Profiles of Ohio

2018

Fifth Edition

Profiles of Ohio

A Universal Reference Book

Grey House Publishing

PUBLISHER: Leslie Mackenzie
EDITORIAL DIRECTOR: Laura Mars
SENIOR EDITOR: David Garoogian
MARKETING DIRECTOR: Jessica Moody

Grey House Publishing, Inc.
4919 Route 22
Amenia, NY 12501
518.789.8700
FAX 845.373.6390
www.greyhouse.com
e-mail: books@greyhouse.com

First edition published 2006
Printed in Canada

Publisher's Cataloging-In-Publication Data
(Prepared by The Donohue Group, Inc.)

Title: Profiles of Ohio.
Description: Millerton, N.Y. : Grey House Pub., 2006- | "A Universal Reference Book." | "History, statistics, demographics for all 1,197 populated places in Ohio including comparative statistics and rankings."
Identifiers: ISSN: 1933-8058
Subjects: LCSH: Cities and towns—Ohio—Statistics—Periodicals. | Cities and towns—Ohio—History—Periodicals.
Classification: LCC HA571 .P76 | DDC 317—dc23

ISBN: 978-1-68217-767-9

Table of Contents

Introduction

This is the fifth edition of *Profiles of Ohio—Facts, Figures & Statistics for 1,346 Populated Places in Ohio.* As with the other titles in our *State Profiles* series, it was built with content from Grey House Publishing's award-winning *Profiles of America*—a 4-volume compilation of data on more than 43,000 places in the United States. We have included a fully updated Ohio chapter from *Profiles of America,* and added several new chapters of demographic information and ranking sections, so that *Profiles of Ohio* is the most comprehensive portrait of the state of Ohio ever published.

Profiles of Ohio provides data on all populated communities and counties in the state of Ohio for which the US Census provides individual statistics. This edition also includes profiles of 132 unincorporated places based on US Census data by zip code.

This premier reference work includes five major sections that cover everything from **Education** to **Ethnic Backgrounds** to **Climate**. All sections include **Comparative Statistics** or **Rankings**. A section called **About Ohio** at the front of the book includes detailed narrative and colorful photos and maps. Here is an overview of each section:

1. About Ohio
This 4-color section gives the researcher a real sense of the state and its history. It includes a Photo Gallery, and comprehensive sections on Ohio's History and Government, Timeline of Ohio History, Land and Natural Resources, Ohio Energy Profile and Demographic Maps. These 42 pages, with the help of photos, maps and charts, anchor the researcher to the state, both physically and politically.

2. Profiles
This section, organized by county, gives detailed profiles of 1,346 places plus 88 counties, based on Census 2010 and data from the 2012-2016 American Community Survey. In addition, we have added current government statistics and original research, so that these profiles pull together statistical and descriptive information on every Census-recognized place in the state. Major fields of information include:

Geography	*Housing*	*Education*	*Religion*
Ancestry	*Transportation*	*Population*	*Climate*
Economy	*Industry*	*Health*	

Categories **NEW** to this edition include dentists per capita and selected monthly owner costs with and without a mortgage. In addition to place and county profiles, this section includes a **Place Name Index**.

3. Comparative Statistics
This section includes tables that compare Ohio's 100 largest incorporated communities by dozens of data points.

4. Community Rankings
This section includes tables that rank the top 150 and bottom 150 incorporated communities with population over 2,500, in dozens of categories.

5. Education
This section begins with an **Educational State Profile,** summarizing number of schools, students, diplomas granted and educational dollars spent. Following the state profile are **School District Rankings** on 16 topics ranging from *Student/Teacher Ratios* to *Current Expenditures per Student.* Following these rankings are statewide *National Assessment of Educational Progress (NAEP)* results and data from the Ohio Department of Education showing a statewide overview of student performance.

6. Ancestry and Ethnicity
This section provides a detailed look at the ancestral, Hispanic and racial makeup of Ohio's 200+ ethnic

categories. Profiles are included for the state, for all counties with 100,000 or more residents, and for all places with 50,000 or more residents. In the ranking section, data is displayed three ways: 1) by number, based on all places regardless of population; 2) by percent, based on all places regardless of population; 3) by percent, based on places with populations of 50,000 or more. You will discover, for example, that the city of Mentor has the greatest number of people reporting Croatian ancestry in the state (1,797), and that 100% of the population of Miamiville are of German ancestry.

7. Climate
This section includes a State Summary, three colorful maps and profiles of both National and Cooperative Weather Stations. In addition, you'll find Weather Station Rankings with hundreds of interesting details, such as Danville 2 W and Millersburg reporting the lowest annual extreme minimum temperatures (-35° F).

This section also includes Significant Storm Event data from January 2000 through December 2009. Here you will learn that a winter storm caused $750 million in property damage in Knox, Stark and Trumbull Counties in March 2008 and that a F4 tornado was responsible for two deaths and 17 injuries in Van Wert in November 2002.

Note: The extensive **User Guide** that follows this introduction is segmented into four sections and examines, in some detail, each data field in the individual profiles and comparative sections for all chapters. It provides sources for all data points and statistical definitions as necessary.

User Guide

Profile Section

Places Covered

All 88 counties.

937 incorporated municipalities. Comprised of 248 cities and 689 villages.

267 Census Designated Places (CDP). The U.S. Bureau of the Census defines a CDP as "a statistical entity, defined for each decennial census according to Census Bureau guidelines, comprising a densely settled concentration of population that is not within an incorporated place, but is locally identified by a name. CDPs are delineated cooperatively by state and local officials and the Census Bureau, following Census Bureau guidelines.

132 unincorporated communities. The communities included have statistics for their ZIP Code Tabulation Area (ZCTA) available from the Census Bureau. They are referred to as "postal areas." "Postal areas" can span multiple ZCTAs. A ZCTA is a statistical entity developed by the Census Bureau to approximate the delivery area for a US Postal Service 5-digit or 3-digit ZIP Code in the US and Puerto Rico. A ZCTA is an aggregation of census blocks that have the same predominant ZIP Code associated with the mailing addresses in the Census Bureau's Master Address File. Thus, the Postal Service's delivery areas have been adjusted to encompass whole census blocks so that the Census Bureau can tabulate census data for the ZCTAs. ZCTAs do not include all ZIP Codes used for mail delivery and therefore do not precisely depict the area within which mail deliveries associated with that ZIP Code occur. Additionally, some areas that are known by a unique name, although they are part of a larger incorporated place, are also included as "postal areas."

For a more in-depth discussion of geographic areas, please refer to the Census Bureau's Geographic Areas Reference Manual at http://www.census.gov/geo/www/garm.html.

IMPORTANT NOTES

- Since the last decennial census, the U.S. Census replaced the long-form sample with the American Community Survey (ACS), which uses a series of monthly samples to produce annually updated estimates for the same areas. ACS estimates are based on data from a sample of housing units and people in the population, not the full population. ACS sampling error (uncertainty of data) is greater for those areas with smaller populations.
- *Profiles of Ohio* uses the term "community" to refer to all places except counties. The term "county" is used to refer to counties and county-equivalents. All places are defined as of the 2010 Census.
- If a community spans multiple counties, the community will be shown in the county that contains its largest population.
- When a county and city are coextensive (occupying the same geographic area and sharing the same government), they are given a single entry.
- In each community profile, only school districts that have schools that are physically located within the community are shown. In addition, statistics for each school district cover the entire district, regardless of the physical location of the schools within the district.
- Special care should be taken when interpreting certain statistics for communities containing large colleges or universities. College students were counted as residents of the area in which they were living while attending college (as they have been since the 1950 census). One effect this may have is skewing the figures for population, income, housing, and educational attainment.
- Some information (e.g. income) is available for both counties and individual communities. Other information is available for just counties (e.g. election results), or just individual communities (e.g. local newspapers). Refer to the "Data Explanation and Sources" section for a complete listing.

- Some statistical information is available only for larger communities. In addition, the larger places are more apt to have services such as newspapers, airports, school districts, etc.
- For the most complete information on any community, users should also check the entry for the county in which the community is located. In addition, more information and services will be listed under the larger places in the county.

Data Explanation and Sources—County Profiles

PHYSICAL AND GEOGRAPHICAL CHARACTERISTICS

Physical Location: Describes the physical location of the county. *Source: Columbia University Press, The Columbia Gazetteer of North America and original research.*

Land and Water Area: Land and water area in square miles. *Source: U.S. Census Bureau, Census 2010*

Latitude and Longitude: Latitude and longitude in degrees. *Source: U.S. Census Bureau, Census 2010*

Time Zone: Lists the time zone. *Source: Original research*

Year Organized: Year the county government was organized. *Source: National Association of Counties*

County Seat: Lists the county seat. If a county has more than one seat, then both are listed. *Source: National Association of Counties*

Metropolitan Area: Indicates the metropolitan area the county is located in. Also lists all the component counties of that metropolitan area. The Office of Management and Budget (OMB) defines metropolitan and micropolitan statistical areas. The most current definitions are as of July 2015. *Source: U.S. Census Bureau*

Climate: Includes all weather stations located within the county. Indicates the station name and elevation as well as the monthly average high and low temperatures, average precipitation, and average snowfall. The period of record is generally 1980-2009, however, certain weather stations contain averages going back as far as 1900. *Source: Grey House Publishing, Weather America: A Thirty-Year Summary of Statistical Weather Data and Rankings, 2010*

POPULATION

Population: Current population. *Source: U.S. Census Bureau, American Community Survey, 2012-2016 Five-Year Estimates*

Population Growth: The increase or decrease in population since 2000. *Source: U.S. Census Bureau, Census 2000; U.S. Census Bureau, American Community Survey, 2012-2016 Five-Year Estimates*

Population Density: Total current population divided by the land area in square miles. *Source: U.S. Census Bureau, Census 2010; U.S. Census Bureau, American Community Survey, 2012-2016 Five-Year Estimates*

Race/Hispanic Origin: Figures include the U.S. Census Bureau categories of White alone; Black/African American alone; Asian alone; American Indian/Alaska Native alone; Native Hawaiian/Other Pacific Islander alone; two or more races; and Hispanic of any race. Alone refers to the fact that these figures are not in combination with any other race. *Source: U.S. Census Bureau, American Community Survey, 2012-2016 Five-Year Estimates*

The concept of race, as used by the Census Bureau, reflects self-identification by people according to the race or races with which they most closely identify. These categories are socio-political constructs and should not be interpreted as being scientific or anthropological in nature. Furthermore, the race categories include both racial and national-origin groups.

- **White.** A person having origins in any of the original peoples of Europe, the Middle East, or North Africa. It includes people who indicated their race(s) as "White" or reported entries such as Irish, German, Italian, Lebanese, Arab, Moroccan, or Caucasian.
- **Black/African American.** A person having origins in any of the Black racial groups of Africa. It includes people who indicated their race(s) as "Black, African Am., or Negro" or reported entries such as African American, Kenyan, Nigerian, or Haitian.
- **Asian.** A person having origins in any of the original peoples of the Far East, Southeast Asia, or the Indian subcontinent, including, for example, Cambodia, China, India, Japan, Korea, Malaysia, Pakistan, the Philippine Islands, Thailand, and Vietnam. It includes people who indicated their race(s) as "Asian" or reported entries such as "Asian Indian," "Chinese," "Filipino," "Korean," "Japanese," "Vietnamese," and "Other Asian" or provided other detailed Asian responses.
- **American Indian/Alaska Native.** A person having origins in any of the original peoples of North and South America (including Central America) and who maintains tribal affiliation or community attachment. This category includes people who indicated their race(s) as "American Indian or Alaska Native" or

reported their enrolled or principal tribe, such as Navajo, Blackfeet, Inupiat, Yup'ik, or Central American Indian groups or South American Indian groups.

- **Native Hawaiian/Other Pacific Islander.** A person having origins in any of the original peoples of Hawaii, Guam, Samoa, or other Pacific Islands. It includes people who indicated their race(s) as "Pacific Islander" or reported entries such as "Native Hawaiian," "Guamanian or Chamorro," "Samoan," and "Other Pacific Islander" or provided other detailed Pacific Islander responses..
- **Two or More Races.** People may choose to provide two or more races either by checking two or more race response check boxes, by providing multiple responses, or by some combination of check boxes and other responses. The race response categories shown on the questionnaire are collapsed into the five minimum race groups identified by OMB, and the Census Bureau's "Some Other Race" category.
- **Hispanic.** The data on the Hispanic or Latino population were derived from answers to a question that was asked of all people. The terms "Spanish," "Hispanic origin," and "Latino" are used interchangeably. Some respondents identify with all three terms while others may identify with only one of these three specific terms. Hispanics or Latinos who identify with the terms "Spanish," "Hispanic," or "Latino" are those who classify themselves in one of the specific Spanish, Hispanic, or Latino categories listed on the questionnaire ("Mexican," "Puerto Rican," or "Cuban") as well as those who indicate that they are "other Spanish/Hispanic/Latino." People who do not identify with one of the specific origins listed on the questionnaire but indicate that they are "other Spanish/Hispanic/Latino" are those whose origins are from Spain, the Spanish-speaking countries of Central or South America, the Dominican Republic, or people identifying themselves generally as Spanish, Spanish-American, Hispanic, Hispano, Latino, and so on. All write-in responses to the "other Spanish/Hispanic/Latino" category were coded. Origin can be viewed as the heritage, nationality group, lineage, or country of birth of the person or the person's parents or ancestors before their arrival in the United States. People who identify their origin as Spanish, Hispanic, or Latino may be of any race.

Average Household Size: Number of persons in the average household. *Source: U.S. Census Bureau, American Community Survey, 2012-2016 Five-Year Estimates*

Median Age: Median age of the population. *Source: U.S. Census Bureau, American Community Survey, 2012-2016 Five-Year Estimates*

Age Under 18: Percent of the total population under 18 years old. *Source: U.S. Census Bureau, American Community Survey, 2012-2016 Five-Year Estimates*

Age 65 and Over: Percent of the total population age 65 and over. *Source: U.S. Census Bureau, American Community Survey, 2012-2016 Five-Year Estimates*

Males per 100 Females: Number of males per 100 females. *Source: U.S. Census Bureau, American Community Survey, 2012-2016 Five-Year Estimates*

Marital Status: Percentage of population never married, now married, separated, widowed, or divorced. *Source: U.S. Census Bureau, American Community Survey, 2012-2016 Five-Year Estimates*

The marital status classification refers to the status at the time of enumeration. Data on marital status are tabulated only for the population 15 years old and over. Each person was asked whether they were "Now married," "Widowed," "Separated," "Divorced," or "Never married." Couples who live together (for example, people in common-law marriages) were able to report the marital status they considered to be the most appropriate.

- **Never married.** Never married includes all people who have never been married, including people whose only marriage(s) was annulled.
- **Now married.** All people whose current marriage has not ended by widowhood or divorce. This category includes people defined as "separated."
- **Separated.** Includes people legally separated or otherwise absent from their spouse because of marital discord. Those without a final divorce decree are classified as "separated." This category also includes people who have been deserted or who have parted because they no longer want to live together, but who have not obtained a divorce.
- **Widowed**. This category includes widows and widowers who have not remarried.
- **Divorced.** This category includes people who are legally divorced and who have not remarried.

Foreign Born: Percentage of population who were not U.S. citizens at birth. Foreign-born people are those who indicated they were either a U.S. citizen by naturalization or they were not a citizen of the United States. *Source: U.S. Census Bureau, American Community Survey, 2012-2016 Five-Year Estimates*

Speak English Only: Percent of population that reported speaking only English at home. *Source: U.S. Census Bureau, American Community Survey, 2012-2016 Five-Year Estimates*

With Disability: Percent of the civilian noninstitutionalized population that reported having a disability. Disability status is determined from from six types of difficulty: vision, hearing, cognitive, ambulatory, self-care, and independent living. For children under 5 years old, hearing and vision difficulty are used to determine disability status. For children between the ages of 5 and 14, disability status is determined from hearing, vision, cognitive, ambulatory, and self-care difficulties. For people aged 15 years and older, they are considered to have a disability if they have difficulty with any one of the six difficulty types. *Source: U.S. Census Bureau, American Community Survey, 2012-2016 Five-Year Estimates*

Veterans: Percent of the civilian population 18 years and over who have served (even for a short time), but are not currently serving, on active duty in the U.S. Army, Navy, Air Force, Marine Corps, or the Coast Guard, or who served in the U.S. Merchant Marine during World War II. People who served in the National Guard or Reserves are classified as veterans only if they were ever called or ordered to active duty, not counting the 4-6 months for initial training or yearly summer camps. All other civilians are classified as nonveterans. Note: While it is possible for 17 year olds to be veterans of the Armed Forces, ACS data products are restricted to the population 18 years and older. *Source: U.S. Census Bureau, American Community Survey, 2012-2016 Five-Year Estimates*

Ancestry: Largest ancestry groups reported (up to five). The data includes persons who report multiple ancestries. For example, if a person reported being Irish and Italian, they would be included in both categories. Thus, the sum of the percentages may be greater than 100%. *Source: U.S. Census Bureau, American Community Survey, 2012-2016 Five-Year Estimates*

The data represent self-classification by people according to the ancestry group or groups with which they most closely identify. Ancestry refers to a person's ethnic origin or descent, "roots," heritage, or the place of birth of the person, the person's parents, or their ancestors before their arrival in the United States. Some ethnic identities, such as Egyptian or Polish, can be traced to geographic areas outside the United States, while other ethnicities such as Pennsylvania German or Cajun evolved in the United States.

The ancestry question was intended to provide data for groups that were not included in the Hispanic origin and race questions. Therefore, although data on all groups are collected, the ancestry data shown in these tabulations are for non-Hispanic and non-race groups. *See* Race/Hispanic Origin for information on Hispanic and race groups.

RELIGION

Religion: Lists the largest religious groups (up to six) based on the number of adherents divided by the population of the county. Adherents are defined as "all members, including full members, their children and the estimated number of other regular participants who are not considered as communicant, confirmed or full members." *Source: American Religious Bodies, 2010 U.S. Religion Census: Religious Congregations & Membership Study*

ECONOMY

Unemployment Rate: Unemployment rate as of October 2017. Includes all civilians age 16 or over who were unemployed and looking for work. *Source: U.S. Department of Labor, Bureau of Labor Statistics, Local Area Unemployment Statistics*

Leading Industries: Lists the three leading industries (excluding government) based on the number of establishments. *Source: U.S. Census Bureau, County Business Patterns 2015*

Farms: The total number of farms and the total acreage they occupy. *Source: U.S. Department of Agriculture, National Agricultural Statistics Service, 2012 Census of Agriculture*

Company Size: The numbers of companies at various employee headcounts. Includes private employers only. *Source: U.S. Census Bureau, County Business Patterns 2015*

- **Employ 1,000 or more persons.** The numbers of companies that employ 1,000 or more persons.
- **Employ 500-999 persons.** The numbers of companies that employ 500 to 999 persons.

- **Employ 100-499 persons.** The numbers of companies that employ 100 to 499 persons.
- **Employ 1-99 persons.** The numbers of companies that employ 1 to 99 persons.

Business Ownership: Number of businesses that are majority-owned by women or various minority groups. *Source: U.S. Census Bureau, 2012 Economic Census, Survey of Business Owners*

- **Women-Owned.** Number of businesses that are majority-owned by a woman. Majority ownership is defined as having 51 percent or more of the stock or equity in the business.
- **Black-Owned.** Number of businesses that are majority-owned by a Black or African American person(s). Majority ownership is defined as having 51 percent or more of the stock or equity in the business. Black or African American is defined as a person having origins in any of the black racial groups of Africa, including those who consider themselves to be "Haitian."
- **Asian-Owned.** Number of businesses that are majority-owned by an Asian person(s). Majority ownership is defined as having 51 percent or more of the stock or equity in the business.
- **American Indian/Alaska Native-Owned.** Number of businesses that are majority-owned by an American Indian or Alaska Native person(s). Majority ownership is defined as having 51 percent or more of the stock or equity in the business.
- **Hispanic-Owned.** Number of businesses that are majority-owned by a person(s) of Hispanic or Latino origin. Majority ownership is defined as having 51 percent or more of the stock or equity in the business. Hispanic or Latino origin is defined as a person of Cuban, Mexican, Puerto Rican, South or Central American, or other Spanish culture or origin, regardless of race.

EMPLOYMENT

Employment by Occupation: Percentage of the employed civilian population 16 years and over in management, professional, service, sales, farming, construction, and production occupations. *Source: U.S. Census Bureau, American Community Survey, 2012-2016 Five-Year Estimates*

- Management, business, and financial occupations include:
  - Management occupations
  - Business and financial operations occupations
- Computer, engineering, and science occupations include:
  - Computer and mathematical occupations
  - Architecture and engineering occupations
  - Life, physical, and social science occupations
- Education, legal, community service, arts, and media occupations include:
  - Community and social service occupations
  - Legal occupations
  - Education, training, and library occupations
  - Arts, design, entertainment, sports, and media occupations
- Healthcare practitioners and technical occupations include:
  - Health diagnosing and treating practitioners and other technical occupations
  - Health technologists and technicians
- Service occupations include:
  - Healthcare support occupations
  - Protective service occupations:
    - Fire fighting and prevention, and other protective service workers including supervisors
    - Law enforcement workers including supervisors
  - Food preparation and serving related occupations
  - Building and grounds cleaning and maintenance occupations
  - Personal care and service occupations
- Sales and office occupations include:
  - Sales and related occupations
  - Office and administrative support occupations

- Natural resources, construction, and maintenance occupations include:
  Farming, fishing, and forestry occupations
  Construction and extraction occupations
  Installation, maintenance, and repair occupations

- Production, transportation, and material moving occupations include:
  Production occupations
  Transportation occupations
  Material moving occupations

INCOME

Per Capita Income: Per capita income is the mean income computed for every man, woman, and child in a particular group. It is derived by dividing the total income of a particular group by the total population in that group. Per capita income is rounded to the nearest whole dollar. *Source: U.S. Census Bureau, American Community Survey, 2012-2016 Five-Year Estimates*

Median Household Income: Includes the income of the householder and all other individuals 15 years old and over in the household, whether they are related to the householder or not. The median divides the income distribution into two equal parts: one-half of the cases falling below the median income and one-half above the median. For households, the median income is based on the distribution of the total number of households including those with no income. Median income for households is computed on the basis of a standard distribution and is rounded to the nearest whole dollar. *Source: U.S. Census Bureau, American Community Survey, 2012-2016 Five-Year Estimates*

Average Household Income: Average household income is obtained by dividing total household income by the total number of households. *Source: U.S. Census Bureau, American Community Survey, 2012-2016 Five-Year Estimates*

Percent of Households with Income of $100,000 or more: Percent of households with income of $100,000 or more. *Source: U.S. Census Bureau, American Community Survey, 2012-2016 Five-Year Estimates*

Poverty Rate: Percentage of population with income below the poverty level. Based on individuals for whom poverty status is determined. Poverty status was determined for all people except institutionalized people, people in military group quarters, people in college dormitories, and unrelated individuals under 15 years old. *Source: U.S. Census Bureau, American Community Survey, 2012-2016 Five-Year Estimates*

EDUCATIONAL ATTAINMENT

Figures show the percent of population age 25 and over with the following levels of educational attainment. *Source: U.S. Census Bureau, American Community Survey, 2012-2016 Five-Year Estimates*

- **High school diploma or higher.** Includes people whose highest degree is a high school diploma or its equivalent (GED), people who attended college but did not receive a degree, and people who received a college, university, or professional degree.
- **Bachelor's degree or higher.** Includes people who received a bachelor's, master's, doctorate, or professional degree.
- **Graduate/professional degree or higher.** Includes people who received a master's, doctorate, or professional degree.

HOUSING

Homeownership Rate: Percentage of housing units that are owner-occupied. *Source: U.S. Census Bureau, American Community Survey, 2012-2016 Five-Year Estimates*

Median Home Value: Median value in dollars of all owner-occupied housing units as reported by the owner. *Source: U.S. Census Bureau, American Community Survey, 2012-2016 Five-Year Estimates*

Median Year Structure Built: Year structure built refers to when the building was first constructed, not when it was remodeled, added to, or converted. For mobile homes, houseboats, RVs, etc, the manufacturer's model year was assumed to be the year built. The data relate to the number of units built during the specified periods that were still in existence at the time of enumeration. *Source: U.S. Census Bureau, American Community Survey, 2012-2016 Five-Year Estimates*

Homeowner Vacancy Rate: Proportion of the homeowner inventory that is vacant "for sale." It is computed by dividing the number of vacant units "for sale only" by the sum of the owner-occupied units, vacant units that are "for sale only," and vacant units that have been sold but not yet occupied, and then multiplying by 100. This measure is rounded to the nearest tenth. *Source: U.S. Census Bureau, American Community Survey, 2012-2016 Five-Year Estimates*

Median Selected Monthly Owner Costs: Selected monthly owner costs are the sum of payments for mortgages, deeds of trust, contracts to purchase, or similar debts on the property (including payments for the first mortgage, second mortgages, home equity loans, and other junior mortgages); real estate taxes; fire, hazard, and flood insurance on the property; utilities (electricity, gas, and water and sewer); and fuels (oil, coal, kerosene, wood, etc.). It also includes, where appropriate, the monthly condominium fee for condominiums and mobile home costs (personal property taxes, site rent, registration fees, and license fees). Selected monthly owner costs were tabulated for all owner-occupied units, and are shown separately for units "with a mortgage" and for units "not mortgaged." *Source: U.S. Census Bureau, American Community Survey, 2012-2016 Five-Year Estimates*

Median Gross Rent: Median monthly gross rent in dollars on specified renter-occupied and specified vacant-for-rent units. Specified renter-occupied and specified vacant-for-rent units exclude 1-family houses on 10 acres or more. Gross rent is the contract rent plus the estimated average monthly cost of utilities (electricity, gas, and water and sewer) and fuels (oil, coal, kerosene, wood, etc.) if these are paid by the renter (or paid for the renter by someone else). Gross rent is intended to eliminate differentials that result from varying practices with respect to the inclusion of utilities and fuels as part of the rental payment. Contract rent is the monthly rent agreed to or contracted for, regardless of any furnishings, utilities, fees, meals, or services that may be included. For vacant units, it is the monthly rent asked for the rental unit at the time of enumeration. *Source: U.S. Census Bureau, American Community Survey, 2012-2016 Five-Year Estimates*

Rental Vacancy Rate: Proportion of the rental inventory that is vacant "for rent." It is computed by dividing the number of vacant units "for rent" by the sum of the renter-occupied units, vacant units that are "for rent," and vacant units that have been rented but not yet occupied, and then multiplying by 100. This measure is rounded to the nearest tenth. *Source: U.S. Census Bureau, American Community Survey, 2012-2016 Five-Year Estimates*

VITAL STATISTICS

Birth Rate: Estimated number of births per 10,000 population in 2016. *Source: U.S. Census Bureau, Annual Components of Population Change, July 1, 2010 - July 1, 2016*

Death Rate: Estimated number of deaths per 10,000 population in 2016. *Source: U.S. Census Bureau, Annual Components of Population Change, July 1, 2010 - July 1, 2016*

Age-adjusted Cancer Mortality Rate: Number of age-adjusted deaths from cancer per 100,000 population in 2016. Cancer is defined as International Classification of Disease (ICD) codes C00–D48.9 Neoplasms. *Source: Centers for Disease Control, CDC Wonder, 2016*

Age-adjusted death rates are weighted averages of the age-specific death rates, where the weights represent a fixed population by age. They are used because the rates of almost all causes of death vary by age. Age adjustment is a technique for "removing" the effects of age from crude rates, so as to allow meaningful comparisons across populations with different underlying age structures. For example, comparing the crude rate of heart disease in Virginia to that of California is misleading, because the relatively older population in Virginia will lead to a higher crude death rate, even if the age-specific rates of heart disease in Virginia and California are the same. For such a comparison, age-adjusted rates would be preferable. Age-adjusted rates should be viewed as relative indexes rather than as direct or actual measures of mortality risk.

Death rates based on counts of twenty or less (≤ 20) are flagged as "Unreliable". Death rates based on fewer than three years of data for counties with populations of less than 100,000 in the 2000 Census counts, are also flagged as "Unreliable" if the number of deaths is five or less (≤ 5).

HEALTH INSURANCE

Health insurance coverage in the ACS and other Census Bureau surveys define coverage to include plans and programs that provide comprehensive health coverage. Plans that provide insurance for specific conditions or situations such as cancer and long-term care policies are not considered coverage. Likewise, other types of insurance like dental, vision, life, and disability insurance are not considered health insurance coverage.

For reporting purposes, the Census Bureau broadly classifies health insurance coverage as private health insurance or public coverage. Private health insurance is a plan provided through an employer or union, a plan purchased by an individual from a private company, or TRICARE or other military health care. Public health coverage includes the federal programs Medicare, Medicaid, and VA Health Care (provided through the Department of Veterans Affairs); the Children's Health Insurance Program (CHIP); and individual state health plans. The types of health insurance are not mutually exclusive; people may be covered by more than one at the same time. People who had no reported health coverage, or those whose only health coverage was Indian Health Service, were considered uninsured. *Source: U.S. Census Bureau, American Community Survey, 2012-2016 Five-Year Estimates*

- **Have Insurance:** Percent of the civilian noninstitutionalized population with any type of comprehensive health insurance.
- **Have Private Insurance.** Percent of the civilian noninstitutionalized population with private health insurance. A person may report that they have both public and private health insurance, thus, the sum of the percentages may be greater than 100%.
- **Have Public Insurance.** Percent of the civilian noninstitutionalized population with public health insurance. A person may report that they have both public and private health insurance, thus, the sum of the percentages may be greater than 100%.
- **Do Not Have Insurance.** Percent of the civilian noninstitutionalized population with no health insurance.
- **Children Under 18 With No Insurance.** Percent of the civilian noninstitutionalized population under age 18 with no health insurance.

HEALTH CARE

Number of physicians, hospital beds and hospital admission per 10,000 population. *Source: Area Health Resource File (AHRF) 2016-2017. U.S. Department of Health and Human Services, Health Resources and Services Administration, Bureau of Health Professions, Rockville, MD.*

- **Number of Physicians.** The number of active, non-federal physicians (MDs and DOs) per 10,000 population in 2015.
- **Number of Dentists.** The number of dentists per 10,000 population in 2016.
- **Number of Hospital Beds.** The number of hospital beds per 10,000 population in 2014.
- **Number of Hospital Admissions.** The number of hospital admissions per 10,000 population in 2014.

AIR QUALITY INDEX

The percentage of days in 2016 the AQI fell into the Good (0-50), Moderate (51-100), Unhealthy for Sensitive Groups (101-150), Unhealthy (151-200), Very Unhealthy (201-300), and Hazardous (300+) ranges. If a range does not appear, its value is zero. Data covers January 2016 through December 2016 and only includes counties for which air quality data was available for 100 days or more. *Source: AirData: Access to Air Pollution Data, U.S. Environmental Protection Agency, Office of Air and Radiation*

The AQI is an index for reporting daily air quality. It tells you how clean or polluted your air is, and what associated health concerns you should be aware of. The AQI focuses on health effects that can happen within a few hours or days after breathing polluted air. EPA uses the AQI for five major air pollutants regulated by the Clean Air Act: ground-level ozone, particulate matter, carbon monoxide, sulfur dioxide, and nitrogen dioxide. For each of these pollutants, EPA has established national air quality standards to protect against harmful health effects.

The AQI runs from 0 to 500. The higher the AQI value, the greater the level of air pollution and the greater the health danger. For example, an AQI value of 50 represents good air quality and little potential to affect public health, while an AQI value over 300 represents hazardous air quality. An AQI value of 100 generally corresponds to the national air quality standard for the pollutant, which is the level EPA has set to protect public health. So, AQI values below 100 are generally thought of as satisfactory. When AQI values are above 100, air quality is considered to be unhealthy—at first for certain sensitive groups of people, then for everyone as AQI values get higher. Each category corresponds to a different level of health concern. For example, when the AQI for a pollutant is between 51 and 100, the health concern is "Moderate." Here are the six levels of health concern and what they mean:

- "Good" The AQI value for your community is between 0 and 50. Air quality is considered satisfactory and air pollution poses little or no risk.

- "Moderate" The AQI for your community is between 51 and 100. Air quality is acceptable; however, for some pollutants there may be a moderate health concern for a very small number of individuals. For example, people who are unusually sensitive to ozone may experience respiratory symptoms.
- "Unhealthy for Sensitive Groups" Certain groups of people are particularly sensitive to the harmful effects of certain air pollutants. This means they are likely to be affected at lower levels than the general public. For example, children and adults who are active outdoors and people with respiratory disease are at greater risk from exposure to ozone, while people with heart disease are at greater risk from carbon monoxide. Some people may be sensitive to more than one pollutant. When AQI values are between 101 and 150, members of sensitive groups may experience health effects. The general public is not likely to be affected when the AQI is in this range.
- "Unhealthy" AQI values are between 151 and 200. Everyone may begin to experience health effects. Members of sensitive groups may experience more serious health effects.
- "Very Unhealthy" AQI values between 201 and 300 trigger a health alert, meaning everyone may experience more serious health effects.
- "Hazardous" AQI values over 300 trigger health warnings of emergency conditions. The entire population is more likely to be affected.

TRANSPORTATION

Commute to Work: Percentage of workers 16 years old and over that use the following means of transportation to commute to work: car; public transportation; walk; work from home. The means of transportation data for some areas may show workers using modes of public transportation that are not available in those areas (e.g. subway or elevated riders in a metropolitan area where there actually is no subway or elevated service). This result is largely due to people who worked during the reference week at a location that was different from their usual place of work (such as people away from home on business in an area where subway service was available) and people who used more than one means of transportation each day but whose principal means was unavailable where they lived (e.g. residents of non-metropolitan areas who drove to the fringe of a metropolitan area and took the commuter railroad most of the distance to work). *Source: U.S. Census Bureau, American Community Survey, 2012-2016 Five-Year Estimates*

Mean Travel Time to Work: Mean travel time to work for workers 16 years old and over. Travel time to work refers to the total number of minutes that it usually took the person to get from home to work each day during the reference week. The elapsed time includes time spent waiting for public transportation, picking up passengers in carpools, and time spent in other activities related to getting to work. *Source: U.S. Census Bureau, American Community Survey, 2012-2016 Five-Year Estimates*

PRESIDENTIAL ELECTION

2016 Presidential election results. *Source: Dave Leip's Atlas of U.S. Presidential Elections*

NATIONAL AND STATE PARKS

Lists National/State parks located in the area. *Source: U.S. Geological Survey, Geographic Names Information System*

ADDITIONAL INFORMATION CONTACTS

General telephone number and website address (if available) of local government.

Data Explanation and Sources—Community Profiles

PHYSICAL AND GEOGRAPHICAL CHARACTERISTICS

Place Type: Lists the type of place (city, town, village, borough, Census-Designated Place (CDP), township, charter township, plantation, gore, district, grant, location, purchase, municipality, reservation, unorganized territory, or unincorporated postal area). *Source: U.S. Census Bureau, American Community Survey, 2012-2016 Five-Year Estimates and U.S. Postal Service, City State File*

ZCTA: *This only appears within unincorporated postal areas.* The statistics that follow cover the corresponding ZIP Code Tabulation Area (ZCTA). A ZCTA is a statistical entity developed by the Census Bureau to approximate the delivery area for a US Postal Service 5-digit or 3-digit ZIP Code in the US and Puerto Rico. A ZCTA is an aggregation of census blocks that have the same predominant ZIP Code associated with the mailing addresses in the Census Bureau's Master Address File. Thus, the Postal Service's delivery areas have been adjusted to encompass whole census blocks so that the Census Bureau can tabulate census data for the ZCTAs. ZCTAs do not include all ZIP Codes used for mail delivery and therefore do not precisely depict the area within which mail deliveries associated with that ZIP Code occur. Additionally, some areas that are known by a unique name, although they are part of a larger incorporated place, are also included as "postal areas."

Land and Water Area: Land and water area in square miles. *Source: U.S. Census Bureau, Census 2010*

Latitude and Longitude: Latitude and longitude in degrees. *Source: U.S. Census Bureau, Census 2010*

Elevation: Elevation in feet. *Source: U.S. Geological Survey, Geographic Names Information System (GNIS)*

HISTORY

Historical information. *Source: Columbia University Press, The Columbia Gazetteer of North America; Original research*

POPULATION

Population: Current population. *Source: U.S. Census Bureau, American Community Survey, 2012-2016 Five-Year Estimates*

Population Growth: The increase or decrease in population since 2000. *Source: U.S. Census Bureau, Census 2000; U.S. Census Bureau, American Community Survey, 2012-2016 Five-Year Estimates*

Population Density: Total current population divided by the land area in square miles. *Source: U.S. Census Bureau, Census 2010; U.S. Census Bureau, American Community Survey, 2012-2016 Five-Year Estimates*

Race/Hispanic Origin: Figures include the U.S. Census Bureau categories of White alone; Black/African American alone; Asian alone; American Indian/Alaska Native alone; Native Hawaiian/Other Pacific Islander alone; two or more races; and Hispanic of any race. Alone refers to the fact that these figures are not in combination with any other race. *Source: U.S. Census Bureau, American Community Survey, 2012-2016 Five-Year Estimates*

The concept of race, as used by the Census Bureau, reflects self-identification by people according to the race or races with which they most closely identify. These categories are socio-political constructs and should not be interpreted as being scientific or anthropological in nature. Furthermore, the race categories include both racial and national-origin groups.

- **White.** A person having origins in any of the original peoples of Europe, the Middle East, or North Africa. It includes people who indicated their race(s) as "White" or reported entries such as Irish, German, Italian, Lebanese, Arab, Moroccan, or Caucasian.
- **Black/African American.** A person having origins in any of the Black racial groups of Africa. It includes people who indicated their race(s) as "Black, African Am., or Negro" or reported entries such as African American, Kenyan, Nigerian, or Haitian.
- **Asian.** A person having origins in any of the original peoples of the Far East, Southeast Asia, or the Indian subcontinent, including, for example, Cambodia, China, India, Japan, Korea, Malaysia, Pakistan, the Philippine Islands, Thailand, and Vietnam. It includes people who indicated their race(s) as "Asian" or reported entries such as "Asian Indian," "Chinese," "Filipino," "Korean," "Japanese," "Vietnamese," and "Other Asian" or provided other detailed Asian responses.

- **American Indian/Alaska Native.** A person having origins in any of the original peoples of North and South America (including Central America) and who maintains tribal affiliation or community attachment. This category includes people who indicated their race(s) as "American Indian or Alaska Native" or reported their enrolled or principal tribe, such as Navajo, Blackfeet, Inupiat, Yup'ik, or Central American Indian groups or South American Indian groups.
- **Native Hawaiian/Other Pacific Islander.** A person having origins in any of the original peoples of Hawaii, Guam, Samoa, or other Pacific Islands. It includes people who indicated their race(s) as "Pacific Islander" or reported entries such as "Native Hawaiian," "Guamanian or Chamorro," "Samoan," and "Other Pacific Islander" or provided other detailed Pacific Islander responses..
- **Two or More Races.** People may choose to provide two or more races either by checking two or more race response check boxes, by providing multiple responses, or by some combination of check boxes and other responses. The race response categories shown on the questionnaire are collapsed into the five minimum race groups identified by OMB, and the Census Bureau's "Some Other Race" category.
- **Hispanic.** The data on the Hispanic or Latino population were derived from answers to a question that was asked of all people. The terms "Spanish," "Hispanic origin," and "Latino" are used interchangeably. Some respondents identify with all three terms while others may identify with only one of these three specific terms. Hispanics or Latinos who identify with the terms "Spanish," "Hispanic," or "Latino" are those who classify themselves in one of the specific Spanish, Hispanic, or Latino categories listed on the questionnaire ("Mexican," "Puerto Rican," or "Cuban") as well as those who indicate that they are "other Spanish/Hispanic/Latino." People who do not identify with one of the specific origins listed on the questionnaire but indicate that they are "other Spanish/Hispanic/Latino" are those whose origins are from Spain, the Spanish-speaking countries of Central or South America, the Dominican Republic, or people identifying themselves generally as Spanish, Spanish-American, Hispanic, Hispano, Latino, and so on. All write-in responses to the "other Spanish/Hispanic/Latino" category were coded. Origin can be viewed as the heritage, nationality group, lineage, or country of birth of the person or the person's parents or ancestors before their arrival in the United States. People who identify their origin as Spanish, Hispanic, or Latino may be of any race.

Average Household Size: Number of persons in the average household. *Source: U.S. Census Bureau, American Community Survey, 2012-2016 Five-Year Estimates*

Median Age: Median age of the population. *Source: U.S. Census Bureau, American Community Survey, 2012-2016 Five-Year Estimates*

Age Under 18: Percent of the total population under 18 years old. *Source: U.S. Census Bureau, American Community Survey, 2012-2016 Five-Year Estimates*

Age 65 and Over: Percent of the total population age 65 and over. *Source: U.S. Census Bureau, American Community Survey, 2012-2016 Five-Year Estimates*

Males per 100 Females: Number of males per 100 females. *Source: U.S. Census Bureau, American Community Survey, 2012-2016 Five-Year Estimates*

Marital Status: Percentage of population never married, now married, separated, widowed, or divorced. *Source: U.S. Census Bureau, American Community Survey, 2012-2016 Five-Year Estimates*

The marital status classification refers to the status at the time of enumeration. Data on marital status are tabulated only for the population 15 years old and over. Each person was asked whether they were "Now married," "Widowed," "Separated," "Divorced," or "Never married." Couples who live together (for example, people in common-law marriages) were able to report the marital status they considered to be the most appropriate.

- **Never married**. Never married includes all people who have never been married, including people whose only marriage(s) was annulled.
- **Now married.** All people whose current marriage has not ended by widowhood or divorce. This category includes people defined as "separated."
- **Separated.** Includes people legally separated or otherwise absent from their spouse because of marital discord. Those without a final divorce decree are classified as "separated." This category also includes people who have been deserted or who have parted because they no longer want to live together, but who have not obtained a divorce.
- **Widowed**. This category includes widows and widowers who have not remarried.
- **Divorced.** This category includes people who are legally divorced and who have not remarried.

Foreign Born: Percentage of population who were not U.S. citizens at birth. Foreign-born people are those who indicated they were either a U.S. citizen by naturalization or they were not a citizen of the United States. *Source: U.S. Census Bureau, American Community Survey, 2012-2016 Five-Year Estimates*

Speak English Only: Percent of population that reported speaking only English at home. *Source: U.S. Census Bureau, American Community Survey, 2012-2016 Five-Year Estimates*

With Disability: Percent of the civilian noninstitutionalized population that reported having a disability. Disability status is determined from from six types of difficulty: vision, hearing, cognitive, ambulatory, self-care, and independent living. For children under 5 years old, hearing and vision difficulty are used to determine disability status. For children between the ages of 5 and 14, disability status is determined from hearing, vision, cognitive, ambulatory, and self-care difficulties. For people aged 15 years and older, they are considered to have a disability if they have difficulty with any one of the six difficulty types. *Source: U.S. Census Bureau, American Community Survey, 2012-2016 Five-Year Estimates*

Veterans: Percent of the civilian population 18 years and over who have served (even for a short time), but are not currently serving, on active duty in the U.S. Army, Navy, Air Force, Marine Corps, or the Coast Guard, or who served in the U.S. Merchant Marine during World War II. People who served in the National Guard or Reserves are classified as veterans only if they were ever called or ordered to active duty, not counting the 4-6 months for initial training or yearly summer camps. All other civilians are classified as nonveterans. Note: While it is possible for 17 year olds to be veterans of the Armed Forces, ACS data products are restricted to the population 18 years and older. *Source: U.S. Census Bureau, American Community Survey, 2012-2016 Five-Year Estimates*

Ancestry: Largest ancestry groups reported (up to five). The data includes persons who report multiple ancestries. For example, if a person reported being Irish and Italian, they would be included in both categories. Thus, the sum of the percentages may be greater than 100%. *Source: U.S. Census Bureau, American Community Survey, 2012-2016 Five-Year Estimates*

The data represent self-classification by people according to the ancestry group or groups with which they most closely identify. Ancestry refers to a person's ethnic origin or descent, "roots," heritage, or the place of birth of the person, the person's parents, or their ancestors before their arrival in the United States. Some ethnic identities, such as Egyptian or Polish, can be traced to geographic areas outside the United States, while other ethnicities such as Pennsylvania German or Cajun evolved in the United States.

The ancestry question was intended to provide data for groups that were not included in the Hispanic origin and race questions. Therefore, although data on all groups are collected, the ancestry data shown in these tabulations are for non-Hispanic and non-race groups. *See* Race/Hispanic Origin for information on Hispanic and race groups.

EMPLOYMENT

Employment by Occupation: Percentage of the employed civilian population 16 years and over in management, professional, service, sales, farming, construction, and production occupations. *Source: U.S. Census Bureau, American Community Survey, 2012-2016 Five-Year Estimates*

- Management, business, and financial occupations include:
  - Management occupations
  - Business and financial operations occupations
- Computer, engineering, and science occupations include:
  - Computer and mathematical occupations
  - Architecture and engineering occupations
  - Life, physical, and social science occupations
- Education, legal, community service, arts, and media occupations include:
  - Community and social service occupations
  - Legal occupations
  - Education, training, and library occupations
  - Arts, design, entertainment, sports, and media occupations
- Healthcare practitioners and technical occupations include:
  - Health diagnosing and treating practitioners and other technical occupations
  - Health technologists and technicians

- Service occupations include:
  - Healthcare support occupations
  - Protective service occupations:
    - Fire fighting and prevention, and other protective service workers including supervisors
    - Law enforcement workers including supervisors
  - Food preparation and serving related occupations
  - Building and grounds cleaning and maintenance occupations
  - Personal care and service occupations

- Sales and office occupations include:
  - Sales and related occupations
  - Office and administrative support occupations

- Natural resources, construction, and maintenance occupations include:
  - Farming, fishing, and forestry occupations
  - Construction and extraction occupations
  - Installation, maintenance, and repair occupations

- Production, transportation, and material moving occupations include:
  - Production occupations
  - Transportation occupations
  - Material moving occupations

INCOME

Per Capita Income: Per capita income is the mean income computed for every man, woman, and child in a particular group. It is derived by dividing the total income of a particular group by the total population in that group. Per capita income is rounded to the nearest whole dollar. *Source: U.S. Census Bureau, American Community Survey, 2012-2016 Five-Year Estimates*

Median Household Income: Includes the income of the householder and all other individuals 15 years old and over in the household, whether they are related to the householder or not. The median divides the income distribution into two equal parts: one-half of the cases falling below the median income and one-half above the median. For households, the median income is based on the distribution of the total number of households including those with no income. Median income for households is computed on the basis of a standard distribution and is rounded to the nearest whole dollar. *Source: U.S. Census Bureau, American Community Survey, 2012-2016 Five-Year Estimates*

Average Household Income: Average household income is obtained by dividing total household income by the total number of households. *Source: U.S. Census Bureau, American Community Survey, 2012-2016 Five-Year Estimates*

Percent of Households with Income of $100,000 or more: Percent of households with income of $100,000 or more. *Source: U.S. Census Bureau, American Community Survey, 2012-2016 Five-Year Estimates*

Poverty Rate: Percentage of population with income below the poverty level. Based on individuals for whom poverty status is determined. Poverty status was determined for all people except institutionalized people, people in military group quarters, people in college dormitories, and unrelated individuals under 15 years old. *Source: U.S. Census Bureau, American Community Survey, 2012-2016 Five-Year Estimates*

EDUCATIONAL ATTAINMENT

Figures show the percent of population age 25 and over with the following levels of educational attainment. *Source: U.S. Census Bureau, American Community Survey, 2012-2016 Five-Year Estimates*

- **High school diploma or higher.** Includes people whose highest degree is a high school diploma or its equivalent (GED), people who attended college but did not receive a degree, and people who received a college, university, or professional degree.
- **Bachelor's degree or higher.** Includes people who received a bachelor's, master's, doctorate, or professional degree.
- **Graduate/professional degree or higher.** Includes people who received a master's, doctorate, or professional degree.

SCHOOL DISTRICTS

Lists the name of each school district, the grade range (PK=pre-kindergarten; KG=kindergarten), the student enrollment, and the district headquarters' phone number. In each community profile, only school districts that have schools that are physically located within the community are shown. In addition, statistics for each school district cover the entire district, regardless of the physical location of the schools within the district. *Source: U.S. Department of Education, National Center for Educational Statistics, Directory of Public Elementary and Secondary Education Agencies, 2015-16*

COLLEGES

Four-year Colleges: Lists the name of each four-year college, the type of institution (private or public; for-profit or non-profit; religious affiliation; historically black), the total estimated student enrollment in 2016, the general telephone number, and the annual tuition and fees for full-time, first-time undergraduate students (in-state and out-of-state). *Source: U.S. Department of Education, National Center for Educational Statistics, IPEDS College Data, 2016-17*

Two-year Colleges: Lists the name of each two-year college, the type of institution (private or public; for-profit or non-profit; religious affiliation; historically black), the total estimated student enrollment in 2016, the general telephone number, and the annual tuition and fees for full-time, first-time undergraduate students (in-state and out-of-state). *Source: U.S. Department of Education, National Center for Educational Statistics, IPEDS College Data, 2016-17*

Vocational/Technical Schools: Lists the name of each vocational/technical school, the type of institution (private or public; for-profit or non-profit; religious affiliation; historically black), the total estimated student enrollment in 2016, the general telephone number, and the annual tuition and fees for full-time students. *Source: U.S. Department of Education, National Center for Educational Statistics, IPEDS College Data, 2016-17*

HOUSING

Homeownership Rate: Percentage of housing units that are owner-occupied. *Source: U.S. Census Bureau, American Community Survey, 2012-2016 Five-Year Estimates*

Median Home Value: Median value in dollars of all owner-occupied housing units as reported by the owner. *Source: U.S. Census Bureau, American Community Survey, 2012-2016 Five-Year Estimates*

Median Year Structure Built: Year structure built refers to when the building was first constructed, not when it was remodeled, added to, or converted. For mobile homes, houseboats, RVs, etc, the manufacturer's model year was assumed to be the year built. The data relate to the number of units built during the specified periods that were still in existence at the time of enumeration. *Source: U.S. Census Bureau, American Community Survey, 2012-2016 Five-Year Estimates*

Homeowner Vacancy Rate: Proportion of the homeowner inventory that is vacant "for sale." It is computed by dividing the number of vacant units "for sale only" by the sum of the owner-occupied units, vacant units that are "for sale only," and vacant units that have been sold but not yet occupied, and then multiplying by 100. This measure is rounded to the nearest tenth. *Source: U.S. Census Bureau, American Community Survey, 2012-2016 Five-Year Estimates*

Median Selected Monthly Owner Costs: Selected monthly owner costs are the sum of payments for mortgages, deeds of trust, contracts to purchase, or similar debts on the property (including payments for the first mortgage, second mortgages, home equity loans, and other junior mortgages); real estate taxes; fire, hazard, and flood insurance on the property; utilities (electricity, gas, and water and sewer); and fuels (oil, coal, kerosene, wood, etc.). It also includes, where appropriate, the monthly condominium fee for condominiums and mobile home costs (personal property taxes, site rent, registration fees, and license fees). Selected monthly owner costs were tabulated for all owner-occupied units, and are shown separately for units "with a mortgage" and for units "not mortgaged." *Source: U.S. Census Bureau, American Community Survey, 2012-2016 Five-Year Estimates*

Median Gross Rent: Median monthly gross rent in dollars on specified renter-occupied and specified vacant-for-rent units. Specified renter-occupied and specified vacant-for-rent units exclude 1-family houses on 10 acres or more. Gross rent is the contract rent plus the estimated average monthly cost of utilities (electricity, gas, and water and sewer) and fuels (oil, coal, kerosene, wood, etc.) if these are paid by the renter (or paid for the renter by someone else). Gross rent is intended to eliminate differentials that result from varying practices with respect to the inclusion of utilities and fuels as part of the rental payment. Contract rent is the monthly rent agreed to or contracted for, regardless of any furnishings, utilities, fees, meals, or services that may be included. For vacant units, it is the monthly rent asked for the rental unit at the time of enumeration. *Source: U.S. Census Bureau, American Community Survey, 2012-2016 Five-Year Estimates*

Rental Vacancy Rate: Proportion of the rental inventory that is vacant "for rent." It is computed by dividing the number of vacant units "for rent" by the sum of the renter-occupied units, vacant units that are "for rent," and vacant units that have been rented but not yet occupied, and then multiplying by 100. This measure is rounded to the nearest tenth. *Source: U.S. Census Bureau, American Community Survey, 2012-2016 Five-Year Estimates*

HEALTH INSURANCE

Health insurance coverage in the ACS and other Census Bureau surveys define coverage to include plans and programs that provide comprehensive health coverage. Plans that provide insurance for specific conditions or situations such as cancer and long-term care policies are not considered coverage. Likewise, other types of insurance like dental, vision, life, and disability insurance are not considered health insurance coverage.

For reporting purposes, the Census Bureau broadly classifies health insurance coverage as private health insurance or public coverage. Private health insurance is a plan provided through an employer or union, a plan purchased by an individual from a private company, or TRICARE or other military health care. Public health coverage includes the federal programs Medicare, Medicaid, and VA Health Care (provided through the Department of Veterans Affairs); the Children's Health Insurance Program (CHIP); and individual state health plans. The types of health insurance are not mutually exclusive; people may be covered by more than one at the same time. People who had no reported health coverage, or those whose only health coverage was Indian Health Service, were considered uninsured. *Source: U.S. Census Bureau, American Community Survey, 2012-2016 Five-Year Estimates*

- **Have Insurance:** Percent of the civilian noninstitutionalized population with any type of comprehensive health insurance.
- **Have Private Insurance.** Percent of the civilian noninstitutionalized population with private health insurance. A person may report that they have both public and private health insurance, thus, the sum of the percentages may be greater than 100%.
- **Have Public Insurance.** Percent of the civilian noninstitutionalized population with public health insurance. A person may report that they have both public and private health insurance, thus, the sum of the percentages may be greater than 100%.
- **Do Not Have Insurance.** Percent of the civilian noninstitutionalized population with no health insurance.
- **Children Under 18 With No Insurance.** Percent of the civilian noninstitutionalized population under age 18 with no health insurance.

HOSPITALS

Lists the hospital name and the number of licensed beds. *Source: Grey House Publishing, The Comparative Guide to American Hospitals, 2014*; Original research

NEWSPAPERS

List of daily and weekly newspapers with circulation figures. *Source: Gebbie Press, 2015 All-In-One Media Directory*

SAFETY

Violent Crime Rate: Number of violent crimes reported per 10,000 population. Violent crimes include murder, forcible rape, robbery, and aggravated assault. Statistics include the revised definition of forcible rate if available. Otherwise statistics using the legacy definition are used. *Source: Federal Bureau of Investigation, Uniform Crime Reports 2016*

Property Crime Rate: Number of property crimes reported per 10,000 population. Property crimes include burglary, larceny-theft, and motor vehicle theft. *Source: Federal Bureau of Investigation, Uniform Crime Reports 2016*

TRANSPORTATION

Commute to Work: Percentage of workers 16 years old and over that use the following means of transportation to commute to work: car; public transportation; walk; work from home. The means of transportation data for some areas may show workers using modes of public transportation that are not available in those areas (e.g. subway or elevated riders in a metropolitan area where there actually is no subway or elevated service). This result is largely due to people who worked during the reference week at a location that was different from their usual place of work (such as people away from home on business in an area where subway service was available) and people who used more than one means of transportation each day but whose principal means was unavailable where they lived (e.g. residents of non-metropolitan areas who drove to the fringe of a metropolitan area and took the commuter railroad most of the distance to work). *Source: U.S. Census Bureau, American Community Survey, 2012-2016 Five-Year Estimates*

Mean Travel Time to Work: Mean travel time to work for workers 16 years old and over. Travel time to work refers to the total number of minutes that it usually took the person to get from home to work each day during the reference week. The elapsed time includes time spent waiting for public transportation, picking up passengers in carpools, and time spent in other activities related to getting to work. *Source: U.S. Census Bureau, American Community Survey, 2012-2016 Five-Year Estimates*

Amtrak: Indicates if Amtrak rail or bus service is available. Please note that the cities being served continually change. *Source: National Railroad Passenger Corporation, Amtrak National Timetable, 2018*

AIRPORTS

Lists the local airport(s) along with type of service and hub size. *Source: U.S. Department of Transportation, Bureau of Transportation Statistics*

ADDITIONAL INFORMATION CONTACTS

General telephone number and website address (if available) of local government.

Education Section

State Public School Educational Profile

Schools: Total number of schools in the district. Figures exclude schools with the following status codes: 2 (school has closed since the time of the last report) and 6 (school is temporarily closed and may reopen within three years). *Source: U.S. Department of Education, National Center for Education Statistics, Common Core of Data, Public Elementary/Secondary School Universe Survey: School Year 2013-2014.*

Instructional Level

Primary: Low grade—prekindergarten through 3; high grade—prekindergarten through 8
Middle: Low grade—4 through 7; high grade—4 through 9
High: Low grade—7 through 12; high grade—12 only
Other/Not Reported: Any configuration not falling within the previous three, including ungraded schools

Curriculum

Regular: A regular school is defined as a public elementary/secondary school that does not focus primarily on vocational, special, or alternative education.

Special Education: A special education school is defined as a public elementary/secondary school that focuses primarily on special education, including instruction for any of the following: autism, deaf-blindness, developmental delay, hearing impairment, mental retardation, multiple disabilities, orthopedic impairment, serious emotional disturbance, specific learning disability, speech or language impairment, traumatic brain injury, visual impairment, and other health impairments. These schools adapt curriculum, materials or instruction for students served.

Vocational: A vocational educational school is defined as a public elementary/secondary school that focuses primarily on providing formal preparation for semi-skilled, skilled, technical, or professional occupations for high school-aged students who have opted to develop or expand their employment opportunities, often in lieu of preparing for college entry.

Alternative: A public elementary/secondary school that addresses needs of students which typically cannot be met in a regular school; provides nontraditional education; serves as an adjunct to a regular school; and falls outside of the categories of regular, special education, or vocational education.

Type

Magnet: A special school or program designed to attract students of different racial/ethnic backgrounds for the purpose of reducing, preventing or eliminating racial isolation (50 percent or more minority enrollment); and/or to provide an academic or social focus on a particular theme (e.g., science/math, performing arts, gifted/talented, or foreign language).

Charter: A school providing free public elementary and/or secondary education to eligible students under a specific charter granted by the state legislature or other appropriate authority, and designated by such authority to be a charter school.

Title I Eligible: A school designated under appropriate state and federal regulations as being eligible for participation in programs authorized by Title I of Public Law 103-382.

School-wide Title I: A school in which all the pupils in a school are designated under appropriate state and federal regulations as being eligible for participation in programs authorized by Title I of Public Law 103-382.

Students: A student is an individual for whom instruction is provided in an elementary or secondary education program that is not an adult education program and is under the jurisdiction of a school, school system, or other education institution. *Sources: U.S. Department of Education, National Center for Education Statistics, Common Core of Data, Local Education Agency (School District) Universe Survey: School Year 2013-2014; U.S. Department of Education, National Center for Education Statistics, Common Core of Data, Public Elementary/Secondary School Universe Survey: School Year 2013-2014*

Gender: Percentage of male and female students.

Race/Ethnicity

White: A person having origins in any of the original peoples of Europe, North Africa, or the Middle East. Figures include non-Hispanic whites only.

Black: A person having origins in any of the black racial groups of Africa. Figures include non-Hispanic blacks only.

Asian: A person having origins in any of the original peoples of the Far east, Southeast Asia, and the Indian subcontinent. This includes, for example, China, India, Japan, Korea, and the Philippines. Figures include non-Hispanic Asians only.

American Indian/Alaska Native: A person having origins in any of the original peoples of North America, and who maintains cultural identification through tribal affiliation or community recognition. Figures include non-Hispanic American Indian/Alaska Natives only.

Hawaiian Native/Pacific Islander: A person having origins in any of the original peoples of Hawaii, Guam, Samoa, or other Pacific Islands. Figures include non-Hispanic Hawaiian Native/Pacific Islanders only.

Two or More Races: A person identifying himself or herself as of two or more of the following race groups: White, Black, Asian, Native Hawaiian/Pacific Islander, or American Indian/Alaska Native. Some, but not all, reporting districts use this category. Figures include non-Hispanics, multiple-race students only.

Hispanic: A person of Mexican, Puerto Rican, Cuban, Central or South American, or other Spanish culture or origin, regardless of race.

Special Programs

Individual Education Program (IEP): A written instructional plan for students with disabilities designated as special education students under IDEA-Part B. The written instructional plan includes a statement of present levels of educational performance of a child; statement of annual goals, including short-term instructional objectives; statement of specific educational services to be provided and the extent to which the child will be able to participate in regular educational programs; the projected date for initiation and anticipated duration of services; the appropriate objectives, criteria and evaluation procedures; and the schedules for determining, on at least an annual basis, whether instructional objectives are being achieved. *Source: U.S. Department of Education, National Center for Education Statistics, Common Core of Data, Local Education Agency (School District) Universe Survey: School Year 2013-2014*

English Language Learner (ELL): Formerly referred to as Limited English Proficient (LEP). Students being served in appropriate programs of language assistance (e.g., English as a Second Language, High Intensity Language Training, bilingual education). Does not include pupils enrolled in a class to learn a language other than English. Also Limited-English-Proficient students are individuals who were not born in the United States or whose native language is a language other than English; or individuals who come from environments where a language other than English is dominant; or individuals who are American Indians and Alaskan Natives and who come from environments where a language other than English has had a significant impact on their level of English language proficiency; and who, by reason thereof, have sufficient difficulty speaking, reading, writing, or understanding the English language, to deny such individuals the opportunity to learn successfully in classrooms where the language of instruction is English or to participate fully in our society. *Source: U.S. Department of Education, National Center for Education Statistics, Common Core of Data, Local Education Agency (School District) Universe Survey: School Year 2013-2014*

Eligible for Free Lunch Program: The free lunch program is defined as a program under the National School Lunch Act that provides cash subsidies for free lunches to students based on family size and income criteria. *Source: U.S. Department of Education, National Center for Education Statistics, Common Core of Data, Public Elementary/Secondary School Universe Survey: School Year 2013-2014*

Eligible for Reduced-Price Lunch Program: A student who is eligible to participate in the Reduced-Price Lunch Program under the National School Lunch Act. *Source: U.S. Department of Education, National Center for Education Statistics, Common Core of Data, Public Elementary/Secondary School Universe Survey: School Year 2013-2014*

Adjusted Cohort Graduation Rate (ACGR): The adjusted cohort graduation rate (ACGR) is the percentage of public high school freshmen who graduate with a regular diploma within 4 years of starting 9th grade. Students who are entering 9th grade for the first time form a cohort for the graduating class. This cohort is "adjusted" by adding any students who subsequently transfer into the cohort and subtracting any students who subsequently transfer out, emigrate to another country, or die. Race categories exclude persons of Hispanic ethnicity. *Source: U.S. Department of Education, Office of Elementary and Secondary Education, Consolidated State Performance Report, 2010-11 through 2013-14.*

Averaged Freshman Graduation Rate (AFGR): Public high school averaged freshman graduation rate (AFGR). The AFGR provides an estimate of the percentage of high school students who graduate within 4 years of first starting 9th grade. The rate uses aggregate student enrollment data to estimate the size of an incoming freshman class and aggregate counts of diplomas awarded 4 years later. *Source: U.S. Department of Education, National Center for Education Statistics, Common Core of Data (CCD), "NCES Common Core of Data State Dropout and Graduation Rate Data file," School Year 2011–12, Preliminary Version 1a.*

Caution in interpreting the AFGR. Although the AFGR was selected as the best of the available alternatives, several factors make it fall short of a true on-time graduation rate. First, the AFGR does not take into account any imbalances in the number of students moving in and out of the nation or individual states over the high school years. As a result, the averaged freshman class is at best an approximation of the actual number of freshmen, where differences in the rates of transfers, retention, and dropping out in the three grades affect the average. Second, by including all graduates in a specific year, the graduates may include students who repeated a grade in high school or completed high school early and thus are not on-time graduates in that year.

Difference between ACGR and AFGR. Both rates measure the percentage of public school students who attain a regular high school diploma within 4 years of starting 9th grade for the first time. However, they differ in important ways. The AFGR is an estimate of the on-time 4-year graduation rate derived from aggregate student enrollment data and graduate counts. The ACGR, on the other hand, uses detailed student-level data to determine the percentage of students who graduate within 4 years of starting 9th grade for the first time. In many states, the data required to produce the ACGR have become available only in recent years. The AFGR estimate is less precise than the ACGR, but it can be estimated as far back as the 1960s.

Event Dropout Rate: The public high school event dropout rate indicates the proportion of students who were enrolled at some time during the school year and were expected to be enrolled in grades 9–12 in the following school year but were not enrolled by October 1 of the following school year. Students who have graduated, transferred to another school, died, moved to another country, or who are out of school due to illness are not considered dropouts. The event dropout rate is not comparable to other dropout rates released by the Department or elsewhere. Status dropout rates, for example, measure the percentage of a population that did not complete high school (e.g., some percentage of young adults aged 18–24 dropped out of high school). *Source: U.S. Department of Education, National Center for Education Statistics, Common Core of Data (CCD), "NCES Common Core of Data State Dropout and Graduation Rate Data file," School Year 2011–12, Preliminary Version 1a.*

Staff

Teachers: Teachers are defined as individuals who provide instruction to pre-kindergarten, kindergarten, grades 1 through 12, or ungraded classes, or individuals who teach in an environment other than a classroom setting, and who maintain daily student attendance records. Numbers reported are full-time equivalents (FTE). The students per teacher ratio is shown in parentheses. *Source: U.S. Department of Education, National Center for Education Statistics, Common Core of Data, Local Education Agency (School District) Universe Survey: School Year 2013-2014.*

Teacher Salary: The average classroom teacher salary in 2015-2016. *Source: National Education Association, Rankings & Estimates: Rankings of the States 2015 and Estimates of School Statistics 2016*

Librarians/Media Specialists: Library and media support staff are defined as staff members who render other professional library and media services; also includes library aides and those involved in library/media support. Their duties include selecting, preparing, caring for, and making available to instructional staff, equipment, films, filmstrips, transparencies, tapes, TV programs, and similar materials maintained separately or as part of an instructional materials center. Also included are activities in the audio-visual center, TV studio, related-work-study areas, and services provided by audio-visual personnel. Numbers reported are full-time equivalents (FTE). The students per librarian/media specialist ratio is shown in parentheses. *Source: U.S. Department of Education, National Center for Education Statistics, Common Core of Data, Local Education Agency (School District) Universe Survey: School Year 2013-2014.*

Guidance Counselors: Professional staff assigned specific duties and school time for any of the following activities in an elementary or secondary setting: counseling with students and parents; consulting with other staff members on learning problems; evaluating student abilities; assisting students in making educational and career choices; assisting students in personal and social development; providing referral assistance; and/or working with other staff members in planning and conducting guidance programs for students. The state applies its own standards in apportioning the aggregate of guidance counselors/directors into the elementary and secondary level components. Numbers reported are full-time equivalents (FTE). The students per guidance counselor ratio is shown in parentheses. *Source: U.S. Department of Education, National Center for Education Statistics, Common Core of Data, Local Education Agency (School District) Universe Survey: School Year 2013-2014.*

Ratios

Number of Students per Teacher: The number of students divided by the number of teachers (FTE). See Number of Students and Number of Teachers above for more information. *Source: U.S. Department of Education, National Center for Education Statistics, Common Core of Data, Local Education Agency (School District) Universe Survey: School Year 2013-2014.*

Number of Students per Librarian: The number of students divided by the number of library and media support staff. Library and media support staff are defined as staff members who render other professional library and media services; also includes library aides and those involved in library/media support. Their duties include selecting, preparing, caring for, and making available to instructional staff, equipment, films, filmstrips, transparencies, tapes, TV programs, and similar materials maintained separately or as part of an instructional materials center. Also included are activities in the audio-visual center, TV studio, related-work-study areas, and services provided by audio-visual personnel. Numbers are based on full-time equivalents. *Source: U.S. Department of Education, National Center for Education Statistics, Common Core of Data, Local Education Agency (School District) Universe Survey: School Year 2013-2014.*

Number of Students per Counselor: The number of students divided by the number of guidance counselors. Guidance counselors are professional staff assigned specific duties and school time for any of the following activities in an elementary or secondary setting: counseling with students and parents; consulting with other staff members on learning problems; evaluating student abilities; assisting students in making educational and career choices; assisting students in personal and social development; providing referral assistance; and/or working with other staff members in planning and conducting guidance programs for students. The state applies its own standards in apportioning the aggregate of guidance counselors/directors into the elementary and secondary level components. Numbers reported are full-time equivalents. *Source: U.S. Department of Education, National Center for Education Statistics, Common Core of Data, Local Education Agency (School District) Universe Survey: School Year 2013-2014.*

Finances

Note: *all financial figures are per student and are calculated by dividing the dollar amount by the fall membership.* ***Source:*** *U.S. Department of Education, National Center for Education Statistics, Common Core of Data (CCD), National Public Education Financial Survey (State Fiscal), 2012-13 (FY 2013) v.1a*

Total Expenditures per Pupil: This is the total expenditures divided by the fall membership as reported in the state finance file. The total expenditures is the subtotal of direct state support expenditures for private schools, debt services expenditures—interest and total expenditures for education.

Total Current Expenditures per Pupil: This is the total current expenditures for public elementary and secondary education divided by the fall membership as reported in the state finance file. The expenditures for equipment, non-public education, school construction, debt financing and community services are excluded from this data item.

Instruction Expenditures per Pupil: This is the total of instructional expenditures divided by the fall membership as reported in the state finance file. Instruction expenditures are for services and materials directly related to classroom instruction and the interaction between teachers and students. Teacher salaries and benefits, textbooks, classroom supplies and extra curricular activities are included in Instruction. Expenditures for the library and in-service teacher training are reported as instruction support services. Guidance counselors and nurses are reported under student support services.

Support Services Expenditures per Pupil: This is the total of support services expenditures divided by the fall membership as reported in the state finance file.

Non-Instruction Expenditures per Pupil: This is the total for food services operations expenditures and enterprise operations expenditures divided by the fall membership as reported in the state finance file. This does not include property or community services expenditures.

Net Current Expenditures per Attendance for Title I: Net current expenditures per average daily attendance (ADA) are calculated by NCES. Net current expenditures are calculated by NCES and are equal to current expenditures minus total exclusions. Computation of ADA is defined by state laws or regulations or by NCES. Net current expenditures per ADA (or state per public expenditures—SPPE) are used to calculate allocations for certain federal education programs, including Title I, impact aid, Indian education and individuals with disabilities.

Total Revenues per Pupil: Total revenues per student are the total revenues from all sources divided by the fall membership as reported in the state finance file.

Federal Revenues per Pupil: Federal revenues per student are federal revenues divided by the fall membership as reported in the state finance file.

State Revenues per Pupil: State revenues per student are revenues received by the LEAs from the state, divided by the fall membership as reported in the state finance file.

Local Revenues per Pupil: Local revenues per student are the total of all local revenue categories divided by the fall membership as reported in the state finance file. Local revenues are raised and allocated by local governments.

Intermediate Revenue per Pupil: Intermediate revenue per pupil are intermediate sources of revenue divided by the student membership as reported on the state finance file. Intermediate sources of revenue are from educational agencies that possess independent fund-raising capabilities and that operate between the state and local government levels.

College Entrance Exam Scores

Scholastic Aptitude Test (SAT). Number of test takers and mean scores for 2015. *Source: The College Board, SAT, 2015 College-Bound Seniors, State Profile Reports*

American College Testing Program (ACT). Participation rate and mean scores for 2015. *Source: ACT, Inc., 2015 ACT National and State Scores*

Note: n/a indicates data not available.

School District Rankings

Number of Schools: Total number of schools in the district. *Source: U.S. Department of Education, National Center for Education Statistics, Common Core of Data, Public Elementary/Secondary School Universe Survey: School Year 2013-2014.*

Number of Teachers: Teachers are defined as individuals who provide instruction to pre-kindergarten, kindergarten, grades 1 through 12, or ungraded classes, or individuals who teach in an environment other than a classroom setting, and who maintain daily student attendance records. Numbers reported are full-time equivalents (FTE). *Source: U.S. Department of Education, National Center for Education Statistics, Common Core of Data, Local Education Agency (School District) Universe Survey: School Year 2013-2014.*

Number of Students: A student is an individual for whom instruction is provided in an elementary or secondary education program that is not an adult education program and is under the jurisdiction of a school, school system, or other education institution. *Source: U.S. Department of Education, National Center for Education Statistics, Common Core of Data, Local Education Agency (School District) Universe Survey: School Year 2013-2014*

Male Students: Percentage of students who are male. *Source: U.S. Department of Education, National Center for Education Statistics, Common Core of Data, Local Education Agency (School District) Universe Survey: School Year 2013-2014*

Female Students: Percentage of students who are female. *Source: U.S. Department of Education, National Center for Education Statistics, Common Core of Data, Local Education Agency (School District) Universe Survey: School Year 2013-2014*

White Students: Percentage of students who are white (a person having origins in any of the original peoples of Europe, North Africa, or the Middle East). Figures include non-Hispanic whites only. *Source: U.S. Department of Education, National Center for Education Statistics, Common Core of Data, Local Education Agency (School District) Universe Survey: School Year 2013-2014*

Black Students: Percentage of students who are black (a person having origins in any of the black racial groups of Africa). Figures include non-Hispanic blacks only. *Source: U.S. Department of Education, National Center for Education Statistics, Common Core of Data, Local Education Agency (School District) Universe Survey: School Year 2013-2014*

Asian Students: Percentage of students who are Asian (a person having origins in any of the original peoples of the Far east, Southeast Asia, and the Indian subcontinent. This includes, for example, China, India, Japan, Korea, and the Philippines). Figures include non-Hispanic Asians only. *Source: U.S. Department of Education, National Center for Education Statistics, Common Core of Data, Local Education Agency (School District) Universe Survey: School Year 2013-2014*

American Indian/Alaska Native Students: Percentage of students who are American Indian/Alaska Native Students (a person having origins in any of the original peoples of North America, and who maintains cultural identification through tribal affiliation or community recognition). Figures include non-Hispanic American Indian/Alaska Natives only. *Source: U.S. Department of Education, National Center for Education Statistics, Common Core of Data, Local Education Agency (School District) Universe Survey: School Year 2013-2014*

Hawaiian Native/Pacific Islander Students: Percentage of students who are Hawaiian Native/Pacific Islander (a person having origins in any of the original peoples of Hawaii, Guam, Samoa, or other Pacific Islands). Figures include non-Hispanic Hawaiian Native/Pacific Islanders only. *Source: U.S. Department of Education, National Center for Education Statistics, Common Core of Data, Local Education Agency (School District) Universe Survey: School Year 2013-2014*

Students who are Two or More Races: Percentage of students who are two or more races (a person identifying himself or herself as of two or more of the following race groups: White, Black, Asian, Native Hawaiian/Pacific Islander, or American Indian/Alaska Native). Some, but not all, reporting districts use this category. Figures include non-Hispanic, multiple-race students only. *Source: U.S. Department of Education, National Center for Education Statistics, Common Core of Data, Local Education Agency (School District) Universe Survey: School Year 2013-2014*

Hispanic Students: Percentage of students who are Hispanic (a person of Mexican, Puerto Rican, Cuban, Central or South American, or other Spanish culture or origin, regardless of race). *Source: U.S. Department of Education, National Center for Education Statistics, Common Core of Data, Local Education Agency (School District) Universe Survey: School Year 2013-2014*

Individual Education Program (IEP) Students: Percentage of students who have an Individual Education Program (IEP) which is a written instructional plan for students with disabilities designated as special education students under IDEA-Part B. The written instructional plan includes a statement of present levels of educational performance of a child; statement of annual goals, including short-term instructional objectives; statement of specific educational services to be provided and the extent to which the child will be able to participate in regular educational programs; the projected date for initiation and anticipated duration of services; the appropriate objectives, criteria and evaluation procedures; and the schedules for determining, on at least an annual basis, whether instructional objectives are being achieved. *Source: U.S. Department of Education, National Center for Education Statistics, Common Core of Data, Local Education Agency (School District) Universe Survey: School Year 2013-2014*

English Language Learner (ELL) Students: Percentage of students who are English Language Learners (ELL). Formerly referred to as Limited English Proficient (LEP). Students being served in appropriate programs of language assistance (e.g., English as a Second Language, High Intensity Language Training, bilingual education). Does not include pupils enrolled in a class to learn a language other than English. Also Limited-English-Proficient students are individuals who were not born in the United States or whose native language is a language other than English; or individuals who come from environments where a language other than English is dominant; or individuals who are American Indians and Alaskan Natives and who come from environments where a language other than English has had a significant impact on their level of English language proficiency; and who, by reason thereof, have sufficient difficulty speaking, reading, writing, or understanding the English language, to deny such individuals the opportunity to learn successfully in classrooms where the language of instruction is English or to participate fully in our society. *Source: U.S. Department of Education, National Center for Education Statistics, Common Core of Data, Local Education Agency (School District) Universe Survey: School Year 2013-2014*

Students Eligible for Free Lunch Program: Percentage of students that are eligible for the free lunch program. The free lunch program is defined as a program under the National School Lunch Act that provides cash subsidies for free lunches to students based on family size and income criteria. *Source: U.S. Department of Education, National Center for Education Statistics, Common Core of Data, Public Elementary/Secondary School Universe Survey: School Year 2013-2014*

Students Eligible for Reduced-Price Lunch Program: Percentage of students that are eligible for the reduced-price lunch program. A student who is eligible to participate in the reduced-price lunch program under the National School Lunch Act. *Source: U.S. Department of Education, National Center for Education Statistics, Common Core of Data, Public Elementary/Secondary School Universe Survey: School Year 2013-2014*

Student/Teacher Ratio: The number of students divided by the number of teachers (FTE). See Number of Students and Number of Teachers above for for information. *Source: U.S. Department of Education, National Center for Education Statistics, Common Core of Data, Local Education Agency (School District) Universe Survey: School Year 2013-2014*

Student/Librarian Ratio: The number of students divided by the number of library and media support staff. Library and media support staff are defined as staff members who render other professional library and media services; also includes library aides and those involved in library/media support. Their duties include selecting, preparing, caring for, and making available to instructional staff, equipment, films, filmstrips, transparencies, tapes, TV programs, and similar materials maintained separately or as part of an instructional materials center. Also included are activities in the audio-visual center, TV studio, related-work-study areas, and services provided by audio-visual personnel. Numbers are based on full-time equivalents. *Source: U.S. Department of Education, National Center for Education Statistics, Common Core of Data, Local Education Agency (School District) Universe Survey: School Year 2013-2014.*

Student/Counselor Ratio: The number of students divided by the number of guidance counselors. Guidance counselors are professional staff assigned specific duties and school time for any of the following activities in an elementary or secondary setting: counseling with students and parents; consulting with other staff members on learning problems; evaluating student abilities; assisting students in making educational and career choices; assisting students in personal and social development; providing referral assistance; and/or working with other staff members in planning and conducting guidance programs for students. The state applies its own standards in apportioning the aggregate of guidance counselors/directors into the elementary and secondary level components. Numbers reported are full-time equivalents. *Source: U.S. Department of Education, National Center for Education Statistics, Common Core of Data, Local Education Agency (School District) Universe Survey: School Year 2013-2014.*

Current Spending per Student: Expenditure for Instruction, Support Services, and Other Elementary/Secondary Programs. Includes salaries, employee benefits, purchased services, and supplies, as well as payments made by states on behalf of school districts. Also includes transfers made by school districts into their own retirement system. Excludes expenditure for Non-Elementary/Secondary Programs, debt service, capital outlay, and transfers to other governments or school districts. This item is formally called "Current Expenditures for Public Elementary/Secondary Education."

Values shown are dollars per pupil per year. They were calculated by dividing the total dollar amounts by the fall membership. Fall membership is comprised of the total student enrollment on October 1 (or the closest school day to October 1) for all grade levels (including prekindergarten and kindergarten) and ungraded pupils. Membership includes students both present and absent on the measurement day. *Source: U.S. Department of Education, National Center for Education Statistics, Common Core of Data, School District Finance Survey (F-33), Fiscal Year 2013.*

Total General Revenue per Student: The sum of revenue contributions emerging from local, state, and federal sources as reported in the district finance file.

Values shown are dollars per pupil per year. They were calculated by dividing the total dollar amounts by the fall membership. Fall membership is comprised of the total student enrollment on October 1 (or the closest school day to October 1) for all grade levels (including prekindergarten and kindergarten) and ungraded pupils. Membership includes students both present and absent on the measurement day. *Source: U.S. Department of Education, National Center for Education Statistics, Common Core of Data, School District Finance Survey (F-33), Fiscal Year 2013.*

Long-Term Debt per Student (end of FY): Includes long-term credit obligations of the school system or its parent government and all interest-bearing short-term (repayable within 1 year) credit obligations. Excludes non-interest bearing short-term obligations, interfund obligations, amounts owed in a trust agency capacity, advances and contingent loans from other governments, and rights of individuals to benefits from school system employee retirement funds.

Values shown are dollars per pupil per year. They were calculated by dividing the total dollar amounts at the end of the fiscal year by the fall membership. Fall membership is comprised of the total student enrollment on October 1 (or the closest school day to October 1) for all grade levels (including prekindergarten and kindergarten) and ungraded pupils. Membership includes students both present and absent on the measurement day. *Source: U.S. Department of Education, National Center for Education Statistics, Common Core of Data, School District Finance Survey (F-33), Fiscal Year 2013.*

Note: n/a indicates data not available.

National Assessment of Educational Progress (NAEP)

The National Assessment of Educational Progress (NAEP), also known as "The Nation's Report Card," is the only nationally representative and continuing assessment of what America's students know and can do in various subject areas. As a result of the "No Child Left Behind" legislation, all states are required to participate in NAEP.

For more information, visit the U.S. Department of Education, National Center for Education Statistics at http://nces.ed.gov/nationsreportcard.

Ancestry and Ethnicity Section

Places Covered

The ancestry and ethnicity profile section of this book covers the state and all counties and places with populations of 50,000 or more. Places included fall into one of the following categories:

Incorporated Places. Depending on the state, places are incorporated as either cities, towns, villages, boroughs, municipalities, independent cities, or corporations. A few municipalities have a form of government combined with another entity (e.g. county) and are listed as special cities or consolidated, unified, or metropolitan governments.

Census Designated Places (CDP). The U.S. Census Bureau defines a CDP as "a statistical entity," defined for each decennial census according to Census Bureau guidelines, comprising a densely settled concentration of population that is not within an incorporated place, but is locally identified by a name. CDPs are delineated cooperatively by state and local officials and the Census Bureau, following Census Bureau guidelines.

Minor Civil Divisions (called charter townships, districts, gores, grants, locations, plantations, purchases, reservations, towns, townships, and unorganized territories) for the states where the Census Bureau has determined that they serve as general-purpose governments. Those states are Connecticut, Maine, Massachusetts, Michigan, Minnesota, New Hampshire, New Jersey, New York, Pennsylvania, Rhode Island, Vermont, and Wisconsin. In some states incorporated municipalities are part of minor civil divisions and in some states they are independent of them.

Note: Several states have incorporated municipalities and minor civil divisions in the same county with the same name. Those communities are given separate entries (e.g. Burlington, New Jersey, in Burlington County will be listed under both the city and township of Burlington). A few states have Census Designated Places and minor civil divisions in the same county with the same name. Those communities are given separate entries (e.g. Bridgewater, Massachusetts, in Plymouth County will be listed under both the CDP and town of Bridgewater).

Source of Data

The ethnicities shown in this book were compiled from two different sources. Data for Race and Hispanic Origin was taken from Census 2010 Summary File 1 (SF1) while Ancestry data was taken from the American Community Survey (ACS) 2006-2010 Five-Year Estimate. The distinction is important because SF1 contains 100-percent data, which is the information compiled from the questions asked of all people and about every housing unit. ACS estimates are compiled from a sampling of households. The 2006-2010 Five-Year Estimate is based on data collected from January 1, 2006 to December 31, 2010.

The American Community Survey (ACS) is a relatively new survey conducted by the U.S. Census Bureau. It uses a series of monthly samples to produce annually updated data for the same small areas (census tracts and block groups) formerly surveyed via the decennial census long-form sample. While some version of this survey has been in the field since 1999, it was not fully implemented in terms of coverage until 2006. In 2005 it was expanded to cover all counties in the country and the 1-in-40 households sampling rate was first applied. The full implementation of the (household) sampling strategy for ACS entails having the survey mailed to about 250,000 households nationwide every month of every year and was begun in January 2005. In January 2006 sampling of group quarters was added to complete the sample as planned. In any given year about 2.5% (1 in 40) of U.S. households will receive the survey. Over any 5-year period about 1 in 8 households should receive the survey (as compared to about 1 in 6 that received the census long form in the 2000 census). Since receiving the survey is not the same as responding to it, the Bureau has adopted a strategy of sampling for non-response, resulting in something closer to 1 in 11 households actually participating in the survey over any 5-year period. For more information about the American Community Survey visit http://www.census.gov/acs/www.

Ancestry

Ancestry refers to a person's ethnic origin, heritage, descent, or "roots," which may reflect their place of birth or that of previous generations of their family. Some ethnic identities, such as "Egyptian" or "Polish" can be traced to geographic areas outside the United States, while other ethnicities such as "Pennsylvania German" or "Cajun" evolved in the United States.

The intent of the ancestry question in the ACS was not to measure the degree of attachment the respondent had to a particular ethnicity, but simply to establish that the respondent had a connection to and self-identified with a particular ethnic group. For example, a response of "Irish" might reflect total involvement in an Irish community or only a memory of ancestors several generations removed from the respondent.

The Census Bureau coded the responses into a numeric representation of over 1,000 categories. Responses initially were processed through an automated coding system; then, those that were not automatically assigned a code were coded by individuals trained in coding ancestry responses. The code list reflects the results of the Census Bureau's own research and consultations with many ethnic experts. Many decisions were made to determine the classification of responses. These decisions affected the grouping of the tabulated data. For example, the "Indonesian" category includes the responses of "Indonesian," "Celebesian," "Moluccan," and a number of other responses.

Ancestries Covered

- Afghan
- African, Sub-Saharan
    - African
    - Cape Verdean
    - Ethiopian
    - Ghanaian
    - Kenyan
    - Liberian
    - Nigerian
    - Senegalese
    - Sierra Leonean
    - Somalian
    - South African
    - Sudanese
    - Ugandan
    - Zimbabwean
    - Other Sub-Saharan African
- Albanian
- Alsatian
- American
- Arab
    - Arab
    - Egyptian
    - Iraqi
    - Jordanian
    - Lebanese
    - Moroccan
    - Palestinian
    - Syrian
    - Other Arab
- Armenian
- Assyrian/Chaldean/Syriac
- Australian
- Austrian
- Basque
- Belgian
- Brazilian
- British
- Bulgarian
- Cajun
- Canadian
- Carpatho Rusyn
- Celtic
- Croatian
- Cypriot
- Czech
- Czechoslovakian
- Danish
- Dutch
- Eastern European
- English
- Estonian
- European
- Finnish
- French, ex. Basque
- French Canadian
- German
- German Russian
- Greek
- Guyanese
- Hungarian
- Icelander
- Iranian
- Irish
- Israeli
- Italian
- Latvian
- Lithuanian
- Luxemburger
- Macedonian
- Maltese
- New Zealander
- Northern European
- Norwegian
- Pennsylvania German
- Polish
- Portuguese
- Romanian
- Russian
- Scandinavian
- Scotch-Irish
- Scottish
- Serbian
- Slavic
- Slovak
- Slovene
- Soviet Union
- Swedish
- Swiss
- Turkish
- Ukrainian
- Welsh
- West Indian, ex. Hispanic
    - Bahamian
    - Barbadian
    - Belizean
    - Bermudan
    - British West Indian
    - Dutch West Indian
    - Haitian
    - Jamaican
    - Trinidadian/Tobagonian
    - U.S. Virgin Islander
    - West Indian
    - Other West Indian
- Yugoslavian

The ancestry question allowed respondents to report one or more ancestry groups. Generally, only the first two responses reported were coded. If a response was in terms of a dual ancestry, for example, "Irish English," the person was assigned two codes, in this case one for Irish and another for English. However, in certain cases, multiple responses such as "French Canadian," "Scotch-Irish," "Greek Cypriot," and "Black Dutch" were assigned a single code reflecting their status as unique groups. If a person reported one of these unique groups in addition to another group, for example, "Scotch-Irish English," resulting in three terms, that person received one code for the unique group (Scotch-Irish) and another one for the remaining group (English). If a person reported "English Irish French," only English and Irish were coded. If there were more than two ancestries listed and one of the ancestries was a part of another, such as "German Bavarian Hawaiian," the responses were coded using the more detailed groups (Bavarian and Hawaiian).

The Census Bureau accepted "American" as a unique ethnicity if it was given alone or with one other ancestry. There were some groups such as "American Indian," "Mexican American," and "African American" that were coded and identified separately.

The ancestry question is asked for every person in the American Community Survey, regardless of age, place of birth, Hispanic origin, or race.

Although some people consider religious affiliation a component of ethnic identity, the ancestry question was not designed to collect any information concerning religion. Thus, if a religion was given as an answer to the ancestry question, it was listed in the "Other groups" category which is not shown in this book.

Ancestry should not be confused with a person's place of birth, although a person's place of birth and ancestry may be the same.

Hispanic Origin

The data on the Hispanic or Latino population were derived from answers to a Census 2010 question that was asked of all people. The terms "Spanish," "Hispanic origin," and "Latino" are used interchangeably. Some respondents identify with all three terms while others may identify with only one of these three specific terms. Hispanics or Latinos who identify with the terms "Spanish," "Hispanic," or "Latino" are those who classify themselves in one of the specific Spanish, Hispanic, or Latino categories listed on the questionnaire ("Mexican," "Puerto Rican," or "Cuban") as well as those who indicate that they are "other Spanish/Hispanic/Latino." People who do not identify with one of the specific origins listed on the questionnaire but indicate that they are "other Spanish/Hispanic/Latino" are those whose origins are from Spain, the Spanish-speaking countries of Central or South America, the Dominican Republic, or people identifying themselves generally as Spanish, Spanish-American, Hispanic, Hispano, Latino, and so on. All write-in responses to the "other Spanish/Hispanic/Latino" category were coded.

Hispanic Origins Covered

- Hispanic or Latino
  - Central American, ex. Mexican
    - Costa Rican
    - Guatemalan
    - Honduran
    - Nicaraguan
    - Panamanian
    - Salvadoran
    - Other Central American
  - Cuban
  - Dominican Republic
  - Mexican
  - Puerto Rican
  - South American
    - Argentinean
    - Bolivian
    - Chilean
    - Colombian
    - Ecuadorian
    - Paraguayan
    - Peruvian
    - Uruguayan
    - Venezuelan
    - Other South American
  - Other Hispanic or Latino

Origin can be viewed as the heritage, nationality group, lineage, or country of birth of the person or the person's parents or ancestors before their arrival in the United States. People who identify their origin as Hispanic, Latino, or Spanish may be of any race.

Ethnicities Based on Race

The data on race were derived from answers to the Census 2010 question on race that was asked of individuals in the United States. The Census Bureau collects racial data in accordance with guidelines provided by the U.S. Office of Management and Budget (OMB), and these data are based on self-identification.

The racial categories included in the census questionnaire generally reflect a social definition of race recognized in this country and not an attempt to define race biologically, anthropologically, or genetically. In addition, it is recognized that the categories of the race item include racial and national origin or sociocultural groups. People may choose to report more than one race to indicate their racial mixture, such as "American Indian" and "White." People who identify their origin as Hispanic, Latino, or Spanish may be of any race.

Racial Groups Covered

- **African-American/Black**
  - *Not Hispanic*
  - *Hispanic*
- **American Indian/Alaska Native**
  - *Not Hispanic*
  - *Hispanic*
  - Alaska Athabascan *(Ala. Nat.)*
  - Aleut *(Alaska Native)*
  - Apache
  - Arapaho
  - Blackfeet
  - Canadian/French Am. Indian
  - Central American Indian
  - Cherokee
  - Cheyenne
  - Chickasaw
  - Chippewa
  - Choctaw
  - Colville
  - Comanche
  - Cree
  - Creek
  - Crow
  - Delaware
  - Hopi
  - Houma
  - Inupiat *(Alaska Native)*
  - Iroquois
  - Kiowa
  - Lumbee
  - Menominee
  - Mexican American Indian
  - Navajo
  - Osage
  - Ottawa
  - Paiute
  - Pima
  - Potawatomi
  - Pueblo
  - Puget Sound Salish
  - Seminole
  - Shoshone
  - Sioux
  - South American Indian
  - Spanish American Indian
  - Tlingit-Haida *(Alaska Native)*
  - Tohono O'Odham
  - Tsimshian *(Alaska Native)*
  - Ute
  - Yakama
  - Yaqui
  - Yuman
  - Yup'ik *(Alaska Native)*
- **Asian**
  - *Not Hispanic*
  - *Hispanic*
  - Bangladeshi
  - Bhutanese
  - Burmese
  - Cambodian
  - Chinese, ex. Taiwanese
  - Filipino
  - Hmong
  - Indian
  - Indonesian
  - Japanese
  - Korean
  - Laotian
  - Malaysian
  - Nepalese
  - Pakistani
  - Sri Lankan
  - Taiwanese
  - Thai
  - Vietnamese
- **Hawaii Native/Pacific Islander**
  - *Not Hispanic*
  - *Hispanic*
  - Fijian
  - Guamanian/Chamorro
  - Marshallese
  - Native Hawaiian
  - Samoan
  - Tongan
- **White**
  - *Not Hispanic*
  - *Hispanic*

African American or Black: A person having origins in any of the Black racial groups of Africa. It includes people who indicated their race(s) as "Black, African Am., or Negro" or reported entries such as African American, Kenyan, Nigerian, or Haitian.

American Indian or Alaska Native: A person having origins in any of the original peoples of North and South America (including Central America) and who maintains tribal affiliation or community attachment. This category includes people who indicated their race(s) as "American Indian or Alaska Native" or reported their enrolled or principal tribe, such as Navajo, Blackfeet, Inupiat, Yup'ik, or Central American Indian groups or South American Indian groups.

Asian: A person having origins in any of the original peoples of the Far East, Southeast Asia, or the Indian subcontinent, including, for example, Cambodia, China, India, Japan, Korea, Malaysia, Pakistan, the Philippine Islands, Thailand, and Vietnam. It includes people who indicated their race(s) as "Asian" or reported entries such as "Asian Indian," "Chinese," "Filipino," "Korean," "Japanese," "Vietnamese," and "Other Asian" or provided other detailed Asian responses.

Native Hawaiian or Other Pacific Islander: A person having origins in any of the original peoples of Hawaii, Guam, Samoa, or other Pacific Islands. It includes people who indicated their race(s) as "Pacific Islander" or reported entries such as "Native Hawaiian," "Guamanian or Chamorro," "Samoan," and "Other Pacific Islander" or provided other detailed Pacific Islander responses.

White: A person having origins in any of the original peoples of Europe, the Middle East, or North Africa. It includes people who indicated their race(s) as "White" or reported entries such as Irish, German, Italian, Lebanese, Arab, Moroccan, or Caucasian.

Profiles

Each profile shows the name of the place, the county (if a place spans more than one county, the county that holds the majority of the population is shown), and the 2010 population (based on 100-percent data from Census 2010 Summary File 1). The rest of each profile is comprised of all 218 ethnicities grouped into three sections: ancestry; Hispanic origin; and race.

Column one displays the ancestry/Hispanic origin/race name, column two displays the number of people reporting each ancestry/Hispanic origin/race, and column three is the percent of the total population reporting each ancestry/Hispanic origin/race. The population figure shown is used to calculate the value in the "%" column for ethnicities based on race and Hispanic origin. The 2006-2010 estimated population figure from the American Community Survey (not shown) is used to calculate the value in the "%" column for all other ancestries.

For ethnicities in the ancestries group, the value in the "Number" column includes multiple ancestries reported. For example, if a person reported a multiple ancestry such as "French Danish," that response was counted twice in the tabulations, once in the French category and again in the Danish category. Thus, the sum of the counts is not the total population but the total of all responses. Numbers in parentheses indicate the number of people reporting a single ancestry. People reporting a single ancestry includes all people who reported only one ethnic group such as "German." Also included in this category are people with only a multiple-term response such as "Scotch-Irish" who are assigned a single code because they represent one distinct group. For example, the count for German would be interpreted as "The number of people who reported that German was their only ancestry."

For ethnicities based on Hispanic origin, the value in the "Number" column represents the number of people who reported being Mexican, Puerto Rican, Cuban or other Spanish/Hispanic/ Latino (all written-in responses were coded). All ethnicities based on Hispanic origin can be of any race.

For ethnicities based on race data the value in the "Number" column represents the total number of people who reported each category alone or in combination with one or more other race categories. This number represents the maximum number of people reporting and therefore the individual race categories may add up to more than the total population because people may be included in more than one category. The figures in parentheses show the number of people that reported that particular ethnicity alone, not in combination with any other race. For example, in Alabama, the entry for Korean shows 8,320 in parentheses and 10,624 in the "Number" column. This means that 8,320 people reported being Korean alone and 10,624 people reported being Korean alone or in combination with one or more other races.

Rankings

In the rankings section, each ethnicity has three tables. The first table shows the top 10 places sorted by ethnic population (based on all places, regardless of total population), the second table shows the top 10 places sorted by percent of the total population (based on all places, regardless of total population), the third table shows the top 10 places sorted by percent of the total population (based on places with total population of 50,000 or more).

Within each table, column one displays the place name, the state, and the county (if a place spans more than one county, the county that holds the majority of the population is shown). Column one in the first table displays the state only. Column two displays the number of people reporting each ancestry (includes people reporting multiple ancestries), Hispanic origin, or race (alone or in combination with any other race). Column three is the percent of the total population reporting each ancestry, Hispanic origin or race. For tables representing ethnicities based on race or Hispanic origin, the 100-percent population figure from SF1 is used to calculate the value in the "%" column. For all other ancestries, the 2006-2010 five-year estimated population figure from the American Community Survey is used to calculate the value in the "%" column.

Alphabetical Ethnicity Cross-Reference Guide

Afghan *see* Ancestry–Afghan
African *see* Ancestry–African, Sub-Saharan: African
African-American *see* Race–African-American/Black
African-American: Hispanic *see* Race–African-American/Black: Hispanic
African-American: Not Hispanic *see* Race–African-American/Black: Not Hispanic
Alaska Athabascan *see* Race–Alaska Native: Alaska Athabascan
Alaska Native *see* Race–American Indian/Alaska Native
Alaska Native: Hispanic *see* Race–American Indian/Alaska Native: Hispanic
Alaska Native: Not Hispanic *see* Race–American Indian/Alaska Native: Not Hispanic
Albanian *see* Ancestry–Albanian
Aleut *see* Race–Alaska Native: Aleut
Alsatian *see* Ancestry–Alsatian
American *see* Ancestry–American
American Indian *see* Race–American Indian/Alaska Native
American Indian: Hispanic *see* Race–American Indian/Alaska Native: Hispanic
American Indian: Not Hispanic *see* Race–American Indian/Alaska Native: Not Hispanic
Apache *see* Race–American Indian: Apache
Arab *see* Ancestry–Arab: Arab
Arab: Other *see* Ancestry–Arab: Other
Arapaho *see* Race–American Indian: Arapaho
Argentinean *see* Hispanic Origin–South American: Argentinean
Armenian *see* Ancestry–Armenian
Asian *see* Race–Asian
Asian Indian *see* Race–Asian: Indian
Asian: Hispanic *see* Race–Asian: Hispanic
Asian: Not Hispanic *see* Race–Asian: Not Hispanic
Assyrian *see* Ancestry–Assyrian/Chaldean/Syriac
Australian *see* Ancestry–Australian
Austrian *see* Ancestry–Austrian
Bahamian *see* Ancestry–West Indian: Bahamian, except Hispanic
Bangladeshi *see* Race–Asian: Bangladeshi
Barbadian *see* Ancestry–West Indian: Barbadian, except Hispanic
Basque *see* Ancestry–Basque
Belgian *see* Ancestry–Belgian
Belizean *see* Ancestry–West Indian: Belizean, except Hispanic
Bermudan *see* Ancestry–West Indian: Bermudan, except Hispanic
Bhutanese *see* Race–Asian: Bhutanese
Black *see* Race–African-American/Black
Black: Hispanic *see* Race–African-American/Black: Hispanic
Black: Not Hispanic *see* Race–African-American/Black: Not Hispanic
Blackfeet *see* Race–American Indian: Blackfeet
Bolivian *see* Hispanic Origin–South American: Bolivian
Brazilian *see* Ancestry–Brazilian
British *see* Ancestry–British

British West Indian *see* Ancestry–West Indian: British West Indian, except Hispanic
Bulgarian *see* Ancestry–Bulgarian
Burmese *see* Race–Asian: Burmese
Cajun *see* Ancestry–Cajun
Cambodian *see* Race–Asian: Cambodian
Canadian *see* Ancestry–Canadian
Canadian/French American Indian *see* Race–American Indian: Canadian/French American Indian
Cape Verdean *see* Ancestry–African, Sub-Saharan: Cape Verdean
Carpatho Rusyn *see* Ancestry–Carpatho Rusyn
Celtic *see* Ancestry–Celtic
Central American *see* Hispanic Origin–Central American, except Mexican
Central American Indian *see* Race–American Indian: Central American Indian
Central American: Other *see* Hispanic Origin–Central American: Other Central American
Chaldean *see* Ancestry–Assyrian/Chaldean/Syriac
Chamorro *see* Race–Hawaii Native/Pacific Islander: Guamanian or Chamorro
Cherokee *see* Race–American Indian: Cherokee
Cheyenne *see* Race–American Indian: Cheyenne
Chickasaw *see* Race–American Indian: Chickasaw
Chilean *see* Hispanic Origin–South American: Chilean
Chinese (except Taiwanese) *see* Race–Asian: Chinese, except Taiwanese
Chippewa *see* Race–American Indian: Chippewa
Choctaw *see* Race–American Indian: Choctaw
Colombian *see* Hispanic Origin–South American: Colombian
Colville *see* Race–American Indian: Colville
Comanche *see* Race–American Indian: Comanche
Costa Rican *see* Hispanic Origin–Central American: Costa Rican
Cree *see* Race–American Indian: Cree
Creek *see* Race–American Indian: Creek
Croatian *see* Ancestry–Croatian
Crow *see* Race–American Indian: Crow
Cuban *see* Hispanic Origin–Cuban
Cypriot *see* Ancestry–Cypriot
Czech *see* Ancestry–Czech
Czechoslovakian *see* Ancestry–Czechoslovakian
Danish *see* Ancestry–Danish
Delaware *see* Race–American Indian: Delaware
Dominican Republic *see* Hispanic Origin–Dominican Republic
Dutch *see* Ancestry–Dutch
Dutch West Indian *see* Ancestry–West Indian: Dutch West Indian, except Hispanic
Eastern European *see* Ancestry–Eastern European
Ecuadorian *see* Hispanic Origin–South American: Ecuadorian
Egyptian *see* Ancestry–Arab: Egyptian
English *see* Ancestry–English
Eskimo *see* Race–Alaska Native: Inupiat
Estonian *see* Ancestry–Estonian
Ethiopian *see* Ancestry–African, Sub-Saharan: Ethiopian
European *see* Ancestry–European
Fijian *see* Race–Hawaii Native/Pacific Islander: Fijian
Filipino *see* Race–Asian: Filipino
Finnish *see* Ancestry–Finnish
French (except Basque) *see* Ancestry–French, except Basque
French Canadian *see* Ancestry–French Canadian
German *see* Ancestry–German
German Russian *see* Ancestry–German Russian
Ghanaian *see* Ancestry–African, Sub-Saharan: Ghanaian
Greek *see* Ancestry–Greek
Guamanian *see* Race–Hawaii Native/Pacific Islander: Guamanian or Chamorro
Guatemalan *see* Hispanic Origin–Central American: Guatemalan
Guyanese *see* Ancestry–Guyanese
Haitian *see* Ancestry–West Indian: Haitian, except Hispanic
Hawaii Native *see* Race–Hawaii Native/Pacific Islander
Hawaii Native: Hispanic *see* Race–Hawaii Native/Pacific Islander: Hispanic

Hawaii Native: Not Hispanic *see* Race–Hawaii Native/Pacific Islander: Not Hispanic
Hispanic or Latino: *see* Hispanic Origin–Hispanic or Latino (of any race)
Hispanic or Latino: Other *see* Hispanic Origin–Other Hispanic or Latino
Hmong *see* Race–Asian: Hmong
Honduran *see* Hispanic Origin–Central American: Honduran
Hopi *see* Race–American Indian: Hopi
Houma *see* Race–American Indian: Houma
Hungarian *see* Ancestry–Hungarian
Icelander *see* Ancestry–Icelander
Indonesian *see* Race–Asian: Indonesian
Inupiat *see* Race–Alaska Native: Inupiat
Iranian *see* Ancestry–Iranian
Iraqi *see* Ancestry–Arab: Iraqi
Irish *see* Ancestry–Irish
Iroquois *see* Race–American Indian: Iroquois
Israeli *see* Ancestry–Israeli
Italian *see* Ancestry–Italian
Jamaican *see* Ancestry–West Indian: Jamaican, except Hispanic
Japanese *see* Race–Asian: Japanese
Jordanian *see* Ancestry–Arab: Jordanian
Kenyan *see* Ancestry–African, Sub-Saharan: Kenyan
Kiowa *see* Race–American Indian: Kiowa
Korean *see* Race–Asian: Korean
Laotian *see* Race–Asian: Laotian
Latvian *see* Ancestry–Latvian
Lebanese *see* Ancestry–Arab: Lebanese
Liberian *see* Ancestry–African, Sub-Saharan: Liberian
Lithuanian *see* Ancestry–Lithuanian
Lumbee *see* Race–American Indian: Lumbee
Luxemburger *see* Ancestry–Luxemburger
Macedonian *see* Ancestry–Macedonian
Malaysian *see* Race–Asian: Malaysian
Maltese *see* Ancestry–Maltese
Marshallese *see* Race–Hawaii Native/Pacific Islander: Marshallese
Menominee *see* Race–American Indian: Menominee
Mexican *see* Hispanic Origin–Mexican
Mexican American Indian *see* Race–American Indian: Mexican American Indian
Moroccan *see* Ancestry–Arab: Moroccan
Native Hawaiian *see* Race–Hawaii Native/Pacific Islander: Native Hawaiian
Navajo *see* Race–American Indian: Navajo
Nepalese *see* Race–Asian: Nepalese
New Zealander *see* Ancestry–New Zealander
Nicaraguan *see* Hispanic Origin–Central American: Nicaraguan
Nigerian *see* Ancestry–African, Sub-Saharan: Nigerian
Northern European *see* Ancestry–Northern European
Norwegian *see* Ancestry–Norwegian
Osage *see* Race–American Indian: Osage
Ottawa *see* Race–American Indian: Ottawa
Pacific Islander *see* Race–Hawaii Native/Pacific Islander
Pacific Islander: Hispanic *see* Race–Hawaii Native/Pacific Islander: Hispanic
Pacific Islander: Not Hispanic *see* Race–Hawaii Native/Pacific Islander: Not Hispanic
Paiute *see* Race–American Indian: Paiute
Pakistani *see* Race–Asian: Pakistani
Palestinian *see* Ancestry–Arab: Palestinian
Panamanian *see* Hispanic Origin–Central American: Panamanian
Paraguayan *see* Hispanic Origin–South American: Paraguayan
Pennsylvania German *see* Ancestry–Pennsylvania German
Peruvian *see* Hispanic Origin–South American: Peruvian
Pima *see* Race–American Indian: Pima
Polish *see* Ancestry–Polish
Portuguese *see* Ancestry–Portuguese
Potawatomi *see* Race–American Indian: Potawatomi

Pueblo *see* Race–American Indian: Pueblo
Puerto Rican *see* Hispanic Origin–Puerto Rican
Puget Sound Salish *see* Race–American Indian: Puget Sound Salish
Romanian *see* Ancestry–Romanian
Russian *see* Ancestry–Russian
Salvadoran *see* Hispanic Origin–Central American: Salvadoran
Samoan *see* Race–Hawaii Native/Pacific Islander: Samoan
Scandinavian *see* Ancestry–Scandinavian
Scotch-Irish *see* Ancestry–Scotch-Irish
Scottish *see* Ancestry–Scottish
Seminole *see* Race–American Indian: Seminole
Senegalese *see* Ancestry–African, Sub-Saharan: Senegalese
Serbian *see* Ancestry–Serbian
Shoshone *see* Race–American Indian: Shoshone
Sierra Leonean *see* Ancestry–African, Sub-Saharan: Sierra Leonean
Sioux *see* Race–American Indian: Sioux
Slavic *see* Ancestry–Slavic
Slovak *see* Ancestry–Slovak
Slovene *see* Ancestry–Slovene
Somalian *see* Ancestry–African, Sub-Saharan: Somalian
South African *see* Ancestry–African, Sub-Saharan: South African
South American *see* Hispanic Origin–South American
South American Indian *see* Race–American Indian: South American Indian
South American: Other *see* Hispanic Origin–South American: Other South American
Soviet Union *see* Ancestry–Soviet Union
Spanish American Indian *see* Race–American Indian: Spanish American Indian
Sri Lankan *see* Race–Asian: Sri Lankan
Sub-Saharan African *see* Ancestry–African, Sub-Saharan
Sub-Saharan African: Other *see* Ancestry–African, Sub-Saharan: Other
Sudanese *see* Ancestry–African, Sub-Saharan: Sudanese
Swedish *see* Ancestry–Swedish
Swiss *see* Ancestry–Swiss
Syriac *see* Ancestry–Assyrian/Chaldean/Syriac
Syrian *see* Ancestry–Arab: Syrian
Taiwanese *see* Race–Asian: Taiwanese
Thai *see* Race–Asian: Thai
Tlingit-Haida *see* Race–Alaska Native: Tlingit-Haida
Tohono O'Odham *see* Race–American Indian: Tohono O'Odham
Tongan *see* Race–Hawaii Native/Pacific Islander: Tongan
Trinidadian and Tobagonian *see* Ancestry–West Indian: Trinidadian and Tobagonian, except Hispanic
Tsimshian *see* Race–Alaska Native: Tsimshian
Turkish *see* Ancestry–Turkish
U.S. Virgin Islander *see* Ancestry–West Indian: U.S. Virgin Islander, except Hispanic
Ugandan *see* Ancestry–African, Sub-Saharan: Ugandan
Ukrainian *see* Ancestry–Ukrainian
Uruguayan *see* Hispanic Origin–South American: Uruguayan
Ute *see* Race–American Indian: Ute
Venezuelan *see* Hispanic Origin–South American: Venezuelan
Vietnamese *see* Race–Asian: Vietnamese
Welsh *see* Ancestry–Welsh
West Indian *see* Ancestry–West Indian: West Indian, except Hispanic
West Indian (except Hispanic) *see* Ancestry–West Indian, except Hispanic
West Indian: Other *see* Ancestry–West Indian: Other, except Hispanic
White *see* Race–White
White: Hispanic *see* Race–White: Hispanic
White: Not Hispanic *see* Race–White: Not Hispanic
Yakama *see* Race–American Indian: Yakama
Yaqui *see* Race–American Indian: Yaqui
Yugoslavian *see* Ancestry–Yugoslavian
Yuman *see* Race–American Indian: Yuman
Yup'ik *see* Race–Alaska Native: Yup'ik
Zimbabwean *see* Ancestry–African, Sub-Saharan: Zimbabwean

Climate Section

SOURCES OF THE DATA

The National Climactic Data Center (NCDC) has two main classes or types of weather stations; first-order stations which are staffed by professional meteorologists and cooperative stations which are staffed by volunteers. All National Weather Service (NWS) stations included in this book are first-order stations.

The data in the climate section is compiled from several sources. The majority comes from the original NCDC computer tapes (DSI-3220 Summary of Month Cooperative). This data was used to create the entire table for each cooperative station and part of each National Weather Service station. The remainder of the data for each NWS station comes from the International Station Meteorological Climate Summary, Version 4.0, September 1996, which is also available from the NCDC.

Storm events come from the NCDC Storm Events Database which is accessible over the Internet at https://www.ncdc.noaa.gov/stormevents.

WEATHER STATION TABLES

The weather station tables are grouped by type (National Weather Service and Cooperative) and then arranged alphabetically. The station name is almost always a place name, and is shown here just as it appears in NCDC data. The station name is followed by the county in which the station is located (or by county equivalent name), the elevation of the station (at the time beginning of the thirty year period) and the latitude and longitude.

The National Weather Service Station tables contain 32 data elements which were compiled from two different sources, the International Station Meteorological Climate Summary (ISMCS) and NCDC DSI-3220 data tapes. The following 13 elements are from the ISMCS: maximum precipitation, minimum precipitation, maximum snowfall, maximum 24-hour snowfall, thunderstorm days, foggy days, predominant sky cover, relative humidity (morning and afternoon), dewpoint, wind speed and direction, and maximum wind gust. The remaining 19 elements come from the DSI-3220 data tapes. The period of record (POR) for data from the DSI-3220 data tapes is 1980-2009. The POR for ISMCS data varies from station to station and appears in a note below each station.

The Cooperative Station tables contain 19 data elements which were all compiled from the DSI-3220 data tapes with a POR of 1980-2009.

WEATHER ELEMENTS (NWS AND COOPERATIVE STATIONS)

The following elements were compiled by the editor from the NCDC DSI-3220 data tapes using a period of record of 1980-2009.

The average temperatures (maximum, minimum, and mean) are the average (see Methodology below) of those temperatures for all available values for a given month. For example, for a given station the average maximum temperature for July is the arithmetic average of all available maximum July temperatures for that station. (Maximum means the highest recorded temperature, minimum means the lowest recorded temperature, and mean means an arithmetic average temperature.)

The extreme maximum temperature is the highest temperature recorded in each month over the period 1980-2009. The extreme minimum temperature is the lowest temperature recorded in each month over the same time period. The extreme maximum daily precipitation is the largest amount of precipitation recorded over a 24-hour period in each month from 1980-2009. The maximum snow depth is the maximum snow depth recorded in each month over the period 1980-2009.

The days for maximum temperature and minimum temperature are the average number of days those criteria were met for all available instances. The symbol ≥ means greater than or equal to, the symbol ≤ means less than or equal to. For example, for a given station, the number of days the maximum temperature was greater than or equal to 90°F in July, is just an arithmetic average of the number of days in all the available Julys for that station.

Heating and cooling degree days are based on the median temperature for a given day and its variance from 65°F. For example, for a given station if the day's high temperature was 50°F and the day's low temperature was 30°F, the median (midpoint) temperature was 40°F. 40°F is 25 degrees below 65°F, hence on this day there would be 25 heating degree days. This also applies for cooling degree days. For example, for a given station if the day's high temperature was 80°F and the day's low temperature was 70°F, the median (midpoint) temperature was 75°F. 75°F is 10 degrees above 65°F, hence on this day there would be 10 cooling degree days. All heating and/or cooling degree days in a month are summed for the month giving respective totals for each element for that month. These sums for a given month for a given station over the past thirty years are again summed and then arithmetically averaged. It should be noted that the heating and cooling degree days do not cancel each other out. It is possible to have both for a given station in the same month.

Precipitation data is computed the same as heating and cooling degree days. Mean precipitation and mean snowfall are arithmetic averages of cumulative totals for the month. All available values for the thirty year period for a given month for a given station are summed and then divided by the number of values. The same is true for days of greater than or equal to 0.1", 0.5",and 1.0" of precipitation, and days of greater than or equal to 1.0" of snow depth on the ground. The word trace appears for precipitation and snowfall amounts that are too small to measure.

Finally, remember that all values presented in the tables and the rankings are averages, maximums, or minimums of available data (see Methodology below) for that specific data element for the last thirty years (1980-2009).

WEATHER ELEMENTS (NWS STATIONS ONLY)

The following elements were taken directly from the International Station Meteorological Climate Summary. The periods of records vary per station and are noted at the bottom of each table.

Maximum precipitation, minimum precipitation, maximum snowfall, maximum snow depth, maximum 24-hour snowfall, thunderstorm days, foggy days, relative humidity (morning and afternoon), dewpoint, prevailing wind speed and direction, and maximum wind gust are all self-explanatory.

The word trace appears for precipitation and snowfall amounts that are too small to measure.

Predominant sky cover contains four possible entries: CLR (clear); SCT (scattered); BRK (broken); and OVR (overcast).

INCLUSION CRITERIA—HOW STATIONS WERE SELECTED

The basic criteria is that a station must have data for temperature, precipitation, heating and cooling degree days of sufficient quantity in order to create a meaningful average. More specifically, the definition of sufficiency here has two parts. First, there must be 22 values for a given data element, and second, ten of the nineteen elements included in the table must pass this sufficiency test. For example, in regard to mean maximum temperature (the first element on every data table), a given station needs to have a value for every month of at least 22 of the last thirty years in order to meet the criteria, and, in addition, every station included must have at least ten of the nineteen elements with at least this minimal level of completeness in order to fulfill the criteria. We then removed stations that were geographically close together, giving preference to stations with better data quality.

METHODOLOGY

The following discussion applies only to data compiled from the NCDC DSI-3220 data tapes and excludes weather elements that are extreme maximums or minimums.

The data is based on an arithmetic average of all available data for a specific data element at a given station. For example, the average maximum daily high temperature during July for any given station was abstracted from NCDC source tapes for the thirty Julys, starting in July, 1980 and ending in July, 2009. These thirty figures were then summed and divided by thirty to produce an arithmetic average. As might be expected, there were not thirty values for every data element on every table. For a variety of reasons, NCDC data is sometimes incomplete. Thus the following standards were established.

For those data elements where there were 26-30 values, the data was taken to be essentially complete and an average was computed. For data elements where there were 22-25 values, the data was taken as being partly complete but still valid enough to use to compute an average. Such averages are shown in ***bold italic*** type to indicate that there was less than 26 values. For the few data elements where there were not even 22 values, no average was computed and 'na' appears in the space. If any of the twelve months for a given data element reported a value of 'na', no annual average was computed and the annual average was reported as 'na' as well.

Thus the basic computational methodology used is designed to provide an arithmetic average. Because of this, such a pure arithmetic average is somewhat different from the special type of average (called a "normal") which NCDC procedures produces and appears in federal publications.

Perhaps the best outline of the contrasting normalization methodology is found in the following paragraph (which appears as part of an NCDC technical document titled, CLIM81 1961-1990 NORMALS TD-9641 prepared by Lewis France of NCDC in May, 1992):

Normals have been defined as the arithmetic mean of a climatological element computed over a long time period. International agreements eventually led to the decision that the appropriate time period would be three consecutive decades (Guttman, 1989). The data record should be consistent (have no changes in location, instruments, observation practices, etc.; these are identified here as "exposure changes") and have no missing values so a normal will reflect the actual average climatic conditions. If any significant exposure changes have occurred, the data record is said to be "inhomogeneous," and the normal may not reflect a true climatic average. Such data need to be adjusted to remove the nonclimatic inhomogeneities. The resulting (adjusted) record is then said to be "homogeneous." If no exposure changes have occurred at a station, the normal is calculated simply by averaging the appropriate 30 values from the 1961-1990 record.

In the main, there are two "inhomogeneities" that NCDC is correcting for with normalization: adjusting for variances in time of day of observation (at the so-called First Order stations data is based on midnight to midnight observation times and this practice is not necessarily followed at cooperative stations which are staffed by volunteers), and second, estimating data that is either missing or incongruent.

The editors had some concerns regarding the comparative results of the two methodologies. Would our methodology produce strikingly different results than NCDC's? To allay concerns, results of the two processes were compared for the time period normalized results are available (1971-2000). In short, what was found was that the answer to this question is no. Never the less, users should be aware that because of both the time period covered (1980-2009) and the methodology used, data is not compatible with data from other sources.

POTENTIAL CAUTIONS

First, as with any statistical reference work of this type, users need to be aware of the source of the data. The information here comes from NOAA, and it is the most comprehensive and reliable core data available. Although it is the best, it is not perfect. Most weather stations are staffed by volunteers, times of observation sometimes vary, stations occasionally are moved (especially over a thirty year period), equipment is changed or upgraded, and all of these factors affect the uniformity of the data. The editors do not attempt to correct for these factors, and this data is not intended for either climatologists or atmospheric scientists. Users with concerns about data collection and reporting protocols are both referred to NCDC technical documentation.

Second, users need to be aware of the methodology here which is described above. Although this methodology has produced fully satisfactory results, it is not directly compatible with other methodologies, hence variances in the results published here and those which appear in other publications will doubtlessly arise.

Third, is the trap of that informal logical fallacy known as "hasty generalization," and its corollaries. This may involve presuming the future will be like the past (specifically, next year will be an average year), or it may involve misunderstanding the limitations of an arithmetic average, but more interestingly, it may involve those mistakes made most innocently by generalizing informally on too broad a basis. As weather is highly localized, the data should be taken in that context. A weather station collects data about climatic conditions at that spot, and that spot may or may not be an effective paradigm for an entire town or area.

About Ohio

Governor . . . . John Richard Kasich Jr (R)
Lt Governor . . . . Mary Taylor (R)

State Capital	Columbus
Date of Statehood	March 1, 1803 (17th state)
State Nickname	The Buckeye State
Demonym	Ohioan
Largest City	Columbus
Highest Point	Campbell Hill (1,549 feet)
Lowest Point	Ohio River at Indiana border (455 feet)
Time Zone	Eastern
State Amphibian	Spotted Salamander *(Ambystoma maculatum)*
State Artifact	The Adena Pipe
State Beverage	Tomato Juice
State Bicentennial Bridge	Blaine Hill bridge built in 1828 (Belmont county)
State Bird	Northern Cardinal *(Cardinalis cardinalis)*
State Flower	Red Carnation *(Dianthus caryophyllus)*
State Fossil	Isotelus (Trilobite)
State Frog	Bullfrog *(Rana catesbeiana)*
State Fruit	Tomato
State Gemstone	Ohio Flint
State Insect	Ladybug (no specific species)
State Mammal	White-tailed Deer *(Odocoileus virginianus)*
State Motto	"With God All Things Are Possible"
State Native Fruit	Pawpaw *(Asimina triloba)*
State Prehistoric Monument	Newark Earthworks
State Reptile	Black Racer Snake *(Coluber constrictor constrictor)*
State Rock Song	"Hang on Sloopy"
State Song	"Beautiful Ohio"
State Tree	Ohio Buckeye *(Aesculus glabra)*
State Wildflower	White Trillium *(Trillium grandiflorum)*

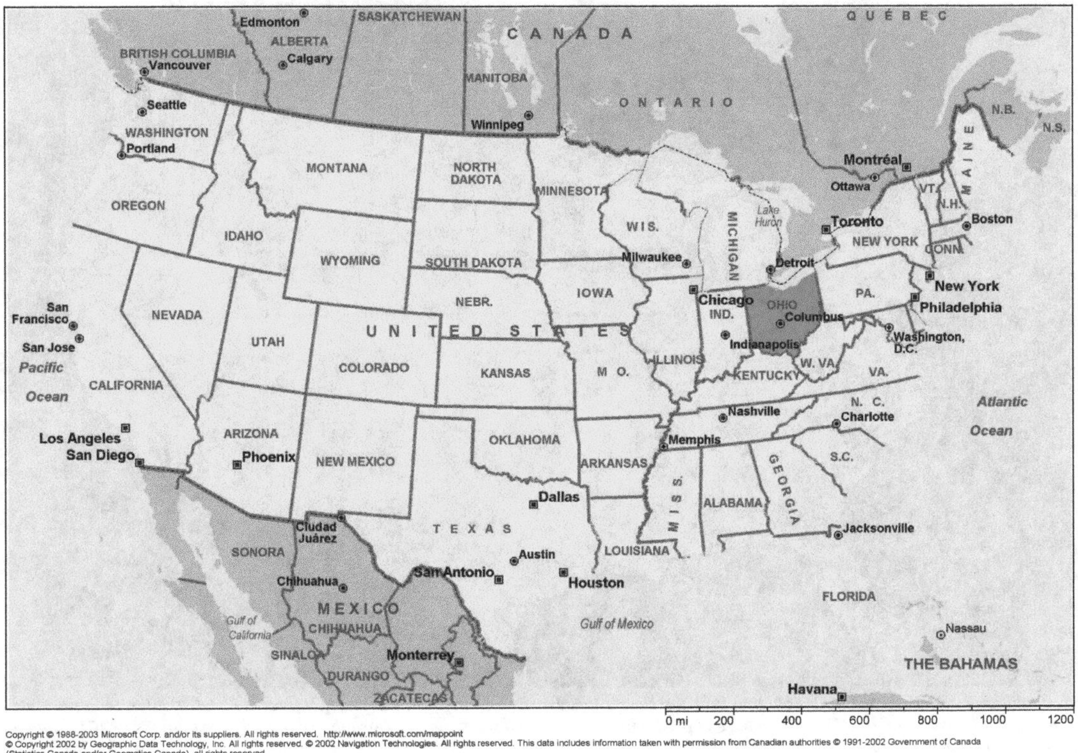

Columbus, pictured above, is the capitol of Ohio. It is the state's largest city and the 32nd largest metropolitan statistical area in the United States. In Greek Revival style, the Ohio Statehouse is predominant at the bottom of the photograph. Columbus was founded in 1812, and named for explorer Christopher Columbus.

Cleveland, shown at top, is the state's second most populous city, located on the southern shore of Lake Erie, about 60 miles west of the Pennsylvania state border. Ohio State University, pictured bottom, in located in the city of Columbus. It was founded in 1873, and is the third largest university campus in the United States.

Toledo, pictured top, on the Maumee River, is the fourth most populous city in Ohio. It is nicknamed "The Glass City" for its glass industry. The skyline of Cincinnati, the third largest city in the state, is shown in the bottom photo. Located on the Ohio River, at the border between Ohio and Kentucky, it is home to major league baseball team the Cincinnati Reds, whose stadium can be seen in the center of the photograph.

Cincinnati's Music Hall, pictured top, was completed in 1878. It is home to the city's ballet, symphony and pops orchestras, and opera. It is both a National Historic Landmark and included on the Nation's Trust for Historic Preservation. The bottom photo showcases the Victorian architecture in Dayton, the state's sixth largest city.

Agriculture is an important piece of Ohio's economy. The state's corn crop, pictured top, ranks ninth in the nation. Soybeans, pictured bottom, ranks sixth in the nation.

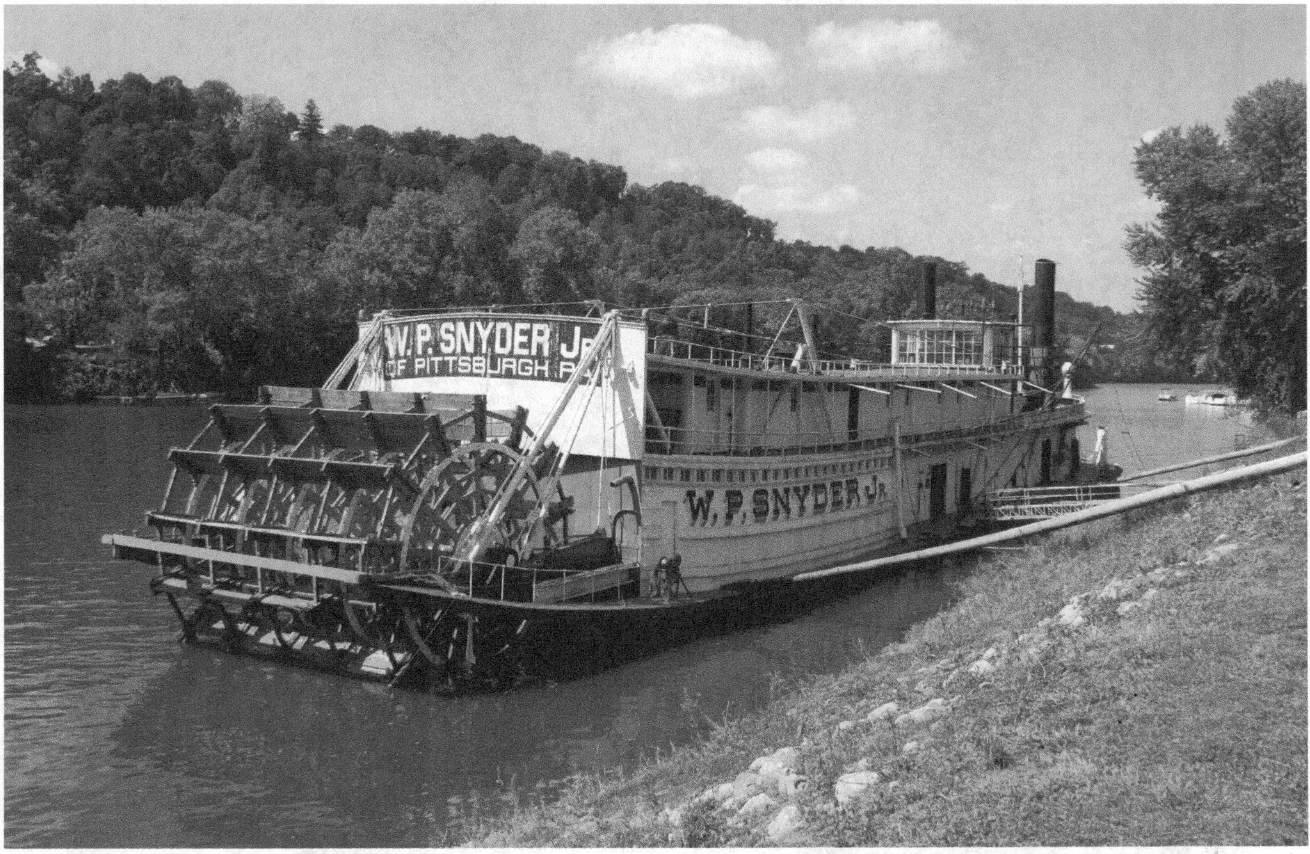

Pictured top is the summer home of Rutherford B. Hayes, 19th U.S. President. Located in Fremont, Ohio, Spiegel Grove, as the site is called, is on the National Register of Historic Places and a National Historic Landmark. W. P. Snyder Jr., *pictured bottom, is a historic towboat moored on the Muskingum River in Marietta, Ohio. A National Historic Landmark, she is the only intact, steam-driven sternwheel towboat still on the nation's river system.*

Pictured here is a towboat pushing coal-laden barges along the Ohio River at Cincinnati, Ohio. Not only the drinking water source for more than 3 million people, the Ohio River is a major transportation route and flows through or along the border of six states.

A Brief History of Ohio

Ohio's earliest occupants probably followed retreating glaciers into the area while hunting mastadon and giant beaver. The earliest inhabitants were followed by the more advanced Mound Builders who ranged over Ohio between 1000 BC and 800 AD. They were noted for their burial practices, evidence of which remains in some 6,000 burial and ceremonial mounds.

Probably the first European to set foot in the Ohio Country was either Robert Cavelier, Sieur de La Salle, or Louis Jolliet. Between 1669 and 1670, La Salle explored the Ohio River area and Jolliet journeyed along Lake Erie. Based on La Salle's exploration and resulting map, the French later laid claim to the entire Ohio Valley. Both French and English hotly contested their control of the Ohio territory before permanent American settlement.

Among the historic Indian groups in Ohio were the Erie, Huron (Wyandot), Ottawa, and Tuscarora in the north; the Mingo (or Iroquois League) in the east; the Delaware and Shawnee in the south; and the Miami in the west. Remnants of these tribes, led by the Shawnee chief Blue Jacket, were defeated at the Battle of Fallen Timbers in 1794. This U.S. Army victory led to the establishment of the Greenville Treaty Line in 1795, which separated the Indian land to the northwest from the settlers' land to the east and south.

The Ohio Country became part of the Northwest Territory in 1787. With the passage of the Ordinances of 1785 and 1787, providing for stable government as well as land survey and sales in the territory, settlement by Anglo-Americans accelerated. Connecticut and Virginia retained title to Ohio land, forming the Connecticut Western Reserve in the northeast and the Virginia Military District between the Little Miami and Scioto rivers in the southwest. The Ohio Company of Associates acquired 1,875 sq miles in southeastern Ohio and in 1788 founded Ohio's first town, Marietta, at the confluence of the Muskingum and Ohio rivers.

Ohio statehood was guaranteed when more than 5,000 adult white males were counted during the area's census of 1797. In 1803, Ohio entered the Union with Edward Tiffin as its first governor. Chillicothe was the state capital from 1803 to 1810, when it was replaced by Zanesville. Chillicothe again was capital from 1812 to 1816, when Columbus assumed the honor.

The state's early years were characterized by dramatic population increases and political and military turmoil. Political intrigue was fomented by the supposedly treasonous activities of Aaron Burr on an Ohio River island owned by Harman Blennerhassett. Military problems resulted from Indian agitation and the campaigns of the War of 1812. Two names forever to be connected with Ohio and its early struggles are Tecumseh and William Henry Harrison. The first was the great Shawnee chief who almost succeeded in rallying the Indians for a last stand against the white man. The latter was the victor in the fight to bring peace to the New West and was the first of several U.S. presidents with strong ties to Ohio.

Transportation opened Ohio to internal development. Favored by navigable waters north and south, overland transportation surged with completion of the National Road through the state in 1838, and of the Ohio-Erie and Miami-Erie canals in 1832 and 1847, respectively. Ohio's railroad network was begun in 1836 but didn't really take off until about 1850. Efficient transportation gave impetus to the coal industry and boosted farm income and land values in the western and northern agricultural areas. By the Civil War period, Ohio had achieved national status as an agricultural and industrial state.

Preceding the Civil War, Ohio was strongly identified with abolitionist causes. The Underground Railroad was active along the Ohio River and on Lake Erie. The abolitionist movement received wide support, and in 1848, Ohio repealed its Black Laws, which had been restrictive of Blacks' civil rights. The Civil War was carried into Ohio during a cavalry foray led by Gen. John Hunt Morgan. The "invasion" lasted from July 13 to July 26, 1863, ending with the surrender of Morgan and his men and their imprisonment as horse thieves rather than combatants.

After the Civil War, Ohio became a political power on the national level. Seven U.S. presidents were born in Ohio: Ulysses S. Grant, Rutherford B. Hayes, James A. Garfield, Benjamin Harrison, William McKinley, William Howard Taft, and Warren G. Harding.

As an industrial state, Ohio was in the forefront of the union- organizing movement. The American Federation of Labor was formed in Columbus in 1886, followed by the United Mine Workers in 1888. Violence connected with labor unrest became commonplace in the mining areas of southeastern Ohio. During a strike in 1884 several mine shafts in Perry County were set afire and have been burning ever since. Many millions of tons of coal have been consumed, and despite a system of barricades and packing mud into the tunnels, some smoke from the fire is still visible.

During the 20th century Ohio moved to the forefront of the industrial states under the business leadership of such men as Benjamin F. Goodrich, Charles Franklin Kettering, and John D. Rockefeller. Two world wars and conflicts in Korea and Vietnam triggered massive industrialization, rapid in-migration, and subsequent urbanization. Ohio's fortunes can, however, be rapidly reversed by economic relocation such as a shift from coal to natural gas or by recession. These trends have had devastating results in the central cities and the traditional coal mining districts in Appalachia, where unemployment and poverty are chronic ills. Beset by overcapitalization and outdated facilities, Ohio struggles to remain an industrial giant. Steel plants with excess capacity have shut down, as have outmoded automobile plants. New Japanese-owned factories have opened in Ohio, however, offsetting gloomy economic developments at least in part.

Text written by Hubert G. H. Wilhelm. Sources: Havighurst, Walter, Ohio: A Bicentennial History (1976); Maizlish, Stephen E., The Triumph of Sectionalism (1983); Roseboom, E. H., and Weisenburger, F. P., A History of Ohio, 2d ed. (1977); Smith, Thomas H., ed., An Ohio Reader, 2 vols. (1975).

Timeline of Ohio History

1670
French explorer, Rene-Robert Cavelier, discovered Ohio region, claimed for France

1748
Ohio Company formed by Virginians

1750
Ohio Company claimed land for England

1754 - 1763
French and Indian War

1763
France ceded all rights to the Ohio Territory to Britain in Treaty of Paris

1768
Iroquois Indians ceded all lands south and east of Ohio River to British in Treaty of Fort Stanwix

1775 - 1783
Revolutionary War

1783
Treaty of Paris ended Revolutionary War; England ceded all lands in Ohio

1785
Methods of surveying, dividing land in Ohio established by Land Ordinance of 1785

1787
Ohio became part of Northwest Territory

1788
First permanent white settlement in Ohio founded at Marietta

1790 - 1794
Ohio Indian Wars

1795
Treaty of Greeneville ended Ohio Indian Wars; Indians gave up most of lands

1800
Chillicothe became capital of Northwest Territory; Division Act created Indian Territory

1802
Formation of state government in Ohio authorized by Congress

1803
Ohio became 17th state, first state west of Allegheny Mountains; Chillicothe named state capital

1810
Zanesville named state capital

1812
Columbus founded; Fort Meigs constructed to protect Ohio from invasion

1812 - 1814
War of 1812

1813
British failed in attempt to overtake Fort Meigs; Oliver Perry Hazard's fleet defeated British fleet at Battle of Lake Erie

1816
State capital relocated to Columbus

1832
Ohio and Lake Erie Canal opened

1834
Anti-Slavery Society founded in Zanesville

1835
Boundary dispute between Ohio and Michigan caused Toledo War; Ohio granted contested lands around Toledo

1840
William Henry Harrison elected U.S. President

1842
Ohio's last Indian tribe, Wyandots, relinquished all claims to land within state; left Ohio

1845
Miami and Erie Canal opened

1851
Current Ohio Constitution adopted

1852
Publication of Uncle Tom's Cabin, written in Ohio by Harriet Beecher Stowe, increased racial tensions between North and South

1859
In an effort to end slavery, abolitionist John Brown's led raid on Harper's Ferry

1861 - 1865
Civil War

1863
Confederate Brigadier General John Hunt Morgan led troops on raid across southern Ohio (Morgan's Raid); Battle of Buffington Island was only Civil War battle fought in Ohio

1864
President Abraham Lincoln promoted Ohioan Ulysses S. Grant to supreme commander of Union forces; Ohioan William T. Sherman's Union forces captured Atlanta; Sherman led troops on "March to the Sea" from Atlanta to Savannah

1865
Robert E. Lee surrendered Army of Northern Virginia to Ulysses S. Grant

1868
Ulysses S. Grant elected U.S. President

1869
Cincinnati Redstockings, first professional baseball team, founded; W. F. Semple of Mount Vernon patented chewing gum

1870
John D. Rockefeller founded Standard Oil; Benjamin Goodrich opened rubber plant in Akron

1876
Rutherford B. Hayes of Ohio, elected U.S. President; Ashtabula train accident killed 83

1878
First cash register developed by James Ritty

1879
Ohioan Thomas Edison invented electric light bulb; Cleveland became first city in world to be lighted electrically by arc lights; National Cash Register Co. founded in Dayton

1880
James Garfield elected U.S. President

1881
President Garfield shot by Charles Guiteau

1884
Three-day riot occurred at Cincinnati Courthouse following verdict of murder trial, 45 townspeople killed, 139 wounded

1888
Benjamin Harrison elected U.S. President

1896
Ohioan William McKinley elected U.S. President; first x-rays used in surgery by John Gilman

1898
Roller bearing invented by Henry Timken

1901
President McKinley assassinated

1903
Wright brothers, Orville and Wilbur, began building airplanes in Dayton

1908
William Howard Taft of Cincinnati elected U.S. President; Collinwood school fire near Cleveland killed 173 students, two teachers, one firefighter

1911
Automobile self-starter invented by Charles Kettering of Loudonville

1913
Flood of 1913 killed 428 people, caused state-wide destruction

1914 - 1918
World War I

1917
Camp Sherman constructed near Chillicothe to train WWI army troops

1918
1,200 troops die of influenza epidemic at Camp Sherman

1920
William G. Harding elected U.S. President

1921
Bing Act passed, required students to remain in school until graduation or age 18

1925
Shenandoan dirigible crashed, killed 14

1929
Steel became Ohio's number one industry

1930
Ohio Penitentiary fire killed 322 prisoners

1937
Ohio River flooded, 750,000 people left homeless; East Ohio Gas Co. explosion killed 131

1938
Teflon invented by Ohioan Roy J. Plunkett

1955
Ohio Turnpike completed

1958
St. Lawrence Seaway completed

1962
John Glenn of New Concord first American to orbit Earth

1969
Neil Armstrong of Wapakoneta became first man to walk on moon

1970
Four Kent State University students killed by National Guardsmen during Vietnam War protests

1973
Voters approved lottery

1974
Tornado in Xenia killed 33

1979
Public schools began busing students to eliminate segregation

1986
Astronaut Judith Resnick of Akron, died in Challenger space shuttle explosion

1993
Lucasville prison riots resulted in nine prisoners and one guard killed

1995
Rock and Roll Hall of Fame opened in Cleveland; Bosnian Peace Agreement signed at Wright-Patterson Air Force Base

1998
John Glenn (from Ohio) became oldest American to travel into space (age 77)

2001
New York terrorist attacks led to flurry of anti-terrorist activities throughout Ohio; steam engine explosion at fair killed four, injured 49

2002
Former representative, James Traficant, sentenced to eight-year prison term for corruption

2003
Electric faults in Cleveland caused power outages to 50 million

2006
Voters passed smoking ban in public places

2009
Six bodies found in home of convicted sex offender in Cleveland; Nazi war crimes suspect John Demjanjuk, deported to Germany from Cleveland home; environmental activist, Marie Mason, sentenced to 22 years in prison for arson, property damage

2010
Three Ohio pension funds filed class action lawsuit against American International Group for fraud, resulted in $725 million fine

2011
Exotic animals escaped from private zoo in Zanesville, owner committed suicide, police killed dozens of the animals; Anthony Sowell found guilty of murder of 11 women, sentenced to death

2012
Gunman killed three, wounded others at high school in Chardon; Tornadoes killed at least three, governor declared state of emergency; Ten US states voted in the Super Tuesday Republican primaries. Republican presidential frontrunner Mitt Romney edged out conservative rival Rick Santorum in the vital battleground of Ohio and won five of the night's other contests; Ohio state regulators said a dozen earthquakes in northeastern Ohio were almost certainly induced by injection of gas-drilling wastewater into the earth and announced tougher regulations for drillers

2013
It was reported that Lake Erie is sick and that a dead zone covers a large portion of the lake bottom due to a poisonous blue-green algae called microcystis enhanced by high levels of phosphorous from fertilizer runoff, a problem compounded by the zebra mussel, a foreign invader discovered in 1988, which excretes phosphorous; A federal judge granted marriage rights to a same-sex couple residing in the state as one of the partners neared death, the first time that Ohio recognized such unions; later in the year a federal judge ordered Ohio authorities to recognize same-sex marriages on death certificates.

2014
James Traficant (b. 1941), former Ohio politican, died in Youngstown. He was expelled from the US Congress in 2002 following conviction on charges of racketeering and corruption; The Sixth US Circuit Court of Appeals upheld antigay marriage laws in Kentucky, Michigan, Ohio and Tennessee; In Ohio Ricky Jackson (59), imprisoned for 39 years for a crime he did not commit, was freed. He had been jailed since 1975 on a murder conviction where the prosecution's case was based on the testimony of a 13-year-old witness, who recanted his story in 2011

2015
Abdirahman Sheik Mohamud (23) was arrested for violating state law by providing support to persons engaged in terrorism in the Middle East. Mohamud had trained with a terrorist group in Syria, and he was charged with planning to carry out attacks in the US; In Ohio, 71 people were arrested, as multiple demonstrators broke away from the peaceful protests following the acquittal of officer Michael Brelo in the Nov 29, 2012, killing of black couple Timothy Russell and Melissa Williams

2016
Ohio native astronaut John Glenn died; Baseball's Cleveland Indians won the American League championship for the first time since 2007; Republican Governor of Ohio, John Kasich, made a failed presidential run

2017
Otto Warmbier, who, after spending nearly 18 months in captivity in North Korea, was released and flown to his home in Cincinnati in a coma, where he died a week later. President Trump accussed North Korea of torture, a claim that has been denied; Baseball's Cleveland Indians captured the nation's attention with an American League record 22-game winning streak, outscoring their opponents 145-41 during the three-week run

2018
Gov. John R. Kasich signed an executive order creating a one-stop shop, DriveOhio, that will bring together those building infrastructure in Ohio with developing new transportation technologies to better coordinate efforts and connect transportation providers with automotive and equipment manufacturers; President Donald Trump approved a disaster declaration for 18 Ohio counties hit by severe storms, flooding and landslides in February

Source: http://www.worldatlas.com/webimage/countrys/namerica/usstates/ohtimeln.htm; http://timelines.ws/states/OHIO.HTML; Original research

Ohio State Government

Organization

Ohio's state government contains three branches elected by Ohio voters. The legislative branch makes laws, the executive branch administers laws and the judicial branch interprets and enforces laws.

The legislative branch consists of the House of Representatives and the Senate, collectively called the General Assembly.

The executive branch includes the Governor, Lieutenant Governor, Attorney General, Auditor of State, Secretary of State, Treasurer of State, State Board of Education, the governor's cabinet, and boards and commissions whose members are appointed by the governor.

Ohio's judicial branch of government is comprised of the Supreme Court of Ohio and lower courts that all perform judicial functions for the people of Ohio.

The following are brief descriptions of the elected offices in Ohio government. These descriptions are not intended to be complete lists of responsibilities, but to give a broad overview of their duties.

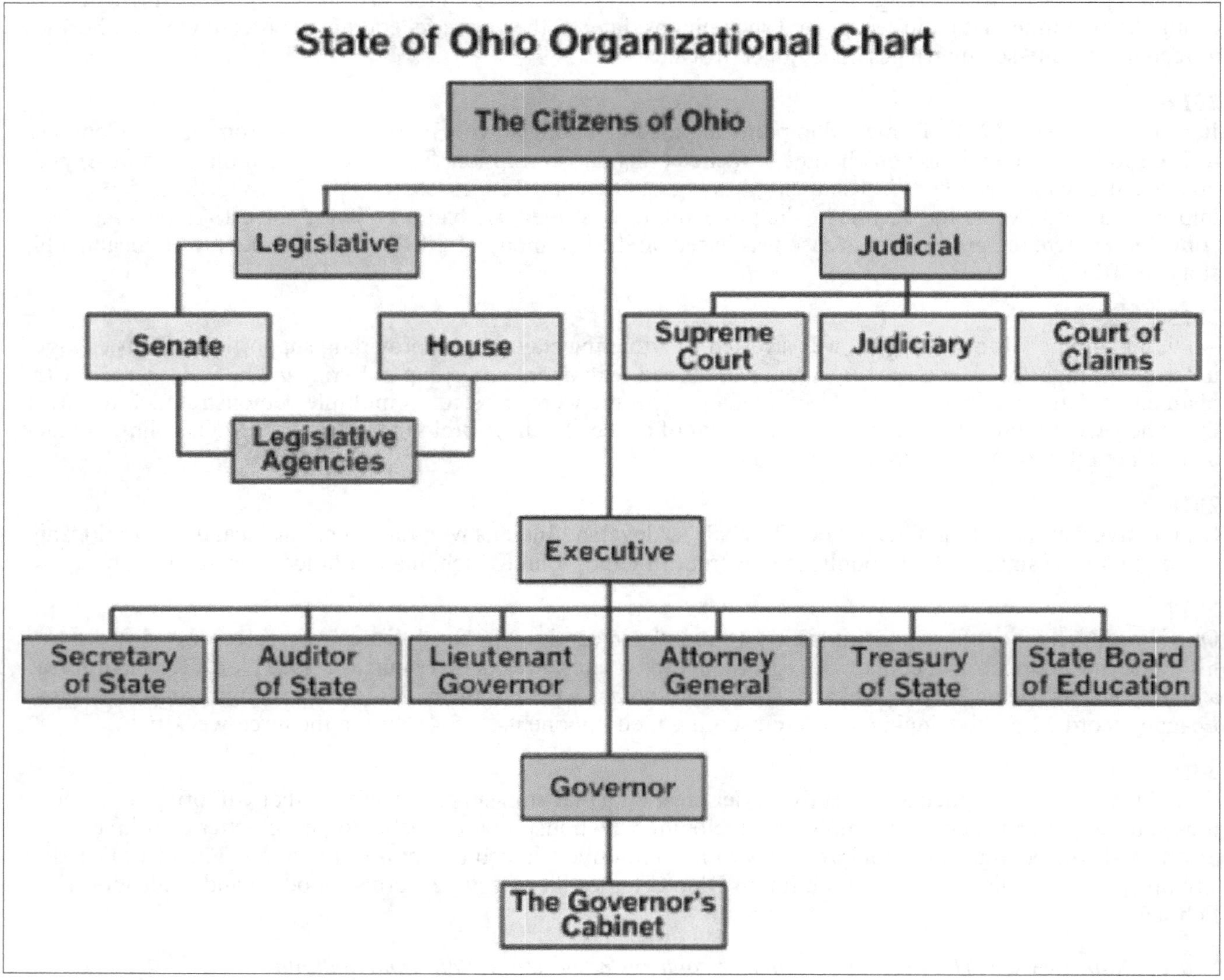

Legislative Branch

Ohio's House of Representatives has 99 members; the Senate has 33 (three House Districts within each Senate District). The General Assembly debates bills proposed for adoption as laws. Most bills require a majority vote in both the Senate and the House to pass. If a bill passes one chamber and is amended by the second chamber, the first chamber must concur with the changes. If there is no concurrence, the bill goes to a conference committee of members selected from both chambers. When both chambers approve a bill, it is then presented to the governor to be signed into law, vetoed or allowed to become law after 10 days without the governor's signature. The Legislature can override a governor's veto with a three-fifths vote of both chambers. When laws are finally adopted, they become part of Ohio Revised Code, and are known as "statutes."

Executive Branch

Governor

The governor is the chief executive officer of state government. The governor is responsible for proposing the state budget, appointing state department directors and members of boards and commissions (except for the state school board, whose members are elected) and signing into law or vetoing bills passed by the Ohio General Assembly. Term limit: two consecutive four-year terms.

Cabinet Offices

- Adjutant General
- Administrative Services
- Aging
- Agriculture
- Alcohol & Drug Addiction Services
- Board of Regents
- Budget & Management
- Commerce
- Development
- Environmental Protection Agency
- Health
- Insurance
- Job & Family Services
- Lottery
- Mental Health
- Mental Retardation & Developmental Disabilities
- Natural Resources
- Public Safety
- Rehabilitation & Correction
- Taxation
- Transportation
- Workers' Compensation
- Youth Services

Lieutenant Governor

The lieutenant governor, elected to a four-year term as a running mate to the governor, is also a member of the governor's cabinet and presides in the absence of the governor. The governor may appoint the lieutenant governor to be the director of one of the departments.

Attorney General

The attorney general is the lawyer for the state and all its departments. The attorney general has enforcement authority as empowered by the General Assembly. The attorney general also provides support to local law enforcement agencies. Term limit: two consecutive four-year terms.

Auditor of State
The auditor of state is the constitutional officer responsible for auditing all public offices in Ohio, including cities and villages, schools and universities, counties and townships, as well as the many departments, agencies and commissions of state government. The auditor's office also has the responsibility of making monthly distributions of state revenues to these entities. Term limit: two consecutive four-year terms.

Secretary of State
The Secretary of State is the chief election officer for the state, appointing members of the 88 county boards of elections and ensuring the integrity of the Ohio voting process. The Secretary is also charged with safely keeping the laws and resolutions passed by the Ohio General Assembly. The Secretary of state's office grants authority to companies to do business in Ohio and provides the public access to a wide variety of records and documents. Term limit: two consecutive four-year terms.

Treasurer of State
In general, the treasurer serves as the state's banker. The state treasurer manages the state's multi-billion dollar investment portfolios. Using sophisticated security measures and procedures, the treasurer maintains an accurate account of all state and custodial funds, including those of the state's five public pension systems. Term limit: two consecutive four-year terms.

State Board of Education
The Ohio State Board of Education regulates every school in the state, whether tax-supported or not, from preschool through high school. The board also sets standards for education and certifying Ohio teachers. The board provides leadership toward the continuous improvement of Ohio schools by making legislative and budgetary recommendations to the governor and the General Assembly. There are 19 board members, 11 elected and eight appointed by the governor. Term limit: two consecutive four-year terms.

Source: Ohio Secretary of State

nationalatlas.gov™ Where We Are

OHIO

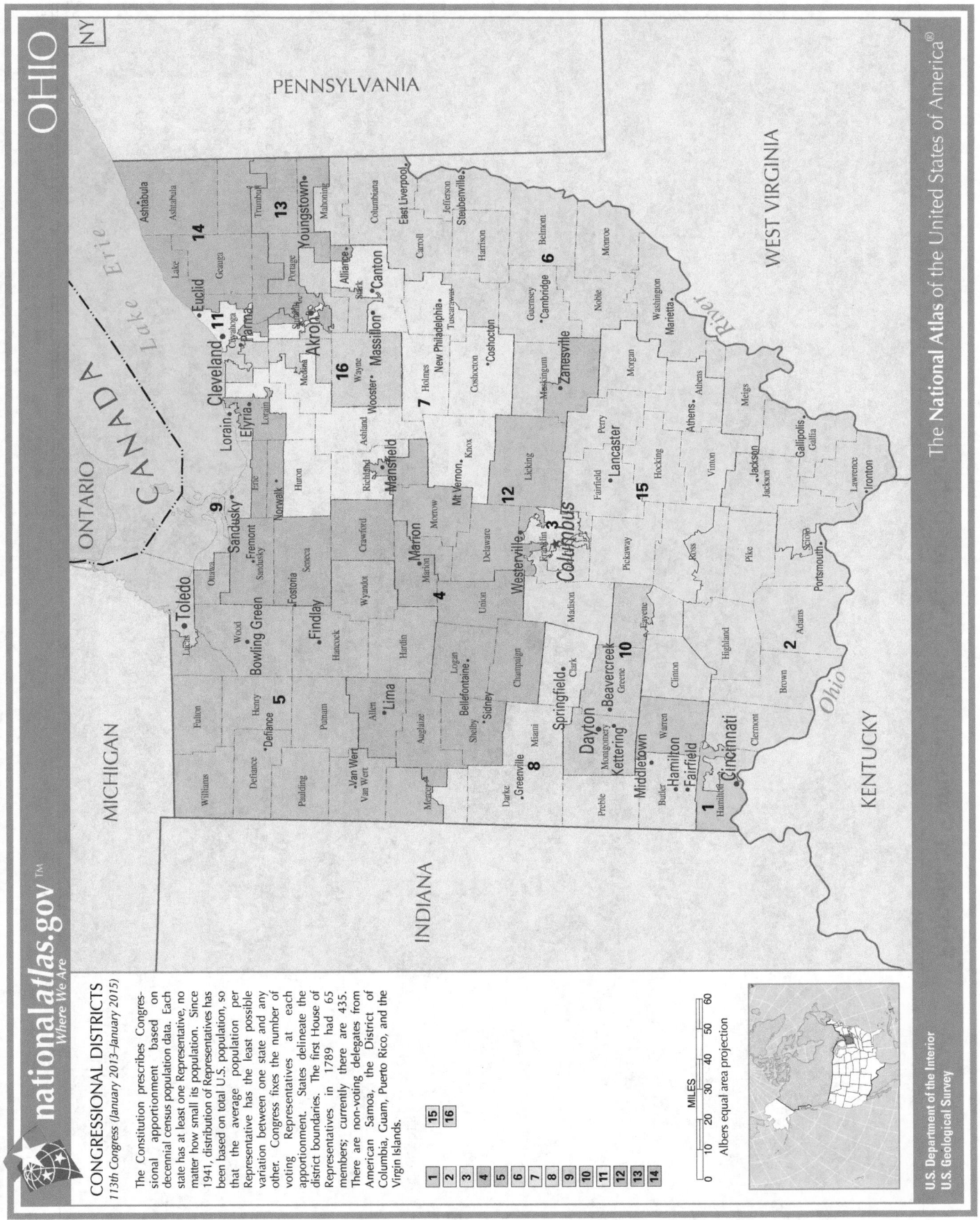

CONGRESSIONAL DISTRICTS

113th Congress (January 2013–January 2015)

The Constitution prescribes Congressional apportionment based on decennial census population data. Each state has at least one Representative, no matter how small its population. Since 1941, distribution of Representatives has been based on total U.S. population, so that the average population per Representative has the least possible variation between one state and any other. Congress fixes the number of voting Representatives at each apportionment. States delineate the district boundaries. The first House of Representatives in 1789 had 65 members; currently there are 435. There are non-voting delegates from American Samoa, the District of Columbia, Guam, Puerto Rico, and the Virgin Islands.

1, 2, 3, 4, 5, 6, 7, 8, 9, 10, 11, 12, 13, 14, 15, 16

MILES
0 10 20 30 40 50 60
Albers equal area projection

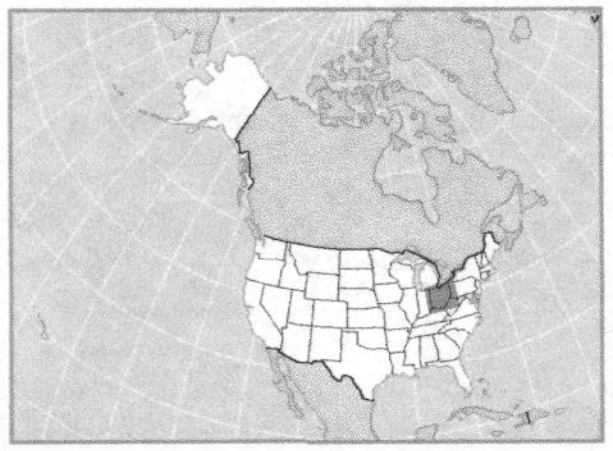

U.S. Department of the Interior
U.S. Geological Survey

The National Atlas of the United States of America®

Percent of Population Who Voted for Donald Trump in 2016

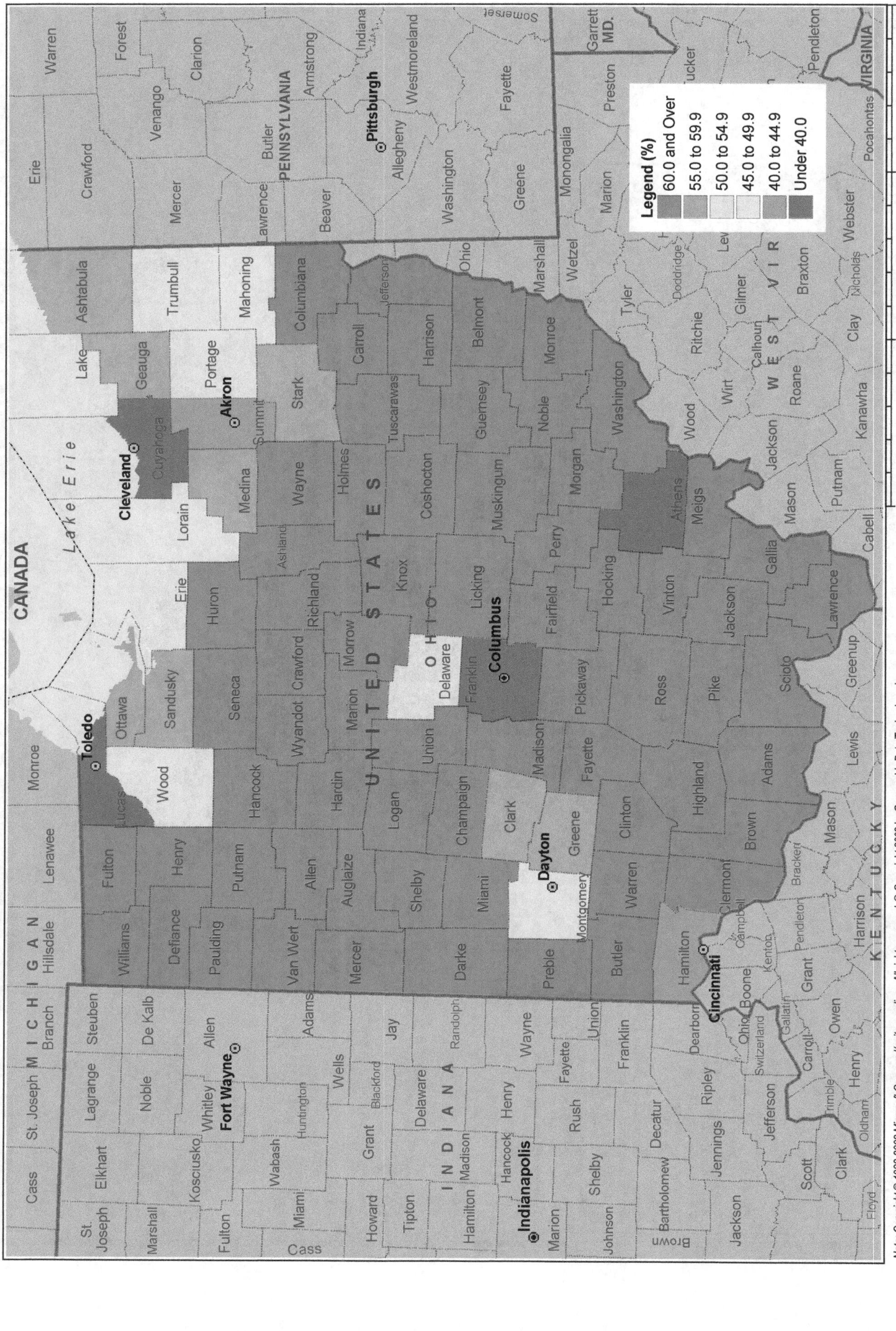

Note: Copyright © 1988-2003 Microsoft Corp. and/or its suppliers. All rights reserved. © Copyright 2002 by Geographic Data Technology, Inc. All rights reserved. © 2002 Navigation Technologies. All rights reserved.

OHIO - Core Based Statistical Areas (CBSAs) and Counties

U.S. DEPARTMENT OF COMMERCE Economics and Statistics Administration U.S. Census Bureau

Ohio Land and Natural Resources

Topic	Value	Time Period
Total Surface Area (acres)	26,444,800	2012
Land	26,021,200	2012
Federal Land	359,100	2012
Owned	144,404	FY 2016
Leased	3,270	FY 2016
Otherwise Managed	1,052	FY 2016
National Wilderness	77	October 15, 2017
Non-Federal Land, Developed	4,178,300	2012
Non-Federal Land, Rural	21,483,800	2012
Cropland	11,098,900	2012
CRP Land	159,200	2012
Pastureland	2,253,000	2012
Rangeland	0	2012
Forest Land	7,098,800	2012
Other Rural Land	873,900	2012
Water	423,600	2012
World Heritage Sites	0	September 30, 2016
National Heritage Areas	2	September 30, 2016
National Natural Landmarks	23	September 30, 2016
National Historic Landmarks	72	September 30, 2016
National Register of Historic Places	3,957	September 30, 2016
National Parks	8	September 30, 2016
Wild and Scenic Rivers Managed by the NPS	3	September 30, 2016
Archeological Sites in National Parks	257	September 30, 2016
Visitors to National Parks	2,766,176	September 30, 2016
Economic Benefit from National Park Tourism (dollars)	96,400,000	September 30, 2016
Land and Water Conservation Fund Grants (dollars)	152,278,866	Since 1965
Community Conservation and Recreation Projects	60	Since 1987
Federal Acres Transferred for Local Parks and Recreation	2,664	Since 1948
Crude Oil Production (thousand barrels per year)	22,010	2016
Crude Oil Reserves, Proved (million barrels)	38	December 31, 2016
Natural Gas Marketed Production (million cubic feet per year)	1,439,905	2016
Natural Gas Reserves, Dry (billion cubic feet)	15,143	December 31, 2016
Coal Production (thousand short tons per year)	12,564	2016
Coal Reserves, Recoverable (million short tons)	231	2016

Sources: *U.S. Department of the Interior, National Park Service, State Profiles, September 30, 2016; United States Department of Agriculture, Natural Resources Conservation Service, 2012 National Resources Inventory; U.S. General Services Administration, Federal Real Property Profile, FY 2016; University of Montana, Wilderness Connect (www.wilderness.net), October 15, 2017; Department of Energy, Energy Information Administration (www.eia.gov), Coal, Natural Gas, Petroleum and Other Liquids*

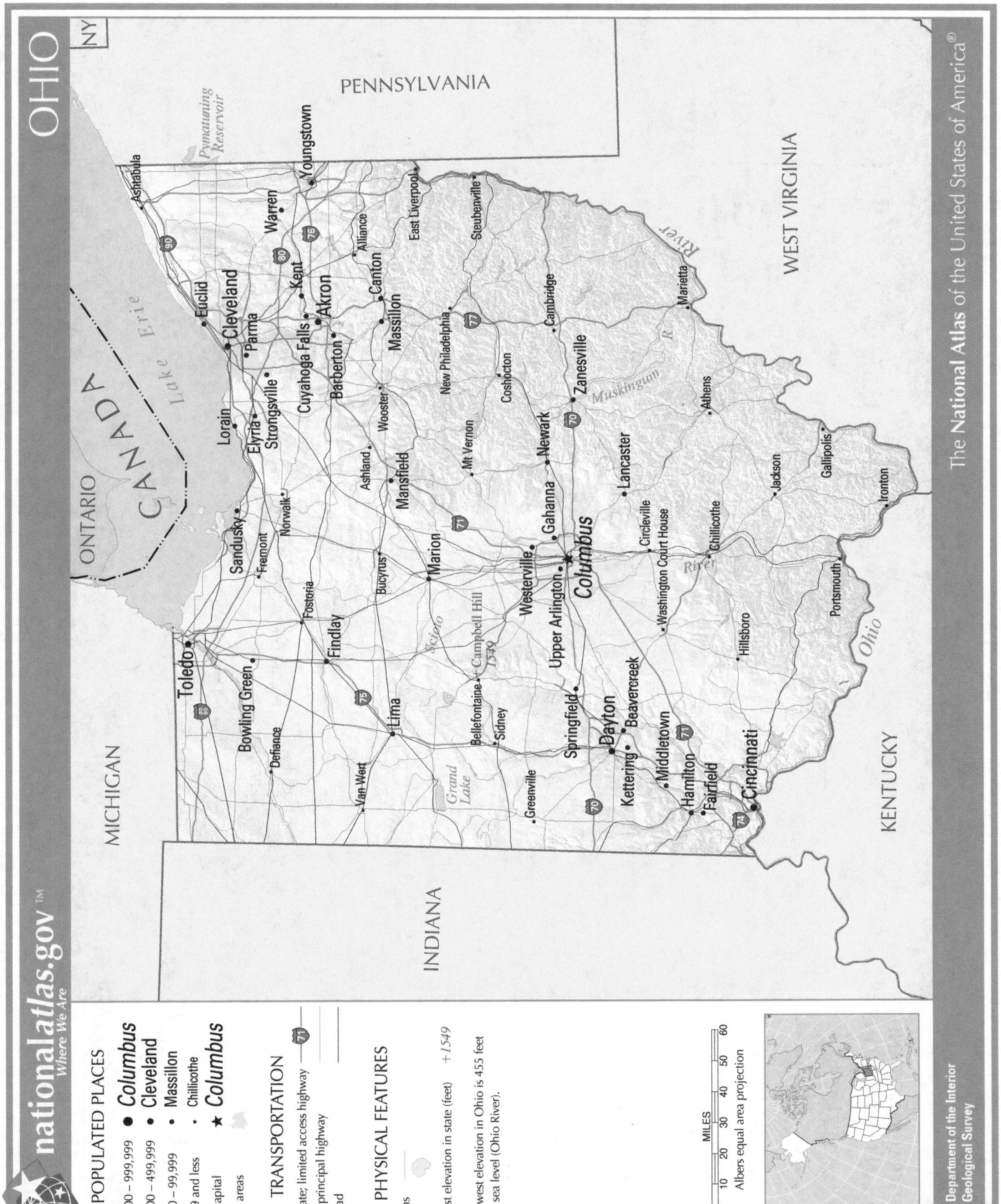
OHIO
nationalatlas.gov™
Where We Are
POPULATED PLACES
500,000 – 999,999 Columbus
100,000 – 499,999 Cleveland
25,000 – 99,999 Massillon
24,999 and less Chillicothe
State capital Columbus
Urban areas
TRANSPORTATION
Interstate; limited access highway 71
Other principal highway
Railroad
PHYSICAL FEATURES
Streams
Lakes
Highest elevation in state (feet) +1549
The lowest elevation in Ohio is 455 feet above sea level (Ohio River).
MILES
0 10 20 30 40 50 60
Albers equal area projection
U.S. Department of the Interior
U.S. Geological Survey
The National Atlas of the United States of America®
MICHIGAN
ONTARIO
CANADA
Lake Erie
NY
PENNSYLVANIA
WEST VIRGINIA
KENTUCKY
INDIANA
Pymatuning Reservoir
Toledo
Bowling Green
Defiance
Sandusky
Fremont
Norwalk
Lorain
Elyria
Strongsville
Cleveland
Euclid
Parma
Cuyahoga Falls
Akron
Kent
Barberton
Warren
Youngstown
Ashtabula
Alliance
Canton
Massillon
East Liverpool
Steubenville
New Philadelphia
Wooster
Ashland
Mansfield
Findlay
Fostoria
Bucyrus
Marion
Lima
Van Wert
Grand Lake
Bellefontaine
Campbell Hill
1549
Sidney
Greenville
Mt Vernon
Coshocton
Cambridge
Zanesville
Muskingum R.
Marietta
Newark
Gahanna
Westerville
Columbus
Upper Arlington
Lancaster
Athens
Circleville
Washington Court House
Chillicothe
Jackson
Gallipolis
Ironton
Portsmouth
Hillsboro
Springfield
Dayton
Beavercreek
Kettering
Middletown
Hamilton
Fairfield
Cincinnati
Scioto
Ohio River
90
80
76
77
70
71
75
74

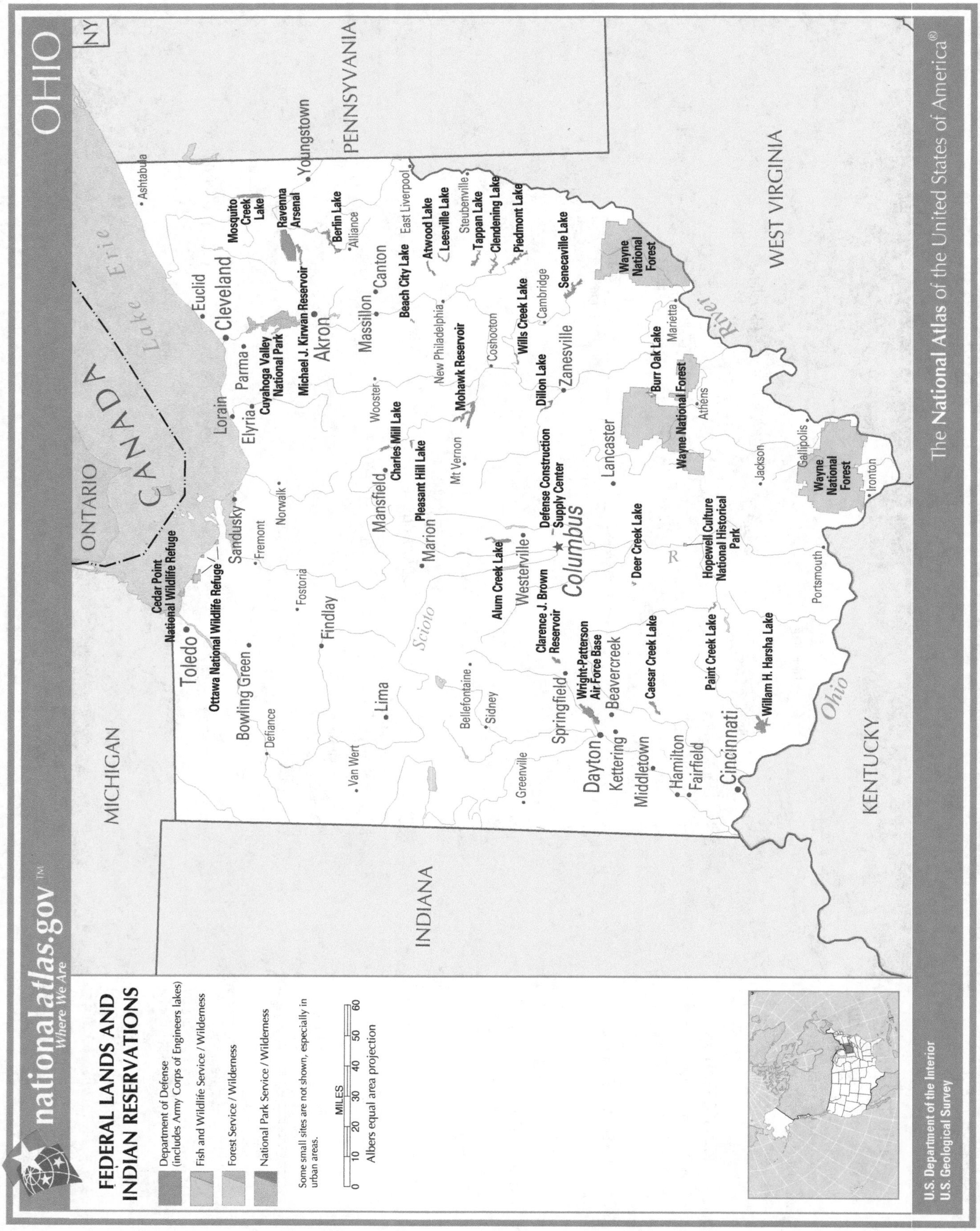
nationalatlas.gov TM
Where We Are
OHIO
FEDERAL LANDS AND INDIAN RESERVATIONS
Department of Defense (includes Army Corps of Engineers lakes)
Fish and Wildlife Service / Wilderness
Forest Service / Wilderness
National Park Service / Wilderness
Some small sites are not shown, especially in urban areas.
MILES
0 10 20 30 40 50 60
Albers equal area projection
U.S. Department of the Interior
U.S. Geological Survey
The National Atlas of the United States of America®
ONTARIO
CANADA
MICHIGAN
INDIANA
KENTUCKY
WEST VIRGINIA
PENNSYVANIA
NY
Lake Erie
Ohio River
Scioto R
Toledo
Cedar Point National Wildlife Refuge
Ottawa National Wildlife Refuge
Sandusky
Fremont
Norwalk
Bowling Green
Defiance
Fostoria
Findlay
Lima
Van Wert
Lorain
Elyria
Parma
Cleveland
Euclid
Cuyahoga Valley National Park
Michael J. Kirwan Reservoir
Akron
Mosquito Creek Lake
Ravenna Arsenal
Youngstown
Ashtabula
Berlin Lake
Alliance
Canton
Massillon
Beach City Lake
East Liverpool
Atwood Lake
Leesville Lake
Steubenville
Tappan Lake
Clendening Lake
Piedmont Lake
Senecaville Lake
Wayne National Forest
Wooster
Charles Mill Lake
Mansfield
Pleasant Hill Lake
New Philadelphia
Mohawk Reservoir
Coshocton
Wills Creek Lake
Cambridge
Dillon Lake
Zanesville
Marietta
Burr Oak Lake
Wayne National Forest
Athens
Mt Vernon
Marion
Defense Construction Supply Center
Columbus
Lancaster
Westerville
Alum Creek Lake
Clarence J. Brown Reservoir
Deer Creek Lake
Hopewell Culture National Historical Park
Jackson
Gallipolis
Wayne National Forest
Ironton
Portsmouth
Bellefontaine
Sidney
Springfield
Wright-Patterson Air Force Base
Beavercreek
Caesar Creek Lake
Paint Creek Lake
Willam H. Harsha Lake
Greenville
Dayton
Kettering
Middletown
Hamilton
Fairfield
Cincinnati

nationalatlas.gov™
Where We Are

OHIO

SATELLITE VIEW

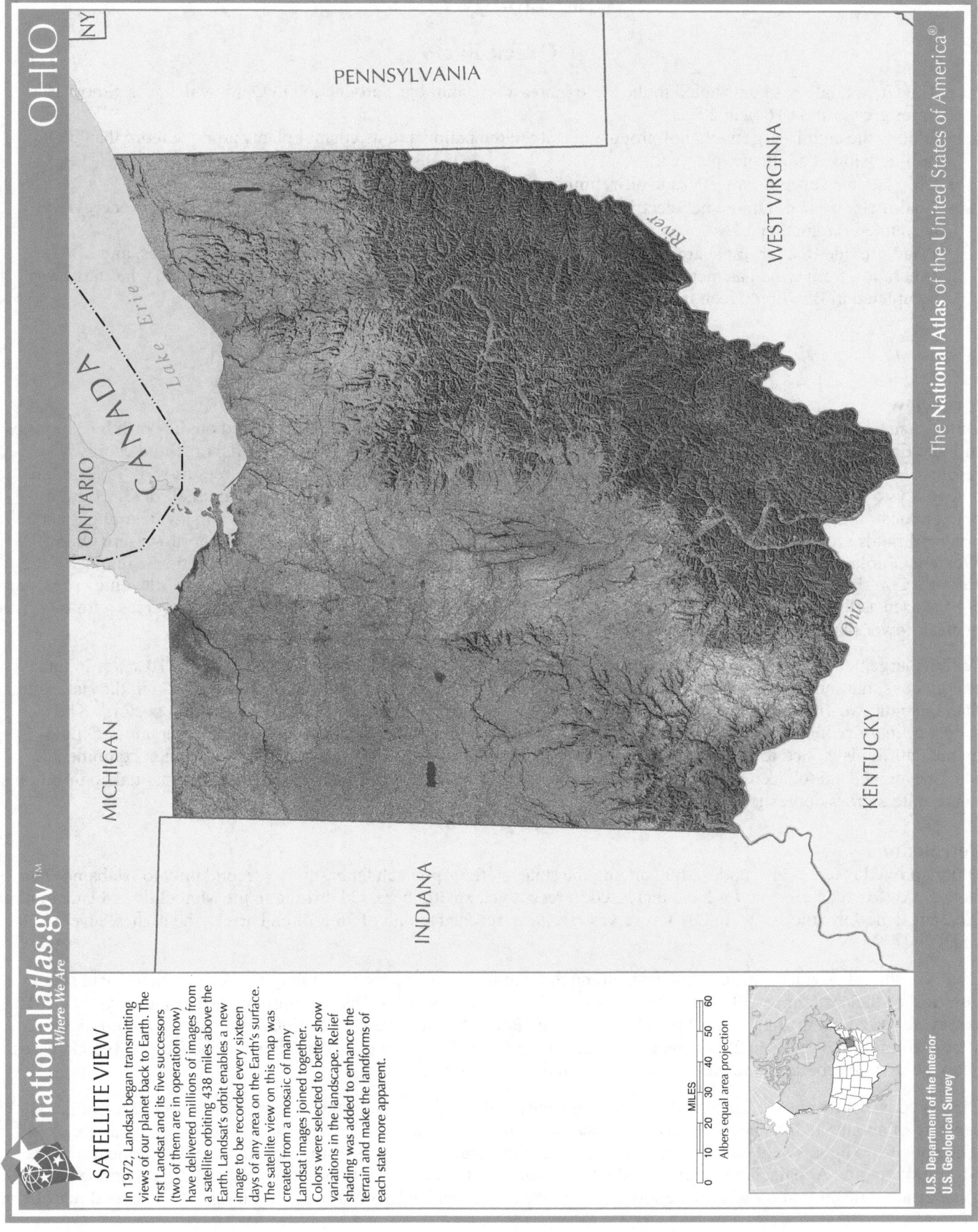

In 1972, Landsat began transmitting views of our planet back to Earth. The first Landsat and its five successors (two of them are in operation now) have delivered millions of images from a satellite orbiting 438 miles above the Earth. Landsat's orbit enables a new image to be recorded every sixteen days of any area on the Earth's surface. The satellite view on this map was created from a mosaic of many Landsat images joined together. Colors were selected to better show variations in the landscape. Relief shading was added to enhance the terrain and make the landforms of each state more apparent.

MILES
0 10 20 30 40 50 60
Albers equal area projection

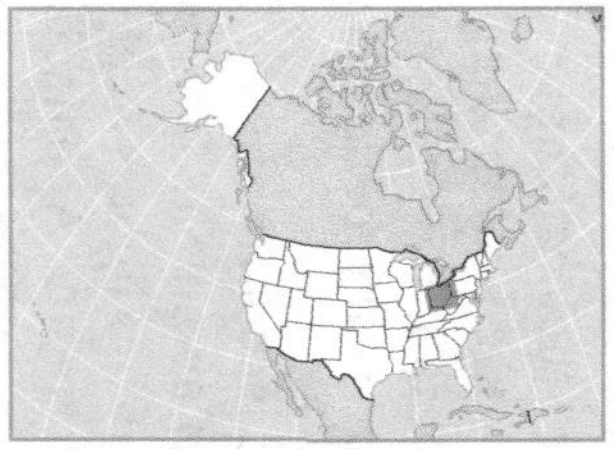

U.S. Department of the Interior
U.S. Geological Survey

The **National Atlas** of the United States of America®

Ohio Energy Profile

Quick Facts

- The Utica Shale has contributed to the rapid increase in natural gas production in Ohio, which was almost 19 times greater in 2016 than 2011.
- Ohio is the eighth-largest ethanol-producing state in the nation and its ethanol plants produce more than 550 million gallons of ethanol per year.
- Ohio had the seventh-largest crude oil-refining capacity in the nation in 2016.
- Coal fueled 58% of Ohio's net electricity generation in 2015, natural gas fueled 24%, and nuclear energy accounted for another 14%.
- Wind provides the largest share (48%) of Ohio's electricity generation from renewable resources, and net generation from wind has increased substantially since construction of Ohio's first utility-scale wind farm was completed in Bowling Green in 2004.

Analysis

Overview

Ohio, named after the river that forms its southern boundary, is a Great Lakes state bordered on the north by 312 miles of Lake Erie shoreline.[1] Lake Erie influences Ohio's weather and provides an important offshore wind energy resource. Prevailing winds that blow across the state from the southwest deliver wind resources as well.[2,3,4] The hills and valleys of the Appalachian Plateau, part of the larger Appalachian Basin, cover the eastern half of Ohio and contain most of the state's fossil fuel resources. Ohio's coal resources and most of the state's many natural gas and crude oil fields are located there. Several oil fields lie further to the west in a belt that crosses northwestern Ohio.[5,6,7] Western Ohio's rolling plains, which have some of the most fertile farmland in the nation, mark the beginning of the nation's Corn Belt, which extends westward across the Midwest.[8] Corn and soybeans are the state's leading crops, and corn is used as feedstock at most of Ohio's ethanol plants.[9,10] The state also has nuclear energy resources with two nuclear power plants located along Lake Erie.[11]

With its large population, heavily industrial economy, and variable climate, Ohio is among the top 10 states in total energy consumption.[12,13,14] But, despite Ohio's strong industrial base, per capita energy consumption in the state is less than in about two-fifths of the states.[15] End-use energy consumption is greatest in Ohio's industrial sector.[16] The state's primary economic activities are in the financial and manufacturing sectors. A significant amount of Ohio's manufacturing is related to petroleum, coal, and chemical products. Motor vehicles and transportation equipment; food, beverage, and tobacco products; fabricated metals; and machinery production also make substantial contributions to the state's gross domestic product.[17]

Petroleum

Ohio's proved reserves are modest, but, among the states in the Appalachian basin, are second only to Alabama. The state's proved crude oil reserves have increased in recent years with increased drilling in the Marcellus and Utica/Point Pleasant shale formations.[18,19] In 2014, reserves estimates reached a high of 78 million barrels, the highest level in 30 years.[20]

Ohio's crude oil production is also modest, although Ohio is first in production among the Appalachian basin states.[21] For most of the past almost 30 years, Ohio's crude oil production was less than 10 million barrels annually.[22] In 2015, however, horizontal drilling in the Marcellus and Utica/Point Pleasant shale formations resulted in a record high of almost 26 million barrels. In 2016, annual production remained high at about 22 million barrels. Despite the increases, Ohio's crude oil production remains below 1% of the nation's total.[23,24,25]

Ohio is consistently among the top 10 oil-refining states in the nation.[26] The state's four refineries have a combined capacity of about 558,000 barrels of crude oil per calendar day.[27] Collectively, they can process a wide variety of crude oils from light, sweet crudes to heavy, sour ones. The crude oils come from Canada, the Midcontinent region, North Dakota, the Appalachian Basin, and the U.S. Gulf Coast. Among the finished products Ohio's refineries produce are transportation fuels, including motor gasoline, jet fuel, and ultra-low sulfur diesel.[28,29,30] Several petroleum product pipelines connect the state's refineries to markets in Ohio and adjacent states and to petroleum product port facilities on Lake Erie.[31,32]

Total petroleum demand in Ohio far exceeds the state's production, and the state is among the top 10 petroleum-consuming states in the nation. Most of the petroleum consumed in Ohio is used as transportation fuels, either as motor gasoline or diesel fuel.[33,34,35] Conventional motor gasoline can be sold throughout most of the state, but the U.S. Environmental Protection Agency requires motor gasoline to be formulated to reduce emissions that contribute to ozone formation in the summer months in the eight counties in southwestern Ohio surrounding Cincinnati and Dayton.[36] Ohio has substantial ethanol production capacity, and the additive is blended into most of the state's motor gasoline.[37] Fewer than 1 in 13 Ohio households heat with petroleum products.[38]

Natural gas

Ohio's natural gas reserves and production have increased substantially in recent years.[39] Ohio was one of two states with the largest annual natural gas production increase from 2015 to 2016, reflecting higher production from the Utica and Marcellus shales.[40] In 2016, natural gas production in Ohio was more than 18 times greater than in 2011, rising from less than 0.3% of the nation's total to nearly 4.5% of the total. Almost two-thirds of gross withdrawals were from shale gas wells.[41,42] Much of the additional natural gas production is from the Utica-Point Pleasant Shale play, and some is from the Marcellus Shale.[43] Ohio's marketed natural gas production equaled state demand for the first time in 2015. Production has increased significantly in the one year since then while consumption has not.[44,45]

Several interstate natural gas pipelines cross Ohio.[46] The 2009 extension of the Rockies Express Pipeline (REX) to Clarington, Ohio, near the border with West Virginia, led to the formation of new natural gas trading points in the state.[47] In August 2015, the eastern section of the REX became bidirectional, allowing delivery of natural gas from the Appalachian Basin to the Midwest, as well as delivery of Rocky Mountain natural gas to the East.[48,49] Since 2015, the state has produced more natural gas than it consumes, and the natural gas leaving Ohio is sent on to Kentucky, Michigan, and Indiana.[50,51,52] To meet peak demand in winter, Ohio withdraws natural gas from storage.[53] The state has 24 natural gas storage fields; all are in depleted oil and natural gas reservoirs. Those fields have a combined total storage capacity of almost 576 billion cubic feet, about 6% of the nation's total.[54,55]

Ohio is among the top 10 natural gas-consuming states.[56] The residential and industrial sectors are the state's largest natural gas consumers, followed by the electric power sector. Natural gas use for electric power generation in Ohio has increased markedly in recent years as domestic natural gas production in the region has increased, bringing prices down.[57,58] Much of the increase in production comes from the Utica Shale in Ohio and the Marcellus Shale in Pennsylvania and West Virginia.[59] Two-thirds of Ohio households use natural gas for home heating.[60]

Coal

Bituminous coal is one of Ohio's primary fossil fuel resources. The state is the 12th-largest coal-producing state in the nation and is the 6th-largest producer of bituminous coal. Although more than half of Ohio's mining operations are surface mines, most of Ohio's coal comes from the state's underground mines.[61,62] The state has 1.3% of the nation's recoverable coal at producing mines.[63] About three-tenths of the coal mined in Ohio is shipped out to other states by barge, truck, and rail.[64] Coal from Ohio and other states is shipped from the state's ports along Lake Erie and on the Ohio River. The state's largest ports are at Cleveland and Toledo.[65] Cleveland is a leading Great Lakes export point for coal.[66] Coal is transferred from rail to vessels at Toledo and shipped from there throughout the Great Lakes region and overseas.[67] Coal is also shipped from Cincinnati, Ohio, on the Ohio River.[68]

Ohio is among the top five coal-consuming states in the nation (third in 2014) along with Texas, Indiana, Pennsylvania, and Illinois.[69] Twice as much coal is consumed in Ohio as is produced there.[70,71] To meet the state's needs, coal is brought in from several surrounding states by barge, rail, and truck. Coal arrives primarily from West Virginia, Illinois, Pennsylvania, and Kentucky. Lesser amounts come from several other states, including from as far away as Wyoming.[72] Almost seven-eighths of the coal consumed in Ohio is used for electric power generation.[73]

Electricity

The primary fuel for electricity generation in Ohio is coal. Eight of Ohio's 10 largest power plants by capacity are coal-fired, although only 6 are among the 10 largest by generation.[74] In recent years, coal's share of generation and the number of coal-fired power plants in the state has decreased. In 2015, 15% of the state's coal-fired generation capacity was retired. However, in 2016, coal still fueled almost three-fifths of the state's power generation.[75,76] Even though natural gas-fired generation has increased greatly since 2008, it accounted for less than one-fourth of the state's net generation in 2016.[77,78] Ohio's two nuclear power plants, located along Lake Erie, supply about one-seventh of the state's net generation.[79,80] Renewable energy resources, petroleum coke, gases derived from fossil fuels, and petroleum are used to produce almost all the remainder of Ohio's net generation.[81]

Ohio is among the top 10 electric power generators in the nation and among the top 5 states in retail sales. The residential sector accounts for the greatest share of retail sales of electricity in Ohio.[82] About two in nine Ohio households rely on electricity as their primary source of energy for home heating.[83] Because net generation does not meet state demand, Ohio is a net recipient of electricity from outside of the state.[84]

Ohio is part of an electric power grid that services all or part of 12 states between the Mississippi River and the Atlantic Ocean.[85] In August 2003, a transmission failure in northeastern Ohio led to the largest blackout to date in North America, affecting more than 50 million people in the northeastern United States and Canada for up to two days.[86] It took only nine seconds for the grid to collapse.[87] A U.S.-Canadian joint task force investigated the causes of the blackout and a number of task force recommendations were incorporated into federal laws that established standards for electricity reliability nationwide.[88]

Renewable energy

Renewable energy resources, including hydroelectric power, supply slightly more than 2% of Ohio's net electricity generation.[89] Wind provides the largest share, and net generation from wind in the state has increased substantially since construction of Ohio's first utility-scale wind farm was completed in Bowling Green in 2004. That wind farm's four turbines generate up to 7.2 megawatts of power.[90] By 2016, Ohio had 34 projects online, and by the fourth quarter of 2016, Ohio had 545 megawatts of installed wind capacity online and more than 100 megawatts of capacity under construction.[91,92] The 304-megawatt Blue Creek Wind Farm, with 152 2-megawatt turbines, became the state's largest wind farm when it was completed in 2012.[93] Offshore wind-powered generation in Lake Erie is planned, and a demonstration project called Icebreaker is in development in Lake Erie northwest of Cleveland.[94,95]

Biomass from wood and wood waste, municipal solid waste, landfill gas, and biodigesters has contributed to Ohio's net electricity generation for some time. There are 19 utility-scale power plants fueled by landfill gas or biomass in Ohio.[96] The state also has two wood pellet manufacturers that produce a combined total of 115,000 short tons of pellets per year, some of which are used for power generation and heating.[97] In 2016, solar photovoltaic (PV) generation contributed almost one-tenth of Ohio's nonhydroelectric renewable generation. More than half of that was distributed (small-scale, customer-sited) generation.[98] However, Ohio has more than a dozen utility-scale solar PV power plants. The two largest solar facilities in the state are the Wyandot Solar Farm and the Napoleon Solar Project, both located in the northwestern part of the state.[99]

Ohio is the eighth-largest ethanol-producing state in the nation.[100] All but one of the state's eight operational ethanol plants use corn as a feedstock. The remaining plant uses waste industrial alcohol.[101] Ohio's ethanol plants produce more than 550 million gallons of ethanol per year, and state fuel ethanol consumption is about 480 million gallons per year.[102] Ohio also has two operational biodiesel plants that process soy oil into biofuels. Those plants have a combined capacity of about 65 million gallons per year.[103]

Ohio has both an alternative energy portfolio standard (AEPS) and an energy efficiency portfolio standard (EEPS). The AEPS requires that the state's investor-owned utilities and retail electricity providers—except municipal utilities and electric cooperatives—obtain 12.5% of their retail electricity sales from alternative energy resources by the end of 2026. The AEPS includes a solar energy requirement.[104] Ohio's EEPS requires that utilities put in place energy efficiency and peak demand reduction programs that achieve a 7.75% reduction in peak demand by 2020 and cumulative energy savings of 22% by 2027.[105]

Endnotes

[1] Ohio Department of Natural Resources, Division of Geological Survey, Lake Erie Facts, updated November 18, 2016.
[2] Ohio State University Department of Geography, Climate of Ohio, accessed April 11, 2017.
[3] U.S. Department of Energy, Energy Efficiency and Renewable Energy, WINDExchange, Ohio Offshore 90-Meter Wind Map and Wind Resource Potential, updated June 13, 2014.
[4] U.S. Department of Energy, Energy Efficiency and Renewable Energy, WINDExchange, Ohio Wind Resource Map and Potential Wind Capacity, updated September 24, 2015.
[5] Ohio Department of Natural Resources, Division of Geological Survey, Physiographic Regions of Ohio (April 1998).
[6] Ohio Department of Natural Resources, Division of Geological Survey, Oil and Gas Fields Map of Ohio (2014).
[7] U.S. Energy Information Administration (EIA), Ohio Profile Overview, Map Layers, All Coal Mines, accessed April 11, 2017.
[8] NETSTATE, Ohio, The Geography of Ohio, updated February 25, 2016.
[9] U.S. Department of Agriculture Economic Research Service, Farm Income and Wealth Statistics, Ohio, 2015.
[10] Ethanol Producer Magazine, U.S. Ethanol Plants, updated January 23, 2016.

[11] U.S. EIA, Ohio Profile Overview, Nuclear Power Plant Map Layer, accessed April 12, 2017.
[12] U.S. Census Bureau, State Population by Characteristics Tables: 2010-2016, Estimates of the Total Resident Population and Resident Population Age 18 Years and Older for the United States, States, and Puerto Rico: July 1, 2016.
[13] Ohio State University Department of Geography, Climate of Ohio, accessed April 11, 2017.
[14] U.S. EIA, State Energy Consumption Estimates 1960 through 2014, DOE/EIA-0214(2014) (June 2016), Table C10, Energy Consumption Estimates by End-Use Sector, Ranked by State, 2014.
[15] U.S. EIA, State Energy Consumption Estimates 1960 through 2014, DOE/EIA-0214(2014) (June 2016), Table C13, Energy Consumption per Capita by End-Use Sector, Ranked by State, 2014.
[16] U.S. EIA, State Energy Consumption Estimates 1960 through 2014, DOE/EIA-0214(2014) (June 2016), Ohio Tables CT4, CT5, CT6, CT7, CT8.
[17] U.S. Bureau of Economic Analysis, Interactive Data, GDP and Personal Income, Regional Data, Annual Gross Domestic Product (GDP) by State, GDP in Current Dollars, All Industries, Ohio, 2014.
[18] Ohio Department of Natural Resources, Shale Well Drilling and Permitting, Shale Development and Activity, accessed May 10, 2017.
[19] U.S. EIA, Crude Oil Proved Reserves, Reserves Changes, and Production, Proved Reserves as of December 31, 2011-15, accessed May 10, 2017.
[20] U.S. EIA, Ohio Crude Oil Proved Reserves, 1986-2015, accessed April 13, 2017.
[21] U.S. EIA, Crude Oil Production, Annual, 2016, accessed April 13, 2017.
[22] U.S. EIA, Ohio Field Production of Crude Oil, 1981-2016, accessed April 13, 2017.
[23] U.S. EIA, Crude Oil Production, Annual, 2011-16, accessed April 13, 2017.
[24] Ohio Department of Natural Resources, "Ohio's Oil and Natural Gas Production Continues Upward Trend in Fourth Quarter," Press Release (March 9, 2016).
[25] Ohio Department of Natural Resources, Oil and Gas Well Production, 2016 Quarterly Horizontal Shale Production, accessed April 27, 2017.
[26] U.S. EIA, Number and Capacity of Petroleum Refineries, Atmospheric Distillation Operable Capacity, 2016, accessed April 13, 2017.
[27] U.S. EIA, Number and Capacity of Petroleum Refineries, Total Number of Operable Refineries, 2016, accessed April 13, 2017.
[28] Husky Energy, U.S. Refineries, Lima Refinery, Toledo Refinery, accessed April 13, 2017.
[29] PBF Energy, Refineries, Toledo Ohio, accessed April 13, 2017.
[30] Marathon Petroleum, Ohio Refining Division, accessed April 13, 2017.
[31] U.S. EIA, Ohio Profile Data, Distribution and Marketing, accessed April 13, 2017.
[32] Toledo Lucas County Port Authority, Terminals and Commodities, Tour the Port, Petroleum, accessed April 13, 2017.
[33] U.S. EIA, Crude Oil Production, Annual, accessed April 13, 2017.
[34] U.S. EIA, State Energy Data System, Table F15, Total Petroleum Consumption Estimates, 2015.
[35] U.S. EIA, State Energy Consumption Estimates 1960 through 2014, DOE/EIA-0214(2014) (June 2016), Table C3, Primary Energy Consumption Estimates, 2014.
[36] U.S. Environmental Protection Agency, Gasoline Standards, Gasoline Reid Vapor Pressure, accessed April 13, 2017.
[37] U.S. EIA, Ohio Profile Data, Environment, accessed April 13, 2017.
[38] U.S. Census Bureau, American FactFinder, Ohio, Table B25040, House Heating Fuel, 2011-2015 American Community Survey 5-Year Estimate.
[39] U.S. EIA, Dry Natural Gas Proved Reserves, accessed April 13, 2017.
[40] U.S. EIA, "Ohio and Pennsylvania increased natural gas production more than other states in 2016," Today in Energy (April 25, 2017).
[41] U.S. EIA, Natural Gas Gross Withdrawals and Production, Gross Withdrawals, Annual, 2011-16 accessed April 13, 2017.
[42] U.S. EIA, Natural Gas Gross Withdrawals and Production, Gross Withdrawals from Shale Gas Wells, Annual, accessed April 13, 2017.
[43] Ohio Department of Natural Resources, Division of Oil and Gas Resources, Shale Well Drilling and Permitting, Activity, through March 8, 2017, accessed April 13, 2017.
[44] U.S. EIA, Natural Gas Consumption by End Use, Ohio, Annual, accessed April 13, 2017.
[45] U.S. EIA, Natural Gas Gross Withdrawals and Production, Marketed Production, Annual, accessed April 13, 2017.
[46] U.S. EIA, Ohio Profile Data, Distribution and Marketing, accessed April 14, 2017.
[47] U.S. EIA, "Market changes contribute to growing Marcellus area spot natural gas trading," Today in Energy (December 15, 2011).
[48] U.S. EIA, "Ohio's Utica Region now included in EIA's monthly Drilling Productivity Report," Today in Energy (August 12, 2014).
[49] Waite, Warren, "Rockies Express-The Aorta of the Central U.S.," PointLogic Energy (October 1, 2015).
[50] U.S. EIA, International and Interstate Movements of Natural Gas by State, Ohio, accessed April 14, 2017.
[51] U.S. EIA, Natural Gas Gross Withdrawals and Production, Marketed Production, Annual, 2011-16.
[52] U.S. EIA, Natural Gas Consumption by End Use, Ohio, Annual, 2011-16.
[53] U.S. EIA, Ohio Natural Gas Underground Storage Withdrawals, Monthly, 1990-2016, accessed April 14, 2017.
[54] U.S. EIA, Underground Natural Gas Storage Capacity, Total Number of Existing Fields, Number of Depleted Fields, 2015, accessed April 14, 2017.
[55] U.S. EIA, Underground Natural Gas Storage Capacity, Total Storage Capacity, accessed April 14, 2017.
[56] U.S. EIA, State Energy Consumption Estimates 1960 through 2014, DOE/EIA-0214(2014) (June 2016), Table C3, Primary Energy Consumption Estimates, 2014.
[57] U.S. EIA, Natural Gas Consumption by End Use, Ohio, Annual, accessed April 14, 2017.
[58] U.S. EIA, Natural Gas Prices, Ohio, Annual, accessed April 14, 2017.
[59] U.S. EIA, Drilling Productivity Report (March 2017), p. 6, 9.
[60] U.S. Census Bureau, American FactFinder, Ohio, Table B25040, House Heating Fuel, 2011-2015 American Community Survey 5-Year Estimate.
[61] U.S. EIA, Annual Coal Report 2015 (November 2016), Table 1, Coal Production and Number of Mines by State and Mine Type, 2015 and 2014.
[62] U.S. EIA, Annual Coal Report 2015 (November 2016), Table 6, Coal Production and Number of Mines by State and Coal Rank, 2015.
[63] U.S. EIA, Annual Coal Report 2015 (November 2016), Table 14, Recoverable Coal Reserves and Average Recovery Percentage at Producing Mines by State, 2015 and 2014.
[64] U.S. EIA, Annual Coal Distribution Report 2015 (November 2016), Ohio, Table OS-19, Domestic Coal Distribution, by Origin State, 2015.
[65] World Port Source, Ohio, Satellite Map of Ports, accessed April 15, 2017.
[66] U.S. EIA, Quarterly Coal Report, July-September 2016 (February 2017), Table 13, U.S. Coal Exports by Customs District.
[67] World Port Source, Port of Toledo, Port Commerce, accessed April 15, 2017.
[68] World Port Source, Port of Cincinnati, Port Commerce, accessed April 15, 2017.
[69] U.S. EIA, State Energy Consumption Estimates 1960 through 2014, DOE/EIA-0214(2014) (June 2016), Table C3, Primary Energy Consumption Estimates, 2014.
[70] U.S. EIA, Annual Coal Report 2015 (November 2016), Table 26, U.S. Coal Consumption by End Use Sector, Census Division, and State, 2015 and 2014.
[71] U.S. EIA, Annual Coal Report 2015 (November 2016), Table 1, Coal Production and Number of Mines by State and Mine Type, 2015 and 2014.
[72] U.S. EIA, Annual Coal Distribution Report 2015 (November 2016), Ohio, Table DS-34, Domestic Coal Distribution by Destination State, 2015.
[73] U.S. EIA, Annual Coal Report 2015 (November 2016), Table 26, U.S. Coal Consumption by End Use Sector, Census Division, and State, 2015 and 2014.
[74] U.S. EIA, Ohio Electricity Profile 2015, Tables 2A, 2B.
[75] U.S. EIA, Electric Power Monthly (February 2017), Tables 1.3.B, 1.4.B.
[76] U.S. EIA, "Coal made up more than 80% of retired electricity generating capacity in 2015," Today in Energy (March 8, 2016).
[77] U.S. EIA, Ohio Natural Gas Deliveries to Electric Power Consumers, accessed April 15, 2017.
[78] U.S. EIA, Electric Power Monthly (February 2017), Tables 1.3.B, 1.7.B.
[79] U.S. EIA, Ohio Nuclear Profile 2010, accessed April 15, 2017.
[80] U.S. EIA, Electric Power Monthly (February 2017), Tables 1.3.B, 1.9.B.
[81] U.S. EIA, Electric Power Monthly (February 2017), Tables 1.3.B, 1.5.B, 1.6.B, 1.8.B, 1.10.B, 1.11.B.
[82] U.S. EIA, Electric Power Monthly (February 2017), Tables 1.3.B, 5.4.B.
[83] U.S. Census Bureau, American FactFinder, Ohio, Table B25040, House Heating Fuel, 2011-2015 American Community Survey 5-Year Estimate.
[84] U.S. EIA, Ohio Electricity Profile 2015, Table 10, Supply and disposition of electricity, 1990 through 2015.
[85] PJM Interconnection, Territory Served, accessed April 17, 2017.
[86] Minkel, J. R., "The 2003 Northeast Blackout Five Years Later," Scientific American (August 13, 2008).
[87] "Blackout by the numbers," CBC News Online (August 15, 2003, updated November 14, 2003).
[88] U.S. Department of Energy, Office of Electricity Delivery and Energy Reliability, "10 Years after the 2003 Northeast Blackout" (August 14, 2013).
[89] U.S. EIA, Electric Power Monthly (February 2017), Tables 1.3.B, 1.10.B, 1.11.B, 1.14.B.
[90] American Municipal Power, Inc., Wind Power, accessed April 17, 2017.
[91] American Wind Energy Association, Ohio Wind Energy, accessed April 17, 2017.
[92] American Wind Energy Association, U.S. Wind Industry Fourth Quarter 2016 Market Report (January 26, 2017), p. 6, 11.

[93] Iberdrola Renewables, Blue Creek Wind Farm, accessed April 17, 2017.
[94] Krouse, Peter, "A close-up look at Lake Erie's wind-energy project (video): Impact 2016: The path to green energy," Cleveland.com (September 20, 2016).
[95] Lake Erie Energy Development Corporation, Icebreaker, Vision and Timeline, accessed April 17, 2017.
[96] U.S. EIA, Electricity, 2015 Form EIA-860 Data - Schedule 3, 'Generator Data' (Operable Units Only), accessed April 17, 2017.
[97] Biomass Magazine, Pellet Plants, updated January 25, 2017.
[98] U.S. EIA, Electric Power Monthly (February 2017), Tables 1.10.B, 1.11.B, 1.17.B.
[99] U.S. EIA, Electricity, 2015 Form EIA-860 Data - Schedule 3, 'Generator Data' (Operable Units Only), accessed April 17, 2017.
[100] Nebraska Energy Office, Ethanol Facilities' Capacity by State, updated October 20, 2016.
[101] Ethanol Producer Magazine, U.S. Ethanol Plants, updated February 14, 2017.
[102] U.S. EIA, Ohio Profile Data, Environment, accessed April 17, 2017.
[103] Biodiesel Magazine, USA Plants, updated December 12, 2016.
[104] NC Clean Technology Center, DSIRE, Ohio Alternative Energy Portfolio Standard, updated February 7, 2017.
[105] NC Clean Technology Center, DSIRE, Ohio Energy Efficiency Portfolio Standard, updated October 6, 2016.

Source: *U.S. Energy Information Administration, State Profile and Energy Estimates, May 18, 2017*

Demographic Maps

Population

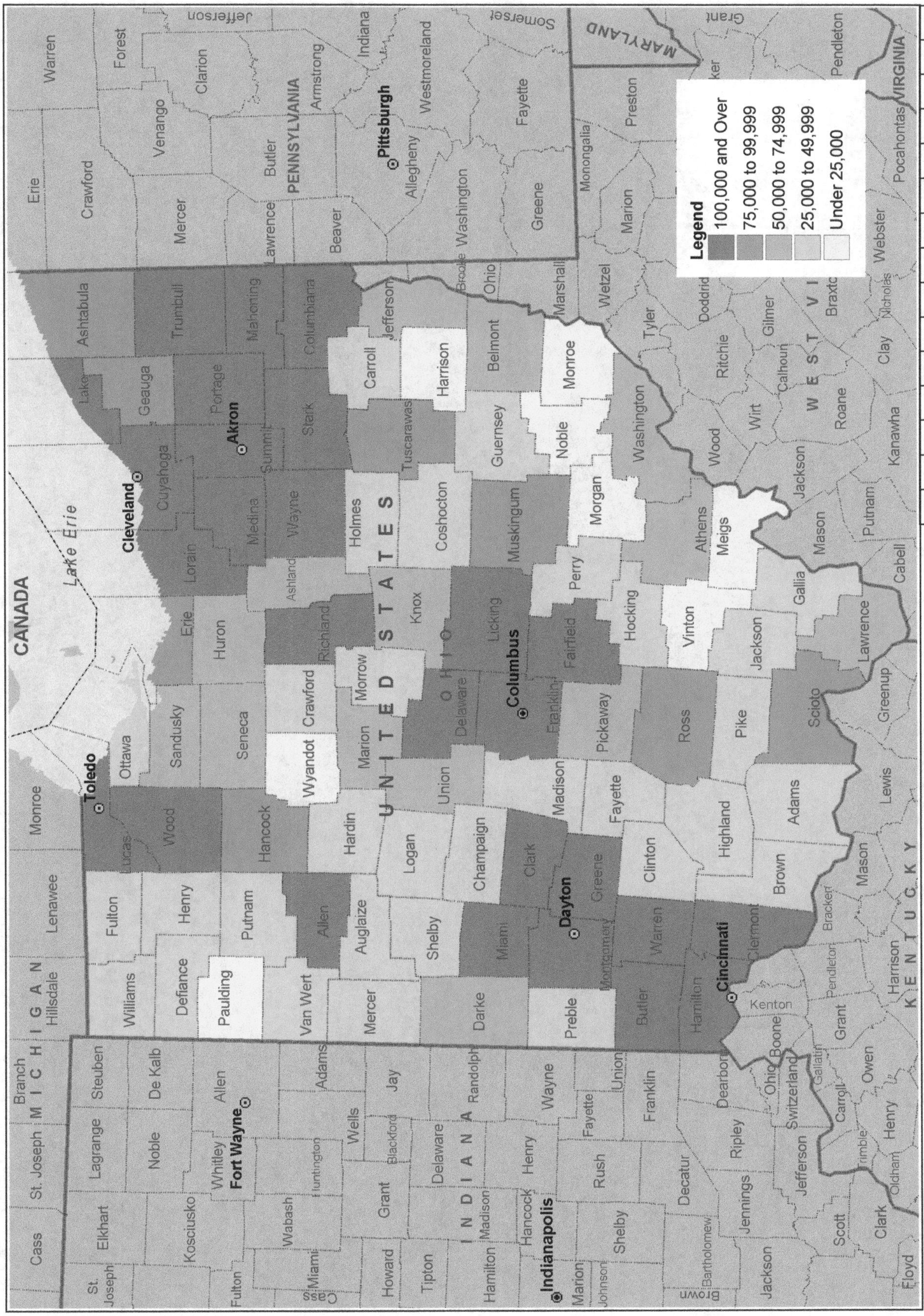

Note: Copyright © 1988-2003 Microsoft Corp. and/or its suppliers. All rights reserved. © Copyright 2002 by Geographic Data Technology, Inc. All rights reserved. © 2002 Navigation Technologies. All rights reserved.

Percent White

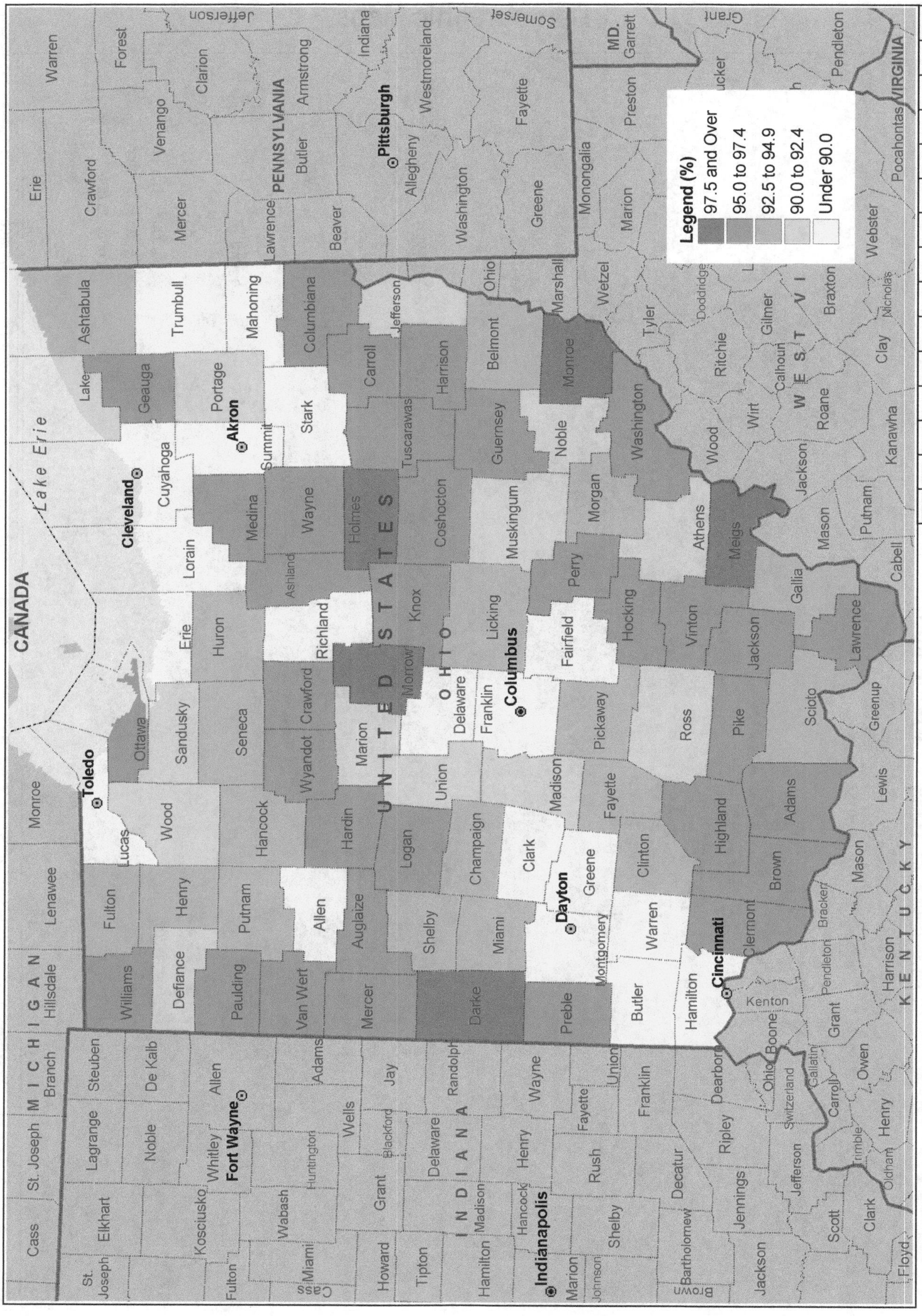

Percent Black

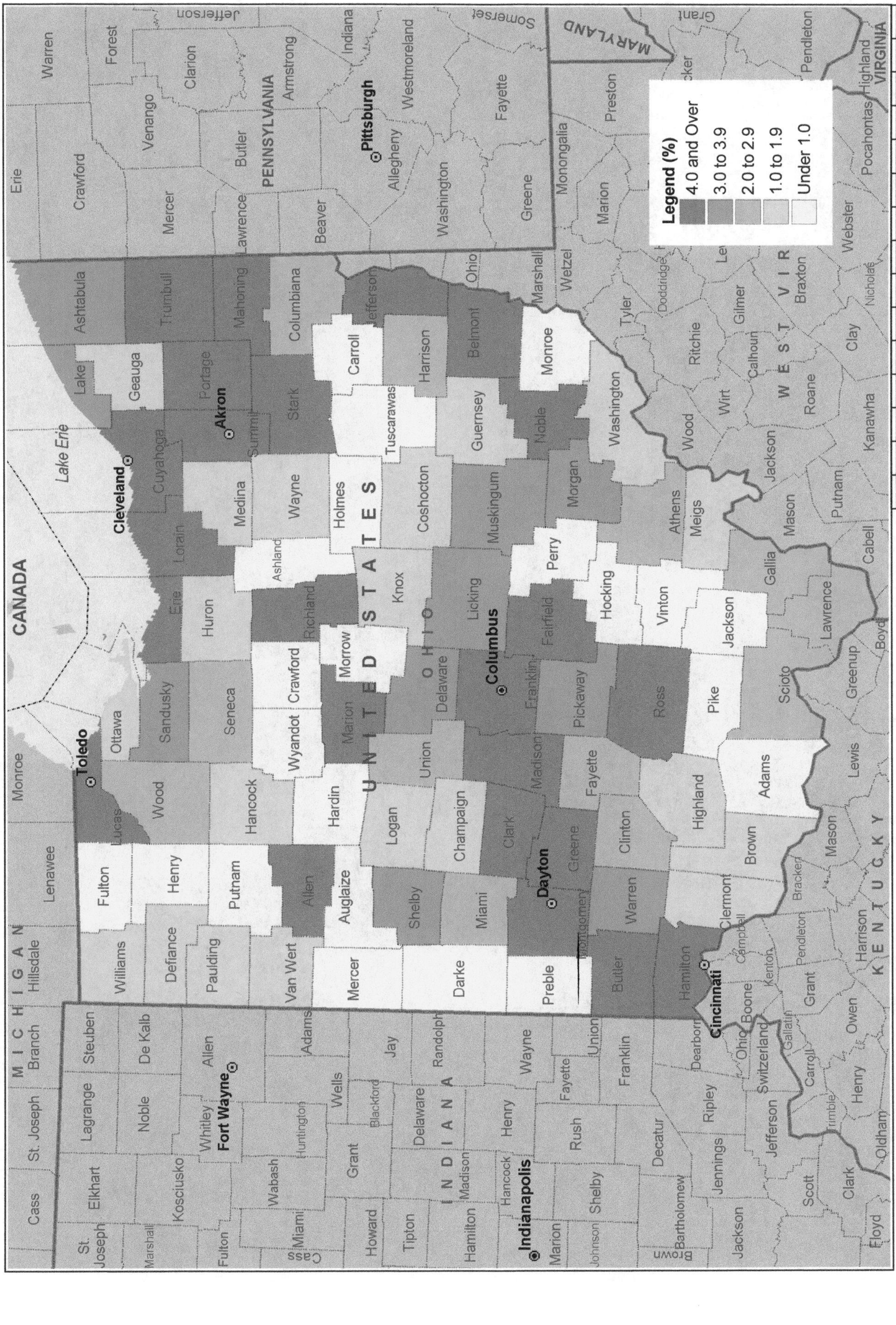

Percent Asian

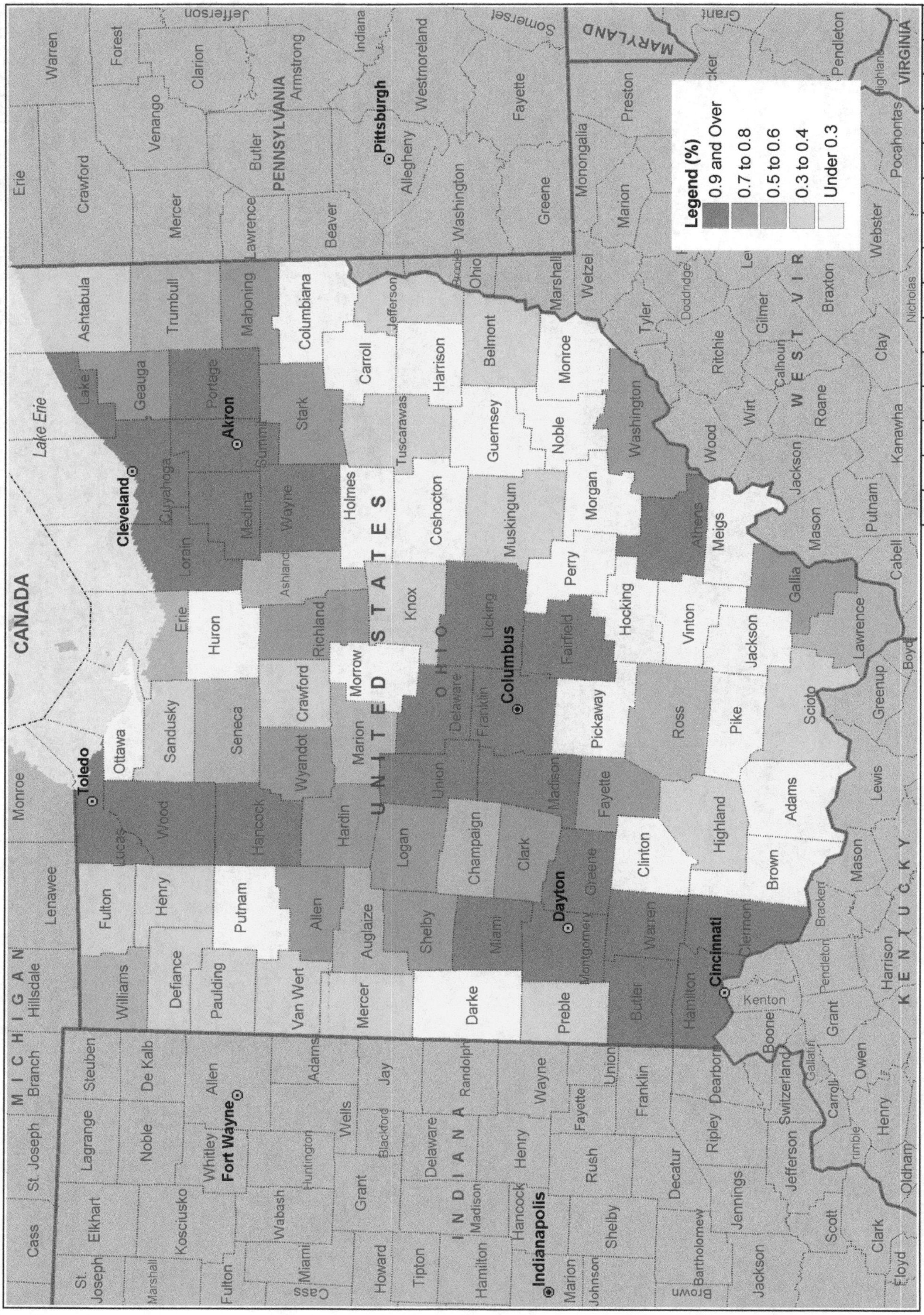

Percent Hispanic

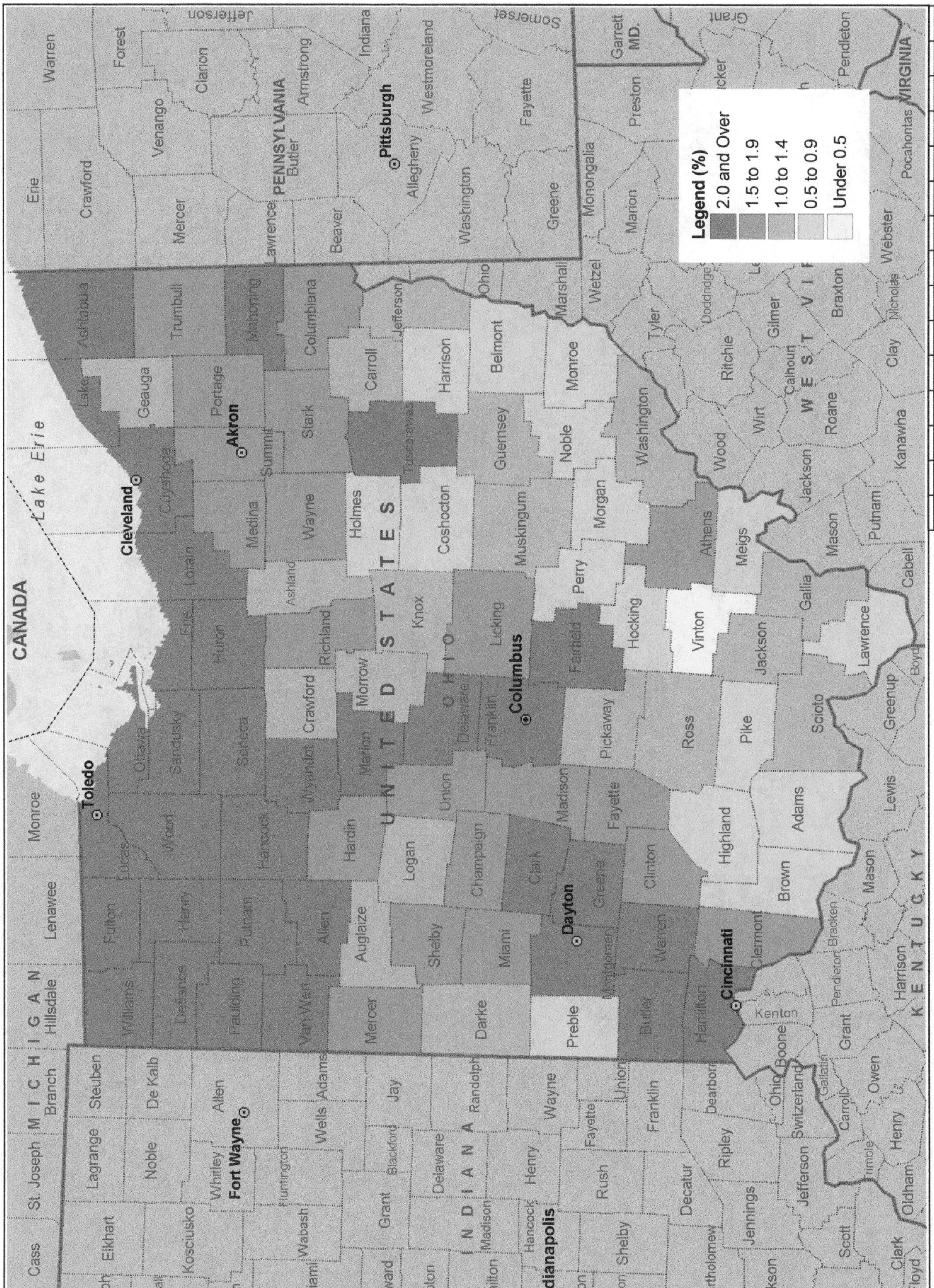

Median Age

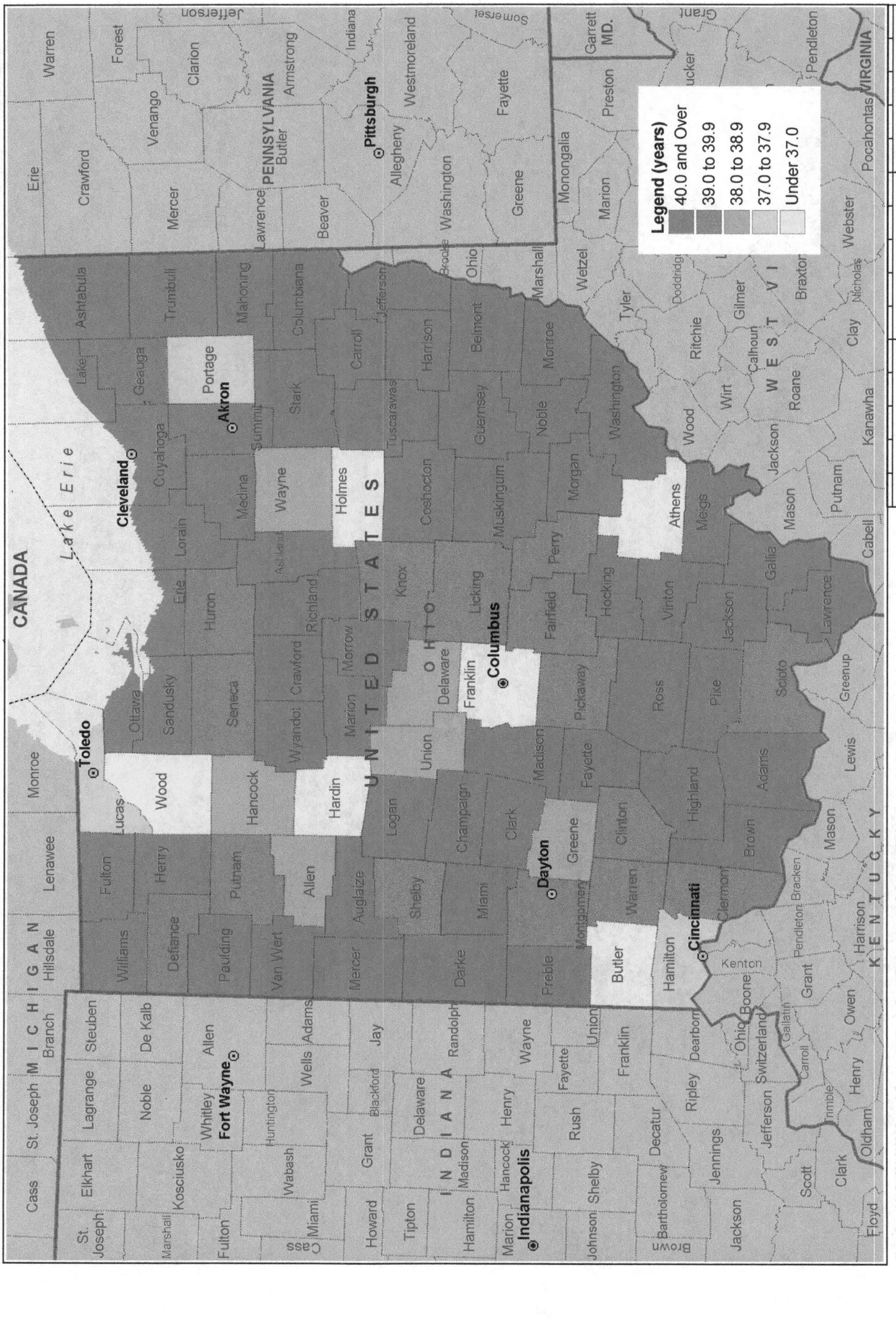
Legend (years)
40.0 and Over
39.0 to 39.9
38.0 to 38.9
37.0 to 37.9
Under 37.0
0 mi
50
100
150
CANADA
Lake Erie
MICHIGAN
INDIANA
OHIO
PENNSYLVANIA
WEST VIRGINIA
KENTUCKY
MD.
UNITED STATES
Toledo
Cleveland
Akron
Columbus
Dayton
Cincinnati
Fort Wayne
Indianapolis
Pittsburgh

Median Household Income

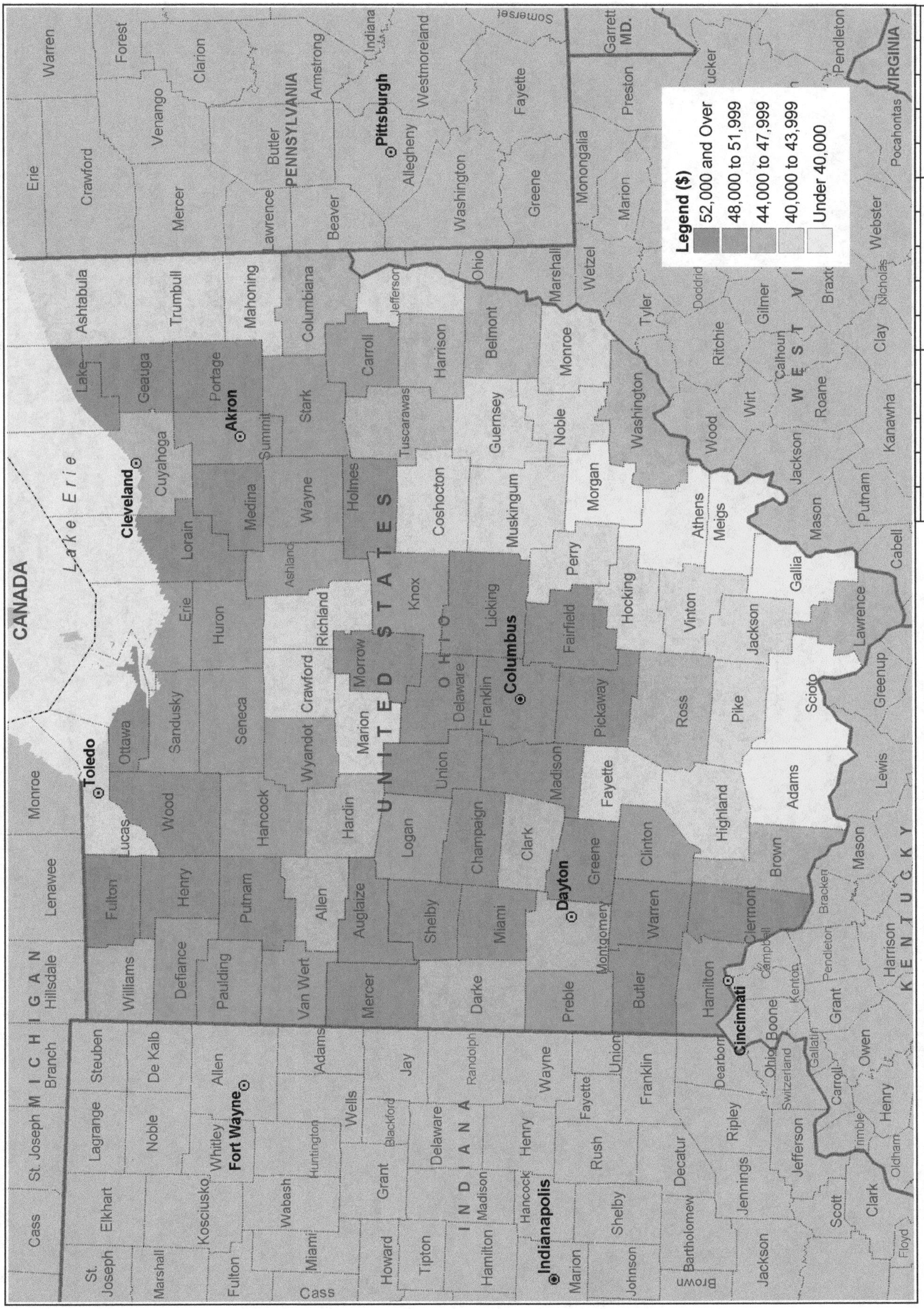

Median Home Value

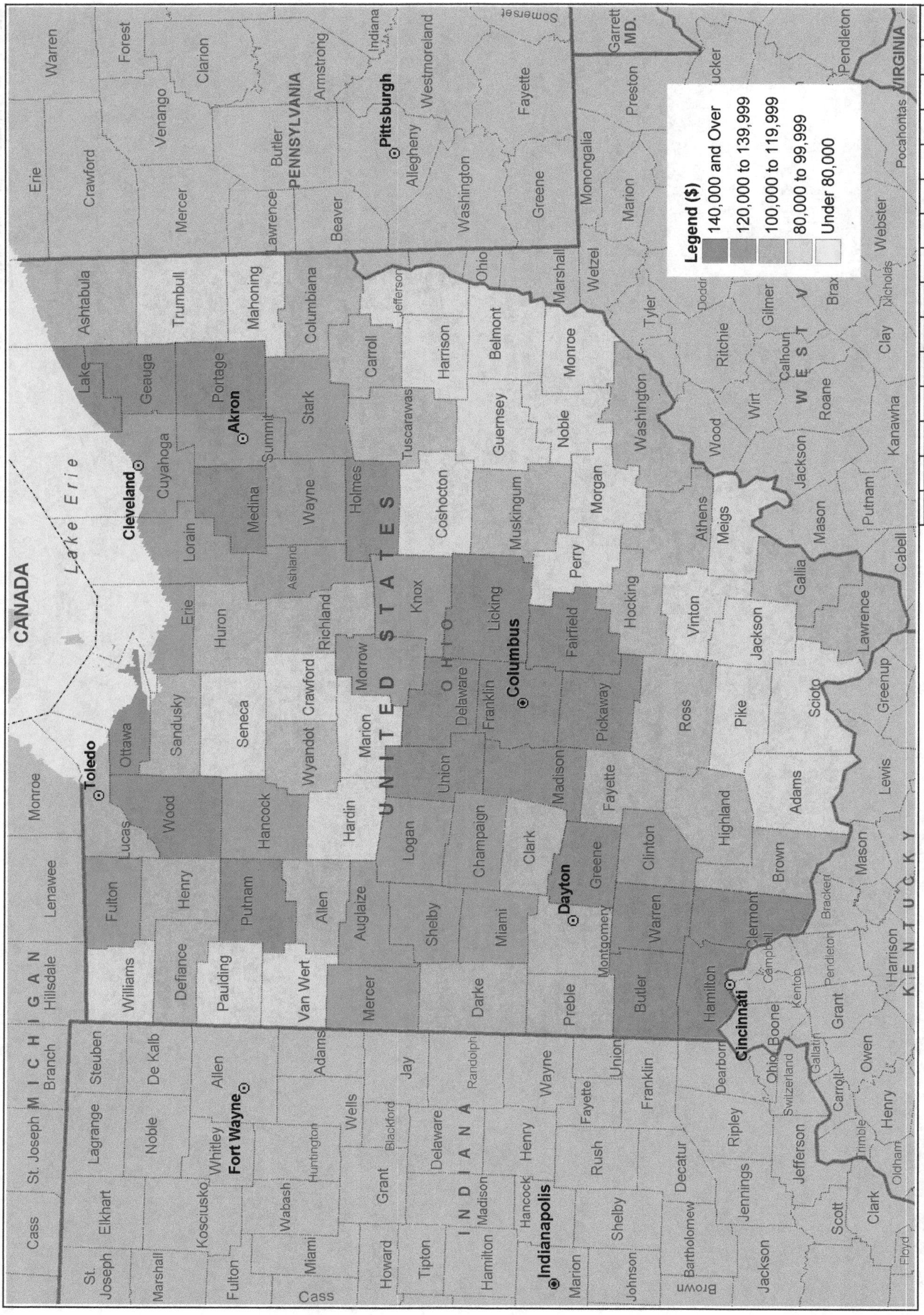

High School Graduates*

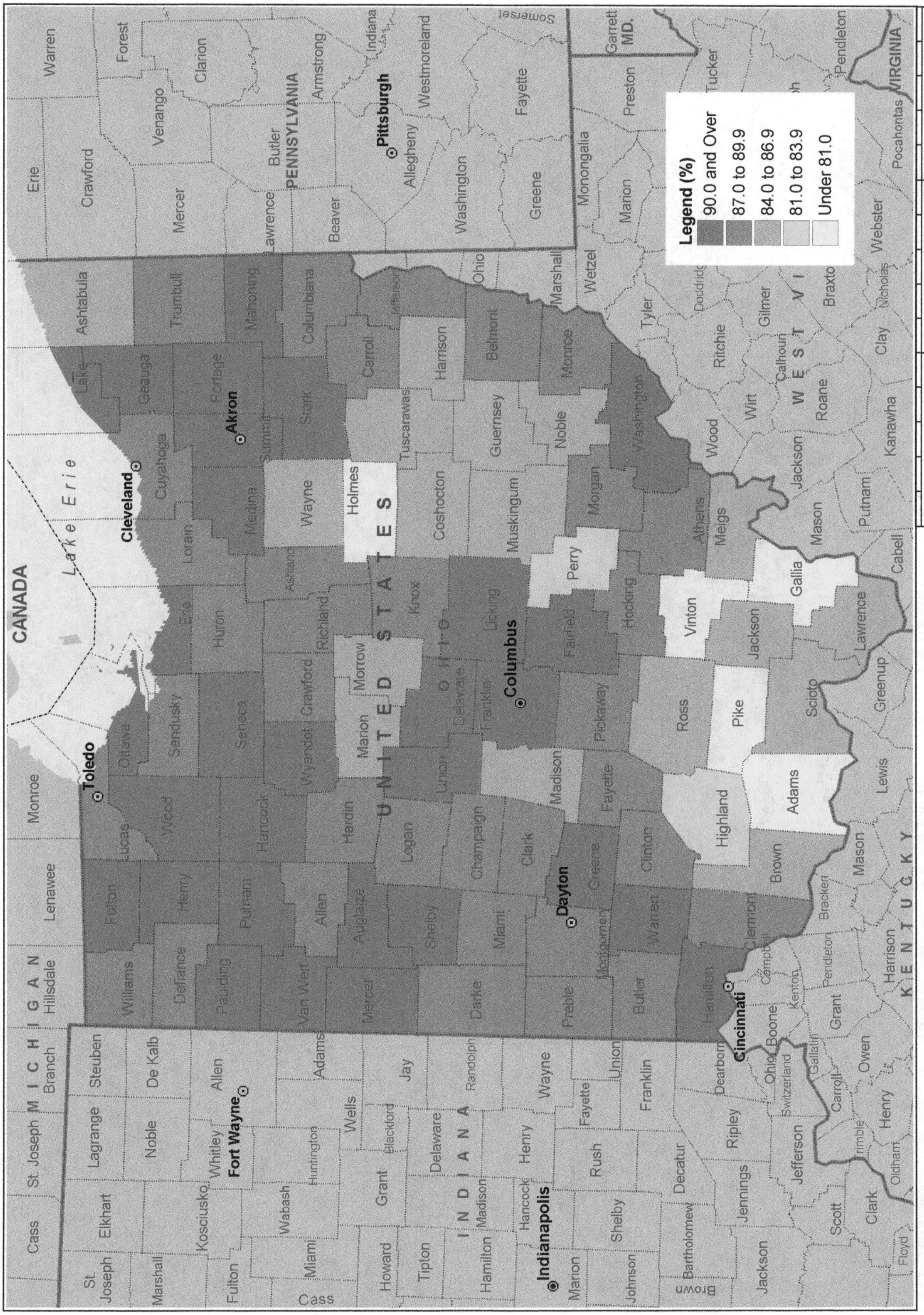

Note: *Percent of population age 25 and over with a high school diploma (including equivalency) or higher.

College Graduates*

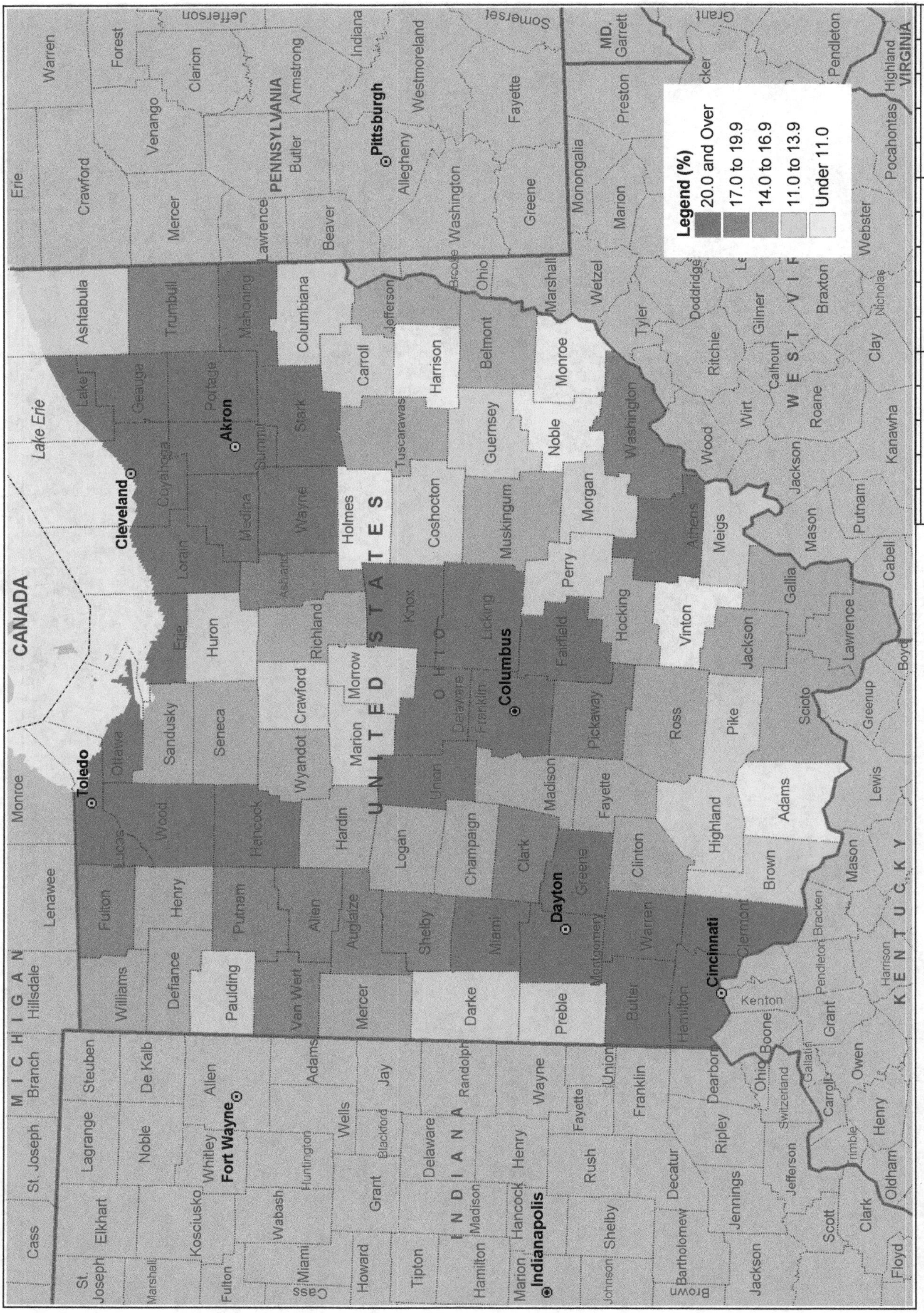

Note: *Percent of population age 25 and over with a Bachelor's Degree or higher.

Profiles

Adams County

Located in southern Ohio; bounded on the south by the Ohio River and the Kentucky border. Covers a land area of 583.867 square miles, a water area of 2.381 square miles, and is located in the Eastern Time Zone at 38.84° N. Lat., 83.47° W. Long. The county was founded in 1797. County seat is West Union.

Population: 28,111; Growth (since 2000): 2.9%; Density: 48.1 persons per square mile; Race: 97.1% White, 0.4% Black/African American, 0.2% Asian, 0.4% American Indian/Alaska Native, 0.0% Native Hawaiian/Other Pacific Islander, 1.9% two or more races, 0.5% Hispanic of any race; Average household size: 2.55; Median age: 42.1; Age under 18: 24.5%; Age 65 and over: 16.4%; Males per 100 females: 97.5; Marriage status: 23.8% never married, 54.8% now married, 2.4% separated, 7.3% widowed, 14.1% divorced; Foreign born: 0.6%; Speak English only: 98.6%; With disability: 20.8%; Veterans: 8.6%; Ancestry: 36.5% American, 12.5% German, 8.4% Irish, 7.5% English, 1.7% French

Religion: Six largest groups: 6.4% Baptist, 5.4% Non-denominational Protestant, 4.4% Methodist/Pietist, 1.8% Catholicism, 1.6% European Free-Church, 1.5% Presbyterian-Reformed

Economy: Unemployment rate: 5.8%; Leading industries: 22.5 % retail trade; 12.3 % health care and social assistance; 11.3 % other services (except public administration); Farms: 1,351 totaling 172,408 acres; Company size: 0 employ 1,000 or more persons, 0 employ 500 to 999 persons, 6 employ 100 to 499 persons, 376 employ less than 100 persons; Business ownership: 669 women-owned, n/a Black-owned, n/a Hispanic-owned, n/a Asian-owned, 45 American Indian/Alaska Native-owned

Employment: 11.2% management, business, and financial, 3.0% computer, engineering, and science, 7.9% education, legal, community service, arts, and media, 6.4% healthcare practitioners, 19.9% service, 16.1% sales and office, 14.4% natural resources, construction, and maintenance, 21.1% production, transportation, and material moving

Income: Per capita: $18,901; Median household: $34,709; Average household: $47,211; Households with income of $100,000 or more: 10.6%; Poverty rate: 24.5%

Educational Attainment: High school diploma or higher: 78.2%; Bachelor's degree or higher: 10.9%; Graduate/professional degree or higher: 4.2%

Housing: Homeownership rate: 68.6%; Median home value: $94,300; Median year structure built: 1981; Homeowner vacancy rate: 2.0%; Median selected monthly owner costs: $980 with a mortgage, $351 without a mortgage; Median gross rent: $575 per month; Rental vacancy rate: 5.8%

Vital Statistics: Birth rate: 111.1 per 10,000 population; Death rate: 119.3 per 10,000 population; Age-adjusted cancer mortality rate: 228.7 deaths per 100,000 population

Health Insurance: 87.3% have insurance; 49.3% have private insurance; 48.7% have public insurance; 12.7% do not have insurance; 5.9% of children under 18 do not have insurance

Health Care: Physicians: 4.3 per 10,000 population; Dentists: 3.6 per 10,000 population; Hospital beds: 8.9 per 10,000 population; Hospital admissions: 297.5 per 10,000 population

Air Quality Index (AQI): Percent of Days: 97.8% good, 2.2% moderate, 0.0% unhealthy for sensitive individuals, 0.0% unhealthy, 0.0% very unhealthy; Annual median: 23; Annual maximum: 80

Transportation: Commute: 90.8% car, 0.7% public transportation, 1.5% walk, 5.7% work from home; Mean travel time to work: 35.5 minutes

2016 Presidential Election: 75.9% Trump, 20.4% Clinton, 2.0% Johnson, 0.4% Stein

National and State Parks: Adams Lake State Park; Johnson Ridge State Nature Preserve; Ohio State Park; Serpent Mound State Memorial; Shawnee State Wilderness; Tranquility State Wildlife Area

Additional Information Contacts

Adams Government . . . . (937) 544-3286
http://www.adamscountyoh.com

Adams County Communities

BENTONVILLE (CDP). Covers a land area of 1.727 square miles and a water area of 0 square miles. Located at 38.75° N. Lat; 83.61° W. Long. Elevation is 915 feet.

Population: 226; Growth (since 2000): n/a; Density: 130.9 persons per square mile; Race: 100.0% White, 0.0% Black/African American, 0.0% Asian, 0.0% American Indian/Alaska Native, 0.0% Native Hawaiian/Other Pacific Islander, 0.0% Two or more races, 0.0% Hispanic of any race; Average household size: 2.04; Median age: 58.7; Age under 18: 16.4%; Age 65 and over: 37.6%; Males per 100 females: 78.3; Marriage status: 11.6% never married, 73.5% now married, 0.0% separated, 7.4% widowed, 7.4% divorced; Foreign born: 0.0%; Speak English only: 100.0%; With disability: 6.2%; Veterans: 4.8%; Ancestry: 26.1% American, 25.2% German, 18.1% Italian, 10.2% Dutch, 4.0% English

Employment: 13.0% management, business, and financial, 0.0% computer, engineering, and science, 13.0% education, legal, community service, arts, and media, 0.0% healthcare practitioners, 21.3% service, 13.0% sales and office, 30.6% natural resources, construction, and maintenance, 9.3% production, transportation, and material moving

Income: Per capita: $40,350; Median household: $86,033; Average household: $83,328; Households with income of $100,000 or more: 37.8%; Poverty rate: n/a

Educational Attainment: High school diploma or higher: 91.6%; Bachelor's degree or higher: 13.8%; Graduate/professional degree or higher: 13.8%

Housing: Homeownership rate: 100.0%; Median home value: $115,600; Median year structure built: 1988; Homeowner vacancy rate: 0.0%; Median selected monthly owner costs: $870 with a mortgage, $341 without a mortgage; Median gross rent: n/a per month; Rental vacancy rate: 0.0%

Health Insurance: 100.0% have insurance; 93.8% have private insurance; 33.6% have public insurance; 0.0% do not have insurance; 0.0% of children under 18 do not have insurance

Transportation: Commute: 100.0% car, 0.0% public transportation, 0.0% walk, 0.0% work from home; Mean travel time to work: 0.0 minutes

BLUE CREEK (unincorporated postal area)

ZCTA: 45616

Covers a land area of 82.330 square miles and a water area of 0.121 square miles. Located at 38.76° N. Lat; 83.31° W. Long. Elevation is 673 feet.

Population: 1,543; Growth (since 2000): 11.6%; Density: 18.7 persons per square mile; Race: 97.2% White, 0.3% Black/African American, 0.0% Asian, 2.1% American Indian/Alaska Native, 0.0% Native Hawaiian/Other Pacific Islander, 0.5% Two or more races, 0.0% Hispanic of any race; Average household size: 2.63; Median age: 41.2; Age under 18: 26.4%; Age 65 and over: 15.6%; Males per 100 females: 98.6; Marriage status: 20.2% never married, 65.0% now married, 2.8% separated, 5.2% widowed, 9.7% divorced; Foreign born: 0.0%; Speak English only: 97.2%; With disability: 20.9%; Veterans: 9.2%; Ancestry: 37.7% American, 12.6% German, 6.2% English, 3.7% Irish, 2.6% Russian

Employment: 14.2% management, business, and financial, 0.0% computer, engineering, and science, 2.6% education, legal, community service, arts, and media, 3.4% healthcare practitioners, 34.3% service, 6.7% sales and office, 9.3% natural resources, construction, and maintenance, 29.6% production, transportation, and material moving

Income: Per capita: $13,501; Median household: $25,917; Average household: $35,189; Households with income of $100,000 or more: 2.1%; Poverty rate: 33.4%

Educational Attainment: High school diploma or higher: 72.9%; Bachelor's degree or higher: 7.8%; Graduate/professional degree or higher: 0.7%

Housing: Homeownership rate: 83.4%; Median home value: $66,600; Median year structure built: 1980; Homeowner vacancy rate: 9.8%; Median selected monthly owner costs: $980 with a mortgage, $232 without a mortgage; Median gross rent: $548 per month; Rental vacancy rate: 19.2%

Health Insurance: 88.8% have insurance; 38.0% have private insurance; 65.8% have public insurance; 11.2% do not have insurance; 4.4% of children under 18 do not have insurance

Transportation: Commute: 96.3% car, 0.2% public transportation, 1.6% walk, 2.0% work from home; Mean travel time to work: 33.3 minutes

CHERRY FORK (village). Covers a land area of 0.122 square miles and a water area of 0 square miles. Located at 38.89° N. Lat; 83.61° W. Long. Elevation is 902 feet.

Population: 220; Growth (since 2000): 73.2%; Density: 1,805.8 persons per square mile; Race: 100.0% White, 0.0% Black/African American, 0.0% Asian, 0.0% American Indian/Alaska Native, 0.0% Native Hawaiian/Other Pacific Islander, 0.0% Two or more races, 0.0% Hispanic of any race; Average household size: 2.97; Median age: 43.1; Age under 18: 24.5%; Age 65 and over: 10.0%; Males per 100 females: 118.3; Marriage status: 25.6% never married, 63.1% now married, 0.6% separated, 4.2% widowed, 7.1% divorced; Foreign born: 0.0%; Speak English only: 100.0%;

With disability: 9.1%; Veterans: 27.1%; Ancestry: 74.1% American, 4.5% German, 2.3% Scottish, 1.8% European, 1.8% Italian
Employment: 9.1% management, business, and financial, 6.1% computer, engineering, and science, 3.0% education, legal, community service, arts, and media, 1.0% healthcare practitioners, 8.1% service, 30.3% sales and office, 0.0% natural resources, construction, and maintenance, 42.4% production, transportation, and material moving
Income: Per capita: $16,535; Median household: $43,548; Average household: $50,664; Households with income of $100,000 or more: 12.2%; Poverty rate: 12.7%
Educational Attainment: High school diploma or higher: 91.9%; Bachelor's degree or higher: 55.1%; Graduate/professional degree or higher: 2.9%
Housing: Homeownership rate: 95.9%; Median home value: $65,700; Median year structure built: 1956; Homeowner vacancy rate: 4.1%; Median selected monthly owner costs: $1,087 with a mortgage, $275 without a mortgage; Median gross rent: n/a per month; Rental vacancy rate: 62.5%
Health Insurance: 91.8% have insurance; 75.5% have private insurance; 35.0% have public insurance; 8.2% do not have insurance; 5.6% of children under 18 do not have insurance
Transportation: Commute: 93.9% car, 0.0% public transportation, 4.0% walk, 2.0% work from home; Mean travel time to work: 30.1 minutes

LYNX (unincorporated postal area)

ZCTA: 45650

Covers a land area of 14.942 square miles and a water area of 0.060 square miles. Located at 38.74° N. Lat; 83.42° W. Long. Elevation is 820 feet.
Population: 274; Growth (since 2000): -42.2%; Density: 18.3 persons per square mile; Race: 91.6% White, 0.0% Black/African American, 0.0% Asian, 8.4% American Indian/Alaska Native, 0.0% Native Hawaiian/Other Pacific Islander, 0.0% Two or more races, 0.0% Hispanic of any race; Average household size: 1.83; Median age: 57.9; Age under 18: 9.1%; Age 65 and over: 21.2%; Males per 100 females: 109.1; Marriage status: 2.4% never married, 66.3% now married, 0.0% separated, 4.0% widowed, 27.3% divorced; Foreign born: 0.0%; Speak English only: 96.6%; With disability: 17.2%; Veterans: 6.0%; Ancestry: 24.1% German, 18.6% Irish, 13.1% English, 12.0% American, 3.3% Bulgarian
Employment: 0.0% management, business, and financial, 0.0% computer, engineering, and science, 0.0% education, legal, community service, arts, and media, 0.0% healthcare practitioners, 41.7% service, 24.2% sales and office, 5.0% natural resources, construction, and maintenance, 29.2% production, transportation, and material moving
Income: Per capita: $19,892; Median household: $28,250; Average household: $35,085; Households with income of $100,000 or more: 9.3%; Poverty rate: 20.1%
Educational Attainment: High school diploma or higher: 59.7%; Bachelor's degree or higher: 5.3%; Graduate/professional degree or higher: 2.5%
Housing: Homeownership rate: 68.7%; Median home value: $65,000; Median year structure built: 1976; Homeowner vacancy rate: 0.0%; Median selected monthly owner costs: $0 with a mortgage, $0 without a mortgage; Median gross rent: n/a per month; Rental vacancy rate: 0.0%
Health Insurance: 97.8% have insurance; 63.9% have private insurance; 43.1% have public insurance; 2.2% do not have insurance; 0.0% of children under 18 do not have insurance
Transportation: Commute: 90.0% car, 5.0% public transportation, 0.0% walk, 0.0% work from home; Mean travel time to work: 39.5 minutes

MANCHESTER (village). Covers a land area of 1.283 square miles and a water area of 0.012 square miles. Located at 38.69° N. Lat; 83.60° W. Long. Elevation is 512 feet.
History: Manchester was founded in 1791 by General Nathaniel Massie. The town was an important steamboat landing in the mid-1800's, and in the later 1800's offered excursions on the river and showboats at the wharf.
Population: 2,234; Growth (since 2000): 9.3%; Density: 1,741.3 persons per square mile; Race: 98.6% White, 0.0% Black/African American, 0.0% Asian, 0.0% American Indian/Alaska Native, 0.0% Native Hawaiian/Other Pacific Islander, 1.3% Two or more races, 2.6% Hispanic of any race; Average household size: 2.65; Median age: 35.1; Age under 18: 24.7%; Age 65 and over: 10.8%; Males per 100 females: 93.2; Marriage status: 33.0% never married, 41.3% now married, 3.2% separated, 9.4% widowed, 16.3% divorced; Foreign born: 0.0%; Speak English only: 99.7%; With disability: 31.8%; Veterans: 7.3%; Ancestry: 42.3% American, 8.8% Irish, 6.4% German, 5.2% English, 1.8% Dutch
Employment: 10.1% management, business, and financial, 4.2% computer, engineering, and science, 4.1% education, legal, community service, arts, and media, 4.2% healthcare practitioners, 24.7% service, 12.3% sales and office, 18.5% natural resources, construction, and maintenance, 21.8% production, transportation, and material moving
Income: Per capita: $16,338; Median household: $29,077; Average household: $41,815; Households with income of $100,000 or more: 7.2%; Poverty rate: 41.8%
Educational Attainment: High school diploma or higher: 72.0%; Bachelor's degree or higher: 9.2%; Graduate/professional degree or higher: 2.4%

School District(s)

Manchester Local (PK-12)
2015-16 Enrollment: 892. . . . . (937) 549-4777
Housing: Homeownership rate: 52.0%; Median home value: $75,000; Median year structure built: 1963; Homeowner vacancy rate: 3.7%; Median selected monthly owner costs: $829 with a mortgage, $311 without a mortgage; Median gross rent: $505 per month; Rental vacancy rate: 8.6%
Health Insurance: 79.8% have insurance; 32.1% have private insurance; 58.9% have public insurance; 20.2% do not have insurance; 12.3% of children under 18 do not have insurance
Newspapers: Manchester Signal (weekly circulation 3,500)
Transportation: Commute: 80.6% car, 0.5% public transportation, 6.7% walk, 12.2% work from home; Mean travel time to work: 27.3 minutes

PEEBLES (village). Covers a land area of 1.182 square miles and a water area of 0 square miles. Located at 38.95° N. Lat; 83.41° W. Long. Elevation is 827 feet.
Population: 1,809; Growth (since 2000): 4.0%; Density: 1,530.6 persons per square mile; Race: 94.1% White, 1.1% Black/African American, 0.3% Asian, 2.0% American Indian/Alaska Native, 0.0% Native Hawaiian/Other Pacific Islander, 2.5% Two or more races, 1.3% Hispanic of any race; Average household size: 2.37; Median age: 42.4; Age under 18: 21.5%; Age 65 and over: 16.0%; Males per 100 females: 89.0; Marriage status: 25.9% never married, 46.7% now married, 2.2% separated, 10.2% widowed, 17.2% divorced; Foreign born: 0.8%; Speak English only: 98.7%; With disability: 25.1%; Veterans: 8.0%; Ancestry: 35.0% American, 10.1% German, 7.5% Irish, 4.4% English, 3.3% Dutch
Employment: 5.7% management, business, and financial, 3.1% computer, engineering, and science, 8.7% education, legal, community service, arts, and media, 6.4% healthcare practitioners, 22.9% service, 20.9% sales and office, 12.7% natural resources, construction, and maintenance, 19.6% production, transportation, and material moving
Income: Per capita: $19,883; Median household: $28,558; Average household: $46,365; Households with income of $100,000 or more: 13.1%; Poverty rate: 27.8%
Educational Attainment: High school diploma or higher: 73.2%; Bachelor's degree or higher: 8.3%; Graduate/professional degree or higher: 4.2%

School District(s)

Adams County Ohio Valley Local (PK-12)
2015-16 Enrollment: 3,960 . . . . (937) 544-5586
Housing: Homeownership rate: 49.1%; Median home value: $80,600; Median year structure built: 1970; Homeowner vacancy rate: 0.0%; Median selected monthly owner costs: $926 with a mortgage, $420 without a mortgage; Median gross rent: $629 per month; Rental vacancy rate: 6.0%
Health Insurance: 86.1% have insurance; 39.1% have private insurance; 56.9% have public insurance; 13.9% do not have insurance; 1.8% of children under 18 do not have insurance
Transportation: Commute: 95.0% car, 0.7% public transportation, 1.5% walk, 1.2% work from home; Mean travel time to work: 31.5 minutes

ROME (village). Covers a land area of 0.230 square miles and a water area of 0.025 square miles. Located at 38.67° N. Lat; 83.38° W. Long. Elevation is 518 feet.
History: Also called Stout.
Population: 79; Growth (since 2000): -32.5%; Density: 343.1 persons per square mile; Race: 100.0% White, 0.0% Black/African American, 0.0% Asian, 0.0% American Indian/Alaska Native, 0.0% Native Hawaiian/Other Pacific Islander, 0.0% Two or more races, 0.0% Hispanic of any race; Average household size: 2.55; Median age: 45.4; Age under 18: 21.5%; Age 65 and over: 20.3%; Males per 100 females: 100.0; Marriage status: 29.9% never married, 31.3% now married, 0.0% separated, 22.4%

widowed, 16.4% divorced; Foreign born: 0.0%; Speak English only: 100.0%; With disability: 32.9%; Veterans: 11.3%; Ancestry: 60.8% American, 8.9% German, 5.1% Irish, 2.5% Scottish
Employment: 4.3% management, business, and financial, 0.0% computer, engineering, and science, 0.0% education, legal, community service, arts, and media, 13.0% healthcare practitioners, 26.1% service, 8.7% sales and office, 0.0% natural resources, construction, and maintenance, 47.8% production, transportation, and material moving
Income: Per capita: $26,433; Median household: n/a; Average household: $62,587; Households with income of $100,000 or more: 16.2%; Poverty rate: 30.4%
Educational Attainment: High school diploma or higher: 66.1%; Bachelor's degree or higher: n/a; Graduate/professional degree or higher: n/a
Housing: Homeownership rate: 64.5%; Median home value: $85,000; Median year structure built: 1950; Homeowner vacancy rate: 0.0%; Median selected monthly owner costs: n/a with a mortgage, $350 without a mortgage; Median gross rent: $535 per month; Rental vacancy rate: 26.7%
Health Insurance: 89.9% have insurance; 35.4% have private insurance; 63.3% have public insurance; 10.1% do not have insurance; 0.0% of children under 18 do not have insurance
Transportation: Commute: 82.6% car, 0.0% public transportation, 0.0% walk, 0.0% work from home; Mean travel time to work: 39.1 minutes

SEAMAN (village). Covers a land area of 1.067 square miles and a water area of 0 square miles. Located at 38.93° N. Lat; 83.57° W. Long. Elevation is 906 feet.
Population: 935; Growth (since 2000): -10.0%; Density: 875.9 persons per square mile; Race: 97.6% White, 0.0% Black/African American, 0.0% Asian, 0.0% American Indian/Alaska Native, 0.0% Native Hawaiian/Other Pacific Islander, 1.8% Two or more races, 1.4% Hispanic of any race; Average household size: 2.69; Median age: 38.2; Age under 18: 26.5%; Age 65 and over: 14.9%; Males per 100 females: 91.1; Marriage status: 23.1% never married, 54.8% now married, 3.7% separated, 7.6% widowed, 14.5% divorced; Foreign born: 0.5%; Speak English only: 98.3%; With disability: 14.9%; Veterans: 9.0%; Ancestry: 49.4% American, 11.3% German, 9.3% Irish, 8.8% English, 2.9% French
Employment: 11.0% management, business, and financial, 3.0% computer, engineering, and science, 3.4% education, legal, community service, arts, and media, 10.7% healthcare practitioners, 17.7% service, 23.8% sales and office, 13.1% natural resources, construction, and maintenance, 17.4% production, transportation, and material moving
Income: Per capita: $17,745; Median household: $31,974; Average household: $45,527; Households with income of $100,000 or more: 7.8%; Poverty rate: 28.1%
Educational Attainment: High school diploma or higher: 81.6%; Bachelor's degree or higher: 14.4%; Graduate/professional degree or higher: 5.6%

School District(s)

Adams County Ohio Valley Local (PK-12)
2015-16 Enrollment: 3,960 . . . . (937) 544-5586
Housing: Homeownership rate: 52.9%; Median home value: $92,700; Median year structure built: 1963; Homeowner vacancy rate: 5.5%; Median selected monthly owner costs: $925 with a mortgage, $362 without a mortgage; Median gross rent: $640 per month; Rental vacancy rate: 7.9%
Health Insurance: 88.3% have insurance; 50.1% have private insurance; 49.6% have public insurance; 11.7% do not have insurance; 2.8% of children under 18 do not have insurance
Hospitals: Adams County Regional Medical Center
Transportation: Commute: 91.4% car, 0.0% public transportation, 1.2% walk, 4.0% work from home; Mean travel time to work: 34.1 minutes

WEST UNION (village). County seat. Covers a land area of 2.831 square miles and a water area of 0 square miles. Located at 38.79° N. Lat; 83.54° W. Long. Elevation is 945 feet.
History: Laid out 1804.
Population: 3,028; Growth (since 2000): 4.3%; Density: 1,069.6 persons per square mile; Race: 98.6% White, 1.1% Black/African American, 0.0% Asian, 0.0% American Indian/Alaska Native, 0.0% Native Hawaiian/Other Pacific Islander, 0.3% Two or more races, 0.0% Hispanic of any race; Average household size: 2.06; Median age: 42.6; Age under 18: 19.6%; Age 65 and over: 21.5%; Males per 100 females: 83.4; Marriage status: 29.4% never married, 38.0% now married, 1.9% separated, 13.0% widowed, 19.6% divorced; Foreign born: 0.4%; Speak English only: 99.2%; With disability: 27.0%; Veterans: 6.1%; Ancestry: 33.0% American, 9.5% English, 9.0% German, 8.0% Irish, 2.2% Italian
Employment: 11.7% management, business, and financial, 0.0% computer, engineering, and science, 5.6% education, legal, community service, arts, and media, 7.9% healthcare practitioners, 13.2% service, 18.0% sales and office, 16.4% natural resources, construction, and maintenance, 27.2% production, transportation, and material moving
Income: Per capita: $16,673; Median household: $20,479; Average household: $34,582; Households with income of $100,000 or more: 5.6%; Poverty rate: 44.1%
Educational Attainment: High school diploma or higher: 78.4%; Bachelor's degree or higher: 11.6%; Graduate/professional degree or higher: 6.1%

School District(s)

Adams County Ohio Valley Local (PK-12)
2015-16 Enrollment: 3,960 . . . . (937) 544-5586
Housing: Homeownership rate: 39.8%; Median home value: $75,200; Median year structure built: 1976; Homeowner vacancy rate: 0.0%; Median selected monthly owner costs: $925 with a mortgage, $346 without a mortgage; Median gross rent: $496 per month; Rental vacancy rate: 0.0%
Health Insurance: 89.1% have insurance; 47.0% have private insurance; 58.5% have public insurance; 10.9% do not have insurance; 0.0% of children under 18 do not have insurance
Safety: Violent crime rate: 15.8 per 10,000 population; Property crime rate: 138.9 per 10,000 population
Newspapers: The Peoples Defender (weekly circulation 7,400)
Transportation: Commute: 95.9% car, 3.1% public transportation, 0.0% walk, 1.0% work from home; Mean travel time to work: 29.4 minutes

WINCHESTER (village). Covers a land area of 2.612 square miles and a water area of 0.017 square miles. Located at 38.94° N. Lat; 83.65° W. Long. Elevation is 971 feet.
History: In agricultural area.
Population: 1,094; Growth (since 2000): 6.7%; Density: 418.8 persons per square mile; Race: 90.6% White, 0.0% Black/African American, 0.0% Asian, 0.0% American Indian/Alaska Native, 0.0% Native Hawaiian/Other Pacific Islander, 8.7% Two or more races, 0.7% Hispanic of any race; Average household size: 2.95; Median age: 32.7; Age under 18: 28.3%; Age 65 and over: 10.2%; Males per 100 females: 96.1; Marriage status: 28.9% never married, 47.7% now married, 3.5% separated, 6.7% widowed, 16.7% divorced; Foreign born: 0.3%; Speak English only: 100.0%; With disability: 22.8%; Veterans: 5.0%; Ancestry: 40.3% American, 17.4% German, 9.7% English, 8.4% Irish, 1.0% Norwegian
Employment: 7.5% management, business, and financial, 0.0% computer, engineering, and science, 6.4% education, legal, community service, arts, and media, 3.1% healthcare practitioners, 26.4% service, 21.9% sales and office, 8.1% natural resources, construction, and maintenance, 26.7% production, transportation, and material moving
Income: Per capita: $16,085; Median household: $28,690; Average household: $43,295; Households with income of $100,000 or more: 9.8%; Poverty rate: 41.5%
Educational Attainment: High school diploma or higher: 86.6%; Bachelor's degree or higher: 5.8%; Graduate/professional degree or higher: 2.7%
Housing: Homeownership rate: 53.3%; Median home value: $95,800; Median year structure built: 1963; Homeowner vacancy rate: 0.0%; Median selected monthly owner costs: $996 with a mortgage, $382 without a mortgage; Median gross rent: $611 per month; Rental vacancy rate: 12.3%
Health Insurance: 87.2% have insurance; 38.5% have private insurance; 56.4% have public insurance; 12.8% do not have insurance; 0.0% of children under 18 do not have insurance
Transportation: Commute: 94.7% car, 0.0% public transportation, 1.9% walk, 3.3% work from home; Mean travel time to work: 37.2 minutes

Allen County

Located in western Ohio; crossed by the Ottawa and Auglaize Rivers. Covers a land area of 402.496 square miles, a water area of 4.353 square miles, and is located in the Eastern Time Zone at 40.77° N. Lat., 84.11° W. Long. The county was founded in 1820. County seat is Lima.

Allen County is part of the Lima, OH Metropolitan Statistical Area. The entire metro area includes: Allen County, OH

Weather Station: Lima WWTP Elevation: 850 feet

	Jan	Feb	Mar	Apr	May	Jun	Jul	Aug	Sep	Oct	Nov	Dec
High	34	38	48	61	72	80	84	82	77	64	51	38
Low	20	22	30	40	51	60	64	63	55	44	35	24
Precip	2.4	2.2	2.7	3.4	4.2	3.9	4.3	3.5	3.2	2.7	3.3	2.8
Snow	na	na	na	tr	0.0	0.0	0.0	0.0	0.0	0.0	0.1	na

High and Low temperatures in degrees Fahrenheit; Precipitation and Snow in inches

Population: 104,664; Growth (since 2000): -3.5%; Density: 260.0 persons per square mile; Race: 83.4% White, 11.9% Black/African American, 0.7% Asian, 0.2% American Indian/Alaska Native, 0.0% Native Hawaiian/Other Pacific Islander, 3.1% two or more races, 2.7% Hispanic of any race; Average household size: 2.51; Median age: 38.2; Age under 18: 23.4%; Age 65 and over: 15.9%; Males per 100 females: 101.8; Marriage status: 32.3% never married, 48.0% now married, 1.3% separated, 6.9% widowed, 12.8% divorced; Foreign born: 1.2%; Speak English only: 97.6%; With disability: 15.2%; Veterans: 9.1%; Ancestry: 32.4% German, 10.7% Irish, 7.3% American, 6.9% English, 4.2% Italian
Religion: Six largest groups: 16.9% Catholicism, 8.3% Baptist, 7.4% Methodist/Pietist, 5.9% Holiness, 4.8% Non-denominational Protestant, 3.0% Lutheran
Economy: Unemployment rate: 4.5%; Leading industries: 16.6 % retail trade; 12.8 % other services (except public administration); 12.5 % health care and social assistance; Farms: 904 totaling 183,186 acres; Company size: 3 employ 1,000 or more persons, 4 employ 500 to 999 persons, 71 employs 100 to 499 persons, 2,326 employ less than 100 persons; Business ownership: 2,179 women-owned, 483 Black-owned, 44 Hispanic-owned, 72 Asian-owned, 27 American Indian/Alaska Native-owned
Employment: 9.3% management, business, and financial, 2.8% computer, engineering, and science, 8.3% education, legal, community service, arts, and media, 6.6% healthcare practitioners, 19.4% service, 22.2% sales and office, 8.4% natural resources, construction, and maintenance, 23.0% production, transportation, and material moving
Income: Per capita: $23,600; Median household: $45,575; Average household: $59,209; Households with income of $100,000 or more: 13.7%; Poverty rate: 16.1%
Educational Attainment: High school diploma or higher: 89.3%; Bachelor's degree or higher: 17.4%; Graduate/professional degree or higher: 7.2%
Housing: Homeownership rate: 66.4%; Median home value: $107,500; Median year structure built: 1963; Homeowner vacancy rate: 1.5%; Median selected monthly owner costs: $1,059 with a mortgage, $406 without a mortgage; Median gross rent: $660 per month; Rental vacancy rate: 5.5%
Vital Statistics: Birth rate: 120.7 per 10,000 population; Death rate: 104.6 per 10,000 population; Age-adjusted cancer mortality rate: 175.5 deaths per 100,000 population
Health Insurance: 90.9% have insurance; 68.7% have private insurance; 37.0% have public insurance; 9.1% do not have insurance; 4.0% of children under 18 do not have insurance
Health Care: Physicians: 28.5 per 10,000 population; Dentists: 6.0 per 10,000 population; Hospital beds: 71.2 per 10,000 population; Hospital admissions: 2,434.4 per 10,000 population
Air Quality Index (AQI): Percent of Days: 86.3% good, 12.8% moderate, 0.8% unhealthy for sensitive individuals, 0.0% unhealthy, 0.0% very unhealthy; Annual median: 34; Annual maximum: 122
Transportation: Commute: 95.1% car, 0.5% public transportation, 1.5% walk, 1.9% work from home; Mean travel time to work: 19.0 minutes
2016 Presidential Election: 65.9% Trump, 28.8% Clinton, 3.2% Johnson, 0.7% Stein
Additional Information Contacts
Allen Government . . . . (419) 228-3700
http://www.co.allen.oh.us

Allen County Communities

BEAVERDAM (village). Covers a land area of 0.612 square miles and a water area of <.001 square miles. Located at 40.83° N. Lat; 83.97° W. Long. Elevation is 856 feet.
Population: 466; Growth (since 2000): 30.9%; Density: 761.1 persons per square mile; Race: 99.1% White, 0.0% Black/African American, 0.0% Asian, 0.0% American Indian/Alaska Native, 0.0% Native Hawaiian/Other Pacific Islander, 0.9% Two or more races, 0.4% Hispanic of any race; Average household size: 2.44; Median age: 30.3; Age under 18: 27.0%; Age 65 and over: 13.1%; Males per 100 females: 106.5; Marriage status: 26.7% never married, 56.5% now married, 1.7% separated, 2.8% widowed, 14.0% divorced; Foreign born: 0.4%; Speak English only: 100.0%; With disability: 8.6%; Veterans: 13.5%; Ancestry: 30.0% German, 14.4% Irish, 7.1% American, 6.7% Italian, 4.7% Swiss
Employment: 3.3% management, business, and financial, 0.8% computer, engineering, and science, 1.2% education, legal, community service, arts, and media, 7.4% healthcare practitioners, 16.0% service, 30.0% sales and office, 9.1% natural resources, construction, and maintenance, 32.1% production, transportation, and material moving
Income: Per capita: $24,251; Median household: $47,344; Average household: $58,548; Households with income of $100,000 or more: 7.8%; Poverty rate: 14.6%
Educational Attainment: High school diploma or higher: 88.7%; Bachelor's degree or higher: 7.6%; Graduate/professional degree or higher: 1.0%
Housing: Homeownership rate: 69.6%; Median home value: $75,000; Median year structure built: 1944; Homeowner vacancy rate: 0.0%; Median selected monthly owner costs: $845 with a mortgage, $288 without a mortgage; Median gross rent: $733 per month; Rental vacancy rate: 0.0%
Health Insurance: 87.6% have insurance; 69.5% have private insurance; 35.0% have public insurance; 12.4% do not have insurance; 3.2% of children under 18 do not have insurance
Transportation: Commute: 100.0% car, 0.0% public transportation, 0.0% walk, 0.0% work from home; Mean travel time to work: 19.4 minutes

BLUFFTON (village). Covers a land area of 3.547 square miles and a water area of 0.069 square miles. Located at 40.89° N. Lat; 83.89° W. Long. Elevation is 837 feet.
History: Bluffton was founded in 1833 and named for a Mennonite community in Indiana. Many of the early residents were Mennonites of Swiss descent. Limestone outcroppings in the vicinity created a crushed stone and lime industry here.
Population: 4,376; Growth (since 2000): 12.3%; Density: 1,233.8 persons per square mile; Race: 95.4% White, 2.9% Black/African American, 0.8% Asian, 0.0% American Indian/Alaska Native, 0.0% Native Hawaiian/Other Pacific Islander, 0.9% Two or more races, 1.3% Hispanic of any race; Average household size: 2.37; Median age: 39.3; Age under 18: 22.4%; Age 65 and over: 20.7%; Males per 100 females: 83.9; Marriage status: 27.0% never married, 55.6% now married, 0.6% separated, 7.7% widowed, 9.7% divorced; Foreign born: 1.8%; Speak English only: 98.2%; With disability: 10.0%; Veterans: 6.5%; Ancestry: 37.9% German, 11.7% Swiss, 8.3% American, 5.4% European, 5.2% Irish
Employment: 17.3% management, business, and financial, 4.0% computer, engineering, and science, 20.1% education, legal, community service, arts, and media, 6.5% healthcare practitioners, 17.7% service, 17.8% sales and office, 4.2% natural resources, construction, and maintenance, 12.4% production, transportation, and material moving
Income: Per capita: $29,729; Median household: $73,132; Average household: $74,464; Households with income of $100,000 or more: 21.7%; Poverty rate: 6.0%
Educational Attainment: High school diploma or higher: 95.8%; Bachelor's degree or higher: 44.0%; Graduate/professional degree or higher: 23.1%

School District(s)
Bluffton Exempted Village (KG-12)
2015-16 Enrollment: 1,163 . . . . (419) 358-5901

Four-year College(s)
Bluffton University (Private, Not-for-profit, Mennonite Church)
Fall 2016 Enrollment: 952 . . . . (419) 358-3000
2016-17 Tuition: In-state $30,762; Out-of-state $30,762
Housing: Homeownership rate: 71.1%; Median home value: $139,900; Median year structure built: 1960; Homeowner vacancy rate: 1.8%; Median selected monthly owner costs: $1,140 with a mortgage, $429 without a mortgage; Median gross rent: $617 per month; Rental vacancy rate: 4.7%
Health Insurance: 94.0% have insurance; 84.5% have private insurance; 24.2% have public insurance; 6.0% do not have insurance; 9.9% of children under 18 do not have insurance
Hospitals: Bluffton Hospital (25 beds)
Safety: Violent crime rate: 2.4 per 10,000 population; Property crime rate: 198.7 per 10,000 population
Newspapers: Bluffton News (weekly circulation 2,900); North Baltimore News (weekly circulation 600)
Transportation: Commute: 83.0% car, 0.0% public transportation, 6.8% walk, 5.7% work from home; Mean travel time to work: 19.2 minutes
Additional Information Contacts

Village of Bluffton . . . . (419) 358-2066
http://www.bluffton-ohio.com

CAIRO (village). Covers a land area of 0.225 square miles and a water area of 0 square miles. Located at 40.83° N. Lat; 84.08° W. Long. Elevation is 814 feet.
Population: 470; Growth (since 2000): -5.8%; Density: 2,089.1 persons per square mile; Race: 98.5% White, 0.0% Black/African American, 0.2% Asian, 0.0% American Indian/Alaska Native, 0.0% Native Hawaiian/Other Pacific Islander, 1.3% Two or more races, 0.6% Hispanic of any race; Average household size: 2.53; Median age: 40.5; Age under 18: 21.7%; Age 65 and over: 20.4%; Males per 100 females: 87.1; Marriage status: 20.5% never married, 51.1% now married, 0.0% separated, 11.1% widowed, 17.4% divorced; Foreign born: 0.2%; Speak English only: 99.5%; With disability: 23.0%; Veterans: 9.0%; Ancestry: 36.2% German, 18.7% Irish, 11.7% American, 8.5% Italian, 6.2% English
Employment: 10.5% management, business, and financial, 0.0% computer, engineering, and science, 7.8% education, legal, community service, arts, and media, 5.0% healthcare practitioners, 16.0% service, 28.3% sales and office, 15.1% natural resources, construction, and maintenance, 17.4% production, transportation, and material moving
Income: Per capita: $27,803; Median household: $46,875; Average household: $67,156; Households with income of $100,000 or more: 9.8%; Poverty rate: 10.0%
Educational Attainment: High school diploma or higher: 90.5%; Bachelor's degree or higher: 9.8%; Graduate/professional degree or higher: 3.0%
Housing: Homeownership rate: 90.3%; Median home value: $82,900; Median year structure built: 1954; Homeowner vacancy rate: 1.1%; Median selected monthly owner costs: $1,100 with a mortgage, $336 without a mortgage; Median gross rent: $675 per month; Rental vacancy rate: 28.0%
Health Insurance: 87.7% have insurance; 75.3% have private insurance; 36.4% have public insurance; 12.3% do not have insurance; 0.0% of children under 18 do not have insurance
Transportation: Commute: 97.5% car, 0.0% public transportation, 0.0% walk, 0.0% work from home; Mean travel time to work: 19.2 minutes

DELPHOS (city). Covers a land area of 3.435 square miles and a water area of 0.044 square miles. Located at 40.85° N. Lat; 84.34° W. Long. Elevation is 774 feet.
History: Delphos was platted in 1845 by Ferdinand Bredeick. Its location on the Miami & Erie Canal and the Pennsylvania Railroad brought it early growth. Large-scale honey production was one of the leading industries.
Population: 7,216; Growth (since 2000): 3.9%; Density: 2,100.5 persons per square mile; Race: 94.0% White, 1.3% Black/African American, 0.2% Asian, 0.0% American Indian/Alaska Native, 0.0% Native Hawaiian/Other Pacific Islander, 1.2% Two or more races, 4.7% Hispanic of any race; Average household size: 2.38; Median age: 40.5; Age under 18: 21.9%; Age 65 and over: 17.8%; Males per 100 females: 94.5; Marriage status: 26.7% never married, 51.9% now married, 1.9% separated, 9.1% widowed, 12.4% divorced; Foreign born: 3.1%; Speak English only: 94.8%; With disability: 16.5%; Veterans: 9.2%; Ancestry: 52.2% German, 10.1% Irish, 8.3% American, 3.2% English, 2.6% Italian
Employment: 7.7% management, business, and financial, 4.5% computer, engineering, and science, 7.7% education, legal, community service, arts, and media, 2.9% healthcare practitioners, 13.9% service, 25.0% sales and office, 6.7% natural resources, construction, and maintenance, 31.6% production, transportation, and material moving
Income: Per capita: $22,261; Median household: $44,528; Average household: $52,858; Households with income of $100,000 or more: 9.3%; Poverty rate: 9.4%
Educational Attainment: High school diploma or higher: 89.2%; Bachelor's degree or higher: 16.4%; Graduate/professional degree or higher: 6.1%

School District(s)

Delphos City (KG-12)
2015-16 Enrollment: 1,042 . . . . (419) 692-2509
Housing: Homeownership rate: 68.8%; Median home value: $86,500; Median year structure built: 1958; Homeowner vacancy rate: 4.5%; Median selected monthly owner costs: $990 with a mortgage, $389 without a mortgage; Median gross rent: $693 per month; Rental vacancy rate: 7.2%
Health Insurance: 89.4% have insurance; 71.5% have private insurance; 33.6% have public insurance; 10.6% do not have insurance; 6.2% of children under 18 do not have insurance
Safety: Violent crime rate: 2.9 per 10,000 population; Property crime rate: 215.4 per 10,000 population
Newspapers: Delphos Daily Herald (daily circulation 3,300)
Transportation: Commute: 95.2% car, 0.0% public transportation, 2.9% walk, 1.0% work from home; Mean travel time to work: 18.1 minutes

ELIDA (village). Covers a land area of 1.220 square miles and a water area of <.001 square miles. Located at 40.79° N. Lat; 84.20° W. Long. Elevation is 797 feet.
Population: 1,935; Growth (since 2000): 0.9%; Density: 1,586.3 persons per square mile; Race: 92.7% White, 4.7% Black/African American, 0.0% Asian, 0.0% American Indian/Alaska Native, 0.0% Native Hawaiian/Other Pacific Islander, 2.6% Two or more races, 3.5% Hispanic of any race; Average household size: 2.82; Median age: 40.8; Age under 18: 27.7%; Age 65 and over: 12.7%; Males per 100 females: 95.0; Marriage status: 20.5% never married, 60.8% now married, 0.2% separated, 3.8% widowed, 14.8% divorced; Foreign born: 0.7%; Speak English only: 98.0%; With disability: 9.4%; Veterans: 7.2%; Ancestry: 42.5% German, 12.7% Irish, 10.7% English, 8.4% American, 2.7% French
Employment: 9.6% management, business, and financial, 2.1% computer, engineering, and science, 10.2% education, legal, community service, arts, and media, 5.5% healthcare practitioners, 21.8% service, 18.2% sales and office, 12.4% natural resources, construction, and maintenance, 20.1% production, transportation, and material moving
Income: Per capita: $29,069; Median household: $70,069; Average household: $78,449; Households with income of $100,000 or more: 29.4%; Poverty rate: 1.8%
Educational Attainment: High school diploma or higher: 97.0%; Bachelor's degree or higher: 22.7%; Graduate/professional degree or higher: 10.7%

School District(s)

Elida Local (KG-12)
2015-16 Enrollment: 2,459 . . . . (419) 331-4155
Housing: Homeownership rate: 89.1%; Median home value: $139,200; Median year structure built: 1975; Homeowner vacancy rate: 2.4%; Median selected monthly owner costs: $1,110 with a mortgage, $440 without a mortgage; Median gross rent: $736 per month; Rental vacancy rate: 0.0%
Health Insurance: 94.0% have insurance; 83.7% have private insurance; 26.5% have public insurance; 6.0% do not have insurance; 4.9% of children under 18 do not have insurance
Transportation: Commute: 98.3% car, 0.0% public transportation, 0.6% walk, 0.6% work from home; Mean travel time to work: 18.1 minutes

FORT SHAWNEE (CDP). Covers a land area of 7.208 square miles and a water area of 0.043 square miles. Located at 40.68° N. Lat; 84.13° W. Long. Elevation is 866 feet.
Population: 6,060; Growth (since 2000): 57.2%; Density: 840.7 persons per square mile; Race: 93.1% White, 1.6% Black/African American, 1.4% Asian, 0.1% American Indian/Alaska Native, 0.0% Native Hawaiian/Other Pacific Islander, 3.8% Two or more races, 0.3% Hispanic of any race; Average household size: 2.46; Median age: 45.9; Age under 18: 20.3%; Age 65 and over: 21.4%; Males per 100 females: 100.5; Marriage status: 18.7% never married, 59.8% now married, 3.1% separated, 8.2% widowed, 13.3% divorced; Foreign born: 1.6%; Speak English only: 97.8%; With disability: 13.4%; Veterans: 10.5%; Ancestry: 37.5% German, 10.2% English, 8.3% American, 8.3% Italian, 7.7% Irish
Employment: 11.3% management, business, and financial, 4.6% computer, engineering, and science, 12.2% education, legal, community service, arts, and media, 9.5% healthcare practitioners, 10.0% service, 24.7% sales and office, 5.9% natural resources, construction, and maintenance, 21.6% production, transportation, and material moving
Income: Per capita: $35,440; Median household: $62,514; Average household: $84,731; Households with income of $100,000 or more: 21.3%; Poverty rate: 11.0%
Educational Attainment: High school diploma or higher: 93.4%; Bachelor's degree or higher: 22.2%; Graduate/professional degree or higher: 9.3%
Housing: Homeownership rate: 87.4%; Median home value: $125,700; Median year structure built: 1967; Homeowner vacancy rate: 0.9%; Median selected monthly owner costs: $1,140 with a mortgage, $427 without a mortgage; Median gross rent: $820 per month; Rental vacancy rate: 22.4%
Health Insurance: 94.1% have insurance; 75.7% have private insurance; 35.3% have public insurance; 5.9% do not have insurance; 7.7% of children under 18 do not have insurance

Transportation: Commute: 98.0% car, 0.0% public transportation, 0.3% walk, 1.3% work from home; Mean travel time to work: 19.1 minutes

GOMER (unincorporated postal area)

ZCTA: 45809

Covers a land area of 0.254 square miles and a water area of 0 square miles. Located at 40.85° N. Lat; 84.19° W. Long. Elevation is 778 feet.
Population: 153; Growth (since 2000): -26.4%; Density: 601.8 persons per square mile; Race: 100.0% White, 0.0% Black/African American, 0.0% Asian, 0.0% American Indian/Alaska Native, 0.0% Native Hawaiian/Other Pacific Islander, 0.0% Two or more races, 30.1% Hispanic of any race; Average household size: 2.68; Median age: 26.8; Age under 18: 37.9%; Age 65 and over: 2.6%; Males per 100 females: 101.3; Marriage status: 6.1% never married, 89.8% now married, 0.0% separated, 0.0% widowed, 4.1% divorced; Foreign born: 0.0%; Speak English only: 100.0%; With disability: 3.3%; Veterans: 5.3%; Ancestry: 36.6% German, 10.5% Irish, 9.2% English, 9.2% French, 7.8% Swiss
Employment: 7.1% management, business, and financial, 3.5% computer, engineering, and science, 4.7% education, legal, community service, arts, and media, 3.5% healthcare practitioners, 5.9% service, 32.9% sales and office, 9.4% natural resources, construction, and maintenance, 32.9% production, transportation, and material moving
Income: Per capita: $23,582; Median household: $66,198; Average household: $68,614; Households with income of $100,000 or more: 12.3%; Poverty rate: n/a
Educational Attainment: High school diploma or higher: 94.7%; Bachelor's degree or higher: 3.2%; Graduate/professional degree or higher: n/a
Housing: Homeownership rate: 84.2%; Median home value: $70,000; Median year structure built: Before 1940; Homeowner vacancy rate: 0.0%; Median selected monthly owner costs: $879 with a mortgage, $0 without a mortgage; Median gross rent: n/a per month; Rental vacancy rate: 0.0%
Health Insurance: 100.0% have insurance; 82.4% have private insurance; 20.3% have public insurance; 0.0% do not have insurance; 0.0% of children under 18 do not have insurance
Transportation: Commute: 100.0% car, 0.0% public transportation, 0.0% walk, 0.0% work from home; Mean travel time to work: 15.7 minutes

HARROD (village).
Covers a land area of 0.239 square miles and a water area of 0.001 square miles. Located at 40.71° N. Lat; 83.92° W. Long. Elevation is 981 feet.
Population: 425; Growth (since 2000): -13.4%; Density: 1,781.0 persons per square mile; Race: 97.4% White, 0.0% Black/African American, 0.0% Asian, 0.0% American Indian/Alaska Native, 0.0% Native Hawaiian/Other Pacific Islander, 0.0% Two or more races, 2.6% Hispanic of any race; Average household size: 2.78; Median age: 32.9; Age under 18: 32.5%; Age 65 and over: 11.1%; Males per 100 females: 97.6; Marriage status: 25.6% never married, 57.5% now married, 0.0% separated, 3.1% widowed, 13.8% divorced; Foreign born: 0.0%; Speak English only: 99.7%; With disability: 11.3%; Veterans: 11.5%; Ancestry: 26.8% German, 15.3% Irish, 12.2% American, 5.2% French, 4.9% English
Employment: 6.7% management, business, and financial, 1.9% computer, engineering, and science, 7.1% education, legal, community service, arts, and media, 8.1% healthcare practitioners, 23.3% service, 24.3% sales and office, 10.0% natural resources, construction, and maintenance, 18.6% production, transportation, and material moving
Income: Per capita: $22,940; Median household: $47,321; Average household: $59,601; Households with income of $100,000 or more: 15.7%; Poverty rate: 17.9%
Educational Attainment: High school diploma or higher: 92.6%; Bachelor's degree or higher: 10.7%; Graduate/professional degree or higher: 1.9%

School District(s)

Allen East Local (KG-12)
2015-16 Enrollment: 1,103 . . . . (419) 648-3333

Housing: Homeownership rate: 81.7%; Median home value: $77,400; Median year structure built: Before 1940; Homeowner vacancy rate: 0.0%; Median selected monthly owner costs: $871 with a mortgage, $332 without a mortgage; Median gross rent: $669 per month; Rental vacancy rate: 6.7%
Health Insurance: 93.4% have insurance; 76.2% have private insurance; 28.9% have public insurance; 6.6% do not have insurance; 2.2% of children under 18 do not have insurance
Transportation: Commute: 94.2% car, 0.0% public transportation, 2.4% walk, 1.0% work from home; Mean travel time to work: 25.9 minutes

LAFAYETTE (village).
Covers a land area of 0.253 square miles and a water area of <.001 square miles. Located at 40.76° N. Lat; 83.95° W. Long. Elevation is 928 feet.
Population: 384; Growth (since 2000): 26.3%; Density: 1,520.5 persons per square mile; Race: 100.0% White, 0.0% Black/African American, 0.0% Asian, 0.0% American Indian/Alaska Native, 0.0% Native Hawaiian/Other Pacific Islander, 0.0% Two or more races, 0.8% Hispanic of any race; Average household size: 2.61; Median age: 39.4; Age under 18: 22.1%; Age 65 and over: 14.6%; Males per 100 females: 91.8; Marriage status: 25.2% never married, 54.8% now married, 2.6% separated, 7.1% widowed, 12.9% divorced; Foreign born: 0.5%; Speak English only: 100.0%; With disability: 12.5%; Veterans: 9.0%; Ancestry: 31.0% German, 13.5% Irish, 7.8% English, 4.2% American, 4.2% French
Employment: 11.2% management, business, and financial, 6.5% computer, engineering, and science, 4.7% education, legal, community service, arts, and media, 2.3% healthcare practitioners, 26.5% service, 22.8% sales and office, 6.5% natural resources, construction, and maintenance, 19.5% production, transportation, and material moving
Income: Per capita: $20,579; Median household: $41,625; Average household: $51,749; Households with income of $100,000 or more: 7.5%; Poverty rate: 17.2%
Educational Attainment: High school diploma or higher: 95.4%; Bachelor's degree or higher: 7.2%; Graduate/professional degree or higher: 0.4%
Housing: Homeownership rate: 74.8%; Median home value: $82,200; Median year structure built: Before 1940; Homeowner vacancy rate: 1.8%; Median selected monthly owner costs: $846 with a mortgage, $328 without a mortgage; Median gross rent: $750 per month; Rental vacancy rate: 0.0%
Health Insurance: 86.7% have insurance; 71.6% have private insurance; 28.4% have public insurance; 13.3% do not have insurance; 2.4% of children under 18 do not have insurance
Transportation: Commute: 85.6% car, 0.0% public transportation, 9.8% walk, 4.7% work from home; Mean travel time to work: 20.5 minutes

LIMA (city).
County seat. Covers a land area of 13.565 square miles and a water area of 0.229 square miles. Located at 40.74° N. Lat; 84.11° W. Long. Elevation is 879 feet.
History: Lima was laid out on the Ottawa River in 1831 as the seat of Allen County. The name, the suggestion of minister and congressman Patrick Good, was drawn from a hat. Lima was incorporated in 1842. Oil was found here in 1885, bringing prosperity for a time until local industry turned to manufacturing railroad locomotives. It was in Lima that the Dillinger gang murdered Sheriff Jesse Sarber, starting a nation-wide hunt that ended in Dillinger's death and the end of his gang.
Population: 37,836; Growth (since 2000): -5.6%; Density: 2,789.3 persons per square mile; Race: 67.1% White, 25.9% Black/African American, 0.7% Asian, 0.4% American Indian/Alaska Native, 0.0% Native Hawaiian/Other Pacific Islander, 5.1% Two or more races, 3.3% Hispanic of any race; Average household size: 2.48; Median age: 33.2; Age under 18: 25.7%; Age 65 and over: 11.2%; Males per 100 females: 112.0; Marriage status: 45.0% never married, 32.1% now married, 2.2% separated, 6.2% widowed, 16.7% divorced; Foreign born: 1.1%; Speak English only: 97.2%; With disability: 18.4%; Veterans: 8.5%; Ancestry: 24.9% German, 10.9% Irish, 5.8% English, 4.8% American, 3.7% Italian
Employment: 6.0% management, business, and financial, 1.5% computer, engineering, and science, 6.5% education, legal, community service, arts, and media, 5.7% healthcare practitioners, 25.9% service, 20.0% sales and office, 6.1% natural resources, construction, and maintenance, 28.1% production, transportation, and material moving
Income: Per capita: $16,705; Median household: $30,953; Average household: $42,178; Households with income of $100,000 or more: 6.2%; Poverty rate: 28.5%
Educational Attainment: High school diploma or higher: 83.7%; Bachelor's degree or higher: 11.5%; Graduate/professional degree or higher: 4.1%

School District(s)

Apollo (07-12)
2015-16 Enrollment: n/a . . . . (419) 998-2910
Auglaize County Educational Academy (03-12)
2015-16 Enrollment: 46. . . . . (419) 738-4572
Bath Local (KG-12)
2015-16 Enrollment: 1,786 . . . . (419) 221-0807
Heir Force Community School (KG-08)
2015-16 Enrollment: 304. . . . . (419) 228-9241

Lima City (PK-12)
2015-16 Enrollment: 3,722 . . . . (419) 996-3400
Perry Local (KG-12)
2015-16 Enrollment: 840. . . . . (419) 221-2770
Shawnee Local (KG-12)
2015-16 Enrollment: 2,466 . . . . (419) 998-8031
West Central Learning Academy II (07-12)
2015-16 Enrollment: 51. . . . . (419) 227-9252

Four-year College(s)

Ohio State University-Lima Campus (Public)
Fall 2016 Enrollment: 1,039 . . . . (419) 995-8600
2016-17 Tuition: In-state $7,140; Out-of-state $25,332
University of Northwestern Ohio (Private, Not-for-profit)
Fall 2016 Enrollment: 3,812 . . . . (419) 227-3141
2016-17 Tuition: In-state $10,440; Out-of-state $10,440

Two-year College(s)

James A Rhodes State College (Public)
Fall 2016 Enrollment: 4,575 . . . . (419) 995-8320
2016-17 Tuition: In-state $3,845; Out-of-state $7,689
Ohio State Beauty Academy (Private, For-profit)
Fall 2016 Enrollment: 116 . . . . (419) 229-7896

Vocational/Technical School(s)

Apollo Career Center (Public)
Fall 2016 Enrollment: 445 . . . . (419) 998-3000
2016-17 Tuition: $9,608

Housing: Homeownership rate: 45.2%; Median home value: $66,600; Median year structure built: 1952; Homeowner vacancy rate: 3.3%; Median selected monthly owner costs: $848 with a mortgage, $336 without a mortgage; Median gross rent: $628 per month; Rental vacancy rate: 7.1%
Health Insurance: 86.4% have insurance; 53.0% have private insurance; 46.2% have public insurance; 13.6% do not have insurance; 4.4% of children under 18 do not have insurance
Hospitals: Institute For Orthopaedic Surgery; Lima Memorial Health System (308 beds); Saint Rita's Medical Center (424 beds)
Safety: Violent crime rate: 94.4 per 10,000 population; Property crime rate: 599.0 per 10,000 population
Newspapers: Lima News (daily circulation 32,900)
Transportation: Commute: 93.9% car, 1.6% public transportation, 2.3% walk, 1.1% work from home; Mean travel time to work: 18.0 minutes
Airports: Lima Allen County (general aviation)
Additional Information Contacts
City of Lima . . . . (419) 228-5462
http://www.cityhall.lima.oh.us

SPENCERVILLE (village). Covers a land area of 0.969 square miles and a water area of <.001 square miles. Located at 40.71° N. Lat; 84.35° W. Long. Elevation is 830 feet.
History: Laid out 1844-1845, incorporated 1866.
Population: 2,339; Growth (since 2000): 4.7%; Density: 2,412.8 persons per square mile; Race: 97.0% White, 1.8% Black/African American, 0.0% Asian, 0.2% American Indian/Alaska Native, 0.0% Native Hawaiian/Other Pacific Islander, 0.6% Two or more races, 0.7% Hispanic of any race; Average household size: 2.55; Median age: 32.3; Age under 18: 28.0%; Age 65 and over: 14.6%; Males per 100 females: 94.8; Marriage status: 27.8% never married, 52.5% now married, 0.7% separated, 7.1% widowed, 12.6% divorced; Foreign born: 0.0%; Speak English only: 98.8%; With disability: 14.4%; Veterans: 9.7%; Ancestry: 40.5% German, 10.1% American, 8.6% Irish, 6.7% English, 2.5% Dutch
Employment: 5.9% management, business, and financial, 3.1% computer, engineering, and science, 4.8% education, legal, community service, arts, and media, 4.8% healthcare practitioners, 22.2% service, 19.1% sales and office, 8.3% natural resources, construction, and maintenance, 31.8% production, transportation, and material moving
Income: Per capita: $23,105; Median household: $40,430; Average household: $54,765; Households with income of $100,000 or more: 9.8%; Poverty rate: 24.4%
Educational Attainment: High school diploma or higher: 89.3%; Bachelor's degree or higher: 10.3%; Graduate/professional degree or higher: 4.1%

School District(s)

Spencerville Local (KG-12)
2015-16 Enrollment: 969. . . . . (419) 647-4111
Housing: Homeownership rate: 67.8%; Median home value: $79,000; Median year structure built: 1956; Homeowner vacancy rate: 0.0%; Median selected monthly owner costs: $790 with a mortgage, $389 without a mortgage; Median gross rent: $717 per month; Rental vacancy rate: 4.0%
Health Insurance: 93.5% have insurance; 65.4% have private insurance; 41.4% have public insurance; 6.5% do not have insurance; 2.6% of children under 18 do not have insurance
Safety: Violent crime rate: 4.6 per 10,000 population; Property crime rate: 127.6 per 10,000 population
Newspapers: The Journal News (weekly circulation 2,100)
Transportation: Commute: 97.1% car, 0.0% public transportation, 1.5% walk, 1.3% work from home; Mean travel time to work: 23.5 minutes

WESTMINSTER (CDP).
Land/water area and latitude/longitude are not available.
Population: 391; Growth (since 2000): n/a; Density: n/a persons per square mile; Race: 100.0% White, 0.0% Black/African American, 0.0% Asian, 0.0% American Indian/Alaska Native, 0.0% Native Hawaiian/Other Pacific Islander, 0.0% Two or more races, 2.6% Hispanic of any race; Average household size: 3.29; Median age: 27.2; Age under 18: 37.1%; Age 65 and over: 0.0%; Males per 100 females: 0.0; Marriage status: 25.8% never married, 59.0% now married, 0.0% separated, 0.0% widowed, 15.2% divorced; Foreign born: 0.0%; Speak English only: 91.2%; With disability: 10.2%; Veterans: 2.8%; Ancestry: 28.9% German, 22.5% American, 11.0% English, 5.6% Irish, 3.8% Scotch-Irish
Employment: 11.9% management, business, and financial, 3.1% computer, engineering, and science, 0.0% education, legal, community service, arts, and media, 14.9% healthcare practitioners, 19.1% service, 33.5% sales and office, 4.1% natural resources, construction, and maintenance, 13.4% production, transportation, and material moving
Income: Per capita: $18,078; Median household: $55,375; Average household: $57,929; Households with income of $100,000 or more: 11.8%; Poverty rate: 19.4%
Educational Attainment: High school diploma or higher: 100.0%; Bachelor's degree or higher: 8.3%; Graduate/professional degree or higher: n/a
Housing: Homeownership rate: 81.5%; Median home value: $98,200; Median year structure built: 1968; Homeowner vacancy rate: 0.0%; Median selected monthly owner costs: $950 with a mortgage, n/a without a mortgage; Median gross rent: n/a per month; Rental vacancy rate: 0.0%
Health Insurance: 97.7% have insurance; 70.8% have private insurance; 30.9% have public insurance; 2.3% do not have insurance; 0.0% of children under 18 do not have insurance
Safety: Violent crime rate: 0.0 per 10,000 population; Property crime rate: 0.0 per 10,000 population
Transportation: Commute: 100.0% car, 0.0% public transportation, 0.0% walk, 0.0% work from home; Mean travel time to work: 18.5 minutes

Ashland County

Located in north central Ohio; drained by forks of the Mohican River. Covers a land area of 422.950 square miles, a water area of 3.849 square miles, and is located in the Eastern Time Zone at 40.84° N. Lat., 82.27° W. Long. The county was founded in 1846. County seat is Ashland.

Ashland County is part of the Ashland, OH Micropolitan Statistical Area. The entire metro area includes: Ashland County, OH

Population: 53,343; Growth (since 2000): 1.6%; Density: 126.1 persons per square mile; Race: 97.0% White, 0.7% Black/African American, 0.6% Asian, 0.0% American Indian/Alaska Native, 0.0% Native Hawaiian/Other Pacific Islander, 1.4% two or more races, 1.2% Hispanic of any race; Average household size: 2.51; Median age: 40.0; Age under 18: 23.0%; Age 65 and over: 17.3%; Males per 100 females: 95.6; Marriage status: 28.6% never married, 53.9% now married, 1.5% separated, 6.4% widowed, 11.2% divorced; Foreign born: 2.1%; Speak English only: 94.1%; With disability: 14.5%; Veterans: 9.1%; Ancestry: 33.1% German, 11.8% Irish, 10.1% American, 9.1% English, 4.6% Italian
Religion: Six largest groups: 12.9% Baptist, 7.4% Methodist/Pietist, 6.2% European Free-Church, 5.9% Non-denominational Protestant, 3.1% Lutheran, 2.8% Catholicism
Economy: Unemployment rate: 4.2%; Leading industries: 16.6 % other services (except public administration); 15.6 % retail trade; 11.5 % health care and social assistance; Farms: 1,034 totaling 152,972 acres; Company size: 0 employ 1,000 or more persons, 3 employ 500 to 999 persons, 24 employ 100 to 499 persons, 986 employ less than 100 persons; Business

ownership: 1,287 women-owned, n/a Black-owned, 34 Hispanic-owned, 32 Asian-owned, n/a American Indian/Alaska Native-owned
Employment: 11.5% management, business, and financial, 2.6% computer, engineering, and science, 8.9% education, legal, community service, arts, and media, 6.0% healthcare practitioners, 17.4% service, 20.7% sales and office, 10.9% natural resources, construction, and maintenance, 22.0% production, transportation, and material moving
Income: Per capita: $22,604; Median household: $48,509; Average household: $57,977; Households with income of $100,000 or more: 13.5%; Poverty rate: 15.4%
Educational Attainment: High school diploma or higher: 87.4%; Bachelor's degree or higher: 19.6%; Graduate/professional degree or higher: 7.0%
Housing: Homeownership rate: 71.5%; Median home value: $120,700; Median year structure built: 1968; Homeowner vacancy rate: 1.2%; Median selected monthly owner costs: $1,028 with a mortgage, $409 without a mortgage; Median gross rent: $682 per month; Rental vacancy rate: 4.1%
Vital Statistics: Birth rate: 113.0 per 10,000 population; Death rate: 107.9 per 10,000 population; Age-adjusted cancer mortality rate: 164.4 deaths per 100,000 population
Health Insurance: 88.9% have insurance; 70.1% have private insurance; 33.8% have public insurance; 11.1% do not have insurance; 13.7% of children under 18 do not have insurance
Health Care: Physicians: 9.6 per 10,000 population; Dentists: 4.7 per 10,000 population; Hospital beds: 9.2 per 10,000 population; Hospital admissions: 423.1 per 10,000 population
Transportation: Commute: 91.6% car, 0.2% public transportation, 4.1% walk, 3.2% work from home; Mean travel time to work: 23.9 minutes
2016 Presidential Election: 70.7% Trump, 23.2% Clinton, 3.7% Johnson, 0.7% Stein
National and State Parks: Mohican State Forest; Mohican State Park
Additional Information Contacts
Ashland Government. . . . . (419) 289-0000
http://www.ashlandcounty.org

Ashland County Communities

ASHLAND (city). County seat. Covers a land area of 11.169 square miles and a water area of 0.062 square miles. Located at 40.87° N. Lat; 82.32° W. Long. Elevation is 1,066 feet.
History: Ashland was platted in 1815 by William Montgomery, who called it Uniontown. In 1822 the town was renamed Ashland, for Henry Clay's estate at Lexington, Kentucky. A memorial to Johnny Appleseed, who often came through Ashland, was erected in 1915 through the donations of Ashland County children.
Population: 20,419; Growth (since 2000): -3.9%; Density: 1,828.2 persons per square mile; Race: 95.1% White, 1.4% Black/African American, 1.0% Asian, 0.0% American Indian/Alaska Native, 0.0% Native Hawaiian/Other Pacific Islander, 2.2% Two or more races, 0.8% Hispanic of any race; Average household size: 2.25; Median age: 37.6; Age under 18: 20.0%; Age 65 and over: 18.3%; Males per 100 females: 88.1; Marriage status: 35.8% never married, 43.9% now married, 1.4% separated, 7.7% widowed, 12.6% divorced; Foreign born: 3.3%; Speak English only: 96.1%; With disability: 16.7%; Veterans: 9.4%; Ancestry: 30.5% German, 11.7% Irish, 9.6% English, 7.6% American, 5.1% Italian
Employment: 12.3% management, business, and financial, 2.9% computer, engineering, and science, 11.6% education, legal, community service, arts, and media, 5.4% healthcare practitioners, 18.5% service, 24.7% sales and office, 5.4% natural resources, construction, and maintenance, 19.3% production, transportation, and material moving
Income: Per capita: $21,897; Median household: $39,417; Average household: $52,911; Households with income of $100,000 or more: 12.0%; Poverty rate: 16.4%
Educational Attainment: High school diploma or higher: 87.0%; Bachelor's degree or higher: 26.8%; Graduate/professional degree or higher: 10.1%

School District(s)

Ashland City (PK-12)
2015-16 Enrollment: 3,270 . . . . (419) 289-1117
Ashland County Community Academy (08-12)
2015-16 Enrollment: 111. . . . . (419) 903-0295
Ashland County-West Holmes (10-12)
2015-16 Enrollment: n/a . . . . (419) 289-3313
Crestview Local (KG-12)
2015-16 Enrollment: 1,099 . . . . (419) 895-1700
Mapleton Local (PK-12)
2015-16 Enrollment: 946. . . . . (419) 945-2188

Four-year College(s)

Ashland University (Private, Not-for-profit, Brethren Church)
Fall 2016 Enrollment: 6,579 . . . . (800) 882-1548
2016-17 Tuition: In-state $20,392; Out-of-state $20,392

Vocational/Technical School(s)

Ashland County-West Holmes Career Center (Public)
Fall 2016 Enrollment: 45 . . . . (419) 289-3313
2016-17 Tuition: $4,941
Housing: Homeownership rate: 60.0%; Median home value: $99,400; Median year structure built: 1961; Homeowner vacancy rate: 2.8%; Median selected monthly owner costs: $999 with a mortgage, $417 without a mortgage; Median gross rent: $680 per month; Rental vacancy rate: 5.6%
Health Insurance: 92.4% have insurance; 72.0% have private insurance; 35.4% have public insurance; 7.6% do not have insurance; 3.0% of children under 18 do not have insurance
Hospitals: Samaritan Regional Health System (110 beds)
Safety: Violent crime rate: 11.8 per 10,000 population; Property crime rate: 199.7 per 10,000 population
Newspapers: Ashland Times-Gazette (daily circulation 11,900)
Transportation: Commute: 89.4% car, 0.0% public transportation, 6.6% walk, 2.3% work from home; Mean travel time to work: 19.6 minutes
Additional Information Contacts
City of Ashland . . . . (419) 289-8622
http://www.ashland-ohio.com

BAILEY LAKES (village). Covers a land area of 0.388 square miles and a water area of 0.075 square miles. Located at 40.95° N. Lat; 82.36° W. Long. Elevation is 1,053 feet.
Population: 440; Growth (since 2000): 10.8%; Density: 1,133.7 persons per square mile; Race: 100.0% White, 0.0% Black/African American, 0.0% Asian, 0.0% American Indian/Alaska Native, 0.0% Native Hawaiian/Other Pacific Islander, 0.0% Two or more races, 0.0% Hispanic of any race; Average household size: 2.53; Median age: 46.3; Age under 18: 19.5%; Age 65 and over: 20.5%; Males per 100 females: 94.2; Marriage status: 15.6% never married, 69.8% now married, 5.0% separated, 5.9% widowed, 8.7% divorced; Foreign born: 0.0%; Speak English only: 99.0%; With disability: 19.5%; Veterans: 13.6%; Ancestry: 48.0% German, 21.6% Irish, 9.8% English, 7.0% American, 7.0% Polish
Employment: 6.0% management, business, and financial, 3.4% computer, engineering, and science, 11.1% education, legal, community service, arts, and media, 10.3% healthcare practitioners, 19.7% service, 15.8% sales and office, 8.5% natural resources, construction, and maintenance, 25.2% production, transportation, and material moving
Income: Per capita: $23,545; Median household: $51,563; Average household: $57,487; Households with income of $100,000 or more: 9.8%; Poverty rate: 6.3%
Educational Attainment: High school diploma or higher: 85.9%; Bachelor's degree or higher: 13.4%; Graduate/professional degree or higher: 7.3%
Housing: Homeownership rate: 66.7%; Median home value: $100,000; Median year structure built: 1963; Homeowner vacancy rate: 0.0%; Median selected monthly owner costs: $1,070 with a mortgage, $348 without a mortgage; Median gross rent: $718 per month; Rental vacancy rate: 3.3%
Health Insurance: 92.7% have insurance; 74.8% have private insurance; 36.6% have public insurance; 7.3% do not have insurance; 7.0% of children under 18 do not have insurance
Transportation: Commute: 94.8% car, 0.9% public transportation, 0.0% walk, 3.9% work from home; Mean travel time to work: 24.9 minutes

CINNAMON LAKE (CDP). Covers a land area of 1.618 square miles and a water area of 0.225 square miles. Located at 40.98° N. Lat; 82.19° W. Long.
Population: 1,103; Growth (since 2000): n/a; Density: 681.7 persons per square mile; Race: 100.0% White, 0.0% Black/African American, 0.0% Asian, 0.0% American Indian/Alaska Native, 0.0% Native Hawaiian/Other Pacific Islander, 0.0% Two or more races, 0.0% Hispanic of any race; Average household size: 2.51; Median age: 39.3; Age under 18: 24.1%; Age 65 and over: 22.3%; Males per 100 females: 97.9; Marriage status: 18.3% never married, 55.5% now married, 2.5% separated, 11.6% widowed, 14.5% divorced; Foreign born: 0.0%; Speak English only: 100.0%; With disability: 24.2%; Veterans: 14.1%; Ancestry: 33.6% German, 22.8% Irish, 10.4% American, 8.5% English, 6.2% Norwegian

Employment: 10.7% management, business, and financial, 0.0% computer, engineering, and science, 6.5% education, legal, community service, arts, and media, 4.2% healthcare practitioners, 26.0% service, 17.4% sales and office, 10.9% natural resources, construction, and maintenance, 24.2% production, transportation, and material moving
Income: Per capita: $21,148; Median household: $49,942; Average household: $52,754; Households with income of $100,000 or more: 4.1%; Poverty rate: 15.0%
Educational Attainment: High school diploma or higher: 95.0%; Bachelor's degree or higher: 10.6%; Graduate/professional degree or higher: 4.1%
Housing: Homeownership rate: 92.7%; Median home value: $102,100; Median year structure built: 1992; Homeowner vacancy rate: 0.0%; Median selected monthly owner costs: $1,064 with a mortgage, $382 without a mortgage; Median gross rent: n/a per month; Rental vacancy rate: 0.0%
Health Insurance: 86.3% have insurance; 66.0% have private insurance; 42.3% have public insurance; 13.7% do not have insurance; 18.4% of children under 18 do not have insurance
Transportation: Commute: 100.0% car, 0.0% public transportation, 0.0% walk, 0.0% work from home; Mean travel time to work: 37.0 minutes

HAYESVILLE (village). Covers a land area of 0.738 square miles and a water area of 0.003 square miles. Located at 40.78° N. Lat; 82.26° W. Long. Elevation is 1,247 feet.
History: Hayesville was laid out in 1830 by Linus Hayes, a tavern owner, and Reverend John Cox. It was in Hayesville that William McKinley pleaded his first law case.
Population: 434; Growth (since 2000): 24.7%; Density: 588.1 persons per square mile; Race: 97.2% White, 0.0% Black/African American, 0.9% Asian, 0.2% American Indian/Alaska Native, 0.0% Native Hawaiian/Other Pacific Islander, 1.6% Two or more races, 3.9% Hispanic of any race; Average household size: 2.58; Median age: 38.0; Age under 18: 23.7%; Age 65 and over: 16.4%; Males per 100 females: 109.3; Marriage status: 20.0% never married, 67.7% now married, 2.0% separated, 3.4% widowed, 8.9% divorced; Foreign born: 0.0%; Speak English only: 97.8%; With disability: 7.1%; Veterans: 11.5%; Ancestry: 37.8% German, 10.8% Irish, 6.7% American, 4.6% English, 3.9% Italian
Employment: 11.2% management, business, and financial, 0.4% computer, engineering, and science, 13.9% education, legal, community service, arts, and media, 6.3% healthcare practitioners, 14.8% service, 22.0% sales and office, 4.9% natural resources, construction, and maintenance, 26.5% production, transportation, and material moving
Income: Per capita: $22,342; Median household: $53,250; Average household: $56,724; Households with income of $100,000 or more: 9.6%; Poverty rate: 8.1%
Educational Attainment: High school diploma or higher: 95.1%; Bachelor's degree or higher: 18.6%; Graduate/professional degree or higher: 5.9%

School District(s)

Hillsdale Local (KG-12)
2015-16 Enrollment: 820 . . . . (419) 368-8231
Housing: Homeownership rate: 86.9%; Median home value: $96,700; Median year structure built: 1961; Homeowner vacancy rate: 0.0%; Median selected monthly owner costs: $1,018 with a mortgage, $400 without a mortgage; Median gross rent: $738 per month; Rental vacancy rate: 0.0%
Health Insurance: 95.9% have insurance; 80.4% have private insurance; 28.8% have public insurance; 4.1% do not have insurance; 0.0% of children under 18 do not have insurance
Transportation: Commute: 95.3% car, 0.0% public transportation, 0.0% walk, 4.2% work from home; Mean travel time to work: 31.2 minutes

JEROMESVILLE (village). Covers a land area of 0.363 square miles and a water area of <.001 square miles. Located at 40.80° N. Lat; 82.20° W. Long. Elevation is 1,007 feet.
History: Jeromesville was named for a French trader, Jean Baptiste Jerome, who lived here. The town grew as a rural trading center.
Population: 578; Growth (since 2000): 20.9%; Density: 1,592.9 persons per square mile; Race: 100.0% White, 0.0% Black/African American, 0.0% Asian, 0.0% American Indian/Alaska Native, 0.0% Native Hawaiian/Other Pacific Islander, 0.0% Two or more races, 0.7% Hispanic of any race; Average household size: 2.59; Median age: 33.6; Age under 18: 29.2%; Age 65 and over: 11.4%; Males per 100 females: 98.6; Marriage status: 25.5% never married, 55.5% now married, 4.4% separated, 3.7% widowed, 15.4% divorced; Foreign born: 0.9%; Speak English only: 97.5%; With disability: 13.3%; Veterans: 9.5%; Ancestry: 49.7% German, 16.8% Irish, 12.8% English, 6.4% American, 2.1% Polish
Employment: 6.8% management, business, and financial, 3.8% computer, engineering, and science, 4.8% education, legal, community service, arts, and media, 9.9% healthcare practitioners, 11.6% service, 23.3% sales and office, 24.0% natural resources, construction, and maintenance, 15.8% production, transportation, and material moving
Income: Per capita: $23,888; Median household: $53,750; Average household: $58,402; Households with income of $100,000 or more: 11.7%; Poverty rate: 11.8%
Educational Attainment: High school diploma or higher: 92.6%; Bachelor's degree or higher: 12.8%; Graduate/professional degree or higher: 4.8%

School District(s)

Hillsdale Local (KG-12)
2015-16 Enrollment: 820 . . . . (419) 368-8231
Housing: Homeownership rate: 61.0%; Median home value: $86,400; Median year structure built: Before 1940; Homeowner vacancy rate: 12.8%; Median selected monthly owner costs: $928 with a mortgage, $367 without a mortgage; Median gross rent: $737 per month; Rental vacancy rate: 0.0%
Health Insurance: 88.2% have insurance; 67.8% have private insurance; 32.2% have public insurance; 11.8% do not have insurance; 1.8% of children under 18 do not have insurance
Transportation: Commute: 93.1% car, 0.0% public transportation, 4.2% walk, 2.8% work from home; Mean travel time to work: 29.9 minutes

LOUDONVILLE (village). Covers a land area of 2.599 square miles and a water area of 0.024 square miles. Located at 40.63° N. Lat; 82.23° W. Long. Elevation is 971 feet.
History: Loudonville was laid out in 1814 and named for a Revolutionary War soldier, James Louden Priest, who helped to survey the town. An early industry was the building of buses and ambulances.
Population: 2,634; Growth (since 2000): -9.4%; Density: 1,013.5 persons per square mile; Race: 97.6% White, 0.6% Black/African American, 0.8% Asian, 0.0% American Indian/Alaska Native, 0.0% Native Hawaiian/Other Pacific Islander, 0.9% Two or more races, 0.4% Hispanic of any race; Average household size: 2.17; Median age: 49.3; Age under 18: 16.2%; Age 65 and over: 23.7%; Males per 100 females: 87.6; Marriage status: 21.8% never married, 53.0% now married, 2.3% separated, 10.3% widowed, 14.9% divorced; Foreign born: 0.4%; Speak English only: 99.6%; With disability: 17.8%; Veterans: 13.2%; Ancestry: 36.6% German, 15.5% Irish, 11.1% American, 8.8% English, 5.4% French
Employment: 8.6% management, business, and financial, 2.7% computer, engineering, and science, 9.1% education, legal, community service, arts, and media, 2.8% healthcare practitioners, 18.4% service, 17.3% sales and office, 12.3% natural resources, construction, and maintenance, 28.8% production, transportation, and material moving
Income: Per capita: $20,886; Median household: $37,344; Average household: $45,897; Households with income of $100,000 or more: 9.3%; Poverty rate: 16.4%
Educational Attainment: High school diploma or higher: 88.8%; Bachelor's degree or higher: 12.8%; Graduate/professional degree or higher: 3.9%

School District(s)

Loudonville-Perrysville Exempted Village (KG-12)
2015-16 Enrollment: 1,121 . . . . (419) 994-3912
Housing: Homeownership rate: 64.0%; Median home value: $88,900; Median year structure built: 1951; Homeowner vacancy rate: 0.7%; Median selected monthly owner costs: $793 with a mortgage, $341 without a mortgage; Median gross rent: $580 per month; Rental vacancy rate: 2.1%
Health Insurance: 90.4% have insurance; 65.6% have private insurance; 46.5% have public insurance; 9.6% do not have insurance; 1.2% of children under 18 do not have insurance
Safety: Violent crime rate: 53.4 per 10,000 population; Property crime rate: 179.3 per 10,000 population
Newspapers: Loudonville Times (weekly circulation 2,500)
Transportation: Commute: 95.2% car, 0.0% public transportation, 2.5% walk, 1.8% work from home; Mean travel time to work: 23.9 minutes

MIFFLIN (village). Covers a land area of 0.183 square miles and a water area of 0 square miles. Located at 40.77° N. Lat; 82.36° W. Long. Elevation is 1,066 feet.
Population: 121; Growth (since 2000): -16.0%; Density: 662.1 persons per square mile; Race: 100.0% White, 0.0% Black/African American, 0.0%

Asian, 0.0% American Indian/Alaska Native, 0.0% Native Hawaiian/Other Pacific Islander, 0.0% Two or more races, 0.0% Hispanic of any race; Average household size: 2.12; Median age: 46.2; Age under 18: 18.2%; Age 65 and over: 12.4%; Males per 100 females: 93.0; Marriage status: 15.4% never married, 48.1% now married, 7.7% separated, 13.5% widowed, 23.1% divorced; Foreign born: 0.0%; Speak English only: 100.0%; With disability: 15.7%; Veterans: 7.1%; Ancestry: 40.5% German, 13.2% Irish, 9.1% Italian, 6.6% English, 4.1% American
Employment: 3.5% management, business, and financial, 0.0% computer, engineering, and science, 7.0% education, legal, community service, arts, and media, 14.0% healthcare practitioners, 12.3% service, 15.8% sales and office, 10.5% natural resources, construction, and maintenance, 36.8% production, transportation, and material moving
Income: Per capita: $20,697; Median household: $36,250; Average household: $40,828; Households with income of $100,000 or more: 7.0%; Poverty rate: 23.1%
Educational Attainment: High school diploma or higher: 76.1%; Bachelor's degree or higher: 7.6%; Graduate/professional degree or higher: 4.3%
Housing: Homeownership rate: 73.7%; Median home value: $66,400; Median year structure built: Before 1940; Homeowner vacancy rate: 0.0%; Median selected monthly owner costs: $740 with a mortgage, $307 without a mortgage; Median gross rent: $538 per month; Rental vacancy rate: 0.0%
Health Insurance: 94.2% have insurance; 73.6% have private insurance; 36.4% have public insurance; 5.8% do not have insurance; 0.0% of children under 18 do not have insurance
Transportation: Commute: 94.7% car, 0.0% public transportation, 5.3% walk, 0.0% work from home; Mean travel time to work: 24.4 minutes

NOVA (unincorporated postal area)

ZCTA: 44859

Covers a land area of 30.319 square miles and a water area of 0.204 square miles. Located at 41.02° N. Lat; 82.33° W. Long. Elevation is 1,129 feet.
Population: 1,515; Growth (since 2000): -13.9%; Density: 50.0 persons per square mile; Race: 96.2% White, 0.5% Black/African American, 0.0% Asian, 0.0% American Indian/Alaska Native, 0.0% Native Hawaiian/Other Pacific Islander, 0.0% Two or more races, 4.9% Hispanic of any race; Average household size: 2.96; Median age: 43.0; Age under 18: 22.1%; Age 65 and over: 15.1%; Males per 100 females: 103.4; Marriage status: 25.4% never married, 58.8% now married, 0.0% separated, 5.4% widowed, 10.4% divorced; Foreign born: 0.3%; Speak English only: 97.3%; With disability: 20.5%; Veterans: 3.9%; Ancestry: 20.2% German, 16.6% Italian, 15.8% English, 13.1% Hungarian, 7.6% American
Employment: 13.5% management, business, and financial, 4.4% computer, engineering, and science, 10.3% education, legal, community service, arts, and media, 1.8% healthcare practitioners, 7.2% service, 19.3% sales and office, 20.0% natural resources, construction, and maintenance, 23.5% production, transportation, and material moving
Income: Per capita: $22,709; Median household: $61,188; Average household: $65,550; Households with income of $100,000 or more: 20.4%; Poverty rate: 15.7%
Educational Attainment: High school diploma or higher: 78.6%; Bachelor's degree or higher: 18.4%; Graduate/professional degree or higher: 9.5%
Housing: Homeownership rate: 80.2%; Median home value: $143,300; Median year structure built: 1975; Homeowner vacancy rate: 0.0%; Median selected monthly owner costs: $1,330 with a mortgage, $429 without a mortgage; Median gross rent: $681 per month; Rental vacancy rate: 0.0%
Health Insurance: 90.6% have insurance; 67.5% have private insurance; 33.9% have public insurance; 9.4% do not have insurance; 0.0% of children under 18 do not have insurance
Transportation: Commute: 91.4% car, 0.1% public transportation, 0.6% walk, 7.9% work from home; Mean travel time to work: 39.3 minutes

PERRYSVILLE (village). Covers a land area of 0.787 square miles and a water area of 0 square miles. Located at 40.66° N. Lat; 82.31° W. Long. Elevation is 988 feet.
Population: 864; Growth (since 2000): 5.9%; Density: 1,097.2 persons per square mile; Race: 98.0% White, 0.5% Black/African American, 0.0% Asian, 0.6% American Indian/Alaska Native, 0.0% Native Hawaiian/Other Pacific Islander, 0.9% Two or more races, 0.2% Hispanic of any race; Average household size: 2.89; Median age: 33.3; Age under 18: 26.3%; Age 65 and over: 8.8%; Males per 100 females: 95.5; Marriage status: 33.6% never married, 45.9% now married, 1.8% separated, 3.1% widowed, 17.4% divorced; Foreign born: 0.7%; Speak English only: 99.8%; With disability: 14.2%; Veterans: 8.6%; Ancestry: 45.4% German, 17.4% Irish, 11.9% English, 3.4% American, 2.9% Swedish
Employment: 2.8% management, business, and financial, 1.0% computer, engineering, and science, 1.5% education, legal, community service, arts, and media, 5.8% healthcare practitioners, 27.0% service, 18.5% sales and office, 9.3% natural resources, construction, and maintenance, 34.3% production, transportation, and material moving
Income: Per capita: $16,407; Median household: $32,366; Average household: $45,425; Households with income of $100,000 or more: 8.3%; Poverty rate: 23.2%
Educational Attainment: High school diploma or higher: 89.1%; Bachelor's degree or higher: 6.2%; Graduate/professional degree or higher: 0.6%

School District(s)

Loudonville-Perrysville Exempted Village (KG-12)
2015-16 Enrollment: 1,121 . . . . (419) 994-3912
Housing: Homeownership rate: 63.2%; Median home value: $76,000; Median year structure built: 1948; Homeowner vacancy rate: 5.0%; Median selected monthly owner costs: $846 with a mortgage, $291 without a mortgage; Median gross rent: $575 per month; Rental vacancy rate: 13.5%
Health Insurance: 86.0% have insurance; 58.0% have private insurance; 35.8% have public insurance; 14.0% do not have insurance; 3.5% of children under 18 do not have insurance
Transportation: Commute: 90.4% car, 0.0% public transportation, 7.3% walk, 2.3% work from home; Mean travel time to work: 24.0 minutes

POLK (village). Covers a land area of 1.012 square miles and a water area of 0.024 square miles. Located at 40.95° N. Lat; 82.21° W. Long. Elevation is 1,263 feet.
Population: 293; Growth (since 2000): -17.9%; Density: 289.5 persons per square mile; Race: 100.0% White, 0.0% Black/African American, 0.0% Asian, 0.0% American Indian/Alaska Native, 0.0% Native Hawaiian/Other Pacific Islander, 0.0% Two or more races, 1.0% Hispanic of any race; Average household size: 2.71; Median age: 46.5; Age under 18: 17.1%; Age 65 and over: 16.4%; Males per 100 females: 90.9; Marriage status: 23.2% never married, 60.6% now married, 2.4% separated, 7.5% widowed, 8.7% divorced; Foreign born: 0.0%; Speak English only: 99.6%; With disability: 15.9%; Veterans: 8.8%; Ancestry: 42.7% German, 15.4% American, 13.0% Irish, 4.8% Dutch, 4.1% Hungarian
Employment: 11.5% management, business, and financial, 2.7% computer, engineering, and science, 4.1% education, legal, community service, arts, and media, 2.7% healthcare practitioners, 21.6% service, 20.9% sales and office, 8.1% natural resources, construction, and maintenance, 28.4% production, transportation, and material moving
Income: Per capita: $22,594; Median household: $49,500; Average household: $61,121; Households with income of $100,000 or more: 14.0%; Poverty rate: 8.3%
Educational Attainment: High school diploma or higher: 82.1%; Bachelor's degree or higher: 9.0%; Graduate/professional degree or higher: 2.4%
Housing: Homeownership rate: 81.5%; Median home value: $95,000; Median year structure built: Before 1940; Homeowner vacancy rate: 0.0%; Median selected monthly owner costs: $944 with a mortgage, $338 without a mortgage; Median gross rent: $864 per month; Rental vacancy rate: 0.0%
Health Insurance: 96.6% have insurance; 74.5% have private insurance; 35.5% have public insurance; 3.4% do not have insurance; 0.0% of children under 18 do not have insurance
Transportation: Commute: 86.7% car, 0.0% public transportation, 7.7% walk, 2.8% work from home; Mean travel time to work: 26.7 minutes

SAVANNAH (village). Covers a land area of 0.572 square miles and a water area of 0.009 square miles. Located at 40.97° N. Lat; 82.37° W. Long. Elevation is 1,102 feet.
Population: 425; Growth (since 2000): 14.2%; Density: 743.0 persons per square mile; Race: 98.1% White, 0.0% Black/African American, 0.0% Asian, 0.2% American Indian/Alaska Native, 0.0% Native Hawaiian/Other Pacific Islander, 1.6% Two or more races, 0.0% Hispanic of any race; Average household size: 2.85; Median age: 35.1; Age under 18: 24.0%; Age 65 and over: 8.9%; Males per 100 females: 97.6; Marriage status: 28.6% never married, 57.8% now married, 3.2% separated, 5.6% widowed, 8.0% divorced; Foreign born: 0.0%; Speak English only: 98.0%;

With disability: 16.0%; Veterans: 8.4%; Ancestry: 36.9% German, 19.5% Irish, 17.6% English, 5.2% American, 4.2% Czech
Employment: 10.9% management, business, and financial, 2.6% computer, engineering, and science, 6.7% education, legal, community service, arts, and media, 2.1% healthcare practitioners, 16.1% service, 17.6% sales and office, 8.3% natural resources, construction, and maintenance, 35.8% production, transportation, and material moving
Income: Per capita: $18,201; Median household: $42,266; Average household: $53,630; Households with income of $100,000 or more: 11.4%; Poverty rate: 6.6%
Educational Attainment: High school diploma or higher: 89.7%; Bachelor's degree or higher: 14.4%; Graduate/professional degree or higher: 4.1%
Housing: Homeownership rate: 81.9%; Median home value: $89,600; Median year structure built: Before 1940; Homeowner vacancy rate: 0.0%; Median selected monthly owner costs: $988 with a mortgage, $400 without a mortgage; Median gross rent: $625 per month; Rental vacancy rate: 0.0%
Health Insurance: 80.2% have insurance; 61.6% have private insurance; 28.2% have public insurance; 19.8% do not have insurance; 9.8% of children under 18 do not have insurance
Transportation: Commute: 87.6% car, 0.0% public transportation, 6.7% walk, 5.7% work from home; Mean travel time to work: 22.0 minutes

SULLIVAN (unincorporated postal area)

ZCTA: 44880

Covers a land area of 30.787 square miles and a water area of 0.229 square miles. Located at 41.03° N. Lat; 82.22° W. Long. Elevation is 1,125 feet.
Population: 2,975; Growth (since 2000): 26.1%; Density: 96.6 persons per square mile; Race: 96.0% White, 0.0% Black/African American, 0.0% Asian, 0.0% American Indian/Alaska Native, 0.0% Native Hawaiian/Other Pacific Islander, 4.0% Two or more races, 4.0% Hispanic of any race; Average household size: 2.93; Median age: 43.3; Age under 18: 26.6%; Age 65 and over: 14.7%; Males per 100 females: 105.2; Marriage status: 25.7% never married, 62.9% now married, 0.9% separated, 4.1% widowed, 7.3% divorced; Foreign born: 3.4%; Speak English only: 87.2%; With disability: 11.2%; Veterans: 9.8%; Ancestry: 24.1% German, 13.8% Irish, 11.2% American, 9.5% Polish, 4.8% English
Employment: 12.9% management, business, and financial, 0.0% computer, engineering, and science, 5.1% education, legal, community service, arts, and media, 4.5% healthcare practitioners, 15.6% service, 12.9% sales and office, 8.4% natural resources, construction, and maintenance, 40.7% production, transportation, and material moving
Income: Per capita: $22,123; Median household: $54,500; Average household: $63,480; Households with income of $100,000 or more: 19.6%; Poverty rate: 23.8%
Educational Attainment: High school diploma or higher: 82.5%; Bachelor's degree or higher: 6.8%; Graduate/professional degree or higher: 3.5%

School District(s)

Black River Local (PK-12)
2015-16 Enrollment: 1,202 . . . . (419) 736-3300
Housing: Homeownership rate: 89.8%; Median home value: $143,300; Median year structure built: 1991; Homeowner vacancy rate: 0.0%; Median selected monthly owner costs: $1,205 with a mortgage, $390 without a mortgage; Median gross rent: $1,147 per month; Rental vacancy rate: 0.0%
Health Insurance: 80.8% have insurance; 57.4% have private insurance; 34.9% have public insurance; 19.2% do not have insurance; 24.7% of children under 18 do not have insurance
Transportation: Commute: 89.2% car, 1.7% public transportation, 4.2% walk, 4.9% work from home; Mean travel time to work: 34.1 minutes

Ashtabula County

Located in northeastern Ohio; bounded on the north by Lake Erie; crossed by the Grand and Ashtabula Rivers. Covers a land area of 701.931 square miles, a water area of 665.971 square miles, and is located in the Eastern Time Zone at 41.91° N. Lat., 80.75° W. Long. The county was founded in 1807. County seat is Jefferson.

Ashtabula County is part of the Ashtabula, OH Micropolitan Statistical Area. The entire metro area includes: Ashtabula County, OH

Weather Station: Dorset — Elevation: 979 feet

	Jan	Feb	Mar	Apr	May	Jun	Jul	Aug	Sep	Oct	Nov	Dec
High	33	35	45	58	68	77	81	80	74	61	49	37
Low	16	17	25	35	44	54	58	57	50	40	33	22
Precip	2.6	2.2	2.9	3.6	3.9	4.5	4.8	3.8	4.4	4.0	3.7	3.2
Snow	21.2	13.5	11.6	3.5	tr	0.0	0.0	0.0	0.0	0.5	8.3	20.4

High and Low temperatures in degrees Fahrenheit; Precipitation and Snow in inches

Population: 99,175; Growth (since 2000): -3.5%; Density: 141.3 persons per square mile; Race: 93.0% White, 3.5% Black/African American, 0.4% Asian, 0.2% American Indian/Alaska Native, 0.0% Native Hawaiian/Other Pacific Islander, 2.4% two or more races, 3.9% Hispanic of any race; Average household size: 2.47; Median age: 42.2; Age under 18: 22.6%; Age 65 and over: 17.3%; Males per 100 females: 99.8; Marriage status: 28.0% never married, 49.4% now married, 1.3% separated, 7.6% widowed, 15.0% divorced; Foreign born: 1.4%; Speak English only: 93.7%; With disability: 16.0%; Veterans: 11.1%; Ancestry: 22.2% German, 15.4% Irish, 13.6% American, 10.9% English, 10.1% Italian
Religion: Six largest groups: 13.9% Catholicism, 5.0% Methodist/Pietist, 3.7% Baptist, 2.7% Presbyterian-Reformed, 2.5% Lutheran, 2.2% European Free-Church
Economy: Unemployment rate: 5.3%; Leading industries: 16.1 % retail trade; 12.3 % other services (except public administration); 12.2 % accommodation and food services; Farms: 1,099 totaling 165,967 acres; Company size: 0 employ 1,000 or more persons, 1 employs 500 to 999 persons, 40 employ 100 to 499 persons, 1,868 employ less than 100 persons; Business ownership: 1,916 women-owned, 85 Black-owned, 109 Hispanic-owned, 96 Asian-owned, 48 American Indian/Alaska Native-owned
Employment: 10.0% management, business, and financial, 2.2% computer, engineering, and science, 6.9% education, legal, community service, arts, and media, 5.8% healthcare practitioners, 19.0% service, 21.9% sales and office, 9.4% natural resources, construction, and maintenance, 24.7% production, transportation, and material moving
Income: Per capita: $20,978; Median household: $41,158; Average household: $51,525; Households with income of $100,000 or more: 11.5%; Poverty rate: 19.6%
Educational Attainment: High school diploma or higher: 85.4%; Bachelor's degree or higher: 13.1%; Graduate/professional degree or higher: 4.6%
Housing: Homeownership rate: 71.5%; Median home value: $104,700; Median year structure built: 1959; Homeowner vacancy rate: 2.2%; Median selected monthly owner costs: $1,062 with a mortgage, $375 without a mortgage; Median gross rent: $637 per month; Rental vacancy rate: 7.0%
Vital Statistics: Birth rate: 105.4 per 10,000 population; Death rate: 113.8 per 10,000 population; Age-adjusted cancer mortality rate: 194.1 deaths per 100,000 population
Health Insurance: 89.0% have insurance; 62.1% have private insurance; 41.0% have public insurance; 11.0% do not have insurance; 8.6% of children under 18 do not have insurance
Health Care: Physicians: 7.2 per 10,000 population; Dentists: 3.8 per 10,000 population; Hospital beds: 31.8 per 10,000 population; Hospital admissions: 1,064.5 per 10,000 population
Air Quality Index (AQI): Percent of Days: 88.5% good, 9.8% moderate, 1.6% unhealthy for sensitive individuals, 0.0% unhealthy, 0.0% very unhealthy; Annual median: 30; Annual maximum: 126
Transportation: Commute: 93.1% car, 0.6% public transportation, 1.8% walk, 2.9% work from home; Mean travel time to work: 25.3 minutes
2016 Presidential Election: 56.6% Trump, 37.8% Clinton, 2.9% Johnson, 1.0% Stein
National and State Parks: Geneva-On-The-Lake State Park; Orwell State Wildlife Area; Pymatuning State Park
Additional Information Contacts
Ashtabula Government . . . . (440) 576-3750
http://www.co.ashtabula.oh.us

Ashtabula County Communities

ANDOVER (village). Covers a land area of 1.366 square miles and a water area of 0 square miles. Located at 41.61° N. Lat; 80.57° W. Long. Elevation is 1,093 feet.
Population: 1,056; Growth (since 2000): -16.8%; Density: 773.0 persons per square mile; Race: 95.6% White, 0.0% Black/African American, 0.0% Asian, 0.0% American Indian/Alaska Native, 0.0% Native Hawaiian/Other Pacific Islander, 4.4% Two or more races, 3.4% Hispanic of any race;

Average household size: 2.13; Median age: 48.5; Age under 18: 19.4%; Age 65 and over: 27.9%; Males per 100 females: 83.2; Marriage status: 21.2% never married, 33.2% now married, 0.6% separated, 21.1% widowed, 24.5% divorced; Foreign born: 1.5%; Speak English only: 97.5%; With disability: 19.2%; Veterans: 12.7%; Ancestry: 32.3% American, 20.4% Irish, 18.0% German, 8.9% English, 7.2% Polish
Employment: 0.0% management, business, and financial, 5.4% computer, engineering, and science, 16.5% education, legal, community service, arts, and media, 5.4% healthcare practitioners, 28.4% service, 18.7% sales and office, 4.3% natural resources, construction, and maintenance, 21.2% production, transportation, and material moving
Income: Per capita: $16,457; Median household: $22,688; Average household: $35,667; Households with income of $100,000 or more: 5.1%; Poverty rate: 19.3%
Educational Attainment: High school diploma or higher: 82.6%; Bachelor's degree or higher: 14.7%; Graduate/professional degree or higher: 3.6%

School District(s)

Pymatuning Valley Local (PK-12)
2015-16 Enrollment: 1,234 . . . . (440) 293-6488
Housing: Homeownership rate: 52.0%; Median home value: $81,100; Median year structure built: Before 1940; Homeowner vacancy rate: 0.0%; Median selected monthly owner costs: $717 with a mortgage, $297 without a mortgage; Median gross rent: $520 per month; Rental vacancy rate: 0.0%
Health Insurance: 93.3% have insurance; 57.8% have private insurance; 52.2% have public insurance; 6.7% do not have insurance; 0.0% of children under 18 do not have insurance
Newspapers: Pymatuning Area News (weekly circulation 2,200)
Transportation: Commute: 93.4% car, 0.0% public transportation, 4.4% walk, 2.2% work from home; Mean travel time to work: 30.2 minutes

ASHTABULA (city). Covers a land area of 7.735 square miles and a water area of 0.171 square miles. Located at 41.88° N. Lat; 80.80° W. Long. Elevation is 669 feet.
History: The surveying party of Moses Cleaveland stopped here in 1796, and two members of the group remained as settlers. The town that was incorporated in 1831 was named Ashtabula for the river that emptied into Lake Erie at the site. Ashtabula developed as a shipping center for coal and iron ore, and as a fishing and farm trading center. Strong abolitionist sentiment made it a key station on the Underground Railroad.
Population: 18,540; Growth (since 2000): -11.6%; Density: 2,397.0 persons per square mile; Race: 85.0% White, 8.6% Black/African American, 0.2% Asian, 0.3% American Indian/Alaska Native, 0.2% Native Hawaiian/Other Pacific Islander, 5.0% Two or more races, 8.7% Hispanic of any race; Average household size: 2.37; Median age: 38.8; Age under 18: 25.1%; Age 65 and over: 15.9%; Males per 100 females: 90.9; Marriage status: 33.8% never married, 39.1% now married, 1.9% separated, 8.1% widowed, 19.0% divorced; Foreign born: 2.2%; Speak English only: 93.3%; With disability: 18.1%; Veterans: 10.9%; Ancestry: 18.2% German, 14.1% Italian, 13.8% Irish, 12.8% American, 8.2% English
Employment: 8.8% management, business, and financial, 2.0% computer, engineering, and science, 5.6% education, legal, community service, arts, and media, 3.8% healthcare practitioners, 27.2% service, 22.3% sales and office, 5.9% natural resources, construction, and maintenance, 24.5% production, transportation, and material moving
Income: Per capita: $16,171; Median household: $28,865; Average household: $37,516; Households with income of $100,000 or more: 4.2%; Poverty rate: 34.3%
Educational Attainment: High school diploma or higher: 80.0%; Bachelor's degree or higher: 9.4%; Graduate/professional degree or higher: 4.2%

School District(s)

Ashtabula Area City (PK-12)
2015-16 Enrollment: 3,640 . . . . (440) 992-1201
Buckeye Local (KG-12)
2015-16 Enrollment: 1,740 . . . . (440) 998-4411

Four-year College(s)

Kent State University at Ashtabula (Public)
Fall 2016 Enrollment: 2,074 . . . . (440) 964-3322
2016-17 Tuition: In-state $5,664; Out-of-state $14,028
Housing: Homeownership rate: 47.4%; Median home value: $70,600; Median year structure built: 1951; Homeowner vacancy rate: 4.2%; Median selected monthly owner costs: $841 with a mortgage, $336 without a mortgage; Median gross rent: $621 per month; Rental vacancy rate: 7.8%
Health Insurance: 89.8% have insurance; 45.7% have private insurance; 56.7% have public insurance; 10.2% do not have insurance; 2.2% of children under 18 do not have insurance
Hospitals: Ashtabula County Medical Center (234 beds)
Newspapers: Star-Beacon (daily circulation 17,600)
Transportation: Commute: 93.0% car, 0.4% public transportation, 1.7% walk, 2.9% work from home; Mean travel time to work: 19.6 minutes
Additional Information Contacts
City of Ashtabula . . . . (440) 992-7103
http://ci.ashtabula.oh.us

AUSTINBURG (CDP). Covers a land area of 3.283 square miles and a water area of 0 square miles. Located at 41.77° N. Lat; 80.86° W. Long. Elevation is 810 feet.
Population: 459; Growth (since 2000): n/a; Density: 139.8 persons per square mile; Race: 98.7% White, 0.9% Black/African American, 0.4% Asian, 0.0% American Indian/Alaska Native, 0.0% Native Hawaiian/Other Pacific Islander, 0.0% Two or more races, 4.8% Hispanic of any race; Average household size: 2.10; Median age: 47.5; Age under 18: 10.9%; Age 65 and over: 31.4%; Males per 100 females: 76.1; Marriage status: 30.6% never married, 27.1% now married, 0.0% separated, 19.8% widowed, 22.5% divorced; Foreign born: 10.0%; Speak English only: 90.0%; With disability: 25.8%; Veterans: 7.6%; Ancestry: 32.0% Irish, 19.0% German, 14.8% American, 12.4% Italian, 5.4% Ukrainian
Employment: 11.4% management, business, and financial, 0.0% computer, engineering, and science, 7.6% education, legal, community service, arts, and media, 8.7% healthcare practitioners, 1.1% service, 19.6% sales and office, 0.0% natural resources, construction, and maintenance, 51.6% production, transportation, and material moving
Income: Per capita: $14,541; Median household: $19,350; Average household: $30,301; Households with income of $100,000 or more: n/a; Poverty rate: 46.2%
Educational Attainment: High school diploma or higher: 88.7%; Bachelor's degree or higher: 10.4%; Graduate/professional degree or higher: 9.1%

School District(s)

Geneva Area City (PK-12)
2015-16 Enrollment: 2,491 . . . . (440) 466-4831
Housing: Homeownership rate: 38.7%; Median home value: $156,600; Median year structure built: Before 1940; Homeowner vacancy rate: 30.0%; Median selected monthly owner costs: $1,132 with a mortgage, n/a without a mortgage; Median gross rent: $613 per month; Rental vacancy rate: 0.0%
Health Insurance: 77.2% have insurance; 37.2% have private insurance; 40.0% have public insurance; 22.8% do not have insurance; 0.0% of children under 18 do not have insurance
Transportation: Commute: 86.4% car, 3.8% public transportation, 8.7% walk, 1.1% work from home; Mean travel time to work: 17.7 minutes

CONNEAUT (city). Covers a land area of 26.355 square miles and a water area of 0.066 square miles. Located at 41.93° N. Lat; 80.57° W. Long. Elevation is 650 feet.
History: Conneaut was settled in 1799 by Thomas Montgomery and Aaron Wright. The village grew around the natural harbor, which attracted shipping of coal and ores.
Population: 12,782; Growth (since 2000): 2.4%; Density: 485.0 persons per square mile; Race: 89.1% White, 8.5% Black/African American, 0.1% Asian, 0.2% American Indian/Alaska Native, 0.0% Native Hawaiian/Other Pacific Islander, 1.7% Two or more races, 3.0% Hispanic of any race; Average household size: 2.28; Median age: 41.9; Age under 18: 17.7%; Age 65 and over: 18.3%; Males per 100 females: 119.5; Marriage status: 30.4% never married, 47.4% now married, 2.0% separated, 7.8% widowed, 14.3% divorced; Foreign born: 1.1%; Speak English only: 97.8%; With disability: 15.3%; Veterans: 10.3%; Ancestry: 23.1% German, 17.0% American, 16.9% Irish, 12.2% Italian, 10.1% English
Employment: 7.6% management, business, and financial, 2.7% computer, engineering, and science, 6.0% education, legal, community service, arts, and media, 6.2% healthcare practitioners, 18.6% service, 23.1% sales and office, 10.6% natural resources, construction, and maintenance, 25.2% production, transportation, and material moving
Income: Per capita: $18,287; Median household: $34,856; Average household: $44,406; Households with income of $100,000 or more: 7.0%; Poverty rate: 18.4%

Educational Attainment: High school diploma or higher: 86.5%; Bachelor's degree or higher: 10.2%; Graduate/professional degree or higher: 3.4%

School District(s)

Conneaut Area City (PK-12)
2015-16 Enrollment: 1,668 . . . . (440) 593-7200

Housing: Homeownership rate: 67.1%; Median home value: $87,900; Median year structure built: 1948; Homeowner vacancy rate: 3.9%; Median selected monthly owner costs: $924 with a mortgage, $338 without a mortgage; Median gross rent: $591 per month; Rental vacancy rate: 7.4%
Health Insurance: 91.3% have insurance; 63.9% have private insurance; 42.9% have public insurance; 8.7% do not have insurance; 3.7% of children under 18 do not have insurance
Hospitals: University Hospitals Conneaut Medical Center (86 beds)
Transportation: Commute: 92.0% car, 0.6% public transportation, 3.5% walk, 3.7% work from home; Mean travel time to work: 23.9 minutes
Additional Information Contacts
City of Conneaut . . . . (440) 593-7401
http://www.conneaut.net

DORSET (unincorporated postal area)

ZCTA: 44032

Covers a land area of 40.250 square miles and a water area of 0.028 square miles. Located at 41.67° N. Lat; 80.67° W. Long. Elevation is 981 feet.
Population: 2,427; Growth (since 2000): 62.4%; Density: 60.3 persons per square mile; Race: 88.3% White, 4.3% Black/African American, 0.0% Asian, 0.0% American Indian/Alaska Native, 0.0% Native Hawaiian/Other Pacific Islander, 1.5% Two or more races, 6.3% Hispanic of any race; Average household size: 3.32; Median age: 34.5; Age under 18: 31.9%; Age 65 and over: 11.6%; Males per 100 females: 105.4; Marriage status: 25.9% never married, 55.3% now married, 0.0% separated, 7.5% widowed, 11.3% divorced; Foreign born: 0.2%; Speak English only: 82.2%; With disability: 16.1%; Veterans: 9.9%; Ancestry: 17.3% Irish, 16.9% American, 16.8% German, 11.5% English, 8.2% Polish
Employment: 2.6% management, business, and financial, 1.4% computer, engineering, and science, 6.6% education, legal, community service, arts, and media, 4.1% healthcare practitioners, 9.0% service, 26.7% sales and office, 21.6% natural resources, construction, and maintenance, 28.0% production, transportation, and material moving
Income: Per capita: $14,738; Median household: $36,316; Average household: $48,699; Households with income of $100,000 or more: 9.2%; Poverty rate: 27.6%
Educational Attainment: High school diploma or higher: 74.0%; Bachelor's degree or higher: 3.5%; Graduate/professional degree or higher: n/a
Housing: Homeownership rate: 94.5%; Median home value: $105,000; Median year structure built: 1962; Homeowner vacancy rate: 0.0%; Median selected monthly owner costs: $1,140 with a mortgage, $298 without a mortgage; Median gross rent: $841 per month; Rental vacancy rate: 0.0%
Health Insurance: 87.6% have insurance; 60.4% have private insurance; 41.7% have public insurance; 12.4% do not have insurance; 22.1% of children under 18 do not have insurance
Transportation: Commute: 95.9% car, 1.0% public transportation, 0.0% walk, 3.1% work from home; Mean travel time to work: 28.8 minutes

EDGEWOOD (CDP). Covers a land area of 6.831 square miles and a water area of 0.006 square miles. Located at 41.88° N. Lat; 80.75° W. Long. Elevation is 682 feet.

Population: 4,389; Growth (since 2000): -7.8%; Density: 642.5 persons per square mile; Race: 91.9% White, 3.4% Black/African American, 0.0% Asian, 0.2% American Indian/Alaska Native, 0.2% Native Hawaiian/Other Pacific Islander, 3.7% Two or more races, 3.8% Hispanic of any race; Average household size: 2.34; Median age: 41.7; Age under 18: 21.3%; Age 65 and over: 16.2%; Males per 100 females: 97.7; Marriage status: 34.6% never married, 45.7% now married, 0.3% separated, 5.6% widowed, 14.2% divorced; Foreign born: 0.6%; Speak English only: 99.0%; With disability: 16.1%; Veterans: 10.0%; Ancestry: 23.1% German, 16.2% American, 13.6% Italian, 11.6% Irish, 9.5% English
Employment: 8.6% management, business, and financial, 5.7% computer, engineering, and science, 4.4% education, legal, community service, arts, and media, 8.7% healthcare practitioners, 22.2% service, 24.8% sales and office, 3.0% natural resources, construction, and maintenance, 22.6% production, transportation, and material moving
Income: Per capita: $21,281; Median household: $34,688; Average household: $48,862; Households with income of $100,000 or more: 13.0%; Poverty rate: 23.2%
Educational Attainment: High school diploma or higher: 89.7%; Bachelor's degree or higher: 13.6%; Graduate/professional degree or higher: 3.6%
Housing: Homeownership rate: 68.6%; Median home value: $81,700; Median year structure built: 1957; Homeowner vacancy rate: 0.8%; Median selected monthly owner costs: $984 with a mortgage, $393 without a mortgage; Median gross rent: $624 per month; Rental vacancy rate: 5.9%
Health Insurance: 90.7% have insurance; 68.5% have private insurance; 42.1% have public insurance; 9.3% do not have insurance; 3.9% of children under 18 do not have insurance
Transportation: Commute: 95.2% car, 2.2% public transportation, 1.7% walk, 0.6% work from home; Mean travel time to work: 17.0 minutes

GENEVA (city). Covers a land area of 4.136 square miles and a water area of 0 square miles. Located at 41.80° N. Lat; 80.95° W. Long. Elevation is 673 feet.

History: Geneva was founded in 1805. In Geneva's cemetery is a monument to Platt R. Spencer (1800-1864) who founded business schools in many cities and created the Spencerian penmanship system.
Population: 6,077; Growth (since 2000): -7.9%; Density: 1,469.4 persons per square mile; Race: 97.2% White, 0.3% Black/African American, 0.0% Asian, 0.0% American Indian/Alaska Native, 0.0% Native Hawaiian/Other Pacific Islander, 2.5% Two or more races, 8.2% Hispanic of any race; Average household size: 2.37; Median age: 40.9; Age under 18: 24.7%; Age 65 and over: 18.7%; Males per 100 females: 95.5; Marriage status: 25.1% never married, 51.1% now married, 2.0% separated, 9.0% widowed, 14.7% divorced; Foreign born: 0.7%; Speak English only: 91.9%; With disability: 17.3%; Veterans: 12.0%; Ancestry: 26.1% German, 15.1% Irish, 13.4% English, 7.0% Italian, 6.5% Polish
Employment: 8.6% management, business, and financial, 0.7% computer, engineering, and science, 5.8% education, legal, community service, arts, and media, 8.6% healthcare practitioners, 20.0% service, 23.4% sales and office, 9.1% natural resources, construction, and maintenance, 23.9% production, transportation, and material moving
Income: Per capita: $22,276; Median household: $41,640; Average household: $52,053; Households with income of $100,000 or more: 11.4%; Poverty rate: 15.3%
Educational Attainment: High school diploma or higher: 89.2%; Bachelor's degree or higher: 11.2%; Graduate/professional degree or higher: 3.7%

School District(s)

Geneva Area City (PK-12)
2015-16 Enrollment: 2,491 . . . . (440) 466-4831

Housing: Homeownership rate: 68.0%; Median home value: $95,500; Median year structure built: 1948; Homeowner vacancy rate: 0.0%; Median selected monthly owner costs: $973 with a mortgage, $380 without a mortgage; Median gross rent: $593 per month; Rental vacancy rate: 3.2%
Health Insurance: 91.2% have insurance; 69.6% have private insurance; 35.0% have public insurance; 8.8% do not have insurance; 5.4% of children under 18 do not have insurance
Hospitals: UHHS Memorial Hospital of Geneva (46 beds)
Transportation: Commute: 94.1% car, 2.1% public transportation, 0.4% walk, 1.8% work from home; Mean travel time to work: 27.1 minutes

GENEVA-ON-THE-LAKE (village). Covers a land area of 2.257 square miles and a water area of 0.021 square miles. Located at 41.86° N. Lat; 80.95° W. Long. Elevation is 604 feet.

Population: 1,352; Growth (since 2000): -12.5%; Density: 598.9 persons per square mile; Race: 93.1% White, 0.0% Black/African American, 1.4% Asian, 4.4% American Indian/Alaska Native, 0.0% Native Hawaiian/Other Pacific Islander, 1.0% Two or more races, 3.8% Hispanic of any race; Average household size: 2.08; Median age: 43.3; Age under 18: 19.9%; Age 65 and over: 17.8%; Males per 100 females: 102.8; Marriage status: 24.5% never married, 42.7% now married, 1.9% separated, 7.5% widowed, 25.2% divorced; Foreign born: 3.6%; Speak English only: 95.2%; With disability: 22.1%; Veterans: 10.5%; Ancestry: 24.6% German, 19.2% Irish, 12.3% Italian, 9.8% American, 9.7% English
Employment: 7.9% management, business, and financial, 3.7% computer, engineering, and science, 4.5% education, legal, community service, arts, and media, 5.0% healthcare practitioners, 25.3% service, 22.0% sales and office, 4.4% natural resources, construction, and maintenance, 27.2% production, transportation, and material moving

Income: Per capita: $19,808; Median household: $31,633; Average household: $41,476; Households with income of $100,000 or more: 8.1%; Poverty rate: 16.3%
Educational Attainment: High school diploma or higher: 85.6%; Bachelor's degree or higher: 17.0%; Graduate/professional degree or higher: 7.4%
Housing: Homeownership rate: 56.6%; Median home value: $96,700; Median year structure built: 1957; Homeowner vacancy rate: 3.1%; Median selected monthly owner costs: $988 with a mortgage, $353 without a mortgage; Median gross rent: $617 per month; Rental vacancy rate: 22.9%
Health Insurance: 90.2% have insurance; 58.4% have private insurance; 48.7% have public insurance; 9.8% do not have insurance; 0.0% of children under 18 do not have insurance
Safety: Violent crime rate: 58.0 per 10,000 population; Property crime rate: 223.7 per 10,000 population
Transportation: Commute: 90.9% car, 0.0% public transportation, 5.7% walk, 0.8% work from home; Mean travel time to work: 29.3 minutes

JEFFERSON (village). County seat. Covers a land area of 2.519 square miles and a water area of 0 square miles. Located at 41.74° N. Lat; 80.77° W. Long. Elevation is 961 feet.
History: Jefferson was named by Gideon Granger, Postmaster General in Jefferson's cabinet. The Republican Party's first national platform was written here at the law office of Joshua R. Giddings.
Population: 3,295; Growth (since 2000): -7.8%; Density: 1,308.0 persons per square mile; Race: 96.7% White, 0.9% Black/African American, 1.2% Asian, 0.0% American Indian/Alaska Native, 0.0% Native Hawaiian/Other Pacific Islander, 0.5% Two or more races, 2.0% Hispanic of any race; Average household size: 2.52; Median age: 36.9; Age under 18: 24.5%; Age 65 and over: 16.1%; Males per 100 females: 83.9; Marriage status: 30.0% never married, 43.4% now married, 0.5% separated, 11.2% widowed, 15.5% divorced; Foreign born: 1.6%; Speak English only: 96.4%; With disability: 13.1%; Veterans: 7.7%; Ancestry: 26.6% German, 22.3% Irish, 14.5% American, 13.0% English, 9.3% Italian
Employment: 4.6% management, business, and financial, 2.1% computer, engineering, and science, 7.8% education, legal, community service, arts, and media, 6.9% healthcare practitioners, 26.3% service, 25.8% sales and office, 5.4% natural resources, construction, and maintenance, 21.1% production, transportation, and material moving
Income: Per capita: $20,497; Median household: $50,523; Average household: $52,563; Households with income of $100,000 or more: 11.6%; Poverty rate: 21.2%
Educational Attainment: High school diploma or higher: 91.6%; Bachelor's degree or higher: 12.7%; Graduate/professional degree or higher: 6.3%

School District(s)

Ashtabula County Technical and Career Center (06-12)
2015-16 Enrollment: n/a . . . . (877) 644-6338
Jefferson Area Local (KG-12)
2015-16 Enrollment: 1,682 . . . . (440) 576-9180

Vocational/Technical School(s)

Ashtabula County Technical and Career Campus (Public)
Fall 2016 Enrollment: 153 . . . . (440) 576-6015
2016-17 Tuition: $10,750

Housing: Homeownership rate: 68.5%; Median home value: $95,900; Median year structure built: 1972; Homeowner vacancy rate: 0.0%; Median selected monthly owner costs: $1,016 with a mortgage, $369 without a mortgage; Median gross rent: $564 per month; Rental vacancy rate: 19.4%
Health Insurance: 90.8% have insurance; 59.9% have private insurance; 43.1% have public insurance; 9.2% do not have insurance; 0.0% of children under 18 do not have insurance
Newspapers: Gazette Newspapers (weekly circulation 13,000); Gazette Newspapers (weekly circulation 31,000)
Transportation: Commute: 93.2% car, 0.0% public transportation, 4.9% walk, 1.9% work from home; Mean travel time to work: 22.7 minutes

KINGSVILLE (unincorporated postal area)

ZCTA: 44048

Covers a land area of 30.431 square miles and a water area of 0.042 square miles. Located at 41.85° N. Lat; 80.64° W. Long. Elevation is 791 feet.
Population: 2,704; Growth (since 2000): 5.9%; Density: 88.9 persons per square mile; Race: 96.2% White, 2.3% Black/African American, 0.0% Asian, 0.0% American Indian/Alaska Native, 0.0% Native Hawaiian/Other Pacific Islander, 1.3% Two or more races, 0.5% Hispanic of any race; Average household size: 2.77; Median age: 38.3; Age under 18: 28.9%; Age 65 and over: 24.0%; Males per 100 females: 100.5; Marriage status: 21.1% never married, 47.7% now married, 0.6% separated, 14.1% widowed, 17.1% divorced; Foreign born: 0.8%; Speak English only: 98.8%; With disability: 14.8%; Veterans: 15.4%; Ancestry: 27.6% American, 16.4% German, 11.3% English, 10.9% Polish, 8.3% Irish
Employment: 9.9% management, business, and financial, 2.3% computer, engineering, and science, 12.0% education, legal, community service, arts, and media, 5.3% healthcare practitioners, 22.7% service, 13.4% sales and office, 9.6% natural resources, construction, and maintenance, 24.8% production, transportation, and material moving
Income: Per capita: $19,208; Median household: $48,696; Average household: $53,522; Households with income of $100,000 or more: 12.8%; Poverty rate: 24.0%
Educational Attainment: High school diploma or higher: 90.9%; Bachelor's degree or higher: 17.3%; Graduate/professional degree or higher: 3.6%

School District(s)

Buckeye Local (KG-12)
2015-16 Enrollment: 1,740 . . . . (440) 998-4411

Housing: Homeownership rate: 76.2%; Median home value: $103,200; Median year structure built: 1963; Homeowner vacancy rate: 2.6%; Median selected monthly owner costs: $1,015 with a mortgage, $391 without a mortgage; Median gross rent: $823 per month; Rental vacancy rate: 0.0%
Health Insurance: 98.4% have insurance; 59.0% have private insurance; 51.9% have public insurance; 1.6% do not have insurance; 1.7% of children under 18 do not have insurance
Transportation: Commute: 98.7% car, 0.0% public transportation, 0.0% walk, 0.9% work from home; Mean travel time to work: 26.7 minutes

NORTH KINGSVILLE (village). Covers a land area of 8.887 square miles and a water area of 0.019 square miles. Located at 41.93° N. Lat; 80.68° W. Long. Elevation is 709 feet.
Population: 2,859; Growth (since 2000): 7.6%; Density: 321.7 persons per square mile; Race: 91.1% White, 1.6% Black/African American, 5.3% Asian, 0.0% American Indian/Alaska Native, 0.0% Native Hawaiian/Other Pacific Islander, 1.8% Two or more races, 4.6% Hispanic of any race; Average household size: 2.44; Median age: 44.3; Age under 18: 23.5%; Age 65 and over: 15.0%; Males per 100 females: 95.3; Marriage status: 22.9% never married, 59.0% now married, 1.0% separated, 5.4% widowed, 12.7% divorced; Foreign born: 2.4%; Speak English only: 96.8%; With disability: 11.1%; Veterans: 12.4%; Ancestry: 19.5% German, 19.4% Irish, 14.9% Italian, 12.9% American, 10.8% English
Employment: 15.7% management, business, and financial, 3.1% computer, engineering, and science, 7.3% education, legal, community service, arts, and media, 6.9% healthcare practitioners, 14.8% service, 20.4% sales and office, 9.3% natural resources, construction, and maintenance, 22.5% production, transportation, and material moving
Income: Per capita: $28,495; Median household: $61,555; Average household: $68,760; Households with income of $100,000 or more: 19.2%; Poverty rate: 6.9%
Educational Attainment: High school diploma or higher: 89.8%; Bachelor's degree or higher: 21.2%; Graduate/professional degree or higher: 7.0%
Housing: Homeownership rate: 86.1%; Median home value: $132,400; Median year structure built: 1970; Homeowner vacancy rate: 0.0%; Median selected monthly owner costs: $1,160 with a mortgage, $357 without a mortgage; Median gross rent: $834 per month; Rental vacancy rate: 0.0%
Health Insurance: 95.5% have insurance; 79.6% have private insurance; 27.9% have public insurance; 4.5% do not have insurance; 0.0% of children under 18 do not have insurance
Transportation: Commute: 95.6% car, 0.4% public transportation, 0.3% walk, 3.4% work from home; Mean travel time to work: 18.1 minutes

ORWELL (village). Covers a land area of 1.966 square miles and a water area of 0 square miles. Located at 41.54° N. Lat; 80.86° W. Long. Elevation is 889 feet.
Population: 1,448; Growth (since 2000): -4.7%; Density: 736.6 persons per square mile; Race: 99.1% White, 0.6% Black/African American, 0.3% Asian, 0.0% American Indian/Alaska Native, 0.0% Native Hawaiian/Other Pacific Islander, 0.0% Two or more races, 1.0% Hispanic of any race; Average household size: 2.19; Median age: 42.1; Age under 18: 22.8%; Age 65 and over: 19.5%; Males per 100 females: 93.7; Marriage status: 27.0% never married, 39.7% now married, 0.6% separated, 12.8% widowed, 20.5% divorced; Foreign born: 0.8%; Speak English only: 97.3%;

With disability: 17.5%; Veterans: 11.9%; Ancestry: 21.9% German, 20.7% American, 18.0% Irish, 11.4% English, 6.8% Italian
Employment: 5.3% management, business, and financial, 2.0% computer, engineering, and science, 7.2% education, legal, community service, arts, and media, 2.8% healthcare practitioners, 15.6% service, 24.0% sales and office, 7.5% natural resources, construction, and maintenance, 35.6% production, transportation, and material moving
Income: Per capita: $20,460; Median household: $37,635; Average household: $44,755; Households with income of $100,000 or more: 7.5%; Poverty rate: 19.4%
Educational Attainment: High school diploma or higher: 84.5%; Bachelor's degree or higher: 8.4%; Graduate/professional degree or higher: 4.0%

School District(s)

Grand Valley Local (KG-12)
2015-16 Enrollment: 1,196 . . . . (440) 437-6260
Housing: Homeownership rate: 53.0%; Median home value: $92,700; Median year structure built: 1975; Homeowner vacancy rate: 0.0%; Median selected monthly owner costs: $1,115 with a mortgage, $332 without a mortgage; Median gross rent: $637 per month; Rental vacancy rate: 0.0%
Health Insurance: 88.9% have insurance; 63.1% have private insurance; 38.9% have public insurance; 11.1% do not have insurance; 7.0% of children under 18 do not have insurance
Transportation: Commute: 93.1% car, 0.0% public transportation, 4.7% walk, 2.2% work from home; Mean travel time to work: 26.7 minutes
Additional Information Contacts
Village of Orwell . . . . (440) 437-6459
http://www.orwellvillage.org

PIERPONT (unincorporated postal area)

ZCTA: 44082

Covers a land area of 33.880 square miles and a water area of 0.020 square miles. Located at 41.76° N. Lat; 80.57° W. Long. Elevation is 997 feet.
Population: 1,799; Growth (since 2000): 22.5%; Density: 53.1 persons per square mile; Race: 98.7% White, 0.0% Black/African American, 0.0% Asian, 1.3% American Indian/Alaska Native, 0.0% Native Hawaiian/Other Pacific Islander, 0.0% Two or more races, 1.4% Hispanic of any race; Average household size: 3.56; Median age: 41.3; Age under 18: 34.7%; Age 65 and over: 17.2%; Males per 100 females: 105.2; Marriage status: 39.7% never married, 46.2% now married, 1.7% separated, 6.0% widowed, 8.1% divorced; Foreign born: 0.0%; Speak English only: 63.9%; With disability: 12.1%; Veterans: 5.5%; Ancestry: 31.3% Pennsylvania German, 17.5% German, 9.9% Irish, 8.9% English, 4.6% Slovak
Employment: 14.4% management, business, and financial, 3.4% computer, engineering, and science, 3.8% education, legal, community service, arts, and media, 2.7% healthcare practitioners, 6.7% service, 33.0% sales and office, 11.5% natural resources, construction, and maintenance, 24.5% production, transportation, and material moving
Income: Per capita: $14,918; Median household: $46,908; Average household: $51,142; Households with income of $100,000 or more: 8.9%; Poverty rate: 37.2%
Educational Attainment: High school diploma or higher: 81.8%; Bachelor's degree or higher: 8.9%; Graduate/professional degree or higher: n/a
Housing: Homeownership rate: 84.8%; Median home value: $153,000; Median year structure built: 1956; Homeowner vacancy rate: 0.0%; Median selected monthly owner costs: $1,026 with a mortgage, $408 without a mortgage; Median gross rent: $649 per month; Rental vacancy rate: 0.0%
Health Insurance: 66.3% have insurance; 50.0% have private insurance; 31.3% have public insurance; 33.7% do not have insurance; 61.5% of children under 18 do not have insurance
Transportation: Commute: 70.9% car, 4.5% public transportation, 3.9% walk, 11.1% work from home; Mean travel time to work: 49.1 minutes

ROAMING SHORES (village). Covers a land area of 2.098 square miles and a water area of 0.719 square miles. Located at 41.64° N. Lat; 80.83° W. Long. Elevation is 869 feet.
Population: 1,546; Growth (since 2000): 24.8%; Density: 736.9 persons per square mile; Race: 99.7% White, 0.0% Black/African American, 0.0% Asian, 0.0% American Indian/Alaska Native, 0.0% Native Hawaiian/Other Pacific Islander, 0.3% Two or more races, 0.2% Hispanic of any race; Average household size: 2.74; Median age: 40.2; Age under 18: 27.7%; Age 65 and over: 15.2%; Males per 100 females: 102.4; Marriage status: 14.5% never married, 70.0% now married, 0.0% separated, 3.6% widowed, 11.9% divorced; Foreign born: 1.6%; Speak English only: 98.0%; With disability: 8.2%; Veterans: 10.4%; Ancestry: 22.9% German, 22.0% Irish, 16.9% American, 13.8% Italian, 9.4% English
Employment: 16.0% management, business, and financial, 4.6% computer, engineering, and science, 12.2% education, legal, community service, arts, and media, 9.2% healthcare practitioners, 13.8% service, 14.7% sales and office, 9.1% natural resources, construction, and maintenance, 20.5% production, transportation, and material moving
Income: Per capita: $32,901; Median household: $76,761; Average household: $89,087; Households with income of $100,000 or more: 26.4%; Poverty rate: 5.8%
Educational Attainment: High school diploma or higher: 93.6%; Bachelor's degree or higher: 32.4%; Graduate/professional degree or higher: 9.3%
Housing: Homeownership rate: 95.9%; Median home value: $150,000; Median year structure built: 1994; Homeowner vacancy rate: 0.5%; Median selected monthly owner costs: $1,287 with a mortgage, $506 without a mortgage; Median gross rent: $1,180 per month; Rental vacancy rate: 0.0%
Health Insurance: 95.3% have insurance; 79.8% have private insurance; 31.1% have public insurance; 4.7% do not have insurance; 4.4% of children under 18 do not have insurance
Transportation: Commute: 93.3% car, 0.3% public transportation, 1.2% walk, 5.2% work from home; Mean travel time to work: 38.3 minutes

ROCK CREEK (village). Covers a land area of 0.889 square miles and a water area of 0 square miles. Located at 41.66° N. Lat; 80.85° W. Long. Elevation is 804 feet.
Population: 333; Growth (since 2000): -43.0%; Density: 374.4 persons per square mile; Race: 98.8% White, 0.0% Black/African American, 0.0% Asian, 0.0% American Indian/Alaska Native, 0.0% Native Hawaiian/Other Pacific Islander, 1.2% Two or more races, 0.0% Hispanic of any race; Average household size: 2.35; Median age: 51.7; Age under 18: 15.3%; Age 65 and over: 16.2%; Males per 100 females: 101.9; Marriage status: 24.0% never married, 55.7% now married, 2.0% separated, 4.3% widowed, 16.0% divorced; Foreign born: 0.0%; Speak English only: 100.0%; With disability: 21.6%; Veterans: 17.4%; Ancestry: 30.9% German, 16.5% Irish, 12.6% American, 11.7% English, 7.2% Italian
Employment: 7.4% management, business, and financial, 4.0% computer, engineering, and science, 8.1% education, legal, community service, arts, and media, 2.7% healthcare practitioners, 10.7% service, 15.4% sales and office, 14.1% natural resources, construction, and maintenance, 37.6% production, transportation, and material moving
Income: Per capita: $22,305; Median household: $49,375; Average household: $52,124; Households with income of $100,000 or more: 12.7%; Poverty rate: 12.6%
Educational Attainment: High school diploma or higher: 85.9%; Bachelor's degree or higher: 3.8%; Graduate/professional degree or higher: 1.5%

School District(s)

Jefferson Area Local (KG-12)
2015-16 Enrollment: 1,682 . . . . (440) 576-9180
Housing: Homeownership rate: 73.2%; Median home value: $84,600; Median year structure built: Before 1940; Homeowner vacancy rate: 0.0%; Median selected monthly owner costs: $1,050 with a mortgage, $450 without a mortgage; Median gross rent: $846 per month; Rental vacancy rate: 0.0%
Health Insurance: 87.7% have insurance; 60.7% have private insurance; 38.1% have public insurance; 12.3% do not have insurance; 5.9% of children under 18 do not have insurance
Hospitals: Glenbeigh (80 beds)
Transportation: Commute: 93.2% car, 0.0% public transportation, 2.0% walk, 4.7% work from home; Mean travel time to work: 32.7 minutes

WILLIAMSFIELD (unincorporated postal area)

ZCTA: 44093

Covers a land area of 32.164 square miles and a water area of 0.110 square miles. Located at 41.53° N. Lat; 80.61° W. Long. Elevation is 1,135 feet.
Population: 1,317; Growth (since 2000): -13.6%; Density: 40.9 persons per square mile; Race: 85.7% White, 0.0% Black/African American, 0.0% Asian, 0.0% American Indian/Alaska Native, 0.0% Native Hawaiian/Other Pacific Islander, 14.3% Two or more races, 0.0% Hispanic of any race; Average household size: 2.76; Median age: 40.8; Age under 18: 24.5%; Age 65 and over: 12.8%; Males per 100 females: 104.6; Marriage status:

27.4% never married, 58.4% now married, 2.1% separated, 2.5% widowed, 11.7% divorced; Foreign born: 0.8%; Speak English only: 99.0%; With disability: 10.6%; Veterans: 8.7%; Ancestry: 34.8% German, 19.4% Irish, 13.1% English, 9.8% American, 8.9% Hungarian
Employment: 18.3% management, business, and financial, 0.0% computer, engineering, and science, 18.6% education, legal, community service, arts, and media, 3.4% healthcare practitioners, 15.2% service, 13.8% sales and office, 10.7% natural resources, construction, and maintenance, 19.9% production, transportation, and material moving
Income: Per capita: $27,551; Median household: $54,063; Average household: $76,495; Households with income of $100,000 or more: 22.6%; Poverty rate: 29.8%
Educational Attainment: High school diploma or higher: 93.4%; Bachelor's degree or higher: 14.7%; Graduate/professional degree or higher: 3.2%
Housing: Homeownership rate: 93.5%; Median home value: $110,500; Median year structure built: 1964; Homeowner vacancy rate: 5.9%; Median selected monthly owner costs: $1,154 with a mortgage, $458 without a mortgage; Median gross rent: $850 per month; Rental vacancy rate: 0.0%
Health Insurance: 84.1% have insurance; 64.1% have private insurance; 30.8% have public insurance; 15.9% do not have insurance; 11.8% of children under 18 do not have insurance
Transportation: Commute: 94.5% car, 0.0% public transportation, 1.7% walk, 3.8% work from home; Mean travel time to work: 25.2 minutes

WINDSOR (unincorporated postal area)

ZCTA: 44099

Covers a land area of 21.981 square miles and a water area of 0.085 square miles. Located at 41.55° N. Lat; 80.98° W. Long. Elevation is 827 feet.
Population: 2,120; Growth (since 2000): 28.7%; Density: 96.4 persons per square mile; Race: 98.0% White, 2.0% Black/African American, 0.0% Asian, 0.0% American Indian/Alaska Native, 0.0% Native Hawaiian/Other Pacific Islander, 0.0% Two or more races, 0.0% Hispanic of any race; Average household size: 2.97; Median age: 37.7; Age under 18: 32.7%; Age 65 and over: 10.4%; Males per 100 females: 98.3; Marriage status: 21.2% never married, 65.0% now married, 0.0% separated, 4.8% widowed, 9.0% divorced; Foreign born: 1.4%; Speak English only: 64.3%; With disability: 11.1%; Veterans: 3.6%; Ancestry: 20.3% German, 15.2% Pennsylvania German, 11.7% American, 10.6% Irish, 7.3% English
Employment: 13.5% management, business, and financial, 3.0% computer, engineering, and science, 12.7% education, legal, community service, arts, and media, 1.2% healthcare practitioners, 15.5% service, 20.7% sales and office, 9.9% natural resources, construction, and maintenance, 23.5% production, transportation, and material moving
Income: Per capita: $21,655; Median household: $61,528; Average household: $64,530; Households with income of $100,000 or more: 10.8%; Poverty rate: 2.1%
Educational Attainment: High school diploma or higher: 73.4%; Bachelor's degree or higher: 9.4%; Graduate/professional degree or higher: 2.3%
Housing: Homeownership rate: 97.9%; Median home value: $160,000; Median year structure built: 1976; Homeowner vacancy rate: 0.0%; Median selected monthly owner costs: $1,301 with a mortgage, $313 without a mortgage; Median gross rent: n/a per month; Rental vacancy rate: 0.0%
Health Insurance: 65.8% have insurance; 59.4% have private insurance; 18.2% have public insurance; 34.2% do not have insurance; 39.6% of children under 18 do not have insurance
Transportation: Commute: 82.2% car, 0.0% public transportation, 4.0% walk, 5.9% work from home; Mean travel time to work: 44.5 minutes

Athens County

Located in southeastern Ohio; bounded on the southeast by the Ohio River and the West Virginia border. Covers a land area of 503.598 square miles, a water area of 4.843 square miles, and is located in the Eastern Time Zone at 39.33° N. Lat., 82.05° W. Long. The county was founded in 1805. County seat is Athens.

Athens County is part of the Athens, OH Micropolitan Statistical Area. The entire metro area includes: Athens County, OH

Population: 65,103; Growth (since 2000): 4.6%; Density: 129.3 persons per square mile; Race: 91.0% White, 2.5% Black/African American, 3.1% Asian, 0.3% American Indian/Alaska Native, 0.0% Native Hawaiian/Other Pacific Islander, 2.6% two or more races, 1.8% Hispanic of any race; Average household size: 2.48; Median age: 28.2; Age under 18: 15.2%; Age 65 and over: 11.4%; Males per 100 females: 100.3; Marriage status: 50.7% never married, 35.1% now married, 1.5% separated, 4.6% widowed, 9.5% divorced; Foreign born: 4.5%; Speak English only: 94.5%; With disability: 15.7%; Veterans: 6.3%; Ancestry: 21.0% German, 13.6% Irish, 9.5% English, 9.0% American, 4.1% Italian
Religion: Six largest groups: 4.7% Methodist/Pietist, 4.2% Baptist, 3.0% Catholicism, 2.8% Non-denominational Protestant, 2.0% Holiness, 0.7% Presbyterian-Reformed
Economy: Unemployment rate: 4.9%; Leading industries: 18.3 % retail trade; 14.4 % health care and social assistance; 12.5 % accommodation and food services; Farms: 722 totaling 90,473 acres; Company size: 0 employ 1,000 or more persons, 1 employs 500 to 999 persons, 13 employ 100 to 499 persons, 1,026 employ less than 100 persons; Business ownership: 1,216 women-owned, 53 Black-owned, 26 Hispanic-owned, 61 Asian-owned, 42 American Indian/Alaska Native-owned
Employment: 9.1% management, business, and financial, 4.2% computer, engineering, and science, 18.7% education, legal, community service, arts, and media, 5.2% healthcare practitioners, 23.8% service, 22.1% sales and office, 7.9% natural resources, construction, and maintenance, 8.9% production, transportation, and material moving
Income: Per capita: $18,602; Median household: $34,221; Average household: $50,089; Households with income of $100,000 or more: 12.4%; Poverty rate: 31.2%
Educational Attainment: High school diploma or higher: 89.7%; Bachelor's degree or higher: 29.1%; Graduate/professional degree or higher: 15.2%
Housing: Homeownership rate: 56.1%; Median home value: $113,900; Median year structure built: 1976; Homeowner vacancy rate: 2.4%; Median selected monthly owner costs: $1,080 with a mortgage, $389 without a mortgage; Median gross rent: $726 per month; Rental vacancy rate: 7.2%
Vital Statistics: Birth rate: 83.7 per 10,000 population; Death rate: 74.2 per 10,000 population; Age-adjusted cancer mortality rate: 184.9 deaths per 100,000 population
Health Insurance: 92.4% have insurance; 69.1% have private insurance; 32.8% have public insurance; 7.6% do not have insurance; 3.7% of children under 18 do not have insurance
Health Care: Physicians: 28.0 per 10,000 population; Dentists: 2.3 per 10,000 population; Hospital beds: 44.6 per 10,000 population; Hospital admissions: 1,073.2 per 10,000 population
Air Quality Index (AQI): Percent of Days: 96.7% good, 3.3% moderate, 0.0% unhealthy for sensitive individuals, 0.0% unhealthy, 0.0% very unhealthy; Annual median: 27; Annual maximum: 56
Transportation: Commute: 77.8% car, 0.7% public transportation, 14.8% walk, 4.5% work from home; Mean travel time to work: 20.1 minutes
2016 Presidential Election: 38.2% Trump, 55.1% Clinton, 3.4% Johnson, 1.8% Stein
National and State Parks: Gifford State Forest; Strouds Run State Park; Trimble State Wildlife Area; Waterloo State Forest
Additional Information Contacts
Athens Government . . . . (740) 592-3219
http://www.co.athensoh.org

Athens County Communities

ALBANY (village). Covers a land area of 1.248 square miles and a water area of 0.015 square miles. Located at 39.22° N. Lat; 82.20° W. Long. Elevation is 761 feet.
History: Albany was laid out in 1831 and named for Albany, New York.
Population: 1,011; Growth (since 2000): 25.1%; Density: 809.8 persons per square mile; Race: 96.9% White, 2.2% Black/African American, 0.5% Asian, 0.0% American Indian/Alaska Native, 0.0% Native Hawaiian/Other Pacific Islander, 0.4% Two or more races, 0.3% Hispanic of any race; Average household size: 2.39; Median age: 41.6; Age under 18: 21.9%; Age 65 and over: 18.3%; Males per 100 females: 84.8; Marriage status: 22.1% never married, 46.7% now married, 0.9% separated, 7.3% widowed, 23.9% divorced; Foreign born: 2.3%; Speak English only: 97.3%; With disability: 19.7%; Veterans: 9.5%; Ancestry: 17.9% Irish, 15.1% German, 14.2% English, 11.8% American, 8.9% Polish
Employment: 6.1% management, business, and financial, 4.5% computer, engineering, and science, 15.8% education, legal, community service, arts, and media, 8.1% healthcare practitioners, 16.7% service, 26.0% sales and office, 9.0% natural resources, construction, and maintenance, 13.8% production, transportation, and material moving

Income: Per capita: $21,009; Median household: $41,339; Average household: $48,177; Households with income of $100,000 or more: 7.0%; Poverty rate: 14.7%

Educational Attainment: High school diploma or higher: 89.7%; Bachelor's degree or higher: 20.8%; Graduate/professional degree or higher: 6.2%

School District(s)

Alexander Local (PK-12)
2015-16 Enrollment: 1,533 . . . . (740) 698-8831

Housing: Homeownership rate: 70.0%; Median home value: $113,300; Median year structure built: 1974; Homeowner vacancy rate: 11.6%; Median selected monthly owner costs: $981 with a mortgage, $338 without a mortgage; Median gross rent: $714 per month; Rental vacancy rate: 15.1%

Health Insurance: 88.2% have insurance; 58.2% have private insurance; 40.7% have public insurance; 11.8% do not have insurance; 1.4% of children under 18 do not have insurance

Transportation: Commute: 97.9% car, 0.0% public transportation, 0.5% walk, 1.6% work from home; Mean travel time to work: 23.5 minutes

AMESVILLE (village). Covers a land area of 0.219 square miles and a water area of 0 square miles. Located at 39.40° N. Lat; 81.95° W. Long. Elevation is 633 feet.

Population: 120; Growth (since 2000): -34.8%; Density: 548.4 persons per square mile; Race: 100.0% White, 0.0% Black/African American, 0.0% Asian, 0.0% American Indian/Alaska Native, 0.0% Native Hawaiian/Other Pacific Islander, 0.0% Two or more races, 0.0% Hispanic of any race; Average household size: 3.08; Median age: 41.5; Age under 18: 27.5%; Age 65 and over: 24.2%; Males per 100 females: 94.9; Marriage status: 20.4% never married, 46.2% now married, 0.0% separated, 20.4% widowed, 12.9% divorced; Foreign born: 0.0%; Speak English only: 100.0%; With disability: 38.3%; Veterans: 12.6%; Ancestry: 23.3% German, 15.0% American, 15.0% English, 13.3% Irish, 10.0% Welsh

Employment: 7.7% management, business, and financial, 3.8% computer, engineering, and science, 17.3% education, legal, community service, arts, and media, 5.8% healthcare practitioners, 19.2% service, 23.1% sales and office, 7.7% natural resources, construction, and maintenance, 15.4% production, transportation, and material moving

Income: Per capita: $25,851; Median household: $56,875; Average household: $74,382; Households with income of $100,000 or more: 33.3%; Poverty rate: 13.0%

Educational Attainment: High school diploma or higher: 95.2%; Bachelor's degree or higher: 37.3%; Graduate/professional degree or higher: 20.5%

School District(s)

Federal Hocking Local (PK-12)
2015-16 Enrollment: 987. . . . . (740) 662-6691

Housing: Homeownership rate: 100.0%; Median home value: $91,300; Median year structure built: 1950; Homeowner vacancy rate: 11.4%; Median selected monthly owner costs: $878 with a mortgage, $385 without a mortgage; Median gross rent: n/a per month; Rental vacancy rate: 100.0%

Health Insurance: 86.7% have insurance; 57.5% have private insurance; 59.2% have public insurance; 13.3% do not have insurance; 21.2% of children under 18 do not have insurance

Transportation: Commute: 79.6% car, 0.0% public transportation, 16.3% walk, 4.1% work from home; Mean travel time to work: 19.6 minutes

ATHENS (city). County seat. Covers a land area of 9.827 square miles and a water area of 0.219 square miles. Located at 39.33° N. Lat; 82.10° W. Long. Elevation is 718 feet.

History: Athens was selected by the territorial legislature as the site of a university, which was chartered in 1804 and became Ohio University. Athens was incorporated as a city in 1912.

Population: 24,365; Growth (since 2000): 14.2%; Density: 2,479.4 persons per square mile; Race: 83.7% White, 4.0% Black/African American, 7.5% Asian, 0.0% American Indian/Alaska Native, 0.1% Native Hawaiian/Other Pacific Islander, 3.8% Two or more races, 3.4% Hispanic of any race; Average household size: 2.32; Median age: 21.4; Age under 18: 6.7%; Age 65 and over: 5.0%; Males per 100 females: 100.0; Marriage status: 80.1% never married, 14.7% now married, 0.3% separated, 1.6% widowed, 3.6% divorced; Foreign born: 10.2%; Speak English only: 88.5%; With disability: 7.3%; Veterans: 2.8%; Ancestry: 23.6% German, 14.1% Irish, 7.2% Italian, 7.2% English, 5.0% Polish

Employment: 7.5% management, business, and financial, 5.7% computer, engineering, and science, 25.6% education, legal, community service, arts, and media, 3.0% healthcare practitioners, 28.4% service, 21.8% sales and office, 2.5% natural resources, construction, and maintenance, 5.4% production, transportation, and material moving

Income: Per capita: $13,758; Median household: $22,204; Average household: $42,562; Households with income of $100,000 or more: 11.6%; Poverty rate: 54.7%

Educational Attainment: High school diploma or higher: 96.2%; Bachelor's degree or higher: 63.2%; Graduate/professional degree or higher: 38.7%

School District(s)

Athens City (PK-12)
2015-16 Enrollment: 2,692 . . . . (740) 797-4544

Four-year College(s)

Ohio University-Main Campus (Public)
Fall 2016 Enrollment: 29,509 . . . . (740) 593-1000
2016-17 Tuition: In-state $11,744; Out-of-state $21,208

Housing: Homeownership rate: 29.4%; Median home value: $164,300; Median year structure built: 1970; Homeowner vacancy rate: 1.8%; Median selected monthly owner costs: $1,234 with a mortgage, $461 without a mortgage; Median gross rent: $754 per month; Rental vacancy rate: 6.6%

Health Insurance: 95.0% have insurance; 86.0% have private insurance; 13.8% have public insurance; 5.0% do not have insurance; 2.0% of children under 18 do not have insurance

Hospitals: O'Bleness Memorial Hospital (114 beds)

Safety: Violent crime rate: 10.7 per 10,000 population; Property crime rate: 183.3 per 10,000 population

Newspapers: Athens Messenger (daily circulation 11,300); Athens News (weekly circulation 18,000)

Transportation: Commute: 51.6% car, 1.4% public transportation, 35.9% walk, 6.7% work from home; Mean travel time to work: 13.9 minutes

Airports: Ohio University Snyder Field (general aviation)

Additional Information Contacts

City of Athens . . . . (740) 592-3338
http://www.ci.athens.oh.us

BUCHTEL (village). Covers a land area of 0.486 square miles and a water area of 0.001 square miles. Located at 39.46° N. Lat; 82.18° W. Long. Elevation is 689 feet.

Population: 574; Growth (since 2000): 0.0%; Density: 1,180.6 persons per square mile; Race: 99.7% White, 0.0% Black/African American, 0.0% Asian, 0.0% American Indian/Alaska Native, 0.0% Native Hawaiian/Other Pacific Islander, 0.3% Two or more races, 0.3% Hispanic of any race; Average household size: 2.67; Median age: 41.3; Age under 18: 20.6%; Age 65 and over: 16.6%; Males per 100 females: 94.4; Marriage status: 29.8% never married, 58.3% now married, 0.0% separated, 4.0% widowed, 7.9% divorced; Foreign born: 0.3%; Speak English only: 97.9%; With disability: 19.7%; Veterans: 14.0%; Ancestry: 21.4% English, 20.6% German, 13.6% Irish, 11.3% American, 5.1% Italian

Employment: 11.4% management, business, and financial, 0.8% computer, engineering, and science, 14.4% education, legal, community service, arts, and media, 3.4% healthcare practitioners, 22.4% service, 28.5% sales and office, 8.0% natural resources, construction, and maintenance, 11.0% production, transportation, and material moving

Income: Per capita: $25,191; Median household: $60,859; Average household: $66,146; Households with income of $100,000 or more: 26.1%; Poverty rate: 11.0%

Educational Attainment: High school diploma or higher: 88.3%; Bachelor's degree or higher: 16.0%; Graduate/professional degree or higher: 9.6%

Housing: Homeownership rate: 75.3%; Median home value: $84,300; Median year structure built: 1985; Homeowner vacancy rate: 4.7%; Median selected monthly owner costs: $994 with a mortgage, $322 without a mortgage; Median gross rent: $738 per month; Rental vacancy rate: 0.0%

Health Insurance: 94.4% have insurance; 72.6% have private insurance; 33.8% have public insurance; 5.6% do not have insurance; 6.8% of children under 18 do not have insurance

Transportation: Commute: 92.0% car, 0.8% public transportation, 1.9% walk, 5.3% work from home; Mean travel time to work: 19.5 minutes

CHAUNCEY (village). Covers a land area of 0.664 square miles and a water area of 0.002 square miles. Located at 39.40° N. Lat; 82.13° W. Long. Elevation is 653 feet.

History: Chauncey was first a salt town, and later a coal town.

Population: 1,232; Growth (since 2000): 15.5%; Density: 1,854.1 persons per square mile; Race: 92.4% White, 0.7% Black/African American, 0.4% Asian, 0.0% American Indian/Alaska Native, 0.0% Native Hawaiian/Other Pacific Islander, 6.5% Two or more races, 0.0% Hispanic of any race; Average household size: 2.62; Median age: 36.7; Age under 18: 24.0%; Age 65 and over: 18.3%; Males per 100 females: 101.7; Marriage status: 29.6% never married, 40.8% now married, 3.1% separated, 10.1% widowed, 19.5% divorced; Foreign born: 0.4%; Speak English only: 99.6%; With disability: 31.3%; Veterans: 14.9%; Ancestry: 21.1% American, 19.3% Irish, 17.6% German, 6.9% English, 3.4% French
Employment: 6.0% management, business, and financial, 1.3% computer, engineering, and science, 16.6% education, legal, community service, arts, and media, 6.4% healthcare practitioners, 25.7% service, 16.8% sales and office, 14.8% natural resources, construction, and maintenance, 12.4% production, transportation, and material moving
Income: Per capita: $13,576; Median household: $28,000; Average household: $33,402; Households with income of $100,000 or more: 0.9%; Poverty rate: 33.0%
Educational Attainment: High school diploma or higher: 78.9%; Bachelor's degree or higher: 8.7%; Graduate/professional degree or higher: 2.5%

School District(s)

Athens City (PK-12)
2015-16 Enrollment: 2,692 . . . . (740) 797-4544
Housing: Homeownership rate: 52.8%; Median home value: $49,600; Median year structure built: 1955; Homeowner vacancy rate: 2.4%; Median selected monthly owner costs: $814 with a mortgage, $294 without a mortgage; Median gross rent: $636 per month; Rental vacancy rate: 3.8%
Health Insurance: 82.2% have insurance; 33.0% have private insurance; 57.4% have public insurance; 17.8% do not have insurance; 18.6% of children under 18 do not have insurance
Transportation: Commute: 94.5% car, 1.6% public transportation, 1.6% walk, 2.3% work from home; Mean travel time to work: 20.3 minutes

COOLVILLE (village). Covers a land area of 0.833 square miles and a water area of 0.024 square miles. Located at 39.22° N. Lat; 81.80° W. Long. Elevation is 699 feet.
Population: 610; Growth (since 2000): 15.5%; Density: 732.4 persons per square mile; Race: 99.8% White, 0.0% Black/African American, 0.0% Asian, 0.0% American Indian/Alaska Native, 0.0% Native Hawaiian/Other Pacific Islander, 0.2% Two or more races, 0.0% Hispanic of any race; Average household size: 3.61; Median age: 35.4; Age under 18: 30.0%; Age 65 and over: 11.6%; Males per 100 females: 92.2; Marriage status: 33.0% never married, 46.5% now married, 0.2% separated, 7.1% widowed, 13.5% divorced; Foreign born: 0.0%; Speak English only: 100.0%; With disability: 22.6%; Veterans: 6.1%; Ancestry: 21.6% German, 13.6% Irish, 12.0% English, 6.4% American, 4.3% Polish
Employment: 15.6% management, business, and financial, 0.5% computer, engineering, and science, 5.2% education, legal, community service, arts, and media, 7.6% healthcare practitioners, 9.0% service, 21.8% sales and office, 16.1% natural resources, construction, and maintenance, 24.2% production, transportation, and material moving
Income: Per capita: $14,529; Median household: $37,321; Average household: $47,493; Households with income of $100,000 or more: 6.5%; Poverty rate: 9.3%
Educational Attainment: High school diploma or higher: 79.9%; Bachelor's degree or higher: 5.3%; Graduate/professional degree or higher: 1.9%

School District(s)

Federal Hocking Local (PK-12)
2015-16 Enrollment: 987. . . . . (740) 662-6691
Housing: Homeownership rate: 85.2%; Median home value: $78,800; Median year structure built: 1963; Homeowner vacancy rate: 3.4%; Median selected monthly owner costs: $867 with a mortgage, $345 without a mortgage; Median gross rent: $950 per month; Rental vacancy rate: 0.0%
Health Insurance: 88.5% have insurance; 39.0% have private insurance; 58.9% have public insurance; 11.5% do not have insurance; 4.9% of children under 18 do not have insurance
Transportation: Commute: 96.6% car, 0.0% public transportation, 0.5% walk, 0.0% work from home; Mean travel time to work: 31.6 minutes

GLOUSTER (village). Covers a land area of 1.327 square miles and a water area of 0.012 square miles. Located at 39.50° N. Lat; 82.08° W. Long. Elevation is 673 feet.
Population: 1,737; Growth (since 2000): -11.9%; Density: 1,308.6 persons per square mile; Race: 96.3% White, 1.1% Black/African American, 0.0% Asian, 0.3% American Indian/Alaska Native, 0.0% Native Hawaiian/Other Pacific Islander, 2.2% Two or more races, 0.5% Hispanic of any race; Average household size: 2.76; Median age: 37.4; Age under 18: 30.7%; Age 65 and over: 12.3%; Males per 100 females: 91.6; Marriage status: 31.4% never married, 45.0% now married, 3.3% separated, 7.4% widowed, 16.1% divorced; Foreign born: 0.0%; Speak English only: 99.5%; With disability: 23.7%; Veterans: 8.3%; Ancestry: 19.6% Irish, 14.6% German, 10.1% English, 8.2% American, 4.7% Polish
Employment: 5.5% management, business, and financial, 0.0% computer, engineering, and science, 3.8% education, legal, community service, arts, and media, 4.6% healthcare practitioners, 31.5% service, 27.7% sales and office, 6.7% natural resources, construction, and maintenance, 20.2% production, transportation, and material moving
Income: Per capita: $13,095; Median household: $26,450; Average household: $34,883; Households with income of $100,000 or more: 4.6%; Poverty rate: 37.5%
Educational Attainment: High school diploma or higher: 73.7%; Bachelor's degree or higher: 4.5%; Graduate/professional degree or higher: 1.5%

School District(s)

Trimble Local (PK-12)
2015-16 Enrollment: 841. . . . . (740) 767-4444
Housing: Homeownership rate: 60.7%; Median home value: $53,000; Median year structure built: Before 1940; Homeowner vacancy rate: 5.5%; Median selected monthly owner costs: $792 with a mortgage, $357 without a mortgage; Median gross rent: $641 per month; Rental vacancy rate: 8.2%
Health Insurance: 90.3% have insurance; 39.3% have private insurance; 62.8% have public insurance; 9.7% do not have insurance; 5.1% of children under 18 do not have insurance
Safety: Violent crime rate: 16.7 per 10,000 population; Property crime rate: 216.9 per 10,000 population
Transportation: Commute: 95.5% car, 0.0% public transportation, 2.6% walk, 0.8% work from home; Mean travel time to work: 31.9 minutes

GUYSVILLE (unincorporated postal area)

ZCTA: 45735

Covers a land area of 50.061 square miles and a water area of 0.177 square miles. Located at 39.26° N. Lat; 81.93° W. Long. Elevation is 643 feet.
Population: 1,745; Growth (since 2000): 3.1%; Density: 34.9 persons per square mile; Race: 95.6% White, 3.6% Black/African American, 0.8% Asian, 0.0% American Indian/Alaska Native, 0.0% Native Hawaiian/Other Pacific Islander, 0.0% Two or more races, 0.0% Hispanic of any race; Average household size: 2.49; Median age: 50.7; Age under 18: 18.3%; Age 65 and over: 20.5%; Males per 100 females: 103.8; Marriage status: 19.7% never married, 65.1% now married, 1.2% separated, 4.4% widowed, 10.9% divorced; Foreign born: 0.8%; Speak English only: 100.0%; With disability: 16.2%; Veterans: 12.8%; Ancestry: 21.0% English, 15.9% Irish, 14.3% German, 8.1% American, 4.7% European
Employment: 10.8% management, business, and financial, 6.2% computer, engineering, and science, 11.5% education, legal, community service, arts, and media, 5.6% healthcare practitioners, 21.7% service, 15.7% sales and office, 18.0% natural resources, construction, and maintenance, 10.4% production, transportation, and material moving
Income: Per capita: $30,460; Median household: $45,875; Average household: $64,614; Households with income of $100,000 or more: 14.6%; Poverty rate: 16.8%
Educational Attainment: High school diploma or higher: 92.9%; Bachelor's degree or higher: 19.3%; Graduate/professional degree or higher: 10.7%
Housing: Homeownership rate: 87.6%; Median home value: $133,800; Median year structure built: 1986; Homeowner vacancy rate: 4.1%; Median selected monthly owner costs: $1,154 with a mortgage, $371 without a mortgage; Median gross rent: $639 per month; Rental vacancy rate: 0.0%
Health Insurance: 97.6% have insurance; 76.8% have private insurance; 46.3% have public insurance; 2.4% do not have insurance; 0.0% of children under 18 do not have insurance
Transportation: Commute: 93.6% car, 0.0% public transportation, 0.0% walk, 4.1% work from home; Mean travel time to work: 32.7 minutes

HOCKINGPORT (CDP). Covers a land area of 0.426 square miles and a water area of 0.044 square miles. Located at 39.19° N. Lat; 81.74° W. Long. Elevation is 617 feet.

Population: 93; Growth (since 2000): n/a; Density: 218.2 persons per square mile; Race: 100.0% White, 0.0% Black/African American, 0.0% Asian, 0.0% American Indian/Alaska Native, 0.0% Native Hawaiian/Other Pacific Islander, 0.0% Two or more races, 0.0% Hispanic of any race; Average household size: 1.45; Median age: 66.6; Age under 18: 9.7%; Age 65 and over: 61.3%; Males per 100 females: 84.3; Marriage status: 18.3% never married, 62.4% now married, 20.4% separated, 19.4% widowed, 0.0% divorced; Foreign born: 0.0%; Speak English only: 100.0%; With disability: 100.0%; Veterans: 21.4%; Ancestry: 41.9% German, 41.9% Irish, 19.4% Welsh

Employment: 0.0% management, business, and financial, 0.0% computer, engineering, and science, 0.0% education, legal, community service, arts, and media, 0.0% healthcare practitioners, 0.0% service, 0.0% sales and office, 0.0% natural resources, construction, and maintenance, 100.0% production, transportation, and material moving

Income: Per capita: $16,103; Median household: n/a; Average household: $23,108; Households with income of $100,000 or more: n/a; Poverty rate: 37.6%

Educational Attainment: High school diploma or higher: 32.1%; Bachelor's degree or higher: n/a; Graduate/professional degree or higher: n/a

Housing: Homeownership rate: 87.5%; Median home value: n/a; Median year structure built: 1985; Homeowner vacancy rate: 0.0%; Median selected monthly owner costs: n/a with a mortgage, n/a without a mortgage; Median gross rent: n/a per month; Rental vacancy rate: 0.0%

Health Insurance: 100.0% have insurance; 81.7% have private insurance; 79.6% have public insurance; 0.0% do not have insurance; 0.0% of children under 18 do not have insurance

Transportation: Commute: 100.0% car, 0.0% public transportation, 0.0% walk, 0.0% work from home; Mean travel time to work: 0.0 minutes

JACKSONVILLE (village). Covers a land area of 0.242 square miles and a water area of 0.002 square miles. Located at 39.48° N. Lat; 82.08° W. Long. Elevation is 679 feet.

Population: 495; Growth (since 2000): -9.0%; Density: 2,044.8 persons per square mile; Race: 100.0% White, 0.0% Black/African American, 0.0% Asian, 0.0% American Indian/Alaska Native, 0.0% Native Hawaiian/Other Pacific Islander, 0.0% Two or more races, 0.0% Hispanic of any race; Average household size: 2.68; Median age: 39.5; Age under 18: 20.2%; Age 65 and over: 10.1%; Males per 100 females: 91.6; Marriage status: 35.4% never married, 45.5% now married, 0.7% separated, 6.5% widowed, 12.7% divorced; Foreign born: 0.0%; Speak English only: 100.0%; With disability: 32.1%; Veterans: 9.1%; Ancestry: 19.6% German, 17.2% English, 14.9% American, 13.7% Irish, 11.1% Dutch

Employment: 14.9% management, business, and financial, 0.0% computer, engineering, and science, 5.1% education, legal, community service, arts, and media, 5.1% healthcare practitioners, 35.7% service, 17.4% sales and office, 3.0% natural resources, construction, and maintenance, 18.7% production, transportation, and material moving

Income: Per capita: $22,143; Median household: $43,523; Average household: $55,523; Households with income of $100,000 or more: 12.4%; Poverty rate: 25.9%

Educational Attainment: High school diploma or higher: 86.8%; Bachelor's degree or higher: 9.9%; Graduate/professional degree or higher: 3.6%

Housing: Homeownership rate: 71.9%; Median home value: $63,900; Median year structure built: Before 1940; Homeowner vacancy rate: 2.9%; Median selected monthly owner costs: $785 with a mortgage, $300 without a mortgage; Median gross rent: $693 per month; Rental vacancy rate: 11.3%

Health Insurance: 87.9% have insurance; 53.3% have private insurance; 44.4% have public insurance; 12.1% do not have insurance; 0.0% of children under 18 do not have insurance

Transportation: Commute: 97.0% car, 0.0% public transportation, 0.0% walk, 3.0% work from home; Mean travel time to work: 23.3 minutes

MILLFIELD (CDP). Covers a land area of 0.567 square miles and a water area of 0.011 square miles. Located at 39.44° N. Lat; 82.10° W. Long. Elevation is 679 feet.

Population: 343; Growth (since 2000): n/a; Density: 604.6 persons per square mile; Race: 100.0% White, 0.0% Black/African American, 0.0% Asian, 0.0% American Indian/Alaska Native, 0.0% Native Hawaiian/Other Pacific Islander, 0.0% Two or more races, 0.0% Hispanic of any race; Average household size: 2.32; Median age: 55.6; Age under 18: 8.2%; Age 65 and over: 22.4%; Males per 100 females: 104.2; Marriage status: 11.7% never married, 63.5% now married, 8.9% separated, 2.9% widowed, 21.9% divorced; Foreign born: 0.0%; Speak English only: 100.0%; With disability: 17.8%; Veterans: 5.1%; Ancestry: 54.5% American, 12.8% German, 5.2% Irish, 2.6% English, 2.3% Lithuanian

Employment: 5.6% management, business, and financial, 0.0% computer, engineering, and science, 0.0% education, legal, community service, arts, and media, 5.0% healthcare practitioners, 21.1% service, 50.9% sales and office, 17.4% natural resources, construction, and maintenance, 0.0% production, transportation, and material moving

Income: Per capita: $17,940; Median household: $24,408; Average household: $35,491; Households with income of $100,000 or more: n/a; Poverty rate: 2.6%

Educational Attainment: High school diploma or higher: 79.9%; Bachelor's degree or higher: n/a; Graduate/professional degree or higher: n/a

Housing: Homeownership rate: 100.0%; Median home value: n/a; Median year structure built: 1973; Homeowner vacancy rate: 0.0%; Median selected monthly owner costs: n/a with a mortgage, $337 without a mortgage; Median gross rent: n/a per month; Rental vacancy rate: 0.0%

Health Insurance: 79.6% have insurance; 66.5% have private insurance; 32.1% have public insurance; 20.4% do not have insurance; 0.0% of children under 18 do not have insurance

Transportation: Commute: 100.0% car, 0.0% public transportation, 0.0% walk, 0.0% work from home; Mean travel time to work: 19.8 minutes

NELSONVILLE (city). Covers a land area of 4.892 square miles and a water area of 0.111 square miles. Located at 39.46° N. Lat; 82.22° W. Long. Elevation is 679 feet.

History: First called Englishtown, the name was changed in 1824 to Nelsonville, in honor of Daniel Nelson, an enterprising citizen. Nelsonville developed as a coal town.

Population: 5,249; Growth (since 2000): 0.4%; Density: 1,072.9 persons per square mile; Race: 91.7% White, 4.2% Black/African American, 0.6% Asian, 0.4% American Indian/Alaska Native, 0.0% Native Hawaiian/Other Pacific Islander, 3.0% Two or more races, 1.2% Hispanic of any race; Average household size: 2.36; Median age: 28.2; Age under 18: 18.3%; Age 65 and over: 8.5%; Males per 100 females: 121.2; Marriage status: 55.0% never married, 27.8% now married, 4.3% separated, 5.5% widowed, 11.7% divorced; Foreign born: 1.3%; Speak English only: 97.9%; With disability: 20.8%; Veterans: 7.6%; Ancestry: 22.7% German, 13.7% Irish, 12.8% American, 6.2% English, 4.6% Italian

Employment: 7.2% management, business, and financial, 1.4% computer, engineering, and science, 6.2% education, legal, community service, arts, and media, 3.3% healthcare practitioners, 29.7% service, 31.3% sales and office, 5.8% natural resources, construction, and maintenance, 15.0% production, transportation, and material moving

Income: Per capita: $13,218; Median household: $25,735; Average household: $34,119; Households with income of $100,000 or more: 4.6%; Poverty rate: 40.0%

Educational Attainment: High school diploma or higher: 85.5%; Bachelor's degree or higher: 10.9%; Graduate/professional degree or higher: 2.1%

School District(s)

Nelsonville-York City (PK-12)
2015-16 Enrollment: 1,266 . . . . (740) 753-4441
Tri-County Career Center (10-12)
2015-16 Enrollment: n/a . . . . (740) 753-3511

Two-year College(s)

Hocking College (Public)
Fall 2016 Enrollment: 2,940 . . . . (740) 753-3591
2016-17 Tuition: In-state $4,390; Out-of-state $8,780
Tri-County Adult Career Center (Public)
Fall 2016 Enrollment: 53 . . . . (740) 753-5464

Housing: Homeownership rate: 42.3%; Median home value: $77,700; Median year structure built: 1963; Homeowner vacancy rate: 3.1%; Median selected monthly owner costs: $969 with a mortgage, $361 without a mortgage; Median gross rent: $653 per month; Rental vacancy rate: 19.2%

Health Insurance: 89.1% have insurance; 51.3% have private insurance; 48.6% have public insurance; 10.9% do not have insurance; 6.9% of children under 18 do not have insurance

Hospitals: Doctors Hospital of Nelsonville (50 beds)

Safety: Violent crime rate: 21.3 per 10,000 population; Property crime rate: 378.0 per 10,000 population
Transportation: Commute: 87.4% car, 0.3% public transportation, 9.0% walk, 2.9% work from home; Mean travel time to work: 19.9 minutes

NEW MARSHFIELD (CDP). Covers a land area of 0.392 square miles and a water area of 0.001 square miles. Located at 39.32° N. Lat; 82.22° W. Long. Elevation is 820 feet.
Population: 367; Growth (since 2000): n/a; Density: 936.4 persons per square mile; Race: 100.0% White, 0.0% Black/African American, 0.0% Asian, 0.0% American Indian/Alaska Native, 0.0% Native Hawaiian/Other Pacific Islander, 0.0% Two or more races, 0.0% Hispanic of any race; Average household size: 2.72; Median age: 53.1; Age under 18: 20.7%; Age 65 and over: 29.7%; Males per 100 females: 88.4; Marriage status: 31.3% never married, 43.6% now married, 0.0% separated, 5.2% widowed, 19.9% divorced; Foreign born: 0.0%; Speak English only: 95.1%; With disability: 12.5%; Veterans: 5.2%; Ancestry: 16.6% American, 13.4% German, 8.4% English, 4.1% Welsh
Employment: 0.0% management, business, and financial, 0.0% computer, engineering, and science, 23.4% education, legal, community service, arts, and media, 0.0% healthcare practitioners, 76.6% service, 0.0% sales and office, 0.0% natural resources, construction, and maintenance, 0.0% production, transportation, and material moving
Income: Per capita: $18,629; Median household: $31,417; Average household: $48,815; Households with income of $100,000 or more: 11.9%; Poverty rate: 9.3%
Educational Attainment: High school diploma or higher: 79.4%; Bachelor's degree or higher: 16.2%; Graduate/professional degree or higher: 10.7%
Housing: Homeownership rate: 77.8%; Median home value: n/a; Median year structure built: 1963; Homeowner vacancy rate: 0.0%; Median selected monthly owner costs: n/a with a mortgage, $388 without a mortgage; Median gross rent: n/a per month; Rental vacancy rate: 0.0%
Health Insurance: 67.6% have insurance; 37.6% have private insurance; 55.6% have public insurance; 32.4% do not have insurance; 0.0% of children under 18 do not have insurance
Transportation: Commute: 100.0% car, 0.0% public transportation, 0.0% walk, 0.0% work from home; Mean travel time to work: 0.0 minutes

STEWART (CDP). Covers a land area of 0.296 square miles and a water area of 0 square miles. Located at 39.31° N. Lat; 81.90° W. Long. Elevation is 669 feet.
Population: 268; Growth (since 2000): n/a; Density: 906.2 persons per square mile; Race: 93.7% White, 0.0% Black/African American, 0.0% Asian, 0.0% American Indian/Alaska Native, 0.0% Native Hawaiian/Other Pacific Islander, 6.3% Two or more races, 0.0% Hispanic of any race; Average household size: 2.50; Median age: 26.5; Age under 18: 23.1%; Age 65 and over: 8.6%; Males per 100 females: 96.0; Marriage status: 35.7% never married, 50.2% now married, 0.0% separated, 4.7% widowed, 9.4% divorced; Foreign born: 0.0%; Speak English only: 100.0%; With disability: 14.2%; Veterans: 0.0%; Ancestry: 18.3% Irish, 15.7% English, 7.8% Polish, 6.3% African, 2.6% Dutch
Employment: 0.0% management, business, and financial, 4.8% computer, engineering, and science, 0.0% education, legal, community service, arts, and media, 11.4% healthcare practitioners, 8.4% service, 53.6% sales and office, 18.1% natural resources, construction, and maintenance, 3.6% production, transportation, and material moving
Income: Per capita: $25,963; Median household: n/a; Average household: $62,870; Households with income of $100,000 or more: 13.1%; Poverty rate: 21.6%
Educational Attainment: High school diploma or higher: 100.0%; Bachelor's degree or higher: 14.3%; Graduate/professional degree or higher: 8.8%

School District(s)

Federal Hocking Local (PK-12)
2015-16 Enrollment: 987 . . . . (740) 662-6691
Housing: Homeownership rate: 77.6%; Median home value: n/a; Median year structure built: 1992; Homeowner vacancy rate: 0.0%; Median selected monthly owner costs: $1,045 with a mortgage, n/a without a mortgage; Median gross rent: n/a per month; Rental vacancy rate: 0.0%
Health Insurance: 92.2% have insurance; 54.9% have private insurance; 41.0% have public insurance; 7.8% do not have insurance; 16.1% of children under 18 do not have insurance
Transportation: Commute: 100.0% car, 0.0% public transportation, 0.0% walk, 0.0% work from home; Mean travel time to work: 19.2 minutes

THE PLAINS (CDP). Covers a land area of 2.277 square miles and a water area of 0.006 square miles. Located at 39.37° N. Lat; 82.13° W. Long. Elevation is 715 feet.
Population: 2,918; Growth (since 2000): -0.4%; Density: 1,281.4 persons per square mile; Race: 89.3% White, 2.1% Black/African American, 3.0% Asian, 2.7% American Indian/Alaska Native, 0.0% Native Hawaiian/Other Pacific Islander, 3.0% Two or more races, 1.6% Hispanic of any race; Average household size: 2.27; Median age: 37.8; Age under 18: 21.7%; Age 65 and over: 20.0%; Males per 100 females: 80.0; Marriage status: 34.5% never married, 40.5% now married, 0.5% separated, 8.4% widowed, 16.5% divorced; Foreign born: 2.2%; Speak English only: 95.1%; With disability: 27.0%; Veterans: 8.2%; Ancestry: 22.6% German, 14.1% Irish, 12.7% English, 12.5% American, 3.9% Polish
Employment: 4.3% management, business, and financial, 7.3% computer, engineering, and science, 20.7% education, legal, community service, arts, and media, 3.7% healthcare practitioners, 13.5% service, 26.6% sales and office, 11.1% natural resources, construction, and maintenance, 12.9% production, transportation, and material moving
Income: Per capita: $17,733; Median household: $33,207; Average household: $40,827; Households with income of $100,000 or more: 7.1%; Poverty rate: 30.6%
Educational Attainment: High school diploma or higher: 85.3%; Bachelor's degree or higher: 21.5%; Graduate/professional degree or higher: 11.1%

School District(s)

Athens City (PK-12)
2015-16 Enrollment: 2,692 . . . . (740) 797-4544
Housing: Homeownership rate: 43.9%; Median home value: $111,300; Median year structure built: 1988; Homeowner vacancy rate: 0.0%; Median selected monthly owner costs: $1,176 with a mortgage, $292 without a mortgage; Median gross rent: $691 per month; Rental vacancy rate: 7.0%
Health Insurance: 95.7% have insurance; 47.9% have private insurance; 58.7% have public insurance; 4.3% do not have insurance; 0.0% of children under 18 do not have insurance
Transportation: Commute: 94.9% car, 0.0% public transportation, 3.8% walk, 1.3% work from home; Mean travel time to work: 15.0 minutes

TRIMBLE (village). Covers a land area of 0.662 square miles and a water area of 0.010 square miles. Located at 39.49° N. Lat; 82.08° W. Long. Elevation is 679 feet.
Population: 523; Growth (since 2000): 12.2%; Density: 789.6 persons per square mile; Race: 93.3% White, 0.0% Black/African American, 0.0% Asian, 2.1% American Indian/Alaska Native, 0.0% Native Hawaiian/Other Pacific Islander, 4.6% Two or more races, 2.3% Hispanic of any race; Average household size: 2.99; Median age: 39.5; Age under 18: 29.8%; Age 65 and over: 11.1%; Males per 100 females: 109.7; Marriage status: 28.3% never married, 46.1% now married, 4.8% separated, 10.4% widowed, 15.2% divorced; Foreign born: 0.0%; Speak English only: 100.0%; With disability: 31.0%; Veterans: 16.3%; Ancestry: 28.1% German, 11.7% English, 11.5% Irish, 8.0% Dutch, 5.4% Welsh
Employment: 4.1% management, business, and financial, 0.0% computer, engineering, and science, 16.6% education, legal, community service, arts, and media, 4.8% healthcare practitioners, 42.8% service, 11.0% sales and office, 4.8% natural resources, construction, and maintenance, 15.9% production, transportation, and material moving
Income: Per capita: $11,493; Median household: $25,375; Average household: $32,911; Households with income of $100,000 or more: 6.9%; Poverty rate: 42.0%
Educational Attainment: High school diploma or higher: 75.4%; Bachelor's degree or higher: 5.6%; Graduate/professional degree or higher: 1.2%
Housing: Homeownership rate: 69.1%; Median home value: $46,300; Median year structure built: Before 1940; Homeowner vacancy rate: 3.0%; Median selected monthly owner costs: $756 with a mortgage, $325 without a mortgage; Median gross rent: $565 per month; Rental vacancy rate: 14.3%
Health Insurance: 83.4% have insurance; 37.9% have private insurance; 57.0% have public insurance; 16.6% do not have insurance; 21.2% of children under 18 do not have insurance
Transportation: Commute: 89.0% car, 0.0% public transportation, 3.4% walk, 0.0% work from home; Mean travel time to work: 23.5 minutes

Auglaize County

Located in western Ohio; drained by the Auglaize and Saint Marys Rivers; includes part of Grand Lake. Covers a land area of 401.386 square miles, a water area of 0.519 square miles, and is located in the Eastern Time Zone at 40.56° N. Lat., 84.22° W. Long. The county was founded in 1848. County seat is Wapakoneta.

Auglaize County is part of the Wapakoneta, OH Micropolitan Statistical Area. The entire metro area includes: Auglaize County, OH

Population: 45,871; Growth (since 2000): -1.6%; Density: 114.3 persons per square mile; Race: 97.0% White, 0.4% Black/African American, 0.6% Asian, 0.2% American Indian/Alaska Native, 0.0% Native Hawaiian/Other Pacific Islander, 1.1% two or more races, 1.4% Hispanic of any race; Average household size: 2.49; Median age: 41.2; Age under 18: 24.3%; Age 65 and over: 16.9%; Males per 100 females: 98.4; Marriage status: 24.1% never married, 58.7% now married, 0.6% separated, 7.5% widowed, 9.7% divorced; Foreign born: 1.0%; Speak English only: 97.7%; With disability: 11.8%; Veterans: 8.0%; Ancestry: 48.1% German, 11.1% Irish, 8.5% American, 6.5% English, 2.5% French
Religion: Six largest groups: 25.3% Catholicism, 8.1% Presbyterian-Reformed, 7.1% Methodist/Pietist, 6.5% Holiness, 5.4% Lutheran, 1.9% Baptist
Economy: Unemployment rate: 3.3%; Leading industries: 16.0 % retail trade; 13.5 % other services (except public administration); 10.3 % construction; Farms: 1,040 totaling 210,084 acres; Company size: 1 employs 1,000 or more persons, 2 employ 500 to 999 persons, 30 employ 100 to 499 persons, 957 employ less than 100 persons; Business ownership: 984 women-owned, n/a Black-owned, n/a Hispanic-owned, 59 Asian-owned, n/a American Indian/Alaska Native-owned
Employment: 12.2% management, business, and financial, 4.0% computer, engineering, and science, 8.3% education, legal, community service, arts, and media, 5.6% healthcare practitioners, 15.0% service, 19.9% sales and office, 9.2% natural resources, construction, and maintenance, 25.7% production, transportation, and material moving
Income: Per capita: $26,690; Median household: $55,914; Average household: $66,672; Households with income of $100,000 or more: 19.0%; Poverty rate: 8.8%
Educational Attainment: High school diploma or higher: 92.8%; Bachelor's degree or higher: 17.8%; Graduate/professional degree or higher: 6.0%
Housing: Homeownership rate: 75.2%; Median home value: $138,700; Median year structure built: 1968; Homeowner vacancy rate: 1.1%; Median selected monthly owner costs: $1,146 with a mortgage, $403 without a mortgage; Median gross rent: $651 per month; Rental vacancy rate: 5.1%
Vital Statistics: Birth rate: 115.9 per 10,000 population; Death rate: 108.9 per 10,000 population; Age-adjusted cancer mortality rate: 154.4 deaths per 100,000 population
Health Insurance: 94.5% have insurance; 79.2% have private insurance; 30.7% have public insurance; 5.5% do not have insurance; 1.7% of children under 18 do not have insurance
Health Care: Physicians: 7.9 per 10,000 population; Dentists: 3.5 per 10,000 population; Hospital beds: 11.6 per 10,000 population; Hospital admissions: 365.2 per 10,000 population
Transportation: Commute: 93.6% car, 0.1% public transportation, 2.0% walk, 2.8% work from home; Mean travel time to work: 19.6 minutes
2016 Presidential Election: 78.4% Trump, 16.7% Clinton, 2.9% Johnson, 0.5% Stein
National and State Parks: Fort Amanda State Park
Additional Information Contacts
Auglaize Government . . . . (419) 739-6710
http://www2.auglaizecounty.org

Auglaize County Communities

BUCKLAND (village). Covers a land area of 0.258 square miles and a water area of 0 square miles. Located at 40.62° N. Lat; 84.26° W. Long. Elevation is 850 feet.
Population: 290; Growth (since 2000): 13.7%; Density: 1,125.2 persons per square mile; Race: 98.6% White, 0.3% Black/African American, 0.0% Asian, 0.0% American Indian/Alaska Native, 0.0% Native Hawaiian/Other Pacific Islander, 1.0% Two or more races, 0.0% Hispanic of any race; Average household size: 2.46; Median age: 31.3; Age under 18: 34.1%; Age 65 and over: 11.4%; Males per 100 females: 102.6; Marriage status: 22.5% never married, 52.5% now married, 1.0% separated, 9.3% widowed, 15.7% divorced; Foreign born: 0.3%; Speak English only: 98.8%; With disability: 11.7%; Veterans: 5.2%; Ancestry: 50.7% German, 15.2% Irish, 11.7% American, 10.0% Dutch, 3.1% English
Employment: 2.4% management, business, and financial, 0.0% computer, engineering, and science, 9.5% education, legal, community service, arts, and media, 11.1% healthcare practitioners, 13.5% service, 19.0% sales and office, 7.1% natural resources, construction, and maintenance, 37.3% production, transportation, and material moving
Income: Per capita: $20,948; Median household: $45,000; Average household: $53,658; Households with income of $100,000 or more: 13.6%; Poverty rate: 14.0%
Educational Attainment: High school diploma or higher: 92.0%; Bachelor's degree or higher: 4.6%; Graduate/professional degree or higher: 1.7%
Housing: Homeownership rate: 62.7%; Median home value: $81,400; Median year structure built: 1944; Homeowner vacancy rate: 0.0%; Median selected monthly owner costs: $931 with a mortgage, $315 without a mortgage; Median gross rent: $864 per month; Rental vacancy rate: 0.0%
Health Insurance: 91.7% have insurance; 67.9% have private insurance; 33.8% have public insurance; 8.3% do not have insurance; 4.0% of children under 18 do not have insurance
Transportation: Commute: 96.8% car, 0.0% public transportation, 3.2% walk, 0.0% work from home; Mean travel time to work: 22.3 minutes

CRIDERSVILLE (village). Covers a land area of 0.897 square miles and a water area of 0 square miles. Located at 40.65° N. Lat; 84.15° W. Long. Elevation is 883 feet.
Population: 1,896; Growth (since 2000): 4.3%; Density: 2,114.6 persons per square mile; Race: 99.2% White, 0.0% Black/African American, 0.0% Asian, 0.0% American Indian/Alaska Native, 0.0% Native Hawaiian/Other Pacific Islander, 0.6% Two or more races, 1.9% Hispanic of any race; Average household size: 2.27; Median age: 45.8; Age under 18: 20.9%; Age 65 and over: 23.7%; Males per 100 females: 87.3; Marriage status: 19.6% never married, 53.5% now married, 1.6% separated, 11.7% widowed, 15.2% divorced; Foreign born: 0.5%; Speak English only: 98.9%; With disability: 18.2%; Veterans: 10.7%; Ancestry: 29.9% German, 11.2% American, 9.7% Irish, 6.9% English, 5.8% Italian
Employment: 4.7% management, business, and financial, 2.2% computer, engineering, and science, 8.9% education, legal, community service, arts, and media, 7.5% healthcare practitioners, 18.8% service, 24.6% sales and office, 5.3% natural resources, construction, and maintenance, 28.1% production, transportation, and material moving
Income: Per capita: $21,682; Median household: $37,434; Average household: $49,620; Households with income of $100,000 or more: 11.2%; Poverty rate: 20.5%
Educational Attainment: High school diploma or higher: 91.4%; Bachelor's degree or higher: 13.9%; Graduate/professional degree or higher: 5.0%

School District(s)

Wapakoneta City (PK-12)
2015-16 Enrollment: 3,083 . . . . (419) 739-2900
Housing: Homeownership rate: 62.2%; Median home value: $86,900; Median year structure built: 1972; Homeowner vacancy rate: 0.0%; Median selected monthly owner costs: $917 with a mortgage, $378 without a mortgage; Median gross rent: $752 per month; Rental vacancy rate: 14.8%
Health Insurance: 89.1% have insurance; 60.6% have private insurance; 46.1% have public insurance; 10.9% do not have insurance; 0.8% of children under 18 do not have insurance
Transportation: Commute: 97.1% car, 0.0% public transportation, 1.7% walk, 0.8% work from home; Mean travel time to work: 21.2 minutes

MINSTER (village). Covers a land area of 1.932 square miles and a water area of 0 square miles. Located at 40.40° N. Lat; 84.38° W. Long. Elevation is 965 feet.
History: Incorporated 1833.
Population: 2,898; Growth (since 2000): 3.7%; Density: 1,500.3 persons per square mile; Race: 97.1% White, 0.0% Black/African American, 1.2% Asian, 0.0% American Indian/Alaska Native, 0.0% Native Hawaiian/Other Pacific Islander, 0.0% Two or more races, 2.0% Hispanic of any race; Average household size: 2.57; Median age: 40.3; Age under 18: 28.4%; Age 65 and over: 19.2%; Males per 100 females: 98.7; Marriage status: 20.6% never married, 65.6% now married, 0.3% separated, 9.2% widowed, 4.6% divorced; Foreign born: 1.5%; Speak English only: 97.5%;

With disability: 9.8%; Veterans: 5.8%; Ancestry: 69.4% German, 8.1% Irish, 6.0% American, 5.0% French, 1.9% English
Employment: 13.2% management, business, and financial, 7.2% computer, engineering, and science, 12.1% education, legal, community service, arts, and media, 9.0% healthcare practitioners, 12.3% service, 22.2% sales and office, 6.5% natural resources, construction, and maintenance, 17.5% production, transportation, and material moving
Income: Per capita: $29,060; Median household: $70,478; Average household: $75,526; Households with income of $100,000 or more: 28.1%; Poverty rate: 6.1%
Educational Attainment: High school diploma or higher: 94.3%; Bachelor's degree or higher: 29.9%; Graduate/professional degree or higher: 10.6%

School District(s)

Minster Local (KG-12)
2015-16 Enrollment: 866 .... (419) 628-3397

Housing: Homeownership rate: 80.4%; Median home value: $169,100; Median year structure built: 1970; Homeowner vacancy rate: 0.0%; Median selected monthly owner costs: $1,325 with a mortgage, $379 without a mortgage; Median gross rent: $650 per month; Rental vacancy rate: 6.6%
Health Insurance: 98.4% have insurance; 87.7% have private insurance; 24.1% have public insurance; 1.6% do not have insurance; 0.0% of children under 18 do not have insurance
Newspapers: Community Post (weekly circulation 6,800)
Transportation: Commute: 91.2% car, 1.4% public transportation, 2.8% walk, 2.0% work from home; Mean travel time to work: 16.5 minutes
Additional Information Contacts
Village of Minster .... (419) 628-3497
http://www.minsteroh.com

NEW BREMEN (village). Covers a land area of 2.145 square miles and a water area of 0 square miles. Located at 40.43° N. Lat; 84.38° W. Long. Elevation is 945 feet.
History: Incorporated 1833.
Population: 3,159; Growth (since 2000): 8.6%; Density: 1,473.0 persons per square mile; Race: 96.5% White, 0.0% Black/African American, 1.6% Asian, 0.0% American Indian/Alaska Native, 0.0% Native Hawaiian/Other Pacific Islander, 1.8% Two or more races, 2.4% Hispanic of any race; Average household size: 2.42; Median age: 40.2; Age under 18: 25.9%; Age 65 and over: 13.6%; Males per 100 females: 99.3; Marriage status: 24.1% never married, 62.7% now married, 0.0% separated, 3.8% widowed, 9.5% divorced; Foreign born: 1.8%; Speak English only: 97.0%; With disability: 8.5%; Veterans: 6.2%; Ancestry: 67.0% German, 9.5% English, 6.9% Irish, 4.7% American, 3.2% French
Employment: 17.7% management, business, and financial, 9.3% computer, engineering, and science, 10.6% education, legal, community service, arts, and media, 5.8% healthcare practitioners, 12.1% service, 18.1% sales and office, 4.5% natural resources, construction, and maintenance, 22.0% production, transportation, and material moving
Income: Per capita: $32,879; Median household: $70,122; Average household: $79,393; Households with income of $100,000 or more: 30.3%; Poverty rate: 6.1%
Educational Attainment: High school diploma or higher: 97.1%; Bachelor's degree or higher: 30.7%; Graduate/professional degree or higher: 11.2%

School District(s)

New Bremen Local (KG-12)
2015-16 Enrollment: 761 .... (419) 629-8606

Housing: Homeownership rate: 79.9%; Median home value: $162,000; Median year structure built: 1967; Homeowner vacancy rate: 0.0%; Median selected monthly owner costs: $1,185 with a mortgage, $384 without a mortgage; Median gross rent: $594 per month; Rental vacancy rate: 0.0%
Health Insurance: 98.0% have insurance; 89.5% have private insurance; 20.1% have public insurance; 2.0% do not have insurance; 0.0% of children under 18 do not have insurance
Transportation: Commute: 91.0% car, 0.0% public transportation, 3.0% walk, 2.8% work from home; Mean travel time to work: 18.2 minutes
Additional Information Contacts
Village of New Bremen .... (419) 629-2827
http://www.newbremen.com

NEW HAMPSHIRE (CDP). Covers a land area of 0.610 square miles and a water area of 0 square miles. Located at 40.55° N. Lat; 83.95° W. Long. Elevation is 1,037 feet.
Population: 196; Growth (since 2000): n/a; Density: 321.2 persons per square mile; Race: 100.0% White, 0.0% Black/African American, 0.0% Asian, 0.0% American Indian/Alaska Native, 0.0% Native Hawaiian/Other Pacific Islander, 0.0% Two or more races, 0.0% Hispanic of any race; Average household size: 3.16; Median age: 45.4; Age under 18: 22.4%; Age 65 and over: 30.1%; Males per 100 females: 95.5; Marriage status: 16.0% never married, 67.9% now married, 0.0% separated, 2.6% widowed, 13.5% divorced; Foreign born: 0.0%; Speak English only: 100.0%; With disability: 11.7%; Veterans: 21.1%; Ancestry: 56.1% German, 13.3% English, 9.2% Dutch, 7.7% Irish, 6.1% American
Employment: 22.2% management, business, and financial, 0.0% computer, engineering, and science, 8.9% education, legal, community service, arts, and media, 0.0% healthcare practitioners, 0.0% service, 57.8% sales and office, 0.0% natural resources, construction, and maintenance, 11.1% production, transportation, and material moving
Income: Per capita: $23,070; Median household: $58,750; Average household: $70,839; Households with income of $100,000 or more: 17.8%; Poverty rate: 2.0%
Educational Attainment: High school diploma or higher: 86.9%; Bachelor's degree or higher: 15.2%; Graduate/professional degree or higher: 11.7%
Housing: Homeownership rate: 74.2%; Median home value: $74,500; Median year structure built: Before 1940; Homeowner vacancy rate: 0.0%; Median selected monthly owner costs: $1,136 with a mortgage, <$100 without a mortgage; Median gross rent: n/a per month; Rental vacancy rate: 0.0%
Health Insurance: 75.5% have insurance; 44.4% have private insurance; 56.6% have public insurance; 24.5% do not have insurance; 29.5% of children under 18 do not have insurance
Transportation: Commute: 75.6% car, 0.0% public transportation, 24.4% walk, 0.0% work from home; Mean travel time to work: 19.0 minutes

NEW KNOXVILLE (village). Covers a land area of 0.885 square miles and a water area of 0 square miles. Located at 40.49° N. Lat; 84.32° W. Long. Elevation is 899 feet.
Population: 942; Growth (since 2000): 5.7%; Density: 1,064.5 persons per square mile; Race: 97.5% White, 0.0% Black/African American, 0.0% Asian, 0.0% American Indian/Alaska Native, 0.0% Native Hawaiian/Other Pacific Islander, 2.5% Two or more races, 0.7% Hispanic of any race; Average household size: 2.55; Median age: 38.4; Age under 18: 29.9%; Age 65 and over: 14.3%; Males per 100 females: 97.5; Marriage status: 22.1% never married, 63.6% now married, 0.4% separated, 6.7% widowed, 7.6% divorced; Foreign born: 0.0%; Speak English only: 99.3%; With disability: 8.6%; Veterans: 10.0%; Ancestry: 56.1% German, 12.1% Irish, 9.7% English, 8.5% American, 2.8% Scottish
Employment: 12.3% management, business, and financial, 3.6% computer, engineering, and science, 11.5% education, legal, community service, arts, and media, 5.3% healthcare practitioners, 12.9% service, 19.8% sales and office, 6.9% natural resources, construction, and maintenance, 27.7% production, transportation, and material moving
Income: Per capita: $28,866; Median household: $61,875; Average household: $72,857; Households with income of $100,000 or more: 18.7%; Poverty rate: 2.9%
Educational Attainment: High school diploma or higher: 95.3%; Bachelor's degree or higher: 22.4%; Graduate/professional degree or higher: 4.7%

School District(s)

New Knoxville Local (KG-12)
2015-16 Enrollment: 408 .... (419) 753-2431

Housing: Homeownership rate: 65.4%; Median home value: $118,300; Median year structure built: 1951; Homeowner vacancy rate: 0.0%; Median selected monthly owner costs: $1,033 with a mortgage, $342 without a mortgage; Median gross rent: $710 per month; Rental vacancy rate: 0.0%
Health Insurance: 97.2% have insurance; 87.3% have private insurance; 22.3% have public insurance; 2.8% do not have insurance; 2.8% of children under 18 do not have insurance
Transportation: Commute: 95.0% car, 0.0% public transportation, 2.9% walk, 0.8% work from home; Mean travel time to work: 18.2 minutes
Additional Information Contacts
Village of New Knoxville .... (419) 753-2160
http://www.newknoxville.com

SAINT JOHNS (CDP). Covers a land area of 0.384 square miles and a water area of 0.007 square miles. Located at 40.56° N. Lat; 84.08° W. Long. Elevation is 1,007 feet.
Population: 197; Growth (since 2000): n/a; Density: 513.3 persons per square mile; Race: 91.9% White, 0.0% Black/African American, 0.0% Asian, 0.0% American Indian/Alaska Native, 0.0% Native Hawaiian/Other Pacific Islander, 8.1% Two or more races, 0.0% Hispanic of any race; Average household size: 3.18; Median age: 27.0; Age under 18: 41.6%; Age 65 and over: 0.0%; Males per 100 females: 105.6; Marriage status: 37.7% never married, 48.4% now married, 0.0% separated, 0.0% widowed, 13.8% divorced; Foreign born: 0.0%; Speak English only: 100.0%; With disability: 0.0%; Veterans: 0.0%; Ancestry: 30.5% German, 23.4% Irish, 17.3% Austrian
Employment: 0.0% management, business, and financial, 16.0% computer, engineering, and science, 0.0% education, legal, community service, arts, and media, 0.0% healthcare practitioners, 14.3% service, 35.3% sales and office, 34.5% natural resources, construction, and maintenance, 0.0% production, transportation, and material moving
Income: Per capita: $17,662; Median household: $63,684; Average household: $56,963; Households with income of $100,000 or more: n/a; Poverty rate: n/a
Educational Attainment: High school diploma or higher: 100.0%; Bachelor's degree or higher: n/a; Graduate/professional degree or higher: n/a
Housing: Homeownership rate: 30.6%; Median home value: n/a; Median year structure built: Before 1940; Homeowner vacancy rate: 0.0%; Median selected monthly owner costs: n/a with a mortgage, n/a without a mortgage; Median gross rent: n/a per month; Rental vacancy rate: 0.0%
Health Insurance: 100.0% have insurance; 100.0% have private insurance; 0.0% have public insurance; 0.0% do not have insurance; 0.0% of children under 18 do not have insurance
Transportation: Commute: 100.0% car, 0.0% public transportation, 0.0% walk, 0.0% work from home; Mean travel time to work: 0.0 minutes

SAINT MARYS (city). Covers a land area of 4.589 square miles and a water area of 0.030 square miles. Located at 40.55° N. Lat; 84.39° W. Long. Elevation is 869 feet.
History: St. Marys began as a trading post, and was organized as a town after 1818. It was called Girty's Town when it served as headquarters and supply depot for Generals Harmar, Wayne, and Harrison. Later, its location on the Miami & Erie Canal made it a shipping center for farm produce, which arrived in St. Marys by boat and was transferred to wagons for the overland haul to the Ohio River.
Population: 8,169; Growth (since 2000): -2.1%; Density: 1,780.3 persons per square mile; Race: 95.2% White, 0.6% Black/African American, 0.8% Asian, 1.2% American Indian/Alaska Native, 0.0% Native Hawaiian/Other Pacific Islander, 2.0% Two or more races, 0.6% Hispanic of any race; Average household size: 2.42; Median age: 38.5; Age under 18: 24.5%; Age 65 and over: 15.6%; Males per 100 females: 96.9; Marriage status: 27.1% never married, 51.0% now married, 1.6% separated, 9.9% widowed, 12.1% divorced; Foreign born: 1.1%; Speak English only: 97.8%; With disability: 12.6%; Veterans: 7.9%; Ancestry: 40.1% German, 13.5% Irish, 8.1% English, 6.6% American, 2.9% Italian
Employment: 9.3% management, business, and financial, 2.4% computer, engineering, and science, 6.9% education, legal, community service, arts, and media, 5.5% healthcare practitioners, 16.4% service, 19.5% sales and office, 7.4% natural resources, construction, and maintenance, 32.5% production, transportation, and material moving
Income: Per capita: $22,176; Median household: $41,841; Average household: $54,180; Households with income of $100,000 or more: 14.4%; Poverty rate: 12.9%
Educational Attainment: High school diploma or higher: 88.8%; Bachelor's degree or higher: 11.6%; Graduate/professional degree or higher: 2.9%

School District(s)

St Marys City (KG-12)
2015-16 Enrollment: 2,137 . . . . (419) 394-4312
Housing: Homeownership rate: 62.2%; Median home value: $103,100; Median year structure built: 1958; Homeowner vacancy rate: 4.3%; Median selected monthly owner costs: $1,060 with a mortgage, $351 without a mortgage; Median gross rent: $663 per month; Rental vacancy rate: 7.6%
Health Insurance: 92.5% have insurance; 72.6% have private insurance; 36.9% have public insurance; 7.5% do not have insurance; 1.9% of children under 18 do not have insurance
Hospitals: Grand Lake Health System (130 beds)
Safety: Violent crime rate: 6.1 per 10,000 population; Property crime rate: 157.5 per 10,000 population
Newspapers: The Evening Leader (daily circulation 4,500)
Transportation: Commute: 92.5% car, 0.1% public transportation, 2.1% walk, 1.9% work from home; Mean travel time to work: 16.2 minutes

UNIOPOLIS (village). Covers a land area of 0.156 square miles and a water area of 0 square miles. Located at 40.60° N. Lat; 84.09° W. Long. Elevation is 935 feet.
Population: 173; Growth (since 2000): -32.4%; Density: 1,111.0 persons per square mile; Race: 100.0% White, 0.0% Black/African American, 0.0% Asian, 0.0% American Indian/Alaska Native, 0.0% Native Hawaiian/Other Pacific Islander, 0.0% Two or more races, 0.0% Hispanic of any race; Average household size: 2.47; Median age: 41.3; Age under 18: 23.1%; Age 65 and over: 19.7%; Males per 100 females: 109.4; Marriage status: 27.3% never married, 56.1% now married, 0.0% separated, 3.6% widowed, 12.9% divorced; Foreign born: 0.6%; Speak English only: 99.4%; With disability: 20.2%; Veterans: 15.8%; Ancestry: 48.0% German, 14.5% American, 8.1% English, 5.2% Irish, 2.3% European
Employment: 8.5% management, business, and financial, 0.0% computer, engineering, and science, 1.4% education, legal, community service, arts, and media, 2.8% healthcare practitioners, 14.1% service, 21.1% sales and office, 4.2% natural resources, construction, and maintenance, 47.9% production, transportation, and material moving
Income: Per capita: $19,882; Median household: $49,167; Average household: $50,803; Households with income of $100,000 or more: 1.4%; Poverty rate: 10.0%
Educational Attainment: High school diploma or higher: 87.9%; Bachelor's degree or higher: 2.6%; Graduate/professional degree or higher: 0.9%
Housing: Homeownership rate: 80.0%; Median home value: $78,300; Median year structure built: Before 1940; Homeowner vacancy rate: 0.0%; Median selected monthly owner costs: $950 with a mortgage, $400 without a mortgage; Median gross rent: $1,063 per month; Rental vacancy rate: 12.5%
Health Insurance: 91.9% have insurance; 70.5% have private insurance; 41.6% have public insurance; 8.1% do not have insurance; 0.0% of children under 18 do not have insurance
Transportation: Commute: 100.0% car, 0.0% public transportation, 0.0% walk, 0.0% work from home; Mean travel time to work: 20.7 minutes

WAPAKONETA (city). County seat. Covers a land area of 6.206 square miles and a water area of 0.053 square miles. Located at 40.57° N. Lat; 84.19° W. Long. Elevation is 892 feet.
History: Wapakoneta was platted in 1833 and settled by people of German heritage. Woodworking industries provided the economic base in the late 1800's. The town's name was first Wapaghkonetta, a combination of two Indian names, Wapaugh and Konetta.
Population: 9,786; Growth (since 2000): 3.3%; Density: 1,576.9 persons per square mile; Race: 96.6% White, 0.5% Black/African American, 0.9% Asian, 0.0% American Indian/Alaska Native, 0.0% Native Hawaiian/Other Pacific Islander, 0.8% Two or more races, 2.9% Hispanic of any race; Average household size: 2.41; Median age: 36.2; Age under 18: 26.1%; Age 65 and over: 16.6%; Males per 100 females: 91.6; Marriage status: 28.2% never married, 51.3% now married, 0.7% separated, 9.2% widowed, 11.3% divorced; Foreign born: 1.2%; Speak English only: 97.1%; With disability: 12.5%; Veterans: 7.6%; Ancestry: 42.1% German, 11.7% Irish, 8.3% American, 6.8% English, 3.9% Italian
Employment: 10.5% management, business, and financial, 3.6% computer, engineering, and science, 6.8% education, legal, community service, arts, and media, 4.7% healthcare practitioners, 17.1% service, 20.5% sales and office, 8.1% natural resources, construction, and maintenance, 28.8% production, transportation, and material moving
Income: Per capita: $22,508; Median household: $49,934; Average household: $54,980; Households with income of $100,000 or more: 10.6%; Poverty rate: 10.1%
Educational Attainment: High school diploma or higher: 90.6%; Bachelor's degree or higher: 13.7%; Graduate/professional degree or higher: 4.8%

School District(s)

Wapakoneta City (PK-12)
2015-16 Enrollment: 3,083 . . . . (419) 739-2900
Housing: Homeownership rate: 66.1%; Median home value: $104,100; Median year structure built: 1966; Homeowner vacancy rate: 0.0%; Median

selected monthly owner costs: $973 with a mortgage, $392 without a mortgage; Median gross rent: $589 per month; Rental vacancy rate: 1.7%
Health Insurance: 93.7% have insurance; 73.9% have private insurance; 33.7% have public insurance; 6.3% do not have insurance; 2.6% of children under 18 do not have insurance
Safety: Violent crime rate: 10.2 per 10,000 population; Property crime rate: 146.7 per 10,000 population
Newspapers: Wapakoneta Daily News (daily circulation 5,000)
Transportation: Commute: 93.3% car, 0.0% public transportation, 2.5% walk, 1.9% work from home; Mean travel time to work: 20.2 minutes
Airports: Neil Armstrong (general aviation)
Additional Information Contacts
City of Wapakoneta . . . . (419) 738-3011
http://www.wapakoneta.net

WAYNESFIELD (village). Covers a land area of 0.740 square miles and a water area of 0 square miles. Located at 40.60° N. Lat; 83.97° W. Long. Elevation is 1,063 feet.
Population: 744; Growth (since 2000): -7.3%; Density: 1,005.4 persons per square mile; Race: 86.2% White, 0.1% Black/African American, 0.8% Asian, 0.0% American Indian/Alaska Native, 0.0% Native Hawaiian/Other Pacific Islander, 3.1% Two or more races, 11.0% Hispanic of any race; Average household size: 2.57; Median age: 40.7; Age under 18: 20.6%; Age 65 and over: 11.7%; Males per 100 females: 92.1; Marriage status: 24.1% never married, 57.9% now married, 1.4% separated, 6.3% widowed, 11.7% divorced; Foreign born: 0.8%; Speak English only: 88.9%; With disability: 9.3%; Veterans: 4.9%; Ancestry: 28.0% German, 9.7% American, 9.3% English, 7.0% Irish, 4.3% Dutch
Employment: 9.2% management, business, and financial, 2.2% computer, engineering, and science, 3.2% education, legal, community service, arts, and media, 8.4% healthcare practitioners, 11.9% service, 16.9% sales and office, 14.9% natural resources, construction, and maintenance, 33.3% production, transportation, and material moving
Income: Per capita: $25,349; Median household: $55,598; Average household: $65,345; Households with income of $100,000 or more: 21.8%; Poverty rate: 10.3%
Educational Attainment: High school diploma or higher: 86.9%; Bachelor's degree or higher: 11.4%; Graduate/professional degree or higher: 2.9%

School District(s)

Waynesfield-Goshen Local (PK-12)
2015-16 Enrollment: 536. . . . . (419) 568-9100
Housing: Homeownership rate: 81.0%; Median home value: $86,100; Median year structure built: 1966; Homeowner vacancy rate: 0.0%; Median selected monthly owner costs: $1,057 with a mortgage, $432 without a mortgage; Median gross rent: $915 per month; Rental vacancy rate: 0.0%
Health Insurance: 91.3% have insurance; 80.6% have private insurance; 23.0% have public insurance; 8.7% do not have insurance; 5.2% of children under 18 do not have insurance
Transportation: Commute: 98.2% car, 0.0% public transportation, 0.0% walk, 0.0% work from home; Mean travel time to work: 22.5 minutes

Belmont County

Located in eastern Ohio; bounded on the east by the Ohio River and the West Virginia border. Covers a land area of 532.129 square miles, a water area of 9.145 square miles, and is located in the Eastern Time Zone at 40.02° N. Lat., 80.97° W. Long. The county was founded in 1801. County seat is Saint Clairsville.

Belmont County is part of the Wheeling, WV-OH Metropolitan Statistical Area. The entire metro area includes: Belmont County, OH; Marshall County, WV; Ohio County, WV

Weather Station: Barnesville Elevation: 1,240 feet

	Jan	Feb	Mar	Apr	May	Jun	Jul	Aug	Sep	Oct	Nov	Dec
High	36	39	49	61	70	79	83	81	74	63	51	39
Low	20	21	28	39	48	57	62	60	52	41	33	24
Precip	3.0	2.6	3.5	3.9	4.5	4.6	4.4	3.7	3.2	3.1	4.0	3.0
Snow	10.1	7.7	4.9	1.2	tr	0.0	0.0	tr	0.0	0.1	1.8	5.8

High and Low temperatures in degrees Fahrenheit; Precipitation and Snow in inches

Population: 69,228; Growth (since 2000): -1.4%; Density: 130.1 persons per square mile; Race: 93.5% White, 4.1% Black/African American, 0.4% Asian, 0.3% American Indian/Alaska Native, 0.0% Native Hawaiian/Other Pacific Islander, 1.3% two or more races, 0.8% Hispanic of any race; Average household size: 2.35; Median age: 44.1; Age under 18: 19.1%; Age 65 and over: 18.9%; Males per 100 females: 101.7; Marriage status: 27.3% never married, 51.2% now married, 1.8% separated, 8.3% widowed, 13.3% divorced; Foreign born: 1.1%; Speak English only: 98.0%; With disability: 16.8%; Veterans: 10.0%; Ancestry: 25.6% German, 19.1% Irish, 10.4% Italian, 10.0% Polish, 10.0% English
Religion: Six largest groups: 11.6% Catholicism, 8.7% Methodist/Pietist, 6.4% Baptist, 3.5% Presbyterian-Reformed, 1.8% Non-denominational Protestant, 1.5% Lutheran
Economy: Unemployment rate: 5.5%; Leading industries: 20.7 % retail trade; 13.6 % health care and social assistance; 12.9 % other services (except public administration); Farms: 700 totaling 113,233 acres; Company size: 0 employ 1,000 or more persons, 1 employs 500 to 999 persons, 25 employ 100 to 499 persons, 1,420 employ less than 100 persons; Business ownership: 1,457 women-owned, 84 Black-owned, 28 Hispanic-owned, 63 Asian-owned, n/a American Indian/Alaska Native-owned
Employment: 8.8% management, business, and financial, 1.8% computer, engineering, and science, 8.9% education, legal, community service, arts, and media, 7.9% healthcare practitioners, 19.8% service, 23.2% sales and office, 14.3% natural resources, construction, and maintenance, 15.1% production, transportation, and material moving
Income: Per capita: $24,533; Median household: $44,719; Average household: $58,872; Households with income of $100,000 or more: 15.2%; Poverty rate: 15.1%
Educational Attainment: High school diploma or higher: 89.9%; Bachelor's degree or higher: 16.4%; Graduate/professional degree or higher: 6.0%
Housing: Homeownership rate: 74.0%; Median home value: $94,300; Median year structure built: 1959; Homeowner vacancy rate: 0.9%; Median selected monthly owner costs: $988 with a mortgage, $350 without a mortgage; Median gross rent: $564 per month; Rental vacancy rate: 4.6%
Vital Statistics: Birth rate: 100.2 per 10,000 population; Death rate: 124.2 per 10,000 population; Age-adjusted cancer mortality rate: 182.6 deaths per 100,000 population
Health Insurance: 91.5% have insurance; 69.5% have private insurance; 38.5% have public insurance; 8.5% do not have insurance; 4.1% of children under 18 do not have insurance
Health Care: Physicians: 11.0 per 10,000 population; Dentists: 3.8 per 10,000 population; Hospital beds: 33.2 per 10,000 population; Hospital admissions: 809.2 per 10,000 population
Air Quality Index (AQI): Percent of Days: 94.3% good, 5.7% moderate, 0.0% unhealthy for sensitive individuals, 0.0% unhealthy, 0.0% very unhealthy; Annual median: 17; Annual maximum: 100
Transportation: Commute: 93.9% car, 0.5% public transportation, 2.7% walk, 1.9% work from home; Mean travel time to work: 22.9 minutes
2016 Presidential Election: 67.4% Trump, 28.0% Clinton, 2.5% Johnson, 0.6% Stein
National and State Parks: Belmont Lake State Reserve
Additional Information Contacts
Belmont Government . . . . (740) 699-2155
http://www.belcc.com

Belmont County Communities

ALLEDONIA (unincorporated postal area)

ZCTA: 43902

Covers a land area of 17.276 square miles and a water area of 0.327 square miles. Located at 39.88° N. Lat; 80.95° W. Long. Elevation is 830 feet.
Population: 20; Growth (since 2000): -90.6%; Density: 1.2 persons per square mile; Race: 100.0% White, 0.0% Black/African American, 0.0% Asian, 0.0% American Indian/Alaska Native, 0.0% Native Hawaiian/Other Pacific Islander, 0.0% Two or more races, 0.0% Hispanic of any race; Average household size: 2.00; Median age: n/a; Age under 18: 0.0%; Age 65 and over: 50.0%; Males per 100 females: 119.6; Marriage status: 0.0% never married, 100.0% now married, 0.0% separated, 0.0% widowed, 0.0% divorced; Foreign born: 0.0%; Speak English only: 100.0%; With disability: 0.0%; Veterans: 50.0%; Ancestry: 50.0% Irish, 50.0% Portuguese
Employment: n/a management, business, and financial, n/a computer, engineering, and science, n/a education, legal, community service, arts, and media, n/a healthcare practitioners, n/a service, n/a sales and office, n/a natural resources, construction, and maintenance, n/a production, transportation, and material moving

Income: Per capita: n/a; Median household: n/a; Average household: n/a; Households with income of $100,000 or more: n/a; Poverty rate: n/a
Educational Attainment: High school diploma or higher: 50.0%; Bachelor's degree or higher: n/a; Graduate/professional degree or higher: n/a
Housing: Homeownership rate: 100.0%; Median home value: n/a; Median year structure built: n/a; Homeowner vacancy rate: 0.0%; Median selected monthly owner costs: $0 with a mortgage, $0 without a mortgage; Median gross rent: n/a per month; Rental vacancy rate: 0.0%
Health Insurance: 100.0% have insurance; 100.0% have private insurance; 100.0% have public insurance; 0.0% do not have insurance; 0.0% of children under 18 do not have insurance
Transportation: Commute: n/a car, n/a public transportation, n/a walk, n/a work from home; Mean travel time to work: 0.0 minutes

BANNOCK (CDP). Covers a land area of 0.296 square miles and a water area of <.001 square miles. Located at 40.10° N. Lat; 80.98° W. Long. Elevation is 1,004 feet.
Population: 231; Growth (since 2000): n/a; Density: 780.8 persons per square mile; Race: 100.0% White, 0.0% Black/African American, 0.0% Asian, 0.0% American Indian/Alaska Native, 0.0% Native Hawaiian/Other Pacific Islander, 0.0% Two or more races, 0.0% Hispanic of any race; Average household size: 3.00; Median age: 46.1; Age under 18: 4.3%; Age 65 and over: 1.7%; Males per 100 females: 111.0; Marriage status: 31.7% never married, 68.3% now married, 1.4% separated, 0.0% widowed, 0.0% divorced; Foreign born: 0.0%; Speak English only: 99.1%; With disability: 0.0%; Veterans: 0.0%; Ancestry: 52.8% Polish, 13.9% Irish, 11.7% Scotch-Irish, 7.8% Syrian, 7.8% British
Employment: 0.0% management, business, and financial, 0.0% computer, engineering, and science, 17.4% education, legal, community service, arts, and media, 7.1% healthcare practitioners, 21.3% service, 36.8% sales and office, 9.0% natural resources, construction, and maintenance, 8.4% production, transportation, and material moving
Income: Per capita: $27,786; Median household: $83,487; Average household: $77,827; Households with income of $100,000 or more: 35.1%; Poverty rate: 2.6%
Educational Attainment: High school diploma or higher: 97.4%; Bachelor's degree or higher: 6.0%; Graduate/professional degree or higher: 6.0%
Housing: Homeownership rate: 92.2%; Median home value: $83,600; Median year structure built: Before 1940; Homeowner vacancy rate: 0.0%; Median selected monthly owner costs: n/a with a mortgage, n/a without a mortgage; Median gross rent: n/a per month; Rental vacancy rate: 0.0%
Health Insurance: 94.8% have insurance; 90.9% have private insurance; 5.6% have public insurance; 5.2% do not have insurance; 0.0% of children under 18 do not have insurance
Transportation: Commute: 91.0% car, 0.0% public transportation, 9.0% walk, 0.0% work from home; Mean travel time to work: 16.5 minutes

BARNESVILLE (village). Covers a land area of 1.943 square miles and a water area of 0.012 square miles. Located at 39.99° N. Lat; 81.17° W. Long. Elevation is 1,273 feet.
Population: 3,923; Growth (since 2000): -7.1%; Density: 2,018.8 persons per square mile; Race: 97.9% White, 0.3% Black/African American, 0.8% Asian, 0.0% American Indian/Alaska Native, 0.0% Native Hawaiian/Other Pacific Islander, 1.1% Two or more races, 0.1% Hispanic of any race; Average household size: 2.28; Median age: 45.1; Age under 18: 21.5%; Age 65 and over: 20.1%; Males per 100 females: 85.9; Marriage status: 17.1% never married, 51.5% now married, 0.4% separated, 11.4% widowed, 20.1% divorced; Foreign born: 0.0%; Speak English only: 100.0%; With disability: 24.3%; Veterans: 10.2%; Ancestry: 27.2% German, 22.7% Irish, 8.6% English, 7.5% American, 4.4% Italian
Employment: 5.9% management, business, and financial, 1.3% computer, engineering, and science, 9.4% education, legal, community service, arts, and media, 12.3% healthcare practitioners, 14.3% service, 24.6% sales and office, 15.3% natural resources, construction, and maintenance, 16.9% production, transportation, and material moving
Income: Per capita: $20,742; Median household: $33,355; Average household: $46,530; Households with income of $100,000 or more: 8.0%; Poverty rate: 16.8%
Educational Attainment: High school diploma or higher: 89.5%; Bachelor's degree or higher: 17.0%; Graduate/professional degree or higher: 3.7%

School District(s)
Barnesville Exempted Village (PK-12)
2015-16 Enrollment: 1,363 . . . . (740) 425-3615
Housing: Homeownership rate: 67.1%; Median home value: $83,200; Median year structure built: 1946; Homeowner vacancy rate: 0.0%; Median selected monthly owner costs: $815 with a mortgage, $298 without a mortgage; Median gross rent: $506 per month; Rental vacancy rate: 7.0%
Health Insurance: 90.3% have insurance; 64.8% have private insurance; 37.0% have public insurance; 9.7% do not have insurance; 1.9% of children under 18 do not have insurance
Hospitals: Barnesville Hospital Association (25 beds)
Safety: Violent crime rate: 2.4 per 10,000 population; Property crime rate: 34.0 per 10,000 population
Newspapers: Barnesville Enterprise (weekly circulation 4,500)
Transportation: Commute: 93.8% car, 0.0% public transportation, 6.2% walk, 0.0% work from home; Mean travel time to work: 25.4 minutes

BARTON (unincorporated postal area)
ZCTA: 43905
Covers a land area of 0.387 square miles and a water area of 0.006 square miles. Located at 40.10° N. Lat; 80.84° W. Long. Elevation is 797 feet.
Population: 138; Growth (since 2000): -41.0%; Density: 356.9 persons per square mile; Race: 100.0% White, 0.0% Black/African American, 0.0% Asian, 0.0% American Indian/Alaska Native, 0.0% Native Hawaiian/Other Pacific Islander, 0.0% Two or more races, 0.0% Hispanic of any race; Average household size: 1.53; Median age: 77.3; Age under 18: 0.0%; Age 65 and over: 77.5%; Males per 100 females: 94.3; Marriage status: 15.2% never married, 44.9% now married, 0.0% separated, 26.1% widowed, 13.8% divorced; Foreign born: 0.0%; Speak English only: 100.0%; With disability: 43.5%; Veterans: 42.0%; Ancestry: 45.7% German, 41.3% Irish, 19.6% Polish, 15.2% Slovak, 5.8% English
Employment: 15.6% management, business, and financial, 0.0% computer, engineering, and science, 18.8% education, legal, community service, arts, and media, 0.0% healthcare practitioners, 37.5% service, 28.1% sales and office, 0.0% natural resources, construction, and maintenance, 0.0% production, transportation, and material moving
Income: Per capita: $21,587; Median household: $21,000; Average household: $31,961; Households with income of $100,000 or more: n/a; Poverty rate: 25.4%
Educational Attainment: High school diploma or higher: 44.2%; Bachelor's degree or higher: 8.7%; Graduate/professional degree or higher: 4.3%
Housing: Homeownership rate: 65.6%; Median home value: n/a; Median year structure built: Before 1940; Homeowner vacancy rate: 0.0%; Median selected monthly owner costs: $539 with a mortgage, $0 without a mortgage; Median gross rent: n/a per month; Rental vacancy rate: 0.0%
Health Insurance: 100.0% have insurance; 58.0% have private insurance; 83.3% have public insurance; 0.0% do not have insurance; 0.0% of children under 18 do not have insurance
Transportation: Commute: 71.9% car, 0.0% public transportation, 0.0% walk, 28.1% work from home; Mean travel time to work: 32.0 minutes

BELLAIRE (village). Covers a land area of 1.650 square miles and a water area of 0.026 square miles. Located at 40.02° N. Lat; 80.75° W. Long. Elevation is 666 feet.
History: Bellaire was named for the home of a Maryland settler who purchased part of the townsite in 1802. After 1900, coal mining and the manufacture of glass and enamel ware became the leading industries.
Population: 4,189; Growth (since 2000): -14.4%; Density: 2,538.6 persons per square mile; Race: 90.9% White, 7.4% Black/African American, 0.5% Asian, 0.3% American Indian/Alaska Native, 0.0% Native Hawaiian/Other Pacific Islander, 0.9% Two or more races, 0.6% Hispanic of any race; Average household size: 2.28; Median age: 40.1; Age under 18: 21.5%; Age 65 and over: 16.3%; Males per 100 females: 92.1; Marriage status: 32.3% never married, 42.5% now married, 5.4% separated, 9.1% widowed, 16.1% divorced; Foreign born: 0.5%; Speak English only: 97.9%; With disability: 20.2%; Veterans: 9.4%; Ancestry: 24.7% German, 21.8% Irish, 15.2% Italian, 11.5% Polish, 9.2% English
Employment: 4.8% management, business, and financial, 0.3% computer, engineering, and science, 4.2% education, legal, community service, arts, and media, 9.8% healthcare practitioners, 28.2% service, 20.2% sales and office, 15.2% natural resources, construction, and maintenance, 17.4% production, transportation, and material moving

Income: Per capita: $17,892; Median household: $25,594; Average household: $39,237; Households with income of $100,000 or more: 7.2%; Poverty rate: 33.8%

Educational Attainment: High school diploma or higher: 79.6%; Bachelor's degree or higher: 7.2%; Graduate/professional degree or higher: 2.6%

School District(s)

Bellaire Local (PK-12)
2015-16 Enrollment: 1,166 . . . . (740) 676-1826

Housing: Homeownership rate: 52.4%; Median home value: $51,200; Median year structure built: Before 1940; Homeowner vacancy rate: 0.0%; Median selected monthly owner costs: $881 with a mortgage, $306 without a mortgage; Median gross rent: $563 per month; Rental vacancy rate: 4.2%

Health Insurance: 87.5% have insurance; 51.8% have private insurance; 50.2% have public insurance; 12.5% do not have insurance; 2.7% of children under 18 do not have insurance

Hospitals: Belmont Community Hospital (99 beds)

Safety: Violent crime rate: 21.6 per 10,000 population; Property crime rate: 110.3 per 10,000 population

Transportation: Commute: 88.1% car, 1.0% public transportation, 9.7% walk, 1.0% work from home; Mean travel time to work: 17.9 minutes

BELMONT (village). Covers a land area of 0.266 square miles and a water area of 0 square miles. Located at 40.03° N. Lat; 81.04° W. Long. Elevation is 1,191 feet.

Population: 430; Growth (since 2000): -19.2%; Density: 1,615.0 persons per square mile; Race: 97.0% White, 0.0% Black/African American, 0.7% Asian, 0.0% American Indian/Alaska Native, 0.0% Native Hawaiian/Other Pacific Islander, 2.3% Two or more races, 0.0% Hispanic of any race; Average household size: 2.28; Median age: 42.0; Age under 18: 15.3%; Age 65 and over: 9.3%; Males per 100 females: 85.7; Marriage status: 33.0% never married, 49.5% now married, 0.5% separated, 8.9% widowed, 8.6% divorced; Foreign born: 0.0%; Speak English only: 97.4%; With disability: 15.6%; Veterans: 8.0%; Ancestry: 27.2% German, 17.4% Irish, 11.4% English, 8.6% Polish, 7.9% American

Employment: 7.8% management, business, and financial, 3.0% computer, engineering, and science, 3.9% education, legal, community service, arts, and media, 5.2% healthcare practitioners, 26.7% service, 26.7% sales and office, 15.9% natural resources, construction, and maintenance, 10.8% production, transportation, and material moving

Income: Per capita: $21,059; Median household: $37,143; Average household: $47,926; Households with income of $100,000 or more: 9.8%; Poverty rate: 12.8%

Educational Attainment: High school diploma or higher: 90.5%; Bachelor's degree or higher: 18.0%; Graduate/professional degree or higher: 6.1%

School District(s)

Union Local (PK-12)
2015-16 Enrollment: 1,513 . . . . (740) 782-1978

Housing: Homeownership rate: 75.5%; Median home value: $80,200; Median year structure built: Before 1940; Homeowner vacancy rate: 4.0%; Median selected monthly owner costs: $768 with a mortgage, $290 without a mortgage; Median gross rent: $538 per month; Rental vacancy rate: 0.0%

Health Insurance: 88.1% have insurance; 74.4% have private insurance; 20.5% have public insurance; 11.9% do not have insurance; 12.1% of children under 18 do not have insurance

Transportation: Commute: 94.6% car, 0.0% public transportation, 0.9% walk, 1.8% work from home; Mean travel time to work: 25.3 minutes

BETHESDA (village). Covers a land area of 0.624 square miles and a water area of 0.020 square miles. Located at 40.02° N. Lat; 81.07° W. Long. Elevation is 1,227 feet.

Population: 1,194; Growth (since 2000): -15.5%; Density: 1,913.8 persons per square mile; Race: 95.1% White, 0.0% Black/African American, 0.0% Asian, 0.0% American Indian/Alaska Native, 0.0% Native Hawaiian/Other Pacific Islander, 4.9% Two or more races, 0.0% Hispanic of any race; Average household size: 2.50; Median age: 40.8; Age under 18: 24.0%; Age 65 and over: 14.9%; Males per 100 females: 87.2; Marriage status: 24.6% never married, 53.8% now married, 0.8% separated, 6.8% widowed, 14.8% divorced; Foreign born: 0.0%; Speak English only: 99.3%; With disability: 16.8%; Veterans: 11.5%; Ancestry: 24.9% German, 17.6% Irish, 11.6% English, 8.5% Italian, 3.9% Scotch-Irish

Employment: 3.5% management, business, and financial, 0.8% computer, engineering, and science, 8.3% education, legal, community service, arts, and media, 6.4% healthcare practitioners, 36.3% service, 17.4% sales and office, 15.1% natural resources, construction, and maintenance, 12.4% production, transportation, and material moving

Income: Per capita: $19,229; Median household: $39,423; Average household: $47,658; Households with income of $100,000 or more: 8.8%; Poverty rate: 18.4%

Educational Attainment: High school diploma or higher: 92.9%; Bachelor's degree or higher: 12.2%; Graduate/professional degree or higher: 5.3%

Housing: Homeownership rate: 75.1%; Median home value: $78,700; Median year structure built: 1940; Homeowner vacancy rate: 4.7%; Median selected monthly owner costs: $990 with a mortgage, $344 without a mortgage; Median gross rent: $428 per month; Rental vacancy rate: 11.9%

Health Insurance: 85.8% have insurance; 60.6% have private insurance; 39.7% have public insurance; 14.2% do not have insurance; 6.6% of children under 18 do not have insurance

Transportation: Commute: 92.7% car, 0.0% public transportation, 4.9% walk, 1.2% work from home; Mean travel time to work: 22.0 minutes

BRIDGEPORT (village). Covers a land area of 1.366 square miles and a water area of 0.010 square miles. Located at 40.06° N. Lat; 80.75° W. Long. Elevation is 656 feet.

History: Bridgeport was platted by Ebenezer Zane in 1806, when it was called Canton. The present name was given in 1836. An early boatbuilding industry was replaced by glass-making in the late 1800's.

Population: 1,769; Growth (since 2000): -19.1%; Density: 1,294.6 persons per square mile; Race: 83.7% White, 13.2% Black/African American, 1.1% Asian, 0.0% American Indian/Alaska Native, 0.0% Native Hawaiian/Other Pacific Islander, 2.0% Two or more races, 0.4% Hispanic of any race; Average household size: 2.51; Median age: 41.7; Age under 18: 21.4%; Age 65 and over: 14.0%; Males per 100 females: 95.2; Marriage status: 31.1% never married, 48.0% now married, 2.5% separated, 7.8% widowed, 13.1% divorced; Foreign born: 2.0%; Speak English only: 96.4%; With disability: 17.1%; Veterans: 12.7%; Ancestry: 22.5% German, 20.4% Irish, 8.3% Polish, 7.3% American, 6.9% Italian

Employment: 7.3% management, business, and financial, 2.6% computer, engineering, and science, 4.2% education, legal, community service, arts, and media, 14.0% healthcare practitioners, 22.8% service, 21.1% sales and office, 10.9% natural resources, construction, and maintenance, 17.0% production, transportation, and material moving

Income: Per capita: $19,013; Median household: $37,692; Average household: $47,595; Households with income of $100,000 or more: 5.9%; Poverty rate: 22.0%

Educational Attainment: High school diploma or higher: 88.0%; Bachelor's degree or higher: 10.5%; Graduate/professional degree or higher: 4.0%

School District(s)

Bridgeport Exempted Village (PK-12)
2015-16 Enrollment: 813 . . . . (740) 635-1713

Housing: Homeownership rate: 72.7%; Median home value: $63,500; Median year structure built: Before 1940; Homeowner vacancy rate: 2.4%; Median selected monthly owner costs: $766 with a mortgage, $323 without a mortgage; Median gross rent: $633 per month; Rental vacancy rate: 0.0%

Health Insurance: 92.6% have insurance; 47.8% have private insurance; 52.2% have public insurance; 7.4% do not have insurance; 2.9% of children under 18 do not have insurance

Safety: Violent crime rate: 16.8 per 10,000 population; Property crime rate: 100.8 per 10,000 population

Transportation: Commute: 91.9% car, 2.9% public transportation, 2.1% walk, 1.8% work from home; Mean travel time to work: 20.5 minutes

BROOKSIDE (village). Covers a land area of 0.173 square miles and a water area of 0.003 square miles. Located at 40.07° N. Lat; 80.76° W. Long. Elevation is 650 feet.

History: Brookside was settled along Wheeling Creek, where grist mills, sawmills, and woolen mills were established. Later it became a coal mining town.

Population: 720; Growth (since 2000): 11.8%; Density: 4,157.9 persons per square mile; Race: 86.8% White, 7.5% Black/African American, 0.0% Asian, 0.0% American Indian/Alaska Native, 0.0% Native Hawaiian/Other Pacific Islander, 0.7% Two or more races, 5.0% Hispanic of any race; Average household size: 2.29; Median age: 44.8; Age under 18: 14.4%;

Age 65 and over: 21.1%; Males per 100 females: 93.9; Marriage status: 26.6% never married, 53.1% now married, 0.8% separated, 8.4% widowed, 11.9% divorced; Foreign born: 0.3%; Speak English only: 97.6%; With disability: 16.5%; Veterans: 9.4%; Ancestry: 33.8% German, 18.2% Irish, 12.6% Polish, 9.6% English, 6.5% Slovak
Employment: 12.0% management, business, and financial, 0.0% computer, engineering, and science, 9.6% education, legal, community service, arts, and media, 4.9% healthcare practitioners, 17.5% service, 31.4% sales and office, 7.1% natural resources, construction, and maintenance, 17.5% production, transportation, and material moving
Income: Per capita: $26,888; Median household: $50,323; Average household: $59,534; Households with income of $100,000 or more: 11.1%; Poverty rate: 10.4%
Educational Attainment: High school diploma or higher: 97.3%; Bachelor's degree or higher: 19.0%; Graduate/professional degree or higher: 4.9%
Housing: Homeownership rate: 80.3%; Median home value: $81,700; Median year structure built: 1942; Homeowner vacancy rate: 0.0%; Median selected monthly owner costs: $921 with a mortgage, $335 without a mortgage; Median gross rent: $663 per month; Rental vacancy rate: 17.3%
Health Insurance: 93.6% have insurance; 77.9% have private insurance; 34.9% have public insurance; 6.4% do not have insurance; 4.8% of children under 18 do not have insurance
Transportation: Commute: 98.0% car, 0.0% public transportation, 0.0% walk, 1.7% work from home; Mean travel time to work: 19.0 minutes

FAIRPOINT (unincorporated postal area)

ZCTA: 43927

Covers a land area of 0.410 square miles and a water area of 0.008 square miles. Located at 40.12° N. Lat; 80.94° W. Long. Elevation is 948 feet.
Population: 155; Growth (since 2000): 252.3%; Density: 378.2 persons per square mile; Race: 100.0% White, 0.0% Black/African American, 0.0% Asian, 0.0% American Indian/Alaska Native, 0.0% Native Hawaiian/Other Pacific Islander, 0.0% Two or more races, 0.0% Hispanic of any race; Average household size: 2.72; Median age: 36.6; Age under 18: 21.9%; Age 65 and over: 18.1%; Males per 100 females: 94.7; Marriage status: 37.2% never married, 56.2% now married, 0.0% separated, 6.6% widowed, 0.0% divorced; Foreign born: 0.0%; Speak English only: 100.0%; With disability: 5.2%; Veterans: 7.4%; Ancestry: 38.1% Polish, 13.5% German, 12.3% Italian, 7.1% Swedish
Employment: 0.0% management, business, and financial, 0.0% computer, engineering, and science, 0.0% education, legal, community service, arts, and media, 0.0% healthcare practitioners, 25.8% service, 41.9% sales and office, 8.6% natural resources, construction, and maintenance, 23.7% production, transportation, and material moving
Income: Per capita: $19,491; Median household: $50,139; Average household: $53,988; Households with income of $100,000 or more: n/a; Poverty rate: 11.6%
Educational Attainment: High school diploma or higher: 92.2%; Bachelor's degree or higher: n/a; Graduate/professional degree or higher: n/a
Housing: Homeownership rate: 84.2%; Median home value: $62,400; Median year structure built: 1941; Homeowner vacancy rate: 0.0%; Median selected monthly owner costs: $0 with a mortgage, $360 without a mortgage; Median gross rent: n/a per month; Rental vacancy rate: 0.0%
Health Insurance: 93.5% have insurance; 93.5% have private insurance; 25.2% have public insurance; 6.5% do not have insurance; 0.0% of children under 18 do not have insurance
Transportation: Commute: 100.0% car, 0.0% public transportation, 0.0% walk, 0.0% work from home; Mean travel time to work: 16.6 minutes

FLUSHING (village). Covers a land area of 0.614 square miles and a water area of 0 square miles. Located at 40.15° N. Lat; 81.06° W. Long. Elevation is 1,286 feet.
Population: 868; Growth (since 2000): -3.6%; Density: 1,414.7 persons per square mile; Race: 96.7% White, 1.8% Black/African American, 0.0% Asian, 0.8% American Indian/Alaska Native, 0.0% Native Hawaiian/Other Pacific Islander, 0.7% Two or more races, 0.8% Hispanic of any race; Average household size: 2.49; Median age: 40.6; Age under 18: 23.4%; Age 65 and over: 19.5%; Males per 100 females: 96.6; Marriage status: 23.4% never married, 54.1% now married, 0.4% separated, 8.1% widowed, 14.4% divorced; Foreign born: 0.0%; Speak English only: 99.1%; With disability: 17.7%; Veterans: 10.1%; Ancestry: 20.6% German, 19.6% Irish, 12.9% Polish, 11.4% English, 9.9% Italian
Employment: 6.6% management, business, and financial, 0.5% computer, engineering, and science, 4.8% education, legal, community service, arts, and media, 6.1% healthcare practitioners, 22.4% service, 27.0% sales and office, 15.6% natural resources, construction, and maintenance, 16.8% production, transportation, and material moving
Income: Per capita: $21,338; Median household: $41,875; Average household: $53,495; Households with income of $100,000 or more: 11.4%; Poverty rate: 14.8%
Educational Attainment: High school diploma or higher: 94.8%; Bachelor's degree or higher: 8.8%; Graduate/professional degree or higher: 3.3%
Housing: Homeownership rate: 70.5%; Median home value: $68,800; Median year structure built: 1944; Homeowner vacancy rate: 3.4%; Median selected monthly owner costs: $888 with a mortgage, $350 without a mortgage; Median gross rent: $638 per month; Rental vacancy rate: 0.0%
Health Insurance: 89.7% have insurance; 60.7% have private insurance; 43.2% have public insurance; 10.3% do not have insurance; 3.0% of children under 18 do not have insurance
Transportation: Commute: 95.6% car, 0.0% public transportation, 0.0% walk, 4.4% work from home; Mean travel time to work: 28.6 minutes

GLENCOE (CDP). Covers a land area of 1.223 square miles and a water area of 0.011 square miles. Located at 40.01° N. Lat; 80.88° W. Long. Elevation is 830 feet.
Population: 137; Growth (since 2000): n/a; Density: 112.1 persons per square mile; Race: 100.0% White, 0.0% Black/African American, 0.0% Asian, 0.0% American Indian/Alaska Native, 0.0% Native Hawaiian/Other Pacific Islander, 0.0% Two or more races, 0.0% Hispanic of any race; Average household size: 2.80; Median age: 51.0; Age under 18: 0.0%; Age 65 and over: 12.4%; Males per 100 females: 109.5; Marriage status: 29.9% never married, 8.8% now married, 0.0% separated, 17.5% widowed, 43.8% divorced; Foreign born: 0.0%; Speak English only: 100.0%; With disability: 24.8%; Veterans: 4.4%; Ancestry: 66.4% German, 46.0% French, 20.4% Irish, 7.3% Czech, 7.3% Polish
Employment: 0.0% management, business, and financial, 0.0% computer, engineering, and science, 0.0% education, legal, community service, arts, and media, 0.0% healthcare practitioners, 0.0% service, 100.0% sales and office, 0.0% natural resources, construction, and maintenance, 0.0% production, transportation, and material moving
Income: Per capita: $16,674; Median household: $38,705; Average household: $43,794; Households with income of $100,000 or more: n/a; Poverty rate: 46.0%
Educational Attainment: High school diploma or higher: 91.6%; Bachelor's degree or higher: n/a; Graduate/professional degree or higher: n/a
Housing: Homeownership rate: 100.0%; Median home value: $43,400; Median year structure built: Before 1940; Homeowner vacancy rate: 0.0%; Median selected monthly owner costs: n/a with a mortgage, n/a without a mortgage; Median gross rent: n/a per month; Rental vacancy rate: 0.0%
Health Insurance: 79.6% have insurance; 79.6% have private insurance; 26.3% have public insurance; 20.4% do not have insurance; 0.0% of children under 18 do not have insurance
Transportation: Commute: 100.0% car, 0.0% public transportation, 0.0% walk, 0.0% work from home; Mean travel time to work: 0.0 minutes

HOLLOWAY (village). Covers a land area of 0.949 square miles and a water area of 0.011 square miles. Located at 40.16° N. Lat; 81.13° W. Long. Elevation is 925 feet.
Population: 315; Growth (since 2000): -8.7%; Density: 331.9 persons per square mile; Race: 99.0% White, 0.0% Black/African American, 0.0% Asian, 1.0% American Indian/Alaska Native, 0.0% Native Hawaiian/Other Pacific Islander, 0.0% Two or more races, 0.3% Hispanic of any race; Average household size: 2.50; Median age: 40.8; Age under 18: 25.1%; Age 65 and over: 18.4%; Males per 100 females: 100.0; Marriage status: 25.3% never married, 55.3% now married, 5.9% separated, 2.0% widowed, 17.4% divorced; Foreign born: 0.0%; Speak English only: 99.7%; With disability: 17.5%; Veterans: 6.0%; Ancestry: 27.6% Irish, 14.6% German, 13.3% Italian, 8.3% English, 7.9% Polish
Employment: 15.9% management, business, and financial, 0.0% computer, engineering, and science, 0.0% education, legal, community service, arts, and media, 0.0% healthcare practitioners, 27.5% service, 21.0% sales and office, 17.4% natural resources, construction, and maintenance, 18.1% production, transportation, and material moving

Income: Per capita: $19,057; Median household: $43,000; Average household: $48,599; Households with income of $100,000 or more: 8.8%; Poverty rate: 23.2%
Educational Attainment: High school diploma or higher: 77.4%; Bachelor's degree or higher: n/a; Graduate/professional degree or higher: n/a
Housing: Homeownership rate: 73.8%; Median home value: $53,100; Median year structure built: Before 1940; Homeowner vacancy rate: 4.0%; Median selected monthly owner costs: $800 with a mortgage, $367 without a mortgage; Median gross rent: $758 per month; Rental vacancy rate: 0.0%
Health Insurance: 95.9% have insurance; 60.8% have private insurance; 49.7% have public insurance; 4.1% do not have insurance; 0.0% of children under 18 do not have insurance
Transportation: Commute: 97.7% car, 0.0% public transportation, 0.0% walk, 2.3% work from home; Mean travel time to work: 29.7 minutes

JACOBSBURG (unincorporated postal area)
ZCTA: 43933
Covers a land area of 47.582 square miles and a water area of 0.371 square miles. Located at 39.94° N. Lat; 80.90° W. Long. Elevation is 1,296 feet.
Population: 2,020; Growth (since 2000): 15.8%; Density: 42.5 persons per square mile; Race: 100.0% White, 0.0% Black/African American, 0.0% Asian, 0.0% American Indian/Alaska Native, 0.0% Native Hawaiian/Other Pacific Islander, 0.0% Two or more races, 0.0% Hispanic of any race; Average household size: 2.43; Median age: 45.6; Age under 18: 18.4%; Age 65 and over: 21.4%; Males per 100 females: 103.3; Marriage status: 23.3% never married, 55.4% now married, 2.3% separated, 6.7% widowed, 14.6% divorced; Foreign born: 0.7%; Speak English only: 98.9%; With disability: 19.6%; Veterans: 7.4%; Ancestry: 26.9% German, 24.2% Irish, 10.0% American, 8.9% English, 5.6% Polish
Employment: 5.0% management, business, and financial, 0.0% computer, engineering, and science, 1.1% education, legal, community service, arts, and media, 13.8% healthcare practitioners, 20.8% service, 17.2% sales and office, 20.2% natural resources, construction, and maintenance, 21.7% production, transportation, and material moving
Income: Per capita: $21,664; Median household: $42,266; Average household: $52,052; Households with income of $100,000 or more: 10.2%; Poverty rate: 15.3%
Educational Attainment: High school diploma or higher: 94.9%; Bachelor's degree or higher: 1.8%; Graduate/professional degree or higher: 0.7%
Housing: Homeownership rate: 79.5%; Median home value: $84,700; Median year structure built: 1972; Homeowner vacancy rate: 1.6%; Median selected monthly owner costs: $1,005 with a mortgage, $392 without a mortgage; Median gross rent: $544 per month; Rental vacancy rate: 7.6%
Health Insurance: 91.5% have insurance; 70.8% have private insurance; 35.8% have public insurance; 8.5% do not have insurance; 0.0% of children under 18 do not have insurance
Transportation: Commute: 93.4% car, 0.0% public transportation, 0.0% walk, 2.5% work from home; Mean travel time to work: 29.5 minutes

LAFFERTY (CDP). Covers a land area of 0.936 square miles and a water area of 0.014 square miles. Located at 40.12° N. Lat; 81.02° W. Long. Elevation is 1,060 feet.
Population: 348; Growth (since 2000): n/a; Density: 372.0 persons per square mile; Race: 100.0% White, 0.0% Black/African American, 0.0% Asian, 0.0% American Indian/Alaska Native, 0.0% Native Hawaiian/Other Pacific Islander, 0.0% Two or more races, 0.0% Hispanic of any race; Average household size: 2.05; Median age: 49.3; Age under 18: 11.2%; Age 65 and over: 12.6%; Males per 100 females: 97.4; Marriage status: 35.7% never married, 39.8% now married, 0.0% separated, 0.0% widowed, 24.5% divorced; Foreign born: 0.0%; Speak English only: 100.0%; With disability: 23.3%; Veterans: 11.7%; Ancestry: 33.9% Irish, 29.3% German, 21.0% English, 12.4% Italian, 10.9% Polish
Employment: 0.0% management, business, and financial, 0.0% computer, engineering, and science, 3.4% education, legal, community service, arts, and media, 8.1% healthcare practitioners, 23.0% service, 39.6% sales and office, 10.2% natural resources, construction, and maintenance, 15.7% production, transportation, and material moving
Income: Per capita: $17,493; Median household: $18,229; Average household: $35,288; Households with income of $100,000 or more: 5.9%; Poverty rate: 47.4%
Educational Attainment: High school diploma or higher: 93.7%; Bachelor's degree or higher: 7.6%; Graduate/professional degree or higher: n/a
Housing: Homeownership rate: 50.6%; Median home value: $68,600; Median year structure built: 1975; Homeowner vacancy rate: 0.0%; Median selected monthly owner costs: n/a with a mortgage, $271 without a mortgage; Median gross rent: $706 per month; Rental vacancy rate: 0.0%
Health Insurance: 80.7% have insurance; 58.3% have private insurance; 29.6% have public insurance; 19.3% do not have insurance; 0.0% of children under 18 do not have insurance
Transportation: Commute: 100.0% car, 0.0% public transportation, 0.0% walk, 0.0% work from home; Mean travel time to work: 17.4 minutes

LANSING (CDP). Covers a land area of 0.281 square miles and a water area of 0.003 square miles. Located at 40.08° N. Lat; 80.79° W. Long. Elevation is 705 feet.
Population: 841; Growth (since 2000): n/a; Density: 2,988.1 persons per square mile; Race: 100.0% White, 0.0% Black/African American, 0.0% Asian, 0.0% American Indian/Alaska Native, 0.0% Native Hawaiian/Other Pacific Islander, 0.0% Two or more races, 0.0% Hispanic of any race; Average household size: 2.69; Median age: 34.9; Age under 18: 30.1%; Age 65 and over: 9.5%; Males per 100 females: 93.3; Marriage status: 21.9% never married, 49.8% now married, 0.0% separated, 2.6% widowed, 25.7% divorced; Foreign born: 0.0%; Speak English only: 100.0%; With disability: 15.8%; Veterans: 7.3%; Ancestry: 22.8% German, 20.3% Irish, 10.6% Hungarian, 10.6% Slavic, 9.0% English
Employment: 11.7% management, business, and financial, 0.0% computer, engineering, and science, 17.8% education, legal, community service, arts, and media, 7.4% healthcare practitioners, 17.6% service, 14.4% sales and office, 8.8% natural resources, construction, and maintenance, 22.3% production, transportation, and material moving
Income: Per capita: $17,390; Median household: $40,145; Average household: $45,122; Households with income of $100,000 or more: 6.7%; Poverty rate: 29.1%
Educational Attainment: High school diploma or higher: 85.2%; Bachelor's degree or higher: 8.8%; Graduate/professional degree or higher: 7.8%
Housing: Homeownership rate: 65.5%; Median home value: $82,600; Median year structure built: 1951; Homeowner vacancy rate: 0.0%; Median selected monthly owner costs: $643 with a mortgage, $340 without a mortgage; Median gross rent: n/a per month; Rental vacancy rate: 0.0%
Health Insurance: 88.2% have insurance; 62.9% have private insurance; 35.0% have public insurance; 11.8% do not have insurance; 4.7% of children under 18 do not have insurance
Transportation: Commute: 100.0% car, 0.0% public transportation, 0.0% walk, 0.0% work from home; Mean travel time to work: 18.0 minutes

MARTINS FERRY (city). Covers a land area of 2.329 square miles and a water area of 0.002 square miles. Located at 40.11° N. Lat; 80.73° W. Long. Elevation is 709 feet.
History: The settlement that formed here in the 1780's was known as Norristown. In 1795 Absalom Martin laid out a town that he called Jefferson, but he later voided his town plat when he failed to get the county seat. Settlers continued to come, and in 1835 Absalom's son, Ebenezer Martin, replatted the town and named it Martinsville. Because Martin owned the ferry, the town became known as Martins Ferry. Writer William Dean Howells was born here in 1837.
Population: 6,813; Growth (since 2000): -5.7%; Density: 2,925.7 persons per square mile; Race: 88.3% White, 6.6% Black/African American, 0.0% Asian, 0.0% American Indian/Alaska Native, 0.0% Native Hawaiian/Other Pacific Islander, 5.1% Two or more races, 1.2% Hispanic of any race; Average household size: 2.27; Median age: 44.1; Age under 18: 20.6%; Age 65 and over: 19.1%; Males per 100 females: 88.1; Marriage status: 28.1% never married, 49.4% now married, 3.7% separated, 8.6% widowed, 13.8% divorced; Foreign born: 1.8%; Speak English only: 98.3%; With disability: 16.3%; Veterans: 7.1%; Ancestry: 25.6% German, 16.1% Irish, 13.8% Italian, 13.5% English, 8.3% Polish
Employment: 7.3% management, business, and financial, 2.6% computer, engineering, and science, 6.7% education, legal, community service, arts, and media, 5.8% healthcare practitioners, 25.9% service, 26.3% sales and office, 10.5% natural resources, construction, and maintenance, 15.0% production, transportation, and material moving
Income: Per capita: $20,753; Median household: $33,456; Average household: $44,318; Households with income of $100,000 or more: 8.7%; Poverty rate: 22.8%

Educational Attainment: High school diploma or higher: 88.9%; Bachelor's degree or higher: 15.1%; Graduate/professional degree or higher: 5.5%

School District(s)

Martins Ferry City (PK-12)
2015-16 Enrollment: 1,410 . . . . (740) 633-1732

Housing: Homeownership rate: 61.8%; Median home value: $76,000; Median year structure built: 1945; Homeowner vacancy rate: 0.3%; Median selected monthly owner costs: $901 with a mortgage, $338 without a mortgage; Median gross rent: $456 per month; Rental vacancy rate: 5.4%
Health Insurance: 90.8% have insurance; 58.2% have private insurance; 48.1% have public insurance; 9.2% do not have insurance; 1.8% of children under 18 do not have insurance
Hospitals: East Ohio Regional Hospital (250 beds)
Safety: Violent crime rate: 17.7 per 10,000 population; Property crime rate: 162.7 per 10,000 population
Newspapers: Times-Leader (daily circulation 16,100)
Transportation: Commute: 89.8% car, 1.9% public transportation, 4.5% walk, 2.0% work from home; Mean travel time to work: 19.5 minutes

MORRISTOWN (village). Covers a land area of 0.505 square miles and a water area of 0.002 square miles. Located at 40.06° N. Lat; 81.07° W. Long. Elevation is 1,260 feet.
History: Morristown was laid out in 1802 and served as a toll station on the National Road.
Population: 271; Growth (since 2000): -9.4%; Density: 537.1 persons per square mile; Race: 96.3% White, 1.8% Black/African American, 0.0% Asian, 0.0% American Indian/Alaska Native, 0.0% Native Hawaiian/Other Pacific Islander, 0.0% Two or more races, 0.4% Hispanic of any race; Average household size: 2.11; Median age: 44.9; Age under 18: 19.9%; Age 65 and over: 13.7%; Males per 100 females: 118.0; Marriage status: 30.2% never married, 43.4% now married, 2.1% separated, 8.3% widowed, 18.2% divorced; Foreign born: 0.4%; Speak English only: 99.6%; With disability: 16.1%; Veterans: 7.4%; Ancestry: 27.7% Irish, 26.6% German, 13.3% Welsh, 10.3% Italian, 5.9% English
Employment: 3.3% management, business, and financial, 0.0% computer, engineering, and science, 5.8% education, legal, community service, arts, and media, 16.5% healthcare practitioners, 24.8% service, 15.7% sales and office, 19.0% natural resources, construction, and maintenance, 14.9% production, transportation, and material moving
Income: Per capita: $22,290; Median household: $41,364; Average household: $50,889; Households with income of $100,000 or more: 6.7%; Poverty rate: 6.4%
Educational Attainment: High school diploma or higher: 90.3%; Bachelor's degree or higher: 12.3%; Graduate/professional degree or higher: 4.6%
Housing: Homeownership rate: 81.4%; Median home value: $95,000; Median year structure built: 1941; Homeowner vacancy rate: 3.8%; Median selected monthly owner costs: $993 with a mortgage, $352 without a mortgage; Median gross rent: $613 per month; Rental vacancy rate: 18.5%
Health Insurance: 92.4% have insurance; 79.5% have private insurance; 25.7% have public insurance; 7.6% do not have insurance; 0.0% of children under 18 do not have insurance
Transportation: Commute: 100.0% car, 0.0% public transportation, 0.0% walk, 0.0% work from home; Mean travel time to work: 19.7 minutes

NEFFS (CDP). Covers a land area of 3.986 square miles and a water area of 0.038 square miles. Located at 40.04° N. Lat; 80.82° W. Long. Elevation is 735 feet.
Population: 719; Growth (since 2000): -36.8%; Density: 180.4 persons per square mile; Race: 100.0% White, 0.0% Black/African American, 0.0% Asian, 0.0% American Indian/Alaska Native, 0.0% Native Hawaiian/Other Pacific Islander, 0.0% Two or more races, 0.0% Hispanic of any race; Average household size: 2.11; Median age: 59.3; Age under 18: 6.4%; Age 65 and over: 24.9%; Males per 100 females: 98.2; Marriage status: 27.8% never married, 47.5% now married, 0.0% separated, 11.4% widowed, 13.3% divorced; Foreign born: 0.0%; Speak English only: 100.0%; With disability: 28.5%; Veterans: 12.5%; Ancestry: 25.5% German, 19.5% Irish, 13.6% Polish, 12.0% English, 11.0% Italian
Employment: 17.1% management, business, and financial, 0.0% computer, engineering, and science, 15.5% education, legal, community service, arts, and media, 3.5% healthcare practitioners, 24.0% service, 6.2% sales and office, 16.7% natural resources, construction, and maintenance, 17.1% production, transportation, and material moving
Income: Per capita: $28,290; Median household: $42,500; Average household: $57,855; Households with income of $100,000 or more: 20.9%; Poverty rate: 13.1%
Educational Attainment: High school diploma or higher: 92.7%; Bachelor's degree or higher: 22.9%; Graduate/professional degree or higher: 12.0%
Housing: Homeownership rate: 89.7%; Median home value: $85,800; Median year structure built: 1942; Homeowner vacancy rate: 0.0%; Median selected monthly owner costs: $780 with a mortgage, $319 without a mortgage; Median gross rent: n/a per month; Rental vacancy rate: 0.0%
Health Insurance: 90.4% have insurance; 78.3% have private insurance; 44.2% have public insurance; 9.6% do not have insurance; 0.0% of children under 18 do not have insurance
Transportation: Commute: 100.0% car, 0.0% public transportation, 0.0% walk, 0.0% work from home; Mean travel time to work: 20.8 minutes

PIEDMONT (unincorporated postal area)

ZCTA: 43983

Covers a land area of 20.556 square miles and a water area of 1.980 square miles. Located at 40.14° N. Lat; 81.20° W. Long..
Population: 513; Growth (since 2000): 18.5%; Density: 25.0 persons per square mile; Race: 93.4% White, 0.0% Black/African American, 0.0% Asian, 0.0% American Indian/Alaska Native, 0.0% Native Hawaiian/Other Pacific Islander, 6.6% Two or more races, 13.1% Hispanic of any race; Average household size: 2.09; Median age: 44.1; Age under 18: 19.3%; Age 65 and over: 22.6%; Males per 100 females: 116.7; Marriage status: 27.0% never married, 49.0% now married, 0.0% separated, 7.2% widowed, 16.9% divorced; Foreign born: 4.1%; Speak English only: 94.2%; With disability: 16.4%; Veterans: 13.0%; Ancestry: 15.2% German, 14.2% Italian, 12.9% Irish, 12.3% English, 10.5% Dutch
Employment: 23.3% management, business, and financial, 3.1% computer, engineering, and science, 8.1% education, legal, community service, arts, and media, 3.6% healthcare practitioners, 0.0% service, 21.5% sales and office, 19.7% natural resources, construction, and maintenance, 20.6% production, transportation, and material moving
Income: Per capita: $22,273; Median household: $40,227; Average household: $45,998; Households with income of $100,000 or more: n/a; Poverty rate: 24.0%
Educational Attainment: High school diploma or higher: 93.1%; Bachelor's degree or higher: 13.4%; Graduate/professional degree or higher: 9.9%
Housing: Homeownership rate: 67.5%; Median home value: $60,000; Median year structure built: 1955; Homeowner vacancy rate: 0.0%; Median selected monthly owner costs: $855 with a mortgage, $214 without a mortgage; Median gross rent: $863 per month; Rental vacancy rate: 0.0%
Health Insurance: 87.9% have insurance; 83.2% have private insurance; 29.8% have public insurance; 12.1% do not have insurance; 0.0% of children under 18 do not have insurance
Transportation: Commute: 100.0% car, 0.0% public transportation, 0.0% walk, 0.0% work from home; Mean travel time to work: 24.6 minutes

POWHATAN POINT (village). Covers a land area of 1.470 square miles and a water area of 0.163 square miles. Located at 39.86° N. Lat; 80.81° W. Long. Elevation is 679 feet.
History: Powhatan Point was established in the 1820's along the Ohio River. A coal boom during the 1920's brought growth to the town.
Population: 1,603; Growth (since 2000): -8.1%; Density: 1,090.8 persons per square mile; Race: 98.6% White, 0.1% Black/African American, 0.0% Asian, 0.0% American Indian/Alaska Native, 0.0% Native Hawaiian/Other Pacific Islander, 1.3% Two or more races, 0.0% Hispanic of any race; Average household size: 2.02; Median age: 48.6; Age under 18: 16.7%; Age 65 and over: 17.8%; Males per 100 females: 91.6; Marriage status: 25.9% never married, 47.9% now married, 1.2% separated, 9.1% widowed, 17.0% divorced; Foreign born: 0.4%; Speak English only: 99.1%; With disability: 20.6%; Veterans: 7.7%; Ancestry: 22.3% German, 19.9% Irish, 11.7% American, 9.4% English, 5.9% Italian
Employment: 6.2% management, business, and financial, 0.9% computer, engineering, and science, 4.3% education, legal, community service, arts, and media, 6.2% healthcare practitioners, 22.5% service, 21.6% sales and office, 18.3% natural resources, construction, and maintenance, 19.9% production, transportation, and material moving
Income: Per capita: $30,279; Median household: $39,565; Average household: $60,676; Households with income of $100,000 or more: 10.7%; Poverty rate: 21.6%

Educational Attainment: High school diploma or higher: 88.7%; Bachelor's degree or higher: 9.4%; Graduate/professional degree or higher: 3.3%

School District(s)

Switzerland of Ohio Local (PK-12)
2015-16 Enrollment: 2,227 . . . . (740) 472-5801

Housing: Homeownership rate: 69.1%; Median home value: $78,500; Median year structure built: 1958; Homeowner vacancy rate: 1.9%; Median selected monthly owner costs: $850 with a mortgage, $354 without a mortgage; Median gross rent: $514 per month; Rental vacancy rate: 0.0%
Health Insurance: 98.0% have insurance; 67.7% have private insurance; 47.1% have public insurance; 2.0% do not have insurance; 1.1% of children under 18 do not have insurance
Transportation: Commute: 98.0% car, 0.0% public transportation, 0.8% walk, 1.2% work from home; Mean travel time to work: 27.9 minutes

SAINT CLAIRSVILLE (city). County seat. Covers a land area of 2.418 square miles and a water area of 0.019 square miles. Located at 40.08° N. Lat; 80.90° W. Long. Elevation is 1,266 feet.
History: St. Clairsville was named for Arthur St. Clair, first governor of the Northwest Territory. It became the seat of Belmont County in 1804.
Population: 5,117; Growth (since 2000): 1.2%; Density: 2,116.1 persons per square mile; Race: 91.2% White, 6.3% Black/African American, 0.7% Asian, 0.0% American Indian/Alaska Native, 0.0% Native Hawaiian/Other Pacific Islander, 1.0% Two or more races, 0.4% Hispanic of any race; Average household size: 2.16; Median age: 49.7; Age under 18: 17.6%; Age 65 and over: 27.9%; Males per 100 females: 84.9; Marriage status: 21.1% never married, 55.6% now married, 1.1% separated, 10.4% widowed, 12.9% divorced; Foreign born: 1.4%; Speak English only: 97.9%; With disability: 13.9%; Veterans: 14.4%; Ancestry: 20.5% German, 17.1% Irish, 15.1% Italian, 11.6% English, 10.8% Polish
Employment: 10.1% management, business, and financial, 4.2% computer, engineering, and science, 13.6% education, legal, community service, arts, and media, 12.6% healthcare practitioners, 13.9% service, 24.6% sales and office, 10.9% natural resources, construction, and maintenance, 10.2% production, transportation, and material moving
Income: Per capita: $34,635; Median household: $68,234; Average household: $77,056; Households with income of $100,000 or more: 28.0%; Poverty rate: 4.8%
Educational Attainment: High school diploma or higher: 95.1%; Bachelor's degree or higher: 29.2%; Graduate/professional degree or higher: 10.8%

School District(s)

Belmont-Harrison (08-12)
2015-16 Enrollment: n/a . . . . (740) 695-9130
St Clairsville-richland City (PK-12)
2015-16 Enrollment: 1,691 . . . . (740) 695-1624

Four-year College(s)

Ohio University-Eastern Campus (Public)
Fall 2016 Enrollment: 647 . . . . (740) 695-1720
2016-17 Tuition: In-state $4,872; Out-of-state $6,718

Two-year College(s)

Belmont College (Public)
Fall 2016 Enrollment: 1,202 . . . . (740) 695-9500
2016-17 Tuition: In-state $3,541; Out-of-state $6,020

Housing: Homeownership rate: 71.4%; Median home value: $143,900; Median year structure built: 1970; Homeowner vacancy rate: 0.0%; Median selected monthly owner costs: $1,107 with a mortgage, $430 without a mortgage; Median gross rent: $744 per month; Rental vacancy rate: 4.6%
Health Insurance: 90.7% have insurance; 80.1% have private insurance; 32.8% have public insurance; 9.3% do not have insurance; 14.5% of children under 18 do not have insurance
Safety: Violent crime rate: 7.9 per 10,000 population; Property crime rate: 17.7 per 10,000 population
Transportation: Commute: 94.4% car, 0.7% public transportation, 1.5% walk, 1.4% work from home; Mean travel time to work: 18.6 minutes
Additional Information Contacts
City of Saint Clairsville. . . . . (740) 695-1410
http://www.stclairsville.com

SHADYSIDE (village). Covers a land area of 1.011 square miles and a water area of 0.020 square miles. Located at 39.97° N. Lat; 80.75° W. Long. Elevation is 689 feet.
History: Shadyside was platted in 1901. It developed as a residential town, with casket making as a primary industry.
Population: 3,637; Growth (since 2000): -1.0%; Density: 3,598.8 persons per square mile; Race: 99.3% White, 0.2% Black/African American, 0.4% Asian, 0.0% American Indian/Alaska Native, 0.0% Native Hawaiian/Other Pacific Islander, 0.0% Two or more races, 0.0% Hispanic of any race; Average household size: 2.15; Median age: 45.7; Age under 18: 16.1%; Age 65 and over: 23.0%; Males per 100 females: 84.7; Marriage status: 28.1% never married, 47.5% now married, 2.5% separated, 10.0% widowed, 14.4% divorced; Foreign born: 1.4%; Speak English only: 97.2%; With disability: 17.3%; Veterans: 13.7%; Ancestry: 32.5% German, 16.3% Irish, 14.6% English, 12.0% Italian, 9.2% Polish
Employment: 9.8% management, business, and financial, 1.6% computer, engineering, and science, 9.5% education, legal, community service, arts, and media, 9.0% healthcare practitioners, 21.3% service, 17.6% sales and office, 14.8% natural resources, construction, and maintenance, 16.5% production, transportation, and material moving
Income: Per capita: $26,212; Median household: $48,385; Average household: $55,637; Households with income of $100,000 or more: 14.0%; Poverty rate: 10.0%
Educational Attainment: High school diploma or higher: 96.0%; Bachelor's degree or higher: 19.8%; Graduate/professional degree or higher: 6.3%

School District(s)

Shadyside Local (PK-12)
2015-16 Enrollment: 830. . . . . (740) 676-3235

Housing: Homeownership rate: 73.7%; Median home value: $92,600; Median year structure built: 1951; Homeowner vacancy rate: 0.0%; Median selected monthly owner costs: $866 with a mortgage, $311 without a mortgage; Median gross rent: $612 per month; Rental vacancy rate: 10.5%
Health Insurance: 88.7% have insurance; 72.1% have private insurance; 34.7% have public insurance; 11.3% do not have insurance; 3.4% of children under 18 do not have insurance
Safety: Violent crime rate: 0.0 per 10,000 population; Property crime rate: 16.2 per 10,000 population
Transportation: Commute: 90.5% car, 0.0% public transportation, 4.4% walk, 2.4% work from home; Mean travel time to work: 21.8 minutes

WOLFHURST (CDP). Covers a land area of 0.486 square miles and a water area of 0.017 square miles. Located at 40.07° N. Lat; 80.78° W. Long. Elevation is 676 feet.
Population: 1,185; Growth (since 2000): n/a; Density: 2,438.7 persons per square mile; Race: 96.8% White, 1.0% Black/African American, 0.0% Asian, 1.3% American Indian/Alaska Native, 0.0% Native Hawaiian/Other Pacific Islander, 0.9% Two or more races, 0.0% Hispanic of any race; Average household size: 1.92; Median age: 52.9; Age under 18: 20.2%; Age 65 and over: 28.1%; Males per 100 females: 85.5; Marriage status: 33.5% never married, 33.0% now married, 0.9% separated, 22.0% widowed, 11.5% divorced; Foreign born: 0.6%; Speak English only: 96.8%; With disability: 23.0%; Veterans: 14.4%; Ancestry: 37.6% German, 28.6% Irish, 11.7% Polish, 4.6% Italian, 4.1% English
Employment: 0.0% management, business, and financial, 1.7% computer, engineering, and science, 19.2% education, legal, community service, arts, and media, 1.9% healthcare practitioners, 24.2% service, 25.0% sales and office, 15.8% natural resources, construction, and maintenance, 12.2% production, transportation, and material moving
Income: Per capita: $17,667; Median household: $20,357; Average household: $33,460; Households with income of $100,000 or more: 3.8%; Poverty rate: 39.1%
Educational Attainment: High school diploma or higher: 78.4%; Bachelor's degree or higher: 12.0%; Graduate/professional degree or higher: 1.7%
Housing: Homeownership rate: 51.6%; Median home value: $70,500; Median year structure built: 1967; Homeowner vacancy rate: 0.0%; Median selected monthly owner costs: $723 with a mortgage, $305 without a mortgage; Median gross rent: $302 per month; Rental vacancy rate: 0.0%
Health Insurance: 90.4% have insurance; 48.5% have private insurance; 64.7% have public insurance; 9.6% do not have insurance; 0.0% of children under 18 do not have insurance
Transportation: Commute: 88.3% car, 0.0% public transportation, 10.0% walk, 0.0% work from home; Mean travel time to work: 16.0 minutes

Brown County

Located in southwestern Ohio; bounded on the south by the Ohio River and the Kentucky border. Covers a land area of 490.016 square miles, a water area of 3.436 square miles, and is located in the Eastern Time Zone at 38.93° N. Lat., 83.87° W. Long. The county was founded in 1817. County seat is Georgetown.

Brown County is part of the Cincinnati, OH-KY-IN Metropolitan Statistical Area. The entire metro area includes: Dearborn County, IN; Ohio County, IN; Union County, IN; Boone County, KY; Bracken County, KY; Campbell County, KY; Gallatin County, KY; Grant County, KY; Kenton County, KY; Pendleton County, KY; Brown County, OH; Butler County, OH; Clermont County, OH; Hamilton County, OH; Warren County, OH

Weather Station: Ripley Exp Farm Elevation: 879 feet

	Jan	Feb	Mar	Apr	May	Jun	Jul	Aug	Sep	Oct	Nov	Dec
High	39	44	52	64	74	82	86	85	78	67	54	43
Low	20	23	30	40	50	59	63	61	53	41	33	24
Precip	2.9	2.9	4.2	4.0	5.4	4.1	5.0	3.8	2.9	3.2	3.5	3.4
Snow	6.4	5.1	3.0	0.4	tr	0.0	0.0	0.0	0.0	0.1	0.5	3.2

High and Low temperatures in degrees Fahrenheit; Precipitation and Snow in inches

Population: 44,059; Growth (since 2000): 4.2%; Density: 89.9 persons per square mile; Race: 97.1% White, 1.0% Black/African American, 0.2% Asian, 0.1% American Indian/Alaska Native, 0.0% Native Hawaiian/Other Pacific Islander, 1.2% two or more races, 0.8% Hispanic of any race; Average household size: 2.55; Median age: 41.1; Age under 18: 23.3%; Age 65 and over: 16.8%; Males per 100 females: 98.5; Marriage status: 23.6% never married, 55.5% now married, 1.8% separated, 7.5% widowed, 13.5% divorced; Foreign born: 0.7%; Speak English only: 98.5%; With disability: 15.6%; Veterans: 9.5%; Ancestry: 27.8% American, 20.3% German, 11.1% Irish, 8.2% English, 2.9% Italian
Religion: Six largest groups: 10.6% Baptist, 8.0% Non-denominational Protestant, 6.4% Catholicism, 3.4% Methodist/Pietist, 1.3% Presbyterian-Reformed, 1.0% Holiness
Economy: Unemployment rate: 5.2%; Leading industries: 17.5 % retail trade; 13.1 % health care and social assistance; 10.8 % other services (except public administration); Farms: 1,379 totaling 206,446 acres; Company size: 0 employ 1,000 or more persons, 0 employ 500 to 999 persons, 8 employ 100 to 499 persons, 528 employ less than 100 persons; Business ownership: 796 women-owned, n/a Black-owned, n/a Hispanic-owned, n/a Asian-owned, 54 American Indian/Alaska Native-owned
Employment: 10.5% management, business, and financial, 2.8% computer, engineering, and science, 6.8% education, legal, community service, arts, and media, 6.2% healthcare practitioners, 20.5% service, 20.8% sales and office, 12.2% natural resources, construction, and maintenance, 20.2% production, transportation, and material moving
Income: Per capita: $23,776; Median household: $47,999; Average household: $60,376; Households with income of $100,000 or more: 13.8%; Poverty rate: 16.7%
Educational Attainment: High school diploma or higher: 85.3%; Bachelor's degree or higher: 12.4%; Graduate/professional degree or higher: 3.9%
Housing: Homeownership rate: 75.0%; Median home value: $116,500; Median year structure built: 1981; Homeowner vacancy rate: 2.7%; Median selected monthly owner costs: $1,108 with a mortgage, $396 without a mortgage; Median gross rent: $640 per month; Rental vacancy rate: 7.2%
Vital Statistics: Birth rate: 104.7 per 10,000 population; Death rate: 110.6 per 10,000 population; Age-adjusted cancer mortality rate: 214.7 deaths per 100,000 population
Health Insurance: 89.8% have insurance; 63.1% have private insurance; 39.1% have public insurance; 10.2% do not have insurance; 4.9% of children under 18 do not have insurance
Health Care: Physicians: 4.1 per 10,000 population; Dentists: 1.6 per 10,000 population; Hospital beds: 0.0 per 10,000 population; Hospital admissions: 0.0 per 10,000 population
Transportation: Commute: 92.4% car, 0.1% public transportation, 1.1% walk, 5.4% work from home; Mean travel time to work: 36.3 minutes
2016 Presidential Election: 74.0% Trump, 22.1% Clinton, 2.2% Johnson, 0.5% Stein
National and State Parks: Rankin House State Memorial
Additional Information Contacts
Brown Government . . . . (937) 378-3956
http://www.browncountyohio.gov

Brown County Communities

ABERDEEN (village). Covers a land area of 1.347 square miles and a water area of 0.284 square miles. Located at 38.67° N. Lat; 83.77° W. Long. Elevation is 515 feet.
History: Aberdeen was the Ohio River terminus of Zane's Trace, and a ferry point for people and goods going across the river to Kentucky.
Population: 1,509; Growth (since 2000): -5.9%; Density: 1,120.2 persons per square mile; Race: 97.3% White, 0.9% Black/African American, 0.0% Asian, 0.0% American Indian/Alaska Native, 0.0% Native Hawaiian/Other Pacific Islander, 1.9% Two or more races, 0.9% Hispanic of any race; Average household size: 2.02; Median age: 47.5; Age under 18: 19.4%; Age 65 and over: 19.0%; Males per 100 females: 87.2; Marriage status: 22.8% never married, 45.1% now married, 1.0% separated, 11.1% widowed, 21.0% divorced; Foreign born: 0.3%; Speak English only: 97.7%; With disability: 25.7%; Veterans: 10.4%; Ancestry: 37.4% American, 16.7% German, 11.6% English, 11.2% Irish, 3.0% Scottish
Employment: 7.8% management, business, and financial, 3.0% computer, engineering, and science, 4.9% education, legal, community service, arts, and media, 9.3% healthcare practitioners, 15.2% service, 22.1% sales and office, 15.0% natural resources, construction, and maintenance, 22.6% production, transportation, and material moving
Income: Per capita: $21,803; Median household: $27,125; Average household: $43,943; Households with income of $100,000 or more: 11.2%; Poverty rate: 27.9%
Educational Attainment: High school diploma or higher: 81.4%; Bachelor's degree or higher: 11.1%; Graduate/professional degree or higher: 2.6%

School District(s)

Ripley-Union-Lewis-Huntington Local (PK-12)
2015-16 Enrollment: 925. . . . . (937) 392-4396

Housing: Homeownership rate: 50.5%; Median home value: $96,900; Median year structure built: 1978; Homeowner vacancy rate: 4.5%; Median selected monthly owner costs: $1,102 with a mortgage, $394 without a mortgage; Median gross rent: $512 per month; Rental vacancy rate: 12.1%
Health Insurance: 89.4% have insurance; 57.4% have private insurance; 44.5% have public insurance; 10.6% do not have insurance; 8.9% of children under 18 do not have insurance
Transportation: Commute: 97.1% car, 0.0% public transportation, 1.9% walk, 1.0% work from home; Mean travel time to work: 31.6 minutes

DECATUR (unincorporated postal area)
ZCTA: 45115
Covers a land area of 1.041 square miles and a water area of 0 square miles. Located at 38.82° N. Lat; 83.70° W. Long. Elevation is 922 feet.
Population: 80; Growth (since 2000): 185.7%; Density: 76.9 persons per square mile; Race: 50.0% White, 0.0% Black/African American, 0.0% Asian, 0.0% American Indian/Alaska Native, 0.0% Native Hawaiian/Other Pacific Islander, 50.0% Two or more races, 0.0% Hispanic of any race; Average household size: 1.40; Median age: 50.8; Age under 18: 0.0%; Age 65 and over: 0.0%; Males per 100 females: 100.0; Marriage status: 12.5% never married, 87.5% now married, 8.8% separated, 0.0% widowed, 0.0% divorced; Foreign born: 0.0%; Speak English only: 100.0%; With disability: 37.5%; Veterans: 0.0%; Ancestry: 8.8% Dutch
Employment: 100.0% management, business, and financial, 0.0% computer, engineering, and science, 0.0% education, legal, community service, arts, and media, 0.0% healthcare practitioners, 0.0% service, 0.0% sales and office, 0.0% natural resources, construction, and maintenance, 0.0% production, transportation, and material moving
Income: Per capita: $75,869; Median household: $250,000+; Average household: $182,642; Households with income of $100,000 or more: 70.2%; Poverty rate: 8.8%
Educational Attainment: High school diploma or higher: 100.0%; Bachelor's degree or higher: n/a; Graduate/professional degree or higher: n/a
Housing: Homeownership rate: 87.7%; Median home value: n/a; Median year structure built: 1993; Homeowner vacancy rate: 0.0%; Median selected monthly owner costs: $0 with a mortgage, $0 without a mortgage; Median gross rent: n/a per month; Rental vacancy rate: 0.0%
Health Insurance: 100.0% have insurance; 78.8% have private insurance; 21.3% have public insurance; 0.0% do not have insurance; 0.0% of children under 18 do not have insurance
Transportation: Commute: 100.0% car, 0.0% public transportation, 0.0% walk, 0.0% work from home; Mean travel time to work: 0.0 minutes

FAYETTEVILLE (village). Covers a land area of 0.521 square miles and a water area of 0 square miles. Located at 39.18° N. Lat; 83.93° W. Long. Elevation is 948 feet.

History: Fayetteville was settled in 1811 and became a village in 1868. St. Aloysius Academy, a Catholic school for boys, was founded here in 1850.

Population: 324; Growth (since 2000): -12.9%; Density: 622.2 persons per square mile; Race: 87.3% White, 0.0% Black/African American, 0.6% Asian, 0.0% American Indian/Alaska Native, 0.0% Native Hawaiian/Other Pacific Islander, 12.0% Two or more races, 1.5% Hispanic of any race; Average household size: 2.53; Median age: 42.1; Age under 18: 27.8%; Age 65 and over: 12.0%; Males per 100 females: 96.4; Marriage status: 19.5% never married, 58.2% now married, 2.4% separated, 3.6% widowed, 18.7% divorced; Foreign born: 0.3%; Speak English only: 99.4%; With disability: 16.0%; Veterans: 9.0%; Ancestry: 26.9% German, 15.4% Irish, 7.7% French, 7.1% American, 5.6% Dutch

Employment: 7.2% management, business, and financial, 1.3% computer, engineering, and science, 3.3% education, legal, community service, arts, and media, 2.6% healthcare practitioners, 13.1% service, 23.5% sales and office, 17.0% natural resources, construction, and maintenance, 32.0% production, transportation, and material moving

Income: Per capita: $24,240; Median household: $55,000; Average household: $59,832; Households with income of $100,000 or more: 14.0%; Poverty rate: 8.7%

Educational Attainment: High school diploma or higher: 91.2%; Bachelor's degree or higher: 13.7%; Graduate/professional degree or higher: 4.4%

School District(s)

Fayetteville-Perry Local (KG-12)
2015-16 Enrollment: 866. . . . . (513) 875-2423

Housing: Homeownership rate: 53.1%; Median home value: $112,500; Median year structure built: 1962; Homeowner vacancy rate: 8.1%; Median selected monthly owner costs: $1,077 with a mortgage, $500 without a mortgage; Median gross rent: $758 per month; Rental vacancy rate: 0.0%

Health Insurance: 92.6% have insurance; 76.2% have private insurance; 30.9% have public insurance; 7.4% do not have insurance; 0.0% of children under 18 do not have insurance

Transportation: Commute: 96.7% car, 2.0% public transportation, 0.0% walk, 1.3% work from home; Mean travel time to work: 42.0 minutes

GEORGETOWN (village). County seat. Covers a land area of 4.044 square miles and a water area of 0 square miles. Located at 38.87° N. Lat; 83.90° W. Long. Elevation is 922 feet.

History: Georgetown was surveyed in 1819 and named for Georgetown, Kentucky. In the second half of the 1800's, the town was a distribution point for tobacco grown in the area.

Population: 4,810; Growth (since 2000): 30.3%; Density: 1,189.3 persons per square mile; Race: 94.0% White, 4.0% Black/African American, 1.1% Asian, 0.0% American Indian/Alaska Native, 0.0% Native Hawaiian/Other Pacific Islander, 1.0% Two or more races, 0.3% Hispanic of any race; Average household size: 2.39; Median age: 36.2; Age under 18: 27.9%; Age 65 and over: 15.2%; Males per 100 females: 93.1; Marriage status: 24.3% never married, 48.5% now married, 6.2% separated, 12.3% widowed, 14.9% divorced; Foreign born: 1.1%; Speak English only: 97.9%; With disability: 16.6%; Veterans: 10.0%; Ancestry: 28.9% American, 20.1% German, 16.1% Irish, 8.4% English, 7.0% Italian

Employment: 6.4% management, business, and financial, 3.4% computer, engineering, and science, 9.4% education, legal, community service, arts, and media, 8.7% healthcare practitioners, 27.9% service, 24.5% sales and office, 7.6% natural resources, construction, and maintenance, 12.1% production, transportation, and material moving

Income: Per capita: $17,578; Median household: $34,569; Average household: $41,724; Households with income of $100,000 or more: 5.4%; Poverty rate: 25.2%

Educational Attainment: High school diploma or higher: 85.3%; Bachelor's degree or higher: 11.8%; Graduate/professional degree or higher: 4.5%

School District(s)

Georgetown Exempted Village (PK-12)
2015-16 Enrollment: 1,020 . . . . (937) 378-3565
Southern Hills (07-12)
2015-16 Enrollment: n/a . . . . (937) 378-6131

Housing: Homeownership rate: 49.8%; Median home value: $101,300; Median year structure built: 1973; Homeowner vacancy rate: 2.2%; Median selected monthly owner costs: $888 with a mortgage, $322 without a mortgage; Median gross rent: $529 per month; Rental vacancy rate: 4.2%

Health Insurance: 90.7% have insurance; 49.9% have private insurance; 49.6% have public insurance; 9.3% do not have insurance; 1.5% of children under 18 do not have insurance

Hospitals: Southwest Regional Medical Center (127 beds)

Safety: Violent crime rate: 11.3 per 10,000 population; Property crime rate: 229.9 per 10,000 population

Newspapers: The News Democrat (weekly circulation 4,000)

Transportation: Commute: 96.4% car, 0.1% public transportation, 3.5% walk, 0.0% work from home; Mean travel time to work: 33.2 minutes

HAMERSVILLE (village). Covers a land area of 0.393 square miles and a water area of 0 square miles. Located at 38.92° N. Lat; 83.99° W. Long. Elevation is 965 feet.

Population: 795; Growth (since 2000): 54.4%; Density: 2,024.9 persons per square mile; Race: 97.6% White, 0.0% Black/African American, 0.0% Asian, 0.0% American Indian/Alaska Native, 0.0% Native Hawaiian/Other Pacific Islander, 2.4% Two or more races, 0.0% Hispanic of any race; Average household size: 2.88; Median age: 37.8; Age under 18: 25.9%; Age 65 and over: 6.8%; Males per 100 females: 100.0; Marriage status: 23.2% never married, 63.3% now married, 1.6% separated, 4.0% widowed, 9.5% divorced; Foreign born: 0.0%; Speak English only: 99.7%; With disability: 10.4%; Veterans: 7.6%; Ancestry: 52.5% American, 14.3% German, 8.6% Irish, 5.0% English, 4.2% Scottish

Employment: 10.6% management, business, and financial, 0.0% computer, engineering, and science, 11.8% education, legal, community service, arts, and media, 0.0% healthcare practitioners, 22.6% service, 24.1% sales and office, 8.1% natural resources, construction, and maintenance, 22.9% production, transportation, and material moving

Income: Per capita: $22,278; Median household: $51,667; Average household: $64,428; Households with income of $100,000 or more: 14.8%; Poverty rate: 14.9%

Educational Attainment: High school diploma or higher: 89.6%; Bachelor's degree or higher: 12.9%; Graduate/professional degree or higher: 1.7%

School District(s)

Western Brown Local (KG-12)
2015-16 Enrollment: 3,056 . . . . (937) 444-2044

Housing: Homeownership rate: 61.2%; Median home value: $98,200; Median year structure built: 1956; Homeowner vacancy rate: 0.0%; Median selected monthly owner costs: $857 with a mortgage, $343 without a mortgage; Median gross rent: $739 per month; Rental vacancy rate: 4.5%

Health Insurance: 90.9% have insurance; 62.5% have private insurance; 32.8% have public insurance; 9.1% do not have insurance; 0.0% of children under 18 do not have insurance

Transportation: Commute: 92.9% car, 0.5% public transportation, 2.2% walk, 4.4% work from home; Mean travel time to work: 32.0 minutes

HIGGINSPORT (village). Covers a land area of 0.251 square miles and a water area of 0.043 square miles. Located at 38.79° N. Lat; 83.97° W. Long. Elevation is 512 feet.

Population: 279; Growth (since 2000): -4.1%; Density: 1,112.3 persons per square mile; Race: 100.0% White, 0.0% Black/African American, 0.0% Asian, 0.0% American Indian/Alaska Native, 0.0% Native Hawaiian/Other Pacific Islander, 0.0% Two or more races, 0.0% Hispanic of any race; Average household size: 2.16; Median age: 46.5; Age under 18: 24.7%; Age 65 and over: 22.2%; Males per 100 females: 96.1; Marriage status: 17.0% never married, 54.3% now married, 2.7% separated, 18.4% widowed, 10.3% divorced; Foreign born: 0.0%; Speak English only: 100.0%; With disability: 30.1%; Veterans: 8.1%; Ancestry: 51.3% American, 20.4% German, 9.7% Irish, 7.5% English, 2.9% Lebanese

Employment: 1.2% management, business, and financial, 1.2% computer, engineering, and science, 2.3% education, legal, community service, arts, and media, 7.0% healthcare practitioners, 20.9% service, 27.9% sales and office, 5.8% natural resources, construction, and maintenance, 33.7% production, transportation, and material moving

Income: Per capita: $16,218; Median household: $30,875; Average household: $35,702; Households with income of $100,000 or more: 0.8%; Poverty rate: 25.4%

Educational Attainment: High school diploma or higher: 75.2%; Bachelor's degree or higher: 8.4%; Graduate/professional degree or higher: 2.0%

Housing: Homeownership rate: 76.7%; Median home value: $80,900; Median year structure built: Before 1940; Homeowner vacancy rate: 3.9%; Median selected monthly owner costs: $872 with a mortgage, $331 without

a mortgage; Median gross rent: $826 per month; Rental vacancy rate: 12.5%
Health Insurance: 82.1% have insurance; 41.2% have private insurance; 47.0% have public insurance; 17.9% do not have insurance; 21.7% of children under 18 do not have insurance
Transportation: Commute: 84.7% car, 0.0% public transportation, 5.9% walk, 9.4% work from home; Mean travel time to work: 33.4 minutes

---

LAKE LORELEI (CDP). Covers a land area of 2.201 square miles and a water area of 0.249 square miles. Located at 39.19° N. Lat; 83.97° W. Long.
Population: 1,129; Growth (since 2000): n/a; Density: 512.9 persons per square mile; Race: 98.1% White, 1.9% Black/African American, 0.0% Asian, 0.0% American Indian/Alaska Native, 0.0% Native Hawaiian/Other Pacific Islander, 0.0% Two or more races, 2.0% Hispanic of any race; Average household size: 2.42; Median age: 46.0; Age under 18: 22.0%; Age 65 and over: 26.8%; Males per 100 females: 99.3; Marriage status: 16.6% never married, 65.4% now married, 0.0% separated, 2.9% widowed, 15.1% divorced; Foreign born: 0.0%; Speak English only: 99.0%; With disability: 16.0%; Veterans: 13.8%; Ancestry: 35.6% American, 29.3% German, 8.6% Irish, 3.8% English, 2.8% Polish
Employment: 11.8% management, business, and financial, 3.0% computer, engineering, and science, 4.3% education, legal, community service, arts, and media, 5.9% healthcare practitioners, 29.8% service, 20.7% sales and office, 10.7% natural resources, construction, and maintenance, 13.9% production, transportation, and material moving
Income: Per capita: $27,276; Median household: $53,929; Average household: $64,755; Households with income of $100,000 or more: 19.7%; Poverty rate: 10.3%
Educational Attainment: High school diploma or higher: 95.9%; Bachelor's degree or higher: 18.1%; Graduate/professional degree or higher: 8.4%
Housing: Homeownership rate: 84.1%; Median home value: $171,700; Median year structure built: 1982; Homeowner vacancy rate: 10.1%; Median selected monthly owner costs: $1,417 with a mortgage, $461 without a mortgage; Median gross rent: $684 per month; Rental vacancy rate: 0.0%
Health Insurance: 96.7% have insurance; 81.6% have private insurance; 34.1% have public insurance; 3.3% do not have insurance; 0.0% of children under 18 do not have insurance
Safety: Violent crime rate: 5.6 per 10,000 population; Property crime rate: 146.1 per 10,000 population
Transportation: Commute: 90.4% car, 0.0% public transportation, 0.0% walk, 5.5% work from home; Mean travel time to work: 48.6 minutes

---

LAKE WAYNOKA (CDP). Covers a land area of 4.281 square miles and a water area of 0.521 square miles. Located at 38.94° N. Lat; 83.78° W. Long.
Population: 970; Growth (since 2000): n/a; Density: 226.6 persons per square mile; Race: 100.0% White, 0.0% Black/African American, 0.0% Asian, 0.0% American Indian/Alaska Native, 0.0% Native Hawaiian/Other Pacific Islander, 0.0% Two or more races, 0.0% Hispanic of any race; Average household size: 2.00; Median age: 55.4; Age under 18: 12.4%; Age 65 and over: 26.8%; Males per 100 females: 99.8; Marriage status: 14.7% never married, 65.0% now married, 2.7% separated, 10.4% widowed, 9.9% divorced; Foreign born: 0.0%; Speak English only: 100.0%; With disability: 6.6%; Veterans: 18.1%; Ancestry: 36.6% German, 19.1% English, 16.9% Irish, 12.9% American, 1.9% French
Employment: 22.7% management, business, and financial, 10.0% computer, engineering, and science, 8.3% education, legal, community service, arts, and media, 8.5% healthcare practitioners, 6.3% service, 21.0% sales and office, 5.0% natural resources, construction, and maintenance, 18.1% production, transportation, and material moving
Income: Per capita: $68,431; Median household: $86,250; Average household: $136,602; Households with income of $100,000 or more: 37.4%; Poverty rate: 1.4%
Educational Attainment: High school diploma or higher: 100.0%; Bachelor's degree or higher: 26.1%; Graduate/professional degree or higher: 12.0%
Housing: Homeownership rate: 93.6%; Median home value: $262,500; Median year structure built: 2001; Homeowner vacancy rate: 3.0%; Median selected monthly owner costs: $1,487 with a mortgage, $466 without a mortgage; Median gross rent: n/a per month; Rental vacancy rate: 0.0%
Health Insurance: 100.0% have insurance; 92.7% have private insurance; 29.5% have public insurance; 0.0% do not have insurance; 0.0% of children under 18 do not have insurance
Transportation: Commute: 89.6% car, 0.0% public transportation, 0.0% walk, 10.4% work from home; Mean travel time to work: 38.7 minutes

---

MOUNT ORAB (village). Covers a land area of 8.887 square miles and a water area of 0 square miles. Located at 39.03° N. Lat; 83.92° W. Long. Elevation is 942 feet.
History: The name of Mount Orab was derived from the biblical Horeb.
Population: 4,159; Growth (since 2000): 80.3%; Density: 468.0 persons per square mile; Race: 96.3% White, 1.0% Black/African American, 0.6% Asian, 0.5% American Indian/Alaska Native, 0.0% Native Hawaiian/Other Pacific Islander, 1.7% Two or more races, 0.8% Hispanic of any race; Average household size: 2.86; Median age: 34.1; Age under 18: 31.2%; Age 65 and over: 14.2%; Males per 100 females: 91.0; Marriage status: 29.5% never married, 52.6% now married, 0.9% separated, 7.6% widowed, 10.3% divorced; Foreign born: 0.8%; Speak English only: 99.2%; With disability: 12.2%; Veterans: 8.1%; Ancestry: 33.0% American, 10.9% Irish, 10.7% German, 3.3% English, 3.1% Italian
Employment: 5.2% management, business, and financial, 1.1% computer, engineering, and science, 7.7% education, legal, community service, arts, and media, 7.7% healthcare practitioners, 25.5% service, 25.2% sales and office, 11.8% natural resources, construction, and maintenance, 16.0% production, transportation, and material moving
Income: Per capita: $19,277; Median household: $42,415; Average household: $55,539; Households with income of $100,000 or more: 14.1%; Poverty rate: 17.3%
Educational Attainment: High school diploma or higher: 81.2%; Bachelor's degree or higher: 11.1%; Graduate/professional degree or higher: 2.0%

School District(s)

Western Brown Local (KG-12)
2015-16 Enrollment: 3,056 . . . . (937) 444-2044
Housing: Homeownership rate: 64.6%; Median home value: $116,400; Median year structure built: 1994; Homeowner vacancy rate: 3.3%; Median selected monthly owner costs: $1,175 with a mortgage, $370 without a mortgage; Median gross rent: $716 per month; Rental vacancy rate: 0.0%
Health Insurance: 80.9% have insurance; 57.5% have private insurance; 35.3% have public insurance; 19.1% do not have insurance; 5.9% of children under 18 do not have insurance
Safety: Violent crime rate: 13.7 per 10,000 population; Property crime rate: 257.6 per 10,000 population
Newspapers: Brown County Press (weekly circulation 16,500)
Transportation: Commute: 84.5% car, 1.0% public transportation, 0.0% walk, 14.5% work from home; Mean travel time to work: 34.8 minutes

---

RIPLEY (village). Covers a land area of 1.988 square miles and a water area of 0.305 square miles. Located at 38.73° N. Lat; 83.83° W. Long. Elevation is 505 feet.
History: Ripley was laid out in 1812 by Colonel James Poage of Virginia. It was an early center for steamboat building, and for piano manufacturing. The 1937 flooding of the Ohio River ruined Ripley's wharf area. The Rankin House in Ripley was a station on the Underground Railroad.
Population: 1,933; Growth (since 2000): 10.8%; Density: 972.5 persons per square mile; Race: 92.0% White, 5.9% Black/African American, 0.0% Asian, 0.0% American Indian/Alaska Native, 0.0% Native Hawaiian/Other Pacific Islander, 2.0% Two or more races, 0.0% Hispanic of any race; Average household size: 2.38; Median age: 45.1; Age under 18: 23.2%; Age 65 and over: 17.7%; Males per 100 females: 90.6; Marriage status: 26.1% never married, 48.6% now married, 3.1% separated, 7.8% widowed, 17.5% divorced; Foreign born: 0.1%; Speak English only: 99.5%; With disability: 19.8%; Veterans: 8.0%; Ancestry: 36.3% American, 20.3% German, 10.6% Irish, 9.8% English, 5.0% Italian
Employment: 7.9% management, business, and financial, 0.5% computer, engineering, and science, 9.2% education, legal, community service, arts, and media, 4.9% healthcare practitioners, 30.4% service, 24.2% sales and office, 8.6% natural resources, construction, and maintenance, 14.4% production, transportation, and material moving
Income: Per capita: $17,794; Median household: $33,603; Average household: $41,727; Households with income of $100,000 or more: 4.1%; Poverty rate: 22.8%
Educational Attainment: High school diploma or higher: 77.9%; Bachelor's degree or higher: 12.0%; Graduate/professional degree or higher: 4.8%

School District(s)

Ripley-Union-Lewis-Huntington Local (PK-12)
2015-16 Enrollment: 925 . . . . (937) 392-4396

Housing: Homeownership rate: 55.5%; Median home value: $75,200; Median year structure built: 1953; Homeowner vacancy rate: 8.0%; Median selected monthly owner costs: $857 with a mortgage, $337 without a mortgage; Median gross rent: $584 per month; Rental vacancy rate: 19.1%
Health Insurance: 93.1% have insurance; 56.1% have private insurance; 51.5% have public insurance; 6.9% do not have insurance; 3.6% of children under 18 do not have insurance
Newspapers: Ripley Bee (weekly circulation 1,300)
Transportation: Commute: 93.9% car, 0.0% public transportation, 2.7% walk, 2.5% work from home; Mean travel time to work: 28.9 minutes

RUSSELLVILLE (village). Covers a land area of 0.729 square miles and a water area of 0 square miles. Located at 38.87° N. Lat; 83.79° W. Long. Elevation is 971 feet.
Population: 639; Growth (since 2000): 41.1%; Density: 876.1 persons per square mile; Race: 96.6% White, 0.0% Black/African American, 0.0% Asian, 0.6% American Indian/Alaska Native, 0.0% Native Hawaiian/Other Pacific Islander, 0.0% Two or more races, 3.3% Hispanic of any race; Average household size: 2.64; Median age: 40.1; Age under 18: 21.8%; Age 65 and over: 18.6%; Males per 100 females: 92.8; Marriage status: 25.0% never married, 53.3% now married, 3.1% separated, 5.8% widowed, 15.9% divorced; Foreign born: 0.5%; Speak English only: 99.8%; With disability: 14.9%; Veterans: 10.0%; Ancestry: 50.4% American, 15.8% German, 8.1% English, 4.1% Irish, 2.5% Scottish
Employment: 4.6% management, business, and financial, 0.0% computer, engineering, and science, 3.6% education, legal, community service, arts, and media, 5.0% healthcare practitioners, 22.1% service, 22.8% sales and office, 14.2% natural resources, construction, and maintenance, 27.8% production, transportation, and material moving
Income: Per capita: $21,472; Median household: $46,875; Average household: $56,789; Households with income of $100,000 or more: 8.7%; Poverty rate: 10.2%
Educational Attainment: High school diploma or higher: 78.4%; Bachelor's degree or higher: 6.7%; Graduate/professional degree or higher: 4.1%

School District(s)

Eastern Local (KG-12)
2015-16 Enrollment: 1,279 . . . . (937) 695-1399

Housing: Homeownership rate: 66.5%; Median home value: $82,100; Median year structure built: Before 1940; Homeowner vacancy rate: 10.1%; Median selected monthly owner costs: $898 with a mortgage, $375 without a mortgage; Median gross rent: $894 per month; Rental vacancy rate: 0.0%
Health Insurance: 83.7% have insurance; 56.2% have private insurance; 36.9% have public insurance; 16.3% do not have insurance; 20.1% of children under 18 do not have insurance
Transportation: Commute: 87.8% car, 0.7% public transportation, 5.4% walk, 6.1% work from home; Mean travel time to work: 43.6 minutes

SAINT MARTIN (village). Covers a land area of 1.093 square miles and a water area of 0 square miles. Located at 39.21° N. Lat; 83.89° W. Long. Elevation is 978 feet.
Population: 294; Growth (since 2000): 223.1%; Density: 269.0 persons per square mile; Race: 99.7% White, 0.0% Black/African American, 0.0% Asian, 0.3% American Indian/Alaska Native, 0.0% Native Hawaiian/Other Pacific Islander, 0.0% Two or more races, 0.0% Hispanic of any race; Average household size: 2.11; Median age: 48.9; Age under 18: 8.5%; Age 65 and over: 19.0%; Males per 100 females: 95.5; Marriage status: 17.5% never married, 57.1% now married, 1.1% separated, 4.3% widowed, 21.1% divorced; Foreign born: 0.3%; Speak English only: 99.7%; With disability: 12.6%; Veterans: 11.2%; Ancestry: 24.1% German, 18.7% American, 10.9% English, 5.1% British, 5.1% Irish
Employment: 0.0% management, business, and financial, 9.2% computer, engineering, and science, 7.6% education, legal, community service, arts, and media, 3.8% healthcare practitioners, 7.0% service, 27.0% sales and office, 13.0% natural resources, construction, and maintenance, 32.4% production, transportation, and material moving
Income: Per capita: $27,738; Median household: $41,594; Average household: $58,371; Households with income of $100,000 or more: 14.6%; Poverty rate: 9.2%
Educational Attainment: High school diploma or higher: 99.1%; Bachelor's degree or higher: 22.1%; Graduate/professional degree or higher: 13.2%

Two-year College(s)

Chatfield College (Private, Not-for-profit, Roman Catholic)
Fall 2016 Enrollment: 379 . . . . (513) 875-3344
2016-17 Tuition: In-state $10,523; Out-of-state $10,523

Housing: Homeownership rate: 66.4%; Median home value: $126,600; Median year structure built: 1977; Homeowner vacancy rate: 0.0%; Median selected monthly owner costs: $1,758 with a mortgage, $295 without a mortgage; Median gross rent: n/a per month; Rental vacancy rate: 0.0%
Health Insurance: 96.9% have insurance; 96.3% have private insurance; 22.8% have public insurance; 3.1% do not have insurance; 0.0% of children under 18 do not have insurance
Transportation: Commute: 91.9% car, 0.0% public transportation, 0.0% walk, 8.1% work from home; Mean travel time to work: 39.0 minutes

SARDINIA (village). Covers a land area of 1.239 square miles and a water area of 0 square miles. Located at 39.01° N. Lat; 83.80° W. Long. Elevation is 958 feet.
Population: 1,442; Growth (since 2000): 67.3%; Density: 1,164.3 persons per square mile; Race: 98.7% White, 0.0% Black/African American, 0.0% Asian, 0.0% American Indian/Alaska Native, 0.1% Native Hawaiian/Other Pacific Islander, 0.5% Two or more races, 0.0% Hispanic of any race; Average household size: 3.20; Median age: 27.5; Age under 18: 38.0%; Age 65 and over: 8.9%; Males per 100 females: 86.3; Marriage status: 33.3% never married, 51.7% now married, 0.5% separated, 2.3% widowed, 12.8% divorced; Foreign born: 0.0%; Speak English only: 100.0%; With disability: 15.4%; Veterans: 7.4%; Ancestry: 40.9% American, 15.7% German, 5.5% English, 4.9% Irish, 1.9% Dutch
Employment: 6.4% management, business, and financial, 2.8% computer, engineering, and science, 2.8% education, legal, community service, arts, and media, 7.0% healthcare practitioners, 26.6% service, 20.0% sales and office, 12.1% natural resources, construction, and maintenance, 22.3% production, transportation, and material moving
Income: Per capita: $13,087; Median household: $31,667; Average household: $42,289; Households with income of $100,000 or more: 5.5%; Poverty rate: 34.2%
Educational Attainment: High school diploma or higher: 81.6%; Bachelor's degree or higher: 7.8%; Graduate/professional degree or higher: 2.8%

School District(s)

Eastern Local (KG-12)
2015-16 Enrollment: 1,279 . . . . (937) 695-1399
Eastern Local (PK-12)
2015-16 Enrollment: 859 . . . . (740) 226-4851

Housing: Homeownership rate: 48.9%; Median home value: $71,900; Median year structure built: 1957; Homeowner vacancy rate: 4.0%; Median selected monthly owner costs: $954 with a mortgage, $375 without a mortgage; Median gross rent: $795 per month; Rental vacancy rate: 3.4%
Health Insurance: 90.4% have insurance; 38.4% have private insurance; 60.3% have public insurance; 9.6% do not have insurance; 3.6% of children under 18 do not have insurance
Transportation: Commute: 87.7% car, 0.0% public transportation, 5.8% walk, 5.6% work from home; Mean travel time to work: 30.2 minutes

Butler County

Located in southwestern Ohio; bounded on the west by Indiana; crossed by the Great Miami River. Covers a land area of 467.056 square miles, a water area of 3.077 square miles, and is located in the Eastern Time Zone at 39.44° N. Lat., 84.57° W. Long. The county was founded in 1803. County seat is Hamilton.

Butler County is part of the Cincinnati, OH-KY-IN Metropolitan Statistical Area. The entire metro area includes: Dearborn County, IN; Ohio County, IN; Union County, IN; Boone County, KY; Bracken County, KY; Campbell County, KY; Gallatin County, KY; Grant County, KY; Kenton County, KY; Pendleton County, KY; Brown County, OH; Butler County, OH; Clermont County, OH; Hamilton County, OH; Warren County, OH

Weather Station: Fairfield Elevation: 575 feet

	Jan	Feb	Mar	Apr	May	Jun	Jul	Aug	Sep	Oct	Nov	Dec
High	40	43	54	66	75	84	88	87	80	68	55	42
Low	22	24	31	41	51	61	65	63	55	43	34	26
Precip	3.2	2.9	3.8	4.5	5.0	4.1	4.2	3.2	3.1	3.2	3.0	3.7
Snow	3.1	2.1	0.8	0.0	0.0	0.0	0.0	0.0	0.0	0.2	0.1	1.5

High and Low temperatures in degrees Fahrenheit; Precipitation and Snow in inches

Population: 373,638; Growth (since 2000): 12.3%; Density: 800.0 persons per square mile; Race: 85.8% White, 7.8% Black/African American, 2.7% Asian, 0.2% American Indian/Alaska Native, 0.1% Native Hawaiian/Other Pacific Islander, 2.4% two or more races, 4.4% Hispanic of any race; Average household size: 2.68; Median age: 36.5; Age under 18: 24.2%; Age 65 and over: 13.2%; Males per 100 females: 95.8; Marriage status: 31.4% never married, 51.9% now married, 1.8% separated, 5.4% widowed, 11.3% divorced; Foreign born: 5.4%; Speak English only: 92.9%; With disability: 11.7%; Veterans: 7.9%; Ancestry: 27.4% German, 12.9% Irish, 8.8% English, 8.0% American, 4.3% Italian
Religion: Six largest groups: 12.1% Catholicism, 7.4% Baptist, 4.4% Non-denominational Protestant, 3.7% Pentecostal, 3.0% Methodist/Pietist, 2.2% Holiness
Economy: Unemployment rate: 4.2%; Leading industries: 14.4 % retail trade; 10.7 % health care and social assistance; 10.3 % other services (except public administration); Farms: 865 totaling 146,054 acres; Company size: 6 employ 1,000 or more persons, 12 employ 500 to 999 persons, 195 employ 100 to 499 persons, 6,902 employ less than 100 persons; Business ownership: 8,682 women-owned, 1,750 Black-owned, 695 Hispanic-owned, 1,015 Asian-owned, 101 American Indian/Alaska Native-owned
Employment: 15.5% management, business, and financial, 6.1% computer, engineering, and science, 9.4% education, legal, community service, arts, and media, 6.8% healthcare practitioners, 16.7% service, 24.1% sales and office, 7.0% natural resources, construction, and maintenance, 14.4% production, transportation, and material moving
Income: Per capita: $28,556; Median household: $59,652; Average household: $76,687; Households with income of $100,000 or more: 26.0%; Poverty rate: 13.6%
Educational Attainment: High school diploma or higher: 89.7%; Bachelor's degree or higher: 29.1%; Graduate/professional degree or higher: 10.3%
Housing: Homeownership rate: 68.7%; Median home value: $159,800; Median year structure built: 1977; Homeowner vacancy rate: 1.6%; Median selected monthly owner costs: $1,380 with a mortgage, $477 without a mortgage; Median gross rent: $823 per month; Rental vacancy rate: 6.1%
Vital Statistics: Birth rate: 117.4 per 10,000 population; Death rate: 90.2 per 10,000 population; Age-adjusted cancer mortality rate: 178.4 deaths per 100,000 population
Health Insurance: 92.2% have insurance; 73.5% have private insurance; 29.0% have public insurance; 7.8% do not have insurance; 3.5% of children under 18 do not have insurance
Health Care: Physicians: 13.6 per 10,000 population; Dentists: 4.8 per 10,000 population; Hospital beds: 16.8 per 10,000 population; Hospital admissions: 929.9 per 10,000 population
Air Quality Index (AQI): Percent of Days: 70.8% good, 26.2% moderate, 3.0% unhealthy for sensitive individuals, 0.0% unhealthy, 0.0% very unhealthy; Annual median: 42; Annual maximum: 136
Transportation: Commute: 92.5% car, 0.6% public transportation, 2.2% walk, 3.9% work from home; Mean travel time to work: 24.2 minutes
2016 Presidential Election: 61.1% Trump, 33.5% Clinton, 3.3% Johnson, 0.7% Stein
Additional Information Contacts
Butler Government . . . . (513) 887-3247
http://www.butlercountyohio.org

Butler County Communities

BECKETT RIDGE (CDP). Covers a land area of 4.802 square miles and a water area of 0 square miles. Located at 39.34° N. Lat; 84.44° W. Long. Elevation is 820 feet.
History: Beckett Ridge's planning began in 1976 with the purchase of 1,800 acres of farmland from the Beckett family who owned the land since 1810.
Population: 8,724; Growth (since 2000): 0.7%; Density: 1,816.6 persons per square mile; Race: 82.6% White, 8.3% Black/African American, 5.8% Asian, 0.3% American Indian/Alaska Native, 0.1% Native Hawaiian/Other Pacific Islander, 2.0% Two or more races, 4.3% Hispanic of any race; Average household size: 2.46; Median age: 41.3; Age under 18: 21.5%; Age 65 and over: 11.7%; Males per 100 females: 96.7; Marriage status: 25.6% never married, 60.3% now married, 0.8% separated, 3.7% widowed, 10.4% divorced; Foreign born: 10.1%; Speak English only: 91.6%; With disability: 5.8%; Veterans: 7.1%; Ancestry: 27.3% German, 11.0% English, 10.5% Irish, 5.8% Italian, 5.7% American
Employment: 24.6% management, business, and financial, 12.9% computer, engineering, and science, 10.3% education, legal, community service, arts, and media, 9.1% healthcare practitioners, 12.2% service, 23.6% sales and office, 2.5% natural resources, construction, and maintenance, 4.8% production, transportation, and material moving
Income: Per capita: $47,706; Median household: $84,958; Average household: $116,170; Households with income of $100,000 or more: 44.1%; Poverty rate: 3.5%
Educational Attainment: High school diploma or higher: 98.3%; Bachelor's degree or higher: 56.3%; Graduate/professional degree or higher: 19.8%
Housing: Homeownership rate: 77.2%; Median home value: $204,200; Median year structure built: 1991; Homeowner vacancy rate: 0.7%; Median selected monthly owner costs: $1,560 with a mortgage, $646 without a mortgage; Median gross rent: $1,196 per month; Rental vacancy rate: 1.2%
Health Insurance: 95.9% have insurance; 86.5% have private insurance; 19.2% have public insurance; 4.1% do not have insurance; 3.6% of children under 18 do not have insurance
Transportation: Commute: 89.5% car, 0.4% public transportation, 1.5% walk, 8.2% work from home; Mean travel time to work: 23.1 minutes

DARRTOWN (CDP). Covers a land area of 2.356 square miles and a water area of 0 square miles. Located at 39.50° N. Lat; 84.67° W. Long. Elevation is 738 feet.
Population: 369; Growth (since 2000): n/a; Density: 156.6 persons per square mile; Race: 92.7% White, 2.2% Black/African American, 2.4% Asian, 0.0% American Indian/Alaska Native, 0.0% Native Hawaiian/Other Pacific Islander, 0.0% Two or more races, 0.0% Hispanic of any race; Average household size: 2.18; Median age: 46.1; Age under 18: 19.2%; Age 65 and over: 16.3%; Males per 100 females: 94.0; Marriage status: 11.8% never married, 76.1% now married, 0.0% separated, 5.9% widowed, 6.2% divorced; Foreign born: 2.4%; Speak English only: 100.0%; With disability: 13.6%; Veterans: 8.7%; Ancestry: 18.7% English, 13.8% German, 8.7% American, 4.9% Irish, 2.7% Polish
Employment: 17.9% management, business, and financial, 3.3% computer, engineering, and science, 22.1% education, legal, community service, arts, and media, 0.0% healthcare practitioners, 14.2% service, 17.9% sales and office, 6.7% natural resources, construction, and maintenance, 17.9% production, transportation, and material moving
Income: Per capita: $50,464; Median household: $87,422; Average household: $109,583; Households with income of $100,000 or more: 46.1%; Poverty rate: n/a
Educational Attainment: High school diploma or higher: 92.3%; Bachelor's degree or higher: 26.2%; Graduate/professional degree or higher: 10.1%
Housing: Homeownership rate: 100.0%; Median home value: $113,600; Median year structure built: 1975; Homeowner vacancy rate: 0.0%; Median selected monthly owner costs: $944 with a mortgage, n/a without a mortgage; Median gross rent: n/a per month; Rental vacancy rate: 0.0%
Health Insurance: 90.8% have insurance; 88.6% have private insurance; 22.8% have public insurance; 9.2% do not have insurance; 29.6% of children under 18 do not have insurance
Transportation: Commute: 100.0% car, 0.0% public transportation, 0.0% walk, 0.0% work from home; Mean travel time to work: 28.1 minutes

FAIRFIELD (city). Covers a land area of 20.939 square miles and a water area of 0.121 square miles. Located at 39.33° N. Lat; 84.54° W. Long. Elevation is 594 feet.
Population: 42,640; Growth (since 2000): 1.3%; Density: 2,036.4 persons per square mile; Race: 80.1% White, 13.1% Black/African American, 2.3% Asian, 0.2% American Indian/Alaska Native, 0.0% Native Hawaiian/Other Pacific Islander, 2.6% Two or more races, 7.8% Hispanic of any race; Average household size: 2.50; Median age: 38.1; Age under 18: 20.9%; Age 65 and over: 14.5%; Males per 100 females: 92.9; Marriage status: 29.7% never married, 51.8% now married, 2.1% separated, 6.0% widowed, 12.4% divorced; Foreign born: 9.4%; Speak English only: 87.5%;

With disability: 10.4%; Veterans: 7.8%; Ancestry: 26.8% German, 11.1% Irish, 8.0% American, 7.1% English, 5.6% Italian
Employment: 15.4% management, business, and financial, 4.7% computer, engineering, and science, 9.0% education, legal, community service, arts, and media, 6.6% healthcare practitioners, 16.3% service, 24.6% sales and office, 6.3% natural resources, construction, and maintenance, 17.1% production, transportation, and material moving
Income: Per capita: $28,653; Median household: $60,336; Average household: $70,398; Households with income of $100,000 or more: 20.9%; Poverty rate: 7.6%
Educational Attainment: High school diploma or higher: 91.3%; Bachelor's degree or higher: 28.2%; Graduate/professional degree or higher: 10.1%

School District(s)

Fairfield City (PK-12)
2015-16 Enrollment: 9,884 . . . . (513) 829-6300

Two-year College(s)

Moler-Pickens Beauty Academy (Private, For-profit)
Fall 2016 Enrollment: 78 . . . . (513) 874-5116

Housing: Homeownership rate: 62.2%; Median home value: $146,800; Median year structure built: 1979; Homeowner vacancy rate: 2.3%; Median selected monthly owner costs: $1,233 with a mortgage, $472 without a mortgage; Median gross rent: $844 per month; Rental vacancy rate: 6.8%
Health Insurance: 88.7% have insurance; 73.4% have private insurance; 25.7% have public insurance; 11.3% do not have insurance; 3.8% of children under 18 do not have insurance
Hospitals: Mercy Hospital Fairfield (167 beds)
Safety: Violent crime rate: 25.7 per 10,000 population; Property crime rate: 244.1 per 10,000 population
Transportation: Commute: 96.5% car, 0.3% public transportation, 0.7% walk, 2.0% work from home; Mean travel time to work: 22.9 minutes
Additional Information Contacts
City of Fairfield . . . . (513) 867-5300
http://www.fairfield-city.org

FOUR BRIDGES (CDP). Covers a land area of 2.194 square miles and a water area of 0.003 square miles. Located at 39.38° N. Lat; 84.36° W. Long.
Population: 3,359; Growth (since 2000): n/a; Density: 1,530.7 persons per square mile; Race: 85.9% White, 5.3% Black/African American, 3.7% Asian, 0.0% American Indian/Alaska Native, 0.0% Native Hawaiian/Other Pacific Islander, 4.7% Two or more races, 2.1% Hispanic of any race; Average household size: 2.56; Median age: 41.2; Age under 18: 29.0%; Age 65 and over: 18.6%; Males per 100 females: 92.8; Marriage status: 18.5% never married, 64.6% now married, 1.4% separated, 10.9% widowed, 6.0% divorced; Foreign born: 7.1%; Speak English only: 95.0%; With disability: 10.6%; Veterans: 8.4%; Ancestry: 29.7% German, 14.6% English, 13.8% Irish, 5.1% American, 4.0% Italian
Employment: 26.5% management, business, and financial, 9.8% computer, engineering, and science, 12.3% education, legal, community service, arts, and media, 8.0% healthcare practitioners, 6.0% service, 25.8% sales and office, 6.9% natural resources, construction, and maintenance, 4.9% production, transportation, and material moving
Income: Per capita: $47,960; Median household: $105,000; Average household: $127,450; Households with income of $100,000 or more: 54.8%; Poverty rate: 2.7%
Educational Attainment: High school diploma or higher: 96.0%; Bachelor's degree or higher: 56.5%; Graduate/professional degree or higher: 22.5%
Housing: Homeownership rate: 64.1%; Median home value: $383,800; Median year structure built: 2004; Homeowner vacancy rate: 0.0%; Median selected monthly owner costs: $2,529 with a mortgage, $1,058 without a mortgage; Median gross rent: $1,377 per month; Rental vacancy rate: 0.0%
Health Insurance: 98.5% have insurance; 92.1% have private insurance; 18.6% have public insurance; 1.5% do not have insurance; 0.9% of children under 18 do not have insurance
Transportation: Commute: 88.6% car, 0.6% public transportation, 0.0% walk, 10.8% work from home; Mean travel time to work: 23.9 minutes

HAMILTON (city). County seat. Covers a land area of 21.596 square miles and a water area of 0.479 square miles. Located at 39.39° N. Lat; 84.57° W. Long. Elevation is 597 feet.
History: Settlement at Hamilton began in 1791 when General St. Clair built Fort Hamilton as a military and trading post. The town was platted in 1794 by Colonel Israel Ludlow, and named Fairfield, but the site was abandoned in 1796. When the plat was recorded in 1802, the town was named Hamilton for the fort, and became the seat of Butler County. In 1854 Rossville, settled in 1804 on the other side of the Great Miami River, became part of Hamilton. It was the Hamilton Hydraulic water-power plant completed in 1852 that changed Hamilton into an industrial center. A resident here at that time was William Dean Howells, who describes the city in "A Boy's Town."
Population: 62,259; Growth (since 2000): 2.6%; Density: 2,882.9 persons per square mile; Race: 84.7% White, 10.3% Black/African American, 0.8% Asian, 0.5% American Indian/Alaska Native, 0.2% Native Hawaiian/Other Pacific Islander, 2.8% Two or more races, 5.0% Hispanic of any race; Average household size: 2.49; Median age: 37.2; Age under 18: 24.3%; Age 65 and over: 14.9%; Males per 100 females: 95.4; Marriage status: 33.4% never married, 42.7% now married, 3.0% separated, 7.3% widowed, 16.6% divorced; Foreign born: 3.4%; Speak English only: 94.4%; With disability: 16.4%; Veterans: 8.3%; Ancestry: 29.8% German, 15.8% Irish, 8.7% English, 8.3% American, 3.7% Italian
Employment: 8.9% management, business, and financial, 3.0% computer, engineering, and science, 6.7% education, legal, community service, arts, and media, 6.5% healthcare practitioners, 21.8% service, 25.9% sales and office, 8.7% natural resources, construction, and maintenance, 18.6% production, transportation, and material moving
Income: Per capita: $22,113; Median household: $40,401; Average household: $53,972; Households with income of $100,000 or more: 12.1%; Poverty rate: 21.9%
Educational Attainment: High school diploma or higher: 84.7%; Bachelor's degree or higher: 15.1%; Graduate/professional degree or higher: 4.6%

School District(s)

Butler Technology & Career Development Schools (07-12)
2015-16 Enrollment: n/a . . . . (513) 868-1911
Edgewood City (PK-12)
2015-16 Enrollment: 3,624 . . . . (513) 863-4692
Fairfield City (PK-12)
2015-16 Enrollment: 9,884 . . . . (513) 829-6300
Hamilton City (PK-12)
2015-16 Enrollment: 10,190 . . . . (513) 887-5000
New Miami Local (PK-12)
2015-16 Enrollment: 687. . . . . (513) 863-0833
Richard Allen Academy III (KG-06)
2015-16 Enrollment: 166. . . . . (513) 868-2900
Ross Local (PK-12)
2015-16 Enrollment: 2,774 . . . . (513) 863-1253

Four-year College(s)

Miami University-Hamilton (Public)
Fall 2016 Enrollment: 2,894 . . . . (513) 785-3000
2016-17 Tuition: In-state $5,173; Out-of-state $15,031

Vocational/Technical School(s)

Butler Tech-D Russel Lee Career Center (Public)
Fall 2016 Enrollment: 317. . . . . (513) 645-8205
2016-17 Tuition: $6,592

Housing: Homeownership rate: 56.0%; Median home value: $99,900; Median year structure built: 1954; Homeowner vacancy rate: 2.5%; Median selected monthly owner costs: $1,027 with a mortgage, $371 without a mortgage; Median gross rent: $749 per month; Rental vacancy rate: 6.9%
Health Insurance: 88.6% have insurance; 57.3% have private insurance; 42.6% have public insurance; 11.4% do not have insurance; 3.7% of children under 18 do not have insurance
Hospitals: Fort Hamilton Hughes Memorial Hospital (310 beds)
Safety: Violent crime rate: 51.3 per 10,000 population; Property crime rate: 531.2 per 10,000 population
Newspapers: Journal-News (daily circulation 20,300)
Transportation: Commute: 94.2% car, 0.4% public transportation, 2.4% walk, 1.7% work from home; Mean travel time to work: 25.3 minutes
Airports: Butler Co Regional-Hogan Field (general aviation)
Additional Information Contacts
City of Hamilton. . . . . (513) 785-7000
http://www.hamilton-city.org

JACKSONBURG (village). Covers a land area of 0.020 square miles and a water area of 0 square miles. Located at 39.54° N. Lat; 84.50° W. Long. Elevation is 955 feet.
History: Sometimes spelled Jacksonburgh.

Population: 44; Growth (since 2000): -34.3%; Density: 2,206.7 persons per square mile; Race: 100.0% White, 0.0% Black/African American, 0.0% Asian, 0.0% American Indian/Alaska Native, 0.0% Native Hawaiian/Other Pacific Islander, 0.0% Two or more races, 0.0% Hispanic of any race; Average household size: 2.20; Median age: 42.0; Age under 18: 20.5%; Age 65 and over: 13.6%; Males per 100 females: 117.2; Marriage status: 25.0% never married, 44.4% now married, 0.0% separated, 8.3% widowed, 22.2% divorced; Foreign born: 0.0%; Speak English only: 100.0%; With disability: 27.3%; Veterans: 5.7%; Ancestry: 18.2% German, 13.6% American, 13.6% Irish, 4.5% English
Employment: 22.2% management, business, and financial, 0.0% computer, engineering, and science, 0.0% education, legal, community service, arts, and media, 0.0% healthcare practitioners, 11.1% service, 22.2% sales and office, 22.2% natural resources, construction, and maintenance, 22.2% production, transportation, and material moving
Income: Per capita: $23,568; Median household: $41,250; Average household: $52,505; Households with income of $100,000 or more: 5.0%; Poverty rate: 2.3%
Educational Attainment: High school diploma or higher: 72.7%; Bachelor's degree or higher: 6.1%; Graduate/professional degree or higher: n/a
Housing: Homeownership rate: 90.0%; Median home value: $106,300; Median year structure built: 1956; Homeowner vacancy rate: 0.0%; Median selected monthly owner costs: $1,281 with a mortgage, $425 without a mortgage; Median gross rent: n/a per month; Rental vacancy rate: 0.0%
Health Insurance: 95.5% have insurance; 88.6% have private insurance; 13.6% have public insurance; 4.5% do not have insurance; 0.0% of children under 18 do not have insurance
Transportation: Commute: 88.9% car, 0.0% public transportation, 11.1% walk, 0.0% work from home; Mean travel time to work: 19.4 minutes

MIDDLETOWN (city). Covers a land area of 26.185 square miles and a water area of 0.235 square miles. Located at 39.50° N. Lat; 84.36° W. Long. Elevation is 656 feet.
History: Middletown was platted in 1802 by Stephen Vail and James Sutton, who named it for its position midway between Cincinnati and Dayton. It was in Middletown in 1825 that Governor DeWitt Clinton of New York took the first shovelful of dirt to signify the beginning of the Miami & Erie Canal.
Population: 48,527; Growth (since 2000): -6.0%; Density: 1,853.2 persons per square mile; Race: 81.8% White, 11.9% Black/African American, 1.0% Asian, 0.2% American Indian/Alaska Native, 0.0% Native Hawaiian/Other Pacific Islander, 4.0% Two or more races, 5.1% Hispanic of any race; Average household size: 2.45; Median age: 37.8; Age under 18: 24.0%; Age 65 and over: 15.0%; Males per 100 females: 90.6; Marriage status: 31.3% never married, 45.1% now married, 3.3% separated, 7.2% widowed, 16.4% divorced; Foreign born: 3.1%; Speak English only: 94.6%; With disability: 19.6%; Veterans: 7.8%; Ancestry: 21.0% German, 11.3% Irish, 8.2% American, 7.3% English, 3.7% Italian
Employment: 9.9% management, business, and financial, 3.4% computer, engineering, and science, 7.7% education, legal, community service, arts, and media, 5.0% healthcare practitioners, 20.1% service, 25.1% sales and office, 8.1% natural resources, construction, and maintenance, 20.8% production, transportation, and material moving
Income: Per capita: $20,786; Median household: $36,898; Average household: $49,634; Households with income of $100,000 or more: 10.0%; Poverty rate: 24.2%
Educational Attainment: High school diploma or higher: 82.5%; Bachelor's degree or higher: 16.8%; Graduate/professional degree or higher: 4.5%

School District(s)

Madison Local (PK-12)
2015-16 Enrollment: 1,543 . . . . (513) 420-4750
Marshall High School (09-12)
2015-16 Enrollment: 248. . . . . (513) 318-7078
Middletown City (PK-12)
2015-16 Enrollment: 6,298 . . . . (513) 423-0781
Middletown Fitness & Prep Academy (KG-08)
2015-16 Enrollment: 248. . . . . (513) 424-6110
Summit Academy Secondary School - Middletown (07-12)
2015-16 Enrollment: 90. . . . . (513) 420-9767
Summit Acdy Comm Schl For Alternative Learners Of Middletown (KG-06)
2015-16 Enrollment: 89. . . . . (513) 422-8540

Four-year College(s)

Miami University-Middletown (Public)
Fall 2016 Enrollment: 1,914 . . . . (513) 727-3200
2016-17 Tuition: In-state $5,173; Out-of-state $15,031
Housing: Homeownership rate: 52.6%; Median home value: $91,300; Median year structure built: 1959; Homeowner vacancy rate: 1.9%; Median selected monthly owner costs: $1,052 with a mortgage, $390 without a mortgage; Median gross rent: $745 per month; Rental vacancy rate: 7.5%
Health Insurance: 88.5% have insurance; 51.7% have private insurance; 48.9% have public insurance; 11.5% do not have insurance; 4.2% of children under 18 do not have insurance
Safety: Violent crime rate: 52.3 per 10,000 population; Property crime rate: 675.9 per 10,000 population
Newspapers: Middletown Journal (daily circulation 18,300)
Transportation: Commute: 94.2% car, 0.9% public transportation, 1.1% walk, 1.9% work from home; Mean travel time to work: 21.8 minutes
Airports: Middletown Regional/Hook Field (general aviation)
Additional Information Contacts
City of Middletown. . . . . (513) 425-7730
http://www.ci.middletown.oh.us

MILLVILLE (village). Covers a land area of 0.583 square miles and a water area of 0 square miles. Located at 39.39° N. Lat; 84.65° W. Long. Elevation is 623 feet.
Population: 765; Growth (since 2000): -6.4%; Density: 1,311.5 persons per square mile; Race: 99.1% White, 0.0% Black/African American, 0.0% Asian, 0.0% American Indian/Alaska Native, 0.0% Native Hawaiian/Other Pacific Islander, 0.9% Two or more races, 1.7% Hispanic of any race; Average household size: 2.43; Median age: 40.6; Age under 18: 19.7%; Age 65 and over: 17.4%; Males per 100 females: 92.9; Marriage status: 20.0% never married, 56.6% now married, 2.7% separated, 6.8% widowed, 16.5% divorced; Foreign born: 0.8%; Speak English only: 99.2%; With disability: 8.4%; Veterans: 8.3%; Ancestry: 49.8% German, 12.9% Irish, 9.2% American, 7.8% English, 5.6% Italian
Employment: 7.8% management, business, and financial, 2.8% computer, engineering, and science, 10.9% education, legal, community service, arts, and media, 7.3% healthcare practitioners, 15.0% service, 26.4% sales and office, 9.3% natural resources, construction, and maintenance, 20.5% production, transportation, and material moving
Income: Per capita: $29,284; Median household: $56,705; Average household: $68,345; Households with income of $100,000 or more: 23.8%; Poverty rate: 5.2%
Educational Attainment: High school diploma or higher: 89.5%; Bachelor's degree or higher: 16.2%; Graduate/professional degree or higher: 6.3%
Housing: Homeownership rate: 81.3%; Median home value: $136,000; Median year structure built: 1958; Homeowner vacancy rate: 3.8%; Median selected monthly owner costs: $1,129 with a mortgage, $411 without a mortgage; Median gross rent: $685 per month; Rental vacancy rate: 0.0%
Health Insurance: 91.2% have insurance; 75.3% have private insurance; 27.8% have public insurance; 8.8% do not have insurance; 17.2% of children under 18 do not have insurance
Transportation: Commute: 98.4% car, 0.0% public transportation, 1.1% walk, 0.0% work from home; Mean travel time to work: 30.3 minutes

MONROE (city). Covers a land area of 15.873 square miles and a water area of 0.023 square miles. Located at 39.45° N. Lat; 84.37° W. Long. Elevation is 830 feet.
Population: 13,552; Growth (since 2000): 90.0%; Density: 853.8 persons per square mile; Race: 92.4% White, 3.4% Black/African American, 2.1% Asian, 0.0% American Indian/Alaska Native, 0.0% Native Hawaiian/Other Pacific Islander, 1.5% Two or more races, 3.4% Hispanic of any race; Average household size: 2.81; Median age: 34.7; Age under 18: 28.8%; Age 65 and over: 14.5%; Males per 100 females: 95.1; Marriage status: 22.3% never married, 60.1% now married, 1.2% separated, 8.6% widowed, 8.9% divorced; Foreign born: 2.7%; Speak English only: 93.9%; With disability: 9.7%; Veterans: 9.9%; Ancestry: 34.9% German, 13.5% Irish, 9.5% American, 9.5% English, 5.1% Italian
Employment: 20.8% management, business, and financial, 8.0% computer, engineering, and science, 6.8% education, legal, community service, arts, and media, 9.1% healthcare practitioners, 15.5% service, 23.7% sales and office, 4.2% natural resources, construction, and maintenance, 12.0% production, transportation, and material moving

Income: Per capita: $30,368; Median household: $72,982; Average household: $84,423; Households with income of $100,000 or more: 30.5%; Poverty rate: 5.9%

Educational Attainment: High school diploma or higher: 93.0%; Bachelor's degree or higher: 30.8%; Graduate/professional degree or higher: 7.9%

School District(s)

Butler Technology & Career Development Schools (07-12)
2015-16 Enrollment: n/a . . . . (513) 868-1911

Monroe Local (PK-12)
2015-16 Enrollment: 2,627 . . . . (513) 539-2536

Housing: Homeownership rate: 75.3%; Median home value: $162,800; Median year structure built: 1997; Homeowner vacancy rate: 2.1%; Median selected monthly owner costs: $1,408 with a mortgage, $484 without a mortgage; Median gross rent: $977 per month; Rental vacancy rate: 4.1%

Health Insurance: 94.7% have insurance; 83.1% have private insurance; 23.4% have public insurance; 5.3% do not have insurance; 3.1% of children under 18 do not have insurance

Safety: Violent crime rate: 15.1 per 10,000 population; Property crime rate: 273.6 per 10,000 population

Transportation: Commute: 91.7% car, 0.4% public transportation, 0.9% walk, 7.0% work from home; Mean travel time to work: 26.9 minutes

Additional Information Contacts

City of Monroe . . . . (513) 539-7374
http://www.monroeohio.org

NEW MIAMI (village). Covers a land area of 0.905 square miles and a water area of 0.036 square miles. Located at 39.43° N. Lat; 84.54° W. Long. Elevation is 594 feet.

Population: 2,126; Growth (since 2000): -13.9%; Density: 2,349.5 persons per square mile; Race: 96.3% White, 2.1% Black/African American, 0.0% Asian, 0.0% American Indian/Alaska Native, 0.0% Native Hawaiian/Other Pacific Islander, 1.5% Two or more races, 3.0% Hispanic of any race; Average household size: 2.82; Median age: 37.6; Age under 18: 25.5%; Age 65 and over: 13.0%; Males per 100 females: 101.5; Marriage status: 29.7% never married, 48.4% now married, 5.6% separated, 6.8% widowed, 15.1% divorced; Foreign born: 0.4%; Speak English only: 99.1%; With disability: 16.7%; Veterans: 8.6%; Ancestry: 17.5% German, 17.3% English, 12.0% American, 8.0% Irish, 2.0% Dutch

Employment: 8.8% management, business, and financial, 1.9% computer, engineering, and science, 1.9% education, legal, community service, arts, and media, 1.9% healthcare practitioners, 13.1% service, 29.7% sales and office, 14.2% natural resources, construction, and maintenance, 28.4% production, transportation, and material moving

Income: Per capita: $18,707; Median household: $40,625; Average household: $50,697; Households with income of $100,000 or more: 7.5%; Poverty rate: 16.1%

Educational Attainment: High school diploma or higher: 72.9%; Bachelor's degree or higher: 6.3%; Graduate/professional degree or higher: 2.8%

Housing: Homeownership rate: 59.7%; Median home value: $73,500; Median year structure built: 1957; Homeowner vacancy rate: 3.4%; Median selected monthly owner costs: $874 with a mortgage, $384 without a mortgage; Median gross rent: $920 per month; Rental vacancy rate: 4.7%

Health Insurance: 82.0% have insurance; 48.5% have private insurance; 43.0% have public insurance; 18.0% do not have insurance; 13.6% of children under 18 do not have insurance

Transportation: Commute: 91.8% car, 0.0% public transportation, 3.5% walk, 4.7% work from home; Mean travel time to work: 26.9 minutes

OKEANA (unincorporated postal area)

ZCTA: 45053

Covers a land area of 27.128 square miles and a water area of <.001 square miles. Located at 39.35° N. Lat; 84.79° W. Long. Elevation is 640 feet.

Population: 3,642; Growth (since 2000): 19.5%; Density: 134.3 persons per square mile; Race: 100.0% White, 0.0% Black/African American, 0.0% Asian, 0.0% American Indian/Alaska Native, 0.0% Native Hawaiian/Other Pacific Islander, 0.0% Two or more races, 0.0% Hispanic of any race; Average household size: 3.00; Median age: 41.4; Age under 18: 27.5%; Age 65 and over: 11.5%; Males per 100 females: 104.7; Marriage status: 23.1% never married, 63.5% now married, 0.5% separated, 4.9% widowed, 8.6% divorced; Foreign born: 0.3%; Speak English only: 99.3%; With disability: 7.2%; Veterans: 7.6%; Ancestry: 42.1% German, 11.0% Irish, 10.7% American, 5.8% English, 2.2% French

Employment: 20.3% management, business, and financial, 3.4% computer, engineering, and science, 10.1% education, legal, community service, arts, and media, 7.4% healthcare practitioners, 18.0% service, 16.3% sales and office, 13.4% natural resources, construction, and maintenance, 11.1% production, transportation, and material moving

Income: Per capita: $32,886; Median household: $82,417; Average household: $96,981; Households with income of $100,000 or more: 41.1%; Poverty rate: 1.0%

Educational Attainment: High school diploma or higher: 95.7%; Bachelor's degree or higher: 26.1%; Graduate/professional degree or higher: 7.1%

Housing: Homeownership rate: 96.0%; Median home value: $250,600; Median year structure built: 1985; Homeowner vacancy rate: 0.7%; Median selected monthly owner costs: $1,623 with a mortgage, $642 without a mortgage; Median gross rent: $599 per month; Rental vacancy rate: 0.0%

Health Insurance: 94.8% have insurance; 87.1% have private insurance; 17.9% have public insurance; 5.2% do not have insurance; 3.6% of children under 18 do not have insurance

Transportation: Commute: 91.3% car, 0.0% public transportation, 1.7% walk, 7.0% work from home; Mean travel time to work: 32.5 minutes

OLDE WEST CHESTER (CDP). Covers a land area of 0.357 square miles and a water area of 0 square miles. Located at 39.34° N. Lat; 84.40° W. Long. Elevation is 676 feet.

Population: 245; Growth (since 2000): 5.6%; Density: 685.9 persons per square mile; Race: 100.0% White, 0.0% Black/African American, 0.0% Asian, 0.0% American Indian/Alaska Native, 0.0% Native Hawaiian/Other Pacific Islander, 0.0% Two or more races, 50.6% Hispanic of any race; Average household size: 3.89; Median age: 33.2; Age under 18: 29.4%; Age 65 and over: 6.1%; Males per 100 females: 103.4; Marriage status: 25.8% never married, 65.7% now married, 0.0% separated, 8.4% widowed, 0.0% divorced; Foreign born: 32.2%; Speak English only: 42.2%; With disability: 0.0%; Veterans: 2.9%; Ancestry: 13.9% European, 9.4% Greek, 5.7% American, 4.5% Italian, 4.5% Polish

Employment: 7.9% management, business, and financial, 0.0% computer, engineering, and science, 28.6% education, legal, community service, arts, and media, 0.0% healthcare practitioners, 11.1% service, 10.3% sales and office, 42.1% natural resources, construction, and maintenance, 0.0% production, transportation, and material moving

Income: Per capita: $27,199; Median household: n/a; Average household: $96,976; Households with income of $100,000 or more: 42.9%; Poverty rate: n/a

Educational Attainment: High school diploma or higher: 67.8%; Bachelor's degree or higher: 36.2%; Graduate/professional degree or higher: 14.5%

Housing: Homeownership rate: 100.0%; Median home value: $159,900; Median year structure built: 1963; Homeowner vacancy rate: 0.0%; Median selected monthly owner costs: $1,302 with a mortgage, n/a without a mortgage; Median gross rent: n/a per month; Rental vacancy rate: 0.0%

Health Insurance: 65.3% have insurance; 51.8% have private insurance; 15.5% have public insurance; 34.7% do not have insurance; 40.3% of children under 18 do not have insurance

Transportation: Commute: 96.0% car, 0.0% public transportation, 0.0% walk, 4.0% work from home; Mean travel time to work: 26.7 minutes

OXFORD (city). Covers a land area of 6.676 square miles and a water area of 0.002 square miles. Located at 39.51° N. Lat; 84.75° W. Long. Elevation is 922 feet.

History: Named for Oxford, the university town in Oxfordshire, England. Oxford was planned, even before the land had been surveyed and cleared, as the site of Miami University, authorized by the Ohio Legislature in 1809. The University actually opened in 1824, and the town grew around it. It was joined in 1848 by the Oxford College for Women, which flourished for 80 years before it was absorbed by Miami University. One of the instructors at the University was William Holmes McGuffey, whose name became synonymous with the "Eclectic Readers" that he compiled to help children learn to read.

Population: 21,941; Growth (since 2000): 0.0%; Density: 3,286.3 persons per square mile; Race: 88.9% White, 4.0% Black/African American, 6.1% Asian, 0.0% American Indian/Alaska Native, 0.0% Native Hawaiian/Other Pacific Islander, 0.9% Two or more races, 2.4% Hispanic of any race; Average household size: 2.42; Median age: 21.2; Age under 18: 5.7%; Age 65 and over: 6.9%; Males per 100 females: 90.7; Marriage status: 78.9% never married, 16.2% now married, 0.8% separated, 1.6% widowed, 3.4% divorced; Foreign born: 7.8%; Speak English only: 91.4%;

With disability: 5.8%; Veterans: 2.4%; Ancestry: 20.2% German, 10.4% Irish, 6.3% Italian, 5.8% English, 5.1% American
Employment: 10.3% management, business, and financial, 4.0% computer, engineering, and science, 22.6% education, legal, community service, arts, and media, 2.8% healthcare practitioners, 32.2% service, 18.0% sales and office, 3.1% natural resources, construction, and maintenance, 6.9% production, transportation, and material moving
Income: Per capita: $16,197; Median household: $29,451; Average household: $53,876; Households with income of $100,000 or more: 17.5%; Poverty rate: 46.1%
Educational Attainment: High school diploma or higher: 90.7%; Bachelor's degree or higher: 58.8%; Graduate/professional degree or higher: 33.1%

School District(s)

Talawanda City (KG-12)
2015-16 Enrollment: 2,949 . . . . (513) 273-3333

Four-year College(s)

Miami University-Oxford (Public)
Fall 2016 Enrollment: 19,697 . . . . (513) 529-1809
2016-17 Tuition: In-state $14,736; Out-of-state $32,555

Housing: Homeownership rate: 32.3%; Median home value: $185,900; Median year structure built: 1978; Homeowner vacancy rate: 4.1%; Median selected monthly owner costs: $1,329 with a mortgage, $473 without a mortgage; Median gross rent: $772 per month; Rental vacancy rate: 6.8%
Health Insurance: 95.6% have insurance; 89.2% have private insurance; 11.6% have public insurance; 4.4% do not have insurance; 1.7% of children under 18 do not have insurance
Hospitals: McCullough - Hyde Memorial Hospital (60 beds)
Newspapers: Oxford Press (weekly circulation 3,700)
Transportation: Commute: 63.4% car, 4.0% public transportation, 25.5% walk, 5.5% work from home; Mean travel time to work: 14.2 minutes
Airports: Miami University (general aviation)
Additional Information Contacts
City of Oxford . . . . (513) 524-5200
http://www.cityofoxford.org

ROSS (CDP). Covers a land area of 3.117 square miles and a water area of 0.027 square miles. Located at 39.31° N. Lat; 84.66° W. Long. Elevation is 554 feet.
Population: 3,693; Growth (since 2000): 87.4%; Density: 1,184.9 persons per square mile; Race: 98.7% White, 0.0% Black/African American, 0.0% Asian, 0.0% American Indian/Alaska Native, 0.0% Native Hawaiian/Other Pacific Islander, 1.3% Two or more races, 0.6% Hispanic of any race; Average household size: 2.83; Median age: 36.0; Age under 18: 29.7%; Age 65 and over: 13.0%; Males per 100 females: 99.1; Marriage status: 23.5% never married, 61.5% now married, 0.0% separated, 8.9% widowed, 6.1% divorced; Foreign born: 0.0%; Speak English only: 100.0%; With disability: 12.1%; Veterans: 12.6%; Ancestry: 41.3% German, 12.2% Irish, 10.8% English, 4.6% American, 3.6% French
Employment: 8.9% management, business, and financial, 4.4% computer, engineering, and science, 4.1% education, legal, community service, arts, and media, 7.2% healthcare practitioners, 19.3% service, 23.5% sales and office, 16.4% natural resources, construction, and maintenance, 16.2% production, transportation, and material moving
Income: Per capita: $26,842; Median household: $70,731; Average household: $74,744; Households with income of $100,000 or more: 26.7%; Poverty rate: 2.5%
Educational Attainment: High school diploma or higher: 89.0%; Bachelor's degree or higher: 24.4%; Graduate/professional degree or higher: 5.1%
Housing: Homeownership rate: 87.5%; Median home value: $158,700; Median year structure built: 1978; Homeowner vacancy rate: 0.0%; Median selected monthly owner costs: $1,200 with a mortgage, $399 without a mortgage; Median gross rent: $824 per month; Rental vacancy rate: 0.0%
Health Insurance: 94.9% have insurance; 85.7% have private insurance; 23.3% have public insurance; 5.1% do not have insurance; 5.3% of children under 18 do not have insurance
Transportation: Commute: 98.5% car, 1.3% public transportation, 0.0% walk, 0.2% work from home; Mean travel time to work: 26.1 minutes

---

SEVEN MILE (village). Covers a land area of 0.723 square miles and a water area of 0 square miles. Located at 39.49° N. Lat; 84.55° W. Long. Elevation is 653 feet.
Population: 821; Growth (since 2000): 21.1%; Density: 1,135.4 persons per square mile; Race: 95.5% White, 0.0% Black/African American, 1.5% Asian, 0.0% American Indian/Alaska Native, 0.0% Native Hawaiian/Other Pacific Islander, 3.0% Two or more races, 0.4% Hispanic of any race; Average household size: 2.57; Median age: 44.1; Age under 18: 20.3%; Age 65 and over: 16.2%; Males per 100 females: 94.1; Marriage status: 25.7% never married, 53.3% now married, 1.0% separated, 6.4% widowed, 14.6% divorced; Foreign born: 2.7%; Speak English only: 97.0%; With disability: 14.6%; Veterans: 15.4%; Ancestry: 30.6% American, 16.4% German, 11.9% English, 5.5% Irish, 2.2% Italian
Employment: 10.1% management, business, and financial, 4.7% computer, engineering, and science, 5.4% education, legal, community service, arts, and media, 3.5% healthcare practitioners, 8.9% service, 30.6% sales and office, 16.0% natural resources, construction, and maintenance, 20.7% production, transportation, and material moving
Income: Per capita: $23,928; Median household: $49,911; Average household: $59,800; Households with income of $100,000 or more: 16.9%; Poverty rate: 14.9%
Educational Attainment: High school diploma or higher: 88.9%; Bachelor's degree or higher: 14.9%; Graduate/professional degree or higher: 6.2%

School District(s)

Edgewood City (PK-12)
2015-16 Enrollment: 3,624 . . . . (513) 863-4692

Housing: Homeownership rate: 69.3%; Median home value: $109,500; Median year structure built: 1960; Homeowner vacancy rate: 5.2%; Median selected monthly owner costs: $1,222 with a mortgage, $482 without a mortgage; Median gross rent: $777 per month; Rental vacancy rate: 16.9%
Health Insurance: 93.4% have insurance; 75.8% have private insurance; 30.9% have public insurance; 6.6% do not have insurance; 2.4% of children under 18 do not have insurance
Transportation: Commute: 91.6% car, 0.0% public transportation, 5.0% walk, 3.5% work from home; Mean travel time to work: 28.0 minutes

---

SOMERVILLE (village). Covers a land area of 0.252 square miles and a water area of 0 square miles. Located at 39.56° N. Lat; 84.64° W. Long. Elevation is 768 feet.
Population: 259; Growth (since 2000): -11.9%; Density: 1,026.0 persons per square mile; Race: 100.0% White, 0.0% Black/African American, 0.0% Asian, 0.0% American Indian/Alaska Native, 0.0% Native Hawaiian/Other Pacific Islander, 0.0% Two or more races, 0.0% Hispanic of any race; Average household size: 2.59; Median age: 42.6; Age under 18: 20.8%; Age 65 and over: 18.1%; Males per 100 females: 112.9; Marriage status: 30.6% never married, 47.9% now married, 1.8% separated, 6.4% widowed, 15.1% divorced; Foreign born: 0.0%; Speak English only: 100.0%; With disability: 19.7%; Veterans: 14.6%; Ancestry: 16.6% German, 5.8% English, 3.9% American, 3.9% Irish, 1.5% Dutch
Employment: 6.0% management, business, and financial, 1.2% computer, engineering, and science, 0.0% education, legal, community service, arts, and media, 10.8% healthcare practitioners, 19.3% service, 31.3% sales and office, 19.3% natural resources, construction, and maintenance, 12.0% production, transportation, and material moving
Income: Per capita: $17,368; Median household: $40,833; Average household: $44,709; Households with income of $100,000 or more: 2.0%; Poverty rate: 26.3%
Educational Attainment: High school diploma or higher: 79.4%; Bachelor's degree or higher: 8.5%; Graduate/professional degree or higher: n/a
Housing: Homeownership rate: 71.0%; Median home value: $63,900; Median year structure built: 1972; Homeowner vacancy rate: 13.4%; Median selected monthly owner costs: $1,083 with a mortgage, $333 without a mortgage; Median gross rent: $779 per month; Rental vacancy rate: 0.0%
Health Insurance: 87.3% have insurance; 63.7% have private insurance; 36.7% have public insurance; 12.7% do not have insurance; 0.0% of children under 18 do not have insurance
Transportation: Commute: 97.6% car, 0.0% public transportation, 2.4% walk, 0.0% work from home; Mean travel time to work: 29.5 minutes

---

TRENTON (city). Covers a land area of 4.563 square miles and a water area of 0 square miles. Located at 39.48° N. Lat; 84.46° W. Long. Elevation is 650 feet.
Population: 12,477; Growth (since 2000): 42.7%; Density: 2,734.2 persons per square mile; Race: 93.7% White, 2.4% Black/African American, 0.0% Asian, 0.0% American Indian/Alaska Native, 0.0% Native Hawaiian/Other Pacific Islander, 2.2% Two or more races, 2.8% Hispanic of any race; Average household size: 2.96; Median age: 30.9; Age under

18: 31.1%; Age 65 and over: 10.0%; Males per 100 females: 94.6; Marriage status: 23.2% never married, 59.0% now married, 2.9% separated, 4.2% widowed, 13.6% divorced; Foreign born: 0.7%; Speak English only: 98.9%; With disability: 12.1%; Veterans: 10.6%; Ancestry: 25.5% German, 15.5% Irish, 8.3% American, 6.3% English, 3.4% Italian
Employment: 11.2% management, business, and financial, 4.0% computer, engineering, and science, 7.6% education, legal, community service, arts, and media, 6.5% healthcare practitioners, 13.2% service, 26.0% sales and office, 9.0% natural resources, construction, and maintenance, 22.5% production, transportation, and material moving
Income: Per capita: $24,273; Median household: $63,618; Average household: $70,754; Households with income of $100,000 or more: 20.8%; Poverty rate: 11.8%
Educational Attainment: High school diploma or higher: 90.0%; Bachelor's degree or higher: 14.8%; Graduate/professional degree or higher: 3.9%

School District(s)

Edgewood City (PK-12)
2015-16 Enrollment: 3,624 . . . . (513) 863-4692

Housing: Homeownership rate: 64.3%; Median home value: $123,700; Median year structure built: 1985; Homeowner vacancy rate: 1.3%; Median selected monthly owner costs: $1,229 with a mortgage, $432 without a mortgage; Median gross rent: $936 per month; Rental vacancy rate: 0.0%
Health Insurance: 93.7% have insurance; 75.7% have private insurance; 26.3% have public insurance; 6.3% do not have insurance; 2.5% of children under 18 do not have insurance
Transportation: Commute: 95.8% car, 0.0% public transportation, 1.6% walk, 2.6% work from home; Mean travel time to work: 28.5 minutes
Additional Information Contacts
City of Trenton. . . . . (513) 988-6304
http://www.ci.trenton.oh.us

WEST CHESTER (unincorporated postal area)

ZCTA: 45069

Covers a land area of 28.438 square miles and a water area of 0.019 square miles. Located at 39.35° N. Lat; 84.41° W. Long..
Population: 50,167; Growth (since 2000): 17.2%; Density: 1,764.1 persons per square mile; Race: 81.9% White, 7.0% Black/African American, 8.4% Asian, 0.2% American Indian/Alaska Native, 0.0% Native Hawaiian/Other Pacific Islander, 2.2% Two or more races, 3.3% Hispanic of any race; Average household size: 2.73; Median age: 39.4; Age under 18: 24.7%; Age 65 and over: 13.5%; Males per 100 females: 96.9; Marriage status: 24.6% never married, 61.7% now married, 1.4% separated, 4.8% widowed, 8.8% divorced; Foreign born: 10.9%; Speak English only: 88.0%; With disability: 8.1%; Veterans: 7.7%; Ancestry: 26.0% German, 11.4% Irish, 9.2% English, 6.1% American, 4.7% Italian
Employment: 22.4% management, business, and financial, 12.3% computer, engineering, and science, 9.8% education, legal, community service, arts, and media, 6.7% healthcare practitioners, 12.8% service, 23.2% sales and office, 4.4% natural resources, construction, and maintenance, 8.3% production, transportation, and material moving
Income: Per capita: $39,303; Median household: $84,771; Average household: $106,130; Households with income of $100,000 or more: 42.5%; Poverty rate: 6.2%
Educational Attainment: High school diploma or higher: 95.0%; Bachelor's degree or higher: 49.5%; Graduate/professional degree or higher: 18.2%

School District(s)

Lakota Local (PK-12)
2015-16 Enrollment: 15,937 . . . . (513) 874-5505

Four-year College(s)

Aveda Fredric's Institute-Cincinnati (Private, For-profit)
Fall 2016 Enrollment: 211 . . . . (513) 533-0700

Two-year College(s)

Aveda Fredric's Institute-Cincinnati (Private, For-profit)
Fall 2016 Enrollment: 211 . . . . (513) 533-0700

Vocational/Technical School(s)

Aveda Fredric's Institute-Cincinnati (Private, For-profit)
Fall 2016 Enrollment: 211 . . . . (513) 533-0700
2016-17 Tuition: $18,700

Housing: Homeownership rate: 79.5%; Median home value: $202,700; Median year structure built: 1989; Homeowner vacancy rate: 1.1%; Median selected monthly owner costs: $1,592 with a mortgage, $590 without a mortgage; Median gross rent: $1,115 per month; Rental vacancy rate: 2.9%
Health Insurance: 95.0% have insurance; 84.5% have private insurance; 21.3% have public insurance; 5.0% do not have insurance; 3.4% of children under 18 do not have insurance
Hospitals: West Chester Hospital
Transportation: Commute: 91.0% car, 0.7% public transportation, 0.8% walk, 6.6% work from home; Mean travel time to work: 23.4 minutes

WETHERINGTON (CDP). Covers a land area of 0.906 square miles and a water area of 0 square miles. Located at 39.36° N. Lat; 84.38° W. Long. Elevation is 860 feet.

Population: 1,527; Growth (since 2000): 51.2%; Density: 1,685.5 persons per square mile; Race: 92.5% White, 1.6% Black/African American, 2.2% Asian, 0.0% American Indian/Alaska Native, 0.0% Native Hawaiian/Other Pacific Islander, 3.8% Two or more races, 5.6% Hispanic of any race; Average household size: 2.64; Median age: 48.8; Age under 18: 13.8%; Age 65 and over: 20.0%; Males per 100 females: 95.5; Marriage status: 26.3% never married, 66.9% now married, 0.5% separated, 3.5% widowed, 3.3% divorced; Foreign born: 7.2%; Speak English only: 90.8%; With disability: 8.3%; Veterans: 9.6%; Ancestry: 30.3% German, 15.0% Irish, 6.3% English, 4.3% Italian, 3.9% American
Employment: 19.8% management, business, and financial, 3.1% computer, engineering, and science, 5.2% education, legal, community service, arts, and media, 10.7% healthcare practitioners, 10.0% service, 41.5% sales and office, 5.8% natural resources, construction, and maintenance, 4.0% production, transportation, and material moving
Income: Per capita: $63,746; Median household: $120,530; Average household: $165,728; Households with income of $100,000 or more: 59.4%; Poverty rate: 3.1%
Educational Attainment: High school diploma or higher: 98.1%; Bachelor's degree or higher: 57.6%; Graduate/professional degree or higher: 19.9%
Housing: Homeownership rate: 94.3%; Median home value: $420,200; Median year structure built: 1996; Homeowner vacancy rate: 1.4%; Median selected monthly owner costs: $2,417 with a mortgage, $1,020 without a mortgage; Median gross rent: n/a per month; Rental vacancy rate: 0.0%
Health Insurance: 98.0% have insurance; 90.1% have private insurance; 19.3% have public insurance; 2.0% do not have insurance; 0.0% of children under 18 do not have insurance
Transportation: Commute: 85.3% car, 0.0% public transportation, 1.4% walk, 13.3% work from home; Mean travel time to work: 24.6 minutes

WILLIAMSDALE (CDP). Covers a land area of 0.174 square miles and a water area of 0 square miles. Located at 39.44° N. Lat; 84.53° W. Long. Elevation is 600 feet.

Population: 796; Growth (since 2000): n/a; Density: 4,569.6 persons per square mile; Race: 100.0% White, 0.0% Black/African American, 0.0% Asian, 0.0% American Indian/Alaska Native, 0.0% Native Hawaiian/Other Pacific Islander, 0.0% Two or more races, 0.0% Hispanic of any race; Average household size: 2.97; Median age: 34.2; Age under 18: 28.6%; Age 65 and over: 7.8%; Males per 100 females: 106.8; Marriage status: 33.7% never married, 53.9% now married, 0.0% separated, 1.9% widowed, 10.5% divorced; Foreign born: 0.0%; Speak English only: 100.0%; With disability: 5.8%; Veterans: 8.1%; Ancestry: 15.5% German, 8.8% French, 7.2% Irish, 6.2% Scottish, 4.8% English
Employment: 2.5% management, business, and financial, 0.0% computer, engineering, and science, 0.0% education, legal, community service, arts, and media, 4.7% healthcare practitioners, 12.1% service, 38.5% sales and office, 12.4% natural resources, construction, and maintenance, 29.8% production, transportation, and material moving
Income: Per capita: $17,709; Median household: $44,516; Average household: $51,806; Households with income of $100,000 or more: 8.2%; Poverty rate: 23.2%
Educational Attainment: High school diploma or higher: 70.1%; Bachelor's degree or higher: 3.4%; Graduate/professional degree or higher: n/a
Housing: Homeownership rate: 55.2%; Median home value: $76,200; Median year structure built: 1956; Homeowner vacancy rate: 0.0%; Median selected monthly owner costs: $782 with a mortgage, $340 without a mortgage; Median gross rent: $688 per month; Rental vacancy rate: 0.0%
Health Insurance: 88.3% have insurance; 58.4% have private insurance; 36.7% have public insurance; 11.7% do not have insurance; 0.0% of children under 18 do not have insurance
Transportation: Commute: 100.0% car, 0.0% public transportation, 0.0% walk, 0.0% work from home; Mean travel time to work: 23.1 minutes

Carroll County

Located in eastern Ohio; drained by Small Sandy, Conotton, and Yellow Creeks. Covers a land area of 394.609 square miles, a water area of 4.322 square miles, and is located in the Eastern Time Zone at 40.58° N. Lat., 81.09° W. Long. The county was founded in 1832. County seat is Carrollton.

Carroll County is part of the Canton-Massillon, OH Metropolitan Statistical Area. The entire metro area includes: Carroll County, OH; Stark County, OH

Population: 28,108; Growth (since 2000): -2.5%; Density: 71.2 persons per square mile; Race: 97.2% White, 0.8% Black/African American, 0.3% Asian, 0.1% American Indian/Alaska Native, 0.0% Native Hawaiian/Other Pacific Islander, 1.3% two or more races, 1.2% Hispanic of any race; Average household size: 2.54; Median age: 44.7; Age under 18: 21.3%; Age 65 and over: 19.2%; Males per 100 females: 99.7; Marriage status: 22.5% never married, 59.4% now married, 2.4% separated, 6.8% widowed, 11.3% divorced; Foreign born: 0.9%; Speak English only: 96.9%; With disability: 14.0%; Veterans: 9.5%; Ancestry: 27.7% German, 17.1% American, 13.8% Irish, 9.8% English, 7.5% Italian
Religion: Six largest groups: 9.0% Methodist/Pietist, 6.3% Catholicism, 4.0% Lutheran, 3.4% Baptist, 2.1% European Free-Church, 2.1% Non-denominational Protestant
Economy: Unemployment rate: 5.2%; Leading industries: 14.9 % retail trade; 14.0 % other services (except public administration); 10.4 % construction; Farms: 733 totaling 106,256 acres; Company size: 0 employ 1,000 or more persons, 0 employ 500 to 999 persons, 6 employ 100 to 499 persons, 465 employ less than 100 persons; Business ownership: 548 women-owned, n/a Black-owned, 36 Hispanic-owned, 29 Asian-owned, n/a American Indian/Alaska Native-owned
Employment: 11.2% management, business, and financial, 2.1% computer, engineering, and science, 6.0% education, legal, community service, arts, and media, 6.4% healthcare practitioners, 17.0% service, 22.5% sales and office, 13.2% natural resources, construction, and maintenance, 21.7% production, transportation, and material moving
Income: Per capita: $25,093; Median household: $48,545; Average household: $63,061; Households with income of $100,000 or more: 15.5%; Poverty rate: 14.0%
Educational Attainment: High school diploma or higher: 87.0%; Bachelor's degree or higher: 11.4%; Graduate/professional degree or higher: 4.4%
Housing: Homeownership rate: 79.6%; Median home value: $113,300; Median year structure built: 1972; Homeowner vacancy rate: 2.5%; Median selected monthly owner costs: $1,072 with a mortgage, $371 without a mortgage; Median gross rent: $633 per month; Rental vacancy rate: 4.1%
Vital Statistics: Birth rate: 95.8 per 10,000 population; Death rate: 104.4 per 10,000 population; Age-adjusted cancer mortality rate: 150.1 deaths per 100,000 population
Health Insurance: 88.4% have insurance; 66.1% have private insurance; 35.8% have public insurance; 11.6% do not have insurance; 11.4% of children under 18 do not have insurance
Health Care: Physicians: 4.3 per 10,000 population; Dentists: 4.0 per 10,000 population; Hospital beds: 0.0 per 10,000 population; Hospital admissions: 0.0 per 10,000 population
Transportation: Commute: 92.3% car, 0.1% public transportation, 1.7% walk, 5.2% work from home; Mean travel time to work: 29.7 minutes
2016 Presidential Election: 70.4% Trump, 24.0% Clinton, 3.4% Johnson, 0.7% Stein
National and State Parks: Leesville State Wildlife Area
Additional Information Contacts
Carroll Government . . . . (330) 627-4869
http://www.carrollcountyohio.us

Carroll County Communities

AUGUSTA (unincorporated postal area)
ZCTA: 44607
Covers a land area of 2.094 square miles and a water area of 0 square miles. Located at 40.69° N. Lat; 81.03° W. Long. Elevation is 1,230 feet.
Population: 176; Growth (since 2000): n/a; Density: 84.1 persons per square mile; Race: 83.5% White, 0.0% Black/African American, 16.5% Asian, 0.0% American Indian/Alaska Native, 0.0% Native Hawaiian/Other Pacific Islander, 0.0% Two or more races, 0.0% Hispanic of any race; Average household size: 3.26; Median age: 29.6; Age under 18: 32.4%; Age 65 and over: 3.4%; Males per 100 females: 105.3; Marriage status: 35.1% never married, 48.1% now married, 0.0% separated, 4.6% widowed, 12.2% divorced; Foreign born: 9.7%; Speak English only: 60.4%; With disability: 9.7%; Veterans: 0.0%; Ancestry: 34.7% German, 32.4% American, 11.4% English
Employment: 12.5% management, business, and financial, 0.0% computer, engineering, and science, 0.0% education, legal, community service, arts, and media, 11.1% healthcare practitioners, 0.0% service, 0.0% sales and office, 23.6% natural resources, construction, and maintenance, 52.8% production, transportation, and material moving
Income: Per capita: $21,151; Median household: $61,111; Average household: $66,250; Households with income of $100,000 or more: 25.9%; Poverty rate: 4.5%
Educational Attainment: High school diploma or higher: 79.8%; Bachelor's degree or higher: 8.5%; Graduate/professional degree or higher: n/a
Housing: Homeownership rate: 85.2%; Median home value: $77,000; Median year structure built: 1941; Homeowner vacancy rate: 0.0%; Median selected monthly owner costs: $1,125 with a mortgage, $0 without a mortgage; Median gross rent: n/a per month; Rental vacancy rate: 0.0%
Health Insurance: 54.0% have insurance; 50.6% have private insurance; 3.4% have public insurance; 46.0% do not have insurance; 66.7% of children under 18 do not have insurance
Transportation: Commute: 100.0% car, 0.0% public transportation, 0.0% walk, 0.0% work from home; Mean travel time to work: 0.0 minutes

CARROLLTON (village). County seat. Covers a land area of 2.447 square miles and a water area of 0 square miles. Located at 40.58° N. Lat; 81.09° W. Long. Elevation is 1,106 feet.
History: Laid out 1815.
Population: 2,952; Growth (since 2000): -7.5%; Density: 1,206.5 persons per square mile; Race: 98.1% White, 0.3% Black/African American, 1.6% Asian, 0.0% American Indian/Alaska Native, 0.0% Native Hawaiian/Other Pacific Islander, 0.0% Two or more races, 1.4% Hispanic of any race; Average household size: 2.13; Median age: 48.7; Age under 18: 14.2%; Age 65 and over: 26.0%; Males per 100 females: 79.2; Marriage status: 26.9% never married, 53.9% now married, 4.6% separated, 5.3% widowed, 13.9% divorced; Foreign born: 2.1%; Speak English only: 96.7%; With disability: 13.2%; Veterans: 7.1%; Ancestry: 25.1% German, 20.4% American, 14.2% Irish, 9.5% English, 4.7% Italian
Employment: 11.0% management, business, and financial, 1.7% computer, engineering, and science, 8.0% education, legal, community service, arts, and media, 2.8% healthcare practitioners, 22.1% service, 28.8% sales and office, 6.4% natural resources, construction, and maintenance, 19.3% production, transportation, and material moving
Income: Per capita: $24,852; Median household: $46,556; Average household: $54,294; Households with income of $100,000 or more: 10.9%; Poverty rate: 10.7%
Educational Attainment: High school diploma or higher: 91.7%; Bachelor's degree or higher: 17.5%; Graduate/professional degree or higher: 8.8%

School District(s)
Carrollton Exempted Village (PK-12)
2015-16 Enrollment: 2,157 . . . . (330) 627-2181
Housing: Homeownership rate: 65.0%; Median home value: $104,800; Median year structure built: 1960; Homeowner vacancy rate: 0.0%; Median selected monthly owner costs: $963 with a mortgage, $347 without a mortgage; Median gross rent: $483 per month; Rental vacancy rate: 7.9%
Health Insurance: 93.9% have insurance; 76.9% have private insurance; 34.7% have public insurance; 6.1% do not have insurance; 0.0% of children under 18 do not have insurance
Newspapers: Free Press Standard (weekly circulation 8,500)
Transportation: Commute: 92.6% car, 0.0% public transportation, 4.5% walk, 2.9% work from home; Mean travel time to work: 18.3 minutes
Airports: Carroll County-Tolson (general aviation)

DELLROY (village). Covers a land area of 0.180 square miles and a water area of 0.032 square miles. Located at 40.56° N. Lat; 81.20° W. Long. Elevation is 958 feet.
Population: 355; Growth (since 2000): 20.7%; Density: 1,974.5 persons per square mile; Race: 99.2% White, 0.8% Black/African American, 0.0% Asian, 0.0% American Indian/Alaska Native, 0.0% Native Hawaiian/Other Pacific Islander, 0.0% Two or more races, 6.8% Hispanic of any race; Average household size: 3.11; Median age: 34.7; Age under 18: 32.4%;

Age 65 and over: 10.4%; Males per 100 females: 94.5; Marriage status: 22.7% never married, 59.4% now married, 4.4% separated, 4.4% widowed, 13.5% divorced; Foreign born: 0.0%; Speak English only: 100.0%; With disability: 9.0%; Veterans: 10.0%; Ancestry: 29.6% American, 21.1% German, 20.3% Irish, 5.9% English, 5.1% Hungarian
Employment: 8.9% management, business, and financial, 3.0% computer, engineering, and science, 1.5% education, legal, community service, arts, and media, 3.0% healthcare practitioners, 23.7% service, 20.7% sales and office, 14.8% natural resources, construction, and maintenance, 24.4% production, transportation, and material moving
Income: Per capita: $16,006; Median household: $41,250; Average household: $47,489; Households with income of $100,000 or more: 4.4%; Poverty rate: 14.1%
Educational Attainment: High school diploma or higher: 93.7%; Bachelor's degree or higher: 8.6%; Graduate/professional degree or higher: 3.6%

School District(s)

Carrollton Exempted Village (PK-12)
2015-16 Enrollment: 2,157 . . . . (330) 627-2181
Housing: Homeownership rate: 61.4%; Median home value: $91,300; Median year structure built: Before 1940; Homeowner vacancy rate: 0.0%; Median selected monthly owner costs: $769 with a mortgage, $354 without a mortgage; Median gross rent: $725 per month; Rental vacancy rate: 8.3%
Health Insurance: 96.6% have insurance; 61.7% have private insurance; 54.1% have public insurance; 3.4% do not have insurance; 1.7% of children under 18 do not have insurance
Transportation: Commute: 94.0% car, 0.0% public transportation, 1.7% walk, 4.3% work from home; Mean travel time to work: 28.1 minutes

LAKE MOHAWK (CDP). Covers a land area of 3.670 square miles and a water area of 0.805 square miles. Located at 40.66° N. Lat; 81.19° W. Long. Elevation is 1,204 feet.
Population: 1,604; Growth (since 2000): n/a; Density: 437.1 persons per square mile; Race: 100.0% White, 0.0% Black/African American, 0.0% Asian, 0.0% American Indian/Alaska Native, 0.0% Native Hawaiian/Other Pacific Islander, 0.0% Two or more races, 0.0% Hispanic of any race; Average household size: 2.61; Median age: 50.3; Age under 18: 23.7%; Age 65 and over: 21.8%; Males per 100 females: 102.0; Marriage status: 16.1% never married, 63.9% now married, 1.3% separated, 5.0% widowed, 15.0% divorced; Foreign born: 0.6%; Speak English only: 100.0%; With disability: 8.5%; Veterans: 7.7%; Ancestry: 41.1% German, 16.6% Irish, 8.0% Italian, 7.7% English, 6.8% American
Employment: 27.5% management, business, and financial, 2.3% computer, engineering, and science, 4.9% education, legal, community service, arts, and media, 12.9% healthcare practitioners, 3.6% service, 23.4% sales and office, 11.0% natural resources, construction, and maintenance, 14.5% production, transportation, and material moving
Income: Per capita: $43,580; Median household: $83,750; Average household: $112,890; Households with income of $100,000 or more: 41.7%; Poverty rate: 1.9%
Educational Attainment: High school diploma or higher: 100.0%; Bachelor's degree or higher: 28.1%; Graduate/professional degree or higher: 10.6%
Housing: Homeownership rate: 100.0%; Median home value: $197,600; Median year structure built: 1990; Homeowner vacancy rate: 2.1%; Median selected monthly owner costs: $1,375 with a mortgage, $540 without a mortgage; Median gross rent: n/a per month; Rental vacancy rate: 0.0%
Health Insurance: 98.0% have insurance; 88.2% have private insurance; 28.5% have public insurance; 2.0% do not have insurance; 0.0% of children under 18 do not have insurance
Transportation: Commute: 86.7% car, 0.0% public transportation, 0.0% walk, 12.0% work from home; Mean travel time to work: 37.0 minutes

LEESVILLE (village). Covers a land area of 0.257 square miles and a water area of 0 square miles. Located at 40.45° N. Lat; 81.21° W. Long. Elevation is 994 feet.
Population: 195; Growth (since 2000): 6.0%; Density: 759.5 persons per square mile; Race: 100.0% White, 0.0% Black/African American, 0.0% Asian, 0.0% American Indian/Alaska Native, 0.0% Native Hawaiian/Other Pacific Islander, 0.0% Two or more races, 0.0% Hispanic of any race; Average household size: 2.47; Median age: 43.8; Age under 18: 11.3%; Age 65 and over: 23.1%; Males per 100 females: 92.7; Marriage status: 17.9% never married, 61.8% now married, 1.7% separated, 9.8% widowed, 10.4% divorced; Foreign born: 0.0%; Speak English only: 98.9%; With disability: 18.5%; Veterans: 5.8%; Ancestry: 34.4% German, 14.4% American, 11.8% Irish, 7.7% Swedish, 6.7% Portuguese
Employment: 9.6% management, business, and financial, 0.0% computer, engineering, and science, 7.7% education, legal, community service, arts, and media, 4.8% healthcare practitioners, 20.2% service, 11.5% sales and office, 15.4% natural resources, construction, and maintenance, 30.8% production, transportation, and material moving
Income: Per capita: $24,974; Median household: $50,938; Average household: $59,353; Households with income of $100,000 or more: 8.9%; Poverty rate: 4.6%
Educational Attainment: High school diploma or higher: 93.1%; Bachelor's degree or higher: 0.7%; Graduate/professional degree or higher: n/a
Housing: Homeownership rate: 91.1%; Median home value: $82,100; Median year structure built: 1965; Homeowner vacancy rate: 0.0%; Median selected monthly owner costs: $838 with a mortgage, $369 without a mortgage; Median gross rent: n/a per month; Rental vacancy rate: 0.0%
Health Insurance: 91.3% have insurance; 68.7% have private insurance; 37.4% have public insurance; 8.7% do not have insurance; 0.0% of children under 18 do not have insurance
Transportation: Commute: 100.0% car, 0.0% public transportation, 0.0% walk, 0.0% work from home; Mean travel time to work: 27.6 minutes

MALVERN (village). Covers a land area of 0.668 square miles and a water area of 0 square miles. Located at 40.69° N. Lat; 81.18° W. Long. Elevation is 994 feet.
Population: 1,159; Growth (since 2000): -4.8%; Density: 1,735.2 persons per square mile; Race: 95.2% White, 1.7% Black/African American, 0.0% Asian, 0.0% American Indian/Alaska Native, 0.0% Native Hawaiian/Other Pacific Islander, 3.1% Two or more races, 1.7% Hispanic of any race; Average household size: 2.38; Median age: 38.5; Age under 18: 24.0%; Age 65 and over: 14.8%; Males per 100 females: 93.6; Marriage status: 32.5% never married, 44.1% now married, 1.0% separated, 6.6% widowed, 16.7% divorced; Foreign born: 0.0%; Speak English only: 98.3%; With disability: 17.7%; Veterans: 5.3%; Ancestry: 33.1% German, 18.8% American, 17.0% Italian, 12.3% Irish, 6.6% English
Employment: 5.8% management, business, and financial, 0.5% computer, engineering, and science, 3.1% education, legal, community service, arts, and media, 2.2% healthcare practitioners, 27.6% service, 24.5% sales and office, 8.7% natural resources, construction, and maintenance, 27.6% production, transportation, and material moving
Income: Per capita: $20,564; Median household: $41,094; Average household: $47,626; Households with income of $100,000 or more: 9.6%; Poverty rate: 23.3%
Educational Attainment: High school diploma or higher: 91.1%; Bachelor's degree or higher: 12.5%; Graduate/professional degree or higher: 3.7%

School District(s)

Brown Local (KG-12)
2015-16 Enrollment: 629. . . . . (330) 863-1170
Housing: Homeownership rate: 56.3%; Median home value: $96,500; Median year structure built: 1953; Homeowner vacancy rate: 1.1%; Median selected monthly owner costs: $1,058 with a mortgage, $441 without a mortgage; Median gross rent: $555 per month; Rental vacancy rate: 3.7%
Health Insurance: 90.5% have insurance; 59.0% have private insurance; 46.2% have public insurance; 9.5% do not have insurance; 0.0% of children under 18 do not have insurance
Transportation: Commute: 93.8% car, 0.0% public transportation, 2.2% walk, 3.9% work from home; Mean travel time to work: 22.2 minutes

MECHANICSTOWN (unincorporated postal area)

ZCTA: 44651

Covers a land area of 24.093 square miles and a water area of 0.009 square miles. Located at 40.63° N. Lat; 80.95° W. Long. Elevation is 1,253 feet.
Population: 538; Growth (since 2000): -35.4%; Density: 22.3 persons per square mile; Race: 100.0% White, 0.0% Black/African American, 0.0% Asian, 0.0% American Indian/Alaska Native, 0.0% Native Hawaiian/Other Pacific Islander, 0.0% Two or more races, 0.0% Hispanic of any race; Average household size: 2.50; Median age: 30.0; Age under 18: 28.3%; Age 65 and over: 11.7%; Males per 100 females: 108.0; Marriage status: 23.8% never married, 57.5% now married, 0.0% separated, 4.6% widowed, 14.1% divorced; Foreign born: 0.0%; Speak English only: 91.0%; With disability: 16.5%; Veterans: 4.1%; Ancestry: 33.1% American, 12.1% German, 4.8% Irish, 3.9% Hungarian, 3.9% Polish

Employment: 16.4% management, business, and financial, 2.8% computer, engineering, and science, 2.8% education, legal, community service, arts, and media, 0.0% healthcare practitioners, 3.3% service, 9.8% sales and office, 29.9% natural resources, construction, and maintenance, 35.0% production, transportation, and material moving
Income: Per capita: $23,155; Median household: $31,875; Average household: $54,788; Households with income of $100,000 or more: 17.2%; Poverty rate: 15.2%
Educational Attainment: High school diploma or higher: 81.5%; Bachelor's degree or higher: 8.2%; Graduate/professional degree or higher: 3.6%
Housing: Homeownership rate: 73.5%; Median home value: $116,700; Median year structure built: 1955; Homeowner vacancy rate: 0.0%; Median selected monthly owner costs: $1,111 with a mortgage, $342 without a mortgage; Median gross rent: $588 per month; Rental vacancy rate: 0.0%
Health Insurance: 77.1% have insurance; 58.4% have private insurance; 30.7% have public insurance; 22.9% do not have insurance; 26.3% of children under 18 do not have insurance
Transportation: Commute: 93.7% car, 0.0% public transportation, 0.0% walk, 0.0% work from home; Mean travel time to work: 42.4 minutes

SHERRODSVILLE (village). Covers a land area of 0.316 square miles and a water area of 0 square miles. Located at 40.49° N. Lat; 81.24° W. Long. Elevation is 909 feet.
Population: 281; Growth (since 2000): -11.1%; Density: 890.4 persons per square mile; Race: 98.6% White, 0.0% Black/African American, 0.0% Asian, 1.4% American Indian/Alaska Native, 0.0% Native Hawaiian/Other Pacific Islander, 0.0% Two or more races, 0.0% Hispanic of any race; Average household size: 2.84; Median age: 33.3; Age under 18: 27.8%; Age 65 and over: 15.7%; Males per 100 females: 108.2; Marriage status: 29.2% never married, 46.7% now married, 3.3% separated, 7.5% widowed, 16.5% divorced; Foreign born: 0.0%; Speak English only: 99.2%; With disability: 15.3%; Veterans: 14.3%; Ancestry: 27.8% American, 25.6% German, 14.9% Irish, 6.0% Dutch, 5.0% Italian
Employment: 5.2% management, business, and financial, 3.7% computer, engineering, and science, 1.5% education, legal, community service, arts, and media, 11.9% healthcare practitioners, 23.9% service, 18.7% sales and office, 14.9% natural resources, construction, and maintenance, 20.1% production, transportation, and material moving
Income: Per capita: $18,262; Median household: $40,469; Average household: $50,922; Households with income of $100,000 or more: 7.1%; Poverty rate: 14.7%
Educational Attainment: High school diploma or higher: 83.4%; Bachelor's degree or higher: 3.4%; Graduate/professional degree or higher: n/a

School District(s)

Conotton Valley Union Local (PK-12)
2015-16 Enrollment: 384. . . . . (740) 269-2000
Housing: Homeownership rate: 70.7%; Median home value: $61,100; Median year structure built: Before 1940; Homeowner vacancy rate: 0.0%; Median selected monthly owner costs: $825 with a mortgage, $371 without a mortgage; Median gross rent: $925 per month; Rental vacancy rate: 0.0%
Health Insurance: 85.4% have insurance; 52.7% have private insurance; 49.1% have public insurance; 14.6% do not have insurance; 14.1% of children under 18 do not have insurance
Transportation: Commute: 97.0% car, 0.0% public transportation, 3.0% walk, 0.0% work from home; Mean travel time to work: 28.6 minutes

Champaign County

Located in west central Ohio; crossed by the Mad River, and Darby, Small Buck, and Little Darby Creeks. Covers a land area of 428.669 square miles, a water area of 1.164 square miles, and is located in the Eastern Time Zone at 40.13° N. Lat., 83.77° W. Long. The county was founded in 1805. County seat is Urbana.

Champaign County is part of the Urbana, OH Micropolitan Statistical Area. The entire metro area includes: Champaign County, OH

Weather Station: Urbana WWTP Elevation: 1,000 feet

	Jan	Feb	Mar	Apr	May	Jun	Jul	Aug	Sep	Oct	Nov	Dec
High	34	39	48	61	71	80	84	83	76	64	51	38
Low	19	22	29	39	49	59	62	60	52	41	33	23
Precip	2.6	2.1	2.8	3.8	4.8	4.5	5.5	3.4	3.1	2.9	3.2	3.0
Snow	na	na	na	0.1	0.0	0.0	0.0	0.0	0.0	0.0	tr	na

High and Low temperatures in degrees Fahrenheit; Precipitation and Snow in inches

Population: 39,175; Growth (since 2000): 0.7%; Density: 91.4 persons per square mile; Race: 94.4% White, 1.7% Black/African American, 0.5% Asian, 0.1% American Indian/Alaska Native, 0.1% Native Hawaiian/Other Pacific Islander, 2.8% two or more races, 1.5% Hispanic of any race; Average household size: 2.53; Median age: 41.6; Age under 18: 23.3%; Age 65 and over: 16.6%; Males per 100 females: 98.0; Marriage status: 24.9% never married, 55.8% now married, 1.5% separated, 7.1% widowed, 12.2% divorced; Foreign born: 0.9%; Speak English only: 98.1%; With disability: 15.1%; Veterans: 9.7%; Ancestry: 25.6% German, 13.8% Irish, 11.0% English, 10.8% American, 2.5% Dutch
Religion: Six largest groups: 8.3% Methodist/Pietist, 4.9% Non-denominational Protestant, 4.3% Baptist, 3.7% Catholicism, 2.8% Holiness, 1.7% Lutheran
Economy: Unemployment rate: 3.8%; Leading industries: 15.2 % retail trade; 14.9 % other services (except public administration); 10.3 % construction; Farms: 873 totaling 190,060 acres; Company size: 0 employ 1,000 or more persons, 2 employ 500 to 999 persons, 16 employ 100 to 499 persons, 547 employ less than 100 persons; Business ownership: 1,078 women-owned, 33 Black-owned, 25 Hispanic-owned, n/a Asian-owned, n/a American Indian/Alaska Native-owned
Employment: 11.5% management, business, and financial, 2.6% computer, engineering, and science, 8.6% education, legal, community service, arts, and media, 4.0% healthcare practitioners, 15.0% service, 21.3% sales and office, 9.4% natural resources, construction, and maintenance, 27.7% production, transportation, and material moving
Income: Per capita: $24,715; Median household: $53,673; Average household: $62,738; Households with income of $100,000 or more: 16.7%; Poverty rate: 11.2%
Educational Attainment: High school diploma or higher: 89.1%; Bachelor's degree or higher: 16.5%; Graduate/professional degree or higher: 5.5%
Housing: Homeownership rate: 73.1%; Median home value: $124,400; Median year structure built: 1968; Homeowner vacancy rate: 2.6%; Median selected monthly owner costs: $1,141 with a mortgage, $432 without a mortgage; Median gross rent: $687 per month; Rental vacancy rate: 5.0%
Vital Statistics: Birth rate: 96.0 per 10,000 population; Death rate: 103.0 per 10,000 population; Age-adjusted cancer mortality rate: 206.2 deaths per 100,000 population
Health Insurance: 93.1% have insurance; 74.0% have private insurance; 34.4% have public insurance; 6.9% do not have insurance; 3.6% of children under 18 do not have insurance
Health Care: Physicians: 3.1 per 10,000 population; Dentists: 3.4 per 10,000 population; Hospital beds: 6.4 per 10,000 population; Hospital admissions: 250.2 per 10,000 population
Transportation: Commute: 94.2% car, 0.1% public transportation, 2.1% walk, 3.0% work from home; Mean travel time to work: 27.0 minutes
2016 Presidential Election: 69.2% Trump, 25.2% Clinton, 3.2% Johnson, 0.8% Stein
National and State Parks: Cedar Bog State Nature Preserve; Kiser Lake State Park; Siegenthaler-Kaestner Esker State Nature Preserve
Additional Information Contacts
Champaign Government . . . . (937) 484-1611
http://www.co.champaign.oh.us

Champaign County Communities

CABLE (unincorporated postal area)

ZCTA: 43009

Covers a land area of 34.470 square miles and a water area of 0.018 square miles. Located at 40.17° N. Lat; 83.64° W. Long. Elevation is 1,184 feet.
Population: 2,161; Growth (since 2000): 21.7%; Density: 62.7 persons per square mile; Race: 98.9% White, 0.2% Black/African American, 0.1% Asian, 0.0% American Indian/Alaska Native, 0.0% Native Hawaiian/Other Pacific Islander, 0.7% Two or more races, 0.7% Hispanic of any race; Average household size: 2.94; Median age: 37.3; Age under 18: 29.3%; Age 65 and over: 11.5%; Males per 100 females: 102.2; Marriage status:

18.9% never married, 68.8% now married, 0.9% separated, 3.6% widowed, 8.8% divorced; Foreign born: 0.2%; Speak English only: 98.1%; With disability: 11.7%; Veterans: 9.3%; Ancestry: 28.9% German, 25.7% English, 15.5% Irish, 12.4% American, 6.2% French
Employment: 10.8% management, business, and financial, 1.2% computer, engineering, and science, 19.3% education, legal, community service, arts, and media, 4.8% healthcare practitioners, 13.6% service, 20.2% sales and office, 14.5% natural resources, construction, and maintenance, 15.6% production, transportation, and material moving
Income: Per capita: $27,631; Median household: $78,571; Average household: $80,542; Households with income of $100,000 or more: 27.5%; Poverty rate: 5.2%
Educational Attainment: High school diploma or higher: 93.2%; Bachelor's degree or higher: 25.8%; Graduate/professional degree or higher: 6.6%
Housing: Homeownership rate: 87.6%; Median home value: $180,300; Median year structure built: 1992; Homeowner vacancy rate: 0.0%; Median selected monthly owner costs: $1,449 with a mortgage, $448 without a mortgage; Median gross rent: $1,104 per month; Rental vacancy rate: 0.0%
Health Insurance: 94.7% have insurance; 89.9% have private insurance; 17.9% have public insurance; 5.3% do not have insurance; 3.2% of children under 18 do not have insurance
Transportation: Commute: 94.8% car, 0.0% public transportation, 1.6% walk, 1.3% work from home; Mean travel time to work: 27.0 minutes

CHRISTIANSBURG (village). Covers a land area of 0.216 square miles and a water area of 0 square miles. Located at 40.06° N. Lat; 84.03° W. Long. Elevation is 1,115 feet.
Population: 556; Growth (since 2000): 0.5%; Density: 2,574.3 persons per square mile; Race: 97.3% White, 1.3% Black/African American, 0.0% Asian, 0.0% American Indian/Alaska Native, 0.0% Native Hawaiian/Other Pacific Islander, 1.4% Two or more races, 0.0% Hispanic of any race; Average household size: 2.67; Median age: 37.3; Age under 18: 23.7%; Age 65 and over: 18.2%; Males per 100 females: 97.0; Marriage status: 26.8% never married, 54.1% now married, 1.1% separated, 8.1% widowed, 11.0% divorced; Foreign born: 1.8%; Speak English only: 99.3%; With disability: 16.0%; Veterans: 8.3%; Ancestry: 29.1% German, 17.8% Irish, 14.9% American, 9.4% English, 2.9% Northern European
Employment: 2.7% management, business, and financial, 0.0% computer, engineering, and science, 3.6% education, legal, community service, arts, and media, 8.1% healthcare practitioners, 17.2% service, 24.0% sales and office, 20.8% natural resources, construction, and maintenance, 23.5% production, transportation, and material moving
Income: Per capita: $18,403; Median household: $45,000; Average household: $48,118; Households with income of $100,000 or more: 4.3%; Poverty rate: 15.5%
Educational Attainment: High school diploma or higher: 85.6%; Bachelor's degree or higher: 6.4%; Graduate/professional degree or higher: 1.4%
Housing: Homeownership rate: 70.2%; Median home value: $73,900; Median year structure built: Before 1940; Homeowner vacancy rate: 0.0%; Median selected monthly owner costs: $897 with a mortgage, $368 without a mortgage; Median gross rent: $869 per month; Rental vacancy rate: 8.8%
Health Insurance: 87.2% have insurance; 67.3% have private insurance; 33.8% have public insurance; 12.8% do not have insurance; 12.1% of children under 18 do not have insurance
Transportation: Commute: 93.7% car, 0.0% public transportation, 5.4% walk, 0.9% work from home; Mean travel time to work: 28.4 minutes

CONOVER (unincorporated postal area)

ZCTA: 45317

Covers a land area of 24.688 square miles and a water area of 0.004 square miles. Located at 40.21° N. Lat; 83.99° W. Long..
Population: 1,112; Growth (since 2000): 3.2%; Density: 45.0 persons per square mile; Race: 98.6% White, 0.0% Black/African American, 0.0% Asian, 0.0% American Indian/Alaska Native, 0.0% Native Hawaiian/Other Pacific Islander, 1.4% Two or more races, 0.0% Hispanic of any race; Average household size: 3.53; Median age: 31.6; Age under 18: 41.5%; Age 65 and over: 6.3%; Males per 100 females: 108.1; Marriage status: 18.6% never married, 62.8% now married, 0.0% separated, 3.5% widowed, 15.0% divorced; Foreign born: 0.5%; Speak English only: 100.0%; With disability: 11.8%; Veterans: 9.2%; Ancestry: 35.9% German, 14.6% English, 8.5% Irish, 5.1% American, 1.8% French
Employment: 6.4% management, business, and financial, 1.7% computer, engineering, and science, 10.2% education, legal, community service, arts, and media, 17.8% healthcare practitioners, 9.3% service, 15.1% sales and office, 10.8% natural resources, construction, and maintenance, 28.7% production, transportation, and material moving
Income: Per capita: $18,519; Median household: $64,917; Average household: $64,095; Households with income of $100,000 or more: 4.4%; Poverty rate: 2.8%
Educational Attainment: High school diploma or higher: 91.9%; Bachelor's degree or higher: 16.0%; Graduate/professional degree or higher: 7.6%
Housing: Homeownership rate: 80.3%; Median home value: $134,400; Median year structure built: 1955; Homeowner vacancy rate: 9.0%; Median selected monthly owner costs: $1,395 with a mortgage, $490 without a mortgage; Median gross rent: $674 per month; Rental vacancy rate: 0.0%
Health Insurance: 98.4% have insurance; 90.6% have private insurance; 26.2% have public insurance; 1.6% do not have insurance; 1.5% of children under 18 do not have insurance
Transportation: Commute: 93.2% car, 0.0% public transportation, 3.8% walk, 3.0% work from home; Mean travel time to work: 35.9 minutes

MECHANICSBURG (village). Covers a land area of 1.010 square miles and a water area of 0.007 square miles. Located at 40.07° N. Lat; 83.56° W. Long. Elevation is 1,083 feet.
Population: 1,902; Growth (since 2000): 9.1%; Density: 1,884.0 persons per square mile; Race: 94.6% White, 2.4% Black/African American, 0.0% Asian, 0.0% American Indian/Alaska Native, 0.0% Native Hawaiian/Other Pacific Islander, 2.3% Two or more races, 0.9% Hispanic of any race; Average household size: 2.74; Median age: 33.1; Age under 18: 29.2%; Age 65 and over: 10.4%; Males per 100 females: 109.4; Marriage status: 27.1% never married, 47.8% now married, 1.9% separated, 5.6% widowed, 19.5% divorced; Foreign born: 0.0%; Speak English only: 98.2%; With disability: 11.5%; Veterans: 8.4%; Ancestry: 20.2% German, 9.9% Irish, 9.1% American, 7.4% English, 4.5% Dutch
Employment: 14.1% management, business, and financial, 4.3% computer, engineering, and science, 6.2% education, legal, community service, arts, and media, 5.1% healthcare practitioners, 18.7% service, 16.3% sales and office, 11.1% natural resources, construction, and maintenance, 24.2% production, transportation, and material moving
Income: Per capita: $20,201; Median household: $51,750; Average household: $56,645; Households with income of $100,000 or more: 8.5%; Poverty rate: 10.9%
Educational Attainment: High school diploma or higher: 80.2%; Bachelor's degree or higher: 10.7%; Graduate/professional degree or higher: 3.1%

School District(s)

Mechanicsburg Exempted Village (PK-12)
2015-16 Enrollment: 884. . . . . (937) 834-2453
Housing: Homeownership rate: 57.9%; Median home value: $86,200; Median year structure built: Before 1940; Homeowner vacancy rate: 4.5%; Median selected monthly owner costs: $976 with a mortgage, $404 without a mortgage; Median gross rent: $774 per month; Rental vacancy rate: 2.4%
Health Insurance: 84.2% have insurance; 66.2% have private insurance; 29.3% have public insurance; 15.8% do not have insurance; 18.3% of children under 18 do not have insurance
Safety: Violent crime rate: 18.9 per 10,000 population; Property crime rate: 282.8 per 10,000 population
Transportation: Commute: 93.2% car, 0.0% public transportation, 4.8% walk, 1.7% work from home; Mean travel time to work: 29.1 minutes

MUTUAL (village). Covers a land area of 0.133 square miles and a water area of 0 square miles. Located at 40.08° N. Lat; 83.64° W. Long. Elevation is 1,194 feet.
Population: 127; Growth (since 2000): -3.8%; Density: 953.7 persons per square mile; Race: 100.0% White, 0.0% Black/African American, 0.0% Asian, 0.0% American Indian/Alaska Native, 0.0% Native Hawaiian/Other Pacific Islander, 0.0% Two or more races, 0.0% Hispanic of any race; Average household size: 2.70; Median age: 37.7; Age under 18: 34.6%; Age 65 and over: 19.7%; Males per 100 females: 103.9; Marriage status: 4.8% never married, 80.7% now married, 0.0% separated, 7.2% widowed, 7.2% divorced; Foreign born: 0.0%; Speak English only: 100.0%; With disability: 13.4%; Veterans: 8.4%; Ancestry: 32.3% Irish, 12.6% German, 6.3% American, 3.9% English, 2.4% Scottish

Employment: 5.3% management, business, and financial, 1.8% computer, engineering, and science, 14.0% education, legal, community service, arts, and media, 0.0% healthcare practitioners, 10.5% service, 38.6% sales and office, 0.0% natural resources, construction, and maintenance, 29.8% production, transportation, and material moving
Income: Per capita: $23,411; Median household: $61,250; Average household: $66,272; Households with income of $100,000 or more: 12.7%; Poverty rate: 2.4%
Educational Attainment: High school diploma or higher: 82.3%; Bachelor's degree or higher: 16.5%; Graduate/professional degree or higher: 1.3%
Housing: Homeownership rate: 68.1%; Median home value: $135,700; Median year structure built: 1953; Homeowner vacancy rate: 12.2%; Median selected monthly owner costs: $983 with a mortgage, $388 without a mortgage; Median gross rent: $1,200 per month; Rental vacancy rate: 0.0%
Health Insurance: 100.0% have insurance; 87.4% have private insurance; 22.0% have public insurance; 0.0% do not have insurance; 0.0% of children under 18 do not have insurance
Transportation: Commute: 100.0% car, 0.0% public transportation, 0.0% walk, 0.0% work from home; Mean travel time to work: 33.8 minutes

NORTH LEWISBURG (village). Covers a land area of 1.151 square miles and a water area of 0 square miles. Located at 40.22° N. Lat; 83.56° W. Long. Elevation is 1,089 feet.
Population: 1,552; Growth (since 2000): -2.3%; Density: 1,348.9 persons per square mile; Race: 94.9% White, 0.1% Black/African American, 0.0% Asian, 0.7% American Indian/Alaska Native, 0.0% Native Hawaiian/Other Pacific Islander, 2.4% Two or more races, 2.6% Hispanic of any race; Average household size: 2.59; Median age: 34.9; Age under 18: 29.4%; Age 65 and over: 8.5%; Males per 100 females: 101.9; Marriage status: 25.6% never married, 49.5% now married, 1.8% separated, 6.1% widowed, 18.8% divorced; Foreign born: 1.2%; Speak English only: 97.7%; With disability: 14.3%; Veterans: 8.9%; Ancestry: 28.8% German, 16.1% Irish, 10.3% American, 7.9% English, 2.5% Polish
Employment: 6.2% management, business, and financial, 5.2% computer, engineering, and science, 4.0% education, legal, community service, arts, and media, 4.3% healthcare practitioners, 14.4% service, 22.0% sales and office, 6.7% natural resources, construction, and maintenance, 37.2% production, transportation, and material moving
Income: Per capita: $24,253; Median household: $51,346; Average household: $61,938; Households with income of $100,000 or more: 14.6%; Poverty rate: 5.3%
Educational Attainment: High school diploma or higher: 91.4%; Bachelor's degree or higher: 11.3%; Graduate/professional degree or higher: 0.8%

School District(s)

Triad Local (PK-12)
2015-16 Enrollment: 859. . . . . (937) 826-4961
Housing: Homeownership rate: 69.7%; Median home value: $103,900; Median year structure built: 1985; Homeowner vacancy rate: 2.0%; Median selected monthly owner costs: $1,078 with a mortgage, $553 without a mortgage; Median gross rent: $753 per month; Rental vacancy rate: 8.7%
Health Insurance: 88.7% have insurance; 76.0% have private insurance; 20.9% have public insurance; 11.3% do not have insurance; 9.2% of children under 18 do not have insurance
Transportation: Commute: 94.8% car, 0.5% public transportation, 0.9% walk, 2.6% work from home; Mean travel time to work: 22.8 minutes

ROSEWOOD (CDP). Covers a land area of 1.354 square miles and a water area of 0 square miles. Located at 40.22° N. Lat; 83.96° W. Long. Elevation is 1,132 feet.
Population: 431; Growth (since 2000): n/a; Density: 318.2 persons per square mile; Race: 100.0% White, 0.0% Black/African American, 0.0% Asian, 0.0% American Indian/Alaska Native, 0.0% Native Hawaiian/Other Pacific Islander, 0.0% Two or more races, 0.0% Hispanic of any race; Average household size: 4.18; Median age: 24.8; Age under 18: 47.1%; Age 65 and over: 2.8%; Males per 100 females: 116.0; Marriage status: 23.2% never married, 71.5% now married, 0.0% separated, 5.3% widowed, 0.0% divorced; Foreign born: 0.0%; Speak English only: 100.0%; With disability: 10.4%; Veterans: 0.0%; Ancestry: 72.4% German, 14.6% Irish, 10.9% English, 2.8% American
Employment: 0.0% management, business, and financial, 0.0% computer, engineering, and science, 0.0% education, legal, community service, arts, and media, 28.7% healthcare practitioners, 0.0% service, 7.5% sales and office, 38.5% natural resources, construction, and maintenance, 25.3% production, transportation, and material moving
Income: Per capita: $16,758; Median household: $80,613; Average household: $67,985; Households with income of $100,000 or more: 12.6%; Poverty rate: 2.9%
Educational Attainment: High school diploma or higher: 87.7%; Bachelor's degree or higher: n/a; Graduate/professional degree or higher: n/a
Housing: Homeownership rate: 100.0%; Median home value: n/a; Median year structure built: 1961; Homeowner vacancy rate: 0.0%; Median selected monthly owner costs: n/a with a mortgage, $227 without a mortgage; Median gross rent: n/a per month; Rental vacancy rate: 0.0%
Health Insurance: 100.0% have insurance; 87.2% have private insurance; 12.8% have public insurance; 0.0% do not have insurance; 0.0% of children under 18 do not have insurance
Transportation: Commute: 83.3% car, 0.0% public transportation, 0.0% walk, 7.5% work from home; Mean travel time to work: 0.0 minutes

SAINT PARIS (village). Covers a land area of 1.677 square miles and a water area of 0 square miles. Located at 40.13° N. Lat; 83.96° W. Long. Elevation is 1,204 feet.
History: St. Paris was settled in 1813 by David Huffman, when it was called simply Paris.
Population: 2,143; Growth (since 2000): 7.3%; Density: 1,277.7 persons per square mile; Race: 99.1% White, 0.0% Black/African American, 0.2% Asian, 0.0% American Indian/Alaska Native, 0.0% Native Hawaiian/Other Pacific Islander, 0.7% Two or more races, 0.6% Hispanic of any race; Average household size: 2.66; Median age: 40.2; Age under 18: 24.3%; Age 65 and over: 14.8%; Males per 100 females: 91.7; Marriage status: 27.7% never married, 53.3% now married, 0.7% separated, 8.2% widowed, 10.8% divorced; Foreign born: 1.2%; Speak English only: 99.0%; With disability: 14.0%; Veterans: 12.5%; Ancestry: 38.7% German, 12.2% Irish, 6.4% American, 6.3% English, 5.5% Dutch
Employment: 7.1% management, business, and financial, 5.0% computer, engineering, and science, 7.4% education, legal, community service, arts, and media, 1.0% healthcare practitioners, 17.5% service, 28.3% sales and office, 6.9% natural resources, construction, and maintenance, 27.0% production, transportation, and material moving
Income: Per capita: $23,323; Median household: $51,518; Average household: $60,307; Households with income of $100,000 or more: 18.5%; Poverty rate: 10.5%
Educational Attainment: High school diploma or higher: 86.1%; Bachelor's degree or higher: 13.2%; Graduate/professional degree or higher: 3.5%

School District(s)

Graham Local (PK-12)
2015-16 Enrollment: 2,003 . . . . (937) 663-4123
Housing: Homeownership rate: 68.5%; Median home value: $97,400; Median year structure built: 1968; Homeowner vacancy rate: 2.6%; Median selected monthly owner costs: $973 with a mortgage, $417 without a mortgage; Median gross rent: $634 per month; Rental vacancy rate: 6.6%
Health Insurance: 97.7% have insurance; 78.9% have private insurance; 33.1% have public insurance; 2.3% do not have insurance; 2.5% of children under 18 do not have insurance
Safety: Violent crime rate: 0.0 per 10,000 population; Property crime rate: 79.4 per 10,000 population
Transportation: Commute: 95.7% car, 0.0% public transportation, 2.4% walk, 0.6% work from home; Mean travel time to work: 29.3 minutes

URBANA (city). County seat. Covers a land area of 7.753 square miles and a water area of 0.023 square miles. Located at 40.11° N. Lat; 83.75° W. Long. Elevation is 1,050 feet.
History: Urbana was laid out in 1805, and selected in 1812 by General Hull as the site of a training camp. After the war, many of the soldiers who had trained here remained as residents.
Population: 11,586; Growth (since 2000): -0.2%; Density: 1,494.3 persons per square mile; Race: 90.7% White, 4.0% Black/African American, 0.3% Asian, 0.2% American Indian/Alaska Native, 0.2% Native Hawaiian/Other Pacific Islander, 3.6% Two or more races, 3.4% Hispanic of any race; Average household size: 2.24; Median age: 38.8; Age under 18: 23.1%; Age 65 and over: 18.3%; Males per 100 females: 89.1; Marriage status: 31.0% never married, 43.1% now married, 2.7% separated, 10.7% widowed, 15.3% divorced; Foreign born: 1.3%; Speak English only: 97.2%; With disability: 19.3%; Veterans: 7.1%; Ancestry: 21.9% German, 15.6% Irish, 10.0% English, 9.5% American, 2.7% Italian

Employment: 6.4% management, business, and financial, 1.5% computer, engineering, and science, 9.6% education, legal, community service, arts, and media, 4.7% healthcare practitioners, 16.9% service, 21.0% sales and office, 7.7% natural resources, construction, and maintenance, 32.2% production, transportation, and material moving
Income: Per capita: $20,074; Median household: $36,736; Average household: $46,550; Households with income of $100,000 or more: 7.8%; Poverty rate: 20.7%
Educational Attainment: High school diploma or higher: 85.1%; Bachelor's degree or higher: 15.4%; Graduate/professional degree or higher: 5.5%

School District(s)

Urbana City (PK-12)
2015-16 Enrollment: 1,985 . . . . (937) 653-1402
Urbana Community School (06-12)
2015-16 Enrollment: 38. . . . . (937) 653-1402

Four-year College(s)

Urbana University (Private, Not-for-profit)
Fall 2016 Enrollment: 2,235 . . . . (937) 772-9200
2016-17 Tuition: In-state $22,452; Out-of-state $22,452
Housing: Homeownership rate: 53.4%; Median home value: $98,500; Median year structure built: 1957; Homeowner vacancy rate: 5.3%; Median selected monthly owner costs: $962 with a mortgage, $405 without a mortgage; Median gross rent: $645 per month; Rental vacancy rate: 5.7%
Health Insurance: 93.2% have insurance; 65.0% have private insurance; 44.3% have public insurance; 6.8% do not have insurance; 0.0% of children under 18 do not have insurance
Hospitals: Mercy Memorial Hospital (73 beds)
Safety: Violent crime rate: 12.2 per 10,000 population; Property crime rate: 365.8 per 10,000 population
Newspapers: Urbana Daily Citizen (daily circulation 5,600)
Transportation: Commute: 94.7% car, 0.0% public transportation, 3.8% walk, 1.4% work from home; Mean travel time to work: 18.1 minutes
Additional Information Contacts
City of Urbana . . . . (937) 652-4300
http://urbanaohio.com

WOODSTOCK (village). Covers a land area of 0.293 square miles and a water area of 0 square miles. Located at 40.17° N. Lat; 83.53° W. Long. Elevation is 1,043 feet.
Population: 295; Growth (since 2000): -6.9%; Density: 1,008.4 persons per square mile; Race: 99.3% White, 0.0% Black/African American, 0.0% Asian, 0.0% American Indian/Alaska Native, 0.0% Native Hawaiian/Other Pacific Islander, 0.7% Two or more races, 5.4% Hispanic of any race; Average household size: 3.39; Median age: 30.9; Age under 18: 33.9%; Age 65 and over: 8.5%; Males per 100 females: 111.8; Marriage status: 26.9% never married, 54.6% now married, 2.8% separated, 3.2% widowed, 15.3% divorced; Foreign born: 1.0%; Speak English only: 97.4%; With disability: 10.5%; Veterans: 11.3%; Ancestry: 34.9% Irish, 28.5% German, 13.6% English, 10.2% American, 3.1% Dutch
Employment: 13.3% management, business, and financial, 1.6% computer, engineering, and science, 1.6% education, legal, community service, arts, and media, 0.0% healthcare practitioners, 10.9% service, 29.7% sales and office, 12.5% natural resources, construction, and maintenance, 30.5% production, transportation, and material moving
Income: Per capita: $18,501; Median household: $55,313; Average household: $59,444; Households with income of $100,000 or more: 14.9%; Poverty rate: 5.4%
Educational Attainment: High school diploma or higher: 84.9%; Bachelor's degree or higher: 3.9%; Graduate/professional degree or higher: n/a
Housing: Homeownership rate: 78.2%; Median home value: $98,600; Median year structure built: Before 1940; Homeowner vacancy rate: 0.0%; Median selected monthly owner costs: $979 with a mortgage, $494 without a mortgage; Median gross rent: $700 per month; Rental vacancy rate: 17.4%
Health Insurance: 90.5% have insurance; 66.4% have private insurance; 32.5% have public insurance; 9.5% do not have insurance; 2.0% of children under 18 do not have insurance
Transportation: Commute: 100.0% car, 0.0% public transportation, 0.0% walk, 0.0% work from home; Mean travel time to work: 28.7 minutes

Clark County

Located in west central Ohio; crossed by the Mad and Little Miami Rivers. Covers a land area of 397.473 square miles, a water area of 5.054 square miles, and is located in the Eastern Time Zone at 39.92° N. Lat., 83.78° W. Long. The county was founded in 1817. County seat is Springfield.

Clark County is part of the Springfield, OH Metropolitan Statistical Area. The entire metro area includes: Clark County, OH

Weather Station: Springfield New Water Works Elevation: 930 feet

	Jan	Feb	Mar	Apr	May	Jun	Jul	Aug	Sep	Oct	Nov	Dec
High	35	39	49	61	72	80	84	83	77	64	52	39
Low	19	21	29	38	49	59	62	60	52	41	32	23
Precip	2.4	1.8	2.4	3.4	4.7	4.4	4.6	3.3	3.1	2.8	2.9	2.7
Snow	na	2.7	na	tr	0.0	0.0	0.0	0.0	0.0	tr	tr	1.4

High and Low temperatures in degrees Fahrenheit; Precipitation and Snow in inches

Population: 136,175; Growth (since 2000): -5.9%; Density: 342.6 persons per square mile; Race: 86.4% White, 8.2% Black/African American, 0.7% Asian, 0.2% American Indian/Alaska Native, 0.1% Native Hawaiian/Other Pacific Islander, 3.4% two or more races, 3.1% Hispanic of any race; Average household size: 2.43; Median age: 41.2; Age under 18: 22.9%; Age 65 and over: 17.8%; Males per 100 females: 93.9; Marriage status: 28.8% never married, 49.8% now married, 2.1% separated, 7.5% widowed, 13.9% divorced; Foreign born: 2.0%; Speak English only: 96.1%; With disability: 16.5%; Veterans: 12.1%; Ancestry: 23.6% German, 14.9% Irish, 9.1% English, 9.0% American, 3.2% Italian
Religion: Six largest groups: 7.0% Baptist, 6.6% Catholicism, 4.3% Methodist/Pietist, 2.7% Non-denominational Protestant, 2.5% Lutheran, 2.4% Holiness
Economy: Unemployment rate: 4.4%; Leading industries: 16.7 % retail trade; 13.5 % health care and social assistance; 13.4 % other services (except public administration); Farms: 785 totaling 174,337 acres; Company size: 4 employ 1,000 or more persons, 2 employ 500 to 999 persons, 61 employs 100 to 499 persons, 2,214 employ less than 100 persons; Business ownership: 3,107 women-owned, 436 Black-owned, 64 Hispanic-owned, 161 Asian-owned, 48 American Indian/Alaska Native-owned
Employment: 10.3% management, business, and financial, 3.5% computer, engineering, and science, 8.5% education, legal, community service, arts, and media, 6.3% healthcare practitioners, 18.3% service, 23.7% sales and office, 8.4% natural resources, construction, and maintenance, 21.0% production, transportation, and material moving
Income: Per capita: $23,992; Median household: $44,154; Average household: $58,346; Households with income of $100,000 or more: 14.1%; Poverty rate: 17.9%
Educational Attainment: High school diploma or higher: 87.2%; Bachelor's degree or higher: 18.0%; Graduate/professional degree or higher: 6.7%
Housing: Homeownership rate: 65.4%; Median home value: $103,200; Median year structure built: 1960; Homeowner vacancy rate: 1.9%; Median selected monthly owner costs: $1,055 with a mortgage, $392 without a mortgage; Median gross rent: $691 per month; Rental vacancy rate: 5.0%
Vital Statistics: Birth rate: 116.2 per 10,000 population; Death rate: 124.3 per 10,000 population; Age-adjusted cancer mortality rate: 187.9 deaths per 100,000 population
Health Insurance: 91.5% have insurance; 63.7% have private insurance; 43.2% have public insurance; 8.5% do not have insurance; 3.1% of children under 18 do not have insurance
Health Care: Physicians: 14.3 per 10,000 population; Dentists: 4.9 per 10,000 population; Hospital beds: 20.2 per 10,000 population; Hospital admissions: 1,074.7 per 10,000 population
Air Quality Index (AQI): Percent of Days: 73.8% good, 24.6% moderate, 1.6% unhealthy for sensitive individuals, 0.0% unhealthy, 0.0% very unhealthy; Annual median: 42; Annual maximum: 119
Transportation: Commute: 92.1% car, 0.8% public transportation, 2.5% walk, 3.4% work from home; Mean travel time to work: 22.1 minutes
2016 Presidential Election: 56.9% Trump, 37.7% Clinton, 3.1% Johnson, 0.8% Stein
National and State Parks: Buck Creek State Park; Prairie Road Fen State Nature Preserve
Additional Information Contacts
Clark Government . . . . (937) 328-2405
http://www.clarkcountyohio.gov

Clark County Communities

CATAWBA (village). Covers a land area of 0.255 square miles and a water area of 0 square miles. Located at 40.00° N. Lat; 83.62° W. Long. Elevation is 1,234 feet.
Population: 390; Growth (since 2000): 25.0%; Density: 1,527.0 persons per square mile; Race: 100.0% White, 0.0% Black/African American, 0.0% Asian, 0.0% American Indian/Alaska Native, 0.0% Native Hawaiian/Other Pacific Islander, 0.0% Two or more races, 0.0% Hispanic of any race; Average household size: 3.05; Median age: 29.4; Age under 18: 29.2%; Age 65 and over: 17.2%; Males per 100 females: 107.6; Marriage status: 32.5% never married, 48.4% now married, 0.0% separated, 5.3% widowed, 13.8% divorced; Foreign born: 0.0%; Speak English only: 100.0%; With disability: 14.4%; Veterans: 11.2%; Ancestry: 32.8% German, 19.7% English, 16.4% Irish, 6.9% American, 6.7% French
Employment: 6.6% management, business, and financial, 5.1% computer, engineering, and science, 1.5% education, legal, community service, arts, and media, 2.2% healthcare practitioners, 22.8% service, 25.0% sales and office, 10.3% natural resources, construction, and maintenance, 26.5% production, transportation, and material moving
Income: Per capita: $17,503; Median household: $45,000; Average household: $52,360; Households with income of $100,000 or more: 5.5%; Poverty rate: 22.6%
Educational Attainment: High school diploma or higher: 91.1%; Bachelor's degree or higher: 3.8%; Graduate/professional degree or higher: 0.9%
Housing: Homeownership rate: 64.1%; Median home value: $83,700; Median year structure built: Before 1940; Homeowner vacancy rate: 0.0%; Median selected monthly owner costs: $1,038 with a mortgage, $410 without a mortgage; Median gross rent: $775 per month; Rental vacancy rate: 0.0%
Health Insurance: 89.5% have insurance; 56.9% have private insurance; 47.2% have public insurance; 10.5% do not have insurance; 6.1% of children under 18 do not have insurance
Transportation: Commute: 96.0% car, 0.0% public transportation, 1.6% walk, 0.8% work from home; Mean travel time to work: 27.6 minutes

CRYSTAL LAKES (CDP). Covers a land area of 0.474 square miles and a water area of 0.031 square miles. Located at 39.89° N. Lat; 84.02° W. Long. Elevation is 850 feet.
Population: 1,316; Growth (since 2000): -6.7%; Density: 2,776.7 persons per square mile; Race: 95.5% White, 0.0% Black/African American, 0.0% Asian, 0.0% American Indian/Alaska Native, 0.0% Native Hawaiian/Other Pacific Islander, 4.5% Two or more races, 19.8% Hispanic of any race; Average household size: 2.53; Median age: 34.9; Age under 18: 32.1%; Age 65 and over: 10.3%; Males per 100 females: 107.7; Marriage status: 19.0% never married, 60.8% now married, 5.0% separated, 5.3% widowed, 14.8% divorced; Foreign born: 4.4%; Speak English only: 88.9%; With disability: 12.0%; Veterans: 19.0%; Ancestry: 15.3% German, 12.1% American, 11.3% English, 7.9% Irish, 7.6% French
Employment: 5.2% management, business, and financial, 1.7% computer, engineering, and science, 6.7% education, legal, community service, arts, and media, 9.4% healthcare practitioners, 3.7% service, 21.0% sales and office, 15.0% natural resources, construction, and maintenance, 37.3% production, transportation, and material moving
Income: Per capita: $15,507; Median household: $35,735; Average household: $38,490; Households with income of $100,000 or more: 3.3%; Poverty rate: 31.8%
Educational Attainment: High school diploma or higher: 89.5%; Bachelor's degree or higher: 5.9%; Graduate/professional degree or higher: 0.7%
Housing: Homeownership rate: 75.4%; Median home value: $60,000; Median year structure built: 1957; Homeowner vacancy rate: 3.9%; Median selected monthly owner costs: $915 with a mortgage, $384 without a mortgage; Median gross rent: $772 per month; Rental vacancy rate: 0.0%
Health Insurance: 88.8% have insurance; 49.5% have private insurance; 48.4% have public insurance; 11.2% do not have insurance; 0.0% of children under 18 do not have insurance
Transportation: Commute: 94.9% car, 0.0% public transportation, 1.3% walk, 3.9% work from home; Mean travel time to work: 22.9 minutes

DONNELSVILLE (village). Covers a land area of 0.389 square miles and a water area of 0 square miles. Located at 39.92° N. Lat; 83.94° W. Long. Elevation is 928 feet.
Population: 462; Growth (since 2000): 57.7%; Density: 1,187.5 persons per square mile; Race: 99.6% White, 0.0% Black/African American, 0.0% Asian, 0.0% American Indian/Alaska Native, 0.0% Native Hawaiian/Other Pacific Islander, 0.4% Two or more races, 0.9% Hispanic of any race; Average household size: 3.00; Median age: 33.8; Age under 18: 28.4%; Age 65 and over: 6.9%; Males per 100 females: 102.7; Marriage status: 26.2% never married, 57.3% now married, 0.3% separated, 2.8% widowed, 13.7% divorced; Foreign born: 1.1%; Speak English only: 99.1%; With disability: 11.9%; Veterans: 22.1%; Ancestry: 30.5% German, 25.8% Irish, 9.3% American, 4.3% Italian, 4.1% Dutch
Employment: 12.6% management, business, and financial, 10.8% computer, engineering, and science, 11.7% education, legal, community service, arts, and media, 2.7% healthcare practitioners, 23.0% service, 24.3% sales and office, 3.6% natural resources, construction, and maintenance, 11.3% production, transportation, and material moving
Income: Per capita: $23,691; Median household: $55,227; Average household: $67,583; Households with income of $100,000 or more: 24.0%; Poverty rate: 11.3%
Educational Attainment: High school diploma or higher: 93.1%; Bachelor's degree or higher: 23.9%; Graduate/professional degree or higher: 12.0%

School District(s)

Tecumseh Local (KG-12)
2015-16 Enrollment: 2,980 . . . . (937) 845-3576
Housing: Homeownership rate: 66.2%; Median home value: $123,300; Median year structure built: Before 1940; Homeowner vacancy rate: 4.7%; Median selected monthly owner costs: $1,096 with a mortgage, $400 without a mortgage; Median gross rent: $772 per month; Rental vacancy rate: 10.3%
Health Insurance: 91.1% have insurance; 63.6% have private insurance; 35.5% have public insurance; 8.9% do not have insurance; 0.0% of children under 18 do not have insurance
Transportation: Commute: 94.5% car, 0.0% public transportation, 0.0% walk, 4.6% work from home; Mean travel time to work: 22.8 minutes

ENON (village). Covers a land area of 1.276 square miles and a water area of 0 square miles. Located at 39.87° N. Lat; 83.93° W. Long. Elevation is 896 feet.
Population: 2,648; Growth (since 2000): 0.4%; Density: 2,074.6 persons per square mile; Race: 96.6% White, 0.0% Black/African American, 0.9% Asian, 0.8% American Indian/Alaska Native, 0.0% Native Hawaiian/Other Pacific Islander, 1.6% Two or more races, 2.9% Hispanic of any race; Average household size: 2.18; Median age: 51.7; Age under 18: 15.4%; Age 65 and over: 25.3%; Males per 100 females: 94.9; Marriage status: 20.7% never married, 57.8% now married, 1.3% separated, 8.3% widowed, 13.2% divorced; Foreign born: 2.8%; Speak English only: 97.4%; With disability: 21.5%; Veterans: 21.6%; Ancestry: 25.6% German, 17.5% Irish, 9.6% English, 7.0% American, 4.9% Italian
Employment: 13.0% management, business, and financial, 8.3% computer, engineering, and science, 11.3% education, legal, community service, arts, and media, 3.8% healthcare practitioners, 16.6% service, 20.4% sales and office, 6.8% natural resources, construction, and maintenance, 20.0% production, transportation, and material moving
Income: Per capita: $32,358; Median household: $55,795; Average household: $69,539; Households with income of $100,000 or more: 25.8%; Poverty rate: 12.8%
Educational Attainment: High school diploma or higher: 90.5%; Bachelor's degree or higher: 28.9%; Graduate/professional degree or higher: 13.8%

School District(s)

Greenon Local (KG-12)
2015-16 Enrollment: 1,569 . . . . (937) 864-1202
Housing: Homeownership rate: 74.5%; Median home value: $142,700; Median year structure built: 1971; Homeowner vacancy rate: 0.0%; Median selected monthly owner costs: $1,280 with a mortgage, $460 without a mortgage; Median gross rent: $650 per month; Rental vacancy rate: 0.0%
Health Insurance: 94.6% have insurance; 75.2% have private insurance; 41.0% have public insurance; 5.4% do not have insurance; 12.5% of children under 18 do not have insurance
Transportation: Commute: 91.4% car, 1.3% public transportation, 1.6% walk, 5.0% work from home; Mean travel time to work: 21.2 minutes

GREEN MEADOWS (CDP). Covers a land area of 0.798 square miles and a water area of 0 square miles. Located at 39.87° N. Lat; 83.95° W. Long. Elevation is 892 feet.
Population: 2,514; Growth (since 2000): 8.5%; Density: 3,149.8 persons per square mile; Race: 94.8% White, 0.8% Black/African American, 2.0% Asian, 0.4% American Indian/Alaska Native, 0.0% Native Hawaiian/Other Pacific Islander, 2.1% Two or more races, 2.1% Hispanic of any race; Average household size: 2.41; Median age: 42.9; Age under 18: 21.2%; Age 65 and over: 20.4%; Males per 100 females: 96.2; Marriage status: 29.0% never married, 46.4% now married, 0.2% separated, 7.4% widowed, 17.3% divorced; Foreign born: 2.3%; Speak English only: 96.1%; With disability: 17.5%; Veterans: 17.1%; Ancestry: 29.6% German, 20.2% Irish, 12.7% English, 10.9% American, 5.8% Canadian
Employment: 10.6% management, business, and financial, 7.1% computer, engineering, and science, 9.1% education, legal, community service, arts, and media, 0.7% healthcare practitioners, 18.0% service, 18.8% sales and office, 17.1% natural resources, construction, and maintenance, 18.7% production, transportation, and material moving
Income: Per capita: $32,834; Median household: $57,357; Average household: $78,144; Households with income of $100,000 or more: 17.4%; Poverty rate: 3.7%
Educational Attainment: High school diploma or higher: 93.5%; Bachelor's degree or higher: 18.2%; Graduate/professional degree or higher: 5.3%
Housing: Homeownership rate: 82.0%; Median home value: $108,300; Median year structure built: 1965; Homeowner vacancy rate: 0.0%; Median selected monthly owner costs: $1,034 with a mortgage, $413 without a mortgage; Median gross rent: $740 per month; Rental vacancy rate: 8.7%
Health Insurance: 90.2% have insurance; 72.0% have private insurance; 38.1% have public insurance; 9.8% do not have insurance; 4.3% of children under 18 do not have insurance
Transportation: Commute: 92.5% car, 0.0% public transportation, 1.4% walk, 6.1% work from home; Mean travel time to work: 25.2 minutes

HOLIDAY VALLEY (CDP). Covers a land area of 1.820 square miles and a water area of 0 square miles. Located at 39.85° N. Lat; 83.96° W. Long. Elevation is 866 feet.
Population: 1,379; Growth (since 2000): -19.5%; Density: 757.6 persons per square mile; Race: 95.9% White, 1.2% Black/African American, 0.0% Asian, 0.0% American Indian/Alaska Native, 0.0% Native Hawaiian/Other Pacific Islander, 2.3% Two or more races, 2.2% Hispanic of any race; Average household size: 2.54; Median age: 45.0; Age under 18: 18.7%; Age 65 and over: 22.7%; Males per 100 females: 90.2; Marriage status: 15.7% never married, 64.1% now married, 1.8% separated, 8.6% widowed, 11.6% divorced; Foreign born: 0.0%; Speak English only: 97.8%; With disability: 8.5%; Veterans: 18.0%; Ancestry: 28.1% German, 21.5% Irish, 14.6% English, 7.2% American, 5.4% Polish
Employment: 14.3% management, business, and financial, 10.4% computer, engineering, and science, 9.4% education, legal, community service, arts, and media, 10.5% healthcare practitioners, 6.1% service, 22.7% sales and office, 5.1% natural resources, construction, and maintenance, 21.6% production, transportation, and material moving
Income: Per capita: $32,396; Median household: $75,652; Average household: $82,985; Households with income of $100,000 or more: 19.9%; Poverty rate: 0.5%
Educational Attainment: High school diploma or higher: 91.2%; Bachelor's degree or higher: 27.4%; Graduate/professional degree or higher: 11.9%
Housing: Homeownership rate: 85.4%; Median home value: $119,900; Median year structure built: 1973; Homeowner vacancy rate: 0.0%; Median selected monthly owner costs: $1,181 with a mortgage, $417 without a mortgage; Median gross rent: n/a per month; Rental vacancy rate: 0.0%
Health Insurance: 96.0% have insurance; 85.1% have private insurance; 29.1% have public insurance; 4.0% do not have insurance; 4.7% of children under 18 do not have insurance
Transportation: Commute: 98.8% car, 1.2% public transportation, 0.0% walk, 0.0% work from home; Mean travel time to work: 21.6 minutes

MEDWAY (unincorporated postal area)

ZCTA: 45341

Covers a land area of 6.062 square miles and a water area of 0.364 square miles. Located at 39.88° N. Lat; 84.02° W. Long. Elevation is 846 feet.
Population: 3,748; Growth (since 2000): -8.8%; Density: 618.3 persons per square mile; Race: 91.4% White, 0.0% Black/African American, 0.0% Asian, 2.0% American Indian/Alaska Native, 0.0% Native Hawaiian/Other Pacific Islander, 2.9% Two or more races, 14.4% Hispanic of any race; Average household size: 2.41; Median age: 43.8; Age under 18: 23.2%; Age 65 and over: 22.7%; Males per 100 females: 103.0; Marriage status: 20.6% never married, 56.7% now married, 2.5% separated, 6.0% widowed, 16.6% divorced; Foreign born: 2.3%; Speak English only: 92.7%; With disability: 14.9%; Veterans: 17.6%; Ancestry: 23.6% German, 12.0% English, 11.6% Irish, 9.8% American, 5.9% French
Employment: 11.8% management, business, and financial, 5.8% computer, engineering, and science, 4.8% education, legal, community service, arts, and media, 7.9% healthcare practitioners, 7.3% service, 27.1% sales and office, 12.3% natural resources, construction, and maintenance, 23.0% production, transportation, and material moving
Income: Per capita: $21,380; Median household: $42,127; Average household: $51,387; Households with income of $100,000 or more: 10.2%; Poverty rate: 17.6%
Educational Attainment: High school diploma or higher: 87.2%; Bachelor's degree or higher: 12.8%; Graduate/professional degree or higher: 4.2%

School District(s)

Tecumseh Local (KG-12)
2015-16 Enrollment: 2,980 . . . . (937) 845-3576
Housing: Homeownership rate: 79.8%; Median home value: $75,500; Median year structure built: 1963; Homeowner vacancy rate: 1.7%; Median selected monthly owner costs: $1,024 with a mortgage, $382 without a mortgage; Median gross rent: $712 per month; Rental vacancy rate: 0.0%
Health Insurance: 91.7% have insurance; 66.9% have private insurance; 44.4% have public insurance; 8.3% do not have insurance; 7.5% of children under 18 do not have insurance
Transportation: Commute: 94.0% car, 0.0% public transportation, 0.4% walk, 3.1% work from home; Mean travel time to work: 23.8 minutes

NEW CARLISLE (city). Covers a land area of 2.738 square miles and a water area of 0.016 square miles. Located at 39.95° N. Lat; 84.03° W. Long. Elevation is 899 feet.
History: Founded 1810.
Population: 5,690; Growth (since 2000): -0.8%; Density: 2,078.4 persons per square mile; Race: 95.1% White, 0.0% Black/African American, 0.1% Asian, 0.1% American Indian/Alaska Native, 0.0% Native Hawaiian/Other Pacific Islander, 1.2% Two or more races, 19.1% Hispanic of any race; Average household size: 2.68; Median age: 35.9; Age under 18: 29.3%; Age 65 and over: 14.8%; Males per 100 females: 91.2; Marriage status: 26.4% never married, 44.3% now married, 1.1% separated, 8.5% widowed, 20.8% divorced; Foreign born: 9.3%; Speak English only: 82.8%; With disability: 14.8%; Veterans: 10.2%; Ancestry: 21.9% German, 10.3% Irish, 8.0% American, 7.6% English, 4.5% Italian
Employment: 7.3% management, business, and financial, 4.0% computer, engineering, and science, 4.0% education, legal, community service, arts, and media, 4.2% healthcare practitioners, 20.4% service, 20.7% sales and office, 15.5% natural resources, construction, and maintenance, 23.9% production, transportation, and material moving
Income: Per capita: $16,556; Median household: $37,798; Average household: $43,475; Households with income of $100,000 or more: 7.5%; Poverty rate: 20.8%
Educational Attainment: High school diploma or higher: 80.8%; Bachelor's degree or higher: 11.8%; Graduate/professional degree or higher: 1.9%

School District(s)

Tecumseh Local (KG-12)
2015-16 Enrollment: 2,980 . . . . (937) 845-3576
Housing: Homeownership rate: 62.7%; Median home value: $90,800; Median year structure built: 1964; Homeowner vacancy rate: 6.4%; Median selected monthly owner costs: $895 with a mortgage, $332 without a mortgage; Median gross rent: $792 per month; Rental vacancy rate: 6.3%
Health Insurance: 81.3% have insurance; 48.3% have private insurance; 44.9% have public insurance; 18.7% do not have insurance; 15.2% of children under 18 do not have insurance
Transportation: Commute: 93.4% car, 0.0% public transportation, 4.6% walk, 1.1% work from home; Mean travel time to work: 24.1 minutes

NORTH HAMPTON (village). Covers a land area of 0.432 square miles and a water area of 0 square miles. Located at 39.99° N. Lat; 83.94° W. Long. Elevation is 1,096 feet.
Population: 426; Growth (since 2000): 15.1%; Density: 986.8 persons per square mile; Race: 96.7% White, 0.9% Black/African American, 0.5%

Asian, 0.0% American Indian/Alaska Native, 0.0% Native Hawaiian/Other Pacific Islander, 1.6% Two or more races, 0.5% Hispanic of any race; Average household size: 2.61; Median age: 42.5; Age under 18: 25.4%; Age 65 and over: 19.5%; Males per 100 females: 93.5; Marriage status: 27.6% never married, 55.6% now married, 0.0% separated, 7.5% widowed, 9.3% divorced; Foreign born: 0.5%; Speak English only: 98.3%; With disability: 13.2%; Veterans: 12.0%; Ancestry: 35.4% German, 14.6% American, 13.6% Irish, 8.7% English, 3.3% Dutch
Employment: 7.8% management, business, and financial, 3.2% computer, engineering, and science, 0.9% education, legal, community service, arts, and media, 2.3% healthcare practitioners, 22.0% service, 31.7% sales and office, 16.1% natural resources, construction, and maintenance, 16.1% production, transportation, and material moving
Income: Per capita: $28,493; Median household: $51,458; Average household: $71,751; Households with income of $100,000 or more: 11.7%; Poverty rate: 4.8%
Educational Attainment: High school diploma or higher: 91.3%; Bachelor's degree or higher: 14.2%; Graduate/professional degree or higher: 4.0%
Housing: Homeownership rate: 65.6%; Median home value: $107,100; Median year structure built: Before 1940; Homeowner vacancy rate: 0.0%; Median selected monthly owner costs: $1,159 with a mortgage, $441 without a mortgage; Median gross rent: $827 per month; Rental vacancy rate: 7.8%
Health Insurance: 92.7% have insurance; 69.4% have private insurance; 40.0% have public insurance; 7.3% do not have insurance; 7.4% of children under 18 do not have insurance
Transportation: Commute: 94.9% car, 0.0% public transportation, 0.0% walk, 3.7% work from home; Mean travel time to work: 23.4 minutes

NORTHRIDGE (CDP). Covers a land area of 3.051 square miles and a water area of 0 square miles. Located at 40.00° N. Lat; 83.78° W. Long. Elevation is 1,079 feet.
Population: 7,188; Growth (since 2000): 4.9%; Density: 2,356.0 persons per square mile; Race: 96.0% White, 0.2% Black/African American, 1.5% Asian, 0.2% American Indian/Alaska Native, 0.0% Native Hawaiian/Other Pacific Islander, 2.2% Two or more races, 0.4% Hispanic of any race; Average household size: 2.24; Median age: 46.7; Age under 18: 20.7%; Age 65 and over: 23.8%; Males per 100 females: 89.4; Marriage status: 21.7% never married, 57.4% now married, 1.3% separated, 7.6% widowed, 13.4% divorced; Foreign born: 1.7%; Speak English only: 96.6%; With disability: 16.3%; Veterans: 17.7%; Ancestry: 21.5% German, 18.7% Irish, 11.3% American, 9.1% English, 5.6% Italian
Employment: 9.2% management, business, and financial, 3.3% computer, engineering, and science, 10.6% education, legal, community service, arts, and media, 9.0% healthcare practitioners, 13.9% service, 24.8% sales and office, 7.4% natural resources, construction, and maintenance, 21.8% production, transportation, and material moving
Income: Per capita: $28,531; Median household: $56,986; Average household: $63,098; Households with income of $100,000 or more: 14.2%; Poverty rate: 4.8%
Educational Attainment: High school diploma or higher: 94.3%; Bachelor's degree or higher: 23.4%; Graduate/professional degree or higher: 5.7%
Housing: Homeownership rate: 80.1%; Median home value: $120,300; Median year structure built: 1973; Homeowner vacancy rate: 0.4%; Median selected monthly owner costs: $1,062 with a mortgage, $384 without a mortgage; Median gross rent: $678 per month; Rental vacancy rate: 0.0%
Health Insurance: 95.1% have insurance; 82.8% have private insurance; 35.1% have public insurance; 4.9% do not have insurance; 2.3% of children under 18 do not have insurance
Transportation: Commute: 98.0% car, 0.3% public transportation, 0.0% walk, 1.7% work from home; Mean travel time to work: 24.3 minutes

PARK LAYNE (CDP). Covers a land area of 1.465 square miles and a water area of 0 square miles. Located at 39.89° N. Lat; 84.04° W. Long. Elevation is 840 feet.
Population: 4,481; Growth (since 2000): -0.8%; Density: 3,059.6 persons per square mile; Race: 93.2% White, 0.7% Black/African American, 0.3% Asian, 2.2% American Indian/Alaska Native, 0.0% Native Hawaiian/Other Pacific Islander, 2.9% Two or more races, 2.9% Hispanic of any race; Average household size: 2.92; Median age: 33.9; Age under 18: 29.4%; Age 65 and over: 10.8%; Males per 100 females: 97.1; Marriage status: 27.0% never married, 56.2% now married, 3.7% separated, 7.1% widowed, 9.7% divorced; Foreign born: 0.8%; Speak English only: 98.5%; With disability: 12.6%; Veterans: 10.9%; Ancestry: 24.7% German, 19.1% Irish, 11.4% American, 9.1% English, 5.1% Dutch
Employment: 4.0% management, business, and financial, 4.3% computer, engineering, and science, 1.9% education, legal, community service, arts, and media, 4.7% healthcare practitioners, 24.0% service, 30.9% sales and office, 9.5% natural resources, construction, and maintenance, 20.6% production, transportation, and material moving
Income: Per capita: $18,132; Median household: $43,586; Average household: $52,369; Households with income of $100,000 or more: 13.1%; Poverty rate: 16.6%
Educational Attainment: High school diploma or higher: 79.8%; Bachelor's degree or higher: 7.5%; Graduate/professional degree or higher: 0.6%
Housing: Homeownership rate: 68.8%; Median home value: $73,600; Median year structure built: 1964; Homeowner vacancy rate: 0.0%; Median selected monthly owner costs: $885 with a mortgage, $334 without a mortgage; Median gross rent: $716 per month; Rental vacancy rate: 0.0%
Health Insurance: 90.4% have insurance; 56.7% have private insurance; 41.3% have public insurance; 9.6% do not have insurance; 1.6% of children under 18 do not have insurance
Transportation: Commute: 92.5% car, 0.0% public transportation, 3.6% walk, 0.7% work from home; Mean travel time to work: 22.2 minutes

SOUTH CHARLESTON (village). Covers a land area of 1.284 square miles and a water area of <.001 square miles. Located at 39.82° N. Lat; 83.64° W. Long. Elevation is 1,129 feet.
History: South Charleston developed as a rural distributing center.
Population: 1,879; Growth (since 2000): 1.6%; Density: 1,463.6 persons per square mile; Race: 96.6% White, 0.0% Black/African American, 0.0% Asian, 0.0% American Indian/Alaska Native, 0.2% Native Hawaiian/Other Pacific Islander, 1.5% Two or more races, 1.9% Hispanic of any race; Average household size: 2.52; Median age: 34.2; Age under 18: 27.4%; Age 65 and over: 13.8%; Males per 100 females: 90.7; Marriage status: 22.9% never married, 54.8% now married, 2.0% separated, 7.6% widowed, 14.6% divorced; Foreign born: 1.8%; Speak English only: 97.8%; With disability: 17.8%; Veterans: 8.2%; Ancestry: 29.0% German, 18.5% Irish, 12.2% English, 7.6% American, 3.4% French
Employment: 8.5% management, business, and financial, 2.9% computer, engineering, and science, 5.0% education, legal, community service, arts, and media, 5.9% healthcare practitioners, 19.7% service, 23.9% sales and office, 5.1% natural resources, construction, and maintenance, 29.0% production, transportation, and material moving
Income: Per capita: $18,908; Median household: $35,375; Average household: $47,129; Households with income of $100,000 or more: 6.3%; Poverty rate: 18.7%
Educational Attainment: High school diploma or higher: 87.6%; Bachelor's degree or higher: 16.9%; Graduate/professional degree or higher: 5.6%

School District(s)

Southeastern Local (KG-12)
2015-16 Enrollment: 706. . . . . (888) 627-6745
Housing: Homeownership rate: 51.8%; Median home value: $97,800; Median year structure built: 1958; Homeowner vacancy rate: 0.0%; Median selected monthly owner costs: $932 with a mortgage, $363 without a mortgage; Median gross rent: $585 per month; Rental vacancy rate: 3.0%
Health Insurance: 90.8% have insurance; 63.6% have private insurance; 41.1% have public insurance; 9.2% do not have insurance; 0.0% of children under 18 do not have insurance
Safety: Violent crime rate: 12.1 per 10,000 population; Property crime rate: 139.0 per 10,000 population
Transportation: Commute: 90.5% car, 0.0% public transportation, 3.7% walk, 4.4% work from home; Mean travel time to work: 22.5 minutes

SOUTH VIENNA (village). Covers a land area of 0.523 square miles and a water area of 0 square miles. Located at 39.93° N. Lat; 83.61° W. Long. Elevation is 1,191 feet.
Population: 406; Growth (since 2000): -13.4%; Density: 776.4 persons per square mile; Race: 100.0% White, 0.0% Black/African American, 0.0% Asian, 0.0% American Indian/Alaska Native, 0.0% Native Hawaiian/Other Pacific Islander, 0.0% Two or more races, 2.0% Hispanic of any race; Average household size: 2.52; Median age: 42.8; Age under 18: 15.3%; Age 65 and over: 14.3%; Males per 100 females: 93.9; Marriage status: 31.9% never married, 51.5% now married, 1.1% separated, 4.4% widowed, 12.3% divorced; Foreign born: 0.0%; Speak English only: 96.0%;

With disability: 13.1%; Veterans: 9.3%; Ancestry: 41.4% German, 28.3% Irish, 15.5% English, 8.6% French, 6.2% Scottish
Employment: 9.0% management, business, and financial, 2.0% computer, engineering, and science, 5.3% education, legal, community service, arts, and media, 4.5% healthcare practitioners, 20.0% service, 22.0% sales and office, 19.2% natural resources, construction, and maintenance, 18.0% production, transportation, and material moving
Income: Per capita: $26,490; Median household: $60,074; Average household: $65,767; Households with income of $100,000 or more: 17.3%; Poverty rate: 6.2%
Educational Attainment: High school diploma or higher: 94.3%; Bachelor's degree or higher: 14.5%; Graduate/professional degree or higher: 5.7%

School District(s)

Northeastern Local (PK-12)
2015-16 Enrollment: 3,369 . . . . (937) 325-7615
Housing: Homeownership rate: 70.2%; Median home value: $92,100; Median year structure built: Before 1940; Homeowner vacancy rate: 0.0%; Median selected monthly owner costs: $926 with a mortgage, $343 without a mortgage; Median gross rent: $807 per month; Rental vacancy rate: 5.9%
Health Insurance: 90.6% have insurance; 77.3% have private insurance; 25.6% have public insurance; 9.4% do not have insurance; 0.0% of children under 18 do not have insurance
Transportation: Commute: 97.0% car, 0.0% public transportation, 2.1% walk, 0.8% work from home; Mean travel time to work: 24.7 minutes

SPRINGFIELD (city). County seat. Covers a land area of 25.294 square miles and a water area of 0.205 square miles. Located at 39.93° N. Lat; 83.80° W. Long. Elevation is 974 feet.
History: Springfield's first settler was James Demint, who came in 1799. Surveyor John Daugherty platted a town in 1801. The settlement was called Springfield for the spring water coming down the cliffs that bordered the valley of Buck Creek. Simon Kenton from Kentucky set up a gristmill and sawmill on the site that was later the International Harvester plant. The National Road, completed in 1838, put Springfield on the route of the Ohio Stage Company and provided a means for the area's produce to get to a market. In the 1850's the Champion Binder Company was producing farm machinery here, its facility later purchased by the McCormick interests, which were subsequently acquired by International Harvester Company.
Population: 59,761; Growth (since 2000): -8.6%; Density: 2,362.6 persons per square mile; Race: 74.7% White, 17.4% Black/African American, 0.6% Asian, 0.2% American Indian/Alaska Native, 0.0% Native Hawaiian/Other Pacific Islander, 5.6% Two or more races, 3.1% Hispanic of any race; Average household size: 2.32; Median age: 36.7; Age under 18: 23.9%; Age 65 and over: 16.2%; Males per 100 females: 90.9; Marriage status: 36.4% never married, 38.6% now married, 3.1% separated, 8.8% widowed, 16.1% divorced; Foreign born: 1.7%; Speak English only: 95.7%; With disability: 18.5%; Veterans: 10.0%; Ancestry: 19.9% German, 13.4% Irish, 7.1% English, 6.8% American, 3.1% Italian
Employment: 9.2% management, business, and financial, 2.1% computer, engineering, and science, 8.9% education, legal, community service, arts, and media, 4.5% healthcare practitioners, 23.4% service, 23.8% sales and office, 5.7% natural resources, construction, and maintenance, 22.3% production, transportation, and material moving
Income: Per capita: $19,608; Median household: $32,165; Average household: $45,891; Households with income of $100,000 or more: 7.8%; Poverty rate: 27.9%
Educational Attainment: High school diploma or higher: 83.1%; Bachelor's degree or higher: 14.9%; Graduate/professional degree or higher: 5.5%

School District(s)

Clark-Shawnee Local (PK-12)
2015-16 Enrollment: 1,966 . . . . (937) 328-5378
Cliff Park High School (09-12)
2015-16 Enrollment: 151. . . . . (937) 342-3006
Greenon Local (KG-12)
2015-16 Enrollment: 1,569 . . . . (937) 864-1202
Northeastern Local (PK-12)
2015-16 Enrollment: 3,369 . . . . (937) 325-7615
Northwestern Local (PK-12)
2015-16 Enrollment: 1,747 . . . . (937) 964-1318
Springfield Academy of Excellence
2015-16 Enrollment: n/a . . . . (937) 325-0933
Springfield City School District (PK-12)
2015-16 Enrollment: 7,809 . . . . (937) 505-2800
Springfield Preparatory and Fitness Academy (KG-08)
2015-16 Enrollment: 178. . . . . (937) 323-6250
Springfield-Clark County (07-12)
2015-16 Enrollment: n/a . . . . (937) 325-7368

Four-year College(s)

Wittenberg University (Private, Not-for-profit, Lutheran Church in America)
Fall 2016 Enrollment: 1,988 . . . . (937) 327-6231
2016-17 Tuition: In-state $38,090; Out-of-state $38,090

Two-year College(s)

Clark State Community College (Public)
Fall 2016 Enrollment: 5,915 . . . . (937) 325-0691
2016-17 Tuition: In-state $3,359; Out-of-state $6,271
Housing: Homeownership rate: 47.8%; Median home value: $77,000; Median year structure built: 1950; Homeowner vacancy rate: 3.4%; Median selected monthly owner costs: $871 with a mortgage, $338 without a mortgage; Median gross rent: $675 per month; Rental vacancy rate: 4.8%
Health Insurance: 90.5% have insurance; 53.1% have private insurance; 51.3% have public insurance; 9.5% do not have insurance; 1.6% of children under 18 do not have insurance
Hospitals: Ohio Valley Medical Center; Springfield Regional Medical Center (324 beds)
Safety: Violent crime rate: 69.1 per 10,000 population; Property crime rate: 679.0 per 10,000 population
Newspapers: Springfield News-Sun (daily circulation 25,700)
Transportation: Commute: 89.9% car, 1.5% public transportation, 4.7% walk, 2.8% work from home; Mean travel time to work: 19.5 minutes
Airports: Springfield-Beckley Municipal (general aviation)
Additional Information Contacts
City of Springfield . . . . (937) 324-7700
http://www.ci.springfield.oh.us

TREMONT CITY (village). Covers a land area of 0.256 square miles and a water area of 0 square miles. Located at 40.02° N. Lat; 83.84° W. Long. Elevation is 955 feet.
Population: 368; Growth (since 2000): 5.4%; Density: 1,436.0 persons per square mile; Race: 96.7% White, 0.0% Black/African American, 0.0% Asian, 0.0% American Indian/Alaska Native, 0.0% Native Hawaiian/Other Pacific Islander, 3.3% Two or more races, 0.5% Hispanic of any race; Average household size: 2.45; Median age: 37.1; Age under 18: 23.9%; Age 65 and over: 14.7%; Males per 100 females: 108.3; Marriage status: 36.2% never married, 46.5% now married, 1.0% separated, 3.7% widowed, 13.6% divorced; Foreign born: 0.0%; Speak English only: 98.9%; With disability: 13.6%; Veterans: 15.4%; Ancestry: 38.9% German, 17.9% Irish, 9.0% American, 8.2% Polish, 7.6% English
Employment: 9.5% management, business, and financial, 3.7% computer, engineering, and science, 7.4% education, legal, community service, arts, and media, 5.3% healthcare practitioners, 24.9% service, 19.0% sales and office, 4.8% natural resources, construction, and maintenance, 25.4% production, transportation, and material moving
Income: Per capita: $23,441; Median household: $42,500; Average household: $55,209; Households with income of $100,000 or more: 12.0%; Poverty rate: 12.0%
Educational Attainment: High school diploma or higher: 91.6%; Bachelor's degree or higher: 10.1%; Graduate/professional degree or higher: 1.7%
Housing: Homeownership rate: 61.3%; Median home value: $83,500; Median year structure built: Before 1940; Homeowner vacancy rate: 0.0%; Median selected monthly owner costs: $868 with a mortgage, $368 without a mortgage; Median gross rent: $691 per month; Rental vacancy rate: 7.9%
Health Insurance: 88.6% have insurance; 67.1% have private insurance; 35.3% have public insurance; 11.4% do not have insurance; 15.9% of children under 18 do not have insurance
Transportation: Commute: 95.7% car, 0.5% public transportation, 0.5% walk, 1.6% work from home; Mean travel time to work: 24.6 minutes

Clermont County

Located in southwestern Ohio; bounded on the southwest by the Ohio River and the Kentucky border, and on the northwest by the Little Miami River. Covers a land area of 452.100 square miles, a water area of 7.666 square miles, and is located in the Eastern Time Zone at 39.05° N. Lat., 84.15° W. Long. The county was founded in 1800. County seat is Batavia.

Clermont County is part of the Cincinnati, OH-KY-IN Metropolitan Statistical Area. The entire metro area includes: Dearborn County, IN; Ohio County, IN; Union County, IN; Boone County, KY; Bracken County, KY; Campbell County, KY; Gallatin County, KY; Grant County, KY; Kenton County, KY; Pendleton County, KY; Brown County, OH; Butler County, OH; Clermont County, OH; Hamilton County, OH; Warren County, OH

Weather Station: Chilo Meldahl L&D Elevation: 500 feet

	Jan	Feb	Mar	Apr	May	Jun	Jul	Aug	Sep	Oct	Nov	Dec
High	40	44	54	65	74	82	86	86	80	68	56	44
Low	23	24	32	42	51	60	65	64	56	45	36	27
Precip	2.9	2.8	4.3	3.4	4.6	3.6	3.9	3.2	2.8	3.1	2.9	3.0
Snow	0.6	na	0.7	0.0	0.0	0.0	0.0	0.0	0.0	0.0	tr	1.4

High and Low temperatures in degrees Fahrenheit; Precipitation and Snow in inches

Weather Station: Milford Elevation: 520 feet

	Jan	Feb	Mar	Apr	May	Jun	Jul	Aug	Sep	Oct	Nov	Dec
High	38	43	53	65	75	83	87	86	79	68	55	43
Low	20	23	30	40	50	59	63	62	53	41	33	25
Precip	3.1	2.6	3.7	4.1	5.6	4.4	4.3	4.1	3.0	3.0	3.6	3.3
Snow	na	4.5	1.3	0.3	tr	0.0	0.0	tr	0.0	0.2	0.1	2.6

High and Low temperatures in degrees Fahrenheit; Precipitation and Snow in inches

Population: 201,092; Growth (since 2000): 13.0%; Density: 444.8 persons per square mile; Race: 95.4% White, 1.3% Black/African American, 1.1% Asian, 0.2% American Indian/Alaska Native, 0.0% Native Hawaiian/Other Pacific Islander, 1.6% two or more races, 1.7% Hispanic of any race; Average household size: 2.65; Median age: 39.7; Age under 18: 24.3%; Age 65 and over: 14.0%; Males per 100 females: 97.3; Marriage status: 26.3% never married, 57.1% now married, 1.7% separated, 5.5% widowed, 11.1% divorced; Foreign born: 2.1%; Speak English only: 97.0%; With disability: 12.8%; Veterans: 9.3%; Ancestry: 27.0% German, 22.2% American, 13.0% Irish, 9.7% English, 3.5% Italian
Religion: Six largest groups: 15.9% Catholicism, 8.0% Baptist, 5.1% Methodist/Pietist, 3.3% Non-denominational Protestant, 1.7% Pentecostal, 0.9% Holiness
Economy: Unemployment rate: 4.1%; Leading industries: 14.9 % retail trade; 12.0 % construction; 10.4 % other services (except public administration); Farms: 822 totaling 121,125 acres; Company size: 1 employs 1,000 or more persons, 5 employ 500 to 999 persons, 79 employ 100 to 499 persons, 3,501 employs less than 100 persons; Business ownership: 4,029 women-owned, 136 Black-owned, 130 Hispanic-owned, 242 Asian-owned, 45 American Indian/Alaska Native-owned
Employment: 15.0% management, business, and financial, 5.6% computer, engineering, and science, 9.0% education, legal, community service, arts, and media, 6.0% healthcare practitioners, 15.8% service, 25.8% sales and office, 9.2% natural resources, construction, and maintenance, 13.6% production, transportation, and material moving
Income: Per capita: $30,060; Median household: $61,265; Average household: $78,529; Households with income of $100,000 or more: 26.4%; Poverty rate: 10.5%
Educational Attainment: High school diploma or higher: 89.6%; Bachelor's degree or higher: 27.6%; Graduate/professional degree or higher: 9.2%
Housing: Homeownership rate: 73.6%; Median home value: $159,100; Median year structure built: 1983; Homeowner vacancy rate: 1.9%; Median selected monthly owner costs: $1,374 with a mortgage, $474 without a mortgage; Median gross rent: $774 per month; Rental vacancy rate: 7.0%
Vital Statistics: Birth rate: 112.5 per 10,000 population; Death rate: 84.6 per 10,000 population; Age-adjusted cancer mortality rate: 175.8 deaths per 100,000 population
Health Insurance: 92.7% have insurance; 74.1% have private insurance; 29.2% have public insurance; 7.3% do not have insurance; 3.3% of children under 18 do not have insurance
Health Care: Physicians: 21.5 per 10,000 population; Dentists: 3.8 per 10,000 population; Hospital beds: 5.9 per 10,000 population; Hospital admissions: 275.7 per 10,000 population
Air Quality Index (AQI): Percent of Days: 66.1% good, 32.5% moderate, 1.4% unhealthy for sensitive individuals, 0.0% unhealthy, 0.0% very unhealthy; Annual median: 44; Annual maximum: 133
Transportation: Commute: 93.0% car, 0.6% public transportation, 0.9% walk, 4.7% work from home; Mean travel time to work: 27.8 minutes
2016 Presidential Election: 67.5% Trump, 26.7% Clinton, 3.5% Johnson, 0.7% Stein
National and State Parks: East Fork State Park; East Fork Tailwater State Wildlife Area; Stonelick Lake State Park

Additional Information Contacts
Clermont Government. . . . . (513) 732-7300
http://www.clermontcountyohio.gov

Clermont County Communities

AMELIA (village). Covers a land area of 1.791 square miles and a water area of 0 square miles. Located at 39.02° N. Lat; 84.22° W. Long. Elevation is 876 feet.
Population: 5,132; Growth (since 2000): 86.5%; Density: 2,865.4 persons per square mile; Race: 95.8% White, 0.3% Black/African American, 1.3% Asian, 0.8% American Indian/Alaska Native, 1.0% Native Hawaiian/Other Pacific Islander, 0.9% Two or more races, 0.0% Hispanic of any race; Average household size: 2.81; Median age: 32.1; Age under 18: 30.2%; Age 65 and over: 6.8%; Males per 100 females: 94.1; Marriage status: 26.6% never married, 55.7% now married, 0.4% separated, 5.0% widowed, 12.8% divorced; Foreign born: 2.8%; Speak English only: 96.6%; With disability: 14.0%; Veterans: 10.2%; Ancestry: 23.5% American, 20.0% German, 14.2% Irish, 8.2% English, 3.0% Italian
Employment: 8.5% management, business, and financial, 6.9% computer, engineering, and science, 8.3% education, legal, community service, arts, and media, 3.7% healthcare practitioners, 17.2% service, 27.7% sales and office, 15.2% natural resources, construction, and maintenance, 12.3% production, transportation, and material moving
Income: Per capita: $21,658; Median household: $52,628; Average household: $58,719; Households with income of $100,000 or more: 19.7%; Poverty rate: 13.0%
Educational Attainment: High school diploma or higher: 86.7%; Bachelor's degree or higher: 15.0%; Graduate/professional degree or higher: 2.4%

School District(s)

West Clermont Local (PK-12)
2015-16 Enrollment: 8,027 . . . . (513) 943-5000
Housing: Homeownership rate: 59.7%; Median home value: $141,200; Median year structure built: 1997; Homeowner vacancy rate: 0.0%; Median selected monthly owner costs: $1,200 with a mortgage, $402 without a mortgage; Median gross rent: $822 per month; Rental vacancy rate: 8.6%
Health Insurance: 91.9% have insurance; 63.3% have private insurance; 36.0% have public insurance; 8.1% do not have insurance; 3.7% of children under 18 do not have insurance
Safety: Violent crime rate: 0.0 per 10,000 population; Property crime rate: 50.4 per 10,000 population
Transportation: Commute: 92.9% car, 1.8% public transportation, 1.4% walk, 3.9% work from home; Mean travel time to work: 33.5 minutes

BATAVIA (village). County seat. Covers a land area of 1.590 square miles and a water area of 0.030 square miles. Located at 39.08° N. Lat; 84.18° W. Long. Elevation is 594 feet.
History: Settled c.1797, laid out 1814, incorporated 1842.
Population: 1,796; Growth (since 2000): 11.1%; Density: 1,129.5 persons per square mile; Race: 90.1% White, 6.1% Black/African American, 0.0% Asian, 0.0% American Indian/Alaska Native, 0.0% Native Hawaiian/Other Pacific Islander, 3.7% Two or more races, 1.9% Hispanic of any race; Average household size: 2.44; Median age: 40.6; Age under 18: 18.6%; Age 65 and over: 18.0%; Males per 100 females: 89.1; Marriage status: 39.8% never married, 43.7% now married, 2.7% separated, 4.8% widowed, 11.7% divorced; Foreign born: 0.1%; Speak English only: 99.3%; With disability: 24.6%; Veterans: 6.3%; Ancestry: 22.7% German, 17.1% American, 13.6% Irish, 12.1% English, 3.1% Welsh
Employment: 10.9% management, business, and financial, 5.8% computer, engineering, and science, 11.6% education, legal, community service, arts, and media, 4.6% healthcare practitioners, 23.1% service, 19.7% sales and office, 7.6% natural resources, construction, and maintenance, 16.7% production, transportation, and material moving
Income: Per capita: $24,236; Median household: $49,398; Average household: $62,245; Households with income of $100,000 or more: 14.2%; Poverty rate: 21.5%
Educational Attainment: High school diploma or higher: 77.7%; Bachelor's degree or higher: 18.6%; Graduate/professional degree or higher: 8.7%

School District(s)

Batavia Local (PK-12)
2015-16 Enrollment: 2,244 . . . . (513) 732-2343
Clermont Northeastern Local (PK-12)
2015-16 Enrollment: 1,460 . . . . (513) 625-5478

West Clermont Local (PK-12)
2015-16 Enrollment: 8,027 . . . . (513) 943-5000

Four-year College(s)

University of Cincinnati-Clermont College (Public)
Fall 2016 Enrollment: 2,883 . . . . (513) 732-5200
2016-17 Tuition: In-state $5,316; Out-of-state $12,548

Housing: Homeownership rate: 67.5%; Median home value: $119,700; Median year structure built: 1955; Homeowner vacancy rate: 2.6%; Median selected monthly owner costs: $1,107 with a mortgage, $450 without a mortgage; Median gross rent: $672 per month; Rental vacancy rate: 22.3%

Health Insurance: 89.0% have insurance; 51.7% have private insurance; 47.0% have public insurance; 11.0% do not have insurance; 14.7% of children under 18 do not have insurance

Hospitals: Mercy Hospital Clermont (114 beds)

Safety: Violent crime rate: 36.3 per 10,000 population; Property crime rate: 332.5 per 10,000 population

Newspapers: Clermont Sun (weekly circulation 3,000)

Transportation: Commute: 91.9% car, 1.1% public transportation, 1.2% walk, 5.3% work from home; Mean travel time to work: 25.6 minutes

---

BETHEL (village). Covers a land area of 1.395 square miles and a water area of 0.005 square miles. Located at 38.96° N. Lat; 84.08° W. Long. Elevation is 889 feet.

History: Settled 1797.

Population: 2,763; Growth (since 2000): 4.8%; Density: 1,980.0 persons per square mile; Race: 97.7% White, 0.1% Black/African American, 0.0% Asian, 0.0% American Indian/Alaska Native, 0.0% Native Hawaiian/Other Pacific Islander, 1.9% Two or more races, 0.9% Hispanic of any race; Average household size: 2.52; Median age: 41.6; Age under 18: 20.4%; Age 65 and over: 15.7%; Males per 100 females: 86.8; Marriage status: 31.8% never married, 44.2% now married, 1.9% separated, 7.4% widowed, 16.6% divorced; Foreign born: 0.3%; Speak English only: 98.6%; With disability: 19.8%; Veterans: 7.9%; Ancestry: 33.3% American, 23.4% German, 13.0% Irish, 9.0% English, 1.6% Scottish

Employment: 3.9% management, business, and financial, 4.0% computer, engineering, and science, 8.9% education, legal, community service, arts, and media, 5.0% healthcare practitioners, 22.7% service, 26.1% sales and office, 9.7% natural resources, construction, and maintenance, 19.6% production, transportation, and material moving

Income: Per capita: $19,538; Median household: $40,677; Average household: $46,831; Households with income of $100,000 or more: 8.5%; Poverty rate: 14.5%

Educational Attainment: High school diploma or higher: 85.3%; Bachelor's degree or higher: 12.8%; Graduate/professional degree or higher: 3.5%

School District(s)

Bethel-Tate Local (KG-12)
2015-16 Enrollment: 1,604 . . . . (513) 734-2271
U S Grant (07-12)
2015-16 Enrollment: n/a . . . . (513) 734-6222

Two-year College(s)

U S Grant Joint Vocational School (Public)
Fall 2016 Enrollment: 42 . . . . (513) 734-6222
2016-17 Tuition: In-state $6,300; Out-of-state $6,300

Housing: Homeownership rate: 48.2%; Median home value: $84,700; Median year structure built: 1958; Homeowner vacancy rate: 2.0%; Median selected monthly owner costs: $900 with a mortgage, $354 without a mortgage; Median gross rent: $573 per month; Rental vacancy rate: 7.2%

Health Insurance: 88.5% have insurance; 56.8% have private insurance; 46.0% have public insurance; 11.5% do not have insurance; 3.0% of children under 18 do not have insurance

Safety: Violent crime rate: 21.6 per 10,000 population; Property crime rate: 341.5 per 10,000 population

Transportation: Commute: 92.1% car, 0.0% public transportation, 3.7% walk, 4.2% work from home; Mean travel time to work: 32.1 minutes

Additional Information Contacts

Village of Bethel . . . . (513) 734-2243
http://bethel-oh.gov

CHILO (village). Covers a land area of 0.202 square miles and a water area of 0.043 square miles. Located at 38.79° N. Lat; 84.14° W. Long. Elevation is 502 feet.

History: Chilo was a boat-building center and river port before the 1937 floods destroyed most of the town.

Population: 92; Growth (since 2000): -5.2%; Density: 454.5 persons per square mile; Race: 97.8% White, 0.0% Black/African American, 0.0% Asian, 0.0% American Indian/Alaska Native, 0.0% Native Hawaiian/Other Pacific Islander, 2.2% Two or more races, 0.0% Hispanic of any race; Average household size: 3.29; Median age: 46.0; Age under 18: 22.8%; Age 65 and over: 21.7%; Males per 100 females: 70.3; Marriage status: 40.7% never married, 43.2% now married, 0.0% separated, 9.9% widowed, 6.2% divorced; Foreign born: 0.0%; Speak English only: 100.0%; With disability: 26.1%; Veterans: 12.7%; Ancestry: 34.8% American, 6.5% Irish, 2.2% French, 2.2% German

Employment: 0.0% management, business, and financial, 0.0% computer, engineering, and science, 17.9% education, legal, community service, arts, and media, 0.0% healthcare practitioners, 32.1% service, 25.0% sales and office, 0.0% natural resources, construction, and maintenance, 25.0% production, transportation, and material moving

Income: Per capita: $18,399; Median household: $39,375; Average household: $57,118; Households with income of $100,000 or more: 21.5%; Poverty rate: 25.0%

Educational Attainment: High school diploma or higher: 51.6%; Bachelor's degree or higher: 1.6%; Graduate/professional degree or higher: n/a

Housing: Homeownership rate: 85.7%; Median home value: $125,000; Median year structure built: 1977; Homeowner vacancy rate: 0.0%; Median selected monthly owner costs: $1,150 with a mortgage, $233 without a mortgage; Median gross rent: n/a per month; Rental vacancy rate: 0.0%

Health Insurance: 90.2% have insurance; 34.8% have private insurance; 78.3% have public insurance; 9.8% do not have insurance; 23.8% of children under 18 do not have insurance

Transportation: Commute: 100.0% car, 0.0% public transportation, 0.0% walk, 0.0% work from home; Mean travel time to work: 0.0 minutes

---

DAY HEIGHTS (CDP). Covers a land area of 1.178 square miles and a water area of 0 square miles. Located at 39.18° N. Lat; 84.23° W. Long. Elevation is 873 feet.

Population: 2,599; Growth (since 2000): -7.9%; Density: 2,206.0 persons per square mile; Race: 99.5% White, 0.0% Black/African American, 0.0% Asian, 0.5% American Indian/Alaska Native, 0.0% Native Hawaiian/Other Pacific Islander, 0.0% Two or more races, 0.5% Hispanic of any race; Average household size: 2.89; Median age: 39.4; Age under 18: 30.4%; Age 65 and over: 21.2%; Males per 100 females: 102.3; Marriage status: 21.3% never married, 68.5% now married, 1.7% separated, 3.8% widowed, 6.4% divorced; Foreign born: 1.0%; Speak English only: 98.3%; With disability: 14.7%; Veterans: 11.0%; Ancestry: 24.3% American, 21.0% Irish, 18.5% German, 6.0% English, 3.9% European

Employment: 25.7% management, business, and financial, 6.3% computer, engineering, and science, 4.2% education, legal, community service, arts, and media, 7.3% healthcare practitioners, 11.8% service, 30.0% sales and office, 2.0% natural resources, construction, and maintenance, 12.7% production, transportation, and material moving

Income: Per capita: $31,182; Median household: $72,318; Average household: $88,626; Households with income of $100,000 or more: 34.0%; Poverty rate: 10.4%

Educational Attainment: High school diploma or higher: 95.5%; Bachelor's degree or higher: 21.0%; Graduate/professional degree or higher: 9.0%

Housing: Homeownership rate: 93.1%; Median home value: $155,100; Median year structure built: 1962; Homeowner vacancy rate: 0.0%; Median selected monthly owner costs: $1,311 with a mortgage, $548 without a mortgage; Median gross rent: $1,161 per month; Rental vacancy rate: 0.0%

Health Insurance: 98.4% have insurance; 86.4% have private insurance; 24.7% have public insurance; 1.6% do not have insurance; 0.0% of children under 18 do not have insurance

Transportation: Commute: 93.5% car, 0.0% public transportation, 1.9% walk, 4.6% work from home; Mean travel time to work: 26.9 minutes

---

FELICITY (village). Covers a land area of 0.272 square miles and a water area of 0 square miles. Located at 38.84° N. Lat; 84.10° W. Long. Elevation is 919 feet.

Population: 983; Growth (since 2000): 6.6%; Density: 3,618.7 persons per square mile; Race: 94.5% White, 1.0% Black/African American, 0.0% Asian, 0.0% American Indian/Alaska Native, 0.0% Native Hawaiian/Other Pacific Islander, 4.5% Two or more races, 7.8% Hispanic of any race; Average household size: 2.43; Median age: 38.5; Age under 18: 26.2%; Age 65 and over: 12.7%; Males per 100 females: 87.2; Marriage status:

31.8% never married, 43.8% now married, 1.4% separated, 9.1% widowed, 15.2% divorced; Foreign born: 0.0%; Speak English only: 97.1%; With disability: 26.4%; Veterans: 5.9%; Ancestry: 42.8% American, 11.8% German, 11.4% Irish, 4.6% Italian, 2.6% German Russian
Employment: 12.2% management, business, and financial, 0.0% computer, engineering, and science, 14.9% education, legal, community service, arts, and media, 5.4% healthcare practitioners, 16.9% service, 23.0% sales and office, 2.4% natural resources, construction, and maintenance, 25.3% production, transportation, and material moving
Income: Per capita: $13,051; Median household: $23,942; Average household: $31,172; Households with income of $100,000 or more: 2.5%; Poverty rate: 35.2%
Educational Attainment: High school diploma or higher: 68.8%; Bachelor's degree or higher: 9.2%; Graduate/professional degree or higher: 1.5%

School District(s)

Felicity-Franklin Local (KG-12)
2015-16 Enrollment: 840 . . . . (513) 362-5348
Housing: Homeownership rate: 40.1%; Median home value: $86,000; Median year structure built: 1956; Homeowner vacancy rate: 4.1%; Median selected monthly owner costs: $794 with a mortgage, $317 without a mortgage; Median gross rent: $545 per month; Rental vacancy rate: 5.5%
Health Insurance: 88.1% have insurance; 45.8% have private insurance; 47.3% have public insurance; 11.9% do not have insurance; 4.3% of children under 18 do not have insurance
Safety: Violent crime rate: 24.1 per 10,000 population; Property crime rate: 506.0 per 10,000 population
Transportation: Commute: 80.1% car, 0.0% public transportation, 4.8% walk, 15.1% work from home; Mean travel time to work: 33.2 minutes

GOSHEN (CDP).
Land/water area and latitude/longitude are not available.
Population: 546; Growth (since 2000): n/a; Density: n/a persons per square mile; Race: 100.0% White, 0.0% Black/African American, 0.0% Asian, 0.0% American Indian/Alaska Native, 0.0% Native Hawaiian/Other Pacific Islander, 0.0% Two or more races, 7.1% Hispanic of any race; Average household size: 2.54; Median age: 53.4; Age under 18: 13.7%; Age 65 and over: 25.8%; Males per 100 females: 0.0; Marriage status: 20.8% never married, 56.9% now married, 5.2% separated, 11.5% widowed, 10.7% divorced; Foreign born: 0.0%; Speak English only: 100.0%; With disability: 26.7%; Veterans: 9.8%; Ancestry: 26.6% German, 14.3% Irish, 13.9% American, 4.4% Dutch, 4.4% Swedish
Employment: 22.0% management, business, and financial, 0.0% computer, engineering, and science, 18.0% education, legal, community service, arts, and media, 0.0% healthcare practitioners, 8.0% service, 45.5% sales and office, 0.0% natural resources, construction, and maintenance, 6.5% production, transportation, and material moving
Income: Per capita: $26,334; Median household: n/a; Average household: $60,731; Households with income of $100,000 or more: 20.5%; Poverty rate: 16.3%
Educational Attainment: High school diploma or higher: 83.3%; Bachelor's degree or higher: 11.2%; Graduate/professional degree or higher: 4.1%
Housing: Homeownership rate: 68.4%; Median home value: $159,800; Median year structure built: 1968; Homeowner vacancy rate: 0.0%; Median selected monthly owner costs: $1,717 with a mortgage, $473 without a mortgage; Median gross rent: n/a per month; Rental vacancy rate: 0.0%
Health Insurance: 91.2% have insurance; 48.9% have private insurance; 55.3% have public insurance; 8.8% do not have insurance; 18.7% of children under 18 do not have insurance
Safety: Violent crime rate: 0.0 per 10,000 population; Property crime rate: 0.0 per 10,000 population
Transportation: Commute: 78.5% car, 0.0% public transportation, 0.0% walk, 21.5% work from home; Mean travel time to work: 0.0 minutes

MIAMIVILLE (CDP). Covers a land area of 0.338 square miles and a water area of 0.030 square miles. Located at 39.21° N. Lat; 84.30° W. Long. Elevation is 584 feet.
Population: 75; Growth (since 2000): n/a; Density: 221.8 persons per square mile; Race: 100.0% White, 0.0% Black/African American, 0.0% Asian, 0.0% American Indian/Alaska Native, 0.0% Native Hawaiian/Other Pacific Islander, 0.0% Two or more races, 0.0% Hispanic of any race; Average household size: 1.88; Median age: 49.7; Age under 18: 0.0%; Age 65 and over: 28.0%; Males per 100 females: 112.3; Marriage status: 45.3% never married, 28.0% now married, 0.0% separated, 0.0% widowed, 26.7% divorced; Foreign born: 0.0%; Speak English only: 100.0%; With disability: 0.0%; Veterans: 0.0%; Ancestry: 38.7% German, 30.7% English, 14.7% Irish, 13.3% American
Employment: 70.0% management, business, and financial, 0.0% computer, engineering, and science, 0.0% education, legal, community service, arts, and media, 0.0% healthcare practitioners, 15.0% service, 0.0% sales and office, 0.0% natural resources, construction, and maintenance, 15.0% production, transportation, and material moving
Income: Per capita: $60,207; Median household: $86,750; Average household: $110,545; Households with income of $100,000 or more: 25.0%; Poverty rate: n/a
Educational Attainment: High school diploma or higher: 100.0%; Bachelor's degree or higher: 56.9%; Graduate/professional degree or higher: 39.2%
Housing: Homeownership rate: 77.5%; Median home value: $153,800; Median year structure built: 1980; Homeowner vacancy rate: 0.0%; Median selected monthly owner costs: $1,169 with a mortgage, n/a without a mortgage; Median gross rent: n/a per month; Rental vacancy rate: 0.0%
Health Insurance: 100.0% have insurance; 100.0% have private insurance; 28.0% have public insurance; 0.0% do not have insurance; 0.0% of children under 18 do not have insurance
Transportation: Commute: 83.3% car, 0.0% public transportation, 0.0% walk, 16.7% work from home; Mean travel time to work: 0.0 minutes

MILFORD (city). Covers a land area of 3.727 square miles and a water area of 0.124 square miles. Located at 39.17° N. Lat; 84.28° W. Long. Elevation is 551 feet.
History: Milford was settled in an area of glacial moraines, on the Little Miami River. A prehistoric civilization left mounds in this region.
Population: 6,833; Growth (since 2000): 8.7%; Density: 1,833.3 persons per square mile; Race: 93.2% White, 1.7% Black/African American, 0.8% Asian, 0.0% American Indian/Alaska Native, 0.0% Native Hawaiian/Other Pacific Islander, 3.8% Two or more races, 4.3% Hispanic of any race; Average household size: 2.18; Median age: 42.2; Age under 18: 23.0%; Age 65 and over: 20.7%; Males per 100 females: 82.6; Marriage status: 29.6% never married, 44.2% now married, 4.1% separated, 11.7% widowed, 14.5% divorced; Foreign born: 4.1%; Speak English only: 95.2%; With disability: 17.9%; Veterans: 10.6%; Ancestry: 27.2% German, 20.0% American, 14.2% English, 12.4% Irish, 3.9% Italian
Employment: 5.0% management, business, and financial, 6.8% computer, engineering, and science, 10.5% education, legal, community service, arts, and media, 8.9% healthcare practitioners, 22.2% service, 29.2% sales and office, 4.4% natural resources, construction, and maintenance, 13.0% production, transportation, and material moving
Income: Per capita: $28,412; Median household: $38,418; Average household: $61,868; Households with income of $100,000 or more: 18.2%; Poverty rate: 21.2%
Educational Attainment: High school diploma or higher: 87.5%; Bachelor's degree or higher: 30.4%; Graduate/professional degree or higher: 11.3%

School District(s)

Great Oaks Career Campuses (05-12)
2015-16 Enrollment: n/a . . . . (513) 771-8840
Milford Exempted Village (PK-12)
2015-16 Enrollment: 6,565 . . . . (513) 831-1314
Housing: Homeownership rate: 44.6%; Median home value: $152,700; Median year structure built: 1973; Homeowner vacancy rate: 2.8%; Median selected monthly owner costs: $1,491 with a mortgage, $459 without a mortgage; Median gross rent: $655 per month; Rental vacancy rate: 1.7%
Health Insurance: 88.2% have insurance; 64.0% have private insurance; 37.9% have public insurance; 11.8% do not have insurance; 3.2% of children under 18 do not have insurance
Safety: Violent crime rate: 13.0 per 10,000 population; Property crime rate: 334.3 per 10,000 population
Transportation: Commute: 84.4% car, 1.1% public transportation, 3.7% walk, 9.7% work from home; Mean travel time to work: 21.4 minutes

MOSCOW (village). Covers a land area of 0.367 square miles and a water area of 0.022 square miles. Located at 38.86° N. Lat; 84.23° W. Long. Elevation is 499 feet.
History: Moscow was one of the first stations on the Underground Railroad. During the Reconstruction Period, Moscow was a busy shipping point, and a producer of large quantities of brandy.
Population: 89; Growth (since 2000): -63.5%; Density: 242.6 persons per square mile; Race: 100.0% White, 0.0% Black/African American, 0.0%

Asian, 0.0% American Indian/Alaska Native, 0.0% Native Hawaiian/Other Pacific Islander, 0.0% Two or more races, 0.0% Hispanic of any race; Average household size: 1.89; Median age: 50.9; Age under 18: 6.7%; Age 65 and over: 21.3%; Males per 100 females: 107.9; Marriage status: 38.6% never married, 51.8% now married, 0.0% separated, 2.4% widowed, 7.2% divorced; Foreign born: 0.0%; Speak English only: 100.0%; With disability: 36.0%; Veterans: 12.0%; Ancestry: 38.2% American, 22.5% German, 4.5% Dutch, 4.5% Scotch-Irish, 3.4% English

Employment: 5.3% management, business, and financial, 0.0% computer, engineering, and science, 5.3% education, legal, community service, arts, and media, 0.0% healthcare practitioners, 2.6% service, 28.9% sales and office, 23.7% natural resources, construction, and maintenance, 34.2% production, transportation, and material moving

Income: Per capita: $23,736; Median household: n/a; Average household: $46,506; Households with income of $100,000 or more: 14.9%; Poverty rate: 30.3%

Educational Attainment: High school diploma or higher: 93.1%; Bachelor's degree or higher: 1.4%; Graduate/professional degree or higher: n/a

Housing: Homeownership rate: 78.7%; Median home value: $87,000; Median year structure built: 1948; Homeowner vacancy rate: 2.6%; Median selected monthly owner costs: $1,016 with a mortgage, $319 without a mortgage; Median gross rent: n/a per month; Rental vacancy rate: 28.6%

Health Insurance: 91.0% have insurance; 66.3% have private insurance; 47.2% have public insurance; 9.0% do not have insurance; 0.0% of children under 18 do not have insurance

Transportation: Commute: 92.1% car, 0.0% public transportation, 0.0% walk, 7.9% work from home; Mean travel time to work: 33.0 minutes

MOUNT CARMEL (CDP). Covers a land area of 1.834 square miles and a water area of 0.002 square miles. Located at 39.10° N. Lat; 84.30° W. Long. Elevation is 883 feet.

Population: 5,063; Growth (since 2000): 17.5%; Density: 2,760.6 persons per square mile; Race: 98.0% White, 0.0% Black/African American, 0.0% Asian, 0.1% American Indian/Alaska Native, 0.0% Native Hawaiian/Other Pacific Islander, 1.6% Two or more races, 0.0% Hispanic of any race; Average household size: 2.71; Median age: 31.8; Age under 18: 25.2%; Age 65 and over: 13.2%; Males per 100 females: 95.4; Marriage status: 37.3% never married, 43.2% now married, 3.6% separated, 6.4% widowed, 13.0% divorced; Foreign born: 0.0%; Speak English only: 98.6%; With disability: 12.5%; Veterans: 7.6%; Ancestry: 29.6% American, 25.7% German, 17.2% Irish, 5.5% English, 3.8% French

Employment: 14.5% management, business, and financial, 2.4% computer, engineering, and science, 10.4% education, legal, community service, arts, and media, 4.2% healthcare practitioners, 21.6% service, 25.2% sales and office, 6.7% natural resources, construction, and maintenance, 14.9% production, transportation, and material moving

Income: Per capita: $24,024; Median household: $43,415; Average household: $62,981; Households with income of $100,000 or more: 14.0%; Poverty rate: 19.6%

Educational Attainment: High school diploma or higher: 84.6%; Bachelor's degree or higher: 17.2%; Graduate/professional degree or higher: 4.2%

Housing: Homeownership rate: 49.6%; Median home value: $118,200; Median year structure built: 1968; Homeowner vacancy rate: 0.0%; Median selected monthly owner costs: $1,177 with a mortgage, $445 without a mortgage; Median gross rent: $725 per month; Rental vacancy rate: 4.8%

Health Insurance: 93.1% have insurance; 68.7% have private insurance; 32.5% have public insurance; 6.9% do not have insurance; 3.5% of children under 18 do not have insurance

Transportation: Commute: 93.1% car, 0.0% public transportation, 2.7% walk, 3.0% work from home; Mean travel time to work: 20.6 minutes

MOUNT REPOSE (CDP). Covers a land area of 2.033 square miles and a water area of <.001 square miles. Located at 39.19° N. Lat; 84.22° W. Long. Elevation is 866 feet.

Population: 4,691; Growth (since 2000): 14.4%; Density: 2,306.9 persons per square mile; Race: 97.5% White, 0.7% Black/African American, 0.0% Asian, 0.5% American Indian/Alaska Native, 0.0% Native Hawaiian/Other Pacific Islander, 0.3% Two or more races, 2.7% Hispanic of any race; Average household size: 2.68; Median age: 39.3; Age under 18: 28.8%; Age 65 and over: 15.9%; Males per 100 females: 96.1; Marriage status: 29.0% never married, 52.8% now married, 1.1% separated, 7.4% widowed, 10.8% divorced; Foreign born: 2.1%; Speak English only: 94.8%; With disability: 8.3%; Veterans: 10.7%; Ancestry: 30.4% German, 25.7% American, 14.6% Irish, 8.8% English, 3.1% Italian

Employment: 15.6% management, business, and financial, 7.0% computer, engineering, and science, 9.8% education, legal, community service, arts, and media, 5.1% healthcare practitioners, 19.5% service, 22.4% sales and office, 5.9% natural resources, construction, and maintenance, 14.7% production, transportation, and material moving

Income: Per capita: $27,679; Median household: $59,959; Average household: $72,005; Households with income of $100,000 or more: 22.5%; Poverty rate: 6.9%

Educational Attainment: High school diploma or higher: 93.8%; Bachelor's degree or higher: 30.2%; Graduate/professional degree or higher: 12.0%

Housing: Homeownership rate: 84.3%; Median home value: $142,000; Median year structure built: 1977; Homeowner vacancy rate: 5.2%; Median selected monthly owner costs: $1,290 with a mortgage, $527 without a mortgage; Median gross rent: $803 per month; Rental vacancy rate: 0.0%

Health Insurance: 95.9% have insurance; 82.7% have private insurance; 25.4% have public insurance; 4.1% do not have insurance; 3.0% of children under 18 do not have insurance

Transportation: Commute: 91.4% car, 0.0% public transportation, 1.0% walk, 6.4% work from home; Mean travel time to work: 25.9 minutes

MULBERRY (CDP). Covers a land area of 1.590 square miles and a water area of 0 square miles. Located at 39.20° N. Lat; 84.25° W. Long. Elevation is 843 feet.

Population: 3,802; Growth (since 2000): 21.1%; Density: 2,391.0 persons per square mile; Race: 95.8% White, 1.6% Black/African American, 1.3% Asian, 0.0% American Indian/Alaska Native, 0.0% Native Hawaiian/Other Pacific Islander, 1.2% Two or more races, 0.7% Hispanic of any race; Average household size: 2.15; Median age: 53.5; Age under 18: 15.6%; Age 65 and over: 33.0%; Males per 100 females: 80.6; Marriage status: 19.7% never married, 52.3% now married, 0.7% separated, 12.6% widowed, 15.4% divorced; Foreign born: 3.4%; Speak English only: 97.9%; With disability: 13.9%; Veterans: 14.4%; Ancestry: 32.6% German, 20.3% Irish, 18.8% English, 10.5% American, 5.3% Scottish

Employment: 15.1% management, business, and financial, 6.3% computer, engineering, and science, 13.4% education, legal, community service, arts, and media, 6.2% healthcare practitioners, 15.5% service, 25.8% sales and office, 5.9% natural resources, construction, and maintenance, 11.8% production, transportation, and material moving

Income: Per capita: $36,228; Median household: $64,167; Average household: $81,082; Households with income of $100,000 or more: 28.3%; Poverty rate: 4.4%

Educational Attainment: High school diploma or higher: 93.6%; Bachelor's degree or higher: 37.2%; Graduate/professional degree or higher: 17.6%

Housing: Homeownership rate: 71.9%; Median home value: $148,200; Median year structure built: 1989; Homeowner vacancy rate: 4.2%; Median selected monthly owner costs: $1,243 with a mortgage, $530 without a mortgage; Median gross rent: $835 per month; Rental vacancy rate: 25.8%

Health Insurance: 98.3% have insurance; 80.9% have private insurance; 35.3% have public insurance; 1.7% do not have insurance; 0.0% of children under 18 do not have insurance

Transportation: Commute: 94.5% car, 0.0% public transportation, 0.6% walk, 4.9% work from home; Mean travel time to work: 25.5 minutes

NEVILLE (village). Covers a land area of 0.395 square miles and a water area of 0.064 square miles. Located at 38.81° N. Lat; 84.21° W. Long. Elevation is 499 feet.

History: Neville was founded in 1808 and named for a Virginia officer in the Revolutionary War who was given land here for his military service. More than half of the houses in Neville were destroyed by the 1937 flooding of the Ohio River.

Population: 73; Growth (since 2000): -42.5%; Density: 185.0 persons per square mile; Race: 94.5% White, 0.0% Black/African American, 0.0% Asian, 0.0% American Indian/Alaska Native, 0.0% Native Hawaiian/Other Pacific Islander, 5.5% Two or more races, 0.0% Hispanic of any race; Average household size: 2.15; Median age: 47.8; Age under 18: 6.8%; Age 65 and over: 20.5%; Males per 100 females: 100.0; Marriage status: 32.4% never married, 42.6% now married, 7.4% separated, 4.4% widowed, 20.6% divorced; Foreign born: 0.0%; Speak English only: 100.0%; With disability: 13.7%; Veterans: 4.4%; Ancestry: 21.9% German, 12.3% Irish, 4.1% Dutch, 2.7% British, 2.7% Hungarian

Employment: 12.1% management, business, and financial, 6.1% computer, engineering, and science, 0.0% education, legal, community service, arts, and media, 6.1% healthcare practitioners, 6.1% service, 15.2% sales and office, 18.2% natural resources, construction, and maintenance, 36.4% production, transportation, and material moving
Income: Per capita: $31,274; Median household: $31,667; Average household: $70,506; Households with income of $100,000 or more: 14.7%; Poverty rate: 20.5%
Educational Attainment: High school diploma or higher: 76.9%; Bachelor's degree or higher: 32.7%; Graduate/professional degree or higher: 3.8%
Housing: Homeownership rate: 67.6%; Median home value: n/a; Median year structure built: 1968; Homeowner vacancy rate: 0.0%; Median selected monthly owner costs: n/a with a mortgage, $413 without a mortgage; Median gross rent: n/a per month; Rental vacancy rate: 26.7%
Health Insurance: 68.5% have insurance; 58.9% have private insurance; 26.0% have public insurance; 31.5% do not have insurance; 0.0% of children under 18 do not have insurance
Transportation: Commute: 82.8% car, 0.0% public transportation, 0.0% walk, 17.2% work from home; Mean travel time to work: 40.0 minutes

---

NEW RICHMOND (village). Covers a land area of 3.413 square miles and a water area of 0.309 square miles. Located at 38.97° N. Lat; 84.28° W. Long. Elevation is 492 feet.
History: New Richmond was created when two villages were joined. One of them, Susanna, had been laid out in 1816 by Thomas Ashburn as a model town. The 1937 flooding of the Ohio River devastated New Richmond.
Population: 2,645; Growth (since 2000): 19.2%; Density: 774.9 persons per square mile; Race: 95.5% White, 1.4% Black/African American, 0.1% Asian, 0.0% American Indian/Alaska Native, 0.0% Native Hawaiian/Other Pacific Islander, 2.7% Two or more races, 0.3% Hispanic of any race; Average household size: 2.67; Median age: 38.0; Age under 18: 27.1%; Age 65 and over: 14.7%; Males per 100 females: 100.5; Marriage status: 26.1% never married, 51.3% now married, 1.7% separated, 6.5% widowed, 16.1% divorced; Foreign born: 0.1%; Speak English only: 98.4%; With disability: 16.3%; Veterans: 10.3%; Ancestry: 33.7% American, 20.5% German, 10.8% Irish, 4.5% English, 2.4% Greek
Employment: 11.4% management, business, and financial, 7.2% computer, engineering, and science, 6.8% education, legal, community service, arts, and media, 6.8% healthcare practitioners, 18.8% service, 20.7% sales and office, 17.6% natural resources, construction, and maintenance, 10.5% production, transportation, and material moving
Income: Per capita: $23,722; Median household: $47,245; Average household: $62,309; Households with income of $100,000 or more: 19.2%; Poverty rate: 16.1%
Educational Attainment: High school diploma or higher: 81.6%; Bachelor's degree or higher: 17.4%; Graduate/professional degree or higher: 4.2%

School District(s)

New Richmond Exempted Village (PK-12)
2015-16 Enrollment: 2,407 . . . . (513) 553-2616

Housing: Homeownership rate: 64.0%; Median home value: $146,700; Median year structure built: 1971; Homeowner vacancy rate: 0.0%; Median selected monthly owner costs: $1,259 with a mortgage, $455 without a mortgage; Median gross rent: $647 per month; Rental vacancy rate: 4.6%
Health Insurance: 89.1% have insurance; 63.3% have private insurance; 37.4% have public insurance; 10.9% do not have insurance; 0.7% of children under 18 do not have insurance
Safety: Violent crime rate: 45.3 per 10,000 population; Property crime rate: 279.1 per 10,000 population
Transportation: Commute: 91.9% car, 0.4% public transportation, 0.2% walk, 7.2% work from home; Mean travel time to work: 28.2 minutes

---

NEWTONSVILLE (village). Covers a land area of 0.254 square miles and a water area of 0 square miles. Located at 39.18° N. Lat; 84.09° W. Long. Elevation is 906 feet.
Population: 442; Growth (since 2000): -10.2%; Density: 1,742.0 persons per square mile; Race: 98.0% White, 0.0% Black/African American, 0.0% Asian, 0.5% American Indian/Alaska Native, 0.0% Native Hawaiian/Other Pacific Islander, 1.6% Two or more races, 8.6% Hispanic of any race; Average household size: 3.07; Median age: 34.8; Age under 18: 26.9%; Age 65 and over: 10.6%; Males per 100 females: 92.2; Marriage status: 29.6% never married, 46.2% now married, 3.9% separated, 4.5% widowed, 19.6% divorced; Foreign born: 0.0%; Speak English only: 98.3%; With disability: 11.5%; Veterans: 9.0%; Ancestry: 37.6% American, 14.0% German, 6.3% Irish, 5.0% Dutch, 3.8% English
Employment: 14.6% management, business, and financial, 1.5% computer, engineering, and science, 3.4% education, legal, community service, arts, and media, 2.4% healthcare practitioners, 14.6% service, 27.3% sales and office, 15.1% natural resources, construction, and maintenance, 21.0% production, transportation, and material moving
Income: Per capita: $18,846; Median household: $46,250; Average household: $55,481; Households with income of $100,000 or more: 15.3%; Poverty rate: 15.0%
Educational Attainment: High school diploma or higher: 83.8%; Bachelor's degree or higher: 5.1%; Graduate/professional degree or higher: 0.4%
Housing: Homeownership rate: 60.4%; Median home value: $87,000; Median year structure built: 1959; Homeowner vacancy rate: 0.0%; Median selected monthly owner costs: $1,031 with a mortgage, $346 without a mortgage; Median gross rent: $700 per month; Rental vacancy rate: 0.0%
Health Insurance: 90.5% have insurance; 57.2% have private insurance; 39.6% have public insurance; 9.5% do not have insurance; 0.0% of children under 18 do not have insurance
Transportation: Commute: 97.1% car, 0.0% public transportation, 2.9% walk, 0.0% work from home; Mean travel time to work: 27.2 minutes

---

OWENSVILLE (village). Covers a land area of 0.430 square miles and a water area of 0 square miles. Located at 39.12° N. Lat; 84.14° W. Long. Elevation is 860 feet.
Population: 892; Growth (since 2000): 9.3%; Density: 2,073.3 persons per square mile; Race: 98.9% White, 0.0% Black/African American, 0.0% Asian, 1.1% American Indian/Alaska Native, 0.0% Native Hawaiian/Other Pacific Islander, 0.0% Two or more races, 1.1% Hispanic of any race; Average household size: 2.05; Median age: 46.8; Age under 18: 20.5%; Age 65 and over: 27.0%; Males per 100 females: 82.9; Marriage status: 21.7% never married, 44.7% now married, 5.0% separated, 11.6% widowed, 22.1% divorced; Foreign born: 0.0%; Speak English only: 98.0%; With disability: 33.1%; Veterans: 9.0%; Ancestry: 44.2% American, 15.4% German, 14.1% Irish, 3.9% Dutch, 2.6% English
Employment: 8.8% management, business, and financial, 0.0% computer, engineering, and science, 5.3% education, legal, community service, arts, and media, 2.9% healthcare practitioners, 24.2% service, 28.9% sales and office, 12.1% natural resources, construction, and maintenance, 17.7% production, transportation, and material moving
Income: Per capita: $20,090; Median household: $25,938; Average household: $39,722; Households with income of $100,000 or more: 8.5%; Poverty rate: 22.8%
Educational Attainment: High school diploma or higher: 79.2%; Bachelor's degree or higher: 9.0%; Graduate/professional degree or higher: 1.8%
Housing: Homeownership rate: 36.6%; Median home value: $112,100; Median year structure built: 1972; Homeowner vacancy rate: 0.0%; Median selected monthly owner costs: $943 with a mortgage, $384 without a mortgage; Median gross rent: $504 per month; Rental vacancy rate: 13.2%
Health Insurance: 89.0% have insurance; 51.6% have private insurance; 51.0% have public insurance; 11.0% do not have insurance; 1.1% of children under 18 do not have insurance
Transportation: Commute: 98.5% car, 0.0% public transportation, 0.6% walk, 0.9% work from home; Mean travel time to work: 25.3 minutes

---

SUMMERSIDE (CDP). Covers a land area of 2.087 square miles and a water area of 0.007 square miles. Located at 39.12° N. Lat; 84.29° W. Long. Elevation is 873 feet.
Population: 5,161; Growth (since 2000): -6.6%; Density: 2,473.2 persons per square mile; Race: 97.4% White, 2.3% Black/African American, 0.0% Asian, 0.0% American Indian/Alaska Native, 0.0% Native Hawaiian/Other Pacific Islander, 0.0% Two or more races, 0.7% Hispanic of any race; Average household size: 2.61; Median age: 33.2; Age under 18: 28.0%; Age 65 and over: 14.1%; Males per 100 females: 87.4; Marriage status: 27.3% never married, 51.8% now married, 1.0% separated, 6.2% widowed, 14.7% divorced; Foreign born: 1.0%; Speak English only: 97.6%; With disability: 13.1%; Veterans: 9.5%; Ancestry: 31.1% German, 15.1% American, 14.1% English, 11.6% Irish, 3.5% Italian
Employment: 17.3% management, business, and financial, 8.0% computer, engineering, and science, 6.7% education, legal, community service, arts, and media, 1.0% healthcare practitioners, 16.5% service, 25.9% sales and office, 7.6% natural resources, construction, and maintenance, 17.0% production, transportation, and material moving

Income: Per capita: $24,295; Median household: $57,091; Average household: $62,575; Households with income of $100,000 or more: 14.1%; Poverty rate: 12.8%
Educational Attainment: High school diploma or higher: 87.0%; Bachelor's degree or higher: 24.1%; Graduate/professional degree or higher: 6.2%
Housing: Homeownership rate: 70.8%; Median home value: $119,500; Median year structure built: 1977; Homeowner vacancy rate: 0.0%; Median selected monthly owner costs: $1,174 with a mortgage, $450 without a mortgage; Median gross rent: $691 per month; Rental vacancy rate: 19.4%
Health Insurance: 97.3% have insurance; 69.9% have private insurance; 37.6% have public insurance; 2.7% do not have insurance; 1.0% of children under 18 do not have insurance
Transportation: Commute: 95.1% car, 1.6% public transportation, 0.0% walk, 2.7% work from home; Mean travel time to work: 26.2 minutes

WILLIAMSBURG (village). Covers a land area of 1.947 square miles and a water area of 0.020 square miles. Located at 39.05° N. Lat; 84.05° W. Long. Elevation is 814 feet.
History: Incorporated 1800.
Population: 2,543; Growth (since 2000): 7.8%; Density: 1,306.4 persons per square mile; Race: 95.3% White, 3.1% Black/African American, 0.0% Asian, 0.0% American Indian/Alaska Native, 0.0% Native Hawaiian/Other Pacific Islander, 1.4% Two or more races, 0.2% Hispanic of any race; Average household size: 2.81; Median age: 35.7; Age under 18: 25.5%; Age 65 and over: 12.0%; Males per 100 females: 93.8; Marriage status: 31.5% never married, 47.8% now married, 2.8% separated, 5.0% widowed, 15.8% divorced; Foreign born: 0.2%; Speak English only: 98.6%; With disability: 16.4%; Veterans: 8.8%; Ancestry: 32.9% American, 18.2% German, 12.7% Irish, 7.9% English, 1.8% Italian
Employment: 5.1% management, business, and financial, 4.6% computer, engineering, and science, 10.1% education, legal, community service, arts, and media, 5.0% healthcare practitioners, 17.6% service, 20.3% sales and office, 14.6% natural resources, construction, and maintenance, 22.7% production, transportation, and material moving
Income: Per capita: $20,650; Median household: $48,102; Average household: $57,284; Households with income of $100,000 or more: 14.6%; Poverty rate: 23.6%
Educational Attainment: High school diploma or higher: 82.7%; Bachelor's degree or higher: 14.6%; Graduate/professional degree or higher: 5.0%

School District(s)

Williamsburg Local (PK-12)
2015-16 Enrollment: 968. . . . . (513) 724-3077
Housing: Homeownership rate: 47.6%; Median home value: $106,700; Median year structure built: 1955; Homeowner vacancy rate: 2.7%; Median selected monthly owner costs: $1,166 with a mortgage, $358 without a mortgage; Median gross rent: $645 per month; Rental vacancy rate: 2.7%
Health Insurance: 87.8% have insurance; 56.1% have private insurance; 42.8% have public insurance; 12.2% do not have insurance; 2.8% of children under 18 do not have insurance
Safety: Violent crime rate: 11.7 per 10,000 population; Property crime rate: 246.1 per 10,000 population
Transportation: Commute: 94.4% car, 0.9% public transportation, 1.4% walk, 1.4% work from home; Mean travel time to work: 32.0 minutes

WITHAMSVILLE (CDP). Covers a land area of 3.117 square miles and a water area of 0 square miles. Located at 39.06° N. Lat; 84.28° W. Long. Elevation is 879 feet.
Population: 7,087; Growth (since 2000): 125.3%; Density: 2,273.9 persons per square mile; Race: 96.5% White, 1.4% Black/African American, 1.3% Asian, 0.0% American Indian/Alaska Native, 0.0% Native Hawaiian/Other Pacific Islander, 0.8% Two or more races, 0.6% Hispanic of any race; Average household size: 2.25; Median age: 42.7; Age under 18: 15.2%; Age 65 and over: 15.6%; Males per 100 females: 95.9; Marriage status: 30.3% never married, 52.7% now married, 2.4% separated, 5.1% widowed, 11.8% divorced; Foreign born: 2.3%; Speak English only: 98.1%; With disability: 18.4%; Veterans: 8.8%; Ancestry: 31.1% American, 24.2% German, 10.0% Irish, 7.8% English, 4.1% Polish
Employment: 17.1% management, business, and financial, 3.5% computer, engineering, and science, 6.7% education, legal, community service, arts, and media, 7.0% healthcare practitioners, 17.0% service, 25.5% sales and office, 9.7% natural resources, construction, and maintenance, 13.4% production, transportation, and material moving
Income: Per capita: $27,836; Median household: $56,481; Average household: $61,866; Households with income of $100,000 or more: 13.0%; Poverty rate: 9.8%
Educational Attainment: High school diploma or higher: 91.1%; Bachelor's degree or higher: 20.8%; Graduate/professional degree or higher: 4.1%
Housing: Homeownership rate: 55.1%; Median home value: $145,100; Median year structure built: 1977; Homeowner vacancy rate: 0.0%; Median selected monthly owner costs: $1,181 with a mortgage, $461 without a mortgage; Median gross rent: $744 per month; Rental vacancy rate: 3.3%
Health Insurance: 92.2% have insurance; 74.7% have private insurance; 27.3% have public insurance; 7.8% do not have insurance; 1.4% of children under 18 do not have insurance
Transportation: Commute: 94.4% car, 0.9% public transportation, 0.4% walk, 2.5% work from home; Mean travel time to work: 28.3 minutes

Clinton County

Located in southwestern Ohio; drained by forks of the Little Miami River and Caesar Creek. Covers a land area of 408.684 square miles, a water area of 3.610 square miles, and is located in the Eastern Time Zone at 39.41° N. Lat., 83.81° W. Long. The county was founded in 1810. County seat is Wilmington.

Clinton County is part of the Wilmington, OH Micropolitan Statistical Area. The entire metro area includes: Clinton County, OH

Weather Station: Wilmington 3 N Elevation: 1,029 feet

	Jan	Feb	Mar	Apr	May	Jun	Jul	Aug	Sep	Oct	Nov	Dec
High	36	39	50	62	72	80	84	83	77	65	52	39
Low	20	22	30	40	50	59	62	60	53	42	34	24
Precip	2.8	2.4	3.5	3.9	5.2	3.8	4.2	3.0	2.8	3.1	3.1	3.0
Snow	6.9	5.8	3.3	0.4	tr	0.0	0.0	0.0	0.0	0.2	0.9	3.5

High and Low temperatures in degrees Fahrenheit; Precipitation and Snow in inches

Population: 41,854; Growth (since 2000): 3.2%; Density: 102.4 persons per square mile; Race: 94.5% White, 2.4% Black/African American, 0.3% Asian, 0.1% American Indian/Alaska Native, 0.0% Native Hawaiian/Other Pacific Islander, 2.3% two or more races, 1.6% Hispanic of any race; Average household size: 2.53; Median age: 39.4; Age under 18: 24.0%; Age 65 and over: 15.2%; Males per 100 females: 96.2; Marriage status: 26.2% never married, 54.3% now married, 1.8% separated, 6.8% widowed, 12.7% divorced; Foreign born: 1.1%; Speak English only: 98.5%; With disability: 14.9%; Veterans: 9.9%; Ancestry: 21.8% German, 13.5% Irish, 10.7% American, 10.1% English, 2.0% Italian
Religion: Six largest groups: 11.5% Baptist, 5.8% Non-denominational Protestant, 5.2% Catholicism, 4.7% Methodist/Pietist, 2.0% Holiness, 1.8% European Free-Church
Economy: Unemployment rate: 4.9%; Leading industries: 18.6 % retail trade; 12.3 % health care and social assistance; 12.1 % other services (except public administration); Farms: 759 totaling 208,142 acres; Company size: 0 employ 1,000 or more persons, 5 employ 500 to 999 persons, 20 employ 100 to 499 persons, 705 employ less than 100 persons; Business ownership: 983 women-owned, 25 Black-owned, n/a Hispanic-owned, 29 Asian-owned, n/a American Indian/Alaska Native-owned
Employment: 11.1% management, business, and financial, 4.1% computer, engineering, and science, 7.2% education, legal, community service, arts, and media, 4.7% healthcare practitioners, 16.0% service, 26.3% sales and office, 9.8% natural resources, construction, and maintenance, 20.7% production, transportation, and material moving
Income: Per capita: $23,612; Median household: $48,675; Average household: $60,583; Households with income of $100,000 or more: 16.6%; Poverty rate: 15.2%
Educational Attainment: High school diploma or higher: 88.5%; Bachelor's degree or higher: 16.5%; Graduate/professional degree or higher: 5.6%
Housing: Homeownership rate: 64.1%; Median home value: $121,700; Median year structure built: 1975; Homeowner vacancy rate: 2.7%; Median selected monthly owner costs: $1,123 with a mortgage, $405 without a mortgage; Median gross rent: $696 per month; Rental vacancy rate: 4.9%
Vital Statistics: Birth rate: 123.9 per 10,000 population; Death rate: 107.2 per 10,000 population; Age-adjusted cancer mortality rate: 165.3 deaths per 100,000 population

Health Insurance: 91.4% have insurance; 67.2% have private insurance; 37.3% have public insurance; 8.6% do not have insurance; 3.5% of children under 18 do not have insurance
Health Care: Physicians: 15.3 per 10,000 population; Dentists: 2.9 per 10,000 population; Hospital beds: 24.4 per 10,000 population; Hospital admissions: 935.5 per 10,000 population
Air Quality Index (AQI): Percent of Days: 73.0% good, 25.1% moderate, 1.9% unhealthy for sensitive individuals, 0.0% unhealthy, 0.0% very unhealthy; Annual median: 44; Annual maximum: 112
Transportation: Commute: 91.3% car, 0.5% public transportation, 3.4% walk, 3.6% work from home; Mean travel time to work: 26.4 minutes
2016 Presidential Election: 73.7% Trump, 21.7% Clinton, 2.7% Johnson, 0.7% Stein
National and State Parks: Cowan State Park
Additional Information Contacts
Clinton Government .... (937) 382-2103
http://co.clinton.oh.us

Clinton County Communities

BLANCHESTER (village). Covers a land area of 4.148 square miles and a water area of 0.097 square miles. Located at 39.30° N. Lat; 83.97° W. Long. Elevation is 968 feet.
Population: 4,163; Growth (since 2000): -1.4%; Density: 1,003.5 persons per square mile; Race: 96.9% White, 0.5% Black/African American, 0.8% Asian, 0.0% American Indian/Alaska Native, 0.0% Native Hawaiian/Other Pacific Islander, 1.8% Two or more races, 0.0% Hispanic of any race; Average household size: 2.56; Median age: 37.7; Age under 18: 25.3%; Age 65 and over: 15.9%; Males per 100 females: 89.0; Marriage status: 28.5% never married, 50.1% now married, 3.1% separated, 7.9% widowed, 13.5% divorced; Foreign born: 0.6%; Speak English only: 99.2%; With disability: 15.1%; Veterans: 13.7%; Ancestry: 15.9% German, 13.1% Irish, 12.6% American, 11.0% English, 2.5% Welsh
Employment: 5.2% management, business, and financial, 1.5% computer, engineering, and science, 5.2% education, legal, community service, arts, and media, 2.8% healthcare practitioners, 16.8% service, 24.3% sales and office, 12.6% natural resources, construction, and maintenance, 31.7% production, transportation, and material moving
Income: Per capita: $21,370; Median household: $41,080; Average household: $54,991; Households with income of $100,000 or more: 12.9%; Poverty rate: 16.5%
Educational Attainment: High school diploma or higher: 84.0%; Bachelor's degree or higher: 5.5%; Graduate/professional degree or higher: 1.9%

School District(s)

Blanchester Local (PK-12)
2015-16 Enrollment: 1,631 .... (937) 783-3523
Housing: Homeownership rate: 59.9%; Median home value: $88,200; Median year structure built: 1971; Homeowner vacancy rate: 0.0%; Median selected monthly owner costs: $1,118 with a mortgage, $372 without a mortgage; Median gross rent: $659 per month; Rental vacancy rate: 8.2%
Health Insurance: 88.4% have insurance; 59.9% have private insurance; 41.6% have public insurance; 11.6% do not have insurance; 6.6% of children under 18 do not have insurance
Safety: Violent crime rate: 14.1 per 10,000 population; Property crime rate: 176.5 per 10,000 population
Transportation: Commute: 90.3% car, 0.0% public transportation, 7.9% walk, 1.4% work from home; Mean travel time to work: 29.1 minutes

CLARKSVILLE (village). Covers a land area of 0.463 square miles and a water area of 0.030 square miles. Located at 39.40° N. Lat; 83.99° W. Long. Elevation is 814 feet.
Population: 634; Growth (since 2000): 27.6%; Density: 1,370.7 persons per square mile; Race: 97.8% White, 0.0% Black/African American, 0.0% Asian, 0.0% American Indian/Alaska Native, 0.0% Native Hawaiian/Other Pacific Islander, 2.2% Two or more races, 0.0% Hispanic of any race; Average household size: 2.84; Median age: 35.1; Age under 18: 34.7%; Age 65 and over: 6.8%; Males per 100 females: 105.2; Marriage status: 34.3% never married, 47.2% now married, 2.1% separated, 7.4% widowed, 11.1% divorced; Foreign born: 0.0%; Speak English only: 100.0%; With disability: 17.8%; Veterans: 11.1%; Ancestry: 27.6% German, 24.9% Irish, 4.1% Scotch-Irish, 2.5% American, 2.2% English
Employment: 8.8% management, business, and financial, 2.6% computer, engineering, and science, 5.5% education, legal, community service, arts, and media, 5.9% healthcare practitioners, 20.1% service, 27.8% sales and office, 6.2% natural resources, construction, and maintenance, 23.1% production, transportation, and material moving
Income: Per capita: $18,640; Median household: $45,625; Average household: $52,239; Households with income of $100,000 or more: 11.6%; Poverty rate: 25.6%
Educational Attainment: High school diploma or higher: 89.6%; Bachelor's degree or higher: 7.7%; Graduate/professional degree or higher: 2.2%

School District(s)

Clinton-Massie Local (PK-12)
2015-16 Enrollment: 1,831 .... (937) 289-2471
Housing: Homeownership rate: 60.5%; Median home value: $85,400; Median year structure built: 1962; Homeowner vacancy rate: 0.0%; Median selected monthly owner costs: $1,003 with a mortgage, $354 without a mortgage; Median gross rent: $815 per month; Rental vacancy rate: 0.0%
Health Insurance: 89.7% have insurance; 61.8% have private insurance; 38.8% have public insurance; 10.3% do not have insurance; 8.2% of children under 18 do not have insurance
Transportation: Commute: 84.0% car, 1.2% public transportation, 3.9% walk, 8.6% work from home; Mean travel time to work: 28.0 minutes

MARTINSVILLE (village). Covers a land area of 0.439 square miles and a water area of 0.002 square miles. Located at 39.32° N. Lat; 83.81° W. Long. Elevation is 1,089 feet.
Population: 425; Growth (since 2000): -3.4%; Density: 967.4 persons per square mile; Race: 97.4% White, 0.0% Black/African American, 0.0% Asian, 0.0% American Indian/Alaska Native, 0.0% Native Hawaiian/Other Pacific Islander, 2.6% Two or more races, 0.0% Hispanic of any race; Average household size: 2.99; Median age: 32.5; Age under 18: 34.6%; Age 65 and over: 10.4%; Males per 100 females: 98.7; Marriage status: 26.6% never married, 51.5% now married, 3.6% separated, 7.2% widowed, 14.8% divorced; Foreign born: 0.0%; Speak English only: 100.0%; With disability: 16.0%; Veterans: 10.8%; Ancestry: 24.7% German, 12.0% Portuguese, 10.6% American, 9.6% English, 8.9% Irish
Employment: 9.3% management, business, and financial, 6.6% computer, engineering, and science, 11.3% education, legal, community service, arts, and media, 1.3% healthcare practitioners, 10.6% service, 24.5% sales and office, 15.2% natural resources, construction, and maintenance, 21.2% production, transportation, and material moving
Income: Per capita: $15,316; Median household: $35,000; Average household: $44,175; Households with income of $100,000 or more: 6.3%; Poverty rate: 26.8%
Educational Attainment: High school diploma or higher: 81.9%; Bachelor's degree or higher: 7.7%; Graduate/professional degree or higher: 1.2%
Housing: Homeownership rate: 63.4%; Median home value: $76,000; Median year structure built: 1943; Homeowner vacancy rate: 0.0%; Median selected monthly owner costs: $950 with a mortgage, $408 without a mortgage; Median gross rent: $854 per month; Rental vacancy rate: 0.0%
Health Insurance: 89.4% have insurance; 41.2% have private insurance; 57.4% have public insurance; 10.6% do not have insurance; 2.7% of children under 18 do not have insurance
Transportation: Commute: 90.7% car, 0.0% public transportation, 4.0% walk, 4.7% work from home; Mean travel time to work: 26.2 minutes

MIDLAND (village). Covers a land area of 0.352 square miles and a water area of 0 square miles. Located at 39.31° N. Lat; 83.91° W. Long. Elevation is 988 feet.
History: Midland developed as a junction town for two branches of the Baltimore & Ohio Railroad.
Population: 352; Growth (since 2000): 32.8%; Density: 998.9 persons per square mile; Race: 98.9% White, 0.0% Black/African American, 0.0% Asian, 0.0% American Indian/Alaska Native, 0.0% Native Hawaiian/Other Pacific Islander, 1.1% Two or more races, 0.0% Hispanic of any race; Average household size: 3.63; Median age: 24.5; Age under 18: 42.9%; Age 65 and over: 4.8%; Males per 100 females: 92.1; Marriage status: 27.0% never married, 50.9% now married, 5.8% separated, 5.3% widowed, 16.8% divorced; Foreign born: 0.0%; Speak English only: 100.0%; With disability: 10.5%; Veterans: 7.0%; Ancestry: 33.0% German, 23.6% Irish, 17.0% American, 11.4% English, 2.8% Scotch-Irish
Employment: 5.1% management, business, and financial, 1.7% computer, engineering, and science, 2.6% education, legal, community service, arts, and media, 6.0% healthcare practitioners, 12.0% service, 33.3% sales and office, 12.0% natural resources, construction, and maintenance, 27.4% production, transportation, and material moving

Income: Per capita: $12,276; Median household: $40,750; Average household: $41,532; Households with income of $100,000 or more: 2.1%; Poverty rate: 34.3%
Educational Attainment: High school diploma or higher: 82.4%; Bachelor's degree or higher: 1.1%; Graduate/professional degree or higher: 0.6%
Housing: Homeownership rate: 54.6%; Median home value: $81,700; Median year structure built: 1960; Homeowner vacancy rate: 5.0%; Median selected monthly owner costs: $981 with a mortgage, $425 without a mortgage; Median gross rent: $735 per month; Rental vacancy rate: 0.0%
Health Insurance: 89.8% have insurance; 55.4% have private insurance; 46.0% have public insurance; 10.2% do not have insurance; 2.0% of children under 18 do not have insurance
Transportation: Commute: 100.0% car, 0.0% public transportation, 0.0% walk, 0.0% work from home; Mean travel time to work: 34.1 minutes

NEW VIENNA (village). Covers a land area of 0.853 square miles and a water area of 0.019 square miles. Located at 39.33° N. Lat; 83.69° W. Long. Elevation is 1,122 feet.
Population: 1,377; Growth (since 2000): 6.4%; Density: 1,614.6 persons per square mile; Race: 96.2% White, 0.3% Black/African American, 0.0% Asian, 0.0% American Indian/Alaska Native, 0.0% Native Hawaiian/Other Pacific Islander, 2.2% Two or more races, 5.4% Hispanic of any race; Average household size: 2.79; Median age: 29.5; Age under 18: 31.2%; Age 65 and over: 8.5%; Males per 100 females: 91.8; Marriage status: 28.5% never married, 45.4% now married, 1.2% separated, 5.8% widowed, 20.3% divorced; Foreign born: 0.0%; Speak English only: 99.7%; With disability: 14.7%; Veterans: 7.0%; Ancestry: 24.0% German, 11.6% Irish, 9.2% American, 3.4% English, 3.4% Swedish
Employment: 6.0% management, business, and financial, 3.2% computer, engineering, and science, 7.7% education, legal, community service, arts, and media, 3.0% healthcare practitioners, 12.1% service, 21.1% sales and office, 15.4% natural resources, construction, and maintenance, 31.5% production, transportation, and material moving
Income: Per capita: $15,180; Median household: $37,727; Average household: $42,859; Households with income of $100,000 or more: 5.7%; Poverty rate: 28.1%
Educational Attainment: High school diploma or higher: 91.4%; Bachelor's degree or higher: 4.9%; Graduate/professional degree or higher: 2.3%

School District(s)

East Clinton Local (PK-12)
2015-16 Enrollment: 1,398 . . . . (937) 584-2461

Housing: Homeownership rate: 47.6%; Median home value: $81,800; Median year structure built: 1976; Homeowner vacancy rate: 6.4%; Median selected monthly owner costs: $864 with a mortgage, $384 without a mortgage; Median gross rent: $701 per month; Rental vacancy rate: 2.6%
Health Insurance: 90.6% have insurance; 49.0% have private insurance; 50.2% have public insurance; 9.4% do not have insurance; 0.0% of children under 18 do not have insurance
Transportation: Commute: 97.1% car, 0.4% public transportation, 0.0% walk, 2.1% work from home; Mean travel time to work: 29.8 minutes

PORT WILLIAM (village). Covers a land area of 0.116 square miles and a water area of 0.003 square miles. Located at 39.55° N. Lat; 83.79° W. Long. Elevation is 1,020 feet.
Population: 283; Growth (since 2000): 9.7%; Density: 2,434.5 persons per square mile; Race: 88.3% White, 0.0% Black/African American, 0.0% Asian, 0.0% American Indian/Alaska Native, 0.0% Native Hawaiian/Other Pacific Islander, 11.7% Two or more races, 0.0% Hispanic of any race; Average household size: 2.95; Median age: 26.3; Age under 18: 32.2%; Age 65 and over: 7.1%; Males per 100 females: 96.9; Marriage status: 37.3% never married, 44.6% now married, 0.0% separated, 2.5% widowed, 15.7% divorced; Foreign born: 0.4%; Speak English only: 99.2%; With disability: 18.7%; Veterans: 13.0%; Ancestry: 19.1% German, 10.6% Irish, 9.9% American, 5.3% Scottish, 3.5% English
Employment: 8.3% management, business, and financial, 0.0% computer, engineering, and science, 3.7% education, legal, community service, arts, and media, 0.9% healthcare practitioners, 24.8% service, 29.4% sales and office, 4.6% natural resources, construction, and maintenance, 28.4% production, transportation, and material moving
Income: Per capita: $12,578; Median household: $31,000; Average household: $40,238; Households with income of $100,000 or more: 3.1%; Poverty rate: 29.7%
Educational Attainment: High school diploma or higher: 78.1%; Bachelor's degree or higher: 11.0%; Graduate/professional degree or higher: 1.9%
Housing: Homeownership rate: 65.6%; Median home value: $65,000; Median year structure built: 1940; Homeowner vacancy rate: 8.7%; Median selected monthly owner costs: $900 with a mortgage, $388 without a mortgage; Median gross rent: $811 per month; Rental vacancy rate: 0.0%
Health Insurance: 87.6% have insurance; 46.3% have private insurance; 51.6% have public insurance; 12.4% do not have insurance; 8.8% of children under 18 do not have insurance
Transportation: Commute: 92.7% car, 0.0% public transportation, 6.4% walk, 0.9% work from home; Mean travel time to work: 23.0 minutes

REESVILLE (unincorporated postal area)

ZCTA: 45166

Covers a land area of 0.740 square miles and a water area of 0 square miles. Located at 39.48° N. Lat; 83.69° W. Long. Elevation is 1,083 feet.
Population: 60; Growth (since 2000): n/a; Density: 81.1 persons per square mile; Race: 100.0% White, 0.0% Black/African American, 0.0% Asian, 0.0% American Indian/Alaska Native, 0.0% Native Hawaiian/Other Pacific Islander, 0.0% Two or more races, 0.0% Hispanic of any race; Average household size: 3.16; Median age: 29.4; Age under 18: 33.3%; Age 65 and over: 20.0%; Males per 100 females: 127.9; Marriage status: 20.0% never married, 65.0% now married, 0.0% separated, 15.0% widowed, 0.0% divorced; Foreign born: 0.0%; Speak English only: 100.0%; With disability: 0.0%; Veterans: 0.0%; Ancestry: 43.3% American
Employment: 0.0% management, business, and financial, 0.0% computer, engineering, and science, 0.0% education, legal, community service, arts, and media, 0.0% healthcare practitioners, 0.0% service, 65.0% sales and office, 0.0% natural resources, construction, and maintenance, 35.0% production, transportation, and material moving
Income: Per capita: $15,208; Median household: $46,250; Average household: $47,937; Households with income of $100,000 or more: n/a; Poverty rate: n/a
Educational Attainment: High school diploma or higher: 100.0%; Bachelor's degree or higher: n/a; Graduate/professional degree or higher: n/a
Housing: Homeownership rate: 100.0%; Median home value: $82,700; Median year structure built: 1968; Homeowner vacancy rate: 0.0%; Median selected monthly owner costs: $0 with a mortgage, $0 without a mortgage; Median gross rent: n/a per month; Rental vacancy rate: 0.0%
Health Insurance: 76.7% have insurance; 76.7% have private insurance; 20.0% have public insurance; 23.3% do not have insurance; 0.0% of children under 18 do not have insurance
Transportation: Commute: 100.0% car, 0.0% public transportation, 0.0% walk, 0.0% work from home; Mean travel time to work: 0.0 minutes

SABINA (village). Covers a land area of 1.282 square miles and a water area of 0.008 square miles. Located at 39.49° N. Lat; 83.63° W. Long. Elevation is 1,050 feet.
Population: 2,399; Growth (since 2000): -13.7%; Density: 1,871.0 persons per square mile; Race: 90.5% White, 0.2% Black/African American, 0.3% Asian, 1.4% American Indian/Alaska Native, 0.0% Native Hawaiian/Other Pacific Islander, 6.3% Two or more races, 4.3% Hispanic of any race; Average household size: 2.53; Median age: 38.8; Age under 18: 23.9%; Age 65 and over: 15.0%; Males per 100 females: 94.8; Marriage status: 24.3% never married, 49.2% now married, 2.1% separated, 7.7% widowed, 18.8% divorced; Foreign born: 1.7%; Speak English only: 95.9%; With disability: 19.3%; Veterans: 9.6%; Ancestry: 21.3% German, 13.4% Irish, 10.6% American, 7.5% English, 2.9% Scottish
Employment: 7.6% management, business, and financial, 2.2% computer, engineering, and science, 2.8% education, legal, community service, arts, and media, 1.9% healthcare practitioners, 20.9% service, 30.2% sales and office, 7.7% natural resources, construction, and maintenance, 26.8% production, transportation, and material moving
Income: Per capita: $16,496; Median household: $34,706; Average household: $41,297; Households with income of $100,000 or more: 3.2%; Poverty rate: 28.0%
Educational Attainment: High school diploma or higher: 83.7%; Bachelor's degree or higher: 7.5%; Graduate/professional degree or higher: 1.2%

School District(s)

East Clinton Local (PK-12)
2015-16 Enrollment: 1,398 . . . . (937) 584-2461

Housing: Homeownership rate: 55.5%; Median home value: $82,900; Median year structure built: 1962; Homeowner vacancy rate: 3.0%; Median selected monthly owner costs: $854 with a mortgage, $322 without a mortgage; Median gross rent: $632 per month; Rental vacancy rate: 0.0%
Health Insurance: 89.2% have insurance; 55.8% have private insurance; 43.4% have public insurance; 10.8% do not have insurance; 5.4% of children under 18 do not have insurance
Safety: Violent crime rate: 7.9 per 10,000 population; Property crime rate: 249.0 per 10,000 population
Transportation: Commute: 95.9% car, 0.8% public transportation, 2.2% walk, 0.5% work from home; Mean travel time to work: 21.4 minutes

WILMINGTON (city). County seat. Covers a land area of 10.889 square miles and a water area of 0.041 square miles. Located at 39.44° N. Lat; 83.82° W. Long. Elevation is 1,017 feet.
History: Seat of Wilmington College. Settled 1810, incorporated 1828.
Population: 12,441; Growth (since 2000): 4.4%; Density: 1,142.5 persons per square mile; Race: 89.1% White, 7.5% Black/African American, 0.2% Asian, 0.0% American Indian/Alaska Native, 0.1% Native Hawaiian/Other Pacific Islander, 2.8% Two or more races, 2.5% Hispanic of any race; Average household size: 2.21; Median age: 35.6; Age under 18: 21.9%; Age 65 and over: 16.3%; Males per 100 females: 87.7; Marriage status: 33.0% never married, 45.2% now married, 2.3% separated, 8.4% widowed, 13.4% divorced; Foreign born: 2.3%; Speak English only: 96.7%; With disability: 18.5%; Veterans: 8.7%; Ancestry: 19.6% German, 13.3% Irish, 12.0% English, 10.0% American, 2.5% Italian
Employment: 9.5% management, business, and financial, 4.6% computer, engineering, and science, 7.9% education, legal, community service, arts, and media, 4.9% healthcare practitioners, 21.9% service, 26.6% sales and office, 7.0% natural resources, construction, and maintenance, 17.7% production, transportation, and material moving
Income: Per capita: $20,898; Median household: $33,845; Average household: $49,145; Households with income of $100,000 or more: 11.3%; Poverty rate: 21.4%
Educational Attainment: High school diploma or higher: 85.6%; Bachelor's degree or higher: 17.9%; Graduate/professional degree or higher: 6.0%

School District(s)

Great Oaks Career Campuses (05-12)
2015-16 Enrollment: n/a . . . . (513) 771-8840
Wilmington City (PK-12)
2015-16 Enrollment: 2,946 . . . . (937) 382-1641

Four-year College(s)

Wilmington College (Private, Not-for-profit, Friends)
Fall 2016 Enrollment: 1,140 . . . . (800) 341-9318
2016-17 Tuition: In-state $25,000; Out-of-state $25,000
Housing: Homeownership rate: 42.5%; Median home value: $98,800; Median year structure built: 1971; Homeowner vacancy rate: 7.9%; Median selected monthly owner costs: $934 with a mortgage, $348 without a mortgage; Median gross rent: $673 per month; Rental vacancy rate: 5.8%
Health Insurance: 92.5% have insurance; 63.1% have private insurance; 44.6% have public insurance; 7.5% do not have insurance; 0.8% of children under 18 do not have insurance
Hospitals: Clinton Memorial Hospital (150 beds)
Safety: Violent crime rate: 14.5 per 10,000 population; Property crime rate: 464.5 per 10,000 population
Newspapers: Wilmington News Journal (daily circulation 7,400)
Transportation: Commute: 89.1% car, 0.5% public transportation, 6.1% walk, 2.8% work from home; Mean travel time to work: 19.9 minutes
Airports: Wilmington Air Park (general aviation)
Additional Information Contacts
City of Wilmington . . . . (937) 382-5458
http://ci.wilmington.oh.us

Columbiana County

Located in eastern Ohio; bounded on the east by Pennsylvania, and on the southeast by the Ohio River; drained by the Little Beaver River. Covers a land area of 531.893 square miles, a water area of 2.795 square miles, and is located in the Eastern Time Zone at 40.77° N. Lat., 80.78° W. Long. The county was founded in 1803. County seat is Lisbon.

Columbiana County is part of the Salem, OH Micropolitan Statistical Area. The entire metro area includes: Columbiana County, OH

Weather Station: Millport 2 NW — Elevation: 1,149 feet

	Jan	Feb	Mar	Apr	May	Jun	Jul	Aug	Sep	Oct	Nov	Dec
High	36	40	50	62	72	80	84	82	76	64	51	39
Low	18	20	27	37	46	55	59	57	50	39	31	22
Precip	2.5	2.2	2.8	3.3	4.0	3.8	4.0	3.3	3.3	2.6	3.1	2.8
Snow	8.0	6.6	5.1	1.5	tr	0.0	0.0	0.0	0.0	tr	1.6	6.0

High and Low temperatures in degrees Fahrenheit; Precipitation and Snow in inches

Population: 105,230; Growth (since 2000): -6.1%; Density: 197.8 persons per square mile; Race: 95.0% White, 2.3% Black/African American, 0.3% Asian, 0.1% American Indian/Alaska Native, 0.0% Native Hawaiian/Other Pacific Islander, 1.6% two or more races, 1.5% Hispanic of any race; Average household size: 2.43; Median age: 43.4; Age under 18: 20.9%; Age 65 and over: 18.2%; Males per 100 females: 101.0; Marriage status: 25.8% never married, 54.5% now married, 1.9% separated, 7.5% widowed, 12.2% divorced; Foreign born: 1.1%; Speak English only: 97.8%; With disability: 15.9%; Veterans: 11.1%; Ancestry: 25.0% German, 17.8% American, 15.9% Irish, 11.4% English, 8.1% Italian
Religion: Six largest groups: 9.0% Catholicism, 7.1% Methodist/Pietist, 6.2% Baptist, 4.5% Non-denominational Protestant, 3.8% Presbyterian-Reformed, 2.9% Lutheran
Economy: Unemployment rate: 5.2%; Leading industries: 16.3 % retail trade; 14.1 % other services (except public administration); 13.9 % health care and social assistance; Farms: 1,045 totaling 127,846 acres; Company size: 0 employ 1,000 or more persons, 3 employ 500 to 999 persons, 30 employ 100 to 499 persons, 2,006 employ less than 100 persons; Business ownership: 2,499 women-owned, 27 Black-owned, n/a Hispanic-owned, 56 Asian-owned, n/a American Indian/Alaska Native-owned
Employment: 10.4% management, business, and financial, 2.7% computer, engineering, and science, 7.0% education, legal, community service, arts, and media, 5.7% healthcare practitioners, 18.6% service, 22.2% sales and office, 10.1% natural resources, construction, and maintenance, 23.4% production, transportation, and material moving
Income: Per capita: $23,785; Median household: $45,389; Average household: $58,570; Households with income of $100,000 or more: 13.6%; Poverty rate: 15.8%
Educational Attainment: High school diploma or higher: 87.6%; Bachelor's degree or higher: 13.9%; Graduate/professional degree or higher: 4.6%
Housing: Homeownership rate: 71.7%; Median home value: $104,100; Median year structure built: 1963; Homeowner vacancy rate: 1.8%; Median selected monthly owner costs: $1,003 with a mortgage, $377 without a mortgage; Median gross rent: $621 per month; Rental vacancy rate: 5.1%
Vital Statistics: Birth rate: 97.8 per 10,000 population; Death rate: 112.5 per 10,000 population; Age-adjusted cancer mortality rate: 198.9 deaths per 100,000 population
Health Insurance: 90.2% have insurance; 64.4% have private insurance; 40.3% have public insurance; 9.8% do not have insurance; 5.6% of children under 18 do not have insurance
Health Care: Physicians: 10.1 per 10,000 population; Dentists: 2.3 per 10,000 population; Hospital beds: 22.4 per 10,000 population; Hospital admissions: 846.9 per 10,000 population
Air Quality Index (AQI): Percent of Days: 99.7% good, 0.3% moderate, 0.0% unhealthy for sensitive individuals, 0.0% unhealthy, 0.0% very unhealthy; Annual median: 1; Annual maximum: 52
Transportation: Commute: 93.8% car, 0.4% public transportation, 2.2% walk, 2.8% work from home; Mean travel time to work: 25.3 minutes
2016 Presidential Election: 68.1% Trump, 26.7% Clinton, 3.0% Johnson, 0.7% Stein
National and State Parks: Beaver Creek State Forest; Guilford Lake State Park
Additional Information Contacts
Columbiana Government . . . . (330) 424-9511
http://www.columbianacounty.org

Columbiana County Communities

CALCUTTA (CDP). Covers a land area of 11.865 square miles and a water area of 0.013 square miles. Located at 40.69° N. Lat; 80.55° W. Long. Elevation is 1,112 feet.
Population: 3,543; Growth (since 2000): 1.5%; Density: 298.6 persons per square mile; Race: 98.5% White, 0.6% Black/African American, 0.0% Asian, 0.0% American Indian/Alaska Native, 0.0% Native Hawaiian/Other Pacific Islander, 1.0% Two or more races, 1.4% Hispanic of any race;

Average household size: 2.49; Median age: 47.3; Age under 18: 21.2%; Age 65 and over: 25.5%; Males per 100 females: 91.7; Marriage status: 21.7% never married, 55.3% now married, 1.2% separated, 13.1% widowed, 9.9% divorced; Foreign born: 2.1%; Speak English only: 97.4%; With disability: 14.5%; Veterans: 11.9%; Ancestry: 28.5% American, 21.8% German, 16.9% Irish, 12.7% English, 9.3% Italian
Employment: 7.0% management, business, and financial, 0.5% computer, engineering, and science, 11.9% education, legal, community service, arts, and media, 4.0% healthcare practitioners, 18.1% service, 27.0% sales and office, 4.3% natural resources, construction, and maintenance, 27.2% production, transportation, and material moving
Income: Per capita: $23,722; Median household: $52,019; Average household: $59,933; Households with income of $100,000 or more: 16.0%; Poverty rate: 7.3%
Educational Attainment: High school diploma or higher: 87.8%; Bachelor's degree or higher: 15.4%; Graduate/professional degree or higher: 9.4%
Housing: Homeownership rate: 79.4%; Median home value: $124,100; Median year structure built: 1970; Homeowner vacancy rate: 0.0%; Median selected monthly owner costs: $1,193 with a mortgage, $451 without a mortgage; Median gross rent: $618 per month; Rental vacancy rate: 7.8%
Health Insurance: 94.3% have insurance; 75.1% have private insurance; 37.2% have public insurance; 5.7% do not have insurance; 3.2% of children under 18 do not have insurance
Transportation: Commute: 95.9% car, 0.0% public transportation, 1.6% walk, 1.4% work from home; Mean travel time to work: 25.1 minutes

COLUMBIANA (city). Covers a land area of 6.000 square miles and a water area of 0.143 square miles. Located at 40.89° N. Lat; 80.67° W. Long. Elevation is 1,148 feet.
History: Columbiana was laid out in 1805, when it was called Dixonville for its founder, Joshua Dixon. Harvey S. Firestone (1868-1938), who had the idea of making rubber tires for buggies, was born in Columbiana.
Population: 6,463; Growth (since 2000): 14.7%; Density: 1,077.2 persons per square mile; Race: 99.0% White, 0.6% Black/African American, 0.3% Asian, 0.0% American Indian/Alaska Native, 0.0% Native Hawaiian/Other Pacific Islander, 0.0% Two or more races, 1.0% Hispanic of any race; Average household size: 2.09; Median age: 53.9; Age under 18: 16.8%; Age 65 and over: 30.9%; Males per 100 females: 87.4; Marriage status: 18.1% never married, 59.6% now married, 0.7% separated, 10.7% widowed, 11.7% divorced; Foreign born: 0.5%; Speak English only: 98.7%; With disability: 16.0%; Veterans: 14.9%; Ancestry: 29.5% German, 21.9% Irish, 11.5% American, 11.1% Italian, 9.5% English
Employment: 15.7% management, business, and financial, 5.0% computer, engineering, and science, 7.7% education, legal, community service, arts, and media, 9.3% healthcare practitioners, 17.5% service, 22.9% sales and office, 5.0% natural resources, construction, and maintenance, 16.9% production, transportation, and material moving
Income: Per capita: $30,493; Median household: $49,930; Average household: $64,913; Households with income of $100,000 or more: 18.2%; Poverty rate: 10.0%
Educational Attainment: High school diploma or higher: 94.9%; Bachelor's degree or higher: 26.5%; Graduate/professional degree or higher: 8.3%

School District(s)

Columbiana Exempted Village (PK-12)
2015-16 Enrollment: 1,037 . . . . (330) 482-5353
Crestview Local (KG-12)
2015-16 Enrollment: 1,300 . . . . (330) 482-5526

Housing: Homeownership rate: 68.0%; Median home value: $141,100; Median year structure built: 1970; Homeowner vacancy rate: 0.0%; Median selected monthly owner costs: $1,170 with a mortgage, $417 without a mortgage; Median gross rent: $626 per month; Rental vacancy rate: 7.1%
Health Insurance: 96.6% have insurance; 74.2% have private insurance; 44.1% have public insurance; 3.4% do not have insurance; 0.0% of children under 18 do not have insurance
Safety: Violent crime rate: 4.8 per 10,000 population; Property crime rate: 140.4 per 10,000 population
Transportation: Commute: 94.4% car, 0.0% public transportation, 2.8% walk, 2.8% work from home; Mean travel time to work: 19.7 minutes

EAST LIVERPOOL (city). Covers a land area of 4.563 square miles and a water area of 0.196 square miles. Located at 40.63° N. Lat; 80.57° W. Long. Elevation is 768 feet.
History: East Liverpool was called St. Clair in 1798 by its founder, Thomas Fawcett of Ireland. Early residents called it Fawcett's Town, but in 1860 the name became Liverpool, because many of the residents had come from the English pottery city. James Bennett, a young potter from England, arrived here in 1838, and East Liverpool began the pottery production that shaped its character for many years.
Population: 10,919; Growth (since 2000): -16.6%; Density: 2,393.2 persons per square mile; Race: 90.2% White, 5.6% Black/African American, 0.0% Asian, 0.0% American Indian/Alaska Native, 0.0% Native Hawaiian/Other Pacific Islander, 3.2% Two or more races, 1.4% Hispanic of any race; Average household size: 2.42; Median age: 38.6; Age under 18: 25.9%; Age 65 and over: 14.1%; Males per 100 females: 90.7; Marriage status: 29.1% never married, 50.1% now married, 2.9% separated, 7.8% widowed, 13.0% divorced; Foreign born: 1.0%; Speak English only: 98.3%; With disability: 21.4%; Veterans: 10.2%; Ancestry: 19.3% German, 18.3% American, 16.3% Irish, 10.0% English, 5.4% Italian
Employment: 8.8% management, business, and financial, 2.8% computer, engineering, and science, 7.6% education, legal, community service, arts, and media, 4.8% healthcare practitioners, 27.0% service, 18.8% sales and office, 7.8% natural resources, construction, and maintenance, 22.5% production, transportation, and material moving
Income: Per capita: $17,324; Median household: $30,291; Average household: $42,213; Households with income of $100,000 or more: 8.3%; Poverty rate: 26.3%
Educational Attainment: High school diploma or higher: 82.0%; Bachelor's degree or higher: 10.7%; Graduate/professional degree or higher: 3.7%

School District(s)

Beaver Local (KG-12)
2015-16 Enrollment: 1,890 . . . . (330) 385-6831
Buckeye On-line School For Success (KG-12)
2015-16 Enrollment: 853. . . . . (330) 385-1987
East Liverpool City (PK-12)
2015-16 Enrollment: 2,075 . . . . (330) 385-7132

Four-year College(s)

Kent State University at East Liverpool (Public)
Fall 2016 Enrollment: 1,302 . . . . (330) 385-3805
2016-17 Tuition: In-state $5,664; Out-of-state $14,028

Two-year College(s)

Ohio Valley College of Technology (Private, For-profit)
Fall 2016 Enrollment: 204 . . . . (330) 385-1070
2016-17 Tuition: In-state $11,698; Out-of-state $11,698

Housing: Homeownership rate: 54.9%; Median home value: $55,300; Median year structure built: 1941; Homeowner vacancy rate: 3.1%; Median selected monthly owner costs: $790 with a mortgage, $332 without a mortgage; Median gross rent: $559 per month; Rental vacancy rate: 4.0%
Health Insurance: 88.5% have insurance; 49.6% have private insurance; 51.6% have public insurance; 11.5% do not have insurance; 6.1% of children under 18 do not have insurance
Hospitals: East Liverpool City Hospital (199 beds)
Newspapers: The Review (daily circulation 9,300)
Transportation: Commute: 95.1% car, 0.9% public transportation, 2.6% walk, 1.0% work from home; Mean travel time to work: 23.6 minutes
Additional Information Contacts
City of East Liverpool . . . . (330) 385-3381
http://www.eastliverpool.com

EAST PALESTINE (village). Covers a land area of 3.152 square miles and a water area of 0 square miles. Located at 40.84° N. Lat; 80.55° W. Long. Elevation is 997 feet.
History: East Palestine was established in 1828 by Thomas McCalla and William Grate. It developed as a pottery town, first using deposits of local clay, but later employing finer materials.
Population: 4,598; Growth (since 2000): -6.5%; Density: 1,458.7 persons per square mile; Race: 94.8% White, 1.2% Black/African American, 0.8% Asian, 0.2% American Indian/Alaska Native, 0.0% Native Hawaiian/Other Pacific Islander, 2.3% Two or more races, 2.0% Hispanic of any race; Average household size: 2.53; Median age: 38.6; Age under 18: 25.5%; Age 65 and over: 16.3%; Males per 100 females: 96.2; Marriage status: 28.0% never married, 49.5% now married, 3.4% separated, 8.9% widowed, 13.6% divorced; Foreign born: 1.4%; Speak English only: 99.1%;

With disability: 17.5%; Veterans: 9.5%; Ancestry: 29.2% German, 17.3% Irish, 13.5% Italian, 13.2% English, 9.3% American
Employment: 8.3% management, business, and financial, 3.0% computer, engineering, and science, 6.3% education, legal, community service, arts, and media, 6.9% healthcare practitioners, 15.6% service, 23.1% sales and office, 12.5% natural resources, construction, and maintenance, 24.4% production, transportation, and material moving
Income: Per capita: $20,175; Median household: $40,854; Average household: $50,630; Households with income of $100,000 or more: 10.2%; Poverty rate: 17.6%
Educational Attainment: High school diploma or higher: 88.4%; Bachelor's degree or higher: 12.7%; Graduate/professional degree or higher: 3.0%

School District(s)

East Palestine City (KG-12)
2015-16 Enrollment: 1,107 . . . . (330) 426-4191
Housing: Homeownership rate: 65.4%; Median home value: $81,100; Median year structure built: Before 1940; Homeowner vacancy rate: 2.8%; Median selected monthly owner costs: $848 with a mortgage, $376 without a mortgage; Median gross rent: $756 per month; Rental vacancy rate: 4.0%
Health Insurance: 93.2% have insurance; 62.3% have private insurance; 44.1% have public insurance; 6.8% do not have insurance; 0.6% of children under 18 do not have insurance
Safety: Violent crime rate: 13.2 per 10,000 population; Property crime rate: 136.3 per 10,000 population
Transportation: Commute: 93.4% car, 0.3% public transportation, 3.8% walk, 0.5% work from home; Mean travel time to work: 27.2 minutes
Additional Information Contacts
City of East Palestine . . . . (330) 426-4367
http://www.eastpalestine-oh.gov

EAST ROCHESTER (CDP). Covers a land area of 0.426 square miles and a water area of 0 square miles. Located at 40.75° N. Lat; 81.04° W. Long. Elevation is 1,093 feet.
Population: 279; Growth (since 2000): n/a; Density: 654.9 persons per square mile; Race: 100.0% White, 0.0% Black/African American, 0.0% Asian, 0.0% American Indian/Alaska Native, 0.0% Native Hawaiian/Other Pacific Islander, 0.0% Two or more races, 0.0% Hispanic of any race; Average household size: 1.94; Median age: 39.3; Age under 18: 16.8%; Age 65 and over: 17.6%; Males per 100 females: 104.4; Marriage status: 48.4% never married, 21.6% now married, 0.0% separated, 6.4% widowed, 23.6% divorced; Foreign born: 0.0%; Speak English only: 100.0%; With disability: 17.9%; Veterans: 0.0%; Ancestry: 40.1% German, 33.0% Irish, 15.1% English, 13.3% Dutch, 5.7% American
Employment: 11.6% management, business, and financial, 0.0% computer, engineering, and science, 0.0% education, legal, community service, arts, and media, 0.0% healthcare practitioners, 11.0% service, 22.6% sales and office, 29.5% natural resources, construction, and maintenance, 25.3% production, transportation, and material moving
Income: Per capita: $20,073; Median household: n/a; Average household: $38,537; Households with income of $100,000 or more: n/a; Poverty rate: 6.1%
Educational Attainment: High school diploma or higher: 91.9%; Bachelor's degree or higher: 8.6%; Graduate/professional degree or higher: n/a
Housing: Homeownership rate: 75.7%; Median home value: $75,600; Median year structure built: 1981; Homeowner vacancy rate: 0.0%; Median selected monthly owner costs: $951 with a mortgage, n/a without a mortgage; Median gross rent: n/a per month; Rental vacancy rate: 0.0%
Health Insurance: 91.0% have insurance; 73.1% have private insurance; 35.1% have public insurance; 9.0% do not have insurance; 0.0% of children under 18 do not have insurance
Transportation: Commute: 100.0% car, 0.0% public transportation, 0.0% walk, 0.0% work from home; Mean travel time to work: 32.4 minutes

GLENMOOR (CDP). Covers a land area of 2.796 square miles and a water area of <.001 square miles. Located at 40.66° N. Lat; 80.61° W. Long. Elevation is 1,122 feet.
Population: 1,987; Growth (since 2000): -9.4%; Density: 710.7 persons per square mile; Race: 98.2% White, 0.0% Black/African American, 0.0% Asian, 0.0% American Indian/Alaska Native, 0.0% Native Hawaiian/Other Pacific Islander, 1.8% Two or more races, 0.0% Hispanic of any race; Average household size: 2.70; Median age: 35.9; Age under 18: 33.5%; Age 65 and over: 16.2%; Males per 100 females: 103.0; Marriage status: 18.4% never married, 59.7% now married, 5.6% separated, 6.4% widowed, 15.4% divorced; Foreign born: 0.0%; Speak English only: 100.0%; With disability: 15.2%; Veterans: 7.3%; Ancestry: 20.6% American, 16.2% German, 14.0% Irish, 7.4% English, 2.1% Scotch-Irish
Employment: 3.6% management, business, and financial, 2.1% computer, engineering, and science, 3.5% education, legal, community service, arts, and media, 2.9% healthcare practitioners, 25.0% service, 28.9% sales and office, 6.0% natural resources, construction, and maintenance, 28.0% production, transportation, and material moving
Income: Per capita: $17,851; Median household: $39,620; Average household: $47,983; Households with income of $100,000 or more: 5.6%; Poverty rate: 22.7%
Educational Attainment: High school diploma or higher: 76.9%; Bachelor's degree or higher: 4.6%; Graduate/professional degree or higher: 2.3%
Housing: Homeownership rate: 78.6%; Median home value: $85,400; Median year structure built: 1962; Homeowner vacancy rate: 9.1%; Median selected monthly owner costs: $899 with a mortgage, $431 without a mortgage; Median gross rent: $785 per month; Rental vacancy rate: 0.0%
Health Insurance: 84.0% have insurance; 54.7% have private insurance; 42.8% have public insurance; 16.0% do not have insurance; 21.2% of children under 18 do not have insurance
Transportation: Commute: 92.1% car, 0.0% public transportation, 3.8% walk, 4.1% work from home; Mean travel time to work: 25.5 minutes

HANOVERTON (village). Covers a land area of 0.695 square miles and a water area of 0 square miles. Located at 40.75° N. Lat; 80.94° W. Long. Elevation is 1,132 feet.
Population: 372; Growth (since 2000): -3.9%; Density: 535.4 persons per square mile; Race: 93.5% White, 0.0% Black/African American, 1.3% Asian, 0.0% American Indian/Alaska Native, 0.0% Native Hawaiian/Other Pacific Islander, 5.1% Two or more races, 0.5% Hispanic of any race; Average household size: 2.40; Median age: 45.3; Age under 18: 21.8%; Age 65 and over: 18.8%; Males per 100 females: 91.5; Marriage status: 26.3% never married, 54.3% now married, 2.5% separated, 6.7% widowed, 12.7% divorced; Foreign born: 1.1%; Speak English only: 96.9%; With disability: 13.4%; Veterans: 10.0%; Ancestry: 28.2% German, 23.1% Irish, 14.0% American, 13.4% English, 3.2% Polish
Employment: 2.6% management, business, and financial, 1.0% computer, engineering, and science, 9.8% education, legal, community service, arts, and media, 5.2% healthcare practitioners, 13.5% service, 27.5% sales and office, 15.5% natural resources, construction, and maintenance, 24.9% production, transportation, and material moving
Income: Per capita: $23,679; Median household: $44,688; Average household: $56,249; Households with income of $100,000 or more: 13.5%; Poverty rate: 13.4%
Educational Attainment: High school diploma or higher: 86.5%; Bachelor's degree or higher: 13.1%; Graduate/professional degree or higher: 6.6%

School District(s)

United Local (KG-12)
2015-16 Enrollment: 1,194 . . . . (330) 223-1521
Housing: Homeownership rate: 74.8%; Median home value: $105,900; Median year structure built: 1951; Homeowner vacancy rate: 4.1%; Median selected monthly owner costs: $968 with a mortgage, $295 without a mortgage; Median gross rent: $613 per month; Rental vacancy rate: 0.0%
Health Insurance: 92.2% have insurance; 71.2% have private insurance; 37.6% have public insurance; 7.8% do not have insurance; 4.9% of children under 18 do not have insurance
Transportation: Commute: 95.3% car, 0.0% public transportation, 2.6% walk, 1.1% work from home; Mean travel time to work: 28.8 minutes

HOMEWORTH (CDP). Covers a land area of 1.239 square miles and a water area of 0.015 square miles. Located at 40.84° N. Lat; 81.07° W. Long. Elevation is 1,142 feet.
Population: 298; Growth (since 2000): n/a; Density: 240.6 persons per square mile; Race: 100.0% White, 0.0% Black/African American, 0.0% Asian, 0.0% American Indian/Alaska Native, 0.0% Native Hawaiian/Other Pacific Islander, 0.0% Two or more races, 0.0% Hispanic of any race; Average household size: 2.31; Median age: 51.5; Age under 18: 12.1%; Age 65 and over: 14.4%; Males per 100 females: 104.7; Marriage status: 29.8% never married, 53.8% now married, 3.8% separated, 8.4% widowed, 8.0% divorced; Foreign born: 0.0%; Speak English only: 100.0%; With disability: 12.1%; Veterans: 11.8%; Ancestry: 43.6% German, 18.5% Irish, 16.1% English, 10.1% American, 5.7% Dutch

Employment: 5.6% management, business, and financial, 4.4% computer, engineering, and science, 0.0% education, legal, community service, arts, and media, 0.0% healthcare practitioners, 20.6% service, 21.1% sales and office, 5.6% natural resources, construction, and maintenance, 42.8% production, transportation, and material moving
Income: Per capita: $28,763; Median household: $78,281; Average household: $66,721; Households with income of $100,000 or more: 16.3%; Poverty rate: 2.3%
Educational Attainment: High school diploma or higher: 93.4%; Bachelor's degree or higher: 16.2%; Graduate/professional degree or higher: 8.3%
Housing: Homeownership rate: 71.3%; Median home value: $109,400; Median year structure built: 1957; Homeowner vacancy rate: 0.0%; Median selected monthly owner costs: $1,006 with a mortgage, $359 without a mortgage; Median gross rent: n/a per month; Rental vacancy rate: 0.0%
Health Insurance: 100.0% have insurance; 59.4% have private insurance; 49.7% have public insurance; 0.0% do not have insurance; 0.0% of children under 18 do not have insurance
Transportation: Commute: 94.4% car, 0.0% public transportation, 5.6% walk, 0.0% work from home; Mean travel time to work: 25.1 minutes

KENSINGTON (unincorporated postal area)

ZCTA: 44427

Covers a land area of 30.596 square miles and a water area of 0.043 square miles. Located at 40.71° N. Lat; 80.95° W. Long. Elevation is 1,115 feet.
Population: 1,798; Growth (since 2000): 4.1%; Density: 58.8 persons per square mile; Race: 95.3% White, 0.0% Black/African American, 0.0% Asian, 0.0% American Indian/Alaska Native, 0.0% Native Hawaiian/Other Pacific Islander, 0.0% Two or more races, 4.7% Hispanic of any race; Average household size: 2.82; Median age: 42.5; Age under 18: 26.5%; Age 65 and over: 11.1%; Males per 100 females: 99.5; Marriage status: 27.3% never married, 64.6% now married, 2.4% separated, 3.3% widowed, 4.8% divorced; Foreign born: 3.6%; Speak English only: 90.3%; With disability: 12.6%; Veterans: 12.5%; Ancestry: 28.6% German, 22.0% American, 16.3% Irish, 9.8% Italian, 8.1% Swiss
Employment: 8.7% management, business, and financial, 0.0% computer, engineering, and science, 10.6% education, legal, community service, arts, and media, 2.9% healthcare practitioners, 21.7% service, 13.6% sales and office, 16.7% natural resources, construction, and maintenance, 25.8% production, transportation, and material moving
Income: Per capita: $21,091; Median household: $47,150; Average household: $60,996; Households with income of $100,000 or more: 11.2%; Poverty rate: 8.9%
Educational Attainment: High school diploma or higher: 84.4%; Bachelor's degree or higher: 14.9%; Graduate/professional degree or higher: 7.3%
Housing: Homeownership rate: 79.0%; Median home value: $106,400; Median year structure built: 1981; Homeowner vacancy rate: 0.0%; Median selected monthly owner costs: $1,178 with a mortgage, $375 without a mortgage; Median gross rent: $770 per month; Rental vacancy rate: 0.0%
Health Insurance: 89.1% have insurance; 72.8% have private insurance; 27.3% have public insurance; 10.9% do not have insurance; 8.6% of children under 18 do not have insurance
Transportation: Commute: 91.0% car, 1.8% public transportation, 0.7% walk, 6.6% work from home; Mean travel time to work: 29.6 minutes

LA CROFT (CDP). Covers a land area of 1.145 square miles and a water area of 0 square miles. Located at 40.65° N. Lat; 80.60° W. Long. Elevation is 1,168 feet.

Population: 1,237; Growth (since 2000): -5.4%; Density: 1,080.6 persons per square mile; Race: 94.4% White, 3.6% Black/African American, 0.0% Asian, 0.0% American Indian/Alaska Native, 0.0% Native Hawaiian/Other Pacific Islander, 1.9% Two or more races, 0.0% Hispanic of any race; Average household size: 2.66; Median age: 33.0; Age under 18: 23.3%; Age 65 and over: 10.9%; Males per 100 females: 89.7; Marriage status: 35.6% never married, 43.9% now married, 0.0% separated, 5.5% widowed, 14.9% divorced; Foreign born: 0.0%; Speak English only: 100.0%; With disability: 21.7%; Veterans: 7.4%; Ancestry: 42.2% American, 15.0% English, 12.4% German, 8.6% Irish, 4.6% Scottish
Employment: 8.4% management, business, and financial, 0.0% computer, engineering, and science, 6.1% education, legal, community service, arts, and media, 3.3% healthcare practitioners, 20.0% service, 23.5% sales and office, 5.5% natural resources, construction, and maintenance, 33.2% production, transportation, and material moving
Income: Per capita: $22,224; Median household: $44,879; Average household: $58,659; Households with income of $100,000 or more: 3.6%; Poverty rate: 11.3%
Educational Attainment: High school diploma or higher: 94.9%; Bachelor's degree or higher: 9.7%; Graduate/professional degree or higher: 7.4%
Housing: Homeownership rate: 72.5%; Median home value: $70,200; Median year structure built: 1951; Homeowner vacancy rate: 0.0%; Median selected monthly owner costs: $955 with a mortgage, $331 without a mortgage; Median gross rent: $708 per month; Rental vacancy rate: 0.0%
Health Insurance: 83.2% have insurance; 61.4% have private insurance; 34.5% have public insurance; 16.8% do not have insurance; 3.1% of children under 18 do not have insurance
Transportation: Commute: 92.5% car, 0.0% public transportation, 0.0% walk, 7.5% work from home; Mean travel time to work: 23.8 minutes

LAKE TOMAHAWK (CDP). Covers a land area of 0.829 square miles and a water area of 0.197 square miles. Located at 40.76° N. Lat; 80.60° W. Long.

Population: 788; Growth (since 2000): n/a; Density: 950.7 persons per square mile; Race: 98.9% White, 0.0% Black/African American, 0.0% Asian, 1.1% American Indian/Alaska Native, 0.0% Native Hawaiian/Other Pacific Islander, 0.0% Two or more races, 0.0% Hispanic of any race; Average household size: 2.47; Median age: 49.3; Age under 18: 17.0%; Age 65 and over: 28.2%; Males per 100 females: 106.4; Marriage status: 24.3% never married, 65.5% now married, 0.0% separated, 3.4% widowed, 6.7% divorced; Foreign born: 2.9%; Speak English only: 97.7%; With disability: 13.8%; Veterans: 2.8%; Ancestry: 22.1% German, 17.9% American, 13.3% Irish, 11.0% English, 7.6% Italian
Employment: 11.2% management, business, and financial, 24.4% computer, engineering, and science, 24.2% education, legal, community service, arts, and media, 12.6% healthcare practitioners, 2.5% service, 20.8% sales and office, 0.0% natural resources, construction, and maintenance, 4.2% production, transportation, and material moving
Income: Per capita: $60,704; Median household: $57,042; Average household: $156,587; Households with income of $100,000 or more: 34.8%; Poverty rate: 2.9%
Educational Attainment: High school diploma or higher: 100.0%; Bachelor's degree or higher: 37.8%; Graduate/professional degree or higher: 8.1%
Housing: Homeownership rate: 100.0%; Median home value: $207,400; Median year structure built: 1985; Homeowner vacancy rate: 0.0%; Median selected monthly owner costs: $1,604 with a mortgage, $570 without a mortgage; Median gross rent: n/a per month; Rental vacancy rate: 0.0%
Health Insurance: 98.9% have insurance; 82.5% have private insurance; 40.9% have public insurance; 1.1% do not have insurance; 0.0% of children under 18 do not have insurance
Transportation: Commute: 80.7% car, 0.0% public transportation, 13.3% walk, 6.0% work from home; Mean travel time to work: 24.7 minutes

LEETONIA (village). Covers a land area of 2.263 square miles and a water area of 0.007 square miles. Located at 40.88° N. Lat; 80.76° W. Long. Elevation is 1,017 feet.

History: Laid out 1866.
Population: 2,105; Growth (since 2000): 3.0%; Density: 930.2 persons per square mile; Race: 97.8% White, 0.4% Black/African American, 0.2% Asian, 0.4% American Indian/Alaska Native, 0.0% Native Hawaiian/Other Pacific Islander, 1.2% Two or more races, 1.0% Hispanic of any race; Average household size: 2.44; Median age: 43.7; Age under 18: 20.3%; Age 65 and over: 16.2%; Males per 100 females: 96.1; Marriage status: 28.4% never married, 49.5% now married, 3.5% separated, 6.8% widowed, 15.3% divorced; Foreign born: 0.3%; Speak English only: 99.0%; With disability: 15.6%; Veterans: 11.2%; Ancestry: 29.5% German, 16.3% Italian, 16.2% Irish, 11.6% American, 11.5% English
Employment: 8.5% management, business, and financial, 0.6% computer, engineering, and science, 3.6% education, legal, community service, arts, and media, 4.7% healthcare practitioners, 23.2% service, 19.0% sales and office, 10.5% natural resources, construction, and maintenance, 29.9% production, transportation, and material moving
Income: Per capita: $22,098; Median household: $42,917; Average household: $53,371; Households with income of $100,000 or more: 11.6%; Poverty rate: 12.1%
Educational Attainment: High school diploma or higher: 90.2%; Bachelor's degree or higher: 11.6%; Graduate/professional degree or higher: 3.4%

School District(s)

Leetonia Exempted Village (KG-12)
2015-16 Enrollment: 686. . . . . (330) 427-6594

Housing: Homeownership rate: 73.9%; Median home value: $80,800; Median year structure built: Before 1940; Homeowner vacancy rate: 0.5%; Median selected monthly owner costs: $886 with a mortgage, $354 without a mortgage; Median gross rent: $771 per month; Rental vacancy rate: 1.7%

Health Insurance: 85.2% have insurance; 62.5% have private insurance; 35.1% have public insurance; 14.8% do not have insurance; 13.3% of children under 18 do not have insurance

Transportation: Commute: 93.8% car, 1.0% public transportation, 1.9% walk, 2.1% work from home; Mean travel time to work: 20.2 minutes

LISBON (village). County seat. Covers a land area of 1.687 square miles and a water area of 0 square miles. Located at 40.78° N. Lat; 80.76° W. Long. Elevation is 965 feet.

History: Lisbon was founded in 1802, and grew as a coal and pottery town. This was the birthplace of politicians Marcus A. Hanna (1837-1904) and Clement L. Vallandigham (1820-1871).

Population: 2,741; Growth (since 2000): -1.7%; Density: 1,624.4 persons per square mile; Race: 97.5% White, 1.1% Black/African American, 0.0% Asian, 0.0% American Indian/Alaska Native, 0.0% Native Hawaiian/Other Pacific Islander, 0.7% Two or more races, 1.7% Hispanic of any race; Average household size: 2.40; Median age: 39.4; Age under 18: 21.6%; Age 65 and over: 16.1%; Males per 100 females: 89.7; Marriage status: 31.6% never married, 46.7% now married, 2.3% separated, 9.0% widowed, 12.7% divorced; Foreign born: 0.6%; Speak English only: 98.0%; With disability: 19.3%; Veterans: 8.4%; Ancestry: 27.5% German, 26.5% American, 21.7% Irish, 13.4% English, 5.8% Italian

Employment: 8.5% management, business, and financial, 2.2% computer, engineering, and science, 9.1% education, legal, community service, arts, and media, 4.0% healthcare practitioners, 22.7% service, 20.4% sales and office, 11.2% natural resources, construction, and maintenance, 21.9% production, transportation, and material moving

Income: Per capita: $19,042; Median household: $36,581; Average household: $47,135; Households with income of $100,000 or more: 11.1%; Poverty rate: 32.3%

Educational Attainment: High school diploma or higher: 84.3%; Bachelor's degree or higher: 13.6%; Graduate/professional degree or higher: 5.5%

School District(s)

Beaver Local (KG-12)
2015-16 Enrollment: 1,890 . . . . (330) 385-6831
Columbiana County (11-12)
2015-16 Enrollment: n/a . . . . (330) 424-9561
Lisbon Exempted Village (PK-12)
2015-16 Enrollment: 901. . . . . (330) 424-7714

Vocational/Technical School(s)

Columbiana County Career and Technical Center (Public)
Fall 2016 Enrollment: 156 . . . . (330) 424-9561
2016-17 Tuition: $6,600

Housing: Homeownership rate: 58.8%; Median home value: $78,600; Median year structure built: Before 1940; Homeowner vacancy rate: 1.5%; Median selected monthly owner costs: $870 with a mortgage, $352 without a mortgage; Median gross rent: $594 per month; Rental vacancy rate: 9.7%

Health Insurance: 90.3% have insurance; 53.0% have private insurance; 48.5% have public insurance; 9.7% do not have insurance; 1.0% of children under 18 do not have insurance

Safety: Violent crime rate: 0.0 per 10,000 population; Property crime rate: 144.0 per 10,000 population

Newspapers: Morning Journal (daily circulation 11,800)

Transportation: Commute: 92.5% car, 0.0% public transportation, 4.6% walk, 2.8% work from home; Mean travel time to work: 18.9 minutes

NEGLEY (CDP). Covers a land area of 0.891 square miles and a water area of 0 square miles. Located at 40.79° N. Lat; 80.54° W. Long. Elevation is 856 feet.

Population: 146; Growth (since 2000): n/a; Density: 163.8 persons per square mile; Race: 100.0% White, 0.0% Black/African American, 0.0% Asian, 0.0% American Indian/Alaska Native, 0.0% Native Hawaiian/Other Pacific Islander, 0.0% Two or more races, 0.0% Hispanic of any race; Average household size: 1.70; Median age: 62.3; Age under 18: 0.0%; Age 65 and over: 36.3%; Males per 100 females: 102.2; Marriage status: 0.0% never married, 85.6% now married, 0.0% separated, 6.8% widowed, 7.5% divorced; Foreign born: 0.0%; Speak English only: 100.0%; With disability: 34.2%; Veterans: 11.6%; Ancestry: 40.4% Irish, 39.0% German, 17.1% Italian, 15.1% Scottish, 14.4% American

Employment: 0.0% management, business, and financial, 0.0% computer, engineering, and science, 22.4% education, legal, community service, arts, and media, 11.2% healthcare practitioners, 29.6% service, 0.0% sales and office, 25.5% natural resources, construction, and maintenance, 11.2% production, transportation, and material moving

Income: Per capita: $33,330; Median household: $53,125; Average household: $58,181; Households with income of $100,000 or more: 14.0%; Poverty rate: 7.5%

Educational Attainment: High school diploma or higher: 85.6%; Bachelor's degree or higher: n/a; Graduate/professional degree or higher: n/a

Housing: Homeownership rate: 88.4%; Median home value: $54,700; Median year structure built: Before 1940; Homeowner vacancy rate: 0.0%; Median selected monthly owner costs: $927 with a mortgage, n/a without a mortgage; Median gross rent: n/a per month; Rental vacancy rate: 0.0%

Health Insurance: 100.0% have insurance; 92.5% have private insurance; 36.3% have public insurance; 0.0% do not have insurance; 0.0% of children under 18 do not have insurance

Transportation: Commute: 100.0% car, 0.0% public transportation, 0.0% walk, 0.0% work from home; Mean travel time to work: 0.0 minutes

NEW WATERFORD (village). Covers a land area of 0.887 square miles and a water area of 0 square miles. Located at 40.85° N. Lat; 80.62° W. Long. Elevation is 1,047 feet.

Population: 1,289; Growth (since 2000): -7.3%; Density: 1,452.5 persons per square mile; Race: 96.9% White, 1.1% Black/African American, 0.3% Asian, 0.0% American Indian/Alaska Native, 0.0% Native Hawaiian/Other Pacific Islander, 1.7% Two or more races, 0.0% Hispanic of any race; Average household size: 2.44; Median age: 43.4; Age under 18: 23.9%; Age 65 and over: 15.2%; Males per 100 females: 89.0; Marriage status: 21.0% never married, 58.6% now married, 1.3% separated, 8.0% widowed, 12.4% divorced; Foreign born: 0.5%; Speak English only: 99.4%; With disability: 12.9%; Veterans: 10.8%; Ancestry: 25.5% German, 19.6% Irish, 12.4% Italian, 11.0% American, 5.5% English

Employment: 14.7% management, business, and financial, 0.9% computer, engineering, and science, 3.1% education, legal, community service, arts, and media, 6.6% healthcare practitioners, 18.5% service, 18.3% sales and office, 7.9% natural resources, construction, and maintenance, 30.0% production, transportation, and material moving

Income: Per capita: $20,244; Median household: $40,119; Average household: $48,637; Households with income of $100,000 or more: 11.9%; Poverty rate: 23.2%

Educational Attainment: High school diploma or higher: 85.8%; Bachelor's degree or higher: 8.2%; Graduate/professional degree or higher: 2.7%

Housing: Homeownership rate: 77.5%; Median home value: $88,900; Median year structure built: 1975; Homeowner vacancy rate: 5.5%; Median selected monthly owner costs: $970 with a mortgage, $422 without a mortgage; Median gross rent: $563 per month; Rental vacancy rate: 0.0%

Health Insurance: 92.6% have insurance; 63.4% have private insurance; 44.7% have public insurance; 7.4% do not have insurance; 3.2% of children under 18 do not have insurance

Transportation: Commute: 97.9% car, 0.0% public transportation, 0.0% walk, 0.5% work from home; Mean travel time to work: 24.1 minutes

ROGERS (village). Covers a land area of 0.227 square miles and a water area of 0 square miles. Located at 40.79° N. Lat; 80.63° W. Long. Elevation is 1,027 feet.

Population: 232; Growth (since 2000): -12.8%; Density: 1,020.2 persons per square mile; Race: 99.1% White, 0.0% Black/African American, 0.0% Asian, 0.0% American Indian/Alaska Native, 0.0% Native Hawaiian/Other Pacific Islander, 0.9% Two or more races, 0.0% Hispanic of any race; Average household size: 2.52; Median age: 45.2; Age under 18: 13.4%; Age 65 and over: 16.8%; Males per 100 females: 91.1; Marriage status: 34.0% never married, 50.0% now married, 3.4% separated, 3.9% widowed, 12.1% divorced; Foreign born: 0.9%; Speak English only: 98.7%; With disability: 14.7%; Veterans: 7.0%; Ancestry: 32.3% German, 25.9% Irish, 21.6% American, 14.2% Italian, 6.0% English

Employment: 3.1% management, business, and financial, 0.0% computer, engineering, and science, 0.8% education, legal, community service, arts, and media, 4.7% healthcare practitioners, 26.6% service, 24.2% sales and

office, 17.2% natural resources, construction, and maintenance, 23.4% production, transportation, and material moving
Income: Per capita: $18,496; Median household: $36,000; Average household: $47,432; Households with income of $100,000 or more: 12.0%; Poverty rate: 13.8%
Educational Attainment: High school diploma or higher: 78.4%; Bachelor's degree or higher: 5.4%; Graduate/professional degree or higher: 1.2%
Housing: Homeownership rate: 83.7%; Median home value: $69,200; Median year structure built: 1947; Homeowner vacancy rate: 6.1%; Median selected monthly owner costs: $917 with a mortgage, $433 without a mortgage; Median gross rent: $644 per month; Rental vacancy rate: 0.0%
Health Insurance: 91.4% have insurance; 55.2% have private insurance; 47.0% have public insurance; 8.6% do not have insurance; 6.5% of children under 18 do not have insurance
Transportation: Commute: 96.7% car, 0.0% public transportation, 0.0% walk, 0.0% work from home; Mean travel time to work: 20.6 minutes

SALEM (city). Covers a land area of 6.425 square miles and a water area of 0.003 square miles. Located at 40.90° N. Lat; 80.85° W. Long. Elevation is 1,227 feet.
History: The Quakers came to Salem in 1801 from Salem, New Jersey, and were joined by others from Pennsylvania and Virginia. The town was a station on the Underground Railroad.
Population: 12,071; Growth (since 2000): -1.0%; Density: 1,878.9 persons per square mile; Race: 95.5% White, 1.3% Black/African American, 0.1% Asian, 0.1% American Indian/Alaska Native, 0.0% Native Hawaiian/Other Pacific Islander, 1.0% Two or more races, 3.8% Hispanic of any race; Average household size: 2.38; Median age: 37.7; Age under 18: 23.6%; Age 65 and over: 16.7%; Males per 100 females: 91.8; Marriage status: 27.9% never married, 49.7% now married, 1.7% separated, 8.6% widowed, 13.8% divorced; Foreign born: 2.9%; Speak English only: 95.9%; With disability: 13.2%; Veterans: 10.4%; Ancestry: 21.0% German, 17.8% American, 15.9% Irish, 9.0% Italian, 7.6% English
Employment: 9.5% management, business, and financial, 2.1% computer, engineering, and science, 6.2% education, legal, community service, arts, and media, 6.7% healthcare practitioners, 21.8% service, 24.7% sales and office, 7.4% natural resources, construction, and maintenance, 21.6% production, transportation, and material moving
Income: Per capita: $23,340; Median household: $38,624; Average household: $55,506; Households with income of $100,000 or more: 11.6%; Poverty rate: 23.3%
Educational Attainment: High school diploma or higher: 86.0%; Bachelor's degree or higher: 13.3%; Graduate/professional degree or higher: 4.4%

School District(s)

Salem City (KG-12)
2015-16 Enrollment: 2,061 . . . . (330) 332-0316
West Branch Local (PK-12)
2015-16 Enrollment: 2,110 . . . . (330) 938-9324

Four-year College(s)

Allegheny Wesleyan College (Private, Not-for-profit, Other Protestant)
Fall 2016 Enrollment: 79 . . . . (330) 337-6403
2016-17 Tuition: In-state $5,000; Out-of-state $5,000
Kent State University at Salem (Public)
Fall 2016 Enrollment: 1,675 . . . . (330) 332-0361
2016-17 Tuition: In-state $5,664; Out-of-state $14,028

Vocational/Technical School(s)

Hannah E Mullins School of Practical Nursing (Public)
Fall 2016 Enrollment: 50 . . . . (330) 332-8940
2016-17 Tuition: $12,499
Housing: Homeownership rate: 58.6%; Median home value: $93,500; Median year structure built: 1958; Homeowner vacancy rate: 3.0%; Median selected monthly owner costs: $931 with a mortgage, $341 without a mortgage; Median gross rent: $646 per month; Rental vacancy rate: 7.1%
Health Insurance: 87.3% have insurance; 57.9% have private insurance; 41.6% have public insurance; 12.7% do not have insurance; 5.2% of children under 18 do not have insurance
Hospitals: Salem Regional Medical Center (183 beds)
Safety: Violent crime rate: 7.5 per 10,000 population; Property crime rate: 259.6 per 10,000 population
Newspapers: Salem News (daily circulation 6,100)
Transportation: Commute: 91.6% car, 0.2% public transportation, 3.8% walk, 3.7% work from home; Mean travel time to work: 22.4 minutes
Additional Information Contacts
City of Salem . . . . (330) 332-4241
http://www.cityofsalemohio.org

SALINEVILLE (village). Covers a land area of 2.208 square miles and a water area of 0 square miles. Located at 40.62° N. Lat; 80.83° W. Long. Elevation is 909 feet.
History: Salineville was named for the salt springs nearby. A salt well was sunk here in 1809, and by 1835 twenty wells were operating along Little Yellow Creek. The arrival of the railroad in 1852 led to the opening of drift coal mines, bringing prosperity to Salineville after the Civil War.
Population: 1,119; Growth (since 2000): -19.9%; Density: 506.9 persons per square mile; Race: 97.9% White, 0.4% Black/African American, 0.0% Asian, 0.0% American Indian/Alaska Native, 0.0% Native Hawaiian/Other Pacific Islander, 1.3% Two or more races, 0.8% Hispanic of any race; Average household size: 2.43; Median age: 36.9; Age under 18: 26.4%; Age 65 and over: 14.6%; Males per 100 females: 91.7; Marriage status: 29.4% never married, 47.0% now married, 1.1% separated, 7.7% widowed, 15.9% divorced; Foreign born: 0.0%; Speak English only: 99.5%; With disability: 16.8%; Veterans: 10.2%; Ancestry: 25.8% German, 20.3% Irish, 15.2% American, 7.7% English, 7.4% Polish
Employment: 1.5% management, business, and financial, 3.0% computer, engineering, and science, 5.8% education, legal, community service, arts, and media, 1.3% healthcare practitioners, 24.9% service, 18.8% sales and office, 11.8% natural resources, construction, and maintenance, 32.9% production, transportation, and material moving
Income: Per capita: $16,703; Median household: $32,260; Average household: $40,920; Households with income of $100,000 or more: 4.2%; Poverty rate: 25.2%
Educational Attainment: High school diploma or higher: 82.0%; Bachelor's degree or higher: 4.5%; Graduate/professional degree or higher: 1.3%

School District(s)

Southern Local (KG-12)
2015-16 Enrollment: 857 . . . . (330) 679-2343
Housing: Homeownership rate: 66.1%; Median home value: $46,300; Median year structure built: Before 1940; Homeowner vacancy rate: 3.4%; Median selected monthly owner costs: $800 with a mortgage, $343 without a mortgage; Median gross rent: $631 per month; Rental vacancy rate: 4.8%
Health Insurance: 90.9% have insurance; 49.1% have private insurance; 53.8% have public insurance; 9.1% do not have insurance; 0.0% of children under 18 do not have insurance
Safety: Violent crime rate: 7.9 per 10,000 population; Property crime rate: 181.7 per 10,000 population
Transportation: Commute: 91.6% car, 0.0% public transportation, 2.7% walk, 0.8% work from home; Mean travel time to work: 36.0 minutes

SUMMITVILLE (village). Covers a land area of 0.924 square miles and a water area of 0.027 square miles. Located at 40.67° N. Lat; 80.89° W. Long. Elevation is 1,106 feet.
Population: 123; Growth (since 2000): 13.9%; Density: 133.1 persons per square mile; Race: 100.0% White, 0.0% Black/African American, 0.0% Asian, 0.0% American Indian/Alaska Native, 0.0% Native Hawaiian/Other Pacific Islander, 0.0% Two or more races, 0.0% Hispanic of any race; Average household size: 3.08; Median age: 40.3; Age under 18: 26.8%; Age 65 and over: 25.2%; Males per 100 females: 101.5; Marriage status: 12.0% never married, 79.3% now married, 0.0% separated, 2.2% widowed, 6.5% divorced; Foreign born: 0.0%; Speak English only: 96.2%; With disability: 6.5%; Veterans: 15.6%; Ancestry: 45.5% American, 24.4% Irish, 18.7% German, 11.4% Italian, 3.3% English
Employment: 3.3% management, business, and financial, 0.0% computer, engineering, and science, 5.0% education, legal, community service, arts, and media, 6.7% healthcare practitioners, 16.7% service, 20.0% sales and office, 16.7% natural resources, construction, and maintenance, 31.7% production, transportation, and material moving
Income: Per capita: $25,760; Median household: $65,417; Average household: $67,908; Households with income of $100,000 or more: 7.5%; Poverty rate: n/a
Educational Attainment: High school diploma or higher: 90.5%; Bachelor's degree or higher: 7.1%; Graduate/professional degree or higher: 7.1%
Housing: Homeownership rate: 95.0%; Median home value: $84,300; Median year structure built: 1951; Homeowner vacancy rate: 0.0%; Median selected monthly owner costs: $1,146 with a mortgage, $305 without a mortgage; Median gross rent: n/a per month; Rental vacancy rate: 0.0%

Health Insurance: 96.7% have insurance; 85.4% have private insurance; 34.1% have public insurance; 3.3% do not have insurance; 3.0% of children under 18 do not have insurance
Transportation: Commute: 90.0% car, 0.0% public transportation, 1.7% walk, 8.3% work from home; Mean travel time to work: 33.3 minutes

WASHINGTONVILLE (village). Covers a land area of 0.668 square miles and a water area of <.001 square miles. Located at 40.90° N. Lat; 80.77° W. Long. Elevation is 1,056 feet.
Population: 864; Growth (since 2000): 9.5%; Density: 1,292.6 persons per square mile; Race: 95.3% White, 0.2% Black/African American, 3.7% Asian, 0.0% American Indian/Alaska Native, 0.0% Native Hawaiian/Other Pacific Islander, 0.1% Two or more races, 2.7% Hispanic of any race; Average household size: 2.35; Median age: 38.9; Age under 18: 18.6%; Age 65 and over: 16.4%; Males per 100 females: 94.9; Marriage status: 34.0% never married, 49.0% now married, 6.0% separated, 3.8% widowed, 13.2% divorced; Foreign born: 2.4%; Speak English only: 97.0%; With disability: 16.6%; Veterans: 11.9%; Ancestry: 28.5% German, 21.3% Irish, 14.9% American, 8.7% Italian, 8.2% English
Employment: 5.5% management, business, and financial, 0.5% computer, engineering, and science, 6.4% education, legal, community service, arts, and media, 3.2% healthcare practitioners, 16.1% service, 21.3% sales and office, 17.2% natural resources, construction, and maintenance, 29.8% production, transportation, and material moving
Income: Per capita: $19,035; Median household: $37,321; Average household: $44,774; Households with income of $100,000 or more: 6.9%; Poverty rate: 24.6%
Educational Attainment: High school diploma or higher: 88.5%; Bachelor's degree or higher: 10.7%; Graduate/professional degree or higher: 4.4%
Housing: Homeownership rate: 59.2%; Median home value: $75,700; Median year structure built: 1967; Homeowner vacancy rate: 0.0%; Median selected monthly owner costs: $833 with a mortgage, $355 without a mortgage; Median gross rent: $693 per month; Rental vacancy rate: 3.7%
Health Insurance: 86.7% have insurance; 57.4% have private insurance; 40.3% have public insurance; 13.3% do not have insurance; 4.3% of children under 18 do not have insurance
Transportation: Commute: 92.4% car, 0.0% public transportation, 6.2% walk, 1.4% work from home; Mean travel time to work: 27.0 minutes

WELLSVILLE (village). Covers a land area of 1.802 square miles and a water area of 0.109 square miles. Located at 40.60° N. Lat; 80.65° W. Long. Elevation is 696 feet.
History: Wellsville was founded in 1797 by William Wells, and grew as a stagecoach stop, a shipping center during the steamboat era, and the location of brickyards, potteries, and tile plants.
Population: 3,436; Growth (since 2000): -16.9%; Density: 1,906.7 persons per square mile; Race: 87.6% White, 6.4% Black/African American, 0.0% Asian, 0.0% American Indian/Alaska Native, 0.0% Native Hawaiian/Other Pacific Islander, 6.0% Two or more races, 1.4% Hispanic of any race; Average household size: 2.28; Median age: 34.5; Age under 18: 28.8%; Age 65 and over: 13.2%; Males per 100 females: 88.2; Marriage status: 35.8% never married, 39.5% now married, 3.7% separated, 7.9% widowed, 16.8% divorced; Foreign born: 0.0%; Speak English only: 98.0%; With disability: 18.1%; Veterans: 10.7%; Ancestry: 32.4% American, 20.1% German, 14.5% Irish, 8.4% Italian, 6.1% English
Employment: 3.5% management, business, and financial, 0.0% computer, engineering, and science, 2.8% education, legal, community service, arts, and media, 8.9% healthcare practitioners, 21.3% service, 24.6% sales and office, 15.1% natural resources, construction, and maintenance, 23.9% production, transportation, and material moving
Income: Per capita: $15,282; Median household: $28,171; Average household: $34,838; Households with income of $100,000 or more: 2.9%; Poverty rate: 33.5%
Educational Attainment: High school diploma or higher: 85.1%; Bachelor's degree or higher: 5.4%; Graduate/professional degree or higher: 0.3%

School District(s)

Wellsville Local (PK-12)
2015-16 Enrollment: 763. . . . . (330) 532-2643
Housing: Homeownership rate: 49.8%; Median home value: $54,200; Median year structure built: Before 1940; Homeowner vacancy rate: 6.9%; Median selected monthly owner costs: $773 with a mortgage, $343 without a mortgage; Median gross rent: $442 per month; Rental vacancy rate: 0.0%
Health Insurance: 88.0% have insurance; 47.0% have private insurance; 54.4% have public insurance; 12.0% do not have insurance; 2.3% of children under 18 do not have insurance
Transportation: Commute: 91.8% car, 0.5% public transportation, 5.3% walk, 0.6% work from home; Mean travel time to work: 25.1 minutes

WINONA (unincorporated postal area)
ZCTA: 44493
Covers a land area of 0.251 square miles and a water area of 0 square miles. Located at 40.83° N. Lat; 80.89° W. Long. Elevation is 1,194 feet.
Population: 31; Growth (since 2000): n/a; Density: 123.7 persons per square mile; Race: 100.0% White, 0.0% Black/African American, 0.0% Asian, 0.0% American Indian/Alaska Native, 0.0% Native Hawaiian/Other Pacific Islander, 0.0% Two or more races, 0.0% Hispanic of any race; Average household size: 1.94; Median age: n/a; Age under 18: 0.0%; Age 65 and over: 51.6%; Males per 100 females: 92.3; Marriage status: 0.0% never married, 100.0% now married, 0.0% separated, 0.0% widowed, 0.0% divorced; Foreign born: 0.0%; Speak English only: 100.0%; With disability: 0.0%; Veterans: 0.0%; Ancestry: 51.6% German, 48.4% English
Employment: 0.0% management, business, and financial, 0.0% computer, engineering, and science, 0.0% education, legal, community service, arts, and media, 0.0% healthcare practitioners, 0.0% service, 100.0% sales and office, 0.0% natural resources, construction, and maintenance, 0.0% production, transportation, and material moving
Income: Per capita: n/a; Median household: n/a; Average household: n/a; Households with income of $100,000 or more: n/a; Poverty rate: n/a
Educational Attainment: High school diploma or higher: 100.0%; Bachelor's degree or higher: 51.6%; Graduate/professional degree or higher: n/a
Housing: Homeownership rate: 100.0%; Median home value: n/a; Median year structure built: n/a; Homeowner vacancy rate: 0.0%; Median selected monthly owner costs: $0 with a mortgage, $0 without a mortgage; Median gross rent: n/a per month; Rental vacancy rate: 0.0%
Health Insurance: 100.0% have insurance; 48.4% have private insurance; 51.6% have public insurance; 0.0% do not have insurance; 0.0% of children under 18 do not have insurance
Transportation: Commute: 100.0% car, 0.0% public transportation, 0.0% walk, 0.0% work from home; Mean travel time to work: 0.0 minutes

Coshocton County

Located in central Ohio; drained by the Muskingum, Tuscarawas, and Walhonding Rivers. Covers a land area of 563.913 square miles, a water area of 3.569 square miles, and is located in the Eastern Time Zone at 40.30° N. Lat., 81.93° W. Long. The county was founded in 1811. County seat is Coshocton.

Coshocton County is part of the Coshocton, OH Micropolitan Statistical Area. The entire metro area includes: Coshocton County, OH

Weather Station: Coshocton Agr Res Stn — Elevation: 1,140 feet

	Jan	Feb	Mar	Apr	May	Jun	Jul	Aug	Sep	Oct	Nov	Dec
High	35	38	48	61	70	79	83	82	75	63	51	39
Low	19	22	29	41	51	59	63	62	55	43	34	24
Precip	2.5	2.1	3.0	3.4	4.1	4.0	4.4	3.8	3.0	2.6	3.0	2.8
Snow	na	na	na	tr	tr	0.0	0.0	0.0	0.0	tr	tr	na

High and Low temperatures in degrees Fahrenheit; Precipitation and Snow in inches

Weather Station: Coshocton Wpc Plant — Elevation: 759 feet

	Jan	Feb	Mar	Apr	May	Jun	Jul	Aug	Sep	Oct	Nov	Dec
High	37	41	51	63	72	80	84	83	76	64	53	41
Low	20	22	30	39	49	58	62	61	53	41	33	24
Precip	2.9	2.4	3.4	3.9	4.6	4.0	4.5	4.0	3.1	2.9	3.4	3.1
Snow	7.8	5.4	3.0	0.8	tr	0.0	0.0	0.0	0.0	tr	0.8	3.5

High and Low temperatures in degrees Fahrenheit; Precipitation and Snow in inches

Population: 36,665; Growth (since 2000): 0.0%; Density: 65.0 persons per square mile; Race: 96.9% White, 1.0% Black/African American, 0.3% Asian, 0.2% American Indian/Alaska Native, 0.0% Native Hawaiian/Other Pacific Islander, 1.5% two or more races, 0.9% Hispanic of any race; Average household size: 2.51; Median age: 41.2; Age under 18: 23.7%; Age 65 and over: 17.6%; Males per 100 females: 97.6; Marriage status: 23.8% never married, 56.1% now married, 1.1% separated, 7.5% widowed, 12.7% divorced; Foreign born: 0.6%; Speak English only: 91.7%; With disability: 13.8%; Veterans: 9.6%; Ancestry: 26.2% German, 11.5% American, 10.7% Irish, 8.5% English, 3.6% Italian

Religion: Six largest groups: 13.6% Methodist/Pietist, 5.4% Baptist, 5.2% European Free-Church, 3.9% Holiness, 3.9% Non-denominational Protestant, 3.7% Catholicism
Economy: Unemployment rate: 5.8%; Leading industries: 16.4 % retail trade; 14.8 % other services (except public administration); 13.1 % health care and social assistance; Farms: 1,122 totaling 169,762 acres; Company size: 0 employ 1,000 or more persons, 0 employ 500 to 999 persons, 16 employ 100 to 499 persons, 611 employs less than 100 persons; Business ownership: 859 women-owned, n/a Black-owned, n/a Hispanic-owned, n/a Asian-owned, n/a American Indian/Alaska Native-owned
Employment: 8.9% management, business, and financial, 1.9% computer, engineering, and science, 6.9% education, legal, community service, arts, and media, 4.8% healthcare practitioners, 17.6% service, 18.2% sales and office, 13.9% natural resources, construction, and maintenance, 27.9% production, transportation, and material moving
Income: Per capita: $21,521; Median household: $43,380; Average household: $53,636; Households with income of $100,000 or more: 12.5%; Poverty rate: 14.0%
Educational Attainment: High school diploma or higher: 85.7%; Bachelor's degree or higher: 12.1%; Graduate/professional degree or higher: 3.7%
Housing: Homeownership rate: 74.7%; Median home value: $97,100; Median year structure built: 1962; Homeowner vacancy rate: 1.0%; Median selected monthly owner costs: $972 with a mortgage, $346 without a mortgage; Median gross rent: $574 per month; Rental vacancy rate: 6.3%
Vital Statistics: Birth rate: 125.1 per 10,000 population; Death rate: 103.5 per 10,000 population; Age-adjusted cancer mortality rate: 181.1 deaths per 100,000 population
Health Insurance: 87.1% have insurance; 64.0% have private insurance; 37.9% have public insurance; 12.9% do not have insurance; 16.2% of children under 18 do not have insurance
Health Care: Physicians: 6.8 per 10,000 population; Dentists: 3.0 per 10,000 population; Hospital beds: 29.8 per 10,000 population; Hospital admissions: 677.1 per 10,000 population
Transportation: Commute: 89.3% car, 0.5% public transportation, 2.7% walk, 5.4% work from home; Mean travel time to work: 24.0 minutes
2016 Presidential Election: 68.9% Trump, 25.6% Clinton, 3.0% Johnson, 0.8% Stein
Additional Information Contacts
Coshocton Government . . . . (740) 622-1753
http://www.coshoctoncounty.net

Coshocton County Communities

BLISSFIELD (unincorporated postal area)
ZCTA: 43805
Covers a land area of 1.193 square miles and a water area of 0.014 square miles. Located at 40.39° N. Lat; 81.97° W. Long. Elevation is 823 feet.
Population: 16; Growth (since 2000): n/a; Density: 13.4 persons per square mile; Race: 100.0% White, 0.0% Black/African American, 0.0% Asian, 0.0% American Indian/Alaska Native, 0.0% Native Hawaiian/Other Pacific Islander, 0.0% Two or more races, 0.0% Hispanic of any race; Average household size: 0.00; Median age: n/a; Age under 18: 0.0%; Age 65 and over: 100.0%; Males per 100 females: 129.0; Marriage status: 0.0% never married, 0.0% now married, 0.0% separated, 100.0% widowed, 0.0% divorced; Foreign born: 0.0%; Speak English only: 100.0%; With disability: 56.3%; Veterans: 56.3%; Ancestry: 43.8% French, 43.8% German
Employment: n/a management, business, and financial, n/a computer, engineering, and science, n/a education, legal, community service, arts, and media, n/a healthcare practitioners, n/a service, n/a sales and office, n/a natural resources, construction, and maintenance, n/a production, transportation, and material moving
Income: Per capita: n/a; Median household: n/a; Average household: n/a; Households with income of $100,000 or more: n/a; Poverty rate: 43.8%
Educational Attainment: High school diploma or higher: 43.8%; Bachelor's degree or higher: n/a; Graduate/professional degree or higher: n/a
Housing: Homeownership rate: 100.0%; Median home value: n/a; Median year structure built: n/a; Homeowner vacancy rate: 0.0%; Median selected monthly owner costs: $0 with a mortgage, $0 without a mortgage; Median gross rent: n/a per month; Rental vacancy rate: 0.0%
Health Insurance: 100.0% have insurance; 43.8% have private insurance; 100.0% have public insurance; 0.0% do not have insurance; 0.0% of children under 18 do not have insurance
Transportation: Commute: n/a car, n/a public transportation, n/a walk, n/a work from home; Mean travel time to work: 0.0 minutes

CANAL LEWISVILLE (CDP). Covers a land area of 0.418 square miles and a water area of 0 square miles. Located at 40.30° N. Lat; 81.84° W. Long. Elevation is 761 feet.
Population: 263; Growth (since 2000): n/a; Density: 629.5 persons per square mile; Race: 100.0% White, 0.0% Black/African American, 0.0% Asian, 0.0% American Indian/Alaska Native, 0.0% Native Hawaiian/Other Pacific Islander, 0.0% Two or more races, 0.0% Hispanic of any race; Average household size: 2.10; Median age: 48.0; Age under 18: 17.9%; Age 65 and over: 29.3%; Males per 100 females: 78.8; Marriage status: 7.9% never married, 63.9% now married, 0.0% separated, 17.1% widowed, 11.1% divorced; Foreign born: 0.0%; Speak English only: 100.0%; With disability: 25.1%; Veterans: 9.7%; Ancestry: 28.1% German, 19.8% Irish, 15.6% American, 10.3% Swedish, 9.5% Dutch
Employment: 8.1% management, business, and financial, 0.0% computer, engineering, and science, 15.2% education, legal, community service, arts, and media, 0.0% healthcare practitioners, 20.2% service, 29.3% sales and office, 20.2% natural resources, construction, and maintenance, 7.1% production, transportation, and material moving
Income: Per capita: $15,495; Median household: $26,875; Average household: $32,621; Households with income of $100,000 or more: n/a; Poverty rate: 16.3%
Educational Attainment: High school diploma or higher: 92.9%; Bachelor's degree or higher: 16.7%; Graduate/professional degree or higher: 5.7%
Housing: Homeownership rate: 78.4%; Median home value: $63,300; Median year structure built: 1959; Homeowner vacancy rate: 0.0%; Median selected monthly owner costs: $668 with a mortgage, $139 without a mortgage; Median gross rent: $618 per month; Rental vacancy rate: 0.0%
Health Insurance: 93.9% have insurance; 68.4% have private insurance; 56.7% have public insurance; 6.1% do not have insurance; 0.0% of children under 18 do not have insurance
Transportation: Commute: 100.0% car, 0.0% public transportation, 0.0% walk, 0.0% work from home; Mean travel time to work: 22.1 minutes

CONESVILLE (village). Covers a land area of 0.160 square miles and a water area of 0 square miles. Located at 40.18° N. Lat; 81.89° W. Long. Elevation is 741 feet.
Population: 349; Growth (since 2000): -4.1%; Density: 2,181.9 persons per square mile; Race: 100.0% White, 0.0% Black/African American, 0.0% Asian, 0.0% American Indian/Alaska Native, 0.0% Native Hawaiian/Other Pacific Islander, 0.0% Two or more races, 0.6% Hispanic of any race; Average household size: 2.30; Median age: 37.6; Age under 18: 22.3%; Age 65 and over: 18.3%; Males per 100 females: 87.6; Marriage status: 20.7% never married, 56.6% now married, 0.7% separated, 9.0% widowed, 13.8% divorced; Foreign born: 0.0%; Speak English only: 98.8%; With disability: 18.3%; Veterans: 5.2%; Ancestry: 25.5% German, 12.6% English, 10.9% Irish, 8.9% American, 3.2% Italian
Employment: 5.2% management, business, and financial, 2.6% computer, engineering, and science, 5.2% education, legal, community service, arts, and media, 3.9% healthcare practitioners, 19.6% service, 15.0% sales and office, 14.4% natural resources, construction, and maintenance, 34.0% production, transportation, and material moving
Income: Per capita: $20,388; Median household: $40,833; Average household: $47,433; Households with income of $100,000 or more: 8.6%; Poverty rate: 16.6%
Educational Attainment: High school diploma or higher: 91.9%; Bachelor's degree or higher: 5.6%; Graduate/professional degree or higher: 0.8%

School District(s)
River View Local (PK-12)
2015-16 Enrollment: 2,014 . . . . (740) 824-3521
Housing: Homeownership rate: 71.7%; Median home value: $80,800; Median year structure built: Before 1940; Homeowner vacancy rate: 5.2%; Median selected monthly owner costs: $761 with a mortgage, $310 without a mortgage; Median gross rent: $610 per month; Rental vacancy rate: 0.0%
Health Insurance: 87.1% have insurance; 69.6% have private insurance; 30.7% have public insurance; 12.9% do not have insurance; 14.1% of children under 18 do not have insurance

Transportation: Commute: 97.4% car, 0.0% public transportation, 2.0% walk, 0.7% work from home; Mean travel time to work: 21.7 minutes

COSHOCTON (city). County seat. Covers a land area of 8.084 square miles and a water area of 0.124 square miles. Located at 40.26° N. Lat; 81.85° W. Long. Elevation is 774 feet.

History: Coshocton was established on a plateau southeast of the juncture of the Walhonding and Tuscarawas Rivers, and developed as an industrial city. The town's name is of Indian origin. An advertising novelty plant built in 1887 by J.F. Meek was a leading industry. Coshocton suffered repeated floodings from the rivers until Wills Creek Dam and Mohawk Dam were built on the Walhonding in the 1930's.

Population: 11,190; Growth (since 2000): -4.2%; Density: 1,384.3 persons per square mile; Race: 95.1% White, 2.2% Black/African American, 0.6% Asian, 0.3% American Indian/Alaska Native, 0.0% Native Hawaiian/Other Pacific Islander, 1.9% Two or more races, 1.8% Hispanic of any race; Average household size: 2.29; Median age: 42.5; Age under 18: 20.0%; Age 65 and over: 20.3%; Males per 100 females: 88.0; Marriage status: 25.2% never married, 49.4% now married, 1.6% separated, 9.8% widowed, 15.6% divorced; Foreign born: 1.0%; Speak English only: 98.1%; With disability: 15.8%; Veterans: 11.6%; Ancestry: 23.7% German, 12.3% Irish, 11.8% American, 9.7% English, 4.2% Italian

Employment: 7.7% management, business, and financial, 2.1% computer, engineering, and science, 7.8% education, legal, community service, arts, and media, 4.6% healthcare practitioners, 22.5% service, 20.0% sales and office, 9.6% natural resources, construction, and maintenance, 25.7% production, transportation, and material moving

Income: Per capita: $22,250; Median household: $38,310; Average household: $50,790; Households with income of $100,000 or more: 12.9%; Poverty rate: 15.6%

Educational Attainment: High school diploma or higher: 88.4%; Bachelor's degree or higher: 16.0%; Graduate/professional degree or higher: 4.8%

School District(s)

Coshocton City (PK-12)
2015-16 Enrollment: 1,492 . . . . (740) 622-1901
Coshocton County (11-12)
2015-16 Enrollment: n/a . . . . (740) 622-0211
Coshocton Opportunity School (09-12)
2015-16 Enrollment: 45. . . . . (740) 622-3600

Housing: Homeownership rate: 61.3%; Median home value: $84,000; Median year structure built: 1944; Homeowner vacancy rate: 1.7%; Median selected monthly owner costs: $868 with a mortgage, $360 without a mortgage; Median gross rent: $585 per month; Rental vacancy rate: 8.6%

Health Insurance: 94.4% have insurance; 65.1% have private insurance; 46.4% have public insurance; 5.6% do not have insurance; 0.0% of children under 18 do not have insurance

Hospitals: Coshocton County Memorial Hospital (61 beds)

Newspapers: Coshocton Tribune (daily circulation 6,200)

Transportation: Commute: 90.5% car, 0.4% public transportation, 3.8% walk, 3.6% work from home; Mean travel time to work: 15.2 minutes

Airports: Richard Downing (general aviation)

Additional Information Contacts

City of Coshocton . . . . (740) 622-1373

FRESNO (CDP). Covers a land area of 0.230 square miles and a water area of 0 square miles. Located at 40.33° N. Lat; 81.74° W. Long. Elevation is 794 feet.

Population: 235; Growth (since 2000): n/a; Density: 1,022.8 persons per square mile; Race: 100.0% White, 0.0% Black/African American, 0.0% Asian, 0.0% American Indian/Alaska Native, 0.0% Native Hawaiian/Other Pacific Islander, 0.0% Two or more races, 0.0% Hispanic of any race; Average household size: 2.90; Median age: 33.7; Age under 18: 26.8%; Age 65 and over: 8.1%; Males per 100 females: 97.2; Marriage status: 28.5% never married, 65.1% now married, 0.0% separated, 0.0% widowed, 6.4% divorced; Foreign born: 0.0%; Speak English only: 100.0%; With disability: 4.3%; Veterans: 12.2%; Ancestry: 34.9% German, 18.3% Irish, 16.2% American, 15.3% English, 14.5% Italian

Employment: 0.0% management, business, and financial, 0.0% computer, engineering, and science, 0.0% education, legal, community service, arts, and media, 7.6% healthcare practitioners, 23.5% service, 22.7% sales and office, 37.0% natural resources, construction, and maintenance, 9.2% production, transportation, and material moving

Income: Per capita: $20,898; Median household: $60,688; Average household: $59,942; Households with income of $100,000 or more: 12.3%; Poverty rate: n/a

Educational Attainment: High school diploma or higher: 74.7%; Bachelor's degree or higher: n/a; Graduate/professional degree or higher: n/a

Housing: Homeownership rate: 86.4%; Median home value: $76,300; Median year structure built: Before 1940; Homeowner vacancy rate: 0.0%; Median selected monthly owner costs: $947 with a mortgage, n/a without a mortgage; Median gross rent: n/a per month; Rental vacancy rate: 0.0%

Health Insurance: 70.2% have insurance; 46.8% have private insurance; 43.8% have public insurance; 29.8% do not have insurance; 0.0% of children under 18 do not have insurance

Transportation: Commute: 100.0% car, 0.0% public transportation, 0.0% walk, 0.0% work from home; Mean travel time to work: 30.4 minutes

NELLIE (village). Covers a land area of 0.714 square miles and a water area of 0 square miles. Located at 40.34° N. Lat; 82.07° W. Long. Elevation is 817 feet.

Population: 96; Growth (since 2000): -28.4%; Density: 134.4 persons per square mile; Race: 100.0% White, 0.0% Black/African American, 0.0% Asian, 0.0% American Indian/Alaska Native, 0.0% Native Hawaiian/Other Pacific Islander, 0.0% Two or more races, 0.0% Hispanic of any race; Average household size: 2.59; Median age: 33.6; Age under 18: 25.0%; Age 65 and over: 26.0%; Males per 100 females: 111.3; Marriage status: 14.9% never married, 68.9% now married, 0.0% separated, 5.4% widowed, 10.8% divorced; Foreign born: 0.0%; Speak English only: 96.3%; With disability: 12.5%; Veterans: 5.6%; Ancestry: 34.4% German, 10.4% English, 8.3% American, 5.2% Swedish, 4.2% Austrian

Employment: 6.5% management, business, and financial, 0.0% computer, engineering, and science, 26.1% education, legal, community service, arts, and media, 0.0% healthcare practitioners, 32.6% service, 10.9% sales and office, 8.7% natural resources, construction, and maintenance, 15.2% production, transportation, and material moving

Income: Per capita: $16,779; Median household: $39,028; Average household: $43,789; Households with income of $100,000 or more: 2.7%; Poverty rate: 11.5%

Educational Attainment: High school diploma or higher: 83.1%; Bachelor's degree or higher: 4.6%; Graduate/professional degree or higher: 3.1%

Housing: Homeownership rate: 70.3%; Median home value: $65,700; Median year structure built: Before 1940; Homeowner vacancy rate: 0.0%; Median selected monthly owner costs: $750 with a mortgage, $269 without a mortgage; Median gross rent: n/a per month; Rental vacancy rate: 0.0%

Health Insurance: 96.9% have insurance; 69.8% have private insurance; 44.8% have public insurance; 3.1% do not have insurance; 4.2% of children under 18 do not have insurance

Transportation: Commute: 82.2% car, 0.0% public transportation, 4.4% walk, 2.2% work from home; Mean travel time to work: 27.3 minutes

PLAINFIELD (village). Covers a land area of 0.410 square miles and a water area of 0 square miles. Located at 40.21° N. Lat; 81.72° W. Long. Elevation is 797 feet.

Population: 147; Growth (since 2000): -7.0%; Density: 358.8 persons per square mile; Race: 97.3% White, 0.0% Black/African American, 0.0% Asian, 0.0% American Indian/Alaska Native, 0.0% Native Hawaiian/Other Pacific Islander, 2.7% Two or more races, 0.0% Hispanic of any race; Average household size: 2.26; Median age: 43.5; Age under 18: 21.1%; Age 65 and over: 15.6%; Males per 100 females: 96.3; Marriage status: 10.2% never married, 73.7% now married, 2.5% separated, 5.1% widowed, 11.0% divorced; Foreign born: 0.0%; Speak English only: 99.3%; With disability: 11.6%; Veterans: 9.5%; Ancestry: 28.6% German, 24.5% Irish, 9.5% American, 8.8% English, 2.0% Hungarian

Employment: 12.5% management, business, and financial, 0.0% computer, engineering, and science, 6.9% education, legal, community service, arts, and media, 4.2% healthcare practitioners, 6.9% service, 30.6% sales and office, 6.9% natural resources, construction, and maintenance, 31.9% production, transportation, and material moving

Income: Per capita: $23,061; Median household: $50,417; Average household: $50,743; Households with income of $100,000 or more: 3.0%; Poverty rate: 14.0%

Educational Attainment: High school diploma or higher: 94.6%; Bachelor's degree or higher: 10.8%; Graduate/professional degree or higher: 0.9%

Housing: Homeownership rate: 81.5%; Median home value: $69,200; Median year structure built: Before 1940; Homeowner vacancy rate: 0.0%; Median selected monthly owner costs: $800 with a mortgage, $338 without a mortgage; Median gross rent: $494 per month; Rental vacancy rate: 0.0%
Health Insurance: 89.1% have insurance; 64.6% have private insurance; 34.0% have public insurance; 10.9% do not have insurance; 9.7% of children under 18 do not have insurance
Transportation: Commute: 97.2% car, 0.0% public transportation, 0.0% walk, 2.8% work from home; Mean travel time to work: 25.7 minutes

WALHONDING (unincorporated postal area)

ZCTA: 43843

Covers a land area of 42.303 square miles and a water area of 0.045 square miles. Located at 40.35° N. Lat; 82.18° W. Long. Elevation is 889 feet.
Population: 1,645; Growth (since 2000): 84.8%; Density: 38.9 persons per square mile; Race: 96.8% White, 0.0% Black/African American, 1.6% Asian, 0.0% American Indian/Alaska Native, 0.0% Native Hawaiian/Other Pacific Islander, 1.6% Two or more races, 2.6% Hispanic of any race; Average household size: 3.17; Median age: 26.5; Age under 18: 35.0%; Age 65 and over: 4.5%; Males per 100 females: 106.8; Marriage status: 26.3% never married, 60.2% now married, 0.0% separated, 6.1% widowed, 7.3% divorced; Foreign born: 1.5%; Speak English only: 79.9%; With disability: 6.1%; Veterans: 5.2%; Ancestry: 43.8% German, 20.9% English, 7.4% Welsh, 6.3% Scottish, 6.0% French
Employment: 6.1% management, business, and financial, 4.9% computer, engineering, and science, 1.0% education, legal, community service, arts, and media, 8.8% healthcare practitioners, 25.6% service, 12.4% sales and office, 10.2% natural resources, construction, and maintenance, 30.9% production, transportation, and material moving
Income: Per capita: $17,732; Median household: $60,402; Average household: $56,276; Households with income of $100,000 or more: 4.8%; Poverty rate: 10.3%
Educational Attainment: High school diploma or higher: 81.5%; Bachelor's degree or higher: 13.9%; Graduate/professional degree or higher: 6.8%
Housing: Homeownership rate: 93.3%; Median home value: $151,100; Median year structure built: 1990; Homeowner vacancy rate: 0.0%; Median selected monthly owner costs: $1,059 with a mortgage, $336 without a mortgage; Median gross rent: n/a per month; Rental vacancy rate: 0.0%
Health Insurance: 67.5% have insurance; 53.4% have private insurance; 18.7% have public insurance; 32.5% do not have insurance; 37.0% of children under 18 do not have insurance
Transportation: Commute: 87.3% car, 0.0% public transportation, 1.4% walk, 11.3% work from home; Mean travel time to work: 39.1 minutes

WARSAW (village). Covers a land area of 0.438 square miles and a water area of 0.016 square miles. Located at 40.34° N. Lat; 82.00° W. Long. Elevation is 801 feet.
Population: 683; Growth (since 2000): -12.5%; Density: 1,560.5 persons per square mile; Race: 95.2% White, 0.7% Black/African American, 0.3% Asian, 0.0% American Indian/Alaska Native, 0.0% Native Hawaiian/Other Pacific Islander, 3.8% Two or more races, 0.0% Hispanic of any race; Average household size: 2.55; Median age: 41.6; Age under 18: 25.0%; Age 65 and over: 8.6%; Males per 100 females: 99.4; Marriage status: 25.3% never married, 45.9% now married, 1.1% separated, 7.3% widowed, 21.5% divorced; Foreign born: 0.0%; Speak English only: 99.2%; With disability: 13.3%; Veterans: 7.8%; Ancestry: 25.9% German, 11.9% English, 9.4% Irish, 3.8% American, 2.2% French
Employment: 3.9% management, business, and financial, 2.5% computer, engineering, and science, 1.7% education, legal, community service, arts, and media, 9.0% healthcare practitioners, 25.2% service, 17.1% sales and office, 10.1% natural resources, construction, and maintenance, 30.5% production, transportation, and material moving
Income: Per capita: $20,700; Median household: $41,250; Average household: $51,193; Households with income of $100,000 or more: 19.0%; Poverty rate: 15.5%
Educational Attainment: High school diploma or higher: 86.6%; Bachelor's degree or higher: 5.9%; Graduate/professional degree or higher: 1.3%

School District(s)

River View Local (PK-12)
2015-16 Enrollment: 2,014 . . . . (740) 824-3521

Housing: Homeownership rate: 72.4%; Median home value: $80,000; Median year structure built: 1951; Homeowner vacancy rate: 0.0%; Median selected monthly owner costs: $1,004 with a mortgage, $316 without a mortgage; Median gross rent: $697 per month; Rental vacancy rate: 17.7%
Health Insurance: 88.6% have insurance; 70.7% have private insurance; 24.9% have public insurance; 11.4% do not have insurance; 5.3% of children under 18 do not have insurance
Transportation: Commute: 90.1% car, 1.4% public transportation, 2.0% walk, 6.4% work from home; Mean travel time to work: 24.9 minutes

WEST LAFAYETTE (village). Covers a land area of 0.885 square miles and a water area of 0 square miles. Located at 40.28° N. Lat; 81.75° W. Long. Elevation is 804 feet.
History: West Lafayette began when John Coles, an Englishman, opened a store here in 1850. The town prospered with the arrival of the Pennsylvania Railroad. Early industries were an enameling plant, a metal-products company, and a novelty factory.
Population: 2,272; Growth (since 2000): -1.8%; Density: 2,568.5 persons per square mile; Race: 94.3% White, 0.2% Black/African American, 0.0% Asian, 0.0% American Indian/Alaska Native, 0.0% Native Hawaiian/Other Pacific Islander, 5.5% Two or more races, 1.3% Hispanic of any race; Average household size: 2.39; Median age: 45.2; Age under 18: 25.0%; Age 65 and over: 21.7%; Males per 100 females: 86.7; Marriage status: 26.2% never married, 45.1% now married, 1.6% separated, 12.6% widowed, 16.0% divorced; Foreign born: 0.5%; Speak English only: 97.9%; With disability: 20.5%; Veterans: 10.0%; Ancestry: 25.7% German, 14.4% American, 14.2% Irish, 8.2% English, 5.5% Italian
Employment: 6.5% management, business, and financial, 2.6% computer, engineering, and science, 7.0% education, legal, community service, arts, and media, 6.3% healthcare practitioners, 20.5% service, 19.0% sales and office, 8.3% natural resources, construction, and maintenance, 29.7% production, transportation, and material moving
Income: Per capita: $20,031; Median household: $39,348; Average household: $48,212; Households with income of $100,000 or more: 8.8%; Poverty rate: 17.2%
Educational Attainment: High school diploma or higher: 83.9%; Bachelor's degree or higher: 11.9%; Graduate/professional degree or higher: 3.0%

School District(s)

Ridgewood Local (PK-12)
2015-16 Enrollment: 1,267 . . . . (740) 545-6354

Housing: Homeownership rate: 71.5%; Median home value: $73,400; Median year structure built: 1961; Homeowner vacancy rate: 1.8%; Median selected monthly owner costs: $857 with a mortgage, $364 without a mortgage; Median gross rent: $589 per month; Rental vacancy rate: 4.4%
Health Insurance: 92.3% have insurance; 61.2% have private insurance; 48.1% have public insurance; 7.7% do not have insurance; 3.3% of children under 18 do not have insurance
Safety: Violent crime rate: 13.2 per 10,000 population; Property crime rate: 35.1 per 10,000 population
Transportation: Commute: 94.7% car, 1.9% public transportation, 1.7% walk, 1.2% work from home; Mean travel time to work: 24.3 minutes

Crawford County

Located in north central Ohio; drained by the Sandusky and Olentangy Rivers. Covers a land area of 401.786 square miles, a water area of 0.911 square miles, and is located in the Eastern Time Zone at 40.85° N. Lat., 82.92° W. Long. The county was founded in 1820. County seat is Bucyrus.

Crawford County is part of the Bucyrus, OH Micropolitan Statistical Area. The entire metro area includes: Crawford County, OH

Weather Station: Bucyrus — Elevation: 955 feet

	Jan	Feb	Mar	Apr	May	Jun	Jul	Aug	Sep	Oct	Nov	Dec
High	33	36	46	60	70	80	83	81	75	62	49	37
Low	18	20	27	37	47	57	61	60	52	41	32	23
Precip	2.5	2.0	2.7	3.4	4.3	4.2	4.4	3.8	3.2	2.6	3.1	2.9
Snow	7.4	4.6	3.4	0.9	0.1	0.0	0.0	0.0	0.0	0.1	0.9	5.1

High and Low temperatures in degrees Fahrenheit; Precipitation and Snow in inches

Population: 42,485; Growth (since 2000): -9.5%; Density: 105.7 persons per square mile; Race: 96.9% White, 0.6% Black/African American, 0.4% Asian, 0.0% American Indian/Alaska Native, 0.0% Native Hawaiian/Other Pacific Islander, 1.7% two or more races, 1.4% Hispanic of any race; Average household size: 2.38; Median age: 42.9; Age under 18: 22.2%;

Age 65 and over: 19.5%; Males per 100 females: 94.4; Marriage status: 24.8% never married, 54.8% now married, 2.0% separated, 8.6% widowed, 11.7% divorced; Foreign born: 1.0%; Speak English only: 98.6%; With disability: 17.1%; Veterans: 10.5%; Ancestry: 36.6% German, 13.8% Irish, 10.8% American, 9.3% English, 3.3% Italian
Religion: Six largest groups: 13.3% Catholicism, 10.5% Lutheran, 8.1% Methodist/Pietist, 4.9% Non-denominational Protestant, 4.2% Presbyterian-Reformed, 4.2% Holiness
Economy: Unemployment rate: 5.0%; Leading industries: 15.7 % retail trade; 14.5 % other services (except public administration); 10.2 % accommodation and food services; Farms: 634 totaling 240,022 acres; Company size: 0 employ 1,000 or more persons, 2 employ 500 to 999 persons, 17 employ 100 to 499 persons, 801 employs less than 100 persons; Business ownership: 849 women-owned, n/a Black-owned, n/a Hispanic-owned, 33 Asian-owned, n/a American Indian/Alaska Native-owned
Employment: 10.3% management, business, and financial, 2.4% computer, engineering, and science, 8.2% education, legal, community service, arts, and media, 5.7% healthcare practitioners, 19.0% service, 20.2% sales and office, 8.8% natural resources, construction, and maintenance, 25.5% production, transportation, and material moving
Income: Per capita: $22,631; Median household: $40,563; Average household: $53,755; Households with income of $100,000 or more: 10.7%; Poverty rate: 15.7%
Educational Attainment: High school diploma or higher: 88.5%; Bachelor's degree or higher: 12.7%; Graduate/professional degree or higher: 4.3%
Housing: Homeownership rate: 69.8%; Median home value: $85,200; Median year structure built: 1958; Homeowner vacancy rate: 1.8%; Median selected monthly owner costs: $926 with a mortgage, $369 without a mortgage; Median gross rent: $633 per month; Rental vacancy rate: 5.0%
Vital Statistics: Birth rate: 116.7 per 10,000 population; Death rate: 111.9 per 10,000 population; Age-adjusted cancer mortality rate: 193.5 deaths per 100,000 population
Health Insurance: 91.7% have insurance; 69.0% have private insurance; 39.5% have public insurance; 8.3% do not have insurance; 3.6% of children under 18 do not have insurance
Health Care: Physicians: 7.3 per 10,000 population; Dentists: 5.9 per 10,000 population; Hospital beds: 14.1 per 10,000 population; Hospital admissions: 580.6 per 10,000 population
Transportation: Commute: 93.3% car, 0.4% public transportation, 2.8% walk, 2.1% work from home; Mean travel time to work: 21.1 minutes
2016 Presidential Election: 70.4% Trump, 23.9% Clinton, 3.7% Johnson, 0.6% Stein
National and State Parks: Carmean Woods State Nature Preserve; Paul B Sears Woods State Nature Preserve
Additional Information Contacts
Crawford Government . . . . (419) 562-5876
http://www.crawford-co.org

Crawford County Communities

BUCYRUS (city). County seat. Covers a land area of 7.422 square miles and a water area of 0.014 square miles. Located at 40.81° N. Lat; 82.97° W. Long. Elevation is 994 feet.
History: The site of Bucyrus was purchased by Samuel Norton and Colonel James Kilbourne in 1819, and settled by a group from Pennsylvania. Kilbourne surveyed the village in 1822 and named it for Cyrus, an ancient Persian leader. He prefixed it with "bu" to suggest "beautiful."
Population: 12,011; Growth (since 2000): -9.2%; Density: 1,618.3 persons per square mile; Race: 96.7% White, 0.9% Black/African American, 0.9% Asian, 0.1% American Indian/Alaska Native, 0.1% Native Hawaiian/Other Pacific Islander, 1.3% Two or more races, 1.0% Hispanic of any race; Average household size: 2.18; Median age: 43.7; Age under 18: 21.6%; Age 65 and over: 21.7%; Males per 100 females: 91.4; Marriage status: 27.4% never married, 46.2% now married, 1.6% separated, 11.1% widowed, 15.2% divorced; Foreign born: 1.2%; Speak English only: 98.4%; With disability: 17.2%; Veterans: 10.4%; Ancestry: 35.9% German, 17.6% Irish, 11.3% American, 9.2% English, 2.3% Italian
Employment: 8.0% management, business, and financial, 2.8% computer, engineering, and science, 8.0% education, legal, community service, arts, and media, 5.6% healthcare practitioners, 21.1% service, 22.0% sales and office, 3.6% natural resources, construction, and maintenance, 28.9% production, transportation, and material moving
Income: Per capita: $21,550; Median household: $36,230; Average household: $47,512; Households with income of $100,000 or more: 7.9%; Poverty rate: 17.8%
Educational Attainment: High school diploma or higher: 87.8%; Bachelor's degree or higher: 12.5%; Graduate/professional degree or higher: 3.1%

School District(s)

Bucyrus City (PK-12)
2015-16 Enrollment: 1,373 . . . . (419) 562-4045
Wynford Local (PK-12)
2015-16 Enrollment: 1,116 . . . . (419) 562-7828
Housing: Homeownership rate: 61.8%; Median home value: $79,600; Median year structure built: 1958; Homeowner vacancy rate: 2.1%; Median selected monthly owner costs: $857 with a mortgage, $339 without a mortgage; Median gross rent: $631 per month; Rental vacancy rate: 5.1%
Health Insurance: 90.1% have insurance; 65.5% have private insurance; 44.5% have public insurance; 9.9% do not have insurance; 0.5% of children under 18 do not have insurance
Hospitals: Bucyrus Community Hospital (25 beds)
Safety: Violent crime rate: 20.3 per 10,000 population; Property crime rate: 415.0 per 10,000 population
Newspapers: Telegraph-Forum (daily circulation 6,200)
Transportation: Commute: 94.1% car, 0.0% public transportation, 2.9% walk, 1.9% work from home; Mean travel time to work: 18.4 minutes

CHATFIELD (village). Covers a land area of 0.300 square miles and a water area of 0 square miles. Located at 40.95° N. Lat; 82.94° W. Long. Elevation is 978 feet.
Population: 255; Growth (since 2000): 17.0%; Density: 849.3 persons per square mile; Race: 100.0% White, 0.0% Black/African American, 0.0% Asian, 0.0% American Indian/Alaska Native, 0.0% Native Hawaiian/Other Pacific Islander, 0.0% Two or more races, 3.5% Hispanic of any race; Average household size: 2.77; Median age: 28.8; Age under 18: 25.9%; Age 65 and over: 10.6%; Males per 100 females: 101.1; Marriage status: 13.2% never married, 76.5% now married, 2.5% separated, 2.0% widowed, 8.3% divorced; Foreign born: 1.2%; Speak English only: 98.7%; With disability: 19.6%; Veterans: 7.4%; Ancestry: 32.5% German, 7.8% Irish, 7.5% English, 3.5% American, 1.6% Scottish
Employment: 4.5% management, business, and financial, 4.5% computer, engineering, and science, 7.1% education, legal, community service, arts, and media, 6.3% healthcare practitioners, 9.8% service, 4.5% sales and office, 13.4% natural resources, construction, and maintenance, 50.0% production, transportation, and material moving
Income: Per capita: $19,328; Median household: $45,938; Average household: $49,121; Households with income of $100,000 or more: 5.4%; Poverty rate: 6.3%
Educational Attainment: High school diploma or higher: 86.4%; Bachelor's degree or higher: 10.0%; Graduate/professional degree or higher: 1.4%
Housing: Homeownership rate: 77.2%; Median home value: $74,500; Median year structure built: Before 1940; Homeowner vacancy rate: 0.0%; Median selected monthly owner costs: $860 with a mortgage, $483 without a mortgage; Median gross rent: $548 per month; Rental vacancy rate: 0.0%
Health Insurance: 94.9% have insurance; 82.0% have private insurance; 27.8% have public insurance; 5.1% do not have insurance; 0.0% of children under 18 do not have insurance
Transportation: Commute: 92.5% car, 0.0% public transportation, 0.0% walk, 7.5% work from home; Mean travel time to work: 31.7 minutes

CRESTLINE (village). Covers a land area of 3.166 square miles and a water area of 0.005 square miles. Located at 40.78° N. Lat; 82.75° W. Long. Elevation is 1,145 feet.
History: Crestline (Crest Line) was established when the Pennsylvania Railroad became the second line in the area. It joined Livingston, founded two years earlier when the first railroad came through. When the two villages grew to the point where their borders touched, they joined as Crestline.
Population: 4,463; Growth (since 2000): -12.3%; Density: 1,409.7 persons per square mile; Race: 93.2% White, 1.5% Black/African American, 0.8% Asian, 0.0% American Indian/Alaska Native, 0.0% Native Hawaiian/Other Pacific Islander, 4.5% Two or more races, 1.4% Hispanic of any race; Average household size: 2.37; Median age: 38.6; Age under 18: 24.5%; Age 65 and over: 16.6%; Males per 100 females: 90.7; Marriage status: 27.9% never married, 50.6% now married, 3.2% separated, 9.6%

widowed, 12.0% divorced; Foreign born: 0.4%; Speak English only: 99.0%; With disability: 17.0%; Veterans: 12.2%; Ancestry: 29.8% German, 14.6% Irish, 11.0% American, 9.5% English, 6.7% Italian
Employment: 8.2% management, business, and financial, 1.9% computer, engineering, and science, 10.0% education, legal, community service, arts, and media, 5.9% healthcare practitioners, 23.7% service, 15.3% sales and office, 9.3% natural resources, construction, and maintenance, 25.8% production, transportation, and material moving
Income: Per capita: $19,962; Median household: $37,143; Average household: $46,498; Households with income of $100,000 or more: 8.3%; Poverty rate: 25.8%
Educational Attainment: High school diploma or higher: 84.9%; Bachelor's degree or higher: 10.5%; Graduate/professional degree or higher: 2.6%

School District(s)

Colonel Crawford Local (PK-12)
2015-16 Enrollment: 932. . . . . (419) 562-4666
Crestline Exempted Village (PK-12)
2015-16 Enrollment: 627. . . . . (419) 683-3647

Housing: Homeownership rate: 62.7%; Median home value: $68,800; Median year structure built: 1962; Homeowner vacancy rate: 3.0%; Median selected monthly owner costs: $929 with a mortgage, $382 without a mortgage; Median gross rent: $578 per month; Rental vacancy rate: 7.1%
Health Insurance: 94.8% have insurance; 61.5% have private insurance; 47.8% have public insurance; 5.2% do not have insurance; 0.0% of children under 18 do not have insurance
Safety: Violent crime rate: 20.4 per 10,000 population; Property crime rate: 222.6 per 10,000 population
Newspapers: Crestline Advocate (weekly circulation 2,300)
Transportation: Commute: 94.0% car, 1.5% public transportation, 3.3% walk, 0.6% work from home; Mean travel time to work: 19.8 minutes
Additional Information Contacts
Village of Crestline . . . . (419) 683-3800
http://www.crestlineoh.com

GALION (city). Covers a land area of 7.607 square miles and a water area of 0.018 square miles. Located at 40.74° N. Lat; 82.78° W. Long. Elevation is 1,168 feet.
History: Galion was setttled by German Lutherans from Pennsylvania in 1831. In the 1890's C.H. North organized a company for the manufacture of telephone equipment, inventing improvements that made Galion a pioneering center for this industry.
Population: 10,245; Growth (since 2000): -9.7%; Density: 1,346.8 persons per square mile; Race: 97.4% White, 0.1% Black/African American, 0.2% Asian, 0.0% American Indian/Alaska Native, 0.0% Native Hawaiian/Other Pacific Islander, 1.2% Two or more races, 2.4% Hispanic of any race; Average household size: 2.33; Median age: 41.2; Age under 18: 22.6%; Age 65 and over: 19.3%; Males per 100 females: 88.9; Marriage status: 25.5% never married, 52.3% now married, 3.6% separated, 8.6% widowed, 13.6% divorced; Foreign born: 1.9%; Speak English only: 98.3%; With disability: 21.7%; Veterans: 10.3%; Ancestry: 36.9% German, 16.0% Irish, 11.6% American, 10.2% English, 2.9% Dutch
Employment: 10.8% management, business, and financial, 3.0% computer, engineering, and science, 8.7% education, legal, community service, arts, and media, 5.2% healthcare practitioners, 20.2% service, 20.3% sales and office, 9.4% natural resources, construction, and maintenance, 22.3% production, transportation, and material moving
Income: Per capita: $20,291; Median household: $32,721; Average household: $47,844; Households with income of $100,000 or more: 7.1%; Poverty rate: 17.7%
Educational Attainment: High school diploma or higher: 88.4%; Bachelor's degree or higher: 9.9%; Graduate/professional degree or higher: 4.2%

School District(s)

Galion City (PK-12)
2015-16 Enrollment: 1,771 . . . . (419) 468-3432
Northmor Local (PK-12)
2015-16 Enrollment: 1,072 . . . . (419) 946-8861

Housing: Homeownership rate: 61.1%; Median home value: $68,600; Median year structure built: 1954; Homeowner vacancy rate: 3.3%; Median selected monthly owner costs: $853 with a mortgage, $347 without a mortgage; Median gross rent: $614 per month; Rental vacancy rate: 4.8%
Health Insurance: 90.1% have insurance; 61.2% have private insurance; 43.7% have public insurance; 9.9% do not have insurance; 4.7% of children under 18 do not have insurance
Hospitals: Galion Community Hospital (25 beds)
Safety: Violent crime rate: 16.9 per 10,000 population; Property crime rate: 339.2 per 10,000 population
Newspapers: Galion Inquirer (daily circulation 3,900)
Transportation: Commute: 90.5% car, 0.0% public transportation, 5.4% walk, 1.8% work from home; Mean travel time to work: 22.8 minutes
Additional Information Contacts
City of Galion. . . . . (419) 468-1857
http://www.ci.galion.oh.us

NEW WASHINGTON (village). Covers a land area of 1.373 square miles and a water area of 0 square miles. Located at 40.96° N. Lat; 82.85° W. Long. Elevation is 994 feet.
Population: 940; Growth (since 2000): -4.8%; Density: 684.4 persons per square mile; Race: 92.6% White, 1.3% Black/African American, 0.0% Asian, 0.0% American Indian/Alaska Native, 0.0% Native Hawaiian/Other Pacific Islander, 6.2% Two or more races, 0.0% Hispanic of any race; Average household size: 2.53; Median age: 36.9; Age under 18: 27.6%; Age 65 and over: 15.2%; Males per 100 females: 97.8; Marriage status: 23.5% never married, 58.7% now married, 1.4% separated, 8.1% widowed, 9.6% divorced; Foreign born: 0.0%; Speak English only: 98.2%; With disability: 10.0%; Veterans: 10.4%; Ancestry: 50.4% German, 14.1% Irish, 8.3% American, 4.9% Italian, 4.5% Dutch
Employment: 11.8% management, business, and financial, 0.7% computer, engineering, and science, 4.8% education, legal, community service, arts, and media, 7.5% healthcare practitioners, 15.8% service, 19.2% sales and office, 7.9% natural resources, construction, and maintenance, 32.4% production, transportation, and material moving
Income: Per capita: $23,332; Median household: $49,063; Average household: $59,135; Households with income of $100,000 or more: 15.3%; Poverty rate: 8.8%
Educational Attainment: High school diploma or higher: 97.2%; Bachelor's degree or higher: 19.5%; Graduate/professional degree or higher: 6.4%

School District(s)

Buckeye Central Local (KG-12)
2015-16 Enrollment: 676. . . . . (419) 492-2864

Housing: Homeownership rate: 75.3%; Median home value: $87,100; Median year structure built: 1949; Homeowner vacancy rate: 0.0%; Median selected monthly owner costs: $958 with a mortgage, $390 without a mortgage; Median gross rent: $654 per month; Rental vacancy rate: 8.9%
Health Insurance: 93.4% have insurance; 81.4% have private insurance; 25.7% have public insurance; 6.6% do not have insurance; 4.6% of children under 18 do not have insurance
Newspapers: New Washington Herald (weekly circulation 1,600)
Transportation: Commute: 97.7% car, 0.0% public transportation, 1.4% walk, 0.9% work from home; Mean travel time to work: 26.5 minutes

NORTH ROBINSON (village). Covers a land area of 0.097 square miles and a water area of 0 square miles. Located at 40.79° N. Lat; 82.86° W. Long. Elevation is 1,070 feet.
Population: 243; Growth (since 2000): 15.2%; Density: 2,496.0 persons per square mile; Race: 100.0% White, 0.0% Black/African American, 0.0% Asian, 0.0% American Indian/Alaska Native, 0.0% Native Hawaiian/Other Pacific Islander, 0.0% Two or more races, 0.0% Hispanic of any race; Average household size: 2.13; Median age: 58.0; Age under 18: 13.2%; Age 65 and over: 35.8%; Males per 100 females: 103.0; Marriage status: 12.0% never married, 62.5% now married, 1.9% separated, 8.3% widowed, 17.1% divorced; Foreign born: 0.0%; Speak English only: 100.0%; With disability: 9.1%; Veterans: 15.2%; Ancestry: 23.9% German, 17.7% English, 14.8% Dutch, 7.0% Polish, 5.3% Irish
Employment: 0.0% management, business, and financial, 1.9% computer, engineering, and science, 4.7% education, legal, community service, arts, and media, 2.8% healthcare practitioners, 28.3% service, 12.3% sales and office, 2.8% natural resources, construction, and maintenance, 47.2% production, transportation, and material moving
Income: Per capita: $20,753; Median household: $47,750; Average household: $41,695; Households with income of $100,000 or more: 0.9%; Poverty rate: 9.5%
Educational Attainment: High school diploma or higher: 78.2%; Bachelor's degree or higher: 5.8%; Graduate/professional degree or higher: n/a

School District(s)

Colonel Crawford Local (PK-12)
2015-16 Enrollment: 932. . . . . (419) 562-4666

Housing: Homeownership rate: 89.5%; Median home value: $66,900; Median year structure built: 1942; Homeowner vacancy rate: 0.0%; Median selected monthly owner costs: $975 with a mortgage, $338 without a mortgage; Median gross rent: $925 per month; Rental vacancy rate: 0.0%
Health Insurance: 95.1% have insurance; 74.9% have private insurance; 48.6% have public insurance; 4.9% do not have insurance; 0.0% of children under 18 do not have insurance
Transportation: Commute: 95.3% car, 0.0% public transportation, 0.0% walk, 4.7% work from home; Mean travel time to work: 22.5 minutes

OCEOLA (CDP). Covers a land area of 0.501 square miles and a water area of 0 square miles. Located at 40.84° N. Lat; 83.09° W. Long. Elevation is 932 feet.
Population: 16; Growth (since 2000): n/a; Density: 31.9 persons per square mile; Race: 100.0% White, 0.0% Black/African American, 0.0% Asian, 0.0% American Indian/Alaska Native, 0.0% Native Hawaiian/Other Pacific Islander, 0.0% Two or more races, 0.0% Hispanic of any race; Average household size: 2.00; Median age: n/a; Age under 18: 0.0%; Age 65 and over: 0.0%; Males per 100 females: 95.9; Marriage status: 0.0% never married, 100.0% now married, 0.0% separated, 0.0% widowed, 0.0% divorced; Foreign born: 0.0%; Speak English only: 100.0%; With disability: 0.0%; Veterans: 0.0%; Ancestry: 100.0% American
Employment: 0.0% management, business, and financial, 0.0% computer, engineering, and science, 0.0% education, legal, community service, arts, and media, 0.0% healthcare practitioners, 0.0% service, 100.0% sales and office, 0.0% natural resources, construction, and maintenance, 0.0% production, transportation, and material moving
Income: Per capita: n/a; Median household: n/a; Average household: n/a; Households with income of $100,000 or more: n/a; Poverty rate: n/a
Educational Attainment: High school diploma or higher: 100.0%; Bachelor's degree or higher: n/a; Graduate/professional degree or higher: n/a
Housing: Homeownership rate: n/a; Median home value: n/a; Median year structure built: n/a; Homeowner vacancy rate: 0.0%; Median selected monthly owner costs: n/a with a mortgage, n/a without a mortgage; Median gross rent: n/a per month; Rental vacancy rate: 0.0%
Health Insurance: 100.0% have insurance; 100.0% have private insurance; 0.0% have public insurance; 0.0% do not have insurance; 0.0% of children under 18 do not have insurance
Transportation: Commute: 100.0% car, 0.0% public transportation, 0.0% walk, 0.0% work from home; Mean travel time to work: 0.0 minutes

SULPHUR SPRINGS (CDP). Covers a land area of 0.241 square miles and a water area of 0 square miles. Located at 40.87° N. Lat; 82.88° W. Long. Elevation is 1,027 feet.
Population: 93; Growth (since 2000): n/a; Density: 386.5 persons per square mile; Race: 100.0% White, 0.0% Black/African American, 0.0% Asian, 0.0% American Indian/Alaska Native, 0.0% Native Hawaiian/Other Pacific Islander, 0.0% Two or more races, 0.0% Hispanic of any race; Average household size: 1.94; Median age: 49.9; Age under 18: 0.0%; Age 65 and over: 11.8%; Males per 100 females: 104.2; Marriage status: 30.1% never married, 60.2% now married, 0.0% separated, 0.0% widowed, 9.7% divorced; Foreign born: 0.0%; Speak English only: 100.0%; With disability: 9.7%; Veterans: 11.8%; Ancestry: 21.5% American, 20.4% German, 11.8% English, 11.8% Swiss, 9.7% Irish
Employment: 13.1% management, business, and financial, 0.0% computer, engineering, and science, 0.0% education, legal, community service, arts, and media, 0.0% healthcare practitioners, 13.1% service, 20.2% sales and office, 0.0% natural resources, construction, and maintenance, 53.6% production, transportation, and material moving
Income: Per capita: $30,231; Median household: n/a; Average household: $53,638; Households with income of $100,000 or more: n/a; Poverty rate: n/a
Educational Attainment: High school diploma or higher: 100.0%; Bachelor's degree or higher: n/a; Graduate/professional degree or higher: n/a
Housing: Homeownership rate: 100.0%; Median home value: $77,900; Median year structure built: Before 1940; Homeowner vacancy rate: 0.0%; Median selected monthly owner costs: $1,125 with a mortgage, n/a without a mortgage; Median gross rent: n/a per month; Rental vacancy rate: 0.0%
Health Insurance: 81.7% have insurance; 69.9% have private insurance; 11.8% have public insurance; 18.3% do not have insurance; 0.0% of children under 18 do not have insurance
Transportation: Commute: 100.0% car, 0.0% public transportation, 0.0% walk, 0.0% work from home; Mean travel time to work: 12.1 minutes

TIRO (village). Covers a land area of 0.411 square miles and a water area of 0 square miles. Located at 40.91° N. Lat; 82.77° W. Long. Elevation is 1,053 feet.
Population: 197; Growth (since 2000): -29.9%; Density: 478.8 persons per square mile; Race: 97.5% White, 0.0% Black/African American, 0.0% Asian, 0.0% American Indian/Alaska Native, 0.0% Native Hawaiian/Other Pacific Islander, 2.5% Two or more races, 11.7% Hispanic of any race; Average household size: 3.18; Median age: 32.5; Age under 18: 33.5%; Age 65 and over: 11.7%; Males per 100 females: 98.6; Marriage status: 19.1% never married, 58.1% now married, 0.0% separated, 5.1% widowed, 17.6% divorced; Foreign born: 1.0%; Speak English only: 95.7%; With disability: 21.8%; Veterans: 9.9%; Ancestry: 24.4% German, 14.2% English, 12.7% American, 6.6% Dutch, 4.1% Irish
Employment: 0.0% management, business, and financial, 0.0% computer, engineering, and science, 1.9% education, legal, community service, arts, and media, 5.6% healthcare practitioners, 18.5% service, 13.0% sales and office, 11.1% natural resources, construction, and maintenance, 50.0% production, transportation, and material moving
Income: Per capita: $14,107; Median household: $37,500; Average household: $42,152; Households with income of $100,000 or more: 4.8%; Poverty rate: 35.7%
Educational Attainment: High school diploma or higher: 81.4%; Bachelor's degree or higher: 5.1%; Graduate/professional degree or higher: 1.7%
Housing: Homeownership rate: 71.0%; Median home value: $68,800; Median year structure built: 1943; Homeowner vacancy rate: 20.0%; Median selected monthly owner costs: $786 with a mortgage, $292 without a mortgage; Median gross rent: $630 per month; Rental vacancy rate: 0.0%
Health Insurance: 91.4% have insurance; 49.7% have private insurance; 53.8% have public insurance; 8.6% do not have insurance; 1.5% of children under 18 do not have insurance
Transportation: Commute: 88.5% car, 0.0% public transportation, 0.0% walk, 7.7% work from home; Mean travel time to work: 23.3 minutes

Cuyahoga County

Located in northern Ohio; bounded on the north by Lake Erie; drained by the Cuyahoga and Rocky Rivers. Covers a land area of 457.191 square miles, a water area of 788.396 square miles, and is located in the Eastern Time Zone at 41.76° N. Lat., 81.72° W. Long. The county was founded in 1808. County seat is Cleveland.

Cuyahoga County is part of the Cleveland-Elyria, OH Metropolitan Statistical Area. The entire metro area includes: Cuyahoga County, OH; Geauga County, OH; Lake County, OH; Lorain County, OH; Medina County, OH

Weather Station: Cleveland Hopkins Intl Arpt Elevation: 770 feet

	Jan	Feb	Mar	Apr	May	Jun	Jul	Aug	Sep	Oct	Nov	Dec
High	34	37	46	59	69	78	82	81	74	62	50	38
Low	20	22	29	39	49	58	63	62	55	44	36	25
Precip	2.7	2.3	3.0	3.5	3.6	3.4	3.5	3.5	3.8	3.1	3.5	3.1
Snow	18.4	14.5	12.6	3.4	tr	tr	tr	tr	tr	0.2	4.5	14.1

High and Low temperatures in degrees Fahrenheit; Precipitation and Snow in inches

Population: 1,258,710; Growth (since 2000): -9.7%; Density: 2,753.1 persons per square mile; Race: 63.2% White, 29.7% Black/African American, 2.8% Asian, 0.3% American Indian/Alaska Native, 0.0% Native Hawaiian/Other Pacific Islander, 2.6% two or more races, 5.4% Hispanic of any race; Average household size: 2.30; Median age: 40.4; Age under 18: 21.6%; Age 65 and over: 16.5%; Males per 100 females: 90.3; Marriage status: 38.3% never married, 42.3% now married, 2.0% separated, 7.0% widowed, 12.4% divorced; Foreign born: 7.0%; Speak English only: 88.7%; With disability: 14.8%; Veterans: 7.5%; Ancestry: 16.1% German, 12.6% Irish, 8.7% Italian, 7.6% Polish, 5.6% English
Religion: Six largest groups: 28.6% Catholicism, 5.3% Baptist, 3.3% Non-denominational Protestant, 2.5% Lutheran, 2.4% Methodist/Pietist, 2.4% Judaism
Economy: Unemployment rate: 5.4%; Leading industries: 12.8 % retail trade; 12.1 % professional, scientific, and technical services; 11.2 % health care and social assistance; Farms: 114 totaling 2,608 acres; Company size: 37 employ 1,000 or more persons, 72 employ 500 to 999 persons, 973 employ 100 to 499 persons, 32,079 employ less than 100 persons; Business ownership: 42,859 women-owned, 22,812 Black-owned, 3,577

Hispanic-owned, 3,718 Asian-owned, 413 American Indian/Alaska Native-owned
Employment: 15.3% management, business, and financial, 5.3% computer, engineering, and science, 11.1% education, legal, community service, arts, and media, 7.3% healthcare practitioners, 18.5% service, 24.4% sales and office, 5.4% natural resources, construction, and maintenance, 12.7% production, transportation, and material moving
Income: Per capita: $29,143; Median household: $45,289; Average household: $66,851; Households with income of $100,000 or more: 18.9%; Poverty rate: 18.5%
Educational Attainment: High school diploma or higher: 88.5%; Bachelor's degree or higher: 30.9%; Graduate/professional degree or higher: 12.7%
Housing: Homeownership rate: 58.9%; Median home value: $122,200; Median year structure built: 1955; Homeowner vacancy rate: 2.2%; Median selected monthly owner costs: $1,287 with a mortgage, $505 without a mortgage; Median gross rent: $742 per month; Rental vacancy rate: 7.4%
Vital Statistics: Birth rate: 119.6 per 10,000 population; Death rate: 108.6 per 10,000 population; Age-adjusted cancer mortality rate: 185.1 deaths per 100,000 population
Health Insurance: 91.8% have insurance; 65.2% have private insurance; 38.9% have public insurance; 8.2% do not have insurance; 3.3% of children under 18 do not have insurance
Health Care: Physicians: 75.2 per 10,000 population; Dentists: 10.2 per 10,000 population; Hospital beds: 55.4 per 10,000 population; Hospital admissions: 2,220.6 per 10,000 population
Air Quality Index (AQI): Percent of Days: 56.6% good, 40.4% moderate, 1.6% unhealthy for sensitive individuals, 1.4% unhealthy, 0.0% very unhealthy; Annual median: 47; Annual maximum: 200
Transportation: Commute: 87.3% car, 5.0% public transportation, 2.7% walk, 3.8% work from home; Mean travel time to work: 24.3 minutes
2016 Presidential Election: 30.3% Trump, 65.4% Clinton, 2.1% Johnson, 0.9% Stein
National and State Parks: Chagrin State Scenic River; Cleveland Lakefront State Park; Cuyahoga Valley National Recreation Area; Edgewater State Park
Additional Information Contacts
Cuyahoga Government . . . . (216) 443-7000
http://www.cuyahogacounty.us

Cuyahoga County Communities

BAY VILLAGE (city). Covers a land area of 4.566 square miles and a water area of 2.488 square miles. Located at 41.49° N. Lat; 81.93° W. Long. Elevation is 633 feet.
History: Named for its location on a bay of Lake Erie. Incorporated 1903.
Population: 15,414; Growth (since 2000): -4.2%; Density: 3,376.0 persons per square mile; Race: 95.9% White, 0.6% Black/African American, 0.9% Asian, 0.0% American Indian/Alaska Native, 0.1% Native Hawaiian/Other Pacific Islander, 2.3% Two or more races, 1.8% Hispanic of any race; Average household size: 2.53; Median age: 43.8; Age under 18: 24.9%; Age 65 and over: 17.5%; Males per 100 females: 90.4; Marriage status: 22.0% never married, 63.3% now married, 0.5% separated, 5.0% widowed, 9.6% divorced; Foreign born: 3.4%; Speak English only: 96.0%; With disability: 8.2%; Veterans: 7.7%; Ancestry: 31.2% German, 27.4% Irish, 14.5% English, 12.1% Italian, 7.0% Polish
Employment: 26.6% management, business, and financial, 4.4% computer, engineering, and science, 19.4% education, legal, community service, arts, and media, 7.6% healthcare practitioners, 9.0% service, 23.9% sales and office, 4.1% natural resources, construction, and maintenance, 5.0% production, transportation, and material moving
Income: Per capita: $47,990; Median household: $93,220; Average household: $121,516; Households with income of $100,000 or more: 46.2%; Poverty rate: 3.5%
Educational Attainment: High school diploma or higher: 97.5%; Bachelor's degree or higher: 64.0%; Graduate/professional degree or higher: 25.0%

School District(s)

Bay Village City (PK-12)
2015-16 Enrollment: 2,494 . . . . (440) 617-7300
Housing: Homeownership rate: 91.1%; Median home value: $215,100; Median year structure built: 1957; Homeowner vacancy rate: 0.9%; Median selected monthly owner costs: $1,641 with a mortgage, $730 without a mortgage; Median gross rent: $976 per month; Rental vacancy rate: 4.3%
Health Insurance: 97.5% have insurance; 88.4% have private insurance; 22.2% have public insurance; 2.5% do not have insurance; 2.3% of children under 18 do not have insurance
Newspapers: Gottschalk Publishing (weekly circulation 19,000)
Transportation: Commute: 86.5% car, 2.2% public transportation, 0.7% walk, 9.8% work from home; Mean travel time to work: 25.0 minutes
Additional Information Contacts
City of Bay Village . . . . (440) 899-3415
http://www.cityofbayvillage.com

BEACHWOOD (city). Covers a land area of 5.325 square miles and a water area of 0.014 square miles. Located at 41.48° N. Lat; 81.50° W. Long. Elevation is 1,184 feet.
History: On June 26, 1915, the trustees of Warrensville Township ordered the incorporation of Beachwood Village; in 1960, Beachwood attained "City" status.
Population: 11,786; Growth (since 2000): -3.3%; Density: 2,213.3 persons per square mile; Race: 77.8% White, 10.2% Black/African American, 9.5% Asian, 0.0% American Indian/Alaska Native, 0.2% Native Hawaiian/Other Pacific Islander, 1.9% Two or more races, 2.0% Hispanic of any race; Average household size: 2.34; Median age: 50.3; Age under 18: 20.4%; Age 65 and over: 30.3%; Males per 100 females: 79.6; Marriage status: 20.2% never married, 57.0% now married, 0.6% separated, 13.6% widowed, 9.2% divorced; Foreign born: 16.3%; Speak English only: 79.2%; With disability: 13.8%; Veterans: 6.7%; Ancestry: 10.4% Russian, 9.8% German, 7.2% Polish, 6.5% American, 6.2% Eastern European
Employment: 30.9% management, business, and financial, 8.7% computer, engineering, and science, 16.2% education, legal, community service, arts, and media, 10.0% healthcare practitioners, 9.8% service, 20.8% sales and office, 1.8% natural resources, construction, and maintenance, 1.9% production, transportation, and material moving
Income: Per capita: $50,525; Median household: $88,287; Average household: $124,009; Households with income of $100,000 or more: 43.0%; Poverty rate: 2.9%
Educational Attainment: High school diploma or higher: 95.6%; Bachelor's degree or higher: 56.9%; Graduate/professional degree or higher: 32.3%

School District(s)

Beachwood City (PK-12)
2015-16 Enrollment: 1,502 . . . . (216) 464-2600

Four-year College(s)

University of Phoenix-Ohio (Private, For-profit)
Fall 2016 Enrollment: 102 . . . . (866) 766-0766
Housing: Homeownership rate: 63.0%; Median home value: $274,400; Median year structure built: 1969; Homeowner vacancy rate: 0.0%; Median selected monthly owner costs: $2,010 with a mortgage, $818 without a mortgage; Median gross rent: $1,546 per month; Rental vacancy rate: 14.8%
Health Insurance: 98.8% have insurance; 87.8% have private insurance; 29.1% have public insurance; 1.2% do not have insurance; 0.2% of children under 18 do not have insurance
Hospitals: University Hospitals Ahuja Medical Center
Transportation: Commute: 90.1% car, 3.6% public transportation, 0.7% walk, 5.2% work from home; Mean travel time to work: 23.0 minutes
Additional Information Contacts
City of Beachwood . . . . (216) 464-1070
http://www.beachwoodohio.com

BEDFORD (city). Covers a land area of 5.351 square miles and a water area of 0.048 square miles. Located at 41.39° N. Lat; 81.54° W. Long. Elevation is 948 feet.
History: Named for Bedford in Bedfordshire, England. The first settlement at Bedford was made in 1786 by a group of Moravian missionaries, and was called Pilgerruh, meaning pilgrim's rest. In 1810 the town site was surveyed by the Connecticut Land Company, and in 1813 permanent settlers arrived. Benjamin Fitch, who began the manufacture of chairs in Bedford, was one of the first settlers.
Population: 12,782; Growth (since 2000): -10.1%; Density: 2,388.7 persons per square mile; Race: 41.1% White, 55.2% Black/African American, 1.5% Asian, 0.0% American Indian/Alaska Native, 0.0% Native Hawaiian/Other Pacific Islander, 1.3% Two or more races, 2.4% Hispanic of any race; Average household size: 2.23; Median age: 40.2; Age under 18: 23.6%; Age 65 and over: 15.2%; Males per 100 females: 84.4; Marriage status: 34.1% never married, 43.1% now married, 2.1% separated, 7.4% widowed, 15.3% divorced; Foreign born: 2.6%; Speak

English only: 96.5%; With disability: 12.2%; Veterans: 8.3%; Ancestry: 9.8% German, 7.8% Polish, 6.7% Irish, 5.6% Italian, 4.3% English
Employment: 8.5% management, business, and financial, 2.8% computer, engineering, and science, 9.7% education, legal, community service, arts, and media, 4.3% healthcare practitioners, 18.5% service, 28.7% sales and office, 7.2% natural resources, construction, and maintenance, 20.4% production, transportation, and material moving
Income: Per capita: $24,271; Median household: $41,285; Average household: $52,981; Households with income of $100,000 or more: 12.8%; Poverty rate: 10.9%
Educational Attainment: High school diploma or higher: 92.0%; Bachelor's degree or higher: 19.5%; Graduate/professional degree or higher: 7.1%

School District(s)

Bedford City (PK-12)
2015-16 Enrollment: 3,329 . . . . (440) 439-1500
Housing: Homeownership rate: 50.8%; Median home value: $91,500; Median year structure built: 1958; Homeowner vacancy rate: 4.3%; Median selected monthly owner costs: $1,135 with a mortgage, $427 without a mortgage; Median gross rent: $787 per month; Rental vacancy rate: 13.6%
Health Insurance: 92.4% have insurance; 73.3% have private insurance; 33.0% have public insurance; 7.6% do not have insurance; 3.8% of children under 18 do not have insurance
Safety: Violent crime rate: 23.7 per 10,000 population; Property crime rate: 201.1 per 10,000 population
Transportation: Commute: 92.1% car, 3.0% public transportation, 1.6% walk, 1.9% work from home; Mean travel time to work: 22.9 minutes
Additional Information Contacts
City of Bedford. . . . . (440) 232-1600
http://www.bedfordoh.gov

BEDFORD HEIGHTS (city). Covers a land area of 4.535 square miles and a water area of 0.012 square miles. Located at 41.40° N. Lat; 81.50° W. Long. Elevation is 1,040 feet.
History: Named for Bedford in Bedfordshire, England. Incorporated 1951.
Population: 10,640; Growth (since 2000): -6.5%; Density: 2,346.4 persons per square mile; Race: 20.0% White, 72.7% Black/African American, 1.4% Asian, 0.1% American Indian/Alaska Native, 0.0% Native Hawaiian/Other Pacific Islander, 4.7% Two or more races, 3.3% Hispanic of any race; Average household size: 2.05; Median age: 45.5; Age under 18: 17.9%; Age 65 and over: 20.6%; Males per 100 females: 84.9; Marriage status: 37.2% never married, 36.6% now married, 4.5% separated, 6.9% widowed, 19.3% divorced; Foreign born: 4.6%; Speak English only: 92.7%; With disability: 14.7%; Veterans: 10.3%; Ancestry: 5.1% German, 4.3% Irish, 2.8% American, 2.6% European, 2.2% English
Employment: 10.5% management, business, and financial, 3.8% computer, engineering, and science, 7.7% education, legal, community service, arts, and media, 5.8% healthcare practitioners, 17.8% service, 25.5% sales and office, 5.7% natural resources, construction, and maintenance, 23.1% production, transportation, and material moving
Income: Per capita: $24,313; Median household: $37,692; Average household: $48,410; Households with income of $100,000 or more: 9.9%; Poverty rate: 16.4%
Educational Attainment: High school diploma or higher: 88.7%; Bachelor's degree or higher: 16.5%; Graduate/professional degree or higher: 5.0%
Housing: Homeownership rate: 49.1%; Median home value: $97,800; Median year structure built: 1967; Homeowner vacancy rate: 4.9%; Median selected monthly owner costs: $1,133 with a mortgage, $459 without a mortgage; Median gross rent: $718 per month; Rental vacancy rate: 14.6%
Health Insurance: 89.5% have insurance; 63.2% have private insurance; 42.3% have public insurance; 10.5% do not have insurance; 4.8% of children under 18 do not have insurance
Safety: Violent crime rate: 26.4 per 10,000 population; Property crime rate: 273.7 per 10,000 population
Transportation: Commute: 91.5% car, 5.0% public transportation, 1.0% walk, 1.1% work from home; Mean travel time to work: 23.3 minutes
Additional Information Contacts
City of Bedford Heights . . . . (440) 786-3200
http://www.bedfordheights.gov

BENTLEYVILLE (village). Covers a land area of 2.557 square miles and a water area of 0.043 square miles. Located at 41.41° N. Lat; 81.41° W. Long. Elevation is 938 feet.
Population: 905; Growth (since 2000): -4.4%; Density: 353.9 persons per square mile; Race: 96.9% White, 0.4% Black/African American, 1.3% Asian, 0.0% American Indian/Alaska Native, 0.1% Native Hawaiian/Other Pacific Islander, 0.7% Two or more races, 1.9% Hispanic of any race; Average household size: 2.95; Median age: 49.1; Age under 18: 24.4%; Age 65 and over: 12.2%; Males per 100 females: 98.2; Marriage status: 21.4% never married, 72.5% now married, 0.0% separated, 1.1% widowed, 5.0% divorced; Foreign born: 6.0%; Speak English only: 97.3%; With disability: 4.8%; Veterans: 3.7%; Ancestry: 21.9% German, 18.9% Italian, 16.6% English, 11.8% Irish, 9.7% Polish
Employment: 30.4% management, business, and financial, 3.0% computer, engineering, and science, 12.4% education, legal, community service, arts, and media, 17.3% healthcare practitioners, 5.4% service, 25.3% sales and office, 2.4% natural resources, construction, and maintenance, 3.9% production, transportation, and material moving
Income: Per capita: $101,089; Median household: $173,250; Average household: $294,039; Households with income of $100,000 or more: 78.2%; Poverty rate: 3.1%
Educational Attainment: High school diploma or higher: 99.2%; Bachelor's degree or higher: 80.0%; Graduate/professional degree or higher: 49.9%
Housing: Homeownership rate: 97.1%; Median home value: $563,900; Median year structure built: 1988; Homeowner vacancy rate: 0.0%; Median selected monthly owner costs: $3,500 with a mortgage, $1,390 without a mortgage; Median gross rent: n/a per month; Rental vacancy rate: 0.0%
Health Insurance: 98.0% have insurance; 93.7% have private insurance; 13.6% have public insurance; 2.0% do not have insurance; 0.9% of children under 18 do not have insurance
Transportation: Commute: 90.1% car, 0.9% public transportation, 1.1% walk, 7.7% work from home; Mean travel time to work: 27.0 minutes
Additional Information Contacts
Village of Bentleyville . . . . (440) 247-5055
http://www.villageofbentleyville.com

BEREA (city). Covers a land area of 5.718 square miles and a water area of 0.109 square miles. Located at 41.37° N. Lat; 81.86° W. Long. Elevation is 755 feet.
History: Named for the city in ancient Syria, mentioned in the Bible. Berea was founded by John Baldwin in 1827, on land owned by Gideon Granger, Postmaster General under President Jefferson. Baldwin discovered the vein of abrasive sandstone that provided the early industry for the community.
Population: 18,949; Growth (since 2000): -0.1%; Density: 3,314.2 persons per square mile; Race: 88.1% White, 6.4% Black/African American, 2.5% Asian, 0.4% American Indian/Alaska Native, 0.0% Native Hawaiian/Other Pacific Islander, 2.1% Two or more races, 3.3% Hispanic of any race; Average household size: 2.30; Median age: 38.2; Age under 18: 18.3%; Age 65 and over: 15.9%; Males per 100 females: 91.3; Marriage status: 40.5% never married, 40.2% now married, 0.9% separated, 5.4% widowed, 13.9% divorced; Foreign born: 2.9%; Speak English only: 94.1%; With disability: 13.3%; Veterans: 6.3%; Ancestry: 28.0% German, 20.9% Irish, 11.4% English, 10.3% Italian, 9.7% Polish
Employment: 14.6% management, business, and financial, 6.8% computer, engineering, and science, 12.7% education, legal, community service, arts, and media, 4.5% healthcare practitioners, 15.9% service, 27.2% sales and office, 6.7% natural resources, construction, and maintenance, 11.6% production, transportation, and material moving
Income: Per capita: $27,862; Median household: $57,896; Average household: $70,665; Households with income of $100,000 or more: 21.6%; Poverty rate: 11.3%
Educational Attainment: High school diploma or higher: 92.1%; Bachelor's degree or higher: 32.9%; Graduate/professional degree or higher: 12.3%

School District(s)

Berea City (PK-12)
2015-16 Enrollment: 6,598 . . . . (216) 898-8300
Columbia Local (KG-12)
2015-16 Enrollment: 836. . . . . (440) 236-5008

Four-year College(s)

Baldwin Wallace University (Private, Not-for-profit, United Methodist)
Fall 2016 Enrollment: 3,933 . . . . (440) 826-2900
2016-17 Tuition: In-state $30,776; Out-of-state $30,776

Housing: Homeownership rate: 67.7%; Median home value: $129,000; Median year structure built: 1960; Homeowner vacancy rate: 0.5%; Median selected monthly owner costs: $1,296 with a mortgage, $490 without a mortgage; Median gross rent: $753 per month; Rental vacancy rate: 7.2%
Health Insurance: 94.3% have insurance; 81.4% have private insurance; 25.4% have public insurance; 5.7% do not have insurance; 2.2% of children under 18 do not have insurance
Safety: Violent crime rate: 5.9 per 10,000 population; Property crime rate: 96.3 per 10,000 population
Transportation: Commute: 86.5% car, 0.7% public transportation, 6.1% walk, 4.6% work from home; Mean travel time to work: 22.0 minutes
Additional Information Contacts
City of Berea . . . . (440) 826-5800
http://www.bereaohio.com

BRATENAHL (village). Covers a land area of 1.023 square miles and a water area of 0.581 square miles. Located at 41.56° N. Lat; 81.61° W. Long. Elevation is 614 feet.
Population: 1,203; Growth (since 2000): -10.0%; Density: 1,176.5 persons per square mile; Race: 83.5% White, 13.5% Black/African American, 1.2% Asian, 0.2% American Indian/Alaska Native, 0.0% Native Hawaiian/Other Pacific Islander, 1.5% Two or more races, 0.2% Hispanic of any race; Average household size: 1.78; Median age: 62.2; Age under 18: 9.2%; Age 65 and over: 42.4%; Males per 100 females: 94.6; Marriage status: 19.5% never married, 59.9% now married, 0.6% separated, 5.8% widowed, 14.8% divorced; Foreign born: 5.3%; Speak English only: 93.4%; With disability: 12.7%; Veterans: 9.4%; Ancestry: 18.2% German, 13.2% Irish, 11.3% English, 6.4% Polish, 6.2% Italian
Employment: 32.9% management, business, and financial, 3.5% computer, engineering, and science, 26.3% education, legal, community service, arts, and media, 14.2% healthcare practitioners, 7.2% service, 11.7% sales and office, 1.7% natural resources, construction, and maintenance, 2.5% production, transportation, and material moving
Income: Per capita: $97,187; Median household: $82,500; Average household: $171,810; Households with income of $100,000 or more: 45.3%; Poverty rate: 8.0%
Educational Attainment: High school diploma or higher: 98.8%; Bachelor's degree or higher: 67.4%; Graduate/professional degree or higher: 36.3%
Housing: Homeownership rate: 81.3%; Median home value: $266,500; Median year structure built: 1964; Homeowner vacancy rate: 2.4%; Median selected monthly owner costs: $2,403 with a mortgage, $1,328 without a mortgage; Median gross rent: $1,222 per month; Rental vacancy rate: 12.0%
Health Insurance: 95.9% have insurance; 84.4% have private insurance; 43.5% have public insurance; 4.1% do not have insurance; 1.8% of children under 18 do not have insurance
Transportation: Commute: 90.2% car, 0.3% public transportation, 0.5% walk, 8.3% work from home; Mean travel time to work: 17.7 minutes

BRECKSVILLE (city). Covers a land area of 19.574 square miles and a water area of 0.113 square miles. Located at 41.31° N. Lat; 81.62° W. Long. Elevation is 889 feet.
History: Brecksville was settled about 1811 and named for John and Robert Breck, early residents.
Population: 13,470; Growth (since 2000): 0.7%; Density: 688.2 persons per square mile; Race: 95.7% White, 0.9% Black/African American, 3.2% Asian, 0.0% American Indian/Alaska Native, 0.0% Native Hawaiian/Other Pacific Islander, 0.2% Two or more races, 0.4% Hispanic of any race; Average household size: 2.51; Median age: 47.9; Age under 18: 22.8%; Age 65 and over: 20.0%; Males per 100 females: 99.5; Marriage status: 25.6% never married, 60.1% now married, 0.6% separated, 4.6% widowed, 9.7% divorced; Foreign born: 6.8%; Speak English only: 91.4%; With disability: 6.7%; Veterans: 8.6%; Ancestry: 26.4% German, 15.2% Irish, 14.5% Polish, 14.0% Italian, 9.3% English
Employment: 25.3% management, business, and financial, 7.0% computer, engineering, and science, 14.2% education, legal, community service, arts, and media, 9.3% healthcare practitioners, 11.9% service, 21.9% sales and office, 4.9% natural resources, construction, and maintenance, 5.5% production, transportation, and material moving
Income: Per capita: $50,988; Median household: $98,345; Average household: $126,923; Households with income of $100,000 or more: 49.1%; Poverty rate: 2.8%
Educational Attainment: High school diploma or higher: 97.4%; Bachelor's degree or higher: 53.8%; Graduate/professional degree or higher: 22.4%

School District(s)

Brecksville-Broadview Heights City (PK-12)
2015-16 Enrollment: 3,961 . . . . (440) 740-4000
Cuyahoga Valley Career Center (09-12)
2015-16 Enrollment: n/a . . . . (440) 526-5200

Two-year College(s)

Stautzenberger College-Brecksville (Private, For-profit)
Fall 2016 Enrollment: 408 . . . . (440) 838-1999
2016-17 Tuition: In-state $12,090; Out-of-state $12,090

Vocational/Technical School(s)

Cuyahoga Valley Career Center (Public)
Fall 2016 Enrollment: 119 . . . . (440) 746-8230
2016-17 Tuition: $13,238

Housing: Homeownership rate: 84.5%; Median home value: $256,000; Median year structure built: 1978; Homeowner vacancy rate: 1.5%; Median selected monthly owner costs: $1,851 with a mortgage, $758 without a mortgage; Median gross rent: $1,452 per month; Rental vacancy rate: 2.3%
Health Insurance: 97.3% have insurance; 87.9% have private insurance; 21.9% have public insurance; 2.7% do not have insurance; 0.0% of children under 18 do not have insurance
Safety: Violent crime rate: 3.0 per 10,000 population; Property crime rate: 40.3 per 10,000 population
Newspapers: Gazette Newspaper (weekly circulation 10,000)
Transportation: Commute: 90.9% car, 1.9% public transportation, 0.8% walk, 6.0% work from home; Mean travel time to work: 23.4 minutes
Additional Information Contacts
City of Brecksville . . . . (440) 526-4351
http://www.brecksville.oh.us

BROADVIEW HEIGHTS (city). Covers a land area of 13.048 square miles and a water area of 0.021 square miles. Located at 41.32° N. Lat; 81.68° W. Long. Elevation is 1,191 feet.
History: Named for the beautiful local views. Incorporated 1926.
Population: 19,257; Growth (since 2000): 20.6%; Density: 1,475.8 persons per square mile; Race: 86.0% White, 4.6% Black/African American, 6.0% Asian, 0.4% American Indian/Alaska Native, 0.0% Native Hawaiian/Other Pacific Islander, 2.6% Two or more races, 2.7% Hispanic of any race; Average household size: 2.52; Median age: 41.7; Age under 18: 23.2%; Age 65 and over: 14.8%; Males per 100 females: 92.7; Marriage status: 27.1% never married, 56.2% now married, 0.5% separated, 6.6% widowed, 10.1% divorced; Foreign born: 9.9%; Speak English only: 87.8%; With disability: 7.0%; Veterans: 6.0%; Ancestry: 23.5% German, 16.6% Irish, 16.0% Italian, 15.8% Polish, 5.6% Slovak
Employment: 20.6% management, business, and financial, 8.9% computer, engineering, and science, 9.5% education, legal, community service, arts, and media, 10.0% healthcare practitioners, 12.7% service, 23.5% sales and office, 4.3% natural resources, construction, and maintenance, 10.6% production, transportation, and material moving
Income: Per capita: $42,092; Median household: $77,480; Average household: $105,617; Households with income of $100,000 or more: 38.0%; Poverty rate: 4.1%
Educational Attainment: High school diploma or higher: 96.2%; Bachelor's degree or higher: 45.7%; Graduate/professional degree or higher: 19.9%

School District(s)

Brecksville-Broadview Heights City (PK-12)
2015-16 Enrollment: 3,961 . . . . (440) 740-4000
North Royalton City (PK-12)
2015-16 Enrollment: 4,387 . . . . (440) 237-8800

Two-year College(s)

Vatterott College-Cleveland (Private, For-profit)
Fall 2016 Enrollment: 184 . . . . (440) 526-1660
2016-17 Tuition: In-state $12,419; Out-of-state $12,419

Housing: Homeownership rate: 81.0%; Median home value: $217,600; Median year structure built: 1981; Homeowner vacancy rate: 2.4%; Median selected monthly owner costs: $1,734 with a mortgage, $609 without a mortgage; Median gross rent: $843 per month; Rental vacancy rate: 0.0%
Health Insurance: 93.9% have insurance; 83.1% have private insurance; 22.2% have public insurance; 6.1% do not have insurance; 3.7% of children under 18 do not have insurance

Transportation: Commute: 93.0% car, 0.4% public transportation, 0.1% walk, 6.4% work from home; Mean travel time to work: 28.2 minutes
Additional Information Contacts
City of Broadview Heights . . . . (440) 526-4357
http://www.broadview-heights.org

BROOK PARK (city). Covers a land area of 7.530 square miles and a water area of 0.003 square miles. Located at 41.40° N. Lat; 81.82° W. Long. Elevation is 797 feet.
History: Named for its location near a branch of the Rocky River. Incorporated 1914.
Population: 18,875; Growth (since 2000): -11.0%; Density: 2,506.7 persons per square mile; Race: 90.2% White, 5.1% Black/African American, 1.3% Asian, 0.1% American Indian/Alaska Native, 0.0% Native Hawaiian/Other Pacific Islander, 2.1% Two or more races, 3.6% Hispanic of any race; Average household size: 2.46; Median age: 44.5; Age under 18: 19.8%; Age 65 and over: 20.0%; Males per 100 females: 92.4; Marriage status: 30.0% never married, 47.6% now married, 1.1% separated, 8.7% widowed, 13.7% divorced; Foreign born: 4.8%; Speak English only: 92.4%; With disability: 17.7%; Veterans: 10.8%; Ancestry: 25.8% German, 19.3% Irish, 12.8% Italian, 10.7% Polish, 8.2% English
Employment: 8.8% management, business, and financial, 2.6% computer, engineering, and science, 6.7% education, legal, community service, arts, and media, 5.7% healthcare practitioners, 17.6% service, 29.8% sales and office, 9.2% natural resources, construction, and maintenance, 19.7% production, transportation, and material moving
Income: Per capita: $24,384; Median household: $48,813; Average household: $58,454; Households with income of $100,000 or more: 15.4%; Poverty rate: 9.7%
Educational Attainment: High school diploma or higher: 87.0%; Bachelor's degree or higher: 12.6%; Graduate/professional degree or higher: 3.5%

School District(s)

Berea City (PK-12)
2015-16 Enrollment: 6,598 . . . . (216) 898-8300
Quest Community School (09-12)
2015-16 Enrollment: 74. . . . . (216) 220-4412
Housing: Homeownership rate: 76.7%; Median home value: $111,800; Median year structure built: 1961; Homeowner vacancy rate: 1.2%; Median selected monthly owner costs: $1,146 with a mortgage, $407 without a mortgage; Median gross rent: $850 per month; Rental vacancy rate: 5.0%
Health Insurance: 92.1% have insurance; 72.5% have private insurance; 34.8% have public insurance; 7.9% do not have insurance; 3.0% of children under 18 do not have insurance
Transportation: Commute: 94.9% car, 1.1% public transportation, 1.6% walk, 1.8% work from home; Mean travel time to work: 21.8 minutes
Additional Information Contacts
City of Brook Park . . . . (216) 433-1300
http://www.cityofbrookpark.com

BROOKLYN (city). Covers a land area of 4.248 square miles and a water area of 0.036 square miles. Located at 41.43° N. Lat; 81.75° W. Long. Elevation is 764 feet.
History: Brooklyn is a city in Cuyahoga County, Ohio, and a suburb of Cleveland.
Population: 10,936; Growth (since 2000): -5.6%; Density: 2,574.1 persons per square mile; Race: 79.5% White, 7.5% Black/African American, 5.4% Asian, 0.5% American Indian/Alaska Native, 0.1% Native Hawaiian/Other Pacific Islander, 2.8% Two or more races, 11.8% Hispanic of any race; Average household size: 2.20; Median age: 43.5; Age under 18: 16.1%; Age 65 and over: 20.4%; Males per 100 females: 93.1; Marriage status: 35.7% never married, 43.3% now married, 1.4% separated, 8.1% widowed, 13.0% divorced; Foreign born: 13.8%; Speak English only: 77.5%; With disability: 17.4%; Veterans: 8.9%; Ancestry: 22.3% German, 14.9% Irish, 8.4% Italian, 8.1% Polish, 5.0% English
Employment: 10.4% management, business, and financial, 4.2% computer, engineering, and science, 10.6% education, legal, community service, arts, and media, 4.1% healthcare practitioners, 19.2% service, 24.3% sales and office, 9.9% natural resources, construction, and maintenance, 17.2% production, transportation, and material moving
Income: Per capita: $24,069; Median household: $45,102; Average household: $51,627; Households with income of $100,000 or more: 10.2%; Poverty rate: 12.9%
Educational Attainment: High school diploma or higher: 86.1%; Bachelor's degree or higher: 16.7%; Graduate/professional degree or higher: 5.5%

School District(s)

Brooklyn City (PK-12)
2015-16 Enrollment: 1,366 . . . . (216) 485-8100
Housing: Homeownership rate: 57.5%; Median home value: $103,400; Median year structure built: 1959; Homeowner vacancy rate: 0.3%; Median selected monthly owner costs: $1,100 with a mortgage, $425 without a mortgage; Median gross rent: $677 per month; Rental vacancy rate: 3.2%
Health Insurance: 92.7% have insurance; 69.9% have private insurance; 39.1% have public insurance; 7.3% do not have insurance; 3.9% of children under 18 do not have insurance
Safety: Violent crime rate: 26.8 per 10,000 population; Property crime rate: 620.8 per 10,000 population
Transportation: Commute: 93.9% car, 2.4% public transportation, 1.2% walk, 2.0% work from home; Mean travel time to work: 22.5 minutes
Additional Information Contacts
City of Brooklyn . . . . (216) 351-2133
http://www.brooklynohio.gov

BROOKLYN HEIGHTS (village). Covers a land area of 1.744 square miles and a water area of 0.019 square miles. Located at 41.42° N. Lat; 81.67° W. Long. Elevation is 764 feet.
Population: 1,603; Growth (since 2000): 2.9%; Density: 919.4 persons per square mile; Race: 98.0% White, 1.7% Black/African American, 0.0% Asian, 0.0% American Indian/Alaska Native, 0.0% Native Hawaiian/Other Pacific Islander, 0.3% Two or more races, 2.5% Hispanic of any race; Average household size: 2.73; Median age: 43.8; Age under 18: 23.4%; Age 65 and over: 16.3%; Males per 100 females: 89.3; Marriage status: 24.2% never married, 59.5% now married, 0.6% separated, 5.8% widowed, 10.5% divorced; Foreign born: 2.2%; Speak English only: 97.1%; With disability: 14.0%; Veterans: 6.4%; Ancestry: 22.5% Polish, 20.1% German, 19.6% Irish, 15.6% Italian, 7.0% English
Employment: 9.7% management, business, and financial, 4.4% computer, engineering, and science, 10.2% education, legal, community service, arts, and media, 6.7% healthcare practitioners, 23.3% service, 27.0% sales and office, 7.5% natural resources, construction, and maintenance, 11.2% production, transportation, and material moving
Income: Per capita: $29,623; Median household: $64,722; Average household: $79,091; Households with income of $100,000 or more: 25.1%; Poverty rate: 4.4%
Educational Attainment: High school diploma or higher: 93.0%; Bachelor's degree or higher: 28.3%; Graduate/professional degree or higher: 9.7%
Housing: Homeownership rate: 87.5%; Median home value: $146,400; Median year structure built: 1958; Homeowner vacancy rate: 1.4%; Median selected monthly owner costs: $1,339 with a mortgage, $492 without a mortgage; Median gross rent: $1,240 per month; Rental vacancy rate: 5.1%
Health Insurance: 96.3% have insurance; 82.4% have private insurance; 28.6% have public insurance; 3.7% do not have insurance; 1.1% of children under 18 do not have insurance
Transportation: Commute: 94.9% car, 0.0% public transportation, 2.4% walk, 1.1% work from home; Mean travel time to work: 20.0 minutes

CHAGRIN FALLS (village). Covers a land area of 2.075 square miles and a water area of 0.058 square miles. Located at 41.43° N. Lat; 81.39° W. Long. Elevation is 1,001 feet.
History: Noah Graves from Massachusetts built a grist mill here in 1833, and the town of Chagrin Falls developed as a residential community. The town was named for the Chagrin River, said to have been named by surveyor Moses Cleaveland to express his embarrassment at mistaking it for the Cuyahoga River.
Population: 4,056; Growth (since 2000): 0.8%; Density: 1,954.6 persons per square mile; Race: 97.5% White, 0.3% Black/African American, 0.7% Asian, 0.0% American Indian/Alaska Native, 0.0% Native Hawaiian/Other Pacific Islander, 1.0% Two or more races, 0.9% Hispanic of any race; Average household size: 2.16; Median age: 47.9; Age under 18: 23.9%; Age 65 and over: 25.1%; Males per 100 females: 86.0; Marriage status: 19.6% never married, 56.0% now married, 1.3% separated, 9.7% widowed, 14.7% divorced; Foreign born: 3.3%; Speak English only: 93.1%; With disability: 12.0%; Veterans: 7.6%; Ancestry: 26.9% German, 25.0% English, 20.5% Irish, 14.8% Italian, 10.8% Polish

Employment: 30.8% management, business, and financial, 3.4% computer, engineering, and science, 12.1% education, legal, community service, arts, and media, 7.3% healthcare practitioners, 12.1% service, 28.5% sales and office, 2.5% natural resources, construction, and maintenance, 3.4% production, transportation, and material moving
Income: Per capita: $63,340; Median household: $75,260; Average household: $138,885; Households with income of $100,000 or more: 39.3%; Poverty rate: 2.7%
Educational Attainment: High school diploma or higher: 97.3%; Bachelor's degree or higher: 65.4%; Graduate/professional degree or higher: 26.7%

School District(s)

Chagrin Falls Exempted Village (PK-12)
2015-16 Enrollment: 2,052 . . . . (440) 247-5500
Kenston Local (KG-12)
2015-16 Enrollment: 2,782 . . . . (440) 543-9677

Housing: Homeownership rate: 64.0%; Median home value: $328,100; Median year structure built: 1958; Homeowner vacancy rate: 2.7%; Median selected monthly owner costs: $2,224 with a mortgage, $895 without a mortgage; Median gross rent: $1,309 per month; Rental vacancy rate: 5.7%
Health Insurance: 97.8% have insurance; 89.2% have private insurance; 26.9% have public insurance; 2.2% do not have insurance; 0.0% of children under 18 do not have insurance
Safety: Violent crime rate: 10.0 per 10,000 population; Property crime rate: 67.4 per 10,000 population
Newspapers: Chagrin Valley Publishing (weekly circulation 30,000)
Transportation: Commute: 87.5% car, 1.5% public transportation, 1.6% walk, 8.7% work from home; Mean travel time to work: 25.4 minutes
Additional Information Contacts
Village of Chagrin Falls . . . . (440) 247-5050
http://www.chagrin-falls.org

CLEVELAND (city). County seat. Covers a land area of 77.697 square miles and a water area of 4.769 square miles. Located at 41.48° N. Lat; 81.68° W. Long. Elevation is 653 feet.
History: Moses Cleaveland platted the city of Cleveland on the shores of Lake Erie in 1796 for the Connecticut Land Company, but stayed only a few months in the town that would bear his name. It was Lorenzo Carter who pulled the community together, and launched the first boat from Cleveland harbor in 1804, a prophesy of the many freighters and passenger steamers that would one day enter this harbor. The spelling of the town's name changed from Cleaveland to Cleveland about 1832, when a newspaper editor had to drop one letter from his masthead to make it fit the space, and decided to drop the "a" from Cleaveland. Cleveland expanded when the Ohio & Erie Canal was completed, becoming a commercial center. In 1836 it was incorporated as a city, and over the next half-century developed into an industrial giant. The Cuyahoga Steam Furnace Company began making locomotives, the Cleveland Iron Company and the Standard Oil Company were organized, along with many other industries.
Population: 389,165; Growth (since 2000): -18.7%; Density: 5,008.8 persons per square mile; Race: 40.3% White, 50.8% Black/African American, 2.0% Asian, 0.5% American Indian/Alaska Native, 0.0% Native Hawaiian/Other Pacific Islander, 3.5% Two or more races, 10.8% Hispanic of any race; Average household size: 2.25; Median age: 35.8; Age under 18: 23.0%; Age 65 and over: 13.0%; Males per 100 females: 92.1; Marriage status: 50.3% never married, 28.8% now married, 3.5% separated, 6.6% widowed, 14.3% divorced; Foreign born: 4.9%; Speak English only: 87.4%; With disability: 20.0%; Veterans: 7.0%; Ancestry: 9.4% German, 8.8% Irish, 4.6% Italian, 4.1% Polish, 3.0% English
Employment: 10.1% management, business, and financial, 3.2% computer, engineering, and science, 8.6% education, legal, community service, arts, and media, 5.1% healthcare practitioners, 26.4% service, 22.9% sales and office, 6.0% natural resources, construction, and maintenance, 17.7% production, transportation, and material moving
Income: Per capita: $18,003; Median household: $26,583; Average household: $40,057; Households with income of $100,000 or more: 7.0%; Poverty rate: 36.0%
Educational Attainment: High school diploma or higher: 78.4%; Bachelor's degree or higher: 16.1%; Graduate/professional degree or higher: 5.9%

School District(s)

Apex Academy (KG-08)
2015-16 Enrollment: 637 . . . . (216) 451-1725
Bella Academy of Excellence (KG-06)
2015-16 Enrollment: 306 . . . . (216) 481-1500
Broadway Academy (KG-08)
2015-16 Enrollment: 321 . . . . (216) 271-7747
Citizens Academy (KG-05)
2015-16 Enrollment: 452 . . . . (216) 791-4195
Citizens Leadership Academy (06-08)
2015-16 Enrollment: 260 . . . . (216) 229-8185
Cleveland Academy For Scholarship Technology And Leadership (09-12)
2015-16 Enrollment: 169 . . . . (216) 443-5400
Cleveland Arts and Social Sciences Academy (KG-08)
2015-16 Enrollment: 332 . . . . (216) 229-3000
Cleveland College Preparatory School (KG-08)
2015-16 Enrollment: 278 . . . . (216) 341-1347
Cleveland Community School
2015-16 Enrollment: n/a . . . . (216) 523-1133
Cleveland Entrepreneurship Preparatory School (05-08)
2015-16 Enrollment: 308 . . . . (216) 456-2080
Cleveland Municipal (PK-12)
2015-16 Enrollment: 39,410 . . . . (216) 838-0000
Constellation Schools: Collinwood Village Academy (KG-06)
2015-16 Enrollment: 140 . . . . (216) 451-4022
Constellation Schools: Eastside Arts Academy (KG-06)
2015-16 Enrollment: 135 . . . . (216) 441-9830
Constellation Schools: Madison Community Elementary (KG-08)
2015-16 Enrollment: 330 . . . . (216) 651-5212
Constellation Schools: Old Brooklyn Community Elementary (KG-04)
2015-16 Enrollment: 336 . . . . (216) 661-7888
Constellation Schools: Old Brooklyn Community Middle (05-08)
2015-16 Enrollment: 245 . . . . (216) 351-0280
Constellation Schools: Outreach Academy For Students With Disabilities (01-12)
2015-16 Enrollment: 27 . . . . (216) 688-1900
Constellation Schools: Puritas Community Elementary (KG-04)
2015-16 Enrollment: 203 . . . . (216) 688-0680
Constellation Schools: Puritas Community Middle (05-08)
2015-16 Enrollment: 137 . . . . (216) 688-0680
Constellation Schools: Stockyard Community Elementary (KG-06)
2015-16 Enrollment: 276 . . . . (216) 651-5143
Constellation Schools: Westpark Community Elementary (KG-04)
2015-16 Enrollment: 321 . . . . (216) 688-0271
Constellation Schools: Westpark Community Middle (05-08)
2015-16 Enrollment: 205 . . . . (216) 251-7200
Constellation Schools: Westside Community School Of The Arts (KG-08)
2015-16 Enrollment: 370 . . . . (216) 688-1900
Entrepreneurship Preparatory School - Woodland Hills Campus (05-08)
2015-16 Enrollment: 291 . . . . (216) 298-1164
Frederick Douglass Reclamation Academy (09-12)
2015-16 Enrollment: 128 . . . . (216) 941-9661
George V. Voinovich Reclamation Academy (09-12)
2015-16 Enrollment: 148 . . . . (216) 295-1493
Green Inspiration Academy (KG-08)
2015-16 Enrollment: 202 . . . . (216) 378-9573
Harvard Avenue Performance Academy (KG-08)
2015-16 Enrollment: 589 . . . . (216) 283-5100
Hbcu Preparatory School 1 (03-08)
2015-16 Enrollment: 143 . . . . (216) 812-0244
Hbcu Preparatory School 2 (KG-02)
2015-16 Enrollment: 111 . . . . (216) 812-0244
Hope Academy Northcoast (KG-08)
2015-16 Enrollment: 286 . . . . (216) 429-0232
Hope Academy Northwest Campus (KG-08)
2015-16 Enrollment: 251 . . . . (216) 226-6800
Horizon Science Acad Cleveland (09-12)
2015-16 Enrollment: 474 . . . . (216) 432-3660
Horizon Science Academy Denison Elementary School (KG-05)
2015-16 Enrollment: 159 . . . . (216) 661-8840
Horizon Science Academy-Cleveland Middle School (KG-08)
2015-16 Enrollment: 328 . . . . (216) 432-9940
Horizon Science Academy-Denison Middle School (KG-08)
2015-16 Enrollment: 289 . . . . (216) 739-9911
Imagine Cleveland Academy
2015-16 Enrollment: n/a . . . . (216) 641-1500
Intergenerational School the (KG-08)
2015-16 Enrollment: 253 . . . . (216) 721-0120

Invictus High School (09-12)
2015-16 Enrollment: 397. . . . . (216) 539-7200
Lake Erie International High School (09-12)
2015-16 Enrollment: 275. . . . . (216) 539-7229
Life Skills of Northeast Ohio (09-12)
2015-16 Enrollment: 72. . . . . (216) 421-7587
Lincoln Preparatory Academy (KG-08)
2015-16 Enrollment: 195. . . . . (216) 772-1336
Mayfield City (KG-12)
2015-16 Enrollment: 4,269 . . . . (440) 995-7201
Menlo Park Academy (KG-08)
2015-16 Enrollment: 364. . . . . (440) 925-6365
Near West Intergenerational School (KG-08)
2015-16 Enrollment: 194. . . . . (216) 961-4308
Northeast Ohio College Preparatory School (KG-12)
2015-16 Enrollment: 568. . . . . (216) 965-0580
Oak Leadership Institute (KG-08)
2015-16 Enrollment: 95. . . . . (877) 644-6338
Ohio Connections Academy Inc (KG-12)
2015-16 Enrollment: 3,417 . . . . (513) 234-4900
Old Brook High School (09-12)
2015-16 Enrollment: 41. . . . . (216) 721-0845
Pearl Academy (KG-08)
2015-16 Enrollment: 227. . . . . (216) 741-2991
Promise Academy (09-12)
2015-16 Enrollment: 289. . . . . (216) 443-0500
Regent High School (09-12)
2015-16 Enrollment: 40. . . . . (216) 512-0076
South Euclid-Lyndhurst City (PK-12)
2015-16 Enrollment: 3,531 . . . . (216) 691-2000
University of Cleveland Preparatory School (KG-08)
2015-16 Enrollment: 384. . . . . (877) 644-6338
Village Preparatory School (KG-04)
2015-16 Enrollment: 446. . . . . (216) 456-2070
Villaview Community School
2015-16 Enrollment: n/a . . . . (216) 523-1133
Virtual Schoolhouse Inc. (KG-12)
2015-16 Enrollment: 330. . . . . (216) 541-2048
West Preparatory Academy (KG-08)
2015-16 Enrollment: 253. . . . . (216) 772-1340
Woodland Academy
2015-16 Enrollment: n/a . . . . (216) 721-6909

Four-year College(s)

Bryant & Stratton College-Cleveland (Private, For-profit)
Fall 2016 Enrollment: 321 . . . . (216) 771-1700
2016-17 Tuition: In-state $16,918; Out-of-state $16,918
Case Western Reserve University (Private, Not-for-profit)
Fall 2016 Enrollment: 11,664 . . . . (216) 368-2000
2016-17 Tuition: In-state $46,006; Out-of-state $46,006
Cleveland Institute of Art (Private, Not-for-profit)
Fall 2016 Enrollment: 624 . . . . (216) 421-7000
2016-17 Tuition: In-state $39,585; Out-of-state $39,585
Cleveland Institute of Music (Private, Not-for-profit)
Fall 2016 Enrollment: 431 . . . . (216) 791-5000
2016-17 Tuition: In-state $49,106; Out-of-state $49,106
Cleveland State University (Public)
Fall 2016 Enrollment: 16,864 . . . . (216) 687-2000
2016-17 Tuition: In-state $9,768; Out-of-state $13,819
Notre Dame College (Private, Not-for-profit, Roman Catholic)
Fall 2016 Enrollment: 1,985 . . . . (216) 381-1680
2016-17 Tuition: In-state $28,300; Out-of-state $28,300
South University-Cleveland (Private, For-profit)
Fall 2016 Enrollment: 401 . . . . (855) 398-9280
2016-17 Tuition: In-state $17,330; Out-of-state $17,330

Two-year College(s)

Allstate Hairstyling & Barber College (Private, For-profit)
Fall 2016 Enrollment: 31 . . . . (216) 241-6684
Cuyahoga Community College District (Public)
Fall 2016 Enrollment: 23,987 . . . . (800) 954-8742
2016-17 Tuition: In-state $3,953; Out-of-state $7,648
Merrillville Beauty College-Flawless Barber Academy (Private, For-profit)
Fall 2016 Enrollment: n/a . . . . (216) 641-9338
Ohio Technical College (Private, For-profit)
Fall 2016 Enrollment: 1,023 . . . . (216) 881-1700
Remington College-Cleveland Campus (Private, Not-for-profit)
Fall 2016 Enrollment: 564 . . . . (216) 475-7520
2016-17 Tuition: In-state $14,953; Out-of-state $14,953

Vocational/Technical School(s)

Cleveland Institute of Dental-Medical Assistants-Cleveland (Private, For-profit)
Fall 2016 Enrollment: 98 . . . . (216) 241-2930
2016-17 Tuition: $10,800

Housing: Homeownership rate: 41.9%; Median home value: $67,500; Median year structure built: Before 1940; Homeowner vacancy rate: 3.0%; Median selected monthly owner costs: $1,000 with a mortgage, $369 without a mortgage; Median gross rent: $660 per month; Rental vacancy rate: 6.9%

Health Insurance: 87.8% have insurance; 43.1% have private insurance; 53.9% have public insurance; 12.2% do not have insurance; 3.7% of children under 18 do not have insurance

Hospitals: Cleveland - Wade Park VA Medical Center (688 beds); Cleveland Clinic (1,113 beds); Fairview Hospital (511 beds); Lutheran Hospital (209 beds); Metrohealth System (728 beds); Saint Vincent Charity Medical Center (492 beds); University Hospitals Case Medical Center (1,032 beds)

Safety: Violent crime rate: 163.1 per 10,000 population; Property crime rate: 531.6 per 10,000 population

Newspapers: Call & Post (weekly circulation 34,000); Cleveland Scene (weekly circulation 90,000); Plain Dealer (daily circulation 292,000)

Transportation: Commute: 79.5% car, 10.6% public transportation, 5.3% walk, 2.8% work from home; Mean travel time to work: 24.3 minutes; Amtrak: Train service available.

Airports: Burke Lakefront (general aviation); Cleveland-Hopkins International (primary service/medium hub); Cuyahoga County (general aviation)

Additional Information Contacts

City of Cleveland . . . . (216) 664-2000
http://www.city.cleveland.oh.us

CLEVELAND HEIGHTS (city). Covers a land area of 8.107 square miles and a water area of 0.018 square miles. Located at 41.51° N. Lat; 81.56° W. Long. Elevation is 942 feet.

History: Named for Moses Cleaveland (1754-1806), surveyor of the Western Reserve. Cleveland Heights was established in 1905, and became a city in 1921. It grew as a collection of neighborhoods serving as residential suburbs for Cleveland.

Population: 45,160; Growth (since 2000): -9.6%; Density: 5,570.8 persons per square mile; Race: 49.3% White, 42.7% Black/African American, 4.2% Asian, 0.2% American Indian/Alaska Native, 0.0% Native Hawaiian/Other Pacific Islander, 2.9% Two or more races, 2.3% Hispanic of any race; Average household size: 2.32; Median age: 36.1; Age under 18: 21.9%; Age 65 and over: 15.0%; Males per 100 females: 87.2; Marriage status: 43.3% never married, 40.5% now married, 1.4% separated, 4.9% widowed, 11.3% divorced; Foreign born: 8.1%; Speak English only: 89.7%; With disability: 12.0%; Veterans: 5.5%; Ancestry: 12.1% German, 8.4% Irish, 5.5% English, 5.3% Italian, 4.3% Polish

Employment: 15.7% management, business, and financial, 7.8% computer, engineering, and science, 22.4% education, legal, community service, arts, and media, 11.6% healthcare practitioners, 13.7% service, 19.0% sales and office, 3.4% natural resources, construction, and maintenance, 6.5% production, transportation, and material moving

Income: Per capita: $31,887; Median household: $53,901; Average household: $73,782; Households with income of $100,000 or more: 22.9%; Poverty rate: 20.2%

Educational Attainment: High school diploma or higher: 93.7%; Bachelor's degree or higher: 51.0%; Graduate/professional degree or higher: 26.8%

School District(s)

Cleveland Heights-University Heights City (PK-12)
2015-16 Enrollment: 5,349 . . . . (216) 371-7171

Housing: Homeownership rate: 56.2%; Median home value: $127,700; Median year structure built: Before 1940; Homeowner vacancy rate: 3.3%; Median selected monthly owner costs: $1,465 with a mortgage, $635 without a mortgage; Median gross rent: $871 per month; Rental vacancy rate: 9.0%

Health Insurance: 93.2% have insurance; 69.3% have private insurance; 35.9% have public insurance; 6.8% do not have insurance; 4.7% of children under 18 do not have insurance

Safety: Violent crime rate: 32.4 per 10,000 population; Property crime rate: 223.1 per 10,000 population
Transportation: Commute: 82.1% car, 5.3% public transportation, 5.7% walk, 5.0% work from home; Mean travel time to work: 23.2 minutes
Additional Information Contacts
City of Cleveland Heights .... (216) 291-4444
http://www.clevelandheights.com

CUYAHOGA HEIGHTS (village). Covers a land area of 3.072 square miles and a water area of 0.142 square miles. Located at 41.44° N. Lat; 81.65° W. Long. Elevation is 715 feet.
Population: 603; Growth (since 2000): 0.7%; Density: 196.3 persons per square mile; Race: 92.9% White, 0.7% Black/African American, 4.0% Asian, 0.0% American Indian/Alaska Native, 0.0% Native Hawaiian/Other Pacific Islander, 2.5% Two or more races, 0.3% Hispanic of any race; Average household size: 2.47; Median age: 40.8; Age under 18: 27.9%; Age 65 and over: 16.6%; Males per 100 females: 83.9; Marriage status: 35.6% never married, 36.1% now married, 1.8% separated, 11.7% widowed, 16.6% divorced; Foreign born: 4.5%; Speak English only: 90.4%; With disability: 8.1%; Veterans: 8.0%; Ancestry: 29.9% Polish, 20.4% Italian, 13.8% German, 11.8% Irish, 7.3% Czech
Employment: 7.3% management, business, and financial, 4.0% computer, engineering, and science, 8.0% education, legal, community service, arts, and media, 5.8% healthcare practitioners, 16.4% service, 37.2% sales and office, 8.4% natural resources, construction, and maintenance, 12.8% production, transportation, and material moving
Income: Per capita: $26,496; Median household: $49,286; Average household: $64,962; Households with income of $100,000 or more: 16.4%; Poverty rate: 12.4%
Educational Attainment: High school diploma or higher: 85.5%; Bachelor's degree or higher: 17.7%; Graduate/professional degree or higher: 4.7%

School District(s)

Cuyahoga Heights Local (PK-12)
2015-16 Enrollment: 818 .... (216) 429-5700
Housing: Homeownership rate: 63.9%; Median home value: $140,200; Median year structure built: 1949; Homeowner vacancy rate: 0.0%; Median selected monthly owner costs: $1,302 with a mortgage, $379 without a mortgage; Median gross rent: $980 per month; Rental vacancy rate: 14.6%
Health Insurance: 89.1% have insurance; 64.8% have private insurance; 35.3% have public insurance; 10.9% do not have insurance; 4.8% of children under 18 do not have insurance
Transportation: Commute: 94.8% car, 0.0% public transportation, 0.7% walk, 4.5% work from home; Mean travel time to work: 19.4 minutes

EAST CLEVELAND (city). Covers a land area of 3.086 square miles and a water area of 0.007 square miles. Located at 41.53° N. Lat; 81.58° W. Long. Elevation is 686 feet.
History: Named for its location east of Cleveland. The original East Cleveland was annexed by Cleveland in 1872, and the name disappeared from the map until 1892, when the neighboring Collamer became East Cleveland Hamlet. In 1911 the village became a city.
Population: 17,413; Growth (since 2000): -36.0%; Density: 5,643.1 persons per square mile; Race: 6.6% White, 90.3% Black/African American, 0.2% Asian, 0.4% American Indian/Alaska Native, 0.0% Native Hawaiian/Other Pacific Islander, 2.4% Two or more races, 0.9% Hispanic of any race; Average household size: 2.07; Median age: 43.9; Age under 18: 20.7%; Age 65 and over: 19.2%; Males per 100 females: 82.1; Marriage status: 49.3% never married, 25.5% now married, 4.0% separated, 8.3% widowed, 16.9% divorced; Foreign born: 2.3%; Speak English only: 96.9%; With disability: 21.8%; Veterans: 8.7%; Ancestry: 2.1% Irish, 1.2% German, 1.1% English, 0.9% American, 0.8% Jamaican
Employment: 6.5% management, business, and financial, 1.6% computer, engineering, and science, 9.3% education, legal, community service, arts, and media, 6.7% healthcare practitioners, 30.7% service, 24.4% sales and office, 4.2% natural resources, construction, and maintenance, 16.6% production, transportation, and material moving
Income: Per capita: $15,089; Median household: $19,953; Average household: $30,188; Households with income of $100,000 or more: 3.6%; Poverty rate: 41.8%
Educational Attainment: High school diploma or higher: 82.1%; Bachelor's degree or higher: 12.4%; Graduate/professional degree or higher: 4.6%

School District(s)

Cleveland Municipal (PK-12)
2015-16 Enrollment: 39,410 .... (216) 838-0000
East Cleveland City School District (PK-12)
2015-16 Enrollment: 2,282 .... (216) 268-6570
Housing: Homeownership rate: 32.7%; Median home value: $58,500; Median year structure built: Before 1940; Homeowner vacancy rate: 5.2%; Median selected monthly owner costs: $1,084 with a mortgage, $377 without a mortgage; Median gross rent: $575 per month; Rental vacancy rate: 14.9%
Health Insurance: 88.4% have insurance; 34.8% have private insurance; 66.5% have public insurance; 11.6% do not have insurance; 6.2% of children under 18 do not have insurance
Safety: Violent crime rate: 64.4 per 10,000 population; Property crime rate: 198.4 per 10,000 population
Transportation: Commute: 71.0% car, 20.1% public transportation, 5.0% walk, 3.3% work from home; Mean travel time to work: 25.6 minutes
Additional Information Contacts
City of East Cleveland .... (216) 681-2208
http://www.eastcleveland.org

EUCLID (city). Covers a land area of 10.630 square miles and a water area of 0.852 square miles. Located at 41.59° N. Lat; 81.52° W. Long. Elevation is 617 feet.
History: Euclid was settled in 1798 and named for the Greek mathematician by surveyors in the party of Moses Cleaveland. Euclid developed as a residential community near Cleveland.
Population: 47,863; Growth (since 2000): -9.2%; Density: 4,502.6 persons per square mile; Race: 37.3% White, 59.5% Black/African American, 0.7% Asian, 0.1% American Indian/Alaska Native, 0.0% Native Hawaiian/Other Pacific Islander, 2.2% Two or more races, 1.4% Hispanic of any race; Average household size: 2.12; Median age: 40.6; Age under 18: 22.2%; Age 65 and over: 15.2%; Males per 100 females: 81.1; Marriage status: 43.2% never married, 34.6% now married, 2.8% separated, 8.1% widowed, 14.1% divorced; Foreign born: 3.3%; Speak English only: 95.3%; With disability: 16.2%; Veterans: 8.4%; Ancestry: 9.0% German, 7.1% Irish, 5.1% Italian, 4.1% Slovene, 3.5% English
Employment: 10.3% management, business, and financial, 3.5% computer, engineering, and science, 7.8% education, legal, community service, arts, and media, 6.3% healthcare practitioners, 22.7% service, 29.8% sales and office, 4.4% natural resources, construction, and maintenance, 15.4% production, transportation, and material moving
Income: Per capita: $22,471; Median household: $35,949; Average household: $46,671; Households with income of $100,000 or more: 9.3%; Poverty rate: 21.5%
Educational Attainment: High school diploma or higher: 89.3%; Bachelor's degree or higher: 20.6%; Graduate/professional degree or higher: 6.6%

School District(s)

Euclid City (PK-12)
2015-16 Enrollment: 5,527 .... (216) 261-2900
New Day Academy Boarding & Day School (KG-12)
2015-16 Enrollment: 165 .... (216) 797-1602
Noble Academy-Cleveland (KG-08)
2015-16 Enrollment: 410 .... (216) 486-8866
Pinnacle Academy (KG-08)
2015-16 Enrollment: 744 .... (216) 731-0127

Two-year College(s)

Cleveland Clinic Health System-School of Diagnostic Imaging (Private, Not-for-profit)
Fall 2016 Enrollment: 38 .... (216) 692-7512
Housing: Homeownership rate: 48.6%; Median home value: $80,700; Median year structure built: 1956; Homeowner vacancy rate: 3.8%; Median selected monthly owner costs: $1,083 with a mortgage, $428 without a mortgage; Median gross rent: $734 per month; Rental vacancy rate: 13.1%
Health Insurance: 89.8% have insurance; 61.3% have private insurance; 40.8% have public insurance; 10.2% do not have insurance; 5.3% of children under 18 do not have insurance
Hospitals: Euclid Hospital (371 beds)
Transportation: Commute: 88.4% car, 6.3% public transportation, 1.4% walk, 2.8% work from home; Mean travel time to work: 24.6 minutes
Additional Information Contacts
City of Euclid .... (216) 289-2751
http://www.ci.euclid.oh.us

FAIRVIEW PARK (city). Covers a land area of 4.678 square miles and a water area of 0 square miles. Located at 41.44° N. Lat; 81.85° W. Long. Elevation is 745 feet.
History: Named to promote the town as a good place to live. Incorporated 1950.
Population: 16,473; Growth (since 2000): -6.3%; Density: 3,521.2 persons per square mile; Race: 94.1% White, 2.2% Black/African American, 1.0% Asian, 0.2% American Indian/Alaska Native, 0.0% Native Hawaiian/Other Pacific Islander, 1.7% Two or more races, 4.2% Hispanic of any race; Average household size: 2.25; Median age: 42.0; Age under 18: 20.2%; Age 65 and over: 17.8%; Males per 100 females: 92.1; Marriage status: 31.4% never married, 49.9% now married, 0.6% separated, 5.9% widowed, 12.8% divorced; Foreign born: 7.5%; Speak English only: 88.8%; With disability: 11.8%; Veterans: 7.8%; Ancestry: 28.0% German, 27.7% Irish, 10.3% Italian, 9.8% English, 7.6% Polish
Employment: 16.8% management, business, and financial, 6.9% computer, engineering, and science, 11.3% education, legal, community service, arts, and media, 6.8% healthcare practitioners, 14.8% service, 26.5% sales and office, 5.7% natural resources, construction, and maintenance, 11.2% production, transportation, and material moving
Income: Per capita: $32,171; Median household: $54,431; Average household: $71,401; Households with income of $100,000 or more: 22.1%; Poverty rate: 8.8%
Educational Attainment: High school diploma or higher: 95.4%; Bachelor's degree or higher: 36.9%; Graduate/professional degree or higher: 12.7%

School District(s)

Fairview Park City (PK-12)
2015-16 Enrollment: 1,810 . . . . (440) 331-5500

Two-year College(s)

Fairview Beauty Academy (Private, For-profit)
Fall 2016 Enrollment: 38 . . . . (440) 734-5555

Housing: Homeownership rate: 72.9%; Median home value: $145,500; Median year structure built: 1957; Homeowner vacancy rate: 1.2%; Median selected monthly owner costs: $1,326 with a mortgage, $551 without a mortgage; Median gross rent: $703 per month; Rental vacancy rate: 4.9%
Health Insurance: 92.9% have insurance; 78.2% have private insurance; 28.8% have public insurance; 7.1% do not have insurance; 3.4% of children under 18 do not have insurance
Safety: Violent crime rate: 19.6 per 10,000 population; Property crime rate: 139.1 per 10,000 population
Transportation: Commute: 91.2% car, 1.5% public transportation, 1.5% walk, 4.1% work from home; Mean travel time to work: 24.9 minutes
Additional Information Contacts
City of Fairview Park . . . . (440) 356-4411
http://www.fairviewpark.org

GARFIELD HEIGHTS (city). Covers a land area of 7.230 square miles and a water area of 0.061 square miles. Located at 41.42° N. Lat; 81.60° W. Long. Elevation is 955 feet.
History: Founded 1904, incorporated 1932.
Population: 28,207; Growth (since 2000): -8.2%; Density: 3,901.5 persons per square mile; Race: 50.5% White, 45.3% Black/African American, 0.8% Asian, 0.3% American Indian/Alaska Native, 0.0% Native Hawaiian/Other Pacific Islander, 2.2% Two or more races, 2.2% Hispanic of any race; Average household size: 2.38; Median age: 38.9; Age under 18: 23.2%; Age 65 and over: 15.9%; Males per 100 females: 85.2; Marriage status: 41.8% never married, 37.0% now married, 2.0% separated, 7.3% widowed, 13.9% divorced; Foreign born: 2.9%; Speak English only: 93.9%; With disability: 14.4%; Veterans: 8.8%; Ancestry: 13.8% Polish, 11.8% German, 9.7% Irish, 7.6% Italian, 3.2% English
Employment: 10.0% management, business, and financial, 3.5% computer, engineering, and science, 8.1% education, legal, community service, arts, and media, 5.6% healthcare practitioners, 19.6% service, 29.9% sales and office, 7.1% natural resources, construction, and maintenance, 16.2% production, transportation, and material moving
Income: Per capita: $21,332; Median household: $40,376; Average household: $49,500; Households with income of $100,000 or more: 9.3%; Poverty rate: 17.4%
Educational Attainment: High school diploma or higher: 85.5%; Bachelor's degree or higher: 14.1%; Graduate/professional degree or higher: 5.3%

School District(s)

Cleveland Municipal (PK-12)
2015-16 Enrollment: 39,410 . . . . (216) 838-0000
Garfield Heights City Schools (PK-12)
2015-16 Enrollment: 3,648 . . . . (216) 475-8100

Housing: Homeownership rate: 67.0%; Median home value: $73,600; Median year structure built: 1954; Homeowner vacancy rate: 1.1%; Median selected monthly owner costs: $1,080 with a mortgage, $428 without a mortgage; Median gross rent: $807 per month; Rental vacancy rate: 8.8%
Health Insurance: 90.6% have insurance; 62.3% have private insurance; 42.8% have public insurance; 9.4% do not have insurance; 2.4% of children under 18 do not have insurance
Hospitals: Marymount Hospital (322 beds)
Transportation: Commute: 91.6% car, 4.0% public transportation, 1.6% walk, 2.2% work from home; Mean travel time to work: 23.7 minutes
Additional Information Contacts
City of Garfield Heights . . . . (216) 475-1100
http://www.garfieldhts.org

GATES MILLS (village). Covers a land area of 8.968 square miles and a water area of 0.129 square miles. Located at 41.53° N. Lat; 81.41° W. Long. Elevation is 718 feet.
Population: 2,229; Growth (since 2000): -10.6%; Density: 248.5 persons per square mile; Race: 92.9% White, 2.1% Black/African American, 2.5% Asian, 0.0% American Indian/Alaska Native, 0.0% Native Hawaiian/Other Pacific Islander, 2.0% Two or more races, 2.4% Hispanic of any race; Average household size: 2.45; Median age: 54.7; Age under 18: 16.0%; Age 65 and over: 27.3%; Males per 100 females: 103.0; Marriage status: 21.6% never married, 60.7% now married, 0.8% separated, 8.3% widowed, 9.5% divorced; Foreign born: 9.7%; Speak English only: 93.2%; With disability: 9.9%; Veterans: 10.0%; Ancestry: 28.0% German, 16.6% Irish, 16.0% English, 12.4% Italian, 8.3% Polish
Employment: 32.8% management, business, and financial, 4.1% computer, engineering, and science, 12.8% education, legal, community service, arts, and media, 15.4% healthcare practitioners, 9.7% service, 19.3% sales and office, 1.9% natural resources, construction, and maintenance, 3.9% production, transportation, and material moving
Income: Per capita: $86,133; Median household: $132,167; Average household: $208,787; Households with income of $100,000 or more: 61.7%; Poverty rate: 8.2%
Educational Attainment: High school diploma or higher: 98.7%; Bachelor's degree or higher: 70.9%; Graduate/professional degree or higher: 36.3%

School District(s)

Mayfield City (KG-12)
2015-16 Enrollment: 4,269 . . . . (440) 995-7201

Housing: Homeownership rate: 95.0%; Median home value: $437,400; Median year structure built: 1958; Homeowner vacancy rate: 4.4%; Median selected monthly owner costs: $2,785 with a mortgage, $1,396 without a mortgage; Median gross rent: $1,354 per month; Rental vacancy rate: 0.0%
Health Insurance: 91.2% have insurance; 78.9% have private insurance; 29.5% have public insurance; 8.8% do not have insurance; 8.7% of children under 18 do not have insurance
Transportation: Commute: 86.8% car, 0.0% public transportation, 0.7% walk, 12.5% work from home; Mean travel time to work: 27.3 minutes

GLENWILLOW (village). Covers a land area of 2.720 square miles and a water area of 0.061 square miles. Located at 41.36° N. Lat; 81.47° W. Long. Elevation is 942 feet.
Population: 1,129; Growth (since 2000): 151.4%; Density: 415.1 persons per square mile; Race: 50.4% White, 23.6% Black/African American, 22.0% Asian, 0.0% American Indian/Alaska Native, 0.0% Native Hawaiian/Other Pacific Islander, 1.8% Two or more races, 1.2% Hispanic of any race; Average household size: 2.93; Median age: 42.2; Age under 18: 29.8%; Age 65 and over: 17.2%; Males per 100 females: 91.9; Marriage status: 18.6% never married, 56.3% now married, 1.3% separated, 14.5% widowed, 10.6% divorced; Foreign born: 15.9%; Speak English only: 78.6%; With disability: 11.8%; Veterans: 6.9%; Ancestry: 12.7% German, 12.2% Polish, 8.6% Irish, 6.6% Italian, 3.6% English
Employment: 29.4% management, business, and financial, 10.6% computer, engineering, and science, 7.5% education, legal, community service, arts, and media, 11.2% healthcare practitioners, 5.8% service, 20.1% sales and office, 5.6% natural resources, construction, and maintenance, 9.9% production, transportation, and material moving
Income: Per capita: $31,117; Median household: $87,375; Average household: $93,740; Households with income of $100,000 or more: 42.1%; Poverty rate: 6.5%

Educational Attainment: High school diploma or higher: 90.3%; Bachelor's degree or higher: 48.3%; Graduate/professional degree or higher: 29.8%
Housing: Homeownership rate: 91.1%; Median home value: $252,400; Median year structure built: 1993; Homeowner vacancy rate: 3.7%; Median selected monthly owner costs: $1,918 with a mortgage, $464 without a mortgage; Median gross rent: $689 per month; Rental vacancy rate: 21.7%
Health Insurance: 92.7% have insurance; 84.3% have private insurance; 16.4% have public insurance; 7.3% do not have insurance; 2.1% of children under 18 do not have insurance
Transportation: Commute: 91.5% car, 0.0% public transportation, 0.9% walk, 6.4% work from home; Mean travel time to work: 22.6 minutes

HIGHLAND HEIGHTS (city). Covers a land area of 5.152 square miles and a water area of 0 square miles. Located at 41.55° N. Lat; 81.47° W. Long. Elevation is 935 feet.
History: Originally part of Mayfield Township, the City of Highland Heights was founded in 1920 and incorporated in 1967. It was the first city in Cuyahoga County to require new residential neighborhoods to have underground wiring and ornamental lamp posts.
Population: 8,366; Growth (since 2000): 3.5%; Density: 1,623.7 persons per square mile; Race: 89.8% White, 2.2% Black/African American, 5.1% Asian, 0.0% American Indian/Alaska Native, 0.0% Native Hawaiian/Other Pacific Islander, 2.2% Two or more races, 3.2% Hispanic of any race; Average household size: 2.63; Median age: 48.5; Age under 18: 20.8%; Age 65 and over: 19.7%; Males per 100 females: 97.0; Marriage status: 27.6% never married, 62.0% now married, 0.7% separated, 5.2% widowed, 5.2% divorced; Foreign born: 11.8%; Speak English only: 83.1%; With disability: 6.9%; Veterans: 7.5%; Ancestry: 22.9% Italian, 15.5% German, 13.9% Irish, 7.9% English, 4.4% Russian
Employment: 23.3% management, business, and financial, 7.9% computer, engineering, and science, 11.8% education, legal, community service, arts, and media, 15.3% healthcare practitioners, 11.4% service, 21.8% sales and office, 2.0% natural resources, construction, and maintenance, 6.6% production, transportation, and material moving
Income: Per capita: $46,864; Median household: $101,875; Average household: $122,786; Households with income of $100,000 or more: 52.0%; Poverty rate: 3.6%
Educational Attainment: High school diploma or higher: 95.4%; Bachelor's degree or higher: 55.1%; Graduate/professional degree or higher: 27.8%

Two-year College(s)

ATS Institute of Technology (Private, For-profit)
Fall 2016 Enrollment: 292 . . . . (440) 449-1700
2016-17 Tuition: In-state $25,580; Out-of-state $25,580
Housing: Homeownership rate: 93.1%; Median home value: $246,700; Median year structure built: 1975; Homeowner vacancy rate: 2.3%; Median selected monthly owner costs: $1,943 with a mortgage, $841 without a mortgage; Median gross rent: $1,022 per month; Rental vacancy rate: 0.0%
Health Insurance: 97.2% have insurance; 87.0% have private insurance; 25.7% have public insurance; 2.8% do not have insurance; 0.0% of children under 18 do not have insurance
Safety: Violent crime rate: 1.2 per 10,000 population; Property crime rate: 117.8 per 10,000 population
Transportation: Commute: 94.3% car, 0.0% public transportation, 0.8% walk, 4.3% work from home; Mean travel time to work: 22.1 minutes

HIGHLAND HILLS (village). Covers a land area of 1.959 square miles and a water area of 0.007 square miles. Located at 41.45° N. Lat; 81.52° W. Long. Elevation is 1,086 feet.
Population: 967; Growth (since 2000): -40.2%; Density: 493.7 persons per square mile; Race: 18.8% White, 77.0% Black/African American, 0.0% Asian, 0.4% American Indian/Alaska Native, 0.0% Native Hawaiian/Other Pacific Islander, 2.6% Two or more races, 3.9% Hispanic of any race; Average household size: 1.80; Median age: 40.7; Age under 18: 12.7%; Age 65 and over: 21.3%; Males per 100 females: 206.2; Marriage status: 58.5% never married, 12.8% now married, 1.6% separated, 7.4% widowed, 21.3% divorced; Foreign born: 1.7%; Speak English only: 93.6%; With disability: 25.1%; Veterans: 8.5%; Ancestry: 5.0% German, 4.3% Irish, 2.6% Italian, 1.7% Polish, 1.1% British
Employment: 8.6% management, business, and financial, 5.4% computer, engineering, and science, 4.7% education, legal, community service, arts, and media, 7.0% healthcare practitioners, 26.8% service, 28.8% sales and office, 2.7% natural resources, construction, and maintenance, 16.0% production, transportation, and material moving
Income: Per capita: $15,948; Median household: $23,984; Average household: $38,282; Households with income of $100,000 or more: 8.1%; Poverty rate: 30.9%
Educational Attainment: High school diploma or higher: 85.9%; Bachelor's degree or higher: 15.4%; Graduate/professional degree or higher: 6.2%

School District(s)

Buckeye United School District (07-12)
2015-16 Enrollment: 311 . . . . (614) 466-0720
Housing: Homeownership rate: 38.8%; Median home value: $76,200; Median year structure built: 1964; Homeowner vacancy rate: 0.0%; Median selected monthly owner costs: $1,005 with a mortgage, $507 without a mortgage; Median gross rent: $492 per month; Rental vacancy rate: 12.6%
Health Insurance: 81.2% have insurance; 33.8% have private insurance; 64.2% have public insurance; 18.8% do not have insurance; 0.0% of children under 18 do not have insurance
Transportation: Commute: 86.4% car, 1.2% public transportation, 1.6% walk, 7.4% work from home; Mean travel time to work: 25.1 minutes

HUNTING VALLEY (village). Covers a land area of 7.892 square miles and a water area of 0.121 square miles. Located at 41.48° N. Lat; 81.41° W. Long. Elevation is 761 feet.
Population: 787; Growth (since 2000): 7.1%; Density: 99.7 persons per square mile; Race: 93.8% White, 1.4% Black/African American, 3.0% Asian, 0.0% American Indian/Alaska Native, 0.0% Native Hawaiian/Other Pacific Islander, 1.8% Two or more races, 2.0% Hispanic of any race; Average household size: 2.68; Median age: 50.3; Age under 18: 24.1%; Age 65 and over: 27.7%; Males per 100 females: 96.9; Marriage status: 18.4% never married, 72.4% now married, 0.5% separated, 4.9% widowed, 4.4% divorced; Foreign born: 6.7%; Speak English only: 95.2%; With disability: 10.0%; Veterans: 5.0%; Ancestry: 21.2% German, 16.1% English, 12.5% Irish, 8.5% Italian, 8.5% Polish
Employment: 58.6% management, business, and financial, 2.1% computer, engineering, and science, 7.4% education, legal, community service, arts, and media, 10.7% healthcare practitioners, 6.0% service, 11.0% sales and office, 1.2% natural resources, construction, and maintenance, 3.0% production, transportation, and material moving
Income: Per capita: $156,212; Median household: $250,000+; Average household: $420,730; Households with income of $100,000 or more: 73.1%; Poverty rate: 6.1%
Educational Attainment: High school diploma or higher: 98.9%; Bachelor's degree or higher: 84.3%; Graduate/professional degree or higher: 47.5%
Housing: Homeownership rate: 90.5%; Median home value: $1,222,200; Median year structure built: 1960; Homeowner vacancy rate: 1.5%; Median selected monthly owner costs: $4,000+ with a mortgage, $1,500+ without a mortgage; Median gross rent: n/a per month; Rental vacancy rate: 0.0%
Health Insurance: 99.4% have insurance; 92.6% have private insurance; 28.1% have public insurance; 0.6% do not have insurance; 2.6% of children under 18 do not have insurance
Transportation: Commute: 82.4% car, 0.0% public transportation, 1.2% walk, 15.8% work from home; Mean travel time to work: 26.9 minutes

INDEPENDENCE (city). Covers a land area of 9.540 square miles and a water area of 0.103 square miles. Located at 41.38° N. Lat; 81.63° W. Long. Elevation is 860 feet.
Population: 7,115; Growth (since 2000): 0.1%; Density: 745.8 persons per square mile; Race: 97.4% White, 0.3% Black/African American, 0.9% Asian, 0.0% American Indian/Alaska Native, 0.0% Native Hawaiian/Other Pacific Islander, 1.1% Two or more races, 1.6% Hispanic of any race; Average household size: 2.64; Median age: 46.9; Age under 18: 21.7%; Age 65 and over: 19.6%; Males per 100 females: 94.2; Marriage status: 26.1% never married, 60.0% now married, 0.7% separated, 8.0% widowed, 6.0% divorced; Foreign born: 5.7%; Speak English only: 91.5%; With disability: 10.7%; Veterans: 9.6%; Ancestry: 28.2% Polish, 25.3% German, 16.4% Italian, 14.4% Irish, 9.7% English
Employment: 25.8% management, business, and financial, 4.3% computer, engineering, and science, 9.4% education, legal, community service, arts, and media, 8.0% healthcare practitioners, 13.6% service, 22.6% sales and office, 7.4% natural resources, construction, and maintenance, 9.0% production, transportation, and material moving

Income: Per capita: $41,425; Median household: $84,900; Average household: $107,851; Households with income of $100,000 or more: 42.0%; Poverty rate: 2.5%
Educational Attainment: High school diploma or higher: 94.5%; Bachelor's degree or higher: 40.3%; Graduate/professional degree or higher: 14.4%

School District(s)

Independence Local (PK-12)
2015-16 Enrollment: 1,034 . . . . (216) 642-5850

Two-year College(s)

Miami-Jacobs Career College-Independence (Private, For-profit)
Fall 2016 Enrollment: 141 . . . . (216) 861-3222
2016-17 Tuition: In-state $11,540; Out-of-state $11,540

Vocational/Technical School(s)

Central School of Practical Nursing (Private, Not-for-profit)
Fall 2016 Enrollment: 112 . . . . (216) 901-4400
2016-17 Tuition: $15,810

Housing: Homeownership rate: 94.2%; Median home value: $222,600; Median year structure built: 1962; Homeowner vacancy rate: 0.0%; Median selected monthly owner costs: $1,768 with a mortgage, $562 without a mortgage; Median gross rent: $779 per month; Rental vacancy rate: 0.0%
Health Insurance: 98.9% have insurance; 89.2% have private insurance; 22.8% have public insurance; 1.1% do not have insurance; 1.1% of children under 18 do not have insurance
Safety: Violent crime rate: 15.4 per 10,000 population; Property crime rate: 168.3 per 10,000 population
Transportation: Commute: 95.6% car, 1.1% public transportation, 0.6% walk, 2.7% work from home; Mean travel time to work: 20.6 minutes
Additional Information Contacts
City of Independence . . . . (216) 524-4131
http://www.independenceohio.org

LAKEWOOD (city). Covers a land area of 5.534 square miles and a water area of 1.159 square miles. Located at 41.48° N. Lat; 81.80° W. Long. Elevation is 702 feet.
History: Named for its location on the wooded shores of Lake Erie. Lakewood was known as East Rockport until 1889, when its name was changed to Lakewood, refering to its location on the wooded shore of Lake Erie. Lakewood was incorporated as a city in 1911.
Population: 50,866; Growth (since 2000): -10.2%; Density: 9,190.8 persons per square mile; Race: 86.8% White, 6.9% Black/African American, 1.6% Asian, 0.1% American Indian/Alaska Native, 0.1% Native Hawaiian/Other Pacific Islander, 4.1% Two or more races, 4.9% Hispanic of any race; Average household size: 2.07; Median age: 34.7; Age under 18: 18.4%; Age 65 and over: 11.3%; Males per 100 females: 96.6; Marriage status: 43.8% never married, 38.6% now married, 1.5% separated, 4.9% widowed, 12.7% divorced; Foreign born: 7.3%; Speak English only: 89.9%; With disability: 11.8%; Veterans: 6.2%; Ancestry: 24.8% German, 24.5% Irish, 10.0% Italian, 9.0% English, 7.4% Polish
Employment: 18.0% management, business, and financial, 5.6% computer, engineering, and science, 15.9% education, legal, community service, arts, and media, 7.9% healthcare practitioners, 15.1% service, 23.2% sales and office, 5.5% natural resources, construction, and maintenance, 8.8% production, transportation, and material moving
Income: Per capita: $31,122; Median household: $47,145; Average household: $63,217; Households with income of $100,000 or more: 19.0%; Poverty rate: 14.4%
Educational Attainment: High school diploma or higher: 93.9%; Bachelor's degree or higher: 43.7%; Graduate/professional degree or higher: 16.0%

School District(s)

Lakewood City (PK-12)
2015-16 Enrollment: 5,331 . . . . (216) 529-4092
Lakewood City Academy (06-12)
2015-16 Enrollment: 149 . . . . (216) 529-4037

Two-year College(s)

Virginia Marti College of Art and Design (Private, For-profit)
Fall 2016 Enrollment: 169 . . . . (216) 221-8584
2016-17 Tuition: In-state $17,980; Out-of-state $17,980

Housing: Homeownership rate: 45.0%; Median home value: $134,000; Median year structure built: Before 1940; Homeowner vacancy rate: 2.1%; Median selected monthly owner costs: $1,393 with a mortgage, $592 without a mortgage; Median gross rent: $715 per month; Rental vacancy rate: 4.8%
Health Insurance: 90.4% have insurance; 70.1% have private insurance; 28.4% have public insurance; 9.6% do not have insurance; 3.4% of children under 18 do not have insurance
Hospitals: Lakewood Hospital (400 beds)
Safety: Violent crime rate: 12.5 per 10,000 population; Property crime rate: 174.0 per 10,000 population
Transportation: Commute: 86.2% car, 5.2% public transportation, 2.8% walk, 3.8% work from home; Mean travel time to work: 23.4 minutes
Additional Information Contacts
City of Lakewood . . . . (216) 529-6600
http://www.ci.lakewood.oh.us

LINNDALE (village). Covers a land area of 0.081 square miles and a water area of 0 square miles. Located at 41.44° N. Lat; 81.77° W. Long. Elevation is 755 feet.
Population: 125; Growth (since 2000): 6.8%; Density: 1,552.4 persons per square mile; Race: 69.6% White, 28.0% Black/African American, 0.0% Asian, 0.0% American Indian/Alaska Native, 0.0% Native Hawaiian/Other Pacific Islander, 0.0% Two or more races, 26.4% Hispanic of any race; Average household size: 2.23; Median age: 38.5; Age under 18: 33.6%; Age 65 and over: 12.8%; Males per 100 females: 94.6; Marriage status: 28.2% never married, 44.7% now married, 4.7% separated, 10.6% widowed, 16.5% divorced; Foreign born: 0.0%; Speak English only: 70.8%; With disability: 8.8%; Veterans: 9.6%; Ancestry: 17.6% Irish, 16.8% German, 9.6% Italian, 9.6% Polish, 4.0% Slovak
Employment: 1.5% management, business, and financial, 4.6% computer, engineering, and science, 9.2% education, legal, community service, arts, and media, 0.0% healthcare practitioners, 43.1% service, 15.4% sales and office, 12.3% natural resources, construction, and maintenance, 13.8% production, transportation, and material moving
Income: Per capita: $14,267; Median household: $32,857; Average household: $32,146; Households with income of $100,000 or more: n/a; Poverty rate: 36.0%
Educational Attainment: High school diploma or higher: 77.1%; Bachelor's degree or higher: 3.6%; Graduate/professional degree or higher: n/a
Housing: Homeownership rate: 53.6%; Median home value: $54,000; Median year structure built: 1952; Homeowner vacancy rate: 11.8%; Median selected monthly owner costs: $713 with a mortgage, $325 without a mortgage; Median gross rent: $713 per month; Rental vacancy rate: 0.0%
Health Insurance: 80.0% have insurance; 50.4% have private insurance; 37.6% have public insurance; 20.0% do not have insurance; 0.0% of children under 18 do not have insurance
Transportation: Commute: 88.9% car, 1.6% public transportation, 9.5% walk, 0.0% work from home; Mean travel time to work: 18.7 minutes

---

LYNDHURST (city). Covers a land area of 4.432 square miles and a water area of 0.006 square miles. Located at 41.52° N. Lat; 81.49° W. Long. Elevation is 1,033 feet.
History: Incorporated 1917.
Population: 13,736; Growth (since 2000): -10.1%; Density: 3,099.5 persons per square mile; Race: 87.3% White, 10.0% Black/African American, 1.1% Asian, 0.3% American Indian/Alaska Native, 0.0% Native Hawaiian/Other Pacific Islander, 1.3% Two or more races, 1.1% Hispanic of any race; Average household size: 2.20; Median age: 46.7; Age under 18: 17.9%; Age 65 and over: 24.1%; Males per 100 females: 85.3; Marriage status: 23.0% never married, 57.2% now married, 0.7% separated, 8.7% widowed, 11.1% divorced; Foreign born: 7.7%; Speak English only: 89.9%; With disability: 12.1%; Veterans: 9.7%; Ancestry: 21.1% Italian, 20.3% German, 15.3% Irish, 7.3% English, 5.8% Polish
Employment: 18.6% management, business, and financial, 8.1% computer, engineering, and science, 12.5% education, legal, community service, arts, and media, 11.3% healthcare practitioners, 13.0% service, 24.4% sales and office, 4.3% natural resources, construction, and maintenance, 7.8% production, transportation, and material moving
Income: Per capita: $38,049; Median household: $65,921; Average household: $82,891; Households with income of $100,000 or more: 28.1%; Poverty rate: 4.7%
Educational Attainment: High school diploma or higher: 95.4%; Bachelor's degree or higher: 48.3%; Graduate/professional degree or higher: 19.9%

School District(s)

South Euclid-Lyndhurst City (PK-12)
2015-16 Enrollment: 3,531 . . . . (216) 691-2000

Two-year College(s)

Inner State Beauty School (Private, For-profit)
Fall 2016 Enrollment: 105 . . . . (440) 442-4500

Vocational/Technical School(s)

Cleveland Institute of Dental-Medical Assistants-Lyndhurst (Private, For-profit)
Fall 2016 Enrollment: 19 . . . . (216) 241-2930
2016-17 Tuition: $10,800

Housing: Homeownership rate: 81.6%; Median home value: $138,800; Median year structure built: 1957; Homeowner vacancy rate: 1.8%; Median selected monthly owner costs: $1,373 with a mortgage, $615 without a mortgage; Median gross rent: $1,106 per month; Rental vacancy rate: 8.6%

Health Insurance: 96.1% have insurance; 83.2% have private insurance; 31.7% have public insurance; 3.9% do not have insurance; 0.6% of children under 18 do not have insurance

Safety: Violent crime rate: 10.3 per 10,000 population; Property crime rate: 142.4 per 10,000 population

Transportation: Commute: 90.1% car, 1.8% public transportation, 1.1% walk, 6.2% work from home; Mean travel time to work: 22.8 minutes

Additional Information Contacts

City of Lyndhurst . . . . (440) 442-5777
http://www.lyndhurst-oh.com

MAPLE HEIGHTS (city). Covers a land area of 5.172 square miles and a water area of <.001 square miles. Located at 41.41° N. Lat; 81.56° W. Long. Elevation is 896 feet.

History: Named for its abundance of maple trees. Incorporated 1932.

Population: 22,685; Growth (since 2000): -13.3%; Density: 4,386.0 persons per square mile; Race: 23.9% White, 72.1% Black/African American, 1.1% Asian, 0.2% American Indian/Alaska Native, 0.0% Native Hawaiian/Other Pacific Islander, 2.4% Two or more races, 1.8% Hispanic of any race; Average household size: 2.41; Median age: 37.6; Age under 18: 22.8%; Age 65 and over: 13.5%; Males per 100 females: 86.1; Marriage status: 44.5% never married, 32.6% now married, 2.3% separated, 7.6% widowed, 15.3% divorced; Foreign born: 2.5%; Speak English only: 97.0%; With disability: 19.2%; Veterans: 7.8%; Ancestry: 5.1% Polish, 5.0% German, 3.6% Irish, 3.3% Italian, 1.9% Czech

Employment: 10.9% management, business, and financial, 3.2% computer, engineering, and science, 6.0% education, legal, community service, arts, and media, 5.9% healthcare practitioners, 23.8% service, 27.0% sales and office, 5.5% natural resources, construction, and maintenance, 17.6% production, transportation, and material moving

Income: Per capita: $19,983; Median household: $37,911; Average household: $46,843; Households with income of $100,000 or more: 7.9%; Poverty rate: 21.1%

Educational Attainment: High school diploma or higher: 89.0%; Bachelor's degree or higher: 15.4%; Graduate/professional degree or higher: 4.6%

School District(s)

Maple Heights City (PK-12)
2015-16 Enrollment: 3,557 . . . . (216) 587-6100

Housing: Homeownership rate: 63.5%; Median home value: $71,800; Median year structure built: 1956; Homeowner vacancy rate: 4.7%; Median selected monthly owner costs: $1,031 with a mortgage, $387 without a mortgage; Median gross rent: $841 per month; Rental vacancy rate: 7.3%

Health Insurance: 92.1% have insurance; 57.9% have private insurance; 47.1% have public insurance; 7.9% do not have insurance; 0.9% of children under 18 do not have insurance

Transportation: Commute: 89.6% car, 7.2% public transportation, 1.3% walk, 1.0% work from home; Mean travel time to work: 25.3 minutes

Additional Information Contacts

City of Maple Heights . . . . (216) 662-6000
http://mapleheights.cuyahogacounty.us

MAYFIELD (village). Covers a land area of 3.950 square miles and a water area of 0.008 square miles. Located at 41.55° N. Lat; 81.43° W. Long. Elevation is 925 feet.

Population: 3,401; Growth (since 2000): -1.0%; Density: 860.9 persons per square mile; Race: 90.8% White, 0.5% Black/African American, 7.7% Asian, 0.0% American Indian/Alaska Native, 0.0% Native Hawaiian/Other Pacific Islander, 1.0% Two or more races, 1.0% Hispanic of any race; Average household size: 2.28; Median age: 51.3; Age under 18: 15.9%; Age 65 and over: 27.0%; Males per 100 females: 98.3; Marriage status: 27.3% never married, 56.4% now married, 1.6% separated, 10.5% widowed, 5.7% divorced; Foreign born: 18.2%; Speak English only: 80.0%; With disability: 8.9%; Veterans: 8.2%; Ancestry: 24.2% Italian, 18.3% Irish, 17.2% German, 8.3% English, 5.4% Polish

Employment: 20.5% management, business, and financial, 7.2% computer, engineering, and science, 20.2% education, legal, community service, arts, and media, 9.8% healthcare practitioners, 7.4% service, 23.9% sales and office, 7.5% natural resources, construction, and maintenance, 3.5% production, transportation, and material moving

Income: Per capita: $48,498; Median household: $72,156; Average household: $108,189; Households with income of $100,000 or more: 33.6%; Poverty rate: 2.9%

Educational Attainment: High school diploma or higher: 94.9%; Bachelor's degree or higher: 52.4%; Graduate/professional degree or higher: 23.1%

School District(s)

Mayfield City (KG-12)
2015-16 Enrollment: 4,269 . . . . (440) 995-7201

Housing: Homeownership rate: 67.8%; Median home value: $234,200; Median year structure built: 1965; Homeowner vacancy rate: 5.1%; Median selected monthly owner costs: $1,953 with a mortgage, $656 without a mortgage; Median gross rent: $998 per month; Rental vacancy rate: 0.0%

Health Insurance: 97.7% have insurance; 84.3% have private insurance; 30.9% have public insurance; 2.3% do not have insurance; 0.0% of children under 18 do not have insurance

Transportation: Commute: 94.5% car, 0.0% public transportation, 0.0% walk, 3.4% work from home; Mean travel time to work: 23.0 minutes

Additional Information Contacts

Village of Mayfield . . . . (440) 461-2210
http://www.mayfieldvillage.com

MAYFIELD HEIGHTS (city). Covers a land area of 4.168 square miles and a water area of 0.009 square miles. Located at 41.52° N. Lat; 81.45° W. Long. Elevation is 1,086 feet.

History: Named either for Mayfield in Derby, England, or for the month of May. Incorporated 1925.

Population: 18,878; Growth (since 2000): -2.6%; Density: 4,528.9 persons per square mile; Race: 79.3% White, 13.9% Black/African American, 4.5% Asian, 0.2% American Indian/Alaska Native, 0.0% Native Hawaiian/Other Pacific Islander, 1.6% Two or more races, 1.4% Hispanic of any race; Average household size: 1.99; Median age: 43.1; Age under 18: 18.3%; Age 65 and over: 24.2%; Males per 100 females: 82.7; Marriage status: 32.8% never married, 42.9% now married, 1.1% separated, 10.8% widowed, 13.4% divorced; Foreign born: 15.8%; Speak English only: 80.5%; With disability: 14.9%; Veterans: 7.3%; Ancestry: 20.0% Italian, 17.0% German, 11.8% Irish, 7.8% Polish, 6.6% Russian

Employment: 16.6% management, business, and financial, 12.4% computer, engineering, and science, 10.6% education, legal, community service, arts, and media, 8.1% healthcare practitioners, 18.0% service, 23.9% sales and office, 4.4% natural resources, construction, and maintenance, 6.1% production, transportation, and material moving

Income: Per capita: $29,955; Median household: $45,875; Average household: $58,682; Households with income of $100,000 or more: 14.2%; Poverty rate: 9.3%

Educational Attainment: High school diploma or higher: 93.5%; Bachelor's degree or higher: 37.2%; Graduate/professional degree or higher: 15.3%

Two-year College(s)

LaBarberia Institute of Hair (Private, For-profit)
Fall 2016 Enrollment: 164 . . . . (440) 565-7525

Housing: Homeownership rate: 50.7%; Median home value: $141,700; Median year structure built: 1962; Homeowner vacancy rate: 3.1%; Median selected monthly owner costs: $1,323 with a mortgage, $531 without a mortgage; Median gross rent: $861 per month; Rental vacancy rate: 11.4%

Health Insurance: 92.2% have insurance; 73.0% have private insurance; 35.1% have public insurance; 7.8% do not have insurance; 8.1% of children under 18 do not have insurance

Hospitals: Hillcrest Hospital (424 beds)

Transportation: Commute: 93.5% car, 1.5% public transportation, 1.1% walk, 3.6% work from home; Mean travel time to work: 20.9 minutes

Additional Information Contacts

City of Mayfield Heights. . . . . (440) 442-2626
http://www.mayfieldheights.org

MIDDLEBURG HEIGHTS (city). Covers a land area of 8.065 square miles and a water area of 0.011 square miles. Located at 41.37° N. Lat; 81.81° W. Long. Elevation is 853 feet.

Population: 15,724; Growth (since 2000): 1.2%; Density: 1,949.7 persons per square mile; Race: 85.7% White, 2.7% Black/African American, 8.5% Asian, 0.6% American Indian/Alaska Native, 0.0% Native Hawaiian/Other Pacific Islander, 0.7% Two or more races, 5.8% Hispanic of any race; Average household size: 2.24; Median age: 46.2; Age under 18: 18.5%; Age 65 and over: 23.5%; Males per 100 females: 89.6; Marriage status: 26.9% never married, 52.7% now married, 1.2% separated, 8.5% widowed, 11.8% divorced; Foreign born: 13.9%; Speak English only: 80.5%; With disability: 12.2%; Veterans: 10.2%; Ancestry: 23.1% German, 14.1% Irish, 12.7% Italian, 11.0% Polish, 7.4% English

Employment: 17.8% management, business, and financial, 8.8% computer, engineering, and science, 8.6% education, legal, community service, arts, and media, 5.3% healthcare practitioners, 15.4% service, 25.1% sales and office, 5.1% natural resources, construction, and maintenance, 13.9% production, transportation, and material moving

Income: Per capita: $31,346; Median household: $58,810; Average household: $69,522; Households with income of $100,000 or more: 23.2%; Poverty rate: 4.1%

Educational Attainment: High school diploma or higher: 92.2%; Bachelor's degree or higher: 34.6%; Graduate/professional degree or higher: 13.0%

School District(s)

Berea City (PK-12)
2015-16 Enrollment: 6,598 . . . . (216) 898-8300
Polaris (07-12)
2015-16 Enrollment: n/a . . . . (440) 891-7600

Vocational/Technical School(s)

Heritage College-Cleveland (Private, For-profit)
Fall 2016 Enrollment: n/a . . . . (440) 243-6726
2016-17 Tuition: $14,381
Polaris Career Center (Public)
Fall 2016 Enrollment: 204 . . . . (440) 891-7600
2016-17 Tuition: $8,589

Housing: Homeownership rate: 70.3%; Median home value: $157,500; Median year structure built: 1972; Homeowner vacancy rate: 0.8%; Median selected monthly owner costs: $1,315 with a mortgage, $557 without a mortgage; Median gross rent: $824 per month; Rental vacancy rate: 1.4%

Health Insurance: 95.8% have insurance; 81.0% have private insurance; 30.6% have public insurance; 4.2% do not have insurance; 1.6% of children under 18 do not have insurance

Hospitals: Southwest General Health Center (336 beds)

Transportation: Commute: 94.0% car, 0.8% public transportation, 1.9% walk, 2.0% work from home; Mean travel time to work: 22.1 minutes

Additional Information Contacts

City of Middleburg Heights . . . . (440) 234-8811
http://www.middleburgheights.com

MORELAND HILLS (village). Covers a land area of 7.149 square miles and a water area of 0.078 square miles. Located at 41.44° N. Lat; 81.44° W. Long. Elevation is 1,040 feet.

History: In 1815, settlement began near the point where State Route 87 crosses the Chagrin River. The village, which in 1831 was still part of Orange Township, was the birthplace of James A. Garfield, the 20th President of the United States.

Population: 3,297; Growth (since 2000): 0.0%; Density: 461.2 persons per square mile; Race: 90.2% White, 2.4% Black/African American, 3.2% Asian, 0.0% American Indian/Alaska Native, 0.0% Native Hawaiian/Other Pacific Islander, 4.2% Two or more races, 4.7% Hispanic of any race; Average household size: 2.58; Median age: 48.0; Age under 18: 22.3%; Age 65 and over: 21.2%; Males per 100 females: 97.1; Marriage status: 18.1% never married, 69.1% now married, 0.4% separated, 3.7% widowed, 9.0% divorced; Foreign born: 11.2%; Speak English only: 88.8%; With disability: 10.6%; Veterans: 6.0%; Ancestry: 18.5% German, 11.3% Irish, 9.9% English, 9.1% Italian, 8.4% Russian

Employment: 36.3% management, business, and financial, 6.3% computer, engineering, and science, 8.3% education, legal, community service, arts, and media, 11.8% healthcare practitioners, 10.0% service, 23.4% sales and office, 1.8% natural resources, construction, and maintenance, 2.1% production, transportation, and material moving

Income: Per capita: $78,776; Median household: $139,539; Average household: $203,660; Households with income of $100,000 or more: 61.7%; Poverty rate: 2.8%

Educational Attainment: High school diploma or higher: 99.3%; Bachelor's degree or higher: 74.5%; Graduate/professional degree or higher: 34.6%

Housing: Homeownership rate: 92.9%; Median home value: $379,400; Median year structure built: 1965; Homeowner vacancy rate: 0.8%; Median selected monthly owner costs: $2,405 with a mortgage, $1,160 without a mortgage; Median gross rent: $1,375 per month; Rental vacancy rate: 0.0%

Health Insurance: 96.4% have insurance; 88.1% have private insurance; 27.1% have public insurance; 3.6% do not have insurance; 2.2% of children under 18 do not have insurance

Safety: Violent crime rate: 3.0 per 10,000 population; Property crime rate: 30.3 per 10,000 population

Transportation: Commute: 78.8% car, 3.8% public transportation, 1.1% walk, 14.3% work from home; Mean travel time to work: 26.3 minutes

Additional Information Contacts

Village of Moreland Hills . . . . (440) 248-1188
http://www.morelandhills.com

NEWBURGH HEIGHTS (village). Covers a land area of 0.583 square miles and a water area of <.001 square miles. Located at 41.45° N. Lat; 81.66° W. Long. Elevation is 692 feet.

Population: 1,869; Growth (since 2000): -21.8%; Density: 3,208.0 persons per square mile; Race: 71.3% White, 19.7% Black/African American, 2.7% Asian, 0.0% American Indian/Alaska Native, 0.0% Native Hawaiian/Other Pacific Islander, 3.9% Two or more races, 3.2% Hispanic of any race; Average household size: 2.10; Median age: 41.4; Age under 18: 22.3%; Age 65 and over: 14.9%; Males per 100 females: 104.0; Marriage status: 33.7% never married, 38.1% now married, 2.0% separated, 7.5% widowed, 20.7% divorced; Foreign born: 4.8%; Speak English only: 93.5%; With disability: 13.6%; Veterans: 8.8%; Ancestry: 20.6% German, 17.4% Polish, 16.1% Irish, 5.9% Italian, 5.1% Slovak

Employment: 7.0% management, business, and financial, 1.6% computer, engineering, and science, 10.6% education, legal, community service, arts, and media, 2.4% healthcare practitioners, 27.1% service, 24.6% sales and office, 4.8% natural resources, construction, and maintenance, 21.9% production, transportation, and material moving

Income: Per capita: $20,080; Median household: $33,750; Average household: $41,416; Households with income of $100,000 or more: 4.1%; Poverty rate: 19.7%

Educational Attainment: High school diploma or higher: 81.7%; Bachelor's degree or higher: 14.5%; Graduate/professional degree or higher: 1.9%

School District(s)

Cleveland Municipal (PK-12)
2015-16 Enrollment: 39,410 . . . . (216) 838-0000
Washington Park Community School (KG-08)
2015-16 Enrollment: 212. . . . . (216) 271-6055

Housing: Homeownership rate: 49.0%; Median home value: $65,700; Median year structure built: Before 1940; Homeowner vacancy rate: 8.3%; Median selected monthly owner costs: $981 with a mortgage, $398 without a mortgage; Median gross rent: $690 per month; Rental vacancy rate: 2.9%

Health Insurance: 84.4% have insurance; 57.6% have private insurance; 41.5% have public insurance; 15.6% do not have insurance; 6.7% of children under 18 do not have insurance

Transportation: Commute: 91.4% car, 1.5% public transportation, 2.2% walk, 3.4% work from home; Mean travel time to work: 20.3 minutes

NORTH OLMSTED (city). Covers a land area of 11.674 square miles and a water area of 0 square miles. Located at 41.41° N. Lat; 81.92° W. Long. Elevation is 761 feet.

History: Named for Charles H. Olmsted. First U.S. municipal bus line began operations in North Olmstead in 1931. Incorporated as a city 1951.

Population: 32,108; Growth (since 2000): -5.9%; Density: 2,750.4 persons per square mile; Race: 92.0% White, 2.6% Black/African American, 3.4% Asian, 0.1% American Indian/Alaska Native, 0.0% Native Hawaiian/Other Pacific Islander, 1.5% Two or more races, 3.5% Hispanic of any race; Average household size: 2.42; Median age: 45.2; Age under 18: 18.9%; Age 65 and over: 19.9%; Males per 100 females: 93.4; Marriage status: 29.6% never married, 54.2% now married, 1.2% separated, 6.5% widowed, 9.6% divorced; Foreign born: 9.1%; Speak English only: 87.1%; With disability: 12.7%; Veterans: 8.0%; Ancestry: 26.8% German, 22.7% Irish, 11.4% Italian, 9.3% Polish, 8.7% English

Employment: 14.6% management, business, and financial, 6.9% computer, engineering, and science, 9.6% education, legal, community service, arts, and media, 6.1% healthcare practitioners, 16.7% service, 26.8% sales and office, 7.2% natural resources, construction, and maintenance, 12.1% production, transportation, and material moving
Income: Per capita: $31,172; Median household: $61,444; Average household: $74,465; Households with income of $100,000 or more: 23.7%; Poverty rate: 7.2%
Educational Attainment: High school diploma or higher: 92.6%; Bachelor's degree or higher: 29.0%; Graduate/professional degree or higher: 9.0%

School District(s)

North Olmsted City (PK-12)
2015-16 Enrollment: 3,868 . . . . (440) 779-3549
Housing: Homeownership rate: 74.0%; Median home value: $146,900; Median year structure built: 1966; Homeowner vacancy rate: 1.5%; Median selected monthly owner costs: $1,407 with a mortgage, $572 without a mortgage; Median gross rent: $867 per month; Rental vacancy rate: 4.9%
Health Insurance: 92.9% have insurance; 77.1% have private insurance; 31.5% have public insurance; 7.1% do not have insurance; 4.3% of children under 18 do not have insurance
Transportation: Commute: 90.8% car, 2.8% public transportation, 1.8% walk, 3.3% work from home; Mean travel time to work: 24.1 minutes
Additional Information Contacts
City of North Olmsted . . . . (440) 777-8000
http://www.north-olmsted.com

NORTH RANDALL (village). Covers a land area of 0.769 square miles and a water area of 0.001 square miles. Located at 41.43° N. Lat; 81.53° W. Long. Elevation is 1,043 feet.
Population: 998; Growth (since 2000): 10.2%; Density: 1,297.8 persons per square mile; Race: 15.2% White, 82.9% Black/African American, 0.4% Asian, 0.0% American Indian/Alaska Native, 0.0% Native Hawaiian/Other Pacific Islander, 0.8% Two or more races, 1.2% Hispanic of any race; Average household size: 1.78; Median age: 56.2; Age under 18: 11.7%; Age 65 and over: 35.0%; Males per 100 females: 75.0; Marriage status: 36.6% never married, 32.3% now married, 6.1% separated, 10.9% widowed, 20.1% divorced; Foreign born: 0.6%; Speak English only: 96.9%; With disability: 17.4%; Veterans: 11.2%; Ancestry: 5.8% American, 2.2% Polish, 1.6% English, 1.5% German, 1.2% Italian
Employment: 5.6% management, business, and financial, 1.7% computer, engineering, and science, 11.2% education, legal, community service, arts, and media, 10.7% healthcare practitioners, 30.1% service, 13.6% sales and office, 4.9% natural resources, construction, and maintenance, 22.3% production, transportation, and material moving
Income: Per capita: $20,414; Median household: $35,288; Average household: $37,411; Households with income of $100,000 or more: 3.7%; Poverty rate: 20.5%
Educational Attainment: High school diploma or higher: 85.1%; Bachelor's degree or higher: 13.6%; Graduate/professional degree or higher: 6.3%

Two-year College(s)

Ohio Technical College-PowerSport Institute (Private, For-profit)
Fall 2016 Enrollment: 212 . . . . (216) 881-1700
Housing: Homeownership rate: 24.8%; Median home value: $82,000; Median year structure built: 1963; Homeowner vacancy rate: 5.8%; Median selected monthly owner costs: $1,053 with a mortgage, $371 without a mortgage; Median gross rent: $697 per month; Rental vacancy rate: 4.9%
Health Insurance: 89.0% have insurance; 56.1% have private insurance; 47.9% have public insurance; 11.0% do not have insurance; 0.0% of children under 18 do not have insurance
Transportation: Commute: 71.0% car, 14.8% public transportation, 8.0% walk, 2.8% work from home; Mean travel time to work: 27.5 minutes

---

NORTH ROYALTON (city). Covers a land area of 21.310 square miles and a water area of 0.013 square miles. Located at 41.31° N. Lat; 81.75° W. Long. Elevation is 1,197 feet.
History: Dairy-processing and sawmilling center in the 19th century, North Royalton has since developed a variety of light industries. Settled 1811, incorporated as a village 1927, as a city 1960.
Population: 30,302; Growth (since 2000): 5.8%; Density: 1,422.0 persons per square mile; Race: 93.4% White, 1.5% Black/African American, 3.5% Asian, 0.1% American Indian/Alaska Native, 0.0% Native Hawaiian/Other Pacific Islander, 1.4% Two or more races, 2.0% Hispanic of any race; Average household size: 2.35; Median age: 43.1; Age under 18: 19.5%; Age 65 and over: 17.0%; Males per 100 females: 95.3; Marriage status: 28.8% never married, 53.9% now married, 0.6% separated, 6.5% widowed, 10.8% divorced; Foreign born: 10.3%; Speak English only: 86.7%; With disability: 10.8%; Veterans: 6.9%; Ancestry: 24.4% German, 17.2% Italian, 16.6% Polish, 14.7% Irish, 8.3% English
Employment: 20.2% management, business, and financial, 5.0% computer, engineering, and science, 8.6% education, legal, community service, arts, and media, 9.4% healthcare practitioners, 14.2% service, 25.6% sales and office, 6.9% natural resources, construction, and maintenance, 10.1% production, transportation, and material moving
Income: Per capita: $36,649; Median household: $66,189; Average household: $85,697; Households with income of $100,000 or more: 30.6%; Poverty rate: 5.3%
Educational Attainment: High school diploma or higher: 93.1%; Bachelor's degree or higher: 36.0%; Graduate/professional degree or higher: 13.7%

School District(s)

North Royalton City (PK-12)
2015-16 Enrollment: 4,387 . . . . (440) 237-8800
Housing: Homeownership rate: 70.7%; Median home value: $193,100; Median year structure built: 1982; Homeowner vacancy rate: 1.5%; Median selected monthly owner costs: $1,550 with a mortgage, $618 without a mortgage; Median gross rent: $820 per month; Rental vacancy rate: 0.8%
Health Insurance: 91.8% have insurance; 79.2% have private insurance; 25.8% have public insurance; 8.2% do not have insurance; 3.4% of children under 18 do not have insurance
Transportation: Commute: 93.8% car, 0.6% public transportation, 0.5% walk, 4.6% work from home; Mean travel time to work: 27.3 minutes
Additional Information Contacts
City of North Royalton . . . . (440) 237-5686
http://www.northroyalton.org

OAKWOOD (village). Covers a land area of 3.436 square miles and a water area of 0.008 square miles. Located at 41.37° N. Lat; 81.50° W. Long. Elevation is 1,047 feet.
Population: 3,684; Growth (since 2000): 0.5%; Density: 1,072.0 persons per square mile; Race: 36.1% White, 59.2% Black/African American, 0.6% Asian, 0.2% American Indian/Alaska Native, 0.0% Native Hawaiian/Other Pacific Islander, 2.8% Two or more races, 2.4% Hispanic of any race; Average household size: 2.39; Median age: 43.1; Age under 18: 19.3%; Age 65 and over: 19.8%; Males per 100 females: 90.8; Marriage status: 34.7% never married, 43.6% now married, 1.6% separated, 7.2% widowed, 14.5% divorced; Foreign born: 4.5%; Speak English only: 92.5%; With disability: 13.1%; Veterans: 8.3%; Ancestry: 5.7% Irish, 5.5% German, 5.1% English, 4.9% Italian, 4.5% Polish
Employment: 11.3% management, business, and financial, 4.7% computer, engineering, and science, 13.6% education, legal, community service, arts, and media, 8.6% healthcare practitioners, 13.7% service, 21.9% sales and office, 9.4% natural resources, construction, and maintenance, 16.7% production, transportation, and material moving
Income: Per capita: $25,993; Median household: $51,667; Average household: $62,390; Households with income of $100,000 or more: 18.3%; Poverty rate: 16.4%
Educational Attainment: High school diploma or higher: 84.8%; Bachelor's degree or higher: 24.4%; Graduate/professional degree or higher: 10.4%
Housing: Homeownership rate: 72.5%; Median home value: $140,800; Median year structure built: 1972; Homeowner vacancy rate: 6.8%; Median selected monthly owner costs: $1,386 with a mortgage, $483 without a mortgage; Median gross rent: $628 per month; Rental vacancy rate: 0.0%
Health Insurance: 88.6% have insurance; 67.1% have private insurance; 34.9% have public insurance; 11.4% do not have insurance; 8.3% of children under 18 do not have insurance
Transportation: Commute: 95.0% car, 2.1% public transportation, 0.0% walk, 2.0% work from home; Mean travel time to work: 22.9 minutes

---

OLMSTED FALLS (city). Covers a land area of 4.122 square miles and a water area of 0 square miles. Located at 41.37° N. Lat; 81.90° W. Long. Elevation is 774 feet.
Population: 8,889; Growth (since 2000): 11.6%; Density: 2,156.3 persons per square mile; Race: 97.4% White, 0.8% Black/African American, 0.1% Asian, 0.0% American Indian/Alaska Native, 0.0% Native Hawaiian/Other Pacific Islander, 1.7% Two or more races, 1.7% Hispanic of any race; Average household size: 2.40; Median age: 43.9; Age under 18: 23.8%; Age 65 and over: 16.8%; Males per 100 females: 87.6; Marriage status:

24.7% never married, 57.0% now married, 1.1% separated, 6.6% widowed, 11.8% divorced; Foreign born: 3.3%; Speak English only: 95.4%; With disability: 10.1%; Veterans: 8.4%; Ancestry: 32.4% German, 18.9% Italian, 17.9% Irish, 12.1% English, 10.4% Polish
Employment: 17.4% management, business, and financial, 6.1% computer, engineering, and science, 11.3% education, legal, community service, arts, and media, 8.8% healthcare practitioners, 10.8% service, 28.1% sales and office, 7.1% natural resources, construction, and maintenance, 10.5% production, transportation, and material moving
Income: Per capita: $32,842; Median household: $62,058; Average household: $78,199; Households with income of $100,000 or more: 28.3%; Poverty rate: 3.0%
Educational Attainment: High school diploma or higher: 95.0%; Bachelor's degree or higher: 34.0%; Graduate/professional degree or higher: 11.3%

School District(s)

Olmsted Falls City (PK-12)
2015-16 Enrollment: 3,705 . . . . (440) 427-6000
Housing: Homeownership rate: 80.8%; Median home value: $145,700; Median year structure built: 1978; Homeowner vacancy rate: 0.4%; Median selected monthly owner costs: $1,415 with a mortgage, $578 without a mortgage; Median gross rent: $812 per month; Rental vacancy rate: 0.0%
Health Insurance: 94.5% have insurance; 80.9% have private insurance; 27.1% have public insurance; 5.5% do not have insurance; 1.8% of children under 18 do not have insurance
Safety: Violent crime rate: 3.4 per 10,000 population; Property crime rate: 33.9 per 10,000 population
Transportation: Commute: 93.3% car, 1.3% public transportation, 1.4% walk, 2.3% work from home; Mean travel time to work: 29.2 minutes
Additional Information Contacts
City of Olmsted Falls . . . . (440) 235-5550
http://www.olmstedfalls.org

ORANGE (village). Covers a land area of 3.803 square miles and a water area of 0.019 square miles. Located at 41.44° N. Lat; 81.47° W. Long. Elevation is 1,158 feet.
History: Orange Village, the southwest quadrant of the original Orange township, was incorporated as a village in 1929.
Population: 3,288; Growth (since 2000): 1.6%; Density: 864.6 persons per square mile; Race: 71.3% White, 18.5% Black/African American, 7.2% Asian, 0.0% American Indian/Alaska Native, 0.0% Native Hawaiian/Other Pacific Islander, 2.7% Two or more races, 1.9% Hispanic of any race; Average household size: 2.53; Median age: 45.7; Age under 18: 23.5%; Age 65 and over: 19.4%; Males per 100 females: 92.5; Marriage status: 19.3% never married, 61.0% now married, 0.8% separated, 5.5% widowed, 14.2% divorced; Foreign born: 12.9%; Speak English only: 81.7%; With disability: 9.4%; Veterans: 9.2%; Ancestry: 10.5% Russian, 10.5% Polish, 8.8% German, 7.0% Hungarian, 6.9% English
Employment: 24.7% management, business, and financial, 11.2% computer, engineering, and science, 13.9% education, legal, community service, arts, and media, 13.0% healthcare practitioners, 4.8% service, 24.3% sales and office, 2.6% natural resources, construction, and maintenance, 5.5% production, transportation, and material moving
Income: Per capita: $57,619; Median household: $102,109; Average household: $145,301; Households with income of $100,000 or more: 51.1%; Poverty rate: 2.8%
Educational Attainment: High school diploma or higher: 97.6%; Bachelor's degree or higher: 69.3%; Graduate/professional degree or higher: 33.2%
Housing: Homeownership rate: 88.3%; Median home value: $291,800; Median year structure built: 1973; Homeowner vacancy rate: 0.0%; Median selected monthly owner costs: $2,039 with a mortgage, $915 without a mortgage; Median gross rent: $1,625 per month; Rental vacancy rate: 0.0%
Health Insurance: 97.9% have insurance; 84.1% have private insurance; 27.3% have public insurance; 2.1% do not have insurance; 0.0% of children under 18 do not have insurance
Transportation: Commute: 91.1% car, 0.0% public transportation, 0.0% walk, 8.2% work from home; Mean travel time to work: 20.4 minutes
Additional Information Contacts
Village of Orange . . . . (440) 498-4400
http://www.orangevillage.com

PARMA (city). Covers a land area of 20.024 square miles and a water area of 0.049 square miles. Located at 41.38° N. Lat; 81.73° W. Long. Elevation is 863 feet.
History: Named for the Italian city of Parma. Population declined between 1970 and 1990, reflecting the pattern in conjunction with the greater Northern Ohio area. Settled 1816. Incorporated 1924.
Population: 80,088; Growth (since 2000): -6.5%; Density: 3,999.5 persons per square mile; Race: 91.6% White, 3.1% Black/African American, 2.0% Asian, 0.2% American Indian/Alaska Native, 0.0% Native Hawaiian/Other Pacific Islander, 2.0% Two or more races, 5.6% Hispanic of any race; Average household size: 2.36; Median age: 41.9; Age under 18: 19.9%; Age 65 and over: 17.8%; Males per 100 females: 92.8; Marriage status: 31.6% never married, 48.8% now married, 1.1% separated, 8.0% widowed, 11.6% divorced; Foreign born: 9.9%; Speak English only: 84.5%; With disability: 14.2%; Veterans: 8.6%; Ancestry: 24.1% German, 15.9% Polish, 15.2% Irish, 13.1% Italian, 6.3% Slovak
Employment: 11.1% management, business, and financial, 4.6% computer, engineering, and science, 7.3% education, legal, community service, arts, and media, 7.3% healthcare practitioners, 17.5% service, 27.4% sales and office, 8.1% natural resources, construction, and maintenance, 16.6% production, transportation, and material moving
Income: Per capita: $25,715; Median household: $51,383; Average household: $59,920; Households with income of $100,000 or more: 15.1%; Poverty rate: 10.2%
Educational Attainment: High school diploma or higher: 90.1%; Bachelor's degree or higher: 20.0%; Graduate/professional degree or higher: 6.4%

School District(s)

Avon Local (PK-12)
2015-16 Enrollment: 4,286 . . . . (440) 937-4680
Constellation Schools: Parma Community (KG-12)
2015-16 Enrollment: 1,296 . . . . (440) 888-5490
Constellation Schools: Stockyard Community Middle (07-08)
2015-16 Enrollment: 87. . . . . (216) 961-5052
Global Village Academy (KG-06)
2015-16 Enrollment: 152. . . . . (216) 767-5956
Parma City (PK-12)
2015-16 Enrollment: 10,832 . . . . (440) 842-5300
Summit Academy Community School-Parma (KG-12)
2015-16 Enrollment: 201. . . . . (440) 888-5407

Four-year College(s)

Bryant & Stratton College-Parma (Private, For-profit)
Fall 2016 Enrollment: 334 . . . . (216) 265-3151
2016-17 Tuition: In-state $17,431; Out-of-state $17,431
Housing: Homeownership rate: 73.2%; Median home value: $107,500; Median year structure built: 1958; Homeowner vacancy rate: 1.4%; Median selected monthly owner costs: $1,154 with a mortgage, $466 without a mortgage; Median gross rent: $778 per month; Rental vacancy rate: 5.6%
Health Insurance: 92.3% have insurance; 72.1% have private insurance; 34.4% have public insurance; 7.7% do not have insurance; 5.0% of children under 18 do not have insurance
Hospitals: Parma Community General Hospital (348 beds)
Safety: Violent crime rate: 13.6 per 10,000 population; Property crime rate: 138.5 per 10,000 population
Transportation: Commute: 93.5% car, 1.7% public transportation, 1.4% walk, 2.4% work from home; Mean travel time to work: 24.8 minutes
Additional Information Contacts
City of Parma. . . . . (440) 885-8000
http://www.cityofparma-oh.gov

PARMA HEIGHTS (city). Covers a land area of 4.186 square miles and a water area of <.001 square miles. Located at 41.38° N. Lat; 81.76° W. Long. Elevation is 856 feet.
History: Named for the city in Italy. Settled 1818; set off from Parma and incorporated 1912.
Population: 20,311; Growth (since 2000): -6.2%; Density: 4,852.6 persons per square mile; Race: 86.7% White, 7.3% Black/African American, 2.8% Asian, 0.2% American Indian/Alaska Native, 0.0% Native Hawaiian/Other Pacific Islander, 2.6% Two or more races, 4.7% Hispanic of any race; Average household size: 2.22; Median age: 40.0; Age under 18: 20.4%; Age 65 and over: 18.8%; Males per 100 females: 87.0; Marriage status: 32.7% never married, 45.8% now married, 0.5% separated, 8.4% widowed, 13.1% divorced; Foreign born: 10.4%; Speak English only: 86.2%; With disability: 15.5%; Veterans: 7.0%; Ancestry: 21.0% German, 14.2% Irish, 13.3% Polish, 12.0% Italian, 7.7% English

Employment: 11.9% management, business, and financial, 6.5% computer, engineering, and science, 7.6% education, legal, community service, arts, and media, 6.0% healthcare practitioners, 18.2% service, 29.6% sales and office, 6.8% natural resources, construction, and maintenance, 13.4% production, transportation, and material moving
Income: Per capita: $24,654; Median household: $44,564; Average household: $53,903; Households with income of $100,000 or more: 11.2%; Poverty rate: 11.2%
Educational Attainment: High school diploma or higher: 90.9%; Bachelor's degree or higher: 22.6%; Graduate/professional degree or higher: 6.5%

School District(s)

Parma City (PK-12)
2015-16 Enrollment: 10,832 . . . . (440) 842-5300
Housing: Homeownership rate: 55.2%; Median home value: $110,700; Median year structure built: 1960; Homeowner vacancy rate: 1.4%; Median selected monthly owner costs: $1,155 with a mortgage, $469 without a mortgage; Median gross rent: $738 per month; Rental vacancy rate: 3.5%
Health Insurance: 93.5% have insurance; 71.0% have private insurance; 36.8% have public insurance; 6.5% do not have insurance; 3.6% of children under 18 do not have insurance
Transportation: Commute: 94.2% car, 1.1% public transportation, 2.0% walk, 2.2% work from home; Mean travel time to work: 26.4 minutes
Additional Information Contacts
City of Parma Heights . . . . (440) 884-9600
http://www.parmaheightsoh.gov

PEPPER PIKE (city). Covers a land area of 7.059 square miles and a water area of 0.033 square miles. Located at 41.48° N. Lat; 81.46° W. Long. Elevation is 1,056 feet.
History: In 1820, Orange Township was established, which included the present municipalities of Pepper Pike, Hunting Valley, Moreland Hills, Orange Village and Woodmere. The name "Pepper Pike" was selected after the Pepper family, who lived and worked along the primary transportation corridor (i.e., turnpike).
Population: 6,150; Growth (since 2000): 1.8%; Density: 871.3 persons per square mile; Race: 82.8% White, 5.8% Black/African American, 9.0% Asian, 0.2% American Indian/Alaska Native, 0.0% Native Hawaiian/Other Pacific Islander, 1.9% Two or more races, 2.0% Hispanic of any race; Average household size: 2.71; Median age: 49.2; Age under 18: 25.3%; Age 65 and over: 25.3%; Males per 100 females: 87.0; Marriage status: 22.4% never married, 68.8% now married, 1.9% separated, 5.5% widowed, 3.2% divorced; Foreign born: 13.1%; Speak English only: 82.9%; With disability: 10.6%; Veterans: 4.1%; Ancestry: 16.6% German, 10.2% English, 10.2% Irish, 9.3% Polish, 7.3% Russian
Employment: 23.5% management, business, and financial, 4.0% computer, engineering, and science, 17.9% education, legal, community service, arts, and media, 15.9% healthcare practitioners, 7.0% service, 24.3% sales and office, 2.7% natural resources, construction, and maintenance, 4.7% production, transportation, and material moving
Income: Per capita: $86,786; Median household: $164,471; Average household: $248,753; Households with income of $100,000 or more: 70.2%; Poverty rate: 4.1%
Educational Attainment: High school diploma or higher: 97.6%; Bachelor's degree or higher: 75.3%; Graduate/professional degree or higher: 43.3%

School District(s)

Orange City (PK-12)
2015-16 Enrollment: 2,111 . . . . (216) 831-8600

Four-year College(s)

Ursuline College (Private, Not-for-profit, Roman Catholic)
Fall 2016 Enrollment: 1,136 . . . . (440) 449-4200
2016-17 Tuition: In-state $29,940; Out-of-state $29,940
Housing: Homeownership rate: 96.5%; Median home value: $421,500; Median year structure built: 1966; Homeowner vacancy rate: 2.3%; Median selected monthly owner costs: $3,286 with a mortgage, $1,117 without a mortgage; Median gross rent: $1,241 per month; Rental vacancy rate: 0.0%
Health Insurance: 98.7% have insurance; 91.8% have private insurance; 25.9% have public insurance; 1.3% do not have insurance; 0.7% of children under 18 do not have insurance
Safety: Violent crime rate: 1.6 per 10,000 population; Property crime rate: 51.2 per 10,000 population
Transportation: Commute: 88.0% car, 1.1% public transportation, 1.5% walk, 8.4% work from home; Mean travel time to work: 21.8 minutes
Additional Information Contacts
City of Pepper Pike . . . . (216) 831-8500
http://www.pepperpike.org

RICHMOND HEIGHTS (city). Covers a land area of 4.436 square miles and a water area of 0.008 square miles. Located at 41.56° N. Lat; 81.51° W. Long. Elevation is 869 feet.
Population: 10,476; Growth (since 2000): -4.3%; Density: 2,361.8 persons per square mile; Race: 45.7% White, 45.7% Black/African American, 4.3% Asian, 0.6% American Indian/Alaska Native, 0.0% Native Hawaiian/Other Pacific Islander, 3.2% Two or more races, 2.8% Hispanic of any race; Average household size: 2.14; Median age: 48.5; Age under 18: 15.2%; Age 65 and over: 22.1%; Males per 100 females: 81.5; Marriage status: 37.9% never married, 43.8% now married, 2.1% separated, 7.9% widowed, 10.5% divorced; Foreign born: 10.4%; Speak English only: 87.7%; With disability: 15.8%; Veterans: 8.1%; Ancestry: 9.1% Italian, 9.0% German, 5.3% Irish, 3.3% English, 2.8% Slovak
Employment: 11.8% management, business, and financial, 7.4% computer, engineering, and science, 10.3% education, legal, community service, arts, and media, 5.8% healthcare practitioners, 20.9% service, 25.5% sales and office, 3.6% natural resources, construction, and maintenance, 14.6% production, transportation, and material moving
Income: Per capita: $28,592; Median household: $51,212; Average household: $60,001; Households with income of $100,000 or more: 15.8%; Poverty rate: 10.6%
Educational Attainment: High school diploma or higher: 92.1%; Bachelor's degree or higher: 34.6%; Graduate/professional degree or higher: 13.5%

School District(s)

Richmond Heights Local (PK-12)
2015-16 Enrollment: 758. . . . . (216) 692-8485
Housing: Homeownership rate: 64.8%; Median home value: $137,700; Median year structure built: 1967; Homeowner vacancy rate: 2.5%; Median selected monthly owner costs: $1,587 with a mortgage, $574 without a mortgage; Median gross rent: $758 per month; Rental vacancy rate: 18.3%
Health Insurance: 94.1% have insurance; 72.6% have private insurance; 36.0% have public insurance; 5.9% do not have insurance; 2.9% of children under 18 do not have insurance
Hospitals: UHHS Richmond Heights Hospital (250 beds)
Safety: Violent crime rate: 25.9 per 10,000 population; Property crime rate: 238.4 per 10,000 population
Transportation: Commute: 89.4% car, 4.3% public transportation, 0.5% walk, 5.3% work from home; Mean travel time to work: 24.9 minutes
Additional Information Contacts
City of Richmond Heights . . . . (216) 383-6300
http://www.richmondheightsohio.org

ROCKY RIVER (city). Covers a land area of 4.738 square miles and a water area of 0.873 square miles. Located at 41.47° N. Lat; 81.85° W. Long. Elevation is 692 feet.
History: Named for its location at the mouth of the Rocky River, so named because of its rocky river bed. The town of Rocky River was established in 1815 on Lake Erie at the mouth of the Rocky River.
Population: 20,211; Growth (since 2000): -2.5%; Density: 4,265.8 persons per square mile; Race: 96.1% White, 1.8% Black/African American, 0.7% Asian, 0.0% American Indian/Alaska Native, 0.0% Native Hawaiian/Other Pacific Islander, 1.2% Two or more races, 2.8% Hispanic of any race; Average household size: 2.25; Median age: 46.2; Age under 18: 20.8%; Age 65 and over: 23.0%; Males per 100 females: 85.5; Marriage status: 29.9% never married, 49.7% now married, 1.6% separated, 10.2% widowed, 10.1% divorced; Foreign born: 9.1%; Speak English only: 88.5%; With disability: 11.1%; Veterans: 8.8%; Ancestry: 28.2% Irish, 26.6% German, 10.7% Italian, 10.4% English, 7.6% Polish
Employment: 26.8% management, business, and financial, 7.4% computer, engineering, and science, 13.9% education, legal, community service, arts, and media, 8.9% healthcare practitioners, 12.6% service, 19.8% sales and office, 2.7% natural resources, construction, and maintenance, 7.9% production, transportation, and material moving
Income: Per capita: $48,301; Median household: $65,226; Average household: $108,531; Households with income of $100,000 or more: 34.3%; Poverty rate: 4.7%
Educational Attainment: High school diploma or higher: 95.7%; Bachelor's degree or higher: 55.2%; Graduate/professional degree or higher: 25.7%

School District(s)

Rocky River City (PK-12)
2015-16 Enrollment: 2,736 . . . . (440) 333-6000

Two-year College(s)

Brown Aveda Institute-Rocky River (Private, For-profit)
Fall 2016 Enrollment: 113 . . . . (440) 255-9494

Housing: Homeownership rate: 72.7%; Median home value: $215,800; Median year structure built: 1958; Homeowner vacancy rate: 1.7%; Median selected monthly owner costs: $1,623 with a mortgage, $689 without a mortgage; Median gross rent: $838 per month; Rental vacancy rate: 1.7%

Health Insurance: 95.0% have insurance; 84.7% have private insurance; 28.3% have public insurance; 5.0% do not have insurance; 3.0% of children under 18 do not have insurance

Safety: Violent crime rate: 3.4 per 10,000 population; Property crime rate: 39.7 per 10,000 population

Transportation: Commute: 88.0% car, 4.1% public transportation, 1.1% walk, 5.8% work from home; Mean travel time to work: 24.3 minutes

Additional Information Contacts

City of Rocky River . . . . (440) 331-0600
http://www.rrcity.com

SEVEN HILLS (city). Covers a land area of 4.907 square miles and a water area of 0.007 square miles. Located at 41.38° N. Lat; 81.68° W. Long. Elevation is 883 feet.

History: Named for the seven hills of Rome. Incorporated as a city 1961. Part of its city hall is an old schoolhouse, built in 1861.

Population: 11,697; Growth (since 2000): -3.2%; Density: 2,383.5 persons per square mile; Race: 95.5% White, 1.4% Black/African American, 1.9% Asian, 0.1% American Indian/Alaska Native, 0.0% Native Hawaiian/Other Pacific Islander, 1.1% Two or more races, 1.4% Hispanic of any race; Average household size: 2.39; Median age: 50.9; Age under 18: 16.0%; Age 65 and over: 25.4%; Males per 100 females: 95.0; Marriage status: 25.6% never married, 58.4% now married, 0.4% separated, 8.6% widowed, 7.4% divorced; Foreign born: 9.5%; Speak English only: 87.2%; With disability: 13.6%; Veterans: 7.6%; Ancestry: 21.9% Polish, 20.4% Italian, 19.5% German, 14.1% Irish, 8.4% Slovak

Employment: 19.9% management, business, and financial, 9.9% computer, engineering, and science, 11.7% education, legal, community service, arts, and media, 8.4% healthcare practitioners, 10.8% service, 25.2% sales and office, 5.8% natural resources, construction, and maintenance, 8.3% production, transportation, and material moving

Income: Per capita: $36,283; Median household: $73,948; Average household: $85,048; Households with income of $100,000 or more: 34.0%; Poverty rate: 4.5%

Educational Attainment: High school diploma or higher: 93.1%; Bachelor's degree or higher: 34.5%; Graduate/professional degree or higher: 11.5%

School District(s)

Parma City (PK-12)
2015-16 Enrollment: 10,832 . . . . (440) 842-5300

Housing: Homeownership rate: 95.4%; Median home value: $164,100; Median year structure built: 1966; Homeowner vacancy rate: 0.4%; Median selected monthly owner costs: $1,435 with a mortgage, $590 without a mortgage; Median gross rent: $1,165 per month; Rental vacancy rate: 2.6%

Health Insurance: 98.2% have insurance; 86.9% have private insurance; 30.2% have public insurance; 1.8% do not have insurance; 1.3% of children under 18 do not have insurance

Safety: Violent crime rate: 3.4 per 10,000 population; Property crime rate: 54.9 per 10,000 population

Transportation: Commute: 96.0% car, 0.7% public transportation, 0.4% walk, 2.4% work from home; Mean travel time to work: 26.4 minutes

Additional Information Contacts

City of Seven Hills . . . . (216) 524-4421
http://www.sevenhillsohio.org

SHAKER HEIGHTS (city). Covers a land area of 6.282 square miles and a water area of 0.042 square miles. Located at 41.48° N. Lat; 81.55° W. Long. Elevation is 1,050 feet.

History: Named for a community of Shakers founded in the region in the early 1800s. The Shakers founded a religious community here in the early 1800's. The site was acquired in 1905 by O.P. and M.J. VanSweringen, railroad tycoons, who connected it with downtown Cleveland by a rapid transit line. Shaker Heights grew as a residential area.

Population: 27,773; Growth (since 2000): -5.6%; Density: 4,420.7 persons per square mile; Race: 54.7% White, 34.3% Black/African American, 5.9% Asian, 0.2% American Indian/Alaska Native, 0.0% Native Hawaiian/Other Pacific Islander, 4.3% Two or more races, 2.4% Hispanic of any race; Average household size: 2.48; Median age: 40.5; Age under 18: 25.8%; Age 65 and over: 16.6%; Males per 100 females: 82.5; Marriage status: 31.8% never married, 53.5% now married, 1.5% separated, 4.9% widowed, 9.7% divorced; Foreign born: 9.2%; Speak English only: 89.6%; With disability: 9.6%; Veterans: 6.2%; Ancestry: 12.6% German, 9.9% Irish, 8.6% English, 7.1% Italian, 4.0% Polish

Employment: 20.4% management, business, and financial, 7.2% computer, engineering, and science, 23.4% education, legal, community service, arts, and media, 14.0% healthcare practitioners, 10.5% service, 17.3% sales and office, 2.3% natural resources, construction, and maintenance, 4.9% production, transportation, and material moving

Income: Per capita: $52,441; Median household: $79,519; Average household: $130,025; Households with income of $100,000 or more: 39.7%; Poverty rate: 8.1%

Educational Attainment: High school diploma or higher: 96.2%; Bachelor's degree or higher: 64.9%; Graduate/professional degree or higher: 39.9%

School District(s)

Shaker Heights City (PK-12)
2015-16 Enrollment: 5,254 . . . . (216) 295-4000

Housing: Homeownership rate: 63.1%; Median home value: $213,100; Median year structure built: 1941; Homeowner vacancy rate: 3.7%; Median selected monthly owner costs: $2,033 with a mortgage, $1,021 without a mortgage; Median gross rent: $945 per month; Rental vacancy rate: 8.8%

Health Insurance: 96.5% have insurance; 82.6% have private insurance; 26.9% have public insurance; 3.5% do not have insurance; 1.1% of children under 18 do not have insurance

Transportation: Commute: 83.7% car, 5.0% public transportation, 1.4% walk, 7.9% work from home; Mean travel time to work: 22.8 minutes

Additional Information Contacts

City of Shaker Heights. . . . . (216) 491-1400
http://www.shakeronline.com

SOLON (city). Covers a land area of 20.361 square miles and a water area of 0.130 square miles. Located at 41.39° N. Lat; 81.44° W. Long. Elevation is 1,040 feet.

History: Named for Solon Bull, one of the town's early settlers. Founded 1820. Incorporated as a city 1960.

Population: 23,085; Growth (since 2000): 5.9%; Density: 1,133.8 persons per square mile; Race: 72.6% White, 11.4% Black/African American, 12.5% Asian, 0.2% American Indian/Alaska Native, 0.1% Native Hawaiian/Other Pacific Islander, 3.1% Two or more races, 1.3% Hispanic of any race; Average household size: 2.75; Median age: 44.0; Age under 18: 27.4%; Age 65 and over: 15.8%; Males per 100 females: 95.1; Marriage status: 21.6% never married, 64.8% now married, 0.8% separated, 5.8% widowed, 7.9% divorced; Foreign born: 14.9%; Speak English only: 82.7%; With disability: 7.2%; Veterans: 4.8%; Ancestry: 14.4% German, 10.6% Italian, 9.2% Irish, 6.0% Polish, 5.4% English

Employment: 23.5% management, business, and financial, 7.7% computer, engineering, and science, 15.3% education, legal, community service, arts, and media, 10.4% healthcare practitioners, 14.0% service, 21.3% sales and office, 3.2% natural resources, construction, and maintenance, 4.6% production, transportation, and material moving

Income: Per capita: $49,223; Median household: $96,976; Average household: $134,570; Households with income of $100,000 or more: 48.7%; Poverty rate: 4.8%

Educational Attainment: High school diploma or higher: 96.9%; Bachelor's degree or higher: 62.0%; Graduate/professional degree or higher: 31.6%

School District(s)

Solon City (PK-12)
2015-16 Enrollment: 4,652 . . . . (440) 248-1600

Housing: Homeownership rate: 83.7%; Median home value: $273,800; Median year structure built: 1981; Homeowner vacancy rate: 1.8%; Median selected monthly owner costs: $1,996 with a mortgage, $737 without a mortgage; Median gross rent: $1,200 per month; Rental vacancy rate: 1.2%

Health Insurance: 97.5% have insurance; 86.9% have private insurance; 22.0% have public insurance; 2.5% do not have insurance; 1.4% of children under 18 do not have insurance

Safety: Violent crime rate: 4.8 per 10,000 population; Property crime rate: 76.2 per 10,000 population
Transportation: Commute: 92.9% car, 0.4% public transportation, 0.4% walk, 5.9% work from home; Mean travel time to work: 25.3 minutes
Additional Information Contacts
City of Solon . . . . (440) 248-1155
http://www.solonohio.org

SOUTH EUCLID (city). Covers a land area of 4.651 square miles and a water area of 0 square miles. Located at 41.52° N. Lat; 81.52° W. Long. Elevation is 958 feet.
History: Named for Euclid, the mathematician of Alexandria. Site of Notre Dame College, a Roman Catholic school for women. Incorporated as a city 1940.
Population: 21,865; Growth (since 2000): -7.1%; Density: 4,701.5 persons per square mile; Race: 52.1% White, 41.0% Black/African American, 2.1% Asian, 0.1% American Indian/Alaska Native, 0.0% Native Hawaiian/Other Pacific Islander, 3.9% Two or more races, 2.8% Hispanic of any race; Average household size: 2.41; Median age: 38.0; Age under 18: 20.4%; Age 65 and over: 14.0%; Males per 100 females: 83.9; Marriage status: 40.8% never married, 43.7% now married, 1.4% separated, 5.2% widowed, 10.3% divorced; Foreign born: 6.7%; Speak English only: 92.5%; With disability: 9.0%; Veterans: 6.4%; Ancestry: 11.3% German, 10.0% Irish, 9.6% Italian, 4.8% Polish, 3.5% American
Employment: 15.0% management, business, and financial, 5.5% computer, engineering, and science, 11.5% education, legal, community service, arts, and media, 8.3% healthcare practitioners, 19.5% service, 25.1% sales and office, 4.7% natural resources, construction, and maintenance, 10.2% production, transportation, and material moving
Income: Per capita: $27,731; Median household: $59,734; Average household: $67,205; Households with income of $100,000 or more: 20.4%; Poverty rate: 9.2%
Educational Attainment: High school diploma or higher: 92.8%; Bachelor's degree or higher: 39.5%; Graduate/professional degree or higher: 17.0%

School District(s)

South Euclid-Lyndhurst City (PK-12)
2015-16 Enrollment: 3,531 . . . . (216) 691-2000
Housing: Homeownership rate: 73.9%; Median home value: $100,100; Median year structure built: 1954; Homeowner vacancy rate: 2.8%; Median selected monthly owner costs: $1,218 with a mortgage, $499 without a mortgage; Median gross rent: $943 per month; Rental vacancy rate: 5.1%
Health Insurance: 92.1% have insurance; 75.9% have private insurance; 26.5% have public insurance; 7.9% do not have insurance; 3.8% of children under 18 do not have insurance
Safety: Violent crime rate: 16.1 per 10,000 population; Property crime rate: 262.8 per 10,000 population
Transportation: Commute: 89.7% car, 2.4% public transportation, 3.8% walk, 3.1% work from home; Mean travel time to work: 23.2 minutes
Additional Information Contacts
City of South Euclid. . . . . (216) 381-0400
http://www.cityofsoutheuclid.com

STRONGSVILLE (city). Covers a land area of 24.627 square miles and a water area of 0.007 square miles. Located at 41.31° N. Lat; 81.83° W. Long. Elevation is 932 feet.
History: Named for Caleb Strong (1745-1819), a Massachusetts statesman. The city's population doubled between 1970 and 1990. Settled 1816. Incorporated 1927.
Population: 44,622; Growth (since 2000): 1.7%; Density: 1,811.9 persons per square mile; Race: 90.5% White, 2.7% Black/African American, 4.4% Asian, 0.3% American Indian/Alaska Native, 0.0% Native Hawaiian/Other Pacific Islander, 1.3% Two or more races, 2.8% Hispanic of any race; Average household size: 2.52; Median age: 45.9; Age under 18: 21.2%; Age 65 and over: 19.1%; Males per 100 females: 94.7; Marriage status: 22.6% never married, 60.6% now married, 0.6% separated, 7.0% widowed, 9.8% divorced; Foreign born: 8.6%; Speak English only: 88.2%; With disability: 9.8%; Veterans: 8.5%; Ancestry: 24.5% German, 16.6% Irish, 13.2% Italian, 12.1% Polish, 9.3% English
Employment: 21.8% management, business, and financial, 7.8% computer, engineering, and science, 10.6% education, legal, community service, arts, and media, 7.5% healthcare practitioners, 12.8% service, 26.8% sales and office, 4.2% natural resources, construction, and maintenance, 8.5% production, transportation, and material moving
Income: Per capita: $40,133; Median household: $80,323; Average household: $100,415; Households with income of $100,000 or more: 39.8%; Poverty rate: 4.2%
Educational Attainment: High school diploma or higher: 95.9%; Bachelor's degree or higher: 44.6%; Graduate/professional degree or higher: 17.3%

School District(s)

Strongsville City (PK-12)
2015-16 Enrollment: 5,459 . . . . (440) 572-7000

Four-year College(s)

ITT Technical Institute-Strongsville (Private, For-profit)
Fall 2016 Enrollment: n/a . . . . (440) 234-9091
Housing: Homeownership rate: 80.4%; Median home value: $194,000; Median year structure built: 1981; Homeowner vacancy rate: 1.1%; Median selected monthly owner costs: $1,651 with a mortgage, $617 without a mortgage; Median gross rent: $908 per month; Rental vacancy rate: 2.3%
Health Insurance: 96.3% have insurance; 84.5% have private insurance; 25.7% have public insurance; 3.7% do not have insurance; 1.0% of children under 18 do not have insurance
Safety: Violent crime rate: 4.3 per 10,000 population; Property crime rate: 197.6 per 10,000 population
Transportation: Commute: 91.8% car, 1.9% public transportation, 0.7% walk, 4.9% work from home; Mean travel time to work: 27.4 minutes
Additional Information Contacts
City of Strongsville. . . . . (440) 580-3100
http://www.strongsville.org

UNIVERSITY HEIGHTS (city). Covers a land area of 1.820 square miles and a water area of 0 square miles. Located at 41.49° N. Lat; 81.53° W. Long. Elevation is 1,027 feet.
History: Named for it being home to John Carroll University. University Heights grew as a residential community. It took its name from John Carroll University, a liberal arts college founded here by the Jesuit Order in 1886.
Population: 13,273; Growth (since 2000): -6.2%; Density: 7,291.7 persons per square mile; Race: 73.9% White, 20.6% Black/African American, 2.1% Asian, 0.1% American Indian/Alaska Native, 0.0% Native Hawaiian/Other Pacific Islander, 2.3% Two or more races, 2.6% Hispanic of any race; Average household size: 2.56; Median age: 29.9; Age under 18: 21.9%; Age 65 and over: 10.3%; Males per 100 females: 91.0; Marriage status: 43.2% never married, 46.4% now married, 0.6% separated, 3.9% widowed, 6.5% divorced; Foreign born: 8.0%; Speak English only: 90.0%; With disability: 7.8%; Veterans: 4.2%; Ancestry: 16.9% German, 14.3% Irish, 10.7% Italian, 8.4% Polish, 4.1% American
Employment: 20.0% management, business, and financial, 6.3% computer, engineering, and science, 21.0% education, legal, community service, arts, and media, 9.8% healthcare practitioners, 14.0% service, 21.3% sales and office, 1.3% natural resources, construction, and maintenance, 6.3% production, transportation, and material moving
Income: Per capita: $30,298; Median household: $65,143; Average household: $87,172; Households with income of $100,000 or more: 29.8%; Poverty rate: 13.6%
Educational Attainment: High school diploma or higher: 96.3%; Bachelor's degree or higher: 57.0%; Graduate/professional degree or higher: 30.3%

School District(s)

Cleveland Heights-University Heights City (PK-12)
2015-16 Enrollment: 5,349 . . . . (216) 371-7171

Four-year College(s)

John Carroll University (Private, Not-for-profit, Roman Catholic)
Fall 2016 Enrollment: 3,523 . . . . (216) 397-1886
2016-17 Tuition: In-state $38,490; Out-of-state $38,490
Housing: Homeownership rate: 63.8%; Median home value: $154,600; Median year structure built: 1949; Homeowner vacancy rate: 2.5%; Median selected monthly owner costs: $1,574 with a mortgage, $699 without a mortgage; Median gross rent: $987 per month; Rental vacancy rate: 9.8%
Health Insurance: 95.9% have insurance; 81.6% have private insurance; 23.2% have public insurance; 4.1% do not have insurance; 2.4% of children under 18 do not have insurance
Safety: Violent crime rate: 34.3 per 10,000 population; Property crime rate: 232.3 per 10,000 population
Transportation: Commute: 82.2% car, 2.8% public transportation, 8.7% walk, 5.3% work from home; Mean travel time to work: 21.9 minutes
Additional Information Contacts

City of University Heights .... (216) 932-7800
http://www.universityheights.com

VALLEY VIEW (village). Covers a land area of 5.437 square miles and a water area of 0.134 square miles. Located at 41.38° N. Lat; 81.61° W. Long. Elevation is 643 feet.

Population: 1,974; Growth (since 2000): -9.4%; Density: 363.1 persons per square mile; Race: 93.8% White, 3.3% Black/African American, 0.2% Asian, 0.0% American Indian/Alaska Native, 0.0% Native Hawaiian/Other Pacific Islander, 2.7% Two or more races, 0.4% Hispanic of any race; Average household size: 2.75; Median age: 46.7; Age under 18: 21.2%; Age 65 and over: 18.8%; Males per 100 females: 102.6; Marriage status: 28.8% never married, 57.7% now married, 1.0% separated, 6.7% widowed, 6.9% divorced; Foreign born: 2.0%; Speak English only: 97.8%; With disability: 12.3%; Veterans: 8.7%; Ancestry: 21.7% German, 20.0% Polish, 19.7% Italian, 17.7% Irish, 8.1% English

Employment: 18.7% management, business, and financial, 6.7% computer, engineering, and science, 10.0% education, legal, community service, arts, and media, 7.3% healthcare practitioners, 15.0% service, 25.8% sales and office, 6.3% natural resources, construction, and maintenance, 10.1% production, transportation, and material moving

Income: Per capita: $36,382; Median household: $86,071; Average household: $98,843; Households with income of $100,000 or more: 44.3%; Poverty rate: 5.7%

Educational Attainment: High school diploma or higher: 94.6%; Bachelor's degree or higher: 33.5%; Graduate/professional degree or higher: 11.0%

Vocational/Technical School(s)

Ohio Media School-Valley View (Private, For-profit)
Fall 2016 Enrollment: 130 .... (216) 503-5900
2016-17 Tuition: $16,965

Housing: Homeownership rate: 89.8%; Median home value: $245,600; Median year structure built: 1973; Homeowner vacancy rate: 0.0%; Median selected monthly owner costs: $1,736 with a mortgage, $577 without a mortgage; Median gross rent: $827 per month; Rental vacancy rate: 8.8%

Health Insurance: 96.6% have insurance; 87.2% have private insurance; 28.1% have public insurance; 3.4% do not have insurance; 0.0% of children under 18 do not have insurance

Safety: Violent crime rate: 0.0 per 10,000 population; Property crime rate: 174.4 per 10,000 population

Newspapers: Sun Newspapers (weekly circulation 355,000)

Transportation: Commute: 93.9% car, 0.0% public transportation, 1.4% walk, 4.0% work from home; Mean travel time to work: 22.8 minutes

Additional Information Contacts

Village of Valley View .... (216) 524-6511
http://www.valleyview.net

WALTON HILLS (village). Covers a land area of 6.756 square miles and a water area of 0.046 square miles. Located at 41.37° N. Lat; 81.55° W. Long. Elevation is 988 feet.

Population: 2,236; Growth (since 2000): -6.8%; Density: 331.0 persons per square mile; Race: 88.5% White, 9.4% Black/African American, 0.6% Asian, 0.0% American Indian/Alaska Native, 0.0% Native Hawaiian/Other Pacific Islander, 1.0% Two or more races, 1.4% Hispanic of any race; Average household size: 2.25; Median age: 58.6; Age under 18: 8.5%; Age 65 and over: 32.5%; Males per 100 females: 91.7; Marriage status: 21.2% never married, 55.8% now married, 0.8% separated, 12.8% widowed, 10.2% divorced; Foreign born: 4.7%; Speak English only: 93.6%; With disability: 14.6%; Veterans: 9.9%; Ancestry: 19.5% Polish, 17.9% German, 16.7% Italian, 12.6% Irish, 9.1% Slovak

Employment: 18.5% management, business, and financial, 5.5% computer, engineering, and science, 7.8% education, legal, community service, arts, and media, 7.3% healthcare practitioners, 17.5% service, 22.2% sales and office, 8.6% natural resources, construction, and maintenance, 12.7% production, transportation, and material moving

Income: Per capita: $34,347; Median household: $69,167; Average household: $78,656; Households with income of $100,000 or more: 28.8%; Poverty rate: 4.5%

Educational Attainment: High school diploma or higher: 93.4%; Bachelor's degree or higher: 28.7%; Graduate/professional degree or higher: 9.7%

Housing: Homeownership rate: 97.2%; Median home value: $206,600; Median year structure built: 1965; Homeowner vacancy rate: 0.0%; Median selected monthly owner costs: $1,577 with a mortgage, $541 without a mortgage; Median gross rent: $1,179 per month; Rental vacancy rate: 0.0%

Health Insurance: 96.3% have insurance; 81.1% have private insurance; 35.7% have public insurance; 3.7% do not have insurance; 2.1% of children under 18 do not have insurance

Safety: Violent crime rate: 0.0 per 10,000 population; Property crime rate: 129.7 per 10,000 population

Transportation: Commute: 91.8% car, 0.3% public transportation, 0.0% walk, 7.9% work from home; Mean travel time to work: 25.2 minutes

WARRENSVILLE HEIGHTS (city). Covers a land area of 4.132 square miles and a water area of 0.005 square miles. Located at 41.44° N. Lat; 81.52° W. Long. Elevation is 1,037 feet.

History: Named for the David Warren family. Incorporated 1927.

Population: 13,293; Growth (since 2000): -12.0%; Density: 3,217.5 persons per square mile; Race: 4.6% White, 92.1% Black/African American, 0.8% Asian, 0.1% American Indian/Alaska Native, 0.0% Native Hawaiian/Other Pacific Islander, 2.0% Two or more races, 0.9% Hispanic of any race; Average household size: 2.16; Median age: 38.0; Age under 18: 23.1%; Age 65 and over: 18.6%; Males per 100 females: 74.4; Marriage status: 45.8% never married, 30.2% now married, 2.3% separated, 7.5% widowed, 16.5% divorced; Foreign born: 4.0%; Speak English only: 96.4%; With disability: 13.5%; Veterans: 9.2%; Ancestry: 2.7% African, 2.5% Jamaican, 2.4% American, 0.8% Italian, 0.8% German

Employment: 10.3% management, business, and financial, 1.2% computer, engineering, and science, 9.0% education, legal, community service, arts, and media, 3.8% healthcare practitioners, 25.0% service, 30.3% sales and office, 5.1% natural resources, construction, and maintenance, 15.5% production, transportation, and material moving

Income: Per capita: $20,830; Median household: $35,733; Average household: $43,469; Households with income of $100,000 or more: 4.7%; Poverty rate: 19.9%

Educational Attainment: High school diploma or higher: 89.3%; Bachelor's degree or higher: 17.2%; Graduate/professional degree or higher: 6.3%

School District(s)

Warrensville Heights City (PK-12)
2015-16 Enrollment: 1,579 .... (216) 865-4717

Four-year College(s)

ITT Technical Institute-Warrensville Heights (Private, For-profit)
Fall 2016 Enrollment: n/a .... (216) 896-6500

Housing: Homeownership rate: 41.3%; Median home value: $80,400; Median year structure built: 1960; Homeowner vacancy rate: 3.0%; Median selected monthly owner costs: $1,063 with a mortgage, $460 without a mortgage; Median gross rent: $786 per month; Rental vacancy rate: 11.6%

Health Insurance: 92.4% have insurance; 56.7% have private insurance; 50.6% have public insurance; 7.6% do not have insurance; 1.0% of children under 18 do not have insurance

Hospitals: South Pointe Hospital (232 beds)

Transportation: Commute: 83.3% car, 11.9% public transportation, 1.1% walk, 2.8% work from home; Mean travel time to work: 25.9 minutes

Additional Information Contacts

City of Warrensville Heights .... (216) 587-6500
http://www.cityofwarrensville.com

WESTLAKE (city). Covers a land area of 15.926 square miles and a water area of 0.004 square miles. Located at 41.45° N. Lat; 81.93° W. Long. Elevation is 709 feet.

History: Named for its location southwest of Lakewood. Incorporated as a city 1956.

Population: 32,408; Growth (since 2000): 2.2%; Density: 2,034.9 persons per square mile; Race: 89.9% White, 2.1% Black/African American, 5.1% Asian, 0.0% American Indian/Alaska Native, 0.1% Native Hawaiian/Other Pacific Islander, 2.2% Two or more races, 3.2% Hispanic of any race; Average household size: 2.29; Median age: 47.2; Age under 18: 21.1%; Age 65 and over: 22.2%; Males per 100 females: 90.2; Marriage status: 24.8% never married, 56.0% now married, 1.4% separated, 8.4% widowed, 10.8% divorced; Foreign born: 7.8%; Speak English only: 89.0%; With disability: 9.7%; Veterans: 8.3%; Ancestry: 26.7% German, 19.3% Irish, 10.8% Italian, 10.4% English, 7.0% Polish

Employment: 25.2% management, business, and financial, 6.5% computer, engineering, and science, 12.9% education, legal, community service, arts, and media, 10.6% healthcare practitioners, 11.8% service, 24.4% sales and office, 3.5% natural resources, construction, and maintenance, 5.0% production, transportation, and material moving

Income: Per capita: $51,230; Median household: $80,989; Average household: $118,080; Households with income of $100,000 or more: 39.4%; Poverty rate: 4.9%
Educational Attainment: High school diploma or higher: 96.4%; Bachelor's degree or higher: 52.5%; Graduate/professional degree or higher: 21.1%

School District(s)

Westlake City (PK-12)
2015-16 Enrollment: 3,685 . . . . (440) 871-7300
Housing: Homeownership rate: 75.2%; Median home value: $236,400; Median year structure built: 1982; Homeowner vacancy rate: 1.1%; Median selected monthly owner costs: $1,789 with a mortgage, $657 without a mortgage; Median gross rent: $1,066 per month; Rental vacancy rate: 9.0%
Health Insurance: 96.0% have insurance; 83.1% have private insurance; 28.1% have public insurance; 4.0% do not have insurance; 3.5% of children under 18 do not have insurance
Hospitals: Saint John Medical Center (200 beds)
Safety: Violent crime rate: 4.3 per 10,000 population; Property crime rate: 142.5 per 10,000 population
Transportation: Commute: 90.0% car, 1.5% public transportation, 0.9% walk, 7.1% work from home; Mean travel time to work: 25.3 minutes
Additional Information Contacts
City of Westlake . . . . (440) 871-3300
http://www.cityofwestlake.org

WOODMERE (village). Covers a land area of 0.334 square miles and a water area of 0 square miles. Located at 41.46° N. Lat; 81.48° W. Long. Elevation is 1,171 feet.
Population: 847; Growth (since 2000): 2.3%; Density: 2,539.4 persons per square mile; Race: 24.4% White, 56.8% Black/African American, 13.1% Asian, 0.0% American Indian/Alaska Native, 0.0% Native Hawaiian/Other Pacific Islander, 3.1% Two or more races, 8.0% Hispanic of any race; Average household size: 2.19; Median age: 39.1; Age under 18: 25.1%; Age 65 and over: 8.0%; Males per 100 females: 72.0; Marriage status: 38.9% never married, 37.6% now married, 0.6% separated, 5.0% widowed, 18.5% divorced; Foreign born: 18.7%; Speak English only: 77.3%; With disability: 13.6%; Veterans: 5.0%; Ancestry: 4.4% German, 3.9% Portuguese, 3.3% Irish, 2.8% English, 2.1% Slovak
Employment: 23.6% management, business, and financial, 5.2% computer, engineering, and science, 5.9% education, legal, community service, arts, and media, 6.8% healthcare practitioners, 21.6% service, 21.2% sales and office, 2.8% natural resources, construction, and maintenance, 12.9% production, transportation, and material moving
Income: Per capita: $29,539; Median household: $44,333; Average household: $63,040; Households with income of $100,000 or more: 11.7%; Poverty rate: 17.9%
Educational Attainment: High school diploma or higher: 96.6%; Bachelor's degree or higher: 42.8%; Graduate/professional degree or higher: 23.7%
Housing: Homeownership rate: 37.6%; Median home value: $219,500; Median year structure built: 1967; Homeowner vacancy rate: 0.0%; Median selected monthly owner costs: $1,670 with a mortgage, $800 without a mortgage; Median gross rent: $760 per month; Rental vacancy rate: 3.8%
Health Insurance: 96.9% have insurance; 83.7% have private insurance; 21.4% have public insurance; 3.1% do not have insurance; 3.3% of children under 18 do not have insurance
Safety: Violent crime rate: 23.3 per 10,000 population; Property crime rate: 651.9 per 10,000 population
Transportation: Commute: 87.6% car, 5.1% public transportation, 3.1% walk, 3.1% work from home; Mean travel time to work: 22.6 minutes

Darke County

Located in western Ohio; bounded on the west by Indiana; drained by Greenville Creek and the Stillwater and Mississinewa Rivers. Covers a land area of 598.100 square miles, a water area of 1.657 square miles, and is located in the Eastern Time Zone at 40.13° N. Lat., 84.62° W. Long. The county was founded in 1809. County seat is Greenville.

Darke County is part of the Greenville, OH Micropolitan Statistical Area. The entire metro area includes: Darke County, OH

Weather Station: Greenville Water Plant Elevation: 1,023 feet

	Jan	Feb	Mar	Apr	May	Jun	Jul	Aug	Sep	Oct	Nov	Dec
High	33	37	48	61	71	80	83	82	77	64	51	38
Low	17	19	28	38	49	59	62	59	51	40	32	22
Precip	2.4	2.1	3.0	3.7	4.5	4.2	4.3	3.2	2.6	2.9	3.2	2.8
Snow	7.3	6.0	3.0	0.5	tr	0.0	0.0	0.0	0.0	0.2	0.7	4.3

High and Low temperatures in degrees Fahrenheit; Precipitation and Snow in inches

Population: 52,185; Growth (since 2000): -2.1%; Density: 87.3 persons per square mile; Race: 97.7% White, 0.7% Black/African American, 0.3% Asian, 0.3% American Indian/Alaska Native, 0.0% Native Hawaiian/Other Pacific Islander, 0.8% two or more races, 1.4% Hispanic of any race; Average household size: 2.47; Median age: 42.0; Age under 18: 24.4%; Age 65 and over: 18.4%; Males per 100 females: 96.6; Marriage status: 23.5% never married, 57.8% now married, 1.4% separated, 7.4% widowed, 11.3% divorced; Foreign born: 1.0%; Speak English only: 98.1%; With disability: 14.8%; Veterans: 9.4%; Ancestry: 39.4% German, 12.2% American, 11.2% Irish, 8.3% English, 5.2% French
Religion: Six largest groups: 13.4% Catholicism, 6.5% Methodist/Pietist, 4.3% European Free-Church, 4.0% Lutheran, 3.6% Baptist, 3.5% Non-denominational Protestant
Economy: Unemployment rate: 3.7%; Leading industries: 15.4 % retail trade; 15.1 % other services (except public administration); 14.5 % construction; Farms: 1,693 totaling 339,981 acres; Company size: 1 employs 1,000 or more persons, 2 employ 500 to 999 persons, 22 employ 100 to 499 persons, 1,122 employ less than 100 persons; Business ownership: 1,120 women-owned, n/a Black-owned, n/a Hispanic-owned, n/a Asian-owned, n/a American Indian/Alaska Native-owned
Employment: 11.7% management, business, and financial, 2.7% computer, engineering, and science, 5.8% education, legal, community service, arts, and media, 4.6% healthcare practitioners, 15.5% service, 20.2% sales and office, 12.5% natural resources, construction, and maintenance, 27.1% production, transportation, and material moving
Income: Per capita: $23,589; Median household: $47,043; Average household: $58,006; Households with income of $100,000 or more: 13.3%; Poverty rate: 12.4%
Educational Attainment: High school diploma or higher: 88.9%; Bachelor's degree or higher: 13.1%; Graduate/professional degree or higher: 4.7%
Housing: Homeownership rate: 72.2%; Median home value: $112,100; Median year structure built: 1957; Homeowner vacancy rate: 1.3%; Median selected monthly owner costs: $1,045 with a mortgage, $387 without a mortgage; Median gross rent: $624 per month; Rental vacancy rate: 6.0%
Vital Statistics: Birth rate: 126.5 per 10,000 population; Death rate: 115.9 per 10,000 population; Age-adjusted cancer mortality rate: 184.3 deaths per 100,000 population
Health Insurance: 92.3% have insurance; 71.6% have private insurance; 36.4% have public insurance; 7.7% do not have insurance; 3.1% of children under 18 do not have insurance
Health Care: Physicians: 8.3 per 10,000 population; Dentists: 3.3 per 10,000 population; Hospital beds: 12.1 per 10,000 population; Hospital admissions: 391.8 per 10,000 population
Transportation: Commute: 91.4% car, 0.7% public transportation, 2.4% walk, 4.3% work from home; Mean travel time to work: 22.6 minutes
2016 Presidential Election: 78.2% Trump, 17.5% Clinton, 2.5% Johnson, 0.6% Stein
National and State Parks: Fort Jefferson State Memorial; Treaty of Greenville State Park
Additional Information Contacts
Darke Government . . . . (937) 547-7370
http://www.co.darke.oh.us

Darke County Communities

ANSONIA (village). Covers a land area of 0.785 square miles and a water area of 0.021 square miles. Located at 40.21° N. Lat; 84.63° W. Long. Elevation is 1,001 feet.
Population: 1,214; Growth (since 2000): 6.0%; Density: 1,546.3 persons per square mile; Race: 98.4% White, 1.2% Black/African American, 0.0% Asian, 0.0% American Indian/Alaska Native, 0.0% Native Hawaiian/Other Pacific Islander, 0.2% Two or more races, 1.2% Hispanic of any race; Average household size: 2.66; Median age: 35.3; Age under 18: 28.0%; Age 65 and over: 14.3%; Males per 100 females: 94.0; Marriage status: 26.6% never married, 54.9% now married, 0.3% separated, 5.3% widowed, 13.2% divorced; Foreign born: 1.2%; Speak English only: 99.3%;

With disability: 15.7%; Veterans: 10.3%; Ancestry: 18.5% German, 12.5% American, 9.3% Irish, 8.0% English, 2.8% French
Employment: 10.2% management, business, and financial, 1.2% computer, engineering, and science, 4.4% education, legal, community service, arts, and media, 0.6% healthcare practitioners, 12.4% service, 19.5% sales and office, 20.3% natural resources, construction, and maintenance, 31.5% production, transportation, and material moving
Income: Per capita: $16,417; Median household: $37,596; Average household: $42,686; Households with income of $100,000 or more: 3.5%; Poverty rate: 27.2%
Educational Attainment: High school diploma or higher: 82.5%; Bachelor's degree or higher: 7.7%; Graduate/professional degree or higher: 2.3%

School District(s)

Ansonia Local (PK-12)
2015-16 Enrollment: 809. . . . . (937) 337-4000

Housing: Homeownership rate: 62.6%; Median home value: $78,000; Median year structure built: 1959; Homeowner vacancy rate: 0.0%; Median selected monthly owner costs: $845 with a mortgage, $332 without a mortgage; Median gross rent: $627 per month; Rental vacancy rate: 4.5%
Health Insurance: 90.0% have insurance; 67.8% have private insurance; 36.4% have public insurance; 10.0% do not have insurance; 1.5% of children under 18 do not have insurance
Transportation: Commute: 92.2% car, 0.8% public transportation, 4.3% walk, 1.0% work from home; Mean travel time to work: 18.2 minutes

ARCANUM (village). Covers a land area of 1.299 square miles and a water area of 0 square miles. Located at 39.99° N. Lat; 84.55° W. Long. Elevation is 1,047 feet.
Population: 2,272; Growth (since 2000): 9.4%; Density: 1,748.4 persons per square mile; Race: 99.9% White, 0.0% Black/African American, 0.0% Asian, 0.0% American Indian/Alaska Native, 0.0% Native Hawaiian/Other Pacific Islander, 0.1% Two or more races, 1.4% Hispanic of any race; Average household size: 2.43; Median age: 37.2; Age under 18: 25.8%; Age 65 and over: 14.3%; Males per 100 females: 89.9; Marriage status: 22.3% never married, 59.0% now married, 4.1% separated, 6.5% widowed, 12.1% divorced; Foreign born: 0.5%; Speak English only: 99.1%; With disability: 11.1%; Veterans: 8.0%; Ancestry: 33.9% German, 12.7% American, 10.0% Irish, 8.2% Italian, 7.4% English
Employment: 10.9% management, business, and financial, 3.3% computer, engineering, and science, 9.8% education, legal, community service, arts, and media, 4.2% healthcare practitioners, 14.2% service, 23.4% sales and office, 9.7% natural resources, construction, and maintenance, 24.4% production, transportation, and material moving
Income: Per capita: $23,464; Median household: $49,392; Average household: $56,042; Households with income of $100,000 or more: 13.2%; Poverty rate: 10.2%
Educational Attainment: High school diploma or higher: 92.5%; Bachelor's degree or higher: 16.2%; Graduate/professional degree or higher: 5.5%

School District(s)

Arcanum-Butler Local (KG-12)
2015-16 Enrollment: 1,054 . . . . (937) 692-5174
Franklin Monroe Local (KG-12)
2015-16 Enrollment: 738. . . . . (937) 947-1212

Housing: Homeownership rate: 67.1%; Median home value: $102,300; Median year structure built: 1953; Homeowner vacancy rate: 1.7%; Median selected monthly owner costs: $1,067 with a mortgage, $374 without a mortgage; Median gross rent: $637 per month; Rental vacancy rate: 0.0%
Health Insurance: 94.4% have insurance; 83.8% have private insurance; 26.4% have public insurance; 5.6% do not have insurance; 0.0% of children under 18 do not have insurance
Transportation: Commute: 93.3% car, 0.0% public transportation, 4.5% walk, 1.7% work from home; Mean travel time to work: 24.7 minutes

CASTINE (village). Covers a land area of 0.076 square miles and a water area of 0 square miles. Located at 39.93° N. Lat; 84.62° W. Long. Elevation is 1,076 feet.
Population: 127; Growth (since 2000): -1.6%; Density: 1,675.4 persons per square mile; Race: 97.6% White, 0.0% Black/African American, 0.0% Asian, 1.6% American Indian/Alaska Native, 0.0% Native Hawaiian/Other Pacific Islander, 0.8% Two or more races, 1.6% Hispanic of any race; Average household size: 2.49; Median age: 34.5; Age under 18: 14.2%; Age 65 and over: 14.2%; Males per 100 females: 97.0; Marriage status: 38.5% never married, 45.0% now married, 1.8% separated, 3.7% widowed, 12.8% divorced; Foreign born: 1.6%; Speak English only: 98.3%; With disability: 26.8%; Veterans: 17.4%; Ancestry: 19.7% German, 7.1% American, 4.7% English, 3.1% Irish, 1.6% French
Employment: 10.3% management, business, and financial, 0.0% computer, engineering, and science, 2.9% education, legal, community service, arts, and media, 0.0% healthcare practitioners, 2.9% service, 23.5% sales and office, 1.5% natural resources, construction, and maintenance, 58.8% production, transportation, and material moving
Income: Per capita: $18,130; Median household: $46,250; Average household: $43,151; Households with income of $100,000 or more: n/a; Poverty rate: 15.7%
Educational Attainment: High school diploma or higher: 89.9%; Bachelor's degree or higher: 1.4%; Graduate/professional degree or higher: n/a
Housing: Homeownership rate: 56.9%; Median home value: $80,400; Median year structure built: Before 1940; Homeowner vacancy rate: 0.0%; Median selected monthly owner costs: $750 with a mortgage, $185 without a mortgage; Median gross rent: $540 per month; Rental vacancy rate: 0.0%
Health Insurance: 100.0% have insurance; 56.7% have private insurance; 52.8% have public insurance; 0.0% do not have insurance; 0.0% of children under 18 do not have insurance
Transportation: Commute: 91.2% car, 0.0% public transportation, 0.0% walk, 8.8% work from home; Mean travel time to work: 21.1 minutes

GETTYSBURG (village). Covers a land area of 0.436 square miles and a water area of <.001 square miles. Located at 40.12° N. Lat; 84.50° W. Long. Elevation is 994 feet.
Population: 613; Growth (since 2000): 9.9%; Density: 1,406.7 persons per square mile; Race: 99.5% White, 0.0% Black/African American, 0.0% Asian, 0.0% American Indian/Alaska Native, 0.0% Native Hawaiian/Other Pacific Islander, 0.5% Two or more races, 1.5% Hispanic of any race; Average household size: 2.77; Median age: 32.8; Age under 18: 27.9%; Age 65 and over: 11.1%; Males per 100 females: 96.6; Marriage status: 27.5% never married, 51.5% now married, 3.2% separated, 5.4% widowed, 15.7% divorced; Foreign born: 0.3%; Speak English only: 98.2%; With disability: 23.5%; Veterans: 7.9%; Ancestry: 42.6% German, 14.5% Irish, 7.0% American, 4.6% French, 3.4% English
Employment: 4.2% management, business, and financial, 4.2% computer, engineering, and science, 6.9% education, legal, community service, arts, and media, 3.4% healthcare practitioners, 15.3% service, 23.4% sales and office, 10.3% natural resources, construction, and maintenance, 32.2% production, transportation, and material moving
Income: Per capita: $14,974; Median household: $34,583; Average household: $41,538; Households with income of $100,000 or more: 2.7%; Poverty rate: 34.0%
Educational Attainment: High school diploma or higher: 88.2%; Bachelor's degree or higher: 3.9%; Graduate/professional degree or higher: 0.8%
Housing: Homeownership rate: 67.4%; Median home value: $76,300; Median year structure built: Before 1940; Homeowner vacancy rate: 3.2%; Median selected monthly owner costs: $808 with a mortgage, $412 without a mortgage; Median gross rent: $753 per month; Rental vacancy rate: 6.5%
Health Insurance: 89.7% have insurance; 58.7% have private insurance; 45.2% have public insurance; 10.3% do not have insurance; 11.1% of children under 18 do not have insurance
Transportation: Commute: 97.3% car, 1.9% public transportation, 0.0% walk, 0.8% work from home; Mean travel time to work: 21.4 minutes

GORDON (village). Covers a land area of 0.165 square miles and a water area of 0 square miles. Located at 39.93° N. Lat; 84.51° W. Long. Elevation is 1,047 feet.
Population: 213; Growth (since 2000): 12.1%; Density: 1,294.3 persons per square mile; Race: 92.0% White, 0.9% Black/African American, 0.0% Asian, 2.3% American Indian/Alaska Native, 0.0% Native Hawaiian/Other Pacific Islander, 4.7% Two or more races, 1.9% Hispanic of any race; Average household size: 2.70; Median age: 45.3; Age under 18: 16.4%; Age 65 and over: 8.5%; Males per 100 females: 114.1; Marriage status: 31.3% never married, 53.3% now married, 0.5% separated, 6.0% widowed, 9.3% divorced; Foreign born: 0.0%; Speak English only: 98.1%; With disability: 10.8%; Veterans: 7.9%; Ancestry: 17.8% German, 12.2% Irish, 6.1% American, 6.1% English, 5.2% Scotch-Irish
Employment: 16.7% management, business, and financial, 2.6% computer, engineering, and science, 7.0% education, legal, community

service, arts, and media, 7.0% healthcare practitioners, 12.3% service, 8.8% sales and office, 15.8% natural resources, construction, and maintenance, 29.8% production, transportation, and material moving
Income: Per capita: $24,453; Median household: $51,563; Average household: $61,797; Households with income of $100,000 or more: 17.8%; Poverty rate: 11.0%
Educational Attainment: High school diploma or higher: 96.8%; Bachelor's degree or higher: 9.7%; Graduate/professional degree or higher: 3.9%
Housing: Homeownership rate: 83.5%; Median home value: $83,600; Median year structure built: Before 1940; Homeowner vacancy rate: 0.0%; Median selected monthly owner costs: $770 with a mortgage, $375 without a mortgage; Median gross rent: $775 per month; Rental vacancy rate: 0.0%
Health Insurance: 89.2% have insurance; 75.6% have private insurance; 22.5% have public insurance; 10.8% do not have insurance; 0.0% of children under 18 do not have insurance
Transportation: Commute: 92.0% car, 0.0% public transportation, 1.8% walk, 4.4% work from home; Mean travel time to work: 25.5 minutes

---

GREENVILLE (city). County seat. Covers a land area of 6.604 square miles and a water area of 0.063 square miles. Located at 40.10° N. Lat; 84.62° W. Long. Elevation is 1,043 feet.
History: Fort Greenville, established here and named for General Nathanael Greene, was abandoned in 1795. A town was founded here in 1805 by the Swawnee chieftain, Tecumseh, and his brother, Tenakwatawa, known as The Prophet. After Prophet's Town was moved to Indiana, other settlers came and the town of Greenville was founded.
Population: 12,979; Growth (since 2000): -2.4%; Density: 1,965.3 persons per square mile; Race: 96.6% White, 1.5% Black/African American, 0.5% Asian, 0.5% American Indian/Alaska Native, 0.0% Native Hawaiian/Other Pacific Islander, 0.7% Two or more races, 1.1% Hispanic of any race; Average household size: 2.09; Median age: 43.8; Age under 18: 21.3%; Age 65 and over: 23.8%; Males per 100 females: 85.4; Marriage status: 27.2% never married, 42.9% now married, 2.0% separated, 13.4% widowed, 16.5% divorced; Foreign born: 0.6%; Speak English only: 98.2%; With disability: 21.2%; Veterans: 10.2%; Ancestry: 36.7% German, 14.9% Irish, 10.8% American, 9.0% English, 3.0% French
Employment: 8.2% management, business, and financial, 2.2% computer, engineering, and science, 4.5% education, legal, community service, arts, and media, 3.7% healthcare practitioners, 17.8% service, 25.9% sales and office, 10.3% natural resources, construction, and maintenance, 27.4% production, transportation, and material moving
Income: Per capita: $21,434; Median household: $35,471; Average household: $44,367; Households with income of $100,000 or more: 6.9%; Poverty rate: 17.7%
Educational Attainment: High school diploma or higher: 87.5%; Bachelor's degree or higher: 11.7%; Graduate/professional degree or higher: 3.8%

School District(s)

Greenville City (KG-12)
2015-16 Enrollment: 2,592 . . . . (937) 548-3185
Housing: Homeownership rate: 52.5%; Median home value: $87,600; Median year structure built: 1958; Homeowner vacancy rate: 2.5%; Median selected monthly owner costs: $870 with a mortgage, $356 without a mortgage; Median gross rent: $609 per month; Rental vacancy rate: 6.9%
Health Insurance: 92.0% have insurance; 60.9% have private insurance; 49.8% have public insurance; 8.0% do not have insurance; 0.6% of children under 18 do not have insurance
Hospitals: Wayne Hospital (92 beds)
Safety: Violent crime rate: 33.9 per 10,000 population; Property crime rate: 243.0 per 10,000 population
Newspapers: Daily Advocate (daily circulation 6,500); The Early Bird (weekly circulation 22,400)
Transportation: Commute: 90.6% car, 1.8% public transportation, 2.6% walk, 2.9% work from home; Mean travel time to work: 18.8 minutes
Additional Information Contacts
City of Greenville . . . . (937) 548-1819
http://www.cityofgreenville.org

HOLLANSBURG (village). Covers a land area of 0.121 square miles and a water area of 0 square miles. Located at 40.00° N. Lat; 84.79° W. Long. Elevation is 1,161 feet.
Population: 253; Growth (since 2000): 18.2%; Density: 2,092.3 persons per square mile; Race: 99.6% White, 0.0% Black/African American, 0.4% Asian, 0.0% American Indian/Alaska Native, 0.0% Native Hawaiian/Other Pacific Islander, 0.0% Two or more races, 0.0% Hispanic of any race; Average household size: 2.56; Median age: 42.4; Age under 18: 25.7%; Age 65 and over: 17.4%; Males per 100 females: 116.2; Marriage status: 20.7% never married, 59.1% now married, 0.0% separated, 8.3% widowed, 11.9% divorced; Foreign born: 0.0%; Speak English only: 98.3%; With disability: 17.8%; Veterans: 8.0%; Ancestry: 34.0% German, 11.5% Irish, 7.9% American, 5.5% English, 5.1% Dutch
Employment: 5.8% management, business, and financial, 0.0% computer, engineering, and science, 9.7% education, legal, community service, arts, and media, 6.8% healthcare practitioners, 14.6% service, 13.6% sales and office, 28.2% natural resources, construction, and maintenance, 21.4% production, transportation, and material moving
Income: Per capita: $17,100; Median household: $33,438; Average household: $42,174; Households with income of $100,000 or more: 2.0%; Poverty rate: 19.6%
Educational Attainment: High school diploma or higher: 81.3%; Bachelor's degree or higher: 11.4%; Graduate/professional degree or higher: 1.7%
Housing: Homeownership rate: 74.7%; Median home value: $50,000; Median year structure built: Before 1940; Homeowner vacancy rate: 0.0%; Median selected monthly owner costs: $800 with a mortgage, $280 without a mortgage; Median gross rent: $575 per month; Rental vacancy rate: 16.7%
Health Insurance: 94.5% have insurance; 55.3% have private insurance; 54.9% have public insurance; 5.5% do not have insurance; 0.0% of children under 18 do not have insurance
Transportation: Commute: 95.1% car, 0.0% public transportation, 2.9% walk, 0.0% work from home; Mean travel time to work: 27.3 minutes

---

ITHACA (village). Covers a land area of 0.031 square miles and a water area of 0 square miles. Located at 39.94° N. Lat; 84.55° W. Long. Elevation is 1,033 feet.
Population: 132; Growth (since 2000): 29.4%; Density: 4,227.0 persons per square mile; Race: 97.0% White, 0.0% Black/African American, 0.0% Asian, 0.0% American Indian/Alaska Native, 0.0% Native Hawaiian/Other Pacific Islander, 1.5% Two or more races, 0.0% Hispanic of any race; Average household size: 2.54; Median age: 36.0; Age under 18: 31.1%; Age 65 and over: 6.1%; Males per 100 females: 86.3; Marriage status: 31.0% never married, 56.0% now married, 0.0% separated, 3.4% widowed, 9.5% divorced; Foreign born: 0.0%; Speak English only: 100.0%; With disability: 9.8%; Veterans: 9.9%; Ancestry: 33.3% German, 10.6% English, 4.5% Russian, 2.3% Irish
Employment: 0.0% management, business, and financial, 0.0% computer, engineering, and science, 17.6% education, legal, community service, arts, and media, 0.0% healthcare practitioners, 5.4% service, 39.2% sales and office, 4.1% natural resources, construction, and maintenance, 33.8% production, transportation, and material moving
Income: Per capita: $15,174; Median household: $31,964; Average household: $38,227; Households with income of $100,000 or more: n/a; Poverty rate: 2.3%
Educational Attainment: High school diploma or higher: 91.3%; Bachelor's degree or higher: 2.5%; Graduate/professional degree or higher: 1.3%
Housing: Homeownership rate: 46.2%; Median home value: $48,000; Median year structure built: Before 1940; Homeowner vacancy rate: 17.2%; Median selected monthly owner costs: $664 with a mortgage, n/a without a mortgage; Median gross rent: $617 per month; Rental vacancy rate: 0.0%
Health Insurance: 97.0% have insurance; 82.6% have private insurance; 20.5% have public insurance; 3.0% do not have insurance; 0.0% of children under 18 do not have insurance
Transportation: Commute: 100.0% car, 0.0% public transportation, 0.0% walk, 0.0% work from home; Mean travel time to work: 22.8 minutes

---

NEW MADISON (village). Covers a land area of 0.410 square miles and a water area of 0 square miles. Located at 39.97° N. Lat; 84.71° W. Long. Elevation is 1,106 feet.
Population: 954; Growth (since 2000): 16.8%; Density: 2,325.9 persons per square mile; Race: 94.7% White, 0.0% Black/African American, 0.6% Asian, 0.1% American Indian/Alaska Native, 0.0% Native Hawaiian/Other Pacific Islander, 4.6% Two or more races, 1.0% Hispanic of any race; Average household size: 2.53; Median age: 32.3; Age under 18: 27.1%; Age 65 and over: 17.5%; Males per 100 females: 91.0; Marriage status: 27.0% never married, 51.8% now married, 1.5% separated, 8.0%

widowed, 13.2% divorced; Foreign born: 0.6%; Speak English only: 97.7%; With disability: 13.3%; Veterans: 10.2%; Ancestry: 26.1% German, 12.5% Irish, 10.6% American, 7.9% English, 2.3% French
Employment: 5.7% management, business, and financial, 2.4% computer, engineering, and science, 5.5% education, legal, community service, arts, and media, 5.5% healthcare practitioners, 15.7% service, 16.9% sales and office, 12.9% natural resources, construction, and maintenance, 35.5% production, transportation, and material moving
Income: Per capita: $22,507; Median household: $45,865; Average household: $55,350; Households with income of $100,000 or more: 5.9%; Poverty rate: 14.9%
Educational Attainment: High school diploma or higher: 90.7%; Bachelor's degree or higher: 10.4%; Graduate/professional degree or higher: 3.5%

School District(s)

Tri-Village Local (PK-12)
2015-16 Enrollment: 744. . . . . (937) 996-6261
Housing: Homeownership rate: 71.6%; Median home value: $77,400; Median year structure built: 1940; Homeowner vacancy rate: 0.0%; Median selected monthly owner costs: $914 with a mortgage, $351 without a mortgage; Median gross rent: $693 per month; Rental vacancy rate: 11.6%
Health Insurance: 91.9% have insurance; 70.9% have private insurance; 41.6% have public insurance; 8.1% do not have insurance; 5.4% of children under 18 do not have insurance
Transportation: Commute: 96.6% car, 0.5% public transportation, 1.7% walk, 0.5% work from home; Mean travel time to work: 27.1 minutes

NEW WESTON (village). Covers a land area of 0.256 square miles and a water area of 0 square miles. Located at 40.34° N. Lat; 84.64° W. Long. Elevation is 1,010 feet.
Population: 110; Growth (since 2000): -18.5%; Density: 430.1 persons per square mile; Race: 96.4% White, 0.0% Black/African American, 0.0% Asian, 0.9% American Indian/Alaska Native, 0.0% Native Hawaiian/Other Pacific Islander, 2.7% Two or more races, 0.9% Hispanic of any race; Average household size: 2.75; Median age: 30.6; Age under 18: 23.6%; Age 65 and over: 10.9%; Males per 100 females: 106.1; Marriage status: 43.5% never married, 31.8% now married, 0.0% separated, 17.6% widowed, 7.1% divorced; Foreign born: 0.0%; Speak English only: 96.8%; With disability: 20.0%; Veterans: 7.1%; Ancestry: 30.0% German, 29.1% Portuguese, 10.9% American, 10.0% English, 7.3% Scottish
Employment: 0.0% management, business, and financial, 4.5% computer, engineering, and science, 0.0% education, legal, community service, arts, and media, 0.0% healthcare practitioners, 6.8% service, 4.5% sales and office, 4.5% natural resources, construction, and maintenance, 79.5% production, transportation, and material moving
Income: Per capita: $16,166; Median household: $41,667; Average household: $43,210; Households with income of $100,000 or more: 2.5%; Poverty rate: 3.6%
Educational Attainment: High school diploma or higher: 51.4%; Bachelor's degree or higher: 2.7%; Graduate/professional degree or higher: 2.7%
Housing: Homeownership rate: 65.0%; Median home value: $71,800; Median year structure built: 1941; Homeowner vacancy rate: 0.0%; Median selected monthly owner costs: $818 with a mortgage, $375 without a mortgage; Median gross rent: $708 per month; Rental vacancy rate: 0.0%
Health Insurance: 86.4% have insurance; 44.5% have private insurance; 48.2% have public insurance; 13.6% do not have insurance; 0.0% of children under 18 do not have insurance
Transportation: Commute: 95.5% car, 0.0% public transportation, 0.0% walk, 0.0% work from home; Mean travel time to work: 18.8 minutes

NORTH STAR (village). Covers a land area of 0.525 square miles and a water area of 0 square miles. Located at 40.32° N. Lat; 84.57° W. Long. Elevation is 1,007 feet.
History: North Star was founded in 1844 by John Houston and Heronimus Star. This was the birthplace of Annie Oakley, born in 1860, who became an expert markswoman.
Population: 269; Growth (since 2000): 28.7%; Density: 512.6 persons per square mile; Race: 100.0% White, 0.0% Black/African American, 0.0% Asian, 0.0% American Indian/Alaska Native, 0.0% Native Hawaiian/Other Pacific Islander, 0.0% Two or more races, 0.0% Hispanic of any race; Average household size: 2.89; Median age: 32.3; Age under 18: 28.6%; Age 65 and over: 18.2%; Males per 100 females: 90.3; Marriage status: 26.1% never married, 59.9% now married, 0.0% separated, 10.6% widowed, 3.4% divorced; Foreign born: 0.0%; Speak English only: 99.6%; With disability: 9.3%; Veterans: 7.3%; Ancestry: 74.3% German, 23.8% French, 7.4% Irish, 4.8% American, 1.5% English
Employment: 10.6% management, business, and financial, 5.7% computer, engineering, and science, 9.9% education, legal, community service, arts, and media, 5.0% healthcare practitioners, 12.8% service, 19.9% sales and office, 14.9% natural resources, construction, and maintenance, 21.3% production, transportation, and material moving
Income: Per capita: $22,916; Median household: $56,250; Average household: $64,596; Households with income of $100,000 or more: 18.3%; Poverty rate: 3.0%
Educational Attainment: High school diploma or higher: 90.9%; Bachelor's degree or higher: 17.6%; Graduate/professional degree or higher: 7.9%
Housing: Homeownership rate: 89.2%; Median home value: $123,400; Median year structure built: 1962; Homeowner vacancy rate: 0.0%; Median selected monthly owner costs: $1,026 with a mortgage, $414 without a mortgage; Median gross rent: $838 per month; Rental vacancy rate: 0.0%
Health Insurance: 97.8% have insurance; 95.2% have private insurance; 22.3% have public insurance; 2.2% do not have insurance; 0.0% of children under 18 do not have insurance
Transportation: Commute: 99.3% car, 0.0% public transportation, 0.7% walk, 0.0% work from home; Mean travel time to work: 21.0 minutes

OSGOOD (village). Covers a land area of 0.341 square miles and a water area of 0 square miles. Located at 40.34° N. Lat; 84.50° W. Long. Elevation is 958 feet.
Population: 291; Growth (since 2000): 14.1%; Density: 853.2 persons per square mile; Race: 99.3% White, 0.7% Black/African American, 0.0% Asian, 0.0% American Indian/Alaska Native, 0.0% Native Hawaiian/Other Pacific Islander, 0.0% Two or more races, 0.0% Hispanic of any race; Average household size: 2.81; Median age: 38.3; Age under 18: 28.5%; Age 65 and over: 22.0%; Males per 100 females: 111.2; Marriage status: 23.0% never married, 63.8% now married, 0.0% separated, 10.8% widowed, 2.3% divorced; Foreign born: 0.3%; Speak English only: 98.9%; With disability: 7.9%; Veterans: 9.1%; Ancestry: 69.8% German, 13.4% American, 13.1% French, 2.4% English, 1.4% Irish
Employment: 11.9% management, business, and financial, 6.7% computer, engineering, and science, 11.9% education, legal, community service, arts, and media, 8.9% healthcare practitioners, 4.4% service, 8.9% sales and office, 14.1% natural resources, construction, and maintenance, 33.3% production, transportation, and material moving
Income: Per capita: $26,232; Median household: $66,563; Average household: $72,123; Households with income of $100,000 or more: 17.5%; Poverty rate: 2.1%
Educational Attainment: High school diploma or higher: 92.4%; Bachelor's degree or higher: 18.5%; Graduate/professional degree or higher: 10.9%
Housing: Homeownership rate: 92.2%; Median home value: $136,700; Median year structure built: 1958; Homeowner vacancy rate: 2.0%; Median selected monthly owner costs: $1,146 with a mortgage, $450 without a mortgage; Median gross rent: $700 per month; Rental vacancy rate: 0.0%
Health Insurance: 95.9% have insurance; 89.0% have private insurance; 26.1% have public insurance; 4.1% do not have insurance; 0.0% of children under 18 do not have insurance
Transportation: Commute: 90.4% car, 0.0% public transportation, 0.7% walk, 7.4% work from home; Mean travel time to work: 22.5 minutes

PALESTINE (village). Covers a land area of 0.146 square miles and a water area of 0 square miles. Located at 40.05° N. Lat; 84.74° W. Long. Elevation is 1,109 feet.
Population: 229; Growth (since 2000): 34.7%; Density: 1,567.7 persons per square mile; Race: 82.1% White, 17.9% Black/African American, 0.0% Asian, 0.0% American Indian/Alaska Native, 0.0% Native Hawaiian/Other Pacific Islander, 0.0% Two or more races, 0.0% Hispanic of any race; Average household size: 2.63; Median age: 37.4; Age under 18: 31.9%; Age 65 and over: 14.8%; Males per 100 females: 100.0; Marriage status: 22.7% never married, 59.7% now married, 0.0% separated, 6.3% widowed, 11.4% divorced; Foreign born: 0.0%; Speak English only: 83.3%; With disability: 15.3%; Veterans: 18.6%; Ancestry: 30.6% German, 17.9% African, 16.2% Irish, 7.4% English, 3.9% American
Employment: 7.8% management, business, and financial, 0.0% computer, engineering, and science, 1.0% education, legal, community service, arts, and media, 9.7% healthcare practitioners, 17.5% service, 7.8% sales and office, 17.5% natural resources, construction, and maintenance, 38.8% production, transportation, and material moving

Income: Per capita: $18,333; Median household: $31,250; Average household: $44,367; Households with income of $100,000 or more: 3.4%; Poverty rate: 28.9%
Educational Attainment: High school diploma or higher: 87.9%; Bachelor's degree or higher: 1.3%; Graduate/professional degree or higher: 1.3%
Housing: Homeownership rate: 66.7%; Median home value: $61,300; Median year structure built: Before 1940; Homeowner vacancy rate: 0.0%; Median selected monthly owner costs: $736 with a mortgage, $289 without a mortgage; Median gross rent: $642 per month; Rental vacancy rate: 0.0%
Health Insurance: 93.4% have insurance; 72.9% have private insurance; 34.5% have public insurance; 6.6% do not have insurance; 0.0% of children under 18 do not have insurance
Transportation: Commute: 99.0% car, 0.0% public transportation, 1.0% walk, 0.0% work from home; Mean travel time to work: 25.8 minutes

PITSBURG (village). Covers a land area of 0.189 square miles and a water area of 0 square miles. Located at 39.99° N. Lat; 84.49° W. Long. Elevation is 1,024 feet.
History: Also spelled Pittsburg.
Population: 418; Growth (since 2000): 6.6%; Density: 2,208.7 persons per square mile; Race: 96.9% White, 0.0% Black/African American, 0.2% Asian, 0.2% American Indian/Alaska Native, 0.0% Native Hawaiian/Other Pacific Islander, 2.6% Two or more races, 0.0% Hispanic of any race; Average household size: 2.73; Median age: 36.3; Age under 18: 24.6%; Age 65 and over: 13.4%; Males per 100 females: 92.1; Marriage status: 20.7% never married, 64.9% now married, 1.2% separated, 3.3% widowed, 11.1% divorced; Foreign born: 0.2%; Speak English only: 97.5%; With disability: 9.6%; Veterans: 8.3%; Ancestry: 45.9% German, 16.0% Irish, 10.3% English, 9.1% American, 4.8% Italian
Employment: 11.5% management, business, and financial, 4.1% computer, engineering, and science, 5.5% education, legal, community service, arts, and media, 7.8% healthcare practitioners, 20.2% service, 20.6% sales and office, 11.9% natural resources, construction, and maintenance, 18.3% production, transportation, and material moving
Income: Per capita: $27,333; Median household: $57,321; Average household: $73,443; Households with income of $100,000 or more: 17.7%; Poverty rate: 10.1%
Educational Attainment: High school diploma or higher: 93.5%; Bachelor's degree or higher: 7.3%; Graduate/professional degree or higher: 0.8%
Housing: Homeownership rate: 77.8%; Median home value: $93,100; Median year structure built: Before 1940; Homeowner vacancy rate: 0.0%; Median selected monthly owner costs: $1,039 with a mortgage, $492 without a mortgage; Median gross rent: $595 per month; Rental vacancy rate: 2.9%
Health Insurance: 85.6% have insurance; 65.8% have private insurance; 28.5% have public insurance; 14.4% do not have insurance; 13.6% of children under 18 do not have insurance
Transportation: Commute: 95.3% car, 0.0% public transportation, 2.3% walk, 2.3% work from home; Mean travel time to work: 25.5 minutes

ROSSBURG (village). Covers a land area of 0.140 square miles and a water area of 0 square miles. Located at 40.28° N. Lat; 84.64° W. Long. Elevation is 1,030 feet.
Population: 249; Growth (since 2000): 11.2%; Density: 1,776.0 persons per square mile; Race: 98.8% White, 0.0% Black/African American, 0.4% Asian, 0.0% American Indian/Alaska Native, 0.0% Native Hawaiian/Other Pacific Islander, 0.8% Two or more races, 0.0% Hispanic of any race; Average household size: 2.71; Median age: 39.6; Age under 18: 20.9%; Age 65 and over: 9.6%; Males per 100 females: 103.0; Marriage status: 27.8% never married, 51.2% now married, 0.5% separated, 5.4% widowed, 15.6% divorced; Foreign born: 0.4%; Speak English only: 99.1%; With disability: 10.0%; Veterans: 3.0%; Ancestry: 41.0% German, 11.2% American, 8.8% Irish, 6.4% English, 2.8% Swiss
Employment: 7.6% management, business, and financial, 0.7% computer, engineering, and science, 1.4% education, legal, community service, arts, and media, 6.9% healthcare practitioners, 6.9% service, 13.8% sales and office, 24.8% natural resources, construction, and maintenance, 37.9% production, transportation, and material moving
Income: Per capita: $20,090; Median household: $49,500; Average household: $51,258; Households with income of $100,000 or more: 8.7%; Poverty rate: 8.5%
Educational Attainment: High school diploma or higher: 89.2%; Bachelor's degree or higher: 9.7%; Graduate/professional degree or higher: 2.8%
Housing: Homeownership rate: 76.1%; Median home value: $62,500; Median year structure built: 1953; Homeowner vacancy rate: 0.0%; Median selected monthly owner costs: $767 with a mortgage, $407 without a mortgage; Median gross rent: $563 per month; Rental vacancy rate: 0.0%
Health Insurance: 89.2% have insurance; 78.7% have private insurance; 19.7% have public insurance; 10.8% do not have insurance; 15.4% of children under 18 do not have insurance
Transportation: Commute: 97.9% car, 0.0% public transportation, 0.0% walk, 1.4% work from home; Mean travel time to work: 23.8 minutes

UNION CITY (village). Covers a land area of 0.919 square miles and a water area of 0.047 square miles. Located at 40.20° N. Lat; 84.79° W. Long. Elevation is 1,106 feet.
Population: 1,803; Growth (since 2000): 2.0%; Density: 1,961.1 persons per square mile; Race: 95.2% White, 1.1% Black/African American, 0.0% Asian, 0.0% American Indian/Alaska Native, 0.0% Native Hawaiian/Other Pacific Islander, 1.4% Two or more races, 12.0% Hispanic of any race; Average household size: 2.45; Median age: 36.6; Age under 18: 28.5%; Age 65 and over: 17.0%; Males per 100 females: 90.0; Marriage status: 34.1% never married, 38.2% now married, 4.6% separated, 7.9% widowed, 19.8% divorced; Foreign born: 3.3%; Speak English only: 89.5%; With disability: 20.4%; Veterans: 7.4%; Ancestry: 39.5% German, 16.1% Irish, 9.2% American, 7.9% English, 3.1% Italian
Employment: 3.8% management, business, and financial, 1.3% computer, engineering, and science, 2.9% education, legal, community service, arts, and media, 7.5% healthcare practitioners, 22.5% service, 13.3% sales and office, 7.3% natural resources, construction, and maintenance, 41.4% production, transportation, and material moving
Income: Per capita: $15,084; Median household: $27,206; Average household: $35,762; Households with income of $100,000 or more: 4.0%; Poverty rate: 34.1%
Educational Attainment: High school diploma or higher: 76.4%; Bachelor's degree or higher: 5.4%; Graduate/professional degree or higher: 0.5%

School District(s)

Mississinawa Valley Local (PK-12)
2015-16 Enrollment: 686. . . . . (937) 968-5656
Housing: Homeownership rate: 49.0%; Median home value: $57,100; Median year structure built: 1955; Homeowner vacancy rate: 2.6%; Median selected monthly owner costs: $684 with a mortgage, $315 without a mortgage; Median gross rent: $463 per month; Rental vacancy rate: 0.0%
Health Insurance: 88.5% have insurance; 47.1% have private insurance; 55.7% have public insurance; 11.5% do not have insurance; 4.1% of children under 18 do not have insurance
Transportation: Commute: 92.7% car, 0.5% public transportation, 4.6% walk, 1.2% work from home; Mean travel time to work: 22.0 minutes

VERSAILLES (village). Covers a land area of 1.867 square miles and a water area of 0.006 square miles. Located at 40.22° N. Lat; 84.48° W. Long. Elevation is 981 feet.
History: Settled 1819, incorporated 1855.
Population: 2,690; Growth (since 2000): 3.9%; Density: 1,441.0 persons per square mile; Race: 99.4% White, 0.0% Black/African American, 0.0% Asian, 0.0% American Indian/Alaska Native, 0.0% Native Hawaiian/Other Pacific Islander, 0.6% Two or more races, 0.0% Hispanic of any race; Average household size: 2.44; Median age: 43.0; Age under 18: 24.9%; Age 65 and over: 23.2%; Males per 100 females: 91.4; Marriage status: 20.9% never married, 57.6% now married, 2.0% separated, 9.6% widowed, 11.8% divorced; Foreign born: 0.1%; Speak English only: 99.8%; With disability: 11.6%; Veterans: 11.8%; Ancestry: 45.8% German, 25.7% French, 12.9% Irish, 8.4% American, 8.2% English
Employment: 15.6% management, business, and financial, 3.4% computer, engineering, and science, 6.9% education, legal, community service, arts, and media, 6.0% healthcare practitioners, 12.2% service, 16.1% sales and office, 8.9% natural resources, construction, and maintenance, 30.9% production, transportation, and material moving
Income: Per capita: $27,823; Median household: $47,199; Average household: $70,205; Households with income of $100,000 or more: 19.1%; Poverty rate: 7.8%
Educational Attainment: High school diploma or higher: 90.3%; Bachelor's degree or higher: 18.6%; Graduate/professional degree or higher: 6.7%

School District(s)

Versailles Exempted Village (KG-12)
2015-16 Enrollment: 1,458 . . . . (937) 526-4773

Housing: Homeownership rate: 75.5%; Median home value: $135,700; Median year structure built: 1952; Homeowner vacancy rate: 2.3%; Median selected monthly owner costs: $1,087 with a mortgage, $384 without a mortgage; Median gross rent: $571 per month; Rental vacancy rate: 11.6%

Health Insurance: 95.6% have insurance; 79.9% have private insurance; 31.2% have public insurance; 4.4% do not have insurance; 0.0% of children under 18 do not have insurance

Newspapers: Versailles Policy (weekly circulation 2,400)

Transportation: Commute: 92.7% car, 0.7% public transportation, 3.1% walk, 0.9% work from home; Mean travel time to work: 18.0 minutes

Additional Information Contacts

Village of Versailles . . . . (937) 526-3294
http://www.versaillesohio.cc

WAYNE LAKES (village). Covers a land area of 0.530 square miles and a water area of 0.119 square miles. Located at 40.02° N. Lat; 84.66° W. Long. Elevation is 1,047 feet.

Population: 642; Growth (since 2000): -6.1%; Density: 1,210.3 persons per square mile; Race: 88.2% White, 2.6% Black/African American, 0.0% Asian, 1.1% American Indian/Alaska Native, 0.0% Native Hawaiian/Other Pacific Islander, 7.8% Two or more races, 0.3% Hispanic of any race; Average household size: 2.24; Median age: 49.2; Age under 18: 19.8%; Age 65 and over: 20.9%; Males per 100 females: 97.8; Marriage status: 18.1% never married, 60.6% now married, 2.8% separated, 8.5% widowed, 12.8% divorced; Foreign born: 0.6%; Speak English only: 97.7%; With disability: 15.1%; Veterans: 13.6%; Ancestry: 29.6% German, 18.8% American, 10.1% Irish, 10.0% English, 3.3% Dutch

Employment: 16.7% management, business, and financial, 3.5% computer, engineering, and science, 7.6% education, legal, community service, arts, and media, 2.2% healthcare practitioners, 15.5% service, 15.1% sales and office, 7.3% natural resources, construction, and maintenance, 32.2% production, transportation, and material moving

Income: Per capita: $24,324; Median household: $47,917; Average household: $52,432; Households with income of $100,000 or more: 9.8%; Poverty rate: 5.2%

Educational Attainment: High school diploma or higher: 94.4%; Bachelor's degree or higher: 15.6%; Graduate/professional degree or higher: 5.2%

Housing: Homeownership rate: 75.6%; Median home value: $98,000; Median year structure built: 1963; Homeowner vacancy rate: 8.1%; Median selected monthly owner costs: $939 with a mortgage, $409 without a mortgage; Median gross rent: $627 per month; Rental vacancy rate: 0.0%

Health Insurance: 94.7% have insurance; 74.1% have private insurance; 38.5% have public insurance; 5.3% do not have insurance; 4.7% of children under 18 do not have insurance

Transportation: Commute: 97.5% car, 0.0% public transportation, 0.0% walk, 0.9% work from home; Mean travel time to work: 28.9 minutes

---

YORKSHIRE (village). Covers a land area of 0.283 square miles and a water area of 0 square miles. Located at 40.33° N. Lat; 84.50° W. Long. Elevation is 981 feet.

Population: 100; Growth (since 2000): -9.1%; Density: 353.9 persons per square mile; Race: 100.0% White, 0.0% Black/African American, 0.0% Asian, 0.0% American Indian/Alaska Native, 0.0% Native Hawaiian/Other Pacific Islander, 0.0% Two or more races, 0.0% Hispanic of any race; Average household size: 2.70; Median age: 29.0; Age under 18: 35.0%; Age 65 and over: 6.0%; Males per 100 females: 113.3; Marriage status: 46.5% never married, 42.3% now married, 0.0% separated, 7.0% widowed, 4.2% divorced; Foreign born: 0.0%; Speak English only: 100.0%; With disability: 8.0%; Veterans: 4.6%; Ancestry: 44.0% German, 14.0% American, 5.0% French

Employment: 12.3% management, business, and financial, 0.0% computer, engineering, and science, 0.0% education, legal, community service, arts, and media, 1.8% healthcare practitioners, 1.8% service, 21.1% sales and office, 15.8% natural resources, construction, and maintenance, 47.4% production, transportation, and material moving

Income: Per capita: $19,684; Median household: $54,688; Average household: $52,781; Households with income of $100,000 or more: 5.4%; Poverty rate: 3.1%

Educational Attainment: High school diploma or higher: 68.6%; Bachelor's degree or higher: 2.0%; Graduate/professional degree or higher: n/a

Housing: Homeownership rate: 78.4%; Median home value: $67,500; Median year structure built: Before 1940; Homeowner vacancy rate: 0.0%; Median selected monthly owner costs: $779 with a mortgage, $400 without a mortgage; Median gross rent: n/a per month; Rental vacancy rate: 0.0%

Health Insurance: 83.0% have insurance; 57.0% have private insurance; 37.0% have public insurance; 17.0% do not have insurance; 14.3% of children under 18 do not have insurance

Transportation: Commute: 94.4% car, 0.0% public transportation, 0.0% walk, 0.0% work from home; Mean travel time to work: 20.1 minutes

Defiance County

Located in northwestern Ohio; bounded on the west by Indiana; intersected by the Maumee, Auglize, and Tiffin Rivers. Covers a land area of 411.460 square miles, a water area of 2.730 square miles, and is located in the Eastern Time Zone at 41.32° N. Lat., 84.49° W. Long. The county was founded in 1845. County seat is Defiance.

Defiance County is part of the Defiance, OH Micropolitan Statistical Area. The entire metro area includes: Defiance County, OH

Weather Station: Defiance Elevation: 700 feet

	Jan	Feb	Mar	Apr	May	Jun	Jul	Aug	Sep	Oct	Nov	Dec
High	32	35	46	60	71	81	84	82	76	63	49	36
Low	17	19	27	38	48	58	62	61	53	42	32	22
Precip	2.0	2.1	2.5	3.4	3.9	3.6	4.1	3.2	3.3	3.0	3.0	2.7
Snow	6.7	5.6	2.5	0.5	tr	0.0	0.0	0.0	0.0	0.1	0.9	4.5

High and Low temperatures in degrees Fahrenheit; Precipitation and Snow in inches

Population: 38,488; Growth (since 2000): -2.6%; Density: 93.5 persons per square mile; Race: 91.7% White, 1.9% Black/African American, 0.4% Asian, 0.4% American Indian/Alaska Native, 0.0% Native Hawaiian/Other Pacific Islander, 2.1% two or more races, 9.5% Hispanic of any race; Average household size: 2.46; Median age: 39.9; Age under 18: 23.6%; Age 65 and over: 16.8%; Males per 100 females: 97.0; Marriage status: 26.2% never married, 56.4% now married, 2.0% separated, 6.2% widowed, 11.2% divorced; Foreign born: 1.8%; Speak English only: 95.4%; With disability: 13.2%; Veterans: 9.3%; Ancestry: 40.7% German, 12.5% Irish, 9.0% English, 7.4% American, 3.0% Italian

Religion: Six largest groups: 20.5% Catholicism, 15.7% Lutheran, 7.5% Methodist/Pietist, 5.5% Baptist, 4.7% Non-denominational Protestant, 2.6% Holiness

Economy: Unemployment rate: 4.3%; Leading industries: 17.3 % retail trade; 14.6 % other services (except public administration); 10.7 % health care and social assistance; Farms: 1,030 totaling 225,250 acres; Company size: 1 employs 1,000 or more persons, 1 employs 500 to 999 persons, 22 employ 100 to 499 persons, 789 employ less than 100 persons; Business ownership: 766 women-owned, n/a Black-owned, 44 Hispanic-owned, n/a Asian-owned, n/a American Indian/Alaska Native-owned

Employment: 10.2% management, business, and financial, 2.9% computer, engineering, and science, 7.4% education, legal, community service, arts, and media, 5.3% healthcare practitioners, 16.4% service, 22.8% sales and office, 9.4% natural resources, construction, and maintenance, 25.7% production, transportation, and material moving

Income: Per capita: $24,703; Median household: $50,822; Average household: $61,324; Households with income of $100,000 or more: 14.2%; Poverty rate: 13.6%

Educational Attainment: High school diploma or higher: 89.8%; Bachelor's degree or higher: 15.8%; Graduate/professional degree or higher: 5.3%

Housing: Homeownership rate: 74.7%; Median home value: $109,400; Median year structure built: 1965; Homeowner vacancy rate: 1.0%; Median selected monthly owner costs: $1,083 with a mortgage, $415 without a mortgage; Median gross rent: $669 per month; Rental vacancy rate: 6.2%

Vital Statistics: Birth rate: 110.9 per 10,000 population; Death rate: 107.2 per 10,000 population; Age-adjusted cancer mortality rate: 184.7 deaths per 100,000 population

Health Insurance: 90.9% have insurance; 73.1% have private insurance; 34.2% have public insurance; 9.1% do not have insurance; 6.1% of children under 18 do not have insurance

Health Care: Physicians: 12.3 per 10,000 population; Dentists: 3.4 per 10,000 population; Hospital beds: 21.5 per 10,000 population; Hospital admissions: 1,011.0 per 10,000 population

Transportation: Commute: 94.0% car, 0.3% public transportation, 2.1% walk, 2.8% work from home; Mean travel time to work: 20.3 minutes

2016 Presidential Election: 63.7% Trump, 29.3% Clinton, 4.3% Johnson, 0.8% Stein
National and State Parks: Independence Dam State Park; Oxbow Lake State Wildlife Area
Additional Information Contacts
Defiance Government . . . . (419) 782-4761
http://www.defiance-county.com

Defiance County Communities

DEFIANCE (city). County seat. Covers a land area of 11.617 square miles and a water area of 0.509 square miles. Located at 41.28° N. Lat; 84.37° W. Long. Elevation is 676 feet.
History: General Anthony Wayne built a fort here in 1794 and called it Fort Defiance. It was replaced in 1812 by General William Henry Harrison, who built Fort Winchester near Wayne's old fort. The town that developed after the War of 1812 was spurred by the Wabash & Erie Canal and the Miami & Erie Canal, which joined near here.
Population: 16,725; Growth (since 2000): 1.6%; Density: 1,439.6 persons per square mile; Race: 87.0% White, 3.5% Black/African American, 0.4% Asian, 0.4% American Indian/Alaska Native, 0.0% Native Hawaiian/Other Pacific Islander, 3.2% Two or more races, 14.7% Hispanic of any race; Average household size: 2.31; Median age: 37.5; Age under 18: 22.8%; Age 65 and over: 17.7%; Males per 100 females: 93.4; Marriage status: 31.5% never married, 49.3% now married, 1.9% separated, 8.0% widowed, 11.2% divorced; Foreign born: 1.8%; Speak English only: 94.1%; With disability: 14.9%; Veterans: 9.0%; Ancestry: 36.4% German, 11.6% Irish, 7.1% English, 6.9% American, 3.8% Italian
Employment: 9.9% management, business, and financial, 2.2% computer, engineering, and science, 9.5% education, legal, community service, arts, and media, 4.3% healthcare practitioners, 17.6% service, 24.5% sales and office, 6.6% natural resources, construction, and maintenance, 25.4% production, transportation, and material moving
Income: Per capita: $23,883; Median household: $43,855; Average household: $56,816; Households with income of $100,000 or more: 12.1%; Poverty rate: 18.8%
Educational Attainment: High school diploma or higher: 89.6%; Bachelor's degree or higher: 18.9%; Graduate/professional degree or higher: 6.2%

School District(s)

Ayersville Local (KG-12)
2015-16 Enrollment: 762. . . . . (419) 395-1111
Defiance City (KG-12)
2015-16 Enrollment: 2,452 . . . . (419) 782-0070
Northeastern Local (PK-12)
2015-16 Enrollment: 1,113 . . . . (419) 497-3461

Four-year College(s)

Defiance College (Private, Not-for-profit, United Church of Christ)
Fall 2016 Enrollment: 648 . . . . (419) 784-4010
2016-17 Tuition: In-state $31,680; Out-of-state $31,680
Housing: Homeownership rate: 63.0%; Median home value: $98,900; Median year structure built: 1960; Homeowner vacancy rate: 2.5%; Median selected monthly owner costs: $1,035 with a mortgage, $389 without a mortgage; Median gross rent: $684 per month; Rental vacancy rate: 4.9%
Health Insurance: 91.6% have insurance; 68.7% have private insurance; 40.7% have public insurance; 8.4% do not have insurance; 2.1% of children under 18 do not have insurance
Hospitals: Defiance Regional Medical Center (61 beds); Mercy Hospital of Defiance
Safety: Violent crime rate: 15.0 per 10,000 population; Property crime rate: 204.2 per 10,000 population
Newspapers: Crescent-News (daily circulation 17,300)
Transportation: Commute: 92.2% car, 0.4% public transportation, 3.7% walk, 2.1% work from home; Mean travel time to work: 16.9 minutes
Additional Information Contacts
City of Defiance . . . . (419) 784-2101
http://www.cityofdefiance.com

EVANSPORT (unincorporated postal area)

ZCTA: 43519

Covers a land area of 1.289 square miles and a water area of 0.003 square miles. Located at 41.42° N. Lat; 84.41° W. Long. Elevation is 696 feet.
Population: 301; Growth (since 2000): n/a; Density: 233.4 persons per square mile; Race: 100.0% White, 0.0% Black/African American, 0.0% Asian, 0.0% American Indian/Alaska Native, 0.0% Native Hawaiian/Other Pacific Islander, 0.0% Two or more races, 0.0% Hispanic of any race; Average household size: 3.38; Median age: 23.7; Age under 18: 38.5%; Age 65 and over: 14.3%; Males per 100 females: 100.0; Marriage status: 54.8% never married, 22.3% now married, 0.0% separated, 7.6% widowed, 15.2% divorced; Foreign born: 0.0%; Speak English only: 100.0%; With disability: 10.0%; Veterans: 3.8%; Ancestry: 49.5% German, 43.2% Irish, 9.3% Canadian, 7.0% French, 5.6% English
Employment: 0.0% management, business, and financial, 0.0% computer, engineering, and science, 0.0% education, legal, community service, arts, and media, 7.5% healthcare practitioners, 19.5% service, 12.8% sales and office, 0.0% natural resources, construction, and maintenance, 60.2% production, transportation, and material moving
Income: Per capita: $41,420; Median household: $61,490; Average household: $138,178; Households with income of $100,000 or more: 9.0%; Poverty rate: 10.3%
Educational Attainment: High school diploma or higher: 92.2%; Bachelor's degree or higher: 16.3%; Graduate/professional degree or higher: n/a
Housing: Homeownership rate: 70.8%; Median home value: $63,200; Median year structure built: Before 1940; Homeowner vacancy rate: 0.0%; Median selected monthly owner costs: $657 with a mortgage, $275 without a mortgage; Median gross rent: n/a per month; Rental vacancy rate: 0.0%
Health Insurance: 100.0% have insurance; 55.1% have private insurance; 63.8% have public insurance; 0.0% do not have insurance; 0.0% of children under 18 do not have insurance
Transportation: Commute: 92.5% car, 0.0% public transportation, 0.0% walk, 7.5% work from home; Mean travel time to work: 28.1 minutes

HICKSVILLE (village). Covers a land area of 2.656 square miles and a water area of 0 square miles. Located at 41.29° N. Lat; 84.76° W. Long. Elevation is 761 feet.
History: Hicksville was founded in 1836 by Henry Hicks, Isaac Smith, and John Bryan as a trading post dealing in furs. The town's industry passed from lumber, to mills and tanneries, and to canning and wood products.
Population: 3,110; Growth (since 2000): -14.8%; Density: 1,170.8 persons per square mile; Race: 89.0% White, 0.0% Black/African American, 0.4% Asian, 1.1% American Indian/Alaska Native, 0.3% Native Hawaiian/Other Pacific Islander, 2.8% Two or more races, 11.6% Hispanic of any race; Average household size: 2.14; Median age: 38.3; Age under 18: 21.5%; Age 65 and over: 18.2%; Males per 100 females: 92.7; Marriage status: 18.7% never married, 54.7% now married, 3.1% separated, 8.5% widowed, 18.0% divorced; Foreign born: 4.3%; Speak English only: 93.1%; With disability: 12.2%; Veterans: 11.0%; Ancestry: 32.2% German, 11.2% Irish, 10.9% English, 10.5% American, 3.1% Dutch
Employment: 10.0% management, business, and financial, 3.7% computer, engineering, and science, 3.1% education, legal, community service, arts, and media, 1.7% healthcare practitioners, 16.2% service, 20.3% sales and office, 11.1% natural resources, construction, and maintenance, 34.0% production, transportation, and material moving
Income: Per capita: $19,916; Median household: $41,372; Average household: $42,966; Households with income of $100,000 or more: 2.5%; Poverty rate: 12.2%
Educational Attainment: High school diploma or higher: 80.4%; Bachelor's degree or higher: 8.2%; Graduate/professional degree or higher: 1.2%

School District(s)

Hicksville Exempted Village (PK-12)
2015-16 Enrollment: 897. . . . . (419) 542-7665
Housing: Homeownership rate: 66.2%; Median home value: $82,500; Median year structure built: 1958; Homeowner vacancy rate: 0.0%; Median selected monthly owner costs: $988 with a mortgage, $443 without a mortgage; Median gross rent: $539 per month; Rental vacancy rate: 4.9%
Health Insurance: 89.3% have insurance; 67.5% have private insurance; 35.2% have public insurance; 10.7% do not have insurance; 1.5% of children under 18 do not have insurance
Hospitals: Community Memorial Hospital
Newspapers: Hicksville News-Tribune (weekly circulation 2,500)
Transportation: Commute: 94.1% car, 1.5% public transportation, 3.7% walk, 0.7% work from home; Mean travel time to work: 21.8 minutes

MARK CENTER (unincorporated postal area)

ZCTA: 43536

Covers a land area of 15.402 square miles and a water area of 0 square miles. Located at 41.31° N. Lat; 84.63° W. Long. Elevation is 718 feet.

Population: 518; Growth (since 2000): 14.9%; Density: 33.6 persons per square mile; Race: 100.0% White, 0.0% Black/African American, 0.0% Asian, 0.0% American Indian/Alaska Native, 0.0% Native Hawaiian/Other Pacific Islander, 0.0% Two or more races, 0.0% Hispanic of any race; Average household size: 3.24; Median age: 36.2; Age under 18: 35.7%; Age 65 and over: 10.6%; Males per 100 females: 110.7; Marriage status: 15.6% never married, 77.6% now married, 2.6% separated, 6.8% widowed, 0.0% divorced; Foreign born: 0.0%; Speak English only: 100.0%; With disability: 3.3%; Veterans: 6.9%; Ancestry: 37.1% German, 27.6% Dutch, 18.3% Irish, 9.1% English, 2.9% American
Employment: 3.9% management, business, and financial, 3.9% computer, engineering, and science, 0.0% education, legal, community service, arts, and media, 11.0% healthcare practitioners, 29.8% service, 42.1% sales and office, 6.6% natural resources, construction, and maintenance, 2.6% production, transportation, and material moving
Income: Per capita: $20,026; Median household: $65,517; Average household: $62,425; Households with income of $100,000 or more: 5.6%; Poverty rate: 5.4%
Educational Attainment: High school diploma or higher: 94.4%; Bachelor's degree or higher: 10.9%; Graduate/professional degree or higher: n/a
Housing: Homeownership rate: 95.6%; Median home value: $125,700; Median year structure built: Before 1940; Homeowner vacancy rate: 0.0%; Median selected monthly owner costs: $1,116 with a mortgage, $223 without a mortgage; Median gross rent: n/a per month; Rental vacancy rate: 0.0%
Health Insurance: 100.0% have insurance; 90.2% have private insurance; 17.2% have public insurance; 0.0% do not have insurance; 0.0% of children under 18 do not have insurance
Transportation: Commute: 100.0% car, 0.0% public transportation, 0.0% walk, 0.0% work from home; Mean travel time to work: 19.7 minutes

NEY (village). Covers a land area of 0.408 square miles and a water area of 0 square miles. Located at 41.38° N. Lat; 84.52° W. Long. Elevation is 712 feet.
Population: 282; Growth (since 2000): -22.5%; Density: 690.4 persons per square mile; Race: 96.5% White, 1.4% Black/African American, 0.4% Asian, 0.0% American Indian/Alaska Native, 0.0% Native Hawaiian/Other Pacific Islander, 1.8% Two or more races, 2.1% Hispanic of any race; Average household size: 2.43; Median age: 39.0; Age under 18: 25.9%; Age 65 and over: 11.0%; Males per 100 females: 104.6; Marriage status: 24.9% never married, 52.1% now married, 0.9% separated, 8.3% widowed, 14.7% divorced; Foreign born: 0.4%; Speak English only: 99.3%; With disability: 11.7%; Veterans: 8.1%; Ancestry: 35.5% German, 8.5% English, 8.5% Irish, 6.7% American, 6.7% Swedish
Employment: 5.8% management, business, and financial, 0.0% computer, engineering, and science, 2.2% education, legal, community service, arts, and media, 1.4% healthcare practitioners, 17.4% service, 16.7% sales and office, 20.3% natural resources, construction, and maintenance, 36.2% production, transportation, and material moving
Income: Per capita: $18,977; Median household: $40,000; Average household: $47,039; Households with income of $100,000 or more: 2.6%; Poverty rate: 7.4%
Educational Attainment: High school diploma or higher: 89.3%; Bachelor's degree or higher: 7.5%; Graduate/professional degree or higher: 1.1%
Housing: Homeownership rate: 81.9%; Median home value: $70,300; Median year structure built: Before 1940; Homeowner vacancy rate: 0.0%; Median selected monthly owner costs: $888 with a mortgage, $392 without a mortgage; Median gross rent: n/a per month; Rental vacancy rate: 0.0%
Health Insurance: 77.3% have insurance; 56.4% have private insurance; 34.0% have public insurance; 22.7% do not have insurance; 31.5% of children under 18 do not have insurance
Transportation: Commute: 94.2% car, 0.0% public transportation, 5.8% walk, 0.0% work from home; Mean travel time to work: 19.6 minutes

SHERWOOD (village). Covers a land area of 1.467 square miles and a water area of 0.015 square miles. Located at 41.29° N. Lat; 84.55° W. Long. Elevation is 709 feet.
Population: 778; Growth (since 2000): -2.9%; Density: 530.4 persons per square mile; Race: 96.3% White, 0.3% Black/African American, 1.3% Asian, 0.5% American Indian/Alaska Native, 0.0% Native Hawaiian/Other Pacific Islander, 1.7% Two or more races, 3.1% Hispanic of any race; Average household size: 2.48; Median age: 37.2; Age under 18: 27.1%; Age 65 and over: 14.8%; Males per 100 females: 88.4; Marriage status: 22.0% never married, 52.3% now married, 0.3% separated, 7.1% widowed, 18.6% divorced; Foreign born: 0.1%; Speak English only: 97.7%; With disability: 15.5%; Veterans: 8.5%; Ancestry: 50.3% German, 18.8% Irish, 9.4% English, 8.1% American, 4.0% Dutch
Employment: 17.5% management, business, and financial, 0.6% computer, engineering, and science, 5.7% education, legal, community service, arts, and media, 7.7% healthcare practitioners, 17.5% service, 22.1% sales and office, 8.0% natural resources, construction, and maintenance, 20.9% production, transportation, and material moving
Income: Per capita: $20,220; Median household: $43,846; Average household: $49,798; Households with income of $100,000 or more: 10.5%; Poverty rate: 19.9%
Educational Attainment: High school diploma or higher: 89.6%; Bachelor's degree or higher: 14.9%; Graduate/professional degree or higher: 4.3%

School District(s)

Central Local (KG-12)
2015-16 Enrollment: 1,002 . . . . (419) 658-2808
Housing: Homeownership rate: 70.7%; Median home value: $86,700; Median year structure built: 1951; Homeowner vacancy rate: 2.6%; Median selected monthly owner costs: $825 with a mortgage, $347 without a mortgage; Median gross rent: $663 per month; Rental vacancy rate: 0.0%
Health Insurance: 94.6% have insurance; 64.9% have private insurance; 41.9% have public insurance; 5.4% do not have insurance; 0.9% of children under 18 do not have insurance
Transportation: Commute: 96.3% car, 0.0% public transportation, 2.8% walk, 0.8% work from home; Mean travel time to work: 23.3 minutes

Delaware County

Located in central Ohio; crossed by the Olentangy and Scioto Rivers. Covers a land area of 443.098 square miles, a water area of 14.231 square miles, and is located in the Eastern Time Zone at 40.28° N. Lat., 83.01° W. Long. The county was founded in 1808. County seat is Delaware.

Delaware County is part of the Columbus, OH Metropolitan Statistical Area. The entire metro area includes: Delaware County, OH; Fairfield County, OH; Franklin County, OH; Hocking County, OH; Licking County, OH; Madison County, OH; Morrow County, OH; Perry County, OH; Pickaway County, OH; Union County, OH

Population: 188,996; Growth (since 2000): 71.8%; Density: 426.5 persons per square mile; Race: 88.8% White, 3.5% Black/African American, 5.1% Asian, 0.1% American Indian/Alaska Native, 0.0% Native Hawaiian/Other Pacific Islander, 2.0% two or more races, 2.4% Hispanic of any race; Average household size: 2.80; Median age: 38.0; Age under 18: 27.6%; Age 65 and over: 11.5%; Males per 100 females: 97.3; Marriage status: 23.6% never married, 63.4% now married, 0.9% separated, 4.3% widowed, 8.8% divorced; Foreign born: 6.5%; Speak English only: 92.0%; With disability: 7.4%; Veterans: 7.1%; Ancestry: 29.8% German, 15.6% Irish, 12.4% English, 8.0% Italian, 7.4% American
Religion: Six largest groups: 12.7% Catholicism, 4.5% Methodist/Pietist, 3.6% Hindu, 2.9% Presbyterian-Reformed, 2.5% Baptist, 1.7% Non-denominational Protestant
Economy: Unemployment rate: 3.3%; Leading industries: 14.1 % retail trade; 14.0 % professional, scientific, and technical services; 10.1 % accommodation and food services; Farms: 755 totaling 140,902 acres; Company size: 3 employ 1,000 or more persons, 9 employ 500 to 999 persons, 106 employ 100 to 499 persons, 4,139 employ less than 100 persons; Business ownership: 5,113 women-owned, 425 Black-owned, 197 Hispanic-owned, 959 Asian-owned, 80 American Indian/Alaska Native-owned
Employment: 24.7% management, business, and financial, 8.6% computer, engineering, and science, 11.2% education, legal, community service, arts, and media, 7.8% healthcare practitioners, 12.3% service, 23.9% sales and office, 4.7% natural resources, construction, and maintenance, 6.7% production, transportation, and material moving
Income: Per capita: $42,985; Median household: $94,234; Average household: $119,897; Households with income of $100,000 or more: 46.9%; Poverty rate: 4.9%
Educational Attainment: High school diploma or higher: 96.6%; Bachelor's degree or higher: 52.5%; Graduate/professional degree or higher: 18.9%

Housing: Homeownership rate: 81.2%; Median home value: $267,600; Median year structure built: 1996; Homeowner vacancy rate: 1.2%; Median selected monthly owner costs: $1,965 with a mortgage, $695 without a mortgage; Median gross rent: $969 per month; Rental vacancy rate: 5.3%
Vital Statistics: Birth rate: 113.5 per 10,000 population; Death rate: 58.7 per 10,000 population; Age-adjusted cancer mortality rate: 135.9 deaths per 100,000 population
Health Insurance: 95.9% have insurance; 86.7% have private insurance; 18.2% have public insurance; 4.1% do not have insurance; 1.7% of children under 18 do not have insurance
Health Care: Physicians: 41.3 per 10,000 population; Dentists: 5.8 per 10,000 population; Hospital beds: 3.2 per 10,000 population; Hospital admissions: 141.6 per 10,000 population
Air Quality Index (AQI): Percent of Days: 84.4% good, 15.1% moderate, 0.5% unhealthy for sensitive individuals, 0.0% unhealthy, 0.0% very unhealthy; Annual median: 41; Annual maximum: 112
Transportation: Commute: 90.8% car, 0.3% public transportation, 1.1% walk, 6.9% work from home; Mean travel time to work: 26.0 minutes
2016 Presidential Election: 54.5% Trump, 38.7% Clinton, 3.9% Johnson, 0.6% Stein
National and State Parks: Alum Creek State Park
Additional Information Contacts
Delaware Government . . . . (740) 833-2100
http://www.co.delaware.oh.us

Delaware County Communities

ASHLEY (village). Covers a land area of 0.659 square miles and a water area of 0 square miles. Located at 40.41° N. Lat; 82.95° W. Long. Elevation is 984 feet.
Population: 1,426; Growth (since 2000): 17.3%; Density: 2,164.6 persons per square mile; Race: 98.5% White, 0.0% Black/African American, 0.1% Asian, 0.0% American Indian/Alaska Native, 0.0% Native Hawaiian/Other Pacific Islander, 1.2% Two or more races, 2.9% Hispanic of any race; Average household size: 2.70; Median age: 38.4; Age under 18: 22.2%; Age 65 and over: 12.9%; Males per 100 females: 89.2; Marriage status: 27.6% never married, 44.4% now married, 1.5% separated, 6.3% widowed, 21.7% divorced; Foreign born: 0.0%; Speak English only: 99.3%; With disability: 14.7%; Veterans: 6.8%; Ancestry: 20.1% German, 17.2% American, 8.6% English, 7.9% Irish, 3.9% French
Employment: 8.3% management, business, and financial, 2.0% computer, engineering, and science, 3.2% education, legal, community service, arts, and media, 0.7% healthcare practitioners, 23.3% service, 26.8% sales and office, 14.7% natural resources, construction, and maintenance, 21.0% production, transportation, and material moving
Income: Per capita: $19,701; Median household: $45,560; Average household: $49,244; Households with income of $100,000 or more: 9.3%; Poverty rate: 20.1%
Educational Attainment: High school diploma or higher: 82.8%; Bachelor's degree or higher: 11.5%; Graduate/professional degree or higher: 2.7%

School District(s)
Buckeye Valley Local (PK-12)
2015-16 Enrollment: 2,195 . . . . (740) 369-8735
Housing: Homeownership rate: 63.9%; Median home value: $91,200; Median year structure built: 1958; Homeowner vacancy rate: 3.5%; Median selected monthly owner costs: $1,147 with a mortgage, $399 without a mortgage; Median gross rent: $710 per month; Rental vacancy rate: 5.5%
Health Insurance: 87.9% have insurance; 55.3% have private insurance; 40.7% have public insurance; 12.1% do not have insurance; 3.2% of children under 18 do not have insurance
Transportation: Commute: 93.0% car, 0.3% public transportation, 0.9% walk, 2.0% work from home; Mean travel time to work: 27.8 minutes

DELAWARE (city). County seat. Covers a land area of 18.952 square miles and a water area of 0.122 square miles. Located at 40.29° N. Lat; 83.07° W. Long. Elevation is 869 feet.
History: Named for Thomas West, Lord Delaware, first British governor of the colony of Virginia. Delaware was established around a sulphur spring, called Medicine Waters by the Mingo and Delaware tribes who lived here in the early 1800's. Joseph Barber settled on the present town site in 1807 and opened a tavern, and the town was platted in 1808. In 1833 a company, formed to exploit the local mineral springs, built a resort hotel. The resort was unsuccessful, but the hotel became the first building of Ohio Wesleyan University, chartered in 1842.
Population: 37,554; Growth (since 2000): 48.8%; Density: 1,981.5 persons per square mile; Race: 90.8% White, 4.6% Black/African American, 1.6% Asian, 0.1% American Indian/Alaska Native, 0.0% Native Hawaiian/Other Pacific Islander, 2.2% Two or more races, 2.3% Hispanic of any race; Average household size: 2.52; Median age: 34.0; Age under 18: 25.5%; Age 65 and over: 11.2%; Males per 100 females: 92.2; Marriage status: 30.9% never married, 51.8% now married, 1.7% separated, 5.1% widowed, 12.2% divorced; Foreign born: 3.5%; Speak English only: 96.0%; With disability: 9.7%; Veterans: 8.1%; Ancestry: 29.7% German, 14.7% Irish, 12.5% English, 7.4% American, 6.1% Italian
Employment: 15.5% management, business, and financial, 6.3% computer, engineering, and science, 12.9% education, legal, community service, arts, and media, 6.3% healthcare practitioners, 17.7% service, 22.7% sales and office, 6.6% natural resources, construction, and maintenance, 12.0% production, transportation, and material moving
Income: Per capita: $28,129; Median household: $58,472; Average household: $73,259; Households with income of $100,000 or more: 23.5%; Poverty rate: 9.8%
Educational Attainment: High school diploma or higher: 93.6%; Bachelor's degree or higher: 34.3%; Graduate/professional degree or higher: 13.3%

School District(s)
Buckeye United School District (07-12)
2015-16 Enrollment: 311 . . . . (614) 466-0720
Buckeye Valley Local (PK-12)
2015-16 Enrollment: 2,195 . . . . (740) 369-8735
Delaware Area Career Center (07-12)
2015-16 Enrollment: n/a . . . . (740) 548-0708
Delaware City (PK-12)
2015-16 Enrollment: 5,429 . . . . (740) 833-1100
Olentangy Local (PK-12)
2015-16 Enrollment: 19,658 . . . . (740) 657-4050

Four-year College(s)
Methodist Theological School in Ohio (Private, Not-for-profit, United Methodist)
Fall 2016 Enrollment: 153 . . . . (740) 363-1146
Ohio Wesleyan University (Private, Not-for-profit, United Methodist)
Fall 2016 Enrollment: 1,638 . . . . (740) 368-2000
2016-17 Tuition: In-state $44,090; Out-of-state $44,090

Vocational/Technical School(s)
Delaware Area Career Center (Public)
Fall 2016 Enrollment: n/a . . . . (740) 201-3206
2016-17 Tuition: $5,200
Housing: Homeownership rate: 62.5%; Median home value: $161,100; Median year structure built: 1988; Homeowner vacancy rate: 1.2%; Median selected monthly owner costs: $1,441 with a mortgage, $513 without a mortgage; Median gross rent: $861 per month; Rental vacancy rate: 3.7%
Health Insurance: 92.9% have insurance; 77.5% have private insurance; 25.4% have public insurance; 7.1% do not have insurance; 3.0% of children under 18 do not have insurance
Hospitals: Grady Memorial Hospital (135 beds)
Safety: Violent crime rate: 18.9 per 10,000 population; Property crime rate: 230.2 per 10,000 population
Newspapers: Delaware Gazette (daily circulation 8,400)
Transportation: Commute: 89.5% car, 0.4% public transportation, 3.9% walk, 5.3% work from home; Mean travel time to work: 27.0 minutes
Airports: Delaware Municipal - Jim Moore Field (general aviation)
Additional Information Contacts
City of Delaware . . . . (740) 203-1000
http://www.delawareohio.net

GALENA (village). Covers a land area of 1.598 square miles and a water area of 0.102 square miles. Located at 40.23° N. Lat; 82.88° W. Long. Elevation is 919 feet.
Population: 719; Growth (since 2000): 135.7%; Density: 450.0 persons per square mile; Race: 91.4% White, 1.1% Black/African American, 2.9% Asian, 1.4% American Indian/Alaska Native, 0.0% Native Hawaiian/Other Pacific Islander, 3.2% Two or more races, 2.4% Hispanic of any race; Average household size: 3.15; Median age: 34.6; Age under 18: 27.1%; Age 65 and over: 10.6%; Males per 100 females: 97.9; Marriage status: 26.0% never married, 60.1% now married, 0.7% separated, 2.2% widowed, 11.7% divorced; Foreign born: 3.9%; Speak English only: 93.8%; With disability: 9.2%; Veterans: 4.8%; Ancestry: 24.8% German, 19.6% English, 9.3% Italian, 8.6% Irish, 5.3% American

Employment: 14.6% management, business, and financial, 6.2% computer, engineering, and science, 10.0% education, legal, community service, arts, and media, 7.8% healthcare practitioners, 16.5% service, 27.8% sales and office, 9.5% natural resources, construction, and maintenance, 7.6% production, transportation, and material moving
Income: Per capita: $30,907; Median household: $86,250; Average household: $95,129; Households with income of $100,000 or more: 43.9%; Poverty rate: 8.9%
Educational Attainment: High school diploma or higher: 93.4%; Bachelor's degree or higher: 38.5%; Graduate/professional degree or higher: 10.8%

School District(s)

Big Walnut Local (PK-12)
2015-16 Enrollment: 3,426 . . . . (740) 965-3010
Olentangy Local (PK-12)
2015-16 Enrollment: 19,658 . . . . (740) 657-4050

Housing: Homeownership rate: 77.6%; Median home value: $211,900; Median year structure built: 1974; Homeowner vacancy rate: 0.0%; Median selected monthly owner costs: $1,560 with a mortgage, $525 without a mortgage; Median gross rent: $1,156 per month; Rental vacancy rate: 0.0%
Health Insurance: 94.0% have insurance; 84.1% have private insurance; 17.7% have public insurance; 6.0% do not have insurance; 1.0% of children under 18 do not have insurance
Transportation: Commute: 88.0% car, 0.0% public transportation, 3.3% walk, 7.7% work from home; Mean travel time to work: 23.8 minutes

KILBOURNE (CDP). Covers a land area of 0.449 square miles and a water area of 0 square miles. Located at 40.33° N. Lat; 82.96° W. Long. Elevation is 915 feet.
Population: 151; Growth (since 2000): n/a; Density: 336.2 persons per square mile; Race: 100.0% White, 0.0% Black/African American, 0.0% Asian, 0.0% American Indian/Alaska Native, 0.0% Native Hawaiian/Other Pacific Islander, 0.0% Two or more races, 0.0% Hispanic of any race; Average household size: 2.44; Median age: 24.9; Age under 18: 24.5%; Age 65 and over: 9.3%; Males per 100 females: 127.9; Marriage status: 36.8% never married, 32.5% now married, 0.0% separated, 20.2% widowed, 10.5% divorced; Foreign born: 7.9%; Speak English only: 100.0%; With disability: 48.3%; Veterans: 0.0%; Ancestry: 62.3% American, 33.1% Scottish, 12.6% English, 5.3% Welsh
Employment: 0.0% management, business, and financial, 0.0% computer, engineering, and science, 24.0% education, legal, community service, arts, and media, 0.0% healthcare practitioners, 14.0% service, 0.0% sales and office, 0.0% natural resources, construction, and maintenance, 62.0% production, transportation, and material moving
Income: Per capita: $17,403; Median household: n/a; Average household: $40,708; Households with income of $100,000 or more: n/a; Poverty rate: 54.3%
Educational Attainment: High school diploma or higher: 73.6%; Bachelor's degree or higher: n/a; Graduate/professional degree or higher: n/a
Housing: Homeownership rate: 43.5%; Median home value: $104,700; Median year structure built: 1962; Homeowner vacancy rate: 0.0%; Median selected monthly owner costs: n/a with a mortgage, n/a without a mortgage; Median gross rent: n/a per month; Rental vacancy rate: 0.0%
Health Insurance: 84.8% have insurance; 45.7% have private insurance; 48.3% have public insurance; 15.2% do not have insurance; 0.0% of children under 18 do not have insurance
Transportation: Commute: 100.0% car, 0.0% public transportation, 0.0% walk, 0.0% work from home; Mean travel time to work: 0.0 minutes

LEWIS CENTER (unincorporated postal area)

ZCTA: 43035

Covers a land area of 19.590 square miles and a water area of 3.102 square miles. Located at 40.19° N. Lat; 83.00° W. Long. Elevation is 938 feet.
Population: 26,421; Growth (since 2000): 134.6%; Density: 1,348.7 persons per square mile; Race: 78.5% White, 6.1% Black/African American, 12.0% Asian, 0.0% American Indian/Alaska Native, 0.0% Native Hawaiian/Other Pacific Islander, 3.1% Two or more races, 4.0% Hispanic of any race; Average household size: 3.06; Median age: 33.4; Age under 18: 33.6%; Age 65 and over: 5.1%; Males per 100 females: 99.4; Marriage status: 24.9% never married, 65.0% now married, 1.0% separated, 2.2% widowed, 7.9% divorced; Foreign born: 14.5%; Speak English only: 81.0%; With disability: 4.9%; Veterans: 4.7%; Ancestry: 29.0% German, 16.3% Irish, 8.6% Italian, 8.5% English, 4.8% American
Employment: 27.5% management, business, and financial, 11.3% computer, engineering, and science, 9.9% education, legal, community service, arts, and media, 7.7% healthcare practitioners, 12.1% service, 24.7% sales and office, 2.4% natural resources, construction, and maintenance, 4.4% production, transportation, and material moving
Income: Per capita: $40,600; Median household: $108,948; Average household: $123,358; Households with income of $100,000 or more: 54.9%; Poverty rate: 5.3%
Educational Attainment: High school diploma or higher: 97.8%; Bachelor's degree or higher: 62.6%; Graduate/professional degree or higher: 20.8%

School District(s)

Olentangy Local (PK-12)
2015-16 Enrollment: 19,658 . . . . (740) 657-4050

Housing: Homeownership rate: 80.3%; Median home value: $277,000; Median year structure built: 2000; Homeowner vacancy rate: 1.1%; Median selected monthly owner costs: $2,079 with a mortgage, $752 without a mortgage; Median gross rent: $1,025 per month; Rental vacancy rate: 7.9%
Health Insurance: 95.1% have insurance; 87.5% have private insurance; 12.5% have public insurance; 4.9% do not have insurance; 3.2% of children under 18 do not have insurance
Newspapers: Grove City Record (weekly circulation 3,500); ThisWeek Newspapers (weekly circulation 307,000)
Transportation: Commute: 92.2% car, 0.2% public transportation, 0.5% walk, 6.8% work from home; Mean travel time to work: 23.2 minutes

OSTRANDER (village). Covers a land area of 0.842 square miles and a water area of 0 square miles. Located at 40.26° N. Lat; 83.22° W. Long. Elevation is 928 feet.
Population: 1,041; Growth (since 2000): 157.0%; Density: 1,236.3 persons per square mile; Race: 98.9% White, 0.0% Black/African American, 0.0% Asian, 0.0% American Indian/Alaska Native, 0.0% Native Hawaiian/Other Pacific Islander, 1.1% Two or more races, 8.4% Hispanic of any race; Average household size: 3.41; Median age: 33.8; Age under 18: 36.3%; Age 65 and over: 7.2%; Males per 100 females: 108.8; Marriage status: 25.4% never married, 57.9% now married, 1.2% separated, 3.9% widowed, 12.8% divorced; Foreign born: 3.5%; Speak English only: 92.7%; With disability: 6.7%; Veterans: 5.4%; Ancestry: 29.7% German, 13.7% Irish, 10.7% American, 8.7% English, 4.6% Scottish
Employment: 23.4% management, business, and financial, 2.8% computer, engineering, and science, 7.8% education, legal, community service, arts, and media, 4.6% healthcare practitioners, 10.2% service, 23.8% sales and office, 19.4% natural resources, construction, and maintenance, 8.2% production, transportation, and material moving
Income: Per capita: $23,765; Median household: $70,469; Average household: $78,314; Households with income of $100,000 or more: 27.5%; Poverty rate: 14.3%
Educational Attainment: High school diploma or higher: 91.5%; Bachelor's degree or higher: 26.1%; Graduate/professional degree or higher: 5.8%

School District(s)

Buckeye Valley Local (PK-12)
2015-16 Enrollment: 2,195 . . . . (740) 369-8735

Housing: Homeownership rate: 83.0%; Median home value: $163,900; Median year structure built: 1972; Homeowner vacancy rate: 5.6%; Median selected monthly owner costs: $1,411 with a mortgage, $617 without a mortgage; Median gross rent: $896 per month; Rental vacancy rate: 0.0%
Health Insurance: 93.6% have insurance; 78.1% have private insurance; 20.9% have public insurance; 6.4% do not have insurance; 0.0% of children under 18 do not have insurance
Transportation: Commute: 91.9% car, 0.4% public transportation, 0.0% walk, 5.8% work from home; Mean travel time to work: 28.4 minutes

POWELL (city). Covers a land area of 4.932 square miles and a water area of 0.004 square miles. Located at 40.17° N. Lat; 83.08° W. Long. Elevation is 906 feet.
History: It was named "Middlebury" at the time, because the first settlers came from the Middlebury, Connecticut area. In 1857, Judge Thomas Powell established the first post office in the community, and the residents decided to adopt his name. Powell was finally incorporated as a municipality in 1947.

Population: 12,436; Growth (since 2000): 99.1%; Density: 2,521.7 persons per square mile; Race: 86.0% White, 3.2% Black/African American, 9.2% Asian, 0.0% American Indian/Alaska Native, 0.1% Native Hawaiian/Other Pacific Islander, 1.3% Two or more races, 0.6% Hispanic of any race; Average household size: 3.01; Median age: 38.5; Age under 18: 33.7%; Age 65 and over: 10.4%; Males per 100 females: 97.0; Marriage status: 17.7% never married, 73.1% now married, 1.0% separated, 2.1% widowed, 7.0% divorced; Foreign born: 8.6%; Speak English only: 89.8%; With disability: 4.7%; Veterans: 6.0%; Ancestry: 24.1% German, 17.8% Irish, 15.6% Italian, 14.6% English, 8.4% American
Employment: 31.1% management, business, and financial, 9.6% computer, engineering, and science, 10.4% education, legal, community service, arts, and media, 11.0% healthcare practitioners, 4.9% service, 26.5% sales and office, 2.3% natural resources, construction, and maintenance, 4.1% production, transportation, and material moving
Income: Per capita: $52,991; Median household: $132,917; Average household: $159,361; Households with income of $100,000 or more: 69.5%; Poverty rate: 0.3%
Educational Attainment: High school diploma or higher: 99.8%; Bachelor's degree or higher: 73.4%; Graduate/professional degree or higher: 32.1%

School District(s)

Dublin City (PK-12)
2015-16 Enrollment: 15,432 . . . . (614) 764-5913
Olentangy Local (PK-12)
2015-16 Enrollment: 19,658 . . . . (740) 657-4050
Worthington City (PK-12)
2015-16 Enrollment: 9,885 . . . . (614) 450-6000

Housing: Homeownership rate: 95.8%; Median home value: $348,000; Median year structure built: 2000; Homeowner vacancy rate: 1.0%; Median selected monthly owner costs: $2,342 with a mortgage, $948 without a mortgage; Median gross rent: $1,675 per month; Rental vacancy rate: 11.3%
Health Insurance: 99.6% have insurance; 95.9% have private insurance; 12.1% have public insurance; 0.4% do not have insurance; 0.3% of children under 18 do not have insurance
Safety: Violent crime rate: 0.0 per 10,000 population; Property crime rate: 79.9 per 10,000 population
Transportation: Commute: 87.5% car, 0.7% public transportation, 0.4% walk, 10.6% work from home; Mean travel time to work: 24.9 minutes
Additional Information Contacts
Village of Powell . . . . (614) 885-5380
http://www.cityofpowell.us

RADNOR (CDP). Covers a land area of 0.721 square miles and a water area of 0 square miles. Located at 40.39° N. Lat; 83.15° W. Long. Elevation is 935 feet.
Population: 205; Growth (since 2000): n/a; Density: 284.4 persons per square mile; Race: 100.0% White, 0.0% Black/African American, 0.0% Asian, 0.0% American Indian/Alaska Native, 0.0% Native Hawaiian/Other Pacific Islander, 0.0% Two or more races, 0.0% Hispanic of any race; Average household size: 1.86; Median age: 54.7; Age under 18: 9.8%; Age 65 and over: 33.2%; Males per 100 females: 105.1; Marriage status: 14.1% never married, 73.0% now married, 0.0% separated, 0.0% widowed, 13.0% divorced; Foreign born: 0.0%; Speak English only: 100.0%; With disability: 8.8%; Veterans: 10.8%; Ancestry: 36.1% German, 22.0% Irish, 20.5% Welsh, 15.6% English, 7.8% Italian
Employment: 14.7% management, business, and financial, 0.0% computer, engineering, and science, 0.0% education, legal, community service, arts, and media, 0.0% healthcare practitioners, 9.2% service, 49.5% sales and office, 0.0% natural resources, construction, and maintenance, 26.6% production, transportation, and material moving
Income: Per capita: $28,967; Median household: $46,000; Average household: $53,984; Households with income of $100,000 or more: 8.2%; Poverty rate: n/a
Educational Attainment: High school diploma or higher: 95.1%; Bachelor's degree or higher: 4.3%; Graduate/professional degree or higher: n/a

School District(s)

Buckeye Valley Local (PK-12)
2015-16 Enrollment: 2,195 . . . . (740) 369-8735

Housing: Homeownership rate: 70.0%; Median home value: $152,000; Median year structure built: Before 1940; Homeowner vacancy rate: 0.0%; Median selected monthly owner costs: $1,633 with a mortgage, $320 without a mortgage; Median gross rent: n/a per month; Rental vacancy rate: 0.0%
Health Insurance: 100.0% have insurance; 100.0% have private insurance; 33.2% have public insurance; 0.0% do not have insurance; 0.0% of children under 18 do not have insurance
Transportation: Commute: 100.0% car, 0.0% public transportation, 0.0% walk, 0.0% work from home; Mean travel time to work: 26.6 minutes

SHAWNEE HILLS (village). Covers a land area of 0.442 square miles and a water area of 0 square miles. Located at 40.16° N. Lat; 83.14° W. Long. Elevation is 892 feet.
Population: 775; Growth (since 2000): 85.0%; Density: 1,753.1 persons per square mile; Race: 92.0% White, 1.3% Black/African American, 3.7% Asian, 0.0% American Indian/Alaska Native, 0.0% Native Hawaiian/Other Pacific Islander, 2.2% Two or more races, 2.2% Hispanic of any race; Average household size: 2.68; Median age: 40.4; Age under 18: 28.9%; Age 65 and over: 9.8%; Males per 100 females: 108.9; Marriage status: 20.3% never married, 64.8% now married, 3.0% separated, 4.2% widowed, 10.7% divorced; Foreign born: 6.1%; Speak English only: 90.7%; With disability: 7.7%; Veterans: 8.0%; Ancestry: 35.1% German, 14.7% Irish, 12.1% English, 10.1% American, 4.9% Italian
Employment: 14.4% management, business, and financial, 9.5% computer, engineering, and science, 14.7% education, legal, community service, arts, and media, 9.5% healthcare practitioners, 13.2% service, 25.5% sales and office, 5.0% natural resources, construction, and maintenance, 8.3% production, transportation, and material moving
Income: Per capita: $47,024; Median household: $97,813; Average household: $122,926; Households with income of $100,000 or more: 48.8%; Poverty rate: 1.9%
Educational Attainment: High school diploma or higher: 98.7%; Bachelor's degree or higher: 50.5%; Graduate/professional degree or higher: 19.2%
Housing: Homeownership rate: 89.3%; Median home value: $262,700; Median year structure built: 1990; Homeowner vacancy rate: 0.0%; Median selected monthly owner costs: $1,948 with a mortgage, $627 without a mortgage; Median gross rent: $1,125 per month; Rental vacancy rate: 0.0%
Health Insurance: 93.8% have insurance; 87.6% have private insurance; 14.6% have public insurance; 6.2% do not have insurance; 1.8% of children under 18 do not have insurance
Transportation: Commute: 88.4% car, 0.0% public transportation, 0.0% walk, 8.2% work from home; Mean travel time to work: 24.3 minutes
Additional Information Contacts
Village of Shawnee Hills . . . . (614) 889-2824
http://www.shawneehillsoh.com

SUNBURY (village). Covers a land area of 3.278 square miles and a water area of 0.018 square miles. Located at 40.25° N. Lat; 82.87° W. Long. Elevation is 968 feet.
Population: 4,926; Growth (since 2000): 87.3%; Density: 1,502.8 persons per square mile; Race: 95.0% White, 1.1% Black/African American, 1.1% Asian, 0.3% American Indian/Alaska Native, 0.0% Native Hawaiian/Other Pacific Islander, 2.0% Two or more races, 1.4% Hispanic of any race; Average household size: 2.92; Median age: 35.8; Age under 18: 30.6%; Age 65 and over: 11.8%; Males per 100 females: 90.1; Marriage status: 22.4% never married, 61.4% now married, 1.4% separated, 5.4% widowed, 10.8% divorced; Foreign born: 1.9%; Speak English only: 96.2%; With disability: 10.8%; Veterans: 5.8%; Ancestry: 36.1% German, 17.6% Irish, 13.6% English, 6.7% Italian, 4.3% European
Employment: 22.3% management, business, and financial, 5.7% computer, engineering, and science, 13.6% education, legal, community service, arts, and media, 8.2% healthcare practitioners, 14.5% service, 22.1% sales and office, 3.1% natural resources, construction, and maintenance, 10.6% production, transportation, and material moving
Income: Per capita: $26,433; Median household: $69,671; Average household: $75,604; Households with income of $100,000 or more: 30.4%; Poverty rate: 8.1%
Educational Attainment: High school diploma or higher: 95.7%; Bachelor's degree or higher: 36.8%; Graduate/professional degree or higher: 12.6%

School District(s)

Big Walnut Local (PK-12)
2015-16 Enrollment: 3,426 . . . . (740) 965-3010

Housing: Homeownership rate: 74.1%; Median home value: $186,400; Median year structure built: 1991; Homeowner vacancy rate: 3.5%; Median

selected monthly owner costs: $1,428 with a mortgage, $457 without a mortgage; Median gross rent: $1,004 per month; Rental vacancy rate: 0.0%
Health Insurance: 96.9% have insurance; 84.2% have private insurance; 23.3% have public insurance; 3.1% do not have insurance; 1.1% of children under 18 do not have insurance
Safety: Violent crime rate: 0.0 per 10,000 population; Property crime rate: 106.8 per 10,000 population
Newspapers: Sunbury News (weekly circulation 3,200)
Transportation: Commute: 93.0% car, 0.0% public transportation, 0.0% walk, 6.1% work from home; Mean travel time to work: 25.4 minutes

Erie County

Located in northern Ohio; bounded on the north by Lake Erie; drained by the Huron and Vermilion Rivers; includes Kelleys Island. Covers a land area of 251.558 square miles, a water area of 374.429 square miles, and is located in the Eastern Time Zone at 41.55° N. Lat., 82.53° W. Long. The county was founded in 1838. County seat is Sandusky.

Erie County is part of the Sandusky, OH Micropolitan Statistical Area. The entire metro area includes: Erie County, OH

Weather Station: Sandusky Elevation: 583 feet

	Jan	Feb	Mar	Apr	May	Jun	Jul	Aug	Sep	Oct	Nov	Dec
High	33	36	44	57	67	78	82	80	74	62	50	37
Low	20	22	29	40	52	61	66	65	57	45	36	25
Precip	1.8	1.7	2.4	3.2	3.3	3.8	3.5	3.3	2.8	2.4	2.7	2.3
Snow	6.7	4.3	2.6	0.5	tr	0.0	0.0	0.0	0.0	0.0	0.2	2.9

High and Low temperatures in degrees Fahrenheit; Precipitation and Snow in inches

Population: 75,808; Growth (since 2000): -4.7%; Density: 301.4 persons per square mile; Race: 86.4% White, 8.0% Black/African American, 0.6% Asian, 0.5% American Indian/Alaska Native, 0.1% Native Hawaiian/Other Pacific Islander, 3.5% two or more races, 4.0% Hispanic of any race; Average household size: 2.35; Median age: 44.5; Age under 18: 20.9%; Age 65 and over: 19.6%; Males per 100 females: 96.1; Marriage status: 27.9% never married, 51.2% now married, 1.8% separated, 7.8% widowed, 13.1% divorced; Foreign born: 2.1%; Speak English only: 96.6%; With disability: 14.1%; Veterans: 11.1%; Ancestry: 34.7% German, 14.9% Irish, 8.8% Italian, 8.8% English, 4.7% American
Religion: Six largest groups: 25.6% Catholicism, 6.0% Non-denominational Protestant, 5.9% Lutheran, 5.2% Presbyterian-Reformed, 3.7% Methodist/Pietist, 3.5% Baptist
Economy: Unemployment rate: 5.9%; Leading industries: 16.5 % retail trade; 14.4 % accommodation and food services; 11.9 % health care and social assistance; Farms: 345 totaling 83,330 acres; Company size: 3 employ 1,000 or more persons, 2 employ 500 to 999 persons, 41 employs 100 to 499 persons, 1,808 employ less than 100 persons; Business ownership: 1,616 women-owned, 252 Black-owned, 68 Hispanic-owned, 55 Asian-owned, n/a American Indian/Alaska Native-owned
Employment: 11.3% management, business, and financial, 2.5% computer, engineering, and science, 9.0% education, legal, community service, arts, and media, 7.4% healthcare practitioners, 22.0% service, 21.8% sales and office, 8.1% natural resources, construction, and maintenance, 18.0% production, transportation, and material moving
Income: Per capita: $28,684; Median household: $48,276; Average household: $66,588; Households with income of $100,000 or more: 18.5%; Poverty rate: 12.8%
Educational Attainment: High school diploma or higher: 90.6%; Bachelor's degree or higher: 21.6%; Graduate/professional degree or higher: 8.1%
Housing: Homeownership rate: 69.3%; Median home value: $130,900; Median year structure built: 1964; Homeowner vacancy rate: 3.1%; Median selected monthly owner costs: $1,160 with a mortgage, $439 without a mortgage; Median gross rent: $708 per month; Rental vacancy rate: 6.6%
Vital Statistics: Birth rate: 103.2 per 10,000 population; Death rate: 121.4 per 10,000 population; Age-adjusted cancer mortality rate: 169.3 deaths per 100,000 population
Health Insurance: 91.8% have insurance; 71.2% have private insurance; 38.2% have public insurance; 8.2% do not have insurance; 3.9% of children under 18 do not have insurance
Health Care: Physicians: 26.0 per 10,000 population; Dentists: 6.7 per 10,000 population; Hospital beds: 31.1 per 10,000 population; Hospital admissions: 1,122.9 per 10,000 population
Transportation: Commute: 92.8% car, 0.9% public transportation, 2.1% walk, 2.9% work from home; Mean travel time to work: 21.0 minutes
2016 Presidential Election: 51.9% Trump, 42.4% Clinton, 3.2% Johnson, 0.9% Stein
National and State Parks: Glacial Grooves State Memorial; Kelleys Island State Park
Additional Information Contacts
Erie Government . . . . (419) 627-7682
http://www.eriecounty.oh.gov

Erie County Communities

BAY VIEW (village). Covers a land area of 0.276 square miles and a water area of 0.002 square miles. Located at 41.47° N. Lat; 82.82° W. Long. Elevation is 577 feet.
History: Bay View developed as a resort community with swimming, boating, and camping facilities.
Population: 629; Growth (since 2000): -9.1%; Density: 2,278.1 persons per square mile; Race: 98.4% White, 0.0% Black/African American, 1.6% Asian, 0.0% American Indian/Alaska Native, 0.0% Native Hawaiian/Other Pacific Islander, 0.0% Two or more races, 1.0% Hispanic of any race; Average household size: 2.22; Median age: 50.8; Age under 18: 12.7%; Age 65 and over: 27.5%; Males per 100 females: 98.7; Marriage status: 22.5% never married, 55.6% now married, 1.2% separated, 8.5% widowed, 13.4% divorced; Foreign born: 2.1%; Speak English only: 97.4%; With disability: 18.1%; Veterans: 15.8%; Ancestry: 35.1% German, 9.5% Irish, 8.3% American, 6.2% English, 5.2% Italian
Employment: 17.3% management, business, and financial, 3.3% computer, engineering, and science, 6.0% education, legal, community service, arts, and media, 4.0% healthcare practitioners, 25.9% service, 12.6% sales and office, 7.6% natural resources, construction, and maintenance, 23.3% production, transportation, and material moving
Income: Per capita: $26,069; Median household: $44,135; Average household: $59,612; Households with income of $100,000 or more: 14.1%; Poverty rate: 8.3%
Educational Attainment: High school diploma or higher: 81.8%; Bachelor's degree or higher: 14.2%; Graduate/professional degree or higher: 3.2%
Housing: Homeownership rate: 85.5%; Median home value: $111,700; Median year structure built: 1964; Homeowner vacancy rate: 3.2%; Median selected monthly owner costs: $1,010 with a mortgage, $376 without a mortgage; Median gross rent: $911 per month; Rental vacancy rate: 4.7%
Health Insurance: 94.3% have insurance; 75.0% have private insurance; 43.2% have public insurance; 5.7% do not have insurance; 3.8% of children under 18 do not have insurance
Transportation: Commute: 95.3% car, 0.3% public transportation, 1.0% walk, 3.0% work from home; Mean travel time to work: 19.7 minutes

BERLIN HEIGHTS (village). Covers a land area of 1.603 square miles and a water area of 0.001 square miles. Located at 41.32° N. Lat; 82.49° W. Long. Elevation is 774 feet.
History: Berlin Heights developed as the center of an apple and peach district, begun in 1812 when John Hoak and John Fleming brought from Canada a number of young fruit trees.
Population: 504; Growth (since 2000): -26.4%; Density: 314.5 persons per square mile; Race: 98.6% White, 0.0% Black/African American, 0.0% Asian, 0.0% American Indian/Alaska Native, 1.4% Native Hawaiian/Other Pacific Islander, 0.0% Two or more races, 0.0% Hispanic of any race; Average household size: 2.01; Median age: 55.5; Age under 18: 12.5%; Age 65 and over: 32.3%; Males per 100 females: 89.9; Marriage status: 22.2% never married, 53.8% now married, 0.4% separated, 14.2% widowed, 9.8% divorced; Foreign born: 1.8%; Speak English only: 100.0%; With disability: 21.2%; Veterans: 13.8%; Ancestry: 38.9% German, 19.4% Irish, 10.7% English, 8.3% American, 6.2% Italian
Employment: 14.9% management, business, and financial, 0.4% computer, engineering, and science, 12.0% education, legal, community service, arts, and media, 2.9% healthcare practitioners, 20.3% service, 11.2% sales and office, 14.1% natural resources, construction, and maintenance, 24.1% production, transportation, and material moving
Income: Per capita: $31,641; Median household: $38,542; Average household: $62,669; Households with income of $100,000 or more: 18.4%; Poverty rate: 11.1%
Educational Attainment: High school diploma or higher: 82.2%; Bachelor's degree or higher: 16.8%; Graduate/professional degree or higher: 5.9%

School District(s)

Edison Local (Formerly Berlin-Milan) (PK-12)
2015-16 Enrollment: 1,485 . . . . (419) 499-3000

Housing: Homeownership rate: 76.1%; Median home value: $123,000; Median year structure built: Before 1940; Homeowner vacancy rate: 7.7%; Median selected monthly owner costs: $1,160 with a mortgage, $343 without a mortgage; Median gross rent: $592 per month; Rental vacancy rate: 3.2%

Health Insurance: 95.2% have insurance; 75.4% have private insurance; 44.2% have public insurance; 4.8% do not have insurance; 0.0% of children under 18 do not have insurance

Transportation: Commute: 93.4% car, 0.0% public transportation, 2.1% walk, 4.6% work from home; Mean travel time to work: 23.1 minutes

BEULAH BEACH (CDP). Covers a land area of 0.046 square miles and a water area of 0 square miles. Located at 41.39° N. Lat; 82.44° W. Long. Elevation is 600 feet.

Population: 58; Growth (since 2000): n/a; Density: 1,263.6 persons per square mile; Race: 100.0% White, 0.0% Black/African American, 0.0% Asian, 0.0% American Indian/Alaska Native, 0.0% Native Hawaiian/Other Pacific Islander, 0.0% Two or more races, 0.0% Hispanic of any race; Average household size: 1.93; Median age: 83.2; Age under 18: 0.0%; Age 65 and over: 72.4%; Males per 100 females: 82.8; Marriage status: 0.0% never married, 58.6% now married, 0.0% separated, 41.4% widowed, 0.0% divorced; Foreign born: 0.0%; Speak English only: 100.0%; With disability: 19.0%; Veterans: 15.5%; Ancestry: 48.3% English, 29.3% German, 22.4% Czech, 19.0% Scotch-Irish, 13.8% Scottish

Employment: 0.0% management, business, and financial, 0.0% computer, engineering, and science, 64.0% education, legal, community service, arts, and media, 0.0% healthcare practitioners, 0.0% service, 36.0% sales and office, 0.0% natural resources, construction, and maintenance, 0.0% production, transportation, and material moving

Income: Per capita: $35,174; Median household: n/a; Average household: $64,760; Households with income of $100,000 or more: 26.7%; Poverty rate: n/a

Educational Attainment: High school diploma or higher: 100.0%; Bachelor's degree or higher: 13.8%; Graduate/professional degree or higher: 13.8%

Housing: Homeownership rate: 56.7%; Median home value: n/a; Median year structure built: 1960; Homeowner vacancy rate: 0.0%; Median selected monthly owner costs: n/a with a mortgage, n/a without a mortgage; Median gross rent: n/a per month; Rental vacancy rate: 0.0%

Health Insurance: 100.0% have insurance; 69.0% have private insurance; 72.4% have public insurance; 0.0% do not have insurance; 0.0% of children under 18 do not have insurance

Transportation: Commute: 64.0% car, 0.0% public transportation, 36.0% walk, 0.0% work from home; Mean travel time to work: 0.0 minutes

BIRMINGHAM (unincorporated postal area)

ZCTA: 44816

Covers a land area of 0.026 square miles and a water area of 0 square miles. Located at 41.33° N. Lat; 82.35° W. Long. Elevation is 784 feet.

Population: 37; Growth (since 2000): -64.8%; Density: 1,434.9 persons per square mile; Race: 100.0% White, 0.0% Black/African American, 0.0% Asian, 0.0% American Indian/Alaska Native, 0.0% Native Hawaiian/Other Pacific Islander, 0.0% Two or more races, 0.0% Hispanic of any race; Average household size: 0.00; Median age: n/a; Age under 18: 0.0%; Age 65 and over: 51.4%; Males per 100 females: 100.0; Marriage status: 0.0% never married, 0.0% now married, 0.0% separated, 51.4% widowed, 48.6% divorced; Foreign born: 0.0%; Speak English only: 100.0%; With disability: 100.0%; Veterans: 0.0%; Ancestry: 51.4% Hungarian, 48.6% French Canadian, 48.6% Italian

Employment: n/a management, business, and financial, n/a computer, engineering, and science, n/a education, legal, community service, arts, and media, n/a healthcare practitioners, n/a service, n/a sales and office, n/a natural resources, construction, and maintenance, n/a production, transportation, and material moving

Income: Per capita: n/a; Median household: n/a; Average household: n/a; Households with income of $100,000 or more: n/a; Poverty rate: n/a

Educational Attainment: High school diploma or higher: 100.0%; Bachelor's degree or higher: n/a; Graduate/professional degree or higher: n/a

Housing: Homeownership rate: 100.0%; Median home value: n/a; Median year structure built: n/a; Homeowner vacancy rate: 0.0%; Median selected monthly owner costs: $0 with a mortgage, $0 without a mortgage; Median gross rent: n/a per month; Rental vacancy rate: 0.0%

Health Insurance: 100.0% have insurance; 48.6% have private insurance; 51.4% have public insurance; 0.0% do not have insurance; 0.0% of children under 18 do not have insurance

Transportation: Commute: n/a car, n/a public transportation, n/a walk, n/a work from home; Mean travel time to work: 0.0 minutes

CASTALIA (village). Covers a land area of 1.044 square miles and a water area of 0.009 square miles. Located at 41.40° N. Lat; 82.80° W. Long. Elevation is 636 feet.

Population: 853; Growth (since 2000): -8.8%; Density: 817.0 persons per square mile; Race: 98.2% White, 1.1% Black/African American, 0.0% Asian, 0.0% American Indian/Alaska Native, 0.0% Native Hawaiian/Other Pacific Islander, 0.2% Two or more races, 5.6% Hispanic of any race; Average household size: 2.60; Median age: 45.5; Age under 18: 18.9%; Age 65 and over: 17.4%; Males per 100 females: 96.3; Marriage status: 29.5% never married, 53.0% now married, 0.0% separated, 7.6% widowed, 9.9% divorced; Foreign born: 1.8%; Speak English only: 95.2%; With disability: 12.1%; Veterans: 8.2%; Ancestry: 41.7% German, 19.3% Irish, 8.8% English, 8.3% Italian, 4.8% Hungarian

Employment: 7.3% management, business, and financial, 3.5% computer, engineering, and science, 8.2% education, legal, community service, arts, and media, 3.5% healthcare practitioners, 18.8% service, 20.7% sales and office, 11.2% natural resources, construction, and maintenance, 26.8% production, transportation, and material moving

Income: Per capita: $28,574; Median household: $66,154; Average household: $72,387; Households with income of $100,000 or more: 25.2%; Poverty rate: 7.5%

Educational Attainment: High school diploma or higher: 91.4%; Bachelor's degree or higher: 17.6%; Graduate/professional degree or higher: 4.7%

School District(s)

Margaretta Local (PK-12)
2015-16 Enrollment: 1,146 . . . . (419) 684-5322
Townsend North Community School (09-12)
2015-16 Enrollment: 740. . . . . (419) 684-5402

Housing: Homeownership rate: 72.0%; Median home value: $125,000; Median year structure built: 1954; Homeowner vacancy rate: 5.1%; Median selected monthly owner costs: $1,283 with a mortgage, $451 without a mortgage; Median gross rent: $675 per month; Rental vacancy rate: 0.0%

Health Insurance: 96.5% have insurance; 82.6% have private insurance; 30.7% have public insurance; 3.5% do not have insurance; 0.6% of children under 18 do not have insurance

Transportation: Commute: 95.0% car, 0.0% public transportation, 3.7% walk, 1.3% work from home; Mean travel time to work: 19.1 minutes

CRYSTAL ROCK (CDP). Covers a land area of 0.106 square miles and a water area of 0 square miles. Located at 41.45° N. Lat; 82.84° W. Long. Elevation is 581 feet.

Population: 113; Growth (since 2000): n/a; Density: 1,061.6 persons per square mile; Race: 100.0% White, 0.0% Black/African American, 0.0% Asian, 0.0% American Indian/Alaska Native, 0.0% Native Hawaiian/Other Pacific Islander, 0.0% Two or more races, 0.0% Hispanic of any race; Average household size: 2.46; Median age: 40.0; Age under 18: 35.4%; Age 65 and over: 12.4%; Males per 100 females: 100.0; Marriage status: 37.0% never married, 38.0% now married, 20.7% separated, 15.2% widowed, 9.8% divorced; Foreign born: 0.0%; Speak English only: 100.0%; With disability: 29.2%; Veterans: 0.0%; Ancestry: 34.5% German, 14.2% Polish

Employment: 0.0% management, business, and financial, 20.0% computer, engineering, and science, 0.0% education, legal, community service, arts, and media, 20.0% healthcare practitioners, 37.5% service, 0.0% sales and office, 0.0% natural resources, construction, and maintenance, 22.5% production, transportation, and material moving

Income: Per capita: $17,038; Median household: $36,250; Average household: $41,854; Households with income of $100,000 or more: n/a; Poverty rate: 8.0%

Educational Attainment: High school diploma or higher: 80.8%; Bachelor's degree or higher: 11.0%; Graduate/professional degree or higher: n/a

Housing: Homeownership rate: 67.4%; Median home value: $23,400; Median year structure built: Before 1940; Homeowner vacancy rate: 0.0%; Median selected monthly owner costs: n/a with a mortgage, n/a without a mortgage; Median gross rent: n/a per month; Rental vacancy rate: 0.0%

Health Insurance: 100.0% have insurance; 21.2% have private insurance; 78.8% have public insurance; 0.0% do not have insurance; 0.0% of children under 18 do not have insurance
Transportation: Commute: 100.0% car, 0.0% public transportation, 0.0% walk, 0.0% work from home; Mean travel time to work: 0.0 minutes

HURON (city). Covers a land area of 4.837 square miles and a water area of 2.891 square miles. Located at 41.40° N. Lat; 82.56° W. Long. Elevation is 587 feet.
History: A French trading post was established here about 1749. In 1805, trader B.F. Flemond arrived, and the town of Huron soon grew up around the harbor at the mouth of the Huron River. Shipping and shipbuilding supported the town.
Population: 7,038; Growth (since 2000): -11.6%; Density: 1,455.1 persons per square mile; Race: 96.6% White, 0.9% Black/African American, 0.0% Asian, 0.0% American Indian/Alaska Native, 0.0% Native Hawaiian/Other Pacific Islander, 2.4% Two or more races, 1.4% Hispanic of any race; Average household size: 2.32; Median age: 45.1; Age under 18: 21.6%; Age 65 and over: 23.2%; Males per 100 females: 92.7; Marriage status: 29.3% never married, 50.9% now married, 1.3% separated, 8.4% widowed, 11.4% divorced; Foreign born: 1.2%; Speak English only: 98.9%; With disability: 13.4%; Veterans: 11.2%; Ancestry: 41.1% German, 21.0% Irish, 13.7% Italian, 10.2% English, 4.9% French
Employment: 17.7% management, business, and financial, 1.3% computer, engineering, and science, 9.2% education, legal, community service, arts, and media, 7.6% healthcare practitioners, 21.8% service, 21.6% sales and office, 7.1% natural resources, construction, and maintenance, 13.6% production, transportation, and material moving
Income: Per capita: $34,784; Median household: $51,633; Average household: $80,134; Households with income of $100,000 or more: 22.4%; Poverty rate: 15.8%
Educational Attainment: High school diploma or higher: 94.4%; Bachelor's degree or higher: 33.8%; Graduate/professional degree or higher: 12.3%

School District(s)

Huron City Schools (PK-12)
2015-16 Enrollment: 1,376 . . . . (419) 433-1234

Two-year College(s)

Bowling Green State University-Firelands (Public)
Fall 2016 Enrollment: 2,162 . . . . (419) 433-5560
2016-17 Tuition: In-state $5,260; Out-of-state $12,596
Housing: Homeownership rate: 71.2%; Median home value: $152,200; Median year structure built: 1964; Homeowner vacancy rate: 5.3%; Median selected monthly owner costs: $1,165 with a mortgage, $491 without a mortgage; Median gross rent: $785 per month; Rental vacancy rate: 0.0%
Health Insurance: 94.5% have insurance; 70.1% have private insurance; 45.3% have public insurance; 5.5% do not have insurance; 0.7% of children under 18 do not have insurance
Transportation: Commute: 94.5% car, 0.0% public transportation, 1.5% walk, 3.6% work from home; Mean travel time to work: 22.7 minutes
Additional Information Contacts
City of Huron . . . . (419) 433-5000
http://www.cityofhuron.org

KELLEYS ISLAND (village). Covers a land area of 4.348 square miles and a water area of 0.058 square miles. Located at 41.60° N. Lat; 82.71° W. Long. Elevation is 594 feet.
History: In 1833 Irad and Datus Kelley acquired the island in Lake Erie, and settled here. They first harvested the forests of red cedar. In 1846 they planted an acre of grapes, and the island was soon known for its wine, as well as its peaches and grapes. Later, quarrying of the limestone became an important industry.
Population: 158; Growth (since 2000): -56.9%; Density: 36.3 persons per square mile; Race: 100.0% White, 0.0% Black/African American, 0.0% Asian, 0.0% American Indian/Alaska Native, 0.0% Native Hawaiian/Other Pacific Islander, 0.0% Two or more races, 0.6% Hispanic of any race; Average household size: 1.78; Median age: 67.0; Age under 18: 0.0%; Age 65 and over: 62.0%; Males per 100 females: 110.8; Marriage status: 16.5% never married, 65.2% now married, 0.0% separated, 8.2% widowed, 10.1% divorced; Foreign born: 0.0%; Speak English only: 98.1%; With disability: 17.1%; Veterans: 8.9%; Ancestry: 43.0% German, 15.8% Irish, 15.2% English, 7.0% Dutch, 5.7% British
Employment: 10.2% management, business, and financial, 0.0% computer, engineering, and science, 6.8% education, legal, community service, arts, and media, 3.4% healthcare practitioners, 18.6% service, 42.4% sales and office, 0.0% natural resources, construction, and maintenance, 18.6% production, transportation, and material moving
Income: Per capita: $31,944; Median household: $56,458; Average household: $57,819; Households with income of $100,000 or more: 4.4%; Poverty rate: 2.5%
Educational Attainment: High school diploma or higher: 92.8%; Bachelor's degree or higher: 26.8%; Graduate/professional degree or higher: 6.5%

School District(s)

Kelleys Island Local
2015-16 Enrollment: n/a . . . . (419) 746-2730
Housing: Homeownership rate: 93.3%; Median home value: $289,700; Median year structure built: 1983; Homeowner vacancy rate: 9.8%; Median selected monthly owner costs: $993 with a mortgage, $623 without a mortgage; Median gross rent: n/a per month; Rental vacancy rate: 0.0%
Health Insurance: 92.4% have insurance; 80.4% have private insurance; 71.5% have public insurance; 7.6% do not have insurance; 0.0% of children under 18 do not have insurance
Transportation: Commute: 74.6% car, 0.0% public transportation, 0.0% walk, 18.6% work from home; Mean travel time to work: 8.3 minutes
Airports: Kelleys Island Land Field (general aviation)

MILAN (village). Covers a land area of 1.185 square miles and a water area of 0.019 square miles. Located at 41.29° N. Lat; 82.60° W. Long. Elevation is 663 feet.
History: Several villages occupied this site on the Huron River before the permanent settlement of Milan was laid out in 1816 by Ebenezer Merry. The town became a shipping port in 1839, when residents completed a canal to the Huron River, three miles away. Wheat was the principal cargo of the ships that left Milan. Milan prospered until the river became unnavigable for lake boats and the canal ceased to be used in the 1880 's.
Population: 1,263; Growth (since 2000): -12.6%; Density: 1,066.0 persons per square mile; Race: 93.8% White, 1.0% Black/African American, 4.0% Asian, 0.0% American Indian/Alaska Native, 0.0% Native Hawaiian/Other Pacific Islander, 0.9% Two or more races, 3.2% Hispanic of any race; Average household size: 2.56; Median age: 44.0; Age under 18: 18.4%; Age 65 and over: 17.5%; Males per 100 females: 98.1; Marriage status: 32.4% never married, 49.7% now married, 0.7% separated, 8.3% widowed, 9.6% divorced; Foreign born: 3.0%; Speak English only: 94.1%; With disability: 11.0%; Veterans: 8.9%; Ancestry: 47.5% German, 21.6% Irish, 12.4% English, 5.1% Italian, 3.8% Swiss
Employment: 12.1% management, business, and financial, 2.2% computer, engineering, and science, 11.6% education, legal, community service, arts, and media, 5.4% healthcare practitioners, 15.5% service, 28.0% sales and office, 3.3% natural resources, construction, and maintenance, 21.9% production, transportation, and material moving
Income: Per capita: $26,900; Median household: $66,250; Average household: $72,608; Households with income of $100,000 or more: 20.8%; Poverty rate: 5.6%
Educational Attainment: High school diploma or higher: 93.5%; Bachelor's degree or higher: 24.7%; Graduate/professional degree or higher: 9.5%

School District(s)

Edison Local (Formerly Berlin-Milan) (PK-12)
2015-16 Enrollment: 1,485 . . . . (419) 499-3000
Ehove Career Center (10-12)
2015-16 Enrollment: n/a . . . . (866) 256-9707

Two-year College(s)

EHOVE Career Center (Public)
Fall 2016 Enrollment: 382 . . . . (419) 499-4663
Housing: Homeownership rate: 75.1%; Median home value: $136,900; Median year structure built: 1954; Homeowner vacancy rate: 2.8%; Median selected monthly owner costs: $1,226 with a mortgage, $438 without a mortgage; Median gross rent: $767 per month; Rental vacancy rate: 5.0%
Health Insurance: 96.8% have insurance; 90.3% have private insurance; 21.0% have public insurance; 3.2% do not have insurance; 3.0% of children under 18 do not have insurance
Safety: Violent crime rate: 7.4 per 10,000 population; Property crime rate: 186.2 per 10,000 population
Transportation: Commute: 88.7% car, 0.0% public transportation, 5.1% walk, 2.6% work from home; Mean travel time to work: 25.5 minutes

MITIWANGA (CDP).
Land/water area and latitude/longitude are not available.

Population: 158; Growth (since 2000): n/a; Density: n/a persons per square mile; Race: 82.3% White, 0.0% Black/African American, 0.0% Asian, 0.0% American Indian/Alaska Native, 0.0% Native Hawaiian/Other Pacific Islander, 17.7% Two or more races, 0.0% Hispanic of any race; Average household size: 1.74; Median age: 53.1; Age under 18: 15.2%; Age 65 and over: 12.7%; Males per 100 females: 0.0; Marriage status: 20.3% never married, 63.5% now married, 18.9% separated, 0.0% widowed, 16.2% divorced; Foreign born: 4.4%; Speak English only: 95.6%; With disability: 27.2%; Veterans: 19.4%; Ancestry: 38.6% German, 22.8% American, 17.7% Iranian, 17.1% Polish, 5.7% French
Employment: 5.8% management, business, and financial, 7.4% computer, engineering, and science, 53.7% education, legal, community service, arts, and media, 0.0% healthcare practitioners, 0.0% service, 15.7% sales and office, 5.8% natural resources, construction, and maintenance, 11.6% production, transportation, and material moving
Income: Per capita: $45,894; Median household: $67,875; Average household: $79,796; Households with income of $100,000 or more: 25.3%; Poverty rate: 27.2%
Educational Attainment: High school diploma or higher: 90.6%; Bachelor's degree or higher: 43.4%; Graduate/professional degree or higher: 34.9%
Housing: Homeownership rate: 61.5%; Median home value: $143,800; Median year structure built: 1953; Homeowner vacancy rate: 0.0%; Median selected monthly owner costs: n/a with a mortgage, $537 without a mortgage; Median gross rent: n/a per month; Rental vacancy rate: 0.0%
Health Insurance: 75.9% have insurance; 55.1% have private insurance; 38.0% have public insurance; 24.1% do not have insurance; 0.0% of children under 18 do not have insurance
Safety: Violent crime rate: 0.0 per 10,000 population; Property crime rate: 0.0 per 10,000 population
Transportation: Commute: 45.5% car, 0.0% public transportation, 0.0% walk, 54.5% work from home; Mean travel time to work: 0.0 minutes

SANDUSKY (city). County seat. Covers a land area of 9.726 square miles and a water area of 12.175 square miles. Located at 41.46° N. Lat; 82.71° W. Long. Elevation is 594 feet.
History: Sandusky was platted in 1818, replacing a smaller tract laid out in 1816 and called Portland. Its location on the southeastern corner of Sandusky Bay (named Lac Sandouske by French explorers, after the Wyandotte San-doos-tee) made the town a tourist and vacation destination, as well as an industrial community. The town was a port of entry and a shipping center, a stopping place for all vessels that sailed the Great Lakes. Sandusky became the seat of Erie County in 1838, but the 1840's brought epidemics of cholera that killed hundreds of people. In the 1850's Sandusky was an important station on the Underground Railroad.
Population: 25,338; Growth (since 2000): -9.0%; Density: 2,605.3 persons per square mile; Race: 69.2% White, 21.2% Black/African American, 0.3% Asian, 0.9% American Indian/Alaska Native, 0.3% Native Hawaiian/Other Pacific Islander, 6.0% Two or more races, 6.1% Hispanic of any race; Average household size: 2.20; Median age: 39.4; Age under 18: 22.3%; Age 65 and over: 17.0%; Males per 100 females: 91.0; Marriage status: 37.7% never married, 38.2% now married, 2.9% separated, 8.6% widowed, 15.5% divorced; Foreign born: 2.4%; Speak English only: 96.3%; With disability: 17.0%; Veterans: 10.4%; Ancestry: 30.2% German, 14.3% Irish, 7.9% Italian, 5.9% English, 4.3% American
Employment: 8.6% management, business, and financial, 1.1% computer, engineering, and science, 7.3% education, legal, community service, arts, and media, 4.7% healthcare practitioners, 29.5% service, 22.4% sales and office, 5.2% natural resources, construction, and maintenance, 21.3% production, transportation, and material moving
Income: Per capita: $20,793; Median household: $33,817; Average household: $44,919; Households with income of $100,000 or more: 6.2%; Poverty rate: 22.4%
Educational Attainment: High school diploma or higher: 85.3%; Bachelor's degree or higher: 16.2%; Graduate/professional degree or higher: 4.8%

School District(s)

Perkins Local (PK-12)
2015-16 Enrollment: 2,201 . . . . (419) 625-0484
Sandusky City (PK-12)
2015-16 Enrollment: 3,372 . . . . (419) 626-6940

Two-year College(s)

Firelands Regional Medical Center School of Nursing (Private, Not-for-profit)
Fall 2016 Enrollment: 66 . . . . (419) 557-7110
Ohio Business College-Sandusky (Private, For-profit)
Fall 2016 Enrollment: 217 . . . . (419) 627-8345
2016-17 Tuition: In-state $9,000; Out-of-state $9,000

Vocational/Technical School(s)

Sandusky Career Center (Public)
Fall 2016 Enrollment: 60 . . . . (419) 984-1100
2016-17 Tuition: $10,547

Housing: Homeownership rate: 52.0%; Median home value: $81,600; Median year structure built: 1952; Homeowner vacancy rate: 4.8%; Median selected monthly owner costs: $885 with a mortgage, $348 without a mortgage; Median gross rent: $640 per month; Rental vacancy rate: 9.5%
Health Insurance: 89.4% have insurance; 54.5% have private insurance; 50.0% have public insurance; 10.6% do not have insurance; 4.5% of children under 18 do not have insurance
Hospitals: Firelands Regional Medical Center (325 beds)
Safety: Violent crime rate: 17.9 per 10,000 population; Property crime rate: 363.3 per 10,000 population
Newspapers: Sandusky Register (daily circulation 22,200)
Transportation: Commute: 89.8% car, 2.4% public transportation, 3.3% walk, 2.0% work from home; Mean travel time to work: 17.1 minutes; Amtrak: Train service available.
Airports: Griffing Sandusky (general aviation)
Additional Information Contacts
City of Sandusky . . . . (419) 627-5844
http://www.ci.sandusky.oh.us

WHITES LANDING (CDP). Covers a land area of 0.293 square miles and a water area of <.001 square miles. Located at 41.43° N. Lat; 82.89° W. Long. Elevation is 577 feet.
Population: 341; Growth (since 2000): n/a; Density: 1,164.0 persons per square mile; Race: 100.0% White, 0.0% Black/African American, 0.0% Asian, 0.0% American Indian/Alaska Native, 0.0% Native Hawaiian/Other Pacific Islander, 0.0% Two or more races, 0.0% Hispanic of any race; Average household size: 2.73; Median age: 39.8; Age under 18: 17.9%; Age 65 and over: 7.6%; Males per 100 females: 115.5; Marriage status: 44.6% never married, 52.1% now married, 0.0% separated, 3.2% widowed, 0.0% divorced; Foreign born: 0.0%; Speak English only: 100.0%; With disability: 20.2%; Veterans: 10.7%; Ancestry: 61.3% German, 45.7% Irish, 4.1% Italian
Employment: 9.7% management, business, and financial, 0.0% computer, engineering, and science, 23.4% education, legal, community service, arts, and media, 0.0% healthcare practitioners, 0.0% service, 10.3% sales and office, 35.2% natural resources, construction, and maintenance, 21.4% production, transportation, and material moving
Income: Per capita: $21,861; Median household: n/a; Average household: $58,886; Households with income of $100,000 or more: 12.0%; Poverty rate: 32.0%
Educational Attainment: High school diploma or higher: 91.6%; Bachelor's degree or higher: 32.7%; Graduate/professional degree or higher: n/a
Housing: Homeownership rate: 65.6%; Median home value: $83,200; Median year structure built: 1962; Homeowner vacancy rate: 0.0%; Median selected monthly owner costs: $1,265 with a mortgage, n/a without a mortgage; Median gross rent: n/a per month; Rental vacancy rate: 0.0%
Health Insurance: 80.6% have insurance; 68.0% have private insurance; 24.6% have public insurance; 19.4% do not have insurance; 0.0% of children under 18 do not have insurance
Transportation: Commute: 100.0% car, 0.0% public transportation, 0.0% walk, 0.0% work from home; Mean travel time to work: 26.3 minutes

Fairfield County

Located in central Ohio; drained by the Hocking River; includes part of Buckeye Lake. Covers a land area of 504.411 square miles, a water area of 4.150 square miles, and is located in the Eastern Time Zone at 39.75° N. Lat., 82.63° W. Long. The county was founded in 1800. County seat is Lancaster.

Fairfield County is part of the Columbus, OH Metropolitan Statistical Area. The entire metro area includes: Delaware County, OH; Fairfield County, OH; Franklin County, OH; Hocking County, OH; Licking County, OH; Madison County, OH; Morrow County, OH; Perry County, OH; Pickaway County, OH; Union County, OH

Population: 150,163; Growth (since 2000): 22.3%; Density: 297.7 persons per square mile; Race: 89.0% White, 6.7% Black/African American, 1.3% Asian, 0.1% American Indian/Alaska Native, 0.0% Native Hawaiian/Other Pacific Islander, 2.3% two or more races, 2.0% Hispanic of any race; Average household size: 2.67; Median age: 39.3; Age under 18: 24.5%; Age 65 and over: 14.4%; Males per 100 females: 98.3; Marriage status: 26.3% never married, 56.7% now married, 1.8% separated, 5.4% widowed, 11.6% divorced; Foreign born: 2.6%; Speak English only: 96.6%; With disability: 13.4%; Veterans: 9.9%; Ancestry: 30.9% German, 16.1% Irish, 10.1% English, 8.4% American, 4.3% Italian
Religion: Six largest groups: 12.0% Catholicism, 6.8% Methodist/Pietist, 6.4% Baptist, 3.9% Lutheran, 3.8% Non-denominational Protestant, 2.0% Pentecostal
Economy: Unemployment rate: 3.8%; Leading industries: 15.4 % retail trade; 12.9 % health care and social assistance; 10.9 % other services (except public administration); Farms: 1,184 totaling 206,699 acres; Company size: 2 employ 1,000 or more persons, 1 employs 500 to 999 persons, 48 employ 100 to 499 persons, 2,593 employ less than 100 persons; Business ownership: 3,635 women-owned, 548 Black-owned, 167 Hispanic-owned, 210 Asian-owned, 61 American Indian/Alaska Native-owned
Employment: 16.1% management, business, and financial, 4.4% computer, engineering, and science, 9.3% education, legal, community service, arts, and media, 6.5% healthcare practitioners, 17.3% service, 25.0% sales and office, 8.4% natural resources, construction, and maintenance, 13.1% production, transportation, and material moving
Income: Per capita: $28,746; Median household: $61,473; Average household: $76,365; Households with income of $100,000 or more: 26.2%; Poverty rate: 10.2%
Educational Attainment: High school diploma or higher: 91.7%; Bachelor's degree or higher: 26.4%; Graduate/professional degree or higher: 8.5%
Housing: Homeownership rate: 71.2%; Median home value: $164,400; Median year structure built: 1979; Homeowner vacancy rate: 1.3%; Median selected monthly owner costs: $1,399 with a mortgage, $464 without a mortgage; Median gross rent: $814 per month; Rental vacancy rate: 4.9%
Vital Statistics: Birth rate: 104.4 per 10,000 population; Death rate: 88.2 per 10,000 population; Age-adjusted cancer mortality rate: 151.8 deaths per 100,000 population
Health Insurance: 93.4% have insurance; 73.6% have private insurance; 31.6% have public insurance; 6.6% do not have insurance; 2.3% of children under 18 do not have insurance
Health Care: Physicians: 17.1 per 10,000 population; Dentists: 4.8 per 10,000 population; Hospital beds: 14.8 per 10,000 population; Hospital admissions: 630.5 per 10,000 population
Transportation: Commute: 93.6% car, 0.3% public transportation, 1.3% walk, 4.0% work from home; Mean travel time to work: 27.6 minutes
2016 Presidential Election: 60.2% Trump, 33.8% Clinton, 3.3% Johnson, 0.8% Stein
National and State Parks: Rock Mill Dam State Wildlife Area; Shallenberger State Nature Reserve; Sherman House State Memorial; Tarlton State Park
Additional Information Contacts
Fairfield Government . . . . (740) 687-7190
http://www.co.fairfield.oh.us

Fairfield County Communities

AMANDA (village). Covers a land area of 0.300 square miles and a water area of 0 square miles. Located at 39.65° N. Lat; 82.74° W. Long. Elevation is 922 feet.
Population: 750; Growth (since 2000): 6.1%; Density: 2,497.1 persons per square mile; Race: 96.8% White, 0.1% Black/African American, 0.0% Asian, 0.0% American Indian/Alaska Native, 0.0% Native Hawaiian/Other Pacific Islander, 3.1% Two or more races, 2.3% Hispanic of any race; Average household size: 2.64; Median age: 38.9; Age under 18: 28.7%; Age 65 and over: 14.1%; Males per 100 females: 106.4; Marriage status: 24.7% never married, 54.1% now married, 1.4% separated, 5.6% widowed, 15.7% divorced; Foreign born: 0.9%; Speak English only: 97.6%; With disability: 13.2%; Veterans: 13.1%; Ancestry: 31.9% German, 22.8% Irish, 8.3% Italian, 7.5% English, 6.3% American
Employment: 9.2% management, business, and financial, 1.1% computer, engineering, and science, 4.9% education, legal, community service, arts, and media, 6.5% healthcare practitioners, 20.5% service, 20.5% sales and office, 12.2% natural resources, construction, and maintenance, 25.1% production, transportation, and material moving
Income: Per capita: $23,197; Median household: $50,682; Average household: $59,548; Households with income of $100,000 or more: 16.9%; Poverty rate: 11.5%
Educational Attainment: High school diploma or higher: 90.9%; Bachelor's degree or higher: 10.2%; Graduate/professional degree or higher: 2.5%

School District(s)

Amanda-Clearcreek Local (PK-12)
2015-16 Enrollment: 1,547 . . . . (740) 969-7250
Housing: Homeownership rate: 64.8%; Median home value: $105,800; Median year structure built: Before 1940; Homeowner vacancy rate: 0.0%; Median selected monthly owner costs: $1,088 with a mortgage, $429 without a mortgage; Median gross rent: $725 per month; Rental vacancy rate: 0.0%
Health Insurance: 94.1% have insurance; 75.7% have private insurance; 29.6% have public insurance; 5.9% do not have insurance; 1.4% of children under 18 do not have insurance
Transportation: Commute: 83.4% car, 0.0% public transportation, 8.0% walk, 3.6% work from home; Mean travel time to work: 28.2 minutes

BALTIMORE (village). Covers a land area of 2.090 square miles and a water area of 0 square miles. Located at 39.85° N. Lat; 82.61° W. Long. Elevation is 866 feet.
Population: 2,963; Growth (since 2000): 2.8%; Density: 1,417.7 persons per square mile; Race: 98.2% White, 0.0% Black/African American, 0.0% Asian, 0.2% American Indian/Alaska Native, 0.0% Native Hawaiian/Other Pacific Islander, 1.2% Two or more races, 2.8% Hispanic of any race; Average household size: 2.66; Median age: 34.5; Age under 18: 34.2%; Age 65 and over: 14.2%; Males per 100 females: 90.1; Marriage status: 27.3% never married, 49.3% now married, 3.0% separated, 7.3% widowed, 16.1% divorced; Foreign born: 0.3%; Speak English only: 97.3%; With disability: 12.9%; Veterans: 11.2%; Ancestry: 31.4% German, 13.8% English, 12.2% Irish, 11.0% American, 6.9% Italian
Employment: 9.5% management, business, and financial, 3.4% computer, engineering, and science, 8.7% education, legal, community service, arts, and media, 4.3% healthcare practitioners, 26.2% service, 21.8% sales and office, 8.6% natural resources, construction, and maintenance, 17.5% production, transportation, and material moving
Income: Per capita: $19,894; Median household: $43,208; Average household: $51,774; Households with income of $100,000 or more: 13.9%; Poverty rate: 17.2%
Educational Attainment: High school diploma or higher: 92.6%; Bachelor's degree or higher: 11.6%; Graduate/professional degree or higher: 3.0%

School District(s)

Liberty Union-Thurston Local (KG-12)
2015-16 Enrollment: 1,315 . . . . (740) 862-4171
Housing: Homeownership rate: 57.2%; Median home value: $129,900; Median year structure built: 1960; Homeowner vacancy rate: 0.0%; Median selected monthly owner costs: $1,147 with a mortgage, $451 without a mortgage; Median gross rent: $904 per month; Rental vacancy rate: 3.8%
Health Insurance: 95.9% have insurance; 63.5% have private insurance; 45.0% have public insurance; 4.1% do not have insurance; 0.0% of children under 18 do not have insurance
Safety: Violent crime rate: 3.4 per 10,000 population; Property crime rate: 84.2 per 10,000 population
Newspapers: Towne Crier (weekly circulation 30,000)
Transportation: Commute: 93.6% car, 0.0% public transportation, 1.8% walk, 4.5% work from home; Mean travel time to work: 31.0 minutes
Additional Information Contacts
Village of Baltimore . . . . (740) 862-4491
http://www.baltimoreohio.org

BREMEN (village). Covers a land area of 0.861 square miles and a water area of 0.002 square miles. Located at 39.71° N. Lat; 82.43° W. Long. Elevation is 794 feet.
Population: 1,826; Growth (since 2000): 44.3%; Density: 2,119.6 persons per square mile; Race: 98.8% White, 0.6% Black/African American, 0.0% Asian, 0.4% American Indian/Alaska Native, 0.0% Native Hawaiian/Other Pacific Islander, 0.2% Two or more races, 0.0% Hispanic of any race; Average household size: 2.95; Median age: 34.3; Age under 18: 27.7%; Age 65 and over: 13.6%; Males per 100 females: 99.0; Marriage status: 28.8% never married, 55.0% now married, 4.2% separated, 6.1%

widowed, 10.2% divorced; Foreign born: 0.0%; Speak English only: 99.9%; With disability: 14.2%; Veterans: 9.1%; Ancestry: 42.0% German, 18.6% Irish, 12.7% English, 7.2% Italian, 6.8% American
Employment: 14.6% management, business, and financial, 2.0% computer, engineering, and science, 6.1% education, legal, community service, arts, and media, 3.7% healthcare practitioners, 24.6% service, 23.4% sales and office, 10.8% natural resources, construction, and maintenance, 14.6% production, transportation, and material moving
Income: Per capita: $20,535; Median household: $47,989; Average household: $60,042; Households with income of $100,000 or more: 15.1%; Poverty rate: 12.8%
Educational Attainment: High school diploma or higher: 91.1%; Bachelor's degree or higher: 13.6%; Graduate/professional degree or higher: 4.6%

School District(s)

Fairfield Union Local (KG-12)
2015-16 Enrollment: 1,924 . . . . (740) 536-7384
Housing: Homeownership rate: 74.4%; Median home value: $111,000; Median year structure built: Before 1940; Homeowner vacancy rate: 0.0%; Median selected monthly owner costs: $1,059 with a mortgage, $346 without a mortgage; Median gross rent: $745 per month; Rental vacancy rate: 4.1%
Health Insurance: 89.8% have insurance; 60.6% have private insurance; 38.4% have public insurance; 10.2% do not have insurance; 4.0% of children under 18 do not have insurance
Transportation: Commute: 89.7% car, 0.7% public transportation, 2.9% walk, 6.3% work from home; Mean travel time to work: 31.7 minutes

---

CARROLL (village). Covers a land area of 0.315 square miles and a water area of 0 square miles. Located at 39.80° N. Lat; 82.70° W. Long. Elevation is 833 feet.
Population: 381; Growth (since 2000): -21.9%; Density: 1,207.9 persons per square mile; Race: 98.7% White, 0.0% Black/African American, 0.0% Asian, 0.0% American Indian/Alaska Native, 0.0% Native Hawaiian/Other Pacific Islander, 1.3% Two or more races, 0.0% Hispanic of any race; Average household size: 2.28; Median age: 41.1; Age under 18: 15.7%; Age 65 and over: 22.0%; Males per 100 females: 103.9; Marriage status: 26.4% never married, 55.3% now married, 4.2% separated, 5.1% widowed, 13.2% divorced; Foreign born: 0.5%; Speak English only: 100.0%; With disability: 21.0%; Veterans: 10.0%; Ancestry: 39.1% German, 26.0% Irish, 17.8% English, 7.3% Hungarian, 3.9% Italian
Employment: 3.8% management, business, and financial, 6.0% computer, engineering, and science, 3.8% education, legal, community service, arts, and media, 9.3% healthcare practitioners, 19.7% service, 26.8% sales and office, 22.4% natural resources, construction, and maintenance, 8.2% production, transportation, and material moving
Income: Per capita: $26,432; Median household: $46,719; Average household: $58,135; Households with income of $100,000 or more: 10.2%; Poverty rate: 4.8%
Educational Attainment: High school diploma or higher: 85.9%; Bachelor's degree or higher: 10.5%; Graduate/professional degree or higher: 1.6%

School District(s)

Bloom-Carroll Local (KG-12)
2015-16 Enrollment: 1,931 . . . . (614) 837-6560
Eastland-Fairfield Career/Tech (09-12)
2015-16 Enrollment: n/a . . . . (614) 836-4530
Housing: Homeownership rate: 59.3%; Median home value: $109,700; Median year structure built: 1963; Homeowner vacancy rate: 0.0%; Median selected monthly owner costs: $1,045 with a mortgage, $324 without a mortgage; Median gross rent: $683 per month; Rental vacancy rate: 6.8%
Health Insurance: 89.0% have insurance; 69.6% have private insurance; 36.7% have public insurance; 11.0% do not have insurance; 13.3% of children under 18 do not have insurance
Transportation: Commute: 95.1% car, 0.0% public transportation, 1.1% walk, 3.8% work from home; Mean travel time to work: 31.3 minutes

---

FAIRFIELD BEACH (CDP). Covers a land area of 0.653 square miles and a water area of 0.315 square miles. Located at 39.92° N. Lat; 82.48° W. Long. Elevation is 925 feet.
Population: 850; Growth (since 2000): -26.9%; Density: 1,301.2 persons per square mile; Race: 92.7% White, 1.5% Black/African American, 0.0% Asian, 0.0% American Indian/Alaska Native, 0.0% Native Hawaiian/Other Pacific Islander, 5.8% Two or more races, 2.7% Hispanic of any race; Average household size: 2.04; Median age: 52.7; Age under 18: 15.4%; Age 65 and over: 27.2%; Males per 100 females: 111.1; Marriage status: 22.9% never married, 50.7% now married, 0.0% separated, 5.8% widowed, 20.6% divorced; Foreign born: 0.0%; Speak English only: 98.3%; With disability: 21.9%; Veterans: 16.7%; Ancestry: 35.1% German, 23.2% American, 12.7% Irish, 6.7% English, 5.5% Hungarian
Employment: 8.3% management, business, and financial, 2.0% computer, engineering, and science, 4.7% education, legal, community service, arts, and media, 20.3% healthcare practitioners, 23.3% service, 13.3% sales and office, 5.7% natural resources, construction, and maintenance, 22.3% production, transportation, and material moving
Income: Per capita: $28,362; Median household: $51,406; Average household: $58,158; Households with income of $100,000 or more: 5.0%; Poverty rate: 10.0%
Educational Attainment: High school diploma or higher: 86.1%; Bachelor's degree or higher: 12.9%; Graduate/professional degree or higher: 5.5%
Housing: Homeownership rate: 70.0%; Median home value: $101,700; Median year structure built: 1958; Homeowner vacancy rate: 9.3%; Median selected monthly owner costs: $985 with a mortgage, $429 without a mortgage; Median gross rent: $931 per month; Rental vacancy rate: 0.0%
Health Insurance: 90.0% have insurance; 64.7% have private insurance; 38.2% have public insurance; 10.0% do not have insurance; 0.0% of children under 18 do not have insurance
Transportation: Commute: 100.0% car, 0.0% public transportation, 0.0% walk, 0.0% work from home; Mean travel time to work: 40.4 minutes

---

LANCASTER (city). County seat. Covers a land area of 18.841 square miles and a water area of 0.064 square miles. Located at 39.72° N. Lat; 82.61° W. Long. Elevation is 886 feet.
History: Lancaster was established on one of the three sections of land given to Ebenezer Zane for his work in laying out Zane's Trace. In 1800 the settlement on the banks of the Hocking River was named New Lancaster, because settlers had come from Lancaster, Pennsylvania. The first newspaper was printed in German, which was the language used in the early schools.
Population: 39,483; Growth (since 2000): 11.7%; Density: 2,095.6 persons per square mile; Race: 94.9% White, 1.9% Black/African American, 0.5% Asian, 0.2% American Indian/Alaska Native, 0.0% Native Hawaiian/Other Pacific Islander, 2.3% Two or more races, 2.1% Hispanic of any race; Average household size: 2.40; Median age: 38.8; Age under 18: 22.5%; Age 65 and over: 16.7%; Males per 100 females: 92.2; Marriage status: 29.2% never married, 46.9% now married, 2.8% separated, 7.7% widowed, 16.2% divorced; Foreign born: 1.2%; Speak English only: 98.5%; With disability: 19.6%; Veterans: 10.5%; Ancestry: 29.5% German, 16.7% Irish, 10.3% American, 9.4% English, 3.9% Italian
Employment: 11.5% management, business, and financial, 2.4% computer, engineering, and science, 7.5% education, legal, community service, arts, and media, 5.7% healthcare practitioners, 22.1% service, 27.2% sales and office, 7.8% natural resources, construction, and maintenance, 15.7% production, transportation, and material moving
Income: Per capita: $21,740; Median household: $38,625; Average household: $51,321; Households with income of $100,000 or more: 12.5%; Poverty rate: 20.5%
Educational Attainment: High school diploma or higher: 87.6%; Bachelor's degree or higher: 16.5%; Graduate/professional degree or higher: 5.3%

School District(s)

Fairfield Union Local (KG-12)
2015-16 Enrollment: 1,924 . . . . (740) 536-7384
Lancaster City (PK-12)
2015-16 Enrollment: 6,301 . . . . (740) 687-7300

Four-year College(s)

Ohio University-Lancaster Campus (Public)
Fall 2016 Enrollment: 1,829 . . . . (740) 654-6711
2016-17 Tuition: In-state $5,060; Out-of-state $9,596
Housing: Homeownership rate: 52.3%; Median home value: $117,100; Median year structure built: 1963; Homeowner vacancy rate: 1.8%; Median selected monthly owner costs: $1,110 with a mortgage, $395 without a mortgage; Median gross rent: $748 per month; Rental vacancy rate: 5.9%
Health Insurance: 91.4% have insurance; 59.5% have private insurance; 45.1% have public insurance; 8.6% do not have insurance; 1.1% of children under 18 do not have insurance
Hospitals: Fairfield Medical Center (229 beds)
Safety: Violent crime rate: 35.3 per 10,000 population; Property crime rate: 457.0 per 10,000 population

Newspapers: Eagle-Gazette (daily circulation 13,200)
Transportation: Commute: 93.4% car, 0.7% public transportation, 3.4% walk, 1.4% work from home; Mean travel time to work: 25.7 minutes
Airports: Fairfield County (general aviation)
Additional Information Contacts
City of Lancaster . . . . (740) 687-6600
http://www.ci.lancaster.oh.us

LITHOPOLIS (village). Covers a land area of 2.024 square miles and a water area of 0.004 square miles. Located at 39.82° N. Lat; 82.82° W. Long. Elevation is 942 feet.
History: The name of Lithopolis means "stone city" in the Greek, an appropriate name for a town that grew around sandstone quarries.
Population: 1,439; Growth (since 2000): 139.8%; Density: 710.9 persons per square mile; Race: 83.3% White, 8.0% Black/African American, 2.3% Asian, 0.1% American Indian/Alaska Native, 0.0% Native Hawaiian/Other Pacific Islander, 3.7% Two or more races, 2.5% Hispanic of any race; Average household size: 2.84; Median age: 38.0; Age under 18: 27.3%; Age 65 and over: 17.6%; Males per 100 females: 93.4; Marriage status: 23.3% never married, 59.6% now married, 2.3% separated, 6.0% widowed, 11.2% divorced; Foreign born: 4.4%; Speak English only: 90.4%; With disability: 17.2%; Veterans: 12.9%; Ancestry: 31.4% German, 18.2% Irish, 13.7% English, 5.3% American, 4.0% Italian
Employment: 17.5% management, business, and financial, 4.8% computer, engineering, and science, 7.0% education, legal, community service, arts, and media, 10.0% healthcare practitioners, 16.5% service, 20.6% sales and office, 3.5% natural resources, construction, and maintenance, 20.1% production, transportation, and material moving
Income: Per capita: $29,769; Median household: $70,069; Average household: $81,537; Households with income of $100,000 or more: 29.9%; Poverty rate: 2.4%
Educational Attainment: High school diploma or higher: 91.0%; Bachelor's degree or higher: 23.6%; Graduate/professional degree or higher: 10.9%

School District(s)

Bloom-Carroll Local (KG-12)
2015-16 Enrollment: 1,931 . . . . (614) 837-6560
Housing: Homeownership rate: 75.1%; Median home value: $184,900; Median year structure built: 1987; Homeowner vacancy rate: 0.0%; Median selected monthly owner costs: $1,641 with a mortgage, $459 without a mortgage; Median gross rent: $907 per month; Rental vacancy rate: 8.0%
Health Insurance: 91.7% have insurance; 80.6% have private insurance; 25.6% have public insurance; 8.3% do not have insurance; 12.5% of children under 18 do not have insurance
Safety: Violent crime rate: 0.0 per 10,000 population; Property crime rate: 92.8 per 10,000 population
Transportation: Commute: 96.3% car, 0.6% public transportation, 0.5% walk, 2.6% work from home; Mean travel time to work: 26.6 minutes

MILLERSPORT (village). Covers a land area of 0.873 square miles and a water area of 0.031 square miles. Located at 39.90° N. Lat; 82.54° W. Long. Elevation is 899 feet.
Population: 1,348; Growth (since 2000): 40.0%; Density: 1,544.3 persons per square mile; Race: 100.0% White, 0.0% Black/African American, 0.0% Asian, 0.0% American Indian/Alaska Native, 0.0% Native Hawaiian/Other Pacific Islander, 0.0% Two or more races, 0.0% Hispanic of any race; Average household size: 2.86; Median age: 35.9; Age under 18: 30.2%; Age 65 and over: 11.1%; Males per 100 females: 89.5; Marriage status: 26.2% never married, 51.6% now married, 1.0% separated, 3.8% widowed, 18.5% divorced; Foreign born: 0.7%; Speak English only: 98.6%; With disability: 15.7%; Veterans: 7.2%; Ancestry: 29.9% German, 20.6% English, 13.9% Irish, 6.6% American, 6.6% Polish
Employment: 7.0% management, business, and financial, 2.5% computer, engineering, and science, 11.7% education, legal, community service, arts, and media, 4.8% healthcare practitioners, 14.8% service, 26.8% sales and office, 14.1% natural resources, construction, and maintenance, 18.3% production, transportation, and material moving
Income: Per capita: $23,293; Median household: $52,813; Average household: $64,632; Households with income of $100,000 or more: 16.8%; Poverty rate: 9.4%
Educational Attainment: High school diploma or higher: 88.7%; Bachelor's degree or higher: 20.8%; Graduate/professional degree or higher: 6.7%

School District(s)

Walnut Township Local (KG-12)
2015-16 Enrollment: 528. . . . . (740) 467-2802
Housing: Homeownership rate: 69.4%; Median home value: $136,500; Median year structure built: 1963; Homeowner vacancy rate: 3.0%; Median selected monthly owner costs: $1,114 with a mortgage, $471 without a mortgage; Median gross rent: $717 per month; Rental vacancy rate: 10.0%
Health Insurance: 94.1% have insurance; 81.0% have private insurance; 24.6% have public insurance; 5.9% do not have insurance; 5.2% of children under 18 do not have insurance
Transportation: Commute: 94.7% car, 0.0% public transportation, 1.7% walk, 3.6% work from home; Mean travel time to work: 29.7 minutes

PICKERINGTON (city). Covers a land area of 9.745 square miles and a water area of 0.001 square miles. Located at 39.89° N. Lat; 82.77° W. Long. Elevation is 840 feet.
Population: 19,379; Growth (since 2000): 97.9%; Density: 1,988.6 persons per square mile; Race: 73.6% White, 18.4% Black/African American, 3.6% Asian, 0.0% American Indian/Alaska Native, 0.1% Native Hawaiian/Other Pacific Islander, 3.2% Two or more races, 2.9% Hispanic of any race; Average household size: 2.91; Median age: 35.5; Age under 18: 30.5%; Age 65 and over: 9.3%; Males per 100 females: 94.7; Marriage status: 26.1% never married, 59.8% now married, 1.2% separated, 4.4% widowed, 9.7% divorced; Foreign born: 5.2%; Speak English only: 93.3%; With disability: 8.0%; Veterans: 10.3%; Ancestry: 24.0% German, 14.3% Irish, 11.6% English, 5.5% Italian, 4.5% American
Employment: 19.4% management, business, and financial, 5.4% computer, engineering, and science, 10.4% education, legal, community service, arts, and media, 8.2% healthcare practitioners, 16.9% service, 25.9% sales and office, 5.6% natural resources, construction, and maintenance, 8.2% production, transportation, and material moving
Income: Per capita: $32,626; Median household: $84,410; Average household: $93,283; Households with income of $100,000 or more: 38.5%; Poverty rate: 5.2%
Educational Attainment: High school diploma or higher: 94.9%; Bachelor's degree or higher: 38.6%; Graduate/professional degree or higher: 12.3%

School District(s)

Pickerington Community School (09-12)
2015-16 Enrollment: 66. . . . . (877) 644-6338
Pickerington Local (PK-12)
2015-16 Enrollment: 10,181 . . . . (614) 833-2110
Housing: Homeownership rate: 75.1%; Median home value: $184,500; Median year structure built: 2000; Homeowner vacancy rate: 1.0%; Median selected monthly owner costs: $1,686 with a mortgage, $600 without a mortgage; Median gross rent: $1,033 per month; Rental vacancy rate: 0.0%
Health Insurance: 96.9% have insurance; 86.0% have private insurance; 19.8% have public insurance; 3.1% do not have insurance; 1.2% of children under 18 do not have insurance
Safety: Violent crime rate: 8.0 per 10,000 population; Property crime rate: 214.6 per 10,000 population
Transportation: Commute: 95.5% car, 0.1% public transportation, 0.0% walk, 3.6% work from home; Mean travel time to work: 26.4 minutes
Additional Information Contacts
City of Pickerington . . . . (614) 837-3974
http://www.ci.pickerington.oh.us

PLEASANTVILLE (village). Covers a land area of 0.266 square miles and a water area of 0 square miles. Located at 39.81° N. Lat; 82.52° W. Long. Elevation is 915 feet.
Population: 1,206; Growth (since 2000): 37.5%; Density: 4,539.7 persons per square mile; Race: 94.5% White, 2.7% Black/African American, 0.0% Asian, 0.0% American Indian/Alaska Native, 0.0% Native Hawaiian/Other Pacific Islander, 2.6% Two or more races, 0.5% Hispanic of any race; Average household size: 2.82; Median age: 31.8; Age under 18: 32.4%; Age 65 and over: 9.1%; Males per 100 females: 100.0; Marriage status: 33.5% never married, 48.0% now married, 2.0% separated, 5.7% widowed, 12.7% divorced; Foreign born: 0.0%; Speak English only: 98.4%; With disability: 22.1%; Veterans: 6.7%; Ancestry: 33.7% German, 15.3% Irish, 13.0% American, 7.5% English, 5.6% Dutch
Employment: 9.9% management, business, and financial, 2.2% computer, engineering, and science, 5.8% education, legal, community service, arts, and media, 3.9% healthcare practitioners, 23.5% service, 16.4% sales and

office, 20.1% natural resources, construction, and maintenance, 18.1% production, transportation, and material moving
Income: Per capita: $17,773; Median household: $35,000; Average household: $49,956; Households with income of $100,000 or more: 9.5%; Poverty rate: 29.8%
Educational Attainment: High school diploma or higher: 79.8%; Bachelor's degree or higher: 5.5%; Graduate/professional degree or higher: 1.3%

School District(s)

Fairfield Union Local (KG-12)
2015-16 Enrollment: 1,924 . . . . (740) 536-7384
Housing: Homeownership rate: 54.4%; Median home value: $93,800; Median year structure built: 1954; Homeowner vacancy rate: 3.0%; Median selected monthly owner costs: $1,012 with a mortgage, $419 without a mortgage; Median gross rent: $659 per month; Rental vacancy rate: 6.9%
Health Insurance: 84.4% have insurance; 47.3% have private insurance; 48.1% have public insurance; 15.6% do not have insurance; 6.9% of children under 18 do not have insurance
Transportation: Commute: 85.8% car, 3.1% public transportation, 1.8% walk, 6.4% work from home; Mean travel time to work: 31.3 minutes

RUSHVILLE (village). Covers a land area of 0.240 square miles and a water area of 0 square miles. Located at 39.76° N. Lat; 82.43° W. Long. Elevation is 1,053 feet.
History: Rushville was the birthplace of Benjamin Russell Hanby (1833-1867), who wrote the song "Darling Nellie Gray." Though it was published and became popular across the country, Hanby never received royalties for his work.
Population: 459; Growth (since 2000): 71.3%; Density: 1,915.7 persons per square mile; Race: 92.8% White, 0.7% Black/African American, 0.0% Asian, 2.2% American Indian/Alaska Native, 0.0% Native Hawaiian/Other Pacific Islander, 4.4% Two or more races, 0.0% Hispanic of any race; Average household size: 3.45; Median age: 26.4; Age under 18: 37.3%; Age 65 and over: 7.0%; Males per 100 females: 89.9; Marriage status: 32.9% never married, 50.0% now married, 1.9% separated, 6.2% widowed, 10.9% divorced; Foreign born: 0.0%; Speak English only: 100.0%; With disability: 10.5%; Veterans: 8.3%; Ancestry: 33.3% Irish, 25.5% German, 7.8% English, 3.5% Italian, 2.8% European
Employment: 7.8% management, business, and financial, 1.2% computer, engineering, and science, 4.8% education, legal, community service, arts, and media, 3.0% healthcare practitioners, 18.0% service, 31.1% sales and office, 12.6% natural resources, construction, and maintenance, 21.6% production, transportation, and material moving
Income: Per capita: $14,430; Median household: $39,107; Average household: $50,421; Households with income of $100,000 or more: 12.0%; Poverty rate: 29.4%
Educational Attainment: High school diploma or higher: 86.8%; Bachelor's degree or higher: 16.2%; Graduate/professional degree or higher: 0.4%
Housing: Homeownership rate: 67.7%; Median home value: $118,300; Median year structure built: Before 1940; Homeowner vacancy rate: 0.0%; Median selected monthly owner costs: $1,038 with a mortgage, $375 without a mortgage; Median gross rent: $900 per month; Rental vacancy rate: 4.4%
Health Insurance: 90.8% have insurance; 54.7% have private insurance; 40.1% have public insurance; 9.2% do not have insurance; 0.6% of children under 18 do not have insurance
Transportation: Commute: 90.4% car, 0.0% public transportation, 1.2% walk, 3.6% work from home; Mean travel time to work: 32.5 minutes

STOUTSVILLE (village). Covers a land area of 1.156 square miles and a water area of 0 square miles. Located at 39.60° N. Lat; 82.82° W. Long. Elevation is 968 feet.
Population: 544; Growth (since 2000): -6.4%; Density: 470.7 persons per square mile; Race: 96.0% White, 0.0% Black/African American, 0.0% Asian, 0.0% American Indian/Alaska Native, 0.0% Native Hawaiian/Other Pacific Islander, 4.0% Two or more races, 0.6% Hispanic of any race; Average household size: 2.72; Median age: 39.0; Age under 18: 21.0%; Age 65 and over: 15.1%; Males per 100 females: 102.2; Marriage status: 24.3% never married, 59.7% now married, 1.1% separated, 3.8% widowed, 12.2% divorced; Foreign born: 0.0%; Speak English only: 99.2%; With disability: 14.9%; Veterans: 7.9%; Ancestry: 21.5% German, 14.9% Irish, 13.6% American, 10.8% English, 3.9% Scottish
Employment: 12.3% management, business, and financial, 2.1% computer, engineering, and science, 4.5% education, legal, community service, arts, and media, 4.9% healthcare practitioners, 15.6% service, 16.0% sales and office, 18.9% natural resources, construction, and maintenance, 25.5% production, transportation, and material moving
Income: Per capita: $20,838; Median household: $47,500; Average household: $55,409; Households with income of $100,000 or more: 7.0%; Poverty rate: 12.1%
Educational Attainment: High school diploma or higher: 88.9%; Bachelor's degree or higher: 6.7%; Graduate/professional degree or higher: 3.0%
Housing: Homeownership rate: 80.0%; Median home value: $106,100; Median year structure built: 1948; Homeowner vacancy rate: 0.0%; Median selected monthly owner costs: $967 with a mortgage, $453 without a mortgage; Median gross rent: $732 per month; Rental vacancy rate: 0.0%
Health Insurance: 90.3% have insurance; 70.2% have private insurance; 33.6% have public insurance; 9.7% do not have insurance; 3.5% of children under 18 do not have insurance
Transportation: Commute: 92.6% car, 0.0% public transportation, 4.5% walk, 2.1% work from home; Mean travel time to work: 32.5 minutes

SUGAR GROVE (village). Covers a land area of 0.289 square miles and a water area of 0.012 square miles. Located at 39.63° N. Lat; 82.55° W. Long. Elevation is 778 feet.
Population: 480; Growth (since 2000): 7.1%; Density: 1,660.0 persons per square mile; Race: 99.6% White, 0.0% Black/African American, 0.0% Asian, 0.0% American Indian/Alaska Native, 0.0% Native Hawaiian/Other Pacific Islander, 0.4% Two or more races, 0.0% Hispanic of any race; Average household size: 3.02; Median age: 36.2; Age under 18: 29.0%; Age 65 and over: 10.2%; Males per 100 females: 100.9; Marriage status: 35.2% never married, 40.3% now married, 3.7% separated, 5.3% widowed, 19.2% divorced; Foreign born: 0.0%; Speak English only: 99.6%; With disability: 11.0%; Veterans: 5.0%; Ancestry: 43.1% German, 19.6% Irish, 7.9% Hungarian, 7.5% French, 7.3% English
Employment: 18.8% management, business, and financial, 0.5% computer, engineering, and science, 11.5% education, legal, community service, arts, and media, 8.7% healthcare practitioners, 10.1% service, 20.7% sales and office, 15.4% natural resources, construction, and maintenance, 14.4% production, transportation, and material moving
Income: Per capita: $19,260; Median household: $49,464; Average household: $55,881; Households with income of $100,000 or more: 8.1%; Poverty rate: 19.2%
Educational Attainment: High school diploma or higher: 96.5%; Bachelor's degree or higher: 11.4%; Graduate/professional degree or higher: 2.4%

School District(s)

Berne Union Local (PK-12)
2015-16 Enrollment: 876. . . . . (740) 746-8341
Housing: Homeownership rate: 50.3%; Median home value: $93,300; Median year structure built: Before 1940; Homeowner vacancy rate: 0.0%; Median selected monthly owner costs: $1,078 with a mortgage, $292 without a mortgage; Median gross rent: $800 per month; Rental vacancy rate: 0.0%
Health Insurance: 86.9% have insurance; 61.5% have private insurance; 36.3% have public insurance; 13.1% do not have insurance; 9.4% of children under 18 do not have insurance
Transportation: Commute: 93.5% car, 0.0% public transportation, 5.9% walk, 0.5% work from home; Mean travel time to work: 30.4 minutes

THURSTON (village). Covers a land area of 0.260 square miles and a water area of 0 square miles. Located at 39.84° N. Lat; 82.54° W. Long. Elevation is 886 feet.
Population: 473; Growth (since 2000): -14.8%; Density: 1,819.3 persons per square mile; Race: 99.4% White, 0.0% Black/African American, 0.0% Asian, 0.0% American Indian/Alaska Native, 0.0% Native Hawaiian/Other Pacific Islander, 0.0% Two or more races, 2.1% Hispanic of any race; Average household size: 2.44; Median age: 43.2; Age under 18: 26.0%; Age 65 and over: 13.5%; Males per 100 females: 92.4; Marriage status: 19.6% never married, 59.2% now married, 0.0% separated, 8.2% widowed, 13.0% divorced; Foreign born: 0.0%; Speak English only: 99.6%; With disability: 19.9%; Veterans: 10.3%; Ancestry: 27.1% German, 15.0% Irish, 9.3% English, 8.2% American, 5.5% Scottish
Employment: 10.7% management, business, and financial, 2.3% computer, engineering, and science, 4.7% education, legal, community service, arts, and media, 6.0% healthcare practitioners, 23.7% service, 24.7% sales and office, 11.6% natural resources, construction, and maintenance, 16.3% production, transportation, and material moving

Income: Per capita: $17,782; Median household: $37,500; Average household: $43,428; Households with income of $100,000 or more: 3.6%; Poverty rate: 19.0%
Educational Attainment: High school diploma or higher: 82.8%; Bachelor's degree or higher: 7.2%; Graduate/professional degree or higher: 1.3%
Housing: Homeownership rate: 58.8%; Median home value: $86,000; Median year structure built: 1976; Homeowner vacancy rate: 0.0%; Median selected monthly owner costs: $1,073 with a mortgage, $433 without a mortgage; Median gross rent: $833 per month; Rental vacancy rate: 11.1%
Health Insurance: 85.4% have insurance; 48.0% have private insurance; 46.7% have public insurance; 14.6% do not have insurance; 8.9% of children under 18 do not have insurance
Transportation: Commute: 91.0% car, 0.0% public transportation, 1.9% walk, 7.1% work from home; Mean travel time to work: 34.8 minutes
Additional Information Contacts
Village of Thurston . . . . (740) 862-6003
http://www.thurstonohio.com

WEST RUSHVILLE (village). Covers a land area of 0.065 square miles and a water area of <.001 square miles. Located at 39.76° N. Lat; 82.45° W. Long. Elevation is 1,020 feet.
Population: 267; Growth (since 2000): 102.3%; Density: 4,118.0 persons per square mile; Race: 88.0% White, 8.2% Black/African American, 0.0% Asian, 0.0% American Indian/Alaska Native, 0.0% Native Hawaiian/Other Pacific Islander, 3.7% Two or more races, 0.0% Hispanic of any race; Average household size: 3.66; Median age: 31.6; Age under 18: 34.1%; Age 65 and over: 5.2%; Males per 100 females: 103.0; Marriage status: 30.2% never married, 61.5% now married, 3.6% separated, 3.1% widowed, 5.2% divorced; Foreign born: 0.0%; Speak English only: 99.2%; With disability: 17.2%; Veterans: 8.0%; Ancestry: 31.8% German, 22.5% Irish, 7.5% American, 7.1% Dutch, 3.7% Italian
Employment: 13.3% management, business, and financial, 4.8% computer, engineering, and science, 9.6% education, legal, community service, arts, and media, 10.8% healthcare practitioners, 8.4% service, 16.9% sales and office, 10.8% natural resources, construction, and maintenance, 25.3% production, transportation, and material moving
Income: Per capita: $14,512; Median household: $48,750; Average household: $48,993; Households with income of $100,000 or more: 4.1%; Poverty rate: 15.0%
Educational Attainment: High school diploma or higher: 75.4%; Bachelor's degree or higher: 10.8%; Graduate/professional degree or higher: 0.6%
Housing: Homeownership rate: 65.8%; Median home value: $68,800; Median year structure built: Before 1940; Homeowner vacancy rate: 0.0%; Median selected monthly owner costs: $879 with a mortgage, $241 without a mortgage; Median gross rent: $681 per month; Rental vacancy rate: 0.0%
Health Insurance: 86.5% have insurance; 48.7% have private insurance; 55.1% have public insurance; 13.5% do not have insurance; 7.7% of children under 18 do not have insurance
Transportation: Commute: 98.8% car, 0.0% public transportation, 1.3% walk, 0.0% work from home; Mean travel time to work: 32.6 minutes

Fayette County

Located in south central Ohio; drained by Paint, Sugar, and Rattlesnakes Creeks. Covers a land area of 406.357 square miles, a water area of 0.658 square miles, and is located in the Eastern Time Zone at 39.55° N. Lat., 83.46° W. Long. The county was founded in 1810. County seat is Washington Court House.

Fayette County is part of the Washington Court House, OH Micropolitan Statistical Area. The entire metro area includes: Fayette County, OH

Population: 28,719; Growth (since 2000): 1.0%; Density: 70.7 persons per square mile; Race: 94.2% White, 2.0% Black/African American, 0.8% Asian, 0.1% American Indian/Alaska Native, 0.0% Native Hawaiian/Other Pacific Islander, 2.3% two or more races, 1.9% Hispanic of any race; Average household size: 2.42; Median age: 41.3; Age under 18: 23.9%; Age 65 and over: 16.5%; Males per 100 females: 96.7; Marriage status: 23.8% never married, 54.4% now married, 3.0% separated, 6.0% widowed, 15.9% divorced; Foreign born: 1.5%; Speak English only: 97.0%; With disability: 16.3%; Veterans: 10.0%; Ancestry: 14.6% American, 13.7% German, 8.8% Irish, 7.8% English, 1.7% Dutch
Religion: Six largest groups: 7.0% Methodist/Pietist, 6.2% Baptist, 5.9% Non-denominational Protestant, 2.2% Catholicism, 1.5% Presbyterian-Reformed, 0.8% Episcopalianism/Anglicanism
Economy: Unemployment rate: 3.8%; Leading industries: 29.5 % retail trade; 11.3 % accommodation and food services; 10.8 % other services (except public administration); Farms: 504 totaling 196,529 acres; Company size: 0 employ 1,000 or more persons, 1 employs 500 to 999 persons, 15 employ 100 to 499 persons, 568 employ less than 100 persons; Business ownership: 581 women-owned, 31 Black-owned, n/a Hispanic-owned, 33 Asian-owned, n/a American Indian/Alaska Native-owned
Employment: 10.7% management, business, and financial, 1.8% computer, engineering, and science, 7.1% education, legal, community service, arts, and media, 5.7% healthcare practitioners, 16.8% service, 25.1% sales and office, 10.3% natural resources, construction, and maintenance, 22.5% production, transportation, and material moving
Income: Per capita: $22,728; Median household: $41,954; Average household: $55,529; Households with income of $100,000 or more: 12.5%; Poverty rate: 18.6%
Educational Attainment: High school diploma or higher: 87.4%; Bachelor's degree or higher: 14.5%; Graduate/professional degree or higher: 3.3%
Housing: Homeownership rate: 61.5%; Median home value: $107,100; Median year structure built: 1971; Homeowner vacancy rate: 1.5%; Median selected monthly owner costs: $1,040 with a mortgage, $379 without a mortgage; Median gross rent: $691 per month; Rental vacancy rate: 2.6%
Vital Statistics: Birth rate: 109.8 per 10,000 population; Death rate: 108.1 per 10,000 population; Age-adjusted cancer mortality rate: 219.7 deaths per 100,000 population
Health Insurance: 89.9% have insurance; 59.9% have private insurance; 42.7% have public insurance; 10.1% do not have insurance; 4.7% of children under 18 do not have insurance
Health Care: Physicians: 5.2 per 10,000 population; Dentists: 4.2 per 10,000 population; Hospital beds: 8.7 per 10,000 population; Hospital admissions: 294.9 per 10,000 population
Air Quality Index (AQI): Percent of Days: 87.8% good, 11.9% moderate, 0.3% unhealthy for sensitive individuals, 0.0% unhealthy, 0.0% very unhealthy; Annual median: 37; Annual maximum: 108
Transportation: Commute: 94.5% car, 0.1% public transportation, 1.7% walk, 3.3% work from home; Mean travel time to work: 24.0 minutes
2016 Presidential Election: 71.2% Trump, 24.4% Clinton, 2.6% Johnson, 0.5% Stein
Additional Information Contacts
Fayette Government . . . . (740) 335-0720
http://www.fayette-co-oh.com

Fayette County Communities

BLOOMINGBURG (village). Covers a land area of 0.701 square miles and a water area of 0 square miles. Located at 39.61° N. Lat; 83.40° W. Long. Elevation is 994 feet.
Population: 1,006; Growth (since 2000): 15.1%; Density: 1,434.7 persons per square mile; Race: 92.8% White, 4.4% Black/African American, 0.0% Asian, 1.5% American Indian/Alaska Native, 0.0% Native Hawaiian/Other Pacific Islander, 0.0% Two or more races, 10.2% Hispanic of any race; Average household size: 2.42; Median age: 34.4; Age under 18: 26.7%; Age 65 and over: 10.4%; Males per 100 females: 107.1; Marriage status: 28.9% never married, 50.9% now married, 1.0% separated, 5.1% widowed, 15.0% divorced; Foreign born: 6.3%; Speak English only: 91.3%; With disability: 16.6%; Veterans: 8.1%; Ancestry: 10.1% American, 8.3% Irish, 5.8% German, 5.4% English, 1.5% Dutch
Employment: 3.6% management, business, and financial, 5.9% computer, engineering, and science, 2.0% education, legal, community service, arts, and media, 2.3% healthcare practitioners, 12.0% service, 23.7% sales and office, 20.2% natural resources, construction, and maintenance, 30.4% production, transportation, and material moving
Income: Per capita: $17,867; Median household: $34,861; Average household: $42,994; Households with income of $100,000 or more: 6.0%; Poverty rate: 26.6%
Educational Attainment: High school diploma or higher: 89.7%; Bachelor's degree or higher: 9.8%; Graduate/professional degree or higher: n/a
Housing: Homeownership rate: 61.1%; Median home value: $74,500; Median year structure built: 1972; Homeowner vacancy rate: 0.0%; Median

selected monthly owner costs: $800 with a mortgage, $319 without a mortgage; Median gross rent: $672 per month; Rental vacancy rate: 3.6%
Health Insurance: 78.6% have insurance; 53.8% have private insurance; 37.2% have public insurance; 21.4% do not have insurance; 10.8% of children under 18 do not have insurance
Transportation: Commute: 94.6% car, 0.0% public transportation, 4.1% walk, 1.3% work from home; Mean travel time to work: 24.0 minutes

GOOD HOPE (CDP). Covers a land area of 0.753 square miles and a water area of 0 square miles. Located at 39.45° N. Lat; 83.36° W. Long. Elevation is 922 feet.
Population: 327; Growth (since 2000): n/a; Density: 434.4 persons per square mile; Race: 98.8% White, 0.0% Black/African American, 0.0% Asian, 0.0% American Indian/Alaska Native, 0.0% Native Hawaiian/Other Pacific Islander, 1.2% Two or more races, 0.0% Hispanic of any race; Average household size: 3.17; Median age: 27.0; Age under 18: 38.5%; Age 65 and over: 15.3%; Males per 100 females: 91.8; Marriage status: 6.7% never married, 85.6% now married, 0.0% separated, 0.0% widowed, 7.7% divorced; Foreign born: 0.0%; Speak English only: 100.0%; With disability: 32.1%; Veterans: 13.9%; Ancestry: 29.4% English, 4.9% American, 4.9% German, 3.4% Hungarian, 2.4% Irish
Employment: 0.0% management, business, and financial, 0.0% computer, engineering, and science, 14.1% education, legal, community service, arts, and media, 0.0% healthcare practitioners, 23.4% service, 23.4% sales and office, 39.1% natural resources, construction, and maintenance, 0.0% production, transportation, and material moving
Income: Per capita: $12,396; Median household: $40,815; Average household: $40,086; Households with income of $100,000 or more: 9.7%; Poverty rate: 42.2%
Educational Attainment: High school diploma or higher: 100.0%; Bachelor's degree or higher: 10.7%; Graduate/professional degree or higher: 6.2%
Housing: Homeownership rate: 62.1%; Median home value: $85,000; Median year structure built: 1978; Homeowner vacancy rate: 0.0%; Median selected monthly owner costs: $838 with a mortgage, $424 without a mortgage; Median gross rent: n/a per month; Rental vacancy rate: 0.0%
Health Insurance: 97.6% have insurance; 40.1% have private insurance; 60.9% have public insurance; 2.4% do not have insurance; 0.0% of children under 18 do not have insurance
Transportation: Commute: 100.0% car, 0.0% public transportation, 0.0% walk, 0.0% work from home; Mean travel time to work: 14.6 minutes

JEFFERSONVILLE (village). Covers a land area of 1.700 square miles and a water area of 0.035 square miles. Located at 39.65° N. Lat; 83.56° W. Long. Elevation is 1,050 feet.
Population: 1,212; Growth (since 2000): -5.9%; Density: 713.1 persons per square mile; Race: 89.3% White, 7.3% Black/African American, 0.0% Asian, 0.0% American Indian/Alaska Native, 0.0% Native Hawaiian/Other Pacific Islander, 3.4% Two or more races, 2.2% Hispanic of any race; Average household size: 2.50; Median age: 31.7; Age under 18: 29.3%; Age 65 and over: 13.3%; Males per 100 females: 95.0; Marriage status: 30.0% never married, 44.7% now married, 4.6% separated, 4.5% widowed, 20.8% divorced; Foreign born: 0.0%; Speak English only: 99.2%; With disability: 12.3%; Veterans: 8.4%; Ancestry: 11.7% German, 9.4% American, 8.3% Irish, 5.0% English, 1.7% Italian
Employment: 6.4% management, business, and financial, 3.1% computer, engineering, and science, 3.1% education, legal, community service, arts, and media, 0.8% healthcare practitioners, 16.6% service, 29.1% sales and office, 9.6% natural resources, construction, and maintenance, 31.4% production, transportation, and material moving
Income: Per capita: $18,013; Median household: $38,276; Average household: $45,156; Households with income of $100,000 or more: 4.3%; Poverty rate: 26.5%
Educational Attainment: High school diploma or higher: 83.9%; Bachelor's degree or higher: 9.7%; Graduate/professional degree or higher: 3.9%
Housing: Homeownership rate: 51.9%; Median home value: $77,500; Median year structure built: 1971; Homeowner vacancy rate: 4.6%; Median selected monthly owner costs: $845 with a mortgage, $372 without a mortgage; Median gross rent: $652 per month; Rental vacancy rate: 9.7%
Health Insurance: 91.5% have insurance; 52.6% have private insurance; 49.7% have public insurance; 8.5% do not have insurance; 0.6% of children under 18 do not have insurance
Transportation: Commute: 98.2% car, 0.0% public transportation, 1.2% walk, 0.0% work from home; Mean travel time to work: 23.4 minutes

MILLEDGEVILLE (village). Covers a land area of 0.101 square miles and a water area of 0 square miles. Located at 39.59° N. Lat; 83.59° W. Long. Elevation is 1,050 feet.
Population: 140; Growth (since 2000): 14.8%; Density: 1,382.9 persons per square mile; Race: 72.1% White, 0.0% Black/African American, 0.0% Asian, 0.0% American Indian/Alaska Native, 0.0% Native Hawaiian/Other Pacific Islander, 27.9% Two or more races, 0.7% Hispanic of any race; Average household size: 2.37; Median age: 35.0; Age under 18: 35.7%; Age 65 and over: 17.1%; Males per 100 females: 133.3; Marriage status: 30.1% never married, 34.4% now married, 0.0% separated, 10.8% widowed, 24.7% divorced; Foreign born: 0.0%; Speak English only: 100.0%; With disability: 12.1%; Veterans: 24.4%; Ancestry: 25.7% American, 5.7% Irish, 5.0% German, 3.6% Dutch, 2.9% English
Employment: 15.0% management, business, and financial, 0.0% computer, engineering, and science, 5.0% education, legal, community service, arts, and media, 0.0% healthcare practitioners, 25.0% service, 25.0% sales and office, 2.5% natural resources, construction, and maintenance, 27.5% production, transportation, and material moving
Income: Per capita: $16,349; Median household: $41,250; Average household: $39,105; Households with income of $100,000 or more: 6.8%; Poverty rate: 16.4%
Educational Attainment: High school diploma or higher: 74.0%; Bachelor's degree or higher: 5.5%; Graduate/professional degree or higher: 2.7%
Housing: Homeownership rate: 52.5%; Median home value: $63,000; Median year structure built: Before 1940; Homeowner vacancy rate: 3.1%; Median selected monthly owner costs: $950 with a mortgage, $370 without a mortgage; Median gross rent: $710 per month; Rental vacancy rate: 0.0%
Health Insurance: 97.9% have insurance; 79.3% have private insurance; 28.6% have public insurance; 2.1% do not have insurance; 0.0% of children under 18 do not have insurance
Transportation: Commute: 85.0% car, 0.0% public transportation, 0.0% walk, 15.0% work from home; Mean travel time to work: 29.7 minutes

OCTA (village). Covers a land area of 0.278 square miles and a water area of 0 square miles. Located at 39.61° N. Lat; 83.61° W. Long. Elevation is 1,040 feet.
Population: 34; Growth (since 2000): -59.0%; Density: 122.5 persons per square mile; Race: 100.0% White, 0.0% Black/African American, 0.0% Asian, 0.0% American Indian/Alaska Native, 0.0% Native Hawaiian/Other Pacific Islander, 0.0% Two or more races, 11.8% Hispanic of any race; Average household size: 1.48; Median age: 62.5; Age under 18: 0.0%; Age 65 and over: 47.1%; Males per 100 females: 96.7; Marriage status: 17.6% never married, 32.4% now married, 5.9% separated, 26.5% widowed, 23.5% divorced; Foreign born: 0.0%; Speak English only: 100.0%; With disability: 23.5%; Veterans: 14.7%; Ancestry: 17.6% German, 11.8% English, 5.9% Irish, 2.9% American, 2.9% Dutch
Employment: 27.8% management, business, and financial, 0.0% computer, engineering, and science, 0.0% education, legal, community service, arts, and media, 0.0% healthcare practitioners, 38.9% service, 0.0% sales and office, 11.1% natural resources, construction, and maintenance, 22.2% production, transportation, and material moving
Income: Per capita: $21,121; Median household: $29,375; Average household: $31,396; Households with income of $100,000 or more: n/a; Poverty rate: 32.4%
Educational Attainment: High school diploma or higher: 73.5%; Bachelor's degree or higher: 5.9%; Graduate/professional degree or higher: n/a
Housing: Homeownership rate: 60.9%; Median home value: $55,000; Median year structure built: 1986; Homeowner vacancy rate: 0.0%; Median selected monthly owner costs: n/a with a mortgage, $200 without a mortgage; Median gross rent: $465 per month; Rental vacancy rate: 0.0%
Health Insurance: 85.3% have insurance; 52.9% have private insurance; 52.9% have public insurance; 14.7% do not have insurance; 0.0% of children under 18 do not have insurance
Transportation: Commute: 72.2% car, 0.0% public transportation, 27.8% walk, 0.0% work from home; Mean travel time to work: 15.0 minutes

PANCOASTBURG (CDP). Covers a land area of 0.341 square miles and a water area of 0.006 square miles. Located at 39.62° N. Lat; 83.27° W. Long. Elevation is 866 feet.
Population: 106; Growth (since 2000): n/a; Density: 311.2 persons per square mile; Race: 95.3% White, 0.0% Black/African American, 0.0% Asian, 0.0% American Indian/Alaska Native, 0.0% Native Hawaiian/Other

Pacific Islander, 4.7% Two or more races, 0.0% Hispanic of any race; Average household size: 2.26; Median age: 45.4; Age under 18: 8.5%; Age 65 and over: 4.7%; Males per 100 females: 107.1; Marriage status: 5.2% never married, 86.6% now married, 20.6% separated, 0.0% widowed, 8.2% divorced; Foreign born: 0.0%; Speak English only: 100.0%; With disability: 0.0%; Veterans: 20.6%; Ancestry: 7.5% German, 4.7% Scottish
Employment: 0.0% management, business, and financial, 32.8% computer, engineering, and science, 0.0% education, legal, community service, arts, and media, 0.0% healthcare practitioners, 18.0% service, 0.0% sales and office, 0.0% natural resources, construction, and maintenance, 49.2% production, transportation, and material moving
Income: Per capita: $21,746; Median household: n/a; Average household: $55,238; Households with income of $100,000 or more: n/a; Poverty rate: 7.5%
Educational Attainment: High school diploma or higher: 76.3%; Bachelor's degree or higher: n/a; Graduate/professional degree or higher: n/a
Housing: Homeownership rate: 51.1%; Median home value: $47,500; Median year structure built: Before 1940; Homeowner vacancy rate: 0.0%; Median selected monthly owner costs: $580 with a mortgage, n/a without a mortgage; Median gross rent: n/a per month; Rental vacancy rate: 0.0%
Health Insurance: 80.2% have insurance; 67.0% have private insurance; 13.2% have public insurance; 19.8% do not have insurance; 0.0% of children under 18 do not have insurance
Transportation: Commute: 100.0% car, 0.0% public transportation, 0.0% walk, 0.0% work from home; Mean travel time to work: 0.0 minutes

WASHINGTON COURT HOUSE (city). County seat. Covers a land area of 8.739 square miles and a water area of 0.060 square miles. Located at 39.54° N. Lat; 83.43° W. Long. Elevation is 978 feet.
Population: 14,115; Growth (since 2000): n/a; Density: 1,615.2 persons per square mile; Race: 93.4% White, 1.9% Black/African American, 1.2% Asian, 0.0% American Indian/Alaska Native, 0.0% Native Hawaiian/Other Pacific Islander, 3.0% Two or more races, 1.4% Hispanic of any race; Average household size: 2.32; Median age: 41.0; Age under 18: 24.5%; Age 65 and over: 16.6%; Males per 100 females: 91.1; Marriage status: 25.5% never married, 48.0% now married, 3.5% separated, 7.6% widowed, 18.9% divorced; Foreign born: 1.9%; Speak English only: 96.7%; With disability: 17.6%; Veterans: 9.9%; Ancestry: 16.1% American, 13.9% German, 10.3% Irish, 6.9% English, 2.2% Dutch
Employment: 9.0% management, business, and financial, 1.0% computer, engineering, and science, 7.4% education, legal, community service, arts, and media, 5.7% healthcare practitioners, 19.3% service, 26.5% sales and office, 8.8% natural resources, construction, and maintenance, 22.4% production, transportation, and material moving
Income: Per capita: $21,773; Median household: $37,905; Average household: $51,401; Households with income of $100,000 or more: 9.4%; Poverty rate: 22.4%
Educational Attainment: High school diploma or higher: 86.6%; Bachelor's degree or higher: 15.0%; Graduate/professional degree or higher: 2.9%

School District(s)

Miami Trace Local (PK-12)
2015-16 Enrollment: 2,595 . . . . (740) 335-3010
Washington Court House City (PK-12)
2015-16 Enrollment: 2,232 . . . . (740) 335-6620

Housing: Homeownership rate: 49.9%; Median home value: $95,600; Median year structure built: 1966; Homeowner vacancy rate: 1.7%; Median selected monthly owner costs: $1,005 with a mortgage, $353 without a mortgage; Median gross rent: $689 per month; Rental vacancy rate: 2.9%
Health Insurance: 89.5% have insurance; 54.4% have private insurance; 48.3% have public insurance; 10.5% do not have insurance; 5.8% of children under 18 do not have insurance
Hospitals: Fayette County Memorial Hospital (70 beds)
Safety: Violent crime rate: 26.5 per 10,000 population; Property crime rate: 437.6 per 10,000 population
Newspapers: Record-Herald (daily circulation 5,200)
Transportation: Commute: 95.2% car, 0.0% public transportation, 1.7% walk, 2.8% work from home; Mean travel time to work: 23.7 minutes
Airports: Fayette County (general aviation)
Additional Information Contacts
City of Washington Court House . . . . (740) 636-2340
http://www.ci.washington-court-house.oh.us

Franklin County

Located in central Ohio; crossed by the Scioto and Olentangy Rivers. Covers a land area of 532.188 square miles, a water area of 11.320 square miles, and is located in the Eastern Time Zone at 39.97° N. Lat., 83.01° W. Long. The county was founded in 1803. County seat is Columbus.

Franklin County is part of the Columbus, OH Metropolitan Statistical Area. The entire metro area includes: Delaware County, OH; Fairfield County, OH; Franklin County, OH; Hocking County, OH; Licking County, OH; Madison County, OH; Morrow County, OH; Perry County, OH; Pickaway County, OH; Union County, OH

Weather Station: Columbus Valley Crossing — Elevation: 734 feet

	Jan	Feb	Mar	Apr	May	Jun	Jul	Aug	Sep	Oct	Nov	Dec
High	37	41	52	64	73	82	85	84	78	66	54	41
Low	21	23	31	41	51	60	64	62	54	43	34	25
Precip	2.9	2.1	3.3	3.7	4.5	4.0	4.5	3.3	3.0	2.9	3.2	3.0
Snow	5.7	4.0	1.6	0.5	tr	0.0	0.0	0.0	0.0	tr	0.4	2.7

High and Low temperatures in degrees Fahrenheit; Precipitation and Snow in inches

Weather Station: Columbus-Port Columbus Intl — Elevation: 810 feet

	Jan	Feb	Mar	Apr	May	Jun	Jul	Aug	Sep	Oct	Nov	Dec
High	37	41	51	63	73	81	85	84	77	65	52	40
Low	22	24	32	42	51	61	65	63	56	44	35	26
Precip	2.7	2.2	3.1	3.4	4.2	4.0	4.7	3.5	2.9	2.6	3.1	3.0
Snow	9.3	6.3	4.4	1.1	tr	tr	tr	tr	tr	0.2	1.2	5.4

High and Low temperatures in degrees Fahrenheit; Precipitation and Snow in inches

Weather Station: Westerville — Elevation: 810 feet

	Jan	Feb	Mar	Apr	May	Jun	Jul	Aug	Sep	Oct	Nov	Dec
High	37	41	52	65	74	82	85	84	78	66	53	41
Low	21	23	31	41	50	59	63	62	54	43	35	26
Precip	2.7	2.2	2.9	3.5	4.4	4.5	4.3	3.2	2.8	2.8	3.1	2.9
Snow	6.9	4.6	2.5	0.5	tr	0.0	0.0	0.0	0.0	tr	0.3	3.7

High and Low temperatures in degrees Fahrenheit; Precipitation and Snow in inches

Population: 1,232,118; Growth (since 2000): 15.3%; Density: 2,315.2 persons per square mile; Race: 68.3% White, 21.7% Black/African American, 4.6% Asian, 0.2% American Indian/Alaska Native, 0.0% Native Hawaiian/Other Pacific Islander, 3.7% two or more races, 5.1% Hispanic of any race; Average household size: 2.46; Median age: 33.9; Age under 18: 23.7%; Age 65 and over: 10.8%; Males per 100 females: 94.9; Marriage status: 38.9% never married, 44.5% now married, 2.0% separated, 4.6% widowed, 12.0% divorced; Foreign born: 9.9%; Speak English only: 87.5%; With disability: 11.5%; Veterans: 7.1%; Ancestry: 21.7% German, 12.5% Irish, 7.9% English, 5.7% Italian, 5.1% American
Religion: Six largest groups: 13.2% Catholicism, 5.3% Baptist, 4.4% Non-denominational Protestant, 4.0% Methodist/Pietist, 2.6% Lutheran, 2.2% Pentecostal
Economy: Unemployment rate: 3.8%; Leading industries: 13.3 % retail trade; 13.2 % health care and social assistance; 12.9 % professional, scientific, and technical services; Farms: 388 totaling 62,017 acres; Company size: 39 employ 1,000 or more persons, 71 employs 500 to 999 persons, 987 employ 100 to 499 persons, 26,661 employs less than 100 persons; Business ownership: 40,290 women-owned, 19,001 Black-owned, 2,985 Hispanic-owned, 4,633 Asian-owned, 665 American Indian/Alaska Native-owned
Employment: 17.2% management, business, and financial, 7.0% computer, engineering, and science, 11.6% education, legal, community service, arts, and media, 6.3% healthcare practitioners, 16.8% service, 24.9% sales and office, 5.1% natural resources, construction, and maintenance, 11.1% production, transportation, and material moving
Income: Per capita: $30,098; Median household: $54,037; Average household: $73,666; Households with income of $100,000 or more: 22.6%; Poverty rate: 17.1%
Educational Attainment: High school diploma or higher: 90.4%; Bachelor's degree or higher: 38.4%; Graduate/professional degree or higher: 14.0%
Housing: Homeownership rate: 53.3%; Median home value: $153,100; Median year structure built: 1975; Homeowner vacancy rate: 1.5%; Median selected monthly owner costs: $1,405 with a mortgage, $549 without a mortgage; Median gross rent: $869 per month; Rental vacancy rate: 5.5%
Vital Statistics: Birth rate: 149.8 per 10,000 population; Death rate: 77.4 per 10,000 population; Age-adjusted cancer mortality rate: 168.3 deaths per 100,000 population

Health Insurance: 89.8% have insurance; 68.6% have private insurance; 29.8% have public insurance; 10.2% do not have insurance; 4.9% of children under 18 do not have insurance
Health Care: Physicians: 48.1 per 10,000 population; Dentists: 8.5 per 10,000 population; Hospital beds: 41.3 per 10,000 population; Hospital admissions: 1,840.2 per 10,000 population
Air Quality Index (AQI): Percent of Days: 74.9% good, 22.7% moderate, 2.5% unhealthy for sensitive individuals, 0.0% unhealthy, 0.0% very unhealthy; Annual median: 42; Annual maximum: 126
Transportation: Commute: 89.3% car, 2.5% public transportation, 2.5% walk, 4.1% work from home; Mean travel time to work: 21.7 minutes
2016 Presidential Election: 33.9% Trump, 59.8% Clinton, 3.4% Johnson, 1.0% Stein
National and State Parks: Olentangy River State Wildlife Access Area; Sawmill State Wildlife Education Area
Additional Information Contacts
Franklin Government. . . . . (614) 462-3322
http://www.co.franklin.oh.us

Franklin County Communities

AMLIN (unincorporated postal area)

ZCTA: 43002

Covers a land area of 0.994 square miles and a water area of 0.002 square miles. Located at 40.06° N. Lat; 83.17° W. Long. Elevation is 945 feet.
Population: 2,858; Growth (since 2000): 119.2%; Density: 2,874.7 persons per square mile; Race: 89.6% White, 4.7% Black/African American, 2.3% Asian, 0.0% American Indian/Alaska Native, 0.0% Native Hawaiian/Other Pacific Islander, 3.5% Two or more races, 4.6% Hispanic of any race; Average household size: 1.73; Median age: 33.9; Age under 18: 6.7%; Age 65 and over: 5.0%; Males per 100 females: 91.5; Marriage status: 37.7% never married, 46.5% now married, 0.0% separated, 2.0% widowed, 13.8% divorced; Foreign born: 5.1%; Speak English only: 88.4%; With disability: 5.4%; Veterans: 4.9%; Ancestry: 40.2% German, 28.9% Irish, 7.8% European, 7.2% Italian, 5.8% Hungarian
Employment: 23.6% management, business, and financial, 13.7% computer, engineering, and science, 10.9% education, legal, community service, arts, and media, 12.8% healthcare practitioners, 10.1% service, 21.5% sales and office, 4.3% natural resources, construction, and maintenance, 3.1% production, transportation, and material moving
Income: Per capita: $52,333; Median household: $79,060; Average household: $88,888; Households with income of $100,000 or more: 41.3%; Poverty rate: 0.5%
Educational Attainment: High school diploma or higher: 98.7%; Bachelor's degree or higher: 61.5%; Graduate/professional degree or higher: 17.6%
Housing: Homeownership rate: 85.9%; Median home value: $155,600; Median year structure built: 2007; Homeowner vacancy rate: 2.9%; Median selected monthly owner costs: $1,357 with a mortgage, $0 without a mortgage; Median gross rent: $1,280 per month; Rental vacancy rate: 0.0%
Health Insurance: 99.5% have insurance; 97.4% have private insurance; 6.5% have public insurance; 0.5% do not have insurance; 0.0% of children under 18 do not have insurance
Transportation: Commute: 95.5% car, 0.0% public transportation, 0.0% walk, 4.5% work from home; Mean travel time to work: 21.7 minutes

BEXLEY (city). Covers a land area of 2.431 square miles and a water area of 0.020 square miles. Located at 39.97° N. Lat; 82.93° W. Long. Elevation is 794 feet.
History: Named for Bexley, England. Bexley developed as a residential suburb of Columbus, and as the location of Capital University, founded in 1830 as a Lutheran divinity school.
Population: 13,534; Growth (since 2000): 2.5%; Density: 5,567.1 persons per square mile; Race: 88.8% White, 6.0% Black/African American, 1.1% Asian, 0.1% American Indian/Alaska Native, 0.1% Native Hawaiian/Other Pacific Islander, 2.8% Two or more races, 1.9% Hispanic of any race; Average household size: 2.71; Median age: 34.1; Age under 18: 25.9%; Age 65 and over: 11.0%; Males per 100 females: 88.4; Marriage status: 36.7% never married, 52.0% now married, 0.6% separated, 3.0% widowed, 8.2% divorced; Foreign born: 5.9%; Speak English only: 94.9%; With disability: 6.4%; Veterans: 4.9%; Ancestry: 30.8% German, 17.9% Irish, 12.5% English, 7.3% Italian, 5.4% American
Employment: 26.1% management, business, and financial, 5.4% computer, engineering, and science, 23.1% education, legal, community service, arts, and media, 6.7% healthcare practitioners, 12.2% service, 21.5% sales and office, 1.8% natural resources, construction, and maintenance, 3.2% production, transportation, and material moving
Income: Per capita: $46,821; Median household: $101,736; Average household: $137,652; Households with income of $100,000 or more: 50.8%; Poverty rate: 9.7%
Educational Attainment: High school diploma or higher: 97.8%; Bachelor's degree or higher: 74.1%; Graduate/professional degree or higher: 35.8%

School District(s)

Bexley City (PK-12)
2015-16 Enrollment: 2,282 . . . . (614) 231-7611
Housing: Homeownership rate: 76.0%; Median home value: $291,900; Median year structure built: 1943; Homeowner vacancy rate: 1.3%; Median selected monthly owner costs: $2,100 with a mortgage, $868 without a mortgage; Median gross rent: $913 per month; Rental vacancy rate: 5.3%
Health Insurance: 97.2% have insurance; 89.7% have private insurance; 15.7% have public insurance; 2.8% do not have insurance; 1.2% of children under 18 do not have insurance
Safety: Violent crime rate: 18.9 per 10,000 population; Property crime rate: 260.6 per 10,000 population
Transportation: Commute: 83.0% car, 1.4% public transportation, 6.4% walk, 7.0% work from home; Mean travel time to work: 18.2 minutes
Additional Information Contacts
City of Bexley . . . . (614) 559-4200
http://www.bexley.org

BLACKLICK ESTATES (CDP). Covers a land area of 1.891 square miles and a water area of 0.024 square miles. Located at 39.90° N. Lat; 82.87° W. Long. Elevation is 758 feet.
Population: 9,022; Growth (since 2000): -5.2%; Density: 4,772.2 persons per square mile; Race: 63.7% White, 31.3% Black/African American, 0.1% Asian, 0.0% American Indian/Alaska Native, 0.0% Native Hawaiian/Other Pacific Islander, 4.8% Two or more races, 2.0% Hispanic of any race; Average household size: 2.74; Median age: 34.4; Age under 18: 30.1%; Age 65 and over: 10.6%; Males per 100 females: 95.0; Marriage status: 35.1% never married, 42.6% now married, 3.2% separated, 6.5% widowed, 15.8% divorced; Foreign born: 2.9%; Speak English only: 96.1%; With disability: 14.2%; Veterans: 9.9%; Ancestry: 16.9% German, 10.8% Irish, 8.9% English, 5.2% American, 4.0% Italian
Employment: 12.4% management, business, and financial, 2.1% computer, engineering, and science, 4.2% education, legal, community service, arts, and media, 4.3% healthcare practitioners, 17.5% service, 29.2% sales and office, 5.5% natural resources, construction, and maintenance, 24.7% production, transportation, and material moving
Income: Per capita: $20,180; Median household: $48,538; Average household: $53,849; Households with income of $100,000 or more: 8.1%; Poverty rate: 14.3%
Educational Attainment: High school diploma or higher: 88.9%; Bachelor's degree or higher: 11.4%; Graduate/professional degree or higher: 1.2%

School District(s)

Gahanna-Jefferson City (PK-12)
2015-16 Enrollment: 7,407 . . . . (614) 471-7065
Licking Heights Local (PK-12)
2015-16 Enrollment: 4,024 . . . . (740) 927-6926
Housing: Homeownership rate: 63.7%; Median home value: $89,500; Median year structure built: 1970; Homeowner vacancy rate: 1.1%; Median selected monthly owner costs: $1,095 with a mortgage, $448 without a mortgage; Median gross rent: $1,040 per month; Rental vacancy rate: 2.2%
Health Insurance: 83.4% have insurance; 55.3% have private insurance; 36.6% have public insurance; 16.6% do not have insurance; 12.5% of children under 18 do not have insurance
Transportation: Commute: 94.0% car, 2.0% public transportation, 1.4% walk, 2.6% work from home; Mean travel time to work: 23.0 minutes

BRICE (village). Covers a land area of 0.098 square miles and a water area of <.001 square miles. Located at 39.92° N. Lat; 82.83° W. Long. Elevation is 781 feet.
Population: 123; Growth (since 2000): 75.7%; Density: 1,255.2 persons per square mile; Race: 95.9% White, 1.6% Black/African American, 0.0% Asian, 0.0% American Indian/Alaska Native, 0.0% Native Hawaiian/Other

Pacific Islander, 2.4% Two or more races, 0.0% Hispanic of any race; Average household size: 2.46; Median age: 49.5; Age under 18: 19.5%; Age 65 and over: 13.8%; Males per 100 females: 93.2; Marriage status: 28.2% never married, 44.7% now married, 4.9% separated, 8.7% widowed, 18.4% divorced; Foreign born: 0.0%; Speak English only: 98.4%; With disability: 16.3%; Veterans: 8.1%; Ancestry: 42.3% German, 19.5% Irish, 14.6% English, 12.2% American, 4.9% Italian

Employment: 26.0% management, business, and financial, 0.0% computer, engineering, and science, 2.0% education, legal, community service, arts, and media, 2.0% healthcare practitioners, 20.0% service, 18.0% sales and office, 14.0% natural resources, construction, and maintenance, 18.0% production, transportation, and material moving

Income: Per capita: $26,622; Median household: $53,750; Average household: $61,896; Households with income of $100,000 or more: 18.0%; Poverty rate: 8.9%

Educational Attainment: High school diploma or higher: 79.3%; Bachelor's degree or higher: 18.5%; Graduate/professional degree or higher: 6.5%

Housing: Homeownership rate: 76.0%; Median home value: $92,200; Median year structure built: Before 1940; Homeowner vacancy rate: 0.0%; Median selected monthly owner costs: $1,153 with a mortgage, $470 without a mortgage; Median gross rent: $1,104 per month; Rental vacancy rate: 0.0%

Health Insurance: 74.8% have insurance; 58.5% have private insurance; 29.3% have public insurance; 25.2% do not have insurance; 33.3% of children under 18 do not have insurance

Transportation: Commute: 100.0% car, 0.0% public transportation, 0.0% walk, 0.0% work from home; Mean travel time to work: 26.9 minutes

---

CANAL WINCHESTER (city). Covers a land area of 7.465 square miles and a water area of 0.136 square miles. Located at 39.84° N. Lat; 82.82° W. Long. Elevation is 761 feet.

History: The town of Canal Winchester developed as a produce center on the Ohio & Erie Canal.

Population: 7,774; Growth (since 2000): 73.6%; Density: 1,041.3 persons per square mile; Race: 89.6% White, 5.9% Black/African American, 2.6% Asian, 0.0% American Indian/Alaska Native, 0.0% Native Hawaiian/Other Pacific Islander, 1.8% Two or more races, 1.5% Hispanic of any race; Average household size: 2.64; Median age: 43.2; Age under 18: 25.0%; Age 65 and over: 19.6%; Males per 100 females: 89.3; Marriage status: 23.9% never married, 59.8% now married, 0.4% separated, 6.6% widowed, 9.8% divorced; Foreign born: 2.5%; Speak English only: 96.8%; With disability: 11.6%; Veterans: 13.1%; Ancestry: 27.0% German, 19.5% Irish, 11.6% English, 10.3% American, 10.2% Italian

Employment: 24.3% management, business, and financial, 6.4% computer, engineering, and science, 9.3% education, legal, community service, arts, and media, 9.7% healthcare practitioners, 17.9% service, 20.6% sales and office, 2.5% natural resources, construction, and maintenance, 9.3% production, transportation, and material moving

Income: Per capita: $32,165; Median household: $78,718; Average household: $84,383; Households with income of $100,000 or more: 32.9%; Poverty rate: 2.8%

Educational Attainment: High school diploma or higher: 94.6%; Bachelor's degree or higher: 35.8%; Graduate/professional degree or higher: 17.7%

School District(s)

Canal Winchester Local (PK-12)
2015-16 Enrollment: 3,729 . . . . (614) 837-4533

Two-year College(s)

Ohio State School of Cosmetology-Canal Winchester (Private, For-profit)
Fall 2016 Enrollment: 138 . . . . (614) 252-5252
Valor Christian College (Private, Not-for-profit, Other Protestant)
Fall 2016 Enrollment: 263 . . . . (614) 837-4088
2016-17 Tuition: In-state $4,490; Out-of-state $4,490

Housing: Homeownership rate: 82.2%; Median home value: $173,900; Median year structure built: 1999; Homeowner vacancy rate: 1.6%; Median selected monthly owner costs: $1,613 with a mortgage, $705 without a mortgage; Median gross rent: $721 per month; Rental vacancy rate: 0.0%

Health Insurance: 97.0% have insurance; 86.2% have private insurance; 22.7% have public insurance; 3.0% do not have insurance; 0.4% of children under 18 do not have insurance

Hospitals: Diley Ridge Medical Center

Transportation: Commute: 92.9% car, 0.4% public transportation, 0.9% walk, 5.5% work from home; Mean travel time to work: 26.8 minutes

Additional Information Contacts

Village of Canal Winchester . . . . (614) 837-7493
http://www.canalwinchesterohio.gov

COLUMBUS (city). State capital. County seat. Covers a land area of 217.169 square miles and a water area of 5.936 square miles. Located at 39.98° N. Lat; 82.99° W. Long. Elevation is 781 feet.

History: The site of Columbus was selected for the capital of Ohio in 1812, and the town was laid out. Columbus' early problems of cholera and lack of transportation were solved by draining the nearby swamps, and by the the Ohio & Erie Canal connected to Columbus by a feeder canal. The National Road reached Columbus in 1833, with stagecoaches arriving daily from the east. By 1872 transportation was being provided by five rail lines, and in 1873 Ohio State University was founded in Columbus.

Population: 837,038; Growth (since 2000): 17.6%; Density: 3,854.3 persons per square mile; Race: 61.1% White, 28.0% Black/African American, 4.9% Asian, 0.2% American Indian/Alaska Native, 0.0% Native Hawaiian/Other Pacific Islander, 4.1% Two or more races, 5.8% Hispanic of any race; Average household size: 2.39; Median age: 32.1; Age under 18: 22.7%; Age 65 and over: 9.4%; Males per 100 females: 95.4; Marriage status: 44.3% never married, 38.8% now married, 2.3% separated, 4.4% widowed, 12.5% divorced; Foreign born: 11.6%; Speak English only: 85.3%; With disability: 11.9%; Veterans: 6.4%; Ancestry: 19.3% German, 11.2% Irish, 6.5% English, 5.1% Italian, 4.3% American

Employment: 15.5% management, business, and financial, 6.9% computer, engineering, and science, 11.1% education, legal, community service, arts, and media, 5.9% healthcare practitioners, 18.2% service, 25.4% sales and office, 5.0% natural resources, construction, and maintenance, 12.1% production, transportation, and material moving

Income: Per capita: $25,781; Median household: $47,156; Average household: $61,050; Households with income of $100,000 or more: 16.5%; Poverty rate: 21.2%

Educational Attainment: High school diploma or higher: 88.8%; Bachelor's degree or higher: 34.8%; Graduate/professional degree or higher: 11.9%

School District(s)

A+ Arts Academy (KG-10)
2015-16 Enrollment: 692. . . . . (614) 725-1305
Arts & College Preparatory Academy (09-12)
2015-16 Enrollment: 393. . . . . (614) 986-9974
C.m. Grant Leadership Academy (KG-06)
2015-16 Enrollment: 109. . . . . (614) 478-3875
Capital High School (09-12)
2015-16 Enrollment: 258. . . . . (614) 228-2854
Central High School (09-12)
2015-16 Enrollment: 40. . . . . (614) 299-9802
Cesar Chavez College Preparatory School (KG-05)
2015-16 Enrollment: 348. . . . . (614) 297-8801
Charles School At Ohio Dominican University (09-12)
2015-16 Enrollment: 402. . . . . (614) 258-8588
Columbus Arts & Technology Academy (KG-10)
2015-16 Enrollment: 539. . . . . (614) 577-0900
Columbus Bilingual Academy (KG-07)
2015-16 Enrollment: 176. . . . . (614) 324-1492
Columbus Bilingual Academy-North (KG-08)
2015-16 Enrollment: 386. . . . . (877) 644-6338
Columbus City School District (PK-12)
2015-16 Enrollment: 50,028 . . . . (614) 365-5000
Columbus Collegiate Academy (06-08)
2015-16 Enrollment: 238. . . . . (614) 299-5284
Columbus Humanities Arts and Technology Academy (KG-08)
2015-16 Enrollment: 382. . . . . (614) 261-1200
Columbus Performance Academy (KG-08)
2015-16 Enrollment: 184. . . . . (614) 318-0720
Columbus Preparatory Academy (KG-09)
2015-16 Enrollment: 684. . . . . (614) 275-3600
Columbus Preparatory and Fitness Academy (KG-08)
2015-16 Enrollment: 293. . . . . (614) 318-0606
Cruiser Academy (09-12)
2015-16 Enrollment: 170. . . . . (614) 237-8756
Dublin City (PK-12)
2015-16 Enrollment: 15,432 . . . . (614) 764-5913
Early College Academy (10-12)
2015-16 Enrollment: 202. . . . . (614) 298-4742
Educational Academy for Boys & Girls (KG-06)
2015-16 Enrollment: 128. . . . . (614) 294-3020

Electronic Classroom of Tomorrow (KG-12)
2015-16 Enrollment: 14,153 .... (614) 492-8884
Fci Academy
2015-16 Enrollment: n/a .... (614) 471-4527
Focus Learning Academy of Northern Columbus (KG-08)
2015-16 Enrollment: 396....................... (614) 547-0927
Focus Learning Academy of Southeastern Columbus (09-12)
2015-16 Enrollment: 181....................... (614) 269-0150
Focus Learning Academy of Southwest Columbus (09-12)
2015-16 Enrollment: 270....................... (614) 545-2000
Focus North High School (09-12)
2015-16 Enrollment: 187....................... (614) 310-0430
Gateway Academy Of Ohio (07-12)
2015-16 Enrollment: 45....................... (614) 856-1149
Graham Expeditionary Middle School (06-08)
2015-16 Enrollment: 127....................... (614) 262-1111
Graham School the (09-12)
2015-16 Enrollment: 266....................... (614) 262-1111
Grandview Heights Schools (PK-12)
2015-16 Enrollment: 1,069 .... (614) 481-3600
Great Western Academy (KG-08)
2015-16 Enrollment: 718....................... (614) 276-1028
Groveport Madison Local (PK-12)
2015-16 Enrollment: 5,639 .... (614) 492-2520
Hamilton Alternative Academy (08-12)
2015-16 Enrollment: 36....................... (614) 491-8044
Hamilton Local (PK-12)
2015-16 Enrollment: 3,137 .... (614) 491-8044
Harrisburg Pike Community School (KG-06)
2015-16 Enrollment: 333....................... (614) 223-1510
Hilliard City (PK-12)
2015-16 Enrollment: 15,910 .... (614) 921-7000
Horizon Science Academy Columbus (09-12)
2015-16 Enrollment: 507....................... (614) 846-7616
Horizon Science Academy Columbus Middle School (06-08)
2015-16 Enrollment: 470....................... (614) 428-6564
Horizon Science Academy Elementary School (KG-05)
2015-16 Enrollment: 562....................... (614) 475-4585
Imagine Integrity Academy (KG-05)
2015-16 Enrollment: 81....................... (614) 464-1500
International Acad of Columbus (KG-08)
2015-16 Enrollment: 219....................... (614) 794-0643
Kipp Columbus (KG-08)
2015-16 Enrollment: 729....................... (614) 263-6137
Life Skills Center of Columbus North (09-12)
2015-16 Enrollment: 96....................... (614) 891-9041
Life Skills Center of Columbus Southeast (09-12)
2015-16 Enrollment: 151....................... (614) 863-9175
Mason Run High School (09-12)
2015-16 Enrollment: 29....................... (614) 237-9540
Midnimo Cross Cultural Community School (06-08)
2015-16 Enrollment: 103....................... (614) 261-7480
Millennium Community School (KG-08)
2015-16 Enrollment: 595....................... (614) 255-5585
Newbridge Math & Reading Preparatory Academy (KG-06)
2015-16 Enrollment: 180....................... (614) 279-6000
Noble Academy-Columbus (KG-08)
2015-16 Enrollment: 323....................... (614) 326-0687
Northland Preparatory and Fitness Academy (KG-08)
2015-16 Enrollment: 321....................... (614) 318-0600
Oakstone Community School (KG-12)
2015-16 Enrollment: 291....................... (614) 458-1085
Ohio School For The Blind (KG-12)
2015-16 Enrollment: 105....................... (614) 752-1152
Ohio School for the Deaf (PK-12)
2015-16 Enrollment: 135....................... (614) 728-1556
Patriot Preparatory Academy (KG-12)
2015-16 Enrollment: 581....................... (614) 864-5332
Performance Academy Eastland (KG-08)
2015-16 Enrollment: 323....................... (614) 314-6301
Renaissance Academy (KG-08)
2015-16 Enrollment: 178....................... (614) 866-7277
Road To Success Academy (09-12)
2015-16 Enrollment: 130....................... (614) 421-5838
South Scioto Academy (KG-08)
2015-16 Enrollment: 235....................... (614) 445-7684
South-Western City (PK-12)
2015-16 Enrollment: 21,866 .... (614) 801-3000
Sullivant Avenue Community School (KG-06)
2015-16 Enrollment: 365....................... (614) 308-5991
Summit Academy Community School-Columbus (KG-05)
2015-16 Enrollment: 48....................... (614) 237-5497
Summit Academy Middle School - Columbus (06-08)
2015-16 Enrollment: 106....................... (614) 237-5497
Summit Academy Transition High School-Columbus (09-12)
2015-16 Enrollment: 228....................... (614) 880-0714
The Academy For Urban Scholars (09-12)
2015-16 Enrollment: 314....................... (614) 545-9890
Virtual Community School of Ohio (KG-12)
2015-16 Enrollment: 856....................... (614) 501-9473
Westerville City (PK-12)
2015-16 Enrollment: 14,802 .... (614) 797-5700
Westside Academy (KG-06)
2015-16 Enrollment: 208....................... (614) 272-9392
Whitehall Preparatory and Fitness Academy (KG-08)
2015-16 Enrollment: 277....................... (614) 324-4585
Worthington City (PK-12)
2015-16 Enrollment: 9,885 .... (614) 450-6000
Youthbuild Columbus Community (10-12)
2015-16 Enrollment: 209....................... (614) 291-0805
Zenith Academy (KG-12)
2015-16 Enrollment: 411....................... (614) 419-6753
Zenith Academy East (KG-08)
2015-16 Enrollment: 304....................... (614) 577-0997

Four-year College(s)

American National University-Columbus (Private, For-profit)
Fall 2016 Enrollment: 6....................... (614) 212-2800
2016-17 Tuition: In-state $14,886; Out-of-state $14,886
Capital University (Private, Not-for-profit, Evangelical Lutheran Church)
Fall 2016 Enrollment: 3,367 .... (614) 236-6011
2016-17 Tuition: In-state $33,492; Out-of-state $33,492
Chamberlain College of Nursing-Ohio (Private, For-profit)
Fall 2016 Enrollment: 718....................... (614) 252-8890
2016-17 Tuition: In-state $19,230; Out-of-state $19,230
Columbus College of Art and Design (Private, Not-for-profit)
Fall 2016 Enrollment: 1,095 .... (614) 224-9101
2016-17 Tuition: In-state $32,880; Out-of-state $32,880
DeVry University-Ohio (Private, For-profit)
Fall 2016 Enrollment: 1,635 .... (614) 253-1525
2016-17 Tuition: In-state $19,948; Out-of-state $19,948
Franklin University (Private, Not-for-profit)
Fall 2016 Enrollment: 5,006 .... (614) 797-4700
2016-17 Tuition: In-state $11,881; Out-of-state $11,881
ITT Technical Institute-Columbus (Private, For-profit)
Fall 2016 Enrollment: n/a .... (614) 868-2000
Mount Carmel College of Nursing (Private, Not-for-profit, Roman Catholic)
Fall 2016 Enrollment: 1,105 .... (614) 234-5800
2016-17 Tuition: In-state $12,673; Out-of-state $12,673
Ohio Dominican University (Private, Not-for-profit, Roman Catholic)
Fall 2016 Enrollment: 2,406 .... (614) 253-2741
2016-17 Tuition: In-state $31,080; Out-of-state $31,080
Ohio State University-Main Campus (Public)
Fall 2016 Enrollment: 59,482 .... (292) 646-8600
2016-17 Tuition: In-state $10,037; Out-of-state $28,229
Pontifical College Josephinum (Private, Not-for-profit, Roman Catholic)
Fall 2016 Enrollment: 161....................... (614) 885-5585
2016-17 Tuition: In-state $22,092; Out-of-state $22,092
Trinity Lutheran Seminary (Private, Not-for-profit, Evangelical Lutheran Church)
Fall 2016 Enrollment: 80....................... (614) 235-4136

Two-year College(s)

American Institute of Alternative Medicine (Private, For-profit)
Fall 2016 Enrollment: 384....................... (614) 825-6255
Bradford School (Private, For-profit)
Fall 2016 Enrollment: 397....................... (614) 416-6200
2016-17 Tuition: In-state $13,980; Out-of-state $13,980
Columbus State Community College (Public)
Fall 2016 Enrollment: 27,109 .... (614) 287-5353
2016-17 Tuition: In-state $3,808; Out-of-state $8,430

Daymar College-Columbus (Private, For-profit)
Fall 2016 Enrollment: 114 . . . . (614) 643-6680
2016-17 Tuition: In-state $15,000; Out-of-state $15,000
Felbry College School of Nursing (Private, For-profit)
Fall 2016 Enrollment: 86 . . . . (614) 781-1085
Miami-Jacobs Career College-Columbus (Private, For-profit)
Fall 2016 Enrollment: 381 . . . . (614) 221-7770
2016-17 Tuition: In-state $11,140; Out-of-state $11,140
Nationwide Beauty Academy (Private, For-profit)
Fall 2016 Enrollment: 71 . . . . (614) 252-5252
Ohio State College of Barber Styling (Private, For-profit)
Fall 2016 Enrollment: 233 . . . . (614) 868-1015
The Spa School (Private, For-profit)
Fall 2016 Enrollment: 127 . . . . (614) 252-5252

Vocational/Technical School(s)

Adult and Community Education-Hudson (Public)
Fall 2016 Enrollment: 113 . . . . (614) 365-6000
2016-17 Tuition: $15,000
American School of Technology (Private, For-profit)
Fall 2016 Enrollment: n/a . . . . (614) 436-4820
2016-17 Tuition: $15,235
Aveda Institute-Columbus (Private, For-profit)
Fall 2016 Enrollment: 284 . . . . (614) 291-2421
2016-17 Tuition: $22,775
Dental Assistant Pro LLC-Columbus (Private, For-profit)
Fall 2016 Enrollment: 19 . . . . (513) 932-3413
Heritage College-Columbus (Private, For-profit)
Fall 2016 Enrollment: n/a . . . . (614) 328-4700
2016-17 Tuition: $14,380
National Personal Training Institute of Columbus (Private, For-profit)
Fall 2016 Enrollment: 41 . . . . (614) 336-2664
Paul Mitchell the School-Columbus (Private, For-profit)
Fall 2016 Enrollment: 139 . . . . (614) 478-0922
2016-17 Tuition: $17,050
The Ohio Media School-Columbus (Private, For-profit)
Fall 2016 Enrollment: 83 . . . . (614) 655-5250
2016-17 Tuition: In-state $15,705; Out-of-state $15,705

Housing: Homeownership rate: 45.0%; Median home value: $131,800; Median year structure built: 1976; Homeowner vacancy rate: 1.8%; Median selected monthly owner costs: $1,277 with a mortgage, $485 without a mortgage; Median gross rent: $856 per month; Rental vacancy rate: 5.7%
Health Insurance: 88.1% have insurance; 63.7% have private insurance; 32.0% have public insurance; 11.9% do not have insurance; 5.8% of children under 18 do not have insurance
Hospitals: Doctors Hospital (478 beds); Grant Medical Center (337 beds); James Cancer Hospital & Solove Research Institute; Mount Carmel West (523 beds); Ohio State University Hospitals (156 beds); Riverside Methodist Hospital (1,049 beds)
Safety: Violent crime rate: 52.2 per 10,000 population; Property crime rate: 407.0 per 10,000 population
Newspapers: Columbus Alive (weekly circulation 46,000); Columbus Dispatch (daily circulation 217,000); Columbus Messenger Company (weekly circulation 100,000); Suburban News Publications (weekly circulation 293,000)
Transportation: Commute: 88.6% car, 3.2% public transportation, 3.0% walk, 3.5% work from home; Mean travel time to work: 21.5 minutes; Amtrak: Bus service available.
Airports: Bolton Field (general aviation); Ohio State University (general aviation); Port Columbus International (primary service/medium hub); Rickenbacker International (primary service/non-hub)
Additional Information Contacts
City of Columbus . . . . (614) 645-8100
http://www.ci.columbus.oh.us

DARBYDALE (CDP). Covers a land area of 0.987 square miles and a water area of 0.002 square miles. Located at 39.86° N. Lat; 83.17° W. Long. Elevation is 873 feet.
Population: 674; Growth (since 2000): n/a; Density: 683.0 persons per square mile; Race: 100.0% White, 0.0% Black/African American, 0.0% Asian, 0.0% American Indian/Alaska Native, 0.0% Native Hawaiian/Other Pacific Islander, 0.0% Two or more races, 0.0% Hispanic of any race; Average household size: 2.91; Median age: 37.9; Age under 18: 23.6%; Age 65 and over: 20.8%; Males per 100 females: 99.2; Marriage status: 36.1% never married, 52.9% now married, 0.0% separated, 0.0% widowed, 11.0% divorced; Foreign born: 0.0%; Speak English only: 100.0%; With disability: 21.4%; Veterans: 6.0%; Ancestry: 22.6% American, 16.0% English, 14.4% Irish, 8.2% German, 3.3% Polish
Employment: 6.7% management, business, and financial, 0.0% computer, engineering, and science, 0.0% education, legal, community service, arts, and media, 0.0% healthcare practitioners, 10.4% service, 12.5% sales and office, 28.6% natural resources, construction, and maintenance, 41.8% production, transportation, and material moving
Income: Per capita: $22,270; Median household: $48,875; Average household: $58,853; Households with income of $100,000 or more: 23.7%; Poverty rate: 22.6%
Educational Attainment: High school diploma or higher: 73.0%; Bachelor's degree or higher: n/a; Graduate/professional degree or higher: n/a
Housing: Homeownership rate: 92.7%; Median home value: $113,800; Median year structure built: 1970; Homeowner vacancy rate: 0.0%; Median selected monthly owner costs: $1,098 with a mortgage, n/a without a mortgage; Median gross rent: n/a per month; Rental vacancy rate: 0.0%
Health Insurance: 98.1% have insurance; 85.8% have private insurance; 29.5% have public insurance; 1.9% do not have insurance; 0.0% of children under 18 do not have insurance
Transportation: Commute: 100.0% car, 0.0% public transportation, 0.0% walk, 0.0% work from home; Mean travel time to work: 25.0 minutes

---

DUBLIN (city). Covers a land area of 24.437 square miles and a water area of 0.361 square miles. Located at 40.11° N. Lat; 83.14° W. Long. Elevation is 830 feet.
History: Named for Dublin, Ireland. Dublin was laid out in 1818 by John Sells, whose descendants organized the Sells Brothers' Circus. At one time, Dublin was selected to be the state capital by a commission appointed for that purpose, but "political horse trading" changed the selection.
Population: 43,874; Growth (since 2000): 39.8%; Density: 1,795.4 persons per square mile; Race: 76.4% White, 2.3% Black/African American, 16.9% Asian, 0.3% American Indian/Alaska Native, 0.0% Native Hawaiian/Other Pacific Islander, 3.3% Two or more races, 5.5% Hispanic of any race; Average household size: 2.80; Median age: 39.6; Age under 18: 29.7%; Age 65 and over: 9.4%; Males per 100 females: 97.6; Marriage status: 21.6% never married, 68.2% now married, 0.4% separated, 3.0% widowed, 7.2% divorced; Foreign born: 16.5%; Speak English only: 81.8%; With disability: 5.7%; Veterans: 6.8%; Ancestry: 27.3% German, 14.1% Irish, 10.7% English, 7.2% Italian, 6.3% American
Employment: 30.1% management, business, and financial, 15.6% computer, engineering, and science, 10.8% education, legal, community service, arts, and media, 9.2% healthcare practitioners, 7.9% service, 21.1% sales and office, 1.5% natural resources, construction, and maintenance, 3.8% production, transportation, and material moving
Income: Per capita: $58,698; Median household: $125,540; Average household: $163,872; Households with income of $100,000 or more: 61.9%; Poverty rate: 2.7%
Educational Attainment: High school diploma or higher: 98.5%; Bachelor's degree or higher: 75.3%; Graduate/professional degree or higher: 30.7%

School District(s)

Dublin City (PK-12)
2015-16 Enrollment: 15,432 . . . . (614) 764-5913
Hilliard City (PK-12)
2015-16 Enrollment: 15,910 . . . . (614) 921-7000

Housing: Homeownership rate: 75.7%; Median home value: $352,300; Median year structure built: 1993; Homeowner vacancy rate: 0.7%; Median selected monthly owner costs: $2,460 with a mortgage, $1,029 without a mortgage; Median gross rent: $1,266 per month; Rental vacancy rate: 5.7%
Health Insurance: 97.9% have insurance; 93.5% have private insurance; 11.4% have public insurance; 2.1% do not have insurance; 1.2% of children under 18 do not have insurance
Hospitals: Dublin Methodist Hospital
Safety: Violent crime rate: 4.8 per 10,000 population; Property crime rate: 112.7 per 10,000 population
Transportation: Commute: 90.3% car, 0.4% public transportation, 0.5% walk, 7.2% work from home; Mean travel time to work: 24.4 minutes
Additional Information Contacts
City of Dublin . . . . (614) 410-4400
http://www.dublin.oh.us

GAHANNA (city). Covers a land area of 12.427 square miles and a water area of 0.171 square miles. Located at 40.04° N. Lat; 82.88° W. Long. Elevation is 797 feet.

History: Named for an Algonquian Indian translation of "stream". Incorporated 1881.

Population: 34,373; Growth (since 2000): 5.3%; Density: 2,766.0 persons per square mile; Race: 81.4% White, 12.9% Black/African American, 2.6% Asian, 0.1% American Indian/Alaska Native, 0.0% Native Hawaiian/Other Pacific Islander, 2.6% Two or more races, 1.9% Hispanic of any race; Average household size: 2.59; Median age: 39.0; Age under 18: 24.2%; Age 65 and over: 13.5%; Males per 100 females: 91.9; Marriage status: 26.4% never married, 55.6% now married, 1.6% separated, 5.0% widowed, 13.1% divorced; Foreign born: 5.6%; Speak English only: 93.7%; With disability: 9.5%; Veterans: 7.9%; Ancestry: 27.6% German, 16.3% Irish, 11.0% English, 7.5% Italian, 5.6% American

Employment: 24.0% management, business, and financial, 7.6% computer, engineering, and science, 13.8% education, legal, community service, arts, and media, 5.1% healthcare practitioners, 16.0% service, 22.5% sales and office, 3.8% natural resources, construction, and maintenance, 7.2% production, transportation, and material moving

Income: Per capita: $37,283; Median household: $73,535; Average household: $96,031; Households with income of $100,000 or more: 35.0%; Poverty rate: 6.3%

Educational Attainment: High school diploma or higher: 95.2%; Bachelor's degree or higher: 46.1%; Graduate/professional degree or higher: 17.1%

School District(s)

Gahanna-Jefferson City (PK-12)
2015-16 Enrollment: 7,407 . . . . (614) 471-7065

Vocational/Technical School(s)

Everest Institute-Gahanna (Private, Not-for-profit)
Fall 2016 Enrollment: 138 . . . . (614) 322-3414
2016-17 Tuition: $15,450

Housing: Homeownership rate: 71.5%; Median home value: $195,100; Median year structure built: 1984; Homeowner vacancy rate: 0.6%; Median selected monthly owner costs: $1,659 with a mortgage, $641 without a mortgage; Median gross rent: $984 per month; Rental vacancy rate: 2.8%

Health Insurance: 94.7% have insurance; 81.6% have private insurance; 23.4% have public insurance; 5.3% do not have insurance; 3.3% of children under 18 do not have insurance

Safety: Violent crime rate: 5.7 per 10,000 population; Property crime rate: 226.3 per 10,000 population

Transportation: Commute: 90.4% car, 0.4% public transportation, 1.2% walk, 7.7% work from home; Mean travel time to work: 20.3 minutes

Additional Information Contacts

City of Gahanna . . . . (614) 342-4000
http://www.gahanna.gov

GALLOWAY (unincorporated postal area)

ZCTA: 43119

Covers a land area of 31.791 square miles and a water area of 0.317 square miles. Located at 39.94° N. Lat; 83.21° W. Long. Elevation is 899 feet.

Population: 28,100; Growth (since 2000): 29.5%; Density: 883.9 persons per square mile; Race: 83.2% White, 8.0% Black/African American, 4.0% Asian, 0.1% American Indian/Alaska Native, 0.0% Native Hawaiian/Other Pacific Islander, 4.5% Two or more races, 6.9% Hispanic of any race; Average household size: 2.79; Median age: 33.0; Age under 18: 27.0%; Age 65 and over: 8.2%; Males per 100 females: 95.2; Marriage status: 30.5% never married, 55.4% now married, 1.3% separated, 2.7% widowed, 11.4% divorced; Foreign born: 8.2%; Speak English only: 86.6%; With disability: 9.6%; Veterans: 7.5%; Ancestry: 27.7% German, 14.3% Irish, 8.8% English, 6.1% American, 5.2% Italian

Employment: 16.4% management, business, and financial, 5.6% computer, engineering, and science, 7.5% education, legal, community service, arts, and media, 5.5% healthcare practitioners, 18.3% service, 25.6% sales and office, 5.5% natural resources, construction, and maintenance, 15.6% production, transportation, and material moving

Income: Per capita: $26,327; Median household: $62,423; Average household: $71,897; Households with income of $100,000 or more: 22.2%; Poverty rate: 12.6%

Educational Attainment: High school diploma or higher: 90.2%; Bachelor's degree or higher: 27.2%; Graduate/professional degree or higher: 7.1%

School District(s)

South-Western City (PK-12)
2015-16 Enrollment: 21,866 . . . . (614) 801-3000

Housing: Homeownership rate: 69.1%; Median home value: $137,900; Median year structure built: 1992; Homeowner vacancy rate: 2.3%; Median selected monthly owner costs: $1,323 with a mortgage, $529 without a mortgage; Median gross rent: $864 per month; Rental vacancy rate: 0.0%

Health Insurance: 92.2% have insurance; 75.3% have private insurance; 24.6% have public insurance; 7.8% do not have insurance; 2.8% of children under 18 do not have insurance

Transportation: Commute: 95.0% car, 0.3% public transportation, 1.4% walk, 2.9% work from home; Mean travel time to work: 23.4 minutes

GRANDVIEW HEIGHTS (city). Covers a land area of 1.332 square miles and a water area of 0.004 square miles. Located at 39.98° N. Lat; 83.04° W. Long. Elevation is 771 feet.

Population: 7,191; Growth (since 2000): 7.4%; Density: 5,400.0 persons per square mile; Race: 93.6% White, 0.8% Black/African American, 2.6% Asian, 0.0% American Indian/Alaska Native, 0.0% Native Hawaiian/Other Pacific Islander, 2.6% Two or more races, 1.6% Hispanic of any race; Average household size: 2.37; Median age: 34.0; Age under 18: 19.4%; Age 65 and over: 10.0%; Males per 100 females: 94.3; Marriage status: 35.4% never married, 52.3% now married, 0.4% separated, 2.8% widowed, 9.5% divorced; Foreign born: 3.3%; Speak English only: 96.1%; With disability: 6.0%; Veterans: 5.8%; Ancestry: 30.9% German, 17.0% Irish, 13.2% Italian, 11.5% English, 5.4% American

Employment: 28.2% management, business, and financial, 8.0% computer, engineering, and science, 19.3% education, legal, community service, arts, and media, 10.5% healthcare practitioners, 9.4% service, 17.1% sales and office, 2.4% natural resources, construction, and maintenance, 5.2% production, transportation, and material moving

Income: Per capita: $55,306; Median household: $95,938; Average household: $126,923; Households with income of $100,000 or more: 48.4%; Poverty rate: 2.0%

Educational Attainment: High school diploma or higher: 99.3%; Bachelor's degree or higher: 71.0%; Graduate/professional degree or higher: 30.7%

Housing: Homeownership rate: 65.7%; Median home value: $295,400; Median year structure built: Before 1940; Homeowner vacancy rate: 1.4%; Median selected monthly owner costs: $1,931 with a mortgage, $818 without a mortgage; Median gross rent: $1,092 per month; Rental vacancy rate: 9.2%

Health Insurance: 95.1% have insurance; 90.8% have private insurance; 11.2% have public insurance; 4.9% do not have insurance; 0.9% of children under 18 do not have insurance

Safety: Violent crime rate: 1.3 per 10,000 population; Property crime rate: 191.9 per 10,000 population

Transportation: Commute: 90.2% car, 1.3% public transportation, 2.2% walk, 4.8% work from home; Mean travel time to work: 17.4 minutes

Additional Information Contacts

City of Grandview Heights. . . . . (614) 481-6211
http://www.grandviewheights.org

GROVE CITY (city). Covers a land area of 16.196 square miles and a water area of 0.157 square miles. Located at 39.87° N. Lat; 83.07° W. Long. Elevation is 846 feet.

History: Named for its many tree groves, by William F. Brock. Grove City developed around an agricultural and truck gardening region. Many of its early residents were of German ancestry.

Population: 38,374; Growth (since 2000): 41.7%; Density: 2,369.3 persons per square mile; Race: 92.8% White, 3.3% Black/African American, 1.3% Asian, 0.0% American Indian/Alaska Native, 0.0% Native Hawaiian/Other Pacific Islander, 2.2% Two or more races, 1.3% Hispanic of any race; Average household size: 2.57; Median age: 39.0; Age under 18: 25.4%; Age 65 and over: 13.6%; Males per 100 females: 93.5; Marriage status: 25.7% never married, 57.0% now married, 1.7% separated, 5.3% widowed, 12.0% divorced; Foreign born: 2.6%; Speak English only: 96.5%; With disability: 12.1%; Veterans: 9.7%; Ancestry: 32.3% German, 17.5% Irish, 8.7% English, 8.6% American, 5.4% Italian

Employment: 14.5% management, business, and financial, 5.2% computer, engineering, and science, 10.4% education, legal, community service, arts, and media, 7.9% healthcare practitioners, 14.9% service, 28.1% sales and office, 8.1% natural resources, construction, and maintenance, 10.9% production, transportation, and material moving

Income: Per capita: $30,632; Median household: $65,277; Average household: $77,947; Households with income of $100,000 or more: 27.2%; Poverty rate: 7.8%
Educational Attainment: High school diploma or higher: 94.5%; Bachelor's degree or higher: 29.9%; Graduate/professional degree or higher: 8.4%

School District(s)

South-Western City (PK-12)
2015-16 Enrollment: 21,866 . . . . (614) 801-3000

Four-year College(s)

Harrison College-Grove City (Private, For-profit)
Fall 2016 Enrollment: 237 . . . . (888) 544-4422
2016-17 Tuition: In-state $16,275; Out-of-state $16,275

Housing: Homeownership rate: 68.4%; Median home value: $162,400; Median year structure built: 1990; Homeowner vacancy rate: 2.7%; Median selected monthly owner costs: $1,504 with a mortgage, $574 without a mortgage; Median gross rent: $912 per month; Rental vacancy rate: 3.0%
Health Insurance: 93.6% have insurance; 80.7% have private insurance; 23.7% have public insurance; 6.4% do not have insurance; 3.3% of children under 18 do not have insurance
Safety: Violent crime rate: 10.7 per 10,000 population; Property crime rate: 417.8 per 10,000 population
Transportation: Commute: 94.7% car, 0.5% public transportation, 0.6% walk, 3.3% work from home; Mean travel time to work: 23.0 minutes
Additional Information Contacts
City of Grove City . . . . (614) 277-3000
http://www.grovecityohio.gov

GROVEPORT (city). Covers a land area of 8.560 square miles and a water area of 0.227 square miles. Located at 39.86° N. Lat; 82.89° W. Long. Elevation is 741 feet.
Population: 5,500; Growth (since 2000): 42.3%; Density: 642.5 persons per square mile; Race: 73.8% White, 21.5% Black/African American, 3.2% Asian, 0.2% American Indian/Alaska Native, 0.0% Native Hawaiian/Other Pacific Islander, 0.9% Two or more races, 1.3% Hispanic of any race; Average household size: 2.50; Median age: 42.8; Age under 18: 22.5%; Age 65 and over: 15.4%; Males per 100 females: 92.8; Marriage status: 26.8% never married, 53.1% now married, 2.8% separated, 6.8% widowed, 13.3% divorced; Foreign born: 3.7%; Speak English only: 94.9%; With disability: 14.3%; Veterans: 9.7%; Ancestry: 22.1% German, 14.1% Irish, 7.5% English, 5.6% American, 3.9% Italian
Employment: 12.4% management, business, and financial, 5.1% computer, engineering, and science, 9.7% education, legal, community service, arts, and media, 5.6% healthcare practitioners, 13.5% service, 29.6% sales and office, 7.7% natural resources, construction, and maintenance, 16.4% production, transportation, and material moving
Income: Per capita: $26,548; Median household: $56,750; Average household: $64,799; Households with income of $100,000 or more: 21.3%; Poverty rate: 5.1%
Educational Attainment: High school diploma or higher: 93.8%; Bachelor's degree or higher: 19.7%; Graduate/professional degree or higher: 6.0%

School District(s)

Eastland-Fairfield Career/Tech (09-12)
2015-16 Enrollment: n/a . . . . (614) 836-4530
Groveport Community School (KG-08)
2015-16 Enrollment: 785. . . . . (614) 574-4100
Groveport Madison Local (PK-12)
2015-16 Enrollment: 5,639 . . . . (614) 492-2520

Vocational/Technical School(s)

Eastland-Fairfield Career and Technical Schools (Public)
Fall 2016 Enrollment: 115 . . . . (614) 836-4541
2016-17 Tuition: $5,775

Housing: Homeownership rate: 72.9%; Median home value: $144,300; Median year structure built: 1977; Homeowner vacancy rate: 0.0%; Median selected monthly owner costs: $1,383 with a mortgage, $513 without a mortgage; Median gross rent: $673 per month; Rental vacancy rate: 0.0%
Health Insurance: 93.4% have insurance; 73.5% have private insurance; 33.6% have public insurance; 6.6% do not have insurance; 6.2% of children under 18 do not have insurance
Safety: Violent crime rate: 8.6 per 10,000 population; Property crime rate: 306.2 per 10,000 population
Transportation: Commute: 93.7% car, 0.3% public transportation, 0.7% walk, 4.9% work from home; Mean travel time to work: 20.6 minutes
Additional Information Contacts
Village of Groveport. . . . . (614) 836-5301
http://www.groveport.org

HARRISBURG (village). Covers a land area of 0.154 square miles and a water area of 0 square miles. Located at 39.81° N. Lat; 83.17° W. Long. Elevation is 794 feet.
Population: 457; Growth (since 2000): 37.7%; Density: 2,966.3 persons per square mile; Race: 100.0% White, 0.0% Black/African American, 0.0% Asian, 0.0% American Indian/Alaska Native, 0.0% Native Hawaiian/Other Pacific Islander, 0.0% Two or more races, 0.4% Hispanic of any race; Average household size: 2.69; Median age: 39.5; Age under 18: 22.3%; Age 65 and over: 17.1%; Males per 100 females: 103.8; Marriage status: 28.5% never married, 48.8% now married, 1.3% separated, 8.8% widowed, 13.9% divorced; Foreign born: 0.0%; Speak English only: 100.0%; With disability: 16.2%; Veterans: 8.5%; Ancestry: 45.1% German, 20.1% Irish, 7.0% American, 6.1% French, 5.7% Scottish
Employment: 26.6% management, business, and financial, 3.5% computer, engineering, and science, 7.0% education, legal, community service, arts, and media, 6.5% healthcare practitioners, 15.1% service, 18.1% sales and office, 5.5% natural resources, construction, and maintenance, 17.6% production, transportation, and material moving
Income: Per capita: $24,562; Median household: $51,250; Average household: $64,094; Households with income of $100,000 or more: 13.5%; Poverty rate: 16.9%
Educational Attainment: High school diploma or higher: 87.2%; Bachelor's degree or higher: 15.2%; Graduate/professional degree or higher: 2.4%
Housing: Homeownership rate: 67.6%; Median home value: $111,000; Median year structure built: Before 1940; Homeowner vacancy rate: 0.0%; Median selected monthly owner costs: $1,197 with a mortgage, $556 without a mortgage; Median gross rent: $784 per month; Rental vacancy rate: 0.0%
Health Insurance: 87.1% have insurance; 58.4% have private insurance; 38.9% have public insurance; 12.9% do not have insurance; 0.0% of children under 18 do not have insurance
Transportation: Commute: 89.6% car, 0.0% public transportation, 2.1% walk, 8.3% work from home; Mean travel time to work: 24.1 minutes

HILLIARD (city). Covers a land area of 13.167 square miles and a water area of 0.168 square miles. Located at 40.04° N. Lat; 83.15° W. Long. Elevation is 932 feet.
Population: 33,108; Growth (since 2000): 36.6%; Density: 2,514.5 persons per square mile; Race: 88.2% White, 3.4% Black/African American, 6.5% Asian, 0.1% American Indian/Alaska Native, 0.1% Native Hawaiian/Other Pacific Islander, 1.4% Two or more races, 2.6% Hispanic of any race; Average household size: 2.75; Median age: 35.9; Age under 18: 28.5%; Age 65 and over: 10.2%; Males per 100 females: 95.5; Marriage status: 26.7% never married, 60.4% now married, 1.3% separated, 5.0% widowed, 8.0% divorced; Foreign born: 6.2%; Speak English only: 89.8%; With disability: 7.7%; Veterans: 7.3%; Ancestry: 28.6% German, 14.5% Irish, 11.2% English, 8.4% Italian, 5.8% American
Employment: 22.8% management, business, and financial, 10.3% computer, engineering, and science, 12.4% education, legal, community service, arts, and media, 8.4% healthcare practitioners, 12.4% service, 24.4% sales and office, 2.4% natural resources, construction, and maintenance, 6.8% production, transportation, and material moving
Income: Per capita: $40,964; Median household: $92,727; Average household: $111,490; Households with income of $100,000 or more: 46.1%; Poverty rate: 4.0%
Educational Attainment: High school diploma or higher: 96.3%; Bachelor's degree or higher: 52.1%; Graduate/professional degree or higher: 20.5%

School District(s)

Hilliard City (PK-12)
2015-16 Enrollment: 15,910 . . . . (614) 921-7000

Four-year College(s)

ITT Technical Institute-Hilliard (Private, For-profit)
Fall 2016 Enrollment: n/a . . . . (614) 771-4888

Two-year College(s)

Ohio Business College-Hilliard (Private, For-profit)
Fall 2016 Enrollment: 55 . . . . (614) 891-5030
2016-17 Tuition: In-state $9,025; Out-of-state $9,025

Housing: Homeownership rate: 77.3%; Median home value: $213,000; Median year structure built: 1993; Homeowner vacancy rate: 0.8%; Median selected monthly owner costs: $1,771 with a mortgage, $750 without a

mortgage; Median gross rent: $1,004 per month; Rental vacancy rate: 2.5%
Health Insurance: 94.6% have insurance; 84.7% have private insurance; 18.3% have public insurance; 5.4% do not have insurance; 2.2% of children under 18 do not have insurance
Safety: Violent crime rate: 9.5 per 10,000 population; Property crime rate: 98.8 per 10,000 population
Transportation: Commute: 92.5% car, 0.4% public transportation, 1.0% walk, 5.2% work from home; Mean travel time to work: 22.1 minutes
Additional Information Contacts
City of Hilliard . . . . (614) 876-7361
http://hilliardohio.gov

HUBER RIDGE (CDP). Covers a land area of 1.041 square miles and a water area of 0.010 square miles. Located at 40.09° N. Lat; 82.92° W. Long. Elevation is 830 feet.
Population: 4,569; Growth (since 2000): -6.4%; Density: 4,387.8 persons per square mile; Race: 78.8% White, 11.8% Black/African American, 0.3% Asian, 0.0% American Indian/Alaska Native, 0.0% Native Hawaiian/Other Pacific Islander, 8.7% Two or more races, 2.9% Hispanic of any race; Average household size: 2.88; Median age: 31.6; Age under 18: 28.6%; Age 65 and over: 9.8%; Males per 100 females: 93.5; Marriage status: 34.8% never married, 50.2% now married, 1.1% separated, 3.7% widowed, 11.3% divorced; Foreign born: 5.3%; Speak English only: 91.5%; With disability: 10.1%; Veterans: 9.3%; Ancestry: 27.6% German, 12.7% Irish, 8.8% American, 7.9% Italian, 6.9% English
Employment: 18.4% management, business, and financial, 5.7% computer, engineering, and science, 8.0% education, legal, community service, arts, and media, 4.5% healthcare practitioners, 18.9% service, 24.6% sales and office, 5.9% natural resources, construction, and maintenance, 14.0% production, transportation, and material moving
Income: Per capita: $23,883; Median household: $60,563; Average household: $67,151; Households with income of $100,000 or more: 19.7%; Poverty rate: 10.8%
Educational Attainment: High school diploma or higher: 93.0%; Bachelor's degree or higher: 25.8%; Graduate/professional degree or higher: 5.5%
Housing: Homeownership rate: 67.9%; Median home value: $121,700; Median year structure built: 1968; Homeowner vacancy rate: 0.0%; Median selected monthly owner costs: $1,318 with a mortgage, $545 without a mortgage; Median gross rent: $1,119 per month; Rental vacancy rate: 1.4%
Health Insurance: 92.3% have insurance; 70.4% have private insurance; 34.1% have public insurance; 7.7% do not have insurance; 2.6% of children under 18 do not have insurance
Transportation: Commute: 95.7% car, 0.0% public transportation, 0.0% walk, 3.6% work from home; Mean travel time to work: 21.0 minutes

LAKE DARBY (CDP). Covers a land area of 3.463 square miles and a water area of 0.040 square miles. Located at 39.96° N. Lat; 83.22° W. Long. Elevation is 925 feet.
Population: 4,392; Growth (since 2000): 17.8%; Density: 1,268.2 persons per square mile; Race: 90.7% White, 1.6% Black/African American, 3.5% Asian, 0.3% American Indian/Alaska Native, 0.0% Native Hawaiian/Other Pacific Islander, 4.0% Two or more races, 2.8% Hispanic of any race; Average household size: 3.09; Median age: 35.2; Age under 18: 29.9%; Age 65 and over: 5.9%; Males per 100 females: 100.6; Marriage status: 19.8% never married, 67.2% now married, 0.6% separated, 2.5% widowed, 10.5% divorced; Foreign born: 5.9%; Speak English only: 90.8%; With disability: 8.6%; Veterans: 9.4%; Ancestry: 28.4% German, 16.3% Irish, 8.9% English, 7.2% Italian, 6.7% American
Employment: 17.2% management, business, and financial, 6.7% computer, engineering, and science, 11.0% education, legal, community service, arts, and media, 5.2% healthcare practitioners, 15.6% service, 25.4% sales and office, 6.5% natural resources, construction, and maintenance, 12.6% production, transportation, and material moving
Income: Per capita: $31,279; Median household: $87,152; Average household: $96,327; Households with income of $100,000 or more: 33.6%; Poverty rate: 6.3%
Educational Attainment: High school diploma or higher: 96.5%; Bachelor's degree or higher: 34.8%; Graduate/professional degree or higher: 9.1%
Housing: Homeownership rate: 93.4%; Median home value: $140,400; Median year structure built: 1990; Homeowner vacancy rate: 7.1%; Median selected monthly owner costs: $1,558 with a mortgage, $608 without a mortgage; Median gross rent: $1,385 per month; Rental vacancy rate: 0.0%
Health Insurance: 90.8% have insurance; 78.1% have private insurance; 15.8% have public insurance; 9.2% do not have insurance; 7.2% of children under 18 do not have insurance
Transportation: Commute: 97.7% car, 0.3% public transportation, 0.4% walk, 1.7% work from home; Mean travel time to work: 28.2 minutes

LINCOLN VILLAGE (CDP). Covers a land area of 1.836 square miles and a water area of <.001 square miles. Located at 39.95° N. Lat; 83.13° W. Long. Elevation is 909 feet.
Population: 9,882; Growth (since 2000): 4.2%; Density: 5,382.8 persons per square mile; Race: 85.5% White, 8.7% Black/African American, 0.2% Asian, 0.0% American Indian/Alaska Native, 0.0% Native Hawaiian/Other Pacific Islander, 2.3% Two or more races, 12.4% Hispanic of any race; Average household size: 2.61; Median age: 37.8; Age under 18: 26.2%; Age 65 and over: 12.8%; Males per 100 females: 96.8; Marriage status: 32.6% never married, 46.1% now married, 3.9% separated, 6.4% widowed, 14.9% divorced; Foreign born: 7.6%; Speak English only: 86.2%; With disability: 18.3%; Veterans: 11.5%; Ancestry: 16.9% German, 12.8% Irish, 10.2% American, 10.1% English, 4.3% Italian
Employment: 9.2% management, business, and financial, 2.6% computer, engineering, and science, 3.4% education, legal, community service, arts, and media, 3.6% healthcare practitioners, 23.7% service, 27.7% sales and office, 10.7% natural resources, construction, and maintenance, 19.0% production, transportation, and material moving
Income: Per capita: $21,475; Median household: $43,616; Average household: $54,203; Households with income of $100,000 or more: 10.6%; Poverty rate: 15.0%
Educational Attainment: High school diploma or higher: 80.3%; Bachelor's degree or higher: 10.5%; Graduate/professional degree or higher: 2.2%
Housing: Homeownership rate: 63.7%; Median home value: $90,800; Median year structure built: 1960; Homeowner vacancy rate: 0.8%; Median selected monthly owner costs: $1,112 with a mortgage, $468 without a mortgage; Median gross rent: $766 per month; Rental vacancy rate: 17.1%
Health Insurance: 84.8% have insurance; 57.5% have private insurance; 38.3% have public insurance; 15.2% do not have insurance; 10.0% of children under 18 do not have insurance
Transportation: Commute: 86.8% car, 2.5% public transportation, 1.1% walk, 6.5% work from home; Mean travel time to work: 22.5 minutes

LOCKBOURNE (village). Covers a land area of 0.750 square miles and a water area of 0.046 square miles. Located at 39.81° N. Lat; 82.99° W. Long. Elevation is 712 feet.
Population: 181; Growth (since 2000): -35.4%; Density: 241.2 persons per square mile; Race: 100.0% White, 0.0% Black/African American, 0.0% Asian, 0.0% American Indian/Alaska Native, 0.0% Native Hawaiian/Other Pacific Islander, 0.0% Two or more races, 0.6% Hispanic of any race; Average household size: 2.59; Median age: 42.2; Age under 18: 19.9%; Age 65 and over: 21.0%; Males per 100 females: 91.1; Marriage status: 28.8% never married, 45.1% now married, 1.3% separated, 7.2% widowed, 19.0% divorced; Foreign born: 0.0%; Speak English only: 100.0%; With disability: 27.6%; Veterans: 5.5%; Ancestry: 22.7% English, 17.7% American, 11.0% Irish, 9.9% German, 5.0% Italian
Employment: 3.3% management, business, and financial, 0.0% computer, engineering, and science, 1.7% education, legal, community service, arts, and media, 0.0% healthcare practitioners, 20.0% service, 41.7% sales and office, 10.0% natural resources, construction, and maintenance, 23.3% production, transportation, and material moving
Income: Per capita: $16,094; Median household: $38,929; Average household: $39,321; Households with income of $100,000 or more: 1.4%; Poverty rate: 28.7%
Educational Attainment: High school diploma or higher: 68.3%; Bachelor's degree or higher: 6.5%; Graduate/professional degree or higher: n/a
Housing: Homeownership rate: 38.6%; Median home value: $95,000; Median year structure built: Before 1940; Homeowner vacancy rate: 0.0%; Median selected monthly owner costs: $1,063 with a mortgage, $513 without a mortgage; Median gross rent: $1,083 per month; Rental vacancy rate: 0.0%
Health Insurance: 81.2% have insurance; 50.3% have private insurance; 47.5% have public insurance; 18.8% do not have insurance; 47.2% of children under 18 do not have insurance

Transportation: Commute: 95.0% car, 0.0% public transportation, 1.7% walk, 3.3% work from home; Mean travel time to work: 23.4 minutes

MARBLE CLIFF (village). Covers a land area of 0.266 square miles and a water area of 0 square miles. Located at 39.99° N. Lat; 83.06° W. Long. Elevation is 794 feet.
History: Limestone quarry gave its name.
Population: 556; Growth (since 2000): -13.9%; Density: 2,091.3 persons per square mile; Race: 96.0% White, 2.2% Black/African American, 1.6% Asian, 0.0% American Indian/Alaska Native, 0.0% Native Hawaiian/Other Pacific Islander, 0.2% Two or more races, 1.4% Hispanic of any race; Average household size: 2.09; Median age: 46.8; Age under 18: 19.4%; Age 65 and over: 17.3%; Males per 100 females: 97.6; Marriage status: 32.4% never married, 53.9% now married, 0.0% separated, 5.6% widowed, 8.1% divorced; Foreign born: 3.8%; Speak English only: 97.0%; With disability: 8.6%; Veterans: 5.6%; Ancestry: 45.0% German, 18.9% English, 16.7% Irish, 13.3% Italian, 7.2% Polish
Employment: 29.6% management, business, and financial, 6.0% computer, engineering, and science, 22.2% education, legal, community service, arts, and media, 6.0% healthcare practitioners, 7.5% service, 27.5% sales and office, 1.2% natural resources, construction, and maintenance, 0.0% production, transportation, and material moving
Income: Per capita: $71,732; Median household: $102,917; Average household: $134,829; Households with income of $100,000 or more: 50.3%; Poverty rate: 2.2%
Educational Attainment: High school diploma or higher: 96.9%; Bachelor's degree or higher: 73.5%; Graduate/professional degree or higher: 36.4%
Housing: Homeownership rate: 56.4%; Median home value: $565,600; Median year structure built: 1961; Homeowner vacancy rate: 5.1%; Median selected monthly owner costs: $2,981 with a mortgage, $1,081 without a mortgage; Median gross rent: $865 per month; Rental vacancy rate: 4.0%
Health Insurance: 97.7% have insurance; 88.7% have private insurance; 21.8% have public insurance; 2.3% do not have insurance; 0.0% of children under 18 do not have insurance
Transportation: Commute: 86.1% car, 3.0% public transportation, 2.7% walk, 6.3% work from home; Mean travel time to work: 18.3 minutes

MINERVA PARK (village). Covers a land area of 0.506 square miles and a water area of 0.011 square miles. Located at 40.08° N. Lat; 82.95° W. Long. Elevation is 846 feet.
Population: 1,299; Growth (since 2000): 0.9%; Density: 2,565.6 persons per square mile; Race: 85.0% White, 4.3% Black/African American, 1.3% Asian, 0.0% American Indian/Alaska Native, 0.0% Native Hawaiian/Other Pacific Islander, 3.5% Two or more races, 7.7% Hispanic of any race; Average household size: 2.56; Median age: 40.5; Age under 18: 24.2%; Age 65 and over: 15.9%; Males per 100 females: 92.1; Marriage status: 24.8% never married, 59.8% now married, 0.4% separated, 4.4% widowed, 11.0% divorced; Foreign born: 5.5%; Speak English only: 92.5%; With disability: 10.9%; Veterans: 9.9%; Ancestry: 33.9% German, 16.5% Irish, 10.2% American, 9.2% English, 8.6% Dutch
Employment: 23.8% management, business, and financial, 10.0% computer, engineering, and science, 18.1% education, legal, community service, arts, and media, 8.6% healthcare practitioners, 6.3% service, 21.6% sales and office, 2.8% natural resources, construction, and maintenance, 8.8% production, transportation, and material moving
Income: Per capita: $35,585; Median household: $84,896; Average household: $90,539; Households with income of $100,000 or more: 30.9%; Poverty rate: 7.2%
Educational Attainment: High school diploma or higher: 92.3%; Bachelor's degree or higher: 50.4%; Graduate/professional degree or higher: 18.8%
Housing: Homeownership rate: 87.6%; Median home value: $163,400; Median year structure built: 1957; Homeowner vacancy rate: 2.0%; Median selected monthly owner costs: $1,442 with a mortgage, $673 without a mortgage; Median gross rent: $1,400 per month; Rental vacancy rate: 0.0%
Health Insurance: 96.2% have insurance; 79.8% have private insurance; 27.4% have public insurance; 3.8% do not have insurance; 0.0% of children under 18 do not have insurance
Transportation: Commute: 94.8% car, 0.3% public transportation, 0.2% walk, 4.3% work from home; Mean travel time to work: 20.9 minutes

NEW ALBANY (city). Covers a land area of 11.557 square miles and a water area of 0.144 square miles. Located at 40.08° N. Lat; 82.80° W. Long. Elevation is 1,024 feet.
History: Founded in 1837, it is now a growing suburb in the Columbus area. The Village of New Albany is a master planned community built upon the best traditions of small town America.
Population: 9,384; Growth (since 2000): 152.9%; Density: 812.0 persons per square mile; Race: 83.7% White, 5.5% Black/African American, 8.2% Asian, 0.4% American Indian/Alaska Native, 0.0% Native Hawaiian/Other Pacific Islander, 1.4% Two or more races, 1.6% Hispanic of any race; Average household size: 3.17; Median age: 38.6; Age under 18: 36.3%; Age 65 and over: 9.0%; Males per 100 females: 98.3; Marriage status: 19.3% never married, 69.6% now married, 0.3% separated, 3.4% widowed, 7.7% divorced; Foreign born: 6.8%; Speak English only: 91.8%; With disability: 3.9%; Veterans: 5.7%; Ancestry: 21.9% German, 18.3% Irish, 11.6% English, 8.0% Italian, 6.8% American
Employment: 32.2% management, business, and financial, 5.7% computer, engineering, and science, 15.1% education, legal, community service, arts, and media, 9.8% healthcare practitioners, 9.6% service, 20.9% sales and office, 1.5% natural resources, construction, and maintenance, 5.3% production, transportation, and material moving
Income: Per capita: $73,900; Median household: $191,375; Average household: $232,615; Households with income of $100,000 or more: 73.9%; Poverty rate: 2.7%
Educational Attainment: High school diploma or higher: 98.7%; Bachelor's degree or higher: 77.0%; Graduate/professional degree or higher: 36.2%

School District(s)

New Albany-Plain Local (KG-12)
2015-16 Enrollment: 4,856 . . . . (614) 855-2040
Housing: Homeownership rate: 88.1%; Median home value: $492,400; Median year structure built: 2003; Homeowner vacancy rate: 0.0%; Median selected monthly owner costs: $3,220 with a mortgage, $1,354 without a mortgage; Median gross rent: $1,667 per month; Rental vacancy rate: 20.2%
Health Insurance: 98.0% have insurance; 92.8% have private insurance; 13.6% have public insurance; 2.0% do not have insurance; 1.1% of children under 18 do not have insurance
Hospitals: Mount Carmel New Albany Surgical Hospital
Safety: Violent crime rate: 4.8 per 10,000 population; Property crime rate: 164.4 per 10,000 population
Transportation: Commute: 90.4% car, 0.0% public transportation, 0.9% walk, 7.5% work from home; Mean travel time to work: 20.6 minutes
Additional Information Contacts
Village of New Albany . . . . (614) 855-3913
http://www.villageofnewalbany.org

OBETZ (village). Covers a land area of 5.784 square miles and a water area of 0.144 square miles. Located at 39.86° N. Lat; 82.94° W. Long. Elevation is 748 feet.
Population: 4,421; Growth (since 2000): 11.2%; Density: 764.4 persons per square mile; Race: 85.7% White, 7.7% Black/African American, 1.4% Asian, 0.0% American Indian/Alaska Native, 0.0% Native Hawaiian/Other Pacific Islander, 3.2% Two or more races, 3.8% Hispanic of any race; Average household size: 2.83; Median age: 35.9; Age under 18: 29.1%; Age 65 and over: 8.8%; Males per 100 females: 96.0; Marriage status: 26.1% never married, 55.3% now married, 2.5% separated, 3.5% widowed, 15.1% divorced; Foreign born: 2.9%; Speak English only: 95.0%; With disability: 18.1%; Veterans: 12.9%; Ancestry: 26.0% German, 13.0% Irish, 8.9% American, 8.7% English, 7.1% Italian
Employment: 10.0% management, business, and financial, 3.4% computer, engineering, and science, 8.0% education, legal, community service, arts, and media, 4.9% healthcare practitioners, 13.8% service, 25.1% sales and office, 14.2% natural resources, construction, and maintenance, 20.6% production, transportation, and material moving
Income: Per capita: $18,756; Median household: $43,462; Average household: $51,686; Households with income of $100,000 or more: 12.7%; Poverty rate: 21.0%
Educational Attainment: High school diploma or higher: 83.4%; Bachelor's degree or higher: 11.9%; Graduate/professional degree or higher: 2.4%
Housing: Homeownership rate: 65.5%; Median home value: $108,000; Median year structure built: 1980; Homeowner vacancy rate: 0.0%; Median selected monthly owner costs: $1,150 with a mortgage, $499 without a mortgage; Median gross rent: $829 per month; Rental vacancy rate: 0.0%

Health Insurance: 89.1% have insurance; 59.5% have private insurance; 37.2% have public insurance; 10.9% do not have insurance; 3.5% of children under 18 do not have insurance
Transportation: Commute: 96.3% car, 0.0% public transportation, 0.4% walk, 2.2% work from home; Mean travel time to work: 19.2 minutes
Additional Information Contacts
Village of Obetz . . . . (614) 491-1080
http://www.obetz.oh.us

REYNOLDSBURG (city). Covers a land area of 11.157 square miles and a water area of 0.083 square miles. Located at 39.96° N. Lat; 82.80° W. Long. Elevation is 879 feet.
Population: 36,995; Growth (since 2000): 15.4%; Density: 3,315.8 persons per square mile; Race: 64.3% White, 26.9% Black/African American, 2.4% Asian, 0.0% American Indian/Alaska Native, 0.1% Native Hawaiian/Other Pacific Islander, 4.5% Two or more races, 3.9% Hispanic of any race; Average household size: 2.55; Median age: 35.9; Age under 18: 24.4%; Age 65 and over: 11.2%; Males per 100 females: 90.0; Marriage status: 33.6% never married, 47.2% now married, 1.8% separated, 4.5% widowed, 14.6% divorced; Foreign born: 6.0%; Speak English only: 93.0%; With disability: 10.5%; Veterans: 10.0%; Ancestry: 20.2% German, 13.5% Irish, 7.3% English, 5.1% American, 5.0% Italian
Employment: 14.9% management, business, and financial, 6.8% computer, engineering, and science, 10.3% education, legal, community service, arts, and media, 4.3% healthcare practitioners, 16.6% service, 30.2% sales and office, 7.2% natural resources, construction, and maintenance, 9.7% production, transportation, and material moving
Income: Per capita: $29,184; Median household: $61,648; Average household: $72,886; Households with income of $100,000 or more: 24.2%; Poverty rate: 9.8%
Educational Attainment: High school diploma or higher: 93.8%; Bachelor's degree or higher: 31.4%; Graduate/professional degree or higher: 10.8%

School District(s)

Everest High School (09-12)
2015-16 Enrollment: 96. . . . . (614) 367-1980
Pickerington Local (PK-12)
2015-16 Enrollment: 10,181 . . . . (614) 833-2110
Reynoldsburg City (PK-12)
2015-16 Enrollment: 6,865 . . . . (614) 501-1020

Housing: Homeownership rate: 58.9%; Median home value: $142,600; Median year structure built: 1983; Homeowner vacancy rate: 1.3%; Median selected monthly owner costs: $1,416 with a mortgage, $545 without a mortgage; Median gross rent: $948 per month; Rental vacancy rate: 5.2%
Health Insurance: 92.3% have insurance; 76.2% have private insurance; 27.1% have public insurance; 7.7% do not have insurance; 4.2% of children under 18 do not have insurance
Safety: Violent crime rate: 21.9 per 10,000 population; Property crime rate: 359.6 per 10,000 population
Transportation: Commute: 91.9% car, 1.0% public transportation, 2.0% walk, 4.2% work from home; Mean travel time to work: 24.3 minutes
Additional Information Contacts
City of Reynoldsburg . . . . (614) 322-6800
http://www.ci.reynoldsburg.oh.us

RIVERLEA (village). Covers a land area of 0.153 square miles and a water area of 0 square miles. Located at 40.08° N. Lat; 83.02° W. Long. Elevation is 787 feet.
Population: 583; Growth (since 2000): 16.8%; Density: 3,821.3 persons per square mile; Race: 97.3% White, 0.7% Black/African American, 0.0% Asian, 0.0% American Indian/Alaska Native, 0.0% Native Hawaiian/Other Pacific Islander, 2.1% Two or more races, 0.0% Hispanic of any race; Average household size: 2.59; Median age: 42.5; Age under 18: 29.3%; Age 65 and over: 14.8%; Males per 100 females: 81.7; Marriage status: 19.2% never married, 64.2% now married, 0.9% separated, 5.3% widowed, 11.3% divorced; Foreign born: 2.7%; Speak English only: 97.0%; With disability: 6.5%; Veterans: 7.8%; Ancestry: 33.8% German, 15.1% English, 12.3% Irish, 8.6% Italian, 6.3% Scottish
Employment: 24.9% management, business, and financial, 7.2% computer, engineering, and science, 28.2% education, legal, community service, arts, and media, 10.8% healthcare practitioners, 7.5% service, 18.7% sales and office, 0.7% natural resources, construction, and maintenance, 2.0% production, transportation, and material moving
Income: Per capita: $53,005; Median household: $109,688; Average household: $133,229; Households with income of $100,000 or more: 56.0%; Poverty rate: 0.7%
Educational Attainment: High school diploma or higher: 98.7%; Bachelor's degree or higher: 77.9%; Graduate/professional degree or higher: 39.9%
Housing: Homeownership rate: 80.4%; Median home value: $354,600; Median year structure built: 1955; Homeowner vacancy rate: 0.0%; Median selected monthly owner costs: $2,288 with a mortgage, $1,020 without a mortgage; Median gross rent: $825 per month; Rental vacancy rate: 0.0%
Health Insurance: 96.2% have insurance; 92.1% have private insurance; 15.1% have public insurance; 3.8% do not have insurance; 2.9% of children under 18 do not have insurance
Transportation: Commute: 87.2% car, 3.0% public transportation, 0.0% walk, 9.8% work from home; Mean travel time to work: 21.2 minutes

UPPER ARLINGTON (city). Covers a land area of 9.839 square miles and a water area of 0.030 square miles. Located at 40.03° N. Lat; 83.07° W. Long. Elevation is 814 feet.
History: Named for the Upper Arlington Company, a development organization. Incorporated 1918.
Population: 34,675; Growth (since 2000): 2.9%; Density: 3,524.3 persons per square mile; Race: 91.9% White, 1.3% Black/African American, 4.3% Asian, 0.2% American Indian/Alaska Native, 0.0% Native Hawaiian/Other Pacific Islander, 2.1% Two or more races, 2.5% Hispanic of any race; Average household size: 2.53; Median age: 42.1; Age under 18: 26.6%; Age 65 and over: 17.0%; Males per 100 females: 91.7; Marriage status: 23.1% never married, 63.9% now married, 0.8% separated, 4.8% widowed, 8.1% divorced; Foreign born: 7.5%; Speak English only: 90.9%; With disability: 8.6%; Veterans: 6.9%; Ancestry: 31.7% German, 17.6% Irish, 15.5% English, 9.3% Italian, 6.5% American
Employment: 25.3% management, business, and financial, 9.0% computer, engineering, and science, 20.1% education, legal, community service, arts, and media, 12.8% healthcare practitioners, 7.8% service, 20.4% sales and office, 2.2% natural resources, construction, and maintenance, 2.4% production, transportation, and material moving
Income: Per capita: $57,331; Median household: $102,094; Average household: $144,048; Households with income of $100,000 or more: 50.9%; Poverty rate: 5.1%
Educational Attainment: High school diploma or higher: 98.7%; Bachelor's degree or higher: 74.0%; Graduate/professional degree or higher: 35.4%

School District(s)

Upper Arlington City (KG-12)
2015-16 Enrollment: 5,892 . . . . (614) 487-5000

Housing: Homeownership rate: 80.4%; Median home value: $338,000; Median year structure built: 1958; Homeowner vacancy rate: 0.9%; Median selected monthly owner costs: $2,127 with a mortgage, $873 without a mortgage; Median gross rent: $1,074 per month; Rental vacancy rate: 7.2%
Health Insurance: 96.8% have insurance; 88.4% have private insurance; 21.4% have public insurance; 3.2% do not have insurance; 1.6% of children under 18 do not have insurance
Safety: Violent crime rate: 4.6 per 10,000 population; Property crime rate: 152.2 per 10,000 population
Transportation: Commute: 90.1% car, 0.8% public transportation, 1.5% walk, 5.9% work from home; Mean travel time to work: 19.7 minutes
Additional Information Contacts
City of Upper Arlington . . . . (614) 583-5000
http://www.ua-ohio.net

URBANCREST (village). Covers a land area of 0.598 square miles and a water area of <.001 square miles. Located at 39.90° N. Lat; 83.09° W. Long. Elevation is 840 feet.
Population: 894; Growth (since 2000): 3.0%; Density: 1,495.7 persons per square mile; Race: 25.7% White, 60.6% Black/African American, 9.6% Asian, 0.8% American Indian/Alaska Native, 0.0% Native Hawaiian/Other Pacific Islander, 2.6% Two or more races, 3.1% Hispanic of any race; Average household size: 2.53; Median age: 29.2; Age under 18: 29.6%; Age 65 and over: 8.2%; Males per 100 females: 81.8; Marriage status: 45.5% never married, 35.2% now married, 2.0% separated, 9.9% widowed, 9.4% divorced; Foreign born: 12.4%; Speak English only: 82.1%; With disability: 24.6%; Veterans: 4.5%; Ancestry: 11.7% Somalian, 7.7% Irish, 3.8% American, 3.6% African, 3.4% German

Employment: 8.0% management, business, and financial, 2.5% computer, engineering, and science, 10.1% education, legal, community service, arts, and media, 1.4% healthcare practitioners, 16.7% service, 20.3% sales and office, 6.2% natural resources, construction, and maintenance, 34.8% production, transportation, and material moving
Income: Per capita: $13,356; Median household: $16,480; Average household: $30,760; Households with income of $100,000 or more: 5.1%; Poverty rate: 40.9%
Educational Attainment: High school diploma or higher: 76.5%; Bachelor's degree or higher: 7.4%; Graduate/professional degree or higher: 4.8%
Housing: Homeownership rate: 41.0%; Median home value: $76,500; Median year structure built: 1974; Homeowner vacancy rate: 0.0%; Median selected monthly owner costs: $838 with a mortgage, $366 without a mortgage; Median gross rent: $555 per month; Rental vacancy rate: 9.8%
Health Insurance: 84.7% have insurance; 28.3% have private insurance; 62.4% have public insurance; 15.3% do not have insurance; 2.3% of children under 18 do not have insurance
Transportation: Commute: 85.2% car, 0.0% public transportation, 10.0% walk, 0.0% work from home; Mean travel time to work: 18.4 minutes

VALLEYVIEW (village). Covers a land area of 0.149 square miles and a water area of 0.003 square miles. Located at 39.96° N. Lat; 83.07° W. Long. Elevation is 778 feet.
Population: 623; Growth (since 2000): 3.7%; Density: 4,188.1 persons per square mile; Race: 88.9% White, 6.6% Black/African American, 1.9% Asian, 0.0% American Indian/Alaska Native, 0.0% Native Hawaiian/Other Pacific Islander, 2.6% Two or more races, 1.3% Hispanic of any race; Average household size: 2.45; Median age: 40.6; Age under 18: 20.1%; Age 65 and over: 11.4%; Males per 100 females: 98.7; Marriage status: 33.1% never married, 45.3% now married, 2.1% separated, 6.7% widowed, 14.9% divorced; Foreign born: 3.0%; Speak English only: 96.4%; With disability: 15.4%; Veterans: 6.4%; Ancestry: 27.6% Irish, 26.5% German, 8.8% English, 8.2% Italian, 7.7% American
Employment: 9.5% management, business, and financial, 4.4% computer, engineering, and science, 6.8% education, legal, community service, arts, and media, 3.7% healthcare practitioners, 28.7% service, 20.9% sales and office, 12.2% natural resources, construction, and maintenance, 13.9% production, transportation, and material moving
Income: Per capita: $18,290; Median household: $40,441; Average household: $44,207; Households with income of $100,000 or more: 5.5%; Poverty rate: 13.5%
Educational Attainment: High school diploma or higher: 88.6%; Bachelor's degree or higher: 10.1%; Graduate/professional degree or higher: 1.1%
Housing: Homeownership rate: 59.8%; Median home value: $90,000; Median year structure built: 1950; Homeowner vacancy rate: 3.8%; Median selected monthly owner costs: $1,042 with a mortgage, $417 without a mortgage; Median gross rent: $991 per month; Rental vacancy rate: 0.0%
Health Insurance: 78.8% have insurance; 60.2% have private insurance; 29.4% have public insurance; 21.2% do not have insurance; 24.8% of children under 18 do not have insurance
Transportation: Commute: 93.9% car, 3.4% public transportation, 0.0% walk, 1.0% work from home; Mean travel time to work: 25.9 minutes

WESTERVILLE (city). Covers a land area of 12.473 square miles and a water area of 0.138 square miles. Located at 40.12° N. Lat; 82.91° W. Long. Elevation is 869 feet.
History: Named for the Westervelt family, prominent farmers in the area. Westerville was settled in 1813 by Virginia Cavalier families and Quakers from Pennsylvania, and became the headquarters of the Anti-Saloon League in 1909.
Population: 38,089; Growth (since 2000): 7.8%; Density: 3,053.7 persons per square mile; Race: 86.3% White, 7.8% Black/African American, 2.0% Asian, 0.0% American Indian/Alaska Native, 0.1% Native Hawaiian/Other Pacific Islander, 3.2% Two or more races, 2.4% Hispanic of any race; Average household size: 2.49; Median age: 41.4; Age under 18: 21.9%; Age 65 and over: 17.7%; Males per 100 females: 88.5; Marriage status: 26.9% never married, 56.4% now married, 1.3% separated, 6.7% widowed, 10.0% divorced; Foreign born: 5.2%; Speak English only: 94.0%; With disability: 11.3%; Veterans: 8.1%; Ancestry: 29.5% German, 16.5% Irish, 13.2% English, 7.5% Italian, 5.3% American
Employment: 25.3% management, business, and financial, 7.3% computer, engineering, and science, 15.3% education, legal, community service, arts, and media, 5.9% healthcare practitioners, 12.3% service, 24.4% sales and office, 3.8% natural resources, construction, and maintenance, 5.6% production, transportation, and material moving
Income: Per capita: $38,779; Median household: $85,230; Average household: $99,308; Households with income of $100,000 or more: 42.0%; Poverty rate: 6.5%
Educational Attainment: High school diploma or higher: 96.7%; Bachelor's degree or higher: 52.5%; Graduate/professional degree or higher: 19.5%

School District(s)

Cornerstone Academy Community School (KG-08)
2015-16 Enrollment: 674 . . . . (614) 775-0615
Westerville City (PK-12)
2015-16 Enrollment: 14,802 . . . . (614) 797-5700
Worthington City (PK-12)
2015-16 Enrollment: 9,885 . . . . (614) 450-6000

Four-year College(s)

Hondros College of Nursing (Private, For-profit)
Fall 2016 Enrollment: 1,642 . . . . (855) 906-8773
2016-17 Tuition: In-state $18,235; Out-of-state $18,235
Otterbein University (Private, Not-for-profit, United Methodist)
Fall 2016 Enrollment: 2,928 . . . . (614) 890-3000
2016-17 Tuition: In-state $31,874; Out-of-state $31,874

Two-year College(s)

Fortis College-Columbus (Private, For-profit)
Fall 2016 Enrollment: 789 . . . . (614) 882-2551
2016-17 Tuition: In-state $14,900; Out-of-state $14,900
MyComputerCareer.com-Columbus (Private, For-profit)
Fall 2016 Enrollment: 246 . . . . (919) 813-6266

Housing: Homeownership rate: 76.6%; Median home value: $207,900; Median year structure built: 1980; Homeowner vacancy rate: 0.4%; Median selected monthly owner costs: $1,701 with a mortgage, $677 without a mortgage; Median gross rent: $927 per month; Rental vacancy rate: 4.1%
Health Insurance: 95.5% have insurance; 85.5% have private insurance; 22.5% have public insurance; 4.5% do not have insurance; 1.2% of children under 18 do not have insurance
Hospitals: Mount Carmel Saint Ann's (180 beds)
Safety: Violent crime rate: 5.4 per 10,000 population; Property crime rate: 240.9 per 10,000 population
Transportation: Commute: 90.1% car, 0.6% public transportation, 2.1% walk, 6.1% work from home; Mean travel time to work: 21.1 minutes
Additional Information Contacts
City of Westerville . . . . (614) 901-6400
http://www.westerville.org

WHITEHALL (city). Covers a land area of 5.257 square miles and a water area of 0.028 square miles. Located at 39.97° N. Lat; 82.88° W. Long. Elevation is 791 feet.
History: Named for Whitehall, site of government offices in London, England. Incorporated 1948.
Population: 18,596; Growth (since 2000): -3.2%; Density: 3,537.3 persons per square mile; Race: 52.2% White, 32.0% Black/African American, 1.2% Asian, 0.1% American Indian/Alaska Native, 0.0% Native Hawaiian/Other Pacific Islander, 7.7% Two or more races, 14.0% Hispanic of any race; Average household size: 2.46; Median age: 33.0; Age under 18: 28.5%; Age 65 and over: 11.0%; Males per 100 females: 94.6; Marriage status: 40.5% never married, 40.0% now married, 3.3% separated, 4.8% widowed, 14.7% divorced; Foreign born: 12.5%; Speak English only: 80.8%; With disability: 14.6%; Veterans: 8.2%; Ancestry: 11.2% German, 8.0% Irish, 6.3% American, 4.1% Italian, 3.2% English
Employment: 8.4% management, business, and financial, 3.0% computer, engineering, and science, 6.1% education, legal, community service, arts, and media, 2.7% healthcare practitioners, 22.0% service, 26.1% sales and office, 8.2% natural resources, construction, and maintenance, 23.6% production, transportation, and material moving
Income: Per capita: $19,342; Median household: $37,671; Average household: $45,678; Households with income of $100,000 or more: 7.0%; Poverty rate: 22.9%
Educational Attainment: High school diploma or higher: 80.7%; Bachelor's degree or higher: 12.7%; Graduate/professional degree or higher: 3.2%

School District(s)

Whitehall City (PK-12)
2015-16 Enrollment: 3,495 . . . . (614) 417-5000

Housing: Homeownership rate: 36.4%; Median home value: $83,200; Median year structure built: 1961; Homeowner vacancy rate: 1.3%; Median

selected monthly owner costs: $1,027 with a mortgage, $386 without a mortgage; Median gross rent: $796 per month; Rental vacancy rate: 5.9%
Health Insurance: 84.1% have insurance; 46.3% have private insurance; 46.8% have public insurance; 15.9% do not have insurance; 6.0% of children under 18 do not have insurance
Safety: Violent crime rate: 81.4 per 10,000 population; Property crime rate: 618.5 per 10,000 population
Transportation: Commute: 90.1% car, 3.9% public transportation, 3.4% walk, 1.6% work from home; Mean travel time to work: 20.8 minutes
Additional Information Contacts
City of Whitehall . . . . (614) 338-3106
http://whitehall-oh.us

WORTHINGTON (city). Covers a land area of 5.545 square miles and a water area of 0.076 square miles. Located at 40.10° N. Lat; 83.02° W. Long. Elevation is 863 feet.
History: Worthington was settled in 1803 by a group led by Colonel James Kilbourne, who named the place after a parish in Connecticut. A series of educational institutions opened and closed in Worthington over the next century.
Population: 14,155; Growth (since 2000): 0.2%; Density: 2,552.8 persons per square mile; Race: 93.4% White, 1.2% Black/African American, 1.4% Asian, 0.1% American Indian/Alaska Native, 0.0% Native Hawaiian/Other Pacific Islander, 2.3% Two or more races, 2.3% Hispanic of any race; Average household size: 2.41; Median age: 43.1; Age under 18: 25.4%; Age 65 and over: 20.0%; Males per 100 females: 89.3; Marriage status: 20.1% never married, 61.2% now married, 0.9% separated, 6.4% widowed, 12.2% divorced; Foreign born: 3.5%; Speak English only: 95.6%; With disability: 7.3%; Veterans: 7.7%; Ancestry: 35.8% German, 18.9% Irish, 15.4% English, 7.6% Italian, 5.5% American
Employment: 23.6% management, business, and financial, 7.9% computer, engineering, and science, 22.3% education, legal, community service, arts, and media, 8.5% healthcare practitioners, 8.6% service, 23.1% sales and office, 2.4% natural resources, construction, and maintenance, 3.5% production, transportation, and material moving
Income: Per capita: $49,654; Median household: $91,075; Average household: $120,388; Households with income of $100,000 or more: 47.1%; Poverty rate: 3.8%
Educational Attainment: High school diploma or higher: 98.4%; Bachelor's degree or higher: 68.4%; Graduate/professional degree or higher: 29.8%

School District(s)

Worthington City (PK-12)
2015-16 Enrollment: 9,885 . . . . (614) 450-6000
Housing: Homeownership rate: 79.5%; Median home value: $251,400; Median year structure built: 1965; Homeowner vacancy rate: 0.7%; Median selected monthly owner costs: $1,829 with a mortgage, $769 without a mortgage; Median gross rent: $882 per month; Rental vacancy rate: 0.9%
Health Insurance: 97.1% have insurance; 88.9% have private insurance; 24.4% have public insurance; 2.9% do not have insurance; 1.0% of children under 18 do not have insurance
Safety: Violent crime rate: 3.4 per 10,000 population; Property crime rate: 158.6 per 10,000 population
Transportation: Commute: 88.9% car, 0.6% public transportation, 0.8% walk, 8.3% work from home; Mean travel time to work: 21.6 minutes
Additional Information Contacts
City of Worthington . . . . (614) 436-3100
http://www.worthington.org

Fulton County

Located in northwestern Ohio; bounded on the north by Michigan; drained by the Tiffin River. Covers a land area of 405.443 square miles, a water area of 1.784 square miles, and is located in the Eastern Time Zone at 41.60° N. Lat., 84.12° W. Long. The county was founded in 1850. County seat is Wauseon.

Fulton County is part of the Toledo, OH Metropolitan Statistical Area. The entire metro area includes: Fulton County, OH; Lucas County, OH; Wood County, OH

Weather Station: Wauseon Water Plant Elevation: 750 feet

	Jan	Feb	Mar	Apr	May	Jun	Jul	Aug	Sep	Oct	Nov	Dec
High	32	36	46	60	71	81	84	82	76	63	49	36
Low	17	19	27	38	48	58	61	60	52	41	32	22
Precip	1.9	1.6	2.3	3.1	3.7	3.4	3.7	3.7	3.2	2.9	2.9	2.5
Snow	8.2	6.1	4.1	0.6	tr	0.0	0.0	0.0	0.0	0.1	1.2	5.3

High and Low temperatures in degrees Fahrenheit; Precipitation and Snow in inches

Population: 42,466; Growth (since 2000): 0.9%; Density: 104.7 persons per square mile; Race: 94.2% White, 0.5% Black/African American, 0.4% Asian, 0.1% American Indian/Alaska Native, 0.0% Native Hawaiian/Other Pacific Islander, 1.3% two or more races, 8.2% Hispanic of any race; Average household size: 2.59; Median age: 40.0; Age under 18: 24.6%; Age 65 and over: 16.2%; Males per 100 females: 96.6; Marriage status: 23.9% never married, 58.3% now married, 1.1% separated, 6.6% widowed, 11.3% divorced; Foreign born: 1.5%; Speak English only: 95.3%; With disability: 13.4%; Veterans: 8.3%; Ancestry: 44.1% German, 12.7% Irish, 9.2% English, 6.8% Polish, 5.7% American
Religion: Six largest groups: 17.8% Catholicism, 9.2% European Free-Church, 8.5% Lutheran, 6.1% Baptist, 4.9% Holiness, 4.6% Methodist/Pietist
Economy: Unemployment rate: 4.0%; Leading industries: 17.1 % retail trade; 13.1 % other services (except public administration); 12.8 % construction; Farms: 825 totaling 195,356 acres; Company size: 1 employs 1,000 or more persons, 2 employ 500 to 999 persons, 20 employ 100 to 499 persons, 928 employ less than 100 persons; Business ownership: 1,132 women-owned, n/a Black-owned, 90 Hispanic-owned, 41 Asian-owned, n/a American Indian/Alaska Native-owned
Employment: 11.2% management, business, and financial, 2.4% computer, engineering, and science, 6.9% education, legal, community service, arts, and media, 5.9% healthcare practitioners, 16.0% service, 22.0% sales and office, 12.7% natural resources, construction, and maintenance, 22.9% production, transportation, and material moving
Income: Per capita: $27,010; Median household: $55,860; Average household: $69,615; Households with income of $100,000 or more: 18.9%; Poverty rate: 11.2%
Educational Attainment: High school diploma or higher: 90.4%; Bachelor's degree or higher: 17.0%; Graduate/professional degree or higher: 6.1%
Housing: Homeownership rate: 78.0%; Median home value: $131,100; Median year structure built: 1969; Homeowner vacancy rate: 0.6%; Median selected monthly owner costs: $1,170 with a mortgage, $423 without a mortgage; Median gross rent: $647 per month; Rental vacancy rate: 3.1%
Vital Statistics: Birth rate: 120.2 per 10,000 population; Death rate: 99.7 per 10,000 population; Age-adjusted cancer mortality rate: 196.1 deaths per 100,000 population
Health Insurance: 94.8% have insurance; 77.2% have private insurance; 32.0% have public insurance; 5.2% do not have insurance; 1.7% of children under 18 do not have insurance
Health Care: Physicians: 8.0 per 10,000 population; Dentists: 3.8 per 10,000 population; Hospital beds: 24.9 per 10,000 population; Hospital admissions: 383.5 per 10,000 population
Transportation: Commute: 94.7% car, 0.1% public transportation, 1.6% walk, 2.6% work from home; Mean travel time to work: 24.3 minutes
2016 Presidential Election: 64.2% Trump, 28.4% Clinton, 4.8% Johnson, 0.8% Stein
National and State Parks: Harrison Lake State Reservation
Additional Information Contacts
Fulton Government . . . . (419) 337-9255
http://www.fultoncountyoh.com

Fulton County Communities

ARCHBOLD (village). Covers a land area of 4.932 square miles and a water area of 0.139 square miles. Located at 41.52° N. Lat; 84.30° W. Long. Elevation is 732 feet.
Population: 4,368; Growth (since 2000): 1.8%; Density: 885.7 persons per square mile; Race: 86.5% White, 0.8% Black/African American, 0.0% Asian, 0.0% American Indian/Alaska Native, 0.0% Native Hawaiian/Other Pacific Islander, 2.3% Two or more races, 17.1% Hispanic of any race; Average household size: 2.54; Median age: 38.0; Age under 18: 27.4%; Age 65 and over: 19.3%; Males per 100 females: 88.5; Marriage status: 23.8% never married, 60.7% now married, 1.9% separated, 7.4% widowed, 8.0% divorced; Foreign born: 2.7%; Speak English only: 92.8%;

With disability: 12.5%; Veterans: 7.4%; Ancestry: 43.6% German, 8.5% English, 7.0% Irish, 4.7% Swiss, 4.7% French
Employment: 10.3% management, business, and financial, 2.3% computer, engineering, and science, 12.4% education, legal, community service, arts, and media, 7.2% healthcare practitioners, 20.4% service, 17.1% sales and office, 5.3% natural resources, construction, and maintenance, 25.0% production, transportation, and material moving
Income: Per capita: $26,696; Median household: $55,203; Average household: $68,013; Households with income of $100,000 or more: 21.1%; Poverty rate: 12.5%
Educational Attainment: High school diploma or higher: 89.3%; Bachelor's degree or higher: 24.2%; Graduate/professional degree or higher: 9.4%

School District(s)

Archbold-Area Local (KG-12)
2015-16 Enrollment: 1,210 . . . . (419) 446-2728
Four County Career Center (07-12)
2015-16 Enrollment: n/a . . . . (419) 267-3331

Two-year College(s)

Northwest State Community College (Public)
Fall 2016 Enrollment: 3,102 . . . . (419) 267-5511
2016-17 Tuition: In-state $3,858; Out-of-state $7,490

Vocational/Technical School(s)

Four County Career Center (Public)
Fall 2016 Enrollment: 152 . . . . (419) 267-3331

Housing: Homeownership rate: 68.8%; Median home value: $126,400; Median year structure built: 1968; Homeowner vacancy rate: 0.0%; Median selected monthly owner costs: $1,067 with a mortgage, $407 without a mortgage; Median gross rent: $607 per month; Rental vacancy rate: 4.7%
Health Insurance: 94.9% have insurance; 73.9% have private insurance; 36.9% have public insurance; 5.1% do not have insurance; 3.8% of children under 18 do not have insurance
Safety: Violent crime rate: 9.2 per 10,000 population; Property crime rate: 133.6 per 10,000 population
Newspapers: Archbold Buckeye (weekly circulation 3,200); Farmland News (weekly circulation 3,500)
Transportation: Commute: 90.6% car, 0.0% public transportation, 2.5% walk, 2.0% work from home; Mean travel time to work: 16.4 minutes
Additional Information Contacts
Village of Archbold . . . . (419) 445-4726
http://www.archbold.com

DELTA (village). Covers a land area of 2.670 square miles and a water area of 0.001 square miles. Located at 41.58° N. Lat; 84.00° W. Long. Elevation is 722 feet.
Population: 3,271; Growth (since 2000): 11.6%; Density: 1,225.2 persons per square mile; Race: 96.5% White, 0.8% Black/African American, 2.1% Asian, 0.2% American Indian/Alaska Native, 0.0% Native Hawaiian/Other Pacific Islander, 0.0% Two or more races, 8.3% Hispanic of any race; Average household size: 2.44; Median age: 38.7; Age under 18: 26.5%; Age 65 and over: 17.3%; Males per 100 females: 93.9; Marriage status: 26.0% never married, 51.8% now married, 0.5% separated, 6.7% widowed, 15.4% divorced; Foreign born: 1.1%; Speak English only: 94.7%; With disability: 12.9%; Veterans: 9.9%; Ancestry: 43.3% German, 11.5% English, 10.8% Irish, 7.6% American, 6.0% Polish
Employment: 12.1% management, business, and financial, 2.7% computer, engineering, and science, 4.8% education, legal, community service, arts, and media, 8.4% healthcare practitioners, 20.2% service, 25.9% sales and office, 8.0% natural resources, construction, and maintenance, 17.9% production, transportation, and material moving
Income: Per capita: $25,712; Median household: $50,924; Average household: $62,063; Households with income of $100,000 or more: 16.5%; Poverty rate: 12.5%
Educational Attainment: High school diploma or higher: 93.2%; Bachelor's degree or higher: 18.2%; Graduate/professional degree or higher: 6.8%

School District(s)

Pike-Delta-York Local (PK-12)
2015-16 Enrollment: 1,276 . . . . (419) 822-3391

Housing: Homeownership rate: 79.3%; Median home value: $113,200; Median year structure built: 1959; Homeowner vacancy rate: 0.0%; Median selected monthly owner costs: $1,056 with a mortgage, $353 without a mortgage; Median gross rent: $605 per month; Rental vacancy rate: 7.7%
Health Insurance: 98.2% have insurance; 76.4% have private insurance; 39.7% have public insurance; 1.8% do not have insurance; 0.0% of children under 18 do not have insurance
Newspapers: Delta Atlas (weekly circulation 2,000)
Transportation: Commute: 94.2% car, 0.1% public transportation, 0.8% walk, 4.8% work from home; Mean travel time to work: 26.9 minutes

FAYETTE (village). Covers a land area of 0.984 square miles and a water area of 0 square miles. Located at 41.67° N. Lat; 84.33° W. Long. Elevation is 791 feet.
History: Fayette developed as a grain and livestock shipping center.
Population: 1,461; Growth (since 2000): 9.0%; Density: 1,484.5 persons per square mile; Race: 94.9% White, 0.0% Black/African American, 1.9% Asian, 1.0% American Indian/Alaska Native, 0.0% Native Hawaiian/Other Pacific Islander, 1.1% Two or more races, 6.2% Hispanic of any race; Average household size: 2.45; Median age: 32.1; Age under 18: 32.2%; Age 65 and over: 8.8%; Males per 100 females: 90.1; Marriage status: 28.9% never married, 49.6% now married, 0.0% separated, 3.3% widowed, 18.1% divorced; Foreign born: 4.4%; Speak English only: 94.3%; With disability: 14.0%; Veterans: 9.6%; Ancestry: 39.6% German, 14.8% Irish, 10.4% English, 6.8% Dutch, 5.8% American
Employment: 4.9% management, business, and financial, 3.9% computer, engineering, and science, 8.5% education, legal, community service, arts, and media, 3.2% healthcare practitioners, 12.5% service, 18.0% sales and office, 18.8% natural resources, construction, and maintenance, 30.2% production, transportation, and material moving
Income: Per capita: $17,896; Median household: $39,125; Average household: $43,853; Households with income of $100,000 or more: 3.7%; Poverty rate: 21.2%
Educational Attainment: High school diploma or higher: 89.4%; Bachelor's degree or higher: 14.0%; Graduate/professional degree or higher: 6.1%

School District(s)

Fayette Local (PK-12)
2015-16 Enrollment: 408 . . . . (877) 644-6338

Housing: Homeownership rate: 59.3%; Median home value: $75,300; Median year structure built: 1950; Homeowner vacancy rate: 1.1%; Median selected monthly owner costs: $817 with a mortgage, $395 without a mortgage; Median gross rent: $575 per month; Rental vacancy rate: 10.0%
Health Insurance: 94.2% have insurance; 66.0% have private insurance; 37.6% have public insurance; 5.8% do not have insurance; 0.0% of children under 18 do not have insurance
Transportation: Commute: 97.7% car, 0.0% public transportation, 1.9% walk, 0.5% work from home; Mean travel time to work: 23.1 minutes

LYONS (village). Covers a land area of 0.708 square miles and a water area of <.001 square miles. Located at 41.70° N. Lat; 84.07° W. Long. Elevation is 768 feet.
Population: 465; Growth (since 2000): -16.8%; Density: 657.2 persons per square mile; Race: 98.5% White, 0.0% Black/African American, 0.0% Asian, 0.0% American Indian/Alaska Native, 0.0% Native Hawaiian/Other Pacific Islander, 0.0% Two or more races, 5.2% Hispanic of any race; Average household size: 2.38; Median age: 41.5; Age under 18: 21.7%; Age 65 and over: 18.5%; Males per 100 females: 95.1; Marriage status: 28.0% never married, 50.4% now married, 1.0% separated, 9.6% widowed, 12.1% divorced; Foreign born: 0.0%; Speak English only: 99.8%; With disability: 21.3%; Veterans: 10.7%; Ancestry: 36.1% German, 26.0% Irish, 6.9% English, 5.6% American, 4.7% Polish
Employment: 8.6% management, business, and financial, 0.9% computer, engineering, and science, 4.5% education, legal, community service, arts, and media, 5.4% healthcare practitioners, 19.8% service, 20.7% sales and office, 19.8% natural resources, construction, and maintenance, 20.3% production, transportation, and material moving
Income: Per capita: $22,964; Median household: $45,938; Average household: $54,369; Households with income of $100,000 or more: 7.2%; Poverty rate: 9.3%
Educational Attainment: High school diploma or higher: 88.5%; Bachelor's degree or higher: 11.5%; Graduate/professional degree or higher: 2.1%
Housing: Homeownership rate: 68.7%; Median home value: $90,000; Median year structure built: Before 1940; Homeowner vacancy rate: 5.0%; Median selected monthly owner costs: $966 with a mortgage, $348 without a mortgage; Median gross rent: $665 per month; Rental vacancy rate: 0.0%

Health Insurance: 90.1% have insurance; 72.3% have private insurance; 36.6% have public insurance; 9.9% do not have insurance; 0.0% of children under 18 do not have insurance
Transportation: Commute: 95.0% car, 0.0% public transportation, 1.4% walk, 3.6% work from home; Mean travel time to work: 32.5 minutes

METAMORA (village). Covers a land area of 0.825 square miles and a water area of 0.014 square miles. Located at 41.71° N. Lat; 83.91° W. Long. Elevation is 718 feet.
Population: 592; Growth (since 2000): 5.2%; Density: 717.8 persons per square mile; Race: 94.4% White, 0.0% Black/African American, 0.5% Asian, 0.0% American Indian/Alaska Native, 0.0% Native Hawaiian/Other Pacific Islander, 1.7% Two or more races, 6.3% Hispanic of any race; Average household size: 2.55; Median age: 34.3; Age under 18: 27.5%; Age 65 and over: 11.7%; Males per 100 females: 97.2; Marriage status: 29.2% never married, 52.8% now married, 2.6% separated, 6.3% widowed, 11.7% divorced; Foreign born: 1.2%; Speak English only: 98.7%; With disability: 9.3%; Veterans: 6.3%; Ancestry: 45.9% German, 12.0% Irish, 10.6% English, 9.6% Polish, 5.1% French
Employment: 3.9% management, business, and financial, 3.9% computer, engineering, and science, 11.0% education, legal, community service, arts, and media, 14.2% healthcare practitioners, 16.0% service, 29.9% sales and office, 7.5% natural resources, construction, and maintenance, 13.5% production, transportation, and material moving
Income: Per capita: $23,501; Median household: $48,636; Average household: $60,964; Households with income of $100,000 or more: 14.6%; Poverty rate: 7.8%
Educational Attainment: High school diploma or higher: 93.5%; Bachelor's degree or higher: 24.2%; Graduate/professional degree or higher: 7.3%

School District(s)

Evergreen Local (PK-12)
2015-16 Enrollment: 1,177 . . . . (419) 644-3521
Housing: Homeownership rate: 74.6%; Median home value: $113,900; Median year structure built: Before 1940; Homeowner vacancy rate: 0.0%; Median selected monthly owner costs: $1,141 with a mortgage, $414 without a mortgage; Median gross rent: $790 per month; Rental vacancy rate: 6.3%
Health Insurance: 94.3% have insurance; 73.8% have private insurance; 31.4% have public insurance; 5.7% do not have insurance; 3.7% of children under 18 do not have insurance
Transportation: Commute: 91.4% car, 0.0% public transportation, 3.6% walk, 3.6% work from home; Mean travel time to work: 29.5 minutes

PETTISVILLE (CDP). Covers a land area of 0.952 square miles and a water area of <.001 square miles. Located at 41.53° N. Lat; 84.22° W. Long. Elevation is 758 feet.
Population: 505; Growth (since 2000): n/a; Density: 530.7 persons per square mile; Race: 91.7% White, 5.7% Black/African American, 1.0% Asian, 0.0% American Indian/Alaska Native, 0.0% Native Hawaiian/Other Pacific Islander, 1.6% Two or more races, 12.5% Hispanic of any race; Average household size: 2.64; Median age: 46.4; Age under 18: 25.9%; Age 65 and over: 18.6%; Males per 100 females: 93.8; Marriage status: 25.0% never married, 63.8% now married, 0.5% separated, 5.6% widowed, 5.6% divorced; Foreign born: 2.4%; Speak English only: 98.8%; With disability: 16.4%; Veterans: 7.5%; Ancestry: 51.1% German, 5.7% French, 4.0% Irish, 4.0% Swiss, 3.6% English
Employment: 14.0% management, business, and financial, 2.2% computer, engineering, and science, 7.9% education, legal, community service, arts, and media, 13.2% healthcare practitioners, 12.7% service, 19.3% sales and office, 9.6% natural resources, construction, and maintenance, 21.1% production, transportation, and material moving
Income: Per capita: $21,069; Median household: $57,250; Average household: $55,010; Households with income of $100,000 or more: 7.9%; Poverty rate: 4.8%
Educational Attainment: High school diploma or higher: 93.3%; Bachelor's degree or higher: 24.5%; Graduate/professional degree or higher: 9.3%

School District(s)

Pettisville Local (KG-12)
2015-16 Enrollment: 486. . . . . (419) 446-2705
Housing: Homeownership rate: 78.0%; Median home value: $113,900; Median year structure built: 1953; Homeowner vacancy rate: 0.0%; Median selected monthly owner costs: $886 with a mortgage, $386 without a mortgage; Median gross rent: $790 per month; Rental vacancy rate: 0.0%
Health Insurance: 97.6% have insurance; 90.7% have private insurance; 25.7% have public insurance; 2.4% do not have insurance; 1.5% of children under 18 do not have insurance
Transportation: Commute: 90.1% car, 0.0% public transportation, 9.9% walk, 0.0% work from home; Mean travel time to work: 13.7 minutes

SWANTON (village). Covers a land area of 3.094 square miles and a water area of 0.037 square miles. Located at 41.58° N. Lat; 83.89° W. Long. Elevation is 682 feet.
Population: 3,755; Growth (since 2000): 13.5%; Density: 1,213.6 persons per square mile; Race: 97.0% White, 1.2% Black/African American, 0.0% Asian, 0.2% American Indian/Alaska Native, 0.0% Native Hawaiian/Other Pacific Islander, 0.0% Two or more races, 7.8% Hispanic of any race; Average household size: 2.59; Median age: 36.0; Age under 18: 23.3%; Age 65 and over: 18.4%; Males per 100 females: 95.1; Marriage status: 24.8% never married, 55.7% now married, 2.3% separated, 9.6% widowed, 9.9% divorced; Foreign born: 1.0%; Speak English only: 96.9%; With disability: 12.2%; Veterans: 8.6%; Ancestry: 39.7% German, 14.9% Irish, 10.5% Polish, 9.9% English, 4.6% American
Employment: 11.3% management, business, and financial, 4.5% computer, engineering, and science, 8.5% education, legal, community service, arts, and media, 5.6% healthcare practitioners, 17.7% service, 22.0% sales and office, 12.0% natural resources, construction, and maintenance, 18.5% production, transportation, and material moving
Income: Per capita: $24,067; Median household: $52,452; Average household: $60,816; Households with income of $100,000 or more: 16.4%; Poverty rate: 10.5%
Educational Attainment: High school diploma or higher: 93.4%; Bachelor's degree or higher: 19.4%; Graduate/professional degree or higher: 7.2%

School District(s)

Swanton Local (PK-12)
2015-16 Enrollment: 1,296 . . . . (419) 826-7085
Housing: Homeownership rate: 71.4%; Median home value: $127,600; Median year structure built: 1963; Homeowner vacancy rate: 0.0%; Median selected monthly owner costs: $1,172 with a mortgage, $401 without a mortgage; Median gross rent: $658 per month; Rental vacancy rate: 0.0%
Health Insurance: 94.7% have insurance; 83.3% have private insurance; 25.3% have public insurance; 5.3% do not have insurance; 4.5% of children under 18 do not have insurance
Safety: Violent crime rate: 7.7 per 10,000 population; Property crime rate: 72.0 per 10,000 population
Newspapers: Swanton Enterprise (weekly circulation 1,900)
Transportation: Commute: 98.9% car, 0.0% public transportation, 0.0% walk, 0.6% work from home; Mean travel time to work: 24.4 minutes
Additional Information Contacts
Village of Swanton. . . . . (419) 826-9515
http://www.villageofswantonohio.us

TEDROW (CDP). Covers a land area of 0.321 square miles and a water area of 0 square miles. Located at 41.60° N. Lat; 84.20° W. Long. Elevation is 768 feet.
Population: 245; Growth (since 2000): n/a; Density: 764.1 persons per square mile; Race: 82.0% White, 16.7% Black/African American, 0.0% Asian, 0.0% American Indian/Alaska Native, 0.0% Native Hawaiian/Other Pacific Islander, 1.2% Two or more races, 24.5% Hispanic of any race; Average household size: 3.31; Median age: 43.1; Age under 18: 23.3%; Age 65 and over: 10.6%; Males per 100 females: 111.0; Marriage status: 42.4% never married, 41.0% now married, 3.9% separated, 8.3% widowed, 8.3% divorced; Foreign born: 2.4%; Speak English only: 94.6%; With disability: 11.8%; Veterans: 7.4%; Ancestry: 11.8% English, 10.6% German, 9.8% Hungarian, 8.2% Czech, 8.2% Slovene
Employment: 13.9% management, business, and financial, 3.7% computer, engineering, and science, 8.3% education, legal, community service, arts, and media, 0.0% healthcare practitioners, 14.8% service, 21.3% sales and office, 0.0% natural resources, construction, and maintenance, 38.0% production, transportation, and material moving
Income: Per capita: $19,281; Median household: $57,500; Average household: $64,861; Households with income of $100,000 or more: 21.6%; Poverty rate: 27.8%
Educational Attainment: High school diploma or higher: 86.6%; Bachelor's degree or higher: 6.3%; Graduate/professional degree or higher: n/a
Housing: Homeownership rate: 78.4%; Median home value: $90,000; Median year structure built: 1947; Homeowner vacancy rate: 0.0%; Median

selected monthly owner costs: $1,250 with a mortgage, $283 without a mortgage; Median gross rent: n/a per month; Rental vacancy rate: 0.0%
Health Insurance: 100.0% have insurance; 55.1% have private insurance; 51.4% have public insurance; 0.0% do not have insurance; 0.0% of children under 18 do not have insurance
Transportation: Commute: 100.0% car, 0.0% public transportation, 0.0% walk, 0.0% work from home; Mean travel time to work: 23.8 minutes

WAUSEON (city). County seat. Covers a land area of 5.168 square miles and a water area of 0.023 square miles. Located at 41.55° N. Lat; 84.14° W. Long. Elevation is 768 feet.
History: Settled 1835, incorporated 1852.
Population: 7,059; Growth (since 2000): -0.5%; Density: 1,365.8 persons per square mile; Race: 85.6% White, 0.1% Black/African American, 0.7% Asian, 0.3% American Indian/Alaska Native, 0.0% Native Hawaiian/Other Pacific Islander, 3.6% Two or more races, 17.8% Hispanic of any race; Average household size: 2.48; Median age: 36.3; Age under 18: 25.9%; Age 65 and over: 17.1%; Males per 100 females: 92.1; Marriage status: 25.9% never married, 47.7% now married, 2.8% separated, 9.2% widowed, 17.2% divorced; Foreign born: 3.1%; Speak English only: 89.1%; With disability: 17.2%; Veterans: 9.6%; Ancestry: 41.7% German, 12.6% Irish, 10.7% English, 5.5% American, 5.5% Polish
Employment: 7.5% management, business, and financial, 1.6% computer, engineering, and science, 4.2% education, legal, community service, arts, and media, 5.2% healthcare practitioners, 18.8% service, 17.8% sales and office, 7.8% natural resources, construction, and maintenance, 37.1% production, transportation, and material moving
Income: Per capita: $22,434; Median household: $48,750; Average household: $55,963; Households with income of $100,000 or more: 12.9%; Poverty rate: 16.5%
Educational Attainment: High school diploma or higher: 85.2%; Bachelor's degree or higher: 17.5%; Graduate/professional degree or higher: 4.5%

School District(s)

Wauseon Exempted Village (PK-12)
2015-16 Enrollment: 1,806 . . . . (419) 335-6616
Housing: Homeownership rate: 58.5%; Median home value: $119,100; Median year structure built: 1963; Homeowner vacancy rate: 0.0%; Median selected monthly owner costs: $1,170 with a mortgage, $383 without a mortgage; Median gross rent: $631 per month; Rental vacancy rate: 1.0%
Health Insurance: 92.3% have insurance; 69.4% have private insurance; 37.3% have public insurance; 7.7% do not have insurance; 1.6% of children under 18 do not have insurance
Hospitals: Fulton County Health Center (119 beds)
Safety: Violent crime rate: 9.6 per 10,000 population; Property crime rate: 269.5 per 10,000 population
Newspapers: Fulton County Expositor (weekly circulation 13,000)
Transportation: Commute: 94.2% car, 0.2% public transportation, 2.9% walk, 1.2% work from home; Mean travel time to work: 22.3 minutes

Gallia County

Located in southern Ohio; bounded on the east by the Ohio River and the West Virginia border; crossed by Raccoon Creek. Covers a land area of 466.530 square miles, a water area of 4.666 square miles, and is located in the Eastern Time Zone at 38.82° N. Lat., 82.30° W. Long. The county was founded in 1803. County seat is Gallipolis.

Gallia County is part of the Point Pleasant, WV-OH Micropolitan Statistical Area. The entire metro area includes: Gallia County, OH; Mason County, WV

Weather Station: Gallipolis Elevation: 568 feet

	Jan	Feb	Mar	Apr	May	Jun	Jul	Aug	Sep	Oct	Nov	Dec
High	43	47	57	68	76	84	87	87	80	69	58	46
Low	23	25	32	41	51	60	65	63	56	44	35	27
Precip	2.8	3.0	3.8	3.5	4.4	3.7	4.1	3.4	3.0	2.8	3.1	3.2
Snow	4.2	2.9	1.2	tr	0.0	0.0	0.0	0.0	0.0	0.0	tr	1.0

High and Low temperatures in degrees Fahrenheit; Precipitation and Snow in inches

Population: 30,376; Growth (since 2000): -2.2%; Density: 65.1 persons per square mile; Race: 94.8% White, 2.7% Black/African American, 0.7% Asian, 0.3% American Indian/Alaska Native, 0.1% Native Hawaiian/Other Pacific Islander, 1.3% two or more races, 1.2% Hispanic of any race; Average household size: 2.57; Median age: 40.5; Age under 18: 23.6%; Age 65 and over: 17.2%; Males per 100 females: 97.1; Marriage status: 23.5% never married, 55.5% now married, 1.7% separated, 7.1% widowed, 13.8% divorced; Foreign born: 0.9%; Speak English only: 96.8%; With disability: 19.8%; Veterans: 9.2%; Ancestry: 16.0% German, 11.0% Irish, 10.9% American, 10.7% English, 2.6% French
Religion: Six largest groups: 9.7% Baptist, 4.6% Methodist/Pietist, 3.3% Non-denominational Protestant, 2.4% European Free-Church, 2.0% Holiness, 1.6% Catholicism
Economy: Unemployment rate: 5.4%; Leading industries: 22.8 % retail trade; 13.3 % health care and social assistance; 12.7 % other services (except public administration); Farms: 957 totaling 115,838 acres; Company size: 1 employs 1,000 or more persons, 0 employ 500 to 999 persons, 11 employs 100 to 499 persons, 545 employ less than 100 persons; Business ownership: 687 women-owned, n/a Black-owned, n/a Hispanic-owned, n/a Asian-owned, n/a American Indian/Alaska Native-owned
Employment: 9.7% management, business, and financial, 2.3% computer, engineering, and science, 8.8% education, legal, community service, arts, and media, 7.2% healthcare practitioners, 18.1% service, 23.7% sales and office, 10.9% natural resources, construction, and maintenance, 19.3% production, transportation, and material moving
Income: Per capita: $20,914; Median household: $39,423; Average household: $53,749; Households with income of $100,000 or more: 13.8%; Poverty rate: 21.4%
Educational Attainment: High school diploma or higher: 80.5%; Bachelor's degree or higher: 15.4%; Graduate/professional degree or higher: 6.4%
Housing: Homeownership rate: 74.8%; Median home value: $101,200; Median year structure built: 1980; Homeowner vacancy rate: 1.3%; Median selected monthly owner costs: $1,067 with a mortgage, $393 without a mortgage; Median gross rent: $642 per month; Rental vacancy rate: 9.7%
Vital Statistics: Birth rate: 125.6 per 10,000 population; Death rate: 116.3 per 10,000 population; Age-adjusted cancer mortality rate: 238.0 deaths per 100,000 population
Health Insurance: 87.9% have insurance; 58.5% have private insurance; 44.6% have public insurance; 12.1% do not have insurance; 8.4% of children under 18 do not have insurance
Health Care: Physicians: 30.9 per 10,000 population; Dentists: 3.3 per 10,000 population; Hospital beds: 59.6 per 10,000 population; Hospital admissions: 2,140.1 per 10,000 population
Transportation: Commute: 92.5% car, 0.2% public transportation, 2.6% walk, 3.6% work from home; Mean travel time to work: 27.8 minutes
2016 Presidential Election: 75.5% Trump, 20.2% Clinton, 2.2% Johnson, 0.8% Stein
National and State Parks: Tycoon Lake State Wildlife Area
Additional Information Contacts
Gallia Government . . . . (740) 446-8510
http://www.gallianet.net

Gallia County Communities

BIDWELL (unincorporated postal area)
ZCTA: 45614
Covers a land area of 73.163 square miles and a water area of 0.725 square miles. Located at 38.93° N. Lat; 82.28° W. Long. Elevation is 686 feet.
Population: 4,884; Growth (since 2000): 10.3%; Density: 66.8 persons per square mile; Race: 91.9% White, 6.1% Black/African American, 0.9% Asian, 0.0% American Indian/Alaska Native, 0.0% Native Hawaiian/Other Pacific Islander, 1.2% Two or more races, 2.5% Hispanic of any race; Average household size: 2.48; Median age: 44.7; Age under 18: 24.3%; Age 65 and over: 19.6%; Males per 100 females: 91.5; Marriage status: 19.3% never married, 57.5% now married, 1.1% separated, 10.3% widowed, 13.0% divorced; Foreign born: 0.9%; Speak English only: 98.6%; With disability: 18.4%; Veterans: 9.6%; Ancestry: 11.8% German, 10.6% Irish, 10.2% American, 9.4% English, 1.4% Scotch-Irish
Employment: 10.0% management, business, and financial, 4.0% computer, engineering, and science, 5.4% education, legal, community service, arts, and media, 10.2% healthcare practitioners, 10.0% service, 23.2% sales and office, 15.2% natural resources, construction, and maintenance, 21.8% production, transportation, and material moving
Income: Per capita: $22,045; Median household: $41,250; Average household: $55,748; Households with income of $100,000 or more: 19.7%; Poverty rate: 19.0%

Educational Attainment: High school diploma or higher: 82.7%; Bachelor's degree or higher: 16.5%; Graduate/professional degree or higher: 4.7%

School District(s)

Gallia County Local (PK-12)
2015-16 Enrollment: 2,167 . . . . (740) 379-9085

Housing: Homeownership rate: 79.7%; Median home value: $101,500; Median year structure built: 1979; Homeowner vacancy rate: 1.8%; Median selected monthly owner costs: $994 with a mortgage, $453 without a mortgage; Median gross rent: $620 per month; Rental vacancy rate: 21.3%
Health Insurance: 91.2% have insurance; 63.5% have private insurance; 44.5% have public insurance; 8.8% do not have insurance; 1.4% of children under 18 do not have insurance
Transportation: Commute: 94.0% car, 0.0% public transportation, 2.4% walk, 2.9% work from home; Mean travel time to work: 27.8 minutes

CENTERVILLE (village). Covers a land area of 0.100 square miles and a water area of 0 square miles. Located at 38.90° N. Lat; 82.45° W. Long. Elevation is 679 feet.
Population: 69; Growth (since 2000): -48.5%; Density: 688.3 persons per square mile; Race: 94.2% White, 0.0% Black/African American, 0.0% Asian, 0.0% American Indian/Alaska Native, 0.0% Native Hawaiian/Other Pacific Islander, 0.0% Two or more races, 0.0% Hispanic of any race; Average household size: 2.16; Median age: 47.8; Age under 18: 11.6%; Age 65 and over: 18.8%; Males per 100 females: 110.2; Marriage status: 11.1% never married, 81.0% now married, 0.0% separated, 7.9% widowed, 0.0% divorced; Foreign born: 0.0%; Speak English only: 100.0%; With disability: 2.9%; Veterans: 3.3%; Ancestry: 39.1% Irish, 29.0% German, 15.9% American, 4.3% English
Employment: 0.0% management, business, and financial, 0.0% computer, engineering, and science, 22.6% education, legal, community service, arts, and media, 12.9% healthcare practitioners, 16.1% service, 22.6% sales and office, 19.4% natural resources, construction, and maintenance, 6.5% production, transportation, and material moving
Income: Per capita: $29,043; Median household: n/a; Average household: $61,634; Households with income of $100,000 or more: 25.0%; Poverty rate: 2.9%
Educational Attainment: High school diploma or higher: 82.7%; Bachelor's degree or higher: 26.9%; Graduate/professional degree or higher: 13.5%
Housing: Homeownership rate: 100.0%; Median home value: $67,800; Median year structure built: 1955; Homeowner vacancy rate: 7.5%; Median selected monthly owner costs: $1,275 with a mortgage, $363 without a mortgage; Median gross rent: n/a per month; Rental vacancy rate: 0.0%
Health Insurance: 97.1% have insurance; 91.3% have private insurance; 24.6% have public insurance; 2.9% do not have insurance; 0.0% of children under 18 do not have insurance
Transportation: Commute: 96.6% car, 0.0% public transportation, 0.0% walk, 3.4% work from home; Mean travel time to work: 52.3 minutes

CHESHIRE (village). Covers a land area of 0.770 square miles and a water area of 0.012 square miles. Located at 38.95° N. Lat; 82.11° W. Long. Elevation is 571 feet.
Population: 193; Growth (since 2000): -12.7%; Density: 250.6 persons per square mile; Race: 100.0% White, 0.0% Black/African American, 0.0% Asian, 0.0% American Indian/Alaska Native, 0.0% Native Hawaiian/Other Pacific Islander, 0.0% Two or more races, 1.0% Hispanic of any race; Average household size: 2.14; Median age: 46.5; Age under 18: 22.3%; Age 65 and over: 18.7%; Males per 100 females: 112.9; Marriage status: 26.4% never married, 56.6% now married, 4.4% separated, 6.3% widowed, 10.7% divorced; Foreign born: 2.6%; Speak English only: 96.1%; With disability: 17.1%; Veterans: 13.3%; Ancestry: 10.9% German, 5.7% Irish, 5.2% English, 4.7% American, 3.6% Scottish
Employment: 0.0% management, business, and financial, 0.0% computer, engineering, and science, 3.9% education, legal, community service, arts, and media, 2.6% healthcare practitioners, 22.1% service, 45.5% sales and office, 16.9% natural resources, construction, and maintenance, 9.1% production, transportation, and material moving
Income: Per capita: $21,052; Median household: $36,944; Average household: $47,069; Households with income of $100,000 or more: 10.0%; Poverty rate: 13.0%
Educational Attainment: High school diploma or higher: 95.5%; Bachelor's degree or higher: 2.3%; Graduate/professional degree or higher: n/a
Housing: Homeownership rate: 88.9%; Median home value: $86,300; Median year structure built: 1963; Homeowner vacancy rate: 5.9%; Median selected monthly owner costs: $906 with a mortgage, $385 without a mortgage; Median gross rent: n/a per month; Rental vacancy rate: 0.0%
Health Insurance: 82.9% have insurance; 58.5% have private insurance; 50.8% have public insurance; 17.1% do not have insurance; 16.3% of children under 18 do not have insurance
Transportation: Commute: 100.0% car, 0.0% public transportation, 0.0% walk, 0.0% work from home; Mean travel time to work: 29.0 minutes

CROWN CITY (village). Covers a land area of 1.161 square miles and a water area of 0.036 square miles. Located at 38.59° N. Lat; 82.30° W. Long. Elevation is 568 feet.
Population: 391; Growth (since 2000): -4.9%; Density: 336.8 persons per square mile; Race: 97.4% White, 0.0% Black/African American, 2.3% Asian, 0.0% American Indian/Alaska Native, 0.0% Native Hawaiian/Other Pacific Islander, 0.3% Two or more races, 0.0% Hispanic of any race; Average household size: 2.30; Median age: 42.3; Age under 18: 17.6%; Age 65 and over: 15.1%; Males per 100 females: 90.3; Marriage status: 20.3% never married, 50.6% now married, 3.2% separated, 8.2% widowed, 20.9% divorced; Foreign born: 1.5%; Speak English only: 98.4%; With disability: 16.4%; Veterans: 6.2%; Ancestry: 15.3% American, 8.4% Irish, 6.1% German, 5.6% English, 2.3% Italian
Employment: 5.5% management, business, and financial, 0.6% computer, engineering, and science, 5.5% education, legal, community service, arts, and media, 9.1% healthcare practitioners, 11.6% service, 29.3% sales and office, 25.6% natural resources, construction, and maintenance, 12.8% production, transportation, and material moving
Income: Per capita: $20,016; Median household: $28,750; Average household: $46,134; Households with income of $100,000 or more: 16.5%; Poverty rate: 29.7%
Educational Attainment: High school diploma or higher: 85.6%; Bachelor's degree or higher: 10.7%; Graduate/professional degree or higher: 1.5%

School District(s)

Gallia County Local (PK-12)
2015-16 Enrollment: 2,167 . . . . (740) 379-9085

Housing: Homeownership rate: 65.3%; Median home value: $79,400; Median year structure built: 1972; Homeowner vacancy rate: 0.0%; Median selected monthly owner costs: $831 with a mortgage, $388 without a mortgage; Median gross rent: $695 per month; Rental vacancy rate: 0.0%
Health Insurance: 84.1% have insurance; 49.1% have private insurance; 45.8% have public insurance; 15.9% do not have insurance; 5.8% of children under 18 do not have insurance
Transportation: Commute: 94.8% car, 0.0% public transportation, 2.6% walk, 1.9% work from home; Mean travel time to work: 37.1 minutes

GALLIPOLIS (village). County seat. Covers a land area of 3.597 square miles and a water area of 0.228 square miles. Located at 38.82° N. Lat; 82.19° W. Long. Elevation is 571 feet.
History: Gallipolis was settled in 1790 by French immigrants who had been induced to leave France and purchase land in Ohio. After their long journey, they found that the deeds they had purchased were worthless, and those who stayed in Gallipolis had to buy their land all over again.
Population: 3,555; Growth (since 2000): -15.0%; Density: 988.2 persons per square mile; Race: 92.8% White, 3.0% Black/African American, 0.0% Asian, 2.0% American Indian/Alaska Native, 0.8% Native Hawaiian/Other Pacific Islander, 1.4% Two or more races, 3.0% Hispanic of any race; Average household size: 2.30; Median age: 39.0; Age under 18: 21.9%; Age 65 and over: 16.5%; Males per 100 females: 93.3; Marriage status: 32.5% never married, 33.7% now married, 1.2% separated, 8.5% widowed, 25.3% divorced; Foreign born: 1.0%; Speak English only: 98.3%; With disability: 27.1%; Veterans: 8.6%; Ancestry: 17.4% German, 11.3% English, 10.1% Irish, 8.9% American, 7.1% Scottish
Employment: 10.2% management, business, and financial, 2.0% computer, engineering, and science, 9.7% education, legal, community service, arts, and media, 8.1% healthcare practitioners, 15.5% service, 30.6% sales and office, 11.1% natural resources, construction, and maintenance, 12.8% production, transportation, and material moving
Income: Per capita: $23,451; Median household: $33,704; Average household: $52,641; Households with income of $100,000 or more: 10.0%; Poverty rate: 32.6%
Educational Attainment: High school diploma or higher: 81.5%; Bachelor's degree or higher: 16.8%; Graduate/professional degree or higher: 8.8%

School District(s)

Gallia County Local (PK-12)
2015-16 Enrollment: 2,167 . . . . (740) 379-9085
Gallipolis City (PK-12)
2015-16 Enrollment: 2,165 . . . . (740) 446-3211

Two-year College(s)

Gallipolis Career College (Private, For-profit)
Fall 2016 Enrollment: 54 . . . . (740) 446-4367
2016-17 Tuition: In-state $12,530; Out-of-state $12,530

Housing: Homeownership rate: 47.7%; Median home value: $126,700; Median year structure built: 1953; Homeowner vacancy rate: 2.5%; Median selected monthly owner costs: $1,283 with a mortgage, $337 without a mortgage; Median gross rent: $641 per month; Rental vacancy rate: 2.0%

Health Insurance: 91.7% have insurance; 56.0% have private insurance; 49.3% have public insurance; 8.3% do not have insurance; 2.1% of children under 18 do not have insurance

Hospitals: Holzer Medical Center (269 beds)

Safety: Violent crime rate: 29.1 per 10,000 population; Property crime rate: 1,286.8 per 10,000 population

Newspapers: Gallipolis Daily Tribune (daily circulation 4,500)

Transportation: Commute: 92.5% car, 1.6% public transportation, 2.9% walk, 3.1% work from home; Mean travel time to work: 20.1 minutes

Airports: Gallia-Meigs Regional (general aviation)

Additional Information Contacts

City of Gallipolis. . . . . (740) 446-1789
http://www.gallianet.net/Gallipolis/index.htm

KANAUGA (CDP). Covers a land area of 0.289 square miles and a water area of 0.031 square miles. Located at 38.84° N. Lat; 82.15° W. Long. Elevation is 571 feet.

Population: 142; Growth (since 2000): n/a; Density: 490.6 persons per square mile; Race: 100.0% White, 0.0% Black/African American, 0.0% Asian, 0.0% American Indian/Alaska Native, 0.0% Native Hawaiian/Other Pacific Islander, 0.0% Two or more races, 0.0% Hispanic of any race; Average household size: 2.15; Median age: 43.8; Age under 18: 28.9%; Age 65 and over: 0.0%; Males per 100 females: 110.8; Marriage status: 15.8% never married, 67.3% now married, 0.0% separated, 0.0% widowed, 16.8% divorced; Foreign born: 0.0%; Speak English only: 100.0%; With disability: 18.3%; Veterans: 27.7%; Ancestry: 44.4% Irish, 28.2% American, 16.2% German, 6.3% Dutch, 5.6% English

Employment: 46.3% management, business, and financial, 0.0% computer, engineering, and science, 0.0% education, legal, community service, arts, and media, 0.0% healthcare practitioners, 14.6% service, 24.4% sales and office, 0.0% natural resources, construction, and maintenance, 14.6% production, transportation, and material moving

Income: Per capita: $11,481; Median household: n/a; Average household: $24,355; Households with income of $100,000 or more: n/a; Poverty rate: 70.4%

Educational Attainment: High school diploma or higher: 54.4%; Bachelor's degree or higher: n/a; Graduate/professional degree or higher: n/a

Housing: Homeownership rate: 40.9%; Median home value: n/a; Median year structure built: 1974; Homeowner vacancy rate: 0.0%; Median selected monthly owner costs: n/a with a mortgage, n/a without a mortgage; Median gross rent: $625 per month; Rental vacancy rate: 0.0%

Health Insurance: 87.3% have insurance; 4.2% have private insurance; 83.1% have public insurance; 12.7% do not have insurance; 0.0% of children under 18 do not have insurance

Transportation: Commute: 100.0% car, 0.0% public transportation, 0.0% walk, 0.0% work from home; Mean travel time to work: 0.0 minutes

PATRIOT (unincorporated postal area)

ZCTA: 45658

Covers a land area of 97.157 square miles and a water area of 0.391 square miles. Located at 38.76° N. Lat; 82.41° W. Long. Elevation is 718 feet.

Population: 2,718; Growth (since 2000): 17.4%; Density: 28.0 persons per square mile; Race: 91.7% White, 6.4% Black/African American, 1.1% Asian, 0.0% American Indian/Alaska Native, 0.0% Native Hawaiian/Other Pacific Islander, 0.8% Two or more races, 1.2% Hispanic of any race; Average household size: 3.32; Median age: 30.0; Age under 18: 32.3%; Age 65 and over: 11.1%; Males per 100 females: 108.1; Marriage status: 28.3% never married, 58.2% now married, 2.3% separated, 4.4% widowed, 9.1% divorced; Foreign born: 2.6%; Speak English only: 91.0%; With disability: 20.6%; Veterans: 6.8%; Ancestry: 18.1% English, 16.6% German, 13.1% Irish, 7.1% American, 5.5% Welsh

Employment: 10.6% management, business, and financial, 4.8% computer, engineering, and science, 7.3% education, legal, community service, arts, and media, 4.3% healthcare practitioners, 14.6% service, 19.3% sales and office, 12.9% natural resources, construction, and maintenance, 26.2% production, transportation, and material moving

Income: Per capita: $13,878; Median household: $32,245; Average household: $45,715; Households with income of $100,000 or more: 10.1%; Poverty rate: 36.3%

Educational Attainment: High school diploma or higher: 66.9%; Bachelor's degree or higher: 10.6%; Graduate/professional degree or higher: 4.8%

School District(s)

Gallia County Local (PK-12)
2015-16 Enrollment: 2,167 . . . . (740) 379-9085

Housing: Homeownership rate: 72.8%; Median home value: $108,800; Median year structure built: 1985; Homeowner vacancy rate: 1.9%; Median selected monthly owner costs: $1,036 with a mortgage, $389 without a mortgage; Median gross rent: $678 per month; Rental vacancy rate: 12.6%

Health Insurance: 78.3% have insurance; 33.2% have private insurance; 56.2% have public insurance; 21.7% do not have insurance; 20.2% of children under 18 do not have insurance

Transportation: Commute: 81.4% car, 0.0% public transportation, 5.2% walk, 9.9% work from home; Mean travel time to work: 36.3 minutes

RIO GRANDE (village). Covers a land area of 1.357 square miles and a water area of 0.011 square miles. Located at 38.88° N. Lat; 82.38° W. Long. Elevation is 656 feet.

History: Rio Grande was settled by Nehemiah Atwood, who served under General William Henry Harrison in the War of 1812 and, in 1818, opened a tavern at this site. Atwood provided the endowment for Rio Grande College, established in 1876 under the supervision of the Baptist church.

Population: 881; Growth (since 2000): -3.7%; Density: 649.4 persons per square mile; Race: 80.4% White, 12.5% Black/African American, 0.3% Asian, 0.0% American Indian/Alaska Native, 0.0% Native Hawaiian/Other Pacific Islander, 4.3% Two or more races, 2.5% Hispanic of any race; Average household size: 3.04; Median age: 21.2; Age under 18: 20.0%; Age 65 and over: 1.9%; Males per 100 females: 101.5; Marriage status: 71.0% never married, 21.1% now married, 2.6% separated, 2.2% widowed, 5.7% divorced; Foreign born: 2.7%; Speak English only: 96.6%; With disability: 18.3%; Veterans: 4.7%; Ancestry: 25.8% German, 11.7% Irish, 9.2% English, 8.7% Scottish, 2.8% Polish

Employment: 6.8% management, business, and financial, 2.9% computer, engineering, and science, 26.3% education, legal, community service, arts, and media, 1.9% healthcare practitioners, 36.4% service, 19.8% sales and office, 4.5% natural resources, construction, and maintenance, 1.3% production, transportation, and material moving

Income: Per capita: $7,773; Median household: $21,932; Average household: $31,429; Households with income of $100,000 or more: n/a; Poverty rate: 44.4%

Educational Attainment: High school diploma or higher: 93.0%; Bachelor's degree or higher: 20.5%; Graduate/professional degree or higher: 14.0%

School District(s)

Gallia-Jackson-Vinton (07-12)
2015-16 Enrollment: n/a . . . . (740) 245-5334
Gallipolis City (PK-12)
2015-16 Enrollment: 2,165 . . . . (740) 446-3211

Four-year College(s)

University of Rio Grande (Private, Not-for-profit)
Fall 2016 Enrollment: 1,903 . . . . (740) 245-7206
2016-17 Tuition: In-state $23,860; Out-of-state $23,860

Vocational/Technical School(s)

Buckeye Hills Career Center (Public)
Fall 2016 Enrollment: 192 . . . . (740) 245-5334
2016-17 Tuition: $8,500

Housing: Homeownership rate: 39.2%; Median home value: $145,800; Median year structure built: 1984; Homeowner vacancy rate: 8.2%; Median selected monthly owner costs: $1,400 with a mortgage, $349 without a mortgage; Median gross rent: $543 per month; Rental vacancy rate: 0.0%

Health Insurance: 87.6% have insurance; 62.0% have private insurance; 27.9% have public insurance; 12.4% do not have insurance; 1.7% of children under 18 do not have insurance

Safety: Violent crime rate: 35.8 per 10,000 population; Property crime rate: 190.7 per 10,000 population
Transportation: Commute: 60.5% car, 0.0% public transportation, 29.9% walk, 8.6% work from home; Mean travel time to work: 21.0 minutes

THURMAN (unincorporated postal area)

ZCTA: 45685

Covers a land area of 30.275 square miles and a water area of 0.019 square miles. Located at 38.93° N. Lat; 82.46° W. Long. Elevation is 682 feet.
Population: 735; Growth (since 2000): -19.9%; Density: 24.3 persons per square mile; Race: 94.3% White, 2.7% Black/African American, 0.0% Asian, 0.0% American Indian/Alaska Native, 0.0% Native Hawaiian/Other Pacific Islander, 2.4% Two or more races, 0.0% Hispanic of any race; Average household size: 2.12; Median age: 33.2; Age under 18: 21.4%; Age 65 and over: 11.6%; Males per 100 females: 92.2; Marriage status: 21.7% never married, 66.6% now married, 3.4% separated, 4.8% widowed, 7.0% divorced; Foreign born: 0.0%; Speak English only: 100.0%; With disability: 10.9%; Veterans: 3.6%; Ancestry: 25.9% German, 14.7% American, 8.8% Irish, 5.0% Italian, 4.9% English
Employment: 4.5% management, business, and financial, 3.6% computer, engineering, and science, 13.1% education, legal, community service, arts, and media, 4.5% healthcare practitioners, 19.3% service, 29.4% sales and office, 10.4% natural resources, construction, and maintenance, 15.4% production, transportation, and material moving
Income: Per capita: $21,887; Median household: $31,350; Average household: $45,009; Households with income of $100,000 or more: 10.7%; Poverty rate: 28.0%
Educational Attainment: High school diploma or higher: 91.5%; Bachelor's degree or higher: 21.7%; Graduate/professional degree or higher: 11.4%
Housing: Homeownership rate: 64.0%; Median home value: $127,500; Median year structure built: 1990; Homeowner vacancy rate: 1.3%; Median selected monthly owner costs: $1,196 with a mortgage, $419 without a mortgage; Median gross rent: $515 per month; Rental vacancy rate: 0.0%
Health Insurance: 86.7% have insurance; 62.2% have private insurance; 35.1% have public insurance; 13.3% do not have insurance; 8.3% of children under 18 do not have insurance
Transportation: Commute: 96.3% car, 0.0% public transportation, 2.5% walk, 0.3% work from home; Mean travel time to work: 34.0 minutes

VINTON (village). Covers a land area of 1.177 square miles and a water area of 0.033 square miles. Located at 38.98° N. Lat; 82.33° W. Long. Elevation is 610 feet.
Population: 239; Growth (since 2000): -26.2%; Density: 203.0 persons per square mile; Race: 99.2% White, 0.8% Black/African American, 0.0% Asian, 0.0% American Indian/Alaska Native, 0.0% Native Hawaiian/Other Pacific Islander, 0.0% Two or more races, 0.0% Hispanic of any race; Average household size: 2.37; Median age: 45.4; Age under 18: 21.3%; Age 65 and over: 19.2%; Males per 100 females: 89.7; Marriage status: 8.7% never married, 72.3% now married, 6.2% separated, 8.2% widowed, 10.8% divorced; Foreign born: 0.8%; Speak English only: 97.8%; With disability: 23.0%; Veterans: 11.7%; Ancestry: 17.6% German, 17.2% English, 13.8% Irish, 6.7% American, 4.2% Welsh
Employment: 15.8% management, business, and financial, 0.0% computer, engineering, and science, 15.8% education, legal, community service, arts, and media, 11.8% healthcare practitioners, 11.8% service, 28.9% sales and office, 7.9% natural resources, construction, and maintenance, 7.9% production, transportation, and material moving
Income: Per capita: $16,345; Median household: $33,750; Average household: $37,809; Households with income of $100,000 or more: 1.0%; Poverty rate: 19.8%
Educational Attainment: High school diploma or higher: 79.1%; Bachelor's degree or higher: 12.4%; Graduate/professional degree or higher: 2.3%

School District(s)

Gallia County Local (PK-12)
2015-16 Enrollment: 2,167 . . . . (740) 379-9085
Housing: Homeownership rate: 82.2%; Median home value: $70,700; Median year structure built: 1964; Homeowner vacancy rate: 0.0%; Median selected monthly owner costs: $919 with a mortgage, $331 without a mortgage; Median gross rent: n/a per month; Rental vacancy rate: 21.7%
Health Insurance: 94.6% have insurance; 53.1% have private insurance; 56.1% have public insurance; 5.4% do not have insurance; 0.0% of children under 18 do not have insurance
Transportation: Commute: 82.9% car, 0.0% public transportation, 9.2% walk, 6.6% work from home; Mean travel time to work: 31.7 minutes

Geauga County

Located in northeastern Ohio; drained by the Cuyahoga, Chagrin, and Grand Rivers; includes several lakes. Covers a land area of 400.164 square miles, a water area of 8.129 square miles, and is located in the Eastern Time Zone at 41.50° N. Lat., 81.17° W. Long. The county was founded in 1805. County seat is Chardon.

Geauga County is part of the Cleveland-Elyria, OH Metropolitan Statistical Area. The entire metro area includes: Cuyahoga County, OH; Geauga County, OH; Lake County, OH; Lorain County, OH; Medina County, OH

Weather Station: Chardon Elevation: 1,129 feet

	Jan	Feb	Mar	Apr	May	Jun	Jul	Aug	Sep	Oct	Nov	Dec
High	32	35	44	57	68	77	80	79	72	60	49	37
Low	16	17	24	35	45	54	58	57	50	40	32	22
Precip	3.6	2.8	3.3	4.0	4.4	4.5	4.4	4.2	4.3	4.1	4.3	4.4
Snow	28.6	19.2	14.4	4.5	tr	0.0	0.0	0.0	0.0	0.9	9.5	25.7

High and Low temperatures in degrees Fahrenheit; Precipitation and Snow in inches

Population: 94,020; Growth (since 2000): 3.4%; Density: 235.0 persons per square mile; Race: 96.7% White, 1.3% Black/African American, 0.7% Asian, 0.1% American Indian/Alaska Native, 0.0% Native Hawaiian/Other Pacific Islander, 1.2% two or more races, 1.3% Hispanic of any race; Average household size: 2.67; Median age: 44.2; Age under 18: 24.2%; Age 65 and over: 18.0%; Males per 100 females: 96.7; Marriage status: 24.1% never married, 62.1% now married, 1.0% separated, 5.3% widowed, 8.5% divorced; Foreign born: 2.6%; Speak English only: 88.4%; With disability: 10.5%; Veterans: 8.3%; Ancestry: 26.0% German, 14.3% Irish, 13.6% Italian, 12.0% English, 8.6% Polish
Religion: Six largest groups: 33.1% Catholicism, 9.6% European Free-Church, 3.6% Methodist/Pietist, 3.1% Presbyterian-Reformed, 2.3% Lutheran, 1.9% Baptist
Economy: Unemployment rate: 4.2%; Leading industries: 14.0 % construction; 12.4 % professional, scientific, and technical services; 10.5 % retail trade; Farms: 959 totaling 66,809 acres; Company size: 1 employs 1,000 or more persons, 3 employ 500 to 999 persons, 36 employ 100 to 499 persons, 2,710 employ less than 100 persons; Business ownership: 3,137 women-owned, 43 Black-owned, 76 Hispanic-owned, 79 Asian-owned, n/a American Indian/Alaska Native-owned
Employment: 18.4% management, business, and financial, 5.9% computer, engineering, and science, 9.6% education, legal, community service, arts, and media, 6.2% healthcare practitioners, 14.4% service, 24.3% sales and office, 9.7% natural resources, construction, and maintenance, 11.6% production, transportation, and material moving
Income: Per capita: $37,537; Median household: $74,165; Average household: $100,733; Households with income of $100,000 or more: 36.2%; Poverty rate: 6.9%
Educational Attainment: High school diploma or higher: 91.1%; Bachelor's degree or higher: 37.3%; Graduate/professional degree or higher: 13.1%
Housing: Homeownership rate: 85.4%; Median home value: $221,500; Median year structure built: 1974; Homeowner vacancy rate: 1.3%; Median selected monthly owner costs: $1,569 with a mortgage, $556 without a mortgage; Median gross rent: $815 per month; Rental vacancy rate: 1.9%
Vital Statistics: Birth rate: 96.9 per 10,000 population; Death rate: 86.0 per 10,000 population; Age-adjusted cancer mortality rate: 145.2 deaths per 100,000 population
Health Insurance: 89.3% have insurance; 77.1% have private insurance; 26.0% have public insurance; 10.7% do not have insurance; 15.7% of children under 18 do not have insurance
Health Care: Physicians: 25.6 per 10,000 population; Dentists: 4.4 per 10,000 population; Hospital beds: 36.1 per 10,000 population; Hospital admissions: 1,273.8 per 10,000 population
Air Quality Index (AQI): Percent of Days: 72.4% good, 22.9% moderate, 4.7% unhealthy for sensitive individuals, 0.0% unhealthy, 0.0% very unhealthy; Annual median: 44; Annual maximum: 140
Transportation: Commute: 88.4% car, 0.4% public transportation, 2.0% walk, 7.2% work from home; Mean travel time to work: 28.2 minutes
2016 Presidential Election: 59.7% Trump, 34.7% Clinton, 3.0% Johnson, 0.7% Stein
National and State Parks: Auburn State Wildlife Area; Punderson State Park

Additional Information Contacts
Geauga Government . . . . (440) 285-2222
http://www.co.geauga.oh.us

Geauga County Communities

AQUILLA (village). Covers a land area of 0.147 square miles and a water area of 0 square miles. Located at 41.55° N. Lat; 81.17° W. Long. Elevation is 1,266 feet.
Population: 306; Growth (since 2000): -17.7%; Density: 2,075.0 persons per square mile; Race: 99.7% White, 0.0% Black/African American, 0.3% Asian, 0.0% American Indian/Alaska Native, 0.0% Native Hawaiian/Other Pacific Islander, 0.0% Two or more races, 1.6% Hispanic of any race; Average household size: 2.57; Median age: 37.6; Age under 18: 21.9%; Age 65 and over: 10.5%; Males per 100 females: 97.7; Marriage status: 30.0% never married, 48.2% now married, 1.6% separated, 9.3% widowed, 12.6% divorced; Foreign born: 1.6%; Speak English only: 98.2%; With disability: 13.7%; Veterans: 6.7%; Ancestry: 26.1% German, 17.6% Irish, 14.1% English, 9.2% American, 5.9% Polish
Employment: 8.0% management, business, and financial, 3.1% computer, engineering, and science, 4.9% education, legal, community service, arts, and media, 6.2% healthcare practitioners, 27.2% service, 19.1% sales and office, 11.7% natural resources, construction, and maintenance, 19.8% production, transportation, and material moving
Income: Per capita: $21,174; Median household: $52,708; Average household: $53,232; Households with income of $100,000 or more: 10.1%; Poverty rate: 13.3%
Educational Attainment: High school diploma or higher: 88.5%; Bachelor's degree or higher: 11.1%; Graduate/professional degree or higher: 4.1%
Housing: Homeownership rate: 64.7%; Median home value: $104,700; Median year structure built: 1947; Homeowner vacancy rate: 8.3%; Median selected monthly owner costs: $1,017 with a mortgage, $450 without a mortgage; Median gross rent: $879 per month; Rental vacancy rate: 0.0%
Health Insurance: 88.9% have insurance; 57.5% have private insurance; 35.6% have public insurance; 11.1% do not have insurance; 3.0% of children under 18 do not have insurance
Transportation: Commute: 96.1% car, 0.0% public transportation, 0.0% walk, 3.9% work from home; Mean travel time to work: 24.5 minutes

BAINBRIDGE (CDP). Covers a land area of 3.392 square miles and a water area of 0.072 square miles. Located at 41.40° N. Lat; 81.34° W. Long. Elevation is 1,168 feet.
History: In 1817, Bainbridge Township was established and named for a well-known naval hero of the War of 1812, Commodore William Bainbridge.
Population: 3,096; Growth (since 2000): -9.4%; Density: 912.9 persons per square mile; Race: 97.7% White, 1.6% Black/African American, 0.0% Asian, 0.0% American Indian/Alaska Native, 0.0% Native Hawaiian/Other Pacific Islander, 0.7% Two or more races, 1.1% Hispanic of any race; Average household size: 2.56; Median age: 44.0; Age under 18: 26.7%; Age 65 and over: 15.1%; Males per 100 females: 91.5; Marriage status: 22.1% never married, 63.0% now married, 0.0% separated, 5.2% widowed, 9.7% divorced; Foreign born: 2.5%; Speak English only: 94.6%; With disability: 4.0%; Veterans: 5.6%; Ancestry: 24.6% German, 23.6% Italian, 20.0% Irish, 13.9% English, 13.2% Polish
Employment: 17.5% management, business, and financial, 7.0% computer, engineering, and science, 18.6% education, legal, community service, arts, and media, 8.9% healthcare practitioners, 8.3% service, 28.2% sales and office, 6.3% natural resources, construction, and maintenance, 5.2% production, transportation, and material moving
Income: Per capita: $44,499; Median household: $103,208; Average household: $114,249; Households with income of $100,000 or more: 52.9%; Poverty rate: 2.3%
Educational Attainment: High school diploma or higher: 99.2%; Bachelor's degree or higher: 64.4%; Graduate/professional degree or higher: 28.5%
Housing: Homeownership rate: 90.6%; Median home value: $263,100; Median year structure built: 1973; Homeowner vacancy rate: 0.0%; Median selected monthly owner costs: $1,791 with a mortgage, $846 without a mortgage; Median gross rent: $1,324 per month; Rental vacancy rate: 0.0%
Health Insurance: 96.1% have insurance; 91.3% have private insurance; 15.5% have public insurance; 3.9% do not have insurance; 0.0% of children under 18 do not have insurance
Transportation: Commute: 87.1% car, 0.0% public transportation, 1.9% walk, 10.4% work from home; Mean travel time to work: 25.4 minutes

BURTON (village). Covers a land area of 1.047 square miles and a water area of 0.002 square miles. Located at 41.47° N. Lat; 81.15° W. Long. Elevation is 1,312 feet.
Population: 1,217; Growth (since 2000): -16.1%; Density: 1,161.9 persons per square mile; Race: 97.2% White, 1.2% Black/African American, 0.2% Asian, 0.0% American Indian/Alaska Native, 0.0% Native Hawaiian/Other Pacific Islander, 1.2% Two or more races, 2.3% Hispanic of any race; Average household size: 1.99; Median age: 43.9; Age under 18: 18.1%; Age 65 and over: 26.1%; Males per 100 females: 93.7; Marriage status: 30.6% never married, 46.1% now married, 1.4% separated, 12.9% widowed, 10.4% divorced; Foreign born: 1.5%; Speak English only: 96.8%; With disability: 19.7%; Veterans: 8.8%; Ancestry: 29.1% German, 17.6% English, 15.4% Irish, 10.1% Italian, 5.6% Scottish
Employment: 11.0% management, business, and financial, 4.1% computer, engineering, and science, 13.9% education, legal, community service, arts, and media, 7.1% healthcare practitioners, 17.1% service, 26.7% sales and office, 6.9% natural resources, construction, and maintenance, 13.2% production, transportation, and material moving
Income: Per capita: $26,067; Median household: $44,091; Average household: $52,514; Households with income of $100,000 or more: 10.7%; Poverty rate: 13.9%
Educational Attainment: High school diploma or higher: 89.5%; Bachelor's degree or higher: 27.1%; Graduate/professional degree or higher: 13.1%

School District(s)

Berkshire Local (KG-12)
2015-16 Enrollment: 1,207 . . . . (440) 834-3380

Four-year College(s)

Kent State University at Geauga (Public)
Fall 2016 Enrollment: 2,416 . . . . (440) 834-4187
2016-17 Tuition: In-state $5,664; Out-of-state $14,028
Housing: Homeownership rate: 50.5%; Median home value: $145,300; Median year structure built: 1970; Homeowner vacancy rate: 0.0%; Median selected monthly owner costs: $1,125 with a mortgage, $514 without a mortgage; Median gross rent: $801 per month; Rental vacancy rate: 11.0%
Health Insurance: 93.4% have insurance; 78.0% have private insurance; 32.9% have public insurance; 6.6% do not have insurance; 3.2% of children under 18 do not have insurance
Transportation: Commute: 91.4% car, 0.5% public transportation, 4.1% walk, 2.7% work from home; Mean travel time to work: 24.8 minutes

CHARDON (city). County seat. Covers a land area of 4.580 square miles and a water area of 0.035 square miles. Located at 41.58° N. Lat; 81.21° W. Long. Elevation is 1,309 feet.
History: Chardon was named for Peter Chardon Brooks, first owner of the site. The town developed as the maple syrup and sugar center of Ohio, from its location on the crest of a hill, surrounded by maple groves.
Population: 5,194; Growth (since 2000): 0.7%; Density: 1,134.1 persons per square mile; Race: 94.0% White, 3.1% Black/African American, 2.3% Asian, 0.0% American Indian/Alaska Native, 0.0% Native Hawaiian/Other Pacific Islander, 0.6% Two or more races, 2.3% Hispanic of any race; Average household size: 2.22; Median age: 40.8; Age under 18: 22.9%; Age 65 and over: 18.1%; Males per 100 females: 82.2; Marriage status: 30.4% never married, 50.6% now married, 1.7% separated, 4.8% widowed, 14.1% divorced; Foreign born: 3.4%; Speak English only: 94.9%; With disability: 15.6%; Veterans: 14.1%; Ancestry: 24.6% German, 14.2% Irish, 13.1% Italian, 13.1% Polish, 10.8% English
Employment: 15.8% management, business, and financial, 2.3% computer, engineering, and science, 9.2% education, legal, community service, arts, and media, 7.0% healthcare practitioners, 11.6% service, 37.3% sales and office, 8.1% natural resources, construction, and maintenance, 8.7% production, transportation, and material moving
Income: Per capita: $32,118; Median household: $60,845; Average household: $72,300; Households with income of $100,000 or more: 21.2%; Poverty rate: 11.0%
Educational Attainment: High school diploma or higher: 93.3%; Bachelor's degree or higher: 27.9%; Graduate/professional degree or higher: 9.2%

School District(s)

Chardon Local (KG-12)
2015-16 Enrollment: 2,889 . . . . (440) 285-4052

Housing: Homeownership rate: 58.5%; Median home value: $167,500; Median year structure built: 1966; Homeowner vacancy rate: 5.0%; Median selected monthly owner costs: $1,349 with a mortgage, $535 without a mortgage; Median gross rent: $699 per month; Rental vacancy rate: 0.0%
Health Insurance: 96.7% have insurance; 79.1% have private insurance; 34.8% have public insurance; 3.3% do not have insurance; 4.4% of children under 18 do not have insurance
Hospitals: UH Geauga Medical Center
Safety: Violent crime rate: 13.6 per 10,000 population; Property crime rate: 127.9 per 10,000 population
Newspapers: Geauga County Maple Leaf (weekly circulation 3,000)
Transportation: Commute: 87.6% car, 0.4% public transportation, 5.8% walk, 2.1% work from home; Mean travel time to work: 24.4 minutes
Additional Information Contacts
Village of Chardon . . . . (440) 286-2600
http://www.chardon.cc

CHESTERLAND (CDP). Covers a land area of 4.377 square miles and a water area of 0.014 square miles. Located at 41.52° N. Lat; 81.34° W. Long. Elevation is 1,211 feet.
Population: 2,040; Growth (since 2000): -22.9%; Density: 466.0 persons per square mile; Race: 99.6% White, 0.4% Black/African American, 0.0% Asian, 0.0% American Indian/Alaska Native, 0.0% Native Hawaiian/Other Pacific Islander, 0.0% Two or more races, 0.0% Hispanic of any race; Average household size: 2.25; Median age: 52.3; Age under 18: 20.1%; Age 65 and over: 27.1%; Males per 100 females: 93.5; Marriage status: 21.2% never married, 56.6% now married, 1.9% separated, 10.7% widowed, 11.4% divorced; Foreign born: 3.2%; Speak English only: 96.5%; With disability: 14.1%; Veterans: 9.1%; Ancestry: 22.9% Italian, 20.1% German, 16.3% Polish, 10.0% Irish, 9.5% English
Employment: 11.2% management, business, and financial, 3.6% computer, engineering, and science, 12.7% education, legal, community service, arts, and media, 1.0% healthcare practitioners, 23.2% service, 33.3% sales and office, 8.4% natural resources, construction, and maintenance, 6.6% production, transportation, and material moving
Income: Per capita: $32,809; Median household: $57,159; Average household: $74,819; Households with income of $100,000 or more: 23.3%; Poverty rate: 6.2%
Educational Attainment: High school diploma or higher: 94.6%; Bachelor's degree or higher: 39.1%; Graduate/professional degree or higher: 11.9%

School District(s)
West Geauga Local (KG-12)
2015-16 Enrollment: 1,956 . . . . (440) 729-5900

Vocational/Technical School(s)
International Culinary Arts and Sciences Institute (Private, For-profit)
Fall 2016 Enrollment: 20 . . . . (440) 729-7340
2016-17 Tuition: $21,905

Housing: Homeownership rate: 94.2%; Median home value: $177,900; Median year structure built: 1960; Homeowner vacancy rate: 0.0%; Median selected monthly owner costs: $1,487 with a mortgage, $534 without a mortgage; Median gross rent: $755 per month; Rental vacancy rate: 32.9%
Health Insurance: 94.5% have insurance; 81.6% have private insurance; 32.5% have public insurance; 5.5% do not have insurance; 0.0% of children under 18 do not have insurance
Newspapers: Chesterland News (weekly circulation 6,400)
Transportation: Commute: 93.4% car, 0.0% public transportation, 3.9% walk, 2.7% work from home; Mean travel time to work: 31.7 minutes

HUNTSBURG (unincorporated postal area)
ZCTA: 44046
Covers a land area of 15.412 square miles and a water area of 0.731 square miles. Located at 41.54° N. Lat; 81.07° W. Long. Elevation is 1,253 feet.
Population: 2,107; Growth (since 2000): 4.2%; Density: 136.7 persons per square mile; Race: 97.9% White, 0.6% Black/African American, 0.0% Asian, 0.0% American Indian/Alaska Native, 0.0% Native Hawaiian/Other Pacific Islander, 1.5% Two or more races, 0.0% Hispanic of any race; Average household size: 2.81; Median age: 37.0; Age under 18: 28.7%; Age 65 and over: 16.3%; Males per 100 females: 90.4; Marriage status: 17.7% never married, 61.9% now married, 1.0% separated, 9.3% widowed, 11.2% divorced; Foreign born: 1.3%; Speak English only: 71.8%; With disability: 9.8%; Veterans: 7.6%; Ancestry: 22.3% German, 16.1% Pennsylvania German, 13.8% English, 10.7% Irish, 5.7% Polish
Employment: 9.1% management, business, and financial, 3.4% computer, engineering, and science, 1.7% education, legal, community service, arts, and media, 3.7% healthcare practitioners, 22.6% service, 31.7% sales and office, 14.2% natural resources, construction, and maintenance, 13.7% production, transportation, and material moving
Income: Per capita: $23,441; Median household: $57,214; Average household: $66,303; Households with income of $100,000 or more: 14.5%; Poverty rate: 4.9%
Educational Attainment: High school diploma or higher: 86.5%; Bachelor's degree or higher: 21.6%; Graduate/professional degree or higher: 7.0%
Housing: Homeownership rate: 93.3%; Median home value: $177,800; Median year structure built: 1974; Homeowner vacancy rate: 0.0%; Median selected monthly owner costs: $1,273 with a mortgage, $386 without a mortgage; Median gross rent: $883 per month; Rental vacancy rate: 0.0%
Health Insurance: 78.2% have insurance; 70.1% have private insurance; 15.2% have public insurance; 21.8% do not have insurance; 48.3% of children under 18 do not have insurance
Transportation: Commute: 94.5% car, 0.0% public transportation, 0.0% walk, 2.1% work from home; Mean travel time to work: 31.0 minutes

MIDDLEFIELD (village). Covers a land area of 3.021 square miles and a water area of 0.022 square miles. Located at 41.46° N. Lat; 81.07° W. Long. Elevation is 1,125 feet.
Population: 2,709; Growth (since 2000): 21.3%; Density: 896.7 persons per square mile; Race: 96.2% White, 0.3% Black/African American, 1.8% Asian, 0.0% American Indian/Alaska Native, 0.0% Native Hawaiian/Other Pacific Islander, 1.8% Two or more races, 3.0% Hispanic of any race; Average household size: 2.12; Median age: 40.8; Age under 18: 21.8%; Age 65 and over: 21.3%; Males per 100 females: 82.9; Marriage status: 27.1% never married, 46.2% now married, 0.7% separated, 11.3% widowed, 15.4% divorced; Foreign born: 2.1%; Speak English only: 94.8%; With disability: 15.1%; Veterans: 8.1%; Ancestry: 25.4% German, 24.0% Irish, 13.7% English, 9.5% Italian, 6.7% American
Employment: 11.1% management, business, and financial, 2.3% computer, engineering, and science, 10.3% education, legal, community service, arts, and media, 6.5% healthcare practitioners, 26.4% service, 21.2% sales and office, 6.3% natural resources, construction, and maintenance, 15.9% production, transportation, and material moving
Income: Per capita: $23,578; Median household: $41,556; Average household: $50,781; Households with income of $100,000 or more: 11.8%; Poverty rate: 8.1%
Educational Attainment: High school diploma or higher: 89.7%; Bachelor's degree or higher: 21.2%; Graduate/professional degree or higher: 4.2%

School District(s)
Cardinal Local (KG-12)
2015-16 Enrollment: 1,100 . . . . (440) 632-0261

Housing: Homeownership rate: 53.8%; Median home value: $157,500; Median year structure built: 1981; Homeowner vacancy rate: 0.0%; Median selected monthly owner costs: $1,137 with a mortgage, $475 without a mortgage; Median gross rent: $735 per month; Rental vacancy rate: 1.5%
Health Insurance: 94.8% have insurance; 72.4% have private insurance; 38.2% have public insurance; 5.2% do not have insurance; 3.4% of children under 18 do not have insurance
Safety: Violent crime rate: 0.0 per 10,000 population; Property crime rate: 163.3 per 10,000 population
Transportation: Commute: 94.1% car, 0.0% public transportation, 1.8% walk, 3.0% work from home; Mean travel time to work: 21.9 minutes
Airports: Geauga County (general aviation)
Additional Information Contacts
Village of Middlefield . . . . (440) 632-5248
http://www.middlefieldohio.com

MONTVILLE (unincorporated postal area)
ZCTA: 44064
Covers a land area of 22.510 square miles and a water area of 0.324 square miles. Located at 41.60° N. Lat; 81.03° W. Long. Elevation is 1,204 feet.
Population: 1,641; Growth (since 2000): -1.1%; Density: 72.9 persons per square mile; Race: 90.1% White, 0.0% Black/African American, 1.2% Asian, 0.0% American Indian/Alaska Native, 0.0% Native Hawaiian/Other Pacific Islander, 8.7% Two or more races, 0.1% Hispanic of any race; Average household size: 2.53; Median age: 41.2; Age under 18: 23.6%; Age 65 and over: 15.2%; Males per 100 females: 110.3; Marriage status:

19.7% never married, 65.1% now married, 0.5% separated, 4.0% widowed, 11.2% divorced; Foreign born: 2.5%; Speak English only: 92.1%; With disability: 9.3%; Veterans: 12.7%; Ancestry: 25.4% German, 18.4% Italian, 17.9% Irish, 12.1% Polish, 11.0% English

Employment: 11.7% management, business, and financial, 2.8% computer, engineering, and science, 6.6% education, legal, community service, arts, and media, 7.0% healthcare practitioners, 17.5% service, 27.4% sales and office, 9.1% natural resources, construction, and maintenance, 18.0% production, transportation, and material moving

Income: Per capita: $29,152; Median household: $69,630; Average household: $74,237; Households with income of $100,000 or more: 22.2%; Poverty rate: 6.3%

Educational Attainment: High school diploma or higher: 93.3%; Bachelor's degree or higher: 16.3%; Graduate/professional degree or higher: 4.3%

Housing: Homeownership rate: 92.0%; Median home value: $172,600; Median year structure built: 1971; Homeowner vacancy rate: 0.0%; Median selected monthly owner costs: $1,320 with a mortgage, $417 without a mortgage; Median gross rent: $1,036 per month; Rental vacancy rate: 0.0%

Health Insurance: 92.6% have insurance; 82.1% have private insurance; 26.8% have public insurance; 7.4% do not have insurance; 5.9% of children under 18 do not have insurance

Transportation: Commute: 93.5% car, 0.0% public transportation, 0.0% walk, 6.5% work from home; Mean travel time to work: 29.2 minutes

NEWBURY (unincorporated postal area)

ZCTA: 44065

Covers a land area of 21.752 square miles and a water area of 0.633 square miles. Located at 41.48° N. Lat; 81.22° W. Long..

Population: 4,633; Growth (since 2000): 12.0%; Density: 213.0 persons per square mile; Race: 95.9% White, 0.9% Black/African American, 2.2% Asian, 0.4% American Indian/Alaska Native, 0.0% Native Hawaiian/Other Pacific Islander, 0.6% Two or more races, 0.6% Hispanic of any race; Average household size: 2.75; Median age: 48.7; Age under 18: 20.2%; Age 65 and over: 20.5%; Males per 100 females: 95.3; Marriage status: 29.4% never married, 55.0% now married, 2.2% separated, 6.1% widowed, 9.6% divorced; Foreign born: 4.5%; Speak English only: 94.9%; With disability: 13.6%; Veterans: 6.4%; Ancestry: 36.2% German, 16.5% Italian, 16.2% Irish, 13.3% English, 8.2% Hungarian

Employment: 19.2% management, business, and financial, 6.9% computer, engineering, and science, 7.8% education, legal, community service, arts, and media, 3.1% healthcare practitioners, 19.6% service, 22.3% sales and office, 8.6% natural resources, construction, and maintenance, 12.5% production, transportation, and material moving

Income: Per capita: $31,430; Median household: $61,429; Average household: $87,178; Households with income of $100,000 or more: 28.2%; Poverty rate: 8.4%

Educational Attainment: High school diploma or higher: 92.8%; Bachelor's degree or higher: 22.0%; Graduate/professional degree or higher: 6.7%

School District(s)

Newbury Local (KG-12)
2015-16 Enrollment: 427 . . . . (440) 564-5501

Housing: Homeownership rate: 77.6%; Median home value: $216,100; Median year structure built: 1960; Homeowner vacancy rate: 0.0%; Median selected monthly owner costs: $1,425 with a mortgage, $566 without a mortgage; Median gross rent: $865 per month; Rental vacancy rate: 0.0%

Health Insurance: 93.2% have insurance; 66.6% have private insurance; 39.3% have public insurance; 6.8% do not have insurance; 0.0% of children under 18 do not have insurance

Transportation: Commute: 92.6% car, 1.5% public transportation, 0.6% walk, 5.3% work from home; Mean travel time to work: 25.9 minutes

NOVELTY (unincorporated postal area)

ZCTA: 44072

Covers a land area of 18.750 square miles and a water area of 0.188 square miles. Located at 41.47° N. Lat; 81.32° W. Long. Elevation is 1,063 feet.

Population: 4,404; Growth (since 2000): 7.9%; Density: 234.9 persons per square mile; Race: 97.6% White, 0.0% Black/African American, 2.3% Asian, 0.0% American Indian/Alaska Native, 0.0% Native Hawaiian/Other Pacific Islander, 0.0% Two or more races, 1.1% Hispanic of any race; Average household size: 2.41; Median age: 50.2; Age under 18: 18.7%; Age 65 and over: 24.9%; Males per 100 females: 98.8; Marriage status: 21.2% never married, 69.6% now married, 0.2% separated, 1.9% widowed, 7.3% divorced; Foreign born: 3.5%; Speak English only: 98.5%; With disability: 5.3%; Veterans: 8.8%; Ancestry: 24.6% German, 18.1% Italian, 16.9% English, 10.6% Irish, 8.0% Polish

Employment: 25.2% management, business, and financial, 8.7% computer, engineering, and science, 13.2% education, legal, community service, arts, and media, 9.3% healthcare practitioners, 11.4% service, 19.3% sales and office, 5.5% natural resources, construction, and maintenance, 7.4% production, transportation, and material moving

Income: Per capita: $49,441; Median household: $83,821; Average household: $119,635; Households with income of $100,000 or more: 40.1%; Poverty rate: 1.7%

Educational Attainment: High school diploma or higher: 98.7%; Bachelor's degree or higher: 50.8%; Graduate/professional degree or higher: 18.1%

School District(s)

West Geauga Local (KG-12)
2015-16 Enrollment: 1,956 . . . . (440) 729-5900

Housing: Homeownership rate: 90.0%; Median home value: $267,500; Median year structure built: 1968; Homeowner vacancy rate: 0.8%; Median selected monthly owner costs: $1,859 with a mortgage, $641 without a mortgage; Median gross rent: $929 per month; Rental vacancy rate: 0.0%

Health Insurance: 96.4% have insurance; 86.5% have private insurance; 25.5% have public insurance; 3.6% do not have insurance; 0.0% of children under 18 do not have insurance

Transportation: Commute: 90.8% car, 0.7% public transportation, 2.5% walk, 6.0% work from home; Mean travel time to work: 29.1 minutes

PARKMAN (CDP).

Land/water area and latitude/longitude are not available.

Population: 71; Growth (since 2000): n/a; Density: n/a persons per square mile; Race: 100.0% White, 0.0% Black/African American, 0.0% Asian, 0.0% American Indian/Alaska Native, 0.0% Native Hawaiian/Other Pacific Islander, 0.0% Two or more races, 0.0% Hispanic of any race; Average household size: 1.42; Median age: 60.3; Age under 18: 0.0%; Age 65 and over: 26.8%; Males per 100 females: 0.0; Marriage status: 28.2% never married, 57.7% now married, 0.0% separated, 0.0% widowed, 14.1% divorced; Foreign born: 0.0%; Speak English only: 100.0%; With disability: 26.8%; Veterans: 0.0%; Ancestry: 32.4% Polish, 26.8% European, 16.9% German, 15.5% Slovene, 15.5% Welsh

Employment: 0.0% management, business, and financial, 0.0% computer, engineering, and science, 33.3% education, legal, community service, arts, and media, 36.4% healthcare practitioners, 0.0% service, 0.0% sales and office, 0.0% natural resources, construction, and maintenance, 30.3% production, transportation, and material moving

Income: Per capita: $51,065; Median household: $73,214; Average household: $71,584; Households with income of $100,000 or more: 20.0%; Poverty rate: n/a

Educational Attainment: High school diploma or higher: 100.0%; Bachelor's degree or higher: 26.8%; Graduate/professional degree or higher: n/a

Housing: Homeownership rate: 80.0%; Median home value: $152,100; Median year structure built: 1958; Homeowner vacancy rate: 0.0%; Median selected monthly owner costs: n/a with a mortgage, n/a without a mortgage; Median gross rent: n/a per month; Rental vacancy rate: 0.0%

Health Insurance: 100.0% have insurance; 100.0% have private insurance; 26.8% have public insurance; 0.0% do not have insurance; 0.0% of children under 18 do not have insurance

Safety: Violent crime rate: 0.0 per 10,000 population; Property crime rate: 0.0 per 10,000 population

Transportation: Commute: 100.0% car, 0.0% public transportation, 0.0% walk, 0.0% work from home; Mean travel time to work: 0.0 minutes

SOUTH RUSSELL (village). Covers a land area of 3.754 square miles and a water area of 0.079 square miles. Located at 41.43° N. Lat; 81.33° W. Long. Elevation is 1,122 feet.

History: The southern part of the township had incorporated early in 1923 as South Russell Village and had asked for annexation to Chagrin Falls School District and had been accepted. South Russell students began attending Chagrin Falls Schools in 1926. Thus South Russell was born in controversy over educational issues, proving that still, as over one hundred years before, people in the Western Reserve considered a good education paramount. After World War II, rapid growth in South Russell led to the opening in 1966 of Gurney Elementary School on Bell Road.

Population: 3,839; Growth (since 2000): -4.5%; Density: 1,022.6 persons per square mile; Race: 99.0% White, 0.0% Black/African American, 0.0% Asian, 0.0% American Indian/Alaska Native, 0.0% Native Hawaiian/Other Pacific Islander, 1.0% Two or more races, 1.3% Hispanic of any race; Average household size: 2.65; Median age: 45.6; Age under 18: 28.4%; Age 65 and over: 14.7%; Males per 100 females: 99.0; Marriage status: 15.0% never married, 73.5% now married, 0.3% separated, 5.1% widowed, 6.5% divorced; Foreign born: 0.8%; Speak English only: 98.7%; With disability: 5.6%; Veterans: 5.3%; Ancestry: 20.2% German, 20.1% English, 17.4% Irish, 10.3% Italian, 9.1% Polish

Employment: 30.0% management, business, and financial, 5.4% computer, engineering, and science, 16.8% education, legal, community service, arts, and media, 9.2% healthcare practitioners, 10.9% service, 23.4% sales and office, 1.1% natural resources, construction, and maintenance, 3.2% production, transportation, and material moving

Income: Per capita: $61,700; Median household: $107,250; Average household: $161,216; Households with income of $100,000 or more: 52.7%; Poverty rate: 0.7%

Educational Attainment: High school diploma or higher: 98.8%; Bachelor's degree or higher: 78.4%; Graduate/professional degree or higher: 25.9%

Housing: Homeownership rate: 91.2%; Median home value: $317,800; Median year structure built: 1975; Homeowner vacancy rate: 1.4%; Median selected monthly owner costs: $1,967 with a mortgage, $824 without a mortgage; Median gross rent: $898 per month; Rental vacancy rate: 0.0%

Health Insurance: 97.4% have insurance; 92.4% have private insurance; 15.3% have public insurance; 2.6% do not have insurance; 0.0% of children under 18 do not have insurance

Safety: Violent crime rate: 5.2 per 10,000 population; Property crime rate: 10.5 per 10,000 population

Transportation: Commute: 86.6% car, 0.0% public transportation, 0.0% walk, 13.4% work from home; Mean travel time to work: 30.6 minutes

Additional Information Contacts

Village of South Russell . . . . (440) 338-6700
http://www.southrussell.com

THOMPSON (unincorporated postal area)

ZCTA: 44086

Covers a land area of 27.571 square miles and a water area of 0.213 square miles. Located at 41.68° N. Lat; 81.06° W. Long. Elevation is 1,270 feet.

Population: 2,564; Growth (since 2000): 11.0%; Density: 93.0 persons per square mile; Race: 96.3% White, 1.6% Black/African American, 0.2% Asian, 0.0% American Indian/Alaska Native, 0.0% Native Hawaiian/Other Pacific Islander, 1.9% Two or more races, 0.0% Hispanic of any race; Average household size: 2.64; Median age: 45.8; Age under 18: 21.7%; Age 65 and over: 16.1%; Males per 100 females: 102.1; Marriage status: 21.2% never married, 66.1% now married, 1.5% separated, 3.1% widowed, 9.6% divorced; Foreign born: 1.0%; Speak English only: 98.4%; With disability: 11.3%; Veterans: 12.4%; Ancestry: 26.1% German, 17.4% Irish, 13.7% English, 10.5% Slovene, 8.5% Polish

Employment: 13.7% management, business, and financial, 5.1% computer, engineering, and science, 7.2% education, legal, community service, arts, and media, 5.1% healthcare practitioners, 13.1% service, 29.9% sales and office, 11.9% natural resources, construction, and maintenance, 14.0% production, transportation, and material moving

Income: Per capita: $25,748; Median household: $58,207; Average household: $68,674; Households with income of $100,000 or more: 23.1%; Poverty rate: 13.2%

Educational Attainment: High school diploma or higher: 93.4%; Bachelor's degree or higher: 16.7%; Graduate/professional degree or higher: 6.2%

School District(s)

Ledgemont Local
2015-16 Enrollment: n/a . . . . (440) 298-3341

Housing: Homeownership rate: 87.5%; Median home value: $178,100; Median year structure built: 1980; Homeowner vacancy rate: 1.3%; Median selected monthly owner costs: $1,443 with a mortgage, $441 without a mortgage; Median gross rent: $863 per month; Rental vacancy rate: 0.0%

Health Insurance: 94.1% have insurance; 81.0% have private insurance; 26.8% have public insurance; 5.9% do not have insurance; 9.2% of children under 18 do not have insurance

Transportation: Commute: 95.4% car, 0.0% public transportation, 1.3% walk, 2.8% work from home; Mean travel time to work: 29.3 minutes

Greene County

Located in southwest central Ohio; crossed by the Little Miami and Mad Rivers. Covers a land area of 413.729 square miles, a water area of 2.526 square miles, and is located in the Eastern Time Zone at 39.69° N. Lat., 83.89° W. Long. The county was founded in 1803. County seat is Xenia.

Greene County is part of the Dayton, OH Metropolitan Statistical Area. The entire metro area includes: Greene County, OH; Miami County, OH; Montgomery County, OH

Weather Station: Xenia 6 SSE Elevation: 967 feet

	Jan	Feb	Mar	Apr	May	Jun	Jul	Aug	Sep	Oct	Nov	Dec
High	37	41	52	64	73	80	83	82	77	65	53	41
Low	21	24	32	42	51	60	63	61	54	44	35	25
Precip	2.9	2.4	3.4	3.9	4.9	4.2	4.4	3.1	2.6	3.1	3.2	3.1
Snow	7.0	5.4	2.6	0.4	tr	0.0	0.0	0.0	0.0	0.2	0.6	4.1

High and Low temperatures in degrees Fahrenheit; Precipitation and Snow in inches

Population: 164,325; Growth (since 2000): 11.1%; Density: 397.2 persons per square mile; Race: 86.3% White, 7.1% Black/African American, 2.9% Asian, 0.1% American Indian/Alaska Native, 0.0% Native Hawaiian/Other Pacific Islander, 3.1% two or more races, 2.6% Hispanic of any race; Average household size: 2.41; Median age: 38.0; Age under 18: 20.8%; Age 65 and over: 15.5%; Males per 100 females: 95.9; Marriage status: 31.7% never married, 52.3% now married, 1.1% separated, 5.7% widowed, 10.3% divorced; Foreign born: 4.7%; Speak English only: 93.7%; With disability: 12.4%; Veterans: 13.0%; Ancestry: 23.9% German, 13.0% Irish, 11.2% American, 10.1% English, 3.8% Italian

Religion: Six largest groups: 8.7% Catholicism, 7.2% Baptist, 3.9% Non-denominational Protestant, 3.6% Methodist/Pietist, 3.0% Presbyterian-Reformed, 2.5% Hindu

Economy: Unemployment rate: 4.0%; Leading industries: 16.5 % retail trade; 16.1 % professional, scientific, and technical services; 12.0 % health care and social assistance; Farms: 800 totaling 145,790 acres; Company size: 3 employ 1,000 or more persons, 3 employ 500 to 999 persons, 76 employ 100 to 499 persons, 2,989 employ less than 100 persons; Business ownership: 3,521 women-owned, 444 Black-owned, 118 Hispanic-owned, 349 Asian-owned, 68 American Indian/Alaska Native-owned

Employment: 16.2% management, business, and financial, 9.1% computer, engineering, and science, 11.1% education, legal, community service, arts, and media, 7.8% healthcare practitioners, 15.3% service, 24.2% sales and office, 6.0% natural resources, construction, and maintenance, 10.4% production, transportation, and material moving

Income: Per capita: $31,877; Median household: $61,116; Average household: $79,602; Households with income of $100,000 or more: 28.1%; Poverty rate: 12.8%

Educational Attainment: High school diploma or higher: 92.6%; Bachelor's degree or higher: 37.6%; Graduate/professional degree or higher: 17.7%

Housing: Homeownership rate: 66.8%; Median home value: $161,600; Median year structure built: 1974; Homeowner vacancy rate: 1.3%; Median selected monthly owner costs: $1,403 with a mortgage, $534 without a mortgage; Median gross rent: $853 per month; Rental vacancy rate: 4.0%

Vital Statistics: Birth rate: 108.3 per 10,000 population; Death rate: 87.9 per 10,000 population; Age-adjusted cancer mortality rate: 144.8 deaths per 100,000 population

Health Insurance: 93.6% have insurance; 76.5% have private insurance; 30.4% have public insurance; 6.4% do not have insurance; 3.2% of children under 18 do not have insurance

Health Care: Physicians: 38.3 per 10,000 population; Dentists: 8.3 per 10,000 population; Hospital beds: 12.9 per 10,000 population; Hospital admissions: 638.0 per 10,000 population

Air Quality Index (AQI): Percent of Days: 77.9% good, 21.9% moderate, 0.3% unhealthy for sensitive individuals, 0.0% unhealthy, 0.0% very unhealthy; Annual median: 40; Annual maximum: 105

Transportation: Commute: 91.7% car, 0.4% public transportation, 3.2% walk, 3.9% work from home; Mean travel time to work: 20.9 minutes

2016 Presidential Election: 58.5% Trump, 34.9% Clinton, 4.0% Johnson, 0.8% Stein

National and State Parks: Beaver Creek State Wildlife Area; Charles Young Buffalo Soldiers National Monument; Clifton Gorge State Nature Preserve; Dayton Aviation Heritage National Historical Park; Glen Thompson State Reserve; Huffman Prairie National Historic Landmark;

John Bryan State Park; Little Miami State Forest Preserve; The Narrows State Scenic River Reserve; Williamson Mound State Memorial
Additional Information Contacts
Greene Government . . . . (937) 562-5006
http://www.co.greene.oh.us

Greene County Communities

ALPHA (unincorporated postal area)

ZCTA: 45301

Covers a land area of 0.092 square miles and a water area of 0 square miles. Located at 39.71° N. Lat; 84.02° W. Long. Elevation is 801 feet.
Population: 65; Growth (since 2000): -52.6%; Density: 703.7 persons per square mile; Race: 100.0% White, 0.0% Black/African American, 0.0% Asian, 0.0% American Indian/Alaska Native, 0.0% Native Hawaiian/Other Pacific Islander, 0.0% Two or more races, 0.0% Hispanic of any race; Average household size: 1.81; Median age: 54.8; Age under 18: 0.0%; Age 65 and over: 0.0%; Males per 100 females: 94.0; Marriage status: 21.5% never married, 44.6% now married, 0.0% separated, 0.0% widowed, 33.8% divorced; Foreign born: 0.0%; Speak English only: 100.0%; With disability: 44.6%; Veterans: 21.5%; Ancestry: 33.8% French, 33.8% Polish
Employment: 0.0% management, business, and financial, 0.0% computer, engineering, and science, 0.0% education, legal, community service, arts, and media, 0.0% healthcare practitioners, 100.0% service, 0.0% sales and office, 0.0% natural resources, construction, and maintenance, 0.0% production, transportation, and material moving
Income: Per capita: n/a; Median household: n/a; Average household: n/a; Households with income of $100,000 or more: n/a; Poverty rate: n/a
Educational Attainment: High school diploma or higher: 100.0%; Bachelor's degree or higher: 56.9%; Graduate/professional degree or higher: 29.4%
Housing: Homeownership rate: 38.9%; Median home value: n/a; Median year structure built: n/a; Homeowner vacancy rate: 0.0%; Median selected monthly owner costs: $0 with a mortgage, $0 without a mortgage; Median gross rent: n/a per month; Rental vacancy rate: 0.0%
Health Insurance: 100.0% have insurance; 100.0% have private insurance; 0.0% have public insurance; 0.0% do not have insurance; 0.0% of children under 18 do not have insurance
Transportation: Commute: 100.0% car, 0.0% public transportation, 0.0% walk, 0.0% work from home; Mean travel time to work: 0.0 minutes

BEAVERCREEK (city). Covers a land area of 26.399 square miles and a water area of 0.037 square miles. Located at 39.73° N. Lat; 84.06° W. Long. Elevation is 876 feet.

Population: 46,086; Growth (since 2000): 21.3%; Density: 1,745.8 persons per square mile; Race: 87.4% White, 3.0% Black/African American, 5.3% Asian, 0.2% American Indian/Alaska Native, 0.0% Native Hawaiian/Other Pacific Islander, 3.6% Two or more races, 2.8% Hispanic of any race; Average household size: 2.45; Median age: 41.1; Age under 18: 20.4%; Age 65 and over: 16.4%; Males per 100 females: 99.7; Marriage status: 26.4% never married, 60.5% now married, 0.8% separated, 4.9% widowed, 8.2% divorced; Foreign born: 7.9%; Speak English only: 89.4%; With disability: 9.6%; Veterans: 16.7%; Ancestry: 24.5% German, 13.2% Irish, 10.6% English, 10.0% American, 4.8% Italian
Employment: 22.1% management, business, and financial, 12.0% computer, engineering, and science, 11.0% education, legal, community service, arts, and media, 9.9% healthcare practitioners, 12.5% service, 21.5% sales and office, 4.0% natural resources, construction, and maintenance, 7.1% production, transportation, and material moving
Income: Per capita: $40,639; Median household: $82,956; Average household: $99,010; Households with income of $100,000 or more: 39.7%; Poverty rate: 4.8%
Educational Attainment: High school diploma or higher: 97.3%; Bachelor's degree or higher: 50.0%; Graduate/professional degree or higher: 25.0%

School District(s)

Beavercreek City (PK-12)
2015-16 Enrollment: 7,586 . . . . (937) 426-1522
Housing: Homeownership rate: 71.2%; Median home value: $175,100; Median year structure built: 1980; Homeowner vacancy rate: 1.2%; Median selected monthly owner costs: $1,604 with a mortgage, $632 without a mortgage; Median gross rent: $1,135 per month; Rental vacancy rate: 3.3%
Health Insurance: 96.6% have insurance; 88.0% have private insurance; 23.4% have public insurance; 3.4% do not have insurance; 3.2% of children under 18 do not have insurance
Hospitals: Indu & Raj Soin Medical Center
Safety: Violent crime rate: 6.9 per 10,000 population; Property crime rate: 229.1 per 10,000 population
Transportation: Commute: 93.9% car, 0.1% public transportation, 1.3% walk, 4.0% work from home; Mean travel time to work: 19.4 minutes
Additional Information Contacts
City of Beavercreek . . . . (937) 427-5510
http://www.ci.beavercreek.oh.us

BELLBROOK (city). Covers a land area of 3.125 square miles and a water area of 0.001 square miles. Located at 39.64° N. Lat; 84.09° W. Long. Elevation is 778 feet.

Population: 7,082; Growth (since 2000): 1.0%; Density: 2,265.9 persons per square mile; Race: 97.8% White, 0.2% Black/African American, 1.0% Asian, 0.0% American Indian/Alaska Native, 0.0% Native Hawaiian/Other Pacific Islander, 0.5% Two or more races, 0.9% Hispanic of any race; Average household size: 2.52; Median age: 42.2; Age under 18: 23.2%; Age 65 and over: 17.9%; Males per 100 females: 97.7; Marriage status: 19.5% never married, 63.5% now married, 1.1% separated, 5.5% widowed, 11.5% divorced; Foreign born: 1.7%; Speak English only: 97.8%; With disability: 8.4%; Veterans: 14.3%; Ancestry: 29.9% German, 14.8% Irish, 12.8% American, 10.4% English, 4.3% Scotch-Irish
Employment: 16.9% management, business, and financial, 16.1% computer, engineering, and science, 13.9% education, legal, community service, arts, and media, 8.3% healthcare practitioners, 9.4% service, 21.9% sales and office, 5.5% natural resources, construction, and maintenance, 8.0% production, transportation, and material moving
Income: Per capita: $35,998; Median household: $76,576; Average household: $89,457; Households with income of $100,000 or more: 34.9%; Poverty rate: 3.2%
Educational Attainment: High school diploma or higher: 96.9%; Bachelor's degree or higher: 44.5%; Graduate/professional degree or higher: 18.7%

School District(s)

Bellbrook-sugarcreek Local (PK-12)
2015-16 Enrollment: 2,696 . . . . (937) 848-5001
Housing: Homeownership rate: 86.0%; Median home value: $160,200; Median year structure built: 1968; Homeowner vacancy rate: 0.0%; Median selected monthly owner costs: $1,506 with a mortgage, $595 without a mortgage; Median gross rent: $988 per month; Rental vacancy rate: 0.0%
Health Insurance: 96.3% have insurance; 84.4% have private insurance; 22.8% have public insurance; 3.7% do not have insurance; 0.0% of children under 18 do not have insurance
Safety: Violent crime rate: 4.2 per 10,000 population; Property crime rate: 80.6 per 10,000 population
Transportation: Commute: 93.4% car, 0.0% public transportation, 1.7% walk, 4.4% work from home; Mean travel time to work: 20.5 minutes
Additional Information Contacts
City of Bellbrook . . . . (937) 848-4666
http://www.cityofbellbrook.org

BOWERSVILLE (village). Covers a land area of 0.150 square miles and a water area of 0 square miles. Located at 39.58° N. Lat; 83.72° W. Long. Elevation is 1,089 feet.

Population: 295; Growth (since 2000): 1.7%; Density: 1,969.2 persons per square mile; Race: 98.6% White, 0.0% Black/African American, 0.0% Asian, 0.0% American Indian/Alaska Native, 0.0% Native Hawaiian/Other Pacific Islander, 1.4% Two or more races, 0.0% Hispanic of any race; Average household size: 2.68; Median age: 34.3; Age under 18: 31.2%; Age 65 and over: 14.2%; Males per 100 females: 96.2; Marriage status: 23.6% never married, 56.4% now married, 2.2% separated, 4.9% widowed, 15.1% divorced; Foreign born: 0.0%; Speak English only: 98.9%; With disability: 15.6%; Veterans: 7.9%; Ancestry: 23.4% German, 11.5% American, 7.1% English, 6.8% Irish, 4.7% European
Employment: 4.2% management, business, and financial, 1.7% computer, engineering, and science, 2.5% education, legal, community service, arts, and media, 2.5% healthcare practitioners, 21.2% service, 24.6% sales and office, 18.6% natural resources, construction, and maintenance, 24.6% production, transportation, and material moving
Income: Per capita: $16,307; Median household: $35,000; Average household: $43,575; Households with income of $100,000 or more: 7.3%; Poverty rate: 23.5%

Educational Attainment: High school diploma or higher: 81.7%; Bachelor's degree or higher: 3.9%; Graduate/professional degree or higher: 0.6%
Housing: Homeownership rate: 70.9%; Median home value: $83,000; Median year structure built: 1944; Homeowner vacancy rate: 0.0%; Median selected monthly owner costs: $860 with a mortgage, $336 without a mortgage; Median gross rent: $824 per month; Rental vacancy rate: 0.0%
Health Insurance: 84.1% have insurance; 59.3% have private insurance; 42.4% have public insurance; 15.9% do not have insurance; 13.0% of children under 18 do not have insurance
Transportation: Commute: 91.4% car, 0.9% public transportation, 3.4% walk, 4.3% work from home; Mean travel time to work: 29.1 minutes

CEDARVILLE (village). Covers a land area of 1.282 square miles and a water area of 0.043 square miles. Located at 39.75° N. Lat; 83.81° W. Long. Elevation is 1,050 feet.
History: Cedarville was settled in 1805 and developed around Cedarville College, chartered in 1887 and opened in 1894 under the Reformed Presbyterian Church.
Population: 4,011; Growth (since 2000): 4.8%; Density: 3,128.6 persons per square mile; Race: 83.5% White, 10.7% Black/African American, 1.9% Asian, 0.3% American Indian/Alaska Native, 0.0% Native Hawaiian/Other Pacific Islander, 1.8% Two or more races, 2.6% Hispanic of any race; Average household size: 2.21; Median age: 20.9; Age under 18: 6.4%; Age 65 and over: 7.8%; Males per 100 females: 87.0; Marriage status: 77.5% never married, 16.5% now married, 0.0% separated, 2.7% widowed, 3.3% divorced; Foreign born: 2.7%; Speak English only: 96.8%; With disability: 7.1%; Veterans: 2.6%; Ancestry: 27.3% German, 13.7% Irish, 11.5% English, 5.7% American, 4.6% Italian
Employment: 7.0% management, business, and financial, 2.1% computer, engineering, and science, 19.9% education, legal, community service, arts, and media, 4.4% healthcare practitioners, 31.4% service, 24.3% sales and office, 4.9% natural resources, construction, and maintenance, 6.0% production, transportation, and material moving
Income: Per capita: $11,724; Median household: $42,609; Average household: $50,188; Households with income of $100,000 or more: 11.0%; Poverty rate: 21.7%
Educational Attainment: High school diploma or higher: 96.0%; Bachelor's degree or higher: 42.3%; Graduate/professional degree or higher: 16.6%

School District(s)

Cedar Cliff Local (KG-12)
2015-16 Enrollment: 612. . . . . (937) 766-6000

Four-year College(s)

Cedarville University (Private, Not-for-profit, Baptist)
Fall 2016 Enrollment: 3,714 . . . . (937) 766-7700
2016-17 Tuition: In-state $28,110; Out-of-state $28,110

Housing: Homeownership rate: 48.1%; Median home value: $121,500; Median year structure built: 1957; Homeowner vacancy rate: 0.0%; Median selected monthly owner costs: $997 with a mortgage, $435 without a mortgage; Median gross rent: $633 per month; Rental vacancy rate: 2.1%
Health Insurance: 93.7% have insurance; 83.3% have private insurance; 15.6% have public insurance; 6.3% do not have insurance; 8.6% of children under 18 do not have insurance
Transportation: Commute: 50.8% car, 0.2% public transportation, 30.6% walk, 18.2% work from home; Mean travel time to work: 15.0 minutes

CLIFTON (village). Covers a land area of 0.179 square miles and a water area of 0.007 square miles. Located at 39.80° N. Lat; 83.83° W. Long. Elevation is 1,004 feet.
History: Clifton was settled on the Little Miami River where water-power was plentiful. Isaac Kaufman Funk, who formed a partnership with college classmate Adam Willis Wagnalls, was born in Clifton in 1839. Funk was the editor of "A Standard Dictionary of the English Language."
Population: 121; Growth (since 2000): -32.4%; Density: 676.4 persons per square mile; Race: 94.2% White, 1.7% Black/African American, 0.0% Asian, 0.0% American Indian/Alaska Native, 0.0% Native Hawaiian/Other Pacific Islander, 4.1% Two or more races, 3.3% Hispanic of any race; Average household size: 1.95; Median age: 48.6; Age under 18: 12.4%; Age 65 and over: 17.4%; Males per 100 females: 85.4; Marriage status: 35.8% never married, 52.8% now married, 5.7% separated, 5.7% widowed, 5.7% divorced; Foreign born: 0.0%; Speak English only: 94.0%; With disability: 34.7%; Veterans: 9.4%; Ancestry: 19.8% German, 16.5% Irish, 14.0% English, 7.4% Dutch, 7.4% Norwegian
Employment: 14.8% management, business, and financial, 0.0% computer, engineering, and science, 9.3% education, legal, community service, arts, and media, 11.1% healthcare practitioners, 27.8% service, 5.6% sales and office, 9.3% natural resources, construction, and maintenance, 22.2% production, transportation, and material moving
Income: Per capita: $32,027; Median household: $42,500; Average household: $65,518; Households with income of $100,000 or more: 12.8%; Poverty rate: 17.4%
Educational Attainment: High school diploma or higher: 91.3%; Bachelor's degree or higher: 27.2%; Graduate/professional degree or higher: 6.5%
Housing: Homeownership rate: 72.6%; Median home value: $118,800; Median year structure built: Before 1940; Homeowner vacancy rate: 0.0%; Median selected monthly owner costs: $858 with a mortgage, $433 without a mortgage; Median gross rent: $700 per month; Rental vacancy rate: 0.0%
Health Insurance: 91.7% have insurance; 67.8% have private insurance; 43.0% have public insurance; 8.3% do not have insurance; 0.0% of children under 18 do not have insurance
Transportation: Commute: 83.0% car, 0.0% public transportation, 11.3% walk, 5.7% work from home; Mean travel time to work: 18.9 minutes

FAIRBORN (city). Covers a land area of 13.160 square miles and a water area of 0.009 square miles. Located at 39.80° N. Lat; 84.01° W. Long. Elevation is 837 feet.
History: Air Force Museum nearby. Settled 1799, incorporated 1950 with the merging of Osborn and Fairborn.
Population: 33,487; Growth (since 2000): 4.5%; Density: 2,544.7 persons per square mile; Race: 82.0% White, 8.1% Black/African American, 4.3% Asian, 0.2% American Indian/Alaska Native, 0.1% Native Hawaiian/Other Pacific Islander, 4.6% Two or more races, 3.9% Hispanic of any race; Average household size: 2.24; Median age: 33.8; Age under 18: 20.4%; Age 65 and over: 14.3%; Males per 100 females: 95.8; Marriage status: 36.4% never married, 43.8% now married, 1.9% separated, 6.1% widowed, 13.7% divorced; Foreign born: 6.0%; Speak English only: 92.5%; With disability: 15.7%; Veterans: 14.3%; Ancestry: 21.8% German, 13.3% American, 12.9% Irish, 10.1% English, 3.8% Italian
Employment: 11.0% management, business, and financial, 7.6% computer, engineering, and science, 8.8% education, legal, community service, arts, and media, 5.7% healthcare practitioners, 17.3% service, 29.4% sales and office, 6.6% natural resources, construction, and maintenance, 13.6% production, transportation, and material moving
Income: Per capita: $24,646; Median household: $41,529; Average household: $55,141; Households with income of $100,000 or more: 14.9%; Poverty rate: 22.1%
Educational Attainment: High school diploma or higher: 87.5%; Bachelor's degree or higher: 26.8%; Graduate/professional degree or higher: 11.7%

School District(s)

Fairborn City (PK-12)
2015-16 Enrollment: 4,189 . . . . (937) 878-3961
Fairborn Digital Academy (09-12)
2015-16 Enrollment: 163. . . . . (937) 879-0511

Housing: Homeownership rate: 48.0%; Median home value: $109,700; Median year structure built: 1969; Homeowner vacancy rate: 2.0%; Median selected monthly owner costs: $1,098 with a mortgage, $407 without a mortgage; Median gross rent: $762 per month; Rental vacancy rate: 5.3%
Health Insurance: 89.4% have insurance; 63.1% have private insurance; 38.8% have public insurance; 10.6% do not have insurance; 4.7% of children under 18 do not have insurance
Safety: Violent crime rate: 25.0 per 10,000 population; Property crime rate: 270.3 per 10,000 population
Transportation: Commute: 93.6% car, 0.3% public transportation, 3.0% walk, 2.3% work from home; Mean travel time to work: 19.8 minutes
Additional Information Contacts
City of Fairborn . . . . (937) 754-3030
http://www.ci.fairborn.oh.us

JAMESTOWN (village). Covers a land area of 1.207 square miles and a water area of 0.004 square miles. Located at 39.66° N. Lat; 83.74° W. Long. Elevation is 1,060 feet.
History: Jamestown was settled near the old route of Chiuxso's Trail, a wagon road through the forest connecting Ripley on the Ohio River with the Mad River Valley. The town was rebuilt after a cyclone destroyed the buildings in 1844.

Population: 1,954; Growth (since 2000): 1.9%; Density: 1,618.6 persons per square mile; Race: 96.4% White, 1.3% Black/African American, 0.2% Asian, 0.0% American Indian/Alaska Native, 0.0% Native Hawaiian/Other Pacific Islander, 2.2% Two or more races, 0.5% Hispanic of any race; Average household size: 2.43; Median age: 45.4; Age under 18: 23.5%; Age 65 and over: 17.5%; Males per 100 females: 82.8; Marriage status: 22.3% never married, 54.5% now married, 3.1% separated, 9.9% widowed, 13.4% divorced; Foreign born: 0.6%; Speak English only: 98.7%; With disability: 19.8%; Veterans: 8.4%; Ancestry: 16.5% German, 14.8% English, 14.0% American, 10.1% Irish, 3.7% European
Employment: 8.7% management, business, and financial, 2.4% computer, engineering, and science, 12.6% education, legal, community service, arts, and media, 8.1% healthcare practitioners, 17.4% service, 21.3% sales and office, 9.7% natural resources, construction, and maintenance, 19.8% production, transportation, and material moving
Income: Per capita: $20,834; Median household: $44,028; Average household: $49,814; Households with income of $100,000 or more: 7.1%; Poverty rate: 16.1%
Educational Attainment: High school diploma or higher: 85.3%; Bachelor's degree or higher: 12.8%; Graduate/professional degree or higher: 4.8%

School District(s)

Greeneview Local (KG-12)
2015-16 Enrollment: 1,307 . . . . (937) 675-2728
Housing: Homeownership rate: 63.6%; Median home value: $92,900; Median year structure built: 1953; Homeowner vacancy rate: 2.0%; Median selected monthly owner costs: $971 with a mortgage, $366 without a mortgage; Median gross rent: $643 per month; Rental vacancy rate: 2.7%
Health Insurance: 95.6% have insurance; 72.3% have private insurance; 40.6% have public insurance; 4.4% do not have insurance; 0.0% of children under 18 do not have insurance
Safety: Violent crime rate: 4.9 per 10,000 population; Property crime rate: 354.0 per 10,000 population
Transportation: Commute: 95.6% car, 1.0% public transportation, 0.8% walk, 1.6% work from home; Mean travel time to work: 28.5 minutes

SHAWNEE HILLS (CDP). Covers a land area of 2.670 square miles and a water area of 0.284 square miles. Located at 39.65° N. Lat; 83.79° W. Long. Elevation is 1,047 feet.
Population: 2,165; Growth (since 2000): -8.1%; Density: 810.9 persons per square mile; Race: 99.8% White, 0.0% Black/African American, 0.0% Asian, 0.0% American Indian/Alaska Native, 0.0% Native Hawaiian/Other Pacific Islander, 0.2% Two or more races, 0.2% Hispanic of any race; Average household size: 2.55; Median age: 40.7; Age under 18: 22.5%; Age 65 and over: 15.8%; Males per 100 females: 100.8; Marriage status: 20.1% never married, 66.6% now married, 1.3% separated, 5.0% widowed, 8.3% divorced; Foreign born: 0.4%; Speak English only: 99.1%; With disability: 10.7%; Veterans: 13.0%; Ancestry: 21.1% German, 15.7% American, 11.7% English, 7.8% European, 7.5% Irish
Employment: 8.4% management, business, and financial, 4.2% computer, engineering, and science, 10.6% education, legal, community service, arts, and media, 4.1% healthcare practitioners, 13.7% service, 32.1% sales and office, 12.6% natural resources, construction, and maintenance, 14.2% production, transportation, and material moving
Income: Per capita: $28,647; Median household: $64,423; Average household: $72,320; Households with income of $100,000 or more: 22.3%; Poverty rate: 2.2%
Educational Attainment: High school diploma or higher: 92.2%; Bachelor's degree or higher: 16.2%; Graduate/professional degree or higher: 7.1%
Housing: Homeownership rate: 92.5%; Median home value: $138,700; Median year structure built: 1977; Homeowner vacancy rate: 0.6%; Median selected monthly owner costs: $1,239 with a mortgage, $494 without a mortgage; Median gross rent: $1,028 per month; Rental vacancy rate: 0.0%
Health Insurance: 96.4% have insurance; 83.9% have private insurance; 27.6% have public insurance; 3.6% do not have insurance; 0.0% of children under 18 do not have insurance
Transportation: Commute: 97.9% car, 0.0% public transportation, 0.0% walk, 2.1% work from home; Mean travel time to work: 29.1 minutes

SPRING VALLEY (village). Covers a land area of 0.266 square miles and a water area of 0.002 square miles. Located at 39.61° N. Lat; 84.01° W. Long. Elevation is 764 feet.
History: Spring Valley was named for the nearby springs, whose water was bottled and shipped from the town. Spring Valley developed as a farming community, with tobacco grown here as early as 1825.
Population: 499; Growth (since 2000): -2.2%; Density: 1,879.0 persons per square mile; Race: 100.0% White, 0.0% Black/African American, 0.0% Asian, 0.0% American Indian/Alaska Native, 0.0% Native Hawaiian/Other Pacific Islander, 0.0% Two or more races, 0.0% Hispanic of any race; Average household size: 2.24; Median age: 46.9; Age under 18: 16.6%; Age 65 and over: 16.4%; Males per 100 females: 101.3; Marriage status: 23.5% never married, 51.8% now married, 0.9% separated, 12.7% widowed, 12.0% divorced; Foreign born: 1.4%; Speak English only: 100.0%; With disability: 21.8%; Veterans: 12.7%; Ancestry: 33.1% German, 21.4% Irish, 12.6% English, 9.6% American, 3.8% Dutch
Employment: 4.3% management, business, and financial, 3.9% computer, engineering, and science, 16.5% education, legal, community service, arts, and media, 3.9% healthcare practitioners, 22.9% service, 28.3% sales and office, 14.7% natural resources, construction, and maintenance, 5.4% production, transportation, and material moving
Income: Per capita: $25,530; Median household: $55,694; Average household: $55,866; Households with income of $100,000 or more: 11.2%; Poverty rate: 8.4%
Educational Attainment: High school diploma or higher: 93.1%; Bachelor's degree or higher: 23.1%; Graduate/professional degree or higher: 11.4%
Housing: Homeownership rate: 81.6%; Median home value: $92,400; Median year structure built: Before 1940; Homeowner vacancy rate: 0.0%; Median selected monthly owner costs: $1,064 with a mortgage, $428 without a mortgage; Median gross rent: $850 per month; Rental vacancy rate: 0.0%
Health Insurance: 92.6% have insurance; 70.1% have private insurance; 36.7% have public insurance; 7.4% do not have insurance; 0.0% of children under 18 do not have insurance
Transportation: Commute: 84.6% car, 0.0% public transportation, 1.1% walk, 10.9% work from home; Mean travel time to work: 27.2 minutes

WILBERFORCE (CDP). Covers a land area of 3.081 square miles and a water area of 0.024 square miles. Located at 39.71° N. Lat; 83.88° W. Long. Elevation is 1,007 feet.
History: Wilberforce was named for William Wilberforce, an English reformer. The town grew around Wilberforce University, opened in 1856 by the Methodist Episcopal Church and purchased in 1863 by the African M.E. Church.
Population: 2,295; Growth (since 2000): 45.3%; Density: 744.9 persons per square mile; Race: 40.3% White, 52.5% Black/African American, 1.2% Asian, 3.1% American Indian/Alaska Native, 0.0% Native Hawaiian/Other Pacific Islander, 2.8% Two or more races, 4.8% Hispanic of any race; Average household size: 2.99; Median age: 20.2; Age under 18: 9.2%; Age 65 and over: 1.7%; Males per 100 females: 94.4; Marriage status: 85.8% never married, 11.0% now married, 0.0% separated, 1.0% widowed, 2.2% divorced; Foreign born: 2.7%; Speak English only: 93.5%; With disability: 6.6%; Veterans: 2.1%; Ancestry: 10.5% German, 8.1% Irish, 4.1% Polish, 3.2% English, 2.4% French
Employment: 7.6% management, business, and financial, 2.7% computer, engineering, and science, 15.5% education, legal, community service, arts, and media, 3.2% healthcare practitioners, 26.6% service, 32.9% sales and office, 1.0% natural resources, construction, and maintenance, 10.6% production, transportation, and material moving
Income: Per capita: $10,619; Median household: $83,320; Average household: $83,526; Households with income of $100,000 or more: 39.7%; Poverty rate: 3.7%
Educational Attainment: High school diploma or higher: 94.0%; Bachelor's degree or higher: 34.6%; Graduate/professional degree or higher: 16.8%

Four-year College(s)

Central State University (Public, Historically black)
Fall 2016 Enrollment: 1,741 . . . . (937) 376-6011
2016-17 Tuition: In-state $6,246; Out-of-state $8,096
Payne Theological Seminary (Private, Not-for-profit, African Methodist Episcopal)
Fall 2016 Enrollment: 190 . . . . (937) 376-2946
Wilberforce University (Private, Not-for-profit, Historically black, African Methodist Episcopal)

Fall 2016 Enrollment: 645 . . . . (937) 376-2911
2016-17 Tuition: In-state $13,250; Out-of-state $13,250
Housing: Homeownership rate: 74.6%; Median home value: $169,300; Median year structure built: 1970; Homeowner vacancy rate: 0.0%; Median selected monthly owner costs: $1,826 with a mortgage, n/a without a mortgage; Median gross rent: $586 per month; Rental vacancy rate: 0.0%
Health Insurance: 94.6% have insurance; 75.9% have private insurance; 23.8% have public insurance; 5.4% do not have insurance; 2.4% of children under 18 do not have insurance
Transportation: Commute: 50.2% car, 0.7% public transportation, 37.5% walk, 11.6% work from home; Mean travel time to work: 14.0 minutes

WRIGHT-PATTERSON AFB (CDP). Covers a land area of 9.929 square miles and a water area of 0.080 square miles. Located at 39.82° N. Lat; 84.05° W. Long.
Population: 2,596; Growth (since 2000): -61.0%; Density: 261.5 persons per square mile; Race: 83.0% White, 11.8% Black/African American, 2.5% Asian, 0.0% American Indian/Alaska Native, 0.0% Native Hawaiian/Other Pacific Islander, 1.5% Two or more races, 12.3% Hispanic of any race; Average household size: 3.12; Median age: 22.8; Age under 18: 22.4%; Age 65 and over: 3.9%; Males per 100 females: 128.2; Marriage status: 51.3% never married, 42.6% now married, 0.0% separated, 1.2% widowed, 4.9% divorced; Foreign born: 4.4%; Speak English only: 92.6%; With disability: 12.7%; Veterans: 32.5%; Ancestry: 21.8% German, 18.9% Irish, 6.4% English, 6.4% American, 6.3% European
Employment: 13.8% management, business, and financial, 11.2% computer, engineering, and science, 11.2% education, legal, community service, arts, and media, 12.6% healthcare practitioners, 15.9% service, 23.1% sales and office, 1.4% natural resources, construction, and maintenance, 10.7% production, transportation, and material moving
Income: Per capita: $26,803; Median household: $82,763; Average household: $92,029; Households with income of $100,000 or more: 38.1%; Poverty rate: 6.8%
Educational Attainment: High school diploma or higher: 91.9%; Bachelor's degree or higher: 45.1%; Graduate/professional degree or higher: 24.6%

Four-year College(s)

Air Force Institute of Technology-Graduate School of Engineering & Mgmt (Public)
Fall 2016 Enrollment: 966 . . . . (937) 255-3636
Housing: Homeownership rate: 1.0%; Median home value: n/a; Median year structure built: 1965; Homeowner vacancy rate: 0.0%; Median selected monthly owner costs: n/a with a mortgage, n/a without a mortgage; Median gross rent: $1,247 per month; Rental vacancy rate: 0.0%
Health Insurance: 91.5% have insurance; 88.8% have private insurance; 15.8% have public insurance; 8.5% do not have insurance; 12.2% of children under 18 do not have insurance
Transportation: Commute: 96.4% car, 0.0% public transportation, 3.4% walk, 0.1% work from home; Mean travel time to work: 12.6 minutes

XENIA (city). County seat. Covers a land area of 13.281 square miles and a water area of 0.014 square miles. Located at 39.68° N. Lat; 83.94° W. Long. Elevation is 935 feet.
History: Xenia developed around an agricultural area. An early industry was the production of rope and twine.
Population: 26,105; Growth (since 2000): 8.0%; Density: 1,965.5 persons per square mile; Race: 81.9% White, 14.5% Black/African American, 0.3% Asian, 0.0% American Indian/Alaska Native, 0.0% Native Hawaiian/Other Pacific Islander, 3.2% Two or more races, 1.6% Hispanic of any race; Average household size: 2.34; Median age: 37.2; Age under 18: 24.8%; Age 65 and over: 16.8%; Males per 100 females: 89.3; Marriage status: 30.9% never married, 45.3% now married, 1.6% separated, 8.6% widowed, 15.2% divorced; Foreign born: 1.0%; Speak English only: 98.1%; With disability: 16.6%; Veterans: 10.4%; Ancestry: 21.6% German, 13.7% Irish, 13.2% American, 7.3% English, 3.0% European
Employment: 11.6% management, business, and financial, 4.2% computer, engineering, and science, 9.5% education, legal, community service, arts, and media, 6.3% healthcare practitioners, 18.1% service, 27.6% sales and office, 9.1% natural resources, construction, and maintenance, 13.4% production, transportation, and material moving
Income: Per capita: $21,867; Median household: $38,426; Average household: $51,563; Households with income of $100,000 or more: 9.6%; Poverty rate: 24.6%
Educational Attainment: High school diploma or higher: 87.9%; Bachelor's degree or higher: 19.5%; Graduate/professional degree or higher: 7.6%

School District(s)

Greene County Vocational School District (07-12)
2015-16 Enrollment: n/a . . . . (937) 372-6941
Summit Academy Community School Alternative Learners-Xenia (KG-09)
2015-16 Enrollment: 162 . . . . (937) 372-5210
Xenia Community City (PK-12)
2015-16 Enrollment: 4,318 . . . . (937) 376-2961

Vocational/Technical School(s)

Greene County Vocational School District (Public)
Fall 2016 Enrollment: 35 . . . . (937) 426-6636
2016-17 Tuition: $4,498
Housing: Homeownership rate: 61.6%; Median home value: $93,800; Median year structure built: 1969; Homeowner vacancy rate: 2.4%; Median selected monthly owner costs: $996 with a mortgage, $377 without a mortgage; Median gross rent: $665 per month; Rental vacancy rate: 3.0%
Health Insurance: 91.5% have insurance; 59.3% have private insurance; 46.1% have public insurance; 8.5% do not have insurance; 1.6% of children under 18 do not have insurance
Hospitals: Greene Memorial Hospital (231 beds)
Safety: Violent crime rate: 20.4 per 10,000 population; Property crime rate: 315.3 per 10,000 population
Newspapers: Fairborn Daily Herald (daily circulation 4,000); Xenia Daily Gazette (daily circulation 5,900)
Transportation: Commute: 93.3% car, 1.3% public transportation, 2.6% walk, 1.9% work from home; Mean travel time to work: 22.2 minutes
Airports: Greene County-Lewis A. Jackson Regional (general aviation)
Additional Information Contacts
City of Xenia . . . . (937) 376-7232
http://www.ci.xenia.oh.us

YELLOW SPRINGS (village). Covers a land area of 2.016 square miles and a water area of <.001 square miles. Located at 39.80° N. Lat; 83.89° W. Long. Elevation is 961 feet.
History: Yellow Springs was founded in 1804 and named for the yellowed water of the nearby iron springs. Antioch College was founded here in 1853 with Horace Mann as its first president.
Population: 3,784; Growth (since 2000): 0.6%; Density: 1,876.9 persons per square mile; Race: 84.0% White, 12.3% Black/African American, 0.3% Asian, 0.0% American Indian/Alaska Native, 0.0% Native Hawaiian/Other Pacific Islander, 3.4% Two or more races, 1.7% Hispanic of any race; Average household size: 2.03; Median age: 48.4; Age under 18: 18.9%; Age 65 and over: 21.5%; Males per 100 females: 85.1; Marriage status: 30.9% never married, 43.9% now married, 1.4% separated, 6.9% widowed, 18.3% divorced; Foreign born: 3.1%; Speak English only: 96.1%; With disability: 15.7%; Veterans: 7.4%; Ancestry: 26.7% German, 14.7% Irish, 12.1% English, 5.4% American, 4.8% European
Employment: 10.7% management, business, and financial, 11.9% computer, engineering, and science, 27.2% education, legal, community service, arts, and media, 11.2% healthcare practitioners, 16.5% service, 11.5% sales and office, 4.1% natural resources, construction, and maintenance, 6.9% production, transportation, and material moving
Income: Per capita: $42,659; Median household: $62,500; Average household: $88,030; Households with income of $100,000 or more: 33.3%; Poverty rate: 16.1%
Educational Attainment: High school diploma or higher: 96.7%; Bachelor's degree or higher: 61.2%; Graduate/professional degree or higher: 36.3%

School District(s)

Yellow Springs Exempted Village (KG-12)
2015-16 Enrollment: 707 . . . . (937) 767-7381

Four-year College(s)

Antioch College (Private, Not-for-profit)
Fall 2016 Enrollment: 223 . . . . (937) 319-6082
2016-17 Tuition: In-state $35,568; Out-of-state $35,568
Antioch University Online (Private, Not-for-profit)
Fall 2016 Enrollment: 163 . . . . (937) 769-1352
Antioch University-Midwest (Private, Not-for-profit)
Fall 2016 Enrollment: 156 . . . . (937) 769-1800
Antioch University-PhD Program in Leadership and Change (Private, Not-for-profit)
Fall 2016 Enrollment: 164 . . . . (937) 769-1360

Housing: Homeownership rate: 68.8%; Median home value: $210,900; Median year structure built: 1960; Homeowner vacancy rate: 0.0%; Median selected monthly owner costs: $1,456 with a mortgage, $560 without a mortgage; Median gross rent: $778 per month; Rental vacancy rate: 0.0%
Health Insurance: 92.7% have insurance; 74.4% have private insurance; 33.9% have public insurance; 7.3% do not have insurance; 0.6% of children under 18 do not have insurance
Safety: Violent crime rate: 5.2 per 10,000 population; Property crime rate: 204.8 per 10,000 population
Newspapers: Yellow Springs News (weekly circulation 1,800)
Transportation: Commute: 76.6% car, 0.1% public transportation, 6.9% walk, 12.1% work from home; Mean travel time to work: 21.7 minutes
Additional Information Contacts
Village of Yellow Springs . . . . (937) 767-7202
http://www.yso.com

Guernsey County

Located in eastern Ohio; drained by Wills Creek; includes Salt Fork Lake. Covers a land area of 522.254 square miles, a water area of 6.049 square miles, and is located in the Eastern Time Zone at 40.06° N. Lat., 81.50° W. Long. The county was founded in 1810. County seat is Cambridge.

Guernsey County is part of the Cambridge, OH Micropolitan Statistical Area. The entire metro area includes: Guernsey County, OH

Weather Station: Cambridge Elevation: 799 feet

	Jan	Feb	Mar	Apr	May	Jun	Jul	Aug	Sep	Oct	Nov	Dec
High	38	43	53	66	74	82	85	84	78	66	54	42
Low	22	24	31	41	50	58	63	62	54	43	34	26
Precip	3.0	2.2	3.1	3.5	4.2	3.9	4.3	3.6	3.3	2.8	3.3	2.8
Snow	6.3	4.5	2.8	0.7	tr	0.0	0.0	0.0	0.0	tr	0.7	3.2

High and Low temperatures in degrees Fahrenheit; Precipitation and Snow in inches

Population: 39,478; Growth (since 2000): -3.2%; Density: 75.6 persons per square mile; Race: 95.8% White, 1.3% Black/African American, 0.3% Asian, 0.2% American Indian/Alaska Native, 0.0% Native Hawaiian/Other Pacific Islander, 2.1% two or more races, 1.1% Hispanic of any race; Average household size: 2.45; Median age: 42.3; Age under 18: 23.0%; Age 65 and over: 17.5%; Males per 100 females: 96.1; Marriage status: 24.9% never married, 52.7% now married, 2.5% separated, 7.7% widowed, 14.7% divorced; Foreign born: 0.8%; Speak English only: 97.0%; With disability: 18.0%; Veterans: 10.3%; Ancestry: 20.0% German, 16.4% Irish, 11.9% English, 9.1% American, 2.8% Dutch
Religion: Six largest groups: 10.4% Methodist/Pietist, 7.8% Baptist, 5.3% Catholicism, 2.1% Presbyterian-Reformed, 2.0% European Free-Church, 1.8% Pentecostal
Economy: Unemployment rate: 5.4%; Leading industries: 16.4 % retail trade; 14.7 % health care and social assistance; 13.1 % other services (except public administration); Farms: 1,228 totaling 143,763 acres; Company size: 0 employ 1,000 or more persons, 2 employ 500 to 999 persons, 27 employ 100 to 499 persons, 826 employ less than 100 persons; Business ownership: 668 women-owned, n/a Black-owned, n/a Hispanic-owned, 26 Asian-owned, n/a American Indian/Alaska Native-owned
Employment: 8.9% management, business, and financial, 2.6% computer, engineering, and science, 7.9% education, legal, community service, arts, and media, 6.8% healthcare practitioners, 18.3% service, 22.2% sales and office, 12.3% natural resources, construction, and maintenance, 21.1% production, transportation, and material moving
Income: Per capita: $22,280; Median household: $41,566; Average household: $53,875; Households with income of $100,000 or more: 12.2%; Poverty rate: 19.8%
Educational Attainment: High school diploma or higher: 84.5%; Bachelor's degree or higher: 13.6%; Graduate/professional degree or higher: 5.0%
Housing: Homeownership rate: 72.5%; Median home value: $98,600; Median year structure built: 1970; Homeowner vacancy rate: 1.9%; Median selected monthly owner costs: $978 with a mortgage, $350 without a mortgage; Median gross rent: $595 per month; Rental vacancy rate: 9.4%
Vital Statistics: Birth rate: 116.7 per 10,000 population; Death rate: 114.4 per 10,000 population; Age-adjusted cancer mortality rate: 189.4 deaths per 100,000 population
Health Insurance: 90.3% have insurance; 61.3% have private insurance; 42.9% have public insurance; 9.7% do not have insurance; 6.4% of children under 18 do not have insurance
Health Care: Physicians: 12.5 per 10,000 population; Dentists: 5.1 per 10,000 population; Hospital beds: 24.0 per 10,000 population; Hospital admissions: 900.1 per 10,000 population
Transportation: Commute: 92.7% car, 0.4% public transportation, 2.1% walk, 3.6% work from home; Mean travel time to work: 23.8 minutes
2016 Presidential Election: 68.8% Trump, 26.2% Clinton, 3.3% Johnson, 0.6% Stein
National and State Parks: Salt Fork State Park and Wildlife Area
Additional Information Contacts
Guernsey Government . . . . (740) 432-9200
http://www.guernseycounty.org

Guernsey County Communities

BUFFALO (CDP). Covers a land area of 0.490 square miles and a water area of 0 square miles. Located at 39.92° N. Lat; 81.52° W. Long. Elevation is 856 feet.
Population: 335; Growth (since 2000): n/a; Density: 683.5 persons per square mile; Race: 97.3% White, 0.0% Black/African American, 0.0% Asian, 0.0% American Indian/Alaska Native, 0.0% Native Hawaiian/Other Pacific Islander, 2.7% Two or more races, 0.0% Hispanic of any race; Average household size: 2.16; Median age: 43.7; Age under 18: 13.7%; Age 65 and over: 10.1%; Males per 100 females: 100.5; Marriage status: 17.9% never married, 72.8% now married, 0.0% separated, 6.3% widowed, 3.0% divorced; Foreign born: 0.0%; Speak English only: 100.0%; With disability: 30.7%; Veterans: 4.5%; Ancestry: 17.6% German, 17.6% Irish, 5.7% English, 4.2% American, 4.2% French
Employment: 5.0% management, business, and financial, 0.0% computer, engineering, and science, 12.6% education, legal, community service, arts, and media, 6.3% healthcare practitioners, 30.8% service, 5.0% sales and office, 34.6% natural resources, construction, and maintenance, 5.7% production, transportation, and material moving
Income: Per capita: $20,113; Median household: $31,713; Average household: $44,972; Households with income of $100,000 or more: 7.1%; Poverty rate: n/a
Educational Attainment: High school diploma or higher: 79.3%; Bachelor's degree or higher: 4.0%; Graduate/professional degree or higher: n/a
Housing: Homeownership rate: 87.1%; Median home value: $55,800; Median year structure built: Before 1940; Homeowner vacancy rate: 0.0%; Median selected monthly owner costs: $589 with a mortgage, $375 without a mortgage; Median gross rent: n/a per month; Rental vacancy rate: 0.0%
Health Insurance: 87.8% have insurance; 57.6% have private insurance; 38.5% have public insurance; 12.2% do not have insurance; 0.0% of children under 18 do not have insurance
Transportation: Commute: 100.0% car, 0.0% public transportation, 0.0% walk, 0.0% work from home; Mean travel time to work: 37.3 minutes

BYESVILLE (village). Covers a land area of 1.187 square miles and a water area of 0 square miles. Located at 39.97° N. Lat; 81.55° W. Long. Elevation is 810 feet.
History: Byesville was named for Jonathan Bye, who built a flour mill here in the early 1800's. Later, the town's economy depended on coal mining.
Population: 2,179; Growth (since 2000): -15.3%; Density: 1,835.9 persons per square mile; Race: 99.7% White, 0.0% Black/African American, 0.0% Asian, 0.0% American Indian/Alaska Native, 0.0% Native Hawaiian/Other Pacific Islander, 0.3% Two or more races, 1.4% Hispanic of any race; Average household size: 2.41; Median age: 39.9; Age under 18: 22.6%; Age 65 and over: 16.4%; Males per 100 females: 87.1; Marriage status: 28.4% never married, 47.9% now married, 2.9% separated, 8.8% widowed, 15.0% divorced; Foreign born: 0.1%; Speak English only: 99.1%; With disability: 19.7%; Veterans: 10.2%; Ancestry: 15.9% German, 14.8% Irish, 12.7% American, 11.6% English, 3.6% French
Employment: 2.8% management, business, and financial, 2.2% computer, engineering, and science, 9.0% education, legal, community service, arts, and media, 3.9% healthcare practitioners, 20.9% service, 23.7% sales and office, 11.4% natural resources, construction, and maintenance, 26.1% production, transportation, and material moving
Income: Per capita: $19,216; Median household: $32,267; Average household: $44,975; Households with income of $100,000 or more: 5.8%; Poverty rate: 26.1%
Educational Attainment: High school diploma or higher: 85.4%; Bachelor's degree or higher: 7.6%; Graduate/professional degree or higher: 3.0%

School District(s)

Rolling Hills Local (KG-12)
2015-16 Enrollment: 1,610 . . . . (740) 432-5370

Housing: Homeownership rate: 60.5%; Median home value: $74,300; Median year structure built: 1962; Homeowner vacancy rate: 0.0%; Median selected monthly owner costs: $949 with a mortgage, $317 without a mortgage; Median gross rent: $624 per month; Rental vacancy rate: 3.4%
Health Insurance: 95.0% have insurance; 60.3% have private insurance; 49.1% have public insurance; 5.0% do not have insurance; 0.0% of children under 18 do not have insurance
Transportation: Commute: 97.3% car, 0.0% public transportation, 0.0% walk, 2.0% work from home; Mean travel time to work: 19.6 minutes

---

CAMBRIDGE (city). County seat. Covers a land area of 6.352 square miles and a water area of 0.004 square miles. Located at 40.02° N. Lat; 81.59° W. Long. Elevation is 814 feet.
History: Cambridge was laid out in 1806 by Jacob Gomber and Zacheus Beatty, and named for Cambridge, Maryland, the former home of many of the first settlers. Oil and gas discovered in the area in the 1880 's led to industrial development, including a glass factory founded in 1901.
Population: 10,495; Growth (since 2000): -8.9%; Density: 1,652.2 persons per square mile; Race: 93.1% White, 3.0% Black/African American, 0.7% Asian, 0.2% American Indian/Alaska Native, 0.0% Native Hawaiian/Other Pacific Islander, 2.3% Two or more races, 2.0% Hispanic of any race; Average household size: 2.26; Median age: 40.3; Age under 18: 23.0%; Age 65 and over: 19.0%; Males per 100 females: 87.4; Marriage status: 26.1% never married, 45.6% now married, 4.4% separated, 9.7% widowed, 18.6% divorced; Foreign born: 1.4%; Speak English only: 97.7%; With disability: 19.6%; Veterans: 10.9%; Ancestry: 22.6% German, 19.2% Irish, 9.6% English, 8.4% American, 3.0% Scottish
Employment: 8.6% management, business, and financial, 2.9% computer, engineering, and science, 7.1% education, legal, community service, arts, and media, 7.0% healthcare practitioners, 21.4% service, 23.8% sales and office, 7.0% natural resources, construction, and maintenance, 22.1% production, transportation, and material moving
Income: Per capita: $18,398; Median household: $30,795; Average household: $41,292; Households with income of $100,000 or more: 8.5%; Poverty rate: 31.2%
Educational Attainment: High school diploma or higher: 85.4%; Bachelor's degree or higher: 12.8%; Graduate/professional degree or higher: 4.8%

School District(s)

Cambridge City (PK-12)
2015-16 Enrollment: 1,972 . . . . (740) 439-5021
East Muskingum Local (PK-12)
2015-16 Enrollment: 2,087 . . . . (740) 826-7655

Housing: Homeownership rate: 53.7%; Median home value: $85,000; Median year structure built: 1950; Homeowner vacancy rate: 0.8%; Median selected monthly owner costs: $885 with a mortgage, $339 without a mortgage; Median gross rent: $576 per month; Rental vacancy rate: 10.7%
Health Insurance: 92.7% have insurance; 51.9% have private insurance; 55.3% have public insurance; 7.3% do not have insurance; 1.4% of children under 18 do not have insurance
Hospitals: Southeastern Ohio Regional Medical Center (209 beds)
Safety: Violent crime rate: 13.5 per 10,000 population; Property crime rate: 468.0 per 10,000 population
Newspapers: Daily Jeffersonian (daily circulation 12,700); New Concord Leader (weekly circulation 1,200); Village Reporter (weekly circulation 1,000)
Transportation: Commute: 93.3% car, 1.1% public transportation, 3.9% walk, 1.2% work from home; Mean travel time to work: 15.6 minutes
Additional Information Contacts
City of Cambridge . . . . (740) 439-1050
http://www.cambridgeoh.org

CUMBERLAND (village). Covers a land area of 0.486 square miles and a water area of 0 square miles. Located at 39.85° N. Lat; 81.66° W. Long. Elevation is 856 feet.
Population: 409; Growth (since 2000): 1.7%; Density: 842.2 persons per square mile; Race: 96.6% White, 0.2% Black/African American, 0.0% Asian, 0.0% American Indian/Alaska Native, 0.0% Native Hawaiian/Other Pacific Islander, 3.2% Two or more races, 1.2% Hispanic of any race; Average household size: 2.96; Median age: 41.1; Age under 18: 27.6%; Age 65 and over: 11.7%; Males per 100 females: 96.3; Marriage status: 30.4% never married, 57.2% now married, 1.2% separated, 4.4% widowed, 8.0% divorced; Foreign born: 0.5%; Speak English only: 99.0%; With disability: 16.4%; Veterans: 6.8%; Ancestry: 25.4% Irish, 10.0% English, 9.3% Dutch, 8.8% American, 7.1% German
Employment: 2.5% management, business, and financial, 1.2% computer, engineering, and science, 3.7% education, legal, community service, arts, and media, 4.3% healthcare practitioners, 16.0% service, 27.0% sales and office, 13.5% natural resources, construction, and maintenance, 31.9% production, transportation, and material moving
Income: Per capita: $16,949; Median household: $42,500; Average household: $46,881; Households with income of $100,000 or more: 7.2%; Poverty rate: 22.7%
Educational Attainment: High school diploma or higher: 83.1%; Bachelor's degree or higher: 7.7%; Graduate/professional degree or higher: 1.9%
Housing: Homeownership rate: 88.4%; Median home value: $62,000; Median year structure built: Before 1940; Homeowner vacancy rate: 0.0%; Median selected monthly owner costs: $775 with a mortgage, $394 without a mortgage; Median gross rent: $533 per month; Rental vacancy rate: 23.8%
Health Insurance: 89.0% have insurance; 57.0% have private insurance; 41.1% have public insurance; 11.0% do not have insurance; 3.5% of children under 18 do not have insurance
Transportation: Commute: 96.8% car, 0.0% public transportation, 1.3% walk, 1.3% work from home; Mean travel time to work: 40.5 minutes

---

DERWENT (unincorporated postal area)
ZCTA: 43733
Covers a land area of 0.923 square miles and a water area of 0 square miles. Located at 39.93° N. Lat; 81.54° W. Long. Elevation is 814 feet.
Population: n/a; Growth (since 2000): n/a; Density: <0.1 persons per square mile; Race: 0.0% White, 0.0% Black/African American, 0.0% Asian, 0.0% American Indian/Alaska Native, 0.0% Native Hawaiian/Other Pacific Islander, 0.0% Two or more races, 0.0% Hispanic of any race; Average household size: 0.00; Median age: n/a; Age under 18: 100.0%; Age 65 and over: 0.0%; Males per 100 females: 102.1
Housing: Homeownership rate: n/a; Homeowner vacancy rate: 0.0%; Rental vacancy rate: 0.0%

FAIRVIEW (village). Covers a land area of 0.401 square miles and a water area of 0 square miles. Located at 40.06° N. Lat; 81.23° W. Long. Elevation is 1,217 feet.
History: Fairview was once the leading U.S. producer of pennyroyal, an herb used in early medicines.
Population: 82; Growth (since 2000): 1.2%; Density: 204.3 persons per square mile; Race: 100.0% White, 0.0% Black/African American, 0.0% Asian, 0.0% American Indian/Alaska Native, 0.0% Native Hawaiian/Other Pacific Islander, 0.0% Two or more races, 0.0% Hispanic of any race; Average household size: 2.73; Median age: 45.5; Age under 18: 18.3%; Age 65 and over: 24.4%; Males per 100 females: 130.6; Marriage status: 31.9% never married, 41.7% now married, 0.0% separated, 18.1% widowed, 8.3% divorced; Foreign born: 0.0%; Speak English only: 100.0%; With disability: 12.2%; Veterans: 14.9%; Ancestry: 19.5% German, 17.1% Irish, 15.9% English, 15.9% Scottish, 13.4% Portuguese
Employment: 0.0% management, business, and financial, 0.0% computer, engineering, and science, 0.0% education, legal, community service, arts, and media, 0.0% healthcare practitioners, 40.0% service, 28.0% sales and office, 8.0% natural resources, construction, and maintenance, 24.0% production, transportation, and material moving
Income: Per capita: $16,273; Median household: n/a; Average household: $43,320; Households with income of $100,000 or more: 16.7%; Poverty rate: 36.6%
Educational Attainment: High school diploma or higher: 75.5%; Bachelor's degree or higher: n/a; Graduate/professional degree or higher: n/a
Housing: Homeownership rate: 90.0%; Median home value: $52,500; Median year structure built: Before 1940; Homeowner vacancy rate: 0.0%; Median selected monthly owner costs: $472 with a mortgage, $358 without a mortgage; Median gross rent: n/a per month; Rental vacancy rate: 0.0%
Health Insurance: 76.8% have insurance; 54.9% have private insurance; 45.1% have public insurance; 23.2% do not have insurance; 0.0% of children under 18 do not have insurance
Transportation: Commute: 100.0% car, 0.0% public transportation, 0.0% walk, 0.0% work from home; Mean travel time to work: 28.8 minutes

KIMBOLTON (CDP). Covers a land area of 0.498 square miles and a water area of 0 square miles. Located at 40.15° N. Lat; 81.58° W. Long. Elevation is 801 feet.

Population: 71; Growth (since 2000): -62.6%; Density: 142.7 persons per square mile; Race: 100.0% White, 0.0% Black/African American, 0.0% Asian, 0.0% American Indian/Alaska Native, 0.0% Native Hawaiian/Other Pacific Islander, 0.0% Two or more races, 0.0% Hispanic of any race; Average household size: 1.61; Median age: 60.1; Age under 18: 0.0%; Age 65 and over: 42.3%; Males per 100 females: 105.7; Marriage status: 0.0% never married, 33.8% now married, 0.0% separated, 53.5% widowed, 12.7% divorced; Foreign born: 0.0%; Speak English only: 100.0%; With disability: 46.5%; Veterans: 8.5%; Ancestry: 54.9% American

Employment: 0.0% management, business, and financial, 0.0% computer, engineering, and science, 0.0% education, legal, community service, arts, and media, 0.0% healthcare practitioners, 0.0% service, 100.0% sales and office, 0.0% natural resources, construction, and maintenance, 0.0% production, transportation, and material moving

Income: Per capita: $31,662; Median household: $60,385; Average household: $50,277; Households with income of $100,000 or more: n/a; Poverty rate: n/a

Educational Attainment: High school diploma or higher: 70.4%; Bachelor's degree or higher: n/a; Graduate/professional degree or higher: n/a

Housing: Homeownership rate: 86.4%; Median home value: n/a; Median year structure built: 1986; Homeowner vacancy rate: 0.0%; Median selected monthly owner costs: n/a with a mortgage, n/a without a mortgage; Median gross rent: n/a per month; Rental vacancy rate: 0.0%

Health Insurance: 63.4% have insurance; 42.3% have private insurance; 63.4% have public insurance; 36.6% do not have insurance; 0.0% of children under 18 do not have insurance

Transportation: Commute: 100.0% car, 0.0% public transportation, 0.0% walk, 0.0% work from home; Mean travel time to work: 0.0 minutes

KIPLING (unincorporated postal area)

ZCTA: 43750

Covers a land area of 1.079 square miles and a water area of 0.003 square miles. Located at 40.00° N. Lat; 81.51° W. Long. Elevation is 820 feet.

Population: 171; Growth (since 2000): n/a; Density: 158.5 persons per square mile; Race: 100.0% White, 0.0% Black/African American, 0.0% Asian, 0.0% American Indian/Alaska Native, 0.0% Native Hawaiian/Other Pacific Islander, 0.0% Two or more races, 0.0% Hispanic of any race; Average household size: 2.14; Median age: 40.6; Age under 18: 24.6%; Age 65 and over: 4.1%; Males per 100 females: 90.7; Marriage status: 39.4% never married, 27.5% now married, 0.0% separated, 4.9% widowed, 28.2% divorced; Foreign born: 0.0%; Speak English only: 100.0%; With disability: 9.9%; Veterans: 20.2%; Ancestry: 19.9% German, 17.0% Irish, 9.4% English, 4.7% Scottish

Employment: 7.6% management, business, and financial, 0.0% computer, engineering, and science, 38.1% education, legal, community service, arts, and media, 0.0% healthcare practitioners, 35.2% service, 19.0% sales and office, 0.0% natural resources, construction, and maintenance, 0.0% production, transportation, and material moving

Income: Per capita: $30,116; Median household: n/a; Average household: $64,135; Households with income of $100,000 or more: 25.0%; Poverty rate: 26.9%

Educational Attainment: High school diploma or higher: 94.6%; Bachelor's degree or higher: 37.2%; Graduate/professional degree or higher: 31.0%

Housing: Homeownership rate: 100.0%; Median home value: $72,000; Median year structure built: Before 1940; Homeowner vacancy rate: 0.0%; Median selected monthly owner costs: $871 with a mortgage, $0 without a mortgage; Median gross rent: n/a per month; Rental vacancy rate: 0.0%

Health Insurance: 100.0% have insurance; 73.1% have private insurance; 31.0% have public insurance; 0.0% do not have insurance; 0.0% of children under 18 do not have insurance

Transportation: Commute: 100.0% car, 0.0% public transportation, 0.0% walk, 0.0% work from home; Mean travel time to work: 21.0 minutes

LORE CITY (village). Covers a land area of 0.328 square miles and a water area of 0 square miles. Located at 39.98° N. Lat; 81.46° W. Long. Elevation is 817 feet.

History: Lore City grew around the coal mines. Morgan's Confederate raiders burned buildings here on their flight across Ohio.

Population: 289; Growth (since 2000): -5.2%; Density: 881.4 persons per square mile; Race: 98.3% White, 0.0% Black/African American, 0.0% Asian, 0.7% American Indian/Alaska Native, 0.0% Native Hawaiian/Other Pacific Islander, 1.0% Two or more races, 1.0% Hispanic of any race; Average household size: 2.43; Median age: 48.5; Age under 18: 20.4%; Age 65 and over: 19.7%; Males per 100 females: 91.2; Marriage status: 24.4% never married, 55.0% now married, 3.8% separated, 2.9% widowed, 17.6% divorced; Foreign born: 0.7%; Speak English only: 97.8%; With disability: 17.4%; Veterans: 14.3%; Ancestry: 26.0% German, 14.2% Irish, 13.1% Dutch, 10.4% French, 6.6% English

Employment: 6.5% management, business, and financial, 0.0% computer, engineering, and science, 12.3% education, legal, community service, arts, and media, 6.5% healthcare practitioners, 22.5% service, 27.5% sales and office, 15.2% natural resources, construction, and maintenance, 9.4% production, transportation, and material moving

Income: Per capita: $26,884; Median household: $39,327; Average household: $58,482; Households with income of $100,000 or more: 10.9%; Poverty rate: 7.3%

Educational Attainment: High school diploma or higher: 79.7%; Bachelor's degree or higher: 10.8%; Graduate/professional degree or higher: 6.6%

School District(s)

East Guernsey Local (KG-12)

2015-16 Enrollment: 991. . . . . (740) 489-5190

Housing: Homeownership rate: 81.5%; Median home value: $69,000; Median year structure built: Before 1940; Homeowner vacancy rate: 2.9%; Median selected monthly owner costs: $786 with a mortgage, $388 without a mortgage; Median gross rent: $588 per month; Rental vacancy rate: 12.0%

Health Insurance: 83.3% have insurance; 68.8% have private insurance; 27.3% have public insurance; 16.7% do not have insurance; 8.5% of children under 18 do not have insurance

Transportation: Commute: 93.1% car, 0.0% public transportation, 2.8% walk, 1.4% work from home; Mean travel time to work: 18.5 minutes

OLD WASHINGTON (village). Covers a land area of 0.672 square miles and a water area of 0 square miles. Located at 40.04° N. Lat; 81.44° W. Long. Elevation is 1,017 feet.

History: Old Washington was a stagecoach stop on the National Road, with several inns providing rooms and meals for travelers.

Population: 351; Growth (since 2000): 32.5%; Density: 522.5 persons per square mile; Race: 97.2% White, 0.9% Black/African American, 0.0% Asian, 0.0% American Indian/Alaska Native, 0.0% Native Hawaiian/Other Pacific Islander, 2.0% Two or more races, 0.0% Hispanic of any race; Average household size: 2.54; Median age: 38.5; Age under 18: 18.2%; Age 65 and over: 20.8%; Males per 100 females: 109.8; Marriage status: 27.2% never married, 52.7% now married, 5.8% separated, 9.5% widowed, 10.5% divorced; Foreign born: 0.0%; Speak English only: 100.0%; With disability: 11.7%; Veterans: 7.7%; Ancestry: 23.6% German, 13.4% English, 7.7% French, 7.4% Irish, 7.1% American

Employment: 8.9% management, business, and financial, 1.7% computer, engineering, and science, 12.8% education, legal, community service, arts, and media, 10.0% healthcare practitioners, 22.2% service, 16.1% sales and office, 7.8% natural resources, construction, and maintenance, 20.6% production, transportation, and material moving

Income: Per capita: $21,823; Median household: $51,731; Average household: $53,147; Households with income of $100,000 or more: 3.6%; Poverty rate: 10.6%

Educational Attainment: High school diploma or higher: 93.8%; Bachelor's degree or higher: 10.5%; Graduate/professional degree or higher: 4.3%

Housing: Homeownership rate: 69.6%; Median home value: $86,300; Median year structure built: 1953; Homeowner vacancy rate: 0.0%; Median selected monthly owner costs: $864 with a mortgage, $339 without a mortgage; Median gross rent: $900 per month; Rental vacancy rate: 6.0%

Health Insurance: 83.5% have insurance; 64.7% have private insurance; 35.0% have public insurance; 16.5% do not have insurance; 26.6% of children under 18 do not have insurance

Transportation: Commute: 95.7% car, 0.0% public transportation, 3.1% walk, 1.2% work from home; Mean travel time to work: 24.7 minutes

PLEASANT CITY (village). Covers a land area of 0.176 square miles and a water area of 0 square miles. Located at 39.90° N. Lat; 81.54° W. Long. Elevation is 823 feet.
History: Pleasant City, first called Point Pleasant, developed around the coal mines in the 1890's.
Population: 478; Growth (since 2000): 8.9%; Density: 2,709.8 persons per square mile; Race: 92.7% White, 0.6% Black/African American, 0.0% Asian, 0.0% American Indian/Alaska Native, 0.0% Native Hawaiian/Other Pacific Islander, 6.7% Two or more races, 0.0% Hispanic of any race; Average household size: 2.93; Median age: 30.4; Age under 18: 30.5%; Age 65 and over: 8.4%; Males per 100 females: 93.5; Marriage status: 36.4% never married, 43.1% now married, 3.5% separated, 3.5% widowed, 16.9% divorced; Foreign born: 0.2%; Speak English only: 94.5%; With disability: 19.5%; Veterans: 8.4%; Ancestry: 23.4% German, 9.2% Irish, 7.5% English, 6.7% Hungarian, 4.4% Slovak
Employment: 5.9% management, business, and financial, 2.5% computer, engineering, and science, 7.4% education, legal, community service, arts, and media, 7.4% healthcare practitioners, 20.6% service, 17.2% sales and office, 15.7% natural resources, construction, and maintenance, 23.5% production, transportation, and material moving
Income: Per capita: $18,234; Median household: $37,063; Average household: $51,474; Households with income of $100,000 or more: 11.0%; Poverty rate: 22.8%
Educational Attainment: High school diploma or higher: 79.8%; Bachelor's degree or higher: 12.1%; Graduate/professional degree or higher: 4.3%
Housing: Homeownership rate: 60.7%; Median home value: $71,300; Median year structure built: Before 1940; Homeowner vacancy rate: 6.6%; Median selected monthly owner costs: $943 with a mortgage, $294 without a mortgage; Median gross rent: $755 per month; Rental vacancy rate: 5.9%
Health Insurance: 84.9% have insurance; 44.4% have private insurance; 51.0% have public insurance; 15.1% do not have insurance; 0.0% of children under 18 do not have insurance
Transportation: Commute: 93.9% car, 0.0% public transportation, 0.5% walk, 5.6% work from home; Mean travel time to work: 21.6 minutes

QUAKER CITY (village). Covers a land area of 0.526 square miles and a water area of 0 square miles. Located at 39.97° N. Lat; 81.30° W. Long. Elevation is 863 feet.
Population: 332; Growth (since 2000): -41.0%; Density: 631.8 persons per square mile; Race: 97.3% White, 0.0% Black/African American, 0.0% Asian, 0.0% American Indian/Alaska Native, 0.0% Native Hawaiian/Other Pacific Islander, 1.8% Two or more races, 0.0% Hispanic of any race; Average household size: 2.09; Median age: 52.5; Age under 18: 19.0%; Age 65 and over: 26.2%; Males per 100 females: 94.6; Marriage status: 15.2% never married, 52.4% now married, 7.1% separated, 14.1% widowed, 18.2% divorced; Foreign born: 0.0%; Speak English only: 99.4%; With disability: 15.7%; Veterans: 8.2%; Ancestry: 22.0% German, 12.3% Irish, 12.0% English, 10.8% American, 8.7% Dutch
Employment: 2.6% management, business, and financial, 4.3% computer, engineering, and science, 12.0% education, legal, community service, arts, and media, 4.3% healthcare practitioners, 11.1% service, 22.2% sales and office, 18.8% natural resources, construction, and maintenance, 24.8% production, transportation, and material moving
Income: Per capita: $17,298; Median household: $29,479; Average household: $35,472; Households with income of $100,000 or more: 1.3%; Poverty rate: 16.9%
Educational Attainment: High school diploma or higher: 90.2%; Bachelor's degree or higher: 3.5%; Graduate/professional degree or higher: 0.8%
Housing: Homeownership rate: 74.8%; Median home value: $73,200; Median year structure built: Before 1940; Homeowner vacancy rate: 12.2%; Median selected monthly owner costs: $850 with a mortgage, $349 without a mortgage; Median gross rent: $440 per month; Rental vacancy rate: 14.9%
Health Insurance: 88.9% have insurance; 64.8% have private insurance; 42.8% have public insurance; 11.1% do not have insurance; 7.9% of children under 18 do not have insurance
Transportation: Commute: 97.4% car, 0.0% public transportation, 0.0% walk, 2.6% work from home; Mean travel time to work: 30.4 minutes

SALESVILLE (village). Covers a land area of 0.096 square miles and a water area of 0 square miles. Located at 39.97° N. Lat; 81.34° W. Long. Elevation is 866 feet.
History: Salesville was established near Leatherwood Creek, and was the setting for William Dean Howells' novel "The Leatherwood God."
Population: 103; Growth (since 2000): -33.1%; Density: 1,076.7 persons per square mile; Race: 100.0% White, 0.0% Black/African American, 0.0% Asian, 0.0% American Indian/Alaska Native, 0.0% Native Hawaiian/Other Pacific Islander, 0.0% Two or more races, 0.0% Hispanic of any race; Average household size: 2.58; Median age: 32.3; Age under 18: 19.4%; Age 65 and over: 13.6%; Males per 100 females: 98.5; Marriage status: 23.3% never married, 65.1% now married, 9.3% separated, 2.3% widowed, 9.3% divorced; Foreign born: 0.0%; Speak English only: 100.0%; With disability: 12.6%; Veterans: 14.5%; Ancestry: 20.4% Irish, 16.5% German, 4.9% American, 4.9% English, 2.9% Dutch
Employment: 3.8% management, business, and financial, 0.0% computer, engineering, and science, 0.0% education, legal, community service, arts, and media, 1.9% healthcare practitioners, 19.2% service, 26.9% sales and office, 30.8% natural resources, construction, and maintenance, 17.3% production, transportation, and material moving
Income: Per capita: $20,841; Median household: $45,000; Average household: $49,883; Households with income of $100,000 or more: 5.0%; Poverty rate: 5.8%
Educational Attainment: High school diploma or higher: 85.1%; Bachelor's degree or higher: n/a; Graduate/professional degree or higher: n/a
Housing: Homeownership rate: 87.5%; Median home value: $68,800; Median year structure built: Before 1940; Homeowner vacancy rate: 0.0%; Median selected monthly owner costs: $836 with a mortgage, $225 without a mortgage; Median gross rent: n/a per month; Rental vacancy rate: 0.0%
Health Insurance: 90.3% have insurance; 67.0% have private insurance; 29.1% have public insurance; 9.7% do not have insurance; 0.0% of children under 18 do not have insurance
Transportation: Commute: 100.0% car, 0.0% public transportation, 0.0% walk, 0.0% work from home; Mean travel time to work: 39.0 minutes

SENECAVILLE (village). Covers a land area of 0.475 square miles and a water area of 0 square miles. Located at 39.93° N. Lat; 81.46° W. Long. Elevation is 896 feet.
Population: 428; Growth (since 2000): -5.5%; Density: 901.1 persons per square mile; Race: 95.6% White, 0.0% Black/African American, 0.0% Asian, 0.5% American Indian/Alaska Native, 0.0% Native Hawaiian/Other Pacific Islander, 4.0% Two or more races, 1.2% Hispanic of any race; Average household size: 2.58; Median age: 31.8; Age under 18: 22.7%; Age 65 and over: 14.3%; Males per 100 females: 104.9; Marriage status: 34.4% never married, 44.7% now married, 0.3% separated, 7.6% widowed, 13.2% divorced; Foreign born: 0.0%; Speak English only: 100.0%; With disability: 19.9%; Veterans: 11.5%; Ancestry: 25.7% German, 17.3% Irish, 10.5% American, 7.7% English, 2.3% Italian
Employment: 3.6% management, business, and financial, 4.7% computer, engineering, and science, 5.2% education, legal, community service, arts, and media, 8.9% healthcare practitioners, 20.3% service, 18.8% sales and office, 18.8% natural resources, construction, and maintenance, 19.8% production, transportation, and material moving
Income: Per capita: $24,664; Median household: $43,611; Average household: $63,201; Households with income of $100,000 or more: 12.6%; Poverty rate: 17.7%
Educational Attainment: High school diploma or higher: 91.9%; Bachelor's degree or higher: 10.0%; Graduate/professional degree or higher: 4.2%

School District(s)

Mid-East Career and Technology Centers (10-12)
2015-16 Enrollment: n/a . . . . (740) 454-0105
Rolling Hills Local (KG-12)
2015-16 Enrollment: 1,610 . . . . (740) 432-5370

Housing: Homeownership rate: 75.3%; Median home value: $81,300; Median year structure built: Before 1940; Homeowner vacancy rate: 5.3%; Median selected monthly owner costs: $940 with a mortgage, $416 without a mortgage; Median gross rent: $725 per month; Rental vacancy rate: 16.3%
Health Insurance: 87.1% have insurance; 58.6% have private insurance; 39.0% have public insurance; 12.9% do not have insurance; 4.1% of children under 18 do not have insurance
Transportation: Commute: 95.5% car, 0.0% public transportation, 4.5% walk, 0.0% work from home; Mean travel time to work: 21.3 minutes

Hamilton County

Located in southwestern Ohio; bounded on the west by Indiana, and on the south by the Ohio River and the Kentucky border; drained by Great Miami, Little Miami, and Whitewater Rivers. Covers a land area of 405.910 square miles, a water area of 6.721 square miles, and is located in the Eastern Time Zone at 39.20° N. Lat., 84.54° W. Long. The county was founded in 1790. County seat is Cincinnati.

Hamilton County is part of the Cincinnati, OH-KY-IN Metropolitan Statistical Area. The entire metro area includes: Dearborn County, IN; Ohio County, IN; Union County, IN; Boone County, KY; Bracken County, KY; Campbell County, KY; Gallatin County, KY; Grant County, KY; Kenton County, KY; Pendleton County, KY; Brown County, OH; Butler County, OH; Clermont County, OH; Hamilton County, OH; Warren County, OH

Weather Station: Cincinnati Fernbank Elevation: 500 feet

	Jan	Feb	Mar	Apr	May	Jun	Jul	Aug	Sep	Oct	Nov	Dec
High	40	44	54	65	74	82	86	85	79	67	56	43
Low	22	24	32	41	51	61	65	64	56	44	36	27
Precip	3.3	3.0	4.4	4.4	5.8	4.3	4.5	3.7	3.0	3.6	3.5	3.8
Snow	4.4	4.5	2.3	tr	tr	0.0	0.0	0.0	0.0	tr	0.2	2.9

High and Low temperatures in degrees Fahrenheit; Precipitation and Snow in inches

Population: 805,965; Growth (since 2000): -4.7%; Density: 1,985.6 persons per square mile; Race: 68.2% White, 25.8% Black/African American, 2.4% Asian, 0.1% American Indian/Alaska Native, 0.0% Native Hawaiian/Other Pacific Islander, 2.5% two or more races, 2.9% Hispanic of any race; Average household size: 2.35; Median age: 37.0; Age under 18: 23.3%; Age 65 and over: 14.2%; Males per 100 females: 92.3; Marriage status: 38.0% never married, 44.6% now married, 2.1% separated, 6.1% widowed, 11.3% divorced; Foreign born: 5.1%; Speak English only: 92.9%; With disability: 12.6%; Veterans: 7.3%; Ancestry: 28.4% German, 13.2% Irish, 6.7% English, 5.4% American, 4.7% Italian
Religion: Six largest groups: 25.6% Catholicism, 6.3% Baptist, 4.9% Non-denominational Protestant, 4.5% Methodist/Pietist, 2.6% Pentecostal, 2.4% Presbyterian-Reformed
Economy: Unemployment rate: 4.2%; Leading industries: 13.4 % retail trade; 12.2 % professional, scientific, and technical services; 11.2 % health care and social assistance; Farms: 295 totaling 21,618 acres; Company size: 34 employ 1,000 or more persons, 55 employ 500 to 999 persons, 734 employ 100 to 499 persons, 20,102 employ less than 100 persons; Business ownership: 25,296 women-owned, 11,324 Black-owned, 1,206 Hispanic-owned, 1,813 Asian-owned, 461 American Indian/Alaska Native-owned
Employment: 16.0% management, business, and financial, 6.2% computer, engineering, and science, 11.1% education, legal, community service, arts, and media, 7.2% healthcare practitioners, 18.0% service, 24.3% sales and office, 5.6% natural resources, construction, and maintenance, 11.5% production, transportation, and material moving
Income: Per capita: $31,303; Median household: $50,399; Average household: $73,587; Households with income of $100,000 or more: 22.4%; Poverty rate: 17.8%
Educational Attainment: High school diploma or higher: 90.1%; Bachelor's degree or higher: 35.6%; Graduate/professional degree or higher: 14.0%
Housing: Homeownership rate: 57.7%; Median home value: $143,700; Median year structure built: 1960; Homeowner vacancy rate: 1.9%; Median selected monthly owner costs: $1,346 with a mortgage, $531 without a mortgage; Median gross rent: $725 per month; Rental vacancy rate: 6.7%
Vital Statistics: Birth rate: 135.8 per 10,000 population; Death rate: 98.3 per 10,000 population; Age-adjusted cancer mortality rate: 183.6 deaths per 100,000 population
Health Insurance: 91.7% have insurance; 68.4% have private insurance; 33.8% have public insurance; 8.3% do not have insurance; 3.5% of children under 18 do not have insurance
Health Care: Physicians: 62.1 per 10,000 population; Dentists: 7.2 per 10,000 population; Hospital beds: 51.0 per 10,000 population; Hospital admissions: 1,989.1 per 10,000 population
Air Quality Index (AQI): Percent of Days: 54.4% good, 42.3% moderate, 3.3% unhealthy for sensitive individuals, 0.0% unhealthy, 0.0% very unhealthy; Annual median: 49; Annual maximum: 140
Transportation: Commute: 87.8% car, 3.7% public transportation, 2.9% walk, 4.5% work from home; Mean travel time to work: 23.2 minutes
2016 Presidential Election: 42.4% Trump, 52.7% Clinton, 3.2% Johnson, 0.9% Stein
National and State Parks: Harrison State Park; Kroger Hills State Reserve; LIttle Miami State Scenic River; Little Miami Scenic State Park; National Steamboat Monument; National Underground Railroad Freedom Center; William Howard Taft National Historic Site
Additional Information Contacts
Hamilton Government . . . . (513) 946-4400
http://www.hamilton-co.org

Hamilton County Communities

ADDYSTON (village). Covers a land area of 0.852 square miles and a water area of 0.056 square miles. Located at 39.14° N. Lat; 84.71° W. Long. Elevation is 482 feet.
History: Addyston became a town in 1871 when Matthew Addy of Cincinnati established a pipe foundry.
Population: 983; Growth (since 2000): -2.7%; Density: 1,153.9 persons per square mile; Race: 91.6% White, 4.1% Black/African American, 0.0% Asian, 0.0% American Indian/Alaska Native, 0.0% Native Hawaiian/Other Pacific Islander, 4.4% Two or more races, 2.0% Hispanic of any race; Average household size: 2.48; Median age: 36.3; Age under 18: 22.9%; Age 65 and over: 10.7%; Males per 100 females: 102.2; Marriage status: 37.9% never married, 41.3% now married, 2.7% separated, 6.9% widowed, 13.9% divorced; Foreign born: 0.5%; Speak English only: 99.1%; With disability: 14.9%; Veterans: 7.9%; Ancestry: 46.6% German, 20.1% Irish, 5.0% Italian, 4.3% English, 2.4% Welsh
Employment: 11.9% management, business, and financial, 0.4% computer, engineering, and science, 3.4% education, legal, community service, arts, and media, 0.9% healthcare practitioners, 29.1% service, 19.6% sales and office, 20.7% natural resources, construction, and maintenance, 14.0% production, transportation, and material moving
Income: Per capita: $20,093; Median household: $36,313; Average household: $48,657; Households with income of $100,000 or more: 8.6%; Poverty rate: 17.0%
Educational Attainment: High school diploma or higher: 80.2%; Bachelor's degree or higher: 9.0%; Graduate/professional degree or higher: 1.7%
Housing: Homeownership rate: 31.2%; Median home value: $85,700; Median year structure built: 1953; Homeowner vacancy rate: 3.6%; Median selected monthly owner costs: $1,121 with a mortgage, $332 without a mortgage; Median gross rent: $663 per month; Rental vacancy rate: 2.2%
Health Insurance: 82.1% have insurance; 47.5% have private insurance; 39.8% have public insurance; 17.9% do not have insurance; 5.3% of children under 18 do not have insurance
Transportation: Commute: 95.3% car, 0.4% public transportation, 1.5% walk, 2.8% work from home; Mean travel time to work: 25.1 minutes

AMBERLEY (village). Covers a land area of 3.499 square miles and a water area of 0 square miles. Located at 39.20° N. Lat; 84.43° W. Long. Elevation is 801 feet.
History: Amberley Village was incorporated as a village on April 5, 1940. It was designated a Tree City USA by the National Arbor Day Foundation.
Population: 3,595; Growth (since 2000): 5.0%; Density: 1,027.5 persons per square mile; Race: 88.4% White, 9.5% Black/African American, 0.2% Asian, 0.0% American Indian/Alaska Native, 0.0% Native Hawaiian/Other Pacific Islander, 1.3% Two or more races, 4.4% Hispanic of any race; Average household size: 2.89; Median age: 43.5; Age under 18: 29.6%; Age 65 and over: 18.9%; Males per 100 females: 92.0; Marriage status: 19.2% never married, 73.0% now married, 1.5% separated, 4.3% widowed, 3.5% divorced; Foreign born: 7.8%; Speak English only: 91.0%; With disability: 10.0%; Veterans: 8.3%; Ancestry: 26.5% German, 11.1% Russian, 10.1% Irish, 8.0% American, 7.9% Polish
Employment: 28.9% management, business, and financial, 3.8% computer, engineering, and science, 18.1% education, legal, community service, arts, and media, 14.9% healthcare practitioners, 4.7% service, 22.8% sales and office, 2.0% natural resources, construction, and maintenance, 4.8% production, transportation, and material moving
Income: Per capita: $58,054; Median household: $115,703; Average household: $166,166; Households with income of $100,000 or more: 59.6%; Poverty rate: 3.3%
Educational Attainment: High school diploma or higher: 98.4%; Bachelor's degree or higher: 68.5%; Graduate/professional degree or higher: 33.2%
Housing: Homeownership rate: 93.6%; Median home value: $305,500; Median year structure built: 1959; Homeowner vacancy rate: 2.4%; Median selected monthly owner costs: $2,097 with a mortgage, $1,018 without a

mortgage; Median gross rent: $1,165 per month; Rental vacancy rate: 0.0%
Health Insurance: 96.5% have insurance; 83.3% have private insurance; 30.7% have public insurance; 3.5% do not have insurance; 3.4% of children under 18 do not have insurance
Safety: Violent crime rate: 2.8 per 10,000 population; Property crime rate: 119.7 per 10,000 population
Transportation: Commute: 92.1% car, 0.9% public transportation, 0.9% walk, 5.5% work from home; Mean travel time to work: 23.1 minutes

ARLINGTON HEIGHTS (village). Covers a land area of 0.268 square miles and a water area of 0 square miles. Located at 39.22° N. Lat; 84.46° W. Long. Elevation is 554 feet.
Population: 923; Growth (since 2000): 2.7%; Density: 3,446.8 persons per square mile; Race: 76.9% White, 20.3% Black/African American, 0.0% Asian, 0.0% American Indian/Alaska Native, 0.0% Native Hawaiian/Other Pacific Islander, 2.8% Two or more races, 0.7% Hispanic of any race; Average household size: 2.48; Median age: 33.5; Age under 18: 27.7%; Age 65 and over: 7.6%; Males per 100 females: 99.2; Marriage status: 37.0% never married, 44.8% now married, 1.7% separated, 4.5% widowed, 13.7% divorced; Foreign born: 1.0%; Speak English only: 96.6%; With disability: 12.7%; Veterans: 3.7%; Ancestry: 18.4% Irish, 16.5% German, 5.5% English, 5.4% American, 3.8% Arab
Employment: 7.6% management, business, and financial, 8.3% computer, engineering, and science, 1.2% education, legal, community service, arts, and media, 2.1% healthcare practitioners, 21.0% service, 24.9% sales and office, 8.5% natural resources, construction, and maintenance, 26.3% production, transportation, and material moving
Income: Per capita: $19,371; Median household: $40,139; Average household: $47,650; Households with income of $100,000 or more: 4.8%; Poverty rate: 15.9%
Educational Attainment: High school diploma or higher: 84.7%; Bachelor's degree or higher: 5.3%; Graduate/professional degree or higher: 0.8%
Housing: Homeownership rate: 37.6%; Median home value: $73,500; Median year structure built: Before 1940; Homeowner vacancy rate: 4.1%; Median selected monthly owner costs: $1,134 with a mortgage, $442 without a mortgage; Median gross rent: $903 per month; Rental vacancy rate: 7.9%
Health Insurance: 90.4% have insurance; 57.1% have private insurance; 39.0% have public insurance; 9.6% do not have insurance; 5.9% of children under 18 do not have insurance
Transportation: Commute: 92.6% car, 4.6% public transportation, 0.7% walk, 0.5% work from home; Mean travel time to work: 20.6 minutes

BLUE ASH (city). Covers a land area of 7.580 square miles and a water area of 0.014 square miles. Located at 39.25° N. Lat; 84.39° W. Long. Elevation is 846 feet.
History: The Carpenter's Run Baptist Church (1797-1828) served the earliest settlers of Blue Ash. Built of logs from the blue ash tree, the church gave the community its name.
Population: 12,154; Growth (since 2000): -2.9%; Density: 1,603.5 persons per square mile; Race: 78.3% White, 6.9% Black/African American, 11.2% Asian, 0.0% American Indian/Alaska Native, 0.1% Native Hawaiian/Other Pacific Islander, 2.3% Two or more races, 3.5% Hispanic of any race; Average household size: 2.34; Median age: 42.7; Age under 18: 20.3%; Age 65 and over: 18.0%; Males per 100 females: 96.0; Marriage status: 24.3% never married, 59.6% now married, 0.5% separated, 5.7% widowed, 10.4% divorced; Foreign born: 14.1%; Speak English only: 85.0%; With disability: 10.6%; Veterans: 6.7%; Ancestry: 27.7% German, 14.4% Irish, 8.5% English, 6.5% American, 3.6% Italian
Employment: 19.6% management, business, and financial, 11.6% computer, engineering, and science, 14.2% education, legal, community service, arts, and media, 9.4% healthcare practitioners, 13.5% service, 20.3% sales and office, 3.1% natural resources, construction, and maintenance, 8.2% production, transportation, and material moving
Income: Per capita: $44,374; Median household: $72,628; Average household: $103,655; Households with income of $100,000 or more: 35.4%; Poverty rate: 5.6%
Educational Attainment: High school diploma or higher: 95.7%; Bachelor's degree or higher: 55.4%; Graduate/professional degree or higher: 26.2%

Four-year College(s)
University of Cincinnati-Blue Ash College (Public)
Fall 2016 Enrollment: 4,818 . . . . (513) 745-5600
2016-17 Tuition: In-state $6,010; Out-of-state $14,808
Housing: Homeownership rate: 71.8%; Median home value: $233,200; Median year structure built: 1979; Homeowner vacancy rate: 2.5%; Median selected monthly owner costs: $1,542 with a mortgage, $628 without a mortgage; Median gross rent: $1,054 per month; Rental vacancy rate: 2.2%
Health Insurance: 95.9% have insurance; 84.4% have private insurance; 24.3% have public insurance; 4.1% do not have insurance; 0.9% of children under 18 do not have insurance
Safety: Violent crime rate: 9.0 per 10,000 population; Property crime rate: 263.0 per 10,000 population
Transportation: Commute: 92.7% car, 0.7% public transportation, 0.9% walk, 4.9% work from home; Mean travel time to work: 21.2 minutes
Additional Information Contacts
City of Blue Ash. . . . . (513) 745-8500
http://www.blueash.com

BLUE JAY (CDP). Covers a land area of 4.373 square miles and a water area of 0.035 square miles. Located at 39.24° N. Lat; 84.74° W. Long. Elevation is 781 feet.
Population: 1,225; Growth (since 2000): n/a; Density: 280.1 persons per square mile; Race: 95.8% White, 4.2% Black/African American, 0.0% Asian, 0.0% American Indian/Alaska Native, 0.0% Native Hawaiian/Other Pacific Islander, 0.0% Two or more races, 0.0% Hispanic of any race; Average household size: 2.72; Median age: 44.1; Age under 18: 20.7%; Age 65 and over: 22.7%; Males per 100 females: 103.6; Marriage status: 23.2% never married, 69.8% now married, 0.0% separated, 2.6% widowed, 4.3% divorced; Foreign born: 0.0%; Speak English only: 100.0%; With disability: 8.5%; Veterans: 10.4%; Ancestry: 40.7% German, 34.6% Irish, 12.5% English, 8.0% American, 2.0% Scottish
Employment: 11.7% management, business, and financial, 11.2% computer, engineering, and science, 7.8% education, legal, community service, arts, and media, 9.8% healthcare practitioners, 14.5% service, 26.5% sales and office, 7.3% natural resources, construction, and maintenance, 11.2% production, transportation, and material moving
Income: Per capita: $34,103; Median household: $99,107; Average household: $91,517; Households with income of $100,000 or more: 48.8%; Poverty rate: n/a
Educational Attainment: High school diploma or higher: 90.0%; Bachelor's degree or higher: 26.3%; Graduate/professional degree or higher: 4.7%
Housing: Homeownership rate: 90.7%; Median home value: $202,200; Median year structure built: 1979; Homeowner vacancy rate: 0.0%; Median selected monthly owner costs: $1,828 with a mortgage, $542 without a mortgage; Median gross rent: n/a per month; Rental vacancy rate: 0.0%
Health Insurance: 95.6% have insurance; 82.0% have private insurance; 24.6% have public insurance; 4.4% do not have insurance; 4.3% of children under 18 do not have insurance
Transportation: Commute: 85.5% car, 0.0% public transportation, 0.0% walk, 13.7% work from home; Mean travel time to work: 30.2 minutes

BRECON (CDP). Covers a land area of 0.560 square miles and a water area of <.001 square miles. Located at 39.28° N. Lat; 84.35° W. Long. Elevation is 869 feet.
Population: 309; Growth (since 2000): n/a; Density: 552.1 persons per square mile; Race: 44.0% White, 0.0% Black/African American, 0.0% Asian, 0.0% American Indian/Alaska Native, 0.0% Native Hawaiian/Other Pacific Islander, 0.0% Two or more races, 56.0% Hispanic of any race; Average household size: 2.36; Median age: 27.7; Age under 18: 27.5%; Age 65 and over: 32.7%; Males per 100 females: 101.7; Marriage status: 8.0% never married, 46.4% now married, 7.1% separated, 29.0% widowed, 16.5% divorced; Foreign born: 28.5%; Speak English only: 52.3%; With disability: 17.5%; Veterans: 0.0%; Ancestry: 17.2% German, 5.8% Italian
Employment: 0.0% management, business, and financial, 0.0% computer, engineering, and science, 0.0% education, legal, community service, arts, and media, 0.0% healthcare practitioners, 100.0% service, 0.0% sales and office, 0.0% natural resources, construction, and maintenance, 0.0% production, transportation, and material moving
Income: Per capita: $7,316; Median household: $15,859; Average household: $16,724; Households with income of $100,000 or more: n/a; Poverty rate: 77.7%

Educational Attainment: High school diploma or higher: 46.0%; Bachelor's degree or higher: n/a; Graduate/professional degree or higher: n/a
Housing: Homeownership rate: 38.2%; Median home value: n/a; Median year structure built: 1992; Homeowner vacancy rate: 0.0%; Median selected monthly owner costs: n/a with a mortgage, n/a without a mortgage; Median gross rent: n/a per month; Rental vacancy rate: 0.0%
Health Insurance: 60.2% have insurance; 0.0% have private insurance; 60.2% have public insurance; 39.8% do not have insurance; 0.0% of children under 18 do not have insurance
Transportation: Commute: 65.3% car, 0.0% public transportation, 0.0% walk, 0.0% work from home; Mean travel time to work: 0.0 minutes

BRIDGETOWN (CDP). Covers a land area of 4.323 square miles and a water area of 0 square miles. Located at 39.16° N. Lat; 84.64° W. Long. Elevation is 899 feet.
Population: 14,150; Growth (since 2000): n/a; Density: 3,273.6 persons per square mile; Race: 96.9% White, 1.5% Black/African American, 0.2% Asian, 0.0% American Indian/Alaska Native, 0.0% Native Hawaiian/Other Pacific Islander, 1.3% Two or more races, 0.2% Hispanic of any race; Average household size: 2.44; Median age: 41.6; Age under 18: 22.7%; Age 65 and over: 20.8%; Males per 100 females: 90.0; Marriage status: 29.9% never married, 48.8% now married, 1.0% separated, 10.7% widowed, 10.6% divorced; Foreign born: 1.0%; Speak English only: 97.6%; With disability: 13.3%; Veterans: 10.0%; Ancestry: 50.6% German, 22.4% Irish, 7.1% English, 6.8% Italian, 6.7% American
Employment: 12.8% management, business, and financial, 3.6% computer, engineering, and science, 6.5% education, legal, community service, arts, and media, 8.6% healthcare practitioners, 18.9% service, 30.0% sales and office, 7.7% natural resources, construction, and maintenance, 11.9% production, transportation, and material moving
Income: Per capita: $28,891; Median household: $60,318; Average household: $69,572; Households with income of $100,000 or more: 17.8%; Poverty rate: 8.4%
Educational Attainment: High school diploma or higher: 92.4%; Bachelor's degree or higher: 23.1%; Graduate/professional degree or higher: 8.5%
Housing: Homeownership rate: 80.4%; Median home value: $119,200; Median year structure built: 1960; Homeowner vacancy rate: 2.3%; Median selected monthly owner costs: $1,188 with a mortgage, $455 without a mortgage; Median gross rent: $785 per month; Rental vacancy rate: 2.7%
Health Insurance: 94.8% have insurance; 78.6% have private insurance; 32.5% have public insurance; 5.2% do not have insurance; 5.4% of children under 18 do not have insurance
Transportation: Commute: 95.2% car, 0.7% public transportation, 1.0% walk, 2.2% work from home; Mean travel time to work: 23.7 minutes

CAMP DENNISON (CDP). Covers a land area of 0.401 square miles and a water area of 0 square miles. Located at 39.20° N. Lat; 84.29° W. Long. Elevation is 574 feet.
Population: 255; Growth (since 2000): n/a; Density: 636.3 persons per square mile; Race: 71.0% White, 29.0% Black/African American, 0.0% Asian, 0.0% American Indian/Alaska Native, 0.0% Native Hawaiian/Other Pacific Islander, 0.0% Two or more races, 0.0% Hispanic of any race; Average household size: 2.11; Median age: 60.6; Age under 18: 7.5%; Age 65 and over: 30.6%; Males per 100 females: 107.2; Marriage status: 25.4% never married, 47.9% now married, 0.0% separated, 5.8% widowed, 20.8% divorced; Foreign born: 0.0%; Speak English only: 100.0%; With disability: 21.6%; Veterans: 9.7%; Ancestry: 30.6% German, 12.5% American, 10.6% English, 9.0% Irish, 4.7% European
Employment: 9.0% management, business, and financial, 0.0% computer, engineering, and science, 9.0% education, legal, community service, arts, and media, 12.3% healthcare practitioners, 22.1% service, 18.0% sales and office, 12.3% natural resources, construction, and maintenance, 17.2% production, transportation, and material moving
Income: Per capita: $40,031; Median household: $66,838; Average household: $83,521; Households with income of $100,000 or more: 20.7%; Poverty rate: 15.8%
Educational Attainment: High school diploma or higher: 85.2%; Bachelor's degree or higher: 31.5%; Graduate/professional degree or higher: 23.1%
Housing: Homeownership rate: 96.7%; Median home value: $170,500; Median year structure built: 1950; Homeowner vacancy rate: 0.0%; Median selected monthly owner costs: $1,195 with a mortgage, $277 without a mortgage; Median gross rent: n/a per month; Rental vacancy rate: 0.0%
Health Insurance: 91.8% have insurance; 72.9% have private insurance; 38.8% have public insurance; 8.2% do not have insurance; 0.0% of children under 18 do not have insurance
Transportation: Commute: 90.8% car, 4.2% public transportation, 0.0% walk, 5.0% work from home; Mean travel time to work: 19.7 minutes

CHERRY GROVE (CDP). Covers a land area of 1.132 square miles and a water area of 0 square miles. Located at 39.08° N. Lat; 84.32° W. Long. Elevation is 876 feet.
Population: 4,539; Growth (since 2000): -0.4%; Density: 4,008.0 persons per square mile; Race: 93.4% White, 0.3% Black/African American, 4.2% Asian, 0.0% American Indian/Alaska Native, 0.0% Native Hawaiian/Other Pacific Islander, 1.8% Two or more races, 2.4% Hispanic of any race; Average household size: 2.98; Median age: 36.4; Age under 18: 28.1%; Age 65 and over: 12.4%; Males per 100 females: 91.8; Marriage status: 26.9% never married, 64.3% now married, 1.1% separated, 4.9% widowed, 3.8% divorced; Foreign born: 5.6%; Speak English only: 94.9%; With disability: 8.3%; Veterans: 8.6%; Ancestry: 43.6% German, 14.2% Irish, 11.7% English, 9.8% American, 4.9% Italian
Employment: 12.4% management, business, and financial, 9.7% computer, engineering, and science, 14.2% education, legal, community service, arts, and media, 10.8% healthcare practitioners, 13.2% service, 27.6% sales and office, 6.5% natural resources, construction, and maintenance, 5.7% production, transportation, and material moving
Income: Per capita: $31,649; Median household: $78,173; Average household: $93,087; Households with income of $100,000 or more: 39.2%; Poverty rate: 4.7%
Educational Attainment: High school diploma or higher: 97.7%; Bachelor's degree or higher: 43.1%; Graduate/professional degree or higher: 11.5%
Housing: Homeownership rate: 92.0%; Median home value: $168,700; Median year structure built: 1972; Homeowner vacancy rate: 3.0%; Median selected monthly owner costs: $1,466 with a mortgage, $486 without a mortgage; Median gross rent: $1,750 per month; Rental vacancy rate: 0.0%
Health Insurance: 96.9% have insurance; 85.7% have private insurance; 26.6% have public insurance; 3.1% do not have insurance; 0.0% of children under 18 do not have insurance
Transportation: Commute: 91.2% car, 0.7% public transportation, 0.5% walk, 7.6% work from home; Mean travel time to work: 26.7 minutes

CHEVIOT (city). Covers a land area of 1.168 square miles and a water area of <.001 square miles. Located at 39.16° N. Lat; 84.61° W. Long. Elevation is 909 feet.
History: Settled early 1800s; incorporated 1904.
Population: 8,318; Growth (since 2000): -7.7%; Density: 7,123.2 persons per square mile; Race: 83.2% White, 13.6% Black/African American, 0.2% Asian, 0.1% American Indian/Alaska Native, 0.0% Native Hawaiian/Other Pacific Islander, 2.2% Two or more races, 1.9% Hispanic of any race; Average household size: 2.15; Median age: 36.0; Age under 18: 20.9%; Age 65 and over: 13.3%; Males per 100 females: 92.9; Marriage status: 39.3% never married, 41.8% now married, 5.0% separated, 5.3% widowed, 13.6% divorced; Foreign born: 3.3%; Speak English only: 93.7%; With disability: 20.4%; Veterans: 4.6%; Ancestry: 41.3% German, 22.2% Irish, 6.9% Italian, 3.7% English, 3.3% American
Employment: 10.5% management, business, and financial, 4.2% computer, engineering, and science, 6.1% education, legal, community service, arts, and media, 6.6% healthcare practitioners, 23.6% service, 27.4% sales and office, 8.3% natural resources, construction, and maintenance, 13.3% production, transportation, and material moving
Income: Per capita: $22,572; Median household: $41,289; Average household: $47,899; Households with income of $100,000 or more: 11.3%; Poverty rate: 20.7%
Educational Attainment: High school diploma or higher: 87.5%; Bachelor's degree or higher: 22.6%; Graduate/professional degree or higher: 8.1%
Housing: Homeownership rate: 47.8%; Median home value: $90,100; Median year structure built: 1942; Homeowner vacancy rate: 1.9%; Median selected monthly owner costs: $1,100 with a mortgage, $452 without a mortgage; Median gross rent: $655 per month; Rental vacancy rate: 7.9%
Health Insurance: 90.9% have insurance; 63.6% have private insurance; 38.0% have public insurance; 9.1% do not have insurance; 4.1% of children under 18 do not have insurance
Safety: Violent crime rate: 36.2 per 10,000 population; Property crime rate: 306.7 per 10,000 population

Transportation: Commute: 93.8% car, 3.6% public transportation, 1.2% walk, 0.6% work from home; Mean travel time to work: 26.0 minutes
Additional Information Contacts
City of Cheviot. . . . . (513) 661-2700
http://www.cheviot.org

CINCINNATI (city). County seat. Covers a land area of 77.942 square miles and a water area of 1.604 square miles. Located at 39.14° N. Lat; 84.51° W. Long. Elevation is 627 feet.
History: Cincinnati was settled at an Ohio River crossroads in 1788 when developers platted a village that they named Losantiville. In 1790 the name was changed to Cincinnati by General Arthur St. Clair, Governor of the Northwest Territory, in honor of the Revolutionary Officers' Society. The Ohio River was the avenue down which settlers came to find space to establish farms, and Cincinnati became the center of commerce. Immigrants from Germany and Ireland joined other Europeans who came straight to Cincinnati. Steamboat travel on the Ohio River and the opening of the Miami & Erie Canal spurred trading. When Charles Dickens visited Cincinnati in 1842, he described it as "a place that commends itself... favorably and pleasantly to a stranger." The Civil War tore Cincinnati apart. Its sympathies were with the North, but its trade was with the South, and there was great rejoicing when the war ended.
Population: 298,011; Growth (since 2000): -10.0%; Density: 3,823.5 persons per square mile; Race: 50.7% White, 43.1% Black/African American, 1.8% Asian, 0.2% American Indian/Alaska Native, 0.0% Native Hawaiian/Other Pacific Islander, 3.1% Two or more races, 3.2% Hispanic of any race; Average household size: 2.12; Median age: 32.3; Age under 18: 22.1%; Age 65 and over: 11.6%; Males per 100 females: 92.5; Marriage status: 51.6% never married, 30.5% now married, 2.7% separated, 5.5% widowed, 12.5% divorced; Foreign born: 5.1%; Speak English only: 92.4%; With disability: 14.1%; Veterans: 5.9%; Ancestry: 19.5% German, 10.4% Irish, 5.0% English, 3.7% Italian, 3.7% American
Employment: 14.3% management, business, and financial, 6.5% computer, engineering, and science, 12.5% education, legal, community service, arts, and media, 6.4% healthcare practitioners, 21.4% service, 22.2% sales and office, 4.7% natural resources, construction, and maintenance, 12.0% production, transportation, and material moving
Income: Per capita: $26,152; Median household: $34,629; Average household: $55,931; Households with income of $100,000 or more: 13.8%; Poverty rate: 29.9%
Educational Attainment: High school diploma or higher: 86.2%; Bachelor's degree or higher: 33.8%; Graduate/professional degree or higher: 14.1%

School District(s)

Accelerated Achievement Academy Of Cincinnati (09-12)
2015-16 Enrollment: 99. . . . . (513) 246-4102
Alliance Academy of Cincinnati (KG-08)
2015-16 Enrollment: 463. . . . . (513) 751-5555
Cincinnati City (PK-12)
2015-16 Enrollment: 34,227 . . . . (513) 363-0000
Cincinnati College Preparatory Academy (KG-12)
2015-16 Enrollment: 994. . . . . (513) 684-0777
Cincinnati Leadership Academy
2015-16 Enrollment: n/a . . . . (513) 351-5737
Cincinnati Speech & Reading Intervention Center (KG-08)
2015-16 Enrollment: 272. . . . . (513) 651-9624
Deer Park Community City (KG-12)
2015-16 Enrollment: 1,280 . . . . (513) 891-0222
Dohn Community (09-12)
2015-16 Enrollment: 373. . . . . (513) 281-6100
Finneytown Local (KG-12)
2015-16 Enrollment: 1,436 . . . . (513) 728-3700
Forest Hills Local (PK-12)
2015-16 Enrollment: 7,356 . . . . (513) 231-3600
Great Oaks Career Campuses (05-12)
2015-16 Enrollment: n/a . . . . (513) 771-8840
Hamilton Cnty Math & Science (KG-08)
2015-16 Enrollment: 643. . . . . (513) 728-8620
Horizon Science Academy-Cincinnati (KG-08)
2015-16 Enrollment: 357. . . . . (513) 242-0099
Impact Academy Cincinnati (KG-05)
2015-16 Enrollment: 124. . . . . (513) 751-2000
Indian Hill Exempted Village (PK-12)
2015-16 Enrollment: 1,945 . . . . (513) 272-4500
King Academy Community School (KG-08)
2015-16 Enrollment: 152. . . . . (513) 421-7519
Lakota Local (PK-12)
2015-16 Enrollment: 15,937 . . . . (513) 874-5505
Life Skills Center of Hamilton County
2015-16 Enrollment: n/a . . . . (513) 821-6695
Life Skills Ctr of Cincinnati (09-12)
2015-16 Enrollment: 148. . . . . (513) 475-0222
Lighthouse Community Sch Inc (07-12)
2015-16 Enrollment: 66. . . . . (513) 561-7888
Lockland Local (PK-12)
2015-16 Enrollment: 520. . . . . (513) 563-5000
Madeira City (PK-12)
2015-16 Enrollment: 1,496 . . . . (513) 985-6070
Madisonville Smart Elementary (KG-06)
2015-16 Enrollment: 239. . . . . (513) 241-1101
Mariemont City (KG-12)
2015-16 Enrollment: 1,757 . . . . (513) 272-7500
Mount Auburn International Academy (KG-12)
2015-16 Enrollment: 561. . . . . (513) 241-5500
Mt Healthy City (PK-12)
2015-16 Enrollment: 3,368 . . . . (513) 729-0077
Mt. Healthy Preparatory and Fitness Academy (KG-08)
2015-16 Enrollment: 299. . . . . (513) 587-6280
New Richmond Exempted Village (PK-12)
2015-16 Enrollment: 2,407 . . . . (513) 553-2616
North College Hill City (PK-12)
2015-16 Enrollment: 1,633 . . . . (513) 931-8181
Northwest Local (PK-12)
2015-16 Enrollment: 8,944 . . . . (513) 923-1000
Oak Hills Local (PK-12)
2015-16 Enrollment: 7,674 . . . . (513) 574-3200
Orion Academy (KG-08)
2015-16 Enrollment: 552. . . . . (513) 251-6000
Phoenix Community Learning Ctr (KG-08)
2015-16 Enrollment: 408. . . . . (513) 351-5801
Princeton City (PK-12)
2015-16 Enrollment: 5,606 . . . . (513) 864-1000
Riverside Academy (KG-08)
2015-16 Enrollment: 260. . . . . (513) 921-7777
St Bernard-elmwood Place City (PK-12)
2015-16 Enrollment: 999. . . . . (513) 482-7121
Summit Academy Community School - Cincinnati (KG-08)
2015-16 Enrollment: 122. . . . . (513) 321-0561
Summit Academy Transition High School-Cincinnati (09-12)
2015-16 Enrollment: 84. . . . . (513) 541-4000
Sycamore Community City (PK-12)
2015-16 Enrollment: 5,280 . . . . (513) 686-1700
T.c.p. World Academy (KG-06)
2015-16 Enrollment: 535. . . . . (513) 531-9500
Three Rivers Local (PK-12)
2015-16 Enrollment: 1,973 . . . . (877) 644-6338
West Clermont Local (PK-12)
2015-16 Enrollment: 8,027 . . . . (513) 943-5000
Winton Woods City (PK-12)
2015-16 Enrollment: 3,517 . . . . (513) 619-2300

Four-year College(s)

Art Academy of Cincinnati (Private, Not-for-profit)
Fall 2016 Enrollment: 207 . . . . (513) 562-6262
2016-17 Tuition: In-state $29,752; Out-of-state $29,752
Athenaeum of Ohio (Private, Not-for-profit, Roman Catholic)
Fall 2016 Enrollment: 188 . . . . (513) 231-2223
Brown Mackie College-Cincinnati (Private, For-profit)
Fall 2016 Enrollment: 249 . . . . (513) 771-2424
Cincinnati Christian University (Private, Not-for-profit, Christian Churches and Churches of Christ)
Fall 2016 Enrollment: 887 . . . . (513) 244-8100
2016-17 Tuition: In-state $16,414; Out-of-state $16,414
Cincinnati College of Mortuary Science (Private, Not-for-profit)
Fall 2016 Enrollment: 128 . . . . (513) 761-2020
2016-17 Tuition: In-state $20,025; Out-of-state $20,025
Gods Bible School and College (Private, Not-for-profit, Other Protestant)
Fall 2016 Enrollment: 294 . . . . (513) 721-7944
2016-17 Tuition: In-state $7,040; Out-of-state $7,040

Good Samaritan College of Nursing and Health Science (Private, Not-for-profit, Roman Catholic)
Fall 2016 Enrollment: 403 . . . . (513) 862-2631
2016-17 Tuition: In-state $15,530; Out-of-state $15,530
Mount Saint Joseph University (Private, Not-for-profit, Roman Catholic)
Fall 2016 Enrollment: 2,045 . . . . (513) 244-4200
2016-17 Tuition: In-state $28,300; Out-of-state $28,300
The Art Institute of Cincinnati-AIC College of Design (Private, For-profit)
Fall 2016 Enrollment: 31 . . . . (513) 751-1206
2016-17 Tuition: In-state $23,341; Out-of-state $23,341
The Art Institute of Ohio-Cincinnati (Private, For-profit)
Fall 2016 Enrollment: 98 . . . . (513) 833-2400
The Christ College of Nursing and Health Sciences (Private, Not-for-profit)
Fall 2016 Enrollment: 852 . . . . (513) 585-0032
2016-17 Tuition: In-state $15,882; Out-of-state $15,882
Union Institute & University (Private, Not-for-profit)
Fall 2016 Enrollment: 1,133 . . . . (800) 861-6400
2016-17 Tuition: In-state $12,416; Out-of-state $12,416
University of Cincinnati-Main Campus (Public)
Fall 2016 Enrollment: 36,596 . . . . (513) 556-6000
2016-17 Tuition: In-state $11,000; Out-of-state $26,334
Xavier University (Private, Not-for-profit, Roman Catholic)
Fall 2016 Enrollment: 6,509 . . . . (513) 745-3000
2016-17 Tuition: In-state $36,150; Out-of-state $36,150

Two-year College(s)

American National University-Cincinnati (Private, For-profit)
Fall 2016 Enrollment: 38 . . . . (513) 761-1291
2016-17 Tuition: In-state $14,886; Out-of-state $14,886
Antonelli College-Cincinnati (Private, For-profit)
Fall 2016 Enrollment: 79 . . . . (513) 241-4338
2016-17 Tuition: In-state $15,980; Out-of-state $15,980
Cincinnati State Technical and Community College (Public)
Fall 2016 Enrollment: 9,056 . . . . (513) 569-1500
2016-17 Tuition: In-state $3,825; Out-of-state $7,393
Fortis College-Cincinnati (Private, For-profit)
Fall 2016 Enrollment: 409 . . . . (513) 771-2795
2016-17 Tuition: In-state $15,124; Out-of-state $15,124
Galen College of Nursing-Cincinnati (Private, For-profit)
Fall 2016 Enrollment: 407 . . . . (513) 475-3600
Moler Hollywood Beauty Academy (Private, For-profit)
Fall 2016 Enrollment: 93 . . . . (513) 621-5262
Western Hills School of Beauty and Hair Design (Private, For-profit)
Fall 2016 Enrollment: 180 . . . . (513) 574-3818

Vocational/Technical School(s)

Elite Welding Academy LLC (Private, For-profit)
Fall 2016 Enrollment: 79 . . . . (513) 874-1410
2016-17 Tuition: $11,860
Empire Beauty School-Cincinnati (Private, For-profit)
Fall 2016 Enrollment: 164 . . . . (800) 920-4593
2016-17 Tuition: $17,070
Great Oaks Career Campuses (Public)
Fall 2016 Enrollment: 336 . . . . (513) 771-8881
2016-17 Tuition: $7,250
Ohio Media School-Cincinnati (Private, For-profit)
Fall 2016 Enrollment: 85 . . . . (513) 271-6060
2016-17 Tuition: $15,705
Paul Mitchell the School-Cincinnati (Private, For-profit)
Fall 2016 Enrollment: 233 . . . . (513) 769-7699
2016-17 Tuition: $15,970
Ross Medical Education Center-Cincinnati (Private, For-profit)
Fall 2016 Enrollment: 111 . . . . (513) 851-8500
2016-17 Tuition: $15,740
Summit Salon Academy-Cincinnati (Private, For-profit)
Fall 2016 Enrollment: n/a . . . . (859) 263-1075
2016-17 Tuition: $14,500

Housing: Homeownership rate: 37.7%; Median home value: $120,300; Median year structure built: 1949; Homeowner vacancy rate: 2.7%; Median selected monthly owner costs: $1,239 with a mortgage, $511 without a mortgage; Median gross rent: $662 per month; Rental vacancy rate: 7.5%
Health Insurance: 89.1% have insurance; 57.4% have private insurance; 39.7% have public insurance; 10.9% do not have insurance; 4.2% of children under 18 do not have insurance
Hospitals: Bethesda North (314 beds); Christ Hospital; Cincinnati VA Medical Center (378 beds); Good Samaritan Hospital (700 beds); Jewish Hospital; Mercy Health - West Hospital (269 beds); Mercy Hospital Anderson (186 beds); Trihealth Evendale Hospital; University of Cincinnati Medical Center
Safety: Violent crime rate: 91.0 per 10,000 population; Property crime rate: 514.7 per 10,000 population
Newspapers: CIN Weekly (weekly circulation 65,000); Cincinnati Enquirer (daily circulation 198,000); City Beat (weekly circulation 53,000); Community Press (weekly circulation 72,000); Pulse (weekly circulation 18,000); Valley Courier (weekly circulation 2,200)
Transportation: Commute: 80.3% car, 7.9% public transportation, 5.7% walk, 4.4% work from home; Mean travel time to work: 22.6 minutes; Amtrak: Train service available.
Airports: Cincinnati Municipal Airport Lunken Field (general aviation); Cincinnati/Northern Kentucky International (primary service/medium hub)
Additional Information Contacts
City of Cincinnati . . . . (513) 591-6000
http://www.cincinnati-oh.gov

CLEVES (village). Covers a land area of 1.583 square miles and a water area of 0.003 square miles. Located at 39.16° N. Lat; 84.74° W. Long. Elevation is 499 feet.
History: Cleves was platted in 1818 and named for John Cleves Symmes, a pioneer who had founded North Bend.
Population: 3,371; Growth (since 2000): 20.8%; Density: 2,129.0 persons per square mile; Race: 97.4% White, 0.3% Black/African American, 0.0% Asian, 0.7% American Indian/Alaska Native, 0.0% Native Hawaiian/Other Pacific Islander, 1.5% Two or more races, 1.6% Hispanic of any race; Average household size: 2.98; Median age: 34.0; Age under 18: 32.7%; Age 65 and over: 8.1%; Males per 100 females: 101.2; Marriage status: 28.6% never married, 55.8% now married, 1.8% separated, 3.3% widowed, 12.4% divorced; Foreign born: 0.8%; Speak English only: 98.8%; With disability: 7.7%; Veterans: 9.2%; Ancestry: 45.6% German, 18.7% Irish, 6.9% English, 6.3% Italian, 5.0% American
Employment: 15.6% management, business, and financial, 4.8% computer, engineering, and science, 8.9% education, legal, community service, arts, and media, 3.0% healthcare practitioners, 18.6% service, 25.0% sales and office, 12.8% natural resources, construction, and maintenance, 11.2% production, transportation, and material moving
Income: Per capita: $26,883; Median household: $64,848; Average household: $79,398; Households with income of $100,000 or more: 28.6%; Poverty rate: 11.7%
Educational Attainment: High school diploma or higher: 90.7%; Bachelor's degree or higher: 25.7%; Graduate/professional degree or higher: 7.8%

School District(s)

Three Rivers Local (PK-12)
2015-16 Enrollment: 1,973 . . . . (877) 644-6338
Housing: Homeownership rate: 68.3%; Median home value: $142,400; Median year structure built: 1966; Homeowner vacancy rate: 0.5%; Median selected monthly owner costs: $1,355 with a mortgage, $427 without a mortgage; Median gross rent: $713 per month; Rental vacancy rate: 8.7%
Health Insurance: 90.9% have insurance; 69.6% have private insurance; 30.7% have public insurance; 9.1% do not have insurance; 0.5% of children under 18 do not have insurance
Transportation: Commute: 95.3% car, 0.0% public transportation, 0.7% walk, 2.1% work from home; Mean travel time to work: 26.0 minutes
Additional Information Contacts
Village of Cleves . . . . (513) 941-5127
http://www.cleves.org

COLDSTREAM (CDP). Covers a land area of 2.766 square miles and a water area of 0.084 square miles. Located at 39.04° N. Lat; 84.34° W. Long.
Population: 1,236; Growth (since 2000): n/a; Density: 446.9 persons per square mile; Race: 99.3% White, 0.0% Black/African American, 0.5% Asian, 0.2% American Indian/Alaska Native, 0.0% Native Hawaiian/Other Pacific Islander, 0.0% Two or more races, 0.6% Hispanic of any race; Average household size: 2.82; Median age: 47.7; Age under 18: 23.5%; Age 65 and over: 21.6%; Males per 100 females: 99.8; Marriage status: 18.0% never married, 73.7% now married, 0.0% separated, 3.3% widowed, 4.9% divorced; Foreign born: 1.7%; Speak English only: 96.5%; With disability: 4.0%; Veterans: 4.9%; Ancestry: 39.2% German, 26.0% Irish, 11.4% English, 10.3% American, 9.1% Italian
Employment: 34.0% management, business, and financial, 1.3% computer, engineering, and science, 13.2% education, legal, community service, arts, and media, 18.2% healthcare practitioners, 7.5% service,

22.4% sales and office, 2.0% natural resources, construction, and maintenance, 1.3% production, transportation, and material moving
Income: Per capita: $83,149; Median household: $151,765; Average household: $235,395; Households with income of $100,000 or more: 70.1%; Poverty rate: 7.9%
Educational Attainment: High school diploma or higher: 98.2%; Bachelor's degree or higher: 72.2%; Graduate/professional degree or higher: 26.8%
Housing: Homeownership rate: 98.9%; Median home value: $572,900; Median year structure built: 1983; Homeowner vacancy rate: 5.5%; Median selected monthly owner costs: $3,216 with a mortgage, $1,450 without a mortgage; Median gross rent: n/a per month; Rental vacancy rate: 0.0%
Health Insurance: 96.8% have insurance; 86.6% have private insurance; 23.1% have public insurance; 3.2% do not have insurance; 0.0% of children under 18 do not have insurance
Transportation: Commute: 89.4% car, 0.0% public transportation, 1.3% walk, 9.3% work from home; Mean travel time to work: 23.0 minutes

CONCORDE HILLS (CDP). Covers a land area of 0.383 square miles and a water area of 0 square miles. Located at 39.21° N. Lat; 84.36° W. Long.
Population: 681; Growth (since 2000): n/a; Density: 1,776.3 persons per square mile; Race: 95.2% White, 0.0% Black/African American, 4.8% Asian, 0.0% American Indian/Alaska Native, 0.0% Native Hawaiian/Other Pacific Islander, 0.0% Two or more races, 0.0% Hispanic of any race; Average household size: 2.63; Median age: 54.0; Age under 18: 16.6%; Age 65 and over: 26.9%; Males per 100 females: 83.7; Marriage status: 31.8% never married, 57.4% now married, 0.0% separated, 5.4% widowed, 5.4% divorced; Foreign born: 3.8%; Speak English only: 96.1%; With disability: 18.0%; Veterans: 8.6%; Ancestry: 37.7% German, 19.2% Irish, 12.2% American, 11.6% English, 7.8% Italian
Employment: 31.7% management, business, and financial, 12.7% computer, engineering, and science, 19.7% education, legal, community service, arts, and media, 24.7% healthcare practitioners, 4.7% service, 6.7% sales and office, 0.0% natural resources, construction, and maintenance, 0.0% production, transportation, and material moving
Income: Per capita: $91,283; Median household: $144,036; Average household: $239,775; Households with income of $100,000 or more: 79.4%; Poverty rate: n/a
Educational Attainment: High school diploma or higher: 100.0%; Bachelor's degree or higher: 82.3%; Graduate/professional degree or higher: 46.5%
Housing: Homeownership rate: 76.7%; Median home value: $417,600; Median year structure built: 1963; Homeowner vacancy rate: 0.0%; Median selected monthly owner costs: $2,648 with a mortgage, $950 without a mortgage; Median gross rent: n/a per month; Rental vacancy rate: 0.0%
Health Insurance: 97.0% have insurance; 91.4% have private insurance; 27.8% have public insurance; 3.0% do not have insurance; 0.0% of children under 18 do not have insurance
Transportation: Commute: 100.0% car, 0.0% public transportation, 0.0% walk, 0.0% work from home; Mean travel time to work: 19.6 minutes

COVEDALE (CDP). Covers a land area of 2.800 square miles and a water area of 0 square miles. Located at 39.13° N. Lat; 84.64° W. Long. Elevation is 886 feet.
Population: 6,195; Growth (since 2000): -2.6%; Density: 2,212.4 persons per square mile; Race: 91.9% White, 4.6% Black/African American, 1.6% Asian, 0.0% American Indian/Alaska Native, 0.0% Native Hawaiian/Other Pacific Islander, 1.9% Two or more races, 0.7% Hispanic of any race; Average household size: 2.55; Median age: 42.1; Age under 18: 23.2%; Age 65 and over: 17.6%; Males per 100 females: 89.0; Marriage status: 23.9% never married, 58.8% now married, 0.9% separated, 6.9% widowed, 10.4% divorced; Foreign born: 2.3%; Speak English only: 94.9%; With disability: 12.2%; Veterans: 7.9%; Ancestry: 50.5% German, 18.1% Irish, 8.0% English, 6.2% American, 5.0% Italian
Employment: 18.2% management, business, and financial, 8.6% computer, engineering, and science, 11.8% education, legal, community service, arts, and media, 9.6% healthcare practitioners, 10.7% service, 27.7% sales and office, 6.8% natural resources, construction, and maintenance, 6.6% production, transportation, and material moving
Income: Per capita: $33,037; Median household: $74,545; Average household: $82,979; Households with income of $100,000 or more: 35.6%; Poverty rate: 6.8%
Educational Attainment: High school diploma or higher: 93.3%; Bachelor's degree or higher: 39.6%; Graduate/professional degree or higher: 13.0%
Housing: Homeownership rate: 86.0%; Median home value: $155,100; Median year structure built: 1958; Homeowner vacancy rate: 3.5%; Median selected monthly owner costs: $1,359 with a mortgage, $525 without a mortgage; Median gross rent: $1,021 per month; Rental vacancy rate: 0.0%
Health Insurance: 95.9% have insurance; 77.5% have private insurance; 28.6% have public insurance; 4.1% do not have insurance; 3.5% of children under 18 do not have insurance
Transportation: Commute: 88.3% car, 0.9% public transportation, 3.1% walk, 6.3% work from home; Mean travel time to work: 29.0 minutes

DEER PARK (city). Covers a land area of 0.874 square miles and a water area of 0 square miles. Located at 39.20° N. Lat; 84.40° W. Long. Elevation is 873 feet.
Population: 5,707; Growth (since 2000): -4.6%; Density: 6,531.0 persons per square mile; Race: 85.6% White, 6.5% Black/African American, 2.0% Asian, 0.1% American Indian/Alaska Native, 0.0% Native Hawaiian/Other Pacific Islander, 4.1% Two or more races, 3.1% Hispanic of any race; Average household size: 2.15; Median age: 39.4; Age under 18: 19.6%; Age 65 and over: 14.7%; Males per 100 females: 90.1; Marriage status: 35.3% never married, 41.8% now married, 1.7% separated, 9.1% widowed, 13.9% divorced; Foreign born: 3.6%; Speak English only: 95.4%; With disability: 14.4%; Veterans: 8.5%; Ancestry: 34.2% German, 14.3% Irish, 10.8% English, 5.1% Italian, 4.1% American
Employment: 18.2% management, business, and financial, 9.1% computer, engineering, and science, 9.1% education, legal, community service, arts, and media, 6.1% healthcare practitioners, 15.7% service, 24.0% sales and office, 8.2% natural resources, construction, and maintenance, 9.5% production, transportation, and material moving
Income: Per capita: $30,153; Median household: $49,102; Average household: $64,507; Households with income of $100,000 or more: 15.7%; Poverty rate: 8.1%
Educational Attainment: High school diploma or higher: 91.1%; Bachelor's degree or higher: 27.9%; Graduate/professional degree or higher: 8.4%
Housing: Homeownership rate: 62.9%; Median home value: $121,400; Median year structure built: 1947; Homeowner vacancy rate: 2.0%; Median selected monthly owner costs: $1,184 with a mortgage, $484 without a mortgage; Median gross rent: $737 per month; Rental vacancy rate: 5.4%
Health Insurance: 93.1% have insurance; 74.6% have private insurance; 27.3% have public insurance; 6.9% do not have insurance; 5.0% of children under 18 do not have insurance
Safety: Violent crime rate: 15.9 per 10,000 population; Property crime rate: 130.5 per 10,000 population
Transportation: Commute: 93.2% car, 2.9% public transportation, 1.2% walk, 2.1% work from home; Mean travel time to work: 19.9 minutes

DELHI HILLS (CDP). Covers a land area of 1.488 square miles and a water area of 0 square miles. Located at 39.09° N. Lat; 84.62° W. Long. Elevation is 873 feet.
Population: 5,290; Growth (since 2000): n/a; Density: 3,556.1 persons per square mile; Race: 95.5% White, 1.9% Black/African American, 1.1% Asian, 0.1% American Indian/Alaska Native, 0.4% Native Hawaiian/Other Pacific Islander, 0.9% Two or more races, 0.3% Hispanic of any race; Average household size: 2.92; Median age: 37.0; Age under 18: 20.5%; Age 65 and over: 12.8%; Males per 100 females: 97.3; Marriage status: 29.2% never married, 61.1% now married, 0.7% separated, 4.8% widowed, 4.9% divorced; Foreign born: 1.7%; Speak English only: 97.9%; With disability: 9.5%; Veterans: 7.4%; Ancestry: 58.9% German, 19.9% Irish, 6.8% English, 6.4% Italian, 3.9% American
Employment: 13.8% management, business, and financial, 4.9% computer, engineering, and science, 7.4% education, legal, community service, arts, and media, 8.6% healthcare practitioners, 9.7% service, 35.9% sales and office, 9.4% natural resources, construction, and maintenance, 10.3% production, transportation, and material moving
Income: Per capita: $33,144; Median household: $89,632; Average household: $94,974; Households with income of $100,000 or more: 40.3%; Poverty rate: 4.2%
Educational Attainment: High school diploma or higher: 94.0%; Bachelor's degree or higher: 25.4%; Graduate/professional degree or higher: 9.6%

Housing: Homeownership rate: 92.7%; Median home value: $141,500; Median year structure built: 1972; Homeowner vacancy rate: 2.0%; Median selected monthly owner costs: $1,247 with a mortgage, $469 without a mortgage; Median gross rent: $1,185 per month; Rental vacancy rate: 0.0%
Health Insurance: 92.7% have insurance; 80.2% have private insurance; 19.3% have public insurance; 7.3% do not have insurance; 7.0% of children under 18 do not have insurance
Transportation: Commute: 95.1% car, 0.8% public transportation, 0.0% walk, 3.9% work from home; Mean travel time to work: 27.4 minutes

DELSHIRE (CDP). Covers a land area of 0.699 square miles and a water area of 0 square miles. Located at 39.09° N. Lat; 84.59° W. Long.
Population: 3,092; Growth (since 2000): n/a; Density: 4,424.0 persons per square mile; Race: 91.1% White, 0.0% Black/African American, 0.0% Asian, 0.3% American Indian/Alaska Native, 0.0% Native Hawaiian/Other Pacific Islander, 1.6% Two or more races, 7.4% Hispanic of any race; Average household size: 2.98; Median age: 35.4; Age under 18: 26.4%; Age 65 and over: 11.2%; Males per 100 females: 97.6; Marriage status: 30.9% never married, 54.5% now married, 1.0% separated, 5.2% widowed, 9.4% divorced; Foreign born: 4.2%; Speak English only: 89.9%; With disability: 14.1%; Veterans: 8.0%; Ancestry: 38.7% German, 14.9% Irish, 11.7% Italian, 8.6% American, 2.2% Russian
Employment: 10.5% management, business, and financial, 5.3% computer, engineering, and science, 8.8% education, legal, community service, arts, and media, 3.5% healthcare practitioners, 25.2% service, 28.3% sales and office, 10.5% natural resources, construction, and maintenance, 7.8% production, transportation, and material moving
Income: Per capita: $22,691; Median household: $55,196; Average household: $65,954; Households with income of $100,000 or more: 19.5%; Poverty rate: 10.3%
Educational Attainment: High school diploma or higher: 92.9%; Bachelor's degree or higher: 17.8%; Graduate/professional degree or higher: 6.1%
Housing: Homeownership rate: 72.5%; Median home value: $120,700; Median year structure built: 1968; Homeowner vacancy rate: 4.8%; Median selected monthly owner costs: $1,198 with a mortgage, $465 without a mortgage; Median gross rent: $692 per month; Rental vacancy rate: 0.0%
Health Insurance: 87.9% have insurance; 63.8% have private insurance; 33.2% have public insurance; 12.1% do not have insurance; 12.7% of children under 18 do not have insurance
Transportation: Commute: 92.7% car, 2.1% public transportation, 2.4% walk, 1.7% work from home; Mean travel time to work: 27.1 minutes

DENT (CDP). Covers a land area of 5.930 square miles and a water area of 0 square miles. Located at 39.19° N. Lat; 84.66° W. Long. Elevation is 840 feet.
Population: 10,963; Growth (since 2000): 44.0%; Density: 1,848.8 persons per square mile; Race: 94.2% White, 3.3% Black/African American, 1.2% Asian, 0.2% American Indian/Alaska Native, 0.0% Native Hawaiian/Other Pacific Islander, 1.2% Two or more races, 2.4% Hispanic of any race; Average household size: 2.48; Median age: 40.3; Age under 18: 23.1%; Age 65 and over: 16.9%; Males per 100 females: 91.9; Marriage status: 24.6% never married, 60.1% now married, 1.2% separated, 5.1% widowed, 10.2% divorced; Foreign born: 2.9%; Speak English only: 95.6%; With disability: 9.7%; Veterans: 8.6%; Ancestry: 52.6% German, 16.1% Irish, 8.2% Italian, 7.6% American, 6.3% English
Employment: 17.7% management, business, and financial, 7.2% computer, engineering, and science, 12.1% education, legal, community service, arts, and media, 9.2% healthcare practitioners, 13.1% service, 30.9% sales and office, 4.2% natural resources, construction, and maintenance, 5.6% production, transportation, and material moving
Income: Per capita: $37,657; Median household: $72,176; Average household: $91,566; Households with income of $100,000 or more: 36.0%; Poverty rate: 6.6%
Educational Attainment: High school diploma or higher: 94.7%; Bachelor's degree or higher: 37.1%; Graduate/professional degree or higher: 11.3%
Housing: Homeownership rate: 78.2%; Median home value: $180,500; Median year structure built: 1992; Homeowner vacancy rate: 0.0%; Median selected monthly owner costs: $1,493 with a mortgage, $518 without a mortgage; Median gross rent: $875 per month; Rental vacancy rate: 0.0%
Health Insurance: 97.7% have insurance; 85.7% have private insurance; 24.5% have public insurance; 2.3% do not have insurance; 1.6% of children under 18 do not have insurance
Transportation: Commute: 94.0% car, 1.0% public transportation, 0.2% walk, 4.9% work from home; Mean travel time to work: 24.2 minutes

DILLONVALE (CDP). Covers a land area of 0.891 square miles and a water area of 0 square miles. Located at 39.22° N. Lat; 84.40° W. Long. Elevation is 784 feet.
Population: 3,414; Growth (since 2000): -8.1%; Density: 3,833.2 persons per square mile; Race: 96.5% White, 1.1% Black/African American, 1.8% Asian, 0.0% American Indian/Alaska Native, 0.0% Native Hawaiian/Other Pacific Islander, 0.7% Two or more races, 0.7% Hispanic of any race; Average household size: 2.33; Median age: 39.7; Age under 18: 22.1%; Age 65 and over: 18.3%; Males per 100 females: 92.3; Marriage status: 28.8% never married, 53.0% now married, 1.1% separated, 7.2% widowed, 11.0% divorced; Foreign born: 1.7%; Speak English only: 94.9%; With disability: 10.4%; Veterans: 8.6%; Ancestry: 46.0% German, 22.4% Irish, 11.6% English, 9.6% Italian, 7.9% American
Employment: 27.0% management, business, and financial, 6.5% computer, engineering, and science, 5.2% education, legal, community service, arts, and media, 2.0% healthcare practitioners, 14.1% service, 31.2% sales and office, 3.5% natural resources, construction, and maintenance, 10.5% production, transportation, and material moving
Income: Per capita: $28,680; Median household: $64,337; Average household: $66,452; Households with income of $100,000 or more: 19.8%; Poverty rate: 5.9%
Educational Attainment: High school diploma or higher: 91.1%; Bachelor's degree or higher: 31.4%; Graduate/professional degree or higher: 8.8%
Housing: Homeownership rate: 83.1%; Median home value: $135,900; Median year structure built: 1955; Homeowner vacancy rate: 1.7%; Median selected monthly owner costs: $1,235 with a mortgage, $488 without a mortgage; Median gross rent: $767 per month; Rental vacancy rate: 0.0%
Health Insurance: 91.6% have insurance; 75.9% have private insurance; 28.6% have public insurance; 8.4% do not have insurance; 7.5% of children under 18 do not have insurance
Transportation: Commute: 91.6% car, 1.4% public transportation, 1.2% walk, 5.0% work from home; Mean travel time to work: 21.8 minutes

DRY RIDGE (CDP). Covers a land area of 4.141 square miles and a water area of 0 square miles. Located at 39.26° N. Lat; 84.63° W. Long. Elevation is 919 feet.
Population: 2,573; Growth (since 2000): n/a; Density: 621.4 persons per square mile; Race: 87.3% White, 2.8% Black/African American, 7.7% Asian, 0.0% American Indian/Alaska Native, 0.0% Native Hawaiian/Other Pacific Islander, 1.6% Two or more races, 1.4% Hispanic of any race; Average household size: 2.26; Median age: 53.1; Age under 18: 17.1%; Age 65 and over: 26.5%; Males per 100 females: 90.0; Marriage status: 21.9% never married, 63.2% now married, 0.7% separated, 8.3% widowed, 6.6% divorced; Foreign born: 5.6%; Speak English only: 90.4%; With disability: 9.7%; Veterans: 8.4%; Ancestry: 43.2% German, 10.7% Irish, 7.5% English, 7.1% American, 5.0% Italian
Employment: 23.1% management, business, and financial, 8.8% computer, engineering, and science, 10.4% education, legal, community service, arts, and media, 7.8% healthcare practitioners, 9.8% service, 27.3% sales and office, 3.6% natural resources, construction, and maintenance, 9.1% production, transportation, and material moving
Income: Per capita: $50,461; Median household: $66,419; Average household: $113,102; Households with income of $100,000 or more: 38.3%; Poverty rate: 4.7%
Educational Attainment: High school diploma or higher: 94.3%; Bachelor's degree or higher: 41.7%; Graduate/professional degree or higher: 15.9%
Housing: Homeownership rate: 96.7%; Median home value: $194,800; Median year structure built: 1992; Homeowner vacancy rate: 0.0%; Median selected monthly owner costs: $1,576 with a mortgage, $589 without a mortgage; Median gross rent: $1,222 per month; Rental vacancy rate: 0.0%
Health Insurance: 91.7% have insurance; 80.3% have private insurance; 31.5% have public insurance; 8.3% do not have insurance; 20.0% of children under 18 do not have insurance
Transportation: Commute: 96.1% car, 0.0% public transportation, 0.0% walk, 3.9% work from home; Mean travel time to work: 23.7 minutes

DRY RUN (CDP). Covers a land area of 4.671 square miles and a water area of 0.009 square miles. Located at 39.10° N. Lat; 84.33° W. Long. Elevation is 860 feet.
History: Dry Run is a part of the village of Newtown, which was founded in 1792. The original fort, Fort Mercer, was settled near the current Jones Fish Hatchery on Church Street. It was originally called Mercersburg, named after early settler Captain Aaron Mercer.
Population: 7,785; Growth (since 2000): 18.8%; Density: 1,666.5 persons per square mile; Race: 93.0% White, 0.0% Black/African American, 5.0% Asian, 0.0% American Indian/Alaska Native, 0.0% Native Hawaiian/Other Pacific Islander, 2.0% Two or more races, 2.9% Hispanic of any race; Average household size: 3.20; Median age: 38.8; Age under 18: 32.9%; Age 65 and over: 9.1%; Males per 100 females: 99.5; Marriage status: 22.3% never married, 71.8% now married, 0.6% separated, 3.0% widowed, 2.9% divorced; Foreign born: 6.0%; Speak English only: 93.8%; With disability: 5.9%; Veterans: 5.1%; Ancestry: 36.2% German, 19.2% Irish, 10.7% American, 10.2% English, 10.1% Italian
Employment: 31.3% management, business, and financial, 4.5% computer, engineering, and science, 16.2% education, legal, community service, arts, and media, 10.5% healthcare practitioners, 8.3% service, 22.4% sales and office, 2.4% natural resources, construction, and maintenance, 4.5% production, transportation, and material moving
Income: Per capita: $55,133; Median household: $137,543; Average household: $176,372; Households with income of $100,000 or more: 69.2%; Poverty rate: 0.2%
Educational Attainment: High school diploma or higher: 97.8%; Bachelor's degree or higher: 73.9%; Graduate/professional degree or higher: 28.5%
Housing: Homeownership rate: 97.2%; Median home value: $311,300; Median year structure built: 1985; Homeowner vacancy rate: 0.0%; Median selected monthly owner costs: $2,479 with a mortgage, $752 without a mortgage; Median gross rent: n/a per month; Rental vacancy rate: 0.0%
Health Insurance: 98.2% have insurance; 93.8% have private insurance; 12.7% have public insurance; 1.8% do not have insurance; 0.0% of children under 18 do not have insurance
Transportation: Commute: 90.6% car, 1.5% public transportation, 0.3% walk, 7.0% work from home; Mean travel time to work: 27.3 minutes

DUNLAP (CDP). Covers a land area of 6.533 square miles and a water area of 0.160 square miles. Located at 39.29° N. Lat; 84.64° W. Long. Elevation is 856 feet.
Population: 1,926; Growth (since 2000): n/a; Density: 294.8 persons per square mile; Race: 84.7% White, 13.9% Black/African American, 0.0% Asian, 0.0% American Indian/Alaska Native, 0.0% Native Hawaiian/Other Pacific Islander, 0.3% Two or more races, 1.7% Hispanic of any race; Average household size: 2.72; Median age: 52.3; Age under 18: 14.5%; Age 65 and over: 13.8%; Males per 100 females: 102.7; Marriage status: 25.8% never married, 61.6% now married, 0.0% separated, 4.2% widowed, 8.4% divorced; Foreign born: 0.7%; Speak English only: 97.3%; With disability: 12.7%; Veterans: 11.2%; Ancestry: 45.9% German, 12.1% English, 12.1% Irish, 7.1% American, 4.3% Scottish
Employment: 18.3% management, business, and financial, 5.2% computer, engineering, and science, 11.8% education, legal, community service, arts, and media, 4.8% healthcare practitioners, 9.0% service, 35.5% sales and office, 10.1% natural resources, construction, and maintenance, 5.4% production, transportation, and material moving
Income: Per capita: $44,489; Median household: $116,667; Average household: $119,515; Households with income of $100,000 or more: 53.2%; Poverty rate: 3.1%
Educational Attainment: High school diploma or higher: 92.9%; Bachelor's degree or higher: 37.7%; Graduate/professional degree or higher: 12.7%
Housing: Homeownership rate: 89.4%; Median home value: $230,700; Median year structure built: 1987; Homeowner vacancy rate: 0.0%; Median selected monthly owner costs: $2,011 with a mortgage, $590 without a mortgage; Median gross rent: $1,210 per month; Rental vacancy rate: 0.0%
Health Insurance: 94.8% have insurance; 85.8% have private insurance; 19.9% have public insurance; 5.2% do not have insurance; 9.0% of children under 18 do not have insurance
Transportation: Commute: 93.0% car, 1.9% public transportation, 0.7% walk, 2.9% work from home; Mean travel time to work: 24.1 minutes

ELIZABETHTOWN (CDP). Covers a land area of 0.890 square miles and a water area of 0.014 square miles. Located at 39.16° N. Lat; 84.80° W. Long. Elevation is 492 feet.
Population: 251; Growth (since 2000): n/a; Density: 282.0 persons per square mile; Race: 88.0% White, 0.0% Black/African American, 0.0% Asian, 0.0% American Indian/Alaska Native, 0.0% Native Hawaiian/Other Pacific Islander, 12.0% Two or more races, 4.4% Hispanic of any race; Average household size: 2.06; Median age: 33.8; Age under 18: 19.9%; Age 65 and over: 9.6%; Males per 100 females: 112.1; Marriage status: 34.5% never married, 9.4% now married, 3.0% separated, 17.7% widowed, 38.4% divorced; Foreign born: 0.0%; Speak English only: 100.0%; With disability: 14.7%; Veterans: 6.0%; Ancestry: 23.9% German, 8.4% Irish, 5.6% American, 2.8% Portuguese, 2.4% French Canadian
Employment: 0.0% management, business, and financial, 0.0% computer, engineering, and science, 19.7% education, legal, community service, arts, and media, 0.0% healthcare practitioners, 13.1% service, 33.6% sales and office, 21.3% natural resources, construction, and maintenance, 12.3% production, transportation, and material moving
Income: Per capita: $24,552; Median household: n/a; Average household: $50,834; Households with income of $100,000 or more: 19.7%; Poverty rate: 6.4%
Educational Attainment: High school diploma or higher: 67.6%; Bachelor's degree or higher: 3.2%; Graduate/professional degree or higher: n/a
Housing: Homeownership rate: 50.0%; Median home value: n/a; Median year structure built: 1963; Homeowner vacancy rate: 0.0%; Median selected monthly owner costs: $754 with a mortgage, $392 without a mortgage; Median gross rent: $629 per month; Rental vacancy rate: 0.0%
Health Insurance: 96.0% have insurance; 56.2% have private insurance; 45.4% have public insurance; 4.0% do not have insurance; 0.0% of children under 18 do not have insurance
Transportation: Commute: 100.0% car, 0.0% public transportation, 0.0% walk, 0.0% work from home; Mean travel time to work: 24.1 minutes

ELMWOOD PLACE (village). Covers a land area of 0.319 square miles and a water area of 0 square miles. Located at 39.19° N. Lat; 84.49° W. Long. Elevation is 525 feet.
History: Settled 1875, incorporated 1890.
Population: 1,831; Growth (since 2000): -31.7%; Density: 5,734.9 persons per square mile; Race: 71.2% White, 21.0% Black/African American, 0.0% Asian, 0.9% American Indian/Alaska Native, 0.0% Native Hawaiian/Other Pacific Islander, 1.4% Two or more races, 6.6% Hispanic of any race; Average household size: 2.29; Median age: 38.6; Age under 18: 21.2%; Age 65 and over: 10.0%; Males per 100 females: 103.0; Marriage status: 37.2% never married, 38.8% now married, 0.8% separated, 8.6% widowed, 15.5% divorced; Foreign born: 2.0%; Speak English only: 94.8%; With disability: 21.1%; Veterans: 7.5%; Ancestry: 21.4% German, 11.0% Irish, 10.2% English, 8.9% American, 2.8% African
Employment: 6.7% management, business, and financial, 1.4% computer, engineering, and science, 3.1% education, legal, community service, arts, and media, 3.1% healthcare practitioners, 16.4% service, 33.7% sales and office, 8.1% natural resources, construction, and maintenance, 27.5% production, transportation, and material moving
Income: Per capita: $20,649; Median household: $28,672; Average household: $47,068; Households with income of $100,000 or more: 4.9%; Poverty rate: 30.0%
Educational Attainment: High school diploma or higher: 72.1%; Bachelor's degree or higher: 4.9%; Graduate/professional degree or higher: 2.0%
Housing: Homeownership rate: 42.9%; Median home value: $58,400; Median year structure built: Before 1940; Homeowner vacancy rate: 0.0%; Median selected monthly owner costs: $985 with a mortgage, $401 without a mortgage; Median gross rent: $607 per month; Rental vacancy rate: 17.3%
Health Insurance: 82.6% have insurance; 34.1% have private insurance; 55.9% have public insurance; 17.4% do not have insurance; 3.3% of children under 18 do not have insurance
Safety: Violent crime rate: 46.3 per 10,000 population; Property crime rate: 162.0 per 10,000 population
Transportation: Commute: 86.4% car, 8.9% public transportation, 0.0% walk, 0.7% work from home; Mean travel time to work: 19.4 minutes

EVENDALE (village). Covers a land area of 4.742 square miles and a water area of 0 square miles. Located at 39.25° N. Lat; 84.43° W. Long. Elevation is 594 feet.

Population: 2,769; Growth (since 2000): -10.4%; Density: 583.9 persons per square mile; Race: 87.5% White, 5.5% Black/African American, 4.4% Asian, 0.0% American Indian/Alaska Native, 0.0% Native Hawaiian/Other Pacific Islander, 1.7% Two or more races, 0.4% Hispanic of any race; Average household size: 2.66; Median age: 50.6; Age under 18: 19.8%; Age 65 and over: 20.9%; Males per 100 females: 97.5; Marriage status: 21.5% never married, 68.5% now married, 0.4% separated, 3.9% widowed, 6.1% divorced; Foreign born: 6.1%; Speak English only: 93.5%; With disability: 7.4%; Veterans: 7.3%; Ancestry: 35.8% German, 13.3% Irish, 12.2% English, 9.7% Italian, 8.5% American

Employment: 26.7% management, business, and financial, 5.8% computer, engineering, and science, 13.3% education, legal, community service, arts, and media, 7.3% healthcare practitioners, 14.2% service, 24.3% sales and office, 1.0% natural resources, construction, and maintenance, 7.4% production, transportation, and material moving

Income: Per capita: $56,653; Median household: $113,875; Average household: $148,986; Households with income of $100,000 or more: 56.0%; Poverty rate: 1.9%

Educational Attainment: High school diploma or higher: 97.0%; Bachelor's degree or higher: 60.0%; Graduate/professional degree or higher: 24.9%

Housing: Homeownership rate: 92.5%; Median home value: $264,200; Median year structure built: 1979; Homeowner vacancy rate: 1.0%; Median selected monthly owner costs: $1,787 with a mortgage, $638 without a mortgage; Median gross rent: $1,250 per month; Rental vacancy rate: 0.0%

Health Insurance: 98.3% have insurance; 89.2% have private insurance; 24.8% have public insurance; 1.7% do not have insurance; 1.8% of children under 18 do not have insurance

Safety: Violent crime rate: 21.7 per 10,000 population; Property crime rate: 860.4 per 10,000 population

Transportation: Commute: 92.1% car, 1.2% public transportation, 1.7% walk, 3.6% work from home; Mean travel time to work: 19.5 minutes

FAIRFAX (village). Covers a land area of 0.763 square miles and a water area of 0 square miles. Located at 39.14° N. Lat; 84.40° W. Long. Elevation is 568 feet.

Population: 1,689; Growth (since 2000): -12.8%; Density: 2,214.9 persons per square mile; Race: 94.3% White, 3.3% Black/African American, 1.7% Asian, 0.1% American Indian/Alaska Native, 0.0% Native Hawaiian/Other Pacific Islander, 0.4% Two or more races, 1.1% Hispanic of any race; Average household size: 2.38; Median age: 39.4; Age under 18: 22.2%; Age 65 and over: 12.9%; Males per 100 females: 86.9; Marriage status: 27.5% never married, 48.9% now married, 2.3% separated, 8.6% widowed, 15.0% divorced; Foreign born: 3.0%; Speak English only: 96.0%; With disability: 12.3%; Veterans: 7.2%; Ancestry: 32.1% German, 18.5% Irish, 10.2% English, 7.7% American, 7.2% Italian

Employment: 15.8% management, business, and financial, 5.6% computer, engineering, and science, 7.3% education, legal, community service, arts, and media, 5.4% healthcare practitioners, 13.5% service, 28.6% sales and office, 8.1% natural resources, construction, and maintenance, 15.8% production, transportation, and material moving

Income: Per capita: $27,387; Median household: $51,189; Average household: $63,649; Households with income of $100,000 or more: 20.7%; Poverty rate: 8.9%

Educational Attainment: High school diploma or higher: 92.1%; Bachelor's degree or higher: 30.2%; Graduate/professional degree or higher: 8.9%

Housing: Homeownership rate: 77.6%; Median home value: $118,200; Median year structure built: 1945; Homeowner vacancy rate: 1.2%; Median selected monthly owner costs: $1,250 with a mortgage, $476 without a mortgage; Median gross rent: $833 per month; Rental vacancy rate: 0.0%

Health Insurance: 93.3% have insurance; 77.3% have private insurance; 26.9% have public insurance; 6.7% do not have insurance; 1.9% of children under 18 do not have insurance

Safety: Violent crime rate: 17.6 per 10,000 population; Property crime rate: 1,531.7 per 10,000 population

Transportation: Commute: 92.2% car, 2.0% public transportation, 2.7% walk, 2.4% work from home; Mean travel time to work: 22.7 minutes

Additional Information Contacts

Village of Fairfax . . . . (513) 527-6503
http://www.fairfaxohio.org

FINNEYTOWN (CDP). Covers a land area of 4.057 square miles and a water area of 0 square miles. Located at 39.22° N. Lat; 84.51° W. Long. Elevation is 889 feet.

Population: 12,279; Growth (since 2000): -9.0%; Density: 3,026.3 persons per square mile; Race: 57.1% White, 36.5% Black/African American, 2.6% Asian, 0.0% American Indian/Alaska Native, 0.0% Native Hawaiian/Other Pacific Islander, 3.5% Two or more races, 1.1% Hispanic of any race; Average household size: 2.54; Median age: 40.9; Age under 18: 22.7%; Age 65 and over: 15.7%; Males per 100 females: 87.1; Marriage status: 34.9% never married, 48.8% now married, 2.7% separated, 6.4% widowed, 10.0% divorced; Foreign born: 4.8%; Speak English only: 95.4%; With disability: 12.2%; Veterans: 8.3%; Ancestry: 26.9% German, 11.3% Irish, 7.6% English, 4.9% American, 4.1% Italian

Employment: 14.0% management, business, and financial, 6.3% computer, engineering, and science, 10.6% education, legal, community service, arts, and media, 5.5% healthcare practitioners, 18.4% service, 26.4% sales and office, 4.2% natural resources, construction, and maintenance, 14.6% production, transportation, and material moving

Income: Per capita: $27,285; Median household: $57,546; Average household: $67,352; Households with income of $100,000 or more: 23.9%; Poverty rate: 9.9%

Educational Attainment: High school diploma or higher: 92.7%; Bachelor's degree or higher: 34.6%; Graduate/professional degree or higher: 15.1%

Housing: Homeownership rate: 75.5%; Median home value: $122,400; Median year structure built: 1959; Homeowner vacancy rate: 0.8%; Median selected monthly owner costs: $1,263 with a mortgage, $571 without a mortgage; Median gross rent: $813 per month; Rental vacancy rate: 3.8%

Health Insurance: 92.5% have insurance; 71.7% have private insurance; 34.2% have public insurance; 7.5% do not have insurance; 3.0% of children under 18 do not have insurance

Transportation: Commute: 90.3% car, 3.7% public transportation, 2.1% walk, 2.8% work from home; Mean travel time to work: 22.3 minutes

FOREST PARK (city). Covers a land area of 6.480 square miles and a water area of 0 square miles. Located at 39.29° N. Lat; 84.53° W. Long. Elevation is 833 feet.

Population: 18,679; Growth (since 2000): -4.0%; Density: 2,882.6 persons per square mile; Race: 26.0% White, 60.0% Black/African American, 5.4% Asian, 0.0% American Indian/Alaska Native, 0.1% Native Hawaiian/Other Pacific Islander, 5.1% Two or more races, 6.2% Hispanic of any race; Average household size: 2.61; Median age: 37.1; Age under 18: 24.9%; Age 65 and over: 13.0%; Males per 100 females: 86.6; Marriage status: 34.9% never married, 47.6% now married, 1.9% separated, 4.9% widowed, 12.6% divorced; Foreign born: 10.6%; Speak English only: 85.0%; With disability: 13.4%; Veterans: 8.9%; Ancestry: 8.9% German, 3.8% Irish, 2.6% English, 2.5% American, 1.8% Other Subsaharan African

Employment: 11.9% management, business, and financial, 3.8% computer, engineering, and science, 7.9% education, legal, community service, arts, and media, 5.9% healthcare practitioners, 18.9% service, 26.7% sales and office, 7.3% natural resources, construction, and maintenance, 17.7% production, transportation, and material moving

Income: Per capita: $23,286; Median household: $52,750; Average household: $59,749; Households with income of $100,000 or more: 14.1%; Poverty rate: 16.4%

Educational Attainment: High school diploma or higher: 89.1%; Bachelor's degree or higher: 27.2%; Graduate/professional degree or higher: 8.1%

Housing: Homeownership rate: 56.8%; Median home value: $111,300; Median year structure built: 1972; Homeowner vacancy rate: 0.6%; Median selected monthly owner costs: $1,240 with a mortgage, $436 without a mortgage; Median gross rent: $881 per month; Rental vacancy rate: 9.0%

Health Insurance: 89.7% have insurance; 65.8% have private insurance; 34.1% have public insurance; 10.3% do not have insurance; 0.9% of children under 18 do not have insurance

Safety: Violent crime rate: 25.2 per 10,000 population; Property crime rate: 339.1 per 10,000 population

Transportation: Commute: 92.6% car, 2.5% public transportation, 0.9% walk, 3.4% work from home; Mean travel time to work: 22.7 minutes

Additional Information Contacts

City of Forest Park. . . . . (513) 595-5200
http://www.forestpark.org

FORESTVILLE (CDP). Covers a land area of 3.724 square miles and a water area of <.001 square miles. Located at 39.07° N. Lat; 84.34° W. Long. Elevation is 820 feet.

Population: 10,617; Growth (since 2000): -3.3%; Density: 2,850.7 persons per square mile; Race: 94.0% White, 2.1% Black/African American, 2.2% Asian, 0.1% American Indian/Alaska Native, 0.0% Native Hawaiian/Other Pacific Islander, 1.4% Two or more races, 0.2% Hispanic of any race; Average household size: 2.40; Median age: 43.2; Age under 18: 24.7%; Age 65 and over: 18.8%; Males per 100 females: 86.1; Marriage status: 24.0% never married, 58.0% now married, 2.1% separated, 7.2% widowed, 10.8% divorced; Foreign born: 5.3%; Speak English only: 93.1%; With disability: 13.4%; Veterans: 8.7%; Ancestry: 35.3% German, 18.4% Irish, 13.7% English, 10.1% American, 6.9% Italian

Employment: 24.6% management, business, and financial, 7.8% computer, engineering, and science, 15.9% education, legal, community service, arts, and media, 8.1% healthcare practitioners, 10.5% service, 23.4% sales and office, 3.1% natural resources, construction, and maintenance, 6.7% production, transportation, and material moving

Income: Per capita: $37,951; Median household: $70,265; Average household: $91,234; Households with income of $100,000 or more: 39.1%; Poverty rate: 8.4%

Educational Attainment: High school diploma or higher: 94.8%; Bachelor's degree or higher: 51.8%; Graduate/professional degree or higher: 21.7%

Housing: Homeownership rate: 74.2%; Median home value: $204,000; Median year structure built: 1981; Homeowner vacancy rate: 2.0%; Median selected monthly owner costs: $1,613 with a mortgage, $629 without a mortgage; Median gross rent: $947 per month; Rental vacancy rate: 0.0%

Health Insurance: 96.3% have insurance; 82.5% have private insurance; 27.5% have public insurance; 3.7% do not have insurance; 4.7% of children under 18 do not have insurance

Transportation: Commute: 86.7% car, 3.2% public transportation, 1.5% walk, 7.6% work from home; Mean travel time to work: 24.6 minutes

FRUIT HILL (CDP). Covers a land area of 1.275 square miles and a water area of 0 square miles. Located at 39.07° N. Lat; 84.37° W. Long. Elevation is 732 feet.

Population: 3,743; Growth (since 2000): -5.1%; Density: 2,934.9 persons per square mile; Race: 94.5% White, 2.2% Black/African American, 2.7% Asian, 0.0% American Indian/Alaska Native, 0.0% Native Hawaiian/Other Pacific Islander, 0.6% Two or more races, 1.6% Hispanic of any race; Average household size: 2.72; Median age: 37.2; Age under 18: 32.4%; Age 65 and over: 12.6%; Males per 100 females: 91.4; Marriage status: 22.6% never married, 58.8% now married, 4.7% separated, 4.0% widowed, 14.6% divorced; Foreign born: 2.9%; Speak English only: 96.7%; With disability: 7.2%; Veterans: 7.2%; Ancestry: 31.5% German, 23.7% Irish, 9.5% English, 6.2% Italian, 4.1% American

Employment: 22.8% management, business, and financial, 5.1% computer, engineering, and science, 20.7% education, legal, community service, arts, and media, 7.4% healthcare practitioners, 20.6% service, 18.2% sales and office, 1.2% natural resources, construction, and maintenance, 4.1% production, transportation, and material moving

Income: Per capita: $37,674; Median household: $73,618; Average household: $100,803; Households with income of $100,000 or more: 37.7%; Poverty rate: 24.9%

Educational Attainment: High school diploma or higher: 98.8%; Bachelor's degree or higher: 47.3%; Graduate/professional degree or higher: 15.2%

Housing: Homeownership rate: 83.3%; Median home value: $164,800; Median year structure built: 1963; Homeowner vacancy rate: 1.1%; Median selected monthly owner costs: $1,573 with a mortgage, $701 without a mortgage; Median gross rent: $1,143 per month; Rental vacancy rate: 0.0%

Health Insurance: 94.6% have insurance; 75.2% have private insurance; 30.0% have public insurance; 5.4% do not have insurance; 2.6% of children under 18 do not have insurance

Transportation: Commute: 89.0% car, 0.0% public transportation, 1.8% walk, 9.2% work from home; Mean travel time to work: 21.6 minutes

GLENDALE (village). Covers a land area of 1.686 square miles and a water area of 0 square miles. Located at 39.27° N. Lat; 84.46° W. Long. Elevation is 633 feet.

History: Incorporated 1855.

Population: 2,246; Growth (since 2000): 2.7%; Density: 1,332.1 persons per square mile; Race: 80.2% White, 13.4% Black/African American, 3.5% Asian, 0.0% American Indian/Alaska Native, 0.2% Native Hawaiian/Other Pacific Islander, 1.2% Two or more races, 1.6% Hispanic of any race; Average household size: 2.31; Median age: 48.1; Age under 18: 21.8%; Age 65 and over: 20.0%; Males per 100 females: 94.0; Marriage status: 19.2% never married, 65.0% now married, 1.7% separated, 7.4% widowed, 8.4% divorced; Foreign born: 5.8%; Speak English only: 94.3%; With disability: 8.6%; Veterans: 6.5%; Ancestry: 29.3% German, 15.5% Irish, 14.4% English, 7.0% Scottish, 4.9% Italian

Employment: 21.1% management, business, and financial, 8.7% computer, engineering, and science, 11.4% education, legal, community service, arts, and media, 10.2% healthcare practitioners, 12.9% service, 25.2% sales and office, 3.4% natural resources, construction, and maintenance, 7.0% production, transportation, and material moving

Income: Per capita: $59,158; Median household: $96,964; Average household: $138,997; Households with income of $100,000 or more: 47.4%; Poverty rate: 4.6%

Educational Attainment: High school diploma or higher: 96.6%; Bachelor's degree or higher: 58.6%; Graduate/professional degree or higher: 27.4%

Housing: Homeownership rate: 84.2%; Median home value: $245,300; Median year structure built: 1945; Homeowner vacancy rate: 3.4%; Median selected monthly owner costs: $1,939 with a mortgage, $845 without a mortgage; Median gross rent: $998 per month; Rental vacancy rate: 0.0%

Health Insurance: 97.1% have insurance; 86.3% have private insurance; 25.9% have public insurance; 2.9% do not have insurance; 2.7% of children under 18 do not have insurance

Transportation: Commute: 87.0% car, 0.4% public transportation, 2.9% walk, 8.2% work from home; Mean travel time to work: 22.9 minutes

Additional Information Contacts

Village of Glendale . . . . (513) 771-7200
http://www.glendaleohio.org

GOLF MANOR (village). Covers a land area of 0.575 square miles and a water area of 0 square miles. Located at 39.19° N. Lat; 84.45° W. Long. Elevation is 663 feet.

History: Incorporated 1947.

Population: 3,588; Growth (since 2000): -10.3%; Density: 6,235.5 persons per square mile; Race: 25.1% White, 69.4% Black/African American, 0.8% Asian, 1.2% American Indian/Alaska Native, 0.0% Native Hawaiian/Other Pacific Islander, 3.6% Two or more races, 0.8% Hispanic of any race; Average household size: 2.46; Median age: 32.9; Age under 18: 27.9%; Age 65 and over: 11.5%; Males per 100 females: 80.5; Marriage status: 43.7% never married, 36.4% now married, 1.8% separated, 5.8% widowed, 14.1% divorced; Foreign born: 2.1%; Speak English only: 97.8%; With disability: 12.5%; Veterans: 6.3%; Ancestry: 12.0% German, 3.0% Irish, 2.9% Italian, 2.4% French, 2.1% English

Employment: 6.2% management, business, and financial, 6.5% computer, engineering, and science, 8.4% education, legal, community service, arts, and media, 8.1% healthcare practitioners, 23.8% service, 25.2% sales and office, 1.9% natural resources, construction, and maintenance, 19.9% production, transportation, and material moving

Income: Per capita: $21,061; Median household: $40,361; Average household: $49,653; Households with income of $100,000 or more: 11.5%; Poverty rate: 21.2%

Educational Attainment: High school diploma or higher: 91.8%; Bachelor's degree or higher: 24.5%; Graduate/professional degree or higher: 5.3%

Housing: Homeownership rate: 49.3%; Median home value: $89,200; Median year structure built: 1954; Homeowner vacancy rate: 0.0%; Median selected monthly owner costs: $1,100 with a mortgage, $494 without a mortgage; Median gross rent: $722 per month; Rental vacancy rate: 8.1%

Health Insurance: 93.0% have insurance; 58.6% have private insurance; 45.7% have public insurance; 7.0% do not have insurance; 1.0% of children under 18 do not have insurance

Transportation: Commute: 85.6% car, 6.3% public transportation, 3.1% walk, 3.2% work from home; Mean travel time to work: 29.2 minutes

Additional Information Contacts

Village of Golf Manor. . . . . (513) 531-7418
http://www.golfmanor.org

GRANDVIEW (CDP). Covers a land area of 4.349 square miles and a water area of 0.309 square miles. Located at 39.20° N. Lat; 84.72° W. Long. Elevation is 646 feet.

Population: 1,389; Growth (since 2000): -0.1%; Density: 319.4 persons per square mile; Race: 100.0% White, 0.0% Black/African American, 0.0%

Asian, 0.0% American Indian/Alaska Native, 0.0% Native Hawaiian/Other Pacific Islander, 0.0% Two or more races, 0.0% Hispanic of any race; Average household size: 3.05; Median age: 37.3; Age under 18: 25.9%; Age 65 and over: 5.8%; Males per 100 females: 105.0; Marriage status: 29.4% never married, 63.4% now married, 1.6% separated, 1.5% widowed, 5.6% divorced; Foreign born: 0.0%; Speak English only: 97.5%; With disability: 3.1%; Veterans: 6.1%; Ancestry: 43.8% German, 25.0% Irish, 8.3% Italian, 7.6% English, 3.7% Dutch
Employment: 33.3% management, business, and financial, 1.9% computer, engineering, and science, 2.6% education, legal, community service, arts, and media, 10.7% healthcare practitioners, 5.3% service, 27.4% sales and office, 9.5% natural resources, construction, and maintenance, 9.3% production, transportation, and material moving
Income: Per capita: $37,369; Median household: $80,489; Average household: $112,964; Households with income of $100,000 or more: 30.3%; Poverty rate: 3.4%
Educational Attainment: High school diploma or higher: 100.0%; Bachelor's degree or higher: 29.9%; Graduate/professional degree or higher: 9.2%
Housing: Homeownership rate: 74.5%; Median home value: $178,700; Median year structure built: 1980; Homeowner vacancy rate: 0.0%; Median selected monthly owner costs: $1,576 with a mortgage, $536 without a mortgage; Median gross rent: $982 per month; Rental vacancy rate: 0.0%
Health Insurance: 85.5% have insurance; 83.4% have private insurance; 6.8% have public insurance; 14.5% do not have insurance; 13.3% of children under 18 do not have insurance
Transportation: Commute: 98.2% car, 0.0% public transportation, 0.0% walk, 0.0% work from home; Mean travel time to work: 24.5 minutes

GREENHILLS (village). Covers a land area of 1.246 square miles and a water area of 0 square miles. Located at 39.27° N. Lat; 84.52° W. Long. Elevation is 804 feet.
History: Greenhills was completed in 1937 as a Resettlement Administration project to provide housing.
Population: 3,591; Growth (since 2000): -12.5%; Density: 2,882.7 persons per square mile; Race: 83.0% White, 14.4% Black/African American, 0.6% Asian, 0.3% American Indian/Alaska Native, 0.0% Native Hawaiian/Other Pacific Islander, 1.7% Two or more races, 4.3% Hispanic of any race; Average household size: 2.43; Median age: 41.9; Age under 18: 23.3%; Age 65 and over: 15.9%; Males per 100 females: 89.4; Marriage status: 28.6% never married, 54.4% now married, 0.3% separated, 6.7% widowed, 10.3% divorced; Foreign born: 3.5%; Speak English only: 94.0%; With disability: 10.2%; Veterans: 6.3%; Ancestry: 28.1% German, 16.0% Irish, 7.4% English, 3.5% Scottish, 3.3% American
Employment: 17.2% management, business, and financial, 3.5% computer, engineering, and science, 14.1% education, legal, community service, arts, and media, 6.2% healthcare practitioners, 19.1% service, 22.1% sales and office, 11.1% natural resources, construction, and maintenance, 6.7% production, transportation, and material moving
Income: Per capita: $29,534; Median household: $56,537; Average household: $70,591; Households with income of $100,000 or more: 18.0%; Poverty rate: 12.6%
Educational Attainment: High school diploma or higher: 94.8%; Bachelor's degree or higher: 33.3%; Graduate/professional degree or higher: 11.4%
Housing: Homeownership rate: 68.8%; Median home value: $114,700; Median year structure built: 1954; Homeowner vacancy rate: 0.0%; Median selected monthly owner costs: $1,228 with a mortgage, $517 without a mortgage; Median gross rent: $857 per month; Rental vacancy rate: 4.9%
Health Insurance: 90.2% have insurance; 77.2% have private insurance; 25.4% have public insurance; 9.8% do not have insurance; 0.7% of children under 18 do not have insurance
Safety: Violent crime rate: 2.8 per 10,000 population; Property crime rate: 100.3 per 10,000 population
Transportation: Commute: 96.2% car, 0.2% public transportation, 0.5% walk, 2.3% work from home; Mean travel time to work: 22.3 minutes
Additional Information Contacts
Village of Greenhills . . . . (513) 825-2100
http://www.greenhillsohio.org

GROESBECK (CDP). Covers a land area of 2.945 square miles and a water area of 0 square miles. Located at 39.23° N. Lat; 84.60° W. Long. Elevation is 863 feet.
Population: 6,957; Growth (since 2000): -3.4%; Density: 2,362.5 persons per square mile; Race: 75.2% White, 17.3% Black/African American, 0.2% Asian, 0.0% American Indian/Alaska Native, 0.4% Native Hawaiian/Other Pacific Islander, 6.2% Two or more races, 5.7% Hispanic of any race; Average household size: 2.66; Median age: 36.0; Age under 18: 26.4%; Age 65 and over: 12.6%; Males per 100 females: 96.0; Marriage status: 30.7% never married, 50.8% now married, 2.4% separated, 6.3% widowed, 12.2% divorced; Foreign born: 2.3%; Speak English only: 96.4%; With disability: 13.0%; Veterans: 9.2%; Ancestry: 35.8% German, 13.9% Irish, 6.6% American, 6.1% Italian, 6.0% English
Employment: 14.3% management, business, and financial, 5.7% computer, engineering, and science, 7.4% education, legal, community service, arts, and media, 9.8% healthcare practitioners, 18.0% service, 28.6% sales and office, 5.2% natural resources, construction, and maintenance, 10.9% production, transportation, and material moving
Income: Per capita: $25,446; Median household: $53,425; Average household: $66,107; Households with income of $100,000 or more: 25.0%; Poverty rate: 15.3%
Educational Attainment: High school diploma or higher: 86.6%; Bachelor's degree or higher: 22.5%; Graduate/professional degree or higher: 6.9%
Housing: Homeownership rate: 76.2%; Median home value: $120,800; Median year structure built: 1968; Homeowner vacancy rate: 0.4%; Median selected monthly owner costs: $1,154 with a mortgage, $469 without a mortgage; Median gross rent: $819 per month; Rental vacancy rate: 3.9%
Health Insurance: 92.6% have insurance; 70.6% have private insurance; 33.0% have public insurance; 7.4% do not have insurance; 0.4% of children under 18 do not have insurance
Transportation: Commute: 93.2% car, 0.8% public transportation, 1.6% walk, 3.5% work from home; Mean travel time to work: 24.6 minutes

HARRISON (city). Covers a land area of 4.921 square miles and a water area of 0.038 square miles. Located at 39.26° N. Lat; 84.79° W. Long. Elevation is 522 feet.
History: Harrison was settled before 1800, and the town was laid out in 1813 on the Ohio-Indiana border. It was named for William Henry Harrison.
Population: 10,522; Growth (since 2000): 40.5%; Density: 2,138.1 persons per square mile; Race: 98.6% White, 0.1% Black/African American, 0.0% Asian, 0.1% American Indian/Alaska Native, 0.0% Native Hawaiian/Other Pacific Islander, 0.8% Two or more races, 1.6% Hispanic of any race; Average household size: 2.56; Median age: 36.3; Age under 18: 27.1%; Age 65 and over: 11.5%; Males per 100 females: 94.9; Marriage status: 21.9% never married, 64.2% now married, 1.7% separated, 4.6% widowed, 9.2% divorced; Foreign born: 0.3%; Speak English only: 97.8%; With disability: 12.4%; Veterans: 11.0%; Ancestry: 52.2% German, 20.6% Irish, 9.6% English, 4.8% Italian, 3.4% American
Employment: 14.5% management, business, and financial, 4.7% computer, engineering, and science, 6.0% education, legal, community service, arts, and media, 6.8% healthcare practitioners, 16.5% service, 29.4% sales and office, 9.0% natural resources, construction, and maintenance, 13.2% production, transportation, and material moving
Income: Per capita: $27,469; Median household: $61,343; Average household: $69,882; Households with income of $100,000 or more: 24.7%; Poverty rate: 6.6%
Educational Attainment: High school diploma or higher: 93.4%; Bachelor's degree or higher: 22.9%; Graduate/professional degree or higher: 6.6%

School District(s)

Southwest Local (PK-12)
2015-16 Enrollment: 3,764 . . . . (513) 367-4139
Housing: Homeownership rate: 75.0%; Median home value: $139,500; Median year structure built: 1982; Homeowner vacancy rate: 4.7%; Median selected monthly owner costs: $1,241 with a mortgage, $408 without a mortgage; Median gross rent: $709 per month; Rental vacancy rate: 11.2%
Health Insurance: 95.6% have insurance; 84.2% have private insurance; 23.3% have public insurance; 4.4% do not have insurance; 3.8% of children under 18 do not have insurance
Safety: Violent crime rate: 0.0 per 10,000 population; Property crime rate: 282.8 per 10,000 population
Newspapers: Harrison Press (weekly circulation 5,400)
Transportation: Commute: 97.6% car, 0.1% public transportation, 0.0% walk, 2.3% work from home; Mean travel time to work: 25.9 minutes
Additional Information Contacts
City of Harrison . . . . (513) 367-2111
http://www.harrisonoh.org

HIGHPOINT (CDP). Covers a land area of 0.344 square miles and a water area of 0 square miles. Located at 39.29° N. Lat; 84.35° W. Long. Elevation is 873 feet.

Population: 1,248; Growth (since 2000): n/a; Density: 3,625.4 persons per square mile; Race: 90.9% White, 2.2% Black/African American, 0.0% Asian, 0.0% American Indian/Alaska Native, 0.0% Native Hawaiian/Other Pacific Islander, 0.0% Two or more races, 7.0% Hispanic of any race; Average household size: 2.53; Median age: 36.6; Age under 18: 24.4%; Age 65 and over: 16.6%; Males per 100 females: 96.5; Marriage status: 20.6% never married, 64.4% now married, 0.0% separated, 3.9% widowed, 11.1% divorced; Foreign born: 14.9%; Speak English only: 77.5%; With disability: 10.3%; Veterans: 10.8%; Ancestry: 21.7% American, 12.4% German, 8.9% English, 8.1% Irish, 5.4% Russian

Employment: 4.6% management, business, and financial, 3.2% computer, engineering, and science, 11.6% education, legal, community service, arts, and media, 3.3% healthcare practitioners, 20.1% service, 27.6% sales and office, 8.7% natural resources, construction, and maintenance, 20.9% production, transportation, and material moving

Income: Per capita: $29,226; Median household: $70,078; Average household: $71,390; Households with income of $100,000 or more: 24.9%; Poverty rate: 7.0%

Educational Attainment: High school diploma or higher: 84.8%; Bachelor's degree or higher: 37.0%; Graduate/professional degree or higher: 20.8%

Housing: Homeownership rate: 79.1%; Median home value: $116,300; Median year structure built: 1982; Homeowner vacancy rate: 0.0%; Median selected monthly owner costs: $1,061 with a mortgage, $473 without a mortgage; Median gross rent: $896 per month; Rental vacancy rate: 0.0%

Health Insurance: 93.3% have insurance; 55.6% have private insurance; 40.1% have public insurance; 6.7% do not have insurance; 0.0% of children under 18 do not have insurance

Transportation: Commute: 83.8% car, 0.0% public transportation, 0.0% walk, 16.2% work from home; Mean travel time to work: 40.2 minutes

HOOVEN (CDP). Covers a land area of 2.566 square miles and a water area of 0.078 square miles. Located at 39.18° N. Lat; 84.77° W. Long. Elevation is 502 feet.

Population: 567; Growth (since 2000): n/a; Density: 220.9 persons per square mile; Race: 100.0% White, 0.0% Black/African American, 0.0% Asian, 0.0% American Indian/Alaska Native, 0.0% Native Hawaiian/Other Pacific Islander, 0.0% Two or more races, 0.0% Hispanic of any race; Average household size: 2.58; Median age: 40.2; Age under 18: 19.6%; Age 65 and over: 14.1%; Males per 100 females: 117.1; Marriage status: 39.9% never married, 41.6% now married, 2.5% separated, 8.7% widowed, 9.8% divorced; Foreign born: 0.0%; Speak English only: 100.0%; With disability: 19.2%; Veterans: 2.6%; Ancestry: 46.6% German, 24.9% Irish, 17.3% Welsh, 13.1% American, 6.0% Scottish

Employment: 11.1% management, business, and financial, 0.0% computer, engineering, and science, 12.5% education, legal, community service, arts, and media, 0.0% healthcare practitioners, 12.2% service, 13.3% sales and office, 17.0% natural resources, construction, and maintenance, 33.9% production, transportation, and material moving

Income: Per capita: $24,690; Median household: $57,083; Average household: $61,905; Households with income of $100,000 or more: 22.3%; Poverty rate: 4.9%

Educational Attainment: High school diploma or higher: 62.5%; Bachelor's degree or higher: 1.7%; Graduate/professional degree or higher: 0.8%

Housing: Homeownership rate: 62.3%; Median home value: $71,900; Median year structure built: Before 1940; Homeowner vacancy rate: 0.0%; Median selected monthly owner costs: $875 with a mortgage, $406 without a mortgage; Median gross rent: $918 per month; Rental vacancy rate: 0.0%

Health Insurance: 85.7% have insurance; 56.4% have private insurance; 42.0% have public insurance; 14.3% do not have insurance; 0.0% of children under 18 do not have insurance

Transportation: Commute: 96.9% car, 0.0% public transportation, 3.1% walk, 0.0% work from home; Mean travel time to work: 20.1 minutes

KENWOOD (CDP). Covers a land area of 2.304 square miles and a water area of <.001 square miles. Located at 39.21° N. Lat; 84.38° W. Long. Elevation is 801 feet.

History: Sycamore Township remained virtually unnoticed until after World War II when developers moved in to build subdivisions known as Kenwood and Dillionvale and the township's population grew from only a few thousand to well over 20,000 in just a few short years. Kenwood stands as the commercial district, the "downtown" of Sycamore township.

Population: 6,922; Growth (since 2000): -6.7%; Density: 3,005.0 persons per square mile; Race: 83.8% White, 9.3% Black/African American, 4.0% Asian, 0.4% American Indian/Alaska Native, 0.0% Native Hawaiian/Other Pacific Islander, 2.4% Two or more races, 2.5% Hispanic of any race; Average household size: 2.23; Median age: 44.6; Age under 18: 22.8%; Age 65 and over: 23.1%; Males per 100 females: 84.1; Marriage status: 27.2% never married, 49.8% now married, 0.5% separated, 10.5% widowed, 12.5% divorced; Foreign born: 6.6%; Speak English only: 92.5%; With disability: 13.3%; Veterans: 5.9%; Ancestry: 30.1% German, 16.5% Irish, 10.6% English, 6.5% Italian, 5.9% American

Employment: 22.8% management, business, and financial, 4.7% computer, engineering, and science, 14.7% education, legal, community service, arts, and media, 11.3% healthcare practitioners, 9.1% service, 27.4% sales and office, 4.6% natural resources, construction, and maintenance, 5.4% production, transportation, and material moving

Income: Per capita: $43,623; Median household: $66,386; Average household: $99,000; Households with income of $100,000 or more: 32.7%; Poverty rate: 7.7%

Educational Attainment: High school diploma or higher: 96.3%; Bachelor's degree or higher: 58.1%; Graduate/professional degree or higher: 28.5%

Housing: Homeownership rate: 59.8%; Median home value: $274,400; Median year structure built: 1966; Homeowner vacancy rate: 0.0%; Median selected monthly owner costs: $1,642 with a mortgage, $620 without a mortgage; Median gross rent: $1,311 per month; Rental vacancy rate: 4.8%

Health Insurance: 93.5% have insurance; 80.7% have private insurance; 29.1% have public insurance; 6.5% do not have insurance; 4.6% of children under 18 do not have insurance

Transportation: Commute: 83.5% car, 2.5% public transportation, 0.4% walk, 9.8% work from home; Mean travel time to work: 22.2 minutes

LINCOLN HEIGHTS (village). Covers a land area of 0.757 square miles and a water area of 0 square miles. Located at 39.24° N. Lat; 84.46° W. Long. Elevation is 597 feet.

History: Incorporated 1946.

Population: 3,360; Growth (since 2000): -18.3%; Density: 4,441.3 persons per square mile; Race: 8.8% White, 87.4% Black/African American, 0.0% Asian, 0.0% American Indian/Alaska Native, 0.0% Native Hawaiian/Other Pacific Islander, 3.8% Two or more races, 2.7% Hispanic of any race; Average household size: 2.42; Median age: 38.1; Age under 18: 26.1%; Age 65 and over: 13.3%; Males per 100 females: 76.3; Marriage status: 45.9% never married, 23.1% now married, 6.2% separated, 8.8% widowed, 22.2% divorced; Foreign born: 0.8%; Speak English only: 98.0%; With disability: 15.6%; Veterans: 10.1%; Ancestry: 7.4% American, 4.0% Italian, 2.6% German, 1.8% Irish, 0.7% Dutch

Employment: 5.4% management, business, and financial, 0.0% computer, engineering, and science, 5.2% education, legal, community service, arts, and media, 1.9% healthcare practitioners, 31.7% service, 15.8% sales and office, 7.4% natural resources, construction, and maintenance, 32.7% production, transportation, and material moving

Income: Per capita: $12,019; Median household: $23,494; Average household: $28,357; Households with income of $100,000 or more: 2.3%; Poverty rate: 41.8%

Educational Attainment: High school diploma or higher: 82.8%; Bachelor's degree or higher: 9.6%; Graduate/professional degree or higher: 2.3%

Housing: Homeownership rate: 34.5%; Median home value: $75,400; Median year structure built: 1968; Homeowner vacancy rate: 0.0%; Median selected monthly owner costs: $1,094 with a mortgage, $361 without a mortgage; Median gross rent: $638 per month; Rental vacancy rate: 12.4%

Health Insurance: 85.2% have insurance; 34.9% have private insurance; 61.9% have public insurance; 14.8% do not have insurance; 0.0% of children under 18 do not have insurance

Transportation: Commute: 98.2% car, 0.0% public transportation, 1.0% walk, 0.8% work from home; Mean travel time to work: 25.9 minutes

LOCKLAND (village). Covers a land area of 1.231 square miles and a water area of 0 square miles. Located at 39.23° N. Lat; 84.46° W. Long. Elevation is 581 feet.

History: Plotted 1828, incorporated 1865.

Population: 3,435; Growth (since 2000): -7.3%; Density: 2,790.1 persons per square mile; Race: 53.3% White, 37.6% Black/African American, 0.0%

Asian, 0.0% American Indian/Alaska Native, 0.0% Native Hawaiian/Other Pacific Islander, 2.8% Two or more races, 13.7% Hispanic of any race; Average household size: 2.37; Median age: 36.0; Age under 18: 23.3%; Age 65 and over: 10.9%; Males per 100 females: 105.5; Marriage status: 42.8% never married, 27.8% now married, 2.6% separated, 6.5% widowed, 22.9% divorced; Foreign born: 14.8%; Speak English only: 75.2%; With disability: 14.3%; Veterans: 7.4%; Ancestry: 9.3% German, 8.0% American, 7.5% Irish, 5.1% Other Subsaharan African, 4.8% Dutch
Employment: 6.5% management, business, and financial, 2.5% computer, engineering, and science, 1.1% education, legal, community service, arts, and media, 2.4% healthcare practitioners, 18.8% service, 22.4% sales and office, 7.5% natural resources, construction, and maintenance, 38.7% production, transportation, and material moving
Income: Per capita: $16,670; Median household: $31,742; Average household: $37,580; Households with income of $100,000 or more: 6.2%; Poverty rate: 35.6%
Educational Attainment: High school diploma or higher: 75.6%; Bachelor's degree or higher: 5.4%; Graduate/professional degree or higher: 1.3%

School District(s)

Lockland Local (PK-12)
2015-16 Enrollment: 520. . . . . (513) 563-5000
Housing: Homeownership rate: 40.4%; Median home value: $81,100; Median year structure built: 1943; Homeowner vacancy rate: 4.6%; Median selected monthly owner costs: $969 with a mortgage, $384 without a mortgage; Median gross rent: $616 per month; Rental vacancy rate: 7.0%
Health Insurance: 84.2% have insurance; 41.8% have private insurance; 53.6% have public insurance; 15.8% do not have insurance; 4.0% of children under 18 do not have insurance
Safety: Violent crime rate: 58.4 per 10,000 population; Property crime rate: 353.6 per 10,000 population
Transportation: Commute: 86.9% car, 3.9% public transportation, 5.7% walk, 1.8% work from home; Mean travel time to work: 26.8 minutes
Additional Information Contacts
Village of Lockland . . . . (513) 761-1124
http://www.lockland.com

LOVELAND (city). Covers a land area of 4.927 square miles and a water area of 0.074 square miles. Located at 39.27° N. Lat; 84.27° W. Long. Elevation is 600 feet.
Population: 12,641; Growth (since 2000): 8.3%; Density: 2,565.7 persons per square mile; Race: 95.8% White, 2.0% Black/African American, 0.3% Asian, 0.0% American Indian/Alaska Native, 0.0% Native Hawaiian/Other Pacific Islander, 1.4% Two or more races, 2.5% Hispanic of any race; Average household size: 2.56; Median age: 39.7; Age under 18: 22.9%; Age 65 and over: 13.5%; Males per 100 females: 91.8; Marriage status: 30.6% never married, 51.5% now married, 1.5% separated, 7.6% widowed, 10.3% divorced; Foreign born: 3.5%; Speak English only: 95.2%; With disability: 9.4%; Veterans: 8.1%; Ancestry: 40.2% German, 14.6% Irish, 10.5% American, 10.1% English, 4.0% Italian
Employment: 20.0% management, business, and financial, 6.6% computer, engineering, and science, 10.7% education, legal, community service, arts, and media, 4.1% healthcare practitioners, 16.7% service, 23.4% sales and office, 7.5% natural resources, construction, and maintenance, 11.0% production, transportation, and material moving
Income: Per capita: $36,838; Median household: $69,355; Average household: $93,425; Households with income of $100,000 or more: 33.7%; Poverty rate: 8.6%
Educational Attainment: High school diploma or higher: 94.6%; Bachelor's degree or higher: 41.6%; Graduate/professional degree or higher: 15.5%

School District(s)

Loveland City (PK-12)
2015-16 Enrollment: 4,679 . . . . (513) 683-5600
Milford Exempted Village (PK-12)
2015-16 Enrollment: 6,565 . . . . (513) 831-1314
Sycamore Community City (PK-12)
2015-16 Enrollment: 5,280 . . . . (513) 686-1700
Housing: Homeownership rate: 72.7%; Median home value: $172,900; Median year structure built: 1976; Homeowner vacancy rate: 0.0%; Median selected monthly owner costs: $1,493 with a mortgage, $529 without a mortgage; Median gross rent: $793 per month; Rental vacancy rate: 3.5%
Health Insurance: 92.7% have insurance; 77.9% have private insurance; 25.8% have public insurance; 7.3% do not have insurance; 3.9% of children under 18 do not have insurance
Safety: Violent crime rate: 4.7 per 10,000 population; Property crime rate: 104.0 per 10,000 population
Newspapers: Community Press (weekly circulation 113,000)
Transportation: Commute: 95.0% car, 0.0% public transportation, 1.1% walk, 3.9% work from home; Mean travel time to work: 22.7 minutes
Additional Information Contacts
City of Loveland. . . . . (513) 683-0150
http://www.lovelandoh.com

MACK (CDP). Covers a land area of 9.273 square miles and a water area of 0 square miles. Located at 39.15° N. Lat; 84.68° W. Long. Elevation is 906 feet.
Population: 11,495; Growth (since 2000): n/a; Density: 1,239.7 persons per square mile; Race: 96.3% White, 0.3% Black/African American, 0.7% Asian, 0.0% American Indian/Alaska Native, 0.0% Native Hawaiian/Other Pacific Islander, 1.5% Two or more races, 1.6% Hispanic of any race; Average household size: 2.87; Median age: 44.9; Age under 18: 24.2%; Age 65 and over: 14.5%; Males per 100 females: 100.1; Marriage status: 24.0% never married, 64.9% now married, 0.2% separated, 4.5% widowed, 6.7% divorced; Foreign born: 2.3%; Speak English only: 96.9%; With disability: 8.8%; Veterans: 7.2%; Ancestry: 51.6% German, 18.8% Irish, 10.7% Italian, 9.0% American, 6.2% English
Employment: 20.0% management, business, and financial, 9.4% computer, engineering, and science, 9.0% education, legal, community service, arts, and media, 9.5% healthcare practitioners, 10.7% service, 26.0% sales and office, 6.6% natural resources, construction, and maintenance, 8.9% production, transportation, and material moving
Income: Per capita: $38,216; Median household: $85,994; Average household: $108,723; Households with income of $100,000 or more: 43.2%; Poverty rate: 6.0%
Educational Attainment: High school diploma or higher: 97.0%; Bachelor's degree or higher: 40.5%; Graduate/professional degree or higher: 11.8%
Housing: Homeownership rate: 95.2%; Median home value: $215,300; Median year structure built: 1975; Homeowner vacancy rate: 0.0%; Median selected monthly owner costs: $1,683 with a mortgage, $594 without a mortgage; Median gross rent: $971 per month; Rental vacancy rate: 0.0%
Health Insurance: 96.7% have insurance; 86.6% have private insurance; 21.2% have public insurance; 3.3% do not have insurance; 0.0% of children under 18 do not have insurance
Transportation: Commute: 93.3% car, 0.7% public transportation, 0.0% walk, 5.4% work from home; Mean travel time to work: 27.5 minutes

---

MADEIRA (city). Covers a land area of 3.377 square miles and a water area of 0.003 square miles. Located at 39.19° N. Lat; 84.37° W. Long. Elevation is 764 feet.
Population: 8,924; Growth (since 2000): 0.0%; Density: 2,642.6 persons per square mile; Race: 95.1% White, 1.0% Black/African American, 1.6% Asian, 0.0% American Indian/Alaska Native, 0.0% Native Hawaiian/Other Pacific Islander, 2.0% Two or more races, 4.3% Hispanic of any race; Average household size: 2.61; Median age: 41.3; Age under 18: 26.0%; Age 65 and over: 16.9%; Males per 100 females: 92.8; Marriage status: 23.7% never married, 62.7% now married, 0.8% separated, 5.5% widowed, 8.1% divorced; Foreign born: 5.2%; Speak English only: 92.1%; With disability: 7.1%; Veterans: 7.2%; Ancestry: 32.8% German, 14.5% Irish, 12.6% English, 10.4% Italian, 7.7% American
Employment: 25.0% management, business, and financial, 8.3% computer, engineering, and science, 16.7% education, legal, community service, arts, and media, 6.5% healthcare practitioners, 10.5% service, 24.1% sales and office, 3.1% natural resources, construction, and maintenance, 5.8% production, transportation, and material moving
Income: Per capita: $41,507; Median household: $91,810; Average household: $110,765; Households with income of $100,000 or more: 45.3%; Poverty rate: 2.1%
Educational Attainment: High school diploma or higher: 95.9%; Bachelor's degree or higher: 61.1%; Graduate/professional degree or higher: 27.3%

School District(s)

Madeira City (PK-12)
2015-16 Enrollment: 1,496 . . . . (513) 985-6070
Housing: Homeownership rate: 87.3%; Median home value: $249,700; Median year structure built: 1956; Homeowner vacancy rate: 2.2%; Median selected monthly owner costs: $1,709 with a mortgage, $743 without a mortgage; Median gross rent: $1,102 per month; Rental vacancy rate: 0.0%

Health Insurance: 97.0% have insurance; 88.1% have private insurance; 18.9% have public insurance; 3.0% do not have insurance; 1.5% of children under 18 do not have insurance
Transportation: Commute: 87.3% car, 1.3% public transportation, 2.5% walk, 8.2% work from home; Mean travel time to work: 20.0 minutes
Additional Information Contacts
City of Madeira . . . . (513) 561-7228
http://www.madeiracity.com

MARIEMONT (village). Covers a land area of 0.864 square miles and a water area of 0.029 square miles. Located at 39.14° N. Lat; 84.38° W. Long. Elevation is 584 feet.
History: Mariemont was laid out in 1922 along the Little Miami River on land owned by Marie Emery of Cincinnati. A large stone tower on a knoll above the town housed the Bells of Mariemont, 23 bells weighing from 100 pounds to two tons.
Population: 3,400; Growth (since 2000): -0.2%; Density: 3,935.5 persons per square mile; Race: 97.0% White, 0.3% Black/African American, 0.2% Asian, 0.0% American Indian/Alaska Native, 0.0% Native Hawaiian/Other Pacific Islander, 2.6% Two or more races, 1.9% Hispanic of any race; Average household size: 2.37; Median age: 38.0; Age under 18: 27.7%; Age 65 and over: 15.9%; Males per 100 females: 82.5; Marriage status: 26.7% never married, 59.4% now married, 2.2% separated, 6.6% widowed, 7.2% divorced; Foreign born: 3.9%; Speak English only: 96.4%; With disability: 2.9%; Veterans: 5.8%; Ancestry: 41.1% German, 16.7% Irish, 16.4% English, 10.8% American, 6.5% Italian
Employment: 23.0% management, business, and financial, 5.7% computer, engineering, and science, 10.9% education, legal, community service, arts, and media, 12.0% healthcare practitioners, 9.0% service, 30.4% sales and office, 3.3% natural resources, construction, and maintenance, 5.8% production, transportation, and material moving
Income: Per capita: $54,162; Median household: $92,216; Average household: $129,583; Households with income of $100,000 or more: 45.9%; Poverty rate: 2.3%
Educational Attainment: High school diploma or higher: 99.6%; Bachelor's degree or higher: 76.7%; Graduate/professional degree or higher: 33.7%
Housing: Homeownership rate: 61.4%; Median home value: $364,900; Median year structure built: 1945; Homeowner vacancy rate: 0.0%; Median selected monthly owner costs: $2,344 with a mortgage, $1,325 without a mortgage; Median gross rent: $1,019 per month; Rental vacancy rate: 11.3%
Health Insurance: 98.4% have insurance; 87.7% have private insurance; 20.8% have public insurance; 1.6% do not have insurance; 0.0% of children under 18 do not have insurance
Safety: Violent crime rate: 2.9 per 10,000 population; Property crime rate: 131.2 per 10,000 population
Transportation: Commute: 86.6% car, 0.9% public transportation, 2.4% walk, 8.2% work from home; Mean travel time to work: 24.5 minutes

MIAMI HEIGHTS (CDP). Covers a land area of 3.513 square miles and a water area of 0 square miles. Located at 39.17° N. Lat; 84.72° W. Long. Elevation is 823 feet.
Population: 4,740; Growth (since 2000): n/a; Density: 1,349.5 persons per square mile; Race: 96.4% White, 0.2% Black/African American, 0.6% Asian, 0.0% American Indian/Alaska Native, 0.0% Native Hawaiian/Other Pacific Islander, 0.4% Two or more races, 3.6% Hispanic of any race; Average household size: 2.58; Median age: 44.5; Age under 18: 24.7%; Age 65 and over: 17.1%; Males per 100 females: 95.4; Marriage status: 18.9% never married, 66.2% now married, 1.6% separated, 7.3% widowed, 7.6% divorced; Foreign born: 1.4%; Speak English only: 95.6%; With disability: 7.9%; Veterans: 9.2%; Ancestry: 51.9% German, 28.8% Irish, 10.6% English, 6.4% American, 5.6% Italian
Employment: 21.3% management, business, and financial, 7.4% computer, engineering, and science, 8.5% education, legal, community service, arts, and media, 8.7% healthcare practitioners, 14.7% service, 25.6% sales and office, 4.7% natural resources, construction, and maintenance, 9.0% production, transportation, and material moving
Income: Per capita: $34,929; Median household: $81,204; Average household: $90,768; Households with income of $100,000 or more: 38.2%; Poverty rate: 3.2%
Educational Attainment: High school diploma or higher: 92.6%; Bachelor's degree or higher: 34.6%; Graduate/professional degree or higher: 11.5%
Housing: Homeownership rate: 94.4%; Median home value: $208,500; Median year structure built: 1997; Homeowner vacancy rate: 0.0%; Median selected monthly owner costs: $1,560 with a mortgage, $593 without a mortgage; Median gross rent: $875 per month; Rental vacancy rate: 0.0%
Health Insurance: 97.9% have insurance; 86.1% have private insurance; 25.3% have public insurance; 2.1% do not have insurance; 0.9% of children under 18 do not have insurance
Transportation: Commute: 92.3% car, 0.5% public transportation, 2.2% walk, 5.0% work from home; Mean travel time to work: 27.6 minutes

MIAMITOWN (CDP). Covers a land area of 1.343 square miles and a water area of 0.024 square miles. Located at 39.21° N. Lat; 84.71° W. Long. Elevation is 522 feet.
Population: 1,343; Growth (since 2000): n/a; Density: 999.8 persons per square mile; Race: 89.0% White, 3.5% Black/African American, 0.0% Asian, 0.0% American Indian/Alaska Native, 6.6% Native Hawaiian/Other Pacific Islander, 0.0% Two or more races, 2.1% Hispanic of any race; Average household size: 2.61; Median age: 27.2; Age under 18: 27.6%; Age 65 and over: 7.4%; Males per 100 females: 101.1; Marriage status: 38.0% never married, 45.8% now married, 5.8% separated, 3.9% widowed, 12.3% divorced; Foreign born: 1.1%; Speak English only: 92.2%; With disability: 11.1%; Veterans: 16.6%; Ancestry: 26.1% German, 13.9% American, 13.2% Irish, 6.0% French, 4.2% Scottish
Employment: 3.6% management, business, and financial, 1.7% computer, engineering, and science, 0.0% education, legal, community service, arts, and media, 0.0% healthcare practitioners, 36.3% service, 26.0% sales and office, 14.0% natural resources, construction, and maintenance, 18.4% production, transportation, and material moving
Income: Per capita: $19,832; Median household: $45,099; Average household: $49,868; Households with income of $100,000 or more: 6.8%; Poverty rate: 13.0%
Educational Attainment: High school diploma or higher: 82.9%; Bachelor's degree or higher: 11.1%; Graduate/professional degree or higher: 1.8%

School District(s)

Southwest Local (PK-12)
2015-16 Enrollment: 3,764 . . . . (513) 367-4139
Housing: Homeownership rate: 8.0%; Median home value: $157,800; Median year structure built: 1978; Homeowner vacancy rate: 0.0%; Median selected monthly owner costs: $1,469 with a mortgage, n/a without a mortgage; Median gross rent: $766 per month; Rental vacancy rate: 0.0%
Health Insurance: 83.2% have insurance; 58.4% have private insurance; 35.9% have public insurance; 16.8% do not have insurance; 22.6% of children under 18 do not have insurance
Transportation: Commute: 93.5% car, 0.0% public transportation, 2.0% walk, 4.5% work from home; Mean travel time to work: 21.7 minutes

MONFORT HEIGHTS (CDP). Covers a land area of 5.913 square miles and a water area of <.001 square miles. Located at 39.18° N. Lat; 84.61° W. Long. Elevation is 899 feet.
Population: 12,850; Growth (since 2000): n/a; Density: 2,173.2 persons per square mile; Race: 87.2% White, 10.4% Black/African American, 1.6% Asian, 0.0% American Indian/Alaska Native, 0.0% Native Hawaiian/Other Pacific Islander, 0.7% Two or more races, 0.2% Hispanic of any race; Average household size: 2.63; Median age: 42.3; Age under 18: 22.4%; Age 65 and over: 17.0%; Males per 100 females: 92.7; Marriage status: 27.1% never married, 59.2% now married, 0.9% separated, 5.8% widowed, 7.9% divorced; Foreign born: 2.0%; Speak English only: 97.2%; With disability: 11.7%; Veterans: 8.3%; Ancestry: 47.4% German, 21.3% Irish, 8.0% Italian, 6.3% American, 6.0% English
Employment: 19.7% management, business, and financial, 4.6% computer, engineering, and science, 9.1% education, legal, community service, arts, and media, 10.3% healthcare practitioners, 15.1% service, 23.0% sales and office, 5.9% natural resources, construction, and maintenance, 12.4% production, transportation, and material moving
Income: Per capita: $36,568; Median household: $74,197; Average household: $94,836; Households with income of $100,000 or more: 28.4%; Poverty rate: 6.5%
Educational Attainment: High school diploma or higher: 94.2%; Bachelor's degree or higher: 35.3%; Graduate/professional degree or higher: 13.0%
Housing: Homeownership rate: 77.4%; Median home value: $165,700; Median year structure built: 1976; Homeowner vacancy rate: 2.1%; Median selected monthly owner costs: $1,477 with a mortgage, $564 without a

mortgage; Median gross rent: $1,036 per month; Rental vacancy rate: 0.0%
Health Insurance: 95.5% have insurance; 80.6% have private insurance; 26.8% have public insurance; 4.5% do not have insurance; 2.6% of children under 18 do not have insurance
Transportation: Commute: 94.0% car, 0.3% public transportation, 1.2% walk, 4.0% work from home; Mean travel time to work: 22.5 minutes

MONTGOMERY (city). Covers a land area of 5.286 square miles and a water area of 0.013 square miles. Located at 39.25° N. Lat; 84.35° W. Long. Elevation is 801 feet.
History: Montgomery was named after the town of Montgomery, New York, where the original settlers came from. Montgomery, New York was named in honor of Richard Montgomery, Brigadier General of the Continental Army during the American Revolution.
Population: 10,440; Growth (since 2000): 2.7%; Density: 1,974.8 persons per square mile; Race: 88.8% White, 2.9% Black/African American, 6.4% Asian, 0.0% American Indian/Alaska Native, 0.0% Native Hawaiian/Other Pacific Islander, 1.3% Two or more races, 3.4% Hispanic of any race; Average household size: 2.66; Median age: 46.5; Age under 18: 25.9%; Age 65 and over: 21.5%; Males per 100 females: 92.7; Marriage status: 16.8% never married, 70.6% now married, 0.4% separated, 7.4% widowed, 5.3% divorced; Foreign born: 9.4%; Speak English only: 89.1%; With disability: 9.7%; Veterans: 7.6%; Ancestry: 29.5% German, 18.0% Irish, 13.1% English, 6.9% American, 5.8% Italian
Employment: 28.1% management, business, and financial, 8.0% computer, engineering, and science, 16.2% education, legal, community service, arts, and media, 9.7% healthcare practitioners, 9.1% service, 21.6% sales and office, 3.0% natural resources, construction, and maintenance, 4.3% production, transportation, and material moving
Income: Per capita: $54,809; Median household: $108,469; Average household: $148,522; Households with income of $100,000 or more: 54.3%; Poverty rate: 3.9%
Educational Attainment: High school diploma or higher: 97.7%; Bachelor's degree or higher: 69.1%; Graduate/professional degree or higher: 30.8%
Housing: Homeownership rate: 88.3%; Median home value: $332,900; Median year structure built: 1975; Homeowner vacancy rate: 0.5%; Median selected monthly owner costs: $2,146 with a mortgage, $702 without a mortgage; Median gross rent: $1,116 per month; Rental vacancy rate: 4.3%
Health Insurance: 98.3% have insurance; 90.0% have private insurance; 25.0% have public insurance; 1.7% do not have insurance; 1.5% of children under 18 do not have insurance
Safety: Violent crime rate: 3.8 per 10,000 population; Property crime rate: 140.2 per 10,000 population
Transportation: Commute: 84.6% car, 1.5% public transportation, 1.5% walk, 11.7% work from home; Mean travel time to work: 22.3 minutes
Additional Information Contacts
City of Montgomery . . . . (513) 891-2424
http://www.ci.montgomery.oh.us

MOUNT HEALTHY (city). Covers a land area of 1.406 square miles and a water area of 0 square miles. Located at 39.23° N. Lat; 84.55° W. Long. Elevation is 837 feet.
History: Mount Healthy was founded in 1817 by John Laboyteaux and Samuel Hill. It was first called Mount Pleasant, but the name was later changed to reflect the village's escape from the cholera epidemic of the 1850's.
Population: 6,054; Growth (since 2000): -15.3%; Density: 4,305.2 persons per square mile; Race: 53.4% White, 39.7% Black/African American, 2.7% Asian, 0.0% American Indian/Alaska Native, 0.0% Native Hawaiian/Other Pacific Islander, 3.9% Two or more races, 0.6% Hispanic of any race; Average household size: 2.02; Median age: 40.2; Age under 18: 24.4%; Age 65 and over: 18.4%; Males per 100 females: 81.4; Marriage status: 36.9% never married, 33.3% now married, 0.7% separated, 12.4% widowed, 17.3% divorced; Foreign born: 3.1%; Speak English only: 96.7%; With disability: 18.9%; Veterans: 6.6%; Ancestry: 26.1% German, 10.3% Irish, 6.3% English, 3.0% American, 2.3% Italian
Employment: 5.7% management, business, and financial, 7.3% computer, engineering, and science, 9.0% education, legal, community service, arts, and media, 5.3% healthcare practitioners, 21.8% service, 26.9% sales and office, 6.6% natural resources, construction, and maintenance, 17.4% production, transportation, and material moving
Income: Per capita: $21,057; Median household: $34,404; Average household: $42,420; Households with income of $100,000 or more: 8.3%; Poverty rate: 19.4%
Educational Attainment: High school diploma or higher: 90.2%; Bachelor's degree or higher: 18.1%; Graduate/professional degree or higher: 7.0%
Housing: Homeownership rate: 43.7%; Median home value: $84,600; Median year structure built: 1957; Homeowner vacancy rate: 2.0%; Median selected monthly owner costs: $1,077 with a mortgage, $469 without a mortgage; Median gross rent: $659 per month; Rental vacancy rate: 1.3%
Health Insurance: 93.0% have insurance; 60.8% have private insurance; 44.1% have public insurance; 7.0% do not have insurance; 1.3% of children under 18 do not have insurance
Safety: Violent crime rate: 51.4 per 10,000 population; Property crime rate: 429.7 per 10,000 population
Transportation: Commute: 89.7% car, 3.6% public transportation, 6.3% walk, 0.4% work from home; Mean travel time to work: 23.3 minutes
Additional Information Contacts
City of Mount Healthy . . . . (513) 931-8840
http://www.mthealthy.org

MOUNT HEALTHY HEIGHTS (CDP). Covers a land area of 0.777 square miles and a water area of 0 square miles. Located at 39.27° N. Lat; 84.57° W. Long. Elevation is 846 feet.
Population: 3,068; Growth (since 2000): -11.1%; Density: 3,947.0 persons per square mile; Race: 51.5% White, 44.6% Black/African American, 0.0% Asian, 0.0% American Indian/Alaska Native, 0.0% Native Hawaiian/Other Pacific Islander, 3.1% Two or more races, 0.0% Hispanic of any race; Average household size: 2.48; Median age: 34.6; Age under 18: 28.7%; Age 65 and over: 12.2%; Males per 100 females: 83.2; Marriage status: 32.7% never married, 46.2% now married, 5.7% separated, 8.4% widowed, 12.7% divorced; Foreign born: 0.0%; Speak English only: 100.0%; With disability: 12.0%; Veterans: 8.8%; Ancestry: 20.8% German, 8.9% Irish, 5.2% Italian, 4.1% English, 3.7% American
Employment: 4.1% management, business, and financial, 2.8% computer, engineering, and science, 0.4% education, legal, community service, arts, and media, 6.8% healthcare practitioners, 21.7% service, 28.5% sales and office, 13.2% natural resources, construction, and maintenance, 22.5% production, transportation, and material moving
Income: Per capita: $20,185; Median household: $42,442; Average household: $49,309; Households with income of $100,000 or more: 11.7%; Poverty rate: 20.4%
Educational Attainment: High school diploma or higher: 85.0%; Bachelor's degree or higher: 9.3%; Graduate/professional degree or higher: 1.2%
Housing: Homeownership rate: 58.8%; Median home value: $93,100; Median year structure built: 1968; Homeowner vacancy rate: 6.9%; Median selected monthly owner costs: $1,064 with a mortgage, $396 without a mortgage; Median gross rent: $843 per month; Rental vacancy rate: 11.0%
Health Insurance: 92.7% have insurance; 62.8% have private insurance; 41.5% have public insurance; 7.3% do not have insurance; 6.3% of children under 18 do not have insurance
Transportation: Commute: 97.8% car, 0.0% public transportation, 0.0% walk, 2.2% work from home; Mean travel time to work: 24.4 minutes

MOUNT SAINT JOSEPH (unincorporated postal area)
ZCTA: 45051
Covers a land area of 0.086 square miles and a water area of 0 square miles. Located at 39.10° N. Lat; 84.65° W. Long. Elevation is 817 feet.
Population: 204; Growth (since 2000): n/a; Density: 2,360.2 persons per square mile; Race: 68.6% White, 21.6% Black/African American, 0.0% Asian, 9.8% American Indian/Alaska Native, 0.0% Native Hawaiian/Other Pacific Islander, 0.0% Two or more races, 0.0% Hispanic of any race; Average household size: 0.00; Median age: 67.9; Age under 18: 7.8%; Age 65 and over: 58.3%; Males per 100 females: 0.0; Marriage status: 31.9% never married, 12.2% now married, 0.0% separated, 29.8% widowed, 26.1% divorced; Foreign born: 0.0%; Speak English only: 100.0%; With disability: 63.0%; Veterans: 0.0%; Ancestry: 16.7% Irish, 13.2% German, 9.8% American, 9.8% Ethiopian, 8.8% Croatian
Employment: 0.0% management, business, and financial, 0.0% computer, engineering, and science, 0.0% education, legal, community service, arts, and media, 0.0% healthcare practitioners, 0.0% service, 100.0% sales and office, 0.0% natural resources, construction, and maintenance, 0.0% production, transportation, and material moving

Income: Per capita: $9,719; Median household: n/a; Average household: n/a; Households with income of $100,000 or more: n/a; Poverty rate: 76.3%
Educational Attainment: High school diploma or higher: 71.3%; Bachelor's degree or higher: 9.6%; Graduate/professional degree or higher: 9.6%
Housing: Homeownership rate: n/a; Median home value: n/a; Median year structure built: n/a; Homeowner vacancy rate: 0.0%; Median selected monthly owner costs: $0 with a mortgage, $0 without a mortgage; Median gross rent: n/a per month; Rental vacancy rate: 0.0%
Health Insurance: 78.3% have insurance; 19.6% have private insurance; 78.3% have public insurance; 21.7% do not have insurance; 0.0% of children under 18 do not have insurance
Transportation: Commute: 52.6% car, 47.4% public transportation, 0.0% walk, 0.0% work from home; Mean travel time to work: 0.0 minutes

NEW BALTIMORE (CDP). Covers a land area of 1.371 square miles and a water area of 0.017 square miles. Located at 39.28° N. Lat; 84.67° W. Long. Elevation is 564 feet.
Population: 723; Growth (since 2000): n/a; Density: 527.3 persons per square mile; Race: 100.0% White, 0.0% Black/African American, 0.0% Asian, 0.0% American Indian/Alaska Native, 0.0% Native Hawaiian/Other Pacific Islander, 0.0% Two or more races, 0.0% Hispanic of any race; Average household size: 2.65; Median age: 38.4; Age under 18: 31.0%; Age 65 and over: 7.5%; Males per 100 females: 94.4; Marriage status: 25.6% never married, 66.2% now married, 0.0% separated, 5.3% widowed, 2.9% divorced; Foreign born: 0.0%; Speak English only: 98.5%; With disability: 11.2%; Veterans: 8.0%; Ancestry: 59.3% German, 18.3% Italian, 17.6% English, 12.3% Irish, 6.6% American
Employment: 22.8% management, business, and financial, 0.0% computer, engineering, and science, 9.2% education, legal, community service, arts, and media, 4.2% healthcare practitioners, 32.5% service, 16.5% sales and office, 8.7% natural resources, construction, and maintenance, 6.0% production, transportation, and material moving
Income: Per capita: $23,315; Median household: $55,590; Average household: $61,376; Households with income of $100,000 or more: 20.1%; Poverty rate: 5.5%
Educational Attainment: High school diploma or higher: 86.9%; Bachelor's degree or higher: 21.3%; Graduate/professional degree or higher: 9.5%
Housing: Homeownership rate: 91.9%; Median home value: n/a; Median year structure built: 1990; Homeowner vacancy rate: 0.0%; Median selected monthly owner costs: $1,569 with a mortgage, $418 without a mortgage; Median gross rent: $1,042 per month; Rental vacancy rate: 0.0%
Health Insurance: 94.5% have insurance; 78.6% have private insurance; 18.5% have public insurance; 5.5% do not have insurance; 0.0% of children under 18 do not have insurance
Transportation: Commute: 100.0% car, 0.0% public transportation, 0.0% walk, 0.0% work from home; Mean travel time to work: 29.9 minutes

NEW BURLINGTON (CDP). Covers a land area of 3.068 square miles and a water area of 0 square miles. Located at 39.26° N. Lat; 84.55° W. Long. Elevation is 823 feet.
Population: 4,506; Growth (since 2000): n/a; Density: 1,468.6 persons per square mile; Race: 50.7% White, 45.1% Black/African American, 0.0% Asian, 0.0% American Indian/Alaska Native, 0.0% Native Hawaiian/Other Pacific Islander, 4.2% Two or more races, 1.7% Hispanic of any race; Average household size: 2.55; Median age: 46.1; Age under 18: 22.9%; Age 65 and over: 20.5%; Males per 100 females: 85.9; Marriage status: 28.2% never married, 52.5% now married, 3.0% separated, 6.3% widowed, 13.0% divorced; Foreign born: 3.5%; Speak English only: 97.4%; With disability: 18.9%; Veterans: 10.9%; Ancestry: 28.5% German, 9.0% Irish, 5.9% English, 3.0% American, 2.8% West Indian
Employment: 13.2% management, business, and financial, 2.6% computer, engineering, and science, 3.6% education, legal, community service, arts, and media, 2.6% healthcare practitioners, 22.6% service, 30.0% sales and office, 6.7% natural resources, construction, and maintenance, 18.7% production, transportation, and material moving
Income: Per capita: $25,282; Median household: $56,401; Average household: $64,166; Households with income of $100,000 or more: 18.5%; Poverty rate: 23.7%
Educational Attainment: High school diploma or higher: 89.7%; Bachelor's degree or higher: 18.2%; Graduate/professional degree or higher: 6.2%
Housing: Homeownership rate: 69.0%; Median home value: $118,500; Median year structure built: 1972; Homeowner vacancy rate: 8.5%; Median selected monthly owner costs: $1,180 with a mortgage, $558 without a mortgage; Median gross rent: $887 per month; Rental vacancy rate: 0.0%
Health Insurance: 94.2% have insurance; 60.8% have private insurance; 47.1% have public insurance; 5.8% do not have insurance; 1.5% of children under 18 do not have insurance
Transportation: Commute: 97.6% car, 1.5% public transportation, 0.0% walk, 0.9% work from home; Mean travel time to work: 25.7 minutes

NEW HAVEN (CDP). Covers a land area of 1.294 square miles and a water area of 0.005 square miles. Located at 39.28° N. Lat; 84.75° W. Long. Elevation is 561 feet.
Population: 623; Growth (since 2000): n/a; Density: 481.3 persons per square mile; Race: 90.5% White, 0.0% Black/African American, 0.0% Asian, 1.4% American Indian/Alaska Native, 0.0% Native Hawaiian/Other Pacific Islander, 0.0% Two or more races, 8.0% Hispanic of any race; Average household size: 2.47; Median age: 35.9; Age under 18: 18.8%; Age 65 and over: 12.7%; Males per 100 females: 105.3; Marriage status: 27.2% never married, 63.2% now married, 0.0% separated, 4.6% widowed, 5.0% divorced; Foreign born: 1.4%; Speak English only: 98.4%; With disability: 11.4%; Veterans: 9.5%; Ancestry: 59.7% German, 15.2% American, 13.0% Irish, 6.3% Scottish, 4.8% Dutch
Employment: 17.5% management, business, and financial, 0.0% computer, engineering, and science, 6.5% education, legal, community service, arts, and media, 14.6% healthcare practitioners, 2.4% service, 24.0% sales and office, 22.9% natural resources, construction, and maintenance, 12.1% production, transportation, and material moving
Income: Per capita: $24,774; Median household: $61,731; Average household: $61,707; Households with income of $100,000 or more: 13.9%; Poverty rate: n/a
Educational Attainment: High school diploma or higher: 95.0%; Bachelor's degree or higher: 18.6%; Graduate/professional degree or higher: 4.6%
Housing: Homeownership rate: 100.0%; Median home value: $106,900; Median year structure built: 1972; Homeowner vacancy rate: 0.0%; Median selected monthly owner costs: $1,228 with a mortgage, $441 without a mortgage; Median gross rent: n/a per month; Rental vacancy rate: 0.0%
Health Insurance: 98.2% have insurance; 86.8% have private insurance; 25.2% have public insurance; 1.8% do not have insurance; 0.0% of children under 18 do not have insurance
Transportation: Commute: 95.1% car, 0.0% public transportation, 0.0% walk, 4.9% work from home; Mean travel time to work: 20.1 minutes

NEWTOWN (village). Covers a land area of 2.172 square miles and a water area of 0.199 square miles. Located at 39.12° N. Lat; 84.35° W. Long. Elevation is 499 feet.
History: Laid out 1801.
Population: 2,683; Growth (since 2000): 10.9%; Density: 1,235.4 persons per square mile; Race: 92.1% White, 2.7% Black/African American, 0.9% Asian, 0.0% American Indian/Alaska Native, 0.0% Native Hawaiian/Other Pacific Islander, 0.5% Two or more races, 7.3% Hispanic of any race; Average household size: 2.48; Median age: 39.0; Age under 18: 26.1%; Age 65 and over: 12.1%; Males per 100 females: 93.1; Marriage status: 27.6% never married, 54.1% now married, 1.3% separated, 4.7% widowed, 13.6% divorced; Foreign born: 2.8%; Speak English only: 94.0%; With disability: 9.2%; Veterans: 8.1%; Ancestry: 26.2% German, 18.6% American, 11.9% Irish, 10.7% English, 4.8% Italian
Employment: 24.5% management, business, and financial, 6.0% computer, engineering, and science, 15.9% education, legal, community service, arts, and media, 6.4% healthcare practitioners, 13.8% service, 19.4% sales and office, 5.8% natural resources, construction, and maintenance, 8.2% production, transportation, and material moving
Income: Per capita: $41,364; Median household: $70,473; Average household: $102,624; Households with income of $100,000 or more: 32.1%; Poverty rate: 8.5%
Educational Attainment: High school diploma or higher: 91.7%; Bachelor's degree or higher: 43.8%; Graduate/professional degree or higher: 13.5%
Housing: Homeownership rate: 61.2%; Median home value: $145,900; Median year structure built: 1980; Homeowner vacancy rate: 0.0%; Median selected monthly owner costs: $1,400 with a mortgage, $581 without a mortgage; Median gross rent: $1,075 per month; Rental vacancy rate: 9.7%

Health Insurance: 90.9% have insurance; 76.7% have private insurance; 25.2% have public insurance; 9.1% do not have insurance; 9.4% of children under 18 do not have insurance
Safety: Violent crime rate: 11.3 per 10,000 population; Property crime rate: 116.4 per 10,000 population
Transportation: Commute: 91.3% car, 0.7% public transportation, 1.7% walk, 4.4% work from home; Mean travel time to work: 26.3 minutes

NORTH BEND (village). Covers a land area of 1.070 square miles and a water area of 0.075 square miles. Located at 39.15° N. Lat; 84.74° W. Long. Elevation is 574 feet.
History: North Bend was founded in 1789 by John Cleves Symmes. William Henry Harrison lived here until he became the 9th President of the U.S. in 1841. This was the birthplace of his grandson, William Henry Harrison (1833-1901), the 23rd U.S. President.
Population: 825; Growth (since 2000): 36.8%; Density: 770.7 persons per square mile; Race: 98.2% White, 0.0% Black/African American, 0.2% Asian, 1.1% American Indian/Alaska Native, 0.0% Native Hawaiian/Other Pacific Islander, 0.5% Two or more races, 0.0% Hispanic of any race; Average household size: 2.10; Median age: 61.0; Age under 18: 7.5%; Age 65 and over: 36.5%; Males per 100 females: 100.2; Marriage status: 17.3% never married, 63.4% now married, 1.0% separated, 5.2% widowed, 14.1% divorced; Foreign born: 1.5%; Speak English only: 97.9%; With disability: 11.2%; Veterans: 9.7%; Ancestry: 53.8% German, 18.9% Irish, 11.4% Italian, 7.0% American, 6.8% English
Employment: 20.7% management, business, and financial, 0.6% computer, engineering, and science, 9.4% education, legal, community service, arts, and media, 8.8% healthcare practitioners, 6.6% service, 39.1% sales and office, 3.0% natural resources, construction, and maintenance, 11.8% production, transportation, and material moving
Income: Per capita: $48,817; Median household: $65,417; Average household: $102,711; Households with income of $100,000 or more: 36.9%; Poverty rate: 8.7%
Educational Attainment: High school diploma or higher: 95.0%; Bachelor's degree or higher: 38.7%; Graduate/professional degree or higher: 14.1%

School District(s)

Three Rivers Local (PK-12)
2015-16 Enrollment: 1,973 . . . . (877) 644-6338
Housing: Homeownership rate: 82.4%; Median home value: $283,800; Median year structure built: 1998; Homeowner vacancy rate: 0.0%; Median selected monthly owner costs: $1,908 with a mortgage, $844 without a mortgage; Median gross rent: $588 per month; Rental vacancy rate: 0.0%
Health Insurance: 94.8% have insurance; 73.1% have private insurance; 44.7% have public insurance; 5.2% do not have insurance; 0.0% of children under 18 do not have insurance
Transportation: Commute: 98.0% car, 0.0% public transportation, 0.0% walk, 1.4% work from home; Mean travel time to work: 23.4 minutes

NORTH COLLEGE HILL (city). Covers a land area of 1.826 square miles and a water area of 0.001 square miles. Located at 39.22° N. Lat; 84.55° W. Long. Elevation is 823 feet.
History: Named for its location north of Cincinnati. Revolutionary War cemetery is in the city. Incorporated as a city 1940.
Population: 9,351; Growth (since 2000): -7.3%; Density: 5,120.1 persons per square mile; Race: 50.4% White, 46.2% Black/African American, 0.0% Asian, 0.3% American Indian/Alaska Native, 0.0% Native Hawaiian/Other Pacific Islander, 3.0% Two or more races, 0.8% Hispanic of any race; Average household size: 2.21; Median age: 38.5; Age under 18: 23.2%; Age 65 and over: 13.0%; Males per 100 females: 89.8; Marriage status: 41.3% never married, 34.0% now married, 5.2% separated, 8.4% widowed, 16.3% divorced; Foreign born: 3.0%; Speak English only: 96.7%; With disability: 13.2%; Veterans: 8.7%; Ancestry: 21.6% German, 9.5% Irish, 4.9% American, 4.1% English, 2.5% African
Employment: 9.1% management, business, and financial, 2.4% computer, engineering, and science, 10.4% education, legal, community service, arts, and media, 6.5% healthcare practitioners, 23.4% service, 23.9% sales and office, 5.4% natural resources, construction, and maintenance, 18.9% production, transportation, and material moving
Income: Per capita: $22,493; Median household: $41,841; Average household: $48,851; Households with income of $100,000 or more: 8.6%; Poverty rate: 19.2%
Educational Attainment: High school diploma or higher: 92.4%; Bachelor's degree or higher: 17.5%; Graduate/professional degree or higher: 5.0%

School District(s)

North College Hill City (PK-12)
2015-16 Enrollment: 1,633 . . . . (513) 931-8181
Housing: Homeownership rate: 52.6%; Median home value: $83,400; Median year structure built: 1952; Homeowner vacancy rate: 2.9%; Median selected monthly owner costs: $1,027 with a mortgage, $390 without a mortgage; Median gross rent: $823 per month; Rental vacancy rate: 5.2%
Health Insurance: 87.0% have insurance; 57.2% have private insurance; 39.9% have public insurance; 13.0% do not have insurance; 5.5% of children under 18 do not have insurance
Safety: Violent crime rate: 32.2 per 10,000 population; Property crime rate: 333.7 per 10,000 population
Transportation: Commute: 89.8% car, 6.0% public transportation, 2.7% walk, 1.1% work from home; Mean travel time to work: 28.4 minutes
Additional Information Contacts
City of North College Hill . . . . (513) 521-7413
http://www.northcollegehill.org

NORTHBROOK (CDP). Covers a land area of 1.949 square miles and a water area of 0 square miles. Located at 39.25° N. Lat; 84.58° W. Long. Elevation is 833 feet.
Population: 10,297; Growth (since 2000): -7.0%; Density: 5,284.1 persons per square mile; Race: 60.1% White, 31.3% Black/African American, 1.2% Asian, 0.0% American Indian/Alaska Native, 0.0% Native Hawaiian/Other Pacific Islander, 7.1% Two or more races, 4.1% Hispanic of any race; Average household size: 2.53; Median age: 34.2; Age under 18: 26.8%; Age 65 and over: 13.3%; Males per 100 females: 88.4; Marriage status: 34.8% never married, 45.7% now married, 2.8% separated, 5.4% widowed, 14.1% divorced; Foreign born: 4.6%; Speak English only: 93.9%; With disability: 13.7%; Veterans: 9.7%; Ancestry: 21.1% German, 9.8% Irish, 7.5% American, 3.7% Italian, 3.5% English
Employment: 6.9% management, business, and financial, 2.1% computer, engineering, and science, 5.6% education, legal, community service, arts, and media, 7.3% healthcare practitioners, 21.2% service, 31.6% sales and office, 7.3% natural resources, construction, and maintenance, 18.0% production, transportation, and material moving
Income: Per capita: $21,605; Median household: $43,875; Average household: $53,610; Households with income of $100,000 or more: 9.8%; Poverty rate: 13.7%
Educational Attainment: High school diploma or higher: 87.2%; Bachelor's degree or higher: 15.8%; Graduate/professional degree or higher: 4.4%
Housing: Homeownership rate: 63.5%; Median home value: $78,700; Median year structure built: 1968; Homeowner vacancy rate: 3.9%; Median selected monthly owner costs: $998 with a mortgage, $426 without a mortgage; Median gross rent: $939 per month; Rental vacancy rate: 2.1%
Health Insurance: 90.0% have insurance; 56.7% have private insurance; 43.1% have public insurance; 10.0% do not have insurance; 1.9% of children under 18 do not have insurance
Transportation: Commute: 95.4% car, 0.6% public transportation, 1.3% walk, 2.7% work from home; Mean travel time to work: 23.7 minutes

NORTHGATE (CDP). Covers a land area of 2.530 square miles and a water area of 0.021 square miles. Located at 39.25° N. Lat; 84.59° W. Long. Elevation is 879 feet.
Population: 7,563; Growth (since 2000): -5.7%; Density: 2,989.3 persons per square mile; Race: 76.0% White, 18.8% Black/African American, 1.2% Asian, 0.0% American Indian/Alaska Native, 0.0% Native Hawaiian/Other Pacific Islander, 3.0% Two or more races, 1.7% Hispanic of any race; Average household size: 2.66; Median age: 42.8; Age under 18: 22.3%; Age 65 and over: 16.8%; Males per 100 females: 94.2; Marriage status: 31.0% never married, 48.6% now married, 2.2% separated, 7.3% widowed, 13.1% divorced; Foreign born: 2.2%; Speak English only: 95.4%; With disability: 12.2%; Veterans: 10.0%; Ancestry: 31.5% German, 12.9% Irish, 6.9% American, 4.7% Italian, 3.4% French
Employment: 13.3% management, business, and financial, 2.5% computer, engineering, and science, 6.5% education, legal, community service, arts, and media, 3.9% healthcare practitioners, 18.5% service, 23.6% sales and office, 12.7% natural resources, construction, and maintenance, 19.1% production, transportation, and material moving
Income: Per capita: $26,588; Median household: $63,864; Average household: $69,900; Households with income of $100,000 or more: 20.0%; Poverty rate: 7.5%

Educational Attainment: High school diploma or higher: 90.4%; Bachelor's degree or higher: 17.0%; Graduate/professional degree or higher: 4.7%
Housing: Homeownership rate: 70.6%; Median home value: $122,800; Median year structure built: 1969; Homeowner vacancy rate: 0.0%; Median selected monthly owner costs: $1,192 with a mortgage, $497 without a mortgage; Median gross rent: $935 per month; Rental vacancy rate: 0.0%
Health Insurance: 88.8% have insurance; 70.4% have private insurance; 34.4% have public insurance; 11.2% do not have insurance; 0.8% of children under 18 do not have insurance
Transportation: Commute: 94.5% car, 1.4% public transportation, 0.7% walk, 3.4% work from home; Mean travel time to work: 26.5 minutes

NORWOOD (city). Covers a land area of 3.147 square miles and a water area of 0 square miles. Located at 39.16° N. Lat; 84.45° W. Long. Elevation is 653 feet.
History: Named for the shortened form of north woods. Norwood began in the early 1800's, and until 1888 was called Sharpsburg, for early settler John Sharp. The U.S. Playing Card Company was established here, and maintained a Playing Card Museum.
Population: 19,462; Growth (since 2000): -10.2%; Density: 6,183.8 persons per square mile; Race: 87.8% White, 9.3% Black/African American, 0.4% Asian, 0.0% American Indian/Alaska Native, 0.0% Native Hawaiian/Other Pacific Islander, 1.5% Two or more races, 4.1% Hispanic of any race; Average household size: 2.20; Median age: 33.3; Age under 18: 18.6%; Age 65 and over: 10.6%; Males per 100 females: 99.5; Marriage status: 47.5% never married, 33.4% now married, 2.3% separated, 6.6% widowed, 12.5% divorced; Foreign born: 3.3%; Speak English only: 94.8%; With disability: 14.4%; Veterans: 7.6%; Ancestry: 26.8% German, 16.5% Irish, 7.9% English, 7.4% American, 5.1% Italian
Employment: 15.4% management, business, and financial, 5.9% computer, engineering, and science, 8.6% education, legal, community service, arts, and media, 6.0% healthcare practitioners, 20.2% service, 26.4% sales and office, 6.4% natural resources, construction, and maintenance, 11.2% production, transportation, and material moving
Income: Per capita: $25,030; Median household: $40,306; Average household: $54,207; Households with income of $100,000 or more: 13.5%; Poverty rate: 22.0%
Educational Attainment: High school diploma or higher: 84.0%; Bachelor's degree or higher: 28.3%; Graduate/professional degree or higher: 8.2%

School District(s)

Norwood City (PK-12)
2015-16 Enrollment: 2,021 . . . . (513) 924-2500

Four-year College(s)

ITT Technical Institute-Norwood (Private, For-profit)
Fall 2016 Enrollment: n/a . . . . (513) 531-8300

Housing: Homeownership rate: 47.8%; Median home value: $118,700; Median year structure built: Before 1940; Homeowner vacancy rate: 2.0%; Median selected monthly owner costs: $1,176 with a mortgage, $473 without a mortgage; Median gross rent: $706 per month; Rental vacancy rate: 4.8%
Health Insurance: 88.2% have insurance; 63.1% have private insurance; 33.4% have public insurance; 11.8% do not have insurance; 7.2% of children under 18 do not have insurance
Safety: Violent crime rate: 25.9 per 10,000 population; Property crime rate: 504.9 per 10,000 population
Transportation: Commute: 91.9% car, 2.3% public transportation, 2.1% walk, 1.5% work from home; Mean travel time to work: 19.6 minutes
Additional Information Contacts
City of Norwood. . . . . (513) 458-4500
http://www.norwood-ohio.com

PLAINVILLE (CDP). Covers a land area of 0.093 square miles and a water area of 0 square miles. Located at 39.14° N. Lat; 84.36° W. Long. Elevation is 499 feet.
Population: 26; Growth (since 2000): n/a; Density: 279.1 persons per square mile; Race: 100.0% White, 0.0% Black/African American, 0.0% Asian, 0.0% American Indian/Alaska Native, 0.0% Native Hawaiian/Other Pacific Islander, 0.0% Two or more races, 0.0% Hispanic of any race; Average household size: 2.00; Median age: n/a; Age under 18: 0.0%; Age 65 and over: 0.0%; Males per 100 females: 74.0; Marriage status: 50.0% never married, 50.0% now married, 50.0% separated, 0.0% widowed, 0.0% divorced; Foreign born: 0.0%; Speak English only: 100.0%; With disability: 0.0%; Veterans: 0.0%; Ancestry: n/a.
Employment: 50.0% management, business, and financial, 0.0% computer, engineering, and science, 0.0% education, legal, community service, arts, and media, 0.0% healthcare practitioners, 0.0% service, 50.0% sales and office, 0.0% natural resources, construction, and maintenance, 0.0% production, transportation, and material moving
Income: Per capita: n/a; Median household: n/a; Average household: n/a; Households with income of $100,000 or more: 100.0%; Poverty rate: 50.0%
Educational Attainment: High school diploma or higher: 100.0%; Bachelor's degree or higher: 100.0%; Graduate/professional degree or higher: 50.0%
Housing: Homeownership rate: 100.0%; Median home value: n/a; Median year structure built: n/a; Homeowner vacancy rate: 0.0%; Median selected monthly owner costs: n/a with a mortgage, n/a without a mortgage; Median gross rent: n/a per month; Rental vacancy rate: 0.0%
Health Insurance: 50.0% have insurance; 50.0% have private insurance; 0.0% have public insurance; 50.0% do not have insurance; 0.0% of children under 18 do not have insurance
Transportation: Commute: 100.0% car, 0.0% public transportation, 0.0% walk, 0.0% work from home; Mean travel time to work: 0.0 minutes

PLEASANT HILLS (CDP). Covers a land area of 0.330 square miles and a water area of 0 square miles. Located at 39.24° N. Lat; 84.52° W. Long. Elevation is 787 feet.
Population: 564; Growth (since 2000): n/a; Density: 1,711.1 persons per square mile; Race: 32.6% White, 67.4% Black/African American, 0.0% Asian, 0.0% American Indian/Alaska Native, 0.0% Native Hawaiian/Other Pacific Islander, 0.0% Two or more races, 0.0% Hispanic of any race; Average household size: 2.32; Median age: 33.8; Age under 18: 11.9%; Age 65 and over: 12.2%; Males per 100 females: 90.0; Marriage status: 62.8% never married, 20.4% now married, 0.0% separated, 8.6% widowed, 8.2% divorced; Foreign born: 0.0%; Speak English only: 98.4%; With disability: 12.1%; Veterans: 3.8%; Ancestry: 8.2% German, 5.1% Irish, 1.8% American, 1.6% Scottish, 1.6% Swedish
Employment: 13.2% management, business, and financial, 8.3% computer, engineering, and science, 6.6% education, legal, community service, arts, and media, 0.0% healthcare practitioners, 28.4% service, 9.3% sales and office, 13.5% natural resources, construction, and maintenance, 20.6% production, transportation, and material moving
Income: Per capita: $29,951; Median household: $55,150; Average household: $67,889; Households with income of $100,000 or more: 18.1%; Poverty rate: 17.0%
Educational Attainment: High school diploma or higher: 99.3%; Bachelor's degree or higher: 25.3%; Graduate/professional degree or higher: 5.1%
Housing: Homeownership rate: 76.1%; Median home value: $97,600; Median year structure built: 1966; Homeowner vacancy rate: 0.0%; Median selected monthly owner costs: $1,201 with a mortgage, $434 without a mortgage; Median gross rent: n/a per month; Rental vacancy rate: 0.0%
Health Insurance: 66.1% have insurance; 55.5% have private insurance; 19.1% have public insurance; 33.9% do not have insurance; 0.0% of children under 18 do not have insurance
Transportation: Commute: 73.0% car, 23.8% public transportation, 0.0% walk, 3.2% work from home; Mean travel time to work: 24.0 minutes

PLEASANT RUN (CDP). Covers a land area of 2.069 square miles and a water area of 0 square miles. Located at 39.29° N. Lat; 84.58° W. Long. Elevation is 748 feet.
Population: 4,592; Growth (since 2000): -12.8%; Density: 2,219.3 persons per square mile; Race: 78.3% White, 15.7% Black/African American, 1.7% Asian, 0.0% American Indian/Alaska Native, 0.0% Native Hawaiian/Other Pacific Islander, 2.4% Two or more races, 4.6% Hispanic of any race; Average household size: 2.75; Median age: 37.4; Age under 18: 24.5%; Age 65 and over: 12.0%; Males per 100 females: 94.3; Marriage status: 32.3% never married, 51.0% now married, 0.7% separated, 6.1% widowed, 10.5% divorced; Foreign born: 2.7%; Speak English only: 94.2%; With disability: 10.9%; Veterans: 8.5%; Ancestry: 39.5% German, 15.2% Irish, 7.5% English, 6.3% American, 2.0% Italian
Employment: 11.3% management, business, and financial, 3.9% computer, engineering, and science, 3.1% education, legal, community service, arts, and media, 9.3% healthcare practitioners, 22.2% service, 28.3% sales and office, 12.4% natural resources, construction, and maintenance, 9.6% production, transportation, and material moving

Income: Per capita: $25,682; Median household: $65,222; Average household: $71,460; Households with income of $100,000 or more: 20.9%; Poverty rate: 4.7%
Educational Attainment: High school diploma or higher: 93.4%; Bachelor's degree or higher: 16.7%; Graduate/professional degree or higher: 3.1%
Housing: Homeownership rate: 88.8%; Median home value: $108,000; Median year structure built: 1973; Homeowner vacancy rate: 4.0%; Median selected monthly owner costs: $1,122 with a mortgage, $465 without a mortgage; Median gross rent: $1,189 per month; Rental vacancy rate: 0.0%
Health Insurance: 93.8% have insurance; 78.9% have private insurance; 21.6% have public insurance; 6.2% do not have insurance; 9.0% of children under 18 do not have insurance
Transportation: Commute: 92.6% car, 0.1% public transportation, 3.1% walk, 4.1% work from home; Mean travel time to work: 23.2 minutes

PLEASANT RUN FARM (CDP). Covers a land area of 1.058 square miles and a water area of 0 square miles. Located at 39.30° N. Lat; 84.55° W. Long. Elevation is 764 feet.
Population: 5,085; Growth (since 2000): 7.5%; Density: 4,804.2 persons per square mile; Race: 51.8% White, 44.6% Black/African American, 0.3% Asian, 0.0% American Indian/Alaska Native, 0.0% Native Hawaiian/Other Pacific Islander, 2.4% Two or more races, 0.8% Hispanic of any race; Average household size: 2.89; Median age: 36.2; Age under 18: 29.0%; Age 65 and over: 13.9%; Males per 100 females: 91.1; Marriage status: 30.2% never married, 50.9% now married, 1.3% separated, 7.5% widowed, 11.3% divorced; Foreign born: 1.3%; Speak English only: 98.2%; With disability: 11.8%; Veterans: 11.9%; Ancestry: 17.8% German, 8.7% English, 8.2% Irish, 3.6% American, 2.8% Polish
Employment: 13.7% management, business, and financial, 9.4% computer, engineering, and science, 12.3% education, legal, community service, arts, and media, 12.9% healthcare practitioners, 14.2% service, 23.1% sales and office, 3.6% natural resources, construction, and maintenance, 10.8% production, transportation, and material moving
Income: Per capita: $27,389; Median household: $65,060; Average household: $78,169; Households with income of $100,000 or more: 25.0%; Poverty rate: 14.3%
Educational Attainment: High school diploma or higher: 92.9%; Bachelor's degree or higher: 30.4%; Graduate/professional degree or higher: 10.2%
Housing: Homeownership rate: 82.3%; Median home value: $134,800; Median year structure built: 1975; Homeowner vacancy rate: 2.8%; Median selected monthly owner costs: $1,256 with a mortgage, $529 without a mortgage; Median gross rent: $914 per month; Rental vacancy rate: 0.0%
Health Insurance: 95.4% have insurance; 75.1% have private insurance; 34.0% have public insurance; 4.6% do not have insurance; 0.0% of children under 18 do not have insurance
Transportation: Commute: 87.2% car, 3.6% public transportation, 0.9% walk, 8.3% work from home; Mean travel time to work: 24.4 minutes

READING (city). Covers a land area of 2.892 square miles and a water area of 0 square miles. Located at 39.22° N. Lat; 84.43° W. Long. Elevation is 561 feet.
History: Reading was platted in 1798 by Adam Vorhees, and named Vorheestown. The name was changed to honor Redingbo, William Penn 's son-in-law.
Population: 10,342; Growth (since 2000): -8.4%; Density: 3,576.7 persons per square mile; Race: 88.6% White, 9.2% Black/African American, 1.1% Asian, 0.0% American Indian/Alaska Native, 0.0% Native Hawaiian/Other Pacific Islander, 0.8% Two or more races, 1.2% Hispanic of any race; Average household size: 2.34; Median age: 38.5; Age under 18: 22.5%; Age 65 and over: 13.7%; Males per 100 females: 96.4; Marriage status: 37.1% never married, 43.5% now married, 2.5% separated, 7.1% widowed, 12.4% divorced; Foreign born: 4.5%; Speak English only: 95.4%; With disability: 13.0%; Veterans: 10.6%; Ancestry: 31.0% German, 16.2% Irish, 10.3% American, 10.0% English, 3.5% Italian
Employment: 12.2% management, business, and financial, 6.7% computer, engineering, and science, 8.2% education, legal, community service, arts, and media, 7.4% healthcare practitioners, 19.3% service, 21.2% sales and office, 8.5% natural resources, construction, and maintenance, 16.5% production, transportation, and material moving
Income: Per capita: $24,842; Median household: $44,271; Average household: $57,487; Households with income of $100,000 or more: 15.3%; Poverty rate: 13.5%
Educational Attainment: High school diploma or higher: 87.5%; Bachelor's degree or higher: 20.3%; Graduate/professional degree or higher: 5.9%

School District(s)
Reading Community City (PK-12)
2015-16 Enrollment: 1,674 . . . . (513) 554-1800
Housing: Homeownership rate: 61.9%; Median home value: $116,800; Median year structure built: 1959; Homeowner vacancy rate: 0.0%; Median selected monthly owner costs: $1,108 with a mortgage, $446 without a mortgage; Median gross rent: $657 per month; Rental vacancy rate: 7.6%
Health Insurance: 90.4% have insurance; 65.3% have private insurance; 35.2% have public insurance; 9.6% do not have insurance; 3.7% of children under 18 do not have insurance
Transportation: Commute: 96.1% car, 0.0% public transportation, 2.2% walk, 1.0% work from home; Mean travel time to work: 19.1 minutes
Additional Information Contacts
City of Reading . . . . (513) 733-3725
http://www.readingohio.org

REMINGTON (CDP). Covers a land area of 0.211 square miles and a water area of 0.003 square miles. Located at 39.23° N. Lat; 84.32° W. Long. Elevation is 577 feet.
Population: 221; Growth (since 2000): n/a; Density: 1,045.2 persons per square mile; Race: 100.0% White, 0.0% Black/African American, 0.0% Asian, 0.0% American Indian/Alaska Native, 0.0% Native Hawaiian/Other Pacific Islander, 0.0% Two or more races, 0.0% Hispanic of any race; Average household size: 1.78; Median age: 50.8; Age under 18: 18.6%; Age 65 and over: 14.9%; Males per 100 females: 108.9; Marriage status: 23.2% never married, 43.3% now married, 0.0% separated, 8.8% widowed, 24.7% divorced; Foreign born: 0.0%; Speak English only: 100.0%; With disability: 7.2%; Veterans: 0.0%; Ancestry: 41.2% Irish, 40.3% German, 14.5% English, 14.0% Russian, 12.7% Polish
Employment: 19.0% management, business, and financial, 0.0% computer, engineering, and science, 20.4% education, legal, community service, arts, and media, 0.0% healthcare practitioners, 32.0% service, 28.6% sales and office, 0.0% natural resources, construction, and maintenance, 0.0% production, transportation, and material moving
Income: Per capita: $42,971; Median household: n/a; Average household: $76,585; Households with income of $100,000 or more: 22.6%; Poverty rate: n/a
Educational Attainment: High school diploma or higher: 100.0%; Bachelor's degree or higher: 80.1%; Graduate/professional degree or higher: 8.4%
Housing: Homeownership rate: 73.4%; Median home value: $239,700; Median year structure built: 1977; Homeowner vacancy rate: 0.0%; Median selected monthly owner costs: $1,923 with a mortgage, n/a without a mortgage; Median gross rent: n/a per month; Rental vacancy rate: 0.0%
Health Insurance: 92.3% have insurance; 85.1% have private insurance; 14.9% have public insurance; 7.7% do not have insurance; 0.0% of children under 18 do not have insurance
Transportation: Commute: 89.1% car, 0.0% public transportation, 0.0% walk, 0.0% work from home; Mean travel time to work: 18.9 minutes

ROSSMOYNE (CDP). Covers a land area of 0.591 square miles and a water area of 0 square miles. Located at 39.21° N. Lat; 84.39° W. Long. Elevation is 833 feet.
Population: 2,287; Growth (since 2000): n/a; Density: 3,872.2 persons per square mile; Race: 64.1% White, 26.7% Black/African American, 8.0% Asian, 0.0% American Indian/Alaska Native, 0.0% Native Hawaiian/Other Pacific Islander, 1.3% Two or more races, 0.6% Hispanic of any race; Average household size: 2.36; Median age: 31.0; Age under 18: 22.8%; Age 65 and over: 6.8%; Males per 100 females: 94.3; Marriage status: 45.4% never married, 35.2% now married, 2.8% separated, 4.3% widowed, 15.1% divorced; Foreign born: 6.9%; Speak English only: 91.6%; With disability: 11.5%; Veterans: 3.6%; Ancestry: 23.2% German, 10.3% Irish, 8.8% American, 5.1% Scottish, 3.8% English
Employment: 14.4% management, business, and financial, 6.9% computer, engineering, and science, 8.0% education, legal, community service, arts, and media, 3.2% healthcare practitioners, 24.1% service, 19.8% sales and office, 9.6% natural resources, construction, and maintenance, 14.1% production, transportation, and material moving
Income: Per capita: $23,530; Median household: $48,576; Average household: $53,531; Households with income of $100,000 or more: 9.0%; Poverty rate: 14.7%

Educational Attainment: High school diploma or higher: 89.7%; Bachelor's degree or higher: 23.6%; Graduate/professional degree or higher: 5.7%
Housing: Homeownership rate: 53.5%; Median home value: $109,500; Median year structure built: 1952; Homeowner vacancy rate: 0.0%; Median selected monthly owner costs: $1,160 with a mortgage, $383 without a mortgage; Median gross rent: $996 per month; Rental vacancy rate: 5.6%
Health Insurance: 87.2% have insurance; 63.5% have private insurance; 28.6% have public insurance; 12.8% do not have insurance; 0.0% of children under 18 do not have insurance
Transportation: Commute: 88.5% car, 6.3% public transportation, 1.1% walk, 2.6% work from home; Mean travel time to work: 22.9 minutes

SAINT BERNARD (city). Covers a land area of 1.546 square miles and a water area of 0.012 square miles. Located at 39.17° N. Lat; 84.49° W. Long. Elevation is 568 feet.
Population: 4,352; Growth (since 2000): -11.6%; Density: 2,815.1 persons per square mile; Race: 78.4% White, 17.6% Black/African American, 0.0% Asian, 0.0% American Indian/Alaska Native, 0.0% Native Hawaiian/Other Pacific Islander, 3.5% Two or more races, 0.6% Hispanic of any race; Average household size: 2.39; Median age: 37.9; Age under 18: 21.5%; Age 65 and over: 12.4%; Males per 100 females: 89.4; Marriage status: 37.3% never married, 45.1% now married, 2.0% separated, 7.4% widowed, 10.3% divorced; Foreign born: 0.8%; Speak English only: 96.8%; With disability: 14.6%; Veterans: 7.0%; Ancestry: 34.9% German, 14.2% Irish, 10.4% American, 7.7% English, 4.0% French
Employment: 7.8% management, business, and financial, 3.9% computer, engineering, and science, 7.6% education, legal, community service, arts, and media, 6.0% healthcare practitioners, 28.9% service, 26.5% sales and office, 6.4% natural resources, construction, and maintenance, 12.9% production, transportation, and material moving
Income: Per capita: $24,169; Median household: $48,305; Average household: $56,946; Households with income of $100,000 or more: 15.8%; Poverty rate: 13.0%
Educational Attainment: High school diploma or higher: 90.8%; Bachelor's degree or higher: 17.2%; Graduate/professional degree or higher: 6.4%

School District(s)

St Bernard-elmwood Place City (PK-12)
2015-16 Enrollment: 999. . . . . (513) 482-7121

Housing: Homeownership rate: 59.5%; Median home value: $93,700; Median year structure built: Before 1940; Homeowner vacancy rate: 6.1%; Median selected monthly owner costs: $1,073 with a mortgage, $497 without a mortgage; Median gross rent: $734 per month; Rental vacancy rate: 8.1%
Health Insurance: 90.7% have insurance; 66.7% have private insurance; 34.7% have public insurance; 9.3% do not have insurance; 6.3% of children under 18 do not have insurance
Transportation: Commute: 91.9% car, 0.7% public transportation, 2.6% walk, 4.8% work from home; Mean travel time to work: 20.6 minutes

SALEM HEIGHTS (CDP). Covers a land area of 1.645 square miles and a water area of 0 square miles. Located at 39.07° N. Lat; 84.38° W. Long. Elevation is 745 feet.
Population: 3,175; Growth (since 2000): n/a; Density: 1,930.1 persons per square mile; Race: 98.3% White, 0.7% Black/African American, 0.0% Asian, 0.0% American Indian/Alaska Native, 0.0% Native Hawaiian/Other Pacific Islander, 1.0% Two or more races, 0.0% Hispanic of any race; Average household size: 2.36; Median age: 45.1; Age under 18: 20.9%; Age 65 and over: 19.1%; Males per 100 females: 96.3; Marriage status: 23.1% never married, 59.6% now married, 2.8% separated, 7.1% widowed, 10.3% divorced; Foreign born: 0.9%; Speak English only: 97.6%; With disability: 7.4%; Veterans: 6.9%; Ancestry: 45.1% German, 19.3% Irish, 11.7% English, 10.2% American, 6.9% Italian
Employment: 19.8% management, business, and financial, 4.5% computer, engineering, and science, 17.2% education, legal, community service, arts, and media, 5.7% healthcare practitioners, 13.1% service, 24.4% sales and office, 5.8% natural resources, construction, and maintenance, 9.4% production, transportation, and material moving
Income: Per capita: $39,714; Median household: $80,203; Average household: $95,116; Households with income of $100,000 or more: 31.2%; Poverty rate: 2.7%
Educational Attainment: High school diploma or higher: 96.1%; Bachelor's degree or higher: 40.8%; Graduate/professional degree or higher: 10.1%
Housing: Homeownership rate: 91.7%; Median home value: $150,000; Median year structure built: 1961; Homeowner vacancy rate: 0.0%; Median selected monthly owner costs: $1,421 with a mortgage, $606 without a mortgage; Median gross rent: $1,442 per month; Rental vacancy rate: 16.3%
Health Insurance: 91.8% have insurance; 82.8% have private insurance; 23.8% have public insurance; 8.2% do not have insurance; 4.8% of children under 18 do not have insurance
Transportation: Commute: 86.7% car, 0.1% public transportation, 0.0% walk, 11.1% work from home; Mean travel time to work: 22.1 minutes

SHARONVILLE (city). Covers a land area of 9.832 square miles and a water area of 0.058 square miles. Located at 39.28° N. Lat; 84.41° W. Long. Elevation is 587 feet.
History: Named for Sharon, Pennsylvania, which was named for the region in Palestine mentioned in the Bible. Sharonville was surveyed in 1796 by Simon Hegerman, and became a transportation center when the New York Central Lines built their freight yards and shops here.
Population: 13,782; Growth (since 2000): -0.2%; Density: 1,401.8 persons per square mile; Race: 75.1% White, 13.7% Black/African American, 6.4% Asian, 0.0% American Indian/Alaska Native, 0.0% Native Hawaiian/Other Pacific Islander, 2.9% Two or more races, 4.4% Hispanic of any race; Average household size: 2.29; Median age: 37.6; Age under 18: 23.6%; Age 65 and over: 16.9%; Males per 100 females: 91.5; Marriage status: 31.8% never married, 48.9% now married, 0.7% separated, 7.4% widowed, 11.9% divorced; Foreign born: 11.0%; Speak English only: 85.1%; With disability: 11.9%; Veterans: 9.4%; Ancestry: 24.6% German, 11.8% Irish, 9.1% English, 7.0% American, 4.7% Italian
Employment: 18.6% management, business, and financial, 10.4% computer, engineering, and science, 8.1% education, legal, community service, arts, and media, 6.1% healthcare practitioners, 13.2% service, 22.2% sales and office, 4.0% natural resources, construction, and maintenance, 17.4% production, transportation, and material moving
Income: Per capita: $31,498; Median household: $52,934; Average household: $71,516; Households with income of $100,000 or more: 21.8%; Poverty rate: 11.4%
Educational Attainment: High school diploma or higher: 91.9%; Bachelor's degree or higher: 39.0%; Graduate/professional degree or higher: 15.5%

Two-year College(s)

Miami-Jacobs Career College-Sharonville (Private, For-profit)
Fall 2016 Enrollment: n/a . . . . (513) 693-4400
2016-17 Tuition: In-state $10,720; Out-of-state $10,720

Housing: Homeownership rate: 60.5%; Median home value: $141,900; Median year structure built: 1980; Homeowner vacancy rate: 0.0%; Median selected monthly owner costs: $1,262 with a mortgage, $510 without a mortgage; Median gross rent: $908 per month; Rental vacancy rate: 1.8%
Health Insurance: 88.4% have insurance; 71.7% have private insurance; 29.6% have public insurance; 11.6% do not have insurance; 8.6% of children under 18 do not have insurance
Transportation: Commute: 92.4% car, 0.0% public transportation, 3.1% walk, 4.2% work from home; Mean travel time to work: 20.1 minutes
Additional Information Contacts
City of Sharonville . . . . (513) 563-1144
http://www.sharonville.org

SHAWNEE (CDP). Covers a land area of 6.418 square miles and a water area of 0.530 square miles. Located at 39.14° N. Lat; 84.78° W. Long.
Population: 756; Growth (since 2000): n/a; Density: 117.8 persons per square mile; Race: 100.0% White, 0.0% Black/African American, 0.0% Asian, 0.0% American Indian/Alaska Native, 0.0% Native Hawaiian/Other Pacific Islander, 0.0% Two or more races, 0.0% Hispanic of any race; Average household size: 2.28; Median age: 51.7; Age under 18: 8.5%; Age 65 and over: 20.4%; Males per 100 females: 101.1; Marriage status: 31.0% never married, 57.5% now married, 0.0% separated, 2.5% widowed, 9.0% divorced; Foreign born: 2.4%; Speak English only: 97.6%; With disability: 15.5%; Veterans: 12.3%; Ancestry: 44.3% German, 12.2% Irish, 12.0% English, 8.5% Scotch-Irish, 7.0% American
Employment: 8.4% management, business, and financial, 2.9% computer, engineering, and science, 18.9% education, legal, community service, arts, and media, 0.0% healthcare practitioners, 15.7% service, 24.6% sales and office, 8.1% natural resources, construction, and maintenance, 21.4% production, transportation, and material moving

Income: Per capita: $29,405; Median household: $65,625; Average household: $67,253; Households with income of $100,000 or more: 30.0%; Poverty rate: 15.6%
Educational Attainment: High school diploma or higher: 87.8%; Bachelor's degree or higher: 23.3%; Graduate/professional degree or higher: 14.3%
Housing: Homeownership rate: 77.3%; Median home value: $216,900; Median year structure built: 1963; Homeowner vacancy rate: 0.0%; Median selected monthly owner costs: $1,161 with a mortgage, $785 without a mortgage; Median gross rent: $954 per month; Rental vacancy rate: 0.0%
Health Insurance: 89.8% have insurance; 78.0% have private insurance; 29.0% have public insurance; 10.2% do not have insurance; 0.0% of children under 18 do not have insurance
Transportation: Commute: 91.4% car, 5.3% public transportation, 0.0% walk, 3.3% work from home; Mean travel time to work: 22.6 minutes

SHERWOOD (CDP). Covers a land area of 1.069 square miles and a water area of 0 square miles. Located at 39.09° N. Lat; 84.36° W. Long. Elevation is 725 feet.
History: During the Civil War, Morgan's Raid (a Confederate cavalry assault) passed through this part of Hamilton County in 1863.
Population: 3,342; Growth (since 2000): n/a; Density: 3,125.6 persons per square mile; Race: 94.3% White, 0.9% Black/African American, 0.0% Asian, 0.0% American Indian/Alaska Native, 0.0% Native Hawaiian/Other Pacific Islander, 3.9% Two or more races, 3.9% Hispanic of any race; Average household size: 2.58; Median age: 43.9; Age under 18: 23.6%; Age 65 and over: 14.7%; Males per 100 females: 93.9; Marriage status: 20.0% never married, 65.9% now married, 1.2% separated, 2.2% widowed, 11.8% divorced; Foreign born: 4.8%; Speak English only: 90.9%; With disability: 9.2%; Veterans: 6.6%; Ancestry: 39.7% German, 16.9% Irish, 11.9% English, 8.4% Italian, 6.8% French
Employment: 18.6% management, business, and financial, 8.3% computer, engineering, and science, 10.2% education, legal, community service, arts, and media, 7.6% healthcare practitioners, 13.2% service, 31.4% sales and office, 4.6% natural resources, construction, and maintenance, 6.1% production, transportation, and material moving
Income: Per capita: $44,056; Median household: $90,139; Average household: $111,898; Households with income of $100,000 or more: 42.4%; Poverty rate: 4.4%
Educational Attainment: High school diploma or higher: 95.7%; Bachelor's degree or higher: 54.1%; Graduate/professional degree or higher: 19.2%
Housing: Homeownership rate: 91.9%; Median home value: $184,400; Median year structure built: 1968; Homeowner vacancy rate: 0.0%; Median selected monthly owner costs: $1,681 with a mortgage, $593 without a mortgage; Median gross rent: $1,074 per month; Rental vacancy rate: 0.0%
Health Insurance: 95.4% have insurance; 85.0% have private insurance; 20.3% have public insurance; 4.6% do not have insurance; 4.4% of children under 18 do not have insurance
Transportation: Commute: 88.0% car, 0.7% public transportation, 0.7% walk, 9.9% work from home; Mean travel time to work: 24.3 minutes

SILVERTON (village). Covers a land area of 1.112 square miles and a water area of 0 square miles. Located at 39.19° N. Lat; 84.40° W. Long. Elevation is 853 feet.
History: Silverton developed as a residential community on the outskirts of Cincinnati.
Population: 4,766; Growth (since 2000): -8.0%; Density: 4,287.4 persons per square mile; Race: 43.3% White, 50.4% Black/African American, 0.0% Asian, 0.0% American Indian/Alaska Native, 0.0% Native Hawaiian/Other Pacific Islander, 6.2% Two or more races, 0.0% Hispanic of any race; Average household size: 1.90; Median age: 44.2; Age under 18: 18.3%; Age 65 and over: 18.2%; Males per 100 females: 85.7; Marriage status: 41.0% never married, 32.5% now married, 2.1% separated, 9.1% widowed, 17.4% divorced; Foreign born: 0.9%; Speak English only: 98.7%; With disability: 12.7%; Veterans: 3.2%; Ancestry: 22.4% German, 9.3% Irish, 2.7% English, 2.5% American, 2.3% Polish
Employment: 7.6% management, business, and financial, 5.6% computer, engineering, and science, 12.1% education, legal, community service, arts, and media, 7.8% healthcare practitioners, 24.3% service, 25.7% sales and office, 8.5% natural resources, construction, and maintenance, 8.4% production, transportation, and material moving
Income: Per capita: $25,674; Median household: $34,750; Average household: $48,826; Households with income of $100,000 or more: 14.6%; Poverty rate: 14.6%
Educational Attainment: High school diploma or higher: 88.0%; Bachelor's degree or higher: 29.9%; Graduate/professional degree or higher: 7.3%
Housing: Homeownership rate: 56.2%; Median home value: $113,800; Median year structure built: 1951; Homeowner vacancy rate: 2.4%; Median selected monthly owner costs: $1,160 with a mortgage, $540 without a mortgage; Median gross rent: $604 per month; Rental vacancy rate: 13.7%
Health Insurance: 91.1% have insurance; 69.9% have private insurance; 34.3% have public insurance; 8.9% do not have insurance; 0.0% of children under 18 do not have insurance
Transportation: Commute: 89.2% car, 2.2% public transportation, 5.4% walk, 3.3% work from home; Mean travel time to work: 22.1 minutes
Additional Information Contacts
City of Silverton . . . . (513) 936-6240
http://silvertonohio.us

SIXTEEN MILE STAND (CDP). Covers a land area of 1.116 square miles and a water area of 0.003 square miles. Located at 39.28° N. Lat; 84.33° W. Long. Elevation is 807 feet.
Population: 3,185; Growth (since 2000): n/a; Density: 2,854.7 persons per square mile; Race: 69.0% White, 10.7% Black/African American, 15.3% Asian, 0.0% American Indian/Alaska Native, 0.0% Native Hawaiian/Other Pacific Islander, 4.0% Two or more races, 2.6% Hispanic of any race; Average household size: 2.53; Median age: 38.8; Age under 18: 19.2%; Age 65 and over: 7.6%; Males per 100 females: 102.3; Marriage status: 30.1% never married, 58.3% now married, 1.7% separated, 2.2% widowed, 9.4% divorced; Foreign born: 16.5%; Speak English only: 78.0%; With disability: 9.0%; Veterans: 5.6%; Ancestry: 25.5% German, 16.8% Irish, 10.0% English, 9.8% Italian, 4.9% American
Employment: 27.0% management, business, and financial, 10.4% computer, engineering, and science, 13.1% education, legal, community service, arts, and media, 8.4% healthcare practitioners, 13.4% service, 23.1% sales and office, 1.4% natural resources, construction, and maintenance, 3.2% production, transportation, and material moving
Income: Per capita: $55,024; Median household: $85,930; Average household: $138,147; Households with income of $100,000 or more: 44.7%; Poverty rate: 4.1%
Educational Attainment: High school diploma or higher: 99.2%; Bachelor's degree or higher: 68.3%; Graduate/professional degree or higher: 29.1%
Housing: Homeownership rate: 50.1%; Median home value: $353,200; Median year structure built: 1987; Homeowner vacancy rate: 0.0%; Median selected monthly owner costs: $2,231 with a mortgage, $928 without a mortgage; Median gross rent: $1,158 per month; Rental vacancy rate: 0.0%
Health Insurance: 94.8% have insurance; 89.5% have private insurance; 14.2% have public insurance; 5.2% do not have insurance; 3.1% of children under 18 do not have insurance
Transportation: Commute: 90.5% car, 1.3% public transportation, 2.4% walk, 5.8% work from home; Mean travel time to work: 24.2 minutes

SKYLINE ACRES (CDP). Covers a land area of 0.657 square miles and a water area of 0 square miles. Located at 39.23° N. Lat; 84.57° W. Long. Elevation is 827 feet.
Population: 2,266; Growth (since 2000): n/a; Density: 3,447.0 persons per square mile; Race: 11.7% White, 87.1% Black/African American, 0.0% Asian, 0.0% American Indian/Alaska Native, 0.0% Native Hawaiian/Other Pacific Islander, 1.1% Two or more races, 0.0% Hispanic of any race; Average household size: 3.32; Median age: 27.8; Age under 18: 34.6%; Age 65 and over: 10.5%; Males per 100 females: 87.4; Marriage status: 52.4% never married, 27.4% now married, 3.4% separated, 6.2% widowed, 14.0% divorced; Foreign born: 0.4%; Speak English only: 100.0%; With disability: 24.8%; Veterans: 4.1%; Ancestry: 5.8% German, 5.4% Irish, 1.1% Italian, 1.0% American, 0.9% Welsh
Employment: 5.5% management, business, and financial, 2.2% computer, engineering, and science, 10.0% education, legal, community service, arts, and media, 5.6% healthcare practitioners, 35.4% service, 20.2% sales and office, 10.4% natural resources, construction, and maintenance, 10.8% production, transportation, and material moving
Income: Per capita: $13,099; Median household: $32,500; Average household: $42,523; Households with income of $100,000 or more: 4.1%; Poverty rate: 40.2%

Educational Attainment: High school diploma or higher: 93.1%; Bachelor's degree or higher: 13.2%; Graduate/professional degree or higher: 4.6%
Housing: Homeownership rate: 53.5%; Median home value: $87,200; Median year structure built: 1963; Homeowner vacancy rate: 0.0%; Median selected monthly owner costs: $1,138 with a mortgage, $456 without a mortgage; Median gross rent: $902 per month; Rental vacancy rate: 12.2%
Health Insurance: 89.7% have insurance; 38.7% have private insurance; 58.9% have public insurance; 10.3% do not have insurance; 1.7% of children under 18 do not have insurance
Transportation: Commute: 92.4% car, 0.0% public transportation, 0.0% walk, 7.6% work from home; Mean travel time to work: 22.4 minutes

SPRINGDALE (city). Covers a land area of 4.963 square miles and a water area of 0.011 square miles. Located at 39.29° N. Lat; 84.48° W. Long. Elevation is 738 feet.
History: Springdale was the site in 1801-1802 of a meeting of the religious sect called the New Lights, who evidenced pronounced physical manifestations of jerking, rolling, whirling, falling, and barking.
Population: 11,205; Growth (since 2000): 6.1%; Density: 2,257.8 persons per square mile; Race: 54.8% White, 33.2% Black/African American, 5.4% Asian, 0.0% American Indian/Alaska Native, 0.0% Native Hawaiian/Other Pacific Islander, 1.1% Two or more races, 17.5% Hispanic of any race; Average household size: 2.54; Median age: 40.2; Age under 18: 28.9%; Age 65 and over: 19.8%; Males per 100 females: 86.8; Marriage status: 30.6% never married, 49.1% now married, 2.3% separated, 10.3% widowed, 10.0% divorced; Foreign born: 15.7%; Speak English only: 77.2%; With disability: 12.3%; Veterans: 10.1%; Ancestry: 14.7% German, 7.5% English, 6.1% Irish, 5.2% American, 5.1% Other Subsaharan African
Employment: 9.3% management, business, and financial, 8.9% computer, engineering, and science, 9.2% education, legal, community service, arts, and media, 6.1% healthcare practitioners, 20.2% service, 24.9% sales and office, 6.3% natural resources, construction, and maintenance, 15.1% production, transportation, and material moving
Income: Per capita: $26,889; Median household: $49,200; Average household: $66,325; Households with income of $100,000 or more: 16.6%; Poverty rate: 18.8%
Educational Attainment: High school diploma or higher: 86.6%; Bachelor's degree or higher: 32.1%; Graduate/professional degree or higher: 9.9%

Two-year College(s)

Beckfield College-Tri-County (Private, For-profit)
Fall 2016 Enrollment: 348 . . . . (513) 671-1920
2016-17 Tuition: In-state $13,281; Out-of-state $13,281

Housing: Homeownership rate: 50.3%; Median home value: $126,300; Median year structure built: 1971; Homeowner vacancy rate: 2.5%; Median selected monthly owner costs: $1,287 with a mortgage, $447 without a mortgage; Median gross rent: $880 per month; Rental vacancy rate: 5.8%
Health Insurance: 88.1% have insurance; 60.0% have private insurance; 43.6% have public insurance; 11.9% do not have insurance; 2.7% of children under 18 do not have insurance
Transportation: Commute: 96.6% car, 0.4% public transportation, 0.8% walk, 1.6% work from home; Mean travel time to work: 19.5 minutes
Additional Information Contacts
City of Springdale . . . . (513) 346-5700
http://www.springdale.org

TAYLOR CREEK (CDP). Covers a land area of 8.435 square miles and a water area of 0 square miles. Located at 39.24° N. Lat; 84.68° W. Long.
Population: 3,229; Growth (since 2000): n/a; Density: 382.8 persons per square mile; Race: 93.4% White, 3.2% Black/African American, 0.0% Asian, 0.1% American Indian/Alaska Native, 0.0% Native Hawaiian/Other Pacific Islander, 3.3% Two or more races, 0.0% Hispanic of any race; Average household size: 2.58; Median age: 42.9; Age under 18: 22.0%; Age 65 and over: 15.1%; Males per 100 females: 98.4; Marriage status: 22.5% never married, 61.3% now married, 1.9% separated, 3.7% widowed, 12.5% divorced; Foreign born: 0.6%; Speak English only: 97.1%; With disability: 13.3%; Veterans: 11.1%; Ancestry: 45.9% German, 20.2% Irish, 8.7% Italian, 5.4% English, 4.1% American
Employment: 17.7% management, business, and financial, 5.5% computer, engineering, and science, 4.7% education, legal, community service, arts, and media, 8.8% healthcare practitioners, 11.1% service, 24.4% sales and office, 14.3% natural resources, construction, and maintenance, 13.6% production, transportation, and material moving
Income: Per capita: $37,046; Median household: $72,946; Average household: $94,959; Households with income of $100,000 or more: 36.0%; Poverty rate: 6.3%
Educational Attainment: High school diploma or higher: 92.9%; Bachelor's degree or higher: 26.4%; Graduate/professional degree or higher: 6.9%
Housing: Homeownership rate: 85.5%; Median home value: $201,100; Median year structure built: 1984; Homeowner vacancy rate: 1.2%; Median selected monthly owner costs: $1,506 with a mortgage, $622 without a mortgage; Median gross rent: $891 per month; Rental vacancy rate: 9.4%
Health Insurance: 93.0% have insurance; 75.2% have private insurance; 28.5% have public insurance; 7.0% do not have insurance; 1.0% of children under 18 do not have insurance
Transportation: Commute: 93.1% car, 0.6% public transportation, 2.1% walk, 2.7% work from home; Mean travel time to work: 23.4 minutes

TERRACE PARK (village). Covers a land area of 1.174 square miles and a water area of 0.054 square miles. Located at 39.16° N. Lat; 84.31° W. Long. Elevation is 568 feet.
History: Terrace Park developed as a suburban community near Cincinnati.
Population: 2,356; Growth (since 2000): 3.7%; Density: 2,007.5 persons per square mile; Race: 98.7% White, 0.3% Black/African American, 0.5% Asian, 0.0% American Indian/Alaska Native, 0.0% Native Hawaiian/Other Pacific Islander, 0.6% Two or more races, 2.5% Hispanic of any race; Average household size: 3.00; Median age: 40.3; Age under 18: 33.4%; Age 65 and over: 10.4%; Males per 100 females: 101.0; Marriage status: 19.4% never married, 72.6% now married, 0.2% separated, 2.3% widowed, 5.7% divorced; Foreign born: 4.0%; Speak English only: 96.9%; With disability: 3.7%; Veterans: 5.2%; Ancestry: 31.1% German, 18.7% English, 16.5% Irish, 11.5% American, 6.5% Italian
Employment: 39.0% management, business, and financial, 5.3% computer, engineering, and science, 14.2% education, legal, community service, arts, and media, 8.7% healthcare practitioners, 5.4% service, 22.8% sales and office, 2.0% natural resources, construction, and maintenance, 2.5% production, transportation, and material moving
Income: Per capita: $67,987; Median household: $145,625; Average household: $203,170; Households with income of $100,000 or more: 67.5%; Poverty rate: 5.3%
Educational Attainment: High school diploma or higher: 98.4%; Bachelor's degree or higher: 80.4%; Graduate/professional degree or higher: 34.9%

School District(s)

Mariemont City (KG-12)
2015-16 Enrollment: 1,757 . . . . (513) 272-7500

Housing: Homeownership rate: 93.5%; Median home value: $496,700; Median year structure built: 1956; Homeowner vacancy rate: 2.4%; Median selected monthly owner costs: $2,991 with a mortgage, $1,075 without a mortgage; Median gross rent: $1,917 per month; Rental vacancy rate: 0.0%
Health Insurance: 97.4% have insurance; 94.0% have private insurance; 12.8% have public insurance; 2.6% do not have insurance; 2.2% of children under 18 do not have insurance
Transportation: Commute: 89.0% car, 0.9% public transportation, 1.0% walk, 7.9% work from home; Mean travel time to work: 24.7 minutes

THE VILLAGE OF INDIAN HILL (city). Covers a land area of 18.554 square miles and a water area of 0.095 square miles. Located at 39.19° N. Lat; 84.34° W. Long. Elevation is 564 feet.
History: Indian Hill began as a farming community, which from about 1904 began to attract Cincinnatians, who bought up its farmhouses as rural weekend designations. The rolling country appealed to a group of four Cincinnati businessmen who had built homes there in the early 1920s and envisioned a more ambitious rural settlement, persuading friends to join them in 1924 in forming the Camargo Realty Co.
Population: 5,803; Growth (since 2000): -1.8%; Density: 312.8 persons per square mile; Race: 88.0% White, 1.5% Black/African American, 10.2% Asian, 0.0% American Indian/Alaska Native, 0.0% Native Hawaiian/Other Pacific Islander, 0.0% Two or more races, 2.0% Hispanic of any race; Average household size: 2.78; Median age: 51.1; Age under 18: 27.7%; Age 65 and over: 20.3%; Males per 100 females: 93.9; Marriage status: 12.7% never married, 80.7% now married, 0.3% separated, 2.6% widowed, 4.0% divorced; Foreign born: 9.9%; Speak English only: 90.1%; With disability: 9.4%; Veterans: 6.3%; Ancestry: 28.8% German, 16.8% Irish, 16.7% English, 5.5% Polish, 4.9% Italian

Employment: 35.4% management, business, and financial, 5.9% computer, engineering, and science, 17.6% education, legal, community service, arts, and media, 21.0% healthcare practitioners, 2.9% service, 14.9% sales and office, 0.6% natural resources, construction, and maintenance, 1.7% production, transportation, and material moving
Income: Per capita: $112,391; Median household: $205,221; Average household: $314,077; Households with income of $100,000 or more: 74.6%; Poverty rate: 3.1%
Educational Attainment: High school diploma or higher: 98.7%; Bachelor's degree or higher: 88.1%; Graduate/professional degree or higher: 45.0%
Housing: Homeownership rate: 96.6%; Median home value: $922,500; Median year structure built: 1967; Homeowner vacancy rate: 0.0%; Median selected monthly owner costs: $4,000+ with a mortgage, $1,366 without a mortgage; Median gross rent: n/a per month; Rental vacancy rate: 19.5%
Health Insurance: 98.9% have insurance; 90.5% have private insurance; 24.6% have public insurance; 1.1% do not have insurance; 0.0% of children under 18 do not have insurance
Transportation: Commute: 79.4% car, 0.0% public transportation, 2.0% walk, 16.0% work from home; Mean travel time to work: 21.1 minutes

TURPIN HILLS (CDP). Covers a land area of 2.978 square miles and a water area of 0.003 square miles. Located at 39.11° N. Lat; 84.38° W. Long. Elevation is 650 feet.
History: The development of Turpin Hills (TH) began in the spring of 1956. A sign appeared on the site announcing lots "for sale" and the current name.
Population: 5,176; Growth (since 2000): 4.4%; Density: 1,738.4 persons per square mile; Race: 97.7% White, 0.8% Black/African American, 0.3% Asian, 0.0% American Indian/Alaska Native, 0.0% Native Hawaiian/Other Pacific Islander, 1.2% Two or more races, 5.7% Hispanic of any race; Average household size: 2.73; Median age: 42.6; Age under 18: 28.3%; Age 65 and over: 14.2%; Males per 100 females: 96.7; Marriage status: 23.5% never married, 64.5% now married, 0.3% separated, 2.4% widowed, 9.6% divorced; Foreign born: 1.2%; Speak English only: 97.3%; With disability: 8.8%; Veterans: 9.2%; Ancestry: 42.0% German, 20.9% Irish, 11.3% American, 7.9% Italian, 6.6% English
Employment: 29.2% management, business, and financial, 7.3% computer, engineering, and science, 17.1% education, legal, community service, arts, and media, 9.3% healthcare practitioners, 9.3% service, 25.4% sales and office, 0.0% natural resources, construction, and maintenance, 2.5% production, transportation, and material moving
Income: Per capita: $50,415; Median household: $114,973; Average household: $136,838; Households with income of $100,000 or more: 58.1%; Poverty rate: 2.0%
Educational Attainment: High school diploma or higher: 99.5%; Bachelor's degree or higher: 68.0%; Graduate/professional degree or higher: 25.8%
Housing: Homeownership rate: 79.2%; Median home value: $299,800; Median year structure built: 1976; Homeowner vacancy rate: 0.0%; Median selected monthly owner costs: $2,087 with a mortgage, $756 without a mortgage; Median gross rent: $854 per month; Rental vacancy rate: 0.0%
Health Insurance: 98.6% have insurance; 89.0% have private insurance; 19.3% have public insurance; 1.4% do not have insurance; 1.2% of children under 18 do not have insurance
Transportation: Commute: 90.0% car, 1.2% public transportation, 0.0% walk, 8.8% work from home; Mean travel time to work: 28.1 minutes

WHITE OAK (CDP). Covers a land area of 6.167 square miles and a water area of 0 square miles. Located at 39.21° N. Lat; 84.61° W. Long. Elevation is 915 feet.
Population: 19,068; Growth (since 2000): 43.6%; Density: 3,092.1 persons per square mile; Race: 83.8% White, 8.7% Black/African American, 5.4% Asian, 0.0% American Indian/Alaska Native, 0.0% Native Hawaiian/Other Pacific Islander, 1.9% Two or more races, 0.9% Hispanic of any race; Average household size: 2.47; Median age: 41.1; Age under 18: 23.2%; Age 65 and over: 16.8%; Males per 100 females: 93.0; Marriage status: 28.1% never married, 53.1% now married, 1.7% separated, 6.4% widowed, 12.4% divorced; Foreign born: 6.9%; Speak English only: 92.6%; With disability: 12.0%; Veterans: 8.6%; Ancestry: 37.0% German, 15.5% Irish, 5.3% American, 5.2% English, 4.9% Italian
Employment: 12.9% management, business, and financial, 4.1% computer, engineering, and science, 8.4% education, legal, community service, arts, and media, 10.0% healthcare practitioners, 21.3% service, 25.9% sales and office, 5.3% natural resources, construction, and maintenance, 12.1% production, transportation, and material moving
Income: Per capita: $30,620; Median household: $60,264; Average household: $74,749; Households with income of $100,000 or more: 23.3%; Poverty rate: 12.6%
Educational Attainment: High school diploma or higher: 88.6%; Bachelor's degree or higher: 25.4%; Graduate/professional degree or higher: 9.0%
Housing: Homeownership rate: 72.3%; Median home value: $136,300; Median year structure built: 1967; Homeowner vacancy rate: 2.3%; Median selected monthly owner costs: $1,322 with a mortgage, $492 without a mortgage; Median gross rent: $709 per month; Rental vacancy rate: 12.5%
Health Insurance: 92.5% have insurance; 68.7% have private insurance; 35.4% have public insurance; 7.5% do not have insurance; 3.2% of children under 18 do not have insurance
Transportation: Commute: 93.9% car, 0.6% public transportation, 1.1% walk, 3.2% work from home; Mean travel time to work: 23.3 minutes

WOODLAWN (village). Covers a land area of 2.570 square miles and a water area of 0 square miles. Located at 39.26° N. Lat; 84.47° W. Long. Elevation is 587 feet.
Population: 3,279; Growth (since 2000): 16.4%; Density: 1,275.6 persons per square mile; Race: 27.6% White, 59.1% Black/African American, 4.9% Asian, 0.2% American Indian/Alaska Native, 0.0% Native Hawaiian/Other Pacific Islander, 8.2% Two or more races, 3.3% Hispanic of any race; Average household size: 2.24; Median age: 37.2; Age under 18: 22.4%; Age 65 and over: 14.4%; Males per 100 females: 81.8; Marriage status: 41.5% never married, 37.2% now married, 2.4% separated, 7.2% widowed, 14.1% divorced; Foreign born: 6.5%; Speak English only: 92.8%; With disability: 11.4%; Veterans: 5.2%; Ancestry: 6.7% German, 5.6% American, 2.7% English, 2.1% African, 2.0% Irish
Employment: 13.2% management, business, and financial, 15.1% computer, engineering, and science, 7.0% education, legal, community service, arts, and media, 6.2% healthcare practitioners, 14.6% service, 27.1% sales and office, 5.3% natural resources, construction, and maintenance, 11.4% production, transportation, and material moving
Income: Per capita: $26,619; Median household: $55,028; Average household: $59,152; Households with income of $100,000 or more: 11.3%; Poverty rate: 17.4%
Educational Attainment: High school diploma or higher: 90.0%; Bachelor's degree or higher: 36.9%; Graduate/professional degree or higher: 7.7%
Housing: Homeownership rate: 45.3%; Median home value: $96,200; Median year structure built: 1984; Homeowner vacancy rate: 0.0%; Median selected monthly owner costs: $1,174 with a mortgage, $441 without a mortgage; Median gross rent: $1,058 per month; Rental vacancy rate: 7.9%
Health Insurance: 93.6% have insurance; 71.4% have private insurance; 29.0% have public insurance; 6.4% do not have insurance; 1.9% of children under 18 do not have insurance
Safety: Violent crime rate: 18.2 per 10,000 population; Property crime rate: 349.3 per 10,000 population
Transportation: Commute: 98.2% car, 0.7% public transportation, 0.0% walk, 1.2% work from home; Mean travel time to work: 19.1 minutes

WYOMING (city). Covers a land area of 2.868 square miles and a water area of 0 square miles. Located at 39.23° N. Lat; 84.48° W. Long. Elevation is 577 feet.
History: Settled 1865, incorporated 1874.
Population: 8,484; Growth (since 2000): 2.7%; Density: 2,958.3 persons per square mile; Race: 77.5% White, 14.8% Black/African American, 3.1% Asian, 0.1% American Indian/Alaska Native, 0.0% Native Hawaiian/Other Pacific Islander, 4.2% Two or more races, 2.1% Hispanic of any race; Average household size: 2.76; Median age: 44.2; Age under 18: 27.2%; Age 65 and over: 16.1%; Males per 100 females: 90.4; Marriage status: 24.0% never married, 64.6% now married, 1.4% separated, 4.1% widowed, 7.4% divorced; Foreign born: 8.4%; Speak English only: 88.1%; With disability: 8.1%; Veterans: 4.1%; Ancestry: 31.2% German, 11.8% Irish, 10.5% English, 5.2% Russian, 5.0% American
Employment: 27.8% management, business, and financial, 7.9% computer, engineering, and science, 20.4% education, legal, community service, arts, and media, 8.6% healthcare practitioners, 10.0% service, 21.1% sales and office, 1.4% natural resources, construction, and maintenance, 2.9% production, transportation, and material moving

Income: Per capita: $57,789; Median household: $120,676; Average household: $159,435; Households with income of $100,000 or more: 59.2%; Poverty rate: 2.0%
Educational Attainment: High school diploma or higher: 98.1%; Bachelor's degree or higher: 69.6%; Graduate/professional degree or higher: 37.4%

School District(s)

Wyoming City (KG-12)
2015-16 Enrollment: 1,924 . . . . (513) 206-7000
Housing: Homeownership rate: 86.2%; Median home value: $305,900; Median year structure built: 1953; Homeowner vacancy rate: 2.6%; Median selected monthly owner costs: $2,149 with a mortgage, $874 without a mortgage; Median gross rent: $1,103 per month; Rental vacancy rate: 16.4%
Health Insurance: 97.9% have insurance; 85.5% have private insurance; 22.9% have public insurance; 2.1% do not have insurance; 0.7% of children under 18 do not have insurance
Safety: Violent crime rate: 5.9 per 10,000 population; Property crime rate: 189.1 per 10,000 population
Transportation: Commute: 87.7% car, 0.6% public transportation, 0.6% walk, 10.9% work from home; Mean travel time to work: 21.0 minutes
Additional Information Contacts
City of Wyoming . . . . (513) 821-7600
http://www.wyoming.oh.us

Hancock County

Located in northwestern Ohio; crossed by the Blanchard River. Covers a land area of 531.358 square miles, a water area of 2.301 square miles, and is located in the Eastern Time Zone at 41.00° N. Lat., 83.67° W. Long. The county was founded in 1820. County seat is Findlay.

Hancock County is part of the Findlay, OH Micropolitan Statistical Area. The entire metro area includes: Hancock County, OH

Weather Station: Findlay Airport Elevation: 799 feet

	Jan	Feb	Mar	Apr	May	Jun	Jul	Aug	Sep	Oct	Nov	Dec
High	33	36	47	60	70	79	83	81	75	63	50	37
Low	19	22	29	39	50	59	63	61	54	43	34	24
Precip	1.9	1.7	2.4	3.2	3.8	3.9	3.7	3.4	2.5	2.4	2.8	2.4
Snow	na	na	na	na	na	na	na	na	na	na	na	na

High and Low temperatures in degrees Fahrenheit; Precipitation and Snow in inches

Weather Station: Findlay Wpcc Elevation: 768 feet

	Jan	Feb	Mar	Apr	May	Jun	Jul	Aug	Sep	Oct	Nov	Dec
High	33	37	47	60	71	80	84	82	76	63	50	37
Low	19	22	29	40	50	60	64	63	55	44	34	24
Precip	2.3	2.1	2.6	3.4	4.1	4.2	4.0	3.8	2.7	2.7	2.9	2.8
Snow	8.4	5.5	4.4	1.1	0.1	0.0	0.0	0.0	0.0	0.2	1.3	5.9

High and Low temperatures in degrees Fahrenheit; Precipitation and Snow in inches

Population: 75,672; Growth (since 2000): 6.1%; Density: 142.4 persons per square mile; Race: 93.0% White, 1.4% Black/African American, 1.7% Asian, 0.1% American Indian/Alaska Native, 0.0% Native Hawaiian/Other Pacific Islander, 2.5% two or more races, 5.1% Hispanic of any race; Average household size: 2.34; Median age: 38.9; Age under 18: 22.7%; Age 65 and over: 15.8%; Males per 100 females: 94.2; Marriage status: 26.7% never married, 54.7% now married, 1.6% separated, 6.9% widowed, 11.7% divorced; Foreign born: 3.3%; Speak English only: 95.0%; With disability: 11.4%; Veterans: 9.1%; Ancestry: 36.9% German, 16.1% American, 10.8% Irish, 8.5% English, 3.8% Italian
Religion: Six largest groups: 12.6% Catholicism, 11.3% Methodist/Pietist, 7.4% Lutheran, 4.0% Presbyterian-Reformed, 2.6% Non-denominational Protestant, 2.3% Baptist
Economy: Unemployment rate: 3.3%; Leading industries: 15.2 % retail trade; 12.2 % other services (except public administration); 10.9 % health care and social assistance; Farms: 831 totaling 230,261 acres; Company size: 6 employ 1,000 or more persons, 4 employ 500 to 999 persons, 65 employ 100 to 499 persons, 1,640 employ less than 100 persons; Business ownership: 1,473 women-owned, 77 Black-owned, 64 Hispanic-owned, 35 Asian-owned, n/a American Indian/Alaska Native-owned
Employment: 15.0% management, business, and financial, 5.3% computer, engineering, and science, 7.7% education, legal, community service, arts, and media, 4.5% healthcare practitioners, 16.5% service, 20.0% sales and office, 7.8% natural resources, construction, and maintenance, 23.3% production, transportation, and material moving
Income: Per capita: $28,244; Median household: $51,604; Average household: $67,317; Households with income of $100,000 or more: 20.1%; Poverty rate: 13.5%
Educational Attainment: High school diploma or higher: 92.5%; Bachelor's degree or higher: 25.8%; Graduate/professional degree or higher: 9.2%
Housing: Homeownership rate: 69.4%; Median home value: $130,700; Median year structure built: 1970; Homeowner vacancy rate: 0.8%; Median selected monthly owner costs: $1,175 with a mortgage, $426 without a mortgage; Median gross rent: $711 per month; Rental vacancy rate: 4.6%
Vital Statistics: Birth rate: 126.4 per 10,000 population; Death rate: 90.2 per 10,000 population; Age-adjusted cancer mortality rate: 171.6 deaths per 100,000 population
Health Insurance: 92.9% have insurance; 76.2% have private insurance; 31.1% have public insurance; 7.1% do not have insurance; 3.5% of children under 18 do not have insurance
Health Care: Physicians: 16.8 per 10,000 population; Dentists: 4.7 per 10,000 population; Hospital beds: 21.1 per 10,000 population; Hospital admissions: 968.8 per 10,000 population
Transportation: Commute: 92.8% car, 0.3% public transportation, 2.4% walk, 3.5% work from home; Mean travel time to work: 17.1 minutes
2016 Presidential Election: 66.7% Trump, 26.5% Clinton, 4.2% Johnson, 0.9% Stein
National and State Parks: Van Buren Lake State Park
Additional Information Contacts
Hancock Government . . . . (419) 424-7044
http://www.co.hancock.oh.us

Hancock County Communities

ARCADIA (village). Covers a land area of 0.577 square miles and a water area of 0 square miles. Located at 41.11° N. Lat; 83.51° W. Long. Elevation is 807 feet.
Population: 598; Growth (since 2000): 11.4%; Density: 1,037.0 persons per square mile; Race: 99.5% White, 0.0% Black/African American, 0.0% Asian, 0.0% American Indian/Alaska Native, 0.0% Native Hawaiian/Other Pacific Islander, 0.5% Two or more races, 1.5% Hispanic of any race; Average household size: 2.56; Median age: 35.4; Age under 18: 24.4%; Age 65 and over: 12.9%; Males per 100 females: 100.0; Marriage status: 24.4% never married, 59.1% now married, 0.8% separated, 2.9% widowed, 13.6% divorced; Foreign born: 0.0%; Speak English only: 100.0%; With disability: 14.5%; Veterans: 6.0%; Ancestry: 46.8% German, 19.6% American, 7.0% English, 5.5% Irish, 2.0% Italian
Employment: 7.1% management, business, and financial, 2.5% computer, engineering, and science, 1.2% education, legal, community service, arts, and media, 3.4% healthcare practitioners, 15.2% service, 23.9% sales and office, 13.0% natural resources, construction, and maintenance, 33.5% production, transportation, and material moving
Income: Per capita: $24,973; Median household: $54,167; Average household: $62,837; Households with income of $100,000 or more: 19.3%; Poverty rate: 5.6%
Educational Attainment: High school diploma or higher: 95.4%; Bachelor's degree or higher: 13.9%; Graduate/professional degree or higher: 3.9%

School District(s)

Arcadia Local (KG-12)
2015-16 Enrollment: 596 . . . . (419) 894-6431
Housing: Homeownership rate: 82.1%; Median home value: $90,000; Median year structure built: 1948; Homeowner vacancy rate: 0.0%; Median selected monthly owner costs: $974 with a mortgage, $386 without a mortgage; Median gross rent: $775 per month; Rental vacancy rate: 0.0%
Health Insurance: 97.5% have insurance; 83.8% have private insurance; 29.9% have public insurance; 2.5% do not have insurance; 2.7% of children under 18 do not have insurance
Transportation: Commute: 94.9% car, 0.0% public transportation, 4.5% walk, 0.6% work from home; Mean travel time to work: 22.6 minutes

ARLINGTON (village). Covers a land area of 0.804 square miles and a water area of 0 square miles. Located at 40.89° N. Lat; 83.65° W. Long. Elevation is 863 feet.
Population: 1,439; Growth (since 2000): 6.5%; Density: 1,788.7 persons per square mile; Race: 97.4% White, 1.3% Black/African American, 0.0% Asian, 0.0% American Indian/Alaska Native, 0.0% Native Hawaiian/Other

Pacific Islander, 1.3% Two or more races, 1.3% Hispanic of any race; Average household size: 2.31; Median age: 43.1; Age under 18: 24.0%; Age 65 and over: 20.9%; Males per 100 females: 87.7; Marriage status: 21.4% never married, 55.9% now married, 2.0% separated, 10.9% widowed, 11.8% divorced; Foreign born: 0.7%; Speak English only: 99.3%; With disability: 14.2%; Veterans: 9.0%; Ancestry: 47.5% German, 14.8% American, 10.9% Irish, 9.4% English, 7.3% Italian
Employment: 8.6% management, business, and financial, 6.1% computer, engineering, and science, 9.9% education, legal, community service, arts, and media, 10.1% healthcare practitioners, 19.0% service, 19.9% sales and office, 8.7% natural resources, construction, and maintenance, 17.7% production, transportation, and material moving
Income: Per capita: $24,154; Median household: $44,830; Average household: $57,025; Households with income of $100,000 or more: 18.5%; Poverty rate: 11.9%
Educational Attainment: High school diploma or higher: 93.2%; Bachelor's degree or higher: 28.2%; Graduate/professional degree or higher: 8.3%

School District(s)

Arlington Local (KG-12)
2015-16 Enrollment: 575 . . . . (419) 365-5121

Housing: Homeownership rate: 71.2%; Median home value: $123,500; Median year structure built: 1960; Homeowner vacancy rate: 3.2%; Median selected monthly owner costs: $1,086 with a mortgage, $414 without a mortgage; Median gross rent: $544 per month; Rental vacancy rate: 4.5%
Health Insurance: 94.6% have insurance; 84.4% have private insurance; 34.2% have public insurance; 5.4% do not have insurance; 1.2% of children under 18 do not have insurance
Transportation: Commute: 92.8% car, 1.6% public transportation, 0.5% walk, 1.9% work from home; Mean travel time to work: 21.3 minutes

---

BENTON RIDGE (village). Covers a land area of 0.343 square miles and a water area of 0 square miles. Located at 41.00° N. Lat; 83.79° W. Long. Elevation is 791 feet.
Population: 296; Growth (since 2000): -6.0%; Density: 863.3 persons per square mile; Race: 99.3% White, 0.0% Black/African American, 0.0% Asian, 0.0% American Indian/Alaska Native, 0.0% Native Hawaiian/Other Pacific Islander, 0.7% Two or more races, 0.0% Hispanic of any race; Average household size: 1.96; Median age: 49.3; Age under 18: 14.2%; Age 65 and over: 16.2%; Males per 100 females: 103.4; Marriage status: 20.6% never married, 55.3% now married, 2.3% separated, 3.5% widowed, 20.6% divorced; Foreign born: 0.0%; Speak English only: 100.0%; With disability: 23.0%; Veterans: 15.4%; Ancestry: 49.3% German, 24.7% American, 14.2% English, 6.8% Irish, 5.4% Dutch
Employment: 0.0% management, business, and financial, 3.5% computer, engineering, and science, 6.9% education, legal, community service, arts, and media, 0.7% healthcare practitioners, 17.4% service, 19.4% sales and office, 29.9% natural resources, construction, and maintenance, 22.2% production, transportation, and material moving
Income: Per capita: $24,825; Median household: $43,068; Average household: $49,769; Households with income of $100,000 or more: 6.0%; Poverty rate: 4.4%
Educational Attainment: High school diploma or higher: 90.8%; Bachelor's degree or higher: 7.1%; Graduate/professional degree or higher: 4.2%
Housing: Homeownership rate: 81.5%; Median home value: $96,600; Median year structure built: Before 1940; Homeowner vacancy rate: 2.4%; Median selected monthly owner costs: $1,052 with a mortgage, $394 without a mortgage; Median gross rent: $629 per month; Rental vacancy rate: 0.0%
Health Insurance: 85.8% have insurance; 71.6% have private insurance; 32.8% have public insurance; 14.2% do not have insurance; 0.0% of children under 18 do not have insurance
Transportation: Commute: 100.0% car, 0.0% public transportation, 0.0% walk, 0.0% work from home; Mean travel time to work: 21.5 minutes

---

FINDLAY (city). County seat. Covers a land area of 19.134 square miles and a water area of 0.120 square miles. Located at 41.05° N. Lat; 83.64° W. Long. Elevation is 774 feet.
History: Findlay was laid out in 1821 by Joseph Vance and Elnathan Cory, and named for Fort Findlay, an outpost built under the direction of General Hull during the War of 1812. After the Civil War, the Findlay Natural Gas Company began to make commercial use of the gas and oil beneath the city. It was in the Findlay "Jeffersonian" in 1860 that Petroleum V. Nasby (pen name of David Ross Locke, the editor) wrote satirical letters attacking the institution of slavery.
Population: 41,412; Growth (since 2000): 6.3%; Density: 2,164.3 persons per square mile; Race: 89.6% White, 2.2% Black/African American, 2.6% Asian, 0.1% American Indian/Alaska Native, 0.0% Native Hawaiian/Other Pacific Islander, 3.6% Two or more races, 7.3% Hispanic of any race; Average household size: 2.20; Median age: 36.7; Age under 18: 21.0%; Age 65 and over: 17.1%; Males per 100 females: 90.7; Marriage status: 31.9% never married, 47.4% now married, 2.0% separated, 7.9% widowed, 12.8% divorced; Foreign born: 4.9%; Speak English only: 92.7%; With disability: 13.0%; Veterans: 8.9%; Ancestry: 32.2% German, 16.3% American, 11.2% Irish, 8.3% English, 3.9% Italian
Employment: 15.4% management, business, and financial, 5.8% computer, engineering, and science, 8.1% education, legal, community service, arts, and media, 4.2% healthcare practitioners, 19.1% service, 19.1% sales and office, 6.8% natural resources, construction, and maintenance, 21.4% production, transportation, and material moving
Income: Per capita: $26,052; Median household: $45,364; Average household: $59,210; Households with income of $100,000 or more: 15.5%; Poverty rate: 18.5%
Educational Attainment: High school diploma or higher: 91.0%; Bachelor's degree or higher: 26.8%; Graduate/professional degree or higher: 9.6%

School District(s)

Findlay City (PK-12)
2015-16 Enrollment: 5,812 . . . . (419) 425-8212
Findlay Digital Academy (09-12)
2015-16 Enrollment: 147 . . . . (419) 425-3598
Liberty-Benton Local (KG-12)
2015-16 Enrollment: 1,410 . . . . (419) 422-8526

Four-year College(s)

Brown Mackie College-Findlay (Private, For-profit)
Fall 2016 Enrollment: 214 . . . . (419) 423-2211
The University of Findlay (Private, Not-for-profit, Church of God)
Fall 2016 Enrollment: 5,078 . . . . (419) 422-8313
2016-17 Tuition: In-state $32,402; Out-of-state $32,402
Winebrenner Theological Seminary (Private, Not-for-profit, Other Protestant)
Fall 2016 Enrollment: 66 . . . . (419) 434-4200

Two-year College(s)

The Artisan College of Cosmetology (Private, For-profit)
Fall 2016 Enrollment: 24 . . . . (419) 425-1485

Housing: Homeownership rate: 58.1%; Median home value: $123,800; Median year structure built: 1966; Homeowner vacancy rate: 0.6%; Median selected monthly owner costs: $1,139 with a mortgage, $417 without a mortgage; Median gross rent: $715 per month; Rental vacancy rate: 4.9%
Health Insurance: 90.5% have insurance; 70.7% have private insurance; 34.7% have public insurance; 9.5% do not have insurance; 4.9% of children under 18 do not have insurance
Hospitals: Blanchard Valley Hospital (150 beds)
Newspapers: The Courier (daily circulation 21,200)
Transportation: Commute: 92.2% car, 0.4% public transportation, 3.2% walk, 3.3% work from home; Mean travel time to work: 15.5 minutes
Airports: Findlay (general aviation)
Additional Information Contacts
City of Findlay . . . . (419) 424-7137
http://www.ci.findlay.oh.us

JENERA (village). Covers a land area of 0.270 square miles and a water area of 0 square miles. Located at 40.90° N. Lat; 83.73° W. Long. Elevation is 850 feet.
Population: 202; Growth (since 2000): -14.0%; Density: 748.6 persons per square mile; Race: 88.6% White, 0.0% Black/African American, 0.0% Asian, 0.0% American Indian/Alaska Native, 0.0% Native Hawaiian/Other Pacific Islander, 11.4% Two or more races, 2.0% Hispanic of any race; Average household size: 2.97; Median age: 30.8; Age under 18: 33.7%; Age 65 and over: 6.9%; Males per 100 females: 102.8; Marriage status: 23.2% never married, 67.1% now married, 0.0% separated, 0.0% widowed, 9.7% divorced; Foreign born: 0.0%; Speak English only: 100.0%; With disability: 4.0%; Veterans: 8.2%; Ancestry: 40.6% German, 17.8% American, 7.4% Scottish, 3.0% English, 3.0% French
Employment: 0.8% management, business, and financial, 4.7% computer, engineering, and science, 7.8% education, legal, community service, arts, and media, 4.7% healthcare practitioners, 17.1% service, 32.6% sales and

office, 10.9% natural resources, construction, and maintenance, 21.7% production, transportation, and material moving
Income: Per capita: $18,464; Median household: $50,833; Average household: $53,028; Households with income of $100,000 or more: 5.9%; Poverty rate: 9.9%
Educational Attainment: High school diploma or higher: 94.3%; Bachelor's degree or higher: 19.7%; Graduate/professional degree or higher: 1.6%
Housing: Homeownership rate: 69.1%; Median home value: $80,700; Median year structure built: Before 1940; Homeowner vacancy rate: 0.0%; Median selected monthly owner costs: $900 with a mortgage, $430 without a mortgage; Median gross rent: $615 per month; Rental vacancy rate: 0.0%
Health Insurance: 91.1% have insurance; 66.8% have private insurance; 31.2% have public insurance; 8.9% do not have insurance; 5.9% of children under 18 do not have insurance
Transportation: Commute: 90.2% car, 0.0% public transportation, 0.0% walk, 9.8% work from home; Mean travel time to work: 21.7 minutes

MCCOMB (village). Covers a land area of 0.887 square miles and a water area of 0.036 square miles. Located at 41.11° N. Lat; 83.79° W. Long. Elevation is 771 feet.
Population: 1,699; Growth (since 2000): 1.4%; Density: 1,916.3 persons per square mile; Race: 92.5% White, 0.0% Black/African American, 0.2% Asian, 0.3% American Indian/Alaska Native, 0.0% Native Hawaiian/Other Pacific Islander, 3.6% Two or more races, 11.5% Hispanic of any race; Average household size: 2.55; Median age: 39.2; Age under 18: 25.5%; Age 65 and over: 12.2%; Males per 100 females: 95.3; Marriage status: 25.8% never married, 55.6% now married, 2.1% separated, 3.8% widowed, 14.9% divorced; Foreign born: 1.7%; Speak English only: 92.6%; With disability: 14.6%; Veterans: 6.9%; Ancestry: 35.6% German, 25.2% American, 9.9% Irish, 8.3% English, 4.6% French
Employment: 8.9% management, business, and financial, 5.3% computer, engineering, and science, 3.6% education, legal, community service, arts, and media, 3.4% healthcare practitioners, 16.7% service, 17.6% sales and office, 7.0% natural resources, construction, and maintenance, 37.5% production, transportation, and material moving
Income: Per capita: $21,290; Median household: $47,917; Average household: $54,955; Households with income of $100,000 or more: 9.9%; Poverty rate: 11.4%
Educational Attainment: High school diploma or higher: 89.7%; Bachelor's degree or higher: 8.0%; Graduate/professional degree or higher: 3.3%

School District(s)

Mccomb Local (PK-12)
2015-16 Enrollment: 725. . . . . (419) 293-3979
Housing: Homeownership rate: 73.2%; Median home value: $111,600; Median year structure built: 1962; Homeowner vacancy rate: 2.2%; Median selected monthly owner costs: $925 with a mortgage, $338 without a mortgage; Median gross rent: $723 per month; Rental vacancy rate: 10.6%
Health Insurance: 96.0% have insurance; 77.8% have private insurance; 33.3% have public insurance; 4.0% do not have insurance; 2.3% of children under 18 do not have insurance
Transportation: Commute: 95.9% car, 0.6% public transportation, 1.2% walk, 0.4% work from home; Mean travel time to work: 19.7 minutes

MOUNT BLANCHARD (village). Covers a land area of 0.538 square miles and a water area of 0 square miles. Located at 40.90° N. Lat; 83.56° W. Long. Elevation is 846 feet.
Population: 478; Growth (since 2000): -1.2%; Density: 889.0 persons per square mile; Race: 90.0% White, 4.0% Black/African American, 0.0% Asian, 0.0% American Indian/Alaska Native, 0.0% Native Hawaiian/Other Pacific Islander, 5.9% Two or more races, 1.0% Hispanic of any race; Average household size: 2.72; Median age: 36.3; Age under 18: 34.7%; Age 65 and over: 14.9%; Males per 100 females: 97.6; Marriage status: 28.2% never married, 55.1% now married, 5.0% separated, 4.4% widowed, 12.3% divorced; Foreign born: 0.0%; Speak English only: 96.7%; With disability: 13.4%; Veterans: 10.6%; Ancestry: 34.5% German, 16.3% American, 10.7% English, 10.0% Irish, 5.6% Italian
Employment: 9.3% management, business, and financial, 2.6% computer, engineering, and science, 8.2% education, legal, community service, arts, and media, 5.2% healthcare practitioners, 15.5% service, 17.5% sales and office, 14.4% natural resources, construction, and maintenance, 27.3% production, transportation, and material moving
Income: Per capita: $20,289; Median household: $53,750; Average household: $57,398; Households with income of $100,000 or more: 13.0%; Poverty rate: 17.0%
Educational Attainment: High school diploma or higher: 92.9%; Bachelor's degree or higher: 22.0%; Graduate/professional degree or higher: 4.1%

School District(s)

Riverdale Local (KG-12)
2015-16 Enrollment: 1,007 . . . . (419) 694-4994
Housing: Homeownership rate: 64.5%; Median home value: $87,000; Median year structure built: Before 1940; Homeowner vacancy rate: 0.0%; Median selected monthly owner costs: $953 with a mortgage, $400 without a mortgage; Median gross rent: $700 per month; Rental vacancy rate: 6.3%
Health Insurance: 92.1% have insurance; 68.0% have private insurance; 36.0% have public insurance; 7.9% do not have insurance; 7.8% of children under 18 do not have insurance
Transportation: Commute: 95.5% car, 0.0% public transportation, 2.2% walk, 1.7% work from home; Mean travel time to work: 28.1 minutes

MOUNT CORY (village). Covers a land area of 0.384 square miles and a water area of 0 square miles. Located at 40.93° N. Lat; 83.82° W. Long. Elevation is 814 feet.
Population: 214; Growth (since 2000): 5.4%; Density: 557.1 persons per square mile; Race: 98.1% White, 0.0% Black/African American, 0.0% Asian, 0.0% American Indian/Alaska Native, 0.0% Native Hawaiian/Other Pacific Islander, 1.9% Two or more races, 4.2% Hispanic of any race; Average household size: 2.64; Median age: 34.5; Age under 18: 36.4%; Age 65 and over: 15.0%; Males per 100 females: 102.0; Marriage status: 19.0% never married, 63.3% now married, 4.1% separated, 4.8% widowed, 12.9% divorced; Foreign born: 0.0%; Speak English only: 99.0%; With disability: 14.5%; Veterans: 6.6%; Ancestry: 29.4% German, 15.9% Irish, 14.5% American, 10.7% English, 4.2% Swiss
Employment: 16.5% management, business, and financial, 5.1% computer, engineering, and science, 1.3% education, legal, community service, arts, and media, 3.8% healthcare practitioners, 20.3% service, 21.5% sales and office, 10.1% natural resources, construction, and maintenance, 21.5% production, transportation, and material moving
Income: Per capita: $20,028; Median household: $50,313; Average household: $52,175; Households with income of $100,000 or more: 2.5%; Poverty rate: 17.1%
Educational Attainment: High school diploma or higher: 81.1%; Bachelor's degree or higher: 7.4%; Graduate/professional degree or higher: 1.6%
Housing: Homeownership rate: 77.8%; Median home value: $78,300; Median year structure built: Before 1940; Homeowner vacancy rate: 0.0%; Median selected monthly owner costs: $1,000 with a mortgage, $432 without a mortgage; Median gross rent: $938 per month; Rental vacancy rate: 0.0%
Health Insurance: 93.5% have insurance; 61.7% have private insurance; 43.0% have public insurance; 6.5% do not have insurance; 3.8% of children under 18 do not have insurance
Transportation: Commute: 98.7% car, 0.0% public transportation, 0.0% walk, 1.3% work from home; Mean travel time to work: 21.1 minutes

RAWSON (village). Covers a land area of 0.396 square miles and a water area of 0 square miles. Located at 40.96° N. Lat; 83.78° W. Long. Elevation is 810 feet.
Population: 513; Growth (since 2000): 10.3%; Density: 1,297.1 persons per square mile; Race: 87.9% White, 1.6% Black/African American, 0.2% Asian, 0.0% American Indian/Alaska Native, 0.0% Native Hawaiian/Other Pacific Islander, 10.1% Two or more races, 3.7% Hispanic of any race; Average household size: 2.95; Median age: 30.4; Age under 18: 35.7%; Age 65 and over: 9.7%; Males per 100 females: 96.6; Marriage status: 22.8% never married, 62.8% now married, 2.9% separated, 5.2% widowed, 9.2% divorced; Foreign born: 0.4%; Speak English only: 99.6%; With disability: 11.1%; Veterans: 11.8%; Ancestry: 35.9% German, 16.6% American, 12.1% Irish, 4.1% Italian, 3.7% English
Employment: 7.3% management, business, and financial, 3.0% computer, engineering, and science, 3.0% education, legal, community service, arts, and media, 1.7% healthcare practitioners, 20.9% service, 23.9% sales and office, 8.5% natural resources, construction, and maintenance, 31.6% production, transportation, and material moving

Income: Per capita: $17,313; Median household: $45,833; Average household: $51,922; Households with income of $100,000 or more: 10.3%; Poverty rate: 17.5%
Educational Attainment: High school diploma or higher: 91.2%; Bachelor's degree or higher: 12.1%; Graduate/professional degree or higher: 2.4%

School District(s)

Cory-Rawson Local (KG-12)
2015-16 Enrollment: 537. . . . . (419) 963-3415
Housing: Homeownership rate: 56.9%; Median home value: $79,600; Median year structure built: 1942; Homeowner vacancy rate: 3.7%; Median selected monthly owner costs: $831 with a mortgage, $450 without a mortgage; Median gross rent: $883 per month; Rental vacancy rate: 0.0%
Health Insurance: 95.3% have insurance; 71.2% have private insurance; 37.2% have public insurance; 4.7% do not have insurance; 0.0% of children under 18 do not have insurance
Transportation: Commute: 99.6% car, 0.0% public transportation, 0.0% walk, 0.4% work from home; Mean travel time to work: 24.6 minutes

VAN BUREN (village). Covers a land area of 0.258 square miles and a water area of 0 square miles. Located at 41.14° N. Lat; 83.65° W. Long. Elevation is 768 feet.
History: Van Buren was named for President Martin Van Buren. For a time, Van Buren was an oil center.
Population: 346; Growth (since 2000): 10.5%; Density: 1,340.3 persons per square mile; Race: 96.8% White, 0.0% Black/African American, 0.0% Asian, 0.0% American Indian/Alaska Native, 0.0% Native Hawaiian/Other Pacific Islander, 3.2% Two or more races, 7.2% Hispanic of any race; Average household size: 2.93; Median age: 37.4; Age under 18: 23.1%; Age 65 and over: 15.9%; Males per 100 females: 98.8; Marriage status: 17.1% never married, 74.5% now married, 0.0% separated, 2.2% widowed, 6.2% divorced; Foreign born: 0.0%; Speak English only: 96.4%; With disability: 9.2%; Veterans: 12.0%; Ancestry: 34.1% German, 21.1% American, 15.9% Irish, 6.1% English, 4.6% Italian
Employment: 7.6% management, business, and financial, 1.7% computer, engineering, and science, 11.6% education, legal, community service, arts, and media, 10.5% healthcare practitioners, 19.2% service, 16.9% sales and office, 9.9% natural resources, construction, and maintenance, 22.7% production, transportation, and material moving
Income: Per capita: $27,499; Median household: $73,333; Average household: $81,641; Households with income of $100,000 or more: 17.7%; Poverty rate: 1.7%
Educational Attainment: High school diploma or higher: 97.4%; Bachelor's degree or higher: 17.5%; Graduate/professional degree or higher: 6.0%

School District(s)

Van Buren Local (KG-12)
2015-16 Enrollment: 1,021 . . . . (419) 299-3578
Housing: Homeownership rate: 99.2%; Median home value: $122,800; Median year structure built: Before 1940; Homeowner vacancy rate: 1.7%; Median selected monthly owner costs: $1,203 with a mortgage, $544 without a mortgage; Median gross rent: n/a per month; Rental vacancy rate: 0.0%
Health Insurance: 91.0% have insurance; 80.6% have private insurance; 24.6% have public insurance; 9.0% do not have insurance; 0.0% of children under 18 do not have insurance
Transportation: Commute: 100.0% car, 0.0% public transportation, 0.0% walk, 0.0% work from home; Mean travel time to work: 17.3 minutes

VANLUE (village). Covers a land area of 0.349 square miles and a water area of 0.007 square miles. Located at 40.97° N. Lat; 83.48° W. Long. Elevation is 820 feet.
Population: 312; Growth (since 2000): -15.9%; Density: 894.1 persons per square mile; Race: 95.8% White, 1.3% Black/African American, 0.0% Asian, 0.0% American Indian/Alaska Native, 0.0% Native Hawaiian/Other Pacific Islander, 0.6% Two or more races, 2.9% Hispanic of any race; Average household size: 2.50; Median age: 37.3; Age under 18: 25.0%; Age 65 and over: 15.7%; Males per 100 females: 88.9; Marriage status: 18.1% never married, 61.4% now married, 0.8% separated, 5.2% widowed, 15.3% divorced; Foreign born: 0.6%; Speak English only: 98.6%; With disability: 12.5%; Veterans: 8.1%; Ancestry: 47.1% German, 21.2% American, 8.7% Irish, 5.1% English, 4.8% French
Employment: 9.2% management, business, and financial, 4.0% computer, engineering, and science, 9.8% education, legal, community service, arts, and media, 5.7% healthcare practitioners, 12.1% service, 21.3% sales and office, 9.8% natural resources, construction, and maintenance, 28.2% production, transportation, and material moving
Income: Per capita: $25,844; Median household: $48,958; Average household: $62,912; Households with income of $100,000 or more: 12.8%; Poverty rate: 0.3%
Educational Attainment: High school diploma or higher: 92.4%; Bachelor's degree or higher: 22.2%; Graduate/professional degree or higher: 8.0%

School District(s)

Vanlue Local (KG-12)
2015-16 Enrollment: 239. . . . . (419) 387-7724
Housing: Homeownership rate: 88.0%; Median home value: $83,200; Median year structure built: Before 1940; Homeowner vacancy rate: 0.0%; Median selected monthly owner costs: $938 with a mortgage, $356 without a mortgage; Median gross rent: $754 per month; Rental vacancy rate: 0.0%
Health Insurance: 93.9% have insurance; 89.4% have private insurance; 19.6% have public insurance; 6.1% do not have insurance; 7.7% of children under 18 do not have insurance
Transportation: Commute: 85.4% car, 0.0% public transportation, 10.5% walk, 2.3% work from home; Mean travel time to work: 17.8 minutes

WILLIAMSTOWN (unincorporated postal area)
ZCTA: 45897
Covers a land area of 1.376 square miles and a water area of 0.007 square miles. Located at 40.83° N. Lat; 83.66° W. Long. Elevation is 932 feet.
Population: 39; Growth (since 2000): -42.6%; Density: 28.3 persons per square mile; Race: 100.0% White, 0.0% Black/African American, 0.0% Asian, 0.0% American Indian/Alaska Native, 0.0% Native Hawaiian/Other Pacific Islander, 0.0% Two or more races, 0.0% Hispanic of any race; Average household size: 1.44; Median age: 61.7; Age under 18: 0.0%; Age 65 and over: 0.0%; Males per 100 females: 83.6; Marriage status: 0.0% never married, 59.0% now married, 0.0% separated, 41.0% widowed, 0.0% divorced; Foreign born: 0.0%; Speak English only: 100.0%; With disability: 41.0%; Veterans: 0.0%; Ancestry: 59.0% German
Employment: 100.0% management, business, and financial, 0.0% computer, engineering, and science, 0.0% education, legal, community service, arts, and media, 0.0% healthcare practitioners, 0.0% service, 0.0% sales and office, 0.0% natural resources, construction, and maintenance, 0.0% production, transportation, and material moving
Income: Per capita: $50,044; Median household: n/a; Average household: n/a; Households with income of $100,000 or more: 40.7%; Poverty rate: n/a
Educational Attainment: High school diploma or higher: 59.0%; Bachelor's degree or higher: n/a; Graduate/professional degree or higher: n/a
Housing: Homeownership rate: 100.0%; Median home value: n/a; Median year structure built: n/a; Homeowner vacancy rate: 0.0%; Median selected monthly owner costs: $0 with a mortgage, $0 without a mortgage; Median gross rent: n/a per month; Rental vacancy rate: 0.0%
Health Insurance: 100.0% have insurance; 59.0% have private insurance; 41.0% have public insurance; 0.0% do not have insurance; 0.0% of children under 18 do not have insurance
Transportation: Commute: 0.0% car, 0.0% public transportation, 0.0% walk, 100.0% work from home; Mean travel time to work: 0.0 minutes

Hardin County

Located in west central Ohio; crossed by the Sciota, Blanchard, and Ottawa Rivers. Covers a land area of 470.405 square miles, a water area of 0.243 square miles, and is located in the Eastern Time Zone at 40.66° N. Lat., 83.66° W. Long. The county was founded in 1820. County seat is Kenton.

Weather Station: Kenton Elevation: 995 feet

	Jan	Feb	Mar	Apr	May	Jun	Jul	Aug	Sep	Oct	Nov	Dec
High	33	37	47	60	71	81	85	83	76	63	50	37
Low	18	20	28	39	50	59	63	61	53	42	33	23
Precip	2.3	2.1	2.6	3.3	4.1	3.6	3.9	3.1	2.7	2.4	2.9	2.7
Snow	8.3	6.6	3.9	0.4	0.0	0.0	0.0	0.0	0.0	tr	1.0	5.0

High and Low temperatures in degrees Fahrenheit; Precipitation and Snow in inches

Population: 31,652; Growth (since 2000): -0.9%; Density: 67.3 persons per square mile; Race: 96.4% White, 0.6% Black/African American, 0.8%

Asian, 0.1% American Indian/Alaska Native, 0.0% Native Hawaiian/Other Pacific Islander, 1.7% two or more races, 1.5% Hispanic of any race; Average household size: 2.53; Median age: 35.8; Age under 18: 23.1%; Age 65 and over: 14.8%; Males per 100 females: 98.5; Marriage status: 29.6% never married, 50.9% now married, 1.2% separated, 6.7% widowed, 12.8% divorced; Foreign born: 1.5%; Speak English only: 95.4%; With disability: 13.6%; Veterans: 8.2%; Ancestry: 28.6% German, 15.2% American, 12.9% Irish, 7.5% English, 2.1% Italian
Religion: Six largest groups: 10.7% Methodist/Pietist, 5.6% Catholicism, 5.2% Presbyterian-Reformed, 4.3% Baptist, 2.9% European Free-Church, 2.8% Pentecostal
Economy: Unemployment rate: 4.4%; Leading industries: 19.4 % retail trade; 13.8 % other services (except public administration); 10.7 % accommodation and food services; Farms: 793 totaling 247,839 acres; Company size: 1 employs 1,000 or more persons, 1 employs 500 to 999 persons, 6 employ 100 to 499 persons, 440 employ less than 100 persons; Business ownership: 593 women-owned, n/a Black-owned, 25 Hispanic-owned, n/a Asian-owned, n/a American Indian/Alaska Native-owned
Employment: 9.6% management, business, and financial, 2.6% computer, engineering, and science, 9.8% education, legal, community service, arts, and media, 4.6% healthcare practitioners, 19.6% service, 19.7% sales and office, 7.3% natural resources, construction, and maintenance, 26.8% production, transportation, and material moving
Income: Per capita: $20,994; Median household: $44,842; Average household: $55,951; Households with income of $100,000 or more: 12.4%; Poverty rate: 15.6%
Educational Attainment: High school diploma or higher: 89.4%; Bachelor's degree or higher: 14.4%; Graduate/professional degree or higher: 6.3%
Housing: Homeownership rate: 72.1%; Median home value: $93,500; Median year structure built: 1963; Homeowner vacancy rate: 1.7%; Median selected monthly owner costs: $978 with a mortgage, $395 without a mortgage; Median gross rent: $635 per month; Rental vacancy rate: 7.4%
Vital Statistics: Birth rate: 117.6 per 10,000 population; Death rate: 102.6 per 10,000 population; Age-adjusted cancer mortality rate: 237.7 deaths per 100,000 population
Health Insurance: 89.4% have insurance; 68.3% have private insurance; 34.1% have public insurance; 10.6% do not have insurance; 9.3% of children under 18 do not have insurance
Health Care: Physicians: 3.5 per 10,000 population; Dentists: 2.2 per 10,000 population; Hospital beds: 7.9 per 10,000 population; Hospital admissions: 225.3 per 10,000 population
Transportation: Commute: 90.5% car, 0.2% public transportation, 3.0% walk, 4.9% work from home; Mean travel time to work: 23.8 minutes
2016 Presidential Election: 70.6% Trump, 23.6% Clinton, 3.8% Johnson, 0.6% Stein
Additional Information Contacts
Hardin Government. . . . . (419) 674-2205
http://www.hardincountyoh.com

Hardin County Communities

ADA (village). Covers a land area of 2.078 square miles and a water area of 0 square miles. Located at 40.77° N. Lat; 83.82° W. Long. Elevation is 961 feet.
History: Ada grew up around Ohio Northern University, founded in 1871 as the Northwestern Ohio Normal School by Henry Solomon Lehr.
Population: 6,046; Growth (since 2000): 8.3%; Density: 2,909.3 persons per square mile; Race: 91.3% White, 1.6% Black/African American, 4.2% Asian, 0.0% American Indian/Alaska Native, 0.0% Native Hawaiian/Other Pacific Islander, 2.8% Two or more races, 2.1% Hispanic of any race; Average household size: 2.16; Median age: 21.6; Age under 18: 16.0%; Age 65 and over: 8.5%; Males per 100 females: 103.4; Marriage status: 57.7% never married, 25.0% now married, 0.0% separated, 5.1% widowed, 12.1% divorced; Foreign born: 4.3%; Speak English only: 93.4%; With disability: 8.3%; Veterans: 4.2%; Ancestry: 37.8% German, 16.0% Irish, 11.1% American, 7.0% English, 5.3% Italian
Employment: 7.3% management, business, and financial, 5.5% computer, engineering, and science, 14.2% education, legal, community service, arts, and media, 4.9% healthcare practitioners, 28.7% service, 20.1% sales and office, 4.3% natural resources, construction, and maintenance, 15.1% production, transportation, and material moving
Income: Per capita: $15,485; Median household: $35,022; Average household: $46,422; Households with income of $100,000 or more: 6.7%; Poverty rate: 23.4%
Educational Attainment: High school diploma or higher: 88.3%; Bachelor's degree or higher: 26.7%; Graduate/professional degree or higher: 14.4%

School District(s)

Ada Exempted Village (KG-12)
2015-16 Enrollment: 850. . . . . (419) 634-6421

Four-year College(s)

Ohio Northern University (Private, Not-for-profit, United Methodist)
Fall 2016 Enrollment: 3,108 . . . . (419) 772-2000
2016-17 Tuition: In-state $29,820; Out-of-state $29,820
Housing: Homeownership rate: 46.0%; Median home value: $83,500; Median year structure built: 1964; Homeowner vacancy rate: 0.0%; Median selected monthly owner costs: $1,020 with a mortgage, $435 without a mortgage; Median gross rent: $694 per month; Rental vacancy rate: 8.2%
Health Insurance: 91.7% have insurance; 77.0% have private insurance; 23.5% have public insurance; 8.3% do not have insurance; 2.2% of children under 18 do not have insurance
Safety: Violent crime rate: 1.7 per 10,000 population; Property crime rate: 65.7 per 10,000 population
Newspapers: Ada Herald (weekly circulation 2,800)
Transportation: Commute: 77.4% car, 0.1% public transportation, 8.0% walk, 13.9% work from home; Mean travel time to work: 18.2 minutes

ALGER (village). Covers a land area of 0.285 square miles and a water area of 0 square miles. Located at 40.71° N. Lat; 83.84° W. Long. Elevation is 974 feet.
Population: 947; Growth (since 2000): 6.6%; Density: 3,325.4 persons per square mile; Race: 96.1% White, 0.2% Black/African American, 0.0% Asian, 0.5% American Indian/Alaska Native, 0.0% Native Hawaiian/Other Pacific Islander, 2.3% Two or more races, 3.9% Hispanic of any race; Average household size: 2.53; Median age: 39.5; Age under 18: 25.7%; Age 65 and over: 15.9%; Males per 100 females: 85.7; Marriage status: 28.7% never married, 43.5% now married, 5.1% separated, 11.5% widowed, 16.3% divorced; Foreign born: 0.0%; Speak English only: 99.1%; With disability: 18.8%; Veterans: 7.1%; Ancestry: 26.1% German, 20.7% English, 19.9% American, 17.4% Irish, 5.4% Italian
Employment: 4.9% management, business, and financial, 0.5% computer, engineering, and science, 4.4% education, legal, community service, arts, and media, 2.7% healthcare practitioners, 20.3% service, 19.5% sales and office, 5.8% natural resources, construction, and maintenance, 41.9% production, transportation, and material moving
Income: Per capita: $14,357; Median household: $32,629; Average household: $36,175; Households with income of $100,000 or more: 1.1%; Poverty rate: 28.8%
Educational Attainment: High school diploma or higher: 73.6%; Bachelor's degree or higher: 6.8%; Graduate/professional degree or higher: 1.9%
Housing: Homeownership rate: 59.5%; Median home value: $52,200; Median year structure built: 1972; Homeowner vacancy rate: 3.0%; Median selected monthly owner costs: $708 with a mortgage, $312 without a mortgage; Median gross rent: $529 per month; Rental vacancy rate: 3.6%
Health Insurance: 90.6% have insurance; 59.5% have private insurance; 47.3% have public insurance; 9.4% do not have insurance; 0.0% of children under 18 do not have insurance
Transportation: Commute: 97.3% car, 0.8% public transportation, 0.0% walk, 1.9% work from home; Mean travel time to work: 26.7 minutes

DOLA (CDP). Covers a land area of 0.832 square miles and a water area of 0 square miles. Located at 40.78° N. Lat; 83.70° W. Long. Elevation is 948 feet.
Population: 158; Growth (since 2000): n/a; Density: 190.0 persons per square mile; Race: 84.8% White, 0.0% Black/African American, 0.0% Asian, 0.0% American Indian/Alaska Native, 0.0% Native Hawaiian/Other Pacific Islander, 15.2% Two or more races, 0.0% Hispanic of any race; Average household size: 2.16; Median age: 51.5; Age under 18: 15.8%; Age 65 and over: 24.7%; Males per 100 females: 94.4; Marriage status: 24.8% never married, 67.8% now married, 3.4% separated, 4.7% widowed, 2.7% divorced; Foreign born: 0.0%; Speak English only: 100.0%; With disability: 13.3%; Veterans: 15.8%; Ancestry: 45.6% American, 16.5% English, 8.2% Irish
Employment: 17.1% management, business, and financial, 0.0% computer, engineering, and science, 0.0% education, legal, community

service, arts, and media, 0.0% healthcare practitioners, 6.6% service, 44.7% sales and office, 0.0% natural resources, construction, and maintenance, 31.6% production, transportation, and material moving
Income: Per capita: $19,412; Median household: n/a; Average household: $44,463; Households with income of $100,000 or more: 17.8%; Poverty rate: 28.5%
Educational Attainment: High school diploma or higher: 83.8%; Bachelor's degree or higher: 10.0%; Graduate/professional degree or higher: n/a

School District(s)

Hardin Northern Local (KG-12)
2015-16 Enrollment: 432. . . . . (419) 759-2331
Housing: Homeownership rate: 100.0%; Median home value: $48,800; Median year structure built: Before 1940; Homeowner vacancy rate: 0.0%; Median selected monthly owner costs: $813 with a mortgage, $300 without a mortgage; Median gross rent: n/a per month; Rental vacancy rate: 0.0%
Health Insurance: 92.4% have insurance; 55.1% have private insurance; 50.6% have public insurance; 7.6% do not have insurance; 0.0% of children under 18 do not have insurance
Transportation: Commute: 100.0% car, 0.0% public transportation, 0.0% walk, 0.0% work from home; Mean travel time to work: 29.7 minutes

DUNKIRK (village). Covers a land area of 0.664 square miles and a water area of 0.059 square miles. Located at 40.79° N. Lat; 83.64° W. Long. Elevation is 945 feet.
Population: 818; Growth (since 2000): -14.1%; Density: 1,232.5 persons per square mile; Race: 96.7% White, 1.7% Black/African American, 0.1% Asian, 0.0% American Indian/Alaska Native, 0.0% Native Hawaiian/Other Pacific Islander, 1.5% Two or more races, 0.4% Hispanic of any race; Average household size: 2.44; Median age: 34.9; Age under 18: 26.4%; Age 65 and over: 13.3%; Males per 100 females: 100.7; Marriage status: 28.0% never married, 52.5% now married, 1.7% separated, 7.2% widowed, 12.3% divorced; Foreign born: 0.1%; Speak English only: 99.5%; With disability: 19.1%; Veterans: 14.6%; Ancestry: 30.2% German, 18.1% American, 8.6% English, 5.3% Irish, 3.3% French
Employment: 3.8% management, business, and financial, 4.1% computer, engineering, and science, 3.5% education, legal, community service, arts, and media, 4.3% healthcare practitioners, 10.4% service, 24.1% sales and office, 7.8% natural resources, construction, and maintenance, 42.0% production, transportation, and material moving
Income: Per capita: $18,383; Median household: $41,000; Average household: $44,839; Households with income of $100,000 or more: 6.4%; Poverty rate: 27.5%
Educational Attainment: High school diploma or higher: 89.3%; Bachelor's degree or higher: 9.0%; Graduate/professional degree or higher: 3.9%
Housing: Homeownership rate: 75.0%; Median home value: $65,000; Median year structure built: 1956; Homeowner vacancy rate: 0.0%; Median selected monthly owner costs: $921 with a mortgage, $366 without a mortgage; Median gross rent: $622 per month; Rental vacancy rate: 6.6%
Health Insurance: 88.8% have insurance; 67.4% have private insurance; 44.1% have public insurance; 11.2% do not have insurance; 3.2% of children under 18 do not have insurance
Transportation: Commute: 93.4% car, 0.9% public transportation, 3.0% walk, 1.8% work from home; Mean travel time to work: 28.0 minutes

FOREST (village). Covers a land area of 1.605 square miles and a water area of 0 square miles. Located at 40.81° N. Lat; 83.51° W. Long. Elevation is 928 feet.
Population: 1,575; Growth (since 2000): 5.8%; Density: 981.5 persons per square mile; Race: 95.0% White, 1.0% Black/African American, 0.0% Asian, 0.0% American Indian/Alaska Native, 0.0% Native Hawaiian/Other Pacific Islander, 3.9% Two or more races, 2.9% Hispanic of any race; Average household size: 2.77; Median age: 36.2; Age under 18: 28.2%; Age 65 and over: 8.4%; Males per 100 females: 102.1; Marriage status: 22.4% never married, 51.5% now married, 3.4% separated, 4.7% widowed, 21.5% divorced; Foreign born: 0.4%; Speak English only: 99.3%; With disability: 14.3%; Veterans: 8.4%; Ancestry: 41.5% German, 18.1% Irish, 9.0% American, 7.9% English, 3.5% Swiss
Employment: 9.0% management, business, and financial, 1.6% computer, engineering, and science, 5.0% education, legal, community service, arts, and media, 4.8% healthcare practitioners, 13.4% service, 15.3% sales and office, 6.8% natural resources, construction, and maintenance, 44.1% production, transportation, and material moving
Income: Per capita: $20,579; Median household: $45,035; Average household: $55,608; Households with income of $100,000 or more: 13.7%; Poverty rate: 14.1%
Educational Attainment: High school diploma or higher: 90.6%; Bachelor's degree or higher: 13.3%; Graduate/professional degree or higher: 7.3%
Housing: Homeownership rate: 69.8%; Median home value: $79,500; Median year structure built: 1954; Homeowner vacancy rate: 1.0%; Median selected monthly owner costs: $850 with a mortgage, $384 without a mortgage; Median gross rent: $657 per month; Rental vacancy rate: 6.5%
Health Insurance: 93.3% have insurance; 70.9% have private insurance; 30.1% have public insurance; 6.7% do not have insurance; 5.6% of children under 18 do not have insurance
Transportation: Commute: 98.1% car, 0.0% public transportation, 0.6% walk, 0.0% work from home; Mean travel time to work: 28.2 minutes

KENTON (city). County seat. Covers a land area of 5.038 square miles and a water area of 0.094 square miles. Located at 40.64° N. Lat; 83.61° W. Long. Elevation is 991 feet.
History: Kenton was platted in 1833 on the Scioto River, and named for pioneer Simon Kenton. The town's economic base moved from agriculture to ornamental iron fences and then back to agriculture.
Population: 7,719; Growth (since 2000): -7.4%; Density: 1,532.0 persons per square mile; Race: 97.2% White, 0.6% Black/African American, 0.0% Asian, 0.0% American Indian/Alaska Native, 0.0% Native Hawaiian/Other Pacific Islander, 1.7% Two or more races, 1.9% Hispanic of any race; Average household size: 2.36; Median age: 39.1; Age under 18: 22.6%; Age 65 and over: 16.5%; Males per 100 females: 88.9; Marriage status: 23.8% never married, 47.8% now married, 1.5% separated, 10.1% widowed, 18.3% divorced; Foreign born: 0.5%; Speak English only: 98.4%; With disability: 17.7%; Veterans: 9.4%; Ancestry: 20.2% German, 18.7% American, 12.7% Irish, 5.1% English, 1.7% Polish
Employment: 7.9% management, business, and financial, 1.0% computer, engineering, and science, 11.5% education, legal, community service, arts, and media, 1.4% healthcare practitioners, 18.4% service, 25.2% sales and office, 8.1% natural resources, construction, and maintenance, 26.4% production, transportation, and material moving
Income: Per capita: $20,345; Median household: $40,026; Average household: $47,844; Households with income of $100,000 or more: 7.4%; Poverty rate: 18.6%
Educational Attainment: High school diploma or higher: 88.3%; Bachelor's degree or higher: 8.7%; Graduate/professional degree or higher: 2.6%

School District(s)

Hardin Community School (06-12)
2015-16 Enrollment: 44. . . . . (419) 673-3210
Kenton City (PK-12)
2015-16 Enrollment: 1,940 . . . . (419) 673-0775
Housing: Homeownership rate: 62.6%; Median home value: $74,300; Median year structure built: 1955; Homeowner vacancy rate: 4.4%; Median selected monthly owner costs: $813 with a mortgage, $345 without a mortgage; Median gross rent: $595 per month; Rental vacancy rate: 10.8%
Health Insurance: 88.7% have insurance; 56.8% have private insurance; 45.0% have public insurance; 11.3% do not have insurance; 4.7% of children under 18 do not have insurance
Hospitals: Hardin Memorial Hospital (103 beds)
Safety: Violent crime rate: 23.2 per 10,000 population; Property crime rate: 506.2 per 10,000 population
Newspapers: Kenton Times (daily circulation 7,200)
Transportation: Commute: 96.2% car, 0.3% public transportation, 2.4% walk, 1.1% work from home; Mean travel time to work: 20.9 minutes

MCGUFFEY (village). Covers a land area of 0.364 square miles and a water area of 0 square miles. Located at 40.69° N. Lat; 83.79° W. Long. Elevation is 971 feet.
History: McGuffey was settled in a marshy region, and took to the growing of onions. Those who tended the onion fields were sometimes called "marsh rats."
Population: 483; Growth (since 2000): -7.5%; Density: 1,325.1 persons per square mile; Race: 89.9% White, 0.0% Black/African American, 0.0% Asian, 0.0% American Indian/Alaska Native, 0.8% Native Hawaiian/Other Pacific Islander, 1.0% Two or more races, 8.7% Hispanic of any race; Average household size: 2.79; Median age: 36.4; Age under 18: 22.8%; Age 65 and over: 12.4%; Males per 100 females: 85.6; Marriage status: 35.4% never married, 44.0% now married, 1.8% separated, 6.6%

widowed, 14.0% divorced; Foreign born: 5.4%; Speak English only: 93.2%; With disability: 19.7%; Veterans: 6.4%; Ancestry: 16.6% German, 12.4% American, 11.0% Irish, 9.3% English, 1.9% Dutch
Employment: 5.7% management, business, and financial, 5.7% computer, engineering, and science, 3.1% education, legal, community service, arts, and media, 1.6% healthcare practitioners, 19.2% service, 10.9% sales and office, 11.4% natural resources, construction, and maintenance, 42.5% production, transportation, and material moving
Income: Per capita: $16,901; Median household: $38,295; Average household: $46,261; Households with income of $100,000 or more: 7.5%; Poverty rate: 17.7%
Educational Attainment: High school diploma or higher: 84.0%; Bachelor's degree or higher: 6.6%; Graduate/professional degree or higher: 3.1%

School District(s)

Upper Scioto Valley Local (KG-12)
2015-16 Enrollment: 497 . . . . (419) 757-3231
Housing: Homeownership rate: 68.8%; Median home value: $61,100; Median year structure built: 1957; Homeowner vacancy rate: 9.8%; Median selected monthly owner costs: $771 with a mortgage, $375 without a mortgage; Median gross rent: $608 per month; Rental vacancy rate: 0.0%
Health Insurance: 78.3% have insurance; 53.8% have private insurance; 39.3% have public insurance; 21.7% do not have insurance; 16.4% of children under 18 do not have insurance
Transportation: Commute: 95.2% car, 0.0% public transportation, 1.6% walk, 0.5% work from home; Mean travel time to work: 21.9 minutes

MOUNT VICTORY (village). Covers a land area of 0.766 square miles and a water area of 0 square miles. Located at 40.53° N. Lat; 83.52° W. Long. Elevation is 1,040 feet.
Population: 591; Growth (since 2000): -1.5%; Density: 772.0 persons per square mile; Race: 97.0% White, 0.2% Black/African American, 0.0% Asian, 1.0% American Indian/Alaska Native, 0.0% Native Hawaiian/Other Pacific Islander, 1.5% Two or more races, 0.0% Hispanic of any race; Average household size: 2.49; Median age: 36.7; Age under 18: 26.1%; Age 65 and over: 15.9%; Males per 100 females: 97.2; Marriage status: 16.0% never married, 68.0% now married, 2.4% separated, 4.0% widowed, 12.0% divorced; Foreign born: 0.3%; Speak English only: 99.6%; With disability: 15.4%; Veterans: 10.3%; Ancestry: 39.4% German, 13.4% American, 12.4% Irish, 9.3% English, 4.7% European
Employment: 6.1% management, business, and financial, 2.7% computer, engineering, and science, 9.9% education, legal, community service, arts, and media, 4.2% healthcare practitioners, 24.8% service, 16.4% sales and office, 10.3% natural resources, construction, and maintenance, 25.6% production, transportation, and material moving
Income: Per capita: $19,446; Median household: $39,375; Average household: $48,570; Households with income of $100,000 or more: 5.9%; Poverty rate: 7.3%
Educational Attainment: High school diploma or higher: 90.3%; Bachelor's degree or higher: 9.9%; Graduate/professional degree or higher: 6.2%

School District(s)

Ridgemont Local (KG-12)
2015-16 Enrollment: 488 . . . . (937) 354-2441
Housing: Homeownership rate: 67.1%; Median home value: $80,700; Median year structure built: 1952; Homeowner vacancy rate: 0.0%; Median selected monthly owner costs: $925 with a mortgage, $336 without a mortgage; Median gross rent: $745 per month; Rental vacancy rate: 0.0%
Health Insurance: 85.6% have insurance; 63.8% have private insurance; 38.1% have public insurance; 14.4% do not have insurance; 9.7% of children under 18 do not have insurance
Transportation: Commute: 95.0% car, 0.0% public transportation, 3.1% walk, 0.8% work from home; Mean travel time to work: 26.8 minutes

PATTERSON (village). Covers a land area of 0.107 square miles and a water area of 0 square miles. Located at 40.78° N. Lat; 83.53° W. Long. Elevation is 925 feet.
Population: 127; Growth (since 2000): -8.0%; Density: 1,191.8 persons per square mile; Race: 100.0% White, 0.0% Black/African American, 0.0% Asian, 0.0% American Indian/Alaska Native, 0.0% Native Hawaiian/Other Pacific Islander, 0.0% Two or more races, 0.0% Hispanic of any race; Average household size: 2.59; Median age: 37.3; Age under 18: 29.9%; Age 65 and over: 14.2%; Males per 100 females: 80.5; Marriage status: 19.4% never married, 60.2% now married, 7.5% separated, 9.7% widowed, 10.8% divorced; Foreign born: 0.0%; Speak English only: 99.2%; With disability: 29.1%; Veterans: 11.2%; Ancestry: 40.9% German, 15.0% American, 12.6% Irish, 5.5% Welsh, 4.7% English
Employment: 2.4% management, business, and financial, 0.0% computer, engineering, and science, 2.4% education, legal, community service, arts, and media, 4.8% healthcare practitioners, 7.1% service, 2.4% sales and office, 19.0% natural resources, construction, and maintenance, 61.9% production, transportation, and material moving
Income: Per capita: $16,676; Median household: $42,917; Average household: $44,945; Households with income of $100,000 or more: 4.1%; Poverty rate: 34.1%
Educational Attainment: High school diploma or higher: 84.3%; Bachelor's degree or higher: 6.0%; Graduate/professional degree or higher: 4.8%
Housing: Homeownership rate: 65.3%; Median home value: $47,500; Median year structure built: 1952; Homeowner vacancy rate: 0.0%; Median selected monthly owner costs: $788 with a mortgage, $363 without a mortgage; Median gross rent: $675 per month; Rental vacancy rate: 0.0%
Health Insurance: 93.7% have insurance; 50.4% have private insurance; 59.8% have public insurance; 6.3% do not have insurance; 0.0% of children under 18 do not have insurance
Transportation: Commute: 100.0% car, 0.0% public transportation, 0.0% walk, 0.0% work from home; Mean travel time to work: 22.9 minutes

RIDGEWAY (village). Covers a land area of 0.592 square miles and a water area of 0 square miles. Located at 40.51° N. Lat; 83.57° W. Long. Elevation is 1,060 feet.
Population: 357; Growth (since 2000): 0.8%; Density: 602.7 persons per square mile; Race: 95.8% White, 3.4% Black/African American, 0.0% Asian, 0.0% American Indian/Alaska Native, 0.0% Native Hawaiian/Other Pacific Islander, 0.8% Two or more races, 0.0% Hispanic of any race; Average household size: 2.86; Median age: 37.6; Age under 18: 29.1%; Age 65 and over: 12.0%; Males per 100 females: 88.8; Marriage status: 19.9% never married, 59.2% now married, 2.6% separated, 3.7% widowed, 17.3% divorced; Foreign born: 0.8%; Speak English only: 99.4%; With disability: 18.2%; Veterans: 14.6%; Ancestry: 32.2% Irish, 31.7% German, 12.0% American, 7.0% English, 3.9% Scottish
Employment: 8.0% management, business, and financial, 2.9% computer, engineering, and science, 2.2% education, legal, community service, arts, and media, 0.7% healthcare practitioners, 32.8% service, 13.1% sales and office, 11.7% natural resources, construction, and maintenance, 28.5% production, transportation, and material moving
Income: Per capita: $17,727; Median household: $46,458; Average household: $51,638; Households with income of $100,000 or more: 8.0%; Poverty rate: 13.4%
Educational Attainment: High school diploma or higher: 90.1%; Bachelor's degree or higher: 9.0%; Graduate/professional degree or higher: 2.1%

School District(s)

Ridgemont Local (KG-12)
2015-16 Enrollment: 488 . . . . (937) 354-2441
Housing: Homeownership rate: 84.0%; Median home value: $83,500; Median year structure built: 1956; Homeowner vacancy rate: 0.0%; Median selected monthly owner costs: $925 with a mortgage, $388 without a mortgage; Median gross rent: n/a per month; Rental vacancy rate: 0.0%
Health Insurance: 90.5% have insurance; 58.5% have private insurance; 42.6% have public insurance; 9.5% do not have insurance; 0.0% of children under 18 do not have insurance
Transportation: Commute: 94.9% car, 0.0% public transportation, 0.0% walk, 5.1% work from home; Mean travel time to work: 22.3 minutes

Harrison County

Located in eastern Ohio; drained by Stillwater and Conotton Creeks; includes Tappan and Clendening Lakes. Covers a land area of 402.339 square miles, a water area of 8.428 square miles, and is located in the Eastern Time Zone at 40.29° N. Lat., 81.09° W. Long. The county was founded in 1813. County seat is Cadiz.

Weather Station: Cadiz Elevation: 1,259 feet

	Jan	Feb	Mar	Apr	May	Jun	Jul	Aug	Sep	Oct	Nov	Dec
High	35	39	48	61	70	79	82	81	75	63	51	39
Low	19	22	29	40	49	58	63	61	54	43	34	24
Precip	3.0	2.4	3.2	3.5	4.4	4.3	4.3	3.8	3.4	2.8	3.4	2.9
Snow	8.8	6.1	4.9	1.3	0.0	0.0	0.0	0.0	0.0	0.1	1.5	5.6

High and Low temperatures in degrees Fahrenheit; Precipitation and Snow in inches

Population: 15,521; Growth (since 2000): -2.1%; Density: 38.6 persons per square mile; Race: 95.9% White, 2.0% Black/African American, 0.3% Asian, 0.2% American Indian/Alaska Native, 0.0% Native Hawaiian/Other Pacific Islander, 1.4% two or more races, 0.8% Hispanic of any race; Average household size: 2.44; Median age: 46.2; Age under 18: 21.1%; Age 65 and over: 20.1%; Males per 100 females: 98.4; Marriage status: 22.1% never married, 58.1% now married, 1.0% separated, 7.4% widowed, 12.4% divorced; Foreign born: 0.4%; Speak English only: 97.0%; With disability: 16.9%; Veterans: 11.8%; Ancestry: 20.0% German, 15.3% Irish, 8.7% English, 7.3% Italian, 7.1% Polish
Religion: Six largest groups: 12.9% Methodist/Pietist, 3.7% Presbyterian-Reformed, 3.6% Baptist, 3.4% Catholicism, 2.4% European Free-Church, 0.9% Holiness
Economy: Unemployment rate: 5.1%; Leading industries: 14.6 % other services (except public administration); 13.9 % retail trade; 12.4 % construction; Farms: 444 totaling 95,387 acres; Company size: 0 employ 1,000 or more persons, 0 employ 500 to 999 persons, 8 employ 100 to 499 persons, 259 employ less than 100 persons; Business ownership: 235 women-owned, n/a Black-owned, n/a Hispanic-owned, n/a Asian-owned, n/a American Indian/Alaska Native-owned
Employment: 7.5% management, business, and financial, 1.7% computer, engineering, and science, 5.3% education, legal, community service, arts, and media, 8.7% healthcare practitioners, 17.2% service, 20.5% sales and office, 17.8% natural resources, construction, and maintenance, 21.2% production, transportation, and material moving
Income: Per capita: $22,639; Median household: $44,000; Average household: $55,798; Households with income of $100,000 or more: 13.2%; Poverty rate: 18.1%
Educational Attainment: High school diploma or higher: 85.9%; Bachelor's degree or higher: 9.7%; Graduate/professional degree or higher: 3.2%
Housing: Homeownership rate: 80.8%; Median home value: $85,300; Median year structure built: 1963; Homeowner vacancy rate: 1.5%; Median selected monthly owner costs: $884 with a mortgage, $341 without a mortgage; Median gross rent: $598 per month; Rental vacancy rate: 6.3%
Vital Statistics: Birth rate: 112.4 per 10,000 population; Death rate: 133.3 per 10,000 population; Age-adjusted cancer mortality rate: 144.8 deaths per 100,000 population
Health Insurance: 89.7% have insurance; 65.6% have private insurance; 39.3% have public insurance; 10.3% do not have insurance; 9.2% of children under 18 do not have insurance
Health Care: Physicians: 3.2 per 10,000 population; Dentists: 0.7 per 10,000 population; Hospital beds: 16.1 per 10,000 population; Hospital admissions: 251.5 per 10,000 population
Transportation: Commute: 92.4% car, 0.1% public transportation, 4.0% walk, 2.8% work from home; Mean travel time to work: 27.9 minutes
2016 Presidential Election: 71.8% Trump, 23.8% Clinton, 2.5% Johnson, 0.7% Stein
National and State Parks: Harrison County State Forest
Additional Information Contacts
Harrison Government . . . . (740) 942-4623
http://www.harrisoncountyohio.org

Harrison County Communities

BOWERSTON (village). Covers a land area of 0.506 square miles and a water area of 0 square miles. Located at 40.43° N. Lat; 81.19° W. Long. Elevation is 955 feet.
Population: 422; Growth (since 2000): 1.9%; Density: 833.4 persons per square mile; Race: 96.2% White, 2.4% Black/African American, 0.0% Asian, 0.7% American Indian/Alaska Native, 0.0% Native Hawaiian/Other Pacific Islander, 0.7% Two or more races, 0.5% Hispanic of any race; Average household size: 2.25; Median age: 43.4; Age under 18: 23.5%; Age 65 and over: 23.0%; Males per 100 females: 81.7; Marriage status: 23.0% never married, 47.5% now married, 0.3% separated, 11.8% widowed, 17.7% divorced; Foreign born: 0.0%; Speak English only: 100.0%; With disability: 22.6%; Veterans: 16.7%; Ancestry: 38.6% German, 20.6% Irish, 6.2% American, 6.2% English, 5.9% Scottish
Employment: 3.8% management, business, and financial, 0.0% computer, engineering, and science, 3.1% education, legal, community service, arts, and media, 3.1% healthcare practitioners, 24.4% service, 22.1% sales and office, 13.0% natural resources, construction, and maintenance, 30.5% production, transportation, and material moving
Income: Per capita: $15,168; Median household: $25,625; Average household: $35,882; Households with income of $100,000 or more: 6.0%; Poverty rate: 39.2%
Educational Attainment: High school diploma or higher: 88.1%; Bachelor's degree or higher: 11.0%; Graduate/professional degree or higher: 1.9%

School District(s)

Conotton Valley Union Local (PK-12)
2015-16 Enrollment: 384. . . . . (740) 269-2000
Housing: Homeownership rate: 52.7%; Median home value: $67,500; Median year structure built: 1960; Homeowner vacancy rate: 4.4%; Median selected monthly owner costs: $938 with a mortgage, $325 without a mortgage; Median gross rent: $407 per month; Rental vacancy rate: 0.0%
Health Insurance: 91.7% have insurance; 48.9% have private insurance; 52.2% have public insurance; 8.3% do not have insurance; 5.1% of children under 18 do not have insurance
Transportation: Commute: 94.5% car, 1.6% public transportation, 2.3% walk, 1.6% work from home; Mean travel time to work: 29.3 minutes

CADIZ (village). County seat. Covers a land area of 8.777 square miles and a water area of 0.163 square miles. Located at 40.26° N. Lat; 80.99° W. Long. Elevation is 1,266 feet.
History: The town of Cadiz, settled at the junction of the Mingo and Moravian trails, was surveyed in 1803, and in 1830 became the seat of Harrison County.
Population: 3,268; Growth (since 2000): -1.2%; Density: 372.3 persons per square mile; Race: 90.5% White, 8.0% Black/African American, 0.0% Asian, 0.0% American Indian/Alaska Native, 0.0% Native Hawaiian/Other Pacific Islander, 1.3% Two or more races, 0.5% Hispanic of any race; Average household size: 2.56; Median age: 41.6; Age under 18: 20.5%; Age 65 and over: 20.0%; Males per 100 females: 89.3; Marriage status: 25.5% never married, 54.2% now married, 2.0% separated, 7.5% widowed, 12.8% divorced; Foreign born: 0.5%; Speak English only: 99.4%; With disability: 13.1%; Veterans: 10.5%; Ancestry: 16.4% German, 15.5% Irish, 9.7% Italian, 9.5% English, 5.4% Polish
Employment: 7.7% management, business, and financial, 1.3% computer, engineering, and science, 5.6% education, legal, community service, arts, and media, 12.6% healthcare practitioners, 18.3% service, 21.6% sales and office, 19.6% natural resources, construction, and maintenance, 13.3% production, transportation, and material moving
Income: Per capita: $25,060; Median household: $43,537; Average household: $62,339; Households with income of $100,000 or more: 17.3%; Poverty rate: 16.3%
Educational Attainment: High school diploma or higher: 88.8%; Bachelor's degree or higher: 14.0%; Graduate/professional degree or higher: 5.9%

School District(s)

Belmont-Harrison (08-12)
2015-16 Enrollment: n/a . . . . (740) 695-9130
Harrison Hills City (PK-12)
2015-16 Enrollment: 1,565 . . . . (740) 942-7800
Housing: Homeownership rate: 70.0%; Median home value: $92,500; Median year structure built: 1954; Homeowner vacancy rate: 0.0%; Median selected monthly owner costs: $1,046 with a mortgage, $344 without a mortgage; Median gross rent: $587 per month; Rental vacancy rate: 6.8%
Health Insurance: 92.3% have insurance; 68.4% have private insurance; 37.6% have public insurance; 7.7% do not have insurance; 0.0% of children under 18 do not have insurance
Hospitals: Harrison Community Hospital (48 beds)
Safety: Violent crime rate: 21.5 per 10,000 population; Property crime rate: 184.3 per 10,000 population
Newspapers: Harrison News-Herald (weekly circulation 6,500)
Transportation: Commute: 91.1% car, 0.0% public transportation, 5.2% walk, 2.7% work from home; Mean travel time to work: 20.7 minutes

DEERSVILLE (village). Covers a land area of 0.345 square miles and a water area of 0 square miles. Located at 40.31° N. Lat; 81.19° W. Long. Elevation is 1,230 feet.
Population: 41; Growth (since 2000): -50.0%; Density: 119.0 persons per square mile; Race: 100.0% White, 0.0% Black/African American, 0.0% Asian, 0.0% American Indian/Alaska Native, 0.0% Native Hawaiian/Other Pacific Islander, 0.0% Two or more races, 0.0% Hispanic of any race; Average household size: 1.58; Median age: 58.6; Age under 18: 9.8%; Age 65 and over: 36.6%; Males per 100 females: 107.9; Marriage status: 14.6% never married, 56.1% now married, 0.0% separated, 29.3%

widowed, 0.0% divorced; Foreign born: 0.0%; Speak English only: 100.0%; With disability: 36.6%; Veterans: 5.4%; Ancestry: 36.6% German, 34.1% Irish, 22.0% Italian, 12.2% English, 4.9% American
Employment: 0.0% management, business, and financial, 0.0% computer, engineering, and science, 4.5% education, legal, community service, arts, and media, 18.2% healthcare practitioners, 40.9% service, 9.1% sales and office, 0.0% natural resources, construction, and maintenance, 27.3% production, transportation, and material moving
Income: Per capita: $24,763; Median household: $43,750; Average household: $39,185; Households with income of $100,000 or more: n/a; Poverty rate: 4.9%
Educational Attainment: High school diploma or higher: 89.2%; Bachelor's degree or higher: 10.8%; Graduate/professional degree or higher: n/a
Housing: Homeownership rate: 100.0%; Median home value: $76,000; Median year structure built: 1989; Homeowner vacancy rate: 0.0%; Median selected monthly owner costs: $850 with a mortgage, $338 without a mortgage; Median gross rent: n/a per month; Rental vacancy rate: 0.0%
Health Insurance: 90.2% have insurance; 68.3% have private insurance; 46.3% have public insurance; 9.8% do not have insurance; 0.0% of children under 18 do not have insurance
Transportation: Commute: 100.0% car, 0.0% public transportation, 0.0% walk, 0.0% work from home; Mean travel time to work: 28.4 minutes

FREEPORT (village). Covers a land area of 0.599 square miles and a water area of 0 square miles. Located at 40.21° N. Lat; 81.27° W. Long. Elevation is 997 feet.
Population: 396; Growth (since 2000): -0.5%; Density: 661.1 persons per square mile; Race: 97.0% White, 0.0% Black/African American, 1.5% Asian, 0.0% American Indian/Alaska Native, 0.0% Native Hawaiian/Other Pacific Islander, 1.5% Two or more races, 0.8% Hispanic of any race; Average household size: 2.19; Median age: 43.5; Age under 18: 17.7%; Age 65 and over: 16.4%; Males per 100 females: 99.5; Marriage status: 24.8% never married, 52.7% now married, 1.5% separated, 11.8% widowed, 10.6% divorced; Foreign born: 1.8%; Speak English only: 97.6%; With disability: 18.2%; Veterans: 12.6%; Ancestry: 24.0% German, 19.9% Irish, 7.6% English, 7.3% Italian, 6.8% American
Employment: 6.0% management, business, and financial, 1.0% computer, engineering, and science, 5.0% education, legal, community service, arts, and media, 11.1% healthcare practitioners, 16.6% service, 25.1% sales and office, 12.6% natural resources, construction, and maintenance, 22.6% production, transportation, and material moving
Income: Per capita: $22,564; Median household: $35,125; Average household: $48,509; Households with income of $100,000 or more: 10.5%; Poverty rate: 15.7%
Educational Attainment: High school diploma or higher: 79.8%; Bachelor's degree or higher: 9.8%; Graduate/professional degree or higher: 2.8%
Housing: Homeownership rate: 66.3%; Median home value: $70,000; Median year structure built: Before 1940; Homeowner vacancy rate: 3.2%; Median selected monthly owner costs: $727 with a mortgage, $267 without a mortgage; Median gross rent: $539 per month; Rental vacancy rate: 4.7%
Health Insurance: 85.6% have insurance; 65.2% have private insurance; 33.6% have public insurance; 14.4% do not have insurance; 2.9% of children under 18 do not have insurance
Transportation: Commute: 89.4% car, 0.0% public transportation, 10.6% walk, 0.0% work from home; Mean travel time to work: 32.5 minutes

HARRISVILLE (village). Covers a land area of 0.152 square miles and a water area of <.001 square miles. Located at 40.18° N. Lat; 80.89° W. Long. Elevation is 1,250 feet.
Population: 253; Growth (since 2000): -2.3%; Density: 1,663.0 persons per square mile; Race: 100.0% White, 0.0% Black/African American, 0.0% Asian, 0.0% American Indian/Alaska Native, 0.0% Native Hawaiian/Other Pacific Islander, 0.0% Two or more races, 0.0% Hispanic of any race; Average household size: 2.22; Median age: 53.5; Age under 18: 19.8%; Age 65 and over: 12.6%; Males per 100 females: 106.1; Marriage status: 11.3% never married, 68.1% now married, 0.0% separated, 8.8% widowed, 11.8% divorced; Foreign born: 0.0%; Speak English only: 100.0%; With disability: 25.7%; Veterans: 23.2%; Ancestry: 33.2% German, 12.6% Polish, 9.1% Hungarian, 7.9% Italian, 3.6% Irish
Employment: 4.6% management, business, and financial, 0.0% computer, engineering, and science, 2.8% education, legal, community service, arts, and media, 1.9% healthcare practitioners, 8.3% service, 23.1% sales and office, 13.9% natural resources, construction, and maintenance, 45.4% production, transportation, and material moving
Income: Per capita: $19,157; Median household: $31,397; Average household: $43,028; Households with income of $100,000 or more: 5.3%; Poverty rate: 8.4%
Educational Attainment: High school diploma or higher: 54.2%; Bachelor's degree or higher: 4.0%; Graduate/professional degree or higher: 1.5%
Housing: Homeownership rate: 88.6%; Median home value: $81,400; Median year structure built: 1943; Homeowner vacancy rate: 2.7%; Median selected monthly owner costs: $767 with a mortgage, $334 without a mortgage; Median gross rent: $908 per month; Rental vacancy rate: 13.3%
Health Insurance: 70.4% have insurance; 51.4% have private insurance; 26.1% have public insurance; 29.6% do not have insurance; 0.0% of children under 18 do not have insurance
Transportation: Commute: 91.6% car, 0.0% public transportation, 0.0% walk, 8.4% work from home; Mean travel time to work: 34.0 minutes

HOPEDALE (village). Covers a land area of 1.117 square miles and a water area of <.001 square miles. Located at 40.33° N. Lat; 80.90° W. Long. Elevation is 1,158 feet.
History: Hopedale was the home of motion picture actor Clark Gable, who spent part of his boyhood here. The town developed around the coal mines.
Population: 1,034; Growth (since 2000): 5.1%; Density: 926.0 persons per square mile; Race: 92.7% White, 4.3% Black/African American, 0.2% Asian, 0.0% American Indian/Alaska Native, 0.0% Native Hawaiian/Other Pacific Islander, 2.8% Two or more races, 0.5% Hispanic of any race; Average household size: 2.38; Median age: 51.3; Age under 18: 18.6%; Age 65 and over: 25.4%; Males per 100 females: 95.9; Marriage status: 19.2% never married, 54.8% now married, 2.8% separated, 13.0% widowed, 13.1% divorced; Foreign born: 1.3%; Speak English only: 97.9%; With disability: 17.8%; Veterans: 11.6%; Ancestry: 20.7% German, 14.8% Irish, 14.8% Italian, 6.9% Polish, 6.2% English
Employment: 7.4% management, business, and financial, 0.7% computer, engineering, and science, 11.8% education, legal, community service, arts, and media, 11.5% healthcare practitioners, 16.6% service, 19.4% sales and office, 15.0% natural resources, construction, and maintenance, 17.6% production, transportation, and material moving
Income: Per capita: $24,221; Median household: $52,083; Average household: $60,937; Households with income of $100,000 or more: 17.1%; Poverty rate: 12.5%
Educational Attainment: High school diploma or higher: 89.4%; Bachelor's degree or higher: 11.7%; Graduate/professional degree or higher: 2.8%

School District(s)

Harrison Hills City (PK-12)
2015-16 Enrollment: 1,565 . . . . (740) 942-7800
Housing: Homeownership rate: 80.6%; Median home value: $88,500; Median year structure built: 1953; Homeowner vacancy rate: 2.1%; Median selected monthly owner costs: $948 with a mortgage, $358 without a mortgage; Median gross rent: $663 per month; Rental vacancy rate: 13.5%
Health Insurance: 94.6% have insurance; 73.5% have private insurance; 39.1% have public insurance; 5.4% do not have insurance; 0.0% of children under 18 do not have insurance
Transportation: Commute: 94.7% car, 0.7% public transportation, 0.7% walk, 3.9% work from home; Mean travel time to work: 24.1 minutes

JEWETT (village). Covers a land area of 0.509 square miles and a water area of 0 square miles. Located at 40.37° N. Lat; 81.00° W. Long. Elevation is 1,007 feet.
History: Laid out 1851, incorporated 1886.
Population: 714; Growth (since 2000): -8.9%; Density: 1,402.8 persons per square mile; Race: 95.5% White, 0.0% Black/African American, 0.6% Asian, 0.0% American Indian/Alaska Native, 0.0% Native Hawaiian/Other Pacific Islander, 3.9% Two or more races, 0.0% Hispanic of any race; Average household size: 2.74; Median age: 33.3; Age under 18: 31.7%; Age 65 and over: 12.5%; Males per 100 females: 102.3; Marriage status: 22.2% never married, 59.1% now married, 0.4% separated, 3.9% widowed, 14.8% divorced; Foreign born: 0.6%; Speak English only: 100.0%; With disability: 23.1%; Veterans: 7.6%; Ancestry: 21.8% German, 17.2% Irish, 11.1% American, 9.7% English, 3.8% Polish
Employment: 0.8% management, business, and financial, 0.8% computer, engineering, and science, 2.7% education, legal, community service, arts, and media, 7.7% healthcare practitioners, 21.6% service, 23.9% sales and

office, 22.8% natural resources, construction, and maintenance, 19.7% production, transportation, and material moving
Income: Per capita: $16,108; Median household: $37,981; Average household: $44,225; Households with income of $100,000 or more: 9.2%; Poverty rate: 21.5%
Educational Attainment: High school diploma or higher: 82.2%; Bachelor's degree or higher: 4.7%; Graduate/professional degree or higher: 0.4%
Housing: Homeownership rate: 69.7%; Median home value: $56,800; Median year structure built: 1942; Homeowner vacancy rate: 4.6%; Median selected monthly owner costs: $781 with a mortgage, $344 without a mortgage; Median gross rent: $638 per month; Rental vacancy rate: 7.1%
Health Insurance: 89.6% have insurance; 49.9% have private insurance; 48.2% have public insurance; 10.4% do not have insurance; 3.5% of children under 18 do not have insurance
Transportation: Commute: 96.3% car, 0.0% public transportation, 3.7% walk, 0.0% work from home; Mean travel time to work: 33.4 minutes

NEW ATHENS (village). Covers a land area of 0.279 square miles and a water area of <.001 square miles. Located at 40.18° N. Lat; 80.99° W. Long. Elevation is 1,184 feet.
Population: 291; Growth (since 2000): -14.9%; Density: 1,041.6 persons per square mile; Race: 100.0% White, 0.0% Black/African American, 0.0% Asian, 0.0% American Indian/Alaska Native, 0.0% Native Hawaiian/Other Pacific Islander, 0.0% Two or more races, 0.0% Hispanic of any race; Average household size: 2.27; Median age: 42.9; Age under 18: 18.6%; Age 65 and over: 23.7%; Males per 100 females: 93.9; Marriage status: 24.7% never married, 47.7% now married, 0.0% separated, 16.3% widowed, 11.3% divorced; Foreign born: 0.0%; Speak English only: 99.3%; With disability: 18.2%; Veterans: 15.2%; Ancestry: 30.9% Irish, 26.8% German, 14.4% Polish, 6.5% English, 5.5% Dutch
Employment: 0.0% management, business, and financial, 1.7% computer, engineering, and science, 13.2% education, legal, community service, arts, and media, 9.9% healthcare practitioners, 28.1% service, 10.7% sales and office, 24.0% natural resources, construction, and maintenance, 12.4% production, transportation, and material moving
Income: Per capita: $22,653; Median household: $53,750; Average household: $52,009; Households with income of $100,000 or more: 9.4%; Poverty rate: 6.5%
Educational Attainment: High school diploma or higher: 84.5%; Bachelor's degree or higher: 9.1%; Graduate/professional degree or higher: 3.7%
Housing: Homeownership rate: 87.5%; Median home value: $76,700; Median year structure built: Before 1940; Homeowner vacancy rate: 0.0%; Median selected monthly owner costs: $868 with a mortgage, $348 without a mortgage; Median gross rent: $600 per month; Rental vacancy rate: 0.0%
Health Insurance: 87.3% have insurance; 64.6% have private insurance; 39.2% have public insurance; 12.7% do not have insurance; 13.0% of children under 18 do not have insurance
Transportation: Commute: 99.2% car, 0.0% public transportation, 0.0% walk, 0.0% work from home; Mean travel time to work: 36.4 minutes

SCIO (village). Covers a land area of 0.557 square miles and a water area of 0 square miles. Located at 40.40° N. Lat; 81.09° W. Long. Elevation is 997 feet.
Population: 981; Growth (since 2000): 22.8%; Density: 1,762.0 persons per square mile; Race: 95.5% White, 0.0% Black/African American, 0.0% Asian, 0.5% American Indian/Alaska Native, 0.0% Native Hawaiian/Other Pacific Islander, 1.4% Two or more races, 9.8% Hispanic of any race; Average household size: 2.47; Median age: 33.8; Age under 18: 25.1%; Age 65 and over: 11.3%; Males per 100 females: 90.3; Marriage status: 23.0% never married, 53.6% now married, 0.3% separated, 7.5% widowed, 15.9% divorced; Foreign born: 1.5%; Speak English only: 91.8%; With disability: 22.2%; Veterans: 8.6%; Ancestry: 22.6% Irish, 20.1% German, 8.4% Italian, 5.2% English, 3.7% American
Employment: 2.4% management, business, and financial, 2.0% computer, engineering, and science, 8.5% education, legal, community service, arts, and media, 10.7% healthcare practitioners, 13.4% service, 15.4% sales and office, 20.5% natural resources, construction, and maintenance, 27.1% production, transportation, and material moving
Income: Per capita: $18,706; Median household: $40,750; Average household: $47,646; Households with income of $100,000 or more: 9.9%; Poverty rate: 23.2%
Educational Attainment: High school diploma or higher: 81.8%; Bachelor's degree or higher: 10.7%; Graduate/professional degree or higher: 3.7%

School District(s)

Harrison Hills City (PK-12)
2015-16 Enrollment: 1,565 . . . . (740) 942-7800
Housing: Homeownership rate: 70.0%; Median home value: $63,100; Median year structure built: Before 1940; Homeowner vacancy rate: 3.4%; Median selected monthly owner costs: $703 with a mortgage, $357 without a mortgage; Median gross rent: $606 per month; Rental vacancy rate: 7.0%
Health Insurance: 87.0% have insurance; 55.1% have private insurance; 40.0% have public insurance; 13.0% do not have insurance; 6.9% of children under 18 do not have insurance
Transportation: Commute: 95.8% car, 0.0% public transportation, 3.2% walk, 1.0% work from home; Mean travel time to work: 29.9 minutes

TIPPECANOE (CDP). Covers a land area of 0.537 square miles and a water area of 0 square miles. Located at 40.27° N. Lat; 81.28° W. Long. Elevation is 902 feet.
Population: 51; Growth (since 2000): n/a; Density: 94.9 persons per square mile; Race: 100.0% White, 0.0% Black/African American, 0.0% Asian, 0.0% American Indian/Alaska Native, 0.0% Native Hawaiian/Other Pacific Islander, 0.0% Two or more races, 0.0% Hispanic of any race; Average household size: 2.55; Median age: 31.3; Age under 18: 45.1%; Age 65 and over: 23.5%; Males per 100 females: 105.1; Marriage status: 0.0% never married, 57.1% now married, 0.0% separated, 42.9% widowed, 0.0% divorced; Foreign born: 0.0%; Speak English only: 100.0%; With disability: 0.0%; Veterans: 0.0%; Ancestry: n/a.
Employment: 0.0% management, business, and financial, 0.0% computer, engineering, and science, 0.0% education, legal, community service, arts, and media, 0.0% healthcare practitioners, 0.0% service, 100.0% sales and office, 0.0% natural resources, construction, and maintenance, 0.0% production, transportation, and material moving
Income: Per capita: n/a; Median household: n/a; Average household: n/a; Households with income of $100,000 or more: n/a; Poverty rate: n/a
Educational Attainment: High school diploma or higher: 100.0%; Bachelor's degree or higher: n/a; Graduate/professional degree or higher: n/a
Housing: Homeownership rate: 40.0%; Median home value: n/a; Median year structure built: Before 1940; Homeowner vacancy rate: 0.0%; Median selected monthly owner costs: n/a with a mortgage, n/a without a mortgage; Median gross rent: n/a per month; Rental vacancy rate: 0.0%
Health Insurance: 84.3% have insurance; 39.2% have private insurance; 68.6% have public insurance; 15.7% do not have insurance; 0.0% of children under 18 do not have insurance
Transportation: Commute: 100.0% car, 0.0% public transportation, 0.0% walk, 0.0% work from home; Mean travel time to work: 0.0 minutes

Henry County

Located in northwestern Ohio; crossed by the Maumee River. Covers a land area of 416.010 square miles, a water area of 3.740 square miles, and is located in the Eastern Time Zone at 41.34° N. Lat., 84.07° W. Long. The county was founded in 1820. County seat is Napoleon.

Weather Station: Napoleon — Elevation: 682 feet

	Jan	Feb	Mar	Apr	May	Jun	Jul	Aug	Sep	Oct	Nov	Dec
High	32	35	47	60	71	81	85	83	76	63	50	36
Low	16	17	27	37	47	58	62	60	52	41	33	22
Precip	2.1	2.0	2.5	3.5	3.8	3.5	3.8	3.4	3.2	2.8	2.9	2.7
Snow	8.1	5.8	2.9	0.5	0.0	0.0	0.0	0.0	0.0	0.1	0.7	5.5

High and Low temperatures in degrees Fahrenheit; Precipitation and Snow in inches

Population: 27,890; Growth (since 2000): -4.5%; Density: 67.0 persons per square mile; Race: 94.6% White, 0.5% Black/African American, 0.4% Asian, 0.1% American Indian/Alaska Native, 0.0% Native Hawaiian/Other Pacific Islander, 2.0% two or more races, 7.3% Hispanic of any race; Average household size: 2.49; Median age: 41.4; Age under 18: 23.8%; Age 65 and over: 17.6%; Males per 100 females: 98.1; Marriage status: 24.6% never married, 57.9% now married, 0.9% separated, 8.0% widowed, 9.5% divorced; Foreign born: 1.4%; Speak English only: 95.9%; With disability: 14.1%; Veterans: 8.9%; Ancestry: 48.2% German, 9.3% Irish, 8.5% English, 7.6% American, 3.4% French

Religion: Six largest groups: 34.1% Lutheran, 12.2% Catholicism, 9.8% Methodist/Pietist, 4.1% Baptist, 2.8% Presbyterian-Reformed, 2.4% Holiness
Economy: Unemployment rate: 4.0%; Leading industries: 14.2 % other services (except public administration); 13.3 % retail trade; 12.4 % construction; Farms: 848 totaling 235,919 acres; Company size: 1 employs 1,000 or more persons, 0 employ 500 to 999 persons, 10 employ 100 to 499 persons, 561 employs less than 100 persons; Business ownership: 523 women-owned, n/a Black-owned, 61 Hispanic-owned, n/a Asian-owned, n/a American Indian/Alaska Native-owned
Employment: 11.0% management, business, and financial, 3.2% computer, engineering, and science, 8.2% education, legal, community service, arts, and media, 6.8% healthcare practitioners, 15.6% service, 17.0% sales and office, 11.6% natural resources, construction, and maintenance, 26.6% production, transportation, and material moving
Income: Per capita: $26,288; Median household: $54,941; Average household: $65,830; Households with income of $100,000 or more: 17.4%; Poverty rate: 10.2%
Educational Attainment: High school diploma or higher: 91.3%; Bachelor's degree or higher: 16.0%; Graduate/professional degree or higher: 5.8%
Housing: Homeownership rate: 79.6%; Median home value: $113,600; Median year structure built: 1958; Homeowner vacancy rate: 1.8%; Median selected monthly owner costs: $1,108 with a mortgage, $415 without a mortgage; Median gross rent: $693 per month; Rental vacancy rate: 4.0%
Vital Statistics: Birth rate: 106.0 per 10,000 population; Death rate: 90.1 per 10,000 population; Age-adjusted cancer mortality rate: 148.6 deaths per 100,000 population
Health Insurance: 93.6% have insurance; 77.1% have private insurance; 32.8% have public insurance; 6.4% do not have insurance; 4.7% of children under 18 do not have insurance
Health Care: Physicians: 5.0 per 10,000 population; Dentists: 4.0 per 10,000 population; Hospital beds: 9.0 per 10,000 population; Hospital admissions: 307.0 per 10,000 population
Transportation: Commute: 95.6% car, 0.3% public transportation, 1.0% walk, 2.0% work from home; Mean travel time to work: 21.8 minutes
2016 Presidential Election: 66.2% Trump, 26.7% Clinton, 4.7% Johnson, 0.8% Stein
National and State Parks: Maumee State Forest; North Turkeyfoot State Park
Additional Information Contacts
Henry Government . . . . (419) 592-4876
http://www.henrycountyohio.com

Henry County Communities

DESHLER (village). Covers a land area of 2.255 square miles and a water area of 0.035 square miles. Located at 41.21° N. Lat; 83.91° W. Long. Elevation is 709 feet.
Population: 1,750; Growth (since 2000): -4.4%; Density: 775.9 persons per square mile; Race: 93.6% White, 0.9% Black/African American, 0.5% Asian, 0.5% American Indian/Alaska Native, 0.0% Native Hawaiian/Other Pacific Islander, 1.3% Two or more races, 7.9% Hispanic of any race; Average household size: 2.54; Median age: 36.1; Age under 18: 28.7%; Age 65 and over: 17.4%; Males per 100 females: 97.9; Marriage status: 25.1% never married, 54.8% now married, 1.5% separated, 7.6% widowed, 12.6% divorced; Foreign born: 0.7%; Speak English only: 96.0%; With disability: 17.7%; Veterans: 9.9%; Ancestry: 52.3% German, 12.3% Irish, 7.0% English, 6.7% American, 4.2% French
Employment: 6.6% management, business, and financial, 5.1% computer, engineering, and science, 9.1% education, legal, community service, arts, and media, 8.0% healthcare practitioners, 12.8% service, 17.6% sales and office, 8.9% natural resources, construction, and maintenance, 32.0% production, transportation, and material moving
Income: Per capita: $22,071; Median household: $45,093; Average household: $57,611; Households with income of $100,000 or more: 16.7%; Poverty rate: 15.0%
Educational Attainment: High school diploma or higher: 89.5%; Bachelor's degree or higher: 12.5%; Graduate/professional degree or higher: 4.6%

School District(s)

Patrick Henry Local (KG-12)
2015-16 Enrollment: 861 . . . . (419) 274-5451
Housing: Homeownership rate: 78.3%; Median home value: $86,000; Median year structure built: 1952; Homeowner vacancy rate: 5.4%; Median selected monthly owner costs: $971 with a mortgage, $406 without a mortgage; Median gross rent: $706 per month; Rental vacancy rate: 9.7%
Health Insurance: 94.3% have insurance; 75.1% have private insurance; 35.3% have public insurance; 5.7% do not have insurance; 0.0% of children under 18 do not have insurance
Newspapers: Deshler Flag (weekly circulation 1,500)
Transportation: Commute: 92.7% car, 0.0% public transportation, 2.8% walk, 2.5% work from home; Mean travel time to work: 26.3 minutes

FLORIDA (village). Covers a land area of 0.225 square miles and a water area of 0 square miles. Located at 41.32° N. Lat; 84.20° W. Long. Elevation is 669 feet.
Population: 241; Growth (since 2000): -2.0%; Density: 1,071.6 persons per square mile; Race: 96.7% White, 0.4% Black/African American, 0.0% Asian, 0.0% American Indian/Alaska Native, 0.0% Native Hawaiian/Other Pacific Islander, 2.1% Two or more races, 7.5% Hispanic of any race; Average household size: 2.43; Median age: 39.1; Age under 18: 25.3%; Age 65 and over: 14.1%; Males per 100 females: 85.6; Marriage status: 31.6% never married, 47.4% now married, 0.0% separated, 7.1% widowed, 13.8% divorced; Foreign born: 0.0%; Speak English only: 97.4%; With disability: 12.4%; Veterans: 12.2%; Ancestry: 53.1% German, 9.5% Irish, 7.9% American, 6.6% English, 5.4% French
Employment: 13.6% management, business, and financial, 0.9% computer, engineering, and science, 7.3% education, legal, community service, arts, and media, 4.5% healthcare practitioners, 10.9% service, 21.8% sales and office, 12.7% natural resources, construction, and maintenance, 28.2% production, transportation, and material moving
Income: Per capita: $24,669; Median household: $51,042; Average household: $58,805; Households with income of $100,000 or more: 9.1%; Poverty rate: 20.5%
Educational Attainment: High school diploma or higher: 92.4%; Bachelor's degree or higher: 15.3%; Graduate/professional degree or higher: 6.4%
Housing: Homeownership rate: 65.7%; Median home value: $76,400; Median year structure built: 1946; Homeowner vacancy rate: 0.0%; Median selected monthly owner costs: $958 with a mortgage, $344 without a mortgage; Median gross rent: $694 per month; Rental vacancy rate: 0.0%
Health Insurance: 95.4% have insurance; 71.8% have private insurance; 39.4% have public insurance; 4.6% do not have insurance; 4.9% of children under 18 do not have insurance
Transportation: Commute: 95.4% car, 0.0% public transportation, 0.0% walk, 0.0% work from home; Mean travel time to work: 19.0 minutes

HAMLER (village). Covers a land area of 0.797 square miles and a water area of 0.005 square miles. Located at 41.23° N. Lat; 84.04° W. Long. Elevation is 709 feet.
Population: 647; Growth (since 2000): -0.5%; Density: 811.4 persons per square mile; Race: 93.0% White, 0.0% Black/African American, 0.0% Asian, 0.2% American Indian/Alaska Native, 0.0% Native Hawaiian/Other Pacific Islander, 2.5% Two or more races, 14.1% Hispanic of any race; Average household size: 2.70; Median age: 29.8; Age under 18: 31.7%; Age 65 and over: 11.1%; Males per 100 females: 100.0; Marriage status: 32.9% never married, 53.5% now married, 2.8% separated, 6.5% widowed, 7.1% divorced; Foreign born: 0.6%; Speak English only: 93.1%; With disability: 12.1%; Veterans: 8.1%; Ancestry: 44.8% German, 14.5% Irish, 8.2% English, 4.3% American, 3.6% Swedish
Employment: 12.9% management, business, and financial, 1.2% computer, engineering, and science, 7.4% education, legal, community service, arts, and media, 3.5% healthcare practitioners, 18.4% service, 13.3% sales and office, 13.3% natural resources, construction, and maintenance, 30.1% production, transportation, and material moving
Income: Per capita: $20,311; Median household: $46,316; Average household: $53,638; Households with income of $100,000 or more: 10.8%; Poverty rate: 21.1%
Educational Attainment: High school diploma or higher: 87.7%; Bachelor's degree or higher: 16.4%; Graduate/professional degree or higher: 6.6%

School District(s)

Patrick Henry Local (KG-12)
2015-16 Enrollment: 861 . . . . (419) 274-5451
Housing: Homeownership rate: 72.9%; Median home value: $82,700; Median year structure built: 1944; Homeowner vacancy rate: 8.9%; Median selected monthly owner costs: $1,010 with a mortgage, $377 without a mortgage; Median gross rent: $536 per month; Rental vacancy rate: 12.2%

Health Insurance: 94.1% have insurance; 70.2% have private insurance; 40.3% have public insurance; 5.9% do not have insurance; 0.0% of children under 18 do not have insurance
Transportation: Commute: 97.6% car, 0.0% public transportation, 0.0% walk, 0.0% work from home; Mean travel time to work: 24.7 minutes

HOLGATE (village). Covers a land area of 1.154 square miles and a water area of 0 square miles. Located at 41.25° N. Lat; 84.13° W. Long. Elevation is 709 feet.
Population: 1,080; Growth (since 2000): -9.5%; Density: 935.9 persons per square mile; Race: 85.3% White, 0.1% Black/African American, 0.6% Asian, 0.3% American Indian/Alaska Native, 0.0% Native Hawaiian/Other Pacific Islander, 1.2% Two or more races, 25.0% Hispanic of any race; Average household size: 2.28; Median age: 48.4; Age under 18: 20.3%; Age 65 and over: 20.2%; Males per 100 females: 94.9; Marriage status: 17.1% never married, 61.8% now married, 1.5% separated, 9.3% widowed, 11.8% divorced; Foreign born: 6.5%; Speak English only: 84.2%; With disability: 15.0%; Veterans: 11.5%; Ancestry: 32.8% German, 12.6% Irish, 6.5% English, 4.5% American, 4.0% Italian
Employment: 9.3% management, business, and financial, 3.3% computer, engineering, and science, 5.6% education, legal, community service, arts, and media, 5.6% healthcare practitioners, 9.1% service, 17.6% sales and office, 17.2% natural resources, construction, and maintenance, 32.2% production, transportation, and material moving
Income: Per capita: $22,851; Median household: $50,714; Average household: $52,566; Households with income of $100,000 or more: 9.5%; Poverty rate: 11.9%
Educational Attainment: High school diploma or higher: 81.0%; Bachelor's degree or higher: 6.0%; Graduate/professional degree or higher: 2.3%

School District(s)

Holgate Local (KG-12)
2015-16 Enrollment: 411 . . . . (419) 264-5141
Housing: Homeownership rate: 80.0%; Median home value: $79,300; Median year structure built: 1945; Homeowner vacancy rate: 2.6%; Median selected monthly owner costs: $872 with a mortgage, $364 without a mortgage; Median gross rent: $726 per month; Rental vacancy rate: 16.5%
Health Insurance: 83.8% have insurance; 64.9% have private insurance; 35.9% have public insurance; 16.2% do not have insurance; 5.5% of children under 18 do not have insurance
Transportation: Commute: 93.4% car, 0.0% public transportation, 2.6% walk, 0.9% work from home; Mean travel time to work: 24.4 minutes

LIBERTY CENTER (village). Covers a land area of 1.037 square miles and a water area of 0 square miles. Located at 41.44° N. Lat; 84.01° W. Long. Elevation is 679 feet.
Population: 1,159; Growth (since 2000): 4.5%; Density: 1,117.9 persons per square mile; Race: 97.1% White, 0.0% Black/African American, 0.0% Asian, 0.0% American Indian/Alaska Native, 0.4% Native Hawaiian/Other Pacific Islander, 1.4% Two or more races, 5.2% Hispanic of any race; Average household size: 2.33; Median age: 44.7; Age under 18: 23.3%; Age 65 and over: 14.5%; Males per 100 females: 97.3; Marriage status: 21.5% never married, 51.3% now married, 1.3% separated, 11.1% widowed, 16.1% divorced; Foreign born: 1.6%; Speak English only: 94.7%; With disability: 15.3%; Veterans: 10.1%; Ancestry: 45.6% German, 12.5% Irish, 7.9% English, 7.3% Polish, 5.6% French
Employment: 4.9% management, business, and financial, 0.2% computer, engineering, and science, 4.9% education, legal, community service, arts, and media, 8.9% healthcare practitioners, 16.4% service, 16.6% sales and office, 18.5% natural resources, construction, and maintenance, 29.8% production, transportation, and material moving
Income: Per capita: $27,463; Median household: $59,583; Average household: $64,625; Households with income of $100,000 or more: 18.5%; Poverty rate: 7.5%
Educational Attainment: High school diploma or higher: 94.3%; Bachelor's degree or higher: 10.2%; Graduate/professional degree or higher: 2.6%

School District(s)

Liberty Center Local (KG-12)
2015-16 Enrollment: 1,064 . . . . (419) 533-5011
Housing: Homeownership rate: 79.5%; Median home value: $99,200; Median year structure built: 1950; Homeowner vacancy rate: 5.0%; Median selected monthly owner costs: $1,062 with a mortgage, $380 without a mortgage; Median gross rent: $725 per month; Rental vacancy rate: 7.3%
Health Insurance: 93.1% have insurance; 75.0% have private insurance; 33.2% have public insurance; 6.9% do not have insurance; 1.9% of children under 18 do not have insurance
Newspapers: The Liberty Press (weekly circulation 1,200)
Transportation: Commute: 95.7% car, 0.0% public transportation, 3.7% walk, 0.5% work from home; Mean travel time to work: 24.0 minutes

MALINTA (village). Covers a land area of 0.770 square miles and a water area of 0 square miles. Located at 41.32° N. Lat; 84.04° W. Long. Elevation is 682 feet.
Population: 328; Growth (since 2000): 15.1%; Density: 426.1 persons per square mile; Race: 88.1% White, 0.0% Black/African American, 0.0% Asian, 1.5% American Indian/Alaska Native, 0.0% Native Hawaiian/Other Pacific Islander, 3.0% Two or more races, 17.4% Hispanic of any race; Average household size: 2.43; Median age: 39.9; Age under 18: 23.2%; Age 65 and over: 14.3%; Males per 100 females: 92.0; Marriage status: 31.0% never married, 48.7% now married, 2.2% separated, 6.6% widowed, 13.7% divorced; Foreign born: 6.1%; Speak English only: 89.7%; With disability: 14.0%; Veterans: 7.9%; Ancestry: 48.8% German, 9.1% Irish, 4.9% American, 2.7% Swiss, 2.1% English
Employment: 7.4% management, business, and financial, 2.1% computer, engineering, and science, 4.8% education, legal, community service, arts, and media, 4.8% healthcare practitioners, 24.5% service, 20.7% sales and office, 7.4% natural resources, construction, and maintenance, 28.2% production, transportation, and material moving
Income: Per capita: $24,164; Median household: $62,083; Average household: $60,290; Households with income of $100,000 or more: 10.4%; Poverty rate: 9.9%
Educational Attainment: High school diploma or higher: 90.8%; Bachelor's degree or higher: 7.2%; Graduate/professional degree or higher: 3.4%

School District(s)

Patrick Henry Local (KG-12)
2015-16 Enrollment: 861 . . . . (419) 274-5451
Housing: Homeownership rate: 83.0%; Median home value: $82,600; Median year structure built: Before 1940; Homeowner vacancy rate: 0.0%; Median selected monthly owner costs: $927 with a mortgage, $420 without a mortgage; Median gross rent: $736 per month; Rental vacancy rate: 20.7%
Health Insurance: 98.8% have insurance; 82.3% have private insurance; 25.6% have public insurance; 1.2% do not have insurance; 0.0% of children under 18 do not have insurance
Transportation: Commute: 98.9% car, 1.1% public transportation, 0.0% walk, 0.0% work from home; Mean travel time to work: 23.5 minutes

MCCLURE (village). Covers a land area of 0.498 square miles and a water area of 0 square miles. Located at 41.37° N. Lat; 83.94° W. Long. Elevation is 676 feet.
Population: 611; Growth (since 2000): -19.7%; Density: 1,226.7 persons per square mile; Race: 96.4% White, 1.1% Black/African American, 0.0% Asian, 0.0% American Indian/Alaska Native, 0.0% Native Hawaiian/Other Pacific Islander, 1.3% Two or more races, 3.1% Hispanic of any race; Average household size: 2.16; Median age: 44.1; Age under 18: 21.6%; Age 65 and over: 21.8%; Males per 100 females: 100.3; Marriage status: 23.3% never married, 55.8% now married, 1.0% separated, 8.8% widowed, 12.0% divorced; Foreign born: 0.8%; Speak English only: 97.2%; With disability: 21.8%; Veterans: 11.5%; Ancestry: 36.3% German, 12.6% American, 10.3% Irish, 8.0% English, 4.4% Dutch
Employment: 10.8% management, business, and financial, 1.6% computer, engineering, and science, 7.2% education, legal, community service, arts, and media, 1.6% healthcare practitioners, 14.5% service, 20.1% sales and office, 15.3% natural resources, construction, and maintenance, 28.9% production, transportation, and material moving
Income: Per capita: $19,631; Median household: $34,779; Average household: $42,726; Households with income of $100,000 or more: 4.6%; Poverty rate: 12.2%
Educational Attainment: High school diploma or higher: 86.2%; Bachelor's degree or higher: 8.4%; Graduate/professional degree or higher: 3.1%
Housing: Homeownership rate: 85.2%; Median home value: $71,700; Median year structure built: 1957; Homeowner vacancy rate: 7.7%; Median selected monthly owner costs: $780 with a mortgage, $341 without a mortgage; Median gross rent: $637 per month; Rental vacancy rate: 12.5%

Health Insurance: 91.3% have insurance; 64.6% have private insurance; 46.5% have public insurance; 8.7% do not have insurance; 2.3% of children under 18 do not have insurance
Transportation: Commute: 97.9% car, 0.0% public transportation, 0.0% walk, 2.1% work from home; Mean travel time to work: 28.6 minutes

NAPOLEON (city). County seat. Covers a land area of 6.186 square miles and a water area of 0.400 square miles. Located at 41.40° N. Lat; 84.13° W. Long. Elevation is 679 feet.
History: Napoleon was named by a group of Frenchmen who settled here in the midst of a predominantly German population. Napoleon developed as the seat of Henry County, and as the market center for a rural area.
Population: 8,659; Growth (since 2000): -7.1%; Density: 1,399.8 persons per square mile; Race: 93.2% White, 0.8% Black/African American, 0.9% Asian, 0.0% American Indian/Alaska Native, 0.0% Native Hawaiian/Other Pacific Islander, 2.5% Two or more races, 7.8% Hispanic of any race; Average household size: 2.30; Median age: 41.2; Age under 18: 22.3%; Age 65 and over: 20.5%; Males per 100 females: 89.9; Marriage status: 29.9% never married, 46.9% now married, 1.4% separated, 10.9% widowed, 12.4% divorced; Foreign born: 1.4%; Speak English only: 96.6%; With disability: 18.1%; Veterans: 10.2%; Ancestry: 41.9% German, 9.7% English, 7.2% Irish, 6.9% American, 4.1% Dutch
Employment: 10.3% management, business, and financial, 1.9% computer, engineering, and science, 7.8% education, legal, community service, arts, and media, 6.5% healthcare practitioners, 19.0% service, 13.9% sales and office, 9.9% natural resources, construction, and maintenance, 30.7% production, transportation, and material moving
Income: Per capita: $25,486; Median household: $45,417; Average household: $59,015; Households with income of $100,000 or more: 13.2%; Poverty rate: 16.7%
Educational Attainment: High school diploma or higher: 89.9%; Bachelor's degree or higher: 15.1%; Graduate/professional degree or higher: 6.2%

School District(s)

Napoleon Area City (PK-12)
2015-16 Enrollment: 1,962 . . . . (419) 599-7015
Housing: Homeownership rate: 65.4%; Median home value: $103,100; Median year structure built: 1964; Homeowner vacancy rate: 2.3%; Median selected monthly owner costs: $976 with a mortgage, $431 without a mortgage; Median gross rent: $671 per month; Rental vacancy rate: 0.0%
Health Insurance: 89.2% have insurance; 68.6% have private insurance; 39.7% have public insurance; 10.8% do not have insurance; 9.0% of children under 18 do not have insurance
Hospitals: Henry County Hospital (52 beds)
Safety: Violent crime rate: 12.8 per 10,000 population; Property crime rate: 230.0 per 10,000 population
Newspapers: Northwest Signal (daily circulation 5,700)
Transportation: Commute: 95.4% car, 0.8% public transportation, 1.1% walk, 0.3% work from home; Mean travel time to work: 18.1 minutes
Additional Information Contacts
City of Napoleon . . . . (419) 592-4010
http://www.napoleonohio.com

NEW BAVARIA (village). Covers a land area of 0.070 square miles and a water area of 0 square miles. Located at 41.20° N. Lat; 84.17° W. Long. Elevation is 735 feet.
Population: 119; Growth (since 2000): 52.6%; Density: 1,701.2 persons per square mile; Race: 95.0% White, 0.0% Black/African American, 5.0% Asian, 0.0% American Indian/Alaska Native, 0.0% Native Hawaiian/Other Pacific Islander, 0.0% Two or more races, 0.0% Hispanic of any race; Average household size: 2.38; Median age: 35.6; Age under 18: 28.6%; Age 65 and over: 7.6%; Males per 100 females: 115.2; Marriage status: 20.0% never married, 65.6% now married, 0.0% separated, 1.1% widowed, 13.3% divorced; Foreign born: 5.0%; Speak English only: 94.8%; With disability: 5.9%; Veterans: 3.5%; Ancestry: 64.7% German, 16.0% French, 14.3% Irish, 5.0% Greek, 3.4% Swedish
Employment: 21.0% management, business, and financial, 4.8% computer, engineering, and science, 3.2% education, legal, community service, arts, and media, 0.0% healthcare practitioners, 12.9% service, 38.7% sales and office, 0.0% natural resources, construction, and maintenance, 19.4% production, transportation, and material moving
Income: Per capita: $23,787; Median household: $48,750; Average household: $52,810; Households with income of $100,000 or more: 4.0%; Poverty rate: 5.9%
Educational Attainment: High school diploma or higher: 91.3%; Bachelor's degree or higher: 38.8%; Graduate/professional degree or higher: 11.3%
Housing: Homeownership rate: 84.0%; Median home value: $87,500; Median year structure built: 1959; Homeowner vacancy rate: 0.0%; Median selected monthly owner costs: $895 with a mortgage, $338 without a mortgage; Median gross rent: n/a per month; Rental vacancy rate: 0.0%
Health Insurance: 100.0% have insurance; 100.0% have private insurance; 11.8% have public insurance; 0.0% do not have insurance; 0.0% of children under 18 do not have insurance
Transportation: Commute: 93.4% car, 0.0% public transportation, 3.3% walk, 0.0% work from home; Mean travel time to work: 22.5 minutes

RIDGEVILLE CORNERS (CDP). Covers a land area of 0.914 square miles and a water area of 0 square miles. Located at 41.44° N. Lat; 84.26° W. Long. Elevation is 735 feet.
Population: 381; Growth (since 2000): n/a; Density: 416.6 persons per square mile; Race: 99.5% White, 0.0% Black/African American, 0.0% Asian, 0.0% American Indian/Alaska Native, 0.0% Native Hawaiian/Other Pacific Islander, 0.5% Two or more races, 0.0% Hispanic of any race; Average household size: 2.59; Median age: 31.0; Age under 18: 26.5%; Age 65 and over: 6.6%; Males per 100 females: 106.2; Marriage status: 13.2% never married, 83.6% now married, 0.0% separated, 3.1% widowed, 0.0% divorced; Foreign born: 0.0%; Speak English only: 100.0%; With disability: 4.5%; Veterans: 6.4%; Ancestry: 73.8% German, 15.7% American, 13.1% Polish, 4.7% English, 2.4% French
Employment: 11.1% management, business, and financial, 0.0% computer, engineering, and science, 11.1% education, legal, community service, arts, and media, 15.0% healthcare practitioners, 11.5% service, 15.4% sales and office, 13.7% natural resources, construction, and maintenance, 22.2% production, transportation, and material moving
Income: Per capita: $25,044; Median household: $64,188; Average household: $66,154; Households with income of $100,000 or more: 5.4%; Poverty rate: n/a
Educational Attainment: High school diploma or higher: 93.4%; Bachelor's degree or higher: 21.9%; Graduate/professional degree or higher: 5.4%
Housing: Homeownership rate: 93.2%; Median home value: $111,700; Median year structure built: 1954; Homeowner vacancy rate: 0.0%; Median selected monthly owner costs: $1,079 with a mortgage, $397 without a mortgage; Median gross rent: n/a per month; Rental vacancy rate: 0.0%
Health Insurance: 100.0% have insurance; 97.9% have private insurance; 8.9% have public insurance; 0.0% do not have insurance; 0.0% of children under 18 do not have insurance
Transportation: Commute: 92.3% car, 0.0% public transportation, 7.7% walk, 0.0% work from home; Mean travel time to work: 12.7 minutes

Highland County

Located in southwestern Ohio; drained by the East Fork of Little Miami River, and by several creeks. Covers a land area of 553.084 square miles, a water area of 4.709 square miles, and is located in the Eastern Time Zone at 39.18° N. Lat., 83.60° W. Long. The county was founded in 1805. County seat is Hillsboro.

Weather Station: Hillsboro Elevation: 1,100 feet

	Jan	Feb	Mar	Apr	May	Jun	Jul	Aug	Sep	Oct	Nov	Dec
High	37	41	51	62	71	79	83	82	76	65	53	40
Low	21	23	31	41	51	60	64	62	55	44	35	25
Precip	3.1	2.9	3.7	4.1	5.1	3.9	3.8	3.5	3.1	3.1	3.1	3.0
Snow	6.0	4.8	2.8	0.5	tr	0.0	0.0	0.0	0.0	0.2	0.4	2.6

High and Low temperatures in degrees Fahrenheit; Precipitation and Snow in inches

Population: 43,109; Growth (since 2000): 5.5%; Density: 77.9 persons per square mile; Race: 96.1% White, 1.2% Black/African American, 0.4% Asian, 0.1% American Indian/Alaska Native, 0.0% Native Hawaiian/Other Pacific Islander, 2.1% two or more races, 0.9% Hispanic of any race; Average household size: 2.56; Median age: 40.2; Age under 18: 24.2%; Age 65 and over: 17.1%; Males per 100 females: 96.0; Marriage status: 25.5% never married, 52.7% now married, 2.4% separated, 7.9% widowed, 13.9% divorced; Foreign born: 0.8%; Speak English only: 98.2%; With disability: 18.8%; Veterans: 10.6%; Ancestry: 18.7% German, 17.7% American, 11.9% Irish, 9.3% English, 1.9% Scottish

Religion: Six largest groups: 11.3% Baptist, 6.5% Methodist/Pietist, 6.3% Non-denominational Protestant, 2.1% European Free-Church, 1.8% Pentecostal, 1.8% Catholicism
Economy: Unemployment rate: 5.4%; Leading industries: 20.6 % retail trade; 14.2 % health care and social assistance; 12.0 % other services (except public administration); Farms: 1,412 totaling 264,521 acres; Company size: 0 employ 1,000 or more persons, 0 employ 500 to 999 persons, 18 employ 100 to 499 persons, 643 employ less than 100 persons; Business ownership: 1,298 women-owned, n/a Black-owned, 57 Hispanic-owned, 33 Asian-owned, n/a American Indian/Alaska Native-owned
Employment: 10.7% management, business, and financial, 2.9% computer, engineering, and science, 7.0% education, legal, community service, arts, and media, 6.0% healthcare practitioners, 15.7% service, 19.1% sales and office, 13.5% natural resources, construction, and maintenance, 25.2% production, transportation, and material moving
Income: Per capita: $21,134; Median household: $40,593; Average household: $53,290; Households with income of $100,000 or more: 11.2%; Poverty rate: 20.7%
Educational Attainment: High school diploma or higher: 83.9%; Bachelor's degree or higher: 12.0%; Graduate/professional degree or higher: 5.0%
Housing: Homeownership rate: 70.3%; Median home value: $102,300; Median year structure built: 1977; Homeowner vacancy rate: 1.5%; Median selected monthly owner costs: $1,002 with a mortgage, $369 without a mortgage; Median gross rent: $664 per month; Rental vacancy rate: 3.2%
Vital Statistics: Birth rate: 119.2 per 10,000 population; Death rate: 112.7 per 10,000 population; Age-adjusted cancer mortality rate: 157.6 deaths per 100,000 population
Health Insurance: 88.7% have insurance; 56.9% have private insurance; 45.9% have public insurance; 11.3% do not have insurance; 6.1% of children under 18 do not have insurance
Health Care: Physicians: 5.1 per 10,000 population; Dentists: 4.6 per 10,000 population; Hospital beds: 11.6 per 10,000 population; Hospital admissions: 573.2 per 10,000 population
Transportation: Commute: 92.3% car, 0.8% public transportation, 2.2% walk, 3.9% work from home; Mean travel time to work: 29.7 minutes
2016 Presidential Election: 75.4% Trump, 20.3% Clinton, 2.5% Johnson, 0.6% Stein
National and State Parks: Fallsville State Wildlife Area; Fort Hill State Memorial; Oldaker State Wildlife Area; Rocky Fork State Park
Additional Information Contacts
Highland Government . . . . (937) 393-1911
http://www.co.highland.oh.us

Highland County Communities

BUFORD (CDP). Covers a land area of 1.483 square miles and a water area of 0 square miles. Located at 39.07° N. Lat; 83.84° W. Long. Elevation is 948 feet.
Population: 251; Growth (since 2000): n/a; Density: 169.2 persons per square mile; Race: 100.0% White, 0.0% Black/African American, 0.0% Asian, 0.0% American Indian/Alaska Native, 0.0% Native Hawaiian/Other Pacific Islander, 0.0% Two or more races, 0.0% Hispanic of any race; Average household size: 2.59; Median age: 41.8; Age under 18: 11.6%; Age 65 and over: 17.9%; Males per 100 females: 93.4; Marriage status: 22.9% never married, 65.6% now married, 0.0% separated, 3.5% widowed, 7.9% divorced; Foreign born: 0.0%; Speak English only: 100.0%; With disability: 3.6%; Veterans: 0.0%; Ancestry: 33.5% German, 25.5% American, 16.7% English, 14.7% Irish, 3.6% Dutch
Employment: 0.0% management, business, and financial, 8.5% computer, engineering, and science, 0.0% education, legal, community service, arts, and media, 0.0% healthcare practitioners, 0.0% service, 20.8% sales and office, 35.8% natural resources, construction, and maintenance, 34.9% production, transportation, and material moving
Income: Per capita: $20,857; Median household: $39,861; Average household: $50,527; Households with income of $100,000 or more: 9.3%; Poverty rate: 3.6%
Educational Attainment: High school diploma or higher: 85.5%; Bachelor's degree or higher: 11.8%; Graduate/professional degree or higher: n/a
Housing: Homeownership rate: 100.0%; Median home value: $57,600; Median year structure built: 1978; Homeowner vacancy rate: 0.0%; Median selected monthly owner costs: $919 with a mortgage, $460 without a mortgage; Median gross rent: n/a per month; Rental vacancy rate: 0.0%
Health Insurance: 88.4% have insurance; 53.4% have private insurance; 41.8% have public insurance; 11.6% do not have insurance; 0.0% of children under 18 do not have insurance
Transportation: Commute: 91.5% car, 0.0% public transportation, 0.0% walk, 8.5% work from home; Mean travel time to work: 0.0 minutes

GREENFIELD (village). Covers a land area of 2.061 square miles and a water area of 0 square miles. Located at 39.35° N. Lat; 83.39° W. Long. Elevation is 909 feet.
History: Platted 1798, incorporated 1841.
Population: 4,794; Growth (since 2000): -2.3%; Density: 2,325.9 persons per square mile; Race: 97.4% White, 2.1% Black/African American, 0.1% Asian, 0.0% American Indian/Alaska Native, 0.0% Native Hawaiian/Other Pacific Islander, 0.5% Two or more races, 0.0% Hispanic of any race; Average household size: 2.40; Median age: 38.1; Age under 18: 24.6%; Age 65 and over: 15.8%; Males per 100 females: 90.4; Marriage status: 28.5% never married, 41.1% now married, 4.3% separated, 11.4% widowed, 19.0% divorced; Foreign born: 0.1%; Speak English only: 98.8%; With disability: 23.0%; Veterans: 11.0%; Ancestry: 20.6% German, 14.8% Irish, 12.8% American, 8.7% English, 2.7% Scottish
Employment: 6.7% management, business, and financial, 2.0% computer, engineering, and science, 7.8% education, legal, community service, arts, and media, 3.6% healthcare practitioners, 15.5% service, 27.2% sales and office, 7.1% natural resources, construction, and maintenance, 30.1% production, transportation, and material moving
Income: Per capita: $15,002; Median household: $26,361; Average household: $34,930; Households with income of $100,000 or more: 4.7%; Poverty rate: 33.7%
Educational Attainment: High school diploma or higher: 83.5%; Bachelor's degree or higher: 9.9%; Graduate/professional degree or higher: 3.5%

School District(s)

Greenfield Exempted Village (PK-12)
2015-16 Enrollment: 2,019 . . . . (937) 981-2152
Housing: Homeownership rate: 46.7%; Median home value: $74,900; Median year structure built: 1952; Homeowner vacancy rate: 0.0%; Median selected monthly owner costs: $811 with a mortgage, $324 without a mortgage; Median gross rent: $609 per month; Rental vacancy rate: 2.3%
Health Insurance: 89.5% have insurance; 41.4% have private insurance; 59.7% have public insurance; 10.5% do not have insurance; 0.0% of children under 18 do not have insurance
Hospitals: Greenfield Area Medical Center (46 beds)
Safety: Violent crime rate: 13.2 per 10,000 population; Property crime rate: 223.7 per 10,000 population
Transportation: Commute: 83.9% car, 2.0% public transportation, 10.3% walk, 3.7% work from home; Mean travel time to work: 25.8 minutes

HIGHLAND (village). Covers a land area of 0.170 square miles and a water area of 0 square miles. Located at 39.34° N. Lat; 83.60° W. Long. Elevation is 1,066 feet.
Population: 286; Growth (since 2000): 1.1%; Density: 1,683.3 persons per square mile; Race: 95.8% White, 0.0% Black/African American, 1.7% Asian, 0.0% American Indian/Alaska Native, 0.0% Native Hawaiian/Other Pacific Islander, 2.4% Two or more races, 5.2% Hispanic of any race; Average household size: 2.80; Median age: 32.3; Age under 18: 35.7%; Age 65 and over: 13.3%; Males per 100 females: 88.1; Marriage status: 31.5% never married, 41.5% now married, 2.5% separated, 6.5% widowed, 20.5% divorced; Foreign born: 1.4%; Speak English only: 97.7%; With disability: 15.4%; Veterans: 6.5%; Ancestry: 13.3% German, 12.9% American, 7.3% Irish, 5.2% Italian, 3.8% English
Employment: 10.5% management, business, and financial, 2.3% computer, engineering, and science, 5.8% education, legal, community service, arts, and media, 2.3% healthcare practitioners, 14.0% service, 20.9% sales and office, 14.0% natural resources, construction, and maintenance, 30.2% production, transportation, and material moving
Income: Per capita: $13,885; Median household: $32,206; Average household: $38,335; Households with income of $100,000 or more: 2.0%; Poverty rate: 39.2%
Educational Attainment: High school diploma or higher: 81.0%; Bachelor's degree or higher: 4.4%; Graduate/professional degree or higher: 0.6%
Housing: Homeownership rate: 69.6%; Median home value: $66,800; Median year structure built: 1946; Homeowner vacancy rate: 0.0%; Median selected monthly owner costs: $817 with a mortgage, $375 without a mortgage; Median gross rent: $573 per month; Rental vacancy rate: 23.3%

Health Insurance: 93.4% have insurance; 47.6% have private insurance; 54.9% have public insurance; 6.6% do not have insurance; 0.0% of children under 18 do not have insurance
Transportation: Commute: 97.6% car, 0.0% public transportation, 2.4% walk, 0.0% work from home; Mean travel time to work: 26.1 minutes

HIGHLAND HOLIDAY (CDP). Covers a land area of 0.604 square miles and a water area of 0.493 square miles. Located at 39.19° N. Lat; 83.47° W. Long. Elevation is 938 feet.
Population: 470; Growth (since 2000): n/a; Density: 777.9 persons per square mile; Race: 100.0% White, 0.0% Black/African American, 0.0% Asian, 0.0% American Indian/Alaska Native, 0.0% Native Hawaiian/Other Pacific Islander, 0.0% Two or more races, 0.0% Hispanic of any race; Average household size: 2.61; Median age: 48.4; Age under 18: 22.1%; Age 65 and over: 20.4%; Males per 100 females: 103.0; Marriage status: 21.1% never married, 54.5% now married, 5.3% separated, 10.2% widowed, 14.2% divorced; Foreign born: 0.0%; Speak English only: 96.3%; With disability: 51.1%; Veterans: 11.5%; Ancestry: 31.3% American, 13.4% German, 5.1% English, 3.8% Irish, 3.2% Scotch-Irish
Employment: 31.1% management, business, and financial, 0.0% computer, engineering, and science, 0.0% education, legal, community service, arts, and media, 0.0% healthcare practitioners, 29.5% service, 11.5% sales and office, 18.0% natural resources, construction, and maintenance, 9.8% production, transportation, and material moving
Income: Per capita: $11,433; Median household: $20,667; Average household: $28,956; Households with income of $100,000 or more: n/a; Poverty rate: 51.1%
Educational Attainment: High school diploma or higher: 50.9%; Bachelor's degree or higher: 2.6%; Graduate/professional degree or higher: n/a
Housing: Homeownership rate: 71.1%; Median home value: $33,500; Median year structure built: 1977; Homeowner vacancy rate: 0.0%; Median selected monthly owner costs: $876 with a mortgage, $242 without a mortgage; Median gross rent: $832 per month; Rental vacancy rate: 0.0%
Health Insurance: 96.8% have insurance; 35.1% have private insurance; 81.3% have public insurance; 3.2% do not have insurance; 0.0% of children under 18 do not have insurance
Transportation: Commute: 100.0% car, 0.0% public transportation, 0.0% walk, 0.0% work from home; Mean travel time to work: 65.8 minutes

HILLSBORO (city). County seat. Covers a land area of 5.429 square miles and a water area of 0 square miles. Located at 39.21° N. Lat; 83.61° W. Long. Elevation is 1,132 feet.
History: Hillsboro was platted in 1807, and developed around brickyards, tanneries, and grist and woolen mills. In 1873, The Women 's Temperance Crusade was organized and managed to close all of the saloons in the town when the women marched into each in turn and held a prayer meeting.
Population: 6,572; Growth (since 2000): 3.2%; Density: 1,210.6 persons per square mile; Race: 92.1% White, 3.6% Black/African American, 1.3% Asian, 0.3% American Indian/Alaska Native, 0.0% Native Hawaiian/Other Pacific Islander, 2.2% Two or more races, 1.8% Hispanic of any race; Average household size: 2.21; Median age: 41.2; Age under 18: 22.2%; Age 65 and over: 19.7%; Males per 100 females: 81.6; Marriage status: 27.5% never married, 45.8% now married, 3.0% separated, 9.7% widowed, 17.0% divorced; Foreign born: 1.5%; Speak English only: 97.4%; With disability: 21.2%; Veterans: 10.9%; Ancestry: 16.3% German, 15.1% Irish, 9.9% American, 8.1% English, 3.8% Scottish
Employment: 9.9% management, business, and financial, 0.9% computer, engineering, and science, 7.3% education, legal, community service, arts, and media, 9.7% healthcare practitioners, 22.3% service, 25.8% sales and office, 4.7% natural resources, construction, and maintenance, 19.4% production, transportation, and material moving
Income: Per capita: $19,561; Median household: $33,051; Average household: $43,819; Households with income of $100,000 or more: 6.7%; Poverty rate: 25.5%
Educational Attainment: High school diploma or higher: 82.7%; Bachelor's degree or higher: 16.9%; Graduate/professional degree or higher: 5.9%

School District(s)

Bright Local (PK-12)
2015-16 Enrollment: 660. . . . . (937) 442-3114
Hillsboro City (PK-12)
2015-16 Enrollment: 2,568 . . . . (937) 393-3475

Two-year College(s)

Southern State Community College (Public)
Fall 2016 Enrollment: 2,721 . . . . (937) 393-3431
2016-17 Tuition: In-state $4,412; Out-of-state $8,118
Housing: Homeownership rate: 50.2%; Median home value: $85,000; Median year structure built: 1966; Homeowner vacancy rate: 0.0%; Median selected monthly owner costs: $884 with a mortgage, $345 without a mortgage; Median gross rent: $632 per month; Rental vacancy rate: 8.2%
Health Insurance: 88.9% have insurance; 53.2% have private insurance; 49.5% have public insurance; 11.1% do not have insurance; 4.2% of children under 18 do not have insurance
Hospitals: Highland District Hospital (65 beds)
Safety: Violent crime rate: 12.2 per 10,000 population; Property crime rate: 310.1 per 10,000 population
Newspapers: Times Gazette (daily circulation 5,000)
Transportation: Commute: 95.9% car, 0.0% public transportation, 1.2% walk, 2.9% work from home; Mean travel time to work: 26.2 minutes

LEESBURG (village). Covers a land area of 1.168 square miles and a water area of 0 square miles. Located at 39.34° N. Lat; 83.55° W. Long. Elevation is 1,014 feet.
History: Shortly after Leesburg was founded in 1802, Quakers from Pennsylvania settled here. Prior to 1900, Leesburg hosted the annual meeting of the Society of Friends, attended by members from all parts of the United States.
Population: 1,421; Growth (since 2000): 13.4%; Density: 1,216.3 persons per square mile; Race: 98.9% White, 0.0% Black/African American, 0.1% Asian, 0.0% American Indian/Alaska Native, 0.0% Native Hawaiian/Other Pacific Islander, 0.9% Two or more races, 0.0% Hispanic of any race; Average household size: 2.45; Median age: 38.9; Age under 18: 23.5%; Age 65 and over: 12.2%; Males per 100 females: 90.2; Marriage status: 28.6% never married, 46.3% now married, 5.0% separated, 5.3% widowed, 19.8% divorced; Foreign born: 0.1%; Speak English only: 97.6%; With disability: 17.4%; Veterans: 7.7%; Ancestry: 23.7% German, 22.3% American, 15.8% Irish, 8.0% English, 3.4% French
Employment: 6.2% management, business, and financial, 4.2% computer, engineering, and science, 6.1% education, legal, community service, arts, and media, 2.9% healthcare practitioners, 21.1% service, 19.5% sales and office, 5.6% natural resources, construction, and maintenance, 34.5% production, transportation, and material moving
Income: Per capita: $16,267; Median household: $30,913; Average household: $38,913; Households with income of $100,000 or more: 6.0%; Poverty rate: 28.1%
Educational Attainment: High school diploma or higher: 83.3%; Bachelor's degree or higher: 7.5%; Graduate/professional degree or higher: 3.5%

School District(s)

Fairfield Local (KG-12)
2015-16 Enrollment: 929. . . . . (937) 780-2221
Housing: Homeownership rate: 47.4%; Median home value: $83,300; Median year structure built: 1976; Homeowner vacancy rate: 4.5%; Median selected monthly owner costs: $811 with a mortgage, $383 without a mortgage; Median gross rent: $637 per month; Rental vacancy rate: 0.0%
Health Insurance: 82.3% have insurance; 49.6% have private insurance; 42.0% have public insurance; 17.7% do not have insurance; 3.6% of children under 18 do not have insurance
Safety: Violent crime rate: 0.0 per 10,000 population; Property crime rate: 356.9 per 10,000 population
Transportation: Commute: 92.0% car, 0.8% public transportation, 1.1% walk, 6.1% work from home; Mean travel time to work: 25.7 minutes

LYNCHBURG (village). Covers a land area of 0.940 square miles and a water area of 0.007 square miles. Located at 39.24° N. Lat; 83.79° W. Long. Elevation is 1,007 feet.
Population: 1,310; Growth (since 2000): -3.0%; Density: 1,394.3 persons per square mile; Race: 97.9% White, 0.6% Black/African American, 0.0% Asian, 0.0% American Indian/Alaska Native, 0.0% Native Hawaiian/Other Pacific Islander, 1.5% Two or more races, 0.4% Hispanic of any race; Average household size: 2.68; Median age: 38.2; Age under 18: 31.8%; Age 65 and over: 15.8%; Males per 100 females: 90.0; Marriage status: 27.5% never married, 48.3% now married, 1.1% separated, 6.9% widowed, 17.3% divorced; Foreign born: 0.2%; Speak English only: 99.2%; With disability: 16.6%; Veterans: 12.2%; Ancestry: 28.2% American, 22.4% German, 7.5% Irish, 5.4% English, 1.5% Norwegian

Employment: 8.1% management, business, and financial, 1.1% computer, engineering, and science, 6.4% education, legal, community service, arts, and media, 2.1% healthcare practitioners, 30.4% service, 10.9% sales and office, 7.1% natural resources, construction, and maintenance, 34.0% production, transportation, and material moving
Income: Per capita: $17,695; Median household: $37,212; Average household: $46,562; Households with income of $100,000 or more: 6.9%; Poverty rate: 15.8%
Educational Attainment: High school diploma or higher: 88.9%; Bachelor's degree or higher: 11.5%; Graduate/professional degree or higher: 2.5%

School District(s)

Lynchburg-Clay Local (PK-12)
2015-16 Enrollment: 1,183 . . . . (937) 364-2338
Housing: Homeownership rate: 59.1%; Median home value: $92,200; Median year structure built: 1961; Homeowner vacancy rate: 4.9%; Median selected monthly owner costs: $1,106 with a mortgage, $480 without a mortgage; Median gross rent: $723 per month; Rental vacancy rate: 0.0%
Health Insurance: 92.7% have insurance; 56.6% have private insurance; 50.3% have public insurance; 7.3% do not have insurance; 0.0% of children under 18 do not have insurance
Safety: Violent crime rate: 27.0 per 10,000 population; Property crime rate: 134.8 per 10,000 population
Transportation: Commute: 95.0% car, 0.0% public transportation, 2.7% walk, 2.3% work from home; Mean travel time to work: 30.1 minutes

MOWRYSTOWN (village). Covers a land area of 0.482 square miles and a water area of 0.007 square miles. Located at 39.04° N. Lat; 83.75° W. Long. Elevation is 997 feet.
Population: 299; Growth (since 2000): -19.8%; Density: 620.1 persons per square mile; Race: 98.3% White, 0.0% Black/African American, 0.0% Asian, 0.0% American Indian/Alaska Native, 0.0% Native Hawaiian/Other Pacific Islander, 1.7% Two or more races, 1.0% Hispanic of any race; Average household size: 2.79; Median age: 37.9; Age under 18: 24.7%; Age 65 and over: 18.7%; Males per 100 females: 102.2; Marriage status: 23.9% never married, 52.3% now married, 6.6% separated, 10.3% widowed, 13.6% divorced; Foreign born: 0.0%; Speak English only: 97.9%; With disability: 27.1%; Veterans: 13.3%; Ancestry: 15.7% German, 10.7% American, 8.7% Irish, 7.0% English, 2.7% Scottish
Employment: 13.8% management, business, and financial, 0.0% computer, engineering, and science, 6.5% education, legal, community service, arts, and media, 2.4% healthcare practitioners, 13.8% service, 17.9% sales and office, 15.4% natural resources, construction, and maintenance, 30.1% production, transportation, and material moving
Income: Per capita: $16,996; Median household: $33,036; Average household: $45,824; Households with income of $100,000 or more: 7.5%; Poverty rate: 23.7%
Educational Attainment: High school diploma or higher: 81.5%; Bachelor's degree or higher: 10.7%; Graduate/professional degree or higher: 2.9%

School District(s)

Bright Local (PK-12)
2015-16 Enrollment: 660. . . . . (937) 442-3114
Housing: Homeownership rate: 76.6%; Median home value: $74,000; Median year structure built: Before 1940; Homeowner vacancy rate: 4.4%; Median selected monthly owner costs: $876 with a mortgage, $478 without a mortgage; Median gross rent: $805 per month; Rental vacancy rate: 12.5%
Health Insurance: 85.6% have insurance; 38.5% have private insurance; 61.2% have public insurance; 14.4% do not have insurance; 0.0% of children under 18 do not have insurance
Transportation: Commute: 90.8% car, 0.0% public transportation, 2.5% walk, 5.0% work from home; Mean travel time to work: 32.3 minutes

ROCKY FORK POINT (CDP). Covers a land area of 0.712 square miles and a water area of 0.512 square miles. Located at 39.19° N. Lat; 83.49° W. Long. Elevation is 974 feet.
Population: 665; Growth (since 2000): n/a; Density: 933.6 persons per square mile; Race: 98.8% White, 0.0% Black/African American, 0.0% Asian, 0.0% American Indian/Alaska Native, 0.0% Native Hawaiian/Other Pacific Islander, 1.2% Two or more races, 0.0% Hispanic of any race; Average household size: 2.22; Median age: 52.9; Age under 18: 15.0%; Age 65 and over: 22.1%; Males per 100 females: 99.1; Marriage status: 18.6% never married, 53.6% now married, 2.9% separated, 7.5% widowed, 20.3% divorced; Foreign born: 0.0%; Speak English only: 100.0%; With disability: 34.0%; Veterans: 13.8%; Ancestry: 21.2% Irish, 18.6% German, 12.8% American, 11.9% English, 2.1% Dutch
Employment: 3.9% management, business, and financial, 0.0% computer, engineering, and science, 0.0% education, legal, community service, arts, and media, 0.0% healthcare practitioners, 14.7% service, 4.9% sales and office, 2.0% natural resources, construction, and maintenance, 74.5% production, transportation, and material moving
Income: Per capita: $17,245; Median household: $22,109; Average household: $36,602; Households with income of $100,000 or more: 13.4%; Poverty rate: 49.4%
Educational Attainment: High school diploma or higher: 77.7%; Bachelor's degree or higher: 7.6%; Graduate/professional degree or higher: 3.0%
Housing: Homeownership rate: 77.3%; Median home value: $54,600; Median year structure built: 1981; Homeowner vacancy rate: 0.0%; Median selected monthly owner costs: $824 with a mortgage, $397 without a mortgage; Median gross rent: $713 per month; Rental vacancy rate: 0.0%
Health Insurance: 88.1% have insurance; 34.0% have private insurance; 64.1% have public insurance; 11.9% do not have insurance; 5.0% of children under 18 do not have insurance
Transportation: Commute: 87.2% car, 0.0% public transportation, 0.0% walk, 0.0% work from home; Mean travel time to work: 37.1 minutes

SINKING SPRING (village). Covers a land area of 0.467 square miles and a water area of 0 square miles. Located at 39.07° N. Lat; 83.39° W. Long. Elevation is 866 feet.
History: Nearby are Fort Hill and Serpent Mound, prehistoric earthworks.
Population: 118; Growth (since 2000): -25.3%; Density: 252.6 persons per square mile; Race: 100.0% White, 0.0% Black/African American, 0.0% Asian, 0.0% American Indian/Alaska Native, 0.0% Native Hawaiian/Other Pacific Islander, 0.0% Two or more races, 0.0% Hispanic of any race; Average household size: 2.46; Median age: 36.2; Age under 18: 18.6%; Age 65 and over: 13.6%; Males per 100 females: 98.5; Marriage status: 43.6% never married, 37.6% now married, 0.0% separated, 6.9% widowed, 11.9% divorced; Foreign born: 0.0%; Speak English only: 100.0%; With disability: 15.3%; Veterans: 0.0%; Ancestry: 22.9% German, 14.4% American, 14.4% English, 6.8% Irish, 5.1% French
Employment: 0.0% management, business, and financial, 0.0% computer, engineering, and science, 5.0% education, legal, community service, arts, and media, 0.0% healthcare practitioners, 18.3% service, 25.0% sales and office, 31.7% natural resources, construction, and maintenance, 20.0% production, transportation, and material moving
Income: Per capita: $23,146; Median household: $45,625; Average household: $51,083; Households with income of $100,000 or more: 6.3%; Poverty rate: 10.2%
Educational Attainment: High school diploma or higher: 90.4%; Bachelor's degree or higher: 9.6%; Graduate/professional degree or higher: 4.1%
Housing: Homeownership rate: 81.3%; Median home value: $77,500; Median year structure built: 1960; Homeowner vacancy rate: 7.1%; Median selected monthly owner costs: $775 with a mortgage, n/a without a mortgage; Median gross rent: n/a per month; Rental vacancy rate: 0.0%
Health Insurance: 97.5% have insurance; 73.7% have private insurance; 37.3% have public insurance; 2.5% do not have insurance; 0.0% of children under 18 do not have insurance
Transportation: Commute: 79.3% car, 0.0% public transportation, 20.7% walk, 0.0% work from home; Mean travel time to work: 37.4 minutes

Hocking County

Located in south central Ohio; crossed by the Hocking River. Covers a land area of 421.323 square miles, a water area of 2.305 square miles, and is located in the Eastern Time Zone at 39.49° N. Lat., 82.48° W. Long. The county was founded in 1818. County seat is Logan.

Hocking County is part of the Columbus, OH Metropolitan Statistical Area. The entire metro area includes: Delaware County, OH; Fairfield County, OH; Franklin County, OH; Hocking County, OH; Licking County, OH; Madison County, OH; Morrow County, OH; Perry County, OH; Pickaway County, OH; Union County, OH

Population: 28,690; Growth (since 2000): 1.6%; Density: 68.1 persons per square mile; Race: 97.4% White, 0.9% Black/African American, 0.3% Asian, 0.0% American Indian/Alaska Native, 0.0% Native Hawaiian/Other Pacific Islander, 1.3% two or more races, 0.9% Hispanic of any race;

Average household size: 2.47; Median age: 42.7; Age under 18: 23.1%; Age 65 and over: 17.4%; Males per 100 females: 99.9; Marriage status: 22.2% never married, 57.5% now married, 2.2% separated, 7.3% widowed, 13.0% divorced; Foreign born: 1.0%; Speak English only: 98.8%; With disability: 17.3%; Veterans: 11.5%; Ancestry: 24.7% German, 13.4% Irish, 11.5% American, 10.4% English, 2.5% Italian
Religion: Six largest groups: 8.1% Methodist/Pietist, 4.2% Baptist, 3.4% Catholicism, 2.7% Holiness, 2.4% Lutheran, 2.0% Non-denominational Protestant
Economy: Unemployment rate: 4.4%; Leading industries: 15.8 % retail trade; 12.9 % accommodation and food services; 12.2 % construction; Farms: 367 totaling 38,085 acres; Company size: 0 employ 1,000 or more persons, 0 employ 500 to 999 persons, 7 employ 100 to 499 persons, 475 employ less than 100 persons; Business ownership: 648 women-owned, n/a Black-owned, n/a Hispanic-owned, n/a Asian-owned, n/a American Indian/Alaska Native-owned
Employment: 9.8% management, business, and financial, 2.4% computer, engineering, and science, 8.8% education, legal, community service, arts, and media, 7.0% healthcare practitioners, 20.7% service, 21.5% sales and office, 12.9% natural resources, construction, and maintenance, 16.8% production, transportation, and material moving
Income: Per capita: $22,091; Median household: $43,382; Average household: $55,110; Households with income of $100,000 or more: 13.4%; Poverty rate: 16.6%
Educational Attainment: High school diploma or higher: 88.4%; Bachelor's degree or higher: 14.1%; Graduate/professional degree or higher: 4.6%
Housing: Homeownership rate: 73.7%; Median home value: $114,400; Median year structure built: 1979; Homeowner vacancy rate: 2.4%; Median selected monthly owner costs: $1,080 with a mortgage, $361 without a mortgage; Median gross rent: $569 per month; Rental vacancy rate: 3.2%
Vital Statistics: Birth rate: 103.7 per 10,000 population; Death rate: 106.6 per 10,000 population; Age-adjusted cancer mortality rate: 164.0 deaths per 100,000 population
Health Insurance: 89.3% have insurance; 60.8% have private insurance; 42.9% have public insurance; 10.7% do not have insurance; 5.5% of children under 18 do not have insurance
Health Care: Physicians: 6.7 per 10,000 population; Dentists: 2.1 per 10,000 population; Hospital beds: 12.2 per 10,000 population; Hospital admissions: 428.9 per 10,000 population
Transportation: Commute: 93.0% car, 0.6% public transportation, 1.8% walk, 3.5% work from home; Mean travel time to work: 31.9 minutes
2016 Presidential Election: 65.7% Trump, 29.2% Clinton, 2.8% Johnson, 0.7% Stein
National and State Parks: Conkles Hollow State Nature Preserve; Hocking Hills State Park; Hocking State Forest; Lake Logan State Park; Sunday Creek State Wildlife Area; Wayne National Forest
Additional Information Contacts
Hocking Government. . . . . (740) 385-5195
http://www.co.hocking.oh.us

Hocking County Communities

CARBON HILL (CDP). Covers a land area of 0.405 square miles and a water area of 0.002 square miles. Located at 39.50° N. Lat; 82.24° W. Long. Elevation is 705 feet.
Population: 350; Growth (since 2000): n/a; Density: 865.3 persons per square mile; Race: 100.0% White, 0.0% Black/African American, 0.0% Asian, 0.0% American Indian/Alaska Native, 0.0% Native Hawaiian/Other Pacific Islander, 0.0% Two or more races, 0.0% Hispanic of any race; Average household size: 2.43; Median age: 40.2; Age under 18: 23.4%; Age 65 and over: 32.0%; Males per 100 females: 102.6; Marriage status: 39.8% never married, 42.2% now married, 0.0% separated, 15.6% widowed, 2.4% divorced; Foreign born: 0.0%; Speak English only: 100.0%; With disability: 24.0%; Veterans: 4.1%; Ancestry: 15.7% English, 14.0% German, 7.1% Scandinavian, 5.1% American, 2.0% Irish
Employment: 0.0% management, business, and financial, 0.0% computer, engineering, and science, 0.0% education, legal, community service, arts, and media, 0.0% healthcare practitioners, 69.9% service, 7.3% sales and office, 0.0% natural resources, construction, and maintenance, 22.8% production, transportation, and material moving
Income: Per capita: $15,641; Median household: $31,400; Average household: $38,440; Households with income of $100,000 or more: 3.5%; Poverty rate: 16.6%
Educational Attainment: High school diploma or higher: 88.7%; Bachelor's degree or higher: 3.6%; Graduate/professional degree or higher: 3.6%
Housing: Homeownership rate: 82.6%; Median home value: $71,200; Median year structure built: 1971; Homeowner vacancy rate: 0.0%; Median selected monthly owner costs: $810 with a mortgage, $462 without a mortgage; Median gross rent: n/a per month; Rental vacancy rate: 0.0%
Health Insurance: 84.0% have insurance; 58.0% have private insurance; 33.7% have public insurance; 16.0% do not have insurance; 0.0% of children under 18 do not have insurance
Transportation: Commute: 100.0% car, 0.0% public transportation, 0.0% walk, 0.0% work from home; Mean travel time to work: 29.0 minutes

HAYDENVILLE (CDP). Covers a land area of 0.856 square miles and a water area of 0.025 square miles. Located at 39.48° N. Lat; 82.32° W. Long. Elevation is 705 feet.
Population: 135; Growth (since 2000): n/a; Density: 157.8 persons per square mile; Race: 100.0% White, 0.0% Black/African American, 0.0% Asian, 0.0% American Indian/Alaska Native, 0.0% Native Hawaiian/Other Pacific Islander, 0.0% Two or more races, 0.0% Hispanic of any race; Average household size: 1.88; Median age: 54.8; Age under 18: 0.0%; Age 65 and over: 25.9%; Males per 100 females: 97.4; Marriage status: 25.9% never married, 44.4% now married, 0.0% separated, 20.0% widowed, 9.6% divorced; Foreign born: 0.0%; Speak English only: 100.0%; With disability: 36.3%; Veterans: 0.0%; Ancestry: 38.5% Irish, 23.7% German, 20.0% Czech, 20.0% Italian, 7.4% American
Employment: 0.0% management, business, and financial, 0.0% computer, engineering, and science, 0.0% education, legal, community service, arts, and media, 10.2% healthcare practitioners, 45.8% service, 35.6% sales and office, 8.5% natural resources, construction, and maintenance, 0.0% production, transportation, and material moving
Income: Per capita: $14,975; Median household: n/a; Average household: $28,726; Households with income of $100,000 or more: 8.3%; Poverty rate: 49.6%
Educational Attainment: High school diploma or higher: 92.1%; Bachelor's degree or higher: 4.7%; Graduate/professional degree or higher: 4.7%
Housing: Homeownership rate: 100.0%; Median home value: $112,800; Median year structure built: Before 1940; Homeowner vacancy rate: 0.0%; Median selected monthly owner costs: $811 with a mortgage, n/a without a mortgage; Median gross rent: n/a per month; Rental vacancy rate: 0.0%
Health Insurance: 90.4% have insurance; 40.7% have private insurance; 65.9% have public insurance; 9.6% do not have insurance; 0.0% of children under 18 do not have insurance
Transportation: Commute: 100.0% car, 0.0% public transportation, 0.0% walk, 0.0% work from home; Mean travel time to work: 0.0 minutes

HIDE-A-WAY HILLS (CDP). Covers a land area of 2.606 square miles and a water area of 0.218 square miles. Located at 39.65° N. Lat; 82.47° W. Long. Elevation is 948 feet.
Population: 662; Growth (since 2000): n/a; Density: 254.0 persons per square mile; Race: 93.7% White, 0.0% Black/African American, 0.0% Asian, 0.0% American Indian/Alaska Native, 0.0% Native Hawaiian/Other Pacific Islander, 6.3% Two or more races, 0.0% Hispanic of any race; Average household size: 2.28; Median age: 56.0; Age under 18: 7.6%; Age 65 and over: 9.1%; Males per 100 females: 105.2; Marriage status: 13.9% never married, 64.8% now married, 0.0% separated, 1.5% widowed, 19.8% divorced; Foreign born: 0.0%; Speak English only: 100.0%; With disability: 15.0%; Veterans: 5.9%; Ancestry: 29.5% German, 28.7% Irish, 10.9% English, 8.8% Italian, 8.3% Dutch
Employment: 13.4% management, business, and financial, 0.0% computer, engineering, and science, 18.7% education, legal, community service, arts, and media, 9.3% healthcare practitioners, 12.1% service, 15.2% sales and office, 12.6% natural resources, construction, and maintenance, 18.7% production, transportation, and material moving
Income: Per capita: $55,433; Median household: $120,347; Average household: $125,505; Households with income of $100,000 or more: 55.2%; Poverty rate: n/a
Educational Attainment: High school diploma or higher: 100.0%; Bachelor's degree or higher: 35.1%; Graduate/professional degree or higher: 2.1%
Housing: Homeownership rate: 100.0%; Median home value: $135,500; Median year structure built: 1975; Homeowner vacancy rate: 0.0%; Median selected monthly owner costs: $1,165 with a mortgage, $650 without a mortgage; Median gross rent: n/a per month; Rental vacancy rate: 0.0%

Health Insurance: 88.5% have insurance; 87.2% have private insurance; 10.6% have public insurance; 11.5% do not have insurance; 0.0% of children under 18 do not have insurance
Transportation: Commute: 89.7% car, 0.0% public transportation, 0.0% walk, 10.3% work from home; Mean travel time to work: 44.5 minutes

LAURELVILLE (village). Covers a land area of 0.209 square miles and a water area of 0.002 square miles. Located at 39.47° N. Lat; 82.74° W. Long. Elevation is 738 feet.
Population: 523; Growth (since 2000): -1.9%; Density: 2,508.0 persons per square mile; Race: 100.0% White, 0.0% Black/African American, 0.0% Asian, 0.0% American Indian/Alaska Native, 0.0% Native Hawaiian/Other Pacific Islander, 0.0% Two or more races, 0.0% Hispanic of any race; Average household size: 2.22; Median age: 37.6; Age under 18: 24.3%; Age 65 and over: 14.1%; Males per 100 females: 80.5; Marriage status: 31.5% never married, 37.4% now married, 5.0% separated, 10.0% widowed, 21.1% divorced; Foreign born: 0.0%; Speak English only: 100.0%; With disability: 27.3%; Veterans: 8.6%; Ancestry: 29.8% German, 24.7% Irish, 12.4% English, 6.5% French, 3.8% American
Employment: 5.7% management, business, and financial, 0.0% computer, engineering, and science, 8.1% education, legal, community service, arts, and media, 6.2% healthcare practitioners, 19.9% service, 29.4% sales and office, 13.7% natural resources, construction, and maintenance, 17.1% production, transportation, and material moving
Income: Per capita: $18,249; Median household: $25,682; Average household: $38,992; Households with income of $100,000 or more: 8.5%; Poverty rate: 27.3%
Educational Attainment: High school diploma or higher: 83.7%; Bachelor's degree or higher: 8.4%; Graduate/professional degree or higher: 0.9%

School District(s)

Logan Elm Local (PK-12)
2015-16 Enrollment: 1,826 . . . . (740) 474-7501
Housing: Homeownership rate: 45.3%; Median home value: $80,900; Median year structure built: 1970; Homeowner vacancy rate: 5.3%; Median selected monthly owner costs: $770 with a mortgage, $403 without a mortgage; Median gross rent: $412 per month; Rental vacancy rate: 0.0%
Health Insurance: 88.1% have insurance; 53.7% have private insurance; 48.8% have public insurance; 11.9% do not have insurance; 3.9% of children under 18 do not have insurance
Transportation: Commute: 93.2% car, 0.0% public transportation, 4.8% walk, 1.4% work from home; Mean travel time to work: 26.2 minutes

LOGAN (city). County seat. Covers a land area of 4.791 square miles and a water area of 0.139 square miles. Located at 39.54° N. Lat; 82.41° W. Long. Elevation is 741 feet.
History: Logan was founded in 1816 by Governor Thomas Worthington, who purchased a tract near the Hocking Falls and set up mills. Logan flourished with the opening of the Hocking Canal in 1840, and the completion of the Hocking Valley Railroad in 1869.
Population: 7,205; Growth (since 2000): 7.5%; Density: 1,503.9 persons per square mile; Race: 96.9% White, 1.2% Black/African American, 0.6% Asian, 0.0% American Indian/Alaska Native, 0.0% Native Hawaiian/Other Pacific Islander, 1.1% Two or more races, 0.2% Hispanic of any race; Average household size: 2.23; Median age: 39.2; Age under 18: 24.5%; Age 65 and over: 18.2%; Males per 100 females: 86.7; Marriage status: 25.7% never married, 48.9% now married, 2.1% separated, 8.8% widowed, 16.5% divorced; Foreign born: 1.4%; Speak English only: 98.8%; With disability: 21.5%; Veterans: 11.7%; Ancestry: 24.3% German, 13.2% Irish, 11.7% American, 11.6% English, 4.6% Italian
Employment: 5.5% management, business, and financial, 2.5% computer, engineering, and science, 12.2% education, legal, community service, arts, and media, 5.7% healthcare practitioners, 24.5% service, 25.8% sales and office, 8.6% natural resources, construction, and maintenance, 15.1% production, transportation, and material moving
Income: Per capita: $18,207; Median household: $31,096; Average household: $41,077; Households with income of $100,000 or more: 7.0%; Poverty rate: 22.6%
Educational Attainment: High school diploma or higher: 87.9%; Bachelor's degree or higher: 14.7%; Graduate/professional degree or higher: 5.0%

School District(s)

Logan-Hocking Local (PK-12)
2015-16 Enrollment: 3,819 . . . . (740) 385-8517
Housing: Homeownership rate: 53.7%; Median home value: $98,600; Median year structure built: 1959; Homeowner vacancy rate: 3.0%; Median selected monthly owner costs: $922 with a mortgage, $365 without a mortgage; Median gross rent: $566 per month; Rental vacancy rate: 1.7%
Health Insurance: 87.9% have insurance; 56.1% have private insurance; 46.5% have public insurance; 12.1% do not have insurance; 8.3% of children under 18 do not have insurance
Hospitals: Hocking Valley Community Hospital (93 beds)
Safety: Violent crime rate: 21.1 per 10,000 population; Property crime rate: 342.0 per 10,000 population
Newspapers: Logan Daily News (daily circulation 4,200)
Transportation: Commute: 91.4% car, 1.1% public transportation, 3.0% walk, 3.3% work from home; Mean travel time to work: 24.5 minutes

MURRAY CITY (village). Covers a land area of 0.317 square miles and a water area of <.001 square miles. Located at 39.51° N. Lat; 82.17° W. Long. Elevation is 712 feet.
Population: 350; Growth (since 2000): -22.6%; Density: 1,102.4 persons per square mile; Race: 98.3% White, 0.9% Black/African American, 0.0% Asian, 0.0% American Indian/Alaska Native, 0.0% Native Hawaiian/Other Pacific Islander, 0.9% Two or more races, 0.0% Hispanic of any race; Average household size: 2.26; Median age: 49.5; Age under 18: 14.9%; Age 65 and over: 26.0%; Males per 100 females: 99.6; Marriage status: 24.1% never married, 53.0% now married, 0.0% separated, 14.1% widowed, 8.8% divorced; Foreign born: 0.0%; Speak English only: 100.0%; With disability: 26.3%; Veterans: 14.4%; Ancestry: 22.0% German, 16.9% Irish, 13.1% English, 6.3% Dutch, 6.0% French
Employment: 4.2% management, business, and financial, 0.7% computer, engineering, and science, 11.3% education, legal, community service, arts, and media, 2.8% healthcare practitioners, 28.9% service, 27.5% sales and office, 12.0% natural resources, construction, and maintenance, 12.7% production, transportation, and material moving
Income: Per capita: $19,063; Median household: $34,554; Average household: $43,278; Households with income of $100,000 or more: 3.2%; Poverty rate: 10.0%
Educational Attainment: High school diploma or higher: 91.9%; Bachelor's degree or higher: 1.1%; Graduate/professional degree or higher: 0.4%
Housing: Homeownership rate: 69.7%; Median home value: $46,000; Median year structure built: Before 1940; Homeowner vacancy rate: 0.0%; Median selected monthly owner costs: $750 with a mortgage, $256 without a mortgage; Median gross rent: $517 per month; Rental vacancy rate: 4.1%
Health Insurance: 87.4% have insurance; 52.0% have private insurance; 47.7% have public insurance; 12.6% do not have insurance; 3.8% of children under 18 do not have insurance
Transportation: Commute: 98.6% car, 0.0% public transportation, 0.0% walk, 1.4% work from home; Mean travel time to work: 33.9 minutes

ROCKBRIDGE (CDP). Covers a land area of 0.378 square miles and a water area of 0 square miles. Located at 39.59° N. Lat; 82.53° W. Long. Elevation is 751 feet.
Population: 202; Growth (since 2000): n/a; Density: 534.8 persons per square mile; Race: 100.0% White, 0.0% Black/African American, 0.0% Asian, 0.0% American Indian/Alaska Native, 0.0% Native Hawaiian/Other Pacific Islander, 0.0% Two or more races, 0.0% Hispanic of any race; Average household size: 2.43; Median age: 43.1; Age under 18: 35.6%; Age 65 and over: 10.9%; Males per 100 females: 102.2; Marriage status: 27.5% never married, 16.9% now married, 0.0% separated, 20.6% widowed, 35.0% divorced; Foreign born: 4.0%; Speak English only: 100.0%; With disability: 15.8%; Veterans: 0.0%; Ancestry: 60.9% German, 14.9% Irish, 14.4% British, 6.9% English, 6.4% American
Employment: 0.0% management, business, and financial, 0.0% computer, engineering, and science, 0.0% education, legal, community service, arts, and media, 8.4% healthcare practitioners, 8.4% service, 50.6% sales and office, 0.0% natural resources, construction, and maintenance, 32.5% production, transportation, and material moving
Income: Per capita: $12,292; Median household: n/a; Average household: $30,776; Households with income of $100,000 or more: n/a; Poverty rate: 55.9%
Educational Attainment: High school diploma or higher: 93.8%; Bachelor's degree or higher: n/a; Graduate/professional degree or higher: n/a
Housing: Homeownership rate: 56.6%; Median home value: n/a; Median year structure built: 1942; Homeowner vacancy rate: 0.0%; Median

selected monthly owner costs: n/a with a mortgage, n/a without a mortgage; Median gross rent: n/a per month; Rental vacancy rate: 0.0%
Health Insurance: 65.3% have insurance; 23.8% have private insurance; 52.5% have public insurance; 34.7% do not have insurance; 0.0% of children under 18 do not have insurance
Transportation: Commute: 67.5% car, 0.0% public transportation, 0.0% walk, 0.0% work from home; Mean travel time to work: 23.1 minutes

SOUTH BLOOMINGVILLE (unincorporated postal area)

ZCTA: 43152

Covers a land area of 43.495 square miles and a water area of 0.169 square miles. Located at 39.40° N. Lat; 82.62° W. Long. Elevation is 702 feet.
Population: 780; Growth (since 2000): -29.0%; Density: 17.9 persons per square mile; Race: 92.4% White, 0.0% Black/African American, 0.0% Asian, 0.0% American Indian/Alaska Native, 0.0% Native Hawaiian/Other Pacific Islander, 7.6% Two or more races, 0.0% Hispanic of any race; Average household size: 2.51; Median age: 40.3; Age under 18: 26.7%; Age 65 and over: 17.6%; Males per 100 females: 101.5; Marriage status: 27.5% never married, 56.6% now married, 1.5% separated, 7.4% widowed, 8.5% divorced; Foreign born: 1.3%; Speak English only: 97.6%; With disability: 14.7%; Veterans: 14.0%; Ancestry: 32.6% German, 28.3% Irish, 5.1% American, 2.7% Dutch, 1.7% Swedish
Employment: 3.0% management, business, and financial, 1.5% computer, engineering, and science, 3.7% education, legal, community service, arts, and media, 11.9% healthcare practitioners, 17.5% service, 24.6% sales and office, 10.8% natural resources, construction, and maintenance, 26.9% production, transportation, and material moving
Income: Per capita: $20,397; Median household: $33,906; Average household: $50,907; Households with income of $100,000 or more: 15.8%; Poverty rate: 37.8%
Educational Attainment: High school diploma or higher: 89.5%; Bachelor's degree or higher: 8.1%; Graduate/professional degree or higher: 4.8%
Housing: Homeownership rate: 60.5%; Median home value: $81,600; Median year structure built: 1983; Homeowner vacancy rate: 0.0%; Median selected monthly owner costs: $736 with a mortgage, $321 without a mortgage; Median gross rent: $611 per month; Rental vacancy rate: 0.0%
Health Insurance: 99.1% have insurance; 43.7% have private insurance; 62.9% have public insurance; 0.9% do not have insurance; 0.0% of children under 18 do not have insurance
Transportation: Commute: 100.0% car, 0.0% public transportation, 0.0% walk, 0.0% work from home; Mean travel time to work: 47.1 minutes

UNION FURNACE (unincorporated postal area)

ZCTA: 43158

Covers a land area of 2.039 square miles and a water area of 0.009 square miles. Located at 39.45° N. Lat; 82.36° W. Long. Elevation is 748 feet.
Population: 227; Growth (since 2000): 86.1%; Density: 111.3 persons per square mile; Race: 95.6% White, 0.0% Black/African American, 0.0% Asian, 0.0% American Indian/Alaska Native, 0.0% Native Hawaiian/Other Pacific Islander, 4.4% Two or more races, 0.0% Hispanic of any race; Average household size: 2.41; Median age: 55.2; Age under 18: 17.6%; Age 65 and over: 7.0%; Males per 100 females: 103.0; Marriage status: 15.8% never married, 71.4% now married, 0.0% separated, 0.0% widowed, 12.8% divorced; Foreign born: 0.0%; Speak English only: 100.0%; With disability: 9.7%; Veterans: 20.9%; Ancestry: 12.3% English, 12.3% Irish, 11.9% German, 6.2% Welsh, 5.3% Scottish
Employment: 8.5% management, business, and financial, 0.0% computer, engineering, and science, 19.7% education, legal, community service, arts, and media, 9.9% healthcare practitioners, 0.0% service, 40.8% sales and office, 0.0% natural resources, construction, and maintenance, 21.1% production, transportation, and material moving
Income: Per capita: $14,295; Median household: $36,250; Average household: $34,018; Households with income of $100,000 or more: n/a; Poverty rate: 15.4%
Educational Attainment: High school diploma or higher: 76.3%; Bachelor's degree or higher: n/a; Graduate/professional degree or higher: n/a

School District(s)

Logan-Hocking Local (PK-12)
2015-16 Enrollment: 3,819 . . . . (740) 385-8517
Housing: Homeownership rate: 100.0%; Median home value: $59,300; Median year structure built: Before 1940; Homeowner vacancy rate: 0.0%; Median selected monthly owner costs: $881 with a mortgage, $290 without a mortgage; Median gross rent: n/a per month; Rental vacancy rate: 0.0%
Health Insurance: 89.9% have insurance; 70.9% have private insurance; 46.7% have public insurance; 10.1% do not have insurance; 0.0% of children under 18 do not have insurance
Transportation: Commute: 91.5% car, 0.0% public transportation, 0.0% walk, 8.5% work from home; Mean travel time to work: 19.3 minutes

Holmes County

Located in central Ohio; crossed by Killbuck Creek and Walhonding River. Covers a land area of 422.533 square miles, a water area of 1.446 square miles, and is located in the Eastern Time Zone at 40.57° N. Lat., 81.93° W. Long. The county was founded in 1824. County seat is Millersburg.

Weather Station: Millersburg Elevation: 818 feet

	Jan	Feb	Mar	Apr	May	Jun	Jul	Aug	Sep	Oct	Nov	Dec
High	36	39	49	62	71	80	84	83	76	64	52	39
Low	18	19	27	36	45	56	60	58	50	38	31	22
Precip	2.9	1.8	2.9	3.5	4.6	4.8	4.3	3.5	3.1	2.9	2.8	2.7
Snow	6.3	3.9	2.5	0.3	tr	0.0	0.0	0.0	0.0	tr	0.7	3.9

High and Low temperatures in degrees Fahrenheit; Precipitation and Snow in inches

Population: 43,702; Growth (since 2000): 12.2%; Density: 103.4 persons per square mile; Race: 98.6% White, 0.2% Black/African American, 0.1% Asian, 0.2% American Indian/Alaska Native, 0.0% Native Hawaiian/Other Pacific Islander, 0.9% two or more races, 0.9% Hispanic of any race; Average household size: 3.43; Median age: 30.6; Age under 18: 33.0%; Age 65 and over: 12.5%; Males per 100 females: 99.5; Marriage status: 28.4% never married, 59.8% now married, 0.6% separated, 5.1% widowed, 6.7% divorced; Foreign born: 0.7%; Speak English only: 53.5%; With disability: 8.8%; Veterans: 5.5%; Ancestry: 33.0% German, 10.9% American, 7.9% Swiss, 6.1% Irish, 5.4% Pennsylvania German
Religion: Six largest groups: 51.5% European Free-Church, 4.8% Baptist, 3.7% Methodist/Pietist, 2.8% Non-denominational Protestant, 1.7% Presbyterian-Reformed, 1.5% Catholicism
Economy: Unemployment rate: 3.2%; Leading industries: 24.2 % manufacturing; 18.7 % construction; 13.5 % retail trade; Farms: 1,969 totaling 220,948 acres; Company size: 0 employ 1,000 or more persons, 1 employs 500 to 999 persons, 27 employ 100 to 499 persons, 1,193 employ less than 100 persons; Business ownership: 1,405 women-owned, n/a Black-owned, 37 Hispanic-owned, n/a Asian-owned, n/a American Indian/Alaska Native-owned
Employment: 11.3% management, business, and financial, 1.8% computer, engineering, and science, 3.9% education, legal, community service, arts, and media, 3.0% healthcare practitioners, 14.1% service, 19.2% sales and office, 14.9% natural resources, construction, and maintenance, 31.8% production, transportation, and material moving
Income: Per capita: $19,517; Median household: $53,619; Average household: $66,693; Households with income of $100,000 or more: 16.7%; Poverty rate: 12.9%
Educational Attainment: High school diploma or higher: 58.5%; Bachelor's degree or higher: 7.7%; Graduate/professional degree or higher: 2.6%
Housing: Homeownership rate: 76.0%; Median home value: $170,500; Median year structure built: 1979; Homeowner vacancy rate: 0.4%; Median selected monthly owner costs: $1,114 with a mortgage, $392 without a mortgage; Median gross rent: $577 per month; Rental vacancy rate: 2.5%
Vital Statistics: Birth rate: 172.8 per 10,000 population; Death rate: 75.8 per 10,000 population; Age-adjusted cancer mortality rate: 182.6 deaths per 100,000 population
Health Insurance: 59.3% have insurance; 47.4% have private insurance; 19.9% have public insurance; 40.7% do not have insurance; 48.5% of children under 18 do not have insurance
Health Care: Physicians: 5.2 per 10,000 population; Dentists: 3.2 per 10,000 population; Hospital beds: 9.4 per 10,000 population; Hospital admissions: 328.9 per 10,000 population
Transportation: Commute: 73.6% car, 0.3% public transportation, 6.8% walk, 8.4% work from home; Mean travel time to work: 20.7 minutes
2016 Presidential Election: 78.5% Trump, 16.1% Clinton, 3.4% Johnson, 0.5% Stein
Additional Information Contacts
Holmes Government . . . . (330) 674-0286
http://www.co.holmes.oh.us

Holmes County Communities

BERLIN (CDP). Covers a land area of 1.411 square miles and a water area of <.001 square miles. Located at 40.57° N. Lat; 81.81° W. Long. Elevation is 1,293 feet.
Population: 1,193; Growth (since 2000): n/a; Density: 845.3 persons per square mile; Race: 97.8% White, 0.0% Black/African American, 0.0% Asian, 0.0% American Indian/Alaska Native, 0.0% Native Hawaiian/Other Pacific Islander, 2.2% Two or more races, 1.1% Hispanic of any race; Average household size: 3.03; Median age: 36.5; Age under 18: 19.6%; Age 65 and over: 11.3%; Males per 100 females: 97.8; Marriage status: 33.8% never married, 54.1% now married, 0.0% separated, 6.2% widowed, 5.8% divorced; Foreign born: 0.0%; Speak English only: 72.3%; With disability: 8.0%; Veterans: 0.0%; Ancestry: 39.3% German, 11.6% American, 10.1% Swiss, 9.7% English, 9.5% Pennsylvania German
Employment: 9.7% management, business, and financial, 0.5% computer, engineering, and science, 3.8% education, legal, community service, arts, and media, 0.0% healthcare practitioners, 9.6% service, 31.3% sales and office, 13.8% natural resources, construction, and maintenance, 31.3% production, transportation, and material moving
Income: Per capita: $28,142; Median household: $77,500; Average household: $82,821; Households with income of $100,000 or more: 36.1%; Poverty rate: 8.5%
Educational Attainment: High school diploma or higher: 76.6%; Bachelor's degree or higher: 18.3%; Graduate/professional degree or higher: 4.1%

School District(s)

East Holmes Local (KG-12)
2015-16 Enrollment: 1,690 . . . . (330) 893-2610
Housing: Homeownership rate: 88.3%; Median home value: $184,400; Median year structure built: 1983; Homeowner vacancy rate: 0.0%; Median selected monthly owner costs: $1,634 with a mortgage, $441 without a mortgage; Median gross rent: $704 per month; Rental vacancy rate: 0.0%
Health Insurance: 91.5% have insurance; 86.4% have private insurance; 10.3% have public insurance; 8.5% do not have insurance; 0.0% of children under 18 do not have insurance
Transportation: Commute: 81.9% car, 0.0% public transportation, 6.9% walk, 11.3% work from home; Mean travel time to work: 9.4 minutes

BIG PRAIRIE (unincorporated postal area)
ZCTA: 44611
Covers a land area of 29.071 square miles and a water area of 0.048 square miles. Located at 40.61° N. Lat; 82.07° W. Long. Elevation is 951 feet.
Population: 2,041; Growth (since 2000): 0.6%; Density: 70.2 persons per square mile; Race: 100.0% White, 0.0% Black/African American, 0.0% Asian, 0.0% American Indian/Alaska Native, 0.0% Native Hawaiian/Other Pacific Islander, 0.0% Two or more races, 7.0% Hispanic of any race; Average household size: 2.63; Median age: 44.1; Age under 18: 21.2%; Age 65 and over: 19.2%; Males per 100 females: 100.3; Marriage status: 25.8% never married, 58.4% now married, 0.0% separated, 8.9% widowed, 6.9% divorced; Foreign born: 0.3%; Speak English only: 92.1%; With disability: 15.9%; Veterans: 10.3%; Ancestry: 29.1% German, 9.4% American, 9.4% English, 9.3% Irish, 4.9% European
Employment: 17.2% management, business, and financial, 0.8% computer, engineering, and science, 3.5% education, legal, community service, arts, and media, 2.4% healthcare practitioners, 12.9% service, 24.5% sales and office, 11.7% natural resources, construction, and maintenance, 26.9% production, transportation, and material moving
Income: Per capita: $23,405; Median household: $46,806; Average household: $60,664; Households with income of $100,000 or more: 14.7%; Poverty rate: 21.2%
Educational Attainment: High school diploma or higher: 83.0%; Bachelor's degree or higher: 7.5%; Graduate/professional degree or higher: 3.1%
Housing: Homeownership rate: 83.4%; Median home value: $119,100; Median year structure built: 1973; Homeowner vacancy rate: 4.0%; Median selected monthly owner costs: $1,126 with a mortgage, $342 without a mortgage; Median gross rent: $602 per month; Rental vacancy rate: 0.0%
Health Insurance: 87.5% have insurance; 64.0% have private insurance; 36.1% have public insurance; 12.5% do not have insurance; 11.3% of children under 18 do not have insurance
Transportation: Commute: 87.7% car, 0.0% public transportation, 8.5% walk, 3.8% work from home; Mean travel time to work: 34.3 minutes

BRINKHAVEN (unincorporated postal area)
ZCTA: 43006
Covers a land area of 23.906 square miles and a water area of 0.060 square miles. Located at 40.46° N. Lat; 82.15° W. Long..
Population: 611; Growth (since 2000): 2.3%; Density: 25.6 persons per square mile; Race: 100.0% White, 0.0% Black/African American, 0.0% Asian, 0.0% American Indian/Alaska Native, 0.0% Native Hawaiian/Other Pacific Islander, 0.0% Two or more races, 0.0% Hispanic of any race; Average household size: 2.61; Median age: 50.7; Age under 18: 18.3%; Age 65 and over: 26.2%; Males per 100 females: 102.5; Marriage status: 12.2% never married, 65.9% now married, 0.0% separated, 5.8% widowed, 16.0% divorced; Foreign born: 0.0%; Speak English only: 84.5%; With disability: 21.6%; Veterans: 7.8%; Ancestry: 18.3% German, 9.3% English, 8.2% American, 7.5% Irish, 3.4% Scottish
Employment: 19.3% management, business, and financial, 0.0% computer, engineering, and science, 1.8% education, legal, community service, arts, and media, 4.7% healthcare practitioners, 6.2% service, 15.7% sales and office, 8.0% natural resources, construction, and maintenance, 44.2% production, transportation, and material moving
Income: Per capita: $26,906; Median household: $51,346; Average household: $69,086; Households with income of $100,000 or more: 21.8%; Poverty rate: 15.2%
Educational Attainment: High school diploma or higher: 67.1%; Bachelor's degree or higher: 2.9%; Graduate/professional degree or higher: n/a
Housing: Homeownership rate: 85.5%; Median home value: $90,000; Median year structure built: Before 1940; Homeowner vacancy rate: 5.7%; Median selected monthly owner costs: $731 with a mortgage, $424 without a mortgage; Median gross rent: $800 per month; Rental vacancy rate: 0.0%
Health Insurance: 77.3% have insurance; 67.8% have private insurance; 30.4% have public insurance; 22.7% do not have insurance; 47.3% of children under 18 do not have insurance
Transportation: Commute: 91.4% car, 0.0% public transportation, 0.0% walk, 2.2% work from home; Mean travel time to work: 35.3 minutes

GLENMONT (village). Covers a land area of 0.268 square miles and a water area of 0 square miles. Located at 40.52° N. Lat; 82.09° W. Long. Elevation is 886 feet.
History: Glenmont grew up around the sandstone quarries that furnished the material for some of New York's brownstone houses.
Population: 238; Growth (since 2000): -15.9%; Density: 886.5 persons per square mile; Race: 98.7% White, 0.0% Black/African American, 0.0% Asian, 0.0% American Indian/Alaska Native, 0.0% Native Hawaiian/Other Pacific Islander, 1.3% Two or more races, 0.0% Hispanic of any race; Average household size: 2.43; Median age: 36.3; Age under 18: 23.9%; Age 65 and over: 14.7%; Males per 100 females: 101.5; Marriage status: 19.3% never married, 55.2% now married, 1.0% separated, 9.9% widowed, 15.6% divorced; Foreign born: 1.3%; Speak English only: 99.1%; With disability: 10.9%; Veterans: 9.4%; Ancestry: 38.2% German, 21.8% Irish, 9.2% English, 8.8% American, 3.8% Scottish
Employment: 2.5% management, business, and financial, 5.8% computer, engineering, and science, 2.5% education, legal, community service, arts, and media, 6.6% healthcare practitioners, 10.7% service, 13.2% sales and office, 15.7% natural resources, construction, and maintenance, 43.0% production, transportation, and material moving
Income: Per capita: $21,274; Median household: $41,923; Average household: $52,156; Households with income of $100,000 or more: 10.2%; Poverty rate: 4.2%
Educational Attainment: High school diploma or higher: 84.0%; Bachelor's degree or higher: 6.2%; Graduate/professional degree or higher: 1.9%
Housing: Homeownership rate: 85.7%; Median home value: $73,800; Median year structure built: 1953; Homeowner vacancy rate: 5.6%; Median selected monthly owner costs: $813 with a mortgage, $350 without a mortgage; Median gross rent: $563 per month; Rental vacancy rate: 0.0%
Health Insurance: 87.4% have insurance; 62.6% have private insurance; 37.8% have public insurance; 12.6% do not have insurance; 0.0% of children under 18 do not have insurance
Transportation: Commute: 98.3% car, 0.0% public transportation, 0.0% walk, 1.7% work from home; Mean travel time to work: 29.1 minutes

HOLMESVILLE (village). Covers a land area of 0.226 square miles and a water area of 0.007 square miles. Located at 40.63° N. Lat; 81.92° W. Long. Elevation is 863 feet.

Population: 412; Growth (since 2000): 6.7%; Density: 1,823.9 persons per square mile; Race: 100.0% White, 0.0% Black/African American, 0.0% Asian, 0.0% American Indian/Alaska Native, 0.0% Native Hawaiian/Other Pacific Islander, 0.0% Two or more races, 0.0% Hispanic of any race; Average household size: 2.66; Median age: 37.9; Age under 18: 25.5%; Age 65 and over: 13.1%; Males per 100 females: 98.9; Marriage status: 26.8% never married, 51.6% now married, 0.0% separated, 7.4% widowed, 14.2% divorced; Foreign born: 0.0%; Speak English only: 92.4%; With disability: 17.7%; Veterans: 10.4%; Ancestry: 46.1% German, 17.7% English, 14.8% Irish, 6.8% Dutch, 6.1% Polish

Employment: 5.1% management, business, and financial, 4.3% computer, engineering, and science, 7.3% education, legal, community service, arts, and media, 6.8% healthcare practitioners, 16.2% service, 19.2% sales and office, 21.4% natural resources, construction, and maintenance, 19.7% production, transportation, and material moving

Income: Per capita: $21,070; Median household: $46,964; Average household: $52,528; Households with income of $100,000 or more: 9.7%; Poverty rate: 7.5%

Educational Attainment: High school diploma or higher: 95.1%; Bachelor's degree or higher: 4.2%; Graduate/professional degree or higher: 1.1%

School District(s)

Southeast Local (KG-12)
2015-16 Enrollment: 1,408 . . . . (330) 698-3001

Housing: Homeownership rate: 71.6%; Median home value: $92,200; Median year structure built: 1955; Homeowner vacancy rate: 0.0%; Median selected monthly owner costs: $950 with a mortgage, $361 without a mortgage; Median gross rent: $713 per month; Rental vacancy rate: 8.3%

Health Insurance: 89.6% have insurance; 73.8% have private insurance; 23.5% have public insurance; 10.4% do not have insurance; 4.8% of children under 18 do not have insurance

Transportation: Commute: 93.0% car, 0.0% public transportation, 2.2% walk, 0.0% work from home; Mean travel time to work: 19.7 minutes

KILLBUCK (village). Covers a land area of 0.357 square miles and a water area of 0 square miles. Located at 40.50° N. Lat; 81.98° W. Long. Elevation is 810 feet.

History: Killbuck was settled in 1811, and named for the creek on which it was established.

Population: 1,080; Growth (since 2000): 28.7%; Density: 3,023.3 persons per square mile; Race: 93.2% White, 0.5% Black/African American, 3.0% Asian, 0.0% American Indian/Alaska Native, 0.0% Native Hawaiian/Other Pacific Islander, 3.3% Two or more races, 1.8% Hispanic of any race; Average household size: 2.57; Median age: 36.5; Age under 18: 27.9%; Age 65 and over: 16.9%; Males per 100 females: 80.8; Marriage status: 26.8% never married, 48.3% now married, 2.7% separated, 8.9% widowed, 16.0% divorced; Foreign born: 2.6%; Speak English only: 93.0%; With disability: 19.2%; Veterans: 8.7%; Ancestry: 28.5% German, 13.3% Irish, 6.4% American, 6.2% English, 3.1% Polish

Employment: 3.2% management, business, and financial, 5.6% computer, engineering, and science, 6.5% education, legal, community service, arts, and media, 0.6% healthcare practitioners, 19.4% service, 27.2% sales and office, 10.1% natural resources, construction, and maintenance, 27.4% production, transportation, and material moving

Income: Per capita: $17,151; Median household: $38,500; Average household: $43,499; Households with income of $100,000 or more: 7.9%; Poverty rate: 25.1%

Educational Attainment: High school diploma or higher: 82.9%; Bachelor's degree or higher: 4.3%; Graduate/professional degree or higher: 1.7%

School District(s)

West Holmes Local (KG-12)
2015-16 Enrollment: 2,229 . . . . (330) 674-3546

Housing: Homeownership rate: 57.9%; Median home value: $88,300; Median year structure built: 1958; Homeowner vacancy rate: 0.0%; Median selected monthly owner costs: $1,000 with a mortgage, $359 without a mortgage; Median gross rent: $589 per month; Rental vacancy rate: 3.8%

Health Insurance: 89.6% have insurance; 55.2% have private insurance; 48.0% have public insurance; 10.4% do not have insurance; 4.7% of children under 18 do not have insurance

Transportation: Commute: 98.4% car, 1.6% public transportation, 0.0% walk, 0.0% work from home; Mean travel time to work: 22.7 minutes

LAKE BUCKHORN (CDP). Covers a land area of 1.757 square miles and a water area of 0.255 square miles. Located at 40.47° N. Lat; 81.91° W. Long.

Population: 803; Growth (since 2000): n/a; Density: 457.0 persons per square mile; Race: 91.2% White, 0.0% Black/African American, 0.0% Asian, 0.0% American Indian/Alaska Native, 0.0% Native Hawaiian/Other Pacific Islander, 8.8% Two or more races, 0.0% Hispanic of any race; Average household size: 3.20; Median age: 44.3; Age under 18: 25.7%; Age 65 and over: 15.4%; Males per 100 females: 97.7; Marriage status: 17.8% never married, 77.1% now married, 0.0% separated, 1.4% widowed, 3.7% divorced; Foreign born: 0.0%; Speak English only: 96.6%; With disability: 11.1%; Veterans: 14.9%; Ancestry: 17.7% German, 11.8% English, 6.5% Irish, 5.7% American, 3.2% Scottish

Employment: 13.1% management, business, and financial, 10.4% computer, engineering, and science, 15.7% education, legal, community service, arts, and media, 10.8% healthcare practitioners, 20.1% service, 14.6% sales and office, 0.0% natural resources, construction, and maintenance, 15.3% production, transportation, and material moving

Income: Per capita: $20,535; Median household: $50,637; Average household: $62,257; Households with income of $100,000 or more: 20.7%; Poverty rate: 6.6%

Educational Attainment: High school diploma or higher: 98.5%; Bachelor's degree or higher: 29.2%; Graduate/professional degree or higher: 20.5%

Housing: Homeownership rate: 100.0%; Median home value: $194,400; Median year structure built: 1987; Homeowner vacancy rate: 0.0%; Median selected monthly owner costs: $1,753 with a mortgage, $531 without a mortgage; Median gross rent: n/a per month; Rental vacancy rate: 0.0%

Health Insurance: 81.9% have insurance; 81.9% have private insurance; 21.2% have public insurance; 18.1% do not have insurance; 0.0% of children under 18 do not have insurance

Transportation: Commute: 88.5% car, 0.0% public transportation, 0.0% walk, 11.5% work from home; Mean travel time to work: 18.8 minutes

LAKEVILLE (unincorporated postal area)

ZCTA: 44638

Covers a land area of 28.111 square miles and a water area of 0.420 square miles. Located at 40.65° N. Lat; 82.14° W. Long. Elevation is 961 feet.

Population: 1,422; Growth (since 2000): -7.2%; Density: 50.6 persons per square mile; Race: 97.5% White, 0.0% Black/African American, 0.0% Asian, 0.0% American Indian/Alaska Native, 0.0% Native Hawaiian/Other Pacific Islander, 0.0% Two or more races, 2.5% Hispanic of any race; Average household size: 2.63; Median age: 48.1; Age under 18: 15.2%; Age 65 and over: 22.5%; Males per 100 females: 102.0; Marriage status: 20.3% never married, 64.2% now married, 2.1% separated, 6.3% widowed, 9.1% divorced; Foreign born: 0.0%; Speak English only: 91.6%; With disability: 8.8%; Veterans: 9.2%; Ancestry: 35.7% German, 17.5% Irish, 9.0% American, 6.8% English, 4.2% French

Employment: 10.7% management, business, and financial, 2.1% computer, engineering, and science, 1.2% education, legal, community service, arts, and media, 6.7% healthcare practitioners, 15.0% service, 20.4% sales and office, 13.4% natural resources, construction, and maintenance, 30.3% production, transportation, and material moving

Income: Per capita: $32,125; Median household: $60,100; Average household: $83,589; Households with income of $100,000 or more: 24.5%; Poverty rate: 13.2%

Educational Attainment: High school diploma or higher: 85.2%; Bachelor's degree or higher: 13.3%; Graduate/professional degree or higher: 1.5%

School District(s)

West Holmes Local (KG-12)
2015-16 Enrollment: 2,229 . . . . (330) 674-3546

Housing: Homeownership rate: 76.1%; Median home value: $162,900; Median year structure built: 1975; Homeowner vacancy rate: 0.0%; Median selected monthly owner costs: $952 with a mortgage, $495 without a mortgage; Median gross rent: $634 per month; Rental vacancy rate: 3.7%

Health Insurance: 82.6% have insurance; 63.8% have private insurance; 32.4% have public insurance; 17.4% do not have insurance; 40.7% of children under 18 do not have insurance

Transportation: Commute: 95.1% car, 0.0% public transportation, 1.4% walk, 2.7% work from home; Mean travel time to work: 29.0 minutes

MILLERSBURG (village). County seat. Covers a land area of 2.217 square miles and a water area of 0.009 square miles. Located at 40.55° N. Lat; 81.91° W. Long. Elevation is 892 feet.

History: Settlement in Millersburg began in 1816, when many "Pennsylvania Dutch" came here. The town has been the seat of Holmes County since 1824.

Population: 3,140; Growth (since 2000): -5.6%; Density: 1,416.3 persons per square mile; Race: 96.8% White, 0.5% Black/African American, 0.0% Asian, 0.0% American Indian/Alaska Native, 0.0% Native Hawaiian/Other Pacific Islander, 2.5% Two or more races, 4.6% Hispanic of any race; Average household size: 2.22; Median age: 43.0; Age under 18: 20.6%; Age 65 and over: 17.6%; Males per 100 females: 86.2; Marriage status: 29.2% never married, 41.6% now married, 1.2% separated, 6.3% widowed, 22.9% divorced; Foreign born: 3.2%; Speak English only: 92.1%; With disability: 18.8%; Veterans: 7.6%; Ancestry: 32.0% German, 14.6% Irish, 10.6% American, 7.5% English, 5.8% Swiss

Employment: 8.1% management, business, and financial, 2.7% computer, engineering, and science, 1.5% education, legal, community service, arts, and media, 2.5% healthcare practitioners, 26.0% service, 18.4% sales and office, 9.9% natural resources, construction, and maintenance, 30.8% production, transportation, and material moving

Income: Per capita: $20,225; Median household: $36,829; Average household: $45,402; Households with income of $100,000 or more: 6.4%; Poverty rate: 16.3%

Educational Attainment: High school diploma or higher: 86.2%; Bachelor's degree or higher: 10.0%; Graduate/professional degree or higher: 3.3%

School District(s)

East Holmes Local (KG-12)
2015-16 Enrollment: 1,690 . . . . (330) 893-2610
West Holmes Local (KG-12)
2015-16 Enrollment: 2,229 . . . . (330) 674-3546

Housing: Homeownership rate: 50.0%; Median home value: $100,700; Median year structure built: 1967; Homeowner vacancy rate: 0.0%; Median selected monthly owner costs: $944 with a mortgage, $422 without a mortgage; Median gross rent: $545 per month; Rental vacancy rate: 0.0%

Health Insurance: 86.8% have insurance; 65.0% have private insurance; 35.4% have public insurance; 13.2% do not have insurance; 2.5% of children under 18 do not have insurance

Hospitals: Pomerene Hospital (55 beds)

Safety: Violent crime rate: 9.5 per 10,000 population; Property crime rate: 286.7 per 10,000 population

Newspapers: Holmes County Hub (weekly circulation 4,400)

Transportation: Commute: 95.9% car, 0.0% public transportation, 2.0% walk, 1.4% work from home; Mean travel time to work: 16.8 minutes

Additional Information Contacts

Village of Millersburg . . . . (330) 674-1886
http://www.millersburgohio.com

NASHVILLE (village). Covers a land area of 0.075 square miles and a water area of 0 square miles. Located at 40.60° N. Lat; 82.11° W. Long. Elevation is 1,234 feet.

Population: 200; Growth (since 2000): 16.3%; Density: 2,682.4 persons per square mile; Race: 97.0% White, 0.0% Black/African American, 0.0% Asian, 0.0% American Indian/Alaska Native, 0.0% Native Hawaiian/Other Pacific Islander, 3.0% Two or more races, 0.0% Hispanic of any race; Average household size: 2.63; Median age: 36.0; Age under 18: 33.0%; Age 65 and over: 17.0%; Males per 100 females: 105.2; Marriage status: 23.5% never married, 63.1% now married, 4.7% separated, 5.4% widowed, 8.1% divorced; Foreign born: 0.0%; Speak English only: 100.0%; With disability: 22.5%; Veterans: 13.4%; Ancestry: 43.5% German, 24.0% Irish, 6.0% Scottish, 5.5% Russian, 5.0% English

Employment: 4.3% management, business, and financial, 0.0% computer, engineering, and science, 10.0% education, legal, community service, arts, and media, 2.9% healthcare practitioners, 8.6% service, 28.6% sales and office, 18.6% natural resources, construction, and maintenance, 27.1% production, transportation, and material moving

Income: Per capita: $14,421; Median household: $31,364; Average household: $38,996; Households with income of $100,000 or more: 1.3%; Poverty rate: 25.0%

Educational Attainment: High school diploma or higher: 81.5%; Bachelor's degree or higher: 7.7%; Graduate/professional degree or higher: 1.5%

School District(s)

West Holmes Local (KG-12)
2015-16 Enrollment: 2,229 . . . . (330) 674-3546

Housing: Homeownership rate: 80.3%; Median home value: $73,800; Median year structure built: Before 1940; Homeowner vacancy rate: 0.0%; Median selected monthly owner costs: $925 with a mortgage, $382 without a mortgage; Median gross rent: n/a per month; Rental vacancy rate: 25.0%

Health Insurance: 88.5% have insurance; 54.0% have private insurance; 51.0% have public insurance; 11.5% do not have insurance; 3.0% of children under 18 do not have insurance

Transportation: Commute: 91.4% car, 0.0% public transportation, 2.9% walk, 5.7% work from home; Mean travel time to work: 29.5 minutes

WALNUT CREEK (CDP). Covers a land area of 2.223 square miles and a water area of 0.002 square miles. Located at 40.55° N. Lat; 81.73° W. Long. Elevation is 1,188 feet.

Population: 1,188; Growth (since 2000): n/a; Density: 534.3 persons per square mile; Race: 99.0% White, 1.0% Black/African American, 0.0% Asian, 0.0% American Indian/Alaska Native, 0.0% Native Hawaiian/Other Pacific Islander, 0.0% Two or more races, 0.0% Hispanic of any race; Average household size: 3.22; Median age: 34.4; Age under 18: 31.2%; Age 65 and over: 24.1%; Males per 100 females: 74.6; Marriage status: 12.6% never married, 63.2% now married, 0.7% separated, 13.8% widowed, 10.4% divorced; Foreign born: 0.6%; Speak English only: 57.8%; With disability: 3.2%; Veterans: 9.1%; Ancestry: 32.9% German, 13.2% American, 9.6% Swiss, 4.8% English, 3.9% Irish

Employment: 14.4% management, business, and financial, 0.0% computer, engineering, and science, 5.6% education, legal, community service, arts, and media, 8.6% healthcare practitioners, 6.1% service, 31.1% sales and office, 19.5% natural resources, construction, and maintenance, 14.7% production, transportation, and material moving

Income: Per capita: $18,010; Median household: $48,824; Average household: $63,283; Households with income of $100,000 or more: 6.1%; Poverty rate: 9.3%

Educational Attainment: High school diploma or higher: 57.4%; Bachelor's degree or higher: 6.6%; Graduate/professional degree or higher: 2.9%

School District(s)

East Holmes Local (KG-12)
2015-16 Enrollment: 1,690 . . . . (330) 893-2610

Housing: Homeownership rate: 70.7%; Median home value: $293,500; Median year structure built: 1974; Homeowner vacancy rate: 0.0%; Median selected monthly owner costs: $1,205 with a mortgage, $434 without a mortgage; Median gross rent: $642 per month; Rental vacancy rate: 0.0%

Health Insurance: 69.9% have insurance; 60.8% have private insurance; 14.4% have public insurance; 30.1% do not have insurance; 47.7% of children under 18 do not have insurance

Transportation: Commute: 81.3% car, 2.0% public transportation, 5.1% walk, 4.1% work from home; Mean travel time to work: 23.8 minutes

WINESBURG (CDP). Covers a land area of 0.627 square miles and a water area of 0.003 square miles. Located at 40.62° N. Lat; 81.69° W. Long. Elevation is 1,306 feet.

Population: 345; Growth (since 2000): n/a; Density: 550.0 persons per square mile; Race: 100.0% White, 0.0% Black/African American, 0.0% Asian, 0.0% American Indian/Alaska Native, 0.0% Native Hawaiian/Other Pacific Islander, 0.0% Two or more races, 0.0% Hispanic of any race; Average household size: 2.92; Median age: 48.0; Age under 18: 16.8%; Age 65 and over: 40.0%; Males per 100 females: 91.3; Marriage status: 26.1% never married, 66.9% now married, 0.0% separated, 3.1% widowed, 3.8% divorced; Foreign born: 0.0%; Speak English only: 64.3%; With disability: 8.7%; Veterans: 9.1%; Ancestry: 39.1% German, 31.6% Swiss, 24.9% American, 16.2% English, 13.9% Irish

Employment: 3.3% management, business, and financial, 0.0% computer, engineering, and science, 2.9% education, legal, community service, arts, and media, 3.7% healthcare practitioners, 16.5% service, 14.8% sales and office, 2.5% natural resources, construction, and maintenance, 56.4% production, transportation, and material moving

Income: Per capita: $23,018; Median household: $78,000; Average household: $67,625; Households with income of $100,000 or more: 6.8%; Poverty rate: n/a

Educational Attainment: High school diploma or higher: 77.7%; Bachelor's degree or higher: 5.2%; Graduate/professional degree or higher: n/a

School District(s)

East Holmes Local (KG-12)
2015-16 Enrollment: 1,690 . . . . (330) 893-2610

Housing: Homeownership rate: 83.1%; Median home value: $181,600; Median year structure built: 1975; Homeowner vacancy rate: 0.0%; Median selected monthly owner costs: $1,810 with a mortgage, $248 without a mortgage; Median gross rent: n/a per month; Rental vacancy rate: 0.0%
Health Insurance: 82.6% have insurance; 82.6% have private insurance; 35.1% have public insurance; 17.4% do not have insurance; 67.2% of children under 18 do not have insurance
Transportation: Commute: 80.7% car, 0.0% public transportation, 11.1% walk, 0.0% work from home; Mean travel time to work: 10.4 minutes

Huron County

Located in northern Ohio; drained by the Huron and Vermilion Rivers. Covers a land area of 491.495 square miles, a water area of 3.327 square miles, and is located in the Eastern Time Zone at 41.15° N. Lat., 82.59° W. Long. The county was founded in 1815. County seat is Norwalk.

Huron County is part of the Norwalk, OH Micropolitan Statistical Area. The entire metro area includes: Huron County, OH

Weather Station: Norwalk Wwtp Elevation: 669 feet

	Jan	Feb	Mar	Apr	May	Jun	Jul	Aug	Sep	Oct	Nov	Dec
High	33	36	45	58	69	78	82	81	74	62	50	37
Low	18	20	28	38	49	58	62	61	53	42	34	24
Precip	2.3	2.0	2.7	3.5	3.8	4.2	3.9	3.7	3.3	2.7	3.0	2.8
Snow	8.9	6.0	5.4	1.3	tr	0.0	0.0	tr	0.0	tr	1.4	6.3

High and Low temperatures in degrees Fahrenheit; Precipitation and Snow in inches

Population: 58,704; Growth (since 2000): -1.3%; Density: 119.4 persons per square mile; Race: 94.8% White, 1.5% Black/African American, 0.3% Asian, 0.1% American Indian/Alaska Native, 0.0% Native Hawaiian/Other Pacific Islander, 1.8% two or more races, 6.0% Hispanic of any race; Average household size: 2.57; Median age: 39.4; Age under 18: 24.9%; Age 65 and over: 15.4%; Males per 100 females: 97.1; Marriage status: 27.3% never married, 53.7% now married, 1.5% separated, 6.5% widowed, 12.5% divorced; Foreign born: 2.7%; Speak English only: 93.3%; With disability: 13.6%; Veterans: 8.8%; Ancestry: 34.0% German, 13.7% Irish, 10.2% English, 10.0% American, 4.6% Italian
Religion: Six largest groups: 23.4% Catholicism, 5.4% Methodist/Pietist, 3.8% Lutheran, 3.6% Holiness, 3.0% Baptist, 2.5% Non-denominational Protestant
Economy: Unemployment rate: 4.8%; Leading industries: 15.4 % retail trade; 14.4 % other services (except public administration); 11.3 % construction; Farms: 865 totaling 238,291 acres; Company size: 0 employ 1,000 or more persons, 4 employ 500 to 999 persons, 19 employ 100 to 499 persons, 1,109 employ less than 100 persons; Business ownership: 1,096 women-owned, 88 Black-owned, 119 Hispanic-owned, n/a Asian-owned, n/a American Indian/Alaska Native-owned
Employment: 9.5% management, business, and financial, 2.3% computer, engineering, and science, 6.9% education, legal, community service, arts, and media, 5.2% healthcare practitioners, 16.1% service, 19.6% sales and office, 12.9% natural resources, construction, and maintenance, 27.4% production, transportation, and material moving
Income: Per capita: $23,698; Median household: $48,838; Average household: $60,699; Households with income of $100,000 or more: 14.8%; Poverty rate: 12.9%
Educational Attainment: High school diploma or higher: 87.7%; Bachelor's degree or higher: 13.5%; Graduate/professional degree or higher: 4.5%
Housing: Homeownership rate: 70.7%; Median home value: $117,000; Median year structure built: 1966; Homeowner vacancy rate: 1.7%; Median selected monthly owner costs: $1,089 with a mortgage, $410 without a mortgage; Median gross rent: $634 per month; Rental vacancy rate: 10.3%
Vital Statistics: Birth rate: 124.6 per 10,000 population; Death rate: 96.5 per 10,000 population; Age-adjusted cancer mortality rate: 143.6 deaths per 100,000 population
Health Insurance: 90.7% have insurance; 68.8% have private insurance; 36.1% have public insurance; 9.3% do not have insurance; 6.6% of children under 18 do not have insurance
Health Care: Physicians: 11.1 per 10,000 population; Dentists: 3.3 per 10,000 population; Hospital beds: 37.0 per 10,000 population; Hospital admissions: 1,035.7 per 10,000 population
Transportation: Commute: 92.4% car, 0.8% public transportation, 2.3% walk, 2.7% work from home; Mean travel time to work: 23.1 minutes
2016 Presidential Election: 64.9% Trump, 28.8% Clinton, 3.7% Johnson, 0.8% Stein
Additional Information Contacts
Huron Government . . . . (419) 668-3092
http://www.hccommissioners.com

Huron County Communities

CELERYVILLE (CDP). Covers a land area of 0.516 square miles and a water area of 0 square miles. Located at 41.03° N. Lat; 82.73° W. Long. Elevation is 942 feet.
Population: 271; Growth (since 2000): n/a; Density: 524.8 persons per square mile; Race: 100.0% White, 0.0% Black/African American, 0.0% Asian, 0.0% American Indian/Alaska Native, 0.0% Native Hawaiian/Other Pacific Islander, 0.0% Two or more races, 13.7% Hispanic of any race; Average household size: 2.74; Median age: 22.9; Age under 18: 43.2%; Age 65 and over: 7.0%; Males per 100 females: 114.3; Marriage status: 17.5% never married, 41.6% now married, 0.0% separated, 7.8% widowed, 33.1% divorced; Foreign born: 0.0%; Speak English only: 100.0%; With disability: 12.9%; Veterans: 18.8%; Ancestry: 59.0% German, 13.7% American, 10.0% Irish, 9.2% English, 5.9% Dutch
Employment: 0.0% management, business, and financial, 0.0% computer, engineering, and science, 11.1% education, legal, community service, arts, and media, 0.0% healthcare practitioners, 12.6% service, 4.4% sales and office, 6.7% natural resources, construction, and maintenance, 65.2% production, transportation, and material moving
Income: Per capita: $28,529; Median household: $87,232; Average household: $80,296; Households with income of $100,000 or more: 48.5%; Poverty rate: 16.2%
Educational Attainment: High school diploma or higher: 100.0%; Bachelor's degree or higher: 11.2%; Graduate/professional degree or higher: 11.2%
Housing: Homeownership rate: 52.5%; Median home value: $117,500; Median year structure built: 1965; Homeowner vacancy rate: 0.0%; Median selected monthly owner costs: $1,292 with a mortgage, $445 without a mortgage; Median gross rent: n/a per month; Rental vacancy rate: 0.0%
Health Insurance: 100.0% have insurance; 81.5% have private insurance; 48.0% have public insurance; 0.0% do not have insurance; 0.0% of children under 18 do not have insurance
Transportation: Commute: 100.0% car, 0.0% public transportation, 0.0% walk, 0.0% work from home; Mean travel time to work: 35.3 minutes

COLLINS (CDP). Covers a land area of 4.618 square miles and a water area of 0.005 square miles. Located at 41.25° N. Lat; 82.48° W. Long. Elevation is 876 feet.
Population: 407; Growth (since 2000): n/a; Density: 88.1 persons per square mile; Race: 100.0% White, 0.0% Black/African American, 0.0% Asian, 0.0% American Indian/Alaska Native, 0.0% Native Hawaiian/Other Pacific Islander, 0.0% Two or more races, 17.4% Hispanic of any race; Average household size: 2.29; Median age: 42.2; Age under 18: 24.6%; Age 65 and over: 10.6%; Males per 100 females: 99.1; Marriage status: 22.0% never married, 62.7% now married, 1.8% separated, 3.4% widowed, 11.9% divorced; Foreign born: 1.7%; Speak English only: 100.0%; With disability: 6.6%; Veterans: 6.2%; Ancestry: 37.6% German, 17.7% Italian, 12.5% American, 12.3% Irish, 9.1% Hungarian
Employment: 11.6% management, business, and financial, 0.0% computer, engineering, and science, 0.0% education, legal, community service, arts, and media, 2.8% healthcare practitioners, 0.0% service, 26.9% sales and office, 29.2% natural resources, construction, and maintenance, 29.6% production, transportation, and material moving
Income: Per capita: $33,099; Median household: $70,921; Average household: $73,561; Households with income of $100,000 or more: 29.2%; Poverty rate: 7.6%
Educational Attainment: High school diploma or higher: 91.5%; Bachelor's degree or higher: 2.0%; Graduate/professional degree or higher: n/a

School District(s)

Western Reserve Local (PK-12)
2015-16 Enrollment: 1,103 . . . . (419) 660-8508

Housing: Homeownership rate: 100.0%; Median home value: $153,900; Median year structure built: 1973; Homeowner vacancy rate: 0.0%; Median selected monthly owner costs: $1,193 with a mortgage, $425 without a mortgage; Median gross rent: n/a per month; Rental vacancy rate: 100.0%

Health Insurance: 98.5% have insurance; 98.5% have private insurance; 16.7% have public insurance; 1.5% do not have insurance; 0.0% of children under 18 do not have insurance
Transportation: Commute: 91.2% car, 0.0% public transportation, 0.0% walk, 8.8% work from home; Mean travel time to work: 41.6 minutes

GREENWICH (village). Covers a land area of 1.353 square miles and a water area of 0.016 square miles. Located at 41.03° N. Lat; 82.52° W. Long. Elevation is 1,027 feet.
History: Greenwich was incorporated in 1879 and named for the town in Connecticut.
Population: 1,453; Growth (since 2000): -4.7%; Density: 1,074.2 persons per square mile; Race: 97.6% White, 0.3% Black/African American, 0.0% Asian, 0.5% American Indian/Alaska Native, 0.0% Native Hawaiian/Other Pacific Islander, 0.4% Two or more races, 4.5% Hispanic of any race; Average household size: 2.46; Median age: 37.6; Age under 18: 27.0%; Age 65 and over: 12.6%; Males per 100 females: 101.1; Marriage status: 29.6% never married, 50.0% now married, 3.6% separated, 7.1% widowed, 13.3% divorced; Foreign born: 1.5%; Speak English only: 98.0%; With disability: 15.9%; Veterans: 8.1%; Ancestry: 21.0% German, 19.2% American, 12.9% English, 10.6% Irish, 4.3% French
Employment: 6.3% management, business, and financial, 0.8% computer, engineering, and science, 7.3% education, legal, community service, arts, and media, 3.8% healthcare practitioners, 18.2% service, 14.7% sales and office, 14.2% natural resources, construction, and maintenance, 34.7% production, transportation, and material moving
Income: Per capita: $20,440; Median household: $41,786; Average household: $50,567; Households with income of $100,000 or more: 6.3%; Poverty rate: 15.1%
Educational Attainment: High school diploma or higher: 87.6%; Bachelor's degree or higher: 9.4%; Graduate/professional degree or higher: 4.2%

School District(s)

South Central Local (PK-12)
2015-16 Enrollment: 783. . . . . (419) 752-3815
Housing: Homeownership rate: 69.0%; Median home value: $84,400; Median year structure built: 1953; Homeowner vacancy rate: 9.2%; Median selected monthly owner costs: $893 with a mortgage, $333 without a mortgage; Median gross rent: $582 per month; Rental vacancy rate: 0.0%
Health Insurance: 92.5% have insurance; 71.4% have private insurance; 36.8% have public insurance; 7.5% do not have insurance; 1.5% of children under 18 do not have insurance
Newspapers: Enterprise Review (weekly circulation 14,000)
Transportation: Commute: 93.5% car, 0.0% public transportation, 5.5% walk, 0.3% work from home; Mean travel time to work: 25.6 minutes

HOLIDAY LAKES (CDP). Covers a land area of 1.733 square miles and a water area of 0.350 square miles. Located at 41.10° N. Lat; 82.73° W. Long.
Population: 658; Growth (since 2000): n/a; Density: 379.6 persons per square mile; Race: 95.4% White, 0.0% Black/African American, 1.7% Asian, 0.0% American Indian/Alaska Native, 0.0% Native Hawaiian/Other Pacific Islander, 2.9% Two or more races, 0.0% Hispanic of any race; Average household size: 2.31; Median age: 53.6; Age under 18: 7.1%; Age 65 and over: 17.9%; Males per 100 females: 101.9; Marriage status: 25.2% never married, 60.9% now married, 0.0% separated, 7.0% widowed, 6.9% divorced; Foreign born: 1.7%; Speak English only: 98.3%; With disability: 7.1%; Veterans: 15.1%; Ancestry: 30.2% German, 13.5% American, 13.4% Irish, 12.6% English, 7.9% Polish
Employment: 26.6% management, business, and financial, 4.6% computer, engineering, and science, 15.7% education, legal, community service, arts, and media, 7.1% healthcare practitioners, 5.8% service, 20.3% sales and office, 4.1% natural resources, construction, and maintenance, 15.9% production, transportation, and material moving
Income: Per capita: $46,997; Median household: $78,594; Average household: $108,306; Households with income of $100,000 or more: 40.3%; Poverty rate: 2.0%
Educational Attainment: High school diploma or higher: 95.2%; Bachelor's degree or higher: 24.0%; Graduate/professional degree or higher: 8.1%
Housing: Homeownership rate: 95.4%; Median home value: $171,200; Median year structure built: 1980; Homeowner vacancy rate: 0.0%; Median selected monthly owner costs: $1,272 with a mortgage, $637 without a mortgage; Median gross rent: n/a per month; Rental vacancy rate: 40.9%
Health Insurance: 96.7% have insurance; 88.6% have private insurance; 21.3% have public insurance; 3.3% do not have insurance; 0.0% of children under 18 do not have insurance
Transportation: Commute: 98.0% car, 0.0% public transportation, 0.0% walk, 2.0% work from home; Mean travel time to work: 19.5 minutes

MONROEVILLE (village). Covers a land area of 1.400 square miles and a water area of 0.030 square miles. Located at 41.24° N. Lat; 82.70° W. Long. Elevation is 709 feet.
Population: 1,315; Growth (since 2000): -8.2%; Density: 939.5 persons per square mile; Race: 99.4% White, 0.0% Black/African American, 0.0% Asian, 0.0% American Indian/Alaska Native, 0.0% Native Hawaiian/Other Pacific Islander, 0.0% Two or more races, 1.7% Hispanic of any race; Average household size: 2.57; Median age: 35.4; Age under 18: 27.0%; Age 65 and over: 9.5%; Males per 100 females: 99.4; Marriage status: 19.9% never married, 60.8% now married, 6.7% separated, 7.6% widowed, 11.8% divorced; Foreign born: 0.3%; Speak English only: 99.5%; With disability: 9.3%; Veterans: 13.3%; Ancestry: 43.4% German, 20.2% Irish, 11.0% English, 5.2% Italian, 3.7% American
Employment: 7.6% management, business, and financial, 0.5% computer, engineering, and science, 6.3% education, legal, community service, arts, and media, 4.6% healthcare practitioners, 16.2% service, 27.5% sales and office, 11.9% natural resources, construction, and maintenance, 25.5% production, transportation, and material moving
Income: Per capita: $24,971; Median household: $51,667; Average household: $63,512; Households with income of $100,000 or more: 16.0%; Poverty rate: 8.1%
Educational Attainment: High school diploma or higher: 91.1%; Bachelor's degree or higher: 11.4%; Graduate/professional degree or higher: 2.4%

School District(s)

Monroeville Local (PK-12)
2015-16 Enrollment: 615. . . . . (419) 465-2610
Housing: Homeownership rate: 57.8%; Median home value: $95,500; Median year structure built: 1952; Homeowner vacancy rate: 7.7%; Median selected monthly owner costs: $964 with a mortgage, $413 without a mortgage; Median gross rent: $728 per month; Rental vacancy rate: 10.0%
Health Insurance: 89.4% have insurance; 69.4% have private insurance; 30.1% have public insurance; 10.6% do not have insurance; 7.9% of children under 18 do not have insurance
Transportation: Commute: 95.9% car, 0.0% public transportation, 2.4% walk, 1.7% work from home; Mean travel time to work: 19.0 minutes
Additional Information Contacts
Village of Monroeville . . . . (419) 465-4443
http://www.monroevilleohio.com

NEW HAVEN (CDP). Covers a land area of 1.236 square miles and a water area of 0.003 square miles. Located at 41.03° N. Lat; 82.69° W. Long. Elevation is 932 feet.
Population: 282; Growth (since 2000): n/a; Density: 228.2 persons per square mile; Race: 83.0% White, 7.1% Black/African American, 0.0% Asian, 0.0% American Indian/Alaska Native, 0.0% Native Hawaiian/Other Pacific Islander, 9.9% Two or more races, 0.0% Hispanic of any race; Average household size: 2.33; Median age: 60.2; Age under 18: 16.0%; Age 65 and over: 25.2%; Males per 100 females: 106.7; Marriage status: 20.8% never married, 43.6% now married, 0.0% separated, 11.4% widowed, 24.2% divorced; Foreign born: 0.0%; Speak English only: 100.0%; With disability: 50.4%; Veterans: 32.5%; Ancestry: 28.7% Irish, 16.7% German, 9.6% Czech, 6.4% American, 6.4% English
Employment: 36.4% management, business, and financial, 0.0% computer, engineering, and science, 0.0% education, legal, community service, arts, and media, 0.0% healthcare practitioners, 0.0% service, 0.0% sales and office, 0.0% natural resources, construction, and maintenance, 63.6% production, transportation, and material moving
Income: Per capita: $14,055; Median household: $34,293; Average household: $32,893; Households with income of $100,000 or more: n/a; Poverty rate: 30.1%
Educational Attainment: High school diploma or higher: 85.7%; Bachelor's degree or higher: n/a; Graduate/professional degree or higher: n/a

School District(s)

Willard City (PK-12)
2015-16 Enrollment: 1,610 . . . . (419) 935-1541
Housing: Homeownership rate: 92.6%; Median home value: $85,800; Median year structure built: 1974; Homeowner vacancy rate: 20.6%;

Median selected monthly owner costs: $650 with a mortgage, n/a without a mortgage; Median gross rent: n/a per month; Rental vacancy rate: 0.0%
Health Insurance: 100.0% have insurance; 44.0% have private insurance; 75.2% have public insurance; 0.0% do not have insurance; 0.0% of children under 18 do not have insurance
Transportation: Commute: 100.0% car, 0.0% public transportation, 0.0% walk, 0.0% work from home; Mean travel time to work: 0.0 minutes

NEW LONDON (village). Covers a land area of 2.205 square miles and a water area of 0.331 square miles. Located at 41.08° N. Lat; 82.41° W. Long. Elevation is 981 feet.
History: New London was settled in 1816 and developed as a rural trading and shipping center. The C.E. Ward Company was established here to produce band uniforms, graduation caps and gowns, church vestments, and other regalia for a worldwide market.
Population: 2,614; Growth (since 2000): -3.0%; Density: 1,185.4 persons per square mile; Race: 95.2% White, 3.6% Black/African American, 0.5% Asian, 0.0% American Indian/Alaska Native, 0.1% Native Hawaiian/Other Pacific Islander, 0.6% Two or more races, 2.1% Hispanic of any race; Average household size: 3.01; Median age: 30.1; Age under 18: 31.8%; Age 65 and over: 10.4%; Males per 100 females: 93.3; Marriage status: 31.1% never married, 48.8% now married, 1.4% separated, 4.4% widowed, 15.8% divorced; Foreign born: 0.8%; Speak English only: 98.2%; With disability: 12.1%; Veterans: 8.1%; Ancestry: 31.4% German, 17.7% Irish, 9.1% English, 5.1% American, 5.0% Polish
Employment: 5.8% management, business, and financial, 0.7% computer, engineering, and science, 6.8% education, legal, community service, arts, and media, 5.9% healthcare practitioners, 24.5% service, 17.3% sales and office, 9.1% natural resources, construction, and maintenance, 30.0% production, transportation, and material moving
Income: Per capita: $17,302; Median household: $41,683; Average household: $52,002; Households with income of $100,000 or more: 10.3%; Poverty rate: 23.5%
Educational Attainment: High school diploma or higher: 84.7%; Bachelor's degree or higher: 10.1%; Graduate/professional degree or higher: 2.6%

School District(s)

New London Local (PK-12)
2015-16 Enrollment: 965. . . . . (419) 929-8433
Housing: Homeownership rate: 60.5%; Median home value: $81,100; Median year structure built: 1955; Homeowner vacancy rate: 0.0%; Median selected monthly owner costs: $968 with a mortgage, $360 without a mortgage; Median gross rent: $683 per month; Rental vacancy rate: 7.4%
Health Insurance: 89.6% have insurance; 57.4% have private insurance; 41.9% have public insurance; 10.4% do not have insurance; 1.2% of children under 18 do not have insurance
Newspapers: New London Record (weekly circulation 2,400)
Transportation: Commute: 89.8% car, 0.0% public transportation, 6.5% walk, 2.5% work from home; Mean travel time to work: 27.6 minutes
Additional Information Contacts
Village of New London . . . . (419) 929-1809
http://www.newlondonohio.com

NORTH FAIRFIELD (village). Covers a land area of 0.462 square miles and a water area of 0.002 square miles. Located at 41.10° N. Lat; 82.61° W. Long. Elevation is 928 feet.
Population: 556; Growth (since 2000): -3.0%; Density: 1,203.9 persons per square mile; Race: 90.8% White, 0.0% Black/African American, 0.7% Asian, 0.0% American Indian/Alaska Native, 0.0% Native Hawaiian/Other Pacific Islander, 3.4% Two or more races, 7.4% Hispanic of any race; Average household size: 2.65; Median age: 39.6; Age under 18: 24.3%; Age 65 and over: 14.0%; Males per 100 females: 102.2; Marriage status: 24.9% never married, 56.8% now married, 2.2% separated, 6.9% widowed, 11.4% divorced; Foreign born: 1.3%; Speak English only: 95.4%; With disability: 13.5%; Veterans: 12.4%; Ancestry: 27.3% German, 14.0% Irish, 8.5% American, 6.3% Italian, 5.9% English
Employment: 9.8% management, business, and financial, 0.4% computer, engineering, and science, 1.8% education, legal, community service, arts, and media, 2.9% healthcare practitioners, 11.6% service, 17.1% sales and office, 14.5% natural resources, construction, and maintenance, 41.8% production, transportation, and material moving
Income: Per capita: $22,056; Median household: $54,500; Average household: $58,365; Households with income of $100,000 or more: 10.5%; Poverty rate: 7.6%
Educational Attainment: High school diploma or higher: 87.8%; Bachelor's degree or higher: 6.8%; Graduate/professional degree or higher: 1.9%
Housing: Homeownership rate: 79.0%; Median home value: $83,800; Median year structure built: Before 1940; Homeowner vacancy rate: 0.0%; Median selected monthly owner costs: $1,042 with a mortgage, $346 without a mortgage; Median gross rent: $628 per month; Rental vacancy rate: 10.2%
Health Insurance: 91.3% have insurance; 70.6% have private insurance; 36.3% have public insurance; 8.7% do not have insurance; 0.0% of children under 18 do not have insurance
Transportation: Commute: 94.6% car, 0.0% public transportation, 2.5% walk, 2.2% work from home; Mean travel time to work: 32.4 minutes

NORWALK (city). County seat. Covers a land area of 8.870 square miles and a water area of 0.282 square miles. Located at 41.24° N. Lat; 82.61° W. Long. Elevation is 728 feet.
History: Norwalk was founded in 1816 by Platt Benedict, and named for the Connecticut town which had been the home of many of its first settlers.
Population: 16,862; Growth (since 2000): 3.8%; Density: 1,901.0 persons per square mile; Race: 91.7% White, 3.4% Black/African American, 0.1% Asian, 0.0% American Indian/Alaska Native, 0.0% Native Hawaiian/Other Pacific Islander, 2.5% Two or more races, 9.1% Hispanic of any race; Average household size: 2.46; Median age: 39.0; Age under 18: 25.5%; Age 65 and over: 18.3%; Males per 100 females: 91.7; Marriage status: 31.1% never married, 46.0% now married, 1.5% separated, 6.9% widowed, 16.1% divorced; Foreign born: 4.3%; Speak English only: 92.5%; With disability: 15.6%; Veterans: 10.1%; Ancestry: 34.0% German, 15.1% Irish, 10.0% English, 9.6% American, 4.6% Italian
Employment: 8.2% management, business, and financial, 3.3% computer, engineering, and science, 6.2% education, legal, community service, arts, and media, 5.3% healthcare practitioners, 16.8% service, 22.8% sales and office, 12.4% natural resources, construction, and maintenance, 25.1% production, transportation, and material moving
Income: Per capita: $22,401; Median household: $41,316; Average household: $55,096; Households with income of $100,000 or more: 11.7%; Poverty rate: 17.2%
Educational Attainment: High school diploma or higher: 87.6%; Bachelor's degree or higher: 15.8%; Graduate/professional degree or higher: 6.8%

School District(s)

Norwalk City (PK-12)
2015-16 Enrollment: 2,839 . . . . (419) 668-2779

Two-year College(s)

Elite School of Cosmetology (Private, For-profit)
Fall 2016 Enrollment: 70. . . . . (419) 668-2333
Housing: Homeownership rate: 60.9%; Median home value: $117,200; Median year structure built: 1968; Homeowner vacancy rate: 0.0%; Median selected monthly owner costs: $1,036 with a mortgage, $420 without a mortgage; Median gross rent: $602 per month; Rental vacancy rate: 10.0%
Health Insurance: 92.8% have insurance; 63.7% have private insurance; 43.7% have public insurance; 7.2% do not have insurance; 2.3% of children under 18 do not have insurance
Hospitals: Fisher - Titus Hospital (112 beds)
Safety: Violent crime rate: 6.0 per 10,000 population; Property crime rate: 262.0 per 10,000 population
Newspapers: Norwalk Reflector (daily circulation 8,800)
Transportation: Commute: 91.8% car, 0.6% public transportation, 2.5% walk, 2.9% work from home; Mean travel time to work: 19.5 minutes
Additional Information Contacts
City of Norwalk . . . . (419) 663-6700
http://www.norwalkoh.com

WAKEMAN (village). Covers a land area of 0.825 square miles and a water area of 0.023 square miles. Located at 41.25° N. Lat; 82.40° W. Long. Elevation is 846 feet.
History: Wakeman was the home of the C.S. Clark Seed Company, founded in 1878 and specializing in varieties of seed corn.
Population: 1,355; Growth (since 2000): 42.5%; Density: 1,643.2 persons per square mile; Race: 99.3% White, 0.0% Black/African American, 0.3% Asian, 0.1% American Indian/Alaska Native, 0.0% Native Hawaiian/Other Pacific Islander, 0.3% Two or more races, 0.0% Hispanic of any race; Average household size: 2.46; Median age: 39.5; Age under 18: 24.7%; Age 65 and over: 13.5%; Males per 100 females: 92.5; Marriage status: 24.5% never married, 52.9% now married, 1.5% separated, 4.2%

widowed, 18.4% divorced; Foreign born: 1.9%; Speak English only: 97.0%; With disability: 10.0%; Veterans: 6.1%; Ancestry: 40.2% German, 14.3% Irish, 11.1% English, 6.9% American, 6.5% Hungarian
Employment: 4.8% management, business, and financial, 4.1% computer, engineering, and science, 7.6% education, legal, community service, arts, and media, 9.2% healthcare practitioners, 20.7% service, 21.6% sales and office, 14.5% natural resources, construction, and maintenance, 17.5% production, transportation, and material moving
Income: Per capita: $23,567; Median household: $47,031; Average household: $58,283; Households with income of $100,000 or more: 13.3%; Poverty rate: 9.4%
Educational Attainment: High school diploma or higher: 89.3%; Bachelor's degree or higher: 11.7%; Graduate/professional degree or higher: 3.0%
Housing: Homeownership rate: 66.4%; Median home value: $112,000; Median year structure built: 1971; Homeowner vacancy rate: 0.0%; Median selected monthly owner costs: $1,018 with a mortgage, $389 without a mortgage; Median gross rent: $762 per month; Rental vacancy rate: 13.1%
Health Insurance: 94.5% have insurance; 76.5% have private insurance; 28.7% have public insurance; 5.5% do not have insurance; 3.0% of children under 18 do not have insurance
Transportation: Commute: 97.7% car, 0.0% public transportation, 0.4% walk, 1.9% work from home; Mean travel time to work: 29.3 minutes

WILLARD (city). Covers a land area of 3.549 square miles and a water area of 0.018 square miles. Located at 41.05° N. Lat; 82.72° W. Long. Elevation is 919 feet.
Population: 6,105; Growth (since 2000): -10.3%; Density: 1,720.0 persons per square mile; Race: 93.9% White, 0.9% Black/African American, 0.2% Asian, 0.0% American Indian/Alaska Native, 0.0% Native Hawaiian/Other Pacific Islander, 2.1% Two or more races, 15.0% Hispanic of any race; Average household size: 2.69; Median age: 34.4; Age under 18: 27.5%; Age 65 and over: 15.0%; Males per 100 females: 92.9; Marriage status: 30.9% never married, 49.3% now married, 3.0% separated, 7.1% widowed, 12.6% divorced; Foreign born: 3.6%; Speak English only: 89.0%; With disability: 17.0%; Veterans: 6.6%; Ancestry: 25.2% German, 15.4% Irish, 8.0% American, 6.5% Italian, 5.0% English
Employment: 7.0% management, business, and financial, 0.4% computer, engineering, and science, 7.6% education, legal, community service, arts, and media, 5.0% healthcare practitioners, 18.3% service, 15.2% sales and office, 7.8% natural resources, construction, and maintenance, 38.8% production, transportation, and material moving
Income: Per capita: $18,782; Median household: $40,864; Average household: $49,869; Households with income of $100,000 or more: 10.5%; Poverty rate: 23.2%
Educational Attainment: High school diploma or higher: 79.8%; Bachelor's degree or higher: 11.8%; Graduate/professional degree or higher: 2.8%

School District(s)

Willard City (PK-12)
2015-16 Enrollment: 1,610 . . . . (419) 935-1541
Housing: Homeownership rate: 49.4%; Median home value: $83,000; Median year structure built: 1959; Homeowner vacancy rate: 0.0%; Median selected monthly owner costs: $828 with a mortgage, $356 without a mortgage; Median gross rent: $577 per month; Rental vacancy rate: 12.4%
Health Insurance: 92.1% have insurance; 62.1% have private insurance; 44.9% have public insurance; 7.9% do not have insurance; 0.5% of children under 18 do not have insurance
Hospitals: Mercy Willard Hospital (25 beds)
Safety: Violent crime rate: 6.6 per 10,000 population; Property crime rate: 500.7 per 10,000 population
Newspapers: The Times-Junction (weekly circulation 3,800)
Transportation: Commute: 91.8% car, 0.2% public transportation, 3.6% walk, 1.5% work from home; Mean travel time to work: 20.2 minutes
Additional Information Contacts
City of Willard . . . . (419) 933-2581
http://www.willardohio.com

Jackson County

Located in southern Ohio; drained by the Little Scioto River. Covers a land area of 420.304 square miles, a water area of 1.230 square miles, and is located in the Eastern Time Zone at 39.01° N. Lat., 82.61° W. Long. The county was founded in 1816. County seat is Jackson.

Jackson County is part of the Jackson, OH Micropolitan Statistical Area. The entire metro area includes: Jackson County, OH

Weather Station: Jackson 3 NW — Elevation: 799 feet

	Jan	Feb	Mar	Apr	May	Jun	Jul	Aug	Sep	Oct	Nov	Dec
High	39	43	53	66	74	81	84	84	77	65	54	42
Low	21	23	30	40	49	58	62	61	54	42	33	25
Precip	2.9	2.9	3.9	3.5	4.5	3.9	4.4	3.3	2.9	3.0	3.3	3.2
Snow	na	4.8	2.0	0.7	0.0	0.0	0.0	0.0	0.0	0.0	0.5	2.7

High and Low temperatures in degrees Fahrenheit; Precipitation and Snow in inches

Population: 32,717; Growth (since 2000): 0.2%; Density: 77.8 persons per square mile; Race: 97.1% White, 0.7% Black/African American, 0.2% Asian, 0.0% American Indian/Alaska Native, 0.1% Native Hawaiian/Other Pacific Islander, 1.8% two or more races, 1.0% Hispanic of any race; Average household size: 2.53; Median age: 40.3; Age under 18: 24.2%; Age 65 and over: 15.7%; Males per 100 females: 95.6; Marriage status: 25.6% never married, 52.6% now married, 3.2% separated, 7.2% widowed, 14.7% divorced; Foreign born: 1.3%; Speak English only: 97.5%; With disability: 21.2%; Veterans: 9.4%; Ancestry: 18.5% German, 16.5% Irish, 9.8% American, 7.5% English, 6.1% Welsh
Religion: Six largest groups: 7.9% Methodist/Pietist, 6.2% Baptist, 5.1% Non-denominational Protestant, 2.5% Holiness, 1.9% Latter-day Saints, 1.3% Presbyterian-Reformed
Economy: Unemployment rate: 5.8%; Leading industries: 19.4 % retail trade; 12.7 % other services (except public administration); 12.5 % health care and social assistance; Farms: 526 totaling 71,681 acres; Company size: 2 employ 1,000 or more persons, 0 employ 500 to 999 persons, 9 employ 100 to 499 persons, 588 employ less than 100 persons; Business ownership: 804 women-owned, n/a Black-owned, n/a Hispanic-owned, 27 Asian-owned, n/a American Indian/Alaska Native-owned
Employment: 7.2% management, business, and financial, 2.7% computer, engineering, and science, 12.0% education, legal, community service, arts, and media, 9.8% healthcare practitioners, 14.7% service, 21.0% sales and office, 11.2% natural resources, construction, and maintenance, 21.4% production, transportation, and material moving
Income: Per capita: $20,583; Median household: $40,330; Average household: $50,421; Households with income of $100,000 or more: 9.0%; Poverty rate: 23.0%
Educational Attainment: High school diploma or higher: 84.2%; Bachelor's degree or higher: 16.9%; Graduate/professional degree or higher: 5.4%
Housing: Homeownership rate: 66.5%; Median home value: $90,800; Median year structure built: 1974; Homeowner vacancy rate: 4.0%; Median selected monthly owner costs: $990 with a mortgage, $372 without a mortgage; Median gross rent: $675 per month; Rental vacancy rate: 4.2%
Vital Statistics: Birth rate: 122.8 per 10,000 population; Death rate: 112.3 per 10,000 population; Age-adjusted cancer mortality rate: 201.3 deaths per 100,000 population
Health Insurance: 90.2% have insurance; 59.3% have private insurance; 44.0% have public insurance; 9.8% do not have insurance; 4.5% of children under 18 do not have insurance
Health Care: Physicians: 6.5 per 10,000 population; Dentists: 2.5 per 10,000 population; Hospital beds: 7.3 per 10,000 population; Hospital admissions: 328.4 per 10,000 population
Transportation: Commute: 95.1% car, 0.1% public transportation, 2.0% walk, 2.3% work from home; Mean travel time to work: 27.4 minutes
2016 Presidential Election: 72.2% Trump, 23.4% Clinton, 2.7% Johnson, 0.5% Stein
National and State Parks: Buckeye Furnace State Memorial; Jackson Lake State Reserve; Lake Katharine State Nature Preserve; Leo Petroglyph State Memorial; Richland Furnace State Forest
Additional Information Contacts
Jackson Government . . . . (740) 286-3301
http://www.jacksoncountygovernment.org

Jackson County Communities

COALTON (village). Covers a land area of 0.550 square miles and a water area of 0 square miles. Located at 39.11° N. Lat; 82.61° W. Long. Elevation is 696 feet.
History: During the 1880's, Coalton was a busy coal town.
Population: 570; Growth (since 2000): 4.6%; Density: 1,036.8 persons per square mile; Race: 99.1% White, 0.0% Black/African American, 0.0% Asian, 0.0% American Indian/Alaska Native, 0.0% Native Hawaiian/Other Pacific Islander, 0.9% Two or more races, 0.0% Hispanic of any race;

Average household size: 2.47; Median age: 40.1; Age under 18: 22.5%; Age 65 and over: 10.9%; Males per 100 females: 97.9; Marriage status: 20.6% never married, 45.7% now married, 0.7% separated, 6.0% widowed, 27.7% divorced; Foreign born: 0.0%; Speak English only: 100.0%; With disability: 24.9%; Veterans: 8.4%; Ancestry: 14.9% Irish, 11.6% German, 11.1% American, 8.8% English, 5.1% Italian
Employment: 3.6% management, business, and financial, 0.0% computer, engineering, and science, 4.9% education, legal, community service, arts, and media, 5.4% healthcare practitioners, 20.6% service, 17.5% sales and office, 10.3% natural resources, construction, and maintenance, 37.7% production, transportation, and material moving
Income: Per capita: $14,171; Median household: $29,219; Average household: $33,488; Households with income of $100,000 or more: 4.8%; Poverty rate: 27.4%
Educational Attainment: High school diploma or higher: 77.3%; Bachelor's degree or higher: 6.7%; Graduate/professional degree or higher: n/a
Housing: Homeownership rate: 56.3%; Median home value: $50,000; Median year structure built: 1971; Homeowner vacancy rate: 9.7%; Median selected monthly owner costs: $710 with a mortgage, $350 without a mortgage; Median gross rent: $578 per month; Rental vacancy rate: 0.0%
Health Insurance: 91.4% have insurance; 47.5% have private insurance; 54.4% have public insurance; 8.6% do not have insurance; 0.0% of children under 18 do not have insurance
Transportation: Commute: 95.1% car, 0.0% public transportation, 3.6% walk, 1.3% work from home; Mean travel time to work: 25.4 minutes

JACKSON (city). County seat. Covers a land area of 8.232 square miles and a water area of 0.261 square miles. Located at 39.05° N. Lat; 82.65° W. Long. Elevation is 686 feet.
History: Jackson was platted in 1817, and grew around the railroad that arrived in 1853. Many of Jackson's early settlers were Welsh who came to farm and later worked in the iron furnaces and coal mines.
Population: 6,346; Growth (since 2000): 2.6%; Density: 770.9 persons per square mile; Race: 97.8% White, 1.1% Black/African American, 0.1% Asian, 0.0% American Indian/Alaska Native, 0.0% Native Hawaiian/Other Pacific Islander, 0.7% Two or more races, 4.2% Hispanic of any race; Average household size: 2.17; Median age: 43.3; Age under 18: 19.1%; Age 65 and over: 17.2%; Males per 100 females: 87.0; Marriage status: 25.5% never married, 50.3% now married, 3.1% separated, 7.4% widowed, 16.8% divorced; Foreign born: 2.1%; Speak English only: 94.8%; With disability: 21.8%; Veterans: 7.3%; Ancestry: 18.8% German, 12.6% Irish, 9.2% American, 8.1% English, 5.8% Welsh
Employment: 5.2% management, business, and financial, 3.1% computer, engineering, and science, 15.4% education, legal, community service, arts, and media, 11.5% healthcare practitioners, 15.0% service, 25.9% sales and office, 6.8% natural resources, construction, and maintenance, 17.1% production, transportation, and material moving
Income: Per capita: $21,043; Median household: $37,476; Average household: $44,487; Households with income of $100,000 or more: 7.2%; Poverty rate: 20.8%
Educational Attainment: High school diploma or higher: 90.8%; Bachelor's degree or higher: 20.5%; Graduate/professional degree or higher: 6.2%

School District(s)

Center for Student Achievement (09-12)
2015-16 Enrollment: 48 . . . . (740) 286-7839
Jackson City (PK-12)
2015-16 Enrollment: 2,422 . . . . (740) 286-6442

Two-year College(s)

Daymar College-Jackson (Private, For-profit)
Fall 2016 Enrollment: n/a . . . . (740) 286-1554
2016-17 Tuition: In-state $15,000; Out-of-state $15,000
Housing: Homeownership rate: 56.3%; Median home value: $94,500; Median year structure built: 1955; Homeowner vacancy rate: 6.2%; Median selected monthly owner costs: $948 with a mortgage, $414 without a mortgage; Median gross rent: $728 per month; Rental vacancy rate: 11.1%
Health Insurance: 92.3% have insurance; 68.1% have private insurance; 45.0% have public insurance; 7.7% do not have insurance; 2.3% of children under 18 do not have insurance
Hospitals: Holzer Medical Center Jackson
Safety: Violent crime rate: 16.1 per 10,000 population; Property crime rate: 243.1 per 10,000 population
Newspapers: Jackson Co. Times-Journal (weekly circulation 5,800); Telegram (weekly circulation 6,000)
Transportation: Commute: 95.7% car, 0.2% public transportation, 1.8% walk, 2.2% work from home; Mean travel time to work: 25.2 minutes
Airports: James A Rhodes (general aviation)

OAK HILL (village). Covers a land area of 1.142 square miles and a water area of 0 square miles. Located at 38.90° N. Lat; 82.57° W. Long. Elevation is 702 feet.
Population: 1,890; Growth (since 2000): 12.2%; Density: 1,655.4 persons per square mile; Race: 88.8% White, 0.6% Black/African American, 0.0% Asian, 0.0% American Indian/Alaska Native, 0.0% Native Hawaiian/Other Pacific Islander, 10.6% Two or more races, 0.0% Hispanic of any race; Average household size: 2.67; Median age: 32.8; Age under 18: 29.4%; Age 65 and over: 13.2%; Males per 100 females: 90.8; Marriage status: 32.3% never married, 41.0% now married, 0.7% separated, 10.1% widowed, 16.7% divorced; Foreign born: 0.2%; Speak English only: 98.7%; With disability: 23.3%; Veterans: 8.2%; Ancestry: 17.6% German, 17.0% Irish, 11.1% Welsh, 8.6% English, 7.0% American
Employment: 2.8% management, business, and financial, 0.0% computer, engineering, and science, 12.4% education, legal, community service, arts, and media, 6.4% healthcare practitioners, 18.1% service, 28.3% sales and office, 10.9% natural resources, construction, and maintenance, 21.2% production, transportation, and material moving
Income: Per capita: $15,731; Median household: $30,685; Average household: $40,238; Households with income of $100,000 or more: 6.2%; Poverty rate: 33.9%
Educational Attainment: High school diploma or higher: 87.2%; Bachelor's degree or higher: 10.5%; Graduate/professional degree or higher: 5.8%

School District(s)

Oak Hill Union Local (PK-12)
2015-16 Enrollment: 1,235 . . . . (740) 682-7595
Housing: Homeownership rate: 44.0%; Median home value: $67,000; Median year structure built: 1957; Homeowner vacancy rate: 6.0%; Median selected monthly owner costs: $811 with a mortgage, $361 without a mortgage; Median gross rent: $534 per month; Rental vacancy rate: 1.2%
Health Insurance: 91.4% have insurance; 48.6% have private insurance; 57.5% have public insurance; 8.6% do not have insurance; 2.7% of children under 18 do not have insurance
Safety: Violent crime rate: 13.4 per 10,000 population; Property crime rate: 201.3 per 10,000 population
Transportation: Commute: 95.9% car, 0.7% public transportation, 1.4% walk, 0.0% work from home; Mean travel time to work: 20.2 minutes

WELLSTON (city). Covers a land area of 6.970 square miles and a water area of 0.084 square miles. Located at 39.12° N. Lat; 82.54° W. Long. Elevation is 738 feet.
History: Wellston was named for Harvey Wells, who constructed a blast furnace in 1874 and platted a town around it.
Population: 5,595; Growth (since 2000): -7.9%; Density: 802.7 persons per square mile; Race: 97.2% White, 0.0% Black/African American, 0.0% Asian, 0.0% American Indian/Alaska Native, 0.0% Native Hawaiian/Other Pacific Islander, 2.8% Two or more races, 0.0% Hispanic of any race; Average household size: 2.49; Median age: 38.4; Age under 18: 24.4%; Age 65 and over: 17.8%; Males per 100 females: 88.0; Marriage status: 22.8% never married, 51.6% now married, 3.3% separated, 10.1% widowed, 15.5% divorced; Foreign born: 0.3%; Speak English only: 97.8%; With disability: 20.3%; Veterans: 8.0%; Ancestry: 26.2% Irish, 18.2% German, 7.1% Dutch, 6.3% American, 6.3% English
Employment: 9.5% management, business, and financial, 1.7% computer, engineering, and science, 10.4% education, legal, community service, arts, and media, 9.1% healthcare practitioners, 10.7% service, 20.2% sales and office, 14.0% natural resources, construction, and maintenance, 24.5% production, transportation, and material moving
Income: Per capita: $23,302; Median household: $39,398; Average household: $55,379; Households with income of $100,000 or more: 10.1%; Poverty rate: 25.4%
Educational Attainment: High school diploma or higher: 81.8%; Bachelor's degree or higher: 16.3%; Graduate/professional degree or higher: 5.3%

School District(s)

Wellston City (PK-12)
2015-16 Enrollment: 1,464 . . . . (740) 384-2152
Housing: Homeownership rate: 62.8%; Median home value: $85,700; Median year structure built: 1962; Homeowner vacancy rate: 8.0%; Median

selected monthly owner costs: $986 with a mortgage, $353 without a mortgage; Median gross rent: $535 per month; Rental vacancy rate: 0.0%
Health Insurance: 91.0% have insurance; 56.2% have private insurance; 44.6% have public insurance; 9.0% do not have insurance; 0.4% of children under 18 do not have insurance
Safety: Violent crime rate: 33.0 per 10,000 population; Property crime rate: 294.9 per 10,000 population
Transportation: Commute: 97.5% car, 0.0% public transportation, 1.0% walk, 1.5% work from home; Mean travel time to work: 28.6 minutes

Jefferson County

Located in eastern Ohio; bounded on the east by the Ohio River and the West Virginia border; drained by Yellow and Cross Creeks. Covers a land area of 408.329 square miles, a water area of 2.624 square miles, and is located in the Eastern Time Zone at 40.40° N. Lat., 80.76° W. Long. The county was founded in 1797. County seat is Steubenville.

Jefferson County is part of the Weirton-Steubenville, WV-OH Metropolitan Statistical Area. The entire metro area includes: Jefferson County, OH; Brooke County, WV; Hancock County, WV

Weather Station: Steubenville Elevation: 992 feet

	Jan	Feb	Mar	Apr	May	Jun	Jul	Aug	Sep	Oct	Nov	Dec
High	37	41	50	63	72	80	83	82	76	64	52	41
Low	22	23	30	40	50	59	64	63	55	43	35	25
Precip	3.0	2.3	3.3	3.4	4.4	4.2	4.4	4.0	3.4	2.8	3.5	3.0
Snow	na	na	0.4	tr	0.0	0.0	0.0	0.0	0.0	0.2	0.2	na

High and Low temperatures in degrees Fahrenheit; Precipitation and Snow in inches

Population: 67,607; Growth (since 2000): -8.5%; Density: 165.6 persons per square mile; Race: 91.4% White, 5.6% Black/African American, 0.4% Asian, 0.2% American Indian/Alaska Native, 0.0% Native Hawaiian/Other Pacific Islander, 2.4% two or more races, 1.3% Hispanic of any race; Average household size: 2.35; Median age: 44.5; Age under 18: 19.6%; Age 65 and over: 19.5%; Males per 100 females: 92.3; Marriage status: 29.5% never married, 48.9% now married, 1.6% separated, 8.0% widowed, 13.5% divorced; Foreign born: 1.3%; Speak English only: 97.4%; With disability: 18.4%; Veterans: 10.8%; Ancestry: 20.7% German, 17.9% Irish, 14.4% Italian, 8.4% English, 7.8% Polish
Religion: Six largest groups: 19.9% Catholicism, 11.2% Methodist/Pietist, 3.8% Baptist, 3.2% Presbyterian-Reformed, 2.0% Holiness, 1.9% Non-denominational Protestant
Economy: Unemployment rate: 6.4%; Leading industries: 17.1 % retail trade; 15.3 % other services (except public administration); 13.7 % health care and social assistance; Farms: 493 totaling 68,341 acres; Company size: 2 employ 1,000 or more persons, 2 employ 500 to 999 persons, 17 employ 100 to 499 persons, 1,240 employ less than 100 persons; Business ownership: 1,292 women-owned, 211 Black-owned, 71 Hispanic-owned, 31 Asian-owned, n/a American Indian/Alaska Native-owned
Employment: 10.6% management, business, and financial, 2.5% computer, engineering, and science, 7.7% education, legal, community service, arts, and media, 8.7% healthcare practitioners, 20.8% service, 23.2% sales and office, 11.1% natural resources, construction, and maintenance, 15.4% production, transportation, and material moving
Income: Per capita: $23,356; Median household: $42,327; Average household: $55,269; Households with income of $100,000 or more: 13.6%; Poverty rate: 17.2%
Educational Attainment: High school diploma or higher: 89.9%; Bachelor's degree or higher: 15.4%; Graduate/professional degree or higher: 5.5%
Housing: Homeownership rate: 69.6%; Median home value: $87,100; Median year structure built: 1958; Homeowner vacancy rate: 2.1%; Median selected monthly owner costs: $934 with a mortgage, $390 without a mortgage; Median gross rent: $612 per month; Rental vacancy rate: 8.1%
Vital Statistics: Birth rate: 99.7 per 10,000 population; Death rate: 144.5 per 10,000 population; Age-adjusted cancer mortality rate: 209.1 deaths per 100,000 population
Health Insurance: 91.9% have insurance; 65.4% have private insurance; 42.0% have public insurance; 8.1% do not have insurance; 4.0% of children under 18 do not have insurance
Health Care: Physicians: 11.6 per 10,000 population; Dentists: 4.8 per 10,000 population; Hospital beds: 59.5 per 10,000 population; Hospital admissions: 1,779.5 per 10,000 population
Air Quality Index (AQI): Percent of Days: 53.0% good, 45.9% moderate, 1.1% unhealthy for sensitive individuals, 0.0% unhealthy, 0.0% very unhealthy; Annual median: 49; Annual maximum: 105
Transportation: Commute: 91.6% car, 0.6% public transportation, 3.8% walk, 3.0% work from home; Mean travel time to work: 24.9 minutes
2016 Presidential Election: 65.2% Trump, 29.9% Clinton, 2.6% Johnson, 0.6% Stein
National and State Parks: Fernwood State Forest; Jefferson Lake State Park
Additional Information Contacts
Jefferson Government. . . . . (740) 283-8500
http://www.jeffersoncountyoh.com

Jefferson County Communities

ADENA (village). Covers a land area of 0.537 square miles and a water area of 0 square miles. Located at 40.22° N. Lat; 80.88° W. Long. Elevation is 856 feet.
Population: 743; Growth (since 2000): -8.8%; Density: 1,383.2 persons per square mile; Race: 97.6% White, 1.2% Black/African American, 0.0% Asian, 0.0% American Indian/Alaska Native, 0.0% Native Hawaiian/Other Pacific Islander, 1.2% Two or more races, 0.0% Hispanic of any race; Average household size: 2.34; Median age: 43.5; Age under 18: 17.5%; Age 65 and over: 21.1%; Males per 100 females: 91.7; Marriage status: 37.8% never married, 42.5% now married, 0.6% separated, 9.1% widowed, 10.6% divorced; Foreign born: 0.4%; Speak English only: 98.9%; With disability: 21.5%; Veterans: 9.8%; Ancestry: 23.3% Polish, 17.0% German, 14.7% Irish, 9.7% Italian, 5.8% English
Employment: 4.1% management, business, and financial, 1.0% computer, engineering, and science, 6.7% education, legal, community service, arts, and media, 6.7% healthcare practitioners, 40.1% service, 16.9% sales and office, 10.2% natural resources, construction, and maintenance, 14.3% production, transportation, and material moving
Income: Per capita: $18,380; Median household: $32,708; Average household: $41,708; Households with income of $100,000 or more: 5.0%; Poverty rate: 15.6%
Educational Attainment: High school diploma or higher: 89.6%; Bachelor's degree or higher: 9.8%; Graduate/professional degree or higher: 3.4%

School District(s)

Buckeye Local (PK-12)
2015-16 Enrollment: 1,773 . . . . (740) 769-7395
Housing: Homeownership rate: 75.1%; Median home value: $59,400; Median year structure built: Before 1940; Homeowner vacancy rate: 1.9%; Median selected monthly owner costs: $739 with a mortgage, $372 without a mortgage; Median gross rent: $700 per month; Rental vacancy rate: 0.0%
Health Insurance: 86.8% have insurance; 59.4% have private insurance; 45.5% have public insurance; 13.2% do not have insurance; 7.7% of children under 18 do not have insurance
Transportation: Commute: 98.0% car, 0.0% public transportation, 2.0% walk, 0.0% work from home; Mean travel time to work: 30.5 minutes

AMSTERDAM (village). Covers a land area of 0.319 square miles and a water area of 0 square miles. Located at 40.47° N. Lat; 80.92° W. Long. Elevation is 928 feet.
History: Settled 1830, incorporated 1904.
Population: 440; Growth (since 2000): -22.5%; Density: 1,378.4 persons per square mile; Race: 99.1% White, 0.0% Black/African American, 0.0% Asian, 0.0% American Indian/Alaska Native, 0.0% Native Hawaiian/Other Pacific Islander, 0.9% Two or more races, 0.0% Hispanic of any race; Average household size: 2.42; Median age: 44.5; Age under 18: 23.6%; Age 65 and over: 16.8%; Males per 100 females: 86.5; Marriage status: 18.2% never married, 57.0% now married, 0.6% separated, 10.0% widowed, 14.8% divorced; Foreign born: 0.0%; Speak English only: 99.5%; With disability: 23.9%; Veterans: 9.8%; Ancestry: 20.5% German, 18.4% Irish, 10.5% American, 8.2% English, 6.1% Polish
Employment: 8.9% management, business, and financial, 1.1% computer, engineering, and science, 3.9% education, legal, community service, arts, and media, 11.7% healthcare practitioners, 20.6% service, 22.8% sales and office, 13.3% natural resources, construction, and maintenance, 17.8% production, transportation, and material moving
Income: Per capita: $18,567; Median household: $33,289; Average household: $42,481; Households with income of $100,000 or more: 6.5%; Poverty rate: 15.5%

Educational Attainment: High school diploma or higher: 80.0%; Bachelor's degree or higher: 8.0%; Graduate/professional degree or higher: 0.7%
Housing: Homeownership rate: 60.4%; Median home value: $50,400; Median year structure built: Before 1940; Homeowner vacancy rate: 0.0%; Median selected monthly owner costs: $796 with a mortgage, $316 without a mortgage; Median gross rent: $475 per month; Rental vacancy rate: 0.0%
Health Insurance: 83.2% have insurance; 50.5% have private insurance; 48.0% have public insurance; 16.8% do not have insurance; 19.2% of children under 18 do not have insurance
Transportation: Commute: 95.2% car, 0.0% public transportation, 0.0% walk, 3.6% work from home; Mean travel time to work: 34.8 minutes

BERGHOLZ (village). Covers a land area of 0.563 square miles and a water area of 0 square miles. Located at 40.52° N. Lat; 80.89° W. Long. Elevation is 925 feet.
History: Settled 1885, incorporated 1906.
Population: 782; Growth (since 2000): 1.7%; Density: 1,387.9 persons per square mile; Race: 99.2% White, 0.8% Black/African American, 0.0% Asian, 0.0% American Indian/Alaska Native, 0.0% Native Hawaiian/Other Pacific Islander, 0.0% Two or more races, 0.0% Hispanic of any race; Average household size: 2.98; Median age: 32.1; Age under 18: 32.1%; Age 65 and over: 6.0%; Males per 100 females: 91.4; Marriage status: 27.0% never married, 54.1% now married, 2.2% separated, 4.9% widowed, 14.0% divorced; Foreign born: 0.0%; Speak English only: 99.4%; With disability: 13.8%; Veterans: 8.5%; Ancestry: 28.0% German, 19.9% Irish, 7.5% English, 4.9% Dutch, 4.7% American
Employment: 9.6% management, business, and financial, 1.2% computer, engineering, and science, 4.1% education, legal, community service, arts, and media, 3.5% healthcare practitioners, 21.0% service, 22.2% sales and office, 14.3% natural resources, construction, and maintenance, 24.2% production, transportation, and material moving
Income: Per capita: $20,592; Median household: $41,094; Average household: $61,031; Households with income of $100,000 or more: 20.2%; Poverty rate: 30.6%
Educational Attainment: High school diploma or higher: 88.9%; Bachelor's degree or higher: 11.3%; Graduate/professional degree or higher: 1.5%

School District(s)

Edison Local (PK-12)
2015-16 Enrollment: 1,551 . . . . (330) 532-3199
Housing: Homeownership rate: 72.1%; Median home value: $60,200; Median year structure built: Before 1940; Homeowner vacancy rate: 0.0%; Median selected monthly owner costs: $720 with a mortgage, $352 without a mortgage; Median gross rent: $628 per month; Rental vacancy rate: 3.9%
Health Insurance: 92.2% have insurance; 57.9% have private insurance; 41.7% have public insurance; 7.8% do not have insurance; 0.0% of children under 18 do not have insurance
Transportation: Commute: 95.8% car, 0.0% public transportation, 2.7% walk, 1.5% work from home; Mean travel time to work: 29.9 minutes

BLOOMINGDALE (village). Covers a land area of 0.088 square miles and a water area of 0 square miles. Located at 40.34° N. Lat; 80.82° W. Long. Elevation is 1,263 feet.
History: Laid out 1816. Also called Bloomfield.
Population: 197; Growth (since 2000): -10.9%; Density: 2,229.4 persons per square mile; Race: 100.0% White, 0.0% Black/African American, 0.0% Asian, 0.0% American Indian/Alaska Native, 0.0% Native Hawaiian/Other Pacific Islander, 0.0% Two or more races, 0.0% Hispanic of any race; Average household size: 2.81; Median age: 42.4; Age under 18: 29.4%; Age 65 and over: 10.2%; Males per 100 females: 112.6; Marriage status: 16.0% never married, 65.3% now married, 3.5% separated, 8.3% widowed, 10.4% divorced; Foreign born: 0.0%; Speak English only: 100.0%; With disability: 15.7%; Veterans: 12.2%; Ancestry: 25.9% German, 16.8% Irish, 13.2% American, 9.6% Italian, 7.1% English
Employment: 5.4% management, business, and financial, 1.1% computer, engineering, and science, 8.7% education, legal, community service, arts, and media, 31.5% healthcare practitioners, 13.0% service, 22.8% sales and office, 9.8% natural resources, construction, and maintenance, 7.6% production, transportation, and material moving
Income: Per capita: $27,264; Median household: $56,250; Average household: $82,216; Households with income of $100,000 or more: 31.4%; Poverty rate: 20.3%
Educational Attainment: High school diploma or higher: 88.1%; Bachelor's degree or higher: 17.9%; Graduate/professional degree or higher: 9.7%

School District(s)

Indian Creek Local (PK-12)
2015-16 Enrollment: 2,166 . . . . (740) 264-3502
Jefferson County (10-12)
2015-16 Enrollment: n/a . . . . (740) 264-5545
Housing: Homeownership rate: 87.1%; Median home value: $82,300; Median year structure built: 1954; Homeowner vacancy rate: 0.0%; Median selected monthly owner costs: $750 with a mortgage, $375 without a mortgage; Median gross rent: n/a per month; Rental vacancy rate: 18.2%
Health Insurance: 94.9% have insurance; 79.2% have private insurance; 21.8% have public insurance; 5.1% do not have insurance; 0.0% of children under 18 do not have insurance
Transportation: Commute: 98.9% car, 0.0% public transportation, 0.0% walk, 0.0% work from home; Mean travel time to work: 21.4 minutes

BRILLIANT (CDP). Covers a land area of 1.754 square miles and a water area of 0.014 square miles. Located at 40.27° N. Lat; 80.64° W. Long. Elevation is 689 feet.
Population: 1,830; Growth (since 2000): n/a; Density: 1,043.5 persons per square mile; Race: 100.0% White, 0.0% Black/African American, 0.0% Asian, 0.0% American Indian/Alaska Native, 0.0% Native Hawaiian/Other Pacific Islander, 0.0% Two or more races, 0.0% Hispanic of any race; Average household size: 2.52; Median age: 41.0; Age under 18: 24.3%; Age 65 and over: 14.4%; Males per 100 females: 90.5; Marriage status: 27.5% never married, 46.0% now married, 4.1% separated, 8.5% widowed, 17.9% divorced; Foreign born: 0.0%; Speak English only: 99.6%; With disability: 19.9%; Veterans: 14.9%; Ancestry: 31.3% German, 30.4% Irish, 10.1% Italian, 9.7% English, 6.2% American
Employment: 3.6% management, business, and financial, 0.7% computer, engineering, and science, 1.1% education, legal, community service, arts, and media, 11.8% healthcare practitioners, 21.9% service, 39.9% sales and office, 9.0% natural resources, construction, and maintenance, 12.1% production, transportation, and material moving
Income: Per capita: $21,082; Median household: $41,349; Average household: $51,134; Households with income of $100,000 or more: 13.6%; Poverty rate: 18.1%
Educational Attainment: High school diploma or higher: 95.1%; Bachelor's degree or higher: 5.8%; Graduate/professional degree or higher: 0.7%

School District(s)

Buckeye Local (PK-12)
2015-16 Enrollment: 1,773 . . . . (740) 769-7395
Housing: Homeownership rate: 57.4%; Median home value: $66,700; Median year structure built: 1954; Homeowner vacancy rate: 6.7%; Median selected monthly owner costs: $819 with a mortgage, $330 without a mortgage; Median gross rent: $481 per month; Rental vacancy rate: 1.9%
Health Insurance: 88.9% have insurance; 64.5% have private insurance; 41.4% have public insurance; 11.1% do not have insurance; 0.0% of children under 18 do not have insurance
Transportation: Commute: 96.3% car, 0.0% public transportation, 1.2% walk, 2.5% work from home; Mean travel time to work: 21.3 minutes

CONNORVILLE (CDP).
Land/water area and latitude/longitude are not available.
Population: 207; Growth (since 2000): n/a; Density: n/a persons per square mile; Race: 100.0% White, 0.0% Black/African American, 0.0% Asian, 0.0% American Indian/Alaska Native, 0.0% Native Hawaiian/Other Pacific Islander, 0.0% Two or more races, 0.0% Hispanic of any race; Average household size: 2.44; Median age: 46.3; Age under 18: 22.7%; Age 65 and over: 11.6%; Males per 100 females: 0.0; Marriage status: 26.2% never married, 57.3% now married, 0.0% separated, 5.5% widowed, 11.0% divorced; Foreign born: 0.0%; Speak English only: 96.9%; With disability: 20.3%; Veterans: 3.1%; Ancestry: 35.3% Italian, 17.4% Polish, 15.9% Irish, 12.6% English, 7.2% American
Employment: 9.9% management, business, and financial, 0.0% computer, engineering, and science, 12.9% education, legal, community service, arts, and media, 10.9% healthcare practitioners, 14.9% service, 6.9% sales and office, 29.7% natural resources, construction, and maintenance, 14.9% production, transportation, and material moving
Income: Per capita: $33,041; Median household: $68,750; Average household: $79,604; Households with income of $100,000 or more: 27.0%; Poverty rate: 14.0%

Educational Attainment: High school diploma or higher: 97.1%; Bachelor's degree or higher: 18.8%; Graduate/professional degree or higher: 7.2%
Housing: Homeownership rate: 100.0%; Median home value: $136,300; Median year structure built: 1965; Homeowner vacancy rate: 0.0%; Median selected monthly owner costs: $991 with a mortgage, $347 without a mortgage; Median gross rent: n/a per month; Rental vacancy rate: 0.0%
Health Insurance: 100.0% have insurance; 77.8% have private insurance; 42.5% have public insurance; 0.0% do not have insurance; 0.0% of children under 18 do not have insurance
Safety: Violent crime rate: 0.0 per 10,000 population; Property crime rate: 0.0 per 10,000 population
Transportation: Commute: 93.1% car, 0.0% public transportation, 0.0% walk, 6.9% work from home; Mean travel time to work: 28.2 minutes

DILLONVALE (village). Covers a land area of 0.386 square miles and a water area of 0.008 square miles. Located at 40.20° N. Lat; 80.78° W. Long. Elevation is 735 feet.
History: Dillonvale grew in the center of a large coal-mining region.
Population: 645; Growth (since 2000): -17.4%; Density: 1,670.6 persons per square mile; Race: 90.7% White, 1.7% Black/African American, 0.6% Asian, 0.0% American Indian/Alaska Native, 0.0% Native Hawaiian/Other Pacific Islander, 7.0% Two or more races, 0.0% Hispanic of any race; Average household size: 2.32; Median age: 46.3; Age under 18: 20.0%; Age 65 and over: 18.3%; Males per 100 females: 89.5; Marriage status: 21.1% never married, 64.0% now married, 1.1% separated, 4.7% widowed, 10.2% divorced; Foreign born: 0.3%; Speak English only: 99.0%; With disability: 22.0%; Veterans: 13.0%; Ancestry: 20.2% German, 17.7% Polish, 14.0% Irish, 9.1% Italian, 6.8% English
Employment: 9.5% management, business, and financial, 1.6% computer, engineering, and science, 6.3% education, legal, community service, arts, and media, 10.5% healthcare practitioners, 15.1% service, 21.4% sales and office, 16.4% natural resources, construction, and maintenance, 19.1% production, transportation, and material moving
Income: Per capita: $22,619; Median household: $40,833; Average household: $52,509; Households with income of $100,000 or more: 10.4%; Poverty rate: 22.0%
Educational Attainment: High school diploma or higher: 91.2%; Bachelor's degree or higher: 12.9%; Graduate/professional degree or higher: 4.1%
Housing: Homeownership rate: 82.4%; Median home value: $56,900; Median year structure built: 1941; Homeowner vacancy rate: 0.8%; Median selected monthly owner costs: $864 with a mortgage, $425 without a mortgage; Median gross rent: $604 per month; Rental vacancy rate: 10.9%
Health Insurance: 95.8% have insurance; 63.9% have private insurance; 49.8% have public insurance; 4.2% do not have insurance; 0.0% of children under 18 do not have insurance
Transportation: Commute: 90.5% car, 0.0% public transportation, 8.8% walk, 0.7% work from home; Mean travel time to work: 30.0 minutes

EAST SPRINGFIELD (CDP).
Land/water area and latitude/longitude are not available.
Population: 574; Growth (since 2000): n/a; Density: n/a persons per square mile; Race: 100.0% White, 0.0% Black/African American, 0.0% Asian, 0.0% American Indian/Alaska Native, 0.0% Native Hawaiian/Other Pacific Islander, 0.0% Two or more races, 0.0% Hispanic of any race; Average household size: 3.40; Median age: 28.7; Age under 18: 31.4%; Age 65 and over: 0.0%; Males per 100 females: 0.0; Marriage status: 48.0% never married, 52.0% now married, 0.0% separated, 0.0% widowed, 0.0% divorced; Foreign born: 0.0%; Speak English only: 100.0%; With disability: 0.0%; Veterans: 6.6%; Ancestry: 35.7% American, 4.5% Czech, 4.0% German, 4.0% Italian, 3.5% Irish
Employment: 26.8% management, business, and financial, 16.0% computer, engineering, and science, 0.0% education, legal, community service, arts, and media, 16.0% healthcare practitioners, 18.3% service, 20.2% sales and office, 0.0% natural resources, construction, and maintenance, 2.7% production, transportation, and material moving
Income: Per capita: $18,294; Median household: n/a; Average household: $62,353; Households with income of $100,000 or more: 28.4%; Poverty rate: 35.7%
Educational Attainment: High school diploma or higher: 100.0%; Bachelor's degree or higher: 17.8%; Graduate/professional degree or higher: n/a
Housing: Homeownership rate: 61.5%; Median home value: $59,600; Median year structure built: Before 1940; Homeowner vacancy rate: 0.0%; Median selected monthly owner costs: $991 with a mortgage, n/a without a mortgage; Median gross rent: n/a per month; Rental vacancy rate: 0.0%
Health Insurance: 97.9% have insurance; 59.9% have private insurance; 38.0% have public insurance; 2.1% do not have insurance; 0.0% of children under 18 do not have insurance
Safety: Violent crime rate: 0.0 per 10,000 population; Property crime rate: 0.0 per 10,000 population
Transportation: Commute: 100.0% car, 0.0% public transportation, 0.0% walk, 0.0% work from home; Mean travel time to work: 36.9 minutes

EMPIRE (village). Covers a land area of 0.300 square miles and a water area of 0 square miles. Located at 40.51° N. Lat; 80.63° W. Long. Elevation is 682 feet.
Population: 242; Growth (since 2000): -19.3%; Density: 805.9 persons per square mile; Race: 100.0% White, 0.0% Black/African American, 0.0% Asian, 0.0% American Indian/Alaska Native, 0.0% Native Hawaiian/Other Pacific Islander, 0.0% Two or more races, 0.0% Hispanic of any race; Average household size: 2.12; Median age: 39.0; Age under 18: 20.7%; Age 65 and over: 10.7%; Males per 100 females: 88.1; Marriage status: 35.6% never married, 45.7% now married, 4.8% separated, 9.1% widowed, 9.6% divorced; Foreign born: 0.0%; Speak English only: 100.0%; With disability: 9.5%; Veterans: 9.9%; Ancestry: 21.5% Irish, 16.5% German, 11.2% English, 7.9% Swedish, 7.4% Polish
Employment: 6.1% management, business, and financial, 0.0% computer, engineering, and science, 2.6% education, legal, community service, arts, and media, 4.3% healthcare practitioners, 36.5% service, 10.4% sales and office, 10.4% natural resources, construction, and maintenance, 29.6% production, transportation, and material moving
Income: Per capita: $23,302; Median household: $30,625; Average household: $48,851; Households with income of $100,000 or more: 15.7%; Poverty rate: 26.9%
Educational Attainment: High school diploma or higher: 88.6%; Bachelor's degree or higher: 5.7%; Graduate/professional degree or higher: n/a
Housing: Homeownership rate: 64.9%; Median home value: $63,300; Median year structure built: 1961; Homeowner vacancy rate: 0.0%; Median selected monthly owner costs: $680 with a mortgage, $350 without a mortgage; Median gross rent: $507 per month; Rental vacancy rate: 9.1%
Health Insurance: 86.8% have insurance; 66.1% have private insurance; 40.5% have public insurance; 13.2% do not have insurance; 0.0% of children under 18 do not have insurance
Transportation: Commute: 87.8% car, 0.0% public transportation, 10.4% walk, 1.7% work from home; Mean travel time to work: 23.0 minutes

HAMMONDSVILLE (unincorporated postal area)
ZCTA: 43930
Covers a land area of 37.618 square miles and a water area of 0.121 square miles. Located at 40.56° N. Lat; 80.76° W. Long. Elevation is 689 feet.
Population: 860; Growth (since 2000): 15.7%; Density: 22.9 persons per square mile; Race: 98.6% White, 0.0% Black/African American, 0.0% Asian, 0.0% American Indian/Alaska Native, 0.0% Native Hawaiian/Other Pacific Islander, 1.4% Two or more races, 0.0% Hispanic of any race; Average household size: 2.39; Median age: 40.9; Age under 18: 26.7%; Age 65 and over: 27.2%; Males per 100 females: 101.4; Marriage status: 19.2% never married, 61.8% now married, 0.9% separated, 5.4% widowed, 13.7% divorced; Foreign born: 0.0%; Speak English only: 99.4%; With disability: 20.5%; Veterans: 21.0%; Ancestry: 33.1% German, 16.7% English, 13.0% American, 11.7% Irish, 11.0% Scottish
Employment: 10.6% management, business, and financial, 4.2% computer, engineering, and science, 3.9% education, legal, community service, arts, and media, 3.9% healthcare practitioners, 10.2% service, 18.4% sales and office, 23.7% natural resources, construction, and maintenance, 25.1% production, transportation, and material moving
Income: Per capita: $29,067; Median household: $43,854; Average household: $69,798; Households with income of $100,000 or more: 24.2%; Poverty rate: 11.4%
Educational Attainment: High school diploma or higher: 95.4%; Bachelor's degree or higher: 9.8%; Graduate/professional degree or higher: 0.8%

School District(s)

Edison Local (PK-12)
2015-16 Enrollment: 1,551 . . . . (330) 532-3199
Housing: Homeownership rate: 72.8%; Median home value: $85,000; Median year structure built: 1975; Homeowner vacancy rate: 0.0%; Median

selected monthly owner costs: $980 with a mortgage, $330 without a mortgage; Median gross rent: $680 per month; Rental vacancy rate: 14.8%
Health Insurance: 95.5% have insurance; 58.1% have private insurance; 46.5% have public insurance; 4.5% do not have insurance; 0.0% of children under 18 do not have insurance
Transportation: Commute: 94.0% car, 0.0% public transportation, 1.8% walk, 4.2% work from home; Mean travel time to work: 37.6 minutes

IRONDALE (village). Covers a land area of 1.449 square miles and a water area of 0.027 square miles. Located at 40.57° N. Lat; 80.73° W. Long. Elevation is 712 feet.
Population: 322; Growth (since 2000): -23.0%; Density: 222.2 persons per square mile; Race: 100.0% White, 0.0% Black/African American, 0.0% Asian, 0.0% American Indian/Alaska Native, 0.0% Native Hawaiian/Other Pacific Islander, 0.0% Two or more races, 0.0% Hispanic of any race; Average household size: 2.56; Median age: 33.5; Age under 18: 27.6%; Age 65 and over: 11.2%; Males per 100 females: 112.6; Marriage status: 26.3% never married, 55.6% now married, 3.3% separated, 5.8% widowed, 12.3% divorced; Foreign born: 0.0%; Speak English only: 100.0%; With disability: 15.8%; Veterans: 14.6%; Ancestry: 32.3% Irish, 26.1% German, 12.4% English, 6.5% Polish, 5.6% American
Employment: 1.6% management, business, and financial, 0.0% computer, engineering, and science, 7.0% education, legal, community service, arts, and media, 9.4% healthcare practitioners, 25.8% service, 3.1% sales and office, 17.2% natural resources, construction, and maintenance, 35.9% production, transportation, and material moving
Income: Per capita: $17,871; Median household: $38,750; Average household: $44,688; Households with income of $100,000 or more: 7.2%; Poverty rate: 16.7%
Educational Attainment: High school diploma or higher: 82.9%; Bachelor's degree or higher: 2.0%; Graduate/professional degree or higher: n/a
Housing: Homeownership rate: 79.4%; Median home value: $43,500; Median year structure built: Before 1940; Homeowner vacancy rate: 8.9%; Median selected monthly owner costs: $719 with a mortgage, $299 without a mortgage; Median gross rent: $607 per month; Rental vacancy rate: 0.0%
Health Insurance: 81.4% have insurance; 59.0% have private insurance; 42.2% have public insurance; 18.6% do not have insurance; 20.2% of children under 18 do not have insurance
Transportation: Commute: 98.4% car, 0.0% public transportation, 1.6% walk, 0.0% work from home; Mean travel time to work: 37.4 minutes

MINGO JUNCTION (village). Covers a land area of 2.690 square miles and a water area of 0.171 square miles. Located at 40.33° N. Lat; 80.62° W. Long. Elevation is 794 feet.
History: Mingo Junction developed near Steubenville as a steel town.
Population: 3,253; Growth (since 2000): -10.4%; Density: 1,209.5 persons per square mile; Race: 85.3% White, 5.1% Black/African American, 1.5% Asian, 2.2% American Indian/Alaska Native, 0.0% Native Hawaiian/Other Pacific Islander, 5.9% Two or more races, 3.6% Hispanic of any race; Average household size: 2.30; Median age: 50.5; Age under 18: 15.7%; Age 65 and over: 21.3%; Males per 100 females: 90.6; Marriage status: 28.0% never married, 46.4% now married, 1.2% separated, 8.9% widowed, 16.7% divorced; Foreign born: 1.5%; Speak English only: 96.6%; With disability: 20.1%; Veterans: 15.3%; Ancestry: 21.6% Italian, 19.7% German, 14.2% Irish, 6.9% English, 6.2% Slovak
Employment: 12.7% management, business, and financial, 2.0% computer, engineering, and science, 4.0% education, legal, community service, arts, and media, 9.4% healthcare practitioners, 23.6% service, 23.1% sales and office, 8.8% natural resources, construction, and maintenance, 16.3% production, transportation, and material moving
Income: Per capita: $24,745; Median household: $44,387; Average household: $56,699; Households with income of $100,000 or more: 20.4%; Poverty rate: 12.2%
Educational Attainment: High school diploma or higher: 95.9%; Bachelor's degree or higher: 13.9%; Graduate/professional degree or higher: 5.8%

School District(s)

Indian Creek Local (PK-12)
2015-16 Enrollment: 2,166 . . . . (740) 264-3502
Housing: Homeownership rate: 80.1%; Median home value: $79,700; Median year structure built: 1958; Homeowner vacancy rate: 6.6%; Median selected monthly owner costs: $868 with a mortgage, $364 without a mortgage; Median gross rent: $567 per month; Rental vacancy rate: 12.4%
Health Insurance: 90.8% have insurance; 63.5% have private insurance; 45.0% have public insurance; 9.2% do not have insurance; 11.6% of children under 18 do not have insurance
Safety: Violent crime rate: 45.5 per 10,000 population; Property crime rate: 133.4 per 10,000 population
Transportation: Commute: 96.3% car, 0.0% public transportation, 0.8% walk, 2.9% work from home; Mean travel time to work: 27.2 minutes

MOUNT PLEASANT (village). Covers a land area of 0.255 square miles and a water area of 0 square miles. Located at 40.18° N. Lat; 80.80° W. Long. Elevation is 1,247 feet.
History: Mount Pleasant began in the early 1800's as a Quaker community. The town was an abolitionist stronghold, and a refuge for fugitive slaves from the south long before the Civil War. The first abolitionist newspaper, the "Philanthopist," was published here in 1817 by Charles Osborn.
Population: 512; Growth (since 2000): -4.3%; Density: 2,008.0 persons per square mile; Race: 98.8% White, 0.6% Black/African American, 0.0% Asian, 0.0% American Indian/Alaska Native, 0.0% Native Hawaiian/Other Pacific Islander, 0.6% Two or more races, 0.0% Hispanic of any race; Average household size: 3.01; Median age: 40.0; Age under 18: 24.0%; Age 65 and over: 15.6%; Males per 100 females: 93.5; Marriage status: 23.9% never married, 55.1% now married, 0.5% separated, 4.6% widowed, 16.3% divorced; Foreign born: 0.8%; Speak English only: 99.0%; With disability: 15.4%; Veterans: 10.5%; Ancestry: 33.0% German, 19.5% Irish, 13.5% Polish, 13.3% Italian, 10.5% English
Employment: 12.0% management, business, and financial, 2.8% computer, engineering, and science, 10.1% education, legal, community service, arts, and media, 8.8% healthcare practitioners, 18.0% service, 12.0% sales and office, 12.9% natural resources, construction, and maintenance, 23.5% production, transportation, and material moving
Income: Per capita: $21,444; Median household: $44,286; Average household: $60,945; Households with income of $100,000 or more: 14.1%; Poverty rate: 19.8%
Educational Attainment: High school diploma or higher: 89.7%; Bachelor's degree or higher: 12.9%; Graduate/professional degree or higher: 6.9%
Housing: Homeownership rate: 87.1%; Median home value: $70,800; Median year structure built: Before 1940; Homeowner vacancy rate: 0.0%; Median selected monthly owner costs: $889 with a mortgage, $450 without a mortgage; Median gross rent: $1,094 per month; Rental vacancy rate: 8.3%
Health Insurance: 97.3% have insurance; 66.8% have private insurance; 42.4% have public insurance; 2.7% do not have insurance; 0.0% of children under 18 do not have insurance
Transportation: Commute: 94.4% car, 0.0% public transportation, 5.6% walk, 0.0% work from home; Mean travel time to work: 29.8 minutes

NEW ALEXANDRIA (village). Covers a land area of 0.367 square miles and a water area of 0 square miles. Located at 40.29° N. Lat; 80.68° W. Long. Elevation is 1,224 feet.
Population: 252; Growth (since 2000): 13.5%; Density: 686.9 persons per square mile; Race: 97.6% White, 0.0% Black/African American, 0.0% Asian, 0.0% American Indian/Alaska Native, 0.0% Native Hawaiian/Other Pacific Islander, 2.4% Two or more races, 0.0% Hispanic of any race; Average household size: 2.60; Median age: 49.3; Age under 18: 16.7%; Age 65 and over: 25.8%; Males per 100 females: 114.2; Marriage status: 29.4% never married, 55.7% now married, 5.4% separated, 5.9% widowed, 9.0% divorced; Foreign born: 0.0%; Speak English only: 99.6%; With disability: 26.6%; Veterans: 9.5%; Ancestry: 21.0% German, 13.1% Irish, 8.7% English, 7.1% Italian, 6.7% Hungarian
Employment: 6.9% management, business, and financial, 3.0% computer, engineering, and science, 6.9% education, legal, community service, arts, and media, 3.0% healthcare practitioners, 29.7% service, 19.8% sales and office, 10.9% natural resources, construction, and maintenance, 19.8% production, transportation, and material moving
Income: Per capita: $24,717; Median household: $43,125; Average household: $60,198; Households with income of $100,000 or more: 10.3%; Poverty rate: 18.7%
Educational Attainment: High school diploma or higher: 74.6%; Bachelor's degree or higher: 10.0%; Graduate/professional degree or higher: 5.0%
Housing: Homeownership rate: 73.2%; Median home value: $62,300; Median year structure built: 1944; Homeowner vacancy rate: 0.0%; Median

selected monthly owner costs: $870 with a mortgage, $370 without a mortgage; Median gross rent: $811 per month; Rental vacancy rate: 0.0%
Health Insurance: 90.1% have insurance; 50.8% have private insurance; 56.3% have public insurance; 9.9% do not have insurance; 4.8% of children under 18 do not have insurance
Transportation: Commute: 86.9% car, 5.1% public transportation, 0.0% walk, 7.1% work from home; Mean travel time to work: 36.7 minutes

POTTERY ADDITION (CDP). Covers a land area of 0.908 square miles and a water area of 0.185 square miles. Located at 40.40° N. Lat; 80.62° W. Long. Elevation is 686 feet.
Population: 119; Growth (since 2000): n/a; Density: 131.1 persons per square mile; Race: 100.0% White, 0.0% Black/African American, 0.0% Asian, 0.0% American Indian/Alaska Native, 0.0% Native Hawaiian/Other Pacific Islander, 0.0% Two or more races, 0.0% Hispanic of any race; Average household size: 2.16; Median age: 54.3; Age under 18: 0.0%; Age 65 and over: 22.7%; Males per 100 females: 102.1; Marriage status: 39.5% never married, 42.9% now married, 16.8% separated, 0.0% widowed, 17.6% divorced; Foreign born: 0.0%; Speak English only: 100.0%; With disability: 42.0%; Veterans: 15.1%; Ancestry: 15.1% Italian, 8.4% American, 8.4% German, 8.4% Polish, 7.6% Welsh
Employment: 11.1% management, business, and financial, 0.0% computer, engineering, and science, 0.0% education, legal, community service, arts, and media, 0.0% healthcare practitioners, 14.3% service, 15.9% sales and office, 28.6% natural resources, construction, and maintenance, 30.2% production, transportation, and material moving
Income: Per capita: $23,412; Median household: n/a; Average household: $48,602; Households with income of $100,000 or more: n/a; Poverty rate: 26.1%
Educational Attainment: High school diploma or higher: 90.0%; Bachelor's degree or higher: n/a; Graduate/professional degree or higher: n/a
Housing: Homeownership rate: 83.6%; Median home value: $67,900; Median year structure built: 1950; Homeowner vacancy rate: 27.0%; Median selected monthly owner costs: $1,107 with a mortgage, n/a without a mortgage; Median gross rent: n/a per month; Rental vacancy rate: 0.0%
Health Insurance: 91.6% have insurance; 58.8% have private insurance; 45.4% have public insurance; 8.4% do not have insurance; 0.0% of children under 18 do not have insurance
Transportation: Commute: 64.2% car, 0.0% public transportation, 0.0% walk, 35.8% work from home; Mean travel time to work: 0.0 minutes

RAYLAND (village). Covers a land area of 0.472 square miles and a water area of 0.027 square miles. Located at 40.18° N. Lat; 80.69° W. Long. Elevation is 679 feet.
Population: 412; Growth (since 2000): -5.1%; Density: 872.1 persons per square mile; Race: 98.1% White, 0.5% Black/African American, 0.0% Asian, 0.0% American Indian/Alaska Native, 0.0% Native Hawaiian/Other Pacific Islander, 1.5% Two or more races, 0.0% Hispanic of any race; Average household size: 2.33; Median age: 45.4; Age under 18: 23.3%; Age 65 and over: 19.4%; Males per 100 females: 95.8; Marriage status: 26.8% never married, 44.0% now married, 0.3% separated, 11.1% widowed, 18.1% divorced; Foreign born: 0.0%; Speak English only: 99.5%; With disability: 18.4%; Veterans: 11.1%; Ancestry: 18.7% German, 15.0% Polish, 14.8% Irish, 12.1% Italian, 11.9% English
Employment: 6.1% management, business, and financial, 0.0% computer, engineering, and science, 4.5% education, legal, community service, arts, and media, 5.1% healthcare practitioners, 34.3% service, 22.2% sales and office, 17.7% natural resources, construction, and maintenance, 10.1% production, transportation, and material moving
Income: Per capita: $18,724; Median household: $36,875; Average household: $42,040; Households with income of $100,000 or more: 5.1%; Poverty rate: 13.6%
Educational Attainment: High school diploma or higher: 88.9%; Bachelor's degree or higher: 10.4%; Graduate/professional degree or higher: 3.4%

School District(s)

Buckeye Local (PK-12)
2015-16 Enrollment: 1,773 . . . . (740) 769-7395
Housing: Homeownership rate: 76.8%; Median home value: $70,000; Median year structure built: Before 1940; Homeowner vacancy rate: 0.0%; Median selected monthly owner costs: $767 with a mortgage, $354 without a mortgage; Median gross rent: $638 per month; Rental vacancy rate: 0.0%
Health Insurance: 92.5% have insurance; 50.2% have private insurance; 54.9% have public insurance; 7.5% do not have insurance; 0.0% of children under 18 do not have insurance
Transportation: Commute: 87.8% car, 0.5% public transportation, 5.3% walk, 5.3% work from home; Mean travel time to work: 27.7 minutes

RICHMOND (village). Covers a land area of 0.553 square miles and a water area of 0 square miles. Located at 40.43° N. Lat; 80.77° W. Long. Elevation is 1,240 feet.
Population: 390; Growth (since 2000): -17.2%; Density: 705.2 persons per square mile; Race: 97.2% White, 0.0% Black/African American, 0.5% Asian, 0.0% American Indian/Alaska Native, 0.0% Native Hawaiian/Other Pacific Islander, 2.3% Two or more races, 2.3% Hispanic of any race; Average household size: 2.29; Median age: 51.8; Age under 18: 10.5%; Age 65 and over: 27.4%; Males per 100 females: 87.9; Marriage status: 17.4% never married, 66.9% now married, 2.2% separated, 3.4% widowed, 12.4% divorced; Foreign born: 1.5%; Speak English only: 99.0%; With disability: 16.9%; Veterans: 14.6%; Ancestry: 34.1% German, 19.2% Irish, 9.2% English, 7.4% Polish, 5.1% Italian
Employment: 8.6% management, business, and financial, 2.2% computer, engineering, and science, 6.5% education, legal, community service, arts, and media, 6.5% healthcare practitioners, 10.8% service, 28.1% sales and office, 10.3% natural resources, construction, and maintenance, 27.0% production, transportation, and material moving
Income: Per capita: $29,727; Median household: $46,719; Average household: $65,782; Households with income of $100,000 or more: 12.4%; Poverty rate: 7.4%
Educational Attainment: High school diploma or higher: 90.0%; Bachelor's degree or higher: 10.0%; Graduate/professional degree or higher: 2.7%

School District(s)

Edison Local (PK-12)
2015-16 Enrollment: 1,551 . . . . (330) 532-3199
Housing: Homeownership rate: 74.7%; Median home value: $86,100; Median year structure built: 1955; Homeowner vacancy rate: 0.0%; Median selected monthly owner costs: $979 with a mortgage, $272 without a mortgage; Median gross rent: $589 per month; Rental vacancy rate: 0.0%
Health Insurance: 91.8% have insurance; 72.6% have private insurance; 41.3% have public insurance; 8.2% do not have insurance; 0.0% of children under 18 do not have insurance
Transportation: Commute: 95.6% car, 0.0% public transportation, 1.1% walk, 1.7% work from home; Mean travel time to work: 26.0 minutes

SMITHFIELD (village). Covers a land area of 0.945 square miles and a water area of 0 square miles. Located at 40.27° N. Lat; 80.78° W. Long. Elevation is 1,247 feet.
Population: 827; Growth (since 2000): -4.6%; Density: 874.8 persons per square mile; Race: 84.6% White, 5.0% Black/African American, 0.0% Asian, 0.0% American Indian/Alaska Native, 0.0% Native Hawaiian/Other Pacific Islander, 10.2% Two or more races, 1.3% Hispanic of any race; Average household size: 2.51; Median age: 37.7; Age under 18: 25.5%; Age 65 and over: 20.1%; Males per 100 females: 90.6; Marriage status: 22.9% never married, 57.4% now married, 0.0% separated, 5.8% widowed, 13.9% divorced; Foreign born: 0.0%; Speak English only: 100.0%; With disability: 20.4%; Veterans: 16.6%; Ancestry: 28.7% German, 26.0% Irish, 10.2% English, 10.0% Polish, 8.2% Italian
Employment: 3.7% management, business, and financial, 1.2% computer, engineering, and science, 1.8% education, legal, community service, arts, and media, 7.3% healthcare practitioners, 17.4% service, 32.7% sales and office, 16.5% natural resources, construction, and maintenance, 19.3% production, transportation, and material moving
Income: Per capita: $19,455; Median household: $43,819; Average household: $49,216; Households with income of $100,000 or more: 10.3%; Poverty rate: 16.8%
Educational Attainment: High school diploma or higher: 90.5%; Bachelor's degree or higher: 16.2%; Graduate/professional degree or higher: 5.1%
Housing: Homeownership rate: 77.3%; Median home value: $68,600; Median year structure built: 1951; Homeowner vacancy rate: 4.0%; Median selected monthly owner costs: $931 with a mortgage, $394 without a mortgage; Median gross rent: $339 per month; Rental vacancy rate: 18.4%
Health Insurance: 95.2% have insurance; 66.6% have private insurance; 47.8% have public insurance; 4.8% do not have insurance; 0.0% of children under 18 do not have insurance

Transportation: Commute: 94.9% car, 1.3% public transportation, 1.9% walk, 1.9% work from home; Mean travel time to work: 26.0 minutes

STEUBENVILLE (city). County seat. Covers a land area of 10.545 square miles and a water area of 0.082 square miles. Located at 40.37° N. Lat; 80.66° W. Long. Elevation is 1,050 feet.

History: Jacob Walker came to the Ohio River in 1765. He was followed in 1786 by government scouts who selected this site for a fort, called Fort Steuben for Baron Frederick William von Steuben, a Prussian drillmaster who aided the colonies in the Revolutionary War. A community called La Belle sprang up around the fort, and when the fort was destroyed in 1790, the settlement remained. Bezaleel Wells and James Ross laid out the town in 1797. It was named Steubenville, and became the seat of Jefferson County. Industries began in the early 1800's with a pottery, a drift coal mine, nail factory and foundry. As river traffic increased, Steubenville became an important port. The Frazier, Kilgore and Company rolling mill, using the labels of Wheeling Steel and Weirton Steel, was erected in 1856.

Population: 18,305; Growth (since 2000): -3.7%; Density: 1,735.9 persons per square mile; Race: 80.8% White, 13.9% Black/African American, 0.8% Asian, 0.1% American Indian/Alaska Native, 0.0% Native Hawaiian/Other Pacific Islander, 4.2% Two or more races, 2.2% Hispanic of any race; Average household size: 2.22; Median age: 42.6; Age under 18: 18.1%; Age 65 and over: 20.9%; Males per 100 females: 85.7; Marriage status: 38.3% never married, 38.6% now married, 2.0% separated, 8.7% widowed, 14.4% divorced; Foreign born: 1.9%; Speak English only: 96.0%; With disability: 20.7%; Veterans: 8.4%; Ancestry: 19.6% German, 18.7% Irish, 16.9% Italian, 7.8% Polish, 6.8% English

Employment: 13.1% management, business, and financial, 2.4% computer, engineering, and science, 12.5% education, legal, community service, arts, and media, 7.5% healthcare practitioners, 22.1% service, 25.4% sales and office, 4.9% natural resources, construction, and maintenance, 12.1% production, transportation, and material moving

Income: Per capita: $20,584; Median household: $33,369; Average household: $48,861; Households with income of $100,000 or more: 11.2%; Poverty rate: 26.9%

Educational Attainment: High school diploma or higher: 87.6%; Bachelor's degree or higher: 20.9%; Graduate/professional degree or higher: 8.6%

School District(s)

Edison Local (PK-12)
 2015-16 Enrollment: 1,551 . . . . (330) 532-3199

Steubenville City (PK-12)
 2015-16 Enrollment: 2,425 . . . . (740) 283-3767

Four-year College(s)

Franciscan University of Steubenville (Private, Not-for-profit, Roman Catholic)
 Fall 2016 Enrollment: 2,759 . . . . (740) 283-3771
 2016-17 Tuition: In-state $25,680; Out-of-state $25,680

Two-year College(s)

Eastern Gateway Community College (Public)
 Fall 2016 Enrollment: 4,527 . . . . (740) 264-5591
 2016-17 Tuition: In-state $3,605; Out-of-state $4,445

Trinity Health System School of Nursing (Private, Not-for-profit, Roman Catholic)
 Fall 2016 Enrollment: 84 . . . . (740) 283-7467
 2016-17 Tuition: In-state $8,396; Out-of-state $8,620

Housing: Homeownership rate: 55.1%; Median home value: $86,800; Median year structure built: 1954; Homeowner vacancy rate: 0.7%; Median selected monthly owner costs: $944 with a mortgage, $411 without a mortgage; Median gross rent: $585 per month; Rental vacancy rate: 12.3%

Health Insurance: 92.4% have insurance; 60.7% have private insurance; 46.8% have public insurance; 7.6% do not have insurance; 4.0% of children under 18 do not have insurance

Hospitals: Trinity Medical Center East & Trinity Medical Center West (401 beds)

Safety: Violent crime rate: 33.1 per 10,000 population; Property crime rate: 598.2 per 10,000 population

Newspapers: Herald-Star (daily circulation 13,200)

Transportation: Commute: 82.3% car, 1.9% public transportation, 10.5% walk, 4.7% work from home; Mean travel time to work: 17.9 minutes

Airports: Jefferson County Airpark (general aviation)

Additional Information Contacts

City of Steubenville . . . . (740) 283-6000
 http://www.ci.steubenville.oh.us

STRATTON (village). Covers a land area of 0.537 square miles and a water area of 0 square miles. Located at 40.53° N. Lat; 80.63° W. Long. Elevation is 650 feet.

Population: 333; Growth (since 2000): 20.2%; Density: 620.5 persons per square mile; Race: 91.3% White, 2.7% Black/African American, 0.0% Asian, 0.0% American Indian/Alaska Native, 0.0% Native Hawaiian/Other Pacific Islander, 6.0% Two or more races, 0.0% Hispanic of any race; Average household size: 2.07; Median age: 47.4; Age under 18: 18.9%; Age 65 and over: 15.6%; Males per 100 females: 88.5; Marriage status: 17.1% never married, 52.7% now married, 0.7% separated, 5.8% widowed, 24.4% divorced; Foreign born: 0.0%; Speak English only: 99.4%; With disability: 24.9%; Veterans: 8.1%; Ancestry: 21.0% Irish, 17.1% German, 10.5% English, 6.9% Slovak, 6.6% Polish

Employment: 6.9% management, business, and financial, 0.0% computer, engineering, and science, 3.1% education, legal, community service, arts, and media, 7.5% healthcare practitioners, 18.8% service, 21.3% sales and office, 13.8% natural resources, construction, and maintenance, 28.8% production, transportation, and material moving

Income: Per capita: $19,679; Median household: $27,396; Average household: $39,083; Households with income of $100,000 or more: 8.1%; Poverty rate: 20.9%

Educational Attainment: High school diploma or higher: 91.9%; Bachelor's degree or higher: 6.5%; Graduate/professional degree or higher: n/a

Housing: Homeownership rate: 57.1%; Median home value: $47,500; Median year structure built: 1966; Homeowner vacancy rate: 0.0%; Median selected monthly owner costs: $667 with a mortgage, $270 without a mortgage; Median gross rent: $625 per month; Rental vacancy rate: 5.5%

Health Insurance: 94.6% have insurance; 65.2% have private insurance; 42.6% have public insurance; 5.4% do not have insurance; 0.0% of children under 18 do not have insurance

Transportation: Commute: 88.8% car, 0.0% public transportation, 6.9% walk, 0.0% work from home; Mean travel time to work: 19.0 minutes

TILTONSVILLE (village). Covers a land area of 0.525 square miles and a water area of 0.031 square miles. Located at 40.17° N. Lat; 80.70° W. Long. Elevation is 673 feet.

Population: 1,297; Growth (since 2000): -2.4%; Density: 2,470.9 persons per square mile; Race: 98.1% White, 0.5% Black/African American, 0.0% Asian, 0.0% American Indian/Alaska Native, 0.0% Native Hawaiian/Other Pacific Islander, 1.5% Two or more races, 0.0% Hispanic of any race; Average household size: 2.37; Median age: 43.7; Age under 18: 20.2%; Age 65 and over: 17.9%; Males per 100 females: 85.9; Marriage status: 27.5% never married, 51.4% now married, 1.7% separated, 6.9% widowed, 14.2% divorced; Foreign born: 0.0%; Speak English only: 99.0%; With disability: 18.5%; Veterans: 9.4%; Ancestry: 16.5% German, 15.8% Italian, 15.1% Irish, 12.6% English, 10.1% Polish

Employment: 7.8% management, business, and financial, 0.0% computer, engineering, and science, 9.6% education, legal, community service, arts, and media, 7.3% healthcare practitioners, 30.1% service, 24.6% sales and office, 11.3% natural resources, construction, and maintenance, 9.4% production, transportation, and material moving

Income: Per capita: $21,012; Median household: $31,154; Average household: $48,119; Households with income of $100,000 or more: 10.6%; Poverty rate: 18.7%

Educational Attainment: High school diploma or higher: 87.3%; Bachelor's degree or higher: 13.9%; Graduate/professional degree or higher: 5.8%

School District(s)

Buckeye Local (PK-12)
 2015-16 Enrollment: 1,773 . . . . (740) 769-7395

Housing: Homeownership rate: 60.9%; Median home value: $79,600; Median year structure built: 1950; Homeowner vacancy rate: 4.6%; Median selected monthly owner costs: $871 with a mortgage, $367 without a mortgage; Median gross rent: $611 per month; Rental vacancy rate: 0.0%

Health Insurance: 94.7% have insurance; 65.1% have private insurance; 46.4% have public insurance; 5.3% do not have insurance; 0.0% of children under 18 do not have insurance

Transportation: Commute: 94.9% car, 1.1% public transportation, 1.1% walk, 2.3% work from home; Mean travel time to work: 24.4 minutes

TORONTO (city). Covers a land area of 1.858 square miles and a water area of 0.276 square miles. Located at 40.46° N. Lat; 80.61° W. Long. Elevation is 696 feet.
History: Toronto was laid out in 1818 by John Depuy when it was called Newburg, and later Sloan's Station. In 1881 it was renamed Toronto for a prominent citizen who had come from Toronto, Canada.
Population: 5,087; Growth (since 2000): -10.4%; Density: 2,737.5 persons per square mile; Race: 93.6% White, 1.7% Black/African American, 0.2% Asian, 0.7% American Indian/Alaska Native, 0.0% Native Hawaiian/Other Pacific Islander, 3.7% Two or more races, 0.6% Hispanic of any race; Average household size: 2.26; Median age: 41.5; Age under 18: 20.4%; Age 65 and over: 19.0%; Males per 100 females: 88.2; Marriage status: 30.7% never married, 47.6% now married, 1.4% separated, 8.0% widowed, 13.6% divorced; Foreign born: 0.6%; Speak English only: 98.4%; With disability: 20.0%; Veterans: 9.8%; Ancestry: 23.8% Irish, 19.9% German, 9.1% English, 8.2% Italian, 6.3% American
Employment: 10.9% management, business, and financial, 1.1% computer, engineering, and science, 5.3% education, legal, community service, arts, and media, 7.7% healthcare practitioners, 29.4% service, 23.8% sales and office, 8.9% natural resources, construction, and maintenance, 12.9% production, transportation, and material moving
Income: Per capita: $20,464; Median household: $38,438; Average household: $45,434; Households with income of $100,000 or more: 9.8%; Poverty rate: 20.9%
Educational Attainment: High school diploma or higher: 92.2%; Bachelor's degree or higher: 9.6%; Graduate/professional degree or higher: 2.9%

School District(s)

Toronto City (PK-12)
2015-16 Enrollment: 940. . . . . (740) 537-2456
Housing: Homeownership rate: 63.1%; Median home value: $82,200; Median year structure built: 1955; Homeowner vacancy rate: 4.1%; Median selected monthly owner costs: $792 with a mortgage, $338 without a mortgage; Median gross rent: $589 per month; Rental vacancy rate: 0.0%
Health Insurance: 89.9% have insurance; 60.7% have private insurance; 43.3% have public insurance; 10.1% do not have insurance; 1.3% of children under 18 do not have insurance
Safety: Violent crime rate: 12.4 per 10,000 population; Property crime rate: 33.0 per 10,000 population
Transportation: Commute: 93.2% car, 0.0% public transportation, 2.3% walk, 2.8% work from home; Mean travel time to work: 24.5 minutes

WINTERSVILLE (village). Covers a land area of 3.119 square miles and a water area of <.001 square miles. Located at 40.38° N. Lat; 80.71° W. Long. Elevation is 1,260 feet.
History: Land office here for first land sales in Northwest Territory. Incorporated 1947.
Population: 4,077; Growth (since 2000): 0.2%; Density: 1,307.0 persons per square mile; Race: 90.7% White, 8.8% Black/African American, 0.0% Asian, 0.0% American Indian/Alaska Native, 0.0% Native Hawaiian/Other Pacific Islander, 0.5% Two or more races, 3.8% Hispanic of any race; Average household size: 2.41; Median age: 45.0; Age under 18: 20.1%; Age 65 and over: 23.1%; Males per 100 females: 87.9; Marriage status: 29.5% never married, 47.9% now married, 0.4% separated, 7.8% widowed, 14.8% divorced; Foreign born: 4.6%; Speak English only: 97.1%; With disability: 12.8%; Veterans: 9.7%; Ancestry: 20.5% Italian, 16.2% Irish, 13.6% German, 6.9% English, 6.5% Polish
Employment: 14.3% management, business, and financial, 4.7% computer, engineering, and science, 7.3% education, legal, community service, arts, and media, 10.6% healthcare practitioners, 17.7% service, 24.4% sales and office, 11.3% natural resources, construction, and maintenance, 9.8% production, transportation, and material moving
Income: Per capita: $26,782; Median household: $52,984; Average household: $64,330; Households with income of $100,000 or more: 15.3%; Poverty rate: 10.7%
Educational Attainment: High school diploma or higher: 93.6%; Bachelor's degree or higher: 20.2%; Graduate/professional degree or higher: 6.7%

School District(s)

Indian Creek Local (PK-12)
2015-16 Enrollment: 2,166 . . . . (740) 264-3502
Housing: Homeownership rate: 60.2%; Median home value: $111,200; Median year structure built: 1964; Homeowner vacancy rate: 0.0%; Median selected monthly owner costs: $1,011 with a mortgage, $445 without a mortgage; Median gross rent: $738 per month; Rental vacancy rate: 9.0%
Health Insurance: 94.7% have insurance; 72.8% have private insurance; 38.5% have public insurance; 5.3% do not have insurance; 1.5% of children under 18 do not have insurance
Safety: Violent crime rate: 2.7 per 10,000 population; Property crime rate: 151.2 per 10,000 population
Transportation: Commute: 96.0% car, 0.1% public transportation, 0.0% walk, 3.8% work from home; Mean travel time to work: 29.6 minutes

YORKVILLE (village). Covers a land area of 0.595 square miles and a water area of 0.002 square miles. Located at 40.15° N. Lat; 80.71° W. Long. Elevation is 659 feet.
History: Yorkville grew around the Wheeling Steel Corporation's mill. It was named for York, Pennsylvania, the former home of many of the early settlers.
Population: 1,127; Growth (since 2000): -8.4%; Density: 1,894.1 persons per square mile; Race: 99.1% White, 0.9% Black/African American, 0.0% Asian, 0.0% American Indian/Alaska Native, 0.0% Native Hawaiian/Other Pacific Islander, 0.0% Two or more races, 0.5% Hispanic of any race; Average household size: 2.13; Median age: 42.4; Age under 18: 16.3%; Age 65 and over: 20.1%; Males per 100 females: 90.3; Marriage status: 29.7% never married, 49.9% now married, 2.4% separated, 10.2% widowed, 10.2% divorced; Foreign born: 1.6%; Speak English only: 98.4%; With disability: 20.9%; Veterans: 10.0%; Ancestry: 19.1% German, 18.7% Italian, 14.4% Irish, 12.4% English, 9.2% Hungarian
Employment: 6.8% management, business, and financial, 0.4% computer, engineering, and science, 12.0% education, legal, community service, arts, and media, 5.9% healthcare practitioners, 23.9% service, 22.5% sales and office, 10.1% natural resources, construction, and maintenance, 18.4% production, transportation, and material moving
Income: Per capita: $20,958; Median household: $33,313; Average household: $44,589; Households with income of $100,000 or more: 5.6%; Poverty rate: 17.9%
Educational Attainment: High school diploma or higher: 90.1%; Bachelor's degree or higher: 14.6%; Graduate/professional degree or higher: 3.0%
Housing: Homeownership rate: 54.5%; Median home value: $79,200; Median year structure built: 1951; Homeowner vacancy rate: 0.0%; Median selected monthly owner costs: $763 with a mortgage, $319 without a mortgage; Median gross rent: $555 per month; Rental vacancy rate: 0.0%
Health Insurance: 91.4% have insurance; 57.7% have private insurance; 50.4% have public insurance; 8.6% do not have insurance; 0.0% of children under 18 do not have insurance
Transportation: Commute: 92.4% car, 2.7% public transportation, 2.9% walk, 1.1% work from home; Mean travel time to work: 28.5 minutes

Knox County

Located in central Ohio; drained by the Kokosing and Mohican Rivers and the North Fork of the Licking River. Covers a land area of 525.494 square miles, a water area of 4.139 square miles, and is located in the Eastern Time Zone at 40.40° N. Lat., 82.42° W. Long. The county was founded in 1808. County seat is Mount Vernon.

Knox County is part of the Mount Vernon, OH Micropolitan Statistical Area. The entire metro area includes: Knox County, OH

Weather Station: Centerburg 2 SE — Elevation: 1,205 feet

	Jan	Feb	Mar	Apr	May	Jun	Jul	Aug	Sep	Oct	Nov	Dec
High	34	37	48	61	71	79	83	81	75	63	50	37
Low	17	20	28	39	49	58	62	60	52	41	32	22
Precip	2.9	2.4	3.1	3.8	4.5	4.6	4.4	3.7	3.2	2.9	3.5	3.1
Snow	4.6	2.1	2.1	0.2	tr	0.0	0.0	0.0	0.0	0.1	0.8	2.5

High and Low temperatures in degrees Fahrenheit; Precipitation and Snow in inches

Weather Station: Danville 2 W — Elevation: 970 feet

	Jan	Feb	Mar	Apr	May	Jun	Jul	Aug	Sep	Oct	Nov	Dec
High	35	39	49	61	71	80	83	82	76	64	51	39
Low	17	19	26	35	45	55	59	57	49	37	30	22
Precip	2.8	2.4	3.2	3.6	4.7	4.6	4.6	3.7	3.1	2.8	3.2	3.2
Snow	12.2	8.5	6.2	1.8	tr	0.0	0.0	0.0	0.0	tr	2.2	8.2

High and Low temperatures in degrees Fahrenheit; Precipitation and Snow in inches

Weather Station: Fredericktown 4 S Elevation: 1,049 feet

	Jan	Feb	Mar	Apr	May	Jun	Jul	Aug	Sep	Oct	Nov	Dec
High	33	37	47	60	70	79	82	81	75	63	51	39
Low	15	18	26	36	46	55	59	56	49	37	30	22
Precip	2.4	1.9	3.0	3.4	4.3	4.1	4.3	3.4	3.1	2.7	3.0	2.7
Snow	8.7	5.6	3.5	0.7	tr	0.0	0.0	0.0	0.0	0.0	1.1	5.4

High and Low temperatures in degrees Fahrenheit; Precipitation and Snow in inches

Population: 60,878; Growth (since 2000): 11.7%; Density: 115.8 persons per square mile; Race: 96.5% White, 1.0% Black/African American, 0.4% Asian, 0.1% American Indian/Alaska Native, 0.0% Native Hawaiian/Other Pacific Islander, 1.8% two or more races, 1.4% Hispanic of any race; Average household size: 2.49; Median age: 39.0; Age under 18: 23.2%; Age 65 and over: 16.3%; Males per 100 females: 95.4; Marriage status: 28.3% never married, 53.1% now married, 1.6% separated, 7.7% widowed, 10.9% divorced; Foreign born: 1.3%; Speak English only: 95.4%; With disability: 14.1%; Veterans: 9.3%; Ancestry: 28.7% German, 14.2% Irish, 13.2% English, 8.4% American, 4.1% Italian
Religion: Six largest groups: 7.3% Baptist, 6.1% Methodist/Pietist, 5.3% Catholicism, 4.7% Holiness, 4.2% European Free-Church, 2.6% Pentecostal
Economy: Unemployment rate: 4.1%; Leading industries: 17.1 % retail trade; 13.7 % other services (except public administration); 12.9 % health care and social assistance; Farms: 1,374 totaling 186,047 acres; Company size: 3 employ 1,000 or more persons, 3 employ 500 to 999 persons, 16 employ 100 to 499 persons, 1,038 employ less than 100 persons; Business ownership: 1,365 women-owned, 37 Black-owned, 33 Hispanic-owned, 59 Asian-owned, n/a American Indian/Alaska Native-owned
Employment: 13.4% management, business, and financial, 3.4% computer, engineering, and science, 9.6% education, legal, community service, arts, and media, 5.1% healthcare practitioners, 19.3% service, 20.5% sales and office, 10.0% natural resources, construction, and maintenance, 18.7% production, transportation, and material moving
Income: Per capita: $23,426; Median household: $48,619; Average household: $60,027; Households with income of $100,000 or more: 14.7%; Poverty rate: 15.6%
Educational Attainment: High school diploma or higher: 89.6%; Bachelor's degree or higher: 21.9%; Graduate/professional degree or higher: 7.2%
Housing: Homeownership rate: 70.7%; Median home value: $135,600; Median year structure built: 1973; Homeowner vacancy rate: 1.5%; Median selected monthly owner costs: $1,145 with a mortgage, $420 without a mortgage; Median gross rent: $692 per month; Rental vacancy rate: 3.2%
Vital Statistics: Birth rate: 114.6 per 10,000 population; Death rate: 103.3 per 10,000 population; Age-adjusted cancer mortality rate: 175.0 deaths per 100,000 population
Health Insurance: 89.1% have insurance; 67.0% have private insurance; 34.8% have public insurance; 10.9% do not have insurance; 12.6% of children under 18 do not have insurance
Health Care: Physicians: 8.9 per 10,000 population; Dentists: 3.8 per 10,000 population; Hospital beds: 10.0 per 10,000 population; Hospital admissions: 484.0 per 10,000 population
Air Quality Index (AQI): Percent of Days: 82.2% good, 17.8% moderate, 0.0% unhealthy for sensitive individuals, 0.0% unhealthy, 0.0% very unhealthy; Annual median: 41; Annual maximum: 100
Transportation: Commute: 87.5% car, 0.5% public transportation, 4.7% walk, 6.0% work from home; Mean travel time to work: 25.6 minutes
2016 Presidential Election: 66.1% Trump, 28.2% Clinton, 3.2% Johnson, 0.7% Stein
National and State Parks: Knox Lake State Wildlife Area; Knox Woods State Nature Preserve
Additional Information Contacts
Knox Government . . . . (740) 393-6703
http://www.co.knox.oh.us

Knox County Communities

APPLE VALLEY (CDP). Covers a land area of 6.013 square miles and a water area of 0.795 square miles. Located at 40.44° N. Lat; 82.35° W. Long. Elevation is 1,125 feet.
Population: 5,565; Growth (since 2000): n/a; Density: 925.4 persons per square mile; Race: 97.1% White, 1.0% Black/African American, 0.8% Asian, 0.3% American Indian/Alaska Native, 0.0% Native Hawaiian/Other Pacific Islander, 1.0% Two or more races, 0.4% Hispanic of any race; Average household size: 2.49; Median age: 45.6; Age under 18: 21.3%; Age 65 and over: 24.7%; Males per 100 females: 101.4; Marriage status: 15.5% never married, 68.2% now married, 0.1% separated, 9.1% widowed, 7.3% divorced; Foreign born: 3.6%; Speak English only: 98.4%; With disability: 15.1%; Veterans: 12.4%; Ancestry: 21.6% German, 15.0% Irish, 12.9% English, 10.9% American, 4.1% Dutch
Employment: 17.1% management, business, and financial, 3.6% computer, engineering, and science, 14.2% education, legal, community service, arts, and media, 8.8% healthcare practitioners, 9.3% service, 23.9% sales and office, 6.5% natural resources, construction, and maintenance, 16.6% production, transportation, and material moving
Income: Per capita: $29,644; Median household: $60,656; Average household: $73,577; Households with income of $100,000 or more: 16.6%; Poverty rate: 7.7%
Educational Attainment: High school diploma or higher: 91.9%; Bachelor's degree or higher: 28.2%; Graduate/professional degree or higher: 7.5%
Housing: Homeownership rate: 92.4%; Median home value: $144,800; Median year structure built: 1995; Homeowner vacancy rate: 0.0%; Median selected monthly owner costs: $1,164 with a mortgage, $437 without a mortgage; Median gross rent: $1,188 per month; Rental vacancy rate: 0.0%
Health Insurance: 96.7% have insurance; 77.1% have private insurance; 37.7% have public insurance; 3.3% do not have insurance; 1.9% of children under 18 do not have insurance
Transportation: Commute: 92.1% car, 0.1% public transportation, 0.0% walk, 7.8% work from home; Mean travel time to work: 35.2 minutes

BLADENSBURG (CDP). Covers a land area of 0.330 square miles and a water area of 0.002 square miles. Located at 40.29° N. Lat; 82.28° W. Long. Elevation is 961 feet.
Population: 111; Growth (since 2000): n/a; Density: 336.2 persons per square mile; Race: 100.0% White, 0.0% Black/African American, 0.0% Asian, 0.0% American Indian/Alaska Native, 0.0% Native Hawaiian/Other Pacific Islander, 0.0% Two or more races, 0.0% Hispanic of any race; Average household size: 2.06; Median age: 59.3; Age under 18: 17.1%; Age 65 and over: 16.2%; Males per 100 females: 83.7; Marriage status: 42.4% never married, 50.0% now married, 0.0% separated, 7.6% widowed, 0.0% divorced; Foreign born: 0.0%; Speak English only: 100.0%; With disability: 56.8%; Veterans: 0.0%; Ancestry: 27.9% German, 18.0% American, 9.9% English, 6.3% Irish, 4.5% Welsh
Employment: 0.0% management, business, and financial, 0.0% computer, engineering, and science, 0.0% education, legal, community service, arts, and media, 0.0% healthcare practitioners, 46.7% service, 0.0% sales and office, 30.0% natural resources, construction, and maintenance, 23.3% production, transportation, and material moving
Income: Per capita: $19,018; Median household: $42,045; Average household: $39,709; Households with income of $100,000 or more: n/a; Poverty rate: 37.8%
Educational Attainment: High school diploma or higher: 90.2%; Bachelor's degree or higher: n/a; Graduate/professional degree or higher: n/a

School District(s)

East Knox Local (KG-12)
2015-16 Enrollment: 923. . . . . (740) 599-7493
Housing: Homeownership rate: 63.0%; Median home value: $84,500; Median year structure built: 1972; Homeowner vacancy rate: 0.0%; Median selected monthly owner costs: n/a with a mortgage, n/a without a mortgage; Median gross rent: n/a per month; Rental vacancy rate: 0.0%
Health Insurance: 88.3% have insurance; 48.6% have private insurance; 55.9% have public insurance; 11.7% do not have insurance; 0.0% of children under 18 do not have insurance
Transportation: Commute: 100.0% car, 0.0% public transportation, 0.0% walk, 0.0% work from home; Mean travel time to work: 0.0 minutes

CENTERBURG (village). Covers a land area of 0.895 square miles and a water area of 0.003 square miles. Located at 40.30° N. Lat; 82.70° W. Long. Elevation is 1,227 feet.
History: Centerburg was settled in 1806 and named for its position near the geographical center of the state.
Population: 1,796; Growth (since 2000): 25.4%; Density: 2,007.0 persons per square mile; Race: 94.9% White, 3.7% Black/African American, 0.0% Asian, 0.0% American Indian/Alaska Native, 0.0% Native Hawaiian/Other Pacific Islander, 1.2% Two or more races, 0.2% Hispanic of any race; Average household size: 2.61; Median age: 37.4; Age under 18: 25.2%;

Age 65 and over: 13.8%; Males per 100 females: 89.8; Marriage status: 26.4% never married, 46.4% now married, 4.6% separated, 13.1% widowed, 14.1% divorced; Foreign born: 0.1%; Speak English only: 99.0%; With disability: 15.8%; Veterans: 10.2%; Ancestry: 28.8% German, 17.3% Irish, 14.3% English, 9.2% Italian, 7.3% American

Employment: 18.0% management, business, and financial, 4.8% computer, engineering, and science, 3.8% education, legal, community service, arts, and media, 7.6% healthcare practitioners, 22.4% service, 25.5% sales and office, 9.0% natural resources, construction, and maintenance, 8.9% production, transportation, and material moving

Income: Per capita: $20,723; Median household: $36,667; Average household: $53,538; Households with income of $100,000 or more: 15.2%; Poverty rate: 19.7%

Educational Attainment: High school diploma or higher: 90.8%; Bachelor's degree or higher: 16.4%; Graduate/professional degree or higher: 3.7%

School District(s)

Centerburg Local (KG-12)
2015-16 Enrollment: 1,068 . . . . (740) 625-6346

Housing: Homeownership rate: 48.9%; Median home value: $150,800; Median year structure built: 1963; Homeowner vacancy rate: 0.0%; Median selected monthly owner costs: $1,261 with a mortgage, $458 without a mortgage; Median gross rent: $636 per month; Rental vacancy rate: 3.7%

Health Insurance: 89.2% have insurance; 63.9% have private insurance; 32.5% have public insurance; 10.8% do not have insurance; 5.3% of children under 18 do not have insurance

Transportation: Commute: 88.1% car, 0.0% public transportation, 5.6% walk, 5.9% work from home; Mean travel time to work: 28.7 minutes

DANVILLE (village). Covers a land area of 0.553 square miles and a water area of 0.005 square miles. Located at 40.45° N. Lat; 82.26° W. Long. Elevation is 988 feet.

Population: 1,138; Growth (since 2000): 3.1%; Density: 2,056.0 persons per square mile; Race: 95.1% White, 0.6% Black/African American, 0.0% Asian, 0.0% American Indian/Alaska Native, 0.0% Native Hawaiian/Other Pacific Islander, 3.3% Two or more races, 3.5% Hispanic of any race; Average household size: 2.26; Median age: 40.3; Age under 18: 19.9%; Age 65 and over: 17.9%; Males per 100 females: 97.0; Marriage status: 31.0% never married, 43.9% now married, 4.0% separated, 11.5% widowed, 13.6% divorced; Foreign born: 0.0%; Speak English only: 97.4%; With disability: 14.2%; Veterans: 12.4%; Ancestry: 30.6% German, 20.3% Irish, 6.9% American, 5.1% English, 2.9% Italian

Employment: 12.6% management, business, and financial, 0.9% computer, engineering, and science, 5.6% education, legal, community service, arts, and media, 4.8% healthcare practitioners, 26.8% service, 18.4% sales and office, 14.1% natural resources, construction, and maintenance, 16.7% production, transportation, and material moving

Income: Per capita: $19,890; Median household: $36,850; Average household: $44,109; Households with income of $100,000 or more: 5.8%; Poverty rate: 17.8%

Educational Attainment: High school diploma or higher: 85.4%; Bachelor's degree or higher: 15.4%; Graduate/professional degree or higher: 3.3%

School District(s)

Danville Local (PK-12)
2015-16 Enrollment: 646. . . . . (740) 599-6116

Housing: Homeownership rate: 51.3%; Median home value: $83,700; Median year structure built: Before 1940; Homeowner vacancy rate: 0.0%; Median selected monthly owner costs: $785 with a mortgage, $350 without a mortgage; Median gross rent: $593 per month; Rental vacancy rate: 9.3%

Health Insurance: 88.3% have insurance; 56.7% have private insurance; 41.9% have public insurance; 11.7% do not have insurance; 6.2% of children under 18 do not have insurance

Transportation: Commute: 90.6% car, 0.0% public transportation, 3.9% walk, 3.7% work from home; Mean travel time to work: 28.6 minutes

FREDERICKTOWN (village). Covers a land area of 1.974 square miles and a water area of 0.102 square miles. Located at 40.48° N. Lat; 82.55° W. Long. Elevation is 1,096 feet.

Population: 3,084; Growth (since 2000): 27.0%; Density: 1,561.9 persons per square mile; Race: 97.6% White, 0.8% Black/African American, 0.0% Asian, 0.0% American Indian/Alaska Native, 0.0% Native Hawaiian/Other Pacific Islander, 1.0% Two or more races, 0.8% Hispanic of any race; Average household size: 2.49; Median age: 36.8; Age under 18: 25.8%; Age 65 and over: 16.2%; Males per 100 females: 94.9; Marriage status: 25.5% never married, 55.9% now married, 2.1% separated, 7.6% widowed, 10.9% divorced; Foreign born: 0.0%; Speak English only: 98.9%; With disability: 13.1%; Veterans: 10.0%; Ancestry: 36.0% German, 17.3% Irish, 16.2% English, 8.7% American, 5.3% Italian

Employment: 11.6% management, business, and financial, 4.9% computer, engineering, and science, 9.1% education, legal, community service, arts, and media, 3.8% healthcare practitioners, 22.6% service, 23.2% sales and office, 6.8% natural resources, construction, and maintenance, 18.0% production, transportation, and material moving

Income: Per capita: $24,728; Median household: $40,673; Average household: $60,165; Households with income of $100,000 or more: 9.6%; Poverty rate: 12.3%

Educational Attainment: High school diploma or higher: 92.2%; Bachelor's degree or higher: 20.8%; Graduate/professional degree or higher: 8.9%

School District(s)

Fredericktown Local (KG-12)
2015-16 Enrollment: 1,209 . . . . (740) 694-2956

Housing: Homeownership rate: 67.6%; Median home value: $100,600; Median year structure built: 1959; Homeowner vacancy rate: 1.1%; Median selected monthly owner costs: $1,046 with a mortgage, $421 without a mortgage; Median gross rent: $748 per month; Rental vacancy rate: 0.0%

Health Insurance: 86.2% have insurance; 61.4% have private insurance; 38.8% have public insurance; 13.8% do not have insurance; 14.3% of children under 18 do not have insurance

Safety: Violent crime rate: 24.1 per 10,000 population; Property crime rate: 164.9 per 10,000 population

Newspapers: Knox County Citizen (weekly circulation 1,400)

Transportation: Commute: 91.9% car, 0.1% public transportation, 3.8% walk, 2.9% work from home; Mean travel time to work: 25.6 minutes

GAMBIER (village). Covers a land area of 0.935 square miles and a water area of <.001 square miles. Located at 40.38° N. Lat; 82.39° W. Long. Elevation is 1,076 feet.

History: Gambier was the site of the founding of Kenyon College, established in 1824 by Philander Chase, first Episcopal bishop of Ohio, as a Theological Seminary. The college was located on land donated by Lord Gambier, for whom the town was named.

Population: 2,469; Growth (since 2000): 32.0%; Density: 2,640.6 persons per square mile; Race: 92.2% White, 2.3% Black/African American, 1.7% Asian, 0.0% American Indian/Alaska Native, 0.0% Native Hawaiian/Other Pacific Islander, 3.0% Two or more races, 3.4% Hispanic of any race; Average household size: 2.05; Median age: 21.0; Age under 18: 2.8%; Age 65 and over: 7.7%; Males per 100 females: 89.9; Marriage status: 80.7% never married, 14.0% now married, 0.6% separated, 1.2% widowed, 4.1% divorced; Foreign born: 3.3%; Speak English only: 91.2%; With disability: 5.0%; Veterans: 1.2%; Ancestry: 29.3% German, 14.3% Irish, 8.3% English, 5.4% Italian, 4.7% Scottish

Employment: 19.2% management, business, and financial, 1.5% computer, engineering, and science, 31.9% education, legal, community service, arts, and media, 1.5% healthcare practitioners, 21.1% service, 19.9% sales and office, 3.1% natural resources, construction, and maintenance, 1.7% production, transportation, and material moving

Income: Per capita: $14,487; Median household: $70,368; Average household: $77,139; Households with income of $100,000 or more: 34.4%; Poverty rate: 24.1%

Educational Attainment: High school diploma or higher: 99.5%; Bachelor's degree or higher: 76.5%; Graduate/professional degree or higher: 52.6%

School District(s)

Mount Vernon City (PK-12)
2015-16 Enrollment: 3,817 . . . . (740) 397-7422

Four-year College(s)

Kenyon College (Private, Not-for-profit)
Fall 2016 Enrollment: 1,708 . . . . (740) 427-5000
2016-17 Tuition: In-state $51,200; Out-of-state $51,200

Housing: Homeownership rate: 62.8%; Median home value: $216,500; Median year structure built: 1968; Homeowner vacancy rate: 0.0%; Median selected monthly owner costs: $1,516 with a mortgage, $431 without a mortgage; Median gross rent: $563 per month; Rental vacancy rate: 9.0%

Health Insurance: 95.9% have insurance; 92.4% have private insurance; 10.2% have public insurance; 4.1% do not have insurance; 0.0% of children under 18 do not have insurance

Transportation: Commute: 33.5% car, 0.0% public transportation, 50.0% walk, 16.1% work from home; Mean travel time to work: 17.0 minutes

GANN (village). Covers a land area of 0.187 square miles and a water area of 0.012 square miles. Located at 40.47° N. Lat; 82.19° W. Long. Elevation is 902 feet.
Population: 127; Growth (since 2000): -11.2%; Density: 679.9 persons per square mile; Race: 100.0% White, 0.0% Black/African American, 0.0% Asian, 0.0% American Indian/Alaska Native, 0.0% Native Hawaiian/Other Pacific Islander, 0.0% Two or more races, 0.0% Hispanic of any race; Average household size: 2.19; Median age: 45.1; Age under 18: 15.0%; Age 65 and over: 13.4%; Males per 100 females: 104.9; Marriage status: 41.7% never married, 32.4% now married, 0.0% separated, 6.5% widowed, 19.4% divorced; Foreign born: 0.0%; Speak English only: 100.0%; With disability: 11.0%; Veterans: 12.0%; Ancestry: 22.0% Irish, 20.5% German, 11.8% English, 8.7% American, 3.9% Greek
Employment: 1.5% management, business, and financial, 0.0% computer, engineering, and science, 7.4% education, legal, community service, arts, and media, 4.4% healthcare practitioners, 25.0% service, 10.3% sales and office, 20.6% natural resources, construction, and maintenance, 30.9% production, transportation, and material moving
Income: Per capita: $22,136; Median household: $46,000; Average household: $47,022; Households with income of $100,000 or more: 12.1%; Poverty rate: 18.9%
Educational Attainment: High school diploma or higher: 91.3%; Bachelor's degree or higher: 7.6%; Graduate/professional degree or higher: n/a
Housing: Homeownership rate: 58.6%; Median home value: $65,000; Median year structure built: Before 1940; Homeowner vacancy rate: 10.5%; Median selected monthly owner costs: $580 with a mortgage, $350 without a mortgage; Median gross rent: $769 per month; Rental vacancy rate: 0.0%
Health Insurance: 90.6% have insurance; 77.2% have private insurance; 33.9% have public insurance; 9.4% do not have insurance; 0.0% of children under 18 do not have insurance
Transportation: Commute: 91.2% car, 0.0% public transportation, 0.0% walk, 8.8% work from home; Mean travel time to work: 28.6 minutes

HOWARD (CDP). Covers a land area of 0.224 square miles and a water area of 0 square miles. Located at 40.41° N. Lat; 82.33° W. Long. Elevation is 902 feet.
Population: 164; Growth (since 2000): n/a; Density: 732.8 persons per square mile; Race: 100.0% White, 0.0% Black/African American, 0.0% Asian, 0.0% American Indian/Alaska Native, 0.0% Native Hawaiian/Other Pacific Islander, 0.0% Two or more races, 0.0% Hispanic of any race; Average household size: 2.38; Median age: 51.0; Age under 18: 16.5%; Age 65 and over: 24.4%; Males per 100 females: 112.3; Marriage status: 7.3% never married, 65.0% now married, 0.0% separated, 8.8% widowed, 19.0% divorced; Foreign born: 0.0%; Speak English only: 100.0%; With disability: 12.8%; Veterans: 21.9%; Ancestry: 30.5% Irish, 26.2% English, 16.5% Italian, 7.3% German, 6.1% American
Employment: 0.0% management, business, and financial, 10.6% computer, engineering, and science, 0.0% education, legal, community service, arts, and media, 0.0% healthcare practitioners, 45.9% service, 11.8% sales and office, 0.0% natural resources, construction, and maintenance, 31.8% production, transportation, and material moving
Income: Per capita: $14,564; Median household: $31,940; Average household: $34,754; Households with income of $100,000 or more: n/a; Poverty rate: 29.9%
Educational Attainment: High school diploma or higher: 100.0%; Bachelor's degree or higher: n/a; Graduate/professional degree or higher: n/a

School District(s)

East Knox Local (KG-12)
2015-16 Enrollment: 923 . . . . (740) 599-7493
Housing: Homeownership rate: 68.1%; Median home value: $84,300; Median year structure built: Before 1940; Homeowner vacancy rate: 0.0%; Median selected monthly owner costs: n/a with a mortgage, n/a without a mortgage; Median gross rent: n/a per month; Rental vacancy rate: 0.0%
Health Insurance: 100.0% have insurance; 79.9% have private insurance; 37.2% have public insurance; 0.0% do not have insurance; 0.0% of children under 18 do not have insurance
Transportation: Commute: 68.2% car, 0.0% public transportation, 0.0% walk, 31.8% work from home; Mean travel time to work: 0.0 minutes

MARTINSBURG (village). Covers a land area of 0.177 square miles and a water area of <.001 square miles. Located at 40.27° N. Lat; 82.35° W. Long. Elevation is 1,175 feet.
Population: 248; Growth (since 2000): 34.1%; Density: 1,404.1 persons per square mile; Race: 99.2% White, 0.8% Black/African American, 0.0% Asian, 0.0% American Indian/Alaska Native, 0.0% Native Hawaiian/Other Pacific Islander, 0.0% Two or more races, 0.0% Hispanic of any race; Average household size: 2.70; Median age: 29.1; Age under 18: 29.8%; Age 65 and over: 13.3%; Males per 100 females: 107.9; Marriage status: 39.8% never married, 38.7% now married, 1.0% separated, 4.2% widowed, 17.3% divorced; Foreign born: 0.0%; Speak English only: 99.6%; With disability: 13.7%; Veterans: 4.6%; Ancestry: 19.0% German, 19.0% Irish, 8.5% American, 6.9% English, 5.2% French Canadian
Employment: 7.3% management, business, and financial, 0.0% computer, engineering, and science, 0.0% education, legal, community service, arts, and media, 0.0% healthcare practitioners, 31.2% service, 20.2% sales and office, 23.9% natural resources, construction, and maintenance, 17.4% production, transportation, and material moving
Income: Per capita: $15,882; Median household: $40,893; Average household: $41,550; Households with income of $100,000 or more: n/a; Poverty rate: 9.3%
Educational Attainment: High school diploma or higher: 88.7%; Bachelor's degree or higher: 2.8%; Graduate/professional degree or higher: n/a
Housing: Homeownership rate: 43.5%; Median home value: $105,800; Median year structure built: 1951; Homeowner vacancy rate: 0.0%; Median selected monthly owner costs: $820 with a mortgage, n/a without a mortgage; Median gross rent: $530 per month; Rental vacancy rate: 0.0%
Health Insurance: 86.3% have insurance; 50.8% have private insurance; 43.5% have public insurance; 13.7% do not have insurance; 8.1% of children under 18 do not have insurance
Transportation: Commute: 90.8% car, 0.0% public transportation, 0.0% walk, 9.2% work from home; Mean travel time to work: 29.5 minutes

MOUNT VERNON (city). County seat. Covers a land area of 9.408 square miles and a water area of 0.185 square miles. Located at 40.39° N. Lat; 82.47° W. Long. Elevation is 1,004 feet.
History: Mount Vernon was laid out in 1805 by Benjamin Butler, Thomas Patterson, and Joseph Walker, all of whom became prominent citizens here. The town developed as a rural commercial center, and later as a manufacturer of steam, diesel, and gas engines. John Chapman, known as Johnny Appleseed, owned lots in Mount Vernon. This was the birthplace of Daniel Decatur Emmett (1815-1904) who wrote the song "Dixie."
Population: 16,777; Growth (since 2000): 16.7%; Density: 1,783.3 persons per square mile; Race: 95.5% White, 1.4% Black/African American, 0.1% Asian, 0.0% American Indian/Alaska Native, 0.0% Native Hawaiian/Other Pacific Islander, 2.7% Two or more races, 1.7% Hispanic of any race; Average household size: 2.22; Median age: 35.8; Age under 18: 21.2%; Age 65 and over: 17.5%; Males per 100 females: 86.9; Marriage status: 33.0% never married, 43.7% now married, 3.0% separated, 8.8% widowed, 14.5% divorced; Foreign born: 1.2%; Speak English only: 97.9%; With disability: 18.9%; Veterans: 8.4%; Ancestry: 27.8% German, 14.2% English, 13.2% Irish, 7.7% American, 4.9% Italian
Employment: 11.7% management, business, and financial, 3.7% computer, engineering, and science, 10.6% education, legal, community service, arts, and media, 5.3% healthcare practitioners, 24.6% service, 18.5% sales and office, 5.8% natural resources, construction, and maintenance, 19.7% production, transportation, and material moving
Income: Per capita: $19,728; Median household: $34,698; Average household: $45,712; Households with income of $100,000 or more: 7.4%; Poverty rate: 23.5%
Educational Attainment: High school diploma or higher: 87.7%; Bachelor's degree or higher: 22.2%; Graduate/professional degree or higher: 8.9%

School District(s)

Knox County Jvsd (09-12)
2015-16 Enrollment: n/a . . . . (740) 397-5820
Mount Vernon City (PK-12)
2015-16 Enrollment: 3,817 . . . . (740) 397-7422

Four-year College(s)

Mount Vernon Nazarene University (Private, Not-for-profit, Church of the Nazarene)
Fall 2016 Enrollment: 2,245 . . . . (740) 392-6868
2016-17 Tuition: In-state $26,950; Out-of-state $26,950

Vocational/Technical School(s)

Knox County Career Center (Public)
Fall 2016 Enrollment: 205 . . . . (740) 393-2933
2016-17 Tuition: $13,452

Housing: Homeownership rate: 49.7%; Median home value: $101,900; Median year structure built: 1960; Homeowner vacancy rate: 3.7%; Median selected monthly owner costs: $989 with a mortgage, $409 without a mortgage; Median gross rent: $676 per month; Rental vacancy rate: 4.6%
Health Insurance: 92.0% have insurance; 55.0% have private insurance; 49.8% have public insurance; 8.0% do not have insurance; 2.7% of children under 18 do not have insurance
Hospitals: Knox Community Hospital (115 beds)
Safety: Violent crime rate: 10.2 per 10,000 population; Property crime rate: 407.6 per 10,000 population
Newspapers: Mount Vernon News (daily circulation 9,200)
Transportation: Commute: 87.3% car, 0.3% public transportation, 7.2% walk, 3.2% work from home; Mean travel time to work: 17.6 minutes
Airports: Knox County (general aviation)
Additional Information Contacts
City of Mount Vernon. . . . . (740) 393-9517
http://www.mountvernonohio.org

Lake County

Located in northeastern Ohio; bounded on the north by Lake Erie; drained by the Grand and Chagrin Rivers. Covers a land area of 227.493 square miles, a water area of 751.705 square miles, and is located in the Eastern Time Zone at 41.92° N. Lat., 81.39° W. Long. The county was founded in 1840. County seat is Painesville.

Lake County is part of the Cleveland-Elyria, OH Metropolitan Statistical Area. The entire metro area includes: Cuyahoga County, OH; Geauga County, OH; Lake County, OH; Lorain County, OH; Medina County, OH

Weather Station: Painesville 4 NW — Elevation: 600 feet

	Jan	Feb	Mar	Apr	May	Jun	Jul	Aug	Sep	Oct	Nov	Dec
High	35	37	45	57	67	77	81	80	74	63	52	40
Low	22	23	29	40	50	60	65	64	57	47	38	28
Precip	2.4	2.0	2.8	3.3	3.3	3.7	3.8	3.4	4.0	3.5	3.5	3.0
Snow	11.5	8.1	6.5	1.2	tr	0.0	0.0	0.0	0.0	tr	2.2	9.7

High and Low temperatures in degrees Fahrenheit; Precipitation and Snow in inches

Population: 229,266; Growth (since 2000): 0.8%; Density: 1,007.8 persons per square mile; Race: 92.2% White, 3.8% Black/African American, 1.3% Asian, 0.1% American Indian/Alaska Native, 0.0% Native Hawaiian/Other Pacific Islander, 2.0% two or more races, 3.9% Hispanic of any race; Average household size: 2.37; Median age: 43.3; Age under 18: 21.0%; Age 65 and over: 17.9%; Males per 100 females: 95.1; Marriage status: 28.0% never married, 53.4% now married, 1.2% separated, 7.0% widowed, 11.5% divorced; Foreign born: 5.4%; Speak English only: 92.8%; With disability: 12.2%; Veterans: 8.8%; Ancestry: 24.8% German, 18.1% Irish, 16.0% Italian, 9.8% English, 7.0% Polish
Religion: Six largest groups: 35.2% Catholicism, 3.9% Methodist/Pietist, 2.4% Lutheran, 2.0% Non-denominational Protestant, 1.6% Pentecostal, 1.4% Baptist
Economy: Unemployment rate: 4.5%; Leading industries: 13.4 % retail trade; 10.1 % finance and insurance; 10.0 % health care and social assistance; Farms: 214 totaling 17,125 acres; Company size: 3 employ 1,000 or more persons, 9 employ 500 to 999 persons, 136 employ 100 to 499 persons, 5,911 employs less than 100 persons; Business ownership: 5,763 women-owned, 523 Black-owned, 193 Hispanic-owned, 294 Asian-owned, 45 American Indian/Alaska Native-owned
Employment: 14.9% management, business, and financial, 6.0% computer, engineering, and science, 8.8% education, legal, community service, arts, and media, 6.8% healthcare practitioners, 16.4% service, 24.7% sales and office, 7.3% natural resources, construction, and maintenance, 15.1% production, transportation, and material moving
Income: Per capita: $31,053; Median household: $59,958; Average household: $74,249; Households with income of $100,000 or more: 23.8%; Poverty rate: 8.5%
Educational Attainment: High school diploma or higher: 91.9%; Bachelor's degree or higher: 27.0%; Graduate/professional degree or higher: 9.7%
Housing: Homeownership rate: 73.8%; Median home value: $149,300; Median year structure built: 1970; Homeowner vacancy rate: 1.5%; Median selected monthly owner costs: $1,301 with a mortgage, $478 without a mortgage; Median gross rent: $844 per month; Rental vacancy rate: 5.5%
Vital Statistics: Birth rate: 95.4 per 10,000 population; Death rate: 108.2 per 10,000 population; Age-adjusted cancer mortality rate: 176.0 deaths per 100,000 population
Health Insurance: 93.3% have insurance; 77.0% have private insurance; 29.8% have public insurance; 6.7% do not have insurance; 3.6% of children under 18 do not have insurance
Health Care: Physicians: 16.2 per 10,000 population; Dentists: 6.8 per 10,000 population; Hospital beds: 22.2 per 10,000 population; Hospital admissions: 920.8 per 10,000 population
Air Quality Index (AQI): Percent of Days: 75.1% good, 21.3% moderate, 3.6% unhealthy for sensitive individuals, 0.0% unhealthy, 0.0% very unhealthy; Annual median: 39; Annual maximum: 143
Transportation: Commute: 94.1% car, 0.9% public transportation, 1.4% walk, 3.2% work from home; Mean travel time to work: 23.2 minutes
2016 Presidential Election: 54.8% Trump, 39.6% Clinton, 3.3% Johnson, 0.8% Stein
National and State Parks: Chaplin State Forest; Hach-Otis Sanctuary State Nature Preserve; Headlands Beach State Park; Headlands Dunes State Nature Preserve; James A Garfield National Historic Site; Mentor Marsh State Nature Preserve
Additional Information Contacts
Lake Government . . . . (440) 350-2500
http://www.lakecountyohio.gov

Lake County Communities

EASTLAKE (city). Covers a land area of 6.395 square miles and a water area of 0.130 square miles. Located at 41.66° N. Lat; 81.43° W. Long. Elevation is 617 feet.
Population: 18,342; Growth (since 2000): -9.4%; Density: 2,868.2 persons per square mile; Race: 93.5% White, 4.8% Black/African American, 0.8% Asian, 0.1% American Indian/Alaska Native, 0.0% Native Hawaiian/Other Pacific Islander, 0.8% Two or more races, 2.0% Hispanic of any race; Average household size: 2.35; Median age: 43.4; Age under 18: 20.3%; Age 65 and over: 17.2%; Males per 100 females: 97.2; Marriage status: 30.7% never married, 50.1% now married, 1.0% separated, 6.5% widowed, 12.6% divorced; Foreign born: 4.3%; Speak English only: 94.0%; With disability: 12.5%; Veterans: 9.2%; Ancestry: 28.9% German, 19.8% Irish, 17.0% Italian, 8.7% English, 7.5% Polish
Employment: 12.9% management, business, and financial, 5.4% computer, engineering, and science, 6.0% education, legal, community service, arts, and media, 5.8% healthcare practitioners, 19.5% service, 23.5% sales and office, 9.4% natural resources, construction, and maintenance, 17.4% production, transportation, and material moving
Income: Per capita: $25,767; Median household: $51,462; Average household: $60,599; Households with income of $100,000 or more: 15.7%; Poverty rate: 9.9%
Educational Attainment: High school diploma or higher: 89.6%; Bachelor's degree or higher: 16.3%; Graduate/professional degree or higher: 5.8%

School District(s)

Willoughby-Eastlake City (PK-12)
2015-16 Enrollment: 8,207 . . . . (440) 946-5000

Four-year College(s)

Bryant & Stratton College-Eastlake (Private, For-profit)
Fall 2016 Enrollment: 254 . . . . (440) 510-1112
2016-17 Tuition: In-state $16,679; Out-of-state $16,679

Vocational/Technical School(s)

Willoughby-Eastlake School of Practical Nursing (Public)
Fall 2016 Enrollment: 103 . . . . (440) 602-5094
2016-17 Tuition: In-state $12,120; Out-of-state $12,120

Housing: Homeownership rate: 71.1%; Median home value: $122,300; Median year structure built: 1967; Homeowner vacancy rate: 3.0%; Median selected monthly owner costs: $1,164 with a mortgage, $424 without a mortgage; Median gross rent: $781 per month; Rental vacancy rate: 0.0%
Health Insurance: 92.4% have insurance; 73.3% have private insurance; 31.8% have public insurance; 7.6% do not have insurance; 3.6% of children under 18 do not have insurance
Safety: Violent crime rate: 5.5 per 10,000 population; Property crime rate: 243.9 per 10,000 population
Transportation: Commute: 95.7% car, 0.9% public transportation, 1.3% walk, 1.8% work from home; Mean travel time to work: 23.1 minutes
Additional Information Contacts

City of Eastlake . . . . (330) 426-4367
http://www.eastlakeohio.com

FAIRPORT HARBOR (village). Covers a land area of 1.027 square miles and a water area of 0.081 square miles. Located at 41.75° N. Lat; 81.27° W. Long. Elevation is 610 feet.
History: Fairport Harbor grew around fishing, salt-making, and the shipping of iron ore. Many of the early residents were Hungarians and Finns.
Population: 3,081; Growth (since 2000): -3.1%; Density: 2,999.8 persons per square mile; Race: 98.8% White, 0.6% Black/African American, 0.0% Asian, 0.0% American Indian/Alaska Native, 0.0% Native Hawaiian/Other Pacific Islander, 0.6% Two or more races, 6.5% Hispanic of any race; Average household size: 2.20; Median age: 44.8; Age under 18: 23.0%; Age 65 and over: 14.5%; Males per 100 females: 94.7; Marriage status: 34.5% never married, 41.1% now married, 2.9% separated, 8.1% widowed, 16.4% divorced; Foreign born: 1.6%; Speak English only: 91.5%; With disability: 13.2%; Veterans: 8.4%; Ancestry: 24.9% German, 16.3% Irish, 12.5% English, 9.7% Hungarian, 9.2% Italian
Employment: 14.4% management, business, and financial, 3.4% computer, engineering, and science, 9.2% education, legal, community service, arts, and media, 7.0% healthcare practitioners, 12.7% service, 24.3% sales and office, 5.6% natural resources, construction, and maintenance, 23.5% production, transportation, and material moving
Income: Per capita: $26,886; Median household: $48,346; Average household: $59,291; Households with income of $100,000 or more: 14.1%; Poverty rate: 17.2%
Educational Attainment: High school diploma or higher: 92.1%; Bachelor's degree or higher: 19.2%; Graduate/professional degree or higher: 6.6%

School District(s)

Fairport Harbor Exempted Village (KG-12)
2015-16 Enrollment: 671. . . . . (440) 354-5400
Housing: Homeownership rate: 65.9%; Median home value: $104,700; Median year structure built: 1954; Homeowner vacancy rate: 0.0%; Median selected monthly owner costs: $1,331 with a mortgage, $478 without a mortgage; Median gross rent: $780 per month; Rental vacancy rate: 5.9%
Health Insurance: 87.9% have insurance; 58.7% have private insurance; 38.9% have public insurance; 12.1% do not have insurance; 7.5% of children under 18 do not have insurance
Safety: Violent crime rate: 16.2 per 10,000 population; Property crime rate: 329.8 per 10,000 population
Transportation: Commute: 93.6% car, 0.0% public transportation, 0.9% walk, 4.2% work from home; Mean travel time to work: 20.5 minutes

GRAND RIVER (village). Covers a land area of 0.541 square miles and a water area of 0.094 square miles. Located at 41.74° N. Lat; 81.29° W. Long. Elevation is 610 feet.
History: Formerly Richmond.
Population: 348; Growth (since 2000): 0.9%; Density: 642.7 persons per square mile; Race: 96.6% White, 2.3% Black/African American, 1.1% Asian, 0.0% American Indian/Alaska Native, 0.0% Native Hawaiian/Other Pacific Islander, 0.0% Two or more races, 2.3% Hispanic of any race; Average household size: 2.37; Median age: 39.8; Age under 18: 19.3%; Age 65 and over: 21.0%; Males per 100 females: 106.7; Marriage status: 28.4% never married, 50.3% now married, 1.0% separated, 11.8% widowed, 9.5% divorced; Foreign born: 3.2%; Speak English only: 96.9%; With disability: 17.8%; Veterans: 8.5%; Ancestry: 25.9% German, 22.4% Irish, 17.2% English, 14.4% Hungarian, 11.5% Polish
Employment: 9.7% management, business, and financial, 5.1% computer, engineering, and science, 8.2% education, legal, community service, arts, and media, 2.1% healthcare practitioners, 28.7% service, 22.6% sales and office, 6.7% natural resources, construction, and maintenance, 16.9% production, transportation, and material moving
Income: Per capita: $23,438; Median household: $47,083; Average household: $55,819; Households with income of $100,000 or more: 14.3%; Poverty rate: 13.5%
Educational Attainment: High school diploma or higher: 77.2%; Bachelor's degree or higher: 11.0%; Graduate/professional degree or higher: 0.8%
Housing: Homeownership rate: 51.0%; Median home value: $123,500; Median year structure built: 1959; Homeowner vacancy rate: 0.0%; Median selected monthly owner costs: $1,264 with a mortgage, $450 without a mortgage; Median gross rent: $871 per month; Rental vacancy rate: 0.0%
Health Insurance: 92.5% have insurance; 59.5% have private insurance; 44.5% have public insurance; 7.5% do not have insurance; 3.0% of children under 18 do not have insurance
Transportation: Commute: 96.9% car, 0.0% public transportation, 0.0% walk, 3.1% work from home; Mean travel time to work: 20.9 minutes

KIRTLAND (city). Covers a land area of 16.671 square miles and a water area of 0.130 square miles. Located at 41.60° N. Lat; 81.34° W. Long. Elevation is 666 feet.
History: Kirtland was the location in 1831 where Joseph Smith led a group of his followers. The town flourished as a Mormon stronghold until 1838, when Smith moved on. The Kirtland Temple built by the group remained a dominant factor in the town.
Population: 6,802; Growth (since 2000): 2.0%; Density: 408.0 persons per square mile; Race: 98.9% White, 0.2% Black/African American, 0.3% Asian, 0.1% American Indian/Alaska Native, 0.0% Native Hawaiian/Other Pacific Islander, 0.6% Two or more races, 1.0% Hispanic of any race; Average household size: 2.50; Median age: 49.4; Age under 18: 19.0%; Age 65 and over: 21.9%; Males per 100 females: 97.1; Marriage status: 23.4% never married, 62.6% now married, 2.3% separated, 7.4% widowed, 6.6% divorced; Foreign born: 4.7%; Speak English only: 93.6%; With disability: 10.1%; Veterans: 9.1%; Ancestry: 21.7% German, 17.9% Irish, 15.9% Italian, 11.7% English, 9.1% Polish
Employment: 19.7% management, business, and financial, 8.9% computer, engineering, and science, 10.9% education, legal, community service, arts, and media, 7.8% healthcare practitioners, 11.6% service, 22.0% sales and office, 7.1% natural resources, construction, and maintenance, 12.0% production, transportation, and material moving
Income: Per capita: $45,454; Median household: $76,691; Average household: $114,894; Households with income of $100,000 or more: 41.5%; Poverty rate: 2.8%
Educational Attainment: High school diploma or higher: 94.5%; Bachelor's degree or higher: 41.0%; Graduate/professional degree or higher: 19.5%

School District(s)

Kirtland Local (KG-12)
2015-16 Enrollment: 1,143 . . . . (440) 256-3360

Two-year College(s)

Lakeland Community College (Public)
Fall 2016 Enrollment: 7,997 . . . . (440) 525-7000
2016-17 Tuition: In-state $4,165; Out-of-state $9,205
Housing: Homeownership rate: 81.7%; Median home value: $271,400; Median year structure built: 1971; Homeowner vacancy rate: 0.9%; Median selected monthly owner costs: $1,995 with a mortgage, $589 without a mortgage; Median gross rent: $762 per month; Rental vacancy rate: 0.0%
Health Insurance: 98.3% have insurance; 90.1% have private insurance; 23.2% have public insurance; 1.7% do not have insurance; 0.0% of children under 18 do not have insurance
Safety: Violent crime rate: 4.4 per 10,000 population; Property crime rate: 39.8 per 10,000 population
Transportation: Commute: 93.1% car, 0.5% public transportation, 1.0% walk, 5.2% work from home; Mean travel time to work: 25.6 minutes
Additional Information Contacts
City of Kirtland. . . . . (440) 256-3332
http://kirtlandohio.com

KIRTLAND HILLS (village). Covers a land area of 5.567 square miles and a water area of 0.076 square miles. Located at 41.64° N. Lat; 81.33° W. Long. Elevation is 843 feet.
History: The first Mormon temple was built here (1833-1836) by Joseph Smith and his followers. Settled 1808, incorporated 1926.
Population: 717; Growth (since 2000): 20.1%; Density: 128.8 persons per square mile; Race: 95.7% White, 0.0% Black/African American, 0.3% Asian, 0.0% American Indian/Alaska Native, 0.0% Native Hawaiian/Other Pacific Islander, 3.3% Two or more races, 2.8% Hispanic of any race; Average household size: 2.67; Median age: 50.2; Age under 18: 21.9%; Age 65 and over: 20.9%; Males per 100 females: 94.6; Marriage status: 19.2% never married, 71.2% now married, 0.5% separated, 5.1% widowed, 4.6% divorced; Foreign born: 5.4%; Speak English only: 94.6%; With disability: 8.1%; Veterans: 5.4%; Ancestry: 29.0% German, 22.2% Irish, 16.0% Italian, 13.2% English, 9.6% Hungarian
Employment: 29.6% management, business, and financial, 3.0% computer, engineering, and science, 10.9% education, legal, community service, arts, and media, 13.6% healthcare practitioners, 8.0% service,

19.8% sales and office, 3.6% natural resources, construction, and maintenance, 11.5% production, transportation, and material moving
Income: Per capita: $69,081; Median household: $116,875; Average household: $183,149; Households with income of $100,000 or more: 58.0%; Poverty rate: 1.8%
Educational Attainment: High school diploma or higher: 96.5%; Bachelor's degree or higher: 54.1%; Graduate/professional degree or higher: 28.0%
Housing: Homeownership rate: 89.6%; Median home value: $533,700; Median year structure built: 1985; Homeowner vacancy rate: 3.2%; Median selected monthly owner costs: $3,067 with a mortgage, $1,131 without a mortgage; Median gross rent: $1,042 per month; Rental vacancy rate: 0.0%
Health Insurance: 96.4% have insurance; 88.4% have private insurance; 22.6% have public insurance; 3.6% do not have insurance; 0.0% of children under 18 do not have insurance
Safety: Violent crime rate: 15.6 per 10,000 population; Property crime rate: 0.0 per 10,000 population
Transportation: Commute: 90.4% car, 0.0% public transportation, 0.6% walk, 6.0% work from home; Mean travel time to work: 26.6 minutes

LAKELINE (village). Covers a land area of 0.088 square miles and a water area of 0 square miles. Located at 41.66° N. Lat; 81.45° W. Long. Elevation is 617 feet.
Population: 243; Growth (since 2000): 47.3%; Density: 2,772.2 persons per square mile; Race: 96.7% White, 1.6% Black/African American, 0.0% Asian, 0.0% American Indian/Alaska Native, 0.0% Native Hawaiian/Other Pacific Islander, 1.6% Two or more races, 0.0% Hispanic of any race; Average household size: 2.25; Median age: 41.1; Age under 18: 16.9%; Age 65 and over: 9.9%; Males per 100 females: 105.5; Marriage status: 23.4% never married, 54.1% now married, 2.4% separated, 5.7% widowed, 16.7% divorced; Foreign born: 8.2%; Speak English only: 90.7%; With disability: 7.0%; Veterans: 10.9%; Ancestry: 22.2% German, 21.0% Irish, 19.8% Italian, 12.3% Slovene, 11.1% English
Employment: 9.2% management, business, and financial, 5.2% computer, engineering, and science, 14.4% education, legal, community service, arts, and media, 9.2% healthcare practitioners, 17.0% service, 22.2% sales and office, 8.5% natural resources, construction, and maintenance, 14.4% production, transportation, and material moving
Income: Per capita: $30,975; Median household: $55,625; Average household: $70,443; Households with income of $100,000 or more: 25.0%; Poverty rate: 4.5%
Educational Attainment: High school diploma or higher: 98.4%; Bachelor's degree or higher: 28.0%; Graduate/professional degree or higher: 6.9%
Housing: Homeownership rate: 86.1%; Median home value: $126,300; Median year structure built: 1950; Homeowner vacancy rate: 4.1%; Median selected monthly owner costs: $1,211 with a mortgage, $536 without a mortgage; Median gross rent: $933 per month; Rental vacancy rate: 0.0%
Health Insurance: 91.8% have insurance; 78.2% have private insurance; 17.3% have public insurance; 8.2% do not have insurance; 0.0% of children under 18 do not have insurance
Transportation: Commute: 96.0% car, 0.0% public transportation, 0.0% walk, 4.0% work from home; Mean travel time to work: 21.3 minutes

MADISON (village). Covers a land area of 5.087 square miles and a water area of 0 square miles. Located at 41.77° N. Lat; 81.05° W. Long. Elevation is 728 feet.
History: Madison grew around its orchards, nurseries, and potato fields. It was known for Madison Willowcraft, the product of its basket-making industry.
Population: 3,166; Growth (since 2000): 8.4%; Density: 622.4 persons per square mile; Race: 98.2% White, 1.0% Black/African American, 0.5% Asian, 0.0% American Indian/Alaska Native, 0.0% Native Hawaiian/Other Pacific Islander, 0.3% Two or more races, 1.1% Hispanic of any race; Average household size: 2.51; Median age: 40.0; Age under 18: 26.3%; Age 65 and over: 14.4%; Males per 100 females: 90.3; Marriage status: 28.4% never married, 55.4% now married, 0.0% separated, 8.3% widowed, 7.9% divorced; Foreign born: 2.5%; Speak English only: 97.7%; With disability: 14.4%; Veterans: 6.9%; Ancestry: 31.2% German, 18.6% Irish, 17.8% Italian, 17.4% English, 6.1% American
Employment: 13.9% management, business, and financial, 4.8% computer, engineering, and science, 11.9% education, legal, community service, arts, and media, 5.5% healthcare practitioners, 17.5% service, 18.8% sales and office, 8.8% natural resources, construction, and maintenance, 18.8% production, transportation, and material moving
Income: Per capita: $24,890; Median household: $52,222; Average household: $62,815; Households with income of $100,000 or more: 14.7%; Poverty rate: 9.1%
Educational Attainment: High school diploma or higher: 93.2%; Bachelor's degree or higher: 25.2%; Graduate/professional degree or higher: 8.9%

School District(s)

Madison Local (PK-12)
 2015-16 Enrollment: 3,199 . . . . (440) 428-2166
Housing: Homeownership rate: 74.0%; Median home value: $136,200; Median year structure built: 1973; Homeowner vacancy rate: 0.0%; Median selected monthly owner costs: $1,288 with a mortgage, $471 without a mortgage; Median gross rent: $764 per month; Rental vacancy rate: 14.0%
Health Insurance: 91.2% have insurance; 76.4% have private insurance; 27.9% have public insurance; 8.8% do not have insurance; 7.7% of children under 18 do not have insurance
Transportation: Commute: 91.4% car, 2.6% public transportation, 3.3% walk, 1.5% work from home; Mean travel time to work: 26.6 minutes
Additional Information Contacts
Village of Madison . . . . (440) 428-7526
 http://www.madisonvillage.org

MENTOR (city). Covers a land area of 26.645 square miles and a water area of 1.353 square miles. Located at 41.69° N. Lat; 81.34° W. Long. Elevation is 692 feet.
History: Named, possibly, for Hiram Mentor, an early settler. Mentor was founded in 1799. James A. Garfield lived in Mentor prior to his time as president of the U.S.
Population: 46,896; Growth (since 2000): -6.7%; Density: 1,760.0 persons per square mile; Race: 96.6% White, 0.6% Black/African American, 1.6% Asian, 0.1% American Indian/Alaska Native, 0.0% Native Hawaiian/Other Pacific Islander, 0.8% Two or more races, 0.9% Hispanic of any race; Average household size: 2.38; Median age: 46.7; Age under 18: 19.2%; Age 65 and over: 19.1%; Males per 100 females: 93.7; Marriage status: 24.5% never married, 57.5% now married, 0.6% separated, 7.3% widowed, 10.7% divorced; Foreign born: 4.1%; Speak English only: 95.1%; With disability: 11.8%; Veterans: 8.7%; Ancestry: 27.9% German, 19.9% Irish, 15.9% Italian, 10.8% English, 8.0% Polish
Employment: 17.8% management, business, and financial, 7.2% computer, engineering, and science, 9.1% education, legal, community service, arts, and media, 6.7% healthcare practitioners, 14.3% service, 26.9% sales and office, 6.2% natural resources, construction, and maintenance, 11.7% production, transportation, and material moving
Income: Per capita: $34,819; Median household: $70,058; Average household: $83,165; Households with income of $100,000 or more: 32.1%; Poverty rate: 5.6%
Educational Attainment: High school diploma or higher: 94.7%; Bachelor's degree or higher: 32.2%; Graduate/professional degree or higher: 11.9%

School District(s)

Mentor Exempted Village (PK-12)
 2015-16 Enrollment: 7,874 . . . . (440) 255-4444

Two-year College(s)

Brown Aveda Institute-Mentor (Private, For-profit)
 Fall 2016 Enrollment: 139 . . . . (440) 255-9494

Vocational/Technical School(s)

Cleveland Institute of Dental-Medical Assistants-Mentor (Private, For-profit)
 Fall 2016 Enrollment: 92 . . . . (216) 241-2930
 2016-17 Tuition: $10,800
Housing: Homeownership rate: 85.0%; Median home value: $167,100; Median year structure built: 1973; Homeowner vacancy rate: 1.3%; Median selected monthly owner costs: $1,341 with a mortgage, $486 without a mortgage; Median gross rent: $925 per month; Rental vacancy rate: 8.4%
Health Insurance: 95.8% have insurance; 84.1% have private insurance; 27.3% have public insurance; 4.2% do not have insurance; 2.2% of children under 18 do not have insurance
Safety: Violent crime rate: 10.9 per 10,000 population; Property crime rate: 220.7 per 10,000 population
Transportation: Commute: 91.9% car, 1.1% public transportation, 2.6% walk, 3.9% work from home; Mean travel time to work: 23.2 minutes
Additional Information Contacts

City of Mentor . . . . (440) 255-1100
http://www.cityofmentor.com

MENTOR-ON-THE-LAKE (city). Covers a land area of 1.613 square miles and a water area of 0.040 square miles. Located at 41.71° N. Lat; 81.37° W. Long. Elevation is 627 feet.

History: Mentor-on-the-Lake is a city in Lake County, Ohio. Established October 22, 1924, it was incorporated city on February 12, 1971. A vast majority of its land was originally deeded as the Dickey-Moore tract and property known as Mooreland, once owned by the Moore family, is situated on land that now houses Lakeland Community College.

Population: 7,404; Growth (since 2000): -8.9%; Density: 4,589.8 persons per square mile; Race: 95.1% White, 0.7% Black/African American, 1.2% Asian, 0.1% American Indian/Alaska Native, 0.0% Native Hawaiian/Other Pacific Islander, 2.4% Two or more races, 2.7% Hispanic of any race; Average household size: 2.30; Median age: 41.2; Age under 18: 19.1%; Age 65 and over: 16.1%; Males per 100 females: 96.0; Marriage status: 29.4% never married, 49.2% now married, 1.5% separated, 6.3% widowed, 15.1% divorced; Foreign born: 3.0%; Speak English only: 94.5%; With disability: 16.8%; Veterans: 10.9%; Ancestry: 19.4% Irish, 19.2% Italian, 19.1% German, 11.8% English, 7.6% Polish

Employment: 11.8% management, business, and financial, 3.3% computer, engineering, and science, 6.7% education, legal, community service, arts, and media, 4.8% healthcare practitioners, 21.5% service, 23.3% sales and office, 9.6% natural resources, construction, and maintenance, 19.0% production, transportation, and material moving

Income: Per capita: $26,639; Median household: $50,040; Average household: $61,188; Households with income of $100,000 or more: 17.9%; Poverty rate: 9.1%

Educational Attainment: High school diploma or higher: 91.8%; Bachelor's degree or higher: 15.8%; Graduate/professional degree or higher: 3.7%

School District(s)

Mentor Exempted Village (PK-12)
2015-16 Enrollment: 7,874 . . . . (440) 255-4444

Housing: Homeownership rate: 61.8%; Median home value: $125,400; Median year structure built: 1970; Homeowner vacancy rate: 0.0%; Median selected monthly owner costs: $1,139 with a mortgage, $449 without a mortgage; Median gross rent: $853 per month; Rental vacancy rate: 4.5%

Health Insurance: 90.1% have insurance; 64.1% have private insurance; 38.8% have public insurance; 9.9% do not have insurance; 5.0% of children under 18 do not have insurance

Safety: Violent crime rate: 13.6 per 10,000 population; Property crime rate: 123.4 per 10,000 population

Transportation: Commute: 95.5% car, 0.9% public transportation, 0.9% walk, 2.0% work from home; Mean travel time to work: 25.0 minutes

NORTH MADISON (CDP). Covers a land area of 3.907 square miles and a water area of 0 square miles. Located at 41.83° N. Lat; 81.05° W. Long. Elevation is 673 feet.

Population: 8,473; Growth (since 2000): 0.3%; Density: 2,168.4 persons per square mile; Race: 97.8% White, 0.3% Black/African American, 0.4% Asian, 0.0% American Indian/Alaska Native, 0.0% Native Hawaiian/Other Pacific Islander, 1.3% Two or more races, 0.5% Hispanic of any race; Average household size: 2.65; Median age: 38.8; Age under 18: 29.1%; Age 65 and over: 14.7%; Males per 100 females: 97.1; Marriage status: 25.7% never married, 56.0% now married, 1.9% separated, 4.5% widowed, 13.7% divorced; Foreign born: 1.3%; Speak English only: 98.3%; With disability: 13.2%; Veterans: 10.8%; Ancestry: 33.6% German, 16.3% Italian, 15.7% Irish, 12.4% English, 7.6% Polish

Employment: 11.6% management, business, and financial, 4.4% computer, engineering, and science, 4.5% education, legal, community service, arts, and media, 9.3% healthcare practitioners, 12.9% service, 22.9% sales and office, 11.3% natural resources, construction, and maintenance, 23.1% production, transportation, and material moving

Income: Per capita: $22,520; Median household: $51,039; Average household: $59,279; Households with income of $100,000 or more: 15.8%; Poverty rate: 5.8%

Educational Attainment: High school diploma or higher: 92.9%; Bachelor's degree or higher: 16.3%; Graduate/professional degree or higher: 7.1%

Housing: Homeownership rate: 74.1%; Median home value: $113,600; Median year structure built: 1968; Homeowner vacancy rate: 2.0%; Median selected monthly owner costs: $1,039 with a mortgage, $412 without a mortgage; Median gross rent: $916 per month; Rental vacancy rate: 5.3%

Health Insurance: 91.9% have insurance; 72.7% have private insurance; 30.8% have public insurance; 8.1% do not have insurance; 4.3% of children under 18 do not have insurance

Transportation: Commute: 97.5% car, 0.0% public transportation, 0.1% walk, 1.0% work from home; Mean travel time to work: 30.8 minutes

NORTH PERRY (village). Covers a land area of 3.867 square miles and a water area of 0 square miles. Located at 41.80° N. Lat; 81.12° W. Long. Elevation is 679 feet.

Population: 713; Growth (since 2000): -14.9%; Density: 184.4 persons per square mile; Race: 99.3% White, 0.0% Black/African American, 0.4% Asian, 0.0% American Indian/Alaska Native, 0.0% Native Hawaiian/Other Pacific Islander, 0.0% Two or more races, 0.3% Hispanic of any race; Average household size: 2.42; Median age: 50.9; Age under 18: 15.6%; Age 65 and over: 21.3%; Males per 100 females: 106.7; Marriage status: 20.4% never married, 61.5% now married, 1.1% separated, 6.7% widowed, 11.3% divorced; Foreign born: 1.1%; Speak English only: 98.0%; With disability: 14.2%; Veterans: 9.8%; Ancestry: 31.4% German, 21.6% Irish, 15.8% English, 9.8% Italian, 8.3% Polish

Employment: 16.0% management, business, and financial, 5.1% computer, engineering, and science, 8.6% education, legal, community service, arts, and media, 2.9% healthcare practitioners, 16.8% service, 21.7% sales and office, 10.2% natural resources, construction, and maintenance, 18.7% production, transportation, and material moving

Income: Per capita: $32,119; Median household: $67,188; Average household: $76,246; Households with income of $100,000 or more: 25.4%; Poverty rate: 6.5%

Educational Attainment: High school diploma or higher: 95.1%; Bachelor's degree or higher: 23.9%; Graduate/professional degree or higher: 6.7%

Housing: Homeownership rate: 84.1%; Median home value: $167,400; Median year structure built: 1961; Homeowner vacancy rate: 0.0%; Median selected monthly owner costs: $1,272 with a mortgage, $450 without a mortgage; Median gross rent: $870 per month; Rental vacancy rate: 0.0%

Health Insurance: 94.7% have insurance; 83.6% have private insurance; 29.3% have public insurance; 5.3% do not have insurance; 5.4% of children under 18 do not have insurance

Transportation: Commute: 89.2% car, 0.0% public transportation, 2.4% walk, 7.5% work from home; Mean travel time to work: 24.2 minutes

Additional Information Contacts

Village of North Perry . . . . (440) 259-4994
http://www.northperry.org

PAINESVILLE (city). County seat. Covers a land area of 6.285 square miles and a water area of 0.726 square miles. Located at 41.72° N. Lat; 81.25° W. Long. Elevation is 676 feet.

History: Named for Edward Paine, first settler, who had been a general in the American Revolution. Painesville was settled in the early 1800's by pioneers from Connecticut. Architect-builder Jonathan Goldsmith lived in Painesville from 1811 until his death in 1847, and the town had several examples of Goldsmith's work.

Population: 19,735; Growth (since 2000): 12.8%; Density: 3,140.1 persons per square mile; Race: 72.6% White, 13.9% Black/African American, 0.7% Asian, 0.2% American Indian/Alaska Native, 0.0% Native Hawaiian/Other Pacific Islander, 9.0% Two or more races, 24.3% Hispanic of any race; Average household size: 2.54; Median age: 32.5; Age under 18: 25.7%; Age 65 and over: 10.4%; Males per 100 females: 101.2; Marriage status: 40.3% never married, 42.4% now married, 2.4% separated, 4.8% widowed, 12.5% divorced; Foreign born: 12.3%; Speak English only: 79.7%; With disability: 14.2%; Veterans: 8.1%; Ancestry: 16.4% German, 13.8% Irish, 11.1% Italian, 4.7% English, 4.0% Hungarian

Employment: 8.7% management, business, and financial, 3.5% computer, engineering, and science, 8.4% education, legal, community service, arts, and media, 3.0% healthcare practitioners, 24.0% service, 20.5% sales and office, 8.6% natural resources, construction, and maintenance, 23.3% production, transportation, and material moving

Income: Per capita: $20,666; Median household: $41,652; Average household: $54,069; Households with income of $100,000 or more: 12.0%; Poverty rate: 21.7%

Educational Attainment: High school diploma or higher: 79.2%; Bachelor's degree or higher: 14.7%; Graduate/professional degree or higher: 4.2%

School District(s)

Auburn (11-12)
2015-16 Enrollment: n/a . . . . (440) 358-8006

Painesville City Local (PK-12)
2015-16 Enrollment: 3,096 . . . . (440) 392-5060
Riverside Local (PK-12)
2015-16 Enrollment: 4,268 . . . . (440) 352-0668
Summit Academy Community School - Painesville (KG-08)
2015-16 Enrollment: 74. . . . . (440) 358-0877

Four-year College(s)

Lake Erie College (Private, Not-for-profit)
Fall 2016 Enrollment: 1,201 . . . . (440) 375-7000
2016-17 Tuition: In-state $29,960; Out-of-state $29,960

Vocational/Technical School(s)

Auburn Career Center (Public)
Fall 2016 Enrollment: 155 . . . . (440) 357-7542
2016-17 Tuition: $13,950

Housing: Homeownership rate: 49.1%; Median home value: $100,300; Median year structure built: 1963; Homeowner vacancy rate: 0.6%; Median selected monthly owner costs: $1,120 with a mortgage, $348 without a mortgage; Median gross rent: $734 per month; Rental vacancy rate: 5.9%
Health Insurance: 87.3% have insurance; 56.9% have private insurance; 38.2% have public insurance; 12.7% do not have insurance; 6.7% of children under 18 do not have insurance
Hospitals: TriPoint Medical center
Transportation: Commute: 92.9% car, 1.6% public transportation, 2.4% walk, 2.4% work from home; Mean travel time to work: 19.5 minutes
Additional Information Contacts
City of Painesville . . . . (440) 352-9301
http://www.painesville.com

PERRY (village). Covers a land area of 2.181 square miles and a water area of 0 square miles. Located at 41.76° N. Lat; 81.14° W. Long. Elevation is 699 feet.
Population: 1,591; Growth (since 2000): 33.1%; Density: 729.6 persons per square mile; Race: 97.1% White, 0.6% Black/African American, 1.7% Asian, 0.0% American Indian/Alaska Native, 0.0% Native Hawaiian/Other Pacific Islander, 0.6% Two or more races, 0.6% Hispanic of any race; Average household size: 2.73; Median age: 41.7; Age under 18: 26.2%; Age 65 and over: 13.8%; Males per 100 females: 98.4; Marriage status: 22.7% never married, 60.1% now married, 2.6% separated, 6.4% widowed, 10.9% divorced; Foreign born: 2.8%; Speak English only: 96.2%; With disability: 13.6%; Veterans: 11.3%; Ancestry: 23.4% German, 17.3% Italian, 15.7% Irish, 9.9% English, 9.0% Hungarian
Employment: 17.5% management, business, and financial, 7.1% computer, engineering, and science, 11.0% education, legal, community service, arts, and media, 6.1% healthcare practitioners, 15.3% service, 24.5% sales and office, 7.0% natural resources, construction, and maintenance, 11.4% production, transportation, and material moving
Income: Per capita: $28,296; Median household: $71,172; Average household: $76,582; Households with income of $100,000 or more: 33.9%; Poverty rate: 10.8%
Educational Attainment: High school diploma or higher: 91.8%; Bachelor's degree or higher: 24.3%; Graduate/professional degree or higher: 10.3%

School District(s)

Perry Local (KG-12)
2015-16 Enrollment: 1,722 . . . . (440) 259-9200

Housing: Homeownership rate: 86.0%; Median home value: $170,300; Median year structure built: 1986; Homeowner vacancy rate: 3.7%; Median selected monthly owner costs: $1,486 with a mortgage, $555 without a mortgage; Median gross rent: $588 per month; Rental vacancy rate: 12.0%
Health Insurance: 94.9% have insurance; 77.4% have private insurance; 27.9% have public insurance; 5.1% do not have insurance; 3.4% of children under 18 do not have insurance
Transportation: Commute: 95.5% car, 0.4% public transportation, 0.7% walk, 3.5% work from home; Mean travel time to work: 25.0 minutes

TIMBERLAKE (village). Covers a land area of 0.211 square miles and a water area of 0 square miles. Located at 41.67° N. Lat; 81.44° W. Long. Elevation is 617 feet.
Population: 673; Growth (since 2000): -13.2%; Density: 3,189.6 persons per square mile; Race: 96.7% White, 0.0% Black/African American, 1.5% Asian, 0.0% American Indian/Alaska Native, 0.0% Native Hawaiian/Other Pacific Islander, 1.8% Two or more races, 0.0% Hispanic of any race; Average household size: 2.31; Median age: 52.0; Age under 18: 15.5%; Age 65 and over: 24.4%; Males per 100 females: 96.8; Marriage status: 29.7% never married, 51.0% now married, 0.8% separated, 6.5% widowed, 12.8% divorced; Foreign born: 3.9%; Speak English only: 97.2%; With disability: 15.0%; Veterans: 13.0%; Ancestry: 21.8% Italian, 19.8% Irish, 17.7% German, 10.7% English, 9.8% Polish
Employment: 11.3% management, business, and financial, 5.6% computer, engineering, and science, 6.2% education, legal, community service, arts, and media, 8.5% healthcare practitioners, 18.3% service, 31.5% sales and office, 9.9% natural resources, construction, and maintenance, 8.7% production, transportation, and material moving
Income: Per capita: $28,852; Median household: $65,313; Average household: $67,052; Households with income of $100,000 or more: 17.1%; Poverty rate: 11.0%
Educational Attainment: High school diploma or higher: 95.8%; Bachelor's degree or higher: 22.5%; Graduate/professional degree or higher: 8.1%
Housing: Homeownership rate: 91.1%; Median home value: $150,100; Median year structure built: 1957; Homeowner vacancy rate: 3.3%; Median selected monthly owner costs: $1,225 with a mortgage, $486 without a mortgage; Median gross rent: $1,083 per month; Rental vacancy rate: 21.2%
Health Insurance: 91.5% have insurance; 72.8% have private insurance; 34.9% have public insurance; 8.5% do not have insurance; 11.5% of children under 18 do not have insurance
Transportation: Commute: 94.9% car, 1.4% public transportation, 0.0% walk, 2.0% work from home; Mean travel time to work: 22.8 minutes

WAITE HILL (village). Covers a land area of 4.182 square miles and a water area of 0.066 square miles. Located at 41.61° N. Lat; 81.39° W. Long. Elevation is 768 feet.
Population: 495; Growth (since 2000): 11.0%; Density: 118.4 persons per square mile; Race: 95.6% White, 0.0% Black/African American, 2.4% Asian, 0.4% American Indian/Alaska Native, 0.4% Native Hawaiian/Other Pacific Islander, 0.8% Two or more races, 1.0% Hispanic of any race; Average household size: 2.51; Median age: 56.6; Age under 18: 18.2%; Age 65 and over: 29.5%; Males per 100 females: 102.1; Marriage status: 16.1% never married, 71.0% now married, 0.7% separated, 5.3% widowed, 7.6% divorced; Foreign born: 5.9%; Speak English only: 94.5%; With disability: 9.7%; Veterans: 8.1%; Ancestry: 20.2% German, 20.2% Irish, 13.3% Italian, 11.1% English, 10.3% Croatian
Employment: 50.8% management, business, and financial, 1.0% computer, engineering, and science, 13.5% education, legal, community service, arts, and media, 7.8% healthcare practitioners, 6.7% service, 13.0% sales and office, 3.6% natural resources, construction, and maintenance, 3.6% production, transportation, and material moving
Income: Per capita: $88,413; Median household: $131,875; Average household: $217,361; Households with income of $100,000 or more: 60.0%; Poverty rate: 10.5%
Educational Attainment: High school diploma or higher: 98.1%; Bachelor's degree or higher: 65.0%; Graduate/professional degree or higher: 34.7%
Housing: Homeownership rate: 90.9%; Median home value: $573,100; Median year structure built: 1961; Homeowner vacancy rate: 0.0%; Median selected monthly owner costs: $3,688 with a mortgage, $1,338 without a mortgage; Median gross rent: $750 per month; Rental vacancy rate: 14.3%
Health Insurance: 90.1% have insurance; 75.4% have private insurance; 33.1% have public insurance; 9.9% do not have insurance; 15.6% of children under 18 do not have insurance
Transportation: Commute: 93.8% car, 2.1% public transportation, 1.0% walk, 2.1% work from home; Mean travel time to work: 24.5 minutes

WICKLIFFE (city). Covers a land area of 4.639 square miles and a water area of 0.021 square miles. Located at 41.61° N. Lat; 81.47° W. Long. Elevation is 764 feet.
History: Named for Charles A. Wickliffe, a Kentucky lawyer. Borromeo College of Ohio and the Rabbinical College of Telshe are here. Incorporated 1916.
Population: 12,718; Growth (since 2000): -5.7%; Density: 2,741.8 persons per square mile; Race: 91.2% White, 5.6% Black/African American, 1.1% Asian, 0.0% American Indian/Alaska Native, 0.0% Native Hawaiian/Other Pacific Islander, 1.5% Two or more races, 1.5% Hispanic of any race; Average household size: 2.19; Median age: 44.4; Age under 18: 19.0%; Age 65 and over: 21.2%; Males per 100 females: 93.7; Marriage status: 26.6% never married, 51.1% now married, 1.0% separated, 9.1% widowed, 13.2% divorced; Foreign born: 4.5%; Speak English only: 93.8%; With disability: 12.7%; Veterans: 10.0%; Ancestry: 19.8% Italian, 19.3% German, 17.4% Irish, 10.6% Slovene, 7.2% Polish

Employment: 13.0% management, business, and financial, 6.5% computer, engineering, and science, 11.3% education, legal, community service, arts, and media, 7.1% healthcare practitioners, 18.1% service, 22.8% sales and office, 7.2% natural resources, construction, and maintenance, 14.1% production, transportation, and material moving
Income: Per capita: $27,800; Median household: $51,018; Average household: $61,631; Households with income of $100,000 or more: 16.5%; Poverty rate: 6.8%
Educational Attainment: High school diploma or higher: 91.9%; Bachelor's degree or higher: 26.5%; Graduate/professional degree or higher: 8.1%

School District(s)

Wickliffe City (PK-12)
2015-16 Enrollment: 1,431 . . . . (440) 943-6900

Four-year College(s)

Rabbinical College Telshe (Private, Not-for-profit, Jewish)
Fall 2016 Enrollment: 73 . . . . (440) 943-5300
2016-17 Tuition: In-state $10,500; Out-of-state $10,500

Housing: Homeownership rate: 81.0%; Median home value: $117,200; Median year structure built: 1957; Homeowner vacancy rate: 2.2%; Median selected monthly owner costs: $1,096 with a mortgage, $428 without a mortgage; Median gross rent: $876 per month; Rental vacancy rate: 4.0%
Health Insurance: 94.9% have insurance; 78.9% have private insurance; 31.1% have public insurance; 5.1% do not have insurance; 3.9% of children under 18 do not have insurance
Safety: Violent crime rate: 13.6 per 10,000 population; Property crime rate: 186.3 per 10,000 population
Transportation: Commute: 95.1% car, 0.9% public transportation, 1.0% walk, 2.8% work from home; Mean travel time to work: 21.3 minutes
Additional Information Contacts
City of Wickliffe . . . . (440) 943-7100
http://www.cityofwickliffe.com

WILLOUGHBY (city). Covers a land area of 10.249 square miles and a water area of 0.090 square miles. Located at 41.65° N. Lat; 81.41° W. Long. Elevation is 659 feet.
History: Willoughby was first called Chagrin, but was renamed for an instructor in the Willoughby Medical College, established in 1834. The college had a good reputation until 1843, when a local resident discovered her newly-buried husband was missing from his grave. The medical school's method of acquiring cadavers for research soon brought about its own demise.
Population: 22,495; Growth (since 2000): -0.6%; Density: 2,194.8 persons per square mile; Race: 91.0% White, 5.1% Black/African American, 1.5% Asian, 0.2% American Indian/Alaska Native, 0.0% Native Hawaiian/Other Pacific Islander, 1.3% Two or more races, 1.7% Hispanic of any race; Average household size: 2.06; Median age: 44.0; Age under 18: 18.3%; Age 65 and over: 20.4%; Males per 100 females: 88.1; Marriage status: 30.7% never married, 47.0% now married, 1.2% separated, 8.8% widowed, 13.5% divorced; Foreign born: 5.0%; Speak English only: 93.6%; With disability: 13.0%; Veterans: 8.9%; Ancestry: 23.0% German, 20.8% Irish, 19.4% Italian, 9.9% English, 7.1% Polish
Employment: 14.8% management, business, and financial, 6.2% computer, engineering, and science, 10.3% education, legal, community service, arts, and media, 7.8% healthcare practitioners, 16.4% service, 24.7% sales and office, 6.5% natural resources, construction, and maintenance, 13.2% production, transportation, and material moving
Income: Per capita: $31,754; Median household: $53,324; Average household: $65,810; Households with income of $100,000 or more: 18.1%; Poverty rate: 7.6%
Educational Attainment: High school diploma or higher: 93.3%; Bachelor's degree or higher: 30.7%; Graduate/professional degree or higher: 9.5%

School District(s)

Willoughby-Eastlake City (PK-12)
2015-16 Enrollment: 8,207 . . . . (440) 946-5000

Housing: Homeownership rate: 60.2%; Median home value: $144,300; Median year structure built: 1972; Homeowner vacancy rate: 1.1%; Median selected monthly owner costs: $1,323 with a mortgage, $479 without a mortgage; Median gross rent: $864 per month; Rental vacancy rate: 6.1%
Health Insurance: 93.2% have insurance; 78.4% have private insurance; 28.9% have public insurance; 6.8% do not have insurance; 3.0% of children under 18 do not have insurance
Safety: Violent crime rate: 19.8 per 10,000 population; Property crime rate: 210.6 per 10,000 population
Newspapers: News-Herald (daily circulation 40,600)
Transportation: Commute: 95.7% car, 0.6% public transportation, 1.1% walk, 2.4% work from home; Mean travel time to work: 22.0 minutes
Airports: Willoughby Lost Nation Municipal (general aviation)
Additional Information Contacts
City of Willoughby . . . . (440) 951-2800
http://www.willoughbyohio.com

WILLOUGHBY HILLS (city). Covers a land area of 10.729 square miles and a water area of 0.085 square miles. Located at 41.58° N. Lat; 81.43° W. Long. Elevation is 804 feet.
History: Willoughby Hills, incorporated as a village in Lake County, Ohio, in 1954, became a city in 1970.
Population: 9,497; Growth (since 2000): 10.5%; Density: 885.2 persons per square mile; Race: 77.5% White, 15.0% Black/African American, 5.2% Asian, 0.1% American Indian/Alaska Native, 0.0% Native Hawaiian/Other Pacific Islander, 2.2% Two or more races, 2.1% Hispanic of any race; Average household size: 2.11; Median age: 44.8; Age under 18: 15.5%; Age 65 and over: 18.8%; Males per 100 females: 92.9; Marriage status: 32.1% never married, 51.0% now married, 2.4% separated, 4.9% widowed, 11.9% divorced; Foreign born: 17.8%; Speak English only: 80.6%; With disability: 10.2%; Veterans: 8.2%; Ancestry: 13.4% German, 13.1% Italian, 9.7% Irish, 9.1% Slovene, 6.9% English
Employment: 12.3% management, business, and financial, 10.7% computer, engineering, and science, 7.9% education, legal, community service, arts, and media, 12.2% healthcare practitioners, 13.5% service, 25.3% sales and office, 4.6% natural resources, construction, and maintenance, 13.5% production, transportation, and material moving
Income: Per capita: $35,911; Median household: $61,276; Average household: $76,276; Households with income of $100,000 or more: 25.5%; Poverty rate: 9.2%
Educational Attainment: High school diploma or higher: 92.2%; Bachelor's degree or higher: 37.8%; Graduate/professional degree or higher: 14.7%

Two-year College(s)

American National University-Willoughby Hills (Private, For-profit)
Fall 2016 Enrollment: 10 . . . . (440) 944-0825
2016-17 Tuition: In-state $14,886; Out-of-state $14,886

Housing: Homeownership rate: 50.2%; Median home value: $244,100; Median year structure built: 1973; Homeowner vacancy rate: 0.0%; Median selected monthly owner costs: $1,722 with a mortgage, $682 without a mortgage; Median gross rent: $833 per month; Rental vacancy rate: 9.0%
Health Insurance: 93.0% have insurance; 82.6% have private insurance; 25.2% have public insurance; 7.0% do not have insurance; 3.1% of children under 18 do not have insurance
Transportation: Commute: 95.5% car, 0.8% public transportation, 0.0% walk, 2.6% work from home; Mean travel time to work: 21.8 minutes

---

WILLOWICK (city). Covers a land area of 2.536 square miles and a water area of 0 square miles. Located at 41.63° N. Lat; 81.47° W. Long. Elevation is 623 feet.
History: Named for the Willoughby and Wickliff families. Incorporated 1924.
Population: 14,131; Growth (since 2000): -1.6%; Density: 5,571.2 persons per square mile; Race: 93.7% White, 2.1% Black/African American, 1.3% Asian, 0.2% American Indian/Alaska Native, 0.1% Native Hawaiian/Other Pacific Islander, 2.5% Two or more races, 2.3% Hispanic of any race; Average household size: 2.36; Median age: 40.9; Age under 18: 22.4%; Age 65 and over: 18.3%; Males per 100 females: 93.8; Marriage status: 31.5% never married, 48.6% now married, 0.7% separated, 8.2% widowed, 11.8% divorced; Foreign born: 5.3%; Speak English only: 94.1%; With disability: 12.2%; Veterans: 8.1%; Ancestry: 24.6% German, 22.1% Italian, 18.1% Irish, 11.9% Polish, 8.4% Slovene
Employment: 12.4% management, business, and financial, 5.7% computer, engineering, and science, 7.8% education, legal, community service, arts, and media, 7.0% healthcare practitioners, 14.8% service, 25.3% sales and office, 8.7% natural resources, construction, and maintenance, 18.3% production, transportation, and material moving
Income: Per capita: $27,750; Median household: $54,493; Average household: $65,358; Households with income of $100,000 or more: 16.4%; Poverty rate: 6.5%
Educational Attainment: High school diploma or higher: 91.9%; Bachelor's degree or higher: 22.2%; Graduate/professional degree or higher: 7.1%

School District(s)

Willoughby-Eastlake City (PK-12)
2015-16 Enrollment: 8,207 . . . . (440) 946-5000

Housing: Homeownership rate: 76.5%; Median home value: $117,400; Median year structure built: 1957; Homeowner vacancy rate: 1.6%; Median selected monthly owner costs: $1,157 with a mortgage, $447 without a mortgage; Median gross rent: $781 per month; Rental vacancy rate: 6.2%
Health Insurance: 93.2% have insurance; 76.4% have private insurance; 30.4% have public insurance; 6.8% do not have insurance; 5.4% of children under 18 do not have insurance
Transportation: Commute: 93.4% car, 1.7% public transportation, 1.4% walk, 3.0% work from home; Mean travel time to work: 20.6 minutes
Additional Information Contacts
City of Willowick . . . . (440) 585-3700
http://www.cityofwillowick.com

Lawrence County

Located in southern Ohio; bounded on the south by the Ohio River and the Kentucky and West Virginia borders. Covers a land area of 453.371 square miles, a water area of 3.904 square miles, and is located in the Eastern Time Zone at 38.60° N. Lat., 82.52° W. Long. The county was founded in 1815. County seat is Ironton.

Lawrence County is part of the Huntington-Ashland, WV-KY-OH Metropolitan Statistical Area. The entire metro area includes: Boyd County, KY; Greenup County, KY; Lawrence County, OH; Cabell County, WV; Lincoln County, WV; Putnam County, WV; Wayne County, WV

Population: 61,503; Growth (since 2000): -1.3%; Density: 135.7 persons per square mile; Race: 95.4% White, 2.3% Black/African American, 0.5% Asian, 0.1% American Indian/Alaska Native, 0.0% Native Hawaiian/Other Pacific Islander, 1.6% two or more races, 0.9% Hispanic of any race; Average household size: 2.62; Median age: 41.4; Age under 18: 22.7%; Age 65 and over: 17.4%; Males per 100 females: 94.6; Marriage status: 26.2% never married, 51.9% now married, 2.5% separated, 8.4% widowed, 13.6% divorced; Foreign born: 0.6%; Speak English only: 98.4%; With disability: 21.5%; Veterans: 9.5%; Ancestry: 15.3% German, 11.8% Irish, 11.6% American, 8.8% English, 1.5% Scottish
Religion: Six largest groups: 11.4% Baptist, 3.1% Catholicism, 2.9% Methodist/Pietist, 2.4% Non-denominational Protestant, 1.6% Holiness, 0.7% Pentecostal
Economy: Unemployment rate: 5.2%; Leading industries: 17.5 % retail trade; 15.7 % health care and social assistance; 12.1 % other services (except public administration); Farms: 592 totaling 64,575 acres; Company size: 0 employ 1,000 or more persons, 0 employ 500 to 999 persons, 18 employ 100 to 499 persons, 776 employ less than 100 persons; Business ownership: 1,137 women-owned, 37 Black-owned, 30 Hispanic-owned, 27 Asian-owned, n/a American Indian/Alaska Native-owned
Employment: 9.4% management, business, and financial, 2.5% computer, engineering, and science, 9.3% education, legal, community service, arts, and media, 8.9% healthcare practitioners, 19.1% service, 24.8% sales and office, 7.7% natural resources, construction, and maintenance, 18.2% production, transportation, and material moving
Income: Per capita: $22,567; Median household: $44,256; Average household: $56,062; Households with income of $100,000 or more: 12.0%; Poverty rate: 18.4%
Educational Attainment: High school diploma or higher: 85.7%; Bachelor's degree or higher: 14.1%; Graduate/professional degree or higher: 5.3%
Housing: Homeownership rate: 73.6%; Median home value: $101,600; Median year structure built: 1974; Homeowner vacancy rate: 2.6%; Median selected monthly owner costs: $1,005 with a mortgage, $382 without a mortgage; Median gross rent: $664 per month; Rental vacancy rate: 9.3%
Vital Statistics: Birth rate: 113.2 per 10,000 population; Death rate: 118.0 per 10,000 population; Age-adjusted cancer mortality rate: 234.5 deaths per 100,000 population
Health Insurance: 90.8% have insurance; 61.6% have private insurance; 44.6% have public insurance; 9.2% do not have insurance; 2.9% of children under 18 do not have insurance
Health Care: Physicians: 10.5 per 10,000 population; Dentists: 3.4 per 10,000 population; Hospital beds: 1.3 per 10,000 population; Hospital admissions: 36.4 per 10,000 population
Air Quality Index (AQI): Percent of Days: 78.7% good, 20.5% moderate, 0.8% unhealthy for sensitive individuals, 0.0% unhealthy, 0.0% very unhealthy; Annual median: 39; Annual maximum: 119
Transportation: Commute: 94.4% car, 0.4% public transportation, 1.7% walk, 2.2% work from home; Mean travel time to work: 23.1 minutes
2016 Presidential Election: 69.8% Trump, 26.0% Clinton, 2.2% Johnson, 0.6% Stein
National and State Parks: Dean State Forest; Wayne National Forest; Wayne National Forest - Ironton Ranger District
Additional Information Contacts
Lawrence Government . . . . (740) 533-4300
http://www.lawrencecountyohio.org

Lawrence County Communities

ATHALIA (village). Covers a land area of 0.686 square miles and a water area of <.001 square miles. Located at 38.51° N. Lat; 82.31° W. Long. Elevation is 558 feet.
Population: 267; Growth (since 2000): -18.6%; Density: 389.4 persons per square mile; Race: 92.5% White, 1.1% Black/African American, 0.0% Asian, 0.0% American Indian/Alaska Native, 0.0% Native Hawaiian/Other Pacific Islander, 6.4% Two or more races, 1.1% Hispanic of any race; Average household size: 2.21; Median age: 45.1; Age under 18: 20.6%; Age 65 and over: 21.0%; Males per 100 females: 91.3; Marriage status: 27.4% never married, 53.1% now married, 5.8% separated, 9.7% widowed, 9.7% divorced; Foreign born: 0.0%; Speak English only: 95.7%; With disability: 31.1%; Veterans: 13.2%; Ancestry: 15.7% American, 13.1% English, 11.6% German, 5.2% Scottish, 3.7% Scotch-Irish
Employment: 9.9% management, business, and financial, 0.0% computer, engineering, and science, 4.9% education, legal, community service, arts, and media, 0.0% healthcare practitioners, 21.0% service, 29.6% sales and office, 7.4% natural resources, construction, and maintenance, 27.2% production, transportation, and material moving
Income: Per capita: $18,257; Median household: $31,750; Average household: $38,689; Households with income of $100,000 or more: 6.6%; Poverty rate: 28.5%
Educational Attainment: High school diploma or higher: 80.3%; Bachelor's degree or higher: 15.7%; Graduate/professional degree or higher: 5.1%
Housing: Homeownership rate: 64.5%; Median home value: $95,000; Median year structure built: 1974; Homeowner vacancy rate: 9.3%; Median selected monthly owner costs: $1,054 with a mortgage, $339 without a mortgage; Median gross rent: $543 per month; Rental vacancy rate: 0.0%
Health Insurance: 87.6% have insurance; 47.2% have private insurance; 58.8% have public insurance; 12.4% do not have insurance; 0.0% of children under 18 do not have insurance
Transportation: Commute: 97.5% car, 0.0% public transportation, 0.0% walk, 1.3% work from home; Mean travel time to work: 38.5 minutes

BURLINGTON (CDP). Covers a land area of 1.393 square miles and a water area of 0.025 square miles. Located at 38.41° N. Lat; 82.53° W. Long. Elevation is 558 feet.
History: Burlington was founded by Reverend Plymale, a Baptist minister in Virginia who had been a slave-holder. He purchased the land in Ohio and presented each of his former slaves with an equal portion of it. In 1817 Burlington became the first seat of Lawrence County.
Population: 2,514; Growth (since 2000): -10.0%; Density: 1,804.8 persons per square mile; Race: 92.5% White, 5.1% Black/African American, 0.0% Asian, 0.0% American Indian/Alaska Native, 0.0% Native Hawaiian/Other Pacific Islander, 2.4% Two or more races, 0.0% Hispanic of any race; Average household size: 2.39; Median age: 44.1; Age under 18: 21.8%; Age 65 and over: 25.8%; Males per 100 females: 85.8; Marriage status: 22.9% never married, 40.2% now married, 1.0% separated, 17.4% widowed, 19.4% divorced; Foreign born: 1.0%; Speak English only: 98.9%; With disability: 19.1%; Veterans: 9.0%; Ancestry: 18.0% Irish, 17.8% German, 14.9% American, 9.1% English, 1.7% Dutch
Employment: 5.0% management, business, and financial, 6.1% computer, engineering, and science, 5.2% education, legal, community service, arts, and media, 11.4% healthcare practitioners, 21.1% service, 30.4% sales and office, 6.8% natural resources, construction, and maintenance, 14.1% production, transportation, and material moving
Income: Per capita: $25,281; Median household: $50,775; Average household: $59,107; Households with income of $100,000 or more: 11.0%; Poverty rate: 15.5%

Educational Attainment: High school diploma or higher: 90.9%; Bachelor's degree or higher: 9.4%; Graduate/professional degree or higher: 2.9%
Housing: Homeownership rate: 68.8%; Median home value: $102,500; Median year structure built: 1977; Homeowner vacancy rate: 2.0%; Median selected monthly owner costs: $965 with a mortgage, $434 without a mortgage; Median gross rent: $527 per month; Rental vacancy rate: 9.1%
Health Insurance: 90.0% have insurance; 63.9% have private insurance; 42.0% have public insurance; 10.0% do not have insurance; 0.0% of children under 18 do not have insurance
Transportation: Commute: 95.8% car, 0.0% public transportation, 0.0% walk, 4.2% work from home; Mean travel time to work: 20.0 minutes

CHESAPEAKE (village). Covers a land area of 0.472 square miles and a water area of 0.086 square miles. Located at 38.43° N. Lat; 82.46° W. Long. Elevation is 558 feet.
History: Chesapeake developed as a residential community, with many of its citizens commuting to Huntington, across the Ohio River in West Virginia.
Population: 833; Growth (since 2000): -1.1%; Density: 1,763.0 persons per square mile; Race: 96.2% White, 0.7% Black/African American, 0.0% Asian, 0.0% American Indian/Alaska Native, 0.0% Native Hawaiian/Other Pacific Islander, 1.9% Two or more races, 4.4% Hispanic of any race; Average household size: 2.56; Median age: 33.6; Age under 18: 21.5%; Age 65 and over: 14.2%; Males per 100 females: 90.1; Marriage status: 37.8% never married, 44.8% now married, 1.2% separated, 7.4% widowed, 10.0% divorced; Foreign born: 0.4%; Speak English only: 99.4%; With disability: 19.8%; Veterans: 8.7%; Ancestry: 19.8% German, 18.6% Irish, 8.6% American, 7.7% English, 3.4% Scottish
Employment: 7.0% management, business, and financial, 1.1% computer, engineering, and science, 13.3% education, legal, community service, arts, and media, 6.8% healthcare practitioners, 15.2% service, 30.4% sales and office, 14.9% natural resources, construction, and maintenance, 11.4% production, transportation, and material moving
Income: Per capita: $17,988; Median household: $37,500; Average household: $46,603; Households with income of $100,000 or more: 8.9%; Poverty rate: 16.6%
Educational Attainment: High school diploma or higher: 84.2%; Bachelor's degree or higher: 17.4%; Graduate/professional degree or higher: 5.1%

School District(s)

Chesapeake Union Exempted Village (PK-12)
2015-16 Enrollment: 1,352 . . . . (740) 867-3135
Lawrence County (07-12)
2015-16 Enrollment: n/a . . . . (740) 867-6641

Two-year College(s)

O C Collins Career Center (Public)
Fall 2016 Enrollment: 443 . . . . (740) 867-6641
Housing: Homeownership rate: 52.1%; Median home value: $86,200; Median year structure built: 1962; Homeowner vacancy rate: 2.9%; Median selected monthly owner costs: $965 with a mortgage, $358 without a mortgage; Median gross rent: $715 per month; Rental vacancy rate: 4.9%
Health Insurance: 86.9% have insurance; 52.8% have private insurance; 52.1% have public insurance; 13.1% do not have insurance; 1.1% of children under 18 do not have insurance
Transportation: Commute: 92.3% car, 0.0% public transportation, 1.6% walk, 4.6% work from home; Mean travel time to work: 21.3 minutes
Airports: Lawrence County Airpark (general aviation)

COAL GROVE (village). Covers a land area of 1.902 square miles and a water area of 0.144 square miles. Located at 38.49° N. Lat; 82.64° W. Long. Elevation is 571 feet.
Population: 1,884; Growth (since 2000): -7.1%; Density: 990.7 persons per square mile; Race: 98.4% White, 0.6% Black/African American, 0.0% Asian, 0.0% American Indian/Alaska Native, 0.0% Native Hawaiian/Other Pacific Islander, 0.5% Two or more races, 1.1% Hispanic of any race; Average household size: 2.51; Median age: 44.1; Age under 18: 15.4%; Age 65 and over: 20.8%; Males per 100 females: 88.9; Marriage status: 28.6% never married, 44.3% now married, 0.5% separated, 9.4% widowed, 17.6% divorced; Foreign born: 0.0%; Speak English only: 97.8%; With disability: 31.5%; Veterans: 7.8%; Ancestry: 20.3% German, 13.3% Irish, 10.8% American, 8.8% English, 3.3% French
Employment: 8.5% management, business, and financial, 0.6% computer, engineering, and science, 9.3% education, legal, community service, arts, and media, 11.6% healthcare practitioners, 12.3% service, 22.9% sales and office, 5.5% natural resources, construction, and maintenance, 29.3% production, transportation, and material moving
Income: Per capita: $20,174; Median household: $39,474; Average household: $47,675; Households with income of $100,000 or more: 6.8%; Poverty rate: 22.1%
Educational Attainment: High school diploma or higher: 79.2%; Bachelor's degree or higher: 12.9%; Graduate/professional degree or higher: 4.6%

School District(s)

Dawson-Bryant Local (PK-12)
2015-16 Enrollment: 1,113 . . . . (740) 532-6451
Housing: Homeownership rate: 68.9%; Median home value: $79,600; Median year structure built: 1955; Homeowner vacancy rate: 10.1%; Median selected monthly owner costs: $918 with a mortgage, $319 without a mortgage; Median gross rent: $589 per month; Rental vacancy rate: 9.5%
Health Insurance: 91.7% have insurance; 56.0% have private insurance; 46.9% have public insurance; 8.3% do not have insurance; 3.8% of children under 18 do not have insurance
Transportation: Commute: 94.3% car, 0.0% public transportation, 0.9% walk, 0.6% work from home; Mean travel time to work: 18.8 minutes

HANGING ROCK (village). Covers a land area of 0.556 square miles and a water area of 0.086 square miles. Located at 38.56° N. Lat; 82.73° W. Long. Elevation is 538 feet.
History: Hanging Rock was named for the sandstone cliff, 400 feet high, which has an overhang at the top. Hanging Rock was founded in 1820 and developed around an iron furnace.
Population: 222; Growth (since 2000): -20.4%; Density: 399.0 persons per square mile; Race: 98.2% White, 0.0% Black/African American, 0.0% Asian, 0.0% American Indian/Alaska Native, 0.0% Native Hawaiian/Other Pacific Islander, 1.8% Two or more races, 0.0% Hispanic of any race; Average household size: 2.09; Median age: 50.4; Age under 18: 12.6%; Age 65 and over: 16.7%; Males per 100 females: 90.5; Marriage status: 17.7% never married, 48.0% now married, 1.0% separated, 15.2% widowed, 19.2% divorced; Foreign born: 0.0%; Speak English only: 99.5%; With disability: 23.0%; Veterans: 9.3%; Ancestry: 15.3% German, 14.4% Irish, 13.5% English, 8.1% American, 1.8% Scotch-Irish
Employment: 10.5% management, business, and financial, 0.0% computer, engineering, and science, 12.8% education, legal, community service, arts, and media, 12.8% healthcare practitioners, 22.1% service, 20.9% sales and office, 10.5% natural resources, construction, and maintenance, 10.5% production, transportation, and material moving
Income: Per capita: $23,782; Median household: $43,333; Average household: $50,562; Households with income of $100,000 or more: 11.3%; Poverty rate: 13.1%
Educational Attainment: High school diploma or higher: 88.0%; Bachelor's degree or higher: 7.1%; Graduate/professional degree or higher: 1.6%
Housing: Homeownership rate: 81.1%; Median home value: $84,000; Median year structure built: 1978; Homeowner vacancy rate: 4.4%; Median selected monthly owner costs: $1,139 with a mortgage, $463 without a mortgage; Median gross rent: $625 per month; Rental vacancy rate: 4.8%
Health Insurance: 91.0% have insurance; 62.2% have private insurance; 43.2% have public insurance; 9.0% do not have insurance; 0.0% of children under 18 do not have insurance
Transportation: Commute: 90.7% car, 2.3% public transportation, 0.0% walk, 4.7% work from home; Mean travel time to work: 21.0 minutes

IRONTON (city). County seat. Covers a land area of 4.161 square miles and a water area of 0.296 square miles. Located at 38.53° N. Lat; 82.68° W. Long. Elevation is 551 feet.
History: Ironton was founded in 1848 by John Campbell, one of the first ironmasters of the region. The ore deposits in the Ironton district were discovered about 1826, and a charcoal furnace was set up to make pigiron. The iron industry supported Ironton for a century.
Population: 11,049; Growth (since 2000): -1.4%; Density: 2,655.2 persons per square mile; Race: 90.4% White, 6.2% Black/African American, 0.1% Asian, 0.0% American Indian/Alaska Native, 0.0% Native Hawaiian/Other Pacific Islander, 3.2% Two or more races, 2.7% Hispanic of any race; Average household size: 2.50; Median age: 40.0; Age under 18: 22.8%; Age 65 and over: 18.9%; Males per 100 females: 89.1; Marriage status: 30.2% never married, 44.2% now married, 3.8% separated, 11.3% widowed, 14.3% divorced; Foreign born: 0.5%; Speak English only: 96.7%;

With disability: 24.4%; Veterans: 8.0%; Ancestry: 16.8% German, 11.8% Irish, 9.3% American, 8.9% English, 1.3% French
Employment: 5.8% management, business, and financial, 1.9% computer, engineering, and science, 11.8% education, legal, community service, arts, and media, 6.7% healthcare practitioners, 24.2% service, 27.4% sales and office, 6.8% natural resources, construction, and maintenance, 15.6% production, transportation, and material moving
Income: Per capita: $19,347; Median household: $34,140; Average household: $45,561; Households with income of $100,000 or more: 9.7%; Poverty rate: 21.0%
Educational Attainment: High school diploma or higher: 86.6%; Bachelor's degree or higher: 15.2%; Graduate/professional degree or higher: 5.0%

School District(s)

Dawson-Bryant Local (PK-12)
2015-16 Enrollment: 1,113 . . . . (740) 532-6451
Ironton City (PK-12)
2015-16 Enrollment: 1,462 . . . . (740) 532-4133
Rock Hill Local (PK-12)
2015-16 Enrollment: 1,425 . . . . (740) 532-7030

Four-year College(s)

Ohio University-Southern Campus (Public)
Fall 2016 Enrollment: 1,372 . . . . (740) 533-4600
2016-17 Tuition: In-state $4,872; Out-of-state $6,718

Housing: Homeownership rate: 62.6%; Median home value: $91,400; Median year structure built: 1952; Homeowner vacancy rate: 2.5%; Median selected monthly owner costs: $870 with a mortgage, $368 without a mortgage; Median gross rent: $579 per month; Rental vacancy rate: 12.2%
Health Insurance: 87.6% have insurance; 54.2% have private insurance; 47.8% have public insurance; 12.4% do not have insurance; 4.3% of children under 18 do not have insurance
Safety: Violent crime rate: 19.3 per 10,000 population; Property crime rate: 248.7 per 10,000 population
Newspapers: Ironton Tribune (daily circulation 5,200)
Transportation: Commute: 92.3% car, 0.0% public transportation, 2.6% walk, 2.7% work from home; Mean travel time to work: 15.8 minutes

Additional Information Contacts

City of Ironton . . . . (740) 532-3833
http://ironton-ohio.com

KITTS HILL (unincorporated postal area)

ZCTA: 45645

Covers a land area of 46.737 square miles and a water area of 0.134 square miles. Located at 38.57° N. Lat; 82.53° W. Long. Elevation is 955 feet.
Population: 3,115; Growth (since 2000): 7.0%; Density: 66.6 persons per square mile; Race: 93.2% White, 0.0% Black/African American, 1.4% Asian, 0.0% American Indian/Alaska Native, 0.0% Native Hawaiian/Other Pacific Islander, 5.5% Two or more races, 1.4% Hispanic of any race; Average household size: 2.39; Median age: 50.4; Age under 18: 18.7%; Age 65 and over: 31.5%; Males per 100 females: 99.6; Marriage status: 20.3% never married, 63.8% now married, 4.0% separated, 11.7% widowed, 4.3% divorced; Foreign born: 2.0%; Speak English only: 97.7%; With disability: 24.8%; Veterans: 11.0%; Ancestry: 25.6% German, 12.5% English, 9.5% Irish, 6.1% American, 5.5% Swedish
Employment: 12.7% management, business, and financial, 1.6% computer, engineering, and science, 4.0% education, legal, community service, arts, and media, 13.8% healthcare practitioners, 4.5% service, 35.1% sales and office, 5.6% natural resources, construction, and maintenance, 22.6% production, transportation, and material moving
Income: Per capita: $24,228; Median household: $46,844; Average household: $53,325; Households with income of $100,000 or more: 9.9%; Poverty rate: 6.1%
Educational Attainment: High school diploma or higher: 82.7%; Bachelor's degree or higher: 7.7%; Graduate/professional degree or higher: 3.2%
Housing: Homeownership rate: 94.2%; Median home value: $82,400; Median year structure built: 1979; Homeowner vacancy rate: 0.0%; Median selected monthly owner costs: $999 with a mortgage, $396 without a mortgage; Median gross rent: n/a per month; Rental vacancy rate: 0.0%
Health Insurance: 95.2% have insurance; 66.1% have private insurance; 50.2% have public insurance; 4.8% do not have insurance; 0.0% of children under 18 do not have insurance
Transportation: Commute: 97.8% car, 0.0% public transportation, 0.0% walk, 2.2% work from home; Mean travel time to work: 28.3 minutes

PEDRO (unincorporated postal area)

ZCTA: 45659

Covers a land area of 98.267 square miles and a water area of 0.608 square miles. Located at 38.65° N. Lat; 82.64° W. Long. Elevation is 610 feet.
Population: 2,632; Growth (since 2000): -16.6%; Density: 26.8 persons per square mile; Race: 99.7% White, 0.3% Black/African American, 0.0% Asian, 0.0% American Indian/Alaska Native, 0.0% Native Hawaiian/Other Pacific Islander, 0.0% Two or more races, 0.0% Hispanic of any race; Average household size: 2.70; Median age: 44.1; Age under 18: 19.4%; Age 65 and over: 14.6%; Males per 100 females: 100.9; Marriage status: 23.9% never married, 49.8% now married, 1.1% separated, 8.1% widowed, 18.2% divorced; Foreign born: 0.0%; Speak English only: 100.0%; With disability: 27.3%; Veterans: 5.9%; Ancestry: 21.2% American, 14.7% German, 6.9% Irish, 5.1% English, 4.1% Scottish
Employment: 4.2% management, business, and financial, 2.7% computer, engineering, and science, 10.0% education, legal, community service, arts, and media, 8.1% healthcare practitioners, 17.1% service, 24.9% sales and office, 10.0% natural resources, construction, and maintenance, 23.1% production, transportation, and material moving
Income: Per capita: $21,907; Median household: $34,565; Average household: $53,008; Households with income of $100,000 or more: 15.2%; Poverty rate: 21.8%
Educational Attainment: High school diploma or higher: 77.2%; Bachelor's degree or higher: 15.8%; Graduate/professional degree or higher: 7.6%
Housing: Homeownership rate: 68.9%; Median home value: $88,500; Median year structure built: 1985; Homeowner vacancy rate: 7.0%; Median selected monthly owner costs: $855 with a mortgage, $375 without a mortgage; Median gross rent: $671 per month; Rental vacancy rate: 0.0%
Health Insurance: 87.7% have insurance; 49.3% have private insurance; 46.4% have public insurance; 12.3% do not have insurance; 0.0% of children under 18 do not have insurance
Transportation: Commute: 96.7% car, 1.7% public transportation, 1.2% walk, 0.5% work from home; Mean travel time to work: 36.5 minutes

PROCTORVILLE (village). Covers a land area of 0.238 square miles and a water area of 0.034 square miles. Located at 38.44° N. Lat; 82.38° W. Long. Elevation is 551 feet.

Population: 519; Growth (since 2000): -16.3%; Density: 2,182.5 persons per square mile; Race: 100.0% White, 0.0% Black/African American, 0.0% Asian, 0.0% American Indian/Alaska Native, 0.0% Native Hawaiian/Other Pacific Islander, 0.0% Two or more races, 1.2% Hispanic of any race; Average household size: 2.22; Median age: 43.5; Age under 18: 19.8%; Age 65 and over: 27.9%; Males per 100 females: 93.3; Marriage status: 26.9% never married, 37.6% now married, 3.5% separated, 13.7% widowed, 21.8% divorced; Foreign born: 0.0%; Speak English only: 99.6%; With disability: 34.9%; Veterans: 6.0%; Ancestry: 9.1% German, 8.1% English, 7.7% American, 7.3% Irish, 2.3% Scottish
Employment: 8.1% management, business, and financial, 0.0% computer, engineering, and science, 5.8% education, legal, community service, arts, and media, 5.2% healthcare practitioners, 25.4% service, 22.0% sales and office, 17.3% natural resources, construction, and maintenance, 16.2% production, transportation, and material moving
Income: Per capita: $16,903; Median household: $26,333; Average household: $33,594; Households with income of $100,000 or more: 2.6%; Poverty rate: 19.1%
Educational Attainment: High school diploma or higher: 82.3%; Bachelor's degree or higher: 6.0%; Graduate/professional degree or higher: 0.5%

School District(s)

Fairland Local (PK-12)
2015-16 Enrollment: 1,656 . . . . (740) 886-3100

Housing: Homeownership rate: 56.8%; Median home value: $80,300; Median year structure built: 1967; Homeowner vacancy rate: 0.0%; Median selected monthly owner costs: $775 with a mortgage, $348 without a mortgage; Median gross rent: $591 per month; Rental vacancy rate: 9.2%
Health Insurance: 88.4% have insurance; 48.0% have private insurance; 62.6% have public insurance; 11.6% do not have insurance; 1.9% of children under 18 do not have insurance
Hospitals: Three Gables Surgery Center
Transportation: Commute: 87.3% car, 2.9% public transportation, 6.4% walk, 0.0% work from home; Mean travel time to work: 32.0 minutes

SCOTTOWN (unincorporated postal area)

ZCTA: 45678

Covers a land area of 40.737 square miles and a water area of 0.239 square miles. Located at 38.61° N. Lat; 82.38° W. Long. Elevation is 594 feet.

Population: 1,242; Growth (since 2000): 15.2%; Density: 30.5 persons per square mile; Race: 98.7% White, 0.0% Black/African American, 0.0% Asian, 0.0% American Indian/Alaska Native, 0.0% Native Hawaiian/Other Pacific Islander, 1.3% Two or more races, 0.0% Hispanic of any race; Average household size: 2.59; Median age: 41.5; Age under 18: 35.7%; Age 65 and over: 8.0%; Males per 100 females: 108.9; Marriage status: 18.3% never married, 63.6% now married, 3.5% separated, 1.9% widowed, 16.3% divorced; Foreign born: 0.0%; Speak English only: 100.0%; With disability: 12.7%; Veterans: 11.6%; Ancestry: 15.1% American, 3.4% German, 1.4% Dutch, 1.4% Italian, 1.4% French

Employment: 10.8% management, business, and financial, 11.6% computer, engineering, and science, 0.0% education, legal, community service, arts, and media, 15.7% healthcare practitioners, 11.2% service, 17.6% sales and office, 11.0% natural resources, construction, and maintenance, 22.0% production, transportation, and material moving

Income: Per capita: $25,571; Median household: $51,518; Average household: $64,969; Households with income of $100,000 or more: 15.7%; Poverty rate: 9.7%

Educational Attainment: High school diploma or higher: 86.7%; Bachelor's degree or higher: n/a; Graduate/professional degree or higher: n/a

Housing: Homeownership rate: 89.2%; Median home value: $93,800; Median year structure built: 1984; Homeowner vacancy rate: 0.0%; Median selected monthly owner costs: $1,084 with a mortgage, $378 without a mortgage; Median gross rent: n/a per month; Rental vacancy rate: 0.0%

Health Insurance: 96.6% have insurance; 80.9% have private insurance; 40.2% have public insurance; 3.4% do not have insurance; 0.0% of children under 18 do not have insurance

Transportation: Commute: 100.0% car, 0.0% public transportation, 0.0% walk, 0.0% work from home; Mean travel time to work: 28.4 minutes

SOUTH POINT (village). Covers a land area of 2.939 square miles and a water area of 0.289 square miles. Located at 38.42° N. Lat; 82.58° W. Long. Elevation is 561 feet.

History: South Point was named for its location at the southern tip of Ohio. The residents of South Point enjoyed a view of three states: Kentucky, West Virginia, and Ohio.

Population: 3,639; Growth (since 2000): -2.8%; Density: 1,238.2 persons per square mile; Race: 95.8% White, 2.3% Black/African American, 1.4% Asian, 0.0% American Indian/Alaska Native, 0.0% Native Hawaiian/Other Pacific Islander, 0.5% Two or more races, 1.6% Hispanic of any race; Average household size: 2.38; Median age: 40.6; Age under 18: 22.2%; Age 65 and over: 15.5%; Males per 100 females: 88.1; Marriage status: 25.3% never married, 53.4% now married, 0.6% separated, 7.5% widowed, 13.8% divorced; Foreign born: 0.2%; Speak English only: 98.7%; With disability: 18.0%; Veterans: 9.5%; Ancestry: 15.7% German, 13.9% Irish, 7.5% American, 4.5% English, 3.3% French

Employment: 17.3% management, business, and financial, 1.8% computer, engineering, and science, 13.5% education, legal, community service, arts, and media, 10.0% healthcare practitioners, 20.8% service, 20.4% sales and office, 6.6% natural resources, construction, and maintenance, 9.6% production, transportation, and material moving

Income: Per capita: $27,684; Median household: $46,612; Average household: $65,520; Households with income of $100,000 or more: 16.3%; Poverty rate: 9.6%

Educational Attainment: High school diploma or higher: 89.2%; Bachelor's degree or higher: 18.5%; Graduate/professional degree or higher: 7.5%

School District(s)

South Point Local (PK-12)
 2015-16 Enrollment: 1,563 . . . . (740) 377-4315

Four-year College(s)

Tri-State Bible College (Private, Not-for-profit, Undenominational)
 Fall 2016 Enrollment: 43 . . . . (740) 377-2520
 2016-17 Tuition: In-state $9,100; Out-of-state $9,100

Housing: Homeownership rate: 64.6%; Median home value: $127,600; Median year structure built: 1976; Homeowner vacancy rate: 0.0%; Median selected monthly owner costs: $1,222 with a mortgage, $389 without a mortgage; Median gross rent: $751 per month; Rental vacancy rate: 4.6%

Health Insurance: 91.0% have insurance; 73.0% have private insurance; 32.3% have public insurance; 9.0% do not have insurance; 1.2% of children under 18 do not have insurance

Transportation: Commute: 95.8% car, 0.0% public transportation, 0.0% walk, 2.2% work from home; Mean travel time to work: 20.8 minutes

Additional Information Contacts

Village of South Point . . . . (740) 377-4838
 http://www.villageofsouthpoint.com

WATERLOO (unincorporated postal area)

ZCTA: 45688

Covers a land area of 36.711 square miles and a water area of 0.124 square miles. Located at 38.73° N. Lat; 82.54° W. Long. Elevation is 636 feet.

Population: 615; Growth (since 2000): 39.8%; Density: 16.8 persons per square mile; Race: 99.3% White, 0.0% Black/African American, 0.7% Asian, 0.0% American Indian/Alaska Native, 0.0% Native Hawaiian/Other Pacific Islander, 0.0% Two or more races, 0.0% Hispanic of any race; Average household size: 2.66; Median age: 37.8; Age under 18: 24.9%; Age 65 and over: 20.5%; Males per 100 females: 96.3; Marriage status: 20.0% never married, 50.8% now married, 0.0% separated, 10.5% widowed, 18.6% divorced; Foreign born: 0.7%; Speak English only: 100.0%; With disability: 15.4%; Veterans: 10.6%; Ancestry: 11.5% American, 7.8% Irish, 5.7% English, 2.9% German, 2.0% Welsh

Employment: 2.2% management, business, and financial, 0.0% computer, engineering, and science, 4.4% education, legal, community service, arts, and media, 4.0% healthcare practitioners, 34.4% service, 6.6% sales and office, 6.2% natural resources, construction, and maintenance, 42.3% production, transportation, and material moving

Income: Per capita: $18,733; Median household: $36,477; Average household: $44,492; Households with income of $100,000 or more: 2.2%; Poverty rate: 8.2%

Educational Attainment: High school diploma or higher: 83.3%; Bachelor's degree or higher: 4.5%; Graduate/professional degree or higher: 1.2%

Housing: Homeownership rate: 74.0%; Median home value: $63,900; Median year structure built: 1984; Homeowner vacancy rate: 0.0%; Median selected monthly owner costs: $957 with a mortgage, $272 without a mortgage; Median gross rent: $1,053 per month; Rental vacancy rate: 0.0%

Health Insurance: 92.0% have insurance; 62.8% have private insurance; 41.1% have public insurance; 8.0% do not have insurance; 0.0% of children under 18 do not have insurance

Transportation: Commute: 97.7% car, 0.0% public transportation, 2.3% walk, 0.0% work from home; Mean travel time to work: 62.1 minutes

WILLOW WOOD (unincorporated postal area)

ZCTA: 45696

Covers a land area of 36.009 square miles and a water area of 0.168 square miles. Located at 38.60° N. Lat; 82.45° W. Long. Elevation is 620 feet.

Population: 1,398; Growth (since 2000): 2.3%; Density: 38.8 persons per square mile; Race: 98.8% White, 0.0% Black/African American, 0.0% Asian, 0.0% American Indian/Alaska Native, 0.0% Native Hawaiian/Other Pacific Islander, 1.2% Two or more races, 0.0% Hispanic of any race; Average household size: 2.69; Median age: 37.6; Age under 18: 20.8%; Age 65 and over: 18.0%; Males per 100 females: 101.4; Marriage status: 26.8% never married, 49.7% now married, 5.6% separated, 10.0% widowed, 13.5% divorced; Foreign born: 0.0%; Speak English only: 100.0%; With disability: 14.3%; Veterans: 8.2%; Ancestry: 17.7% German, 13.7% Irish, 12.3% American, 6.2% Polish, 5.6% French

Employment: 12.8% management, business, and financial, 2.4% computer, engineering, and science, 16.7% education, legal, community service, arts, and media, 7.1% healthcare practitioners, 17.5% service, 10.7% sales and office, 9.4% natural resources, construction, and maintenance, 23.5% production, transportation, and material moving

Income: Per capita: $23,621; Median household: $62,991; Average household: $57,422; Households with income of $100,000 or more: 16.0%; Poverty rate: 20.7%

Educational Attainment: High school diploma or higher: 95.3%; Bachelor's degree or higher: 19.4%; Graduate/professional degree or higher: 3.7%

School District(s)

Symmes Valley Local (PK-12)
 2015-16 Enrollment: 765. . . . . (740) 643-2451

Housing: Homeownership rate: 86.5%; Median home value: $147,700; Median year structure built: 1992; Homeowner vacancy rate: 9.5%; Median selected monthly owner costs: $1,255 with a mortgage, $518 without a mortgage; Median gross rent: n/a per month; Rental vacancy rate: 13.6%
Health Insurance: 90.4% have insurance; 64.1% have private insurance; 37.6% have public insurance; 9.6% do not have insurance; 0.0% of children under 18 do not have insurance
Transportation: Commute: 97.3% car, 0.0% public transportation, 0.0% walk, 0.0% work from home; Mean travel time to work: 30.0 minutes

Licking County

Located in central Ohio; drained by the Licking River and Raccoon Creek; includes part of Buckeye Lake. Covers a land area of 682.500 square miles, a water area of 4.991 square miles, and is located in the Eastern Time Zone at 40.09° N. Lat., 82.48° W. Long. The county was founded in 1808. County seat is Newark.

Licking County is part of the Columbus, OH Metropolitan Statistical Area. The entire metro area includes: Delaware County, OH; Fairfield County, OH; Franklin County, OH; Hocking County, OH; Licking County, OH; Madison County, OH; Morrow County, OH; Perry County, OH; Pickaway County, OH; Union County, OH

Weather Station: Newark Water Works — Elevation: 834 feet

	Jan	Feb	Mar	Apr	May	Jun	Jul	Aug	Sep	Oct	Nov	Dec
High	36	40	50	63	72	81	84	83	76	64	52	40
Low	20	22	29	39	48	58	62	60	53	41	33	24
Precip	3.0	2.5	3.2	3.7	4.4	4.5	4.4	3.7	2.9	3.0	3.2	3.2
Snow	6.8	4.7	2.2	0.7	tr	0.0	0.0	0.0	0.0	tr	0.4	2.6

High and Low temperatures in degrees Fahrenheit; Precipitation and Snow in inches

Population: 169,762; Growth (since 2000): 16.7%; Density: 248.7 persons per square mile; Race: 92.6% White, 3.4% Black/African American, 1.1% Asian, 0.1% American Indian/Alaska Native, 0.0% Native Hawaiian/Other Pacific Islander, 2.4% two or more races, 1.7% Hispanic of any race; Average household size: 2.59; Median age: 39.8; Age under 18: 23.8%; Age 65 and over: 15.1%; Males per 100 females: 95.9; Marriage status: 27.1% never married, 54.8% now married, 1.8% separated, 5.9% widowed, 12.2% divorced; Foreign born: 1.9%; Speak English only: 96.7%; With disability: 13.9%; Veterans: 10.4%; Ancestry: 27.7% German, 15.5% Irish, 10.0% English, 9.3% American, 5.7% Italian
Religion: Six largest groups: 9.6% Catholicism, 8.9% Baptist, 5.4% Methodist/Pietist, 2.3% Presbyterian-Reformed, 2.2% Non-denominational Protestant, 1.7% Pentecostal
Economy: Unemployment rate: 3.7%; Leading industries: 15.4 % retail trade; 11.0 % other services (except public administration); 10.8 % construction; Farms: 1,484 totaling 224,015 acres; Company size: 3 employ 1,000 or more persons, 5 employ 500 to 999 persons, 78 employ 100 to 499 persons, 2,856 employ less than 100 persons; Business ownership: 4,400 women-owned, 325 Black-owned, 149 Hispanic-owned, 130 Asian-owned, 89 American Indian/Alaska Native-owned
Employment: 14.7% management, business, and financial, 4.9% computer, engineering, and science, 9.4% education, legal, community service, arts, and media, 6.3% healthcare practitioners, 16.3% service, 25.4% sales and office, 9.0% natural resources, construction, and maintenance, 14.1% production, transportation, and material moving
Income: Per capita: $27,934; Median household: $57,571; Average household: $72,360; Households with income of $100,000 or more: 23.0%; Poverty rate: 12.6%
Educational Attainment: High school diploma or higher: 90.4%; Bachelor's degree or higher: 23.3%; Graduate/professional degree or higher: 8.2%
Housing: Homeownership rate: 71.6%; Median home value: $153,900; Median year structure built: 1976; Homeowner vacancy rate: 2.3%; Median selected monthly owner costs: $1,329 with a mortgage, $446 without a mortgage; Median gross rent: $784 per month; Rental vacancy rate: 5.0%
Vital Statistics: Birth rate: 121.5 per 10,000 population; Death rate: 92.6 per 10,000 population; Age-adjusted cancer mortality rate: 177.4 deaths per 100,000 population
Health Insurance: 91.8% have insurance; 71.4% have private insurance; 33.0% have public insurance; 8.2% do not have insurance; 4.6% of children under 18 do not have insurance
Health Care: Physicians: 10.3 per 10,000 population; Dentists: 3.5 per 10,000 population; Hospital beds: 11.7 per 10,000 population; Hospital admissions: 473.0 per 10,000 population
Air Quality Index (AQI): Percent of Days: 80.4% good, 18.2% moderate, 1.4% unhealthy for sensitive individuals, 0.0% unhealthy, 0.0% very unhealthy; Annual median: 43; Annual maximum: 108
Transportation: Commute: 91.6% car, 0.3% public transportation, 2.4% walk, 4.5% work from home; Mean travel time to work: 25.1 minutes
2016 Presidential Election: 61.3% Trump, 32.7% Clinton, 3.2% Johnson, 0.9% Stein
National and State Parks: Black Hand State Nature Preserve; Cranberry Bog State Nature Preserve; Morris Woods State Nature Preserve; Moundbuilders State Memorial; Octagon State Memorial
Additional Information Contacts
Licking Government . . . . (740) 349-6066
http://www.lcounty.com

Licking County Communities

ALEXANDRIA (village). Covers a land area of 0.245 square miles and a water area of <.001 square miles. Located at 40.09° N. Lat; 82.61° W. Long. Elevation is 974 feet.
Population: 612; Growth (since 2000): 620.0%; Density: 2,497.3 persons per square mile; Race: 99.0% White, 0.0% Black/African American, 0.0% Asian, 0.0% American Indian/Alaska Native, 0.0% Native Hawaiian/Other Pacific Islander, 1.0% Two or more races, 0.2% Hispanic of any race; Average household size: 2.99; Median age: 34.7; Age under 18: 24.7%; Age 65 and over: 10.5%; Males per 100 females: 98.1; Marriage status: 29.1% never married, 42.6% now married, 3.8% separated, 10.5% widowed, 17.8% divorced; Foreign born: 0.0%; Speak English only: 99.7%; With disability: 16.5%; Veterans: 7.6%; Ancestry: 42.3% German, 27.6% English, 21.4% Irish, 6.5% Italian, 5.2% Dutch
Employment: 10.1% management, business, and financial, 3.0% computer, engineering, and science, 18.9% education, legal, community service, arts, and media, 3.4% healthcare practitioners, 17.9% service, 18.2% sales and office, 17.2% natural resources, construction, and maintenance, 11.1% production, transportation, and material moving
Income: Per capita: $22,883; Median household: $61,442; Average household: $65,846; Households with income of $100,000 or more: 14.2%; Poverty rate: 8.0%
Educational Attainment: High school diploma or higher: 95.5%; Bachelor's degree or higher: 22.8%; Graduate/professional degree or higher: 10.8%

School District(s)

Northridge Local (KG-12)
2015-16 Enrollment: 1,186 . . . . (740) 967-6631
Housing: Homeownership rate: 65.9%; Median home value: $132,000; Median year structure built: Before 1940; Homeowner vacancy rate: 2.8%; Median selected monthly owner costs: $1,055 with a mortgage, $442 without a mortgage; Median gross rent: $1,063 per month; Rental vacancy rate: 0.0%
Health Insurance: 89.1% have insurance; 69.3% have private insurance; 28.6% have public insurance; 10.9% do not have insurance; 0.0% of children under 18 do not have insurance
Transportation: Commute: 88.6% car, 3.6% public transportation, 5.3% walk, 2.5% work from home; Mean travel time to work: 25.3 minutes

BEECHWOOD TRAILS (CDP). Covers a land area of 3.910 square miles and a water area of 0.013 square miles. Located at 40.03° N. Lat; 82.66° W. Long. Elevation is 1,207 feet.
Population: 2,994; Growth (since 2000): 32.6%; Density: 765.7 persons per square mile; Race: 98.3% White, 1.4% Black/African American, 0.3% Asian, 0.0% American Indian/Alaska Native, 0.0% Native Hawaiian/Other Pacific Islander, 0.0% Two or more races, 0.9% Hispanic of any race; Average household size: 2.44; Median age: 52.2; Age under 18: 15.2%; Age 65 and over: 16.3%; Males per 100 females: 95.1; Marriage status: 15.9% never married, 72.3% now married, 0.6% separated, 3.4% widowed, 8.4% divorced; Foreign born: 2.2%; Speak English only: 96.4%; With disability: 6.5%; Veterans: 9.3%; Ancestry: 29.1% German, 11.5% English, 11.4% Irish, 9.5% American, 4.6% Dutch
Employment: 16.2% management, business, and financial, 5.6% computer, engineering, and science, 15.3% education, legal, community service, arts, and media, 7.9% healthcare practitioners, 14.6% service, 16.9% sales and office, 12.8% natural resources, construction, and maintenance, 10.8% production, transportation, and material moving
Income: Per capita: $37,498; Median household: $88,478; Average household: $89,858; Households with income of $100,000 or more: 37.1%; Poverty rate: n/a

Educational Attainment: High school diploma or higher: 96.6%; Bachelor's degree or higher: 35.2%; Graduate/professional degree or higher: 12.6%
Housing: Homeownership rate: 100.0%; Median home value: $187,100; Median year structure built: 1988; Homeowner vacancy rate: 0.0%; Median selected monthly owner costs: $1,570 with a mortgage, $679 without a mortgage; Median gross rent: n/a per month; Rental vacancy rate: 0.0%
Health Insurance: 97.2% have insurance; 86.0% have private insurance; 22.2% have public insurance; 2.8% do not have insurance; 0.0% of children under 18 do not have insurance
Transportation: Commute: 91.3% car, 1.1% public transportation, 0.0% walk, 7.6% work from home; Mean travel time to work: 28.4 minutes

BROWNSVILLE (CDP). Covers a land area of 0.892 square miles and a water area of <.001 square miles. Located at 39.94° N. Lat; 82.25° W. Long. Elevation is 948 feet.
Population: 20; Growth (since 2000): n/a; Density: 22.4 persons per square mile; Race: 100.0% White, 0.0% Black/African American, 0.0% Asian, 0.0% American Indian/Alaska Native, 0.0% Native Hawaiian/Other Pacific Islander, 0.0% Two or more races, 0.0% Hispanic of any race; Average household size: 0.00; Median age: n/a; Age under 18: 0.0%; Age 65 and over: 100.0%; Males per 100 females: 105.6; Marriage status: 0.0% never married, 0.0% now married, 0.0% separated, 0.0% widowed, 100.0% divorced; Foreign born: 0.0%; Speak English only: 100.0%; With disability: 0.0%; Veterans: 100.0%; Ancestry: n/a.
Employment: n/a management, business, and financial, n/a computer, engineering, and science, n/a education, legal, community service, arts, and media, n/a healthcare practitioners, n/a service, n/a sales and office, n/a natural resources, construction, and maintenance, n/a production, transportation, and material moving
Income: Per capita: n/a; Median household: n/a; Average household: n/a; Households with income of $100,000 or more: n/a; Poverty rate: n/a
Educational Attainment: High school diploma or higher: n/a; Bachelor's degree or higher: n/a; Graduate/professional degree or higher: n/a
Housing: Homeownership rate: 100.0%; Median home value: n/a; Median year structure built: n/a; Homeowner vacancy rate: 0.0%; Median selected monthly owner costs: n/a with a mortgage, n/a without a mortgage; Median gross rent: n/a per month; Rental vacancy rate: 0.0%
Health Insurance: 100.0% have insurance; 0.0% have private insurance; 100.0% have public insurance; 0.0% do not have insurance; 0.0% of children under 18 do not have insurance
Transportation: Commute: n/a car, n/a public transportation, n/a walk, n/a work from home; Mean travel time to work: 0.0 minutes

BUCKEYE LAKE (village). Covers a land area of 2.000 square miles and a water area of 0.020 square miles. Located at 39.94° N. Lat; 82.49° W. Long. Elevation is 899 feet.
History: Beside lake created for Ohio Canal c.1827.
Population: 2,725; Growth (since 2000): -10.6%; Density: 1,362.6 persons per square mile; Race: 92.6% White, 0.0% Black/African American, 2.7% Asian, 1.6% American Indian/Alaska Native, 0.0% Native Hawaiian/Other Pacific Islander, 2.5% Two or more races, 7.6% Hispanic of any race; Average household size: 2.39; Median age: 38.4; Age under 18: 26.6%; Age 65 and over: 15.9%; Males per 100 females: 94.6; Marriage status: 29.7% never married, 48.0% now married, 0.9% separated, 5.7% widowed, 16.6% divorced; Foreign born: 0.8%; Speak English only: 98.4%; With disability: 18.0%; Veterans: 13.5%; Ancestry: 29.2% Irish, 23.7% German, 7.0% Dutch, 4.6% American, 4.5% English
Employment: 10.1% management, business, and financial, 1.4% computer, engineering, and science, 8.7% education, legal, community service, arts, and media, 5.6% healthcare practitioners, 14.7% service, 23.9% sales and office, 12.1% natural resources, construction, and maintenance, 23.4% production, transportation, and material moving
Income: Per capita: $24,780; Median household: $38,359; Average household: $57,365; Households with income of $100,000 or more: 12.3%; Poverty rate: 22.9%
Educational Attainment: High school diploma or higher: 80.2%; Bachelor's degree or higher: 15.6%; Graduate/professional degree or higher: 6.2%
Housing: Homeownership rate: 63.6%; Median home value: $85,800; Median year structure built: 1982; Homeowner vacancy rate: 0.0%; Median selected monthly owner costs: $786 with a mortgage, $444 without a mortgage; Median gross rent: $710 per month; Rental vacancy rate: 6.8%
Health Insurance: 87.4% have insurance; 45.5% have private insurance; 52.7% have public insurance; 12.6% do not have insurance; 5.8% of children under 18 do not have insurance
Newspapers: Buckeye Lake Beacon (weekly circulation 14,800)
Transportation: Commute: 91.2% car, 0.0% public transportation, 2.2% walk, 2.5% work from home; Mean travel time to work: 24.5 minutes

CROTON (unincorporated postal area)
ZCTA: 43013
Covers a land area of 19.222 square miles and a water area of 0.043 square miles. Located at 40.23° N. Lat; 82.69° W. Long. Elevation is 1,168 feet.
Population: 1,004; Growth (since 2000): 2.6%; Density: 52.2 persons per square mile; Race: 98.4% White, 0.0% Black/African American, 0.0% Asian, 0.0% American Indian/Alaska Native, 0.0% Native Hawaiian/Other Pacific Islander, 1.2% Two or more races, 0.0% Hispanic of any race; Average household size: 2.19; Median age: 48.3; Age under 18: 14.1%; Age 65 and over: 16.4%; Males per 100 females: 100.5; Marriage status: 18.7% never married, 67.4% now married, 0.7% separated, 6.8% widowed, 7.2% divorced; Foreign born: 0.0%; Speak English only: 98.6%; With disability: 8.6%; Veterans: 5.3%; Ancestry: 21.2% German, 20.2% Irish, 12.0% English, 9.1% American, 7.0% Italian
Employment: 12.0% management, business, and financial, 7.2% computer, engineering, and science, 6.1% education, legal, community service, arts, and media, 8.2% healthcare practitioners, 22.6% service, 20.5% sales and office, 13.5% natural resources, construction, and maintenance, 9.9% production, transportation, and material moving
Income: Per capita: $47,348; Median household: $63,333; Average household: $106,260; Households with income of $100,000 or more: 27.3%; Poverty rate: 6.2%
Educational Attainment: High school diploma or higher: 93.8%; Bachelor's degree or higher: 19.1%; Graduate/professional degree or higher: 5.9%
Housing: Homeownership rate: 90.8%; Median home value: $135,600; Median year structure built: 1968; Homeowner vacancy rate: 0.0%; Median selected monthly owner costs: $1,500 with a mortgage, $468 without a mortgage; Median gross rent: $548 per month; Rental vacancy rate: 8.7%
Health Insurance: 96.2% have insurance; 77.3% have private insurance; 29.1% have public insurance; 3.8% do not have insurance; 14.8% of children under 18 do not have insurance
Transportation: Commute: 97.5% car, 0.0% public transportation, 0.0% walk, 2.2% work from home; Mean travel time to work: 30.3 minutes

ETNA (CDP). Covers a land area of 0.630 square miles and a water area of 0.004 square miles. Located at 39.96° N. Lat; 82.69° W. Long. Elevation is 1,060 feet.
Population: 1,130; Growth (since 2000): n/a; Density: 1,793.3 persons per square mile; Race: 94.4% White, 0.0% Black/African American, 2.0% Asian, 0.0% American Indian/Alaska Native, 0.0% Native Hawaiian/Other Pacific Islander, 3.5% Two or more races, 0.0% Hispanic of any race; Average household size: 2.93; Median age: 32.6; Age under 18: 26.8%; Age 65 and over: 6.3%; Males per 100 females: 109.5; Marriage status: 36.3% never married, 51.1% now married, 0.0% separated, 0.0% widowed, 12.6% divorced; Foreign born: 0.9%; Speak English only: 98.1%; With disability: 9.8%; Veterans: 15.4%; Ancestry: 31.6% Irish, 25.7% German, 15.1% English, 6.3% Italian, 5.9% American
Employment: 22.6% management, business, and financial, 7.7% computer, engineering, and science, 3.9% education, legal, community service, arts, and media, 6.7% healthcare practitioners, 17.0% service, 24.9% sales and office, 3.4% natural resources, construction, and maintenance, 13.8% production, transportation, and material moving
Income: Per capita: $31,375; Median household: $68,500; Average household: $90,657; Households with income of $100,000 or more: 23.5%; Poverty rate: 11.7%
Educational Attainment: High school diploma or higher: 91.1%; Bachelor's degree or higher: 15.1%; Graduate/professional degree or higher: 4.1%
Housing: Homeownership rate: 71.0%; Median home value: $154,800; Median year structure built: 2002; Homeowner vacancy rate: 0.0%; Median selected monthly owner costs: $1,322 with a mortgage, $490 without a mortgage; Median gross rent: $1,067 per month; Rental vacancy rate: 0.0%
Health Insurance: 90.3% have insurance; 73.9% have private insurance; 25.2% have public insurance; 9.7% do not have insurance; 0.0% of children under 18 do not have insurance

Transportation: Commute: 92.2% car, 0.0% public transportation, 2.3% walk, 5.5% work from home; Mean travel time to work: 20.4 minutes

GRANVILLE (village). Covers a land area of 4.675 square miles and a water area of 0.029 square miles. Located at 40.06° N. Lat; 82.50° W. Long. Elevation is 958 feet.
History: Granville was laid out in 1806 and named for the Massachusetts home of its early settlers. In 1831 the Granville Literary and Theological Institute was established, becoming Denison University in 1856.
Population: 5,725; Growth (since 2000): 80.8%; Density: 1,224.6 persons per square mile; Race: 88.1% White, 5.7% Black/African American, 3.5% Asian, 0.0% American Indian/Alaska Native, 0.0% Native Hawaiian/Other Pacific Islander, 2.5% Two or more races, 3.9% Hispanic of any race; Average household size: 2.56; Median age: 21.6; Age under 18: 16.7%; Age 65 and over: 11.0%; Males per 100 females: 86.1; Marriage status: 55.0% never married, 39.5% now married, 0.2% separated, 1.2% widowed, 4.3% divorced; Foreign born: 4.7%; Speak English only: 88.7%; With disability: 4.7%; Veterans: 4.1%; Ancestry: 27.5% German, 12.7% Irish, 11.3% English, 7.1% Polish, 6.3% Swedish
Employment: 17.4% management, business, and financial, 4.5% computer, engineering, and science, 29.3% education, legal, community service, arts, and media, 5.1% healthcare practitioners, 16.1% service, 21.4% sales and office, 2.3% natural resources, construction, and maintenance, 3.8% production, transportation, and material moving
Income: Per capita: $32,832; Median household: $92,109; Average household: $128,428; Households with income of $100,000 or more: 46.8%; Poverty rate: 8.9%
Educational Attainment: High school diploma or higher: 98.8%; Bachelor's degree or higher: 66.0%; Graduate/professional degree or higher: 40.2%

School District(s)

Granville Exempted Village (PK-12)
2015-16 Enrollment: 2,450 . . . . (740) 587-8101

Four-year College(s)

Denison University (Private, Not-for-profit)
Fall 2016 Enrollment: 2,277 . . . . (740) 587-0810
2016-17 Tuition: In-state $48,960; Out-of-state $48,960

Housing: Homeownership rate: 73.5%; Median home value: $323,400; Median year structure built: 1965; Homeowner vacancy rate: 4.7%; Median selected monthly owner costs: $2,139 with a mortgage, $782 without a mortgage; Median gross rent: $900 per month; Rental vacancy rate: 0.0%
Health Insurance: 96.7% have insurance; 90.9% have private insurance; 12.9% have public insurance; 3.3% do not have insurance; 3.0% of children under 18 do not have insurance
Safety: Violent crime rate: 0.0 per 10,000 population; Property crime rate: 71.2 per 10,000 population
Newspapers: Granville Sentinel (weekly circulation 2,400)
Transportation: Commute: 50.9% car, 0.7% public transportation, 31.8% walk, 16.6% work from home; Mean travel time to work: 19.1 minutes
Additional Information Contacts
Village of Granville . . . . (740) 587-0707
http://www.granville.oh.us

GRANVILLE SOUTH (CDP). Covers a land area of 6.096 square miles and a water area of 0.055 square miles. Located at 40.05° N. Lat; 82.55° W. Long.
Population: 1,326; Growth (since 2000): 11.1%; Density: 217.5 persons per square mile; Race: 94.0% White, 0.0% Black/African American, 6.0% Asian, 0.0% American Indian/Alaska Native, 0.0% Native Hawaiian/Other Pacific Islander, 0.0% Two or more races, 0.0% Hispanic of any race; Average household size: 2.74; Median age: 44.1; Age under 18: 30.4%; Age 65 and over: 16.0%; Males per 100 females: 93.2; Marriage status: 14.0% never married, 74.1% now married, 1.3% separated, 4.4% widowed, 7.5% divorced; Foreign born: 6.0%; Speak English only: 87.7%; With disability: 4.4%; Veterans: 16.3%; Ancestry: 37.4% German, 16.1% American, 11.5% Irish, 9.4% English, 7.8% Italian
Employment: 16.4% management, business, and financial, 8.7% computer, engineering, and science, 16.0% education, legal, community service, arts, and media, 10.6% healthcare practitioners, 19.3% service, 16.0% sales and office, 6.4% natural resources, construction, and maintenance, 6.6% production, transportation, and material moving
Income: Per capita: $45,932; Median household: $110,833; Average household: $126,833; Households with income of $100,000 or more: 61.1%; Poverty rate: 2.1%
Educational Attainment: High school diploma or higher: 96.4%; Bachelor's degree or higher: 60.5%; Graduate/professional degree or higher: 26.9%
Housing: Homeownership rate: 88.7%; Median home value: $236,100; Median year structure built: 1974; Homeowner vacancy rate: 0.0%; Median selected monthly owner costs: $1,873 with a mortgage, $651 without a mortgage; Median gross rent: n/a per month; Rental vacancy rate: 0.0%
Health Insurance: 99.1% have insurance; 94.4% have private insurance; 21.3% have public insurance; 0.9% do not have insurance; 0.0% of children under 18 do not have insurance
Transportation: Commute: 84.2% car, 0.0% public transportation, 0.0% walk, 15.8% work from home; Mean travel time to work: 27.7 minutes

GRATIOT (village). Covers a land area of 0.131 square miles and a water area of 0 square miles. Located at 39.95° N. Lat; 82.22° W. Long. Elevation is 984 feet.
Population: 348; Growth (since 2000): 86.1%; Density: 2,658.7 persons per square mile; Race: 86.8% White, 0.0% Black/African American, 0.0% Asian, 0.0% American Indian/Alaska Native, 0.0% Native Hawaiian/Other Pacific Islander, 13.2% Two or more races, 0.0% Hispanic of any race; Average household size: 3.08; Median age: 27.5; Age under 18: 35.6%; Age 65 and over: 12.9%; Males per 100 females: 90.5; Marriage status: 29.5% never married, 44.4% now married, 1.2% separated, 7.9% widowed, 18.3% divorced; Foreign born: 0.6%; Speak English only: 98.4%; With disability: 12.9%; Veterans: 11.2%; Ancestry: 37.4% German, 28.4% Irish, 9.8% Scotch-Irish, 2.9% French, 2.6% American
Employment: 7.6% management, business, and financial, 0.0% computer, engineering, and science, 3.8% education, legal, community service, arts, and media, 13.7% healthcare practitioners, 9.2% service, 10.7% sales and office, 16.8% natural resources, construction, and maintenance, 38.2% production, transportation, and material moving
Income: Per capita: $17,719; Median household: $45,625; Average household: $50,169; Households with income of $100,000 or more: 7.1%; Poverty rate: 33.6%
Educational Attainment: High school diploma or higher: 83.4%; Bachelor's degree or higher: 3.7%; Graduate/professional degree or higher: 0.5%
Housing: Homeownership rate: 76.1%; Median home value: $108,800; Median year structure built: 1949; Homeowner vacancy rate: 10.4%; Median selected monthly owner costs: $1,071 with a mortgage, $379 without a mortgage; Median gross rent: $805 per month; Rental vacancy rate: 0.0%
Health Insurance: 89.7% have insurance; 58.9% have private insurance; 41.7% have public insurance; 10.3% do not have insurance; 4.0% of children under 18 do not have insurance
Transportation: Commute: 93.9% car, 0.0% public transportation, 0.0% walk, 2.3% work from home; Mean travel time to work: 29.5 minutes

HANOVER (village). Covers a land area of 1.663 square miles and a water area of 0.018 square miles. Located at 40.08° N. Lat; 82.27° W. Long. Elevation is 823 feet.
Population: 1,262; Growth (since 2000): 42.6%; Density: 759.0 persons per square mile; Race: 97.1% White, 0.4% Black/African American, 0.2% Asian, 0.2% American Indian/Alaska Native, 0.0% Native Hawaiian/Other Pacific Islander, 2.1% Two or more races, 0.0% Hispanic of any race; Average household size: 3.01; Median age: 31.1; Age under 18: 30.1%; Age 65 and over: 12.0%; Males per 100 females: 107.4; Marriage status: 29.1% never married, 55.6% now married, 1.3% separated, 4.7% widowed, 10.7% divorced; Foreign born: 0.2%; Speak English only: 99.4%; With disability: 14.1%; Veterans: 10.0%; Ancestry: 38.2% German, 12.8% Irish, 12.7% English, 8.2% American, 4.9% Italian
Employment: 11.7% management, business, and financial, 4.1% computer, engineering, and science, 11.5% education, legal, community service, arts, and media, 7.0% healthcare practitioners, 23.2% service, 17.7% sales and office, 8.2% natural resources, construction, and maintenance, 16.7% production, transportation, and material moving
Income: Per capita: $22,004; Median household: $62,159; Average household: $65,602; Households with income of $100,000 or more: 20.7%; Poverty rate: 10.2%
Educational Attainment: High school diploma or higher: 92.7%; Bachelor's degree or higher: 21.1%; Graduate/professional degree or higher: 4.2%
Housing: Homeownership rate: 75.2%; Median home value: $147,800; Median year structure built: 1976; Homeowner vacancy rate: 0.0%; Median

selected monthly owner costs: $1,436 with a mortgage, $405 without a mortgage; Median gross rent: $719 per month; Rental vacancy rate: 16.0%
Health Insurance: 94.0% have insurance; 78.2% have private insurance; 28.2% have public insurance; 6.0% do not have insurance; 0.8% of children under 18 do not have insurance
Transportation: Commute: 90.7% car, 0.0% public transportation, 0.6% walk, 6.7% work from home; Mean travel time to work: 24.8 minutes

HARBOR HILLS (CDP). Covers a land area of 2.764 square miles and a water area of 0.729 square miles. Located at 39.94° N. Lat; 82.43° W. Long. Elevation is 928 feet.
Population: 1,593; Growth (since 2000): 22.3%; Density: 576.3 persons per square mile; Race: 100.0% White, 0.0% Black/African American, 0.0% Asian, 0.0% American Indian/Alaska Native, 0.0% Native Hawaiian/Other Pacific Islander, 0.0% Two or more races, 0.0% Hispanic of any race; Average household size: 2.35; Median age: 55.5; Age under 18: 20.8%; Age 65 and over: 25.9%; Males per 100 females: 101.7; Marriage status: 18.5% never married, 57.5% now married, 0.9% separated, 8.9% widowed, 15.1% divorced; Foreign born: 0.8%; Speak English only: 98.2%; With disability: 15.0%; Veterans: 12.2%; Ancestry: 19.5% English, 16.8% Irish, 16.0% American, 15.4% German, 3.2% French
Employment: 23.7% management, business, and financial, 0.0% computer, engineering, and science, 6.5% education, legal, community service, arts, and media, 15.7% healthcare practitioners, 10.4% service, 25.0% sales and office, 9.1% natural resources, construction, and maintenance, 9.7% production, transportation, and material moving
Income: Per capita: $33,254; Median household: $68,967; Average household: $77,539; Households with income of $100,000 or more: 26.6%; Poverty rate: 18.9%
Educational Attainment: High school diploma or higher: 93.1%; Bachelor's degree or higher: 25.6%; Graduate/professional degree or higher: 11.7%
Housing: Homeownership rate: 74.8%; Median home value: $170,900; Median year structure built: 1977; Homeowner vacancy rate: 0.0%; Median selected monthly owner costs: $1,490 with a mortgage, $365 without a mortgage; Median gross rent: $1,281 per month; Rental vacancy rate: 0.0%
Health Insurance: 86.8% have insurance; 58.3% have private insurance; 49.1% have public insurance; 13.2% do not have insurance; 0.0% of children under 18 do not have insurance
Transportation: Commute: 94.3% car, 0.0% public transportation, 0.0% walk, 5.7% work from home; Mean travel time to work: 28.7 minutes

HARTFORD (village). Covers a land area of 0.549 square miles and a water area of 0.004 square miles. Located at 40.24° N. Lat; 82.69° W. Long. Elevation is 1,168 feet.
Population: 355; Growth (since 2000): -13.8%; Density: 646.5 persons per square mile; Race: 92.1% White, 3.4% Black/African American, 0.0% Asian, 0.0% American Indian/Alaska Native, 0.0% Native Hawaiian/Other Pacific Islander, 3.4% Two or more races, 0.0% Hispanic of any race; Average household size: 3.01; Median age: 35.2; Age under 18: 30.4%; Age 65 and over: 15.8%; Males per 100 females: 91.8; Marriage status: 29.6% never married, 46.4% now married, 2.2% separated, 7.1% widowed, 16.9% divorced; Foreign born: 0.0%; Speak English only: 99.4%; With disability: 16.9%; Veterans: 8.5%; Ancestry: 30.7% German, 18.3% Irish, 10.1% American, 9.9% English, 6.8% Italian
Employment: 5.0% management, business, and financial, 2.5% computer, engineering, and science, 6.9% education, legal, community service, arts, and media, 5.0% healthcare practitioners, 20.6% service, 16.9% sales and office, 25.6% natural resources, construction, and maintenance, 17.5% production, transportation, and material moving
Income: Per capita: $19,846; Median household: $46,667; Average household: $56,075; Households with income of $100,000 or more: 10.9%; Poverty rate: 15.7%
Educational Attainment: High school diploma or higher: 90.1%; Bachelor's degree or higher: 9.5%; Graduate/professional degree or higher: 1.4%
Housing: Homeownership rate: 75.4%; Median home value: $102,500; Median year structure built: Before 1940; Homeowner vacancy rate: 0.0%; Median selected monthly owner costs: $1,033 with a mortgage, $421 without a mortgage; Median gross rent: $706 per month; Rental vacancy rate: 12.1%
Health Insurance: 94.4% have insurance; 64.2% have private insurance; 44.2% have public insurance; 5.6% do not have insurance; 2.8% of children under 18 do not have insurance
Transportation: Commute: 92.0% car, 0.0% public transportation, 0.0% walk, 6.7% work from home; Mean travel time to work: 31.3 minutes

HEATH (city). Covers a land area of 10.922 square miles and a water area of 0.078 square miles. Located at 40.02° N. Lat; 82.44° W. Long. Elevation is 860 feet.
History: Former Newark Air Force Base nearby that specialized in guidance of navigation systems; closed base scheduled for privatization.
Population: 10,471; Growth (since 2000): 22.8%; Density: 958.7 persons per square mile; Race: 90.7% White, 1.8% Black/African American, 2.9% Asian, 0.2% American Indian/Alaska Native, 0.0% Native Hawaiian/Other Pacific Islander, 4.3% Two or more races, 0.9% Hispanic of any race; Average household size: 2.45; Median age: 39.2; Age under 18: 22.0%; Age 65 and over: 20.2%; Males per 100 females: 91.9; Marriage status: 25.8% never married, 51.3% now married, 2.5% separated, 7.0% widowed, 15.9% divorced; Foreign born: 1.9%; Speak English only: 97.3%; With disability: 18.8%; Veterans: 10.6%; Ancestry: 26.3% German, 15.8% Irish, 12.1% American, 9.6% English, 4.4% Italian
Employment: 11.5% management, business, and financial, 4.4% computer, engineering, and science, 9.0% education, legal, community service, arts, and media, 3.8% healthcare practitioners, 21.5% service, 24.2% sales and office, 6.3% natural resources, construction, and maintenance, 19.3% production, transportation, and material moving
Income: Per capita: $23,700; Median household: $44,656; Average household: $57,500; Households with income of $100,000 or more: 11.2%; Poverty rate: 13.4%
Educational Attainment: High school diploma or higher: 89.3%; Bachelor's degree or higher: 17.4%; Graduate/professional degree or higher: 5.1%

School District(s)

Heath City (KG-12)
2015-16 Enrollment: 1,666 . . . . (740) 522-2816

Two-year College(s)

Ohio State School of Cosmetology-Heath (Private, For-profit)
Fall 2016 Enrollment: 83 . . . . (614) 252-5252
Housing: Homeownership rate: 63.2%; Median home value: $128,700; Median year structure built: 1979; Homeowner vacancy rate: 2.5%; Median selected monthly owner costs: $1,154 with a mortgage, $449 without a mortgage; Median gross rent: $836 per month; Rental vacancy rate: 4.9%
Health Insurance: 91.2% have insurance; 69.6% have private insurance; 38.2% have public insurance; 8.8% do not have insurance; 8.2% of children under 18 do not have insurance
Safety: Violent crime rate: 21.8 per 10,000 population; Property crime rate: 630.7 per 10,000 population
Newspapers: Heath News (weekly circulation 4,500)
Transportation: Commute: 88.3% car, 0.8% public transportation, 1.8% walk, 4.0% work from home; Mean travel time to work: 18.2 minutes

HEBRON (village). Covers a land area of 3.065 square miles and a water area of 0.004 square miles. Located at 39.97° N. Lat; 82.49° W. Long. Elevation is 889 feet.
History: Hebron developed as a commercial center on the Ohio & Erie Canal and the old National Road.
Population: 2,254; Growth (since 2000): 10.8%; Density: 735.5 persons per square mile; Race: 98.3% White, 0.0% Black/African American, 1.3% Asian, 0.0% American Indian/Alaska Native, 0.0% Native Hawaiian/Other Pacific Islander, 0.0% Two or more races, 2.1% Hispanic of any race; Average household size: 2.43; Median age: 42.3; Age under 18: 25.6%; Age 65 and over: 16.5%; Males per 100 females: 88.1; Marriage status: 26.3% never married, 44.1% now married, 2.6% separated, 8.2% widowed, 21.4% divorced; Foreign born: 0.9%; Speak English only: 98.7%; With disability: 22.4%; Veterans: 13.3%; Ancestry: 29.9% German, 20.3% Irish, 12.5% English, 5.6% American, 3.5% Italian
Employment: 8.1% management, business, and financial, 1.9% computer, engineering, and science, 4.4% education, legal, community service, arts, and media, 3.3% healthcare practitioners, 16.0% service, 32.5% sales and office, 6.5% natural resources, construction, and maintenance, 27.3% production, transportation, and material moving
Income: Per capita: $22,053; Median household: $40,068; Average household: $50,125; Households with income of $100,000 or more: 5.5%; Poverty rate: 16.0%
Educational Attainment: High school diploma or higher: 81.7%; Bachelor's degree or higher: 9.8%; Graduate/professional degree or higher: 2.7%

School District(s)

Lakewood Digital Academy (01-12)
2015-16 Enrollment: 30 . . . . (740) 928-1915
Lakewood Local (PK-12)
2015-16 Enrollment: 1,851 . . . . (740) 928-5878

Housing: Homeownership rate: 54.7%; Median home value: $101,600; Median year structure built: 1970; Homeowner vacancy rate: 0.6%; Median selected monthly owner costs: $1,094 with a mortgage, $411 without a mortgage; Median gross rent: $610 per month; Rental vacancy rate: 0.0%
Health Insurance: 93.5% have insurance; 62.6% have private insurance; 45.1% have public insurance; 6.5% do not have insurance; 0.7% of children under 18 do not have insurance
Transportation: Commute: 96.0% car, 1.8% public transportation, 0.6% walk, 0.0% work from home; Mean travel time to work: 21.6 minutes
Additional Information Contacts
Village of Hebron. . . . . (740) 928-2261
http://www.hebronvillage.com

JACKSONTOWN (unincorporated postal area)

ZCTA: 43030

Covers a land area of 0.092 square miles and a water area of 0 square miles. Located at 39.96° N. Lat; 82.42° W. Long. Elevation is 991 feet.
Population: n/a; Growth (since 2000): n/a; Density: <0.1 persons per square mile; Race: 0.0% White, 0.0% Black/African American, 0.0% Asian, 0.0% American Indian/Alaska Native, 0.0% Native Hawaiian/Other Pacific Islander, 0.0% Two or more races, 0.0% Hispanic of any race; Average household size: 0.00; Median age: n/a; Age under 18: 100.0%; Age 65 and over: 0.0%; Males per 100 females: 93.2
Housing: Homeownership rate: n/a; Homeowner vacancy rate: 100.0%; Rental vacancy rate: 0.0%

JOHNSTOWN (village). Covers a land area of 2.904 square miles and a water area of 0.009 square miles. Located at 40.15° N. Lat; 82.69° W. Long. Elevation is 1,158 feet.
History: Johnstown was the site of the discovery in 1926 of the skeleton of a mastodon. A farmer digging in his garden uncovered the bones of an animal that had been 8 feet tall and 15 feet long. The skeleton was purchased by the Cleveland Museum of Natural History.
Population: 4,999; Growth (since 2000): 45.3%; Density: 1,721.3 persons per square mile; Race: 98.6% White, 0.0% Black/African American, 0.0% Asian, 0.0% American Indian/Alaska Native, 0.0% Native Hawaiian/Other Pacific Islander, 1.4% Two or more races, 6.6% Hispanic of any race; Average household size: 2.69; Median age: 32.7; Age under 18: 26.0%; Age 65 and over: 15.1%; Males per 100 females: 90.3; Marriage status: 31.8% never married, 51.1% now married, 0.5% separated, 6.0% widowed, 11.0% divorced; Foreign born: 1.5%; Speak English only: 97.2%; With disability: 14.4%; Veterans: 10.5%; Ancestry: 23.3% German, 17.6% Irish, 9.9% American, 9.9% Italian, 8.6% English
Employment: 10.7% management, business, and financial, 4.2% computer, engineering, and science, 5.6% education, legal, community service, arts, and media, 5.5% healthcare practitioners, 21.3% service, 21.8% sales and office, 14.8% natural resources, construction, and maintenance, 16.2% production, transportation, and material moving
Income: Per capita: $23,756; Median household: $47,978; Average household: $62,626; Households with income of $100,000 or more: 21.7%; Poverty rate: 9.0%
Educational Attainment: High school diploma or higher: 90.4%; Bachelor's degree or higher: 21.5%; Graduate/professional degree or higher: 7.7%

School District(s)

Johnstown-Monroe Local (KG-12)
2015-16 Enrollment: 1,569 . . . . (740) 967-6846
Northridge Local (KG-12)
2015-16 Enrollment: 1,186 . . . . (740) 967-6631

Housing: Homeownership rate: 61.1%; Median home value: $150,600; Median year structure built: 1974; Homeowner vacancy rate: 7.2%; Median selected monthly owner costs: $1,276 with a mortgage, $431 without a mortgage; Median gross rent: $717 per month; Rental vacancy rate: 11.8%
Health Insurance: 91.7% have insurance; 72.2% have private insurance; 30.1% have public insurance; 8.3% do not have insurance; 2.0% of children under 18 do not have insurance
Safety: Violent crime rate: 12.1 per 10,000 population; Property crime rate: 158.9 per 10,000 population
Newspapers: Johnstown Independent (weekly circulation 2,400)
Transportation: Commute: 93.3% car, 0.0% public transportation, 5.0% walk, 1.7% work from home; Mean travel time to work: 28.9 minutes
Additional Information Contacts
Village of Johnstown . . . . (740) 967-3177
http://www.villageofjohnstown.org

KIRKERSVILLE (village). Covers a land area of 2.237 square miles and a water area of <.001 square miles. Located at 39.95° N. Lat; 82.60° W. Long. Elevation is 935 feet.
Population: 507; Growth (since 2000): -2.5%; Density: 226.6 persons per square mile; Race: 98.8% White, 0.0% Black/African American, 0.8% Asian, 0.0% American Indian/Alaska Native, 0.0% Native Hawaiian/Other Pacific Islander, 0.4% Two or more races, 0.0% Hispanic of any race; Average household size: 2.25; Median age: 48.4; Age under 18: 17.0%; Age 65 and over: 16.6%; Males per 100 females: 106.7; Marriage status: 17.8% never married, 48.0% now married, 0.5% separated, 10.9% widowed, 23.3% divorced; Foreign born: 0.8%; Speak English only: 98.5%; With disability: 17.5%; Veterans: 15.4%; Ancestry: 35.5% German, 22.3% Irish, 8.9% English, 7.9% Italian, 5.3% American
Employment: 18.8% management, business, and financial, 1.2% computer, engineering, and science, 8.6% education, legal, community service, arts, and media, 3.7% healthcare practitioners, 9.0% service, 25.7% sales and office, 17.1% natural resources, construction, and maintenance, 15.9% production, transportation, and material moving
Income: Per capita: $28,205; Median household: $52,308; Average household: $65,239; Households with income of $100,000 or more: 10.8%; Poverty rate: 13.4%
Educational Attainment: High school diploma or higher: 94.3%; Bachelor's degree or higher: 13.0%; Graduate/professional degree or higher: 4.8%

School District(s)

Southwest Licking Local (KG-12)
2015-16 Enrollment: 3,884 . . . . (740) 927-3941

Housing: Homeownership rate: 72.0%; Median home value: $111,700; Median year structure built: 1947; Homeowner vacancy rate: 0.0%; Median selected monthly owner costs: $1,076 with a mortgage, $315 without a mortgage; Median gross rent: $648 per month; Rental vacancy rate: 0.0%
Health Insurance: 86.7% have insurance; 64.4% have private insurance; 34.5% have public insurance; 13.3% do not have insurance; 9.3% of children under 18 do not have insurance
Transportation: Commute: 98.3% car, 0.0% public transportation, 1.7% walk, 0.0% work from home; Mean travel time to work: 29.8 minutes

MARNE (CDP). Covers a land area of 0.884 square miles and a water area of 0.001 square miles. Located at 40.07° N. Lat; 82.30° W. Long. Elevation is 801 feet.
Population: 641; Growth (since 2000): n/a; Density: 725.0 persons per square mile; Race: 92.8% White, 2.3% Black/African American, 0.0% Asian, 0.0% American Indian/Alaska Native, 0.0% Native Hawaiian/Other Pacific Islander, 4.8% Two or more races, 0.0% Hispanic of any race; Average household size: 2.93; Median age: 35.3; Age under 18: 32.8%; Age 65 and over: 7.3%; Males per 100 females: 99.2; Marriage status: 29.3% never married, 60.3% now married, 0.0% separated, 5.0% widowed, 5.4% divorced; Foreign born: 0.0%; Speak English only: 100.0%; With disability: 4.8%; Veterans: 6.5%; Ancestry: 25.0% German, 18.9% English, 8.7% American, 8.7% Greek, 8.7% Irish
Employment: 29.7% management, business, and financial, 0.0% computer, engineering, and science, 10.7% education, legal, community service, arts, and media, 10.7% healthcare practitioners, 9.3% service, 27.7% sales and office, 0.0% natural resources, construction, and maintenance, 12.0% production, transportation, and material moving
Income: Per capita: $27,617; Median household: $62,396; Average household: $77,487; Households with income of $100,000 or more: 15.0%; Poverty rate: 11.1%
Educational Attainment: High school diploma or higher: 93.3%; Bachelor's degree or higher: 37.1%; Graduate/professional degree or higher: 11.3%
Housing: Homeownership rate: 87.2%; Median home value: $137,500; Median year structure built: 1962; Homeowner vacancy rate: 0.0%; Median selected monthly owner costs: $1,192 with a mortgage, $531 without a mortgage; Median gross rent: n/a per month; Rental vacancy rate: 0.0%
Health Insurance: 100.0% have insurance; 87.8% have private insurance; 21.7% have public insurance; 0.0% do not have insurance; 0.0% of children under 18 do not have insurance

Transportation: Commute: 95.3% car, 0.0% public transportation, 0.0% walk, 4.7% work from home; Mean travel time to work: 29.4 minutes

NEWARK (city). County seat. Covers a land area of 20.884 square miles and a water area of 0.486 square miles. Located at 40.07° N. Lat; 82.42° W. Long. Elevation is 833 feet.
History: In 1802, near the ancient mounds of a vanished people, General William Schenck platted a settlement and named it for his hometown in New Jersey. When Newark became the seat of Licking County in 1808, its citizens hammered together a one-room log cabin, with slab benches on a sawdust floor, as the courthouse. The canal came to Newark in 1832, and the population tripled, only to be cut again by a cholera epidemic in 1849. Natural gas discovered here in 1887 attracted iron and glass industries with its cheap fuel, and Newark again grew.
Population: 48,477; Growth (since 2000): 4.7%; Density: 2,321.3 persons per square mile; Race: 92.8% White, 2.9% Black/African American, 0.6% Asian, 0.1% American Indian/Alaska Native, 0.0% Native Hawaiian/Other Pacific Islander, 3.2% Two or more races, 1.0% Hispanic of any race; Average household size: 2.40; Median age: 37.0; Age under 18: 24.6%; Age 65 and over: 15.5%; Males per 100 females: 91.5; Marriage status: 32.1% never married, 44.5% now married, 2.4% separated, 7.8% widowed, 15.7% divorced; Foreign born: 1.5%; Speak English only: 97.7%; With disability: 18.2%; Veterans: 9.7%; Ancestry: 25.5% German, 14.8% Irish, 10.0% American, 9.1% English, 6.2% Italian
Employment: 12.3% management, business, and financial, 3.8% computer, engineering, and science, 8.5% education, legal, community service, arts, and media, 5.2% healthcare practitioners, 21.9% service, 24.7% sales and office, 7.1% natural resources, construction, and maintenance, 16.7% production, transportation, and material moving
Income: Per capita: $22,226; Median household: $38,913; Average household: $53,000; Households with income of $100,000 or more: 12.6%; Poverty rate: 21.8%
Educational Attainment: High school diploma or higher: 87.1%; Bachelor's degree or higher: 18.1%; Graduate/professional degree or higher: 6.0%

School District(s)

Career and Technology Educational Centers (07-12)
2015-16 Enrollment: n/a . . . . (740) 366-3351
Licking Valley Local (KG-12)
2015-16 Enrollment: 1,954 . . . . (740) 763-3525
Newark City (PK-12)
2015-16 Enrollment: 6,250 . . . . (740) 670-7000
Newark Digital Academy (02-12)
2015-16 Enrollment: 368. . . . . (740) 328-2022
North Fork Local (KG-12)
2015-16 Enrollment: 1,573 . . . . (740) 892-3666
Par Excellence Academy (KG-05)
2015-16 Enrollment: 150. . . . . (740) 344-7279

Four-year College(s)

Ohio State University-Newark Campus (Public)
Fall 2016 Enrollment: 2,536 . . . . (740) 366-9333
2016-17 Tuition: In-state $7,140; Out-of-state $25,332

Two-year College(s)

Career and Technology Education Centers of Licking County (Public)
Fall 2016 Enrollment: 286 . . . . (740) 364-2333
Central Ohio Technical College (Public)
Fall 2016 Enrollment: 3,337 . . . . (740) 366-1351
2016-17 Tuition: In-state $4,296; Out-of-state $7,056

Housing: Homeownership rate: 54.0%; Median home value: $114,500; Median year structure built: 1964; Homeowner vacancy rate: 3.0%; Median selected monthly owner costs: $1,051 with a mortgage, $373 without a mortgage; Median gross rent: $702 per month; Rental vacancy rate: 5.4%
Health Insurance: 89.8% have insurance; 58.8% have private insurance; 44.3% have public insurance; 10.2% do not have insurance; 2.0% of children under 18 do not have insurance
Hospitals: Licking Memorial Hospital (195 beds)
Newspapers: The Advocate (daily circulation 19,400)
Transportation: Commute: 92.8% car, 0.5% public transportation, 2.4% walk, 2.7% work from home; Mean travel time to work: 21.1 minutes
Airports: Newark-Heath (general aviation)
Additional Information Contacts
City of Newark. . . . . (740) 670-7500
http://www.ci.newark.oh.us

PATASKALA (city). Covers a land area of 28.617 square miles and a water area of 0.096 square miles. Located at 40.01° N. Lat; 82.71° W. Long. Elevation is 1,001 feet.
Population: 15,225; Growth (since 2000): 48.6%; Density: 532.0 persons per square mile; Race: 89.3% White, 7.4% Black/African American, 0.7% Asian, 0.3% American Indian/Alaska Native, 0.0% Native Hawaiian/Other Pacific Islander, 2.2% Two or more races, 1.2% Hispanic of any race; Average household size: 2.71; Median age: 37.5; Age under 18: 25.6%; Age 65 and over: 12.6%; Males per 100 females: 96.5; Marriage status: 27.8% never married, 53.5% now married, 2.2% separated, 5.4% widowed, 13.3% divorced; Foreign born: 2.9%; Speak English only: 96.2%; With disability: 11.3%; Veterans: 11.2%; Ancestry: 28.0% German, 13.8% Irish, 9.5% American, 8.8% English, 8.0% Italian
Employment: 18.0% management, business, and financial, 4.4% computer, engineering, and science, 7.7% education, legal, community service, arts, and media, 7.3% healthcare practitioners, 16.0% service, 27.8% sales and office, 8.7% natural resources, construction, and maintenance, 10.1% production, transportation, and material moving
Income: Per capita: $30,488; Median household: $69,574; Average household: $81,925; Households with income of $100,000 or more: 27.9%; Poverty rate: 8.9%
Educational Attainment: High school diploma or higher: 92.5%; Bachelor's degree or higher: 27.0%; Graduate/professional degree or higher: 8.4%

School District(s)

Licking Heights Local (PK-12)
2015-16 Enrollment: 4,024 . . . . (740) 927-6926
Southwest Licking Digital Acad (KG-12)
2015-16 Enrollment: 25. . . . . (740) 927-3941
Southwest Licking Local (KG-12)
2015-16 Enrollment: 3,884 . . . . (740) 927-3941

Housing: Homeownership rate: 71.6%; Median home value: $162,900; Median year structure built: 1993; Homeowner vacancy rate: 2.4%; Median selected monthly owner costs: $1,462 with a mortgage, $543 without a mortgage; Median gross rent: $1,009 per month; Rental vacancy rate: 3.4%
Health Insurance: 91.0% have insurance; 74.3% have private insurance; 27.1% have public insurance; 9.0% do not have insurance; 6.0% of children under 18 do not have insurance
Newspapers: Pataskala Post (weekly circulation 11,100); Pataskala Standard (weekly circulation 5,200)
Transportation: Commute: 94.7% car, 0.2% public transportation, 1.1% walk, 3.4% work from home; Mean travel time to work: 26.0 minutes
Additional Information Contacts
City of Pataskala . . . . (740) 927-2021
http://www.ci.pataskala.oh.us

SAINT LOUISVILLE (village). Covers a land area of 0.249 square miles and a water area of 0 square miles. Located at 40.17° N. Lat; 82.42° W. Long. Elevation is 902 feet.
Population: 429; Growth (since 2000): 24.0%; Density: 1,723.3 persons per square mile; Race: 97.2% White, 0.0% Black/African American, 0.0% Asian, 0.0% American Indian/Alaska Native, 0.0% Native Hawaiian/Other Pacific Islander, 2.8% Two or more races, 0.2% Hispanic of any race; Average household size: 2.92; Median age: 37.0; Age under 18: 31.5%; Age 65 and over: 13.5%; Males per 100 females: 91.3; Marriage status: 29.7% never married, 49.5% now married, 1.2% separated, 10.1% widowed, 10.7% divorced; Foreign born: 0.0%; Speak English only: 99.0%; With disability: 21.7%; Veterans: 10.5%; Ancestry: 28.0% German, 18.2% Irish, 15.2% American, 5.1% English, 4.9% French Canadian
Employment: 14.0% management, business, and financial, 3.0% computer, engineering, and science, 5.0% education, legal, community service, arts, and media, 2.5% healthcare practitioners, 25.0% service, 19.0% sales and office, 10.5% natural resources, construction, and maintenance, 21.0% production, transportation, and material moving
Income: Per capita: $19,839; Median household: $50,938; Average household: $57,685; Households with income of $100,000 or more: 21.7%; Poverty rate: 20.7%
Educational Attainment: High school diploma or higher: 91.3%; Bachelor's degree or higher: 8.3%; Graduate/professional degree or higher: 2.0%
Housing: Homeownership rate: 78.2%; Median home value: $94,500; Median year structure built: Before 1940; Homeowner vacancy rate: 8.7%; Median selected monthly owner costs: $1,083 with a mortgage, $331

without a mortgage; Median gross rent: $875 per month; Rental vacancy rate: 0.0%
Health Insurance: 93.0% have insurance; 66.4% have private insurance; 39.2% have public insurance; 7.0% do not have insurance; 5.9% of children under 18 do not have insurance
Transportation: Commute: 96.6% car, 0.0% public transportation, 1.1% walk, 2.3% work from home; Mean travel time to work: 30.7 minutes

UTICA (village). Covers a land area of 1.691 square miles and a water area of 0.016 square miles. Located at 40.24° N. Lat; 82.44° W. Long. Elevation is 958 feet.
Population: 1,982; Growth (since 2000): -6.9%; Density: 1,172.3 persons per square mile; Race: 97.2% White, 0.4% Black/African American, 0.5% Asian, 0.8% American Indian/Alaska Native, 0.0% Native Hawaiian/Other Pacific Islander, 1.2% Two or more races, 1.8% Hispanic of any race; Average household size: 2.39; Median age: 39.8; Age under 18: 21.0%; Age 65 and over: 18.2%; Males per 100 females: 87.3; Marriage status: 29.9% never married, 46.5% now married, 1.8% separated, 7.3% widowed, 16.4% divorced; Foreign born: 1.9%; Speak English only: 98.3%; With disability: 19.3%; Veterans: 13.4%; Ancestry: 29.7% German, 13.2% Irish, 9.0% American, 6.2% English, 5.2% Italian
Employment: 9.7% management, business, and financial, 3.0% computer, engineering, and science, 3.1% education, legal, community service, arts, and media, 2.4% healthcare practitioners, 19.1% service, 23.9% sales and office, 10.5% natural resources, construction, and maintenance, 28.2% production, transportation, and material moving
Income: Per capita: $20,398; Median household: $42,500; Average household: $48,081; Households with income of $100,000 or more: 6.7%; Poverty rate: 15.0%
Educational Attainment: High school diploma or higher: 84.6%; Bachelor's degree or higher: 9.3%; Graduate/professional degree or higher: 1.8%

School District(s)

North Fork Local (KG-12)
2015-16 Enrollment: 1,573 . . . . (740) 892-3666
Housing: Homeownership rate: 65.2%; Median home value: $87,700; Median year structure built: 1956; Homeowner vacancy rate: 9.2%; Median selected monthly owner costs: $882 with a mortgage, $338 without a mortgage; Median gross rent: $562 per month; Rental vacancy rate: 12.9%
Health Insurance: 87.8% have insurance; 65.4% have private insurance; 34.7% have public insurance; 12.2% do not have insurance; 0.0% of children under 18 do not have insurance
Safety: Violent crime rate: 22.7 per 10,000 population; Property crime rate: 72.5 per 10,000 population
Newspapers: Utica Herald (weekly circulation 2,300)
Transportation: Commute: 97.8% car, 0.0% public transportation, 0.3% walk, 1.4% work from home; Mean travel time to work: 28.2 minutes

Logan County

Located in west central Ohio; drained by the Great Miami and Mad Rivers; includes Campbell Hill, the highest point in the state (1,550 ft). Covers a land area of 458.429 square miles, a water area of 8.343 square miles, and is located in the Eastern Time Zone at 40.39° N. Lat., 83.77° W. Long. The county was founded in 1817. County seat is Bellefontaine.

Logan County is part of the Bellefontaine, OH Micropolitan Statistical Area. The entire metro area includes: Logan County, OH

Weather Station: Bellefontaine Elevation: 1,185 feet

	Jan	Feb	Mar	Apr	May	Jun	Jul	Aug	Sep	Oct	Nov	Dec
High	33	37	48	61	71	80	83	82	76	63	50	38
Low	18	20	28	39	50	59	63	61	54	42	33	23
Precip	2.6	2.1	2.9	3.6	4.1	4.4	4.2	3.6	2.8	2.6	3.2	3.0
Snow	na	3.2	1.2	0.2	0.0	0.0	0.0	0.0	0.0	0.2	0.4	2.5

High and Low temperatures in degrees Fahrenheit; Precipitation and Snow in inches

Population: 45,388; Growth (since 2000): -1.3%; Density: 99.0 persons per square mile; Race: 95.0% White, 1.7% Black/African American, 0.7% Asian, 0.1% American Indian/Alaska Native, 0.0% Native Hawaiian/Other Pacific Islander, 2.3% two or more races, 1.4% Hispanic of any race; Average household size: 2.40; Median age: 41.2; Age under 18: 24.1%; Age 65 and over: 16.5%; Males per 100 females: 97.2; Marriage status: 22.8% never married, 57.8% now married, 2.6% separated, 6.5% widowed, 12.8% divorced; Foreign born: 1.3%; Speak English only: 95.6%; With disability: 14.4%; Veterans: 9.5%; Ancestry: 32.0% German, 16.2% American, 15.5% Irish, 9.4% English, 3.1% French
Religion: Six largest groups: 7.2% Methodist/Pietist, 4.9% Catholicism, 4.8% Baptist, 3.4% European Free-Church, 2.8% Presbyterian-Reformed, 2.7% Holiness
Economy: Unemployment rate: 3.7%; Leading industries: 17.2 % retail trade; 13.4 % other services (except public administration); 11.2 % accommodation and food services; Farms: 868 totaling 212,937 acres; Company size: 3 employ 1,000 or more persons, 0 employ 500 to 999 persons, 22 employ 100 to 499 persons, 818 employ less than 100 persons; Business ownership: 1,078 women-owned, 53 Black-owned, n/a Hispanic-owned, 48 Asian-owned, n/a American Indian/Alaska Native-owned
Employment: 12.1% management, business, and financial, 2.6% computer, engineering, and science, 7.4% education, legal, community service, arts, and media, 4.6% healthcare practitioners, 12.9% service, 19.5% sales and office, 9.8% natural resources, construction, and maintenance, 31.1% production, transportation, and material moving
Income: Per capita: $25,877; Median household: $51,136; Average household: $63,112; Households with income of $100,000 or more: 17.5%; Poverty rate: 14.0%
Educational Attainment: High school diploma or higher: 89.6%; Bachelor's degree or higher: 15.6%; Graduate/professional degree or higher: 5.4%
Housing: Homeownership rate: 73.4%; Median home value: $124,400; Median year structure built: 1968; Homeowner vacancy rate: 2.0%; Median selected monthly owner costs: $1,102 with a mortgage, $420 without a mortgage; Median gross rent: $704 per month; Rental vacancy rate: 4.0%
Vital Statistics: Birth rate: 114.0 per 10,000 population; Death rate: 112.5 per 10,000 population; Age-adjusted cancer mortality rate: 220.8 deaths per 100,000 population
Health Insurance: 89.4% have insurance; 69.7% have private insurance; 34.9% have public insurance; 10.6% do not have insurance; 8.1% of children under 18 do not have insurance
Health Care: Physicians: 11.7 per 10,000 population; Dentists: 4.2 per 10,000 population; Hospital beds: 22.0 per 10,000 population; Hospital admissions: 361.7 per 10,000 population
Transportation: Commute: 92.4% car, 0.2% public transportation, 1.4% walk, 5.0% work from home; Mean travel time to work: 22.2 minutes
2016 Presidential Election: 73.5% Trump, 21.4% Clinton, 3.0% Johnson, 0.6% Stein
National and State Parks: Fox Island State Park; Indian Lake State Park; Indian Lake State Wildlife Area
Additional Information Contacts
Logan Government . . . . (937) 599-7283
http://www.co.logan.oh.us

Logan County Communities

BELLE CENTER (village). Covers a land area of 0.695 square miles and a water area of 0.013 square miles. Located at 40.51° N. Lat; 83.75° W. Long. Elevation is 1,043 feet.
History: Belle Center developed as a rural trading village. A large butter and cheese plant was established here.
Population: 793; Growth (since 2000): -1.7%; Density: 1,141.2 persons per square mile; Race: 98.1% White, 0.0% Black/African American, 0.0% Asian, 0.0% American Indian/Alaska Native, 0.0% Native Hawaiian/Other Pacific Islander, 1.1% Two or more races, 2.4% Hispanic of any race; Average household size: 2.42; Median age: 38.9; Age under 18: 24.0%; Age 65 and over: 16.9%; Males per 100 females: 92.7; Marriage status: 25.3% never married, 52.4% now married, 1.4% separated, 11.4% widowed, 11.0% divorced; Foreign born: 0.4%; Speak English only: 97.3%; With disability: 15.4%; Veterans: 10.8%; Ancestry: 33.2% German, 19.5% American, 14.5% Irish, 11.2% English, 5.2% Scottish
Employment: 7.5% management, business, and financial, 1.3% computer, engineering, and science, 7.8% education, legal, community service, arts, and media, 2.3% healthcare practitioners, 15.8% service, 16.0% sales and office, 10.3% natural resources, construction, and maintenance, 39.0% production, transportation, and material moving
Income: Per capita: $21,563; Median household: $48,750; Average household: $53,527; Households with income of $100,000 or more: 10.0%; Poverty rate: 11.6%
Educational Attainment: High school diploma or higher: 90.5%; Bachelor's degree or higher: 9.1%; Graduate/professional degree or higher: 3.8%

Housing: Homeownership rate: 86.0%; Median home value: $82,600; Median year structure built: Before 1940; Homeowner vacancy rate: 2.1%; Median selected monthly owner costs: $904 with a mortgage, $377 without a mortgage; Median gross rent: $725 per month; Rental vacancy rate: 0.0%
Health Insurance: 93.3% have insurance; 73.4% have private insurance; 33.7% have public insurance; 6.7% do not have insurance; 4.2% of children under 18 do not have insurance
Transportation: Commute: 97.6% car, 0.0% public transportation, 1.3% walk, 0.5% work from home; Mean travel time to work: 24.3 minutes

BELLEFONTAINE (city). County seat. Covers a land area of 10.036 square miles and a water area of 0 square miles. Located at 40.36° N. Lat; 83.76° W. Long. Elevation is 1,243 feet.
History: Bellefontaine was settled in 1806, and became the seat of Logan County in 1820. The name means "beautiful fountain," referring to the natural springs at the site.
Population: 13,211; Growth (since 2000): 1.1%; Density: 1,316.3 persons per square mile; Race: 90.3% White, 4.0% Black/African American, 1.0% Asian, 0.0% American Indian/Alaska Native, 0.0% Native Hawaiian/Other Pacific Islander, 3.9% Two or more races, 2.5% Hispanic of any race; Average household size: 2.37; Median age: 33.3; Age under 18: 26.5%; Age 65 and over: 13.4%; Males per 100 females: 93.9; Marriage status: 30.6% never married, 47.0% now married, 5.0% separated, 7.0% widowed, 15.4% divorced; Foreign born: 2.2%; Speak English only: 96.2%; With disability: 16.3%; Veterans: 7.6%; Ancestry: 30.3% German, 17.3% Irish, 16.2% American, 10.0% English, 3.7% Italian
Employment: 9.4% management, business, and financial, 3.7% computer, engineering, and science, 8.5% education, legal, community service, arts, and media, 5.3% healthcare practitioners, 15.1% service, 19.0% sales and office, 7.6% natural resources, construction, and maintenance, 31.3% production, transportation, and material moving
Income: Per capita: $23,232; Median household: $42,471; Average household: $56,002; Households with income of $100,000 or more: 14.7%; Poverty rate: 20.9%
Educational Attainment: High school diploma or higher: 88.1%; Bachelor's degree or higher: 17.9%; Graduate/professional degree or higher: 6.2%

School District(s)

Bellefontaine City (KG-12)
2015-16 Enrollment: 2,434 . . . . (937) 593-9060
Benjamin Logan Local (KG-12)
2015-16 Enrollment: 1,730 . . . . (937) 593-9211
Ohio Hi-Point Career Center (07-12)
2015-16 Enrollment: n/a . . . . (937) 599-3010

Housing: Homeownership rate: 55.0%; Median home value: $101,300; Median year structure built: 1960; Homeowner vacancy rate: 0.5%; Median selected monthly owner costs: $965 with a mortgage, $380 without a mortgage; Median gross rent: $738 per month; Rental vacancy rate: 4.7%
Health Insurance: 90.3% have insurance; 63.6% have private insurance; 40.6% have public insurance; 9.7% do not have insurance; 1.8% of children under 18 do not have insurance
Hospitals: Mary Rutan Hospital (105 beds)
Safety: Violent crime rate: 17.6 per 10,000 population; Property crime rate: 309.0 per 10,000 population
Newspapers: Bellefontaine Examiner (daily circulation 8,900)
Transportation: Commute: 95.7% car, 0.1% public transportation, 1.6% walk, 1.9% work from home; Mean travel time to work: 18.9 minutes
Airports: Bellefontaine Regional (general aviation)
Additional Information Contacts
City of Bellefontaine . . . . (937) 592-4376
http://www.ci.bellefontaine.oh.us

CHIPPEWA PARK (CDP). Covers a land area of 0.440 square miles and a water area of 0.053 square miles. Located at 40.52° N. Lat; 83.89° W. Long. Elevation is 1,014 feet.
Population: 708; Growth (since 2000): n/a; Density: 1,608.3 persons per square mile; Race: 100.0% White, 0.0% Black/African American, 0.0% Asian, 0.0% American Indian/Alaska Native, 0.0% Native Hawaiian/Other Pacific Islander, 0.0% Two or more races, 1.1% Hispanic of any race; Average household size: 1.78; Median age: 59.4; Age under 18: 11.2%; Age 65 and over: 39.3%; Males per 100 females: 106.3; Marriage status: 19.9% never married, 45.6% now married, 3.5% separated, 11.6% widowed, 22.9% divorced; Foreign born: 0.0%; Speak English only: 98.4%; With disability: 12.9%; Veterans: 16.7%; Ancestry: 28.2% German, 15.4% American, 14.3% Irish, 13.3% English, 5.4% Swedish
Employment: 4.5% management, business, and financial, 0.0% computer, engineering, and science, 3.8% education, legal, community service, arts, and media, 4.1% healthcare practitioners, 17.9% service, 29.0% sales and office, 24.5% natural resources, construction, and maintenance, 16.2% production, transportation, and material moving
Income: Per capita: $18,093; Median household: $29,432; Average household: $33,120; Households with income of $100,000 or more: n/a; Poverty rate: 22.2%
Educational Attainment: High school diploma or higher: 83.7%; Bachelor's degree or higher: 6.1%; Graduate/professional degree or higher: 3.1%
Housing: Homeownership rate: 90.2%; Median home value: $66,400; Median year structure built: 1964; Homeowner vacancy rate: 24.3%; Median selected monthly owner costs: $717 with a mortgage, $317 without a mortgage; Median gross rent: $613 per month; Rental vacancy rate: 0.0%
Health Insurance: 86.2% have insurance; 51.0% have private insurance; 71.6% have public insurance; 13.8% do not have insurance; 10.1% of children under 18 do not have insurance
Transportation: Commute: 90.0% car, 0.0% public transportation, 4.5% walk, 3.8% work from home; Mean travel time to work: 28.4 minutes

DE GRAFF (village). Covers a land area of 1.010 square miles and a water area of 0 square miles. Located at 40.31° N. Lat; 83.92° W. Long. Elevation is 1,001 feet.
History: Sometimes spelled Degraff.
Population: 1,399; Growth (since 2000): 15.4%; Density: 1,384.8 persons per square mile; Race: 90.9% White, 0.4% Black/African American, 2.6% Asian, 0.6% American Indian/Alaska Native, 0.0% Native Hawaiian/Other Pacific Islander, 5.5% Two or more races, 0.0% Hispanic of any race; Average household size: 2.51; Median age: 35.0; Age under 18: 29.2%; Age 65 and over: 13.4%; Males per 100 females: 95.6; Marriage status: 25.6% never married, 56.7% now married, 0.4% separated, 7.5% widowed, 10.2% divorced; Foreign born: 3.1%; Speak English only: 96.5%; With disability: 15.7%; Veterans: 7.5%; Ancestry: 25.9% German, 19.2% American, 16.8% Irish, 10.6% English, 4.1% Italian
Employment: 8.4% management, business, and financial, 2.2% computer, engineering, and science, 9.7% education, legal, community service, arts, and media, 3.8% healthcare practitioners, 14.2% service, 15.7% sales and office, 7.3% natural resources, construction, and maintenance, 38.8% production, transportation, and material moving
Income: Per capita: $17,688; Median household: $38,281; Average household: $44,568; Households with income of $100,000 or more: 5.9%; Poverty rate: 16.5%
Educational Attainment: High school diploma or higher: 87.1%; Bachelor's degree or higher: 12.4%; Graduate/professional degree or higher: 4.8%

School District(s)

Riverside Local (KG-12)
2015-16 Enrollment: 721. . . . . (937) 585-5981

Housing: Homeownership rate: 65.0%; Median home value: $86,600; Median year structure built: 1954; Homeowner vacancy rate: 1.9%; Median selected monthly owner costs: $1,000 with a mortgage, $442 without a mortgage; Median gross rent: $763 per month; Rental vacancy rate: 11.8%
Health Insurance: 91.7% have insurance; 69.3% have private insurance; 34.5% have public insurance; 8.3% do not have insurance; 0.0% of children under 18 do not have insurance
Transportation: Commute: 92.4% car, 2.3% public transportation, 2.1% walk, 1.9% work from home; Mean travel time to work: 26.0 minutes

EAST LIBERTY (CDP). Covers a land area of 1.577 square miles and a water area of 0 square miles. Located at 40.33° N. Lat; 83.59° W. Long. Elevation is 1,135 feet.
Population: 192; Growth (since 2000): n/a; Density: 121.7 persons per square mile; Race: 100.0% White, 0.0% Black/African American, 0.0% Asian, 0.0% American Indian/Alaska Native, 0.0% Native Hawaiian/Other Pacific Islander, 0.0% Two or more races, 27.6% Hispanic of any race; Average household size: 1.85; Median age: 55.0; Age under 18: 8.3%; Age 65 and over: 18.8%; Males per 100 females: 95.7; Marriage status: 4.0% never married, 80.7% now married, 0.0% separated, 0.0% widowed, 15.3% divorced; Foreign born: 0.0%; Speak English only: 100.0%; With disability: 15.1%; Veterans: 21.0%; Ancestry: 45.3% German, 9.9% English, 9.4% American, 9.4% Irish, 8.9% Dutch

Employment: 9.3% management, business, and financial, 0.0% computer, engineering, and science, 0.0% education, legal, community service, arts, and media, 0.0% healthcare practitioners, 0.0% service, 49.3% sales and office, 0.0% natural resources, construction, and maintenance, 41.3% production, transportation, and material moving
Income: Per capita: $32,227; Median household: $66,389; Average household: $60,371; Households with income of $100,000 or more: n/a; Poverty rate: 9.4%
Educational Attainment: High school diploma or higher: 93.8%; Bachelor's degree or higher: 25.0%; Graduate/professional degree or higher: n/a
Housing: Homeownership rate: 100.0%; Median home value: n/a; Median year structure built: Before 1940; Homeowner vacancy rate: 0.0%; Median selected monthly owner costs: $986 with a mortgage, n/a without a mortgage; Median gross rent: n/a per month; Rental vacancy rate: 0.0%
Health Insurance: 100.0% have insurance; 100.0% have private insurance; 33.3% have public insurance; 0.0% do not have insurance; 0.0% of children under 18 do not have insurance
Transportation: Commute: 100.0% car, 0.0% public transportation, 0.0% walk, 0.0% work from home; Mean travel time to work: 35.2 minutes

HUNTSVILLE (village). Covers a land area of 0.302 square miles and a water area of 0 square miles. Located at 40.44° N. Lat; 83.80° W. Long. Elevation is 1,076 feet.
Population: 535; Growth (since 2000): 17.8%; Density: 1,769.3 persons per square mile; Race: 97.2% White, 0.0% Black/African American, 0.9% Asian, 0.0% American Indian/Alaska Native, 0.0% Native Hawaiian/Other Pacific Islander, 1.9% Two or more races, 6.4% Hispanic of any race; Average household size: 2.52; Median age: 34.1; Age under 18: 22.1%; Age 65 and over: 11.6%; Males per 100 females: 93.3; Marriage status: 27.9% never married, 57.2% now married, 0.5% separated, 3.2% widowed, 11.7% divorced; Foreign born: 2.2%; Speak English only: 95.8%; With disability: 9.9%; Veterans: 7.2%; Ancestry: 36.6% German, 18.1% American, 16.8% Irish, 5.6% Polish, 5.4% English
Employment: 14.7% management, business, and financial, 2.2% computer, engineering, and science, 3.5% education, legal, community service, arts, and media, 5.8% healthcare practitioners, 10.6% service, 14.4% sales and office, 9.3% natural resources, construction, and maintenance, 39.4% production, transportation, and material moving
Income: Per capita: $25,126; Median household: $53,088; Average household: $61,115; Households with income of $100,000 or more: 16.4%; Poverty rate: 14.2%
Educational Attainment: High school diploma or higher: 91.8%; Bachelor's degree or higher: 5.2%; Graduate/professional degree or higher: n/a
Housing: Homeownership rate: 62.7%; Median home value: $104,400; Median year structure built: 1951; Homeowner vacancy rate: 0.0%; Median selected monthly owner costs: $987 with a mortgage, $388 without a mortgage; Median gross rent: $683 per month; Rental vacancy rate: 11.2%
Health Insurance: 88.6% have insurance; 70.3% have private insurance; 30.3% have public insurance; 11.4% do not have insurance; 5.9% of children under 18 do not have insurance
Transportation: Commute: 95.7% car, 0.0% public transportation, 1.0% walk, 0.7% work from home; Mean travel time to work: 24.4 minutes
Additional Information Contacts
Village of Huntsville . . . . (937) 686-7275
http://huntsvilleohio.com

LAKEVIEW (village). Covers a land area of 0.707 square miles and a water area of 0.005 square miles. Located at 40.49° N. Lat; 83.93° W. Long. Elevation is 991 feet.
History: Lakeview developed as a resort on Indian Lake.
Population: 1,187; Growth (since 2000): 10.5%; Density: 1,677.9 persons per square mile; Race: 94.9% White, 0.3% Black/African American, 0.4% Asian, 0.0% American Indian/Alaska Native, 0.0% Native Hawaiian/Other Pacific Islander, 4.5% Two or more races, 0.9% Hispanic of any race; Average household size: 2.17; Median age: 46.7; Age under 18: 20.4%; Age 65 and over: 16.2%; Males per 100 females: 92.5; Marriage status: 20.8% never married, 47.7% now married, 2.9% separated, 5.4% widowed, 26.1% divorced; Foreign born: 1.3%; Speak English only: 98.0%; With disability: 22.4%; Veterans: 16.0%; Ancestry: 47.7% German, 16.8% American, 15.5% Irish, 13.9% English, 5.7% Italian
Employment: 5.9% management, business, and financial, 2.1% computer, engineering, and science, 1.0% education, legal, community service, arts, and media, 5.2% healthcare practitioners, 10.7% service, 22.0% sales and office, 8.6% natural resources, construction, and maintenance, 44.6% production, transportation, and material moving
Income: Per capita: $21,176; Median household: $42,462; Average household: $47,379; Households with income of $100,000 or more: 5.7%; Poverty rate: 19.4%
Educational Attainment: High school diploma or higher: 83.5%; Bachelor's degree or higher: 4.8%; Graduate/professional degree or higher: 1.2%
Housing: Homeownership rate: 68.5%; Median home value: $72,400; Median year structure built: 1954; Homeowner vacancy rate: 1.5%; Median selected monthly owner costs: $939 with a mortgage, $367 without a mortgage; Median gross rent: $666 per month; Rental vacancy rate: 0.0%
Health Insurance: 85.2% have insurance; 54.9% have private insurance; 43.5% have public insurance; 14.8% do not have insurance; 9.5% of children under 18 do not have insurance
Transportation: Commute: 95.4% car, 0.0% public transportation, 1.1% walk, 3.4% work from home; Mean travel time to work: 23.9 minutes

LEWISTOWN (CDP). Covers a land area of 0.768 square miles and a water area of 0 square miles. Located at 40.42° N. Lat; 83.88° W. Long. Elevation is 1,014 feet.
Population: 113; Growth (since 2000): n/a; Density: 147.2 persons per square mile; Race: 100.0% White, 0.0% Black/African American, 0.0% Asian, 0.0% American Indian/Alaska Native, 0.0% Native Hawaiian/Other Pacific Islander, 0.0% Two or more races, 0.0% Hispanic of any race; Average household size: 1.92; Median age: 47.1; Age under 18: 23.9%; Age 65 and over: 0.0%; Males per 100 females: 93.0; Marriage status: 32.6% never married, 31.4% now married, 0.0% separated, 0.0% widowed, 36.0% divorced; Foreign born: 0.0%; Speak English only: 100.0%; With disability: 12.4%; Veterans: 16.3%; Ancestry: 76.1% German, 29.2% Irish, 22.1% French
Employment: 15.1% management, business, and financial, 0.0% computer, engineering, and science, 0.0% education, legal, community service, arts, and media, 0.0% healthcare practitioners, 19.8% service, 16.3% sales and office, 16.3% natural resources, construction, and maintenance, 32.6% production, transportation, and material moving
Income: Per capita: $20,696; Median household: n/a; Average household: $40,278; Households with income of $100,000 or more: n/a; Poverty rate: 12.4%
Educational Attainment: High school diploma or higher: 100.0%; Bachelor's degree or higher: n/a; Graduate/professional degree or higher: n/a

School District(s)

Indian Lake Local (KG-12)
2015-16 Enrollment: 1,643 . . . . (937) 686-8601
Housing: Homeownership rate: 76.3%; Median home value: n/a; Median year structure built: Before 1940; Homeowner vacancy rate: 0.0%; Median selected monthly owner costs: n/a with a mortgage, n/a without a mortgage; Median gross rent: n/a per month; Rental vacancy rate: 0.0%
Health Insurance: 87.6% have insurance; 87.6% have private insurance; 9.7% have public insurance; 12.4% do not have insurance; 0.0% of children under 18 do not have insurance
Transportation: Commute: 83.7% car, 0.0% public transportation, 0.0% walk, 16.3% work from home; Mean travel time to work: 0.0 minutes

QUINCY (village). Covers a land area of 1.132 square miles and a water area of 0 square miles. Located at 40.30° N. Lat; 83.97° W. Long. Elevation is 1,056 feet.
Population: 579; Growth (since 2000): -21.1%; Density: 511.3 persons per square mile; Race: 96.0% White, 0.0% Black/African American, 0.0% Asian, 0.0% American Indian/Alaska Native, 0.0% Native Hawaiian/Other Pacific Islander, 4.0% Two or more races, 0.0% Hispanic of any race; Average household size: 2.43; Median age: 40.1; Age under 18: 25.6%; Age 65 and over: 13.8%; Males per 100 females: 99.4; Marriage status: 28.0% never married, 54.7% now married, 0.9% separated, 5.6% widowed, 11.8% divorced; Foreign born: 0.0%; Speak English only: 99.5%; With disability: 21.8%; Veterans: 11.1%; Ancestry: 27.3% German, 19.9% American, 17.1% Irish, 13.0% English, 4.0% Italian
Employment: 11.4% management, business, and financial, 1.8% computer, engineering, and science, 5.0% education, legal, community service, arts, and media, 2.3% healthcare practitioners, 5.9% service, 20.1% sales and office, 16.4% natural resources, construction, and maintenance, 37.0% production, transportation, and material moving

Income: Per capita: $17,885; Median household: $42,500; Average household: $44,598; Households with income of $100,000 or more: 4.2%; Poverty rate: 21.6%
Educational Attainment: High school diploma or higher: 77.7%; Bachelor's degree or higher: 8.0%; Graduate/professional degree or higher: 1.1%
Housing: Homeownership rate: 53.4%; Median home value: $63,800; Median year structure built: 1954; Homeowner vacancy rate: 0.0%; Median selected monthly owner costs: $925 with a mortgage, $446 without a mortgage; Median gross rent: $544 per month; Rental vacancy rate: 1.6%
Health Insurance: 87.6% have insurance; 56.5% have private insurance; 42.1% have public insurance; 12.4% do not have insurance; 6.8% of children under 18 do not have insurance
Transportation: Commute: 92.6% car, 0.0% public transportation, 0.5% walk, 7.0% work from home; Mean travel time to work: 29.6 minutes

RUSHSYLVANIA (village). Covers a land area of 0.784 square miles and a water area of 0 square miles. Located at 40.46° N. Lat; 83.67° W. Long. Elevation is 1,243 feet.
Population: 620; Growth (since 2000): 14.2%; Density: 791.0 persons per square mile; Race: 99.4% White, 0.0% Black/African American, 0.0% Asian, 0.0% American Indian/Alaska Native, 0.0% Native Hawaiian/Other Pacific Islander, 0.6% Two or more races, 0.0% Hispanic of any race; Average household size: 2.57; Median age: 34.0; Age under 18: 26.6%; Age 65 and over: 13.7%; Males per 100 females: 94.0; Marriage status: 24.4% never married, 53.1% now married, 2.9% separated, 8.6% widowed, 13.9% divorced; Foreign born: 0.3%; Speak English only: 100.0%; With disability: 12.9%; Veterans: 6.8%; Ancestry: 31.5% American, 19.2% English, 17.9% German, 11.3% Irish, 3.9% French
Employment: 11.1% management, business, and financial, 1.1% computer, engineering, and science, 3.2% education, legal, community service, arts, and media, 0.0% healthcare practitioners, 18.3% service, 23.3% sales and office, 8.2% natural resources, construction, and maintenance, 34.8% production, transportation, and material moving
Income: Per capita: $19,564; Median household: $41,250; Average household: $49,180; Households with income of $100,000 or more: 8.3%; Poverty rate: 23.2%
Educational Attainment: High school diploma or higher: 91.4%; Bachelor's degree or higher: 6.5%; Graduate/professional degree or higher: 0.8%
Housing: Homeownership rate: 76.3%; Median home value: $80,400; Median year structure built: Before 1940; Homeowner vacancy rate: 0.0%; Median selected monthly owner costs: $1,051 with a mortgage, $370 without a mortgage; Median gross rent: $695 per month; Rental vacancy rate: 0.0%
Health Insurance: 92.9% have insurance; 61.5% have private insurance; 43.9% have public insurance; 7.1% do not have insurance; 0.6% of children under 18 do not have insurance
Transportation: Commute: 95.0% car, 0.0% public transportation, 3.4% walk, 0.8% work from home; Mean travel time to work: 26.5 minutes

RUSSELLS POINT (village). Covers a land area of 0.932 square miles and a water area of 0.079 square miles. Located at 40.47° N. Lat; 83.89° W. Long. Elevation is 1,004 feet.
History: Russells Point developed as a resort and vacation center on Indian Lake.
Population: 1,113; Growth (since 2000): -31.3%; Density: 1,194.1 persons per square mile; Race: 95.4% White, 1.1% Black/African American, 0.4% Asian, 0.7% American Indian/Alaska Native, 0.2% Native Hawaiian/Other Pacific Islander, 2.2% Two or more races, 0.0% Hispanic of any race; Average household size: 2.12; Median age: 38.9; Age under 18: 26.7%; Age 65 and over: 18.1%; Males per 100 females: 94.5; Marriage status: 17.3% never married, 51.3% now married, 2.7% separated, 8.4% widowed, 22.9% divorced; Foreign born: 0.4%; Speak English only: 99.9%; With disability: 21.6%; Veterans: 12.7%; Ancestry: 33.8% German, 19.0% American, 18.1% Irish, 7.5% English, 5.1% French
Employment: 12.2% management, business, and financial, 0.6% computer, engineering, and science, 3.6% education, legal, community service, arts, and media, 0.6% healthcare practitioners, 20.7% service, 28.5% sales and office, 10.5% natural resources, construction, and maintenance, 23.2% production, transportation, and material moving
Income: Per capita: $20,535; Median household: $30,446; Average household: $44,214; Households with income of $100,000 or more: 9.3%; Poverty rate: 26.1%
Educational Attainment: High school diploma or higher: 83.4%; Bachelor's degree or higher: 6.8%; Graduate/professional degree or higher: 1.7%
Housing: Homeownership rate: 54.7%; Median home value: $82,700; Median year structure built: 1973; Homeowner vacancy rate: 13.5%; Median selected monthly owner costs: $764 with a mortgage, $467 without a mortgage; Median gross rent: $531 per month; Rental vacancy rate: 8.1%
Health Insurance: 88.4% have insurance; 53.9% have private insurance; 49.4% have public insurance; 11.6% do not have insurance; 7.4% of children under 18 do not have insurance
Safety: Violent crime rate: 0.0 per 10,000 population; Property crime rate: 191.9 per 10,000 population
Transportation: Commute: 94.8% car, 0.0% public transportation, 0.7% walk, 4.1% work from home; Mean travel time to work: 23.6 minutes

VALLEY HI (village). Covers a land area of 0.617 square miles and a water area of 0 square miles. Located at 40.32° N. Lat; 83.68° W. Long. Elevation is 1,270 feet.
Population: 267; Growth (since 2000): 9.4%; Density: 433.1 persons per square mile; Race: 97.4% White, 0.0% Black/African American, 0.0% Asian, 2.6% American Indian/Alaska Native, 0.0% Native Hawaiian/Other Pacific Islander, 0.0% Two or more races, 0.0% Hispanic of any race; Average household size: 2.28; Median age: 30.5; Age under 18: 25.1%; Age 65 and over: 7.9%; Males per 100 females: 107.8; Marriage status: 17.7% never married, 63.1% now married, 9.4% separated, 2.0% widowed, 17.2% divorced; Foreign born: 0.0%; Speak English only: 100.0%; With disability: 6.4%; Veterans: 11.0%; Ancestry: 27.3% German, 21.0% Irish, 14.6% American, 9.4% English, 3.4% European
Employment: 3.6% management, business, and financial, 0.9% computer, engineering, and science, 0.0% education, legal, community service, arts, and media, 1.8% healthcare practitioners, 4.5% service, 20.0% sales and office, 13.6% natural resources, construction, and maintenance, 55.5% production, transportation, and material moving
Income: Per capita: $18,569; Median household: $36,563; Average household: $41,680; Households with income of $100,000 or more: 3.4%; Poverty rate: 11.2%
Educational Attainment: High school diploma or higher: 91.8%; Bachelor's degree or higher: 5.7%; Graduate/professional degree or higher: n/a
Housing: Homeownership rate: 31.6%; Median home value: n/a; Median year structure built: 1985; Homeowner vacancy rate: 0.0%; Median selected monthly owner costs: $1,047 with a mortgage, $422 without a mortgage; Median gross rent: $765 per month; Rental vacancy rate: 0.0%
Health Insurance: 83.1% have insurance; 48.3% have private insurance; 46.8% have public insurance; 16.9% do not have insurance; 4.5% of children under 18 do not have insurance
Transportation: Commute: 98.1% car, 0.0% public transportation, 0.0% walk, 1.9% work from home; Mean travel time to work: 19.7 minutes

WEST LIBERTY (village). Covers a land area of 1.120 square miles and a water area of 0 square miles. Located at 40.26° N. Lat; 83.76° W. Long. Elevation is 1,086 feet.
History: West Liberty developed as a rural trading center around a milk plant, a flour mill, and grain elevators.
Population: 1,725; Growth (since 2000): -4.9%; Density: 1,539.7 persons per square mile; Race: 91.2% White, 2.3% Black/African American, 0.3% Asian, 0.0% American Indian/Alaska Native, 0.0% Native Hawaiian/Other Pacific Islander, 5.6% Two or more races, 3.1% Hispanic of any race; Average household size: 2.26; Median age: 44.3; Age under 18: 23.9%; Age 65 and over: 25.4%; Males per 100 females: 80.5; Marriage status: 23.4% never married, 53.6% now married, 0.3% separated, 13.2% widowed, 9.8% divorced; Foreign born: 1.8%; Speak English only: 95.1%; With disability: 15.1%; Veterans: 7.5%; Ancestry: 35.4% German, 11.9% Irish, 10.9% American, 10.1% English, 3.9% Swiss
Employment: 10.4% management, business, and financial, 2.2% computer, engineering, and science, 8.0% education, legal, community service, arts, and media, 7.1% healthcare practitioners, 17.8% service, 19.2% sales and office, 7.7% natural resources, construction, and maintenance, 27.6% production, transportation, and material moving
Income: Per capita: $23,195; Median household: $46,181; Average household: $54,566; Households with income of $100,000 or more: 14.5%; Poverty rate: 7.2%

Educational Attainment: High school diploma or higher: 91.8%; Bachelor's degree or higher: 17.1%; Graduate/professional degree or higher: 6.6%

School District(s)

West Liberty-Salem Local (KG-12)
2015-16 Enrollment: 1,203 . . . . (937) 465-1075

Housing: Homeownership rate: 64.6%; Median home value: $112,600; Median year structure built: 1948; Homeowner vacancy rate: 1.8%; Median selected monthly owner costs: $998 with a mortgage, $382 without a mortgage; Median gross rent: $552 per month; Rental vacancy rate: 0.0%
Health Insurance: 96.1% have insurance; 77.9% have private insurance; 37.9% have public insurance; 3.9% do not have insurance; 0.5% of children under 18 do not have insurance
Safety: Violent crime rate: 17.0 per 10,000 population; Property crime rate: 118.7 per 10,000 population
Transportation: Commute: 93.3% car, 0.0% public transportation, 4.8% walk, 1.9% work from home; Mean travel time to work: 21.1 minutes

WEST MANSFIELD (village). Covers a land area of 0.834 square miles and a water area of 0.025 square miles. Located at 40.40° N. Lat; 83.54° W. Long. Elevation is 1,089 feet.
Population: 755; Growth (since 2000): 7.9%; Density: 904.8 persons per square mile; Race: 98.5% White, 0.0% Black/African American, 0.7% Asian, 0.0% American Indian/Alaska Native, 0.0% Native Hawaiian/Other Pacific Islander, 0.8% Two or more races, 0.9% Hispanic of any race; Average household size: 2.40; Median age: 36.0; Age under 18: 23.0%; Age 65 and over: 16.7%; Males per 100 females: 100.0; Marriage status: 15.7% never married, 68.6% now married, 3.3% separated, 7.9% widowed, 7.9% divorced; Foreign born: 0.4%; Speak English only: 99.3%; With disability: 13.2%; Veterans: 7.9%; Ancestry: 42.5% German, 19.3% English, 18.8% Irish, 13.1% American, 4.8% Italian
Employment: 7.5% management, business, and financial, 4.3% computer, engineering, and science, 5.6% education, legal, community service, arts, and media, 2.7% healthcare practitioners, 12.1% service, 28.3% sales and office, 12.8% natural resources, construction, and maintenance, 26.8% production, transportation, and material moving
Income: Per capita: $24,774; Median household: $52,917; Average household: $59,633; Households with income of $100,000 or more: 15.3%; Poverty rate: 8.9%
Educational Attainment: High school diploma or higher: 86.3%; Bachelor's degree or higher: 10.5%; Graduate/professional degree or higher: 2.2%
Housing: Homeownership rate: 72.0%; Median home value: $85,600; Median year structure built: Before 1940; Homeowner vacancy rate: 0.0%; Median selected monthly owner costs: $1,105 with a mortgage, $492 without a mortgage; Median gross rent: $696 per month; Rental vacancy rate: 0.0%
Health Insurance: 94.2% have insurance; 78.9% have private insurance; 39.2% have public insurance; 5.8% do not have insurance; 0.0% of children under 18 do not have insurance
Transportation: Commute: 93.7% car, 0.0% public transportation, 2.3% walk, 4.0% work from home; Mean travel time to work: 24.4 minutes

ZANESFIELD (village). Covers a land area of 0.106 square miles and a water area of 0 square miles. Located at 40.34° N. Lat; 83.68° W. Long. Elevation is 1,171 feet.
History: Zanesfield was settled in 1819 on the site of a blockhouse built by the English during the French and Indian War. The land once belonged to Isaac Zane, who was adopted by the Wyandot tribe when he was nine years old, and married the daughter of Chief Tarhe. He was known as White Eagle.
Population: 302; Growth (since 2000): 37.3%; Density: 2,844.9 persons per square mile; Race: 99.0% White, 0.0% Black/African American, 1.0% Asian, 0.0% American Indian/Alaska Native, 0.0% Native Hawaiian/Other Pacific Islander, 0.0% Two or more races, 0.0% Hispanic of any race; Average household size: 2.77; Median age: 36.8; Age under 18: 36.8%; Age 65 and over: 15.6%; Males per 100 females: 77.5; Marriage status: 31.4% never married, 51.1% now married, 0.9% separated, 4.0% widowed, 13.5% divorced; Foreign born: 0.3%; Speak English only: 100.0%; With disability: 11.3%; Veterans: 7.3%; Ancestry: 35.8% English, 32.5% German, 20.5% Irish, 12.3% Scottish, 8.3% American
Employment: 15.3% management, business, and financial, 1.6% computer, engineering, and science, 8.9% education, legal, community service, arts, and media, 0.8% healthcare practitioners, 16.9% service, 32.3% sales and office, 4.8% natural resources, construction, and maintenance, 19.4% production, transportation, and material moving
Income: Per capita: $22,105; Median household: $59,375; Average household: $58,869; Households with income of $100,000 or more: 10.1%; Poverty rate: 7.6%
Educational Attainment: High school diploma or higher: 93.3%; Bachelor's degree or higher: 16.8%; Graduate/professional degree or higher: 5.6%
Housing: Homeownership rate: 74.3%; Median home value: $97,900; Median year structure built: Before 1940; Homeowner vacancy rate: 0.0%; Median selected monthly owner costs: $863 with a mortgage, $357 without a mortgage; Median gross rent: $756 per month; Rental vacancy rate: 0.0%
Health Insurance: 97.4% have insurance; 76.8% have private insurance; 39.4% have public insurance; 2.6% do not have insurance; 0.0% of children under 18 do not have insurance
Transportation: Commute: 95.6% car, 0.0% public transportation, 0.0% walk, 4.4% work from home; Mean travel time to work: 19.9 minutes

Lorain County

Located in northern Ohio; bounded on the north by Lake Erie; drained by the Black and Vermilion Rivers. Covers a land area of 491.101 square miles, a water area of 432.230 square miles, and is located in the Eastern Time Zone at 41.44° N. Lat., 82.18° W. Long. The county was founded in 1822. County seat is Elyria.

Lorain County is part of the Cleveland-Elyria, OH Metropolitan Statistical Area. The entire metro area includes: Cuyahoga County, OH; Geauga County, OH; Lake County, OH; Lorain County, OH; Medina County, OH

Weather Station: Elyria 3 E Elevation: 729 feet

	Jan	Feb	Mar	Apr	May	Jun	Jul	Aug	Sep	Oct	Nov	Dec
High	35	39	48	61	72	81	85	83	76	64	52	39
Low	21	22	29	39	49	59	63	62	55	44	36	25
Precip	2.6	2.3	2.8	3.4	3.7	3.8	3.8	3.8	3.7	3.1	3.3	3.2
Snow	11.6	9.0	7.2	2.2	tr	tr	0.0	0.0	0.0	tr	2.4	8.6

High and Low temperatures in degrees Fahrenheit; Precipitation and Snow in inches

Weather Station: Oberlin Elevation: 815 feet

	Jan	Feb	Mar	Apr	May	Jun	Jul	Aug	Sep	Oct	Nov	Dec
High	34	37	46	59	70	79	83	81	75	63	50	38
Low	18	19	27	37	47	57	61	59	52	41	33	23
Precip	2.5	2.1	2.7	3.4	3.9	3.7	3.9	3.4	3.3	2.9	3.1	2.8
Snow	13.3	10.0	8.6	2.2	tr	0.0	0.0	0.0	0.0	tr	2.1	9.6

High and Low temperatures in degrees Fahrenheit; Precipitation and Snow in inches

Population: 304,091; Growth (since 2000): 6.8%; Density: 619.2 persons per square mile; Race: 85.4% White, 8.5% Black/African American, 1.0% Asian, 0.3% American Indian/Alaska Native, 0.0% Native Hawaiian/Other Pacific Islander, 3.5% two or more races, 9.3% Hispanic of any race; Average household size: 2.50; Median age: 41.2; Age under 18: 22.8%; Age 65 and over: 16.3%; Males per 100 females: 96.7; Marriage status: 30.5% never married, 50.7% now married, 1.7% separated, 6.8% widowed, 12.0% divorced; Foreign born: 2.9%; Speak English only: 92.2%; With disability: 15.4%; Veterans: 9.2%; Ancestry: 24.6% German, 15.4% Irish, 10.0% English, 8.8% Italian, 8.1% Polish
Religion: Six largest groups: 24.4% Catholicism, 4.9% Non-denominational Protestant, 4.2% Baptist, 2.9% Methodist/Pietist, 2.6% Presbyterian-Reformed, 1.8% Lutheran
Economy: Unemployment rate: 5.7%; Leading industries: 14.9 % retail trade; 11.8 % other services (except public administration); 11.1 % health care and social assistance; Farms: 768 totaling 122,692 acres; Company size: 5 employ 1,000 or more persons, 7 employ 500 to 999 persons, 124 employ 100 to 499 persons, 5,452 employ less than 100 persons; Business ownership: 7,095 women-owned, 1,109 Black-owned, 764 Hispanic-owned, 583 Asian-owned, 132 American Indian/Alaska Native-owned
Employment: 12.8% management, business, and financial, 4.1% computer, engineering, and science, 9.3% education, legal, community service, arts, and media, 6.9% healthcare practitioners, 17.8% service, 24.3% sales and office, 8.4% natural resources, construction, and maintenance, 16.4% production, transportation, and material moving
Income: Per capita: $27,537; Median household: $53,459; Average household: $69,522; Households with income of $100,000 or more: 21.2%; Poverty rate: 14.0%

Educational Attainment: High school diploma or higher: 89.2%; Bachelor's degree or higher: 23.5%; Graduate/professional degree or higher: 8.9%
Housing: Homeownership rate: 71.3%; Median home value: $138,600; Median year structure built: 1970; Homeowner vacancy rate: 1.6%; Median selected monthly owner costs: $1,276 with a mortgage, $460 without a mortgage; Median gross rent: $748 per month; Rental vacancy rate: 5.4%
Vital Statistics: Birth rate: 111.9 per 10,000 population; Death rate: 95.6 per 10,000 population; Age-adjusted cancer mortality rate: 177.8 deaths per 100,000 population
Health Insurance: 93.1% have insurance; 72.0% have private insurance; 35.5% have public insurance; 6.9% do not have insurance; 2.1% of children under 18 do not have insurance
Health Care: Physicians: 16.6 per 10,000 population; Dentists: 4.7 per 10,000 population; Hospital beds: 18.1 per 10,000 population; Hospital admissions: 831.2 per 10,000 population
Air Quality Index (AQI): Percent of Days: 86.6% good, 12.9% moderate, 0.5% unhealthy for sensitive individuals, 0.0% unhealthy, 0.0% very unhealthy; Annual median: 34; Annual maximum: 115
Transportation: Commute: 91.5% car, 0.6% public transportation, 2.3% walk, 3.4% work from home; Mean travel time to work: 24.2 minutes
2016 Presidential Election: 47.5% Trump, 47.6% Clinton, 3.2% Johnson, 0.9% Stein
National and State Parks: Black River State Reservation; Findley State Park; French Creek State Reservation
Additional Information Contacts
Lorain Government . . . . (440) 329-5000
http://www.loraincounty.us

Lorain County Communities

AMHERST (city). Covers a land area of 7.062 square miles and a water area of 0.059 square miles. Located at 41.41° N. Lat; 82.23° W. Long. Elevation is 689 feet.
History: Named for Baron Jeffrey Amherst (1717-1797), British general in the French and Indian Wars. Amherst grew around an extensive sandstone quarry.
Population: 12,058; Growth (since 2000): 2.2%; Density: 1,707.4 persons per square mile; Race: 96.3% White, 0.5% Black/African American, 0.4% Asian, 0.5% American Indian/Alaska Native, 0.0% Native Hawaiian/Other Pacific Islander, 2.0% Two or more races, 5.1% Hispanic of any race; Average household size: 2.56; Median age: 44.5; Age under 18: 21.1%; Age 65 and over: 18.0%; Males per 100 females: 93.4; Marriage status: 24.1% never married, 55.4% now married, 1.2% separated, 7.8% widowed, 12.6% divorced; Foreign born: 2.8%; Speak English only: 96.8%; With disability: 13.1%; Veterans: 8.9%; Ancestry: 30.6% German, 12.7% Irish, 11.2% English, 10.9% Italian, 9.9% Polish
Employment: 11.9% management, business, and financial, 4.2% computer, engineering, and science, 8.7% education, legal, community service, arts, and media, 7.1% healthcare practitioners, 18.8% service, 26.9% sales and office, 10.4% natural resources, construction, and maintenance, 11.9% production, transportation, and material moving
Income: Per capita: $30,656; Median household: $66,731; Average household: $77,712; Households with income of $100,000 or more: 30.0%; Poverty rate: 8.2%
Educational Attainment: High school diploma or higher: 90.6%; Bachelor's degree or higher: 23.5%; Graduate/professional degree or higher: 8.5%

School District(s)

Amherst Exempted Village (PK-12)
2015-16 Enrollment: 3,679 . . . . (440) 988-4406
Housing: Homeownership rate: 81.2%; Median home value: $146,200; Median year structure built: 1966; Homeowner vacancy rate: 0.8%; Median selected monthly owner costs: $1,393 with a mortgage, $457 without a mortgage; Median gross rent: $845 per month; Rental vacancy rate: 0.0%
Health Insurance: 94.2% have insurance; 80.0% have private insurance; 29.5% have public insurance; 5.8% do not have insurance; 5.5% of children under 18 do not have insurance
Safety: Violent crime rate: 5.8 per 10,000 population; Property crime rate: 154.7 per 10,000 population
Newspapers: Amherst News Times (weekly circulation 2,500)
Transportation: Commute: 95.8% car, 0.2% public transportation, 0.2% walk, 3.1% work from home; Mean travel time to work: 21.9 minutes
Additional Information Contacts
City of Amherst . . . . (440) 988-4380
http://www.amherstohio.org

AVON (city). Covers a land area of 20.808 square miles and a water area of 0.057 square miles. Located at 41.45° N. Lat; 82.01° W. Long. Elevation is 669 feet.
History: Named for Avon, New York. Settled c.1814. Incorporated 1918.
Population: 22,289; Growth (since 2000): 94.7%; Density: 1,071.2 persons per square mile; Race: 88.5% White, 8.7% Black/African American, 1.6% Asian, 0.0% American Indian/Alaska Native, 0.0% Native Hawaiian/Other Pacific Islander, 0.8% Two or more races, 3.1% Hispanic of any race; Average household size: 2.78; Median age: 40.5; Age under 18: 30.5%; Age 65 and over: 15.0%; Males per 100 females: 93.8; Marriage status: 26.1% never married, 59.0% now married, 1.1% separated, 6.7% widowed, 8.2% divorced; Foreign born: 3.3%; Speak English only: 92.9%; With disability: 8.2%; Veterans: 7.0%; Ancestry: 26.7% German, 21.3% Irish, 13.9% Italian, 12.1% English, 8.9% Polish
Employment: 23.4% management, business, and financial, 6.5% computer, engineering, and science, 11.2% education, legal, community service, arts, and media, 8.4% healthcare practitioners, 12.7% service, 27.5% sales and office, 4.7% natural resources, construction, and maintenance, 5.7% production, transportation, and material moving
Income: Per capita: $42,594; Median household: $90,846; Average household: $119,947; Households with income of $100,000 or more: 47.1%; Poverty rate: 3.8%
Educational Attainment: High school diploma or higher: 95.7%; Bachelor's degree or higher: 47.2%; Graduate/professional degree or higher: 18.2%

School District(s)

Avon Local (PK-12)
2015-16 Enrollment: 4,286 . . . . (440) 937-4680
Housing: Homeownership rate: 80.9%; Median home value: $262,100; Median year structure built: 2000; Homeowner vacancy rate: 0.6%; Median selected monthly owner costs: $1,831 with a mortgage, $599 without a mortgage; Median gross rent: $1,156 per month; Rental vacancy rate: 9.4%
Health Insurance: 97.8% have insurance; 89.6% have private insurance; 22.3% have public insurance; 2.2% do not have insurance; 0.5% of children under 18 do not have insurance
Transportation: Commute: 88.1% car, 0.3% public transportation, 0.4% walk, 8.9% work from home; Mean travel time to work: 25.1 minutes
Additional Information Contacts
City of Avon . . . . (440) 937-7800
http://www.cityofavon.com

AVON LAKE (city). Covers a land area of 11.129 square miles and a water area of 0 square miles. Located at 41.49° N. Lat; 82.02° W. Long. Elevation is 610 feet.
History: Named for Avon New York, which was named for the river in England. Avon Lake developed as a vacation area, with beaches for water sports.
Population: 23,221; Growth (since 2000): 28.0%; Density: 2,086.5 persons per square mile; Race: 94.3% White, 1.7% Black/African American, 0.7% Asian, 0.1% American Indian/Alaska Native, 0.0% Native Hawaiian/Other Pacific Islander, 2.1% Two or more races, 2.7% Hispanic of any race; Average household size: 2.55; Median age: 43.4; Age under 18: 26.0%; Age 65 and over: 17.2%; Males per 100 females: 93.3; Marriage status: 21.6% never married, 61.1% now married, 0.4% separated, 6.1% widowed, 11.3% divorced; Foreign born: 4.6%; Speak English only: 94.3%; With disability: 10.7%; Veterans: 7.3%; Ancestry: 31.2% German, 21.9% Irish, 13.6% English, 9.6% Italian, 7.4% Polish
Employment: 23.2% management, business, and financial, 4.1% computer, engineering, and science, 14.0% education, legal, community service, arts, and media, 8.9% healthcare practitioners, 11.8% service, 26.5% sales and office, 4.0% natural resources, construction, and maintenance, 7.4% production, transportation, and material moving
Income: Per capita: $41,668; Median household: $80,884; Average household: $106,163; Households with income of $100,000 or more: 40.2%; Poverty rate: 3.8%
Educational Attainment: High school diploma or higher: 96.3%; Bachelor's degree or higher: 51.5%; Graduate/professional degree or higher: 20.0%

School District(s)

Avon Lake City (PK-12)
2015-16 Enrollment: 3,765 . . . . (440) 933-6210

Housing: Homeownership rate: 79.7%; Median home value: $225,600; Median year structure built: 1988; Homeowner vacancy rate: 2.0%; Median selected monthly owner costs: $1,657 with a mortgage, $636 without a mortgage; Median gross rent: $1,122 per month; Rental vacancy rate: 4.1%
Health Insurance: 97.3% have insurance; 87.7% have private insurance; 23.0% have public insurance; 2.7% do not have insurance; 0.7% of children under 18 do not have insurance
Newspapers: North Ridgeville Press (weekly circulation 3,500); The Press (weekly circulation 9,000); West Life (weekly circulation 7,500)
Transportation: Commute: 90.6% car, 1.1% public transportation, 1.5% walk, 5.7% work from home; Mean travel time to work: 26.3 minutes
Additional Information Contacts
City of Avon Lake .... (440) 933-6141
http://www.avonlake.org

COLUMBIA STATION (unincorporated postal area)

ZCTA: 44028

Covers a land area of 33.199 square miles and a water area of 0.220 square miles. Located at 41.30° N. Lat; 81.94° W. Long. Elevation is 804 feet.
Population: 8,908; Growth (since 2000): -12.7%; Density: 268.3 persons per square mile; Race: 96.2% White, 0.0% Black/African American, 1.0% Asian, 0.0% American Indian/Alaska Native, 0.0% Native Hawaiian/Other Pacific Islander, 2.7% Two or more races, 1.0% Hispanic of any race; Average household size: 2.67; Median age: 46.3; Age under 18: 21.1%; Age 65 and over: 14.5%; Males per 100 females: 105.1; Marriage status: 26.5% never married, 55.8% now married, 1.9% separated, 6.3% widowed, 11.4% divorced; Foreign born: 3.4%; Speak English only: 96.9%; With disability: 12.0%; Veterans: 7.9%; Ancestry: 31.4% German, 17.6% Irish, 11.3% Italian, 10.7% Polish, 10.5% English
Employment: 14.1% management, business, and financial, 3.0% computer, engineering, and science, 8.8% education, legal, community service, arts, and media, 6.5% healthcare practitioners, 15.3% service, 19.5% sales and office, 13.4% natural resources, construction, and maintenance, 19.5% production, transportation, and material moving
Income: Per capita: $35,090; Median household: $68,810; Average household: $92,529; Households with income of $100,000 or more: 27.2%; Poverty rate: 7.1%
Educational Attainment: High school diploma or higher: 91.9%; Bachelor's degree or higher: 21.2%; Graduate/professional degree or higher: 9.3%

School District(s)

Columbia Local (KG-12)
2015-16 Enrollment: 836........................ (440) 236-5008
Housing: Homeownership rate: 89.1%; Median home value: $186,200; Median year structure built: 1967; Homeowner vacancy rate: 0.3%; Median selected monthly owner costs: $1,486 with a mortgage, $533 without a mortgage; Median gross rent: $982 per month; Rental vacancy rate: 0.0%
Health Insurance: 94.6% have insurance; 80.0% have private insurance; 26.7% have public insurance; 5.4% do not have insurance; 0.7% of children under 18 do not have insurance
Newspapers: The Rural-Urban Record (weekly circulation 10,000)
Transportation: Commute: 89.2% car, 1.0% public transportation, 0.3% walk, 8.0% work from home; Mean travel time to work: 26.7 minutes

EATON ESTATES (CDP).

Covers a land area of 0.869 square miles and a water area of 0.003 square miles. Located at 41.30° N. Lat; 82.01° W. Long. Elevation is 801 feet.
Population: 997; Growth (since 2000): -29.2%; Density: 1,146.6 persons per square mile; Race: 97.9% White, 0.0% Black/African American, 0.0% Asian, 0.0% American Indian/Alaska Native, 0.0% Native Hawaiian/Other Pacific Islander, 2.1% Two or more races, 3.1% Hispanic of any race; Average household size: 2.54; Median age: 44.7; Age under 18: 19.9%; Age 65 and over: 9.9%; Males per 100 females: 103.0; Marriage status: 26.6% never married, 52.6% now married, 1.0% separated, 1.4% widowed, 19.5% divorced; Foreign born: 0.0%; Speak English only: 100.0%; With disability: 24.3%; Veterans: 13.8%; Ancestry: 25.0% German, 14.9% Irish, 12.3% American, 10.9% English, 7.5% Hungarian
Employment: 3.6% management, business, and financial, 0.0% computer, engineering, and science, 5.4% education, legal, community service, arts, and media, 2.8% healthcare practitioners, 21.3% service, 30.7% sales and office, 15.1% natural resources, construction, and maintenance, 21.1% production, transportation, and material moving
Income: Per capita: $22,733; Median household: $57,037; Average household: $56,159; Households with income of $100,000 or more: 6.1%; Poverty rate: 10.9%
Educational Attainment: High school diploma or higher: 85.3%; Bachelor's degree or higher: 5.3%; Graduate/professional degree or higher: 1.3%
Housing: Homeownership rate: 79.1%; Median home value: $88,600; Median year structure built: 1956; Homeowner vacancy rate: 3.4%; Median selected monthly owner costs: $1,100 with a mortgage, $430 without a mortgage; Median gross rent: $898 per month; Rental vacancy rate: 0.0%
Health Insurance: 90.6% have insurance; 69.9% have private insurance; 30.2% have public insurance; 9.4% do not have insurance; 5.1% of children under 18 do not have insurance
Transportation: Commute: 94.6% car, 0.0% public transportation, 1.0% walk, 0.0% work from home; Mean travel time to work: 23.9 minutes

ELYRIA (city).

County seat. Covers a land area of 20.571 square miles and a water area of 0.274 square miles. Located at 41.37° N. Lat; 82.11° W. Long. Elevation is 738 feet.
History: Named for Herman Ely (1775-1852), merchant and founder of the town. Settlement at Elyria began in 1817 when Heman Ely, a New Englander, acquired land around the falls of the Black River and built a dam, grist mill, sawmill, and house. Novelist Sherwood Anderson managed a paint factory in Elyria before he became a writer.
Population: 53,928; Growth (since 2000): -3.6%; Density: 2,621.5 persons per square mile; Race: 77.8% White, 15.1% Black/African American, 0.9% Asian, 0.2% American Indian/Alaska Native, 0.1% Native Hawaiian/Other Pacific Islander, 5.1% Two or more races, 5.2% Hispanic of any race; Average household size: 2.35; Median age: 37.8; Age under 18: 23.1%; Age 65 and over: 14.4%; Males per 100 females: 91.6; Marriage status: 36.3% never married, 42.6% now married, 1.9% separated, 7.1% widowed, 13.9% divorced; Foreign born: 1.8%; Speak English only: 95.5%; With disability: 18.0%; Veterans: 9.4%; Ancestry: 22.7% German, 13.4% Irish, 9.5% English, 7.4% Polish, 7.4% American
Employment: 8.0% management, business, and financial, 3.6% computer, engineering, and science, 6.8% education, legal, community service, arts, and media, 6.3% healthcare practitioners, 22.2% service, 23.7% sales and office, 8.4% natural resources, construction, and maintenance, 21.0% production, transportation, and material moving
Income: Per capita: $21,727; Median household: $40,967; Average household: $50,422; Households with income of $100,000 or more: 10.7%; Poverty rate: 22.2%
Educational Attainment: High school diploma or higher: 86.7%; Bachelor's degree or higher: 15.4%; Graduate/professional degree or higher: 5.2%

School District(s)

Constellation Schools: Elyria Community (KG-08)
2015-16 Enrollment: 536........................ (440) 366-5225
Elyria City Schools (PK-12)
2015-16 Enrollment: 6,112....................... (440) 284-8201
Life Skills Center of Elyria (09-12)
2015-16 Enrollment: 119........................ (440) 324-1755

Two-year College(s)

Lorain County Community College (Public)
Fall 2016 Enrollment: 11,482 .... (440) 366-5222
2016-17 Tuition: In-state $3,679; Out-of-state $7,302

Vocational/Technical School(s)

Ross Medical Education Center-Elyria (Private, For-profit)
Fall 2016 Enrollment: 61........................ (440) 328-8877
2016-17 Tuition: $15,740
Housing: Homeownership rate: 58.3%; Median home value: $94,800; Median year structure built: 1965; Homeowner vacancy rate: 2.6%; Median selected monthly owner costs: $1,056 with a mortgage, $435 without a mortgage; Median gross rent: $710 per month; Rental vacancy rate: 5.5%
Health Insurance: 90.4% have insurance; 62.5% have private insurance; 41.8% have public insurance; 9.6% do not have insurance; 2.4% of children under 18 do not have insurance
Hospitals: University Hospitals - Elyria Medical Center (348 beds)
Safety: Violent crime rate: 30.0 per 10,000 population; Property crime rate: 276.5 per 10,000 population
Newspapers: Chronicle-Telegram (daily circulation 24,400)
Transportation: Commute: 93.2% car, 0.7% public transportation, 1.0% walk, 1.6% work from home; Mean travel time to work: 21.7 minutes; Amtrak: Train service available.
Additional Information Contacts

City of Elyria . . . . (440) 326-1500
http://www.cityofelyria.org

GRAFTON (village). Covers a land area of 4.712 square miles and a water area of 0.029 square miles. Located at 41.28° N. Lat; 82.03° W. Long. Elevation is 801 feet.

Population: 6,075; Growth (since 2000): 163.9%; Density: 1,289.2 persons per square mile; Race: 64.2% White, 30.4% Black/African American, 0.2% Asian, 1.1% American Indian/Alaska Native, 0.0% Native Hawaiian/Other Pacific Islander, 3.4% Two or more races, 4.0% Hispanic of any race; Average household size: 2.41; Median age: 42.0; Age under 18: 7.6%; Age 65 and over: 8.6%; Males per 100 females: 392.3; Marriage status: 46.8% never married, 31.4% now married, 4.0% separated, 4.1% widowed, 17.8% divorced; Foreign born: 1.1%; Speak English only: 94.2%; With disability: 12.7%; Veterans: 13.5%; Ancestry: 20.3% German, 13.9% Irish, 8.5% English, 7.9% Italian, 5.4% African

Employment: 11.5% management, business, and financial, 4.5% computer, engineering, and science, 11.4% education, legal, community service, arts, and media, 6.2% healthcare practitioners, 13.1% service, 29.7% sales and office, 9.3% natural resources, construction, and maintenance, 14.3% production, transportation, and material moving

Income: Per capita: $14,390; Median household: $52,545; Average household: $62,469; Households with income of $100,000 or more: 18.5%; Poverty rate: 9.6%

Educational Attainment: High school diploma or higher: 79.8%; Bachelor's degree or higher: 6.5%; Graduate/professional degree or higher: 2.2%

School District(s)

Midview Local (PK-12)
2015-16 Enrollment: 2,981 . . . . (877) 644-6338

Housing: Homeownership rate: 73.3%; Median home value: $135,000; Median year structure built: 1973; Homeowner vacancy rate: 0.0%; Median selected monthly owner costs: $1,187 with a mortgage, $471 without a mortgage; Median gross rent: $690 per month; Rental vacancy rate: 0.0%

Health Insurance: 96.0% have insurance; 77.0% have private insurance; 33.2% have public insurance; 4.0% do not have insurance; 2.0% of children under 18 do not have insurance

Safety: Violent crime rate: 6.6 per 10,000 population; Property crime rate: 62.2 per 10,000 population

Transportation: Commute: 94.4% car, 0.9% public transportation, 1.1% walk, 3.2% work from home; Mean travel time to work: 26.2 minutes

KIPTON (village). Covers a land area of 0.440 square miles and a water area of 0.005 square miles. Located at 41.27° N. Lat; 82.30° W. Long. Elevation is 850 feet.

Population: 245; Growth (since 2000): -7.5%; Density: 556.3 persons per square mile; Race: 100.0% White, 0.0% Black/African American, 0.0% Asian, 0.0% American Indian/Alaska Native, 0.0% Native Hawaiian/Other Pacific Islander, 0.0% Two or more races, 0.0% Hispanic of any race; Average household size: 2.31; Median age: 46.6; Age under 18: 16.3%; Age 65 and over: 12.7%; Males per 100 females: 120.9; Marriage status: 25.0% never married, 61.5% now married, 2.4% separated, 5.3% widowed, 8.2% divorced; Foreign born: 2.9%; Speak English only: 93.4%; With disability: 14.3%; Veterans: 13.2%; Ancestry: 21.6% German, 19.6% Irish, 19.2% Italian, 16.7% English, 13.1% American

Employment: 4.8% management, business, and financial, 4.8% computer, engineering, and science, 2.8% education, legal, community service, arts, and media, 2.8% healthcare practitioners, 24.8% service, 16.6% sales and office, 16.6% natural resources, construction, and maintenance, 26.9% production, transportation, and material moving

Income: Per capita: $27,882; Median household: $58,333; Average household: $63,278; Households with income of $100,000 or more: 21.7%; Poverty rate: 6.1%

Educational Attainment: High school diploma or higher: 94.7%; Bachelor's degree or higher: 4.2%; Graduate/professional degree or higher: n/a

Housing: Homeownership rate: 76.4%; Median home value: $92,700; Median year structure built: Before 1940; Homeowner vacancy rate: 0.0%; Median selected monthly owner costs: $983 with a mortgage, $408 without a mortgage; Median gross rent: $721 per month; Rental vacancy rate: 0.0%

Health Insurance: 93.9% have insurance; 84.1% have private insurance; 24.9% have public insurance; 6.1% do not have insurance; 0.0% of children under 18 do not have insurance

Transportation: Commute: 98.6% car, 0.0% public transportation, 0.0% walk, 1.4% work from home; Mean travel time to work: 30.8 minutes

LAGRANGE (village). Covers a land area of 2.010 square miles and a water area of 0.004 square miles. Located at 41.24° N. Lat; 82.12° W. Long. Elevation is 823 feet.

Population: 2,357; Growth (since 2000): 29.9%; Density: 1,172.9 persons per square mile; Race: 98.6% White, 0.9% Black/African American, 0.0% Asian, 0.1% American Indian/Alaska Native, 0.0% Native Hawaiian/Other Pacific Islander, 0.4% Two or more races, 1.9% Hispanic of any race; Average household size: 2.73; Median age: 41.5; Age under 18: 26.4%; Age 65 and over: 14.4%; Males per 100 females: 94.0; Marriage status: 26.9% never married, 52.3% now married, 1.2% separated, 7.7% widowed, 13.1% divorced; Foreign born: 1.1%; Speak English only: 98.6%; With disability: 10.8%; Veterans: 11.2%; Ancestry: 31.7% German, 20.4% Irish, 11.9% English, 8.5% Italian, 8.2% American

Employment: 12.2% management, business, and financial, 2.4% computer, engineering, and science, 13.7% education, legal, community service, arts, and media, 5.2% healthcare practitioners, 16.5% service, 23.8% sales and office, 6.9% natural resources, construction, and maintenance, 19.3% production, transportation, and material moving

Income: Per capita: $25,062; Median household: $58,088; Average household: $68,384; Households with income of $100,000 or more: 20.8%; Poverty rate: 10.5%

Educational Attainment: High school diploma or higher: 92.3%; Bachelor's degree or higher: 18.7%; Graduate/professional degree or higher: 4.5%

School District(s)

Keystone Local (KG-12)
2015-16 Enrollment: 1,519 . . . . (440) 355-2424

Housing: Homeownership rate: 76.4%; Median home value: $153,800; Median year structure built: 1985; Homeowner vacancy rate: 1.4%; Median selected monthly owner costs: $1,256 with a mortgage, $504 without a mortgage; Median gross rent: $748 per month; Rental vacancy rate: 3.4%

Health Insurance: 95.0% have insurance; 82.1% have private insurance; 26.3% have public insurance; 5.0% do not have insurance; 2.1% of children under 18 do not have insurance

Transportation: Commute: 90.5% car, 0.2% public transportation, 3.1% walk, 5.8% work from home; Mean travel time to work: 26.7 minutes

LORAIN (city). Covers a land area of 23.673 square miles and a water area of 0.474 square miles. Located at 41.44° N. Lat; 82.18° W. Long. Elevation is 610 feet.

History: Named for the province of Lorraine in France. Lorain had its beginnings in 1807 when Nathan Perry and the Azariah Beebes established a trading post on the south shore of Lake Erie, at the mouth of the Black River. In 1810 others arrived, including John Reid, whose home became the post office, justice's office, and tavern. By 1819 shipbuilding began in Lorain. The town had first been known as Mouth of Black River, but in 1836 it was incorporated as Charleston. When the Cleveland, Lorain & Wheeling Railroad arrived in 1872, a new charter was granted under the name of Lorain. The first steel company came to Lorain in 1894, and was later acquired by the United States Steel Corporation, bringing immigrants from many countries to work here.

Population: 63,714; Growth (since 2000): -7.2%; Density: 2,691.4 persons per square mile; Race: 73.4% White, 16.2% Black/African American, 0.9% Asian, 0.5% American Indian/Alaska Native, 0.0% Native Hawaiian/Other Pacific Islander, 5.2% Two or more races, 28.3% Hispanic of any race; Average household size: 2.51; Median age: 36.9; Age under 18: 25.2%; Age 65 and over: 15.3%; Males per 100 females: 90.5; Marriage status: 36.7% never married, 42.3% now married, 3.2% separated, 7.3% widowed, 13.7% divorced; Foreign born: 3.0%; Speak English only: 81.6%; With disability: 20.1%; Veterans: 9.0%; Ancestry: 16.0% German, 10.6% Irish, 7.7% Italian, 6.6% Polish, 6.2% English

Employment: 8.7% management, business, and financial, 2.6% computer, engineering, and science, 7.3% education, legal, community service, arts, and media, 4.9% healthcare practitioners, 21.3% service, 23.4% sales and office, 9.3% natural resources, construction, and maintenance, 22.5% production, transportation, and material moving

Income: Per capita: $19,573; Median household: $35,753; Average household: $48,238; Households with income of $100,000 or more: 9.3%; Poverty rate: 26.2%

Educational Attainment: High school diploma or higher: 82.4%; Bachelor's degree or higher: 11.7%; Graduate/professional degree or higher: 4.4%

School District(s)

Academy of Arts and Sciences (KG-01)
2015-16 Enrollment: 171. . . . . (440) 244-0156
Clearview Local (KG-12)
2015-16 Enrollment: 1,601 . . . . (440) 233-5412
Constellation Schools: Lorain Community Elementary (KG-04)
2015-16 Enrollment: 215. . . . . (440) 204-2130
Constellation Schools: Lorain Community Middle (05-08)
2015-16 Enrollment: 131. . . . . (440) 242-2023
Horizon Science Academy Lorain (KG-12)
2015-16 Enrollment: 628. . . . . (440) 282-4277
Lorain City (PK-12)
2015-16 Enrollment: 6,559 . . . . (440) 233-2271
Lorain K-12 Digital Academy (KG-12)
2015-16 Enrollment: 128. . . . . (440) 282-4087
Lorain Preparatory Academy (02-08)
2015-16 Enrollment: 315. . . . . (440) 282-3127
Summit Academy Community School Alternative Learners-Lorain (KG-05)
2015-16 Enrollment: 138. . . . . (440) 277-4110
Summit Academy Middle School - Lorain (06-08)
2015-16 Enrollment: 91. . . . . (440) 288-0448
Summit Academy Secondary - Lorain (09-12)
2015-16 Enrollment: 83. . . . . (440) 288-0448

Vocational/Technical School(s)

Northern Institute of Cosmetology (Private, For-profit)
Fall 2016 Enrollment: 21 . . . . (440) 244-4282
2016-17 Tuition: $8,900

Housing: Homeownership rate: 57.9%; Median home value: $85,700; Median year structure built: 1960; Homeowner vacancy rate: 1.7%; Median selected monthly owner costs: $1,037 with a mortgage, $355 without a mortgage; Median gross rent: $659 per month; Rental vacancy rate: 8.3%
Health Insurance: 90.1% have insurance; 52.7% have private insurance; 49.2% have public insurance; 9.9% do not have insurance; 2.7% of children under 18 do not have insurance
Hospitals: Mercy Regional Medical Center
Newspapers: Morning Journal (daily circulation 26,700)
Transportation: Commute: 92.5% car, 0.7% public transportation, 1.6% walk, 1.7% work from home; Mean travel time to work: 22.4 minutes
Airports: Lorain County Regional (general aviation)
Additional Information Contacts
City of Lorain . . . . (440) 204-2002
http://www.cityoflorain.org

NORTH RIDGEVILLE (city). Covers a land area of 23.438 square miles and a water area of 0.140 square miles. Located at 41.39° N. Lat; 82.02° W. Long. Elevation is 728 feet.
Population: 31,832; Growth (since 2000): 42.5%; Density: 1,358.1 persons per square mile; Race: 92.9% White, 1.6% Black/African American, 1.7% Asian, 0.1% American Indian/Alaska Native, 0.0% Native Hawaiian/Other Pacific Islander, 3.0% Two or more races, 3.8% Hispanic of any race; Average household size: 2.58; Median age: 41.7; Age under 18: 22.9%; Age 65 and over: 19.5%; Males per 100 females: 96.3; Marriage status: 21.7% never married, 61.9% now married, 1.3% separated, 6.7% widowed, 9.6% divorced; Foreign born: 4.7%; Speak English only: 93.5%; With disability: 10.7%; Veterans: 9.8%; Ancestry: 28.4% German, 20.6% Irish, 11.4% Italian, 9.8% Polish, 9.3% English
Employment: 16.3% management, business, and financial, 5.8% computer, engineering, and science, 10.6% education, legal, community service, arts, and media, 8.8% healthcare practitioners, 14.1% service, 26.3% sales and office, 6.5% natural resources, construction, and maintenance, 11.5% production, transportation, and material moving
Income: Per capita: $31,399; Median household: $68,778; Average household: $80,662; Households with income of $100,000 or more: 28.4%; Poverty rate: 4.9%
Educational Attainment: High school diploma or higher: 92.3%; Bachelor's degree or higher: 32.6%; Graduate/professional degree or higher: 11.5%

School District(s)

North Ridgeville City (PK-12)
2015-16 Enrollment: 4,190 . . . . (440) 327-4444

Housing: Homeownership rate: 87.0%; Median home value: $160,300; Median year structure built: 1986; Homeowner vacancy rate: 0.6%; Median selected monthly owner costs: $1,402 with a mortgage, $495 without a mortgage; Median gross rent: $1,071 per month; Rental vacancy rate: 5.1%
Health Insurance: 95.5% have insurance; 83.1% have private insurance; 27.6% have public insurance; 4.5% do not have insurance; 1.6% of children under 18 do not have insurance
Safety: Violent crime rate: 3.6 per 10,000 population; Property crime rate: 58.3 per 10,000 population
Transportation: Commute: 93.9% car, 0.9% public transportation, 0.5% walk, 3.6% work from home; Mean travel time to work: 27.4 minutes
Additional Information Contacts
City of North Ridgeville . . . . (440) 353-0819
http://www.nridgeville.org

OBERLIN (city). Covers a land area of 4.919 square miles and a water area of 0.038 square miles. Located at 41.29° N. Lat; 82.22° W. Long. Elevation is 810 feet.
History: Oberlin College was founded in 1833 by John L. Shipherd, a Presbyterian minister from Elyria, and Philo P. Steward, a missionary. In 1837 four women applied for the regular college course. When they were accepted, Oberlin became the first coeducational college in the country.
Population: 8,353; Growth (since 2000): 1.9%; Density: 1,698.2 persons per square mile; Race: 68.5% White, 15.6% Black/African American, 5.4% Asian, 0.4% American Indian/Alaska Native, 0.0% Native Hawaiian/Other Pacific Islander, 9.0% Two or more races, 4.0% Hispanic of any race; Average household size: 2.22; Median age: 24.5; Age under 18: 15.4%; Age 65 and over: 16.0%; Males per 100 females: 85.1; Marriage status: 54.2% never married, 31.6% now married, 1.4% separated, 6.1% widowed, 8.0% divorced; Foreign born: 7.8%; Speak English only: 90.9%; With disability: 15.8%; Veterans: 5.9%; Ancestry: 16.6% German, 12.4% English, 10.2% Irish, 5.3% Italian, 4.2% Polish
Employment: 8.7% management, business, and financial, 3.9% computer, engineering, and science, 29.7% education, legal, community service, arts, and media, 2.4% healthcare practitioners, 23.9% service, 21.1% sales and office, 4.2% natural resources, construction, and maintenance, 6.2% production, transportation, and material moving
Income: Per capita: $22,298; Median household: $51,404; Average household: $65,528; Households with income of $100,000 or more: 21.7%; Poverty rate: 20.6%
Educational Attainment: High school diploma or higher: 93.5%; Bachelor's degree or higher: 45.8%; Graduate/professional degree or higher: 30.8%

School District(s)

Firelands Local (KG-12)
2015-16 Enrollment: 1,637 . . . . (440) 965-5821
Lorain County Jvs (09-12)
2015-16 Enrollment: n/a . . . . (440) 774-1051
Oberlin City Schools (PK-12)
2015-16 Enrollment: 985. . . . . (440) 774-1458

Four-year College(s)

Oberlin College (Private, Not-for-profit)
Fall 2016 Enrollment: 2,912 . . . . (440) 775-8411
2016-17 Tuition: In-state $52,002; Out-of-state $52,002

Two-year College(s)

Lorain County Joint Vocational School District (Public)
Fall 2016 Enrollment: 122 . . . . (440) 774-1051

Housing: Homeownership rate: 54.9%; Median home value: $145,000; Median year structure built: 1961; Homeowner vacancy rate: 0.0%; Median selected monthly owner costs: $1,270 with a mortgage, $439 without a mortgage; Median gross rent: $752 per month; Rental vacancy rate: 2.8%
Health Insurance: 94.8% have insurance; 80.2% have private insurance; 29.0% have public insurance; 5.2% do not have insurance; 0.3% of children under 18 do not have insurance
Hospitals: Mercy Allen Hospital (25 beds)
Safety: Violent crime rate: 45.6 per 10,000 population; Property crime rate: 254.1 per 10,000 population
Newspapers: Oberlin News Tribune (weekly circulation 3,500)
Transportation: Commute: 50.7% car, 0.3% public transportation, 39.6% walk, 5.2% work from home; Mean travel time to work: 14.9 minutes

---

PHEASANT RUN (CDP). Covers a land area of 0.934 square miles and a water area of 0.036 square miles. Located at 41.21° N. Lat; 82.15° W. Long. Elevation is 833 feet.
Population: 1,459; Growth (since 2000): n/a; Density: 1,562.7 persons per square mile; Race: 98.7% White, 0.0% Black/African American, 0.0% Asian, 0.0% American Indian/Alaska Native, 0.0% Native Hawaiian/Other Pacific Islander, 1.3% Two or more races, 1.3% Hispanic of any race; Average household size: 2.57; Median age: 38.7; Age under 18: 27.9%;

Age 65 and over: 14.1%; Males per 100 females: 101.0; Marriage status: 14.9% never married, 61.6% now married, 5.7% separated, 2.3% widowed, 21.2% divorced; Foreign born: 0.0%; Speak English only: 95.0%; With disability: 11.3%; Veterans: 9.6%; Ancestry: 33.4% German, 23.9% Irish, 7.0% English, 6.8% Dutch, 5.0% Polish
Employment: 9.6% management, business, and financial, 0.0% computer, engineering, and science, 2.3% education, legal, community service, arts, and media, 6.6% healthcare practitioners, 12.4% service, 35.2% sales and office, 20.0% natural resources, construction, and maintenance, 13.8% production, transportation, and material moving
Income: Per capita: $23,099; Median household: $46,629; Average household: $58,522; Households with income of $100,000 or more: 14.6%; Poverty rate: 5.8%
Educational Attainment: High school diploma or higher: 82.2%; Bachelor's degree or higher: 21.1%; Graduate/professional degree or higher: 8.0%
Housing: Homeownership rate: 71.1%; Median home value: $100,500; Median year structure built: 1978; Homeowner vacancy rate: 0.0%; Median selected monthly owner costs: $1,191 with a mortgage, $369 without a mortgage; Median gross rent: $739 per month; Rental vacancy rate: 0.0%
Health Insurance: 89.0% have insurance; 74.4% have private insurance; 39.5% have public insurance; 11.0% do not have insurance; 15.5% of children under 18 do not have insurance
Transportation: Commute: 84.9% car, 0.0% public transportation, 0.0% walk, 4.7% work from home; Mean travel time to work: 35.3 minutes

ROCHESTER (village). Covers a land area of 1.118 square miles and a water area of 0.007 square miles. Located at 41.12° N. Lat; 82.31° W. Long. Elevation is 928 feet.
Population: 185; Growth (since 2000): -2.6%; Density: 165.5 persons per square mile; Race: 98.9% White, 0.0% Black/African American, 0.0% Asian, 0.5% American Indian/Alaska Native, 0.0% Native Hawaiian/Other Pacific Islander, 0.5% Two or more races, 2.2% Hispanic of any race; Average household size: 2.72; Median age: 40.8; Age under 18: 22.2%; Age 65 and over: 23.2%; Males per 100 females: 95.7; Marriage status: 24.5% never married, 59.7% now married, 0.0% separated, 10.1% widowed, 5.7% divorced; Foreign born: 0.0%; Speak English only: 98.8%; With disability: 10.8%; Veterans: 6.9%; Ancestry: 30.3% German, 13.0% English, 12.4% Italian, 10.8% American, 9.2% Irish
Employment: 2.4% management, business, and financial, 8.3% computer, engineering, and science, 11.9% education, legal, community service, arts, and media, 8.3% healthcare practitioners, 3.6% service, 17.9% sales and office, 1.2% natural resources, construction, and maintenance, 46.4% production, transportation, and material moving
Income: Per capita: $26,236; Median household: $62,188; Average household: $67,925; Households with income of $100,000 or more: 16.2%; Poverty rate: 1.1%
Educational Attainment: High school diploma or higher: 84.8%; Bachelor's degree or higher: 11.4%; Graduate/professional degree or higher: 6.1%
Housing: Homeownership rate: 82.4%; Median home value: $130,600; Median year structure built: 1950; Homeowner vacancy rate: 0.0%; Median selected monthly owner costs: $1,375 with a mortgage, $450 without a mortgage; Median gross rent: $950 per month; Rental vacancy rate: 0.0%
Health Insurance: 95.7% have insurance; 76.2% have private insurance; 42.7% have public insurance; 4.3% do not have insurance; 4.9% of children under 18 do not have insurance
Transportation: Commute: 96.2% car, 0.0% public transportation, 0.0% walk, 1.3% work from home; Mean travel time to work: 26.9 minutes

SHEFFIELD (village). Covers a land area of 10.743 square miles and a water area of 0.098 square miles. Located at 41.46° N. Lat; 82.09° W. Long. Elevation is 669 feet.
History: Incorporated 1933.
Population: 4,045; Growth (since 2000): 37.2%; Density: 376.5 persons per square mile; Race: 90.3% White, 6.0% Black/African American, 2.3% Asian, 1.1% American Indian/Alaska Native, 0.0% Native Hawaiian/Other Pacific Islander, 0.3% Two or more races, 8.8% Hispanic of any race; Average household size: 2.44; Median age: 48.0; Age under 18: 18.4%; Age 65 and over: 17.9%; Males per 100 females: 97.4; Marriage status: 21.1% never married, 62.7% now married, 1.3% separated, 6.9% widowed, 9.3% divorced; Foreign born: 4.7%; Speak English only: 91.7%; With disability: 13.9%; Veterans: 10.0%; Ancestry: 24.5% German, 15.7% Irish, 8.6% English, 7.7% Polish, 6.9% American
Employment: 17.9% management, business, and financial, 4.1% computer, engineering, and science, 11.1% education, legal, community service, arts, and media, 6.7% healthcare practitioners, 15.9% service, 26.5% sales and office, 4.4% natural resources, construction, and maintenance, 13.4% production, transportation, and material moving
Income: Per capita: $35,122; Median household: $75,461; Average household: $85,377; Households with income of $100,000 or more: 37.3%; Poverty rate: 5.1%
Educational Attainment: High school diploma or higher: 95.8%; Bachelor's degree or higher: 28.4%; Graduate/professional degree or higher: 13.7%

School District(s)

Sheffield-Sheffield Lake City (PK-12)
2015-16 Enrollment: 1,702 . . . . (440) 949-6181

Two-year College(s)

Ohio Business College-Sheffield (Private, For-profit)
Fall 2016 Enrollment: 309 . . . . (440) 934-3101
2016-17 Tuition: In-state $9,025; Out-of-state $9,025
Vanity School of Cosmetology (Private, For-profit)
Fall 2016 Enrollment: 31 . . . . (440) 934-3353

Housing: Homeownership rate: 71.0%; Median home value: $183,200; Median year structure built: 1994; Homeowner vacancy rate: 0.0%; Median selected monthly owner costs: $1,515 with a mortgage, $543 without a mortgage; Median gross rent: $1,164 per month; Rental vacancy rate: 0.0%
Health Insurance: 94.0% have insurance; 81.9% have private insurance; 31.0% have public insurance; 6.0% do not have insurance; 2.4% of children under 18 do not have insurance
Transportation: Commute: 91.2% car, 0.0% public transportation, 0.1% walk, 7.8% work from home; Mean travel time to work: 22.6 minutes

SHEFFIELD LAKE (city). Covers a land area of 2.477 square miles and a water area of 0 square miles. Located at 41.49° N. Lat; 82.10° W. Long. Elevation is 600 feet.
History: Incorporated 1920.
Population: 9,055; Growth (since 2000): -3.4%; Density: 3,656.2 persons per square mile; Race: 94.6% White, 0.6% Black/African American, 0.2% Asian, 0.4% American Indian/Alaska Native, 0.0% Native Hawaiian/Other Pacific Islander, 4.0% Two or more races, 9.9% Hispanic of any race; Average household size: 2.53; Median age: 38.6; Age under 18: 22.2%; Age 65 and over: 13.8%; Males per 100 females: 97.9; Marriage status: 31.9% never married, 48.2% now married, 1.3% separated, 8.2% widowed, 11.7% divorced; Foreign born: 1.1%; Speak English only: 96.8%; With disability: 16.5%; Veterans: 10.5%; Ancestry: 26.3% German, 14.9% Italian, 14.1% Irish, 10.0% American, 9.7% Polish
Employment: 10.4% management, business, and financial, 3.2% computer, engineering, and science, 9.9% education, legal, community service, arts, and media, 8.7% healthcare practitioners, 16.8% service, 28.4% sales and office, 8.7% natural resources, construction, and maintenance, 13.8% production, transportation, and material moving
Income: Per capita: $24,917; Median household: $58,153; Average household: $61,393; Households with income of $100,000 or more: 12.4%; Poverty rate: 9.4%
Educational Attainment: High school diploma or higher: 91.8%; Bachelor's degree or higher: 21.3%; Graduate/professional degree or higher: 5.0%

School District(s)

Sheffield-Sheffield Lake City (PK-12)
2015-16 Enrollment: 1,702 . . . . (440) 949-6181

Housing: Homeownership rate: 71.8%; Median home value: $109,500; Median year structure built: 1968; Homeowner vacancy rate: 3.9%; Median selected monthly owner costs: $1,101 with a mortgage, $424 without a mortgage; Median gross rent: $921 per month; Rental vacancy rate: 6.3%
Health Insurance: 92.0% have insurance; 71.8% have private insurance; 33.5% have public insurance; 8.0% do not have insurance; 1.2% of children under 18 do not have insurance
Transportation: Commute: 96.7% car, 0.8% public transportation, 2.0% walk, 0.3% work from home; Mean travel time to work: 29.3 minutes

SOUTH AMHERST (village). Covers a land area of 2.472 square miles and a water area of 0.020 square miles. Located at 41.35° N. Lat; 82.24° W. Long. Elevation is 791 feet.
History: South Amherst was at one time called Podunk. The town developed as a quarrying center.

Population: 1,723; Growth (since 2000): -7.5%; Density: 697.0 persons per square mile; Race: 97.9% White, 0.1% Black/African American, 0.6% Asian, 0.0% American Indian/Alaska Native, 0.0% Native Hawaiian/Other Pacific Islander, 1.2% Two or more races, 4.6% Hispanic of any race; Average household size: 2.40; Median age: 50.0; Age under 18: 16.1%; Age 65 and over: 22.3%; Males per 100 females: 95.6; Marriage status: 25.2% never married, 55.7% now married, 0.3% separated, 5.4% widowed, 13.6% divorced; Foreign born: 1.2%; Speak English only: 95.3%; With disability: 14.3%; Veterans: 9.8%; Ancestry: 31.9% German, 18.3% Irish, 15.4% English, 12.1% Polish, 8.8% American
Employment: 10.8% management, business, and financial, 1.6% computer, engineering, and science, 4.9% education, legal, community service, arts, and media, 7.7% healthcare practitioners, 17.7% service, 22.8% sales and office, 12.7% natural resources, construction, and maintenance, 21.7% production, transportation, and material moving
Income: Per capita: $26,035; Median household: $55,250; Average household: $61,697; Households with income of $100,000 or more: 14.7%; Poverty rate: 5.7%
Educational Attainment: High school diploma or higher: 87.7%; Bachelor's degree or higher: 9.0%; Graduate/professional degree or higher: 1.7%

School District(s)

Firelands Local (KG-12)
2015-16 Enrollment: 1,637 . . . . (440) 965-5821
Housing: Homeownership rate: 82.6%; Median home value: $131,900; Median year structure built: 1955; Homeowner vacancy rate: 0.0%; Median selected monthly owner costs: $1,121 with a mortgage, $419 without a mortgage; Median gross rent: $657 per month; Rental vacancy rate: 6.1%
Health Insurance: 95.2% have insurance; 81.4% have private insurance; 34.0% have public insurance; 4.8% do not have insurance; 0.0% of children under 18 do not have insurance
Transportation: Commute: 98.4% car, 0.0% public transportation, 0.0% walk, 1.6% work from home; Mean travel time to work: 22.7 minutes

VERMILION (city). Covers a land area of 10.655 square miles and a water area of 0.166 square miles. Located at 41.41° N. Lat; 82.32° W. Long.
History: Vermilion was settled in 1808 along the Vermilion River, named for the red clay found along the river bottom. Vermilion developed as a fishing center and a tourist resort.
Population: 10,491; Growth (since 2000): -4.0%; Density: 984.6 persons per square mile; Race: 98.2% White, 0.0% Black/African American, 0.3% Asian, 0.0% American Indian/Alaska Native, 0.0% Native Hawaiian/Other Pacific Islander, 1.5% Two or more races, 3.3% Hispanic of any race; Average household size: 2.29; Median age: 48.3; Age under 18: 17.4%; Age 65 and over: 23.2%; Males per 100 females: 94.5; Marriage status: 23.0% never married, 54.5% now married, 0.7% separated, 9.0% widowed, 13.4% divorced; Foreign born: 1.8%; Speak English only: 98.4%; With disability: 17.0%; Veterans: 12.1%; Ancestry: 26.3% German, 14.0% Irish, 13.6% English, 9.0% Italian, 7.8% Polish
Employment: 11.5% management, business, and financial, 1.9% computer, engineering, and science, 7.6% education, legal, community service, arts, and media, 7.9% healthcare practitioners, 18.9% service, 22.6% sales and office, 12.3% natural resources, construction, and maintenance, 17.2% production, transportation, and material moving
Income: Per capita: $29,852; Median household: $51,108; Average household: $68,097; Households with income of $100,000 or more: 21.2%; Poverty rate: 15.1%
Educational Attainment: High school diploma or higher: 88.0%; Bachelor's degree or higher: 21.1%; Graduate/professional degree or higher: 10.3%

School District(s)

Vermilion Local (KG-12)
2015-16 Enrollment: 1,851 . . . . (440) 204-1700
Housing: Homeownership rate: 74.8%; Median home value: $131,900; Median year structure built: 1969; Homeowner vacancy rate: 3.5%; Median selected monthly owner costs: $1,224 with a mortgage, $468 without a mortgage; Median gross rent: $801 per month; Rental vacancy rate: 6.1%
Health Insurance: 92.9% have insurance; 73.2% have private insurance; 38.7% have public insurance; 7.1% do not have insurance; 2.6% of children under 18 do not have insurance
Safety: Violent crime rate: 2.9 per 10,000 population; Property crime rate: 102.8 per 10,000 population
Newspapers: Vermilion Photojournal (weekly circulation 3,000)
Transportation: Commute: 94.4% car, 0.1% public transportation, 3.3% walk, 1.6% work from home; Mean travel time to work: 27.5 minutes

WELLINGTON (village). Covers a land area of 3.595 square miles and a water area of 0.291 square miles. Located at 41.15° N. Lat; 82.23° W. Long. Elevation is 850 feet.
History: Wellington developed in the dairy and grain area of Lorain County. It was an abolitionist center, and in 1858, when a Federal marshal stopped in Wellington with a runaway slave, the residents rescued the slave. Many of them were then arrested and charged with aiding a fugitive slave.
Population: 5,063; Growth (since 2000): 12.2%; Density: 1,408.2 persons per square mile; Race: 92.6% White, 1.0% Black/African American, 0.4% Asian, 0.1% American Indian/Alaska Native, 0.0% Native Hawaiian/Other Pacific Islander, 5.3% Two or more races, 3.9% Hispanic of any race; Average household size: 2.55; Median age: 37.7; Age under 18: 23.9%; Age 65 and over: 18.6%; Males per 100 females: 92.1; Marriage status: 29.1% never married, 50.3% now married, 2.5% separated, 7.8% widowed, 12.8% divorced; Foreign born: 1.3%; Speak English only: 99.0%; With disability: 16.1%; Veterans: 6.2%; Ancestry: 29.2% German, 15.0% English, 11.6% American, 9.9% Irish, 8.0% Polish
Employment: 10.9% management, business, and financial, 4.8% computer, engineering, and science, 4.2% education, legal, community service, arts, and media, 5.7% healthcare practitioners, 18.8% service, 23.4% sales and office, 6.9% natural resources, construction, and maintenance, 25.3% production, transportation, and material moving
Income: Per capita: $23,150; Median household: $46,207; Average household: $58,200; Households with income of $100,000 or more: 16.4%; Poverty rate: 11.8%
Educational Attainment: High school diploma or higher: 90.5%; Bachelor's degree or higher: 16.8%; Graduate/professional degree or higher: 7.0%

School District(s)

Wellington Exempted Village (PK-12)
2015-16 Enrollment: 1,143 . . . . (440) 647-4286
Housing: Homeownership rate: 54.4%; Median home value: $130,900; Median year structure built: 1969; Homeowner vacancy rate: 0.0%; Median selected monthly owner costs: $1,269 with a mortgage, $351 without a mortgage; Median gross rent: $714 per month; Rental vacancy rate: 0.0%
Health Insurance: 92.8% have insurance; 74.2% have private insurance; 35.2% have public insurance; 7.2% do not have insurance; 0.0% of children under 18 do not have insurance
Newspapers: Wellington Enterprise (weekly circulation 3,000)
Transportation: Commute: 85.2% car, 0.6% public transportation, 8.4% walk, 3.3% work from home; Mean travel time to work: 29.4 minutes

Lucas County

Located in northwestern Ohio; bounded on the north by Michigan, on the southeast by the Maumee River, and on the northeast by the west end of Lake Erie. Covers a land area of 340.855 square miles, a water area of 255.022 square miles, and is located in the Eastern Time Zone at 41.68° N. Lat., 83.47° W. Long. The county was founded in 1835. County seat is Toledo.

Lucas County is part of the Toledo, OH Metropolitan Statistical Area. The entire metro area includes: Fulton County, OH; Lucas County, OH; Wood County, OH

Weather Station: Toledo Express Arpt Elevation: 668 feet

	Jan	Feb	Mar	Apr	May	Jun	Jul	Aug	Sep	Oct	Nov	Dec
High	32	36	46	60	71	80	84	82	75	62	49	36
Low	18	20	28	38	48	58	62	61	53	41	33	23
Precip	2.1	2.0	2.5	3.1	3.5	3.5	3.2	3.3	2.8	2.6	2.8	2.7
Snow	11.3	8.6	5.9	1.4	na	na	na	na	na	na	1.9	7.4

High and Low temperatures in degrees Fahrenheit; Precipitation and Snow in inches

Population: 434,800; Growth (since 2000): -4.5%; Density: 1,275.6 persons per square mile; Race: 72.8% White, 19.1% Black/African American, 1.7% Asian, 0.3% American Indian/Alaska Native, 0.0% Native Hawaiian/Other Pacific Islander, 4.0% two or more races, 6.7% Hispanic of any race; Average household size: 2.38; Median age: 37.9; Age under 18: 23.2%; Age 65 and over: 14.6%; Males per 100 females: 93.9; Marriage status: 36.0% never married, 43.4% now married, 1.9% separated, 6.7% widowed, 13.9% divorced; Foreign born: 3.5%; Speak English only: 93.6%;

With disability: 15.2%; Veterans: 7.9%; Ancestry: 26.6% German, 12.2% Irish, 9.1% Polish, 6.7% English, 4.2% French
Religion: Six largest groups: 20.9% Catholicism, 5.5% Lutheran, 4.4% Baptist, 3.0% Non-denominational Protestant, 2.8% Methodist/Pietist, 2.2% Pentecostal
Economy: Unemployment rate: 5.3%; Leading industries: 14.5 % retail trade; 13.8 % health care and social assistance; 10.6 % accommodation and food services; Farms: 330 totaling 63,022 acres; Company size: 13 employ 1,000 or more persons, 19 employ 500 to 999 persons, 290 employ 100 to 499 persons, 9,248 employ less than 100 persons; Business ownership: 10,880 women-owned, 3,658 Black-owned, 892 Hispanic-owned, 1,037 Asian-owned, 159 American Indian/Alaska Native-owned
Employment: 12.1% management, business, and financial, 4.0% computer, engineering, and science, 9.5% education, legal, community service, arts, and media, 7.4% healthcare practitioners, 19.6% service, 23.6% sales and office, 6.9% natural resources, construction, and maintenance, 16.8% production, transportation, and material moving
Income: Per capita: $25,977; Median household: $42,917; Average household: $61,500; Households with income of $100,000 or more: 16.9%; Poverty rate: 20.7%
Educational Attainment: High school diploma or higher: 88.8%; Bachelor's degree or higher: 25.1%; Graduate/professional degree or higher: 9.6%
Housing: Homeownership rate: 60.2%; Median home value: $105,500; Median year structure built: 1959; Homeowner vacancy rate: 2.2%; Median selected monthly owner costs: $1,185 with a mortgage, $437 without a mortgage; Median gross rent: $674 per month; Rental vacancy rate: 7.1%
Vital Statistics: Birth rate: 129.0 per 10,000 population; Death rate: 104.4 per 10,000 population; Age-adjusted cancer mortality rate: 191.7 deaths per 100,000 population
Health Insurance: 91.5% have insurance; 65.3% have private insurance; 39.0% have public insurance; 8.5% do not have insurance; 3.3% of children under 18 do not have insurance
Health Care: Physicians: 45.7 per 10,000 population; Dentists: 6.8 per 10,000 population; Hospital beds: 55.6 per 10,000 population; Hospital admissions: 2,390.1 per 10,000 population
Air Quality Index (AQI): Percent of Days: 78.7% good, 20.2% moderate, 1.1% unhealthy for sensitive individuals, 0.0% unhealthy, 0.0% very unhealthy; Annual median: 39; Annual maximum: 112
Transportation: Commute: 92.5% car, 1.6% public transportation, 2.0% walk, 2.7% work from home; Mean travel time to work: 20.5 minutes
2016 Presidential Election: 38.1% Trump, 55.7% Clinton, 3.7% Johnson, 1.1% Stein
National and State Parks: Cedar Point National Wildlife Refuge; Fallen Timbers State Memorial; Fort Miamis State Memorial; Irwin Prairie State Nature Preserve; Mallard Club Marsh State Wildlife Area; Maumee Bay State Park; Missionary Island State Wildlife Area; West Sister Island National Wildlife Refuge
Additional Information Contacts
Lucas Government . . . . (419) 213-4000
http://www.co.lucas.oh.us

Lucas County Communities

BERKEY (village). Covers a land area of 4.176 square miles and a water area of 0 square miles. Located at 41.71° N. Lat; 83.84° W. Long. Elevation is 702 feet.
Population: 313; Growth (since 2000): 18.1%; Density: 75.0 persons per square mile; Race: 99.7% White, 0.0% Black/African American, 0.0% Asian, 0.3% American Indian/Alaska Native, 0.0% Native Hawaiian/Other Pacific Islander, 0.0% Two or more races, 0.6% Hispanic of any race; Average household size: 2.35; Median age: 44.8; Age under 18: 25.2%; Age 65 and over: 18.2%; Males per 100 females: 104.3; Marriage status: 30.0% never married, 55.9% now married, 4.6% separated, 4.6% widowed, 9.5% divorced; Foreign born: 1.6%; Speak English only: 98.7%; With disability: 6.7%; Veterans: 6.0%; Ancestry: 42.2% German, 14.7% English, 13.1% Irish, 10.2% French, 9.6% Polish
Employment: 14.3% management, business, and financial, 1.9% computer, engineering, and science, 8.1% education, legal, community service, arts, and media, 19.3% healthcare practitioners, 13.0% service, 17.4% sales and office, 9.9% natural resources, construction, and maintenance, 16.1% production, transportation, and material moving
Income: Per capita: $43,645; Median household: $69,583; Average household: $102,878; Households with income of $100,000 or more: 30.1%; Poverty rate: 6.1%
Educational Attainment: High school diploma or higher: 98.2%; Bachelor's degree or higher: 32.6%; Graduate/professional degree or higher: 15.1%
Housing: Homeownership rate: 72.2%; Median home value: $167,200; Median year structure built: Before 1940; Homeowner vacancy rate: 8.6%; Median selected monthly owner costs: $1,420 with a mortgage, $544 without a mortgage; Median gross rent: $742 per month; Rental vacancy rate: 0.0%
Health Insurance: 97.4% have insurance; 89.8% have private insurance; 26.2% have public insurance; 2.6% do not have insurance; 0.0% of children under 18 do not have insurance
Transportation: Commute: 96.0% car, 0.7% public transportation, 0.7% walk, 2.7% work from home; Mean travel time to work: 24.6 minutes

HARBOR VIEW (village). Covers a land area of 0.029 square miles and a water area of 0 square miles. Located at 41.69° N. Lat; 83.44° W. Long. Elevation is 581 feet.
Population: 52; Growth (since 2000): -47.5%; Density: 1,789.7 persons per square mile; Race: 90.4% White, 0.0% Black/African American, 0.0% Asian, 9.6% American Indian/Alaska Native, 0.0% Native Hawaiian/Other Pacific Islander, 0.0% Two or more races, 0.0% Hispanic of any race; Average household size: 2.26; Median age: 57.1; Age under 18: 13.5%; Age 65 and over: 17.3%; Males per 100 females: 89.2; Marriage status: 19.6% never married, 67.4% now married, 2.2% separated, 2.2% widowed, 10.9% divorced; Foreign born: 0.0%; Speak English only: 100.0%; With disability: 28.8%; Veterans: 11.1%; Ancestry: 36.5% German, 11.5% American, 11.5% Polish, 5.8% Irish, 5.8% Italian
Employment: 14.8% management, business, and financial, 0.0% computer, engineering, and science, 0.0% education, legal, community service, arts, and media, 11.1% healthcare practitioners, 40.7% service, 3.7% sales and office, 0.0% natural resources, construction, and maintenance, 29.6% production, transportation, and material moving
Income: Per capita: $25,906; Median household: $42,188; Average household: $55,570; Households with income of $100,000 or more: 4.3%; Poverty rate: 17.3%
Educational Attainment: High school diploma or higher: 77.3%; Bachelor's degree or higher: 2.3%; Graduate/professional degree or higher: n/a
Housing: Homeownership rate: 82.6%; Median home value: $68,300; Median year structure built: Before 1940; Homeowner vacancy rate: 0.0%; Median selected monthly owner costs: $1,042 with a mortgage, $433 without a mortgage; Median gross rent: n/a per month; Rental vacancy rate: 42.9%
Health Insurance: 92.3% have insurance; 71.2% have private insurance; 46.2% have public insurance; 7.7% do not have insurance; 0.0% of children under 18 do not have insurance
Transportation: Commute: 100.0% car, 0.0% public transportation, 0.0% walk, 0.0% work from home; Mean travel time to work: 21.7 minutes

HOLLAND (village). Covers a land area of 0.990 square miles and a water area of 0 square miles. Located at 41.62° N. Lat; 83.71° W. Long. Elevation is 636 feet.
Population: 1,747; Growth (since 2000): 33.8%; Density: 1,765.3 persons per square mile; Race: 80.8% White, 5.8% Black/African American, 6.6% Asian, 0.0% American Indian/Alaska Native, 0.0% Native Hawaiian/Other Pacific Islander, 6.2% Two or more races, 2.3% Hispanic of any race; Average household size: 2.38; Median age: 44.0; Age under 18: 22.4%; Age 65 and over: 24.8%; Males per 100 females: 84.7; Marriage status: 25.6% never married, 44.6% now married, 0.4% separated, 14.2% widowed, 15.6% divorced; Foreign born: 4.9%; Speak English only: 94.0%; With disability: 14.0%; Veterans: 8.3%; Ancestry: 33.2% German, 12.6% Polish, 12.5% Irish, 8.2% English, 5.3% French
Employment: 11.2% management, business, and financial, 5.4% computer, engineering, and science, 5.3% education, legal, community service, arts, and media, 6.9% healthcare practitioners, 17.7% service, 28.1% sales and office, 5.9% natural resources, construction, and maintenance, 19.5% production, transportation, and material moving
Income: Per capita: $25,121; Median household: $46,950; Average household: $60,172; Households with income of $100,000 or more: 18.5%; Poverty rate: 6.7%

Educational Attainment: High school diploma or higher: 87.2%; Bachelor's degree or higher: 19.8%; Graduate/professional degree or higher: 4.4%

School District(s)

Springfield Local (PK-12)
2015-16 Enrollment: 3,666 . . . . (419) 867-5600

Housing: Homeownership rate: 59.5%; Median home value: $147,200; Median year structure built: 1974; Homeowner vacancy rate: 0.0%; Median selected monthly owner costs: $1,365 with a mortgage, $478 without a mortgage; Median gross rent: $638 per month; Rental vacancy rate: 0.0%
Health Insurance: 95.6% have insurance; 73.2% have private insurance; 40.6% have public insurance; 4.4% do not have insurance; 0.8% of children under 18 do not have insurance
Safety: Violent crime rate: 35.3 per 10,000 population; Property crime rate: 1,696.1 per 10,000 population
Transportation: Commute: 93.4% car, 0.0% public transportation, 1.8% walk, 4.3% work from home; Mean travel time to work: 18.8 minutes

MAUMEE (city). Covers a land area of 9.886 square miles and a water area of 0.716 square miles. Located at 41.57° N. Lat; 83.67° W. Long. Elevation is 633 feet.
History: A French-Canadian trading post was here from 1680 to 1693. In 1764 the British built Fort Miami. When a store opened in 1817, the town began to grow around it. Earlier names of Waynesville and South Toledo gave way to the name of Maumee, a corruption of the Indian name Miami.
Population: 14,018; Growth (since 2000): -8.0%; Density: 1,418.0 persons per square mile; Race: 93.6% White, 2.8% Black/African American, 1.9% Asian, 0.1% American Indian/Alaska Native, 0.1% Native Hawaiian/Other Pacific Islander, 1.0% Two or more races, 3.0% Hispanic of any race; Average household size: 2.41; Median age: 41.0; Age under 18: 22.3%; Age 65 and over: 15.8%; Males per 100 females: 95.9; Marriage status: 26.6% never married, 54.9% now married, 1.6% separated, 5.8% widowed, 12.8% divorced; Foreign born: 1.9%; Speak English only: 95.9%; With disability: 10.7%; Veterans: 7.7%; Ancestry: 39.0% German, 15.9% Irish, 11.4% English, 9.9% Polish, 5.7% American
Employment: 14.6% management, business, and financial, 5.2% computer, engineering, and science, 10.2% education, legal, community service, arts, and media, 8.7% healthcare practitioners, 15.2% service, 25.9% sales and office, 7.0% natural resources, construction, and maintenance, 13.3% production, transportation, and material moving
Income: Per capita: $33,612; Median household: $63,043; Average household: $79,574; Households with income of $100,000 or more: 24.4%; Poverty rate: 7.9%
Educational Attainment: High school diploma or higher: 95.8%; Bachelor's degree or higher: 37.1%; Graduate/professional degree or higher: 14.2%

School District(s)

Maumee City (KG-12)
2015-16 Enrollment: 2,372 . . . . (419) 893-3200
Ohio Virtual Academy (KG-12)
2015-16 Enrollment: 9,466 . . . . (877) 648-2512
Wildwood Environmental Academy (KG-12)
2015-16 Enrollment: 321. . . . . (419) 868-9885

Four-year College(s)

ITT Technical Institute-Maumee (Private, For-profit)
Fall 2016 Enrollment: n/a . . . . (419) 861-6500

Two-year College(s)

Professional Skills Institute (Private, For-profit)
Fall 2016 Enrollment: 290 . . . . (419) 720-6670
2016-17 Tuition: In-state $14,611; Out-of-state $14,611
Stautzenberger College-Maumee (Private, For-profit)
Fall 2016 Enrollment: 656 . . . . (419) 866-0261
2016-17 Tuition: In-state $12,090; Out-of-state $12,090

Housing: Homeownership rate: 72.3%; Median home value: $128,900; Median year structure built: 1961; Homeowner vacancy rate: 2.2%; Median selected monthly owner costs: $1,232 with a mortgage, $486 without a mortgage; Median gross rent: $767 per month; Rental vacancy rate: 6.3%
Health Insurance: 95.3% have insurance; 82.6% have private insurance; 27.4% have public insurance; 4.7% do not have insurance; 1.6% of children under 18 do not have insurance
Hospitals: Saint Luke's Hospital (314 beds)
Safety: Violent crime rate: 10.8 per 10,000 population; Property crime rate: 273.9 per 10,000 population
Transportation: Commute: 94.5% car, 0.4% public transportation, 0.9% walk, 2.9% work from home; Mean travel time to work: 19.1 minutes

Additional Information Contacts

City of Maumee . . . . (419) 897-7100
http://www.maumee.org

MONCLOVA (unincorporated postal area)

ZCTA: 43542

Covers a land area of 14.535 square miles and a water area of 0 square miles. Located at 41.57° N. Lat; 83.77° W. Long. Elevation is 633 feet.
Population: 3,459; Growth (since 2000): 44.8%; Density: 238.0 persons per square mile; Race: 99.5% White, 0.5% Black/African American, 0.0% Asian, 0.0% American Indian/Alaska Native, 0.0% Native Hawaiian/Other Pacific Islander, 0.0% Two or more races, 0.0% Hispanic of any race; Average household size: 2.87; Median age: 39.6; Age under 18: 28.4%; Age 65 and over: 10.8%; Males per 100 females: 107.1; Marriage status: 18.0% never married, 71.8% now married, 0.9% separated, 6.0% widowed, 4.2% divorced; Foreign born: 1.1%; Speak English only: 98.6%; With disability: 4.7%; Veterans: 5.0%; Ancestry: 42.3% German, 16.8% Irish, 11.5% Italian, 8.0% French, 7.3% Polish
Employment: 17.7% management, business, and financial, 5.8% computer, engineering, and science, 10.9% education, legal, community service, arts, and media, 9.7% healthcare practitioners, 12.4% service, 28.1% sales and office, 4.9% natural resources, construction, and maintenance, 10.4% production, transportation, and material moving
Income: Per capita: $40,541; Median household: $104,028; Average household: $114,649; Households with income of $100,000 or more: 54.8%; Poverty rate: 2.7%
Educational Attainment: High school diploma or higher: 97.3%; Bachelor's degree or higher: 44.6%; Graduate/professional degree or higher: 23.8%

School District(s)

Anthony Wayne Local (KG-12)
2015-16 Enrollment: 4,205 . . . . (419) 877-5377

Housing: Homeownership rate: 91.3%; Median home value: $258,200; Median year structure built: 1987; Homeowner vacancy rate: 4.6%; Median selected monthly owner costs: $2,247 with a mortgage, $564 without a mortgage; Median gross rent: n/a per month; Rental vacancy rate: 0.0%
Health Insurance: 95.8% have insurance; 92.3% have private insurance; 13.1% have public insurance; 4.2% do not have insurance; 0.0% of children under 18 do not have insurance
Transportation: Commute: 88.3% car, 0.0% public transportation, 0.0% walk, 8.9% work from home; Mean travel time to work: 22.8 minutes

NEAPOLIS (CDP). Covers a land area of 0.710 square miles and a water area of 0 square miles. Located at 41.49° N. Lat; 83.87° W. Long. Elevation is 669 feet.
Population: 371; Growth (since 2000): n/a; Density: 522.8 persons per square mile; Race: 100.0% White, 0.0% Black/African American, 0.0% Asian, 0.0% American Indian/Alaska Native, 0.0% Native Hawaiian/Other Pacific Islander, 0.0% Two or more races, 0.0% Hispanic of any race; Average household size: 2.90; Median age: 53.0; Age under 18: 22.1%; Age 65 and over: 21.8%; Males per 100 females: 104.3; Marriage status: 10.0% never married, 76.3% now married, 2.3% separated, 6.0% widowed, 7.7% divorced; Foreign born: 0.0%; Speak English only: 100.0%; With disability: 32.1%; Veterans: 17.3%; Ancestry: 31.5% English, 22.1% Welsh, 12.1% Irish, 10.2% French, 8.9% Dutch
Employment: 9.9% management, business, and financial, 0.0% computer, engineering, and science, 7.1% education, legal, community service, arts, and media, 7.1% healthcare practitioners, 43.3% service, 14.2% sales and office, 14.2% natural resources, construction, and maintenance, 4.3% production, transportation, and material moving
Income: Per capita: $23,714; Median household: n/a; Average household: $67,097; Households with income of $100,000 or more: 13.3%; Poverty rate: 10.0%
Educational Attainment: High school diploma or higher: 82.6%; Bachelor's degree or higher: 13.3%; Graduate/professional degree or higher: 13.3%
Housing: Homeownership rate: 100.0%; Median home value: $159,600; Median year structure built: 1978; Homeowner vacancy rate: 0.0%; Median selected monthly owner costs: $1,386 with a mortgage, $409 without a mortgage; Median gross rent: n/a per month; Rental vacancy rate: 0.0%
Health Insurance: 94.9% have insurance; 78.2% have private insurance; 41.5% have public insurance; 5.1% do not have insurance; 0.0% of children under 18 do not have insurance
Transportation: Commute: 100.0% car, 0.0% public transportation, 0.0% walk, 0.0% work from home; Mean travel time to work: 33.0 minutes

OREGON (city). Covers a land area of 29.976 square miles and a water area of 8.055 square miles. Located at 41.67° N. Lat; 83.42° W. Long. Elevation is 604 feet.

History: Incorporated 1958.

Population: 20,137; Growth (since 2000): 4.0%; Density: 671.8 persons per square mile; Race: 89.8% White, 2.3% Black/African American, 1.4% Asian, 0.3% American Indian/Alaska Native, 0.0% Native Hawaiian/Other Pacific Islander, 3.6% Two or more races, 7.6% Hispanic of any race; Average household size: 2.44; Median age: 42.8; Age under 18: 22.1%; Age 65 and over: 17.4%; Males per 100 females: 92.7; Marriage status: 30.2% never married, 49.4% now married, 1.4% separated, 6.9% widowed, 13.6% divorced; Foreign born: 2.6%; Speak English only: 95.4%; With disability: 12.7%; Veterans: 8.8%; Ancestry: 35.9% German, 12.8% Irish, 7.9% English, 7.7% Polish, 7.7% Hungarian

Employment: 9.1% management, business, and financial, 3.9% computer, engineering, and science, 7.2% education, legal, community service, arts, and media, 9.2% healthcare practitioners, 17.2% service, 23.3% sales and office, 10.9% natural resources, construction, and maintenance, 19.4% production, transportation, and material moving

Income: Per capita: $28,458; Median household: $55,157; Average household: $68,410; Households with income of $100,000 or more: 22.6%; Poverty rate: 10.7%

Educational Attainment: High school diploma or higher: 90.2%; Bachelor's degree or higher: 18.3%; Graduate/professional degree or higher: 6.4%

School District(s)

Eagle Learning Center (09-12)
2015-16 Enrollment: 103 . . . . (419) 720-2003
Oregon City (PK-12)
2015-16 Enrollment: 3,701 . . . . (419) 693-0661

Two-year College(s)

Toledo Academy of Beauty Culture-East (Private, For-profit)
Fall 2016 Enrollment: 71 . . . . (419) 693-7257

Housing: Homeownership rate: 68.8%; Median home value: $130,200; Median year structure built: 1971; Homeowner vacancy rate: 2.5%; Median selected monthly owner costs: $1,274 with a mortgage, $436 without a mortgage; Median gross rent: $620 per month; Rental vacancy rate: 3.2%

Health Insurance: 93.6% have insurance; 75.1% have private insurance; 34.3% have public insurance; 6.4% do not have insurance; 3.2% of children under 18 do not have insurance

Hospitals: Bay Park Community Hospital (70 beds); Mercy Saint Charles Hospital (390 beds)

Safety: Violent crime rate: 18.4 per 10,000 population; Property crime rate: 331.6 per 10,000 population

Transportation: Commute: 94.9% car, 1.0% public transportation, 1.1% walk, 2.4% work from home; Mean travel time to work: 19.3 minutes

Additional Information Contacts

City of Oregon . . . . (419) 698-7095
http://www.ci.oregon.oh.us

OTTAWA HILLS (village). Covers a land area of 1.846 square miles and a water area of 0.016 square miles. Located at 41.67° N. Lat; 83.64° W. Long. Elevation is 604 feet.

History: Settled 1916, incorporated 1924.

Population: 4,497; Growth (since 2000): -1.5%; Density: 2,435.5 persons per square mile; Race: 88.5% White, 2.0% Black/African American, 6.7% Asian, 0.0% American Indian/Alaska Native, 0.0% Native Hawaiian/Other Pacific Islander, 2.7% Two or more races, 0.6% Hispanic of any race; Average household size: 2.79; Median age: 42.3; Age under 18: 27.9%; Age 65 and over: 14.2%; Males per 100 females: 89.8; Marriage status: 19.8% never married, 67.3% now married, 0.2% separated, 5.0% widowed, 7.8% divorced; Foreign born: 8.6%; Speak English only: 91.5%; With disability: 7.8%; Veterans: 5.1%; Ancestry: 21.5% German, 17.6% Irish, 17.0% English, 6.5% Polish, 5.3% Italian

Employment: 28.2% management, business, and financial, 4.2% computer, engineering, and science, 19.5% education, legal, community service, arts, and media, 13.0% healthcare practitioners, 7.2% service, 22.1% sales and office, 1.8% natural resources, construction, and maintenance, 3.9% production, transportation, and material moving

Income: Per capita: $69,103; Median household: $118,700; Average household: $192,525; Households with income of $100,000 or more: 57.1%; Poverty rate: 2.4%

Educational Attainment: High school diploma or higher: 96.2%; Bachelor's degree or higher: 77.4%; Graduate/professional degree or higher: 39.3%

Housing: Homeownership rate: 83.0%; Median home value: $273,400; Median year structure built: 1954; Homeowner vacancy rate: 2.3%; Median selected monthly owner costs: $2,275 with a mortgage, $1,043 without a mortgage; Median gross rent: $1,192 per month; Rental vacancy rate: 10.8%

Health Insurance: 97.5% have insurance; 91.1% have private insurance; 15.4% have public insurance; 2.5% do not have insurance; 0.0% of children under 18 do not have insurance

Safety: Violent crime rate: 2.3 per 10,000 population; Property crime rate: 83.5 per 10,000 population

Transportation: Commute: 90.7% car, 0.4% public transportation, 1.7% walk, 4.5% work from home; Mean travel time to work: 18.8 minutes

Additional Information Contacts

Village of Ottawa Hills . . . . (419) 536-1111
http://www.ottawahills.org

SYLVANIA (city). Covers a land area of 6.478 square miles and a water area of 0.045 square miles. Located at 41.71° N. Lat; 83.71° W. Long. Elevation is 666 feet.

History: Incorporated 1867.

Population: 18,882; Growth (since 2000): 1.1%; Density: 2,915.0 persons per square mile; Race: 93.2% White, 1.6% Black/African American, 2.7% Asian, 0.1% American Indian/Alaska Native, 0.0% Native Hawaiian/Other Pacific Islander, 2.1% Two or more races, 2.4% Hispanic of any race; Average household size: 2.43; Median age: 42.8; Age under 18: 22.8%; Age 65 and over: 19.6%; Males per 100 females: 89.7; Marriage status: 26.3% never married, 55.6% now married, 0.9% separated, 8.0% widowed, 10.1% divorced; Foreign born: 4.2%; Speak English only: 95.0%; With disability: 10.8%; Veterans: 7.5%; Ancestry: 34.9% German, 15.7% Irish, 13.4% Polish, 12.4% English, 6.1% French

Employment: 20.2% management, business, and financial, 7.2% computer, engineering, and science, 13.9% education, legal, community service, arts, and media, 10.1% healthcare practitioners, 14.1% service, 22.5% sales and office, 3.9% natural resources, construction, and maintenance, 8.1% production, transportation, and material moving

Income: Per capita: $37,235; Median household: $72,936; Average household: $90,620; Households with income of $100,000 or more: 36.2%; Poverty rate: 7.7%

Educational Attainment: High school diploma or higher: 95.8%; Bachelor's degree or higher: 43.1%; Graduate/professional degree or higher: 15.6%

School District(s)

Sylvania City (PK-12)
2015-16 Enrollment: 7,497 . . . . (419) 824-8501

Four-year College(s)

Lourdes University (Private, Not-for-profit, Roman Catholic)
Fall 2016 Enrollment: 1,426 . . . . (419) 885-3211
2016-17 Tuition: In-state $20,620; Out-of-state $20,620

Two-year College(s)

Ross College-Sylvania (Private, For-profit)
Fall 2016 Enrollment: 507 . . . . (419) 882-3203

Vocational/Technical School(s)

Paul Mitchell the School-Toledo (Private, For-profit)
Fall 2016 Enrollment: 180 . . . . (419) 885-5191
2016-17 Tuition: $15,713
Toledo Restaurant Training Center (Private, Not-for-profit)
Fall 2016 Enrollment: n/a . . . . (419) 241-5100

Housing: Homeownership rate: 72.1%; Median home value: $165,900; Median year structure built: 1975; Homeowner vacancy rate: 0.0%; Median selected monthly owner costs: $1,390 with a mortgage, $579 without a mortgage; Median gross rent: $785 per month; Rental vacancy rate: 5.1%

Health Insurance: 96.2% have insurance; 83.4% have private insurance; 27.3% have public insurance; 3.8% do not have insurance; 1.7% of children under 18 do not have insurance

Hospitals: Flower Hospital (279 beds)

Transportation: Commute: 93.2% car, 0.6% public transportation, 1.2% walk, 4.4% work from home; Mean travel time to work: 21.7 minutes

Additional Information Contacts

City of Sylvania . . . . (419) 885-8925
http://www.cityofsylvania.com

TOLEDO (city). County seat. Covers a land area of 80.692 square miles and a water area of 3.432 square miles. Located at 41.66° N. Lat; 83.58° W. Long. Elevation is 610 feet.

History: Toledo was established along the Maumee River on the westernmost tip of Lake Erie. A stockade called Fort Industry was built here around 1800, but was short-lived. In 1833 two small settlements voted to consolidate, and the residents chose the name of Toledo for the new town. The early years were difficult for the town, with cholera, a drought, business failures, and the Toledo War of 1835, a protracted boundary dispute between Ohio and Michigan which ended with Michigan being given the Upper Peninsula in exchange for Ohio keeping the disputed territory. In the 1840's things improved, with Toledo the logical choice as terminus of the Wabash & Erie Canal, followed by the Miami & Erie Canal. When the 1850's came, Toledo was a station on the Underground Railroad for escaping slaves. Among the industries that developed after the Civil War was the Libby Glass Company, which revolutionized the glass industry, and the Owens Bottle Machine Company.

Population: 280,854; Growth (since 2000): -10.4%; Density: 3,480.6 persons per square mile; Race: 63.5% White, 27.2% Black/African American, 1.4% Asian, 0.3% American Indian/Alaska Native, 0.0% Native Hawaiian/Other Pacific Islander, 4.9% Two or more races, 8.2% Hispanic of any race; Average household size: 2.31; Median age: 35.3; Age under 18: 23.3%; Age 65 and over: 13.4%; Males per 100 females: 93.8; Marriage status: 41.2% never married, 36.6% now married, 2.3% separated, 6.7% widowed, 15.6% divorced; Foreign born: 3.4%; Speak English only: 93.1%; With disability: 17.3%; Veterans: 7.5%; Ancestry: 22.5% German, 11.2% Irish, 8.5% Polish, 5.2% English, 3.6% French

Employment: 9.2% management, business, and financial, 3.2% computer, engineering, and science, 8.6% education, legal, community service, arts, and media, 5.9% healthcare practitioners, 22.5% service, 24.1% sales and office, 7.0% natural resources, construction, and maintenance, 19.7% production, transportation, and material moving

Income: Per capita: $20,317; Median household: $34,548; Average household: $46,477; Households with income of $100,000 or more: 9.2%; Poverty rate: 27.5%

Educational Attainment: High school diploma or higher: 85.7%; Bachelor's degree or higher: 18.0%; Graduate/professional degree or higher: 6.4%

School District(s)

Achieve Career Preparatory Academy (08-12)
2015-16 Enrollment: 177 . . . . (419) 243-8559
Alternative Education Academy (KG-12)
2015-16 Enrollment: 1,611 . . . . (330) 253-8680
Aurora Academy (KG-08)
2015-16 Enrollment: 178 . . . . (419) 693-6841
Autism Model School (KG-12)
2015-16 Enrollment: 110 . . . . (419) 897-4400
Bennett Venture Academy (KG-08)
2015-16 Enrollment: 733 . . . . (419) 269-2247
Central Academy of Ohio (KG-06)
2015-16 Enrollment: 179 . . . . (419) 205-9800
Clay Avenue Community School (KG-08)
2015-16 Enrollment: 532 . . . . (419) 727-9900
Eagle Academy (06-12)
2015-16 Enrollment: 224 . . . . (419) 697-2760
Glass City Academy (11-12)
2015-16 Enrollment: 230 . . . . (419) 720-6311
Great Expectations Elementary School (KG-06)
2015-16 Enrollment: 164 . . . . (419) 490-6252
Horizon Science Academy Toledo (KG-12)
2015-16 Enrollment: 581 . . . . (419) 474-3350
Horizon Science Academy-Springfield (KG-08)
2015-16 Enrollment: 375 . . . . (419) 535-0524
L. Hollingworth School for Talented and Gifted (KG-08)
2015-16 Enrollment: 338 . . . . (419) 705-3411
Lake Erie Academy
2015-16 Enrollment: n/a . . . . (419) 475-3786
Life Skills Center of Toledo (09-12)
2015-16 Enrollment: 62 . . . . (419) 241-5504
Madison Avenue School of Arts (KG-05)
2015-16 Enrollment: 624 . . . . (419) 259-4000
Northpointe Academy (KG-08)
2015-16 Enrollment: 387 . . . . (419) 535-1997
Ottawa Hills Local (KG-12)
2015-16 Enrollment: 900 . . . . (419) 536-6371
Phoenix Academy Community School (07-12)
2015-16 Enrollment: 442 . . . . (419) 720-4500
Polly Fox Academy Community School (07-12)
2015-16 Enrollment: 93 . . . . (419) 720-4500
Springfield Local (PK-12)
2015-16 Enrollment: 3,666 . . . . (419) 867-5600
Star Academy of Toledo (KG-08)
2015-16 Enrollment: 184 . . . . (419) 720-6330
Summit Academy Community School-Toledo (KG-08)
2015-16 Enrollment: 108 . . . . (419) 385-5730
Summit Academy Toledo Learning Center (KG-12)
2015-16 Enrollment: 192 . . . . (419) 476-7859
Sylvania City (PK-12)
2015-16 Enrollment: 7,497 . . . . (419) 824-8501
The Autism Academy of Learning (KG-12)
2015-16 Enrollment: 53 . . . . (419) 865-7487
The Maritime Academy of Toledo (05-12)
2015-16 Enrollment: 261 . . . . (419) 244-9999
Toledo City (PK-12)
2015-16 Enrollment: 22,053 . . . . (419) 671-8282
Toledo Preparatory and Fitness Academy (KG-08)
2015-16 Enrollment: 205 . . . . (419) 535-3700
Toledo School for the Arts (06-12)
2015-16 Enrollment: 679 . . . . (419) 246-8732
Washington Local (KG-12)
2015-16 Enrollment: 7,034 . . . . (419) 473-8220
Winterfield Venture Academy (KG-08)
2015-16 Enrollment: 528 . . . . (419) 531-3285

Four-year College(s)

Herzing University-Toledo (Private, For-profit)
Fall 2016 Enrollment: 217 . . . . (419) 776-0300
2016-17 Tuition: In-state $13,390; Out-of-state $13,390
Mercy College of Ohio (Private, Not-for-profit, Roman Catholic)
Fall 2016 Enrollment: 1,351 . . . . (419) 251-1313
2016-17 Tuition: In-state $13,430; Out-of-state $13,430
University of Toledo (Public)
Fall 2016 Enrollment: 20,615 . . . . (800) 586-5336
2016-17 Tuition: In-state $9,547; Out-of-state $18,885

Two-year College(s)

Davis College (Private, For-profit)
Fall 2016 Enrollment: 114 . . . . (419) 473-2700
2016-17 Tuition: In-state $14,130; Out-of-state $14,130
Salon Institute-Toledo Campus (Private, For-profit)
Fall 2016 Enrollment: 89 . . . . (419) 866-4489
Toledo Public Schools Adult and Continuing Education (Public)
Fall 2016 Enrollment: 100 . . . . (419) 671-8700

Vocational/Technical School(s)

Athena Career Academy (Private, For-profit)
Fall 2016 Enrollment: 188 . . . . (419) 472-1150
2016-17 Tuition: $20,600

Housing: Homeownership rate: 52.3%; Median home value: $77,800; Median year structure built: 1953; Homeowner vacancy rate: 2.4%; Median selected monthly owner costs: $1,015 with a mortgage, $387 without a mortgage; Median gross rent: $651 per month; Rental vacancy rate: 7.9%

Health Insurance: 89.6% have insurance; 56.9% have private insurance; 44.6% have public insurance; 10.4% do not have insurance; 3.8% of children under 18 do not have insurance

Hospitals: Mercy Saint Anne Hospital (88 beds); Mercy Saint Vincent Medical Center (588 beds); The Toledo Hospital (794 beds); University of Toledo Medical Center (319 beds)

Safety: Violent crime rate: 119.2 per 10,000 population; Property crime rate: 402.0 per 10,000 population

Newspapers: Herald Newspapers (weekly circulation 10,000); The Blade (daily circulation 123,000); Toledo Free Press (weekly circulation 115,000)

Transportation: Commute: 91.4% car, 2.4% public transportation, 2.6% walk, 2.1% work from home; Mean travel time to work: 19.6 minutes; Amtrak: Train service available.

Airports: Toledo Express (primary service/non-hub)

Additional Information Contacts

City of Toledo . . . . (419) 245-1001
http://www.ci.toledo.oh.us

WATERVILLE (city). Covers a land area of 4.689 square miles and a water area of 0.188 square miles. Located at 41.50° N. Lat; 83.74° W. Long. Elevation is 614 feet.
History: Waterville was platted in 1818 by John Pray. It grew as the center of a garden nursery region.
Population: 5,496; Growth (since 2000): 13.8%; Density: 1,172.1 persons per square mile; Race: 93.7% White, 1.2% Black/African American, 3.0% Asian, 0.2% American Indian/Alaska Native, 0.0% Native Hawaiian/Other Pacific Islander, 1.8% Two or more races, 2.7% Hispanic of any race; Average household size: 2.83; Median age: 39.5; Age under 18: 27.7%; Age 65 and over: 14.4%; Males per 100 females: 92.8; Marriage status: 21.7% never married, 62.1% now married, 0.5% separated, 5.9% widowed, 10.2% divorced; Foreign born: 3.0%; Speak English only: 95.3%; With disability: 6.9%; Veterans: 7.1%; Ancestry: 35.3% German, 20.0% Irish, 11.9% Polish, 11.4% English, 5.6% French
Employment: 17.0% management, business, and financial, 3.9% computer, engineering, and science, 11.4% education, legal, community service, arts, and media, 12.6% healthcare practitioners, 15.3% service, 24.7% sales and office, 5.8% natural resources, construction, and maintenance, 9.4% production, transportation, and material moving
Income: Per capita: $30,951; Median household: $79,293; Average household: $87,295; Households with income of $100,000 or more: 36.8%; Poverty rate: 4.3%
Educational Attainment: High school diploma or higher: 95.9%; Bachelor's degree or higher: 40.8%; Graduate/professional degree or higher: 18.2%

School District(s)

Anthony Wayne Local (KG-12)
2015-16 Enrollment: 4,205 . . . . (419) 877-5377

Housing: Homeownership rate: 82.8%; Median home value: $175,500; Median year structure built: 1974; Homeowner vacancy rate: 2.3%; Median selected monthly owner costs: $1,490 with a mortgage, $507 without a mortgage; Median gross rent: $1,041 per month; Rental vacancy rate: 10.4%
Health Insurance: 95.9% have insurance; 87.4% have private insurance; 17.3% have public insurance; 4.1% do not have insurance; 1.8% of children under 18 do not have insurance
Safety: Violent crime rate: 3.6 per 10,000 population; Property crime rate: 52.6 per 10,000 population
Transportation: Commute: 93.3% car, 0.7% public transportation, 1.7% walk, 4.2% work from home; Mean travel time to work: 24.3 minutes
Additional Information Contacts
Village of Waterville. . . . . (419) 878-8100
http://www.waterville.org

WHITEHOUSE (village). Covers a land area of 4.292 square miles and a water area of 0 square miles. Located at 41.52° N. Lat; 83.80° W. Long. Elevation is 653 feet.
Population: 4,378; Growth (since 2000): 60.2%; Density: 1,020.0 persons per square mile; Race: 97.3% White, 1.4% Black/African American, 0.0% Asian, 0.0% American Indian/Alaska Native, 0.0% Native Hawaiian/Other Pacific Islander, 0.8% Two or more races, 2.2% Hispanic of any race; Average household size: 2.73; Median age: 39.7; Age under 18: 26.8%; Age 65 and over: 14.6%; Males per 100 females: 94.5; Marriage status: 27.3% never married, 53.6% now married, 0.6% separated, 6.4% widowed, 12.6% divorced; Foreign born: 0.0%; Speak English only: 98.1%; With disability: 9.9%; Veterans: 10.4%; Ancestry: 42.4% German, 15.7% Irish, 11.0% English, 10.9% Polish, 4.8% American
Employment: 18.2% management, business, and financial, 5.1% computer, engineering, and science, 14.7% education, legal, community service, arts, and media, 11.8% healthcare practitioners, 15.6% service, 18.9% sales and office, 6.8% natural resources, construction, and maintenance, 8.9% production, transportation, and material moving
Income: Per capita: $36,659; Median household: $76,133; Average household: $99,959; Households with income of $100,000 or more: 35.8%; Poverty rate: 7.8%
Educational Attainment: High school diploma or higher: 97.4%; Bachelor's degree or higher: 36.1%; Graduate/professional degree or higher: 15.4%

School District(s)

Anthony Wayne Local (KG-12)
2015-16 Enrollment: 4,205 . . . . (419) 877-5377

Housing: Homeownership rate: 78.2%; Median home value: $184,900; Median year structure built: 1988; Homeowner vacancy rate: 2.2%; Median selected monthly owner costs: $1,554 with a mortgage, $484 without a mortgage; Median gross rent: $758 per month; Rental vacancy rate: 7.3%
Health Insurance: 98.4% have insurance; 78.4% have private insurance; 31.6% have public insurance; 1.6% do not have insurance; 0.5% of children under 18 do not have insurance
Safety: Violent crime rate: 2.2 per 10,000 population; Property crime rate: 66.3 per 10,000 population
Transportation: Commute: 95.5% car, 0.5% public transportation, 0.7% walk, 3.4% work from home; Mean travel time to work: 24.5 minutes
Additional Information Contacts
Village of Whitehouse . . . . (419) 877-5383
http://whitehouseoh.gov

Madison County

Located in central Ohio; drained by Deer, Paint, and Darby Creeks. Covers a land area of 465.875 square miles, a water area of 0.755 square miles, and is located in the Eastern Time Zone at 39.90° N. Lat., 83.40° W. Long. The county was founded in 1810. County seat is London.

Madison County is part of the Columbus, OH Metropolitan Statistical Area. The entire metro area includes: Delaware County, OH; Fairfield County, OH; Franklin County, OH; Hocking County, OH; Licking County, OH; Madison County, OH; Morrow County, OH; Perry County, OH; Pickaway County, OH; Union County, OH

Population: 43,537; Growth (since 2000): 8.3%; Density: 93.5 persons per square mile; Race: 90.4% White, 5.7% Black/African American, 1.0% Asian, 0.3% American Indian/Alaska Native, 0.0% Native Hawaiian/Other Pacific Islander, 2.3% two or more races, 1.7% Hispanic of any race; Average household size: 2.60; Median age: 40.2; Age under 18: 21.2%; Age 65 and over: 14.1%; Males per 100 females: 120.4; Marriage status: 31.7% never married, 48.2% now married, 2.5% separated, 5.7% widowed, 14.3% divorced; Foreign born: 1.5%; Speak English only: 96.7%; With disability: 15.2%; Veterans: 8.9%; Ancestry: 28.2% German, 15.8% American, 14.5% Irish, 10.5% English, 3.7% Scottish
Religion: Six largest groups: 5.8% Catholicism, 5.6% Methodist/Pietist, 4.0% Baptist, 4.0% Hindu, 2.7% European Free-Church, 2.4% Presbyterian-Reformed
Economy: Unemployment rate: 3.4%; Leading industries: 14.5 % retail trade; 14.4 % construction; 11.7 % other services (except public administration); Farms: 699 totaling 263,275 acres; Company size: 0 employ 1,000 or more persons, 3 employ 500 to 999 persons, 20 employ 100 to 499 persons, 645 employ less than 100 persons; Business ownership: 895 women-owned, n/a Black-owned, n/a Hispanic-owned, n/a Asian-owned, n/a American Indian/Alaska Native-owned
Employment: 13.9% management, business, and financial, 4.6% computer, engineering, and science, 7.2% education, legal, community service, arts, and media, 4.5% healthcare practitioners, 16.4% service, 22.3% sales and office, 11.7% natural resources, construction, and maintenance, 19.4% production, transportation, and material moving
Income: Per capita: $25,687; Median household: $58,326; Average household: $74,065; Households with income of $100,000 or more: 22.7%; Poverty rate: 10.6%
Educational Attainment: High school diploma or higher: 86.7%; Bachelor's degree or higher: 16.4%; Graduate/professional degree or higher: 4.7%
Housing: Homeownership rate: 70.0%; Median home value: $150,900; Median year structure built: 1974; Homeowner vacancy rate: 2.4%; Median selected monthly owner costs: $1,310 with a mortgage, $481 without a mortgage; Median gross rent: $739 per month; Rental vacancy rate: 2.2%
Vital Statistics: Birth rate: 98.1 per 10,000 population; Death rate: 90.3 per 10,000 population; Age-adjusted cancer mortality rate: 188.9 deaths per 100,000 population
Health Insurance: 91.6% have insurance; 71.2% have private insurance; 34.5% have public insurance; 8.4% do not have insurance; 5.2% of children under 18 do not have insurance
Health Care: Physicians: 15.0 per 10,000 population; Dentists: 2.3 per 10,000 population; Hospital beds: 12.5 per 10,000 population; Hospital admissions: 264.6 per 10,000 population
Air Quality Index (AQI): Percent of Days: 75.6% good, 23.5% moderate, 0.9% unhealthy for sensitive individuals, 0.0% unhealthy, 0.0% very unhealthy; Annual median: 43; Annual maximum: 112
Transportation: Commute: 92.8% car, 0.3% public transportation, 1.6% walk, 4.1% work from home; Mean travel time to work: 24.9 minutes

2016 Presidential Election: 66.8% Trump, 27.4% Clinton, 3.4% Johnson, 0.6% Stein
National and State Parks: Bigelow Cemetery State Nature Preserve; Madison Lake State Park; Madison Lake State Reserve
Additional Information Contacts
Madison Government . . . . (740) 852-2972
http://www.co.madison.oh.us

Madison County Communities

CHOCTAW LAKE (CDP). Covers a land area of 0.824 square miles and a water area of 0.386 square miles. Located at 39.96° N. Lat; 83.49° W. Long. Elevation is 1,053 feet.
Population: 1,465; Growth (since 2000): -6.2%; Density: 1,778.8 persons per square mile; Race: 98.6% White, 0.0% Black/African American, 0.0% Asian, 0.0% American Indian/Alaska Native, 0.0% Native Hawaiian/Other Pacific Islander, 1.4% Two or more races, 2.9% Hispanic of any race; Average household size: 2.67; Median age: 48.1; Age under 18: 20.3%; Age 65 and over: 17.1%; Males per 100 females: 98.0; Marriage status: 20.3% never married, 69.5% now married, 0.0% separated, 3.8% widowed, 6.4% divorced; Foreign born: 1.7%; Speak English only: 97.1%; With disability: 6.8%; Veterans: 15.0%; Ancestry: 46.3% German, 14.5% Irish, 10.2% Italian, 9.1% English, 8.7% American
Employment: 22.7% management, business, and financial, 4.6% computer, engineering, and science, 10.0% education, legal, community service, arts, and media, 4.1% healthcare practitioners, 18.7% service, 21.5% sales and office, 7.2% natural resources, construction, and maintenance, 11.2% production, transportation, and material moving
Income: Per capita: $50,044; Median household: $112,731; Average household: $131,987; Households with income of $100,000 or more: 60.9%; Poverty rate: 2.4%
Educational Attainment: High school diploma or higher: 98.2%; Bachelor's degree or higher: 41.0%; Graduate/professional degree or higher: 10.6%
Housing: Homeownership rate: 88.0%; Median home value: $249,600; Median year structure built: 1980; Homeowner vacancy rate: 1.8%; Median selected monthly owner costs: $1,808 with a mortgage, $693 without a mortgage; Median gross rent: $1,361 per month; Rental vacancy rate: 0.0%
Health Insurance: 100.0% have insurance; 93.0% have private insurance; 23.2% have public insurance; 0.0% do not have insurance; 0.0% of children under 18 do not have insurance
Transportation: Commute: 95.7% car, 0.0% public transportation, 0.0% walk, 4.3% work from home; Mean travel time to work: 29.4 minutes

IRWIN (unincorporated postal area)
ZCTA: 43029
Covers a land area of 23.619 square miles and a water area of 0.013 square miles. Located at 40.10° N. Lat; 83.44° W. Long..
Population: 710; Growth (since 2000): 14.3%; Density: 30.1 persons per square mile; Race: 91.1% White, 0.8% Black/African American, 8.0% Asian, 0.0% American Indian/Alaska Native, 0.0% Native Hawaiian/Other Pacific Islander, 0.0% Two or more races, 0.0% Hispanic of any race; Average household size: 3.04; Median age: 28.3; Age under 18: 17.5%; Age 65 and over: 11.8%; Males per 100 females: 90.8; Marriage status: 41.5% never married, 50.7% now married, 2.0% separated, 5.4% widowed, 2.3% divorced; Foreign born: 9.0%; Speak English only: 94.2%; With disability: 8.9%; Veterans: 2.7%; Ancestry: 40.7% German, 14.2% Irish, 13.4% American, 7.6% Swiss, 3.0% English
Employment: 6.8% management, business, and financial, 2.0% computer, engineering, and science, 21.5% education, legal, community service, arts, and media, 8.8% healthcare practitioners, 18.2% service, 16.3% sales and office, 7.2% natural resources, construction, and maintenance, 19.2% production, transportation, and material moving
Income: Per capita: $21,454; Median household: $52,798; Average household: $69,853; Households with income of $100,000 or more: 15.8%; Poverty rate: 10.7%
Educational Attainment: High school diploma or higher: 95.8%; Bachelor's degree or higher: 37.4%; Graduate/professional degree or higher: 11.3%

Four-year College(s)
Rosedale Bible College (Private, Not-for-profit, Mennonite Church)
Fall 2016 Enrollment: 63 . . . . (740) 857-1311
2013-14 Tuition: In-state $8,336; Out-of-state $8,336

Two-year College(s)
Rosedale Bible College (Private, Not-for-profit, Mennonite Church)
Fall 2016 Enrollment: 63 . . . . (740) 857-1311
2013-14 Tuition: In-state $8,336; Out-of-state $8,336

Vocational/Technical School(s)
Rosedale Bible College (Private, Not-for-profit, Mennonite Church)
Fall 2016 Enrollment: 63 . . . . (740) 857-1311
2016-17 Tuition: In-state $8,336; Out-of-state $8,336
Housing: Homeownership rate: 68.4%; Median home value: $158,200; Median year structure built: 1963; Homeowner vacancy rate: 17.3%; Median selected monthly owner costs: $1,211 with a mortgage, $500 without a mortgage; Median gross rent: $845 per month; Rental vacancy rate: 0.0%
Health Insurance: 90.1% have insurance; 83.7% have private insurance; 17.3% have public insurance; 9.9% do not have insurance; 5.6% of children under 18 do not have insurance
Transportation: Commute: 84.7% car, 0.0% public transportation, 14.0% walk, 0.0% work from home; Mean travel time to work: 26.6 minutes

LAFAYETTE (CDP). Covers a land area of 1.048 square miles and a water area of 0 square miles. Located at 39.94° N. Lat; 83.41° W. Long. Elevation is 1,010 feet.
Population: 256; Growth (since 2000): n/a; Density: 244.3 persons per square mile; Race: 90.2% White, 0.0% Black/African American, 3.5% Asian, 0.0% American Indian/Alaska Native, 0.0% Native Hawaiian/Other Pacific Islander, 6.3% Two or more races, 0.0% Hispanic of any race; Average household size: 2.42; Median age: 42.1; Age under 18: 23.4%; Age 65 and over: 11.3%; Males per 100 females: 102.0; Marriage status: 14.8% never married, 68.4% now married, 3.6% separated, 3.1% widowed, 13.8% divorced; Foreign born: 3.5%; Speak English only: 91.1%; With disability: 4.3%; Veterans: 10.7%; Ancestry: 31.3% Irish, 18.8% German, 13.3% American, 10.2% English, 5.1% Dutch
Employment: 0.0% management, business, and financial, 0.0% computer, engineering, and science, 0.0% education, legal, community service, arts, and media, 30.6% healthcare practitioners, 4.6% service, 28.7% sales and office, 3.7% natural resources, construction, and maintenance, 32.4% production, transportation, and material moving
Income: Per capita: $27,849; Median household: $65,938; Average household: $67,970; Households with income of $100,000 or more: 24.5%; Poverty rate: 7.8%
Educational Attainment: High school diploma or higher: 92.4%; Bachelor's degree or higher: 27.9%; Graduate/professional degree or higher: 5.8%
Housing: Homeownership rate: 62.3%; Median home value: $102,300; Median year structure built: 1945; Homeowner vacancy rate: 0.0%; Median selected monthly owner costs: $1,036 with a mortgage, $436 without a mortgage; Median gross rent: $795 per month; Rental vacancy rate: 0.0%
Health Insurance: 98.0% have insurance; 83.2% have private insurance; 27.7% have public insurance; 2.0% do not have insurance; 0.0% of children under 18 do not have insurance
Transportation: Commute: 95.4% car, 0.0% public transportation, 0.0% walk, 4.6% work from home; Mean travel time to work: 20.6 minutes

LONDON (city). County seat. Covers a land area of 8.448 square miles and a water area of 0 square miles. Located at 39.89° N. Lat; 83.44° W. Long. Elevation is 1,053 feet.
History: London was established on a site that had formerly been a swamp, known for malaria and ague. When the swamp was drained, the land was good for farming and livestock raising. The town was incorporated in 1831 and soon became a stockyard and trading center.
Population: 10,058; Growth (since 2000): 14.7%; Density: 1,190.6 persons per square mile; Race: 89.8% White, 4.5% Black/African American, 1.8% Asian, 0.2% American Indian/Alaska Native, 0.0% Native Hawaiian/Other Pacific Islander, 3.0% Two or more races, 2.9% Hispanic of any race; Average household size: 2.41; Median age: 36.4; Age under 18: 22.6%; Age 65 and over: 15.4%; Males per 100 females: 88.3; Marriage status: 34.9% never married, 42.8% now married, 3.8% separated, 6.4% widowed, 15.8% divorced; Foreign born: 2.5%; Speak English only: 96.0%; With disability: 19.4%; Veterans: 8.4%; Ancestry: 24.6% German, 14.7% Irish, 14.6% American, 10.9% English, 4.5% Scottish
Employment: 6.7% management, business, and financial, 3.7% computer, engineering, and science, 7.1% education, legal, community service, arts, and media, 4.1% healthcare practitioners, 22.7% service, 23.1% sales and

office, 9.4% natural resources, construction, and maintenance, 23.1% production, transportation, and material moving
Income: Per capita: $23,305; Median household: $48,504; Average household: $55,285; Households with income of $100,000 or more: 13.8%; Poverty rate: 13.6%
Educational Attainment: High school diploma or higher: 86.1%; Bachelor's degree or higher: 14.0%; Graduate/professional degree or higher: 3.6%

School District(s)

Jonathan Alder Local (PK-12)
2015-16 Enrollment: 2,219 . . . . (614) 873-5621
London Academy (08-12)
2015-16 Enrollment: 248. . . . . (740) 852-5703
London City (PK-12)
2015-16 Enrollment: 2,016 . . . . (740) 852-5700
Madison-Plains Local (KG-12)
2015-16 Enrollment: 1,183 . . . . (740) 852-0290

Housing: Homeownership rate: 51.3%; Median home value: $125,700; Median year structure built: 1974; Homeowner vacancy rate: 4.3%; Median selected monthly owner costs: $1,124 with a mortgage, $403 without a mortgage; Median gross rent: $764 per month; Rental vacancy rate: 3.3%
Health Insurance: 89.2% have insurance; 63.8% have private insurance; 38.5% have public insurance; 10.8% do not have insurance; 6.1% of children under 18 do not have insurance
Hospitals: Madison County Hospital (102 beds)
Safety: Violent crime rate: 6.9 per 10,000 population; Property crime rate: 281.4 per 10,000 population
Newspapers: Madison Press (daily circulation 5,500); Madison Press (weekly circulation 20,000)
Transportation: Commute: 91.7% car, 0.4% public transportation, 2.9% walk, 3.4% work from home; Mean travel time to work: 18.7 minutes
Additional Information Contacts
City of London . . . . (740) 852-3243
http://ci.london.oh.us

MIDWAY (village). Covers a land area of 0.291 square miles and a water area of 0 square miles. Located at 39.73° N. Lat; 83.48° W. Long. Elevation is 1,066 feet.
History: Also called Sedalia.
Population: 283; Growth (since 2000): 3.3%; Density: 973.3 persons per square mile; Race: 99.6% White, 0.0% Black/African American, 0.0% Asian, 0.0% American Indian/Alaska Native, 0.0% Native Hawaiian/Other Pacific Islander, 0.4% Two or more races, 0.0% Hispanic of any race; Average household size: 3.33; Median age: 40.3; Age under 18: 28.6%; Age 65 and over: 19.1%; Males per 100 females: 95.2; Marriage status: 26.3% never married, 47.8% now married, 4.4% separated, 13.2% widowed, 12.7% divorced; Foreign born: 0.7%; Speak English only: 99.6%; With disability: 13.8%; Veterans: 9.4%; Ancestry: 33.2% German, 23.7% American, 14.1% Irish, 11.3% English, 7.8% Scottish
Employment: 8.5% management, business, and financial, 5.4% computer, engineering, and science, 3.9% education, legal, community service, arts, and media, 1.6% healthcare practitioners, 19.4% service, 17.8% sales and office, 17.1% natural resources, construction, and maintenance, 26.4% production, transportation, and material moving
Income: Per capita: $19,781; Median household: $53,750; Average household: $63,547; Households with income of $100,000 or more: 18.9%; Poverty rate: 14.2%
Educational Attainment: High school diploma or higher: 90.2%; Bachelor's degree or higher: 5.5%; Graduate/professional degree or higher: 1.1%
Housing: Homeownership rate: 76.5%; Median home value: $85,500; Median year structure built: Before 1940; Homeowner vacancy rate: 0.0%; Median selected monthly owner costs: $1,158 with a mortgage, $275 without a mortgage; Median gross rent: $840 per month; Rental vacancy rate: 0.0%
Health Insurance: 97.5% have insurance; 70.7% have private insurance; 42.4% have public insurance; 2.5% do not have insurance; 0.0% of children under 18 do not have insurance
Transportation: Commute: 98.4% car, 0.0% public transportation, 0.0% walk, 1.6% work from home; Mean travel time to work: 26.8 minutes

MOUNT STERLING (village). Covers a land area of 1.725 square miles and a water area of 0 square miles. Located at 39.72° N. Lat; 83.26° W. Long. Elevation is 902 feet.
History: Mount Sterling was founded in 1828 by John J. Smith, who named the town after his former home in Kentucky. An early industry was the Ohio Willow Wood Company, manufacturers of artificial limbs, polo balls and mallets.
Population: 1,829; Growth (since 2000): -1.9%; Density: 1,060.1 persons per square mile; Race: 97.8% White, 0.2% Black/African American, 0.2% Asian, 0.2% American Indian/Alaska Native, 0.0% Native Hawaiian/Other Pacific Islander, 1.4% Two or more races, 0.9% Hispanic of any race; Average household size: 2.53; Median age: 35.2; Age under 18: 28.6%; Age 65 and over: 12.2%; Males per 100 females: 90.4; Marriage status: 32.0% never married, 42.1% now married, 1.8% separated, 4.9% widowed, 21.0% divorced; Foreign born: 0.4%; Speak English only: 98.7%; With disability: 22.0%; Veterans: 6.1%; Ancestry: 27.4% American, 26.1% German, 19.7% Irish, 9.0% English, 4.4% Hungarian
Employment: 7.4% management, business, and financial, 3.5% computer, engineering, and science, 5.0% education, legal, community service, arts, and media, 9.8% healthcare practitioners, 11.9% service, 29.8% sales and office, 8.2% natural resources, construction, and maintenance, 24.5% production, transportation, and material moving
Income: Per capita: $18,612; Median household: $33,782; Average household: $46,612; Households with income of $100,000 or more: 8.9%; Poverty rate: 26.3%
Educational Attainment: High school diploma or higher: 87.4%; Bachelor's degree or higher: 7.5%; Graduate/professional degree or higher: 1.0%
Housing: Homeownership rate: 44.1%; Median home value: $98,400; Median year structure built: 1954; Homeowner vacancy rate: 3.1%; Median selected monthly owner costs: $972 with a mortgage, $378 without a mortgage; Median gross rent: $653 per month; Rental vacancy rate: 7.0%
Health Insurance: 89.4% have insurance; 56.4% have private insurance; 46.7% have public insurance; 10.6% do not have insurance; 1.1% of children under 18 do not have insurance
Transportation: Commute: 92.2% car, 0.3% public transportation, 3.2% walk, 3.5% work from home; Mean travel time to work: 28.6 minutes

PLAIN CITY (village). Covers a land area of 2.379 square miles and a water area of 0.016 square miles. Located at 40.11° N. Lat; 83.27° W. Long. Elevation is 935 feet.
History: Plain City was laid out in 1818 by Isaac Bigelow. It was first called Westminster, then Pleasant Valley, and finally named Plain City in 1851 because of its location on Big Darby Plain.
Population: 4,444; Growth (since 2000): 56.9%; Density: 1,868.2 persons per square mile; Race: 96.6% White, 0.2% Black/African American, 1.6% Asian, 0.2% American Indian/Alaska Native, 0.0% Native Hawaiian/Other Pacific Islander, 1.4% Two or more races, 0.2% Hispanic of any race; Average household size: 2.40; Median age: 37.0; Age under 18: 27.3%; Age 65 and over: 15.9%; Males per 100 females: 88.9; Marriage status: 24.1% never married, 52.5% now married, 0.5% separated, 6.5% widowed, 16.9% divorced; Foreign born: 1.6%; Speak English only: 96.2%; With disability: 10.5%; Veterans: 9.6%; Ancestry: 31.9% German, 17.7% American, 13.4% English, 13.1% Irish, 6.7% Scottish
Employment: 24.3% management, business, and financial, 6.5% computer, engineering, and science, 5.1% education, legal, community service, arts, and media, 3.8% healthcare practitioners, 10.2% service, 26.6% sales and office, 10.9% natural resources, construction, and maintenance, 12.5% production, transportation, and material moving
Income: Per capita: $31,155; Median household: $61,958; Average household: $76,710; Households with income of $100,000 or more: 26.6%; Poverty rate: 12.8%
Educational Attainment: High school diploma or higher: 92.4%; Bachelor's degree or higher: 30.4%; Graduate/professional degree or higher: 8.3%

School District(s)

Jonathan Alder Local (PK-12)
2015-16 Enrollment: 2,219 . . . . (614) 873-5621
Tolles Career & Technical Center (07-12)
2015-16 Enrollment: n/a . . . . (614) 873-4666

Housing: Homeownership rate: 72.5%; Median home value: $192,900; Median year structure built: 1990; Homeowner vacancy rate: 0.4%; Median selected monthly owner costs: $1,593 with a mortgage, $458 without a mortgage; Median gross rent: $654 per month; Rental vacancy rate: 0.0%

Health Insurance: 92.7% have insurance; 73.9% have private insurance; 32.1% have public insurance; 7.3% do not have insurance; 4.8% of children under 18 do not have insurance
Transportation: Commute: 90.3% car, 0.5% public transportation, 0.6% walk, 6.9% work from home; Mean travel time to work: 24.7 minutes

PLUMWOOD (CDP). Covers a land area of 0.622 square miles and a water area of 0 square miles. Located at 40.01° N. Lat; 83.41° W. Long. Elevation is 1,007 feet.
Population: 253; Growth (since 2000): n/a; Density: 407.0 persons per square mile; Race: 100.0% White, 0.0% Black/African American, 0.0% Asian, 0.0% American Indian/Alaska Native, 0.0% Native Hawaiian/Other Pacific Islander, 0.0% Two or more races, 0.0% Hispanic of any race; Average household size: 2.18; Median age: 45.8; Age under 18: 20.6%; Age 65 and over: 15.8%; Males per 100 females: 118.5; Marriage status: 22.8% never married, 47.5% now married, 0.0% separated, 15.1% widowed, 14.6% divorced; Foreign born: 0.0%; Speak English only: 100.0%; With disability: 24.5%; Veterans: 0.0%; Ancestry: 36.4% German, 17.8% American, 14.6% English, 8.7% Polish, 4.0% Irish
Employment: 8.3% management, business, and financial, 3.3% computer, engineering, and science, 6.6% education, legal, community service, arts, and media, 9.9% healthcare practitioners, 24.0% service, 17.4% sales and office, 6.6% natural resources, construction, and maintenance, 24.0% production, transportation, and material moving
Income: Per capita: $23,418; Median household: $37,174; Average household: $49,185; Households with income of $100,000 or more: 7.7%; Poverty rate: 5.1%
Educational Attainment: High school diploma or higher: 84.7%; Bachelor's degree or higher: 16.8%; Graduate/professional degree or higher: 14.3%
Housing: Homeownership rate: 63.8%; Median home value: $162,500; Median year structure built: 1981; Homeowner vacancy rate: 0.0%; Median selected monthly owner costs: $1,201 with a mortgage, n/a without a mortgage; Median gross rent: $597 per month; Rental vacancy rate: 0.0%
Health Insurance: 80.6% have insurance; 54.9% have private insurance; 42.3% have public insurance; 19.4% do not have insurance; 25.0% of children under 18 do not have insurance
Transportation: Commute: 100.0% car, 0.0% public transportation, 0.0% walk, 0.0% work from home; Mean travel time to work: 23.5 minutes

SEDALIA (unincorporated postal area)

ZCTA: 43151

Covers a land area of 0.291 square miles and a water area of 0 square miles. Located at 39.73° N. Lat; 83.48° W. Long..
Population: 283; Growth (since 2000): 3.3%; Density: 973.3 persons per square mile; Race: 99.6% White, 0.0% Black/African American, 0.0% Asian, 0.0% American Indian/Alaska Native, 0.0% Native Hawaiian/Other Pacific Islander, 0.4% Two or more races, 0.0% Hispanic of any race; Average household size: 3.33; Median age: 40.3; Age under 18: 28.6%; Age 65 and over: 19.1%; Males per 100 females: 95.2; Marriage status: 26.3% never married, 47.8% now married, 4.4% separated, 13.2% widowed, 12.7% divorced; Foreign born: 0.7%; Speak English only: 99.6%; With disability: 13.8%; Veterans: 9.4%; Ancestry: 33.2% German, 23.7% American, 14.1% Irish, 11.3% English, 7.8% Scottish
Employment: 8.5% management, business, and financial, 5.4% computer, engineering, and science, 3.9% education, legal, community service, arts, and media, 1.6% healthcare practitioners, 19.4% service, 17.8% sales and office, 17.1% natural resources, construction, and maintenance, 26.4% production, transportation, and material moving
Income: Per capita: $19,781; Median household: $53,750; Average household: $63,547; Households with income of $100,000 or more: 18.9%; Poverty rate: 14.2%
Educational Attainment: High school diploma or higher: 90.2%; Bachelor's degree or higher: 5.5%; Graduate/professional degree or higher: 1.1%
Housing: Homeownership rate: 76.5%; Median home value: $85,500; Median year structure built: Before 1940; Homeowner vacancy rate: 0.0%; Median selected monthly owner costs: $1,158 with a mortgage, $275 without a mortgage; Median gross rent: $840 per month; Rental vacancy rate: 0.0%
Health Insurance: 97.5% have insurance; 70.7% have private insurance; 42.4% have public insurance; 2.5% do not have insurance; 0.0% of children under 18 do not have insurance
Transportation: Commute: 98.4% car, 0.0% public transportation, 0.0% walk, 1.6% work from home; Mean travel time to work: 26.8 minutes

SOUTH SOLON (village). Covers a land area of 0.251 square miles and a water area of 0 square miles. Located at 39.74° N. Lat; 83.61° W. Long. Elevation is 1,112 feet.
Population: 311; Growth (since 2000): -23.2%; Density: 1,240.8 persons per square mile; Race: 100.0% White, 0.0% Black/African American, 0.0% Asian, 0.0% American Indian/Alaska Native, 0.0% Native Hawaiian/Other Pacific Islander, 0.0% Two or more races, 0.0% Hispanic of any race; Average household size: 2.64; Median age: 35.7; Age under 18: 19.6%; Age 65 and over: 14.5%; Males per 100 females: 102.9; Marriage status: 34.0% never married, 52.9% now married, 4.2% separated, 7.7% widowed, 5.4% divorced; Foreign born: 1.0%; Speak English only: 98.6%; With disability: 14.1%; Veterans: 1.6%; Ancestry: 32.2% American, 22.5% Irish, 21.2% German, 15.8% English, 4.2% Scotch-Irish
Employment: 10.8% management, business, and financial, 6.2% computer, engineering, and science, 3.8% education, legal, community service, arts, and media, 0.8% healthcare practitioners, 20.8% service, 17.7% sales and office, 11.5% natural resources, construction, and maintenance, 28.5% production, transportation, and material moving
Income: Per capita: $17,102; Median household: $41,250; Average household: $45,108; Households with income of $100,000 or more: 9.3%; Poverty rate: 22.4%
Educational Attainment: High school diploma or higher: 83.4%; Bachelor's degree or higher: 4.0%; Graduate/professional degree or higher: 0.5%
Housing: Homeownership rate: 70.3%; Median home value: $65,000; Median year structure built: Before 1940; Homeowner vacancy rate: 3.5%; Median selected monthly owner costs: $918 with a mortgage, $395 without a mortgage; Median gross rent: $788 per month; Rental vacancy rate: 0.0%
Health Insurance: 79.4% have insurance; 46.6% have private insurance; 37.9% have public insurance; 20.6% do not have insurance; 32.8% of children under 18 do not have insurance
Transportation: Commute: 100.0% car, 0.0% public transportation, 0.0% walk, 0.0% work from home; Mean travel time to work: 30.1 minutes

WEST JEFFERSON (village). Covers a land area of 4.850 square miles and a water area of 0.021 square miles. Located at 39.95° N. Lat; 83.31° W. Long. Elevation is 912 feet.
Population: 4,285; Growth (since 2000): -1.1%; Density: 883.5 persons per square mile; Race: 92.6% White, 0.8% Black/African American, 0.0% Asian, 0.0% American Indian/Alaska Native, 0.0% Native Hawaiian/Other Pacific Islander, 6.6% Two or more races, 0.5% Hispanic of any race; Average household size: 2.64; Median age: 40.1; Age under 18: 23.8%; Age 65 and over: 16.9%; Males per 100 females: 95.6; Marriage status: 28.8% never married, 48.6% now married, 2.3% separated, 7.5% widowed, 15.1% divorced; Foreign born: 0.4%; Speak English only: 99.5%; With disability: 14.1%; Veterans: 8.5%; Ancestry: 28.4% German, 20.1% American, 18.0% Irish, 15.5% English, 6.0% Scottish
Employment: 11.3% management, business, and financial, 2.4% computer, engineering, and science, 6.5% education, legal, community service, arts, and media, 1.7% healthcare practitioners, 16.1% service, 32.2% sales and office, 12.5% natural resources, construction, and maintenance, 17.4% production, transportation, and material moving
Income: Per capita: $22,614; Median household: $51,644; Average household: $59,817; Households with income of $100,000 or more: 12.9%; Poverty rate: 9.0%
Educational Attainment: High school diploma or higher: 86.6%; Bachelor's degree or higher: 7.7%; Graduate/professional degree or higher: 1.7%

School District(s)

Jefferson Local (KG-12)
2015-16 Enrollment: 1,164 . . . . (614) 879-7654
Housing: Homeownership rate: 65.5%; Median home value: $121,100; Median year structure built: 1964; Homeowner vacancy rate: 2.5%; Median selected monthly owner costs: $1,112 with a mortgage, $414 without a mortgage; Median gross rent: $727 per month; Rental vacancy rate: 0.0%
Health Insurance: 88.3% have insurance; 69.1% have private insurance; 33.9% have public insurance; 11.7% do not have insurance; 7.4% of children under 18 do not have insurance
Safety: Violent crime rate: 7.0 per 10,000 population; Property crime rate: 235.4 per 10,000 population
Transportation: Commute: 93.0% car, 0.0% public transportation, 1.6% walk, 3.7% work from home; Mean travel time to work: 22.3 minutes
Additional Information Contacts

Village of West Jefferson . . . . (614) 879-7674
http://www.villageofwestjefferson.com

Mahoning County

Located in eastern Ohio; bounded on the east by Pennsylvania; crossed by the Mahoning and Little Beaver Rivers. Covers a land area of 411.623 square miles, a water area of 13.663 square miles, and is located in the Eastern Time Zone at 41.01° N. Lat., 80.77° W. Long. The county was founded in 1846. County seat is Youngstown.

Mahoning County is part of the Youngstown-Warren-Boardman, OH-PA Metropolitan Statistical Area. The entire metro area includes: Mahoning County, OH; Trumbull County, OH; Mercer County, PA

Population: 233,015; Growth (since 2000): -9.5%; Density: 566.1 persons per square mile; Race: 80.2% White, 15.5% Black/African American, 0.8% Asian, 0.3% American Indian/Alaska Native, 0.0% Native Hawaiian/Other Pacific Islander, 2.5% two or more races, 5.3% Hispanic of any race; Average household size: 2.32; Median age: 43.4; Age under 18: 20.6%; Age 65 and over: 19.1%; Males per 100 females: 93.7; Marriage status: 32.2% never married, 47.2% now married, 1.7% separated, 8.2% widowed, 12.4% divorced; Foreign born: 2.8%; Speak English only: 93.7%; With disability: 15.6%; Veterans: 9.4%; Ancestry: 19.8% German, 18.5% Italian, 16.2% Irish, 7.4% American, 7.3% English
Religion: Six largest groups: 29.8% Catholicism, 7.6% Baptist, 3.9% Pentecostal, 3.6% Methodist/Pietist, 3.5% Lutheran, 2.8% Presbyterian-Reformed
Economy: Unemployment rate: 5.9%; Leading industries: 15.7 % retail trade; 13.6 % health care and social assistance; 11.2 % other services (except public administration); Farms: 578 totaling 74,966 acres; Company size: 1 employs 1,000 or more persons, 7 employ 500 to 999 persons, 136 employ 100 to 499 persons, 5,341 employs less than 100 persons; Business ownership: 7,180 women-owned, 2,305 Black-owned, 565 Hispanic-owned, 412 Asian-owned, 84 American Indian/Alaska Native-owned
Employment: 11.4% management, business, and financial, 2.8% computer, engineering, and science, 9.8% education, legal, community service, arts, and media, 7.7% healthcare practitioners, 19.1% service, 24.8% sales and office, 8.6% natural resources, construction, and maintenance, 15.9% production, transportation, and material moving
Income: Per capita: $24,651; Median household: $41,872; Average household: $57,417; Households with income of $100,000 or more: 14.5%; Poverty rate: 18.1%
Educational Attainment: High school diploma or higher: 90.1%; Bachelor's degree or higher: 22.8%; Graduate/professional degree or higher: 8.0%
Housing: Homeownership rate: 68.3%; Median home value: $98,300; Median year structure built: 1960; Homeowner vacancy rate: 4.5%; Median selected monthly owner costs: $1,047 with a mortgage, $383 without a mortgage; Median gross rent: $637 per month; Rental vacancy rate: 6.1%
Vital Statistics: Birth rate: 103.3 per 10,000 population; Death rate: 130.0 per 10,000 population; Age-adjusted cancer mortality rate: 178.8 deaths per 100,000 population
Health Insurance: 92.2% have insurance; 63.5% have private insurance; 42.1% have public insurance; 7.8% do not have insurance; 3.6% of children under 18 do not have insurance
Health Care: Physicians: 35.8 per 10,000 population; Dentists: 7.1 per 10,000 population; Hospital beds: 46.9 per 10,000 population; Hospital admissions: 2,223.2 per 10,000 population
Air Quality Index (AQI): Percent of Days: 85.0% good, 15.0% moderate, 0.0% unhealthy for sensitive individuals, 0.0% unhealthy, 0.0% very unhealthy; Annual median: 35; Annual maximum: 75
Transportation: Commute: 93.1% car, 1.1% public transportation, 1.5% walk, 3.1% work from home; Mean travel time to work: 21.6 minutes
2016 Presidential Election: 46.2% Trump, 49.5% Clinton, 2.2% Johnson, 0.8% Stein
Additional Information Contacts
Mahoning Government . . . . (330) 740-2130
http://www.mahoningcountyoh.gov

Mahoning County Communities

AUSTINTOWN (CDP). Covers a land area of 11.630 square miles and a water area of 0.034 square miles. Located at 41.09° N. Lat; 80.74° W. Long. Elevation is 1,129 feet.
Population: 28,468; Growth (since 2000): -10.0%; Density: 2,447.9 persons per square mile; Race: 87.5% White, 9.5% Black/African American, 1.0% Asian, 0.2% American Indian/Alaska Native, 0.2% Native Hawaiian/Other Pacific Islander, 1.2% Two or more races, 2.7% Hispanic of any race; Average household size: 2.19; Median age: 43.0; Age under 18: 19.4%; Age 65 and over: 20.2%; Males per 100 females: 90.6; Marriage status: 30.5% never married, 48.7% now married, 0.9% separated, 8.1% widowed, 12.8% divorced; Foreign born: 2.7%; Speak English only: 96.1%; With disability: 14.6%; Veterans: 11.4%; Ancestry: 26.0% German, 21.4% Irish, 19.9% Italian, 8.8% English, 6.8% Slovak
Employment: 11.1% management, business, and financial, 2.4% computer, engineering, and science, 9.6% education, legal, community service, arts, and media, 7.3% healthcare practitioners, 21.2% service, 23.2% sales and office, 8.3% natural resources, construction, and maintenance, 16.8% production, transportation, and material moving
Income: Per capita: $23,717; Median household: $41,789; Average household: $51,740; Households with income of $100,000 or more: 10.4%; Poverty rate: 13.2%
Educational Attainment: High school diploma or higher: 91.4%; Bachelor's degree or higher: 21.1%; Graduate/professional degree or higher: 6.7%

Two-year College(s)

Casal Aveda Institute (Private, For-profit)
Fall 2016 Enrollment: 140 . . . . (330) 792-6504
Housing: Homeownership rate: 63.0%; Median home value: $93,800; Median year structure built: 1966; Homeowner vacancy rate: 6.5%; Median selected monthly owner costs: $1,006 with a mortgage, $358 without a mortgage; Median gross rent: $614 per month; Rental vacancy rate: 13.7%
Health Insurance: 91.4% have insurance; 67.5% have private insurance; 38.7% have public insurance; 8.6% do not have insurance; 6.3% of children under 18 do not have insurance
Safety: Violent crime rate: 14.6 per 10,000 population; Property crime rate: 229.3 per 10,000 population
Transportation: Commute: 96.5% car, 0.4% public transportation, 0.5% walk, 2.2% work from home; Mean travel time to work: 21.7 minutes

BELOIT (village). Covers a land area of 0.975 square miles and a water area of 0.008 square miles. Located at 40.92° N. Lat; 81.00° W. Long. Elevation is 1,125 feet.
Population: 1,045; Growth (since 2000): 2.1%; Density: 1,071.6 persons per square mile; Race: 96.5% White, 1.4% Black/African American, 0.0% Asian, 0.0% American Indian/Alaska Native, 0.0% Native Hawaiian/Other Pacific Islander, 2.1% Two or more races, 1.9% Hispanic of any race; Average household size: 2.31; Median age: 42.1; Age under 18: 20.4%; Age 65 and over: 21.4%; Males per 100 females: 91.0; Marriage status: 27.5% never married, 46.3% now married, 1.7% separated, 8.5% widowed, 17.7% divorced; Foreign born: 0.3%; Speak English only: 99.2%; With disability: 17.1%; Veterans: 7.3%; Ancestry: 40.4% German, 20.2% Irish, 12.2% English, 12.0% Italian, 8.3% American
Employment: 6.1% management, business, and financial, 1.2% computer, engineering, and science, 4.8% education, legal, community service, arts, and media, 6.3% healthcare practitioners, 25.7% service, 23.2% sales and office, 14.3% natural resources, construction, and maintenance, 18.4% production, transportation, and material moving
Income: Per capita: $17,854; Median household: $29,091; Average household: $40,238; Households with income of $100,000 or more: 6.4%; Poverty rate: 12.0%
Educational Attainment: High school diploma or higher: 89.3%; Bachelor's degree or higher: 11.3%; Graduate/professional degree or higher: 3.9%

School District(s)

West Branch Local (PK-12)
2015-16 Enrollment: 2,110 . . . . (330) 938-9324
Housing: Homeownership rate: 70.8%; Median home value: $75,200; Median year structure built: 1960; Homeowner vacancy rate: 1.8%; Median selected monthly owner costs: $899 with a mortgage, $429 without a mortgage; Median gross rent: $502 per month; Rental vacancy rate: 0.0%

Health Insurance: 91.6% have insurance; 62.5% have private insurance; 42.7% have public insurance; 8.4% do not have insurance; 0.0% of children under 18 do not have insurance
Transportation: Commute: 95.0% car, 0.0% public transportation, 2.1% walk, 2.9% work from home; Mean travel time to work: 20.0 minutes

BERLIN CENTER (unincorporated postal area)

ZCTA: 44401

Covers a land area of 32.162 square miles and a water area of 1.922 square miles. Located at 41.02° N. Lat; 80.94° W. Long. Elevation is 1,073 feet.
Population: 2,770; Growth (since 2000): -12.8%; Density: 86.1 persons per square mile; Race: 99.4% White, 0.0% Black/African American, 0.0% Asian, 0.0% American Indian/Alaska Native, 0.0% Native Hawaiian/Other Pacific Islander, 0.6% Two or more races, 1.2% Hispanic of any race; Average household size: 2.43; Median age: 51.1; Age under 18: 15.0%; Age 65 and over: 23.6%; Males per 100 females: 106.7; Marriage status: 23.9% never married, 65.3% now married, 2.5% separated, 5.7% widowed, 5.0% divorced; Foreign born: 0.6%; Speak English only: 98.4%; With disability: 13.5%; Veterans: 11.9%; Ancestry: 30.9% German, 21.3% Irish, 15.9% English, 10.2% Italian, 6.0% American
Employment: 10.5% management, business, and financial, 1.0% computer, engineering, and science, 4.3% education, legal, community service, arts, and media, 6.5% healthcare practitioners, 10.9% service, 25.1% sales and office, 12.2% natural resources, construction, and maintenance, 29.4% production, transportation, and material moving
Income: Per capita: $27,792; Median household: $55,774; Average household: $67,285; Households with income of $100,000 or more: 21.2%; Poverty rate: 6.8%
Educational Attainment: High school diploma or higher: 92.2%; Bachelor's degree or higher: 15.5%; Graduate/professional degree or higher: 4.8%

School District(s)

Western Reserve Local (KG-12)
2015-16 Enrollment: 672. . . . . (330) 547-4100
Housing: Homeownership rate: 86.0%; Median home value: $157,200; Median year structure built: 1973; Homeowner vacancy rate: 1.8%; Median selected monthly owner costs: $1,250 with a mortgage, $528 without a mortgage; Median gross rent: $837 per month; Rental vacancy rate: 0.0%
Health Insurance: 95.0% have insurance; 71.1% have private insurance; 41.1% have public insurance; 5.0% do not have insurance; 1.9% of children under 18 do not have insurance
Transportation: Commute: 95.5% car, 0.0% public transportation, 2.2% walk, 1.5% work from home; Mean travel time to work: 25.5 minutes

BOARDMAN (CDP). Covers a land area of 15.121 square miles and a water area of 0.172 square miles. Located at 41.03° N. Lat; 80.67° W. Long. Elevation is 1,112 feet.
Population: 34,717; Growth (since 2000): -6.7%; Density: 2,295.9 persons per square mile; Race: 89.6% White, 7.0% Black/African American, 0.9% Asian, 0.2% American Indian/Alaska Native, 0.0% Native Hawaiian/Other Pacific Islander, 2.1% Two or more races, 4.1% Hispanic of any race; Average household size: 2.25; Median age: 43.3; Age under 18: 18.8%; Age 65 and over: 19.5%; Males per 100 females: 90.7; Marriage status: 29.6% never married, 49.3% now married, 1.3% separated, 7.9% widowed, 13.1% divorced; Foreign born: 3.5%; Speak English only: 94.1%; With disability: 13.1%; Veterans: 8.8%; Ancestry: 25.7% Italian, 20.7% German, 18.0% Irish, 8.7% Slovak, 8.0% English
Employment: 13.7% management, business, and financial, 3.3% computer, engineering, and science, 10.9% education, legal, community service, arts, and media, 8.8% healthcare practitioners, 16.2% service, 27.6% sales and office, 7.7% natural resources, construction, and maintenance, 11.8% production, transportation, and material moving
Income: Per capita: $28,486; Median household: $51,158; Average household: $63,784; Households with income of $100,000 or more: 17.9%; Poverty rate: 9.6%
Educational Attainment: High school diploma or higher: 93.9%; Bachelor's degree or higher: 29.6%; Graduate/professional degree or higher: 10.2%

Two-year College(s)

Raphael's School of Beauty Culture Inc-Boardman (Private, For-profit)
Fall 2016 Enrollment: 106 . . . . (330) 782-3395
Housing: Homeownership rate: 64.7%; Median home value: $112,100; Median year structure built: 1965; Homeowner vacancy rate: 1.7%; Median selected monthly owner costs: $1,076 with a mortgage, $437 without a mortgage; Median gross rent: $630 per month; Rental vacancy rate: 4.9%
Health Insurance: 92.5% have insurance; 73.9% have private insurance; 33.6% have public insurance; 7.5% do not have insurance; 6.0% of children under 18 do not have insurance
Hospitals: Saint Elizabeth Boardman Health Center
Newspapers: Town Crier Newspapers (weekly circulation 20,000)
Transportation: Commute: 94.8% car, 0.6% public transportation, 0.8% walk, 3.1% work from home; Mean travel time to work: 20.2 minutes

CAMPBELL (city). Covers a land area of 3.712 square miles and a water area of 0.032 square miles. Located at 41.08° N. Lat; 80.59° W. Long. Elevation is 1,033 feet.
History: Until 1926, called East Youngstown.
Population: 8,040; Growth (since 2000): -15.0%; Density: 2,165.8 persons per square mile; Race: 69.3% White, 21.4% Black/African American, 0.0% Asian, 1.0% American Indian/Alaska Native, 0.0% Native Hawaiian/Other Pacific Islander, 7.0% Two or more races, 18.2% Hispanic of any race; Average household size: 2.42; Median age: 40.8; Age under 18: 22.6%; Age 65 and over: 17.8%; Males per 100 females: 90.0; Marriage status: 37.3% never married, 40.3% now married, 2.5% separated, 8.2% widowed, 14.2% divorced; Foreign born: 4.4%; Speak English only: 81.7%; With disability: 22.9%; Veterans: 10.7%; Ancestry: 16.6% Italian, 9.9% Irish, 9.6% German, 7.9% Greek, 6.5% American
Employment: 4.0% management, business, and financial, 0.6% computer, engineering, and science, 5.9% education, legal, community service, arts, and media, 6.4% healthcare practitioners, 22.5% service, 26.4% sales and office, 10.7% natural resources, construction, and maintenance, 23.6% production, transportation, and material moving
Income: Per capita: $16,360; Median household: $28,952; Average household: $38,544; Households with income of $100,000 or more: 4.3%; Poverty rate: 29.2%
Educational Attainment: High school diploma or higher: 83.0%; Bachelor's degree or higher: 8.0%; Graduate/professional degree or higher: 2.5%

School District(s)

Campbell City (PK-12)
2015-16 Enrollment: 1,130 . . . . (330) 799-6726
Housing: Homeownership rate: 67.7%; Median home value: $61,600; Median year structure built: 1952; Homeowner vacancy rate: 1.6%; Median selected monthly owner costs: $769 with a mortgage, $333 without a mortgage; Median gross rent: $633 per month; Rental vacancy rate: 6.4%
Health Insurance: 92.6% have insurance; 44.7% have private insurance; 59.7% have public insurance; 7.4% do not have insurance; 1.2% of children under 18 do not have insurance
Safety: Violent crime rate: 5.0 per 10,000 population; Property crime rate: 51.7 per 10,000 population
Transportation: Commute: 92.2% car, 1.4% public transportation, 0.8% walk, 1.6% work from home; Mean travel time to work: 24.3 minutes
Additional Information Contacts
City of Campbell . . . . (330) 755-1451
http://cityofcampbellohio.org

CANFIELD (city). Covers a land area of 4.579 square miles and a water area of 0.027 square miles. Located at 41.03° N. Lat; 80.77° W. Long. Elevation is 1,148 feet.
History: Canfield was surveyed in 1798. After a brief oil boom, the town turned to lumber, clay, coal, and farm products for its revenue source.
Population: 7,376; Growth (since 2000): 0.0%; Density: 1,610.8 persons per square mile; Race: 92.8% White, 0.0% Black/African American, 4.3% Asian, 0.5% American Indian/Alaska Native, 0.0% Native Hawaiian/Other Pacific Islander, 2.4% Two or more races, 0.9% Hispanic of any race; Average household size: 2.38; Median age: 49.3; Age under 18: 18.8%; Age 65 and over: 21.0%; Males per 100 females: 92.4; Marriage status: 21.2% never married, 66.2% now married, 0.5% separated, 5.8% widowed, 6.8% divorced; Foreign born: 5.4%; Speak English only: 93.1%; With disability: 6.4%; Veterans: 8.3%; Ancestry: 28.3% Italian, 20.5% Irish, 19.7% German, 11.2% Slovak, 8.4% English
Employment: 20.0% management, business, and financial, 3.8% computer, engineering, and science, 16.2% education, legal, community service, arts, and media, 9.9% healthcare practitioners, 10.1% service, 29.1% sales and office, 3.2% natural resources, construction, and maintenance, 7.7% production, transportation, and material moving

Income: Per capita: $39,906; Median household: $66,716; Average household: $94,183; Households with income of $100,000 or more: 32.6%; Poverty rate: 5.7%
Educational Attainment: High school diploma or higher: 97.6%; Bachelor's degree or higher: 43.9%; Graduate/professional degree or higher: 18.0%

School District(s)

Canfield Local (KG-12)
2015-16 Enrollment: 2,664 . . . . (330) 533-3303
Mahoning Co Career & Tech Ctr (07-12)
2015-16 Enrollment: n/a . . . . (330) 729-4000
South Range Local (PK-12)
2015-16 Enrollment: 1,297 . . . . (330) 549-5226

Vocational/Technical School(s)

Mahoning County Career and Technical Center (Public)
Fall 2016 Enrollment: 109 . . . . (330) 729-4100
2016-17 Tuition: $8,653

Housing: Homeownership rate: 79.9%; Median home value: $161,600; Median year structure built: 1977; Homeowner vacancy rate: 5.1%; Median selected monthly owner costs: $1,389 with a mortgage, $501 without a mortgage; Median gross rent: $725 per month; Rental vacancy rate: 0.0%
Health Insurance: 96.2% have insurance; 84.8% have private insurance; 25.1% have public insurance; 3.8% do not have insurance; 1.9% of children under 18 do not have insurance
Safety: Violent crime rate: 1.4 per 10,000 population; Property crime rate: 81.9 per 10,000 population
Transportation: Commute: 94.9% car, 0.1% public transportation, 0.0% walk, 3.9% work from home; Mean travel time to work: 22.3 minutes
Additional Information Contacts
City of Canfield . . . . (330) 533-1101
http://www.ci.canfield.oh.us

CRAIG BEACH (village). Covers a land area of 0.784 square miles and a water area of 0.785 square miles. Located at 41.12° N. Lat; 80.98° W. Long. Elevation is 951 feet.
Population: 1,123; Growth (since 2000): -10.4%; Density: 1,431.7 persons per square mile; Race: 99.4% White, 0.0% Black/African American, 0.0% Asian, 0.4% American Indian/Alaska Native, 0.0% Native Hawaiian/Other Pacific Islander, 0.3% Two or more races, 0.3% Hispanic of any race; Average household size: 2.30; Median age: 41.3; Age under 18: 21.7%; Age 65 and over: 15.8%; Males per 100 females: 94.1; Marriage status: 24.4% never married, 53.1% now married, 2.9% separated, 8.3% widowed, 14.2% divorced; Foreign born: 1.1%; Speak English only: 99.2%; With disability: 21.1%; Veterans: 11.7%; Ancestry: 28.2% Irish, 27.9% German, 11.1% Italian, 6.9% English, 6.5% American
Employment: 13.6% management, business, and financial, 2.5% computer, engineering, and science, 11.4% education, legal, community service, arts, and media, 6.4% healthcare practitioners, 17.1% service, 21.1% sales and office, 10.5% natural resources, construction, and maintenance, 17.4% production, transportation, and material moving
Income: Per capita: $23,859; Median household: $44,643; Average household: $54,263; Households with income of $100,000 or more: 8.8%; Poverty rate: 11.1%
Educational Attainment: High school diploma or higher: 90.0%; Bachelor's degree or higher: 12.2%; Graduate/professional degree or higher: 3.1%
Housing: Homeownership rate: 58.8%; Median home value: $91,300; Median year structure built: 1960; Homeowner vacancy rate: 8.9%; Median selected monthly owner costs: $913 with a mortgage, $360 without a mortgage; Median gross rent: $782 per month; Rental vacancy rate: 0.0%
Health Insurance: 94.9% have insurance; 68.3% have private insurance; 38.5% have public insurance; 5.1% do not have insurance; 4.9% of children under 18 do not have insurance
Transportation: Commute: 96.6% car, 0.0% public transportation, 0.0% walk, 2.2% work from home; Mean travel time to work: 28.3 minutes

DAMASCUS (CDP). Covers a land area of 0.799 square miles and a water area of 0.007 square miles. Located at 40.91° N. Lat; 80.95° W. Long. Elevation is 1,211 feet.
Population: 445; Growth (since 2000): n/a; Density: 556.9 persons per square mile; Race: 100.0% White, 0.0% Black/African American, 0.0% Asian, 0.0% American Indian/Alaska Native, 0.0% Native Hawaiian/Other Pacific Islander, 0.0% Two or more races, 0.0% Hispanic of any race; Average household size: 2.51; Median age: 49.1; Age under 18: 19.1%; Age 65 and over: 15.3%; Males per 100 females: 98.7; Marriage status: 31.1% never married, 46.4% now married, 0.0% separated, 2.2% widowed, 20.3% divorced; Foreign born: 0.0%; Speak English only: 100.0%; With disability: 9.0%; Veterans: 10.6%; Ancestry: 44.7% German, 23.8% Irish, 18.9% Polish, 9.7% American, 5.4% Slovak
Employment: 0.0% management, business, and financial, 9.8% computer, engineering, and science, 3.3% education, legal, community service, arts, and media, 17.7% healthcare practitioners, 12.6% service, 32.6% sales and office, 11.6% natural resources, construction, and maintenance, 12.6% production, transportation, and material moving
Income: Per capita: $23,578; Median household: $43,958; Average household: $58,846; Households with income of $100,000 or more: 5.1%; Poverty rate: n/a
Educational Attainment: High school diploma or higher: 96.9%; Bachelor's degree or higher: 15.0%; Graduate/professional degree or higher: 3.1%
Housing: Homeownership rate: 79.1%; Median home value: $117,500; Median year structure built: 1953; Homeowner vacancy rate: 0.0%; Median selected monthly owner costs: $898 with a mortgage, n/a without a mortgage; Median gross rent: $661 per month; Rental vacancy rate: 0.0%
Health Insurance: 94.6% have insurance; 61.1% have private insurance; 44.0% have public insurance; 5.4% do not have insurance; 10.6% of children under 18 do not have insurance
Transportation: Commute: 91.8% car, 0.0% public transportation, 3.6% walk, 4.6% work from home; Mean travel time to work: 21.9 minutes

LAKE MILTON (CDP).
Land/water area and latitude/longitude are not available.
Population: 547; Growth (since 2000): n/a; Density: n/a persons per square mile; Race: 100.0% White, 0.0% Black/African American, 0.0% Asian, 0.0% American Indian/Alaska Native, 0.0% Native Hawaiian/Other Pacific Islander, 0.0% Two or more races, 0.0% Hispanic of any race; Average household size: 1.98; Median age: 53.2; Age under 18: 14.1%; Age 65 and over: 26.5%; Males per 100 females: 0.0; Marriage status: 13.0% never married, 60.0% now married, 8.3% separated, 5.3% widowed, 21.7% divorced; Foreign born: 0.0%; Speak English only: 100.0%; With disability: 15.9%; Veterans: 8.7%; Ancestry: 34.6% German, 22.5% Irish, 18.5% Slovak, 10.6% American, 8.4% Welsh
Employment: 14.1% management, business, and financial, 4.9% computer, engineering, and science, 2.2% education, legal, community service, arts, and media, 5.4% healthcare practitioners, 0.0% service, 9.2% sales and office, 16.2% natural resources, construction, and maintenance, 48.1% production, transportation, and material moving
Income: Per capita: $24,661; Median household: $37,404; Average household: $48,760; Households with income of $100,000 or more: 8.3%; Poverty rate: 25.0%
Educational Attainment: High school diploma or higher: 94.8%; Bachelor's degree or higher: 18.3%; Graduate/professional degree or higher: 7.7%
Housing: Homeownership rate: 64.1%; Median home value: $139,500; Median year structure built: 1959; Homeowner vacancy rate: 0.0%; Median selected monthly owner costs: $1,152 with a mortgage, $440 without a mortgage; Median gross rent: $818 per month; Rental vacancy rate: 0.0%
Health Insurance: 94.9% have insurance; 68.4% have private insurance; 45.9% have public insurance; 5.1% do not have insurance; 0.0% of children under 18 do not have insurance
Safety: Violent crime rate: 0.0 per 10,000 population; Property crime rate: 0.0 per 10,000 population
Transportation: Commute: 94.9% car, 0.0% public transportation, 5.1% walk, 0.0% work from home; Mean travel time to work: 38.3 minutes

LOWELLVILLE (village). Covers a land area of 1.361 square miles and a water area of 0.082 square miles. Located at 41.04° N. Lat; 80.54° W. Long. Elevation is 823 feet.
History: Lowellville was settled in 1800 and incorporated in 1836. First a coal town, after 1845 the economy depended more on iron and steel.
Population: 1,161; Growth (since 2000): -9.4%; Density: 853.1 persons per square mile; Race: 97.8% White, 1.0% Black/African American, 0.0% Asian, 0.3% American Indian/Alaska Native, 0.0% Native Hawaiian/Other Pacific Islander, 0.5% Two or more races, 2.2% Hispanic of any race; Average household size: 2.46; Median age: 41.3; Age under 18: 25.9%; Age 65 and over: 15.2%; Males per 100 females: 84.2; Marriage status: 32.2% never married, 44.1% now married, 1.5% separated, 8.7% widowed, 15.0% divorced; Foreign born: 0.3%; Speak English only: 94.9%; With disability: 16.7%; Veterans: 10.2%; Ancestry: 40.7% Italian, 23.0% Irish, 18.3% German, 8.7% American, 7.5% Slovak

Employment: 8.3% management, business, and financial, 3.5% computer, engineering, and science, 9.4% education, legal, community service, arts, and media, 4.5% healthcare practitioners, 19.1% service, 18.5% sales and office, 17.1% natural resources, construction, and maintenance, 19.6% production, transportation, and material moving
Income: Per capita: $20,997; Median household: $34,167; Average household: $50,998; Households with income of $100,000 or more: 9.8%; Poverty rate: 18.5%
Educational Attainment: High school diploma or higher: 89.6%; Bachelor's degree or higher: 14.7%; Graduate/professional degree or higher: 3.3%

School District(s)

Lowellville Local (KG-12)
2015-16 Enrollment: 579. . . . . (330) 536-6318
Housing: Homeownership rate: 67.4%; Median home value: $73,500; Median year structure built: Before 1940; Homeowner vacancy rate: 2.4%; Median selected monthly owner costs: $906 with a mortgage, $314 without a mortgage; Median gross rent: $590 per month; Rental vacancy rate: 5.2%
Health Insurance: 94.8% have insurance; 65.3% have private insurance; 45.0% have public insurance; 5.2% do not have insurance; 0.0% of children under 18 do not have insurance
Transportation: Commute: 93.0% car, 0.0% public transportation, 1.6% walk, 2.5% work from home; Mean travel time to work: 21.4 minutes

MAPLE RIDGE (CDP). Covers a land area of 1.840 square miles and a water area of 0.057 square miles. Located at 40.91° N. Lat; 81.05° W. Long. Elevation is 1,102 feet.
Population: 889; Growth (since 2000): -2.3%; Density: 483.2 persons per square mile; Race: 100.0% White, 0.0% Black/African American, 0.0% Asian, 0.0% American Indian/Alaska Native, 0.0% Native Hawaiian/Other Pacific Islander, 0.0% Two or more races, 0.0% Hispanic of any race; Average household size: 2.55; Median age: 41.6; Age under 18: 24.7%; Age 65 and over: 17.5%; Males per 100 females: 96.1; Marriage status: 33.2% never married, 50.2% now married, 0.0% separated, 6.1% widowed, 10.6% divorced; Foreign born: 0.0%; Speak English only: 100.0%; With disability: 15.1%; Veterans: 9.1%; Ancestry: 20.7% German, 20.4% English, 14.7% American, 11.8% Irish, 4.5% Swiss
Employment: 14.2% management, business, and financial, 0.0% computer, engineering, and science, 4.0% education, legal, community service, arts, and media, 3.8% healthcare practitioners, 13.2% service, 24.4% sales and office, 5.8% natural resources, construction, and maintenance, 34.5% production, transportation, and material moving
Income: Per capita: $19,052; Median household: $36,125; Average household: $47,800; Households with income of $100,000 or more: 13.2%; Poverty rate: 14.3%
Educational Attainment: High school diploma or higher: 78.9%; Bachelor's degree or higher: 1.8%; Graduate/professional degree or higher: n/a
Housing: Homeownership rate: 74.7%; Median home value: $83,300; Median year structure built: 1955; Homeowner vacancy rate: 0.0%; Median selected monthly owner costs: $961 with a mortgage, $353 without a mortgage; Median gross rent: $595 per month; Rental vacancy rate: 0.0%
Health Insurance: 88.1% have insurance; 63.8% have private insurance; 38.0% have public insurance; 11.9% do not have insurance; 11.4% of children under 18 do not have insurance
Transportation: Commute: 100.0% car, 0.0% public transportation, 0.0% walk, 0.0% work from home; Mean travel time to work: 17.5 minutes

NEW MIDDLETOWN (village). Covers a land area of 0.873 square miles and a water area of 0.002 square miles. Located at 40.97° N. Lat; 80.56° W. Long. Elevation is 1,253 feet.
Population: 1,536; Growth (since 2000): -8.7%; Density: 1,759.2 persons per square mile; Race: 99.5% White, 0.0% Black/African American, 0.0% Asian, 0.0% American Indian/Alaska Native, 0.0% Native Hawaiian/Other Pacific Islander, 0.5% Two or more races, 1.6% Hispanic of any race; Average household size: 2.33; Median age: 49.6; Age under 18: 18.4%; Age 65 and over: 26.0%; Males per 100 females: 81.7; Marriage status: 25.3% never married, 54.3% now married, 1.1% separated, 7.9% widowed, 12.5% divorced; Foreign born: 0.5%; Speak English only: 98.8%; With disability: 16.1%; Veterans: 11.4%; Ancestry: 27.0% German, 23.1% Italian, 19.3% Irish, 13.9% Slovak, 11.1% American
Employment: 9.1% management, business, and financial, 2.6% computer, engineering, and science, 9.1% education, legal, community service, arts, and media, 9.9% healthcare practitioners, 17.4% service, 24.1% sales and office, 12.2% natural resources, construction, and maintenance, 15.5% production, transportation, and material moving
Income: Per capita: $23,468; Median household: $41,154; Average household: $54,055; Households with income of $100,000 or more: 9.2%; Poverty rate: 12.5%
Educational Attainment: High school diploma or higher: 92.1%; Bachelor's degree or higher: 19.8%; Graduate/professional degree or higher: 6.0%

School District(s)

Springfield Local (KG-12)
2015-16 Enrollment: 1,062 . . . . (330) 542-2929
Housing: Homeownership rate: 86.3%; Median home value: $110,600; Median year structure built: 1963; Homeowner vacancy rate: 1.2%; Median selected monthly owner costs: $991 with a mortgage, $348 without a mortgage; Median gross rent: $500 per month; Rental vacancy rate: 0.0%
Health Insurance: 93.8% have insurance; 70.1% have private insurance; 40.6% have public insurance; 6.2% do not have insurance; 1.1% of children under 18 do not have insurance
Safety: Violent crime rate: 6.4 per 10,000 population; Property crime rate: 63.8 per 10,000 population
Transportation: Commute: 97.8% car, 0.0% public transportation, 0.3% walk, 1.9% work from home; Mean travel time to work: 21.3 minutes

NEW SPRINGFIELD (unincorporated postal area)
ZCTA: 44443
Covers a land area of 12.843 square miles and a water area of 0.222 square miles. Located at 40.93° N. Lat; 80.60° W. Long. Elevation is 1,211 feet.
Population: 1,924; Growth (since 2000): -6.4%; Density: 149.8 persons per square mile; Race: 96.9% White, 0.0% Black/African American, 0.0% Asian, 0.0% American Indian/Alaska Native, 0.0% Native Hawaiian/Other Pacific Islander, 3.1% Two or more races, 2.3% Hispanic of any race; Average household size: 2.87; Median age: 38.2; Age under 18: 32.1%; Age 65 and over: 10.8%; Males per 100 females: 96.5; Marriage status: 36.2% never married, 45.9% now married, 0.8% separated, 5.2% widowed, 12.7% divorced; Foreign born: 0.7%; Speak English only: 98.5%; With disability: 17.5%; Veterans: 10.1%; Ancestry: 20.2% American, 17.2% German, 15.4% Polish, 14.0% Italian, 12.3% Irish
Employment: 2.7% management, business, and financial, 0.0% computer, engineering, and science, 5.2% education, legal, community service, arts, and media, 13.4% healthcare practitioners, 16.5% service, 22.5% sales and office, 13.8% natural resources, construction, and maintenance, 26.0% production, transportation, and material moving
Income: Per capita: $26,123; Median household: $55,543; Average household: $74,398; Households with income of $100,000 or more: 21.8%; Poverty rate: 21.5%
Educational Attainment: High school diploma or higher: 86.3%; Bachelor's degree or higher: 13.8%; Graduate/professional degree or higher: 8.0%
Housing: Homeownership rate: 86.4%; Median home value: $148,000; Median year structure built: 1972; Homeowner vacancy rate: 0.0%; Median selected monthly owner costs: $1,278 with a mortgage, $415 without a mortgage; Median gross rent: $754 per month; Rental vacancy rate: 0.0%
Health Insurance: 95.8% have insurance; 67.1% have private insurance; 36.3% have public insurance; 4.2% do not have insurance; 0.0% of children under 18 do not have insurance
Transportation: Commute: 91.6% car, 0.0% public transportation, 3.6% walk, 0.0% work from home; Mean travel time to work: 28.1 minutes

NORTH JACKSON (unincorporated postal area)
ZCTA: 44451
Covers a land area of 37.483 square miles and a water area of 0.601 square miles. Located at 41.08° N. Lat; 80.87° W. Long. Elevation is 1,020 feet.
Population: 3,047; Growth (since 2000): -1.7%; Density: 81.3 persons per square mile; Race: 98.0% White, 1.1% Black/African American, 0.3% Asian, 0.1% American Indian/Alaska Native, 0.0% Native Hawaiian/Other Pacific Islander, 0.6% Two or more races, 3.0% Hispanic of any race; Average household size: 2.31; Median age: 49.0; Age under 18: 16.2%; Age 65 and over: 22.3%; Males per 100 females: 107.0; Marriage status: 25.8% never married, 55.4% now married, 0.9% separated, 7.1% widowed, 11.7% divorced; Foreign born: 2.5%; Speak English only: 96.1%; With disability: 17.3%; Veterans: 14.0%; Ancestry: 34.3% German, 14.8% Irish, 10.8% Italian, 9.5% American, 8.2% Slovak

Employment: 10.4% management, business, and financial, 2.5% computer, engineering, and science, 6.0% education, legal, community service, arts, and media, 7.0% healthcare practitioners, 14.2% service, 27.6% sales and office, 10.8% natural resources, construction, and maintenance, 21.4% production, transportation, and material moving
Income: Per capita: $26,046; Median household: $51,620; Average household: $59,660; Households with income of $100,000 or more: 14.3%; Poverty rate: 4.7%
Educational Attainment: High school diploma or higher: 92.8%; Bachelor's degree or higher: 18.5%; Graduate/professional degree or higher: 5.8%

School District(s)

Jackson-Milton Local (KG-12)
2015-16 Enrollment: 724. . . . . (330) 538-3232
Housing: Homeownership rate: 77.7%; Median home value: $151,600; Median year structure built: 1971; Homeowner vacancy rate: 3.3%; Median selected monthly owner costs: $1,210 with a mortgage, $447 without a mortgage; Median gross rent: $726 per month; Rental vacancy rate: 0.0%
Health Insurance: 94.9% have insurance; 77.7% have private insurance; 31.3% have public insurance; 5.1% do not have insurance; 0.8% of children under 18 do not have insurance
Transportation: Commute: 90.6% car, 0.0% public transportation, 4.4% walk, 4.5% work from home; Mean travel time to work: 22.6 minutes

NORTH LIMA (unincorporated postal area)

ZCTA: 44452

Covers a land area of 13.354 square miles and a water area of 0.849 square miles. Located at 40.95° N. Lat; 80.66° W. Long. Elevation is 1,102 feet.
Population: 3,610; Growth (since 2000): 32.5%; Density: 270.3 persons per square mile; Race: 97.4% White, 1.0% Black/African American, 1.6% Asian, 0.0% American Indian/Alaska Native, 0.0% Native Hawaiian/Other Pacific Islander, 0.0% Two or more races, 0.0% Hispanic of any race; Average household size: 2.72; Median age: 47.7; Age under 18: 16.6%; Age 65 and over: 27.5%; Males per 100 females: 88.7; Marriage status: 23.8% never married, 53.2% now married, 0.3% separated, 14.2% widowed, 8.8% divorced; Foreign born: 4.0%; Speak English only: 94.6%; With disability: 15.7%; Veterans: 10.2%; Ancestry: 31.2% German, 17.6% Irish, 15.4% Italian, 12.0% American, 9.9% English
Employment: 15.5% management, business, and financial, 4.3% computer, engineering, and science, 6.2% education, legal, community service, arts, and media, 7.0% healthcare practitioners, 15.8% service, 20.1% sales and office, 19.2% natural resources, construction, and maintenance, 11.9% production, transportation, and material moving
Income: Per capita: $26,024; Median household: $58,319; Average household: $69,196; Households with income of $100,000 or more: 25.0%; Poverty rate: 5.1%
Educational Attainment: High school diploma or higher: 91.7%; Bachelor's degree or higher: 20.2%; Graduate/professional degree or higher: 7.6%
Housing: Homeownership rate: 74.9%; Median home value: $178,100; Median year structure built: 1978; Homeowner vacancy rate: 3.8%; Median selected monthly owner costs: $1,465 with a mortgage, $502 without a mortgage; Median gross rent: $777 per month; Rental vacancy rate: 0.0%
Health Insurance: 92.3% have insurance; 76.7% have private insurance; 31.5% have public insurance; 7.7% do not have insurance; 6.0% of children under 18 do not have insurance
Transportation: Commute: 95.9% car, 0.0% public transportation, 1.7% walk, 1.2% work from home; Mean travel time to work: 21.0 minutes

PETERSBURG (unincorporated postal area)

ZCTA: 44454

Covers a land area of 8.286 square miles and a water area of 0.147 square miles. Located at 40.92° N. Lat; 80.55° W. Long. Elevation is 1,129 feet.
Population: 941; Growth (since 2000): -26.3%; Density: 113.6 persons per square mile; Race: 91.9% White, 0.0% Black/African American, 0.0% Asian, 0.0% American Indian/Alaska Native, 0.0% Native Hawaiian/Other Pacific Islander, 0.0% Two or more races, 8.1% Hispanic of any race; Average household size: 2.35; Median age: 35.4; Age under 18: 28.2%; Age 65 and over: 13.8%; Males per 100 females: 100.2; Marriage status: 25.9% never married, 57.6% now married, 0.0% separated, 5.6% widowed, 11.0% divorced; Foreign born: 4.5%; Speak English only: 93.9%; With disability: 20.4%; Veterans: 3.7%; Ancestry: 42.8% German, 16.6% English, 12.3% French, 10.5% Italian, 8.9% Slovak
Employment: 32.4% management, business, and financial, 0.0% computer, engineering, and science, 0.0% education, legal, community service, arts, and media, 0.0% healthcare practitioners, 40.1% service, 6.1% sales and office, 5.4% natural resources, construction, and maintenance, 16.1% production, transportation, and material moving
Income: Per capita: $23,556; Median household: $37,981; Average household: $54,534; Households with income of $100,000 or more: 12.7%; Poverty rate: 12.8%
Educational Attainment: High school diploma or higher: 90.9%; Bachelor's degree or higher: 22.9%; Graduate/professional degree or higher: 8.7%
Housing: Homeownership rate: 75.1%; Median home value: $125,600; Median year structure built: 1973; Homeowner vacancy rate: 0.0%; Median selected monthly owner costs: $1,190 with a mortgage, $456 without a mortgage; Median gross rent: n/a per month; Rental vacancy rate: 0.0%
Health Insurance: 95.5% have insurance; 68.3% have private insurance; 37.2% have public insurance; 4.5% do not have insurance; 0.0% of children under 18 do not have insurance
Transportation: Commute: 97.5% car, 0.0% public transportation, 0.0% walk, 2.5% work from home; Mean travel time to work: 17.6 minutes

POLAND (village). Covers a land area of 1.634 square miles and a water area of 0.022 square miles. Located at 41.02° N. Lat; 80.62° W. Long. Elevation is 1,043 feet.
History: Poland was settled in 1799 by Jonathan Fowler, and originally named for him. Fowler operated the Stone Tavern, a stop on the Pittsburgh to Cleveland stage route. The town became a residential suburb of Youngstown.
Population: 2,671; Growth (since 2000): -6.8%; Density: 1,634.2 persons per square mile; Race: 99.8% White, 0.0% Black/African American, 0.0% Asian, 0.0% American Indian/Alaska Native, 0.0% Native Hawaiian/Other Pacific Islander, 0.2% Two or more races, 2.1% Hispanic of any race; Average household size: 2.43; Median age: 45.4; Age under 18: 22.2%; Age 65 and over: 18.7%; Males per 100 females: 93.1; Marriage status: 19.9% never married, 64.0% now married, 0.7% separated, 7.5% widowed, 8.6% divorced; Foreign born: 1.3%; Speak English only: 96.6%; With disability: 8.4%; Veterans: 8.0%; Ancestry: 28.5% Italian, 24.9% German, 20.1% Irish, 14.1% English, 8.7% Slovak
Employment: 13.1% management, business, and financial, 6.1% computer, engineering, and science, 15.6% education, legal, community service, arts, and media, 10.4% healthcare practitioners, 10.0% service, 23.0% sales and office, 10.9% natural resources, construction, and maintenance, 10.8% production, transportation, and material moving
Income: Per capita: $38,270; Median household: $71,321; Average household: $91,663; Households with income of $100,000 or more: 33.6%; Poverty rate: 4.0%
Educational Attainment: High school diploma or higher: 97.8%; Bachelor's degree or higher: 44.8%; Graduate/professional degree or higher: 22.1%

School District(s)

Poland Local (KG-12)
2015-16 Enrollment: 1,947 . . . . (330) 757-7000
Housing: Homeownership rate: 87.9%; Median home value: $142,300; Median year structure built: 1952; Homeowner vacancy rate: 2.2%; Median selected monthly owner costs: $1,163 with a mortgage, $476 without a mortgage; Median gross rent: $991 per month; Rental vacancy rate: 0.0%
Health Insurance: 97.5% have insurance; 84.8% have private insurance; 25.8% have public insurance; 2.5% do not have insurance; 1.2% of children under 18 do not have insurance
Safety: Violent crime rate: 4.0 per 10,000 population; Property crime rate: 44.5 per 10,000 population
Transportation: Commute: 94.2% car, 0.4% public transportation, 1.1% walk, 3.8% work from home; Mean travel time to work: 25.9 minutes

SEBRING (village). Covers a land area of 2.496 square miles and a water area of 0.016 square miles. Located at 40.92° N. Lat; 81.03° W. Long. Elevation is 1,102 feet.
Population: 4,294; Growth (since 2000): -12.6%; Density: 1,720.6 persons per square mile; Race: 99.6% White, 0.4% Black/African American, 0.0% Asian, 0.0% American Indian/Alaska Native, 0.0% Native Hawaiian/Other Pacific Islander, 0.0% Two or more races, 4.8% Hispanic of any race; Average household size: 2.20; Median age: 46.3; Age under 18: 17.3%; Age 65 and over: 28.1%; Males per 100 females: 84.2; Marriage status: 27.3% never married, 44.2% now married, 1.1% separated, 16.8% widowed, 11.8% divorced; Foreign born: 5.1%; Speak English only: 93.8%;

With disability: 22.0%; Veterans: 9.4%; Ancestry: 23.3% German, 13.9% American, 12.8% Irish, 10.1% Italian, 8.9% English
Employment: 3.6% management, business, and financial, 0.8% computer, engineering, and science, 3.4% education, legal, community service, arts, and media, 5.5% healthcare practitioners, 18.4% service, 20.6% sales and office, 18.6% natural resources, construction, and maintenance, 29.1% production, transportation, and material moving
Income: Per capita: $20,866; Median household: $34,566; Average household: $45,437; Households with income of $100,000 or more: 8.6%; Poverty rate: 15.9%
Educational Attainment: High school diploma or higher: 84.2%; Bachelor's degree or higher: 16.6%; Graduate/professional degree or higher: 4.7%

School District(s)

Sebring Local (KG-12)
2015-16 Enrollment: 532. . . . . (330) 938-6165
Housing: Homeownership rate: 54.4%; Median home value: $79,900; Median year structure built: 1956; Homeowner vacancy rate: 4.6%; Median selected monthly owner costs: $807 with a mortgage, $321 without a mortgage; Median gross rent: $823 per month; Rental vacancy rate: 11.0%
Health Insurance: 90.5% have insurance; 60.9% have private insurance; 52.1% have public insurance; 9.5% do not have insurance; 1.6% of children under 18 do not have insurance
Safety: Violent crime rate: 9.4 per 10,000 population; Property crime rate: 351.4 per 10,000 population
Transportation: Commute: 95.2% car, 0.0% public transportation, 0.0% walk, 4.4% work from home; Mean travel time to work: 20.0 minutes
Additional Information Contacts
Village of Sebring . . . . (330) 938-9340
http://www.sebringohio.net

STRUTHERS (city). Covers a land area of 3.642 square miles and a water area of 0.096 square miles. Located at 41.05° N. Lat; 80.59° W. Long. Elevation is 1,007 feet.
History: Principal steel industry has declined. Founded 1800, incorporated 1922.
Population: 10,445; Growth (since 2000): -11.2%; Density: 2,867.8 persons per square mile; Race: 97.1% White, 1.2% Black/African American, 0.1% Asian, 0.0% American Indian/Alaska Native, 0.0% Native Hawaiian/Other Pacific Islander, 1.4% Two or more races, 2.9% Hispanic of any race; Average household size: 2.50; Median age: 40.7; Age under 18: 22.0%; Age 65 and over: 17.3%; Males per 100 females: 90.9; Marriage status: 32.1% never married, 44.9% now married, 2.4% separated, 9.4% widowed, 13.6% divorced; Foreign born: 1.3%; Speak English only: 96.1%; With disability: 15.8%; Veterans: 6.4%; Ancestry: 26.0% Italian, 23.0% German, 20.6% Irish, 14.9% Slovak, 7.5% Polish
Employment: 8.2% management, business, and financial, 2.9% computer, engineering, and science, 6.4% education, legal, community service, arts, and media, 6.0% healthcare practitioners, 21.6% service, 27.6% sales and office, 7.6% natural resources, construction, and maintenance, 19.7% production, transportation, and material moving
Income: Per capita: $19,701; Median household: $37,431; Average household: $48,336; Households with income of $100,000 or more: 8.3%; Poverty rate: 15.6%
Educational Attainment: High school diploma or higher: 90.2%; Bachelor's degree or higher: 14.7%; Graduate/professional degree or higher: 2.3%

School District(s)

Struthers City (PK-12)
2015-16 Enrollment: 1,893 . . . . (330) 750-1061
Housing: Homeownership rate: 72.5%; Median home value: $71,900; Median year structure built: 1952; Homeowner vacancy rate: 3.2%; Median selected monthly owner costs: $818 with a mortgage, $305 without a mortgage; Median gross rent: $616 per month; Rental vacancy rate: 4.1%
Health Insurance: 89.8% have insurance; 58.3% have private insurance; 43.2% have public insurance; 10.2% do not have insurance; 5.9% of children under 18 do not have insurance
Safety: Violent crime rate: 26.2 per 10,000 population; Property crime rate: 236.6 per 10,000 population
Newspapers: Hometown Journal (weekly circulation 6,000)
Transportation: Commute: 95.8% car, 0.6% public transportation, 1.0% walk, 0.4% work from home; Mean travel time to work: 22.3 minutes
Additional Information Contacts
City of Struthers. . . . . (330) 755-2181
http://www.cityofstruthers.com

YOUNGSTOWN (city). County seat. Covers a land area of 33.955 square miles and a water area of 0.635 square miles. Located at 41.10° N. Lat; 80.65° W. Long. Elevation is 856 feet.
History: Youngstown, established along the Mahoning River, was shaped by the steel industry. In 1797 John Young of New York led a party of settlers to this site. By 1802 James and Daniel Heaton had set up a crude smelter on Yellow Creek, utilizing native bog ores and limestones. The first coal mine in the Mahoning Valley opened in 1826, and Mahoning coal was soon used in the reduction of iron ore. In 1892 the Union Iron & Steel Company built a plant in Youngstown, and the banks of the river were soon lined with Bessemer converters, open-hearth furnaces, strip and rolling mills, pipe plants, and manufactories of steel accessories and products.
Population: 65,161; Growth (since 2000): -20.6%; Density: 1,919.0 persons per square mile; Race: 49.1% White, 43.7% Black/African American, 0.5% Asian, 0.5% American Indian/Alaska Native, 0.0% Native Hawaiian/Other Pacific Islander, 4.7% Two or more races, 10.7% Hispanic of any race; Average household size: 2.23; Median age: 39.0; Age under 18: 22.3%; Age 65 and over: 16.4%; Males per 100 females: 96.9; Marriage status: 44.9% never married, 30.8% now married, 2.9% separated, 8.8% widowed, 15.6% divorced; Foreign born: 3.1%; Speak English only: 90.1%; With disability: 20.6%; Veterans: 8.8%; Ancestry: 10.6% German, 10.4% Irish, 10.2% Italian, 8.2% American, 5.2% African
Employment: 6.6% management, business, and financial, 1.8% computer, engineering, and science, 8.0% education, legal, community service, arts, and media, 5.4% healthcare practitioners, 27.3% service, 24.4% sales and office, 6.9% natural resources, construction, and maintenance, 19.5% production, transportation, and material moving
Income: Per capita: $15,713; Median household: $24,448; Average household: $35,829; Households with income of $100,000 or more: 4.4%; Poverty rate: 38.0%
Educational Attainment: High school diploma or higher: 83.0%; Bachelor's degree or higher: 12.0%; Graduate/professional degree or higher: 3.5%

School District(s)

Austintown Local Schools (KG-12)
2015-16 Enrollment: 4,977 . . . . (330) 797-3900
Boardman Local (KG-12)
2015-16 Enrollment: 4,180 . . . . (330) 726-3404
Horizon Science Academy Youngstown (KG-08)
2015-16 Enrollment: 405. . . . . (330) 782-3003
Liberty Local (PK-12)
2015-16 Enrollment: 1,184 . . . . (330) 759-0807
Life Skills Ctr of Youngstown (09-12)
2015-16 Enrollment: 94. . . . . (330) 743-6698
Mahoning County High School (09-12)
2015-16 Enrollment: 77. . . . . (330) 965-2860
Mahoning Unlimited Classroom (06-12)
2015-16 Enrollment: 132. . . . . (330) 965-7828
Mahoning Valley Opportunity Center (09-12)
2015-16 Enrollment: 74. . . . . (330) 744-7656
Southside Academy (KG-08)
2015-16 Enrollment: 153. . . . . (330) 744-5562
Stambaugh Charter Academy (KG-08)
2015-16 Enrollment: 445. . . . . (330) 792-4806
Steam Academy Of Akron (KG-05)
2015-16 Enrollment: 137. . . . . (330) 773-1100
Summit Academy Secondary - Youngstown (08-12)
2015-16 Enrollment: 251. . . . . (330) 747-0950
Summit Academy-Youngstown (KG-07)
2015-16 Enrollment: 209. . . . . (330) 259-0421
Youngstown Academy of Excellence (KG-08)
2015-16 Enrollment: 143. . . . . (330) 746-3970
Youngstown City (PK-12)
2015-16 Enrollment: 5,252 . . . . (330) 744-6915
Youngstown Community School (KG-06)
2015-16 Enrollment: 337. . . . . (330) 746-2240

Four-year College(s)

ITT Technical Institute-Youngstown (Private, For-profit)
Fall 2016 Enrollment: n/a . . . . (330) 270-1600
Youngstown State University (Public)
Fall 2016 Enrollment: 12,643 . . . . (877) 468-6978
2016-17 Tuition: In-state $8,317; Out-of-state $8,557

Two-year College(s)

American National University-Youngstown (Private, For-profit)
Fall 2016 Enrollment: 102 . . . . (330) 759-0205
2016-17 Tuition: In-state $14,886; Out-of-state $14,886

Vocational/Technical School(s)

Choffin Career and Technical Center (Public)
Fall 2016 Enrollment: 108 . . . . (330) 744-8700
2016-17 Tuition: In-state $8,200; Out-of-state $8,200

Housing: Homeownership rate: 56.5%; Median home value: $43,300; Median year structure built: 1948; Homeowner vacancy rate: 9.0%; Median selected monthly owner costs: $771 with a mortgage, $295 without a mortgage; Median gross rent: $619 per month; Rental vacancy rate: 5.3%
Health Insurance: 89.1% have insurance; 40.0% have private insurance; 60.7% have public insurance; 10.9% do not have insurance; 3.0% of children under 18 do not have insurance
Hospitals: Northside Medical Center (830 beds); Saint Elizabeth Health Center (350 beds); Surgical Hospital at Southwoods
Safety: Violent crime rate: 64.7 per 10,000 population; Property crime rate: 378.0 per 10,000 population
Newspapers: Boardman News (weekly circulation 9,000); The Vindicator (daily circulation 58,300)
Transportation: Commute: 87.2% car, 3.6% public transportation, 3.3% walk, 3.3% work from home; Mean travel time to work: 20.0 minutes
Airports: Youngstown-Warren Regional (primary service/non-hub)
Additional Information Contacts
City of Youngstown . . . . (330) 742-8701
http://www.cityofyoungstownoh.org

Marion County

Located in central Ohio; crossed by the Scioto River; drained by the Olentangy and Little Scioto Rivers. Covers a land area of 403.757 square miles, a water area of 0.351 square miles, and is located in the Eastern Time Zone at 40.59° N. Lat., 83.17° W. Long. The county was founded in 1820. County seat is Marion.

Marion County is part of the Marion, OH Micropolitan Statistical Area. The entire metro area includes: Marion County, OH

Weather Station: Marion 2 N Elevation: 964 feet

	Jan	Feb	Mar	Apr	May	Jun	Jul	Aug	Sep	Oct	Nov	Dec
High	33	37	47	60	71	80	83	82	76	63	50	38
Low	18	20	28	38	49	59	62	60	52	41	33	23
Precip	2.5	1.9	2.3	3.6	4.5	4.4	4.3	3.8	3.2	2.9	3.0	2.8
Snow	7.6	5.2	3.5	0.6	0.0	0.0	0.0	0.0	0.0	tr	0.8	5.3

High and Low temperatures in degrees Fahrenheit; Precipitation and Snow in inches

Population: 65,620; Growth (since 2000): -0.9%; Density: 162.5 persons per square mile; Race: 90.0% White, 5.7% Black/African American, 0.5% Asian, 0.2% American Indian/Alaska Native, 0.0% Native Hawaiian/Other Pacific Islander, 2.7% two or more races, 2.4% Hispanic of any race; Average household size: 2.43; Median age: 40.5; Age under 18: 21.0%; Age 65 and over: 16.0%; Males per 100 females: 110.3; Marriage status: 28.9% never married, 49.6% now married, 2.1% separated, 7.6% widowed, 13.9% divorced; Foreign born: 1.4%; Speak English only: 96.1%; With disability: 20.0%; Veterans: 9.8%; Ancestry: 25.0% German, 13.3% Irish, 11.9% American, 9.3% English, 4.4% Italian
Religion: Six largest groups: 5.5% Methodist/Pietist, 5.3% Baptist, 4.4% Lutheran, 3.8% Catholicism, 3.7% Holiness, 2.3% Non-denominational Protestant
Economy: Unemployment rate: 4.7%; Leading industries: 16.4 % retail trade; 13.7 % health care and social assistance; 13.7 % other services (except public administration); Farms: 578 totaling 189,210 acres; Company size: 2 employ 1,000 or more persons, 1 employs 500 to 999 persons, 28 employ 100 to 499 persons, 1,088 employ less than 100 persons; Business ownership: 1,301 women-owned, 77 Black-owned, n/a Hispanic-owned, 65 Asian-owned, n/a American Indian/Alaska Native-owned
Employment: 10.4% management, business, and financial, 2.4% computer, engineering, and science, 7.4% education, legal, community service, arts, and media, 6.0% healthcare practitioners, 19.0% service, 20.0% sales and office, 8.8% natural resources, construction, and maintenance, 25.9% production, transportation, and material moving
Income: Per capita: $21,177; Median household: $43,557; Average household: $55,671; Households with income of $100,000 or more: 12.9%; Poverty rate: 17.4%
Educational Attainment: High school diploma or higher: 86.6%; Bachelor's degree or higher: 12.3%; Graduate/professional degree or higher: 4.6%
Housing: Homeownership rate: 68.4%; Median home value: $93,400; Median year structure built: 1960; Homeowner vacancy rate: 2.2%; Median selected monthly owner costs: $1,022 with a mortgage, $381 without a mortgage; Median gross rent: $700 per month; Rental vacancy rate: 5.7%
Vital Statistics: Birth rate: 106.5 per 10,000 population; Death rate: 109.1 per 10,000 population; Age-adjusted cancer mortality rate: 224.8 deaths per 100,000 population
Health Insurance: 91.7% have insurance; 63.7% have private insurance; 43.3% have public insurance; 8.3% do not have insurance; 3.9% of children under 18 do not have insurance
Health Care: Physicians: 15.3 per 10,000 population; Dentists: 6.1 per 10,000 population; Hospital beds: 25.9 per 10,000 population; Hospital admissions: 1,117.9 per 10,000 population
Transportation: Commute: 93.8% car, 0.9% public transportation, 1.6% walk, 2.2% work from home; Mean travel time to work: 22.4 minutes
2016 Presidential Election: 64.1% Trump, 29.9% Clinton, 3.7% Johnson, 0.9% Stein
Additional Information Contacts
Marion Government. . . . . (740) 223-4001
http://www.co.marion.oh.us

Marion County Communities

CALEDONIA (village). Covers a land area of 0.230 square miles and a water area of 0 square miles. Located at 40.64° N. Lat; 82.97° W. Long. Elevation is 997 feet.
History: Caledonia was the boyhood home of Warren G. Harding, 29th President of the United States.
Population: 683; Growth (since 2000): 18.2%; Density: 2,965.5 persons per square mile; Race: 99.0% White, 0.0% Black/African American, 0.3% Asian, 0.0% American Indian/Alaska Native, 0.0% Native Hawaiian/Other Pacific Islander, 0.7% Two or more races, 0.6% Hispanic of any race; Average household size: 2.57; Median age: 44.7; Age under 18: 20.5%; Age 65 and over: 16.5%; Males per 100 females: 90.4; Marriage status: 22.9% never married, 55.6% now married, 1.7% separated, 5.9% widowed, 15.6% divorced; Foreign born: 0.3%; Speak English only: 97.8%; With disability: 16.1%; Veterans: 8.5%; Ancestry: 23.7% German, 12.2% English, 11.9% American, 9.5% Irish, 3.7% Swedish
Employment: 13.6% management, business, and financial, 6.6% computer, engineering, and science, 3.9% education, legal, community service, arts, and media, 2.4% healthcare practitioners, 12.7% service, 21.4% sales and office, 13.6% natural resources, construction, and maintenance, 25.9% production, transportation, and material moving
Income: Per capita: $25,065; Median household: $54,091; Average household: $62,826; Households with income of $100,000 or more: 14.3%; Poverty rate: 9.9%
Educational Attainment: High school diploma or higher: 94.0%; Bachelor's degree or higher: 16.5%; Graduate/professional degree or higher: 6.2%

School District(s)

River Valley Local (PK-12)
2015-16 Enrollment: 1,931 . . . . (740) 725-5401
Housing: Homeownership rate: 81.2%; Median home value: $85,600; Median year structure built: 1944; Homeowner vacancy rate: 0.0%; Median selected monthly owner costs: $951 with a mortgage, $368 without a mortgage; Median gross rent: $767 per month; Rental vacancy rate: 13.8%
Health Insurance: 94.6% have insurance; 70.0% have private insurance; 39.1% have public insurance; 5.4% do not have insurance; 0.0% of children under 18 do not have insurance
Transportation: Commute: 96.4% car, 2.4% public transportation, 0.3% walk, 0.9% work from home; Mean travel time to work: 26.4 minutes

GREEN CAMP (village). Covers a land area of 0.338 square miles and a water area of 0 square miles. Located at 40.53° N. Lat; 83.21° W. Long. Elevation is 912 feet.
Population: 349; Growth (since 2000): 2.0%; Density: 1,032.8 persons per square mile; Race: 98.9% White, 0.0% Black/African American, 0.0% Asian, 0.3% American Indian/Alaska Native, 0.0% Native Hawaiian/Other Pacific Islander, 0.9% Two or more races, 2.0% Hispanic of any race; Average household size: 2.59; Median age: 41.8; Age under 18: 23.8%; Age 65 and over: 16.0%; Males per 100 females: 118.7; Marriage status: 22.7% never married, 55.3% now married, 7.3% separated, 8.1%

widowed, 13.9% divorced; Foreign born: 0.6%; Speak English only: 99.7%; With disability: 22.6%; Veterans: 14.3%; Ancestry: 28.7% German, 9.7% American, 8.3% Irish, 3.2% English, 3.2% Scottish
Employment: 7.9% management, business, and financial, 0.0% computer, engineering, and science, 11.3% education, legal, community service, arts, and media, 7.9% healthcare practitioners, 18.5% service, 19.2% sales and office, 8.6% natural resources, construction, and maintenance, 26.5% production, transportation, and material moving
Income: Per capita: $20,845; Median household: $39,844; Average household: $52,742; Households with income of $100,000 or more: 14.1%; Poverty rate: 10.9%
Educational Attainment: High school diploma or higher: 90.1%; Bachelor's degree or higher: 9.1%; Graduate/professional degree or higher: 3.3%

School District(s)

Elgin Local (KG-12)
2015-16 Enrollment: 1,048 . . . . (740) 382-1101
Housing: Homeownership rate: 75.6%; Median home value: $77,800; Median year structure built: 1955; Homeowner vacancy rate: 0.0%; Median selected monthly owner costs: $883 with a mortgage, $335 without a mortgage; Median gross rent: $663 per month; Rental vacancy rate: 0.0%
Health Insurance: 90.8% have insurance; 65.3% have private insurance; 38.1% have public insurance; 9.2% do not have insurance; 3.6% of children under 18 do not have insurance
Transportation: Commute: 93.2% car, 0.0% public transportation, 1.4% walk, 2.7% work from home; Mean travel time to work: 25.6 minutes

LA RUE (village). Covers a land area of 0.478 square miles and a water area of 0 square miles. Located at 40.58° N. Lat; 83.38° W. Long. Elevation is 928 feet.
History: La Rue was the home of the Oorang Dog Kennels, which used Olympic athlete Jim Thorpe and other Indian athletes to play exhibition football games advertising their highly trained dogs.
Population: 718; Growth (since 2000): -7.4%; Density: 1,502.0 persons per square mile; Race: 83.3% White, 0.0% Black/African American, 0.0% Asian, 0.0% American Indian/Alaska Native, 0.0% Native Hawaiian/Other Pacific Islander, 2.1% Two or more races, 16.9% Hispanic of any race; Average household size: 2.52; Median age: 37.0; Age under 18: 32.9%; Age 65 and over: 15.6%; Males per 100 females: 95.5; Marriage status: 22.0% never married, 48.7% now married, 3.6% separated, 8.6% widowed, 20.6% divorced; Foreign born: 4.2%; Speak English only: 85.9%; With disability: 16.7%; Veterans: 11.0%; Ancestry: 17.7% German, 12.1% American, 11.3% Irish, 10.0% English, 2.4% Dutch
Employment: 4.3% management, business, and financial, 0.0% computer, engineering, and science, 3.0% education, legal, community service, arts, and media, 1.7% healthcare practitioners, 15.5% service, 21.5% sales and office, 16.7% natural resources, construction, and maintenance, 37.3% production, transportation, and material moving
Income: Per capita: $17,161; Median household: $34,375; Average household: $42,061; Households with income of $100,000 or more: 6.0%; Poverty rate: 33.2%
Educational Attainment: High school diploma or higher: 80.9%; Bachelor's degree or higher: 7.2%; Graduate/professional degree or higher: 2.7%

School District(s)

Elgin Local (KG-12)
2015-16 Enrollment: 1,048 . . . . (740) 382-1101
Housing: Homeownership rate: 49.8%; Median home value: $72,700; Median year structure built: 1950; Homeowner vacancy rate: 4.7%; Median selected monthly owner costs: $874 with a mortgage, $413 without a mortgage; Median gross rent: $673 per month; Rental vacancy rate: 5.9%
Health Insurance: 90.9% have insurance; 45.0% have private insurance; 59.7% have public insurance; 9.1% do not have insurance; 0.0% of children under 18 do not have insurance
Transportation: Commute: 93.5% car, 0.0% public transportation, 5.2% walk, 1.3% work from home; Mean travel time to work: 32.9 minutes

MARION (city). County seat. Covers a land area of 11.736 square miles and a water area of 0.078 square miles. Located at 40.59° N. Lat; 83.12° W. Long. Elevation is 981 feet.
History: The site of Marion was selected as the seat of Marion County in 1824 because of the abundance of well water, discovered when some thirsty travelers stuck a wooden spade in the ground and named the spot Jacob's Well. The Marion Steam Shovel Company was organized in 1884, sending the name of Marion all over the world on its digging equipment.
Population: 36,568; Growth (since 2000): 3.5%; Density: 3,115.9 persons per square mile; Race: 85.1% White, 9.8% Black/African American, 0.3% Asian, 0.2% American Indian/Alaska Native, 0.0% Native Hawaiian/Other Pacific Islander, 3.4% Two or more races, 3.3% Hispanic of any race; Average household size: 2.40; Median age: 37.8; Age under 18: 20.8%; Age 65 and over: 13.4%; Males per 100 females: 121.6; Marriage status: 34.4% never married, 41.7% now married, 3.0% separated, 7.2% widowed, 16.7% divorced; Foreign born: 1.6%; Speak English only: 95.0%; With disability: 23.2%; Veterans: 10.0%; Ancestry: 22.4% German, 14.2% Irish, 10.1% American, 8.3% English, 4.3% Italian
Employment: 6.8% management, business, and financial, 2.2% computer, engineering, and science, 6.4% education, legal, community service, arts, and media, 5.0% healthcare practitioners, 20.9% service, 21.0% sales and office, 7.3% natural resources, construction, and maintenance, 30.3% production, transportation, and material moving
Income: Per capita: $16,731; Median household: $34,932; Average household: $46,811; Households with income of $100,000 or more: 7.5%; Poverty rate: 21.9%
Educational Attainment: High school diploma or higher: 83.2%; Bachelor's degree or higher: 9.4%; Graduate/professional degree or higher: 3.6%

School District(s)

Elgin Local (KG-12)
2015-16 Enrollment: 1,048 . . . . (740) 382-1101
Marion City (PK-12)
2015-16 Enrollment: 4,194 . . . . (740) 387-3300
Marion City Digital Academy (KG-12)
2015-16 Enrollment: 133. . . . . (740) 223-4417
Pleasant Community Digital (KG-KG)
2015-16 Enrollment: 105. . . . . (740) 389-4476
Pleasant Education Academy (09-12)
2015-16 Enrollment: 21. . . . . (740) 389-4476
Pleasant Local (01-12)
2015-16 Enrollment: 1,238 . . . . (740) 389-4476
River Valley Local (PK-12)
2015-16 Enrollment: 1,931 . . . . (740) 725-5401
Rushmore Academy (09-12)
2015-16 Enrollment: 275. . . . . (740) 387-2043
Treca Digital Academy (KG-12)
2015-16 Enrollment: 1,857 . . . . (740) 389-4798
Tri-Rivers (10-12)
2015-16 Enrollment: n/a . . . . (740) 389-4681

Four-year College(s)

Ohio State University-Marion Campus (Public)
Fall 2016 Enrollment: 1,139 . . . . (740) 389-6786
2016-17 Tuition: In-state $7,140; Out-of-state $25,332

Two-year College(s)

Marion Technical College (Public)
Fall 2016 Enrollment: 2,618 . . . . (740) 389-4636
2016-17 Tuition: In-state $4,480; Out-of-state $6,400

Vocational/Technical School(s)

Tri-Rivers Career Center (Public)
Fall 2016 Enrollment: 163 . . . . (740) 389-4682
2016-17 Tuition: $12,630
Housing: Homeownership rate: 57.2%; Median home value: $73,200; Median year structure built: 1950; Homeowner vacancy rate: 3.1%; Median selected monthly owner costs: $913 with a mortgage, $332 without a mortgage; Median gross rent: $681 per month; Rental vacancy rate: 6.4%
Health Insurance: 89.7% have insurance; 54.3% have private insurance; 49.7% have public insurance; 10.3% do not have insurance; 3.5% of children under 18 do not have insurance
Hospitals: Marion General Hospital
Safety: Violent crime rate: 29.5 per 10,000 population; Property crime rate: 363.9 per 10,000 population
Newspapers: Marion Star (daily circulation 12,400)
Transportation: Commute: 94.0% car, 1.2% public transportation, 1.7% walk, 1.4% work from home; Mean travel time to work: 19.4 minutes
Airports: Marion Municipal (general aviation)
Additional Information Contacts
City of Marion . . . . (740) 387-3591
http://www.marionohio.us

MORRAL (village). Covers a land area of 2.701 square miles and a water area of 0 square miles. Located at 40.69° N. Lat; 83.21° W. Long. Elevation is 909 feet.

Population: 425; Growth (since 2000): 9.5%; Density: 157.4 persons per square mile; Race: 97.6% White, 0.0% Black/African American, 0.0% Asian, 0.2% American Indian/Alaska Native, 0.0% Native Hawaiian/Other Pacific Islander, 2.1% Two or more races, 0.0% Hispanic of any race; Average household size: 2.53; Median age: 37.5; Age under 18: 24.5%; Age 65 and over: 12.5%; Males per 100 females: 98.5; Marriage status: 23.4% never married, 55.1% now married, 0.9% separated, 4.0% widowed, 17.4% divorced; Foreign born: 0.0%; Speak English only: 99.2%; With disability: 13.9%; Veterans: 9.7%; Ancestry: 28.7% German, 18.8% American, 14.4% Irish, 8.2% English, 4.2% Italian

Employment: 10.9% management, business, and financial, 5.2% computer, engineering, and science, 5.7% education, legal, community service, arts, and media, 5.2% healthcare practitioners, 19.6% service, 14.8% sales and office, 9.1% natural resources, construction, and maintenance, 29.6% production, transportation, and material moving

Income: Per capita: $21,923; Median household: $46,000; Average household: $54,718; Households with income of $100,000 or more: 11.3%; Poverty rate: 14.4%

Educational Attainment: High school diploma or higher: 91.0%; Bachelor's degree or higher: 7.9%; Graduate/professional degree or higher: 3.8%

School District(s)

Ridgedale Community School (07-12)
2015-16 Enrollment: 34. . . . . (740) 382-6065
Ridgedale Local (KG-12)
2015-16 Enrollment: 662. . . . . (740) 382-6065

Housing: Homeownership rate: 86.3%; Median home value: $84,200; Median year structure built: Before 1940; Homeowner vacancy rate: 3.3%; Median selected monthly owner costs: $959 with a mortgage, $283 without a mortgage; Median gross rent: $907 per month; Rental vacancy rate: 0.0%

Health Insurance: 94.6% have insurance; 79.1% have private insurance; 33.6% have public insurance; 5.4% do not have insurance; 1.9% of children under 18 do not have insurance

Transportation: Commute: 95.2% car, 0.0% public transportation, 0.4% walk, 3.9% work from home; Mean travel time to work: 21.5 minutes

NEW BLOOMINGTON (village). Covers a land area of 0.440 square miles and a water area of 0 square miles. Located at 40.58° N. Lat; 83.31° W. Long. Elevation is 942 feet.

Population: 382; Growth (since 2000): -30.3%; Density: 867.5 persons per square mile; Race: 90.1% White, 0.0% Black/African American, 0.0% Asian, 8.6% American Indian/Alaska Native, 0.0% Native Hawaiian/Other Pacific Islander, 0.3% Two or more races, 13.4% Hispanic of any race; Average household size: 2.48; Median age: 40.6; Age under 18: 24.6%; Age 65 and over: 16.8%; Males per 100 females: 122.9; Marriage status: 22.0% never married, 48.7% now married, 2.7% separated, 6.0% widowed, 23.3% divorced; Foreign born: 5.0%; Speak English only: 90.7%; With disability: 30.4%; Veterans: 6.3%; Ancestry: 20.9% German, 18.1% English, 13.4% American, 12.8% Irish, 2.1% Italian

Employment: 0.0% management, business, and financial, 0.8% computer, engineering, and science, 2.5% education, legal, community service, arts, and media, 8.5% healthcare practitioners, 16.9% service, 6.8% sales and office, 29.7% natural resources, construction, and maintenance, 34.7% production, transportation, and material moving

Income: Per capita: $23,202; Median household: $31,667; Average household: $51,544; Households with income of $100,000 or more: 4.5%; Poverty rate: 22.0%

Educational Attainment: High school diploma or higher: 53.6%; Bachelor's degree or higher: 2.4%; Graduate/professional degree or higher: 0.8%

Housing: Homeownership rate: 70.8%; Median home value: n/a; Median year structure built: 1979; Homeowner vacancy rate: 4.4%; Median selected monthly owner costs: $761 with a mortgage, $345 without a mortgage; Median gross rent: $695 per month; Rental vacancy rate: 0.0%

Health Insurance: 84.8% have insurance; 38.2% have private insurance; 61.0% have public insurance; 15.2% do not have insurance; 1.1% of children under 18 do not have insurance

Transportation: Commute: 95.6% car, 0.0% public transportation, 2.6% walk, 1.8% work from home; Mean travel time to work: 34.6 minutes

PROSPECT (village). Covers a land area of 0.724 square miles and a water area of 0 square miles. Located at 40.45° N. Lat; 83.18° W. Long. Elevation is 909 feet.

History: Settled 1832, incorporated as village 1876.

Population: 1,152; Growth (since 2000): -3.3%; Density: 1,592.0 persons per square mile; Race: 98.4% White, 0.5% Black/African American, 0.0% Asian, 0.0% American Indian/Alaska Native, 0.0% Native Hawaiian/Other Pacific Islander, 0.7% Two or more races, 1.6% Hispanic of any race; Average household size: 2.52; Median age: 37.8; Age under 18: 27.8%; Age 65 and over: 18.7%; Males per 100 females: 100.0; Marriage status: 21.2% never married, 57.6% now married, 3.6% separated, 4.7% widowed, 16.5% divorced; Foreign born: 1.4%; Speak English only: 96.6%; With disability: 16.1%; Veterans: 10.7%; Ancestry: 42.3% German, 20.1% Irish, 11.7% English, 9.8% American, 4.3% Italian

Employment: 12.9% management, business, and financial, 1.2% computer, engineering, and science, 11.4% education, legal, community service, arts, and media, 5.6% healthcare practitioners, 13.1% service, 20.3% sales and office, 10.6% natural resources, construction, and maintenance, 24.9% production, transportation, and material moving

Income: Per capita: $25,520; Median household: $50,455; Average household: $63,274; Households with income of $100,000 or more: 16.4%; Poverty rate: 6.6%

Educational Attainment: High school diploma or higher: 94.0%; Bachelor's degree or higher: 25.9%; Graduate/professional degree or higher: 9.6%

School District(s)

Elgin Local (KG-12)
2015-16 Enrollment: 1,048 . . . . (740) 382-1101

Housing: Homeownership rate: 65.3%; Median home value: $112,700; Median year structure built: Before 1940; Homeowner vacancy rate: 1.3%; Median selected monthly owner costs: $997 with a mortgage, $335 without a mortgage; Median gross rent: $817 per month; Rental vacancy rate: 17.2%

Health Insurance: 95.5% have insurance; 70.0% have private insurance; 39.1% have public insurance; 4.5% do not have insurance; 2.5% of children under 18 do not have insurance

Transportation: Commute: 97.1% car, 0.0% public transportation, 2.4% walk, 0.4% work from home; Mean travel time to work: 23.7 minutes

WALDO (village). Covers a land area of 0.648 square miles and a water area of 0 square miles. Located at 40.46° N. Lat; 83.08° W. Long. Elevation is 938 feet.

Population: 358; Growth (since 2000): 7.8%; Density: 552.3 persons per square mile; Race: 98.6% White, 0.0% Black/African American, 0.3% Asian, 0.0% American Indian/Alaska Native, 0.0% Native Hawaiian/Other Pacific Islander, 1.1% Two or more races, 1.1% Hispanic of any race; Average household size: 2.12; Median age: 50.4; Age under 18: 16.5%; Age 65 and over: 26.5%; Males per 100 females: 94.3; Marriage status: 17.3% never married, 58.0% now married, 1.6% separated, 12.7% widowed, 12.1% divorced; Foreign born: 0.6%; Speak English only: 98.3%; With disability: 24.3%; Veterans: 13.4%; Ancestry: 29.1% German, 13.1% Irish, 8.4% American, 7.5% English, 4.2% Italian

Employment: 7.1% management, business, and financial, 1.1% computer, engineering, and science, 2.7% education, legal, community service, arts, and media, 8.2% healthcare practitioners, 21.9% service, 23.0% sales and office, 11.5% natural resources, construction, and maintenance, 24.6% production, transportation, and material moving

Income: Per capita: $24,824; Median household: $41,250; Average household: $51,975; Households with income of $100,000 or more: 10.1%; Poverty rate: 5.3%

Educational Attainment: High school diploma or higher: 84.9%; Bachelor's degree or higher: 6.3%; Graduate/professional degree or higher: 1.8%

Housing: Homeownership rate: 78.7%; Median home value: $90,400; Median year structure built: 1945; Homeowner vacancy rate: 7.4%; Median selected monthly owner costs: $978 with a mortgage, $322 without a mortgage; Median gross rent: $788 per month; Rental vacancy rate: 25.0%

Health Insurance: 90.5% have insurance; 72.6% have private insurance; 37.2% have public insurance; 9.5% do not have insurance; 0.0% of children under 18 do not have insurance

Transportation: Commute: 92.8% car, 0.0% public transportation, 4.4% walk, 2.8% work from home; Mean travel time to work: 22.1 minutes

Medina County

Located in northern Ohio; drained by the Rocky and Black Rivers; includes Chippewa Lake. Covers a land area of 421.357 square miles, a water area of 1.658 square miles, and is located in the Eastern Time Zone at 41.12° N. Lat., 81.90° W. Long. The county was founded in 1812. County seat is Medina.

Medina County is part of the Cleveland-Elyria, OH Metropolitan Statistical Area. The entire metro area includes: Cuyahoga County, OH; Geauga County, OH; Lake County, OH; Lorain County, OH; Medina County, OH

Weather Station: Chippewa Lake Elevation: 1,180 feet

	Jan	Feb	Mar	Apr	May	Jun	Jul	Aug	Sep	Oct	Nov	Dec
High	33	37	46	59	70	79	83	81	74	62	50	37
Low	18	19	27	37	47	56	60	59	52	41	33	23
Precip	2.5	2.1	2.9	3.5	4.0	3.9	4.2	3.7	3.4	2.8	3.3	3.0
Snow	9.4	7.1	6.7	1.9	tr	0.0	0.0	0.0	0.0	0.1	2.6	8.1

High and Low temperatures in degrees Fahrenheit; Precipitation and Snow in inches

Population: 175,543; Growth (since 2000): 16.2%; Density: 416.6 persons per square mile; Race: 95.6% White, 1.5% Black/African American, 1.2% Asian, 0.2% American Indian/Alaska Native, 0.0% Native Hawaiian/Other Pacific Islander, 1.2% two or more races, 1.9% Hispanic of any race; Average household size: 2.62; Median age: 41.8; Age under 18: 23.5%; Age 65 and over: 15.6%; Males per 100 females: 97.2; Marriage status: 24.9% never married, 58.8% now married, 1.1% separated, 5.9% widowed, 10.3% divorced; Foreign born: 2.8%; Speak English only: 95.3%; With disability: 10.5%; Veterans: 9.3%; Ancestry: 29.1% German, 16.9% Irish, 10.7% Italian, 9.9% Polish, 9.9% English
Religion: Six largest groups: 28.2% Catholicism, 4.3% Methodist/Pietist, 4.1% Lutheran, 3.9% Non-denominational Protestant, 3.6% Baptist, 2.4% Presbyterian-Reformed
Economy: Unemployment rate: 4.3%; Leading industries: 12.4 % retail trade; 11.9 % construction; 10.4 % professional, scientific, and technical services; Farms: 920 totaling 94,978 acres; Company size: 1 employs 1,000 or more persons, 4 employ 500 to 999 persons, 87 employ 100 to 499 persons, 3,901 employs less than 100 persons; Business ownership: 4,559 women-owned, 142 Black-owned, 133 Hispanic-owned, 288 Asian-owned, 28 American Indian/Alaska Native-owned
Employment: 17.4% management, business, and financial, 5.6% computer, engineering, and science, 8.9% education, legal, community service, arts, and media, 6.8% healthcare practitioners, 14.9% service, 25.4% sales and office, 8.3% natural resources, construction, and maintenance, 12.7% production, transportation, and material moving
Income: Per capita: $32,911; Median household: $69,319; Average household: $85,239; Households with income of $100,000 or more: 30.6%; Poverty rate: 6.6%
Educational Attainment: High school diploma or higher: 93.6%; Bachelor's degree or higher: 31.5%; Graduate/professional degree or higher: 10.1%
Housing: Homeownership rate: 79.7%; Median home value: $182,100; Median year structure built: 1980; Homeowner vacancy rate: 1.8%; Median selected monthly owner costs: $1,435 with a mortgage, $509 without a mortgage; Median gross rent: $833 per month; Rental vacancy rate: 4.0%
Vital Statistics: Birth rate: 105.4 per 10,000 population; Death rate: 81.3 per 10,000 population; Age-adjusted cancer mortality rate: 147.7 deaths per 100,000 population
Health Insurance: 94.1% have insurance; 81.5% have private insurance; 25.3% have public insurance; 5.9% do not have insurance; 3.4% of children under 18 do not have insurance
Health Care: Physicians: 18.1 per 10,000 population; Dentists: 5.1 per 10,000 population; Hospital beds: 8.9 per 10,000 population; Hospital admissions: 361.5 per 10,000 population
Air Quality Index (AQI): Percent of Days: 78.7% good, 21.0% moderate, 0.3% unhealthy for sensitive individuals, 0.0% unhealthy, 0.0% very unhealthy; Annual median: 40; Annual maximum: 105
Transportation: Commute: 93.2% car, 0.5% public transportation, 1.4% walk, 4.1% work from home; Mean travel time to work: 27.4 minutes
2016 Presidential Election: 59.5% Trump, 34.9% Clinton, 3.2% Johnson, 0.8% Stein
National and State Parks: Spencer Lake State Wildlife Area
Additional Information Contacts
Medina Government . . . . (330) 722-9208
http://www.co.medina.oh.us

Medina County Communities

BRUNSWICK (city). Covers a land area of 12.916 square miles and a water area of 0.037 square miles. Located at 41.25° N. Lat; 81.82° W. Long. Elevation is 1,168 feet.
History: Named for its pleasing sound to early residents. Small farm community for many years; population burgeoned with the housing boom after World War II. Settled 1815 as part of the Conn. Western Reserve. Incorporated 1960.
Population: 34,578; Growth (since 2000): 3.6%; Density: 2,677.2 persons per square mile; Race: 95.9% White, 1.2% Black/African American, 1.1% Asian, 0.1% American Indian/Alaska Native, 0.0% Native Hawaiian/Other Pacific Islander, 1.5% Two or more races, 2.1% Hispanic of any race; Average household size: 2.55; Median age: 39.6; Age under 18: 22.4%; Age 65 and over: 14.8%; Males per 100 females: 96.6; Marriage status: 29.8% never married, 51.8% now married, 1.2% separated, 6.2% widowed, 12.2% divorced; Foreign born: 3.3%; Speak English only: 94.6%; With disability: 10.1%; Veterans: 9.0%; Ancestry: 28.2% German, 19.9% Irish, 13.5% Polish, 12.8% Italian, 6.7% English
Employment: 13.4% management, business, and financial, 5.3% computer, engineering, and science, 7.4% education, legal, community service, arts, and media, 6.9% healthcare practitioners, 17.0% service, 27.0% sales and office, 7.7% natural resources, construction, and maintenance, 15.4% production, transportation, and material moving
Income: Per capita: $30,391; Median household: $64,706; Average household: $75,976; Households with income of $100,000 or more: 24.8%; Poverty rate: 8.0%
Educational Attainment: High school diploma or higher: 91.7%; Bachelor's degree or higher: 23.5%; Graduate/professional degree or higher: 6.7%

School District(s)

Brunswick City (PK-12)
2015-16 Enrollment: 7,123 . . . . (330) 225-7731

Two-year College(s)

Raphael's School of Beauty Culture Inc-Brunswick (Private, For-profit)
Fall 2016 Enrollment: 50 . . . . (330) 225-0195
Housing: Homeownership rate: 77.2%; Median home value: $159,400; Median year structure built: 1977; Homeowner vacancy rate: 1.4%; Median selected monthly owner costs: $1,284 with a mortgage, $455 without a mortgage; Median gross rent: $832 per month; Rental vacancy rate: 4.3%
Health Insurance: 94.3% have insurance; 80.5% have private insurance; 26.4% have public insurance; 5.7% do not have insurance; 0.9% of children under 18 do not have insurance
Safety: Violent crime rate: 7.2 per 10,000 population; Property crime rate: 64.4 per 10,000 population
Transportation: Commute: 93.6% car, 1.0% public transportation, 1.6% walk, 3.4% work from home; Mean travel time to work: 28.4 minutes
Additional Information Contacts
City of Brunswick. . . . . (330) 225-9144
http://www.brunswick.oh.us

CHIPPEWA LAKE (village). Covers a land area of 0.247 square miles and a water area of <.001 square miles. Located at 41.07° N. Lat; 81.90° W. Long. Elevation is 1,024 feet.
Population: 656; Growth (since 2000): n/a; Density: 2,658.9 persons per square mile; Race: 94.8% White, 1.1% Black/African American, 1.4% Asian, 0.0% American Indian/Alaska Native, 0.0% Native Hawaiian/Other Pacific Islander, 1.5% Two or more races, 1.5% Hispanic of any race; Average household size: 2.33; Median age: 43.2; Age under 18: 16.3%; Age 65 and over: 24.5%; Males per 100 females: 104.9; Marriage status: 29.4% never married, 46.2% now married, 1.9% separated, 7.6% widowed, 16.8% divorced; Foreign born: 2.7%; Speak English only: 98.4%; With disability: 15.1%; Veterans: 6.8%; Ancestry: 28.5% German, 17.2% Irish, 14.8% English, 11.9% Italian, 6.9% Polish
Employment: 8.5% management, business, and financial, 2.1% computer, engineering, and science, 7.3% education, legal, community service, arts, and media, 1.8% healthcare practitioners, 12.1% service, 29.0% sales and office, 17.5% natural resources, construction, and maintenance, 21.8% production, transportation, and material moving
Income: Per capita: $29,458; Median household: $53,594; Average household: $67,265; Households with income of $100,000 or more: 13.8%; Poverty rate: 9.9%

Educational Attainment: High school diploma or higher: 90.0%; Bachelor's degree or higher: 19.1%; Graduate/professional degree or higher: 7.5%
Housing: Homeownership rate: 75.8%; Median home value: $130,700; Median year structure built: 1955; Homeowner vacancy rate: 3.5%; Median selected monthly owner costs: $1,054 with a mortgage, $398 without a mortgage; Median gross rent: $928 per month; Rental vacancy rate: 0.0%
Health Insurance: 84.8% have insurance; 65.3% have private insurance; 43.0% have public insurance; 15.2% do not have insurance; 4.7% of children under 18 do not have insurance
Transportation: Commute: 94.6% car, 0.0% public transportation, 0.0% walk, 3.3% work from home; Mean travel time to work: 24.3 minutes

GLORIA GLENS PARK (village). Covers a land area of 0.107 square miles and a water area of 0.005 square miles. Located at 41.06° N. Lat; 81.90° W. Long. Elevation is 1,020 feet.
Population: 472; Growth (since 2000): -12.3%; Density: 4,403.7 persons per square mile; Race: 98.7% White, 0.0% Black/African American, 0.6% Asian, 0.0% American Indian/Alaska Native, 0.0% Native Hawaiian/Other Pacific Islander, 0.6% Two or more races, 0.0% Hispanic of any race; Average household size: 2.55; Median age: 36.3; Age under 18: 22.9%; Age 65 and over: 10.6%; Males per 100 females: 107.3; Marriage status: 30.3% never married, 57.0% now married, 0.8% separated, 5.0% widowed, 7.8% divorced; Foreign born: 1.3%; Speak English only: 96.5%; With disability: 10.4%; Veterans: 8.0%; Ancestry: 40.0% German, 21.2% Irish, 12.1% Italian, 8.5% Polish, 5.7% English
Employment: 6.7% management, business, and financial, 2.9% computer, engineering, and science, 7.9% education, legal, community service, arts, and media, 5.4% healthcare practitioners, 22.5% service, 17.5% sales and office, 18.3% natural resources, construction, and maintenance, 18.8% production, transportation, and material moving
Income: Per capita: $29,398; Median household: $48,750; Average household: $79,949; Households with income of $100,000 or more: 15.7%; Poverty rate: 4.2%
Educational Attainment: High school diploma or higher: 83.3%; Bachelor's degree or higher: 17.3%; Graduate/professional degree or higher: 3.9%
Housing: Homeownership rate: 80.0%; Median home value: $105,800; Median year structure built: 1955; Homeowner vacancy rate: 0.0%; Median selected monthly owner costs: $993 with a mortgage, $370 without a mortgage; Median gross rent: $950 per month; Rental vacancy rate: 0.0%
Health Insurance: 92.6% have insurance; 59.7% have private insurance; 40.5% have public insurance; 7.4% do not have insurance; 8.3% of children under 18 do not have insurance
Transportation: Commute: 98.3% car, 0.0% public transportation, 0.0% walk, 1.7% work from home; Mean travel time to work: 27.5 minutes

HINCKLEY (unincorporated postal area)
ZCTA: 44233
Covers a land area of 26.704 square miles and a water area of 0.139 square miles. Located at 41.25° N. Lat; 81.74° W. Long. Elevation is 1,096 feet.
Population: 7,825; Growth (since 2000): 15.5%; Density: 293.0 persons per square mile; Race: 99.0% White, 0.1% Black/African American, 0.6% Asian, 0.2% American Indian/Alaska Native, 0.0% Native Hawaiian/Other Pacific Islander, 0.0% Two or more races, 1.0% Hispanic of any race; Average household size: 2.71; Median age: 46.7; Age under 18: 22.6%; Age 65 and over: 16.4%; Males per 100 females: 101.5; Marriage status: 20.9% never married, 64.3% now married, 0.9% separated, 6.2% widowed, 8.6% divorced; Foreign born: 6.3%; Speak English only: 87.9%; With disability: 8.7%; Veterans: 5.9%; Ancestry: 24.7% German, 17.6% Italian, 12.7% Polish, 10.3% Irish, 7.3% English
Employment: 23.4% management, business, and financial, 4.2% computer, engineering, and science, 6.7% education, legal, community service, arts, and media, 8.6% healthcare practitioners, 9.1% service, 28.6% sales and office, 7.1% natural resources, construction, and maintenance, 12.2% production, transportation, and material moving
Income: Per capita: $41,945; Median household: $88,750; Average household: $112,249; Households with income of $100,000 or more: 43.2%; Poverty rate: 4.4%
Educational Attainment: High school diploma or higher: 96.4%; Bachelor's degree or higher: 35.8%; Graduate/professional degree or higher: 13.2%

School District(s)
Highland Local (PK-12)
2015-16 Enrollment: 3,080 . . . . (330) 239-1901
Housing: Homeownership rate: 98.3%; Median home value: $298,300; Median year structure built: 1982; Homeowner vacancy rate: 0.0%; Median selected monthly owner costs: $1,828 with a mortgage, $666 without a mortgage; Median gross rent: n/a per month; Rental vacancy rate: 0.0%
Health Insurance: 95.8% have insurance; 88.5% have private insurance; 19.1% have public insurance; 4.2% do not have insurance; 1.7% of children under 18 do not have insurance
Transportation: Commute: 91.4% car, 0.0% public transportation, 0.5% walk, 7.4% work from home; Mean travel time to work: 29.4 minutes

HOMERVILLE (unincorporated postal area)
ZCTA: 44235
Covers a land area of 25.034 square miles and a water area of 0.033 square miles. Located at 41.03° N. Lat; 82.12° W. Long. Elevation is 1,073 feet.
Population: 1,964; Growth (since 2000): 4.9%; Density: 78.5 persons per square mile; Race: 99.4% White, 0.0% Black/African American, 0.0% Asian, 0.6% American Indian/Alaska Native, 0.0% Native Hawaiian/Other Pacific Islander, 0.0% Two or more races, 0.0% Hispanic of any race; Average household size: 3.49; Median age: 31.0; Age under 18: 34.4%; Age 65 and over: 12.1%; Males per 100 females: 102.8; Marriage status: 21.0% never married, 66.3% now married, 0.0% separated, 3.8% widowed, 8.9% divorced; Foreign born: 0.0%; Speak English only: 70.3%; With disability: 8.7%; Veterans: 8.8%; Ancestry: 37.8% German, 13.1% Polish, 9.0% English, 7.4% Dutch, 6.1% Irish
Employment: 23.2% management, business, and financial, 3.3% computer, engineering, and science, 5.6% education, legal, community service, arts, and media, 9.3% healthcare practitioners, 18.7% service, 20.5% sales and office, 8.4% natural resources, construction, and maintenance, 11.0% production, transportation, and material moving
Income: Per capita: $20,742; Median household: $58,611; Average household: $70,099; Households with income of $100,000 or more: 29.5%; Poverty rate: 12.9%
Educational Attainment: High school diploma or higher: 73.8%; Bachelor's degree or higher: 19.8%; Graduate/professional degree or higher: 4.2%
Housing: Homeownership rate: 86.7%; Median home value: $172,900; Median year structure built: 1970; Homeowner vacancy rate: 0.0%; Median selected monthly owner costs: $1,333 with a mortgage, $410 without a mortgage; Median gross rent: n/a per month; Rental vacancy rate: 0.0%
Health Insurance: 65.0% have insurance; 52.8% have private insurance; 23.4% have public insurance; 35.0% do not have insurance; 48.6% of children under 18 do not have insurance
Transportation: Commute: 81.7% car, 0.0% public transportation, 3.2% walk, 14.1% work from home; Mean travel time to work: 33.1 minutes

LITCHFIELD (unincorporated postal area)
ZCTA: 44253
Covers a land area of 24.631 square miles and a water area of 0.018 square miles. Located at 41.17° N. Lat; 82.03° W. Long. Elevation is 1,004 feet.
Population: 3,201; Growth (since 2000): -3.4%; Density: 130.0 persons per square mile; Race: 99.4% White, 0.0% Black/African American, 0.0% Asian, 0.0% American Indian/Alaska Native, 0.0% Native Hawaiian/Other Pacific Islander, 0.6% Two or more races, 0.0% Hispanic of any race; Average household size: 2.85; Median age: 47.6; Age under 18: 19.0%; Age 65 and over: 15.5%; Males per 100 females: 106.3; Marriage status: 21.7% never married, 66.1% now married, 0.3% separated, 4.9% widowed, 7.2% divorced; Foreign born: 1.1%; Speak English only: 98.8%; With disability: 10.0%; Veterans: 7.8%; Ancestry: 30.4% German, 16.7% Irish, 14.1% Polish, 10.5% English, 6.5% Italian
Employment: 14.5% management, business, and financial, 3.6% computer, engineering, and science, 5.0% education, legal, community service, arts, and media, 4.7% healthcare practitioners, 16.3% service, 28.9% sales and office, 11.7% natural resources, construction, and maintenance, 15.2% production, transportation, and material moving
Income: Per capita: $29,406; Median household: $83,594; Average household: $81,413; Households with income of $100,000 or more: 32.8%; Poverty rate: 6.1%
Educational Attainment: High school diploma or higher: 87.5%; Bachelor's degree or higher: 18.3%; Graduate/professional degree or higher: 6.0%

Housing: Homeownership rate: 93.7%; Median home value: $188,700; Median year structure built: 1977; Homeowner vacancy rate: 0.0%; Median selected monthly owner costs: $1,434 with a mortgage, $532 without a mortgage; Median gross rent: $945 per month; Rental vacancy rate: 0.0%
Health Insurance: 94.9% have insurance; 86.5% have private insurance; 21.6% have public insurance; 5.1% do not have insurance; 0.0% of children under 18 do not have insurance
Transportation: Commute: 93.2% car, 0.0% public transportation, 3.7% walk, 3.2% work from home; Mean travel time to work: 30.7 minutes

LODI (village). Covers a land area of 2.246 square miles and a water area of 0.008 square miles. Located at 41.04° N. Lat; 82.01° W. Long. Elevation is 925 feet.
History: Lodi was founded in 1824 by Judge Joseph Harris, who built his house on an ancient Indian mound. The town developed as a distribution center for dairy products and fertilizers.
Population: 2,789; Growth (since 2000): -8.9%; Density: 1,241.8 persons per square mile; Race: 96.3% White, 2.2% Black/African American, 0.0% Asian, 0.3% American Indian/Alaska Native, 0.0% Native Hawaiian/Other Pacific Islander, 0.8% Two or more races, 1.4% Hispanic of any race; Average household size: 2.34; Median age: 44.3; Age under 18: 19.4%; Age 65 and over: 18.7%; Males per 100 females: 92.4; Marriage status: 27.8% never married, 46.6% now married, 1.3% separated, 7.8% widowed, 17.7% divorced; Foreign born: 1.1%; Speak English only: 96.0%; With disability: 22.3%; Veterans: 12.6%; Ancestry: 24.6% German, 16.3% Irish, 10.7% English, 9.8% Polish, 8.0% Italian
Employment: 4.8% management, business, and financial, 0.3% computer, engineering, and science, 6.2% education, legal, community service, arts, and media, 2.1% healthcare practitioners, 30.2% service, 26.2% sales and office, 10.3% natural resources, construction, and maintenance, 19.9% production, transportation, and material moving
Income: Per capita: $20,925; Median household: $36,207; Average household: $47,749; Households with income of $100,000 or more: 6.5%; Poverty rate: 24.1%
Educational Attainment: High school diploma or higher: 89.6%; Bachelor's degree or higher: 9.3%; Graduate/professional degree or higher: 2.9%

School District(s)

Cloverleaf Local (PK-12)
2015-16 Enrollment: 2,377 . . . . (330) 948-2500
Housing: Homeownership rate: 55.7%; Median home value: $88,300; Median year structure built: 1969; Homeowner vacancy rate: 1.2%; Median selected monthly owner costs: $1,008 with a mortgage, $439 without a mortgage; Median gross rent: $573 per month; Rental vacancy rate: 0.0%
Health Insurance: 90.4% have insurance; 55.6% have private insurance; 46.3% have public insurance; 9.6% do not have insurance; 0.0% of children under 18 do not have insurance
Hospitals: Lodi Community Hospital (25 beds)
Transportation: Commute: 93.0% car, 0.0% public transportation, 4.5% walk, 2.1% work from home; Mean travel time to work: 21.8 minutes

MEDINA (city). County seat. Covers a land area of 11.572 square miles and a water area of 0.210 square miles. Located at 41.13° N. Lat; 81.87° W. Long. Elevation is 1,089 feet.
History: Named for the city of Hejaz, Saudi Arabia, to which Mohammed made his flight from Mecca in 622. Medina was platted in 1818 by a Captain Badger, who built a log cabin on the site. The town, first called Mecca, became known for its bee culture and honey products, calling itself the "sweetest town on earth."
Population: 26,445; Growth (since 2000): 5.2%; Density: 2,285.3 persons per square mile; Race: 91.9% White, 4.4% Black/African American, 1.2% Asian, 0.4% American Indian/Alaska Native, 0.0% Native Hawaiian/Other Pacific Islander, 1.5% Two or more races, 1.7% Hispanic of any race; Average household size: 2.56; Median age: 37.9; Age under 18: 26.6%; Age 65 and over: 13.1%; Males per 100 females: 92.5; Marriage status: 29.6% never married, 52.1% now married, 1.5% separated, 6.5% widowed, 11.9% divorced; Foreign born: 2.3%; Speak English only: 96.3%; With disability: 10.7%; Veterans: 8.6%; Ancestry: 31.0% German, 19.6% Irish, 11.5% Italian, 10.0% English, 8.9% Polish
Employment: 15.7% management, business, and financial, 5.0% computer, engineering, and science, 10.0% education, legal, community service, arts, and media, 6.1% healthcare practitioners, 14.3% service, 29.7% sales and office, 8.0% natural resources, construction, and maintenance, 11.3% production, transportation, and material moving
Income: Per capita: $29,295; Median household: $60,706; Average household: $74,277; Households with income of $100,000 or more: 26.2%; Poverty rate: 9.8%
Educational Attainment: High school diploma or higher: 94.5%; Bachelor's degree or higher: 35.5%; Graduate/professional degree or higher: 10.9%

School District(s)

Buckeye Local (PK-12)
2015-16 Enrollment: 2,223 . . . . (877) 644-6338
Highland Local (PK-12)
2015-16 Enrollment: 3,080 . . . . (330) 239-1901
Medina City SD (PK-12)
2015-16 Enrollment: 6,812 . . . . (330) 636-3031
Medina County Joint Vocational School District (10-12)
2015-16 Enrollment: n/a . . . . (330) 725-8461

Vocational/Technical School(s)

Hamrick School (Private, For-profit)
Fall 2016 Enrollment: 155 . . . . (330) 239-2229
2016-17 Tuition: $10,845
Medina County Career Center (Public)
Fall 2016 Enrollment: 74 . . . . (330) 725-8461
2016-17 Tuition: $4,570
Housing: Homeownership rate: 65.2%; Median home value: $160,700; Median year structure built: 1979; Homeowner vacancy rate: 3.3%; Median selected monthly owner costs: $1,371 with a mortgage, $513 without a mortgage; Median gross rent: $800 per month; Rental vacancy rate: 0.9%
Health Insurance: 92.9% have insurance; 78.3% have private insurance; 24.6% have public insurance; 7.1% do not have insurance; 4.5% of children under 18 do not have insurance
Hospitals: Medina Hospital (118 beds)
Newspapers: Medina County Gazette (daily circulation 14,400)
Transportation: Commute: 92.4% car, 0.6% public transportation, 1.5% walk, 3.4% work from home; Mean travel time to work: 28.0 minutes
Airports: Medina Municipal (general aviation)
Additional Information Contacts
City of Medina . . . . (330) 725-8861
http://www.medinaoh.org

SEVILLE (village). Covers a land area of 2.603 square miles and a water area of 0 square miles. Located at 41.02° N. Lat; 81.87° W. Long. Elevation is 988 feet.
Population: 2,505; Growth (since 2000): 16.0%; Density: 962.5 persons per square mile; Race: 95.3% White, 0.5% Black/African American, 0.8% Asian, 0.0% American Indian/Alaska Native, 0.0% Native Hawaiian/Other Pacific Islander, 0.0% Two or more races, 4.6% Hispanic of any race; Average household size: 2.45; Median age: 44.2; Age under 18: 22.8%; Age 65 and over: 17.4%; Males per 100 females: 92.0; Marriage status: 26.5% never married, 56.6% now married, 0.9% separated, 6.9% widowed, 10.0% divorced; Foreign born: 1.4%; Speak English only: 97.2%; With disability: 9.7%; Veterans: 8.7%; Ancestry: 26.5% German, 14.1% Irish, 13.4% Italian, 8.3% English, 6.9% Polish
Employment: 14.2% management, business, and financial, 3.1% computer, engineering, and science, 13.8% education, legal, community service, arts, and media, 4.2% healthcare practitioners, 21.6% service, 22.0% sales and office, 7.5% natural resources, construction, and maintenance, 13.6% production, transportation, and material moving
Income: Per capita: $32,111; Median household: $55,188; Average household: $79,519; Households with income of $100,000 or more: 24.3%; Poverty rate: 3.0%
Educational Attainment: High school diploma or higher: 92.1%; Bachelor's degree or higher: 23.5%; Graduate/professional degree or higher: 6.0%

School District(s)

Cloverleaf Local (PK-12)
2015-16 Enrollment: 2,377 . . . . (330) 948-2500
Housing: Homeownership rate: 78.6%; Median home value: $141,400; Median year structure built: 1980; Homeowner vacancy rate: 2.3%; Median selected monthly owner costs: $1,128 with a mortgage, $415 without a mortgage; Median gross rent: $760 per month; Rental vacancy rate: 7.9%
Health Insurance: 97.0% have insurance; 88.1% have private insurance; 22.4% have public insurance; 3.0% do not have insurance; 0.0% of children under 18 do not have insurance
Transportation: Commute: 95.7% car, 0.2% public transportation, 0.5% walk, 3.7% work from home; Mean travel time to work: 26.0 minutes
Additional Information Contacts

Village of Seville . . . . (330) 769-4146
http://www.villageofseville.com

SHARON CENTER (unincorporated postal area)

ZCTA: 44274

Covers a land area of 0.432 square miles and a water area of 0 square miles. Located at 41.10° N. Lat; 81.73° W. Long. Elevation is 1,129 feet.

Population: 351; Growth (since 2000): n/a; Density: 813.1 persons per square mile; Race: 99.1% White, 0.6% Black/African American, 0.0% Asian, 0.0% American Indian/Alaska Native, 0.0% Native Hawaiian/Other Pacific Islander, 0.3% Two or more races, 0.0% Hispanic of any race; Average household size: 2.75; Median age: 31.0; Age under 18: 31.1%; Age 65 and over: 22.2%; Males per 100 females: 106.4; Marriage status: 36.8% never married, 28.1% now married, 0.0% separated, 19.0% widowed, 16.1% divorced; Foreign born: 0.0%; Speak English only: 100.0%; With disability: 40.5%; Veterans: 3.7%; Ancestry: 49.6% German, 24.8% Welsh, 20.8% English, 4.3% American, 3.1% Irish

Employment: 19.4% management, business, and financial, 0.0% computer, engineering, and science, 0.0% education, legal, community service, arts, and media, 7.5% healthcare practitioners, 21.6% service, 0.0% sales and office, 0.0% natural resources, construction, and maintenance, 51.5% production, transportation, and material moving

Income: Per capita: $18,819; Median household: n/a; Average household: $51,303; Households with income of $100,000 or more: 14.2%; Poverty rate: 72.9%

Educational Attainment: High school diploma or higher: 99.6%; Bachelor's degree or higher: 19.4%; Graduate/professional degree or higher: 7.9%

School District(s)

Highland Local (PK-12)
2015-16 Enrollment: 3,080 . . . . (330) 239-1901

Housing: Homeownership rate: 77.8%; Median home value: $182,100; Median year structure built: Before 1940; Homeowner vacancy rate: 0.0%; Median selected monthly owner costs: $1,212 with a mortgage, $0 without a mortgage; Median gross rent: n/a per month; Rental vacancy rate: 0.0%

Health Insurance: 79.5% have insurance; 40.2% have private insurance; 61.5% have public insurance; 20.5% do not have insurance; 0.0% of children under 18 do not have insurance

Transportation: Commute: 99.3% car, 0.0% public transportation, 0.7% walk, 0.0% work from home; Mean travel time to work: 0.0 minutes

SPENCER (village). Covers a land area of 0.986 square miles and a water area of 0.007 square miles. Located at 41.10° N. Lat; 82.12° W. Long. Elevation is 915 feet.

Population: 591; Growth (since 2000): -20.9%; Density: 599.3 persons per square mile; Race: 100.0% White, 0.0% Black/African American, 0.0% Asian, 0.0% American Indian/Alaska Native, 0.0% Native Hawaiian/Other Pacific Islander, 0.0% Two or more races, 0.0% Hispanic of any race; Average household size: 2.53; Median age: 40.4; Age under 18: 23.5%; Age 65 and over: 17.4%; Males per 100 females: 97.6; Marriage status: 22.0% never married, 59.0% now married, 0.9% separated, 7.7% widowed, 11.3% divorced; Foreign born: 0.0%; Speak English only: 100.0%; With disability: 15.7%; Veterans: 11.9%; Ancestry: 33.3% German, 18.8% Irish, 7.8% English, 6.9% Polish, 6.9% Scottish

Employment: 9.8% management, business, and financial, 1.4% computer, engineering, and science, 5.9% education, legal, community service, arts, and media, 8.0% healthcare practitioners, 26.8% service, 14.6% sales and office, 10.5% natural resources, construction, and maintenance, 23.0% production, transportation, and material moving

Income: Per capita: $22,074; Median household: $47,273; Average household: $54,853; Households with income of $100,000 or more: 11.6%; Poverty rate: 6.5%

Educational Attainment: High school diploma or higher: 85.6%; Bachelor's degree or higher: 6.2%; Graduate/professional degree or higher: 1.5%

Housing: Homeownership rate: 65.8%; Median home value: $120,000; Median year structure built: 1954; Homeowner vacancy rate: 0.0%; Median selected monthly owner costs: $1,064 with a mortgage, $420 without a mortgage; Median gross rent: $712 per month; Rental vacancy rate: 5.5%

Health Insurance: 89.7% have insurance; 71.9% have private insurance; 32.7% have public insurance; 10.3% do not have insurance; 0.0% of children under 18 do not have insurance

Transportation: Commute: 92.2% car, 1.5% public transportation, 5.6% walk, 0.7% work from home; Mean travel time to work: 27.7 minutes

VALLEY CITY (CDP).

Land/water area and latitude/longitude are not available.

Population: 527; Growth (since 2000): n/a; Density: n/a persons per square mile; Race: 100.0% White, 0.0% Black/African American, 0.0% Asian, 0.0% American Indian/Alaska Native, 0.0% Native Hawaiian/Other Pacific Islander, 0.0% Two or more races, 0.0% Hispanic of any race; Average household size: 2.44; Median age: 44.9; Age under 18: 14.6%; Age 65 and over: 10.2%; Males per 100 females: 0.0; Marriage status: 28.7% never married, 61.1% now married, 4.9% separated, 1.6% widowed, 8.7% divorced; Foreign born: 0.0%; Speak English only: 100.0%; With disability: 13.1%; Veterans: 14.0%; Ancestry: 27.7% German, 23.9% Polish, 11.6% Italian, 11.4% Irish, 8.3% English

Employment: 17.4% management, business, and financial, 8.5% computer, engineering, and science, 0.0% education, legal, community service, arts, and media, 13.3% healthcare practitioners, 23.9% service, 19.5% sales and office, 6.5% natural resources, construction, and maintenance, 10.9% production, transportation, and material moving

Income: Per capita: $34,659; Median household: $65,694; Average household: $82,645; Households with income of $100,000 or more: 38.9%; Poverty rate: 5.5%

Educational Attainment: High school diploma or higher: 88.9%; Bachelor's degree or higher: 32.3%; Graduate/professional degree or higher: 14.4%

Housing: Homeownership rate: 77.8%; Median home value: $267,400; Median year structure built: 2001; Homeowner vacancy rate: 0.0%; Median selected monthly owner costs: $1,685 with a mortgage, $536 without a mortgage; Median gross rent: $667 per month; Rental vacancy rate: 0.0%

Health Insurance: 98.3% have insurance; 80.5% have private insurance; 41.9% have public insurance; 1.7% do not have insurance; 0.0% of children under 18 do not have insurance

Safety: Violent crime rate: 0.0 per 10,000 population; Property crime rate: 0.0 per 10,000 population

Transportation: Commute: 86.3% car, 0.0% public transportation, 5.8% walk, 7.8% work from home; Mean travel time to work: 29.2 minutes

WADSWORTH (city). Covers a land area of 10.621 square miles and a water area of 0 square miles. Located at 41.03° N. Lat; 81.73° W. Long. Elevation is 1,171 feet.

History: Named for Colonel E. Wadsworth. Wadsworth developed as an industrial town, manufacturing matches, valves, locomotive appliances, and lubricators.

Population: 22,578; Growth (since 2000): 22.5%; Density: 2,125.7 persons per square mile; Race: 95.7% White, 1.4% Black/African American, 0.7% Asian, 0.3% American Indian/Alaska Native, 0.0% Native Hawaiian/Other Pacific Islander, 1.7% Two or more races, 1.3% Hispanic of any race; Average household size: 2.57; Median age: 37.7; Age under 18: 26.3%; Age 65 and over: 16.1%; Males per 100 females: 92.5; Marriage status: 25.2% never married, 55.7% now married, 1.5% separated, 6.6% widowed, 12.6% divorced; Foreign born: 1.3%; Speak English only: 98.0%; With disability: 10.4%; Veterans: 9.4%; Ancestry: 27.3% German, 14.8% Irish, 12.6% English, 8.1% Italian, 6.1% American

Employment: 17.6% management, business, and financial, 6.7% computer, engineering, and science, 10.6% education, legal, community service, arts, and media, 8.0% healthcare practitioners, 14.9% service, 22.1% sales and office, 8.6% natural resources, construction, and maintenance, 11.4% production, transportation, and material moving

Income: Per capita: $29,035; Median household: $62,607; Average household: $74,086; Households with income of $100,000 or more: 24.9%; Poverty rate: 6.8%

Educational Attainment: High school diploma or higher: 94.6%; Bachelor's degree or higher: 35.4%; Graduate/professional degree or higher: 12.1%

School District(s)

Wadsworth City (PK-12)
2015-16 Enrollment: 4,805 . . . . (330) 336-3571

Housing: Homeownership rate: 69.3%; Median home value: $162,300; Median year structure built: 1975; Homeowner vacancy rate: 4.1%; Median selected monthly owner costs: $1,317 with a mortgage, $455 without a mortgage; Median gross rent: $814 per month; Rental vacancy rate: 9.6%

Health Insurance: 93.4% have insurance; 78.3% have private insurance; 28.0% have public insurance; 6.6% do not have insurance; 4.7% of children under 18 do not have insurance

Hospitals: Summa Wadsworth - Rittman Hospital (113 beds)

Safety: Violent crime rate: 11.0 per 10,000 population; Property crime rate: 218.6 per 10,000 population

Transportation: Commute: 95.5% car, 0.3% public transportation, 1.2% walk, 1.9% work from home; Mean travel time to work: 23.7 minutes
Additional Information Contacts
City of Wadsworth . . . . (330) 335-1521
http://www.wadsworthcity.com

WESTFIELD CENTER (village). Covers a land area of 2.108 square miles and a water area of 0 square miles. Located at 41.03° N. Lat; 81.93° W. Long. Elevation is 1,099 feet.
Population: 1,199; Growth (since 2000): 13.8%; Density: 568.9 persons per square mile; Race: 99.6% White, 0.0% Black/African American, 0.0% Asian, 0.0% American Indian/Alaska Native, 0.0% Native Hawaiian/Other Pacific Islander, 0.4% Two or more races, 0.8% Hispanic of any race; Average household size: 2.48; Median age: 48.2; Age under 18: 19.0%; Age 65 and over: 22.3%; Males per 100 females: 102.4; Marriage status: 21.5% never married, 63.6% now married, 0.3% separated, 7.9% widowed, 7.1% divorced; Foreign born: 2.3%; Speak English only: 96.7%; With disability: 11.7%; Veterans: 12.0%; Ancestry: 36.4% German, 18.8% Irish, 13.7% English, 12.3% Italian, 7.7% Hungarian
Employment: 24.2% management, business, and financial, 5.3% computer, engineering, and science, 9.9% education, legal, community service, arts, and media, 7.7% healthcare practitioners, 13.5% service, 23.3% sales and office, 3.2% natural resources, construction, and maintenance, 12.9% production, transportation, and material moving
Income: Per capita: $42,299; Median household: $79,167; Average household: $104,997; Households with income of $100,000 or more: 37.9%; Poverty rate: 3.7%
Educational Attainment: High school diploma or higher: 96.8%; Bachelor's degree or higher: 31.2%; Graduate/professional degree or higher: 8.9%
Housing: Homeownership rate: 86.6%; Median home value: $199,800; Median year structure built: 1975; Homeowner vacancy rate: 0.0%; Median selected monthly owner costs: $1,445 with a mortgage, $557 without a mortgage; Median gross rent: $1,082 per month; Rental vacancy rate: 0.0%
Health Insurance: 97.1% have insurance; 87.0% have private insurance; 31.3% have public insurance; 2.9% do not have insurance; 0.0% of children under 18 do not have insurance
Transportation: Commute: 87.4% car, 0.0% public transportation, 5.6% walk, 6.5% work from home; Mean travel time to work: 23.5 minutes

Meigs County

Located in southeastern Ohio; bounded on the southeast by the Ohio River and the West Virginia border; drained by the Shade River and Leading Creek. Covers a land area of 430.098 square miles, a water area of 2.903 square miles, and is located in the Eastern Time Zone at 39.09° N. Lat., 82.03° W. Long. The county was founded in 1819. County seat is Pomeroy.

Weather Station: Carpenter 2 S — Elevation: 821 feet

	Jan	Feb	Mar	Apr	May	Jun	Jul	Aug	Sep	Oct	Nov	Dec
High	39	43	53	65	73	81	85	84	77	66	55	43
Low	21	23	31	40	49	58	62	60	52	41	33	25
Precip	2.9	2.8	3.7	3.6	4.4	3.8	4.5	3.3	3.2	2.9	3.2	2.8
Snow	6.9	4.4	2.7	0.9	tr	0.0	0.0	0.0	0.0	tr	0.6	3.1

High and Low temperatures in degrees Fahrenheit; Precipitation and Snow in inches

Population: 23,345; Growth (since 2000): 1.2%; Density: 54.3 persons per square mile; Race: 97.5% White, 1.2% Black/African American, 0.2% Asian, 0.1% American Indian/Alaska Native, 0.0% Native Hawaiian/Other Pacific Islander, 1.0% two or more races, 0.6% Hispanic of any race; Average household size: 2.51; Median age: 42.8; Age under 18: 21.9%; Age 65 and over: 17.7%; Males per 100 females: 96.3; Marriage status: 22.7% never married, 53.4% now married, 1.5% separated, 7.8% widowed, 16.1% divorced; Foreign born: 0.3%; Speak English only: 99.4%; With disability: 21.8%; Veterans: 10.1%; Ancestry: 25.2% German, 15.0% Irish, 11.4% American, 9.7% English, 3.4% Dutch
Religion: Six largest groups: 7.4% Baptist, 7.2% Methodist/Pietist, 4.5% Non-denominational Protestant, 3.0% Holiness, 1.2% Catholicism, 1.1% Pentecostal
Economy: Unemployment rate: 6.9%; Leading industries: 20.4 % retail trade; 16.4 % other services (except public administration); 12.8 % health care and social assistance; Farms: 588 totaling 75,801 acres; Company size: 0 employ 1,000 or more persons, 0 employ 500 to 999 persons, 1 employs 100 to 499 persons, 303 employ less than 100 persons; Business ownership: 430 women-owned, n/a Black-owned, n/a Hispanic-owned, n/a Asian-owned, n/a American Indian/Alaska Native-owned
Employment: 8.7% management, business, and financial, 1.8% computer, engineering, and science, 11.9% education, legal, community service, arts, and media, 5.8% healthcare practitioners, 19.8% service, 20.3% sales and office, 13.8% natural resources, construction, and maintenance, 18.0% production, transportation, and material moving
Income: Per capita: $21,317; Median household: $39,640; Average household: $52,529; Households with income of $100,000 or more: 11.3%; Poverty rate: 22.8%
Educational Attainment: High school diploma or higher: 84.0%; Bachelor's degree or higher: 13.4%; Graduate/professional degree or higher: 5.2%
Housing: Homeownership rate: 77.6%; Median home value: $86,300; Median year structure built: 1976; Homeowner vacancy rate: 3.6%; Median selected monthly owner costs: $954 with a mortgage, $355 without a mortgage; Median gross rent: $585 per month; Rental vacancy rate: 2.0%
Vital Statistics: Birth rate: 87.8 per 10,000 population; Death rate: 115.5 per 10,000 population; Age-adjusted cancer mortality rate: 245.9 deaths per 100,000 population
Health Insurance: 89.1% have insurance; 56.5% have private insurance; 47.7% have public insurance; 10.9% do not have insurance; 4.8% of children under 18 do not have insurance
Health Care: Physicians: 2.2 per 10,000 population; Dentists: 2.6 per 10,000 population; Hospital beds: 0.0 per 10,000 population; Hospital admissions: 0.0 per 10,000 population
Air Quality Index (AQI): Percent of Days: 98.9% good, 1.1% moderate, 0.0% unhealthy for sensitive individuals, 0.0% unhealthy, 0.0% very unhealthy; Annual median: 1; Annual maximum: 64
Transportation: Commute: 92.9% car, 0.3% public transportation, 2.1% walk, 4.0% work from home; Mean travel time to work: 30.1 minutes
2016 Presidential Election: 72.8% Trump, 22.5% Clinton, 2.8% Johnson, 0.7% Stein
National and State Parks: Buffington Island State Memorial; Forked Run State Park
Additional Information Contacts
Meigs Government . . . . (740) 992-2895
http://www.meigscountyohio.com

Meigs County Communities

LANGSVILLE (unincorporated postal area)
ZCTA: 45741
Covers a land area of 42.678 square miles and a water area of 0.007 square miles. Located at 39.08° N. Lat; 82.25° W. Long. Elevation is 571 feet.
Population: 905; Growth (since 2000): -1.4%; Density: 21.2 persons per square mile; Race: 100.0% White, 0.0% Black/African American, 0.0% Asian, 0.0% American Indian/Alaska Native, 0.0% Native Hawaiian/Other Pacific Islander, 0.0% Two or more races, 0.0% Hispanic of any race; Average household size: 2.25; Median age: 45.3; Age under 18: 20.7%; Age 65 and over: 11.4%; Males per 100 females: 97.8; Marriage status: 24.0% never married, 45.4% now married, 0.9% separated, 8.9% widowed, 21.7% divorced; Foreign born: 0.0%; Speak English only: 100.0%; With disability: 20.4%; Veterans: 10.0%; Ancestry: 22.1% American, 11.9% German, 9.0% Irish, 5.5% English, 5.0% Dutch
Employment: 3.8% management, business, and financial, 0.0% computer, engineering, and science, 10.4% education, legal, community service, arts, and media, 3.0% healthcare practitioners, 24.6% service, 18.3% sales and office, 13.1% natural resources, construction, and maintenance, 26.8% production, transportation, and material moving
Income: Per capita: $17,861; Median household: $30,000; Average household: $39,991; Households with income of $100,000 or more: 2.7%; Poverty rate: 28.3%
Educational Attainment: High school diploma or higher: 71.6%; Bachelor's degree or higher: 1.7%; Graduate/professional degree or higher: 1.7%
Housing: Homeownership rate: 84.6%; Median home value: $65,200; Median year structure built: 1975; Homeowner vacancy rate: 0.0%; Median selected monthly owner costs: $762 with a mortgage, $305 without a mortgage; Median gross rent: $461 per month; Rental vacancy rate: 0.0%
Health Insurance: 81.0% have insurance; 53.3% have private insurance; 36.8% have public insurance; 19.0% do not have insurance; 0.0% of children under 18 do not have insurance

Transportation: Commute: 100.0% car, 0.0% public transportation, 0.0% walk, 0.0% work from home; Mean travel time to work: 47.0 minutes

LONG BOTTOM (unincorporated postal area)

ZCTA: 45743

Covers a land area of 36.714 square miles and a water area of 0.275 square miles. Located at 39.08° N. Lat; 81.85° W. Long. Elevation is 604 feet.

Population: 1,558; Growth (since 2000): -2.2%; Density: 42.4 persons per square mile; Race: 97.4% White, 1.7% Black/African American, 0.0% Asian, 0.0% American Indian/Alaska Native, 0.0% Native Hawaiian/Other Pacific Islander, 0.8% Two or more races, 0.2% Hispanic of any race; Average household size: 2.86; Median age: 38.5; Age under 18: 26.1%; Age 65 and over: 16.2%; Males per 100 females: 103.5; Marriage status: 20.8% never married, 59.2% now married, 0.0% separated, 4.3% widowed, 15.7% divorced; Foreign born: 0.2%; Speak English only: 99.8%; With disability: 18.9%; Veterans: 10.3%; Ancestry: 22.3% American, 17.1% German, 14.3% English, 9.7% Irish, 6.5% Dutch

Employment: 6.8% management, business, and financial, 7.0% computer, engineering, and science, 6.4% education, legal, community service, arts, and media, 5.9% healthcare practitioners, 27.5% service, 17.9% sales and office, 10.9% natural resources, construction, and maintenance, 17.7% production, transportation, and material moving

Income: Per capita: $21,668; Median household: $58,250; Average household: $61,321; Households with income of $100,000 or more: 19.3%; Poverty rate: 8.9%

Educational Attainment: High school diploma or higher: 89.1%; Bachelor's degree or higher: 16.7%; Graduate/professional degree or higher: 4.6%

Housing: Homeownership rate: 92.5%; Median home value: $116,900; Median year structure built: 1979; Homeowner vacancy rate: 5.2%; Median selected monthly owner costs: $1,108 with a mortgage, $303 without a mortgage; Median gross rent: $591 per month; Rental vacancy rate: 0.0%

Health Insurance: 88.0% have insurance; 70.1% have private insurance; 32.9% have public insurance; 12.0% do not have insurance; 12.6% of children under 18 do not have insurance

Transportation: Commute: 93.4% car, 0.0% public transportation, 0.0% walk, 5.3% work from home; Mean travel time to work: 29.9 minutes

MIDDLEPORT (village).

Covers a land area of 1.798 square miles and a water area of 0.098 square miles. Located at 38.99° N. Lat; 82.07° W. Long. Elevation is 571 feet.

History: Middleport was an active river town along the Ohio River during the last half of the 1800's. The disastrous flooding of the river in 1937 destroyed Middleport's waterfront.

Population: 2,143; Growth (since 2000): -15.1%; Density: 1,191.7 persons per square mile; Race: 93.7% White, 2.2% Black/African American, 0.7% Asian, 0.0% American Indian/Alaska Native, 0.0% Native Hawaiian/Other Pacific Islander, 3.4% Two or more races, 0.0% Hispanic of any race; Average household size: 2.16; Median age: 41.6; Age under 18: 21.0%; Age 65 and over: 22.3%; Males per 100 females: 85.6; Marriage status: 28.0% never married, 37.7% now married, 4.2% separated, 13.8% widowed, 20.5% divorced; Foreign born: 0.4%; Speak English only: 99.5%; With disability: 21.6%; Veterans: 7.3%; Ancestry: 35.7% German, 16.8% Irish, 10.8% American, 8.1% English, 4.4% Dutch

Employment: 11.8% management, business, and financial, 0.8% computer, engineering, and science, 14.4% education, legal, community service, arts, and media, 3.8% healthcare practitioners, 14.8% service, 28.7% sales and office, 10.5% natural resources, construction, and maintenance, 15.2% production, transportation, and material moving

Income: Per capita: $20,154; Median household: $24,263; Average household: $42,992; Households with income of $100,000 or more: 10.0%; Poverty rate: 31.6%

Educational Attainment: High school diploma or higher: 82.9%; Bachelor's degree or higher: 14.6%; Graduate/professional degree or higher: 8.0%

School District(s)

Meigs Local (PK-12)
2015-16 Enrollment: 1,786 . . . . (740) 992-2153

Housing: Homeownership rate: 58.9%; Median home value: $61,100; Median year structure built: 1951; Homeowner vacancy rate: 11.9%; Median selected monthly owner costs: $768 with a mortgage, $340 without a mortgage; Median gross rent: $552 per month; Rental vacancy rate: 3.0%

Health Insurance: 85.3% have insurance; 45.3% have private insurance; 52.4% have public insurance; 14.7% do not have insurance; 4.9% of children under 18 do not have insurance

Safety: Violent crime rate: 16.2 per 10,000 population; Property crime rate: 69.0 per 10,000 population

Transportation: Commute: 89.4% car, 3.1% public transportation, 3.6% walk, 3.9% work from home; Mean travel time to work: 23.5 minutes

POMEROY (village).

County seat. Covers a land area of 3.246 square miles and a water area of 0.063 square miles. Located at 39.03° N. Lat; 82.03° W. Long. Elevation is 574 feet.

History: Pomeroy began in 1804 when Samuel Pomeroy, a Boston merchant, purchased land here. Coal mining began in Pomeroy in the early 1800's, making the town the primary shipper of coal in Ohio prior to 1850. Salt making was also a leading early industry.

Population: 1,961; Growth (since 2000): -0.3%; Density: 604.1 persons per square mile; Race: 92.6% White, 4.5% Black/African American, 0.0% Asian, 0.0% American Indian/Alaska Native, 0.0% Native Hawaiian/Other Pacific Islander, 2.4% Two or more races, 0.1% Hispanic of any race; Average household size: 2.40; Median age: 39.8; Age under 18: 23.4%; Age 65 and over: 12.7%; Males per 100 females: 84.6; Marriage status: 29.0% never married, 46.5% now married, 2.0% separated, 8.9% widowed, 15.6% divorced; Foreign born: 0.2%; Speak English only: 99.1%; With disability: 23.8%; Veterans: 8.8%; Ancestry: 19.3% German, 13.7% Irish, 9.6% American, 8.3% English, 2.4% Scotch-Irish

Employment: 6.2% management, business, and financial, 0.6% computer, engineering, and science, 10.7% education, legal, community service, arts, and media, 4.6% healthcare practitioners, 23.2% service, 30.3% sales and office, 8.8% natural resources, construction, and maintenance, 15.5% production, transportation, and material moving

Income: Per capita: $14,827; Median household: $25,380; Average household: $34,994; Households with income of $100,000 or more: 3.9%; Poverty rate: 38.8%

Educational Attainment: High school diploma or higher: 80.2%; Bachelor's degree or higher: 12.1%; Graduate/professional degree or higher: 2.9%

School District(s)

Meigs Local (PK-12)
2015-16 Enrollment: 1,786 . . . . (740) 992-2153

Housing: Homeownership rate: 53.1%; Median home value: $58,700; Median year structure built: Before 1940; Homeowner vacancy rate: 10.0%; Median selected monthly owner costs: $769 with a mortgage, $310 without a mortgage; Median gross rent: $521 per month; Rental vacancy rate: 2.1%

Health Insurance: 90.5% have insurance; 41.7% have private insurance; 58.9% have public insurance; 9.5% do not have insurance; 1.1% of children under 18 do not have insurance

Newspapers: The Daily Sentinel (daily circulation 3,500)

Transportation: Commute: 92.8% car, 0.0% public transportation, 4.1% walk, 1.0% work from home; Mean travel time to work: 23.5 minutes

PORTLAND (unincorporated postal area)

ZCTA: 45770

Covers a land area of 20.453 square miles and a water area of 0.557 square miles. Located at 38.98° N. Lat; 81.80° W. Long. Elevation is 614 feet.

Population: 487; Growth (since 2000): -10.1%; Density: 23.8 persons per square mile; Race: 100.0% White, 0.0% Black/African American, 0.0% Asian, 0.0% American Indian/Alaska Native, 0.0% Native Hawaiian/Other Pacific Islander, 0.0% Two or more races, 0.0% Hispanic of any race; Average household size: 2.72; Median age: 42.0; Age under 18: 22.2%; Age 65 and over: 17.7%; Males per 100 females: 104.6; Marriage status: 25.1% never married, 49.5% now married, 2.0% separated, 9.0% widowed, 16.3% divorced; Foreign born: 0.0%; Speak English only: 100.0%; With disability: 16.8%; Veterans: 11.9%; Ancestry: 13.1% English, 8.4% Polish, 6.0% Irish, 4.3% German, 3.7% Cajun

Employment: 0.0% management, business, and financial, 7.6% computer, engineering, and science, 11.8% education, legal, community service, arts, and media, 5.9% healthcare practitioners, 0.8% service, 17.6% sales and office, 21.8% natural resources, construction, and maintenance, 34.5% production, transportation, and material moving

Income: Per capita: $18,651; Median household: $30,592; Average household: $49,450; Households with income of $100,000 or more: 21.8%; Poverty rate: 39.2%

Educational Attainment: High school diploma or higher: 78.3%; Bachelor's degree or higher: 11.0%; Graduate/professional degree or higher: n/a
Housing: Homeownership rate: 88.8%; Median home value: $57,300; Median year structure built: 1992; Homeowner vacancy rate: 14.5%; Median selected monthly owner costs: $875 with a mortgage, $231 without a mortgage; Median gross rent: n/a per month; Rental vacancy rate: 0.0%
Health Insurance: 78.4% have insurance; 29.6% have private insurance; 60.4% have public insurance; 21.6% do not have insurance; 0.0% of children under 18 do not have insurance
Transportation: Commute: 85.7% car, 0.0% public transportation, 0.0% walk, 14.3% work from home; Mean travel time to work: 32.8 minutes

RACINE (village). Covers a land area of 0.437 square miles and a water area of 0 square miles. Located at 38.97° N. Lat; 81.91° W. Long. Elevation is 577 feet.
Population: 703; Growth (since 2000): -5.8%; Density: 1,607.4 persons per square mile; Race: 100.0% White, 0.0% Black/African American, 0.0% Asian, 0.0% American Indian/Alaska Native, 0.0% Native Hawaiian/Other Pacific Islander, 0.0% Two or more races, 0.0% Hispanic of any race; Average household size: 2.79; Median age: 39.8; Age under 18: 25.2%; Age 65 and over: 13.7%; Males per 100 females: 87.5; Marriage status: 23.9% never married, 48.2% now married, 2.1% separated, 7.9% widowed, 20.0% divorced; Foreign born: 0.0%; Speak English only: 100.0%; With disability: 15.5%; Veterans: 8.2%; Ancestry: 32.7% German, 15.9% Irish, 5.7% English, 5.5% American, 2.1% Greek
Employment: 10.5% management, business, and financial, 1.1% computer, engineering, and science, 13.0% education, legal, community service, arts, and media, 6.3% healthcare practitioners, 21.8% service, 16.8% sales and office, 17.2% natural resources, construction, and maintenance, 13.3% production, transportation, and material moving
Income: Per capita: $20,564; Median household: $44,000; Average household: $54,686; Households with income of $100,000 or more: 5.2%; Poverty rate: 16.1%
Educational Attainment: High school diploma or higher: 91.9%; Bachelor's degree or higher: 12.5%; Graduate/professional degree or higher: 5.3%

School District(s)

Southern Local (PK-12)
2015-16 Enrollment: 764. . . . . (740) 949-2661
Housing: Homeownership rate: 69.4%; Median home value: $92,300; Median year structure built: 1976; Homeowner vacancy rate: 3.3%; Median selected monthly owner costs: $973 with a mortgage, $398 without a mortgage; Median gross rent: $538 per month; Rental vacancy rate: 0.0%
Health Insurance: 91.2% have insurance; 62.3% have private insurance; 41.5% have public insurance; 8.8% do not have insurance; 8.5% of children under 18 do not have insurance
Transportation: Commute: 97.9% car, 0.0% public transportation, 0.7% walk, 1.4% work from home; Mean travel time to work: 33.4 minutes

REEDSVILLE (unincorporated postal area)
ZCTA: 45772
Covers a land area of 43.164 square miles and a water area of 0.462 square miles. Located at 39.15° N. Lat; 81.82° W. Long. Elevation is 643 feet.
Population: 1,938; Growth (since 2000): -7.0%; Density: 44.9 persons per square mile; Race: 98.3% White, 1.7% Black/African American, 0.0% Asian, 0.0% American Indian/Alaska Native, 0.0% Native Hawaiian/Other Pacific Islander, 0.0% Two or more races, 3.9% Hispanic of any race; Average household size: 2.48; Median age: 45.3; Age under 18: 17.2%; Age 65 and over: 17.1%; Males per 100 females: 95.9; Marriage status: 22.1% never married, 43.9% now married, 0.6% separated, 11.9% widowed, 22.1% divorced; Foreign born: 0.0%; Speak English only: 99.3%; With disability: 23.2%; Veterans: 7.9%; Ancestry: 25.3% German, 10.5% English, 9.6% American, 7.1% Irish, 5.3% Italian
Employment: 8.3% management, business, and financial, 0.9% computer, engineering, and science, 12.9% education, legal, community service, arts, and media, 5.9% healthcare practitioners, 19.1% service, 28.9% sales and office, 6.8% natural resources, construction, and maintenance, 17.1% production, transportation, and material moving
Income: Per capita: $20,186; Median household: $42,697; Average household: $49,038; Households with income of $100,000 or more: 11.4%; Poverty rate: 29.3%
Educational Attainment: High school diploma or higher: 73.9%; Bachelor's degree or higher: 11.8%; Graduate/professional degree or higher: 4.4%

School District(s)

Eastern Local (KG-12)
2015-16 Enrollment: 795. . . . . (740) 667-6079
Housing: Homeownership rate: 84.4%; Median home value: $85,900; Median year structure built: 1986; Homeowner vacancy rate: 4.5%; Median selected monthly owner costs: $940 with a mortgage, $275 without a mortgage; Median gross rent: n/a per month; Rental vacancy rate: 0.0%
Health Insurance: 89.7% have insurance; 47.9% have private insurance; 53.8% have public insurance; 10.3% do not have insurance; 18.0% of children under 18 do not have insurance
Transportation: Commute: 90.5% car, 0.0% public transportation, 3.2% walk, 6.3% work from home; Mean travel time to work: 30.6 minutes

RUTLAND (village). Covers a land area of 0.827 square miles and a water area of 0 square miles. Located at 39.04° N. Lat; 82.13° W. Long. Elevation is 577 feet.
Population: 433; Growth (since 2000): 8.0%; Density: 523.6 persons per square mile; Race: 100.0% White, 0.0% Black/African American, 0.0% Asian, 0.0% American Indian/Alaska Native, 0.0% Native Hawaiian/Other Pacific Islander, 0.0% Two or more races, 0.0% Hispanic of any race; Average household size: 2.72; Median age: 38.9; Age under 18: 27.0%; Age 65 and over: 15.0%; Males per 100 females: 95.5; Marriage status: 33.0% never married, 50.3% now married, 0.9% separated, 10.3% widowed, 6.3% divorced; Foreign born: 0.2%; Speak English only: 99.7%; With disability: 32.3%; Veterans: 12.7%; Ancestry: 20.1% German, 9.2% English, 6.9% Irish, 4.8% Welsh, 4.2% Dutch
Employment: 7.4% management, business, and financial, 0.0% computer, engineering, and science, 8.1% education, legal, community service, arts, and media, 2.2% healthcare practitioners, 12.5% service, 28.7% sales and office, 17.6% natural resources, construction, and maintenance, 23.5% production, transportation, and material moving
Income: Per capita: $15,679; Median household: $33,750; Average household: $40,555; Households with income of $100,000 or more: 1.2%; Poverty rate: 26.1%
Educational Attainment: High school diploma or higher: 84.2%; Bachelor's degree or higher: 3.7%; Graduate/professional degree or higher: 1.1%
Housing: Homeownership rate: 74.8%; Median home value: $77,900; Median year structure built: 1950; Homeowner vacancy rate: 3.2%; Median selected monthly owner costs: $872 with a mortgage, $410 without a mortgage; Median gross rent: $750 per month; Rental vacancy rate: 2.4%
Health Insurance: 87.8% have insurance; 51.0% have private insurance; 49.7% have public insurance; 12.2% do not have insurance; 0.0% of children under 18 do not have insurance
Transportation: Commute: 99.2% car, 0.0% public transportation, 0.0% walk, 0.8% work from home; Mean travel time to work: 32.6 minutes

SHADE (unincorporated postal area)
ZCTA: 45776
Covers a land area of 19.676 square miles and a water area of 0.022 square miles. Located at 39.18° N. Lat; 82.02° W. Long..
Population: 628; Growth (since 2000): -21.3%; Density: 31.9 persons per square mile; Race: 96.8% White, 0.0% Black/African American, 0.0% Asian, 0.0% American Indian/Alaska Native, 0.0% Native Hawaiian/Other Pacific Islander, 3.2% Two or more races, 0.0% Hispanic of any race; Average household size: 2.24; Median age: 39.7; Age under 18: 19.9%; Age 65 and over: 13.5%; Males per 100 females: 105.1; Marriage status: 31.8% never married, 51.0% now married, 0.0% separated, 8.5% widowed, 8.7% divorced; Foreign born: 0.0%; Speak English only: 100.0%; With disability: 22.5%; Veterans: 6.0%; Ancestry: 22.9% German, 17.0% American, 16.6% Irish, 2.9% Dutch, 2.7% English
Employment: 8.5% management, business, and financial, 0.0% computer, engineering, and science, 5.2% education, legal, community service, arts, and media, 5.5% healthcare practitioners, 36.6% service, 21.0% sales and office, 7.0% natural resources, construction, and maintenance, 16.2% production, transportation, and material moving
Income: Per capita: $24,530; Median household: $32,045; Average household: $56,526; Households with income of $100,000 or more: 5.0%; Poverty rate: 32.6%
Educational Attainment: High school diploma or higher: 85.8%; Bachelor's degree or higher: 19.0%; Graduate/professional degree or higher: 5.1%

Housing: Homeownership rate: 68.6%; Median home value: $81,700; Median year structure built: 1976; Homeowner vacancy rate: 0.0%; Median selected monthly owner costs: $930 with a mortgage, $338 without a mortgage; Median gross rent: $624 per month; Rental vacancy rate: 0.0%
Health Insurance: 93.6% have insurance; 56.7% have private insurance; 58.1% have public insurance; 6.4% do not have insurance; 0.0% of children under 18 do not have insurance
Transportation: Commute: 94.5% car, 0.0% public transportation, 0.0% walk, 1.8% work from home; Mean travel time to work: 24.5 minutes

SYRACUSE (village). Covers a land area of 0.927 square miles and a water area of 0.026 square miles. Located at 39.00° N. Lat; 81.97° W. Long. Elevation is 587 feet.
Population: 730; Growth (since 2000): -17.0%; Density: 787.2 persons per square mile; Race: 94.5% White, 3.2% Black/African American, 0.0% Asian, 0.0% American Indian/Alaska Native, 0.0% Native Hawaiian/Other Pacific Islander, 2.3% Two or more races, 0.1% Hispanic of any race; Average household size: 2.60; Median age: 44.6; Age under 18: 18.6%; Age 65 and over: 24.9%; Males per 100 females: 90.8; Marriage status: 21.8% never married, 64.8% now married, 4.0% separated, 4.5% widowed, 9.0% divorced; Foreign born: 0.1%; Speak English only: 99.7%; With disability: 24.7%; Veterans: 11.3%; Ancestry: 24.7% German, 14.2% English, 11.9% Irish, 11.4% American, 2.1% Scottish
Employment: 10.4% management, business, and financial, 5.8% computer, engineering, and science, 8.5% education, legal, community service, arts, and media, 7.7% healthcare practitioners, 20.0% service, 14.2% sales and office, 16.5% natural resources, construction, and maintenance, 16.9% production, transportation, and material moving
Income: Per capita: $21,851; Median household: $45,313; Average household: $54,978; Households with income of $100,000 or more: 15.7%; Poverty rate: 16.5%
Educational Attainment: High school diploma or higher: 81.0%; Bachelor's degree or higher: 10.9%; Graduate/professional degree or higher: 4.2%
Housing: Homeownership rate: 75.4%; Median home value: $87,100; Median year structure built: 1970; Homeowner vacancy rate: 2.3%; Median selected monthly owner costs: $886 with a mortgage, $353 without a mortgage; Median gross rent: $539 per month; Rental vacancy rate: 4.2%
Health Insurance: 97.0% have insurance; 61.9% have private insurance; 53.4% have public insurance; 3.0% do not have insurance; 0.0% of children under 18 do not have insurance
Transportation: Commute: 87.9% car, 0.0% public transportation, 2.7% walk, 9.4% work from home; Mean travel time to work: 31.6 minutes

TUPPERS PLAINS (CDP). Covers a land area of 1.816 square miles and a water area of 0 square miles. Located at 39.17° N. Lat; 81.85° W. Long. Elevation is 735 feet.
Population: 624; Growth (since 2000): n/a; Density: 343.6 persons per square mile; Race: 94.7% White, 5.3% Black/African American, 0.0% Asian, 0.0% American Indian/Alaska Native, 0.0% Native Hawaiian/Other Pacific Islander, 0.0% Two or more races, 12.2% Hispanic of any race; Average household size: 2.99; Median age: 30.1; Age under 18: 31.6%; Age 65 and over: 9.5%; Males per 100 females: 82.4; Marriage status: 25.7% never married, 50.0% now married, 0.0% separated, 4.6% widowed, 19.7% divorced; Foreign born: 0.0%; Speak English only: 100.0%; With disability: 10.9%; Veterans: 2.3%; Ancestry: 12.5% German, 10.6% Irish, 9.1% Italian, 1.6% American, 1.4% English
Employment: 5.9% management, business, and financial, 0.0% computer, engineering, and science, 0.0% education, legal, community service, arts, and media, 3.1% healthcare practitioners, 16.5% service, 40.6% sales and office, 3.9% natural resources, construction, and maintenance, 29.9% production, transportation, and material moving
Income: Per capita: $15,663; Median household: $45,960; Average household: $48,738; Households with income of $100,000 or more: 3.8%; Poverty rate: 36.9%
Educational Attainment: High school diploma or higher: 93.3%; Bachelor's degree or higher: 4.6%; Graduate/professional degree or higher: n/a
Housing: Homeownership rate: 56.9%; Median home value: $107,800; Median year structure built: 1993; Homeowner vacancy rate: 20.7%; Median selected monthly owner costs: $1,086 with a mortgage, n/a without a mortgage; Median gross rent: $1,640 per month; Rental vacancy rate: 0.0%
Health Insurance: 83.2% have insurance; 41.3% have private insurance; 49.5% have public insurance; 16.8% do not have insurance; 30.5% of children under 18 do not have insurance
Transportation: Commute: 83.9% car, 0.0% public transportation, 0.0% walk, 16.1% work from home; Mean travel time to work: 17.6 minutes

Mercer County

Located in western Ohio; bounded on the west by Indiana; drained by the Wabash and Saint Marys Rivers; includes part of Grand Lake. Covers a land area of 462.449 square miles, a water area of 10.976 square miles, and is located in the Eastern Time Zone at 40.54° N. Lat., 84.63° W. Long. The county was founded in 1820. County seat is Celina.

Mercer County is part of the Celina, OH Micropolitan Statistical Area. The entire metro area includes: Mercer County, OH

Weather Station: Celina 3 NE Elevation: 859 feet

	Jan	Feb	Mar	Apr	May	Jun	Jul	Aug	Sep	Oct	Nov	Dec
High	34	38	49	62	72	81	84	82	77	64	50	37
Low	20	22	30	41	51	60	64	62	55	44	35	24
Precip	2.3	2.1	2.6	3.6	4.0	4.0	4.8	3.6	2.6	2.7	3.0	2.6
Snow	10.0	6.8	4.1	0.9	0.0	0.0	0.0	0.0	0.0	0.2	1.3	6.3

High and Low temperatures in degrees Fahrenheit; Precipitation and Snow in inches

Population: 40,886; Growth (since 2000): -0.1%; Density: 88.4 persons per square mile; Race: 97.4% White, 0.5% Black/African American, 0.4% Asian, 0.0% American Indian/Alaska Native, 0.3% Native Hawaiian/Other Pacific Islander, 0.9% two or more races, 1.8% Hispanic of any race; Average household size: 2.51; Median age: 40.0; Age under 18: 25.6%; Age 65 and over: 16.7%; Males per 100 females: 100.1; Marriage status: 23.1% never married, 60.9% now married, 1.0% separated, 7.6% widowed, 8.4% divorced; Foreign born: 0.9%; Speak English only: 98.1%; With disability: 11.0%; Veterans: 8.4%; Ancestry: 56.9% German, 9.7% Irish, 9.2% American, 4.5% English, 3.5% French
Religion: Six largest groups: 58.1% Catholicism, 7.3% Methodist/Pietist, 5.9% Lutheran, 3.1% Presbyterian-Reformed, 2.5% Non-denominational Protestant, 1.7% Holiness
Economy: Unemployment rate: 2.8%; Leading industries: 17.4 % retail trade; 13.8 % other services (except public administration); 11.6 % construction; Farms: 1,208 totaling 273,152 acres; Company size: 0 employ 1,000 or more persons, 2 employ 500 to 999 persons, 24 employ 100 to 499 persons, 948 employ less than 100 persons; Business ownership: 696 women-owned, n/a Black-owned, n/a Hispanic-owned, 29 Asian-owned, n/a American Indian/Alaska Native-owned
Employment: 12.3% management, business, and financial, 3.0% computer, engineering, and science, 6.6% education, legal, community service, arts, and media, 5.1% healthcare practitioners, 13.5% service, 19.6% sales and office, 9.5% natural resources, construction, and maintenance, 30.3% production, transportation, and material moving
Income: Per capita: $26,236; Median household: $55,220; Average household: $67,088; Households with income of $100,000 or more: 18.6%; Poverty rate: 8.3%
Educational Attainment: High school diploma or higher: 91.8%; Bachelor's degree or higher: 16.8%; Graduate/professional degree or higher: 5.9%
Housing: Homeownership rate: 76.0%; Median home value: $134,800; Median year structure built: 1972; Homeowner vacancy rate: 1.2%; Median selected monthly owner costs: $1,114 with a mortgage, $432 without a mortgage; Median gross rent: $647 per month; Rental vacancy rate: 5.0%
Vital Statistics: Birth rate: 135.2 per 10,000 population; Death rate: 94.6 per 10,000 population; Age-adjusted cancer mortality rate: 160.3 deaths per 100,000 population
Health Insurance: 94.4% have insurance; 80.5% have private insurance; 28.2% have public insurance; 5.6% do not have insurance; 3.0% of children under 18 do not have insurance
Health Care: Physicians: 10.5 per 10,000 population; Dentists: 2.9 per 10,000 population; Hospital beds: 14.7 per 10,000 population; Hospital admissions: 458.2 per 10,000 population
Transportation: Commute: 95.1% car, 0.4% public transportation, 1.5% walk, 1.9% work from home; Mean travel time to work: 17.9 minutes
2016 Presidential Election: 80.2% Trump, 15.5% Clinton, 2.6% Johnson, 0.5% Stein
National and State Parks: Grand Lake State Park; Harbor Point State Park
Additional Information Contacts

Mercer Government . . . . (419) 586-3178
http://www.mercercountyohio.org

Mercer County Communities

BURKETTSVILLE (village). Covers a land area of 0.175 square miles and a water area of 0.002 square miles. Located at 40.35° N. Lat; 84.64° W. Long. Elevation is 974 feet.
Population: 267; Growth (since 2000): 5.1%; Density: 1,521.7 persons per square mile; Race: 100.0% White, 0.0% Black/African American, 0.0% Asian, 0.0% American Indian/Alaska Native, 0.0% Native Hawaiian/Other Pacific Islander, 0.0% Two or more races, 0.0% Hispanic of any race; Average household size: 2.41; Median age: 39.2; Age under 18: 24.7%; Age 65 and over: 20.6%; Males per 100 females: 112.2; Marriage status: 13.5% never married, 74.4% now married, 0.0% separated, 7.2% widowed, 4.8% divorced; Foreign born: 0.0%; Speak English only: 100.0%; With disability: 12.7%; Veterans: 11.4%; Ancestry: 73.0% German, 7.1% English, 5.6% French, 3.4% Irish, 3.0% American
Employment: 8.8% management, business, and financial, 13.2% computer, engineering, and science, 4.4% education, legal, community service, arts, and media, 3.1% healthcare practitioners, 14.5% service, 13.8% sales and office, 15.1% natural resources, construction, and maintenance, 27.0% production, transportation, and material moving
Income: Per capita: $39,161; Median household: $58,958; Average household: $92,135; Households with income of $100,000 or more: 18.0%; Poverty rate: 3.0%
Educational Attainment: High school diploma or higher: 92.1%; Bachelor's degree or higher: 15.3%; Graduate/professional degree or higher: 1.6%
Housing: Homeownership rate: 97.3%; Median home value: $107,500; Median year structure built: 1966; Homeowner vacancy rate: 0.0%; Median selected monthly owner costs: $970 with a mortgage, $425 without a mortgage; Median gross rent: n/a per month; Rental vacancy rate: 0.0%
Health Insurance: 99.6% have insurance; 91.0% have private insurance; 27.7% have public insurance; 0.4% do not have insurance; 0.0% of children under 18 do not have insurance
Transportation: Commute: 87.4% car, 0.0% public transportation, 5.0% walk, 6.9% work from home; Mean travel time to work: 18.8 minutes

CELINA (city). County seat. Covers a land area of 4.981 square miles and a water area of 0.289 square miles. Located at 40.56° N. Lat; 84.56° W. Long. Elevation is 873 feet.
History: Celina was settled in 1834 in a densely forested area. Lumber mills soon attracted woodworkers and cabinet makers, and furniture manufacture became the leading industry.
Population: 10,349; Growth (since 2000): 0.4%; Density: 2,077.7 persons per square mile; Race: 93.1% White, 1.2% Black/African American, 1.1% Asian, 0.0% American Indian/Alaska Native, 0.6% Native Hawaiian/Other Pacific Islander, 2.3% Two or more races, 2.3% Hispanic of any race; Average household size: 2.32; Median age: 40.2; Age under 18: 24.1%; Age 65 and over: 15.5%; Males per 100 females: 93.3; Marriage status: 26.0% never married, 51.7% now married, 2.5% separated, 7.8% widowed, 14.5% divorced; Foreign born: 1.0%; Speak English only: 96.9%; With disability: 15.8%; Veterans: 8.6%; Ancestry: 45.3% German, 12.7% Irish, 9.0% American, 6.2% English, 5.3% French
Employment: 10.8% management, business, and financial, 3.1% computer, engineering, and science, 7.8% education, legal, community service, arts, and media, 3.5% healthcare practitioners, 17.3% service, 17.9% sales and office, 9.1% natural resources, construction, and maintenance, 30.5% production, transportation, and material moving
Income: Per capita: $22,534; Median household: $42,263; Average household: $53,031; Households with income of $100,000 or more: 9.3%; Poverty rate: 11.5%
Educational Attainment: High school diploma or higher: 91.4%; Bachelor's degree or higher: 16.0%; Graduate/professional degree or higher: 6.7%

School District(s)

Celina City (PK-12)
2015-16 Enrollment: 2,659 . . . . (419) 586-8300

Four-year College(s)

Wright State University-Lake Campus (Public)
Fall 2016 Enrollment: 1,336 . . . . (419) 586-0300
2016-17 Tuition: In-state $5,842; Out-of-state $14,462
Housing: Homeownership rate: 60.6%; Median home value: $107,000; Median year structure built: 1973; Homeowner vacancy rate: 2.5%; Median selected monthly owner costs: $1,075 with a mortgage, $392 without a mortgage; Median gross rent: $658 per month; Rental vacancy rate: 7.8%
Health Insurance: 91.0% have insurance; 69.2% have private insurance; 34.7% have public insurance; 9.0% do not have insurance; 1.4% of children under 18 do not have insurance
Newspapers: Daily Standard (daily circulation 11,000)
Transportation: Commute: 94.6% car, 0.5% public transportation, 1.5% walk, 0.7% work from home; Mean travel time to work: 16.2 minutes
Airports: Lakefield (general aviation)
Additional Information Contacts
City of Celina . . . . (419) 586-6464
http://www.ci.celina.oh.us

CHICKASAW (village). Covers a land area of 0.234 square miles and a water area of 0.001 square miles. Located at 40.44° N. Lat; 84.49° W. Long. Elevation is 942 feet.
Population: 344; Growth (since 2000): -5.5%; Density: 1,467.2 persons per square mile; Race: 100.0% White, 0.0% Black/African American, 0.0% Asian, 0.0% American Indian/Alaska Native, 0.0% Native Hawaiian/Other Pacific Islander, 0.0% Two or more races, 0.0% Hispanic of any race; Average household size: 2.32; Median age: 38.5; Age under 18: 23.5%; Age 65 and over: 20.3%; Males per 100 females: 98.6; Marriage status: 28.9% never married, 61.5% now married, 0.0% separated, 5.5% widowed, 4.0% divorced; Foreign born: 0.0%; Speak English only: 99.4%; With disability: 9.3%; Veterans: 4.2%; Ancestry: 81.7% German, 6.4% English, 6.1% American, 5.2% Irish, 4.1% French
Employment: 14.4% management, business, and financial, 3.7% computer, engineering, and science, 16.6% education, legal, community service, arts, and media, 3.2% healthcare practitioners, 16.6% service, 14.4% sales and office, 7.0% natural resources, construction, and maintenance, 24.1% production, transportation, and material moving
Income: Per capita: $27,095; Median household: $54,167; Average household: $63,155; Households with income of $100,000 or more: 15.6%; Poverty rate: 3.5%
Educational Attainment: High school diploma or higher: 96.3%; Bachelor's degree or higher: 24.0%; Graduate/professional degree or higher: 6.6%
Housing: Homeownership rate: 75.0%; Median home value: $152,700; Median year structure built: 1972; Homeowner vacancy rate: 0.0%; Median selected monthly owner costs: $1,260 with a mortgage, $478 without a mortgage; Median gross rent: $570 per month; Rental vacancy rate: 0.0%
Health Insurance: 98.5% have insurance; 88.7% have private insurance; 25.0% have public insurance; 1.5% do not have insurance; 0.0% of children under 18 do not have insurance
Transportation: Commute: 88.6% car, 0.0% public transportation, 4.3% walk, 5.4% work from home; Mean travel time to work: 20.7 minutes

COLDWATER (village). Covers a land area of 1.923 square miles and a water area of 0.052 square miles. Located at 40.48° N. Lat; 84.63° W. Long. Elevation is 909 feet.
Population: 4,349; Growth (since 2000): -3.0%; Density: 2,261.1 persons per square mile; Race: 98.0% White, 0.3% Black/African American, 0.0% Asian, 0.0% American Indian/Alaska Native, 1.6% Native Hawaiian/Other Pacific Islander, 0.0% Two or more races, 0.0% Hispanic of any race; Average household size: 2.33; Median age: 42.0; Age under 18: 25.8%; Age 65 and over: 19.8%; Males per 100 females: 92.0; Marriage status: 24.6% never married, 55.4% now married, 0.0% separated, 13.9% widowed, 6.1% divorced; Foreign born: 1.3%; Speak English only: 98.5%; With disability: 9.5%; Veterans: 8.4%; Ancestry: 66.6% German, 9.0% American, 7.4% Irish, 2.7% English, 1.7% Italian
Employment: 13.2% management, business, and financial, 3.1% computer, engineering, and science, 5.5% education, legal, community service, arts, and media, 3.5% healthcare practitioners, 16.5% service, 18.4% sales and office, 12.5% natural resources, construction, and maintenance, 27.4% production, transportation, and material moving
Income: Per capita: $25,177; Median household: $48,250; Average household: $59,997; Households with income of $100,000 or more: 17.8%; Poverty rate: 6.1%
Educational Attainment: High school diploma or higher: 88.2%; Bachelor's degree or higher: 18.3%; Graduate/professional degree or higher: 3.7%

School District(s)

Coldwater Exempted Village (KG-12)
2015-16 Enrollment: 1,404 . . . . (419) 678-2611

Housing: Homeownership rate: 70.4%; Median home value: $120,500; Median year structure built: 1972; Homeowner vacancy rate: 0.0%; Median selected monthly owner costs: $992 with a mortgage, $391 without a mortgage; Median gross rent: $550 per month; Rental vacancy rate: 6.0%
Health Insurance: 92.2% have insurance; 81.7% have private insurance; 26.4% have public insurance; 7.8% do not have insurance; 7.1% of children under 18 do not have insurance
Hospitals: Mercer County Joint Township Community Hospital (76 beds)
Newspapers: Mercer County Chronicle (weekly circulation 3,000)
Transportation: Commute: 95.2% car, 0.0% public transportation, 3.4% walk, 0.6% work from home; Mean travel time to work: 15.0 minutes

FORT RECOVERY (village). Covers a land area of 1.053 square miles and a water area of 0.021 square miles. Located at 40.41° N. Lat; 84.78° W. Long. Elevation is 938 feet.
History: The original Fort Recovery was built by General Anthony Wayne in 1793.
Population: 1,437; Growth (since 2000): 12.9%; Density: 1,365.3 persons per square mile; Race: 96.9% White, 0.0% Black/African American, 0.0% Asian, 0.0% American Indian/Alaska Native, 0.1% Native Hawaiian/Other Pacific Islander, 2.9% Two or more races, 10.6% Hispanic of any race; Average household size: 2.33; Median age: 31.8; Age under 18: 28.5%; Age 65 and over: 16.2%; Males per 100 females: 104.3; Marriage status: 29.2% never married, 54.1% now married, 2.2% separated, 10.0% widowed, 6.8% divorced; Foreign born: 0.2%; Speak English only: 99.1%; With disability: 11.8%; Veterans: 7.3%; Ancestry: 61.9% German, 18.4% Irish, 3.9% English, 3.6% American, 3.5% French
Employment: 5.1% management, business, and financial, 6.7% computer, engineering, and science, 9.6% education, legal, community service, arts, and media, 8.0% healthcare practitioners, 7.0% service, 15.8% sales and office, 7.9% natural resources, construction, and maintenance, 40.0% production, transportation, and material moving
Income: Per capita: $23,618; Median household: $57,250; Average household: $56,123; Households with income of $100,000 or more: 7.9%; Poverty rate: 12.0%
Educational Attainment: High school diploma or higher: 90.7%; Bachelor's degree or higher: 15.6%; Graduate/professional degree or higher: 7.2%

School District(s)

Fort Recovery Local (PK-12)
2015-16 Enrollment: 986. . . . . (419) 375-4139
Housing: Homeownership rate: 71.3%; Median home value: $105,400; Median year structure built: 1959; Homeowner vacancy rate: 0.0%; Median selected monthly owner costs: $1,058 with a mortgage, $345 without a mortgage; Median gross rent: $607 per month; Rental vacancy rate: 4.3%
Health Insurance: 96.8% have insurance; 86.2% have private insurance; 27.1% have public insurance; 3.2% do not have insurance; 0.0% of children under 18 do not have insurance
Transportation: Commute: 95.9% car, 0.0% public transportation, 3.5% walk, 0.6% work from home; Mean travel time to work: 15.6 minutes

MARIA STEIN (unincorporated postal area)

ZCTA: 45860

Covers a land area of 34.984 square miles and a water area of 0.028 square miles. Located at 40.40° N. Lat; 84.52° W. Long. Elevation is 968 feet.
Population: 2,249; Growth (since 2000): -0.9%; Density: 64.3 persons per square mile; Race: 99.2% White, 0.3% Black/African American, 0.5% Asian, 0.0% American Indian/Alaska Native, 0.0% Native Hawaiian/Other Pacific Islander, 0.0% Two or more races, 2.4% Hispanic of any race; Average household size: 2.72; Median age: 35.8; Age under 18: 28.3%; Age 65 and over: 12.1%; Males per 100 females: 105.6; Marriage status: 19.9% never married, 70.6% now married, 0.0% separated, 2.1% widowed, 7.5% divorced; Foreign born: 0.8%; Speak English only: 96.3%; With disability: 4.3%; Veterans: 3.0%; Ancestry: 71.7% German, 9.6% American, 6.2% French, 6.1% English, 2.7% Dutch
Employment: 16.7% management, business, and financial, 2.7% computer, engineering, and science, 9.8% education, legal, community service, arts, and media, 3.4% healthcare practitioners, 9.8% service, 27.1% sales and office, 8.7% natural resources, construction, and maintenance, 21.8% production, transportation, and material moving
Income: Per capita: $27,476; Median household: $74,112; Average household: $76,532; Households with income of $100,000 or more: 35.8%; Poverty rate: 1.3%
Educational Attainment: High school diploma or higher: 95.1%; Bachelor's degree or higher: 16.6%; Graduate/professional degree or higher: 9.1%

School District(s)

Marion Local (KG-12)
2015-16 Enrollment: 876. . . . . (419) 925-4294
Housing: Homeownership rate: 90.1%; Median home value: $172,900; Median year structure built: 1981; Homeowner vacancy rate: 0.0%; Median selected monthly owner costs: $1,187 with a mortgage, $505 without a mortgage; Median gross rent: $580 per month; Rental vacancy rate: 0.0%
Health Insurance: 100.0% have insurance; 89.9% have private insurance; 21.5% have public insurance; 0.0% do not have insurance; 0.0% of children under 18 do not have insurance
Transportation: Commute: 96.4% car, 0.0% public transportation, 0.9% walk, 2.7% work from home; Mean travel time to work: 16.5 minutes

MENDON (village). Covers a land area of 0.555 square miles and a water area of 0.010 square miles. Located at 40.67° N. Lat; 84.52° W. Long. Elevation is 820 feet.
Population: 583; Growth (since 2000): -16.4%; Density: 1,050.6 persons per square mile; Race: 95.4% White, 0.0% Black/African American, 0.0% Asian, 0.5% American Indian/Alaska Native, 0.0% Native Hawaiian/Other Pacific Islander, 4.1% Two or more races, 1.2% Hispanic of any race; Average household size: 2.57; Median age: 33.8; Age under 18: 28.0%; Age 65 and over: 17.8%; Males per 100 females: 100.0; Marriage status: 31.1% never married, 49.1% now married, 0.0% separated, 8.6% widowed, 11.2% divorced; Foreign born: 0.2%; Speak English only: 98.7%; With disability: 14.4%; Veterans: 8.1%; Ancestry: 47.7% German, 20.9% Irish, 13.6% American, 9.9% English, 4.1% Dutch
Employment: 3.1% management, business, and financial, 0.0% computer, engineering, and science, 3.5% education, legal, community service, arts, and media, 1.6% healthcare practitioners, 21.7% service, 23.2% sales and office, 7.5% natural resources, construction, and maintenance, 39.4% production, transportation, and material moving
Income: Per capita: $16,828; Median household: $38,516; Average household: $43,205; Households with income of $100,000 or more: 3.5%; Poverty rate: 24.7%
Educational Attainment: High school diploma or higher: 92.2%; Bachelor's degree or higher: 8.1%; Graduate/professional degree or higher: 2.8%
Housing: Homeownership rate: 78.0%; Median home value: $78,700; Median year structure built: 1953; Homeowner vacancy rate: 3.8%; Median selected monthly owner costs: $891 with a mortgage, $393 without a mortgage; Median gross rent: $690 per month; Rental vacancy rate: 0.0%
Health Insurance: 94.0% have insurance; 63.8% have private insurance; 47.0% have public insurance; 6.0% do not have insurance; 3.7% of children under 18 do not have insurance
Transportation: Commute: 98.0% car, 0.0% public transportation, 1.2% walk, 0.8% work from home; Mean travel time to work: 22.6 minutes

MONTEZUMA (village). Covers a land area of 0.116 square miles and a water area of 0.007 square miles. Located at 40.49° N. Lat; 84.55° W. Long. Elevation is 883 feet.
Population: 169; Growth (since 2000): -11.5%; Density: 1,454.5 persons per square mile; Race: 100.0% White, 0.0% Black/African American, 0.0% Asian, 0.0% American Indian/Alaska Native, 0.0% Native Hawaiian/Other Pacific Islander, 0.0% Two or more races, 0.0% Hispanic of any race; Average household size: 2.01; Median age: 47.8; Age under 18: 20.1%; Age 65 and over: 14.8%; Males per 100 females: 111.5; Marriage status: 12.9% never married, 48.9% now married, 0.0% separated, 10.1% widowed, 28.1% divorced; Foreign born: 0.0%; Speak English only: 98.7%; With disability: 21.3%; Veterans: 13.3%; Ancestry: 66.3% German, 13.0% Irish, 9.5% Italian, 4.7% American, 3.0% French
Employment: 0.0% management, business, and financial, 0.0% computer, engineering, and science, 10.4% education, legal, community service, arts, and media, 1.3% healthcare practitioners, 24.7% service, 20.8% sales and office, 6.5% natural resources, construction, and maintenance, 36.4% production, transportation, and material moving
Income: Per capita: $22,940; Median household: $36,071; Average household: $46,094; Households with income of $100,000 or more: 4.8%; Poverty rate: 9.7%
Educational Attainment: High school diploma or higher: 90.2%; Bachelor's degree or higher: 4.5%; Graduate/professional degree or higher: 1.5%

Housing: Homeownership rate: 64.3%; Median home value: $75,000; Median year structure built: 1947; Homeowner vacancy rate: 0.0%; Median selected monthly owner costs: $768 with a mortgage, $295 without a mortgage; Median gross rent: $713 per month; Rental vacancy rate: 0.0%
Health Insurance: 86.4% have insurance; 69.2% have private insurance; 35.5% have public insurance; 13.6% do not have insurance; 14.7% of children under 18 do not have insurance
Transportation: Commute: 96.1% car, 0.0% public transportation, 1.3% walk, 0.0% work from home; Mean travel time to work: 18.5 minutes

ROCKFORD (village). Covers a land area of 0.819 square miles and a water area of 0.020 square miles. Located at 40.69° N. Lat; 84.65° W. Long. Elevation is 814 feet.
History: Rockford was settled after the Treaty of 1818 on the site of a trading post operated by Anthony Shane. The town was first called Shane's Crossing.
Population: 1,172; Growth (since 2000): 4.1%; Density: 1,430.4 persons per square mile; Race: 98.8% White, 0.9% Black/African American, 0.0% Asian, 0.0% American Indian/Alaska Native, 0.0% Native Hawaiian/Other Pacific Islander, 0.3% Two or more races, 0.9% Hispanic of any race; Average household size: 2.48; Median age: 36.7; Age under 18: 27.6%; Age 65 and over: 16.9%; Males per 100 females: 88.6; Marriage status: 22.8% never married, 54.8% now married, 2.0% separated, 10.1% widowed, 12.4% divorced; Foreign born: 0.1%; Speak English only: 99.7%; With disability: 11.5%; Veterans: 6.7%; Ancestry: 52.4% German, 9.3% Irish, 6.0% American, 5.6% English, 4.4% Dutch
Employment: 7.6% management, business, and financial, 1.7% computer, engineering, and science, 5.6% education, legal, community service, arts, and media, 5.6% healthcare practitioners, 15.8% service, 18.6% sales and office, 9.1% natural resources, construction, and maintenance, 36.2% production, transportation, and material moving
Income: Per capita: $20,718; Median household: $44,236; Average household: $53,993; Households with income of $100,000 or more: 12.3%; Poverty rate: 22.1%
Educational Attainment: High school diploma or higher: 86.9%; Bachelor's degree or higher: 15.6%; Graduate/professional degree or higher: 5.3%

School District(s)

Parkway Local (PK-12)
2015-16 Enrollment: 1,066 . . . . (419) 363-3045
Housing: Homeownership rate: 71.3%; Median home value: $82,000; Median year structure built: 1940; Homeowner vacancy rate: 0.0%; Median selected monthly owner costs: $808 with a mortgage, $375 without a mortgage; Median gross rent: $659 per month; Rental vacancy rate: 9.7%
Health Insurance: 93.9% have insurance; 67.0% have private insurance; 43.3% have public insurance; 6.1% do not have insurance; 0.6% of children under 18 do not have insurance
Transportation: Commute: 94.6% car, 0.0% public transportation, 3.9% walk, 1.5% work from home; Mean travel time to work: 17.5 minutes

SAINT HENRY (village). Covers a land area of 1.604 square miles and a water area of 0.047 square miles. Located at 40.42° N. Lat; 84.63° W. Long. Elevation is 971 feet.
Population: 2,646; Growth (since 2000): 16.5%; Density: 1,649.8 persons per square mile; Race: 99.1% White, 0.4% Black/African American, 0.5% Asian, 0.0% American Indian/Alaska Native, 0.0% Native Hawaiian/Other Pacific Islander, 0.0% Two or more races, 4.3% Hispanic of any race; Average household size: 2.85; Median age: 34.8; Age under 18: 29.3%; Age 65 and over: 11.1%; Males per 100 females: 100.1; Marriage status: 26.7% never married, 65.3% now married, 0.0% separated, 4.6% widowed, 3.4% divorced; Foreign born: 2.8%; Speak English only: 98.1%; With disability: 5.6%; Veterans: 6.0%; Ancestry: 68.7% German, 11.9% American, 4.7% French, 3.4% Irish, 1.7% Polish
Employment: 11.3% management, business, and financial, 4.1% computer, engineering, and science, 7.6% education, legal, community service, arts, and media, 6.9% healthcare practitioners, 12.4% service, 21.6% sales and office, 10.4% natural resources, construction, and maintenance, 25.7% production, transportation, and material moving
Income: Per capita: $30,835; Median household: $75,313; Average household: $89,639; Households with income of $100,000 or more: 30.3%; Poverty rate: 3.7%
Educational Attainment: High school diploma or higher: 91.5%; Bachelor's degree or higher: 22.2%; Graduate/professional degree or higher: 8.0%

School District(s)

St Henry Consolidated Local (KG-12)
2015-16 Enrollment: 953. . . . . (419) 678-4834
Housing: Homeownership rate: 79.0%; Median home value: $166,900; Median year structure built: 1980; Homeowner vacancy rate: 0.6%; Median selected monthly owner costs: $1,131 with a mortgage, $436 without a mortgage; Median gross rent: $678 per month; Rental vacancy rate: 0.0%
Health Insurance: 96.9% have insurance; 90.9% have private insurance; 15.4% have public insurance; 3.1% do not have insurance; 3.4% of children under 18 do not have insurance
Transportation: Commute: 98.0% car, 0.0% public transportation, 0.9% walk, 1.1% work from home; Mean travel time to work: 15.9 minutes

Miami County

Located in western Ohio; crossed by the Great Miami and Stillwater Rivers. Covers a land area of 406.580 square miles, a water area of 3.076 square miles, and is located in the Eastern Time Zone at 40.05° N. Lat., 84.23° W. Long. The county was founded in 1807. County seat is Troy.

Miami County is part of the Dayton, OH Metropolitan Statistical Area. The entire metro area includes: Greene County, OH; Miami County, OH; Montgomery County, OH

Population: 103,864; Growth (since 2000): 5.1%; Density: 255.5 persons per square mile; Race: 94.1% White, 2.0% Black/African American, 1.3% Asian, 0.1% American Indian/Alaska Native, 0.0% Native Hawaiian/Other Pacific Islander, 2.2% two or more races, 1.5% Hispanic of any race; Average household size: 2.50; Median age: 41.4; Age under 18: 23.2%; Age 65 and over: 17.2%; Males per 100 females: 96.7; Marriage status: 25.5% never married, 54.2% now married, 1.1% separated, 7.4% widowed, 12.9% divorced; Foreign born: 1.7%; Speak English only: 97.6%; With disability: 13.2%; Veterans: 9.9%; Ancestry: 32.5% German, 13.5% Irish, 9.6% American, 9.4% English, 3.6% Italian
Religion: Six largest groups: 10.6% Catholicism, 8.8% Methodist/Pietist, 4.3% Baptist, 3.8% Non-denominational Protestant, 2.7% Presbyterian-Reformed, 2.2% Holiness
Economy: Unemployment rate: 3.8%; Leading industries: 14.7 % retail trade; 12.6 % other services (except public administration); 10.0 % manufacturing; Farms: 1,068 totaling 184,233 acres; Company size: 1 employs 1,000 or more persons, 6 employ 500 to 999 persons, 58 employ 100 to 499 persons, 2,039 employ less than 100 persons; Business ownership: 2,700 women-owned, 112 Black-owned, n/a Hispanic-owned, 173 Asian-owned, 97 American Indian/Alaska Native-owned
Employment: 11.7% management, business, and financial, 5.6% computer, engineering, and science, 8.2% education, legal, community service, arts, and media, 5.6% healthcare practitioners, 16.3% service, 22.4% sales and office, 8.7% natural resources, construction, and maintenance, 21.5% production, transportation, and material moving
Income: Per capita: $27,247; Median household: $53,432; Average household: $66,602; Households with income of $100,000 or more: 19.3%; Poverty rate: 11.1%
Educational Attainment: High school diploma or higher: 89.1%; Bachelor's degree or higher: 21.1%; Graduate/professional degree or higher: 7.5%
Housing: Homeownership rate: 69.9%; Median home value: $137,600; Median year structure built: 1967; Homeowner vacancy rate: 1.1%; Median selected monthly owner costs: $1,161 with a mortgage, $395 without a mortgage; Median gross rent: $734 per month; Rental vacancy rate: 4.3%
Vital Statistics: Birth rate: 116.2 per 10,000 population; Death rate: 96.5 per 10,000 population; Age-adjusted cancer mortality rate: 179.0 deaths per 100,000 population
Health Insurance: 92.1% have insurance; 73.6% have private insurance; 32.7% have public insurance; 7.9% do not have insurance; 4.8% of children under 18 do not have insurance
Health Care: Physicians: 12.6 per 10,000 population; Dentists: 4.8 per 10,000 population; Hospital beds: 16.2 per 10,000 population; Hospital admissions: 723.6 per 10,000 population
Air Quality Index (AQI): Percent of Days: 77.0% good, 21.6% moderate, 1.4% unhealthy for sensitive individuals, 0.0% unhealthy, 0.0% very unhealthy; Annual median: 43; Annual maximum: 101
Transportation: Commute: 93.8% car, 0.4% public transportation, 1.7% walk, 3.1% work from home; Mean travel time to work: 20.8 minutes
2016 Presidential Election: 69.8% Trump, 24.7% Clinton, 3.5% Johnson, 0.6% Stein

National and State Parks: Greenville Falls State Nature Preserve
Additional Information Contacts
Miami Government . . . . (937) 332-7000
http://www.co.miami.oh.us

Miami County Communities

BRADFORD (village). Covers a land area of 0.858 square miles and a water area of 0.021 square miles. Located at 40.13° N. Lat; 84.43° W. Long. Elevation is 988 feet.
Population: 1,701; Growth (since 2000): -8.5%; Density: 1,981.4 persons per square mile; Race: 97.8% White, 0.0% Black/African American, 0.6% Asian, 1.1% American Indian/Alaska Native, 0.0% Native Hawaiian/Other Pacific Islander, 0.0% Two or more races, 0.5% Hispanic of any race; Average household size: 2.74; Median age: 37.7; Age under 18: 24.2%; Age 65 and over: 17.3%; Males per 100 females: 91.5; Marriage status: 22.5% never married, 58.9% now married, 0.6% separated, 6.9% widowed, 11.7% divorced; Foreign born: 0.8%; Speak English only: 98.8%; With disability: 14.7%; Veterans: 8.1%; Ancestry: 30.4% German, 13.7% Irish, 11.3% American, 8.7% English, 4.8% Italian
Employment: 5.3% management, business, and financial, 4.2% computer, engineering, and science, 6.2% education, legal, community service, arts, and media, 4.1% healthcare practitioners, 18.6% service, 17.5% sales and office, 10.1% natural resources, construction, and maintenance, 34.0% production, transportation, and material moving
Income: Per capita: $20,287; Median household: $47,969; Average household: $53,681; Households with income of $100,000 or more: 10.3%; Poverty rate: 11.1%
Educational Attainment: High school diploma or higher: 87.4%; Bachelor's degree or higher: 5.9%; Graduate/professional degree or higher: 1.9%

School District(s)

Bradford Exempted Village (KG-12)
2015-16 Enrollment: 495. . . . . (937) 448-2770
Housing: Homeownership rate: 77.9%; Median home value: $83,700; Median year structure built: 1947; Homeowner vacancy rate: 2.4%; Median selected monthly owner costs: $952 with a mortgage, $339 without a mortgage; Median gross rent: $649 per month; Rental vacancy rate: 21.3%
Health Insurance: 91.5% have insurance; 69.4% have private insurance; 38.6% have public insurance; 8.5% do not have insurance; 7.3% of children under 18 do not have insurance
Transportation: Commute: 97.2% car, 0.0% public transportation, 0.8% walk, 1.7% work from home; Mean travel time to work: 24.8 minutes

CASSTOWN (village). Covers a land area of 0.097 square miles and a water area of 0 square miles. Located at 40.05° N. Lat; 84.13° W. Long. Elevation is 935 feet.
Population: 254; Growth (since 2000): -21.1%; Density: 2,616.2 persons per square mile; Race: 99.6% White, 0.0% Black/African American, 0.0% Asian, 0.0% American Indian/Alaska Native, 0.0% Native Hawaiian/Other Pacific Islander, 0.4% Two or more races, 0.8% Hispanic of any race; Average household size: 2.57; Median age: 44.1; Age under 18: 24.0%; Age 65 and over: 21.7%; Males per 100 females: 88.0; Marriage status: 24.5% never married, 52.4% now married, 0.0% separated, 8.5% widowed, 14.6% divorced; Foreign born: 0.4%; Speak English only: 100.0%; With disability: 14.6%; Veterans: 14.5%; Ancestry: 46.5% German, 9.1% Irish, 7.5% French, 6.3% American, 6.3% English
Employment: 11.3% management, business, and financial, 2.8% computer, engineering, and science, 1.9% education, legal, community service, arts, and media, 4.7% healthcare practitioners, 24.5% service, 11.3% sales and office, 13.2% natural resources, construction, and maintenance, 30.2% production, transportation, and material moving
Income: Per capita: $20,069; Median household: $38,854; Average household: $50,715; Households with income of $100,000 or more: 11.1%; Poverty rate: 6.7%
Educational Attainment: High school diploma or higher: 95.2%; Bachelor's degree or higher: 10.2%; Graduate/professional degree or higher: 0.6%

School District(s)

Miami East Local (KG-12)
2015-16 Enrollment: 1,283 . . . . (937) 335-7505
Housing: Homeownership rate: 80.8%; Median home value: $84,600; Median year structure built: Before 1940; Homeowner vacancy rate: 9.0%; Median selected monthly owner costs: $857 with a mortgage, $350 without a mortgage; Median gross rent: $688 per month; Rental vacancy rate: 20.8%
Health Insurance: 90.6% have insurance; 72.8% have private insurance; 36.2% have public insurance; 9.4% do not have insurance; 0.0% of children under 18 do not have insurance
Transportation: Commute: 96.2% car, 0.0% public transportation, 1.9% walk, 1.9% work from home; Mean travel time to work: 22.6 minutes

COVINGTON (village). Covers a land area of 1.324 square miles and a water area of 0.026 square miles. Located at 40.12° N. Lat; 84.35° W. Long. Elevation is 928 feet.
History: Covington was settled in 1807 on the site of an outpost built by General Anthony Wayne.
Population: 2,607; Growth (since 2000): 1.9%; Density: 1,968.8 persons per square mile; Race: 98.6% White, 0.0% Black/African American, 0.2% Asian, 0.0% American Indian/Alaska Native, 0.0% Native Hawaiian/Other Pacific Islander, 1.1% Two or more races, 1.6% Hispanic of any race; Average household size: 2.67; Median age: 36.9; Age under 18: 25.8%; Age 65 and over: 16.4%; Males per 100 females: 93.6; Marriage status: 29.3% never married, 46.1% now married, 0.6% separated, 6.5% widowed, 18.1% divorced; Foreign born: 0.5%; Speak English only: 98.9%; With disability: 10.2%; Veterans: 8.9%; Ancestry: 31.1% German, 14.5% American, 12.5% Irish, 6.0% English, 2.2% Italian
Employment: 5.5% management, business, and financial, 4.4% computer, engineering, and science, 9.6% education, legal, community service, arts, and media, 6.0% healthcare practitioners, 15.7% service, 19.8% sales and office, 8.8% natural resources, construction, and maintenance, 30.3% production, transportation, and material moving
Income: Per capita: $20,379; Median household: $42,614; Average household: $53,088; Households with income of $100,000 or more: 11.1%; Poverty rate: 18.2%
Educational Attainment: High school diploma or higher: 84.1%; Bachelor's degree or higher: 9.6%; Graduate/professional degree or higher: 2.8%

School District(s)

Covington Exempted Village (KG-12)
2015-16 Enrollment: 800. . . . . (937) 473-9816
Housing: Homeownership rate: 61.4%; Median home value: $91,400; Median year structure built: 1950; Homeowner vacancy rate: 0.0%; Median selected monthly owner costs: $921 with a mortgage, $372 without a mortgage; Median gross rent: $679 per month; Rental vacancy rate: 0.0%
Health Insurance: 89.6% have insurance; 70.5% have private insurance; 32.9% have public insurance; 10.4% do not have insurance; 5.8% of children under 18 do not have insurance
Safety: Violent crime rate: 11.4 per 10,000 population; Property crime rate: 110.1 per 10,000 population
Newspapers: Stillwater Advertiser (weekly circulation 11,000)
Transportation: Commute: 91.9% car, 0.4% public transportation, 4.7% walk, 0.5% work from home; Mean travel time to work: 21.0 minutes

FLETCHER (village). Covers a land area of 0.311 square miles and a water area of 0 square miles. Located at 40.14° N. Lat; 84.11° W. Long. Elevation is 1,050 feet.
Population: 489; Growth (since 2000): -4.1%; Density: 1,573.5 persons per square mile; Race: 99.6% White, 0.4% Black/African American, 0.0% Asian, 0.0% American Indian/Alaska Native, 0.0% Native Hawaiian/Other Pacific Islander, 0.0% Two or more races, 3.1% Hispanic of any race; Average household size: 3.13; Median age: 35.4; Age under 18: 32.1%; Age 65 and over: 15.3%; Males per 100 females: 106.6; Marriage status: 21.9% never married, 62.4% now married, 2.4% separated, 5.7% widowed, 10.0% divorced; Foreign born: 1.6%; Speak English only: 99.6%; With disability: 14.9%; Veterans: 10.8%; Ancestry: 24.7% German, 11.2% American, 10.8% Irish, 9.0% Italian, 5.5% English
Employment: 6.9% management, business, and financial, 1.8% computer, engineering, and science, 5.1% education, legal, community service, arts, and media, 7.8% healthcare practitioners, 22.6% service, 16.1% sales and office, 11.1% natural resources, construction, and maintenance, 28.6% production, transportation, and material moving
Income: Per capita: $19,924; Median household: $51,250; Average household: $60,256; Households with income of $100,000 or more: 9.0%; Poverty rate: 10.8%
Educational Attainment: High school diploma or higher: 84.8%; Bachelor's degree or higher: 4.8%; Graduate/professional degree or higher: 1.6%

Housing: Homeownership rate: 76.9%; Median home value: $81,700; Median year structure built: Before 1940; Homeowner vacancy rate: 0.8%; Median selected monthly owner costs: $1,047 with a mortgage, $408 without a mortgage; Median gross rent: $713 per month; Rental vacancy rate: 0.0%
Health Insurance: 92.4% have insurance; 67.9% have private insurance; 41.3% have public insurance; 7.6% do not have insurance; 10.2% of children under 18 do not have insurance
Transportation: Commute: 96.2% car, 0.0% public transportation, 0.5% walk, 2.4% work from home; Mean travel time to work: 23.3 minutes

LAURA (village). Covers a land area of 0.271 square miles and a water area of 0 square miles. Located at 40.00° N. Lat; 84.41° W. Long. Elevation is 991 feet.
Population: 395; Growth (since 2000): -18.9%; Density: 1,458.5 persons per square mile; Race: 98.2% White, 0.5% Black/African American, 0.0% Asian, 0.0% American Indian/Alaska Native, 0.0% Native Hawaiian/Other Pacific Islander, 1.3% Two or more races, 0.0% Hispanic of any race; Average household size: 2.69; Median age: 35.5; Age under 18: 28.6%; Age 65 and over: 15.9%; Males per 100 females: 99.2; Marriage status: 23.2% never married, 56.0% now married, 1.3% separated, 6.7% widowed, 14.1% divorced; Foreign born: 0.5%; Speak English only: 99.0%; With disability: 14.4%; Veterans: 9.2%; Ancestry: 29.4% German, 14.2% American, 11.4% Irish, 10.1% English, 5.3% Dutch
Employment: 4.8% management, business, and financial, 1.2% computer, engineering, and science, 5.4% education, legal, community service, arts, and media, 4.2% healthcare practitioners, 12.0% service, 26.3% sales and office, 16.2% natural resources, construction, and maintenance, 29.9% production, transportation, and material moving
Income: Per capita: $21,416; Median household: $44,063; Average household: $57,386; Households with income of $100,000 or more: 18.3%; Poverty rate: 19.9%
Educational Attainment: High school diploma or higher: 89.6%; Bachelor's degree or higher: 4.6%; Graduate/professional degree or higher: 0.4%
Housing: Homeownership rate: 70.1%; Median home value: $93,100; Median year structure built: 1947; Homeowner vacancy rate: 0.0%; Median selected monthly owner costs: $1,085 with a mortgage, $406 without a mortgage; Median gross rent: $790 per month; Rental vacancy rate: 4.3%
Health Insurance: 92.4% have insurance; 66.6% have private insurance; 37.5% have public insurance; 7.6% do not have insurance; 0.0% of children under 18 do not have insurance
Transportation: Commute: 93.3% car, 0.0% public transportation, 4.9% walk, 1.2% work from home; Mean travel time to work: 24.4 minutes

LUDLOW FALLS (village). Covers a land area of 0.179 square miles and a water area of 0 square miles. Located at 40.00° N. Lat; 84.34° W. Long. Elevation is 902 feet.
Population: 261; Growth (since 2000): 24.3%; Density: 1,462.1 persons per square mile; Race: 100.0% White, 0.0% Black/African American, 0.0% Asian, 0.0% American Indian/Alaska Native, 0.0% Native Hawaiian/Other Pacific Islander, 0.0% Two or more races, 1.9% Hispanic of any race; Average household size: 2.87; Median age: 31.9; Age under 18: 37.2%; Age 65 and over: 5.7%; Males per 100 females: 110.1; Marriage status: 32.1% never married, 47.9% now married, 10.5% separated, 5.8% widowed, 14.2% divorced; Foreign born: 3.4%; Speak English only: 100.0%; With disability: 10.3%; Veterans: 6.7%; Ancestry: 46.7% German, 14.2% Irish, 5.4% American, 5.0% French, 5.0% Russian
Employment: 1.4% management, business, and financial, 3.6% computer, engineering, and science, 8.6% education, legal, community service, arts, and media, 2.9% healthcare practitioners, 24.5% service, 20.1% sales and office, 10.1% natural resources, construction, and maintenance, 28.8% production, transportation, and material moving
Income: Per capita: $17,354; Median household: $46,964; Average household: $48,654; Households with income of $100,000 or more: 11.0%; Poverty rate: 16.9%
Educational Attainment: High school diploma or higher: 89.9%; Bachelor's degree or higher: 8.1%; Graduate/professional degree or higher: 4.7%
Housing: Homeownership rate: 58.2%; Median home value: $82,400; Median year structure built: Before 1940; Homeowner vacancy rate: 3.6%; Median selected monthly owner costs: $892 with a mortgage, $338 without a mortgage; Median gross rent: $850 per month; Rental vacancy rate: 0.0%
Health Insurance: 91.2% have insurance; 56.7% have private insurance; 48.7% have public insurance; 8.8% do not have insurance; 2.1% of children under 18 do not have insurance
Transportation: Commute: 97.0% car, 0.0% public transportation, 0.0% walk, 3.0% work from home; Mean travel time to work: 28.2 minutes

PIQUA (city). Covers a land area of 11.620 square miles and a water area of 0.267 square miles. Located at 40.15° N. Lat; 84.24° W. Long. Elevation is 876 feet.
History: Piqua was settled in 1797 and called Washington until 1816, when the legislature renamed it for a tribe of the Shawnee, who previously had villages near the site. The earlier fur trading was replaced by a flatboat business, as cargoes of lumber and farm products were sent to New Orleans. In 1815 Piqua became a producer of linseed oil. The Miami & Erie Canal and the railroads stimulated Piqua's growth in the later 1800's.
Population: 20,743; Growth (since 2000): 0.0%; Density: 1,785.2 persons per square mile; Race: 90.6% White, 3.2% Black/African American, 1.0% Asian, 0.1% American Indian/Alaska Native, 0.0% Native Hawaiian/Other Pacific Islander, 4.7% Two or more races, 1.4% Hispanic of any race; Average household size: 2.45; Median age: 37.9; Age under 18: 24.4%; Age 65 and over: 17.0%; Males per 100 females: 92.2; Marriage status: 31.4% never married, 42.3% now married, 1.3% separated, 9.3% widowed, 17.0% divorced; Foreign born: 1.1%; Speak English only: 97.5%; With disability: 17.3%; Veterans: 8.4%; Ancestry: 27.3% German, 16.1% Irish, 8.6% American, 7.9% English, 4.2% Italian
Employment: 6.3% management, business, and financial, 4.6% computer, engineering, and science, 7.3% education, legal, community service, arts, and media, 3.9% healthcare practitioners, 19.6% service, 23.8% sales and office, 8.0% natural resources, construction, and maintenance, 26.6% production, transportation, and material moving
Income: Per capita: $20,502; Median household: $40,101; Average household: $48,666; Households with income of $100,000 or more: 8.7%; Poverty rate: 19.8%
Educational Attainment: High school diploma or higher: 85.6%; Bachelor's degree or higher: 11.4%; Graduate/professional degree or higher: 4.3%

School District(s)

Piqua City (PK-12)
2015-16 Enrollment: 3,322 . . . . (937) 773-4321
Upper Valley Career Center (07-12)
2015-16 Enrollment: n/a . . . . (937) 778-1980

Two-year College(s)

Edison State Community College (Public)
Fall 2016 Enrollment: 3,402 . . . . (937) 778-8600
2016-17 Tuition: In-state $4,219; Out-of-state $7,828

Vocational/Technical School(s)

Upper Valley Career Center (Public)
Fall 2016 Enrollment: 232 . . . . (937) 778-1980
2016-17 Tuition: $14,373

Housing: Homeownership rate: 60.4%; Median home value: $85,800; Median year structure built: 1956; Homeowner vacancy rate: 1.3%; Median selected monthly owner costs: $952 with a mortgage, $372 without a mortgage; Median gross rent: $674 per month; Rental vacancy rate: 5.4%
Health Insurance: 90.0% have insurance; 62.9% have private insurance; 44.2% have public insurance; 10.0% do not have insurance; 2.7% of children under 18 do not have insurance
Safety: Violent crime rate: 18.7 per 10,000 population; Property crime rate: 423.1 per 10,000 population
Newspapers: Piqua Daily Call (daily circulation 6,100)
Transportation: Commute: 94.1% car, 0.3% public transportation, 1.6% walk, 2.4% work from home; Mean travel time to work: 18.0 minutes
Additional Information Contacts
City of Piqua . . . . (937) 778-2051
http://www.piquaoh.org

PLEASANT HILL (village). Covers a land area of 0.608 square miles and a water area of 0 square miles. Located at 40.05° N. Lat; 84.35° W. Long. Elevation is 932 feet.
Population: 1,281; Growth (since 2000): 13.0%; Density: 2,107.9 persons per square mile; Race: 100.0% White, 0.0% Black/African American, 0.0% Asian, 0.0% American Indian/Alaska Native, 0.0% Native Hawaiian/Other Pacific Islander, 0.0% Two or more races, 2.0% Hispanic of any race; Average household size: 2.85; Median age: 35.2; Age under 18: 27.2%; Age 65 and over: 12.8%; Males per 100 females: 93.9; Marriage status: 24.1% never married, 61.7% now married, 0.8% separated, 5.5%

widowed, 8.7% divorced; Foreign born: 0.3%; Speak English only: 99.2%; With disability: 11.4%; Veterans: 7.2%; Ancestry: 45.9% German, 18.2% Irish, 8.9% American, 4.8% English, 4.3% French
Employment: 8.9% management, business, and financial, 1.7% computer, engineering, and science, 4.0% education, legal, community service, arts, and media, 6.6% healthcare practitioners, 21.5% service, 18.5% sales and office, 15.3% natural resources, construction, and maintenance, 23.6% production, transportation, and material moving
Income: Per capita: $21,875; Median household: $55,750; Average household: $60,216; Households with income of $100,000 or more: 13.1%; Poverty rate: 6.6%
Educational Attainment: High school diploma or higher: 94.0%; Bachelor's degree or higher: 12.5%; Graduate/professional degree or higher: 4.6%

School District(s)

Newton Local (KG-12)
2015-16 Enrollment: 577 . . . . (937) 676-2002
Housing: Homeownership rate: 76.9%; Median home value: $111,200; Median year structure built: 1943; Homeowner vacancy rate: 6.0%; Median selected monthly owner costs: $1,074 with a mortgage, $373 without a mortgage; Median gross rent: $675 per month; Rental vacancy rate: 7.1%
Health Insurance: 87.1% have insurance; 71.4% have private insurance; 28.8% have public insurance; 12.9% do not have insurance; 13.8% of children under 18 do not have insurance
Transportation: Commute: 94.4% car, 0.0% public transportation, 3.2% walk, 1.9% work from home; Mean travel time to work: 20.7 minutes

POTSDAM (village). Covers a land area of 0.445 square miles and a water area of 0 square miles. Located at 39.96° N. Lat; 84.41° W. Long. Elevation is 1,007 feet.
Population: 310; Growth (since 2000): 52.7%; Density: 696.1 persons per square mile; Race: 99.0% White, 0.0% Black/African American, 0.0% Asian, 0.0% American Indian/Alaska Native, 0.0% Native Hawaiian/Other Pacific Islander, 1.0% Two or more races, 0.0% Hispanic of any race; Average household size: 2.67; Median age: 32.6; Age under 18: 28.1%; Age 65 and over: 10.6%; Males per 100 females: 108.7; Marriage status: 28.1% never married, 55.3% now married, 0.9% separated, 7.9% widowed, 8.8% divorced; Foreign born: 0.0%; Speak English only: 100.0%; With disability: 18.7%; Veterans: 7.6%; Ancestry: 42.3% German, 22.3% Irish, 13.9% American, 4.5% Italian, 3.2% French
Employment: 10.1% management, business, and financial, 12.8% computer, engineering, and science, 9.2% education, legal, community service, arts, and media, 6.4% healthcare practitioners, 11.0% service, 6.4% sales and office, 16.5% natural resources, construction, and maintenance, 27.5% production, transportation, and material moving
Income: Per capita: $17,892; Median household: $45,000; Average household: $47,166; Households with income of $100,000 or more: 2.6%; Poverty rate: 14.2%
Educational Attainment: High school diploma or higher: 91.8%; Bachelor's degree or higher: 10.6%; Graduate/professional degree or higher: 1.9%
Housing: Homeownership rate: 65.5%; Median home value: $87,700; Median year structure built: Before 1940; Homeowner vacancy rate: 0.0%; Median selected monthly owner costs: $894 with a mortgage, $358 without a mortgage; Median gross rent: $775 per month; Rental vacancy rate: 0.0%
Health Insurance: 91.6% have insurance; 64.5% have private insurance; 39.0% have public insurance; 8.4% do not have insurance; 4.6% of children under 18 do not have insurance
Transportation: Commute: 96.2% car, 0.0% public transportation, 0.0% walk, 3.8% work from home; Mean travel time to work: 30.5 minutes

TIPP CITY (city). Covers a land area of 7.529 square miles and a water area of 0.114 square miles. Located at 39.97° N. Lat; 84.19° W. Long. Elevation is 827 feet.
History: Formerly called Tippecanoe City.
Population: 9,834; Growth (since 2000): 6.6%; Density: 1,306.1 persons per square mile; Race: 97.4% White, 0.7% Black/African American, 0.8% Asian, 0.0% American Indian/Alaska Native, 0.0% Native Hawaiian/Other Pacific Islander, 0.8% Two or more races, 0.6% Hispanic of any race; Average household size: 2.40; Median age: 41.6; Age under 18: 23.2%; Age 65 and over: 16.2%; Males per 100 females: 93.2; Marriage status: 24.6% never married, 53.3% now married, 1.4% separated, 7.4% widowed, 14.7% divorced; Foreign born: 1.3%; Speak English only: 98.0%; With disability: 10.7%; Veterans: 9.2%; Ancestry: 31.2% German, 13.4% Irish, 11.3% English, 10.5% American, 4.2% Italian
Employment: 13.9% management, business, and financial, 7.2% computer, engineering, and science, 10.9% education, legal, community service, arts, and media, 5.9% healthcare practitioners, 18.5% service, 17.9% sales and office, 10.6% natural resources, construction, and maintenance, 15.1% production, transportation, and material moving
Income: Per capita: $33,272; Median household: $63,349; Average household: $78,315; Households with income of $100,000 or more: 23.7%; Poverty rate: 6.9%
Educational Attainment: High school diploma or higher: 92.2%; Bachelor's degree or higher: 32.1%; Graduate/professional degree or higher: 12.1%

School District(s)

Bethel Local (PK-12)
2015-16 Enrollment: 1,114 . . . . (937) 845-9414
Tipp City Exempted Village (KG-12)
2015-16 Enrollment: 2,494 . . . . (937) 667-8444
Housing: Homeownership rate: 64.1%; Median home value: $158,100; Median year structure built: 1977; Homeowner vacancy rate: 1.7%; Median selected monthly owner costs: $1,326 with a mortgage, $482 without a mortgage; Median gross rent: $757 per month; Rental vacancy rate: 1.3%
Health Insurance: 91.4% have insurance; 79.5% have private insurance; 24.6% have public insurance; 8.6% do not have insurance; 7.5% of children under 18 do not have insurance
Safety: Violent crime rate: 7.0 per 10,000 population; Property crime rate: 182.1 per 10,000 population
Newspapers: Vandalia Drummer News (weekly circulation 5,000)
Transportation: Commute: 95.9% car, 0.0% public transportation, 0.6% walk, 3.2% work from home; Mean travel time to work: 19.9 minutes
Additional Information Contacts
City of Tipp City . . . . (937) 669-8477
http://www.tippcityohio.gov

TROY (city). County seat. Covers a land area of 11.722 square miles and a water area of 0.219 square miles. Located at 40.04° N. Lat; 84.22° W. Long. Elevation is 837 feet.
History: Troy was settled in 1798 by Michael Garver, who built a cabin here and encouraged other settlers to follow him. The coming of the canal in 1837 and the railroad in 1850 brought industrial growth to Troy.
Population: 25,684; Growth (since 2000): 16.8%; Density: 2,191.2 persons per square mile; Race: 89.6% White, 4.2% Black/African American, 2.7% Asian, 0.3% American Indian/Alaska Native, 0.0% Native Hawaiian/Other Pacific Islander, 3.2% Two or more races, 1.7% Hispanic of any race; Average household size: 2.35; Median age: 40.4; Age under 18: 21.9%; Age 65 and over: 15.7%; Males per 100 females: 94.9; Marriage status: 28.9% never married, 50.0% now married, 1.8% separated, 6.2% widowed, 15.0% divorced; Foreign born: 3.4%; Speak English only: 96.2%; With disability: 14.5%; Veterans: 10.5%; Ancestry: 31.6% German, 14.1% Irish, 9.9% English, 9.1% American, 4.2% French
Employment: 12.2% management, business, and financial, 7.0% computer, engineering, and science, 8.5% education, legal, community service, arts, and media, 4.3% healthcare practitioners, 15.9% service, 22.7% sales and office, 6.2% natural resources, construction, and maintenance, 23.3% production, transportation, and material moving
Income: Per capita: $27,279; Median household: $47,743; Average household: $62,328; Households with income of $100,000 or more: 17.2%; Poverty rate: 12.2%
Educational Attainment: High school diploma or higher: 88.5%; Bachelor's degree or higher: 23.3%; Graduate/professional degree or higher: 6.9%

School District(s)

Troy City (KG-12)
2015-16 Enrollment: 4,314 . . . . (937) 332-6700

Two-year College(s)

Miami-Jacobs Career College-Troy (Private, For-profit)
Fall 2016 Enrollment: 82 . . . . (937) 332-8580
2016-17 Tuition: In-state $10,980; Out-of-state $10,980

Vocational/Technical School(s)

Hobart Institute of Welding Technology (Private, Not-for-profit)
Fall 2016 Enrollment: 438 . . . . (937) 332-9500
2016-17 Tuition: $16,190
Housing: Homeownership rate: 57.8%; Median home value: $123,400; Median year structure built: 1968; Homeowner vacancy rate: 1.4%; Median

selected monthly owner costs: $1,069 with a mortgage, $350 without a mortgage; Median gross rent: $746 per month; Rental vacancy rate: 4.1%
Health Insurance: 92.7% have insurance; 73.6% have private insurance; 32.3% have public insurance; 7.3% do not have insurance; 4.2% of children under 18 do not have insurance
Hospitals: Upper Valley Medical Center (128 beds)
Safety: Violent crime rate: 8.5 per 10,000 population; Property crime rate: 281.2 per 10,000 population
Newspapers: Record Herald (weekly circulation 5,500); Troy Daily News (daily circulation 9,300)
Transportation: Commute: 93.5% car, 0.9% public transportation, 2.6% walk, 2.5% work from home; Mean travel time to work: 19.2 minutes
Additional Information Contacts
City of Troy . . . . (937) 339-1221
http://www.troyohio.gov

WEST MILTON (village). Covers a land area of 3.244 square miles and a water area of 0.098 square miles. Located at 39.96° N. Lat; 84.33° W. Long. Elevation is 902 feet.
History: Settled 1807, incorporated 1835.
Population: 4,690; Growth (since 2000): 1.0%; Density: 1,445.7 persons per square mile; Race: 96.0% White, 0.0% Black/African American, 0.6% Asian, 0.0% American Indian/Alaska Native, 0.0% Native Hawaiian/Other Pacific Islander, 1.8% Two or more races, 2.8% Hispanic of any race; Average household size: 2.44; Median age: 38.9; Age under 18: 21.7%; Age 65 and over: 19.0%; Males per 100 females: 90.5; Marriage status: 30.0% never married, 52.2% now married, 0.5% separated, 8.4% widowed, 9.4% divorced; Foreign born: 0.9%; Speak English only: 97.2%; With disability: 12.0%; Veterans: 10.3%; Ancestry: 44.8% German, 13.1% Irish, 8.5% English, 5.7% French, 4.9% Swiss
Employment: 7.0% management, business, and financial, 1.6% computer, engineering, and science, 3.9% education, legal, community service, arts, and media, 5.2% healthcare practitioners, 23.6% service, 22.3% sales and office, 12.6% natural resources, construction, and maintenance, 23.8% production, transportation, and material moving
Income: Per capita: $23,092; Median household: $44,984; Average household: $54,880; Households with income of $100,000 or more: 14.3%; Poverty rate: 8.0%
Educational Attainment: High school diploma or higher: 87.2%; Bachelor's degree or higher: 17.3%; Graduate/professional degree or higher: 6.7%

School District(s)

Milton-Union Exempted Village (KG-12)
2015-16 Enrollment: 1,441 . . . . (937) 884-7910
Housing: Homeownership rate: 70.1%; Median home value: $108,900; Median year structure built: 1960; Homeowner vacancy rate: 1.4%; Median selected monthly owner costs: $1,088 with a mortgage, $370 without a mortgage; Median gross rent: $828 per month; Rental vacancy rate: 12.9%
Health Insurance: 92.2% have insurance; 70.0% have private insurance; 35.1% have public insurance; 7.8% do not have insurance; 6.8% of children under 18 do not have insurance
Transportation: Commute: 88.5% car, 0.0% public transportation, 6.9% walk, 3.2% work from home; Mean travel time to work: 22.3 minutes

Monroe County

Located in eastern Ohio; bounded on the southeast by the Ohio River and the West Virginia border; drained by Little Muskingum River and Sunfish Creek. Covers a land area of 455.721 square miles, a water area of 1.737 square miles, and is located in the Eastern Time Zone at 39.73° N. Lat., 81.09° W. Long. The county was founded in 1813. County seat is Woodsfield.

Weather Station: Hannibal Lock & Dam — Elevation: 620 feet

	Jan	Feb	Mar	Apr	May	Jun	Jul	Aug	Sep	Oct	Nov	Dec
High	38	42	51	64	72	81	84	83	77	65	54	42
Low	21	23	29	38	48	57	62	62	55	43	34	26
Precip	3.1	2.8	3.7	3.4	4.3	4.0	4.4	3.5	3.2	2.6	3.4	3.1
Snow	na	na	1.9	tr	0.0	0.0	0.0	0.0	0.0	0.0	tr	0.5

High and Low temperatures in degrees Fahrenheit; Precipitation and Snow in inches

Population: 14,442; Growth (since 2000): -4.9%; Density: 31.7 persons per square mile; Race: 98.0% White, 0.3% Black/African American, 0.3% Asian, 0.2% American Indian/Alaska Native, 0.0% Native Hawaiian/Other Pacific Islander, 1.3% two or more races, 0.5% Hispanic of any race; Average household size: 2.39; Median age: 46.3; Age under 18: 20.9%; Age 65 and over: 22.1%; Males per 100 females: 99.1; Marriage status: 21.4% never married, 58.4% now married, 1.9% separated, 8.5% widowed, 11.7% divorced; Foreign born: 0.5%; Speak English only: 96.9%; With disability: 19.8%; Veterans: 10.2%; Ancestry: 34.3% German, 14.1% Irish, 8.8% English, 8.6% American, 3.0% Italian
Religion: Six largest groups: 22.2% Baptist, 10.8% Methodist/Pietist, 6.9% Presbyterian-Reformed, 5.2% Catholicism, 4.2% European Free-Church, 1.1% Holiness
Economy: Unemployment rate: 7.1%; Leading industries: 16.5 % retail trade; 16.5 % other services (except public administration); 13.7 % construction; Farms: 823 totaling 111,161 acres; Company size: 0 employ 1,000 or more persons, 1 employs 500 to 999 persons, 1 employs 100 to 499 persons, 247 employ less than 100 persons; Business ownership: 175 women-owned, n/a Black-owned, n/a Hispanic-owned, n/a Asian-owned, n/a American Indian/Alaska Native-owned
Employment: 7.7% management, business, and financial, 2.0% computer, engineering, and science, 7.9% education, legal, community service, arts, and media, 6.8% healthcare practitioners, 14.3% service, 22.6% sales and office, 23.1% natural resources, construction, and maintenance, 15.7% production, transportation, and material moving
Income: Per capita: $22,100; Median household: $41,368; Average household: $52,242; Households with income of $100,000 or more: 10.5%; Poverty rate: 18.8%
Educational Attainment: High school diploma or higher: 87.5%; Bachelor's degree or higher: 10.7%; Graduate/professional degree or higher: 3.9%
Housing: Homeownership rate: 75.7%; Median home value: $93,200; Median year structure built: 1965; Homeowner vacancy rate: 0.9%; Median selected monthly owner costs: $822 with a mortgage, $339 without a mortgage; Median gross rent: $558 per month; Rental vacancy rate: 6.6%
Vital Statistics: Birth rate: 102.7 per 10,000 population; Death rate: 150.6 per 10,000 population; Age-adjusted cancer mortality rate: 163.9 deaths per 100,000 population
Health Insurance: 89.7% have insurance; 63.4% have private insurance; 45.4% have public insurance; 10.3% do not have insurance; 11.8% of children under 18 do not have insurance
Health Care: Physicians: 2.1 per 10,000 population; Dentists: 1.4 per 10,000 population; Hospital beds: 0.0 per 10,000 population; Hospital admissions: 0.0 per 10,000 population
Transportation: Commute: 93.1% car, 1.6% public transportation, 3.1% walk, 1.9% work from home; Mean travel time to work: 32.6 minutes
2016 Presidential Election: 71.0% Trump, 24.3% Clinton, 2.4% Johnson, 0.5% Stein
National and State Parks: Monroe Lake State Wildlife Area; Sunfish Creek State Forest; Wayne National Forest
Additional Information Contacts
Monroe Government . . . . (740) 472-1341
http://www.monroecountyohio.com

Monroe County Communities

ANTIOCH (village). Covers a land area of 0.106 square miles and a water area of 0 square miles. Located at 39.66° N. Lat; 81.07° W. Long. Elevation is 1,066 feet.
Population: 121; Growth (since 2000): 36.0%; Density: 1,145.0 persons per square mile; Race: 90.1% White, 0.0% Black/African American, 0.0% Asian, 0.0% American Indian/Alaska Native, 0.0% Native Hawaiian/Other Pacific Islander, 9.9% Two or more races, 0.0% Hispanic of any race; Average household size: 2.88; Median age: 33.8; Age under 18: 20.7%; Age 65 and over: 9.1%; Males per 100 females: 109.8; Marriage status: 34.4% never married, 53.1% now married, 2.1% separated, 5.2% widowed, 7.3% divorced; Foreign born: 1.7%; Speak English only: 98.3%; With disability: 19.8%; Veterans: 7.3%; Ancestry: 21.5% German, 11.6% Irish, 7.4% Polish, 4.1% English, 2.5% African
Employment: 18.0% management, business, and financial, 12.0% computer, engineering, and science, 4.0% education, legal, community service, arts, and media, 0.0% healthcare practitioners, 24.0% service, 12.0% sales and office, 18.0% natural resources, construction, and maintenance, 12.0% production, transportation, and material moving
Income: Per capita: $20,270; Median household: $40,625; Average household: $52,776; Households with income of $100,000 or more: 21.4%; Poverty rate: 14.0%

Educational Attainment: High school diploma or higher: 89.4%; Bachelor's degree or higher: 15.3%; Graduate/professional degree or higher: 1.2%
Housing: Homeownership rate: 73.8%; Median home value: $51,700; Median year structure built: Before 1940; Homeowner vacancy rate: 0.0%; Median selected monthly owner costs: $733 with a mortgage, $275 without a mortgage; Median gross rent: $525 per month; Rental vacancy rate: 0.0%
Health Insurance: 85.1% have insurance; 48.8% have private insurance; 43.8% have public insurance; 14.9% do not have insurance; 0.0% of children under 18 do not have insurance
Transportation: Commute: 100.0% car, 0.0% public transportation, 0.0% walk, 0.0% work from home; Mean travel time to work: 32.7 minutes

BEALLSVILLE (village). Covers a land area of 0.363 square miles and a water area of 0 square miles. Located at 39.85° N. Lat; 81.04° W. Long. Elevation is 1,257 feet.
Population: 432; Growth (since 2000): 2.1%; Density: 1,190.6 persons per square mile; Race: 100.0% White, 0.0% Black/African American, 0.0% Asian, 0.0% American Indian/Alaska Native, 0.0% Native Hawaiian/Other Pacific Islander, 0.0% Two or more races, 0.0% Hispanic of any race; Average household size: 2.39; Median age: 38.7; Age under 18: 21.8%; Age 65 and over: 13.4%; Males per 100 females: 95.7; Marriage status: 30.7% never married, 46.7% now married, 1.7% separated, 8.3% widowed, 14.4% divorced; Foreign born: 0.7%; Speak English only: 99.5%; With disability: 26.9%; Veterans: 6.2%; Ancestry: 25.7% German, 8.8% English, 7.4% Irish, 7.4% Italian, 4.2% American
Employment: 1.9% management, business, and financial, 0.0% computer, engineering, and science, 6.5% education, legal, community service, arts, and media, 1.9% healthcare practitioners, 18.8% service, 20.8% sales and office, 29.9% natural resources, construction, and maintenance, 20.1% production, transportation, and material moving
Income: Per capita: $18,280; Median household: $31,750; Average household: $42,220; Households with income of $100,000 or more: 4.5%; Poverty rate: 19.9%
Educational Attainment: High school diploma or higher: 88.4%; Bachelor's degree or higher: 3.8%; Graduate/professional degree or higher: 1.7%

School District(s)

Switzerland of Ohio Local (PK-12)
2015-16 Enrollment: 2,227 . . . . (740) 472-5801
Housing: Homeownership rate: 63.5%; Median home value: $75,400; Median year structure built: 1947; Homeowner vacancy rate: 0.0%; Median selected monthly owner costs: $779 with a mortgage, $313 without a mortgage; Median gross rent: $631 per month; Rental vacancy rate: 5.7%
Health Insurance: 93.5% have insurance; 60.4% have private insurance; 49.5% have public insurance; 6.5% do not have insurance; 0.0% of children under 18 do not have insurance
Transportation: Commute: 87.8% car, 0.0% public transportation, 10.1% walk, 0.0% work from home; Mean travel time to work: 36.7 minutes

CAMERON (unincorporated postal area)

ZCTA: 43914

Covers a land area of 0.580 square miles and a water area of 0 square miles. Located at 39.78° N. Lat; 80.95° W. Long. Elevation is 696 feet.
Population: 169; Growth (since 2000): 128.4%; Density: 291.5 persons per square mile; Race: 100.0% White, 0.0% Black/African American, 0.0% Asian, 0.0% American Indian/Alaska Native, 0.0% Native Hawaiian/Other Pacific Islander, 0.0% Two or more races, 0.0% Hispanic of any race; Average household size: 4.69; Median age: 46.2; Age under 18: 0.0%; Age 65 and over: 8.9%; Males per 100 females: 104.3; Marriage status: 64.5% never married, 9.5% now married, 0.0% separated, 8.9% widowed, 17.2% divorced; Foreign born: 0.0%; Speak English only: 100.0%; With disability: 29.6%; Veterans: 4.7%; Ancestry: 82.2% German, 17.8% English, 8.3% Swiss
Employment: 0.0% management, business, and financial, 0.0% computer, engineering, and science, 9.5% education, legal, community service, arts, and media, 0.0% healthcare practitioners, 6.0% service, 48.8% sales and office, 9.5% natural resources, construction, and maintenance, 26.2% production, transportation, and material moving
Income: Per capita: $12,715; Median household: $56,000; Average household: $53,392; Households with income of $100,000 or more: n/a; Poverty rate: 17.2%
Educational Attainment: High school diploma or higher: 35.8%; Bachelor's degree or higher: n/a; Graduate/professional degree or higher: n/a
Housing: Homeownership rate: 100.0%; Median home value: $104,500; Median year structure built: 1982; Homeowner vacancy rate: 0.0%; Median selected monthly owner costs: $0 with a mortgage, $0 without a mortgage; Median gross rent: n/a per month; Rental vacancy rate: 0.0%
Health Insurance: 100.0% have insurance; 34.3% have private insurance; 74.6% have public insurance; 0.0% do not have insurance; 0.0% of children under 18 do not have insurance
Transportation: Commute: 100.0% car, 0.0% public transportation, 0.0% walk, 0.0% work from home; Mean travel time to work: 0.0 minutes

CLARINGTON (village). Covers a land area of 1.139 square miles and a water area of 0.099 square miles. Located at 39.78° N. Lat; 80.87° W. Long. Elevation is 633 feet.
History: Clarington was originally settled by Swiss immigrants, who engaged in clock-making. Many of the later residents were of Slavic and Italian descent.
Population: 409; Growth (since 2000): -7.9%; Density: 359.0 persons per square mile; Race: 97.1% White, 0.0% Black/African American, 0.0% Asian, 0.0% American Indian/Alaska Native, 0.0% Native Hawaiian/Other Pacific Islander, 2.9% Two or more races, 1.0% Hispanic of any race; Average household size: 2.48; Median age: 43.1; Age under 18: 18.3%; Age 65 and over: 17.8%; Males per 100 females: 80.3; Marriage status: 26.9% never married, 56.7% now married, 0.6% separated, 6.9% widowed, 9.5% divorced; Foreign born: 0.2%; Speak English only: 99.5%; With disability: 17.8%; Veterans: 9.3%; Ancestry: 22.7% German, 13.2% Irish, 6.1% American, 5.9% English, 3.4% Italian
Employment: 2.5% management, business, and financial, 1.9% computer, engineering, and science, 4.4% education, legal, community service, arts, and media, 7.5% healthcare practitioners, 17.6% service, 30.2% sales and office, 22.6% natural resources, construction, and maintenance, 13.2% production, transportation, and material moving
Income: Per capita: $23,629; Median household: $45,313; Average household: $58,738; Households with income of $100,000 or more: 15.1%; Poverty rate: 16.9%
Educational Attainment: High school diploma or higher: 87.0%; Bachelor's degree or higher: 10.9%; Graduate/professional degree or higher: 0.7%
Housing: Homeownership rate: 77.6%; Median home value: $83,300; Median year structure built: 1956; Homeowner vacancy rate: 0.0%; Median selected monthly owner costs: $882 with a mortgage, $377 without a mortgage; Median gross rent: $518 per month; Rental vacancy rate: 0.0%
Health Insurance: 85.6% have insurance; 64.8% have private insurance; 41.1% have public insurance; 14.4% do not have insurance; 6.7% of children under 18 do not have insurance
Transportation: Commute: 97.4% car, 0.0% public transportation, 0.0% walk, 0.0% work from home; Mean travel time to work: 29.4 minutes

GRAYSVILLE (village). Covers a land area of 1.007 square miles and a water area of 0 square miles. Located at 39.66° N. Lat; 81.17° W. Long. Elevation is 1,096 feet.
Population: 62; Growth (since 2000): -45.1%; Density: 61.6 persons per square mile; Race: 90.3% White, 9.7% Black/African American, 0.0% Asian, 0.0% American Indian/Alaska Native, 0.0% Native Hawaiian/Other Pacific Islander, 0.0% Two or more races, 0.0% Hispanic of any race; Average household size: 2.95; Median age: 39.0; Age under 18: 35.5%; Age 65 and over: 14.5%; Males per 100 females: 100.0; Marriage status: 26.0% never married, 68.0% now married, 0.0% separated, 0.0% widowed, 6.0% divorced; Foreign born: 0.0%; Speak English only: 100.0%; With disability: 27.4%; Veterans: 40.0%; Ancestry: 27.4% German, 16.1% Irish, 8.1% English, 6.5% French, 3.2% American
Employment: 0.0% management, business, and financial, 0.0% computer, engineering, and science, 0.0% education, legal, community service, arts, and media, 0.0% healthcare practitioners, 21.1% service, 21.1% sales and office, 10.5% natural resources, construction, and maintenance, 47.4% production, transportation, and material moving
Income: Per capita: $20,435; Median household: $61,875; Average household: $60,900; Households with income of $100,000 or more: 9.5%; Poverty rate: 12.9%
Educational Attainment: High school diploma or higher: 90.0%; Bachelor's degree or higher: 2.5%; Graduate/professional degree or higher: n/a

School District(s)

Switzerland of Ohio Local (PK-12)
2015-16 Enrollment: 2,227 . . . . (740) 472-5801

Housing: Homeownership rate: 71.4%; Median home value: $59,200; Median year structure built: Before 1940; Homeowner vacancy rate: 6.3%; Median selected monthly owner costs: n/a with a mortgage, $325 without a mortgage; Median gross rent: n/a per month; Rental vacancy rate: 0.0%
Health Insurance: 90.3% have insurance; 33.9% have private insurance; 80.6% have public insurance; 9.7% do not have insurance; 0.0% of children under 18 do not have insurance
Transportation: Commute: 68.4% car, 5.3% public transportation, 15.8% walk, 10.5% work from home; Mean travel time to work: 0.0 minutes

HANNIBAL (CDP). Covers a land area of 1.115 square miles and a water area of 0 square miles. Located at 39.67° N. Lat; 80.87° W. Long. Elevation is 653 feet.
Population: 375; Growth (since 2000): n/a; Density: 336.3 persons per square mile; Race: 100.0% White, 0.0% Black/African American, 0.0% Asian, 0.0% American Indian/Alaska Native, 0.0% Native Hawaiian/Other Pacific Islander, 0.0% Two or more races, 0.0% Hispanic of any race; Average household size: 2.66; Median age: 45.8; Age under 18: 22.7%; Age 65 and over: 11.7%; Males per 100 females: 94.8; Marriage status: 23.9% never married, 56.1% now married, 0.0% separated, 6.8% widowed, 13.2% divorced; Foreign born: 0.0%; Speak English only: 100.0%; With disability: 34.9%; Veterans: 7.6%; Ancestry: 58.9% German, 13.3% Irish, 11.5% Swiss, 10.4% American, 6.9% Hungarian
Employment: 13.3% management, business, and financial, 5.8% computer, engineering, and science, 31.8% education, legal, community service, arts, and media, 11.6% healthcare practitioners, 11.6% service, 0.0% sales and office, 15.0% natural resources, construction, and maintenance, 11.0% production, transportation, and material moving
Income: Per capita: $19,524; Median household: $52,604; Average household: $53,023; Households with income of $100,000 or more: 9.2%; Poverty rate: 27.2%
Educational Attainment: High school diploma or higher: 90.3%; Bachelor's degree or higher: 17.2%; Graduate/professional degree or higher: 13.3%

School District(s)

Switzerland of Ohio Local (PK-12)
2015-16 Enrollment: 2,227 . . . . (740) 472-5801

Housing: Homeownership rate: 65.2%; Median home value: $157,500; Median year structure built: 1967; Homeowner vacancy rate: 0.0%; Median selected monthly owner costs: $955 with a mortgage, $416 without a mortgage; Median gross rent: n/a per month; Rental vacancy rate: 0.0%
Health Insurance: 71.5% have insurance; 57.6% have private insurance; 33.6% have public insurance; 28.5% do not have insurance; 0.0% of children under 18 do not have insurance
Transportation: Commute: 87.9% car, 0.0% public transportation, 12.1% walk, 0.0% work from home; Mean travel time to work: 17.3 minutes

JERUSALEM (village). Covers a land area of 0.242 square miles and a water area of 0 square miles. Located at 39.85° N. Lat; 81.10° W. Long. Elevation is 1,263 feet.
Population: 145; Growth (since 2000): -4.6%; Density: 600.3 persons per square mile; Race: 100.0% White, 0.0% Black/African American, 0.0% Asian, 0.0% American Indian/Alaska Native, 0.0% Native Hawaiian/Other Pacific Islander, 0.0% Two or more races, 0.0% Hispanic of any race; Average household size: 2.16; Median age: 39.5; Age under 18: 17.9%; Age 65 and over: 24.1%; Males per 100 females: 106.4; Marriage status: 22.1% never married, 59.0% now married, 1.6% separated, 7.4% widowed, 11.5% divorced; Foreign born: 0.0%; Speak English only: 100.0%; With disability: 29.7%; Veterans: 10.1%; Ancestry: 23.4% German, 22.8% Irish, 17.2% English, 11.0% Dutch, 11.0% French
Employment: 12.1% management, business, and financial, 1.7% computer, engineering, and science, 5.2% education, legal, community service, arts, and media, 3.4% healthcare practitioners, 24.1% service, 13.8% sales and office, 32.8% natural resources, construction, and maintenance, 6.9% production, transportation, and material moving
Income: Per capita: $22,913; Median household: $39,896; Average household: $49,428; Households with income of $100,000 or more: 6.0%; Poverty rate: 10.3%
Educational Attainment: High school diploma or higher: 86.4%; Bachelor's degree or higher: 10.0%; Graduate/professional degree or higher: 0.9%
Housing: Homeownership rate: 74.6%; Median home value: $75,000; Median year structure built: 1950; Homeowner vacancy rate: 7.4%; Median selected monthly owner costs: $735 with a mortgage, $289 without a mortgage; Median gross rent: $425 per month; Rental vacancy rate: 0.0%
Health Insurance: 84.8% have insurance; 67.6% have private insurance; 40.0% have public insurance; 15.2% do not have insurance; 0.0% of children under 18 do not have insurance
Transportation: Commute: 98.2% car, 0.0% public transportation, 0.0% walk, 1.8% work from home; Mean travel time to work: 30.0 minutes

LEWISVILLE (village). Covers a land area of 0.368 square miles and a water area of 0 square miles. Located at 39.77° N. Lat; 81.22° W. Long. Elevation is 1,201 feet.
Population: 236; Growth (since 2000): 1.3%; Density: 642.1 persons per square mile; Race: 97.9% White, 2.1% Black/African American, 0.0% Asian, 0.0% American Indian/Alaska Native, 0.0% Native Hawaiian/Other Pacific Islander, 0.0% Two or more races, 0.0% Hispanic of any race; Average household size: 2.56; Median age: 39.9; Age under 18: 21.6%; Age 65 and over: 19.9%; Males per 100 females: 87.2; Marriage status: 26.6% never married, 55.3% now married, 2.7% separated, 10.1% widowed, 8.0% divorced; Foreign born: 0.0%; Speak English only: 100.0%; With disability: 18.6%; Veterans: 10.8%; Ancestry: 31.8% German, 19.5% American, 11.4% Irish, 3.8% French, 1.3% Scotch-Irish
Employment: 10.0% management, business, and financial, 2.0% computer, engineering, and science, 15.0% education, legal, community service, arts, and media, 1.0% healthcare practitioners, 12.0% service, 17.0% sales and office, 13.0% natural resources, construction, and maintenance, 30.0% production, transportation, and material moving
Income: Per capita: $23,119; Median household: $48,194; Average household: $55,668; Households with income of $100,000 or more: 7.1%; Poverty rate: 8.6%
Educational Attainment: High school diploma or higher: 92.0%; Bachelor's degree or higher: 8.6%; Graduate/professional degree or higher: 1.1%
Housing: Homeownership rate: 83.5%; Median home value: $77,900; Median year structure built: Before 1940; Homeowner vacancy rate: 0.0%; Median selected monthly owner costs: $739 with a mortgage, $270 without a mortgage; Median gross rent: $475 per month; Rental vacancy rate: 41.7%
Health Insurance: 97.0% have insurance; 75.4% have private insurance; 38.6% have public insurance; 3.0% do not have insurance; 0.0% of children under 18 do not have insurance
Transportation: Commute: 95.0% car, 3.0% public transportation, 0.0% walk, 0.0% work from home; Mean travel time to work: 39.3 minutes

MILTONSBURG (village). Covers a land area of 0.073 square miles and a water area of 0 square miles. Located at 39.83° N. Lat; 81.16° W. Long. Elevation is 1,293 feet.
Population: 65; Growth (since 2000): 124.1%; Density: 894.0 persons per square mile; Race: 73.8% White, 26.2% Black/African American, 0.0% Asian, 0.0% American Indian/Alaska Native, 0.0% Native Hawaiian/Other Pacific Islander, 0.0% Two or more races, 0.0% Hispanic of any race; Average household size: 2.95; Median age: 54.8; Age under 18: 16.9%; Age 65 and over: 12.3%; Males per 100 females: 126.3; Marriage status: 27.1% never married, 25.4% now married, 0.0% separated, 6.8% widowed, 40.7% divorced; Foreign born: 0.0%; Speak English only: 100.0%; With disability: 4.6%; Veterans: 1.9%; Ancestry: 30.8% German, 23.1% Irish, 9.2% American, 3.1% Dutch
Employment: 0.0% management, business, and financial, 0.0% computer, engineering, and science, 7.4% education, legal, community service, arts, and media, 0.0% healthcare practitioners, 11.1% service, 37.0% sales and office, 33.3% natural resources, construction, and maintenance, 11.1% production, transportation, and material moving
Income: Per capita: $21,615; Median household: $41,250; Average household: $41,809; Households with income of $100,000 or more: 9.1%; Poverty rate: 18.5%
Educational Attainment: High school diploma or higher: 92.2%; Bachelor's degree or higher: n/a; Graduate/professional degree or higher: n/a
Housing: Homeownership rate: 95.5%; Median home value: $62,500; Median year structure built: 1952; Homeowner vacancy rate: 0.0%; Median selected monthly owner costs: $583 with a mortgage, $417 without a mortgage; Median gross rent: n/a per month; Rental vacancy rate: 0.0%

Health Insurance: 95.4% have insurance; 55.4% have private insurance; 43.1% have public insurance; 4.6% do not have insurance; 0.0% of children under 18 do not have insurance
Transportation: Commute: 100.0% car, 0.0% public transportation, 0.0% walk, 0.0% work from home; Mean travel time to work: 26.7 minutes

NEW MATAMORAS (unincorporated postal area)
ZCTA: 45767
Covers a land area of 113.815 square miles and a water area of 0.672 square miles. Located at 39.54° N. Lat; 81.13° W. Long..
Population: 2,612; Growth (since 2000): -8.0%; Density: 22.9 persons per square mile; Race: 99.7% White, 0.0% Black/African American, 0.0% Asian, 0.0% American Indian/Alaska Native, 0.0% Native Hawaiian/Other Pacific Islander, 0.3% Two or more races, 0.8% Hispanic of any race; Average household size: 2.35; Median age: 40.6; Age under 18: 22.1%; Age 65 and over: 19.4%; Males per 100 females: 102.3; Marriage status: 24.7% never married, 55.6% now married, 1.4% separated, 8.8% widowed, 10.9% divorced; Foreign born: 0.3%; Speak English only: 99.3%; With disability: 24.0%; Veterans: 7.4%; Ancestry: 26.3% German, 11.9% Irish, 9.4% English, 6.9% American, 4.1% Dutch
Employment: 3.8% management, business, and financial, 1.5% computer, engineering, and science, 11.7% education, legal, community service, arts, and media, 9.7% healthcare practitioners, 13.2% service, 18.0% sales and office, 29.5% natural resources, construction, and maintenance, 12.6% production, transportation, and material moving
Income: Per capita: $20,819; Median household: $40,525; Average household: $48,297; Households with income of $100,000 or more: 8.7%; Poverty rate: 22.3%
Educational Attainment: High school diploma or higher: 86.4%; Bachelor's degree or higher: 10.9%; Graduate/professional degree or higher: 2.3%

School District(s)
Frontier Local (KG-12)
2015-16 Enrollment: 638. . . . . (740) 865-3473
Housing: Homeownership rate: 72.7%; Median home value: $96,600; Median year structure built: 1962; Homeowner vacancy rate: 1.1%; Median selected monthly owner costs: $879 with a mortgage, $300 without a mortgage; Median gross rent: $418 per month; Rental vacancy rate: 2.9%
Health Insurance: 94.3% have insurance; 60.4% have private insurance; 50.6% have public insurance; 5.7% do not have insurance; 3.8% of children under 18 do not have insurance
Transportation: Commute: 98.7% car, 0.4% public transportation, 0.5% walk, 0.0% work from home; Mean travel time to work: 28.2 minutes

SARDIS (CDP). Covers a land area of 1.232 square miles and a water area of 0 square miles. Located at 39.63° N. Lat; 80.91° W. Long. Elevation is 666 feet.
Population: 342; Growth (since 2000): n/a; Density: 277.6 persons per square mile; Race: 90.9% White, 0.0% Black/African American, 9.1% Asian, 0.0% American Indian/Alaska Native, 0.0% Native Hawaiian/Other Pacific Islander, 0.0% Two or more races, 0.0% Hispanic of any race; Average household size: 2.12; Median age: 60.9; Age under 18: 15.2%; Age 65 and over: 49.7%; Males per 100 females: 92.8; Marriage status: 7.1% never married, 77.4% now married, 0.0% separated, 4.4% widowed, 11.1% divorced; Foreign born: 9.1%; Speak English only: 90.1%; With disability: 14.0%; Veterans: 6.9%; Ancestry: 31.6% German, 13.7% Irish, 9.6% Swiss, 9.1% Icelander, 6.4% Dutch
Employment: 0.0% management, business, and financial, 0.0% computer, engineering, and science, 5.2% education, legal, community service, arts, and media, 0.0% healthcare practitioners, 8.2% service, 36.6% sales and office, 11.9% natural resources, construction, and maintenance, 38.1% production, transportation, and material moving
Income: Per capita: $19,549; Median household: $41,607; Average household: $40,343; Households with income of $100,000 or more: 5.0%; Poverty rate: n/a
Educational Attainment: High school diploma or higher: 89.6%; Bachelor's degree or higher: 17.5%; Graduate/professional degree or higher: 2.6%

School District(s)
Switzerland of Ohio Local (PK-12)
2015-16 Enrollment: 2,227 . . . . (740) 472-5801
Housing: Homeownership rate: 74.5%; Median home value: $87,600; Median year structure built: Before 1940; Homeowner vacancy rate: 0.0%; Median selected monthly owner costs: $794 with a mortgage, $389 without a mortgage; Median gross rent: n/a per month; Rental vacancy rate: 0.0%
Health Insurance: 91.2% have insurance; 81.6% have private insurance; 58.5% have public insurance; 8.8% do not have insurance; 30.8% of children under 18 do not have insurance
Transportation: Commute: 83.6% car, 0.0% public transportation, 16.4% walk, 0.0% work from home; Mean travel time to work: 14.3 minutes

STAFFORD (village). Covers a land area of 0.340 square miles and a water area of 0 square miles. Located at 39.71° N. Lat; 81.28° W. Long. Elevation is 1,079 feet.
Population: 101; Growth (since 2000): 17.4%; Density: 297.4 persons per square mile; Race: 93.1% White, 0.0% Black/African American, 0.0% Asian, 4.0% American Indian/Alaska Native, 0.0% Native Hawaiian/Other Pacific Islander, 3.0% Two or more races, 0.0% Hispanic of any race; Average household size: 2.53; Median age: 42.9; Age under 18: 25.7%; Age 65 and over: 18.8%; Males per 100 females: 92.9; Marriage status: 19.2% never married, 64.1% now married, 0.0% separated, 15.4% widowed, 1.3% divorced; Foreign born: 0.0%; Speak English only: 99.0%; With disability: 26.7%; Veterans: 5.3%; Ancestry: 52.5% German, 36.6% Irish, 9.9% American, 1.0% English, 1.0% Hungarian
Employment: 3.0% management, business, and financial, 12.1% computer, engineering, and science, 3.0% education, legal, community service, arts, and media, 3.0% healthcare practitioners, 24.2% service, 21.2% sales and office, 15.2% natural resources, construction, and maintenance, 18.2% production, transportation, and material moving
Income: Per capita: $18,303; Median household: $40,000; Average household: $46,178; Households with income of $100,000 or more: 2.5%; Poverty rate: 28.7%
Educational Attainment: High school diploma or higher: 94.4%; Bachelor's degree or higher: 9.7%; Graduate/professional degree or higher: n/a
Housing: Homeownership rate: 70.0%; Median home value: $44,400; Median year structure built: Before 1940; Homeowner vacancy rate: 0.0%; Median selected monthly owner costs: $650 with a mortgage, $238 without a mortgage; Median gross rent: $525 per month; Rental vacancy rate: 0.0%
Health Insurance: 87.1% have insurance; 46.5% have private insurance; 55.4% have public insurance; 12.9% do not have insurance; 7.7% of children under 18 do not have insurance
Transportation: Commute: 90.9% car, 0.0% public transportation, 9.1% walk, 0.0% work from home; Mean travel time to work: 45.3 minutes

WILSON (village). Covers a land area of 0.413 square miles and a water area of 0.058 square miles. Located at 39.86° N. Lat; 81.07° W. Long. Elevation is 1,250 feet.
Population: 117; Growth (since 2000): -0.8%; Density: 283.6 persons per square mile; Race: 100.0% White, 0.0% Black/African American, 0.0% Asian, 0.0% American Indian/Alaska Native, 0.0% Native Hawaiian/Other Pacific Islander, 0.0% Two or more races, 2.6% Hispanic of any race; Average household size: 2.85; Median age: 37.1; Age under 18: 23.9%; Age 65 and over: 21.4%; Males per 100 females: 111.9; Marriage status: 21.1% never married, 65.6% now married, 1.1% separated, 5.6% widowed, 7.8% divorced; Foreign born: 0.0%; Speak English only: 100.0%; With disability: 21.4%; Veterans: 13.5%; Ancestry: 45.3% German, 12.0% Swedish, 9.4% French, 9.4% Irish, 6.8% Italian
Employment: 5.0% management, business, and financial, 5.0% computer, engineering, and science, 17.5% education, legal, community service, arts, and media, 2.5% healthcare practitioners, 15.0% service, 20.0% sales and office, 20.0% natural resources, construction, and maintenance, 15.0% production, transportation, and material moving
Income: Per capita: $21,087; Median household: $47,083; Average household: $62,605; Households with income of $100,000 or more: 14.6%; Poverty rate: 9.7%
Educational Attainment: High school diploma or higher: 88.4%; Bachelor's degree or higher: 10.5%; Graduate/professional degree or higher: 3.5%
Housing: Homeownership rate: 95.1%; Median home value: $95,800; Median year structure built: 1961; Homeowner vacancy rate: 9.3%; Median selected monthly owner costs: $1,000 with a mortgage, $375 without a mortgage; Median gross rent: n/a per month; Rental vacancy rate: 0.0%
Health Insurance: 94.9% have insurance; 67.5% have private insurance; 59.8% have public insurance; 5.1% do not have insurance; 0.0% of children under 18 do not have insurance
Transportation: Commute: 100.0% car, 0.0% public transportation, 0.0% walk, 0.0% work from home; Mean travel time to work: 36.6 minutes

WOODSFIELD (village). County seat. Covers a land area of 2.015 square miles and a water area of 0 square miles. Located at 39.76° N. Lat; 81.12° W. Long. Elevation is 1,207 feet.
History: Settled 1815, incorporated 1834.
Population: 2,370; Growth (since 2000): -8.8%; Density: 1,175.9 persons per square mile; Race: 97.2% White, 0.7% Black/African American, 0.0% Asian, 0.0% American Indian/Alaska Native, 0.0% Native Hawaiian/Other Pacific Islander, 2.2% Two or more races, 1.6% Hispanic of any race; Average household size: 2.10; Median age: 48.4; Age under 18: 18.6%; Age 65 and over: 26.7%; Males per 100 females: 83.5; Marriage status: 20.1% never married, 51.5% now married, 4.9% separated, 12.2% widowed, 16.1% divorced; Foreign born: 0.3%; Speak English only: 99.4%; With disability: 26.3%; Veterans: 11.4%; Ancestry: 30.8% German, 19.0% Irish, 10.9% American, 10.8% English, 4.1% Scottish
Employment: 9.5% management, business, and financial, 2.7% computer, engineering, and science, 11.9% education, legal, community service, arts, and media, 10.3% healthcare practitioners, 17.8% service, 23.2% sales and office, 16.9% natural resources, construction, and maintenance, 7.7% production, transportation, and material moving
Income: Per capita: $19,510; Median household: $34,120; Average household: $39,797; Households with income of $100,000 or more: 5.2%; Poverty rate: 24.1%
Educational Attainment: High school diploma or higher: 88.1%; Bachelor's degree or higher: 12.1%; Graduate/professional degree or higher: 3.9%

School District(s)

Switzerland of Ohio Local (PK-12)
2015-16 Enrollment: 2,227 . . . . (740) 472-5801
Housing: Homeownership rate: 67.3%; Median home value: $78,200; Median year structure built: 1954; Homeowner vacancy rate: 0.0%; Median selected monthly owner costs: $758 with a mortgage, $304 without a mortgage; Median gross rent: $549 per month; Rental vacancy rate: 14.4%
Health Insurance: 94.4% have insurance; 64.7% have private insurance; 51.9% have public insurance; 5.6% do not have insurance; 5.2% of children under 18 do not have insurance
Newspapers: Monroe County Beacon (weekly circulation 5,000)
Transportation: Commute: 92.0% car, 0.0% public transportation, 5.2% walk, 1.9% work from home; Mean travel time to work: 23.4 minutes

Montgomery County

Located in western Ohio; crossed by the Great Miami, Stillwater, and Mad Rivers. Covers a land area of 461.553 square miles, a water area of 2.782 square miles, and is located in the Eastern Time Zone at 39.76° N. Lat., 84.29° W. Long. The county was founded in 1803. County seat is Dayton.

Montgomery County is part of the Dayton, OH Metropolitan Statistical Area. The entire metro area includes: Greene County, OH; Miami County, OH; Montgomery County, OH

Weather Station: Dayton Intl Arpt — Elevation: 1,000 feet

	Jan	Feb	Mar	Apr	May	Jun	Jul	Aug	Sep	Oct	Nov	Dec
High	35	39	50	62	72	81	84	83	76	64	51	39
Low	20	23	31	41	51	61	64	63	55	44	35	24
Precip	2.8	2.3	3.4	4.1	4.6	4.3	4.1	3.1	3.1	3.0	3.3	3.1
Snow	8.0	6.3	4.1	0.6	tr	0.0	tr	tr	tr	0.4	0.8	5.1

High and Low temperatures in degrees Fahrenheit; Precipitation and Snow in inches

Weather Station: Dayton Mcd — Elevation: 745 feet

	Jan	Feb	Mar	Apr	May	Jun	Jul	Aug	Sep	Oct	Nov	Dec
High	36	41	51	64	74	84	87	86	79	66	53	40
Low	22	25	32	43	53	63	67	65	57	45	36	26
Precip	2.9	2.3	3.3	4.0	4.9	4.1	4.4	3.0	2.7	2.9	3.2	3.0
Snow	4.8	2.7	1.6	0.1	0.0	0.0	0.0	0.0	0.0	tr	0.3	2.9

High and Low temperatures in degrees Fahrenheit; Precipitation and Snow in inches

Population: 532,761; Growth (since 2000): -4.7%; Density: 1,154.3 persons per square mile; Race: 73.5% White, 20.7% Black/African American, 2.0% Asian, 0.2% American Indian/Alaska Native, 0.0% Native Hawaiian/Other Pacific Islander, 3.0% two or more races, 2.6% Hispanic of any race; Average household size: 2.32; Median age: 39.4; Age under 18: 22.4%; Age 65 and over: 16.6%; Males per 100 females: 92.4; Marriage status: 33.1% never married, 46.0% now married, 2.1% separated, 7.0% widowed, 13.9% divorced; Foreign born: 4.3%; Speak English only: 94.3%; With disability: 15.3%; Veterans: 10.2%; Ancestry: 22.8% German, 12.5% Irish, 7.9% English, 6.6% American, 3.4% Italian
Religion: Six largest groups: 14.7% Catholicism, 11.5% Baptist, 4.6% Non-denominational Protestant, 4.0% Methodist/Pietist, 3.0% Holiness, 2.2% Lutheran
Economy: Unemployment rate: 4.5%; Leading industries: 14.9 % retail trade; 13.7 % health care and social assistance; 10.7 % other services (except public administration); Farms: 770 totaling 124,105 acres; Company size: 13 employ 1,000 or more persons, 17 employ 500 to 999 persons, 332 employ 100 to 499 persons, 11,039 employ less than 100 persons; Business ownership: 14,676 women-owned, 5,757 Black-owned, 753 Hispanic-owned, 804 Asian-owned, 209 American Indian/Alaska Native-owned
Employment: 13.2% management, business, and financial, 6.0% computer, engineering, and science, 9.9% education, legal, community service, arts, and media, 6.9% healthcare practitioners, 18.8% service, 24.3% sales and office, 6.4% natural resources, construction, and maintenance, 14.5% production, transportation, and material moving
Income: Per capita: $26,392; Median household: $45,394; Average household: $61,666; Households with income of $100,000 or more: 16.9%; Poverty rate: 18.5%
Educational Attainment: High school diploma or higher: 89.6%; Bachelor's degree or higher: 26.1%; Graduate/professional degree or higher: 10.5%
Housing: Homeownership rate: 60.8%; Median home value: $109,600; Median year structure built: 1964; Homeowner vacancy rate: 2.5%; Median selected monthly owner costs: $1,182 with a mortgage, $470 without a mortgage; Median gross rent: $740 per month; Rental vacancy rate: 6.4%
Vital Statistics: Birth rate: 122.1 per 10,000 population; Death rate: 110.0 per 10,000 population; Age-adjusted cancer mortality rate: 182.0 deaths per 100,000 population
Health Insurance: 90.9% have insurance; 64.8% have private insurance; 39.3% have public insurance; 9.1% do not have insurance; 4.1% of children under 18 do not have insurance
Health Care: Physicians: 39.3 per 10,000 population; Dentists: 5.9 per 10,000 population; Hospital beds: 54.3 per 10,000 population; Hospital admissions: 1,972.1 per 10,000 population
Air Quality Index (AQI): Percent of Days: 75.4% good, 23.0% moderate, 1.6% unhealthy for sensitive individuals, 0.0% unhealthy, 0.0% very unhealthy; Annual median: 41; Annual maximum: 112
Transportation: Commute: 90.9% car, 2.4% public transportation, 2.6% walk, 3.2% work from home; Mean travel time to work: 21.4 minutes
2016 Presidential Election: 47.7% Trump, 47.0% Clinton, 3.2% Johnson, 0.9% Stein
National and State Parks: Miamisburg Mound State Memorial; Sycamore State Park
Additional Information Contacts
Montgomery Government . . . . (937) 225-4690
http://www.co.montgomery.oh.us

Montgomery County Communities

BROOKVILLE (city). Covers a land area of 3.822 square miles and a water area of 0 square miles. Located at 39.84° N. Lat; 84.42° W. Long. Elevation is 1,030 feet.
Population: 5,993; Growth (since 2000): 13.3%; Density: 1,567.9 persons per square mile; Race: 98.3% White, 0.4% Black/African American, 0.3% Asian, 0.0% American Indian/Alaska Native, 0.0% Native Hawaiian/Other Pacific Islander, 1.0% Two or more races, 1.0% Hispanic of any race; Average household size: 2.09; Median age: 43.9; Age under 18: 21.1%; Age 65 and over: 28.9%; Males per 100 females: 85.7; Marriage status: 19.8% never married, 54.1% now married, 2.1% separated, 13.2% widowed, 12.8% divorced; Foreign born: 0.6%; Speak English only: 99.3%; With disability: 18.3%; Veterans: 10.0%; Ancestry: 39.5% German, 14.1% Irish, 8.4% American, 7.5% English, 2.3% Italian
Employment: 10.6% management, business, and financial, 6.9% computer, engineering, and science, 14.0% education, legal, community service, arts, and media, 7.3% healthcare practitioners, 14.4% service, 25.6% sales and office, 6.5% natural resources, construction, and maintenance, 14.7% production, transportation, and material moving
Income: Per capita: $27,321; Median household: $44,898; Average household: $57,615; Households with income of $100,000 or more: 14.8%; Poverty rate: 5.6%
Educational Attainment: High school diploma or higher: 90.2%; Bachelor's degree or higher: 17.0%; Graduate/professional degree or higher: 6.5%

School District(s)

Brookville Local (PK-12)
2015-16 Enrollment: 1,481 . . . . (937) 833-2181

Housing: Homeownership rate: 65.9%; Median home value: $117,100; Median year structure built: 1968; Homeowner vacancy rate: 0.0%; Median selected monthly owner costs: $1,022 with a mortgage, $373 without a mortgage; Median gross rent: $788 per month; Rental vacancy rate: 7.9%

Health Insurance: 97.4% have insurance; 81.3% have private insurance; 39.0% have public insurance; 2.6% do not have insurance; 5.6% of children under 18 do not have insurance

Safety: Violent crime rate: 11.9 per 10,000 population; Property crime rate: 100.0 per 10,000 population

Newspapers: Brookville Star (weekly circulation 6,500)

Transportation: Commute: 96.9% car, 0.0% public transportation, 0.4% walk, 0.6% work from home; Mean travel time to work: 21.2 minutes

Additional Information Contacts

Village of Brookville . . . . (937) 833-2135
http://www.brookvilleohio.com

CENTERVILLE (city). Covers a land area of 10.780 square miles and a water area of 0.065 square miles. Located at 39.63° N. Lat; 84.15° W. Long. Elevation is 1,020 feet.

History: Incorporated 1879.

Population: 23,899; Growth (since 2000): 3.8%; Density: 2,216.9 persons per square mile; Race: 87.2% White, 6.0% Black/African American, 3.5% Asian, 0.0% American Indian/Alaska Native, 0.0% Native Hawaiian/Other Pacific Islander, 3.0% Two or more races, 1.5% Hispanic of any race; Average household size: 2.19; Median age: 48.2; Age under 18: 21.0%; Age 65 and over: 27.1%; Males per 100 females: 86.0; Marriage status: 24.3% never married, 56.1% now married, 1.2% separated, 8.7% widowed, 10.9% divorced; Foreign born: 5.8%; Speak English only: 92.7%; With disability: 14.5%; Veterans: 12.0%; Ancestry: 32.5% German, 18.1% Irish, 11.1% English, 7.1% Italian, 6.2% American

Employment: 20.0% management, business, and financial, 7.7% computer, engineering, and science, 13.3% education, legal, community service, arts, and media, 9.6% healthcare practitioners, 13.6% service, 25.1% sales and office, 2.9% natural resources, construction, and maintenance, 7.6% production, transportation, and material moving

Income: Per capita: $38,580; Median household: $63,524; Average household: $85,024; Households with income of $100,000 or more: 32.2%; Poverty rate: 6.4%

Educational Attainment: High school diploma or higher: 95.8%; Bachelor's degree or higher: 51.4%; Graduate/professional degree or higher: 21.9%

School District(s)

Centerville City (PK-12)
2015-16 Enrollment: 8,099 . . . . (937) 433-8841
Springboro Community City (PK-12)
2015-16 Enrollment: 5,985 . . . . (937) 748-3960

Two-year College(s)

Fortis College-Centerville (Private, For-profit)
Fall 2016 Enrollment: 861 . . . . (937) 433-3410
2016-17 Tuition: In-state $18,046; Out-of-state $18,046

Housing: Homeownership rate: 70.5%; Median home value: $179,600; Median year structure built: 1977; Homeowner vacancy rate: 0.0%; Median selected monthly owner costs: $1,522 with a mortgage, $613 without a mortgage; Median gross rent: $853 per month; Rental vacancy rate: 7.9%

Health Insurance: 96.5% have insurance; 80.8% have private insurance; 35.3% have public insurance; 3.5% do not have insurance; 1.5% of children under 18 do not have insurance

Safety: Violent crime rate: 5.5 per 10,000 population; Property crime rate: 147.6 per 10,000 population

Transportation: Commute: 91.9% car, 0.9% public transportation, 0.7% walk, 6.3% work from home; Mean travel time to work: 20.5 minutes

Additional Information Contacts

City of Centerville . . . . (937) 433-7151
http://www.ci.centerville.oh.us

CLAYTON (city). Covers a land area of 18.506 square miles and a water area of 0.089 square miles. Located at 39.87° N. Lat; 84.33° W. Long. Elevation is 1,001 feet.

Population: 13,172; Growth (since 2000): -1.3%; Density: 711.8 persons per square mile; Race: 74.6% White, 20.7% Black/African American, 0.9% Asian, 0.0% American Indian/Alaska Native, 0.0% Native Hawaiian/Other Pacific Islander, 2.8% Two or more races, 1.7% Hispanic of any race; Average household size: 2.63; Median age: 42.3; Age under 18: 23.4%; Age 65 and over: 16.4%; Males per 100 females: 95.9; Marriage status: 26.2% never married, 60.0% now married, 0.9% separated, 4.9% widowed, 8.9% divorced; Foreign born: 5.2%; Speak English only: 95.8%; With disability: 11.3%; Veterans: 11.1%; Ancestry: 23.4% German, 13.1% Irish, 9.0% English, 5.2% American, 3.9% Italian

Employment: 15.7% management, business, and financial, 6.0% computer, engineering, and science, 10.2% education, legal, community service, arts, and media, 7.0% healthcare practitioners, 18.0% service, 23.9% sales and office, 6.9% natural resources, construction, and maintenance, 12.3% production, transportation, and material moving

Income: Per capita: $32,401; Median household: $71,911; Average household: $84,925; Households with income of $100,000 or more: 29.9%; Poverty rate: 7.5%

Educational Attainment: High school diploma or higher: 95.0%; Bachelor's degree or higher: 34.3%; Graduate/professional degree or higher: 14.2%

School District(s)

Miami Valley Career Tech (08-12)
2015-16 Enrollment: n/a . . . . (937) 837-7781
Northmont City (PK-12)
2015-16 Enrollment: 5,074 . . . . (937) 832-5000

Housing: Homeownership rate: 84.5%; Median home value: $133,400; Median year structure built: 1971; Homeowner vacancy rate: 2.8%; Median selected monthly owner costs: $1,380 with a mortgage, $555 without a mortgage; Median gross rent: $789 per month; Rental vacancy rate: 8.0%

Health Insurance: 94.8% have insurance; 80.0% have private insurance; 29.5% have public insurance; 5.2% do not have insurance; 1.4% of children under 18 do not have insurance

Safety: Violent crime rate: 4.6 per 10,000 population; Property crime rate: 102.8 per 10,000 population

Transportation: Commute: 94.9% car, 1.0% public transportation, 0.4% walk, 2.5% work from home; Mean travel time to work: 23.7 minutes

Additional Information Contacts

City of Clayton . . . . (937) 836-3500
http://www.clayton.oh.us

DAYTON (city). County seat. Covers a land area of 55.652 square miles and a water area of 0.853 square miles. Located at 39.78° N. Lat; 84.20° W. Long. Elevation is 738 feet.

History: Settlers began coming in 1795 to the site where the Great Miami River was joined by the Stillwater and Mad Rivers and Wolf Creek. When Ohio became a state in 1803, Dayton became the Montgomery County seat, and two years later the town was incorporated. The opening of the canal system in the 1830's increased Dayton's river traffic, augmented by the railroad traffic that began in 1851. Industries such as the railroad car works and the National Cash Register Company were founded between 1850 and 1890, and by the early 1900's locally-made Stoddard-Dayton, Speedwell, and Big Four automobiles were wheeling around Dayton. Wilbur and Orville Wright used the Dayton Public Library to learn about aerodynamics, and soon established an experimental airplane factory here. Charles F. Kettering came to Dayton to work at the cash register plant, invented a quick-starting electric motor, and started the Dayton Engineering Laboratories Company (Delco). Dayton suffered recurring floods until a system of levees and dams to restrain the rivers was completed in 1921.

Population: 141,143; Growth (since 2000): -15.1%; Density: 2,536.2 persons per square mile; Race: 54.9% White, 39.8% Black/African American, 1.1% Asian, 0.3% American Indian/Alaska Native, 0.0% Native Hawaiian/Other Pacific Islander, 3.3% Two or more races, 3.9% Hispanic of any race; Average household size: 2.25; Median age: 33.3; Age under 18: 22.1%; Age 65 and over: 12.5%; Males per 100 females: 95.0; Marriage status: 47.7% never married, 31.1% now married, 3.0% separated, 6.3% widowed, 15.0% divorced; Foreign born: 4.5%; Speak English only: 93.3%; With disability: 18.5%; Veterans: 8.6%; Ancestry: 15.4% German, 9.5% Irish, 4.6% English, 4.4% American, 3.1% Italian

Employment: 9.2% management, business, and financial, 4.8% computer, engineering, and science, 9.9% education, legal, community service, arts, and media, 4.8% healthcare practitioners, 24.9% service, 23.3% sales and office, 6.8% natural resources, construction, and maintenance, 16.4% production, transportation, and material moving

Income: Per capita: $17,461; Median household: $28,745; Average household: $40,735; Households with income of $100,000 or more: 7.2%; Poverty rate: 34.5%

Educational Attainment: High school diploma or higher: 83.1%; Bachelor's degree or higher: 17.6%; Graduate/professional degree or higher: 6.5%

School District(s)

Centerville City (PK-12)
2015-16 Enrollment: 8,099 . . . . (937) 433-8841
City Day Community School (KG-07)
2015-16 Enrollment: 135. . . . . (937) 223-8130
Dayton Business Technology High School (09-12)
2015-16 Enrollment: 177. . . . . (937) 225-3989
Dayton City (PK-12)
2015-16 Enrollment: 13,846 . . . . (937) 542-3000
Dayton Early College Academy Inc (07-12)
2015-16 Enrollment: 458. . . . . (937) 229-5780
Dayton Leadership Academies-Dayton View Campus (03-08)
2015-16 Enrollment: 238. . . . . (937) 567-9426
Dayton Leadership Academies-early Learning Academy (KG-02)
2015-16 Enrollment: 139. . . . . (937) 567-9426
Emerson Academy (KG-08)
2015-16 Enrollment: 723. . . . . (937) 223-2889
Horizon Science Academy Dayton Downtown (KG-08)
2015-16 Enrollment: 230. . . . . (937) 281-1980
Horizon Science Academy Dayton High School (06-12)
2015-16 Enrollment: 333. . . . . (937) 281-1480
Horizon Science Academy-Dayton (KG-05)
2015-16 Enrollment: 170. . . . . (937) 277-1177
Imagine Woodbury Academy (KG-05)
2015-16 Enrollment: 128. . . . . (877) 644-6338
Jefferson Township Local (PK-12)
2015-16 Enrollment: 375. . . . . (937) 835-5682
Klepinger Community School (KG-08)
2015-16 Enrollment: 431. . . . . (937) 610-1710
Life Skills Center of Dayton (09-12)
2015-16 Enrollment: 195. . . . . (937) 274-2841
Mad River Local (PK-12)
2015-16 Enrollment: 3,961 . . . . (937) 259-6606
Miami Valley Academies (KG-12)
2015-16 Enrollment: 176. . . . . (937) 294-4522
Miami Valley Career Tech (08-12)
2015-16 Enrollment: n/a . . . . (937) 837-7781
Miamisburg City (PK-12)
2015-16 Enrollment: 5,409 . . . . (937) 866-3381
Mound Street Health Careers Acadmy (09-11)
2015-16 Enrollment: 59. . . . . (937) 223-3041
Mound Street It Careers Academy (09-12)
2015-16 Enrollment: 60. . . . . (937) 223-3041
Mound Street Military Careers Academy (09-11)
2015-16 Enrollment: 49. . . . . (937) 223-3041
North Dayton School of Science & Discovery (KG-08)
2015-16 Enrollment: 612. . . . . (937) 278-6671
Northmont City (PK-12)
2015-16 Enrollment: 5,074 . . . . (937) 832-5000
Northridge Local (PK-12)
2015-16 Enrollment: 1,715 . . . . (937) 278-5885
Oakwood City (PK-12)
2015-16 Enrollment: 2,105 . . . . (937) 297-5332
Pathway School of Discovery (KG-08)
2015-16 Enrollment: 782. . . . . (937) 235-5498
Richard Allen Academy (07-08)
2015-16 Enrollment: 75. . . . . (937) 586-9815
Richard Allen Academy II (02-06)
2015-16 Enrollment: 319. . . . . (937) 586-9756
Richard Allen Preparatory (KG-01)
2015-16 Enrollment: 132. . . . . (937) 278-4201
Summit Academy Community School-Dayton (KG-08)
2015-16 Enrollment: 136. . . . . (937) 278-4298
Summit Academy Transition High School Dayton (09-12)
2015-16 Enrollment: 122. . . . . (937) 223-3154
Vandalia-Butler City (PK-12)
2015-16 Enrollment: 2,986 . . . . (937) 415-6400
West Carrollton City (PK-12)
2015-16 Enrollment: 3,864 . . . . (937) 859-5121

Four-year College(s)

ITT Technical Institute-Dayton (Private, For-profit)
Fall 2016 Enrollment: n/a . . . . (937) 264-7700
United Theological Seminary (Private, Not-for-profit, United Methodist)
Fall 2016 Enrollment: 409 . . . . (937) 529-2201
University of Dayton (Private, Not-for-profit, Roman Catholic)
Fall 2016 Enrollment: 10,803 . . . . (937) 229-1000
2016-17 Tuition: In-state $40,940; Out-of-state $40,940
Wright State University-Main Campus (Public)
Fall 2016 Enrollment: 16,655 . . . . (937) 775-3333
2016-17 Tuition: In-state $8,730; Out-of-state $17,098

Two-year College(s)

Brightwood College-Dayton (Private, For-profit)
Fall 2016 Enrollment: 198 . . . . (937) 294-6155
Creative Images Institute of Cosmetology-North Dayton (Private, For-profit)
Fall 2016 Enrollment: 176 . . . . (937) 454-1200
Creative Images Institute of Cosmetology-South Dayton (Private, For-profit)
Fall 2016 Enrollment: 88 . . . . (937) 433-1944
International College of Broadcasting (Private, For-profit)
Fall 2016 Enrollment: 55 . . . . (937) 258-8251
2016-17 Tuition: In-state $12,569; Out-of-state $12,569
Miami-Jacobs Career College-Dayton (Private, For-profit)
Fall 2016 Enrollment: 49 . . . . (937) 668-0203
2016-17 Tuition: In-state $10,740; Out-of-state $10,740
Ohio Medical Career College (Private, For-profit)
Fall 2016 Enrollment: 127 . . . . (937) 567-8880
Sinclair Community College (Public)
Fall 2016 Enrollment: 18,610 . . . . (937) 512-3000
2016-17 Tuition: In-state $3,604; Out-of-state $6,868

Vocational/Technical School(s)

Dayton School of Medical Massage (Private, For-profit)
Fall 2016 Enrollment: 271 . . . . (937) 294-6994
2016-17 Tuition: In-state $15,595; Out-of-state $15,595
Ross Medical Education Center-Dayton (Private, For-profit)
Fall 2016 Enrollment: 72 . . . . (937) 235-0510
2016-17 Tuition: $15,740

Housing: Homeownership rate: 48.4%; Median home value: $66,600; Median year structure built: 1948; Homeowner vacancy rate: 4.5%; Median selected monthly owner costs: $955 with a mortgage, $379 without a mortgage; Median gross rent: $636 per month; Rental vacancy rate: 8.0%

Health Insurance: 87.1% have insurance; 49.0% have private insurance; 48.6% have public insurance; 12.9% do not have insurance; 5.3% of children under 18 do not have insurance

Hospitals: Dayton VA Medical Center (539 beds); Good Samaritan Hospital (560 beds); Grandview Hospital & Medical Center (452 beds); Medical Center at Elizabeth Place (26 beds); Miami Valley Hospital (848 beds)

Safety: Violent crime rate: 100.0 per 10,000 population; Property crime rate: 515.8 per 10,000 population

Newspapers: Dayton City Paper (weekly circulation 23,000); Dayton Daily News (daily circulation 123,000); Dayton Weekly News (weekly circulation 30,000); Oakwood Register (weekly circulation 10,000); Times Community Papers (weekly circulation 78,000)

Transportation: Commute: 82.7% car, 6.1% public transportation, 7.0% walk, 2.5% work from home; Mean travel time to work: 20.8 minutes

Airports: Dayton-Wright Brothers (general aviation); James M Cox Dayton International (primary service/small hub); Wright-Patterson AFB (general aviation)

Additional Information Contacts

City of Dayton . . . . (937) 333-3333
http://www.cityofdayton.org

DREXEL (CDP). Covers a land area of 2.184 square miles and a water area of 0 square miles. Located at 39.74° N. Lat; 84.29° W. Long. Elevation is 951 feet.

Population: 1,677; Growth (since 2000): -18.5%; Density: 767.7 persons per square mile; Race: 54.3% White, 42.9% Black/African American, 0.0% Asian, 0.0% American Indian/Alaska Native, 0.0% Native Hawaiian/Other Pacific Islander, 2.8% Two or more races, 8.6% Hispanic of any race; Average household size: 2.30; Median age: 35.0; Age under 18: 31.9%; Age 65 and over: 12.3%; Males per 100 females: 89.8; Marriage status: 30.9% never married, 40.4% now married, 2.6% separated, 6.5% widowed, 22.2% divorced; Foreign born: 2.9%; Speak English only: 93.2%; With disability: 20.9%; Veterans: 12.3%; Ancestry: 13.2% Irish, 7.1% American, 4.2% English, 2.5% German, 2.4% Italian

Employment: 4.2% management, business, and financial, 6.6% computer, engineering, and science, 6.4% education, legal, community service, arts,

and media, 7.6% healthcare practitioners, 35.0% service, 2.5% sales and office, 10.2% natural resources, construction, and maintenance, 27.5% production, transportation, and material moving
Income: Per capita: $16,240; Median household: $27,418; Average household: $37,811; Households with income of $100,000 or more: 9.1%; Poverty rate: 20.9%
Educational Attainment: High school diploma or higher: 76.2%; Bachelor's degree or higher: 4.9%; Graduate/professional degree or higher: 3.4%
Housing: Homeownership rate: 54.1%; Median home value: $38,700; Median year structure built: 1952; Homeowner vacancy rate: 0.0%; Median selected monthly owner costs: $1,097 with a mortgage, $352 without a mortgage; Median gross rent: $712 per month; Rental vacancy rate: 0.0%
Health Insurance: 85.4% have insurance; 41.6% have private insurance; 50.9% have public insurance; 14.6% do not have insurance; 4.5% of children under 18 do not have insurance
Transportation: Commute: 93.7% car, 3.6% public transportation, 1.6% walk, 1.0% work from home; Mean travel time to work: 22.1 minutes

---

ENGLEWOOD (city). Covers a land area of 6.551 square miles and a water area of 0.041 square miles. Located at 39.87° N. Lat; 84.31° W. Long. Elevation is 919 feet.
History: Englewood was established as a Mennonite community by descendants of a group that had been invited to Pennsylvania by William Penn.
Population: 13,512; Growth (since 2000): 10.4%; Density: 2,062.6 persons per square mile; Race: 82.2% White, 11.7% Black/African American, 2.3% Asian, 0.0% American Indian/Alaska Native, 0.0% Native Hawaiian/Other Pacific Islander, 3.5% Two or more races, 0.4% Hispanic of any race; Average household size: 2.31; Median age: 45.1; Age under 18: 20.3%; Age 65 and over: 21.0%; Males per 100 females: 87.2; Marriage status: 24.4% never married, 52.7% now married, 2.5% separated, 8.6% widowed, 14.3% divorced; Foreign born: 2.9%; Speak English only: 95.6%; With disability: 14.1%; Veterans: 9.4%; Ancestry: 29.2% German, 13.6% Irish, 10.9% English, 8.4% American, 2.9% Italian
Employment: 12.4% management, business, and financial, 5.7% computer, engineering, and science, 10.3% education, legal, community service, arts, and media, 9.8% healthcare practitioners, 16.5% service, 27.3% sales and office, 6.3% natural resources, construction, and maintenance, 11.7% production, transportation, and material moving
Income: Per capita: $28,421; Median household: $55,985; Average household: $65,469; Households with income of $100,000 or more: 18.3%; Poverty rate: 10.6%
Educational Attainment: High school diploma or higher: 93.5%; Bachelor's degree or higher: 28.6%; Graduate/professional degree or higher: 8.5%

School District(s)

Northmont City (PK-12)
2015-16 Enrollment: 5,074 . . . . (937) 832-5000

Vocational/Technical School(s)

Miami Valley Career Technology Center (Public)
Fall 2016 Enrollment: 368 . . . . (800) 716-7161
2016-17 Tuition: $13,660

Housing: Homeownership rate: 71.6%; Median home value: $121,500; Median year structure built: 1974; Homeowner vacancy rate: 1.7%; Median selected monthly owner costs: $1,234 with a mortgage, $460 without a mortgage; Median gross rent: $714 per month; Rental vacancy rate: 9.6%
Health Insurance: 94.0% have insurance; 75.5% have private insurance; 37.0% have public insurance; 6.0% do not have insurance; 1.3% of children under 18 do not have insurance
Safety: Violent crime rate: 9.7 per 10,000 population; Property crime rate: 304.0 per 10,000 population
Newspapers: Englewood Independent (weekly circulation 4,000)
Transportation: Commute: 95.8% car, 0.8% public transportation, 1.0% walk, 2.2% work from home; Mean travel time to work: 21.6 minutes
Additional Information Contacts
City of Englewood . . . . (937) 836-5106
http://www.ci.englewood.oh.us

FARMERSVILLE (village). Covers a land area of 0.715 square miles and a water area of 0 square miles. Located at 39.68° N. Lat; 84.43° W. Long. Elevation is 879 feet.
Population: 1,032; Growth (since 2000): 5.3%; Density: 1,443.9 persons per square mile; Race: 98.0% White, 0.3% Black/African American, 0.0% Asian, 0.0% American Indian/Alaska Native, 0.0% Native Hawaiian/Other Pacific Islander, 1.7% Two or more races, 1.3% Hispanic of any race; Average household size: 2.66; Median age: 44.0; Age under 18: 22.2%; Age 65 and over: 13.0%; Males per 100 females: 88.6; Marriage status: 22.7% never married, 58.1% now married, 2.2% separated, 6.4% widowed, 12.7% divorced; Foreign born: 0.3%; Speak English only: 99.3%; With disability: 8.9%; Veterans: 7.8%; Ancestry: 35.3% German, 13.7% American, 10.3% Irish, 4.3% English, 2.8% Italian
Employment: 10.8% management, business, and financial, 2.7% computer, engineering, and science, 7.1% education, legal, community service, arts, and media, 3.0% healthcare practitioners, 19.5% service, 27.0% sales and office, 11.7% natural resources, construction, and maintenance, 18.1% production, transportation, and material moving
Income: Per capita: $25,199; Median household: $58,750; Average household: $65,003; Households with income of $100,000 or more: 15.5%; Poverty rate: 5.7%
Educational Attainment: High school diploma or higher: 91.3%; Bachelor's degree or higher: 14.0%; Graduate/professional degree or higher: 5.6%

School District(s)

Valley View Local (PK-12)
2015-16 Enrollment: 1,842 . . . . (937) 855-6581

Housing: Homeownership rate: 80.2%; Median home value: $101,800; Median year structure built: 1952; Homeowner vacancy rate: 3.1%; Median selected monthly owner costs: $1,156 with a mortgage, $485 without a mortgage; Median gross rent: $818 per month; Rental vacancy rate: 0.0%
Health Insurance: 96.5% have insurance; 82.9% have private insurance; 26.2% have public insurance; 3.5% do not have insurance; 0.0% of children under 18 do not have insurance
Transportation: Commute: 95.6% car, 0.4% public transportation, 3.5% walk, 0.6% work from home; Mean travel time to work: 28.8 minutes

---

GERMANTOWN (city). Covers a land area of 4.262 square miles and a water area of 0 square miles. Located at 39.63° N. Lat; 84.36° W. Long. Elevation is 718 feet.
History: Laid out 1814.
Population: 5,503; Growth (since 2000): 12.7%; Density: 1,291.1 persons per square mile; Race: 98.0% White, 0.0% Black/African American, 1.2% Asian, 0.0% American Indian/Alaska Native, 0.0% Native Hawaiian/Other Pacific Islander, 0.8% Two or more races, 1.4% Hispanic of any race; Average household size: 2.59; Median age: 40.1; Age under 18: 28.3%; Age 65 and over: 15.4%; Males per 100 females: 92.5; Marriage status: 24.9% never married, 53.6% now married, 2.2% separated, 6.8% widowed, 14.7% divorced; Foreign born: 1.5%; Speak English only: 98.4%; With disability: 13.2%; Veterans: 10.7%; Ancestry: 28.2% German, 20.2% Irish, 10.3% English, 8.8% American, 3.0% Swedish
Employment: 10.5% management, business, and financial, 5.9% computer, engineering, and science, 9.0% education, legal, community service, arts, and media, 9.1% healthcare practitioners, 17.7% service, 28.9% sales and office, 4.6% natural resources, construction, and maintenance, 14.4% production, transportation, and material moving
Income: Per capita: $30,280; Median household: $49,937; Average household: $77,420; Households with income of $100,000 or more: 25.3%; Poverty rate: 14.6%
Educational Attainment: High school diploma or higher: 92.9%; Bachelor's degree or higher: 21.1%; Graduate/professional degree or higher: 9.2%

School District(s)

Valley View Local (PK-12)
2015-16 Enrollment: 1,842 . . . . (937) 855-6581

Housing: Homeownership rate: 67.3%; Median home value: $123,100; Median year structure built: 1962; Homeowner vacancy rate: 0.0%; Median selected monthly owner costs: $1,299 with a mortgage, $383 without a mortgage; Median gross rent: $859 per month; Rental vacancy rate: 0.0%
Health Insurance: 91.3% have insurance; 70.1% have private insurance; 31.8% have public insurance; 8.7% do not have insurance; 2.1% of children under 18 do not have insurance
Safety: Violent crime rate: 10.9 per 10,000 population; Property crime rate: 72.8 per 10,000 population
Transportation: Commute: 96.0% car, 0.0% public transportation, 0.0% walk, 4.0% work from home; Mean travel time to work: 26.9 minutes
Additional Information Contacts
Village of Germantown . . . . (937) 855-7255
http://germantown.oh.us

HUBER HEIGHTS (city). Covers a land area of 22.272 square miles and a water area of 0.095 square miles. Located at 39.86° N. Lat; 84.11° W. Long. Elevation is 932 feet.

Population: 38,795; Growth (since 2000): 1.5%; Density: 1,741.9 persons per square mile; Race: 77.2% White, 13.8% Black/African American, 1.9% Asian, 1.1% American Indian/Alaska Native, 0.0% Native Hawaiian/Other Pacific Islander, 5.0% Two or more races, 3.9% Hispanic of any race; Average household size: 2.57; Median age: 36.8; Age under 18: 26.3%; Age 65 and over: 15.5%; Males per 100 females: 93.4; Marriage status: 27.0% never married, 54.1% now married, 2.1% separated, 6.5% widowed, 12.3% divorced; Foreign born: 4.0%; Speak English only: 93.5%; With disability: 14.1%; Veterans: 14.1%; Ancestry: 22.9% German, 13.9% Irish, 8.6% American, 8.2% English, 2.5% French

Employment: 12.9% management, business, and financial, 6.9% computer, engineering, and science, 7.7% education, legal, community service, arts, and media, 7.6% healthcare practitioners, 18.0% service, 24.0% sales and office, 5.9% natural resources, construction, and maintenance, 17.0% production, transportation, and material moving

Income: Per capita: $25,037; Median household: $54,357; Average household: $63,129; Households with income of $100,000 or more: 15.6%; Poverty rate: 13.0%

Educational Attainment: High school diploma or higher: 92.9%; Bachelor's degree or higher: 23.6%; Graduate/professional degree or higher: 9.2%

School District(s)

Huber Heights City (PK-12)
2015-16 Enrollment: 5,747 . . . . (937) 237-6300

Vocational/Technical School(s)

Ohio Institute of Allied Health (Private, Not-for-profit)
Fall 2016 Enrollment: 75 . . . . (937) 237-1010
2016-17 Tuition: In-state $21,400; Out-of-state $21,400

Housing: Homeownership rate: 68.7%; Median home value: $102,500; Median year structure built: 1973; Homeowner vacancy rate: 1.6%; Median selected monthly owner costs: $1,138 with a mortgage, $451 without a mortgage; Median gross rent: $887 per month; Rental vacancy rate: 4.0%

Health Insurance: 90.1% have insurance; 68.9% have private insurance; 36.0% have public insurance; 9.9% do not have insurance; 6.3% of children under 18 do not have insurance

Safety: Violent crime rate: 22.0 per 10,000 population; Property crime rate: 332.6 per 10,000 population

Newspapers: Huber Heights Courier (weekly circulation 9,000)

Transportation: Commute: 93.7% car, 1.5% public transportation, 1.5% walk, 1.6% work from home; Mean travel time to work: 22.2 minutes

Additional Information Contacts

City of Huber Heights . . . . (937) 233-1423
http://www.hhoh.org

KETTERING (city). Covers a land area of 18.677 square miles and a water area of 0.039 square miles. Located at 39.70° N. Lat; 84.15° W. Long. Elevation is 1,004 feet.

History: Settled c.1812, incorporated 1952.

Population: 55,720; Growth (since 2000): -3.1%; Density: 2,983.3 persons per square mile; Race: 91.2% White, 3.4% Black/African American, 2.2% Asian, 0.2% American Indian/Alaska Native, 0.0% Native Hawaiian/Other Pacific Islander, 2.6% Two or more races, 1.9% Hispanic of any race; Average household size: 2.20; Median age: 40.7; Age under 18: 21.2%; Age 65 and over: 18.2%; Males per 100 females: 91.2; Marriage status: 30.0% never married, 47.8% now married, 1.4% separated, 7.1% widowed, 15.1% divorced; Foreign born: 4.3%; Speak English only: 94.5%; With disability: 13.8%; Veterans: 10.1%; Ancestry: 30.4% German, 14.7% Irish, 11.7% English, 7.5% American, 4.7% Italian

Employment: 13.5% management, business, and financial, 7.1% computer, engineering, and science, 12.0% education, legal, community service, arts, and media, 9.0% healthcare practitioners, 16.6% service, 25.6% sales and office, 5.6% natural resources, construction, and maintenance, 10.7% production, transportation, and material moving

Income: Per capita: $30,579; Median household: $51,441; Average household: $67,143; Households with income of $100,000 or more: 17.7%; Poverty rate: 12.6%

Educational Attainment: High school diploma or higher: 94.1%; Bachelor's degree or higher: 33.6%; Graduate/professional degree or higher: 14.0%

School District(s)

Dayton Regional Stem School (06-12)
2015-16 Enrollment: 635 . . . . (937) 256-3777
Kettering City School District (PK-12)
2015-16 Enrollment: 7,797 . . . . (937) 499-1430

Four-year College(s)

Kettering College (Private, Not-for-profit, Seventh Day Adventist)
Fall 2016 Enrollment: 759 . . . . (937) 395-8601
2016-17 Tuition: In-state $11,808; Out-of-state $11,808

Two-year College(s)

Advertising Art Educational Services DBA School of Advertising Art (Private, For-profit)
Fall 2016 Enrollment: 194 . . . . (937) 294-0592
2016-17 Tuition: In-state $26,181; Out-of-state $26,181
American National University-Dayton (Private, For-profit)
Fall 2016 Enrollment: 99 . . . . (937) 299-9450
2016-17 Tuition: In-state $14,886; Out-of-state $14,886

Housing: Homeownership rate: 61.8%; Median home value: $125,700; Median year structure built: 1960; Homeowner vacancy rate: 2.1%; Median selected monthly owner costs: $1,190 with a mortgage, $485 without a mortgage; Median gross rent: $758 per month; Rental vacancy rate: 3.0%

Health Insurance: 92.2% have insurance; 73.0% have private insurance; 33.1% have public insurance; 7.8% do not have insurance; 4.2% of children under 18 do not have insurance

Hospitals: Kettering Medical Center (522 beds)

Safety: Violent crime rate: 13.2 per 10,000 population; Property crime rate: 182.0 per 10,000 population

Transportation: Commute: 92.6% car, 1.1% public transportation, 1.5% walk, 3.7% work from home; Mean travel time to work: 20.2 minutes

Additional Information Contacts

City of Kettering . . . . (937) 296-2400
http://www.ketteringoh.org

MIAMISBURG (city). Covers a land area of 12.184 square miles and a water area of 0.185 square miles. Located at 39.63° N. Lat; 84.27° W. Long. Elevation is 705 feet.

History: Miamisburg was laid out in 1818 on the site of a blockhouse called Hole's Station, which had been built by Zachariah Hole about 1800. The Hoover and Gamble Company, manufacturer of reapers, was founded here in 1840. Tobacco warehouses were situated in Miamisburg in the late 1800's.

Population: 20,069; Growth (since 2000): 3.0%; Density: 1,647.1 persons per square mile; Race: 92.7% White, 3.2% Black/African American, 1.0% Asian, 0.0% American Indian/Alaska Native, 0.0% Native Hawaiian/Other Pacific Islander, 2.3% Two or more races, 1.5% Hispanic of any race; Average household size: 2.43; Median age: 41.1; Age under 18: 23.3%; Age 65 and over: 17.4%; Males per 100 females: 90.7; Marriage status: 23.0% never married, 53.8% now married, 1.4% separated, 9.0% widowed, 14.2% divorced; Foreign born: 2.3%; Speak English only: 97.3%; With disability: 13.8%; Veterans: 9.0%; Ancestry: 31.3% German, 16.8% Irish, 12.3% English, 8.6% American, 4.0% Scottish

Employment: 16.2% management, business, and financial, 7.4% computer, engineering, and science, 8.6% education, legal, community service, arts, and media, 6.3% healthcare practitioners, 17.4% service, 23.2% sales and office, 5.9% natural resources, construction, and maintenance, 15.0% production, transportation, and material moving

Income: Per capita: $28,437; Median household: $54,557; Average household: $68,211; Households with income of $100,000 or more: 23.7%; Poverty rate: 15.1%

Educational Attainment: High school diploma or higher: 91.6%; Bachelor's degree or higher: 22.6%; Graduate/professional degree or higher: 7.9%

School District(s)

Miamisburg City (PK-12)
2015-16 Enrollment: 5,409 . . . . (937) 866-3381
Miamisburg Secondary Academy (09-12)
2015-16 Enrollment: 63 . . . . (937) 866-3381

Two-year College(s)

Dayton Barber College (Private, For-profit)
Fall 2016 Enrollment: 31 . . . . (937) 222-9101

Housing: Homeownership rate: 70.5%; Median home value: $133,100; Median year structure built: 1970; Homeowner vacancy rate: 2.3%; Median selected monthly owner costs: $1,279 with a mortgage, $524 without a mortgage; Median gross rent: $750 per month; Rental vacancy rate: 6.9%

Health Insurance: 93.8% have insurance; 71.1% have private insurance; 37.0% have public insurance; 6.2% do not have insurance; 1.2% of children under 18 do not have insurance

Hospitals: Sycamore Medical Center (181 beds)

Safety: Violent crime rate: 10.0 per 10,000 population; Property crime rate: 114.0 per 10,000 population
Newspapers: Franklin Chronicle (weekly circulation 8,000); Germantown Press (weekly circulation 2,700); Miamisburg News (weekly circulation 6,500); Springboro Star Press (weekly circulation 12,000)
Transportation: Commute: 94.6% car, 0.7% public transportation, 1.7% walk, 2.9% work from home; Mean travel time to work: 19.8 minutes
Additional Information Contacts
City of Miamisburg. . . . . (937) 866-3303
http://www.ci.miamisburg.oh.us

MORAINE (city). Covers a land area of 9.251 square miles and a water area of 0.266 square miles. Located at 39.70° N. Lat; 84.24° W. Long. Elevation is 738 feet.
Population: 6,343; Growth (since 2000): -8.0%; Density: 685.6 persons per square mile; Race: 84.3% White, 12.8% Black/African American, 1.0% Asian, 0.0% American Indian/Alaska Native, 0.0% Native Hawaiian/Other Pacific Islander, 1.7% Two or more races, 2.1% Hispanic of any race; Average household size: 2.58; Median age: 35.9; Age under 18: 25.9%; Age 65 and over: 12.2%; Males per 100 females: 95.7; Marriage status: 23.3% never married, 55.0% now married, 3.0% separated, 7.7% widowed, 14.0% divorced; Foreign born: 2.1%; Speak English only: 96.9%; With disability: 15.7%; Veterans: 6.9%; Ancestry: 18.3% German, 13.1% Irish, 6.7% American, 4.8% English, 2.3% Polish
Employment: 12.8% management, business, and financial, 2.7% computer, engineering, and science, 2.0% education, legal, community service, arts, and media, 8.2% healthcare practitioners, 20.2% service, 25.5% sales and office, 11.7% natural resources, construction, and maintenance, 16.8% production, transportation, and material moving
Income: Per capita: $20,662; Median household: $46,283; Average household: $52,659; Households with income of $100,000 or more: 12.6%; Poverty rate: 18.6%
Educational Attainment: High school diploma or higher: 85.7%; Bachelor's degree or higher: 13.6%; Graduate/professional degree or higher: 3.0%
Housing: Homeownership rate: 58.6%; Median home value: $81,000; Median year structure built: 1975; Homeowner vacancy rate: 1.3%; Median selected monthly owner costs: $1,103 with a mortgage, $400 without a mortgage; Median gross rent: $759 per month; Rental vacancy rate: 13.5%
Health Insurance: 89.0% have insurance; 56.0% have private insurance; 39.3% have public insurance; 11.0% do not have insurance; 8.7% of children under 18 do not have insurance
Safety: Violent crime rate: 53.3 per 10,000 population; Property crime rate: 1,071.3 per 10,000 population
Transportation: Commute: 88.9% car, 5.3% public transportation, 0.8% walk, 3.9% work from home; Mean travel time to work: 20.8 minutes
Additional Information Contacts
City of Moraine . . . . (937) 535-1000
http://www.ci.moraine.oh.us

NEW LEBANON (village). Covers a land area of 2.045 square miles and a water area of 0 square miles. Located at 39.74° N. Lat; 84.39° W. Long. Elevation is 909 feet.
History: New Lebanon was established as a community of Dunkards. A murder and the burning of the town in 1876 were attributed to a conflict between warring gangs.
Population: 4,130; Growth (since 2000): -2.4%; Density: 2,019.7 persons per square mile; Race: 92.7% White, 1.6% Black/African American, 1.4% Asian, 0.0% American Indian/Alaska Native, 1.2% Native Hawaiian/Other Pacific Islander, 0.6% Two or more races, 1.0% Hispanic of any race; Average household size: 2.61; Median age: 36.0; Age under 18: 26.9%; Age 65 and over: 16.0%; Males per 100 females: 93.3; Marriage status: 32.1% never married, 41.1% now married, 1.3% separated, 8.0% widowed, 18.9% divorced; Foreign born: 3.1%; Speak English only: 98.0%; With disability: 21.5%; Veterans: 9.1%; Ancestry: 22.2% German, 14.8% Irish, 14.0% American, 12.9% English, 3.2% Scottish
Employment: 5.0% management, business, and financial, 1.0% computer, engineering, and science, 2.2% education, legal, community service, arts, and media, 2.2% healthcare practitioners, 18.0% service, 31.2% sales and office, 21.5% natural resources, construction, and maintenance, 18.9% production, transportation, and material moving
Income: Per capita: $19,473; Median household: $37,929; Average household: $50,218; Households with income of $100,000 or more: 11.9%; Poverty rate: 26.3%
Educational Attainment: High school diploma or higher: 88.5%; Bachelor's degree or higher: 6.6%; Graduate/professional degree or higher: 0.8%

School District(s)

New Lebanon Local (PK-12)
2015-16 Enrollment: 1,142 . . . . (937) 687-1301
Housing: Homeownership rate: 50.1%; Median home value: $78,100; Median year structure built: 1966; Homeowner vacancy rate: 9.6%; Median selected monthly owner costs: $937 with a mortgage, $333 without a mortgage; Median gross rent: $640 per month; Rental vacancy rate: 6.6%
Health Insurance: 92.4% have insurance; 58.2% have private insurance; 47.6% have public insurance; 7.6% do not have insurance; 0.0% of children under 18 do not have insurance
Safety: Violent crime rate: 22.5 per 10,000 population; Property crime rate: 289.9 per 10,000 population
Transportation: Commute: 96.6% car, 0.0% public transportation, 3.4% walk, 0.0% work from home; Mean travel time to work: 27.6 minutes
Additional Information Contacts
Village of New Lebanon . . . . (937) 687-1341
http://www.newlebanonoh.com

OAKWOOD (city). Covers a land area of 2.195 square miles and a water area of 0 square miles. Located at 39.72° N. Lat; 84.17° W. Long. Elevation is 988 feet.
History: Incorporated as village in 1907; became city after 1930.
Population: 9,077; Growth (since 2000): -1.5%; Density: 4,135.4 persons per square mile; Race: 96.9% White, 0.0% Black/African American, 0.9% Asian, 0.0% American Indian/Alaska Native, 0.0% Native Hawaiian/Other Pacific Islander, 1.3% Two or more races, 1.4% Hispanic of any race; Average household size: 2.60; Median age: 42.6; Age under 18: 29.2%; Age 65 and over: 14.9%; Males per 100 females: 90.2; Marriage status: 22.5% never married, 61.4% now married, 0.7% separated, 5.7% widowed, 10.4% divorced; Foreign born: 2.9%; Speak English only: 94.5%; With disability: 7.1%; Veterans: 9.8%; Ancestry: 29.5% German, 18.5% Irish, 12.0% English, 8.2% American, 8.0% Italian
Employment: 25.9% management, business, and financial, 9.1% computer, engineering, and science, 21.7% education, legal, community service, arts, and media, 12.9% healthcare practitioners, 4.7% service, 19.0% sales and office, 2.2% natural resources, construction, and maintenance, 4.5% production, transportation, and material moving
Income: Per capita: $50,733; Median household: $96,790; Average household: $130,304; Households with income of $100,000 or more: 48.8%; Poverty rate: 6.3%
Educational Attainment: High school diploma or higher: 98.3%; Bachelor's degree or higher: 70.6%; Graduate/professional degree or higher: 37.3%
Housing: Homeownership rate: 79.1%; Median home value: $228,700; Median year structure built: Before 1940; Homeowner vacancy rate: 3.1%; Median selected monthly owner costs: $2,022 with a mortgage, $762 without a mortgage; Median gross rent: $1,040 per month; Rental vacancy rate: 5.2%
Health Insurance: 96.8% have insurance; 88.5% have private insurance; 20.3% have public insurance; 3.2% do not have insurance; 2.2% of children under 18 do not have insurance
Transportation: Commute: 95.0% car, 0.0% public transportation, 0.0% walk, 4.9% work from home; Mean travel time to work: 19.2 minutes

PHILLIPSBURG (village). Covers a land area of 0.266 square miles and a water area of 0 square miles. Located at 39.90° N. Lat; 84.40° W. Long. Elevation is 1,033 feet.
Population: 447; Growth (since 2000): -28.8%; Density: 1,677.5 persons per square mile; Race: 95.5% White, 1.3% Black/African American, 0.0% Asian, 0.0% American Indian/Alaska Native, 0.7% Native Hawaiian/Other Pacific Islander, 2.0% Two or more races, 3.1% Hispanic of any race; Average household size: 2.18; Median age: 40.9; Age under 18: 22.1%; Age 65 and over: 18.8%; Males per 100 females: 105.5; Marriage status: 24.0% never married, 47.4% now married, 0.0% separated, 11.3% widowed, 17.4% divorced; Foreign born: 0.0%; Speak English only: 97.0%; With disability: 17.2%; Veterans: 13.8%; Ancestry: 38.5% German, 16.1% Irish, 5.1% French, 4.7% English, 4.3% Greek
Employment: 6.3% management, business, and financial, 0.8% computer, engineering, and science, 2.9% education, legal, community service, arts, and media, 6.3% healthcare practitioners, 20.4% service, 22.5% sales and office, 21.7% natural resources, construction, and maintenance, 19.2% production, transportation, and material moving

Income: Per capita: $24,236; Median household: $46,250; Average household: $52,810; Households with income of $100,000 or more: 5.9%; Poverty rate: 0.4%
Educational Attainment: High school diploma or higher: 84.6%; Bachelor's degree or higher: 19.1%; Graduate/professional degree or higher: 2.3%
Housing: Homeownership rate: 81.0%; Median home value: $92,800; Median year structure built: 1943; Homeowner vacancy rate: 2.8%; Median selected monthly owner costs: $1,088 with a mortgage, $458 without a mortgage; Median gross rent: $677 per month; Rental vacancy rate: 11.4%
Health Insurance: 86.6% have insurance; 68.7% have private insurance; 35.1% have public insurance; 13.4% do not have insurance; 17.2% of children under 18 do not have insurance
Transportation: Commute: 94.8% car, 0.9% public transportation, 2.6% walk, 0.9% work from home; Mean travel time to work: 24.0 minutes

RIVERSIDE (city). Covers a land area of 9.720 square miles and a water area of 0.042 square miles. Located at 39.78° N. Lat; 84.12° W. Long. Elevation is 778 feet.
Population: 25,036; Growth (since 2000): 6.3%; Density: 2,575.8 persons per square mile; Race: 85.7% White, 7.8% Black/African American, 2.2% Asian, 0.2% American Indian/Alaska Native, 0.0% Native Hawaiian/Other Pacific Islander, 3.3% Two or more races, 4.0% Hispanic of any race; Average household size: 2.43; Median age: 35.7; Age under 18: 23.7%; Age 65 and over: 14.3%; Males per 100 females: 94.2; Marriage status: 30.6% never married, 47.1% now married, 1.8% separated, 7.7% widowed, 14.6% divorced; Foreign born: 4.5%; Speak English only: 94.4%; With disability: 15.6%; Veterans: 14.0%; Ancestry: 22.6% German, 14.8% Irish, 7.8% American, 5.6% English, 3.6% Italian
Employment: 12.5% management, business, and financial, 7.3% computer, engineering, and science, 5.7% education, legal, community service, arts, and media, 6.5% healthcare practitioners, 19.6% service, 23.3% sales and office, 8.8% natural resources, construction, and maintenance, 16.3% production, transportation, and material moving
Income: Per capita: $22,751; Median household: $43,888; Average household: $54,412; Households with income of $100,000 or more: 11.6%; Poverty rate: 14.9%
Educational Attainment: High school diploma or higher: 86.9%; Bachelor's degree or higher: 18.0%; Graduate/professional degree or higher: 6.6%
Housing: Homeownership rate: 54.7%; Median home value: $84,900; Median year structure built: 1962; Homeowner vacancy rate: 3.4%; Median selected monthly owner costs: $1,039 with a mortgage, $392 without a mortgage; Median gross rent: $798 per month; Rental vacancy rate: 3.4%
Health Insurance: 88.8% have insurance; 63.3% have private insurance; 38.4% have public insurance; 11.2% do not have insurance; 5.6% of children under 18 do not have insurance
Safety: Violent crime rate: 20.5 per 10,000 population; Property crime rate: 248.0 per 10,000 population
Transportation: Commute: 95.4% car, 0.4% public transportation, 1.7% walk, 1.2% work from home; Mean travel time to work: 18.5 minutes
Additional Information Contacts
City of Riverside . . . . (937) 233-1801
http://www.riverside.oh.us

TROTWOOD (city). Covers a land area of 30.494 square miles and a water area of 0.014 square miles. Located at 39.79° N. Lat; 84.32° W. Long. Elevation is 837 feet.
Population: 24,372; Growth (since 2000): -11.1%; Density: 799.2 persons per square mile; Race: 24.3% White, 69.9% Black/African American, 0.3% Asian, 0.1% American Indian/Alaska Native, 0.0% Native Hawaiian/Other Pacific Islander, 4.2% Two or more races, 1.8% Hispanic of any race; Average household size: 2.30; Median age: 41.8; Age under 18: 21.4%; Age 65 and over: 19.4%; Males per 100 females: 79.9; Marriage status: 40.2% never married, 36.0% now married, 2.8% separated, 8.4% widowed, 15.4% divorced; Foreign born: 1.5%; Speak English only: 96.9%; With disability: 19.2%; Veterans: 12.0%; Ancestry: 6.2% German, 3.8% Irish, 3.4% American, 2.1% African, 2.0% English
Employment: 9.7% management, business, and financial, 2.6% computer, engineering, and science, 7.3% education, legal, community service, arts, and media, 5.3% healthcare practitioners, 26.4% service, 23.7% sales and office, 4.5% natural resources, construction, and maintenance, 20.6% production, transportation, and material moving
Income: Per capita: $19,702; Median household: $34,490; Average household: $44,562; Households with income of $100,000 or more: 9.4%; Poverty rate: 25.9%
Educational Attainment: High school diploma or higher: 86.2%; Bachelor's degree or higher: 15.1%; Graduate/professional degree or higher: 5.6%

School District(s)

Trotwood Fitness & Prep Acad (KG-08)
2015-16 Enrollment: 347. . . . . (937) 854-4100
Trotwood-Madison City (PK-12)
2015-16 Enrollment: 2,451 . . . . (937) 854-3050
Housing: Homeownership rate: 50.2%; Median home value: $75,800; Median year structure built: 1966; Homeowner vacancy rate: 2.5%; Median selected monthly owner costs: $1,095 with a mortgage, $435 without a mortgage; Median gross rent: $726 per month; Rental vacancy rate: 6.4%
Health Insurance: 90.0% have insurance; 53.4% have private insurance; 51.9% have public insurance; 10.0% do not have insurance; 4.3% of children under 18 do not have insurance
Safety: Violent crime rate: 37.5 per 10,000 population; Property crime rate: 400.4 per 10,000 population
Transportation: Commute: 91.2% car, 4.9% public transportation, 1.5% walk, 1.5% work from home; Mean travel time to work: 25.9 minutes; Amtrak: Bus service available.
Additional Information Contacts
City of Trotwood . . . . (937) 837-7771
http://www.trotwood.org

UNION (city). Covers a land area of 7.050 square miles and a water area of 0.076 square miles. Located at 39.92° N. Lat; 84.29° W. Long. Elevation is 922 feet.
Population: 6,569; Growth (since 2000): 17.9%; Density: 931.8 persons per square mile; Race: 98.3% White, 0.0% Black/African American, 0.4% Asian, 0.0% American Indian/Alaska Native, 0.0% Native Hawaiian/Other Pacific Islander, 0.2% Two or more races, 2.2% Hispanic of any race; Average household size: 2.63; Median age: 37.6; Age under 18: 25.1%; Age 65 and over: 12.7%; Males per 100 females: 92.6; Marriage status: 20.9% never married, 62.6% now married, 1.9% separated, 4.2% widowed, 12.3% divorced; Foreign born: 0.7%; Speak English only: 98.1%; With disability: 11.9%; Veterans: 12.5%; Ancestry: 38.1% German, 20.6% Irish, 9.0% American, 5.7% French, 5.0% English
Employment: 13.4% management, business, and financial, 1.8% computer, engineering, and science, 9.1% education, legal, community service, arts, and media, 6.0% healthcare practitioners, 20.5% service, 27.7% sales and office, 6.1% natural resources, construction, and maintenance, 15.3% production, transportation, and material moving
Income: Per capita: $28,324; Median household: $64,608; Average household: $74,724; Households with income of $100,000 or more: 17.0%; Poverty rate: 8.2%
Educational Attainment: High school diploma or higher: 95.3%; Bachelor's degree or higher: 16.7%; Graduate/professional degree or higher: 5.0%

School District(s)

Northmont City (PK-12)
2015-16 Enrollment: 5,074 . . . . (937) 832-5000
Housing: Homeownership rate: 84.8%; Median home value: $91,400; Median year structure built: 1974; Homeowner vacancy rate: 2.1%; Median selected monthly owner costs: $1,185 with a mortgage, $518 without a mortgage; Median gross rent: $950 per month; Rental vacancy rate: 3.3%
Health Insurance: 95.5% have insurance; 76.3% have private insurance; 29.3% have public insurance; 4.5% do not have insurance; 1.0% of children under 18 do not have insurance
Transportation: Commute: 95.8% car, 0.4% public transportation, 0.0% walk, 3.1% work from home; Mean travel time to work: 24.7 minutes
Additional Information Contacts
City of Union . . . . (937) 836-8624
http://www.ci.union.oh.us

VANDALIA (city). Covers a land area of 12.344 square miles and a water area of 0.068 square miles. Located at 39.88° N. Lat; 84.19° W. Long. Elevation is 991 feet.
History: Vandalia was settled in 1838 and named for Vandalia, Illinois. Vandalia was known as the site of the largest shotgun tournament in the world, held by the Amateur Trapshooters' Association.
Population: 15,127; Growth (since 2000): 3.6%; Density: 1,225.5 persons per square mile; Race: 89.4% White, 6.2% Black/African American, 1.0%

Asian, 0.0% American Indian/Alaska Native, 0.0% Native Hawaiian/Other Pacific Islander, 3.1% Two or more races, 1.6% Hispanic of any race; Average household size: 2.31; Median age: 43.0; Age under 18: 22.0%; Age 65 and over: 17.8%; Males per 100 females: 93.9; Marriage status: 25.9% never married, 54.4% now married, 1.4% separated, 6.2% widowed, 13.5% divorced; Foreign born: 3.1%; Speak English only: 96.5%; With disability: 13.4%; Veterans: 9.4%; Ancestry: 26.8% German, 17.2% Irish, 9.5% English, 7.5% American, 5.9% Italian

Employment: 14.7% management, business, and financial, 3.3% computer, engineering, and science, 7.9% education, legal, community service, arts, and media, 6.9% healthcare practitioners, 18.0% service, 27.1% sales and office, 4.9% natural resources, construction, and maintenance, 17.2% production, transportation, and material moving

Income: Per capita: $28,867; Median household: $52,700; Average household: $66,615; Households with income of $100,000 or more: 20.6%; Poverty rate: 9.2%

Educational Attainment: High school diploma or higher: 90.4%; Bachelor's degree or higher: 23.8%; Graduate/professional degree or higher: 9.0%

School District(s)

Vandalia-Butler City (PK-12)
2015-16 Enrollment: 2,986 . . . . (937) 415-6400

Housing: Homeownership rate: 61.3%; Median home value: $135,000; Median year structure built: 1971; Homeowner vacancy rate: 2.2%; Median selected monthly owner costs: $1,266 with a mortgage, $438 without a mortgage; Median gross rent: $692 per month; Rental vacancy rate: 2.1%

Health Insurance: 93.2% have insurance; 74.1% have private insurance; 31.2% have public insurance; 6.8% do not have insurance; 2.1% of children under 18 do not have insurance

Safety: Violent crime rate: 9.3 per 10,000 population; Property crime rate: 217.6 per 10,000 population

Transportation: Commute: 94.3% car, 0.9% public transportation, 0.3% walk, 3.4% work from home; Mean travel time to work: 20.0 minutes

Additional Information Contacts

City of Vandalia . . . . (937) 415-2254
http://www.ci.vandalia.oh.us

WEST CARROLLTON (city). Covers a land area of 6.439 square miles and a water area of 0.218 square miles. Located at 39.67° N. Lat; 84.26° W. Long. Elevation is 715 feet.

Population: 13,012; Growth (since 2000): n/a; Density: 2,021.0 persons per square mile; Race: 82.6% White, 12.4% Black/African American, 1.0% Asian, 0.1% American Indian/Alaska Native, 0.1% Native Hawaiian/Other Pacific Islander, 3.3% Two or more races, 3.2% Hispanic of any race; Average household size: 2.15; Median age: 36.6; Age under 18: 19.8%; Age 65 and over: 16.2%; Males per 100 females: 93.0; Marriage status: 34.0% never married, 39.6% now married, 1.5% separated, 7.9% widowed, 18.5% divorced; Foreign born: 6.2%; Speak English only: 92.6%; With disability: 15.2%; Veterans: 9.7%; Ancestry: 18.5% German, 11.3% Irish, 8.4% English, 5.4% American, 2.7% French

Employment: 9.5% management, business, and financial, 4.6% computer, engineering, and science, 4.8% education, legal, community service, arts, and media, 6.8% healthcare practitioners, 19.1% service, 24.7% sales and office, 10.7% natural resources, construction, and maintenance, 19.9% production, transportation, and material moving

Income: Per capita: $21,665; Median household: $37,814; Average household: $45,998; Households with income of $100,000 or more: 8.4%; Poverty rate: 19.9%

Educational Attainment: High school diploma or higher: 89.6%; Bachelor's degree or higher: 13.8%; Graduate/professional degree or higher: 3.2%

School District(s)

West Carrollton City (PK-12)
2015-16 Enrollment: 3,864 . . . . (937) 859-5121

Housing: Homeownership rate: 53.1%; Median home value: $90,700; Median year structure built: 1972; Homeowner vacancy rate: 2.5%; Median selected monthly owner costs: $1,049 with a mortgage, $433 without a mortgage; Median gross rent: $770 per month; Rental vacancy rate: 8.9%

Health Insurance: 89.7% have insurance; 62.3% have private insurance; 42.4% have public insurance; 10.3% do not have insurance; 2.0% of children under 18 do not have insurance

Safety: Violent crime rate: 17.0 per 10,000 population; Property crime rate: 276.6 per 10,000 population

Transportation: Commute: 95.8% car, 0.9% public transportation, 1.6% walk, 1.0% work from home; Mean travel time to work: 20.5 minutes

Additional Information Contacts

City of West Carrollton . . . . (937) 859-5183
http://www.westcarrollton.org

Morgan County

Located in east central Ohio; crossed by the Muskingum River, and Meigs and Wolf Creeks. Covers a land area of 416.423 square miles, a water area of 5.360 square miles, and is located in the Eastern Time Zone at 39.62° N. Lat., 81.86° W. Long. The county was founded in 1817. County seat is McConnelsville.

Weather Station: Mc Connelsville Lock 7 Elevation: 759 feet

	Jan	Feb	Mar	Apr	May	Jun	Jul	Aug	Sep	Oct	Nov	Dec
High	38	42	52	64	73	81	84	83	77	65	54	42
Low	20	21	28	38	47	57	61	60	52	40	32	24
Precip	3.1	2.5	3.7	3.8	4.7	4.1	4.6	3.6	3.2	2.9	3.5	3.2
Snow	6.6	5.4	2.4	0.7	0.0	0.0	0.0	0.0	0.0	tr	0.4	3.3

High and Low temperatures in degrees Fahrenheit; Precipitation and Snow in inches

Population: 14,857; Growth (since 2000): -0.3%; Density: 35.7 persons per square mile; Race: 93.2% White, 3.2% Black/African American, 0.1% Asian, 0.3% American Indian/Alaska Native, 0.0% Native Hawaiian/Other Pacific Islander, 3.0% two or more races, 0.8% Hispanic of any race; Average household size: 2.47; Median age: 43.8; Age under 18: 22.0%; Age 65 and over: 19.3%; Males per 100 females: 99.3; Marriage status: 23.9% never married, 56.6% now married, 2.0% separated, 6.4% widowed, 13.2% divorced; Foreign born: 0.5%; Speak English only: 97.3%; With disability: 20.9%; Veterans: 10.4%; Ancestry: 21.5% German, 13.4% Irish, 12.5% English, 9.7% American, 1.8% Italian

Religion: Six largest groups: 9.9% Methodist/Pietist, 9.2% Baptist, 1.7% European Free-Church, 1.4% Non-denominational Protestant, 0.9% Catholicism, 0.8% Presbyterian-Reformed

Economy: Unemployment rate: 5.2%; Leading industries: 18.9 % retail trade; 17.6 % other services (except public administration); 10.7 % construction; Farms: 510 totaling 95,174 acres; Company size: 0 employ 1,000 or more persons, 0 employ 500 to 999 persons, 4 employ 100 to 499 persons, 155 employ less than 100 persons; Business ownership: 312 women-owned, 29 Black-owned, n/a Hispanic-owned, n/a Asian-owned, n/a American Indian/Alaska Native-owned

Employment: 10.9% management, business, and financial, 2.4% computer, engineering, and science, 8.9% education, legal, community service, arts, and media, 9.4% healthcare practitioners, 14.2% service, 17.6% sales and office, 15.6% natural resources, construction, and maintenance, 21.0% production, transportation, and material moving

Income: Per capita: $20,301; Median household: $38,941; Average household: $49,702; Households with income of $100,000 or more: 9.5%; Poverty rate: 20.3%

Educational Attainment: High school diploma or higher: 87.7%; Bachelor's degree or higher: 12.2%; Graduate/professional degree or higher: 3.8%

Housing: Homeownership rate: 76.7%; Median home value: $91,400; Median year structure built: 1970; Homeowner vacancy rate: 1.5%; Median selected monthly owner costs: $1,025 with a mortgage, $323 without a mortgage; Median gross rent: $536 per month; Rental vacancy rate: 4.3%

Vital Statistics: Birth rate: 102.0 per 10,000 population; Death rate: 100.0 per 10,000 population; Age-adjusted cancer mortality rate: 179.0 deaths per 100,000 population

Health Insurance: 88.9% have insurance; 58.3% have private insurance; 46.9% have public insurance; 11.1% do not have insurance; 7.8% of children under 18 do not have insurance

Health Care: Physicians: 2.0 per 10,000 population; Dentists: 1.4 per 10,000 population; Hospital beds: 0.0 per 10,000 population; Hospital admissions: 0.0 per 10,000 population

Air Quality Index (AQI): Percent of Days: 100.0% good, 0.0% moderate, 0.0% unhealthy for sensitive individuals, 0.0% unhealthy, 0.0% very unhealthy; Annual median: 1; Annual maximum: 40

Transportation: Commute: 92.5% car, 0.6% public transportation, 2.4% walk, 3.1% work from home; Mean travel time to work: 33.1 minutes

2016 Presidential Election: 68.4% Trump, 26.8% Clinton, 3.0% Johnson, 0.7% Stein

National and State Parks: Big Bottom State Memorial Park; Burr Oak State Park; Muskingum River Parkway State Park

Additional Information Contacts

Morgan Government . . . . (740) 962-3183
http://www.morgancounty-oh.gov

Morgan County Communities

CHESTERHILL (village). Covers a land area of 0.539 square miles and a water area of 0.003 square miles. Located at 39.49° N. Lat; 81.87° W. Long. Elevation is 974 feet.
Population: 398; Growth (since 2000): 30.5%; Density: 737.8 persons per square mile; Race: 60.1% White, 26.1% Black/African American, 0.0% Asian, 0.0% American Indian/Alaska Native, 0.0% Native Hawaiian/Other Pacific Islander, 12.3% Two or more races, 1.8% Hispanic of any race; Average household size: 2.67; Median age: 35.0; Age under 18: 27.6%; Age 65 and over: 18.8%; Males per 100 females: 90.1; Marriage status: 24.5% never married, 58.5% now married, 0.7% separated, 10.5% widowed, 6.5% divorced; Foreign born: 0.5%; Speak English only: 100.0%; With disability: 21.9%; Veterans: 9.4%; Ancestry: 19.1% German, 12.6% Irish, 9.0% English, 8.5% American, 4.3% Dutch
Employment: 10.6% management, business, and financial, 2.8% computer, engineering, and science, 6.3% education, legal, community service, arts, and media, 14.8% healthcare practitioners, 16.9% service, 6.3% sales and office, 21.8% natural resources, construction, and maintenance, 20.4% production, transportation, and material moving
Income: Per capita: $17,024; Median household: $37,250; Average household: $44,398; Households with income of $100,000 or more: 4.0%; Poverty rate: 20.3%
Educational Attainment: High school diploma or higher: 83.5%; Bachelor's degree or higher: 5.4%; Graduate/professional degree or higher: 3.4%
Housing: Homeownership rate: 71.8%; Median home value: $53,800; Median year structure built: Before 1940; Homeowner vacancy rate: 5.3%; Median selected monthly owner costs: $841 with a mortgage, $332 without a mortgage; Median gross rent: $529 per month; Rental vacancy rate: 10.6%
Health Insurance: 90.5% have insurance; 60.1% have private insurance; 48.7% have public insurance; 9.5% do not have insurance; 5.5% of children under 18 do not have insurance
Transportation: Commute: 96.2% car, 0.0% public transportation, 3.8% walk, 0.0% work from home; Mean travel time to work: 37.7 minutes

MALTA (village). Covers a land area of 0.343 square miles and a water area of 0.043 square miles. Located at 39.65° N. Lat; 81.86° W. Long. Elevation is 676 feet.
History: Malta was founded in 1816 by Simeon Pool and John Bell, who owned the land. The town was named for the island of Malta in the Mediterranean where Pool had visited.
Population: 837; Growth (since 2000): 20.3%; Density: 2,437.1 persons per square mile; Race: 82.3% White, 11.5% Black/African American, 0.2% Asian, 0.0% American Indian/Alaska Native, 0.0% Native Hawaiian/Other Pacific Islander, 6.0% Two or more races, 0.0% Hispanic of any race; Average household size: 2.67; Median age: 29.4; Age under 18: 37.0%; Age 65 and over: 8.1%; Males per 100 females: 96.2; Marriage status: 25.3% never married, 64.6% now married, 3.5% separated, 1.7% widowed, 8.4% divorced; Foreign born: 0.2%; Speak English only: 99.6%; With disability: 18.2%; Veterans: 8.6%; Ancestry: 15.2% German, 12.5% Irish, 12.1% English, 3.0% American, 2.5% Polish
Employment: 8.3% management, business, and financial, 0.7% computer, engineering, and science, 10.1% education, legal, community service, arts, and media, 2.5% healthcare practitioners, 20.7% service, 18.1% sales and office, 11.6% natural resources, construction, and maintenance, 27.9% production, transportation, and material moving
Income: Per capita: $13,570; Median household: $26,481; Average household: $36,239; Households with income of $100,000 or more: 3.5%; Poverty rate: 28.1%
Educational Attainment: High school diploma or higher: 86.6%; Bachelor's degree or higher: 15.3%; Graduate/professional degree or higher: 3.3%

School District(s)

Morgan Local (PK-12)
2015-16 Enrollment: 1,954 . . . . (740) 962-2782
Housing: Homeownership rate: 63.5%; Median home value: $69,100; Median year structure built: Before 1940; Homeowner vacancy rate: 4.3%; Median selected monthly owner costs: $700 with a mortgage, $320 without a mortgage; Median gross rent: $632 per month; Rental vacancy rate: 4.2%
Health Insurance: 92.0% have insurance; 54.4% have private insurance; 50.8% have public insurance; 8.0% do not have insurance; 4.2% of children under 18 do not have insurance
Transportation: Commute: 90.9% car, 0.7% public transportation, 2.2% walk, 3.6% work from home; Mean travel time to work: 18.7 minutes

MCCONNELSVILLE (village). County seat. Covers a land area of 1.785 square miles and a water area of 0.112 square miles. Located at 39.66° N. Lat; 81.84° W. Long. Elevation is 696 feet.
History: McConnelsville was platted in 1817 by General Robert McConnell, and became a Muskingum River shipping port for salt bound for Pittsburgh by keelboat.
Population: 1,899; Growth (since 2000): 13.3%; Density: 1,064.0 persons per square mile; Race: 90.5% White, 6.2% Black/African American, 0.0% Asian, 0.3% American Indian/Alaska Native, 0.0% Native Hawaiian/Other Pacific Islander, 1.7% Two or more races, 0.0% Hispanic of any race; Average household size: 2.14; Median age: 48.9; Age under 18: 19.6%; Age 65 and over: 29.2%; Males per 100 females: 82.0; Marriage status: 27.3% never married, 37.4% now married, 1.5% separated, 14.3% widowed, 21.0% divorced; Foreign born: 0.7%; Speak English only: 99.1%; With disability: 24.3%; Veterans: 7.6%; Ancestry: 29.4% German, 15.1% Irish, 11.8% English, 10.6% American, 2.5% French
Employment: 6.7% management, business, and financial, 2.9% computer, engineering, and science, 8.9% education, legal, community service, arts, and media, 11.7% healthcare practitioners, 22.2% service, 20.9% sales and office, 12.0% natural resources, construction, and maintenance, 14.6% production, transportation, and material moving
Income: Per capita: $19,740; Median household: $30,000; Average household: $41,966; Households with income of $100,000 or more: 5.4%; Poverty rate: 28.2%
Educational Attainment: High school diploma or higher: 87.9%; Bachelor's degree or higher: 13.9%; Graduate/professional degree or higher: 6.0%

School District(s)

Morgan Local (PK-12)
2015-16 Enrollment: 1,954 . . . . (740) 962-2782
Housing: Homeownership rate: 45.8%; Median home value: $87,700; Median year structure built: 1953; Homeowner vacancy rate: 1.0%; Median selected monthly owner costs: $1,070 with a mortgage, $351 without a mortgage; Median gross rent: $520 per month; Rental vacancy rate: 6.8%
Health Insurance: 92.3% have insurance; 49.4% have private insurance; 61.8% have public insurance; 7.7% do not have insurance; 2.7% of children under 18 do not have insurance
Safety: Violent crime rate: 22.3 per 10,000 population; Property crime rate: 162.0 per 10,000 population
Newspapers: Morgan County Herald (weekly circulation 5,000)
Transportation: Commute: 87.6% car, 1.5% public transportation, 5.7% walk, 4.3% work from home; Mean travel time to work: 20.2 minutes

ROSE FARM (CDP).
Land/water area and latitude/longitude are not available.
Population: 298; Growth (since 2000): n/a; Density: n/a persons per square mile; Race: 100.0% White, 0.0% Black/African American, 0.0% Asian, 0.0% American Indian/Alaska Native, 0.0% Native Hawaiian/Other Pacific Islander, 0.0% Two or more races, 0.0% Hispanic of any race; Average household size: 3.97; Median age: 38.9; Age under 18: 18.5%; Age 65 and over: 17.8%; Males per 100 females: 0.0; Marriage status: 62.9% never married, 17.0% now married, 0.0% separated, 9.5% widowed, 10.6% divorced; Foreign born: 0.0%; Speak English only: 100.0%; With disability: 5.4%; Veterans: 0.0%; Ancestry: 30.9% American, 2.7% French Canadian
Employment: 33.8% management, business, and financial, 0.0% computer, engineering, and science, 0.0% education, legal, community service, arts, and media, 26.2% healthcare practitioners, 0.0% service, 10.8% sales and office, 29.2% natural resources, construction, and maintenance, 0.0% production, transportation, and material moving
Income: Per capita: $11,053; Median household: $37,865; Average household: $40,111; Households with income of $100,000 or more: n/a; Poverty rate: 25.5%
Educational Attainment: High school diploma or higher: 96.2%; Bachelor's degree or higher: 10.4%; Graduate/professional degree or higher: n/a
Housing: Homeownership rate: 100.0%; Median home value: $70,500; Median year structure built: 1992; Homeowner vacancy rate: 0.0%; Median

selected monthly owner costs: n/a with a mortgage, $353 without a mortgage; Median gross rent: n/a per month; Rental vacancy rate: 0.0%
Health Insurance: 80.2% have insurance; 33.2% have private insurance; 64.8% have public insurance; 19.8% do not have insurance; 0.0% of children under 18 do not have insurance
Safety: Violent crime rate: 0.0 per 10,000 population; Property crime rate: 0.0 per 10,000 population
Transportation: Commute: 100.0% car, 0.0% public transportation, 0.0% walk, 0.0% work from home; Mean travel time to work: 0.0 minutes

STOCKPORT (village). Covers a land area of 0.329 square miles and a water area of 0 square miles. Located at 39.55° N. Lat; 81.79° W. Long. Elevation is 692 feet.
Population: 549; Growth (since 2000): 1.7%; Density: 1,670.8 persons per square mile; Race: 86.9% White, 4.2% Black/African American, 1.8% Asian, 0.0% American Indian/Alaska Native, 0.0% Native Hawaiian/Other Pacific Islander, 7.1% Two or more races, 0.0% Hispanic of any race; Average household size: 2.60; Median age: 40.9; Age under 18: 24.0%; Age 65 and over: 20.9%; Males per 100 females: 87.7; Marriage status: 27.1% never married, 54.9% now married, 1.4% separated, 6.4% widowed, 11.6% divorced; Foreign born: 1.1%; Speak English only: 97.8%; With disability: 21.5%; Veterans: 7.0%; Ancestry: 24.4% German, 21.5% Irish, 9.8% English, 5.5% American, 1.6% Italian
Employment: 10.1% management, business, and financial, 2.2% computer, engineering, and science, 12.4% education, legal, community service, arts, and media, 5.1% healthcare practitioners, 24.2% service, 22.5% sales and office, 6.7% natural resources, construction, and maintenance, 16.9% production, transportation, and material moving
Income: Per capita: $15,193; Median household: $26,406; Average household: $38,049; Households with income of $100,000 or more: 5.7%; Poverty rate: 27.0%
Educational Attainment: High school diploma or higher: 77.7%; Bachelor's degree or higher: 5.1%; Graduate/professional degree or higher: 1.4%

School District(s)

Morgan Local (PK-12)
2015-16 Enrollment: 1,954 . . . . (740) 962-2782
Housing: Homeownership rate: 62.1%; Median home value: $79,500; Median year structure built: 1960; Homeowner vacancy rate: 0.0%; Median selected monthly owner costs: $886 with a mortgage, $353 without a mortgage; Median gross rent: $529 per month; Rental vacancy rate: 19.2%
Health Insurance: 89.1% have insurance; 40.1% have private insurance; 64.8% have public insurance; 10.9% do not have insurance; 6.8% of children under 18 do not have insurance
Transportation: Commute: 93.8% car, 0.0% public transportation, 2.8% walk, 1.1% work from home; Mean travel time to work: 32.1 minutes

Morrow County

Located in central Ohio; drained by the Kokosing River and Whetstone and Big Walnut Creeks. Covers a land area of 406.079 square miles, a water area of 1.143 square miles, and is located in the Eastern Time Zone at 40.53° N. Lat., 82.80° W. Long. The county was founded in 1848. County seat is Mount Gilead.

Morrow County is part of the Columbus, OH Metropolitan Statistical Area. The entire metro area includes: Delaware County, OH; Fairfield County, OH; Franklin County, OH; Hocking County, OH; Licking County, OH; Madison County, OH; Morrow County, OH; Perry County, OH; Pickaway County, OH; Union County, OH

Population: 35,032; Growth (since 2000): 10.8%; Density: 86.3 persons per square mile; Race: 97.5% White, 0.6% Black/African American, 0.1% Asian, 0.1% American Indian/Alaska Native, 0.0% Native Hawaiian/Other Pacific Islander, 1.7% two or more races, 1.4% Hispanic of any race; Average household size: 2.75; Median age: 41.5; Age under 18: 24.8%; Age 65 and over: 15.6%; Males per 100 females: 100.5; Marriage status: 23.5% never married, 57.8% now married, 1.3% separated, 7.0% widowed, 11.8% divorced; Foreign born: 0.4%; Speak English only: 97.4%; With disability: 14.4%; Veterans: 9.3%; Ancestry: 28.2% German, 13.1% Irish, 12.2% American, 10.9% English, 2.9% Italian
Religion: Six largest groups: 8.2% Methodist/Pietist, 4.5% Baptist, 3.4% Holiness, 3.1% European Free-Church, 1.9% Non-denominational Protestant, 1.2% Catholicism
Economy: Unemployment rate: 4.3%; Leading industries: 14.4 % construction; 13.3 % retail trade; 13.3 % other services (except public administration); Farms: 824 totaling 167,736 acres; Company size: 0 employ 1,000 or more persons, 1 employs 500 to 999 persons, 3 employ 100 to 499 persons, 371 employs less than 100 persons; Business ownership: 794 women-owned, n/a Black-owned, 36 Hispanic-owned, n/a Asian-owned, n/a American Indian/Alaska Native-owned
Employment: 10.8% management, business, and financial, 3.8% computer, engineering, and science, 6.7% education, legal, community service, arts, and media, 6.3% healthcare practitioners, 15.8% service, 21.0% sales and office, 13.3% natural resources, construction, and maintenance, 22.2% production, transportation, and material moving
Income: Per capita: $23,630; Median household: $53,032; Average household: $63,992; Households with income of $100,000 or more: 18.0%; Poverty rate: 11.0%
Educational Attainment: High school diploma or higher: 86.1%; Bachelor's degree or higher: 13.5%; Graduate/professional degree or higher: 4.1%
Housing: Homeownership rate: 81.4%; Median home value: $137,800; Median year structure built: 1979; Homeowner vacancy rate: 1.1%; Median selected monthly owner costs: $1,190 with a mortgage, $443 without a mortgage; Median gross rent: $639 per month; Rental vacancy rate: 3.7%
Vital Statistics: Birth rate: 106.5 per 10,000 population; Death rate: 91.0 per 10,000 population; Age-adjusted cancer mortality rate: 168.7 deaths per 100,000 population
Health Insurance: 91.1% have insurance; 70.4% have private insurance; 34.2% have public insurance; 8.9% do not have insurance; 5.0% of children under 18 do not have insurance
Health Care: Physicians: 2.8 per 10,000 population; Dentists: 1.4 per 10,000 population; Hospital beds: 6.6 per 10,000 population; Hospital admissions: 138.8 per 10,000 population
Transportation: Commute: 93.5% car, 0.8% public transportation, 1.2% walk, 3.4% work from home; Mean travel time to work: 30.2 minutes
2016 Presidential Election: 71.6% Trump, 22.5% Clinton, 3.4% Johnson, 0.6% Stein
National and State Parks: Mount Gilead State Park
Additional Information Contacts
Morrow Government . . . . (419) 947-4085
http://www.morrowcounty.info

Morrow County Communities

CANDLEWOOD LAKE (CDP). Covers a land area of 2.254 square miles and a water area of 0.309 square miles. Located at 40.62° N. Lat; 82.77° W. Long.
Population: 1,005; Growth (since 2000): n/a; Density: 445.8 persons per square mile; Race: 100.0% White, 0.0% Black/African American, 0.0% Asian, 0.0% American Indian/Alaska Native, 0.0% Native Hawaiian/Other Pacific Islander, 0.0% Two or more races, 8.4% Hispanic of any race; Average household size: 2.75; Median age: 41.7; Age under 18: 22.7%; Age 65 and over: 19.0%; Males per 100 females: 98.8; Marriage status: 12.2% never married, 82.9% now married, 1.0% separated, 0.0% widowed, 4.9% divorced; Foreign born: 0.0%; Speak English only: 100.0%; With disability: 4.5%; Veterans: 6.4%; Ancestry: 29.8% German, 17.6% English, 16.3% American, 5.9% Irish, 5.9% Scottish
Employment: 0.0% management, business, and financial, 0.0% computer, engineering, and science, 17.5% education, legal, community service, arts, and media, 0.0% healthcare practitioners, 0.0% service, 31.1% sales and office, 18.4% natural resources, construction, and maintenance, 33.0% production, transportation, and material moving
Income: Per capita: $28,707; Median household: $62,222; Average household: $77,714; Households with income of $100,000 or more: 26.0%; Poverty rate: 7.9%
Educational Attainment: High school diploma or higher: 86.9%; Bachelor's degree or higher: 28.9%; Graduate/professional degree or higher: 10.7%
Housing: Homeownership rate: 97.8%; Median home value: $114,100; Median year structure built: 1996; Homeowner vacancy rate: 6.8%; Median selected monthly owner costs: $980 with a mortgage, $523 without a mortgage; Median gross rent: n/a per month; Rental vacancy rate: 0.0%
Health Insurance: 87.9% have insurance; 70.6% have private insurance; 34.1% have public insurance; 12.1% do not have insurance; 0.0% of children under 18 do not have insurance
Transportation: Commute: 100.0% car, 0.0% public transportation, 0.0% walk, 0.0% work from home; Mean travel time to work: 33.5 minutes

CARDINGTON (village). Covers a land area of 2.006 square miles and a water area of 0 square miles. Located at 40.50° N. Lat; 82.89° W. Long. Elevation is 1,007 feet.

History: Cardington was founded in 1822 and named for an old carding mill here. After the Civil War, Cardington became a lumber town.

Population: 2,009; Growth (since 2000): 8.7%; Density: 1,001.4 persons per square mile; Race: 98.5% White, 0.3% Black/African American, 0.0% Asian, 0.2% American Indian/Alaska Native, 0.0% Native Hawaiian/Other Pacific Islander, 0.7% Two or more races, 1.1% Hispanic of any race; Average household size: 2.71; Median age: 32.1; Age under 18: 31.4%; Age 65 and over: 9.7%; Males per 100 females: 93.1; Marriage status: 28.8% never married, 43.2% now married, 2.6% separated, 6.3% widowed, 21.8% divorced; Foreign born: 0.3%; Speak English only: 99.4%; With disability: 19.6%; Veterans: 7.6%; Ancestry: 25.6% German, 14.6% Irish, 10.7% American, 9.7% English, 3.4% Italian

Employment: 6.4% management, business, and financial, 0.6% computer, engineering, and science, 5.3% education, legal, community service, arts, and media, 2.1% healthcare practitioners, 20.4% service, 28.1% sales and office, 11.3% natural resources, construction, and maintenance, 25.7% production, transportation, and material moving

Income: Per capita: $15,148; Median household: $30,369; Average household: $40,631; Households with income of $100,000 or more: 7.3%; Poverty rate: 33.2%

Educational Attainment: High school diploma or higher: 86.2%; Bachelor's degree or higher: 7.8%; Graduate/professional degree or higher: 1.9%

School District(s)

Cardington-Lincoln Local (PK-12)
2015-16 Enrollment: 1,089 . . . . (419) 864-3691

Housing: Homeownership rate: 57.1%; Median home value: $87,700; Median year structure built: 1970; Homeowner vacancy rate: 0.0%; Median selected monthly owner costs: $996 with a mortgage, $469 without a mortgage; Median gross rent: $636 per month; Rental vacancy rate: 9.2%

Health Insurance: 89.6% have insurance; 50.5% have private insurance; 48.4% have public insurance; 10.4% do not have insurance; 2.1% of children under 18 do not have insurance

Transportation: Commute: 91.6% car, 2.0% public transportation, 5.0% walk, 0.2% work from home; Mean travel time to work: 31.0 minutes

CHESTERVILLE (village). Covers a land area of 0.205 square miles and a water area of 0.007 square miles. Located at 40.47° N. Lat; 82.68° W. Long. Elevation is 1,145 feet.

Population: 186; Growth (since 2000): -3.6%; Density: 909.3 persons per square mile; Race: 89.8% White, 5.4% Black/African American, 0.0% Asian, 0.0% American Indian/Alaska Native, 0.0% Native Hawaiian/Other Pacific Islander, 2.7% Two or more races, 2.2% Hispanic of any race; Average household size: 2.77; Median age: 45.0; Age under 18: 28.0%; Age 65 and over: 26.3%; Males per 100 females: 83.9; Marriage status: 18.6% never married, 41.4% now married, 0.0% separated, 19.3% widowed, 20.7% divorced; Foreign born: 0.0%; Speak English only: 97.7%; With disability: 22.8%; Veterans: 9.7%; Ancestry: 23.7% German, 15.1% American, 10.8% English, 8.6% Italian, 5.9% Irish

Employment: 15.3% management, business, and financial, 1.7% computer, engineering, and science, 11.9% education, legal, community service, arts, and media, 6.8% healthcare practitioners, 23.7% service, 18.6% sales and office, 10.2% natural resources, construction, and maintenance, 11.9% production, transportation, and material moving

Income: Per capita: $19,512; Median household: $44,063; Average household: $53,837; Households with income of $100,000 or more: 8.8%; Poverty rate: 3.8%

Educational Attainment: High school diploma or higher: 86.5%; Bachelor's degree or higher: 20.6%; Graduate/professional degree or higher: 7.9%

Housing: Homeownership rate: 86.0%; Median home value: $87,000; Median year structure built: Before 1940; Homeowner vacancy rate: 0.0%; Median selected monthly owner costs: $831 with a mortgage, $467 without a mortgage; Median gross rent: $700 per month; Rental vacancy rate: 0.0%

Health Insurance: 96.2% have insurance; 75.3% have private insurance; 52.5% have public insurance; 3.8% do not have insurance; 0.0% of children under 18 do not have insurance

Transportation: Commute: 92.5% car, 0.0% public transportation, 0.0% walk, 7.5% work from home; Mean travel time to work: 34.5 minutes

EDISON (village). Covers a land area of 0.287 square miles and a water area of 0 square miles. Located at 40.56° N. Lat; 82.86° W. Long. Elevation is 1,063 feet.

Population: 415; Growth (since 2000): -5.0%; Density: 1,443.9 persons per square mile; Race: 94.7% White, 0.0% Black/African American, 0.0% Asian, 0.0% American Indian/Alaska Native, 0.0% Native Hawaiian/Other Pacific Islander, 5.3% Two or more races, 7.0% Hispanic of any race; Average household size: 2.75; Median age: 40.6; Age under 18: 23.4%; Age 65 and over: 15.4%; Males per 100 females: 92.5; Marriage status: 27.5% never married, 49.4% now married, 5.0% separated, 8.9% widowed, 14.2% divorced; Foreign born: 1.7%; Speak English only: 96.5%; With disability: 27.5%; Veterans: 7.5%; Ancestry: 21.7% German, 16.9% American, 11.1% Irish, 7.2% English, 5.5% Polish

Employment: 9.4% management, business, and financial, 0.0% computer, engineering, and science, 2.7% education, legal, community service, arts, and media, 4.7% healthcare practitioners, 12.8% service, 22.1% sales and office, 14.8% natural resources, construction, and maintenance, 33.6% production, transportation, and material moving

Income: Per capita: $19,715; Median household: $39,375; Average household: $48,830; Households with income of $100,000 or more: 10.5%; Poverty rate: 22.2%

Educational Attainment: High school diploma or higher: 84.6%; Bachelor's degree or higher: 6.2%; Graduate/professional degree or higher: 2.1%

School District(s)

Tomorrow Center (06-12)
2015-16 Enrollment: 96. . . . . (419) 718-4242

Housing: Homeownership rate: 65.6%; Median home value: $82,200; Median year structure built: Before 1940; Homeowner vacancy rate: 0.0%; Median selected monthly owner costs: $852 with a mortgage, $332 without a mortgage; Median gross rent: $695 per month; Rental vacancy rate: 8.8%

Health Insurance: 92.5% have insurance; 51.8% have private insurance; 52.0% have public insurance; 7.5% do not have insurance; 3.1% of children under 18 do not have insurance

Transportation: Commute: 91.2% car, 3.4% public transportation, 0.0% walk, 2.7% work from home; Mean travel time to work: 33.8 minutes

FULTON (village). Covers a land area of 0.153 square miles and a water area of 0 square miles. Located at 40.46° N. Lat; 82.83° W. Long. Elevation is 1,106 feet.

Population: 224; Growth (since 2000): -15.2%; Density: 1,463.9 persons per square mile; Race: 100.0% White, 0.0% Black/African American, 0.0% Asian, 0.0% American Indian/Alaska Native, 0.0% Native Hawaiian/Other Pacific Islander, 0.0% Two or more races, 5.8% Hispanic of any race; Average household size: 2.57; Median age: 35.8; Age under 18: 28.6%; Age 65 and over: 10.7%; Males per 100 females: 88.3; Marriage status: 29.1% never married, 50.3% now married, 1.1% separated, 6.3% widowed, 14.3% divorced; Foreign born: 0.0%; Speak English only: 100.0%; With disability: 17.4%; Veterans: 8.8%; Ancestry: 27.2% German, 22.3% American, 14.3% Irish, 12.1% English, 4.0% Welsh

Employment: 8.1% management, business, and financial, 5.1% computer, engineering, and science, 4.0% education, legal, community service, arts, and media, 5.1% healthcare practitioners, 29.3% service, 13.1% sales and office, 16.2% natural resources, construction, and maintenance, 19.2% production, transportation, and material moving

Income: Per capita: $17,807; Median household: $43,750; Average household: $44,409; Households with income of $100,000 or more: 4.6%; Poverty rate: 13.0%

Educational Attainment: High school diploma or higher: 89.8%; Bachelor's degree or higher: 5.4%; Graduate/professional degree or higher: 1.4%

Housing: Homeownership rate: 80.5%; Median home value: $96,700; Median year structure built: 1958; Homeowner vacancy rate: 5.4%; Median selected monthly owner costs: $1,019 with a mortgage, $350 without a mortgage; Median gross rent: $813 per month; Rental vacancy rate: 0.0%

Health Insurance: 91.5% have insurance; 62.5% have private insurance; 39.3% have public insurance; 8.5% do not have insurance; 0.0% of children under 18 do not have insurance

Transportation: Commute: 94.7% car, 0.0% public transportation, 1.1% walk, 2.1% work from home; Mean travel time to work: 30.7 minutes

IBERIA (CDP). Covers a land area of 3.854 square miles and a water area of 0.013 square miles. Located at 40.68° N. Lat; 82.83° W. Long. Elevation is 1,079 feet.

Population: 674; Growth (since 2000): n/a; Density: 174.9 persons per square mile; Race: 98.5% White, 0.0% Black/African American, 0.0% Asian, 0.0% American Indian/Alaska Native, 0.0% Native Hawaiian/Other Pacific Islander, 1.5% Two or more races, 0.0% Hispanic of any race; Average household size: 2.77; Median age: 32.8; Age under 18: 21.1%; Age 65 and over: 21.4%; Males per 100 females: 96.5; Marriage status: 19.5% never married, 54.4% now married, 1.9% separated, 11.1% widowed, 15.0% divorced; Foreign born: 0.0%; Speak English only: 100.0%; With disability: 18.4%; Veterans: 7.7%; Ancestry: 38.6% Irish, 20.5% German, 13.4% English, 6.5% American, 4.6% Scottish

Employment: 14.7% management, business, and financial, 0.0% computer, engineering, and science, 0.0% education, legal, community service, arts, and media, 3.9% healthcare practitioners, 6.8% service, 6.2% sales and office, 11.4% natural resources, construction, and maintenance, 57.0% production, transportation, and material moving

Income: Per capita: $19,489; Median household: $42,375; Average household: $53,390; Households with income of $100,000 or more: 18.5%; Poverty rate: 12.3%

Educational Attainment: High school diploma or higher: 85.6%; Bachelor's degree or higher: 5.0%; Graduate/professional degree or higher: n/a

Housing: Homeownership rate: 82.3%; Median home value: $78,200; Median year structure built: 1946; Homeowner vacancy rate: 0.0%; Median selected monthly owner costs: $1,091 with a mortgage, $419 without a mortgage; Median gross rent: n/a per month; Rental vacancy rate: 0.0%

Health Insurance: 87.4% have insurance; 66.2% have private insurance; 38.4% have public insurance; 12.6% do not have insurance; 0.0% of children under 18 do not have insurance

Transportation: Commute: 96.7% car, 0.0% public transportation, 0.0% walk, 3.3% work from home; Mean travel time to work: 36.4 minutes

MARENGO (village). Covers a land area of 0.168 square miles and a water area of 0 square miles. Located at 40.40° N. Lat; 82.81° W. Long. Elevation is 1,158 feet.

Population: 345; Growth (since 2000): 16.2%; Density: 2,049.1 persons per square mile; Race: 99.1% White, 0.0% Black/African American, 0.0% Asian, 0.0% American Indian/Alaska Native, 0.0% Native Hawaiian/Other Pacific Islander, 0.9% Two or more races, 0.6% Hispanic of any race; Average household size: 2.52; Median age: 32.8; Age under 18: 29.6%; Age 65 and over: 9.6%; Males per 100 females: 92.1; Marriage status: 27.4% never married, 44.5% now married, 5.3% separated, 7.6% widowed, 20.5% divorced; Foreign born: 1.2%; Speak English only: 96.3%; With disability: 20.3%; Veterans: 7.0%; Ancestry: 26.1% German, 18.3% Irish, 12.8% Italian, 6.4% Scottish, 6.1% English

Employment: 6.9% management, business, and financial, 0.0% computer, engineering, and science, 5.3% education, legal, community service, arts, and media, 5.3% healthcare practitioners, 23.3% service, 22.2% sales and office, 10.1% natural resources, construction, and maintenance, 27.0% production, transportation, and material moving

Income: Per capita: $18,314; Median household: $33,750; Average household: $45,231; Households with income of $100,000 or more: 8.8%; Poverty rate: 18.8%

Educational Attainment: High school diploma or higher: 89.2%; Bachelor's degree or higher: 8.6%; Graduate/professional degree or higher: 5.2%

School District(s)

Highland Local (PK-12)
2015-16 Enrollment: 1,853 . . . . (419) 768-2206

Housing: Homeownership rate: 43.1%; Median home value: $99,500; Median year structure built: 1953; Homeowner vacancy rate: 1.7%; Median selected monthly owner costs: $978 with a mortgage, $432 without a mortgage; Median gross rent: $670 per month; Rental vacancy rate: 8.2%

Health Insurance: 90.1% have insurance; 60.9% have private insurance; 43.8% have public insurance; 9.9% do not have insurance; 3.9% of children under 18 do not have insurance

Transportation: Commute: 89.0% car, 0.0% public transportation, 11.0% walk, 0.0% work from home; Mean travel time to work: 24.9 minutes

MOUNT GILEAD (village). County seat. Covers a land area of 3.387 square miles and a water area of 0.011 square miles. Located at 40.55° N. Lat; 82.83° W. Long. Elevation is 1,135 feet.

History: Mount Gilead was settled in 1817 by Lewis and Ralph Hardenbrook, whose farm was in a tulip-tree forest. Until 1824 the settlement was called Whetstone, and later Youngstown. In 1832 the Ohio legislature changed the name again to honor Mount Gilead, Virginia.

Population: 3,407; Growth (since 2000): 3.6%; Density: 1,005.9 persons per square mile; Race: 98.3% White, 0.4% Black/African American, 0.0% Asian, 0.0% American Indian/Alaska Native, 0.0% Native Hawaiian/Other Pacific Islander, 1.3% Two or more races, 0.0% Hispanic of any race; Average household size: 2.34; Median age: 49.7; Age under 18: 21.6%; Age 65 and over: 24.1%; Males per 100 females: 89.9; Marriage status: 23.8% never married, 44.4% now married, 1.9% separated, 14.3% widowed, 17.5% divorced; Foreign born: 0.9%; Speak English only: 99.0%; With disability: 22.9%; Veterans: 8.9%; Ancestry: 36.2% German, 16.7% Irish, 13.7% English, 7.7% American, 5.6% Scotch-Irish

Employment: 7.6% management, business, and financial, 6.4% computer, engineering, and science, 12.9% education, legal, community service, arts, and media, 11.6% healthcare practitioners, 14.1% service, 24.8% sales and office, 3.1% natural resources, construction, and maintenance, 19.5% production, transportation, and material moving

Income: Per capita: $22,093; Median household: $36,303; Average household: $51,704; Households with income of $100,000 or more: 14.1%; Poverty rate: 8.8%

Educational Attainment: High school diploma or higher: 93.5%; Bachelor's degree or higher: 19.2%; Graduate/professional degree or higher: 5.2%

School District(s)

Mount Gilead Exempted Village (PK-12)
2015-16 Enrollment: 1,284 . . . . (419) 946-1646

Housing: Homeownership rate: 60.4%; Median home value: $103,200; Median year structure built: 1965; Homeowner vacancy rate: 0.0%; Median selected monthly owner costs: $951 with a mortgage, $410 without a mortgage; Median gross rent: $520 per month; Rental vacancy rate: 0.0%

Health Insurance: 92.0% have insurance; 62.4% have private insurance; 47.3% have public insurance; 8.0% do not have insurance; 0.0% of children under 18 do not have insurance

Hospitals: Morrow County Hospital (79 beds)

Newspapers: Morrow Co. Independent (weekly circulation 1,000); Morrow County Sentinel (weekly circulation 4,800)

Transportation: Commute: 91.5% car, 2.2% public transportation, 1.4% walk, 3.4% work from home; Mean travel time to work: 25.6 minutes

Additional Information Contacts

Village of Mount Gilead . . . . (419) 946-3926
http://www.mountgilead.net

SPARTA (village). Covers a land area of 0.087 square miles and a water area of 0 square miles. Located at 40.39° N. Lat; 82.70° W. Long. Elevation is 1,358 feet.

Population: 157; Growth (since 2000): -17.8%; Density: 1,808.2 persons per square mile; Race: 100.0% White, 0.0% Black/African American, 0.0% Asian, 0.0% American Indian/Alaska Native, 0.0% Native Hawaiian/Other Pacific Islander, 0.0% Two or more races, 1.9% Hispanic of any race; Average household size: 3.14; Median age: 35.6; Age under 18: 33.1%; Age 65 and over: 4.5%; Males per 100 females: 78.9; Marriage status: 29.8% never married, 52.6% now married, 0.0% separated, 4.4% widowed, 13.2% divorced; Foreign born: 0.6%; Speak English only: 96.4%; With disability: 21.7%; Veterans: 6.7%; Ancestry: 48.4% German, 33.8% Irish, 9.6% English, 3.2% Welsh, 1.9% American

Employment: 5.8% management, business, and financial, 0.0% computer, engineering, and science, 0.0% education, legal, community service, arts, and media, 8.7% healthcare practitioners, 17.4% service, 24.6% sales and office, 13.0% natural resources, construction, and maintenance, 30.4% production, transportation, and material moving

Income: Per capita: $15,474; Median household: $41,250; Average household: $49,480; Households with income of $100,000 or more: 4.0%; Poverty rate: 15.3%

Educational Attainment: High school diploma or higher: 98.9%; Bachelor's degree or higher: 7.5%; Graduate/professional degree or higher: 2.2%

School District(s)

Highland Local (PK-12)
2015-16 Enrollment: 1,853 . . . . (419) 768-2206

Housing: Homeownership rate: 68.0%; Median home value: $93,000; Median year structure built: Before 1940; Homeowner vacancy rate: 0.0%; Median selected monthly owner costs: $1,225 with a mortgage, $325 without a mortgage; Median gross rent: $638 per month; Rental vacancy rate: 0.0%
Health Insurance: 95.5% have insurance; 62.4% have private insurance; 42.0% have public insurance; 4.5% do not have insurance; 3.8% of children under 18 do not have insurance
Transportation: Commute: 100.0% car, 0.0% public transportation, 0.0% walk, 0.0% work from home; Mean travel time to work: 32.9 minutes

Muskingum County

Located in central Ohio; crossed by the Muskingum and Licking Rivers, and Salt and Jonathan Creeks. Covers a land area of 664.579 square miles, a water area of 8.004 square miles, and is located in the Eastern Time Zone at 39.97° N. Lat., 81.94° W. Long. The county was founded in 1804. County seat is Zanesville.

Muskingum County is part of the Zanesville, OH Micropolitan Statistical Area. The entire metro area includes: Muskingum County, OH

Weather Station: Philo 3 SW — Elevation: 1,020 feet

	Jan	Feb	Mar	Apr	May	Jun	Jul	Aug	Sep	Oct	Nov	Dec
High	36	40	50	62	70	77	81	81	74	63	51	39
Low	20	23	30	40	49	57	61	60	53	42	34	24
Precip	2.5	2.0	3.0	3.4	4.3	4.1	4.2	3.4	3.2	2.7	3.0	2.6
Snow	8.6	6.3	3.8	0.9	tr	0.0	0.0	0.0	0.0	tr	1.0	4.2

High and Low temperatures in degrees Fahrenheit; Precipitation and Snow in inches

Weather Station: Zanesville Municipal Arpt — Elevation: 879 feet

	Jan	Feb	Mar	Apr	May	Jun	Jul	Aug	Sep	Oct	Nov	Dec
High	37	41	51	63	72	80	84	83	76	64	53	41
Low	22	24	31	40	50	59	63	61	54	42	34	25
Precip	2.7	2.2	3.1	3.5	4.2	4.0	3.9	3.5	3.0	2.6	3.1	2.6
Snow	na	na	na	na	na	na	na	na	na	na	na	na

High and Low temperatures in degrees Fahrenheit; Precipitation and Snow in inches

Population: 85,991; Growth (since 2000): 1.7%; Density: 129.4 persons per square mile; Race: 92.3% White, 3.3% Black/African American, 0.4% Asian, 0.2% American Indian/Alaska Native, 0.0% Native Hawaiian/Other Pacific Islander, 3.5% two or more races, 1.0% Hispanic of any race; Average household size: 2.46; Median age: 40.2; Age under 18: 23.3%; Age 65 and over: 16.6%; Males per 100 females: 93.7; Marriage status: 27.6% never married, 51.4% now married, 1.8% separated, 7.2% widowed, 13.8% divorced; Foreign born: 1.2%; Speak English only: 98.0%; With disability: 16.1%; Veterans: 8.8%; Ancestry: 20.8% German, 13.2% Irish, 10.1% American, 9.4% English, 2.4% Italian
Religion: Six largest groups: 10.6% Methodist/Pietist, 6.6% Baptist, 6.0% Catholicism, 2.8% Non-denominational Protestant, 2.4% Presbyterian-Reformed, 2.4% Lutheran
Economy: Unemployment rate: 4.7%; Leading industries: 18.7 % retail trade; 13.7 % other services (except public administration); 10.9 % health care and social assistance; Farms: 1,259 totaling 173,269 acres; Company size: 1 employs 1,000 or more persons, 1 employs 500 to 999 persons, 38 employ 100 to 499 persons, 1,696 employ less than 100 persons; Business ownership: 1,815 women-owned, 98 Black-owned, n/a Hispanic-owned, 39 Asian-owned, 86 American Indian/Alaska Native-owned
Employment: 8.5% management, business, and financial, 2.2% computer, engineering, and science, 7.9% education, legal, community service, arts, and media, 7.0% healthcare practitioners, 19.9% service, 25.7% sales and office, 9.9% natural resources, construction, and maintenance, 19.0% production, transportation, and material moving
Income: Per capita: $21,945; Median household: $42,464; Average household: $53,831; Households with income of $100,000 or more: 12.9%; Poverty rate: 17.4%
Educational Attainment: High school diploma or higher: 86.5%; Bachelor's degree or higher: 15.1%; Graduate/professional degree or higher: 5.3%
Housing: Homeownership rate: 67.0%; Median home value: $110,500; Median year structure built: 1968; Homeowner vacancy rate: 2.3%; Median selected monthly owner costs: $1,071 with a mortgage, $381 without a mortgage; Median gross rent: $645 per month; Rental vacancy rate: 7.6%
Vital Statistics: Birth rate: 120.6 per 10,000 population; Death rate: 111.8 per 10,000 population; Age-adjusted cancer mortality rate: 195.4 deaths per 100,000 population
Health Insurance: 91.2% have insurance; 62.7% have private insurance; 42.1% have public insurance; 8.8% do not have insurance; 3.5% of children under 18 do not have insurance
Health Care: Physicians: 19.6 per 10,000 population; Dentists: 6.3 per 10,000 population; Hospital beds: 38.7 per 10,000 population; Hospital admissions: 1,780.9 per 10,000 population
Transportation: Commute: 95.0% car, 0.3% public transportation, 1.7% walk, 2.4% work from home; Mean travel time to work: 23.4 minutes
2016 Presidential Election: 64.6% Trump, 29.9% Clinton, 3.3% Johnson, 0.7% Stein
National and State Parks: Blue Rock State Forest; Blue Rock State Park; Dillon State Park; Dillon State Wildlife Area; Monroe Basin State Wildlife Area; Muskingum River Parkway State Park; Powelson State Wildlife Area
Additional Information Contacts
Muskingum Government . . . . (740) 455-7100
http://www.muskingumcounty.org

Muskingum County Communities

ADAMSVILLE (village). Covers a land area of 0.053 square miles and a water area of 0 square miles. Located at 40.07° N. Lat; 81.88° W. Long. Elevation is 1,020 feet.
Population: 168; Growth (since 2000): 32.3%; Density: 3,160.2 persons per square mile; Race: 100.0% White, 0.0% Black/African American, 0.0% Asian, 0.0% American Indian/Alaska Native, 0.0% Native Hawaiian/Other Pacific Islander, 0.0% Two or more races, 0.0% Hispanic of any race; Average household size: 3.00; Median age: 28.7; Age under 18: 37.5%; Age 65 and over: 9.5%; Males per 100 females: 103.6; Marriage status: 24.3% never married, 38.7% now married, 0.9% separated, 9.0% widowed, 27.9% divorced; Foreign born: 0.0%; Speak English only: 96.0%; With disability: 8.9%; Veterans: 12.4%; Ancestry: 31.0% German, 11.3% English, 8.9% French, 8.9% Irish, 3.6% American
Employment: 0.0% management, business, and financial, 0.0% computer, engineering, and science, 10.5% education, legal, community service, arts, and media, 3.9% healthcare practitioners, 11.8% service, 27.6% sales and office, 22.4% natural resources, construction, and maintenance, 23.7% production, transportation, and material moving
Income: Per capita: $15,450; Median household: $31,500; Average household: $46,838; Households with income of $100,000 or more: 16.1%; Poverty rate: 39.9%
Educational Attainment: High school diploma or higher: 85.1%; Bachelor's degree or higher: 5.3%; Graduate/professional degree or higher: n/a

School District(s)

Tri-Valley Local (KG-12)
2015-16 Enrollment: 3,042 . . . . (740) 754-1442
Housing: Homeownership rate: 62.5%; Median home value: $83,800; Median year structure built: Before 1940; Homeowner vacancy rate: 20.5%; Median selected monthly owner costs: $967 with a mortgage, $375 without a mortgage; Median gross rent: $692 per month; Rental vacancy rate: 0.0%
Health Insurance: 95.2% have insurance; 69.0% have private insurance; 38.1% have public insurance; 4.8% do not have insurance; 0.0% of children under 18 do not have insurance
Transportation: Commute: 78.9% car, 0.0% public transportation, 17.1% walk, 2.6% work from home; Mean travel time to work: 25.5 minutes

BLUE ROCK (unincorporated postal area)
ZCTA: 43720
Covers a land area of 45.399 square miles and a water area of 0.550 square miles. Located at 39.80° N. Lat; 81.88° W. Long. Elevation is 715 feet.
Population: 1,474; Growth (since 2000): 22.2%; Density: 32.5 persons per square mile; Race: 100.0% White, 0.0% Black/African American, 0.0% Asian, 0.0% American Indian/Alaska Native, 0.0% Native Hawaiian/Other Pacific Islander, 0.0% Two or more races, 0.0% Hispanic of any race; Average household size: 2.67; Median age: 45.1; Age under 18: 23.8%; Age 65 and over: 16.6%; Males per 100 females: 99.1; Marriage status: 23.4% never married, 45.7% now married, 1.4% separated, 6.0% widowed, 24.8% divorced; Foreign born: 0.0%; Speak English only: 100.0%; With disability: 11.5%; Veterans: 5.3%; Ancestry: 24.4% Irish, 19.7% German, 12.8% English, 9.4% American, 2.0% Italian

Employment: 8.8% management, business, and financial, 0.0% computer, engineering, and science, 2.2% education, legal, community service, arts, and media, 10.7% healthcare practitioners, 17.0% service, 13.8% sales and office, 15.1% natural resources, construction, and maintenance, 32.4% production, transportation, and material moving
Income: Per capita: $21,449; Median household: $56,667; Average household: $56,230; Households with income of $100,000 or more: 5.6%; Poverty rate: 14.7%
Educational Attainment: High school diploma or higher: 86.6%; Bachelor's degree or higher: 11.6%; Graduate/professional degree or higher: 1.9%
Housing: Homeownership rate: 78.4%; Median home value: $103,900; Median year structure built: 1987; Homeowner vacancy rate: 0.0%; Median selected monthly owner costs: $1,125 with a mortgage, $389 without a mortgage; Median gross rent: $732 per month; Rental vacancy rate: 0.0%
Health Insurance: 85.5% have insurance; 59.3% have private insurance; 44.5% have public insurance; 14.5% do not have insurance; 4.8% of children under 18 do not have insurance
Transportation: Commute: 100.0% car, 0.0% public transportation, 0.0% walk, 0.0% work from home; Mean travel time to work: 35.5 minutes

CHANDLERSVILLE (unincorporated postal area)

ZCTA: 43727

Covers a land area of 75.218 square miles and a water area of 0.558 square miles. Located at 39.86° N. Lat; 81.79° W. Long. Elevation is 735 feet.
Population: 1,095; Growth (since 2000): -15.8%; Density: 14.6 persons per square mile; Race: 98.8% White, 0.0% Black/African American, 0.0% Asian, 0.0% American Indian/Alaska Native, 0.0% Native Hawaiian/Other Pacific Islander, 1.2% Two or more races, 1.8% Hispanic of any race; Average household size: 2.34; Median age: 54.0; Age under 18: 12.2%; Age 65 and over: 15.1%; Males per 100 females: 107.2; Marriage status: 14.8% never married, 74.5% now married, 2.0% separated, 6.6% widowed, 4.1% divorced; Foreign born: 0.0%; Speak English only: 100.0%; With disability: 19.7%; Veterans: 2.8%; Ancestry: 20.5% American, 16.8% German, 5.5% Irish, 5.3% English, 4.5% French
Employment: 3.4% management, business, and financial, 7.4% computer, engineering, and science, 4.7% education, legal, community service, arts, and media, 9.3% healthcare practitioners, 24.8% service, 10.2% sales and office, 15.9% natural resources, construction, and maintenance, 24.4% production, transportation, and material moving
Income: Per capita: $26,181; Median household: $55,114; Average household: $60,374; Households with income of $100,000 or more: 19.2%; Poverty rate: 8.7%
Educational Attainment: High school diploma or higher: 87.2%; Bachelor's degree or higher: 3.9%; Graduate/professional degree or higher: 2.1%
Housing: Homeownership rate: 86.8%; Median home value: $93,100; Median year structure built: 1973; Homeowner vacancy rate: 0.0%; Median selected monthly owner costs: $1,071 with a mortgage, $368 without a mortgage; Median gross rent: n/a per month; Rental vacancy rate: 34.7%
Health Insurance: 94.8% have insurance; 79.2% have private insurance; 38.6% have public insurance; 5.2% do not have insurance; 0.0% of children under 18 do not have insurance
Transportation: Commute: 98.1% car, 0.0% public transportation, 0.0% walk, 1.9% work from home; Mean travel time to work: 29.6 minutes

DRESDEN (village). Covers a land area of 1.141 square miles and a water area of 0.035 square miles. Located at 40.12° N. Lat; 82.01° W. Long. Elevation is 741 feet.
Population: 1,531; Growth (since 2000): 7.6%; Density: 1,341.2 persons per square mile; Race: 97.5% White, 0.3% Black/African American, 0.0% Asian, 0.0% American Indian/Alaska Native, 0.0% Native Hawaiian/Other Pacific Islander, 2.2% Two or more races, 0.6% Hispanic of any race; Average household size: 2.43; Median age: 38.6; Age under 18: 24.4%; Age 65 and over: 16.4%; Males per 100 females: 87.1; Marriage status: 31.0% never married, 46.2% now married, 2.2% separated, 9.1% widowed, 13.7% divorced; Foreign born: 1.2%; Speak English only: 98.0%; With disability: 17.0%; Veterans: 7.3%; Ancestry: 22.0% German, 15.6% Irish, 11.8% American, 11.2% English, 3.1% French
Employment: 4.1% management, business, and financial, 1.2% computer, engineering, and science, 6.8% education, legal, community service, arts, and media, 11.2% healthcare practitioners, 23.3% service, 23.6% sales and office, 10.2% natural resources, construction, and maintenance, 19.5% production, transportation, and material moving
Income: Per capita: $17,811; Median household: $37,946; Average household: $42,925; Households with income of $100,000 or more: 3.8%; Poverty rate: 22.1%
Educational Attainment: High school diploma or higher: 90.4%; Bachelor's degree or higher: 13.6%; Graduate/professional degree or higher: 4.9%

School District(s)

Tri-Valley Local (KG-12)
2015-16 Enrollment: 3,042 . . . . (740) 754-1442
Housing: Homeownership rate: 63.4%; Median home value: $82,900; Median year structure built: 1965; Homeowner vacancy rate: 0.0%; Median selected monthly owner costs: $903 with a mortgage, $352 without a mortgage; Median gross rent: $693 per month; Rental vacancy rate: 4.2%
Health Insurance: 90.7% have insurance; 62.1% have private insurance; 42.7% have public insurance; 9.3% do not have insurance; 0.8% of children under 18 do not have insurance
Newspapers: Dresden Transcript (weekly circulation 5,500)
Transportation: Commute: 98.0% car, 0.0% public transportation, 1.5% walk, 0.0% work from home; Mean travel time to work: 25.0 minutes

DUNCAN FALLS (CDP). Covers a land area of 1.240 square miles and a water area of 0.077 square miles. Located at 39.88° N. Lat; 81.91° W. Long. Elevation is 709 feet.
Population: 1,027; Growth (since 2000): n/a; Density: 828.1 persons per square mile; Race: 100.0% White, 0.0% Black/African American, 0.0% Asian, 0.0% American Indian/Alaska Native, 0.0% Native Hawaiian/Other Pacific Islander, 0.0% Two or more races, 0.0% Hispanic of any race; Average household size: 2.47; Median age: 34.6; Age under 18: 20.4%; Age 65 and over: 20.9%; Males per 100 females: 88.8; Marriage status: 28.9% never married, 47.0% now married, 0.0% separated, 11.9% widowed, 12.2% divorced; Foreign born: 0.0%; Speak English only: 100.0%; With disability: 15.3%; Veterans: 8.8%; Ancestry: 18.1% German, 8.8% English, 7.7% American, 7.5% Irish, 3.7% Czechoslovakian
Employment: 0.0% management, business, and financial, 4.5% computer, engineering, and science, 8.0% education, legal, community service, arts, and media, 5.0% healthcare practitioners, 31.3% service, 16.4% sales and office, 11.4% natural resources, construction, and maintenance, 23.5% production, transportation, and material moving
Income: Per capita: $20,937; Median household: $42,188; Average household: $51,049; Households with income of $100,000 or more: 8.4%; Poverty rate: 8.7%
Educational Attainment: High school diploma or higher: 95.9%; Bachelor's degree or higher: 3.0%; Graduate/professional degree or higher: 1.7%

School District(s)

Franklin Local (PK-12)
2015-16 Enrollment: 1,972 . . . . (740) 674-5203
Housing: Homeownership rate: 78.3%; Median home value: $76,700; Median year structure built: 1951; Homeowner vacancy rate: 0.0%; Median selected monthly owner costs: $1,156 with a mortgage, $340 without a mortgage; Median gross rent: $760 per month; Rental vacancy rate: 7.2%
Health Insurance: 90.6% have insurance; 73.4% have private insurance; 33.4% have public insurance; 9.4% do not have insurance; 19.5% of children under 18 do not have insurance
Transportation: Commute: 91.4% car, 0.0% public transportation, 8.6% walk, 0.0% work from home; Mean travel time to work: 37.9 minutes

EAST FULTONHAM (CDP). Covers a land area of 0.466 square miles and a water area of 0.124 square miles. Located at 39.84° N. Lat; 82.12° W. Long. Elevation is 768 feet.
Population: 330; Growth (since 2000): n/a; Density: 708.5 persons per square mile; Race: 100.0% White, 0.0% Black/African American, 0.0% Asian, 0.0% American Indian/Alaska Native, 0.0% Native Hawaiian/Other Pacific Islander, 0.0% Two or more races, 0.0% Hispanic of any race; Average household size: 3.06; Median age: 45.2; Age under 18: 30.9%; Age 65 and over: 5.8%; Males per 100 females: 93.6; Marriage status: 14.8% never married, 85.2% now married, 0.0% separated, 0.0% widowed, 0.0% divorced; Foreign born: 0.0%; Speak English only: 100.0%; With disability: 16.4%; Veterans: 20.2%; Ancestry: 31.2% German, 30.3% English, 10.3% Irish, 9.1% Italian, 5.2% American
Employment: 0.0% management, business, and financial, 9.5% computer, engineering, and science, 11.4% education, legal, community service, arts, and media, 0.0% healthcare practitioners, 0.0% service, 42.9% sales and office, 8.6% natural resources, construction, and maintenance, 27.6% production, transportation, and material moving

Income: Per capita: $16,297; Median household: $53,194; Average household: $51,141; Households with income of $100,000 or more: n/a; Poverty rate: 30.9%
Educational Attainment: High school diploma or higher: 81.2%; Bachelor's degree or higher: 5.6%; Graduate/professional degree or higher: 5.6%
Housing: Homeownership rate: 54.6%; Median home value: $125,600; Median year structure built: 1953; Homeowner vacancy rate: 0.0%; Median selected monthly owner costs: $856 with a mortgage, n/a without a mortgage; Median gross rent: $490 per month; Rental vacancy rate: 0.0%
Health Insurance: 77.0% have insurance; 56.4% have private insurance; 29.4% have public insurance; 23.0% do not have insurance; 0.0% of children under 18 do not have insurance
Transportation: Commute: 100.0% car, 0.0% public transportation, 0.0% walk, 0.0% work from home; Mean travel time to work: 31.3 minutes

---

FRAZEYSBURG (village). Covers a land area of 0.924 square miles and a water area of 0 square miles. Located at 40.12° N. Lat; 82.12° W. Long. Elevation is 751 feet.
Population: 1,754; Growth (since 2000): 46.0%; Density: 1,898.2 persons per square mile; Race: 95.2% White, 0.3% Black/African American, 0.0% Asian, 0.0% American Indian/Alaska Native, 0.0% Native Hawaiian/Other Pacific Islander, 4.3% Two or more races, 0.3% Hispanic of any race; Average household size: 2.96; Median age: 29.3; Age under 18: 32.3%; Age 65 and over: 10.1%; Males per 100 females: 91.3; Marriage status: 36.2% never married, 48.2% now married, 1.4% separated, 4.4% widowed, 11.1% divorced; Foreign born: 0.0%; Speak English only: 99.6%; With disability: 14.7%; Veterans: 7.9%; Ancestry: 20.2% German, 17.7% Irish, 8.3% American, 6.6% English, 2.7% Swiss
Employment: 2.0% management, business, and financial, 0.5% computer, engineering, and science, 7.0% education, legal, community service, arts, and media, 3.9% healthcare practitioners, 19.4% service, 32.7% sales and office, 9.0% natural resources, construction, and maintenance, 25.5% production, transportation, and material moving
Income: Per capita: $14,956; Median household: $37,366; Average household: $43,513; Households with income of $100,000 or more: 5.8%; Poverty rate: 16.9%
Educational Attainment: High school diploma or higher: 84.7%; Bachelor's degree or higher: 7.3%; Graduate/professional degree or higher: 0.2%

School District(s)

Tri-Valley Local (KG-12)
2015-16 Enrollment: 3,042 . . . . (740) 754-1442

Housing: Homeownership rate: 50.8%; Median home value: $85,300; Median year structure built: 1974; Homeowner vacancy rate: 0.0%; Median selected monthly owner costs: $982 with a mortgage, $390 without a mortgage; Median gross rent: $702 per month; Rental vacancy rate: 10.2%
Health Insurance: 88.0% have insurance; 58.2% have private insurance; 39.9% have public insurance; 12.0% do not have insurance; 5.5% of children under 18 do not have insurance
Safety: Violent crime rate: 7.6 per 10,000 population; Property crime rate: 121.1 per 10,000 population
Transportation: Commute: 93.6% car, 0.0% public transportation, 5.2% walk, 0.0% work from home; Mean travel time to work: 27.2 minutes

---

FULTONHAM (village). Covers a land area of 0.156 square miles and a water area of 0 square miles. Located at 39.86° N. Lat; 82.14° W. Long. Elevation is 994 feet.
History: Fultonham developed around the Columbia Cement Company plant, which used the local desposits of limestone.
Population: 120; Growth (since 2000): -20.5%; Density: 768.9 persons per square mile; Race: 100.0% White, 0.0% Black/African American, 0.0% Asian, 0.0% American Indian/Alaska Native, 0.0% Native Hawaiian/Other Pacific Islander, 0.0% Two or more races, 0.0% Hispanic of any race; Average household size: 2.61; Median age: 30.8; Age under 18: 34.2%; Age 65 and over: 6.7%; Males per 100 females: 97.8; Marriage status: 25.9% never married, 50.6% now married, 1.2% separated, 16.0% widowed, 7.4% divorced; Foreign born: 0.0%; Speak English only: 100.0%; With disability: 8.3%; Veterans: 3.8%; Ancestry: 10.0% German, 9.2% American, 9.2% Irish, 7.5% English, 0.8% Polish
Employment: 0.0% management, business, and financial, 11.1% computer, engineering, and science, 9.3% education, legal, community service, arts, and media, 9.3% healthcare practitioners, 14.8% service, 1.9% sales and office, 1.9% natural resources, construction, and maintenance, 51.9% production, transportation, and material moving

Income: Per capita: $17,529; Median household: $45,417; Average household: $45,280; Households with income of $100,000 or more: n/a; Poverty rate: 3.3%
Educational Attainment: High school diploma or higher: 86.5%; Bachelor's degree or higher: 9.5%; Graduate/professional degree or higher: n/a
Housing: Homeownership rate: 58.7%; Median home value: $82,100; Median year structure built: Before 1940; Homeowner vacancy rate: 0.0%; Median selected monthly owner costs: $1,034 with a mortgage, $275 without a mortgage; Median gross rent: $616 per month; Rental vacancy rate: 0.0%
Health Insurance: 95.8% have insurance; 79.2% have private insurance; 25.0% have public insurance; 4.2% do not have insurance; 0.0% of children under 18 do not have insurance
Transportation: Commute: 100.0% car, 0.0% public transportation, 0.0% walk, 0.0% work from home; Mean travel time to work: 32.3 minutes

---

HOPEWELL (unincorporated postal area)

ZCTA: 43746

Covers a land area of 21.020 square miles and a water area of 0.017 square miles. Located at 39.97° N. Lat; 82.18° W. Long. Elevation is 1,089 feet.
Population: 1,299; Growth (since 2000): -3.4%; Density: 61.8 persons per square mile; Race: 95.9% White, 4.1% Black/African American, 0.0% Asian, 0.0% American Indian/Alaska Native, 0.0% Native Hawaiian/Other Pacific Islander, 0.0% Two or more races, 0.0% Hispanic of any race; Average household size: 2.56; Median age: 39.9; Age under 18: 22.8%; Age 65 and over: 21.9%; Males per 100 females: 103.0; Marriage status: 32.3% never married, 54.3% now married, 0.0% separated, 9.1% widowed, 4.2% divorced; Foreign born: 0.0%; Speak English only: 100.0%; With disability: 14.5%; Veterans: 7.2%; Ancestry: 40.4% German, 25.7% Irish, 7.9% American, 7.2% Scottish, 5.0% English
Employment: 12.0% management, business, and financial, 0.0% computer, engineering, and science, 6.8% education, legal, community service, arts, and media, 4.0% healthcare practitioners, 14.1% service, 33.4% sales and office, 8.3% natural resources, construction, and maintenance, 21.3% production, transportation, and material moving
Income: Per capita: $24,604; Median household: $50,268; Average household: $61,126; Households with income of $100,000 or more: 20.0%; Poverty rate: 3.7%
Educational Attainment: High school diploma or higher: 83.5%; Bachelor's degree or higher: 19.7%; Graduate/professional degree or higher: 3.5%

School District(s)

West Muskingum Local (PK-12)
2015-16 Enrollment: 1,496 . . . . (740) 455-4052

Housing: Homeownership rate: 82.2%; Median home value: $163,500; Median year structure built: 1978; Homeowner vacancy rate: 0.0%; Median selected monthly owner costs: $1,256 with a mortgage, $645 without a mortgage; Median gross rent: $805 per month; Rental vacancy rate: 0.0%
Health Insurance: 96.1% have insurance; 78.6% have private insurance; 41.9% have public insurance; 3.9% do not have insurance; 0.0% of children under 18 do not have insurance
Transportation: Commute: 98.3% car, 0.0% public transportation, 0.0% walk, 0.0% work from home; Mean travel time to work: 25.9 minutes

---

NASHPORT (unincorporated postal area)

ZCTA: 43830

Covers a land area of 50.922 square miles and a water area of 1.241 square miles. Located at 40.06° N. Lat; 82.14° W. Long. Elevation is 823 feet.
Population: 6,300; Growth (since 2000): 14.9%; Density: 123.7 persons per square mile; Race: 96.1% White, 0.0% Black/African American, 1.4% Asian, 0.0% American Indian/Alaska Native, 0.0% Native Hawaiian/Other Pacific Islander, 1.5% Two or more races, 1.0% Hispanic of any race; Average household size: 2.54; Median age: 40.4; Age under 18: 26.4%; Age 65 and over: 15.4%; Males per 100 females: 100.9; Marriage status: 22.2% never married, 57.3% now married, 1.9% separated, 7.8% widowed, 12.6% divorced; Foreign born: 0.4%; Speak English only: 99.2%; With disability: 11.2%; Veterans: 8.5%; Ancestry: 22.6% German, 14.0% Irish, 11.2% English, 9.2% American, 3.7% Polish
Employment: 15.4% management, business, and financial, 2.1% computer, engineering, and science, 6.7% education, legal, community service, arts, and media, 7.7% healthcare practitioners, 12.7% service,

27.8% sales and office, 7.9% natural resources, construction, and maintenance, 19.9% production, transportation, and material moving
Income: Per capita: $27,716; Median household: $56,293; Average household: $70,078; Households with income of $100,000 or more: 24.0%; Poverty rate: 7.6%
Educational Attainment: High school diploma or higher: 87.7%; Bachelor's degree or higher: 24.2%; Graduate/professional degree or higher: 7.7%

School District(s)

Tri-Valley Local (KG-12)
2015-16 Enrollment: 3,042 . . . . (740) 754-1442
Housing: Homeownership rate: 74.2%; Median home value: $157,100; Median year structure built: 1979; Homeowner vacancy rate: 0.0%; Median selected monthly owner costs: $1,288 with a mortgage, $456 without a mortgage; Median gross rent: $621 per month; Rental vacancy rate: 5.8%
Health Insurance: 93.3% have insurance; 75.8% have private insurance; 29.8% have public insurance; 6.7% do not have insurance; 1.7% of children under 18 do not have insurance
Transportation: Commute: 98.0% car, 0.0% public transportation, 0.0% walk, 2.0% work from home; Mean travel time to work: 27.1 minutes

NEW CONCORD (village). Covers a land area of 1.626 square miles and a water area of 0 square miles. Located at 39.99° N. Lat; 81.74° W. Long. Elevation is 869 feet.
History: New Concord began in 1807 when the National Road was opened. Muskingum College was founded here in 1836.
Population: 2,604; Growth (since 2000): -1.8%; Density: 1,601.9 persons per square mile; Race: 90.5% White, 2.2% Black/African American, 3.3% Asian, 0.0% American Indian/Alaska Native, 0.0% Native Hawaiian/Other Pacific Islander, 4.0% Two or more races, 2.0% Hispanic of any race; Average household size: 2.54; Median age: 21.4; Age under 18: 14.9%; Age 65 and over: 12.2%; Males per 100 females: 82.4; Marriage status: 62.7% never married, 24.7% now married, 0.5% separated, 7.5% widowed, 5.1% divorced; Foreign born: 5.7%; Speak English only: 93.0%; With disability: 12.4%; Veterans: 3.1%; Ancestry: 28.2% German, 14.7% Irish, 12.4% English, 6.6% Polish, 5.3% American
Employment: 10.8% management, business, and financial, 0.5% computer, engineering, and science, 12.1% education, legal, community service, arts, and media, 5.9% healthcare practitioners, 33.8% service, 23.5% sales and office, 4.2% natural resources, construction, and maintenance, 9.1% production, transportation, and material moving
Income: Per capita: $15,097; Median household: $43,250; Average household: $55,696; Households with income of $100,000 or more: 15.5%; Poverty rate: 24.5%
Educational Attainment: High school diploma or higher: 95.6%; Bachelor's degree or higher: 35.7%; Graduate/professional degree or higher: 15.7%

School District(s)

East Muskingum Local (PK-12)
2015-16 Enrollment: 2,087 . . . . (740) 826-7655

Four-year College(s)

Muskingum University (Private, Not-for-profit, Presbyterian Church (USA))
Fall 2016 Enrollment: 2,121 . . . . (740) 826-8211
2016-17 Tuition: In-state $26,928; Out-of-state $26,928
Housing: Homeownership rate: 55.5%; Median home value: $136,000; Median year structure built: 1964; Homeowner vacancy rate: 4.9%; Median selected monthly owner costs: $1,156 with a mortgage, $481 without a mortgage; Median gross rent: $603 per month; Rental vacancy rate: 0.0%
Health Insurance: 91.0% have insurance; 80.0% have private insurance; 22.4% have public insurance; 9.0% do not have insurance; 13.6% of children under 18 do not have insurance
Safety: Violent crime rate: 0.0 per 10,000 population; Property crime rate: 64.7 per 10,000 population
Transportation: Commute: 70.7% car, 0.0% public transportation, 25.4% walk, 4.0% work from home; Mean travel time to work: 19.1 minutes

NORTH ZANESVILLE (CDP). Covers a land area of 3.552 square miles and a water area of 0.003 square miles. Located at 39.99° N. Lat; 81.99° W. Long. Elevation is 902 feet.
Population: 2,846; Growth (since 2000): -5.5%; Density: 801.2 persons per square mile; Race: 90.0% White, 2.1% Black/African American, 0.9% Asian, 0.0% American Indian/Alaska Native, 0.0% Native Hawaiian/Other Pacific Islander, 6.0% Two or more races, 0.0% Hispanic of any race; Average household size: 2.51; Median age: 47.7; Age under 18: 22.2%; Age 65 and over: 23.3%; Males per 100 females: 90.5; Marriage status: 16.2% never married, 61.4% now married, 1.1% separated, 7.0% widowed, 15.4% divorced; Foreign born: 3.0%; Speak English only: 96.5%; With disability: 20.4%; Veterans: 5.5%; Ancestry: 18.1% American, 14.5% German, 7.3% English, 7.1% Irish, 2.2% Scotch-Irish
Employment: 7.4% management, business, and financial, 4.0% computer, engineering, and science, 19.3% education, legal, community service, arts, and media, 4.9% healthcare practitioners, 15.3% service, 33.9% sales and office, 6.0% natural resources, construction, and maintenance, 9.2% production, transportation, and material moving
Income: Per capita: $31,085; Median household: $60,750; Average household: $76,338; Households with income of $100,000 or more: 25.8%; Poverty rate: 8.5%
Educational Attainment: High school diploma or higher: 93.4%; Bachelor's degree or higher: 33.8%; Graduate/professional degree or higher: 17.4%
Housing: Homeownership rate: 86.4%; Median home value: $156,700; Median year structure built: 1964; Homeowner vacancy rate: 2.9%; Median selected monthly owner costs: $1,472 with a mortgage, $446 without a mortgage; Median gross rent: $514 per month; Rental vacancy rate: 0.0%
Health Insurance: 95.2% have insurance; 81.9% have private insurance; 34.8% have public insurance; 4.8% do not have insurance; 0.0% of children under 18 do not have insurance
Transportation: Commute: 92.6% car, 1.0% public transportation, 2.5% walk, 3.9% work from home; Mean travel time to work: 16.8 minutes

NORWICH (village). Covers a land area of 0.100 square miles and a water area of 0 square miles. Located at 39.98° N. Lat; 81.79° W. Long. Elevation is 968 feet.
History: The village of Norwich was reported in the 1800's to be the home of a headless creature which roamed Stumpy Hollow at night, frightening the residents and leaving them speechless.
Population: 93; Growth (since 2000): -17.7%; Density: 930.9 persons per square mile; Race: 96.8% White, 0.0% Black/African American, 0.0% Asian, 0.0% American Indian/Alaska Native, 0.0% Native Hawaiian/Other Pacific Islander, 2.2% Two or more races, 1.1% Hispanic of any race; Average household size: 2.66; Median age: 52.9; Age under 18: 6.5%; Age 65 and over: 24.7%; Males per 100 females: 104.0; Marriage status: 30.3% never married, 46.1% now married, 4.5% separated, 7.9% widowed, 15.7% divorced; Foreign born: 0.0%; Speak English only: 98.9%; With disability: 28.0%; Veterans: 14.9%; Ancestry: 39.8% German, 26.9% Irish, 24.7% English, 14.0% American, 4.3% French
Employment: 8.3% management, business, and financial, 2.1% computer, engineering, and science, 2.1% education, legal, community service, arts, and media, 2.1% healthcare practitioners, 22.9% service, 18.8% sales and office, 10.4% natural resources, construction, and maintenance, 33.3% production, transportation, and material moving
Income: Per capita: $22,826; Median household: $55,417; Average household: $58,663; Households with income of $100,000 or more: 14.3%; Poverty rate: 7.5%
Educational Attainment: High school diploma or higher: 88.8%; Bachelor's degree or higher: 22.5%; Graduate/professional degree or higher: 15.0%
Housing: Homeownership rate: 94.3%; Median home value: $93,800; Median year structure built: Before 1940; Homeowner vacancy rate: 0.0%; Median selected monthly owner costs: $950 with a mortgage, $296 without a mortgage; Median gross rent: n/a per month; Rental vacancy rate: 0.0%
Health Insurance: 83.9% have insurance; 59.1% have private insurance; 43.0% have public insurance; 16.1% do not have insurance; 0.0% of children under 18 do not have insurance
Transportation: Commute: 89.6% car, 0.0% public transportation, 10.4% walk, 0.0% work from home; Mean travel time to work: 21.7 minutes

PHILO (village). Covers a land area of 0.422 square miles and a water area of 0 square miles. Located at 39.86° N. Lat; 81.91° W. Long. Elevation is 732 feet.
Population: 872; Growth (since 2000): 13.4%; Density: 2,068.5 persons per square mile; Race: 95.6% White, 0.0% Black/African American, 0.0% Asian, 0.0% American Indian/Alaska Native, 0.1% Native Hawaiian/Other Pacific Islander, 3.6% Two or more races, 3.1% Hispanic of any race; Average household size: 3.03; Median age: 36.5; Age under 18: 29.8%; Age 65 and over: 8.5%; Males per 100 females: 93.4; Marriage status: 31.9% never married, 46.4% now married, 1.7% separated, 6.4% widowed, 15.3% divorced; Foreign born: 1.3%; Speak English only: 98.9%; With disability: 16.4%; Veterans: 6.2%; Ancestry: 29.1% German, 19.4% Irish, 11.8% American, 7.2% English, 3.4% Polish

Employment: 1.0% management, business, and financial, 0.7% computer, engineering, and science, 4.8% education, legal, community service, arts, and media, 8.7% healthcare practitioners, 20.0% service, 26.5% sales and office, 12.8% natural resources, construction, and maintenance, 25.5% production, transportation, and material moving
Income: Per capita: $18,426; Median household: $44,000; Average household: $52,305; Households with income of $100,000 or more: 8.3%; Poverty rate: 15.6%
Educational Attainment: High school diploma or higher: 84.6%; Bachelor's degree or higher: 8.9%; Graduate/professional degree or higher: 1.1%

School District(s)

Franklin Local (PK-12)
2015-16 Enrollment: 1,972 . . . . (740) 674-5203
Housing: Homeownership rate: 87.2%; Median home value: $76,400; Median year structure built: 1946; Homeowner vacancy rate: 0.8%; Median selected monthly owner costs: $886 with a mortgage, $280 without a mortgage; Median gross rent: $627 per month; Rental vacancy rate: 0.0%
Health Insurance: 92.9% have insurance; 63.8% have private insurance; 37.5% have public insurance; 7.1% do not have insurance; 0.0% of children under 18 do not have insurance
Transportation: Commute: 97.6% car, 0.0% public transportation, 1.0% walk, 0.5% work from home; Mean travel time to work: 32.7 minutes

PLEASANT GROVE (CDP). Covers a land area of 3.211 square miles and a water area of 0.007 square miles. Located at 39.95° N. Lat; 81.96° W. Long. Elevation is 932 feet.
Population: 1,686; Growth (since 2000): -16.4%; Density: 525.1 persons per square mile; Race: 96.6% White, 1.5% Black/African American, 0.0% Asian, 0.0% American Indian/Alaska Native, 0.0% Native Hawaiian/Other Pacific Islander, 1.8% Two or more races, 0.8% Hispanic of any race; Average household size: 2.24; Median age: 36.6; Age under 18: 28.1%; Age 65 and over: 19.2%; Males per 100 females: 94.4; Marriage status: 24.5% never married, 58.4% now married, 0.0% separated, 4.5% widowed, 12.6% divorced; Foreign born: 0.0%; Speak English only: 98.2%; With disability: 17.1%; Veterans: 14.8%; Ancestry: 19.7% German, 10.1% Irish, 9.4% Italian, 9.0% Czechoslovakian, 8.6% American
Employment: 16.8% management, business, and financial, 4.4% computer, engineering, and science, 8.6% education, legal, community service, arts, and media, 5.6% healthcare practitioners, 11.0% service, 31.6% sales and office, 10.2% natural resources, construction, and maintenance, 11.9% production, transportation, and material moving
Income: Per capita: $26,090; Median household: $54,231; Average household: $58,113; Households with income of $100,000 or more: 17.4%; Poverty rate: 10.3%
Educational Attainment: High school diploma or higher: 95.4%; Bachelor's degree or higher: 23.9%; Graduate/professional degree or higher: 7.0%
Housing: Homeownership rate: 57.7%; Median home value: $143,200; Median year structure built: 1967; Homeowner vacancy rate: 0.0%; Median selected monthly owner costs: $1,074 with a mortgage, $459 without a mortgage; Median gross rent: $634 per month; Rental vacancy rate: 13.8%
Health Insurance: 91.9% have insurance; 72.8% have private insurance; 33.5% have public insurance; 8.1% do not have insurance; 0.0% of children under 18 do not have insurance
Transportation: Commute: 100.0% car, 0.0% public transportation, 0.0% walk, 0.0% work from home; Mean travel time to work: 19.2 minutes

SOUTH ZANESVILLE (village). Covers a land area of 0.828 square miles and a water area of 0 square miles. Located at 39.90° N. Lat; 82.02° W. Long. Elevation is 722 feet.
Population: 2,134; Growth (since 2000): 10.2%; Density: 2,575.7 persons per square mile; Race: 87.7% White, 5.4% Black/African American, 0.0% Asian, 0.0% American Indian/Alaska Native, 0.0% Native Hawaiian/Other Pacific Islander, 6.9% Two or more races, 0.0% Hispanic of any race; Average household size: 2.54; Median age: 34.6; Age under 18: 26.4%; Age 65 and over: 14.2%; Males per 100 females: 93.5; Marriage status: 27.4% never married, 45.0% now married, 2.1% separated, 8.1% widowed, 19.5% divorced; Foreign born: 0.0%; Speak English only: 99.2%; With disability: 15.1%; Veterans: 11.2%; Ancestry: 15.2% German, 13.6% Irish, 12.2% American, 6.0% English, 4.1% Dutch
Employment: 6.4% management, business, and financial, 0.4% computer, engineering, and science, 6.3% education, legal, community service, arts, and media, 1.0% healthcare practitioners, 25.6% service, 29.8% sales and office, 11.6% natural resources, construction, and maintenance, 19.1% production, transportation, and material moving
Income: Per capita: $16,872; Median household: $32,831; Average household: $42,345; Households with income of $100,000 or more: 3.1%; Poverty rate: 17.9%
Educational Attainment: High school diploma or higher: 83.7%; Bachelor's degree or higher: 6.1%; Graduate/professional degree or higher: 3.6%
Housing: Homeownership rate: 66.4%; Median home value: $60,100; Median year structure built: 1969; Homeowner vacancy rate: 0.0%; Median selected monthly owner costs: $841 with a mortgage, $357 without a mortgage; Median gross rent: $624 per month; Rental vacancy rate: 0.0%
Health Insurance: 89.2% have insurance; 47.2% have private insurance; 53.0% have public insurance; 10.8% do not have insurance; 2.8% of children under 18 do not have insurance
Safety: Violent crime rate: 5.1 per 10,000 population; Property crime rate: 111.4 per 10,000 population
Transportation: Commute: 93.2% car, 0.0% public transportation, 3.6% walk, 2.8% work from home; Mean travel time to work: 20.5 minutes

TRINWAY (CDP). Covers a land area of 0.378 square miles and a water area of 0 square miles. Located at 40.14° N. Lat; 82.01° W. Long. Elevation is 738 feet.
Population: 212; Growth (since 2000): n/a; Density: 560.7 persons per square mile; Race: 100.0% White, 0.0% Black/African American, 0.0% Asian, 0.0% American Indian/Alaska Native, 0.0% Native Hawaiian/Other Pacific Islander, 0.0% Two or more races, 0.0% Hispanic of any race; Average household size: 1.86; Median age: 51.6; Age under 18: 0.0%; Age 65 and over: 27.4%; Males per 100 females: 117.3; Marriage status: 33.0% never married, 45.3% now married, 0.0% separated, 7.1% widowed, 14.6% divorced; Foreign born: 0.0%; Speak English only: 100.0%; With disability: 40.1%; Veterans: 0.0%; Ancestry: 45.3% American, 14.6% Irish, 7.5% German
Employment: 0.0% management, business, and financial, 0.0% computer, engineering, and science, 0.0% education, legal, community service, arts, and media, 49.3% healthcare practitioners, 0.0% service, 0.0% sales and office, 50.7% natural resources, construction, and maintenance, 0.0% production, transportation, and material moving
Income: Per capita: $21,695; Median household: $43,500; Average household: $40,627; Households with income of $100,000 or more: n/a; Poverty rate: 7.1%
Educational Attainment: High school diploma or higher: 64.8%; Bachelor's degree or higher: 17.6%; Graduate/professional degree or higher: n/a
Housing: Homeownership rate: 86.8%; Median home value: n/a; Median year structure built: Before 1940; Homeowner vacancy rate: 32.7%; Median selected monthly owner costs: $1,014 with a mortgage, n/a without a mortgage; Median gross rent: n/a per month; Rental vacancy rate: 0.0%
Health Insurance: 89.6% have insurance; 60.8% have private insurance; 56.1% have public insurance; 10.4% do not have insurance; 0.0% of children under 18 do not have insurance
Transportation: Commute: 100.0% car, 0.0% public transportation, 0.0% walk, 0.0% work from home; Mean travel time to work: 0.0 minutes

ZANESVILLE (city). County seat. Covers a land area of 11.768 square miles and a water area of 0.373 square miles. Located at 39.96° N. Lat; 82.01° W. Long. Elevation is 676 feet.
History: Zanesville, situated at the confluence of the Licking and Muskingum Rivers, was established in the late 1790's. Clay suitable for pottery-making was discovered in the vicinity, and by 1808 dishes, stoneware, and bricks were bearing the Zanesville imprint. Local sands were used in the glass plant started in Zanesville in 1815, making goblets and water pitchers that became prized collectors items. Zanesville was named for Ebenezer Zane, who surveyed Zane's Trace, an overland route through Ohio, in 1797. A descendant of Zane was western writer Zane Grey, who was born in Zanesville in 1875.
Population: 25,467; Growth (since 2000): -0.5%; Density: 2,164.1 persons per square mile; Race: 85.0% White, 8.0% Black/African American, 0.5% Asian, 0.3% American Indian/Alaska Native, 0.0% Native Hawaiian/Other Pacific Islander, 6.0% Two or more races, 1.3% Hispanic of any race; Average household size: 2.26; Median age: 35.5; Age under 18: 23.2%; Age 65 and over: 16.5%; Males per 100 females: 87.3; Marriage status: 32.8% never married, 39.3% now married, 3.3% separated, 9.1% widowed, 18.8% divorced; Foreign born: 1.5%; Speak English only: 97.5%;

With disability: 22.1%; Veterans: 9.5%; Ancestry: 18.1% German, 12.1% Irish, 7.8% English, 7.5% American, 2.4% Italian
Employment: 6.2% management, business, and financial, 2.5% computer, engineering, and science, 7.0% education, legal, community service, arts, and media, 7.4% healthcare practitioners, 25.4% service, 26.6% sales and office, 6.8% natural resources, construction, and maintenance, 18.2% production, transportation, and material moving
Income: Per capita: $16,858; Median household: $26,039; Average household: $37,551; Households with income of $100,000 or more: 4.9%; Poverty rate: 30.8%
Educational Attainment: High school diploma or higher: 80.8%; Bachelor's degree or higher: 12.1%; Graduate/professional degree or higher: 4.3%

School District(s)

East Muskingum Local (PK-12)
2015-16 Enrollment: 2,087 . . . . (740) 826-7655
Foxfire High School (09-12)
2015-16 Enrollment: 235. . . . . (740) 453-4509
Foxfire Intermediate School (01-08)
2015-16 Enrollment: 119. . . . . (740) 453-4509
Maysville Local (PK-12)
2015-16 Enrollment: 2,328 . . . . (740) 453-0754
Mid-East Career and Technology Centers (10-12)
2015-16 Enrollment: n/a . . . . (740) 454-0105
West Muskingum Local (PK-12)
2015-16 Enrollment: 1,496 . . . . (740) 455-4052
Zanesville City (PK-12)
2015-16 Enrollment: 3,287 . . . . (740) 454-9751
Zanesville Community School (09-12)
2015-16 Enrollment: 78. . . . . (740) 588-5685

Four-year College(s)

Ohio University-Zanesville Campus (Public)
Fall 2016 Enrollment: 1,279 . . . . (740) 453-0762
2016-17 Tuition: In-state $5,076; Out-of-state $9,612

Two-year College(s)

Zane State College (Public)
Fall 2016 Enrollment: 3,145 . . . . (740) 454-2501
2016-17 Tuition: In-state $4,646; Out-of-state $9,206

Vocational/Technical School(s)

Mid-EastCTC-Adult Education (Public)
Fall 2016 Enrollment: 235 . . . . (740) 455-3111
2016-17 Tuition: $8,548

Housing: Homeownership rate: 43.3%; Median home value: $76,600; Median year structure built: 1946; Homeowner vacancy rate: 3.8%; Median selected monthly owner costs: $827 with a mortgage, $340 without a mortgage; Median gross rent: $632 per month; Rental vacancy rate: 9.4%
Health Insurance: 90.7% have insurance; 44.8% have private insurance; 59.2% have public insurance; 9.3% do not have insurance; 1.3% of children under 18 do not have insurance
Hospitals: Genesis Healthcare System (352 beds)
Safety: Violent crime rate: 36.5 per 10,000 population; Property crime rate: 505.2 per 10,000 population
Newspapers: Times Recorder (daily circulation 18,000)
Transportation: Commute: 93.8% car, 0.6% public transportation, 1.1% walk, 2.6% work from home; Mean travel time to work: 20.3 minutes
Airports: Zanesville Municipal (general aviation)
Additional Information Contacts
City of Zanesville . . . . (740) 455-0603
http://www.coz.org

Noble County

Located in eastern Ohio; drained by Wills, Duck, and Seneca Creeks. Covers a land area of 398.012 square miles, a water area of 6.558 square miles, and is located in the Eastern Time Zone at 39.77° N. Lat., 81.45° W. Long. The county was founded in 1851. County seat is Caldwell.
Population: 14,429; Growth (since 2000): 2.6%; Density: 36.3 persons per square mile; Race: 91.7% White, 5.5% Black/African American, 0.1% Asian, 0.1% American Indian/Alaska Native, 0.0% Native Hawaiian/Other Pacific Islander, 2.0% two or more races, 0.8% Hispanic of any race; Average household size: 2.43; Median age: 47.9; Age under 18: 18.6%; Age 65 and over: 23.5%; Males per 100 females: 137.2; Marriage status: 28.0% never married, 53.7% now married, 2.1% separated, 7.4% widowed, 11.0% divorced; Foreign born: 0.8%; Speak English only: 96.5%; With disability: 16.0%; Veterans: 13.0%; Ancestry: 26.2% German, 12.2% Irish, 7.7% American, 6.2% English, 2.9% Italian
Religion: Six largest groups: 10.5% Catholicism, 7.7% Baptist, 6.5% Methodist/Pietist, 2.2% Holiness, 0.5% Presbyterian-Reformed, 0.0% Other Groups
Economy: Unemployment rate: 6.2%; Leading industries: 16.6 % retail trade; 15.2 % other services (except public administration); 12.0 % construction; Farms: 595 totaling 86,117 acres; Company size: 0 employ 1,000 or more persons, 0 employ 500 to 999 persons, 1 employs 100 to 499 persons, 216 employ less than 100 persons; Business ownership: 269 women-owned, n/a Black-owned, n/a Hispanic-owned, n/a Asian-owned, n/a American Indian/Alaska Native-owned
Employment: 7.9% management, business, and financial, 1.1% computer, engineering, and science, 7.6% education, legal, community service, arts, and media, 5.0% healthcare practitioners, 17.8% service, 25.8% sales and office, 8.8% natural resources, construction, and maintenance, 26.0% production, transportation, and material moving
Income: Per capita: $21,188; Median household: $41,398; Average household: $53,284; Households with income of $100,000 or more: 8.7%; Poverty rate: 11.9%
Educational Attainment: High school diploma or higher: 84.1%; Bachelor's degree or higher: 9.5%; Graduate/professional degree or higher: 4.0%
Housing: Homeownership rate: 83.4%; Median home value: $88,100; Median year structure built: 1973; Homeowner vacancy rate: 0.5%; Median selected monthly owner costs: $847 with a mortgage, $340 without a mortgage; Median gross rent: $607 per month; Rental vacancy rate: 5.0%
Vital Statistics: Birth rate: 95.8 per 10,000 population; Death rate: 91.6 per 10,000 population; Age-adjusted cancer mortality rate: 138.1 deaths per 100,000 population
Health Insurance: 92.8% have insurance; 67.2% have private insurance; 46.4% have public insurance; 7.2% do not have insurance; 8.4% of children under 18 do not have insurance
Health Care: Physicians: 2.8 per 10,000 population; Dentists: 2.8 per 10,000 population; Hospital beds: 0.0 per 10,000 population; Hospital admissions: 0.0 per 10,000 population
Air Quality Index (AQI): Percent of Days: 88.8% good, 10.6% moderate, 0.6% unhealthy for sensitive individuals, 0.0% unhealthy, 0.0% very unhealthy; Annual median: 37; Annual maximum: 105
Transportation: Commute: 94.1% car, 0.0% public transportation, 1.5% walk, 4.4% work from home; Mean travel time to work: 28.8 minutes
2016 Presidential Election: 75.3% Trump, 20.2% Clinton, 2.5% Johnson, 0.6% Stein
National and State Parks: Wolf Run State Park
Additional Information Contacts
Noble Government . . . . (740) 732-2969
http://www.noblecountyohio.com

Noble County Communities

AVA (unincorporated postal area)

ZCTA: 43711

Covers a land area of 0.213 square miles and a water area of <.001 square miles. Located at 39.84° N. Lat; 81.58° W. Long. Elevation is 774 feet.
Population: 94; Growth (since 2000): n/a; Density: 441.8 persons per square mile; Race: 100.0% White, 0.0% Black/African American, 0.0% Asian, 0.0% American Indian/Alaska Native, 0.0% Native Hawaiian/Other Pacific Islander, 0.0% Two or more races, 0.0% Hispanic of any race; Average household size: 3.92; Median age: 17.5; Age under 18: 64.9%; Age 65 and over: 0.0%; Males per 100 females: 111.6; Marriage status: 45.0% never married, 18.3% now married, 0.0% separated, 0.0% widowed, 36.7% divorced; Foreign born: 0.0%; Speak English only: 100.0%; With disability: 0.0%; Veterans: 6.1%; Ancestry: 14.9% French, 2.1% French Canadian
Employment: 0.0% management, business, and financial, 0.0% computer, engineering, and science, 0.0% education, legal, community service, arts, and media, 29.0% healthcare practitioners, 0.0% service, 71.0% sales and office, 0.0% natural resources, construction, and maintenance, 0.0% production, transportation, and material moving
Income: Per capita: $11,920; Median household: n/a; Average household: n/a; Households with income of $100,000 or more: n/a; Poverty rate: n/a
Educational Attainment: High school diploma or higher: 100.0%; Bachelor's degree or higher: n/a; Graduate/professional degree or higher: n/a

Housing: Homeownership rate: n/a; Median home value: n/a; Median year structure built: n/a; Homeowner vacancy rate: 0.0%; Median selected monthly owner costs: $0 with a mortgage, $0 without a mortgage; Median gross rent: n/a per month; Rental vacancy rate: 0.0%
Health Insurance: 100.0% have insurance; 83.0% have private insurance; 26.6% have public insurance; 0.0% do not have insurance; 0.0% of children under 18 do not have insurance
Transportation: Commute: 100.0% car, 0.0% public transportation, 0.0% walk, 0.0% work from home; Mean travel time to work: 0.0 minutes

BATESVILLE (village). Covers a land area of 0.136 square miles and a water area of 0 square miles. Located at 39.91° N. Lat; 81.28° W. Long. Elevation is 912 feet.
Population: 98; Growth (since 2000): -2.0%; Density: 718.8 persons per square mile; Race: 87.8% White, 1.0% Black/African American, 0.0% Asian, 0.0% American Indian/Alaska Native, 0.0% Native Hawaiian/Other Pacific Islander, 11.2% Two or more races, 2.0% Hispanic of any race; Average household size: 3.16; Median age: 45.3; Age under 18: 24.5%; Age 65 and over: 17.3%; Males per 100 females: 91.9; Marriage status: 29.1% never married, 51.9% now married, 0.0% separated, 5.1% widowed, 13.9% divorced; Foreign born: 0.0%; Speak English only: 100.0%; With disability: 22.4%; Veterans: 12.2%; Ancestry: 18.4% Italian, 10.2% German, 8.2% Irish, 6.1% English, 3.1% American
Employment: 0.0% management, business, and financial, 0.0% computer, engineering, and science, 10.0% education, legal, community service, arts, and media, 7.5% healthcare practitioners, 5.0% service, 17.5% sales and office, 17.5% natural resources, construction, and maintenance, 42.5% production, transportation, and material moving
Income: Per capita: $19,635; Median household: $49,375; Average household: $50,832; Households with income of $100,000 or more: 12.9%; Poverty rate: 16.5%
Educational Attainment: High school diploma or higher: 83.6%; Bachelor's degree or higher: 6.0%; Graduate/professional degree or higher: n/a
Housing: Homeownership rate: 83.9%; Median home value: $70,000; Median year structure built: Before 1940; Homeowner vacancy rate: 16.1%; Median selected monthly owner costs: $750 with a mortgage, $244 without a mortgage; Median gross rent: n/a per month; Rental vacancy rate: 0.0%
Health Insurance: 75.5% have insurance; 54.1% have private insurance; 37.8% have public insurance; 24.5% do not have insurance; 0.0% of children under 18 do not have insurance
Transportation: Commute: 100.0% car, 0.0% public transportation, 0.0% walk, 0.0% work from home; Mean travel time to work: 33.3 minutes

BELLE VALLEY (village). Covers a land area of 0.407 square miles and a water area of 0 square miles. Located at 39.79° N. Lat; 81.56° W. Long. Elevation is 748 feet.
History: Belle Valley developed around a large coal mine. In the early 1900's the mine attracted many Eastern European immigrants who found work here.
Population: 267; Growth (since 2000): 1.5%; Density: 656.6 persons per square mile; Race: 93.6% White, 0.0% Black/African American, 0.0% Asian, 0.7% American Indian/Alaska Native, 0.0% Native Hawaiian/Other Pacific Islander, 4.9% Two or more races, 0.7% Hispanic of any race; Average household size: 1.96; Median age: 58.0; Age under 18: 21.0%; Age 65 and over: 26.6%; Males per 100 females: 102.7; Marriage status: 36.5% never married, 41.9% now married, 2.5% separated, 7.9% widowed, 13.7% divorced; Foreign born: 0.0%; Speak English only: 96.9%; With disability: 16.9%; Veterans: 12.3%; Ancestry: 28.1% German, 13.1% Irish, 12.7% Polish, 7.5% English, 6.7% Austrian
Employment: 0.0% management, business, and financial, 0.0% computer, engineering, and science, 4.5% education, legal, community service, arts, and media, 9.8% healthcare practitioners, 23.2% service, 24.1% sales and office, 23.2% natural resources, construction, and maintenance, 15.2% production, transportation, and material moving
Income: Per capita: $18,491; Median household: $26,667; Average household: $37,901; Households with income of $100,000 or more: 0.7%; Poverty rate: 19.5%
Educational Attainment: High school diploma or higher: 88.0%; Bachelor's degree or higher: 8.5%; Graduate/professional degree or higher: 8.5%
Housing: Homeownership rate: 84.6%; Median home value: $79,200; Median year structure built: Before 1940; Homeowner vacancy rate: 0.0%; Median selected monthly owner costs: $610 with a mortgage, $286 without a mortgage; Median gross rent: $550 per month; Rental vacancy rate: 19.2%
Health Insurance: 97.0% have insurance; 67.4% have private insurance; 49.8% have public insurance; 3.0% do not have insurance; 0.0% of children under 18 do not have insurance
Transportation: Commute: 100.0% car, 0.0% public transportation, 0.0% walk, 0.0% work from home; Mean travel time to work: 19.1 minutes

CALDWELL (village). County seat. Covers a land area of 0.889 square miles and a water area of 0.013 square miles. Located at 39.75° N. Lat; 81.51° W. Long. Elevation is 745 feet.
History: Caldwell was founded in 1857 as the seat of Noble County, and named for the owners of the town site. Coal mining was Caldwell's primary industry.
Population: 1,781; Growth (since 2000): -8.9%; Density: 2,003.5 persons per square mile; Race: 99.3% White, 0.0% Black/African American, 0.0% Asian, 0.3% American Indian/Alaska Native, 0.0% Native Hawaiian/Other Pacific Islander, 0.2% Two or more races, 0.2% Hispanic of any race; Average household size: 2.05; Median age: 56.6; Age under 18: 20.9%; Age 65 and over: 28.5%; Males per 100 females: 83.6; Marriage status: 20.0% never married, 50.8% now married, 2.2% separated, 13.5% widowed, 15.8% divorced; Foreign born: 0.0%; Speak English only: 98.6%; With disability: 13.7%; Veterans: 13.6%; Ancestry: 27.5% German, 11.6% Irish, 9.3% English, 6.6% American, 4.9% Polish
Employment: 9.2% management, business, and financial, 0.7% computer, engineering, and science, 12.2% education, legal, community service, arts, and media, 5.3% healthcare practitioners, 15.5% service, 31.6% sales and office, 5.8% natural resources, construction, and maintenance, 19.8% production, transportation, and material moving
Income: Per capita: $23,266; Median household: $30,071; Average household: $45,418; Households with income of $100,000 or more: 11.5%; Poverty rate: 24.6%
Educational Attainment: High school diploma or higher: 90.6%; Bachelor's degree or higher: 15.7%; Graduate/professional degree or higher: 8.2%

School District(s)

Caldwell Exempted Village (KG-12)
2015-16 Enrollment: 799. . . . . (740) 732-5637
Housing: Homeownership rate: 60.4%; Median home value: $73,900; Median year structure built: 1958; Homeowner vacancy rate: 1.1%; Median selected monthly owner costs: $837 with a mortgage, $310 without a mortgage; Median gross rent: $609 per month; Rental vacancy rate: 6.1%
Health Insurance: 93.2% have insurance; 55.2% have private insurance; 59.5% have public insurance; 6.8% do not have insurance; 12.4% of children under 18 do not have insurance
Newspapers: Journal & Noble Co. Leader (weekly circulation 4,500)
Transportation: Commute: 91.8% car, 0.0% public transportation, 5.2% walk, 3.0% work from home; Mean travel time to work: 18.7 minutes

DEXTER CITY (village). Covers a land area of 0.167 square miles and a water area of 0.006 square miles. Located at 39.66° N. Lat; 81.47° W. Long. Elevation is 709 feet.
Population: 107; Growth (since 2000): -35.5%; Density: 642.0 persons per square mile; Race: 100.0% White, 0.0% Black/African American, 0.0% Asian, 0.0% American Indian/Alaska Native, 0.0% Native Hawaiian/Other Pacific Islander, 0.0% Two or more races, 0.0% Hispanic of any race; Average household size: 2.68; Median age: 25.5; Age under 18: 36.4%; Age 65 and over: 9.3%; Males per 100 females: 98.5; Marriage status: 49.4% never married, 29.1% now married, 0.0% separated, 10.1% widowed, 11.4% divorced; Foreign born: 0.0%; Speak English only: 97.8%; With disability: 10.3%; Veterans: 1.5%; Ancestry: 43.9% German, 28.0% Swedish, 5.6% Dutch, 5.6% Irish, 4.7% Polish
Employment: 0.0% management, business, and financial, 0.0% computer, engineering, and science, 20.0% education, legal, community service, arts, and media, 0.0% healthcare practitioners, 36.0% service, 26.0% sales and office, 6.0% natural resources, construction, and maintenance, 12.0% production, transportation, and material moving
Income: Per capita: $13,846; Median household: n/a; Average household: $35,303; Households with income of $100,000 or more: n/a; Poverty rate: 22.4%
Educational Attainment: High school diploma or higher: 72.2%; Bachelor's degree or higher: 1.9%; Graduate/professional degree or higher: n/a
Housing: Homeownership rate: 62.5%; Median home value: $65,000; Median year structure built: Before 1940; Homeowner vacancy rate: 0.0%;

Median selected monthly owner costs: $683 with a mortgage, n/a without a mortgage; Median gross rent: $542 per month; Rental vacancy rate: 0.0%
Health Insurance: 89.7% have insurance; 34.6% have private insurance; 63.6% have public insurance; 10.3% do not have insurance; 10.3% of children under 18 do not have insurance
Transportation: Commute: 82.0% car, 0.0% public transportation, 16.0% walk, 2.0% work from home; Mean travel time to work: 14.1 minutes

SARAHSVILLE (village). Covers a land area of 0.154 square miles and a water area of <.001 square miles. Located at 39.81° N. Lat; 81.47° W. Long. Elevation is 978 feet.
Population: 177; Growth (since 2000): -10.6%; Density: 1,146.0 persons per square mile; Race: 100.0% White, 0.0% Black/African American, 0.0% Asian, 0.0% American Indian/Alaska Native, 0.0% Native Hawaiian/Other Pacific Islander, 0.0% Two or more races, 0.0% Hispanic of any race; Average household size: 2.24; Median age: 55.4; Age under 18: 24.3%; Age 65 and over: 39.5%; Males per 100 females: 100.0; Marriage status: 11.4% never married, 60.7% now married, 0.0% separated, 11.4% widowed, 16.4% divorced; Foreign born: 0.0%; Speak English only: 100.0%; With disability: 15.3%; Veterans: 26.1%; Ancestry: 17.5% German, 8.5% English, 7.9% Irish, 6.2% American, 2.8% French
Employment: 3.4% management, business, and financial, 0.0% computer, engineering, and science, 0.0% education, legal, community service, arts, and media, 6.9% healthcare practitioners, 36.2% service, 6.9% sales and office, 34.5% natural resources, construction, and maintenance, 12.1% production, transportation, and material moving
Income: Per capita: $18,940; Median household: $41,161; Average household: $44,261; Households with income of $100,000 or more: 7.6%; Poverty rate: 9.0%
Educational Attainment: High school diploma or higher: 96.1%; Bachelor's degree or higher: 7.8%; Graduate/professional degree or higher: n/a

School District(s)

Noble Local (KG-12)
2015-16 Enrollment: 873. . . . . (740) 732-2084
Housing: Homeownership rate: 88.6%; Median home value: $71,400; Median year structure built: 1956; Homeowner vacancy rate: 0.0%; Median selected monthly owner costs: $792 with a mortgage, $338 without a mortgage; Median gross rent: n/a per month; Rental vacancy rate: 30.8%
Health Insurance: 88.1% have insurance; 67.8% have private insurance; 55.9% have public insurance; 11.9% do not have insurance; 18.6% of children under 18 do not have insurance
Transportation: Commute: 100.0% car, 0.0% public transportation, 0.0% walk, 0.0% work from home; Mean travel time to work: 22.7 minutes

SUMMERFIELD (village). Covers a land area of 0.371 square miles and a water area of <.001 square miles. Located at 39.80° N. Lat; 81.34° W. Long. Elevation is 1,204 feet.
Population: 232; Growth (since 2000): -21.6%; Density: 624.5 persons per square mile; Race: 93.5% White, 0.0% Black/African American, 0.0% Asian, 0.0% American Indian/Alaska Native, 0.0% Native Hawaiian/Other Pacific Islander, 6.5% Two or more races, 0.0% Hispanic of any race; Average household size: 2.27; Median age: 57.2; Age under 18: 17.2%; Age 65 and over: 34.9%; Males per 100 females: 96.9; Marriage status: 17.8% never married, 47.6% now married, 1.0% separated, 8.2% widowed, 26.4% divorced; Foreign born: 0.0%; Speak English only: 100.0%; With disability: 34.9%; Veterans: 25.0%; Ancestry: 28.4% Irish, 22.8% German, 7.8% Italian, 6.9% English, 5.6% American
Employment: 3.1% management, business, and financial, 0.0% computer, engineering, and science, 10.9% education, legal, community service, arts, and media, 6.3% healthcare practitioners, 29.7% service, 21.9% sales and office, 12.5% natural resources, construction, and maintenance, 15.6% production, transportation, and material moving
Income: Per capita: $22,563; Median household: $31,250; Average household: $52,336; Households with income of $100,000 or more: 10.8%; Poverty rate: 18.5%
Educational Attainment: High school diploma or higher: 79.6%; Bachelor's degree or higher: 5.0%; Graduate/professional degree or higher: 4.4%
Housing: Homeownership rate: 74.5%; Median home value: $56,500; Median year structure built: Before 1940; Homeowner vacancy rate: 0.0%; Median selected monthly owner costs: $600 with a mortgage, $278 without a mortgage; Median gross rent: $719 per month; Rental vacancy rate: 0.0%
Health Insurance: 91.4% have insurance; 50.0% have private insurance; 58.6% have public insurance; 8.6% do not have insurance; 0.0% of children under 18 do not have insurance
Transportation: Commute: 98.4% car, 0.0% public transportation, 1.6% walk, 0.0% work from home; Mean travel time to work: 31.5 minutes

Ottawa County

Located in northern Ohio; bounded on the northeast by Lake Erie; drained by Portage River; includes the Bass Islands. Covers a land area of 254.917 square miles, a water area of 330.146 square miles, and is located in the Eastern Time Zone at 41.54° N. Lat., 83.01° W. Long. The county was founded in 1840. County seat is Port Clinton.

Ottawa County is part of the Port Clinton, OH Micropolitan Statistical Area. The entire metro area includes: Ottawa County, OH

Population: 40,981; Growth (since 2000): 0.0%; Density: 160.8 persons per square mile; Race: 95.9% White, 1.2% Black/African American, 0.3% Asian, 0.1% American Indian/Alaska Native, 0.0% Native Hawaiian/Other Pacific Islander, 1.4% two or more races, 4.8% Hispanic of any race; Average household size: 2.31; Median age: 47.8; Age under 18: 19.5%; Age 65 and over: 22.1%; Males per 100 females: 97.4; Marriage status: 23.6% never married, 56.9% now married, 1.2% separated, 7.9% widowed, 11.5% divorced; Foreign born: 0.8%; Speak English only: 97.3%; With disability: 15.5%; Veterans: 10.4%; Ancestry: 43.9% German, 13.8% Irish, 8.2% English, 5.7% Polish, 5.7% American
Religion: Six largest groups: 17.5% Catholicism, 16.7% Lutheran, 6.3% Presbyterian-Reformed, 5.3% Methodist/Pietist, 1.7% Baptist, 1.3% Holiness
Economy: Unemployment rate: 5.2%; Leading industries: 17.3 % accommodation and food services; 13.5 % retail trade; 12.7 % other services (except public administration); Farms: 620 totaling 112,677 acres; Company size: 0 employ 1,000 or more persons, 2 employ 500 to 999 persons, 10 employ 100 to 499 persons, 1,014 employ less than 100 persons; Business ownership: 837 women-owned, n/a Black-owned, 89 Hispanic-owned, n/a Asian-owned, n/a American Indian/Alaska Native-owned
Employment: 12.8% management, business, and financial, 3.0% computer, engineering, and science, 8.3% education, legal, community service, arts, and media, 7.1% healthcare practitioners, 18.0% service, 20.6% sales and office, 10.6% natural resources, construction, and maintenance, 19.5% production, transportation, and material moving
Income: Per capita: $30,403; Median household: $54,580; Average household: $70,873; Households with income of $100,000 or more: 21.7%; Poverty rate: 11.1%
Educational Attainment: High school diploma or higher: 92.3%; Bachelor's degree or higher: 21.3%; Graduate/professional degree or higher: 8.0%
Housing: Homeownership rate: 78.2%; Median home value: $144,200; Median year structure built: 1972; Homeowner vacancy rate: 2.6%; Median selected monthly owner costs: $1,211 with a mortgage, $418 without a mortgage; Median gross rent: $687 per month; Rental vacancy rate: 8.0%
Vital Statistics: Birth rate: 88.1 per 10,000 population; Death rate: 128.0 per 10,000 population; Age-adjusted cancer mortality rate: 193.9 deaths per 100,000 population
Health Insurance: 93.0% have insurance; 75.1% have private insurance; 35.8% have public insurance; 7.0% do not have insurance; 3.0% of children under 18 do not have insurance
Health Care: Physicians: 10.8 per 10,000 population; Dentists: 3.7 per 10,000 population; Hospital beds: 6.1 per 10,000 population; Hospital admissions: 178.0 per 10,000 population
Transportation: Commute: 93.1% car, 1.0% public transportation, 1.0% walk, 4.0% work from home; Mean travel time to work: 23.8 minutes
2016 Presidential Election: 56.5% Trump, 37.0% Clinton, 4.3% Johnson, 0.7% Stein
National and State Parks: Catawba Island State Park; Crane Creek State Park; East Harbor State Park; Lakeside Daisy State Nature Preserve; Ottawa National Wildlife Refuge; South Bass Island State Park
Additional Information Contacts
Ottawa Government . . . . (419) 734-6710
http://www.co.ottawa.oh.us

Ottawa County Communities

CLAY CENTER (village). Covers a land area of 1.037 square miles and a water area of 0 square miles. Located at 41.57° N. Lat; 83.36° W. Long. Elevation is 610 feet.
Population: 337; Growth (since 2000): 14.6%; Density: 325.1 persons per square mile; Race: 100.0% White, 0.0% Black/African American, 0.0% Asian, 0.0% American Indian/Alaska Native, 0.0% Native Hawaiian/Other Pacific Islander, 0.0% Two or more races, 6.5% Hispanic of any race; Average household size: 2.46; Median age: 38.9; Age under 18: 29.1%; Age 65 and over: 13.6%; Males per 100 females: 85.2; Marriage status: 17.2% never married, 54.9% now married, 3.3% separated, 11.5% widowed, 16.4% divorced; Foreign born: 0.0%; Speak English only: 97.8%; With disability: 12.5%; Veterans: 7.1%; Ancestry: 51.3% German, 8.6% French, 7.4% English, 6.2% Hungarian, 5.9% Irish
Employment: 13.2% management, business, and financial, 4.6% computer, engineering, and science, 3.3% education, legal, community service, arts, and media, 1.3% healthcare practitioners, 21.7% service, 19.1% sales and office, 14.5% natural resources, construction, and maintenance, 22.4% production, transportation, and material moving
Income: Per capita: $20,723; Median household: $41,406; Average household: $52,542; Households with income of $100,000 or more: 13.2%; Poverty rate: 13.6%
Educational Attainment: High school diploma or higher: 96.8%; Bachelor's degree or higher: 9.3%; Graduate/professional degree or higher: 4.2%
Housing: Homeownership rate: 96.4%; Median home value: $79,600; Median year structure built: Before 1940; Homeowner vacancy rate: 0.0%; Median selected monthly owner costs: $823 with a mortgage, $296 without a mortgage; Median gross rent: $688 per month; Rental vacancy rate: 54.5%
Health Insurance: 95.8% have insurance; 79.8% have private insurance; 31.8% have public insurance; 4.2% do not have insurance; 5.1% of children under 18 do not have insurance
Transportation: Commute: 99.3% car, 0.0% public transportation, 0.0% walk, 0.0% work from home; Mean travel time to work: 23.7 minutes

CURTICE (CDP). Covers a land area of 3.636 square miles and a water area of 0 square miles. Located at 41.62° N. Lat; 83.37° W. Long. Elevation is 594 feet.
Population: 1,853; Growth (since 2000): n/a; Density: 509.7 persons per square mile; Race: 96.5% White, 0.0% Black/African American, 0.0% Asian, 0.0% American Indian/Alaska Native, 0.0% Native Hawaiian/Other Pacific Islander, 3.1% Two or more races, 2.6% Hispanic of any race; Average household size: 2.67; Median age: 39.8; Age under 18: 26.8%; Age 65 and over: 7.4%; Males per 100 females: 105.1; Marriage status: 34.0% never married, 54.9% now married, 0.8% separated, 3.8% widowed, 7.3% divorced; Foreign born: 0.0%; Speak English only: 99.1%; With disability: 9.7%; Veterans: 5.8%; Ancestry: 56.9% German, 15.8% Irish, 13.3% French, 10.3% English, 9.8% Hungarian
Employment: 6.5% management, business, and financial, 6.4% computer, engineering, and science, 4.6% education, legal, community service, arts, and media, 10.6% healthcare practitioners, 10.6% service, 30.0% sales and office, 13.4% natural resources, construction, and maintenance, 17.9% production, transportation, and material moving
Income: Per capita: $35,970; Median household: $87,417; Average household: $94,215; Households with income of $100,000 or more: 45.9%; Poverty rate: 6.3%
Educational Attainment: High school diploma or higher: 98.4%; Bachelor's degree or higher: 21.8%; Graduate/professional degree or higher: 4.8%

School District(s)

Oregon City (PK-12)
2015-16 Enrollment: 3,701 . . . . (419) 693-0661
Housing: Homeownership rate: 87.2%; Median home value: $166,200; Median year structure built: 1978; Homeowner vacancy rate: 0.0%; Median selected monthly owner costs: $1,596 with a mortgage, $431 without a mortgage; Median gross rent: $660 per month; Rental vacancy rate: 0.0%
Health Insurance: 97.7% have insurance; 89.9% have private insurance; 15.4% have public insurance; 2.3% do not have insurance; 0.0% of children under 18 do not have insurance
Transportation: Commute: 92.5% car, 0.0% public transportation, 1.3% walk, 6.3% work from home; Mean travel time to work: 28.3 minutes

ELMORE (village). Covers a land area of 0.814 square miles and a water area of 0 square miles. Located at 41.47° N. Lat; 83.29° W. Long. Elevation is 604 feet.
Population: 1,261; Growth (since 2000): -11.6%; Density: 1,549.7 persons per square mile; Race: 95.1% White, 0.0% Black/African American, 0.0% Asian, 0.0% American Indian/Alaska Native, 0.2% Native Hawaiian/Other Pacific Islander, 3.6% Two or more races, 4.1% Hispanic of any race; Average household size: 2.62; Median age: 39.8; Age under 18: 29.8%; Age 65 and over: 17.2%; Males per 100 females: 94.8; Marriage status: 20.2% never married, 56.3% now married, 0.9% separated, 9.7% widowed, 13.8% divorced; Foreign born: 0.0%; Speak English only: 98.4%; With disability: 12.4%; Veterans: 7.9%; Ancestry: 57.3% German, 10.2% Irish, 8.8% American, 7.8% Hungarian, 5.9% Polish
Employment: 9.2% management, business, and financial, 5.2% computer, engineering, and science, 13.0% education, legal, community service, arts, and media, 9.0% healthcare practitioners, 17.0% service, 17.7% sales and office, 11.9% natural resources, construction, and maintenance, 16.8% production, transportation, and material moving
Income: Per capita: $25,247; Median household: $58,750; Average household: $65,212; Households with income of $100,000 or more: 26.4%; Poverty rate: 6.5%
Educational Attainment: High school diploma or higher: 96.0%; Bachelor's degree or higher: 25.8%; Graduate/professional degree or higher: 10.7%

School District(s)

Woodmore Local (PK-12)
2015-16 Enrollment: 1,053 . . . . (419) 862-1060
Housing: Homeownership rate: 69.0%; Median home value: $115,500; Median year structure built: 1945; Homeowner vacancy rate: 2.4%; Median selected monthly owner costs: $1,137 with a mortgage, $453 without a mortgage; Median gross rent: $600 per month; Rental vacancy rate: 4.5%
Health Insurance: 97.5% have insurance; 79.0% have private insurance; 30.8% have public insurance; 2.5% do not have insurance; 2.7% of children under 18 do not have insurance
Transportation: Commute: 94.3% car, 0.0% public transportation, 1.1% walk, 4.1% work from home; Mean travel time to work: 24.8 minutes

GENOA (village). Covers a land area of 1.551 square miles and a water area of 0 square miles. Located at 41.52° N. Lat; 83.36° W. Long. Elevation is 623 feet.
History: Settled 1835 as Stony Ridge Station.
Population: 2,352; Growth (since 2000): 5.5%; Density: 1,516.8 persons per square mile; Race: 92.6% White, 1.1% Black/African American, 2.5% Asian, 0.0% American Indian/Alaska Native, 0.0% Native Hawaiian/Other Pacific Islander, 2.6% Two or more races, 4.3% Hispanic of any race; Average household size: 2.33; Median age: 42.6; Age under 18: 25.3%; Age 65 and over: 16.8%; Males per 100 females: 95.8; Marriage status: 26.5% never married, 52.2% now married, 1.2% separated, 9.6% widowed, 11.8% divorced; Foreign born: 0.3%; Speak English only: 95.7%; With disability: 19.2%; Veterans: 8.8%; Ancestry: 47.8% German, 7.8% Irish, 6.9% English, 6.6% French, 5.6% Hungarian
Employment: 11.0% management, business, and financial, 4.1% computer, engineering, and science, 2.7% education, legal, community service, arts, and media, 6.4% healthcare practitioners, 15.1% service, 22.0% sales and office, 13.5% natural resources, construction, and maintenance, 25.3% production, transportation, and material moving
Income: Per capita: $26,222; Median household: $53,169; Average household: $62,690; Households with income of $100,000 or more: 15.4%; Poverty rate: 16.3%
Educational Attainment: High school diploma or higher: 90.3%; Bachelor's degree or higher: 16.3%; Graduate/professional degree or higher: 2.2%

School District(s)

Genoa Area Local (PK-12)
2015-16 Enrollment: 1,340 . . . . (419) 855-7741
Housing: Homeownership rate: 68.4%; Median home value: $98,800; Median year structure built: 1957; Homeowner vacancy rate: 1.9%; Median selected monthly owner costs: $1,064 with a mortgage, $382 without a mortgage; Median gross rent: $724 per month; Rental vacancy rate: 3.4%
Health Insurance: 90.7% have insurance; 68.6% have private insurance; 32.1% have public insurance; 9.3% do not have insurance; 2.5% of children under 18 do not have insurance
Transportation: Commute: 94.7% car, 0.0% public transportation, 1.2% walk, 4.1% work from home; Mean travel time to work: 24.3 minutes
Additional Information Contacts

Village of Genoa . . . . (419) 855-7791
http://www.genoaohio.org

GRAYTOWN (unincorporated postal area)

ZCTA: 43432

Covers a land area of 22.769 square miles and a water area of 0.017 square miles. Located at 41.56° N. Lat; 83.25° W. Long. Elevation is 594 feet.

Population: 1,263; Growth (since 2000): -6.9%; Density: 55.5 persons per square mile; Race: 98.7% White, 0.0% Black/African American, 0.0% Asian, 0.0% American Indian/Alaska Native, 0.0% Native Hawaiian/Other Pacific Islander, 1.3% Two or more races, 4.4% Hispanic of any race; Average household size: 2.51; Median age: 50.1; Age under 18: 12.4%; Age 65 and over: 7.4%; Males per 100 females: 100.9; Marriage status: 26.7% never married, 62.7% now married, 0.0% separated, 7.4% widowed, 3.3% divorced; Foreign born: 0.0%; Speak English only: 100.0%; With disability: 8.0%; Veterans: 3.0%; Ancestry: 56.6% German, 16.2% Irish, 15.0% American, 8.7% Hungarian, 5.7% French

Employment: 8.4% management, business, and financial, 6.3% computer, engineering, and science, 8.4% education, legal, community service, arts, and media, 13.7% healthcare practitioners, 11.9% service, 16.4% sales and office, 11.1% natural resources, construction, and maintenance, 24.0% production, transportation, and material moving

Income: Per capita: $33,793; Median household: $81,094; Average household: $84,495; Households with income of $100,000 or more: 33.6%; Poverty rate: n/a

Educational Attainment: High school diploma or higher: 91.6%; Bachelor's degree or higher: 25.2%; Graduate/professional degree or higher: 4.7%

School District(s)

Benton Carroll Salem Local (PK-12)
2015-16 Enrollment: 1,566 . . . . (419) 898-6210

Housing: Homeownership rate: 96.6%; Median home value: $155,200; Median year structure built: 1974; Homeowner vacancy rate: 0.0%; Median selected monthly owner costs: $1,436 with a mortgage, $450 without a mortgage; Median gross rent: n/a per month; Rental vacancy rate: 0.0%

Health Insurance: 100.0% have insurance; 96.0% have private insurance; 12.7% have public insurance; 0.0% do not have insurance; 0.0% of children under 18 do not have insurance

Transportation: Commute: 95.7% car, 0.0% public transportation, 0.0% walk, 4.3% work from home; Mean travel time to work: 26.9 minutes

GYPSUM (unincorporated postal area)

ZCTA: 43433

Covers a land area of 0.501 square miles and a water area of 0 square miles. Located at 41.50° N. Lat; 82.88° W. Long. Elevation is 581 feet.

Population: 34; Growth (since 2000): n/a; Density: 67.9 persons per square mile; Race: 100.0% White, 0.0% Black/African American, 0.0% Asian, 0.0% American Indian/Alaska Native, 0.0% Native Hawaiian/Other Pacific Islander, 0.0% Two or more races, 0.0% Hispanic of any race; Average household size: 2.00; Median age: 54.9; Age under 18: 0.0%; Age 65 and over: 23.5%; Males per 100 females: 93.9; Marriage status: 20.6% never married, 55.9% now married, 0.0% separated, 23.5% widowed, 0.0% divorced; Foreign born: 0.0%; Speak English only: 79.4%; With disability: 0.0%; Veterans: 0.0%; Ancestry: 29.4% American, 26.5% German, 23.5% Polish, 20.6% English

Employment: 0.0% management, business, and financial, 0.0% computer, engineering, and science, 0.0% education, legal, community service, arts, and media, 0.0% healthcare practitioners, 47.4% service, 52.6% sales and office, 0.0% natural resources, construction, and maintenance, 0.0% production, transportation, and material moving

Income: Per capita: $20,479; Median household: n/a; Average household: n/a; Households with income of $100,000 or more: n/a; Poverty rate: n/a

Educational Attainment: High school diploma or higher: 70.6%; Bachelor's degree or higher: n/a; Graduate/professional degree or higher: n/a

Housing: Homeownership rate: 100.0%; Median home value: n/a; Median year structure built: n/a; Homeowner vacancy rate: 0.0%; Median selected monthly owner costs: $0 with a mortgage, $0 without a mortgage; Median gross rent: n/a per month; Rental vacancy rate: 0.0%

Health Insurance: 44.1% have insurance; 44.1% have private insurance; 23.5% have public insurance; 55.9% do not have insurance; 0.0% of children under 18 do not have insurance

Transportation: Commute: 100.0% car, 0.0% public transportation, 0.0% walk, 0.0% work from home; Mean travel time to work: 0.0 minutes

LACARNE (unincorporated postal area)

ZCTA: 43439

Covers a land area of 0.055 square miles and a water area of 0 square miles. Located at 41.52° N. Lat; 83.04° W. Long. Elevation is 577 feet.

Population: 45; Growth (since 2000): -39.2%; Density: 813.6 persons per square mile; Race: 100.0% White, 0.0% Black/African American, 0.0% Asian, 0.0% American Indian/Alaska Native, 0.0% Native Hawaiian/Other Pacific Islander, 0.0% Two or more races, 0.0% Hispanic of any race; Average household size: 2.25; Median age: 58.1; Age under 18: 8.9%; Age 65 and over: 8.9%; Males per 100 females: 79.4; Marriage status: 9.8% never married, 70.7% now married, 0.0% separated, 0.0% widowed, 19.5% divorced; Foreign born: 0.0%; Speak English only: 100.0%; With disability: 24.4%; Veterans: 0.0%; Ancestry: 46.7% German, 17.8% American

Employment: 0.0% management, business, and financial, 0.0% computer, engineering, and science, 0.0% education, legal, community service, arts, and media, 0.0% healthcare practitioners, 28.9% service, 0.0% sales and office, 0.0% natural resources, construction, and maintenance, 71.1% production, transportation, and material moving

Income: Per capita: $28,167; Median household: n/a; Average household: $69,005; Households with income of $100,000 or more: 20.0%; Poverty rate: n/a

Educational Attainment: High school diploma or higher: 70.3%; Bachelor's degree or higher: n/a; Graduate/professional degree or higher: n/a

Housing: Homeownership rate: 100.0%; Median home value: $62,500; Median year structure built: 1966; Homeowner vacancy rate: 0.0%; Median selected monthly owner costs: $725 with a mortgage, $0 without a mortgage; Median gross rent: n/a per month; Rental vacancy rate: 100.0%

Health Insurance: 100.0% have insurance; 100.0% have private insurance; 8.9% have public insurance; 0.0% do not have insurance; 0.0% of children under 18 do not have insurance

Transportation: Commute: 100.0% car, 0.0% public transportation, 0.0% walk, 0.0% work from home; Mean travel time to work: 0.0 minutes

LAKESIDE (CDP). Covers a land area of 0.688 square miles and a water area of 0 square miles. Located at 41.54° N. Lat; 82.75° W. Long. Elevation is 607 feet.

Population: 643; Growth (since 2000): n/a; Density: 934.5 persons per square mile; Race: 98.6% White, 0.0% Black/African American, 0.0% Asian, 0.0% American Indian/Alaska Native, 0.0% Native Hawaiian/Other Pacific Islander, 1.4% Two or more races, 0.0% Hispanic of any race; Average household size: 1.45; Median age: 69.9; Age under 18: 0.0%; Age 65 and over: 81.5%; Males per 100 females: 76.6; Marriage status: 5.3% never married, 63.3% now married, 0.0% separated, 25.2% widowed, 6.2% divorced; Foreign born: 1.4%; Speak English only: 100.0%; With disability: 36.1%; Veterans: 18.8%; Ancestry: 32.7% German, 28.6% English, 21.0% Irish, 7.0% French, 5.3% Welsh

Employment: 9.4% management, business, and financial, 5.0% computer, engineering, and science, 28.3% education, legal, community service, arts, and media, 5.0% healthcare practitioners, 14.5% service, 25.2% sales and office, 9.4% natural resources, construction, and maintenance, 3.1% production, transportation, and material moving

Income: Per capita: $44,019; Median household: $38,980; Average household: $63,232; Households with income of $100,000 or more: 15.0%; Poverty rate: 5.9%

Educational Attainment: High school diploma or higher: 96.9%; Bachelor's degree or higher: 57.5%; Graduate/professional degree or higher: 21.5%

School District(s)

Danbury Local (PK-12)
2015-16 Enrollment: 474 . . . . (419) 798-5185

Housing: Homeownership rate: 66.7%; Median home value: $263,700; Median year structure built: 1951; Homeowner vacancy rate: 2.7%; Median selected monthly owner costs: $1,393 with a mortgage, $445 without a mortgage; Median gross rent: $1,539 per month; Rental vacancy rate: 10.0%

Health Insurance: 97.6% have insurance; 73.3% have private insurance; 80.4% have public insurance; 2.4% do not have insurance; 0.0% of children under 18 do not have insurance

Transportation: Commute: 84.9% car, 5.0% public transportation, 5.0% walk, 5.0% work from home; Mean travel time to work: 24.5 minutes

LAKESIDE MARBLEHEAD (unincorporated postal area)

ZCTA: 43440

Covers a land area of 16.096 square miles and a water area of 2.544 square miles. Located at 41.53° N. Lat; 82.78° W. Long..

Population: 4,849; Growth (since 2000): 12.3%; Density: 301.3 persons per square mile; Race: 97.5% White, 1.1% Black/African American, 0.0% Asian, 0.1% American Indian/Alaska Native, 0.0% Native Hawaiian/Other Pacific Islander, 1.0% Two or more races, 0.6% Hispanic of any race; Average household size: 1.97; Median age: 58.3; Age under 18: 13.6%; Age 65 and over: 37.8%; Males per 100 females: 95.8; Marriage status: 16.6% never married, 60.4% now married, 0.4% separated, 11.4% widowed, 11.5% divorced; Foreign born: 1.5%; Speak English only: 98.7%; With disability: 17.9%; Veterans: 14.8%; Ancestry: 36.5% German, 15.2% English, 13.4% Irish, 9.3% Polish, 7.5% Italian

Employment: 14.2% management, business, and financial, 3.2% computer, engineering, and science, 9.2% education, legal, community service, arts, and media, 2.5% healthcare practitioners, 16.5% service, 29.0% sales and office, 10.6% natural resources, construction, and maintenance, 14.8% production, transportation, and material moving

Income: Per capita: $35,250; Median household: $47,500; Average household: $69,264; Households with income of $100,000 or more: 19.3%; Poverty rate: 13.5%

Educational Attainment: High school diploma or higher: 94.6%; Bachelor's degree or higher: 25.7%; Graduate/professional degree or higher: 10.5%

School District(s)

Danbury Local (PK-12)
2015-16 Enrollment: 474. . . . . (419) 798-5185

Housing: Homeownership rate: 82.6%; Median home value: $174,000; Median year structure built: 1979; Homeowner vacancy rate: 2.6%; Median selected monthly owner costs: $1,258 with a mortgage, $419 without a mortgage; Median gross rent: $742 per month; Rental vacancy rate: 3.6%

Health Insurance: 92.8% have insurance; 71.9% have private insurance; 49.9% have public insurance; 7.2% do not have insurance; 0.0% of children under 18 do not have insurance

Transportation: Commute: 88.6% car, 0.4% public transportation, 1.7% walk, 6.2% work from home; Mean travel time to work: 23.9 minutes

MARBLEHEAD (village). Covers a land area of 3.305 square miles and a water area of 0.997 square miles. Located at 41.53° N. Lat; 82.72° W. Long. Elevation is 623 feet.

History: The Benajah Wolcott family settled here in 1809 and found three orchards which the French had planted earlier. Quarrying began in 1834 when John Clemens, a relative of Mark Twain, established himself here. Marblehead may have been called Marble Headland by an early visitor, who thought the white limestone cliffs were marble.

Population: 881; Growth (since 2000): 15.6%; Density: 266.6 persons per square mile; Race: 97.0% White, 0.0% Black/African American, 0.0% Asian, 0.3% American Indian/Alaska Native, 0.0% Native Hawaiian/Other Pacific Islander, 0.5% Two or more races, 3.2% Hispanic of any race; Average household size: 2.01; Median age: 53.3; Age under 18: 9.0%; Age 65 and over: 34.7%; Males per 100 females: 98.9; Marriage status: 16.8% never married, 68.0% now married, 0.9% separated, 7.7% widowed, 7.5% divorced; Foreign born: 2.3%; Speak English only: 96.7%; With disability: 11.6%; Veterans: 10.0%; Ancestry: 36.0% German, 14.3% Slovak, 12.7% Irish, 9.8% English, 7.0% Italian

Employment: 21.6% management, business, and financial, 1.3% computer, engineering, and science, 7.1% education, legal, community service, arts, and media, 4.8% healthcare practitioners, 12.6% service, 30.7% sales and office, 6.1% natural resources, construction, and maintenance, 15.8% production, transportation, and material moving

Income: Per capita: $43,044; Median household: $67,750; Average household: $87,816; Households with income of $100,000 or more: 31.2%; Poverty rate: 3.9%

Educational Attainment: High school diploma or higher: 93.5%; Bachelor's degree or higher: 25.7%; Graduate/professional degree or higher: 11.0%

Housing: Homeownership rate: 85.4%; Median home value: $252,800; Median year structure built: 1981; Homeowner vacancy rate: 6.9%; Median selected monthly owner costs: $1,547 with a mortgage, $410 without a mortgage; Median gross rent: $813 per month; Rental vacancy rate: 0.0%

Health Insurance: 97.8% have insurance; 86.8% have private insurance; 39.7% have public insurance; 2.2% do not have insurance; 0.0% of children under 18 do not have insurance

Newspapers: Peninsula News (weekly circulation 1,800)

Transportation: Commute: 74.9% car, 0.0% public transportation, 0.7% walk, 13.8% work from home; Mean travel time to work: 23.1 minutes

MARTIN (unincorporated postal area)

ZCTA: 43445

Covers a land area of 18.882 square miles and a water area of 0.103 square miles. Located at 41.58° N. Lat; 83.30° W. Long. Elevation is 604 feet.

Population: 1,120; Growth (since 2000): -4.3%; Density: 59.3 persons per square mile; Race: 95.0% White, 0.0% Black/African American, 0.0% Asian, 0.0% American Indian/Alaska Native, 0.0% Native Hawaiian/Other Pacific Islander, 3.6% Two or more races, 10.1% Hispanic of any race; Average household size: 2.71; Median age: 46.0; Age under 18: 18.1%; Age 65 and over: 14.7%; Males per 100 females: 110.7; Marriage status: 24.6% never married, 57.0% now married, 0.8% separated, 4.8% widowed, 13.6% divorced; Foreign born: 0.0%; Speak English only: 93.1%; With disability: 16.8%; Veterans: 6.7%; Ancestry: 50.5% German, 12.1% Irish, 9.3% English, 5.5% American, 5.5% Italian

Employment: 14.9% management, business, and financial, 3.3% computer, engineering, and science, 6.6% education, legal, community service, arts, and media, 9.5% healthcare practitioners, 7.4% service, 16.4% sales and office, 16.1% natural resources, construction, and maintenance, 25.8% production, transportation, and material moving

Income: Per capita: $32,789; Median household: $79,167; Average household: $86,505; Households with income of $100,000 or more: 43.2%; Poverty rate: 2.5%

Educational Attainment: High school diploma or higher: 97.0%; Bachelor's degree or higher: 19.5%; Graduate/professional degree or higher: 6.5%

Housing: Homeownership rate: 97.3%; Median home value: $147,800; Median year structure built: 1959; Homeowner vacancy rate: 10.2%; Median selected monthly owner costs: $1,518 with a mortgage, $432 without a mortgage; Median gross rent: n/a per month; Rental vacancy rate: 0.0%

Health Insurance: 90.8% have insurance; 83.5% have private insurance; 21.5% have public insurance; 9.2% do not have insurance; 9.9% of children under 18 do not have insurance

Transportation: Commute: 97.0% car, 0.0% public transportation, 0.0% walk, 3.0% work from home; Mean travel time to work: 32.1 minutes

MIDDLE BASS (unincorporated postal area)

ZCTA: 43446

Covers a land area of 1.258 square miles and a water area of 0.023 square miles. Located at 41.68° N. Lat; 82.81° W. Long. Elevation is 581 feet.

Population: 102; Growth (since 2000): n/a; Density: 81.1 persons per square mile; Race: 100.0% White, 0.0% Black/African American, 0.0% Asian, 0.0% American Indian/Alaska Native, 0.0% Native Hawaiian/Other Pacific Islander, 0.0% Two or more races, 0.0% Hispanic of any race; Average household size: 1.92; Median age: 60.5; Age under 18: 11.8%; Age 65 and over: 47.1%; Males per 100 females: 66.7; Marriage status: 4.3% never married, 80.9% now married, 4.3% separated, 7.4% widowed, 7.4% divorced; Foreign born: 6.9%; Speak English only: 100.0%; With disability: 10.8%; Veterans: 18.9%; Ancestry: 37.3% German, 28.4% Irish, 12.7% Polish, 10.8% English, 6.9% Lebanese

Employment: 16.3% management, business, and financial, 0.0% computer, engineering, and science, 23.3% education, legal, community service, arts, and media, 7.0% healthcare practitioners, 7.0% service, 27.9% sales and office, 18.6% natural resources, construction, and maintenance, 0.0% production, transportation, and material moving

Income: Per capita: $44,951; Median household: $48,125; Average household: $84,849; Households with income of $100,000 or more: 28.3%; Poverty rate: n/a

Educational Attainment: High school diploma or higher: 98.9%; Bachelor's degree or higher: 43.3%; Graduate/professional degree or higher: 23.3%

Housing: Homeownership rate: 100.0%; Median home value: $256,300; Median year structure built: 1972; Homeowner vacancy rate: 7.0%; Median selected monthly owner costs: $1,500 with a mortgage, $325 without a mortgage; Median gross rent: n/a per month; Rental vacancy rate: 0.0%

Health Insurance: 98.0% have insurance; 83.3% have private insurance; 45.1% have public insurance; 2.0% do not have insurance; 0.0% of children under 18 do not have insurance

Transportation: Commute: 74.4% car, 0.0% public transportation, 0.0% walk, 11.6% work from home; Mean travel time to work: 23.2 minutes

Airports: Middle Bass Island (general aviation)

OAK HARBOR (village). Covers a land area of 1.550 square miles and a water area of 0.153 square miles. Located at 41.51° N. Lat; 83.13° W. Long. Elevation is 584 feet.
History: Sometimes spelled Oakharbor.
Population: 2,741; Growth (since 2000): -3.5%; Density: 1,768.1 persons per square mile; Race: 96.4% White, 0.0% Black/African American, 0.2% Asian, 0.0% American Indian/Alaska Native, 0.0% Native Hawaiian/Other Pacific Islander, 0.3% Two or more races, 5.3% Hispanic of any race; Average household size: 2.36; Median age: 40.2; Age under 18: 24.4%; Age 65 and over: 18.1%; Males per 100 females: 86.8; Marriage status: 24.9% never married, 51.8% now married, 1.7% separated, 9.2% widowed, 14.2% divorced; Foreign born: 0.2%; Speak English only: 97.1%; With disability: 15.6%; Veterans: 9.9%; Ancestry: 57.8% German, 13.6% Irish, 7.8% English, 6.3% Polish, 5.3% French
Employment: 15.7% management, business, and financial, 2.1% computer, engineering, and science, 7.4% education, legal, community service, arts, and media, 4.4% healthcare practitioners, 18.2% service, 21.3% sales and office, 9.2% natural resources, construction, and maintenance, 21.8% production, transportation, and material moving
Income: Per capita: $26,201; Median household: $42,394; Average household: $60,341; Households with income of $100,000 or more: 14.9%; Poverty rate: 15.1%
Educational Attainment: High school diploma or higher: 93.7%; Bachelor's degree or higher: 18.9%; Graduate/professional degree or higher: 9.4%

School District(s)

Benton Carroll Salem Local (PK-12)
2015-16 Enrollment: 1,566 . . . . (419) 898-6210
Housing: Homeownership rate: 64.4%; Median home value: $112,300; Median year structure built: 1951; Homeowner vacancy rate: 1.8%; Median selected monthly owner costs: $1,048 with a mortgage, $362 without a mortgage; Median gross rent: $659 per month; Rental vacancy rate: 8.6%
Health Insurance: 88.2% have insurance; 68.9% have private insurance; 37.3% have public insurance; 11.8% do not have insurance; 3.6% of children under 18 do not have insurance
Safety: Violent crime rate: 3.7 per 10,000 population; Property crime rate: 155.3 per 10,000 population
Newspapers: The Exponent (weekly circulation 2,000)
Transportation: Commute: 93.4% car, 0.3% public transportation, 1.4% walk, 1.7% work from home; Mean travel time to work: 21.9 minutes
Additional Information Contacts
Village of Oak Harbor . . . . (419) 898-5561
http://www.oakharbor.oh.us

PORT CLINTON (city). County seat. Covers a land area of 2.078 square miles and a water area of 0.201 square miles. Located at 41.51° N. Lat; 82.94° W. Long. Elevation is 577 feet.
History: Port Clinton was platted in 1828 and settled by some Scotch immigrants, bound for Chicago, who were shipwrecked at this point and settled here. The town was named for DeWitt Clinton.
Population: 6,004; Growth (since 2000): -6.1%; Density: 2,888.9 persons per square mile; Race: 91.3% White, 4.3% Black/African American, 0.0% Asian, 0.4% American Indian/Alaska Native, 0.0% Native Hawaiian/Other Pacific Islander, 1.1% Two or more races, 9.6% Hispanic of any race; Average household size: 2.20; Median age: 43.8; Age under 18: 22.7%; Age 65 and over: 17.1%; Males per 100 females: 91.5; Marriage status: 28.9% never married, 45.7% now married, 2.3% separated, 8.0% widowed, 17.4% divorced; Foreign born: 0.8%; Speak English only: 95.8%; With disability: 15.3%; Veterans: 7.8%; Ancestry: 36.4% German, 15.1% Irish, 7.6% Italian, 6.2% English, 5.0% American
Employment: 10.7% management, business, and financial, 4.0% computer, engineering, and science, 6.7% education, legal, community service, arts, and media, 4.9% healthcare practitioners, 20.2% service, 23.1% sales and office, 10.8% natural resources, construction, and maintenance, 19.6% production, transportation, and material moving
Income: Per capita: $24,037; Median household: $45,244; Average household: $53,996; Households with income of $100,000 or more: 12.3%; Poverty rate: 12.1%
Educational Attainment: High school diploma or higher: 88.4%; Bachelor's degree or higher: 19.1%; Graduate/professional degree or higher: 7.7%

School District(s)

Port Clinton City (PK-12)
2015-16 Enrollment: 1,810 . . . . (419) 732-2102
Housing: Homeownership rate: 67.5%; Median home value: $103,700; Median year structure built: 1956; Homeowner vacancy rate: 0.6%; Median selected monthly owner costs: $1,039 with a mortgage, $394 without a mortgage; Median gross rent: $608 per month; Rental vacancy rate: 12.7%
Health Insurance: 93.1% have insurance; 71.8% have private insurance; 34.9% have public insurance; 6.9% do not have insurance; 0.9% of children under 18 do not have insurance
Hospitals: H B Magruder Memorial Hospital (98 beds)
Safety: Violent crime rate: 21.9 per 10,000 population; Property crime rate: 286.2 per 10,000 population
Newspapers: News-Herald (daily circulation 5,200); The Beacon (weekly circulation 17,000)
Transportation: Commute: 93.4% car, 1.2% public transportation, 1.1% walk, 3.9% work from home; Mean travel time to work: 18.9 minutes
Airports: Carl R Keller Field (general aviation)
Additional Information Contacts
City of Port Clinton . . . . (419) 734-5522

PUT-IN-BAY (village). Covers a land area of 0.453 square miles and a water area of 0.178 square miles. Located at 41.65° N. Lat; 82.82° W. Long. Elevation is 568 feet.
History: Perry's Victory and International Peace Memorial national monument (est. 1936) is near here. A granite column 352 feet high commemorates battle of Lake Erie (1813), in which Admiral Perry's U.S. fleet defeated the British, and symbolizes century of peace between U.S. and Canada.
Population: 103; Growth (since 2000): -19.5%; Density: 227.5 persons per square mile; Race: 100.0% White, 0.0% Black/African American, 0.0% Asian, 0.0% American Indian/Alaska Native, 0.0% Native Hawaiian/Other Pacific Islander, 0.0% Two or more races, 10.7% Hispanic of any race; Average household size: 1.63; Median age: 58.3; Age under 18: 3.9%; Age 65 and over: 33.0%; Males per 100 females: 112.3; Marriage status: 25.0% never married, 63.0% now married, 0.0% separated, 8.0% widowed, 4.0% divorced; Foreign born: 1.0%; Speak English only: 99.0%; With disability: 9.7%; Veterans: 5.1%; Ancestry: 46.6% German, 18.4% Irish, 16.5% English, 7.8% Czechoslovakian, 4.9% Hungarian
Employment: 22.5% management, business, and financial, 0.0% computer, engineering, and science, 12.7% education, legal, community service, arts, and media, 8.5% healthcare practitioners, 39.4% service, 15.5% sales and office, 0.0% natural resources, construction, and maintenance, 1.4% production, transportation, and material moving
Income: Per capita: $44,383; Median household: $64,375; Average household: $72,535; Households with income of $100,000 or more: 22.2%; Poverty rate: 4.9%
Educational Attainment: High school diploma or higher: 93.9%; Bachelor's degree or higher: 40.4%; Graduate/professional degree or higher: 12.1%

School District(s)

Put-In-Bay Local (PK-12)
2015-16 Enrollment: 75. . . . . (419) 285-3614
Housing: Homeownership rate: 58.7%; Median home value: $468,200; Median year structure built: 1970; Homeowner vacancy rate: 0.0%; Median selected monthly owner costs: n/a with a mortgage, $500 without a mortgage; Median gross rent: $532 per month; Rental vacancy rate: 0.0%
Health Insurance: 100.0% have insurance; 90.3% have private insurance; 41.7% have public insurance; 0.0% do not have insurance; 0.0% of children under 18 do not have insurance
Transportation: Commute: 21.0% car, 0.0% public transportation, 24.2% walk, 54.8% work from home; Mean travel time to work: 2.0 minutes
Airports: Put-in-Bay (general aviation)

ROCKY RIDGE (village). Covers a land area of 1.011 square miles and a water area of 0.015 square miles. Located at 41.53° N. Lat; 83.21° W. Long. Elevation is 604 feet.
Population: 520; Growth (since 2000): 33.7%; Density: 514.5 persons per square mile; Race: 98.7% White, 0.0% Black/African American, 0.0% Asian, 0.0% American Indian/Alaska Native, 0.0% Native Hawaiian/Other Pacific Islander, 1.3% Two or more races, 2.7% Hispanic of any race; Average household size: 3.29; Median age: 30.8; Age under 18: 35.2%; Age 65 and over: 8.8%; Males per 100 females: 106.4; Marriage status: 29.7% never married, 51.6% now married, 4.6% separated, 4.6% widowed, 14.1% divorced; Foreign born: 0.2%; Speak English only: 95.1%;

With disability: 12.1%; Veterans: 8.3%; Ancestry: 56.2% German, 19.0% Irish, 8.8% Polish, 6.3% French, 5.6% American
Employment: 7.4% management, business, and financial, 0.9% computer, engineering, and science, 2.2% education, legal, community service, arts, and media, 11.4% healthcare practitioners, 25.3% service, 14.4% sales and office, 19.2% natural resources, construction, and maintenance, 19.2% production, transportation, and material moving
Income: Per capita: $18,900; Median household: $44,375; Average household: $60,116; Households with income of $100,000 or more: 24.7%; Poverty rate: 17.1%
Educational Attainment: High school diploma or higher: 88.2%; Bachelor's degree or higher: 7.3%; Graduate/professional degree or higher: 2.1%
Housing: Homeownership rate: 82.9%; Median home value: $104,900; Median year structure built: 1974; Homeowner vacancy rate: 3.0%; Median selected monthly owner costs: $1,100 with a mortgage, $454 without a mortgage; Median gross rent: $725 per month; Rental vacancy rate: 0.0%
Health Insurance: 89.2% have insurance; 63.7% have private insurance; 32.5% have public insurance; 10.8% do not have insurance; 8.7% of children under 18 do not have insurance
Transportation: Commute: 96.4% car, 3.2% public transportation, 0.5% walk, 0.0% work from home; Mean travel time to work: 24.1 minutes

WILLISTON (CDP). Covers a land area of 0.611 square miles and a water area of 0 square miles. Located at 41.60° N. Lat; 83.34° W. Long. Elevation is 594 feet.
Population: 641; Growth (since 2000): n/a; Density: 1,048.4 persons per square mile; Race: 92.5% White, 1.6% Black/African American, 0.0% Asian, 0.0% American Indian/Alaska Native, 0.0% Native Hawaiian/Other Pacific Islander, 5.9% Two or more races, 16.7% Hispanic of any race; Average household size: 2.48; Median age: 36.1; Age under 18: 10.9%; Age 65 and over: 10.9%; Males per 100 females: 94.8; Marriage status: 48.2% never married, 48.5% now married, 0.0% separated, 0.0% widowed, 3.3% divorced; Foreign born: 0.0%; Speak English only: 100.0%; With disability: 25.5%; Veterans: 6.0%; Ancestry: 26.4% German, 18.1% Irish, 9.0% French, 8.9% Italian, 3.0% Polish
Employment: 0.0% management, business, and financial, 0.0% computer, engineering, and science, 5.2% education, legal, community service, arts, and media, 6.1% healthcare practitioners, 2.9% service, 16.7% sales and office, 6.3% natural resources, construction, and maintenance, 62.8% production, transportation, and material moving
Income: Per capita: $22,552; Median household: $57,639; Average household: $66,405; Households with income of $100,000 or more: 11.2%; Poverty rate: 22.1%
Educational Attainment: High school diploma or higher: 82.4%; Bachelor's degree or higher: 12.1%; Graduate/professional degree or higher: n/a
Housing: Homeownership rate: 49.0%; Median home value: $98,600; Median year structure built: 1958; Homeowner vacancy rate: 0.0%; Median selected monthly owner costs: $986 with a mortgage, $355 without a mortgage; Median gross rent: $811 per month; Rental vacancy rate: 0.0%
Health Insurance: 76.7% have insurance; 55.9% have private insurance; 27.0% have public insurance; 23.3% do not have insurance; 0.0% of children under 18 do not have insurance
Transportation: Commute: 85.6% car, 12.6% public transportation, 1.8% walk, 0.0% work from home; Mean travel time to work: 24.5 minutes

Paulding County

Located in northwestern Ohio; bounded on the west by Indiana; drained by the Auglaize and Maumee Rivers. Covers a land area of 416.438 square miles, a water area of 2.410 square miles, and is located in the Eastern Time Zone at 41.12° N. Lat., 84.58° W. Long. The county was founded in 1820. County seat is Paulding.

Weather Station: Paulding Elevation: 725 feet

	Jan	Feb	Mar	Apr	May	Jun	Jul	Aug	Sep	Oct	Nov	Dec
High	32	35	46	60	71	80	84	82	76	63	49	36
Low	16	18	27	37	48	58	61	59	51	40	31	21
Precip	2.1	2.0	2.5	3.2	4.1	3.4	3.9	3.2	3.0	2.7	2.8	2.6
Snow	5.9	5.8	3.6	0.3	0.0	0.0	0.0	0.0	0.0	0.1	0.6	4.2

High and Low temperatures in degrees Fahrenheit; Precipitation and Snow in inches

Population: 19,057; Growth (since 2000): -6.1%; Density: 45.8 persons per square mile; Race: 95.1% White, 1.1% Black/African American, 0.4% Asian, 0.2% American Indian/Alaska Native, 0.0% Native Hawaiian/Other Pacific Islander, 1.5% two or more races, 4.5% Hispanic of any race; Average household size: 2.48; Median age: 41.3; Age under 18: 23.9%; Age 65 and over: 16.8%; Males per 100 females: 97.9; Marriage status: 22.8% never married, 59.7% now married, 1.3% separated, 7.1% widowed, 10.5% divorced; Foreign born: 1.4%; Speak English only: 96.5%; With disability: 16.5%; Veterans: 10.0%; Ancestry: 36.4% German, 11.9% Irish, 9.3% American, 6.9% English, 2.5% Dutch
Religion: Six largest groups: 23.1% Catholicism, 9.4% Methodist/Pietist, 4.5% Baptist, 4.4% Lutheran, 4.4% Holiness, 2.7% European Free-Church
Economy: Unemployment rate: 4.1%; Leading industries: 16.4 % retail trade; 13.0 % other services (except public administration); 11.0 % manufacturing; Farms: 676 totaling 220,878 acres; Company size: 0 employ 1,000 or more persons, 0 employ 500 to 999 persons, 7 employ 100 to 499 persons, 292 employ less than 100 persons; Business ownership: 476 women-owned, n/a Black-owned, n/a Hispanic-owned, n/a Asian-owned, n/a American Indian/Alaska Native-owned
Employment: 10.2% management, business, and financial, 3.1% computer, engineering, and science, 6.4% education, legal, community service, arts, and media, 5.0% healthcare practitioners, 17.6% service, 17.9% sales and office, 10.1% natural resources, construction, and maintenance, 29.8% production, transportation, and material moving
Income: Per capita: $24,174; Median household: $48,003; Average household: $60,185; Households with income of $100,000 or more: 14.1%; Poverty rate: 11.0%
Educational Attainment: High school diploma or higher: 90.2%; Bachelor's degree or higher: 13.0%; Graduate/professional degree or higher: 4.7%
Housing: Homeownership rate: 77.9%; Median home value: $91,100; Median year structure built: 1970; Homeowner vacancy rate: 2.4%; Median selected monthly owner costs: $934 with a mortgage, $402 without a mortgage; Median gross rent: $619 per month; Rental vacancy rate: 7.0%
Vital Statistics: Birth rate: 116.1 per 10,000 population; Death rate: 102.3 per 10,000 population; Age-adjusted cancer mortality rate: 155.7 deaths per 100,000 population
Health Insurance: 92.0% have insurance; 70.1% have private insurance; 37.3% have public insurance; 8.0% do not have insurance; 4.1% of children under 18 do not have insurance
Health Care: Physicians: 3.2 per 10,000 population; Dentists: 2.1 per 10,000 population; Hospital beds: 13.2 per 10,000 population; Hospital admissions: 244.1 per 10,000 population
Transportation: Commute: 92.1% car, 0.1% public transportation, 2.6% walk, 4.2% work from home; Mean travel time to work: 22.9 minutes
2016 Presidential Election: 71.5% Trump, 23.0% Clinton, 3.1% Johnson, 0.9% Stein
Additional Information Contacts
Paulding Government . . . . (419) 399-8215

Paulding County Communities

ANTWERP (village). Covers a land area of 1.334 square miles and a water area of <.001 square miles. Located at 41.18° N. Lat; 84.74° W. Long. Elevation is 728 feet.
Population: 1,522; Growth (since 2000): -12.5%; Density: 1,141.2 persons per square mile; Race: 95.7% White, 0.4% Black/African American, 0.3% Asian, 0.4% American Indian/Alaska Native, 0.3% Native Hawaiian/Other Pacific Islander, 2.4% Two or more races, 7.9% Hispanic of any race; Average household size: 2.27; Median age: 41.4; Age under 18: 25.9%; Age 65 and over: 19.9%; Males per 100 females: 92.9; Marriage status: 22.4% never married, 50.2% now married, 0.9% separated, 12.6% widowed, 14.7% divorced; Foreign born: 1.3%; Speak English only: 98.2%; With disability: 20.6%; Veterans: 9.6%; Ancestry: 39.5% German, 18.6% Irish, 6.4% Dutch, 6.2% English, 5.7% French
Employment: 12.1% management, business, and financial, 2.6% computer, engineering, and science, 5.1% education, legal, community service, arts, and media, 7.0% healthcare practitioners, 13.6% service, 18.3% sales and office, 4.2% natural resources, construction, and maintenance, 37.1% production, transportation, and material moving
Income: Per capita: $22,662; Median household: $40,184; Average household: $50,394; Households with income of $100,000 or more: 7.9%; Poverty rate: 15.3%
Educational Attainment: High school diploma or higher: 90.2%; Bachelor's degree or higher: 14.1%; Graduate/professional degree or higher: 4.8%

School District(s)

Antwerp Local (PK-12)
2015-16 Enrollment: 701 . . . . (419) 258-5421

Housing: Homeownership rate: 66.0%; Median home value: $78,800; Median year structure built: 1967; Homeowner vacancy rate: 2.8%; Median selected monthly owner costs: $867 with a mortgage, $325 without a mortgage; Median gross rent: $552 per month; Rental vacancy rate: 2.8%

Health Insurance: 97.0% have insurance; 73.1% have private insurance; 42.4% have public insurance; 3.0% do not have insurance; 0.0% of children under 18 do not have insurance

Newspapers: Antwerp Bee-Argus (weekly circulation 1,000)

Transportation: Commute: 93.7% car, 0.0% public transportation, 2.5% walk, 2.5% work from home; Mean travel time to work: 20.6 minutes

---

BROUGHTON (village). Covers a land area of 0.217 square miles and a water area of 0 square miles. Located at 41.09° N. Lat; 84.53° W. Long. Elevation is 725 feet.

Population: 108; Growth (since 2000): -34.9%; Density: 497.1 persons per square mile; Race: 97.2% White, 2.8% Black/African American, 0.0% Asian, 0.0% American Indian/Alaska Native, 0.0% Native Hawaiian/Other Pacific Islander, 0.0% Two or more races, 0.0% Hispanic of any race; Average household size: 2.45; Median age: 38.4; Age under 18: 27.8%; Age 65 and over: 13.9%; Males per 100 females: 100.0; Marriage status: 17.7% never married, 35.4% now married, 5.1% separated, 10.1% widowed, 36.7% divorced; Foreign born: 0.0%; Speak English only: 98.0%; With disability: 20.4%; Veterans: 9.0%; Ancestry: 41.7% German, 7.4% Irish, 6.5% English, 5.6% American, 4.6% French

Employment: 5.6% management, business, and financial, 0.0% computer, engineering, and science, 11.1% education, legal, community service, arts, and media, 0.0% healthcare practitioners, 24.1% service, 20.4% sales and office, 16.7% natural resources, construction, and maintenance, 22.2% production, transportation, and material moving

Income: Per capita: $16,085; Median household: $36,667; Average household: $39,427; Households with income of $100,000 or more: 2.3%; Poverty rate: 22.1%

Educational Attainment: High school diploma or higher: 86.8%; Bachelor's degree or higher: 8.8%; Graduate/professional degree or higher: 1.5%

Housing: Homeownership rate: 95.5%; Median home value: $52,000; Median year structure built: 1978; Homeowner vacancy rate: 0.0%; Median selected monthly owner costs: $775 with a mortgage, $275 without a mortgage; Median gross rent: n/a per month; Rental vacancy rate: 0.0%

Health Insurance: 84.3% have insurance; 50.0% have private insurance; 39.8% have public insurance; 15.7% do not have insurance; 0.0% of children under 18 do not have insurance

Transportation: Commute: 100.0% car, 0.0% public transportation, 0.0% walk, 0.0% work from home; Mean travel time to work: 18.7 minutes

---

CECIL (village). Covers a land area of 1.462 square miles and a water area of <.001 square miles. Located at 41.22° N. Lat; 84.60° W. Long. Elevation is 722 feet.

Population: 179; Growth (since 2000): -17.1%; Density: 122.5 persons per square mile; Race: 97.8% White, 0.0% Black/African American, 0.0% Asian, 0.0% American Indian/Alaska Native, 0.6% Native Hawaiian/Other Pacific Islander, 1.7% Two or more races, 3.4% Hispanic of any race; Average household size: 2.45; Median age: 41.4; Age under 18: 24.0%; Age 65 and over: 16.8%; Males per 100 females: 121.2; Marriage status: 34.2% never married, 46.7% now married, 0.7% separated, 3.3% widowed, 15.8% divorced; Foreign born: 3.9%; Speak English only: 97.1%; With disability: 25.7%; Veterans: 8.1%; Ancestry: 31.3% German, 7.3% English, 3.9% American, 3.4% French, 3.4% Irish

Employment: 5.7% management, business, and financial, 1.4% computer, engineering, and science, 4.3% education, legal, community service, arts, and media, 5.7% healthcare practitioners, 35.7% service, 8.6% sales and office, 7.1% natural resources, construction, and maintenance, 31.4% production, transportation, and material moving

Income: Per capita: $16,089; Median household: $29,904; Average household: $39,832; Households with income of $100,000 or more: 2.7%; Poverty rate: 34.1%

Educational Attainment: High school diploma or higher: 78.2%; Bachelor's degree or higher: 2.4%; Graduate/professional degree or higher: n/a

Housing: Homeownership rate: 78.1%; Median home value: $51,600; Median year structure built: Before 1940; Homeowner vacancy rate: 0.0%; Median selected monthly owner costs: $855 with a mortgage, $258 without a mortgage; Median gross rent: $629 per month; Rental vacancy rate: 15.8%

Health Insurance: 90.5% have insurance; 41.3% have private insurance; 57.0% have public insurance; 9.5% do not have insurance; 4.7% of children under 18 do not have insurance

Transportation: Commute: 89.4% car, 0.0% public transportation, 1.5% walk, 6.1% work from home; Mean travel time to work: 30.6 minutes

---

GROVER HILL (village). Covers a land area of 0.275 square miles and a water area of 0 square miles. Located at 41.02° N. Lat; 84.48° W. Long. Elevation is 725 feet.

Population: 386; Growth (since 2000): -6.3%; Density: 1,403.1 persons per square mile; Race: 98.4% White, 0.8% Black/African American, 0.0% Asian, 0.0% American Indian/Alaska Native, 0.0% Native Hawaiian/Other Pacific Islander, 0.0% Two or more races, 4.4% Hispanic of any race; Average household size: 2.30; Median age: 32.6; Age under 18: 25.9%; Age 65 and over: 13.5%; Males per 100 females: 104.1; Marriage status: 24.5% never married, 55.0% now married, 2.6% separated, 10.9% widowed, 9.6% divorced; Foreign born: 0.3%; Speak English only: 99.7%; With disability: 16.1%; Veterans: 4.2%; Ancestry: 33.7% German, 21.2% Irish, 5.2% English, 5.2% Hungarian, 4.9% American

Employment: 4.1% management, business, and financial, 2.9% computer, engineering, and science, 1.8% education, legal, community service, arts, and media, 7.1% healthcare practitioners, 16.5% service, 18.8% sales and office, 18.2% natural resources, construction, and maintenance, 30.6% production, transportation, and material moving

Income: Per capita: $18,691; Median household: $40,455; Average household: $44,739; Households with income of $100,000 or more: 6.0%; Poverty rate: 15.8%

Educational Attainment: High school diploma or higher: 87.7%; Bachelor's degree or higher: 5.1%; Graduate/professional degree or higher: 2.1%

School District(s)

Wayne Trace Local (KG-12)
2015-16 Enrollment: 932 . . . . (419) 263-2415

Housing: Homeownership rate: 75.6%; Median home value: $50,400; Median year structure built: Before 1940; Homeowner vacancy rate: 0.0%; Median selected monthly owner costs: $759 with a mortgage, $347 without a mortgage; Median gross rent: $722 per month; Rental vacancy rate: 0.0%

Health Insurance: 93.0% have insurance; 56.2% have private insurance; 46.9% have public insurance; 7.0% do not have insurance; 1.0% of children under 18 do not have insurance

Transportation: Commute: 95.8% car, 0.0% public transportation, 0.6% walk, 1.2% work from home; Mean travel time to work: 24.1 minutes

---

HAVILAND (village). Covers a land area of 0.393 square miles and a water area of 0 square miles. Located at 41.02° N. Lat; 84.59° W. Long. Elevation is 735 feet.

Population: 225; Growth (since 2000): 25.0%; Density: 572.2 persons per square mile; Race: 97.8% White, 0.0% Black/African American, 0.0% Asian, 0.0% American Indian/Alaska Native, 0.9% Native Hawaiian/Other Pacific Islander, 0.9% Two or more races, 8.4% Hispanic of any race; Average household size: 2.39; Median age: 34.4; Age under 18: 22.7%; Age 65 and over: 19.1%; Males per 100 females: 92.0; Marriage status: 37.4% never married, 49.7% now married, 0.0% separated, 4.3% widowed, 8.6% divorced; Foreign born: 3.6%; Speak English only: 93.2%; With disability: 27.6%; Veterans: 10.9%; Ancestry: 18.7% Irish, 18.2% German, 14.7% American, 1.8% Polish, 1.3% English

Employment: 13.7% management, business, and financial, 0.0% computer, engineering, and science, 4.2% education, legal, community service, arts, and media, 5.3% healthcare practitioners, 14.7% service, 9.5% sales and office, 5.3% natural resources, construction, and maintenance, 47.4% production, transportation, and material moving

Income: Per capita: $16,837; Median household: $30,938; Average household: $37,552; Households with income of $100,000 or more: 5.3%; Poverty rate: 18.7%

Educational Attainment: High school diploma or higher: 70.3%; Bachelor's degree or higher: 12.4%; Graduate/professional degree or higher: 2.8%

School District(s)

Wayne Trace Local (KG-12)
2015-16 Enrollment: 932 . . . . (419) 263-2415

Housing: Homeownership rate: 54.3%; Median home value: $78,800; Median year structure built: 1955; Homeowner vacancy rate: 6.9%; Median

selected monthly owner costs: $771 with a mortgage, $243 without a mortgage; Median gross rent: $579 per month; Rental vacancy rate: 2.0%
Health Insurance: 83.1% have insurance; 55.1% have private insurance; 39.6% have public insurance; 16.9% do not have insurance; 13.7% of children under 18 do not have insurance
Transportation: Commute: 85.3% car, 0.0% public transportation, 14.7% walk, 0.0% work from home; Mean travel time to work: 18.7 minutes

LATTY (village). Covers a land area of 0.269 square miles and a water area of 0 square miles. Located at 41.09° N. Lat; 84.58° W. Long. Elevation is 728 feet.
Population: 165; Growth (since 2000): -17.5%; Density: 614.0 persons per square mile; Race: 86.1% White, 9.7% Black/African American, 0.0% Asian, 0.0% American Indian/Alaska Native, 0.0% Native Hawaiian/Other Pacific Islander, 4.2% Two or more races, 2.4% Hispanic of any race; Average household size: 2.46; Median age: 44.9; Age under 18: 18.2%; Age 65 and over: 9.1%; Males per 100 females: 101.0; Marriage status: 19.4% never married, 64.6% now married, 4.9% separated, 0.7% widowed, 15.3% divorced; Foreign born: 1.8%; Speak English only: 96.7%; With disability: 17.0%; Veterans: 6.7%; Ancestry: 50.3% German, 20.0% Irish, 9.1% English, 6.7% American, 4.8% Swedish
Employment: 18.6% management, business, and financial, 0.0% computer, engineering, and science, 2.9% education, legal, community service, arts, and media, 10.8% healthcare practitioners, 19.6% service, 9.8% sales and office, 8.8% natural resources, construction, and maintenance, 29.4% production, transportation, and material moving
Income: Per capita: $28,343; Median household: $54,583; Average household: $67,049; Households with income of $100,000 or more: 25.4%; Poverty rate: 11.2%
Educational Attainment: High school diploma or higher: 97.6%; Bachelor's degree or higher: 11.3%; Graduate/professional degree or higher: 2.4%
Housing: Homeownership rate: 89.6%; Median home value: $90,000; Median year structure built: 1972; Homeowner vacancy rate: 0.0%; Median selected monthly owner costs: $995 with a mortgage, $508 without a mortgage; Median gross rent: $708 per month; Rental vacancy rate: 0.0%
Health Insurance: 91.5% have insurance; 76.4% have private insurance; 22.4% have public insurance; 8.5% do not have insurance; 0.0% of children under 18 do not have insurance
Transportation: Commute: 98.0% car, 0.0% public transportation, 2.0% walk, 0.0% work from home; Mean travel time to work: 19.0 minutes

MELROSE (village). Covers a land area of 0.856 square miles and a water area of 0 square miles. Located at 41.09° N. Lat; 84.42° W. Long. Elevation is 709 feet.
Population: 151; Growth (since 2000): -53.1%; Density: 176.3 persons per square mile; Race: 87.4% White, 6.0% Black/African American, 0.0% Asian, 4.0% American Indian/Alaska Native, 0.0% Native Hawaiian/Other Pacific Islander, 2.6% Two or more races, 0.0% Hispanic of any race; Average household size: 2.32; Median age: 48.5; Age under 18: 21.2%; Age 65 and over: 13.9%; Males per 100 females: 93.7; Marriage status: 29.5% never married, 55.8% now married, 0.0% separated, 8.5% widowed, 6.2% divorced; Foreign born: 0.0%; Speak English only: 100.0%; With disability: 17.2%; Veterans: 10.1%; Ancestry: 30.5% German, 14.6% Irish, 6.0% American, 4.0% English, 2.6% Welsh
Employment: 0.0% management, business, and financial, 0.0% computer, engineering, and science, 1.6% education, legal, community service, arts, and media, 8.2% healthcare practitioners, 21.3% service, 32.8% sales and office, 4.9% natural resources, construction, and maintenance, 31.1% production, transportation, and material moving
Income: Per capita: $21,154; Median household: $50,313; Average household: $49,363; Households with income of $100,000 or more: 6.2%; Poverty rate: 20.5%
Educational Attainment: High school diploma or higher: 82.4%; Bachelor's degree or higher: 12.0%; Graduate/professional degree or higher: 5.6%
Housing: Homeownership rate: 81.5%; Median home value: $71,700; Median year structure built: 1976; Homeowner vacancy rate: 16.2%; Median selected monthly owner costs: $1,125 with a mortgage, $244 without a mortgage; Median gross rent: n/a per month; Rental vacancy rate: 40.0%
Health Insurance: 90.7% have insurance; 58.9% have private insurance; 41.1% have public insurance; 9.3% do not have insurance; 0.0% of children under 18 do not have insurance
Transportation: Commute: 89.8% car, 0.0% public transportation, 10.2% walk, 0.0% work from home; Mean travel time to work: 20.8 minutes

OAKWOOD (village). Covers a land area of 0.588 square miles and a water area of 0 square miles. Located at 41.09° N. Lat; 84.38° W. Long. Elevation is 709 feet.
Population: 608; Growth (since 2000): 0.2%; Density: 1,033.9 persons per square mile; Race: 95.1% White, 0.0% Black/African American, 0.0% Asian, 0.0% American Indian/Alaska Native, 0.0% Native Hawaiian/Other Pacific Islander, 1.8% Two or more races, 5.6% Hispanic of any race; Average household size: 2.57; Median age: 33.6; Age under 18: 30.4%; Age 65 and over: 18.1%; Males per 100 females: 101.3; Marriage status: 20.0% never married, 59.4% now married, 3.0% separated, 7.1% widowed, 13.5% divorced; Foreign born: 0.3%; Speak English only: 98.5%; With disability: 18.1%; Veterans: 9.2%; Ancestry: 28.5% German, 11.3% American, 11.0% English, 4.1% Swiss, 3.9% Irish
Employment: 5.0% management, business, and financial, 5.0% computer, engineering, and science, 5.0% education, legal, community service, arts, and media, 6.9% healthcare practitioners, 20.2% service, 19.5% sales and office, 18.7% natural resources, construction, and maintenance, 19.8% production, transportation, and material moving
Income: Per capita: $18,261; Median household: $41,607; Average household: $46,466; Households with income of $100,000 or more: 5.9%; Poverty rate: 8.6%
Educational Attainment: High school diploma or higher: 89.4%; Bachelor's degree or higher: 5.7%; Graduate/professional degree or higher: 2.6%

School District(s)

Paulding Exempted Village (PK-12)
2015-16 Enrollment: 1,486 . . . . (419) 399-4656
Housing: Homeownership rate: 70.5%; Median home value: $62,900; Median year structure built: 1956; Homeowner vacancy rate: 3.3%; Median selected monthly owner costs: $750 with a mortgage, $403 without a mortgage; Median gross rent: $690 per month; Rental vacancy rate: 18.6%
Health Insurance: 95.4% have insurance; 77.0% have private insurance; 47.7% have public insurance; 4.6% do not have insurance; 0.0% of children under 18 do not have insurance
Transportation: Commute: 99.6% car, 0.0% public transportation, 0.0% walk, 0.4% work from home; Mean travel time to work: 24.9 minutes

PAULDING (village). County seat. Covers a land area of 2.364 square miles and a water area of 0.098 square miles. Located at 41.14° N. Lat; 84.58° W. Long. Elevation is 722 feet.
Population: 3,615; Growth (since 2000): 0.6%; Density: 1,529.3 persons per square mile; Race: 86.7% White, 1.9% Black/African American, 1.3% Asian, 0.3% American Indian/Alaska Native, 0.0% Native Hawaiian/Other Pacific Islander, 2.4% Two or more races, 9.7% Hispanic of any race; Average household size: 2.36; Median age: 37.9; Age under 18: 25.0%; Age 65 and over: 17.0%; Males per 100 females: 87.2; Marriage status: 26.6% never married, 53.3% now married, 1.2% separated, 9.7% widowed, 10.4% divorced; Foreign born: 4.1%; Speak English only: 91.4%; With disability: 17.7%; Veterans: 8.9%; Ancestry: 31.3% German, 10.7% American, 9.6% Irish, 5.7% English, 2.4% Dutch
Employment: 5.2% management, business, and financial, 3.8% computer, engineering, and science, 3.2% education, legal, community service, arts, and media, 6.0% healthcare practitioners, 14.9% service, 20.8% sales and office, 15.2% natural resources, construction, and maintenance, 31.0% production, transportation, and material moving
Income: Per capita: $19,843; Median household: $44,191; Average household: $47,125; Households with income of $100,000 or more: 4.8%; Poverty rate: 14.3%
Educational Attainment: High school diploma or higher: 84.5%; Bachelor's degree or higher: 9.9%; Graduate/professional degree or higher: 4.2%

School District(s)

Paulding Exempted Village (PK-12)
2015-16 Enrollment: 1,486 . . . . (419) 399-4656
Housing: Homeownership rate: 62.9%; Median home value: $79,600; Median year structure built: 1966; Homeowner vacancy rate: 0.0%; Median selected monthly owner costs: $889 with a mortgage, $364 without a mortgage; Median gross rent: $598 per month; Rental vacancy rate: 10.7%
Health Insurance: 89.9% have insurance; 63.2% have private insurance; 41.0% have public insurance; 10.1% do not have insurance; 10.3% of children under 18 do not have insurance
Hospitals: Paulding County Hospital (25 beds)

Newspapers: Paulding Progress (weekly circulation 4,200)
Transportation: Commute: 94.6% car, 0.0% public transportation, 2.8% walk, 2.6% work from home; Mean travel time to work: 20.1 minutes

PAYNE (village). Covers a land area of 0.677 square miles and a water area of 0 square miles. Located at 41.08° N. Lat; 84.73° W. Long. Elevation is 748 feet.
Population: 1,167; Growth (since 2000): 0.1%; Density: 1,723.3 persons per square mile; Race: 94.6% White, 1.8% Black/African American, 0.3% Asian, 0.0% American Indian/Alaska Native, 0.0% Native Hawaiian/Other Pacific Islander, 2.7% Two or more races, 3.1% Hispanic of any race; Average household size: 2.19; Median age: 42.3; Age under 18: 18.4%; Age 65 and over: 17.2%; Males per 100 females: 89.5; Marriage status: 30.3% never married, 48.7% now married, 2.4% separated, 8.4% widowed, 12.6% divorced; Foreign born: 0.0%; Speak English only: 98.6%; With disability: 15.7%; Veterans: 10.8%; Ancestry: 35.5% German, 12.1% Irish, 10.0% American, 9.8% English, 4.7% French
Employment: 9.6% management, business, and financial, 0.0% computer, engineering, and science, 7.4% education, legal, community service, arts, and media, 5.4% healthcare practitioners, 14.3% service, 22.7% sales and office, 5.2% natural resources, construction, and maintenance, 35.5% production, transportation, and material moving
Income: Per capita: $23,413; Median household: $48,529; Average household: $53,166; Households with income of $100,000 or more: 8.4%; Poverty rate: 13.7%
Educational Attainment: High school diploma or higher: 87.1%; Bachelor's degree or higher: 8.6%; Graduate/professional degree or higher: 2.0%

School District(s)

Wayne Trace Local (KG-12)
2015-16 Enrollment: 932. . . . . (419) 263-2415
Housing: Homeownership rate: 65.9%; Median home value: $70,300; Median year structure built: 1964; Homeowner vacancy rate: 0.0%; Median selected monthly owner costs: $755 with a mortgage, $348 without a mortgage; Median gross rent: $558 per month; Rental vacancy rate: 0.0%
Health Insurance: 93.2% have insurance; 72.3% have private insurance; 35.4% have public insurance; 6.8% do not have insurance; 2.8% of children under 18 do not have insurance
Transportation: Commute: 88.9% car, 0.0% public transportation, 9.5% walk, 1.5% work from home; Mean travel time to work: 25.3 minutes

Perry County

Located in central Ohio; drained by Rush, Sunday, Jonathan, and Moxahala Creeks; includes part of Buckeye Lake. Covers a land area of 407.971 square miles, a water area of 4.515 square miles, and is located in the Eastern Time Zone at 39.74° N. Lat., 82.24° W. Long. The county was founded in 1817. County seat is New Lexington.

Perry County is part of the Columbus, OH Metropolitan Statistical Area. The entire metro area includes: Delaware County, OH; Fairfield County, OH; Franklin County, OH; Hocking County, OH; Licking County, OH; Madison County, OH; Morrow County, OH; Perry County, OH; Pickaway County, OH; Union County, OH

Weather Station: New Lexington 2 NW Elevation: 890 feet

	Jan	Feb	Mar	Apr	May	Jun	Jul	Aug	Sep	Oct	Nov	Dec
High	37	41	51	64	73	81	84	83	77	65	53	41
Low	18	20	27	37	47	56	61	59	51	39	31	23
Precip	3.0	2.5	3.6	3.9	4.6	4.0	4.7	3.2	3.0	3.0	3.4	3.0
Snow	7.9	5.2	2.8	0.3	tr	0.0	0.0	0.0	0.0	tr	0.5	3.0

High and Low temperatures in degrees Fahrenheit; Precipitation and Snow in inches

Population: 35,947; Growth (since 2000): 5.5%; Density: 88.1 persons per square mile; Race: 97.4% White, 0.3% Black/African American, 0.3% Asian, 0.2% American Indian/Alaska Native, 0.0% Native Hawaiian/Other Pacific Islander, 1.8% two or more races, 0.7% Hispanic of any race; Average household size: 2.63; Median age: 39.8; Age under 18: 24.3%; Age 65 and over: 15.0%; Males per 100 females: 99.4; Marriage status: 24.1% never married, 57.2% now married, 2.5% separated, 6.2% widowed, 12.5% divorced; Foreign born: 0.6%; Speak English only: 98.0%; With disability: 16.8%; Veterans: 9.7%; Ancestry: 22.7% German, 12.6% Irish, 9.9% American, 9.4% English, 4.0% Italian
Religion: Six largest groups: 8.3% Catholicism, 7.1% Methodist/Pietist, 3.4% Baptist, 2.6% Non-denominational Protestant, 1.8% Lutheran, 1.4% Presbyterian-Reformed
Economy: Unemployment rate: 5.1%; Leading industries: 15.9 % retail trade; 15.0 % health care and social assistance; 12.7 % other services (except public administration); Farms: 699 totaling 107,224 acres; Company size: 0 employ 1,000 or more persons, 0 employ 500 to 999 persons, 7 employ 100 to 499 persons, 433 employ less than 100 persons; Business ownership: 834 women-owned, n/a Black-owned, n/a Hispanic-owned, n/a Asian-owned, n/a American Indian/Alaska Native-owned
Employment: 10.6% management, business, and financial, 2.3% computer, engineering, and science, 7.8% education, legal, community service, arts, and media, 6.4% healthcare practitioners, 18.6% service, 19.7% sales and office, 14.7% natural resources, construction, and maintenance, 19.9% production, transportation, and material moving
Income: Per capita: $20,852; Median household: $43,674; Average household: $54,211; Households with income of $100,000 or more: 12.4%; Poverty rate: 20.6%
Educational Attainment: High school diploma or higher: 83.9%; Bachelor's degree or higher: 12.0%; Graduate/professional degree or higher: 3.8%
Housing: Homeownership rate: 73.3%; Median home value: $96,100; Median year structure built: 1974; Homeowner vacancy rate: 2.6%; Median selected monthly owner costs: $1,004 with a mortgage, $382 without a mortgage; Median gross rent: $605 per month; Rental vacancy rate: 2.8%
Vital Statistics: Birth rate: 119.1 per 10,000 population; Death rate: 106.3 per 10,000 population; Age-adjusted cancer mortality rate: 199.3 deaths per 100,000 population
Health Insurance: 90.3% have insurance; 60.9% have private insurance; 42.8% have public insurance; 9.7% do not have insurance; 5.1% of children under 18 do not have insurance
Health Care: Physicians: 2.8 per 10,000 population; Dentists: 2.2 per 10,000 population; Hospital beds: 0.0 per 10,000 population; Hospital admissions: 0.0 per 10,000 population
Transportation: Commute: 95.1% car, 0.8% public transportation, 2.2% walk, 1.3% work from home; Mean travel time to work: 33.1 minutes
2016 Presidential Election: 67.7% Trump, 27.4% Clinton, 2.7% Johnson, 0.7% Stein
National and State Parks: Avondale State Wildlife Area; Perry State Forest
Additional Information Contacts
Perry Government. . . . . (740) 342-2045
http://www.perrycountyohiocofc.com/govnment.htm

Perry County Communities

CORNING (village). Covers a land area of 0.431 square miles and a water area of 0 square miles. Located at 39.60° N. Lat; 82.09° W. Long. Elevation is 732 feet.
Population: 358; Growth (since 2000): -39.6%; Density: 829.7 persons per square mile; Race: 100.0% White, 0.0% Black/African American, 0.0% Asian, 0.0% American Indian/Alaska Native, 0.0% Native Hawaiian/Other Pacific Islander, 0.0% Two or more races, 5.0% Hispanic of any race; Average household size: 2.18; Median age: 35.7; Age under 18: 22.1%; Age 65 and over: 17.0%; Males per 100 females: 95.6; Marriage status: 26.1% never married, 40.4% now married, 3.1% separated, 18.5% widowed, 15.0% divorced; Foreign born: 0.0%; Speak English only: 97.3%; With disability: 26.8%; Veterans: 6.8%; Ancestry: 12.3% Irish, 9.8% German, 8.9% Italian, 7.5% American, 4.7% Hungarian
Employment: 5.6% management, business, and financial, 0.0% computer, engineering, and science, 3.2% education, legal, community service, arts, and media, 12.9% healthcare practitioners, 19.4% service, 16.1% sales and office, 11.3% natural resources, construction, and maintenance, 31.5% production, transportation, and material moving
Income: Per capita: $16,363; Median household: $30,313; Average household: $36,753; Households with income of $100,000 or more: 2.4%; Poverty rate: 22.6%
Educational Attainment: High school diploma or higher: 82.6%; Bachelor's degree or higher: 7.6%; Graduate/professional degree or higher: 2.7%

School District(s)

Southern Local (PK-12)
2015-16 Enrollment: 692. . . . . (740) 721-0520
Housing: Homeownership rate: 70.1%; Median home value: $54,300; Median year structure built: 1944; Homeowner vacancy rate: 12.2%; Median selected monthly owner costs: $875 with a mortgage, $294 without

a mortgage; Median gross rent: $534 per month; Rental vacancy rate: 18.3%
Health Insurance: 84.9% have insurance; 54.2% have private insurance; 43.9% have public insurance; 15.1% do not have insurance; 7.6% of children under 18 do not have insurance
Transportation: Commute: 96.6% car, 0.0% public transportation, 0.0% walk, 3.4% work from home; Mean travel time to work: 40.8 minutes

CROOKSVILLE (village). Covers a land area of 1.624 square miles and a water area of 0.021 square miles. Located at 39.77° N. Lat; 82.10° W. Long. Elevation is 791 feet.
Population: 2,546; Growth (since 2000): 2.5%; Density: 1,567.8 persons per square mile; Race: 97.4% White, 0.0% Black/African American, 0.0% Asian, 0.0% American Indian/Alaska Native, 0.0% Native Hawaiian/Other Pacific Islander, 2.6% Two or more races, 0.6% Hispanic of any race; Average household size: 2.44; Median age: 36.7; Age under 18: 23.3%; Age 65 and over: 13.8%; Males per 100 females: 92.8; Marriage status: 27.4% never married, 51.6% now married, 2.8% separated, 5.8% widowed, 15.2% divorced; Foreign born: 0.2%; Speak English only: 99.2%; With disability: 21.1%; Veterans: 7.3%; Ancestry: 20.0% German, 11.9% Irish, 10.2% English, 8.9% American, 4.7% Italian
Employment: 5.5% management, business, and financial, 1.1% computer, engineering, and science, 4.0% education, legal, community service, arts, and media, 6.2% healthcare practitioners, 19.0% service, 24.7% sales and office, 10.8% natural resources, construction, and maintenance, 28.7% production, transportation, and material moving
Income: Per capita: $16,106; Median household: $31,250; Average household: $38,996; Households with income of $100,000 or more: 4.7%; Poverty rate: 22.4%
Educational Attainment: High school diploma or higher: 85.5%; Bachelor's degree or higher: 8.5%; Graduate/professional degree or higher: 2.2%

School District(s)

Crooksville Exempted Village (PK-12)
2015-16 Enrollment: 1,104 . . . . (740) 982-7040
Housing: Homeownership rate: 52.7%; Median home value: $59,600; Median year structure built: 1941; Homeowner vacancy rate: 0.7%; Median selected monthly owner costs: $742 with a mortgage, $382 without a mortgage; Median gross rent: $557 per month; Rental vacancy rate: 1.0%
Health Insurance: 86.7% have insurance; 57.1% have private insurance; 47.7% have public insurance; 13.3% do not have insurance; 3.9% of children under 18 do not have insurance
Transportation: Commute: 89.6% car, 0.0% public transportation, 7.8% walk, 1.2% work from home; Mean travel time to work: 28.7 minutes
Additional Information Contacts
Village of Crooksville . . . . (740) 982-2656
http://www.crooksville.com

GLENFORD (village). Covers a land area of 0.113 square miles and a water area of 0.002 square miles. Located at 39.89° N. Lat; 82.32° W. Long. Elevation is 846 feet.
History: Glenford was established near a prehistoric fortification known as Glenford Fort. A stone wall 7-10 feet high and 6,600 feet long enclosed an area with a central mound.
Population: 184; Growth (since 2000): -7.1%; Density: 1,631.5 persons per square mile; Race: 96.7% White, 0.0% Black/African American, 0.0% Asian, 0.0% American Indian/Alaska Native, 0.0% Native Hawaiian/Other Pacific Islander, 3.3% Two or more races, 0.0% Hispanic of any race; Average household size: 3.29; Median age: 31.5; Age under 18: 38.0%; Age 65 and over: 10.9%; Males per 100 females: 103.5; Marriage status: 34.8% never married, 39.3% now married, 2.2% separated, 6.7% widowed, 19.3% divorced; Foreign born: 0.0%; Speak English only: 100.0%; With disability: 9.2%; Veterans: 6.1%; Ancestry: 35.9% German, 13.6% American, 7.1% Irish, 4.9% Dutch, 2.2% English
Employment: 11.1% management, business, and financial, 2.5% computer, engineering, and science, 1.2% education, legal, community service, arts, and media, 9.9% healthcare practitioners, 23.5% service, 22.2% sales and office, 18.5% natural resources, construction, and maintenance, 11.1% production, transportation, and material moving
Income: Per capita: $17,891; Median household: $51,250; Average household: $59,059; Households with income of $100,000 or more: 10.8%; Poverty rate: 19.6%
Educational Attainment: High school diploma or higher: 86.0%; Bachelor's degree or higher: 11.0%; Graduate/professional degree or higher: 3.0%

School District(s)

Northern Local (PK-12)
2015-16 Enrollment: 2,188 . . . . (740) 743-1303
Housing: Homeownership rate: 53.6%; Median home value: $98,300; Median year structure built: Before 1940; Homeowner vacancy rate: 0.0%; Median selected monthly owner costs: $1,050 with a mortgage, $400 without a mortgage; Median gross rent: $900 per month; Rental vacancy rate: 0.0%
Health Insurance: 89.7% have insurance; 71.7% have private insurance; 26.1% have public insurance; 10.3% do not have insurance; 2.9% of children under 18 do not have insurance
Transportation: Commute: 97.5% car, 0.0% public transportation, 2.5% walk, 0.0% work from home; Mean travel time to work: 33.2 minutes

HEMLOCK (village). Covers a land area of 0.372 square miles and a water area of 0.002 square miles. Located at 39.59° N. Lat; 82.15° W. Long. Elevation is 764 feet.
Population: 211; Growth (since 2000): 48.6%; Density: 566.8 persons per square mile; Race: 97.2% White, 0.0% Black/African American, 0.0% Asian, 0.0% American Indian/Alaska Native, 0.0% Native Hawaiian/Other Pacific Islander, 2.8% Two or more races, 0.0% Hispanic of any race; Average household size: 3.01; Median age: 29.8; Age under 18: 21.8%; Age 65 and over: 10.9%; Males per 100 females: 98.7; Marriage status: 40.5% never married, 45.7% now married, 2.9% separated, 6.4% widowed, 7.5% divorced; Foreign born: 0.0%; Speak English only: 97.9%; With disability: 20.9%; Veterans: 10.9%; Ancestry: 16.6% Irish, 15.6% American, 15.6% German, 6.2% Scotch-Irish, 3.3% English
Employment: 4.5% management, business, and financial, 0.0% computer, engineering, and science, 13.4% education, legal, community service, arts, and media, 1.5% healthcare practitioners, 22.4% service, 35.8% sales and office, 16.4% natural resources, construction, and maintenance, 6.0% production, transportation, and material moving
Income: Per capita: $14,990; Median household: $38,636; Average household: $43,767; Households with income of $100,000 or more: 4.3%; Poverty rate: 28.4%
Educational Attainment: High school diploma or higher: 86.3%; Bachelor's degree or higher: 11.1%; Graduate/professional degree or higher: 7.7%
Housing: Homeownership rate: 64.3%; Median home value: $77,500; Median year structure built: Before 1940; Homeowner vacancy rate: 0.0%; Median selected monthly owner costs: $1,028 with a mortgage, $242 without a mortgage; Median gross rent: $575 per month; Rental vacancy rate: 0.0%
Health Insurance: 91.5% have insurance; 46.0% have private insurance; 54.5% have public insurance; 8.5% do not have insurance; 0.0% of children under 18 do not have insurance
Transportation: Commute: 100.0% car, 0.0% public transportation, 0.0% walk, 0.0% work from home; Mean travel time to work: 30.7 minutes

JUNCTION CITY (village). Covers a land area of 0.633 square miles and a water area of 0.005 square miles. Located at 39.72° N. Lat; 82.30° W. Long. Elevation is 840 feet.
Population: 913; Growth (since 2000): 11.6%; Density: 1,442.2 persons per square mile; Race: 97.0% White, 0.8% Black/African American, 0.0% Asian, 0.5% American Indian/Alaska Native, 0.0% Native Hawaiian/Other Pacific Islander, 1.6% Two or more races, 1.5% Hispanic of any race; Average household size: 3.00; Median age: 27.9; Age under 18: 34.1%; Age 65 and over: 11.5%; Males per 100 females: 101.7; Marriage status: 38.1% never married, 38.4% now married, 2.7% separated, 4.8% widowed, 18.6% divorced; Foreign born: 0.0%; Speak English only: 100.0%; With disability: 17.1%; Veterans: 9.0%; Ancestry: 23.9% German, 14.1% Irish, 10.3% English, 3.6% Italian, 2.2% Dutch
Employment: 2.4% management, business, and financial, 0.7% computer, engineering, and science, 2.7% education, legal, community service, arts, and media, 6.4% healthcare practitioners, 26.9% service, 20.9% sales and office, 13.8% natural resources, construction, and maintenance, 26.3% production, transportation, and material moving
Income: Per capita: $12,921; Median household: $27,609; Average household: $37,732; Households with income of $100,000 or more: 3.3%; Poverty rate: 45.6%
Educational Attainment: High school diploma or higher: 81.4%; Bachelor's degree or higher: 5.7%; Graduate/professional degree or higher: 1.0%

School District(s)

New Lexington City (PK-12)
2015-16 Enrollment: 1,788 . . . . (740) 342-4133

Housing: Homeownership rate: 59.2%; Median home value: $68,100; Median year structure built: 1942; Homeowner vacancy rate: 0.0%; Median selected monthly owner costs: $879 with a mortgage, $340 without a mortgage; Median gross rent: $591 per month; Rental vacancy rate: 12.1%

Health Insurance: 95.5% have insurance; 42.5% have private insurance; 70.2% have public insurance; 4.5% do not have insurance; 0.0% of children under 18 do not have insurance

Transportation: Commute: 99.3% car, 0.0% public transportation, 0.0% walk, 0.0% work from home; Mean travel time to work: 29.2 minutes

MOUNT PERRY (unincorporated postal area)

ZCTA: 43760

Covers a land area of 34.670 square miles and a water area of 0.059 square miles. Located at 39.89° N. Lat; 82.19° W. Long. Elevation is 846 feet.

Population: 2,310; Growth (since 2000): 32.2%; Density: 66.6 persons per square mile; Race: 92.9% White, 0.5% Black/African American, 1.9% Asian, 0.0% American Indian/Alaska Native, 0.0% Native Hawaiian/Other Pacific Islander, 4.1% Two or more races, 0.0% Hispanic of any race; Average household size: 2.94; Median age: 41.8; Age under 18: 28.7%; Age 65 and over: 12.3%; Males per 100 females: 107.4; Marriage status: 26.8% never married, 56.5% now married, 0.6% separated, 4.0% widowed, 12.7% divorced; Foreign born: 4.7%; Speak English only: 99.0%; With disability: 13.1%; Veterans: 8.0%; Ancestry: 19.8% English, 14.4% German, 10.7% American, 10.3% Irish, 6.3% Hungarian

Employment: 12.0% management, business, and financial, 3.0% computer, engineering, and science, 12.1% education, legal, community service, arts, and media, 6.7% healthcare practitioners, 5.4% service, 27.9% sales and office, 14.6% natural resources, construction, and maintenance, 18.3% production, transportation, and material moving

Income: Per capita: $22,740; Median household: $70,250; Average household: $67,631; Households with income of $100,000 or more: 16.3%; Poverty rate: 16.2%

Educational Attainment: High school diploma or higher: 81.4%; Bachelor's degree or higher: 14.9%; Graduate/professional degree or higher: 7.8%

Housing: Homeownership rate: 86.0%; Median home value: $157,900; Median year structure built: 1987; Homeowner vacancy rate: 0.0%; Median selected monthly owner costs: $1,523 with a mortgage, $395 without a mortgage; Median gross rent: $629 per month; Rental vacancy rate: 31.3%

Health Insurance: 89.8% have insurance; 74.2% have private insurance; 24.9% have public insurance; 10.2% do not have insurance; 0.0% of children under 18 do not have insurance

Transportation: Commute: 98.7% car, 1.3% public transportation, 0.0% walk, 0.0% work from home; Mean travel time to work: 46.3 minutes

MOXAHALA (unincorporated postal area)

ZCTA: 43761

Covers a land area of 0.621 square miles and a water area of 0.007 square miles. Located at 39.67° N. Lat; 82.15° W. Long. Elevation is 817 feet.

Population: 45; Growth (since 2000): n/a; Density: 72.4 persons per square mile; Race: 100.0% White, 0.0% Black/African American, 0.0% Asian, 0.0% American Indian/Alaska Native, 0.0% Native Hawaiian/Other Pacific Islander, 0.0% Two or more races, 0.0% Hispanic of any race; Average household size: 1.96; Median age: n/a; Age under 18: 0.0%; Age 65 and over: 100.0%; Males per 100 females: 101.8; Marriage status: 0.0% never married, 100.0% now married, 0.0% separated, 0.0% widowed, 0.0% divorced; Foreign born: 0.0%; Speak English only: 100.0%; With disability: 0.0%; Veterans: 51.1%; Ancestry: n/a

Employment: n/a management, business, and financial, n/a computer, engineering, and science, n/a education, legal, community service, arts, and media, n/a healthcare practitioners, n/a service, n/a sales and office, n/a natural resources, construction, and maintenance, n/a production, transportation, and material moving

Income: Per capita: n/a; Median household: n/a; Average household: n/a; Households with income of $100,000 or more: n/a; Poverty rate: n/a

Educational Attainment: High school diploma or higher: 48.9%; Bachelor's degree or higher: n/a; Graduate/professional degree or higher: n/a

Housing: Homeownership rate: 100.0%; Median home value: n/a; Median year structure built: n/a; Homeowner vacancy rate: 0.0%; Median selected monthly owner costs: $0 with a mortgage, $0 without a mortgage; Median gross rent: n/a per month; Rental vacancy rate: 0.0%

Health Insurance: 100.0% have insurance; 100.0% have private insurance; 100.0% have public insurance; 0.0% do not have insurance; 0.0% of children under 18 do not have insurance

Transportation: Commute: n/a car, n/a public transportation, n/a walk, n/a work from home; Mean travel time to work: 0.0 minutes

NEW LEXINGTON (village). County seat. Covers a land area of 1.947 square miles and a water area of 0.002 square miles. Located at 39.72° N. Lat; 82.21° W. Long. Elevation is 958 feet.

History: New Lexington developed around the tile and pottery works, which used the excellent clays found in the vicinity.

Population: 4,992; Growth (since 2000): 6.5%; Density: 2,563.6 persons per square mile; Race: 97.4% White, 0.3% Black/African American, 0.0% Asian, 0.0% American Indian/Alaska Native, 0.0% Native Hawaiian/Other Pacific Islander, 2.0% Two or more races, 0.6% Hispanic of any race; Average household size: 2.69; Median age: 34.7; Age under 18: 27.3%; Age 65 and over: 13.2%; Males per 100 females: 89.6; Marriage status: 31.3% never married, 49.8% now married, 2.2% separated, 6.3% widowed, 12.7% divorced; Foreign born: 0.9%; Speak English only: 96.0%; With disability: 12.9%; Veterans: 3.7%; Ancestry: 24.8% German, 15.1% Irish, 8.9% American, 8.1% English, 6.0% Italian

Employment: 8.1% management, business, and financial, 1.3% computer, engineering, and science, 13.0% education, legal, community service, arts, and media, 4.7% healthcare practitioners, 21.4% service, 23.0% sales and office, 8.4% natural resources, construction, and maintenance, 20.2% production, transportation, and material moving

Income: Per capita: $15,746; Median household: $33,563; Average household: $41,646; Households with income of $100,000 or more: 4.3%; Poverty rate: 29.0%

Educational Attainment: High school diploma or higher: 81.6%; Bachelor's degree or higher: 7.9%; Graduate/professional degree or higher: 5.2%

School District(s)

New Lexington City (PK-12)
2015-16 Enrollment: 1,788 . . . . (740) 342-4133

Housing: Homeownership rate: 50.9%; Median home value: $76,000; Median year structure built: 1951; Homeowner vacancy rate: 1.9%; Median selected monthly owner costs: $872 with a mortgage, $372 without a mortgage; Median gross rent: $595 per month; Rental vacancy rate: 0.0%

Health Insurance: 86.3% have insurance; 53.4% have private insurance; 46.6% have public insurance; 13.7% do not have insurance; 12.6% of children under 18 do not have insurance

Safety: Violent crime rate: 25.4 per 10,000 population; Property crime rate: 398.2 per 10,000 population

Newspapers: Perry Co Tribune (weekly circulation 3,800)

Transportation: Commute: 92.4% car, 0.0% public transportation, 6.3% walk, 0.0% work from home; Mean travel time to work: 26.9 minutes

Additional Information Contacts

City of New Lexington . . . . (740) 342-2177
http://www.newlexington.org

NEW STRAITSVILLE (village). Covers a land area of 1.300 square miles and a water area of 0.001 square miles. Located at 39.58° N. Lat; 82.23° W. Long. Elevation is 794 feet.

History: New Straitsville was laid out in 1870 by a mining company. An undergound coal fire began to burn here in 1884, when some desperate miners set fire to loaded coal cars and pushed them down five mine shafts.

Population: 842; Growth (since 2000): 8.8%; Density: 647.9 persons per square mile; Race: 96.4% White, 0.5% Black/African American, 0.0% Asian, 2.3% American Indian/Alaska Native, 0.0% Native Hawaiian/Other Pacific Islander, 0.8% Two or more races, 0.6% Hispanic of any race; Average household size: 2.58; Median age: 34.5; Age under 18: 28.0%; Age 65 and over: 10.5%; Males per 100 females: 84.2; Marriage status: 25.4% never married, 55.8% now married, 4.6% separated, 6.1% widowed, 12.7% divorced; Foreign born: 0.2%; Speak English only: 99.2%; With disability: 19.2%; Veterans: 10.7%; Ancestry: 17.2% German, 16.6% English, 10.3% Irish, 7.6% Welsh, 4.6% Italian

Employment: 1.6% management, business, and financial, 1.0% computer, engineering, and science, 7.4% education, legal, community service, arts, and media, 4.2% healthcare practitioners, 15.4% service, 19.0% sales and office, 23.2% natural resources, construction, and maintenance, 28.3% production, transportation, and material moving

Income: Per capita: $14,101; Median household: $23,929; Average household: $37,181; Households with income of $100,000 or more: 9.5%; Poverty rate: 37.8%
Educational Attainment: High school diploma or higher: 81.1%; Bachelor's degree or higher: 3.4%; Graduate/professional degree or higher: 2.1%
Housing: Homeownership rate: 59.2%; Median home value: $66,100; Median year structure built: 1947; Homeowner vacancy rate: 0.0%; Median selected monthly owner costs: $815 with a mortgage, $305 without a mortgage; Median gross rent: $608 per month; Rental vacancy rate: 11.9%
Health Insurance: 87.5% have insurance; 43.9% have private insurance; 56.8% have public insurance; 12.5% do not have insurance; 6.8% of children under 18 do not have insurance
Transportation: Commute: 90.1% car, 4.6% public transportation, 0.7% walk, 4.0% work from home; Mean travel time to work: 36.9 minutes

RENDVILLE (village). Covers a land area of 0.312 square miles and a water area of 0.001 square miles. Located at 39.62° N. Lat; 82.09° W. Long. Elevation is 748 feet.
Population: 34; Growth (since 2000): -26.1%; Density: 109.1 persons per square mile; Race: 73.5% White, 8.8% Black/African American, 0.0% Asian, 0.0% American Indian/Alaska Native, 0.0% Native Hawaiian/Other Pacific Islander, 17.6% Two or more races, 0.0% Hispanic of any race; Average household size: 2.00; Median age: 48.8; Age under 18: 23.5%; Age 65 and over: 20.6%; Males per 100 females: 80.0; Marriage status: 30.8% never married, 53.8% now married, 0.0% separated, 15.4% widowed, 0.0% divorced; Foreign born: 0.0%; Speak English only: 100.0%; With disability: 17.6%; Veterans: 3.8%; Ancestry: 32.4% Irish, 14.7% German, 11.8% American, 11.8% African, 5.9% Dutch
Employment: 0.0% management, business, and financial, 0.0% computer, engineering, and science, 0.0% education, legal, community service, arts, and media, 0.0% healthcare practitioners, 42.9% service, 28.6% sales and office, 14.3% natural resources, construction, and maintenance, 14.3% production, transportation, and material moving
Income: Per capita: $13,044; Median household: n/a; Average household: $27,906; Households with income of $100,000 or more: n/a; Poverty rate: 8.8%
Educational Attainment: High school diploma or higher: 68.0%; Bachelor's degree or higher: 20.0%; Graduate/professional degree or higher: 4.0%
Housing: Homeownership rate: 88.2%; Median home value: n/a; Median year structure built: 1984; Homeowner vacancy rate: 0.0%; Median selected monthly owner costs: n/a with a mortgage, n/a without a mortgage; Median gross rent: n/a per month; Rental vacancy rate: 0.0%
Health Insurance: 85.3% have insurance; 47.1% have private insurance; 55.9% have public insurance; 14.7% do not have insurance; 0.0% of children under 18 do not have insurance
Transportation: Commute: 85.7% car, 0.0% public transportation, 0.0% walk, 14.3% work from home; Mean travel time to work: 0.0 minutes

ROSEVILLE (village). Covers a land area of 0.700 square miles and a water area of 0.005 square miles. Located at 39.81° N. Lat; 82.08° W. Long.
Population: 2,128; Growth (since 2000): 9.9%; Density: 3,039.1 persons per square mile; Race: 96.2% White, 0.0% Black/African American, 0.0% Asian, 0.0% American Indian/Alaska Native, 0.0% Native Hawaiian/Other Pacific Islander, 3.8% Two or more races, 0.4% Hispanic of any race; Average household size: 2.86; Median age: 32.1; Age under 18: 33.1%; Age 65 and over: 10.3%; Males per 100 females: 94.3; Marriage status: 31.9% never married, 49.3% now married, 3.1% separated, 5.4% widowed, 13.3% divorced; Foreign born: 0.0%; Speak English only: 99.9%; With disability: 15.8%; Veterans: 7.4%; Ancestry: 18.0% German, 12.8% Irish, 8.2% American, 7.8% Italian, 6.3% English
Employment: 7.8% management, business, and financial, 0.4% computer, engineering, and science, 7.0% education, legal, community service, arts, and media, 6.7% healthcare practitioners, 16.8% service, 25.3% sales and office, 9.0% natural resources, construction, and maintenance, 27.0% production, transportation, and material moving
Income: Per capita: $12,395; Median household: $29,107; Average household: $34,324; Households with income of $100,000 or more: 3.5%; Poverty rate: 35.7%
Educational Attainment: High school diploma or higher: 83.2%; Bachelor's degree or higher: 5.7%; Graduate/professional degree or higher: 3.2%

School District(s)

Franklin Local (PK-12)
2015-16 Enrollment: 1,972 . . . . (740) 674-5203
Franklin Local Community School (07-12)
2015-16 Enrollment: 75. . . . . (740) 697-7317

Housing: Homeownership rate: 64.9%; Median home value: $65,400; Median year structure built: 1948; Homeowner vacancy rate: 0.0%; Median selected monthly owner costs: $822 with a mortgage, $343 without a mortgage; Median gross rent: $438 per month; Rental vacancy rate: 9.1%
Health Insurance: 91.6% have insurance; 36.9% have private insurance; 62.6% have public insurance; 8.4% do not have insurance; 1.4% of children under 18 do not have insurance
Safety: Violent crime rate: 43.2 per 10,000 population; Property crime rate: 183.7 per 10,000 population
Transportation: Commute: 93.6% car, 0.0% public transportation, 1.8% walk, 2.5% work from home; Mean travel time to work: 33.0 minutes

SHAWNEE (village). Covers a land area of 2.247 square miles and a water area of 0.014 square miles. Located at 39.61° N. Lat; 82.20° W. Long. Elevation is 850 feet.
Population: 541; Growth (since 2000): -11.0%; Density: 240.7 persons per square mile; Race: 96.3% White, 1.7% Black/African American, 0.0% Asian, 0.0% American Indian/Alaska Native, 0.0% Native Hawaiian/Other Pacific Islander, 2.0% Two or more races, 1.7% Hispanic of any race; Average household size: 2.67; Median age: 33.4; Age under 18: 28.8%; Age 65 and over: 9.4%; Males per 100 females: 110.6; Marriage status: 27.7% never married, 47.3% now married, 2.5% separated, 7.4% widowed, 17.6% divorced; Foreign born: 0.0%; Speak English only: 96.4%; With disability: 24.0%; Veterans: 11.7%; Ancestry: 18.7% German, 14.0% Irish, 11.5% Italian, 10.5% English, 6.1% Dutch
Employment: 13.6% management, business, and financial, 0.0% computer, engineering, and science, 1.1% education, legal, community service, arts, and media, 1.1% healthcare practitioners, 29.4% service, 14.7% sales and office, 22.0% natural resources, construction, and maintenance, 18.1% production, transportation, and material moving
Income: Per capita: $12,358; Median household: $27,303; Average household: $32,420; Households with income of $100,000 or more: n/a; Poverty rate: 35.3%
Educational Attainment: High school diploma or higher: 78.5%; Bachelor's degree or higher: 7.3%; Graduate/professional degree or higher: 1.8%
Housing: Homeownership rate: 66.0%; Median home value: $46,300; Median year structure built: Before 1940; Homeowner vacancy rate: 0.0%; Median selected monthly owner costs: $715 with a mortgage, $306 without a mortgage; Median gross rent: $666 per month; Rental vacancy rate: 14.8%
Health Insurance: 83.7% have insurance; 23.7% have private insurance; 66.7% have public insurance; 16.3% do not have insurance; 0.0% of children under 18 do not have insurance
Transportation: Commute: 84.1% car, 0.0% public transportation, 8.0% walk, 4.5% work from home; Mean travel time to work: 29.1 minutes

SOMERSET (village). Covers a land area of 1.163 square miles and a water area of 0.003 square miles. Located at 39.81° N. Lat; 82.30° W. Long. Elevation is 1,083 feet.
History: Somerset was laid out in 1810 by John Fink and Jacob Miller, and served as the seat of Perry County from 1829 to 1857. Civil War general Philip Henry Sheridan spent his boyhood in Somerset.
Population: 1,499; Growth (since 2000): -3.2%; Density: 1,288.7 persons per square mile; Race: 98.8% White, 0.0% Black/African American, 1.2% Asian, 0.0% American Indian/Alaska Native, 0.0% Native Hawaiian/Other Pacific Islander, 0.0% Two or more races, 0.0% Hispanic of any race; Average household size: 2.49; Median age: 40.2; Age under 18: 25.9%; Age 65 and over: 18.1%; Males per 100 females: 92.3; Marriage status: 26.4% never married, 51.4% now married, 2.0% separated, 11.3% widowed, 10.9% divorced; Foreign born: 1.2%; Speak English only: 97.5%; With disability: 17.7%; Veterans: 10.4%; Ancestry: 28.4% German, 19.6% Irish, 10.0% English, 6.0% American, 3.2% Dutch
Employment: 11.7% management, business, and financial, 3.8% computer, engineering, and science, 6.9% education, legal, community service, arts, and media, 7.7% healthcare practitioners, 22.4% service, 16.6% sales and office, 15.3% natural resources, construction, and maintenance, 15.6% production, transportation, and material moving

Income: Per capita: $22,722; Median household: $52,941; Average household: $55,208; Households with income of $100,000 or more: 9.0%; Poverty rate: 11.1%
Educational Attainment: High school diploma or higher: 92.7%; Bachelor's degree or higher: 16.5%; Graduate/professional degree or higher: 5.1%

School District(s)

Northern Local (PK-12)
2015-16 Enrollment: 2,188 . . . . (740) 743-1303
Housing: Homeownership rate: 63.1%; Median home value: $108,300; Median year structure built: 1947; Homeowner vacancy rate: 0.0%; Median selected monthly owner costs: $1,004 with a mortgage, $377 without a mortgage; Median gross rent: $578 per month; Rental vacancy rate: 3.2%
Health Insurance: 94.3% have insurance; 74.8% have private insurance; 31.6% have public insurance; 5.7% do not have insurance; 4.1% of children under 18 do not have insurance
Transportation: Commute: 92.2% car, 0.5% public transportation, 4.4% walk, 1.7% work from home; Mean travel time to work: 29.1 minutes

THORNPORT (CDP). Covers a land area of 1.221 square miles and a water area of 0.467 square miles. Located at 39.92° N. Lat; 82.43° W. Long. Elevation is 899 feet.
Population: 1,000; Growth (since 2000): n/a; Density: 818.8 persons per square mile; Race: 100.0% White, 0.0% Black/African American, 0.0% Asian, 0.0% American Indian/Alaska Native, 0.0% Native Hawaiian/Other Pacific Islander, 0.0% Two or more races, 0.0% Hispanic of any race; Average household size: 2.00; Median age: 59.3; Age under 18: 14.2%; Age 65 and over: 29.7%; Males per 100 females: 99.6; Marriage status: 9.4% never married, 58.9% now married, 1.9% separated, 6.9% widowed, 24.8% divorced; Foreign born: 4.2%; Speak English only: 94.1%; With disability: 30.5%; Veterans: 18.2%; Ancestry: 12.8% English, 11.9% German, 10.1% American, 9.0% Irish, 8.2% Italian
Employment: 24.4% management, business, and financial, 5.4% computer, engineering, and science, 8.5% education, legal, community service, arts, and media, 7.7% healthcare practitioners, 12.2% service, 12.8% sales and office, 11.6% natural resources, construction, and maintenance, 17.3% production, transportation, and material moving
Income: Per capita: $39,644; Median household: $70,347; Average household: $79,646; Households with income of $100,000 or more: 36.5%; Poverty rate: 3.0%
Educational Attainment: High school diploma or higher: 96.5%; Bachelor's degree or higher: 35.0%; Graduate/professional degree or higher: 21.0%
Housing: Homeownership rate: 85.6%; Median home value: $216,300; Median year structure built: 1978; Homeowner vacancy rate: 4.9%; Median selected monthly owner costs: $1,242 with a mortgage, $715 without a mortgage; Median gross rent: $1,291 per month; Rental vacancy rate: 0.0%
Health Insurance: 88.8% have insurance; 74.4% have private insurance; 42.1% have public insurance; 11.2% do not have insurance; 0.0% of children under 18 do not have insurance
Transportation: Commute: 100.0% car, 0.0% public transportation, 0.0% walk, 0.0% work from home; Mean travel time to work: 44.4 minutes

THORNVILLE (village). Covers a land area of 1.104 square miles and a water area of 0.004 square miles. Located at 39.89° N. Lat; 82.41° W. Long. Elevation is 1,030 feet.
Population: 1,196; Growth (since 2000): 63.6%; Density: 1,083.6 persons per square mile; Race: 98.0% White, 0.0% Black/African American, 0.0% Asian, 0.0% American Indian/Alaska Native, 0.0% Native Hawaiian/Other Pacific Islander, 2.0% Two or more races, 0.5% Hispanic of any race; Average household size: 2.74; Median age: 34.0; Age under 18: 30.5%; Age 65 and over: 15.6%; Males per 100 females: 91.7; Marriage status: 26.8% never married, 52.7% now married, 0.9% separated, 7.9% widowed, 12.5% divorced; Foreign born: 0.0%; Speak English only: 99.5%; With disability: 9.8%; Veterans: 7.1%; Ancestry: 32.7% German, 12.0% Irish, 9.0% American, 7.3% English, 6.2% Dutch
Employment: 15.6% management, business, and financial, 2.1% computer, engineering, and science, 3.9% education, legal, community service, arts, and media, 9.6% healthcare practitioners, 26.3% service, 17.2% sales and office, 8.9% natural resources, construction, and maintenance, 16.3% production, transportation, and material moving
Income: Per capita: $23,164; Median household: $55,259; Average household: $62,190; Households with income of $100,000 or more: 16.1%; Poverty rate: 8.5%
Educational Attainment: High school diploma or higher: 96.0%; Bachelor's degree or higher: 18.5%; Graduate/professional degree or higher: 4.9%

School District(s)

Northern Local (PK-12)
2015-16 Enrollment: 2,188 . . . . (740) 743-1303
Housing: Homeownership rate: 64.9%; Median home value: $166,200; Median year structure built: 1977; Homeowner vacancy rate: 6.6%; Median selected monthly owner costs: $1,402 with a mortgage, $448 without a mortgage; Median gross rent: $763 per month; Rental vacancy rate: 7.8%
Health Insurance: 92.2% have insurance; 75.3% have private insurance; 28.8% have public insurance; 7.8% do not have insurance; 0.8% of children under 18 do not have insurance
Transportation: Commute: 97.1% car, 0.0% public transportation, 1.8% walk, 1.1% work from home; Mean travel time to work: 27.7 minutes

Pickaway County

Located in south central Ohio; crossed by the Scioto River. Covers a land area of 501.320 square miles, a water area of 5.232 square miles, and is located in the Eastern Time Zone at 39.65° N. Lat., 83.05° W. Long. The county was founded in 1810. County seat is Circleville.

Pickaway County is part of the Columbus, OH Metropolitan Statistical Area. The entire metro area includes: Delaware County, OH; Fairfield County, OH; Franklin County, OH; Hocking County, OH; Licking County, OH; Madison County, OH; Morrow County, OH; Perry County, OH; Pickaway County, OH; Union County, OH

Weather Station: Circleville Elevation: 672 feet

	Jan	Feb	Mar	Apr	May	Jun	Jul	Aug	Sep	Oct	Nov	Dec
High	38	41	51	64	73	82	85	84	78	66	54	41
Low	22	23	31	41	51	60	63	62	54	43	34	26
Precip	2.6	2.2	3.0	3.5	4.8	3.7	4.0	3.4	2.9	3.0	3.0	2.8
Snow	5.5	3.9	1.7	0.4	0.0	0.0	0.0	0.0	0.0	0.0	0.3	2.1

High and Low temperatures in degrees Fahrenheit; Precipitation and Snow in inches

Population: 56,804; Growth (since 2000): 7.7%; Density: 113.3 persons per square mile; Race: 93.7% White, 3.2% Black/African American, 0.3% Asian, 0.2% American Indian/Alaska Native, 0.0% Native Hawaiian/Other Pacific Islander, 2.3% two or more races, 1.3% Hispanic of any race; Average household size: 2.72; Median age: 39.3; Age under 18: 22.3%; Age 65 and over: 14.5%; Males per 100 females: 110.4; Marriage status: 29.3% never married, 52.5% now married, 2.2% separated, 5.8% widowed, 12.4% divorced; Foreign born: 1.0%; Speak English only: 97.9%; With disability: 14.8%; Veterans: 8.9%; Ancestry: 28.2% German, 15.7% Irish, 14.7% American, 11.9% English, 2.9% Italian
Religion: Six largest groups: 6.9% Methodist/Pietist, 3.4% Baptist, 3.1% Catholicism, 2.1% Lutheran, 1.8% Holiness, 1.4% Non-denominational Protestant
Economy: Unemployment rate: 4.1%; Leading industries: 16.3 % retail trade; 11.8 % construction; 11.8 % health care and social assistance; Farms: 803 totaling 293,684 acres; Company size: 0 employ 1,000 or more persons, 1 employs 500 to 999 persons, 23 employ 100 to 499 persons, 766 employ less than 100 persons; Business ownership: 1,440 women-owned, n/a Black-owned, 34 Hispanic-owned, 25 Asian-owned, n/a American Indian/Alaska Native-owned
Employment: 14.2% management, business, and financial, 2.5% computer, engineering, and science, 9.3% education, legal, community service, arts, and media, 6.8% healthcare practitioners, 16.2% service, 24.3% sales and office, 10.0% natural resources, construction, and maintenance, 16.7% production, transportation, and material moving
Income: Per capita: $24,779; Median household: $58,706; Average household: $70,332; Households with income of $100,000 or more: 20.8%; Poverty rate: 12.2%
Educational Attainment: High school diploma or higher: 87.1%; Bachelor's degree or higher: 17.3%; Graduate/professional degree or higher: 6.2%
Housing: Homeownership rate: 74.3%; Median home value: $150,100; Median year structure built: 1976; Homeowner vacancy rate: 1.5%; Median selected monthly owner costs: $1,252 with a mortgage, $464 without a mortgage; Median gross rent: $755 per month; Rental vacancy rate: 8.5%
Vital Statistics: Birth rate: 106.7 per 10,000 population; Death rate: 98.5 per 10,000 population; Age-adjusted cancer mortality rate: 217.9 deaths per 100,000 population

Health Insurance: 92.4% have insurance; 72.9% have private insurance; 32.5% have public insurance; 7.6% do not have insurance; 4.3% of children under 18 do not have insurance
Health Care: Physicians: 7.7 per 10,000 population; Dentists: 3.6 per 10,000 population; Hospital beds: 9.9 per 10,000 population; Hospital admissions: 353.5 per 10,000 population
Transportation: Commute: 94.4% car, 0.2% public transportation, 1.0% walk, 3.6% work from home; Mean travel time to work: 28.0 minutes
2016 Presidential Election: 68.5% Trump, 26.2% Clinton, 3.0% Johnson, 0.7% Stein
National and State Parks: A W Marion State Park; Logan Elm State Memorial; Stages Pond State Nature Preserve
Additional Information Contacts
Pickaway Government . . . . (740) 474-6093
http://www.pickaway.org

Pickaway County Communities

ASHVILLE (village). Covers a land area of 2.507 square miles and a water area of 0 square miles. Located at 39.72° N. Lat; 82.95° W. Long. Elevation is 712 feet.
Population: 4,142; Growth (since 2000): 30.5%; Density: 1,652.4 persons per square mile; Race: 92.8% White, 0.0% Black/African American, 0.0% Asian, 0.7% American Indian/Alaska Native, 0.0% Native Hawaiian/Other Pacific Islander, 6.4% Two or more races, 1.3% Hispanic of any race; Average household size: 2.89; Median age: 34.3; Age under 18: 27.6%; Age 65 and over: 9.2%; Males per 100 females: 94.1; Marriage status: 22.6% never married, 67.2% now married, 0.4% separated, 2.9% widowed, 7.4% divorced; Foreign born: 1.4%; Speak English only: 96.0%; With disability: 9.9%; Veterans: 8.7%; Ancestry: 34.4% German, 21.9% Irish, 13.1% American, 10.5% English, 4.6% Italian
Employment: 15.8% management, business, and financial, 3.4% computer, engineering, and science, 8.1% education, legal, community service, arts, and media, 3.3% healthcare practitioners, 15.8% service, 30.4% sales and office, 7.8% natural resources, construction, and maintenance, 15.4% production, transportation, and material moving
Income: Per capita: $25,175; Median household: $65,625; Average household: $71,142; Households with income of $100,000 or more: 22.3%; Poverty rate: 6.5%
Educational Attainment: High school diploma or higher: 92.8%; Bachelor's degree or higher: 21.9%; Graduate/professional degree or higher: 8.1%

School District(s)

Teays Valley Local (PK-12)
2015-16 Enrollment: 3,909 . . . . (740) 983-5000
Housing: Homeownership rate: 62.9%; Median home value: $148,300; Median year structure built: 1992; Homeowner vacancy rate: 0.0%; Median selected monthly owner costs: $1,227 with a mortgage, $437 without a mortgage; Median gross rent: $736 per month; Rental vacancy rate: 7.6%
Health Insurance: 93.2% have insurance; 81.0% have private insurance; 21.1% have public insurance; 6.8% do not have insurance; 0.0% of children under 18 do not have insurance
Safety: Violent crime rate: 2.4 per 10,000 population; Property crime rate: 159.3 per 10,000 population
Transportation: Commute: 93.1% car, 0.0% public transportation, 0.8% walk, 5.5% work from home; Mean travel time to work: 28.9 minutes
Additional Information Contacts
Village of Ashville . . . . (740) 983-6367
http://ashvilleohio.gov

CIRCLEVILLE (city). County seat. Covers a land area of 6.644 square miles and a water area of 0.121 square miles. Located at 39.60° N. Lat; 82.93° W. Long. Elevation is 696 feet.
History: Named for local circular earthworks made by prehistoric mound builders. Circleville was settled in 1810 on the site of two ancient forts erected by the mound builders, one of them a round enclosure from which Circleville took its name.
Population: 13,761; Growth (since 2000): 2.0%; Density: 2,071.2 persons per square mile; Race: 93.6% White, 3.2% Black/African American, 0.1% Asian, 0.2% American Indian/Alaska Native, 0.0% Native Hawaiian/Other Pacific Islander, 2.2% Two or more races, 2.3% Hispanic of any race; Average household size: 2.41; Median age: 38.0; Age under 18: 21.0%; Age 65 and over: 19.5%; Males per 100 females: 92.0; Marriage status: 31.6% never married, 44.5% now married, 2.4% separated, 8.8% widowed, 15.1% divorced; Foreign born: 0.5%; Speak English only: 98.0%; With disability: 17.9%; Veterans: 9.5%; Ancestry: 30.3% German, 15.6% Irish, 13.8% American, 10.2% English, 3.1% Dutch
Employment: 9.6% management, business, and financial, 1.4% computer, engineering, and science, 10.5% education, legal, community service, arts, and media, 7.1% healthcare practitioners, 19.2% service, 24.2% sales and office, 6.1% natural resources, construction, and maintenance, 22.0% production, transportation, and material moving
Income: Per capita: $21,256; Median household: $40,276; Average household: $51,919; Households with income of $100,000 or more: 11.3%; Poverty rate: 20.4%
Educational Attainment: High school diploma or higher: 84.4%; Bachelor's degree or higher: 15.7%; Graduate/professional degree or higher: 5.3%

School District(s)

Buckeye United School District (07-12)
2015-16 Enrollment: 311 . . . . (614) 466-0720
Circleville City (PK-12)
2015-16 Enrollment: 2,176 . . . . (740) 474-4340
Logan Elm Local (PK-12)
2015-16 Enrollment: 1,826 . . . . (740) 474-7501

Four-year College(s)

Ohio Christian University (Private, Not-for-profit, Other Protestant)
Fall 2016 Enrollment: 4,661 . . . . (740) 474-8896
2016-17 Tuition: In-state $19,540; Out-of-state $19,540
Housing: Homeownership rate: 54.4%; Median home value: $121,600; Median year structure built: 1961; Homeowner vacancy rate: 0.7%; Median selected monthly owner costs: $1,106 with a mortgage, $442 without a mortgage; Median gross rent: $746 per month; Rental vacancy rate: 10.3%
Health Insurance: 89.6% have insurance; 61.0% have private insurance; 43.7% have public insurance; 10.4% do not have insurance; 6.3% of children under 18 do not have insurance
Hospitals: Berger Hospital (91 beds)
Safety: Violent crime rate: 26.6 per 10,000 population; Property crime rate: 483.8 per 10,000 population
Newspapers: Circleville Herald (daily circulation 5,000)
Transportation: Commute: 94.0% car, 0.0% public transportation, 2.6% walk, 2.1% work from home; Mean travel time to work: 24.8 minutes
Additional Information Contacts
City of Circleville . . . . (740) 477-2551
http://www.ci.circleville.oh.us

COMMERCIAL POINT (village). Covers a land area of 1.126 square miles and a water area of 0 square miles. Located at 39.77° N. Lat; 83.06° W. Long. Elevation is 791 feet.
Population: 1,844; Growth (since 2000): 137.6%; Density: 1,638.3 persons per square mile; Race: 93.6% White, 0.2% Black/African American, 1.7% Asian, 0.0% American Indian/Alaska Native, 0.0% Native Hawaiian/Other Pacific Islander, 4.5% Two or more races, 2.8% Hispanic of any race; Average household size: 3.29; Median age: 31.1; Age under 18: 37.4%; Age 65 and over: 6.9%; Males per 100 females: 92.5; Marriage status: 22.6% never married, 63.4% now married, 1.0% separated, 3.1% widowed, 10.9% divorced; Foreign born: 3.4%; Speak English only: 94.6%; With disability: 6.4%; Veterans: 8.9%; Ancestry: 29.4% German, 19.2% Irish, 8.6% American, 8.3% English, 7.3% Italian
Employment: 19.4% management, business, and financial, 0.7% computer, engineering, and science, 8.9% education, legal, community service, arts, and media, 7.5% healthcare practitioners, 23.5% service, 21.2% sales and office, 6.9% natural resources, construction, and maintenance, 11.9% production, transportation, and material moving
Income: Per capita: $26,898; Median household: $87,438; Average household: $87,688; Households with income of $100,000 or more: 40.2%; Poverty rate: 3.8%
Educational Attainment: High school diploma or higher: 95.7%; Bachelor's degree or higher: 27.5%; Graduate/professional degree or higher: 11.6%

School District(s)

Teays Valley Local (PK-12)
2015-16 Enrollment: 3,909 . . . . (740) 983-5000
Housing: Homeownership rate: 87.9%; Median home value: $170,800; Median year structure built: 2001; Homeowner vacancy rate: 0.0%; Median selected monthly owner costs: $1,476 with a mortgage, $367 without a mortgage; Median gross rent: $1,035 per month; Rental vacancy rate: 0.0%

Health Insurance: 96.5% have insurance; 88.3% have private insurance; 12.4% have public insurance; 3.5% do not have insurance; 0.0% of children under 18 do not have insurance
Safety: Violent crime rate: 12.4 per 10,000 population; Property crime rate: 61.9 per 10,000 population
Transportation: Commute: 97.8% car, 0.0% public transportation, 0.3% walk, 1.9% work from home; Mean travel time to work: 26.7 minutes

DARBYVILLE (village). Covers a land area of 0.465 square miles and a water area of 0.016 square miles. Located at 39.70° N. Lat; 83.11° W. Long. Elevation is 745 feet.
Population: 191; Growth (since 2000): -34.8%; Density: 410.8 persons per square mile; Race: 100.0% White, 0.0% Black/African American, 0.0% Asian, 0.0% American Indian/Alaska Native, 0.0% Native Hawaiian/Other Pacific Islander, 0.0% Two or more races, 0.0% Hispanic of any race; Average household size: 2.73; Median age: 47.8; Age under 18: 24.6%; Age 65 and over: 16.8%; Males per 100 females: 91.4; Marriage status: 24.0% never married, 53.9% now married, 4.5% separated, 11.0% widowed, 11.0% divorced; Foreign born: 0.0%; Speak English only: 100.0%; With disability: 21.5%; Veterans: 10.4%; Ancestry: 26.7% American, 15.7% English, 11.0% German, 6.8% Irish, 4.2% French
Employment: 7.8% management, business, and financial, 0.0% computer, engineering, and science, 6.3% education, legal, community service, arts, and media, 9.4% healthcare practitioners, 42.2% service, 9.4% sales and office, 10.9% natural resources, construction, and maintenance, 14.1% production, transportation, and material moving
Income: Per capita: $34,317; Median household: $36,667; Average household: $92,737; Households with income of $100,000 or more: 18.6%; Poverty rate: 17.3%
Educational Attainment: High school diploma or higher: 77.4%; Bachelor's degree or higher: 10.5%; Graduate/professional degree or higher: 3.0%
Housing: Homeownership rate: 65.7%; Median home value: $95,000; Median year structure built: 1970; Homeowner vacancy rate: 2.1%; Median selected monthly owner costs: $1,484 with a mortgage, $239 without a mortgage; Median gross rent: $782 per month; Rental vacancy rate: 0.0%
Health Insurance: 89.5% have insurance; 63.9% have private insurance; 52.4% have public insurance; 10.5% do not have insurance; 0.0% of children under 18 do not have insurance
Transportation: Commute: 90.5% car, 0.0% public transportation, 4.8% walk, 4.8% work from home; Mean travel time to work: 33.5 minutes

DERBY (CDP). Covers a land area of 1.333 square miles and a water area of 0 square miles. Located at 39.76° N. Lat; 83.21° W. Long. Elevation is 915 feet.
Population: 363; Growth (since 2000): n/a; Density: 272.4 persons per square mile; Race: 98.1% White, 0.0% Black/African American, 0.0% Asian, 0.0% American Indian/Alaska Native, 0.0% Native Hawaiian/Other Pacific Islander, 1.9% Two or more races, 0.0% Hispanic of any race; Average household size: 2.49; Median age: 53.9; Age under 18: 9.6%; Age 65 and over: 23.1%; Males per 100 females: 101.0; Marriage status: 27.1% never married, 59.9% now married, 0.0% separated, 2.1% widowed, 10.9% divorced; Foreign born: 0.0%; Speak English only: 100.0%; With disability: 18.5%; Veterans: 14.0%; Ancestry: 39.9% American, 20.9% German, 12.4% Italian, 10.7% English, 8.0% French
Employment: 20.0% management, business, and financial, 0.0% computer, engineering, and science, 0.0% education, legal, community service, arts, and media, 7.8% healthcare practitioners, 29.6% service, 24.3% sales and office, 0.0% natural resources, construction, and maintenance, 18.3% production, transportation, and material moving
Income: Per capita: $45,963; Median household: $64,167; Average household: $110,319; Households with income of $100,000 or more: 26.0%; Poverty rate: 1.9%
Educational Attainment: High school diploma or higher: 80.2%; Bachelor's degree or higher: n/a; Graduate/professional degree or higher: n/a
Housing: Homeownership rate: 80.8%; Median home value: $100,500; Median year structure built: Before 1940; Homeowner vacancy rate: 0.0%; Median selected monthly owner costs: $863 with a mortgage, $440 without a mortgage; Median gross rent: n/a per month; Rental vacancy rate: 31.7%
Health Insurance: 100.0% have insurance; 82.9% have private insurance; 39.9% have public insurance; 0.0% do not have insurance; 0.0% of children under 18 do not have insurance
Transportation: Commute: 100.0% car, 0.0% public transportation, 0.0% walk, 0.0% work from home; Mean travel time to work: 30.8 minutes

LOGAN ELM VILLAGE (CDP). Covers a land area of 0.525 square miles and a water area of <.001 square miles. Located at 39.57° N. Lat; 82.95° W. Long. Elevation is 705 feet.
Population: 1,165; Growth (since 2000): 9.7%; Density: 2,219.1 persons per square mile; Race: 88.1% White, 0.3% Black/African American, 11.7% Asian, 0.0% American Indian/Alaska Native, 0.0% Native Hawaiian/Other Pacific Islander, 0.0% Two or more races, 0.0% Hispanic of any race; Average household size: 2.58; Median age: 45.1; Age under 18: 21.5%; Age 65 and over: 20.5%; Males per 100 females: 85.4; Marriage status: 24.7% never married, 49.5% now married, 0.1% separated, 8.9% widowed, 17.0% divorced; Foreign born: 8.6%; Speak English only: 91.2%; With disability: 18.4%; Veterans: 7.3%; Ancestry: 31.5% German, 12.9% American, 11.3% English, 10.2% Irish, 3.3% European
Employment: 13.3% management, business, and financial, 4.5% computer, engineering, and science, 9.9% education, legal, community service, arts, and media, 6.1% healthcare practitioners, 18.0% service, 30.9% sales and office, 10.1% natural resources, construction, and maintenance, 7.2% production, transportation, and material moving
Income: Per capita: $23,037; Median household: $49,079; Average household: $58,889; Households with income of $100,000 or more: 10.7%; Poverty rate: 22.5%
Educational Attainment: High school diploma or higher: 87.8%; Bachelor's degree or higher: 12.6%; Graduate/professional degree or higher: 0.1%
Housing: Homeownership rate: 60.9%; Median home value: $108,000; Median year structure built: 1975; Homeowner vacancy rate: 0.0%; Median selected monthly owner costs: $1,011 with a mortgage, $363 without a mortgage; Median gross rent: $491 per month; Rental vacancy rate: 0.0%
Health Insurance: 83.0% have insurance; 66.7% have private insurance; 34.0% have public insurance; 17.0% do not have insurance; 9.2% of children under 18 do not have insurance
Transportation: Commute: 93.2% car, 0.0% public transportation, 0.0% walk, 6.8% work from home; Mean travel time to work: 13.4 minutes

NEW HOLLAND (village). Covers a land area of 1.880 square miles and a water area of 0 square miles. Located at 39.55° N. Lat; 83.26° W. Long. Elevation is 856 feet.
History: New Holland was founded in 1818, and grew as a center for poultry and hog raising.
Population: 725; Growth (since 2000): -7.6%; Density: 385.6 persons per square mile; Race: 98.6% White, 0.0% Black/African American, 0.4% Asian, 0.0% American Indian/Alaska Native, 0.0% Native Hawaiian/Other Pacific Islander, 0.6% Two or more races, 1.4% Hispanic of any race; Average household size: 2.50; Median age: 45.9; Age under 18: 21.4%; Age 65 and over: 20.7%; Males per 100 females: 101.8; Marriage status: 24.4% never married, 51.2% now married, 1.0% separated, 7.3% widowed, 17.1% divorced; Foreign born: 0.4%; Speak English only: 99.5%; With disability: 25.8%; Veterans: 13.2%; Ancestry: 30.6% German, 16.1% English, 15.2% American, 13.4% Irish, 4.0% Dutch
Employment: 7.6% management, business, and financial, 0.0% computer, engineering, and science, 8.4% education, legal, community service, arts, and media, 6.8% healthcare practitioners, 15.6% service, 38.8% sales and office, 5.5% natural resources, construction, and maintenance, 17.3% production, transportation, and material moving
Income: Per capita: $20,440; Median household: $41,944; Average household: $49,283; Households with income of $100,000 or more: 12.1%; Poverty rate: 18.0%
Educational Attainment: High school diploma or higher: 83.7%; Bachelor's degree or higher: 9.9%; Graduate/professional degree or higher: 3.4%
Housing: Homeownership rate: 72.1%; Median home value: $80,200; Median year structure built: 1952; Homeowner vacancy rate: 1.4%; Median selected monthly owner costs: $1,063 with a mortgage, $329 without a mortgage; Median gross rent: $563 per month; Rental vacancy rate: 17.3%
Health Insurance: 90.2% have insurance; 57.1% have private insurance; 49.7% have public insurance; 9.8% do not have insurance; 6.5% of children under 18 do not have insurance
Transportation: Commute: 90.0% car, 0.0% public transportation, 3.5% walk, 5.2% work from home; Mean travel time to work: 29.4 minutes

ORIENT (village). Covers a land area of 0.119 square miles and a water area of 0 square miles. Located at 39.81° N. Lat; 83.15° W. Long. Elevation is 837 feet.
Population: 259; Growth (since 2000): -3.7%; Density: 2,177.1 persons per square mile; Race: 96.1% White, 0.0% Black/African American, 1.9%

Asian, 0.0% American Indian/Alaska Native, 0.4% Native Hawaiian/Other Pacific Islander, 1.5% Two or more races, 0.0% Hispanic of any race; Average household size: 3.41; Median age: 34.3; Age under 18: 21.2%; Age 65 and over: 13.5%; Males per 100 females: 106.1; Marriage status: 19.8% never married, 61.3% now married, 4.6% separated, 10.1% widowed, 8.8% divorced; Foreign born: 2.3%; Speak English only: 96.7%; With disability: 22.8%; Veterans: 4.4%; Ancestry: 43.6% German, 23.6% Irish, 20.1% English, 12.7% American, 11.6% Scottish
Employment: 10.5% management, business, and financial, 5.3% computer, engineering, and science, 0.0% education, legal, community service, arts, and media, 2.6% healthcare practitioners, 14.9% service, 24.6% sales and office, 10.5% natural resources, construction, and maintenance, 31.6% production, transportation, and material moving
Income: Per capita: $20,280; Median household: $51,875; Average household: $62,404; Households with income of $100,000 or more: 19.7%; Poverty rate: 4.6%
Educational Attainment: High school diploma or higher: 81.7%; Bachelor's degree or higher: 4.1%; Graduate/professional degree or higher: n/a
Housing: Homeownership rate: 72.4%; Median home value: $83,400; Median year structure built: Before 1940; Homeowner vacancy rate: 6.8%; Median selected monthly owner costs: $979 with a mortgage, $275 without a mortgage; Median gross rent: $1,063 per month; Rental vacancy rate: 0.0%
Health Insurance: 86.9% have insurance; 65.3% have private insurance; 31.7% have public insurance; 13.1% do not have insurance; 0.0% of children under 18 do not have insurance
Transportation: Commute: 99.0% car, 0.0% public transportation, 0.0% walk, 1.0% work from home; Mean travel time to work: 23.7 minutes

SOUTH BLOOMFIELD (village). Covers a land area of 4.278 square miles and a water area of 0 square miles. Located at 39.72° N. Lat; 82.99° W. Long. Elevation is 696 feet.
Population: 2,136; Growth (since 2000): 81.2%; Density: 499.3 persons per square mile; Race: 97.0% White, 0.3% Black/African American, 0.0% Asian, 0.2% American Indian/Alaska Native, 0.0% Native Hawaiian/Other Pacific Islander, 2.3% Two or more races, 0.0% Hispanic of any race; Average household size: 2.73; Median age: 32.8; Age under 18: 29.5%; Age 65 and over: 11.5%; Males per 100 females: 95.5; Marriage status: 28.0% never married, 51.9% now married, 1.2% separated, 5.3% widowed, 14.8% divorced; Foreign born: 0.4%; Speak English only: 99.4%; With disability: 8.5%; Veterans: 15.0%; Ancestry: 35.5% German, 22.0% Irish, 13.7% English, 8.7% American, 5.6% Italian
Employment: 13.6% management, business, and financial, 5.6% computer, engineering, and science, 4.1% education, legal, community service, arts, and media, 7.5% healthcare practitioners, 13.5% service, 23.9% sales and office, 10.8% natural resources, construction, and maintenance, 21.0% production, transportation, and material moving
Income: Per capita: $21,803; Median household: $55,532; Average household: $58,184; Households with income of $100,000 or more: 9.7%; Poverty rate: 13.8%
Educational Attainment: High school diploma or higher: 87.5%; Bachelor's degree or higher: 11.3%; Graduate/professional degree or higher: 2.4%

School District(s)

Teays Valley Local (PK-12)
2015-16 Enrollment: 3,909 . . . . (740) 983-5000

Housing: Homeownership rate: 84.5%; Median home value: $106,600; Median year structure built: 1996; Homeowner vacancy rate: 2.6%; Median selected monthly owner costs: $1,129 with a mortgage, $502 without a mortgage; Median gross rent: $888 per month; Rental vacancy rate: 2.3%
Health Insurance: 93.4% have insurance; 77.9% have private insurance; 30.5% have public insurance; 6.6% do not have insurance; 0.0% of children under 18 do not have insurance
Safety: Violent crime rate: 5.3 per 10,000 population; Property crime rate: 186.9 per 10,000 population
Transportation: Commute: 98.8% car, 0.0% public transportation, 0.3% walk, 0.9% work from home; Mean travel time to work: 29.5 minutes

TARLTON (village). Covers a land area of 0.418 square miles and a water area of 0 square miles. Located at 39.55° N. Lat; 82.78° W. Long. Elevation is 902 feet.
History: Tarlton Cross Mound nearby.
Population: 241; Growth (since 2000): -19.1%; Density: 576.7 persons per square mile; Race: 98.8% White, 0.0% Black/African American, 0.0% Asian, 0.0% American Indian/Alaska Native, 0.0% Native Hawaiian/Other Pacific Islander, 1.2% Two or more races, 9.1% Hispanic of any race; Average household size: 2.84; Median age: 42.2; Age under 18: 14.1%; Age 65 and over: 14.5%; Males per 100 females: 90.5; Marriage status: 35.7% never married, 42.7% now married, 3.8% separated, 10.8% widowed, 10.8% divorced; Foreign born: 0.0%; Speak English only: 100.0%; With disability: 15.4%; Veterans: 4.8%; Ancestry: 35.3% German, 17.4% English, 14.1% Irish, 13.7% American, 4.6% Dutch
Employment: 16.5% management, business, and financial, 0.8% computer, engineering, and science, 1.5% education, legal, community service, arts, and media, 3.0% healthcare practitioners, 19.5% service, 17.3% sales and office, 12.0% natural resources, construction, and maintenance, 29.3% production, transportation, and material moving
Income: Per capita: $21,511; Median household: $46,250; Average household: $55,431; Households with income of $100,000 or more: 16.5%; Poverty rate: 3.7%
Educational Attainment: High school diploma or higher: 86.9%; Bachelor's degree or higher: 12.4%; Graduate/professional degree or higher: n/a
Housing: Homeownership rate: 87.1%; Median home value: $84,200; Median year structure built: Before 1940; Homeowner vacancy rate: 8.6%; Median selected monthly owner costs: $1,057 with a mortgage, $386 without a mortgage; Median gross rent: $588 per month; Rental vacancy rate: 0.0%
Health Insurance: 86.7% have insurance; 61.0% have private insurance; 36.1% have public insurance; 13.3% do not have insurance; 0.0% of children under 18 do not have insurance
Transportation: Commute: 88.6% car, 0.0% public transportation, 0.0% walk, 11.4% work from home; Mean travel time to work: 33.3 minutes

WILLIAMSPORT (village). Covers a land area of 1.812 square miles and a water area of 0.030 square miles. Located at 39.58° N. Lat; 83.12° W. Long. Elevation is 768 feet.
Population: 1,132; Growth (since 2000): 13.0%; Density: 624.7 persons per square mile; Race: 97.9% White, 0.0% Black/African American, 0.0% Asian, 0.0% American Indian/Alaska Native, 0.0% Native Hawaiian/Other Pacific Islander, 2.1% Two or more races, 0.8% Hispanic of any race; Average household size: 3.45; Median age: 32.1; Age under 18: 33.8%; Age 65 and over: 9.1%; Males per 100 females: 93.0; Marriage status: 33.0% never married, 47.2% now married, 2.3% separated, 4.9% widowed, 14.8% divorced; Foreign born: 0.0%; Speak English only: 100.0%; With disability: 19.6%; Veterans: 4.7%; Ancestry: 34.5% German, 19.5% American, 14.5% English, 14.2% Irish, 4.6% Polish
Employment: 5.6% management, business, and financial, 1.9% computer, engineering, and science, 5.0% education, legal, community service, arts, and media, 3.7% healthcare practitioners, 25.0% service, 26.5% sales and office, 12.9% natural resources, construction, and maintenance, 19.4% production, transportation, and material moving
Income: Per capita: $14,397; Median household: $43,036; Average household: $46,900; Households with income of $100,000 or more: 3.6%; Poverty rate: 22.3%
Educational Attainment: High school diploma or higher: 85.8%; Bachelor's degree or higher: 5.4%; Graduate/professional degree or higher: 2.6%

School District(s)

Westfall Local (PK-12)
2015-16 Enrollment: 1,427 . . . . (740) 986-3671

Housing: Homeownership rate: 57.9%; Median home value: $91,500; Median year structure built: 1961; Homeowner vacancy rate: 13.2%; Median selected monthly owner costs: $948 with a mortgage, $367 without a mortgage; Median gross rent: $775 per month; Rental vacancy rate: 4.2%
Health Insurance: 88.1% have insurance; 57.0% have private insurance; 41.7% have public insurance; 11.9% do not have insurance; 2.3% of children under 18 do not have insurance
Transportation: Commute: 92.5% car, 2.7% public transportation, 4.3% walk, 0.0% work from home; Mean travel time to work: 29.6 minutes

Pike County

Located in southern Ohio; crossed by the Scioto River. Covers a land area of 440.282 square miles, a water area of 3.694 square miles, and is located in the Eastern Time Zone at 39.07° N. Lat., 83.05° W. Long. The county was founded in 1815. County seat is Waverly.

Weather Station: Waverly Elevation: 560 feet

	Jan	Feb	Mar	Apr	May	Jun	Jul	Aug	Sep	Oct	Nov	Dec
High	40	44	54	66	75	83	86	85	79	68	56	43
Low	20	22	30	39	49	59	63	61	52	40	32	24
Precip	2.8	2.5	3.7	3.6	4.5	3.5	4.2	3.8	2.6	3.0	3.1	2.9
Snow	4.6	3.3	1.7	tr	0.0	0.0	0.0	0.0	0.0	0.0	0.1	2.2

High and Low temperatures in degrees Fahrenheit; Precipitation and Snow in inches

Population: 28,298; Growth (since 2000): 2.2%; Density: 64.3 persons per square mile; Race: 96.0% White, 0.7% Black/African American, 0.3% Asian, 0.2% American Indian/Alaska Native, 0.3% Native Hawaiian/Other Pacific Islander, 2.2% two or more races, 0.9% Hispanic of any race; Average household size: 2.55; Median age: 40.8; Age under 18: 24.2%; Age 65 and over: 16.2%; Males per 100 females: 98.6; Marriage status: 25.0% never married, 51.0% now married, 2.7% separated, 7.8% widowed, 16.2% divorced; Foreign born: 0.5%; Speak English only: 97.0%; With disability: 23.1%; Veterans: 8.1%; Ancestry: 20.3% German, 13.9% Irish, 9.6% English, 9.2% American, 1.9% Dutch
Religion: Six largest groups: 11.3% Baptist, 3.4% Methodist/Pietist, 2.9% Non-denominational Protestant, 1.0% Catholicism, 0.5% Presbyterian-Reformed, 0.3% European Free-Church
Economy: Unemployment rate: 5.7%; Leading industries: 19.6 % retail trade; 13.4 % health care and social assistance; 11.1 % other services (except public administration); Farms: 490 totaling 97,446 acres; Company size: 1 employs 1,000 or more persons, 1 employs 500 to 999 persons, 14 employ 100 to 499 persons, 388 employ less than 100 persons; Business ownership: 515 women-owned, n/a Black-owned, n/a Hispanic-owned, n/a Asian-owned, n/a American Indian/Alaska Native-owned
Employment: 9.4% management, business, and financial, 4.5% computer, engineering, and science, 8.9% education, legal, community service, arts, and media, 8.0% healthcare practitioners, 17.1% service, 19.0% sales and office, 12.5% natural resources, construction, and maintenance, 20.5% production, transportation, and material moving
Income: Per capita: $21,375; Median household: $41,128; Average household: $55,189; Households with income of $100,000 or more: 13.7%; Poverty rate: 20.7%
Educational Attainment: High school diploma or higher: 78.1%; Bachelor's degree or higher: 12.3%; Graduate/professional degree or higher: 5.3%
Housing: Homeownership rate: 68.3%; Median home value: $97,800; Median year structure built: 1981; Homeowner vacancy rate: 1.1%; Median selected monthly owner costs: $1,063 with a mortgage, $357 without a mortgage; Median gross rent: $662 per month; Rental vacancy rate: 7.0%
Vital Statistics: Birth rate: 126.1 per 10,000 population; Death rate: 131.0 per 10,000 population; Age-adjusted cancer mortality rate: 165.4 deaths per 100,000 population
Health Insurance: 88.4% have insurance; 53.5% have private insurance; 49.3% have public insurance; 11.6% do not have insurance; 4.2% of children under 18 do not have insurance
Health Care: Physicians: 5.7 per 10,000 population; Dentists: 3.9 per 10,000 population; Hospital beds: 7.4 per 10,000 population; Hospital admissions: 205.5 per 10,000 population
Transportation: Commute: 94.5% car, 0.4% public transportation, 0.8% walk, 3.5% work from home; Mean travel time to work: 28.2 minutes
2016 Presidential Election: 66.1% Trump, 29.6% Clinton, 2.4% Johnson, 0.5% Stein
National and State Parks: Lake White State Park
Additional Information Contacts
Pike Government. . . . . (740) 947-4817
http://www.pike-co.org

Pike County Communities

BEAVER (village). Covers a land area of 0.390 square miles and a water area of <.001 square miles. Located at 39.03° N. Lat; 82.83° W. Long. Elevation is 689 feet.
Population: 378; Growth (since 2000): -18.5%; Density: 968.7 persons per square mile; Race: 99.7% White, 0.0% Black/African American, 0.0% Asian, 0.0% American Indian/Alaska Native, 0.0% Native Hawaiian/Other Pacific Islander, 0.3% Two or more races, 2.1% Hispanic of any race; Average household size: 2.24; Median age: 40.0; Age under 18: 27.8%; Age 65 and over: 16.7%; Males per 100 females: 84.8; Marriage status: 26.9% never married, 42.5% now married, 2.7% separated, 16.3% widowed, 14.3% divorced; Foreign born: 0.0%; Speak English only: 99.2%; With disability: 31.0%; Veterans: 4.0%; Ancestry: 22.0% German, 14.3% Irish, 13.0% American, 6.6% English, 3.4% Italian
Employment: 7.4% management, business, and financial, 0.8% computer, engineering, and science, 6.6% education, legal, community service, arts, and media, 11.6% healthcare practitioners, 20.7% service, 24.8% sales and office, 6.6% natural resources, construction, and maintenance, 21.5% production, transportation, and material moving
Income: Per capita: $14,973; Median household: $20,750; Average household: $33,349; Households with income of $100,000 or more: 4.2%; Poverty rate: 36.5%
Educational Attainment: High school diploma or higher: 80.6%; Bachelor's degree or higher: 5.4%; Graduate/professional degree or higher: 2.9%

School District(s)

Eastern Local (PK-12)
2015-16 Enrollment: 859. . . . . (740) 226-4851
Housing: Homeownership rate: 43.2%; Median home value: $107,800; Median year structure built: 1977; Homeowner vacancy rate: 5.1%; Median selected monthly owner costs: $1,102 with a mortgage, $433 without a mortgage; Median gross rent: $463 per month; Rental vacancy rate: 6.8%
Health Insurance: 88.6% have insurance; 48.9% have private insurance; 54.0% have public insurance; 11.4% do not have insurance; 6.7% of children under 18 do not have insurance
Transportation: Commute: 88.8% car, 0.0% public transportation, 10.3% walk, 0.9% work from home; Mean travel time to work: 18.2 minutes

LATHAM (unincorporated postal area)
ZCTA: 45646
Covers a land area of 15.673 square miles and a water area of 0.072 square miles. Located at 39.08° N. Lat; 83.32° W. Long. Elevation is 636 feet.
Population: 199; Growth (since 2000): -32.5%; Density: 12.7 persons per square mile; Race: 100.0% White, 0.0% Black/African American, 0.0% Asian, 0.0% American Indian/Alaska Native, 0.0% Native Hawaiian/Other Pacific Islander, 0.0% Two or more races, 0.0% Hispanic of any race; Average household size: 1.99; Median age: 59.6; Age under 18: 7.5%; Age 65 and over: 31.2%; Males per 100 females: 93.7; Marriage status: 14.7% never married, 64.1% now married, 3.8% separated, 4.3% widowed, 16.8% divorced; Foreign born: 0.0%; Speak English only: 100.0%; With disability: 54.3%; Veterans: 22.3%; Ancestry: 14.1% Welsh, 11.6% German, 10.1% American, 5.0% French, 4.0% European
Employment: 0.0% management, business, and financial, 36.7% computer, engineering, and science, 0.0% education, legal, community service, arts, and media, 0.0% healthcare practitioners, 63.3% service, 0.0% sales and office, 0.0% natural resources, construction, and maintenance, 0.0% production, transportation, and material moving
Income: Per capita: $17,902; Median household: $24,833; Average household: $33,838; Households with income of $100,000 or more: n/a; Poverty rate: 35.7%
Educational Attainment: High school diploma or higher: 81.5%; Bachelor's degree or higher: 5.4%; Graduate/professional degree or higher: n/a

School District(s)

Western Local (PK-12)
2015-16 Enrollment: 746. . . . . (740) 493-3113
Housing: Homeownership rate: 85.0%; Median home value: n/a; Median year structure built: 1996; Homeowner vacancy rate: 0.0%; Median selected monthly owner costs: $1,375 with a mortgage, $288 without a mortgage; Median gross rent: n/a per month; Rental vacancy rate: 0.0%
Health Insurance: 74.4% have insurance; 59.3% have private insurance; 43.7% have public insurance; 25.6% do not have insurance; 0.0% of children under 18 do not have insurance
Transportation: Commute: 100.0% car, 0.0% public transportation, 0.0% walk, 0.0% work from home; Mean travel time to work: 0.0 minutes

PIKETON (village). Covers a land area of 2.503 square miles and a water area of 0.054 square miles. Located at 39.06° N. Lat; 82.99° W. Long. Elevation is 577 feet.
History: Piketon was settled in 1814, when it was called Jefferson. Piketon served as the seat of Pike County until 1861.
Population: 1,929; Growth (since 2000): 1.2%; Density: 770.6 persons per square mile; Race: 96.3% White, 0.0% Black/African American, 0.0% Asian, 0.0% American Indian/Alaska Native, 0.0% Native Hawaiian/Other Pacific Islander, 3.7% Two or more races, 0.0% Hispanic of any race; Average household size: 2.53; Median age: 39.0; Age under 18: 25.6%;

Age 65 and over: 14.0%; Males per 100 females: 87.7; Marriage status: 26.3% never married, 46.1% now married, 3.8% separated, 7.5% widowed, 20.0% divorced; Foreign born: 0.0%; Speak English only: 100.0%; With disability: 27.0%; Veterans: 5.8%; Ancestry: 16.2% Irish, 15.7% German, 10.5% American, 6.7% English, 1.8% Welsh
Employment: 8.4% management, business, and financial, 3.7% computer, engineering, and science, 11.1% education, legal, community service, arts, and media, 10.2% healthcare practitioners, 30.0% service, 16.9% sales and office, 5.5% natural resources, construction, and maintenance, 14.3% production, transportation, and material moving
Income: Per capita: $14,766; Median household: $25,500; Average household: $37,523; Households with income of $100,000 or more: 7.8%; Poverty rate: 40.7%
Educational Attainment: High school diploma or higher: 76.1%; Bachelor's degree or higher: 9.2%; Graduate/professional degree or higher: 3.2%

School District(s)

Pike County Area (07-12)
2015-16 Enrollment: n/a . . . . (740) 289-2721
Scioto Valley Local (PK-12)
2015-16 Enrollment: 1,320 . . . . (740) 289-4456

Vocational/Technical School(s)

Pike County Joint Vocational School District (Public)
Fall 2016 Enrollment: 19 . . . . (740) 289-2282

Housing: Homeownership rate: 49.7%; Median home value: $96,200; Median year structure built: 1978; Homeowner vacancy rate: 6.5%; Median selected monthly owner costs: $1,151 with a mortgage, $388 without a mortgage; Median gross rent: $532 per month; Rental vacancy rate: 13.0%
Health Insurance: 91.2% have insurance; 39.4% have private insurance; 59.1% have public insurance; 8.8% do not have insurance; 0.0% of children under 18 do not have insurance
Transportation: Commute: 91.4% car, 0.0% public transportation, 4.5% walk, 4.1% work from home; Mean travel time to work: 21.4 minutes

STOCKDALE (CDP). Covers a land area of 0.534 square miles and a water area of <.001 square miles. Located at 38.96° N. Lat; 82.86° W. Long. Elevation is 718 feet.
Population: 15; Growth (since 2000): n/a; Density: 28.1 persons per square mile; Race: 100.0% White, 0.0% Black/African American, 0.0% Asian, 0.0% American Indian/Alaska Native, 0.0% Native Hawaiian/Other Pacific Islander, 0.0% Two or more races, 0.0% Hispanic of any race; Average household size: 0.00; Median age: n/a; Age under 18: 0.0%; Age 65 and over: 0.0%; Males per 100 females: 84.9; Marriage status: 0.0% never married, 0.0% now married, 0.0% separated, 0.0% widowed, 100.0% divorced; Foreign born: 0.0%; Speak English only: 100.0%; With disability: 0.0%; Veterans: 0.0%; Ancestry: 100.0% English
Employment: 100.0% management, business, and financial, 0.0% computer, engineering, and science, 0.0% education, legal, community service, arts, and media, 0.0% healthcare practitioners, 0.0% service, 0.0% sales and office, 0.0% natural resources, construction, and maintenance, 0.0% production, transportation, and material moving
Income: Per capita: n/a; Median household: n/a; Average household: n/a; Households with income of $100,000 or more: n/a; Poverty rate: n/a
Educational Attainment: High school diploma or higher: 100.0%; Bachelor's degree or higher: 100.0%; Graduate/professional degree or higher: 100.0%
Housing: Homeownership rate: 100.0%; Median home value: n/a; Median year structure built: n/a; Homeowner vacancy rate: 0.0%; Median selected monthly owner costs: n/a with a mortgage, n/a without a mortgage; Median gross rent: n/a per month; Rental vacancy rate: 0.0%
Health Insurance: 100.0% have insurance; 100.0% have private insurance; 0.0% have public insurance; 0.0% do not have insurance; 0.0% of children under 18 do not have insurance
Transportation: Commute: 100.0% car, 0.0% public transportation, 0.0% walk, 0.0% work from home; Mean travel time to work: 0.0 minutes

WAVERLY (village). Aka Waverly City. County seat.
Land/water area and latitude/longitude are not available.
Population: 4,374; Growth (since 2000): n/a; Density: n/a persons per square mile; Race: 94.9% White, 0.9% Black/African American, 1.8% Asian, 0.1% American Indian/Alaska Native, 0.0% Native Hawaiian/Other Pacific Islander, 0.2% Two or more races, 2.2% Hispanic of any race; Average household size: 2.03; Median age: 45.9; Age under 18: 18.2%; Age 65 and over: 26.2%; Males per 100 females: 95.1; Marriage status: 29.6% never married, 40.5% now married, 1.2% separated, 12.7% widowed, 17.2% divorced; Foreign born: 1.7%; Speak English only: 96.0%; With disability: 23.2%; Veterans: 11.2%; Ancestry: 29.2% German, 15.7% English, 14.5% Irish, 7.7% American, 2.4% Scotch-Irish
Employment: 12.3% management, business, and financial, 2.5% computer, engineering, and science, 8.8% education, legal, community service, arts, and media, 8.2% healthcare practitioners, 23.4% service, 23.2% sales and office, 6.4% natural resources, construction, and maintenance, 15.0% production, transportation, and material moving
Income: Per capita: $23,613; Median household: $38,015; Average household: $49,153; Households with income of $100,000 or more: 11.2%; Poverty rate: 17.4%
Educational Attainment: High school diploma or higher: 83.1%; Bachelor's degree or higher: 16.6%; Graduate/professional degree or higher: 7.3%
Housing: Homeownership rate: 45.0%; Median home value: $100,800; Median year structure built: 1965; Homeowner vacancy rate: 0.0%; Median selected monthly owner costs: $984 with a mortgage, $351 without a mortgage; Median gross rent: $707 per month; Rental vacancy rate: 8.1%
Health Insurance: 94.2% have insurance; 64.9% have private insurance; 55.4% have public insurance; 5.8% do not have insurance; 0.0% of children under 18 do not have insurance
Safety: Violent crime rate: 7.1 per 10,000 population; Property crime rate: 218.9 per 10,000 population
Transportation: Commute: 98.4% car, 0.6% public transportation, 0.0% walk, 0.5% work from home; Mean travel time to work: 20.7 minutes

Portage County

Located in northeastern Ohio; crossed by the Cuyahoga River and tributaries of the Mahoning; includes many small lakes. Covers a land area of 487.381 square miles, a water area of 16.683 square miles, and is located in the Eastern Time Zone at 41.17° N. Lat., 81.20° W. Long. The county was founded in 1807. County seat is Ravenna.

Portage County is part of the Akron, OH Metropolitan Statistical Area. The entire metro area includes: Portage County, OH; Summit County, OH

Weather Station: Hiram Elevation: 1,229 feet

	Jan	Feb	Mar	Apr	May	Jun	Jul	Aug	Sep	Oct	Nov	Dec
High	32	36	45	58	68	77	81	80	73	60	49	36
Low	17	19	26	37	47	56	61	60	52	41	33	22
Precip	3.0	2.4	3.3	3.8	4.1	4.0	4.1	3.7	3.8	3.4	3.6	3.5
Snow	18.2	12.7	10.4	1.9	tr	0.0	0.0	0.0	0.0	0.4	5.3	14.3

High and Low temperatures in degrees Fahrenheit; Precipitation and Snow in inches

Population: 161,796; Growth (since 2000): 6.4%; Density: 332.0 persons per square mile; Race: 91.4% White, 4.0% Black/African American, 1.8% Asian, 0.1% American Indian/Alaska Native, 0.0% Native Hawaiian/Other Pacific Islander, 2.3% two or more races, 1.6% Hispanic of any race; Average household size: 2.52; Median age: 37.7; Age under 18: 19.4%; Age 65 and over: 14.5%; Males per 100 females: 95.5; Marriage status: 36.0% never married, 47.6% now married, 1.5% separated, 5.0% widowed, 11.4% divorced; Foreign born: 4.0%; Speak English only: 95.2%; With disability: 12.8%; Veterans: 8.5%; Ancestry: 28.7% German, 18.5% Irish, 10.8% Italian, 10.1% English, 6.0% Polish
Religion: Six largest groups: 12.3% Catholicism, 4.0% Methodist/Pietist, 2.9% Non-denominational Protestant, 2.2% Baptist, 1.5% Presbyterian-Reformed, 1.2% Lutheran
Economy: Unemployment rate: 4.4%; Leading industries: 14.3 % retail trade; 10.7 % other services (except public administration); 10.6 % accommodation and food services; Farms: 847 totaling 83,321 acres; Company size: 1 employs 1,000 or more persons, 3 employ 500 to 999 persons, 80 employ 100 to 499 persons, 2,927 employ less than 100 persons; Business ownership: 3,970 women-owned, 296 Black-owned, 68 Hispanic-owned, 192 Asian-owned, 36 American Indian/Alaska Native-owned
Employment: 12.7% management, business, and financial, 4.1% computer, engineering, and science, 10.9% education, legal, community service, arts, and media, 4.5% healthcare practitioners, 18.4% service, 24.4% sales and office, 7.9% natural resources, construction, and maintenance, 17.1% production, transportation, and material moving
Income: Per capita: $26,769; Median household: $52,427; Average household: $67,854; Households with income of $100,000 or more: 20.2%; Poverty rate: 15.0%

Educational Attainment: High school diploma or higher: 91.9%; Bachelor's degree or higher: 27.3%; Graduate/professional degree or higher: 10.4%
Housing: Homeownership rate: 68.7%; Median home value: $150,400; Median year structure built: 1975; Homeowner vacancy rate: 1.1%; Median selected monthly owner costs: $1,303 with a mortgage, $482 without a mortgage; Median gross rent: $813 per month; Rental vacancy rate: 4.2%
Vital Statistics: Birth rate: 93.0 per 10,000 population; Death rate: 86.7 per 10,000 population; Age-adjusted cancer mortality rate: 181.8 deaths per 100,000 population
Health Insurance: 92.5% have insurance; 74.2% have private insurance; 30.2% have public insurance; 7.5% do not have insurance; 3.6% of children under 18 do not have insurance
Health Care: Physicians: 14.7 per 10,000 population; Dentists: 4.3 per 10,000 population; Hospital beds: 8.7 per 10,000 population; Hospital admissions: 464.5 per 10,000 population
Air Quality Index (AQI): Percent of Days: 90.3% good, 9.7% moderate, 0.0% unhealthy for sensitive individuals, 0.0% unhealthy, 0.0% very unhealthy; Annual median: 37; Annual maximum: 90
Transportation: Commute: 91.5% car, 0.7% public transportation, 2.6% walk, 4.5% work from home; Mean travel time to work: 25.4 minutes
2016 Presidential Election: 52.1% Trump, 42.2% Clinton, 3.1% Johnson, 1.1% Stein
National and State Parks: Charles Tummonds State Nature Preserve; Eagle Creek State Nature Preserve; Marsh Wetlands State Nature Preserve; Nelson-Kennedy Ledges State Park; Tinkers Creek State Park; Tom S Cooperrider-Kent Bog State Nature Preserve; Triangle Lake Bog State Nature Preserve; West Branch State Park
Additional Information Contacts
Portage Government . . . . (330) 297-3600
http://www.co.portage.oh.us

Portage County Communities

ATWATER (CDP). Covers a land area of 0.842 square miles and a water area of 0.011 square miles. Located at 41.03° N. Lat; 81.16° W. Long. Elevation is 1,129 feet.
Population: 1,030; Growth (since 2000): n/a; Density: 1,223.0 persons per square mile; Race: 100.0% White, 0.0% Black/African American, 0.0% Asian, 0.0% American Indian/Alaska Native, 0.0% Native Hawaiian/Other Pacific Islander, 0.0% Two or more races, 1.7% Hispanic of any race; Average household size: 3.41; Median age: 31.5; Age under 18: 27.2%; Age 65 and over: 5.0%; Males per 100 females: 87.6; Marriage status: 36.5% never married, 49.4% now married, 0.0% separated, 1.6% widowed, 12.5% divorced; Foreign born: 0.0%; Speak English only: 99.2%; With disability: 10.7%; Veterans: 6.9%; Ancestry: 30.8% Irish, 17.3% German, 11.9% American, 9.0% Welsh, 8.7% Italian
Employment: 15.3% management, business, and financial, 4.0% computer, engineering, and science, 18.5% education, legal, community service, arts, and media, 6.7% healthcare practitioners, 6.3% service, 27.2% sales and office, 10.3% natural resources, construction, and maintenance, 11.9% production, transportation, and material moving
Income: Per capita: $19,694; Median household: $50,000; Average household: $63,833; Households with income of $100,000 or more: 20.2%; Poverty rate: 11.6%
Educational Attainment: High school diploma or higher: 96.0%; Bachelor's degree or higher: 10.3%; Graduate/professional degree or higher: n/a

School District(s)

Waterloo Local (PK-12)
2015-16 Enrollment: 1,070 . . . . (330) 947-2664
Housing: Homeownership rate: 63.9%; Median home value: $109,900; Median year structure built: 1972; Homeowner vacancy rate: 0.0%; Median selected monthly owner costs: $991 with a mortgage, $385 without a mortgage; Median gross rent: $1,053 per month; Rental vacancy rate: 0.0%
Health Insurance: 93.2% have insurance; 71.7% have private insurance; 25.2% have public insurance; 6.8% do not have insurance; 0.0% of children under 18 do not have insurance
Transportation: Commute: 98.6% car, 0.0% public transportation, 0.0% walk, 1.4% work from home; Mean travel time to work: 36.3 minutes

AURORA (city). Covers a land area of 22.918 square miles and a water area of 1.147 square miles. Located at 41.30° N. Lat; 81.33° W. Long. Elevation is 1,129 feet.
History: Founded in 1799, Aurora was designated a Tree City USA by the National Arbor Day Foundation.
Population: 15,712; Growth (since 2000): 15.9%; Density: 685.6 persons per square mile; Race: 90.9% White, 3.6% Black/African American, 3.5% Asian, 0.0% American Indian/Alaska Native, 0.0% Native Hawaiian/Other Pacific Islander, 1.9% Two or more races, 1.7% Hispanic of any race; Average household size: 2.43; Median age: 48.2; Age under 18: 22.3%; Age 65 and over: 21.0%; Males per 100 females: 92.0; Marriage status: 22.0% never married, 61.3% now married, 1.8% separated, 7.8% widowed, 8.9% divorced; Foreign born: 6.3%; Speak English only: 93.1%; With disability: 10.9%; Veterans: 10.2%; Ancestry: 28.5% German, 21.2% Irish, 13.3% Italian, 11.5% English, 9.3% Polish
Employment: 25.1% management, business, and financial, 6.9% computer, engineering, and science, 11.0% education, legal, community service, arts, and media, 6.3% healthcare practitioners, 13.9% service, 27.4% sales and office, 2.6% natural resources, construction, and maintenance, 6.8% production, transportation, and material moving
Income: Per capita: $45,269; Median household: $84,135; Average household: $110,317; Households with income of $100,000 or more: 40.4%; Poverty rate: 5.2%
Educational Attainment: High school diploma or higher: 94.7%; Bachelor's degree or higher: 50.1%; Graduate/professional degree or higher: 19.0%

School District(s)

Aurora City (PK-12)
2015-16 Enrollment: 2,956 . . . . (330) 562-6106
Housing: Homeownership rate: 80.0%; Median home value: $241,800; Median year structure built: 1986; Homeowner vacancy rate: 1.0%; Median selected monthly owner costs: $1,694 with a mortgage, $703 without a mortgage; Median gross rent: $1,461 per month; Rental vacancy rate: 5.9%
Health Insurance: 96.0% have insurance; 85.0% have private insurance; 26.4% have public insurance; 4.0% do not have insurance; 3.3% of children under 18 do not have insurance
Safety: Violent crime rate: 6.9 per 10,000 population; Property crime rate: 105.7 per 10,000 population
Transportation: Commute: 91.3% car, 0.3% public transportation, 0.9% walk, 6.6% work from home; Mean travel time to work: 27.6 minutes
Additional Information Contacts
City of Aurora . . . . (330) 562-6131
http://www.auroraoh.com

BRADY LAKE (village). Covers a land area of 0.314 square miles and a water area of 0.098 square miles. Located at 41.16° N. Lat; 81.31° W. Long. Elevation is 1,079 feet.
Population: 504; Growth (since 2000): -1.8%; Density: 1,603.0 persons per square mile; Race: 96.0% White, 0.0% Black/African American, 0.0% Asian, 0.6% American Indian/Alaska Native, 0.0% Native Hawaiian/Other Pacific Islander, 3.4% Two or more races, 0.0% Hispanic of any race; Average household size: 2.53; Median age: 42.0; Age under 18: 18.8%; Age 65 and over: 15.5%; Males per 100 females: 108.1; Marriage status: 35.5% never married, 48.0% now married, 3.3% separated, 5.4% widowed, 11.1% divorced; Foreign born: 0.4%; Speak English only: 99.4%; With disability: 16.1%; Veterans: 6.6%; Ancestry: 43.5% German, 23.6% Irish, 12.9% Italian, 12.7% English, 10.1% American
Employment: 6.2% management, business, and financial, 3.1% computer, engineering, and science, 8.1% education, legal, community service, arts, and media, 5.8% healthcare practitioners, 26.6% service, 22.8% sales and office, 8.9% natural resources, construction, and maintenance, 18.5% production, transportation, and material moving
Income: Per capita: $21,419; Median household: $45,417; Average household: $52,056; Households with income of $100,000 or more: 8.0%; Poverty rate: 15.3%
Educational Attainment: High school diploma or higher: 91.7%; Bachelor's degree or higher: 24.3%; Graduate/professional degree or higher: 10.1%
Housing: Homeownership rate: 68.3%; Median home value: $115,700; Median year structure built: 1953; Homeowner vacancy rate: 0.0%; Median selected monthly owner costs: $960 with a mortgage, $450 without a mortgage; Median gross rent: $833 per month; Rental vacancy rate: 0.0%

Health Insurance: 90.9% have insurance; 68.7% have private insurance; 31.9% have public insurance; 9.1% do not have insurance; 7.4% of children under 18 do not have insurance
Safety: Violent crime rate: 21.6 per 10,000 population; Property crime rate: 107.8 per 10,000 population
Transportation: Commute: 95.9% car, 0.0% public transportation, 0.0% walk, 2.4% work from home; Mean travel time to work: 20.5 minutes

BRIMFIELD (CDP). Covers a land area of 3.970 square miles and a water area of 0.037 square miles. Located at 41.10° N. Lat; 81.35° W. Long. Elevation is 1,102 feet.
Population: 3,341; Growth (since 2000): 2.9%; Density: 841.5 persons per square mile; Race: 93.1% White, 2.7% Black/African American, 0.0% Asian, 0.0% American Indian/Alaska Native, 0.0% Native Hawaiian/Other Pacific Islander, 4.3% Two or more races, 2.5% Hispanic of any race; Average household size: 2.75; Median age: 36.1; Age under 18: 25.4%; Age 65 and over: 13.5%; Males per 100 females: 97.6; Marriage status: 37.8% never married, 48.5% now married, 0.9% separated, 4.4% widowed, 9.3% divorced; Foreign born: 1.6%; Speak English only: 95.7%; With disability: 15.0%; Veterans: 11.6%; Ancestry: 31.9% German, 11.5% American, 9.8% Irish, 7.2% English, 5.1% Hungarian
Employment: 12.0% management, business, and financial, 2.8% computer, engineering, and science, 5.7% education, legal, community service, arts, and media, 1.6% healthcare practitioners, 13.4% service, 32.7% sales and office, 12.4% natural resources, construction, and maintenance, 19.4% production, transportation, and material moving
Income: Per capita: $23,128; Median household: $56,250; Average household: $60,715; Households with income of $100,000 or more: 15.3%; Poverty rate: 12.4%
Educational Attainment: High school diploma or higher: 95.8%; Bachelor's degree or higher: 17.2%; Graduate/professional degree or higher: 7.2%
Housing: Homeownership rate: 76.7%; Median home value: $113,800; Median year structure built: 1969; Homeowner vacancy rate: 0.0%; Median selected monthly owner costs: $1,009 with a mortgage, $345 without a mortgage; Median gross rent: $796 per month; Rental vacancy rate: 0.0%
Health Insurance: 91.9% have insurance; 77.8% have private insurance; 24.7% have public insurance; 8.1% do not have insurance; 3.3% of children under 18 do not have insurance
Transportation: Commute: 93.9% car, 1.0% public transportation, 0.0% walk, 2.3% work from home; Mean travel time to work: 23.0 minutes

DEERFIELD (unincorporated postal area)
ZCTA: 44411
Covers a land area of 17.838 square miles and a water area of 1.917 square miles. Located at 41.04° N. Lat; 81.04° W. Long. Elevation is 1,070 feet.
Population: 2,282; Growth (since 2000): -15.6%; Density: 127.9 persons per square mile; Race: 99.5% White, 0.0% Black/African American, 0.0% Asian, 0.0% American Indian/Alaska Native, 0.0% Native Hawaiian/Other Pacific Islander, 0.0% Two or more races, 0.8% Hispanic of any race; Average household size: 2.93; Median age: 38.0; Age under 18: 28.4%; Age 65 and over: 12.5%; Males per 100 females: 101.4; Marriage status: 25.3% never married, 55.8% now married, 0.4% separated, 2.7% widowed, 16.3% divorced; Foreign born: 0.9%; Speak English only: 97.7%; With disability: 11.0%; Veterans: 10.3%; Ancestry: 26.2% German, 25.4% Irish, 12.0% Dutch, 8.8% American, 8.5% Scottish
Employment: 12.8% management, business, and financial, 3.2% computer, engineering, and science, 4.9% education, legal, community service, arts, and media, 7.3% healthcare practitioners, 15.3% service, 29.2% sales and office, 3.7% natural resources, construction, and maintenance, 23.6% production, transportation, and material moving
Income: Per capita: $22,520; Median household: $53,971; Average household: $65,064; Households with income of $100,000 or more: 20.9%; Poverty rate: 21.5%
Educational Attainment: High school diploma or higher: 88.6%; Bachelor's degree or higher: 9.3%; Graduate/professional degree or higher: 2.7%
Housing: Homeownership rate: 81.4%; Median home value: $140,500; Median year structure built: 1985; Homeowner vacancy rate: 6.2%; Median selected monthly owner costs: $1,362 with a mortgage, $360 without a mortgage; Median gross rent: $870 per month; Rental vacancy rate: 0.0%
Health Insurance: 88.0% have insurance; 62.4% have private insurance; 35.4% have public insurance; 12.0% do not have insurance; 5.1% of children under 18 do not have insurance
Transportation: Commute: 98.8% car, 0.0% public transportation, 0.0% walk, 1.2% work from home; Mean travel time to work: 37.3 minutes

DIAMOND (unincorporated postal area)
ZCTA: 44412
Covers a land area of 22.844 square miles and a water area of 0.209 square miles. Located at 41.09° N. Lat; 81.03° W. Long. Elevation is 991 feet.
Population: 2,846; Growth (since 2000): 5.3%; Density: 124.6 persons per square mile; Race: 95.7% White, 3.2% Black/African American, 0.0% Asian, 0.0% American Indian/Alaska Native, 0.0% Native Hawaiian/Other Pacific Islander, 0.4% Two or more races, 2.0% Hispanic of any race; Average household size: 2.77; Median age: 43.7; Age under 18: 19.3%; Age 65 and over: 16.3%; Males per 100 females: 103.5; Marriage status: 33.5% never married, 48.6% now married, 1.9% separated, 2.5% widowed, 15.5% divorced; Foreign born: 0.2%; Speak English only: 98.1%; With disability: 12.1%; Veterans: 10.0%; Ancestry: 40.8% German, 19.6% Irish, 13.2% English, 7.0% Italian, 5.2% French
Employment: 6.3% management, business, and financial, 2.6% computer, engineering, and science, 8.0% education, legal, community service, arts, and media, 3.2% healthcare practitioners, 22.8% service, 21.4% sales and office, 19.9% natural resources, construction, and maintenance, 15.9% production, transportation, and material moving
Income: Per capita: $24,115; Median household: $60,270; Average household: $64,830; Households with income of $100,000 or more: 14.0%; Poverty rate: 12.0%
Educational Attainment: High school diploma or higher: 89.7%; Bachelor's degree or higher: 12.5%; Graduate/professional degree or higher: 2.7%

School District(s)

Southeast Local (PK-12)
2015-16 Enrollment: 1,630 . . . . (330) 654-5841
Housing: Homeownership rate: 78.2%; Median home value: $157,800; Median year structure built: 1972; Homeowner vacancy rate: 3.1%; Median selected monthly owner costs: $1,302 with a mortgage, $414 without a mortgage; Median gross rent: $599 per month; Rental vacancy rate: 0.0%
Health Insurance: 92.8% have insurance; 76.6% have private insurance; 33.5% have public insurance; 7.2% do not have insurance; 1.3% of children under 18 do not have insurance
Transportation: Commute: 96.0% car, 0.1% public transportation, 0.9% walk, 3.1% work from home; Mean travel time to work: 31.9 minutes

GARRETTSVILLE (village). Covers a land area of 2.513 square miles and a water area of 0.016 square miles. Located at 41.28° N. Lat; 81.09° W. Long. Elevation is 1,001 feet.
Population: 2,870; Growth (since 2000): 26.9%; Density: 1,141.9 persons per square mile; Race: 96.7% White, 0.4% Black/African American, 0.5% Asian, 0.0% American Indian/Alaska Native, 0.0% Native Hawaiian/Other Pacific Islander, 1.7% Two or more races, 2.3% Hispanic of any race; Average household size: 2.77; Median age: 36.5; Age under 18: 30.2%; Age 65 and over: 13.0%; Males per 100 females: 93.3; Marriage status: 26.4% never married, 56.2% now married, 0.9% separated, 3.9% widowed, 13.6% divorced; Foreign born: 1.6%; Speak English only: 99.1%; With disability: 10.9%; Veterans: 11.9%; Ancestry: 30.6% German, 17.1% Irish, 16.4% English, 11.3% Italian, 7.8% American
Employment: 11.3% management, business, and financial, 7.5% computer, engineering, and science, 11.9% education, legal, community service, arts, and media, 5.8% healthcare practitioners, 10.8% service, 22.6% sales and office, 8.9% natural resources, construction, and maintenance, 21.1% production, transportation, and material moving
Income: Per capita: $25,259; Median household: $58,250; Average household: $68,798; Households with income of $100,000 or more: 23.4%; Poverty rate: 10.4%
Educational Attainment: High school diploma or higher: 96.5%; Bachelor's degree or higher: 27.9%; Graduate/professional degree or higher: 9.4%

School District(s)

James A Garfield Local (PK-12)
2015-16 Enrollment: 1,486 . . . . (330) 527-4336
Housing: Homeownership rate: 67.1%; Median home value: $151,600; Median year structure built: 1963; Homeowner vacancy rate: 2.9%; Median selected monthly owner costs: $1,390 with a mortgage, $475 without a mortgage; Median gross rent: $682 per month; Rental vacancy rate: 3.5%

Health Insurance: 96.0% have insurance; 79.0% have private insurance; 26.2% have public insurance; 4.0% do not have insurance; 1.0% of children under 18 do not have insurance
Newspapers: Weekly Villager (weekly circulation 13,000)
Transportation: Commute: 96.2% car, 0.4% public transportation, 2.6% walk, 0.9% work from home; Mean travel time to work: 29.2 minutes
Additional Information Contacts
Village of Garrettsville . . . . (330) 527-2682
http://www.garrettsville.org

HIRAM (village). Covers a land area of 0.927 square miles and a water area of 0 square miles. Located at 41.31° N. Lat; 81.14° W. Long. Elevation is 1,250 feet.
History: Hiram grew up around Hiram College, founded in 1850 by the Disciples of Christ as the Western Reserve Eclectic Institute. President James A. Garfield was valedictorian of his class when he graduated from the Institute in 1853.
Population: 1,320; Growth (since 2000): 6.3%; Density: 1,423.4 persons per square mile; Race: 83.9% White, 6.4% Black/African American, 5.8% Asian, 0.1% American Indian/Alaska Native, 0.0% Native Hawaiian/Other Pacific Islander, 2.7% Two or more races, 1.9% Hispanic of any race; Average household size: 2.29; Median age: 20.4; Age under 18: 11.4%; Age 65 and over: 7.1%; Males per 100 females: 95.0; Marriage status: 74.3% never married, 17.8% now married, 0.8% separated, 1.3% widowed, 6.7% divorced; Foreign born: 7.6%; Speak English only: 94.6%; With disability: 9.5%; Veterans: 1.5%; Ancestry: 31.3% German, 23.1% Irish, 19.9% Italian, 9.8% Polish, 5.8% English
Employment: 12.7% management, business, and financial, 2.4% computer, engineering, and science, 23.1% education, legal, community service, arts, and media, 1.1% healthcare practitioners, 31.1% service, 20.2% sales and office, 4.6% natural resources, construction, and maintenance, 4.9% production, transportation, and material moving
Income: Per capita: $16,808; Median household: $49,779; Average household: $78,306; Households with income of $100,000 or more: 19.3%; Poverty rate: 2.7%
Educational Attainment: High school diploma or higher: 99.2%; Bachelor's degree or higher: 61.7%; Graduate/professional degree or higher: 37.2%

Four-year College(s)

Hiram College (Private, Not-for-profit)
Fall 2016 Enrollment: 1,114 . . . . (330) 569-3211
2016-17 Tuition: In-state $33,040; Out-of-state $33,040
Housing: Homeownership rate: 51.9%; Median home value: $187,100; Median year structure built: Before 1940; Homeowner vacancy rate: 0.0%; Median selected monthly owner costs: $1,239 with a mortgage, $444 without a mortgage; Median gross rent: $690 per month; Rental vacancy rate: 6.5%
Health Insurance: 92.0% have insurance; 85.3% have private insurance; 13.6% have public insurance; 8.0% do not have insurance; 4.6% of children under 18 do not have insurance
Transportation: Commute: 54.0% car, 0.0% public transportation, 16.0% walk, 25.9% work from home; Mean travel time to work: 20.5 minutes

KENT (city). Covers a land area of 9.174 square miles and a water area of 0.109 square miles. Located at 41.15° N. Lat; 81.36° W. Long. Elevation is 1,063 feet.
History: Kent developed around Kent State University, founded in 1910 as a state normal school and accredited as a university in 1935.
Population: 29,761; Growth (since 2000): 6.6%; Density: 3,243.9 persons per square mile; Race: 80.0% White, 9.9% Black/African American, 5.5% Asian, 0.0% American Indian/Alaska Native, 0.0% Native Hawaiian/Other Pacific Islander, 4.3% Two or more races, 2.2% Hispanic of any race; Average household size: 2.43; Median age: 23.5; Age under 18: 15.4%; Age 65 and over: 8.1%; Males per 100 females: 86.2; Marriage status: 62.1% never married, 26.6% now married, 1.0% separated, 3.0% widowed, 8.2% divorced; Foreign born: 8.4%; Speak English only: 90.8%; With disability: 11.2%; Veterans: 4.8%; Ancestry: 28.2% German, 17.9% Irish, 11.6% Italian, 7.4% English, 6.4% Polish
Employment: 9.4% management, business, and financial, 3.9% computer, engineering, and science, 17.4% education, legal, community service, arts, and media, 3.7% healthcare practitioners, 23.8% service, 24.4% sales and office, 4.7% natural resources, construction, and maintenance, 12.8% production, transportation, and material moving
Income: Per capita: $19,872; Median household: $36,539; Average household: $53,253; Households with income of $100,000 or more: 13.8%; Poverty rate: 34.4%
Educational Attainment: High school diploma or higher: 94.1%; Bachelor's degree or higher: 42.1%; Graduate/professional degree or higher: 19.9%

School District(s)

Field Local (KG-12)
2015-16 Enrollment: 2,050 . . . . (330) 673-2659
Kent City (PK-12)
2015-16 Enrollment: 3,372 . . . . (330) 673-6515

Four-year College(s)

Kent State University at Kent (Public)
Fall 2016 Enrollment: 30,167 . . . . (330) 672-3000
2016-17 Tuition: In-state $10,012; Out-of-state $18,376

Vocational/Technical School(s)

Northcoast Medical Training Academy (Private, For-profit)
Fall 2016 Enrollment: 206 . . . . (330) 678-6600
2016-17 Tuition: $19,446
Housing: Homeownership rate: 39.6%; Median home value: $139,900; Median year structure built: 1971; Homeowner vacancy rate: 0.9%; Median selected monthly owner costs: $1,291 with a mortgage, $447 without a mortgage; Median gross rent: $770 per month; Rental vacancy rate: 6.2%
Health Insurance: 89.5% have insurance; 70.8% have private insurance; 25.9% have public insurance; 10.5% do not have insurance; 6.4% of children under 18 do not have insurance
Safety: Violent crime rate: 22.3 per 10,000 population; Property crime rate: 165.4 per 10,000 population
Transportation: Commute: 82.0% car, 2.1% public transportation, 9.3% walk, 5.9% work from home; Mean travel time to work: 21.0 minutes
Additional Information Contacts
City of Kent . . . . (330) 676-7500
http://www.kentohio.org

MANTUA (village). Covers a land area of 1.403 square miles and a water area of 0.015 square miles. Located at 41.28° N. Lat; 81.22° W. Long. Elevation is 1,148 feet.
Population: 1,153; Growth (since 2000): 10.2%; Density: 821.7 persons per square mile; Race: 99.5% White, 0.0% Black/African American, 0.0% Asian, 0.0% American Indian/Alaska Native, 0.0% Native Hawaiian/Other Pacific Islander, 0.5% Two or more races, 0.8% Hispanic of any race; Average household size: 2.23; Median age: 45.7; Age under 18: 17.6%; Age 65 and over: 16.2%; Males per 100 females: 92.8; Marriage status: 33.8% never married, 45.6% now married, 3.9% separated, 5.7% widowed, 14.9% divorced; Foreign born: 1.0%; Speak English only: 97.8%; With disability: 10.3%; Veterans: 7.9%; Ancestry: 33.9% German, 25.8% Irish, 9.7% Hungarian, 8.3% English, 8.1% Polish
Employment: 17.4% management, business, and financial, 2.2% computer, engineering, and science, 8.0% education, legal, community service, arts, and media, 1.5% healthcare practitioners, 16.2% service, 26.8% sales and office, 9.7% natural resources, construction, and maintenance, 18.2% production, transportation, and material moving
Income: Per capita: $24,588; Median household: $41,500; Average household: $53,410; Households with income of $100,000 or more: 11.5%; Poverty rate: 18.3%
Educational Attainment: High school diploma or higher: 94.9%; Bachelor's degree or higher: 20.3%; Graduate/professional degree or higher: 5.1%

School District(s)

Crestwood Local (PK-12)
2015-16 Enrollment: 1,797 . . . . (330) 357-8206
Housing: Homeownership rate: 53.5%; Median home value: $134,100; Median year structure built: Before 1940; Homeowner vacancy rate: 0.0%; Median selected monthly owner costs: $1,261 with a mortgage, $413 without a mortgage; Median gross rent: $712 per month; Rental vacancy rate: 4.0%
Health Insurance: 90.9% have insurance; 69.3% have private insurance; 34.5% have public insurance; 9.1% do not have insurance; 5.9% of children under 18 do not have insurance
Transportation: Commute: 94.3% car, 1.6% public transportation, 1.8% walk, 1.6% work from home; Mean travel time to work: 22.1 minutes

NORTH BENTON (unincorporated postal area)

ZCTA: 44449

Covers a land area of 11.841 square miles and a water area of 0.470 square miles. Located at 40.98° N. Lat; 81.04° W. Long..

Population: 927; Growth (since 2000): -29.0%; Density: 78.3 persons per square mile; Race: 100.0% White, 0.0% Black/African American, 0.0% Asian, 0.0% American Indian/Alaska Native, 0.0% Native Hawaiian/Other Pacific Islander, 0.0% Two or more races, 0.0% Hispanic of any race; Average household size: 2.24; Median age: 45.8; Age under 18: 21.9%; Age 65 and over: 23.8%; Males per 100 females: 105.1; Marriage status: 24.9% never married, 47.3% now married, 2.1% separated, 10.4% widowed, 17.3% divorced; Foreign born: 1.7%; Speak English only: 100.0%; With disability: 12.1%; Veterans: 8.3%; Ancestry: 26.6% German, 17.0% American, 12.6% Irish, 8.1% English, 3.8% Italian

Employment: 12.3% management, business, and financial, 4.0% computer, engineering, and science, 8.7% education, legal, community service, arts, and media, 6.3% healthcare practitioners, 23.3% service, 13.5% sales and office, 13.5% natural resources, construction, and maintenance, 18.4% production, transportation, and material moving

Income: Per capita: $25,607; Median household: $45,667; Average household: $56,505; Households with income of $100,000 or more: 13.7%; Poverty rate: 8.2%

Educational Attainment: High school diploma or higher: 83.2%; Bachelor's degree or higher: 13.6%; Graduate/professional degree or higher: 3.0%

Housing: Homeownership rate: 83.1%; Median home value: $141,200; Median year structure built: 1974; Homeowner vacancy rate: 5.8%; Median selected monthly owner costs: $984 with a mortgage, $457 without a mortgage; Median gross rent: $634 per month; Rental vacancy rate: 0.0%

Health Insurance: 95.1% have insurance; 71.0% have private insurance; 43.6% have public insurance; 4.9% do not have insurance; 5.9% of children under 18 do not have insurance

Transportation: Commute: 88.1% car, 0.0% public transportation, 3.4% walk, 6.3% work from home; Mean travel time to work: 36.3 minutes

RAVENNA (city). County seat. Covers a land area of 5.630 square miles and a water area of 0.047 square miles. Located at 41.16° N. Lat; 81.24° W. Long. Elevation is 1,135 feet.

History: Ravenna was settled in 1799 by Benjamin Tappan, Jr., a New Englander and later U.S. senator from Ohio. The town was named for the Italian city.

Population: 11,582; Growth (since 2000): -1.6%; Density: 2,057.2 persons per square mile; Race: 89.3% White, 3.2% Black/African American, 0.5% Asian, 0.0% American Indian/Alaska Native, 0.0% Native Hawaiian/Other Pacific Islander, 6.6% Two or more races, 1.3% Hispanic of any race; Average household size: 2.27; Median age: 40.2; Age under 18: 20.5%; Age 65 and over: 17.1%; Males per 100 females: 92.8; Marriage status: 33.2% never married, 41.2% now married, 3.3% separated, 7.7% widowed, 17.9% divorced; Foreign born: 1.0%; Speak English only: 98.4%; With disability: 17.6%; Veterans: 7.0%; Ancestry: 30.2% German, 18.9% Irish, 11.4% Italian, 10.6% English, 4.9% American

Employment: 9.0% management, business, and financial, 2.5% computer, engineering, and science, 8.1% education, legal, community service, arts, and media, 6.1% healthcare practitioners, 25.4% service, 23.4% sales and office, 6.9% natural resources, construction, and maintenance, 18.7% production, transportation, and material moving

Income: Per capita: $20,391; Median household: $36,087; Average household: $45,046; Households with income of $100,000 or more: 7.0%; Poverty rate: 22.3%

Educational Attainment: High school diploma or higher: 86.1%; Bachelor's degree or higher: 16.0%; Graduate/professional degree or higher: 5.7%

School District(s)

Maplewood Career Center (10-12)
2015-16 Enrollment: n/a . . . . (330) 296-2892
Ravenna City (PK-12)
2015-16 Enrollment: 2,488 . . . . (330) 296-9679
Southeast Local (PK-12)
2015-16 Enrollment: 1,630 . . . . (330) 654-5841

Two-year College(s)

Fortis College-Ravenna (Private, For-profit)
Fall 2016 Enrollment: 173 . . . . (330) 297-7319
2016-17 Tuition: In-state $13,998; Out-of-state $13,998

Vocational/Technical School(s)

Community Technology Learning Center of Portage (Private, Not-for-profit)
Fall 2016 Enrollment: 1 . . . . (330) 296-8720

Housing: Homeownership rate: 49.2%; Median home value: $99,600; Median year structure built: 1952; Homeowner vacancy rate: 0.8%; Median selected monthly owner costs: $905 with a mortgage, $342 without a mortgage; Median gross rent: $657 per month; Rental vacancy rate: 2.9%

Health Insurance: 94.0% have insurance; 60.0% have private insurance; 48.6% have public insurance; 6.0% do not have insurance; 1.6% of children under 18 do not have insurance

Hospitals: Robinson Memorial Hospital (285 beds)

Newspapers: Record-Courier (daily circulation 17,900)

Transportation: Commute: 94.5% car, 1.1% public transportation, 2.2% walk, 2.1% work from home; Mean travel time to work: 21.8 minutes

Additional Information Contacts

City of Ravenna. . . . . (330) 296-3864
http://www.ci.ravenna.oh.us

ROOTSTOWN (unincorporated postal area)

ZCTA: 44272

Covers a land area of 22.423 square miles and a water area of 0.169 square miles. Located at 41.09° N. Lat; 81.18° W. Long. Elevation is 1,125 feet.

Population: 5,062; Growth (since 2000): 25.1%; Density: 225.7 persons per square mile; Race: 97.6% White, 0.6% Black/African American, 0.4% Asian, 0.5% American Indian/Alaska Native, 0.0% Native Hawaiian/Other Pacific Islander, 0.7% Two or more races, 0.8% Hispanic of any race; Average household size: 2.71; Median age: 38.9; Age under 18: 21.2%; Age 65 and over: 11.8%; Males per 100 females: 96.9; Marriage status: 28.8% never married, 57.6% now married, 0.6% separated, 2.7% widowed, 10.8% divorced; Foreign born: 1.1%; Speak English only: 97.7%; With disability: 10.8%; Veterans: 8.1%; Ancestry: 34.6% German, 15.0% Irish, 13.6% English, 9.6% Polish, 9.5% Italian

Employment: 9.6% management, business, and financial, 4.0% computer, engineering, and science, 8.7% education, legal, community service, arts, and media, 5.8% healthcare practitioners, 18.7% service, 17.6% sales and office, 10.2% natural resources, construction, and maintenance, 25.3% production, transportation, and material moving

Income: Per capita: $25,047; Median household: $60,208; Average household: $66,813; Households with income of $100,000 or more: 20.0%; Poverty rate: 8.4%

Educational Attainment: High school diploma or higher: 91.4%; Bachelor's degree or higher: 19.4%; Graduate/professional degree or higher: 5.7%

School District(s)

Rootstown Local (KG-12)
2015-16 Enrollment: 1,195 . . . . (330) 325-9911

Four-year College(s)

Northeast Ohio Medical University (Public)
Fall 2016 Enrollment: 959 . . . . (800) 686-2511

Two-year College(s)

Northeast Ohio Medical University (Public)
Fall 2016 Enrollment: 959 . . . . (800) 686-2511

Vocational/Technical School(s)

Northeast Ohio Medical University (Public)
Fall 2016 Enrollment: 959 . . . . (800) 686-2511

Housing: Homeownership rate: 77.2%; Median home value: $155,800; Median year structure built: 1976; Homeowner vacancy rate: 0.0%; Median selected monthly owner costs: $1,271 with a mortgage, $432 without a mortgage; Median gross rent: $885 per month; Rental vacancy rate: 6.4%

Health Insurance: 95.3% have insurance; 82.5% have private insurance; 25.6% have public insurance; 4.7% do not have insurance; 0.0% of children under 18 do not have insurance

Transportation: Commute: 95.5% car, 0.0% public transportation, 1.0% walk, 3.1% work from home; Mean travel time to work: 29.2 minutes

STREETSBORO (city). Covers a land area of 23.459 square miles and a water area of 0.902 square miles. Located at 41.24° N. Lat; 81.35° W. Long. Elevation is 1,129 feet.

History: Streetsboro was settled in 1822 and named for Titus Street, original owner of the land.

Population: 16,224; Growth (since 2000): 31.8%; Density: 691.6 persons per square mile; Race: 86.6% White, 7.4% Black/African American, 1.7% Asian, 0.0% American Indian/Alaska Native, 0.0% Native Hawaiian/Other Pacific Islander, 1.8% Two or more races, 3.7% Hispanic of any race;

Average household size: 2.43; Median age: 41.2; Age under 18: 20.9%; Age 65 and over: 14.0%; Males per 100 females: 94.2; Marriage status: 30.6% never married, 51.5% now married, 2.2% separated, 6.0% widowed, 11.9% divorced; Foreign born: 6.7%; Speak English only: 93.5%; With disability: 12.6%; Veterans: 8.9%; Ancestry: 22.6% German, 19.1% Irish, 13.3% Italian, 8.3% English, 7.2% Polish
Employment: 13.6% management, business, and financial, 5.0% computer, engineering, and science, 10.7% education, legal, community service, arts, and media, 2.8% healthcare practitioners, 21.6% service, 27.3% sales and office, 4.6% natural resources, construction, and maintenance, 14.5% production, transportation, and material moving
Income: Per capita: $27,760; Median household: $58,511; Average household: $66,132; Households with income of $100,000 or more: 18.5%; Poverty rate: 9.1%
Educational Attainment: High school diploma or higher: 92.4%; Bachelor's degree or higher: 26.9%; Graduate/professional degree or higher: 8.8%

School District(s)

Streetsboro City (PK-12)
2015-16 Enrollment: 2,150 . . . . (330) 626-4900
Housing: Homeownership rate: 68.9%; Median home value: $144,300; Median year structure built: 1987; Homeowner vacancy rate: 0.3%; Median selected monthly owner costs: $1,353 with a mortgage, $537 without a mortgage; Median gross rent: $967 per month; Rental vacancy rate: 6.7%
Health Insurance: 94.2% have insurance; 77.7% have private insurance; 27.8% have public insurance; 5.8% do not have insurance; 4.2% of children under 18 do not have insurance
Safety: Violent crime rate: 3.7 per 10,000 population; Property crime rate: 149.1 per 10,000 population
Transportation: Commute: 96.2% car, 0.2% public transportation, 0.6% walk, 2.2% work from home; Mean travel time to work: 25.0 minutes
Additional Information Contacts
City of Streetsboro. . . . . (330) 626-4942
http://cityofstreetsboro.com

SUGAR BUSH KNOLLS (village). Covers a land area of 0.214 square miles and a water area of 0.017 square miles. Located at 41.20° N. Lat; 81.35° W. Long. Elevation is 1,099 feet.
Population: 193; Growth (since 2000): -15.0%; Density: 901.7 persons per square mile; Race: 100.0% White, 0.0% Black/African American, 0.0% Asian, 0.0% American Indian/Alaska Native, 0.0% Native Hawaiian/Other Pacific Islander, 0.0% Two or more races, 0.0% Hispanic of any race; Average household size: 2.51; Median age: 55.4; Age under 18: 14.5%; Age 65 and over: 32.1%; Males per 100 females: 92.4; Marriage status: 20.1% never married, 65.5% now married, 1.1% separated, 9.2% widowed, 5.2% divorced; Foreign born: 1.0%; Speak English only: 95.2%; With disability: 8.8%; Veterans: 7.9%; Ancestry: 34.7% German, 20.2% Irish, 14.5% Italian, 11.4% English, 7.8% Polish
Employment: 21.8% management, business, and financial, 5.0% computer, engineering, and science, 25.7% education, legal, community service, arts, and media, 12.9% healthcare practitioners, 7.9% service, 18.8% sales and office, 0.0% natural resources, construction, and maintenance, 7.9% production, transportation, and material moving
Income: Per capita: $50,914; Median household: $101,250; Average household: $123,288; Households with income of $100,000 or more: 52.0%; Poverty rate: 3.7%
Educational Attainment: High school diploma or higher: 100.0%; Bachelor's degree or higher: 64.7%; Graduate/professional degree or higher: 47.3%
Housing: Homeownership rate: 92.2%; Median home value: $302,800; Median year structure built: 1976; Homeowner vacancy rate: 0.0%; Median selected monthly owner costs: $2,111 with a mortgage, $925 without a mortgage; Median gross rent: n/a per month; Rental vacancy rate: 0.0%
Health Insurance: 91.2% have insurance; 75.6% have private insurance; 40.4% have public insurance; 8.8% do not have insurance; 7.1% of children under 18 do not have insurance
Transportation: Commute: 89.1% car, 0.0% public transportation, 0.0% walk, 8.9% work from home; Mean travel time to work: 21.4 minutes

WAYLAND (unincorporated postal area)
ZCTA: 44285
Covers a land area of 0.138 square miles and a water area of 0 square miles. Located at 41.16° N. Lat; 81.07° W. Long. Elevation is 942 feet.
Population: 128; Growth (since 2000): n/a; Density: 924.6 persons per square mile; Race: 100.0% White, 0.0% Black/African American, 0.0% Asian, 0.0% American Indian/Alaska Native, 0.0% Native Hawaiian/Other Pacific Islander, 0.0% Two or more races, 0.0% Hispanic of any race; Average household size: 5.57; Median age: 36.6; Age under 18: 27.3%; Age 65 and over: 20.3%; Males per 100 females: 123.7; Marriage status: 0.0% never married, 38.7% now married, 0.0% separated, 0.0% widowed, 61.3% divorced; Foreign born: 0.0%; Speak English only: 100.0%; With disability: 0.0%; Veterans: 28.0%; Ancestry: 14.1% Irish, 14.1% Pennsylvania German, 3.9% Czech, 3.9% Ukrainian
Employment: 0.0% management, business, and financial, 0.0% computer, engineering, and science, 0.0% education, legal, community service, arts, and media, 0.0% healthcare practitioners, 0.0% service, 0.0% sales and office, 100.0% natural resources, construction, and maintenance, 0.0% production, transportation, and material moving
Income: Per capita: $15,057; Median household: n/a; Average household: n/a; Households with income of $100,000 or more: n/a; Poverty rate: n/a
Educational Attainment: High school diploma or higher: 80.6%; Bachelor's degree or higher: 33.3%; Graduate/professional degree or higher: 5.4%
Housing: Homeownership rate: 100.0%; Median home value: n/a; Median year structure built: 1954; Homeowner vacancy rate: 0.0%; Median selected monthly owner costs: $0 with a mortgage, $0 without a mortgage; Median gross rent: n/a per month; Rental vacancy rate: 0.0%
Health Insurance: 24.2% have insurance; 24.2% have private insurance; 0.0% have public insurance; 75.8% do not have insurance; 100.0% of children under 18 do not have insurance
Transportation: Commute: 100.0% car, 0.0% public transportation, 0.0% walk, 0.0% work from home; Mean travel time to work: 23.7 minutes

WINDHAM (village). Covers a land area of 2.057 square miles and a water area of 0.002 square miles. Located at 41.24° N. Lat; 81.04° W. Long. Elevation is 971 feet.
Population: 1,959; Growth (since 2000): -30.2%; Density: 952.5 persons per square mile; Race: 92.1% White, 4.0% Black/African American, 0.0% Asian, 0.2% American Indian/Alaska Native, 0.0% Native Hawaiian/Other Pacific Islander, 3.4% Two or more races, 1.1% Hispanic of any race; Average household size: 2.73; Median age: 34.1; Age under 18: 26.3%; Age 65 and over: 9.9%; Males per 100 females: 87.8; Marriage status: 43.7% never married, 37.1% now married, 2.8% separated, 4.1% widowed, 15.1% divorced; Foreign born: 0.0%; Speak English only: 99.6%; With disability: 15.6%; Veterans: 7.8%; Ancestry: 29.2% German, 23.7% Irish, 11.1% Italian, 8.9% American, 6.1% English
Employment: 5.2% management, business, and financial, 2.9% computer, engineering, and science, 5.8% education, legal, community service, arts, and media, 4.2% healthcare practitioners, 24.4% service, 15.9% sales and office, 8.2% natural resources, construction, and maintenance, 33.4% production, transportation, and material moving
Income: Per capita: $17,749; Median household: $40,370; Average household: $46,019; Households with income of $100,000 or more: 7.6%; Poverty rate: 29.7%
Educational Attainment: High school diploma or higher: 81.1%; Bachelor's degree or higher: 7.2%; Graduate/professional degree or higher: 1.9%

School District(s)

Windham Exempted Village (PK-12)
2015-16 Enrollment: 540. . . . . (330) 326-2711
Housing: Homeownership rate: 42.4%; Median home value: $81,300; Median year structure built: 1968; Homeowner vacancy rate: 10.6%; Median selected monthly owner costs: $955 with a mortgage, $386 without a mortgage; Median gross rent: $710 per month; Rental vacancy rate: 8.7%
Health Insurance: 89.9% have insurance; 52.0% have private insurance; 48.7% have public insurance; 10.1% do not have insurance; 0.6% of children under 18 do not have insurance
Safety: Violent crime rate: 13.6 per 10,000 population; Property crime rate: 145.4 per 10,000 population
Transportation: Commute: 94.8% car, 0.0% public transportation, 3.3% walk, 1.9% work from home; Mean travel time to work: 26.3 minutes

Preble County

Located in western Ohio; bounded on the west by Indiana; drained by the East Fork of the Whitewater River. Covers a land area of 424.120 square miles, a water area of 2.342 square miles, and is located in the Eastern Time Zone at 39.74° N. Lat., 84.65° W. Long. The county was founded in 1808. County seat is Eaton.

Weather Station: Eaton Elevation: 1,001 feet

	Jan	Feb	Mar	Apr	May	Jun	Jul	Aug	Sep	Oct	Nov	Dec
High	35	39	49	62	72	81	84	84	77	65	52	39
Low	18	20	28	38	49	58	62	60	52	41	32	22
Precip	2.7	2.2	3.3	4.0	5.2	4.1	4.3	3.0	2.8	3.1	3.3	3.2
Snow	na	na	1.3	0.2	0.0	0.0	0.0	0.0	0.0	0.0	0.1	2.1

High and Low temperatures in degrees Fahrenheit; Precipitation and Snow in inches

Population: 41,561; Growth (since 2000): -1.8%; Density: 98.0 persons per square mile; Race: 97.3% White, 0.5% Black/African American, 0.4% Asian, 0.3% American Indian/Alaska Native, 0.0% Native Hawaiian/Other Pacific Islander, 1.5% two or more races, 0.7% Hispanic of any race; Average household size: 2.56; Median age: 42.2; Age under 18: 23.2%; Age 65 and over: 17.2%; Males per 100 females: 98.4; Marriage status: 23.4% never married, 57.0% now married, 1.5% separated, 7.0% widowed, 12.6% divorced; Foreign born: 1.1%; Speak English only: 97.9%; With disability: 15.8%; Veterans: 10.1%; Ancestry: 28.7% German, 12.5% Irish, 12.3% American, 11.6% English, 2.2% Italian

Religion: Six largest groups: 8.4% Baptist, 4.2% Methodist/Pietist, 4.0% Presbyterian-Reformed, 3.5% Lutheran, 2.9% European Free-Church, 2.7% Non-denominational Protestant

Economy: Unemployment rate: 4.0%; Leading industries: 15.8 % retail trade; 12.5 % other services (except public administration); 11.9 % construction; Farms: 1,088 totaling 224,243 acres; Company size: 0 employ 1,000 or more persons, 2 employ 500 to 999 persons, 12 employ 100 to 499 persons, 626 employ less than 100 persons; Business ownership: 755 women-owned, n/a Black-owned, 35 Hispanic-owned, 48 Asian-owned, 32 American Indian/Alaska Native-owned

Employment: 10.9% management, business, and financial, 2.9% computer, engineering, and science, 7.0% education, legal, community service, arts, and media, 6.3% healthcare practitioners, 19.4% service, 19.9% sales and office, 10.9% natural resources, construction, and maintenance, 22.7% production, transportation, and material moving

Income: Per capita: $24,605; Median household: $51,356; Average household: $62,242; Households with income of $100,000 or more: 15.0%; Poverty rate: 13.5%

Educational Attainment: High school diploma or higher: 88.8%; Bachelor's degree or higher: 13.5%; Graduate/professional degree or higher: 4.1%

Housing: Homeownership rate: 76.5%; Median home value: $116,600; Median year structure built: 1968; Homeowner vacancy rate: 1.7%; Median selected monthly owner costs: $1,096 with a mortgage, $438 without a mortgage; Median gross rent: $705 per month; Rental vacancy rate: 7.0%

Vital Statistics: Birth rate: 103.8 per 10,000 population; Death rate: 105.2 per 10,000 population; Age-adjusted cancer mortality rate: 213.9 deaths per 100,000 population

Health Insurance: 91.2% have insurance; 68.8% have private insurance; 36.7% have public insurance; 8.8% do not have insurance; 7.3% of children under 18 do not have insurance

Health Care: Physicians: 2.9 per 10,000 population; Dentists: 1.7 per 10,000 population; Hospital beds: 0.0 per 10,000 population; Hospital admissions: 0.0 per 10,000 population

Air Quality Index (AQI): Percent of Days: 80.6% good, 19.1% moderate, 0.3% unhealthy for sensitive individuals, 0.0% unhealthy, 0.0% very unhealthy; Annual median: 40; Annual maximum: 105

Transportation: Commute: 93.5% car, 0.3% public transportation, 1.8% walk, 2.8% work from home; Mean travel time to work: 26.2 minutes

2016 Presidential Election: 74.7% Trump, 20.9% Clinton, 2.7% Johnson, 0.6% Stein

National and State Parks: Fort Saint Clair State Park; Hueston Woods State Nature Preserve; Hueston Woods State Park

Additional Information Contacts

Preble Government . . . . (937) 456-8143
http://www.prebco.org

Preble County Communities

CAMDEN (village). Covers a land area of 1.241 square miles and a water area of 0.007 square miles. Located at 39.64° N. Lat; 84.64° W. Long. Elevation is 837 feet.

Population: 2,013; Growth (since 2000): -12.6%; Density: 1,622.1 persons per square mile; Race: 96.7% White, 0.0% Black/African American, 0.0% Asian, 2.8% American Indian/Alaska Native, 0.0% Native Hawaiian/Other Pacific Islander, 0.4% Two or more races, 1.7% Hispanic of any race; Average household size: 2.78; Median age: 36.7; Age under 18: 23.4%; Age 65 and over: 15.2%; Males per 100 females: 89.6; Marriage status: 28.5% never married, 48.8% now married, 0.8% separated, 8.3% widowed, 14.4% divorced; Foreign born: 0.2%; Speak English only: 99.2%; With disability: 15.8%; Veterans: 12.7%; Ancestry: 18.4% German, 17.1% American, 14.1% Irish, 8.4% English, 1.7% Italian

Employment: 3.9% management, business, and financial, 1.9% computer, engineering, and science, 3.2% education, legal, community service, arts, and media, 3.8% healthcare practitioners, 25.5% service, 27.6% sales and office, 9.5% natural resources, construction, and maintenance, 24.5% production, transportation, and material moving

Income: Per capita: $17,862; Median household: $41,646; Average household: $48,196; Households with income of $100,000 or more: 10.0%; Poverty rate: 21.1%

Educational Attainment: High school diploma or higher: 79.6%; Bachelor's degree or higher: 4.1%; Graduate/professional degree or higher: 2.1%

School District(s)

Preble Shawnee Local (PK-12)
2015-16 Enrollment: 1,349 . . . . (937) 452-1283

Housing: Homeownership rate: 68.1%; Median home value: $78,400; Median year structure built: 1970; Homeowner vacancy rate: 5.1%; Median selected monthly owner costs: $1,020 with a mortgage, $410 without a mortgage; Median gross rent: $652 per month; Rental vacancy rate: 5.7%

Health Insurance: 87.9% have insurance; 58.1% have private insurance; 44.3% have public insurance; 12.1% do not have insurance; 12.7% of children under 18 do not have insurance

Transportation: Commute: 93.7% car, 2.2% public transportation, 0.0% walk, 1.1% work from home; Mean travel time to work: 29.7 minutes

COLLEGE CORNER (village). Covers a land area of 0.250 square miles and a water area of 0.013 square miles. Located at 39.57° N. Lat; 84.81° W. Long. Elevation is 981 feet.

Population: 401; Growth (since 2000): -5.4%; Density: 1,603.3 persons per square mile; Race: 98.5% White, 0.0% Black/African American, 1.0% Asian, 0.0% American Indian/Alaska Native, 0.0% Native Hawaiian/Other Pacific Islander, 0.5% Two or more races, 0.0% Hispanic of any race; Average household size: 2.32; Median age: 42.3; Age under 18: 19.5%; Age 65 and over: 12.5%; Males per 100 females: 101.5; Marriage status: 31.3% never married, 48.0% now married, 1.4% separated, 4.8% widowed, 15.9% divorced; Foreign born: 1.0%; Speak English only: 97.7%; With disability: 17.2%; Veterans: 11.5%; Ancestry: 34.7% German, 18.7% American, 14.7% Irish, 9.0% English, 6.5% Italian

Employment: 4.4% management, business, and financial, 4.4% computer, engineering, and science, 4.4% education, legal, community service, arts, and media, 1.7% healthcare practitioners, 20.4% service, 33.1% sales and office, 8.3% natural resources, construction, and maintenance, 23.2% production, transportation, and material moving

Income: Per capita: $20,339; Median household: $38,977; Average household: $46,925; Households with income of $100,000 or more: 6.9%; Poverty rate: 22.2%

Educational Attainment: High school diploma or higher: 83.8%; Bachelor's degree or higher: 7.2%; Graduate/professional degree or higher: 2.1%

School District(s)

College Corner Local (KG-12)
2015-16 Enrollment: 96. . . . . (765) 732-3183
Union Co/clg Corner Joint Sch Dist (KG-12)
2015-16 Enrollment: 1,339 . . . . (765) 458-7471

Housing: Homeownership rate: 59.0%; Median home value: $80,500; Median year structure built: Before 1940; Homeowner vacancy rate: 11.3%; Median selected monthly owner costs: $863 with a mortgage, $371 without a mortgage; Median gross rent: $721 per month; Rental vacancy rate: 9.0%

Health Insurance: 84.8% have insurance; 62.3% have private insurance; 32.9% have public insurance; 15.2% do not have insurance; 3.8% of children under 18 do not have insurance

Transportation: Commute: 93.9% car, 0.0% public transportation, 4.4% walk, 1.7% work from home; Mean travel time to work: 19.9 minutes

EATON (city). County seat. Covers a land area of 6.194 square miles and a water area of 0.007 square miles. Located at 39.75° N. Lat; 84.63° W. Long. Elevation is 1,040 feet.

History: Eaton was founded in 1806 and named for General William Eaton, who served in the Tripolitan War of 1805.

Population: 8,274; Growth (since 2000): 1.7%; Density: 1,335.7 persons per square mile; Race: 96.0% White, 1.0% Black/African American, 0.7% Asian, 0.4% American Indian/Alaska Native, 0.0% Native Hawaiian/Other Pacific Islander, 1.8% Two or more races, 0.8% Hispanic of any race; Average household size: 2.34; Median age: 40.2; Age under 18: 21.7%; Age 65 and over: 19.8%; Males per 100 females: 89.5; Marriage status: 26.6% never married, 46.3% now married, 2.0% separated, 10.3% widowed, 16.7% divorced; Foreign born: 1.4%; Speak English only: 97.1%; With disability: 20.9%; Veterans: 9.3%; Ancestry: 29.3% German, 11.4% Irish, 9.8% American, 8.1% English, 3.2% Italian
Employment: 6.7% management, business, and financial, 2.2% computer, engineering, and science, 6.9% education, legal, community service, arts, and media, 7.4% healthcare practitioners, 22.5% service, 17.8% sales and office, 7.7% natural resources, construction, and maintenance, 28.8% production, transportation, and material moving
Income: Per capita: $22,673; Median household: $36,487; Average household: $53,100; Households with income of $100,000 or more: 10.7%; Poverty rate: 22.8%
Educational Attainment: High school diploma or higher: 88.1%; Bachelor's degree or higher: 11.8%; Graduate/professional degree or higher: 3.9%

School District(s)

Eaton Community City (KG-12)
2015-16 Enrollment: 2,085 . . . . (937) 456-1107
Housing: Homeownership rate: 58.2%; Median home value: $96,700; Median year structure built: 1969; Homeowner vacancy rate: 2.1%; Median selected monthly owner costs: $957 with a mortgage, $410 without a mortgage; Median gross rent: $612 per month; Rental vacancy rate: 3.4%
Health Insurance: 91.6% have insurance; 61.3% have private insurance; 46.9% have public insurance; 8.4% do not have insurance; 5.8% of children under 18 do not have insurance
Newspapers: The Register-Herald (weekly circulation 7,200)
Transportation: Commute: 94.3% car, 0.1% public transportation, 2.4% walk, 2.2% work from home; Mean travel time to work: 21.2 minutes

ELDORADO (village). Covers a land area of 0.229 square miles and a water area of 0 square miles. Located at 39.90° N. Lat; 84.68° W. Long. Elevation is 1,132 feet.
Population: 576; Growth (since 2000): 6.1%; Density: 2,519.5 persons per square mile; Race: 100.0% White, 0.0% Black/African American, 0.0% Asian, 0.0% American Indian/Alaska Native, 0.0% Native Hawaiian/Other Pacific Islander, 0.0% Two or more races, 0.0% Hispanic of any race; Average household size: 2.69; Median age: 39.5; Age under 18: 23.6%; Age 65 and over: 14.4%; Males per 100 females: 98.1; Marriage status: 29.8% never married, 49.7% now married, 0.0% separated, 8.5% widowed, 12.1% divorced; Foreign born: 0.0%; Speak English only: 98.5%; With disability: 21.7%; Veterans: 8.9%; Ancestry: 27.3% German, 14.9% Irish, 13.0% English, 6.9% American, 6.3% French
Employment: 5.3% management, business, and financial, 3.0% computer, engineering, and science, 10.2% education, legal, community service, arts, and media, 8.3% healthcare practitioners, 13.9% service, 24.1% sales and office, 12.5% natural resources, construction, and maintenance, 22.8% production, transportation, and material moving
Income: Per capita: $20,194; Median household: $47,500; Average household: $53,591; Households with income of $100,000 or more: 10.7%; Poverty rate: 15.6%
Educational Attainment: High school diploma or higher: 92.2%; Bachelor's degree or higher: 9.7%; Graduate/professional degree or higher: 3.6%
Housing: Homeownership rate: 71.0%; Median home value: $87,400; Median year structure built: 1952; Homeowner vacancy rate: 0.0%; Median selected monthly owner costs: $917 with a mortgage, $385 without a mortgage; Median gross rent: $672 per month; Rental vacancy rate: 0.0%
Health Insurance: 93.8% have insurance; 77.8% have private insurance; 34.9% have public insurance; 6.3% do not have insurance; 0.0% of children under 18 do not have insurance
Transportation: Commute: 93.0% car, 0.0% public transportation, 0.7% walk, 0.0% work from home; Mean travel time to work: 30.5 minutes

GRATIS (village). Covers a land area of 0.965 square miles and a water area of <.001 square miles. Located at 39.65° N. Lat; 84.53° W. Long. Elevation is 876 feet.
Population: 1,008; Growth (since 2000): 7.9%; Density: 1,045.0 persons per square mile; Race: 98.8% White, 0.5% Black/African American, 0.0% Asian, 0.0% American Indian/Alaska Native, 0.0% Native Hawaiian/Other Pacific Islander, 0.7% Two or more races, 0.7% Hispanic of any race; Average household size: 2.62; Median age: 43.8; Age under 18: 21.3%; Age 65 and over: 13.9%; Males per 100 females: 98.9; Marriage status: 25.2% never married, 53.8% now married, 3.2% separated, 7.7% widowed, 13.3% divorced; Foreign born: 0.7%; Speak English only: 98.9%; With disability: 32.0%; Veterans: 11.0%; Ancestry: 21.1% Irish, 20.7% German, 20.6% English, 6.3% American, 3.9% Italian
Employment: 8.5% management, business, and financial, 2.2% computer, engineering, and science, 3.9% education, legal, community service, arts, and media, 12.6% healthcare practitioners, 20.0% service, 26.9% sales and office, 9.3% natural resources, construction, and maintenance, 16.7% production, transportation, and material moving
Income: Per capita: $23,505; Median household: $50,208; Average household: $60,341; Households with income of $100,000 or more: 12.7%; Poverty rate: 13.6%
Educational Attainment: High school diploma or higher: 89.3%; Bachelor's degree or higher: 7.6%; Graduate/professional degree or higher: 1.8%
Housing: Homeownership rate: 75.1%; Median home value: $95,100; Median year structure built: 1975; Homeowner vacancy rate: 3.7%; Median selected monthly owner costs: $900 with a mortgage, $447 without a mortgage; Median gross rent: $721 per month; Rental vacancy rate: 6.4%
Health Insurance: 90.8% have insurance; 61.0% have private insurance; 39.2% have public insurance; 9.2% do not have insurance; 0.0% of children under 18 do not have insurance
Transportation: Commute: 94.9% car, 0.2% public transportation, 2.2% walk, 0.7% work from home; Mean travel time to work: 28.6 minutes

LAKE LAKENGREN (CDP). Covers a land area of 2.860 square miles and a water area of 0.327 square miles. Located at 39.69° N. Lat; 84.69° W. Long. Elevation is 1,089 feet.
Population: 3,465; Growth (since 2000): n/a; Density: 1,211.7 persons per square mile; Race: 95.6% White, 0.0% Black/African American, 0.4% Asian, 0.0% American Indian/Alaska Native, 0.0% Native Hawaiian/Other Pacific Islander, 4.0% Two or more races, 0.3% Hispanic of any race; Average household size: 2.68; Median age: 38.1; Age under 18: 27.2%; Age 65 and over: 14.0%; Males per 100 females: 100.8; Marriage status: 18.5% never married, 67.3% now married, 0.7% separated, 6.3% widowed, 7.9% divorced; Foreign born: 2.8%; Speak English only: 98.1%; With disability: 9.1%; Veterans: 8.4%; Ancestry: 21.7% German, 13.7% American, 12.8% English, 9.8% Irish, 3.2% Italian
Employment: 9.7% management, business, and financial, 5.2% computer, engineering, and science, 12.9% education, legal, community service, arts, and media, 8.4% healthcare practitioners, 24.0% service, 16.5% sales and office, 7.7% natural resources, construction, and maintenance, 15.7% production, transportation, and material moving
Income: Per capita: $24,205; Median household: $64,897; Average household: $65,175; Households with income of $100,000 or more: 10.2%; Poverty rate: 6.5%
Educational Attainment: High school diploma or higher: 90.1%; Bachelor's degree or higher: 22.0%; Graduate/professional degree or higher: 7.0%
Housing: Homeownership rate: 88.6%; Median home value: $115,900; Median year structure built: 1993; Homeowner vacancy rate: 1.6%; Median selected monthly owner costs: $1,116 with a mortgage, $524 without a mortgage; Median gross rent: $931 per month; Rental vacancy rate: 0.0%
Health Insurance: 95.7% have insurance; 83.8% have private insurance; 24.0% have public insurance; 4.3% do not have insurance; 1.7% of children under 18 do not have insurance
Transportation: Commute: 91.9% car, 0.0% public transportation, 3.0% walk, 1.9% work from home; Mean travel time to work: 30.3 minutes

LEWISBURG (village). Covers a land area of 1.074 square miles and a water area of 0 square miles. Located at 39.85° N. Lat; 84.54° W. Long. Elevation is 997 feet.
History: Lewisburg developed as a rural trade center. Tobacco was once a leading crop here.
Population: 1,615; Growth (since 2000): -10.2%; Density: 1,503.5 persons per square mile; Race: 99.1% White, 0.4% Black/African American, 0.4% Asian, 0.0% American Indian/Alaska Native, 0.0% Native Hawaiian/Other Pacific Islander, 0.2% Two or more races, 0.0% Hispanic of any race; Average household size: 2.68; Median age: 35.7; Age under 18: 29.7%; Age 65 and over: 16.3%; Males per 100 females: 97.8; Marriage status: 24.6% never married, 52.5% now married, 1.1% separated, 7.4% widowed, 15.5% divorced; Foreign born: 0.6%; Speak English only: 98.5%;

With disability: 13.8%; Veterans: 10.7%; Ancestry: 35.2% German, 18.3% Irish, 14.3% American, 6.0% Italian, 5.4% English
Employment: 8.6% management, business, and financial, 6.4% computer, engineering, and science, 3.5% education, legal, community service, arts, and media, 5.2% healthcare practitioners, 20.8% service, 25.2% sales and office, 10.3% natural resources, construction, and maintenance, 19.9% production, transportation, and material moving
Income: Per capita: $20,692; Median household: $44,886; Average household: $53,970; Households with income of $100,000 or more: 10.9%; Poverty rate: 14.0%
Educational Attainment: High school diploma or higher: 88.7%; Bachelor's degree or higher: 8.5%; Graduate/professional degree or higher: 1.9%

School District(s)

Tri-County North Local (KG-12)
2015-16 Enrollment: 857. . . . . (937) 962-2671
Housing: Homeownership rate: 69.5%; Median home value: $94,800; Median year structure built: 1945; Homeowner vacancy rate: 3.4%; Median selected monthly owner costs: $1,015 with a mortgage, $374 without a mortgage; Median gross rent: $693 per month; Rental vacancy rate: 4.0%
Health Insurance: 92.7% have insurance; 61.9% have private insurance; 43.9% have public insurance; 7.3% do not have insurance; 1.0% of children under 18 do not have insurance
Transportation: Commute: 93.6% car, 0.0% public transportation, 0.4% walk, 1.8% work from home; Mean travel time to work: 28.2 minutes

NEW PARIS (village). Covers a land area of 0.735 square miles and a water area of 0.023 square miles. Located at 39.86° N. Lat; 84.79° W. Long. Elevation is 1,033 feet.
Population: 1,738; Growth (since 2000): 7.1%; Density: 2,363.6 persons per square mile; Race: 96.7% White, 0.9% Black/African American, 0.0% Asian, 0.1% American Indian/Alaska Native, 0.0% Native Hawaiian/Other Pacific Islander, 2.4% Two or more races, 2.4% Hispanic of any race; Average household size: 2.55; Median age: 30.9; Age under 18: 32.4%; Age 65 and over: 12.9%; Males per 100 females: 87.9; Marriage status: 29.9% never married, 42.8% now married, 2.6% separated, 8.5% widowed, 18.7% divorced; Foreign born: 0.4%; Speak English only: 98.3%; With disability: 19.1%; Veterans: 9.6%; Ancestry: 25.6% German, 16.1% Irish, 11.7% American, 11.6% English, 3.7% Italian
Employment: 6.3% management, business, and financial, 3.8% computer, engineering, and science, 5.5% education, legal, community service, arts, and media, 2.9% healthcare practitioners, 23.7% service, 18.9% sales and office, 10.4% natural resources, construction, and maintenance, 28.5% production, transportation, and material moving
Income: Per capita: $20,117; Median household: $31,633; Average household: $50,576; Households with income of $100,000 or more: 8.4%; Poverty rate: 22.9%
Educational Attainment: High school diploma or higher: 81.3%; Bachelor's degree or higher: 9.0%; Graduate/professional degree or higher: 1.4%

School District(s)

National Trail Local (KG-12)
2015-16 Enrollment: 1,026 . . . . (937) 437-3333
Housing: Homeownership rate: 52.7%; Median home value: $70,700; Median year structure built: 1957; Homeowner vacancy rate: 2.4%; Median selected monthly owner costs: $879 with a mortgage, $305 without a mortgage; Median gross rent: $637 per month; Rental vacancy rate: 8.3%
Health Insurance: 90.4% have insurance; 46.8% have private insurance; 54.2% have public insurance; 9.6% do not have insurance; 6.0% of children under 18 do not have insurance
Transportation: Commute: 92.4% car, 1.3% public transportation, 3.1% walk, 0.4% work from home; Mean travel time to work: 17.5 minutes

VERONA (village). Covers a land area of 0.456 square miles and a water area of 0.007 square miles. Located at 39.90° N. Lat; 84.51° W. Long. Elevation is 1,024 feet.
Population: 443; Growth (since 2000): 3.0%; Density: 971.5 persons per square mile; Race: 98.0% White, 0.0% Black/African American, 0.0% Asian, 0.0% American Indian/Alaska Native, 0.0% Native Hawaiian/Other Pacific Islander, 2.0% Two or more races, 0.0% Hispanic of any race; Average household size: 2.75; Median age: 30.1; Age under 18: 27.8%; Age 65 and over: 11.3%; Males per 100 females: 101.6; Marriage status: 34.8% never married, 47.6% now married, 1.5% separated, 2.7% widowed, 14.8% divorced; Foreign born: 0.2%; Speak English only: 100.0%; With disability: 13.3%; Veterans: 7.8%; Ancestry: 40.4% German, 13.3% Irish, 12.0% English, 4.7% Dutch, 3.6% American
Employment: 7.5% management, business, and financial, 4.9% computer, engineering, and science, 1.8% education, legal, community service, arts, and media, 7.1% healthcare practitioners, 15.5% service, 14.6% sales and office, 15.9% natural resources, construction, and maintenance, 32.7% production, transportation, and material moving
Income: Per capita: $21,814; Median household: $55,938; Average household: $59,957; Households with income of $100,000 or more: 9.2%; Poverty rate: 15.5%
Educational Attainment: High school diploma or higher: 92.0%; Bachelor's degree or higher: 5.8%; Graduate/professional degree or higher: 1.4%
Housing: Homeownership rate: 86.3%; Median home value: $74,500; Median year structure built: Before 1940; Homeowner vacancy rate: 0.0%; Median selected monthly owner costs: $985 with a mortgage, $456 without a mortgage; Median gross rent: $763 per month; Rental vacancy rate: 15.4%
Health Insurance: 91.0% have insurance; 69.5% have private insurance; 31.6% have public insurance; 9.0% do not have insurance; 0.0% of children under 18 do not have insurance
Transportation: Commute: 95.5% car, 0.0% public transportation, 1.8% walk, 0.0% work from home; Mean travel time to work: 27.6 minutes

WEST ALEXANDRIA (village). Covers a land area of 0.674 square miles and a water area of 0 square miles. Located at 39.74° N. Lat; 84.53° W. Long. Elevation is 892 feet.
Population: 1,682; Growth (since 2000): 20.6%; Density: 2,496.8 persons per square mile; Race: 95.2% White, 0.0% Black/African American, 1.7% Asian, 0.0% American Indian/Alaska Native, 0.0% Native Hawaiian/Other Pacific Islander, 3.1% Two or more races, 1.0% Hispanic of any race; Average household size: 2.59; Median age: 33.9; Age under 18: 28.7%; Age 65 and over: 11.1%; Males per 100 females: 91.2; Marriage status: 30.1% never married, 48.6% now married, 2.7% separated, 5.7% widowed, 15.6% divorced; Foreign born: 1.7%; Speak English only: 96.8%; With disability: 14.5%; Veterans: 7.9%; Ancestry: 37.5% German, 9.6% Irish, 8.1% English, 6.5% American, 5.2% Scottish
Employment: 8.2% management, business, and financial, 2.9% computer, engineering, and science, 11.4% education, legal, community service, arts, and media, 7.9% healthcare practitioners, 10.8% service, 19.4% sales and office, 10.4% natural resources, construction, and maintenance, 29.1% production, transportation, and material moving
Income: Per capita: $20,789; Median household: $45,469; Average household: $52,942; Households with income of $100,000 or more: 10.2%; Poverty rate: 18.6%
Educational Attainment: High school diploma or higher: 90.8%; Bachelor's degree or higher: 16.4%; Graduate/professional degree or higher: 7.5%

School District(s)

Twin Valley Community Local (KG-12)
2015-16 Enrollment: 849. . . . . (937) 839-4688
Housing: Homeownership rate: 64.6%; Median home value: $89,900; Median year structure built: 1952; Homeowner vacancy rate: 2.6%; Median selected monthly owner costs: $997 with a mortgage, $390 without a mortgage; Median gross rent: $745 per month; Rental vacancy rate: 3.4%
Health Insurance: 89.4% have insurance; 60.3% have private insurance; 38.1% have public insurance; 10.6% do not have insurance; 3.3% of children under 18 do not have insurance
Safety: Violent crime rate: 7.5 per 10,000 population; Property crime rate: 172.4 per 10,000 population
Newspapers: Twin Valley Publications (weekly circulation 8,000)
Transportation: Commute: 94.5% car, 0.0% public transportation, 1.4% walk, 3.2% work from home; Mean travel time to work: 24.6 minutes

WEST ELKTON (village). Covers a land area of 0.583 square miles and a water area of 0 square miles. Located at 39.59° N. Lat; 84.56° W. Long. Elevation is 1,030 feet.
Population: 240; Growth (since 2000): 23.7%; Density: 411.4 persons per square mile; Race: 87.5% White, 0.0% Black/African American, 2.9% Asian, 2.9% American Indian/Alaska Native, 0.0% Native Hawaiian/Other Pacific Islander, 6.7% Two or more races, 1.7% Hispanic of any race; Average household size: 2.96; Median age: 30.5; Age under 18: 32.9%; Age 65 and over: 10.0%; Males per 100 females: 121.3; Marriage status: 19.8% never married, 58.2% now married, 1.7% separated, 10.2% widowed, 11.9% divorced; Foreign born: 3.3%; Speak English only: 96.7%;

With disability: 12.9%; Veterans: 8.1%; Ancestry: 22.5% Irish, 19.6% English, 15.4% German, 13.8% American, 2.5% Dutch
Employment: 1.1% management, business, and financial, 0.0% computer, engineering, and science, 6.4% education, legal, community service, arts, and media, 1.1% healthcare practitioners, 24.5% service, 11.7% sales and office, 26.6% natural resources, construction, and maintenance, 28.7% production, transportation, and material moving
Income: Per capita: $16,957; Median household: $41,250; Average household: $48,572; Households with income of $100,000 or more: 6.2%; Poverty rate: 7.1%
Educational Attainment: High school diploma or higher: 82.6%; Bachelor's degree or higher: n/a; Graduate/professional degree or higher: n/a

School District(s)

Preble Shawnee Local (PK-12)
2015-16 Enrollment: 1,349 . . . . (937) 452-1283

Housing: Homeownership rate: 79.0%; Median home value: $67,800; Median year structure built: Before 1940; Homeowner vacancy rate: 4.5%; Median selected monthly owner costs: $893 with a mortgage, $381 without a mortgage; Median gross rent: $719 per month; Rental vacancy rate: 0.0%
Health Insurance: 61.3% have insurance; 49.6% have private insurance; 17.9% have public insurance; 38.8% do not have insurance; 63.3% of children under 18 do not have insurance
Transportation: Commute: 96.8% car, 0.0% public transportation, 0.0% walk, 3.2% work from home; Mean travel time to work: 32.0 minutes

WEST MANCHESTER (village). Covers a land area of 0.272 square miles and a water area of 0 square miles. Located at 39.90° N. Lat; 84.63° W. Long. Elevation is 1,093 feet.
Population: 529; Growth (since 2000): 22.2%; Density: 1,945.5 persons per square mile; Race: 96.4% White, 0.0% Black/African American, 0.8% Asian, 0.0% American Indian/Alaska Native, 0.0% Native Hawaiian/Other Pacific Islander, 2.8% Two or more races, 0.0% Hispanic of any race; Average household size: 2.81; Median age: 32.1; Age under 18: 31.8%; Age 65 and over: 9.3%; Males per 100 females: 95.1; Marriage status: 24.2% never married, 48.6% now married, 2.3% separated, 7.7% widowed, 19.5% divorced; Foreign born: 0.8%; Speak English only: 98.1%; With disability: 16.6%; Veterans: 13.6%; Ancestry: 33.5% German, 18.5% Irish, 12.1% English, 4.3% Italian, 3.2% American
Employment: 8.5% management, business, and financial, 0.0% computer, engineering, and science, 5.6% education, legal, community service, arts, and media, 2.1% healthcare practitioners, 25.2% service, 16.7% sales and office, 15.4% natural resources, construction, and maintenance, 26.5% production, transportation, and material moving
Income: Per capita: $20,700; Median household: $41,538; Average household: $58,159; Households with income of $100,000 or more: 10.7%; Poverty rate: 28.0%
Educational Attainment: High school diploma or higher: 83.8%; Bachelor's degree or higher: 9.9%; Graduate/professional degree or higher: 3.0%
Housing: Homeownership rate: 64.4%; Median home value: $82,100; Median year structure built: Before 1940; Homeowner vacancy rate: 6.0%; Median selected monthly owner costs: $919 with a mortgage, $388 without a mortgage; Median gross rent: $725 per month; Rental vacancy rate: 4.3%
Health Insurance: 89.4% have insurance; 51.8% have private insurance; 47.4% have public insurance; 10.6% do not have insurance; 3.0% of children under 18 do not have insurance
Transportation: Commute: 94.7% car, 0.0% public transportation, 3.1% walk, 2.2% work from home; Mean travel time to work: 24.3 minutes

Putnam County

Located in northwestern Ohio; crossed by the Auglize and Blanchard Rivers. Covers a land area of 482.522 square miles, a water area of 1.778 square miles, and is located in the Eastern Time Zone at 41.02° N. Lat., 84.13° W. Long. The county was founded in 1820. County seat is Ottawa.

Weather Station: Pandora Elevation: 770 feet

	Jan	Feb	Mar	Apr	May	Jun	Jul	Aug	Sep	Oct	Nov	Dec
High	33	37	47	61	71	80	84	82	76	63	50	37
Low	18	21	28	39	49	59	63	60	53	42	33	23
Precip	2.3	2.0	2.7	3.5	3.9	4.1	4.0	3.4	3.0	2.7	3.1	2.7
Snow	9.4	6.9	4.4	1.2	tr	0.0	0.0	0.0	tr	0.1	1.9	6.6

High and Low temperatures in degrees Fahrenheit; Precipitation and Snow in inches

Population: 34,116; Growth (since 2000): -1.8%; Density: 70.7 persons per square mile; Race: 94.9% White, 0.3% Black/African American, 0.3% Asian, 0.0% American Indian/Alaska Native, 0.0% Native Hawaiian/Other Pacific Islander, 1.3% two or more races, 5.9% Hispanic of any race; Average household size: 2.58; Median age: 39.4; Age under 18: 25.7%; Age 65 and over: 15.6%; Males per 100 females: 99.9; Marriage status: 22.7% never married, 63.9% now married, 0.7% separated, 6.2% widowed, 7.2% divorced; Foreign born: 0.8%; Speak English only: 96.8%; With disability: 10.1%; Veterans: 7.9%; Ancestry: 57.6% German, 11.0% American, 6.5% Irish, 4.0% English, 2.3% French
Religion: Six largest groups: 60.3% Catholicism, 5.0% Methodist/Pietist, 4.4% European Free-Church, 2.4% Non-denominational Protestant, 2.2% Holiness, 1.6% Baptist
Economy: Unemployment rate: 3.0%; Leading industries: 17.0 % construction; 14.0 % retail trade; 12.0 % other services (except public administration); Farms: 1,272 totaling 305,567 acres; Company size: 0 employ 1,000 or more persons, 0 employ 500 to 999 persons, 19 employ 100 to 499 persons, 723 employ less than 100 persons; Business ownership: 549 women-owned, n/a Black-owned, n/a Hispanic-owned, n/a Asian-owned, n/a American Indian/Alaska Native-owned
Employment: 11.1% management, business, and financial, 4.2% computer, engineering, and science, 7.3% education, legal, community service, arts, and media, 8.4% healthcare practitioners, 15.3% service, 17.5% sales and office, 11.3% natural resources, construction, and maintenance, 24.9% production, transportation, and material moving
Income: Per capita: $27,367; Median household: $60,245; Average household: $71,300; Households with income of $100,000 or more: 22.5%; Poverty rate: 7.8%
Educational Attainment: High school diploma or higher: 92.9%; Bachelor's degree or higher: 19.4%; Graduate/professional degree or higher: 7.4%
Housing: Homeownership rate: 80.3%; Median home value: $143,200; Median year structure built: 1972; Homeowner vacancy rate: 0.9%; Median selected monthly owner costs: $1,151 with a mortgage, $433 without a mortgage; Median gross rent: $674 per month; Rental vacancy rate: 3.6%
Vital Statistics: Birth rate: 136.5 per 10,000 population; Death rate: 96.0 per 10,000 population; Age-adjusted cancer mortality rate: 151.4 deaths per 100,000 population
Health Insurance: 96.0% have insurance; 84.9% have private insurance; 25.9% have public insurance; 4.0% do not have insurance; 2.0% of children under 18 do not have insurance
Health Care: Physicians: 7.1 per 10,000 population; Dentists: 2.3 per 10,000 population; Hospital beds: 0.0 per 10,000 population; Hospital admissions: 0.0 per 10,000 population
Transportation: Commute: 94.2% car, 0.7% public transportation, 1.6% walk, 2.8% work from home; Mean travel time to work: 22.2 minutes
2016 Presidential Election: 79.3% Trump, 15.5% Clinton, 3.4% Johnson, 0.4% Stein

Additional Information Contacts

Putnam Government . . . . (419) 523-3656
http://www.putnamcountyohio.gov

Putnam County Communities

BELMORE (village). Covers a land area of 0.434 square miles and a water area of 0 square miles. Located at 41.15° N. Lat; 83.94° W. Long. Elevation is 735 feet.
Population: 120; Growth (since 2000): -29.8%; Density: 276.6 persons per square mile; Race: 85.0% White, 0.0% Black/African American, 0.0% Asian, 0.0% American Indian/Alaska Native, 0.0% Native Hawaiian/Other Pacific Islander, 7.5% Two or more races, 10.8% Hispanic of any race; Average household size: 2.73; Median age: 48.6; Age under 18: 28.3%; Age 65 and over: 30.0%; Males per 100 females: 101.4; Marriage status: 15.6% never married, 77.1% now married, 0.0% separated, 4.2% widowed, 3.1% divorced; Foreign born: 0.0%; Speak English only: 88.3%; With disability: 35.8%; Veterans: 14.0%; Ancestry: 27.5% American, 25.8% Scottish, 18.3% German, 9.2% Irish, 4.2% Dutch
Employment: 0.0% management, business, and financial, 0.0% computer, engineering, and science, 14.7% education, legal, community service, arts, and media, 0.0% healthcare practitioners, 14.7% service, 5.9% sales and office, 11.8% natural resources, construction, and maintenance, 52.9% production, transportation, and material moving

Income: Per capita: $10,557; Median household: $35,000; Average household: $31,652; Households with income of $100,000 or more: n/a; Poverty rate: 19.2%
Educational Attainment: High school diploma or higher: 69.1%; Bachelor's degree or higher: 2.5%; Graduate/professional degree or higher: n/a
Housing: Homeownership rate: 100.0%; Median home value: $19,300; Median year structure built: Before 1940; Homeowner vacancy rate: 0.0%; Median selected monthly owner costs: n/a with a mortgage, n/a without a mortgage; Median gross rent: n/a per month; Rental vacancy rate: 0.0%
Health Insurance: 92.5% have insurance; 66.7% have private insurance; 60.8% have public insurance; 7.5% do not have insurance; 0.0% of children under 18 do not have insurance
Transportation: Commute: 100.0% car, 0.0% public transportation, 0.0% walk, 0.0% work from home; Mean travel time to work: 0.0 minutes

---

CLOVERDALE (village). Covers a land area of 0.564 square miles and a water area of 0.006 square miles. Located at 41.02° N. Lat; 84.30° W. Long. Elevation is 722 feet.
Population: 149; Growth (since 2000): -25.9%; Density: 264.2 persons per square mile; Race: 98.0% White, 0.0% Black/African American, 0.0% Asian, 0.0% American Indian/Alaska Native, 0.0% Native Hawaiian/Other Pacific Islander, 1.3% Two or more races, 0.7% Hispanic of any race; Average household size: 2.61; Median age: 34.9; Age under 18: 28.2%; Age 65 and over: 9.4%; Males per 100 females: 97.6; Marriage status: 21.3% never married, 61.1% now married, 1.9% separated, 5.6% widowed, 12.0% divorced; Foreign born: 2.0%; Speak English only: 97.6%; With disability: 28.2%; Veterans: 5.6%; Ancestry: 41.6% German, 15.4% Italian, 10.1% American, 2.7% Irish, 1.3% Hungarian
Employment: 3.4% management, business, and financial, 0.0% computer, engineering, and science, 1.7% education, legal, community service, arts, and media, 8.6% healthcare practitioners, 12.1% service, 8.6% sales and office, 3.4% natural resources, construction, and maintenance, 62.1% production, transportation, and material moving
Income: Per capita: $18,979; Median household: $44,583; Average household: $50,663; Households with income of $100,000 or more: 10.5%; Poverty rate: 26.8%
Educational Attainment: High school diploma or higher: 87.8%; Bachelor's degree or higher: 7.1%; Graduate/professional degree or higher: 1.0%
Housing: Homeownership rate: 91.2%; Median home value: $77,500; Median year structure built: 1962; Homeowner vacancy rate: 0.0%; Median selected monthly owner costs: $911 with a mortgage, $425 without a mortgage; Median gross rent: n/a per month; Rental vacancy rate: 0.0%
Health Insurance: 97.3% have insurance; 78.5% have private insurance; 30.2% have public insurance; 2.7% do not have insurance; 0.0% of children under 18 do not have insurance
Transportation: Commute: 100.0% car, 0.0% public transportation, 0.0% walk, 0.0% work from home; Mean travel time to work: 29.6 minutes

---

COLUMBUS GROVE (village). Covers a land area of 1.081 square miles and a water area of 0.004 square miles. Located at 40.92° N. Lat; 84.06° W. Long. Elevation is 774 feet.
Population: 2,173; Growth (since 2000): -1.2%; Density: 2,009.3 persons per square mile; Race: 97.0% White, 0.2% Black/African American, 0.0% Asian, 0.2% American Indian/Alaska Native, 0.0% Native Hawaiian/Other Pacific Islander, 1.0% Two or more races, 7.6% Hispanic of any race; Average household size: 2.50; Median age: 37.1; Age under 18: 27.7%; Age 65 and over: 15.3%; Males per 100 females: 94.4; Marriage status: 24.6% never married, 59.9% now married, 0.3% separated, 5.6% widowed, 9.9% divorced; Foreign born: 0.2%; Speak English only: 97.8%; With disability: 11.0%; Veterans: 7.0%; Ancestry: 52.6% German, 11.6% American, 9.2% English, 6.1% Irish, 5.1% Polish
Employment: 9.8% management, business, and financial, 2.5% computer, engineering, and science, 4.9% education, legal, community service, arts, and media, 9.6% healthcare practitioners, 16.3% service, 15.3% sales and office, 7.1% natural resources, construction, and maintenance, 34.4% production, transportation, and material moving
Income: Per capita: $22,965; Median household: $47,750; Average household: $57,889; Households with income of $100,000 or more: 14.6%; Poverty rate: 9.2%
Educational Attainment: High school diploma or higher: 95.2%; Bachelor's degree or higher: 17.0%; Graduate/professional degree or higher: 7.2%

School District(s)

Columbus Grove Local (KG-12)
2015-16 Enrollment: 867. . . . . (419) 659-2639
Housing: Homeownership rate: 79.9%; Median home value: $96,300; Median year structure built: 1963; Homeowner vacancy rate: 2.4%; Median selected monthly owner costs: $981 with a mortgage, $414 without a mortgage; Median gross rent: $735 per month; Rental vacancy rate: 13.8%
Health Insurance: 93.3% have insurance; 77.2% have private insurance; 32.2% have public insurance; 6.7% do not have insurance; 3.0% of children under 18 do not have insurance
Transportation: Commute: 93.8% car, 0.0% public transportation, 3.1% walk, 2.0% work from home; Mean travel time to work: 21.2 minutes

---

CONTINENTAL (village). Covers a land area of 0.890 square miles and a water area of 0.021 square miles. Located at 41.10° N. Lat; 84.27° W. Long. Elevation is 722 feet.
Population: 1,045; Growth (since 2000): -12.0%; Density: 1,174.1 persons per square mile; Race: 96.9% White, 0.1% Black/African American, 0.0% Asian, 0.0% American Indian/Alaska Native, 0.0% Native Hawaiian/Other Pacific Islander, 3.0% Two or more races, 2.2% Hispanic of any race; Average household size: 2.31; Median age: 38.0; Age under 18: 20.2%; Age 65 and over: 14.2%; Males per 100 females: 99.5; Marriage status: 26.1% never married, 56.8% now married, 0.4% separated, 7.4% widowed, 9.7% divorced; Foreign born: 0.0%; Speak English only: 99.1%; With disability: 15.2%; Veterans: 5.8%; Ancestry: 42.8% German, 24.2% American, 6.3% Irish, 5.1% English, 3.2% Italian
Employment: 6.9% management, business, and financial, 1.1% computer, engineering, and science, 4.8% education, legal, community service, arts, and media, 4.8% healthcare practitioners, 15.1% service, 15.3% sales and office, 8.8% natural resources, construction, and maintenance, 43.2% production, transportation, and material moving
Income: Per capita: $23,450; Median household: $45,200; Average household: $54,431; Households with income of $100,000 or more: 13.0%; Poverty rate: 7.7%
Educational Attainment: High school diploma or higher: 91.1%; Bachelor's degree or higher: 9.2%; Graduate/professional degree or higher: 2.2%

School District(s)

Continental Local (KG-12)
2015-16 Enrollment: 441. . . . . (419) 596-3671
Housing: Homeownership rate: 83.0%; Median home value: $79,900; Median year structure built: 1977; Homeowner vacancy rate: 1.8%; Median selected monthly owner costs: $997 with a mortgage, $423 without a mortgage; Median gross rent: $538 per month; Rental vacancy rate: 17.2%
Health Insurance: 94.4% have insurance; 76.7% have private insurance; 29.3% have public insurance; 5.6% do not have insurance; 3.3% of children under 18 do not have insurance
Newspapers: Continental News Review (weekly circulation 1,000)
Transportation: Commute: 94.0% car, 2.2% public transportation, 1.5% walk, 0.0% work from home; Mean travel time to work: 25.7 minutes

---

DUPONT (village). Covers a land area of 0.928 square miles and a water area of 0.003 square miles. Located at 41.05° N. Lat; 84.30° W. Long. Elevation is 725 feet.
Population: 324; Growth (since 2000): 20.9%; Density: 349.0 persons per square mile; Race: 100.0% White, 0.0% Black/African American, 0.0% Asian, 0.0% American Indian/Alaska Native, 0.0% Native Hawaiian/Other Pacific Islander, 0.0% Two or more races, 0.9% Hispanic of any race; Average household size: 2.70; Median age: 39.3; Age under 18: 30.6%; Age 65 and over: 13.0%; Males per 100 females: 107.8; Marriage status: 24.2% never married, 56.0% now married, 0.4% separated, 6.0% widowed, 13.7% divorced; Foreign born: 0.9%; Speak English only: 99.0%; With disability: 15.1%; Veterans: 9.8%; Ancestry: 35.8% German, 18.8% American, 7.7% Irish, 5.2% English, 3.4% French
Employment: 11.0% management, business, and financial, 0.0% computer, engineering, and science, 4.4% education, legal, community service, arts, and media, 5.1% healthcare practitioners, 16.9% service, 22.1% sales and office, 6.6% natural resources, construction, and maintenance, 33.8% production, transportation, and material moving
Income: Per capita: $16,754; Median household: $41,167; Average household: $44,673; Households with income of $100,000 or more: 6.7%; Poverty rate: 13.9%
Educational Attainment: High school diploma or higher: 85.4%; Bachelor's degree or higher: 9.1%; Graduate/professional degree or higher: 2.5%

Housing: Homeownership rate: 89.2%; Median home value: $83,100; Median year structure built: 1968; Homeowner vacancy rate: 0.0%; Median selected monthly owner costs: $858 with a mortgage, $325 without a mortgage; Median gross rent: $800 per month; Rental vacancy rate: 0.0%
Health Insurance: 94.8% have insurance; 69.4% have private insurance; 43.2% have public insurance; 5.2% do not have insurance; 0.0% of children under 18 do not have insurance
Transportation: Commute: 91.7% car, 1.5% public transportation, 3.8% walk, 2.3% work from home; Mean travel time to work: 23.2 minutes

FORT JENNINGS (village). Covers a land area of 0.522 square miles and a water area of 0.009 square miles. Located at 40.91° N. Lat; 84.30° W. Long. Elevation is 748 feet.
Population: 483; Growth (since 2000): 11.8%; Density: 924.8 persons per square mile; Race: 98.8% White, 0.0% Black/African American, 0.0% Asian, 1.0% American Indian/Alaska Native, 0.0% Native Hawaiian/Other Pacific Islander, 0.2% Two or more races, 0.0% Hispanic of any race; Average household size: 2.49; Median age: 40.8; Age under 18: 22.2%; Age 65 and over: 18.0%; Males per 100 females: 91.7; Marriage status: 27.0% never married, 59.5% now married, 0.0% separated, 6.9% widowed, 6.6% divorced; Foreign born: 0.0%; Speak English only: 100.0%; With disability: 12.2%; Veterans: 5.9%; Ancestry: 74.5% German, 9.9% Irish, 7.9% American, 6.0% English, 1.0% Italian
Employment: 11.9% management, business, and financial, 3.5% computer, engineering, and science, 4.2% education, legal, community service, arts, and media, 8.5% healthcare practitioners, 13.1% service, 21.5% sales and office, 11.9% natural resources, construction, and maintenance, 25.4% production, transportation, and material moving
Income: Per capita: $27,483; Median household: $64,000; Average household: $68,431; Households with income of $100,000 or more: 22.6%; Poverty rate: 6.4%
Educational Attainment: High school diploma or higher: 93.8%; Bachelor's degree or higher: 21.6%; Graduate/professional degree or higher: 7.7%

School District(s)

Jennings Local (KG-12)
2015-16 Enrollment: 372. . . . . (419) 286-2238
Housing: Homeownership rate: 85.1%; Median home value: $112,500; Median year structure built: 1963; Homeowner vacancy rate: 0.0%; Median selected monthly owner costs: $984 with a mortgage, $417 without a mortgage; Median gross rent: $663 per month; Rental vacancy rate: 0.0%
Health Insurance: 96.7% have insurance; 90.3% have private insurance; 23.6% have public insurance; 3.3% do not have insurance; 0.0% of children under 18 do not have insurance
Transportation: Commute: 92.7% car, 0.0% public transportation, 4.1% walk, 3.3% work from home; Mean travel time to work: 24.7 minutes

GILBOA (village). Covers a land area of 0.149 square miles and a water area of 0 square miles. Located at 41.02° N. Lat; 83.92° W. Long. Elevation is 748 feet.
Population: 159; Growth (since 2000): -6.5%; Density: 1,065.0 persons per square mile; Race: 88.7% White, 0.6% Black/African American, 0.0% Asian, 0.0% American Indian/Alaska Native, 0.0% Native Hawaiian/Other Pacific Islander, 6.3% Two or more races, 11.9% Hispanic of any race; Average household size: 2.48; Median age: 33.6; Age under 18: 25.8%; Age 65 and over: 20.1%; Males per 100 females: 97.8; Marriage status: 21.8% never married, 58.8% now married, 0.0% separated, 4.2% widowed, 15.1% divorced; Foreign born: 0.0%; Speak English only: 97.0%; With disability: 11.9%; Veterans: 13.6%; Ancestry: 36.5% German, 19.5% Irish, 15.7% American, 6.9% English, 6.3% Swiss
Employment: 4.8% management, business, and financial, 0.0% computer, engineering, and science, 7.2% education, legal, community service, arts, and media, 6.0% healthcare practitioners, 16.9% service, 13.3% sales and office, 21.7% natural resources, construction, and maintenance, 30.1% production, transportation, and material moving
Income: Per capita: $22,824; Median household: $44,000; Average household: $56,450; Households with income of $100,000 or more: 20.3%; Poverty rate: 15.1%
Educational Attainment: High school diploma or higher: 93.2%; Bachelor's degree or higher: 16.5%; Graduate/professional degree or higher: 3.9%
Housing: Homeownership rate: 84.4%; Median home value: $76,700; Median year structure built: Before 1940; Homeowner vacancy rate: 6.9%; Median selected monthly owner costs: $900 with a mortgage, $338 without a mortgage; Median gross rent: $583 per month; Rental vacancy rate: 0.0%
Health Insurance: 97.5% have insurance; 77.4% have private insurance; 42.1% have public insurance; 2.5% do not have insurance; 0.0% of children under 18 do not have insurance
Transportation: Commute: 95.0% car, 0.0% public transportation, 5.0% walk, 0.0% work from home; Mean travel time to work: 28.6 minutes

GLANDORF (village). Covers a land area of 1.615 square miles and a water area of <.001 square miles. Located at 41.03° N. Lat; 84.08° W. Long. Elevation is 732 feet.
Population: 927; Growth (since 2000): 0.9%; Density: 573.9 persons per square mile; Race: 100.0% White, 0.0% Black/African American, 0.0% Asian, 0.0% American Indian/Alaska Native, 0.0% Native Hawaiian/Other Pacific Islander, 0.0% Two or more races, 0.2% Hispanic of any race; Average household size: 2.64; Median age: 42.2; Age under 18: 24.9%; Age 65 and over: 15.7%; Males per 100 females: 89.6; Marriage status: 17.8% never married, 68.1% now married, 0.0% separated, 10.8% widowed, 3.2% divorced; Foreign born: 0.2%; Speak English only: 99.3%; With disability: 9.7%; Veterans: 6.6%; Ancestry: 75.2% German, 9.1% American, 5.3% French, 4.6% Irish, 4.6% Italian
Employment: 10.6% management, business, and financial, 4.9% computer, engineering, and science, 5.5% education, legal, community service, arts, and media, 11.6% healthcare practitioners, 14.9% service, 14.9% sales and office, 13.9% natural resources, construction, and maintenance, 23.7% production, transportation, and material moving
Income: Per capita: $30,636; Median household: $76,000; Average household: $84,079; Households with income of $100,000 or more: 27.9%; Poverty rate: 0.7%
Educational Attainment: High school diploma or higher: 96.6%; Bachelor's degree or higher: 24.4%; Graduate/professional degree or higher: 7.0%

School District(s)

Ottawa-Glandorf Local (PK-12)
2015-16 Enrollment: 1,564 . . . . (419) 523-5261
Housing: Homeownership rate: 92.1%; Median home value: $162,500; Median year structure built: 1969; Homeowner vacancy rate: 0.0%; Median selected monthly owner costs: $1,222 with a mortgage, $426 without a mortgage; Median gross rent: $688 per month; Rental vacancy rate: 0.0%
Health Insurance: 95.3% have insurance; 92.3% have private insurance; 14.9% have public insurance; 4.7% do not have insurance; 12.1% of children under 18 do not have insurance
Transportation: Commute: 97.6% car, 0.0% public transportation, 0.6% walk, 1.8% work from home; Mean travel time to work: 19.9 minutes

KALIDA (village). Covers a land area of 1.440 square miles and a water area of 0.031 square miles. Located at 40.99° N. Lat; 84.19° W. Long. Elevation is 725 feet.
Population: 1,370; Growth (since 2000): 32.9%; Density: 951.2 persons per square mile; Race: 99.4% White, 0.1% Black/African American, 0.0% Asian, 0.0% American Indian/Alaska Native, 0.0% Native Hawaiian/Other Pacific Islander, 0.4% Two or more races, 0.0% Hispanic of any race; Average household size: 2.44; Median age: 39.8; Age under 18: 23.7%; Age 65 and over: 16.3%; Males per 100 females: 95.4; Marriage status: 20.4% never married, 66.3% now married, 0.7% separated, 8.7% widowed, 4.6% divorced; Foreign born: 0.0%; Speak English only: 100.0%; With disability: 8.0%; Veterans: 5.0%; Ancestry: 80.2% German, 9.0% American, 5.5% Italian, 3.7% Irish, 2.4% Scottish
Employment: 18.7% management, business, and financial, 6.1% computer, engineering, and science, 11.1% education, legal, community service, arts, and media, 10.2% healthcare practitioners, 15.5% service, 17.7% sales and office, 3.4% natural resources, construction, and maintenance, 17.2% production, transportation, and material moving
Income: Per capita: $41,374; Median household: $76,250; Average household: $103,819; Households with income of $100,000 or more: 34.2%; Poverty rate: 1.1%
Educational Attainment: High school diploma or higher: 91.9%; Bachelor's degree or higher: 32.9%; Graduate/professional degree or higher: 14.9%

School District(s)

Kalida Local (KG-12)
2015-16 Enrollment: 602. . . . . (419) 532-3534
Housing: Homeownership rate: 76.9%; Median home value: $171,200; Median year structure built: 1975; Homeowner vacancy rate: 0.0%; Median

selected monthly owner costs: $1,345 with a mortgage, $389 without a mortgage; Median gross rent: $688 per month; Rental vacancy rate: 0.0%
Health Insurance: 98.5% have insurance; 94.7% have private insurance; 15.7% have public insurance; 1.5% do not have insurance; 0.0% of children under 18 do not have insurance
Transportation: Commute: 95.1% car, 0.0% public transportation, 3.6% walk, 0.8% work from home; Mean travel time to work: 22.1 minutes

LEIPSIC (village). Covers a land area of 3.651 square miles and a water area of 0.011 square miles. Located at 41.11° N. Lat; 83.97° W. Long. Elevation is 764 feet.
Population: 2,142; Growth (since 2000): -4.2%; Density: 586.6 persons per square mile; Race: 67.3% White, 0.2% Black/African American, 0.0% Asian, 0.0% American Indian/Alaska Native, 0.0% Native Hawaiian/Other Pacific Islander, 4.8% Two or more races, 40.9% Hispanic of any race; Average household size: 2.38; Median age: 41.7; Age under 18: 25.3%; Age 65 and over: 20.1%; Males per 100 females: 90.8; Marriage status: 23.3% never married, 50.5% now married, 0.7% separated, 11.0% widowed, 15.2% divorced; Foreign born: 3.3%; Speak English only: 77.5%; With disability: 21.8%; Veterans: 11.1%; Ancestry: 29.9% German, 8.7% American, 4.3% English, 3.7% Irish, 2.4% Italian
Employment: 5.8% management, business, and financial, 3.3% computer, engineering, and science, 8.7% education, legal, community service, arts, and media, 2.2% healthcare practitioners, 12.9% service, 18.2% sales and office, 6.1% natural resources, construction, and maintenance, 42.8% production, transportation, and material moving
Income: Per capita: $19,870; Median household: $40,543; Average household: $48,909; Households with income of $100,000 or more: 10.2%; Poverty rate: 16.0%
Educational Attainment: High school diploma or higher: 81.7%; Bachelor's degree or higher: 8.9%; Graduate/professional degree or higher: 4.0%

School District(s)

Leipsic Local (KG-12)
2015-16 Enrollment: 655. . . . . (419) 943-2165
Housing: Homeownership rate: 66.2%; Median home value: $89,600; Median year structure built: 1963; Homeowner vacancy rate: 3.8%; Median selected monthly owner costs: $893 with a mortgage, $414 without a mortgage; Median gross rent: $732 per month; Rental vacancy rate: 10.3%
Health Insurance: 90.0% have insurance; 70.5% have private insurance; 43.7% have public insurance; 10.0% do not have insurance; 2.2% of children under 18 do not have insurance
Newspapers: Leipsic Messenger (weekly circulation 1,400)
Transportation: Commute: 96.3% car, 0.0% public transportation, 0.8% walk, 2.9% work from home; Mean travel time to work: 22.2 minutes

MILLER CITY (village). Covers a land area of 0.301 square miles and a water area of 0 square miles. Located at 41.10° N. Lat; 84.13° W. Long. Elevation is 732 feet.
Population: 116; Growth (since 2000): -14.7%; Density: 385.0 persons per square mile; Race: 99.1% White, 0.0% Black/African American, 0.0% Asian, 0.0% American Indian/Alaska Native, 0.0% Native Hawaiian/Other Pacific Islander, 0.9% Two or more races, 0.9% Hispanic of any race; Average household size: 1.81; Median age: 55.8; Age under 18: 5.2%; Age 65 and over: 27.6%; Males per 100 females: 101.5; Marriage status: 22.5% never married, 56.8% now married, 0.0% separated, 11.7% widowed, 9.0% divorced; Foreign born: 0.0%; Speak English only: 99.1%; With disability: 15.5%; Veterans: 11.8%; Ancestry: 69.0% German, 8.6% American, 4.3% French, 3.4% Irish, 0.9% English
Employment: 1.5% management, business, and financial, 0.0% computer, engineering, and science, 1.5% education, legal, community service, arts, and media, 10.8% healthcare practitioners, 10.8% service, 23.1% sales and office, 10.8% natural resources, construction, and maintenance, 41.5% production, transportation, and material moving
Income: Per capita: $32,934; Median household: $53,125; Average household: $58,766; Households with income of $100,000 or more: 15.7%; Poverty rate: 4.3%
Educational Attainment: High school diploma or higher: 91.2%; Bachelor's degree or higher: 5.9%; Graduate/professional degree or higher: 1.0%

School District(s)

Miller City-New Cleveland Local (KG-12)
2015-16 Enrollment: 507. . . . . (419) 876-3172
Housing: Homeownership rate: 89.1%; Median home value: $92,500; Median year structure built: 1964; Homeowner vacancy rate: 0.0%; Median selected monthly owner costs: $875 with a mortgage, $405 without a mortgage; Median gross rent: $825 per month; Rental vacancy rate: 0.0%
Health Insurance: 98.3% have insurance; 97.4% have private insurance; 31.9% have public insurance; 1.7% do not have insurance; 0.0% of children under 18 do not have insurance
Transportation: Commute: 98.3% car, 0.0% public transportation, 1.7% walk, 0.0% work from home; Mean travel time to work: 28.6 minutes

OTTAWA (village). County seat. Covers a land area of 4.696 square miles and a water area of 0.068 square miles. Located at 41.02° N. Lat; 84.03° W. Long. Elevation is 725 feet.
History: Ottawa was established in 1833, and named for the Ottawa Indians. The Ohio Sugar Company, a beet-sugar refinery, was built here.
Population: 4,430; Growth (since 2000): 1.4%; Density: 943.4 persons per square mile; Race: 88.0% White, 0.7% Black/African American, 0.6% Asian, 0.0% American Indian/Alaska Native, 0.0% Native Hawaiian/Other Pacific Islander, 2.1% Two or more races, 12.9% Hispanic of any race; Average household size: 2.25; Median age: 38.7; Age under 18: 25.0%; Age 65 and over: 18.0%; Males per 100 females: 94.1; Marriage status: 28.2% never married, 54.7% now married, 2.2% separated, 7.9% widowed, 9.2% divorced; Foreign born: 1.3%; Speak English only: 96.8%; With disability: 6.9%; Veterans: 10.6%; Ancestry: 54.9% German, 11.2% Irish, 7.7% American, 3.3% English, 3.0% French
Employment: 12.0% management, business, and financial, 5.1% computer, engineering, and science, 8.4% education, legal, community service, arts, and media, 2.8% healthcare practitioners, 15.6% service, 21.4% sales and office, 10.3% natural resources, construction, and maintenance, 24.3% production, transportation, and material moving
Income: Per capita: $26,994; Median household: $44,487; Average household: $61,254; Households with income of $100,000 or more: 15.2%; Poverty rate: 14.7%
Educational Attainment: High school diploma or higher: 89.1%; Bachelor's degree or higher: 19.9%; Graduate/professional degree or higher: 7.9%

School District(s)

Ottawa-Glandorf Local (PK-12)
2015-16 Enrollment: 1,564 . . . . (419) 523-5261
Housing: Homeownership rate: 57.6%; Median home value: $155,800; Median year structure built: 1975; Homeowner vacancy rate: 0.0%; Median selected monthly owner costs: $1,253 with a mortgage, $416 without a mortgage; Median gross rent: $613 per month; Rental vacancy rate: 0.0%
Health Insurance: 90.9% have insurance; 67.2% have private insurance; 36.6% have public insurance; 9.1% do not have insurance; 6.9% of children under 18 do not have insurance
Newspapers: Putnam County Sentinel (weekly circulation 6,000); Putnam County Vidette (weekly circulation 1,100)
Transportation: Commute: 96.1% car, 0.7% public transportation, 1.9% walk, 1.3% work from home; Mean travel time to work: 18.7 minutes
Additional Information Contacts
Village of Ottawa . . . . (419) 523-5020
http://ottawaohio.us

OTTOVILLE (village). Covers a land area of 0.800 square miles and a water area of 0.005 square miles. Located at 40.93° N. Lat; 84.34° W. Long. Elevation is 741 feet.
Population: 923; Growth (since 2000): 5.7%; Density: 1,154.1 persons per square mile; Race: 94.4% White, 0.0% Black/African American, 5.4% Asian, 0.0% American Indian/Alaska Native, 0.0% Native Hawaiian/Other Pacific Islander, 0.2% Two or more races, 0.5% Hispanic of any race; Average household size: 2.45; Median age: 37.5; Age under 18: 28.5%; Age 65 and over: 13.8%; Males per 100 females: 93.7; Marriage status: 20.7% never married, 61.4% now married, 0.9% separated, 6.6% widowed, 11.4% divorced; Foreign born: 2.5%; Speak English only: 96.8%; With disability: 11.5%; Veterans: 8.2%; Ancestry: 77.7% German, 6.1% American, 5.6% Irish, 1.7% French, 1.1% Austrian
Employment: 11.9% management, business, and financial, 6.5% computer, engineering, and science, 8.9% education, legal, community service, arts, and media, 13.1% healthcare practitioners, 10.7% service, 19.6% sales and office, 6.9% natural resources, construction, and maintenance, 22.4% production, transportation, and material moving
Income: Per capita: $29,614; Median household: $60,500; Average household: $73,194; Households with income of $100,000 or more: 27.7%; Poverty rate: 4.0%

Educational Attainment: High school diploma or higher: 93.1%; Bachelor's degree or higher: 22.4%; Graduate/professional degree or higher: 4.7%

School District(s)

Ottoville Local (KG-12)
2015-16 Enrollment: 420. . . . . (419) 453-3356

Housing: Homeownership rate: 78.7%; Median home value: $152,000; Median year structure built: 1962; Homeowner vacancy rate: 0.7%; Median selected monthly owner costs: $1,010 with a mortgage, $443 without a mortgage; Median gross rent: $644 per month; Rental vacancy rate: 0.0%
Health Insurance: 100.0% have insurance; 94.0% have private insurance; 19.6% have public insurance; 0.0% do not have insurance; 0.0% of children under 18 do not have insurance
Transportation: Commute: 92.8% car, 3.1% public transportation, 0.8% walk, 1.2% work from home; Mean travel time to work: 19.3 minutes
Additional Information Contacts
Village of Ottoville . . . . (419) 453-2426
http://www.villageofottoville.org

PANDORA (village). Covers a land area of 0.903 square miles and a water area of 0.024 square miles. Located at 40.95° N. Lat; 83.96° W. Long. Elevation is 774 feet.
Population: 1,183; Growth (since 2000): -0.4%; Density: 1,309.4 persons per square mile; Race: 95.7% White, 0.3% Black/African American, 1.1% Asian, 0.0% American Indian/Alaska Native, 0.0% Native Hawaiian/Other Pacific Islander, 2.6% Two or more races, 0.9% Hispanic of any race; Average household size: 2.28; Median age: 42.3; Age under 18: 20.6%; Age 65 and over: 18.8%; Males per 100 females: 96.4; Marriage status: 24.1% never married, 57.7% now married, 1.0% separated, 7.8% widowed, 10.4% divorced; Foreign born: 2.2%; Speak English only: 100.0%; With disability: 12.6%; Veterans: 8.0%; Ancestry: 42.9% German, 13.2% Swiss, 10.4% American, 7.8% French, 7.5% English
Employment: 14.8% management, business, and financial, 4.3% computer, engineering, and science, 5.0% education, legal, community service, arts, and media, 9.0% healthcare practitioners, 15.9% service, 18.0% sales and office, 13.1% natural resources, construction, and maintenance, 20.0% production, transportation, and material moving
Income: Per capita: $26,087; Median household: $49,931; Average household: $62,115; Households with income of $100,000 or more: 18.8%; Poverty rate: 6.5%
Educational Attainment: High school diploma or higher: 95.1%; Bachelor's degree or higher: 23.4%; Graduate/professional degree or higher: 9.8%

School District(s)

Pandora-Gilboa Local (KG-12)
2015-16 Enrollment: 565. . . . . (419) 384-3227

Housing: Homeownership rate: 74.3%; Median home value: $113,700; Median year structure built: 1956; Homeowner vacancy rate: 1.9%; Median selected monthly owner costs: $942 with a mortgage, $373 without a mortgage; Median gross rent: $659 per month; Rental vacancy rate: 0.0%
Health Insurance: 96.1% have insurance; 80.9% have private insurance; 27.6% have public insurance; 3.9% do not have insurance; 0.0% of children under 18 do not have insurance
Transportation: Commute: 87.7% car, 2.1% public transportation, 5.2% walk, 2.6% work from home; Mean travel time to work: 21.0 minutes

VAUGHNSVILLE (CDP). Covers a land area of 0.171 square miles and a water area of 0.002 square miles. Located at 40.88° N. Lat; 84.15° W. Long. Elevation is 761 feet.
Population: 272; Growth (since 2000): n/a; Density: 1,590.4 persons per square mile; Race: 100.0% White, 0.0% Black/African American, 0.0% Asian, 0.0% American Indian/Alaska Native, 0.0% Native Hawaiian/Other Pacific Islander, 0.0% Two or more races, 0.0% Hispanic of any race; Average household size: 3.13; Median age: 29.9; Age under 18: 33.8%; Age 65 and over: 6.6%; Males per 100 females: 97.0; Marriage status: 4.4% never married, 95.6% now married, 0.0% separated, 0.0% widowed, 0.0% divorced; Foreign born: 0.0%; Speak English only: 100.0%; With disability: 0.0%; Veterans: 5.0%; Ancestry: 39.7% American, 11.8% German, 8.5% French, 6.6% English, 3.3% Irish
Employment: 17.6% management, business, and financial, 0.0% computer, engineering, and science, 0.0% education, legal, community service, arts, and media, 0.0% healthcare practitioners, 23.0% service, 37.2% sales and office, 0.0% natural resources, construction, and maintenance, 22.3% production, transportation, and material moving
Income: Per capita: $18,919; Median household: $67,548; Average household: $60,845; Households with income of $100,000 or more: 10.3%; Poverty rate: 6.6%
Educational Attainment: High school diploma or higher: 100.0%; Bachelor's degree or higher: 23.9%; Graduate/professional degree or higher: n/a
Housing: Homeownership rate: 83.9%; Median home value: $78,300; Median year structure built: 1952; Homeowner vacancy rate: 0.0%; Median selected monthly owner costs: n/a with a mortgage, n/a without a mortgage; Median gross rent: n/a per month; Rental vacancy rate: 0.0%
Health Insurance: 100.0% have insurance; 100.0% have private insurance; 6.6% have public insurance; 0.0% do not have insurance; 0.0% of children under 18 do not have insurance
Transportation: Commute: 100.0% car, 0.0% public transportation, 0.0% walk, 0.0% work from home; Mean travel time to work: 20.5 minutes

WEST LEIPSIC (village). Covers a land area of 0.238 square miles and a water area of 0 square miles. Located at 41.11° N. Lat; 84.00° W. Long. Elevation is 771 feet.
Population: 242; Growth (since 2000): -10.7%; Density: 1,016.7 persons per square mile; Race: 78.1% White, 0.0% Black/African American, 0.0% Asian, 0.0% American Indian/Alaska Native, 0.0% Native Hawaiian/Other Pacific Islander, 12.4% Two or more races, 47.5% Hispanic of any race; Average household size: 2.72; Median age: 39.3; Age under 18: 25.6%; Age 65 and over: 7.9%; Males per 100 females: 92.5; Marriage status: 27.4% never married, 54.2% now married, 0.0% separated, 8.4% widowed, 10.0% divorced; Foreign born: 1.7%; Speak English only: 73.9%; With disability: 14.0%; Veterans: 7.8%; Ancestry: 33.1% German, 6.2% Irish, 4.1% Dutch, 3.7% English, 3.3% American
Employment: 2.8% management, business, and financial, 0.0% computer, engineering, and science, 2.1% education, legal, community service, arts, and media, 2.8% healthcare practitioners, 9.8% service, 36.4% sales and office, 11.9% natural resources, construction, and maintenance, 34.3% production, transportation, and material moving
Income: Per capita: $19,825; Median household: $56,328; Average household: $57,582; Households with income of $100,000 or more: 6.7%; Poverty rate: 14.3%
Educational Attainment: High school diploma or higher: 91.3%; Bachelor's degree or higher: 8.0%; Graduate/professional degree or higher: 1.3%
Housing: Homeownership rate: 82.0%; Median home value: $77,300; Median year structure built: Before 1940; Homeowner vacancy rate: 0.0%; Median selected monthly owner costs: $1,000 with a mortgage, $414 without a mortgage; Median gross rent: $589 per month; Rental vacancy rate: 0.0%
Health Insurance: 88.8% have insurance; 74.0% have private insurance; 22.3% have public insurance; 11.2% do not have insurance; 3.2% of children under 18 do not have insurance
Transportation: Commute: 93.4% car, 0.0% public transportation, 5.1% walk, 0.0% work from home; Mean travel time to work: 20.1 minutes

Richland County

Located in north central Ohio; drained by forks of the Mohican River. Covers a land area of 495.269 square miles, a water area of 4.809 square miles, and is located in the Eastern Time Zone at 40.77° N. Lat., 82.54° W. Long. The county was founded in 1813. County seat is Mansfield.

Richland County is part of the Mansfield, OH Metropolitan Statistical Area. The entire metro area includes: Richland County, OH

Weather Station: Mansfield 5 W Elevation: 1,350 feet

	Jan	Feb	Mar	Apr	May	Jun	Jul	Aug	Sep	Oct	Nov	Dec
High	32	36	46	59	70	78	82	80	74	61	49	37
Low	17	19	27	37	47	56	60	59	52	40	32	22
Precip	2.2	1.8	2.8	3.6	4.6	4.4	4.0	3.8	3.2	2.8	3.1	2.9
Snow	na	na	na	0.4	0.0	0.0	0.0	0.0	0.0	tr	0.4	na

High and Low temperatures in degrees Fahrenheit; Precipitation and Snow in inches

Weather Station: Mansfield Lahm Municipal Arpt Elevation: 1,294 feet

	Jan	Feb	Mar	Apr	May	Jun	Jul	Aug	Sep	Oct	Nov	Dec
High	33	36	46	59	69	78	82	80	73	62	49	37
Low	19	21	28	39	48	58	62	61	53	42	34	24
Precip	2.9	2.3	3.5	4.2	4.5	4.7	4.5	4.4	3.3	2.9	3.7	3.3
Snow	13.1	10.3	8.0	2.7	tr	tr	0.0	0.0	0.0	0.6	2.5	10.5

High and Low temperatures in degrees Fahrenheit; Precipitation and Snow in inches

Population: 121,888; Growth (since 2000): -5.4%; Density: 246.1 persons per square mile; Race: 86.9% White, 7.5% Black/African American, 0.8% Asian, 0.1% American Indian/Alaska Native, 0.0% Native Hawaiian/Other Pacific Islander, 4.1% two or more races, 1.7% Hispanic of any race; Average household size: 2.39; Median age: 41.2; Age under 18: 21.8%; Age 65 and over: 18.0%; Males per 100 females: 102.2; Marriage status: 27.8% never married, 51.5% now married, 2.8% separated, 7.9% widowed, 12.8% divorced; Foreign born: 1.5%; Speak English only: 96.3%; With disability: 15.4%; Veterans: 10.0%; Ancestry: 30.6% German, 12.7% Irish, 12.0% English, 9.0% American, 5.0% Italian
Religion: Six largest groups: 10.4% Non-denominational Protestant, 7.8% Catholicism, 6.1% Baptist, 4.4% Methodist/Pietist, 3.2% Lutheran, 3.1% Pentecostal
Economy: Unemployment rate: 4.9%; Leading industries: 16.2 % retail trade; 12.4 % other services (except public administration); 12.1 % health care and social assistance; Farms: 1,010 totaling 160,623 acres; Company size: 2 employ 1,000 or more persons, 4 employ 500 to 999 persons, 68 employ 100 to 499 persons, 2,544 employ less than 100 persons; Business ownership: 2,610 women-owned, 281 Black-owned, 76 Hispanic-owned, 220 Asian-owned, 46 American Indian/Alaska Native-owned
Employment: 9.8% management, business, and financial, 2.7% computer, engineering, and science, 8.4% education, legal, community service, arts, and media, 5.8% healthcare practitioners, 19.7% service, 24.4% sales and office, 7.5% natural resources, construction, and maintenance, 21.7% production, transportation, and material moving
Income: Per capita: $22,520; Median household: $42,849; Average household: $55,544; Households with income of $100,000 or more: 12.1%; Poverty rate: 16.5%
Educational Attainment: High school diploma or higher: 87.2%; Bachelor's degree or higher: 16.4%; Graduate/professional degree or higher: 5.3%
Housing: Homeownership rate: 67.8%; Median home value: $102,600; Median year structure built: 1962; Homeowner vacancy rate: 1.2%; Median selected monthly owner costs: $1,002 with a mortgage, $379 without a mortgage; Median gross rent: $639 per month; Rental vacancy rate: 5.3%
Vital Statistics: Birth rate: 108.9 per 10,000 population; Death rate: 111.3 per 10,000 population; Age-adjusted cancer mortality rate: 180.0 deaths per 100,000 population
Health Insurance: 90.0% have insurance; 65.2% have private insurance; 41.4% have public insurance; 10.0% do not have insurance; 5.9% of children under 18 do not have insurance
Health Care: Physicians: 16.0 per 10,000 population; Dentists: 6.9 per 10,000 population; Hospital beds: 23.8 per 10,000 population; Hospital admissions: 1,004.1 per 10,000 population
Transportation: Commute: 93.0% car, 1.0% public transportation, 1.9% walk, 3.1% work from home; Mean travel time to work: 21.8 minutes
2016 Presidential Election: 66.0% Trump, 29.0% Clinton, 3.0% Johnson, 0.7% Stein
National and State Parks: Fowler Woods State Nature Preserve; Malabar Farm State Park
Additional Information Contacts
Richland Government . . . . (419) 774-5599
http://www.richlandcountyoh.us

Richland County Communities

BELLVILLE (village). Covers a land area of 2.735 square miles and a water area of 0.013 square miles. Located at 40.62° N. Lat; 82.51° W. Long. Elevation is 1,138 feet.
History: Bellville grew as a farm community surrounded by apple and peach orchards. Twice, the town's hopes for fortune were dashed. In 1853 Dr. James C. Lee, a former California miner, found gold here, but the amount turned out to be very small. In the 1890's it was thought that a spring might be of therapeutic value and a sanitarium was built, but failed to become a popular health spa.
Population: 1,920; Growth (since 2000): 8.3%; Density: 701.9 persons per square mile; Race: 98.5% White, 0.9% Black/African American, 0.2% Asian, 0.0% American Indian/Alaska Native, 0.0% Native Hawaiian/Other Pacific Islander, 0.4% Two or more races, 0.0% Hispanic of any race; Average household size: 2.25; Median age: 42.7; Age under 18: 23.9%; Age 65 and over: 22.6%; Males per 100 females: 92.8; Marriage status: 18.0% never married, 59.9% now married, 1.9% separated, 8.4% widowed, 13.7% divorced; Foreign born: 0.9%; Speak English only: 98.6%; With disability: 10.7%; Veterans: 10.2%; Ancestry: 34.2% German, 14.0% American, 10.2% English, 9.5% Irish, 5.8% Italian
Employment: 16.6% management, business, and financial, 5.5% computer, engineering, and science, 8.6% education, legal, community service, arts, and media, 7.7% healthcare practitioners, 18.3% service, 22.2% sales and office, 6.6% natural resources, construction, and maintenance, 14.6% production, transportation, and material moving
Income: Per capita: $27,190; Median household: $48,021; Average household: $60,384; Households with income of $100,000 or more: 20.7%; Poverty rate: 6.1%
Educational Attainment: High school diploma or higher: 95.3%; Bachelor's degree or higher: 24.7%; Graduate/professional degree or higher: 6.1%

School District(s)

Clear Fork Valley Local (PK-12)
2015-16 Enrollment: 1,643 . . . . (419) 886-3855
Housing: Homeownership rate: 77.3%; Median home value: $115,600; Median year structure built: 1954; Homeowner vacancy rate: 0.0%; Median selected monthly owner costs: $1,047 with a mortgage, $383 without a mortgage; Median gross rent: $607 per month; Rental vacancy rate: 7.2%
Health Insurance: 93.3% have insurance; 82.0% have private insurance; 31.9% have public insurance; 6.7% do not have insurance; 4.1% of children under 18 do not have insurance
Safety: Violent crime rate: 5.4 per 10,000 population; Property crime rate: 155.7 per 10,000 population
Newspapers: Star & Tri-Forks Press (weekly circulation 2,100)
Transportation: Commute: 84.4% car, 0.0% public transportation, 6.9% walk, 5.9% work from home; Mean travel time to work: 21.3 minutes
Additional Information Contacts
Village of Bellville . . . . (419) 886-2245
http://www.bellvilleohio.net/villageadmin.htm

BUTLER (village). Covers a land area of 1.140 square miles and a water area of 0.007 square miles. Located at 40.59° N. Lat; 82.42° W. Long. Elevation is 1,073 feet.
Population: 966; Growth (since 2000): 4.9%; Density: 847.5 persons per square mile; Race: 95.9% White, 0.0% Black/African American, 0.0% Asian, 0.8% American Indian/Alaska Native, 0.0% Native Hawaiian/Other Pacific Islander, 3.3% Two or more races, 0.6% Hispanic of any race; Average household size: 2.38; Median age: 42.8; Age under 18: 23.6%; Age 65 and over: 21.9%; Males per 100 females: 93.6; Marriage status: 25.5% never married, 52.0% now married, 3.0% separated, 7.1% widowed, 15.5% divorced; Foreign born: 0.3%; Speak English only: 99.3%; With disability: 20.3%; Veterans: 13.1%; Ancestry: 43.0% German, 19.8% Irish, 12.3% English, 7.7% Italian, 3.7% American
Employment: 8.7% management, business, and financial, 0.7% computer, engineering, and science, 5.6% education, legal, community service, arts, and media, 5.2% healthcare practitioners, 21.7% service, 24.9% sales and office, 11.9% natural resources, construction, and maintenance, 21.3% production, transportation, and material moving
Income: Per capita: $21,876; Median household: $41,375; Average household: $50,885; Households with income of $100,000 or more: 10.4%; Poverty rate: 11.8%
Educational Attainment: High school diploma or higher: 87.9%; Bachelor's degree or higher: 12.2%; Graduate/professional degree or higher: 2.1%

School District(s)

Clear Fork Valley Local (PK-12)
2015-16 Enrollment: 1,643 . . . . (419) 886-3855
Housing: Homeownership rate: 73.2%; Median home value: $95,700; Median year structure built: Before 1940; Homeowner vacancy rate: 2.0%; Median selected monthly owner costs: $962 with a mortgage, $344 without a mortgage; Median gross rent: $677 per month; Rental vacancy rate: 0.0%
Health Insurance: 95.1% have insurance; 76.7% have private insurance; 37.7% have public insurance; 4.9% do not have insurance; 0.0% of children under 18 do not have insurance
Transportation: Commute: 94.1% car, 0.0% public transportation, 3.0% walk, 2.5% work from home; Mean travel time to work: 29.2 minutes

LEXINGTON (village). Covers a land area of 3.812 square miles and a water area of 0.004 square miles. Located at 40.68° N. Lat; 82.58° W. Long. Elevation is 1,214 feet.
Population: 5,484; Growth (since 2000): 31.7%; Density: 1,438.4 persons per square mile; Race: 91.2% White, 2.6% Black/African American, 0.3%

Asian, 0.2% American Indian/Alaska Native, 0.0% Native Hawaiian/Other Pacific Islander, 4.9% Two or more races, 1.3% Hispanic of any race; Average household size: 2.51; Median age: 37.8; Age under 18: 28.4%; Age 65 and over: 17.8%; Males per 100 females: 90.9; Marriage status: 23.2% never married, 59.4% now married, 4.5% separated, 5.4% widowed, 12.0% divorced; Foreign born: 0.7%; Speak English only: 97.5%; With disability: 9.9%; Veterans: 6.8%; Ancestry: 38.8% German, 14.5% English, 12.5% Irish, 6.4% Italian, 4.9% Polish

Employment: 12.7% management, business, and financial, 1.1% computer, engineering, and science, 9.9% education, legal, community service, arts, and media, 13.1% healthcare practitioners, 18.6% service, 23.1% sales and office, 3.7% natural resources, construction, and maintenance, 17.9% production, transportation, and material moving

Income: Per capita: $25,573; Median household: $52,045; Average household: $63,603; Households with income of $100,000 or more: 23.2%; Poverty rate: 13.6%

Educational Attainment: High school diploma or higher: 95.1%; Bachelor's degree or higher: 25.8%; Graduate/professional degree or higher: 8.4%

School District(s)

Lexington Local (PK-12)
2015-16 Enrollment: 2,369 . . . . (419) 884-2132

Housing: Homeownership rate: 63.6%; Median home value: $134,900; Median year structure built: 1969; Homeowner vacancy rate: 0.0%; Median selected monthly owner costs: $1,170 with a mortgage, $418 without a mortgage; Median gross rent: $702 per month; Rental vacancy rate: 7.7%

Health Insurance: 88.3% have insurance; 69.6% have private insurance; 33.1% have public insurance; 11.7% do not have insurance; 5.4% of children under 18 do not have insurance

Safety: Violent crime rate: 0.0 per 10,000 population; Property crime rate: 10.6 per 10,000 population

Transportation: Commute: 96.6% car, 0.6% public transportation, 0.0% walk, 2.8% work from home; Mean travel time to work: 21.4 minutes

Additional Information Contacts

Village of Lexington . . . . (419) 884-0765
http://www.lexingtonohio.us

LUCAS (village). Covers a land area of 0.688 square miles and a water area of <.001 square miles. Located at 40.70° N. Lat; 82.42° W. Long. Elevation is 1,086 feet.

Population: 527; Growth (since 2000): -15.0%; Density: 765.5 persons per square mile; Race: 98.1% White, 0.0% Black/African American, 0.0% Asian, 0.0% American Indian/Alaska Native, 0.0% Native Hawaiian/Other Pacific Islander, 1.9% Two or more races, 0.0% Hispanic of any race; Average household size: 2.44; Median age: 34.6; Age under 18: 27.7%; Age 65 and over: 13.3%; Males per 100 females: 96.5; Marriage status: 29.1% never married, 51.8% now married, 1.0% separated, 4.4% widowed, 14.7% divorced; Foreign born: 0.6%; Speak English only: 99.6%; With disability: 9.9%; Veterans: 6.8%; Ancestry: 28.5% German, 25.2% English, 12.0% Irish, 8.0% American, 5.1% Welsh

Employment: 11.9% management, business, and financial, 0.0% computer, engineering, and science, 9.4% education, legal, community service, arts, and media, 6.1% healthcare practitioners, 20.9% service, 14.8% sales and office, 12.6% natural resources, construction, and maintenance, 24.2% production, transportation, and material moving

Income: Per capita: $22,674; Median household: $46,250; Average household: $54,599; Households with income of $100,000 or more: 14.3%; Poverty rate: 11.8%

Educational Attainment: High school diploma or higher: 92.4%; Bachelor's degree or higher: 9.7%; Graduate/professional degree or higher: 2.9%

School District(s)

Lucas Local (KG-12)
2015-16 Enrollment: 545. . . . . (419) 892-2338

Housing: Homeownership rate: 56.9%; Median home value: $88,500; Median year structure built: 1954; Homeowner vacancy rate: 8.9%; Median selected monthly owner costs: $1,034 with a mortgage, $296 without a mortgage; Median gross rent: $687 per month; Rental vacancy rate: 5.1%

Health Insurance: 95.6% have insurance; 81.8% have private insurance; 23.3% have public insurance; 4.4% do not have insurance; 0.0% of children under 18 do not have insurance

Transportation: Commute: 92.4% car, 0.0% public transportation, 2.2% walk, 4.3% work from home; Mean travel time to work: 24.0 minutes

MANSFIELD (city). County seat. Covers a land area of 30.872 square miles and a water area of 0.053 square miles. Located at 40.77° N. Lat; 82.53° W. Long. Elevation is 1,240 feet.

History: Mansfield was named for Jared Mansfield, U.S. Surveyor General, who directed the townsite to be laid out in 1808. Mansfield grew as the surrounding lands were cleared of timber and put under cultivation. During the War of 1812, Mansfield was threatened by British allies, but John Chapman (better known as Johnny Appleseed) made the 30-mile trip to bring troops from Mount Vernon, and Mansfield was saved. Mansfield 's growth was slow, spurred only by the arrival of the railroad in 1846, until after the Civil War. By 1900 it was the home of the Ohio Brass Company, the Empire Sheet and Tin Plate Company, Tappan Stove Company, and a plant of the Westinghouse Electric and Manufacturing Company.

Population: 46,902; Growth (since 2000): -5.0%; Density: 1,519.2 persons per square mile; Race: 73.0% White, 17.8% Black/African American, 0.6% Asian, 0.3% American Indian/Alaska Native, 0.0% Native Hawaiian/Other Pacific Islander, 7.5% Two or more races, 2.6% Hispanic of any race; Average household size: 2.28; Median age: 37.7; Age under 18: 20.9%; Age 65 and over: 16.3%; Males per 100 females: 112.6; Marriage status: 35.8% never married, 39.8% now married, 3.7% separated, 8.3% widowed, 16.1% divorced; Foreign born: 1.7%; Speak English only: 96.3%; With disability: 18.9%; Veterans: 9.9%; Ancestry: 27.3% German, 12.1% Irish, 9.5% English, 6.0% American, 5.2% Italian

Employment: 8.7% management, business, and financial, 2.9% computer, engineering, and science, 7.7% education, legal, community service, arts, and media, 5.4% healthcare practitioners, 22.5% service, 28.0% sales and office, 4.5% natural resources, construction, and maintenance, 20.3% production, transportation, and material moving

Income: Per capita: $18,476; Median household: $33,257; Average household: $46,386; Households with income of $100,000 or more: 8.0%; Poverty rate: 25.6%

Educational Attainment: High school diploma or higher: 83.5%; Bachelor's degree or higher: 13.8%; Graduate/professional degree or higher: 4.2%

School District(s)

Foundation Academy (KG-08)
2015-16 Enrollment: 406. . . . . (419) 526-9540
Goal Digital Academy (01-12)
2015-16 Enrollment: 380. . . . . (419) 775-4809
Interactive Media & Construction (LMAC) (09-12)
2015-16 Enrollment: 42. . . . . (419) 525-0105
Madison Local (PK-12)
2015-16 Enrollment: 3,153 . . . . (419) 589-2600
Mansfield City (PK-12)
2015-16 Enrollment: 3,482 . . . . (419) 525-6400
Mansfield Elective Academy (KG-09)
2015-16 Enrollment: 30. . . . . (567) 247-4475
Mansfield Enhancement Academy (09-12)
2015-16 Enrollment: 36. . . . . (419) 525-0105
Ontario Local (KG-12)
2015-16 Enrollment: 1,922 . . . . (419) 747-4311
Richland Academy School of Excellence (KG-08)
2015-16 Enrollment: 199. . . . . (419) 522-8224

Four-year College(s)

Ohio State University-Mansfield Campus (Public)
Fall 2016 Enrollment: 1,128 . . . . (419) 755-4011
2016-17 Tuition: In-state $7,140; Out-of-state $25,332

Two-year College(s)

Madison Adult Career Center (Public)
Fall 2016 Enrollment: 128 . . . . (419) 589-6363
North Central State College (Public)
Fall 2016 Enrollment: 3,094 . . . . (419) 755-4800
2016-17 Tuition: In-state $3,591; Out-of-state $7,181

Housing: Homeownership rate: 52.7%; Median home value: $77,500; Median year structure built: 1958; Homeowner vacancy rate: 2.1%; Median selected monthly owner costs: $878 with a mortgage, $346 without a mortgage; Median gross rent: $592 per month; Rental vacancy rate: 6.4%

Health Insurance: 88.9% have insurance; 54.4% have private insurance; 49.9% have public insurance; 11.1% do not have insurance; 3.9% of children under 18 do not have insurance

Hospitals: Medcentral Health System Mansfield Hospital (398 beds)

Safety: Violent crime rate: 44.8 per 10,000 population; Property crime rate: 558.3 per 10,000 population

Newspapers: News Journal (daily circulation 29,100)

Transportation: Commute: 91.9% car, 2.3% public transportation, 2.8% walk, 2.2% work from home; Mean travel time to work: 19.3 minutes
Airports: Mansfield Lahm Regional (general aviation)
Additional Information Contacts
City of Mansfield . . . . (419) 755-9626
http://www.ci.mansfield.oh.us

ONTARIO (city). Covers a land area of 11.084 square miles and a water area of 0.023 square miles. Located at 40.77° N. Lat; 82.62° W. Long. Elevation is 1,355 feet.
Population: 6,117; Growth (since 2000): 15.3%; Density: 551.9 persons per square mile; Race: 84.9% White, 5.0% Black/African American, 7.9% Asian, 0.2% American Indian/Alaska Native, 0.0% Native Hawaiian/Other Pacific Islander, 1.2% Two or more races, 1.4% Hispanic of any race; Average household size: 2.36; Median age: 45.9; Age under 18: 17.5%; Age 65 and over: 20.2%; Males per 100 females: 88.9; Marriage status: 23.4% never married, 58.4% now married, 0.0% separated, 9.0% widowed, 9.1% divorced; Foreign born: 6.9%; Speak English only: 89.6%; With disability: 12.4%; Veterans: 9.2%; Ancestry: 22.5% German, 16.2% English, 12.1% Irish, 10.9% American, 4.6% Italian
Employment: 10.8% management, business, and financial, 4.0% computer, engineering, and science, 11.3% education, legal, community service, arts, and media, 4.8% healthcare practitioners, 24.0% service, 27.2% sales and office, 4.5% natural resources, construction, and maintenance, 13.4% production, transportation, and material moving
Income: Per capita: $26,812; Median household: $50,000; Average household: $62,384; Households with income of $100,000 or more: 19.3%; Poverty rate: 7.4%
Educational Attainment: High school diploma or higher: 92.7%; Bachelor's degree or higher: 24.4%; Graduate/professional degree or higher: 8.0%

Vocational/Technical School(s)
Ross Medical Education Center-Ontario (Private, For-profit)
Fall 2016 Enrollment: 117 . . . . (419) 747-2206
2016-17 Tuition: $15,740
Housing: Homeownership rate: 71.7%; Median home value: $131,700; Median year structure built: 1984; Homeowner vacancy rate: 0.0%; Median selected monthly owner costs: $1,153 with a mortgage, $423 without a mortgage; Median gross rent: $762 per month; Rental vacancy rate: 0.0%
Health Insurance: 92.7% have insurance; 79.6% have private insurance; 30.5% have public insurance; 7.3% do not have insurance; 3.7% of children under 18 do not have insurance
Safety: Violent crime rate: 8.2 per 10,000 population; Property crime rate: 607.5 per 10,000 population
Newspapers: Tribune-Courier (weekly circulation 2,400)
Transportation: Commute: 97.5% car, 0.0% public transportation, 0.0% walk, 2.0% work from home; Mean travel time to work: 17.3 minutes
Additional Information Contacts
City of Ontario . . . . (419) 529-3818
http://www.ontarioohio.org

PLYMOUTH (village). Covers a land area of 2.465 square miles and a water area of 0.032 square miles. Located at 41.00° N. Lat; 82.67° W. Long. Elevation is 1,017 feet.
Population: 1,814; Growth (since 2000): -2.1%; Density: 735.9 persons per square mile; Race: 93.6% White, 0.0% Black/African American, 0.0% Asian, 0.3% American Indian/Alaska Native, 0.0% Native Hawaiian/Other Pacific Islander, 5.3% Two or more races, 2.9% Hispanic of any race; Average household size: 2.57; Median age: 35.3; Age under 18: 27.7%; Age 65 and over: 16.0%; Males per 100 females: 92.8; Marriage status: 26.8% never married, 52.1% now married, 2.6% separated, 8.3% widowed, 12.7% divorced; Foreign born: 1.0%; Speak English only: 97.6%; With disability: 11.4%; Veterans: 7.9%; Ancestry: 26.9% German, 16.5% English, 12.4% American, 11.2% Irish, 5.4% Italian
Employment: 10.5% management, business, and financial, 2.0% computer, engineering, and science, 8.4% education, legal, community service, arts, and media, 1.6% healthcare practitioners, 17.6% service, 17.3% sales and office, 6.0% natural resources, construction, and maintenance, 36.6% production, transportation, and material moving
Income: Per capita: $23,270; Median household: $49,659; Average household: $59,412; Households with income of $100,000 or more: 12.9%; Poverty rate: 13.6%
Educational Attainment: High school diploma or higher: 87.5%; Bachelor's degree or higher: 14.5%; Graduate/professional degree or higher: 5.4%

School District(s)
Plymouth-Shiloh Local (KG-12)
2015-16 Enrollment: 736. . . . . (419) 687-4733
Housing: Homeownership rate: 67.3%; Median home value: $80,900; Median year structure built: 1944; Homeowner vacancy rate: 3.7%; Median selected monthly owner costs: $1,004 with a mortgage, $388 without a mortgage; Median gross rent: $632 per month; Rental vacancy rate: 7.2%
Health Insurance: 91.1% have insurance; 69.1% have private insurance; 34.2% have public insurance; 8.9% do not have insurance; 5.8% of children under 18 do not have insurance
Transportation: Commute: 96.5% car, 0.0% public transportation, 1.2% walk, 1.8% work from home; Mean travel time to work: 22.8 minutes

SHELBY (city). Covers a land area of 6.348 square miles and a water area of 0.142 square miles. Located at 40.88° N. Lat; 82.66° W. Long. Elevation is 1,099 feet.
Population: 8,751; Growth (since 2000): -10.9%; Density: 1,378.6 persons per square mile; Race: 98.9% White, 0.1% Black/African American, 0.1% Asian, 0.1% American Indian/Alaska Native, 0.0% Native Hawaiian/Other Pacific Islander, 0.7% Two or more races, 2.5% Hispanic of any race; Average household size: 2.20; Median age: 41.9; Age under 18: 22.6%; Age 65 and over: 19.1%; Males per 100 females: 88.6; Marriage status: 24.2% never married, 48.5% now married, 4.5% separated, 11.2% widowed, 16.1% divorced; Foreign born: 0.3%; Speak English only: 98.3%; With disability: 13.8%; Veterans: 8.8%; Ancestry: 31.5% German, 14.8% Irish, 14.1% English, 13.0% American, 5.2% Italian
Employment: 8.7% management, business, and financial, 1.7% computer, engineering, and science, 10.8% education, legal, community service, arts, and media, 3.0% healthcare practitioners, 15.5% service, 24.0% sales and office, 7.5% natural resources, construction, and maintenance, 28.8% production, transportation, and material moving
Income: Per capita: $21,712; Median household: $41,077; Average household: $47,361; Households with income of $100,000 or more: 8.5%; Poverty rate: 10.9%
Educational Attainment: High school diploma or higher: 86.7%; Bachelor's degree or higher: 16.1%; Graduate/professional degree or higher: 6.2%

School District(s)
Pioneer Career & Technology (06-12)
2015-16 Enrollment: n/a . . . . (419) 347-7926
Shelby City (KG-12)
2015-16 Enrollment: 1,816 . . . . (419) 342-3520

Vocational/Technical School(s)
Pioneer Career and Technology Center (Public)
Fall 2016 Enrollment: 11 . . . . (419) 347-7744
2016-17 Tuition: $5,080
Housing: Homeownership rate: 61.4%; Median home value: $90,100; Median year structure built: 1959; Homeowner vacancy rate: 1.8%; Median selected monthly owner costs: $945 with a mortgage, $347 without a mortgage; Median gross rent: $638 per month; Rental vacancy rate: 6.5%
Health Insurance: 91.6% have insurance; 65.1% have private insurance; 42.5% have public insurance; 8.4% do not have insurance; 0.7% of children under 18 do not have insurance
Hospitals: Medcentral Health System Shelby Hospital (68 beds)
Safety: Violent crime rate: 18.9 per 10,000 population; Property crime rate: 286.3 per 10,000 population
Newspapers: Daily Globe (daily circulation 4,000)
Transportation: Commute: 94.0% car, 0.0% public transportation, 4.6% walk, 0.6% work from home; Mean travel time to work: 20.8 minutes

SHILOH (village). Covers a land area of 0.905 square miles and a water area of 0.004 square miles. Located at 40.97° N. Lat; 82.60° W. Long. Elevation is 1,079 feet.
Population: 787; Growth (since 2000): 9.2%; Density: 869.5 persons per square mile; Race: 97.1% White, 0.0% Black/African American, 0.5% Asian, 0.0% American Indian/Alaska Native, 0.0% Native Hawaiian/Other Pacific Islander, 2.4% Two or more races, 1.1% Hispanic of any race; Average household size: 3.21; Median age: 40.6; Age under 18: 29.0%; Age 65 and over: 10.0%; Males per 100 females: 99.7; Marriage status: 24.3% never married, 56.9% now married, 0.7% separated, 8.4% widowed, 10.4% divorced; Foreign born: 2.7%; Speak English only: 95.5%; With disability: 13.7%; Veterans: 5.9%; Ancestry: 25.3% German, 15.8% Irish, 13.1% American, 11.9% English, 5.3% Welsh
Employment: 7.8% management, business, and financial, 2.5% computer, engineering, and science, 5.3% education, legal, community service, arts,

and media, 5.0% healthcare practitioners, 17.6% service, 20.4% sales and office, 11.6% natural resources, construction, and maintenance, 29.8% production, transportation, and material moving
Income: Per capita: $17,188; Median household: $57,813; Average household: $53,275; Households with income of $100,000 or more: 8.6%; Poverty rate: 13.8%
Educational Attainment: High school diploma or higher: 81.7%; Bachelor's degree or higher: 6.3%; Graduate/professional degree or higher: 2.4%
Housing: Homeownership rate: 81.2%; Median home value: $63,600; Median year structure built: Before 1940; Homeowner vacancy rate: 4.8%; Median selected monthly owner costs: $803 with a mortgage, $338 without a mortgage; Median gross rent: $725 per month; Rental vacancy rate: 0.0%
Health Insurance: 91.1% have insurance; 63.9% have private insurance; 35.5% have public insurance; 8.9% do not have insurance; 1.8% of children under 18 do not have insurance
Transportation: Commute: 93.1% car, 0.0% public transportation, 5.7% walk, 0.0% work from home; Mean travel time to work: 24.2 minutes

Ross County

Located in southern Ohio; crossed by the Scioto River and several creeks. Covers a land area of 689.188 square miles, a water area of 3.837 square miles, and is located in the Eastern Time Zone at 39.32° N. Lat., 83.06° W. Long. The county was founded in 1798. County seat is Chillicothe.

Ross County is part of the Chillicothe, OH Micropolitan Statistical Area. The entire metro area includes: Ross County, OH

Weather Station: Chillicothe Mound City Elevation: 649 feet

	Jan	Feb	Mar	Apr	May	Jun	Jul	Aug	Sep	Oct	Nov	Dec
High	38	43	52	65	73	82	86	85	78	67	54	42
Low	20	23	30	40	50	59	63	61	53	41	34	25
Precip	2.6	2.5	3.5	3.6	4.6	3.3	4.0	3.1	2.7	2.6	2.9	2.8
Snow	5.2	4.0	2.4	0.4	tr	0.0	0.0	0.0	0.0	0.1	0.4	2.3

High and Low temperatures in degrees Fahrenheit; Precipitation and Snow in inches

Population: 77,193; Growth (since 2000): 5.2%; Density: 112.0 persons per square mile; Race: 90.3% White, 4.4% Black/African American, 0.5% Asian, 0.1% American Indian/Alaska Native, 0.0% Native Hawaiian/Other Pacific Islander, 4.2% two or more races, 1.2% Hispanic of any race; Average household size: 2.52; Median age: 40.4; Age under 18: 21.8%; Age 65 and over: 15.2%; Males per 100 females: 111.6; Marriage status: 28.2% never married, 50.9% now married, 2.3% separated, 6.3% widowed, 14.6% divorced; Foreign born: 0.9%; Speak English only: 98.0%; With disability: 19.3%; Veterans: 9.8%; Ancestry: 23.7% German, 14.9% Irish, 11.7% American, 9.4% English, 2.2% Italian
Religion: Six largest groups: 5.9% Baptist, 5.5% Methodist/Pietist, 4.2% Non-denominational Protestant, 3.5% Catholicism, 1.9% Holiness, 1.3% Pentecostal
Economy: Unemployment rate: 4.5%; Leading industries: 19.7 % retail trade; 12.5 % health care and social assistance; 11.6 % other services (except public administration); Farms: 980 totaling 221,723 acres; Company size: 4 employ 1,000 or more persons, 0 employ 500 to 999 persons, 28 employ 100 to 499 persons, 1,196 employ less than 100 persons; Business ownership: 1,543 women-owned, 56 Black-owned, 41 Hispanic-owned, 51 Asian-owned, n/a American Indian/Alaska Native-owned
Employment: 8.6% management, business, and financial, 3.2% computer, engineering, and science, 8.5% education, legal, community service, arts, and media, 7.8% healthcare practitioners, 19.6% service, 23.1% sales and office, 8.8% natural resources, construction, and maintenance, 20.3% production, transportation, and material moving
Income: Per capita: $22,158; Median household: $44,587; Average household: $58,839; Households with income of $100,000 or more: 14.3%; Poverty rate: 18.8%
Educational Attainment: High school diploma or higher: 85.7%; Bachelor's degree or higher: 15.3%; Graduate/professional degree or higher: 5.5%
Housing: Homeownership rate: 70.9%; Median home value: $111,700; Median year structure built: 1972; Homeowner vacancy rate: 1.9%; Median selected monthly owner costs: $1,082 with a mortgage, $376 without a mortgage; Median gross rent: $685 per month; Rental vacancy rate: 4.8%
Vital Statistics: Birth rate: 116.0 per 10,000 population; Death rate: 106.2 per 10,000 population; Age-adjusted cancer mortality rate: 198.2 deaths per 100,000 population
Health Insurance: 91.1% have insurance; 62.8% have private insurance; 42.0% have public insurance; 8.9% do not have insurance; 5.3% of children under 18 do not have insurance
Health Care: Physicians: 20.1 per 10,000 population; Dentists: 5.3 per 10,000 population; Hospital beds: 66.4 per 10,000 population; Hospital admissions: 1,819.2 per 10,000 population
Transportation: Commute: 94.2% car, 0.8% public transportation, 1.7% walk, 2.1% work from home; Mean travel time to work: 26.5 minutes
2016 Presidential Election: 61.0% Trump, 33.9% Clinton, 3.1% Johnson, 0.7% Stein
National and State Parks: Adena State Memorial; Great Seal State Park; Hopewell Culture National Historical Park; Paint Creek State Park; Ross County Lake State Wildlife Area; Scioto River Canal Lands Access State Wildlife Area; Scioto Trail State Forest; Scioto Trail State Park; Seip Mound State Memorial; Story Mound State Memorial; Tar Hollow State Forest

Additional Information Contacts
Ross Government . . . . (740) 702-3085
http://www.co.ross.oh.us

Ross County Communities

ADELPHI (village). Covers a land area of 0.274 square miles and a water area of <.001 square miles. Located at 39.46° N. Lat; 82.75° W. Long. Elevation is 837 feet.
Population: 289; Growth (since 2000): -22.1%; Density: 1,054.3 persons per square mile; Race: 96.5% White, 0.0% Black/African American, 0.0% Asian, 0.0% American Indian/Alaska Native, 0.0% Native Hawaiian/Other Pacific Islander, 3.5% Two or more races, 0.0% Hispanic of any race; Average household size: 2.49; Median age: 45.1; Age under 18: 24.9%; Age 65 and over: 20.8%; Males per 100 females: 104.3; Marriage status: 29.2% never married, 45.1% now married, 0.9% separated, 10.3% widowed, 15.5% divorced; Foreign born: 0.0%; Speak English only: 97.1%; With disability: 29.8%; Veterans: 10.6%; Ancestry: 20.1% German, 14.9% American, 13.8% Irish, 10.7% English, 5.9% French
Employment: 5.7% management, business, and financial, 0.0% computer, engineering, and science, 1.9% education, legal, community service, arts, and media, 3.8% healthcare practitioners, 29.2% service, 21.7% sales and office, 16.0% natural resources, construction, and maintenance, 21.7% production, transportation, and material moving
Income: Per capita: $15,877; Median household: $35,500; Average household: $37,831; Households with income of $100,000 or more: 1.7%; Poverty rate: 26.3%
Educational Attainment: High school diploma or higher: 69.0%; Bachelor's degree or higher: 5.5%; Graduate/professional degree or higher: n/a
Housing: Homeownership rate: 72.4%; Median home value: $85,000; Median year structure built: 1955; Homeowner vacancy rate: 0.0%; Median selected monthly owner costs: $1,016 with a mortgage, $346 without a mortgage; Median gross rent: $575 per month; Rental vacancy rate: 11.1%
Health Insurance: 91.3% have insurance; 46.7% have private insurance; 58.1% have public insurance; 8.7% do not have insurance; 0.0% of children under 18 do not have insurance
Transportation: Commute: 76.4% car, 15.1% public transportation, 8.5% walk, 0.0% work from home; Mean travel time to work: 25.2 minutes

ANDERSONVILLE (CDP). Covers a land area of 2.274 square miles and a water area of 0 square miles. Located at 39.43° N. Lat; 83.02° W. Long. Elevation is 653 feet.
Population: 760; Growth (since 2000): n/a; Density: 334.2 persons per square mile; Race: 98.4% White, 1.3% Black/African American, 0.0% Asian, 0.0% American Indian/Alaska Native, 0.0% Native Hawaiian/Other Pacific Islander, 0.3% Two or more races, 0.0% Hispanic of any race; Average household size: 2.63; Median age: 41.9; Age under 18: 18.4%; Age 65 and over: 17.5%; Males per 100 females: 93.3; Marriage status: 22.6% never married, 61.8% now married, 1.7% separated, 2.8% widowed, 12.9% divorced; Foreign born: 0.7%; Speak English only: 97.7%; With disability: 12.0%; Veterans: 14.2%; Ancestry: 31.6% German, 16.8% Irish, 14.1% American, 12.4% English, 5.3% Dutch
Employment: 8.9% management, business, and financial, 9.4% computer, engineering, and science, 9.4% education, legal, community service, arts, and media, 7.3% healthcare practitioners, 22.8% service, 18.3% sales and

office, 7.9% natural resources, construction, and maintenance, 16.0% production, transportation, and material moving
Income: Per capita: $26,971; Median household: $63,875; Average household: $68,248; Households with income of $100,000 or more: 18.3%; Poverty rate: 14.5%
Educational Attainment: High school diploma or higher: 94.7%; Bachelor's degree or higher: 23.2%; Graduate/professional degree or higher: 11.4%
Housing: Homeownership rate: 85.5%; Median home value: $151,300; Median year structure built: 1984; Homeowner vacancy rate: 0.0%; Median selected monthly owner costs: $1,309 with a mortgage, $449 without a mortgage; Median gross rent: $611 per month; Rental vacancy rate: 0.0%
Health Insurance: 93.9% have insurance; 75.5% have private insurance; 32.8% have public insurance; 6.1% do not have insurance; 0.0% of children under 18 do not have insurance
Transportation: Commute: 97.3% car, 0.0% public transportation, 0.0% walk, 2.7% work from home; Mean travel time to work: 24.4 minutes

BAINBRIDGE (village). Covers a land area of 0.512 square miles and a water area of 0 square miles. Located at 39.23° N. Lat; 83.27° W. Long. Elevation is 735 feet.
History: Bainbridge was founded in 1805 by Nathaniel Massie, a landowner and surveyor. In 1826 Dr. John Harris established a school for teaching dentistry here, where Chapin A. Harris was trained. Harris later founded the dental college at Baltimore and the "American Journal of Dental Science."
Population: 729; Growth (since 2000): -28.0%; Density: 1,423.4 persons per square mile; Race: 96.3% White, 0.5% Black/African American, 0.0% Asian, 0.0% American Indian/Alaska Native, 0.0% Native Hawaiian/Other Pacific Islander, 3.2% Two or more races, 0.7% Hispanic of any race; Average household size: 2.29; Median age: 41.3; Age under 18: 20.7%; Age 65 and over: 17.3%; Males per 100 females: 84.9; Marriage status: 22.9% never married, 52.3% now married, 4.2% separated, 9.4% widowed, 15.5% divorced; Foreign born: 1.0%; Speak English only: 99.0%; With disability: 27.8%; Veterans: 4.8%; Ancestry: 18.4% German, 17.1% English, 10.6% Irish, 9.7% Dutch, 5.2% American
Employment: 15.0% management, business, and financial, 1.5% computer, engineering, and science, 6.9% education, legal, community service, arts, and media, 16.5% healthcare practitioners, 18.5% service, 12.7% sales and office, 9.6% natural resources, construction, and maintenance, 19.2% production, transportation, and material moving
Income: Per capita: $16,249; Median household: $30,391; Average household: $37,001; Households with income of $100,000 or more: 4.2%; Poverty rate: 31.1%
Educational Attainment: High school diploma or higher: 74.2%; Bachelor's degree or higher: 9.8%; Graduate/professional degree or higher: 1.5%

School District(s)

Paint Valley Local (PK-12)
2015-16 Enrollment: 862 . . . . (740) 634-2826

Housing: Homeownership rate: 61.7%; Median home value: $84,200; Median year structure built: Before 1940; Homeowner vacancy rate: 2.5%; Median selected monthly owner costs: $880 with a mortgage, $345 without a mortgage; Median gross rent: $558 per month; Rental vacancy rate: 0.0%
Health Insurance: 82.6% have insurance; 42.9% have private insurance; 49.9% have public insurance; 17.4% do not have insurance; 6.6% of children under 18 do not have insurance
Transportation: Commute: 88.5% car, 0.0% public transportation, 4.2% walk, 1.2% work from home; Mean travel time to work: 31.4 minutes

BOURNEVILLE (CDP). Covers a land area of 0.503 square miles and a water area of 0 square miles. Located at 39.28° N. Lat; 83.16° W. Long. Elevation is 679 feet.
Population: 265; Growth (since 2000): n/a; Density: 527.4 persons per square mile; Race: 45.7% White, 0.0% Black/African American, 0.0% Asian, 0.0% American Indian/Alaska Native, 0.0% Native Hawaiian/Other Pacific Islander, 54.3% Two or more races, 37.4% Hispanic of any race; Average household size: 3.12; Median age: 30.7; Age under 18: 40.4%; Age 65 and over: 0.0%; Males per 100 females: 80.9; Marriage status: 0.0% never married, 100.0% now married, 0.0% separated, 0.0% widowed, 0.0% divorced; Foreign born: 0.0%; Speak English only: 100.0%; With disability: 0.0%; Veterans: 0.0%; Ancestry: 95.5% Irish, 23.0% Welsh, 4.5% Dutch West Indian
Employment: 0.0% management, business, and financial, 0.0% computer, engineering, and science, 0.0% education, legal, community service, arts, and media, 0.0% healthcare practitioners, 100.0% service, 0.0% sales and office, 0.0% natural resources, construction, and maintenance, 0.0% production, transportation, and material moving
Income: Per capita: $5,762; Median household: n/a; Average household: n/a; Households with income of $100,000 or more: n/a; Poverty rate: n/a
Educational Attainment: High school diploma or higher: 92.4%; Bachelor's degree or higher: n/a; Graduate/professional degree or higher: n/a
Housing: Homeownership rate: 70.6%; Median home value: n/a; Median year structure built: n/a; Homeowner vacancy rate: 0.0%; Median selected monthly owner costs: n/a with a mortgage, n/a without a mortgage; Median gross rent: n/a per month; Rental vacancy rate: 0.0%
Health Insurance: 77.0% have insurance; 0.0% have private insurance; 77.0% have public insurance; 23.0% do not have insurance; 0.0% of children under 18 do not have insurance
Transportation: Commute: 100.0% car, 0.0% public transportation, 0.0% walk, 0.0% work from home; Mean travel time to work: 0.0 minutes

CHILLICOTHE (city). County seat. Covers a land area of 10.428 square miles and a water area of 0.167 square miles. Located at 39.34° N. Lat; 82.99° W. Long. Elevation is 633 feet.
History: In 1796 Nathaniel Massie established a community of settlers on the Scioto River at the mouth of Paint Creek. When Edward Tiffin and other young men came from Virginia in 1798, the town of Chillicothe was founded and became the capitol of the Northwest Territory. Ohio became a state in 1803, and Chillicothe continued as the capitol until 1810. Then industrial growth replaced the business of state, and the first paper mill was founded in 1812. By 1815 a flour mill was turning out 50 barrels daily, and by 1835, when the canal made agriculture profitable, cereal mills constructed along its banks shipped their products east and south. By 1890 the town had factories manufacturing a variety of items, including the Champion bed lounge, Mosher ratchet jack, Neely razor blade, Scioto grain elevator, and Crown baking powder and spices.
Population: 21,748; Growth (since 2000): -0.2%; Density: 2,085.5 persons per square mile; Race: 87.9% White, 5.0% Black/African American, 0.8% Asian, 0.0% American Indian/Alaska Native, 0.1% Native Hawaiian/Other Pacific Islander, 5.8% Two or more races, 0.9% Hispanic of any race; Average household size: 2.26; Median age: 43.3; Age under 18: 20.5%; Age 65 and over: 20.4%; Males per 100 females: 90.8; Marriage status: 29.0% never married, 42.6% now married, 2.7% separated, 9.2% widowed, 19.2% divorced; Foreign born: 1.1%; Speak English only: 97.9%; With disability: 23.1%; Veterans: 11.9%; Ancestry: 24.3% German, 14.6% Irish, 11.7% American, 9.5% English, 2.5% Italian
Employment: 7.7% management, business, and financial, 2.9% computer, engineering, and science, 8.2% education, legal, community service, arts, and media, 8.0% healthcare practitioners, 23.9% service, 24.8% sales and office, 8.4% natural resources, construction, and maintenance, 16.0% production, transportation, and material moving
Income: Per capita: $22,890; Median household: $37,757; Average household: $51,700; Households with income of $100,000 or more: 11.3%; Poverty rate: 22.5%
Educational Attainment: High school diploma or higher: 85.6%; Bachelor's degree or higher: 18.8%; Graduate/professional degree or higher: 7.3%

School District(s)

Chillicothe City (PK-12)
2015-16 Enrollment: 2,979 . . . . (740) 775-4250
Huntington Local (KG-12)
2015-16 Enrollment: 1,178 . . . . (740) 663-5892
Pickaway-Ross County Jvsd (07-12)
2015-16 Enrollment: n/a . . . . (740) 642-1200
Southeastern Local (PK-12)
2015-16 Enrollment: 1,117 . . . . (740) 774-2003
Union-Scioto Local (PK-12)
2015-16 Enrollment: 2,153 . . . . (740) 773-4102
Zane Trace Local (KG-12)
2015-16 Enrollment: 1,344 . . . . (740) 775-1355

Four-year College(s)

Ohio University-Chillicothe Campus (Public)
Fall 2016 Enrollment: 1,774 . . . . (740) 774-7200
2016-17 Tuition: In-state $5,060; Out-of-state $9,596

Vocational/Technical School(s)

Pickaway Ross Joint Vocational School District (Public)
Fall 2016 Enrollment: 306 . . . . (740) 642-1200
2016-17 Tuition: $539

Housing: Homeownership rate: 58.4%; Median home value: $98,900; Median year structure built: 1954; Homeowner vacancy rate: 4.4%; Median selected monthly owner costs: $1,039 with a mortgage, $365 without a mortgage; Median gross rent: $701 per month; Rental vacancy rate: 6.6%
Health Insurance: 89.4% have insurance; 55.3% have private insurance; 50.6% have public insurance; 10.6% do not have insurance; 4.6% of children under 18 do not have insurance
Hospitals: Adena Regional Medical Center (238 beds); Chillicothe VA Medical Center (297 beds)
Safety: Violent crime rate: 43.3 per 10,000 population; Property crime rate: 805.4 per 10,000 population
Newspapers: Chillicothe Gazette (daily circulation 14,500)
Transportation: Commute: 92.7% car, 0.8% public transportation, 2.9% walk, 2.3% work from home; Mean travel time to work: 20.3 minutes
Airports: Ross County (general aviation)
Additional Information Contacts
City of Chillicothe. . . . . (740) 774-1185
http://ci.chillicothe.oh.us

CLARKSBURG (village). Covers a land area of 0.173 square miles and a water area of 0 square miles. Located at 39.51° N. Lat; 83.15° W. Long. Elevation is 771 feet.
Population: 497; Growth (since 2000): -3.7%; Density: 2,880.8 persons per square mile; Race: 94.8% White, 1.2% Black/African American, 0.0% Asian, 0.0% American Indian/Alaska Native, 0.0% Native Hawaiian/Other Pacific Islander, 4.0% Two or more races, 0.4% Hispanic of any race; Average household size: 2.73; Median age: 28.0; Age under 18: 31.4%; Age 65 and over: 12.7%; Males per 100 females: 89.6; Marriage status: 31.4% never married, 43.9% now married, 1.4% separated, 9.7% widowed, 15.0% divorced; Foreign born: 0.0%; Speak English only: 98.1%; With disability: 31.2%; Veterans: 10.0%; Ancestry: 32.6% German, 14.5% Irish, 7.0% English, 6.4% American, 2.6% Scottish
Employment: 6.5% management, business, and financial, 0.0% computer, engineering, and science, 2.4% education, legal, community service, arts, and media, 5.6% healthcare practitioners, 31.5% service, 12.9% sales and office, 6.5% natural resources, construction, and maintenance, 34.7% production, transportation, and material moving
Income: Per capita: $12,822; Median household: $22,159; Average household: $34,615; Households with income of $100,000 or more: 4.4%; Poverty rate: 45.0%
Educational Attainment: High school diploma or higher: 77.5%; Bachelor's degree or higher: 8.7%; Graduate/professional degree or higher: 0.7%
Housing: Homeownership rate: 51.6%; Median home value: $64,300; Median year structure built: 1948; Homeowner vacancy rate: 4.0%; Median selected monthly owner costs: $940 with a mortgage, $394 without a mortgage; Median gross rent: $511 per month; Rental vacancy rate: 0.0%
Health Insurance: 89.7% have insurance; 34.8% have private insurance; 64.6% have public insurance; 10.3% do not have insurance; 8.3% of children under 18 do not have insurance
Transportation: Commute: 88.7% car, 8.1% public transportation, 0.0% walk, 1.6% work from home; Mean travel time to work: 27.5 minutes

FRANKFORT (village). Covers a land area of 0.564 square miles and a water area of 0 square miles. Located at 39.40° N. Lat; 83.18° W. Long. Elevation is 738 feet.
History: Frankfort was established on the site of a Shawnee village that was burned and plundered by Simon Kenton in 1787.
Population: 1,118; Growth (since 2000): 10.6%; Density: 1,983.7 persons per square mile; Race: 89.8% White, 6.0% Black/African American, 0.0% Asian, 0.0% American Indian/Alaska Native, 0.0% Native Hawaiian/Other Pacific Islander, 4.2% Two or more races, 0.7% Hispanic of any race; Average household size: 2.26; Median age: 42.8; Age under 18: 22.2%; Age 65 and over: 18.4%; Males per 100 females: 88.7; Marriage status: 23.8% never married, 51.5% now married, 1.3% separated, 10.9% widowed, 13.8% divorced; Foreign born: 0.5%; Speak English only: 98.5%; With disability: 18.3%; Veterans: 8.9%; Ancestry: 20.9% German, 14.0% Irish, 11.3% English, 10.3% American, 3.6% Italian
Employment: 5.9% management, business, and financial, 0.0% computer, engineering, and science, 13.0% education, legal, community service, arts, and media, 15.5% healthcare practitioners, 30.4% service, 12.8% sales and office, 4.6% natural resources, construction, and maintenance, 17.8% production, transportation, and material moving
Income: Per capita: $20,098; Median household: $31,477; Average household: $45,418; Households with income of $100,000 or more: 10.1%; Poverty rate: 18.5%
Educational Attainment: High school diploma or higher: 82.7%; Bachelor's degree or higher: 12.7%; Graduate/professional degree or higher: 7.3%

School District(s)

Adena Local (PK-12)
2015-16 Enrollment: 1,217 . . . . (740) 998-4633

Housing: Homeownership rate: 58.4%; Median home value: $106,300; Median year structure built: 1972; Homeowner vacancy rate: 6.5%; Median selected monthly owner costs: $1,100 with a mortgage, $492 without a mortgage; Median gross rent: $615 per month; Rental vacancy rate: 4.3%
Health Insurance: 91.2% have insurance; 65.5% have private insurance; 40.9% have public insurance; 8.8% do not have insurance; 1.6% of children under 18 do not have insurance
Transportation: Commute: 90.3% car, 0.0% public transportation, 3.7% walk, 4.4% work from home; Mean travel time to work: 23.4 minutes

KINGSTON (village). Covers a land area of 0.369 square miles and a water area of 0 square miles. Located at 39.47° N. Lat; 82.91° W. Long. Elevation is 791 feet.
Population: 1,029; Growth (since 2000): -0.3%; Density: 2,789.8 persons per square mile; Race: 95.1% White, 0.0% Black/African American, 0.0% Asian, 0.0% American Indian/Alaska Native, 0.0% Native Hawaiian/Other Pacific Islander, 4.9% Two or more races, 0.7% Hispanic of any race; Average household size: 2.34; Median age: 45.8; Age under 18: 17.1%; Age 65 and over: 21.8%; Males per 100 females: 93.6; Marriage status: 24.1% never married, 52.4% now married, 1.8% separated, 4.3% widowed, 19.2% divorced; Foreign born: 0.6%; Speak English only: 97.8%; With disability: 19.8%; Veterans: 9.4%; Ancestry: 25.3% German, 23.7% Irish, 12.7% English, 7.0% American, 5.5% Welsh
Employment: 5.9% management, business, and financial, 0.0% computer, engineering, and science, 2.8% education, legal, community service, arts, and media, 8.9% healthcare practitioners, 22.5% service, 28.2% sales and office, 5.4% natural resources, construction, and maintenance, 26.3% production, transportation, and material moving
Income: Per capita: $21,706; Median household: $44,313; Average household: $49,361; Households with income of $100,000 or more: 9.1%; Poverty rate: 20.6%
Educational Attainment: High school diploma or higher: 89.0%; Bachelor's degree or higher: 11.6%; Graduate/professional degree or higher: 4.1%

School District(s)

Logan Elm Local (PK-12)
2015-16 Enrollment: 1,826 . . . . (740) 474-7501

Housing: Homeownership rate: 64.9%; Median home value: $95,400; Median year structure built: 1954; Homeowner vacancy rate: 0.0%; Median selected monthly owner costs: $887 with a mortgage, $360 without a mortgage; Median gross rent: $788 per month; Rental vacancy rate: 6.1%
Health Insurance: 90.0% have insurance; 61.2% have private insurance; 45.7% have public insurance; 10.0% do not have insurance; 11.4% of children under 18 do not have insurance
Transportation: Commute: 97.5% car, 0.0% public transportation, 1.8% walk, 0.8% work from home; Mean travel time to work: 31.9 minutes

LONDONDERRY (unincorporated postal area)
ZCTA: 45647
Covers a land area of 66.486 square miles and a water area of 0.144 square miles. Located at 39.29° N. Lat; 82.73° W. Long. Elevation is 686 feet.
Population: 2,448; Growth (since 2000): 29.6%; Density: 36.8 persons per square mile; Race: 96.9% White, 0.0% Black/African American, 0.0% Asian, 0.2% American Indian/Alaska Native, 0.0% Native Hawaiian/Other Pacific Islander, 2.9% Two or more races, 0.0% Hispanic of any race; Average household size: 2.71; Median age: 47.4; Age under 18: 19.0%; Age 65 and over: 20.0%; Males per 100 females: 104.6; Marriage status: 19.2% never married, 62.7% now married, 2.0% separated, 4.5% widowed, 13.6% divorced; Foreign born: 0.4%; Speak English only: 95.1%; With disability: 20.8%; Veterans: 8.2%; Ancestry: 24.4% German, 10.6% Irish, 9.3% English, 7.9% American, 1.8% European
Employment: 11.8% management, business, and financial, 0.0% computer, engineering, and science, 6.1% education, legal, community

service, arts, and media, 0.0% healthcare practitioners, 24.4% service, 18.7% sales and office, 20.0% natural resources, construction, and maintenance, 19.1% production, transportation, and material moving
Income: Per capita: $19,497; Median household: $51,905; Average household: $51,027; Households with income of $100,000 or more: 3.3%; Poverty rate: 6.5%
Educational Attainment: High school diploma or higher: 85.8%; Bachelor's degree or higher: 5.1%; Graduate/professional degree or higher: n/a
Housing: Homeownership rate: 82.4%; Median home value: $79,700; Median year structure built: 1979; Homeowner vacancy rate: 0.0%; Median selected monthly owner costs: $1,099 with a mortgage, $378 without a mortgage; Median gross rent: $547 per month; Rental vacancy rate: 0.0%
Health Insurance: 84.2% have insurance; 65.0% have private insurance; 39.1% have public insurance; 15.8% do not have insurance; 18.7% of children under 18 do not have insurance
Transportation: Commute: 87.5% car, 0.0% public transportation, 1.4% walk, 8.1% work from home; Mean travel time to work: 37.1 minutes

RICHMOND DALE (CDP). Covers a land area of 0.496 square miles and a water area of 0 square miles. Located at 39.20° N. Lat; 82.81° W. Long. Elevation is 594 feet.
Population: 490; Growth (since 2000): n/a; Density: 987.3 persons per square mile; Race: 93.7% White, 0.0% Black/African American, 0.0% Asian, 0.0% American Indian/Alaska Native, 0.0% Native Hawaiian/Other Pacific Islander, 6.3% Two or more races, 0.0% Hispanic of any race; Average household size: 2.83; Median age: 27.4; Age under 18: 37.6%; Age 65 and over: 5.7%; Males per 100 females: 98.4; Marriage status: 26.8% never married, 61.4% now married, 8.3% separated, 0.0% widowed, 11.8% divorced; Foreign born: 0.0%; Speak English only: 96.4%; With disability: 27.8%; Veterans: 16.0%; Ancestry: 33.7% Irish, 29.0% American, 26.7% German, 17.1% English, 13.1% Scottish
Employment: 10.7% management, business, and financial, 20.0% computer, engineering, and science, 10.7% education, legal, community service, arts, and media, 0.0% healthcare practitioners, 0.0% service, 22.7% sales and office, 0.0% natural resources, construction, and maintenance, 36.0% production, transportation, and material moving
Income: Per capita: $15,352; Median household: n/a; Average household: $43,673; Households with income of $100,000 or more: n/a; Poverty rate: 20.0%
Educational Attainment: High school diploma or higher: 83.8%; Bachelor's degree or higher: n/a; Graduate/professional degree or higher: n/a
Housing: Homeownership rate: 55.5%; Median home value: $76,100; Median year structure built: 1951; Homeowner vacancy rate: 0.0%; Median selected monthly owner costs: $1,314 with a mortgage, n/a without a mortgage; Median gross rent: $673 per month; Rental vacancy rate: 0.0%
Health Insurance: 96.7% have insurance; 76.7% have private insurance; 25.7% have public insurance; 3.3% do not have insurance; 0.0% of children under 18 do not have insurance
Transportation: Commute: 100.0% car, 0.0% public transportation, 0.0% walk, 0.0% work from home; Mean travel time to work: 39.6 minutes

SOUTH SALEM (village). Covers a land area of 0.206 square miles and a water area of 0 square miles. Located at 39.34° N. Lat; 83.31° W. Long. Elevation is 928 feet.
Population: 252; Growth (since 2000): 18.3%; Density: 1,223.2 persons per square mile; Race: 98.8% White, 0.0% Black/African American, 0.0% Asian, 0.0% American Indian/Alaska Native, 0.0% Native Hawaiian/Other Pacific Islander, 1.2% Two or more races, 0.0% Hispanic of any race; Average household size: 2.71; Median age: 35.1; Age under 18: 31.3%; Age 65 and over: 9.5%; Males per 100 females: 96.2; Marriage status: 24.5% never married, 58.5% now married, 0.5% separated, 6.4% widowed, 10.6% divorced; Foreign born: 0.0%; Speak English only: 99.1%; With disability: 17.5%; Veterans: 8.7%; Ancestry: 13.1% Irish, 11.9% German, 10.7% English, 7.5% American, 2.4% Scotch-Irish
Employment: 4.3% management, business, and financial, 0.0% computer, engineering, and science, 10.6% education, legal, community service, arts, and media, 2.1% healthcare practitioners, 9.6% service, 16.0% sales and office, 20.2% natural resources, construction, and maintenance, 37.2% production, transportation, and material moving
Income: Per capita: $15,296; Median household: $36,528; Average household: $40,756; Households with income of $100,000 or more: 2.2%; Poverty rate: 27.7%
Educational Attainment: High school diploma or higher: 86.8%; Bachelor's degree or higher: 8.2%; Graduate/professional degree or higher: 5.7%

School District(s)

Greenfield Exempted Village (PK-12)
2015-16 Enrollment: 2,019 . . . . (937) 981-2152
Housing: Homeownership rate: 65.6%; Median home value: $65,000; Median year structure built: Before 1940; Homeowner vacancy rate: 0.0%; Median selected monthly owner costs: $789 with a mortgage, $350 without a mortgage; Median gross rent: $746 per month; Rental vacancy rate: 0.0%
Health Insurance: 90.1% have insurance; 57.9% have private insurance; 45.2% have public insurance; 9.9% do not have insurance; 6.3% of children under 18 do not have insurance
Transportation: Commute: 95.6% car, 0.0% public transportation, 4.4% walk, 0.0% work from home; Mean travel time to work: 26.9 minutes

Sandusky County

Located in northern Ohio; bounded on the northeast by Sandusky Bay of Lake Erie; crossed by the Sandusky and Portage Rivers. Covers a land area of 408.453 square miles, a water area of 9.254 square miles, and is located in the Eastern Time Zone at 41.36° N. Lat., 83.14° W. Long. The county was founded in 1820. County seat is Fremont.

Sandusky County is part of the Fremont, OH Micropolitan Statistical Area. The entire metro area includes: Sandusky County, OH

Weather Station: Fremont — Elevation: 600 feet

	Jan	Feb	Mar	Apr	May	Jun	Jul	Aug	Sep	Oct	Nov	Dec
High	32	36	46	59	70	80	84	82	75	63	50	37
Low	17	20	28	38	49	59	63	61	53	41	33	23
Precip	2.3	2.2	2.6	3.4	4.0	4.1	3.6	3.2	3.1	2.9	2.9	2.9
Snow	8.0	6.3	4.1	0.5	tr	0.0	0.0	0.0	0.0	tr	0.6	5.0

High and Low temperatures in degrees Fahrenheit; Precipitation and Snow in inches

Population: 59,870; Growth (since 2000): -3.1%; Density: 146.6 persons per square mile; Race: 90.5% White, 3.2% Black/African American, 0.4% Asian, 0.2% American Indian/Alaska Native, 0.0% Native Hawaiian/Other Pacific Islander, 2.2% two or more races, 9.5% Hispanic of any race; Average household size: 2.48; Median age: 41.5; Age under 18: 23.2%; Age 65 and over: 17.1%; Males per 100 females: 96.9; Marriage status: 27.9% never married, 53.1% now married, 1.5% separated, 7.0% widowed, 12.0% divorced; Foreign born: 1.5%; Speak English only: 94.8%; With disability: 14.4%; Veterans: 9.1%; Ancestry: 42.6% German, 12.1% Irish, 6.9% English, 6.4% American, 3.9% Polish
Religion: Six largest groups: 20.3% Catholicism, 10.1% Lutheran, 6.2% Methodist/Pietist, 4.1% Non-denominational Protestant, 1.6% Pentecostal, 1.6% Presbyterian-Reformed
Economy: Unemployment rate: 4.1%; Leading industries: 14.9 % retail trade; 13.3 % health care and social assistance; 11.6 % other services (except public administration); Farms: 737 totaling 181,440 acres; Company size: 1 employs 1,000 or more persons, 1 employs 500 to 999 persons, 37 employ 100 to 499 persons, 1,282 employ less than 100 persons; Business ownership: 1,273 women-owned, 101 Black-owned, 165 Hispanic-owned, n/a Asian-owned, 86 American Indian/Alaska Native-owned
Employment: 9.9% management, business, and financial, 3.1% computer, engineering, and science, 7.2% education, legal, community service, arts, and media, 4.5% healthcare practitioners, 15.9% service, 19.7% sales and office, 10.7% natural resources, construction, and maintenance, 28.9% production, transportation, and material moving
Income: Per capita: $24,467; Median household: $49,032; Average household: $59,934; Households with income of $100,000 or more: 14.8%; Poverty rate: 13.2%
Educational Attainment: High school diploma or higher: 89.3%; Bachelor's degree or higher: 14.8%; Graduate/professional degree or higher: 4.8%
Housing: Homeownership rate: 73.6%; Median home value: $111,300; Median year structure built: 1958; Homeowner vacancy rate: 2.2%; Median selected monthly owner costs: $1,069 with a mortgage, $408 without a mortgage; Median gross rent: $646 per month; Rental vacancy rate: 9.8%
Vital Statistics: Birth rate: 103.8 per 10,000 population; Death rate: 102.5 per 10,000 population; Age-adjusted cancer mortality rate: 201.5 deaths per 100,000 population

Health Insurance: 93.1% have insurance; 73.7% have private insurance; 34.3% have public insurance; 6.9% do not have insurance; 4.2% of children under 18 do not have insurance
Health Care: Physicians: 11.8 per 10,000 population; Dentists: 5.2 per 10,000 population; Hospital beds: 8.2 per 10,000 population; Hospital admissions: 233.2 per 10,000 population
Transportation: Commute: 93.9% car, 0.5% public transportation, 2.3% walk, 2.6% work from home; Mean travel time to work: 19.8 minutes
2016 Presidential Election: 57.7% Trump, 35.1% Clinton, 4.5% Johnson, 1.1% Stein
National and State Parks: Green Springs State Nursery; Pfizer State Park; Sandusky Scenic River State Access Area; Spiegel Grove State Park
Additional Information Contacts
Sandusky Government . . . . (419) 334-6100
http://www.sandusky-county.org

Sandusky County Communities

BALLVILLE (CDP). Covers a land area of 2.703 square miles and a water area of 0.205 square miles. Located at 41.33° N. Lat; 83.13° W. Long. Elevation is 623 feet.
Population: 2,881; Growth (since 2000): -11.5%; Density: 1,065.9 persons per square mile; Race: 95.5% White, 2.1% Black/African American, 0.0% Asian, 0.2% American Indian/Alaska Native, 0.0% Native Hawaiian/Other Pacific Islander, 0.0% Two or more races, 6.3% Hispanic of any race; Average household size: 2.26; Median age: 51.5; Age under 18: 18.8%; Age 65 and over: 25.9%; Males per 100 females: 95.5; Marriage status: 17.9% never married, 66.0% now married, 0.0% separated, 6.7% widowed, 9.4% divorced; Foreign born: 0.8%; Speak English only: 96.7%; With disability: 11.9%; Veterans: 9.0%; Ancestry: 53.8% German, 18.2% Irish, 9.1% English, 5.8% American, 3.7% French
Employment: 11.0% management, business, and financial, 3.3% computer, engineering, and science, 10.5% education, legal, community service, arts, and media, 9.9% healthcare practitioners, 13.0% service, 26.1% sales and office, 4.2% natural resources, construction, and maintenance, 21.9% production, transportation, and material moving
Income: Per capita: $29,327; Median household: $53,773; Average household: $65,560; Households with income of $100,000 or more: 18.4%; Poverty rate: 6.1%
Educational Attainment: High school diploma or higher: 94.1%; Bachelor's degree or higher: 27.2%; Graduate/professional degree or higher: 10.9%
Housing: Homeownership rate: 88.6%; Median home value: $147,100; Median year structure built: 1968; Homeowner vacancy rate: 0.0%; Median selected monthly owner costs: $1,259 with a mortgage, $450 without a mortgage; Median gross rent: $719 per month; Rental vacancy rate: 0.0%
Health Insurance: 94.6% have insurance; 81.5% have private insurance; 33.7% have public insurance; 5.4% do not have insurance; 4.6% of children under 18 do not have insurance
Transportation: Commute: 93.6% car, 0.0% public transportation, 4.4% walk, 1.4% work from home; Mean travel time to work: 15.0 minutes

BELLEVUE (city). Covers a land area of 6.136 square miles and a water area of 0.118 square miles. Located at 41.27° N. Lat; 82.84° W. Long. Elevation is 751 feet.
History: Bellevue was established as a railroad town in 1839 and named by James Bell, a railroad employee.
Population: 8,059; Growth (since 2000): -1.6%; Density: 1,313.4 persons per square mile; Race: 98.8% White, 0.2% Black/African American, 0.1% Asian, 0.1% American Indian/Alaska Native, 0.0% Native Hawaiian/Other Pacific Islander, 0.8% Two or more races, 3.3% Hispanic of any race; Average household size: 2.54; Median age: 37.4; Age under 18: 24.6%; Age 65 and over: 14.7%; Males per 100 females: 91.8; Marriage status: 28.5% never married, 51.5% now married, 3.6% separated, 8.5% widowed, 11.5% divorced; Foreign born: 1.6%; Speak English only: 98.4%; With disability: 12.7%; Veterans: 7.2%; Ancestry: 41.4% German, 12.9% Irish, 10.2% English, 9.1% Italian, 7.1% American
Employment: 7.9% management, business, and financial, 3.1% computer, engineering, and science, 9.1% education, legal, community service, arts, and media, 5.8% healthcare practitioners, 18.5% service, 18.2% sales and office, 10.2% natural resources, construction, and maintenance, 27.3% production, transportation, and material moving
Income: Per capita: $23,421; Median household: $49,017; Average household: $58,791; Households with income of $100,000 or more: 14.4%; Poverty rate: 9.1%
Educational Attainment: High school diploma or higher: 92.8%; Bachelor's degree or higher: 13.9%; Graduate/professional degree or higher: 5.4%

School District(s)

Bellevue City (PK-12)
2015-16 Enrollment: 1,973 . . . . (419) 484-5000
Housing: Homeownership rate: 70.4%; Median home value: $96,900; Median year structure built: 1954; Homeowner vacancy rate: 2.3%; Median selected monthly owner costs: $980 with a mortgage, $394 without a mortgage; Median gross rent: $626 per month; Rental vacancy rate: 10.7%
Health Insurance: 94.2% have insurance; 76.9% have private insurance; 31.3% have public insurance; 5.8% do not have insurance; 3.8% of children under 18 do not have insurance
Hospitals: Bellevue Hospital (64 beds)
Newspapers: Bellevue Gazette (daily circulation 2,800)
Transportation: Commute: 92.8% car, 0.0% public transportation, 1.7% walk, 3.3% work from home; Mean travel time to work: 19.3 minutes
Additional Information Contacts
City of Bellevue . . . . (419) 484-8400
http://www.cityofbellevue.com

BURGOON (village). Covers a land area of 0.121 square miles and a water area of 0 square miles. Located at 41.27° N. Lat; 83.25° W. Long. Elevation is 705 feet.
Population: 166; Growth (since 2000): -16.6%; Density: 1,366.9 persons per square mile; Race: 100.0% White, 0.0% Black/African American, 0.0% Asian, 0.0% American Indian/Alaska Native, 0.0% Native Hawaiian/Other Pacific Islander, 0.0% Two or more races, 0.0% Hispanic of any race; Average household size: 3.07; Median age: 33.9; Age under 18: 28.9%; Age 65 and over: 14.5%; Males per 100 females: 95.5; Marriage status: 24.8% never married, 48.8% now married, 6.4% separated, 4.8% widowed, 21.6% divorced; Foreign born: 0.0%; Speak English only: 100.0%; With disability: 10.8%; Veterans: 11.0%; Ancestry: 51.8% German, 9.6% Dutch, 9.6% Irish, 4.2% French, 4.2% Polish
Employment: 14.6% management, business, and financial, 2.4% computer, engineering, and science, 8.5% education, legal, community service, arts, and media, 0.0% healthcare practitioners, 11.0% service, 17.1% sales and office, 14.6% natural resources, construction, and maintenance, 31.7% production, transportation, and material moving
Income: Per capita: $23,748; Median household: $71,250; Average household: $76,824; Households with income of $100,000 or more: 24.1%; Poverty rate: 2.4%
Educational Attainment: High school diploma or higher: 95.4%; Bachelor's degree or higher: 9.2%; Graduate/professional degree or higher: 4.6%
Housing: Homeownership rate: 98.1%; Median home value: $84,500; Median year structure built: Before 1940; Homeowner vacancy rate: 11.7%; Median selected monthly owner costs: $1,131 with a mortgage, $500 without a mortgage; Median gross rent: n/a per month; Rental vacancy rate: 0.0%
Health Insurance: 97.6% have insurance; 86.1% have private insurance; 22.3% have public insurance; 2.4% do not have insurance; 0.0% of children under 18 do not have insurance
Transportation: Commute: 96.3% car, 0.0% public transportation, 0.0% walk, 3.7% work from home; Mean travel time to work: 27.7 minutes

CLYDE (city). Covers a land area of 5.043 square miles and a water area of 0.052 square miles. Located at 41.31° N. Lat; 82.98° W. Long. Elevation is 696 feet.
History: The story of Clyde's beginnings tells of an officer during the War of 1812 who drove a stake into the ground here and said: "At this spot I shall build my future home, which shall be the nucleus of a thriving town." It was 1820 when the soldier returned, recovered his chosen land, and the city of Clyde came into being. Writer Sherwood Anderson spent his boyhood in Clyde, and portrayed the town in the novel "Winesburg, Ohio."
Population: 6,282; Growth (since 2000): 3.6%; Density: 1,245.7 persons per square mile; Race: 95.8% White, 0.0% Black/African American, 0.4% Asian, 0.5% American Indian/Alaska Native, 0.0% Native Hawaiian/Other Pacific Islander, 2.2% Two or more races, 5.6% Hispanic of any race; Average household size: 2.55; Median age: 37.1; Age under 18: 26.4%; Age 65 and over: 15.3%; Males per 100 females: 95.1; Marriage status: 21.8% never married, 60.8% now married, 0.9% separated, 4.8% widowed, 12.6% divorced; Foreign born: 0.7%; Speak English only: 98.4%; With disability: 15.5%; Veterans: 10.8%; Ancestry: 42.9% German, 11.3% Irish, 8.3% English, 5.1% American, 4.2% Italian

Employment: 5.8% management, business, and financial, 1.7% computer, engineering, and science, 6.4% education, legal, community service, arts, and media, 4.7% healthcare practitioners, 18.8% service, 18.8% sales and office, 10.3% natural resources, construction, and maintenance, 33.5% production, transportation, and material moving
Income: Per capita: $24,833; Median household: $50,339; Average household: $62,435; Households with income of $100,000 or more: 13.4%; Poverty rate: 12.3%
Educational Attainment: High school diploma or higher: 92.2%; Bachelor's degree or higher: 13.4%; Graduate/professional degree or higher: 4.4%

School District(s)

Bellevue City (PK-12)
2015-16 Enrollment: 1,973 . . . . (419) 484-5000
Clyde-Green Springs Exempted Village (PK-12)
2015-16 Enrollment: 2,275 . . . . (419) 547-0588

Housing: Homeownership rate: 71.5%; Median home value: $100,000; Median year structure built: 1966; Homeowner vacancy rate: 5.9%; Median selected monthly owner costs: $1,025 with a mortgage, $391 without a mortgage; Median gross rent: $693 per month; Rental vacancy rate: 8.3%
Health Insurance: 95.8% have insurance; 82.0% have private insurance; 31.0% have public insurance; 4.2% do not have insurance; 2.4% of children under 18 do not have insurance
Safety: Violent crime rate: 4.8 per 10,000 population; Property crime rate: 237.4 per 10,000 population
Newspapers: Clyde Enterprise (weekly circulation 1,700)
Transportation: Commute: 94.7% car, 1.4% public transportation, 2.7% walk, 1.2% work from home; Mean travel time to work: 17.8 minutes
Additional Information Contacts
City of Clyde . . . . (419) 547-6898
http://www.clydeohio.org

FREMONT (city). County seat. Covers a land area of 8.346 square miles and a water area of 0.219 square miles. Located at 41.35° N. Lat; 83.12° W. Long. Elevation is 627 feet.
History: Settlement began here after the War of 1812, when the two small towns of Croghansville and Lower Sandusky were established on the Sandusky River. In 1829 the two united, and in 1849 the name was changed to Fremont, for explorer John C. Fremont. Fremont grew as a sugar-beet and cannery center.
Population: 16,388; Growth (since 2000): -5.7%; Density: 1,963.7 persons per square mile; Race: 80.8% White, 9.1% Black/African American, 0.2% Asian, 0.0% American Indian/Alaska Native, 0.0% Native Hawaiian/Other Pacific Islander, 3.8% Two or more races, 17.8% Hispanic of any race; Average household size: 2.37; Median age: 36.1; Age under 18: 26.4%; Age 65 and over: 14.9%; Males per 100 females: 91.7; Marriage status: 37.9% never married, 39.5% now married, 2.5% separated, 7.2% widowed, 15.4% divorced; Foreign born: 2.3%; Speak English only: 91.0%; With disability: 15.5%; Veterans: 9.1%; Ancestry: 34.0% German, 10.6% Irish, 6.0% English, 5.0% American, 4.7% Polish
Employment: 6.3% management, business, and financial, 3.0% computer, engineering, and science, 7.6% education, legal, community service, arts, and media, 2.3% healthcare practitioners, 16.8% service, 19.2% sales and office, 8.3% natural resources, construction, and maintenance, 36.5% production, transportation, and material moving
Income: Per capita: $20,059; Median household: $34,167; Average household: $46,901; Households with income of $100,000 or more: 7.6%; Poverty rate: 23.8%
Educational Attainment: High school diploma or higher: 85.7%; Bachelor's degree or higher: 10.7%; Graduate/professional degree or higher: 3.5%

School District(s)

Fremont City (PK-12)
2015-16 Enrollment: 4,067 . . . . (419) 332-6454
North Central Academy (07-12)
2015-16 Enrollment: 106. . . . . (419) 448-5786
Vanguard-Sentinel Career & Technology Centers (06-12)
2015-16 Enrollment: n/a . . . . (419) 332-2626

Two-year College(s)

Terra State Community College (Public)
Fall 2016 Enrollment: 2,640 . . . . (419) 334-8400
2016-17 Tuition: In-state $4,284; Out-of-state $8,568

Vocational/Technical School(s)

Vanguard-Sentinel Adult Career and Technology Center (Public)
Fall 2016 Enrollment: 47 . . . . (567) 201-2856
2016-17 Tuition: $6,119

Housing: Homeownership rate: 56.9%; Median home value: $80,900; Median year structure built: 1943; Homeowner vacancy rate: 0.7%; Median selected monthly owner costs: $923 with a mortgage, $334 without a mortgage; Median gross rent: $628 per month; Rental vacancy rate: 11.3%
Health Insurance: 91.0% have insurance; 61.9% have private insurance; 42.8% have public insurance; 9.0% do not have insurance; 4.2% of children under 18 do not have insurance
Hospitals: Memorial Hospital (186 beds)
Safety: Violent crime rate: 19.7 per 10,000 population; Property crime rate: 519.3 per 10,000 population
Newspapers: News-Messenger (daily circulation 12,000)
Transportation: Commute: 94.5% car, 0.5% public transportation, 2.2% walk, 2.2% work from home; Mean travel time to work: 16.3 minutes
Additional Information Contacts
City of Fremont . . . . (419) 334-5900
http://www.fremontohio.org

GIBSONBURG (village). Covers a land area of 2.395 square miles and a water area of 0.478 square miles. Located at 41.39° N. Lat; 83.32° W. Long. Elevation is 682 feet.
History: Founded 1871.
Population: 2,717; Growth (since 2000): 8.4%; Density: 1,134.3 persons per square mile; Race: 88.7% White, 0.8% Black/African American, 0.0% Asian, 0.0% American Indian/Alaska Native, 0.0% Native Hawaiian/Other Pacific Islander, 5.3% Two or more races, 12.7% Hispanic of any race; Average household size: 2.75; Median age: 31.6; Age under 18: 30.1%; Age 65 and over: 12.6%; Males per 100 females: 93.3; Marriage status: 34.2% never married, 49.2% now married, 0.8% separated, 6.4% widowed, 10.3% divorced; Foreign born: 0.2%; Speak English only: 95.2%; With disability: 14.4%; Veterans: 6.5%; Ancestry: 47.7% German, 12.3% Irish, 5.8% English, 5.0% American, 4.9% French
Employment: 8.8% management, business, and financial, 4.0% computer, engineering, and science, 8.4% education, legal, community service, arts, and media, 5.7% healthcare practitioners, 15.5% service, 22.4% sales and office, 8.8% natural resources, construction, and maintenance, 26.4% production, transportation, and material moving
Income: Per capita: $20,393; Median household: $50,761; Average household: $55,421; Households with income of $100,000 or more: 10.5%; Poverty rate: 18.6%
Educational Attainment: High school diploma or higher: 86.4%; Bachelor's degree or higher: 13.1%; Graduate/professional degree or higher: 4.2%

School District(s)

Gibsonburg Exempted Village (PK-12)
2015-16 Enrollment: 967. . . . . (419) 637-2479

Housing: Homeownership rate: 68.8%; Median home value: $90,700; Median year structure built: 1946; Homeowner vacancy rate: 2.4%; Median selected monthly owner costs: $992 with a mortgage, $376 without a mortgage; Median gross rent: $658 per month; Rental vacancy rate: 0.0%
Health Insurance: 92.9% have insurance; 71.3% have private insurance; 34.6% have public insurance; 7.1% do not have insurance; 5.1% of children under 18 do not have insurance
Transportation: Commute: 93.8% car, 0.0% public transportation, 2.3% walk, 2.7% work from home; Mean travel time to work: 23.3 minutes

---

GREEN SPRINGS (village). Covers a land area of 1.207 square miles and a water area of 0.003 square miles. Located at 41.26° N. Lat; 83.05° W. Long. Elevation is 709 feet.
Population: 1,637; Growth (since 2000): 31.3%; Density: 1,356.1 persons per square mile; Race: 94.9% White, 0.0% Black/African American, 0.4% Asian, 2.4% American Indian/Alaska Native, 0.0% Native Hawaiian/Other Pacific Islander, 1.9% Two or more races, 4.3% Hispanic of any race; Average household size: 2.77; Median age: 38.5; Age under 18: 29.0%; Age 65 and over: 16.8%; Males per 100 females: 93.5; Marriage status: 30.6% never married, 40.2% now married, 0.9% separated, 14.4% widowed, 14.9% divorced; Foreign born: 0.6%; Speak English only: 99.5%; With disability: 15.1%; Veterans: 8.7%; Ancestry: 41.5% German, 10.4% Irish, 9.3% English, 5.6% Polish, 3.9% Italian
Employment: 7.1% management, business, and financial, 2.3% computer, engineering, and science, 6.3% education, legal, community service, arts, and media, 2.9% healthcare practitioners, 16.9% service, 17.6% sales and

office, 15.1% natural resources, construction, and maintenance, 31.8% production, transportation, and material moving
Income: Per capita: $20,510; Median household: $44,231; Average household: $56,434; Households with income of $100,000 or more: 13.8%; Poverty rate: 19.8%
Educational Attainment: High school diploma or higher: 92.7%; Bachelor's degree or higher: 8.3%; Graduate/professional degree or higher: 2.5%

School District(s)

Clyde-Green Springs Exempted Village (PK-12)
2015-16 Enrollment: 2,275 . . . . (419) 547-0588

Housing: Homeownership rate: 67.7%; Median home value: $82,800; Median year structure built: 1951; Homeowner vacancy rate: 2.3%; Median selected monthly owner costs: $1,055 with a mortgage, $423 without a mortgage; Median gross rent: $664 per month; Rental vacancy rate: 0.0%
Health Insurance: 91.7% have insurance; 70.0% have private insurance; 33.4% have public insurance; 8.3% do not have insurance; 8.4% of children under 18 do not have insurance
Transportation: Commute: 96.1% car, 0.0% public transportation, 3.2% walk, 0.8% work from home; Mean travel time to work: 22.1 minutes

HELENA (village). Covers a land area of 0.295 square miles and a water area of 0 square miles. Located at 41.34° N. Lat; 83.29° W. Long. Elevation is 696 feet.
Population: 282; Growth (since 2000): 19.5%; Density: 955.6 persons per square mile; Race: 97.9% White, 0.0% Black/African American, 0.0% Asian, 0.4% American Indian/Alaska Native, 0.0% Native Hawaiian/Other Pacific Islander, 1.8% Two or more races, 3.2% Hispanic of any race; Average household size: 2.85; Median age: 38.5; Age under 18: 23.8%; Age 65 and over: 19.5%; Males per 100 females: 121.8; Marriage status: 27.6% never married, 53.4% now married, 1.4% separated, 5.4% widowed, 13.6% divorced; Foreign born: 0.0%; Speak English only: 97.4%; With disability: 17.7%; Veterans: 5.1%; Ancestry: 46.5% German, 10.6% Irish, 7.1% English, 4.3% Hungarian, 3.9% Italian
Employment: 0.0% management, business, and financial, 0.9% computer, engineering, and science, 8.8% education, legal, community service, arts, and media, 0.0% healthcare practitioners, 17.5% service, 18.4% sales and office, 13.2% natural resources, construction, and maintenance, 41.2% production, transportation, and material moving
Income: Per capita: $19,977; Median household: $57,708; Average household: $56,544; Households with income of $100,000 or more: 3.0%; Poverty rate: 20.6%
Educational Attainment: High school diploma or higher: 88.7%; Bachelor's degree or higher: 13.9%; Graduate/professional degree or higher: 3.1%
Housing: Homeownership rate: 84.8%; Median home value: $93,800; Median year structure built: Before 1940; Homeowner vacancy rate: 0.0%; Median selected monthly owner costs: $1,018 with a mortgage, $366 without a mortgage; Median gross rent: $631 per month; Rental vacancy rate: 0.0%
Health Insurance: 93.3% have insurance; 65.2% have private insurance; 44.0% have public insurance; 6.7% do not have insurance; 4.5% of children under 18 do not have insurance
Transportation: Commute: 97.3% car, 0.9% public transportation, 0.9% walk, 0.9% work from home; Mean travel time to work: 23.2 minutes

HESSVILLE (CDP). Covers a land area of 0.699 square miles and a water area of 0 square miles. Located at 41.40° N. Lat; 83.24° W. Long. Elevation is 630 feet.
Population: 321; Growth (since 2000): n/a; Density: 459.3 persons per square mile; Race: 89.4% White, 0.0% Black/African American, 2.5% Asian, 0.0% American Indian/Alaska Native, 0.0% Native Hawaiian/Other Pacific Islander, 3.4% Two or more races, 13.7% Hispanic of any race; Average household size: 2.72; Median age: 24.7; Age under 18: 33.6%; Age 65 and over: 10.3%; Males per 100 females: 107.8; Marriage status: 27.7% never married, 42.6% now married, 0.0% separated, 12.3% widowed, 17.4% divorced; Foreign born: 0.0%; Speak English only: 86.4%; With disability: 37.4%; Veterans: 3.3%; Ancestry: 45.5% German, 9.7% Polish, 5.6% American, 5.6% Irish, 5.6% Italian
Employment: 0.0% management, business, and financial, 0.0% computer, engineering, and science, 0.0% education, legal, community service, arts, and media, 8.2% healthcare practitioners, 39.8% service, 0.0% sales and office, 0.0% natural resources, construction, and maintenance, 52.0% production, transportation, and material moving
Income: Per capita: $14,358; Median household: $35,897; Average household: $38,104; Households with income of $100,000 or more: n/a; Poverty rate: 34.6%
Educational Attainment: High school diploma or higher: 58.5%; Bachelor's degree or higher: 5.4%; Graduate/professional degree or higher: n/a
Housing: Homeownership rate: 61.0%; Median home value: $70,800; Median year structure built: 1951; Homeowner vacancy rate: 0.0%; Median selected monthly owner costs: $582 with a mortgage, n/a without a mortgage; Median gross rent: $903 per month; Rental vacancy rate: 0.0%
Health Insurance: 91.6% have insurance; 39.6% have private insurance; 59.2% have public insurance; 8.4% do not have insurance; 0.0% of children under 18 do not have insurance
Transportation: Commute: 100.0% car, 0.0% public transportation, 0.0% walk, 0.0% work from home; Mean travel time to work: 22.6 minutes

LINDSEY (village). Covers a land area of 1.562 square miles and a water area of 0 square miles. Located at 41.42° N. Lat; 83.22° W. Long. Elevation is 620 feet.
Population: 547; Growth (since 2000): 8.5%; Density: 350.3 persons per square mile; Race: 88.3% White, 3.1% Black/African American, 0.7% Asian, 0.0% American Indian/Alaska Native, 0.0% Native Hawaiian/Other Pacific Islander, 7.5% Two or more races, 8.2% Hispanic of any race; Average household size: 2.45; Median age: 41.9; Age under 18: 22.5%; Age 65 and over: 20.3%; Males per 100 females: 92.2; Marriage status: 23.2% never married, 60.7% now married, 0.0% separated, 7.1% widowed, 9.0% divorced; Foreign born: 0.5%; Speak English only: 96.9%; With disability: 12.1%; Veterans: 9.2%; Ancestry: 45.5% German, 10.1% Irish, 8.8% English, 4.0% French, 3.5% American
Employment: 10.6% management, business, and financial, 0.8% computer, engineering, and science, 4.9% education, legal, community service, arts, and media, 6.1% healthcare practitioners, 15.1% service, 24.1% sales and office, 8.6% natural resources, construction, and maintenance, 29.8% production, transportation, and material moving
Income: Per capita: $23,482; Median household: $50,795; Average household: $60,053; Households with income of $100,000 or more: 12.6%; Poverty rate: 13.9%
Educational Attainment: High school diploma or higher: 90.0%; Bachelor's degree or higher: 17.4%; Graduate/professional degree or higher: 6.4%

School District(s)

Fremont City (PK-12)
2015-16 Enrollment: 4,067 . . . . (419) 332-6454

Housing: Homeownership rate: 85.6%; Median home value: $99,400; Median year structure built: Before 1940; Homeowner vacancy rate: 4.2%; Median selected monthly owner costs: $917 with a mortgage, $400 without a mortgage; Median gross rent: $831 per month; Rental vacancy rate: 11.4%
Health Insurance: 97.1% have insurance; 71.5% have private insurance; 40.8% have public insurance; 2.9% do not have insurance; 0.8% of children under 18 do not have insurance
Transportation: Commute: 98.3% car, 0.0% public transportation, 1.3% walk, 0.4% work from home; Mean travel time to work: 22.8 minutes

STONY PRAIRIE (CDP). Covers a land area of 1.699 square miles and a water area of 0 square miles. Located at 41.35° N. Lat; 83.14° W. Long. Elevation is 633 feet.
Population: 1,257; Growth (since 2000): 50.4%; Density: 739.9 persons per square mile; Race: 79.1% White, 3.2% Black/African American, 0.0% Asian, 0.0% American Indian/Alaska Native, 0.0% Native Hawaiian/Other Pacific Islander, 0.0% Two or more races, 21.3% Hispanic of any race; Average household size: 2.54; Median age: 48.4; Age under 18: 16.1%; Age 65 and over: 19.3%; Males per 100 females: 99.1; Marriage status: 33.6% never married, 46.3% now married, 0.0% separated, 9.3% widowed, 10.8% divorced; Foreign born: 6.8%; Speak English only: 74.2%; With disability: 17.0%; Veterans: 8.8%; Ancestry: 29.9% German, 14.0% Italian, 8.4% American, 7.3% Irish, 4.4% English
Employment: 4.6% management, business, and financial, 7.7% computer, engineering, and science, 7.0% education, legal, community service, arts, and media, 7.9% healthcare practitioners, 16.1% service, 8.4% sales and office, 22.7% natural resources, construction, and maintenance, 25.6% production, transportation, and material moving
Income: Per capita: $20,459; Median household: $43,958; Average household: $50,361; Households with income of $100,000 or more: 5.8%; Poverty rate: 10.2%

Educational Attainment: High school diploma or higher: 74.2%; Bachelor's degree or higher: 6.6%; Graduate/professional degree or higher: 2.9%
Housing: Homeownership rate: 70.7%; Median home value: $98,600; Median year structure built: 1954; Homeowner vacancy rate: 5.1%; Median selected monthly owner costs: $1,013 with a mortgage, $397 without a mortgage; Median gross rent: $645 per month; Rental vacancy rate: 7.1%
Health Insurance: 91.1% have insurance; 64.4% have private insurance; 43.4% have public insurance; 8.9% do not have insurance; 7.4% of children under 18 do not have insurance
Transportation: Commute: 94.9% car, 0.0% public transportation, 0.0% walk, 2.9% work from home; Mean travel time to work: 16.5 minutes

VICKERY (CDP). Covers a land area of 0.423 square miles and a water area of 0 square miles. Located at 41.38° N. Lat; 82.94° W. Long. Elevation is 600 feet.
Population: 53; Growth (since 2000): n/a; Density: 125.4 persons per square mile; Race: 100.0% White, 0.0% Black/African American, 0.0% Asian, 0.0% American Indian/Alaska Native, 0.0% Native Hawaiian/Other Pacific Islander, 0.0% Two or more races, 0.0% Hispanic of any race; Average household size: 2.12; Median age: 65.3; Age under 18: 0.0%; Age 65 and over: 54.7%; Males per 100 females: 101.7; Marriage status: 45.3% never married, 35.8% now married, 0.0% separated, 18.9% widowed, 0.0% divorced; Foreign born: 0.0%; Speak English only: 100.0%; With disability: 28.3%; Veterans: 18.9%; Ancestry: 37.7% German, 18.9% English, 17.0% Norwegian
Employment: 33.3% management, business, and financial, 33.3% computer, engineering, and science, 33.3% education, legal, community service, arts, and media, 0.0% healthcare practitioners, 0.0% service, 0.0% sales and office, 0.0% natural resources, construction, and maintenance, 0.0% production, transportation, and material moving
Income: Per capita: $27,830; Median household: $38,375; Average household: $48,700; Households with income of $100,000 or more: n/a; Poverty rate: n/a
Educational Attainment: High school diploma or higher: 100.0%; Bachelor's degree or higher: 52.8%; Graduate/professional degree or higher: 17.0%
Housing: Homeownership rate: 64.0%; Median home value: n/a; Median year structure built: Before 1940; Homeowner vacancy rate: 0.0%; Median selected monthly owner costs: n/a with a mortgage, n/a without a mortgage; Median gross rent: n/a per month; Rental vacancy rate: 74.3%
Health Insurance: 100.0% have insurance; 34.0% have private insurance; 66.0% have public insurance; 0.0% do not have insurance; 0.0% of children under 18 do not have insurance
Transportation: Commute: 66.7% car, 0.0% public transportation, 33.3% walk, 0.0% work from home; Mean travel time to work: 84.1 minutes

WIGHTMANS GROVE (CDP).
Land/water area and latitude/longitude are not available.
Population: 16; Growth (since 2000): n/a; Density: 113.1 persons per square mile; Race: 100.0% White, 0.0% Black/African American, 0.0% Asian, 0.0% American Indian/Alaska Native, 0.0% Native Hawaiian/Other Pacific Islander, 0.0% Two or more races, 0.0% Hispanic of any race; Average household size: 2.00; Median age: n/a; Age under 18: 0.0%; Age 65 and over: 100.0%; Males per 100 females: 0.0; Marriage status: 0.0% never married, 100.0% now married, 0.0% separated, 0.0% widowed, 0.0% divorced; Foreign born: 0.0%; Speak English only: 100.0%; With disability: 50.0%; Veterans: 50.0%; Ancestry: 100.0% German, 50.0% Danish, 50.0% French
Employment: 0.0% management, business, and financial, 0.0% computer, engineering, and science, 0.0% education, legal, community service, arts, and media, 0.0% healthcare practitioners, 0.0% service, 100.0% sales and office, 0.0% natural resources, construction, and maintenance, 0.0% production, transportation, and material moving
Income: Per capita: n/a; Median household: n/a; Average household: n/a; Households with income of $100,000 or more: n/a; Poverty rate: n/a
Educational Attainment: High school diploma or higher: n/a; Bachelor's degree or higher: n/a; Graduate/professional degree or higher: n/a
Housing: Homeownership rate: n/a; Median home value: n/a; Median year structure built: 1974; Homeowner vacancy rate: 0.0%; Median selected monthly owner costs: n/a with a mortgage, n/a without a mortgage; Median gross rent: n/a per month; Rental vacancy rate: 0.0%
Health Insurance: 100.0% have insurance; 0.0% have private insurance; 100.0% have public insurance; 0.0% do not have insurance; 0.0% of children under 18 do not have insurance

Safety: Violent crime rate: 0.0 per 10,000 population; Property crime rate: 0.0 per 10,000 population
Transportation: Commute: 100.0% car, 0.0% public transportation, 0.0% walk, 0.0% work from home; Mean travel time to work: 0.0 minutes

WOODVILLE (village). Covers a land area of 1.325 square miles and a water area of 0 square miles. Located at 41.45° N. Lat; 83.36° W. Long. Elevation is 636 feet.
History: Woodville developed in the center of an extensive limestone area. The lime produced here was noted for its whiteness, plasticity, and sand-carrying qualities.
Population: 2,078; Growth (since 2000): 5.1%; Density: 1,568.8 persons per square mile; Race: 94.7% White, 0.0% Black/African American, 0.4% Asian, 0.4% American Indian/Alaska Native, 0.0% Native Hawaiian/Other Pacific Islander, 2.5% Two or more races, 7.4% Hispanic of any race; Average household size: 2.42; Median age: 37.2; Age under 18: 27.5%; Age 65 and over: 15.4%; Males per 100 females: 95.0; Marriage status: 22.0% never married, 54.2% now married, 0.8% separated, 8.4% widowed, 15.4% divorced; Foreign born: 1.5%; Speak English only: 95.8%; With disability: 14.5%; Veterans: 8.9%; Ancestry: 55.3% German, 15.1% Irish, 5.6% French, 5.1% Swedish, 4.9% English
Employment: 10.0% management, business, and financial, 2.6% computer, engineering, and science, 11.8% education, legal, community service, arts, and media, 10.1% healthcare practitioners, 13.9% service, 22.4% sales and office, 8.2% natural resources, construction, and maintenance, 21.1% production, transportation, and material moving
Income: Per capita: $26,312; Median household: $50,676; Average household: $62,087; Households with income of $100,000 or more: 17.5%; Poverty rate: 10.9%
Educational Attainment: High school diploma or higher: 93.2%; Bachelor's degree or higher: 24.6%; Graduate/professional degree or higher: 8.3%

School District(s)

Woodmore Local (PK-12)
2015-16 Enrollment: 1,053 . . . . (419) 862-1060
Housing: Homeownership rate: 71.2%; Median home value: $128,500; Median year structure built: 1956; Homeowner vacancy rate: 4.4%; Median selected monthly owner costs: $1,149 with a mortgage, $451 without a mortgage; Median gross rent: $738 per month; Rental vacancy rate: 5.7%
Health Insurance: 93.2% have insurance; 79.3% have private insurance; 29.6% have public insurance; 6.8% do not have insurance; 5.4% of children under 18 do not have insurance
Transportation: Commute: 93.1% car, 0.0% public transportation, 4.5% walk, 1.0% work from home; Mean travel time to work: 27.0 minutes

Scioto County

Located in southern Ohio; bounded on the south by the Ohio River and the Kentucky border; crossed by the Scioto and Little Scioto Rivers. Covers a land area of 610.213 square miles, a water area of 5.935 square miles, and is located in the Eastern Time Zone at 38.82° N. Lat., 83.00° W. Long. The county was founded in 1803. County seat is Portsmouth.

Scioto County is part of the Portsmouth, OH Micropolitan Statistical Area. The entire metro area includes: Scioto County, OH

Weather Station: Portsmouth Sciotoville — Elevation: 540 feet

	Jan	Feb	Mar	Apr	May	Jun	Jul	Aug	Sep	Oct	Nov	Dec
High	41	45	55	67	75	83	87	86	80	68	56	44
Low	23	25	33	42	51	60	64	62	54	42	34	26
Precip	3.1	2.8	3.8	3.6	4.7	3.4	4.4	3.8	2.6	2.6	3.1	3.2
Snow	3.4	2.1	1.2	0.2	tr	0.0	0.0	0.0	0.0	0.0	0.1	1.0

High and Low temperatures in degrees Fahrenheit; Precipitation and Snow in inches

Population: 77,366; Growth (since 2000): -2.3%; Density: 126.8 persons per square mile; Race: 94.4% White, 2.8% Black/African American, 0.4% Asian, 0.4% American Indian/Alaska Native, 0.0% Native Hawaiian/Other Pacific Islander, 1.6% two or more races, 1.2% Hispanic of any race; Average household size: 2.48; Median age: 39.7; Age under 18: 22.0%; Age 65 and over: 16.6%; Males per 100 females: 97.6; Marriage status: 28.5% never married, 49.6% now married, 2.3% separated, 7.6% widowed, 14.3% divorced; Foreign born: 1.0%; Speak English only: 98.6%; With disability: 21.6%; Veterans: 9.2%; Ancestry: 19.9% German, 14.3% Irish, 10.7% American, 8.8% English, 2.2% Italian

Religion: Six largest groups: 5.6% Baptist, 4.8% Non-denominational Protestant, 4.1% Catholicism, 3.9% Methodist/Pietist, 2.1% Holiness, 1.1% Pentecostal

Economy: Unemployment rate: 6.0%; Leading industries: 19.1 % retail trade; 17.3 % health care and social assistance; 11.9 % other services (except public administration); Farms: 689 totaling 94,342 acres; Company size: 1 employs 1,000 or more persons, 0 employ 500 to 999 persons, 26 employ 100 to 499 persons, 1,271 employs less than 100 persons; Business ownership: 1,932 women-owned, 57 Black-owned, n/a Hispanic-owned, 57 Asian-owned, 70 American Indian/Alaska Native-owned

Employment: 9.6% management, business, and financial, 3.4% computer, engineering, and science, 9.4% education, legal, community service, arts, and media, 10.9% healthcare practitioners, 21.8% service, 21.0% sales and office, 9.1% natural resources, construction, and maintenance, 14.7% production, transportation, and material moving

Income: Per capita: $20,728; Median household: $37,936; Average household: $51,990; Households with income of $100,000 or more: 12.9%; Poverty rate: 24.0%

Educational Attainment: High school diploma or higher: 84.1%; Bachelor's degree or higher: 15.0%; Graduate/professional degree or higher: 5.9%

Housing: Homeownership rate: 68.4%; Median home value: $92,000; Median year structure built: 1964; Homeowner vacancy rate: 1.7%; Median selected monthly owner costs: $1,043 with a mortgage, $389 without a mortgage; Median gross rent: $571 per month; Rental vacancy rate: 6.1%

Vital Statistics: Birth rate: 107.2 per 10,000 population; Death rate: 119.9 per 10,000 population; Age-adjusted cancer mortality rate: 187.9 deaths per 100,000 population

Health Insurance: 90.1% have insurance; 55.4% have private insurance; 47.4% have public insurance; 9.9% do not have insurance; 3.3% of children under 18 do not have insurance

Health Care: Physicians: 20.8 per 10,000 population; Dentists: 3.7 per 10,000 population; Hospital beds: 31.9 per 10,000 population; Hospital admissions: 1,508.4 per 10,000 population

Air Quality Index (AQI): Percent of Days: 97.0% good, 2.7% moderate, 0.3% unhealthy for sensitive individuals, 0.0% unhealthy, 0.0% very unhealthy; Annual median: 15; Annual maximum: 129

Transportation: Commute: 93.8% car, 0.3% public transportation, 2.7% walk, 2.5% work from home; Mean travel time to work: 25.4 minutes

2016 Presidential Election: 66.3% Trump, 29.5% Clinton, 2.3% Johnson, 0.7% Stein

National and State Parks: Brush Creek State Forest; Shawnee State Forest; Shawnee State Park

Additional Information Contacts

Scioto Government . . . . (740) 355-8313
http://www.sciotocountyohio.com

Scioto County Communities

CLARKTOWN (CDP). Covers a land area of 2.044 square miles and a water area of 0.002 square miles. Located at 38.85° N. Lat; 82.91° W. Long. Elevation is 689 feet.

Population: 656; Growth (since 2000): n/a; Density: 320.9 persons per square mile; Race: 100.0% White, 0.0% Black/African American, 0.0% Asian, 0.0% American Indian/Alaska Native, 0.0% Native Hawaiian/Other Pacific Islander, 0.0% Two or more races, 0.0% Hispanic of any race; Average household size: 1.79; Median age: 57.2; Age under 18: 11.0%; Age 65 and over: 22.6%; Males per 100 females: 98.3; Marriage status: 12.2% never married, 55.7% now married, 5.4% separated, 15.2% widowed, 16.9% divorced; Foreign born: 0.0%; Speak English only: 100.0%; With disability: 16.0%; Veterans: 11.6%; Ancestry: 28.7% Irish, 14.0% German, 13.9% American, 5.8% English, 2.4% Scotch-Irish

Employment: 5.6% management, business, and financial, 0.0% computer, engineering, and science, 12.3% education, legal, community service, arts, and media, 0.0% healthcare practitioners, 25.5% service, 34.8% sales and office, 12.6% natural resources, construction, and maintenance, 9.3% production, transportation, and material moving

Income: Per capita: $25,084; Median household: $31,250; Average household: $44,113; Households with income of $100,000 or more: 10.1%; Poverty rate: 20.1%

Educational Attainment: High school diploma or higher: 83.1%; Bachelor's degree or higher: 6.3%; Graduate/professional degree or higher: 1.6%

Housing: Homeownership rate: 82.3%; Median home value: $81,100; Median year structure built: 1953; Homeowner vacancy rate: 0.0%; Median selected monthly owner costs: $817 with a mortgage, $293 without a mortgage; Median gross rent: $625 per month; Rental vacancy rate: 0.0%

Health Insurance: 89.6% have insurance; 65.1% have private insurance; 43.1% have public insurance; 10.4% do not have insurance; 0.0% of children under 18 do not have insurance

Transportation: Commute: 90.1% car, 6.3% public transportation, 3.6% walk, 0.0% work from home; Mean travel time to work: 29.9 minutes

FRANKLIN FURNACE (CDP). Covers a land area of 2.355 square miles and a water area of 0.395 square miles. Located at 38.61° N. Lat; 82.85° W. Long. Elevation is 574 feet.

Population: 1,599; Growth (since 2000): 4.0%; Density: 678.9 persons per square mile; Race: 86.4% White, 9.3% Black/African American, 0.0% Asian, 1.3% American Indian/Alaska Native, 0.0% Native Hawaiian/Other Pacific Islander, 2.4% Two or more races, 2.3% Hispanic of any race; Average household size: 2.55; Median age: 29.4; Age under 18: 27.5%; Age 65 and over: 15.3%; Males per 100 females: 126.5; Marriage status: 40.4% never married, 40.8% now married, 4.0% separated, 9.3% widowed, 9.5% divorced; Foreign born: 0.0%; Speak English only: 98.5%; With disability: 15.7%; Veterans: 6.8%; Ancestry: 12.1% German, 11.1% American, 8.7% Irish, 6.8% English, 5.6% Scottish

Employment: 11.8% management, business, and financial, 0.0% computer, engineering, and science, 15.9% education, legal, community service, arts, and media, 2.2% healthcare practitioners, 20.7% service, 21.6% sales and office, 7.6% natural resources, construction, and maintenance, 20.1% production, transportation, and material moving

Income: Per capita: $17,232; Median household: $36,750; Average household: $51,105; Households with income of $100,000 or more: 10.2%; Poverty rate: 27.8%

Educational Attainment: High school diploma or higher: 75.3%; Bachelor's degree or higher: 14.3%; Graduate/professional degree or higher: 6.5%

School District(s)

Green Local (PK-12)
2015-16 Enrollment: 607. . . . . (740) 354-9221

Housing: Homeownership rate: 73.4%; Median home value: $80,700; Median year structure built: 1973; Homeowner vacancy rate: 0.0%; Median selected monthly owner costs: $779 with a mortgage, $411 without a mortgage; Median gross rent: $564 per month; Rental vacancy rate: 0.0%

Health Insurance: 96.2% have insurance; 44.9% have private insurance; 62.8% have public insurance; 3.8% do not have insurance; 0.0% of children under 18 do not have insurance

Transportation: Commute: 98.0% car, 0.0% public transportation, 2.0% walk, 0.0% work from home; Mean travel time to work: 29.3 minutes

FRIENDSHIP (CDP). Covers a land area of 1.168 square miles and a water area of 0.013 square miles. Located at 38.70° N. Lat; 83.10° W. Long. Elevation is 548 feet.

Population: 195; Growth (since 2000): n/a; Density: 166.9 persons per square mile; Race: 100.0% White, 0.0% Black/African American, 0.0% Asian, 0.0% American Indian/Alaska Native, 0.0% Native Hawaiian/Other Pacific Islander, 0.0% Two or more races, 18.5% Hispanic of any race; Average household size: 2.51; Median age: 51.8; Age under 18: 7.7%; Age 65 and over: 25.1%; Males per 100 females: 87.7; Marriage status: 12.2% never married, 63.3% now married, 0.0% separated, 15.6% widowed, 8.9% divorced; Foreign born: 18.5%; Speak English only: 80.0%; With disability: 17.0%; Veterans: 7.2%; Ancestry: 29.7% American, 15.9% English, 6.7% German, 5.6% Dutch, 4.1% French

Employment: 0.0% management, business, and financial, 0.0% computer, engineering, and science, 0.0% education, legal, community service, arts, and media, 24.5% healthcare practitioners, 7.5% service, 33.0% sales and office, 2.8% natural resources, construction, and maintenance, 32.1% production, transportation, and material moving

Income: Per capita: $17,548; Median household: n/a; Average household: $49,924; Households with income of $100,000 or more: 10.3%; Poverty rate: 26.9%

Educational Attainment: High school diploma or higher: 85.2%; Bachelor's degree or higher: 5.4%; Graduate/professional degree or higher: n/a

Housing: Homeownership rate: 100.0%; Median home value: $62,500; Median year structure built: Before 1940; Homeowner vacancy rate: 0.0%; Median selected monthly owner costs: $1,211 with a mortgage, $430

without a mortgage; Median gross rent: n/a per month; Rental vacancy rate: 0.0%
Health Insurance: 63.7% have insurance; 48.5% have private insurance; 21.6% have public insurance; 36.3% do not have insurance; 0.0% of children under 18 do not have insurance
Transportation: Commute: 100.0% car, 0.0% public transportation, 0.0% walk, 0.0% work from home; Mean travel time to work: 18.7 minutes

HAVERHILL (unincorporated postal area)

ZCTA: 45636

Covers a land area of 0.648 square miles and a water area of 0.046 square miles. Located at 38.59° N. Lat; 82.83° W. Long. Elevation is 548 feet.
Population: 188; Growth (since 2000): n/a; Density: 290.0 persons per square mile; Race: 96.8% White, 0.0% Black/African American, 0.0% Asian, 0.0% American Indian/Alaska Native, 0.0% Native Hawaiian/Other Pacific Islander, 3.2% Two or more races, 0.0% Hispanic of any race; Average household size: 3.42; Median age: 36.6; Age under 18: 20.2%; Age 65 and over: 12.8%; Males per 100 females: 108.5; Marriage status: 43.0% never married, 49.2% now married, 0.0% separated, 0.0% widowed, 7.8% divorced; Foreign born: 0.0%; Speak English only: 100.0%; With disability: 17.0%; Veterans: 0.0%; Ancestry: 3.2% English, 3.2% German, 3.2% Welsh
Employment: 6.3% management, business, and financial, 0.0% computer, engineering, and science, 0.0% education, legal, community service, arts, and media, 0.0% healthcare practitioners, 0.0% service, 64.6% sales and office, 0.0% natural resources, construction, and maintenance, 29.2% production, transportation, and material moving
Income: Per capita: $24,827; Median household: $63,208; Average household: $80,362; Households with income of $100,000 or more: 10.9%; Poverty rate: 5.3%
Educational Attainment: High school diploma or higher: 83.9%; Bachelor's degree or higher: 10.7%; Graduate/professional degree or higher: 10.7%
Housing: Homeownership rate: 100.0%; Median home value: $82,800; Median year structure built: 1957; Homeowner vacancy rate: 0.0%; Median selected monthly owner costs: $775 with a mortgage, $0 without a mortgage; Median gross rent: n/a per month; Rental vacancy rate: 0.0%
Health Insurance: 100.0% have insurance; 100.0% have private insurance; 12.8% have public insurance; 0.0% do not have insurance; 0.0% of children under 18 do not have insurance
Transportation: Commute: 100.0% car, 0.0% public transportation, 0.0% walk, 0.0% work from home; Mean travel time to work: 0.0 minutes

LUCASVILLE (CDP).

Covers a land area of 2.513 square miles and a water area of 0.040 square miles. Located at 38.87° N. Lat; 82.99° W. Long. Elevation is 554 feet.
History: Lucasville was founded in 1819 by John Lucas on land received by his father, William Lucas, for Revolutionary War service. The founder's son, Robert Lucas, was governor of Ohio (1832-1836) and territorial governor of Iowa (1838-1841).
Population: 1,534; Growth (since 2000): -3.4%; Density: 610.3 persons per square mile; Race: 99.3% White, 0.0% Black/African American, 0.0% Asian, 0.0% American Indian/Alaska Native, 0.0% Native Hawaiian/Other Pacific Islander, 0.7% Two or more races, 0.7% Hispanic of any race; Average household size: 2.70; Median age: 33.6; Age under 18: 20.6%; Age 65 and over: 13.8%; Males per 100 females: 303.1; Marriage status: 32.2% never married, 58.3% now married, 4.2% separated, 1.2% widowed, 8.3% divorced; Foreign born: 1.3%; Speak English only: 100.0%; With disability: 21.5%; Veterans: 10.4%; Ancestry: 18.0% Irish, 17.6% English, 16.7% German, 12.3% American, 4.6% Italian
Employment: 10.5% management, business, and financial, 2.1% computer, engineering, and science, 13.7% education, legal, community service, arts, and media, 14.3% healthcare practitioners, 14.0% service, 22.0% sales and office, 12.2% natural resources, construction, and maintenance, 11.1% production, transportation, and material moving
Income: Per capita: $22,232; Median household: $45,000; Average household: $58,146; Households with income of $100,000 or more: 11.3%; Poverty rate: 26.8%
Educational Attainment: High school diploma or higher: 85.7%; Bachelor's degree or higher: 27.9%; Graduate/professional degree or higher: 12.0%

School District(s)

Scioto County Career Technical Center (06-12)
2015-16 Enrollment: n/a . . . . (740) 259-5522
Valley Local (PK-12)
2015-16 Enrollment: 1,033 . . . . (740) 259-3115

Vocational/Technical School(s)

Scioto County Career Technical Center (Public)
Fall 2016 Enrollment: 198 . . . . (740) 259-5526
2016-17 Tuition: $10,952
Housing: Homeownership rate: 76.4%; Median home value: $134,100; Median year structure built: 1969; Homeowner vacancy rate: 0.0%; Median selected monthly owner costs: $1,122 with a mortgage, $357 without a mortgage; Median gross rent: $545 per month; Rental vacancy rate: 0.0%
Health Insurance: 90.5% have insurance; 62.5% have private insurance; 40.6% have public insurance; 9.5% do not have insurance; 0.0% of children under 18 do not have insurance
Transportation: Commute: 93.4% car, 0.0% public transportation, 1.3% walk, 5.4% work from home; Mean travel time to work: 27.1 minutes

MCDERMOTT (CDP).

Covers a land area of 0.579 square miles and a water area of <.001 square miles. Located at 38.83° N. Lat; 83.06° W. Long. Elevation is 584 feet.
Population: 573; Growth (since 2000): n/a; Density: 989.6 persons per square mile; Race: 100.0% White, 0.0% Black/African American, 0.0% Asian, 0.0% American Indian/Alaska Native, 0.0% Native Hawaiian/Other Pacific Islander, 0.0% Two or more races, 0.0% Hispanic of any race; Average household size: 2.62; Median age: 35.1; Age under 18: 24.3%; Age 65 and over: 20.8%; Males per 100 females: 96.4; Marriage status: 45.4% never married, 51.6% now married, 3.7% separated, 3.0% widowed, 0.0% divorced; Foreign born: 0.0%; Speak English only: 94.6%; With disability: 19.9%; Veterans: 15.4%; Ancestry: 19.5% American, 14.0% Scotch-Irish, 11.5% English, 9.9% German, 5.2% Irish
Employment: 0.0% management, business, and financial, 0.0% computer, engineering, and science, 0.0% education, legal, community service, arts, and media, 0.0% healthcare practitioners, 7.4% service, 24.2% sales and office, 45.8% natural resources, construction, and maintenance, 22.6% production, transportation, and material moving
Income: Per capita: $19,136; Median household: $57,566; Average household: $50,505; Households with income of $100,000 or more: n/a; Poverty rate: 19.7%
Educational Attainment: High school diploma or higher: 59.0%; Bachelor's degree or higher: n/a; Graduate/professional degree or higher: n/a

School District(s)

Northwest Local (PK-12)
2015-16 Enrollment: 1,508 . . . . (877) 644-6338
Housing: Homeownership rate: 54.0%; Median home value: $91,300; Median year structure built: 1948; Homeowner vacancy rate: 0.0%; Median selected monthly owner costs: n/a with a mortgage, $453 without a mortgage; Median gross rent: $523 per month; Rental vacancy rate: 0.0%
Health Insurance: 91.3% have insurance; 65.6% have private insurance; 56.5% have public insurance; 8.7% do not have insurance; 8.6% of children under 18 do not have insurance
Transportation: Commute: 100.0% car, 0.0% public transportation, 0.0% walk, 0.0% work from home; Mean travel time to work: 30.8 minutes

MINFORD (CDP).

Covers a land area of 1.743 square miles and a water area of 0.005 square miles. Located at 38.86° N. Lat; 82.85° W. Long. Elevation is 656 feet.
Population: 469; Growth (since 2000): n/a; Density: 269.0 persons per square mile; Race: 100.0% White, 0.0% Black/African American, 0.0% Asian, 0.0% American Indian/Alaska Native, 0.0% Native Hawaiian/Other Pacific Islander, 0.0% Two or more races, 0.0% Hispanic of any race; Average household size: 1.97; Median age: 60.7; Age under 18: 11.9%; Age 65 and over: 40.5%; Males per 100 females: 80.5; Marriage status: 32.4% never married, 37.8% now married, 0.0% separated, 17.8% widowed, 12.1% divorced; Foreign born: 0.0%; Speak English only: 100.0%; With disability: 20.9%; Veterans: 8.7%; Ancestry: 21.5% American, 21.1% Italian, 18.3% Irish, 11.3% German, 7.5% English
Employment: 29.7% management, business, and financial, 5.5% computer, engineering, and science, 13.1% education, legal, community service, arts, and media, 26.9% healthcare practitioners, 5.5% service, 19.3% sales and office, 0.0% natural resources, construction, and maintenance, 0.0% production, transportation, and material moving
Income: Per capita: $26,983; Median household: n/a; Average household: $56,026; Households with income of $100,000 or more: 12.9%; Poverty rate: 22.3%

Educational Attainment: High school diploma or higher: 84.9%; Bachelor's degree or higher: 15.9%; Graduate/professional degree or higher: 15.9%

School District(s)

Minford Local (PK-12)
2015-16 Enrollment: 1,425 . . . . (740) 820-3896

Housing: Homeownership rate: 79.9%; Median home value: n/a; Median year structure built: 1949; Homeowner vacancy rate: 0.0%; Median selected monthly owner costs: n/a with a mortgage, $439 without a mortgage; Median gross rent: n/a per month; Rental vacancy rate: 0.0%
Health Insurance: 100.0% have insurance; 81.6% have private insurance; 41.7% have public insurance; 0.0% do not have insurance; 0.0% of children under 18 do not have insurance
Transportation: Commute: 94.5% car, 0.0% public transportation, 0.0% walk, 5.5% work from home; Mean travel time to work: 15.6 minutes

NEW BOSTON (village). Covers a land area of 1.111 square miles and a water area of 0.030 square miles. Located at 38.75° N. Lat; 82.93° W. Long. Elevation is 535 feet.
History: New Boston was founded in 1891 and named for Boston, whose capitalists financed a sawmill here. New Boston later became a river steel town.
Population: 2,139; Growth (since 2000): -8.6%; Density: 1,924.8 persons per square mile; Race: 95.3% White, 1.1% Black/African American, 0.0% Asian, 0.0% American Indian/Alaska Native, 0.0% Native Hawaiian/Other Pacific Islander, 1.6% Two or more races, 0.8% Hispanic of any race; Average household size: 2.06; Median age: 41.9; Age under 18: 22.8%; Age 65 and over: 24.9%; Males per 100 females: 84.4; Marriage status: 28.3% never married, 31.6% now married, 1.2% separated, 13.1% widowed, 27.0% divorced; Foreign born: 0.0%; Speak English only: 97.7%; With disability: 35.9%; Veterans: 6.4%; Ancestry: 13.9% German, 12.6% American, 10.6% English, 10.1% Irish, 2.0% Dutch
Employment: 9.2% management, business, and financial, 0.0% computer, engineering, and science, 14.7% education, legal, community service, arts, and media, 7.8% healthcare practitioners, 33.1% service, 21.1% sales and office, 6.4% natural resources, construction, and maintenance, 7.8% production, transportation, and material moving
Income: Per capita: $12,828; Median household: $14,745; Average household: $24,936; Households with income of $100,000 or more: 1.7%; Poverty rate: 44.7%
Educational Attainment: High school diploma or higher: 78.0%; Bachelor's degree or higher: 9.5%; Graduate/professional degree or higher: 3.6%

School District(s)

New Boston Local (PK-12)
2015-16 Enrollment: 462. . . . . (740) 456-4626

Two-year College(s)

Daymar College-New Boston (Private, For-profit)
Fall 2016 Enrollment: n/a . . . . (740) 456-4124
2016-17 Tuition: In-state $15,000; Out-of-state $15,000

Housing: Homeownership rate: 33.3%; Median home value: $62,300; Median year structure built: 1951; Homeowner vacancy rate: 2.9%; Median selected monthly owner costs: $675 with a mortgage, $295 without a mortgage; Median gross rent: $422 per month; Rental vacancy rate: 4.1%
Health Insurance: 95.2% have insurance; 36.7% have private insurance; 70.7% have public insurance; 4.8% do not have insurance; 2.9% of children under 18 do not have insurance
Transportation: Commute: 93.9% car, 0.0% public transportation, 5.5% walk, 0.6% work from home; Mean travel time to work: 15.3 minutes

OTWAY (village). Covers a land area of 0.204 square miles and a water area of 0.004 square miles. Located at 38.86° N. Lat; 83.19° W. Long. Elevation is 600 feet.
Population: 56; Growth (since 2000): -34.9%; Density: 274.5 persons per square mile; Race: 100.0% White, 0.0% Black/African American, 0.0% Asian, 0.0% American Indian/Alaska Native, 0.0% Native Hawaiian/Other Pacific Islander, 0.0% Two or more races, 0.0% Hispanic of any race; Average household size: 1.93; Median age: 27.0; Age under 18: 32.1%; Age 65 and over: 19.6%; Males per 100 females: 67.3; Marriage status: 34.2% never married, 42.1% now married, 0.0% separated, 13.2% widowed, 10.5% divorced; Foreign born: 0.0%; Speak English only: 100.0%; With disability: 10.7%; Veterans: 13.2%; Ancestry: 44.6% German, 39.3% Irish, 8.9% British, 7.1% American, 5.4% English
Employment: 11.8% management, business, and financial, 0.0% computer, engineering, and science, 0.0% education, legal, community service, arts, and media, 23.5% healthcare practitioners, 17.6% service, 29.4% sales and office, 17.6% natural resources, construction, and maintenance, 0.0% production, transportation, and material moving
Income: Per capita: $14,555; Median household: $20,938; Average household: $29,486; Households with income of $100,000 or more: n/a; Poverty rate: 55.4%
Educational Attainment: High school diploma or higher: 92.9%; Bachelor's degree or higher: 7.1%; Graduate/professional degree or higher: n/a
Housing: Homeownership rate: 48.3%; Median home value: $52,500; Median year structure built: Before 1940; Homeowner vacancy rate: 0.0%; Median selected monthly owner costs: $825 with a mortgage, $350 without a mortgage; Median gross rent: $715 per month; Rental vacancy rate: 0.0%
Health Insurance: 64.3% have insurance; 58.9% have private insurance; 28.6% have public insurance; 35.7% do not have insurance; 83.3% of children under 18 do not have insurance
Transportation: Commute: 100.0% car, 0.0% public transportation, 0.0% walk, 0.0% work from home; Mean travel time to work: 53.5 minutes

PORTSMOUTH (city). County seat. Covers a land area of 10.734 square miles and a water area of 0.338 square miles. Located at 38.75° N. Lat; 82.95° W. Long. Elevation is 535 feet.
History: Portsmouth was founded in 1803 by Major Henry Massie, a Virginia land speculator. By 1815 Portsmouth was an incorporated town. Industry moved from lumbering and fur trading, to canal-boat center, to iron works and brickyards. In 1927, a suspension bridge was built across the Ohio River to connect the town with South Portsmouth in Kentucky.
Population: 20,393; Growth (since 2000): -2.5%; Density: 1,899.8 persons per square mile; Race: 90.0% White, 5.7% Black/African American, 1.2% Asian, 0.4% American Indian/Alaska Native, 0.0% Native Hawaiian/Other Pacific Islander, 2.0% Two or more races, 1.1% Hispanic of any race; Average household size: 2.27; Median age: 36.8; Age under 18: 20.1%; Age 65 and over: 17.6%; Males per 100 females: 86.6; Marriage status: 35.5% never married, 37.0% now married, 2.6% separated, 9.9% widowed, 17.6% divorced; Foreign born: 1.8%; Speak English only: 97.8%; With disability: 24.5%; Veterans: 9.1%; Ancestry: 20.6% German, 15.3% Irish, 9.3% American, 7.2% English, 2.3% Italian
Employment: 9.6% management, business, and financial, 3.7% computer, engineering, and science, 9.8% education, legal, community service, arts, and media, 11.0% healthcare practitioners, 28.3% service, 24.0% sales and office, 3.8% natural resources, construction, and maintenance, 9.8% production, transportation, and material moving
Income: Per capita: $18,701; Median household: $27,769; Average household: $43,185; Households with income of $100,000 or more: 7.8%; Poverty rate: 34.2%
Educational Attainment: High school diploma or higher: 80.7%; Bachelor's degree or higher: 16.7%; Graduate/professional degree or higher: 5.9%

School District(s)

Clay Local (PK-12)
2015-16 Enrollment: 665. . . . . (740) 354-6645
Portsmouth City (PK-12)
2015-16 Enrollment: 1,840 . . . . (740) 354-4727
Sciotoville (05-12)
2015-16 Enrollment: 294. . . . . (740) 776-6777
Sciotoville Elementary Academy (KG-04)
2015-16 Enrollment: 140. . . . . (740) 776-2916

Four-year College(s)

Shawnee State University (Public)
Fall 2016 Enrollment: 3,772 . . . . (740) 354-3205
2016-17 Tuition: In-state $7,365; Out-of-state $14,145

Two-year College(s)

Paramount Beauty Academy (Private, For-profit)
Fall 2016 Enrollment: 51 . . . . (740) 353-2436

Housing: Homeownership rate: 49.9%; Median home value: $72,700; Median year structure built: Before 1940; Homeowner vacancy rate: 1.5%; Median selected monthly owner costs: $840 with a mortgage, $353 without a mortgage; Median gross rent: $562 per month; Rental vacancy rate: 8.2%
Health Insurance: 87.7% have insurance; 43.2% have private insurance; 56.0% have public insurance; 12.3% do not have insurance; 4.0% of children under 18 do not have insurance
Hospitals: Kings Daughters Medical Center Ohio; Southern Ohio Medical Center (488 beds)

Newspapers: Community Common (weekly circulation 39,000); Portsmouth Daily Times (daily circulation 12,400)
Transportation: Commute: 87.5% car, 0.4% public transportation, 7.0% walk, 3.3% work from home; Mean travel time to work: 16.0 minutes
Airports: Greater Portsmouth Regional (general aviation)
Additional Information Contacts
City of Portsmouth. . . . . (740) 354-8807
http://www.ci.portsmouth.oh.us

RARDEN (village). Covers a land area of 0.212 square miles and a water area of <.001 square miles. Located at 38.92° N. Lat; 83.24° W. Long. Elevation is 617 feet.
Population: 192; Growth (since 2000): 9.1%; Density: 907.5 persons per square mile; Race: 100.0% White, 0.0% Black/African American, 0.0% Asian, 0.0% American Indian/Alaska Native, 0.0% Native Hawaiian/Other Pacific Islander, 0.0% Two or more races, 0.0% Hispanic of any race; Average household size: 2.78; Median age: 41.5; Age under 18: 9.4%; Age 65 and over: 7.3%; Males per 100 females: 87.1; Marriage status: 25.1% never married, 67.4% now married, 0.0% separated, 1.1% widowed, 6.3% divorced; Foreign born: 0.0%; Speak English only: 98.9%; With disability: 21.9%; Veterans: 6.3%; Ancestry: 25.0% German, 15.6% Irish, 7.8% American, 6.8% Italian, 6.3% English
Employment: 5.8% management, business, and financial, 0.0% computer, engineering, and science, 5.8% education, legal, community service, arts, and media, 0.0% healthcare practitioners, 21.2% service, 35.6% sales and office, 10.6% natural resources, construction, and maintenance, 21.2% production, transportation, and material moving
Income: Per capita: $18,637; Median household: $34,375; Average household: $43,309; Households with income of $100,000 or more: 5.8%; Poverty rate: 13.5%
Educational Attainment: High school diploma or higher: 84.7%; Bachelor's degree or higher: 3.8%; Graduate/professional degree or higher: 3.8%
Housing: Homeownership rate: 66.7%; Median home value: $68,600; Median year structure built: Before 1940; Homeowner vacancy rate: 0.0%; Median selected monthly owner costs: $933 with a mortgage, $325 without a mortgage; Median gross rent: $581 per month; Rental vacancy rate: 14.8%
Health Insurance: 86.5% have insurance; 52.6% have private insurance; 41.7% have public insurance; 13.5% do not have insurance; 0.0% of children under 18 do not have insurance
Transportation: Commute: 89.9% car, 0.0% public transportation, 6.1% walk, 4.0% work from home; Mean travel time to work: 49.7 minutes

ROSEMOUNT (CDP). Covers a land area of 5.748 square miles and a water area of 0.003 square miles. Located at 38.77° N. Lat; 82.97° W. Long. Elevation is 617 feet.
Population: 2,085; Growth (since 2000): 2.1%; Density: 362.7 persons per square mile; Race: 100.0% White, 0.0% Black/African American, 0.0% Asian, 0.0% American Indian/Alaska Native, 0.0% Native Hawaiian/Other Pacific Islander, 0.0% Two or more races, 13.6% Hispanic of any race; Average household size: 2.65; Median age: 42.9; Age under 18: 22.8%; Age 65 and over: 20.9%; Males per 100 females: 85.1; Marriage status: 35.3% never married, 45.6% now married, 0.0% separated, 7.3% widowed, 11.8% divorced; Foreign born: 0.9%; Speak English only: 98.7%; With disability: 22.4%; Veterans: 15.5%; Ancestry: 28.4% German, 24.5% English, 12.4% Irish, 9.3% American, 2.9% Italian
Employment: 14.9% management, business, and financial, 4.1% computer, engineering, and science, 9.6% education, legal, community service, arts, and media, 16.0% healthcare practitioners, 16.7% service, 9.4% sales and office, 4.9% natural resources, construction, and maintenance, 24.2% production, transportation, and material moving
Income: Per capita: $21,400; Median household: $55,817; Average household: $55,422; Households with income of $100,000 or more: 8.0%; Poverty rate: 13.6%
Educational Attainment: High school diploma or higher: 92.3%; Bachelor's degree or higher: 22.2%; Graduate/professional degree or higher: 9.3%
Housing: Homeownership rate: 66.8%; Median home value: $87,100; Median year structure built: 1955; Homeowner vacancy rate: 0.0%; Median selected monthly owner costs: $1,312 with a mortgage, $358 without a mortgage; Median gross rent: $713 per month; Rental vacancy rate: 0.0%
Health Insurance: 95.6% have insurance; 74.0% have private insurance; 37.4% have public insurance; 4.4% do not have insurance; 0.0% of children under 18 do not have insurance
Transportation: Commute: 98.1% car, 0.0% public transportation, 1.9% walk, 0.0% work from home; Mean travel time to work: 21.3 minutes

SCIOTODALE (CDP). Covers a land area of 1.949 square miles and a water area of 0.005 square miles. Located at 38.75° N. Lat; 82.85° W. Long. Elevation is 597 feet.
Population: 1,305; Growth (since 2000): 32.9%; Density: 669.6 persons per square mile; Race: 97.8% White, 0.0% Black/African American, 0.7% Asian, 0.0% American Indian/Alaska Native, 0.0% Native Hawaiian/Other Pacific Islander, 1.5% Two or more races, 0.0% Hispanic of any race; Average household size: 2.53; Median age: 42.3; Age under 18: 14.7%; Age 65 and over: 16.0%; Males per 100 females: 95.8; Marriage status: 24.8% never married, 56.0% now married, 0.0% separated, 4.2% widowed, 15.0% divorced; Foreign born: 0.7%; Speak English only: 98.7%; With disability: 13.1%; Veterans: 14.2%; Ancestry: 35.4% German, 10.6% English, 10.5% Irish, 5.8% American, 4.7% Italian
Employment: 5.5% management, business, and financial, 1.6% computer, engineering, and science, 9.0% education, legal, community service, arts, and media, 2.4% healthcare practitioners, 37.1% service, 4.3% sales and office, 18.4% natural resources, construction, and maintenance, 21.8% production, transportation, and material moving
Income: Per capita: $25,371; Median household: $69,474; Average household: $63,376; Households with income of $100,000 or more: 11.2%; Poverty rate: 23.5%
Educational Attainment: High school diploma or higher: 93.2%; Bachelor's degree or higher: 6.4%; Graduate/professional degree or higher: 3.5%
Housing: Homeownership rate: 81.4%; Median home value: $97,600; Median year structure built: 1958; Homeowner vacancy rate: 0.0%; Median selected monthly owner costs: $1,070 with a mortgage, $394 without a mortgage; Median gross rent: n/a per month; Rental vacancy rate: 0.0%
Health Insurance: 70.6% have insurance; 54.7% have private insurance; 31.6% have public insurance; 29.4% do not have insurance; 17.2% of children under 18 do not have insurance
Transportation: Commute: 100.0% car, 0.0% public transportation, 0.0% walk, 0.0% work from home; Mean travel time to work: 19.3 minutes

SOUTH WEBSTER (village). Covers a land area of 1.311 square miles and a water area of 0.014 square miles. Located at 38.82° N. Lat; 82.73° W. Long. Elevation is 705 feet.
Population: 645; Growth (since 2000): -15.6%; Density: 492.2 persons per square mile; Race: 99.7% White, 0.0% Black/African American, 0.0% Asian, 0.0% American Indian/Alaska Native, 0.0% Native Hawaiian/Other Pacific Islander, 0.3% Two or more races, 0.6% Hispanic of any race; Average household size: 2.36; Median age: 44.8; Age under 18: 20.9%; Age 65 and over: 23.7%; Males per 100 females: 91.2; Marriage status: 20.9% never married, 58.1% now married, 0.0% separated, 6.8% widowed, 14.2% divorced; Foreign born: 0.3%; Speak English only: 99.7%; With disability: 11.6%; Veterans: 17.3%; Ancestry: 29.9% German, 21.7% Irish, 9.5% American, 6.0% English, 3.6% French
Employment: 6.5% management, business, and financial, 2.0% computer, engineering, and science, 12.1% education, legal, community service, arts, and media, 19.4% healthcare practitioners, 14.9% service, 19.0% sales and office, 10.1% natural resources, construction, and maintenance, 16.1% production, transportation, and material moving
Income: Per capita: $26,503; Median household: $49,375; Average household: $62,606; Households with income of $100,000 or more: 16.1%; Poverty rate: 11.5%
Educational Attainment: High school diploma or higher: 83.5%; Bachelor's degree or higher: 16.5%; Graduate/professional degree or higher: 8.5%

School District(s)

Bloom-Vernon Local (PK-12)
2015-16 Enrollment: 890. . . . . (740) 778-2281
Housing: Homeownership rate: 83.2%; Median home value: $100,300; Median year structure built: 1955; Homeowner vacancy rate: 0.0%; Median selected monthly owner costs: $935 with a mortgage, $405 without a mortgage; Median gross rent: $709 per month; Rental vacancy rate: 0.0%
Health Insurance: 89.9% have insurance; 68.2% have private insurance; 37.4% have public insurance; 10.1% do not have insurance; 3.0% of children under 18 do not have insurance
Transportation: Commute: 91.3% car, 0.0% public transportation, 4.6% walk, 2.9% work from home; Mean travel time to work: 27.6 minutes

STOUT (unincorporated postal area)

ZCTA: 45684

Covers a land area of 79.263 square miles and a water area of 1.169 square miles. Located at 38.65° N. Lat; 83.19° W. Long..

Population: 2,177; Growth (since 2000): 19.2%; Density: 27.5 persons per square mile; Race: 95.6% White, 0.0% Black/African American, 0.0% Asian, 1.4% American Indian/Alaska Native, 0.0% Native Hawaiian/Other Pacific Islander, 3.0% Two or more races, 0.0% Hispanic of any race; Average household size: 2.46; Median age: 43.7; Age under 18: 21.8%; Age 65 and over: 11.6%; Males per 100 females: 98.2; Marriage status: 19.1% never married, 60.1% now married, 0.0% separated, 5.5% widowed, 15.4% divorced; Foreign born: 0.5%; Speak English only: 98.9%; With disability: 22.1%; Veterans: 6.0%; Ancestry: 20.0% German, 19.9% American, 7.3% Irish, 4.1% English, 2.3% Scottish

Employment: 4.1% management, business, and financial, 5.7% computer, engineering, and science, 9.8% education, legal, community service, arts, and media, 6.6% healthcare practitioners, 20.3% service, 19.4% sales and office, 9.9% natural resources, construction, and maintenance, 24.1% production, transportation, and material moving

Income: Per capita: $23,886; Median household: $49,044; Average household: $57,590; Households with income of $100,000 or more: 8.0%; Poverty rate: 9.1%

Educational Attainment: High school diploma or higher: 84.0%; Bachelor's degree or higher: 9.8%; Graduate/professional degree or higher: 2.7%

Housing: Homeownership rate: 79.0%; Median home value: $99,300; Median year structure built: 1986; Homeowner vacancy rate: 1.6%; Median selected monthly owner costs: $1,188 with a mortgage, $435 without a mortgage; Median gross rent: $599 per month; Rental vacancy rate: 2.1%

Health Insurance: 87.6% have insurance; 57.0% have private insurance; 39.2% have public insurance; 12.4% do not have insurance; 0.0% of children under 18 do not have insurance

Transportation: Commute: 94.5% car, 1.5% public transportation, 1.3% walk, 0.0% work from home; Mean travel time to work: 42.9 minutes

WEST PORTSMOUTH (CDP). Covers a land area of 4.705 square miles and a water area of 0.003 square miles. Located at 38.77° N. Lat; 83.04° W. Long. Elevation is 617 feet.

Population: 2,784; Growth (since 2000): -19.5%; Density: 591.7 persons per square mile; Race: 98.8% White, 0.0% Black/African American, 0.0% Asian, 1.2% American Indian/Alaska Native, 0.0% Native Hawaiian/Other Pacific Islander, 0.0% Two or more races, 0.0% Hispanic of any race; Average household size: 2.44; Median age: 40.3; Age under 18: 24.6%; Age 65 and over: 16.1%; Males per 100 females: 93.3; Marriage status: 20.1% never married, 55.2% now married, 2.8% separated, 6.1% widowed, 18.6% divorced; Foreign born: 0.0%; Speak English only: 99.7%; With disability: 23.5%; Veterans: 12.2%; Ancestry: 13.8% American, 13.7% German, 8.8% Irish, 8.7% English, 5.4% Italian

Employment: 9.3% management, business, and financial, 3.9% computer, engineering, and science, 8.6% education, legal, community service, arts, and media, 6.8% healthcare practitioners, 20.5% service, 25.4% sales and office, 7.5% natural resources, construction, and maintenance, 18.0% production, transportation, and material moving

Income: Per capita: $18,327; Median household: $33,379; Average household: $43,331; Households with income of $100,000 or more: 10.6%; Poverty rate: 19.9%

Educational Attainment: High school diploma or higher: 84.8%; Bachelor's degree or higher: 7.9%; Graduate/professional degree or higher: 1.6%

School District(s)

Washington-Nile Local (PK-12)
2015-16 Enrollment: 1,497 . . . . (740) 858-1111

Housing: Homeownership rate: 75.7%; Median home value: $71,800; Median year structure built: 1958; Homeowner vacancy rate: 2.8%; Median selected monthly owner costs: $1,025 with a mortgage, $391 without a mortgage; Median gross rent: $590 per month; Rental vacancy rate: 9.2%

Health Insurance: 90.7% have insurance; 55.6% have private insurance; 46.5% have public insurance; 9.3% do not have insurance; 0.0% of children under 18 do not have insurance

Transportation: Commute: 97.0% car, 0.0% public transportation, 1.1% walk, 0.8% work from home; Mean travel time to work: 29.9 minutes

WHEELERSBURG (CDP). Covers a land area of 5.804 square miles and a water area of 0.094 square miles. Located at 38.74° N. Lat; 82.85° W. Long. Elevation is 554 feet.

Population: 5,931; Growth (since 2000): -8.3%; Density: 1,021.9 persons per square mile; Race: 94.2% White, 0.2% Black/African American, 1.1% Asian, 0.0% American Indian/Alaska Native, 0.0% Native Hawaiian/Other Pacific Islander, 4.5% Two or more races, 0.3% Hispanic of any race; Average household size: 2.32; Median age: 41.5; Age under 18: 19.8%; Age 65 and over: 17.8%; Males per 100 females: 89.4; Marriage status: 22.1% never married, 57.7% now married, 0.8% separated, 7.1% widowed, 13.1% divorced; Foreign born: 2.2%; Speak English only: 99.0%; With disability: 15.7%; Veterans: 7.4%; Ancestry: 27.1% German, 12.3% Irish, 9.7% American, 8.3% English, 2.3% French

Employment: 10.0% management, business, and financial, 3.2% computer, engineering, and science, 7.2% education, legal, community service, arts, and media, 11.2% healthcare practitioners, 19.3% service, 22.5% sales and office, 12.6% natural resources, construction, and maintenance, 14.0% production, transportation, and material moving

Income: Per capita: $27,909; Median household: $50,264; Average household: $65,889; Households with income of $100,000 or more: 22.2%; Poverty rate: 11.5%

Educational Attainment: High school diploma or higher: 89.6%; Bachelor's degree or higher: 21.5%; Graduate/professional degree or higher: 8.6%

School District(s)

Wheelersburg Local (PK-12)
2015-16 Enrollment: 1,594 . . . . (740) 574-8484

Housing: Homeownership rate: 68.4%; Median home value: $152,000; Median year structure built: 1973; Homeowner vacancy rate: 2.6%; Median selected monthly owner costs: $1,265 with a mortgage, $453 without a mortgage; Median gross rent: $609 per month; Rental vacancy rate: 10.9%

Health Insurance: 93.4% have insurance; 70.3% have private insurance; 36.8% have public insurance; 6.6% do not have insurance; 4.8% of children under 18 do not have insurance

Newspapers: The Scioto Voice (weekly circulation 3,600)

Transportation: Commute: 94.9% car, 0.0% public transportation, 1.2% walk, 3.2% work from home; Mean travel time to work: 22.2 minutes

Seneca County

Located in northern Ohio; drained by the Sandusky River and its tributaries. Covers a land area of 551.017 square miles, a water area of 1.776 square miles, and is located in the Eastern Time Zone at 41.12° N. Lat., 83.13° W. Long. The county was founded in 1820. County seat is Tiffin.

Seneca County is part of the Tiffin, OH Micropolitan Statistical Area. The entire metro area includes: Seneca County, OH

Weather Station: Tiffin Elevation: 740 feet

	Jan	Feb	Mar	Apr	May	Jun	Jul	Aug	Sep	Oct	Nov	Dec
High	33	36	47	60	71	80	84	83	76	63	50	37
Low	18	21	29	39	49	59	63	61	53	42	34	23
Precip	2.3	2.0	2.5	3.3	3.9	4.1	3.6	3.7	3.4	2.6	3.0	2.9
Snow	9.3	6.0	4.4	1.3	tr	0.0	0.0	0.0	0.0	tr	1.0	7.0

High and Low temperatures in degrees Fahrenheit; Precipitation and Snow in inches

Population: 55,711; Growth (since 2000): -5.1%; Density: 101.1 persons per square mile; Race: 94.1% White, 2.4% Black/African American, 0.5% Asian, 0.1% American Indian/Alaska Native, 0.0% Native Hawaiian/Other Pacific Islander, 2.1% two or more races, 4.8% Hispanic of any race; Average household size: 2.47; Median age: 39.4; Age under 18: 22.5%; Age 65 and over: 16.2%; Males per 100 females: 99.8; Marriage status: 30.4% never married, 50.7% now married, 1.5% separated, 6.2% widowed, 12.7% divorced; Foreign born: 1.3%; Speak English only: 96.9%; With disability: 14.0%; Veterans: 9.3%; Ancestry: 45.1% German, 10.4% Irish, 7.9% American, 6.1% English, 5.1% Italian

Religion: Six largest groups: 33.1% Catholicism, 6.5% Methodist/Pietist, 5.7% Presbyterian-Reformed, 3.0% Lutheran, 2.4% Baptist, 1.8% Pentecostal

Economy: Unemployment rate: 4.2%; Leading industries: 14.9 % retail trade; 14.5 % other services (except public administration); 12.1 % health care and social assistance; Farms: 1,113 totaling 290,511 acres; Company size: 0 employ 1,000 or more persons, 4 employ 500 to 999 persons, 27 employ 100 to 499 persons, 1,097 employ less than 100 persons;

Business ownership: 1,287 women-owned, 26 Black-owned, 71 Hispanic-owned, n/a Asian-owned, n/a American Indian/Alaska Native-owned
Employment: 10.3% management, business, and financial, 2.8% computer, engineering, and science, 8.0% education, legal, community service, arts, and media, 5.2% healthcare practitioners, 17.4% service, 18.9% sales and office, 9.4% natural resources, construction, and maintenance, 27.8% production, transportation, and material moving
Income: Per capita: $23,900; Median household: $48,415; Average household: $60,504; Households with income of $100,000 or more: 14.3%; Poverty rate: 15.6%
Educational Attainment: High school diploma or higher: 90.8%; Bachelor's degree or higher: 14.7%; Graduate/professional degree or higher: 5.3%
Housing: Homeownership rate: 72.2%; Median home value: $97,000; Median year structure built: 1955; Homeowner vacancy rate: 2.1%; Median selected monthly owner costs: $983 with a mortgage, $388 without a mortgage; Median gross rent: $646 per month; Rental vacancy rate: 8.8%
Vital Statistics: Birth rate: 102.4 per 10,000 population; Death rate: 102.6 per 10,000 population; Age-adjusted cancer mortality rate: 180.9 deaths per 100,000 population
Health Insurance: 93.2% have insurance; 72.8% have private insurance; 35.3% have public insurance; 6.8% do not have insurance; 2.6% of children under 18 do not have insurance
Health Care: Physicians: 8.1 per 10,000 population; Dentists: 4.0 per 10,000 population; Hospital beds: 47.0 per 10,000 population; Hospital admissions: 998.8 per 10,000 population
Transportation: Commute: 92.1% car, 0.4% public transportation, 4.3% walk, 2.3% work from home; Mean travel time to work: 20.8 minutes
2016 Presidential Election: 61.3% Trump, 30.6% Clinton, 5.4% Johnson, 1.0% Stein
National and State Parks: Sandusky Scenic River State Access Area; Springville Marsh State Natural Area
Additional Information Contacts
Seneca Government . . . . (419) 447-4550
http://www.seneca-county.com

Seneca County Communities

ALVADA (unincorporated postal area)
ZCTA: 44802
Covers a land area of 28.449 square miles and a water area of 0 square miles. Located at 41.05° N. Lat; 83.42° W. Long. Elevation is 846 feet.
Population: 841; Growth (since 2000): -17.0%; Density: 29.6 persons per square mile; Race: 99.3% White, 0.0% Black/African American, 0.0% Asian, 0.0% American Indian/Alaska Native, 0.0% Native Hawaiian/Other Pacific Islander, 0.7% Two or more races, 1.1% Hispanic of any race; Average household size: 2.43; Median age: 43.5; Age under 18: 22.2%; Age 65 and over: 13.9%; Males per 100 females: 108.1; Marriage status: 19.4% never married, 70.8% now married, 1.3% separated, 4.1% widowed, 5.7% divorced; Foreign born: 0.4%; Speak English only: 99.4%; With disability: 10.8%; Veterans: 9.9%; Ancestry: 57.2% German, 10.8% American, 8.1% Irish, 7.1% English, 2.3% French
Employment: 13.4% management, business, and financial, 3.2% computer, engineering, and science, 4.1% education, legal, community service, arts, and media, 3.2% healthcare practitioners, 11.2% service, 23.2% sales and office, 14.6% natural resources, construction, and maintenance, 27.1% production, transportation, and material moving
Income: Per capita: $25,069; Median household: $55,833; Average household: $61,213; Households with income of $100,000 or more: 11.9%; Poverty rate: 4.9%
Educational Attainment: High school diploma or higher: 88.4%; Bachelor's degree or higher: 13.3%; Graduate/professional degree or higher: 4.3%
Housing: Homeownership rate: 82.1%; Median home value: $122,700; Median year structure built: 1953; Homeowner vacancy rate: 0.0%; Median selected monthly owner costs: $1,305 with a mortgage, $358 without a mortgage; Median gross rent: $567 per month; Rental vacancy rate: 0.0%
Health Insurance: 95.4% have insurance; 85.6% have private insurance; 23.3% have public insurance; 4.6% do not have insurance; 5.9% of children under 18 do not have insurance
Transportation: Commute: 92.7% car, 0.0% public transportation, 0.7% walk, 6.6% work from home; Mean travel time to work: 19.5 minutes

ATTICA (village). Covers a land area of 0.663 square miles and a water area of 0.009 square miles. Located at 41.06° N. Lat; 82.89° W. Long. Elevation is 948 feet.
Population: 1,018; Growth (since 2000): 6.6%; Density: 1,535.0 persons per square mile; Race: 98.0% White, 0.0% Black/African American, 0.0% Asian, 0.0% American Indian/Alaska Native, 0.0% Native Hawaiian/Other Pacific Islander, 1.7% Two or more races, 1.2% Hispanic of any race; Average household size: 2.45; Median age: 36.0; Age under 18: 25.6%; Age 65 and over: 19.8%; Males per 100 females: 95.4; Marriage status: 22.7% never married, 56.2% now married, 0.4% separated, 4.3% widowed, 16.8% divorced; Foreign born: 0.0%; Speak English only: 99.8%; With disability: 13.4%; Veterans: 10.3%; Ancestry: 56.8% German, 11.0% Irish, 6.8% English, 3.5% Italian, 3.0% American
Employment: 6.0% management, business, and financial, 0.6% computer, engineering, and science, 7.3% education, legal, community service, arts, and media, 5.6% healthcare practitioners, 18.9% service, 18.7% sales and office, 13.5% natural resources, construction, and maintenance, 29.3% production, transportation, and material moving
Income: Per capita: $22,254; Median household: $49,567; Average household: $53,765; Households with income of $100,000 or more: 11.1%; Poverty rate: 12.9%
Educational Attainment: High school diploma or higher: 90.2%; Bachelor's degree or higher: 9.1%; Graduate/professional degree or higher: 4.3%

School District(s)
Seneca East Local (KG-12)
2015-16 Enrollment: 936. . . . . (419) 426-7041
Housing: Homeownership rate: 67.0%; Median home value: $83,200; Median year structure built: 1944; Homeowner vacancy rate: 2.4%; Median selected monthly owner costs: $977 with a mortgage, $435 without a mortgage; Median gross rent: $585 per month; Rental vacancy rate: 9.3%
Health Insurance: 96.4% have insurance; 74.1% have private insurance; 40.9% have public insurance; 3.6% do not have insurance; 0.0% of children under 18 do not have insurance
Newspapers: Attica Hub (weekly circulation 4,400)
Transportation: Commute: 92.1% car, 1.3% public transportation, 1.5% walk, 4.4% work from home; Mean travel time to work: 26.5 minutes

BASCOM (CDP). Covers a land area of 1.514 square miles and a water area of 0 square miles. Located at 41.13° N. Lat; 83.29° W. Long. Elevation is 774 feet.
Population: 368; Growth (since 2000): n/a; Density: 243.1 persons per square mile; Race: 87.2% White, 0.0% Black/African American, 9.0% Asian, 0.0% American Indian/Alaska Native, 0.0% Native Hawaiian/Other Pacific Islander, 3.8% Two or more races, 0.0% Hispanic of any race; Average household size: 2.10; Median age: 54.5; Age under 18: 16.3%; Age 65 and over: 27.7%; Males per 100 females: 109.7; Marriage status: 13.0% never married, 62.9% now married, 0.0% separated, 9.5% widowed, 14.6% divorced; Foreign born: 7.9%; Speak English only: 91.9%; With disability: 17.1%; Veterans: 6.5%; Ancestry: 53.8% German, 7.9% Irish, 5.4% Italian, 3.8% English, 2.7% French
Employment: 17.9% management, business, and financial, 0.0% computer, engineering, and science, 9.8% education, legal, community service, arts, and media, 14.7% healthcare practitioners, 3.1% service, 26.3% sales and office, 11.2% natural resources, construction, and maintenance, 17.0% production, transportation, and material moving
Income: Per capita: $31,464; Median household: $58,125; Average household: $65,859; Households with income of $100,000 or more: 17.7%; Poverty rate: n/a
Educational Attainment: High school diploma or higher: 94.4%; Bachelor's degree or higher: 29.9%; Graduate/professional degree or higher: 7.3%

School District(s)
Hopewell-Loudon Local (KG-12)
2015-16 Enrollment: 880. . . . . (419) 937-2216
Housing: Homeownership rate: 90.3%; Median home value: $114,200; Median year structure built: 1953; Homeowner vacancy rate: 0.0%; Median selected monthly owner costs: $1,125 with a mortgage, $563 without a mortgage; Median gross rent: n/a per month; Rental vacancy rate: 0.0%
Health Insurance: 100.0% have insurance; 91.6% have private insurance; 27.7% have public insurance; 0.0% do not have insurance; 0.0% of children under 18 do not have insurance
Transportation: Commute: 92.4% car, 0.0% public transportation, 0.0% walk, 4.5% work from home; Mean travel time to work: 17.6 minutes

BETTSVILLE (village). Covers a land area of 0.521 square miles and a water area of 0 square miles. Located at 41.24° N. Lat; 83.23° W. Long. Elevation is 702 feet.

Population: 666; Growth (since 2000): -15.1%; Density: 1,278.5 persons per square mile; Race: 95.9% White, 0.0% Black/African American, 0.0% Asian, 0.0% American Indian/Alaska Native, 0.0% Native Hawaiian/Other Pacific Islander, 2.4% Two or more races, 4.5% Hispanic of any race; Average household size: 2.34; Median age: 39.2; Age under 18: 25.7%; Age 65 and over: 13.7%; Males per 100 females: 102.8; Marriage status: 23.0% never married, 49.9% now married, 2.9% separated, 11.6% widowed, 15.5% divorced; Foreign born: 0.6%; Speak English only: 96.1%; With disability: 18.6%; Veterans: 11.5%; Ancestry: 51.4% German, 10.8% Irish, 9.8% Italian, 5.1% American, 3.5% Polish

Employment: 8.9% management, business, and financial, 3.0% computer, engineering, and science, 8.2% education, legal, community service, arts, and media, 1.3% healthcare practitioners, 15.4% service, 24.6% sales and office, 9.2% natural resources, construction, and maintenance, 29.5% production, transportation, and material moving

Income: Per capita: $21,480; Median household: $47,898; Average household: $49,969; Households with income of $100,000 or more: 8.4%; Poverty rate: 11.6%

Educational Attainment: High school diploma or higher: 91.2%; Bachelor's degree or higher: 9.9%; Graduate/professional degree or higher: 2.5%

Housing: Homeownership rate: 72.3%; Median home value: $75,200; Median year structure built: 1941; Homeowner vacancy rate: 8.8%; Median selected monthly owner costs: $910 with a mortgage, $318 without a mortgage; Median gross rent: $621 per month; Rental vacancy rate: 0.0%

Health Insurance: 90.5% have insurance; 65.8% have private insurance; 38.9% have public insurance; 9.5% do not have insurance; 2.3% of children under 18 do not have insurance

Transportation: Commute: 94.8% car, 0.0% public transportation, 3.9% walk, 0.7% work from home; Mean travel time to work: 22.9 minutes

BLOOMVILLE (village). Covers a land area of 0.603 square miles and a water area of 0 square miles. Located at 41.05° N. Lat; 83.01° W. Long. Elevation is 928 feet.

Population: 915; Growth (since 2000): -12.4%; Density: 1,516.3 persons per square mile; Race: 98.1% White, 0.0% Black/African American, 0.5% Asian, 0.2% American Indian/Alaska Native, 0.0% Native Hawaiian/Other Pacific Islander, 0.9% Two or more races, 5.2% Hispanic of any race; Average household size: 2.52; Median age: 39.2; Age under 18: 24.3%; Age 65 and over: 17.6%; Males per 100 females: 102.1; Marriage status: 30.3% never married, 46.7% now married, 2.3% separated, 12.1% widowed, 11.0% divorced; Foreign born: 0.7%; Speak English only: 96.9%; With disability: 20.6%; Veterans: 7.8%; Ancestry: 44.5% German, 16.5% Irish, 10.2% English, 9.0% American, 4.6% Italian

Employment: 3.9% management, business, and financial, 1.3% computer, engineering, and science, 3.4% education, legal, community service, arts, and media, 3.1% healthcare practitioners, 24.5% service, 15.5% sales and office, 11.4% natural resources, construction, and maintenance, 37.0% production, transportation, and material moving

Income: Per capita: $18,739; Median household: $39,417; Average household: $46,476; Households with income of $100,000 or more: 9.9%; Poverty rate: 19.8%

Educational Attainment: High school diploma or higher: 88.2%; Bachelor's degree or higher: 9.1%; Graduate/professional degree or higher: 2.7%

Housing: Homeownership rate: 66.0%; Median home value: $70,200; Median year structure built: 1947; Homeowner vacancy rate: 3.3%; Median selected monthly owner costs: $820 with a mortgage, $375 without a mortgage; Median gross rent: $667 per month; Rental vacancy rate: 10.5%

Health Insurance: 93.7% have insurance; 67.8% have private insurance; 41.0% have public insurance; 6.3% do not have insurance; 8.6% of children under 18 do not have insurance

Transportation: Commute: 97.0% car, 0.0% public transportation, 0.5% walk, 2.2% work from home; Mean travel time to work: 32.9 minutes

FLAT ROCK (CDP). Covers a land area of 0.209 square miles and a water area of 0 square miles. Located at 41.24° N. Lat; 82.86° W. Long. Elevation is 797 feet.

Population: 107; Growth (since 2000): n/a; Density: 511.6 persons per square mile; Race: 96.3% White, 3.7% Black/African American, 0.0% Asian, 0.0% American Indian/Alaska Native, 0.0% Native Hawaiian/Other Pacific Islander, 0.0% Two or more races, 0.0% Hispanic of any race; Average household size: 2.96; Median age: 37.1; Age under 18: 20.6%; Age 65 and over: 26.2%; Males per 100 females: 111.8; Marriage status: 44.0% never married, 50.5% now married, 0.0% separated, 4.4% widowed, 1.1% divorced; Foreign born: 0.0%; Speak English only: 100.0%; With disability: 0.0%; Veterans: 15.3%; Ancestry: 45.8% German, 33.6% Italian, 32.7% English, 0.9% Irish

Employment: 50.0% management, business, and financial, 0.0% computer, engineering, and science, 0.0% education, legal, community service, arts, and media, 0.0% healthcare practitioners, 0.0% service, 0.0% sales and office, 42.3% natural resources, construction, and maintenance, 7.7% production, transportation, and material moving

Income: Per capita: $14,561; Median household: n/a; Average household: n/a; Households with income of $100,000 or more: n/a; Poverty rate: 1.4%

Educational Attainment: High school diploma or higher: 90.6%; Bachelor's degree or higher: n/a; Graduate/professional degree or higher: n/a

Housing: Homeownership rate: 100.0%; Median home value: n/a; Median year structure built: Before 1940; Homeowner vacancy rate: 63.1%; Median selected monthly owner costs: n/a with a mortgage, n/a without a mortgage; Median gross rent: n/a per month; Rental vacancy rate: 0.0%

Health Insurance: 100.0% have insurance; 32.4% have private insurance; 100.0% have public insurance; 0.0% do not have insurance; 0.0% of children under 18 do not have insurance

Transportation: Commute: 100.0% car, 0.0% public transportation, 0.0% walk, 0.0% work from home; Mean travel time to work: 25.2 minutes

FORT SENECA (CDP). Covers a land area of 0.625 square miles and a water area of 0 square miles. Located at 41.20° N. Lat; 83.17° W. Long. Elevation is 699 feet.

Population: 235; Growth (since 2000): n/a; Density: 375.7 persons per square mile; Race: 100.0% White, 0.0% Black/African American, 0.0% Asian, 0.0% American Indian/Alaska Native, 0.0% Native Hawaiian/Other Pacific Islander, 0.0% Two or more races, 0.0% Hispanic of any race; Average household size: 2.47; Median age: 53.4; Age under 18: 12.8%; Age 65 and over: 32.3%; Males per 100 females: 92.4; Marriage status: 22.0% never married, 63.9% now married, 2.4% separated, 5.4% widowed, 8.8% divorced; Foreign born: 2.1%; Speak English only: 93.3%; With disability: 23.0%; Veterans: 20.0%; Ancestry: 42.6% German, 11.5% American, 8.5% English, 5.5% Scotch-Irish, 0.9% Norwegian

Employment: 25.0% management, business, and financial, 0.0% computer, engineering, and science, 0.0% education, legal, community service, arts, and media, 0.0% healthcare practitioners, 8.8% service, 26.5% sales and office, 13.2% natural resources, construction, and maintenance, 26.5% production, transportation, and material moving

Income: Per capita: $17,066; Median household: $32,083; Average household: $40,337; Households with income of $100,000 or more: 3.2%; Poverty rate: 8.7%

Educational Attainment: High school diploma or higher: 94.7%; Bachelor's degree or higher: 4.3%; Graduate/professional degree or higher: n/a

Housing: Homeownership rate: 92.6%; Median home value: $75,000; Median year structure built: 1964; Homeowner vacancy rate: 0.0%; Median selected monthly owner costs: $911 with a mortgage, $340 without a mortgage; Median gross rent: n/a per month; Rental vacancy rate: 0.0%

Health Insurance: 96.6% have insurance; 74.9% have private insurance; 55.7% have public insurance; 3.4% do not have insurance; 0.0% of children under 18 do not have insurance

Transportation: Commute: 92.1% car, 7.9% public transportation, 0.0% walk, 0.0% work from home; Mean travel time to work: 23.5 minutes

FOSTORIA (city). Covers a land area of 7.545 square miles and a water area of 0.218 square miles. Located at 41.16° N. Lat; 83.41° W. Long. Elevation is 781 feet.

History: Fostoria grew from the union in 1854 of two rival settlements, Rome and Risdon, which had been established in 1832. The town was named for C.W. Foster, a local real estate developer whose son, Charles, served as governor of Ohio (1880-1884).

Population: 13,397; Growth (since 2000): -3.8%; Density: 1,775.6 persons per square mile; Race: 86.8% White, 5.8% Black/African American, 0.1% Asian, 0.1% American Indian/Alaska Native, 0.0% Native Hawaiian/Other Pacific Islander, 4.9% Two or more races, 9.9% Hispanic of any race; Average household size: 2.38; Median age: 38.4; Age under 18: 26.5%; Age 65 and over: 16.6%; Males per 100 females: 89.7; Marriage status: 31.3% never married, 40.8% now married, 1.6% separated, 10.0% widowed, 17.9% divorced; Foreign born: 0.7%; Speak English only: 96.6%;

With disability: 17.8%; Veterans: 10.8%; Ancestry: 37.4% German, 10.9% Irish, 7.9% American, 4.4% Italian, 4.2% English
Employment: 5.1% management, business, and financial, 1.9% computer, engineering, and science, 6.6% education, legal, community service, arts, and media, 3.7% healthcare practitioners, 21.7% service, 17.4% sales and office, 4.8% natural resources, construction, and maintenance, 38.8% production, transportation, and material moving
Income: Per capita: $20,200; Median household: $35,168; Average household: $47,967; Households with income of $100,000 or more: 7.1%; Poverty rate: 30.6%
Educational Attainment: High school diploma or higher: 87.1%; Bachelor's degree or higher: 9.3%; Graduate/professional degree or higher: 2.8%

School District(s)

Fostoria City (PK-12)
2015-16 Enrollment: 1,858 . . . . (419) 435-8163
Housing: Homeownership rate: 68.0%; Median home value: $62,900; Median year structure built: 1951; Homeowner vacancy rate: 4.3%; Median selected monthly owner costs: $783 with a mortgage, $366 without a mortgage; Median gross rent: $588 per month; Rental vacancy rate: 4.1%
Health Insurance: 90.7% have insurance; 58.9% have private insurance; 50.0% have public insurance; 9.3% do not have insurance; 2.6% of children under 18 do not have insurance
Hospitals: Fostoria Community Hospital (66 beds)
Newspapers: Review Times (daily circulation 4,100); The Focus (weekly circulation 12,000)
Transportation: Commute: 92.5% car, 0.2% public transportation, 5.1% walk, 1.8% work from home; Mean travel time to work: 19.6 minutes
Additional Information Contacts
City of Fostoria . . . . (419) 435-8282
http://www.ci.fostoria.oh.us

KANSAS (CDP). Covers a land area of 0.439 square miles and a water area of 0 square miles. Located at 41.25° N. Lat; 83.28° W. Long. Elevation is 728 feet.
Population: 53; Growth (since 2000): n/a; Density: 120.7 persons per square mile; Race: 100.0% White, 0.0% Black/African American, 0.0% Asian, 0.0% American Indian/Alaska Native, 0.0% Native Hawaiian/Other Pacific Islander, 0.0% Two or more races, 0.0% Hispanic of any race; Average household size: 1.39; Median age: 44.1; Age under 18: 0.0%; Age 65 and over: 15.1%; Males per 100 females: 82.7; Marriage status: 49.1% never married, 50.9% now married, 0.0% separated, 0.0% widowed, 0.0% divorced; Foreign born: 0.0%; Speak English only: 100.0%; With disability: 0.0%; Veterans: 9.4%; Ancestry: 83.0% German, 49.1% Italian
Employment: 0.0% management, business, and financial, 0.0% computer, engineering, and science, 0.0% education, legal, community service, arts, and media, 0.0% healthcare practitioners, 0.0% service, 73.7% sales and office, 26.3% natural resources, construction, and maintenance, 0.0% production, transportation, and material moving
Income: Per capita: $26,249; Median household: n/a; Average household: $34,405; Households with income of $100,000 or more: n/a; Poverty rate: n/a
Educational Attainment: High school diploma or higher: 100.0%; Bachelor's degree or higher: n/a; Graduate/professional degree or higher: n/a

School District(s)

Lakota Local (KG-12)
2015-16 Enrollment: 1,025 . . . . (419) 986-6650
Housing: Homeownership rate: 31.6%; Median home value: n/a; Median year structure built: 1981; Homeowner vacancy rate: 0.0%; Median selected monthly owner costs: n/a with a mortgage, n/a without a mortgage; Median gross rent: n/a per month; Rental vacancy rate: 0.0%
Health Insurance: 100.0% have insurance; 100.0% have private insurance; 15.1% have public insurance; 0.0% do not have insurance; 0.0% of children under 18 do not have insurance
Transportation: Commute: 100.0% car, 0.0% public transportation, 0.0% walk, 0.0% work from home; Mean travel time to work: 0.0 minutes

MELMORE (CDP). Covers a land area of 0.593 square miles and a water area of 0 square miles. Located at 41.03° N. Lat; 83.10° W. Long. Elevation is 863 feet.
Population: 118; Growth (since 2000): n/a; Density: 198.9 persons per square mile; Race: 100.0% White, 0.0% Black/African American, 0.0% Asian, 0.0% American Indian/Alaska Native, 0.0% Native Hawaiian/Other Pacific Islander, 0.0% Two or more races, 0.0% Hispanic of any race; Average household size: 2.57; Median age: 40.7; Age under 18: 33.1%; Age 65 and over: 9.3%; Males per 100 females: 104.0; Marriage status: 60.8% never married, 11.4% now married, 11.4% separated, 0.0% widowed, 27.8% divorced; Foreign born: 0.0%; Speak English only: 100.0%; With disability: 28.0%; Veterans: 0.0%; Ancestry: 50.0% German, 7.6% Irish, 7.6% Italian
Employment: 0.0% management, business, and financial, 0.0% computer, engineering, and science, 0.0% education, legal, community service, arts, and media, 0.0% healthcare practitioners, 0.0% service, 100.0% sales and office, 0.0% natural resources, construction, and maintenance, 0.0% production, transportation, and material moving
Income: Per capita: $14,635; Median household: n/a; Average household: $36,439; Households with income of $100,000 or more: n/a; Poverty rate: 40.7%
Educational Attainment: High school diploma or higher: 64.6%; Bachelor's degree or higher: 11.4%; Graduate/professional degree or higher: n/a
Housing: Homeownership rate: 100.0%; Median home value: $48,000; Median year structure built: Before 1940; Homeowner vacancy rate: 0.0%; Median selected monthly owner costs: n/a with a mortgage, n/a without a mortgage; Median gross rent: n/a per month; Rental vacancy rate: 100.0%
Health Insurance: 100.0% have insurance; 64.4% have private insurance; 68.6% have public insurance; 0.0% do not have insurance; 0.0% of children under 18 do not have insurance
Transportation: Commute: 100.0% car, 0.0% public transportation, 0.0% walk, 0.0% work from home; Mean travel time to work: 0.0 minutes

NEW RIEGEL (village). Covers a land area of 0.200 square miles and a water area of 0 square miles. Located at 41.05° N. Lat; 83.32° W. Long. Elevation is 833 feet.
Population: 269; Growth (since 2000): 19.0%; Density: 1,343.1 persons per square mile; Race: 99.3% White, 0.7% Black/African American, 0.0% Asian, 0.0% American Indian/Alaska Native, 0.0% Native Hawaiian/Other Pacific Islander, 0.0% Two or more races, 1.1% Hispanic of any race; Average household size: 2.20; Median age: 45.3; Age under 18: 16.7%; Age 65 and over: 15.6%; Males per 100 females: 97.6; Marriage status: 22.2% never married, 49.6% now married, 0.0% separated, 10.0% widowed, 18.3% divorced; Foreign born: 1.1%; Speak English only: 100.0%; With disability: 10.0%; Veterans: 3.1%; Ancestry: 74.3% German, 4.8% Italian, 4.1% Belgian, 4.1% French, 3.0% American
Employment: 9.8% management, business, and financial, 3.1% computer, engineering, and science, 1.8% education, legal, community service, arts, and media, 9.2% healthcare practitioners, 14.7% service, 10.4% sales and office, 12.3% natural resources, construction, and maintenance, 38.7% production, transportation, and material moving
Income: Per capita: $25,908; Median household: $41,667; Average household: $53,996; Households with income of $100,000 or more: 14.2%; Poverty rate: 14.1%
Educational Attainment: High school diploma or higher: 98.5%; Bachelor's degree or higher: 14.5%; Graduate/professional degree or higher: 5.0%

School District(s)

New Riegel Local (KG-12)
2015-16 Enrollment: 400. . . . . (419) 595-2265
Housing: Homeownership rate: 58.3%; Median home value: $77,300; Median year structure built: Before 1940; Homeowner vacancy rate: 0.0%; Median selected monthly owner costs: $838 with a mortgage, $346 without a mortgage; Median gross rent: $711 per month; Rental vacancy rate: 0.0%
Health Insurance: 97.8% have insurance; 76.6% have private insurance; 33.1% have public insurance; 2.2% do not have insurance; 0.0% of children under 18 do not have insurance
Transportation: Commute: 93.6% car, 1.3% public transportation, 3.2% walk, 1.9% work from home; Mean travel time to work: 19.0 minutes

OLD FORT (CDP). Covers a land area of 0.577 square miles and a water area of 0 square miles. Located at 41.24° N. Lat; 83.15° W. Long. Elevation is 686 feet.
Population: 197; Growth (since 2000): n/a; Density: 341.1 persons per square mile; Race: 100.0% White, 0.0% Black/African American, 0.0% Asian, 0.0% American Indian/Alaska Native, 0.0% Native Hawaiian/Other Pacific Islander, 0.0% Two or more races, 0.0% Hispanic of any race; Average household size: 2.81; Median age: 41.4; Age under 18: 21.8%; Age 65 and over: 28.4%; Males per 100 females: 93.8; Marriage status:

22.1% never married, 57.8% now married, 0.0% separated, 8.4% widowed, 11.7% divorced; Foreign born: 0.0%; Speak English only: 100.0%; With disability: 11.2%; Veterans: 17.5%; Ancestry: 50.3% German, 11.2% American, 6.6% English, 6.6% Irish, 3.6% Italian
Employment: 0.0% management, business, and financial, 0.0% computer, engineering, and science, 41.9% education, legal, community service, arts, and media, 0.0% healthcare practitioners, 3.8% service, 32.4% sales and office, 3.8% natural resources, construction, and maintenance, 18.1% production, transportation, and material moving
Income: Per capita: $23,982; Median household: $46,250; Average household: $65,346; Households with income of $100,000 or more: 34.3%; Poverty rate: 13.2%
Educational Attainment: High school diploma or higher: 85.9%; Bachelor's degree or higher: 31.9%; Graduate/professional degree or higher: 23.7%

School District(s)

Old Fort Local (PK-12)
2015-16 Enrollment: 606 . . . . (419) 992-4291
Housing: Homeownership rate: 92.9%; Median home value: $83,900; Median year structure built: 1944; Homeowner vacancy rate: 23.5%; Median selected monthly owner costs: $758 with a mortgage, $325 without a mortgage; Median gross rent: n/a per month; Rental vacancy rate: 0.0%
Health Insurance: 89.8% have insurance; 73.1% have private insurance; 34.0% have public insurance; 10.2% do not have insurance; 0.0% of children under 18 do not have insurance
Transportation: Commute: 100.0% car, 0.0% public transportation, 0.0% walk, 0.0% work from home; Mean travel time to work: 28.1 minutes

---

REPUBLIC (village). Covers a land area of 0.863 square miles and a water area of 0 square miles. Located at 41.13° N. Lat; 83.02° W. Long. Elevation is 886 feet.
Population: 612; Growth (since 2000): -0.3%; Density: 709.5 persons per square mile; Race: 97.9% White, 2.1% Black/African American, 0.0% Asian, 0.0% American Indian/Alaska Native, 0.0% Native Hawaiian/Other Pacific Islander, 0.0% Two or more races, 3.8% Hispanic of any race; Average household size: 2.41; Median age: 41.3; Age under 18: 23.2%; Age 65 and over: 14.7%; Males per 100 females: 100.4; Marriage status: 23.5% never married, 52.4% now married, 0.6% separated, 8.1% widowed, 16.0% divorced; Foreign born: 0.3%; Speak English only: 96.7%; With disability: 13.6%; Veterans: 12.3%; Ancestry: 36.4% German, 11.9% American, 10.0% Irish, 7.0% Italian, 3.6% French
Employment: 9.1% management, business, and financial, 3.6% computer, engineering, and science, 2.9% education, legal, community service, arts, and media, 7.6% healthcare practitioners, 14.1% service, 12.7% sales and office, 8.0% natural resources, construction, and maintenance, 42.0% production, transportation, and material moving
Income: Per capita: $25,013; Median household: $46,563; Average household: $59,661; Households with income of $100,000 or more: 11.1%; Poverty rate: 8.1%
Educational Attainment: High school diploma or higher: 93.5%; Bachelor's degree or higher: 7.0%; Graduate/professional degree or higher: 3.0%
Housing: Homeownership rate: 74.0%; Median home value: $76,300; Median year structure built: Before 1940; Homeowner vacancy rate: 2.6%; Median selected monthly owner costs: $984 with a mortgage, $339 without a mortgage; Median gross rent: $753 per month; Rental vacancy rate: 0.0%
Health Insurance: 98.2% have insurance; 83.3% have private insurance; 30.6% have public insurance; 1.8% do not have insurance; 0.0% of children under 18 do not have insurance
Transportation: Commute: 93.8% car, 0.0% public transportation, 4.8% walk, 1.5% work from home; Mean travel time to work: 30.6 minutes

---

TIFFIN (city). County seat. Covers a land area of 6.764 square miles and a water area of 0.136 square miles. Located at 41.12° N. Lat; 83.18° W. Long. Elevation is 745 feet.
History: In 1817, Erastus Bowe built the Pan Yan Tavern on the north side of the Sandusky River, and a town called Oakley grew up around it. In 1820 Josiah Hedges established a settlement on the south side of the river opposite Oakley, calling it Tiffin after Edward Tiffin, the first governor of Ohio. The two villages were united as Tiffin in 1850.
Population: 17,701; Growth (since 2000): -2.4%; Density: 2,617.1 persons per square mile; Race: 93.5% White, 2.8% Black/African American, 1.4% Asian, 0.1% American Indian/Alaska Native, 0.0% Native Hawaiian/Other Pacific Islander, 1.7% Two or more races, 3.9% Hispanic of any race; Average household size: 2.37; Median age: 35.1; Age under 18: 20.6%; Age 65 and over: 15.8%; Males per 100 females: 95.8; Marriage status: 37.9% never married, 42.5% now married, 1.7% separated, 6.1% widowed, 13.5% divorced; Foreign born: 2.9%; Speak English only: 95.7%; With disability: 15.0%; Veterans: 8.6%; Ancestry: 41.7% German, 11.8% Irish, 7.5% American, 6.4% English, 5.5% Italian
Employment: 9.1% management, business, and financial, 2.6% computer, engineering, and science, 9.8% education, legal, community service, arts, and media, 4.1% healthcare practitioners, 23.0% service, 20.3% sales and office, 8.1% natural resources, construction, and maintenance, 23.1% production, transportation, and material moving
Income: Per capita: $20,648; Median household: $41,037; Average household: $52,752; Households with income of $100,000 or more: 9.9%; Poverty rate: 17.0%
Educational Attainment: High school diploma or higher: 90.3%; Bachelor's degree or higher: 16.4%; Graduate/professional degree or higher: 6.0%

School District(s)

Bridges Community Academy (KG-12)
2015-16 Enrollment: 127 . . . . (419) 455-9295
Lakeland Academy Community School (KG-12)
2015-16 Enrollment: 62 . . . . (740) 658-1042
Tiffin City (PK-12)
2015-16 Enrollment: 2,708 . . . . (419) 447-2515
Vanguard-Sentinel Career & Technology Centers (06-12)
2015-16 Enrollment: n/a . . . . (419) 332-2626

Four-year College(s)

Heidelberg University (Private, Not-for-profit, United Church of Christ)
Fall 2016 Enrollment: 1,314 . . . . (419) 448-2000
2016-17 Tuition: In-state $29,200; Out-of-state $29,200
Tiffin University (Private, Not-for-profit)
Fall 2016 Enrollment: 3,350 . . . . (800) 968-6446
2016-17 Tuition: In-state $23,125; Out-of-state $23,125

Two-year College(s)

Tiffin Academy of Hair Design (Private, For-profit)
Fall 2016 Enrollment: 39 . . . . (419) 447-3117
Housing: Homeownership rate: 60.6%; Median home value: $89,300; Median year structure built: 1952; Homeowner vacancy rate: 1.4%; Median selected monthly owner costs: $949 with a mortgage, $368 without a mortgage; Median gross rent: $667 per month; Rental vacancy rate: 13.1%
Health Insurance: 92.0% have insurance; 69.1% have private insurance; 36.4% have public insurance; 8.0% do not have insurance; 3.0% of children under 18 do not have insurance
Hospitals: Mercy Tiffin Hospital (105 beds)
Safety: Violent crime rate: 7.4 per 10,000 population; Property crime rate: 237.0 per 10,000 population
Newspapers: Advertiser-Tribune (daily circulation 9,800)
Transportation: Commute: 87.4% car, 0.7% public transportation, 9.3% walk, 1.3% work from home; Mean travel time to work: 16.5 minutes
Additional Information Contacts
City of Tiffin . . . . (419) 448-5401
http://www.tiffinohio.com

Shelby County

Located in western Ohio; crossed by the Great Miami River; includes Lake Loramie. Covers a land area of 407.675 square miles, a water area of 3.017 square miles, and is located in the Eastern Time Zone at 40.34° N. Lat., 84.20° W. Long. The county was founded in 1819. County seat is Sidney.

Shelby County is part of the Sidney, OH Micropolitan Statistical Area. The entire metro area includes: Shelby County, OH

Weather Station: Sidney 1 S Elevation: 939 feet

	Jan	Feb	Mar	Apr	May	Jun	Jul	Aug	Sep	Oct	Nov	Dec
High	34	38	48	61	71	81	84	83	77	64	51	38
Low	17	20	28	38	48	58	62	60	52	41	32	22
Precip	2.6	2.2	2.8	3.6	4.1	4.5	4.2	3.8	2.7	2.8	3.3	2.9
Snow	na	na	na	tr	0.0	0.0	0.0	0.0	0.0	0.0	tr	na

High and Low temperatures in degrees Fahrenheit; Precipitation and Snow in inches

Population: 48,949; Growth (since 2000): 2.2%; Density: 120.1 persons per square mile; Race: 94.4% White, 3.0% Black/African American, 0.8% Asian, 0.4% American Indian/Alaska Native, 0.0% Native Hawaiian/Other Pacific Islander, 1.1% two or more races, 1.5% Hispanic of any race;

Average household size: 2.63; Median age: 39.5; Age under 18: 25.9%; Age 65 and over: 14.6%; Males per 100 females: 99.5; Marriage status: 25.6% never married, 57.8% now married, 1.1% separated, 6.5% widowed, 10.1% divorced; Foreign born: 1.7%; Speak English only: 97.0%; With disability: 12.5%; Veterans: 9.2%; Ancestry: 38.3% German, 9.8% American, 8.6% Irish, 7.5% English, 5.0% French
Religion: Six largest groups: 27.0% Catholicism, 7.3% Lutheran, 6.0% Non-denominational Protestant, 5.9% Methodist/Pietist, 3.0% Baptist, 2.9% Presbyterian-Reformed
Economy: Unemployment rate: 3.8%; Leading industries: 14.2 % retail trade; 13.1 % manufacturing; 10.6 % other services (except public administration); Farms: 986 totaling 206,283 acres; Company size: 2 employ 1,000 or more persons, 2 employ 500 to 999 persons, 40 employ 100 to 499 persons, 928 employ less than 100 persons; Business ownership: 969 women-owned, 34 Black-owned, n/a Hispanic-owned, n/a Asian-owned, n/a American Indian/Alaska Native-owned
Employment: 12.2% management, business, and financial, 4.5% computer, engineering, and science, 6.3% education, legal, community service, arts, and media, 4.7% healthcare practitioners, 14.8% service, 20.7% sales and office, 8.8% natural resources, construction, and maintenance, 28.0% production, transportation, and material moving
Income: Per capita: $27,330; Median household: $56,169; Average household: $71,318; Households with income of $100,000 or more: 19.4%; Poverty rate: 9.5%
Educational Attainment: High school diploma or higher: 90.7%; Bachelor's degree or higher: 17.1%; Graduate/professional degree or higher: 6.9%
Housing: Homeownership rate: 70.8%; Median home value: $134,400; Median year structure built: 1973; Homeowner vacancy rate: 1.3%; Median selected monthly owner costs: $1,132 with a mortgage, $439 without a mortgage; Median gross rent: $699 per month; Rental vacancy rate: 3.5%
Vital Statistics: Birth rate: 127.3 per 10,000 population; Death rate: 87.8 per 10,000 population; Age-adjusted cancer mortality rate: 200.2 deaths per 100,000 population
Health Insurance: 94.3% have insurance; 77.7% have private insurance; 31.0% have public insurance; 5.7% do not have insurance; 2.7% of children under 18 do not have insurance
Health Care: Physicians: 8.2 per 10,000 population; Dentists: 2.5 per 10,000 population; Hospital beds: 14.5 per 10,000 population; Hospital admissions: 542.7 per 10,000 population
Transportation: Commute: 94.4% car, 0.2% public transportation, 1.9% walk, 2.7% work from home; Mean travel time to work: 17.7 minutes
2016 Presidential Election: 78.0% Trump, 17.8% Clinton, 2.5% Johnson, 0.5% Stein
National and State Parks: Lake Loramie State Park
Additional Information Contacts
Shelby Government. . . . . (937) 498-7226
http://www.co.shelby.oh.us

Shelby County Communities

ANNA (village). Covers a land area of 1.029 square miles and a water area of <.001 square miles. Located at 40.40° N. Lat; 84.18° W. Long. Elevation is 1,027 feet.
Population: 1,633; Growth (since 2000): 23.8%; Density: 1,586.8 persons per square mile; Race: 99.2% White, 0.0% Black/African American, 0.4% Asian, 0.4% American Indian/Alaska Native, 0.0% Native Hawaiian/Other Pacific Islander, 0.0% Two or more races, 0.7% Hispanic of any race; Average household size: 2.95; Median age: 35.3; Age under 18: 32.2%; Age 65 and over: 9.6%; Males per 100 females: 93.7; Marriage status: 24.2% never married, 61.8% now married, 1.0% separated, 3.6% widowed, 10.4% divorced; Foreign born: 0.4%; Speak English only: 98.5%; With disability: 8.7%; Veterans: 8.5%; Ancestry: 42.7% German, 8.1% Irish, 6.4% English, 6.4% American, 5.1% French
Employment: 15.2% management, business, and financial, 4.2% computer, engineering, and science, 5.9% education, legal, community service, arts, and media, 6.0% healthcare practitioners, 16.3% service, 14.8% sales and office, 11.2% natural resources, construction, and maintenance, 26.3% production, transportation, and material moving
Income: Per capita: $26,485; Median household: $69,107; Average household: $77,830; Households with income of $100,000 or more: 27.7%; Poverty rate: 5.4%
Educational Attainment: High school diploma or higher: 94.8%; Bachelor's degree or higher: 18.9%; Graduate/professional degree or higher: 7.6%

School District(s)

Anna Local (KG-12)
2015-16 Enrollment: 1,230 . . . . (937) 394-2011
Housing: Homeownership rate: 71.1%; Median home value: $119,300; Median year structure built: 1975; Homeowner vacancy rate: 0.0%; Median selected monthly owner costs: $1,096 with a mortgage, $389 without a mortgage; Median gross rent: $791 per month; Rental vacancy rate: 5.9%
Health Insurance: 97.1% have insurance; 89.0% have private insurance; 21.3% have public insurance; 2.9% do not have insurance; 1.7% of children under 18 do not have insurance
Transportation: Commute: 95.1% car, 0.0% public transportation, 1.0% walk, 2.3% work from home; Mean travel time to work: 19.8 minutes

BOTKINS (village). Covers a land area of 1.241 square miles and a water area of 0.013 square miles. Located at 40.45° N. Lat; 84.18° W. Long. Elevation is 997 feet.
Population: 1,323; Growth (since 2000): 9.8%; Density: 1,066.3 persons per square mile; Race: 98.6% White, 0.0% Black/African American, 0.0% Asian, 0.0% American Indian/Alaska Native, 0.0% Native Hawaiian/Other Pacific Islander, 1.4% Two or more races, 0.9% Hispanic of any race; Average household size: 2.56; Median age: 35.2; Age under 18: 30.4%; Age 65 and over: 12.4%; Males per 100 females: 98.5; Marriage status: 24.5% never married, 59.2% now married, 3.9% separated, 5.2% widowed, 11.2% divorced; Foreign born: 0.8%; Speak English only: 97.0%; With disability: 12.2%; Veterans: 10.9%; Ancestry: 67.9% German, 10.4% Irish, 4.0% English, 3.3% American, 2.6% Dutch
Employment: 11.6% management, business, and financial, 2.3% computer, engineering, and science, 8.5% education, legal, community service, arts, and media, 4.7% healthcare practitioners, 13.7% service, 17.7% sales and office, 18.0% natural resources, construction, and maintenance, 23.6% production, transportation, and material moving
Income: Per capita: $25,064; Median household: $52,321; Average household: $62,681; Households with income of $100,000 or more: 14.9%; Poverty rate: 5.3%
Educational Attainment: High school diploma or higher: 95.6%; Bachelor's degree or higher: 21.2%; Graduate/professional degree or higher: 7.4%

School District(s)

Botkins Local (KG-12)
2015-16 Enrollment: 670. . . . . (937) 693-3756
Housing: Homeownership rate: 70.8%; Median home value: $114,500; Median year structure built: 1969; Homeowner vacancy rate: 0.0%; Median selected monthly owner costs: $969 with a mortgage, $349 without a mortgage; Median gross rent: $588 per month; Rental vacancy rate: 6.8%
Health Insurance: 99.5% have insurance; 89.6% have private insurance; 20.3% have public insurance; 0.5% do not have insurance; 0.0% of children under 18 do not have insurance
Transportation: Commute: 94.3% car, 0.0% public transportation, 3.2% walk, 1.1% work from home; Mean travel time to work: 17.1 minutes

FORT LORAMIE (village). Covers a land area of 0.957 square miles and a water area of <.001 square miles. Located at 40.35° N. Lat; 84.37° W. Long. Elevation is 951 feet.
History: Fort Loramie built here (1794) by Anthony Wayne.
Population: 1,375; Growth (since 2000): 2.3%; Density: 1,436.6 persons per square mile; Race: 100.0% White, 0.0% Black/African American, 0.0% Asian, 0.0% American Indian/Alaska Native, 0.0% Native Hawaiian/Other Pacific Islander, 0.0% Two or more races, 1.2% Hispanic of any race; Average household size: 2.77; Median age: 35.9; Age under 18: 29.6%; Age 65 and over: 15.3%; Males per 100 females: 96.0; Marriage status: 27.5% never married, 61.4% now married, 1.0% separated, 5.7% widowed, 5.4% divorced; Foreign born: 0.4%; Speak English only: 99.1%; With disability: 7.0%; Veterans: 7.5%; Ancestry: 65.3% German, 7.7% French, 6.3% American, 2.8% Irish, 1.8% Italian
Employment: 14.6% management, business, and financial, 5.4% computer, engineering, and science, 8.7% education, legal, community service, arts, and media, 7.6% healthcare practitioners, 6.4% service, 21.0% sales and office, 6.3% natural resources, construction, and maintenance, 30.0% production, transportation, and material moving
Income: Per capita: $28,565; Median household: $69,886; Average household: $77,025; Households with income of $100,000 or more: 31.7%; Poverty rate: 2.0%
Educational Attainment: High school diploma or higher: 94.2%; Bachelor's degree or higher: 24.4%; Graduate/professional degree or higher: 11.9%

School District(s)

Fort Loramie Local (KG-12)
2015-16 Enrollment: 794. . . . . (937) 295-3931

Housing: Homeownership rate: 81.9%; Median home value: $175,700; Median year structure built: 1977; Homeowner vacancy rate: 1.9%; Median selected monthly owner costs: $1,177 with a mortgage, $394 without a mortgage; Median gross rent: $573 per month; Rental vacancy rate: 0.0%

Health Insurance: 97.7% have insurance; 91.3% have private insurance; 18.1% have public insurance; 2.3% do not have insurance; 0.0% of children under 18 do not have insurance

Transportation: Commute: 96.9% car, 0.0% public transportation, 0.9% walk, 1.9% work from home; Mean travel time to work: 17.2 minutes

HOUSTON (unincorporated postal area)

ZCTA: 45333

Covers a land area of 22.162 square miles and a water area of 0.244 square miles. Located at 40.25° N. Lat; 84.33° W. Long. Elevation is 961 feet.

Population: 1,324; Growth (since 2000): -11.1%; Density: 59.7 persons per square mile; Race: 100.0% White, 0.0% Black/African American, 0.0% Asian, 0.0% American Indian/Alaska Native, 0.0% Native Hawaiian/Other Pacific Islander, 0.0% Two or more races, 0.0% Hispanic of any race; Average household size: 2.84; Median age: 39.0; Age under 18: 31.9%; Age 65 and over: 17.1%; Males per 100 females: 107.6; Marriage status: 27.9% never married, 64.5% now married, 0.5% separated, 3.1% widowed, 4.5% divorced; Foreign born: 0.7%; Speak English only: 99.3%; With disability: 6.0%; Veterans: 7.1%; Ancestry: 34.8% German, 7.9% American, 7.6% Irish, 5.8% Scottish, 5.2% French

Employment: 14.8% management, business, and financial, 4.9% computer, engineering, and science, 3.1% education, legal, community service, arts, and media, 1.4% healthcare practitioners, 6.0% service, 23.5% sales and office, 7.7% natural resources, construction, and maintenance, 38.6% production, transportation, and material moving

Income: Per capita: $24,898; Median household: $63,063; Average household: $69,104; Households with income of $100,000 or more: 19.5%; Poverty rate: 9.6%

Educational Attainment: High school diploma or higher: 93.6%; Bachelor's degree or higher: 11.2%; Graduate/professional degree or higher: 4.1%

School District(s)

Hardin-Houston Local (KG-12)
2015-16 Enrollment: 830. . . . . (937) 295-3010

Housing: Homeownership rate: 87.2%; Median home value: $154,500; Median year structure built: 1977; Homeowner vacancy rate: 0.0%; Median selected monthly owner costs: $1,257 with a mortgage, $465 without a mortgage; Median gross rent: $783 per month; Rental vacancy rate: 0.0%

Health Insurance: 98.0% have insurance; 81.3% have private insurance; 33.5% have public insurance; 2.0% do not have insurance; 0.0% of children under 18 do not have insurance

Transportation: Commute: 99.5% car, 0.0% public transportation, 0.0% walk, 0.5% work from home; Mean travel time to work: 23.5 minutes

JACKSON CENTER (village). Covers a land area of 1.676 square miles and a water area of 0.008 square miles. Located at 40.44° N. Lat; 84.04° W. Long. Elevation is 1,027 feet.

Population: 1,631; Growth (since 2000): 19.1%; Density: 973.1 persons per square mile; Race: 98.3% White, 1.6% Black/African American, 0.0% Asian, 0.0% American Indian/Alaska Native, 0.0% Native Hawaiian/Other Pacific Islander, 0.1% Two or more races, 1.3% Hispanic of any race; Average household size: 2.63; Median age: 34.0; Age under 18: 28.8%; Age 65 and over: 13.6%; Males per 100 females: 99.7; Marriage status: 22.2% never married, 58.4% now married, 0.5% separated, 5.9% widowed, 13.5% divorced; Foreign born: 0.2%; Speak English only: 98.2%; With disability: 12.6%; Veterans: 9.6%; Ancestry: 35.1% German, 8.8% Irish, 5.7% American, 4.4% French, 2.8% English

Employment: 14.2% management, business, and financial, 2.1% computer, engineering, and science, 10.1% education, legal, community service, arts, and media, 2.7% healthcare practitioners, 12.1% service, 14.5% sales and office, 12.6% natural resources, construction, and maintenance, 31.8% production, transportation, and material moving

Income: Per capita: $21,336; Median household: $49,483; Average household: $56,278; Households with income of $100,000 or more: 10.4%; Poverty rate: 11.5%

Educational Attainment: High school diploma or higher: 92.1%; Bachelor's degree or higher: 16.2%; Graduate/professional degree or higher: 7.3%

School District(s)

Jackson Center Local (PK-12)
2015-16 Enrollment: 531. . . . . (937) 596-6053

Housing: Homeownership rate: 71.8%; Median home value: $95,200; Median year structure built: 1972; Homeowner vacancy rate: 2.3%; Median selected monthly owner costs: $865 with a mortgage, $369 without a mortgage; Median gross rent: $640 per month; Rental vacancy rate: 2.2%

Health Insurance: 94.1% have insurance; 70.2% have private insurance; 41.9% have public insurance; 5.9% do not have insurance; 0.0% of children under 18 do not have insurance

Transportation: Commute: 96.1% car, 0.0% public transportation, 0.5% walk, 2.3% work from home; Mean travel time to work: 18.2 minutes

KETTLERSVILLE (village). Covers a land area of 1.021 square miles and a water area of 0.004 square miles. Located at 40.44° N. Lat; 84.26° W. Long. Elevation is 978 feet.

History: Also spelled Kettlerville.

Population: 160; Growth (since 2000): -8.6%; Density: 156.7 persons per square mile; Race: 100.0% White, 0.0% Black/African American, 0.0% Asian, 0.0% American Indian/Alaska Native, 0.0% Native Hawaiian/Other Pacific Islander, 0.0% Two or more races, 0.0% Hispanic of any race; Average household size: 2.86; Median age: 34.7; Age under 18: 26.9%; Age 65 and over: 12.5%; Males per 100 females: 115.7; Marriage status: 16.0% never married, 68.1% now married, 0.0% separated, 8.4% widowed, 7.6% divorced; Foreign born: 0.0%; Speak English only: 100.0%; With disability: 7.5%; Veterans: 9.4%; Ancestry: 56.3% German, 11.3% Dutch, 11.3% English, 6.9% Irish, 6.3% American

Employment: 9.2% management, business, and financial, 0.0% computer, engineering, and science, 11.8% education, legal, community service, arts, and media, 0.0% healthcare practitioners, 18.4% service, 10.5% sales and office, 18.4% natural resources, construction, and maintenance, 31.6% production, transportation, and material moving

Income: Per capita: $26,663; Median household: $72,000; Average household: $73,400; Households with income of $100,000 or more: 16.1%; Poverty rate: 2.0%

Educational Attainment: High school diploma or higher: 96.9%; Bachelor's degree or higher: 19.6%; Graduate/professional degree or higher: 4.1%

Housing: Homeownership rate: 76.8%; Median home value: $122,900; Median year structure built: Before 1940; Homeowner vacancy rate: 8.5%; Median selected monthly owner costs: $1,250 with a mortgage, $394 without a mortgage; Median gross rent: $1,069 per month; Rental vacancy rate: 0.0%

Health Insurance: 93.8% have insurance; 79.4% have private insurance; 23.8% have public insurance; 6.3% do not have insurance; 11.6% of children under 18 do not have insurance

Transportation: Commute: 93.3% car, 2.7% public transportation, 0.0% walk, 0.0% work from home; Mean travel time to work: 23.3 minutes

LOCKINGTON (village). Covers a land area of 0.082 square miles and a water area of 0 square miles. Located at 40.21° N. Lat; 84.24° W. Long. Elevation is 948 feet.

Population: 148; Growth (since 2000): -28.8%; Density: 1,803.4 persons per square mile; Race: 100.0% White, 0.0% Black/African American, 0.0% Asian, 0.0% American Indian/Alaska Native, 0.0% Native Hawaiian/Other Pacific Islander, 0.0% Two or more races, 0.0% Hispanic of any race; Average household size: 2.47; Median age: 42.7; Age under 18: 17.6%; Age 65 and over: 18.2%; Males per 100 females: 116.9; Marriage status: 26.5% never married, 57.4% now married, 0.0% separated, 8.1% widowed, 8.1% divorced; Foreign born: 0.0%; Speak English only: 100.0%; With disability: 27.7%; Veterans: 5.7%; Ancestry: 34.5% German, 10.8% American, 8.8% Irish, 4.1% Italian, 3.4% English

Employment: 0.0% management, business, and financial, 3.8% computer, engineering, and science, 10.3% education, legal, community service, arts, and media, 0.0% healthcare practitioners, 23.1% service, 14.1% sales and office, 16.7% natural resources, construction, and maintenance, 32.1% production, transportation, and material moving

Income: Per capita: $19,964; Median household: $41,000; Average household: $47,400; Households with income of $100,000 or more: 3.3%; Poverty rate: 4.1%

Educational Attainment: High school diploma or higher: 78.0%; Bachelor's degree or higher: 2.8%; Graduate/professional degree or higher: n/a
Housing: Homeownership rate: 60.0%; Median home value: $76,000; Median year structure built: 1941; Homeowner vacancy rate: 0.0%; Median selected monthly owner costs: $838 with a mortgage, $442 without a mortgage; Median gross rent: $545 per month; Rental vacancy rate: 0.0%
Health Insurance: 83.1% have insurance; 60.1% have private insurance; 29.7% have public insurance; 16.9% do not have insurance; 11.5% of children under 18 do not have insurance
Transportation: Commute: 100.0% car, 0.0% public transportation, 0.0% walk, 0.0% work from home; Mean travel time to work: 21.7 minutes

MAPLEWOOD (unincorporated postal area)

ZCTA: 45340

Covers a land area of 23.095 square miles and a water area of 0.052 square miles. Located at 40.37° N. Lat; 84.05° W. Long. Elevation is 1,033 feet.
Population: 732; Growth (since 2000): -0.9%; Density: 31.7 persons per square mile; Race: 100.0% White, 0.0% Black/African American, 0.0% Asian, 0.0% American Indian/Alaska Native, 0.0% Native Hawaiian/Other Pacific Islander, 0.0% Two or more races, 0.0% Hispanic of any race; Average household size: 2.82; Median age: 47.0; Age under 18: 24.0%; Age 65 and over: 13.9%; Males per 100 females: 97.1; Marriage status: 12.8% never married, 70.0% now married, 1.9% separated, 6.3% widowed, 10.9% divorced; Foreign born: 0.0%; Speak English only: 98.4%; With disability: 12.0%; Veterans: 9.2%; Ancestry: 41.5% German, 23.6% English, 14.9% Irish, 13.0% American, 3.3% Scottish
Employment: 6.5% management, business, and financial, 2.0% computer, engineering, and science, 5.1% education, legal, community service, arts, and media, 5.6% healthcare practitioners, 16.3% service, 22.0% sales and office, 14.6% natural resources, construction, and maintenance, 27.9% production, transportation, and material moving
Income: Per capita: $22,881; Median household: $59,038; Average household: $62,953; Households with income of $100,000 or more: 13.5%; Poverty rate: 2.7%
Educational Attainment: High school diploma or higher: 91.6%; Bachelor's degree or higher: 9.9%; Graduate/professional degree or higher: 2.9%
Housing: Homeownership rate: 94.2%; Median home value: $148,300; Median year structure built: 1981; Homeowner vacancy rate: 0.0%; Median selected monthly owner costs: $1,212 with a mortgage, $535 without a mortgage; Median gross rent: n/a per month; Rental vacancy rate: 0.0%
Health Insurance: 92.3% have insurance; 65.8% have private insurance; 41.4% have public insurance; 7.7% do not have insurance; 0.0% of children under 18 do not have insurance
Transportation: Commute: 97.7% car, 0.0% public transportation, 0.0% walk, 0.0% work from home; Mean travel time to work: 23.2 minutes

NEWPORT (CDP). Covers a land area of 0.360 square miles and a water area of 0.033 square miles. Located at 40.30° N. Lat; 84.37° W. Long. Elevation is 971 feet.
Population: 159; Growth (since 2000): n/a; Density: 442.2 persons per square mile; Race: 100.0% White, 0.0% Black/African American, 0.0% Asian, 0.0% American Indian/Alaska Native, 0.0% Native Hawaiian/Other Pacific Islander, 0.0% Two or more races, 0.0% Hispanic of any race; Average household size: 1.89; Median age: 40.2; Age under 18: 18.2%; Age 65 and over: 23.3%; Males per 100 females: 127.6; Marriage status: 35.7% never married, 52.9% now married, 0.0% separated, 5.0% widowed, 6.4% divorced; Foreign born: 0.0%; Speak English only: 100.0%; With disability: 5.0%; Veterans: 0.0%; Ancestry: 44.7% German, 8.2% Dutch, 5.0% American, 3.8% French
Employment: 0.0% management, business, and financial, 0.0% computer, engineering, and science, 0.0% education, legal, community service, arts, and media, 0.0% healthcare practitioners, 20.4% service, 20.4% sales and office, 32.3% natural resources, construction, and maintenance, 26.9% production, transportation, and material moving
Income: Per capita: $29,901; Median household: $46,583; Average household: $57,513; Households with income of $100,000 or more: 19.0%; Poverty rate: n/a
Educational Attainment: High school diploma or higher: 87.5%; Bachelor's degree or higher: n/a; Graduate/professional degree or higher: n/a
Housing: Homeownership rate: 100.0%; Median home value: $135,600; Median year structure built: 1944; Homeowner vacancy rate: 0.0%; Median selected monthly owner costs: $1,336 with a mortgage, $536 without a mortgage; Median gross rent: n/a per month; Rental vacancy rate: 0.0%
Health Insurance: 88.7% have insurance; 83.6% have private insurance; 23.3% have public insurance; 11.3% do not have insurance; 34.5% of children under 18 do not have insurance
Transportation: Commute: 100.0% car, 0.0% public transportation, 0.0% walk, 0.0% work from home; Mean travel time to work: 11.5 minutes

PEMBERTON (unincorporated postal area)

ZCTA: 45353

Covers a land area of 2.812 square miles and a water area of 0 square miles. Located at 40.29° N. Lat; 84.04° W. Long. Elevation is 1,056 feet.
Population: 199; Growth (since 2000): 77.7%; Density: 70.8 persons per square mile; Race: 100.0% White, 0.0% Black/African American, 0.0% Asian, 0.0% American Indian/Alaska Native, 0.0% Native Hawaiian/Other Pacific Islander, 0.0% Two or more races, 0.0% Hispanic of any race; Average household size: 2.62; Median age: 46.0; Age under 18: 3.0%; Age 65 and over: 12.6%; Males per 100 females: 104.2; Marriage status: 13.5% never married, 68.4% now married, 8.3% separated, 11.4% widowed, 6.7% divorced; Foreign born: 0.0%; Speak English only: 100.0%; With disability: 32.2%; Veterans: 9.8%; Ancestry: 21.1% German, 16.6% American, 10.1% Irish, 2.5% English
Employment: 11.0% management, business, and financial, 4.6% computer, engineering, and science, 0.0% education, legal, community service, arts, and media, 0.0% healthcare practitioners, 27.5% service, 10.1% sales and office, 27.5% natural resources, construction, and maintenance, 19.3% production, transportation, and material moving
Income: Per capita: $22,092; Median household: $65,556; Average household: $54,199; Households with income of $100,000 or more: n/a; Poverty rate: 1.5%
Educational Attainment: High school diploma or higher: 85.7%; Bachelor's degree or higher: 3.6%; Graduate/professional degree or higher: n/a
Housing: Homeownership rate: 69.7%; Median home value: n/a; Median year structure built: Before 1940; Homeowner vacancy rate: 0.0%; Median selected monthly owner costs: $850 with a mortgage, $0 without a mortgage; Median gross rent: $694 per month; Rental vacancy rate: 0.0%
Health Insurance: 91.5% have insurance; 73.9% have private insurance; 33.2% have public insurance; 8.5% do not have insurance; 0.0% of children under 18 do not have insurance
Transportation: Commute: 94.5% car, 0.0% public transportation, 5.5% walk, 0.0% work from home; Mean travel time to work: 23.1 minutes

PORT JEFFERSON (village). Covers a land area of 0.166 square miles and a water area of 0.022 square miles. Located at 40.33° N. Lat; 84.09° W. Long. Elevation is 971 feet.
Population: 429; Growth (since 2000): 33.6%; Density: 2,578.0 persons per square mile; Race: 98.8% White, 0.0% Black/African American, 0.5% Asian, 0.7% American Indian/Alaska Native, 0.0% Native Hawaiian/Other Pacific Islander, 0.0% Two or more races, 0.0% Hispanic of any race; Average household size: 2.57; Median age: 36.3; Age under 18: 29.4%; Age 65 and over: 7.7%; Males per 100 females: 105.0; Marriage status: 20.8% never married, 54.7% now married, 0.6% separated, 4.7% widowed, 19.8% divorced; Foreign born: 0.5%; Speak English only: 98.8%; With disability: 15.4%; Veterans: 9.9%; Ancestry: 27.0% German, 15.2% English, 9.6% American, 8.4% Irish, 2.8% Dutch
Employment: 2.5% management, business, and financial, 0.0% computer, engineering, and science, 1.0% education, legal, community service, arts, and media, 6.5% healthcare practitioners, 20.0% service, 20.5% sales and office, 10.5% natural resources, construction, and maintenance, 39.0% production, transportation, and material moving
Income: Per capita: $19,733; Median household: $38,750; Average household: $49,094; Households with income of $100,000 or more: 8.4%; Poverty rate: 13.5%
Educational Attainment: High school diploma or higher: 90.7%; Bachelor's degree or higher: 6.1%; Graduate/professional degree or higher: 1.4%
Housing: Homeownership rate: 66.5%; Median home value: $80,800; Median year structure built: 1966; Homeowner vacancy rate: 0.0%; Median selected monthly owner costs: $1,009 with a mortgage, $330 without a mortgage; Median gross rent: $646 per month; Rental vacancy rate: 8.2%
Health Insurance: 88.8% have insurance; 64.8% have private insurance; 33.8% have public insurance; 11.2% do not have insurance; 5.6% of children under 18 do not have insurance

Transportation: Commute: 99.5% car, 0.0% public transportation, 0.0% walk, 0.5% work from home; Mean travel time to work: 16.3 minutes

RUSSIA (village). Covers a land area of 0.779 square miles and a water area of 0.008 square miles. Located at 40.23° N. Lat; 84.41° W. Long. Elevation is 968 feet.

Population: 617; Growth (since 2000): 12.0%; Density: 791.7 persons per square mile; Race: 98.9% White, 0.3% Black/African American, 0.0% Asian, 0.0% American Indian/Alaska Native, 0.0% Native Hawaiian/Other Pacific Islander, 0.8% Two or more races, 1.1% Hispanic of any race; Average household size: 2.73; Median age: 33.4; Age under 18: 32.1%; Age 65 and over: 14.3%; Males per 100 females: 93.9; Marriage status: 23.0% never married, 66.6% now married, 0.4% separated, 6.4% widowed, 4.0% divorced; Foreign born: 0.5%; Speak English only: 99.5%; With disability: 7.5%; Veterans: 10.3%; Ancestry: 47.5% German, 36.8% French, 13.1% American, 5.7% Irish, 4.1% English

Employment: 11.5% management, business, and financial, 5.9% computer, engineering, and science, 11.5% education, legal, community service, arts, and media, 3.6% healthcare practitioners, 10.9% service, 20.1% sales and office, 5.3% natural resources, construction, and maintenance, 31.3% production, transportation, and material moving

Income: Per capita: $30,547; Median household: $61,000; Average household: $81,680; Households with income of $100,000 or more: 28.3%; Poverty rate: 1.5%

Educational Attainment: High school diploma or higher: 98.4%; Bachelor's degree or higher: 23.8%; Graduate/professional degree or higher: 8.4%

School District(s)

Russia Local (KG-12)
2015-16 Enrollment: 459. . . . . (937) 526-3156

Housing: Homeownership rate: 77.9%; Median home value: $158,300; Median year structure built: 1970; Homeowner vacancy rate: 3.3%; Median selected monthly owner costs: $1,159 with a mortgage, $513 without a mortgage; Median gross rent: $742 per month; Rental vacancy rate: 0.0%

Health Insurance: 94.8% have insurance; 88.3% have private insurance; 23.0% have public insurance; 5.2% do not have insurance; 3.0% of children under 18 do not have insurance

Transportation: Commute: 98.3% car, 0.0% public transportation, 1.7% walk, 0.0% work from home; Mean travel time to work: 19.9 minutes

SIDNEY (city). County seat. Covers a land area of 12.023 square miles and a water area of 0.132 square miles. Located at 40.29° N. Lat; 84.17° W. Long. Elevation is 955 feet.

History: Sidney was platted in 1820 and named for Sir Philip Sidney, the English poet. The town developed around sawmills and woodworking mills. In 1879, Benjamin Slusser built a factory to produce the sheet-steel road scraper that he had invented.

Population: 20,761; Growth (since 2000): 2.7%; Density: 1,726.8 persons per square mile; Race: 88.5% White, 6.7% Black/African American, 1.7% Asian, 0.4% American Indian/Alaska Native, 0.0% Native Hawaiian/Other Pacific Islander, 2.1% Two or more races, 2.7% Hispanic of any race; Average household size: 2.47; Median age: 38.8; Age under 18: 24.4%; Age 65 and over: 14.5%; Males per 100 females: 96.4; Marriage status: 28.4% never married, 49.5% now married, 1.8% separated, 8.4% widowed, 13.8% divorced; Foreign born: 3.2%; Speak English only: 94.6%; With disability: 15.9%; Veterans: 9.4%; Ancestry: 27.3% German, 10.0% American, 8.1% Irish, 7.9% English, 3.5% French

Employment: 10.8% management, business, and financial, 4.6% computer, engineering, and science, 6.8% education, legal, community service, arts, and media, 3.9% healthcare practitioners, 18.5% service, 20.5% sales and office, 5.6% natural resources, construction, and maintenance, 29.4% production, transportation, and material moving

Income: Per capita: $26,219; Median household: $46,697; Average household: $64,212; Households with income of $100,000 or more: 12.5%; Poverty rate: 14.7%

Educational Attainment: High school diploma or higher: 88.0%; Bachelor's degree or higher: 16.2%; Graduate/professional degree or higher: 6.8%

School District(s)

Fairlawn Local (PK-12)
2015-16 Enrollment: 663. . . . . (937) 492-1974
Sidney City (KG-12)
2015-16 Enrollment: 3,311 . . . . (937) 497-2200

Housing: Homeownership rate: 56.6%; Median home value: $109,500; Median year structure built: 1971; Homeowner vacancy rate: 2.4%; Median selected monthly owner costs: $989 with a mortgage, $410 without a mortgage; Median gross rent: $684 per month; Rental vacancy rate: 4.3%

Health Insurance: 92.9% have insurance; 70.7% have private insurance; 37.3% have public insurance; 7.1% do not have insurance; 2.7% of children under 18 do not have insurance

Hospitals: Wilson Memorial Hospital (112 beds)

Safety: Violent crime rate: 21.6 per 10,000 population; Property crime rate: 445.3 per 10,000 population

Newspapers: Sidney Daily News (daily circulation 13,000)

Transportation: Commute: 95.0% car, 0.5% public transportation, 1.6% walk, 1.8% work from home; Mean travel time to work: 16.2 minutes

Additional Information Contacts

City of Sidney . . . . (937) 498-2335
http://www.sidneyoh.com

Stark County

Located in east central Ohio; crossed by the Tuscarawas River. Covers a land area of 575.271 square miles, a water area of 5.262 square miles, and is located in the Eastern Time Zone at 40.81° N. Lat., 81.37° W. Long. The county was founded in 1808. County seat is Canton.

Stark County is part of the Canton-Massillon, OH Metropolitan Statistical Area. The entire metro area includes: Carroll County, OH; Stark County, OH

Population: 374,762; Growth (since 2000): -0.9%; Density: 651.5 persons per square mile; Race: 88.4% White, 7.3% Black/African American, 0.8% Asian, 0.1% American Indian/Alaska Native, 0.0% Native Hawaiian/Other Pacific Islander, 3.1% two or more races, 1.9% Hispanic of any race; Average household size: 2.42; Median age: 41.7; Age under 18: 22.0%; Age 65 and over: 17.7%; Males per 100 females: 93.8; Marriage status: 29.2% never married, 50.7% now married, 1.4% separated, 6.9% widowed, 13.2% divorced; Foreign born: 2.1%; Speak English only: 96.4%; With disability: 13.3%; Veterans: 9.6%; Ancestry: 30.6% German, 14.8% Irish, 10.5% Italian, 8.9% English, 6.6% American

Religion: Six largest groups: 14.9% Catholicism, 7.5% Non-denominational Protestant, 5.8% Baptist, 5.4% Methodist/Pietist, 2.9% Lutheran, 2.9% Presbyterian-Reformed

Economy: Unemployment rate: 4.8%; Leading industries: 15.1 % retail trade; 12.1 % other services (except public administration); 12.0 % health care and social assistance; Farms: 1,168 totaling 135,749 acres; Company size: 7 employ 1,000 or more persons, 10 employ 500 to 999 persons, 196 employ 100 to 499 persons, 7,997 employ less than 100 persons; Business ownership: 9,393 women-owned, 1,425 Black-owned, 372 Hispanic-owned, 412 Asian-owned, 178 American Indian/Alaska Native-owned

Employment: 12.3% management, business, and financial, 4.0% computer, engineering, and science, 8.9% education, legal, community service, arts, and media, 6.8% healthcare practitioners, 19.0% service, 24.0% sales and office, 8.5% natural resources, construction, and maintenance, 16.5% production, transportation, and material moving

Income: Per capita: $26,442; Median household: $48,714; Average household: $64,173; Households with income of $100,000 or more: 17.9%; Poverty rate: 14.1%

Educational Attainment: High school diploma or higher: 90.4%; Bachelor's degree or higher: 22.6%; Graduate/professional degree or higher: 8.1%

Housing: Homeownership rate: 68.7%; Median home value: $124,000; Median year structure built: 1964; Homeowner vacancy rate: 1.4%; Median selected monthly owner costs: $1,132 with a mortgage, $407 without a mortgage; Median gross rent: $689 per month; Rental vacancy rate: 5.2%

Vital Statistics: Birth rate: 111.7 per 10,000 population; Death rate: 108.0 per 10,000 population; Age-adjusted cancer mortality rate: 179.1 deaths per 100,000 population

Health Insurance: 92.6% have insurance; 70.8% have private insurance; 36.3% have public insurance; 7.4% do not have insurance; 4.1% of children under 18 do not have insurance

Health Care: Physicians: 27.1 per 10,000 population; Dentists: 6.4 per 10,000 population; Hospital beds: 36.4 per 10,000 population; Hospital admissions: 1,279.6 per 10,000 population

Air Quality Index (AQI): Percent of Days: 73.0% good, 25.4% moderate, 1.6% unhealthy for sensitive individuals, 0.0% unhealthy, 0.0% very unhealthy; Annual median: 40; Annual maximum: 119

Transportation: Commute: 93.5% car, 1.3% public transportation, 1.6% walk, 3.0% work from home; Mean travel time to work: 21.8 minutes
2016 Presidential Election: 55.8% Trump, 38.7% Clinton, 3.2% Johnson, 0.8% Stein
National and State Parks: First Ladies National Historic Site; Jackson Bog State Nature Preserve; Quail Hollow State Park
Additional Information Contacts
Stark Government . . . . (330) 451-7371
http://www.co.stark.oh.us

Stark County Communities

ALLIANCE (city). Covers a land area of 8.924 square miles and a water area of 0.044 square miles. Located at 40.91° N. Lat; 81.12° W. Long. Elevation is 1,158 feet.
History: Between 1805 and 1835, four small towns were established along the Mahoning River. In 1854 the four communities were united under the name of Alliance. Alliance was incorporated in 1889, and became known for its production of cranes and heavy mill machinery.
Population: 22,121; Growth (since 2000): -4.9%; Density: 2,478.8 persons per square mile; Race: 84.8% White, 9.9% Black/African American, 0.4% Asian, 0.1% American Indian/Alaska Native, 0.0% Native Hawaiian/Other Pacific Islander, 4.4% Two or more races, 3.2% Hispanic of any race; Average household size: 2.37; Median age: 35.6; Age under 18: 22.5%; Age 65 and over: 16.7%; Males per 100 females: 91.9; Marriage status: 36.3% never married, 38.5% now married, 2.6% separated, 8.9% widowed, 16.2% divorced; Foreign born: 2.0%; Speak English only: 97.1%; With disability: 18.8%; Veterans: 8.2%; Ancestry: 23.7% German, 12.7% Irish, 9.9% Italian, 6.8% English, 5.1% American
Employment: 7.3% management, business, and financial, 3.3% computer, engineering, and science, 6.6% education, legal, community service, arts, and media, 3.6% healthcare practitioners, 22.1% service, 23.8% sales and office, 6.7% natural resources, construction, and maintenance, 26.6% production, transportation, and material moving
Income: Per capita: $18,935; Median household: $32,058; Average household: $47,109; Households with income of $100,000 or more: 8.4%; Poverty rate: 23.4%
Educational Attainment: High school diploma or higher: 85.0%; Bachelor's degree or higher: 14.8%; Graduate/professional degree or higher: 5.0%

School District(s)

Alliance City (PK-12)
2015-16 Enrollment: 3,062 . . . . (330) 821-2100
Marlington Local (KG-12)
2015-16 Enrollment: 2,396 . . . . (330) 823-7458
West Branch Local (PK-12)
2015-16 Enrollment: 2,110 . . . . (330) 938-9324

Four-year College(s)

University of Mount Union (Private, Not-for-profit, United Methodist)
Fall 2016 Enrollment: 2,281 . . . . (800) 992-6682
2016-17 Tuition: In-state $29,120; Out-of-state $29,120

Two-year College(s)

Raphael's School of Beauty Culture Inc-Alliance (Private, For-profit)
Fall 2016 Enrollment: 114 . . . . (330) 823-3884

Vocational/Technical School(s)

Community Services Division-Alliance City (Public)
Fall 2016 Enrollment: 73 . . . . (330) 821-2102
2016-17 Tuition: $6,658

Housing: Homeownership rate: 52.1%; Median home value: $79,600; Median year structure built: 1952; Homeowner vacancy rate: 1.9%; Median selected monthly owner costs: $904 with a mortgage, $315 without a mortgage; Median gross rent: $644 per month; Rental vacancy rate: 3.9%
Health Insurance: 90.0% have insurance; 60.1% have private insurance; 45.2% have public insurance; 10.0% do not have insurance; 6.1% of children under 18 do not have insurance
Hospitals: Alliance Community Hospital (184 beds)
Safety: Violent crime rate: 45.0 per 10,000 population; Property crime rate: 349.8 per 10,000 population
Newspapers: The Review (daily circulation 11,800)
Transportation: Commute: 91.1% car, 0.8% public transportation, 4.9% walk, 2.2% work from home; Mean travel time to work: 19.6 minutes; Amtrak: Train service available.
Additional Information Contacts
City of Alliance. . . . . (330) 821-3110
http://www.cityofalliance.com

BEACH CITY (village). Covers a land area of 0.458 square miles and a water area of 0 square miles. Located at 40.65° N. Lat; 81.58° W. Long. Elevation is 1,004 feet.
History: Flood control dam completed in 1937 nearby.
Population: 895; Growth (since 2000): -21.3%; Density: 1,956.1 persons per square mile; Race: 97.7% White, 0.0% Black/African American, 0.7% Asian, 0.6% American Indian/Alaska Native, 0.0% Native Hawaiian/Other Pacific Islander, 1.1% Two or more races, 0.0% Hispanic of any race; Average household size: 2.47; Median age: 37.8; Age under 18: 21.3%; Age 65 and over: 19.9%; Males per 100 females: 92.0; Marriage status: 23.5% never married, 52.9% now married, 3.6% separated, 8.8% widowed, 14.8% divorced; Foreign born: 1.1%; Speak English only: 100.0%; With disability: 11.2%; Veterans: 11.9%; Ancestry: 44.6% German, 18.5% Irish, 9.2% American, 5.0% Swiss, 3.7% Dutch
Employment: 8.4% management, business, and financial, 1.5% computer, engineering, and science, 3.0% education, legal, community service, arts, and media, 2.3% healthcare practitioners, 18.5% service, 21.8% sales and office, 11.6% natural resources, construction, and maintenance, 32.9% production, transportation, and material moving
Income: Per capita: $19,585; Median household: $40,000; Average household: $46,462; Households with income of $100,000 or more: 8.3%; Poverty rate: 13.7%
Educational Attainment: High school diploma or higher: 85.0%; Bachelor's degree or higher: 5.7%; Graduate/professional degree or higher: 1.1%
Housing: Homeownership rate: 70.4%; Median home value: $79,300; Median year structure built: Before 1940; Homeowner vacancy rate: 0.0%; Median selected monthly owner costs: $754 with a mortgage, $279 without a mortgage; Median gross rent: $661 per month; Rental vacancy rate: 0.0%
Health Insurance: 87.8% have insurance; 68.3% have private insurance; 40.9% have public insurance; 12.2% do not have insurance; 11.5% of children under 18 do not have insurance
Transportation: Commute: 91.6% car, 1.8% public transportation, 2.3% walk, 3.1% work from home; Mean travel time to work: 28.2 minutes

BREWSTER (village). Covers a land area of 2.232 square miles and a water area of 0.008 square miles. Located at 40.71° N. Lat; 81.60° W. Long. Elevation is 991 feet.
Population: 2,291; Growth (since 2000): -1.4%; Density: 1,026.2 persons per square mile; Race: 96.7% White, 0.3% Black/African American, 1.1% Asian, 0.3% American Indian/Alaska Native, 0.0% Native Hawaiian/Other Pacific Islander, 1.6% Two or more races, 0.3% Hispanic of any race; Average household size: 2.55; Median age: 45.1; Age under 18: 20.5%; Age 65 and over: 19.7%; Males per 100 females: 95.9; Marriage status: 27.9% never married, 47.1% now married, 2.0% separated, 10.2% widowed, 14.9% divorced; Foreign born: 1.5%; Speak English only: 97.1%; With disability: 18.9%; Veterans: 10.3%; Ancestry: 36.8% German, 18.1% Irish, 13.6% American, 6.8% English, 6.7% Italian
Employment: 5.8% management, business, and financial, 0.6% computer, engineering, and science, 2.5% education, legal, community service, arts, and media, 4.6% healthcare practitioners, 16.4% service, 29.7% sales and office, 9.8% natural resources, construction, and maintenance, 30.5% production, transportation, and material moving
Income: Per capita: $19,731; Median household: $41,727; Average household: $49,978; Households with income of $100,000 or more: 8.6%; Poverty rate: 14.1%
Educational Attainment: High school diploma or higher: 84.4%; Bachelor's degree or higher: 5.2%; Graduate/professional degree or higher: 0.7%
Housing: Homeownership rate: 70.0%; Median home value: $89,500; Median year structure built: 1957; Homeowner vacancy rate: 0.0%; Median selected monthly owner costs: $1,002 with a mortgage, $365 without a mortgage; Median gross rent: $672 per month; Rental vacancy rate: 0.0%
Health Insurance: 92.3% have insurance; 60.6% have private insurance; 44.3% have public insurance; 7.7% do not have insurance; 1.1% of children under 18 do not have insurance
Safety: Violent crime rate: 0.0 per 10,000 population; Property crime rate: 92.2 per 10,000 population
Transportation: Commute: 94.2% car, 0.8% public transportation, 1.8% walk, 2.3% work from home; Mean travel time to work: 24.3 minutes

CANAL FULTON (city). Covers a land area of 3.258 square miles and a water area of 0.057 square miles. Located at 40.89° N. Lat; 81.59° W. Long. Elevation is 951 feet.

History: Canal Fulton was first called Milan, but the name was changed during the construction of the Ohio & Erie Canal to honor Robert Fulton, inventor of the steamboat.

Population: 5,464; Growth (since 2000): 8.0%; Density: 1,677.3 persons per square mile; Race: 95.8% White, 0.7% Black/African American, 0.0% Asian, 0.0% American Indian/Alaska Native, 0.0% Native Hawaiian/Other Pacific Islander, 2.9% Two or more races, 0.9% Hispanic of any race; Average household size: 2.24; Median age: 44.4; Age under 18: 20.8%; Age 65 and over: 21.1%; Males per 100 females: 89.4; Marriage status: 27.9% never married, 51.0% now married, 0.6% separated, 9.6% widowed, 11.5% divorced; Foreign born: 1.4%; Speak English only: 97.9%; With disability: 14.3%; Veterans: 13.0%; Ancestry: 30.6% German, 17.5% Italian, 14.0% Irish, 12.4% English, 7.3% American

Employment: 10.1% management, business, and financial, 3.8% computer, engineering, and science, 6.3% education, legal, community service, arts, and media, 12.4% healthcare practitioners, 24.8% service, 21.8% sales and office, 3.0% natural resources, construction, and maintenance, 17.9% production, transportation, and material moving

Income: Per capita: $25,986; Median household: $44,711; Average household: $58,591; Households with income of $100,000 or more: 20.9%; Poverty rate: 7.9%

Educational Attainment: High school diploma or higher: 91.4%; Bachelor's degree or higher: 25.5%; Graduate/professional degree or higher: 6.7%

School District(s)

Northwest Local (PK-12)
2015-16 Enrollment: 1,851 . . . . (330) 854-2291

Housing: Homeownership rate: 66.2%; Median home value: $138,400; Median year structure built: 1977; Homeowner vacancy rate: 0.0%; Median selected monthly owner costs: $1,183 with a mortgage, $411 without a mortgage; Median gross rent: $695 per month; Rental vacancy rate: 4.8%

Health Insurance: 94.0% have insurance; 80.0% have private insurance; 30.3% have public insurance; 6.0% do not have insurance; 4.7% of children under 18 do not have insurance

Safety: Violent crime rate: 3.6 per 10,000 population; Property crime rate: 133.0 per 10,000 population

Transportation: Commute: 94.7% car, 0.9% public transportation, 1.6% walk, 2.8% work from home; Mean travel time to work: 24.0 minutes

CANTON (city). County seat. Covers a land area of 25.462 square miles and a water area of 0.016 square miles. Located at 40.81° N. Lat; 81.37° W. Long. Elevation is 1,056 feet.

History: Pioneer settlers from New England built homes along Nimishillen Creek in 1805. The town was platted in 1806 by Bezaleel Wells, the "Father of Canton," and incorporated in 1822. Canton's first major industry began in 1827 when Joshua Gibbs developed an improved metal plow. This was the start of Canton's future as a processor of steel, manufacturing reapers, roller bearings, and other products. German and Swiss artisans came to Canton to work in the Dueber-Hampden Watch Company. President William McKinley was a resident of Canton, and conducted his campaign for the presidency from his home here. After his assassination in Buffalo in 1901, his remains were brought back to Canton for burial.

Population: 72,163; Growth (since 2000): -10.7%; Density: 2,834.1 persons per square mile; Race: 68.1% White, 24.3% Black/African American, 0.4% Asian, 0.3% American Indian/Alaska Native, 0.0% Native Hawaiian/Other Pacific Islander, 6.1% Two or more races, 3.2% Hispanic of any race; Average household size: 2.28; Median age: 35.8; Age under 18: 24.7%; Age 65 and over: 14.4%; Males per 100 females: 90.0; Marriage status: 40.7% never married, 35.2% now married, 2.3% separated, 7.5% widowed, 16.6% divorced; Foreign born: 2.4%; Speak English only: 96.1%; With disability: 16.4%; Veterans: 8.5%; Ancestry: 22.0% German, 12.6% Irish, 8.8% Italian, 5.4% English, 4.3% American

Employment: 8.1% management, business, and financial, 2.9% computer, engineering, and science, 8.0% education, legal, community service, arts, and media, 5.4% healthcare practitioners, 26.6% service, 22.6% sales and office, 8.0% natural resources, construction, and maintenance, 18.4% production, transportation, and material moving

Income: Per capita: $17,384; Median household: $30,444; Average household: $39,670; Households with income of $100,000 or more: 5.6%; Poverty rate: 31.8%

Educational Attainment: High school diploma or higher: 84.4%; Bachelor's degree or higher: 14.6%; Graduate/professional degree or higher: 4.9%

School District(s)

Canton City (PK-12)
2015-16 Enrollment: 9,049 . . . . (330) 438-2500
Canton Harbor High School (09-12)
2015-16 Enrollment: 89. . . . . (330) 452-8414
Canton Local (PK-12)
2015-16 Enrollment: 2,088 . . . . (330) 484-8010
Garfield Academy (KG-08)
2015-16 Enrollment: 218. . . . . (330) 454-3128
Imagine On Superior
2015-16 Enrollment: n/a . . . . (330) 451-2050
Jackson Local (KG-12)
2015-16 Enrollment: 5,977 . . . . (330) 830-8000
Life Skills Center of Canton (09-12)
2015-16 Enrollment: 91. . . . . (330) 456-4490
Perry Local (PK-12)
2015-16 Enrollment: 4,863 . . . . (330) 477-8121
Plain Local (KG-12)
2015-16 Enrollment: 6,077 . . . . (330) 492-3500
Summit Academy Community School For Alternative Learning-Canton (KG-08)
2015-16 Enrollment: 152. . . . . (330) 458-0393
Summit Academy Secondary - Canton (09-12)
2015-16 Enrollment: 113. . . . . (877) 644-6338

Four-year College(s)

Aultman College of Nursing and Health Sciences (Private, Not-for-profit)
Fall 2016 Enrollment: 391 . . . . (330) 363-6347
2016-17 Tuition: In-state $17,370; Out-of-state $17,370
Brown Mackie College-North Canton (Private, For-profit)
Fall 2016 Enrollment: 213 . . . . (330) 494-1214
2016-17 Tuition: In-state $12,492; Out-of-state $12,492
Kent State University at Stark (Public)
Fall 2016 Enrollment: 5,015 . . . . (330) 499-9600
2016-17 Tuition: In-state $5,664; Out-of-state $14,028
Malone University (Private, Not-for-profit, Friends)
Fall 2016 Enrollment: 1,667 . . . . (330) 471-8100
2016-17 Tuition: In-state $29,422; Out-of-state $29,422

Two-year College(s)

American National University-Canton (Private, For-profit)
Fall 2016 Enrollment: 8 . . . . (330) 492-5300
2016-17 Tuition: In-state $14,886; Out-of-state $14,886

Vocational/Technical School(s)

Canton City Schools Adult Career and Technical Education (Public)
Fall 2016 Enrollment: 120 . . . . (330) 438-2556
2016-17 Tuition: $12,054
National Beauty College (Private, For-profit)
Fall 2016 Enrollment: 98 . . . . (330) 499-5596
2016-17 Tuition: $15,850

Housing: Homeownership rate: 49.2%; Median home value: $71,000; Median year structure built: 1948; Homeowner vacancy rate: 2.2%; Median selected monthly owner costs: $887 with a mortgage, $326 without a mortgage; Median gross rent: $606 per month; Rental vacancy rate: 7.9%

Health Insurance: 88.9% have insurance; 49.8% have private insurance; 50.7% have public insurance; 11.1% do not have insurance; 4.4% of children under 18 do not have insurance

Hospitals: Aultman Hospital (808 beds); Mercy Medical Center (476 beds)

Safety: Violent crime rate: 94.5 per 10,000 population; Property crime rate: 511.4 per 10,000 population

Newspapers: The Repository (daily circulation 64,100)

Transportation: Commute: 89.4% car, 4.3% public transportation, 2.9% walk, 2.4% work from home; Mean travel time to work: 20.3 minutes

Additional Information Contacts

City of Canton . . . . (330) 489-3283
http://www.ci.canton.oh.us

EAST CANTON (village). Covers a land area of 1.317 square miles and a water area of 0 square miles. Located at 40.79° N. Lat; 81.28° W. Long. Elevation is 1,165 feet.

History: East Canton was founded in 1805 as Osnaburg. The name was changed in 1821. The town developed as a residential suburb for Canton, and as a center for glazed brick making.

Population: 1,506; Growth (since 2000): -7.6%; Density: 1,143.8 persons per square mile; Race: 97.2% White, 1.8% Black/African American, 0.0% Asian, 0.5% American Indian/Alaska Native, 0.0% Native Hawaiian/Other Pacific Islander, 0.5% Two or more races, 0.3% Hispanic of any race; Average household size: 2.42; Median age: 41.7; Age under 18: 23.2%; Age 65 and over: 16.7%; Males per 100 females: 96.7; Marriage status: 26.6% never married, 53.9% now married, 0.2% separated, 5.3% widowed, 14.2% divorced; Foreign born: 0.8%; Speak English only: 98.2%; With disability: 15.3%; Veterans: 9.9%; Ancestry: 36.6% German, 17.2% Irish, 10.0% Italian, 9.0% American, 8.6% English
Employment: 10.6% management, business, and financial, 2.1% computer, engineering, and science, 6.5% education, legal, community service, arts, and media, 10.5% healthcare practitioners, 17.1% service, 21.3% sales and office, 8.3% natural resources, construction, and maintenance, 23.6% production, transportation, and material moving
Income: Per capita: $24,978; Median household: $51,136; Average household: $59,915; Households with income of $100,000 or more: 12.6%; Poverty rate: 6.8%
Educational Attainment: High school diploma or higher: 90.7%; Bachelor's degree or higher: 12.9%; Graduate/professional degree or higher: 6.5%

School District(s)

Osnaburg Local (PK-12)
2015-16 Enrollment: 848. . . . . (330) 488-1609
Housing: Homeownership rate: 73.0%; Median home value: $98,900; Median year structure built: 1958; Homeowner vacancy rate: 0.6%; Median selected monthly owner costs: $983 with a mortgage, $404 without a mortgage; Median gross rent: $805 per month; Rental vacancy rate: 10.2%
Health Insurance: 95.6% have insurance; 78.2% have private insurance; 31.3% have public insurance; 4.4% do not have insurance; 2.0% of children under 18 do not have insurance
Transportation: Commute: 95.1% car, 0.5% public transportation, 0.9% walk, 3.1% work from home; Mean travel time to work: 21.2 minutes

EAST SPARTA (village). Covers a land area of 1.681 square miles and a water area of 0 square miles. Located at 40.66° N. Lat; 81.36° W. Long. Elevation is 971 feet.
Population: 1,015; Growth (since 2000): 25.9%; Density: 603.6 persons per square mile; Race: 98.8% White, 0.0% Black/African American, 0.0% Asian, 0.0% American Indian/Alaska Native, 0.0% Native Hawaiian/Other Pacific Islander, 1.2% Two or more races, 0.0% Hispanic of any race; Average household size: 2.78; Median age: 40.2; Age under 18: 22.9%; Age 65 and over: 15.3%; Males per 100 females: 98.8; Marriage status: 26.2% never married, 53.5% now married, 0.8% separated, 7.0% widowed, 13.3% divorced; Foreign born: 0.0%; Speak English only: 100.0%; With disability: 16.7%; Veterans: 9.2%; Ancestry: 26.3% German, 18.8% Irish, 10.6% Italian, 8.5% American, 7.5% English
Employment: 12.2% management, business, and financial, 4.0% computer, engineering, and science, 5.1% education, legal, community service, arts, and media, 3.8% healthcare practitioners, 19.2% service, 25.7% sales and office, 6.9% natural resources, construction, and maintenance, 23.2% production, transportation, and material moving
Income: Per capita: $22,318; Median household: $54,107; Average household: $64,157; Households with income of $100,000 or more: 12.2%; Poverty rate: 13.6%
Educational Attainment: High school diploma or higher: 89.9%; Bachelor's degree or higher: 9.8%; Graduate/professional degree or higher: 2.5%
Housing: Homeownership rate: 78.8%; Median home value: $92,300; Median year structure built: 1948; Homeowner vacancy rate: 3.9%; Median selected monthly owner costs: $1,031 with a mortgage, $436 without a mortgage; Median gross rent: $709 per month; Rental vacancy rate: 0.0%
Health Insurance: 94.7% have insurance; 81.5% have private insurance; 29.8% have public insurance; 5.3% do not have insurance; 2.2% of children under 18 do not have insurance
Transportation: Commute: 93.8% car, 0.4% public transportation, 2.2% walk, 2.7% work from home; Mean travel time to work: 23.9 minutes

GREENTOWN (CDP). Covers a land area of 2.741 square miles and a water area of 0 square miles. Located at 40.93° N. Lat; 81.40° W. Long. Elevation is 1,197 feet.
Population: 4,088; Growth (since 2000): 29.6%; Density: 1,491.6 persons per square mile; Race: 98.6% White, 0.5% Black/African American, 0.0% Asian, 0.0% American Indian/Alaska Native, 0.0% Native Hawaiian/Other Pacific Islander, 0.9% Two or more races, 1.0% Hispanic of any race; Average household size: 2.98; Median age: 37.9; Age under 18: 25.0%; Age 65 and over: 9.4%; Males per 100 females: 98.7; Marriage status: 22.1% never married, 69.5% now married, 0.3% separated, 3.1% widowed, 5.3% divorced; Foreign born: 1.5%; Speak English only: 98.3%; With disability: 4.5%; Veterans: 11.3%; Ancestry: 39.2% German, 19.3% Italian, 18.2% English, 14.1% Irish, 4.6% American
Employment: 15.0% management, business, and financial, 12.3% computer, engineering, and science, 13.8% education, legal, community service, arts, and media, 8.1% healthcare practitioners, 10.1% service, 28.7% sales and office, 7.7% natural resources, construction, and maintenance, 4.3% production, transportation, and material moving
Income: Per capita: $31,148; Median household: $84,944; Average household: $91,652; Households with income of $100,000 or more: 46.6%; Poverty rate: 4.6%
Educational Attainment: High school diploma or higher: 98.9%; Bachelor's degree or higher: 40.5%; Graduate/professional degree or higher: 13.6%
Housing: Homeownership rate: 85.6%; Median home value: $189,500; Median year structure built: 1990; Homeowner vacancy rate: 0.0%; Median selected monthly owner costs: $1,645 with a mortgage, $517 without a mortgage; Median gross rent: $842 per month; Rental vacancy rate: 0.0%
Health Insurance: 97.6% have insurance; 93.3% have private insurance; 13.2% have public insurance; 2.4% do not have insurance; 0.0% of children under 18 do not have insurance
Transportation: Commute: 99.1% car, 0.0% public transportation, 0.0% walk, 0.9% work from home; Mean travel time to work: 25.0 minutes

HARTVILLE (village). Covers a land area of 2.576 square miles and a water area of 0.001 square miles. Located at 40.96° N. Lat; 81.33° W. Long. Elevation is 1,168 feet.
Population: 2,998; Growth (since 2000): 37.9%; Density: 1,163.8 persons per square mile; Race: 96.2% White, 0.8% Black/African American, 0.0% Asian, 0.0% American Indian/Alaska Native, 0.0% Native Hawaiian/Other Pacific Islander, 2.8% Two or more races, 0.3% Hispanic of any race; Average household size: 2.49; Median age: 38.6; Age under 18: 23.7%; Age 65 and over: 21.6%; Males per 100 females: 89.6; Marriage status: 29.9% never married, 48.5% now married, 0.7% separated, 6.2% widowed, 15.5% divorced; Foreign born: 1.5%; Speak English only: 98.3%; With disability: 10.6%; Veterans: 8.3%; Ancestry: 37.5% German, 15.4% Irish, 9.1% Italian, 8.3% English, 6.4% American
Employment: 14.9% management, business, and financial, 2.8% computer, engineering, and science, 8.4% education, legal, community service, arts, and media, 3.8% healthcare practitioners, 22.8% service, 25.7% sales and office, 8.4% natural resources, construction, and maintenance, 13.1% production, transportation, and material moving
Income: Per capita: $28,616; Median household: $46,204; Average household: $71,393; Households with income of $100,000 or more: 16.1%; Poverty rate: 10.3%
Educational Attainment: High school diploma or higher: 89.6%; Bachelor's degree or higher: 24.1%; Graduate/professional degree or higher: 6.5%

School District(s)

Lake Local (KG-12)
2015-16 Enrollment: 3,475 . . . . (330) 877-9383
Housing: Homeownership rate: 63.5%; Median home value: $141,200; Median year structure built: 1973; Homeowner vacancy rate: 0.0%; Median selected monthly owner costs: $1,142 with a mortgage, $476 without a mortgage; Median gross rent: $682 per month; Rental vacancy rate: 4.8%
Health Insurance: 92.6% have insurance; 71.2% have private insurance; 41.9% have public insurance; 7.4% do not have insurance; 3.9% of children under 18 do not have insurance
Safety: Violent crime rate: 3.4 per 10,000 population; Property crime rate: 178.2 per 10,000 population
Newspapers: Hartville News (weekly circulation 2,900)
Transportation: Commute: 91.2% car, 0.0% public transportation, 0.9% walk, 6.7% work from home; Mean travel time to work: 26.4 minutes

HILLS AND DALES (village). Covers a land area of 0.323 square miles and a water area of 0 square miles. Located at 40.83° N. Lat; 81.44° W. Long. Elevation is 1,122 feet.
Population: 246; Growth (since 2000): -5.4%; Density: 762.4 persons per square mile; Race: 98.4% White, 0.0% Black/African American, 1.6% Asian, 0.0% American Indian/Alaska Native, 0.0% Native Hawaiian/Other Pacific Islander, 0.0% Two or more races, 2.4% Hispanic of any race; Average household size: 2.65; Median age: 55.3; Age under 18: 17.1%;

Age 65 and over: 29.3%; Males per 100 females: 108.5; Marriage status: 24.3% never married, 63.3% now married, 0.0% separated, 2.2% widowed, 10.2% divorced; Foreign born: 3.7%; Speak English only: 94.7%; With disability: 5.7%; Veterans: 7.8%; Ancestry: 28.5% German, 16.3% Italian, 13.8% English, 11.0% Irish, 4.5% Polish
Employment: 21.4% management, business, and financial, 2.9% computer, engineering, and science, 21.4% education, legal, community service, arts, and media, 3.9% healthcare practitioners, 5.8% service, 37.9% sales and office, 5.8% natural resources, construction, and maintenance, 1.0% production, transportation, and material moving
Income: Per capita: $87,554; Median household: $135,313; Average household: $227,876; Households with income of $100,000 or more: 56.0%; Poverty rate: 0.8%
Educational Attainment: High school diploma or higher: 97.8%; Bachelor's degree or higher: 69.2%; Graduate/professional degree or higher: 30.8%
Housing: Homeownership rate: 100.0%; Median home value: $417,900; Median year structure built: 1957; Homeowner vacancy rate: 11.0%; Median selected monthly owner costs: $2,308 with a mortgage, $1,113 without a mortgage; Median gross rent: n/a per month; Rental vacancy rate: 0.0%
Health Insurance: 98.8% have insurance; 86.2% have private insurance; 31.7% have public insurance; 1.2% do not have insurance; 0.0% of children under 18 do not have insurance
Transportation: Commute: 90.9% car, 0.0% public transportation, 0.0% walk, 9.1% work from home; Mean travel time to work: 22.1 minutes

LIMAVILLE (village). Covers a land area of 0.273 square miles and a water area of 0.007 square miles. Located at 40.99° N. Lat; 81.15° W. Long. Elevation is 1,053 feet.
Population: 144; Growth (since 2000): -25.4%; Density: 528.4 persons per square mile; Race: 100.0% White, 0.0% Black/African American, 0.0% Asian, 0.0% American Indian/Alaska Native, 0.0% Native Hawaiian/Other Pacific Islander, 0.0% Two or more races, 1.4% Hispanic of any race; Average household size: 2.03; Median age: 47.4; Age under 18: 11.8%; Age 65 and over: 14.6%; Males per 100 females: 109.7; Marriage status: 18.0% never married, 57.0% now married, 0.8% separated, 12.5% widowed, 12.5% divorced; Foreign born: 1.4%; Speak English only: 96.5%; With disability: 23.6%; Veterans: 17.3%; Ancestry: 30.6% German, 12.5% Irish, 12.5% Polish, 11.1% English, 5.6% Swiss
Employment: 2.3% management, business, and financial, 0.0% computer, engineering, and science, 0.0% education, legal, community service, arts, and media, 0.0% healthcare practitioners, 9.2% service, 24.1% sales and office, 20.7% natural resources, construction, and maintenance, 43.7% production, transportation, and material moving
Income: Per capita: $22,867; Median household: $45,521; Average household: $42,956; Households with income of $100,000 or more: 1.4%; Poverty rate: 14.6%
Educational Attainment: High school diploma or higher: 95.5%; Bachelor's degree or higher: 9.1%; Graduate/professional degree or higher: 7.3%
Housing: Homeownership rate: 73.2%; Median home value: $90,000; Median year structure built: 1944; Homeowner vacancy rate: 0.0%; Median selected monthly owner costs: $792 with a mortgage, $246 without a mortgage; Median gross rent: $845 per month; Rental vacancy rate: 0.0%
Health Insurance: 86.1% have insurance; 69.4% have private insurance; 33.3% have public insurance; 13.9% do not have insurance; 0.0% of children under 18 do not have insurance
Transportation: Commute: 100.0% car, 0.0% public transportation, 0.0% walk, 0.0% work from home; Mean travel time to work: 23.2 minutes

LOUISVILLE (city). Covers a land area of 5.492 square miles and a water area of 0 square miles. Located at 40.84° N. Lat; 81.26° W. Long. Elevation is 1,138 feet.
Population: 9,318; Growth (since 2000): 4.6%; Density: 1,696.5 persons per square mile; Race: 96.5% White, 0.0% Black/African American, 0.0% Asian, 0.6% American Indian/Alaska Native, 0.0% Native Hawaiian/Other Pacific Islander, 2.4% Two or more races, 1.4% Hispanic of any race; Average household size: 2.40; Median age: 39.9; Age under 18: 22.3%; Age 65 and over: 17.7%; Males per 100 females: 86.8; Marriage status: 25.7% never married, 52.9% now married, 0.9% separated, 8.1% widowed, 13.3% divorced; Foreign born: 2.0%; Speak English only: 96.9%; With disability: 13.5%; Veterans: 11.3%; Ancestry: 33.2% German, 12.2% Irish, 10.4% Italian, 9.1% English, 6.4% French
Employment: 14.4% management, business, and financial, 4.6% computer, engineering, and science, 7.1% education, legal, community service, arts, and media, 4.7% healthcare practitioners, 16.8% service, 26.5% sales and office, 9.7% natural resources, construction, and maintenance, 16.3% production, transportation, and material moving
Income: Per capita: $26,717; Median household: $54,087; Average household: $63,010; Households with income of $100,000 or more: 15.5%; Poverty rate: 5.4%
Educational Attainment: High school diploma or higher: 91.0%; Bachelor's degree or higher: 21.5%; Graduate/professional degree or higher: 8.1%

School District(s)

Louisville City (PK-12)
2015-16 Enrollment: 2,902 . . . . (330) 875-9687
Marlington Local (KG-12)
2015-16 Enrollment: 2,396 . . . . (330) 823-7458

Housing: Homeownership rate: 62.6%; Median home value: $131,900; Median year structure built: 1973; Homeowner vacancy rate: 3.6%; Median selected monthly owner costs: $1,192 with a mortgage, $395 without a mortgage; Median gross rent: $710 per month; Rental vacancy rate: 0.0%
Health Insurance: 93.1% have insurance; 73.3% have private insurance; 32.9% have public insurance; 6.9% do not have insurance; 3.3% of children under 18 do not have insurance
Safety: Violent crime rate: 15.4 per 10,000 population; Property crime rate: 125.1 per 10,000 population
Newspapers: Louisville Herald (weekly circulation 3,000)
Transportation: Commute: 94.4% car, 0.2% public transportation, 2.4% walk, 3.0% work from home; Mean travel time to work: 25.0 minutes
Additional Information Contacts
City of Louisville . . . . (330) 875-3321
http://www.louisvilleohio.com

MAGNOLIA (village). Covers a land area of 0.868 square miles and a water area of 0 square miles. Located at 40.65° N. Lat; 81.29° W. Long. Elevation is 948 feet.
Population: 1,114; Growth (since 2000): 19.7%; Density: 1,283.7 persons per square mile; Race: 99.7% White, 0.0% Black/African American, 0.0% Asian, 0.3% American Indian/Alaska Native, 0.0% Native Hawaiian/Other Pacific Islander, 0.0% Two or more races, 1.2% Hispanic of any race; Average household size: 2.90; Median age: 34.3; Age under 18: 32.1%; Age 65 and over: 13.2%; Males per 100 females: 102.1; Marriage status: 25.4% never married, 58.3% now married, 1.3% separated, 5.8% widowed, 10.4% divorced; Foreign born: 0.2%; Speak English only: 98.5%; With disability: 11.4%; Veterans: 8.6%; Ancestry: 33.1% German, 18.8% Italian, 16.8% Irish, 8.8% English, 5.0% American
Employment: 17.9% management, business, and financial, 3.2% computer, engineering, and science, 6.9% education, legal, community service, arts, and media, 3.8% healthcare practitioners, 18.1% service, 20.2% sales and office, 15.9% natural resources, construction, and maintenance, 13.9% production, transportation, and material moving
Income: Per capita: $22,910; Median household: $51,500; Average household: $65,711; Households with income of $100,000 or more: 19.6%; Poverty rate: 18.1%
Educational Attainment: High school diploma or higher: 95.8%; Bachelor's degree or higher: 21.8%; Graduate/professional degree or higher: 7.1%

School District(s)

Sandy Valley Local (PK-12)
2015-16 Enrollment: 1,453 . . . . (330) 866-3339

Housing: Homeownership rate: 76.3%; Median home value: $101,500; Median year structure built: 1950; Homeowner vacancy rate: 0.0%; Median selected monthly owner costs: $1,072 with a mortgage, $429 without a mortgage; Median gross rent: $839 per month; Rental vacancy rate: 6.2%
Health Insurance: 94.8% have insurance; 71.9% have private insurance; 38.1% have public insurance; 5.2% do not have insurance; 3.4% of children under 18 do not have insurance
Safety: Violent crime rate: 20.6 per 10,000 population; Property crime rate: 452.7 per 10,000 population
Transportation: Commute: 97.6% car, 0.0% public transportation, 0.4% walk, 0.8% work from home; Mean travel time to work: 26.0 minutes

MARLBORO (CDP).
Land/water area and latitude/longitude are not available.
Population: 231; Growth (since 2000): n/a; Density: n/a persons per square mile; Race: 100.0% White, 0.0% Black/African American, 0.0%

Asian, 0.0% American Indian/Alaska Native, 0.0% Native Hawaiian/Other Pacific Islander, 0.0% Two or more races, 0.0% Hispanic of any race; Average household size: 3.04; Median age: 36.4; Age under 18: 32.5%; Age 65 and over: 32.0%; Males per 100 females: 0.0; Marriage status: 21.8% never married, 72.7% now married, 0.0% separated, 0.0% widowed, 5.5% divorced; Foreign born: 0.0%; Speak English only: 100.0%; With disability: 17.3%; Veterans: 9.6%; Ancestry: 29.4% English, 13.9% Polish, 10.4% German, 10.4% Italian, 7.4% Ukrainian

Employment: 21.5% management, business, and financial, 0.0% computer, engineering, and science, 8.9% education, legal, community service, arts, and media, 20.3% healthcare practitioners, 11.4% service, 8.9% sales and office, 10.1% natural resources, construction, and maintenance, 19.0% production, transportation, and material moving

Income: Per capita: $17,406; Median household: n/a; Average household: $50,205; Households with income of $100,000 or more: 7.9%; Poverty rate: 11.3%

Educational Attainment: High school diploma or higher: 83.8%; Bachelor's degree or higher: 5.4%; Graduate/professional degree or higher: n/a

Housing: Homeownership rate: 100.0%; Median home value: $88,800; Median year structure built: Before 1940; Homeowner vacancy rate: 0.0%; Median selected monthly owner costs: n/a with a mortgage, $425 without a mortgage; Median gross rent: n/a per month; Rental vacancy rate: 0.0%

Health Insurance: 96.5% have insurance; 67.5% have private insurance; 71.9% have public insurance; 3.5% do not have insurance; 0.0% of children under 18 do not have insurance

Safety: Violent crime rate: 0.0 per 10,000 population; Property crime rate: 0.0 per 10,000 population

Transportation: Commute: 100.0% car, 0.0% public transportation, 0.0% walk, 0.0% work from home; Mean travel time to work: 31.5 minutes

MASSILLON (city). Covers a land area of 18.578 square miles and a water area of 0.181 square miles. Located at 40.78° N. Lat; 81.53° W. Long. Elevation is 948 feet.

History: Massillon came into existence in 1826 when the Ohio & Erie Canal was planned. The town was laid out on both sides of the Tuscarawas River by James Duncan and Ferdinand Hurxthal, and named for Jean Baptiste Massillon, a French divine and Mrs. Duncan's favorite writer. Two years later the canal was completed, and Massillon became a marketing and industrial town.

Population: 32,268; Growth (since 2000): 3.0%; Density: 1,736.9 persons per square mile; Race: 89.4% White, 7.2% Black/African American, 0.5% Asian, 0.0% American Indian/Alaska Native, 0.0% Native Hawaiian/Other Pacific Islander, 2.8% Two or more races, 2.8% Hispanic of any race; Average household size: 2.41; Median age: 40.0; Age under 18: 23.2%; Age 65 and over: 17.6%; Males per 100 females: 94.0; Marriage status: 31.5% never married, 45.7% now married, 1.4% separated, 6.5% widowed, 16.3% divorced; Foreign born: 1.4%; Speak English only: 96.8%; With disability: 15.4%; Veterans: 10.0%; Ancestry: 31.5% German, 16.0% Irish, 9.5% Italian, 8.9% English, 6.2% American

Employment: 8.3% management, business, and financial, 3.1% computer, engineering, and science, 7.9% education, legal, community service, arts, and media, 6.0% healthcare practitioners, 20.1% service, 25.9% sales and office, 8.8% natural resources, construction, and maintenance, 20.0% production, transportation, and material moving

Income: Per capita: $22,548; Median household: $42,808; Average household: $54,490; Households with income of $100,000 or more: 12.5%; Poverty rate: 18.3%

Educational Attainment: High school diploma or higher: 89.3%; Bachelor's degree or higher: 16.3%; Graduate/professional degree or higher: 6.1%

School District(s)

Buckeye United School District (07-12)
2015-16 Enrollment: 311 . . . . (614) 466-0720
Jackson Local (KG-12)
2015-16 Enrollment: 5,977 . . . . (330) 830-8000
Massillon City (PK-12)
2015-16 Enrollment: 4,009 . . . . (330) 830-3900
Massillon Digital Academy Inc (02-12)
2015-16 Enrollment: 71 . . . . (330) 830-3900
Perry Local (PK-12)
2015-16 Enrollment: 4,863 . . . . (330) 477-8121
Stark County Area (09-12)
2015-16 Enrollment: n/a . . . . (330) 832-1591
Tuslaw Local (KG-12)
2015-16 Enrollment: 1,400 . . . . (330) 837-7813

Housing: Homeownership rate: 63.6%; Median home value: $98,700; Median year structure built: 1957; Homeowner vacancy rate: 2.1%; Median selected monthly owner costs: $994 with a mortgage, $403 without a mortgage; Median gross rent: $670 per month; Rental vacancy rate: 3.8%

Health Insurance: 92.5% have insurance; 65.5% have private insurance; 43.4% have public insurance; 7.5% do not have insurance; 4.0% of children under 18 do not have insurance

Hospitals: Affinity Medical Center (451 beds)

Newspapers: The Independent (daily circulation 12,200)

Transportation: Commute: 93.7% car, 1.8% public transportation, 1.3% walk, 2.6% work from home; Mean travel time to work: 20.1 minutes

Additional Information Contacts

City of Massillon . . . . (330) 830-1700
http://www.massillonohio.com

MEYERS LAKE (village). Covers a land area of 0.224 square miles and a water area of 0.210 square miles. Located at 40.81° N. Lat; 81.42° W. Long. Elevation is 1,112 feet.

History: Former site of amusement park at streetcar line terminus.

Population: 614; Growth (since 2000): 8.7%; Density: 2,738.4 persons per square mile; Race: 96.7% White, 3.3% Black/African American, 0.0% Asian, 0.0% American Indian/Alaska Native, 0.0% Native Hawaiian/Other Pacific Islander, 0.0% Two or more races, 2.6% Hispanic of any race; Average household size: 2.06; Median age: 51.8; Age under 18: 11.4%; Age 65 and over: 29.6%; Males per 100 females: 84.1; Marriage status: 31.5% never married, 47.1% now married, 0.2% separated, 5.8% widowed, 15.6% divorced; Foreign born: 2.8%; Speak English only: 97.5%; With disability: 15.8%; Veterans: 6.6%; Ancestry: 44.0% German, 17.4% Italian, 15.0% Irish, 7.8% English, 4.1% American

Employment: 28.1% management, business, and financial, 5.0% computer, engineering, and science, 8.8% education, legal, community service, arts, and media, 6.6% healthcare practitioners, 13.2% service, 29.3% sales and office, 2.8% natural resources, construction, and maintenance, 6.0% production, transportation, and material moving

Income: Per capita: $45,561; Median household: $66,354; Average household: $96,753; Households with income of $100,000 or more: 30.7%; Poverty rate: 21.7%

Educational Attainment: High school diploma or higher: 93.7%; Bachelor's degree or higher: 42.9%; Graduate/professional degree or higher: 16.1%

Housing: Homeownership rate: 82.2%; Median home value: $167,600; Median year structure built: 1986; Homeowner vacancy rate: 6.7%; Median selected monthly owner costs: $1,362 with a mortgage, $581 without a mortgage; Median gross rent: $1,101 per month; Rental vacancy rate: 12.1%

Health Insurance: 97.2% have insurance; 68.1% have private insurance; 48.5% have public insurance; 2.8% do not have insurance; 4.3% of children under 18 do not have insurance

Transportation: Commute: 95.2% car, 0.0% public transportation, 1.6% walk, 2.6% work from home; Mean travel time to work: 20.9 minutes

MINERVA (village). Covers a land area of 2.230 square miles and a water area of 0 square miles. Located at 40.73° N. Lat; 81.10° W. Long. Elevation is 1,056 feet.

History: Minerva was established as a town in 1835, when the Sandy & Beaver Canal was under construction. The town was named for the niece of John Whitacre, the founder.

Population: 4,001; Growth (since 2000): 1.7%; Density: 1,794.0 persons per square mile; Race: 93.6% White, 2.4% Black/African American, 0.0% Asian, 0.0% American Indian/Alaska Native, 0.7% Native Hawaiian/Other Pacific Islander, 3.3% Two or more races, 2.3% Hispanic of any race; Average household size: 2.51; Median age: 37.5; Age under 18: 22.2%; Age 65 and over: 19.0%; Males per 100 females: 90.1; Marriage status: 23.5% never married, 51.5% now married, 2.5% separated, 10.2% widowed, 14.7% divorced; Foreign born: 0.2%; Speak English only: 98.3%; With disability: 14.5%; Veterans: 10.5%; Ancestry: 31.3% German, 17.9% Irish, 15.6% English, 7.7% American, 6.5% Italian

Employment: 6.1% management, business, and financial, 1.9% computer, engineering, and science, 6.7% education, legal, community service, arts, and media, 4.0% healthcare practitioners, 15.5% service, 29.2% sales and office, 6.0% natural resources, construction, and maintenance, 30.8% production, transportation, and material moving

Income: Per capita: $21,162; Median household: $44,722; Average household: $51,317; Households with income of $100,000 or more: 11.8%; Poverty rate: 9.2%
Educational Attainment: High school diploma or higher: 91.3%; Bachelor's degree or higher: 14.4%; Graduate/professional degree or higher: 7.0%

School District(s)

Minerva Local (KG-12)
2015-16 Enrollment: 1,836 . . . . (330) 868-4332

Housing: Homeownership rate: 64.2%; Median home value: $84,700; Median year structure built: 1955; Homeowner vacancy rate: 8.8%; Median selected monthly owner costs: $942 with a mortgage, $366 without a mortgage; Median gross rent: $653 per month; Rental vacancy rate: 4.9%
Health Insurance: 89.9% have insurance; 65.1% have private insurance; 40.1% have public insurance; 10.1% do not have insurance; 6.0% of children under 18 do not have insurance
Safety: Violent crime rate: 13.6 per 10,000 population; Property crime rate: 125.3 per 10,000 population
Newspapers: Press-News (weekly circulation 2,200); The News Leader (weekly circulation 3,900)
Transportation: Commute: 92.6% car, 0.0% public transportation, 4.8% walk, 0.9% work from home; Mean travel time to work: 28.0 minutes

---

NAVARRE (village). Covers a land area of 2.054 square miles and a water area of 0.004 square miles. Located at 40.73° N. Lat; 81.51° W. Long. Elevation is 961 feet.
History: Navarre was founded by James Duncan and named by his wife for a prince of Navarre. A lock of the Ohio & Erie Canal was located in Navarre, which became a shipping center for farm produce.
Population: 1,853; Growth (since 2000): 28.7%; Density: 901.9 persons per square mile; Race: 98.3% White, 1.3% Black/African American, 0.0% Asian, 0.0% American Indian/Alaska Native, 0.0% Native Hawaiian/Other Pacific Islander, 0.3% Two or more races, 0.4% Hispanic of any race; Average household size: 2.16; Median age: 45.4; Age under 18: 17.7%; Age 65 and over: 22.4%; Males per 100 females: 89.3; Marriage status: 26.4% never married, 37.7% now married, 0.5% separated, 15.4% widowed, 20.5% divorced; Foreign born: 0.0%; Speak English only: 98.9%; With disability: 14.6%; Veterans: 11.5%; Ancestry: 32.6% German, 14.1% Irish, 11.5% English, 9.5% American, 8.1% Italian
Employment: 6.5% management, business, and financial, 2.5% computer, engineering, and science, 4.1% education, legal, community service, arts, and media, 3.4% healthcare practitioners, 24.8% service, 22.3% sales and office, 12.7% natural resources, construction, and maintenance, 23.9% production, transportation, and material moving
Income: Per capita: $21,071; Median household: $38,036; Average household: $45,138; Households with income of $100,000 or more: 6.6%; Poverty rate: 17.2%
Educational Attainment: High school diploma or higher: 90.4%; Bachelor's degree or higher: 14.2%; Graduate/professional degree or higher: 4.2%

School District(s)

Fairless Local (KG-12)
2015-16 Enrollment: 1,529 . . . . (330) 767-3577
Perry Local (PK-12)
2015-16 Enrollment: 4,863 . . . . (330) 477-8121

Housing: Homeownership rate: 71.2%; Median home value: $90,100; Median year structure built: Before 1940; Homeowner vacancy rate: 4.5%; Median selected monthly owner costs: $988 with a mortgage, $333 without a mortgage; Median gross rent: $621 per month; Rental vacancy rate: 5.8%
Health Insurance: 93.5% have insurance; 71.5% have private insurance; 36.8% have public insurance; 6.5% do not have insurance; 4.6% of children under 18 do not have insurance
Safety: Violent crime rate: 0.0 per 10,000 population; Property crime rate: 99.2 per 10,000 population
Transportation: Commute: 94.1% car, 0.6% public transportation, 3.7% walk, 0.6% work from home; Mean travel time to work: 20.8 minutes
Additional Information Contacts
Village of Navarre . . . . (330) 879-5508
http://www.navarreohio.net

NORTH CANTON (city). Covers a land area of 6.400 square miles and a water area of 0 square miles. Located at 40.87° N. Lat; 81.40° W. Long. Elevation is 1,158 feet.
History: Settled c.1815, incorporated as a city 1961.
Population: 17,422; Growth (since 2000): 6.4%; Density: 2,722.2 persons per square mile; Race: 96.2% White, 1.5% Black/African American, 0.6% Asian, 0.0% American Indian/Alaska Native, 0.0% Native Hawaiian/Other Pacific Islander, 1.7% Two or more races, 1.9% Hispanic of any race; Average household size: 2.22; Median age: 44.0; Age under 18: 17.4%; Age 65 and over: 24.3%; Males per 100 females: 86.1; Marriage status: 28.5% never married, 48.2% now married, 0.7% separated, 9.6% widowed, 13.7% divorced; Foreign born: 2.9%; Speak English only: 95.8%; With disability: 13.3%; Veterans: 9.6%; Ancestry: 32.6% German, 16.3% Irish, 12.9% Italian, 12.3% English, 7.1% American
Employment: 13.8% management, business, and financial, 5.8% computer, engineering, and science, 14.9% education, legal, community service, arts, and media, 8.4% healthcare practitioners, 19.0% service, 24.5% sales and office, 4.9% natural resources, construction, and maintenance, 8.7% production, transportation, and material moving
Income: Per capita: $30,399; Median household: $55,874; Average household: $70,867; Households with income of $100,000 or more: 18.9%; Poverty rate: 5.6%
Educational Attainment: High school diploma or higher: 94.4%; Bachelor's degree or higher: 35.3%; Graduate/professional degree or higher: 15.1%

School District(s)

North Canton City (PK-12)
2015-16 Enrollment: 4,440 . . . . (330) 497-5600

Four-year College(s)

Walsh University (Private, Not-for-profit, Roman Catholic)
Fall 2016 Enrollment: 2,776 . . . . (330) 499-7090
2016-17 Tuition: In-state $28,720; Out-of-state $28,720

Two-year College(s)

Stark State College (Public)
Fall 2016 Enrollment: 12,364 . . . . (330) 494-6170
2016-17 Tuition: In-state $3,686; Out-of-state $6,794

Housing: Homeownership rate: 70.1%; Median home value: $136,600; Median year structure built: 1967; Homeowner vacancy rate: 0.6%; Median selected monthly owner costs: $1,177 with a mortgage, $454 without a mortgage; Median gross rent: $769 per month; Rental vacancy rate: 8.7%
Health Insurance: 95.1% have insurance; 83.2% have private insurance; 29.1% have public insurance; 4.9% do not have insurance; 1.6% of children under 18 do not have insurance
Safety: Violent crime rate: 5.2 per 10,000 population; Property crime rate: 155.4 per 10,000 population
Transportation: Commute: 89.3% car, 2.2% public transportation, 2.7% walk, 5.5% work from home; Mean travel time to work: 19.6 minutes
Additional Information Contacts
City of North Canton . . . . (330) 499-5081
http://www.northcantonohio.com

NORTH LAWRENCE (CDP). Covers a land area of 0.339 square miles and a water area of 0.011 square miles. Located at 40.84° N. Lat; 81.64° W. Long. Elevation is 1,033 feet.
Population: 302; Growth (since 2000): n/a; Density: 891.9 persons per square mile; Race: 92.7% White, 0.0% Black/African American, 7.3% Asian, 0.0% American Indian/Alaska Native, 0.0% Native Hawaiian/Other Pacific Islander, 0.0% Two or more races, 0.0% Hispanic of any race; Average household size: 2.22; Median age: 44.5; Age under 18: 19.5%; Age 65 and over: 7.6%; Males per 100 females: 106.2; Marriage status: 12.6% never married, 56.5% now married, 7.9% separated, 15.4% widowed, 15.4% divorced; Foreign born: 0.0%; Speak English only: 100.0%; With disability: 17.5%; Veterans: 11.5%; Ancestry: 40.7% German, 25.2% Irish, 17.2% Hungarian, 8.9% American, 8.6% Polish
Employment: 19.6% management, business, and financial, 0.0% computer, engineering, and science, 0.0% education, legal, community service, arts, and media, 15.0% healthcare practitioners, 11.1% service, 17.6% sales and office, 18.3% natural resources, construction, and maintenance, 18.3% production, transportation, and material moving
Income: Per capita: $26,880; Median household: $46,000; Average household: $58,629; Households with income of $100,000 or more: n/a; Poverty rate: 5.3%
Educational Attainment: High school diploma or higher: 79.7%; Bachelor's degree or higher: n/a; Graduate/professional degree or higher: n/a
Housing: Homeownership rate: 85.3%; Median home value: $94,700; Median year structure built: Before 1940; Homeowner vacancy rate: 0.0%; Median selected monthly owner costs: $1,092 with a mortgage, $353

without a mortgage; Median gross rent: n/a per month; Rental vacancy rate: 0.0%
Health Insurance: 89.4% have insurance; 76.2% have private insurance; 20.9% have public insurance; 10.6% do not have insurance; 0.0% of children under 18 do not have insurance
Transportation: Commute: 100.0% car, 0.0% public transportation, 0.0% walk, 0.0% work from home; Mean travel time to work: 25.4 minutes

PARIS (unincorporated postal area)

ZCTA: 44669

Covers a land area of 17.383 square miles and a water area of 0.032 square miles. Located at 40.79° N. Lat; 81.16° W. Long. Elevation is 1,263 feet.
Population: 1,272; Growth (since 2000): -18.7%; Density: 73.2 persons per square mile; Race: 100.0% White, 0.0% Black/African American, 0.0% Asian, 0.0% American Indian/Alaska Native, 0.0% Native Hawaiian/Other Pacific Islander, 0.0% Two or more races, 0.0% Hispanic of any race; Average household size: 2.40; Median age: 43.3; Age under 18: 20.4%; Age 65 and over: 25.9%; Males per 100 females: 103.5; Marriage status: 26.5% never married, 48.6% now married, 0.0% separated, 9.9% widowed, 15.0% divorced; Foreign born: 0.0%; Speak English only: 99.5%; With disability: 10.9%; Veterans: 10.9%; Ancestry: 37.8% German, 6.6% Irish, 5.3% English, 4.7% American, 3.1% Swedish
Employment: 10.9% management, business, and financial, 4.0% computer, engineering, and science, 3.1% education, legal, community service, arts, and media, 4.2% healthcare practitioners, 18.8% service, 36.7% sales and office, 12.4% natural resources, construction, and maintenance, 9.9% production, transportation, and material moving
Income: Per capita: $33,953; Median household: $60,556; Average household: $80,157; Households with income of $100,000 or more: 23.8%; Poverty rate: 18.6%
Educational Attainment: High school diploma or higher: 92.4%; Bachelor's degree or higher: 29.5%; Graduate/professional degree or higher: 7.1%
Housing: Homeownership rate: 91.9%; Median home value: $139,600; Median year structure built: 1949; Homeowner vacancy rate: 0.0%; Median selected monthly owner costs: $1,198 with a mortgage, $443 without a mortgage; Median gross rent: $753 per month; Rental vacancy rate: 0.0%
Health Insurance: 94.9% have insurance; 77.1% have private insurance; 47.6% have public insurance; 5.1% do not have insurance; 0.0% of children under 18 do not have insurance
Transportation: Commute: 98.5% car, 0.0% public transportation, 0.0% walk, 1.5% work from home; Mean travel time to work: 25.9 minutes

PERRY HEIGHTS (CDP). Covers a land area of 2.863 square miles and a water area of 0.041 square miles. Located at 40.80° N. Lat; 81.47° W. Long. Elevation is 1,099 feet.
Population: 8,732; Growth (since 2000): -1.9%; Density: 3,050.4 persons per square mile; Race: 96.1% White, 2.2% Black/African American, 0.3% Asian, 0.0% American Indian/Alaska Native, 0.0% Native Hawaiian/Other Pacific Islander, 1.1% Two or more races, 0.2% Hispanic of any race; Average household size: 2.36; Median age: 43.5; Age under 18: 21.1%; Age 65 and over: 18.1%; Males per 100 females: 92.0; Marriage status: 26.5% never married, 46.8% now married, 1.6% separated, 8.9% widowed, 17.8% divorced; Foreign born: 0.6%; Speak English only: 98.4%; With disability: 10.6%; Veterans: 11.5%; Ancestry: 35.0% German, 15.8% Irish, 12.5% Italian, 6.4% American, 5.8% Polish
Employment: 11.3% management, business, and financial, 4.1% computer, engineering, and science, 5.2% education, legal, community service, arts, and media, 6.4% healthcare practitioners, 23.6% service, 27.4% sales and office, 7.5% natural resources, construction, and maintenance, 14.6% production, transportation, and material moving
Income: Per capita: $23,417; Median household: $41,956; Average household: $54,606; Households with income of $100,000 or more: 12.4%; Poverty rate: 18.5%
Educational Attainment: High school diploma or higher: 89.2%; Bachelor's degree or higher: 10.7%; Graduate/professional degree or higher: 3.3%
Housing: Homeownership rate: 67.8%; Median home value: $98,300; Median year structure built: 1962; Homeowner vacancy rate: 0.0%; Median selected monthly owner costs: $963 with a mortgage, $384 without a mortgage; Median gross rent: $685 per month; Rental vacancy rate: 4.3%
Health Insurance: 89.2% have insurance; 64.1% have private insurance; 40.7% have public insurance; 10.8% do not have insurance; 4.7% of children under 18 do not have insurance
Transportation: Commute: 93.7% car, 0.8% public transportation, 2.5% walk, 2.5% work from home; Mean travel time to work: 20.5 minutes

RICHVILLE (CDP). Covers a land area of 3.128 square miles and a water area of 0.011 square miles. Located at 40.75° N. Lat; 81.47° W. Long. Elevation is 1,060 feet.
Population: 3,304; Growth (since 2000): n/a; Density: 1,056.1 persons per square mile; Race: 95.7% White, 1.2% Black/African American, 1.0% Asian, 0.0% American Indian/Alaska Native, 0.0% Native Hawaiian/Other Pacific Islander, 1.8% Two or more races, 0.3% Hispanic of any race; Average household size: 2.59; Median age: 46.3; Age under 18: 19.7%; Age 65 and over: 19.5%; Males per 100 females: 100.8; Marriage status: 24.0% never married, 60.3% now married, 0.3% separated, 5.9% widowed, 9.9% divorced; Foreign born: 1.6%; Speak English only: 95.6%; With disability: 11.6%; Veterans: 10.9%; Ancestry: 40.2% German, 17.3% Irish, 12.7% Italian, 7.6% American, 7.5% English
Employment: 11.3% management, business, and financial, 4.1% computer, engineering, and science, 3.1% education, legal, community service, arts, and media, 6.8% healthcare practitioners, 15.7% service, 25.1% sales and office, 8.2% natural resources, construction, and maintenance, 25.8% production, transportation, and material moving
Income: Per capita: $23,513; Median household: $56,250; Average household: $60,300; Households with income of $100,000 or more: 13.8%; Poverty rate: 8.2%
Educational Attainment: High school diploma or higher: 89.4%; Bachelor's degree or higher: 11.9%; Graduate/professional degree or higher: 2.6%
Housing: Homeownership rate: 81.4%; Median home value: $123,300; Median year structure built: 1966; Homeowner vacancy rate: 0.0%; Median selected monthly owner costs: $1,175 with a mortgage, $387 without a mortgage; Median gross rent: $715 per month; Rental vacancy rate: 0.0%
Health Insurance: 91.6% have insurance; 75.2% have private insurance; 35.7% have public insurance; 8.4% do not have insurance; 6.9% of children under 18 do not have insurance
Transportation: Commute: 98.0% car, 0.8% public transportation, 0.0% walk, 0.6% work from home; Mean travel time to work: 19.8 minutes

ROBERTSVILLE (CDP). Covers a land area of 0.309 square miles and a water area of 0 square miles. Located at 40.76° N. Lat; 81.19° W. Long. Elevation is 1,086 feet.
Population: 467; Growth (since 2000): n/a; Density: 1,509.0 persons per square mile; Race: 100.0% White, 0.0% Black/African American, 0.0% Asian, 0.0% American Indian/Alaska Native, 0.0% Native Hawaiian/Other Pacific Islander, 0.0% Two or more races, 0.0% Hispanic of any race; Average household size: 3.43; Median age: 25.6; Age under 18: 40.7%; Age 65 and over: 2.6%; Males per 100 females: 93.6; Marriage status: 23.8% never married, 73.3% now married, 0.0% separated, 2.9% widowed, 0.0% divorced; Foreign born: 0.0%; Speak English only: 100.0%; With disability: 2.4%; Veterans: 12.3%; Ancestry: 54.2% German, 29.3% French, 18.8% English, 6.6% Italian, 6.0% Irish
Employment: 14.7% management, business, and financial, 0.0% computer, engineering, and science, 18.9% education, legal, community service, arts, and media, 8.4% healthcare practitioners, 0.0% service, 32.1% sales and office, 11.6% natural resources, construction, and maintenance, 14.2% production, transportation, and material moving
Income: Per capita: $16,072; Median household: $57,321; Average household: $54,818; Households with income of $100,000 or more: 11.8%; Poverty rate: 18.4%
Educational Attainment: High school diploma or higher: 100.0%; Bachelor's degree or higher: 14.4%; Graduate/professional degree or higher: 14.4%
Housing: Homeownership rate: 83.8%; Median home value: $86,800; Median year structure built: Before 1940; Homeowner vacancy rate: 0.0%; Median selected monthly owner costs: $869 with a mortgage, n/a without a mortgage; Median gross rent: n/a per month; Rental vacancy rate: 0.0%
Health Insurance: 100.0% have insurance; 55.0% have private insurance; 47.5% have public insurance; 0.0% do not have insurance; 0.0% of children under 18 do not have insurance
Transportation: Commute: 95.8% car, 0.0% public transportation, 4.2% walk, 0.0% work from home; Mean travel time to work: 22.0 minutes

UNIONTOWN (CDP). Covers a land area of 2.492 square miles and a water area of 0.025 square miles. Located at 40.97° N. Lat; 81.40° W. Long. Elevation is 1,119 feet.

Population: 3,624; Growth (since 2000): 29.3%; Density: 1,454.1 persons per square mile; Race: 98.1% White, 0.4% Black/African American, 0.3% Asian, 0.0% American Indian/Alaska Native, 0.0% Native Hawaiian/Other Pacific Islander, 1.2% Two or more races, 0.0% Hispanic of any race; Average household size: 2.74; Median age: 40.9; Age under 18: 28.9%; Age 65 and over: 15.3%; Males per 100 females: 96.0; Marriage status: 17.7% never married, 60.6% now married, 0.3% separated, 7.2% widowed, 14.6% divorced; Foreign born: 1.7%; Speak English only: 97.6%; With disability: 9.9%; Veterans: 11.0%; Ancestry: 32.6% German, 22.2% Irish, 12.7% English, 8.3% American, 8.0% Italian

Employment: 19.1% management, business, and financial, 3.4% computer, engineering, and science, 11.2% education, legal, community service, arts, and media, 8.1% healthcare practitioners, 12.0% service, 21.9% sales and office, 7.4% natural resources, construction, and maintenance, 17.0% production, transportation, and material moving

Income: Per capita: $29,341; Median household: $62,000; Average household: $79,603; Households with income of $100,000 or more: 26.9%; Poverty rate: 6.1%

Educational Attainment: High school diploma or higher: 92.3%; Bachelor's degree or higher: 28.4%; Graduate/professional degree or higher: 11.7%

School District(s)

Green Local (PK-12)
2015-16 Enrollment: 4,089 . . . . (330) 896-7500
Lake Local (KG-12)
2015-16 Enrollment: 3,475 . . . . (330) 877-9383
Portage Lakes (10-12)
2015-16 Enrollment: n/a . . . . (330) 896-8200

Vocational/Technical School(s)

Portage Lakes Career Center (Public)
Fall 2016 Enrollment: 110 . . . . (330) 896-8200
2016-17 Tuition: $12,995

Housing: Homeownership rate: 83.3%; Median home value: $148,400; Median year structure built: 1972; Homeowner vacancy rate: 0.0%; Median selected monthly owner costs: $1,387 with a mortgage, $468 without a mortgage; Median gross rent: $762 per month; Rental vacancy rate: 9.8%

Health Insurance: 94.5% have insurance; 82.5% have private insurance; 26.4% have public insurance; 5.5% do not have insurance; 0.7% of children under 18 do not have insurance

Safety: Violent crime rate: 6.0 per 10,000 population; Property crime rate: 243.2 per 10,000 population

Transportation: Commute: 94.9% car, 0.0% public transportation, 1.8% walk, 3.3% work from home; Mean travel time to work: 26.6 minutes

WAYNESBURG (village). Covers a land area of 0.517 square miles and a water area of 0 square miles. Located at 40.67° N. Lat; 81.26° W. Long. Elevation is 997 feet.

Population: 892; Growth (since 2000): -11.1%; Density: 1,726.8 persons per square mile; Race: 95.5% White, 0.6% Black/African American, 0.0% Asian, 0.8% American Indian/Alaska Native, 0.0% Native Hawaiian/Other Pacific Islander, 3.1% Two or more races, 1.1% Hispanic of any race; Average household size: 2.53; Median age: 39.3; Age under 18: 21.3%; Age 65 and over: 16.3%; Males per 100 females: 100.7; Marriage status: 32.8% never married, 42.8% now married, 1.5% separated, 9.0% widowed, 15.4% divorced; Foreign born: 1.0%; Speak English only: 97.4%; With disability: 18.7%; Veterans: 13.5%; Ancestry: 41.3% German, 20.2% Italian, 17.3% Irish, 7.1% English, 3.9% Dutch

Employment: 10.8% management, business, and financial, 3.0% computer, engineering, and science, 2.3% education, legal, community service, arts, and media, 7.3% healthcare practitioners, 20.4% service, 18.8% sales and office, 16.3% natural resources, construction, and maintenance, 21.1% production, transportation, and material moving

Income: Per capita: $22,075; Median household: $45,417; Average household: $53,077; Households with income of $100,000 or more: 10.1%; Poverty rate: 16.3%

Educational Attainment: High school diploma or higher: 95.6%; Bachelor's degree or higher: 8.9%; Graduate/professional degree or higher: 3.0%

Housing: Homeownership rate: 77.3%; Median home value: $98,200; Median year structure built: Before 1940; Homeowner vacancy rate: 0.0%; Median selected monthly owner costs: $970 with a mortgage, $403 without a mortgage; Median gross rent: $625 per month; Rental vacancy rate: 0.0%

Health Insurance: 91.4% have insurance; 65.4% have private insurance; 42.0% have public insurance; 8.6% do not have insurance; 2.6% of children under 18 do not have insurance

Transportation: Commute: 95.7% car, 0.0% public transportation, 2.0% walk, 2.3% work from home; Mean travel time to work: 31.0 minutes

WILMOT (village). Covers a land area of 0.139 square miles and a water area of 0 square miles. Located at 40.66° N. Lat; 81.63° W. Long. Elevation is 1,027 feet.

History: Wilmot was platted in 1836, and developed as a trading center in the midst of the Amish country.

Population: 352; Growth (since 2000): 5.1%; Density: 2,524.7 persons per square mile; Race: 99.4% White, 0.0% Black/African American, 0.6% Asian, 0.0% American Indian/Alaska Native, 0.0% Native Hawaiian/Other Pacific Islander, 0.0% Two or more races, 3.1% Hispanic of any race; Average household size: 2.77; Median age: 31.6; Age under 18: 23.6%; Age 65 and over: 13.1%; Males per 100 females: 111.1; Marriage status: 22.5% never married, 57.1% now married, 2.9% separated, 4.6% widowed, 15.7% divorced; Foreign born: 0.6%; Speak English only: 86.9%; With disability: 14.5%; Veterans: 7.8%; Ancestry: 45.2% German, 15.1% Italian, 14.8% French, 12.5% Swiss, 6.0% Irish

Employment: 3.1% management, business, and financial, 0.0% computer, engineering, and science, 4.1% education, legal, community service, arts, and media, 0.5% healthcare practitioners, 21.6% service, 20.6% sales and office, 11.3% natural resources, construction, and maintenance, 38.7% production, transportation, and material moving

Income: Per capita: $20,409; Median household: $40,536; Average household: $53,835; Households with income of $100,000 or more: 11.8%; Poverty rate: 10.8%

Educational Attainment: High school diploma or higher: 87.9%; Bachelor's degree or higher: 6.3%; Graduate/professional degree or higher: n/a

Housing: Homeownership rate: 65.4%; Median home value: $74,100; Median year structure built: Before 1940; Homeowner vacancy rate: 0.0%; Median selected monthly owner costs: $800 with a mortgage, $346 without a mortgage; Median gross rent: $664 per month; Rental vacancy rate: 0.0%

Health Insurance: 91.2% have insurance; 51.7% have private insurance; 43.8% have public insurance; 8.8% do not have insurance; 0.0% of children under 18 do not have insurance

Transportation: Commute: 98.4% car, 0.0% public transportation, 1.1% walk, 0.0% work from home; Mean travel time to work: 19.8 minutes

Summit County

Located in northeastern Ohio; drained by the Cuyahoga and Tuscarawas Rivers; includes Portage Lakes. Covers a land area of 412.748 square miles, a water area of 7.307 square miles, and is located in the Eastern Time Zone at 41.12° N. Lat., 81.53° W. Long. The county was founded in 1840. County seat is Akron.

Summit County is part of the Akron, OH Metropolitan Statistical Area. The entire metro area includes: Portage County, OH; Summit County, OH

Weather Station: Akron Akron-Canton Reg Arpt Elevation: 1,208 feet

	Jan	Feb	Mar	Apr	May	Jun	Jul	Aug	Sep	Oct	Nov	Dec
High	34	37	47	60	70	78	82	81	73	61	50	38
Low	19	21	28	39	49	58	62	61	53	42	34	24
Precip	2.6	2.3	3.0	3.6	4.3	3.8	4.1	3.7	3.4	2.8	3.2	2.8
Snow	12.2	9.6	8.4	2.8	0.1	tr	0.0	tr	tr	0.5	2.9	9.9

High and Low temperatures in degrees Fahrenheit; Precipitation and Snow in inches

Population: 541,372; Growth (since 2000): -0.3%; Density: 1,311.6 persons per square mile; Race: 79.6% White, 14.4% Black/African American, 2.7% Asian, 0.2% American Indian/Alaska Native, 0.0% Native Hawaiian/Other Pacific Islander, 2.7% two or more races, 1.9% Hispanic of any race; Average household size: 2.40; Median age: 40.8; Age under 18: 21.7%; Age 65 and over: 16.2%; Males per 100 females: 93.7; Marriage status: 32.8% never married, 48.8% now married, 1.5% separated, 6.5% widowed, 11.9% divorced; Foreign born: 4.8%; Speak English only: 94.2%; With disability: 12.6%; Veterans: 8.3%; Ancestry: 21.2% German, 13.3% Irish, 9.6% American, 9.0% Italian, 8.3% English

Religion: Six largest groups: 21.6% Catholicism, 8.0% Non-denominational Protestant, 3.9% Methodist/Pietist, 3.1% Baptist, 2.4% Presbyterian-Reformed, 1.9% Lutheran
Economy: Unemployment rate: 4.6%; Leading industries: 12.6 % retail trade; 11.4 % health care and social assistance; 11.0 % other services (except public administration); Farms: 304 totaling 16,545 acres; Company size: 11 employs 1,000 or more persons, 25 employ 500 to 999 persons, 385 employ 100 to 499 persons, 13,054 employ less than 100 persons; Business ownership: 16,202 women-owned, 4,822 Black-owned, 481 Hispanic-owned, 1,221 Asian-owned, 230 American Indian/Alaska Native-owned
Employment: 14.9% management, business, and financial, 5.4% computer, engineering, and science, 10.6% education, legal, community service, arts, and media, 6.6% healthcare practitioners, 17.1% service, 26.0% sales and office, 6.4% natural resources, construction, and maintenance, 12.9% production, transportation, and material moving
Income: Per capita: $29,643; Median household: $51,562; Average household: $70,475; Households with income of $100,000 or more: 21.0%; Poverty rate: 14.3%
Educational Attainment: High school diploma or higher: 91.0%; Bachelor's degree or higher: 30.7%; Graduate/professional degree or higher: 11.0%
Housing: Homeownership rate: 65.6%; Median home value: $134,300; Median year structure built: 1964; Homeowner vacancy rate: 1.9%; Median selected monthly owner costs: $1,234 with a mortgage, $464 without a mortgage; Median gross rent: $760 per month; Rental vacancy rate: 6.7%
Vital Statistics: Birth rate: 113.5 per 10,000 population; Death rate: 107.1 per 10,000 population; Age-adjusted cancer mortality rate: 174.3 deaths per 100,000 population
Health Insurance: 92.1% have insurance; 70.8% have private insurance; 33.5% have public insurance; 7.9% do not have insurance; 4.2% of children under 18 do not have insurance
Health Care: Physicians: 39.9 per 10,000 population; Dentists: 6.1 per 10,000 population; Hospital beds: 34.5 per 10,000 population; Hospital admissions: 1,445.3 per 10,000 population
Air Quality Index (AQI): Percent of Days: 71.0% good, 28.7% moderate, 0.3% unhealthy for sensitive individuals, 0.0% unhealthy, 0.0% very unhealthy; Annual median: 43; Annual maximum: 112
Transportation: Commute: 93.1% car, 1.8% public transportation, 1.5% walk, 3.0% work from home; Mean travel time to work: 22.8 minutes
2016 Presidential Election: 43.0% Trump, 51.6% Clinton, 2.9% Johnson, 0.9% Stein
National and State Parks: Cuyahoga Valley National Park; Portage Lakes State Park; Portage Lakes Wetland State Nature Preserve
Additional Information Contacts
Summit Government . . . . (330) 643-2510
http://www.co.summit.oh.us

Summit County Communities

AKRON (city). County seat. Covers a land area of 62.033 square miles and a water area of 0.340 square miles. Located at 41.08° N. Lat; 81.52° W. Long. Elevation is 961 feet.
History: The first settler in the Akron area was Captain Joseph Hart, who established Middlebury, now East Akron, in 1807. The city of Akron was laid out in 1825 by General Simon Perkins, commissioner of the Ohio Canal Fund, who saw a great future for a town on the summit of the course of the Ohio & Erie Canal. When the canal opened to traffic in 1827, the town grew rapidly. In 1840 trade was improved further with the opening of the Ohio & Pennsylvania Canal. In 1859, former resident John Brown was executed here for his raid at Harper's Ferry. Dr. Benjamin Franklin Goodrich came to Akron in 1870 and founded a plant for manufacturing fire hose and other articles from rubber. Around 1900 Akron was the national center for the manufacture of farm machinery, and the American Cereal Company (Quaker Oats) emerged as a leading cereal producer. But it was the rubber industry that by 1915 made Akron a boom town.
Population: 198,508; Growth (since 2000): -8.6%; Density: 3,200.1 persons per square mile; Race: 61.1% White, 30.5% Black/African American, 3.6% Asian, 0.2% American Indian/Alaska Native, 0.0% Native Hawaiian/Other Pacific Islander, 4.1% Two or more races, 2.3% Hispanic of any race; Average household size: 2.29; Median age: 36.7; Age under 18: 21.6%; Age 65 and over: 13.6%; Males per 100 females: 93.6; Marriage status: 42.8% never married, 36.6% now married, 2.4% separated, 6.3% widowed, 14.3% divorced; Foreign born: 5.5%; Speak English only: 93.3%; With disability: 15.1%; Veterans: 8.4%; Ancestry: 16.1% German, 11.1% Irish, 8.4% American, 6.1% Italian, 5.7% English
Employment: 10.2% management, business, and financial, 3.6% computer, engineering, and science, 9.8% education, legal, community service, arts, and media, 5.1% healthcare practitioners, 21.7% service, 26.8% sales and office, 6.2% natural resources, construction, and maintenance, 16.6% production, transportation, and material moving
Income: Per capita: $21,378; Median household: $35,240; Average household: $48,368; Households with income of $100,000 or more: 9.5%; Poverty rate: 25.4%
Educational Attainment: High school diploma or higher: 86.4%; Bachelor's degree or higher: 20.2%; Graduate/professional degree or higher: 6.8%

School District(s)

Akron City (PK-12)
2015-16 Enrollment: 21,261 . . . . (330) 761-1661
Akron Digital Academy (06-12)
2015-16 Enrollment: 347. . . . . (330) 237-2232
Akros Middle School (06-08)
2015-16 Enrollment: 140. . . . . (330) 374-6704
Colonial Prep Academy (KG-08)
2015-16 Enrollment: 198. . . . . (330) 752-2792
Coventry Local (KG-12)
2015-16 Enrollment: 2,093 . . . . (330) 644-8489
Edge Academy the (KG-05)
2015-16 Enrollment: 246. . . . . (330) 535-4581
Greater Summit County Early Learning Center (KG-04)
2015-16 Enrollment: 126. . . . . (330) 945-5600
Imagine Akron Academy (KG-KG)
2015-16 Enrollment: 67. . . . . (330) 379-1034
Life Skills Center of North Akron (09-12)
2015-16 Enrollment: 151. . . . . (330) 633-5990
Manchester Local (KG-12)
2015-16 Enrollment: 1,326 . . . . (330) 882-6926
Middlebury Academy (KG-08)
2015-16 Enrollment: 282. . . . . (330) 752-2766
Revere Local (PK-12)
2015-16 Enrollment: 2,662 . . . . (330) 666-4155
Springfield Local (PK-12)
2015-16 Enrollment: 2,287 . . . . (330) 798-1111
Summit Academy Akron Elementary School (KG-06)
2015-16 Enrollment: 146. . . . . (330) 253-7441
Summit Academy Akron Middle School (07-08)
2015-16 Enrollment: 42. . . . . (330) 252-1510
Summit Academy Secondary - Akron (09-12)
2015-16 Enrollment: 65. . . . . (330) 434-2343
The Capella Institute (09-12)
2015-16 Enrollment: 77. . . . . (216) 708-9844
Towpath Trail High School (09-12)
2015-16 Enrollment: 285. . . . . (234) 542-0102

Four-year College(s)

Brown Mackie College-Akron (Private, For-profit)
Fall 2016 Enrollment: 152 . . . . (330) 869-3600
2016-17 Tuition: In-state $12,492; Out-of-state $12,492
Bryant & Stratton College-Akron (Private, For-profit)
Fall 2016 Enrollment: 115 . . . . (330) 598-2500
2016-17 Tuition: In-state $17,785; Out-of-state $17,785
Herzing University-Akron (Private, For-profit)
Fall 2016 Enrollment: 478 . . . . (330) 724-1600
2016-17 Tuition: In-state $13,390; Out-of-state $13,390
ITT Technical Institute-Akron (Private, For-profit)
Fall 2016 Enrollment: n/a . . . . (330) 865-8600
University of Akron Main Campus (Public)
Fall 2016 Enrollment: 21,100 . . . . (330) 972-7111
2016-17 Tuition: In-state $10,270; Out-of-state $18,801

Two-year College(s)

National Institute of Massotherapy (Private, For-profit)
Fall 2016 Enrollment: 39 . . . . (330) 867-1996

Vocational/Technical School(s)

Akron School of Practical Nursing (Public)
Fall 2016 Enrollment: 61 . . . . (330) 873-3355
2016-17 Tuition: $11,000
Gerbers Akron Beauty School (Private, For-profit)
Fall 2016 Enrollment: 64 . . . . (330) 867-6200
2016-17 Tuition: $9,520

Housing: Homeownership rate: 51.0%; Median home value: $80,000; Median year structure built: 1952; Homeowner vacancy rate: 2.8%; Median selected monthly owner costs: $970 with a mortgage, $393 without a mortgage; Median gross rent: $693 per month; Rental vacancy rate: 7.8%
Health Insurance: 87.9% have insurance; 55.3% have private insurance; 43.4% have public insurance; 12.1% do not have insurance; 6.1% of children under 18 do not have insurance
Hospitals: Akron General Medical Center (532 beds); Crystal Clinic Orthopaedic Center; Summa Health Systems Hospitals (658 beds)
Safety: Violent crime rate: 61.6 per 10,000 population; Property crime rate: 438.3 per 10,000 population
Newspapers: Akron Beacon Journal (daily circulation 119,000); Akron Suburbanite (weekly circulation 33,000); Jackson Suburbanite (weekly circulation 12,500); South Side News Leader (weekly circulation 23,000); West Side Leader (weekly circulation 43,000)
Transportation: Commute: 90.8% car, 4.2% public transportation, 2.4% walk, 2.0% work from home; Mean travel time to work: 21.4 minutes
Airports: Akron Fulton International (general aviation); Akron-Canton Regional (primary service/small hub)
Additional Information Contacts
City of Akron . . . . (330) 375-2345
http://www.ci.akron.oh.us

BARBERTON (city). Covers a land area of 9.038 square miles and a water area of 0.219 square miles. Located at 41.01° N. Lat; 81.60° W. Long. Elevation is 971 feet.
History: Barberton was laid out in 1891 by Ohio Columbus Barber, the owner of the Diamond Match Company. Barber dominated the town until his death in 1920, spending millions of dollars on the Anna Dean Experimental Farm, known as Barber's Folly, where cows and horses lived in luxury.
Population: 26,266; Growth (since 2000): -5.9%; Density: 2,906.1 persons per square mile; Race: 89.0% White, 7.1% Black/African American, 0.6% Asian, 0.0% American Indian/Alaska Native, 0.0% Native Hawaiian/Other Pacific Islander, 3.1% Two or more races, 1.9% Hispanic of any race; Average household size: 2.44; Median age: 39.8; Age under 18: 22.7%; Age 65 and over: 18.2%; Males per 100 females: 92.0; Marriage status: 34.7% never married, 43.5% now married, 2.2% separated, 8.9% widowed, 12.9% divorced; Foreign born: 3.1%; Speak English only: 96.2%; With disability: 17.2%; Veterans: 8.5%; Ancestry: 18.5% German, 17.2% American, 12.0% Irish, 7.6% English, 4.6% Italian
Employment: 9.0% management, business, and financial, 3.9% computer, engineering, and science, 6.1% education, legal, community service, arts, and media, 5.9% healthcare practitioners, 21.8% service, 25.9% sales and office, 8.8% natural resources, construction, and maintenance, 18.6% production, transportation, and material moving
Income: Per capita: $21,163; Median household: $39,456; Average household: $50,545; Households with income of $100,000 or more: 8.7%; Poverty rate: 18.0%
Educational Attainment: High school diploma or higher: 84.2%; Bachelor's degree or higher: 12.7%; Graduate/professional degree or higher: 3.1%

School District(s)

Barberton City (PK-12)
2015-16 Enrollment: 3,845 . . . . (330) 753-1025
Housing: Homeownership rate: 62.8%; Median home value: $85,800; Median year structure built: 1954; Homeowner vacancy rate: 2.2%; Median selected monthly owner costs: $895 with a mortgage, $356 without a mortgage; Median gross rent: $676 per month; Rental vacancy rate: 7.9%
Health Insurance: 87.4% have insurance; 57.7% have private insurance; 41.9% have public insurance; 12.6% do not have insurance; 10.5% of children under 18 do not have insurance
Hospitals: Summa Health System Barberton Hospital (311 beds)
Safety: Violent crime rate: 28.7 per 10,000 population; Property crime rate: 305.3 per 10,000 population
Newspapers: Barberton Herald (weekly circulation 7,900)
Transportation: Commute: 93.3% car, 1.7% public transportation, 2.4% walk, 1.5% work from home; Mean travel time to work: 21.9 minutes
Additional Information Contacts
City of Barberton . . . . (330) 848-6719
http://www.cityofbarberton.com

BOSTON HEIGHTS (village). Covers a land area of 6.895 square miles and a water area of <.001 square miles. Located at 41.25° N. Lat; 81.51° W. Long. Elevation is 1,070 feet.
Population: 1,208; Growth (since 2000): 1.9%; Density: 175.2 persons per square mile; Race: 94.5% White, 0.7% Black/African American, 3.5% Asian, 0.0% American Indian/Alaska Native, 0.0% Native Hawaiian/Other Pacific Islander, 1.0% Two or more races, 0.9% Hispanic of any race; Average household size: 2.79; Median age: 47.7; Age under 18: 22.1%; Age 65 and over: 17.0%; Males per 100 females: 95.5; Marriage status: 23.1% never married, 66.6% now married, 0.3% separated, 3.8% widowed, 6.5% divorced; Foreign born: 5.1%; Speak English only: 95.3%; With disability: 8.9%; Veterans: 9.0%; Ancestry: 22.4% German, 19.5% Irish, 13.1% Italian, 10.3% English, 9.6% Polish
Employment: 29.4% management, business, and financial, 5.9% computer, engineering, and science, 6.7% education, legal, community service, arts, and media, 6.9% healthcare practitioners, 15.5% service, 23.5% sales and office, 6.1% natural resources, construction, and maintenance, 5.9% production, transportation, and material moving
Income: Per capita: $52,351; Median household: $103,603; Average household: $147,219; Households with income of $100,000 or more: 53.6%; Poverty rate: 3.2%
Educational Attainment: High school diploma or higher: 96.2%; Bachelor's degree or higher: 48.2%; Graduate/professional degree or higher: 21.0%
Housing: Homeownership rate: 93.3%; Median home value: $347,800; Median year structure built: 1991; Homeowner vacancy rate: 2.2%; Median selected monthly owner costs: $2,134 with a mortgage, $683 without a mortgage; Median gross rent: $900 per month; Rental vacancy rate: 0.0%
Health Insurance: 98.0% have insurance; 90.3% have private insurance; 21.4% have public insurance; 2.0% do not have insurance; 0.0% of children under 18 do not have insurance
Transportation: Commute: 91.9% car, 0.3% public transportation, 0.8% walk, 6.4% work from home; Mean travel time to work: 25.8 minutes

CLINTON (village). Covers a land area of 3.549 square miles and a water area of 0.090 square miles. Located at 40.93° N. Lat; 81.63° W. Long. Elevation is 945 feet.
Population: 1,229; Growth (since 2000): -8.1%; Density: 346.3 persons per square mile; Race: 98.1% White, 0.7% Black/African American, 0.3% Asian, 0.0% American Indian/Alaska Native, 0.0% Native Hawaiian/Other Pacific Islander, 0.9% Two or more races, 1.0% Hispanic of any race; Average household size: 2.51; Median age: 42.6; Age under 18: 22.0%; Age 65 and over: 13.6%; Males per 100 females: 106.5; Marriage status: 29.1% never married, 50.7% now married, 0.6% separated, 4.9% widowed, 15.3% divorced; Foreign born: 1.3%; Speak English only: 98.1%; With disability: 11.8%; Veterans: 7.3%; Ancestry: 26.7% German, 24.1% American, 8.0% Irish, 7.6% English, 4.1% Hungarian
Employment: 7.5% management, business, and financial, 4.4% computer, engineering, and science, 4.4% education, legal, community service, arts, and media, 6.1% healthcare practitioners, 19.9% service, 25.5% sales and office, 19.4% natural resources, construction, and maintenance, 12.8% production, transportation, and material moving
Income: Per capita: $25,409; Median household: $58,438; Average household: $62,316; Households with income of $100,000 or more: 17.8%; Poverty rate: 15.6%
Educational Attainment: High school diploma or higher: 84.0%; Bachelor's degree or higher: 14.1%; Graduate/professional degree or higher: 5.4%

School District(s)

Norton City (PK-12)
2015-16 Enrollment: 2,524 . . . . (330) 825-0863
Housing: Homeownership rate: 81.4%; Median home value: $120,900; Median year structure built: 1954; Homeowner vacancy rate: 6.8%; Median selected monthly owner costs: $1,246 with a mortgage, $406 without a mortgage; Median gross rent: $732 per month; Rental vacancy rate: 9.9%
Health Insurance: 89.7% have insurance; 67.4% have private insurance; 34.8% have public insurance; 10.3% do not have insurance; 9.3% of children under 18 do not have insurance
Transportation: Commute: 97.2% car, 0.0% public transportation, 1.2% walk, 1.5% work from home; Mean travel time to work: 23.5 minutes

CUYAHOGA FALLS (city). Covers a land area of 25.648 square miles and a water area of 0.099 square miles. Located at 41.18° N. Lat; 81.55° W. Long. Elevation is 1,027 feet.
History: The city greatly expanded its area by annexing Northampton township in the 1980s. Incorporated 1836.
Population: 49,353; Growth (since 2000): 0.0%; Density: 1,924.2 persons per square mile; Race: 91.9% White, 3.7% Black/African American, 1.9% Asian, 0.1% American Indian/Alaska Native, 0.1% Native Hawaiian/Other Pacific Islander, 1.6% Two or more races, 2.6% Hispanic of any race; Average household size: 2.27; Median age: 39.5; Age under 18: 20.7%; Age 65 and over: 16.0%; Males per 100 females: 89.7; Marriage status: 30.1% never married, 49.8% now married, 1.1% separated, 6.8% widowed, 13.3% divorced; Foreign born: 4.2%; Speak English only: 95.2%; With disability: 12.3%; Veterans: 8.8%; Ancestry: 24.6% German, 15.4% Irish, 12.7% American, 11.1% Italian, 10.2% English
Employment: 13.5% management, business, and financial, 6.8% computer, engineering, and science, 10.9% education, legal, community service, arts, and media, 6.7% healthcare practitioners, 15.5% service, 27.5% sales and office, 7.7% natural resources, construction, and maintenance, 11.4% production, transportation, and material moving
Income: Per capita: $27,531; Median household: $51,586; Average household: $61,871; Households with income of $100,000 or more: 15.5%; Poverty rate: 10.9%
Educational Attainment: High school diploma or higher: 93.8%; Bachelor's degree or higher: 32.4%; Graduate/professional degree or higher: 10.4%

School District(s)

Cuyahoga Falls City (KG-12)
2015-16 Enrollment: 4,938 . . . . (330) 926-3800
Schnee Learning Center (09-12)
2015-16 Enrollment: 118. . . . . (330) 922-1966
Woodridge Local (PK-12)
2015-16 Enrollment: 2,067 . . . . (330) 928-9074

Two-year College(s)

Fortis College-Cuyahoga Falls (Private, For-profit)
Fall 2016 Enrollment: 504 . . . . (330) 923-9959
2016-17 Tuition: In-state $14,994; Out-of-state $14,994
Housing: Homeownership rate: 61.8%; Median home value: $120,000; Median year structure built: 1959; Homeowner vacancy rate: 3.2%; Median selected monthly owner costs: $1,125 with a mortgage, $437 without a mortgage; Median gross rent: $798 per month; Rental vacancy rate: 7.3%
Health Insurance: 93.4% have insurance; 76.6% have private insurance; 29.8% have public insurance; 6.6% do not have insurance; 3.1% of children under 18 do not have insurance
Hospitals: Edwin Shaw Rehab Institute; Summa Western Reserve Hospital (257 beds)
Safety: Violent crime rate: 13.7 per 10,000 population; Property crime rate: 233.0 per 10,000 population
Transportation: Commute: 95.0% car, 0.6% public transportation, 1.5% walk, 2.6% work from home; Mean travel time to work: 22.3 minutes
Additional Information Contacts
City of Cuyahoga Falls . . . . (330) 971-8000
http://cfo.cityofcf.com/web

FAIRLAWN (city). Covers a land area of 4.476 square miles and a water area of 0.011 square miles. Located at 41.13° N. Lat; 81.62° W. Long. Elevation is 1,007 feet.
Population: 7,477; Growth (since 2000): 2.3%; Density: 1,670.5 persons per square mile; Race: 84.6% White, 8.9% Black/African American, 1.9% Asian, 0.0% American Indian/Alaska Native, 0.4% Native Hawaiian/Other Pacific Islander, 4.0% Two or more races, 1.4% Hispanic of any race; Average household size: 2.14; Median age: 46.7; Age under 18: 18.6%; Age 65 and over: 26.6%; Males per 100 females: 88.9; Marriage status: 29.3% never married, 50.8% now married, 1.5% separated, 9.4% widowed, 10.4% divorced; Foreign born: 4.5%; Speak English only: 92.7%; With disability: 10.0%; Veterans: 9.1%; Ancestry: 24.4% German, 16.9% Irish, 13.4% English, 10.9% American, 7.9% Italian
Employment: 18.4% management, business, and financial, 9.9% computer, engineering, and science, 16.8% education, legal, community service, arts, and media, 10.9% healthcare practitioners, 10.8% service, 18.8% sales and office, 4.0% natural resources, construction, and maintenance, 10.4% production, transportation, and material moving
Income: Per capita: $40,881; Median household: $65,521; Average household: $89,852; Households with income of $100,000 or more: 30.4%; Poverty rate: 6.0%
Educational Attainment: High school diploma or higher: 97.1%; Bachelor's degree or higher: 51.4%; Graduate/professional degree or higher: 18.1%

School District(s)

Copley-Fairlawn City (KG-12)
2015-16 Enrollment: 2,951 . . . . (330) 664-4800
Housing: Homeownership rate: 66.3%; Median home value: $174,700; Median year structure built: 1972; Homeowner vacancy rate: 2.7%; Median selected monthly owner costs: $1,400 with a mortgage, $592 without a mortgage; Median gross rent: $1,053 per month; Rental vacancy rate: 3.4%
Health Insurance: 95.3% have insurance; 81.7% have private insurance; 31.1% have public insurance; 4.7% do not have insurance; 0.0% of children under 18 do not have insurance
Transportation: Commute: 92.6% car, 1.2% public transportation, 1.1% walk, 4.7% work from home; Mean travel time to work: 24.8 minutes
Additional Information Contacts
City of Fairlawn . . . . (330) 668-9500
http://www.cityoffairlawn.com

GREEN (city). Covers a land area of 32.055 square miles and a water area of 1.479 square miles. Located at 40.95° N. Lat; 81.47° W. Long. Elevation is 1,142 feet.
Population: 25,713; Growth (since 2000): 12.7%; Density: 802.2 persons per square mile; Race: 93.4% White, 1.9% Black/African American, 1.9% Asian, 0.1% American Indian/Alaska Native, 0.1% Native Hawaiian/Other Pacific Islander, 2.1% Two or more races, 0.9% Hispanic of any race; Average household size: 2.53; Median age: 42.1; Age under 18: 23.1%; Age 65 and over: 16.7%; Males per 100 females: 95.1; Marriage status: 26.0% never married, 58.6% now married, 1.0% separated, 6.5% widowed, 8.9% divorced; Foreign born: 3.7%; Speak English only: 94.1%; With disability: 10.9%; Veterans: 7.8%; Ancestry: 26.8% German, 13.5% Irish, 11.2% Italian, 10.6% English, 7.1% American
Employment: 15.8% management, business, and financial, 5.7% computer, engineering, and science, 12.2% education, legal, community service, arts, and media, 7.2% healthcare practitioners, 15.1% service, 25.9% sales and office, 6.4% natural resources, construction, and maintenance, 11.8% production, transportation, and material moving
Income: Per capita: $34,117; Median household: $66,656; Average household: $85,426; Households with income of $100,000 or more: 30.3%; Poverty rate: 9.6%
Educational Attainment: High school diploma or higher: 94.3%; Bachelor's degree or higher: 35.1%; Graduate/professional degree or higher: 11.7%

School District(s)

Green Local (PK-12)
2015-16 Enrollment: 4,089 . . . . (330) 896-7500
Housing: Homeownership rate: 74.4%; Median home value: $173,600; Median year structure built: 1981; Homeowner vacancy rate: 1.4%; Median selected monthly owner costs: $1,485 with a mortgage, $495 without a mortgage; Median gross rent: $772 per month; Rental vacancy rate: 4.5%
Health Insurance: 94.5% have insurance; 79.4% have private insurance; 26.7% have public insurance; 5.5% do not have insurance; 2.8% of children under 18 do not have insurance
Transportation: Commute: 95.3% car, 0.4% public transportation, 0.2% walk, 3.7% work from home; Mean travel time to work: 21.4 minutes
Additional Information Contacts
City of Green . . . . (330) 896-5510
http://www.cityofgreen.org

HUDSON (city). Covers a land area of 25.596 square miles and a water area of 0.265 square miles. Located at 41.24° N. Lat; 81.44° W. Long. Elevation is 1,066 feet.
History: The city is named after its founder, David Hudson. Hudson moved here from Goshen, Connecticut in 1799. The Underground Railroad passed through Hudson, and Hudson was the childhood home of John Brown after his family moved there in 1805.
Population: 22,282; Growth (since 2000): -0.7%; Density: 870.5 persons per square mile; Race: 92.6% White, 1.9% Black/African American, 3.6% Asian, 0.0% American Indian/Alaska Native, 0.0% Native Hawaiian/Other Pacific Islander, 1.7% Two or more races, 2.3% Hispanic of any race; Average household size: 2.80; Median age: 45.2; Age under 18: 27.1%; Age 65 and over: 15.6%; Males per 100 females: 96.4; Marriage status: 20.3% never married, 69.7% now married, 0.5% separated, 4.2% widowed, 5.8% divorced; Foreign born: 6.6%; Speak English only: 93.1%;

With disability: 6.7%; Veterans: 5.4%; Ancestry: 26.0% German, 16.6% Irish, 12.3% English, 11.9% Italian, 5.4% Polish
Employment: 30.3% management, business, and financial, 7.1% computer, engineering, and science, 16.4% education, legal, community service, arts, and media, 6.5% healthcare practitioners, 10.0% service, 23.0% sales and office, 2.1% natural resources, construction, and maintenance, 4.5% production, transportation, and material moving
Income: Per capita: $55,145; Median household: $126,618; Average household: $155,164; Households with income of $100,000 or more: 61.6%; Poverty rate: 3.2%
Educational Attainment: High school diploma or higher: 97.9%; Bachelor's degree or higher: 70.7%; Graduate/professional degree or higher: 31.0%

School District(s)

Hudson City (PK-12)
2015-16 Enrollment: 4,557 . . . . (330) 653-1200
Housing: Homeownership rate: 86.1%; Median home value: $313,300; Median year structure built: 1981; Homeowner vacancy rate: 1.1%; Median selected monthly owner costs: $2,149 with a mortgage, $810 without a mortgage; Median gross rent: $1,842 per month; Rental vacancy rate: 0.0%
Health Insurance: 97.3% have insurance; 92.6% have private insurance; 16.9% have public insurance; 2.7% do not have insurance; 2.5% of children under 18 do not have insurance
Safety: Violent crime rate: 1.8 per 10,000 population; Property crime rate: 40.9 per 10,000 population
Transportation: Commute: 87.7% car, 0.5% public transportation, 1.9% walk, 9.0% work from home; Mean travel time to work: 27.6 minutes
Additional Information Contacts
City of Hudson. . . . . (330) 650-1799
http://www.hudson.oh.us

LAKEMORE (village). Covers a land area of 1.476 square miles and a water area of 0.191 square miles. Located at 41.02° N. Lat; 81.42° W. Long. Elevation is 1,083 feet.
History: Incorporated 1920.
Population: 3,064; Growth (since 2000): 19.6%; Density: 2,075.8 persons per square mile; Race: 92.8% White, 7.2% Black/African American, 0.0% Asian, 0.0% American Indian/Alaska Native, 0.0% Native Hawaiian/Other Pacific Islander, 0.0% Two or more races, 0.0% Hispanic of any race; Average household size: 2.45; Median age: 44.8; Age under 18: 19.2%; Age 65 and over: 23.9%; Males per 100 females: 89.3; Marriage status: 25.7% never married, 53.2% now married, 0.0% separated, 8.1% widowed, 13.1% divorced; Foreign born: 1.0%; Speak English only: 99.4%; With disability: 17.9%; Veterans: 7.8%; Ancestry: 16.8% Irish, 14.9% English, 12.1% German, 9.6% Italian, 8.8% Scottish
Employment: 13.9% management, business, and financial, 4.7% computer, engineering, and science, 8.0% education, legal, community service, arts, and media, 6.8% healthcare practitioners, 21.0% service, 23.3% sales and office, 4.1% natural resources, construction, and maintenance, 18.2% production, transportation, and material moving
Income: Per capita: $23,346; Median household: $41,844; Average household: $55,401; Households with income of $100,000 or more: 18.2%; Poverty rate: 16.0%
Educational Attainment: High school diploma or higher: 90.1%; Bachelor's degree or higher: 9.1%; Graduate/professional degree or higher: 4.8%
Housing: Homeownership rate: 79.9%; Median home value: $105,500; Median year structure built: 1959; Homeowner vacancy rate: 0.0%; Median selected monthly owner costs: $1,123 with a mortgage, $411 without a mortgage; Median gross rent: $846 per month; Rental vacancy rate: 11.0%
Health Insurance: 95.4% have insurance; 64.7% have private insurance; 50.6% have public insurance; 4.6% do not have insurance; 0.0% of children under 18 do not have insurance
Transportation: Commute: 96.8% car, 0.0% public transportation, 0.0% walk, 3.2% work from home; Mean travel time to work: 24.9 minutes

MACEDONIA (city). Covers a land area of 9.706 square miles and a water area of 0.038 square miles. Located at 41.31° N. Lat; 81.50° W. Long. Elevation is 988 feet.
Population: 11,595; Growth (since 2000): 25.7%; Density: 1,194.6 persons per square mile; Race: 83.6% White, 9.2% Black/African American, 2.9% Asian, 0.0% American Indian/Alaska Native, 0.0% Native Hawaiian/Other Pacific Islander, 4.3% Two or more races, 2.2% Hispanic of any race; Average household size: 2.56; Median age: 44.9; Age under 18: 21.8%; Age 65 and over: 17.5%; Males per 100 females: 94.1; Marriage status: 20.2% never married, 64.4% now married, 0.9% separated, 8.2% widowed, 7.2% divorced; Foreign born: 4.3%; Speak English only: 95.2%; With disability: 10.4%; Veterans: 9.1%; Ancestry: 22.1% German, 14.0% Irish, 13.7% Polish, 13.7% Italian, 9.2% English
Employment: 21.0% management, business, and financial, 6.8% computer, engineering, and science, 13.1% education, legal, community service, arts, and media, 8.6% healthcare practitioners, 10.0% service, 25.1% sales and office, 5.9% natural resources, construction, and maintenance, 9.5% production, transportation, and material moving
Income: Per capita: $43,468; Median household: $86,061; Average household: $110,207; Households with income of $100,000 or more: 43.2%; Poverty rate: 1.9%
Educational Attainment: High school diploma or higher: 96.4%; Bachelor's degree or higher: 44.0%; Graduate/professional degree or higher: 18.3%

School District(s)

Nordonia Hills City (KG-12)
2015-16 Enrollment: 3,630 . . . . (330) 467-0580
Housing: Homeownership rate: 92.3%; Median home value: $189,700; Median year structure built: 1989; Homeowner vacancy rate: 0.8%; Median selected monthly owner costs: $1,523 with a mortgage, $541 without a mortgage; Median gross rent: $1,202 per month; Rental vacancy rate: 0.0%
Health Insurance: 97.2% have insurance; 87.9% have private insurance; 22.2% have public insurance; 2.8% do not have insurance; 2.9% of children under 18 do not have insurance
Safety: Violent crime rate: 6.8 per 10,000 population; Property crime rate: 167.0 per 10,000 population
Transportation: Commute: 93.5% car, 1.7% public transportation, 0.0% walk, 4.6% work from home; Mean travel time to work: 26.1 minutes
Additional Information Contacts
City of Macedonia . . . . (330) 468-8300
http://www.macedonia.oh.us

MOGADORE (village). Covers a land area of 2.094 square miles and a water area of 0.020 square miles. Located at 41.05° N. Lat; 81.41° W. Long. Elevation is 1,145 feet.
Population: 3,662; Growth (since 2000): -5.9%; Density: 1,748.6 persons per square mile; Race: 99.4% White, 0.1% Black/African American, 0.2% Asian, 0.0% American Indian/Alaska Native, 0.0% Native Hawaiian/Other Pacific Islander, 0.3% Two or more races, 0.7% Hispanic of any race; Average household size: 2.88; Median age: 39.7; Age under 18: 24.9%; Age 65 and over: 15.0%; Males per 100 females: 94.2; Marriage status: 31.2% never married, 50.9% now married, 0.4% separated, 8.7% widowed, 9.2% divorced; Foreign born: 1.4%; Speak English only: 99.2%; With disability: 6.6%; Veterans: 12.7%; Ancestry: 37.6% German, 15.6% Irish, 13.5% Italian, 8.2% American, 6.4% English
Employment: 6.7% management, business, and financial, 3.2% computer, engineering, and science, 9.7% education, legal, community service, arts, and media, 3.4% healthcare practitioners, 17.7% service, 30.8% sales and office, 8.6% natural resources, construction, and maintenance, 19.9% production, transportation, and material moving
Income: Per capita: $23,189; Median household: $62,477; Average household: $64,858; Households with income of $100,000 or more: 13.1%; Poverty rate: 9.1%
Educational Attainment: High school diploma or higher: 91.0%; Bachelor's degree or higher: 18.6%; Graduate/professional degree or higher: 7.2%

School District(s)

Falcon Academy of Creative Arts
2015-16 Enrollment: n/a . . . . (330) 673-4514
Field Local (KG-12)
2015-16 Enrollment: 2,050 . . . . (330) 673-2659
Mogadore Local (KG-12)
2015-16 Enrollment: 870. . . . . (330) 628-9945
Housing: Homeownership rate: 72.8%; Median home value: $113,400; Median year structure built: 1959; Homeowner vacancy rate: 0.0%; Median selected monthly owner costs: $1,147 with a mortgage, $392 without a mortgage; Median gross rent: $896 per month; Rental vacancy rate: 0.0%
Health Insurance: 96.3% have insurance; 86.1% have private insurance; 26.7% have public insurance; 3.7% do not have insurance; 0.0% of children under 18 do not have insurance
Safety: Violent crime rate: 2.6 per 10,000 population; Property crime rate: 104.6 per 10,000 population

Transportation: Commute: 98.0% car, 0.0% public transportation, 0.5% walk, 1.4% work from home; Mean travel time to work: 19.8 minutes

MONTROSE-GHENT (CDP). Covers a land area of 9.423 square miles and a water area of 0.091 square miles. Located at 41.16° N. Lat; 81.64° W. Long. Elevation is 915 feet.

History: Montrose-Ghent is composed of the unincorporated communities of Montrose and Ghent. Despite sharing a commercial district with Fairlawn, the regions are administratively separate.

Population: 4,776; Growth (since 2000): -9.2%; Density: 506.8 persons per square mile; Race: 89.9% White, 6.3% Black/African American, 1.2% Asian, 0.0% American Indian/Alaska Native, 0.0% Native Hawaiian/Other Pacific Islander, 1.5% Two or more races, 1.6% Hispanic of any race; Average household size: 2.40; Median age: 49.8; Age under 18: 23.9%; Age 65 and over: 24.8%; Males per 100 females: 98.5; Marriage status: 15.4% never married, 66.2% now married, 0.0% separated, 6.5% widowed, 11.9% divorced; Foreign born: 7.7%; Speak English only: 92.7%; With disability: 10.2%; Veterans: 9.6%; Ancestry: 20.1% German, 15.4% American, 13.6% Italian, 13.3% Irish, 12.2% English

Employment: 25.7% management, business, and financial, 6.4% computer, engineering, and science, 15.3% education, legal, community service, arts, and media, 18.2% healthcare practitioners, 4.9% service, 21.8% sales and office, 3.5% natural resources, construction, and maintenance, 4.2% production, transportation, and material moving

Income: Per capita: $69,113; Median household: $101,884; Average household: $165,574; Households with income of $100,000 or more: 52.6%; Poverty rate: 5.6%

Educational Attainment: High school diploma or higher: 97.8%; Bachelor's degree or higher: 62.6%; Graduate/professional degree or higher: 27.7%

Housing: Homeownership rate: 87.5%; Median home value: $301,000; Median year structure built: 1971; Homeowner vacancy rate: 0.0%; Median selected monthly owner costs: $2,048 with a mortgage, $751 without a mortgage; Median gross rent: $1,597 per month; Rental vacancy rate: 0.0%

Health Insurance: 97.4% have insurance; 83.8% have private insurance; 29.3% have public insurance; 2.6% do not have insurance; 3.9% of children under 18 do not have insurance

Transportation: Commute: 94.4% car, 0.0% public transportation, 0.0% walk, 5.6% work from home; Mean travel time to work: 23.3 minutes

MUNROE FALLS (city). Covers a land area of 2.718 square miles and a water area of 0.092 square miles. Located at 41.14° N. Lat; 81.44° W. Long. Elevation is 1,030 feet.

Population: 5,055; Growth (since 2000): -4.9%; Density: 1,859.6 persons per square mile; Race: 94.7% White, 1.0% Black/African American, 4.3% Asian, 0.0% American Indian/Alaska Native, 0.0% Native Hawaiian/Other Pacific Islander, 0.0% Two or more races, 0.4% Hispanic of any race; Average household size: 2.44; Median age: 46.1; Age under 18: 17.5%; Age 65 and over: 22.9%; Males per 100 females: 94.9; Marriage status: 25.7% never married, 58.3% now married, 0.8% separated, 7.3% widowed, 8.7% divorced; Foreign born: 5.8%; Speak English only: 93.2%; With disability: 10.8%; Veterans: 7.4%; Ancestry: 19.3% German, 15.9% American, 15.8% Italian, 13.9% Irish, 9.5% English

Employment: 21.2% management, business, and financial, 6.2% computer, engineering, and science, 11.3% education, legal, community service, arts, and media, 10.1% healthcare practitioners, 19.4% service, 22.4% sales and office, 3.2% natural resources, construction, and maintenance, 6.3% production, transportation, and material moving

Income: Per capita: $33,817; Median household: $62,855; Average household: $80,284; Households with income of $100,000 or more: 25.8%; Poverty rate: 7.1%

Educational Attainment: High school diploma or higher: 92.6%; Bachelor's degree or higher: 36.4%; Graduate/professional degree or higher: 13.3%

School District(s)

Stow-munroe Falls City School District (KG-12)
2015-16 Enrollment: 5,158 . . . . (330) 689-5445

Housing: Homeownership rate: 73.3%; Median home value: $160,200; Median year structure built: 1974; Homeowner vacancy rate: 0.0%; Median selected monthly owner costs: $1,341 with a mortgage, $474 without a mortgage; Median gross rent: $620 per month; Rental vacancy rate: 0.0%

Health Insurance: 92.9% have insurance; 78.3% have private insurance; 33.0% have public insurance; 7.1% do not have insurance; 6.8% of children under 18 do not have insurance

Safety: Violent crime rate: 4.0 per 10,000 population; Property crime rate: 79.8 per 10,000 population

Transportation: Commute: 93.7% car, 1.1% public transportation, 2.9% walk, 1.3% work from home; Mean travel time to work: 21.4 minutes

Additional Information Contacts

City of Munroe Falls . . . . (330) 688-7491
http://www.munroefalls.com

NEW FRANKLIN (city). Covers a land area of 25.036 square miles and a water area of 1.642 square miles. Located at 40.95° N. Lat; 81.58° W. Long. Elevation is 1,089 feet.

History: In 1997 the village of New Franklin was incorporated from a section of Franklin Township to thwart annexation attempts from neighboring cities. New Franklin expanded significantly in November 2003 when the residents of Franklin Township and New Franklin voted to merge the two entities. The merger took effect January 1, 2005. The village officially became a city on March 6, 2006.

Population: 14,195; Growth (since 2000): 547.9%; Density: 567.0 persons per square mile; Race: 96.6% White, 0.5% Black/African American, 0.4% Asian, 1.2% American Indian/Alaska Native, 0.0% Native Hawaiian/Other Pacific Islander, 1.3% Two or more races, 0.5% Hispanic of any race; Average household size: 2.55; Median age: 47.9; Age under 18: 18.5%; Age 65 and over: 20.2%; Males per 100 females: 98.0; Marriage status: 23.9% never married, 60.0% now married, 1.0% separated, 6.9% widowed, 9.3% divorced; Foreign born: 1.9%; Speak English only: 98.0%; With disability: 12.7%; Veterans: 10.5%; Ancestry: 27.8% German, 16.3% Irish, 16.0% American, 9.3% English, 7.9% Italian

Employment: 13.1% management, business, and financial, 3.6% computer, engineering, and science, 8.3% education, legal, community service, arts, and media, 7.7% healthcare practitioners, 16.1% service, 26.4% sales and office, 11.0% natural resources, construction, and maintenance, 14.0% production, transportation, and material moving

Income: Per capita: $32,602; Median household: $68,161; Average household: $80,798; Households with income of $100,000 or more: 27.4%; Poverty rate: 4.7%

Educational Attainment: High school diploma or higher: 92.8%; Bachelor's degree or higher: 22.7%; Graduate/professional degree or higher: 5.9%

Housing: Homeownership rate: 91.8%; Median home value: $134,600; Median year structure built: 1963; Homeowner vacancy rate: 1.6%; Median selected monthly owner costs: $1,250 with a mortgage, $431 without a mortgage; Median gross rent: $825 per month; Rental vacancy rate: 13.7%

Health Insurance: 95.2% have insurance; 83.3% have private insurance; 28.2% have public insurance; 4.8% do not have insurance; 3.5% of children under 18 do not have insurance

Safety: Violent crime rate: 6.3 per 10,000 population; Property crime rate: 77.0 per 10,000 population

Transportation: Commute: 95.0% car, 0.2% public transportation, 0.3% walk, 2.9% work from home; Mean travel time to work: 23.8 minutes

Additional Information Contacts

City of New Franklin . . . . (330) 882-4324
http://www.newfranklin.org

NORTHFIELD (village). Covers a land area of 1.083 square miles and a water area of 0 square miles. Located at 41.34° N. Lat; 81.53° W. Long. Elevation is 1,050 feet.

Population: 3,679; Growth (since 2000): -3.9%; Density: 3,398.3 persons per square mile; Race: 80.9% White, 4.9% Black/African American, 8.1% Asian, 0.3% American Indian/Alaska Native, 0.0% Native Hawaiian/Other Pacific Islander, 5.6% Two or more races, 0.3% Hispanic of any race; Average household size: 2.38; Median age: 36.9; Age under 18: 18.5%; Age 65 and over: 17.0%; Males per 100 females: 97.8; Marriage status: 36.8% never married, 41.9% now married, 0.9% separated, 7.6% widowed, 13.7% divorced; Foreign born: 6.9%; Speak English only: 90.1%; With disability: 12.9%; Veterans: 7.1%; Ancestry: 16.5% Polish, 14.4% German, 12.8% Italian, 12.6% Irish, 7.4% English

Employment: 13.6% management, business, and financial, 3.3% computer, engineering, and science, 3.9% education, legal, community service, arts, and media, 3.1% healthcare practitioners, 23.8% service, 22.9% sales and office, 6.4% natural resources, construction, and maintenance, 23.0% production, transportation, and material moving

Income: Per capita: $26,706; Median household: $57,344; Average household: $61,142; Households with income of $100,000 or more: 12.1%; Poverty rate: 14.4%

Educational Attainment: High school diploma or higher: 93.0%; Bachelor's degree or higher: 14.8%; Graduate/professional degree or higher: 3.5%

School District(s)

Nordonia Hills City (KG-12)
2015-16 Enrollment: 3,630 . . . . (330) 467-0580

Housing: Homeownership rate: 63.4%; Median home value: $135,900; Median year structure built: 1964; Homeowner vacancy rate: 0.8%; Median selected monthly owner costs: $1,286 with a mortgage, $435 without a mortgage; Median gross rent: $674 per month; Rental vacancy rate: 0.0%

Health Insurance: 90.4% have insurance; 72.0% have private insurance; 32.8% have public insurance; 9.6% do not have insurance; 0.6% of children under 18 do not have insurance

Safety: Violent crime rate: 5.5 per 10,000 population; Property crime rate: 126.7 per 10,000 population

Transportation: Commute: 93.6% car, 0.0% public transportation, 4.0% walk, 2.3% work from home; Mean travel time to work: 23.1 minutes

NORTON (city). Covers a land area of 20.162 square miles and a water area of 0.327 square miles. Located at 41.03° N. Lat; 81.65° W. Long. Elevation is 1,060 feet.

Population: 12,044; Growth (since 2000): 4.5%; Density: 597.4 persons per square mile; Race: 97.5% White, 1.3% Black/African American, 0.4% Asian, 0.1% American Indian/Alaska Native, 0.0% Native Hawaiian/Other Pacific Islander, 0.6% Two or more races, 1.4% Hispanic of any race; Average household size: 2.59; Median age: 43.2; Age under 18: 21.8%; Age 65 and over: 16.8%; Males per 100 females: 97.2; Marriage status: 23.5% never married, 60.5% now married, 1.1% separated, 6.3% widowed, 9.7% divorced; Foreign born: 2.0%; Speak English only: 96.1%; With disability: 13.3%; Veterans: 9.1%; Ancestry: 24.4% German, 15.3% American, 11.5% Irish, 9.4% English, 6.8% Italian

Employment: 10.3% management, business, and financial, 4.8% computer, engineering, and science, 10.8% education, legal, community service, arts, and media, 7.9% healthcare practitioners, 14.7% service, 26.2% sales and office, 11.1% natural resources, construction, and maintenance, 14.2% production, transportation, and material moving

Income: Per capita: $28,759; Median household: $62,355; Average household: $72,901; Households with income of $100,000 or more: 22.7%; Poverty rate: 6.3%

Educational Attainment: High school diploma or higher: 91.3%; Bachelor's degree or higher: 26.2%; Graduate/professional degree or higher: 9.2%

School District(s)

Norton City (PK-12)
2015-16 Enrollment: 2,524 . . . . (330) 825-0863

Housing: Homeownership rate: 84.6%; Median home value: $131,900; Median year structure built: 1963; Homeowner vacancy rate: 0.0%; Median selected monthly owner costs: $1,192 with a mortgage, $415 without a mortgage; Median gross rent: $923 per month; Rental vacancy rate: 7.2%

Health Insurance: 93.8% have insurance; 77.8% have private insurance; 29.1% have public insurance; 6.2% do not have insurance; 1.7% of children under 18 do not have insurance

Safety: Violent crime rate: 4.2 per 10,000 population; Property crime rate: 112.3 per 10,000 population

Transportation: Commute: 95.5% car, 0.0% public transportation, 1.5% walk, 2.4% work from home; Mean travel time to work: 21.3 minutes

Additional Information Contacts

City of Norton . . . . (330) 825-7815
http://www.cityofnorton.org

PENINSULA (village). Covers a land area of 4.671 square miles and a water area of 0.010 square miles. Located at 41.23° N. Lat; 81.55° W. Long. Elevation is 755 feet.

Population: 615; Growth (since 2000): 2.2%; Density: 131.7 persons per square mile; Race: 99.7% White, 0.0% Black/African American, 0.3% Asian, 0.0% American Indian/Alaska Native, 0.0% Native Hawaiian/Other Pacific Islander, 0.0% Two or more races, 3.3% Hispanic of any race; Average household size: 2.46; Median age: 42.8; Age under 18: 21.0%; Age 65 and over: 17.2%; Males per 100 females: 97.6; Marriage status: 24.4% never married, 61.3% now married, 1.0% separated, 5.8% widowed, 8.6% divorced; Foreign born: 2.3%; Speak English only: 97.6%; With disability: 8.5%; Veterans: 5.1%; Ancestry: 33.8% German, 16.6% Italian, 16.3% Irish, 13.7% Polish, 10.6% American

Employment: 25.3% management, business, and financial, 3.3% computer, engineering, and science, 14.7% education, legal, community service, arts, and media, 14.2% healthcare practitioners, 3.3% service, 18.9% sales and office, 9.4% natural resources, construction, and maintenance, 10.8% production, transportation, and material moving

Income: Per capita: $44,776; Median household: $94,167; Average household: $108,973; Households with income of $100,000 or more: 46.4%; Poverty rate: 2.9%

Educational Attainment: High school diploma or higher: 98.3%; Bachelor's degree or higher: 55.5%; Graduate/professional degree or higher: 21.7%

School District(s)

Woodridge Local (PK-12)
2015-16 Enrollment: 2,067 . . . . (330) 928-9074

Housing: Homeownership rate: 82.8%; Median home value: $246,800; Median year structure built: 1944; Homeowner vacancy rate: 1.0%; Median selected monthly owner costs: $1,830 with a mortgage, $727 without a mortgage; Median gross rent: $1,307 per month; Rental vacancy rate: 0.0%

Health Insurance: 97.1% have insurance; 88.8% have private insurance; 22.6% have public insurance; 2.9% do not have insurance; 9.3% of children under 18 do not have insurance

Safety: Violent crime rate: 17.5 per 10,000 population; Property crime rate: 472.0 per 10,000 population

Transportation: Commute: 91.7% car, 0.0% public transportation, 2.5% walk, 5.8% work from home; Mean travel time to work: 23.1 minutes

PIGEON CREEK (CDP). Covers a land area of 0.895 square miles and a water area of 0 square miles. Located at 41.11° N. Lat; 81.67° W. Long. Elevation is 1,040 feet.

Population: 870; Growth (since 2000): -7.9%; Density: 972.4 persons per square mile; Race: 100.0% White, 0.0% Black/African American, 0.0% Asian, 0.0% American Indian/Alaska Native, 0.0% Native Hawaiian/Other Pacific Islander, 0.0% Two or more races, 4.5% Hispanic of any race; Average household size: 2.49; Median age: 54.0; Age under 18: 23.1%; Age 65 and over: 29.9%; Males per 100 females: 100.5; Marriage status: 12.5% never married, 74.6% now married, 0.0% separated, 6.9% widowed, 6.0% divorced; Foreign born: 0.0%; Speak English only: 100.0%; With disability: 3.2%; Veterans: 5.8%; Ancestry: 36.3% German, 17.4% English, 16.7% Polish, 12.8% Irish, 7.2% British

Employment: 31.6% management, business, and financial, 3.8% computer, engineering, and science, 14.7% education, legal, community service, arts, and media, 7.4% healthcare practitioners, 11.8% service, 17.1% sales and office, 4.4% natural resources, construction, and maintenance, 9.1% production, transportation, and material moving

Income: Per capita: $36,804; Median household: $75,469; Average household: $91,351; Households with income of $100,000 or more: 36.6%; Poverty rate: 3.7%

Educational Attainment: High school diploma or higher: 97.2%; Bachelor's degree or higher: 47.5%; Graduate/professional degree or higher: 13.5%

Housing: Homeownership rate: 100.0%; Median home value: $206,900; Median year structure built: 1970; Homeowner vacancy rate: 6.9%; Median selected monthly owner costs: $1,536 with a mortgage, $554 without a mortgage; Median gross rent: n/a per month; Rental vacancy rate: 0.0%

Health Insurance: 98.7% have insurance; 84.0% have private insurance; 32.3% have public insurance; 1.3% do not have insurance; 0.0% of children under 18 do not have insurance

Transportation: Commute: 89.6% car, 0.0% public transportation, 0.0% walk, 10.4% work from home; Mean travel time to work: 27.9 minutes

PORTAGE LAKES (CDP). Covers a land area of 3.945 square miles and a water area of 0.994 square miles. Located at 41.00° N. Lat; 81.54° W. Long. Elevation is 1,053 feet.

Population: 6,785; Growth (since 2000): -31.3%; Density: 1,719.8 persons per square mile; Race: 95.6% White, 1.8% Black/African American, 2.2% Asian, 0.4% American Indian/Alaska Native, 0.0% Native Hawaiian/Other Pacific Islander, 0.0% Two or more races, 1.0% Hispanic of any race; Average household size: 2.13; Median age: 41.0; Age under 18: 13.9%; Age 65 and over: 16.2%; Males per 100 females: 102.1; Marriage status: 34.5% never married, 43.2% now married, 1.7% separated, 5.9% widowed, 16.3% divorced; Foreign born: 2.2%; Speak English only: 97.4%; With disability: 14.1%; Veterans: 9.9%; Ancestry: 27.7% German, 17.0% American, 13.1% Irish, 10.9% English, 9.4% Italian

Employment: 15.8% management, business, and financial, 4.7% computer, engineering, and science, 6.3% education, legal, community service, arts, and media, 7.4% healthcare practitioners, 16.7% service,

27.3% sales and office, 10.0% natural resources, construction, and maintenance, 11.7% production, transportation, and material moving
Income: Per capita: $30,559; Median household: $54,348; Average household: $63,101; Households with income of $100,000 or more: 15.9%; Poverty rate: 9.5%
Educational Attainment: High school diploma or higher: 93.2%; Bachelor's degree or higher: 31.3%; Graduate/professional degree or higher: 6.9%
Housing: Homeownership rate: 58.2%; Median home value: $129,300; Median year structure built: 1960; Homeowner vacancy rate: 1.3%; Median selected monthly owner costs: $1,093 with a mortgage, $487 without a mortgage; Median gross rent: $798 per month; Rental vacancy rate: 9.9%
Health Insurance: 93.7% have insurance; 79.0% have private insurance; 27.3% have public insurance; 6.3% do not have insurance; 0.0% of children under 18 do not have insurance
Transportation: Commute: 97.3% car, 0.0% public transportation, 0.9% walk, 1.7% work from home; Mean travel time to work: 22.3 minutes

REMINDERVILLE (village). Covers a land area of 2.180 square miles and a water area of 0.030 square miles. Located at 41.33° N. Lat; 81.40° W. Long. Elevation is 1,014 feet.
Population: 3,862; Growth (since 2000): 64.6%; Density: 1,771.3 persons per square mile; Race: 78.5% White, 13.4% Black/African American, 6.4% Asian, 0.0% American Indian/Alaska Native, 0.0% Native Hawaiian/Other Pacific Islander, 1.7% Two or more races, 0.5% Hispanic of any race; Average household size: 2.62; Median age: 39.4; Age under 18: 25.2%; Age 65 and over: 10.8%; Males per 100 females: 95.6; Marriage status: 27.9% never married, 53.6% now married, 1.1% separated, 3.3% widowed, 15.1% divorced; Foreign born: 6.3%; Speak English only: 94.0%; With disability: 8.4%; Veterans: 4.1%; Ancestry: 21.0% German, 18.5% Irish, 16.5% Italian, 6.9% English, 6.3% Polish
Employment: 24.4% management, business, and financial, 11.0% computer, engineering, and science, 11.8% education, legal, community service, arts, and media, 7.9% healthcare practitioners, 14.4% service, 19.7% sales and office, 4.9% natural resources, construction, and maintenance, 5.8% production, transportation, and material moving
Income: Per capita: $33,402; Median household: $71,417; Average household: $86,109; Households with income of $100,000 or more: 34.1%; Poverty rate: 4.7%
Educational Attainment: High school diploma or higher: 97.0%; Bachelor's degree or higher: 42.0%; Graduate/professional degree or higher: 20.3%
Housing: Homeownership rate: 83.8%; Median home value: $172,700; Median year structure built: 1980; Homeowner vacancy rate: 2.4%; Median selected monthly owner costs: $1,472 with a mortgage, $540 without a mortgage; Median gross rent: $1,142 per month; Rental vacancy rate: 0.0%
Health Insurance: 96.8% have insurance; 86.1% have private insurance; 20.5% have public insurance; 3.2% do not have insurance; 0.5% of children under 18 do not have insurance
Safety: Violent crime rate: 0.0 per 10,000 population; Property crime rate: 73.2 per 10,000 population
Transportation: Commute: 93.8% car, 1.5% public transportation, 0.6% walk, 4.1% work from home; Mean travel time to work: 27.2 minutes
Additional Information Contacts
Village of Reminderville. . . . . (330) 562-1234
http://www.reminderville.com

RICHFIELD (village). Covers a land area of 9.319 square miles and a water area of 0.003 square miles. Located at 41.23° N. Lat; 81.64° W. Long. Elevation is 1,152 feet.
History: Richfield was the home of John Brown (1800-1859) during the 1840's, when he was a sheep raiser and wool broker. Brown became a symbol of the Northern sympathies in the Civil War after his raid on the arsenal at Harpers Ferry in 1859, for which he was convicted of treason and hung.
Population: 3,651; Growth (since 2000): 11.1%; Density: 391.8 persons per square mile; Race: 97.8% White, 0.8% Black/African American, 0.3% Asian, 0.0% American Indian/Alaska Native, 0.0% Native Hawaiian/Other Pacific Islander, 1.2% Two or more races, 1.5% Hispanic of any race; Average household size: 2.55; Median age: 47.7; Age under 18: 22.6%; Age 65 and over: 18.2%; Males per 100 females: 101.5; Marriage status: 24.2% never married, 59.4% now married, 0.5% separated, 7.2% widowed, 9.3% divorced; Foreign born: 3.1%; Speak English only: 93.0%; With disability: 8.4%; Veterans: 6.7%; Ancestry: 27.2% German, 16.4% Italian, 12.7% Irish, 12.5% Polish, 10.1% English
Employment: 24.4% management, business, and financial, 6.5% computer, engineering, and science, 11.4% education, legal, community service, arts, and media, 6.8% healthcare practitioners, 12.0% service, 25.4% sales and office, 5.1% natural resources, construction, and maintenance, 8.5% production, transportation, and material moving
Income: Per capita: $42,097; Median household: $67,875; Average household: $108,395; Households with income of $100,000 or more: 41.6%; Poverty rate: 2.9%
Educational Attainment: High school diploma or higher: 94.3%; Bachelor's degree or higher: 41.9%; Graduate/professional degree or higher: 15.0%

School District(s)

Revere Local (PK-12)
2015-16 Enrollment: 2,662 . . . . (330) 666-4155
Housing: Homeownership rate: 87.3%; Median home value: $225,900; Median year structure built: 1960; Homeowner vacancy rate: 0.0%; Median selected monthly owner costs: $1,750 with a mortgage, $475 without a mortgage; Median gross rent: $878 per month; Rental vacancy rate: 0.0%
Health Insurance: 96.4% have insurance; 87.4% have private insurance; 22.7% have public insurance; 3.6% do not have insurance; 2.8% of children under 18 do not have insurance
Transportation: Commute: 90.9% car, 0.1% public transportation, 2.3% walk, 5.3% work from home; Mean travel time to work: 25.3 minutes
Additional Information Contacts
Village of Richfield. . . . . (330) 659-9201
http://www.richfieldvillageohio.org

SAWYERWOOD (CDP). Covers a land area of 0.744 square miles and a water area of 0.277 square miles. Located at 41.03° N. Lat; 81.45° W. Long. Elevation is 1,096 feet.
Population: 1,316; Growth (since 2000): n/a; Density: 1,769.4 persons per square mile; Race: 100.0% White, 0.0% Black/African American, 0.0% Asian, 0.0% American Indian/Alaska Native, 0.0% Native Hawaiian/Other Pacific Islander, 0.0% Two or more races, 1.9% Hispanic of any race; Average household size: 2.38; Median age: 41.1; Age under 18: 18.1%; Age 65 and over: 8.7%; Males per 100 females: 106.2; Marriage status: 35.8% never married, 40.1% now married, 1.0% separated, 3.6% widowed, 20.5% divorced; Foreign born: 0.8%; Speak English only: 100.0%; With disability: 18.2%; Veterans: 7.1%; Ancestry: 36.5% German, 35.1% Irish, 10.7% American, 7.7% French, 6.2% Italian
Employment: 0.0% management, business, and financial, 1.0% computer, engineering, and science, 0.0% education, legal, community service, arts, and media, 7.5% healthcare practitioners, 34.3% service, 26.5% sales and office, 9.4% natural resources, construction, and maintenance, 21.3% production, transportation, and material moving
Income: Per capita: $16,737; Median household: $40,130; Average household: $38,191; Households with income of $100,000 or more: n/a; Poverty rate: 19.0%
Educational Attainment: High school diploma or higher: 85.9%; Bachelor's degree or higher: 12.3%; Graduate/professional degree or higher: 0.7%
Housing: Homeownership rate: 65.2%; Median home value: $62,100; Median year structure built: 1956; Homeowner vacancy rate: 0.0%; Median selected monthly owner costs: $708 with a mortgage, $413 without a mortgage; Median gross rent: $709 per month; Rental vacancy rate: 11.8%
Health Insurance: 78.1% have insurance; 49.8% have private insurance; 39.9% have public insurance; 21.9% do not have insurance; 25.2% of children under 18 do not have insurance
Transportation: Commute: 100.0% car, 0.0% public transportation, 0.0% walk, 0.0% work from home; Mean travel time to work: 15.9 minutes

SILVER LAKE (village). Covers a land area of 1.417 square miles and a water area of 0.181 square miles. Located at 41.15° N. Lat; 81.46° W. Long. Elevation is 1,053 feet.
History: Beginning in 1874, the lake and the land surrounding it was a popular amusement park in the Akron area. It was sold in 1917 and subdivided for residential development, leading to the incorporation of the village in 1918.
Population: 2,452; Growth (since 2000): -18.8%; Density: 1,729.9 persons per square mile; Race: 96.0% White, 0.7% Black/African American, 0.5% Asian, 0.7% American Indian/Alaska Native, 0.0% Native Hawaiian/Other Pacific Islander, 2.1% Two or more races, 0.2% Hispanic of any race; Average household size: 2.51; Median age: 49.0; Age under 18: 19.1%;

Age 65 and over: 22.0%; Males per 100 females: 99.1; Marriage status: 22.6% never married, 64.8% now married, 0.8% separated, 5.6% widowed, 6.9% divorced; Foreign born: 4.2%; Speak English only: 97.7%; With disability: 10.6%; Veterans: 8.7%; Ancestry: 27.3% German, 15.6% Irish, 14.5% Italian, 12.2% English, 7.6% American
Employment: 25.9% management, business, and financial, 2.7% computer, engineering, and science, 14.3% education, legal, community service, arts, and media, 9.3% healthcare practitioners, 14.9% service, 26.0% sales and office, 1.6% natural resources, construction, and maintenance, 5.3% production, transportation, and material moving
Income: Per capita: $50,607; Median household: $94,500; Average household: $124,765; Households with income of $100,000 or more: 47.2%; Poverty rate: 2.0%
Educational Attainment: High school diploma or higher: 97.8%; Bachelor's degree or higher: 58.0%; Graduate/professional degree or higher: 22.3%

School District(s)

Cuyahoga Falls City (KG-12)
2015-16 Enrollment: 4,938 . . . . (330) 926-3800
Housing: Homeownership rate: 94.5%; Median home value: $198,100; Median year structure built: 1957; Homeowner vacancy rate: 1.7%; Median selected monthly owner costs: $1,484 with a mortgage, $571 without a mortgage; Median gross rent: $1,083 per month; Rental vacancy rate: 0.0%
Health Insurance: 96.9% have insurance; 85.6% have private insurance; 25.7% have public insurance; 3.1% do not have insurance; 0.9% of children under 18 do not have insurance
Transportation: Commute: 91.6% car, 0.2% public transportation, 0.8% walk, 5.9% work from home; Mean travel time to work: 19.5 minutes

---

STOW (city). Covers a land area of 17.088 square miles and a water area of 0.233 square miles. Located at 41.18° N. Lat; 81.44° W. Long. Elevation is 1,089 feet.
History: Settled 1802, incorporated as a city 1960.
Population: 34,746; Growth (since 2000): 8.1%; Density: 2,033.3 persons per square mile; Race: 92.7% White, 3.1% Black/African American, 2.0% Asian, 0.2% American Indian/Alaska Native, 0.0% Native Hawaiian/Other Pacific Islander, 1.7% Two or more races, 1.7% Hispanic of any race; Average household size: 2.40; Median age: 40.3; Age under 18: 22.0%; Age 65 and over: 16.4%; Males per 100 females: 93.0; Marriage status: 26.4% never married, 56.0% now married, 0.9% separated, 5.9% widowed, 11.7% divorced; Foreign born: 4.6%; Speak English only: 94.6%; With disability: 8.9%; Veterans: 7.8%; Ancestry: 26.9% German, 15.8% Irish, 11.8% English, 11.5% American, 8.9% Italian
Employment: 17.8% management, business, and financial, 8.0% computer, engineering, and science, 12.3% education, legal, community service, arts, and media, 8.2% healthcare practitioners, 14.8% service, 26.7% sales and office, 3.2% natural resources, construction, and maintenance, 9.0% production, transportation, and material moving
Income: Per capita: $33,475; Median household: $66,079; Average household: $79,639; Households with income of $100,000 or more: 27.9%; Poverty rate: 5.5%
Educational Attainment: High school diploma or higher: 94.9%; Bachelor's degree or higher: 42.9%; Graduate/professional degree or higher: 16.1%

School District(s)

Stow-munroe Falls City School District (KG-12)
2015-16 Enrollment: 5,158 . . . . (330) 689-5445

Two-year College(s)

American National University-Stow (Private, For-profit)
Fall 2016 Enrollment: 24 . . . . (330) 676-1351
2016-17 Tuition: In-state $14,886; Out-of-state $14,886
Housing: Homeownership rate: 69.5%; Median home value: $166,200; Median year structure built: 1980; Homeowner vacancy rate: 1.7%; Median selected monthly owner costs: $1,408 with a mortgage, $514 without a mortgage; Median gross rent: $920 per month; Rental vacancy rate: 6.2%
Health Insurance: 96.2% have insurance; 84.4% have private insurance; 22.6% have public insurance; 3.8% do not have insurance; 0.7% of children under 18 do not have insurance
Safety: Violent crime rate: 8.6 per 10,000 population; Property crime rate: 184.5 per 10,000 population
Newspapers: Record Publishing (weekly circulation 25,000)
Transportation: Commute: 95.8% car, 0.6% public transportation, 0.6% walk, 2.9% work from home; Mean travel time to work: 23.9 minutes
Airports: Kent State University (general aviation)

Additional Information Contacts
City of Stow . . . . (330) 689-2700
http://www.stow.oh.us

TALLMADGE (city). Covers a land area of 13.996 square miles and a water area of 0.024 square miles. Located at 41.11° N. Lat; 81.43° W. Long. Elevation is 1,112 feet.
History: Settled 1807, incorporated 1950. Its historic architecture includes a 19th-century Congregational church near the city's center.
Population: 17,488; Growth (since 2000): 6.7%; Density: 1,249.5 persons per square mile; Race: 92.0% White, 3.6% Black/African American, 0.9% Asian, 0.0% American Indian/Alaska Native, 0.0% Native Hawaiian/Other Pacific Islander, 3.3% Two or more races, 0.8% Hispanic of any race; Average household size: 2.52; Median age: 45.3; Age under 18: 22.0%; Age 65 and over: 20.6%; Males per 100 females: 91.5; Marriage status: 27.6% never married, 55.7% now married, 0.9% separated, 7.1% widowed, 9.6% divorced; Foreign born: 3.9%; Speak English only: 94.8%; With disability: 12.0%; Veterans: 9.9%; Ancestry: 28.7% German, 14.9% Irish, 12.4% Italian, 9.8% English, 7.6% American
Employment: 14.6% management, business, and financial, 4.8% computer, engineering, and science, 10.3% education, legal, community service, arts, and media, 5.4% healthcare practitioners, 16.4% service, 27.8% sales and office, 9.0% natural resources, construction, and maintenance, 11.6% production, transportation, and material moving
Income: Per capita: $30,144; Median household: $59,863; Average household: $75,209; Households with income of $100,000 or more: 25.0%; Poverty rate: 9.6%
Educational Attainment: High school diploma or higher: 93.4%; Bachelor's degree or higher: 27.8%; Graduate/professional degree or higher: 8.9%

School District(s)

Tallmadge City (KG-12)
2015-16 Enrollment: 2,385 . . . . (330) 633-3291
Housing: Homeownership rate: 78.4%; Median home value: $156,400; Median year structure built: 1969; Homeowner vacancy rate: 0.6%; Median selected monthly owner costs: $1,345 with a mortgage, $512 without a mortgage; Median gross rent: $726 per month; Rental vacancy rate: 2.0%
Health Insurance: 95.5% have insurance; 76.9% have private insurance; 33.9% have public insurance; 4.5% do not have insurance; 0.7% of children under 18 do not have insurance
Safety: Violent crime rate: 13.1 per 10,000 population; Property crime rate: 230.3 per 10,000 population
Transportation: Commute: 96.5% car, 0.4% public transportation, 0.6% walk, 1.9% work from home; Mean travel time to work: 20.9 minutes

Additional Information Contacts
City of Tallmadge . . . . (330) 633-0857
http://www.tallmadge-ohio.org

TWINSBURG (city). Covers a land area of 13.769 square miles and a water area of 0.032 square miles. Located at 41.32° N. Lat; 81.44° W. Long. Elevation is 1,004 feet.
History: Twinsburg was named for Moses and Aaron Wilcox, twins who built adjacent houses here in 1818.
Population: 18,851; Growth (since 2000): 10.8%; Density: 1,369.0 persons per square mile; Race: 75.5% White, 13.9% Black/African American, 6.3% Asian, 0.2% American Indian/Alaska Native, 0.1% Native Hawaiian/Other Pacific Islander, 2.9% Two or more races, 2.8% Hispanic of any race; Average household size: 2.46; Median age: 42.5; Age under 18: 23.6%; Age 65 and over: 17.4%; Males per 100 females: 88.0; Marriage status: 25.8% never married, 57.9% now married, 0.4% separated, 7.8% widowed, 8.6% divorced; Foreign born: 7.7%; Speak English only: 91.1%; With disability: 8.6%; Veterans: 7.0%; Ancestry: 20.5% German, 15.3% Italian, 13.4% Irish, 8.3% English, 8.1% Polish
Employment: 21.0% management, business, and financial, 9.9% computer, engineering, and science, 10.7% education, legal, community service, arts, and media, 6.6% healthcare practitioners, 12.7% service, 26.7% sales and office, 3.4% natural resources, construction, and maintenance, 9.0% production, transportation, and material moving
Income: Per capita: $35,955; Median household: $73,314; Average household: $87,382; Households with income of $100,000 or more: 35.3%; Poverty rate: 5.9%
Educational Attainment: High school diploma or higher: 95.1%; Bachelor's degree or higher: 45.8%; Graduate/professional degree or higher: 16.8%

School District(s)

Twinsburg City (PK-12)
2015-16 Enrollment: 4,133 . . . . (330) 486-2000

Vocational/Technical School(s)

Paul Mitchell the School-Cleveland (Private, For-profit)
Fall 2016 Enrollment: 161 . . . . (330) 963-0119
2016-17 Tuition: $17,050

Housing: Homeownership rate: 72.5%; Median home value: $210,100; Median year structure built: 1991; Homeowner vacancy rate: 0.4%; Median selected monthly owner costs: $1,591 with a mortgage, $570 without a mortgage; Median gross rent: $1,027 per month; Rental vacancy rate: 1.1%

Health Insurance: 96.7% have insurance; 86.0% have private insurance; 24.7% have public insurance; 3.3% do not have insurance; 2.7% of children under 18 do not have insurance

Safety: Violent crime rate: 10.6 per 10,000 population; Property crime rate: 69.4 per 10,000 population

Transportation: Commute: 92.2% car, 0.1% public transportation, 0.6% walk, 6.0% work from home; Mean travel time to work: 25.5 minutes

Additional Information Contacts

City of Twinsburg. . . . . (330) 425-7161
http://www.mytwinsburg.com

TWINSBURG HEIGHTS (CDP). Covers a land area of 0.288 square miles and a water area of 0 square miles. Located at 41.31° N. Lat; 81.46° W. Long. Elevation is 1,135 feet.

Population: 1,009; Growth (since 2000): n/a; Density: 3,502.3 persons per square mile; Race: 16.6% White, 70.7% Black/African American, 0.0% Asian, 0.0% American Indian/Alaska Native, 0.0% Native Hawaiian/Other Pacific Islander, 12.8% Two or more races, 0.0% Hispanic of any race; Average household size: 2.99; Median age: 22.6; Age under 18: 41.1%; Age 65 and over: 2.0%; Males per 100 females: 76.5; Marriage status: 57.8% never married, 22.6% now married, 3.6% separated, 5.0% widowed, 14.6% divorced; Foreign born: 0.0%; Speak English only: 98.5%; With disability: 8.2%; Veterans: 0.0%; Ancestry: 12.6% Irish, 7.5% German, 6.2% English, 5.4% Hungarian, 5.2% Welsh

Employment: 8.8% management, business, and financial, 3.6% computer, engineering, and science, 5.2% education, legal, community service, arts, and media, 8.8% healthcare practitioners, 24.2% service, 35.6% sales and office, 0.0% natural resources, construction, and maintenance, 13.7% production, transportation, and material moving

Income: Per capita: $14,774; Median household: n/a; Average household: $43,590; Households with income of $100,000 or more: 6.8%; Poverty rate: 52.3%

Educational Attainment: High school diploma or higher: 95.9%; Bachelor's degree or higher: 16.8%; Graduate/professional degree or higher: 4.3%

Housing: Homeownership rate: 56.1%; Median home value: $109,200; Median year structure built: 1983; Homeowner vacancy rate: 0.0%; Median selected monthly owner costs: $1,123 with a mortgage, $450 without a mortgage; Median gross rent: n/a per month; Rental vacancy rate: 0.0%

Health Insurance: 74.3% have insurance; 32.6% have private insurance; 45.5% have public insurance; 25.7% do not have insurance; 26.7% of children under 18 do not have insurance

Transportation: Commute: 94.4% car, 0.0% public transportation, 0.0% walk, 5.6% work from home; Mean travel time to work: 18.7 minutes

Trumbull County

Located in northeastern Ohio; bounded on the east by Pennsylvania; drained by the Mahoning and Grand Rivers. Covers a land area of 618.296 square miles, a water area of 18.271 square miles, and is located in the Eastern Time Zone at 41.31° N. Lat., 80.77° W. Long. The county was founded in 1800. County seat is Warren.

Trumbull County is part of the Youngstown-Warren-Boardman, OH-PA Metropolitan Statistical Area. The entire metro area includes: Mahoning County, OH; Trumbull County, OH; Mercer County, PA

Weather Station: Warren 3 S — Elevation: 899 feet

	Jan	Feb	Mar	Apr	May	Jun	Jul	Aug	Sep	Oct	Nov	Dec
High	35	38	47	61	71	79	83	82	74	63	51	39
Low	17	18	25	35	44	54	58	57	50	39	31	22
Precip	2.6	1.8	3.1	3.5	4.0	4.0	4.8	3.5	3.8	2.9	3.1	2.8
Snow	11.5	6.9	5.2	0.4	0.0	0.0	0.0	0.0	0.0	tr	0.8	7.1

High and Low temperatures in degrees Fahrenheit; Precipitation and Snow in inches

Weather Station: Youngstown Municipal Arpt — Elevation: 1,180 feet

	Jan	Feb	Mar	Apr	May	Jun	Jul	Aug	Sep	Oct	Nov	Dec
High	33	37	46	59	70	78	82	80	73	61	49	37
Low	19	21	27	38	46	55	60	58	51	41	34	24
Precip	2.5	2.1	3.0	3.4	3.7	3.9	4.4	3.4	3.8	2.7	3.1	2.9
Snow	15.9	11.9	10.8	3.0	tr	tr	tr	tr	tr	0.8	4.0	13.3

High and Low temperatures in degrees Fahrenheit; Precipitation and Snow in inches

Population: 204,908; Growth (since 2000): -9.0%; Density: 331.4 persons per square mile; Race: 88.7% White, 8.3% Black/African American, 0.5% Asian, 0.1% American Indian/Alaska Native, 0.0% Native Hawaiian/Other Pacific Islander, 2.1% two or more races, 1.6% Hispanic of any race; Average household size: 2.32; Median age: 43.8; Age under 18: 21.0%; Age 65 and over: 19.4%; Males per 100 females: 94.4; Marriage status: 28.9% never married, 50.6% now married, 1.6% separated, 7.7% widowed, 12.9% divorced; Foreign born: 1.4%; Speak English only: 94.9%; With disability: 14.6%; Veterans: 10.8%; Ancestry: 22.5% American, 17.7% German, 12.5% Italian, 12.2% Irish, 7.8% English

Religion: Six largest groups: 18.9% Catholicism, 5.4% Methodist/Pietist, 4.9% Baptist, 4.1% Non-denominational Protestant, 2.8% Pentecostal, 2.0% Holiness

Economy: Unemployment rate: 6.0%; Leading industries: 16.7 % retail trade; 13.8 % health care and social assistance; 11.9 % other services (except public administration); Farms: 888 totaling 113,896 acres; Company size: 5 employ 1,000 or more persons, 2 employ 500 to 999 persons, 88 employ 100 to 499 persons, 3,979 employ less than 100 persons; Business ownership: 5,359 women-owned, 783 Black-owned, 92 Hispanic-owned, 276 Asian-owned, 97 American Indian/Alaska Native-owned

Employment: 10.7% management, business, and financial, 2.8% computer, engineering, and science, 7.5% education, legal, community service, arts, and media, 6.2% healthcare practitioners, 19.2% service, 23.6% sales and office, 9.3% natural resources, construction, and maintenance, 20.7% production, transportation, and material moving

Income: Per capita: $24,445; Median household: $43,811; Average household: $57,211; Households with income of $100,000 or more: 13.1%; Poverty rate: 17.5%

Educational Attainment: High school diploma or higher: 88.9%; Bachelor's degree or higher: 18.0%; Graduate/professional degree or higher: 5.4%

Housing: Homeownership rate: 70.3%; Median home value: $99,400; Median year structure built: 1963; Homeowner vacancy rate: 2.0%; Median selected monthly owner costs: $1,022 with a mortgage, $387 without a mortgage; Median gross rent: $638 per month; Rental vacancy rate: 6.8%

Vital Statistics: Birth rate: 100.8 per 10,000 population; Death rate: 123.2 per 10,000 population; Age-adjusted cancer mortality rate: 167.6 deaths per 100,000 population

Health Insurance: 89.9% have insurance; 63.5% have private insurance; 40.4% have public insurance; 10.1% do not have insurance; 7.0% of children under 18 do not have insurance

Health Care: Physicians: 14.8 per 10,000 population; Dentists: 5.1 per 10,000 population; Hospital beds: 24.0 per 10,000 population; Hospital admissions: 1,140.4 per 10,000 population

Air Quality Index (AQI): Percent of Days: 82.0% good, 16.7% moderate, 1.4% unhealthy for sensitive individuals, 0.0% unhealthy, 0.0% very unhealthy; Annual median: 39; Annual maximum: 133

Transportation: Commute: 94.8% car, 0.5% public transportation, 0.9% walk, 2.7% work from home; Mean travel time to work: 22.7 minutes

2016 Presidential Election: 50.7% Trump, 44.5% Clinton, 2.6% Johnson, 0.9% Stein

National and State Parks: Grand River State Wildlife Area; Mosquito Creek State Park; Mosquito Creek State Wildlife Area

Additional Information Contacts

Trumbull Government . . . . (330) 675-2451
http://www.co.trumbull.oh.us

Trumbull County Communities

BOLINDALE (CDP). Covers a land area of 0.994 square miles and a water area of 0 square miles. Located at 41.21° N. Lat; 80.78° W. Long. Elevation is 948 feet.

Population: 2,217; Growth (since 2000): -10.9%; Density: 2,231.4 persons per square mile; Race: 92.3% White, 4.1% Black/African American, 0.0% Asian, 0.0% American Indian/Alaska Native, 0.0% Native Hawaiian/Other

Pacific Islander, 2.8% Two or more races, 1.8% Hispanic of any race; Average household size: 2.39; Median age: 41.3; Age under 18: 19.6%; Age 65 and over: 16.8%; Males per 100 females: 95.1; Marriage status: 22.1% never married, 58.9% now married, 2.8% separated, 8.4% widowed, 10.5% divorced; Foreign born: 0.0%; Speak English only: 98.9%; With disability: 18.5%; Veterans: 14.5%; Ancestry: 34.9% American, 17.5% German, 13.7% Irish, 7.9% Italian, 7.3% English
Employment: 5.5% management, business, and financial, 3.5% computer, engineering, and science, 9.0% education, legal, community service, arts, and media, 2.7% healthcare practitioners, 18.9% service, 31.1% sales and office, 6.7% natural resources, construction, and maintenance, 22.7% production, transportation, and material moving
Income: Per capita: $21,578; Median household: $40,194; Average household: $52,296; Households with income of $100,000 or more: 12.0%; Poverty rate: 18.4%
Educational Attainment: High school diploma or higher: 89.0%; Bachelor's degree or higher: 10.4%; Graduate/professional degree or higher: 2.5%
Housing: Homeownership rate: 72.4%; Median home value: $82,500; Median year structure built: 1962; Homeowner vacancy rate: 0.0%; Median selected monthly owner costs: $892 with a mortgage, $362 without a mortgage; Median gross rent: $719 per month; Rental vacancy rate: 8.2%
Health Insurance: 87.2% have insurance; 59.0% have private insurance; 40.6% have public insurance; 12.8% do not have insurance; 2.1% of children under 18 do not have insurance
Transportation: Commute: 98.4% car, 0.0% public transportation, 0.6% walk, 1.0% work from home; Mean travel time to work: 22.2 minutes

BRISTOLVILLE (unincorporated postal area)

ZCTA: 44402

Covers a land area of 36.198 square miles and a water area of 0.583 square miles. Located at 41.38° N. Lat; 80.85° W. Long. Elevation is 899 feet.
Population: 3,080; Growth (since 2000): -7.4%; Density: 85.1 persons per square mile; Race: 98.8% White, 0.2% Black/African American, 0.0% Asian, 0.0% American Indian/Alaska Native, 0.0% Native Hawaiian/Other Pacific Islander, 1.0% Two or more races, 1.4% Hispanic of any race; Average household size: 2.63; Median age: 43.0; Age under 18: 20.7%; Age 65 and over: 14.4%; Males per 100 females: 102.8; Marriage status: 23.9% never married, 62.6% now married, 0.8% separated, 4.5% widowed, 9.0% divorced; Foreign born: 0.0%; Speak English only: 97.5%; With disability: 10.3%; Veterans: 10.6%; Ancestry: 28.7% American, 23.5% German, 14.5% Irish, 10.2% English, 7.6% Polish
Employment: 13.7% management, business, and financial, 0.9% computer, engineering, and science, 5.4% education, legal, community service, arts, and media, 4.4% healthcare practitioners, 15.6% service, 19.4% sales and office, 12.6% natural resources, construction, and maintenance, 28.1% production, transportation, and material moving
Income: Per capita: $24,006; Median household: $56,456; Average household: $62,204; Households with income of $100,000 or more: 14.9%; Poverty rate: 5.6%
Educational Attainment: High school diploma or higher: 89.3%; Bachelor's degree or higher: 15.7%; Graduate/professional degree or higher: 2.5%

School District(s)

Bristol Local (KG-12)
2015-16 Enrollment: 598 . . . . (330) 889-3882
Housing: Homeownership rate: 79.4%; Median home value: $122,500; Median year structure built: 1970; Homeowner vacancy rate: 2.0%; Median selected monthly owner costs: $1,119 with a mortgage, $405 without a mortgage; Median gross rent: $585 per month; Rental vacancy rate: 0.0%
Health Insurance: 93.4% have insurance; 72.2% have private insurance; 33.6% have public insurance; 6.6% do not have insurance; 3.0% of children under 18 do not have insurance
Transportation: Commute: 90.7% car, 0.0% public transportation, 1.8% walk, 6.5% work from home; Mean travel time to work: 30.1 minutes

BROOKFIELD CENTER (CDP). Covers a land area of 2.800 square miles and a water area of 0 square miles. Located at 41.24° N. Lat; 80.56° W. Long. Elevation is 1,063 feet.
Population: 1,475; Growth (since 2000): 14.5%; Density: 526.8 persons per square mile; Race: 93.7% White, 6.3% Black/African American, 0.0% Asian, 0.0% American Indian/Alaska Native, 0.0% Native Hawaiian/Other Pacific Islander, 0.0% Two or more races, 0.0% Hispanic of any race; Average household size: 2.60; Median age: 43.1; Age under 18: 18.2%; Age 65 and over: 16.5%; Males per 100 females: 97.5; Marriage status: 32.8% never married, 41.5% now married, 0.2% separated, 7.9% widowed, 17.9% divorced; Foreign born: 1.9%; Speak English only: 97.1%; With disability: 11.8%; Veterans: 8.4%; Ancestry: 20.9% German, 19.5% Italian, 19.2% American, 9.5% Irish, 9.1% English
Employment: 12.4% management, business, and financial, 3.9% computer, engineering, and science, 15.0% education, legal, community service, arts, and media, 2.7% healthcare practitioners, 22.4% service, 22.2% sales and office, 7.5% natural resources, construction, and maintenance, 13.8% production, transportation, and material moving
Income: Per capita: $28,265; Median household: $69,583; Average household: $73,561; Households with income of $100,000 or more: 36.0%; Poverty rate: 5.1%
Educational Attainment: High school diploma or higher: 95.7%; Bachelor's degree or higher: 27.6%; Graduate/professional degree or higher: 10.8%

School District(s)

Brookfield Local (KG-12)
2015-16 Enrollment: 1,004 . . . . (330) 448-4930
Housing: Homeownership rate: 85.2%; Median home value: $113,300; Median year structure built: 1966; Homeowner vacancy rate: 4.4%; Median selected monthly owner costs: $1,014 with a mortgage, $432 without a mortgage; Median gross rent: $730 per month; Rental vacancy rate: 0.0%
Health Insurance: 95.7% have insurance; 75.1% have private insurance; 31.3% have public insurance; 4.3% do not have insurance; 0.0% of children under 18 do not have insurance
Transportation: Commute: 95.0% car, 0.0% public transportation, 1.3% walk, 3.8% work from home; Mean travel time to work: 23.9 minutes

BURGHILL (unincorporated postal area)

ZCTA: 44404

Covers a land area of 17.040 square miles and a water area of 0.588 square miles. Located at 41.32° N. Lat; 80.56° W. Long. Elevation is 1,030 feet.
Population: 1,751; Growth (since 2000): 2.8%; Density: 102.8 persons per square mile; Race: 99.5% White, 0.0% Black/African American, 0.0% Asian, 0.0% American Indian/Alaska Native, 0.5% Native Hawaiian/Other Pacific Islander, 0.0% Two or more races, 3.6% Hispanic of any race; Average household size: 2.51; Median age: 47.4; Age under 18: 21.5%; Age 65 and over: 22.8%; Males per 100 females: 100.0; Marriage status: 21.0% never married, 57.2% now married, 1.9% separated, 11.1% widowed, 10.7% divorced; Foreign born: 0.0%; Speak English only: 95.9%; With disability: 11.9%; Veterans: 13.3%; Ancestry: 26.4% American, 19.7% German, 17.1% Irish, 12.0% English, 5.3% French
Employment: 11.6% management, business, and financial, 2.5% computer, engineering, and science, 6.5% education, legal, community service, arts, and media, 7.1% healthcare practitioners, 16.5% service, 24.0% sales and office, 10.6% natural resources, construction, and maintenance, 21.1% production, transportation, and material moving
Income: Per capita: $26,444; Median household: $53,571; Average household: $66,604; Households with income of $100,000 or more: 18.5%; Poverty rate: 5.0%
Educational Attainment: High school diploma or higher: 94.4%; Bachelor's degree or higher: 30.9%; Graduate/professional degree or higher: 4.4%
Housing: Homeownership rate: 82.1%; Median home value: $108,600; Median year structure built: 1953; Homeowner vacancy rate: 4.0%; Median selected monthly owner costs: $1,068 with a mortgage, $355 without a mortgage; Median gross rent: $558 per month; Rental vacancy rate: 16.1%
Health Insurance: 88.7% have insurance; 71.8% have private insurance; 31.1% have public insurance; 11.3% do not have insurance; 6.4% of children under 18 do not have insurance
Transportation: Commute: 96.2% car, 1.7% public transportation, 1.0% walk, 1.0% work from home; Mean travel time to work: 27.5 minutes

CHAMPION HEIGHTS (CDP). Covers a land area of 8.367 square miles and a water area of 0 square miles. Located at 41.30° N. Lat; 80.85° W. Long. Elevation is 932 feet.
Population: 6,491; Growth (since 2000): 37.3%; Density: 775.8 persons per square mile; Race: 98.4% White, 1.2% Black/African American, 0.2% Asian, 0.0% American Indian/Alaska Native, 0.0% Native Hawaiian/Other Pacific Islander, 0.0% Two or more races, 1.1% Hispanic of any race; Average household size: 2.32; Median age: 46.4; Age under 18: 21.3%; Age 65 and over: 22.8%; Males per 100 females: 91.5; Marriage status: 18.3% never married, 59.2% now married, 0.5% separated, 8.8%

widowed, 13.7% divorced; Foreign born: 1.1%; Speak English only: 99.4%; With disability: 12.7%; Veterans: 12.4%; Ancestry: 26.9% American, 22.1% German, 11.8% English, 10.3% Irish, 9.0% Italian
Employment: 15.6% management, business, and financial, 4.2% computer, engineering, and science, 6.0% education, legal, community service, arts, and media, 6.0% healthcare practitioners, 13.7% service, 21.5% sales and office, 11.8% natural resources, construction, and maintenance, 21.2% production, transportation, and material moving
Income: Per capita: $28,230; Median household: $51,680; Average household: $65,864; Households with income of $100,000 or more: 18.6%; Poverty rate: 8.4%
Educational Attainment: High school diploma or higher: 92.0%; Bachelor's degree or higher: 18.0%; Graduate/professional degree or higher: 5.0%
Housing: Homeownership rate: 79.0%; Median home value: $112,600; Median year structure built: 1968; Homeowner vacancy rate: 0.9%; Median selected monthly owner costs: $1,084 with a mortgage, $392 without a mortgage; Median gross rent: $772 per month; Rental vacancy rate: 0.0%
Health Insurance: 95.6% have insurance; 77.9% have private insurance; 33.8% have public insurance; 4.4% do not have insurance; 0.6% of children under 18 do not have insurance
Transportation: Commute: 94.7% car, 0.0% public transportation, 0.0% walk, 5.1% work from home; Mean travel time to work: 23.3 minutes

CHURCHILL (CDP). Covers a land area of 2.560 square miles and a water area of 0 square miles. Located at 41.17° N. Lat; 80.67° W. Long. Elevation is 1,063 feet.
Population: 1,806; Growth (since 2000): -30.6%; Density: 705.4 persons per square mile; Race: 79.9% White, 20.1% Black/African American, 0.0% Asian, 0.0% American Indian/Alaska Native, 0.0% Native Hawaiian/Other Pacific Islander, 0.0% Two or more races, 0.0% Hispanic of any race; Average household size: 1.89; Median age: 52.4; Age under 18: 11.7%; Age 65 and over: 28.1%; Males per 100 females: 94.3; Marriage status: 26.7% never married, 57.1% now married, 3.6% separated, 10.6% widowed, 5.6% divorced; Foreign born: 0.0%; Speak English only: 97.7%; With disability: 15.3%; Veterans: 17.4%; Ancestry: 22.1% American, 21.7% German, 16.1% Irish, 12.3% Italian, 4.2% English
Employment: 1.2% management, business, and financial, 0.0% computer, engineering, and science, 1.2% education, legal, community service, arts, and media, 5.3% healthcare practitioners, 32.9% service, 35.1% sales and office, 15.6% natural resources, construction, and maintenance, 8.9% production, transportation, and material moving
Income: Per capita: $24,179; Median household: $37,951; Average household: $45,668; Households with income of $100,000 or more: 10.9%; Poverty rate: 13.7%
Educational Attainment: High school diploma or higher: 88.5%; Bachelor's degree or higher: 7.8%; Graduate/professional degree or higher: 2.4%
Housing: Homeownership rate: 70.6%; Median home value: $94,000; Median year structure built: 1968; Homeowner vacancy rate: 0.0%; Median selected monthly owner costs: $1,393 with a mortgage, $407 without a mortgage; Median gross rent: $565 per month; Rental vacancy rate: 0.0%
Health Insurance: 90.0% have insurance; 60.0% have private insurance; 45.5% have public insurance; 10.0% do not have insurance; 0.0% of children under 18 do not have insurance
Transportation: Commute: 94.4% car, 3.1% public transportation, 0.0% walk, 0.0% work from home; Mean travel time to work: 18.1 minutes

CORTLAND (city). Covers a land area of 4.248 square miles and a water area of 0 square miles. Located at 41.33° N. Lat; 80.72° W. Long. Elevation is 1,024 feet.
Population: 6,974; Growth (since 2000): 2.1%; Density: 1,641.6 persons per square mile; Race: 97.7% White, 0.6% Black/African American, 0.0% Asian, 0.0% American Indian/Alaska Native, 0.0% Native Hawaiian/Other Pacific Islander, 1.8% Two or more races, 0.4% Hispanic of any race; Average household size: 2.26; Median age: 46.0; Age under 18: 18.7%; Age 65 and over: 22.2%; Males per 100 females: 88.8; Marriage status: 21.7% never married, 62.6% now married, 0.5% separated, 8.1% widowed, 7.6% divorced; Foreign born: 2.1%; Speak English only: 96.6%; With disability: 13.9%; Veterans: 9.4%; Ancestry: 23.1% German, 21.1% American, 15.8% Irish, 11.2% Italian, 11.1% English
Employment: 15.7% management, business, and financial, 6.3% computer, engineering, and science, 12.2% education, legal, community service, arts, and media, 9.2% healthcare practitioners, 11.7% service, 24.6% sales and office, 3.9% natural resources, construction, and maintenance, 16.4% production, transportation, and material moving
Income: Per capita: $31,177; Median household: $63,493; Average household: $68,982; Households with income of $100,000 or more: 21.2%; Poverty rate: 10.0%
Educational Attainment: High school diploma or higher: 94.5%; Bachelor's degree or higher: 31.5%; Graduate/professional degree or higher: 9.3%

School District(s)

Lakeview Local (KG-12)
2015-16 Enrollment: 1,730 . . . . (330) 637-8741
Maplewood Local (KG-12)
2015-16 Enrollment: 732. . . . . (330) 637-7506
Mathews Local (KG-12)
2015-16 Enrollment: 689. . . . . (330) 637-7000

Housing: Homeownership rate: 71.8%; Median home value: $141,100; Median year structure built: 1978; Homeowner vacancy rate: 0.0%; Median selected monthly owner costs: $1,209 with a mortgage, $488 without a mortgage; Median gross rent: $715 per month; Rental vacancy rate: 5.7%
Health Insurance: 91.0% have insurance; 74.4% have private insurance; 32.0% have public insurance; 9.0% do not have insurance; 12.3% of children under 18 do not have insurance
Safety: Violent crime rate: 1.5 per 10,000 population; Property crime rate: 111.7 per 10,000 population
Transportation: Commute: 97.2% car, 0.0% public transportation, 0.0% walk, 2.3% work from home; Mean travel time to work: 25.3 minutes
Additional Information Contacts
City of Cortland . . . . (330) 637-4003
http://www.cityofcortland.org

FARMDALE (unincorporated postal area)
ZCTA: 44417
Covers a land area of 33.322 square miles and a water area of 0 square miles. Located at 41.44° N. Lat; 80.66° W. Long. Elevation is 935 feet.
Population: 1,829; Growth (since 2000): 3.5%; Density: 54.9 persons per square mile; Race: 95.4% White, 1.7% Black/African American, 0.9% Asian, 0.0% American Indian/Alaska Native, 0.0% Native Hawaiian/Other Pacific Islander, 2.1% Two or more races, 0.0% Hispanic of any race; Average household size: 2.73; Median age: 41.2; Age under 18: 25.6%; Age 65 and over: 11.7%; Males per 100 females: 98.0; Marriage status: 29.4% never married, 58.7% now married, 3.0% separated, 4.8% widowed, 7.1% divorced; Foreign born: 0.9%; Speak English only: 97.4%; With disability: 10.3%; Veterans: 7.1%; Ancestry: 24.0% American, 15.4% German, 10.6% Irish, 9.0% Italian, 7.4% Slovak
Employment: 12.4% management, business, and financial, 2.9% computer, engineering, and science, 5.5% education, legal, community service, arts, and media, 11.7% healthcare practitioners, 14.5% service, 21.5% sales and office, 13.0% natural resources, construction, and maintenance, 18.5% production, transportation, and material moving
Income: Per capita: $21,799; Median household: $52,163; Average household: $59,596; Households with income of $100,000 or more: 22.4%; Poverty rate: 24.0%
Educational Attainment: High school diploma or higher: 92.0%; Bachelor's degree or higher: 24.8%; Graduate/professional degree or higher: 7.0%
Housing: Homeownership rate: 80.4%; Median home value: $137,800; Median year structure built: 1970; Homeowner vacancy rate: 0.0%; Median selected monthly owner costs: $1,354 with a mortgage, $453 without a mortgage; Median gross rent: $664 per month; Rental vacancy rate: 0.0%
Health Insurance: 91.0% have insurance; 68.0% have private insurance; 36.1% have public insurance; 9.0% do not have insurance; 3.2% of children under 18 do not have insurance
Transportation: Commute: 95.7% car, 0.0% public transportation, 1.0% walk, 1.0% work from home; Mean travel time to work: 28.8 minutes

FOWLER (unincorporated postal area)
ZCTA: 44418
Covers a land area of 17.426 square miles and a water area of 0 square miles. Located at 41.31° N. Lat; 80.60° W. Long. Elevation is 1,142 feet.
Population: 1,502; Growth (since 2000): 21.4%; Density: 86.2 persons per square mile; Race: 100.0% White, 0.0% Black/African American, 0.0% Asian, 0.0% American Indian/Alaska Native, 0.0% Native Hawaiian/Other Pacific Islander, 0.0% Two or more races, 0.0% Hispanic of any race; Average household size: 2.66; Median age: 49.5; Age under 18: 15.4%; Age 65 and over: 17.1%; Males per 100 females: 98.4; Marriage status:

27.2% never married, 59.6% now married, 0.0% separated, 7.4% widowed, 5.7% divorced; Foreign born: 0.0%; Speak English only: 98.7%; With disability: 14.9%; Veterans: 10.7%; Ancestry: 25.2% German, 23.3% American, 20.9% English, 14.1% Irish, 9.0% Italian
Employment: 8.0% management, business, and financial, 1.1% computer, engineering, and science, 6.8% education, legal, community service, arts, and media, 5.1% healthcare practitioners, 25.6% service, 24.7% sales and office, 9.7% natural resources, construction, and maintenance, 19.2% production, transportation, and material moving
Income: Per capita: $27,670; Median household: $59,728; Average household: $75,590; Households with income of $100,000 or more: 29.9%; Poverty rate: 1.9%
Educational Attainment: High school diploma or higher: 93.2%; Bachelor's degree or higher: 19.8%; Graduate/professional degree or higher: 7.1%
Housing: Homeownership rate: 84.0%; Median home value: $162,300; Median year structure built: 1974; Homeowner vacancy rate: 0.0%; Median selected monthly owner costs: $1,220 with a mortgage, $582 without a mortgage; Median gross rent: $525 per month; Rental vacancy rate: 0.0%
Health Insurance: 94.2% have insurance; 85.8% have private insurance; 21.7% have public insurance; 5.8% do not have insurance; 3.0% of children under 18 do not have insurance
Transportation: Commute: 95.7% car, 0.0% public transportation, 2.9% walk, 1.4% work from home; Mean travel time to work: 19.9 minutes

---

GIRARD (city). Covers a land area of 5.875 square miles and a water area of 0.486 square miles. Located at 41.17° N. Lat; 80.70° W. Long. Elevation is 906 feet.
History: Girard was settled about 1800, but growth was slow until the Ohio & Erie Canal was completed. The town was probably named for Stephen Girard, philanthropist and founder of Girard College in Philadelphia, Pennsylvania.
Population: 9,615; Growth (since 2000): -11.8%; Density: 1,636.5 persons per square mile; Race: 92.5% White, 3.4% Black/African American, 1.0% Asian, 0.2% American Indian/Alaska Native, 0.0% Native Hawaiian/Other Pacific Islander, 2.8% Two or more races, 2.9% Hispanic of any race; Average household size: 2.24; Median age: 40.2; Age under 18: 20.5%; Age 65 and over: 17.5%; Males per 100 females: 87.7; Marriage status: 30.2% never married, 49.7% now married, 2.2% separated, 7.5% widowed, 12.5% divorced; Foreign born: 4.5%; Speak English only: 93.5%; With disability: 15.5%; Veterans: 11.0%; Ancestry: 25.5% Italian, 19.3% American, 15.1% German, 14.7% Irish, 4.3% English
Employment: 11.4% management, business, and financial, 2.7% computer, engineering, and science, 7.0% education, legal, community service, arts, and media, 3.7% healthcare practitioners, 20.1% service, 28.7% sales and office, 5.8% natural resources, construction, and maintenance, 20.6% production, transportation, and material moving
Income: Per capita: $23,398; Median household: $37,426; Average household: $52,871; Households with income of $100,000 or more: 9.9%; Poverty rate: 15.5%
Educational Attainment: High school diploma or higher: 86.8%; Bachelor's degree or higher: 19.0%; Graduate/professional degree or higher: 4.9%

School District(s)

Girard City School District (PK-12)
2015-16 Enrollment: 1,690 . . . . (330) 545-2596
Housing: Homeownership rate: 60.6%; Median home value: $81,200; Median year structure built: 1955; Homeowner vacancy rate: 4.3%; Median selected monthly owner costs: $857 with a mortgage, $376 without a mortgage; Median gross rent: $621 per month; Rental vacancy rate: 7.7%
Health Insurance: 91.1% have insurance; 63.3% have private insurance; 41.6% have public insurance; 8.9% do not have insurance; 3.0% of children under 18 do not have insurance
Transportation: Commute: 95.1% car, 0.7% public transportation, 1.4% walk, 2.8% work from home; Mean travel time to work: 22.3 minutes
Additional Information Contacts
City of Girard . . . . (330) 545-3879
http://www.cityofgirard.com

HILLTOP (CDP). Covers a land area of 0.571 square miles and a water area of 0 square miles. Located at 41.16° N. Lat; 80.74° W. Long. Elevation is 974 feet.
Population: 464; Growth (since 2000): -13.1%; Density: 813.0 persons per square mile; Race: 94.0% White, 6.0% Black/African American, 0.0% Asian, 0.0% American Indian/Alaska Native, 0.0% Native Hawaiian/Other Pacific Islander, 0.0% Two or more races, 0.0% Hispanic of any race; Average household size: 2.33; Median age: 53.7; Age under 18: 14.7%; Age 65 and over: 12.1%; Males per 100 females: 108.6; Marriage status: 26.6% never married, 44.1% now married, 0.0% separated, 17.0% widowed, 12.2% divorced; Foreign born: 0.0%; Speak English only: 92.0%; With disability: 13.1%; Veterans: 13.6%; Ancestry: 27.6% American, 16.6% Irish, 12.5% German, 11.9% Italian, 11.6% Polish
Employment: 8.7% management, business, and financial, 7.0% computer, engineering, and science, 5.2% education, legal, community service, arts, and media, 0.0% healthcare practitioners, 16.9% service, 30.8% sales and office, 17.4% natural resources, construction, and maintenance, 14.0% production, transportation, and material moving
Income: Per capita: $20,568; Median household: n/a; Average household: $47,532; Households with income of $100,000 or more: 8.0%; Poverty rate: 21.3%
Educational Attainment: High school diploma or higher: 83.2%; Bachelor's degree or higher: 7.4%; Graduate/professional degree or higher: 2.5%
Housing: Homeownership rate: 89.9%; Median home value: $76,000; Median year structure built: 1949; Homeowner vacancy rate: 0.0%; Median selected monthly owner costs: $794 with a mortgage, $530 without a mortgage; Median gross rent: n/a per month; Rental vacancy rate: 0.0%
Health Insurance: 94.0% have insurance; 58.6% have private insurance; 51.3% have public insurance; 6.0% do not have insurance; 0.0% of children under 18 do not have insurance
Transportation: Commute: 93.7% car, 0.0% public transportation, 0.0% walk, 0.0% work from home; Mean travel time to work: 16.3 minutes

---

HOWLAND CENTER (CDP). Covers a land area of 4.036 square miles and a water area of 0 square miles. Located at 41.25° N. Lat; 80.74° W. Long. Elevation is 892 feet.
Population: 6,453; Growth (since 2000): -0.4%; Density: 1,599.1 persons per square mile; Race: 94.3% White, 1.8% Black/African American, 1.5% Asian, 0.0% American Indian/Alaska Native, 0.0% Native Hawaiian/Other Pacific Islander, 2.3% Two or more races, 0.5% Hispanic of any race; Average household size: 2.41; Median age: 43.0; Age under 18: 21.1%; Age 65 and over: 22.8%; Males per 100 females: 89.6; Marriage status: 26.5% never married, 53.4% now married, 1.3% separated, 7.7% widowed, 12.4% divorced; Foreign born: 2.7%; Speak English only: 93.4%; With disability: 8.9%; Veterans: 10.3%; Ancestry: 19.5% German, 18.7% American, 16.6% Italian, 14.3% Irish, 9.1% English
Employment: 11.6% management, business, and financial, 5.0% computer, engineering, and science, 10.7% education, legal, community service, arts, and media, 7.3% healthcare practitioners, 18.3% service, 22.8% sales and office, 8.6% natural resources, construction, and maintenance, 15.7% production, transportation, and material moving
Income: Per capita: $36,614; Median household: $63,024; Average household: $88,188; Households with income of $100,000 or more: 24.5%; Poverty rate: 8.0%
Educational Attainment: High school diploma or higher: 93.6%; Bachelor's degree or higher: 30.0%; Graduate/professional degree or higher: 12.1%
Housing: Homeownership rate: 75.1%; Median home value: $124,900; Median year structure built: 1971; Homeowner vacancy rate: 4.3%; Median selected monthly owner costs: $1,227 with a mortgage, $446 without a mortgage; Median gross rent: $873 per month; Rental vacancy rate: 2.7%
Health Insurance: 91.6% have insurance; 76.2% have private insurance; 29.5% have public insurance; 8.4% do not have insurance; 4.3% of children under 18 do not have insurance
Transportation: Commute: 96.8% car, 0.3% public transportation, 0.1% walk, 2.8% work from home; Mean travel time to work: 21.4 minutes

---

HUBBARD (city). Covers a land area of 3.902 square miles and a water area of 0.006 square miles. Located at 41.16° N. Lat; 80.57° W. Long. Elevation is 981 feet.
History: Hubbard was named for Nehemiah Hubbard, who purchased the land on which the town was founded in 1801. Until 1880, coal mining was the principal industry.
Population: 7,686; Growth (since 2000): -7.2%; Density: 1,970.0 persons per square mile; Race: 96.4% White, 0.5% Black/African American, 0.0% Asian, 0.0% American Indian/Alaska Native, 0.0% Native Hawaiian/Other Pacific Islander, 2.4% Two or more races, 1.0% Hispanic of any race; Average household size: 2.31; Median age: 43.1; Age under 18: 24.2%; Age 65 and over: 22.4%; Males per 100 females: 90.8; Marriage status: 22.5% never married, 56.0% now married, 1.0% separated, 8.4%

widowed, 13.2% divorced; Foreign born: 1.0%; Speak English only: 97.5%; With disability: 13.7%; Veterans: 11.1%; Ancestry: 23.3% Italian, 20.8% American, 18.5% German, 16.1% Irish, 8.5% English
Employment: 13.2% management, business, and financial, 3.5% computer, engineering, and science, 10.3% education, legal, community service, arts, and media, 7.8% healthcare practitioners, 19.0% service, 25.8% sales and office, 3.6% natural resources, construction, and maintenance, 16.8% production, transportation, and material moving
Income: Per capita: $24,242; Median household: $41,380; Average household: $55,819; Households with income of $100,000 or more: 11.7%; Poverty rate: 14.9%
Educational Attainment: High school diploma or higher: 93.5%; Bachelor's degree or higher: 24.3%; Graduate/professional degree or higher: 5.8%

School District(s)

Hubbard Exempted Village (KG-12)
2015-16 Enrollment: 1,940 . . . . (330) 534-1921
Housing: Homeownership rate: 72.9%; Median home value: $92,900; Median year structure built: 1959; Homeowner vacancy rate: 0.2%; Median selected monthly owner costs: $985 with a mortgage, $395 without a mortgage; Median gross rent: $630 per month; Rental vacancy rate: 6.3%
Health Insurance: 94.2% have insurance; 69.1% have private insurance; 41.0% have public insurance; 5.8% do not have insurance; 1.0% of children under 18 do not have insurance
Safety: Violent crime rate: 13.1 per 10,000 population; Property crime rate: 174.8 per 10,000 population
Transportation: Commute: 95.0% car, 0.8% public transportation, 0.6% walk, 3.4% work from home; Mean travel time to work: 21.6 minutes
Additional Information Contacts
City of Hubbard . . . . (330) 534-3090
http://www.cityofhubbard.com

KINSMAN (unincorporated postal area)

ZCTA: 44428

Covers a land area of 54.467 square miles and a water area of 2.826 square miles. Located at 41.44° N. Lat; 80.57° W. Long. Elevation is 935 feet.
Population: 3,071; Growth (since 2000): -11.9%; Density: 56.4 persons per square mile; Race: 97.3% White, 1.2% Black/African American, 0.2% Asian, 0.0% American Indian/Alaska Native, 0.0% Native Hawaiian/Other Pacific Islander, 0.8% Two or more races, 0.5% Hispanic of any race; Average household size: 2.52; Median age: 51.5; Age under 18: 16.8%; Age 65 and over: 24.3%; Males per 100 females: 98.0; Marriage status: 22.3% never married, 62.2% now married, 1.2% separated, 6.6% widowed, 9.0% divorced; Foreign born: 0.7%; Speak English only: 98.4%; With disability: 17.2%; Veterans: 11.9%; Ancestry: 27.5% American, 21.7% German, 8.6% Irish, 8.2% English, 4.5% Italian
Employment: 8.3% management, business, and financial, 2.8% computer, engineering, and science, 5.9% education, legal, community service, arts, and media, 2.1% healthcare practitioners, 16.1% service, 21.1% sales and office, 14.2% natural resources, construction, and maintenance, 29.7% production, transportation, and material moving
Income: Per capita: $22,824; Median household: $47,475; Average household: $57,826; Households with income of $100,000 or more: 8.2%; Poverty rate: 11.7%
Educational Attainment: High school diploma or higher: 88.8%; Bachelor's degree or higher: 13.2%; Graduate/professional degree or higher: 3.0%

School District(s)

Joseph Badger Local (PK-12)
2015-16 Enrollment: 778. . . . . (330) 876-2800
Housing: Homeownership rate: 87.6%; Median home value: $109,200; Median year structure built: 1960; Homeowner vacancy rate: 3.0%; Median selected monthly owner costs: $1,070 with a mortgage, $415 without a mortgage; Median gross rent: $522 per month; Rental vacancy rate: 0.0%
Health Insurance: 91.0% have insurance; 62.3% have private insurance; 48.7% have public insurance; 9.0% do not have insurance; 1.9% of children under 18 do not have insurance
Transportation: Commute: 96.4% car, 0.9% public transportation, 0.9% walk, 1.9% work from home; Mean travel time to work: 27.7 minutes

KINSMAN CENTER (CDP). Covers a land area of 2.186 square miles and a water area of 0.008 square miles. Located at 41.45° N. Lat; 80.58° W. Long.

Population: 537; Growth (since 2000): n/a; Density: 245.6 persons per square mile; Race: 100.0% White, 0.0% Black/African American, 0.0% Asian, 0.0% American Indian/Alaska Native, 0.0% Native Hawaiian/Other Pacific Islander, 0.0% Two or more races, 0.0% Hispanic of any race; Average household size: 2.37; Median age: 60.4; Age under 18: 17.1%; Age 65 and over: 35.2%; Males per 100 females: 93.7; Marriage status: 18.1% never married, 77.1% now married, 2.6% separated, 4.8% widowed, 0.0% divorced; Foreign born: 0.0%; Speak English only: 100.0%; With disability: 11.9%; Veterans: 19.1%; Ancestry: 33.0% German, 16.9% American, 11.0% Irish, 7.8% English, 7.1% Dutch
Employment: 18.8% management, business, and financial, 0.0% computer, engineering, and science, 13.9% education, legal, community service, arts, and media, 3.8% healthcare practitioners, 13.5% service, 16.3% sales and office, 13.9% natural resources, construction, and maintenance, 19.7% production, transportation, and material moving
Income: Per capita: $23,527; Median household: $46,648; Average household: $55,411; Households with income of $100,000 or more: 4.0%; Poverty rate: 11.4%
Educational Attainment: High school diploma or higher: 96.5%; Bachelor's degree or higher: 22.8%; Graduate/professional degree or higher: 10.0%
Housing: Homeownership rate: 88.5%; Median home value: $88,100; Median year structure built: Before 1940; Homeowner vacancy rate: 0.0%; Median selected monthly owner costs: $940 with a mortgage, $388 without a mortgage; Median gross rent: n/a per month; Rental vacancy rate: 0.0%
Health Insurance: 94.6% have insurance; 48.4% have private insurance; 63.3% have public insurance; 5.4% do not have insurance; 10.9% of children under 18 do not have insurance
Transportation: Commute: 100.0% car, 0.0% public transportation, 0.0% walk, 0.0% work from home; Mean travel time to work: 24.2 minutes

LEAVITTSBURG (CDP). Covers a land area of 1.735 square miles and a water area of 0.062 square miles. Located at 41.25° N. Lat; 80.88° W. Long. Elevation is 912 feet.

Population: 1,520; Growth (since 2000): -30.9%; Density: 876.1 persons per square mile; Race: 94.6% White, 0.7% Black/African American, 2.2% Asian, 1.2% American Indian/Alaska Native, 0.0% Native Hawaiian/Other Pacific Islander, 0.8% Two or more races, 1.2% Hispanic of any race; Average household size: 2.59; Median age: 40.8; Age under 18: 20.4%; Age 65 and over: 16.0%; Males per 100 females: 102.2; Marriage status: 33.4% never married, 41.7% now married, 0.0% separated, 7.6% widowed, 17.2% divorced; Foreign born: 2.8%; Speak English only: 97.0%; With disability: 21.7%; Veterans: 12.1%; Ancestry: 27.2% American, 21.4% German, 8.7% Irish, 8.2% English, 7.2% Italian
Employment: 6.8% management, business, and financial, 0.0% computer, engineering, and science, 5.4% education, legal, community service, arts, and media, 2.6% healthcare practitioners, 33.5% service, 19.5% sales and office, 12.1% natural resources, construction, and maintenance, 20.2% production, transportation, and material moving
Income: Per capita: $19,388; Median household: $37,857; Average household: $48,854; Households with income of $100,000 or more: 9.9%; Poverty rate: 23.3%
Educational Attainment: High school diploma or higher: 91.1%; Bachelor's degree or higher: 10.9%; Graduate/professional degree or higher: 4.5%

School District(s)

Labrae Local (KG-12)
2015-16 Enrollment: 1,220 . . . . (330) 898-1393
Housing: Homeownership rate: 77.7%; Median home value: $60,100; Median year structure built: 1951; Homeowner vacancy rate: 0.0%; Median selected monthly owner costs: $808 with a mortgage, $313 without a mortgage; Median gross rent: $572 per month; Rental vacancy rate: 0.0%
Health Insurance: 89.9% have insurance; 58.5% have private insurance; 44.6% have public insurance; 10.1% do not have insurance; 2.6% of children under 18 do not have insurance
Transportation: Commute: 98.8% car, 0.0% public transportation, 0.0% walk, 0.0% work from home; Mean travel time to work: 34.0 minutes

LORDSTOWN (village). Covers a land area of 23.137 square miles and a water area of 0.001 square miles. Located at 41.17° N. Lat; 80.87° W. Long. Elevation is 955 feet.
Population: 3,325; Growth (since 2000): -8.5%; Density: 143.7 persons per square mile; Race: 92.3% White, 1.6% Black/African American, 1.9% Asian, 1.0% American Indian/Alaska Native, 0.0% Native Hawaiian/Other Pacific Islander, 3.2% Two or more races, 0.2% Hispanic of any race; Average household size: 2.31; Median age: 46.8; Age under 18: 18.3%; Age 65 and over: 21.9%; Males per 100 females: 94.5; Marriage status: 21.7% never married, 61.0% now married, 1.1% separated, 7.0% widowed, 10.3% divorced; Foreign born: 2.6%; Speak English only: 96.3%; With disability: 15.1%; Veterans: 11.0%; Ancestry: 22.4% American, 17.4% German, 14.4% Irish, 13.1% Italian, 10.2% English
Employment: 12.2% management, business, and financial, 0.7% computer, engineering, and science, 6.9% education, legal, community service, arts, and media, 6.2% healthcare practitioners, 19.5% service, 17.4% sales and office, 12.1% natural resources, construction, and maintenance, 25.0% production, transportation, and material moving
Income: Per capita: $28,211; Median household: $53,523; Average household: $64,238; Households with income of $100,000 or more: 16.8%; Poverty rate: 9.9%
Educational Attainment: High school diploma or higher: 91.2%; Bachelor's degree or higher: 15.4%; Graduate/professional degree or higher: 4.4%
Housing: Homeownership rate: 80.8%; Median home value: $131,700; Median year structure built: 1976; Homeowner vacancy rate: 2.3%; Median selected monthly owner costs: $1,355 with a mortgage, $407 without a mortgage; Median gross rent: $543 per month; Rental vacancy rate: 0.0%
Health Insurance: 88.8% have insurance; 73.5% have private insurance; 33.3% have public insurance; 11.2% do not have insurance; 15.2% of children under 18 do not have insurance
Transportation: Commute: 93.7% car, 0.0% public transportation, 0.0% walk, 5.3% work from home; Mean travel time to work: 20.9 minutes

MAPLEWOOD PARK (CDP). Covers a land area of 0.788 square miles and a water area of 0 square miles. Located at 41.14° N. Lat; 80.58° W. Long. Elevation is 1,093 feet.
Population: 334; Growth (since 2000): 4.0%; Density: 423.9 persons per square mile; Race: 62.9% White, 37.1% Black/African American, 0.0% Asian, 0.0% American Indian/Alaska Native, 0.0% Native Hawaiian/Other Pacific Islander, 0.0% Two or more races, 17.7% Hispanic of any race; Average household size: 2.29; Median age: 50.0; Age under 18: 9.6%; Age 65 and over: 23.1%; Males per 100 females: 81.8; Marriage status: 28.8% never married, 51.0% now married, 9.5% separated, 7.8% widowed, 12.4% divorced; Foreign born: 1.8%; Speak English only: 84.5%; With disability: 33.2%; Veterans: 14.6%; Ancestry: 13.5% English, 9.6% German, 8.4% American, 3.3% Croatian, 3.0% African
Employment: 4.9% management, business, and financial, 0.0% computer, engineering, and science, 12.2% education, legal, community service, arts, and media, 0.0% healthcare practitioners, 24.4% service, 18.3% sales and office, 6.1% natural resources, construction, and maintenance, 34.1% production, transportation, and material moving
Income: Per capita: $15,567; Median household: $24,141; Average household: $34,774; Households with income of $100,000 or more: 3.4%; Poverty rate: 25.7%
Educational Attainment: High school diploma or higher: 77.1%; Bachelor's degree or higher: 6.8%; Graduate/professional degree or higher: n/a
Housing: Homeownership rate: 89.7%; Median home value: $29,100; Median year structure built: 1951; Homeowner vacancy rate: 0.0%; Median selected monthly owner costs: $698 with a mortgage, $300 without a mortgage; Median gross rent: n/a per month; Rental vacancy rate: 0.0%
Health Insurance: 85.3% have insurance; 37.7% have private insurance; 61.7% have public insurance; 14.7% do not have insurance; 0.0% of children under 18 do not have insurance
Transportation: Commute: 92.1% car, 0.0% public transportation, 0.0% walk, 0.0% work from home; Mean travel time to work: 28.6 minutes

MASURY (CDP). Covers a land area of 3.422 square miles and a water area of 0.040 square miles. Located at 41.21° N. Lat; 80.54° W. Long. Elevation is 922 feet.
Population: 2,036; Growth (since 2000): -22.2%; Density: 594.9 persons per square mile; Race: 95.7% White, 0.0% Black/African American, 0.0% Asian, 0.0% American Indian/Alaska Native, 0.0% Native Hawaiian/Other Pacific Islander, 4.3% Two or more races, 1.3% Hispanic of any race; Average household size: 2.25; Median age: 42.4; Age under 18: 23.0%; Age 65 and over: 16.9%; Males per 100 females: 96.8; Marriage status: 34.7% never married, 46.3% now married, 0.6% separated, 7.3% widowed, 11.7% divorced; Foreign born: 0.5%; Speak English only: 97.1%; With disability: 11.0%; Veterans: 11.9%; Ancestry: 22.4% American, 18.0% German, 17.5% Italian, 11.5% Irish, 8.9% Slovak
Employment: 6.2% management, business, and financial, 4.8% computer, engineering, and science, 4.9% education, legal, community service, arts, and media, 5.8% healthcare practitioners, 18.4% service, 22.4% sales and office, 26.4% natural resources, construction, and maintenance, 11.2% production, transportation, and material moving
Income: Per capita: $23,468; Median household: $42,396; Average household: $52,847; Households with income of $100,000 or more: 9.3%; Poverty rate: 18.6%
Educational Attainment: High school diploma or higher: 92.9%; Bachelor's degree or higher: 14.3%; Graduate/professional degree or higher: 5.6%
Housing: Homeownership rate: 65.9%; Median home value: $73,800; Median year structure built: 1953; Homeowner vacancy rate: 0.0%; Median selected monthly owner costs: $892 with a mortgage, $364 without a mortgage; Median gross rent: $694 per month; Rental vacancy rate: 0.0%
Health Insurance: 95.6% have insurance; 72.2% have private insurance; 41.2% have public insurance; 4.4% do not have insurance; 0.0% of children under 18 do not have insurance
Transportation: Commute: 98.2% car, 0.0% public transportation, 0.0% walk, 1.8% work from home; Mean travel time to work: 27.3 minutes

MCDONALD (village). Covers a land area of 1.688 square miles and a water area of 0 square miles. Located at 41.16° N. Lat; 80.72° W. Long. Elevation is 961 feet.
Population: 3,173; Growth (since 2000): -8.8%; Density: 1,880.3 persons per square mile; Race: 98.6% White, 0.5% Black/African American, 0.0% Asian, 0.0% American Indian/Alaska Native, 0.0% Native Hawaiian/Other Pacific Islander, 0.9% Two or more races, 0.3% Hispanic of any race; Average household size: 2.39; Median age: 42.1; Age under 18: 25.4%; Age 65 and over: 17.4%; Males per 100 females: 93.9; Marriage status: 26.8% never married, 50.5% now married, 0.9% separated, 7.2% widowed, 15.5% divorced; Foreign born: 1.5%; Speak English only: 97.6%; With disability: 15.2%; Veterans: 8.9%; Ancestry: 29.5% American, 22.2% German, 17.0% Irish, 16.6% Italian, 5.0% Slovak
Employment: 14.2% management, business, and financial, 1.2% computer, engineering, and science, 8.5% education, legal, community service, arts, and media, 5.6% healthcare practitioners, 21.0% service, 27.1% sales and office, 5.7% natural resources, construction, and maintenance, 16.7% production, transportation, and material moving
Income: Per capita: $23,002; Median household: $47,368; Average household: $54,866; Households with income of $100,000 or more: 10.8%; Poverty rate: 11.6%
Educational Attainment: High school diploma or higher: 92.5%; Bachelor's degree or higher: 16.3%; Graduate/professional degree or higher: 4.7%

School District(s)

Mcdonald Local (KG-12)
2015-16 Enrollment: 840. . . . . (330) 530-8051
Housing: Homeownership rate: 77.9%; Median home value: $88,500; Median year structure built: 1959; Homeowner vacancy rate: 0.0%; Median selected monthly owner costs: $987 with a mortgage, $360 without a mortgage; Median gross rent: $720 per month; Rental vacancy rate: 0.0%
Health Insurance: 96.7% have insurance; 72.1% have private insurance; 37.8% have public insurance; 3.3% do not have insurance; 0.0% of children under 18 do not have insurance
Transportation: Commute: 98.1% car, 0.9% public transportation, 0.7% walk, 0.3% work from home; Mean travel time to work: 20.8 minutes

MCKINLEY HEIGHTS (CDP). Covers a land area of 0.871 square miles and a water area of <.001 square miles. Located at 41.19° N. Lat; 80.72° W. Long. Elevation is 991 feet.
Population: 719; Growth (since 2000): n/a; Density: 825.1 persons per square mile; Race: 100.0% White, 0.0% Black/African American, 0.0% Asian, 0.0% American Indian/Alaska Native, 0.0% Native Hawaiian/Other Pacific Islander, 0.0% Two or more races, 0.0% Hispanic of any race; Average household size: 2.22; Median age: 48.1; Age under 18: 20.4%; Age 65 and over: 12.1%; Males per 100 females: 101.1; Marriage status: 20.5% never married, 64.0% now married, 5.9% separated, 1.0% widowed, 14.5% divorced; Foreign born: 1.5%; Speak English only: 98.4%;

With disability: 14.3%; Veterans: 8.2%; Ancestry: 30.3% American, 27.0% Italian, 18.1% Irish, 10.7% German, 9.0% English
Employment: 12.5% management, business, and financial, 11.5% computer, engineering, and science, 4.4% education, legal, community service, arts, and media, 18.8% healthcare practitioners, 5.0% service, 4.4% sales and office, 5.2% natural resources, construction, and maintenance, 38.1% production, transportation, and material moving
Income: Per capita: $30,044; Median household: $44,038; Average household: $66,785; Households with income of $100,000 or more: 20.7%; Poverty rate: 14.7%
Educational Attainment: High school diploma or higher: 92.4%; Bachelor's degree or higher: 24.6%; Graduate/professional degree or higher: 6.0%
Housing: Homeownership rate: 63.9%; Median home value: $84,200; Median year structure built: 1969; Homeowner vacancy rate: 0.0%; Median selected monthly owner costs: $1,204 with a mortgage, $608 without a mortgage; Median gross rent: $618 per month; Rental vacancy rate: 0.0%
Health Insurance: 84.6% have insurance; 65.8% have private insurance; 26.4% have public insurance; 15.4% do not have insurance; 4.1% of children under 18 do not have insurance
Transportation: Commute: 100.0% car, 0.0% public transportation, 0.0% walk, 0.0% work from home; Mean travel time to work: 20.5 minutes

MESOPOTAMIA (unincorporated postal area)

ZCTA: 44439

Covers a land area of 0.174 square miles and a water area of 0 square miles. Located at 41.46° N. Lat; 80.96° W. Long. Elevation is 856 feet.
Population: 141; Growth (since 2000): n/a; Density: 808.1 persons per square mile; Race: 100.0% White, 0.0% Black/African American, 0.0% Asian, 0.0% American Indian/Alaska Native, 0.0% Native Hawaiian/Other Pacific Islander, 0.0% Two or more races, 0.0% Hispanic of any race; Average household size: 2.94; Median age: 34.2; Age under 18: 14.2%; Age 65 and over: 13.5%; Males per 100 females: 101.8; Marriage status: 43.8% never married, 13.2% now married, 0.0% separated, 8.3% widowed, 34.7% divorced; Foreign born: 0.0%; Speak English only: 100.0%; With disability: 39.0%; Veterans: 3.3%; Ancestry: 53.9% American, 38.3% German, 22.0% Irish, 9.9% Italian, 3.5% Hungarian
Employment: 0.0% management, business, and financial, 0.0% computer, engineering, and science, 0.0% education, legal, community service, arts, and media, 7.6% healthcare practitioners, 22.7% service, 0.0% sales and office, 45.5% natural resources, construction, and maintenance, 24.2% production, transportation, and material moving
Income: Per capita: $27,836; Median household: $93,594; Average household: $79,004; Households with income of $100,000 or more: 31.3%; Poverty rate: 34.0%
Educational Attainment: High school diploma or higher: 97.2%; Bachelor's degree or higher: 8.5%; Graduate/professional degree or higher: 3.8%
Housing: Homeownership rate: 35.4%; Median home value: $153,800; Median year structure built: Before 1940; Homeowner vacancy rate: 0.0%; Median selected monthly owner costs: $0 with a mortgage, $0 without a mortgage; Median gross rent: n/a per month; Rental vacancy rate: 0.0%
Health Insurance: 89.4% have insurance; 62.4% have private insurance; 43.3% have public insurance; 10.6% do not have insurance; 0.0% of children under 18 do not have insurance
Transportation: Commute: 100.0% car, 0.0% public transportation, 0.0% walk, 0.0% work from home; Mean travel time to work: 0.0 minutes

MINERAL RIDGE (CDP). Covers a land area of 3.263 square miles and a water area of 0.017 square miles. Located at 41.14° N. Lat; 80.77° W. Long. Elevation is 1,004 feet.
Population: 3,860; Growth (since 2000): -1.0%; Density: 1,183.1 persons per square mile; Race: 96.6% White, 2.8% Black/African American, 0.0% Asian, 0.0% American Indian/Alaska Native, 0.0% Native Hawaiian/Other Pacific Islander, 0.6% Two or more races, 0.5% Hispanic of any race; Average household size: 2.29; Median age: 42.5; Age under 18: 20.0%; Age 65 and over: 19.1%; Males per 100 females: 95.4; Marriage status: 32.3% never married, 44.4% now married, 0.3% separated, 8.3% widowed, 15.0% divorced; Foreign born: 1.0%; Speak English only: 98.2%; With disability: 16.6%; Veterans: 13.4%; Ancestry: 26.7% American, 17.4% German, 15.1% Italian, 11.8% Irish, 9.2% English
Employment: 8.6% management, business, and financial, 3.7% computer, engineering, and science, 14.3% education, legal, community service, arts, and media, 8.9% healthcare practitioners, 16.6% service, 20.8% sales and office, 6.7% natural resources, construction, and maintenance, 20.4% production, transportation, and material moving
Income: Per capita: $25,537; Median household: $53,607; Average household: $61,069; Households with income of $100,000 or more: 13.7%; Poverty rate: 14.4%
Educational Attainment: High school diploma or higher: 85.2%; Bachelor's degree or higher: 22.8%; Graduate/professional degree or higher: 8.6%

School District(s)

Weathersfield Local (KG-12)
2015-16 Enrollment: 932. . . . . (330) 652-0287
Housing: Homeownership rate: 75.1%; Median home value: $116,000; Median year structure built: 1972; Homeowner vacancy rate: 8.8%; Median selected monthly owner costs: $1,073 with a mortgage, $394 without a mortgage; Median gross rent: $539 per month; Rental vacancy rate: 0.0%
Health Insurance: 93.4% have insurance; 74.5% have private insurance; 29.4% have public insurance; 6.6% do not have insurance; 7.6% of children under 18 do not have insurance
Transportation: Commute: 93.6% car, 4.3% public transportation, 0.0% walk, 1.4% work from home; Mean travel time to work: 24.5 minutes

MORGANDALE (CDP). Covers a land area of 2.658 square miles and a water area of 0 square miles. Located at 41.27° N. Lat; 80.80° W. Long. Elevation is 925 feet.
Population: 832; Growth (since 2000): n/a; Density: 313.1 persons per square mile; Race: 94.5% White, 5.5% Black/African American, 0.0% Asian, 0.0% American Indian/Alaska Native, 0.0% Native Hawaiian/Other Pacific Islander, 0.0% Two or more races, 0.0% Hispanic of any race; Average household size: 1.89; Median age: 53.2; Age under 18: 11.9%; Age 65 and over: 20.4%; Males per 100 females: 102.3; Marriage status: 31.9% never married, 35.7% now married, 0.0% separated, 14.6% widowed, 17.7% divorced; Foreign born: 0.0%; Speak English only: 100.0%; With disability: 20.6%; Veterans: 13.2%; Ancestry: 22.6% American, 14.4% German, 9.7% English, 9.5% Irish, 5.6% Italian
Employment: 5.0% management, business, and financial, 0.0% computer, engineering, and science, 10.6% education, legal, community service, arts, and media, 3.0% healthcare practitioners, 23.3% service, 24.3% sales and office, 5.9% natural resources, construction, and maintenance, 28.0% production, transportation, and material moving
Income: Per capita: $21,731; Median household: $33,145; Average household: $41,040; Households with income of $100,000 or more: 1.6%; Poverty rate: 13.8%
Educational Attainment: High school diploma or higher: 86.9%; Bachelor's degree or higher: 11.1%; Graduate/professional degree or higher: 4.4%
Housing: Homeownership rate: 90.0%; Median home value: $66,000; Median year structure built: 1960; Homeowner vacancy rate: 9.8%; Median selected monthly owner costs: $920 with a mortgage, $341 without a mortgage; Median gross rent: $525 per month; Rental vacancy rate: 0.0%
Health Insurance: 94.0% have insurance; 59.1% have private insurance; 49.8% have public insurance; 6.0% do not have insurance; 0.0% of children under 18 do not have insurance
Transportation: Commute: 97.7% car, 0.0% public transportation, 0.0% walk, 2.3% work from home; Mean travel time to work: 21.4 minutes

NEWTON FALLS (village). Covers a land area of 2.307 square miles and a water area of 0.082 square miles. Located at 41.19° N. Lat; 80.97° W. Long. Elevation is 928 feet.
Population: 4,668; Growth (since 2000): -6.7%; Density: 2,023.4 persons per square mile; Race: 97.0% White, 0.0% Black/African American, 0.9% Asian, 0.0% American Indian/Alaska Native, 0.0% Native Hawaiian/Other Pacific Islander, 1.8% Two or more races, 1.6% Hispanic of any race; Average household size: 2.00; Median age: 43.9; Age under 18: 17.3%; Age 65 and over: 21.1%; Males per 100 females: 90.4; Marriage status: 33.2% never married, 40.3% now married, 2.1% separated, 9.9% widowed, 16.6% divorced; Foreign born: 0.6%; Speak English only: 98.5%; With disability: 9.9%; Veterans: 6.5%; Ancestry: 25.6% American, 18.4% German, 13.8% Irish, 8.6% Italian, 8.0% English
Employment: 6.8% management, business, and financial, 1.4% computer, engineering, and science, 2.4% education, legal, community service, arts, and media, 5.9% healthcare practitioners, 11.5% service, 20.2% sales and office, 7.5% natural resources, construction, and maintenance, 44.5% production, transportation, and material moving

Income: Per capita: $23,866; Median household: $39,980; Average household: $47,927; Households with income of $100,000 or more: 5.8%; Poverty rate: 19.5%

Educational Attainment: High school diploma or higher: 87.3%; Bachelor's degree or higher: 6.4%; Graduate/professional degree or higher: 3.3%

School District(s)

Newton Falls Exempted Village (KG-12)
2015-16 Enrollment: 1,127 . . . . (330) 872-5445

Housing: Homeownership rate: 55.5%; Median home value: $85,500; Median year structure built: 1960; Homeowner vacancy rate: 0.0%; Median selected monthly owner costs: $864 with a mortgage, $368 without a mortgage; Median gross rent: $601 per month; Rental vacancy rate: 4.4%

Health Insurance: 89.2% have insurance; 64.4% have private insurance; 39.9% have public insurance; 10.8% do not have insurance; 0.0% of children under 18 do not have insurance

Safety: Violent crime rate: 19.4 per 10,000 population; Property crime rate: 198.8 per 10,000 population

Transportation: Commute: 98.2% car, 0.4% public transportation, 0.9% walk, 0.4% work from home; Mean travel time to work: 28.6 minutes

NILES (city). Covers a land area of 8.611 square miles and a water area of 0.019 square miles. Located at 41.19° N. Lat; 80.75° W. Long. Elevation is 883 feet.

History: Niles was settled in 1806 by James Heaton, who built a gristmill and blast furnace in the area. It was known as Heaton's Furnace until 1834, when the name was changed to Nilestown for a Baltimore newspaper editor whom Heaton admired. The post office later shortened the name. William McKinley, the 25th president of the United States, was born in Niles in 1843.

Population: 18,877; Growth (since 2000): -9.8%; Density: 2,192.2 persons per square mile; Race: 92.5% White, 4.8% Black/African American, 0.3% Asian, 0.0% American Indian/Alaska Native, 0.0% Native Hawaiian/Other Pacific Islander, 2.3% Two or more races, 1.5% Hispanic of any race; Average household size: 2.24; Median age: 42.4; Age under 18: 21.5%; Age 65 and over: 18.4%; Males per 100 females: 90.9; Marriage status: 32.6% never married, 42.5% now married, 2.7% separated, 8.0% widowed, 17.0% divorced; Foreign born: 0.7%; Speak English only: 96.9%; With disability: 17.8%; Veterans: 10.0%; Ancestry: 28.7% American, 19.6% Italian, 18.1% German, 15.8% Irish, 6.0% English

Employment: 7.3% management, business, and financial, 1.7% computer, engineering, and science, 8.4% education, legal, community service, arts, and media, 6.8% healthcare practitioners, 23.6% service, 24.7% sales and office, 9.5% natural resources, construction, and maintenance, 18.1% production, transportation, and material moving

Income: Per capita: $23,050; Median household: $39,311; Average household: $51,765; Households with income of $100,000 or more: 9.7%; Poverty rate: 19.8%

Educational Attainment: High school diploma or higher: 89.3%; Bachelor's degree or higher: 16.8%; Graduate/professional degree or higher: 4.7%

School District(s)

Niles City (KG-12)
2015-16 Enrollment: 2,390 . . . . (330) 989-5095

Two-year College(s)

ETI Technical College (Private, For-profit)
Fall 2016 Enrollment: 144 . . . . (330) 652-9919
2016-17 Tuition: In-state $10,920; Out-of-state $10,920

Raphael's School of Beauty Culture Inc-Niles (Private, For-profit)
Fall 2016 Enrollment: 134 . . . . (330) 652-1559

Vocational/Technical School(s)

Ross Medical Education Center-Niles (Private, For-profit)
Fall 2016 Enrollment: 171 . . . . (330) 505-1436
2016-17 Tuition: $15,740

Housing: Homeownership rate: 55.0%; Median home value: $78,700; Median year structure built: 1958; Homeowner vacancy rate: 5.3%; Median selected monthly owner costs: $871 with a mortgage, $363 without a mortgage; Median gross rent: $649 per month; Rental vacancy rate: 4.4%

Health Insurance: 87.0% have insurance; 59.8% have private insurance; 41.8% have public insurance; 13.0% do not have insurance; 11.3% of children under 18 do not have insurance

Safety: Violent crime rate: 28.6 per 10,000 population; Property crime rate: 282.7 per 10,000 population

Newspapers: The Review Newspapers (weekly circulation 3,000)

Transportation: Commute: 96.7% car, 0.8% public transportation, 1.3% walk, 1.0% work from home; Mean travel time to work: 17.6 minutes

Additional Information Contacts

City of Niles . . . . (330) 544-9000
http://www.thecityofniles.com

NORTH BLOOMFIELD (unincorporated postal area)

ZCTA: 44450

Covers a land area of 45.710 square miles and a water area of 1.533 square miles. Located at 41.45° N. Lat; 80.83° W. Long. Elevation is 896 feet.

Population: 2,021; Growth (since 2000): -4.4%; Density: 44.2 persons per square mile; Race: 93.2% White, 3.6% Black/African American, 0.0% Asian, 0.0% American Indian/Alaska Native, 0.1% Native Hawaiian/Other Pacific Islander, 1.4% Two or more races, 7.5% Hispanic of any race; Average household size: 2.95; Median age: 42.3; Age under 18: 28.7%; Age 65 and over: 13.3%; Males per 100 females: 104.8; Marriage status: 18.8% never married, 67.7% now married, 0.3% separated, 6.5% widowed, 7.1% divorced; Foreign born: 1.0%; Speak English only: 83.9%; With disability: 14.5%; Veterans: 7.3%; Ancestry: 21.7% American, 14.8% German, 11.0% English, 10.7% Irish, 7.0% Dutch

Employment: 9.1% management, business, and financial, 0.0% computer, engineering, and science, 3.1% education, legal, community service, arts, and media, 3.2% healthcare practitioners, 18.8% service, 12.7% sales and office, 14.9% natural resources, construction, and maintenance, 38.2% production, transportation, and material moving

Income: Per capita: $19,862; Median household: $51,154; Average household: $57,504; Households with income of $100,000 or more: 7.1%; Poverty rate: 2.1%

Educational Attainment: High school diploma or higher: 71.9%; Bachelor's degree or higher: 12.3%; Graduate/professional degree or higher: 1.3%

School District(s)

Bloomfield-Mespo Local (PK-12)
2015-16 Enrollment: 264. . . . . (440) 685-4752

Maplewood Local (KG-12)
2015-16 Enrollment: 732. . . . . (330) 637-7506

Housing: Homeownership rate: 81.4%; Median home value: $103,900; Median year structure built: 1960; Homeowner vacancy rate: 4.2%; Median selected monthly owner costs: $1,103 with a mortgage, $351 without a mortgage; Median gross rent: $667 per month; Rental vacancy rate: 0.0%

Health Insurance: 77.4% have insurance; 57.4% have private insurance; 28.9% have public insurance; 22.6% do not have insurance; 29.8% of children under 18 do not have insurance

Transportation: Commute: 80.6% car, 0.0% public transportation, 5.2% walk, 8.1% work from home; Mean travel time to work: 30.3 minutes

ORANGEVILLE (village). Covers a land area of 0.836 square miles and a water area of 0.322 square miles. Located at 41.35° N. Lat; 80.53° W. Long. Elevation is 919 feet.

Population: 196; Growth (since 2000): 3.7%; Density: 234.4 persons per square mile; Race: 100.0% White, 0.0% Black/African American, 0.0% Asian, 0.0% American Indian/Alaska Native, 0.0% Native Hawaiian/Other Pacific Islander, 0.0% Two or more races, 0.0% Hispanic of any race; Average household size: 2.68; Median age: 32.4; Age under 18: 28.1%; Age 65 and over: 11.7%; Males per 100 females: 111.8; Marriage status: 31.4% never married, 47.2% now married, 0.0% separated, 7.5% widowed, 13.8% divorced; Foreign born: 0.0%; Speak English only: 99.5%; With disability: 8.7%; Veterans: 14.2%; Ancestry: 49.0% American, 14.3% German, 11.2% Irish, 7.7% Italian, 7.1% Polish

Employment: 11.1% management, business, and financial, 0.0% computer, engineering, and science, 4.4% education, legal, community service, arts, and media, 5.6% healthcare practitioners, 24.4% service, 25.6% sales and office, 8.9% natural resources, construction, and maintenance, 20.0% production, transportation, and material moving

Income: Per capita: $21,201; Median household: $55,938; Average household: $55,659; Households with income of $100,000 or more: 4.1%; Poverty rate: 7.1%

Educational Attainment: High school diploma or higher: 99.2%; Bachelor's degree or higher: 19.2%; Graduate/professional degree or higher: 6.4%

Housing: Homeownership rate: 75.3%; Median home value: $109,100; Median year structure built: Before 1940; Homeowner vacancy rate: 0.0%; Median selected monthly owner costs: $1,094 with a mortgage, $322

without a mortgage; Median gross rent: $725 per month; Rental vacancy rate: 0.0%
Health Insurance: 91.8% have insurance; 83.7% have private insurance; 19.9% have public insurance; 8.2% do not have insurance; 3.6% of children under 18 do not have insurance
Transportation: Commute: 90.0% car, 0.0% public transportation, 0.0% walk, 8.9% work from home; Mean travel time to work: 24.8 minutes

SOUTH CANAL (CDP). Covers a land area of 1.705 square miles and a water area of 0.036 square miles. Located at 41.18° N. Lat; 80.99° W. Long. Elevation is 935 feet.
Population: 1,122; Growth (since 2000): -16.6%; Density: 658.1 persons per square mile; Race: 100.0% White, 0.0% Black/African American, 0.0% Asian, 0.0% American Indian/Alaska Native, 0.0% Native Hawaiian/Other Pacific Islander, 0.0% Two or more races, 0.0% Hispanic of any race; Average household size: 2.37; Median age: 52.4; Age under 18: 10.6%; Age 65 and over: 19.6%; Males per 100 females: 101.5; Marriage status: 19.2% never married, 72.4% now married, 0.6% separated, 5.4% widowed, 2.9% divorced; Foreign born: 0.8%; Speak English only: 100.0%; With disability: 19.3%; Veterans: 11.4%; Ancestry: 35.1% American, 31.7% German, 12.6% Polish, 10.0% Slovak, 9.3% English
Employment: 8.0% management, business, and financial, 1.0% computer, engineering, and science, 4.7% education, legal, community service, arts, and media, 4.5% healthcare practitioners, 8.9% service, 25.9% sales and office, 8.5% natural resources, construction, and maintenance, 38.5% production, transportation, and material moving
Income: Per capita: $29,002; Median household: $69,375; Average household: $68,171; Households with income of $100,000 or more: 9.3%; Poverty rate: 2.7%
Educational Attainment: High school diploma or higher: 95.9%; Bachelor's degree or higher: 17.9%; Graduate/professional degree or higher: 5.3%
Housing: Homeownership rate: 82.2%; Median home value: $126,500; Median year structure built: 1962; Homeowner vacancy rate: 0.0%; Median selected monthly owner costs: $1,264 with a mortgage, $338 without a mortgage; Median gross rent: $799 per month; Rental vacancy rate: 25.0%
Health Insurance: 90.4% have insurance; 79.6% have private insurance; 25.3% have public insurance; 9.6% do not have insurance; 0.0% of children under 18 do not have insurance
Transportation: Commute: 96.3% car, 0.0% public transportation, 0.0% walk, 3.7% work from home; Mean travel time to work: 26.8 minutes

SOUTHINGTON (unincorporated postal area)

ZCTA: 44470

Covers a land area of 26.769 square miles and a water area of 0.030 square miles. Located at 41.30° N. Lat; 80.97° W. Long. Elevation is 892 feet.
Population: 3,801; Growth (since 2000): 6.9%; Density: 142.0 persons per square mile; Race: 99.8% White, 0.2% Black/African American, 0.0% Asian, 0.0% American Indian/Alaska Native, 0.0% Native Hawaiian/Other Pacific Islander, 0.0% Two or more races, 0.0% Hispanic of any race; Average household size: 2.54; Median age: 45.2; Age under 18: 21.0%; Age 65 and over: 18.4%; Males per 100 females: 101.6; Marriage status: 21.0% never married, 68.2% now married, 0.8% separated, 5.0% widowed, 5.8% divorced; Foreign born: 0.0%; Speak English only: 98.0%; With disability: 10.9%; Veterans: 13.3%; Ancestry: 23.8% American, 23.3% German, 12.8% English, 10.8% Irish, 7.4% Italian
Employment: 7.6% management, business, and financial, 3.3% computer, engineering, and science, 6.7% education, legal, community service, arts, and media, 6.5% healthcare practitioners, 10.8% service, 26.8% sales and office, 17.1% natural resources, construction, and maintenance, 21.2% production, transportation, and material moving
Income: Per capita: $26,188; Median household: $59,605; Average household: $66,756; Households with income of $100,000 or more: 21.7%; Poverty rate: 5.7%
Educational Attainment: High school diploma or higher: 90.8%; Bachelor's degree or higher: 12.3%; Graduate/professional degree or higher: 3.4%

School District(s)

Southington Local (KG-12)
2015-16 Enrollment: 492. . . . . (330) 898-7480
Housing: Homeownership rate: 89.2%; Median home value: $141,600; Median year structure built: 1968; Homeowner vacancy rate: 0.6%; Median selected monthly owner costs: $1,228 with a mortgage, $403 without a mortgage; Median gross rent: $730 per month; Rental vacancy rate: 13.9%
Health Insurance: 93.0% have insurance; 81.2% have private insurance; 27.1% have public insurance; 7.0% do not have insurance; 1.3% of children under 18 do not have insurance
Transportation: Commute: 94.9% car, 2.3% public transportation, 0.4% walk, 1.8% work from home; Mean travel time to work: 28.0 minutes

VIENNA CENTER (CDP). Covers a land area of 0.957 square miles and a water area of 0 square miles. Located at 41.23° N. Lat; 80.65° W. Long. Elevation is 1,148 feet.
Population: 515; Growth (since 2000): -48.2%; Density: 538.3 persons per square mile; Race: 100.0% White, 0.0% Black/African American, 0.0% Asian, 0.0% American Indian/Alaska Native, 0.0% Native Hawaiian/Other Pacific Islander, 0.0% Two or more races, 3.7% Hispanic of any race; Average household size: 2.24; Median age: 44.9; Age under 18: 17.1%; Age 65 and over: 14.8%; Males per 100 females: 98.8; Marriage status: 19.2% never married, 66.5% now married, 3.9% separated, 5.8% widowed, 8.5% divorced; Foreign born: 1.7%; Speak English only: 98.1%; With disability: 11.1%; Veterans: 7.3%; Ancestry: 20.6% German, 18.4% Italian, 15.5% Irish, 12.4% Ukrainian, 8.3% Slovak
Employment: 9.7% management, business, and financial, 2.4% computer, engineering, and science, 6.5% education, legal, community service, arts, and media, 0.0% healthcare practitioners, 39.5% service, 22.6% sales and office, 3.6% natural resources, construction, and maintenance, 15.7% production, transportation, and material moving
Income: Per capita: $28,274; Median household: $49,196; Average household: $62,644; Households with income of $100,000 or more: 21.7%; Poverty rate: 6.7%
Educational Attainment: High school diploma or higher: 86.9%; Bachelor's degree or higher: 18.8%; Graduate/professional degree or higher: 13.9%

School District(s)

Mathews Local (KG-12)
2015-16 Enrollment: 689. . . . . (330) 637-7000
Housing: Homeownership rate: 73.5%; Median home value: $99,000; Median year structure built: 1969; Homeowner vacancy rate: 10.0%; Median selected monthly owner costs: $861 with a mortgage, $453 without a mortgage; Median gross rent: $754 per month; Rental vacancy rate: 0.0%
Health Insurance: 89.9% have insurance; 84.5% have private insurance; 20.2% have public insurance; 10.1% do not have insurance; 0.0% of children under 18 do not have insurance
Transportation: Commute: 87.5% car, 0.0% public transportation, 4.0% walk, 8.5% work from home; Mean travel time to work: 20.4 minutes

WARREN (city). County seat. Covers a land area of 16.127 square miles and a water area of 0.028 square miles. Located at 41.24° N. Lat; 80.82° W. Long. Elevation is 886 feet.
History: Warren was settled in 1798 when Ephraim Quinby and Richard Storr of the Connecticut Land Company came from Pennsylvania. In 1800 the settlement was made the seat of the newly formed Trumbull County. Warren, named for a surveyor, grew slowly, and was incorporated as a village in 1834. The opening of the canal brought a shipping industry, and manufacturing developed. In 1899 J. Ward Packard made the first Packard automobiles in Warren, as well as founding the forerunner of the Peerless Electric Company and other lamp manufacturing companies.
Population: 40,433; Growth (since 2000): -13.7%; Density: 2,507.1 persons per square mile; Race: 66.8% White, 29.0% Black/African American, 0.3% Asian, 0.2% American Indian/Alaska Native, 0.0% Native Hawaiian/Other Pacific Islander, 3.4% Two or more races, 2.6% Hispanic of any race; Average household size: 2.17; Median age: 38.8; Age under 18: 23.5%; Age 65 and over: 17.5%; Males per 100 females: 92.6; Marriage status: 41.0% never married, 34.5% now married, 2.3% separated, 8.7% widowed, 15.8% divorced; Foreign born: 1.4%; Speak English only: 96.5%; With disability: 17.9%; Veterans: 10.9%; Ancestry: 21.6% American, 11.5% German, 8.1% Italian, 8.0% Irish, 5.1% English
Employment: 9.5% management, business, and financial, 2.6% computer, engineering, and science, 7.9% education, legal, community service, arts, and media, 6.5% healthcare practitioners, 23.6% service, 24.9% sales and office, 5.7% natural resources, construction, and maintenance, 19.3% production, transportation, and material moving
Income: Per capita: $17,680; Median household: $29,176; Average household: $39,518; Households with income of $100,000 or more: 5.4%; Poverty rate: 34.9%

Educational Attainment: High school diploma or higher: 84.9%; Bachelor's degree or higher: 12.8%; Graduate/professional degree or higher: 3.2%

School District(s)

Champion Local (KG-12)
2015-16 Enrollment: 1,351 . . . . (330) 847-2330
Howland Local (KG-12)
2015-16 Enrollment: 2,731 . . . . (330) 856-8200
Lakeview Local (KG-12)
2015-16 Enrollment: 1,730 . . . . (330) 637-8741
Lordstown Local (KG-12)
2015-16 Enrollment: 493. . . . . (330) 824-2534
River Gate High School (09-12)
2015-16 Enrollment: 130. . . . . (330) 647-6500
Steam Academy of Warren (KG-08)
2015-16 Enrollment: 245. . . . . (330) 394-3200
Summit Academy Alternative Learners-Warren Middle & Secondary (07-12)
2015-16 Enrollment: 106. . . . . (330) 399-1692
Summit Academy Community School-Warren (KG-06)
2015-16 Enrollment: 103. . . . . (330) 369-4233
Trumbull Career & Tech Ctr (09-12)
2015-16 Enrollment: n/a . . . . (330) 847-0503
Warren City (PK-12)
2015-16 Enrollment: 4,846 . . . . (330) 841-2321

Four-year College(s)

Kent State University at Trumbull (Public)
Fall 2016 Enrollment: 2,379 . . . . (330) 847-0571
2016-17 Tuition: In-state $5,664; Out-of-state $14,028

Two-year College(s)

Trumbull Business College (Private, For-profit)
Fall 2016 Enrollment: 117 . . . . (330) 369-3200
2016-17 Tuition: In-state $12,389; Out-of-state $12,389

Vocational/Technical School(s)

Trumbull Career & Technical Center (Public)
Fall 2016 Enrollment: 77 . . . . (330) 847-0503
2016-17 Tuition: $11,595

Housing: Homeownership rate: 51.2%; Median home value: $61,200; Median year structure built: 1955; Homeowner vacancy rate: 1.8%; Median selected monthly owner costs: $818 with a mortgage, $322 without a mortgage; Median gross rent: $594 per month; Rental vacancy rate: 7.6%
Health Insurance: 90.1% have insurance; 45.9% have private insurance; 56.6% have public insurance; 9.9% do not have insurance; 1.9% of children under 18 do not have insurance
Hospitals: Saint Joseph Health Center (165 beds); Trumbull Memorial Hospital (350 beds)
Safety: Violent crime rate: 57.0 per 10,000 population; Property crime rate: 377.2 per 10,000 population
Newspapers: Tribune Chronicle (daily circulation 30,600)
Transportation: Commute: 94.4% car, 0.6% public transportation, 1.7% walk, 2.5% work from home; Mean travel time to work: 19.6 minutes
Additional Information Contacts
City of Warren . . . . (330) 841-2601
http://www.warren.org

WEST FARMINGTON (village). Covers a land area of 0.878 square miles and a water area of 0 square miles. Located at 41.39° N. Lat; 80.97° W. Long. Elevation is 869 feet.
Population: 517; Growth (since 2000): -0.4%; Density: 588.6 persons per square mile; Race: 97.3% White, 0.0% Black/African American, 0.4% Asian, 2.1% American Indian/Alaska Native, 0.0% Native Hawaiian/Other Pacific Islander, 0.2% Two or more races, 0.0% Hispanic of any race; Average household size: 3.23; Median age: 30.6; Age under 18: 33.8%; Age 65 and over: 4.1%; Males per 100 females: 107.1; Marriage status: 30.4% never married, 59.5% now married, 2.9% separated, 2.1% widowed, 8.0% divorced; Foreign born: 0.4%; Speak English only: 75.1%; With disability: 9.3%; Veterans: 5.8%; Ancestry: 37.9% American, 13.5% German, 13.5% Pennsylvania German, 7.7% Irish, 5.2% English
Employment: 10.2% management, business, and financial, 1.3% computer, engineering, and science, 0.8% education, legal, community service, arts, and media, 6.4% healthcare practitioners, 14.4% service, 22.5% sales and office, 21.6% natural resources, construction, and maintenance, 22.9% production, transportation, and material moving
Income: Per capita: $18,438; Median household: $48,125; Average household: $57,700; Households with income of $100,000 or more: 11.3%; Poverty rate: 18.3%
Educational Attainment: High school diploma or higher: 72.0%; Bachelor's degree or higher: 8.4%; Graduate/professional degree or higher: 2.0%
Housing: Homeownership rate: 65.6%; Median home value: $98,800; Median year structure built: Before 1940; Homeowner vacancy rate: 0.0%; Median selected monthly owner costs: $1,027 with a mortgage, $350 without a mortgage; Median gross rent: $775 per month; Rental vacancy rate: 6.8%
Health Insurance: 71.8% have insurance; 45.8% have private insurance; 28.0% have public insurance; 28.2% do not have insurance; 26.9% of children under 18 do not have insurance
Transportation: Commute: 92.7% car, 0.0% public transportation, 0.4% walk, 2.2% work from home; Mean travel time to work: 31.3 minutes

WEST HILL (CDP). Covers a land area of 1.577 square miles and a water area of 0 square miles. Located at 41.23° N. Lat; 80.53° W. Long. Elevation is 1,043 feet.
Population: 1,884; Growth (since 2000): -25.3%; Density: 1,194.8 persons per square mile; Race: 86.5% White, 11.8% Black/African American, 0.0% Asian, 1.7% American Indian/Alaska Native, 0.0% Native Hawaiian/Other Pacific Islander, 0.0% Two or more races, 0.0% Hispanic of any race; Average household size: 2.17; Median age: 44.1; Age under 18: 23.5%; Age 65 and over: 17.3%; Males per 100 females: 95.3; Marriage status: 28.6% never married, 36.7% now married, 2.6% separated, 17.7% widowed, 17.1% divorced; Foreign born: 2.0%; Speak English only: 95.0%; With disability: 17.2%; Veterans: 16.1%; Ancestry: 25.5% American, 18.4% German, 10.3% Irish, 7.0% English, 6.7% Italian
Employment: 6.7% management, business, and financial, 0.0% computer, engineering, and science, 9.9% education, legal, community service, arts, and media, 7.1% healthcare practitioners, 26.5% service, 27.6% sales and office, 4.9% natural resources, construction, and maintenance, 17.4% production, transportation, and material moving
Income: Per capita: $13,600; Median household: $19,961; Average household: $28,081; Households with income of $100,000 or more: n/a; Poverty rate: 41.0%
Educational Attainment: High school diploma or higher: 90.5%; Bachelor's degree or higher: 10.2%; Graduate/professional degree or higher: 0.7%
Housing: Homeownership rate: 54.3%; Median home value: $37,200; Median year structure built: 1948; Homeowner vacancy rate: 2.3%; Median selected monthly owner costs: $738 with a mortgage, $339 without a mortgage; Median gross rent: $577 per month; Rental vacancy rate: 9.4%
Health Insurance: 75.3% have insurance; 46.8% have private insurance; 33.8% have public insurance; 24.7% do not have insurance; 19.5% of children under 18 do not have insurance
Transportation: Commute: 96.4% car, 1.3% public transportation, 2.4% walk, 0.0% work from home; Mean travel time to work: 22.7 minutes

YANKEE LAKE (village). Covers a land area of 0.508 square miles and a water area of 0 square miles. Located at 41.27° N. Lat; 80.57° W. Long. Elevation is 1,007 feet.
Population: 95; Growth (since 2000): -4.0%; Density: 187.2 persons per square mile; Race: 93.7% White, 0.0% Black/African American, 0.0% Asian, 0.0% American Indian/Alaska Native, 0.0% Native Hawaiian/Other Pacific Islander, 6.3% Two or more races, 0.0% Hispanic of any race; Average household size: 1.94; Median age: 56.9; Age under 18: 9.5%; Age 65 and over: 17.9%; Males per 100 females: 88.1; Marriage status: 13.6% never married, 78.4% now married, 0.0% separated, 2.3% widowed, 5.7% divorced; Foreign born: 1.1%; Speak English only: 97.9%; With disability: 11.6%; Veterans: 14.0%; Ancestry: 23.2% German, 13.7% Slovak, 12.6% Polish, 10.5% English, 9.5% Dutch
Employment: 2.3% management, business, and financial, 16.3% computer, engineering, and science, 14.0% education, legal, community service, arts, and media, 2.3% healthcare practitioners, 18.6% service, 14.0% sales and office, 14.0% natural resources, construction, and maintenance, 18.6% production, transportation, and material moving
Income: Per capita: $27,375; Median household: $48,750; Average household: $58,445; Households with income of $100,000 or more: 8.2%; Poverty rate: 3.2%
Educational Attainment: High school diploma or higher: 98.8%; Bachelor's degree or higher: 24.4%; Graduate/professional degree or higher: 9.3%

Housing: Homeownership rate: 83.7%; Median home value: $104,200; Median year structure built: 1961; Homeowner vacancy rate: 0.0%; Median selected monthly owner costs: $950 with a mortgage, $294 without a mortgage; Median gross rent: n/a per month; Rental vacancy rate: 0.0%
Health Insurance: 95.8% have insurance; 82.1% have private insurance; 24.2% have public insurance; 4.2% do not have insurance; 0.0% of children under 18 do not have insurance
Transportation: Commute: 85.7% car, 0.0% public transportation, 4.8% walk, 9.5% work from home; Mean travel time to work: 28.2 minutes

Tuscarawas County

Located in eastern Ohio; crossed by the Tuscarawas River. Covers a land area of 567.636 square miles, a water area of 3.815 square miles, and is located in the Eastern Time Zone at 40.45° N. Lat., 81.47° W. Long. The county was founded in 1808. County seat is New Philadelphia.

Tuscarawas County is part of the New Philadelphia-Dover, OH Micropolitan Statistical Area. The entire metro area includes: Tuscarawas County, OH

Population: 92,579; Growth (since 2000): 1.8%; Density: 163.1 persons per square mile; Race: 97.0% White, 0.8% Black/African American, 0.4% Asian, 0.3% American Indian/Alaska Native, 0.0% Native Hawaiian/Other Pacific Islander, 1.3% two or more races, 2.3% Hispanic of any race; Average household size: 2.52; Median age: 40.9; Age under 18: 23.0%; Age 65 and over: 17.8%; Males per 100 females: 96.6; Marriage status: 23.9% never married, 55.9% now married, 1.5% separated, 7.5% widowed, 12.6% divorced; Foreign born: 1.7%; Speak English only: 93.3%; With disability: 14.1%; Veterans: 9.5%; Ancestry: 30.3% German, 13.3% Irish, 8.9% English, 8.7% American, 7.5% Italian
Religion: Six largest groups: 10.8% Methodist/Pietist, 9.5% Catholicism, 6.7% Holiness, 5.5% Presbyterian-Reformed, 3.8% Lutheran, 3.5% European Free-Church
Economy: Unemployment rate: 4.5%; Leading industries: 15.9 % retail trade; 14.1 % other services (except public administration); 9.6 % manufacturing; Farms: 1,014 totaling 138,083 acres; Company size: 1 employs 1,000 or more persons, 0 employ 500 to 999 persons, 49 employ 100 to 499 persons, 2,115 employ less than 100 persons; Business ownership: 2,000 women-owned, 43 Black-owned, n/a Hispanic-owned, 63 Asian-owned, 41 American Indian/Alaska Native-owned
Employment: 8.8% management, business, and financial, 2.8% computer, engineering, and science, 7.1% education, legal, community service, arts, and media, 7.0% healthcare practitioners, 17.6% service, 22.4% sales and office, 9.8% natural resources, construction, and maintenance, 24.5% production, transportation, and material moving
Income: Per capita: $24,173; Median household: $46,992; Average household: $59,730; Households with income of $100,000 or more: 13.7%; Poverty rate: 13.6%
Educational Attainment: High school diploma or higher: 85.9%; Bachelor's degree or higher: 15.0%; Graduate/professional degree or higher: 4.8%
Housing: Homeownership rate: 70.2%; Median home value: $114,400; Median year structure built: 1967; Homeowner vacancy rate: 1.3%; Median selected monthly owner costs: $1,059 with a mortgage, $382 without a mortgage; Median gross rent: $694 per month; Rental vacancy rate: 3.6%
Vital Statistics: Birth rate: 121.5 per 10,000 population; Death rate: 109.3 per 10,000 population; Age-adjusted cancer mortality rate: 166.7 deaths per 100,000 population
Health Insurance: 89.0% have insurance; 67.3% have private insurance; 36.2% have public insurance; 11.0% do not have insurance; 9.8% of children under 18 do not have insurance
Health Care: Physicians: 12.0 per 10,000 population; Dentists: 3.6 per 10,000 population; Hospital beds: 19.2 per 10,000 population; Hospital admissions: 631.9 per 10,000 population
Transportation: Commute: 93.3% car, 0.3% public transportation, 1.9% walk, 2.8% work from home; Mean travel time to work: 21.7 minutes
2016 Presidential Election: 64.7% Trump, 29.3% Clinton, 3.9% Johnson, 0.7% Stein
National and State Parks: Fort Laurens State Memorial
Additional Information Contacts
Tuscarawas Government . . . . (330) 364-8811
http://www.co.tuscarawas.oh.us

Tuscarawas County Communities

BALTIC (village). Covers a land area of 0.803 square miles and a water area of 0 square miles. Located at 40.44° N. Lat; 81.70° W. Long. Elevation is 1,060 feet.
Population: 761; Growth (since 2000): 2.4%; Density: 947.9 persons per square mile; Race: 95.5% White, 2.8% Black/African American, 0.3% Asian, 0.0% American Indian/Alaska Native, 0.0% Native Hawaiian/Other Pacific Islander, 1.4% Two or more races, 2.4% Hispanic of any race; Average household size: 2.80; Median age: 40.4; Age under 18: 25.2%; Age 65 and over: 18.9%; Males per 100 females: 100.3; Marriage status: 22.3% never married, 55.7% now married, 0.3% separated, 10.2% widowed, 11.8% divorced; Foreign born: 0.3%; Speak English only: 82.8%; With disability: 15.2%; Veterans: 8.1%; Ancestry: 52.8% German, 12.2% Irish, 8.5% Swiss, 5.7% English, 3.7% American
Employment: 10.9% management, business, and financial, 1.8% computer, engineering, and science, 2.8% education, legal, community service, arts, and media, 6.0% healthcare practitioners, 13.7% service, 14.4% sales and office, 15.8% natural resources, construction, and maintenance, 34.7% production, transportation, and material moving
Income: Per capita: $19,415; Median household: $49,000; Average household: $57,650; Households with income of $100,000 or more: 6.8%; Poverty rate: 4.5%
Educational Attainment: High school diploma or higher: 80.9%; Bachelor's degree or higher: 7.1%; Graduate/professional degree or higher: 2.5%

School District(s)

Garaway Local (KG-12)
2015-16 Enrollment: 1,170 . . . . (330) 852-2421
Housing: Homeownership rate: 72.5%; Median home value: $95,000; Median year structure built: 1961; Homeowner vacancy rate: 0.0%; Median selected monthly owner costs: $873 with a mortgage, $367 without a mortgage; Median gross rent: $644 per month; Rental vacancy rate: 0.0%
Health Insurance: 91.4% have insurance; 72.4% have private insurance; 36.8% have public insurance; 8.6% do not have insurance; 10.9% of children under 18 do not have insurance
Transportation: Commute: 96.5% car, 0.0% public transportation, 1.4% walk, 2.1% work from home; Mean travel time to work: 17.9 minutes

BARNHILL (village). Covers a land area of 0.362 square miles and a water area of 0 square miles. Located at 40.45° N. Lat; 81.37° W. Long. Elevation is 879 feet.
Population: 417; Growth (since 2000): 14.6%; Density: 1,151.6 persons per square mile; Race: 98.6% White, 0.0% Black/African American, 0.0% Asian, 0.0% American Indian/Alaska Native, 0.0% Native Hawaiian/Other Pacific Islander, 1.4% Two or more races, 0.0% Hispanic of any race; Average household size: 2.90; Median age: 38.4; Age under 18: 25.9%; Age 65 and over: 11.0%; Males per 100 females: 101.0; Marriage status: 28.3% never married, 49.4% now married, 3.3% separated, 8.1% widowed, 14.2% divorced; Foreign born: 0.0%; Speak English only: 99.3%; With disability: 21.3%; Veterans: 7.8%; Ancestry: 25.9% German, 11.8% Irish, 9.6% Italian, 8.6% English, 6.0% American
Employment: 6.6% management, business, and financial, 0.0% computer, engineering, and science, 0.0% education, legal, community service, arts, and media, 4.1% healthcare practitioners, 21.3% service, 20.8% sales and office, 15.7% natural resources, construction, and maintenance, 31.5% production, transportation, and material moving
Income: Per capita: $19,782; Median household: $42,222; Average household: $54,169; Households with income of $100,000 or more: 13.9%; Poverty rate: 19.7%
Educational Attainment: High school diploma or higher: 80.7%; Bachelor's degree or higher: 0.7%; Graduate/professional degree or higher: n/a
Housing: Homeownership rate: 73.6%; Median home value: $70,000; Median year structure built: 1982; Homeowner vacancy rate: 3.6%; Median selected monthly owner costs: $917 with a mortgage, $381 without a mortgage; Median gross rent: $638 per month; Rental vacancy rate: 0.0%
Health Insurance: 90.9% have insurance; 61.6% have private insurance; 44.1% have public insurance; 9.1% do not have insurance; 10.2% of children under 18 do not have insurance
Transportation: Commute: 98.4% car, 0.0% public transportation, 0.0% walk, 1.6% work from home; Mean travel time to work: 23.8 minutes

BOLIVAR (village). Covers a land area of 0.694 square miles and a water area of 0.006 square miles. Located at 40.65° N. Lat; 81.46° W. Long. Elevation is 928 feet.

History: Bolivar was an important grain market during the boom days of the Ohio & Erie and the Sandy & Beaver Canals. Near Bolivar was the site of the cabin built in 1761 by Christian Frederick Post, a Moravian missionary.

Population: 1,070; Growth (since 2000): 19.7%; Density: 1,541.3 persons per square mile; Race: 98.8% White, 0.0% Black/African American, 0.0% Asian, 0.0% American Indian/Alaska Native, 0.0% Native Hawaiian/Other Pacific Islander, 1.2% Two or more races, 0.0% Hispanic of any race; Average household size: 2.44; Median age: 44.3; Age under 18: 18.9%; Age 65 and over: 24.3%; Males per 100 females: 88.3; Marriage status: 22.0% never married, 51.9% now married, 1.0% separated, 13.0% widowed, 13.2% divorced; Foreign born: 2.9%; Speak English only: 99.7%; With disability: 12.4%; Veterans: 11.5%; Ancestry: 36.0% German, 16.7% Irish, 11.9% English, 9.7% Italian, 6.8% Scottish

Employment: 7.3% management, business, and financial, 2.8% computer, engineering, and science, 5.1% education, legal, community service, arts, and media, 10.9% healthcare practitioners, 21.2% service, 22.6% sales and office, 14.7% natural resources, construction, and maintenance, 15.4% production, transportation, and material moving

Income: Per capita: $28,434; Median household: $61,375; Average household: $70,546; Households with income of $100,000 or more: 16.3%; Poverty rate: 5.4%

Educational Attainment: High school diploma or higher: 90.1%; Bachelor's degree or higher: 17.5%; Graduate/professional degree or higher: 6.2%

School District(s)

Tuscarawas Valley Local (PK-12)
2015-16 Enrollment: 1,353 . . . . (330) 859-2213

Housing: Homeownership rate: 83.5%; Median home value: $112,500; Median year structure built: 1945; Homeowner vacancy rate: 2.1%; Median selected monthly owner costs: $876 with a mortgage, $425 without a mortgage; Median gross rent: $775 per month; Rental vacancy rate: 0.0%

Health Insurance: 95.7% have insurance; 84.2% have private insurance; 24.1% have public insurance; 4.3% do not have insurance; 2.0% of children under 18 do not have insurance

Transportation: Commute: 95.2% car, 0.0% public transportation, 3.6% walk, 0.8% work from home; Mean travel time to work: 27.5 minutes

DENNISON (village). Covers a land area of 1.349 square miles and a water area of 0 square miles. Located at 40.40° N. Lat; 81.33° W. Long. Elevation is 863 feet.

History: The site of Dennison was selected in 1864 by the Pittsburgh, Columbus & St. Louis Railroad for its division shops. The town was named for William Dennison, a Civil War governor of Ohio.

Population: 2,687; Growth (since 2000): -10.2%; Density: 1,991.9 persons per square mile; Race: 93.6% White, 2.2% Black/African American, 0.4% Asian, 0.0% American Indian/Alaska Native, 0.0% Native Hawaiian/Other Pacific Islander, 3.1% Two or more races, 0.9% Hispanic of any race; Average household size: 2.37; Median age: 32.9; Age under 18: 27.7%; Age 65 and over: 13.7%; Males per 100 females: 95.2; Marriage status: 29.4% never married, 49.7% now married, 4.7% separated, 8.3% widowed, 12.6% divorced; Foreign born: 1.3%; Speak English only: 97.9%; With disability: 15.3%; Veterans: 9.4%; Ancestry: 33.3% German, 16.3% Irish, 10.4% English, 6.1% American, 4.9% Italian

Employment: 8.7% management, business, and financial, 3.0% computer, engineering, and science, 5.3% education, legal, community service, arts, and media, 5.0% healthcare practitioners, 29.5% service, 17.7% sales and office, 6.2% natural resources, construction, and maintenance, 24.7% production, transportation, and material moving

Income: Per capita: $16,191; Median household: $28,917; Average household: $37,762; Households with income of $100,000 or more: 3.9%; Poverty rate: 30.0%

Educational Attainment: High school diploma or higher: 84.0%; Bachelor's degree or higher: 8.7%; Graduate/professional degree or higher: 1.4%

School District(s)

Claymont City (PK-12)
2015-16 Enrollment: 2,006 . . . . (740) 922-5478

Housing: Homeownership rate: 48.8%; Median home value: $70,600; Median year structure built: Before 1940; Homeowner vacancy rate: 4.5%; Median selected monthly owner costs: $799 with a mortgage, $318 without a mortgage; Median gross rent: $629 per month; Rental vacancy rate: 2.5%

Health Insurance: 88.9% have insurance; 53.6% have private insurance; 48.9% have public insurance; 11.1% do not have insurance; 0.0% of children under 18 do not have insurance

Hospitals: Trinity Hospital Twin City (25 beds)

Safety: Violent crime rate: 7.6 per 10,000 population; Property crime rate: 45.5 per 10,000 population

Transportation: Commute: 94.7% car, 0.0% public transportation, 1.1% walk, 3.1% work from home; Mean travel time to work: 23.2 minutes

DOVER (city). Covers a land area of 5.685 square miles and a water area of 0.103 square miles. Located at 40.53° N. Lat; 81.48° W. Long. Elevation is 892 feet.

History: Dover was laid out in 1807 on land owned by Jesse Slingluff and Christian Deardorff, and settled by German immigrants from Pennsylvania. For a time it was known as Canal Dover, and was the collector's port for the Ohio & Erie Canal in Tuscarawas County.

Population: 12,886; Growth (since 2000): 5.5%; Density: 2,266.7 persons per square mile; Race: 94.0% White, 1.6% Black/African American, 0.8% Asian, 0.0% American Indian/Alaska Native, 0.0% Native Hawaiian/Other Pacific Islander, 2.6% Two or more races, 7.6% Hispanic of any race; Average household size: 2.41; Median age: 43.2; Age under 18: 23.0%; Age 65 and over: 25.3%; Males per 100 females: 90.3; Marriage status: 22.4% never married, 51.5% now married, 1.3% separated, 11.3% widowed, 14.8% divorced; Foreign born: 4.6%; Speak English only: 92.7%; With disability: 16.9%; Veterans: 12.4%; Ancestry: 31.7% German, 11.6% Irish, 9.2% English, 9.0% American, 8.0% Italian

Employment: 8.3% management, business, and financial, 5.4% computer, engineering, and science, 8.7% education, legal, community service, arts, and media, 8.2% healthcare practitioners, 17.2% service, 25.5% sales and office, 6.5% natural resources, construction, and maintenance, 20.3% production, transportation, and material moving

Income: Per capita: $26,478; Median household: $47,451; Average household: $63,238; Households with income of $100,000 or more: 12.9%; Poverty rate: 12.0%

Educational Attainment: High school diploma or higher: 86.5%; Bachelor's degree or higher: 19.4%; Graduate/professional degree or higher: 6.3%

School District(s)

Dover City (PK-12)
2015-16 Enrollment: 2,766 . . . . (330) 364-1906

Housing: Homeownership rate: 67.2%; Median home value: $116,600; Median year structure built: 1961; Homeowner vacancy rate: 1.6%; Median selected monthly owner costs: $1,027 with a mortgage, $402 without a mortgage; Median gross rent: $741 per month; Rental vacancy rate: 6.8%

Health Insurance: 89.9% have insurance; 68.5% have private insurance; 42.1% have public insurance; 10.1% do not have insurance; 4.7% of children under 18 do not have insurance

Hospitals: Union Hospital (105 beds)

Safety: Violent crime rate: 9.3 per 10,000 population; Property crime rate: 74.4 per 10,000 population

Transportation: Commute: 93.1% car, 0.9% public transportation, 1.4% walk, 2.4% work from home; Mean travel time to work: 20.1 minutes

Additional Information Contacts

City of Dover . . . . (330) 343-6726
http://www.doverohio.com

DUNDEE (CDP). Covers a land area of 0.779 square miles and a water area of 0 square miles. Located at 40.59° N. Lat; 81.61° W. Long. Elevation is 1,030 feet.

Population: 415; Growth (since 2000): n/a; Density: 532.8 persons per square mile; Race: 100.0% White, 0.0% Black/African American, 0.0% Asian, 0.0% American Indian/Alaska Native, 0.0% Native Hawaiian/Other Pacific Islander, 0.0% Two or more races, 3.4% Hispanic of any race; Average household size: 3.37; Median age: 38.4; Age under 18: 20.7%; Age 65 and over: 1.7%; Males per 100 females: 98.0; Marriage status: 19.6% never married, 68.8% now married, 6.3% separated, 2.7% widowed, 8.9% divorced; Foreign born: 0.0%; Speak English only: 96.0%; With disability: 5.8%; Veterans: 2.1%; Ancestry: 34.5% German, 26.0% Irish, 18.8% English, 7.2% Scottish, 4.3% Swedish

Employment: 0.0% management, business, and financial, 6.1% computer, engineering, and science, 0.0% education, legal, community service, arts, and media, 2.9% healthcare practitioners, 27.9% service, 27.9% sales and

office, 11.1% natural resources, construction, and maintenance, 24.2% production, transportation, and material moving
Income: Per capita: $25,033; Median household: $69,402; Average household: $79,510; Households with income of $100,000 or more: 20.3%; Poverty rate: 1.7%
Educational Attainment: High school diploma or higher: 58.5%; Bachelor's degree or higher: n/a; Graduate/professional degree or higher: n/a

School District(s)

Beacon Hill Academy (07-12)
2015-16 Enrollment: 75. . . . . (330) 359-5600
Garaway Local (KG-12)
2015-16 Enrollment: 1,170 . . . . (330) 852-2421

Housing: Homeownership rate: 66.7%; Median home value: $110,700; Median year structure built: 1949; Homeowner vacancy rate: 0.0%; Median selected monthly owner costs: $667 with a mortgage, n/a without a mortgage; Median gross rent: $782 per month; Rental vacancy rate: 0.0%
Health Insurance: 90.4% have insurance; 50.6% have private insurance; 51.3% have public insurance; 9.6% do not have insurance; 0.0% of children under 18 do not have insurance
Transportation: Commute: 100.0% car, 0.0% public transportation, 0.0% walk, 0.0% work from home; Mean travel time to work: 16.4 minutes

GNADENHUTTEN (village). Covers a land area of 0.966 square miles and a water area of <.001 square miles. Located at 40.36° N. Lat; 81.43° W. Long. Elevation is 850 feet.
History: The name of Gnadenhutten is of German origin, meaning "tents of grace." A community was established here in 1772 by Joshua, a Mohican elder of a group of Indians from the Moravian mission founded by David Zeisberger at Schoenbrunn. The group was massacred by militiamen from Pennsylvania in 1782.
Population: 1,509; Growth (since 2000): 17.9%; Density: 1,562.4 persons per square mile; Race: 99.5% White, 0.1% Black/African American, 0.2% Asian, 0.1% American Indian/Alaska Native, 0.0% Native Hawaiian/Other Pacific Islander, 0.1% Two or more races, 0.0% Hispanic of any race; Average household size: 2.75; Median age: 36.4; Age under 18: 26.8%; Age 65 and over: 14.6%; Males per 100 females: 98.2; Marriage status: 22.5% never married, 58.3% now married, 0.7% separated, 6.9% widowed, 12.3% divorced; Foreign born: 0.2%; Speak English only: 99.2%; With disability: 12.1%; Veterans: 12.1%; Ancestry: 36.6% German, 18.8% Irish, 8.3% English, 4.6% Italian, 4.4% Scottish
Employment: 11.6% management, business, and financial, 2.4% computer, engineering, and science, 6.3% education, legal, community service, arts, and media, 8.7% healthcare practitioners, 19.9% service, 18.6% sales and office, 7.0% natural resources, construction, and maintenance, 25.5% production, transportation, and material moving
Income: Per capita: $21,227; Median household: $54,432; Average household: $57,233; Households with income of $100,000 or more: 13.7%; Poverty rate: 8.4%
Educational Attainment: High school diploma or higher: 93.8%; Bachelor's degree or higher: 16.2%; Graduate/professional degree or higher: 7.6%

School District(s)

Indian Valley Local (KG-12)
2015-16 Enrollment: 1,808 . . . . (740) 254-4334

Housing: Homeownership rate: 85.4%; Median home value: $104,200; Median year structure built: 1957; Homeowner vacancy rate: 5.7%; Median selected monthly owner costs: $968 with a mortgage, $385 without a mortgage; Median gross rent: $682 per month; Rental vacancy rate: 9.1%
Health Insurance: 90.2% have insurance; 74.5% have private insurance; 33.9% have public insurance; 9.8% do not have insurance; 8.9% of children under 18 do not have insurance
Transportation: Commute: 91.1% car, 0.2% public transportation, 3.2% walk, 5.1% work from home; Mean travel time to work: 22.9 minutes

MIDVALE (village). Covers a land area of 0.759 square miles and a water area of 0 square miles. Located at 40.44° N. Lat; 81.37° W. Long. Elevation is 856 feet.
Population: 837; Growth (since 2000): 53.0%; Density: 1,102.5 persons per square mile; Race: 95.6% White, 2.3% Black/African American, 0.0% Asian, 0.0% American Indian/Alaska Native, 0.0% Native Hawaiian/Other Pacific Islander, 0.7% Two or more races, 2.0% Hispanic of any race; Average household size: 2.87; Median age: 35.4; Age under 18: 25.0%; Age 65 and over: 6.3%; Males per 100 females: 98.9; Marriage status: 30.2% never married, 45.9% now married, 2.6% separated, 2.6% widowed, 21.3% divorced; Foreign born: 1.4%; Speak English only: 97.9%; With disability: 15.7%; Veterans: 5.6%; Ancestry: 22.2% German, 16.2% Irish, 8.4% English, 7.5% Italian, 3.6% Polish
Employment: 4.8% management, business, and financial, 0.0% computer, engineering, and science, 5.5% education, legal, community service, arts, and media, 1.7% healthcare practitioners, 22.4% service, 19.5% sales and office, 18.3% natural resources, construction, and maintenance, 27.9% production, transportation, and material moving
Income: Per capita: $20,081; Median household: $48,167; Average household: $56,437; Households with income of $100,000 or more: 16.1%; Poverty rate: 20.3%
Educational Attainment: High school diploma or higher: 86.1%; Bachelor's degree or higher: 7.7%; Graduate/professional degree or higher: 2.1%

School District(s)

Indian Valley Local (KG-12)
2015-16 Enrollment: 1,808 . . . . (740) 254-4334

Housing: Homeownership rate: 58.6%; Median home value: $85,200; Median year structure built: 1948; Homeowner vacancy rate: 0.0%; Median selected monthly owner costs: $1,003 with a mortgage, $312 without a mortgage; Median gross rent: $684 per month; Rental vacancy rate: 0.0%
Health Insurance: 87.5% have insurance; 60.0% have private insurance; 34.3% have public insurance; 12.5% do not have insurance; 0.0% of children under 18 do not have insurance
Transportation: Commute: 95.9% car, 0.0% public transportation, 1.5% walk, 2.7% work from home; Mean travel time to work: 18.8 minutes

MINERAL CITY (village). Covers a land area of 0.818 square miles and a water area of 0 square miles. Located at 40.60° N. Lat; 81.36° W. Long. Elevation is 951 feet.
Population: 632; Growth (since 2000): -24.9%; Density: 772.5 persons per square mile; Race: 94.8% White, 0.0% Black/African American, 2.4% Asian, 0.0% American Indian/Alaska Native, 0.0% Native Hawaiian/Other Pacific Islander, 2.4% Two or more races, 2.8% Hispanic of any race; Average household size: 2.34; Median age: 42.3; Age under 18: 15.7%; Age 65 and over: 10.8%; Males per 100 females: 92.3; Marriage status: 24.4% never married, 50.0% now married, 0.2% separated, 4.9% widowed, 20.7% divorced; Foreign born: 2.8%; Speak English only: 96.7%; With disability: 23.1%; Veterans: 8.3%; Ancestry: 36.6% German, 14.9% Irish, 9.8% Italian, 7.3% French, 3.0% Scottish
Employment: 19.5% management, business, and financial, 1.4% computer, engineering, and science, 10.4% education, legal, community service, arts, and media, 5.8% healthcare practitioners, 18.1% service, 20.3% sales and office, 8.5% natural resources, construction, and maintenance, 16.2% production, transportation, and material moving
Income: Per capita: $26,306; Median household: $51,719; Average household: $58,913; Households with income of $100,000 or more: 7.8%; Poverty rate: 14.9%
Educational Attainment: High school diploma or higher: 91.9%; Bachelor's degree or higher: 7.5%; Graduate/professional degree or higher: 3.5%

School District(s)

Tuscarawas Valley Local (PK-12)
2015-16 Enrollment: 1,353 . . . . (330) 859-2213

Housing: Homeownership rate: 80.4%; Median home value: $68,400; Median year structure built: 1947; Homeowner vacancy rate: 0.0%; Median selected monthly owner costs: $1,000 with a mortgage, $403 without a mortgage; Median gross rent: $659 per month; Rental vacancy rate: 8.6%
Health Insurance: 86.7% have insurance; 70.6% have private insurance; 27.4% have public insurance; 13.3% do not have insurance; 19.2% of children under 18 do not have insurance
Transportation: Commute: 89.0% car, 1.1% public transportation, 6.5% walk, 2.8% work from home; Mean travel time to work: 22.1 minutes

NEW PHILADELPHIA (city). County seat. Covers a land area of 8.216 square miles and a water area of 0.170 square miles. Located at 40.49° N. Lat; 81.44° W. Long. Elevation is 902 feet.
History: New Philadelphia was founded in 1804 by John Knisely, and settled by many Swiss-German immigrants from Pennsylvania.
Population: 17,412; Growth (since 2000): 2.1%; Density: 2,119.3 persons per square mile; Race: 94.1% White, 2.0% Black/African American, 0.7% Asian, 0.5% American Indian/Alaska Native, 0.0% Native Hawaiian/Other Pacific Islander, 2.4% Two or more races, 4.5% Hispanic of any race; Average household size: 2.43; Median age: 37.9; Age under 18: 22.6%; Age 65 and over: 16.9%; Males per 100 females: 94.1; Marriage status:

28.8% never married, 49.5% now married, 2.3% separated, 8.2% widowed, 13.6% divorced; Foreign born: 2.9%; Speak English only: 95.6%; With disability: 14.6%; Veterans: 9.5%; Ancestry: 27.0% German, 14.2% Irish, 10.0% Italian, 8.4% English, 6.6% American
Employment: 9.6% management, business, and financial, 2.5% computer, engineering, and science, 7.5% education, legal, community service, arts, and media, 6.4% healthcare practitioners, 19.8% service, 23.1% sales and office, 6.5% natural resources, construction, and maintenance, 24.7% production, transportation, and material moving
Income: Per capita: $23,217; Median household: $41,753; Average household: $55,617; Households with income of $100,000 or more: 14.1%; Poverty rate: 16.4%
Educational Attainment: High school diploma or higher: 86.8%; Bachelor's degree or higher: 17.7%; Graduate/professional degree or higher: 5.3%

School District(s)

Buckeye (07-12)
2015-16 Enrollment: n/a . . . . (330) 339-2288
New Philadelphia City (PK-12)
2015-16 Enrollment: 3,054 . . . . (330) 364-0600
Quaker Digital Academy (KG-12)
2015-16 Enrollment: 657 . . . . (330) 364-0618

Four-year College(s)

Kent State University at Tuscarawas (Public)
Fall 2016 Enrollment: 2,066 . . . . (330) 339-3391
2016-17 Tuition: In-state $5,664; Out-of-state $14,028

Vocational/Technical School(s)

Buckeye Joint Vocational School (Public)
Fall 2016 Enrollment: 117 . . . . (330) 308-5720
2016-17 Tuition: $6,075

Housing: Homeownership rate: 60.1%; Median home value: $107,300; Median year structure built: 1959; Homeowner vacancy rate: 1.4%; Median selected monthly owner costs: $1,037 with a mortgage, $377 without a mortgage; Median gross rent: $698 per month; Rental vacancy rate: 3.5%
Health Insurance: 89.4% have insurance; 62.3% have private insurance; 39.6% have public insurance; 10.6% do not have insurance; 5.3% of children under 18 do not have insurance
Safety: Violent crime rate: 1.7 per 10,000 population; Property crime rate: 107.3 per 10,000 population
Newspapers: Times Reporter (daily circulation 19,100)
Transportation: Commute: 93.4% car, 0.2% public transportation, 2.5% walk, 1.1% work from home; Mean travel time to work: 20.6 minutes
Additional Information Contacts
City of New Philadelphia . . . . (330) 364-4491
http://www.newphilaoh.com

NEWCOMERSTOWN (village). Covers a land area of 2.843 square miles and a water area of 0.097 square miles. Located at 40.28° N. Lat; 81.60° W. Long. Elevation is 801 feet.
History: First called Neighbor Town when it was settled in 1815 by the Neighbor brothers from New Jersey, the town became Newcomerstown in remembrance of Chief Eagle Feather who was called "the newcomer."
Population: 3,740; Growth (since 2000): -6.7%; Density: 1,315.7 persons per square mile; Race: 97.2% White, 0.4% Black/African American, 1.0% Asian, 0.0% American Indian/Alaska Native, 0.0% Native Hawaiian/Other Pacific Islander, 1.4% Two or more races, 3.1% Hispanic of any race; Average household size: 2.57; Median age: 39.4; Age under 18: 27.6%; Age 65 and over: 18.0%; Males per 100 females: 90.1; Marriage status: 20.5% never married, 53.3% now married, 2.4% separated, 6.0% widowed, 20.2% divorced; Foreign born: 1.4%; Speak English only: 97.4%; With disability: 18.0%; Veterans: 10.3%; Ancestry: 22.9% German, 14.6% Irish, 14.1% English, 11.9% American, 5.5% Scottish
Employment: 7.0% management, business, and financial, 2.4% computer, engineering, and science, 5.3% education, legal, community service, arts, and media, 10.0% healthcare practitioners, 16.2% service, 20.9% sales and office, 10.8% natural resources, construction, and maintenance, 27.3% production, transportation, and material moving
Income: Per capita: $17,333; Median household: $32,266; Average household: $43,614; Households with income of $100,000 or more: 5.3%; Poverty rate: 22.9%
Educational Attainment: High school diploma or higher: 84.9%; Bachelor's degree or higher: 9.3%; Graduate/professional degree or higher: 3.0%

School District(s)

Newcomerstown Exempted Village (PK-12)
2015-16 Enrollment: 997 . . . . (740) 498-8373

Housing: Homeownership rate: 60.5%; Median home value: $76,400; Median year structure built: 1954; Homeowner vacancy rate: 0.0%; Median selected monthly owner costs: $900 with a mortgage, $294 without a mortgage; Median gross rent: $700 per month; Rental vacancy rate: 7.4%
Health Insurance: 89.7% have insurance; 57.1% have private insurance; 50.7% have public insurance; 10.3% do not have insurance; 6.8% of children under 18 do not have insurance
Safety: Violent crime rate: 13.2 per 10,000 population; Property crime rate: 216.4 per 10,000 population
Newspapers: Newcomerstown News (weekly circulation 3,500)
Transportation: Commute: 98.3% car, 0.0% public transportation, 0.0% walk, 0.0% work from home; Mean travel time to work: 27.3 minutes

PARRAL (village). Covers a land area of 0.180 square miles and a water area of 0 square miles. Located at 40.56° N. Lat; 81.49° W. Long. Elevation is 906 feet.
Population: 244; Growth (since 2000): 1.2%; Density: 1,355.0 persons per square mile; Race: 100.0% White, 0.0% Black/African American, 0.0% Asian, 0.0% American Indian/Alaska Native, 0.0% Native Hawaiian/Other Pacific Islander, 0.0% Two or more races, 0.0% Hispanic of any race; Average household size: 2.05; Median age: 51.0; Age under 18: 11.9%; Age 65 and over: 29.9%; Males per 100 females: 107.6; Marriage status: 24.4% never married, 46.2% now married, 4.5% separated, 7.7% widowed, 21.7% divorced; Foreign born: 0.4%; Speak English only: 95.8%; With disability: 6.6%; Veterans: 15.8%; Ancestry: 37.3% German, 12.7% Irish, 9.0% Italian, 8.2% American, 7.8% Swiss
Employment: 0.8% management, business, and financial, 5.0% computer, engineering, and science, 3.4% education, legal, community service, arts, and media, 5.0% healthcare practitioners, 21.0% service, 26.1% sales and office, 12.6% natural resources, construction, and maintenance, 26.1% production, transportation, and material moving
Income: Per capita: $30,999; Median household: $38,906; Average household: $54,490; Households with income of $100,000 or more: 5.8%; Poverty rate: 18.4%
Educational Attainment: High school diploma or higher: 91.4%; Bachelor's degree or higher: 4.6%; Graduate/professional degree or higher: 1.0%
Housing: Homeownership rate: 76.5%; Median home value: $111,200; Median year structure built: 1956; Homeowner vacancy rate: 0.0%; Median selected monthly owner costs: $960 with a mortgage, $339 without a mortgage; Median gross rent: $500 per month; Rental vacancy rate: 0.0%
Health Insurance: 93.4% have insurance; 66.0% have private insurance; 48.4% have public insurance; 6.6% do not have insurance; 10.3% of children under 18 do not have insurance
Transportation: Commute: 98.3% car, 0.0% public transportation, 0.0% walk, 1.7% work from home; Mean travel time to work: 17.7 minutes

PORT WASHINGTON (village). Covers a land area of 0.514 square miles and a water area of 0 square miles. Located at 40.33° N. Lat; 81.52° W. Long. Elevation is 814 feet.
History: Port Washington was once a shipping center on the Ohio & Erie Canal. Nearby was the settlement of Salem, established in 1780 for members of the Lichtenau community.
Population: 519; Growth (since 2000): -6.0%; Density: 1,009.5 persons per square mile; Race: 99.6% White, 0.0% Black/African American, 0.0% Asian, 0.0% American Indian/Alaska Native, 0.0% Native Hawaiian/Other Pacific Islander, 0.4% Two or more races, 0.0% Hispanic of any race; Average household size: 2.62; Median age: 39.7; Age under 18: 23.7%; Age 65 and over: 16.4%; Males per 100 females: 94.9; Marriage status: 18.3% never married, 65.1% now married, 2.1% separated, 7.1% widowed, 9.5% divorced; Foreign born: 0.6%; Speak English only: 97.5%; With disability: 19.7%; Veterans: 13.1%; Ancestry: 20.6% German, 12.9% Irish, 12.3% English, 8.3% Welsh, 6.9% Scottish
Employment: 3.7% management, business, and financial, 2.3% computer, engineering, and science, 6.5% education, legal, community service, arts, and media, 3.7% healthcare practitioners, 17.6% service, 21.8% sales and office, 8.8% natural resources, construction, and maintenance, 35.6% production, transportation, and material moving
Income: Per capita: $17,621; Median household: $40,000; Average household: $45,461; Households with income of $100,000 or more: 3.0%; Poverty rate: 18.1%

Educational Attainment: High school diploma or higher: 81.5%; Bachelor's degree or higher: 6.5%; Graduate/professional degree or higher: 2.8%

School District(s)

Indian Valley Local (KG-12)
2015-16 Enrollment: 1,808 . . . . (740) 254-4334

Housing: Homeownership rate: 79.8%; Median home value: $86,700; Median year structure built: 1947; Homeowner vacancy rate: 3.1%; Median selected monthly owner costs: $983 with a mortgage, $346 without a mortgage; Median gross rent: $675 per month; Rental vacancy rate: 0.0%
Health Insurance: 91.7% have insurance; 69.0% have private insurance; 35.3% have public insurance; 8.3% do not have insurance; 3.3% of children under 18 do not have insurance
Transportation: Commute: 97.2% car, 0.0% public transportation, 0.9% walk, 0.5% work from home; Mean travel time to work: 24.7 minutes

ROSWELL (village). Covers a land area of 0.262 square miles and a water area of 0 square miles. Located at 40.48° N. Lat; 81.35° W. Long. Elevation is 948 feet.
Population: 235; Growth (since 2000): -14.9%; Density: 897.0 persons per square mile; Race: 96.2% White, 0.0% Black/African American, 0.0% Asian, 0.0% American Indian/Alaska Native, 0.0% Native Hawaiian/Other Pacific Islander, 3.8% Two or more races, 2.6% Hispanic of any race; Average household size: 2.37; Median age: 44.7; Age under 18: 21.3%; Age 65 and over: 8.9%; Males per 100 females: 90.4; Marriage status: 21.1% never married, 44.8% now married, 3.1% separated, 11.3% widowed, 22.7% divorced; Foreign born: 0.0%; Speak English only: 100.0%; With disability: 16.6%; Veterans: 9.7%; Ancestry: 27.2% German, 14.5% English, 11.1% Irish, 7.2% Italian, 6.0% Welsh
Employment: 6.4% management, business, and financial, 0.0% computer, engineering, and science, 0.0% education, legal, community service, arts, and media, 0.0% healthcare practitioners, 17.6% service, 16.8% sales and office, 19.2% natural resources, construction, and maintenance, 40.0% production, transportation, and material moving
Income: Per capita: $19,973; Median household: $38,250; Average household: $47,533; Households with income of $100,000 or more: 6.0%; Poverty rate: 16.2%
Educational Attainment: High school diploma or higher: 79.9%; Bachelor's degree or higher: 7.7%; Graduate/professional degree or higher: n/a
Housing: Homeownership rate: 75.8%; Median home value: $71,300; Median year structure built: Before 1940; Homeowner vacancy rate: 0.0%; Median selected monthly owner costs: $850 with a mortgage, $375 without a mortgage; Median gross rent: $675 per month; Rental vacancy rate: 7.7%
Health Insurance: 87.2% have insurance; 55.3% have private insurance; 44.7% have public insurance; 12.8% do not have insurance; 0.0% of children under 18 do not have insurance
Transportation: Commute: 93.6% car, 0.0% public transportation, 4.0% walk, 0.0% work from home; Mean travel time to work: 21.9 minutes

SANDYVILLE (CDP). Covers a land area of 0.628 square miles and a water area of 0 square miles. Located at 40.65° N. Lat; 81.37° W. Long. Elevation is 965 feet.
Population: 298; Growth (since 2000): n/a; Density: 474.6 persons per square mile; Race: 100.0% White, 0.0% Black/African American, 0.0% Asian, 0.0% American Indian/Alaska Native, 0.0% Native Hawaiian/Other Pacific Islander, 0.0% Two or more races, 0.0% Hispanic of any race; Average household size: 2.38; Median age: 35.9; Age under 18: 27.5%; Age 65 and over: 22.1%; Males per 100 females: 95.7; Marriage status: 18.1% never married, 66.2% now married, 17.6% separated, 6.0% widowed, 9.7% divorced; Foreign born: 0.0%; Speak English only: 100.0%; With disability: 4.4%; Veterans: 0.0%; Ancestry: 17.4% German, 16.4% Italian, 13.4% Irish, 9.1% Scottish, 3.7% Dutch
Employment: 9.0% management, business, and financial, 0.0% computer, engineering, and science, 0.0% education, legal, community service, arts, and media, 0.0% healthcare practitioners, 10.8% service, 70.3% sales and office, 9.9% natural resources, construction, and maintenance, 0.0% production, transportation, and material moving
Income: Per capita: $16,638; Median household: $40,083; Average household: $39,223; Households with income of $100,000 or more: n/a; Poverty rate: 23.1%
Educational Attainment: High school diploma or higher: 51.9%; Bachelor's degree or higher: 11.6%; Graduate/professional degree or higher: 5.1%
Housing: Homeownership rate: 68.8%; Median home value: $74,000; Median year structure built: 1967; Homeowner vacancy rate: 0.0%; Median selected monthly owner costs: $1,298 with a mortgage, $263 without a mortgage; Median gross rent: n/a per month; Rental vacancy rate: 0.0%
Health Insurance: 86.9% have insurance; 65.8% have private insurance; 30.9% have public insurance; 13.1% do not have insurance; 0.0% of children under 18 do not have insurance
Transportation: Commute: 100.0% car, 0.0% public transportation, 0.0% walk, 0.0% work from home; Mean travel time to work: 33.4 minutes

SOMERDALE (unincorporated postal area)
ZCTA: 44678
Covers a land area of 0.931 square miles and a water area of 0 square miles. Located at 40.57° N. Lat; 81.35° W. Long. Elevation is 915 feet.
Population: 105; Growth (since 2000): -50.7%; Density: 112.7 persons per square mile; Race: 100.0% White, 0.0% Black/African American, 0.0% Asian, 0.0% American Indian/Alaska Native, 0.0% Native Hawaiian/Other Pacific Islander, 0.0% Two or more races, 0.0% Hispanic of any race; Average household size: 2.02; Median age: 55.6; Age under 18: 0.0%; Age 65 and over: 28.6%; Males per 100 females: 94.9; Marriage status: 0.0% never married, 100.0% now married, 0.0% separated, 0.0% widowed, 0.0% divorced; Foreign born: 0.0%; Speak English only: 100.0%; With disability: 10.5%; Veterans: 28.6%; Ancestry: 58.1% Irish, 10.5% German
Employment: 0.0% management, business, and financial, 0.0% computer, engineering, and science, 0.0% education, legal, community service, arts, and media, 0.0% healthcare practitioners, 20.8% service, 58.5% sales and office, 0.0% natural resources, construction, and maintenance, 20.8% production, transportation, and material moving
Income: Per capita: $38,812; Median household: $102,833; Average household: $76,871; Households with income of $100,000 or more: 57.7%; Poverty rate: 21.0%
Educational Attainment: High school diploma or higher: 89.5%; Bachelor's degree or higher: n/a; Graduate/professional degree or higher: n/a
Housing: Homeownership rate: 78.8%; Median home value: n/a; Median year structure built: 1965; Homeowner vacancy rate: 0.0%; Median selected monthly owner costs: $0 with a mortgage, $0 without a mortgage; Median gross rent: n/a per month; Rental vacancy rate: 0.0%
Health Insurance: 100.0% have insurance; 61.0% have private insurance; 49.5% have public insurance; 0.0% do not have insurance; 0.0% of children under 18 do not have insurance
Transportation: Commute: 100.0% car, 0.0% public transportation, 0.0% walk, 0.0% work from home; Mean travel time to work: 0.0 minutes

STONE CREEK (village). Covers a land area of 0.429 square miles and a water area of <.001 square miles. Located at 40.40° N. Lat; 81.56° W. Long. Elevation is 938 feet.
History: Stone Creek was laid out in 1854 by Phillip Leonard, and first called Phillipsburg. Settlers had come here as early as 1837 from Pennsylvania. The town grew around the iron ore mined in the area, and the clay used in brick plants. Early Swiss settlers also started a Swiss cheese industry.
Population: 170; Growth (since 2000): -7.6%; Density: 396.4 persons per square mile; Race: 100.0% White, 0.0% Black/African American, 0.0% Asian, 0.0% American Indian/Alaska Native, 0.0% Native Hawaiian/Other Pacific Islander, 0.0% Two or more races, 0.0% Hispanic of any race; Average household size: 2.50; Median age: 30.0; Age under 18: 27.1%; Age 65 and over: 10.6%; Males per 100 females: 113.3; Marriage status: 28.3% never married, 46.5% now married, 6.3% separated, 3.1% widowed, 22.0% divorced; Foreign born: 0.0%; Speak English only: 100.0%; With disability: 4.1%; Veterans: 6.5%; Ancestry: 51.2% German, 12.4% Irish, 11.8% Dutch, 11.2% English, 5.3% Scottish
Employment: 7.7% management, business, and financial, 0.0% computer, engineering, and science, 1.1% education, legal, community service, arts, and media, 8.8% healthcare practitioners, 22.0% service, 22.0% sales and office, 17.6% natural resources, construction, and maintenance, 20.9% production, transportation, and material moving
Income: Per capita: $23,538; Median household: $53,214; Average household: $57,021; Households with income of $100,000 or more: 4.4%; Poverty rate: 3.3%
Educational Attainment: High school diploma or higher: 91.4%; Bachelor's degree or higher: 8.6%; Graduate/professional degree or higher: n/a
Housing: Homeownership rate: 77.9%; Median home value: $78,900; Median year structure built: 1941; Homeowner vacancy rate: 7.0%; Median

selected monthly owner costs: $795 with a mortgage, $417 without a mortgage; Median gross rent: $1,063 per month; Rental vacancy rate: 0.0%
Health Insurance: 90.6% have insurance; 72.4% have private insurance; 29.4% have public insurance; 9.4% do not have insurance; 4.3% of children under 18 do not have insurance
Transportation: Commute: 98.9% car, 0.0% public transportation, 1.1% walk, 0.0% work from home; Mean travel time to work: 23.5 minutes

STRASBURG (village). Covers a land area of 1.388 square miles and a water area of 0 square miles. Located at 40.60° N. Lat; 81.53° W. Long. Elevation is 912 feet.
History: Strasburg was notable as the location of the Garver Brothers Store, founded in 1866 by Phillip A. Garver. When his sons, Rudolph and Albert, took over the store in the 1880's, they made it the focal point of the community by keeping a card index record of every man, woman, and child living within 18 miles of Strasburg, and anticipating their needs.
Population: 3,007; Growth (since 2000): 30.2%; Density: 2,166.4 persons per square mile; Race: 100.0% White, 0.0% Black/African American, 0.0% Asian, 0.0% American Indian/Alaska Native, 0.0% Native Hawaiian/Other Pacific Islander, 0.0% Two or more races, 0.0% Hispanic of any race; Average household size: 2.33; Median age: 49.7; Age under 18: 18.7%; Age 65 and over: 25.2%; Males per 100 females: 94.8; Marriage status: 21.2% never married, 61.8% now married, 0.3% separated, 6.1% widowed, 10.9% divorced; Foreign born: 0.7%; Speak English only: 97.1%; With disability: 16.4%; Veterans: 11.1%; Ancestry: 33.6% German, 13.0% Irish, 12.3% English, 7.9% Italian, 6.5% Swiss
Employment: 8.5% management, business, and financial, 1.5% computer, engineering, and science, 9.9% education, legal, community service, arts, and media, 2.9% healthcare practitioners, 13.6% service, 27.4% sales and office, 9.5% natural resources, construction, and maintenance, 26.9% production, transportation, and material moving
Income: Per capita: $26,597; Median household: $51,369; Average household: $61,531; Households with income of $100,000 or more: 14.2%; Poverty rate: 13.0%
Educational Attainment: High school diploma or higher: 92.2%; Bachelor's degree or higher: 16.3%; Graduate/professional degree or higher: 5.9%

School District(s)

Strasburg-Franklin Local (KG-12)
2015-16 Enrollment: 577. . . . . (330) 878-5571
Housing: Homeownership rate: 65.4%; Median home value: $136,200; Median year structure built: 1974; Homeowner vacancy rate: 2.5%; Median selected monthly owner costs: $999 with a mortgage, $462 without a mortgage; Median gross rent: $771 per month; Rental vacancy rate: 0.0%
Health Insurance: 95.4% have insurance; 74.7% have private insurance; 38.6% have public insurance; 4.6% do not have insurance; 0.0% of children under 18 do not have insurance
Safety: Violent crime rate: 0.0 per 10,000 population; Property crime rate: 78.0 per 10,000 population
Transportation: Commute: 93.6% car, 0.0% public transportation, 3.5% walk, 2.9% work from home; Mean travel time to work: 22.1 minutes

SUGARCREEK (village). Covers a land area of 3.790 square miles and a water area of 0 square miles. Located at 40.51° N. Lat; 81.64° W. Long. Elevation is 1,001 feet.
Population: 2,327; Growth (since 2000): 7.0%; Density: 614.0 persons per square mile; Race: 98.7% White, 0.0% Black/African American, 0.6% Asian, 0.0% American Indian/Alaska Native, 0.0% Native Hawaiian/Other Pacific Islander, 0.7% Two or more races, 0.0% Hispanic of any race; Average household size: 2.42; Median age: 38.0; Age under 18: 22.9%; Age 65 and over: 19.1%; Males per 100 females: 98.4; Marriage status: 19.8% never married, 62.4% now married, 0.3% separated, 9.2% widowed, 8.6% divorced; Foreign born: 0.5%; Speak English only: 82.3%; With disability: 10.9%; Veterans: 5.4%; Ancestry: 44.8% German, 19.0% Swiss, 8.3% Irish, 6.8% American, 6.3% English
Employment: 11.9% management, business, and financial, 2.7% computer, engineering, and science, 9.3% education, legal, community service, arts, and media, 3.8% healthcare practitioners, 15.8% service, 25.4% sales and office, 10.0% natural resources, construction, and maintenance, 21.1% production, transportation, and material moving
Income: Per capita: $25,992; Median household: $50,776; Average household: $61,415; Households with income of $100,000 or more: 16.7%; Poverty rate: 2.8%
Educational Attainment: High school diploma or higher: 80.3%; Bachelor's degree or higher: 15.1%; Graduate/professional degree or higher: 3.6%

School District(s)

Garaway Local (KG-12)
2015-16 Enrollment: 1,170 . . . . (330) 852-2421
Housing: Homeownership rate: 73.5%; Median home value: $124,700; Median year structure built: 1967; Homeowner vacancy rate: 0.0%; Median selected monthly owner costs: $1,048 with a mortgage, $314 without a mortgage; Median gross rent: $810 per month; Rental vacancy rate: 0.0%
Health Insurance: 86.6% have insurance; 71.3% have private insurance; 31.0% have public insurance; 13.4% do not have insurance; 15.4% of children under 18 do not have insurance
Newspapers: The Budget (weekly circulation 19,500)
Transportation: Commute: 93.1% car, 0.0% public transportation, 2.9% walk, 2.2% work from home; Mean travel time to work: 16.6 minutes

TUSCARAWAS (village). Covers a land area of 0.711 square miles and a water area of 0.025 square miles. Located at 40.39° N. Lat; 81.40° W. Long. Elevation is 846 feet.
Population: 1,291; Growth (since 2000): 38.2%; Density: 1,815.0 persons per square mile; Race: 97.8% White, 0.0% Black/African American, 0.0% Asian, 0.5% American Indian/Alaska Native, 0.0% Native Hawaiian/Other Pacific Islander, 1.8% Two or more races, 0.0% Hispanic of any race; Average household size: 2.29; Median age: 43.1; Age under 18: 21.5%; Age 65 and over: 13.9%; Males per 100 females: 99.2; Marriage status: 23.9% never married, 57.3% now married, 2.0% separated, 8.0% widowed, 10.8% divorced; Foreign born: 0.0%; Speak English only: 98.6%; With disability: 15.3%; Veterans: 6.1%; Ancestry: 22.4% German, 12.6% Irish, 9.4% Italian, 5.1% English, 3.9% American
Employment: 10.2% management, business, and financial, 2.0% computer, engineering, and science, 3.1% education, legal, community service, arts, and media, 4.3% healthcare practitioners, 25.7% service, 17.1% sales and office, 14.0% natural resources, construction, and maintenance, 23.6% production, transportation, and material moving
Income: Per capita: $26,420; Median household: $47,292; Average household: $58,769; Households with income of $100,000 or more: 9.4%; Poverty rate: 16.7%
Educational Attainment: High school diploma or higher: 90.2%; Bachelor's degree or higher: 10.3%; Graduate/professional degree or higher: 1.2%

School District(s)

Indian Valley Local (KG-12)
2015-16 Enrollment: 1,808 . . . . (740) 254-4334
Housing: Homeownership rate: 68.2%; Median home value: $94,100; Median year structure built: 1974; Homeowner vacancy rate: 0.0%; Median selected monthly owner costs: $926 with a mortgage, $399 without a mortgage; Median gross rent: $458 per month; Rental vacancy rate: 0.0%
Health Insurance: 93.8% have insurance; 71.3% have private insurance; 35.9% have public insurance; 6.2% do not have insurance; 1.8% of children under 18 do not have insurance
Transportation: Commute: 98.6% car, 0.0% public transportation, 0.0% walk, 0.0% work from home; Mean travel time to work: 21.7 minutes

UHRICHSVILLE (city). Covers a land area of 2.811 square miles and a water area of 0.003 square miles. Located at 40.40° N. Lat; 81.35° W. Long. Elevation is 869 feet.
History: Uhrichsville was settled in 1804 by Michael Uhrich of Pennsylvania, who purchased land in the area and built a flour mill. The town was platted in 1833 and became a center for the manufacture of vitrified clay products.
Population: 5,399; Growth (since 2000): -4.6%; Density: 1,920.9 persons per square mile; Race: 97.1% White, 0.9% Black/African American, 0.1% Asian, 0.7% American Indian/Alaska Native, 0.0% Native Hawaiian/Other Pacific Islander, 1.2% Two or more races, 0.4% Hispanic of any race; Average household size: 2.43; Median age: 37.2; Age under 18: 23.7%; Age 65 and over: 15.9%; Males per 100 females: 89.8; Marriage status: 27.3% never married, 44.8% now married, 0.9% separated, 10.5% widowed, 17.3% divorced; Foreign born: 0.4%; Speak English only: 99.5%; With disability: 18.3%; Veterans: 10.3%; Ancestry: 23.5% German, 20.4% Irish, 14.0% Italian, 7.7% American, 5.8% English
Employment: 4.4% management, business, and financial, 1.5% computer, engineering, and science, 7.7% education, legal, community service, arts, and media, 5.1% healthcare practitioners, 23.9% service, 23.6% sales and

office, 6.9% natural resources, construction, and maintenance, 27.0% production, transportation, and material moving
Income: Per capita: $17,412; Median household: $32,663; Average household: $41,566; Households with income of $100,000 or more: 5.4%; Poverty rate: 30.7%
Educational Attainment: High school diploma or higher: 79.8%; Bachelor's degree or higher: 5.4%; Graduate/professional degree or higher: 1.7%

School District(s)

Claymont City (PK-12)
2015-16 Enrollment: 2,006 . . . . (740) 922-5478
Housing: Homeownership rate: 55.9%; Median home value: $68,800; Median year structure built: 1948; Homeowner vacancy rate: 2.0%; Median selected monthly owner costs: $827 with a mortgage, $364 without a mortgage; Median gross rent: $625 per month; Rental vacancy rate: 3.4%
Health Insurance: 90.2% have insurance; 48.1% have private insurance; 52.8% have public insurance; 9.8% do not have insurance; 6.4% of children under 18 do not have insurance
Safety: Violent crime rate: 5.6 per 10,000 population; Property crime rate: 83.3 per 10,000 population
Transportation: Commute: 91.7% car, 0.7% public transportation, 4.2% walk, 3.0% work from home; Mean travel time to work: 20.3 minutes

ZOAR (village). Covers a land area of 0.583 square miles and a water area of 0.090 square miles. Located at 40.61° N. Lat; 81.42° W. Long. Elevation is 906 feet.
History: Named for the biblical city to which Lot fled after leaving Sodom, Zoar was settled in 1817 by a group of Separatists from southern Germany who came seeking religious freedom. They established a communal corporation, chartered in 1832 as the Separatist Society of Zoar, which prospered for 80 years.
Population: 195; Growth (since 2000): 1.0%; Density: 334.6 persons per square mile; Race: 95.9% White, 0.5% Black/African American, 0.0% Asian, 0.0% American Indian/Alaska Native, 0.0% Native Hawaiian/Other Pacific Islander, 3.1% Two or more races, 0.0% Hispanic of any race; Average household size: 1.97; Median age: 56.2; Age under 18: 8.2%; Age 65 and over: 34.4%; Males per 100 females: 108.6; Marriage status: 22.2% never married, 62.2% now married, 2.2% separated, 10.8% widowed, 4.9% divorced; Foreign born: 0.5%; Speak English only: 98.9%; With disability: 20.0%; Veterans: 10.1%; Ancestry: 53.3% German, 24.1% Irish, 17.9% English, 7.2% Italian, 4.1% Scottish
Employment: 22.8% management, business, and financial, 2.0% computer, engineering, and science, 25.7% education, legal, community service, arts, and media, 6.9% healthcare practitioners, 14.9% service, 14.9% sales and office, 2.0% natural resources, construction, and maintenance, 10.9% production, transportation, and material moving
Income: Per capita: $35,639; Median household: $61,875; Average household: $68,912; Households with income of $100,000 or more: 26.2%; Poverty rate: 5.1%
Educational Attainment: High school diploma or higher: 97.7%; Bachelor's degree or higher: 40.0%; Graduate/professional degree or higher: 13.7%

School District(s)

Tuscarawas Valley Local (PK-12)
2015-16 Enrollment: 1,353 . . . . (330) 859-2213
Housing: Homeownership rate: 83.8%; Median home value: $215,600; Median year structure built: 1952; Homeowner vacancy rate: 0.0%; Median selected monthly owner costs: $1,696 with a mortgage, $433 without a mortgage; Median gross rent: $660 per month; Rental vacancy rate: 11.1%
Health Insurance: 95.4% have insurance; 87.7% have private insurance; 40.5% have public insurance; 4.6% do not have insurance; 0.0% of children under 18 do not have insurance
Transportation: Commute: 84.7% car, 1.0% public transportation, 3.1% walk, 10.2% work from home; Mean travel time to work: 25.5 minutes

Union County

Located in central Ohio; drained by Darby Creek. Covers a land area of 431.730 square miles, a water area of 5.142 square miles, and is located in the Eastern Time Zone at 40.30° N. Lat., 83.37° W. Long. The county was founded in 1820. County seat is Marysville.

Union County is part of the Columbus, OH Metropolitan Statistical Area. The entire metro area includes: Delaware County, OH; Fairfield County, OH; Franklin County, OH; Hocking County, OH; Licking County, OH; Madison County, OH; Morrow County, OH; Perry County, OH; Pickaway County, OH; Union County, OH

Weather Station: Marysville — Elevation: 1,000 feet

	Jan	Feb	Mar	Apr	May	Jun	Jul	Aug	Sep	Oct	Nov	Dec
High	34	39	49	62	72	81	84	83	76	64	51	38
Low	20	22	30	40	50	59	64	62	54	43	34	24
Precip	2.4	2.0	2.7	3.3	4.4	4.3	4.3	3.3	2.9	2.6	3.0	2.8
Snow	6.2	4.6	3.8	0.4	0.0	0.0	0.0	0.0	0.0	0.1	0.9	4.5

High and Low temperatures in degrees Fahrenheit; Precipitation and Snow in inches

Population: 53,955; Growth (since 2000): 31.9%; Density: 125.0 persons per square mile; Race: 92.0% White, 2.4% Black/African American, 2.9% Asian, 0.3% American Indian/Alaska Native, 0.0% Native Hawaiian/Other Pacific Islander, 2.0% two or more races, 1.5% Hispanic of any race; Average household size: 2.70; Median age: 38.2; Age under 18: 25.5%; Age 65 and over: 11.2%; Males per 100 females: 89.5; Marriage status: 26.2% never married, 57.3% now married, 1.5% separated, 4.8% widowed, 11.8% divorced; Foreign born: 3.3%; Speak English only: 95.6%; With disability: 11.4%; Veterans: 8.2%; Ancestry: 31.2% German, 15.0% Irish, 11.2% English, 10.7% American, 4.1% Italian
Religion: Six largest groups: 9.7% Methodist/Pietist, 6.3% Lutheran, 4.8% Catholicism, 4.4% Baptist, 1.6% Pentecostal, 1.3% Presbyterian-Reformed
Economy: Unemployment rate: 3.3%; Leading industries: 12.6 % retail trade; 11.9 % other services (except public administration); 10.2 % construction; Farms: 995 totaling 241,935 acres; Company size: 4 employ 1,000 or more persons, 3 employ 500 to 999 persons, 30 employ 100 to 499 persons, 968 employ less than 100 persons; Business ownership: 1,247 women-owned, n/a Black-owned, n/a Hispanic-owned, 63 Asian-owned, n/a American Indian/Alaska Native-owned
Employment: 16.2% management, business, and financial, 8.0% computer, engineering, and science, 7.9% education, legal, community service, arts, and media, 6.0% healthcare practitioners, 15.1% service, 20.7% sales and office, 8.2% natural resources, construction, and maintenance, 17.9% production, transportation, and material moving
Income: Per capita: $30,431; Median household: $71,282; Average household: $85,950; Households with income of $100,000 or more: 33.4%; Poverty rate: 7.9%
Educational Attainment: High school diploma or higher: 91.9%; Bachelor's degree or higher: 29.1%; Graduate/professional degree or higher: 9.1%
Housing: Homeownership rate: 77.5%; Median home value: $174,300; Median year structure built: 1988; Homeowner vacancy rate: 1.3%; Median selected monthly owner costs: $1,501 with a mortgage, $514 without a mortgage; Median gross rent: $830 per month; Rental vacancy rate: 2.7%
Vital Statistics: Birth rate: 114.1 per 10,000 population; Death rate: 62.4 per 10,000 population; Age-adjusted cancer mortality rate: 175.2 deaths per 100,000 population
Health Insurance: 93.6% have insurance; 79.7% have private insurance; 24.7% have public insurance; 6.4% do not have insurance; 3.3% of children under 18 do not have insurance
Health Care: Physicians: 8.1 per 10,000 population; Dentists: 4.5 per 10,000 population; Hospital beds: 13.8 per 10,000 population; Hospital admissions: 371.1 per 10,000 population
Transportation: Commute: 92.4% car, 0.6% public transportation, 0.7% walk, 5.8% work from home; Mean travel time to work: 24.7 minutes
2016 Presidential Election: 65.3% Trump, 27.9% Clinton, 4.0% Johnson, 0.7% Stein
National and State Parks: Milford Center Prairie State Nature Preserve
Additional Information Contacts
Union Government . . . . (937) 645-3012
http://www.co.union.oh.us

Union County Communities

MAGNETIC SPRINGS (village). Covers a land area of 0.231 square miles and a water area of 0.005 square miles. Located at 40.35° N. Lat; 83.26° W. Long. Elevation is 932 feet.
Population: 263; Growth (since 2000): -18.6%; Density: 1,137.0 persons per square mile; Race: 98.1% White, 1.9% Black/African American, 0.0% Asian, 0.0% American Indian/Alaska Native, 0.0% Native Hawaiian/Other Pacific Islander, 0.0% Two or more races, 0.0% Hispanic of any race; Average household size: 2.41; Median age: 42.5; Age under 18: 24.7%; Age 65 and over: 11.4%; Males per 100 females: 107.8; Marriage status: 30.2% never married, 52.5% now married, 4.5% separated, 5.4% widowed, 11.9% divorced; Foreign born: 0.0%; Speak English only:

100.0%; With disability: 19.8%; Veterans: 13.1%; Ancestry: 31.6% German, 15.2% American, 11.8% English, 10.3% Irish, 9.5% French
Employment: 3.7% management, business, and financial, 0.9% computer, engineering, and science, 7.5% education, legal, community service, arts, and media, 2.8% healthcare practitioners, 27.1% service, 26.2% sales and office, 3.7% natural resources, construction, and maintenance, 28.0% production, transportation, and material moving
Income: Per capita: $17,860; Median household: $39,375; Average household: $44,373; Households with income of $100,000 or more: 6.4%; Poverty rate: 23.0%
Educational Attainment: High school diploma or higher: 81.8%; Bachelor's degree or higher: 7.5%; Graduate/professional degree or higher: n/a
Housing: Homeownership rate: 54.1%; Median home value: $82,500; Median year structure built: Before 1940; Homeowner vacancy rate: 1.7%; Median selected monthly owner costs: $914 with a mortgage, $375 without a mortgage; Median gross rent: $654 per month; Rental vacancy rate: 2.0%
Health Insurance: 93.2% have insurance; 54.8% have private insurance; 50.2% have public insurance; 6.8% do not have insurance; 3.1% of children under 18 do not have insurance
Transportation: Commute: 100.0% car, 0.0% public transportation, 0.0% walk, 0.0% work from home; Mean travel time to work: 24.8 minutes

MARYSVILLE (city). County seat. Covers a land area of 16.271 square miles and a water area of 0.291 square miles. Located at 40.23° N. Lat; 83.36° W. Long. Elevation is 994 feet.
History: Marysville was settled in 1816 by Jonathan Summers, and platted in 1820 by Samuel Culbertson, who named the town for his daughter. The log cabin that became a symbol of William Henry Harrison's presidential campaign of 1840 came from Marysville.
Population: 22,860; Growth (since 2000): 43.4%; Density: 1,404.9 persons per square mile; Race: 89.6% White, 3.7% Black/African American, 2.9% Asian, 0.1% American Indian/Alaska Native, 0.0% Native Hawaiian/Other Pacific Islander, 3.1% Two or more races, 1.7% Hispanic of any race; Average household size: 2.59; Median age: 34.8; Age under 18: 24.7%; Age 65 and over: 9.8%; Males per 100 females: 74.9; Marriage status: 31.5% never married, 48.7% now married, 2.1% separated, 5.5% widowed, 14.2% divorced; Foreign born: 3.6%; Speak English only: 96.6%; With disability: 12.2%; Veterans: 8.3%; Ancestry: 29.8% German, 16.4% Irish, 10.8% American, 9.0% English, 4.5% Italian
Employment: 15.8% management, business, and financial, 9.5% computer, engineering, and science, 7.6% education, legal, community service, arts, and media, 4.9% healthcare practitioners, 17.5% service, 21.2% sales and office, 7.4% natural resources, construction, and maintenance, 16.0% production, transportation, and material moving
Income: Per capita: $25,419; Median household: $62,371; Average household: $74,249; Households with income of $100,000 or more: 28.3%; Poverty rate: 9.3%
Educational Attainment: High school diploma or higher: 89.2%; Bachelor's degree or higher: 27.2%; Graduate/professional degree or higher: 7.8%

School District(s)

Marysville Exempted Village (PK-12)
2015-16 Enrollment: 5,286 . . . . (937) 644-8105
Housing: Homeownership rate: 63.0%; Median home value: $166,200; Median year structure built: 1992; Homeowner vacancy rate: 0.7%; Median selected monthly owner costs: $1,468 with a mortgage, $478 without a mortgage; Median gross rent: $855 per month; Rental vacancy rate: 4.1%
Health Insurance: 94.2% have insurance; 79.8% have private insurance; 24.8% have public insurance; 5.8% do not have insurance; 2.1% of children under 18 do not have insurance
Hospitals: Memorial Hospital of Union County (82 beds)
Safety: Violent crime rate: 3.1 per 10,000 population; Property crime rate: 62.7 per 10,000 population
Newspapers: Marysville Journal-Tribune (daily circulation 6,000)
Transportation: Commute: 93.3% car, 1.5% public transportation, 0.7% walk, 3.9% work from home; Mean travel time to work: 21.7 minutes
Airports: Union County (general aviation)
Additional Information Contacts
City of Marysville . . . . (937) 642-6015
http://www.marysvilleohio.org

MILFORD CENTER (village). Covers a land area of 0.409 square miles and a water area of 0.014 square miles. Located at 40.18° N. Lat; 83.44° W. Long. Elevation is 997 feet.
Population: 947; Growth (since 2000): 51.3%; Density: 2,316.5 persons per square mile; Race: 98.1% White, 0.1% Black/African American, 0.2% Asian, 0.5% American Indian/Alaska Native, 0.0% Native Hawaiian/Other Pacific Islander, 1.1% Two or more races, 3.2% Hispanic of any race; Average household size: 2.93; Median age: 36.8; Age under 18: 27.9%; Age 65 and over: 11.2%; Males per 100 females: 88.6; Marriage status: 27.2% never married, 54.2% now married, 0.9% separated, 4.3% widowed, 14.2% divorced; Foreign born: 0.2%; Speak English only: 98.2%; With disability: 11.6%; Veterans: 8.3%; Ancestry: 38.3% German, 20.2% Irish, 9.8% English, 7.8% American, 5.7% Italian
Employment: 10.1% management, business, and financial, 3.9% computer, engineering, and science, 9.0% education, legal, community service, arts, and media, 2.5% healthcare practitioners, 25.1% service, 21.7% sales and office, 15.9% natural resources, construction, and maintenance, 11.8% production, transportation, and material moving
Income: Per capita: $23,165; Median household: $64,107; Average household: $68,358; Households with income of $100,000 or more: 14.5%; Poverty rate: 6.5%
Educational Attainment: High school diploma or higher: 95.5%; Bachelor's degree or higher: 13.0%; Graduate/professional degree or higher: 2.2%

School District(s)

Fairbanks Local (PK-12)
2015-16 Enrollment: 1,047 . . . . (937) 349-3731
Housing: Homeownership rate: 76.5%; Median home value: $104,600; Median year structure built: 1945; Homeowner vacancy rate: 1.2%; Median selected monthly owner costs: $1,124 with a mortgage, $390 without a mortgage; Median gross rent: $979 per month; Rental vacancy rate: 0.0%
Health Insurance: 92.5% have insurance; 77.1% have private insurance; 22.9% have public insurance; 7.5% do not have insurance; 0.0% of children under 18 do not have insurance
Transportation: Commute: 91.6% car, 0.0% public transportation, 2.3% walk, 6.0% work from home; Mean travel time to work: 23.7 minutes

NEW CALIFORNIA (CDP). Covers a land area of 2.065 square miles and a water area of 0.032 square miles. Located at 40.15° N. Lat; 83.24° W. Long. Elevation is 997 feet.
Population: 1,996; Growth (since 2000): n/a; Density: 966.6 persons per square mile; Race: 90.4% White, 8.4% Black/African American, 1.2% Asian, 0.0% American Indian/Alaska Native, 0.0% Native Hawaiian/Other Pacific Islander, 0.0% Two or more races, 0.0% Hispanic of any race; Average household size: 3.59; Median age: 37.2; Age under 18: 31.9%; Age 65 and over: 8.1%; Males per 100 females: 103.6; Marriage status: 17.7% never married, 71.8% now married, 0.0% separated, 6.3% widowed, 4.2% divorced; Foreign born: 1.2%; Speak English only: 98.1%; With disability: 7.8%; Veterans: 0.0%; Ancestry: 45.0% German, 8.7% Irish, 6.4% Italian, 6.1% European, 5.6% Dutch
Employment: 17.1% management, business, and financial, 9.6% computer, engineering, and science, 13.5% education, legal, community service, arts, and media, 10.8% healthcare practitioners, 16.3% service, 24.7% sales and office, 1.2% natural resources, construction, and maintenance, 6.8% production, transportation, and material moving
Income: Per capita: $39,740; Median household: $128,000; Average household: $140,533; Households with income of $100,000 or more: 78.4%; Poverty rate: n/a
Educational Attainment: High school diploma or higher: 100.0%; Bachelor's degree or higher: 67.7%; Graduate/professional degree or higher: 20.0%
Housing: Homeownership rate: 100.0%; Median home value: $324,200; Median year structure built: 2002; Homeowner vacancy rate: 0.0%; Median selected monthly owner costs: $1,847 with a mortgage, $819 without a mortgage; Median gross rent: n/a per month; Rental vacancy rate: 0.0%
Health Insurance: 99.2% have insurance; 95.0% have private insurance; 12.9% have public insurance; 0.8% do not have insurance; 0.0% of children under 18 do not have insurance
Transportation: Commute: 92.7% car, 0.0% public transportation, 0.0% walk, 7.3% work from home; Mean travel time to work: 25.1 minutes

RAYMOND (CDP). Covers a land area of 1.269 square miles and a water area of 0.027 square miles. Located at 40.34° N. Lat; 83.47° W. Long. Elevation is 1,070 feet.
Population: 131; Growth (since 2000): n/a; Density: 103.2 persons per square mile; Race: 100.0% White, 0.0% Black/African American, 0.0% Asian, 0.0% American Indian/Alaska Native, 0.0% Native Hawaiian/Other Pacific Islander, 0.0% Two or more races, 0.0% Hispanic of any race; Average household size: 2.62; Median age: 28.6; Age under 18: 29.0%; Age 65 and over: 9.9%; Males per 100 females: 87.6; Marriage status: 32.4% never married, 56.5% now married, 12.0% separated, 3.7% widowed, 7.4% divorced; Foreign born: 0.0%; Speak English only: 100.0%; With disability: 0.0%; Veterans: 14.0%; Ancestry: 26.7% German, 16.0% European, 6.1% American
Employment: 53.5% management, business, and financial, 0.0% computer, engineering, and science, 9.9% education, legal, community service, arts, and media, 0.0% healthcare practitioners, 22.5% service, 5.6% sales and office, 0.0% natural resources, construction, and maintenance, 8.5% production, transportation, and material moving
Income: Per capita: $30,733; Median household: $94,423; Average household: $80,420; Households with income of $100,000 or more: 44.0%; Poverty rate: 6.6%
Educational Attainment: High school diploma or higher: 89.9%; Bachelor's degree or higher: 45.6%; Graduate/professional degree or higher: 16.5%

School District(s)

Marysville Exempted Village (PK-12)
2015-16 Enrollment: 5,286 . . . . (937) 644-8105
Housing: Homeownership rate: 86.0%; Median home value: $109,600; Median year structure built: Before 1940; Homeowner vacancy rate: 0.0%; Median selected monthly owner costs: $988 with a mortgage, n/a without a mortgage; Median gross rent: n/a per month; Rental vacancy rate: 0.0%
Health Insurance: 93.9% have insurance; 87.0% have private insurance; 16.8% have public insurance; 6.1% do not have insurance; 0.0% of children under 18 do not have insurance
Transportation: Commute: 76.1% car, 0.0% public transportation, 9.9% walk, 14.1% work from home; Mean travel time to work: 0.0 minutes

RICHWOOD (village). Covers a land area of 1.255 square miles and a water area of 0.026 square miles. Located at 40.43° N. Lat; 83.29° W. Long. Elevation is 948 feet.
Population: 2,449; Growth (since 2000): 13.6%; Density: 1,952.1 persons per square mile; Race: 97.3% White, 0.0% Black/African American, 0.0% Asian, 0.0% American Indian/Alaska Native, 0.0% Native Hawaiian/Other Pacific Islander, 2.3% Two or more races, 0.3% Hispanic of any race; Average household size: 2.65; Median age: 31.1; Age under 18: 29.4%; Age 65 and over: 14.4%; Males per 100 females: 90.2; Marriage status: 30.2% never married, 48.0% now married, 1.0% separated, 7.6% widowed, 14.2% divorced; Foreign born: 1.0%; Speak English only: 98.0%; With disability: 18.7%; Veterans: 10.2%; Ancestry: 30.8% German, 12.3% Irish, 11.0% American, 9.9% English, 3.6% Polish
Employment: 3.5% management, business, and financial, 0.0% computer, engineering, and science, 3.2% education, legal, community service, arts, and media, 4.0% healthcare practitioners, 17.6% service, 21.8% sales and office, 15.7% natural resources, construction, and maintenance, 34.3% production, transportation, and material moving
Income: Per capita: $18,098; Median household: $37,724; Average household: $47,704; Households with income of $100,000 or more: 7.1%; Poverty rate: 19.2%
Educational Attainment: High school diploma or higher: 86.3%; Bachelor's degree or higher: 8.7%; Graduate/professional degree or higher: 0.6%

School District(s)

North Union Local (PK-12)
2015-16 Enrollment: 1,498 . . . . (740) 943-2509
Housing: Homeownership rate: 62.7%; Median home value: $89,100; Median year structure built: 1951; Homeowner vacancy rate: 0.0%; Median selected monthly owner costs: $960 with a mortgage, $368 without a mortgage; Median gross rent: $685 per month; Rental vacancy rate: 0.0%
Health Insurance: 90.7% have insurance; 56.1% have private insurance; 46.3% have public insurance; 9.3% do not have insurance; 4.0% of children under 18 do not have insurance
Newspapers: Richwood Gazette (weekly circulation 2,500)
Transportation: Commute: 94.1% car, 0.0% public transportation, 1.3% walk, 3.3% work from home; Mean travel time to work: 26.4 minutes

UNIONVILLE CENTER (village). Covers a land area of 0.159 square miles and a water area of 0.005 square miles. Located at 40.14° N. Lat; 83.34° W. Long. Elevation is 971 feet.
Population: 361; Growth (since 2000): 20.7%; Density: 2,272.0 persons per square mile; Race: 98.3% White, 0.6% Black/African American, 0.0% Asian, 0.0% American Indian/Alaska Native, 0.0% Native Hawaiian/Other Pacific Islander, 0.0% Two or more races, 5.3% Hispanic of any race; Average household size: 2.78; Median age: 46.3; Age under 18: 21.6%; Age 65 and over: 13.9%; Males per 100 females: 106.2; Marriage status: 22.2% never married, 64.9% now married, 1.0% separated, 6.6% widowed, 6.3% divorced; Foreign born: 1.7%; Speak English only: 97.7%; With disability: 17.5%; Veterans: 3.5%; Ancestry: 33.8% German, 12.5% Irish, 11.9% American, 11.1% English, 3.3% French
Employment: 10.0% management, business, and financial, 2.2% computer, engineering, and science, 7.2% education, legal, community service, arts, and media, 0.0% healthcare practitioners, 20.6% service, 17.2% sales and office, 20.6% natural resources, construction, and maintenance, 22.2% production, transportation, and material moving
Income: Per capita: $20,364; Median household: $46,964; Average household: $57,892; Households with income of $100,000 or more: 11.6%; Poverty rate: 7.2%
Educational Attainment: High school diploma or higher: 62.6%; Bachelor's degree or higher: 9.7%; Graduate/professional degree or higher: 3.5%
Housing: Homeownership rate: 66.9%; Median home value: $95,000; Median year structure built: Before 1940; Homeowner vacancy rate: 3.3%; Median selected monthly owner costs: $979 with a mortgage, $455 without a mortgage; Median gross rent: $729 per month; Rental vacancy rate: 0.0%
Health Insurance: 94.7% have insurance; 82.8% have private insurance; 21.6% have public insurance; 5.3% do not have insurance; 0.0% of children under 18 do not have insurance
Transportation: Commute: 90.6% car, 0.0% public transportation, 0.0% walk, 9.4% work from home; Mean travel time to work: 24.4 minutes

Van Wert County

Located in western Ohio; bounded on the west by Indiana; drained by the Little Auglaize River. Covers a land area of 409.158 square miles, a water area of 1.267 square miles, and is located in the Eastern Time Zone at 40.86° N. Lat., 84.59° W. Long. The county was founded in 1820. County seat is Van Wert.

Van Wert County is part of the Van Wert, OH Micropolitan Statistical Area. The entire metro area includes: Van Wert County, OH

Weather Station: Van Wert 1 S Elevation: 790 feet

	Jan	Feb	Mar	Apr	May	Jun	Jul	Aug	Sep	Oct	Nov	Dec
High	33	36	47	60	72	81	85	83	77	63	50	37
Low	18	20	28	39	50	60	64	62	53	42	33	23
Precip	2.2	1.9	2.3	3.4	4.1	4.2	4.3	3.7	2.9	3.0	3.0	2.6
Snow	5.3	4.6	2.2	0.6	0.0	0.0	0.0	0.0	0.0	0.1	1.0	5.6

High and Low temperatures in degrees Fahrenheit; Precipitation and Snow in inches

Population: 28,501; Growth (since 2000): -3.9%; Density: 69.7 persons per square mile; Race: 96.5% White, 1.2% Black/African American, 0.4% Asian, 0.1% American Indian/Alaska Native, 0.0% Native Hawaiian/Other Pacific Islander, 1.2% two or more races, 2.9% Hispanic of any race; Average household size: 2.47; Median age: 41.4; Age under 18: 23.7%; Age 65 and over: 18.0%; Males per 100 females: 95.0; Marriage status: 23.0% never married, 57.5% now married, 1.5% separated, 6.4% widowed, 13.1% divorced; Foreign born: 0.9%; Speak English only: 98.0%; With disability: 14.9%; Veterans: 9.8%; Ancestry: 38.6% German, 12.0% Irish, 9.3% American, 7.5% English, 2.4% French
Religion: Six largest groups: 10.9% Methodist/Pietist, 8.9% Lutheran, 8.4% Catholicism, 6.3% Presbyterian-Reformed, 4.5% Non-denominational Protestant, 1.2% Pentecostal
Economy: Unemployment rate: 3.7%; Leading industries: 15.8 % other services (except public administration); 15.4 % retail trade; 11.4 % health care and social assistance; Farms: 655 totaling 227,277 acres; Company size: 1 employs 1,000 or more persons, 1 employs 500 to 999 persons, 13 employ 100 to 499 persons, 529 employ less than 100 persons; Business ownership: 606 women-owned, n/a Black-owned, n/a Hispanic-owned, n/a Asian-owned, n/a American Indian/Alaska Native-owned
Employment: 8.7% management, business, and financial, 3.6% computer, engineering, and science, 6.9% education, legal, community service, arts,

and media, 5.9% healthcare practitioners, 15.3% service, 19.9% sales and office, 8.3% natural resources, construction, and maintenance, 31.3% production, transportation, and material moving
Income: Per capita: $25,316; Median household: $50,547; Average household: $62,484; Households with income of $100,000 or more: 14.0%; Poverty rate: 12.3%
Educational Attainment: High school diploma or higher: 91.5%; Bachelor's degree or higher: 17.2%; Graduate/professional degree or higher: 6.8%
Housing: Homeownership rate: 76.0%; Median home value: $98,900; Median year structure built: 1959; Homeowner vacancy rate: 3.5%; Median selected monthly owner costs: $972 with a mortgage, $361 without a mortgage; Median gross rent: $653 per month; Rental vacancy rate: 7.3%
Vital Statistics: Birth rate: 120.2 per 10,000 population; Death rate: 107.5 per 10,000 population; Age-adjusted cancer mortality rate: 172.7 deaths per 100,000 population
Health Insurance: 91.8% have insurance; 72.1% have private insurance; 37.1% have public insurance; 8.2% do not have insurance; 6.1% of children under 18 do not have insurance
Health Care: Physicians: 7.4 per 10,000 population; Dentists: 3.2 per 10,000 population; Hospital beds: 24.3 per 10,000 population; Hospital admissions: 346.3 per 10,000 population
Transportation: Commute: 92.5% car, 0.2% public transportation, 2.3% walk, 2.8% work from home; Mean travel time to work: 18.5 minutes
2016 Presidential Election: 76.0% Trump, 19.6% Clinton, 3.1% Johnson, 0.8% Stein
Additional Information Contacts
Van Wert Government . . . . (419) 238-6159
http://www.vanwertcounty.org

Van Wert County Communities

CONVOY (village). Covers a land area of 0.561 square miles and a water area of <.001 square miles. Located at 40.92° N. Lat; 84.71° W. Long. Elevation is 781 feet.
Population: 1,169; Growth (since 2000): 5.3%; Density: 2,083.5 persons per square mile; Race: 96.4% White, 0.0% Black/African American, 0.2% Asian, 0.0% American Indian/Alaska Native, 0.0% Native Hawaiian/Other Pacific Islander, 2.7% Two or more races, 1.3% Hispanic of any race; Average household size: 2.63; Median age: 37.5; Age under 18: 26.9%; Age 65 and over: 15.4%; Males per 100 females: 85.5; Marriage status: 23.9% never married, 53.9% now married, 1.7% separated, 8.0% widowed, 14.1% divorced; Foreign born: 0.2%; Speak English only: 98.1%; With disability: 17.7%; Veterans: 12.9%; Ancestry: 41.7% German, 17.2% Irish, 5.6% English, 4.8% Scottish, 4.5% French
Employment: 5.5% management, business, and financial, 1.8% computer, engineering, and science, 5.7% education, legal, community service, arts, and media, 6.0% healthcare practitioners, 14.6% service, 18.1% sales and office, 10.1% natural resources, construction, and maintenance, 38.2% production, transportation, and material moving
Income: Per capita: $22,572; Median household: $55,000; Average household: $57,895; Households with income of $100,000 or more: 12.3%; Poverty rate: 13.4%
Educational Attainment: High school diploma or higher: 95.1%; Bachelor's degree or higher: 12.5%; Graduate/professional degree or higher: 4.9%

School District(s)

Crestview Local (KG-12)
2015-16 Enrollment: 833. . . . . (877) 644-6338
Housing: Homeownership rate: 80.3%; Median home value: $68,900; Median year structure built: 1950; Homeowner vacancy rate: 4.9%; Median selected monthly owner costs: $805 with a mortgage, $343 without a mortgage; Median gross rent: $588 per month; Rental vacancy rate: 26.1%
Health Insurance: 92.2% have insurance; 67.8% have private insurance; 39.3% have public insurance; 7.8% do not have insurance; 5.4% of children under 18 do not have insurance
Transportation: Commute: 94.2% car, 0.6% public transportation, 1.0% walk, 4.2% work from home; Mean travel time to work: 20.2 minutes

ELGIN (village). Covers a land area of 0.225 square miles and a water area of 0 square miles. Located at 40.74° N. Lat; 84.48° W. Long. Elevation is 814 feet.
Population: 68; Growth (since 2000): 36.0%; Density: 302.8 persons per square mile; Race: 95.6% White, 0.0% Black/African American, 0.0% Asian, 0.0% American Indian/Alaska Native, 0.0% Native Hawaiian/Other Pacific Islander, 4.4% Two or more races, 2.9% Hispanic of any race; Average household size: 2.96; Median age: 34.6; Age under 18: 30.9%; Age 65 and over: 17.6%; Males per 100 females: 128.0; Marriage status: 21.3% never married, 66.0% now married, 10.6% separated, 0.0% widowed, 12.8% divorced; Foreign born: 0.0%; Speak English only: 100.0%; With disability: 13.2%; Veterans: 12.8%; Ancestry: 17.6% English, 13.2% American, 10.3% German, 5.9% Irish, 2.9% Dutch
Employment: 0.0% management, business, and financial, 0.0% computer, engineering, and science, 7.4% education, legal, community service, arts, and media, 3.7% healthcare practitioners, 14.8% service, 7.4% sales and office, 33.3% natural resources, construction, and maintenance, 33.3% production, transportation, and material moving
Income: Per capita: $13,112; Median household: $36,875; Average household: $38,591; Households with income of $100,000 or more: n/a; Poverty rate: 16.4%
Educational Attainment: High school diploma or higher: 75.6%; Bachelor's degree or higher: n/a; Graduate/professional degree or higher: n/a
Housing: Homeownership rate: 100.0%; Median home value: $45,000; Median year structure built: 1968; Homeowner vacancy rate: 0.0%; Median selected monthly owner costs: $725 with a mortgage, $350 without a mortgage; Median gross rent: n/a per month; Rental vacancy rate: 0.0%
Health Insurance: 100.0% have insurance; 41.2% have private insurance; 76.5% have public insurance; 0.0% do not have insurance; 0.0% of children under 18 do not have insurance
Transportation: Commute: 100.0% car, 0.0% public transportation, 0.0% walk, 0.0% work from home; Mean travel time to work: 31.7 minutes

MIDDLE POINT (village). Covers a land area of 0.560 square miles and a water area of 0.008 square miles. Located at 40.86° N. Lat; 84.45° W. Long. Elevation is 778 feet.
Population: 549; Growth (since 2000): -7.4%; Density: 979.8 persons per square mile; Race: 97.4% White, 2.6% Black/African American, 0.0% Asian, 0.0% American Indian/Alaska Native, 0.0% Native Hawaiian/Other Pacific Islander, 0.0% Two or more races, 5.1% Hispanic of any race; Average household size: 2.48; Median age: 42.7; Age under 18: 23.1%; Age 65 and over: 18.8%; Males per 100 females: 99.3; Marriage status: 15.9% never married, 65.2% now married, 2.2% separated, 6.5% widowed, 12.3% divorced; Foreign born: 0.0%; Speak English only: 99.4%; With disability: 16.0%; Veterans: 12.8%; Ancestry: 31.9% German, 11.3% Irish, 6.4% American, 5.5% Polish, 4.2% Dutch
Employment: 7.2% management, business, and financial, 0.0% computer, engineering, and science, 3.4% education, legal, community service, arts, and media, 6.4% healthcare practitioners, 13.6% service, 15.3% sales and office, 12.7% natural resources, construction, and maintenance, 41.5% production, transportation, and material moving
Income: Per capita: $18,863; Median household: $37,250; Average household: $45,769; Households with income of $100,000 or more: 9.5%; Poverty rate: 11.9%
Educational Attainment: High school diploma or higher: 89.1%; Bachelor's degree or higher: 7.3%; Graduate/professional degree or higher: 3.4%
Housing: Homeownership rate: 80.5%; Median home value: $73,100; Median year structure built: 1950; Homeowner vacancy rate: 3.3%; Median selected monthly owner costs: $886 with a mortgage, $353 without a mortgage; Median gross rent: $695 per month; Rental vacancy rate: 8.5%
Health Insurance: 98.7% have insurance; 77.0% have private insurance; 43.7% have public insurance; 1.3% do not have insurance; 0.0% of children under 18 do not have insurance
Transportation: Commute: 89.2% car, 1.7% public transportation, 6.5% walk, 0.0% work from home; Mean travel time to work: 20.0 minutes

OHIO CITY (village). Covers a land area of 0.531 square miles and a water area of 0 square miles. Located at 40.77° N. Lat; 84.62° W. Long. Elevation is 820 feet.
Population: 805; Growth (since 2000): 2.7%; Density: 1,515.7 persons per square mile; Race: 98.8% White, 0.0% Black/African American, 0.0% Asian, 0.4% American Indian/Alaska Native, 0.0% Native Hawaiian/Other Pacific Islander, 0.0% Two or more races, 3.2% Hispanic of any race; Average household size: 2.48; Median age: 37.5; Age under 18: 23.0%; Age 65 and over: 10.3%; Males per 100 females: 95.8; Marriage status: 21.7% never married, 59.5% now married, 1.9% separated, 7.3% widowed, 11.5% divorced; Foreign born: 0.0%; Speak English only: 98.3%; With disability: 16.8%; Veterans: 5.2%; Ancestry: 35.7% German, 10.6% American, 8.7% Irish, 5.7% English, 4.1% European

Employment: 5.9% management, business, and financial, 1.5% computer, engineering, and science, 3.4% education, legal, community service, arts, and media, 2.9% healthcare practitioners, 18.7% service, 20.6% sales and office, 9.1% natural resources, construction, and maintenance, 37.8% production, transportation, and material moving
Income: Per capita: $19,840; Median household: $40,368; Average household: $47,462; Households with income of $100,000 or more: 7.7%; Poverty rate: 15.0%
Educational Attainment: High school diploma or higher: 90.6%; Bachelor's degree or higher: 6.0%; Graduate/professional degree or higher: 0.4%
Housing: Homeownership rate: 75.1%; Median home value: $67,200; Median year structure built: 1947; Homeowner vacancy rate: 3.5%; Median selected monthly owner costs: $879 with a mortgage, $332 without a mortgage; Median gross rent: $623 per month; Rental vacancy rate: 9.0%
Health Insurance: 92.5% have insurance; 69.6% have private insurance; 36.1% have public insurance; 7.5% do not have insurance; 6.5% of children under 18 do not have insurance
Transportation: Commute: 94.6% car, 0.0% public transportation, 2.2% walk, 0.7% work from home; Mean travel time to work: 19.1 minutes

---

SCOTT (village). Covers a land area of 0.811 square miles and a water area of <.001 square miles. Located at 40.99° N. Lat; 84.58° W. Long. Elevation is 738 feet.
Population: 319; Growth (since 2000): -0.9%; Density: 393.3 persons per square mile; Race: 98.4% White, 0.0% Black/African American, 0.0% Asian, 0.0% American Indian/Alaska Native, 0.0% Native Hawaiian/Other Pacific Islander, 0.0% Two or more races, 1.6% Hispanic of any race; Average household size: 2.73; Median age: 36.3; Age under 18: 30.1%; Age 65 and over: 6.3%; Males per 100 females: 90.7; Marriage status: 30.2% never married, 50.4% now married, 0.0% separated, 4.0% widowed, 15.5% divorced; Foreign born: 0.0%; Speak English only: 100.0%; With disability: 11.9%; Veterans: 4.5%; Ancestry: 32.0% German, 15.0% Irish, 11.9% Dutch, 3.1% American, 1.6% Portuguese
Employment: 3.1% management, business, and financial, 1.3% computer, engineering, and science, 0.0% education, legal, community service, arts, and media, 1.9% healthcare practitioners, 14.4% service, 15.0% sales and office, 10.6% natural resources, construction, and maintenance, 53.8% production, transportation, and material moving
Income: Per capita: $18,752; Median household: $45,250; Average household: $49,049; Households with income of $100,000 or more: 7.7%; Poverty rate: 13.8%
Educational Attainment: High school diploma or higher: 90.9%; Bachelor's degree or higher: 4.5%; Graduate/professional degree or higher: 1.0%
Housing: Homeownership rate: 77.8%; Median home value: $41,900; Median year structure built: 1959; Homeowner vacancy rate: 4.9%; Median selected monthly owner costs: $664 with a mortgage, $315 without a mortgage; Median gross rent: $571 per month; Rental vacancy rate: 0.0%
Health Insurance: 90.9% have insurance; 71.2% have private insurance; 35.4% have public insurance; 9.1% do not have insurance; 5.2% of children under 18 do not have insurance
Transportation: Commute: 99.3% car, 0.0% public transportation, 0.0% walk, 0.7% work from home; Mean travel time to work: 17.1 minutes

---

VAN WERT (city). County seat. Covers a land area of 7.325 square miles and a water area of 0.281 square miles. Located at 40.87° N. Lat; 84.59° W. Long. Elevation is 778 feet.
History: The site of Van Wert was chosen in 1835 by Captain James Watson Riley, who correctly foresaw that the location would make it a thoroughfare. The town developed into the peony center of Ohio, raising many flowers.
Population: 10,738; Growth (since 2000): 0.4%; Density: 1,466.0 persons per square mile; Race: 95.1% White, 2.5% Black/African American, 0.7% Asian, 0.2% American Indian/Alaska Native, 0.0% Native Hawaiian/Other Pacific Islander, 1.2% Two or more races, 5.3% Hispanic of any race; Average household size: 2.38; Median age: 39.6; Age under 18: 24.5%; Age 65 and over: 20.3%; Males per 100 females: 88.0; Marriage status: 22.8% never married, 51.2% now married, 2.2% separated, 7.9% widowed, 18.1% divorced; Foreign born: 1.0%; Speak English only: 98.1%; With disability: 18.5%; Veterans: 11.5%; Ancestry: 36.0% German, 15.0% Irish, 8.3% English, 7.8% American, 2.8% French
Employment: 6.0% management, business, and financial, 3.0% computer, engineering, and science, 6.3% education, legal, community service, arts, and media, 5.9% healthcare practitioners, 19.5% service, 19.2% sales and office, 5.3% natural resources, construction, and maintenance, 35.0% production, transportation, and material moving
Income: Per capita: $20,877; Median household: $41,900; Average household: $49,750; Households with income of $100,000 or more: 8.8%; Poverty rate: 20.0%
Educational Attainment: High school diploma or higher: 90.8%; Bachelor's degree or higher: 16.5%; Graduate/professional degree or higher: 7.5%

School District(s)

Lifelinks Community School (06-12)
2015-16 Enrollment: 77 . . . . (419) 623-5380
Lincolnview Local (KG-12)
2015-16 Enrollment: 853 . . . . (419) 968-2226
Van Wert City (PK-12)
2015-16 Enrollment: 2,010 . . . . (419) 238-0648
Vantage Career Center (09-12)
2015-16 Enrollment: n/a . . . . (419) 238-5411

Vocational/Technical School(s)

Ohio Technical Center at Vantage Career Center (Public)
Fall 2016 Enrollment: 27 . . . . (419) 238-5411
2016-17 Tuition: $620

Housing: Homeownership rate: 63.8%; Median home value: $82,400; Median year structure built: 1955; Homeowner vacancy rate: 4.6%; Median selected monthly owner costs: $857 with a mortgage, $302 without a mortgage; Median gross rent: $633 per month; Rental vacancy rate: 6.7%
Health Insurance: 90.3% have insurance; 63.0% have private insurance; 46.7% have public insurance; 9.7% do not have insurance; 6.5% of children under 18 do not have insurance
Hospitals: Van Wert County Hospital (100 beds)
Safety: Violent crime rate: 26.9 per 10,000 population; Property crime rate: 327.0 per 10,000 population
Newspapers: Times-Bulletin (daily circulation 6,400)
Transportation: Commute: 92.6% car, 0.3% public transportation, 2.4% walk, 0.8% work from home; Mean travel time to work: 16.1 minutes
Additional Information Contacts
City of Van Wert . . . . (419) 238-0308
http://vanwert.org

VENEDOCIA (village). Covers a land area of 0.134 square miles and a water area of 0 square miles. Located at 40.79° N. Lat; 84.46° W. Long. Elevation is 804 feet.
Population: 157; Growth (since 2000): -1.9%; Density: 1,168.8 persons per square mile; Race: 94.9% White, 0.0% Black/African American, 0.0% Asian, 0.0% American Indian/Alaska Native, 0.0% Native Hawaiian/Other Pacific Islander, 5.1% Two or more races, 0.0% Hispanic of any race; Average household size: 2.96; Median age: 30.3; Age under 18: 35.0%; Age 65 and over: 10.2%; Males per 100 females: 117.5; Marriage status: 33.3% never married, 45.1% now married, 4.9% separated, 11.8% widowed, 9.8% divorced; Foreign born: 0.0%; Speak English only: 97.9%; With disability: 13.4%; Veterans: 1.0%; Ancestry: 51.0% German, 17.8% Irish, 10.2% Welsh, 5.1% American, 3.2% Dutch
Employment: 29.4% management, business, and financial, 0.0% computer, engineering, and science, 2.9% education, legal, community service, arts, and media, 10.3% healthcare practitioners, 10.3% service, 10.3% sales and office, 7.4% natural resources, construction, and maintenance, 29.4% production, transportation, and material moving
Income: Per capita: $20,466; Median household: $44,896; Average household: $58,211; Households with income of $100,000 or more: 15.1%; Poverty rate: n/a
Educational Attainment: High school diploma or higher: 95.5%; Bachelor's degree or higher: 4.5%; Graduate/professional degree or higher: 4.5%
Housing: Homeownership rate: 73.6%; Median home value: $68,300; Median year structure built: Before 1940; Homeowner vacancy rate: 11.4%; Median selected monthly owner costs: $667 with a mortgage, $335 without a mortgage; Median gross rent: $755 per month; Rental vacancy rate: 0.0%
Health Insurance: 96.2% have insurance; 70.7% have private insurance; 45.9% have public insurance; 3.8% do not have insurance; 0.0% of children under 18 do not have insurance
Transportation: Commute: 100.0% car, 0.0% public transportation, 0.0% walk, 0.0% work from home; Mean travel time to work: 23.8 minutes

WILLSHIRE (village). Covers a land area of 0.371 square miles and a water area of 0.002 square miles. Located at 40.75° N. Lat; 84.79° W. Long. Elevation is 794 feet.
Population: 462; Growth (since 2000): -0.2%; Density: 1,243.9 persons per square mile; Race: 100.0% White, 0.0% Black/African American, 0.0% Asian, 0.0% American Indian/Alaska Native, 0.0% Native Hawaiian/Other Pacific Islander, 0.0% Two or more races, 0.0% Hispanic of any race; Average household size: 2.48; Median age: 41.3; Age under 18: 23.8%; Age 65 and over: 15.4%; Males per 100 females: 98.5; Marriage status: 21.0% never married, 55.6% now married, 1.9% separated, 6.7% widowed, 16.7% divorced; Foreign born: 0.0%; Speak English only: 99.8%; With disability: 19.3%; Veterans: 4.5%; Ancestry: 50.0% German, 16.0% Irish, 7.8% English, 5.6% American, 4.5% Dutch
Employment: 2.6% management, business, and financial, 3.0% computer, engineering, and science, 0.9% education, legal, community service, arts, and media, 6.0% healthcare practitioners, 10.2% service, 28.5% sales and office, 16.2% natural resources, construction, and maintenance, 32.8% production, transportation, and material moving
Income: Per capita: $19,821; Median household: $45,500; Average household: $50,824; Households with income of $100,000 or more: 9.7%; Poverty rate: 21.0%
Educational Attainment: High school diploma or higher: 77.6%; Bachelor's degree or higher: 2.1%; Graduate/professional degree or higher: 0.3%
Housing: Homeownership rate: 89.2%; Median home value: $50,500; Median year structure built: Before 1940; Homeowner vacancy rate: 8.6%; Median selected monthly owner costs: $868 with a mortgage, $388 without a mortgage; Median gross rent: $738 per month; Rental vacancy rate: 0.0%
Health Insurance: 94.4% have insurance; 66.0% have private insurance; 46.3% have public insurance; 5.6% do not have insurance; 0.0% of children under 18 do not have insurance
Newspapers: Photo Star (weekly circulation 11,000)
Transportation: Commute: 88.2% car, 0.0% public transportation, 0.9% walk, 10.0% work from home; Mean travel time to work: 24.1 minutes

WREN (village). Covers a land area of 0.310 square miles and a water area of <.001 square miles. Located at 40.80° N. Lat; 84.77° W. Long. Elevation is 807 feet.
Population: 185; Growth (since 2000): -7.0%; Density: 597.7 persons per square mile; Race: 100.0% White, 0.0% Black/African American, 0.0% Asian, 0.0% American Indian/Alaska Native, 0.0% Native Hawaiian/Other Pacific Islander, 0.0% Two or more races, 5.9% Hispanic of any race; Average household size: 2.10; Median age: 51.5; Age under 18: 10.8%; Age 65 and over: 19.5%; Males per 100 females: 102.1; Marriage status: 32.3% never married, 56.9% now married, 0.0% separated, 5.4% widowed, 5.4% divorced; Foreign born: 0.0%; Speak English only: 100.0%; With disability: 11.4%; Veterans: 3.0%; Ancestry: 44.9% German, 11.9% Irish, 5.9% English, 3.8% Italian, 2.7% American
Employment: 13.4% management, business, and financial, 2.1% computer, engineering, and science, 0.0% education, legal, community service, arts, and media, 19.6% healthcare practitioners, 4.1% service, 10.3% sales and office, 9.3% natural resources, construction, and maintenance, 41.2% production, transportation, and material moving
Income: Per capita: $27,024; Median household: $46,667; Average household: $56,155; Households with income of $100,000 or more: 19.3%; Poverty rate: 1.6%
Educational Attainment: High school diploma or higher: 96.3%; Bachelor's degree or higher: 4.9%; Graduate/professional degree or higher: 3.1%
Housing: Homeownership rate: 89.8%; Median home value: $61,600; Median year structure built: Before 1940; Homeowner vacancy rate: 0.0%; Median selected monthly owner costs: $1,258 with a mortgage, $413 without a mortgage; Median gross rent: n/a per month; Rental vacancy rate: 0.0%
Health Insurance: 91.4% have insurance; 78.9% have private insurance; 32.4% have public insurance; 8.6% do not have insurance; 0.0% of children under 18 do not have insurance
Transportation: Commute: 100.0% car, 0.0% public transportation, 0.0% walk, 0.0% work from home; Mean travel time to work: 22.8 minutes

Vinton County

Located in southern Ohio; drained by Raccoon Creek. Covers a land area of 412.360 square miles, a water area of 2.618 square miles, and is located in the Eastern Time Zone at 39.25° N. Lat., 82.49° W. Long. The county was founded in 1850. County seat is McArthur.
Population: 13,128; Growth (since 2000): 2.5%; Density: 31.8 persons per square mile; Race: 97.1% White, 0.2% Black/African American, 0.0% Asian, 0.0% American Indian/Alaska Native, 0.0% Native Hawaiian/Other Pacific Islander, 2.6% two or more races, 0.2% Hispanic of any race; Average household size: 2.64; Median age: 41.0; Age under 18: 23.0%; Age 65 and over: 15.4%; Males per 100 females: 99.1; Marriage status: 25.3% never married, 52.7% now married, 1.5% separated, 7.5% widowed, 14.5% divorced; Foreign born: 0.2%; Speak English only: 96.9%; With disability: 21.1%; Veterans: 8.5%; Ancestry: 14.7% German, 13.4% Irish, 9.1% English, 8.8% American, 2.8% Scottish
Religion: Six largest groups: 7.4% Baptist, 4.3% Methodist/Pietist, 2.0% Non-denominational Protestant, 1.7% Pentecostal, 1.5% Catholicism, 1.0% Holiness
Economy: Unemployment rate: 5.5%; Leading industries: 17.0 % retail trade; 13.3 % health care and social assistance; 11.1 % manufacturing; Farms: 226 totaling 33,400 acres; Company size: 0 employ 1,000 or more persons, 0 employ 500 to 999 persons, 2 employ 100 to 499 persons, 133 employ less than 100 persons; Business ownership: 254 women-owned, n/a Black-owned, n/a Hispanic-owned, n/a Asian-owned, n/a American Indian/Alaska Native-owned
Employment: 6.0% management, business, and financial, 1.5% computer, engineering, and science, 8.9% education, legal, community service, arts, and media, 5.7% healthcare practitioners, 21.4% service, 16.9% sales and office, 17.4% natural resources, construction, and maintenance, 22.2% production, transportation, and material moving
Income: Per capita: $19,431; Median household: $41,080; Average household: $49,301; Households with income of $100,000 or more: 10.2%; Poverty rate: 21.3%
Educational Attainment: High school diploma or higher: 80.8%; Bachelor's degree or higher: 9.6%; Graduate/professional degree or higher: 3.4%
Housing: Homeownership rate: 76.4%; Median home value: $84,100; Median year structure built: 1983; Homeowner vacancy rate: 2.7%; Median selected monthly owner costs: $983 with a mortgage, $359 without a mortgage; Median gross rent: $620 per month; Rental vacancy rate: 5.0%
Vital Statistics: Birth rate: 99.1 per 10,000 population; Death rate: 120.0 per 10,000 population; Age-adjusted cancer mortality rate: 202.8 deaths per 100,000 population
Health Insurance: 90.0% have insurance; 53.7% have private insurance; 47.1% have public insurance; 10.0% do not have insurance; 5.5% of children under 18 do not have insurance
Health Care: Physicians: 2.3 per 10,000 population; Dentists: 3.9 per 10,000 population; Hospital beds: 0.0 per 10,000 population; Hospital admissions: 0.0 per 10,000 population
Transportation: Commute: 97.4% car, 0.0% public transportation, 0.9% walk, 1.5% work from home; Mean travel time to work: 33.5 minutes
2016 Presidential Election: 70.1% Trump, 24.4% Clinton, 3.0% Johnson, 0.8% Stein
National and State Parks: Lake Alma State Park; Lake Hope State Park; Wellston Reservoir State Wildlife Park; Zaleski State Forest
Additional Information Contacts
Vinton Government . . . . (740) 596-4571
http://www.vintoncounty.com/index.html

Vinton County Communities

CREOLA (unincorporated postal area)
ZCTA: 45622
Covers a land area of 14.474 square miles and a water area of 0.021 square miles. Located at 39.38° N. Lat; 82.49° W. Long. Elevation is 764 feet.
Population: 220; Growth (since 2000): -49.4%; Density: 15.2 persons per square mile; Race: 100.0% White, 0.0% Black/African American, 0.0% Asian, 0.0% American Indian/Alaska Native, 0.0% Native Hawaiian/Other Pacific Islander, 0.0% Two or more races, 0.0% Hispanic of any race; Average household size: 2.97; Median age: 38.3; Age under 18: 29.1%; Age 65 and over: 10.9%; Males per 100 females: 99.4; Marriage status: 29.6% never married, 53.3% now married, 0.0% separated, 0.0% widowed, 17.2% divorced; Foreign born: 0.0%; Speak English only:

100.0%; With disability: 14.1%; Veterans: 5.8%; Ancestry: 38.2% German, 12.3% Dutch, 8.6% English
Employment: 0.0% management, business, and financial, 0.0% computer, engineering, and science, 0.0% education, legal, community service, arts, and media, 16.8% healthcare practitioners, 36.6% service, 46.5% sales and office, 0.0% natural resources, construction, and maintenance, 0.0% production, transportation, and material moving
Income: Per capita: $16,218; Median household: n/a; Average household: $47,712; Households with income of $100,000 or more: n/a; Poverty rate: 39.5%
Educational Attainment: High school diploma or higher: 82.1%; Bachelor's degree or higher: 30.7%; Graduate/professional degree or higher: 12.1%
Housing: Homeownership rate: 100.0%; Median home value: $125,000; Median year structure built: 1983; Homeowner vacancy rate: 0.0%; Median selected monthly owner costs: $960 with a mortgage, $550 without a mortgage; Median gross rent: n/a per month; Rental vacancy rate: 0.0%
Health Insurance: 94.5% have insurance; 12.7% have private insurance; 81.8% have public insurance; 5.5% do not have insurance; 0.0% of children under 18 do not have insurance
Transportation: Commute: 100.0% car, 0.0% public transportation, 0.0% walk, 0.0% work from home; Mean travel time to work: 34.2 minutes

HAMDEN (village). Covers a land area of 0.569 square miles and a water area of <.001 square miles. Located at 39.16° N. Lat; 82.52° W. Long. Elevation is 722 feet.
Population: 951; Growth (since 2000): 9.2%; Density: 1,670.9 persons per square mile; Race: 97.8% White, 0.0% Black/African American, 0.0% Asian, 0.1% American Indian/Alaska Native, 0.0% Native Hawaiian/Other Pacific Islander, 2.1% Two or more races, 0.0% Hispanic of any race; Average household size: 2.62; Median age: 36.4; Age under 18: 25.4%; Age 65 and over: 16.0%; Males per 100 females: 96.6; Marriage status: 30.6% never married, 41.8% now married, 2.9% separated, 11.3% widowed, 16.3% divorced; Foreign born: 0.0%; Speak English only: 98.4%; With disability: 28.5%; Veterans: 4.9%; Ancestry: 20.6% German, 11.7% Irish, 6.6% English, 5.4% American, 3.5% French
Employment: 9.4% management, business, and financial, 0.0% computer, engineering, and science, 2.8% education, legal, community service, arts, and media, 6.6% healthcare practitioners, 19.9% service, 23.4% sales and office, 8.4% natural resources, construction, and maintenance, 29.4% production, transportation, and material moving
Income: Per capita: $13,316; Median household: $24,375; Average household: $33,099; Households with income of $100,000 or more: 1.9%; Poverty rate: 32.1%
Educational Attainment: High school diploma or higher: 68.6%; Bachelor's degree or higher: 1.6%; Graduate/professional degree or higher: 1.0%

School District(s)

Vinton County Local (PK-12)
2015-16 Enrollment: 2,134 . . . . (740) 596-5218
Housing: Homeownership rate: 69.4%; Median home value: $65,200; Median year structure built: 1971; Homeowner vacancy rate: 6.9%; Median selected monthly owner costs: $770 with a mortgage, $299 without a mortgage; Median gross rent: $653 per month; Rental vacancy rate: 4.3%
Health Insurance: 85.3% have insurance; 34.9% have private insurance; 56.7% have public insurance; 14.7% do not have insurance; 5.4% of children under 18 do not have insurance
Transportation: Commute: 96.7% car, 0.0% public transportation, 1.9% walk, 1.5% work from home; Mean travel time to work: 23.6 minutes

MCARTHUR (village). County seat. Covers a land area of 1.328 square miles and a water area of 0.006 square miles. Located at 39.25° N. Lat; 82.48° W. Long. Elevation is 764 feet.
History: McArthur was platted in 1815 and named McArthurstown for Duncan McArthur, later governor of Ohio. It was sited at the junction of two wilderness roads. Local clays were used in brickmaking, the town's early industry.
Population: 1,892; Growth (since 2000): 0.2%; Density: 1,424.9 persons per square mile; Race: 94.0% White, 0.0% Black/African American, 0.1% Asian, 0.0% American Indian/Alaska Native, 0.0% Native Hawaiian/Other Pacific Islander, 5.9% Two or more races, 1.4% Hispanic of any race; Average household size: 2.68; Median age: 34.6; Age under 18: 26.1%; Age 65 and over: 12.7%; Males per 100 females: 84.3; Marriage status: 25.4% never married, 48.9% now married, 0.5% separated, 6.8% widowed, 18.9% divorced; Foreign born: 0.3%; Speak English only: 98.3%; With disability: 15.8%; Veterans: 7.3%; Ancestry: 14.8% Irish, 12.6% German, 9.0% American, 6.2% English, 5.8% Dutch
Employment: 8.7% management, business, and financial, 1.0% computer, engineering, and science, 16.7% education, legal, community service, arts, and media, 4.0% healthcare practitioners, 21.7% service, 19.5% sales and office, 13.7% natural resources, construction, and maintenance, 14.7% production, transportation, and material moving
Income: Per capita: $18,714; Median household: $38,382; Average household: $48,130; Households with income of $100,000 or more: 10.9%; Poverty rate: 21.3%
Educational Attainment: High school diploma or higher: 84.6%; Bachelor's degree or higher: 14.3%; Graduate/professional degree or higher: 7.9%

School District(s)

Vinton County Local (PK-12)
2015-16 Enrollment: 2,134 . . . . (740) 596-5218
Housing: Homeownership rate: 60.9%; Median home value: $94,100; Median year structure built: 1966; Homeowner vacancy rate: 5.3%; Median selected monthly owner costs: $898 with a mortgage, $382 without a mortgage; Median gross rent: $552 per month; Rental vacancy rate: 2.5%
Health Insurance: 88.4% have insurance; 53.1% have private insurance; 44.8% have public insurance; 11.6% do not have insurance; 3.2% of children under 18 do not have insurance
Safety: Violent crime rate: 12.1 per 10,000 population; Property crime rate: 163.0 per 10,000 population
Newspapers: Vinton Co Courier (weekly circulation 2,100)
Transportation: Commute: 94.3% car, 0.0% public transportation, 4.5% walk, 0.8% work from home; Mean travel time to work: 25.3 minutes

NEW PLYMOUTH (unincorporated postal area)
ZCTA: 45654
Covers a land area of 56.066 square miles and a water area of 0.166 square miles. Located at 39.37° N. Lat; 82.38° W. Long. Elevation is 768 feet.
Population: 868; Growth (since 2000): -15.4%; Density: 15.5 persons per square mile; Race: 99.3% White, 0.0% Black/African American, 0.0% Asian, 0.0% American Indian/Alaska Native, 0.0% Native Hawaiian/Other Pacific Islander, 0.7% Two or more races, 0.0% Hispanic of any race; Average household size: 2.74; Median age: 41.5; Age under 18: 25.2%; Age 65 and over: 19.6%; Males per 100 females: 111.3; Marriage status: 9.1% never married, 78.0% now married, 4.0% separated, 4.3% widowed, 8.5% divorced; Foreign born: 0.0%; Speak English only: 96.1%; With disability: 13.1%; Veterans: 16.2%; Ancestry: 25.9% Irish, 21.1% German, 14.3% American, 13.8% English, 4.3% Italian
Employment: 8.9% management, business, and financial, 0.0% computer, engineering, and science, 4.3% education, legal, community service, arts, and media, 2.4% healthcare practitioners, 15.1% service, 8.6% sales and office, 30.5% natural resources, construction, and maintenance, 30.0% production, transportation, and material moving
Income: Per capita: $21,082; Median household: $46,971; Average household: $56,365; Households with income of $100,000 or more: 11.0%; Poverty rate: 13.5%
Educational Attainment: High school diploma or higher: 83.6%; Bachelor's degree or higher: 7.9%; Graduate/professional degree or higher: 1.6%
Housing: Homeownership rate: 95.0%; Median home value: $90,200; Median year structure built: 1979; Homeowner vacancy rate: 0.0%; Median selected monthly owner costs: $982 with a mortgage, $382 without a mortgage; Median gross rent: n/a per month; Rental vacancy rate: 0.0%
Health Insurance: 76.2% have insurance; 49.2% have private insurance; 38.9% have public insurance; 23.8% do not have insurance; 40.2% of children under 18 do not have insurance
Transportation: Commute: 98.9% car, 0.0% public transportation, 0.0% walk, 1.1% work from home; Mean travel time to work: 31.5 minutes

RAY (unincorporated postal area)
ZCTA: 45672
Covers a land area of 53.459 square miles and a water area of 0.153 square miles. Located at 39.19° N. Lat; 82.69° W. Long. Elevation is 614 feet.
Population: 1,569; Growth (since 2000): -12.0%; Density: 29.3 persons per square mile; Race: 99.4% White, 0.0% Black/African American, 0.0% Asian, 0.0% American Indian/Alaska Native, 0.0% Native Hawaiian/Other Pacific Islander, 0.6% Two or more races, 0.0% Hispanic of any race; Average household size: 2.87; Median age: 43.7; Age under 18: 20.7%;

Age 65 and over: 16.3%; Males per 100 females: 106.7; Marriage status: 16.2% never married, 62.7% now married, 3.5% separated, 4.3% widowed, 16.7% divorced; Foreign born: 0.0%; Speak English only: 91.7%; With disability: 24.5%; Veterans: 14.5%; Ancestry: 14.7% German, 11.0% American, 9.9% Irish, 5.4% English, 1.7% French
Employment: 2.1% management, business, and financial, 0.0% computer, engineering, and science, 4.0% education, legal, community service, arts, and media, 19.2% healthcare practitioners, 10.1% service, 10.5% sales and office, 19.8% natural resources, construction, and maintenance, 34.4% production, transportation, and material moving
Income: Per capita: $20,716; Median household: $50,163; Average household: $57,331; Households with income of $100,000 or more: 18.6%; Poverty rate: 16.4%
Educational Attainment: High school diploma or higher: 89.8%; Bachelor's degree or higher: 9.1%; Graduate/professional degree or higher: 0.3%
Housing: Homeownership rate: 83.2%; Median home value: $108,100; Median year structure built: 1983; Homeowner vacancy rate: 0.0%; Median selected monthly owner costs: $1,361 with a mortgage, $324 without a mortgage; Median gross rent: $915 per month; Rental vacancy rate: 0.0%
Health Insurance: 94.1% have insurance; 61.6% have private insurance; 45.8% have public insurance; 5.9% do not have insurance; 0.0% of children under 18 do not have insurance
Transportation: Commute: 100.0% car, 0.0% public transportation, 0.0% walk, 0.0% work from home; Mean travel time to work: 50.7 minutes

WILKESVILLE (village). Covers a land area of 0.292 square miles and a water area of <.001 square miles. Located at 39.08° N. Lat; 82.33° W. Long. Elevation is 705 feet.
Population: 224; Growth (since 2000): 48.3%; Density: 766.7 persons per square mile; Race: 100.0% White, 0.0% Black/African American, 0.0% Asian, 0.0% American Indian/Alaska Native, 0.0% Native Hawaiian/Other Pacific Islander, 0.0% Two or more races, 0.0% Hispanic of any race; Average household size: 2.49; Median age: 35.4; Age under 18: 22.8%; Age 65 and over: 14.3%; Males per 100 females: 122.4; Marriage status: 26.5% never married, 43.4% now married, 0.0% separated, 7.4% widowed, 22.8% divorced; Foreign born: 0.0%; Speak English only: 93.6%; With disability: 26.3%; Veterans: 12.7%; Ancestry: 39.7% German, 35.3% Irish, 8.9% Italian, 7.1% English, 4.5% Polish
Employment: 9.5% management, business, and financial, 0.0% computer, engineering, and science, 8.1% education, legal, community service, arts, and media, 0.0% healthcare practitioners, 21.6% service, 9.5% sales and office, 16.2% natural resources, construction, and maintenance, 35.1% production, transportation, and material moving
Income: Per capita: $16,875; Median household: $38,125; Average household: $42,398; Households with income of $100,000 or more: 6.7%; Poverty rate: 17.0%
Educational Attainment: High school diploma or higher: 87.7%; Bachelor's degree or higher: 11.6%; Graduate/professional degree or higher: 1.4%
Housing: Homeownership rate: 93.3%; Median home value: $52,900; Median year structure built: 1956; Homeowner vacancy rate: 0.0%; Median selected monthly owner costs: $863 with a mortgage, $414 without a mortgage; Median gross rent: n/a per month; Rental vacancy rate: 0.0%
Health Insurance: 86.2% have insurance; 61.2% have private insurance; 38.4% have public insurance; 13.8% do not have insurance; 0.0% of children under 18 do not have insurance
Transportation: Commute: 100.0% car, 0.0% public transportation, 0.0% walk, 0.0% work from home; Mean travel time to work: 27.3 minutes

ZALESKI (village). Covers a land area of 0.440 square miles and a water area of 0.007 square miles. Located at 39.28° N. Lat; 82.39° W. Long. Elevation is 751 feet.
History: Zaleski was settled in a forested area, the site of the Zaleski Resettlement Project that sought to rehabilitate timberlands.
Population: 392; Growth (since 2000): 4.5%; Density: 890.7 persons per square mile; Race: 100.0% White, 0.0% Black/African American, 0.0% Asian, 0.0% American Indian/Alaska Native, 0.0% Native Hawaiian/Other Pacific Islander, 0.0% Two or more races, 0.0% Hispanic of any race; Average household size: 2.40; Median age: 52.1; Age under 18: 19.6%; Age 65 and over: 25.3%; Males per 100 females: 100.0; Marriage status: 26.1% never married, 64.2% now married, 2.0% separated, 6.0% widowed, 3.7% divorced; Foreign born: 0.0%; Speak English only: 99.5%; With disability: 23.5%; Veterans: 7.3%; Ancestry: 30.6% Irish, 20.9% German, 19.6% English, 8.2% Dutch, 6.1% American
Employment: 18.1% management, business, and financial, 1.1% computer, engineering, and science, 4.3% education, legal, community service, arts, and media, 3.7% healthcare practitioners, 18.6% service, 27.1% sales and office, 16.5% natural resources, construction, and maintenance, 10.6% production, transportation, and material moving
Income: Per capita: $21,039; Median household: $52,031; Average household: $49,874; Households with income of $100,000 or more: n/a; Poverty rate: 14.8%
Educational Attainment: High school diploma or higher: 85.7%; Bachelor's degree or higher: 1.7%; Graduate/professional degree or higher: 0.3%
Housing: Homeownership rate: 77.9%; Median home value: $78,300; Median year structure built: 1973; Homeowner vacancy rate: 3.8%; Median selected monthly owner costs: $863 with a mortgage, $407 without a mortgage; Median gross rent: $544 per month; Rental vacancy rate: 0.0%
Health Insurance: 92.9% have insurance; 67.6% have private insurance; 49.7% have public insurance; 7.1% do not have insurance; 10.4% of children under 18 do not have insurance
Transportation: Commute: 96.7% car, 0.0% public transportation, 3.3% walk, 0.0% work from home; Mean travel time to work: 25.5 minutes

Warren County

Located in southwestern Ohio; crossed by the Little Miami River. Covers a land area of 401.314 square miles, a water area of 5.999 square miles, and is located in the Eastern Time Zone at 39.43° N. Lat., 84.17° W. Long. The county was founded in 1803. County seat is Lebanon.

Warren County is part of the Cincinnati, OH-KY-IN Metropolitan Statistical Area. The entire metro area includes: Dearborn County, IN; Ohio County, IN; Union County, IN; Boone County, KY; Bracken County, KY; Campbell County, KY; Gallatin County, KY; Grant County, KY; Kenton County, KY; Pendleton County, KY; Brown County, OH; Butler County, OH; Clermont County, OH; Hamilton County, OH; Warren County, OH

Weather Station: Franklin Elevation: 669 feet

	Jan	Feb	Mar	Apr	May	Jun	Jul	Aug	Sep	Oct	Nov	Dec
High	37	41	52	63	73	82	85	85	78	66	53	41
Low	20	22	30	39	50	59	63	61	53	40	33	24
Precip	2.5	2.4	3.3	3.7	4.7	3.8	4.1	2.9	2.5	3.1	3.2	3.1
Snow	0.9	1.4	0.4	tr	0.0	0.0	0.0	0.0	0.0	0.0	0.2	na

High and Low temperatures in degrees Fahrenheit; Precipitation and Snow in inches

Population: 222,184; Growth (since 2000): 40.3%; Density: 553.6 persons per square mile; Race: 89.3% White, 3.6% Black/African American, 4.8% Asian, 0.1% American Indian/Alaska Native, 0.0% Native Hawaiian/Other Pacific Islander, 1.5% two or more races, 2.5% Hispanic of any race; Average household size: 2.71; Median age: 39.1; Age under 18: 25.9%; Age 65 and over: 12.9%; Males per 100 females: 101.0; Marriage status: 24.2% never married, 61.1% now married, 1.1% separated, 4.8% widowed, 9.9% divorced; Foreign born: 6.1%; Speak English only: 92.5%; With disability: 9.4%; Veterans: 8.4%; Ancestry: 27.9% German, 13.5% Irish, 10.2% English, 8.0% American, 4.3% Italian
Religion: Six largest groups: 9.2% Catholicism, 8.3% Baptist, 3.4% Methodist/Pietist, 2.9% Non-denominational Protestant, 1.7% Presbyterian-Reformed, 1.5% Pentecostal
Economy: Unemployment rate: 3.9%; Leading industries: 12.8 % retail trade; 12.6 % professional, scientific, and technical services; 10.9 % health care and social assistance; Farms: 942 totaling 106,624 acres; Company size: 4 employ 1,000 or more persons, 12 employ 500 to 999 persons, 130 employ 100 to 499 persons, 3,974 employ less than 100 persons; Business ownership: 5,030 women-owned, 233 Black-owned, 159 Hispanic-owned, 716 Asian-owned, 99 American Indian/Alaska Native-owned
Employment: 20.5% management, business, and financial, 8.7% computer, engineering, and science, 10.5% education, legal, community service, arts, and media, 7.6% healthcare practitioners, 13.0% service, 22.3% sales and office, 6.7% natural resources, construction, and maintenance, 10.7% production, transportation, and material moving
Income: Per capita: $36,057; Median household: $76,200; Average household: $100,123; Households with income of $100,000 or more: 36.8%; Poverty rate: 5.4%
Educational Attainment: High school diploma or higher: 92.9%; Bachelor's degree or higher: 41.0%; Graduate/professional degree or higher: 15.2%

Housing: Homeownership rate: 76.9%; Median home value: $196,200; Median year structure built: 1992; Homeowner vacancy rate: 0.5%; Median selected monthly owner costs: $1,583 with a mortgage, $558 without a mortgage; Median gross rent: $957 per month; Rental vacancy rate: 3.7%
Vital Statistics: Birth rate: 103.8 per 10,000 population; Death rate: 79.5 per 10,000 population; Age-adjusted cancer mortality rate: 160.9 deaths per 100,000 population
Health Insurance: 94.9% have insurance; 83.4% have private insurance; 21.6% have public insurance; 5.1% do not have insurance; 2.9% of children under 18 do not have insurance
Health Care: Physicians: 28.3 per 10,000 population; Dentists: 3.6 per 10,000 population; Hospital beds: 15.8 per 10,000 population; Hospital admissions: 464.6 per 10,000 population
Air Quality Index (AQI): Percent of Days: 66.1% good, 31.4% moderate, 2.5% unhealthy for sensitive individuals, 0.0% unhealthy, 0.0% very unhealthy; Annual median: 44; Annual maximum: 129
Transportation: Commute: 93.3% car, 0.4% public transportation, 0.7% walk, 5.2% work from home; Mean travel time to work: 25.0 minutes
2016 Presidential Election: 65.6% Trump, 28.5% Clinton, 3.7% Johnson, 0.6% Stein
National and State Parks: Caesar Creek Gorge State Natural Area; Caesar Creek State Park; Fort Ancient State Memorial
Additional Information Contacts
Warren Government . . . . (513) 695-1250
http://www.co.warren.oh.us

Warren County Communities

BUTLERVILLE (village). Covers a land area of 0.109 square miles and a water area of 0 square miles. Located at 39.30° N. Lat; 84.09° W. Long. Elevation is 866 feet.
Population: 122; Growth (since 2000): -47.2%; Density: 1,117.6 persons per square mile; Race: 99.2% White, 0.8% Black/African American, 0.0% Asian, 0.0% American Indian/Alaska Native, 0.0% Native Hawaiian/Other Pacific Islander, 0.0% Two or more races, 1.6% Hispanic of any race; Average household size: 2.44; Median age: 46.0; Age under 18: 21.3%; Age 65 and over: 15.6%; Males per 100 females: 103.8; Marriage status: 20.0% never married, 47.0% now married, 0.0% separated, 6.0% widowed, 27.0% divorced; Foreign born: 1.6%; Speak English only: 95.7%; With disability: 13.9%; Veterans: 7.3%; Ancestry: 20.5% German, 14.8% English, 9.8% Irish, 6.6% American, 6.6% British
Employment: 1.5% management, business, and financial, 1.5% computer, engineering, and science, 6.2% education, legal, community service, arts, and media, 0.0% healthcare practitioners, 18.5% service, 21.5% sales and office, 23.1% natural resources, construction, and maintenance, 27.7% production, transportation, and material moving
Income: Per capita: $23,630; Median household: $50,000; Average household: $55,062; Households with income of $100,000 or more: 18.0%; Poverty rate: 8.3%
Educational Attainment: High school diploma or higher: 75.0%; Bachelor's degree or higher: 2.3%; Graduate/professional degree or higher: n/a
Housing: Homeownership rate: 86.0%; Median home value: $107,500; Median year structure built: 1961; Homeowner vacancy rate: 0.0%; Median selected monthly owner costs: $983 with a mortgage, n/a without a mortgage; Median gross rent: $1,125 per month; Rental vacancy rate: 0.0%
Health Insurance: 87.7% have insurance; 76.2% have private insurance; 26.2% have public insurance; 12.3% do not have insurance; 19.2% of children under 18 do not have insurance
Transportation: Commute: 98.5% car, 0.0% public transportation, 0.0% walk, 1.5% work from home; Mean travel time to work: 27.1 minutes

CARLISLE (village). Covers a land area of 3.534 square miles and a water area of 0.198 square miles. Located at 39.58° N. Lat; 84.32° W. Long. Elevation is 689 feet.
Population: 5,125; Growth (since 2000): 0.1%; Density: 1,450.0 persons per square mile; Race: 97.5% White, 0.3% Black/African American, 0.3% Asian, 0.3% American Indian/Alaska Native, 0.0% Native Hawaiian/Other Pacific Islander, 1.7% Two or more races, 0.6% Hispanic of any race; Average household size: 2.70; Median age: 40.5; Age under 18: 23.6%; Age 65 and over: 18.4%; Males per 100 females: 94.2; Marriage status: 23.3% never married, 60.5% now married, 1.2% separated, 7.7% widowed, 8.6% divorced; Foreign born: 0.7%; Speak English only: 99.2%; With disability: 15.9%; Veterans: 9.6%; Ancestry: 21.7% German, 10.2% American, 9.7% Irish, 8.3% English, 3.6% Polish
Employment: 6.4% management, business, and financial, 5.7% computer, engineering, and science, 5.4% education, legal, community service, arts, and media, 6.7% healthcare practitioners, 23.2% service, 26.8% sales and office, 8.6% natural resources, construction, and maintenance, 17.2% production, transportation, and material moving
Income: Per capita: $23,768; Median household: $51,892; Average household: $64,011; Households with income of $100,000 or more: 19.1%; Poverty rate: 9.2%
Educational Attainment: High school diploma or higher: 88.5%; Bachelor's degree or higher: 13.0%; Graduate/professional degree or higher: 4.2%

School District(s)

Carlisle Local (PK-12)
2015-16 Enrollment: 1,604 . . . . (937) 746-0710
Housing: Homeownership rate: 75.7%; Median home value: $133,800; Median year structure built: 1976; Homeowner vacancy rate: 2.0%; Median selected monthly owner costs: $1,274 with a mortgage, $414 without a mortgage; Median gross rent: $802 per month; Rental vacancy rate: 9.2%
Health Insurance: 89.9% have insurance; 70.6% have private insurance; 33.7% have public insurance; 10.1% do not have insurance; 3.9% of children under 18 do not have insurance
Safety: Violent crime rate: 7.5 per 10,000 population; Property crime rate: 47.0 per 10,000 population
Transportation: Commute: 96.5% car, 0.2% public transportation, 0.3% walk, 1.8% work from home; Mean travel time to work: 23.5 minutes
Additional Information Contacts
Village of Carlisle . . . . (937) 746-0555
http://www.carlisleoh.org

CORWIN (village). Covers a land area of 0.345 square miles and a water area of 0 square miles. Located at 39.52° N. Lat; 84.07° W. Long. Elevation is 735 feet.
Population: 510; Growth (since 2000): 99.2%; Density: 1,479.2 persons per square mile; Race: 98.0% White, 0.0% Black/African American, 0.0% Asian, 0.0% American Indian/Alaska Native, 0.0% Native Hawaiian/Other Pacific Islander, 0.2% Two or more races, 1.8% Hispanic of any race; Average household size: 2.46; Median age: 42.7; Age under 18: 22.4%; Age 65 and over: 20.4%; Males per 100 females: 117.0; Marriage status: 17.2% never married, 64.4% now married, 1.2% separated, 8.5% widowed, 9.9% divorced; Foreign born: 1.8%; Speak English only: 97.9%; With disability: 17.3%; Veterans: 9.8%; Ancestry: 27.6% German, 13.3% Irish, 8.6% English, 7.1% American, 4.3% Dutch
Employment: 20.8% management, business, and financial, 9.3% computer, engineering, and science, 9.3% education, legal, community service, arts, and media, 8.5% healthcare practitioners, 14.8% service, 19.1% sales and office, 8.9% natural resources, construction, and maintenance, 9.3% production, transportation, and material moving
Income: Per capita: $26,780; Median household: $54,083; Average household: $64,279; Households with income of $100,000 or more: 16.5%; Poverty rate: 6.1%
Educational Attainment: High school diploma or higher: 84.4%; Bachelor's degree or higher: 29.5%; Graduate/professional degree or higher: 10.6%
Housing: Homeownership rate: 87.0%; Median home value: $165,300; Median year structure built: 2001; Homeowner vacancy rate: 0.0%; Median selected monthly owner costs: $1,359 with a mortgage, $455 without a mortgage; Median gross rent: $713 per month; Rental vacancy rate: 0.0%
Health Insurance: 96.1% have insurance; 71.4% have private insurance; 34.5% have public insurance; 3.9% do not have insurance; 1.8% of children under 18 do not have insurance
Transportation: Commute: 93.5% car, 0.9% public transportation, 0.9% walk, 3.9% work from home; Mean travel time to work: 30.0 minutes

FIVE POINTS (CDP). Covers a land area of 2.059 square miles and a water area of 0 square miles. Located at 39.56° N. Lat; 84.19° W. Long. Elevation is 988 feet.
History: Five Points takes its name from the near-five way intersection on the western edge of the area.
Population: 1,905; Growth (since 2000): -13.1%; Density: 925.4 persons per square mile; Race: 100.0% White, 0.0% Black/African American, 0.0% Asian, 0.0% American Indian/Alaska Native, 0.0% Native Hawaiian/Other Pacific Islander, 0.0% Two or more races, 0.0% Hispanic of any race; Average household size: 2.93; Median age: 47.0; Age under 18: 27.3%;

Age 65 and over: 21.8%; Males per 100 females: 101.5; Marriage status: 12.3% never married, 79.1% now married, 2.9% separated, 4.0% widowed, 4.6% divorced; Foreign born: 2.0%; Speak English only: 96.8%; With disability: 6.8%; Veterans: 15.7%; Ancestry: 32.0% German, 15.0% English, 14.8% American, 7.7% Irish, 7.5% Italian
Employment: 23.3% management, business, and financial, 3.0% computer, engineering, and science, 10.6% education, legal, community service, arts, and media, 12.9% healthcare practitioners, 18.9% service, 20.0% sales and office, 0.0% natural resources, construction, and maintenance, 11.3% production, transportation, and material moving
Income: Per capita: $45,314; Median household: $108,304; Average household: $131,109; Households with income of $100,000 or more: 52.6%; Poverty rate: n/a
Educational Attainment: High school diploma or higher: 99.3%; Bachelor's degree or higher: 67.2%; Graduate/professional degree or higher: 29.1%
Housing: Homeownership rate: 100.0%; Median home value: $259,400; Median year structure built: 1993; Homeowner vacancy rate: 0.0%; Median selected monthly owner costs: $1,849 with a mortgage, $679 without a mortgage; Median gross rent: n/a per month; Rental vacancy rate: 0.0%
Health Insurance: 99.2% have insurance; 99.2% have private insurance; 22.3% have public insurance; 0.8% do not have insurance; 0.0% of children under 18 do not have insurance
Transportation: Commute: 86.1% car, 0.0% public transportation, 0.0% walk, 12.9% work from home; Mean travel time to work: 22.4 minutes

FRANKLIN (city). Covers a land area of 9.173 square miles and a water area of 0.170 square miles. Located at 39.55° N. Lat; 84.30° W. Long. Elevation is 682 feet.
History: Named for Benjamin Franklin, American statesman and inventor. Franklin was founded in 1796 by William Schenck, an officer in Harrison 's Army in the War of 1812. The town was a port on the Great Miami River after the Miami & Erie Canal was built. Later, paper mills were established here.
Population: 11,802; Growth (since 2000): 3.6%; Density: 1,286.6 persons per square mile; Race: 95.0% White, 1.3% Black/African American, 1.1% Asian, 0.3% American Indian/Alaska Native, 0.0% Native Hawaiian/Other Pacific Islander, 2.1% Two or more races, 1.7% Hispanic of any race; Average household size: 2.44; Median age: 37.3; Age under 18: 24.5%; Age 65 and over: 13.8%; Males per 100 females: 93.1; Marriage status: 24.5% never married, 50.5% now married, 2.4% separated, 8.6% widowed, 16.4% divorced; Foreign born: 1.6%; Speak English only: 97.6%; With disability: 15.7%; Veterans: 7.6%; Ancestry: 18.4% German, 14.7% Irish, 9.7% American, 7.5% English, 3.3% Italian
Employment: 11.4% management, business, and financial, 5.1% computer, engineering, and science, 5.6% education, legal, community service, arts, and media, 5.8% healthcare practitioners, 13.3% service, 23.1% sales and office, 11.5% natural resources, construction, and maintenance, 24.3% production, transportation, and material moving
Income: Per capita: $23,538; Median household: $46,438; Average household: $57,007; Households with income of $100,000 or more: 14.2%; Poverty rate: 16.9%
Educational Attainment: High school diploma or higher: 81.9%; Bachelor's degree or higher: 12.6%; Graduate/professional degree or higher: 3.4%

School District(s)

Franklin City (KG-12)
2015-16 Enrollment: 2,904 . . . . (937) 746-1699
Housing: Homeownership rate: 56.7%; Median home value: $102,500; Median year structure built: 1964; Homeowner vacancy rate: 1.9%; Median selected monthly owner costs: $1,070 with a mortgage, $368 without a mortgage; Median gross rent: $782 per month; Rental vacancy rate: 2.0%
Health Insurance: 91.6% have insurance; 64.7% have private insurance; 38.6% have public insurance; 8.4% do not have insurance; 2.8% of children under 18 do not have insurance
Hospitals: Atrium Medical Center (250 beds)
Safety: Violent crime rate: 19.5 per 10,000 population; Property crime rate: 460.0 per 10,000 population
Transportation: Commute: 97.9% car, 0.4% public transportation, 0.6% walk, 1.1% work from home; Mean travel time to work: 21.3 minutes
Additional Information Contacts
City of Franklin . . . . (937) 746-9921
http://www.franklinohio.org

HARVEYSBURG (village). Covers a land area of 0.992 square miles and a water area of 0.024 square miles. Located at 39.50° N. Lat; 83.99° W. Long. Elevation is 925 feet.
Population: 576; Growth (since 2000): 2.3%; Density: 580.6 persons per square mile; Race: 98.1% White, 0.0% Black/African American, 1.0% Asian, 0.0% American Indian/Alaska Native, 0.0% Native Hawaiian/Other Pacific Islander, 0.9% Two or more races, 0.0% Hispanic of any race; Average household size: 2.59; Median age: 33.4; Age under 18: 31.9%; Age 65 and over: 6.1%; Males per 100 females: 104.5; Marriage status: 26.1% never married, 63.6% now married, 1.4% separated, 3.0% widowed, 7.3% divorced; Foreign born: 0.0%; Speak English only: 98.5%; With disability: 8.0%; Veterans: 8.4%; Ancestry: 24.8% German, 19.4% Irish, 13.5% English, 4.9% Scottish, 4.2% Italian
Employment: 14.6% management, business, and financial, 4.8% computer, engineering, and science, 3.2% education, legal, community service, arts, and media, 11.1% healthcare practitioners, 15.0% service, 19.4% sales and office, 20.4% natural resources, construction, and maintenance, 11.5% production, transportation, and material moving
Income: Per capita: $26,293; Median household: $56,250; Average household: $67,767; Households with income of $100,000 or more: 23.0%; Poverty rate: 8.7%
Educational Attainment: High school diploma or higher: 93.6%; Bachelor's degree or higher: 23.5%; Graduate/professional degree or higher: 8.4%
Housing: Homeownership rate: 73.9%; Median home value: $119,600; Median year structure built: 1990; Homeowner vacancy rate: 0.0%; Median selected monthly owner costs: $1,212 with a mortgage, $417 without a mortgage; Median gross rent: $704 per month; Rental vacancy rate: 10.8%
Health Insurance: 91.3% have insurance; 76.9% have private insurance; 20.5% have public insurance; 8.7% do not have insurance; 4.3% of children under 18 do not have insurance
Transportation: Commute: 89.6% car, 0.6% public transportation, 0.0% walk, 9.7% work from home; Mean travel time to work: 31.9 minutes

HUNTER (CDP). Covers a land area of 1.626 square miles and a water area of 0 square miles. Located at 39.49° N. Lat; 84.29° W. Long. Elevation is 883 feet.
Population: 2,277; Growth (since 2000): 31.1%; Density: 1,400.0 persons per square mile; Race: 100.0% White, 0.0% Black/African American, 0.0% Asian, 0.0% American Indian/Alaska Native, 0.0% Native Hawaiian/Other Pacific Islander, 0.0% Two or more races, 2.2% Hispanic of any race; Average household size: 2.61; Median age: 49.7; Age under 18: 16.7%; Age 65 and over: 25.7%; Males per 100 females: 97.2; Marriage status: 20.9% never married, 63.1% now married, 0.0% separated, 4.8% widowed, 11.2% divorced; Foreign born: 1.5%; Speak English only: 98.7%; With disability: 14.4%; Veterans: 14.7%; Ancestry: 27.8% German, 15.7% Irish, 10.7% English, 6.9% American, 4.9% Scottish
Employment: 7.0% management, business, and financial, 1.1% computer, engineering, and science, 4.5% education, legal, community service, arts, and media, 6.6% healthcare practitioners, 14.8% service, 28.2% sales and office, 19.3% natural resources, construction, and maintenance, 18.6% production, transportation, and material moving
Income: Per capita: $28,521; Median household: $59,500; Average household: $73,661; Households with income of $100,000 or more: 22.0%; Poverty rate: 1.3%
Educational Attainment: High school diploma or higher: 84.6%; Bachelor's degree or higher: 7.7%; Graduate/professional degree or higher: 4.9%
Housing: Homeownership rate: 84.3%; Median home value: $148,100; Median year structure built: 1964; Homeowner vacancy rate: 0.0%; Median selected monthly owner costs: $1,265 with a mortgage, $396 without a mortgage; Median gross rent: $1,162 per month; Rental vacancy rate: 0.0%
Health Insurance: 90.3% have insurance; 75.2% have private insurance; 32.1% have public insurance; 9.7% do not have insurance; 0.0% of children under 18 do not have insurance
Transportation: Commute: 98.8% car, 0.0% public transportation, 0.0% walk, 1.2% work from home; Mean travel time to work: 24.5 minutes

KINGS MILLS (CDP). Covers a land area of 1.344 square miles and a water area of 0.049 square miles. Located at 39.36° N. Lat; 84.24° W. Long. Elevation is 758 feet.
Population: 1,470; Growth (since 2000): n/a; Density: 1,093.7 persons per square mile; Race: 100.0% White, 0.0% Black/African American, 0.0% Asian, 0.0% American Indian/Alaska Native, 0.0% Native Hawaiian/Other

Pacific Islander, 0.0% Two or more races, 0.0% Hispanic of any race; Average household size: 2.70; Median age: 36.7; Age under 18: 25.0%; Age 65 and over: 6.3%; Males per 100 females: 106.1; Marriage status: 23.1% never married, 65.3% now married, 1.1% separated, 1.5% widowed, 10.1% divorced; Foreign born: 0.0%; Speak English only: 98.9%; With disability: 5.4%; Veterans: 9.6%; Ancestry: 28.4% German, 10.8% Irish, 9.6% American, 7.2% English, 2.8% Hungarian

Employment: 29.3% management, business, and financial, 12.7% computer, engineering, and science, 10.7% education, legal, community service, arts, and media, 1.8% healthcare practitioners, 11.8% service, 15.7% sales and office, 6.9% natural resources, construction, and maintenance, 11.2% production, transportation, and material moving

Income: Per capita: $37,617; Median household: $102,768; Average household: $103,145; Households with income of $100,000 or more: 50.3%; Poverty rate: 2.6%

Educational Attainment: High school diploma or higher: 91.9%; Bachelor's degree or higher: 42.0%; Graduate/professional degree or higher: 10.6%

School District(s)

Kings Local (PK-12)
2015-16 Enrollment: 4,283 . . . . (513) 398-8050

Housing: Homeownership rate: 81.1%; Median home value: $194,200; Median year structure built: 1995; Homeowner vacancy rate: 0.0%; Median selected monthly owner costs: $1,642 with a mortgage, $912 without a mortgage; Median gross rent: $859 per month; Rental vacancy rate: 0.0%

Health Insurance: 98.6% have insurance; 95.1% have private insurance; 9.3% have public insurance; 1.4% do not have insurance; 0.0% of children under 18 do not have insurance

Transportation: Commute: 87.3% car, 0.0% public transportation, 0.0% walk, 12.7% work from home; Mean travel time to work: 20.6 minutes

---

LANDEN (CDP). Covers a land area of 2.028 square miles and a water area of 0.091 square miles. Located at 39.32° N. Lat; 84.28° W. Long. Elevation is 814 feet.

Population: 6,776; Growth (since 2000): -46.9%; Density: 3,340.8 persons per square mile; Race: 92.1% White, 2.9% Black/African American, 3.2% Asian, 0.0% American Indian/Alaska Native, 0.0% Native Hawaiian/Other Pacific Islander, 1.3% Two or more races, 0.4% Hispanic of any race; Average household size: 2.61; Median age: 35.9; Age under 18: 30.2%; Age 65 and over: 8.4%; Males per 100 females: 93.2; Marriage status: 20.7% never married, 58.2% now married, 1.0% separated, 4.6% widowed, 16.5% divorced; Foreign born: 4.8%; Speak English only: 92.2%; With disability: 5.3%; Veterans: 8.3%; Ancestry: 35.7% German, 19.7% Irish, 12.2% English, 7.7% American, 6.7% Italian

Employment: 20.3% management, business, and financial, 7.9% computer, engineering, and science, 15.8% education, legal, community service, arts, and media, 9.5% healthcare practitioners, 10.4% service, 26.7% sales and office, 4.1% natural resources, construction, and maintenance, 5.2% production, transportation, and material moving

Income: Per capita: $38,466; Median household: $79,600; Average household: $99,762; Households with income of $100,000 or more: 41.2%; Poverty rate: 1.3%

Educational Attainment: High school diploma or higher: 98.1%; Bachelor's degree or higher: 53.0%; Graduate/professional degree or higher: 21.3%

Housing: Homeownership rate: 73.2%; Median home value: $188,600; Median year structure built: 1983; Homeowner vacancy rate: 2.4%; Median selected monthly owner costs: $1,406 with a mortgage, $661 without a mortgage; Median gross rent: $1,142 per month; Rental vacancy rate: 4.9%

Health Insurance: 97.0% have insurance; 87.1% have private insurance; 17.1% have public insurance; 3.0% do not have insurance; 0.0% of children under 18 do not have insurance

Transportation: Commute: 93.9% car, 0.7% public transportation, 0.2% walk, 4.7% work from home; Mean travel time to work: 23.4 minutes

---

LEBANON (city). County seat. Covers a land area of 12.963 square miles and a water area of 0.009 square miles. Located at 39.42° N. Lat; 84.22° W. Long. Elevation is 771 feet.

History: Named for the Semitic translation of "to be white". Lebanon was founded in 1803 and grew as the commercial center for the region between the two Miami Rivers. This was the home of Thomas Corwin (1794-1865) who was governor of Ohio, a U.S. senator, Secretary of the Treasury, and Minister to Mexico under Abraham Lincoln.

Population: 20,536; Growth (since 2000): 21.1%; Density: 1,584.1 persons per square mile; Race: 89.6% White, 5.2% Black/African American, 1.6% Asian, 0.2% American Indian/Alaska Native, 0.1% Native Hawaiian/Other Pacific Islander, 1.7% Two or more races, 2.4% Hispanic of any race; Average household size: 2.75; Median age: 33.2; Age under 18: 28.2%; Age 65 and over: 10.7%; Males per 100 females: 96.2; Marriage status: 29.9% never married, 51.6% now married, 1.0% separated, 5.9% widowed, 12.6% divorced; Foreign born: 4.3%; Speak English only: 95.3%; With disability: 10.6%; Veterans: 7.0%; Ancestry: 29.7% German, 21.3% Irish, 11.6% English, 7.3% American, 4.2% Italian

Employment: 12.7% management, business, and financial, 5.8% computer, engineering, and science, 9.3% education, legal, community service, arts, and media, 6.1% healthcare practitioners, 16.7% service, 27.3% sales and office, 8.6% natural resources, construction, and maintenance, 13.4% production, transportation, and material moving

Income: Per capita: $25,194; Median household: $61,669; Average household: $70,089; Households with income of $100,000 or more: 22.4%; Poverty rate: 10.2%

Educational Attainment: High school diploma or higher: 93.1%; Bachelor's degree or higher: 29.2%; Graduate/professional degree or higher: 7.7%

School District(s)

Greater Ohio Virtual School (07-12)
2015-16 Enrollment: 427. . . . . (513) 695-2924
Lebanon City (PK-12)
2015-16 Enrollment: 5,492 . . . . (513) 934-5770
Warren County Vocational School (07-12)
2015-16 Enrollment: n/a . . . . (513) 932-5677

Two-year College(s)

Warren County Career Center (Public)
Fall 2016 Enrollment: 234 . . . . (513) 933-3944

Vocational/Technical School(s)

Dental Assistant Pro-Lebanon (Private, For-profit)
Fall 2016 Enrollment: 13 . . . . (513) 932-3413

Housing: Homeownership rate: 60.4%; Median home value: $163,800; Median year structure built: 1990; Homeowner vacancy rate: 0.0%; Median selected monthly owner costs: $1,310 with a mortgage, $486 without a mortgage; Median gross rent: $790 per month; Rental vacancy rate: 5.3%

Health Insurance: 90.3% have insurance; 70.6% have private insurance; 28.1% have public insurance; 9.7% do not have insurance; 8.9% of children under 18 do not have insurance

Safety: Violent crime rate: 10.6 per 10,000 population; Property crime rate: 174.2 per 10,000 population

Newspapers: Western Star (weekly circulation 23,000)

Transportation: Commute: 94.3% car, 0.3% public transportation, 1.8% walk, 3.6% work from home; Mean travel time to work: 23.1 minutes

Airports: Warren County/John Lane Field (general aviation)

Additional Information Contacts

City of Lebanon . . . . (513) 932-3060
http://www.ci.lebanon.oh.us

LOVELAND PARK (CDP). Covers a land area of 1.145 square miles and a water area of 0.052 square miles. Located at 39.29° N. Lat; 84.26° W. Long. Elevation is 732 feet.

Population: 1,318; Growth (since 2000): -26.7%; Density: 1,150.7 persons per square mile; Race: 95.2% White, 0.0% Black/African American, 2.0% Asian, 0.0% American Indian/Alaska Native, 0.0% Native Hawaiian/Other Pacific Islander, 1.1% Two or more races, 1.7% Hispanic of any race; Average household size: 2.34; Median age: 50.1; Age under 18: 19.3%; Age 65 and over: 22.2%; Males per 100 females: 108.1; Marriage status: 21.4% never married, 66.1% now married, 1.6% separated, 4.2% widowed, 8.3% divorced; Foreign born: 3.7%; Speak English only: 96.8%; With disability: 8.8%; Veterans: 9.9%; Ancestry: 24.9% American, 19.8% Irish, 15.3% German, 5.6% English, 3.9% Greek

Employment: 9.6% management, business, and financial, 6.8% computer, engineering, and science, 6.5% education, legal, community service, arts, and media, 4.4% healthcare practitioners, 13.0% service, 26.1% sales and office, 15.0% natural resources, construction, and maintenance, 18.4% production, transportation, and material moving

Income: Per capita: $32,843; Median household: $64,754; Average household: $75,786; Households with income of $100,000 or more: 32.5%; Poverty rate: 1.9%

Educational Attainment: High school diploma or higher: 92.7%; Bachelor's degree or higher: 14.0%; Graduate/professional degree or higher: 2.3%

Housing: Homeownership rate: 88.8%; Median home value: $156,900; Median year structure built: 1966; Homeowner vacancy rate: 0.0%; Median selected monthly owner costs: $1,140 with a mortgage, $386 without a mortgage; Median gross rent: n/a per month; Rental vacancy rate: 36.4%
Health Insurance: 100.0% have insurance; 86.5% have private insurance; 22.2% have public insurance; 0.0% do not have insurance; 0.0% of children under 18 do not have insurance
Transportation: Commute: 97.3% car, 0.0% public transportation, 0.0% walk, 1.6% work from home; Mean travel time to work: 23.7 minutes

MAINEVILLE (village). Covers a land area of 1.369 square miles and a water area of 0 square miles. Located at 39.31° N. Lat; 84.21° W. Long. Elevation is 807 feet.
Population: 1,249; Growth (since 2000): 41.1%; Density: 912.6 persons per square mile; Race: 95.6% White, 0.0% Black/African American, 3.0% Asian, 0.0% American Indian/Alaska Native, 0.0% Native Hawaiian/Other Pacific Islander, 1.2% Two or more races, 1.8% Hispanic of any race; Average household size: 2.75; Median age: 31.3; Age under 18: 26.9%; Age 65 and over: 9.5%; Males per 100 females: 101.9; Marriage status: 22.2% never married, 59.7% now married, 1.9% separated, 7.5% widowed, 10.5% divorced; Foreign born: 1.0%; Speak English only: 98.7%; With disability: 10.9%; Veterans: 9.9%; Ancestry: 40.4% German, 21.4% Irish, 16.8% English, 6.3% American, 3.8% Italian
Employment: 11.2% management, business, and financial, 7.6% computer, engineering, and science, 9.3% education, legal, community service, arts, and media, 11.3% healthcare practitioners, 12.7% service, 26.0% sales and office, 12.3% natural resources, construction, and maintenance, 9.5% production, transportation, and material moving
Income: Per capita: $29,529; Median household: $71,063; Average household: $78,921; Households with income of $100,000 or more: 34.4%; Poverty rate: 4.4%
Educational Attainment: High school diploma or higher: 90.1%; Bachelor's degree or higher: 33.2%; Graduate/professional degree or higher: 9.9%

School District(s)

Kings Local (PK-12)
2015-16 Enrollment: 4,283 . . . . (513) 398-8050
Little Miami Local (PK-12)
2015-16 Enrollment: 4,322 . . . . (513) 899-2264
Housing: Homeownership rate: 74.6%; Median home value: $155,600; Median year structure built: 1995; Homeowner vacancy rate: 0.0%; Median selected monthly owner costs: $1,246 with a mortgage, $535 without a mortgage; Median gross rent: $784 per month; Rental vacancy rate: 8.9%
Health Insurance: 92.2% have insurance; 82.1% have private insurance; 16.9% have public insurance; 7.8% do not have insurance; 0.9% of children under 18 do not have insurance
Transportation: Commute: 88.7% car, 0.3% public transportation, 0.6% walk, 8.7% work from home; Mean travel time to work: 33.2 minutes

MASON (city). Covers a land area of 18.629 square miles and a water area of 0.036 square miles. Located at 39.35° N. Lat; 84.30° W. Long. Elevation is 807 feet.
Population: 32,025; Growth (since 2000): 45.5%; Density: 1,719.1 persons per square mile; Race: 84.6% White, 3.9% Black/African American, 8.8% Asian, 0.0% American Indian/Alaska Native, 0.0% Native Hawaiian/Other Pacific Islander, 1.8% Two or more races, 3.4% Hispanic of any race; Average household size: 2.65; Median age: 41.9; Age under 18: 27.3%; Age 65 and over: 14.5%; Males per 100 females: 94.1; Marriage status: 24.4% never married, 61.2% now married, 1.4% separated, 5.5% widowed, 8.9% divorced; Foreign born: 11.3%; Speak English only: 86.1%; With disability: 8.3%; Veterans: 7.6%; Ancestry: 29.0% German, 11.8% Irish, 9.4% English, 6.1% Italian, 5.7% American
Employment: 26.6% management, business, and financial, 10.3% computer, engineering, and science, 12.2% education, legal, community service, arts, and media, 6.7% healthcare practitioners, 11.0% service, 22.9% sales and office, 4.0% natural resources, construction, and maintenance, 6.4% production, transportation, and material moving
Income: Per capita: $46,005; Median household: $92,819; Average household: $121,969; Households with income of $100,000 or more: 46.5%; Poverty rate: 2.6%
Educational Attainment: High school diploma or higher: 97.5%; Bachelor's degree or higher: 59.3%; Graduate/professional degree or higher: 26.0%

School District(s)

Mason City (PK-12)
2015-16 Enrollment: 10,605 . . . . (513) 398-0474
Housing: Homeownership rate: 81.4%; Median home value: $230,100; Median year structure built: 1994; Homeowner vacancy rate: 0.0%; Median selected monthly owner costs: $1,709 with a mortgage, $634 without a mortgage; Median gross rent: $1,056 per month; Rental vacancy rate: 0.8%
Health Insurance: 96.7% have insurance; 89.4% have private insurance; 17.1% have public insurance; 3.3% do not have insurance; 2.0% of children under 18 do not have insurance
Safety: Violent crime rate: 1.8 per 10,000 population; Property crime rate: 99.9 per 10,000 population
Transportation: Commute: 92.2% car, 0.6% public transportation, 0.7% walk, 6.2% work from home; Mean travel time to work: 24.5 minutes
Additional Information Contacts
City of Mason . . . . (513) 229-8500
http://www.imaginemason.org

MORROW (village). Covers a land area of 1.925 square miles and a water area of 0.037 square miles. Located at 39.35° N. Lat; 84.12° W. Long. Elevation is 643 feet.
History: Morrow was settled in 1844 and named for Jeremiah Morrow, Governor of Ohio from 1822 to 1826.
Population: 1,490; Growth (since 2000): 15.9%; Density: 774.2 persons per square mile; Race: 97.0% White, 1.2% Black/African American, 0.0% Asian, 0.8% American Indian/Alaska Native, 0.0% Native Hawaiian/Other Pacific Islander, 0.5% Two or more races, 4.1% Hispanic of any race; Average household size: 2.75; Median age: 35.5; Age under 18: 26.3%; Age 65 and over: 15.4%; Males per 100 females: 93.2; Marriage status: 30.8% never married, 53.3% now married, 0.8% separated, 5.3% widowed, 10.7% divorced; Foreign born: 4.0%; Speak English only: 94.7%; With disability: 13.8%; Veterans: 5.6%; Ancestry: 34.4% German, 15.9% Irish, 9.8% American, 8.9% English, 3.0% Italian
Employment: 9.5% management, business, and financial, 3.4% computer, engineering, and science, 9.3% education, legal, community service, arts, and media, 5.8% healthcare practitioners, 22.9% service, 20.5% sales and office, 5.4% natural resources, construction, and maintenance, 23.2% production, transportation, and material moving
Income: Per capita: $26,249; Median household: $60,417; Average household: $70,863; Households with income of $100,000 or more: 21.1%; Poverty rate: 15.0%
Educational Attainment: High school diploma or higher: 86.7%; Bachelor's degree or higher: 21.4%; Graduate/professional degree or higher: 6.4%

School District(s)

Little Miami Local (PK-12)
2015-16 Enrollment: 4,322 . . . . (513) 899-2264
Housing: Homeownership rate: 66.9%; Median home value: $139,400; Median year structure built: 1959; Homeowner vacancy rate: 0.0%; Median selected monthly owner costs: $1,239 with a mortgage, $463 without a mortgage; Median gross rent: $815 per month; Rental vacancy rate: 0.0%
Health Insurance: 89.2% have insurance; 69.8% have private insurance; 35.5% have public insurance; 10.8% do not have insurance; 4.1% of children under 18 do not have insurance
Transportation: Commute: 97.2% car, 0.0% public transportation, 1.0% walk, 0.8% work from home; Mean travel time to work: 29.7 minutes

OREGONIA (unincorporated postal area)
ZCTA: 45054
Covers a land area of 30.857 square miles and a water area of 0.022 square miles. Located at 39.44° N. Lat; 84.08° W. Long. Elevation is 696 feet.
Population: 2,774; Growth (since 2000): 64.2%; Density: 89.9 persons per square mile; Race: 94.5% White, 0.6% Black/African American, 0.3% Asian, 0.0% American Indian/Alaska Native, 0.0% Native Hawaiian/Other Pacific Islander, 4.6% Two or more races, 0.5% Hispanic of any race; Average household size: 2.66; Median age: 37.8; Age under 18: 25.3%; Age 65 and over: 10.2%; Males per 100 females: 106.8; Marriage status: 14.8% never married, 73.0% now married, 2.2% separated, 4.3% widowed, 7.9% divorced; Foreign born: 1.5%; Speak English only: 98.7%; With disability: 11.9%; Veterans: 8.7%; Ancestry: 32.4% German, 16.0% Irish, 11.8% American, 9.9% English, 3.5% Norwegian
Employment: 12.2% management, business, and financial, 12.8% computer, engineering, and science, 9.0% education, legal, community

service, arts, and media, 5.3% healthcare practitioners, 13.1% service, 17.5% sales and office, 18.0% natural resources, construction, and maintenance, 12.1% production, transportation, and material moving
Income: Per capita: $31,367; Median household: $57,248; Average household: $80,885; Households with income of $100,000 or more: 31.4%; Poverty rate: 9.0%
Educational Attainment: High school diploma or higher: 92.4%; Bachelor's degree or higher: 30.5%; Graduate/professional degree or higher: 12.6%
Housing: Homeownership rate: 95.3%; Median home value: $225,000; Median year structure built: 1991; Homeowner vacancy rate: 0.0%; Median selected monthly owner costs: $1,688 with a mortgage, $594 without a mortgage; Median gross rent: $818 per month; Rental vacancy rate: 0.0%
Health Insurance: 94.1% have insurance; 87.2% have private insurance; 16.7% have public insurance; 5.9% do not have insurance; 0.0% of children under 18 do not have insurance
Transportation: Commute: 90.3% car, 0.7% public transportation, 3.1% walk, 5.9% work from home; Mean travel time to work: 28.6 minutes

---

PLEASANT PLAIN (village). Covers a land area of 0.162 square miles and a water area of 0 square miles. Located at 39.28° N. Lat; 84.11° W. Long. Elevation is 886 feet.
Population: 117; Growth (since 2000): -25.0%; Density: 722.3 persons per square mile; Race: 95.7% White, 0.0% Black/African American, 2.6% Asian, 0.0% American Indian/Alaska Native, 0.0% Native Hawaiian/Other Pacific Islander, 1.7% Two or more races, 0.0% Hispanic of any race; Average household size: 2.21; Median age: 49.5; Age under 18: 12.8%; Age 65 and over: 14.5%; Males per 100 females: 108.1; Marriage status: 33.3% never married, 43.1% now married, 2.9% separated, 3.9% widowed, 19.6% divorced; Foreign born: 0.9%; Speak English only: 100.0%; With disability: 27.4%; Veterans: 2.9%; Ancestry: 29.9% German, 12.8% American, 10.3% Irish, 7.7% British, 7.7% Dutch
Employment: 11.9% management, business, and financial, 5.1% computer, engineering, and science, 0.0% education, legal, community service, arts, and media, 8.5% healthcare practitioners, 3.4% service, 25.4% sales and office, 8.5% natural resources, construction, and maintenance, 37.3% production, transportation, and material moving
Income: Per capita: $22,683; Median household: $34,583; Average household: $49,896; Households with income of $100,000 or more: 7.6%; Poverty rate: 19.7%
Educational Attainment: High school diploma or higher: 85.7%; Bachelor's degree or higher: 8.8%; Graduate/professional degree or higher: 2.2%
Housing: Homeownership rate: 56.6%; Median home value: $76,300; Median year structure built: Before 1940; Homeowner vacancy rate: 0.0%; Median selected monthly owner costs: $950 with a mortgage, $358 without a mortgage; Median gross rent: $721 per month; Rental vacancy rate: 0.0%
Health Insurance: 82.9% have insurance; 54.7% have private insurance; 29.9% have public insurance; 17.1% do not have insurance; 20.0% of children under 18 do not have insurance
Transportation: Commute: 88.1% car, 0.0% public transportation, 5.1% walk, 6.8% work from home; Mean travel time to work: 25.8 minutes

---

SOUTH LEBANON (village). Covers a land area of 2.647 square miles and a water area of 0.034 square miles. Located at 39.37° N. Lat; 84.22° W. Long. Elevation is 630 feet.
Population: 4,746; Growth (since 2000): 87.0%; Density: 1,793.2 persons per square mile; Race: 92.2% White, 2.9% Black/African American, 2.8% Asian, 0.0% American Indian/Alaska Native, 0.0% Native Hawaiian/Other Pacific Islander, 1.1% Two or more races, 1.2% Hispanic of any race; Average household size: 2.72; Median age: 40.1; Age under 18: 20.0%; Age 65 and over: 18.8%; Males per 100 females: 93.3; Marriage status: 25.0% never married, 60.0% now married, 1.6% separated, 3.9% widowed, 11.0% divorced; Foreign born: 4.7%; Speak English only: 92.4%; With disability: 10.7%; Veterans: 10.8%; Ancestry: 29.9% German, 20.6% Irish, 10.2% American, 7.4% English, 5.5% Scottish
Employment: 24.3% management, business, and financial, 10.5% computer, engineering, and science, 15.3% education, legal, community service, arts, and media, 4.4% healthcare practitioners, 12.8% service, 15.9% sales and office, 4.0% natural resources, construction, and maintenance, 12.9% production, transportation, and material moving
Income: Per capita: $35,808; Median household: $61,957; Average household: $95,507; Households with income of $100,000 or more: 35.0%; Poverty rate: 11.4%
Educational Attainment: High school diploma or higher: 91.2%; Bachelor's degree or higher: 49.9%; Graduate/professional degree or higher: 6.5%
Housing: Homeownership rate: 71.9%; Median home value: $230,300; Median year structure built: 2003; Homeowner vacancy rate: 0.0%; Median selected monthly owner costs: $2,007 with a mortgage, $581 without a mortgage; Median gross rent: $834 per month; Rental vacancy rate: 0.0%
Health Insurance: 91.2% have insurance; 70.6% have private insurance; 28.7% have public insurance; 8.8% do not have insurance; 0.0% of children under 18 do not have insurance
Transportation: Commute: 95.9% car, 0.1% public transportation, 0.1% walk, 3.5% work from home; Mean travel time to work: 25.2 minutes
Additional Information Contacts
Village of South Lebanon . . . . (513) 494-2296
http://www.southlebanonohio.org

SPRINGBORO (city). Covers a land area of 9.355 square miles and a water area of <.001 square miles. Located at 39.56° N. Lat; 84.23° W. Long. Elevation is 781 feet.
History: Settled as early as 1796, Springboro was founded in 1815 by Jonathan Wright, a relative of the Wright Brothers, as "Springborough." Jonathan Wright's father, Joel Wright, was a surveyor who plotted Columbus, Ohio. Springboro was predominantly Quaker during its earlier years.
Population: 17,978; Growth (since 2000): 45.2%; Density: 1,921.7 persons per square mile; Race: 88.7% White, 2.8% Black/African American, 5.1% Asian, 0.0% American Indian/Alaska Native, 0.0% Native Hawaiian/Other Pacific Islander, 2.8% Two or more races, 2.6% Hispanic of any race; Average household size: 2.88; Median age: 37.6; Age under 18: 30.6%; Age 65 and over: 12.7%; Males per 100 females: 95.6; Marriage status: 20.6% never married, 67.7% now married, 0.4% separated, 3.2% widowed, 8.5% divorced; Foreign born: 4.5%; Speak English only: 96.0%; With disability: 6.6%; Veterans: 9.2%; Ancestry: 27.7% German, 13.2% Irish, 12.1% English, 6.7% American, 3.7% Italian
Employment: 23.0% management, business, and financial, 9.9% computer, engineering, and science, 13.9% education, legal, community service, arts, and media, 9.5% healthcare practitioners, 11.5% service, 21.0% sales and office, 3.3% natural resources, construction, and maintenance, 8.0% production, transportation, and material moving
Income: Per capita: $37,477; Median household: $99,364; Average household: $108,456; Households with income of $100,000 or more: 49.8%; Poverty rate: 2.6%
Educational Attainment: High school diploma or higher: 96.4%; Bachelor's degree or higher: 48.7%; Graduate/professional degree or higher: 17.9%

School District(s)

Springboro Community City (PK-12)
2015-16 Enrollment: 5,985 . . . . (937) 748-3960

Two-year College(s)

Miami-Jacobs Career College-Springboro (Private, For-profit)
Fall 2016 Enrollment: 33 . . . . (937) 746-1830
2016-17 Tuition: In-state $10,785; Out-of-state $10,785
Housing: Homeownership rate: 85.0%; Median home value: $207,500; Median year structure built: 1993; Homeowner vacancy rate: 1.2%; Median selected monthly owner costs: $1,608 with a mortgage, $576 without a mortgage; Median gross rent: $989 per month; Rental vacancy rate: 2.0%
Health Insurance: 98.0% have insurance; 88.8% have private insurance; 20.6% have public insurance; 2.0% do not have insurance; 0.0% of children under 18 do not have insurance
Safety: Violent crime rate: 6.0 per 10,000 population; Property crime rate: 56.0 per 10,000 population
Transportation: Commute: 94.9% car, 0.6% public transportation, 0.2% walk, 3.9% work from home; Mean travel time to work: 22.9 minutes
Additional Information Contacts
City of Springboro . . . . (937) 748-4343
http://www.ci.springboro.oh.us

WAYNESVILLE (village). Covers a land area of 2.377 square miles and a water area of 0.006 square miles. Located at 39.53° N. Lat; 84.09° W. Long. Elevation is 751 feet.
History: Waynesville was laid out in 1796 by Samuel Highway and Dr. Evan Banes, and was named for General Anthony Wayne. Many of the early residents were Quakers from Carolina and Pennsylvania.
Population: 2,967; Growth (since 2000): 16.0%; Density: 1,248.3 persons per square mile; Race: 98.6% White, 0.5% Black/African American, 0.0%

Asian, 0.0% American Indian/Alaska Native, 0.0% Native Hawaiian/Other Pacific Islander, 0.9% Two or more races, 3.9% Hispanic of any race; Average household size: 2.65; Median age: 40.9; Age under 18: 24.0%; Age 65 and over: 19.2%; Males per 100 females: 88.4; Marriage status: 29.7% never married, 46.7% now married, 2.0% separated, 11.5% widowed, 12.1% divorced; Foreign born: 2.4%; Speak English only: 97.0%; With disability: 14.6%; Veterans: 4.1%; Ancestry: 30.2% German, 13.9% Irish, 9.5% English, 5.0% Italian, 4.7% American
Employment: 13.4% management, business, and financial, 3.9% computer, engineering, and science, 8.8% education, legal, community service, arts, and media, 9.0% healthcare practitioners, 24.9% service, 25.0% sales and office, 4.3% natural resources, construction, and maintenance, 10.7% production, transportation, and material moving
Income: Per capita: $25,055; Median household: $61,005; Average household: $67,124; Households with income of $100,000 or more: 19.3%; Poverty rate: 11.0%
Educational Attainment: High school diploma or higher: 91.4%; Bachelor's degree or higher: 29.5%; Graduate/professional degree or higher: 12.8%

School District(s)

Wayne Local (KG-12)
2015-16 Enrollment: 1,472 . . . . (513) 897-6971
Housing: Homeownership rate: 61.0%; Median home value: $160,900; Median year structure built: 1982; Homeowner vacancy rate: 4.1%; Median selected monthly owner costs: $1,296 with a mortgage, $429 without a mortgage; Median gross rent: $796 per month; Rental vacancy rate: 0.0%
Health Insurance: 93.4% have insurance; 75.8% have private insurance; 32.7% have public insurance; 6.6% do not have insurance; 6.0% of children under 18 do not have insurance
Transportation: Commute: 94.8% car, 0.0% public transportation, 2.5% walk, 2.7% work from home; Mean travel time to work: 23.3 minutes

Washington County

Located in southeastern Ohio; bounded on the southeast by the Ohio River and the West Virginia border; crossed by the Muskingum and Little Muskingum Rivers. Covers a land area of 631.972 square miles, a water area of 8.025 square miles, and is located in the Eastern Time Zone at 39.45° N. Lat., 81.49° W. Long. The county was founded in 1788. County seat is Marietta.

Washington County is part of the Marietta, OH Micropolitan Statistical Area. The entire metro area includes: Washington County, OH

Weather Station: Marietta Wwtp Elevation: 580 feet

	Jan	Feb	Mar	Apr	May	Jun	Jul	Aug	Sep	Oct	Nov	Dec
High	40	44	53	66	74	82	85	85	78	67	55	43
Low	23	25	31	41	50	60	64	63	55	43	34	26
Precip	3.1	2.8	3.8	3.4	4.3	4.6	4.5	3.7	3.2	2.9	3.2	3.3
Snow	7.0	4.6	3.0	0.6	0.0	0.0	0.0	0.0	0.0	tr	0.6	3.0

High and Low temperatures in degrees Fahrenheit; Precipitation and Snow in inches

Population: 61,154; Growth (since 2000): -3.3%; Density: 96.8 persons per square mile; Race: 96.2% White, 1.1% Black/African American, 0.7% Asian, 0.4% American Indian/Alaska Native, 0.1% Native Hawaiian/Other Pacific Islander, 1.3% two or more races, 1.0% Hispanic of any race; Average household size: 2.35; Median age: 43.6; Age under 18: 19.9%; Age 65 and over: 19.2%; Males per 100 females: 95.4; Marriage status: 26.5% never married, 54.9% now married, 1.6% separated, 7.7% widowed, 11.0% divorced; Foreign born: 1.4%; Speak English only: 97.8%; With disability: 19.9%; Veterans: 10.6%; Ancestry: 28.3% German, 14.8% Irish, 10.8% English, 9.4% American, 2.7% Italian
Religion: Six largest groups: 11.5% Baptist, 8.8% Catholicism, 7.2% Methodist/Pietist, 3.4% Non-denominational Protestant, 2.4% Presbyterian-Reformed, 1.5% Holiness
Economy: Unemployment rate: 5.4%; Leading industries: 16.5 % retail trade; 11.8 % other services (except public administration); 10.6 % construction; Farms: 1,122 totaling 138,940 acres; Company size: 1 employs 1,000 or more persons, 1 employs 500 to 999 persons, 31 employs 100 to 499 persons, 1,369 employ less than 100 persons; Business ownership: 1,271 women-owned, n/a Black-owned, 33 Hispanic-owned, 36 Asian-owned, n/a American Indian/Alaska Native-owned
Employment: 10.3% management, business, and financial, 4.0% computer, engineering, and science, 9.4% education, legal, community service, arts, and media, 6.5% healthcare practitioners, 17.6% service, 24.6% sales and office, 10.3% natural resources, construction, and maintenance, 17.2% production, transportation, and material moving
Income: Per capita: $25,462; Median household: $44,763; Average household: $59,707; Households with income of $100,000 or more: 14.5%; Poverty rate: 15.7%
Educational Attainment: High school diploma or higher: 90.2%; Bachelor's degree or higher: 18.4%; Graduate/professional degree or higher: 6.0%
Housing: Homeownership rate: 74.6%; Median home value: $114,000; Median year structure built: 1969; Homeowner vacancy rate: 1.0%; Median selected monthly owner costs: $1,031 with a mortgage, $347 without a mortgage; Median gross rent: $625 per month; Rental vacancy rate: 6.9%
Vital Statistics: Birth rate: 92.7 per 10,000 population; Death rate: 119.5 per 10,000 population; Age-adjusted cancer mortality rate: 180.1 deaths per 100,000 population
Health Insurance: 91.4% have insurance; 67.2% have private insurance; 39.6% have public insurance; 8.6% do not have insurance; 3.3% of children under 18 do not have insurance
Health Care: Physicians: 22.8 per 10,000 population; Dentists: 4.5 per 10,000 population; Hospital beds: 28.9 per 10,000 population; Hospital admissions: 1,297.4 per 10,000 population
Air Quality Index (AQI): Percent of Days: 88.3% good, 11.7% moderate, 0.0% unhealthy for sensitive individuals, 0.0% unhealthy, 0.0% very unhealthy; Annual median: 40; Annual maximum: 90
Transportation: Commute: 92.7% car, 0.2% public transportation, 3.4% walk, 2.9% work from home; Mean travel time to work: 22.3 minutes
2016 Presidential Election: 68.1% Trump, 26.6% Clinton, 3.0% Johnson, 0.7% Stein
National and State Parks: Howes State Park; Marietta State Forest Nursery

Additional Information Contacts

Washington Government . . . . (740) 373-6623
http://www.washingtongov.org

Washington County Communities

BELPRE (city). Covers a land area of 3.485 square miles and a water area of 0.083 square miles. Located at 39.28° N. Lat; 81.59° W. Long. Elevation is 614 feet.
History: Belpre was established in 1789 by Captain Jonathan Stone who led a group of Revolutionary War veterans here from Marietta.
Population: 6,450; Growth (since 2000): -3.2%; Density: 1,850.9 persons per square mile; Race: 93.8% White, 2.8% Black/African American, 0.7% Asian, 0.0% American Indian/Alaska Native, 0.0% Native Hawaiian/Other Pacific Islander, 2.4% Two or more races, 1.3% Hispanic of any race; Average household size: 2.10; Median age: 45.6; Age under 18: 16.1%; Age 65 and over: 23.1%; Males per 100 females: 87.5; Marriage status: 24.7% never married, 52.8% now married, 1.3% separated, 8.1% widowed, 14.4% divorced; Foreign born: 1.3%; Speak English only: 96.8%; With disability: 25.9%; Veterans: 12.9%; Ancestry: 22.0% German, 15.1% Irish, 14.1% English, 13.3% American, 2.6% Dutch
Employment: 8.1% management, business, and financial, 4.1% computer, engineering, and science, 7.3% education, legal, community service, arts, and media, 7.7% healthcare practitioners, 13.2% service, 37.3% sales and office, 5.3% natural resources, construction, and maintenance, 16.9% production, transportation, and material moving
Income: Per capita: $25,262; Median household: $37,118; Average household: $52,295; Households with income of $100,000 or more: 9.0%; Poverty rate: 20.4%
Educational Attainment: High school diploma or higher: 86.8%; Bachelor's degree or higher: 15.5%; Graduate/professional degree or higher: 4.1%

School District(s)

Belpre City (KG-12)
2015-16 Enrollment: 958. . . . . (740) 423-9511
Housing: Homeownership rate: 68.5%; Median home value: $98,500; Median year structure built: 1964; Homeowner vacancy rate: 1.0%; Median selected monthly owner costs: $961 with a mortgage, $348 without a mortgage; Median gross rent: $606 per month; Rental vacancy rate: 12.2%
Health Insurance: 90.9% have insurance; 64.1% have private insurance; 48.0% have public insurance; 9.1% do not have insurance; 1.1% of children under 18 do not have insurance
Safety: Violent crime rate: 17.0 per 10,000 population; Property crime rate: 165.0 per 10,000 population

Transportation: Commute: 95.8% car, 0.0% public transportation, 1.1% walk, 1.1% work from home; Mean travel time to work: 23.1 minutes

BEVERLY (village). Covers a land area of 0.682 square miles and a water area of 0.111 square miles. Located at 39.55° N. Lat; 81.64° W. Long. Elevation is 656 feet.

History: Beverly was settled in 1789 by a group of adventurers from Marietta. Fort Frye was erected, but it was abandoned in 1794 and a new community was established on the Muskingum River at the mouth of Olive Green Creek.

Population: 1,255; Growth (since 2000): -2.1%; Density: 1,839.1 persons per square mile; Race: 93.1% White, 0.0% Black/African American, 1.1% Asian, 0.0% American Indian/Alaska Native, 0.0% Native Hawaiian/Other Pacific Islander, 1.0% Two or more races, 4.6% Hispanic of any race; Average household size: 2.41; Median age: 41.8; Age under 18: 24.1%; Age 65 and over: 19.5%; Males per 100 females: 85.7; Marriage status: 26.2% never married, 47.7% now married, 1.0% separated, 12.7% widowed, 13.4% divorced; Foreign born: 3.6%; Speak English only: 97.3%; With disability: 20.6%; Veterans: 13.3%; Ancestry: 26.0% German, 13.2% Irish, 10.1% English, 6.1% Scottish, 5.7% American

Employment: 8.9% management, business, and financial, 2.9% computer, engineering, and science, 8.0% education, legal, community service, arts, and media, 4.3% healthcare practitioners, 19.0% service, 25.4% sales and office, 12.2% natural resources, construction, and maintenance, 19.2% production, transportation, and material moving

Income: Per capita: $28,191; Median household: $39,583; Average household: $69,025; Households with income of $100,000 or more: 11.0%; Poverty rate: 17.8%

Educational Attainment: High school diploma or higher: 86.6%; Bachelor's degree or higher: 15.3%; Graduate/professional degree or higher: 5.1%

School District(s)

Fort Frye Local (KG-12)
2015-16 Enrollment: 942. . . . . (740) 984-2497

Housing: Homeownership rate: 63.5%; Median home value: $101,500; Median year structure built: 1965; Homeowner vacancy rate: 0.6%; Median selected monthly owner costs: $895 with a mortgage, $346 without a mortgage; Median gross rent: $561 per month; Rental vacancy rate: 10.3%

Health Insurance: 88.0% have insurance; 58.5% have private insurance; 43.7% have public insurance; 12.0% do not have insurance; 4.3% of children under 18 do not have insurance

Transportation: Commute: 94.7% car, 0.0% public transportation, 2.8% walk, 1.8% work from home; Mean travel time to work: 21.2 minutes

COAL RUN (unincorporated postal area)

ZCTA: 45721

Covers a land area of 0.051 square miles and a water area of 0 square miles. Located at 39.57° N. Lat; 81.58° W. Long. Elevation is 646 feet.

Population: 40; Growth (since 2000): n/a; Density: 780.8 persons per square mile; Race: 100.0% White, 0.0% Black/African American, 0.0% Asian, 0.0% American Indian/Alaska Native, 0.0% Native Hawaiian/Other Pacific Islander, 0.0% Two or more races, 0.0% Hispanic of any race; Average household size: 1.82; Median age: 78.4; Age under 18: 0.0%; Age 65 and over: 67.5%; Males per 100 females: 222.2; Marriage status: 0.0% never married, 0.0% now married, 0.0% separated, 100.0% widowed, 0.0% divorced; Foreign born: 0.0%; Speak English only: 100.0%; With disability: 67.5%; Veterans: 22.5%; Ancestry: 22.5% English, 22.5% Scottish

Employment: n/a management, business, and financial, n/a computer, engineering, and science, n/a education, legal, community service, arts, and media, n/a healthcare practitioners, n/a service, n/a sales and office, n/a natural resources, construction, and maintenance, n/a production, transportation, and material moving

Income: Per capita: $20,250; Median household: n/a; Average household: n/a; Households with income of $100,000 or more: n/a; Poverty rate: n/a

Educational Attainment: High school diploma or higher: 55.0%; Bachelor's degree or higher: n/a; Graduate/professional degree or higher: n/a

Housing: Homeownership rate: 100.0%; Median home value: n/a; Median year structure built: 1967; Homeowner vacancy rate: 0.0%; Median selected monthly owner costs: $0 with a mortgage, $0 without a mortgage; Median gross rent: n/a per month; Rental vacancy rate: 0.0%

Health Insurance: 100.0% have insurance; 22.5% have private insurance; 100.0% have public insurance; 0.0% do not have insurance; 0.0% of children under 18 do not have insurance

Transportation: Commute: n/a car, n/a public transportation, n/a walk, n/a work from home; Mean travel time to work: 0.0 minutes

CUTLER (unincorporated postal area)

ZCTA: 45724

Covers a land area of 53.286 square miles and a water area of 0.092 square miles. Located at 39.38° N. Lat; 81.80° W. Long. Elevation is 794 feet.

Population: 1,919; Growth (since 2000): 24.0%; Density: 36.0 persons per square mile; Race: 92.6% White, 5.1% Black/African American, 0.0% Asian, 0.0% American Indian/Alaska Native, 0.0% Native Hawaiian/Other Pacific Islander, 2.3% Two or more races, 0.0% Hispanic of any race; Average household size: 2.65; Median age: 52.6; Age under 18: 16.3%; Age 65 and over: 18.3%; Males per 100 females: 104.5; Marriage status: 22.3% never married, 66.1% now married, 4.8% separated, 7.0% widowed, 4.6% divorced; Foreign born: 0.0%; Speak English only: 99.3%; With disability: 35.0%; Veterans: 12.3%; Ancestry: 31.3% German, 11.3% Irish, 10.1% English, 4.1% American, 3.6% Russian

Employment: 8.8% management, business, and financial, 6.2% computer, engineering, and science, 9.9% education, legal, community service, arts, and media, 16.5% healthcare practitioners, 14.8% service, 17.3% sales and office, 14.8% natural resources, construction, and maintenance, 11.6% production, transportation, and material moving

Income: Per capita: $20,510; Median household: $53,507; Average household: $53,009; Households with income of $100,000 or more: 6.6%; Poverty rate: 16.1%

Educational Attainment: High school diploma or higher: 90.3%; Bachelor's degree or higher: 12.9%; Graduate/professional degree or higher: 4.2%

Housing: Homeownership rate: 93.9%; Median home value: $117,800; Median year structure built: 1979; Homeowner vacancy rate: 0.0%; Median selected monthly owner costs: $1,131 with a mortgage, $216 without a mortgage; Median gross rent: n/a per month; Rental vacancy rate: 0.0%

Health Insurance: 95.5% have insurance; 58.7% have private insurance; 55.6% have public insurance; 4.5% do not have insurance; 0.0% of children under 18 do not have insurance

Transportation: Commute: 90.6% car, 0.0% public transportation, 0.0% walk, 9.4% work from home; Mean travel time to work: 33.2 minutes

DEVOLA (CDP). Covers a land area of 5.135 square miles and a water area of 0.233 square miles. Located at 39.47° N. Lat; 81.47° W. Long. Elevation is 686 feet.

History: Also spelled De Vola.

Population: 2,590; Growth (since 2000): -6.5%; Density: 504.4 persons per square mile; Race: 94.7% White, 0.4% Black/African American, 2.9% Asian, 0.0% American Indian/Alaska Native, 0.0% Native Hawaiian/Other Pacific Islander, 2.0% Two or more races, 3.6% Hispanic of any race; Average household size: 2.27; Median age: 50.2; Age under 18: 18.2%; Age 65 and over: 24.2%; Males per 100 females: 89.7; Marriage status: 21.7% never married, 61.2% now married, 0.6% separated, 9.2% widowed, 7.9% divorced; Foreign born: 5.3%; Speak English only: 94.6%; With disability: 9.7%; Veterans: 8.6%; Ancestry: 30.3% German, 12.7% Irish, 10.9% American, 9.8% English, 4.6% Swiss

Employment: 16.6% management, business, and financial, 7.1% computer, engineering, and science, 9.8% education, legal, community service, arts, and media, 4.7% healthcare practitioners, 14.3% service, 27.7% sales and office, 5.9% natural resources, construction, and maintenance, 13.9% production, transportation, and material moving

Income: Per capita: $35,564; Median household: $76,127; Average household: $85,144; Households with income of $100,000 or more: 29.5%; Poverty rate: 3.1%

Educational Attainment: High school diploma or higher: 95.8%; Bachelor's degree or higher: 34.9%; Graduate/professional degree or higher: 14.3%

Housing: Homeownership rate: 87.2%; Median home value: $176,000; Median year structure built: 1973; Homeowner vacancy rate: 0.0%; Median selected monthly owner costs: $1,332 with a mortgage, $463 without a mortgage; Median gross rent: $1,061 per month; Rental vacancy rate: 0.0%

Health Insurance: 97.4% have insurance; 88.4% have private insurance; 24.9% have public insurance; 2.6% do not have insurance; 0.0% of children under 18 do not have insurance

Transportation: Commute: 86.2% car, 0.6% public transportation, 4.9% walk, 8.3% work from home; Mean travel time to work: 17.1 minutes

FLEMING (unincorporated postal area)

ZCTA: 45729

Covers a land area of 25.572 square miles and a water area of 0.040 square miles. Located at 39.42° N. Lat; 81.60° W. Long. Elevation is 791 feet.

Population: 1,513; Growth (since 2000): 7.3%; Density: 59.2 persons per square mile; Race: 100.0% White, 0.0% Black/African American, 0.0% Asian, 0.0% American Indian/Alaska Native, 0.0% Native Hawaiian/Other Pacific Islander, 0.0% Two or more races, 1.6% Hispanic of any race; Average household size: 3.35; Median age: 35.8; Age under 18: 30.1%; Age 65 and over: 14.3%; Males per 100 females: 105.3; Marriage status: 19.0% never married, 65.4% now married, 0.0% separated, 7.1% widowed, 8.5% divorced; Foreign born: 0.0%; Speak English only: 100.0%; With disability: 15.7%; Veterans: 12.1%; Ancestry: 39.4% German, 19.1% English, 9.9% Irish, 7.5% American, 3.2% Dutch

Employment: 19.4% management, business, and financial, 4.2% computer, engineering, and science, 10.3% education, legal, community service, arts, and media, 8.0% healthcare practitioners, 11.8% service, 13.2% sales and office, 7.4% natural resources, construction, and maintenance, 25.7% production, transportation, and material moving

Income: Per capita: $27,247; Median household: $72,708; Average household: $86,207; Households with income of $100,000 or more: 34.5%; Poverty rate: n/a

Educational Attainment: High school diploma or higher: 92.3%; Bachelor's degree or higher: 23.2%; Graduate/professional degree or higher: 8.0%

Housing: Homeownership rate: 85.4%; Median home value: $134,300; Median year structure built: 1977; Homeowner vacancy rate: 7.9%; Median selected monthly owner costs: $1,218 with a mortgage, $396 without a mortgage; Median gross rent: $873 per month; Rental vacancy rate: 0.0%

Health Insurance: 97.2% have insurance; 68.5% have private insurance; 46.2% have public insurance; 2.8% do not have insurance; 0.0% of children under 18 do not have insurance

Transportation: Commute: 95.1% car, 0.0% public transportation, 2.7% walk, 1.4% work from home; Mean travel time to work: 27.1 minutes

LITTLE HOCKING (CDP). Covers a land area of 0.415 square miles and a water area of 0.012 square miles. Located at 39.26° N. Lat; 81.70° W. Long. Elevation is 640 feet.

Population: 298; Growth (since 2000): n/a; Density: 718.2 persons per square mile; Race: 100.0% White, 0.0% Black/African American, 0.0% Asian, 0.0% American Indian/Alaska Native, 0.0% Native Hawaiian/Other Pacific Islander, 0.0% Two or more races, 0.0% Hispanic of any race; Average household size: 1.94; Median age: 35.7; Age under 18: 11.1%; Age 65 and over: 29.2%; Males per 100 females: 96.3; Marriage status: 45.3% never married, 41.1% now married, 0.0% separated, 3.8% widowed, 9.8% divorced; Foreign born: 0.0%; Speak English only: 100.0%; With disability: 12.8%; Veterans: 0.0%; Ancestry: 18.8% English, 14.4% German, 11.4% Greek, 11.4% Scottish, 9.7% Dutch

Employment: 0.0% management, business, and financial, 9.9% computer, engineering, and science, 0.0% education, legal, community service, arts, and media, 0.0% healthcare practitioners, 29.1% service, 39.5% sales and office, 21.5% natural resources, construction, and maintenance, 0.0% production, transportation, and material moving

Income: Per capita: $38,589; Median household: $61,094; Average household: $74,659; Households with income of $100,000 or more: 26.6%; Poverty rate: 21.5%

Educational Attainment: High school diploma or higher: 95.0%; Bachelor's degree or higher: 45.3%; Graduate/professional degree or higher: n/a

School District(s)

Warren Local (PK-12)
2015-16 Enrollment: 2,091 . . . . (740) 678-2366

Housing: Homeownership rate: 61.0%; Median home value: $165,200; Median year structure built: 1978; Homeowner vacancy rate: 0.0%; Median selected monthly owner costs: n/a with a mortgage, $517 without a mortgage; Median gross rent: $656 per month; Rental vacancy rate: 0.0%

Health Insurance: 78.5% have insurance; 78.5% have private insurance; 29.2% have public insurance; 21.5% do not have insurance; 0.0% of children under 18 do not have insurance

Transportation: Commute: 100.0% car, 0.0% public transportation, 0.0% walk, 0.0% work from home; Mean travel time to work: 17.8 minutes

LOWELL (village). Covers a land area of 0.228 square miles and a water area of 0.009 square miles. Located at 39.53° N. Lat; 81.51° W. Long. Elevation is 627 feet.

History: Lowell was founded in 1822 and grew around woolen mills. It was named for the textile town in Massachusetts.

Population: 532; Growth (since 2000): -15.3%; Density: 2,334.9 persons per square mile; Race: 80.1% White, 2.3% Black/African American, 0.0% Asian, 0.0% American Indian/Alaska Native, 0.0% Native Hawaiian/Other Pacific Islander, 17.7% Two or more races, 0.0% Hispanic of any race; Average household size: 2.51; Median age: 37.5; Age under 18: 24.6%; Age 65 and over: 14.7%; Males per 100 females: 84.8; Marriage status: 27.8% never married, 52.5% now married, 3.3% separated, 8.7% widowed, 11.1% divorced; Foreign born: 0.8%; Speak English only: 98.8%; With disability: 24.6%; Veterans: 10.5%; Ancestry: 24.2% German, 14.1% Irish, 11.3% French, 7.7% English, 4.9% American

Employment: 4.2% management, business, and financial, 2.1% computer, engineering, and science, 7.9% education, legal, community service, arts, and media, 5.2% healthcare practitioners, 11.0% service, 41.9% sales and office, 12.0% natural resources, construction, and maintenance, 15.7% production, transportation, and material moving

Income: Per capita: $18,411; Median household: $37,083; Average household: $43,706; Households with income of $100,000 or more: 4.7%; Poverty rate: 14.5%

Educational Attainment: High school diploma or higher: 90.8%; Bachelor's degree or higher: 12.5%; Graduate/professional degree or higher: 5.0%

School District(s)

Fort Frye Local (KG-12)
2015-16 Enrollment: 942. . . . . (740) 984-2497

Housing: Homeownership rate: 70.3%; Median home value: $77,900; Median year structure built: Before 1940; Homeowner vacancy rate: 2.6%; Median selected monthly owner costs: $814 with a mortgage, $331 without a mortgage; Median gross rent: $692 per month; Rental vacancy rate: 8.7%

Health Insurance: 85.5% have insurance; 57.7% have private insurance; 50.6% have public insurance; 14.5% do not have insurance; 2.3% of children under 18 do not have insurance

Transportation: Commute: 92.0% car, 0.0% public transportation, 1.1% walk, 4.8% work from home; Mean travel time to work: 23.6 minutes

LOWER SALEM (village). Covers a land area of 0.059 square miles and a water area of 0.003 square miles. Located at 39.56° N. Lat; 81.39° W. Long. Elevation is 653 feet.

History: Lower Salem was platted in 1850 by James Stanley.

Population: 89; Growth (since 2000): -18.3%; Density: 1,516.0 persons per square mile; Race: 94.4% White, 0.0% Black/African American, 0.0% Asian, 0.0% American Indian/Alaska Native, 0.0% Native Hawaiian/Other Pacific Islander, 0.0% Two or more races, 5.6% Hispanic of any race; Average household size: 2.78; Median age: 33.9; Age under 18: 31.5%; Age 65 and over: 6.7%; Males per 100 females: 79.2; Marriage status: 27.1% never married, 55.7% now married, 5.7% separated, 2.9% widowed, 14.3% divorced; Foreign born: 7.9%; Speak English only: 93.9%; With disability: 21.3%; Veterans: 0.0%; Ancestry: 44.9% German, 16.9% Irish, 9.0% Italian, 7.9% Dutch, 6.7% Lebanese

Employment: 0.0% management, business, and financial, 0.0% computer, engineering, and science, 2.6% education, legal, community service, arts, and media, 0.0% healthcare practitioners, 15.4% service, 28.2% sales and office, 25.6% natural resources, construction, and maintenance, 28.2% production, transportation, and material moving

Income: Per capita: $16,673; Median household: $29,167; Average household: $40,416; Households with income of $100,000 or more: n/a; Poverty rate: 12.4%

Educational Attainment: High school diploma or higher: 90.4%; Bachelor's degree or higher: 1.9%; Graduate/professional degree or higher: n/a

School District(s)

Fort Frye Local (KG-12)
2015-16 Enrollment: 942. . . . . (740) 984-2497

Housing: Homeownership rate: 65.6%; Median home value: $49,400; Median year structure built: Before 1940; Homeowner vacancy rate: 0.0%; Median selected monthly owner costs: $750 with a mortgage, $291 without a mortgage; Median gross rent: n/a per month; Rental vacancy rate: 0.0%

Health Insurance: 86.5% have insurance; 52.8% have private insurance; 38.2% have public insurance; 13.5% do not have insurance; 0.0% of children under 18 do not have insurance

Transportation: Commute: 97.4% car, 2.6% public transportation, 0.0% walk, 0.0% work from home; Mean travel time to work: 43.6 minutes

MACKSBURG (village). Covers a land area of 0.216 square miles and a water area of 0.007 square miles. Located at 39.63° N. Lat; 81.46° W. Long. Elevation is 702 feet.

Population: 191; Growth (since 2000): -5.4%; Density: 884.5 persons per square mile; Race: 96.9% White, 0.0% Black/African American, 0.0% Asian, 0.0% American Indian/Alaska Native, 0.0% Native Hawaiian/Other Pacific Islander, 3.1% Two or more races, 0.0% Hispanic of any race; Average household size: 1.99; Median age: 49.3; Age under 18: 12.0%; Age 65 and over: 18.3%; Males per 100 females: 118.8; Marriage status: 27.5% never married, 41.5% now married, 1.2% separated, 9.9% widowed, 21.1% divorced; Foreign born: 0.0%; Speak English only: 99.0%; With disability: 20.9%; Veterans: 8.3%; Ancestry: 20.9% Irish, 16.2% German, 8.9% French, 6.8% American, 6.8% English

Employment: 0.0% management, business, and financial, 0.0% computer, engineering, and science, 1.2% education, legal, community service, arts, and media, 0.0% healthcare practitioners, 20.0% service, 9.4% sales and office, 23.5% natural resources, construction, and maintenance, 45.9% production, transportation, and material moving

Income: Per capita: $23,932; Median household: $51,136; Average household: $46,356; Households with income of $100,000 or more: 9.4%; Poverty rate: 15.7%

Educational Attainment: High school diploma or higher: 77.0%; Bachelor's degree or higher: 0.7%; Graduate/professional degree or higher: n/a

Housing: Homeownership rate: 78.1%; Median home value: $57,400; Median year structure built: Before 1940; Homeowner vacancy rate: 0.0%; Median selected monthly owner costs: $656 with a mortgage, $367 without a mortgage; Median gross rent: $705 per month; Rental vacancy rate: 0.0%

Health Insurance: 85.9% have insurance; 64.9% have private insurance; 27.7% have public insurance; 14.1% do not have insurance; 4.3% of children under 18 do not have insurance

Transportation: Commute: 100.0% car, 0.0% public transportation, 0.0% walk, 0.0% work from home; Mean travel time to work: 34.1 minutes

MARIETTA (city). County seat. Covers a land area of 8.433 square miles and a water area of 0.319 square miles. Located at 39.43° N. Lat; 81.45° W. Long. Elevation is 614 feet.

History: Marietta was settled at the confluence of the Muskingum and Ohio Rivers in 1788 by the Ohio Company of Associates, a group of New Englanders looking for land to the west. At first they called the settlement Muskingum, but soon the name was officially declared to be Marietta, a tribute to Queen Marie Antoinette of France for her help in the American Revolution.

Population: 13,912; Growth (since 2000): -4.2%; Density: 1,649.7 persons per square mile; Race: 93.7% White, 1.7% Black/African American, 1.0% Asian, 1.4% American Indian/Alaska Native, 0.1% Native Hawaiian/Other Pacific Islander, 2.1% Two or more races, 1.4% Hispanic of any race; Average household size: 2.13; Median age: 37.5; Age under 18: 18.5%; Age 65 and over: 18.6%; Males per 100 females: 88.4; Marriage status: 37.8% never married, 40.0% now married, 2.2% separated, 9.8% widowed, 12.4% divorced; Foreign born: 2.0%; Speak English only: 96.3%; With disability: 22.2%; Veterans: 8.9%; Ancestry: 28.0% German, 15.3% Irish, 8.9% English, 6.9% American, 3.9% Italian

Employment: 11.7% management, business, and financial, 4.1% computer, engineering, and science, 9.9% education, legal, community service, arts, and media, 5.8% healthcare practitioners, 23.7% service, 24.0% sales and office, 6.5% natural resources, construction, and maintenance, 14.2% production, transportation, and material moving

Income: Per capita: $23,511; Median household: $33,670; Average household: $52,157; Households with income of $100,000 or more: 11.2%; Poverty rate: 25.8%

Educational Attainment: High school diploma or higher: 89.8%; Bachelor's degree or higher: 23.6%; Graduate/professional degree or higher: 8.4%

School District(s)

Frontier Local (KG-12)
  2015-16 Enrollment: 638 . . . . (740) 865-3473
Marietta City (KG-12)
  2015-16 Enrollment: 2,604 . . . . (740) 374-6500
Warren Local (PK-12)
  2015-16 Enrollment: 2,091 . . . . (740) 678-2366
Washington County Career Center (11-12)
  2015-16 Enrollment: n/a . . . . (740) 373-2766

Four-year College(s)

Marietta College (Private, Not-for-profit)
  Fall 2016 Enrollment: 1,224 . . . . (740) 376-4643
  2016-17 Tuition: In-state $35,330; Out-of-state $35,330

Two-year College(s)

Washington County Career Center-Adult Technical Training (Public)
  Fall 2016 Enrollment: 298 . . . . (740) 373-6283
Washington State Community College (Public)
  Fall 2016 Enrollment: 1,714 . . . . (740) 374-8716
  2016-17 Tuition: In-state $4,500; Out-of-state $8,670

Housing: Homeownership rate: 54.1%; Median home value: $98,700; Median year structure built: 1947; Homeowner vacancy rate: 2.0%; Median selected monthly owner costs: $902 with a mortgage, $343 without a mortgage; Median gross rent: $663 per month; Rental vacancy rate: 6.1%

Health Insurance: 90.1% have insurance; 59.7% have private insurance; 43.5% have public insurance; 9.9% do not have insurance; 4.5% of children under 18 do not have insurance

Hospitals: Marietta Memorial Hospital (204 beds); Selby General Hospital (80 beds)

Newspapers: Marietta Times (daily circulation 10,700)

Transportation: Commute: 85.8% car, 0.1% public transportation, 9.5% walk, 3.5% work from home; Mean travel time to work: 14.1 minutes

Additional Information Contacts

City of Marietta . . . . (740) 373-1387
  http://www.mariettaoh.net

MATAMORAS (village). Covers a land area of 0.348 square miles and a water area of 0.038 square miles. Located at 39.52° N. Lat; 81.07° W. Long. Elevation is 646 feet.

History: Matamoras, known as New Matamoras, was the center of a gas and oil boom during the latter decades of the 19th century.

Population: 774; Growth (since 2000): -19.1%; Density: 2,226.5 persons per square mile; Race: 99.1% White, 0.0% Black/African American, 0.0% Asian, 0.0% American Indian/Alaska Native, 0.0% Native Hawaiian/Other Pacific Islander, 0.9% Two or more races, 2.7% Hispanic of any race; Average household size: 2.08; Median age: 45.8; Age under 18: 15.4%; Age 65 and over: 25.8%; Males per 100 females: 88.6; Marriage status: 34.3% never married, 42.9% now married, 0.9% separated, 11.6% widowed, 11.2% divorced; Foreign born: 1.2%; Speak English only: 97.6%; With disability: 31.4%; Veterans: 5.5%; Ancestry: 27.4% German, 19.8% Irish, 11.1% English, 5.2% Dutch, 5.2% Italian

Employment: 3.8% management, business, and financial, 1.7% computer, engineering, and science, 14.5% education, legal, community service, arts, and media, 1.3% healthcare practitioners, 13.7% service, 21.8% sales and office, 12.8% natural resources, construction, and maintenance, 30.3% production, transportation, and material moving

Income: Per capita: $17,698; Median household: $27,083; Average household: $35,685; Households with income of $100,000 or more: 7.0%; Poverty rate: 31.7%

Educational Attainment: High school diploma or higher: 80.1%; Bachelor's degree or higher: 10.8%; Graduate/professional degree or higher: 3.1%

School District(s)

Frontier Local (KG-12)
  2015-16 Enrollment: 638 . . . . (740) 865-3473

Housing: Homeownership rate: 50.5%; Median home value: $90,000; Median year structure built: 1956; Homeowner vacancy rate: 4.6%; Median selected monthly owner costs: $967 with a mortgage, $358 without a mortgage; Median gross rent: $411 per month; Rental vacancy rate: 4.7%

Health Insurance: 96.3% have insurance; 46.4% have private insurance; 66.5% have public insurance; 3.7% do not have insurance; 6.7% of children under 18 do not have insurance

Transportation: Commute: 94.9% car, 1.7% public transportation, 2.1% walk, 0.0% work from home; Mean travel time to work: 24.6 minutes

NEWPORT (CDP). Covers a land area of 1.619 square miles and a water area of 0.102 square miles. Located at 39.40° N. Lat; 81.22° W. Long. Elevation is 640 feet.

Population: 997; Growth (since 2000): n/a; Density: 616.0 persons per square mile; Race: 98.5% White, 1.5% Black/African American, 0.0% Asian, 0.0% American Indian/Alaska Native, 0.0% Native Hawaiian/Other Pacific Islander, 0.0% Two or more races, 2.4% Hispanic of any race; Average household size: 2.21; Median age: 46.6; Age under 18: 19.0%;

Age 65 and over: 17.3%; Males per 100 females: 94.4; Marriage status: 24.0% never married, 63.5% now married, 4.7% separated, 7.2% widowed, 5.3% divorced; Foreign born: 0.0%; Speak English only: 100.0%; With disability: 15.1%; Veterans: 7.1%; Ancestry: 27.2% German, 19.6% Irish, 16.2% English, 9.0% American, 2.7% Swiss

Employment: 7.4% management, business, and financial, 8.2% computer, engineering, and science, 4.4% education, legal, community service, arts, and media, 6.0% healthcare practitioners, 29.5% service, 15.7% sales and office, 13.1% natural resources, construction, and maintenance, 15.7% production, transportation, and material moving

Income: Per capita: $26,583; Median household: $62,574; Average household: $58,792; Households with income of $100,000 or more: 14.4%; Poverty rate: 3.9%

Educational Attainment: High school diploma or higher: 95.7%; Bachelor's degree or higher: 16.7%; Graduate/professional degree or higher: 2.4%

School District(s)

Frontier Local (KG-12)
2015-16 Enrollment: 638 . . . . (740) 865-3473

Housing: Homeownership rate: 80.5%; Median home value: $131,800; Median year structure built: 1970; Homeowner vacancy rate: 0.0%; Median selected monthly owner costs: $995 with a mortgage, $365 without a mortgage; Median gross rent: n/a per month; Rental vacancy rate: 0.0%

Health Insurance: 88.7% have insurance; 75.7% have private insurance; 21.6% have public insurance; 11.3% do not have insurance; 0.0% of children under 18 do not have insurance

Transportation: Commute: 97.1% car, 0.0% public transportation, 0.0% walk, 2.9% work from home; Mean travel time to work: 20.0 minutes

RENO (CDP). Covers a land area of 0.768 square miles and a water area of 0.017 square miles. Located at 39.37° N. Lat; 81.39° W. Long. Elevation is 646 feet.

Population: 1,066; Growth (since 2000): n/a; Density: 1,388.0 persons per square mile; Race: 99.6% White, 0.3% Black/African American, 0.0% Asian, 0.0% American Indian/Alaska Native, 0.0% Native Hawaiian/Other Pacific Islander, 0.1% Two or more races, 0.0% Hispanic of any race; Average household size: 1.84; Median age: 45.4; Age under 18: 19.1%; Age 65 and over: 26.5%; Males per 100 females: 89.6; Marriage status: 30.1% never married, 35.9% now married, 0.8% separated, 21.7% widowed, 12.4% divorced; Foreign born: 0.0%; Speak English only: 100.0%; With disability: 32.3%; Veterans: 7.5%; Ancestry: 34.8% German, 18.4% English, 15.9% Irish, 15.6% American, 2.8% Dutch

Employment: 16.1% management, business, and financial, 0.0% computer, engineering, and science, 8.8% education, legal, community service, arts, and media, 7.1% healthcare practitioners, 22.4% service, 30.6% sales and office, 4.4% natural resources, construction, and maintenance, 10.5% production, transportation, and material moving

Income: Per capita: $22,218; Median household: $23,859; Average household: $40,043; Households with income of $100,000 or more: 10.6%; Poverty rate: 33.6%

Educational Attainment: High school diploma or higher: 94.1%; Bachelor's degree or higher: 7.6%; Graduate/professional degree or higher: 1.1%

Housing: Homeownership rate: 54.8%; Median home value: $133,500; Median year structure built: 1975; Homeowner vacancy rate: 0.0%; Median selected monthly owner costs: $1,141 with a mortgage, $358 without a mortgage; Median gross rent: $532 per month; Rental vacancy rate: 7.1%

Health Insurance: 92.2% have insurance; 51.7% have private insurance; 58.3% have public insurance; 7.8% do not have insurance; 0.0% of children under 18 do not have insurance

Transportation: Commute: 95.5% car, 0.0% public transportation, 0.0% walk, 4.5% work from home; Mean travel time to work: 15.1 minutes

VINCENT (CDP). Covers a land area of 0.383 square miles and a water area of 0.001 square miles. Located at 39.38° N. Lat; 81.67° W. Long. Elevation is 771 feet.

Population: 250; Growth (since 2000): n/a; Density: 653.0 persons per square mile; Race: 100.0% White, 0.0% Black/African American, 0.0% Asian, 0.0% American Indian/Alaska Native, 0.0% Native Hawaiian/Other Pacific Islander, 0.0% Two or more races, 0.0% Hispanic of any race; Average household size: 2.78; Median age: 28.2; Age under 18: 38.0%; Age 65 and over: 0.0%; Males per 100 females: 92.6; Marriage status: 0.0% never married, 78.1% now married, 0.0% separated, 0.0% widowed, 21.9% divorced; Foreign born: 0.0%; Speak English only: 100.0%; With disability: 7.6%; Veterans: 0.0%; Ancestry: 21.6% English, 14.8% Dutch, 14.0% German, 7.6% Irish

Employment: 0.0% management, business, and financial, 0.0% computer, engineering, and science, 0.0% education, legal, community service, arts, and media, 0.0% healthcare practitioners, 18.4% service, 36.0% sales and office, 0.0% natural resources, construction, and maintenance, 45.6% production, transportation, and material moving

Income: Per capita: $12,646; Median household: $37,391; Average household: $33,058; Households with income of $100,000 or more: n/a; Poverty rate: n/a

Educational Attainment: High school diploma or higher: 92.9%; Bachelor's degree or higher: n/a; Graduate/professional degree or higher: n/a

School District(s)

Warren Local (PK-12)
2015-16 Enrollment: 2,091 . . . . (740) 678-2366

Housing: Homeownership rate: 100.0%; Median home value: $48,800; Median year structure built: 1951; Homeowner vacancy rate: 0.0%; Median selected monthly owner costs: $866 with a mortgage, n/a without a mortgage; Median gross rent: n/a per month; Rental vacancy rate: 0.0%

Health Insurance: 89.6% have insurance; 77.2% have private insurance; 20.0% have public insurance; 10.4% do not have insurance; 0.0% of children under 18 do not have insurance

Transportation: Commute: 79.2% car, 0.0% public transportation, 0.0% walk, 20.8% work from home; Mean travel time to work: 0.0 minutes

WATERFORD (CDP). Covers a land area of 0.471 square miles and a water area of 0.051 square miles. Located at 39.54° N. Lat; 81.64° W. Long. Elevation is 653 feet.

Population: 439; Growth (since 2000): n/a; Density: 932.5 persons per square mile; Race: 100.0% White, 0.0% Black/African American, 0.0% Asian, 0.0% American Indian/Alaska Native, 0.0% Native Hawaiian/Other Pacific Islander, 0.0% Two or more races, 0.0% Hispanic of any race; Average household size: 3.18; Median age: 35.2; Age under 18: 37.8%; Age 65 and over: 14.8%; Males per 100 females: 94.8; Marriage status: 15.8% never married, 68.8% now married, 0.0% separated, 2.7% widowed, 12.7% divorced; Foreign born: 0.0%; Speak English only: 100.0%; With disability: 31.2%; Veterans: 13.9%; Ancestry: 51.3% German, 13.0% English, 8.4% Dutch, 8.4% Scotch-Irish, 7.3% American

Employment: 0.0% management, business, and financial, 6.7% computer, engineering, and science, 14.1% education, legal, community service, arts, and media, 0.0% healthcare practitioners, 2.7% service, 20.8% sales and office, 14.8% natural resources, construction, and maintenance, 40.9% production, transportation, and material moving

Income: Per capita: $22,305; Median household: $55,833; Average household: $68,807; Households with income of $100,000 or more: 35.5%; Poverty rate: 2.3%

Educational Attainment: High school diploma or higher: 97.3%; Bachelor's degree or higher: 18.3%; Graduate/professional degree or higher: n/a

School District(s)

Wolf Creek Local (KG-12)
2015-16 Enrollment: 595 . . . . (740) 984-2373

Housing: Homeownership rate: 76.8%; Median home value: $99,600; Median year structure built: Before 1940; Homeowner vacancy rate: 0.0%; Median selected monthly owner costs: $965 with a mortgage, n/a without a mortgage; Median gross rent: n/a per month; Rental vacancy rate: 0.0%

Health Insurance: 91.3% have insurance; 76.5% have private insurance; 33.5% have public insurance; 8.7% do not have insurance; 1.8% of children under 18 do not have insurance

Transportation: Commute: 100.0% car, 0.0% public transportation, 0.0% walk, 0.0% work from home; Mean travel time to work: 25.4 minutes

WHIPPLE (unincorporated postal area)

ZCTA: 45788

Covers a land area of 34.525 square miles and a water area of 0.165 square miles. Located at 39.51° N. Lat; 81.37° W. Long. Elevation is 646 feet.

Population: 1,272; Growth (since 2000): 27.1%; Density: 36.8 persons per square mile; Race: 100.0% White, 0.0% Black/African American, 0.0% Asian, 0.0% American Indian/Alaska Native, 0.0% Native Hawaiian/Other Pacific Islander, 0.0% Two or more races, 3.2% Hispanic of any race; Average household size: 2.56; Median age: 43.1; Age under 18: 25.6%; Age 65 and over: 22.8%; Males per 100 females: 101.2; Marriage status: 19.1% never married, 68.8% now married, 2.2% separated, 4.5%

widowed, 7.6% divorced; Foreign born: 0.6%; Speak English only: 100.0%; With disability: 13.8%; Veterans: 6.4%; Ancestry: 33.3% German, 16.4% Irish, 10.1% English, 7.9% American, 3.9% Dutch
Employment: 5.7% management, business, and financial, 2.8% computer, engineering, and science, 11.0% education, legal, community service, arts, and media, 2.7% healthcare practitioners, 14.3% service, 33.7% sales and office, 12.5% natural resources, construction, and maintenance, 17.3% production, transportation, and material moving
Income: Per capita: $24,158; Median household: $55,893; Average household: $61,087; Households with income of $100,000 or more: 10.5%; Poverty rate: 2.3%
Educational Attainment: High school diploma or higher: 89.5%; Bachelor's degree or higher: 17.7%; Graduate/professional degree or higher: 1.9%
Housing: Homeownership rate: 99.0%; Median home value: $116,800; Median year structure built: 1976; Homeowner vacancy rate: 0.0%; Median selected monthly owner costs: $1,093 with a mortgage, $354 without a mortgage; Median gross rent: n/a per month; Rental vacancy rate: 0.0%
Health Insurance: 96.3% have insurance; 87.5% have private insurance; 28.5% have public insurance; 3.7% do not have insurance; 1.8% of children under 18 do not have insurance
Transportation: Commute: 98.6% car, 0.0% public transportation, 0.0% walk, 0.0% work from home; Mean travel time to work: 23.1 minutes

WINGETT RUN (unincorporated postal area)

ZCTA: 45789

Covers a land area of 11.422 square miles and a water area of 0.065 square miles. Located at 39.55° N. Lat; 81.26° W. Long. Elevation is 656 feet.
Population: 106; Growth (since 2000): -65.6%; Density: 9.3 persons per square mile; Race: 100.0% White, 0.0% Black/African American, 0.0% Asian, 0.0% American Indian/Alaska Native, 0.0% Native Hawaiian/Other Pacific Islander, 0.0% Two or more races, 0.0% Hispanic of any race; Average household size: 2.00; Median age: 56.6; Age under 18: 0.0%; Age 65 and over: 0.0%; Males per 100 females: 126.9; Marriage status: 0.0% never married, 100.0% now married, 0.0% separated, 0.0% widowed, 0.0% divorced; Foreign born: 0.0%; Speak English only: 100.0%; With disability: 0.0%; Veterans: 0.0%; Ancestry: 15.1% English, 15.1% German
Employment: 0.0% management, business, and financial, 0.0% computer, engineering, and science, 0.0% education, legal, community service, arts, and media, 0.0% healthcare practitioners, 34.9% service, 15.1% sales and office, 50.0% natural resources, construction, and maintenance, 0.0% production, transportation, and material moving
Income: Per capita: $26,329; Median household: n/a; Average household: n/a; Households with income of $100,000 or more: n/a; Poverty rate: n/a
Educational Attainment: High school diploma or higher: 100.0%; Bachelor's degree or higher: 15.1%; Graduate/professional degree or higher: n/a
Housing: Homeownership rate: 100.0%; Median home value: n/a; Median year structure built: Before 1940; Homeowner vacancy rate: 0.0%; Median selected monthly owner costs: $0 with a mortgage, $0 without a mortgage; Median gross rent: n/a per month; Rental vacancy rate: 0.0%
Health Insurance: 65.1% have insurance; 65.1% have private insurance; 0.0% have public insurance; 34.9% do not have insurance; 0.0% of children under 18 do not have insurance
Transportation: Commute: 100.0% car, 0.0% public transportation, 0.0% walk, 0.0% work from home; Mean travel time to work: 0.0 minutes

Wayne County

Located in north central Ohio; crossed by the Lake Fork of the Mohican River. Covers a land area of 554.929 square miles, a water area of 1.888 square miles, and is located in the Eastern Time Zone at 40.83° N. Lat., 81.89° W. Long. The county was founded in 1786. County seat is Wooster.

Wayne County is part of the Wooster, OH Micropolitan Statistical Area. The entire metro area includes: Wayne County, OH

Weather Station: Wooster Exp Stn Elevation: 1,020 feet

	Jan	Feb	Mar	Apr	May	Jun	Jul	Aug	Sep	Oct	Nov	Dec
High	33	37	47	60	70	78	82	80	73	61	50	37
Low	19	21	28	38	48	57	61	59	52	41	33	24
Precip	2.3	2.0	2.8	3.7	4.4	4.3	4.2	4.1	3.4	3.0	3.1	2.7
Snow	8.4	6.4	5.6	1.1	tr	0.0	0.0	tr	0.0	0.1	1.5	6.2

High and Low temperatures in degrees Fahrenheit; Precipitation and Snow in inches

Population: 115,747; Growth (since 2000): 3.7%; Density: 208.6 persons per square mile; Race: 95.0% White, 1.6% Black/African American, 0.9% Asian, 0.2% American Indian/Alaska Native, 0.0% Native Hawaiian/Other Pacific Islander, 1.6% two or more races, 1.8% Hispanic of any race; Average household size: 2.60; Median age: 38.8; Age under 18: 24.7%; Age 65 and over: 16.1%; Males per 100 females: 97.7; Marriage status: 27.4% never married, 56.5% now married, 1.3% separated, 5.8% widowed, 10.2% divorced; Foreign born: 2.1%; Speak English only: 89.6%; With disability: 11.0%; Veterans: 8.0%; Ancestry: 31.4% German, 10.8% Irish, 8.8% American, 8.6% English, 5.7% Swiss
Religion: Six largest groups: 13.9% European Free-Church, 7.9% Catholicism, 6.3% Baptist, 5.8% Presbyterian-Reformed, 5.6% Non-denominational Protestant, 5.5% Methodist/Pietist
Economy: Unemployment rate: 3.6%; Leading industries: 14.6 % retail trade; 12.7 % construction; 11.9 % other services (except public administration); Farms: 1,928 totaling 271,657 acres; Company size: 1 employs 1,000 or more persons, 7 employ 500 to 999 persons, 55 employ 100 to 499 persons, 2,418 employ less than 100 persons; Business ownership: 2,503 women-owned, 75 Black-owned, 43 Hispanic-owned, 64 Asian-owned, n/a American Indian/Alaska Native-owned
Employment: 11.8% management, business, and financial, 4.9% computer, engineering, and science, 9.6% education, legal, community service, arts, and media, 4.9% healthcare practitioners, 16.1% service, 21.1% sales and office, 10.3% natural resources, construction, and maintenance, 21.4% production, transportation, and material moving
Income: Per capita: $24,311; Median household: $51,363; Average household: $63,923; Households with income of $100,000 or more: 16.9%; Poverty rate: 12.7%
Educational Attainment: High school diploma or higher: 85.4%; Bachelor's degree or higher: 21.5%; Graduate/professional degree or higher: 8.2%
Housing: Homeownership rate: 72.2%; Median home value: $136,400; Median year structure built: 1973; Homeowner vacancy rate: 1.7%; Median selected monthly owner costs: $1,149 with a mortgage, $430 without a mortgage; Median gross rent: $690 per month; Rental vacancy rate: 3.4%
Vital Statistics: Birth rate: 130.8 per 10,000 population; Death rate: 96.8 per 10,000 population; Age-adjusted cancer mortality rate: 168.4 deaths per 100,000 population
Health Insurance: 87.0% have insurance; 69.0% have private insurance; 31.1% have public insurance; 13.0% do not have insurance; 15.7% of children under 18 do not have insurance
Health Care: Physicians: 13.3 per 10,000 population; Dentists: 4.3 per 10,000 population; Hospital beds: 15.3 per 10,000 population; Hospital admissions: 538.5 per 10,000 population
Transportation: Commute: 88.2% car, 0.2% public transportation, 4.5% walk, 4.7% work from home; Mean travel time to work: 20.8 minutes
2016 Presidential Election: 64.3% Trump, 29.9% Clinton, 3.2% Johnson, 0.8% Stein
National and State Parks: Johnson Woods State Nature Preserve; Killbuck Marsh State Wildlife Area
Additional Information Contacts
Wayne Government . . . . (330) 287-5400
http://www.wayneohio.org

Wayne County Communities

APPLE CREEK (village). Covers a land area of 0.581 square miles and a water area of 0.004 square miles. Located at 40.75° N. Lat; 81.83° W. Long. Elevation is 1,050 feet.
Population: 1,128; Growth (since 2000): 12.9%; Density: 1,942.2 persons per square mile; Race: 99.1% White, 0.2% Black/African American, 0.0% Asian, 0.0% American Indian/Alaska Native, 0.0% Native Hawaiian/Other Pacific Islander, 0.7% Two or more races, 2.7% Hispanic of any race; Average household size: 2.64; Median age: 40.3; Age under 18: 25.6%; Age 65 and over: 14.9%; Males per 100 females: 97.8; Marriage status: 23.9% never married, 56.0% now married, 2.7% separated, 8.6% widowed, 11.6% divorced; Foreign born: 1.7%; Speak English only: 95.4%; With disability: 14.0%; Veterans: 8.5%; Ancestry: 37.1% German, 14.5% Irish, 8.1% English, 7.0% Swiss, 5.5% American
Employment: 12.2% management, business, and financial, 3.8% computer, engineering, and science, 9.6% education, legal, community service, arts, and media, 1.6% healthcare practitioners, 15.8% service, 19.5% sales and office, 7.3% natural resources, construction, and maintenance, 30.3% production, transportation, and material moving

Income: Per capita: $21,691; Median household: $51,528; Average household: $56,802; Households with income of $100,000 or more: 12.1%; Poverty rate: 15.0%
Educational Attainment: High school diploma or higher: 87.2%; Bachelor's degree or higher: 13.7%; Graduate/professional degree or higher: 2.7%

School District(s)

Southeast Local (KG-12)
2015-16 Enrollment: 1,408 . . . . (330) 698-3001

Housing: Homeownership rate: 76.6%; Median home value: $107,200; Median year structure built: 1980; Homeowner vacancy rate: 2.4%; Median selected monthly owner costs: $1,127 with a mortgage, $421 without a mortgage; Median gross rent: $690 per month; Rental vacancy rate: 0.0%
Health Insurance: 92.3% have insurance; 71.2% have private insurance; 32.9% have public insurance; 7.7% do not have insurance; 0.7% of children under 18 do not have insurance
Transportation: Commute: 98.7% car, 0.0% public transportation, 0.7% walk, 0.5% work from home; Mean travel time to work: 22.4 minutes

BURBANK (village). Covers a land area of 0.347 square miles and a water area of 0 square miles. Located at 40.99° N. Lat; 81.99° W. Long. Elevation is 955 feet.
Population: 212; Growth (since 2000): -24.0%; Density: 610.6 persons per square mile; Race: 99.1% White, 0.9% Black/African American, 0.0% Asian, 0.0% American Indian/Alaska Native, 0.0% Native Hawaiian/Other Pacific Islander, 0.0% Two or more races, 1.4% Hispanic of any race; Average household size: 2.46; Median age: 46.6; Age under 18: 20.3%; Age 65 and over: 25.9%; Males per 100 females: 107.0; Marriage status: 27.4% never married, 50.9% now married, 4.6% separated, 5.7% widowed, 16.0% divorced; Foreign born: 0.0%; Speak English only: 99.5%; With disability: 25.4%; Veterans: 13.0%; Ancestry: 25.0% German, 9.9% Irish, 7.1% English, 6.1% American, 2.8% French
Employment: 2.2% management, business, and financial, 2.2% computer, engineering, and science, 6.7% education, legal, community service, arts, and media, 1.1% healthcare practitioners, 24.7% service, 18.0% sales and office, 13.5% natural resources, construction, and maintenance, 31.5% production, transportation, and material moving
Income: Per capita: $21,678; Median household: $48,750; Average household: $53,230; Households with income of $100,000 or more: 8.8%; Poverty rate: 15.2%
Educational Attainment: High school diploma or higher: 86.0%; Bachelor's degree or higher: 7.3%; Graduate/professional degree or higher: 1.3%
Housing: Homeownership rate: 68.8%; Median home value: $87,200; Median year structure built: Before 1940; Homeowner vacancy rate: 12.7%; Median selected monthly owner costs: $1,023 with a mortgage, $375 without a mortgage; Median gross rent: $696 per month; Rental vacancy rate: 0.0%
Health Insurance: 89.3% have insurance; 63.5% have private insurance; 38.1% have public insurance; 10.7% do not have insurance; 9.3% of children under 18 do not have insurance
Transportation: Commute: 100.0% car, 0.0% public transportation, 0.0% walk, 0.0% work from home; Mean travel time to work: 24.0 minutes

CONGRESS (village). Covers a land area of 0.158 square miles and a water area of 0 square miles. Located at 40.93° N. Lat; 82.06° W. Long. Elevation is 1,161 feet.
History: Congress was established in 1827.
Population: 78; Growth (since 2000): -59.4%; Density: 492.7 persons per square mile; Race: 98.7% White, 0.0% Black/African American, 0.0% Asian, 0.0% American Indian/Alaska Native, 0.0% Native Hawaiian/Other Pacific Islander, 0.0% Two or more races, 0.0% Hispanic of any race; Average household size: 2.11; Median age: 51.8; Age under 18: 23.1%; Age 65 and over: 25.6%; Males per 100 females: 83.2; Marriage status: 23.2% never married, 58.0% now married, 0.0% separated, 2.9% widowed, 15.9% divorced; Foreign born: 0.0%; Speak English only: 98.7%; With disability: 15.4%; Veterans: 11.7%; Ancestry: 21.8% German, 10.3% American, 9.0% French, 7.7% English, 2.6% Danish
Employment: 0.0% management, business, and financial, 0.0% computer, engineering, and science, 11.4% education, legal, community service, arts, and media, 0.0% healthcare practitioners, 14.3% service, 14.3% sales and office, 22.9% natural resources, construction, and maintenance, 37.1% production, transportation, and material moving
Income: Per capita: $17,188; Median household: $33,125; Average household: $35,843; Households with income of $100,000 or more: 2.7%; Poverty rate: 9.6%
Educational Attainment: High school diploma or higher: 73.3%; Bachelor's degree or higher: 8.3%; Graduate/professional degree or higher: n/a
Housing: Homeownership rate: 67.6%; Median home value: $79,300; Median year structure built: 1972; Homeowner vacancy rate: 0.0%; Median selected monthly owner costs: $1,075 with a mortgage, $325 without a mortgage; Median gross rent: $717 per month; Rental vacancy rate: 29.4%
Health Insurance: 84.6% have insurance; 65.4% have private insurance; 33.3% have public insurance; 15.4% do not have insurance; 33.3% of children under 18 do not have insurance
Transportation: Commute: 96.9% car, 3.1% public transportation, 0.0% walk, 0.0% work from home; Mean travel time to work: 20.6 minutes

CRESTON (village). Covers a land area of 2.255 square miles and a water area of 0 square miles. Located at 40.98° N. Lat; 81.90° W. Long. Elevation is 991 feet.
Population: 2,297; Growth (since 2000): 6.3%; Density: 1,018.7 persons per square mile; Race: 98.3% White, 0.0% Black/African American, 0.0% Asian, 0.0% American Indian/Alaska Native, 0.0% Native Hawaiian/Other Pacific Islander, 1.7% Two or more races, 0.0% Hispanic of any race; Average household size: 2.68; Median age: 38.7; Age under 18: 25.1%; Age 65 and over: 16.0%; Males per 100 females: 92.5; Marriage status: 25.1% never married, 51.6% now married, 2.2% separated, 6.7% widowed, 16.5% divorced; Foreign born: 0.9%; Speak English only: 99.3%; With disability: 13.5%; Veterans: 7.2%; Ancestry: 28.3% German, 13.5% American, 12.6% Irish, 6.7% English, 4.7% Italian
Employment: 9.0% management, business, and financial, 3.0% computer, engineering, and science, 4.2% education, legal, community service, arts, and media, 9.0% healthcare practitioners, 21.7% service, 16.4% sales and office, 9.0% natural resources, construction, and maintenance, 27.7% production, transportation, and material moving
Income: Per capita: $21,625; Median household: $46,765; Average household: $57,320; Households with income of $100,000 or more: 12.5%; Poverty rate: 12.0%
Educational Attainment: High school diploma or higher: 89.2%; Bachelor's degree or higher: 7.1%; Graduate/professional degree or higher: 2.3%

School District(s)

Norwayne Local (PK-12)
2015-16 Enrollment: 1,457 . . . . (330) 435-6382

Housing: Homeownership rate: 73.5%; Median home value: $107,500; Median year structure built: 1971; Homeowner vacancy rate: 2.2%; Median selected monthly owner costs: $989 with a mortgage, $404 without a mortgage; Median gross rent: $755 per month; Rental vacancy rate: 3.2%
Health Insurance: 91.6% have insurance; 70.7% have private insurance; 37.9% have public insurance; 8.4% do not have insurance; 4.2% of children under 18 do not have insurance
Transportation: Commute: 97.3% car, 0.0% public transportation, 1.4% walk, 1.3% work from home; Mean travel time to work: 25.4 minutes

DALTON (village). Covers a land area of 1.505 square miles and a water area of 0 square miles. Located at 40.80° N. Lat; 81.70° W. Long. Elevation is 1,099 feet.
Population: 1,698; Growth (since 2000): 5.8%; Density: 1,128.1 persons per square mile; Race: 96.5% White, 2.0% Black/African American, 0.0% Asian, 0.0% American Indian/Alaska Native, 0.0% Native Hawaiian/Other Pacific Islander, 1.2% Two or more races, 1.7% Hispanic of any race; Average household size: 2.35; Median age: 41.1; Age under 18: 22.3%; Age 65 and over: 25.2%; Males per 100 females: 89.6; Marriage status: 26.7% never married, 47.6% now married, 0.0% separated, 12.7% widowed, 13.0% divorced; Foreign born: 1.7%; Speak English only: 96.5%; With disability: 13.0%; Veterans: 10.3%; Ancestry: 43.1% German, 11.8% Swiss, 10.1% English, 8.5% Irish, 7.5% Italian
Employment: 8.7% management, business, and financial, 1.4% computer, engineering, and science, 12.8% education, legal, community service, arts, and media, 7.7% healthcare practitioners, 20.8% service, 18.0% sales and office, 9.1% natural resources, construction, and maintenance, 21.5% production, transportation, and material moving
Income: Per capita: $24,365; Median household: $48,964; Average household: $57,981; Households with income of $100,000 or more: 12.9%; Poverty rate: 4.5%

Educational Attainment: High school diploma or higher: 89.4%; Bachelor's degree or higher: 24.2%; Graduate/professional degree or higher: 6.0%

School District(s)

Dalton Local (PK-12)
2015-16 Enrollment: 873. . . . . (330) 828-2267

Housing: Homeownership rate: 64.2%; Median home value: $138,800; Median year structure built: 1975; Homeowner vacancy rate: 2.4%; Median selected monthly owner costs: $1,067 with a mortgage, $391 without a mortgage; Median gross rent: $668 per month; Rental vacancy rate: 6.9%
Health Insurance: 94.9% have insurance; 81.6% have private insurance; 31.6% have public insurance; 5.1% do not have insurance; 0.0% of children under 18 do not have insurance
Newspapers: Dalton Gazette (weekly circulation 1,400)
Transportation: Commute: 95.1% car, 0.3% public transportation, 2.2% walk, 1.4% work from home; Mean travel time to work: 19.0 minutes

DOYLESTOWN (village). Covers a land area of 1.875 square miles and a water area of 0.002 square miles. Located at 40.97° N. Lat; 81.70° W. Long. Elevation is 1,247 feet.
Population: 3,089; Growth (since 2000): 10.4%; Density: 1,647.7 persons per square mile; Race: 94.2% White, 3.2% Black/African American, 0.5% Asian, 0.0% American Indian/Alaska Native, 0.0% Native Hawaiian/Other Pacific Islander, 1.5% Two or more races, 2.4% Hispanic of any race; Average household size: 2.39; Median age: 42.2; Age under 18: 24.8%; Age 65 and over: 19.9%; Males per 100 females: 86.2; Marriage status: 19.4% never married, 61.8% now married, 1.2% separated, 8.8% widowed, 10.0% divorced; Foreign born: 2.2%; Speak English only: 94.3%; With disability: 11.8%; Veterans: 14.3%; Ancestry: 26.3% German, 11.1% American, 9.1% English, 8.9% Irish, 3.7% French
Employment: 16.6% management, business, and financial, 11.8% computer, engineering, and science, 5.8% education, legal, community service, arts, and media, 10.5% healthcare practitioners, 20.3% service, 14.6% sales and office, 5.5% natural resources, construction, and maintenance, 14.9% production, transportation, and material moving
Income: Per capita: $29,674; Median household: $61,092; Average household: $72,109; Households with income of $100,000 or more: 22.4%; Poverty rate: 6.5%
Educational Attainment: High school diploma or higher: 89.1%; Bachelor's degree or higher: 28.9%; Graduate/professional degree or higher: 10.5%

School District(s)

Chippewa Local (PK-12)
2015-16 Enrollment: 1,360 . . . . (330) 658-6368

Housing: Homeownership rate: 74.4%; Median home value: $139,500; Median year structure built: 1965; Homeowner vacancy rate: 2.4%; Median selected monthly owner costs: $1,139 with a mortgage, $356 without a mortgage; Median gross rent: $701 per month; Rental vacancy rate: 0.0%
Health Insurance: 96.0% have insurance; 80.7% have private insurance; 28.8% have public insurance; 4.0% do not have insurance; 3.7% of children under 18 do not have insurance
Transportation: Commute: 93.6% car, 0.0% public transportation, 2.6% walk, 2.5% work from home; Mean travel time to work: 21.0 minutes

FREDERICKSBURG (village). Covers a land area of 0.338 square miles and a water area of 0 square miles. Located at 40.68° N. Lat; 81.87° W. Long. Elevation is 974 feet.
Population: 472; Growth (since 2000): -3.1%; Density: 1,396.4 persons per square mile; Race: 100.0% White, 0.0% Black/African American, 0.0% Asian, 0.0% American Indian/Alaska Native, 0.0% Native Hawaiian/Other Pacific Islander, 0.0% Two or more races, 0.0% Hispanic of any race; Average household size: 2.35; Median age: 34.0; Age under 18: 28.6%; Age 65 and over: 14.8%; Males per 100 females: 97.7; Marriage status: 24.3% never married, 60.9% now married, 0.3% separated, 5.9% widowed, 8.9% divorced; Foreign born: 0.0%; Speak English only: 86.9%; With disability: 10.6%; Veterans: 13.9%; Ancestry: 31.4% German, 15.9% Irish, 10.0% American, 8.5% English, 5.9% French
Employment: 11.4% management, business, and financial, 1.8% computer, engineering, and science, 6.4% education, legal, community service, arts, and media, 7.3% healthcare practitioners, 8.7% service, 20.5% sales and office, 13.7% natural resources, construction, and maintenance, 30.1% production, transportation, and material moving
Income: Per capita: $24,970; Median household: $48,750; Average household: $58,684; Households with income of $100,000 or more: 11.1%; Poverty rate: 1.9%

Educational Attainment: High school diploma or higher: 83.3%; Bachelor's degree or higher: 23.1%; Graduate/professional degree or higher: 3.5%

School District(s)

Southeast Local (KG-12)
2015-16 Enrollment: 1,408 . . . . (330) 698-3001

Housing: Homeownership rate: 71.2%; Median home value: $99,700; Median year structure built: Before 1940; Homeowner vacancy rate: 2.8%; Median selected monthly owner costs: $1,030 with a mortgage, $400 without a mortgage; Median gross rent: $492 per month; Rental vacancy rate: 0.0%
Health Insurance: 86.9% have insurance; 72.7% have private insurance; 26.5% have public insurance; 13.1% do not have insurance; 12.6% of children under 18 do not have insurance
Transportation: Commute: 92.2% car, 0.0% public transportation, 1.8% walk, 4.6% work from home; Mean travel time to work: 18.2 minutes

KIDRON (CDP). Covers a land area of 2.927 square miles and a water area of <.001 square miles. Located at 40.75° N. Lat; 81.75° W. Long. Elevation is 1,102 feet.
Population: 970; Growth (since 2000): n/a; Density: 331.4 persons per square mile; Race: 99.1% White, 0.0% Black/African American, 0.9% Asian, 0.0% American Indian/Alaska Native, 0.0% Native Hawaiian/Other Pacific Islander, 0.0% Two or more races, 0.0% Hispanic of any race; Average household size: 3.38; Median age: 26.6; Age under 18: 35.9%; Age 65 and over: 10.9%; Males per 100 females: 99.2; Marriage status: 26.4% never married, 66.9% now married, 0.0% separated, 3.7% widowed, 3.0% divorced; Foreign born: 1.6%; Speak English only: 68.3%; With disability: 4.7%; Veterans: 1.8%; Ancestry: 26.9% German, 17.7% Dutch, 13.4% Swiss, 9.4% American, 7.7% English
Employment: 10.2% management, business, and financial, 1.6% computer, engineering, and science, 3.5% education, legal, community service, arts, and media, 6.7% healthcare practitioners, 11.6% service, 22.5% sales and office, 10.4% natural resources, construction, and maintenance, 33.6% production, transportation, and material moving
Income: Per capita: $22,085; Median household: $63,125; Average household: $75,619; Households with income of $100,000 or more: 21.6%; Poverty rate: 11.2%
Educational Attainment: High school diploma or higher: 72.5%; Bachelor's degree or higher: 21.3%; Graduate/professional degree or higher: 8.8%
Housing: Homeownership rate: 83.3%; Median home value: $155,800; Median year structure built: 1960; Homeowner vacancy rate: 0.0%; Median selected monthly owner costs: $1,277 with a mortgage, $387 without a mortgage; Median gross rent: $848 per month; Rental vacancy rate: 0.0%
Health Insurance: 79.2% have insurance; 55.6% have private insurance; 30.9% have public insurance; 20.8% do not have insurance; 21.6% of children under 18 do not have insurance
Transportation: Commute: 90.4% car, 0.0% public transportation, 1.9% walk, 4.9% work from home; Mean travel time to work: 22.5 minutes

MARSHALLVILLE (village). Covers a land area of 0.572 square miles and a water area of 0 square miles. Located at 40.90° N. Lat; 81.73° W. Long. Elevation is 1,119 feet.
Population: 718; Growth (since 2000): -13.1%; Density: 1,254.9 persons per square mile; Race: 98.3% White, 0.7% Black/African American, 0.6% Asian, 0.0% American Indian/Alaska Native, 0.0% Native Hawaiian/Other Pacific Islander, 0.0% Two or more races, 0.4% Hispanic of any race; Average household size: 2.73; Median age: 37.6; Age under 18: 27.6%; Age 65 and over: 13.5%; Males per 100 females: 98.4; Marriage status: 23.7% never married, 58.5% now married, 1.8% separated, 5.6% widowed, 12.2% divorced; Foreign born: 0.8%; Speak English only: 96.2%; With disability: 13.6%; Veterans: 11.0%; Ancestry: 32.2% German, 20.5% Irish, 9.3% American, 5.8% English, 5.2% French
Employment: 9.7% management, business, and financial, 3.6% computer, engineering, and science, 3.9% education, legal, community service, arts, and media, 4.4% healthcare practitioners, 19.6% service, 24.6% sales and office, 9.4% natural resources, construction, and maintenance, 24.9% production, transportation, and material moving
Income: Per capita: $22,400; Median household: $59,375; Average household: $60,630; Households with income of $100,000 or more: 9.9%; Poverty rate: 8.1%
Educational Attainment: High school diploma or higher: 85.7%; Bachelor's degree or higher: 8.0%; Graduate/professional degree or higher: 1.3%

School District(s)

Green Local (KG-12)
2015-16 Enrollment: 1,079 . . . . (330) 669-3921

Housing: Homeownership rate: 71.1%; Median home value: $112,200; Median year structure built: 1964; Homeowner vacancy rate: 0.0%; Median selected monthly owner costs: $1,086 with a mortgage, $343 without a mortgage; Median gross rent: $805 per month; Rental vacancy rate: 0.0%
Health Insurance: 95.4% have insurance; 66.6% have private insurance; 44.7% have public insurance; 4.6% do not have insurance; 3.0% of children under 18 do not have insurance
Transportation: Commute: 93.2% car, 0.0% public transportation, 5.1% walk, 1.7% work from home; Mean travel time to work: 24.4 minutes

MOUNT EATON (village). Covers a land area of 0.178 square miles and a water area of 0 square miles. Located at 40.70° N. Lat; 81.70° W. Long. Elevation is 1,250 feet.
Population: 197; Growth (since 2000): -19.9%; Density: 1,108.8 persons per square mile; Race: 97.5% White, 0.0% Black/African American, 0.5% Asian, 0.0% American Indian/Alaska Native, 0.0% Native Hawaiian/Other Pacific Islander, 2.0% Two or more races, 0.0% Hispanic of any race; Average household size: 2.46; Median age: 28.9; Age under 18: 24.9%; Age 65 and over: 17.8%; Males per 100 females: 92.8; Marriage status: 35.3% never married, 54.5% now married, 1.9% separated, 4.5% widowed, 5.8% divorced; Foreign born: 0.0%; Speak English only: 65.2%; With disability: 12.2%; Veterans: 10.1%; Ancestry: 27.4% German, 14.2% Swiss, 12.7% Pennsylvania German, 7.1% English, 6.6% Irish
Employment: 12.1% management, business, and financial, 0.0% computer, engineering, and science, 3.3% education, legal, community service, arts, and media, 0.0% healthcare practitioners, 27.5% service, 30.8% sales and office, 4.4% natural resources, construction, and maintenance, 22.0% production, transportation, and material moving
Income: Per capita: $20,785; Median household: $46,875; Average household: $53,849; Households with income of $100,000 or more: 11.3%; Poverty rate: 14.9%
Educational Attainment: High school diploma or higher: 73.7%; Bachelor's degree or higher: 9.6%; Graduate/professional degree or higher: 0.9%

School District(s)

Southeast Local (KG-12)
2015-16 Enrollment: 1,408 . . . . (330) 698-3001

Housing: Homeownership rate: 65.0%; Median home value: $100,000; Median year structure built: 1955; Homeowner vacancy rate: 0.0%; Median selected monthly owner costs: $800 with a mortgage, $392 without a mortgage; Median gross rent: $534 per month; Rental vacancy rate: 0.0%
Health Insurance: 75.6% have insurance; 58.9% have private insurance; 36.5% have public insurance; 24.4% do not have insurance; 12.2% of children under 18 do not have insurance
Transportation: Commute: 94.3% car, 0.0% public transportation, 5.7% walk, 0.0% work from home; Mean travel time to work: 22.0 minutes

NEW PITTSBURG (CDP). Covers a land area of 1.364 square miles and a water area of 0.008 square miles. Located at 40.85° N. Lat; 82.10° W. Long. Elevation is 1,135 feet.
Population: 357; Growth (since 2000): n/a; Density: 261.8 persons per square mile; Race: 100.0% White, 0.0% Black/African American, 0.0% Asian, 0.0% American Indian/Alaska Native, 0.0% Native Hawaiian/Other Pacific Islander, 0.0% Two or more races, 0.0% Hispanic of any race; Average household size: 3.14; Median age: 43.0; Age under 18: 22.1%; Age 65 and over: 23.0%; Males per 100 females: 89.3; Marriage status: 30.4% never married, 41.5% now married, 0.0% separated, 19.0% widowed, 9.2% divorced; Foreign born: 0.0%; Speak English only: 100.0%; With disability: 11.7%; Veterans: 12.9%; Ancestry: 40.6% German, 11.2% Swiss, 10.4% Irish, 5.6% French, 3.4% English
Employment: 14.2% management, business, and financial, 6.1% computer, engineering, and science, 0.0% education, legal, community service, arts, and media, 0.0% healthcare practitioners, 4.7% service, 22.3% sales and office, 0.0% natural resources, construction, and maintenance, 52.7% production, transportation, and material moving
Income: Per capita: $18,386; Median household: $73,375; Average household: $61,465; Households with income of $100,000 or more: 9.5%; Poverty rate: 4.0%
Educational Attainment: High school diploma or higher: 75.0%; Bachelor's degree or higher: 21.6%; Graduate/professional degree or higher: 2.1%
Housing: Homeownership rate: 87.4%; Median home value: $157,600; Median year structure built: 1965; Homeowner vacancy rate: 0.0%; Median selected monthly owner costs: $1,125 with a mortgage, $441 without a mortgage; Median gross rent: n/a per month; Rental vacancy rate: 0.0%
Health Insurance: 91.3% have insurance; 80.9% have private insurance; 19.5% have public insurance; 8.7% do not have insurance; 0.0% of children under 18 do not have insurance
Transportation: Commute: 100.0% car, 0.0% public transportation, 0.0% walk, 0.0% work from home; Mean travel time to work: 29.3 minutes

ORRVILLE (city). Covers a land area of 5.740 square miles and a water area of 0.013 square miles. Located at 40.85° N. Lat; 81.78° W. Long. Elevation is 1,060 feet.
History: Settled c.1850, incorporated 1864.
Population: 8,351; Growth (since 2000): -2.3%; Density: 1,454.8 persons per square mile; Race: 89.6% White, 2.4% Black/African American, 1.4% Asian, 0.5% American Indian/Alaska Native, 0.0% Native Hawaiian/Other Pacific Islander, 3.3% Two or more races, 4.7% Hispanic of any race; Average household size: 2.33; Median age: 40.9; Age under 18: 22.8%; Age 65 and over: 19.7%; Males per 100 females: 95.1; Marriage status: 24.1% never married, 55.0% now married, 0.5% separated, 8.7% widowed, 12.2% divorced; Foreign born: 4.0%; Speak English only: 95.6%; With disability: 12.3%; Veterans: 8.8%; Ancestry: 29.6% German, 13.3% Irish, 8.0% American, 7.4% English, 6.5% Swiss
Employment: 9.2% management, business, and financial, 5.5% computer, engineering, and science, 13.9% education, legal, community service, arts, and media, 5.5% healthcare practitioners, 15.8% service, 21.9% sales and office, 5.6% natural resources, construction, and maintenance, 22.6% production, transportation, and material moving
Income: Per capita: $25,335; Median household: $45,883; Average household: $58,830; Households with income of $100,000 or more: 14.6%; Poverty rate: 16.0%
Educational Attainment: High school diploma or higher: 90.3%; Bachelor's degree or higher: 24.5%; Graduate/professional degree or higher: 10.1%

School District(s)

Orrville City (KG-12)
2015-16 Enrollment: 1,544 . . . . (330) 682-4651

Two-year College(s)

University of Akron Wayne College (Public)
Fall 2016 Enrollment: 1,923 . . . . (800) 221-8308
2016-17 Tuition: In-state $6,116; Out-of-state $12,789

Housing: Homeownership rate: 66.4%; Median home value: $116,500; Median year structure built: 1967; Homeowner vacancy rate: 0.0%; Median selected monthly owner costs: $982 with a mortgage, $423 without a mortgage; Median gross rent: $712 per month; Rental vacancy rate: 1.9%
Health Insurance: 92.0% have insurance; 75.0% have private insurance; 33.1% have public insurance; 8.0% do not have insurance; 3.6% of children under 18 do not have insurance
Hospitals: Aultman Orrville Hospital (51 beds)
Safety: Violent crime rate: 18.8 per 10,000 population; Property crime rate: 130.4 per 10,000 population
Transportation: Commute: 92.7% car, 0.0% public transportation, 2.4% walk, 3.6% work from home; Mean travel time to work: 18.2 minutes
Additional Information Contacts
City of Orrville . . . . (330) 684-5000
http://www.orrville.com

RITTMAN (city). Covers a land area of 6.431 square miles and a water area of 0.064 square miles. Located at 40.97° N. Lat; 81.78° W. Long. Elevation is 981 feet.
Population: 6,528; Growth (since 2000): 3.4%; Density: 1,015.2 persons per square mile; Race: 96.7% White, 0.8% Black/African American, 0.0% Asian, 0.2% American Indian/Alaska Native, 0.0% Native Hawaiian/Other Pacific Islander, 2.1% Two or more races, 0.1% Hispanic of any race; Average household size: 2.59; Median age: 38.6; Age under 18: 24.8%; Age 65 and over: 14.5%; Males per 100 females: 95.7; Marriage status: 25.8% never married, 54.8% now married, 2.2% separated, 8.0% widowed, 11.5% divorced; Foreign born: 1.0%; Speak English only: 97.5%; With disability: 13.3%; Veterans: 9.9%; Ancestry: 28.7% German, 15.0% Irish, 8.8% English, 8.7% American, 5.8% Italian
Employment: 11.1% management, business, and financial, 5.2% computer, engineering, and science, 6.1% education, legal, community service, arts, and media, 5.4% healthcare practitioners, 19.3% service,

21.6% sales and office, 10.1% natural resources, construction, and maintenance, 21.2% production, transportation, and material moving
Income: Per capita: $21,745; Median household: $42,227; Average household: $55,330; Households with income of $100,000 or more: 11.5%; Poverty rate: 16.2%
Educational Attainment: High school diploma or higher: 87.4%; Bachelor's degree or higher: 15.8%; Graduate/professional degree or higher: 4.0%

School District(s)

Rittman Academy (09-12)
2015-16 Enrollment: 30. . . . . (330) 927-7401
Rittman Exempted Village (KG-12)
2015-16 Enrollment: 1,047 . . . . (330) 927-7400
Housing: Homeownership rate: 67.7%; Median home value: $105,600; Median year structure built: 1959; Homeowner vacancy rate: 1.9%; Median selected monthly owner costs: $1,007 with a mortgage, $389 without a mortgage; Median gross rent: $717 per month; Rental vacancy rate: 3.6%
Health Insurance: 91.4% have insurance; 64.2% have private insurance; 41.3% have public insurance; 8.6% do not have insurance; 5.6% of children under 18 do not have insurance
Safety: Violent crime rate: 6.1 per 10,000 population; Property crime rate: 207.6 per 10,000 population
Transportation: Commute: 94.6% car, 0.0% public transportation, 1.5% walk, 2.8% work from home; Mean travel time to work: 25.5 minutes
Additional Information Contacts
City of Rittman. . . . . (330) 925-2045
http://www.rittman.com

SHREVE (village). Covers a land area of 0.849 square miles and a water area of 0 square miles. Located at 40.68° N. Lat; 82.02° W. Long. Elevation is 896 feet.
Population: 1,447; Growth (since 2000): -8.5%; Density: 1,703.5 persons per square mile; Race: 97.4% White, 0.2% Black/African American, 0.6% Asian, 0.0% American Indian/Alaska Native, 0.0% Native Hawaiian/Other Pacific Islander, 1.4% Two or more races, 0.8% Hispanic of any race; Average household size: 2.44; Median age: 37.4; Age under 18: 25.4%; Age 65 and over: 13.2%; Males per 100 females: 92.6; Marriage status: 27.4% never married, 51.8% now married, 0.3% separated, 4.7% widowed, 16.1% divorced; Foreign born: 1.0%; Speak English only: 98.3%; With disability: 17.1%; Veterans: 9.9%; Ancestry: 38.1% German, 16.8% English, 16.7% Irish, 6.4% American, 3.3% French
Employment: 7.7% management, business, and financial, 3.4% computer, engineering, and science, 7.0% education, legal, community service, arts, and media, 3.3% healthcare practitioners, 17.4% service, 20.5% sales and office, 4.5% natural resources, construction, and maintenance, 36.4% production, transportation, and material moving
Income: Per capita: $19,436; Median household: $42,167; Average household: $46,718; Households with income of $100,000 or more: 6.8%; Poverty rate: 11.2%
Educational Attainment: High school diploma or higher: 89.6%; Bachelor's degree or higher: 14.4%; Graduate/professional degree or higher: 6.7%

School District(s)

Triway Local (PK-12)
2015-16 Enrollment: 1,635 . . . . (330) 264-9491
Housing: Homeownership rate: 63.2%; Median home value: $84,200; Median year structure built: 1959; Homeowner vacancy rate: 4.0%; Median selected monthly owner costs: $836 with a mortgage, $343 without a mortgage; Median gross rent: $575 per month; Rental vacancy rate: 4.7%
Health Insurance: 92.3% have insurance; 71.8% have private insurance; 36.4% have public insurance; 7.7% do not have insurance; 2.2% of children under 18 do not have insurance
Transportation: Commute: 92.3% car, 0.0% public transportation, 6.0% walk, 0.6% work from home; Mean travel time to work: 27.2 minutes

SMITHVILLE (village). Covers a land area of 1.238 square miles and a water area of 0.006 square miles. Located at 40.86° N. Lat; 81.86° W. Long. Elevation is 1,060 feet.
Population: 1,249; Growth (since 2000): -6.3%; Density: 1,009.2 persons per square mile; Race: 95.1% White, 2.7% Black/African American, 0.6% Asian, 0.0% American Indian/Alaska Native, 0.0% Native Hawaiian/Other Pacific Islander, 0.0% Two or more races, 2.6% Hispanic of any race; Average household size: 2.48; Median age: 39.4; Age under 18: 23.1%; Age 65 and over: 12.2%; Males per 100 females: 89.1; Marriage status: 28.8% never married, 54.7% now married, 0.7% separated, 6.7% widowed, 9.8% divorced; Foreign born: 0.4%; Speak English only: 98.1%; With disability: 9.9%; Veterans: 5.1%; Ancestry: 35.7% German, 9.8% Irish, 8.7% English, 8.6% American, 6.1% Italian
Employment: 14.5% management, business, and financial, 8.7% computer, engineering, and science, 9.3% education, legal, community service, arts, and media, 5.0% healthcare practitioners, 17.0% service, 16.2% sales and office, 5.2% natural resources, construction, and maintenance, 24.2% production, transportation, and material moving
Income: Per capita: $25,169; Median household: $49,554; Average household: $62,713; Households with income of $100,000 or more: 15.9%; Poverty rate: 8.6%
Educational Attainment: High school diploma or higher: 91.9%; Bachelor's degree or higher: 25.3%; Graduate/professional degree or higher: 6.2%

School District(s)

Green Local (KG-12)
2015-16 Enrollment: 1,079 . . . . (330) 669-3921
Wayne County Jvsd (11-12)
2015-16 Enrollment: n/a . . . . (330) 669-7000

Vocational/Technical School(s)

Wayne County Schools Career Center (Public)
Fall 2016 Enrollment: 180 . . . . (330) 669-7070
2016-17 Tuition: $12,647
Housing: Homeownership rate: 63.3%; Median home value: $126,100; Median year structure built: 1962; Homeowner vacancy rate: 4.5%; Median selected monthly owner costs: $1,095 with a mortgage, $438 without a mortgage; Median gross rent: $743 per month; Rental vacancy rate: 0.0%
Health Insurance: 95.4% have insurance; 83.2% have private insurance; 25.1% have public insurance; 4.6% do not have insurance; 3.1% of children under 18 do not have insurance
Transportation: Commute: 92.6% car, 0.0% public transportation, 1.4% walk, 5.3% work from home; Mean travel time to work: 18.0 minutes

STERLING (CDP). Covers a land area of 0.976 square miles and a water area of 0 square miles. Located at 40.97° N. Lat; 81.84° W. Long. Elevation is 968 feet.
Population: 390; Growth (since 2000): n/a; Density: 399.5 persons per square mile; Race: 94.6% White, 2.8% Black/African American, 0.0% Asian, 0.0% American Indian/Alaska Native, 0.0% Native Hawaiian/Other Pacific Islander, 2.6% Two or more races, 0.0% Hispanic of any race; Average household size: 2.58; Median age: 38.7; Age under 18: 13.6%; Age 65 and over: 14.6%; Males per 100 females: 100.4; Marriage status: 39.9% never married, 36.5% now married, 1.7% separated, 6.7% widowed, 16.9% divorced; Foreign born: 0.0%; Speak English only: 100.0%; With disability: 15.1%; Veterans: 6.8%; Ancestry: 35.6% German, 11.5% Irish, 7.9% English, 7.7% American, 7.7% French
Employment: 6.0% management, business, and financial, 0.0% computer, engineering, and science, 0.0% education, legal, community service, arts, and media, 4.7% healthcare practitioners, 27.2% service, 9.8% sales and office, 20.4% natural resources, construction, and maintenance, 31.9% production, transportation, and material moving
Income: Per capita: $23,340; Median household: n/a; Average household: $58,952; Households with income of $100,000 or more: 24.5%; Poverty rate: 13.8%
Educational Attainment: High school diploma or higher: 84.9%; Bachelor's degree or higher: 6.9%; Graduate/professional degree or higher: 2.2%
Housing: Homeownership rate: 69.5%; Median home value: $93,400; Median year structure built: Before 1940; Homeowner vacancy rate: 0.0%; Median selected monthly owner costs: $1,095 with a mortgage, $272 without a mortgage; Median gross rent: $1,031 per month; Rental vacancy rate: 0.0%
Health Insurance: 87.2% have insurance; 63.8% have private insurance; 31.3% have public insurance; 12.8% do not have insurance; 0.0% of children under 18 do not have insurance
Transportation: Commute: 95.9% car, 0.0% public transportation, 1.8% walk, 2.3% work from home; Mean travel time to work: 21.1 minutes

WEST SALEM (village). Covers a land area of 1.088 square miles and a water area of 0.003 square miles. Located at 40.97° N. Lat; 82.11° W. Long. Elevation is 1,112 feet.
History: West Salem was laid out in 1834 by the Rickel brothers, who came from Wooster.
Population: 1,647; Growth (since 2000): 9.7%; Density: 1,513.7 persons per square mile; Race: 96.0% White, 3.4% Black/African American, 0.0%

Asian, 0.0% American Indian/Alaska Native, 0.0% Native Hawaiian/Other Pacific Islander, 0.6% Two or more races, 1.2% Hispanic of any race; Average household size: 2.69; Median age: 34.3; Age under 18: 25.5%; Age 65 and over: 9.1%; Males per 100 females: 102.5; Marriage status: 30.0% never married, 51.2% now married, 2.7% separated, 6.0% widowed, 12.7% divorced; Foreign born: 1.2%; Speak English only: 98.8%; With disability: 12.1%; Veterans: 5.1%; Ancestry: 28.4% German, 18.8% Irish, 10.3% English, 6.8% Polish, 6.5% Italian
Employment: 6.8% management, business, and financial, 1.9% computer, engineering, and science, 4.6% education, legal, community service, arts, and media, 2.3% healthcare practitioners, 19.6% service, 18.1% sales and office, 15.5% natural resources, construction, and maintenance, 31.1% production, transportation, and material moving
Income: Per capita: $18,295; Median household: $37,270; Average household: $48,269; Households with income of $100,000 or more: 9.3%; Poverty rate: 18.9%
Educational Attainment: High school diploma or higher: 84.8%; Bachelor's degree or higher: 5.7%; Graduate/professional degree or higher: 1.9%

School District(s)

Northwestern Local (KG-12)
2015-16 Enrollment: 1,357 . . . . (419) 846-3151
Housing: Homeownership rate: 68.0%; Median home value: $85,900; Median year structure built: 1960; Homeowner vacancy rate: 0.0%; Median selected monthly owner costs: $1,000 with a mortgage, $441 without a mortgage; Median gross rent: $705 per month; Rental vacancy rate: 0.0%
Health Insurance: 91.4% have insurance; 56.5% have private insurance; 42.4% have public insurance; 8.6% do not have insurance; 0.0% of children under 18 do not have insurance
Transportation: Commute: 94.5% car, 0.5% public transportation, 3.7% walk, 1.3% work from home; Mean travel time to work: 27.3 minutes

WOOSTER (city). County seat. Covers a land area of 16.310 square miles and a water area of 0.051 square miles. Located at 40.82° N. Lat; 81.93° W. Long. Elevation is 994 feet.
History: Wooster was settled in 1807 by the Larwill family. The town that grew after the War of 1812 was named for Revolutionary War general David Wooster. Wooster claims to have had America's first Christmas tree in 1847, when a young German immigrant, August Imgard, cut and decorated a small spruce tree.
Population: 26,773; Growth (since 2000): 7.9%; Density: 1,641.5 persons per square mile; Race: 90.3% White, 3.2% Black/African American, 3.1% Asian, 0.5% American Indian/Alaska Native, 0.0% Native Hawaiian/Other Pacific Islander, 2.5% Two or more races, 2.2% Hispanic of any race; Average household size: 2.22; Median age: 36.2; Age under 18: 20.2%; Age 65 and over: 18.1%; Males per 100 females: 91.0; Marriage status: 34.9% never married, 46.1% now married, 1.3% separated, 6.3% widowed, 12.7% divorced; Foreign born: 4.1%; Speak English only: 93.8%; With disability: 13.5%; Veterans: 7.5%; Ancestry: 29.6% German, 10.8% Irish, 9.1% English, 6.6% American, 5.5% Italian
Employment: 12.0% management, business, and financial, 6.3% computer, engineering, and science, 13.9% education, legal, community service, arts, and media, 4.8% healthcare practitioners, 20.2% service, 20.5% sales and office, 5.9% natural resources, construction, and maintenance, 16.4% production, transportation, and material moving
Income: Per capita: $24,311; Median household: $41,703; Average household: $57,804; Households with income of $100,000 or more: 12.5%; Poverty rate: 19.3%
Educational Attainment: High school diploma or higher: 90.1%; Bachelor's degree or higher: 28.7%; Graduate/professional degree or higher: 12.8%

School District(s)

Triway Local (PK-12)
2015-16 Enrollment: 1,635 . . . . (330) 264-9491
Wooster City (PK-12)
2015-16 Enrollment: 3,601 . . . . (330) 264-0869

Four-year College(s)

The College of Wooster (Private, Not-for-profit)
Fall 2016 Enrollment: 2,003 . . . . (330) 263-2000
2016-17 Tuition: In-state $46,860; Out-of-state $46,860

Two-year College(s)

Ohio State University Agricultural Technical Institute (Public)
Fall 2016 Enrollment: 722 . . . . (330) 287-1330
2016-17 Tuition: In-state $7,203; Out-of-state $25,395
Housing: Homeownership rate: 54.3%; Median home value: $126,300; Median year structure built: 1971; Homeowner vacancy rate: 3.0%; Median selected monthly owner costs: $1,120 with a mortgage, $468 without a mortgage; Median gross rent: $684 per month; Rental vacancy rate: 4.9%
Health Insurance: 92.6% have insurance; 69.6% have private insurance; 38.5% have public insurance; 7.4% do not have insurance; 2.6% of children under 18 do not have insurance
Hospitals: Wooster Community Hospital (130 beds)
Safety: Violent crime rate: 27.2 per 10,000 population; Property crime rate: 288.7 per 10,000 population
Newspapers: Daily Record (daily circulation 21,600)
Transportation: Commute: 84.1% car, 0.0% public transportation, 9.5% walk, 3.5% work from home; Mean travel time to work: 18.1 minutes
Airports: Wayne County (general aviation)
Additional Information Contacts
City of Wooster . . . . (330) 263-5200
http://www.woosteroh.com

Williams County

Located in northwestern Ohio; bounded on the north by Michigan, and on the west by Indiana; crossed by the Saint Joseph and Tiffin Rivers. Covers a land area of 420.965 square miles, a water area of 2.126 square miles, and is located in the Eastern Time Zone at 41.56° N. Lat., 84.58° W. Long. The county was founded in 1820. County seat is Bryan.

Weather Station: Montpelier Elevation: 859 feet

	Jan	Feb	Mar	Apr	May	Jun	Jul	Aug	Sep	Oct	Nov	Dec
High	32	35	46	59	71	80	84	82	75	62	49	36
Low	15	17	25	36	46	56	60	59	50	39	31	21
Precip	2.2	2.0	2.7	3.4	4.0	3.5	3.7	4.0	3.3	3.0	3.1	2.7
Snow	9.1	8.4	4.7	0.9	tr	0.0	0.0	0.0	0.0	0.2	1.4	9.0

High and Low temperatures in degrees Fahrenheit; Precipitation and Snow in inches

Population: 37,270; Growth (since 2000): -4.9%; Density: 88.5 persons per square mile; Race: 95.6% White, 1.1% Black/African American, 0.6% Asian, 0.3% American Indian/Alaska Native, 0.0% Native Hawaiian/Other Pacific Islander, 1.1% two or more races, 4.0% Hispanic of any race; Average household size: 2.39; Median age: 41.6; Age under 18: 22.9%; Age 65 and over: 17.5%; Males per 100 females: 98.5; Marriage status: 25.5% never married, 53.2% now married, 1.5% separated, 7.7% widowed, 13.6% divorced; Foreign born: 1.3%; Speak English only: 96.9%; With disability: 14.4%; Veterans: 8.6%; Ancestry: 38.8% German, 10.6% Irish, 9.4% English, 7.7% American, 3.7% French
Religion: Six largest groups: 10.3% Catholicism, 8.7% Methodist/Pietist, 5.2% Lutheran, 4.8% Baptist, 3.7% Non-denominational Protestant, 2.7% European Free-Church
Economy: Unemployment rate: 4.0%; Leading industries: 16.0 % retail trade; 14.4 % other services (except public administration); 13.9 % manufacturing; Farms: 984 totaling 208,012 acres; Company size: 0 employ 1,000 or more persons, 3 employ 500 to 999 persons, 26 employ 100 to 499 persons, 778 employ less than 100 persons; Business ownership: 769 women-owned, n/a Black-owned, 60 Hispanic-owned, n/a Asian-owned, n/a American Indian/Alaska Native-owned
Employment: 9.8% management, business, and financial, 3.0% computer, engineering, and science, 8.0% education, legal, community service, arts, and media, 3.7% healthcare practitioners, 14.4% service, 20.5% sales and office, 9.3% natural resources, construction, and maintenance, 31.2% production, transportation, and material moving
Income: Per capita: $22,757; Median household: $45,044; Average household: $55,094; Households with income of $100,000 or more: 11.6%; Poverty rate: 14.4%
Educational Attainment: High school diploma or higher: 88.6%; Bachelor's degree or higher: 14.2%; Graduate/professional degree or higher: 4.8%
Housing: Homeownership rate: 74.5%; Median home value: $95,200; Median year structure built: 1962; Homeowner vacancy rate: 0.7%; Median selected monthly owner costs: $985 with a mortgage, $358 without a mortgage; Median gross rent: $645 per month; Rental vacancy rate: 3.4%
Vital Statistics: Birth rate: 111.6 per 10,000 population; Death rate: 106.2 per 10,000 population; Age-adjusted cancer mortality rate: 202.9 deaths per 100,000 population
Health Insurance: 93.4% have insurance; 71.4% have private insurance; 38.1% have public insurance; 6.6% do not have insurance; 1.6% of children under 18 do not have insurance

Health Care: Physicians: 10.0 per 10,000 population; Dentists: 5.4 per 10,000 population; Hospital beds: 39.7 per 10,000 population; Hospital admissions: 1,193.0 per 10,000 population
Transportation: Commute: 94.5% car, 0.4% public transportation, 1.5% walk, 2.1% work from home; Mean travel time to work: 19.2 minutes
2016 Presidential Election: 69.0% Trump, 25.2% Clinton, 4.1% Johnson, 0.8% Stein
Additional Information Contacts
Williams Government . . . . (419) 636-2059
http://www.co.williams.oh.us

Williams County Communities

ALVORDTON (CDP). Covers a land area of 0.252 square miles and a water area of <.001 square miles. Located at 41.66° N. Lat; 84.43° W. Long. Elevation is 856 feet.
Population: 298; Growth (since 2000): -2.3%; Density: 1,182.4 persons per square mile; Race: 96.3% White, 1.3% Black/African American, 2.0% Asian, 0.3% American Indian/Alaska Native, 0.0% Native Hawaiian/Other Pacific Islander, 0.0% Two or more races, 0.3% Hispanic of any race; Average household size: 2.17; Median age: 41.8; Age under 18: 16.8%; Age 65 and over: 11.1%; Males per 100 females: 128.4; Marriage status: 27.4% never married, 37.0% now married, 4.4% separated, 13.7% widowed, 21.9% divorced; Foreign born: 2.0%; Speak English only: 99.6%; With disability: 19.8%; Veterans: 14.5%; Ancestry: 23.5% German, 14.4% English, 13.4% Irish, 4.4% Polish, 3.7% Dutch
Employment: 4.6% management, business, and financial, 0.0% computer, engineering, and science, 17.9% education, legal, community service, arts, and media, 10.6% healthcare practitioners, 23.2% service, 7.9% sales and office, 0.7% natural resources, construction, and maintenance, 35.1% production, transportation, and material moving
Income: Per capita: $17,088; Median household: $21,771; Average household: $39,243; Households with income of $100,000 or more: 6.3%; Poverty rate: 6.4%
Educational Attainment: High school diploma or higher: 88.7%; Bachelor's degree or higher: 15.5%; Graduate/professional degree or higher: 7.2%
Housing: Homeownership rate: 50.4%; Median home value: n/a; Median year structure built: Before 1940; Homeowner vacancy rate: 0.0%; Median selected monthly owner costs: n/a with a mortgage, $433 without a mortgage; Median gross rent: $630 per month; Rental vacancy rate: 0.0%
Health Insurance: 92.6% have insurance; 53.4% have private insurance; 42.6% have public insurance; 7.4% do not have insurance; 0.0% of children under 18 do not have insurance
Transportation: Commute: 82.9% car, 11.4% public transportation, 0.0% walk, 0.0% work from home; Mean travel time to work: 18.0 minutes

BLAKESLEE (village). Covers a land area of 0.108 square miles and a water area of 0 square miles. Located at 41.52° N. Lat; 84.73° W. Long. Elevation is 860 feet.
Population: 66; Growth (since 2000): -49.2%; Density: 613.4 persons per square mile; Race: 93.9% White, 1.5% Black/African American, 0.0% Asian, 0.0% American Indian/Alaska Native, 0.0% Native Hawaiian/Other Pacific Islander, 4.5% Two or more races, 0.0% Hispanic of any race; Average household size: 1.65; Median age: 42.3; Age under 18: 12.1%; Age 65 and over: 30.3%; Males per 100 females: 95.9; Marriage status: 33.3% never married, 45.0% now married, 0.0% separated, 11.7% widowed, 10.0% divorced; Foreign born: 0.0%; Speak English only: 96.9%; With disability: 19.7%; Veterans: 6.9%; Ancestry: 53.0% German, 27.3% Irish, 9.1% American, 7.6% English, 7.6% French
Employment: 0.0% management, business, and financial, 19.4% computer, engineering, and science, 2.8% education, legal, community service, arts, and media, 2.8% healthcare practitioners, 27.8% service, 13.9% sales and office, 5.6% natural resources, construction, and maintenance, 27.8% production, transportation, and material moving
Income: Per capita: $25,229; Median household: $38,929; Average household: $41,193; Households with income of $100,000 or more: 2.5%; Poverty rate: 4.5%
Educational Attainment: High school diploma or higher: 92.3%; Bachelor's degree or higher: 9.6%; Graduate/professional degree or higher: n/a
Housing: Homeownership rate: 67.5%; Median home value: $79,400; Median year structure built: 1944; Homeowner vacancy rate: 0.0%; Median selected monthly owner costs: $1,047 with a mortgage, $325 without a mortgage; Median gross rent: $705 per month; Rental vacancy rate: 0.0%
Health Insurance: 100.0% have insurance; 86.4% have private insurance; 48.5% have public insurance; 0.0% do not have insurance; 0.0% of children under 18 do not have insurance
Transportation: Commute: 91.7% car, 0.0% public transportation, 5.6% walk, 2.8% work from home; Mean travel time to work: 24.9 minutes

BRYAN (city). County seat. Covers a land area of 5.528 square miles and a water area of 0.032 square miles. Located at 41.47° N. Lat; 84.55° W. Long. Elevation is 768 feet.
History: Bryan's early growth was attributed to its artesian wells, their supposed medicinal value creating a temporary business for the town, which became a trading and industrial center and the seat of Williams County.
Population: 8,480; Growth (since 2000): 1.8%; Density: 1,533.9 persons per square mile; Race: 97.1% White, 0.1% Black/African American, 0.2% Asian, 0.2% American Indian/Alaska Native, 0.0% Native Hawaiian/Other Pacific Islander, 1.6% Two or more races, 4.4% Hispanic of any race; Average household size: 2.24; Median age: 41.2; Age under 18: 23.3%; Age 65 and over: 18.4%; Males per 100 females: 90.6; Marriage status: 26.5% never married, 46.5% now married, 2.3% separated, 9.3% widowed, 17.6% divorced; Foreign born: 2.6%; Speak English only: 95.4%; With disability: 17.6%; Veterans: 6.1%; Ancestry: 36.6% German, 11.6% Irish, 10.5% English, 7.8% American, 6.9% Dutch
Employment: 8.7% management, business, and financial, 4.2% computer, engineering, and science, 8.8% education, legal, community service, arts, and media, 4.3% healthcare practitioners, 9.0% service, 23.5% sales and office, 8.3% natural resources, construction, and maintenance, 33.2% production, transportation, and material moving
Income: Per capita: $21,939; Median household: $34,490; Average household: $49,634; Households with income of $100,000 or more: 7.6%; Poverty rate: 16.2%
Educational Attainment: High school diploma or higher: 91.8%; Bachelor's degree or higher: 13.4%; Graduate/professional degree or higher: 4.3%

School District(s)

Bryan City (PK-12)
2015-16 Enrollment: 1,977 . . . . (419) 636-6973
Housing: Homeownership rate: 60.7%; Median home value: $94,100; Median year structure built: 1961; Homeowner vacancy rate: 1.0%; Median selected monthly owner costs: $924 with a mortgage, $320 without a mortgage; Median gross rent: $654 per month; Rental vacancy rate: 5.6%
Health Insurance: 92.5% have insurance; 69.5% have private insurance; 40.5% have public insurance; 7.5% do not have insurance; 1.6% of children under 18 do not have insurance
Hospitals: Community Hospitals & Wellness Centers (131 beds)
Newspapers: Bryan Times (daily circulation 10,200); The Countyline (weekly circulation 21,000)
Transportation: Commute: 93.7% car, 0.4% public transportation, 2.1% walk, 1.3% work from home; Mean travel time to work: 15.8 minutes; Amtrak: Train service available.

EDGERTON (village). Covers a land area of 1.867 square miles and a water area of 0.011 square miles. Located at 41.45° N. Lat; 84.75° W. Long. Elevation is 840 feet.
Population: 2,162; Growth (since 2000): 2.1%; Density: 1,158.1 persons per square mile; Race: 96.6% White, 0.6% Black/African American, 0.1% Asian, 0.0% American Indian/Alaska Native, 0.0% Native Hawaiian/Other Pacific Islander, 1.1% Two or more races, 7.0% Hispanic of any race; Average household size: 2.39; Median age: 46.4; Age under 18: 20.1%; Age 65 and over: 21.9%; Males per 100 females: 89.8; Marriage status: 26.0% never married, 51.6% now married, 1.4% separated, 10.1% widowed, 12.4% divorced; Foreign born: 0.9%; Speak English only: 97.5%; With disability: 16.4%; Veterans: 8.9%; Ancestry: 37.4% German, 10.6% Irish, 7.7% American, 5.4% English, 3.6% Dutch
Employment: 5.5% management, business, and financial, 2.8% computer, engineering, and science, 7.8% education, legal, community service, arts, and media, 5.5% healthcare practitioners, 21.9% service, 21.8% sales and office, 7.7% natural resources, construction, and maintenance, 26.9% production, transportation, and material moving
Income: Per capita: $22,400; Median household: $43,824; Average household: $53,021; Households with income of $100,000 or more: 8.2%; Poverty rate: 15.3%
Educational Attainment: High school diploma or higher: 87.5%; Bachelor's degree or higher: 15.1%; Graduate/professional degree or higher: 4.3%

School District(s)

Edgerton Local (KG-12)
2015-16 Enrollment: 615 . . . . (419) 298-2112

Housing: Homeownership rate: 77.4%; Median home value: $85,300; Median year structure built: 1964; Homeowner vacancy rate: 0.0%; Median selected monthly owner costs: $932 with a mortgage, $332 without a mortgage; Median gross rent: $609 per month; Rental vacancy rate: 3.9%

Health Insurance: 93.9% have insurance; 68.9% have private insurance; 42.9% have public insurance; 6.1% do not have insurance; 0.0% of children under 18 do not have insurance

Newspapers: Edgerton Earth (weekly circulation 1,200)

Transportation: Commute: 96.6% car, 0.0% public transportation, 1.3% walk, 1.5% work from home; Mean travel time to work: 19.6 minutes

EDON (village). Covers a land area of 1.122 square miles and a water area of 0 square miles. Located at 41.56° N. Lat; 84.77° W. Long. Elevation is 899 feet.

Population: 818; Growth (since 2000): -8.9%; Density: 729.1 persons per square mile; Race: 98.2% White, 0.0% Black/African American, 0.0% Asian, 0.4% American Indian/Alaska Native, 0.5% Native Hawaiian/Other Pacific Islander, 1.0% Two or more races, 1.3% Hispanic of any race; Average household size: 2.25; Median age: 43.5; Age under 18: 24.1%; Age 65 and over: 25.8%; Males per 100 females: 92.6; Marriage status: 28.6% never married, 51.5% now married, 1.5% separated, 9.5% widowed, 10.4% divorced; Foreign born: 0.4%; Speak English only: 97.7%; With disability: 15.4%; Veterans: 9.2%; Ancestry: 53.2% German, 13.4% Irish, 10.3% English, 3.8% American, 2.6% Pennsylvania German

Employment: 12.0% management, business, and financial, 3.5% computer, engineering, and science, 7.9% education, legal, community service, arts, and media, 3.2% healthcare practitioners, 9.7% service, 26.1% sales and office, 9.1% natural resources, construction, and maintenance, 28.4% production, transportation, and material moving

Income: Per capita: $21,562; Median household: $42,019; Average household: $47,563; Households with income of $100,000 or more: 4.7%; Poverty rate: 19.4%

Educational Attainment: High school diploma or higher: 87.9%; Bachelor's degree or higher: 14.1%; Graduate/professional degree or higher: 3.2%

School District(s)

Edon Northwest Local (KG-12)
2015-16 Enrollment: 499 . . . . (419) 272-3213

Housing: Homeownership rate: 79.1%; Median home value: $76,600; Median year structure built: 1950; Homeowner vacancy rate: 3.4%; Median selected monthly owner costs: $894 with a mortgage, $337 without a mortgage; Median gross rent: $682 per month; Rental vacancy rate: 0.0%

Health Insurance: 95.7% have insurance; 69.9% have private insurance; 52.1% have public insurance; 4.3% do not have insurance; 3.6% of children under 18 do not have insurance

Transportation: Commute: 93.3% car, 0.0% public transportation, 3.5% walk, 0.9% work from home; Mean travel time to work: 21.6 minutes

HOLIDAY CITY (village). Covers a land area of 2.666 square miles and a water area of 0.021 square miles. Located at 41.62° N. Lat; 84.54° W. Long. Elevation is 902 feet.

Population: 36; Growth (since 2000): -26.5%; Density: 13.5 persons per square mile; Race: 94.4% White, 0.0% Black/African American, 0.0% Asian, 2.8% American Indian/Alaska Native, 0.0% Native Hawaiian/Other Pacific Islander, 2.8% Two or more races, 0.0% Hispanic of any race; Average household size: 2.00; Median age: 46.0; Age under 18: 27.8%; Age 65 and over: 25.0%; Males per 100 females: 116.7; Marriage status: 14.3% never married, 53.6% now married, 0.0% separated, 25.0% widowed, 7.1% divorced; Foreign born: 2.8%; Speak English only: 97.1%; With disability: 25.0%; Veterans: 26.9%; Ancestry: 30.6% American, 16.7% Polish, 16.7% Russian, 2.8% English, 2.8% German

Employment: 33.3% management, business, and financial, 0.0% computer, engineering, and science, 0.0% education, legal, community service, arts, and media, 0.0% healthcare practitioners, 0.0% service, 26.7% sales and office, 26.7% natural resources, construction, and maintenance, 13.3% production, transportation, and material moving

Income: Per capita: $29,353; Median household: n/a; Average household: $67,517; Households with income of $100,000 or more: 16.7%; Poverty rate: 19.4%

Educational Attainment: High school diploma or higher: 100.0%; Bachelor's degree or higher: 24.0%; Graduate/professional degree or higher: 4.0%

Housing: Homeownership rate: 83.3%; Median home value: n/a; Median year structure built: 1980; Homeowner vacancy rate: 0.0%; Median selected monthly owner costs: n/a with a mortgage, $375 without a mortgage; Median gross rent: n/a per month; Rental vacancy rate: 0.0%

Health Insurance: 94.4% have insurance; 58.3% have private insurance; 44.4% have public insurance; 5.6% do not have insurance; 0.0% of children under 18 do not have insurance

Transportation: Commute: 80.0% car, 0.0% public transportation, 0.0% walk, 13.3% work from home; Mean travel time to work: 0.0 minutes

KUNKLE (CDP). Covers a land area of 0.280 square miles and a water area of 0 square miles. Located at 41.64° N. Lat; 84.49° W. Long. Elevation is 879 feet.

Population: 200; Growth (since 2000): n/a; Density: 713.6 persons per square mile; Race: 100.0% White, 0.0% Black/African American, 0.0% Asian, 0.0% American Indian/Alaska Native, 0.0% Native Hawaiian/Other Pacific Islander, 0.0% Two or more races, 0.0% Hispanic of any race; Average household size: 1.71; Median age: 53.4; Age under 18: 7.5%; Age 65 and over: 0.0%; Males per 100 females: 112.1; Marriage status: 27.6% never married, 33.9% now married, 0.0% separated, 13.5% widowed, 25.0% divorced; Foreign born: 0.0%; Speak English only: 100.0%; With disability: 26.0%; Veterans: 13.5%; Ancestry: 48.5% German, 25.0% English, 23.5% French

Employment: 0.0% management, business, and financial, 0.0% computer, engineering, and science, 0.0% education, legal, community service, arts, and media, 0.0% healthcare practitioners, 44.0% service, 0.0% sales and office, 0.0% natural resources, construction, and maintenance, 56.0% production, transportation, and material moving

Income: Per capita: $21,374; Median household: $16,444; Average household: $34,991; Households with income of $100,000 or more: 19.7%; Poverty rate: 38.0%

Educational Attainment: High school diploma or higher: 68.6%; Bachelor's degree or higher: n/a; Graduate/professional degree or higher: n/a

Housing: Homeownership rate: 49.6%; Median home value: $81,300; Median year structure built: Before 1940; Homeowner vacancy rate: 0.0%; Median selected monthly owner costs: n/a with a mortgage, n/a without a mortgage; Median gross rent: n/a per month; Rental vacancy rate: 0.0%

Health Insurance: 88.5% have insurance; 23.5% have private insurance; 65.0% have public insurance; 11.5% do not have insurance; 0.0% of children under 18 do not have insurance

Transportation: Commute: 73.9% car, 0.0% public transportation, 0.0% walk, 0.0% work from home; Mean travel time to work: 10.4 minutes

LAKE SENECA (CDP). Covers a land area of 1.728 square miles and a water area of 0.060 square miles. Located at 41.67° N. Lat; 84.64° W. Long. Elevation is 932 feet.

Population: 561; Growth (since 2000): n/a; Density: 324.6 persons per square mile; Race: 100.0% White, 0.0% Black/African American, 0.0% Asian, 0.0% American Indian/Alaska Native, 0.0% Native Hawaiian/Other Pacific Islander, 0.0% Two or more races, 0.0% Hispanic of any race; Average household size: 2.42; Median age: 55.9; Age under 18: 23.4%; Age 65 and over: 17.1%; Males per 100 females: 108.5; Marriage status: 10.4% never married, 76.8% now married, 0.0% separated, 4.1% widowed, 8.8% divorced; Foreign born: 0.0%; Speak English only: 100.0%; With disability: 11.8%; Veterans: 3.0%; Ancestry: 30.3% English, 20.0% German, 15.3% Irish, 11.9% American, 4.8% Polish

Employment: 8.0% management, business, and financial, 5.3% computer, engineering, and science, 17.3% education, legal, community service, arts, and media, 7.3% healthcare practitioners, 13.3% service, 18.7% sales and office, 5.7% natural resources, construction, and maintenance, 24.3% production, transportation, and material moving

Income: Per capita: $36,699; Median household: $73,750; Average household: $88,697; Households with income of $100,000 or more: 34.5%; Poverty rate: 6.1%

Educational Attainment: High school diploma or higher: 96.7%; Bachelor's degree or higher: 47.0%; Graduate/professional degree or higher: 20.5%

Housing: Homeownership rate: 97.4%; Median home value: $114,700; Median year structure built: 1976; Homeowner vacancy rate: 0.0%; Median selected monthly owner costs: $1,023 with a mortgage, $650 without a mortgage; Median gross rent: n/a per month; Rental vacancy rate: 0.0%

Health Insurance: 100.0% have insurance; 96.4% have private insurance; 18.2% have public insurance; 0.0% do not have insurance; 0.0% of children under 18 do not have insurance

Transportation: Commute: 100.0% car, 0.0% public transportation, 0.0% walk, 0.0% work from home; Mean travel time to work: 25.3 minutes

MONTPELIER (village). Covers a land area of 2.909 square miles and a water area of 0.017 square miles. Located at 41.58° N. Lat; 84.59° W. Long. Elevation is 853 feet.
History: Settled 1855, incorporated 1875.
Population: 4,024; Growth (since 2000): -6.9%; Density: 1,383.2 persons per square mile; Race: 93.7% White, 0.1% Black/African American, 2.9% Asian, 0.5% American Indian/Alaska Native, 0.1% Native Hawaiian/Other Pacific Islander, 1.3% Two or more races, 2.6% Hispanic of any race; Average household size: 2.40; Median age: 39.4; Age under 18: 24.2%; Age 65 and over: 14.2%; Males per 100 females: 90.6; Marriage status: 28.5% never married, 51.7% now married, 1.5% separated, 5.7% widowed, 14.1% divorced; Foreign born: 2.3%; Speak English only: 96.4%; With disability: 14.5%; Veterans: 10.4%; Ancestry: 34.9% German, 14.4% Irish, 8.0% English, 6.6% American, 4.6% French
Employment: 9.5% management, business, and financial, 1.6% computer, engineering, and science, 5.9% education, legal, community service, arts, and media, 2.1% healthcare practitioners, 15.5% service, 17.5% sales and office, 7.5% natural resources, construction, and maintenance, 40.4% production, transportation, and material moving
Income: Per capita: $21,538; Median household: $41,101; Average household: $52,199; Households with income of $100,000 or more: 11.7%; Poverty rate: 19.2%
Educational Attainment: High school diploma or higher: 81.5%; Bachelor's degree or higher: 11.0%; Graduate/professional degree or higher: 3.6%

School District(s)

Montpelier Exempted Village (KG-12)
2015-16 Enrollment: 954. . . . . (419) 485-3676
Housing: Homeownership rate: 64.3%; Median home value: $75,000; Median year structure built: Before 1940; Homeowner vacancy rate: 0.0%; Median selected monthly owner costs: $819 with a mortgage, $317 without a mortgage; Median gross rent: $621 per month; Rental vacancy rate: 5.0%
Health Insurance: 91.7% have insurance; 60.4% have private insurance; 42.7% have public insurance; 8.3% do not have insurance; 0.7% of children under 18 do not have insurance
Hospitals: Community Hospitals & Wellness Centers
Safety: Violent crime rate: 35.2 per 10,000 population; Property crime rate: 366.8 per 10,000 population
Newspapers: Montpelier Leader (weekly circulation 1,800); Village Reporter (weekly circulation 1,900)
Transportation: Commute: 95.5% car, 0.4% public transportation, 3.4% walk, 0.7% work from home; Mean travel time to work: 18.0 minutes
Additional Information Contacts
Village of Montpelier . . . . (419) 485-5543
http://www.montpelieroh.net

NETTLE LAKE (CDP).
Land/water area and latitude/longitude are not available.
Population: 449; Growth (since 2000): n/a; Density: n/a persons per square mile; Race: 97.3% White, 0.0% Black/African American, 0.0% Asian, 0.0% American Indian/Alaska Native, 0.0% Native Hawaiian/Other Pacific Islander, 0.0% Two or more races, 4.2% Hispanic of any race; Average household size: 2.57; Median age: 34.2; Age under 18: 22.0%; Age 65 and over: 7.3%; Males per 100 females: 0.0; Marriage status: 36.2% never married, 49.7% now married, 0.0% separated, 12.2% widowed, 1.9% divorced; Foreign born: 0.0%; Speak English only: 95.3%; With disability: 18.7%; Veterans: 0.0%; Ancestry: 22.7% Irish, 13.1% French, 11.6% Polish, 10.7% German, 5.1% Swedish
Employment: 0.0% management, business, and financial, 0.0% computer, engineering, and science, 0.0% education, legal, community service, arts, and media, 0.0% healthcare practitioners, 24.7% service, 18.1% sales and office, 6.6% natural resources, construction, and maintenance, 50.5% production, transportation, and material moving
Income: Per capita: $16,414; Median household: $15,469; Average household: $42,917; Households with income of $100,000 or more: 18.3%; Poverty rate: 31.4%
Educational Attainment: High school diploma or higher: 100.0%; Bachelor's degree or higher: 11.3%; Graduate/professional degree or higher: 5.8%
Housing: Homeownership rate: 63.4%; Median home value: $70,200; Median year structure built: 1963; Homeowner vacancy rate: 0.0%; Median selected monthly owner costs: $1,328 with a mortgage, $353 without a mortgage; Median gross rent: $391 per month; Rental vacancy rate: 0.0%
Health Insurance: 97.1% have insurance; 53.5% have private insurance; 45.4% have public insurance; 2.9% do not have insurance; 0.0% of children under 18 do not have insurance
Safety: Violent crime rate: 0.0 per 10,000 population; Property crime rate: 0.0 per 10,000 population
Transportation: Commute: 90.1% car, 0.0% public transportation, 0.0% walk, 0.0% work from home; Mean travel time to work: 33.9 minutes

PIONEER (village). Covers a land area of 2.016 square miles and a water area of 0.071 square miles. Located at 41.68° N. Lat; 84.55° W. Long. Elevation is 879 feet.
Population: 1,814; Growth (since 2000): 24.2%; Density: 900.0 persons per square mile; Race: 94.4% White, 0.0% Black/African American, 0.6% Asian, 1.7% American Indian/Alaska Native, 0.0% Native Hawaiian/Other Pacific Islander, 0.2% Two or more races, 4.3% Hispanic of any race; Average household size: 2.44; Median age: 32.0; Age under 18: 25.8%; Age 65 and over: 11.4%; Males per 100 females: 94.9; Marriage status: 32.3% never married, 49.7% now married, 2.1% separated, 6.9% widowed, 11.0% divorced; Foreign born: 1.9%; Speak English only: 96.1%; With disability: 12.3%; Veterans: 8.8%; Ancestry: 38.3% German, 8.9% English, 8.4% American, 7.4% Irish, 7.3% Italian
Employment: 11.4% management, business, and financial, 3.4% computer, engineering, and science, 6.6% education, legal, community service, arts, and media, 3.1% healthcare practitioners, 13.5% service, 17.5% sales and office, 7.5% natural resources, construction, and maintenance, 37.0% production, transportation, and material moving
Income: Per capita: $20,822; Median household: $41,691; Average household: $49,793; Households with income of $100,000 or more: 9.4%; Poverty rate: 17.1%
Educational Attainment: High school diploma or higher: 87.0%; Bachelor's degree or higher: 14.5%; Graduate/professional degree or higher: 5.7%

School District(s)

North Central Local (PK-12)
2015-16 Enrollment: 579. . . . . (419) 737-2392
Housing: Homeownership rate: 57.1%; Median home value: $86,600; Median year structure built: 1960; Homeowner vacancy rate: 3.0%; Median selected monthly owner costs: $950 with a mortgage, $338 without a mortgage; Median gross rent: $725 per month; Rental vacancy rate: 0.0%
Health Insurance: 89.4% have insurance; 68.7% have private insurance; 37.9% have public insurance; 10.6% do not have insurance; 0.6% of children under 18 do not have insurance
Safety: Violent crime rate: 14.2 per 10,000 population; Property crime rate: 163.6 per 10,000 population
Transportation: Commute: 92.4% car, 0.4% public transportation, 2.2% walk, 3.5% work from home; Mean travel time to work: 21.1 minutes

PULASKI (CDP). Covers a land area of 0.157 square miles and a water area of 0 square miles. Located at 41.51° N. Lat; 84.51° W. Long. Elevation is 761 feet.
Population: 74; Growth (since 2000): n/a; Density: 472.7 persons per square mile; Race: 100.0% White, 0.0% Black/African American, 0.0% Asian, 0.0% American Indian/Alaska Native, 0.0% Native Hawaiian/Other Pacific Islander, 0.0% Two or more races, 0.0% Hispanic of any race; Average household size: 1.68; Median age: 32.4; Age under 18: 12.2%; Age 65 and over: 18.9%; Males per 100 females: 106.3; Marriage status: 36.9% never married, 26.2% now married, 0.0% separated, 12.3% widowed, 24.6% divorced; Foreign born: 0.0%; Speak English only: 100.0%; With disability: 0.0%; Veterans: 0.0%; Ancestry: 29.7% German, 23.0% American
Employment: 0.0% management, business, and financial, 0.0% computer, engineering, and science, 0.0% education, legal, community service, arts, and media, 0.0% healthcare practitioners, 32.3% service, 12.3% sales and office, 0.0% natural resources, construction, and maintenance, 55.4% production, transportation, and material moving
Income: Per capita: $30,005; Median household: $50,833; Average household: $50,182; Households with income of $100,000 or more: n/a; Poverty rate: n/a
Educational Attainment: High school diploma or higher: 85.4%; Bachelor's degree or higher: n/a; Graduate/professional degree or higher: n/a
Housing: Homeownership rate: 100.0%; Median home value: $65,000; Median year structure built: Before 1940; Homeowner vacancy rate: 0.0%;

Median selected monthly owner costs: $871 with a mortgage, n/a without a mortgage; Median gross rent: n/a per month; Rental vacancy rate: 0.0%
Health Insurance: 83.8% have insurance; 55.4% have private insurance; 47.3% have public insurance; 16.2% do not have insurance; 0.0% of children under 18 do not have insurance
Transportation: Commute: 100.0% car, 0.0% public transportation, 0.0% walk, 0.0% work from home; Mean travel time to work: 29.2 minutes

STRYKER (village). Covers a land area of 0.868 square miles and a water area of 0.005 square miles. Located at 41.50° N. Lat; 84.42° W. Long. Elevation is 715 feet.
Population: 1,144; Growth (since 2000): -18.6%; Density: 1,318.4 persons per square mile; Race: 86.3% White, 1.0% Black/African American, 0.8% Asian, 0.4% American Indian/Alaska Native, 0.0% Native Hawaiian/Other Pacific Islander, 3.5% Two or more races, 17.0% Hispanic of any race; Average household size: 2.76; Median age: 38.6; Age under 18: 27.5%; Age 65 and over: 12.7%; Males per 100 females: 98.1; Marriage status: 21.3% never married, 59.5% now married, 1.1% separated, 3.5% widowed, 15.7% divorced; Foreign born: 1.0%; Speak English only: 95.8%; With disability: 12.0%; Veterans: 10.6%; Ancestry: 42.5% German, 10.1% Irish, 6.1% English, 4.2% American, 3.2% French
Employment: 4.8% management, business, and financial, 1.5% computer, engineering, and science, 3.6% education, legal, community service, arts, and media, 3.6% healthcare practitioners, 13.5% service, 26.5% sales and office, 11.6% natural resources, construction, and maintenance, 34.9% production, transportation, and material moving
Income: Per capita: $19,342; Median household: $49,375; Average household: $51,534; Households with income of $100,000 or more: 6.5%; Poverty rate: 11.1%
Educational Attainment: High school diploma or higher: 93.9%; Bachelor's degree or higher: 8.7%; Graduate/professional degree or higher: n/a

School District(s)

Stryker Local (PK-12)
2015-16 Enrollment: 356. . . . . (419) 682-6961
Housing: Homeownership rate: 73.3%; Median home value: $77,000; Median year structure built: 1957; Homeowner vacancy rate: 0.0%; Median selected monthly owner costs: $937 with a mortgage, $297 without a mortgage; Median gross rent: $621 per month; Rental vacancy rate: 8.3%
Health Insurance: 89.2% have insurance; 69.1% have private insurance; 32.2% have public insurance; 10.8% do not have insurance; 5.1% of children under 18 do not have insurance
Transportation: Commute: 97.8% car, 0.0% public transportation, 0.9% walk, 0.6% work from home; Mean travel time to work: 19.9 minutes

WEST UNITY (village). Covers a land area of 1.174 square miles and a water area of 0 square miles. Located at 41.59° N. Lat; 84.43° W. Long. Elevation is 787 feet.
Population: 1,777; Growth (since 2000): -0.7%; Density: 1,513.4 persons per square mile; Race: 96.2% White, 0.3% Black/African American, 0.8% Asian, 0.2% American Indian/Alaska Native, 0.0% Native Hawaiian/Other Pacific Islander, 1.2% Two or more races, 4.1% Hispanic of any race; Average household size: 2.47; Median age: 33.7; Age under 18: 28.0%; Age 65 and over: 11.3%; Males per 100 females: 93.2; Marriage status: 24.6% never married, 52.6% now married, 3.0% separated, 5.4% widowed, 17.4% divorced; Foreign born: 0.8%; Speak English only: 98.2%; With disability: 16.0%; Veterans: 7.5%; Ancestry: 44.1% German, 11.1% Irish, 8.3% American, 5.7% English, 5.7% French
Employment: 3.5% management, business, and financial, 2.5% computer, engineering, and science, 8.1% education, legal, community service, arts, and media, 4.7% healthcare practitioners, 14.1% service, 24.8% sales and office, 7.5% natural resources, construction, and maintenance, 34.9% production, transportation, and material moving
Income: Per capita: $17,872; Median household: $35,929; Average household: $43,194; Households with income of $100,000 or more: 4.5%; Poverty rate: 15.0%
Educational Attainment: High school diploma or higher: 86.9%; Bachelor's degree or higher: 9.0%; Graduate/professional degree or higher: 3.2%

School District(s)

Millcreek-West Unity Local (KG-12)
2015-16 Enrollment: 557. . . . . (419) 924-2365
Housing: Homeownership rate: 64.2%; Median home value: $81,500; Median year structure built: 1961; Homeowner vacancy rate: 0.0%; Median selected monthly owner costs: $831 with a mortgage, $358 without a mortgage; Median gross rent: $577 per month; Rental vacancy rate: 0.0%
Health Insurance: 91.2% have insurance; 63.3% have private insurance; 38.9% have public insurance; 8.8% do not have insurance; 3.0% of children under 18 do not have insurance
Newspapers: Village Reporter (weekly circulation 3,300)
Transportation: Commute: 95.5% car, 1.0% public transportation, 2.8% walk, 0.6% work from home; Mean travel time to work: 18.5 minutes

Wood County

Located in northwestern Ohio; bounded on the northwest by the Maumee River; crossed by the Portage River. Covers a land area of 617.205 square miles, a water area of 3.286 square miles, and is located in the Eastern Time Zone at 41.36° N. Lat., 83.62° W. Long. The county was founded in 1820. County seat is Bowling Green.

Wood County is part of the Toledo, OH Metropolitan Statistical Area. The entire metro area includes: Fulton County, OH; Lucas County, OH; Wood County, OH

Weather Station: Bowling Green WWTP Elevation: 674 feet

	Jan	Feb	Mar	Apr	May	Jun	Jul	Aug	Sep	Oct	Nov	Dec
High	32	36	46	59	71	81	84	82	76	63	50	37
Low	18	20	27	38	48	59	62	60	52	41	33	23
Precip	1.9	1.8	2.2	3.1	3.8	3.4	3.7	3.6	2.6	2.8	2.6	2.4
Snow	7.1	5.4	3.2	0.6	tr	0.0	0.0	0.0	0.0	0.0	0.6	4.7

High and Low temperatures in degrees Fahrenheit; Precipitation and Snow in inches

Weather Station: Hoytville 2 NE Elevation: 700 feet

	Jan	Feb	Mar	Apr	May	Jun	Jul	Aug	Sep	Oct	Nov	Dec
High	33	36	46	60	71	81	84	82	76	63	50	37
Low	16	18	26	36	47	57	61	59	51	40	31	21
Precip	2.0	1.9	2.4	3.2	3.6	3.5	3.9	3.6	2.6	2.7	2.8	2.5
Snow	7.2	4.9	3.6	0.9	tr	0.0	0.0	0.0	0.0	tr	1.1	5.0

High and Low temperatures in degrees Fahrenheit; Precipitation and Snow in inches

Population: 129,418; Growth (since 2000): 6.9%; Density: 209.7 persons per square mile; Race: 92.3% White, 2.8% Black/African American, 1.6% Asian, 0.2% American Indian/Alaska Native, 0.0% Native Hawaiian/Other Pacific Islander, 2.2% two or more races, 5.2% Hispanic of any race; Average household size: 2.45; Median age: 34.7; Age under 18: 20.7%; Age 65 and over: 13.9%; Males per 100 females: 95.6; Marriage status: 35.6% never married, 49.6% now married, 1.4% separated, 5.4% widowed, 9.3% divorced; Foreign born: 3.1%; Speak English only: 94.4%; With disability: 10.9%; Veterans: 7.6%; Ancestry: 39.0% German, 14.2% Irish, 8.8% English, 6.9% Polish, 5.5% American
Religion: Six largest groups: 17.2% Catholicism, 9.9% Non-denominational Protestant, 8.5% Lutheran, 6.7% Methodist/Pietist, 2.7% Pentecostal, 2.4% Baptist
Economy: Unemployment rate: 3.9%; Leading industries: 13.6 % retail trade; 11.7 % accommodation and food services; 11.5 % other services (except public administration); Farms: 1,091 totaling 267,957 acres; Company size: 3 employ 1,000 or more persons, 6 employ 500 to 999 persons, 80 employ 100 to 499 persons, 2,655 employ less than 100 persons; Business ownership: 3,033 women-owned, 149 Black-owned, 234 Hispanic-owned, 154 Asian-owned, 79 American Indian/Alaska Native-owned
Employment: 13.5% management, business, and financial, 4.3% computer, engineering, and science, 12.2% education, legal, community service, arts, and media, 5.7% healthcare practitioners, 17.8% service, 22.8% sales and office, 7.6% natural resources, construction, and maintenance, 16.1% production, transportation, and material moving
Income: Per capita: $28,843; Median household: $55,985; Average household: $72,772; Households with income of $100,000 or more: 23.5%; Poverty rate: 13.7%
Educational Attainment: High school diploma or higher: 94.1%; Bachelor's degree or higher: 31.7%; Graduate/professional degree or higher: 13.5%
Housing: Homeownership rate: 66.5%; Median home value: $149,100; Median year structure built: 1975; Homeowner vacancy rate: 1.0%; Median selected monthly owner costs: $1,339 with a mortgage, $485 without a mortgage; Median gross rent: $747 per month; Rental vacancy rate: 3.2%
Vital Statistics: Birth rate: 106.6 per 10,000 population; Death rate: 82.5 per 10,000 population; Age-adjusted cancer mortality rate: 172.4 deaths per 100,000 population

Health Insurance: 94.3% have insurance; 82.2% have private insurance; 24.9% have public insurance; 5.7% do not have insurance; 2.5% of children under 18 do not have insurance
Health Care: Physicians: 26.8 per 10,000 population; Dentists: 3.5 per 10,000 population; Hospital beds: 7.9 per 10,000 population; Hospital admissions: 239.1 per 10,000 population
Air Quality Index (AQI): Percent of Days: 79.4% good, 19.2% moderate, 1.4% unhealthy for sensitive individuals, 0.0% unhealthy, 0.0% very unhealthy; Annual median: 41; Annual maximum: 115
Transportation: Commute: 91.1% car, 0.3% public transportation, 4.4% walk, 2.8% work from home; Mean travel time to work: 20.0 minutes
2016 Presidential Election: 50.1% Trump, 42.1% Clinton, 5.0% Johnson, 1.1% Stein
National and State Parks: Fort Meigs State Memorial; Thurston State Park
Additional Information Contacts
Wood Government .... (419) 354-9100
http://www.co.wood.oh.us

Wood County Communities

BAIRDSTOWN (village). Covers a land area of 0.270 square miles and a water area of 0 square miles. Located at 41.17° N. Lat; 83.61° W. Long. Elevation is 738 feet.
Population: 128; Growth (since 2000): -1.5%; Density: 473.2 persons per square mile; Race: 95.3% White, 0.0% Black/African American, 1.6% Asian, 0.0% American Indian/Alaska Native, 0.0% Native Hawaiian/Other Pacific Islander, 3.1% Two or more races, 0.0% Hispanic of any race; Average household size: 2.42; Median age: 50.1; Age under 18: 19.5%; Age 65 and over: 19.5%; Males per 100 females: 113.1; Marriage status: 25.2% never married, 37.9% now married, 0.0% separated, 7.8% widowed, 29.1% divorced; Foreign born: 1.6%; Speak English only: 98.4%; With disability: 29.7%; Veterans: 7.8%; Ancestry: 34.4% German, 13.3% American, 8.6% Irish, 3.1% Austrian, 1.6% English
Employment: 4.1% management, business, and financial, 2.0% computer, engineering, and science, 0.0% education, legal, community service, arts, and media, 14.3% healthcare practitioners, 4.1% service, 28.6% sales and office, 8.2% natural resources, construction, and maintenance, 38.8% production, transportation, and material moving
Income: Per capita: $18,782; Median household: $48,750; Average household: $43,749; Households with income of $100,000 or more: n/a; Poverty rate: 4.7%
Educational Attainment: High school diploma or higher: 82.8%; Bachelor's degree or higher: 5.4%; Graduate/professional degree or higher: 2.2%
Housing: Homeownership rate: 79.2%; Median home value: $62,500; Median year structure built: 1951; Homeowner vacancy rate: 10.6%; Median selected monthly owner costs: $855 with a mortgage, $288 without a mortgage; Median gross rent: $838 per month; Rental vacancy rate: 0.0%
Health Insurance: 87.5% have insurance; 71.1% have private insurance; 30.5% have public insurance; 12.5% do not have insurance; 0.0% of children under 18 do not have insurance
Transportation: Commute: 93.8% car, 0.0% public transportation, 0.0% walk, 6.3% work from home; Mean travel time to work: 19.2 minutes

BLOOMDALE (village). Covers a land area of 0.665 square miles and a water area of 0.004 square miles. Located at 41.17° N. Lat; 83.55° W. Long. Elevation is 745 feet.
Population: 685; Growth (since 2000): -5.4%; Density: 1,030.2 persons per square mile; Race: 96.5% White, 0.0% Black/African American, 0.0% Asian, 0.0% American Indian/Alaska Native, 0.0% Native Hawaiian/Other Pacific Islander, 1.8% Two or more races, 4.1% Hispanic of any race; Average household size: 2.62; Median age: 43.8; Age under 18: 21.8%; Age 65 and over: 16.6%; Males per 100 females: 107.3; Marriage status: 27.4% never married, 52.4% now married, 1.7% separated, 5.7% widowed, 14.5% divorced; Foreign born: 1.9%; Speak English only: 96.9%; With disability: 9.3%; Veterans: 12.9%; Ancestry: 38.1% German, 16.8% Irish, 5.5% American, 3.6% English, 3.1% French
Employment: 7.4% management, business, and financial, 2.5% computer, engineering, and science, 6.6% education, legal, community service, arts, and media, 4.6% healthcare practitioners, 11.2% service, 21.3% sales and office, 11.7% natural resources, construction, and maintenance, 34.7% production, transportation, and material moving
Income: Per capita: $23,539; Median household: $55,703; Average household: $59,549; Households with income of $100,000 or more: 10.7%; Poverty rate: 7.4%
Educational Attainment: High school diploma or higher: 89.6%; Bachelor's degree or higher: 15.8%; Graduate/professional degree or higher: 3.7%

School District(s)

Elmwood Local (PK-12)
2015-16 Enrollment: 1,200 .... (877) 644-6338
Housing: Homeownership rate: 85.4%; Median home value: $92,600; Median year structure built: 1941; Homeowner vacancy rate: 0.0%; Median selected monthly owner costs: $1,055 with a mortgage, $350 without a mortgage; Median gross rent: $575 per month; Rental vacancy rate: 7.3%
Health Insurance: 91.4% have insurance; 79.7% have private insurance; 34.9% have public insurance; 8.6% do not have insurance; 0.0% of children under 18 do not have insurance
Transportation: Commute: 94.1% car, 0.0% public transportation, 4.5% walk, 0.6% work from home; Mean travel time to work: 20.5 minutes

BOWLING GREEN (city). County seat. Covers a land area of 12.557 square miles and a water area of 0.047 square miles. Located at 41.38° N. Lat; 83.65° W. Long. Elevation is 692 feet.
History: Bowling Green was laid out in 1835 and named by Joseph Gordon for his home town in Kentucky. Oil was found here in 1886, bringing an industrial boom. In 1914 the H.J. Heinz Company established a tomato-products plant in Bowling Green, and the same year Bowling Green State University opened as a normal school.
Population: 31,641; Growth (since 2000): 6.8%; Density: 2,519.7 persons per square mile; Race: 88.4% White, 6.1% Black/African American, 1.6% Asian, 0.1% American Indian/Alaska Native, 0.1% Native Hawaiian/Other Pacific Islander, 2.8% Two or more races, 5.7% Hispanic of any race; Average household size: 2.26; Median age: 22.8; Age under 18: 12.3%; Age 65 and over: 10.0%; Males per 100 females: 92.1; Marriage status: 61.7% never married, 28.5% now married, 1.1% separated, 3.8% widowed, 6.0% divorced; Foreign born: 5.0%; Speak English only: 92.6%; With disability: 8.6%; Veterans: 4.3%; Ancestry: 37.2% German, 16.1% Irish, 8.7% English, 5.5% Polish, 5.1% Italian
Employment: 8.8% management, business, and financial, 3.0% computer, engineering, and science, 17.6% education, legal, community service, arts, and media, 2.6% healthcare practitioners, 27.1% service, 25.0% sales and office, 5.1% natural resources, construction, and maintenance, 10.8% production, transportation, and material moving
Income: Per capita: $20,175; Median household: $33,562; Average household: $53,245; Households with income of $100,000 or more: 14.4%; Poverty rate: 35.8%
Educational Attainment: High school diploma or higher: 93.9%; Bachelor's degree or higher: 42.4%; Graduate/professional degree or higher: 22.5%

School District(s)

Bowling Green City School District (PK-12)
2015-16 Enrollment: 2,912 .... (419) 352-3576

Four-year College(s)

Bowling Green State University-Main Campus (Public)
Fall 2016 Enrollment: 17,644 .... (419) 372-2531
2016-17 Tuition: In-state $11,057; Out-of-state $18,593
Housing: Homeownership rate: 39.3%; Median home value: $157,900; Median year structure built: 1978; Homeowner vacancy rate: 1.5%; Median selected monthly owner costs: $1,400 with a mortgage, $434 without a mortgage; Median gross rent: $667 per month; Rental vacancy rate: 5.2%
Health Insurance: 94.4% have insurance; 84.0% have private insurance; 20.0% have public insurance; 5.6% do not have insurance; 2.5% of children under 18 do not have insurance
Hospitals: Wood County Hospital (162 beds)
Safety: Violent crime rate: 13.4 per 10,000 population; Property crime rate: 178.3 per 10,000 population
Newspapers: Sentinel-Tribune (daily circulation 11,300)
Transportation: Commute: 79.7% car, 0.7% public transportation, 14.6% walk, 2.5% work from home; Mean travel time to work: 15.5 minutes
Airports: Wood County (general aviation)
Additional Information Contacts
City of Bowling Green .... (419) 354-6204
http://www.bgohio.org

BRADNER (village). Covers a land area of 0.616 square miles and a water area of 0.002 square miles. Located at 41.32° N. Lat; 83.44° W. Long. Elevation is 692 feet.

Population: 959; Growth (since 2000): -18.1%; Density: 1,555.8 persons per square mile; Race: 95.9% White, 0.1% Black/African American, 0.4% Asian, 1.0% American Indian/Alaska Native, 0.8% Native Hawaiian/Other Pacific Islander, 1.1% Two or more races, 3.6% Hispanic of any race; Average household size: 2.45; Median age: 38.7; Age under 18: 26.0%; Age 65 and over: 11.6%; Males per 100 females: 102.7; Marriage status: 20.6% never married, 59.0% now married, 4.6% separated, 6.9% widowed, 13.5% divorced; Foreign born: 0.8%; Speak English only: 96.2%; With disability: 17.6%; Veterans: 10.1%; Ancestry: 31.1% German, 19.0% Irish, 11.1% American, 9.9% French, 8.2% English

Employment: 9.2% management, business, and financial, 2.7% computer, engineering, and science, 3.6% education, legal, community service, arts, and media, 1.0% healthcare practitioners, 14.5% service, 29.0% sales and office, 9.2% natural resources, construction, and maintenance, 30.9% production, transportation, and material moving

Income: Per capita: $19,908; Median household: $43,920; Average household: $48,558; Households with income of $100,000 or more: 6.1%; Poverty rate: 8.8%

Educational Attainment: High school diploma or higher: 93.8%; Bachelor's degree or higher: 7.1%; Graduate/professional degree or higher: 1.6%

Housing: Homeownership rate: 70.8%; Median home value: $84,000; Median year structure built: 1953; Homeowner vacancy rate: 2.4%; Median selected monthly owner costs: $938 with a mortgage, $425 without a mortgage; Median gross rent: $827 per month; Rental vacancy rate: 0.0%

Health Insurance: 91.1% have insurance; 66.5% have private insurance; 37.7% have public insurance; 8.9% do not have insurance; 2.4% of children under 18 do not have insurance

Transportation: Commute: 94.1% car, 0.8% public transportation, 2.1% walk, 2.6% work from home; Mean travel time to work: 26.1 minutes

CUSTAR (village). Covers a land area of 0.251 square miles and a water area of 0 square miles. Located at 41.28° N. Lat; 83.84° W. Long. Elevation is 692 feet.

Population: 118; Growth (since 2000): -43.3%; Density: 470.8 persons per square mile; Race: 96.6% White, 0.0% Black/African American, 0.0% Asian, 0.0% American Indian/Alaska Native, 0.0% Native Hawaiian/Other Pacific Islander, 0.8% Two or more races, 2.5% Hispanic of any race; Average household size: 2.19; Median age: 35.7; Age under 18: 14.4%; Age 65 and over: 8.5%; Males per 100 females: 108.1; Marriage status: 29.7% never married, 52.5% now married, 4.0% separated, 5.9% widowed, 11.9% divorced; Foreign born: 0.0%; Speak English only: 98.2%; With disability: 14.4%; Veterans: 7.9%; Ancestry: 61.9% German, 17.8% Irish, 12.7% American, 3.4% Polish, 2.5% Dutch

Employment: 5.6% management, business, and financial, 2.8% computer, engineering, and science, 0.0% education, legal, community service, arts, and media, 1.4% healthcare practitioners, 22.5% service, 15.5% sales and office, 12.7% natural resources, construction, and maintenance, 39.4% production, transportation, and material moving

Income: Per capita: $22,230; Median household: $48,750; Average household: $49,870; Households with income of $100,000 or more: 7.4%; Poverty rate: 11.9%

Educational Attainment: High school diploma or higher: 93.8%; Bachelor's degree or higher: 1.2%; Graduate/professional degree or higher: n/a

Housing: Homeownership rate: 79.6%; Median home value: $76,800; Median year structure built: Before 1940; Homeowner vacancy rate: 14.0%; Median selected monthly owner costs: $943 with a mortgage, $517 without a mortgage; Median gross rent: $695 per month; Rental vacancy rate: 0.0%

Health Insurance: 89.0% have insurance; 72.0% have private insurance; 28.8% have public insurance; 11.0% do not have insurance; 0.0% of children under 18 do not have insurance

Transportation: Commute: 93.0% car, 0.0% public transportation, 0.0% walk, 7.0% work from home; Mean travel time to work: 31.5 minutes

CYGNET (village). Covers a land area of 0.331 square miles and a water area of 0.001 square miles. Located at 41.24° N. Lat; 83.64° W. Long. Elevation is 705 feet.

Population: 750; Growth (since 2000): 33.0%; Density: 2,265.1 persons per square mile; Race: 95.1% White, 1.5% Black/African American, 0.0% Asian, 2.0% American Indian/Alaska Native, 0.0% Native Hawaiian/Other Pacific Islander, 1.5% Two or more races, 4.8% Hispanic of any race; Average household size: 2.94; Median age: 32.6; Age under 18: 33.5%; Age 65 and over: 14.3%; Males per 100 females: 92.0; Marriage status: 22.6% never married, 53.3% now married, 1.3% separated, 11.1% widowed, 13.0% divorced; Foreign born: 1.7%; Speak English only: 95.7%; With disability: 11.6%; Veterans: 7.2%; Ancestry: 47.1% German, 15.3% Irish, 6.4% English, 6.0% American, 4.7% Dutch

Employment: 4.0% management, business, and financial, 3.7% computer, engineering, and science, 4.9% education, legal, community service, arts, and media, 1.7% healthcare practitioners, 14.9% service, 24.6% sales and office, 11.4% natural resources, construction, and maintenance, 34.9% production, transportation, and material moving

Income: Per capita: $18,534; Median household: $51,563; Average household: $54,003; Households with income of $100,000 or more: 7.5%; Poverty rate: 12.8%

Educational Attainment: High school diploma or higher: 89.8%; Bachelor's degree or higher: 12.7%; Graduate/professional degree or higher: 4.6%

Housing: Homeownership rate: 83.5%; Median home value: $84,400; Median year structure built: 1945; Homeowner vacancy rate: 0.0%; Median selected monthly owner costs: $1,033 with a mortgage, $299 without a mortgage; Median gross rent: $738 per month; Rental vacancy rate: 0.0%

Health Insurance: 89.6% have insurance; 75.9% have private insurance; 31.6% have public insurance; 10.4% do not have insurance; 8.4% of children under 18 do not have insurance

Transportation: Commute: 91.9% car, 0.0% public transportation, 0.6% walk, 5.5% work from home; Mean travel time to work: 22.1 minutes

GRAND RAPIDS (village). Covers a land area of 0.879 square miles and a water area of 0.088 square miles. Located at 41.40° N. Lat; 83.87° W. Long. Elevation is 659 feet.

History: Grand Rapids developed as a rural trading center. It was the location of locks on the Miami & Erie Canal.

Population: 971; Growth (since 2000): -3.1%; Density: 1,104.5 persons per square mile; Race: 97.7% White, 0.3% Black/African American, 0.3% Asian, 0.7% American Indian/Alaska Native, 0.0% Native Hawaiian/Other Pacific Islander, 0.6% Two or more races, 7.6% Hispanic of any race; Average household size: 2.44; Median age: 41.7; Age under 18: 20.0%; Age 65 and over: 15.7%; Males per 100 females: 91.8; Marriage status: 27.3% never married, 49.1% now married, 2.1% separated, 9.1% widowed, 14.5% divorced; Foreign born: 4.1%; Speak English only: 95.4%; With disability: 10.9%; Veterans: 8.8%; Ancestry: 42.1% German, 10.0% Irish, 7.5% English, 6.5% French, 5.7% American

Employment: 10.6% management, business, and financial, 4.7% computer, engineering, and science, 12.0% education, legal, community service, arts, and media, 6.5% healthcare practitioners, 17.8% service, 19.0% sales and office, 11.1% natural resources, construction, and maintenance, 18.3% production, transportation, and material moving

Income: Per capita: $28,443; Median household: $55,234; Average household: $68,599; Households with income of $100,000 or more: 20.6%; Poverty rate: 17.1%

Educational Attainment: High school diploma or higher: 91.7%; Bachelor's degree or higher: 25.9%; Graduate/professional degree or higher: 9.5%

School District(s)

Otsego Local (PK-12)
2015-16 Enrollment: 1,535 . . . . (419) 823-4381

Housing: Homeownership rate: 75.5%; Median home value: $114,000; Median year structure built: 1966; Homeowner vacancy rate: 0.0%; Median selected monthly owner costs: $1,090 with a mortgage, $433 without a mortgage; Median gross rent: $681 per month; Rental vacancy rate: 6.0%

Health Insurance: 92.7% have insurance; 70.7% have private insurance; 31.3% have public insurance; 7.3% do not have insurance; 3.6% of children under 18 do not have insurance

Transportation: Commute: 89.2% car, 0.4% public transportation, 4.0% walk, 4.2% work from home; Mean travel time to work: 26.4 minutes

Additional Information Contacts

Village of Grand Rapids . . . . (419) 832-5305
http://www.grandrapidsohio.com

HASKINS (village). Covers a land area of 1.645 square miles and a water area of 0 square miles. Located at 41.46° N. Lat; 83.70° W. Long. Elevation is 659 feet.

Population: 1,435; Growth (since 2000): 124.9%; Density: 872.4 persons per square mile; Race: 95.9% White, 0.0% Black/African American, 0.0%

Asian, 0.0% American Indian/Alaska Native, 0.0% Native Hawaiian/Other Pacific Islander, 1.3% Two or more races, 4.0% Hispanic of any race; Average household size: 3.07; Median age: 33.0; Age under 18: 34.6%; Age 65 and over: 6.9%; Males per 100 females: 100.3; Marriage status: 22.5% never married, 62.5% now married, 0.7% separated, 5.0% widowed, 10.0% divorced; Foreign born: 0.8%; Speak English only: 96.2%; With disability: 9.1%; Veterans: 9.6%; Ancestry: 37.6% German, 15.6% English, 13.6% Polish, 9.6% Irish, 6.9% American

Employment: 14.6% management, business, and financial, 4.8% computer, engineering, and science, 10.4% education, legal, community service, arts, and media, 9.5% healthcare practitioners, 16.3% service, 20.2% sales and office, 8.6% natural resources, construction, and maintenance, 15.7% production, transportation, and material moving

Income: Per capita: $27,000; Median household: $74,792; Average household: $82,376; Households with income of $100,000 or more: 33.4%; Poverty rate: 2.2%

Educational Attainment: High school diploma or higher: 95.0%; Bachelor's degree or higher: 27.0%; Graduate/professional degree or higher: 7.8%

School District(s)

Otsego Local (PK-12)
2015-16 Enrollment: 1,535 . . . . (419) 823-4381

Housing: Homeownership rate: 87.6%; Median home value: $160,200; Median year structure built: 1993; Homeowner vacancy rate: 0.0%; Median selected monthly owner costs: $1,324 with a mortgage, $485 without a mortgage; Median gross rent: $1,214 per month; Rental vacancy rate: 0.0%

Health Insurance: 94.3% have insurance; 89.3% have private insurance; 11.1% have public insurance; 5.7% do not have insurance; 5.0% of children under 18 do not have insurance

Transportation: Commute: 94.5% car, 0.5% public transportation, 0.5% walk, 4.6% work from home; Mean travel time to work: 23.4 minutes

HOYTVILLE (village). Covers a land area of 0.741 square miles and a water area of 0.012 square miles. Located at 41.19° N. Lat; 83.78° W. Long. Elevation is 709 feet.

Population: 330; Growth (since 2000): 11.5%; Density: 445.1 persons per square mile; Race: 80.3% White, 2.1% Black/African American, 0.9% Asian, 0.0% American Indian/Alaska Native, 0.0% Native Hawaiian/Other Pacific Islander, 6.4% Two or more races, 23.0% Hispanic of any race; Average household size: 3.27; Median age: 33.9; Age under 18: 26.4%; Age 65 and over: 10.0%; Males per 100 females: 100.7; Marriage status: 42.6% never married, 35.8% now married, 0.8% separated, 6.0% widowed, 15.5% divorced; Foreign born: 3.6%; Speak English only: 91.1%; With disability: 23.3%; Veterans: 5.8%; Ancestry: 43.0% German, 9.1% Irish, 6.1% English, 3.9% Polish, 1.5% Dutch

Employment: 7.4% management, business, and financial, 0.0% computer, engineering, and science, 0.7% education, legal, community service, arts, and media, 2.0% healthcare practitioners, 18.8% service, 20.8% sales and office, 3.4% natural resources, construction, and maintenance, 47.0% production, transportation, and material moving

Income: Per capita: $15,024; Median household: $37,679; Average household: $44,247; Households with income of $100,000 or more: 11.9%; Poverty rate: 19.7%

Educational Attainment: High school diploma or higher: 79.4%; Bachelor's degree or higher: 5.1%; Graduate/professional degree or higher: n/a

School District(s)

Mccomb Local (PK-12)
2015-16 Enrollment: 725. . . . . (419) 293-3979

Housing: Homeownership rate: 78.2%; Median home value: $56,300; Median year structure built: Before 1940; Homeowner vacancy rate: 0.0%; Median selected monthly owner costs: $864 with a mortgage, $386 without a mortgage; Median gross rent: $736 per month; Rental vacancy rate: 0.0%

Health Insurance: 91.5% have insurance; 55.5% have private insurance; 43.0% have public insurance; 8.5% do not have insurance; 4.6% of children under 18 do not have insurance

Transportation: Commute: 100.0% car, 0.0% public transportation, 0.0% walk, 0.0% work from home; Mean travel time to work: 26.8 minutes

JERRY CITY (village). Covers a land area of 1.006 square miles and a water area of 0 square miles. Located at 41.25° N. Lat; 83.60° W. Long. Elevation is 692 feet.

Population: 535; Growth (since 2000): 18.1%; Density: 531.7 persons per square mile; Race: 93.5% White, 0.0% Black/African American, 0.0% Asian, 0.7% American Indian/Alaska Native, 0.7% Native Hawaiian/Other Pacific Islander, 1.5% Two or more races, 13.1% Hispanic of any race; Average household size: 2.72; Median age: 31.7; Age under 18: 27.9%; Age 65 and over: 9.3%; Males per 100 females: 100.5; Marriage status: 27.8% never married, 51.6% now married, 1.0% separated, 3.1% widowed, 17.4% divorced; Foreign born: 0.4%; Speak English only: 94.4%; With disability: 10.7%; Veterans: 6.5%; Ancestry: 39.4% German, 11.8% Irish, 8.8% Polish, 4.9% American, 3.6% English

Employment: 6.6% management, business, and financial, 1.0% computer, engineering, and science, 5.9% education, legal, community service, arts, and media, 4.5% healthcare practitioners, 15.9% service, 14.5% sales and office, 16.3% natural resources, construction, and maintenance, 35.3% production, transportation, and material moving

Income: Per capita: $20,618; Median household: $47,411; Average household: $53,017; Households with income of $100,000 or more: 7.6%; Poverty rate: 17.9%

Educational Attainment: High school diploma or higher: 82.8%; Bachelor's degree or higher: 11.4%; Graduate/professional degree or higher: 3.9%

Housing: Homeownership rate: 68.0%; Median home value: $97,000; Median year structure built: 1946; Homeowner vacancy rate: 0.7%; Median selected monthly owner costs: $1,115 with a mortgage, $467 without a mortgage; Median gross rent: $803 per month; Rental vacancy rate: 0.0%

Health Insurance: 88.6% have insurance; 62.8% have private insurance; 33.5% have public insurance; 11.4% do not have insurance; 3.4% of children under 18 do not have insurance

Transportation: Commute: 98.3% car, 0.0% public transportation, 0.0% walk, 0.7% work from home; Mean travel time to work: 25.3 minutes

LUCKEY (village). Covers a land area of 0.690 square miles and a water area of 0.001 square miles. Located at 41.45° N. Lat; 83.48° W. Long. Elevation is 669 feet.

Population: 913; Growth (since 2000): -8.5%; Density: 1,323.5 persons per square mile; Race: 95.3% White, 0.0% Black/African American, 0.0% Asian, 0.0% American Indian/Alaska Native, 0.0% Native Hawaiian/Other Pacific Islander, 2.8% Two or more races, 7.1% Hispanic of any race; Average household size: 2.54; Median age: 40.6; Age under 18: 29.7%; Age 65 and over: 12.5%; Males per 100 females: 97.3; Marriage status: 22.8% never married, 54.6% now married, 1.0% separated, 7.2% widowed, 15.4% divorced; Foreign born: 0.5%; Speak English only: 96.2%; With disability: 6.5%; Veterans: 7.8%; Ancestry: 59.5% German, 17.3% Irish, 11.1% English, 5.1% Polish, 4.5% Italian

Employment: 11.6% management, business, and financial, 1.7% computer, engineering, and science, 10.1% education, legal, community service, arts, and media, 4.9% healthcare practitioners, 12.7% service, 25.1% sales and office, 12.9% natural resources, construction, and maintenance, 21.0% production, transportation, and material moving

Income: Per capita: $25,684; Median household: $59,750; Average household: $64,844; Households with income of $100,000 or more: 14.7%; Poverty rate: 6.1%

Educational Attainment: High school diploma or higher: 92.1%; Bachelor's degree or higher: 23.3%; Graduate/professional degree or higher: 7.3%

School District(s)

Eastwood Local (PK-12)
2015-16 Enrollment: 1,403 . . . . (419) 833-6411

Housing: Homeownership rate: 83.6%; Median home value: $122,300; Median year structure built: 1950; Homeowner vacancy rate: 0.0%; Median selected monthly owner costs: $1,148 with a mortgage, $419 without a mortgage; Median gross rent: $641 per month; Rental vacancy rate: 0.0%

Health Insurance: 97.7% have insurance; 88.6% have private insurance; 20.5% have public insurance; 2.3% do not have insurance; 1.1% of children under 18 do not have insurance

Transportation: Commute: 95.0% car, 0.0% public transportation, 0.4% walk, 4.2% work from home; Mean travel time to work: 23.8 minutes

MILLBURY (village). Covers a land area of 0.996 square miles and a water area of 0 square miles. Located at 41.56° N. Lat; 83.43° W. Long. Elevation is 614 feet.

Population: 1,229; Growth (since 2000): 5.9%; Density: 1,233.8 persons per square mile; Race: 95.7% White, 0.5% Black/African American, 0.2% Asian, 0.0% American Indian/Alaska Native, 0.0% Native Hawaiian/Other Pacific Islander, 0.6% Two or more races, 5.9% Hispanic of any race; Average household size: 2.38; Median age: 42.4; Age under 18: 21.2%; Age 65 and over: 23.1%; Males per 100 females: 93.2; Marriage status: 19.8% never married, 59.6% now married, 0.6% separated, 7.0% widowed, 13.6% divorced; Foreign born: 2.3%; Speak English only: 96.1%; With disability: 11.4%; Veterans: 8.9%; Ancestry: 49.3% German, 16.7% Irish, 12.0% English, 10.8% Polish, 8.6% American

Employment: 6.5% management, business, and financial, 3.6% computer, engineering, and science, 10.6% education, legal, community service, arts, and media, 5.8% healthcare practitioners, 17.7% service, 27.3% sales and office, 9.0% natural resources, construction, and maintenance, 19.6% production, transportation, and material moving

Income: Per capita: $27,191; Median household: $56,765; Average household: $63,903; Households with income of $100,000 or more: 16.1%; Poverty rate: 4.7%

Educational Attainment: High school diploma or higher: 95.8%; Bachelor's degree or higher: 14.8%; Graduate/professional degree or higher: 6.5%

School District(s)

Lake Local (PK-12)
2015-16 Enrollment: 1,612 . . . . (419) 661-6690

Housing: Homeownership rate: 82.8%; Median home value: $136,200; Median year structure built: 1976; Homeowner vacancy rate: 0.0%; Median selected monthly owner costs: $1,197 with a mortgage, $449 without a mortgage; Median gross rent: $687 per month; Rental vacancy rate: 0.0%

Health Insurance: 93.5% have insurance; 82.8% have private insurance; 30.5% have public insurance; 6.5% do not have insurance; 2.3% of children under 18 do not have insurance

Newspapers: Press Newspapers (weekly circulation 34,000)

Transportation: Commute: 97.3% car, 0.0% public transportation, 0.0% walk, 2.7% work from home; Mean travel time to work: 23.9 minutes

MILTON CENTER (village). Covers a land area of 0.398 square miles and a water area of 0 square miles. Located at 41.30° N. Lat; 83.83° W. Long. Elevation is 686 feet.

Population: 196; Growth (since 2000): 0.5%; Density: 492.5 persons per square mile; Race: 70.4% White, 3.1% Black/African American, 5.1% Asian, 0.0% American Indian/Alaska Native, 0.0% Native Hawaiian/Other Pacific Islander, 19.9% Two or more races, 39.8% Hispanic of any race; Average household size: 3.02; Median age: 31.9; Age under 18: 25.5%; Age 65 and over: 12.2%; Males per 100 females: 87.0; Marriage status: 27.2% never married, 42.6% now married, 7.4% separated, 9.9% widowed, 20.4% divorced; Foreign born: 0.0%; Speak English only: 100.0%; With disability: 19.4%; Veterans: 13.0%; Ancestry: 16.3% German, 16.3% Irish, 9.2% French, 4.1% Polish, 3.1% English

Employment: 11.0% management, business, and financial, 3.3% computer, engineering, and science, 1.1% education, legal, community service, arts, and media, 5.5% healthcare practitioners, 23.1% service, 6.6% sales and office, 5.5% natural resources, construction, and maintenance, 44.0% production, transportation, and material moving

Income: Per capita: $21,429; Median household: $53,125; Average household: $64,523; Households with income of $100,000 or more: 24.6%; Poverty rate: 3.1%

Educational Attainment: High school diploma or higher: 84.6%; Bachelor's degree or higher: 11.0%; Graduate/professional degree or higher: 0.7%

Housing: Homeownership rate: 92.3%; Median home value: $80,000; Median year structure built: Before 1940; Homeowner vacancy rate: 0.0%; Median selected monthly owner costs: $1,236 with a mortgage, $348 without a mortgage; Median gross rent: n/a per month; Rental vacancy rate: 0.0%

Health Insurance: 88.3% have insurance; 66.8% have private insurance; 31.1% have public insurance; 11.7% do not have insurance; 0.0% of children under 18 do not have insurance

Transportation: Commute: 97.7% car, 0.0% public transportation, 0.0% walk, 2.3% work from home; Mean travel time to work: 32.4 minutes

NORTH BALTIMORE (village). Covers a land area of 2.471 square miles and a water area of 0.028 square miles. Located at 41.18° N. Lat; 83.67° W. Long. Elevation is 732 feet.

History: Settled 1834.

Population: 3,514; Growth (since 2000): 4.6%; Density: 1,422.4 persons per square mile; Race: 95.0% White, 0.0% Black/African American, 0.1% Asian, 0.2% American Indian/Alaska Native, 0.0% Native Hawaiian/Other Pacific Islander, 3.9% Two or more races, 4.9% Hispanic of any race; Average household size: 2.68; Median age: 33.5; Age under 18: 28.3%; Age 65 and over: 13.1%; Males per 100 females: 95.2; Marriage status: 32.4% never married, 45.9% now married, 1.6% separated, 7.1% widowed, 14.6% divorced; Foreign born: 0.5%; Speak English only: 99.0%; With disability: 13.8%; Veterans: 9.2%; Ancestry: 31.5% German, 12.7% Irish, 7.7% American, 5.9% English, 3.1% Dutch

Employment: 9.5% management, business, and financial, 2.4% computer, engineering, and science, 3.4% education, legal, community service, arts, and media, 5.2% healthcare practitioners, 16.3% service, 17.0% sales and office, 6.9% natural resources, construction, and maintenance, 39.3% production, transportation, and material moving

Income: Per capita: $21,700; Median household: $46,458; Average household: $57,740; Households with income of $100,000 or more: 16.9%; Poverty rate: 15.3%

Educational Attainment: High school diploma or higher: 90.3%; Bachelor's degree or higher: 10.5%; Graduate/professional degree or higher: 2.8%

School District(s)

North Baltimore Local (PK-12)
2015-16 Enrollment: 621. . . . . (419) 257-3531

Housing: Homeownership rate: 65.5%; Median home value: $80,000; Median year structure built: 1954; Homeowner vacancy rate: 0.0%; Median selected monthly owner costs: $1,076 with a mortgage, $453 without a mortgage; Median gross rent: $556 per month; Rental vacancy rate: 0.0%

Health Insurance: 90.6% have insurance; 70.9% have private insurance; 33.0% have public insurance; 9.4% do not have insurance; 1.7% of children under 18 do not have insurance

Safety: Violent crime rate: 25.2 per 10,000 population; Property crime rate: 187.8 per 10,000 population

Transportation: Commute: 97.9% car, 0.0% public transportation, 0.4% walk, 1.3% work from home; Mean travel time to work: 20.9 minutes

NORTHWOOD (city). Covers a land area of 8.523 square miles and a water area of 0.013 square miles. Located at 41.61° N. Lat; 83.48° W. Long. Elevation is 610 feet.

Population: 5,337; Growth (since 2000): -2.4%; Density: 626.2 persons per square mile; Race: 96.4% White, 0.4% Black/African American, 0.7% Asian, 0.4% American Indian/Alaska Native, 0.0% Native Hawaiian/Other Pacific Islander, 1.1% Two or more races, 7.8% Hispanic of any race; Average household size: 2.45; Median age: 41.7; Age under 18: 21.6%; Age 65 and over: 13.4%; Males per 100 females: 96.2; Marriage status: 17.8% never married, 65.2% now married, 3.1% separated, 5.8% widowed, 11.3% divorced; Foreign born: 0.7%; Speak English only: 97.2%; With disability: 18.3%; Veterans: 11.1%; Ancestry: 36.7% German, 10.3% Irish, 9.8% French, 9.7% English, 7.6% Polish

Employment: 8.1% management, business, and financial, 2.4% computer, engineering, and science, 7.5% education, legal, community service, arts, and media, 7.7% healthcare practitioners, 15.0% service, 28.3% sales and office, 7.5% natural resources, construction, and maintenance, 23.5% production, transportation, and material moving

Income: Per capita: $28,290; Median household: $57,488; Average household: $68,838; Households with income of $100,000 or more: 15.9%; Poverty rate: 7.6%

Educational Attainment: High school diploma or higher: 90.2%; Bachelor's degree or higher: 15.5%; Graduate/professional degree or higher: 4.3%

School District(s)

Northwood Local Schools (PK-12)
2015-16 Enrollment: 888. . . . . (419) 691-3888

Housing: Homeownership rate: 84.5%; Median home value: $108,300; Median year structure built: 1960; Homeowner vacancy rate: 0.0%; Median selected monthly owner costs: $1,179 with a mortgage, $496 without a mortgage; Median gross rent: $770 per month; Rental vacancy rate: 0.0%

Health Insurance: 91.7% have insurance; 77.0% have private insurance; 30.3% have public insurance; 8.3% do not have insurance; 5.5% of children under 18 do not have insurance

Safety: Violent crime rate: 11.2 per 10,000 population; Property crime rate: 247.4 per 10,000 population
Transportation: Commute: 92.0% car, 0.0% public transportation, 1.9% walk, 3.1% work from home; Mean travel time to work: 19.0 minutes
Additional Information Contacts
City of Northwood . . . . (419) 693-9320
http://www.ci.northwood.oh.us

PEMBERVILLE (village). Covers a land area of 1.160 square miles and a water area of 0 square miles. Located at 41.41° N. Lat; 83.46° W. Long. Elevation is 653 feet.
History: Settled 1834, incorporated 1876.
Population: 1,620; Growth (since 2000): 18.7%; Density: 1,396.4 persons per square mile; Race: 98.5% White, 0.0% Black/African American, 0.6% Asian, 0.2% American Indian/Alaska Native, 0.0% Native Hawaiian/Other Pacific Islander, 0.7% Two or more races, 2.4% Hispanic of any race; Average household size: 2.70; Median age: 37.6; Age under 18: 27.5%; Age 65 and over: 17.8%; Males per 100 females: 92.0; Marriage status: 24.4% never married, 59.5% now married, 2.3% separated, 4.6% widowed, 11.5% divorced; Foreign born: 3.8%; Speak English only: 96.7%; With disability: 11.2%; Veterans: 10.3%; Ancestry: 47.7% German, 20.7% Irish, 14.4% English, 6.4% Polish, 3.5% Dutch
Employment: 7.9% management, business, and financial, 8.2% computer, engineering, and science, 16.0% education, legal, community service, arts, and media, 8.1% healthcare practitioners, 15.9% service, 21.6% sales and office, 15.7% natural resources, construction, and maintenance, 6.6% production, transportation, and material moving
Income: Per capita: $25,035; Median household: $56,438; Average household: $65,922; Households with income of $100,000 or more: 19.0%; Poverty rate: 11.4%
Educational Attainment: High school diploma or higher: 96.2%; Bachelor's degree or higher: 33.4%; Graduate/professional degree or higher: 13.6%

School District(s)

Eastwood Local (PK-12)
2015-16 Enrollment: 1,403 . . . . (419) 833-6411
Housing: Homeownership rate: 84.1%; Median home value: $132,000; Median year structure built: 1946; Homeowner vacancy rate: 0.0%; Median selected monthly owner costs: $1,273 with a mortgage, $409 without a mortgage; Median gross rent: $869 per month; Rental vacancy rate: 0.0%
Health Insurance: 95.4% have insurance; 85.7% have private insurance; 30.9% have public insurance; 4.6% do not have insurance; 1.8% of children under 18 do not have insurance
Transportation: Commute: 92.5% car, 0.0% public transportation, 3.4% walk, 4.0% work from home; Mean travel time to work: 21.9 minutes
Additional Information Contacts
Village of Pemberville . . . . (419) 287-3832
http://www.pemberville.org

PERRYSBURG (city). Covers a land area of 11.514 square miles and a water area of 0 square miles. Located at 41.54° N. Lat; 83.64° W. Long. Elevation is 633 feet.
History: Perrysburg was settled in 1816 and named for Oliver Hazard Perry. Its site on the Maumee River made it a shipping and shipbuilding center. From 1822 to 1866, Perrysburg served as the seat of Wood County.
Population: 21,367; Growth (since 2000): 26.1%; Density: 1,855.7 persons per square mile; Race: 91.3% White, 1.9% Black/African American, 3.7% Asian, 0.2% American Indian/Alaska Native, 0.0% Native Hawaiian/Other Pacific Islander, 2.4% Two or more races, 3.2% Hispanic of any race; Average household size: 2.51; Median age: 38.1; Age under 18: 26.3%; Age 65 and over: 13.7%; Males per 100 females: 94.0; Marriage status: 27.2% never married, 59.3% now married, 1.0% separated, 6.0% widowed, 7.6% divorced; Foreign born: 4.7%; Speak English only: 92.0%; With disability: 8.5%; Veterans: 6.1%; Ancestry: 39.4% German, 16.4% Irish, 10.5% English, 8.5% Polish, 5.4% Italian
Employment: 24.2% management, business, and financial, 6.9% computer, engineering, and science, 14.5% education, legal, community service, arts, and media, 8.6% healthcare practitioners, 13.2% service, 21.9% sales and office, 4.0% natural resources, construction, and maintenance, 6.7% production, transportation, and material moving
Income: Per capita: $41,668; Median household: $84,508; Average household: $104,476; Households with income of $100,000 or more: 40.1%; Poverty rate: 5.0%
Educational Attainment: High school diploma or higher: 97.1%; Bachelor's degree or higher: 51.0%; Graduate/professional degree or higher: 20.9%

School District(s)

Penta Career Center - District (07-12)
2015-16 Enrollment: n/a . . . . (419) 661-6350
Perrysburg Exempted Village (PK-12)
2015-16 Enrollment: 4,871 . . . . (419) 874-9131
Rossford Exempted Village (PK-12)
2015-16 Enrollment: 1,552 . . . . (419) 666-2010

Two-year College(s)

Owens Community College (Public)
Fall 2016 Enrollment: 10,171 . . . . (567) 661-7000
2016-17 Tuition: In-state $4,643; Out-of-state $8,305
Summit Salon Academy-Perrysburg (Private, For-profit)
Fall 2016 Enrollment: 52. . . . . (419) 873-9999

Vocational/Technical School(s)

Orion Institute (Private, For-profit)
Fall 2016 Enrollment: 91 . . . . (419) 874-4496
Penta County Joint Vocational School (Public)
Fall 2016 Enrollment: 59 . . . . (419) 661-6555
2016-17 Tuition: $5,795
Housing: Homeownership rate: 69.1%; Median home value: $194,200; Median year structure built: 1983; Homeowner vacancy rate: 0.0%; Median selected monthly owner costs: $1,635 with a mortgage, $551 without a mortgage; Median gross rent: $888 per month; Rental vacancy rate: 2.5%
Health Insurance: 96.3% have insurance; 88.2% have private insurance; 18.5% have public insurance; 3.7% do not have insurance; 2.6% of children under 18 do not have insurance
Safety: Violent crime rate: 3.7 per 10,000 population; Property crime rate: 113.2 per 10,000 population
Newspapers: Welch Publishing (weekly circulation 33,000)
Transportation: Commute: 94.0% car, 0.2% public transportation, 1.3% walk, 4.1% work from home; Mean travel time to work: 19.8 minutes
Additional Information Contacts
City of Perrysburg . . . . (419) 872-8010
http://www.ci.perrysburg.oh.us

PORTAGE (village). Covers a land area of 1.488 square miles and a water area of 0 square miles. Located at 41.32° N. Lat; 83.65° W. Long. Elevation is 686 feet.
History: Portage began as a trading post in 1824 and grew during the oil and gas boom of the 1880's and 1890's.
Population: 427; Growth (since 2000): -0.2%; Density: 287.0 persons per square mile; Race: 87.4% White, 9.8% Black/African American, 0.0% Asian, 0.0% American Indian/Alaska Native, 0.0% Native Hawaiian/Other Pacific Islander, 1.6% Two or more races, 9.6% Hispanic of any race; Average household size: 2.33; Median age: 31.6; Age under 18: 25.3%; Age 65 and over: 13.1%; Males per 100 females: 99.1; Marriage status: 34.8% never married, 45.2% now married, 0.3% separated, 6.4% widowed, 13.6% divorced; Foreign born: 0.5%; Speak English only: 95.0%; With disability: 21.5%; Veterans: 5.0%; Ancestry: 43.1% German, 10.8% Irish, 8.2% English, 5.4% Polish, 4.4% French
Employment: 14.0% management, business, and financial, 5.0% computer, engineering, and science, 9.0% education, legal, community service, arts, and media, 1.8% healthcare practitioners, 28.4% service, 25.7% sales and office, 7.2% natural resources, construction, and maintenance, 9.0% production, transportation, and material moving
Income: Per capita: $21,815; Median household: $53,158; Average household: $55,880; Households with income of $100,000 or more: 11.3%; Poverty rate: 16.9%
Educational Attainment: High school diploma or higher: 95.2%; Bachelor's degree or higher: 29.9%; Graduate/professional degree or higher: 12.6%
Housing: Homeownership rate: 59.5%; Median home value: $109,800; Median year structure built: Before 1940; Homeowner vacancy rate: 2.9%; Median selected monthly owner costs: $1,275 with a mortgage, $366 without a mortgage; Median gross rent: $755 per month; Rental vacancy rate: 0.0%
Health Insurance: 97.4% have insurance; 82.0% have private insurance; 36.8% have public insurance; 2.6% do not have insurance; 0.0% of children under 18 do not have insurance
Transportation: Commute: 97.7% car, 0.0% public transportation, 0.9% walk, 1.4% work from home; Mean travel time to work: 27.3 minutes

RISINGSUN (village). Covers a land area of 0.570 square miles and a water area of 0 square miles. Located at 41.27° N. Lat; 83.43° W. Long. Elevation is 715 feet.

Population: 639; Growth (since 2000): 3.1%; Density: 1,121.1 persons per square mile; Race: 95.3% White, 0.0% Black/African American, 0.0% Asian, 1.3% American Indian/Alaska Native, 0.0% Native Hawaiian/Other Pacific Islander, 2.0% Two or more races, 7.0% Hispanic of any race; Average household size: 2.78; Median age: 36.2; Age under 18: 25.5%; Age 65 and over: 11.0%; Males per 100 females: 111.9; Marriage status: 24.1% never married, 58.9% now married, 2.2% separated, 4.2% widowed, 12.8% divorced; Foreign born: 0.0%; Speak English only: 95.7%; With disability: 16.7%; Veterans: 5.7%; Ancestry: 44.6% German, 15.2% Irish, 7.2% American, 6.9% English, 6.3% Italian

Employment: 3.5% management, business, and financial, 2.3% computer, engineering, and science, 5.1% education, legal, community service, arts, and media, 7.8% healthcare practitioners, 21.8% service, 19.5% sales and office, 6.6% natural resources, construction, and maintenance, 33.5% production, transportation, and material moving

Income: Per capita: $16,462; Median household: $37,857; Average household: $44,781; Households with income of $100,000 or more: 5.2%; Poverty rate: 19.1%

Educational Attainment: High school diploma or higher: 90.4%; Bachelor's degree or higher: 6.4%; Graduate/professional degree or higher: 0.7%

Housing: Homeownership rate: 67.4%; Median home value: $79,400; Median year structure built: Before 1940; Homeowner vacancy rate: 0.0%; Median selected monthly owner costs: $907 with a mortgage, $357 without a mortgage; Median gross rent: $589 per month; Rental vacancy rate: 3.8%

Health Insurance: 88.7% have insurance; 56.3% have private insurance; 49.6% have public insurance; 11.3% do not have insurance; 0.0% of children under 18 do not have insurance

Transportation: Commute: 95.7% car, 1.2% public transportation, 1.2% walk, 2.0% work from home; Mean travel time to work: 30.7 minutes

ROSSFORD (city). Covers a land area of 5.019 square miles and a water area of 0.306 square miles. Located at 41.60° N. Lat; 83.56° W. Long. Elevation is 617 feet.

History: Rossford began in 1896 when Edward Ford established a glass company that later merged with the Libbey-Owens corporation.

Population: 6,514; Growth (since 2000): 1.7%; Density: 1,298.0 persons per square mile; Race: 95.5% White, 2.1% Black/African American, 0.1% Asian, 0.0% American Indian/Alaska Native, 0.0% Native Hawaiian/Other Pacific Islander, 1.2% Two or more races, 3.9% Hispanic of any race; Average household size: 2.40; Median age: 39.2; Age under 18: 22.0%; Age 65 and over: 13.1%; Males per 100 females: 97.2; Marriage status: 29.6% never married, 53.1% now married, 0.4% separated, 4.8% widowed, 12.5% divorced; Foreign born: 2.8%; Speak English only: 95.8%; With disability: 8.3%; Veterans: 10.5%; Ancestry: 29.9% German, 18.3% Polish, 15.5% Irish, 6.5% English, 4.9% Hungarian

Employment: 10.2% management, business, and financial, 3.8% computer, engineering, and science, 10.5% education, legal, community service, arts, and media, 6.8% healthcare practitioners, 15.5% service, 27.5% sales and office, 10.8% natural resources, construction, and maintenance, 14.8% production, transportation, and material moving

Income: Per capita: $29,987; Median household: $61,485; Average household: $70,678; Households with income of $100,000 or more: 25.3%; Poverty rate: 6.5%

Educational Attainment: High school diploma or higher: 94.8%; Bachelor's degree or higher: 25.8%; Graduate/professional degree or higher: 8.2%

School District(s)

Rossford Exempted Village (PK-12)
2015-16 Enrollment: 1,552 . . . . (419) 666-2010

Housing: Homeownership rate: 72.7%; Median home value: $132,100; Median year structure built: 1957; Homeowner vacancy rate: 2.8%; Median selected monthly owner costs: $1,304 with a mortgage, $504 without a mortgage; Median gross rent: $670 per month; Rental vacancy rate: 4.4%

Health Insurance: 95.6% have insurance; 85.7% have private insurance; 21.2% have public insurance; 4.4% do not have insurance; 2.0% of children under 18 do not have insurance

Transportation: Commute: 95.3% car, 0.7% public transportation, 1.6% walk, 0.6% work from home; Mean travel time to work: 20.1 minutes

Additional Information Contacts

City of Rossford . . . . (419) 666-0210
http://www.rossfordohio.com

RUDOLPH (CDP). Covers a land area of 0.819 square miles and a water area of 0 square miles. Located at 41.30° N. Lat; 83.66° W. Long. Elevation is 682 feet.

Population: 584; Growth (since 2000): n/a; Density: 712.7 persons per square mile; Race: 100.0% White, 0.0% Black/African American, 0.0% Asian, 0.0% American Indian/Alaska Native, 0.0% Native Hawaiian/Other Pacific Islander, 0.0% Two or more races, 6.7% Hispanic of any race; Average household size: 2.74; Median age: 35.8; Age under 18: 31.2%; Age 65 and over: 7.5%; Males per 100 females: 109.1; Marriage status: 29.4% never married, 37.1% now married, 0.0% separated, 6.0% widowed, 27.6% divorced; Foreign born: 0.0%; Speak English only: 99.1%; With disability: 11.3%; Veterans: 4.7%; Ancestry: 30.7% Irish, 21.6% French, 21.4% German, 3.9% American, 3.8% Yugoslavian

Employment: 4.6% management, business, and financial, 0.0% computer, engineering, and science, 0.0% education, legal, community service, arts, and media, 0.0% healthcare practitioners, 18.6% service, 18.9% sales and office, 23.6% natural resources, construction, and maintenance, 34.3% production, transportation, and material moving

Income: Per capita: $20,548; Median household: $36,602; Average household: $55,587; Households with income of $100,000 or more: 4.2%; Poverty rate: 16.8%

Educational Attainment: High school diploma or higher: 88.7%; Bachelor's degree or higher: 1.7%; Graduate/professional degree or higher: 1.7%

Housing: Homeownership rate: 60.6%; Median home value: $53,800; Median year structure built: 1970; Homeowner vacancy rate: 0.0%; Median selected monthly owner costs: $922 with a mortgage, $380 without a mortgage; Median gross rent: $750 per month; Rental vacancy rate: 0.0%

Health Insurance: 98.6% have insurance; 70.4% have private insurance; 39.2% have public insurance; 1.4% do not have insurance; 0.0% of children under 18 do not have insurance

Transportation: Commute: 100.0% car, 0.0% public transportation, 0.0% walk, 0.0% work from home; Mean travel time to work: 19.9 minutes

STONY RIDGE (CDP). Covers a land area of 1.704 square miles and a water area of 0 square miles. Located at 41.51° N. Lat; 83.51° W. Long. Elevation is 643 feet.

Population: 342; Growth (since 2000): n/a; Density: 200.7 persons per square mile; Race: 86.8% White, 0.0% Black/African American, 0.0% Asian, 2.3% American Indian/Alaska Native, 0.0% Native Hawaiian/Other Pacific Islander, 10.8% Two or more races, 10.8% Hispanic of any race; Average household size: 2.41; Median age: 38.5; Age under 18: 17.3%; Age 65 and over: 14.3%; Males per 100 females: 101.5; Marriage status: 34.6% never married, 49.8% now married, 6.7% separated, 4.9% widowed, 10.6% divorced; Foreign born: 0.0%; Speak English only: 97.0%; With disability: 10.8%; Veterans: 11.7%; Ancestry: 15.8% English, 12.0% German, 7.3% Norwegian, 6.7% Swedish, 6.1% Italian

Employment: 4.6% management, business, and financial, 0.0% computer, engineering, and science, 5.3% education, legal, community service, arts, and media, 5.9% healthcare practitioners, 18.4% service, 30.9% sales and office, 19.7% natural resources, construction, and maintenance, 15.1% production, transportation, and material moving

Income: Per capita: $20,973; Median household: $40,469; Average household: $49,141; Households with income of $100,000 or more: 11.3%; Poverty rate: 27.5%

Educational Attainment: High school diploma or higher: 93.8%; Bachelor's degree or higher: 16.5%; Graduate/professional degree or higher: 2.9%

Housing: Homeownership rate: 69.0%; Median home value: $117,700; Median year structure built: 1958; Homeowner vacancy rate: 20.3%; Median selected monthly owner costs: $1,272 with a mortgage, n/a without a mortgage; Median gross rent: n/a per month; Rental vacancy rate: 0.0%

Health Insurance: 89.2% have insurance; 59.9% have private insurance; 42.7% have public insurance; 10.8% do not have insurance; 0.0% of children under 18 do not have insurance

Transportation: Commute: 95.0% car, 0.0% public transportation, 0.0% walk, 0.0% work from home; Mean travel time to work: 16.6 minutes

TONTOGANY (village). Covers a land area of 0.305 square miles and a water area of 0 square miles. Located at 41.42° N. Lat; 83.74° W. Long. Elevation is 666 feet.

Population: 452; Growth (since 2000): 24.2%; Density: 1,482.7 persons per square mile; Race: 92.9% White, 0.7% Black/African American, 0.2% Asian, 0.0% American Indian/Alaska Native, 0.0% Native Hawaiian/Other Pacific Islander, 3.3% Two or more races, 7.7% Hispanic of any race; Average household size: 2.50; Median age: 46.0; Age under 18: 23.9%; Age 65 and over: 12.2%; Males per 100 females: 105.0; Marriage status: 26.7% never married, 62.8% now married, 0.0% separated, 3.0% widowed, 7.5% divorced; Foreign born: 1.8%; Speak English only: 96.3%; With disability: 9.1%; Veterans: 5.2%; Ancestry: 42.9% German, 12.4% English, 12.2% Irish, 8.8% French, 5.8% Dutch

Employment: 14.8% management, business, and financial, 7.0% computer, engineering, and science, 3.9% education, legal, community service, arts, and media, 1.3% healthcare practitioners, 7.4% service, 48.0% sales and office, 6.6% natural resources, construction, and maintenance, 10.9% production, transportation, and material moving

Income: Per capita: $28,227; Median household: $69,464; Average household: $69,377; Households with income of $100,000 or more: 12.7%; Poverty rate: 6.9%

Educational Attainment: High school diploma or higher: 95.6%; Bachelor's degree or higher: 16.7%; Graduate/professional degree or higher: 6.3%

School District(s)

Otsego Local (PK-12)
2015-16 Enrollment: 1,535 . . . . (419) 823-4381

Housing: Homeownership rate: 73.5%; Median home value: $133,600; Median year structure built: 1955; Homeowner vacancy rate: 0.0%; Median selected monthly owner costs: $1,164 with a mortgage, $390 without a mortgage; Median gross rent: $831 per month; Rental vacancy rate: 11.1%

Health Insurance: 97.3% have insurance; 84.5% have private insurance; 25.0% have public insurance; 2.7% do not have insurance; 0.0% of children under 18 do not have insurance

Transportation: Commute: 91.6% car, 0.0% public transportation, 3.9% walk, 4.4% work from home; Mean travel time to work: 23.6 minutes

WALBRIDGE (village). Covers a land area of 2.186 square miles and a water area of 0.015 square miles. Located at 41.59° N. Lat; 83.49° W. Long. Elevation is 617 feet.

Population: 3,072; Growth (since 2000): 20.7%; Density: 1,405.0 persons per square mile; Race: 97.8% White, 0.0% Black/African American, 0.0% Asian, 0.8% American Indian/Alaska Native, 0.0% Native Hawaiian/Other Pacific Islander, 1.1% Two or more races, 4.3% Hispanic of any race; Average household size: 1.92; Median age: 52.6; Age under 18: 12.8%; Age 65 and over: 29.9%; Males per 100 females: 85.4; Marriage status: 25.0% never married, 46.8% now married, 3.4% separated, 12.0% widowed, 16.3% divorced; Foreign born: 0.0%; Speak English only: 97.9%; With disability: 15.7%; Veterans: 10.7%; Ancestry: 44.7% German, 12.2% English, 11.9% Irish, 9.2% Italian, 9.2% Polish

Employment: 7.4% management, business, and financial, 2.7% computer, engineering, and science, 8.3% education, legal, community service, arts, and media, 5.7% healthcare practitioners, 24.4% service, 22.8% sales and office, 4.2% natural resources, construction, and maintenance, 24.4% production, transportation, and material moving

Income: Per capita: $25,735; Median household: $39,826; Average household: $48,176; Households with income of $100,000 or more: 10.5%; Poverty rate: 8.4%

Educational Attainment: High school diploma or higher: 92.3%; Bachelor's degree or higher: 13.5%; Graduate/professional degree or higher: 5.6%

School District(s)

Lake Local (PK-12)
2015-16 Enrollment: 1,612 . . . . (419) 661-6690

Housing: Homeownership rate: 73.9%; Median home value: $89,000; Median year structure built: 1971; Homeowner vacancy rate: 0.0%; Median selected monthly owner costs: $919 with a mortgage, $389 without a mortgage; Median gross rent: $597 per month; Rental vacancy rate: 0.0%

Health Insurance: 92.6% have insurance; 70.0% have private insurance; 44.8% have public insurance; 7.4% do not have insurance; 0.0% of children under 18 do not have insurance

Transportation: Commute: 92.1% car, 0.0% public transportation, 3.3% walk, 2.1% work from home; Mean travel time to work: 15.4 minutes

Airports: Toledo Executive (general aviation)

WAYNE (village). Covers a land area of 0.322 square miles and a water area of 0 square miles. Located at 41.30° N. Lat; 83.47° W. Long. Elevation is 699 feet.

History: Wayne was known as strongly abolitionist in sentiment prior to the Civil War. In the winter of 1858, Wayne was a transfer point for several hundred rifles headed for John Brown's hide-out in Maryland.

Population: 1,039; Growth (since 2000): 23.4%; Density: 3,225.1 persons per square mile; Race: 95.2% White, 0.6% Black/African American, 0.2% Asian, 0.0% American Indian/Alaska Native, 0.0% Native Hawaiian/Other Pacific Islander, 3.7% Two or more races, 4.4% Hispanic of any race; Average household size: 2.52; Median age: 32.2; Age under 18: 29.2%; Age 65 and over: 10.8%; Males per 100 females: 92.8; Marriage status: 30.1% never married, 53.1% now married, 3.1% separated, 5.8% widowed, 11.0% divorced; Foreign born: 0.0%; Speak English only: 98.9%; With disability: 10.4%; Veterans: 9.8%; Ancestry: 32.7% German, 14.8% Irish, 5.7% American, 5.1% English, 4.8% Polish

Employment: 5.2% management, business, and financial, 0.4% computer, engineering, and science, 5.4% education, legal, community service, arts, and media, 4.5% healthcare practitioners, 24.2% service, 13.4% sales and office, 18.1% natural resources, construction, and maintenance, 28.8% production, transportation, and material moving

Income: Per capita: $20,262; Median household: $44,167; Average household: $50,849; Households with income of $100,000 or more: 5.4%; Poverty rate: 11.1%

Educational Attainment: High school diploma or higher: 94.1%; Bachelor's degree or higher: 6.8%; Graduate/professional degree or higher: 1.6%

Housing: Homeownership rate: 60.2%; Median home value: $81,900; Median year structure built: 1959; Homeowner vacancy rate: 6.1%; Median selected monthly owner costs: $957 with a mortgage, $369 without a mortgage; Median gross rent: $820 per month; Rental vacancy rate: 0.0%

Health Insurance: 96.0% have insurance; 80.9% have private insurance; 26.3% have public insurance; 4.0% do not have insurance; 2.0% of children under 18 do not have insurance

Transportation: Commute: 97.6% car, 1.3% public transportation, 1.1% walk, 0.0% work from home; Mean travel time to work: 21.3 minutes

WEST MILLGROVE (village). Covers a land area of 0.260 square miles and a water area of 0 square miles. Located at 41.24° N. Lat; 83.49° W. Long. Elevation is 712 feet.

Population: 123; Growth (since 2000): 57.7%; Density: 473.1 persons per square mile; Race: 100.0% White, 0.0% Black/African American, 0.0% Asian, 0.0% American Indian/Alaska Native, 0.0% Native Hawaiian/Other Pacific Islander, 0.0% Two or more races, 0.0% Hispanic of any race; Average household size: 2.80; Median age: 35.4; Age under 18: 31.7%; Age 65 and over: 14.6%; Males per 100 females: 77.6; Marriage status: 30.9% never married, 37.1% now married, 3.1% separated, 17.5% widowed, 14.4% divorced; Foreign born: 5.7%; Speak English only: 94.2%; With disability: 14.6%; Veterans: 2.4%; Ancestry: 20.3% German, 17.9% English, 9.8% French, 8.9% Arab, 8.9% Other Arab

Employment: 7.0% management, business, and financial, 1.8% computer, engineering, and science, 0.0% education, legal, community service, arts, and media, 8.8% healthcare practitioners, 19.3% service, 14.0% sales and office, 22.8% natural resources, construction, and maintenance, 26.3% production, transportation, and material moving

Income: Per capita: $18,345; Median household: $31,429; Average household: $48,743; Households with income of $100,000 or more: 11.4%; Poverty rate: 15.4%

Educational Attainment: High school diploma or higher: 80.0%; Bachelor's degree or higher: 12.9%; Graduate/professional degree or higher: 5.7%

Housing: Homeownership rate: 75.0%; Median home value: $71,300; Median year structure built: Before 1940; Homeowner vacancy rate: 0.0%; Median selected monthly owner costs: $1,063 with a mortgage, $375 without a mortgage; Median gross rent: $733 per month; Rental vacancy rate: 0.0%

Health Insurance: 77.2% have insurance; 65.9% have private insurance; 28.5% have public insurance; 22.8% do not have insurance; 0.0% of children under 18 do not have insurance

Transportation: Commute: 93.0% car, 0.0% public transportation, 1.8% walk, 5.3% work from home; Mean travel time to work: 30.7 minutes

WESTON (village). Covers a land area of 1.130 square miles and a water area of 0.003 square miles. Located at 41.35° N. Lat; 83.79° W. Long. Elevation is 679 feet.

Population: 1,630; Growth (since 2000): -1.7%; Density: 1,442.3 persons per square mile; Race: 90.5% White, 1.2% Black/African American, 0.3% Asian, 1.7% American Indian/Alaska Native, 0.0% Native Hawaiian/Other Pacific Islander, 5.8% Two or more races, 20.7% Hispanic of any race; Average household size: 2.55; Median age: 39.7; Age under 18: 22.9%; Age 65 and over: 15.1%; Males per 100 females: 97.5; Marriage status: 30.3% never married, 48.4% now married, 2.2% separated, 6.2% widowed, 15.1% divorced; Foreign born: 0.4%; Speak English only: 94.1%; With disability: 17.7%; Veterans: 12.7%; Ancestry: 29.6% German, 9.6% Irish, 9.0% American, 7.5% English, 3.3% French

Employment: 8.4% management, business, and financial, 3.0% computer, engineering, and science, 5.6% education, legal, community service, arts, and media, 2.8% healthcare practitioners, 12.9% service, 24.3% sales and office, 15.5% natural resources, construction, and maintenance, 27.4% production, transportation, and material moving

Income: Per capita: $21,428; Median household: $42,560; Average household: $54,475; Households with income of $100,000 or more: 15.9%; Poverty rate: 17.4%

Educational Attainment: High school diploma or higher: 86.0%; Bachelor's degree or higher: 10.8%; Graduate/professional degree or higher: 2.6%

Housing: Homeownership rate: 76.9%; Median home value: $80,800; Median year structure built: 1963; Homeowner vacancy rate: 0.0%; Median selected monthly owner costs: $995 with a mortgage, $526 without a mortgage; Median gross rent: $681 per month; Rental vacancy rate: 16.9%

Health Insurance: 90.4% have insurance; 67.4% have private insurance; 34.8% have public insurance; 9.6% do not have insurance; 8.8% of children under 18 do not have insurance

Transportation: Commute: 96.2% car, 0.1% public transportation, 1.0% walk, 2.0% work from home; Mean travel time to work: 26.3 minutes

Wyandot County

Located in north central Ohio; drained by the Sandusky River. Covers a land area of 406.865 square miles, a water area of 0.689 square miles, and is located in the Eastern Time Zone at 40.84° N. Lat., 83.31° W. Long. The county was founded in 1845. County seat is Upper Sandusky.

Weather Station: Upper Sandusky Elevation: 854 feet

	Jan	Feb	Mar	Apr	May	Jun	Jul	Aug	Sep	Oct	Nov	Dec
High	33	37	47	61	71	80	84	83	77	64	50	37
Low	18	20	28	38	48	59	62	61	53	41	33	23
Precip	2.0	1.9	2.5	3.5	4.5	3.9	4.5	3.5	3.1	2.4	3.2	2.6
Snow	6.4	3.8	2.2	1.1	tr	0.0	0.0	0.0	0.0	tr	0.8	5.1

High and Low temperatures in degrees Fahrenheit; Precipitation and Snow in inches

Population: 22,359; Growth (since 2000): -2.4%; Density: 55.0 persons per square mile; Race: 97.2% White, 0.4% Black/African American, 0.8% Asian, 0.0% American Indian/Alaska Native, 0.0% Native Hawaiian/Other Pacific Islander, 0.8% two or more races, 2.6% Hispanic of any race; Average household size: 2.41; Median age: 41.7; Age under 18: 23.6%; Age 65 and over: 17.9%; Males per 100 females: 97.9; Marriage status: 23.6% never married, 57.8% now married, 1.8% separated, 7.2% widowed, 11.3% divorced; Foreign born: 1.5%; Speak English only: 97.0%; With disability: 13.2%; Veterans: 9.2%; Ancestry: 43.3% German, 11.0% Irish, 10.2% American, 8.0% English, 3.0% Italian

Religion: Six largest groups: 20.9% Catholicism, 12.1% Methodist/Pietist, 9.7% Lutheran, 6.5% Presbyterian-Reformed, 1.5% Holiness, 1.4% Pentecostal

Economy: Unemployment rate: 3.2%; Leading industries: 16.7 % other services (except public administration); 12.8 % retail trade; 10.9 % construction; Farms: 593 totaling 220,841 acres; Company size: 0 employ 1,000 or more persons, 2 employ 500 to 999 persons, 12 employ 100 to 499 persons, 501 employs less than 100 persons; Business ownership: 546 women-owned, n/a Black-owned, n/a Hispanic-owned, n/a Asian-owned, n/a American Indian/Alaska Native-owned

Employment: 10.8% management, business, and financial, 2.3% computer, engineering, and science, 5.7% education, legal, community service, arts, and media, 6.6% healthcare practitioners, 15.3% service, 17.7% sales and office, 11.8% natural resources, construction, and maintenance, 30.0% production, transportation, and material moving

Income: Per capita: $25,064; Median household: $50,723; Average household: $61,195; Households with income of $100,000 or more: 14.3%; Poverty rate: 11.1%

Educational Attainment: High school diploma or higher: 90.3%; Bachelor's degree or higher: 14.6%; Graduate/professional degree or higher: 4.4%

Housing: Homeownership rate: 73.2%; Median home value: $111,500; Median year structure built: 1960; Homeowner vacancy rate: 0.7%; Median selected monthly owner costs: $1,033 with a mortgage, $383 without a mortgage; Median gross rent: $636 per month; Rental vacancy rate: 3.8%

Vital Statistics: Birth rate: 113.0 per 10,000 population; Death rate: 112.1 per 10,000 population; Age-adjusted cancer mortality rate: 186.6 deaths per 100,000 population

Health Insurance: 92.6% have insurance; 77.4% have private insurance; 29.9% have public insurance; 7.4% do not have insurance; 4.1% of children under 18 do not have insurance

Health Care: Physicians: 3.6 per 10,000 population; Dentists: 2.7 per 10,000 population; Hospital beds: 11.2 per 10,000 population; Hospital admissions: 457.6 per 10,000 population

Transportation: Commute: 94.1% car, 0.2% public transportation, 1.9% walk, 2.4% work from home; Mean travel time to work: 22.3 minutes

2016 Presidential Election: 70.2% Trump, 23.6% Clinton, 4.1% Johnson, 0.8% Stein

Additional Information Contacts

Wyandot Government . . . . (419) 294-3836
http://www.co.wyandot.oh.us

Wyandot County Communities

CAREY (village). Covers a land area of 1.976 square miles and a water area of 0.007 square miles. Located at 40.95° N. Lat; 83.38° W. Long. Elevation is 820 feet.

History: Carey was platted in 1843, and grew as a trading and shipping center for onions and celery. The Shrine of Our Lady of Consolation was established here in 1875 by Father Joseph P. Gloden.

Population: 3,482; Growth (since 2000): -10.7%; Density: 1,762.5 persons per square mile; Race: 95.7% White, 0.7% Black/African American, 2.2% Asian, 0.0% American Indian/Alaska Native, 0.0% Native Hawaiian/Other Pacific Islander, 1.2% Two or more races, 2.4% Hispanic of any race; Average household size: 2.46; Median age: 39.1; Age under 18: 27.0%; Age 65 and over: 14.1%; Males per 100 females: 97.1; Marriage status: 25.5% never married, 58.3% now married, 2.8% separated, 4.8% widowed, 11.3% divorced; Foreign born: 1.5%; Speak English only: 96.1%; With disability: 13.6%; Veterans: 9.7%; Ancestry: 40.9% German, 8.2% Irish, 7.5% American, 4.9% English, 1.6% French

Employment: 8.5% management, business, and financial, 4.6% computer, engineering, and science, 3.8% education, legal, community service, arts, and media, 6.1% healthcare practitioners, 9.7% service, 15.5% sales and office, 6.9% natural resources, construction, and maintenance, 45.0% production, transportation, and material moving

Income: Per capita: $23,625; Median household: $50,417; Average household: $57,865; Households with income of $100,000 or more: 13.6%; Poverty rate: 9.4%

Educational Attainment: High school diploma or higher: 91.2%; Bachelor's degree or higher: 10.9%; Graduate/professional degree or higher: 3.4%

School District(s)

Carey Exempted Village (KG-12)
2015-16 Enrollment: 815. . . . . (419) 396-7922

Housing: Homeownership rate: 69.2%; Median home value: $93,800; Median year structure built: 1959; Homeowner vacancy rate: 0.0%; Median selected monthly owner costs: $929 with a mortgage, $369 without a mortgage; Median gross rent: $568 per month; Rental vacancy rate: 0.0%

Health Insurance: 92.7% have insurance; 81.6% have private insurance; 24.6% have public insurance; 7.3% do not have insurance; 1.2% of children under 18 do not have insurance

Safety: Violent crime rate: 0.0 per 10,000 population; Property crime rate: 14.0 per 10,000 population

Newspapers: Progressor-Times Inc (weekly circulation 4,000)

Transportation: Commute: 94.9% car, 0.0% public transportation, 2.5% walk, 1.0% work from home; Mean travel time to work: 21.4 minutes

HARPSTER (village). Covers a land area of 1.971 square miles and a water area of 0 square miles. Located at 40.74° N. Lat; 83.25° W. Long. Elevation is 902 feet.
Population: 197; Growth (since 2000): -3.0%; Density: 100.0 persons per square mile; Race: 86.8% White, 10.7% Black/African American, 0.0% Asian, 0.0% American Indian/Alaska Native, 0.0% Native Hawaiian/Other Pacific Islander, 2.5% Two or more races, 7.1% Hispanic of any race; Average household size: 2.43; Median age: 47.1; Age under 18: 23.4%; Age 65 and over: 27.9%; Males per 100 females: 92.5; Marriage status: 18.2% never married, 60.4% now married, 1.3% separated, 3.8% widowed, 17.6% divorced; Foreign born: 0.0%; Speak English only: 99.5%; With disability: 17.8%; Veterans: 11.9%; Ancestry: 43.7% German, 13.2% English, 12.7% Irish, 10.7% American, 2.5% Polish
Employment: 6.7% management, business, and financial, 2.2% computer, engineering, and science, 0.0% education, legal, community service, arts, and media, 7.9% healthcare practitioners, 25.8% service, 18.0% sales and office, 3.4% natural resources, construction, and maintenance, 36.0% production, transportation, and material moving
Income: Per capita: $19,638; Median household: $43,295; Average household: $47,837; Households with income of $100,000 or more: 7.4%; Poverty rate: 5.1%
Educational Attainment: High school diploma or higher: 95.7%; Bachelor's degree or higher: 7.9%; Graduate/professional degree or higher: 3.6%
Housing: Homeownership rate: 74.1%; Median home value: $95,000; Median year structure built: Before 1940; Homeowner vacancy rate: 14.3%; Median selected monthly owner costs: $781 with a mortgage, $322 without a mortgage; Median gross rent: $698 per month; Rental vacancy rate: 0.0%
Health Insurance: 88.8% have insurance; 77.2% have private insurance; 38.6% have public insurance; 11.2% do not have insurance; 17.4% of children under 18 do not have insurance
Transportation: Commute: 88.8% car, 0.0% public transportation, 4.5% walk, 1.1% work from home; Mean travel time to work: 27.3 minutes

KIRBY (village). Covers a land area of 0.108 square miles and a water area of 0 square miles. Located at 40.81° N. Lat; 83.42° W. Long. Elevation is 873 feet.
Population: 120; Growth (since 2000): -9.1%; Density: 1,113.6 persons per square mile; Race: 93.3% White, 0.0% Black/African American, 6.7% Asian, 0.0% American Indian/Alaska Native, 0.0% Native Hawaiian/Other Pacific Islander, 0.0% Two or more races, 1.7% Hispanic of any race; Average household size: 1.97; Median age: 30.5; Age under 18: 21.7%; Age 65 and over: 15.8%; Males per 100 females: 151.1; Marriage status: 45.6% never married, 30.1% now married, 0.0% separated, 16.5% widowed, 7.8% divorced; Foreign born: 0.0%; Speak English only: 100.0%; With disability: 4.2%; Veterans: 8.5%; Ancestry: 31.7% German, 19.2% Irish, 11.7% American, 10.8% English, 2.5% French
Employment: 15.7% management, business, and financial, 0.0% computer, engineering, and science, 0.0% education, legal, community service, arts, and media, 7.1% healthcare practitioners, 37.1% service, 10.0% sales and office, 1.4% natural resources, construction, and maintenance, 28.6% production, transportation, and material moving
Income: Per capita: $24,158; Median household: $29,375; Average household: $47,993; Households with income of $100,000 or more: 9.9%; Poverty rate: 3.3%
Educational Attainment: High school diploma or higher: 85.1%; Bachelor's degree or higher: 11.5%; Graduate/professional degree or higher: 9.2%
Housing: Homeownership rate: 60.7%; Median home value: $66,400; Median year structure built: Before 1940; Homeowner vacancy rate: 0.0%; Median selected monthly owner costs: $744 with a mortgage, $256 without a mortgage; Median gross rent: $558 per month; Rental vacancy rate: 0.0%
Health Insurance: 85.8% have insurance; 77.5% have private insurance; 25.0% have public insurance; 14.2% do not have insurance; 0.0% of children under 18 do not have insurance
Transportation: Commute: 97.1% car, 0.0% public transportation, 0.0% walk, 0.0% work from home; Mean travel time to work: 27.1 minutes

MARSEILLES (village). Covers a land area of 0.098 square miles and a water area of 0 square miles. Located at 40.70° N. Lat; 83.39° W. Long. Elevation is 876 feet.
Population: 96; Growth (since 2000): -22.6%; Density: 983.4 persons per square mile; Race: 100.0% White, 0.0% Black/African American, 0.0% Asian, 0.0% American Indian/Alaska Native, 0.0% Native Hawaiian/Other Pacific Islander, 0.0% Two or more races, 0.0% Hispanic of any race; Average household size: 2.23; Median age: 44.8; Age under 18: 21.9%; Age 65 and over: 17.7%; Males per 100 females: 103.6; Marriage status: 17.9% never married, 60.3% now married, 0.0% separated, 10.3% widowed, 11.5% divorced; Foreign born: 0.0%; Speak English only: 100.0%; With disability: 8.3%; Veterans: 9.3%; Ancestry: 34.4% German, 24.0% American, 5.2% English, 3.1% Irish, 2.1% Dutch
Employment: 9.1% management, business, and financial, 3.6% computer, engineering, and science, 3.6% education, legal, community service, arts, and media, 7.3% healthcare practitioners, 21.8% service, 10.9% sales and office, 3.6% natural resources, construction, and maintenance, 40.0% production, transportation, and material moving
Income: Per capita: $23,590; Median household: $48,125; Average household: $54,184; Households with income of $100,000 or more: 7.0%; Poverty rate: 12.5%
Educational Attainment: High school diploma or higher: 100.0%; Bachelor's degree or higher: 5.8%; Graduate/professional degree or higher: 5.8%
Housing: Homeownership rate: 88.4%; Median home value: $62,000; Median year structure built: Before 1940; Homeowner vacancy rate: 20.8%; Median selected monthly owner costs: $788 with a mortgage, $395 without a mortgage; Median gross rent: n/a per month; Rental vacancy rate: 0.0%
Health Insurance: 91.7% have insurance; 77.1% have private insurance; 34.4% have public insurance; 8.3% do not have insurance; 0.0% of children under 18 do not have insurance
Transportation: Commute: 90.9% car, 0.0% public transportation, 5.5% walk, 3.6% work from home; Mean travel time to work: 19.7 minutes

MCCUTCHENVILLE (CDP). Covers a land area of 2.780 square miles and a water area of 0.015 square miles. Located at 40.99° N. Lat; 83.25° W. Long. Elevation is 794 feet.
Population: 389; Growth (since 2000): n/a; Density: 139.9 persons per square mile; Race: 95.1% White, 0.0% Black/African American, 0.0% Asian, 0.0% American Indian/Alaska Native, 0.0% Native Hawaiian/Other Pacific Islander, 4.9% Two or more races, 0.0% Hispanic of any race; Average household size: 2.68; Median age: 34.1; Age under 18: 26.2%; Age 65 and over: 10.8%; Males per 100 females: 105.1; Marriage status: 38.3% never married, 33.5% now married, 0.0% separated, 2.8% widowed, 25.3% divorced; Foreign born: 2.1%; Speak English only: 97.9%; With disability: 4.4%; Veterans: 11.8%; Ancestry: 49.4% German, 24.9% American, 6.9% European, 4.6% English, 4.4% Scotch-Irish
Employment: 0.0% management, business, and financial, 0.0% computer, engineering, and science, 5.3% education, legal, community service, arts, and media, 4.3% healthcare practitioners, 13.8% service, 27.1% sales and office, 13.8% natural resources, construction, and maintenance, 35.6% production, transportation, and material moving
Income: Per capita: $17,216; Median household: $46,306; Average household: $47,997; Households with income of $100,000 or more: 7.6%; Poverty rate: 4.1%
Educational Attainment: High school diploma or higher: 96.0%; Bachelor's degree or higher: 9.0%; Graduate/professional degree or higher: 9.0%
Housing: Homeownership rate: 69.0%; Median home value: $87,200; Median year structure built: Before 1940; Homeowner vacancy rate: 0.0%; Median selected monthly owner costs: $770 with a mortgage, $275 without a mortgage; Median gross rent: $719 per month; Rental vacancy rate: 0.0%
Health Insurance: 95.6% have insurance; 91.5% have private insurance; 18.0% have public insurance; 4.4% do not have insurance; 8.8% of children under 18 do not have insurance
Transportation: Commute: 77.1% car, 0.0% public transportation, 4.3% walk, 0.0% work from home; Mean travel time to work: 26.6 minutes

NEVADA (village). Covers a land area of 1.026 square miles and a water area of 0 square miles. Located at 40.82° N. Lat; 83.13° W. Long. Elevation is 932 feet.
Population: 899; Growth (since 2000): 10.4%; Density: 876.4 persons per square mile; Race: 96.8% White, 0.7% Black/African American, 0.0% Asian, 0.0% American Indian/Alaska Native, 0.0% Native Hawaiian/Other Pacific Islander, 2.1% Two or more races, 6.8% Hispanic of any race; Average household size: 2.70; Median age: 35.9; Age under 18: 34.4%; Age 65 and over: 11.6%; Males per 100 females: 99.0; Marriage status: 21.8% never married, 59.3% now married, 0.8% separated, 5.8%

widowed, 13.0% divorced; Foreign born: 0.2%; Speak English only: 98.9%; With disability: 16.7%; Veterans: 13.9%; Ancestry: 38.6% German, 21.8% Irish, 9.7% American, 5.9% English, 1.3% French
Employment: 7.7% management, business, and financial, 7.2% computer, engineering, and science, 5.7% education, legal, community service, arts, and media, 3.7% healthcare practitioners, 18.2% service, 13.7% sales and office, 12.2% natural resources, construction, and maintenance, 31.4% production, transportation, and material moving
Income: Per capita: $18,430; Median household: $46,042; Average household: $49,718; Households with income of $100,000 or more: 4.2%; Poverty rate: 9.8%
Educational Attainment: High school diploma or higher: 88.8%; Bachelor's degree or higher: 11.5%; Graduate/professional degree or higher: 2.5%
Housing: Homeownership rate: 64.6%; Median home value: $72,800; Median year structure built: Before 1940; Homeowner vacancy rate: 2.7%; Median selected monthly owner costs: $848 with a mortgage, $367 without a mortgage; Median gross rent: $682 per month; Rental vacancy rate: 6.3%
Health Insurance: 89.3% have insurance; 72.7% have private insurance; 31.4% have public insurance; 10.7% do not have insurance; 8.7% of children under 18 do not have insurance
Transportation: Commute: 92.9% car, 0.0% public transportation, 2.5% walk, 3.0% work from home; Mean travel time to work: 22.8 minutes

---

SYCAMORE (village). Covers a land area of 0.637 square miles and a water area of 0 square miles. Located at 40.95° N. Lat; 83.17° W. Long. Elevation is 850 feet.
Population: 1,054; Growth (since 2000): 15.3%; Density: 1,655.5 persons per square mile; Race: 100.0% White, 0.0% Black/African American, 0.0% Asian, 0.0% American Indian/Alaska Native, 0.0% Native Hawaiian/Other Pacific Islander, 0.0% Two or more races, 2.2% Hispanic of any race; Average household size: 2.49; Median age: 42.5; Age under 18: 26.4%; Age 65 and over: 21.4%; Males per 100 females: 96.6; Marriage status: 23.9% never married, 54.0% now married, 0.4% separated, 8.1% widowed, 14.0% divorced; Foreign born: 0.8%; Speak English only: 99.0%; With disability: 15.0%; Veterans: 7.2%; Ancestry: 48.9% German, 12.0% Irish, 10.8% English, 8.6% American, 2.0% Swedish
Employment: 12.3% management, business, and financial, 0.9% computer, engineering, and science, 10.9% education, legal, community service, arts, and media, 2.5% healthcare practitioners, 18.2% service, 18.2% sales and office, 9.8% natural resources, construction, and maintenance, 27.1% production, transportation, and material moving
Income: Per capita: $21,771; Median household: $42,426; Average household: $53,807; Households with income of $100,000 or more: 12.0%; Poverty rate: 8.0%
Educational Attainment: High school diploma or higher: 86.9%; Bachelor's degree or higher: 17.8%; Graduate/professional degree or higher: 3.1%

School District(s)

Mohawk Local (PK-12)
2015-16 Enrollment: 973. . . . . (419) 927-2414
Housing: Homeownership rate: 73.8%; Median home value: $82,200; Median year structure built: Before 1940; Homeowner vacancy rate: 0.6%; Median selected monthly owner costs: $901 with a mortgage, $405 without a mortgage; Median gross rent: $726 per month; Rental vacancy rate: 0.0%
Health Insurance: 95.6% have insurance; 75.5% have private insurance; 37.8% have public insurance; 4.4% do not have insurance; 1.4% of children under 18 do not have insurance
Transportation: Commute: 94.9% car, 0.0% public transportation, 3.0% walk, 1.6% work from home; Mean travel time to work: 24.3 minutes

---

UPPER SANDUSKY (city). County seat. Covers a land area of 7.011 square miles and a water area of 0.183 square miles. Located at 40.83° N. Lat; 83.27° W. Long. Elevation is 853 feet.
History: Upper Sandusky was laid out in 1843 on land that had belonged to the Wyandot tribe. The town of Upper Sandusky was preceded by Fort Ferree, built during the War of 1812 by General William Henry Harrison.
Population: 6,917; Growth (since 2000): 5.9%; Density: 986.6 persons per square mile; Race: 96.1% White, 0.2% Black/African American, 0.4% Asian, 0.0% American Indian/Alaska Native, 0.0% Native Hawaiian/Other Pacific Islander, 1.3% Two or more races, 3.4% Hispanic of any race; Average household size: 2.20; Median age: 37.7; Age under 18: 22.5%; Age 65 and over: 20.5%; Males per 100 females: 88.2; Marriage status: 25.1% never married, 52.3% now married, 2.5% separated, 10.9% widowed, 11.8% divorced; Foreign born: 2.6%; Speak English only: 95.4%; With disability: 13.7%; Veterans: 11.2%; Ancestry: 42.8% German, 13.8% Irish, 9.1% English, 9.0% American, 4.3% Italian
Employment: 10.5% management, business, and financial, 1.2% computer, engineering, and science, 7.4% education, legal, community service, arts, and media, 6.6% healthcare practitioners, 19.3% service, 16.4% sales and office, 12.8% natural resources, construction, and maintenance, 25.8% production, transportation, and material moving
Income: Per capita: $21,978; Median household: $40,397; Average household: $49,177; Households with income of $100,000 or more: 8.9%; Poverty rate: 17.3%
Educational Attainment: High school diploma or higher: 90.0%; Bachelor's degree or higher: 16.7%; Graduate/professional degree or higher: 5.3%

School District(s)

Upper Sandusky Exempted Village (KG-12)
2015-16 Enrollment: 1,688 . . . . (419) 294-2307
Housing: Homeownership rate: 56.3%; Median home value: $95,800; Median year structure built: 1959; Homeowner vacancy rate: 1.3%; Median selected monthly owner costs: $961 with a mortgage, $394 without a mortgage; Median gross rent: $609 per month; Rental vacancy rate: 6.2%
Health Insurance: 91.6% have insurance; 69.6% have private insurance; 36.7% have public insurance; 8.4% do not have insurance; 2.2% of children under 18 do not have insurance
Hospitals: Wyandot Memorial Hospital (45 beds)
Safety: Violent crime rate: 18.4 per 10,000 population; Property crime rate: 234.8 per 10,000 population
Newspapers: Daily Chief-Union (daily circulation 3,800)
Transportation: Commute: 92.5% car, 0.6% public transportation, 3.0% walk, 1.2% work from home; Mean travel time to work: 18.1 minutes

---

WHARTON (village). Covers a land area of 1.257 square miles and a water area of 0 square miles. Located at 40.86° N. Lat; 83.46° W. Long. Elevation is 883 feet.
Population: 399; Growth (since 2000): -2.4%; Density: 317.5 persons per square mile; Race: 100.0% White, 0.0% Black/African American, 0.0% Asian, 0.0% American Indian/Alaska Native, 0.0% Native Hawaiian/Other Pacific Islander, 0.0% Two or more races, 0.0% Hispanic of any race; Average household size: 2.45; Median age: 34.3; Age under 18: 30.8%; Age 65 and over: 8.5%; Males per 100 females: 105.7; Marriage status: 27.7% never married, 54.3% now married, 0.7% separated, 9.0% widowed, 9.0% divorced; Foreign born: 1.5%; Speak English only: 98.2%; With disability: 9.0%; Veterans: 10.1%; Ancestry: 53.1% German, 8.3% Irish, 8.0% English, 7.0% French, 6.5% Italian
Employment: 6.0% management, business, and financial, 3.8% computer, engineering, and science, 5.5% education, legal, community service, arts, and media, 9.3% healthcare practitioners, 15.3% service, 13.1% sales and office, 9.3% natural resources, construction, and maintenance, 37.7% production, transportation, and material moving
Income: Per capita: $19,375; Median household: $42,969; Average household: $46,350; Households with income of $100,000 or more: 3.7%; Poverty rate: 21.9%
Educational Attainment: High school diploma or higher: 96.1%; Bachelor's degree or higher: 13.3%; Graduate/professional degree or higher: 1.2%
Housing: Homeownership rate: 74.8%; Median home value: $69,300; Median year structure built: Before 1940; Homeowner vacancy rate: 0.0%; Median selected monthly owner costs: $731 with a mortgage, $281 without a mortgage; Median gross rent: $578 per month; Rental vacancy rate: 0.0%
Health Insurance: 82.7% have insurance; 73.7% have private insurance; 20.8% have public insurance; 17.3% do not have insurance; 22.0% of children under 18 do not have insurance
Transportation: Commute: 92.3% car, 1.1% public transportation, 0.0% walk, 4.4% work from home; Mean travel time to work: 25.3 minutes;

Place Name Index

CDP = Census Designated Place

CDP = Census Designated Place

CDP = Census Designated Place

CDP = Census Designated Place

CDP = Census Designated Place

CDP = Census Designated Place

CDP = Census Designated Place

Comparative Statistics

This section compares the 100 largest incorporated cities by population in the state, by the following data points:

Population

Place	2000 Census	2010 Census	Current Estimate[1]	Population Growth Since 2000 (%)
Akron city *Summit Co.*	217,074	199,110	198,508	-8.5
Alliance city *Stark Co.*	23,253	22,322	22,121	-4.8
Ashland city *Ashland Co.*	21,249	20,362	20,419	-3.9
Athens city *Athens Co.*	21,342	23,832	24,365	14.1
Austintown CDP *Mahoning Co.*	31,627	29,677	28,468	-9.9
Avon city *Lorain Co.*	11,446	21,193	22,289	94.7
Avon Lake city *Lorain Co.*	18,145	22,581	23,221	27.9
Barberton city *Summit Co.*	27,899	26,550	26,266	-5.8
Beavercreek city *Greene Co.*	37,984	45,193	46,086	21.3
Berea city *Cuyahoga Co.*	18,970	19,093	18,949	-0.1
Boardman CDP *Mahoning Co.*	37,215	35,376	34,717	-6.7
Bowling Green city *Wood Co.*	29,636	30,028	31,641	6.7
Broadview Heights city *Cuyahoga Co.*	15,967	19,400	19,257	20.6
Brook Park city *Cuyahoga Co.*	21,218	19,212	18,875	-11.0
Brunswick city *Medina Co.*	33,388	34,255	34,578	3.5
Canton city *Stark Co.*	80,806	73,007	72,163	-10.6
Centerville city *Montgomery Co.*	23,024	23,999	23,899	3.8
Chillicothe city *Ross Co.*	21,796	21,901	21,748	-0.2
Cincinnati city *Hamilton Co.*	331,285	296,943	298,011	-10.0
Cleveland city *Cuyahoga Co.*	478,403	396,815	389,165	-18.6
Cleveland Heights city *Cuyahoga Co.*	49,958	46,121	45,160	-9.6
Columbus city *Franklin Co.*	711,470	787,033	837,038	17.6
Cuyahoga Falls city *Summit Co.*	49,374	49,652	49,353	-0.0
Dayton city *Montgomery Co.*	166,179	141,527	141,143	-15.0
Delaware city *Delaware Co.*	25,243	34,753	37,554	48.7
Dublin city *Franklin Co.*	31,392	41,751	43,874	39.7
Elyria city *Lorain Co.*	55,953	54,533	53,928	-3.6
Euclid city *Cuyahoga Co.*	52,717	48,920	47,863	-9.2
Fairborn city *Greene Co.*	32,052	32,352	33,487	4.4
Fairfield city *Butler Co.*	42,097	42,510	42,640	1.2
Findlay city *Hancock Co.*	38,967	41,202	41,412	6.2
Forest Park city *Hamilton Co.*	19,463	18,720	18,679	-4.0
Gahanna city *Franklin Co.*	32,636	33,248	34,373	5.3
Garfield Heights city *Cuyahoga Co.*	30,734	28,849	28,207	-8.2
Green city *Summit Co.*	22,817	25,699	25,713	12.6
Grove City city *Franklin Co.*	27,075	35,575	38,374	41.7
Hamilton city *Butler Co.*	60,690	62,477	62,259	2.5
Hilliard city *Franklin Co.*	24,230	28,435	33,108	36.6
Huber Heights city *Montgomery Co.*	38,212	38,101	38,795	1.5
Hudson city *Summit Co.*	22,439	22,262	22,282	-0.7
Kent city *Portage Co.*	27,906	28,904	29,761	6.6
Kettering city *Montgomery Co.*	57,502	56,163	55,720	-3.0
Lakewood city *Cuyahoga Co.*	56,646	52,131	50,866	-10.2
Lancaster city *Fairfield Co.*	35,335	38,780	39,483	11.7
Lebanon city *Warren Co.*	16,962	20,033	20,536	21.0
Lima city *Allen Co.*	40,081	38,771	37,836	-5.6
Lorain city *Lorain Co.*	68,652	64,097	63,714	-7.1
Mansfield city *Richland Co.*	49,346	47,821	46,902	-4.9
Maple Heights city *Cuyahoga Co.*	26,156	23,138	22,685	-13.2
Marion city *Marion Co.*	35,318	36,837	36,568	3.5

Place	2000 Census	2010 Census	Current Estimate[1]	Population Growth Since 2000 (%)
Marysville city *Union Co.*	15,942	22,094	22,860	43.3
Mason city *Warren Co.*	22,016	30,712	32,025	45.4
Massillon city *Stark Co.*	31,325	32,149	32,268	3.0
Mayfield Heights city *Cuyahoga Co.*	19,386	19,155	18,878	-2.6
Medina city *Medina Co.*	25,139	26,678	26,445	5.1
Mentor city *Lake Co.*	50,278	47,159	46,896	-6.7
Miamisburg city *Montgomery Co.*	19,489	20,181	20,069	2.9
Middletown city *Butler Co.*	51,605	48,694	48,527	-5.9
Newark city *Licking Co.*	46,279	47,573	48,477	4.7
Niles city *Trumbull Co.*	20,932	19,266	18,877	-9.8
North Olmsted city *Cuyahoga Co.*	34,113	32,718	32,108	-5.8
North Ridgeville city *Lorain Co.*	22,338	29,465	31,832	42.5
North Royalton city *Cuyahoga Co.*	28,648	30,444	30,302	5.7
Norwood city *Hamilton Co.*	21,675	19,207	19,462	-10.2
Oregon city *Lucas Co.*	19,355	20,291	20,137	4.0
Oxford city *Butler Co.*	21,943	21,371	21,941	-0.0
Painesville city *Lake Co.*	17,503	19,563	19,735	12.7
Parma city *Cuyahoga Co.*	85,655	81,601	80,088	-6.4
Parma Heights city *Cuyahoga Co.*	21,659	20,718	20,311	-6.2
Perrysburg city *Wood Co.*	16,945	20,623	21,367	26.0
Pickerington city *Fairfield Co.*	9,792	18,291	19,379	97.9
Piqua city *Miami Co.*	20,738	20,522	20,743	0.0
Portsmouth city *Scioto Co.*	20,909	20,226	20,393	-2.4
Reynoldsburg city *Franklin Co.*	32,069	35,893	36,995	15.3
Riverside city *Montgomery Co.*	23,545	25,201	25,036	6.3
Rocky River city *Cuyahoga Co.*	20,735	20,213	20,211	-2.5
Sandusky city *Erie Co.*	27,844	25,793	25,338	-9.0
Shaker Heights city *Cuyahoga Co.*	29,405	28,448	27,773	-5.5
Sidney city *Shelby Co.*	20,211	21,229	20,761	2.7
Solon city *Cuyahoga Co.*	21,802	23,348	23,085	5.8
South Euclid city *Cuyahoga Co.*	23,537	22,295	21,865	-7.1
Springfield city *Clark Co.*	65,358	60,608	59,761	-8.5
Stow city *Summit Co.*	32,139	34,837	34,746	8.1
Strongsville city *Cuyahoga Co.*	43,858	44,750	44,622	1.7
Sylvania city *Lucas Co.*	18,670	18,965	18,882	1.1
Toledo city *Lucas Co.*	313,619	287,208	280,854	-10.4
Trotwood city *Montgomery Co.*	27,420	24,431	24,372	-11.1
Troy city *Miami Co.*	21,999	25,058	25,684	16.7
Twinsburg city *Summit Co.*	17,006	18,795	18,851	10.8
Upper Arlington city *Franklin Co.*	33,686	33,771	34,675	2.9
Wadsworth city *Medina Co.*	18,437	21,567	22,578	22.4
Warren city *Trumbull Co.*	46,832	41,557	40,433	-13.6
Westerville city *Franklin Co.*	35,318	36,120	38,089	7.8
Westlake city *Cuyahoga Co.*	31,719	32,729	32,408	2.1
White Oak CDP *Hamilton Co.*	13,277	19,167	19,068	43.6
Willoughby city *Lake Co.*	22,621	22,268	22,495	-0.5
Wooster city *Wayne Co.*	24,811	26,119	26,773	7.9
Xenia city *Greene Co.*	24,164	25,719	26,105	8.0
Youngstown city *Mahoning Co.*	82,026	66,982	65,161	-20.5
Zanesville city *Muskingum Co.*	25,586	25,487	25,467	-0.4

NOTE: (1) Current population is based on the American Community Survey's 2012-2016 Five-Year Estimate.
SOURCE: U.S. Census Bureau, Census 2010, Census 2000; U.S. Census Bureau, American Community Survey, 2012-2016 Five-Year Estimates

Physical Characteristics

Place	Density (persons per square mile)	Land Area (square miles)	Water Area (square miles)	Elevation (feet)
Akron city *Summit Co.*	3,200.1	62.03	0.34	961
Alliance city *Stark Co.*	2,478.8	8.92	0.04	1,158
Ashland city *Ashland Co.*	1,828.2	11.16	0.06	1,066
Athens city *Athens Co.*	2,479.4	9.82	0.21	718
Austintown CDP *Mahoning Co.*	2,447.9	11.63	0.03	1,129
Avon city *Lorain Co.*	1,071.2	20.80	0.05	669
Avon Lake city *Lorain Co.*	2,086.5	11.12	0.00	610
Barberton city *Summit Co.*	2,906.1	9.03	0.21	971
Beavercreek city *Greene Co.*	1,745.8	26.39	0.03	876
Berea city *Cuyahoga Co.*	3,314.2	5.71	0.10	755
Boardman CDP *Mahoning Co.*	2,295.9	15.12	0.17	1,112
Bowling Green city *Wood Co.*	2,519.7	12.55	0.04	692
Broadview Heights city *Cuyahoga Co.*	1,475.8	13.04	0.02	1,191
Brook Park city *Cuyahoga Co.*	2,506.7	7.53	0.00	797
Brunswick city *Medina Co.*	2,677.2	12.91	0.03	1,168
Canton city *Stark Co.*	2,834.1	25.46	0.01	1,056
Centerville city *Montgomery Co.*	2,216.9	10.78	0.06	1,020
Chillicothe city *Ross Co.*	2,085.5	10.42	0.16	633
Cincinnati city *Hamilton Co.*	3,823.5	77.94	1.60	627
Cleveland city *Cuyahoga Co.*	5,008.8	77.69	4.76	653
Cleveland Heights city *Cuyahoga Co.*	5,570.8	8.10	0.01	942
Columbus city *Franklin Co.*	3,854.3	217.16	5.93	781
Cuyahoga Falls city *Summit Co.*	1,924.2	25.64	0.09	1,027
Dayton city *Montgomery Co.*	2,536.2	55.65	0.85	738
Delaware city *Delaware Co.*	1,981.5	18.95	0.12	869
Dublin city *Franklin Co.*	1,795.4	24.43	0.36	830
Elyria city *Lorain Co.*	2,621.5	20.57	0.27	738
Euclid city *Cuyahoga Co.*	4,502.6	10.63	0.85	617
Fairborn city *Greene Co.*	2,544.7	13.16	0.00	837
Fairfield city *Butler Co.*	2,036.4	20.93	0.12	594
Findlay city *Hancock Co.*	2,164.3	19.13	0.12	774
Forest Park city *Hamilton Co.*	2,882.6	6.48	0.00	833
Gahanna city *Franklin Co.*	2,766.0	12.42	0.17	797
Garfield Heights city *Cuyahoga Co.*	3,901.5	7.23	0.06	955
Green city *Summit Co.*	802.2	32.05	1.47	1,142
Grove City city *Franklin Co.*	2,369.3	16.19	0.15	846
Hamilton city *Butler Co.*	2,882.9	21.59	0.47	597
Hilliard city *Franklin Co.*	2,514.5	13.16	0.16	932
Huber Heights city *Montgomery Co.*	1,741.9	22.27	0.09	932
Hudson city *Summit Co.*	870.5	25.59	0.26	1,066
Kent city *Portage Co.*	3,243.9	9.17	0.10	1,063
Kettering city *Montgomery Co.*	2,983.3	18.67	0.03	1,004
Lakewood city *Cuyahoga Co.*	9,190.8	5.53	1.15	702
Lancaster city *Fairfield Co.*	2,095.6	18.84	0.06	886
Lebanon city *Warren Co.*	1,584.1	12.96	0.00	771
Lima city *Allen Co.*	2,789.3	13.56	0.22	879
Lorain city *Lorain Co.*	2,691.4	23.67	0.47	610
Mansfield city *Richland Co.*	1,519.2	30.87	0.05	1,240
Maple Heights city *Cuyahoga Co.*	4,386.0	5.17	0.00	896
Marion city *Marion Co.*	3,115.9	11.73	0.07	981

Place	Density (persons per square mile)	Land Area (square miles)	Water Area (square miles)	Elevation (feet)
Marysville city *Union Co.*	1,404.9	16.27	0.29	994
Mason city *Warren Co.*	1,719.1	18.62	0.03	807
Massillon city *Stark Co.*	1,736.9	18.57	0.18	948
Mayfield Heights city *Cuyahoga Co.*	4,528.9	4.16	0.00	1,086
Medina city *Medina Co.*	2,285.3	11.57	0.21	1,089
Mentor city *Lake Co.*	1,760.0	26.64	1.35	692
Miamisburg city *Montgomery Co.*	1,647.1	12.18	0.18	705
Middletown city *Butler Co.*	1,853.2	26.18	0.23	656
Newark city *Licking Co.*	2,321.3	20.88	0.48	833
Niles city *Trumbull Co.*	2,192.2	8.61	0.01	883
North Olmsted city *Cuyahoga Co.*	2,750.4	11.67	0.00	761
North Ridgeville city *Lorain Co.*	1,358.1	23.43	0.14	728
North Royalton city *Cuyahoga Co.*	1,422.0	21.31	0.01	1,197
Norwood city *Hamilton Co.*	6,183.8	3.14	0.00	653
Oregon city *Lucas Co.*	671.8	29.97	8.05	604
Oxford city *Butler Co.*	3,286.3	6.67	0.00	922
Painesville city *Lake Co.*	3,140.1	6.28	0.72	676
Parma city *Cuyahoga Co.*	3,999.5	20.02	0.04	863
Parma Heights city *Cuyahoga Co.*	4,852.6	4.18	0.00	856
Perrysburg city *Wood Co.*	1,855.7	11.51	0.00	633
Pickerington city *Fairfield Co.*	1,988.6	9.74	0.00	840
Piqua city *Miami Co.*	1,785.2	11.62	0.26	876
Portsmouth city *Scioto Co.*	1,899.8	10.73	0.33	535
Reynoldsburg city *Franklin Co.*	3,315.8	11.15	0.08	879
Riverside city *Montgomery Co.*	2,575.8	9.72	0.04	778
Rocky River city *Cuyahoga Co.*	4,265.8	4.73	0.87	692
Sandusky city *Erie Co.*	2,605.3	9.72	12.17	594
Shaker Heights city *Cuyahoga Co.*	4,420.7	6.28	0.04	1,050
Sidney city *Shelby Co.*	1,726.8	12.02	0.13	955
Solon city *Cuyahoga Co.*	1,133.8	20.36	0.13	1,040
South Euclid city *Cuyahoga Co.*	4,701.5	4.65	0.00	958
Springfield city *Clark Co.*	2,362.6	25.29	0.20	974
Stow city *Summit Co.*	2,033.3	17.08	0.23	1,089
Strongsville city *Cuyahoga Co.*	1,811.9	24.62	0.00	932
Sylvania city *Lucas Co.*	2,915.0	6.47	0.04	666
Toledo city *Lucas Co.*	3,480.6	80.69	3.43	610
Trotwood city *Montgomery Co.*	799.2	30.49	0.01	837
Troy city *Miami Co.*	2,191.2	11.72	0.21	837
Twinsburg city *Summit Co.*	1,369.0	13.76	0.03	1,004
Upper Arlington city *Franklin Co.*	3,524.3	9.83	0.03	814
Wadsworth city *Medina Co.*	2,125.7	10.62	0.00	1,171
Warren city *Trumbull Co.*	2,507.1	16.12	0.02	886
Westerville city *Franklin Co.*	3,053.7	12.47	0.13	869
Westlake city *Cuyahoga Co.*	2,034.9	15.92	0.00	709
White Oak CDP *Hamilton Co.*	3,092.1	6.16	0.00	915
Willoughby city *Lake Co.*	2,194.8	10.24	0.09	659
Wooster city *Wayne Co.*	1,641.5	16.31	0.05	994
Xenia city *Greene Co.*	1,965.5	13.28	0.01	935
Youngstown city *Mahoning Co.*	1,919.0	33.95	0.63	856
Zanesville city *Muskingum Co.*	2,164.1	11.76	0.37	676

SOURCE: U.S. Census Bureau, Census 2010; U.S. Census Bureau, American Community Survey, 2012-2016 Five-Year Estimates

Population by Race/Hispanic Origin

Place	White[1] (%)	Black[1] (%)	Asian[1] (%)	AIAN[1,2] (%)	NHOPI[1,3] (%)	Two or More Races (%)	Hispanic[4] (%)
Akron city *Summit Co.*	61.1	30.5	3.6	0.2	0.0	4.1	2.3
Alliance city *Stark Co.*	84.8	9.9	0.4	0.1	0.0	4.4	3.2
Ashland city *Ashland Co.*	95.1	1.4	1.0	0.0	0.0	2.2	0.8
Athens city *Athens Co.*	83.7	4.0	7.5	0.0	0.1	3.8	3.4
Austintown CDP *Mahoning Co.*	87.5	9.5	1.0	0.2	0.2	1.2	2.7
Avon city *Lorain Co.*	88.5	8.7	1.6	0.0	0.0	0.8	3.1
Avon Lake city *Lorain Co.*	94.3	1.7	0.7	0.1	0.0	2.1	2.7
Barberton city *Summit Co.*	89.0	7.1	0.6	0.0	0.0	3.1	1.9
Beavercreek city *Greene Co.*	87.4	3.0	5.3	0.2	0.0	3.6	2.8
Berea city *Cuyahoga Co.*	88.1	6.4	2.5	0.4	0.0	2.1	3.3
Boardman CDP *Mahoning Co.*	89.6	7.0	0.9	0.2	0.0	2.1	4.1
Bowling Green city *Wood Co.*	88.4	6.1	1.6	0.1	0.1	2.8	5.7
Broadview Heights city *Cuyahoga Co.*	86.0	4.6	6.0	0.4	0.0	2.6	2.7
Brook Park city *Cuyahoga Co.*	90.2	5.1	1.3	0.1	0.0	2.1	3.6
Brunswick city *Medina Co.*	95.9	1.2	1.1	0.1	0.0	1.5	2.1
Canton city *Stark Co.*	68.1	24.3	0.4	0.3	0.0	6.1	3.2
Centerville city *Montgomery Co.*	87.2	6.0	3.5	0.0	0.0	3.0	1.5
Chillicothe city *Ross Co.*	87.9	5.0	0.8	0.0	0.1	5.8	0.9
Cincinnati city *Hamilton Co.*	50.7	43.1	1.8	0.2	0.0	3.1	3.2
Cleveland city *Cuyahoga Co.*	40.3	50.8	2.0	0.5	0.0	3.5	10.8
Cleveland Heights city *Cuyahoga Co.*	49.3	42.7	4.2	0.2	0.0	2.9	2.3
Columbus city *Franklin Co.*	61.1	28.0	4.9	0.2	0.0	4.1	5.8
Cuyahoga Falls city *Summit Co.*	91.9	3.7	1.9	0.1	0.1	1.6	2.6
Dayton city *Montgomery Co.*	54.9	39.8	1.1	0.3	0.0	3.3	3.9
Delaware city *Delaware Co.*	90.8	4.6	1.6	0.1	0.0	2.2	2.3
Dublin city *Franklin Co.*	76.4	2.3	16.9	0.3	0.0	3.3	5.5
Elyria city *Lorain Co.*	77.8	15.1	0.9	0.2	0.1	5.1	5.2
Euclid city *Cuyahoga Co.*	37.3	59.5	0.7	0.1	0.0	2.2	1.4
Fairborn city *Greene Co.*	82.0	8.1	4.3	0.2	0.1	4.6	3.9
Fairfield city *Butler Co.*	80.1	13.1	2.3	0.2	0.0	2.6	7.8
Findlay city *Hancock Co.*	89.6	2.2	2.6	0.1	0.0	3.6	7.3
Forest Park city *Hamilton Co.*	26.0	60.0	5.4	0.0	0.1	5.1	6.2
Gahanna city *Franklin Co.*	81.4	12.9	2.6	0.1	0.0	2.6	1.9
Garfield Heights city *Cuyahoga Co.*	50.5	45.3	0.8	0.3	0.0	2.2	2.2
Green city *Summit Co.*	93.4	1.9	1.9	0.1	0.1	2.1	0.9
Grove City city *Franklin Co.*	92.8	3.3	1.3	0.0	0.0	2.2	1.3
Hamilton city *Butler Co.*	84.7	10.3	0.8	0.5	0.2	2.8	5.0
Hilliard city *Franklin Co.*	88.2	3.4	6.5	0.1	0.1	1.4	2.6
Huber Heights city *Montgomery Co.*	77.2	13.8	1.9	1.1	0.0	5.0	3.9
Hudson city *Summit Co.*	92.6	1.9	3.6	0.0	0.0	1.7	2.3
Kent city *Portage Co.*	80.0	9.9	5.5	0.0	0.0	4.3	2.2
Kettering city *Montgomery Co.*	91.2	3.4	2.2	0.2	0.0	2.6	1.9
Lakewood city *Cuyahoga Co.*	86.8	6.9	1.6	0.1	0.1	4.1	4.9
Lancaster city *Fairfield Co.*	94.9	1.9	0.5	0.2	0.0	2.3	2.1
Lebanon city *Warren Co.*	89.6	5.2	1.6	0.2	0.1	1.7	2.4
Lima city *Allen Co.*	67.1	25.9	0.7	0.4	0.0	5.1	3.3
Lorain city *Lorain Co.*	73.4	16.2	0.9	0.5	0.0	5.2	28.3
Mansfield city *Richland Co.*	73.0	17.8	0.6	0.3	0.0	7.5	2.6
Maple Heights city *Cuyahoga Co.*	23.9	72.1	1.1	0.2	0.0	2.4	1.8
Marion city *Marion Co.*	85.1	9.8	0.3	0.2	0.0	3.4	3.3

Place	White[1] (%)	Black[1] (%)	Asian[1] (%)	AIAN[1,2] (%)	NHOPI[1,3] (%)	Two or More Races (%)	Hispanic[4] (%)
Marysville city *Union Co.*	89.6	3.7	2.9	0.1	0.0	3.1	1.7
Mason city *Warren Co.*	84.6	3.9	8.8	0.0	0.0	1.8	3.4
Massillon city *Stark Co.*	89.4	7.2	0.5	0.0	0.0	2.8	2.8
Mayfield Heights city *Cuyahoga Co.*	79.3	13.9	4.5	0.2	0.0	1.6	1.4
Medina city *Medina Co.*	91.9	4.4	1.2	0.4	0.0	1.5	1.7
Mentor city *Lake Co.*	96.6	0.6	1.6	0.1	0.0	0.8	0.9
Miamisburg city *Montgomery Co.*	92.7	3.2	1.0	0.0	0.0	2.3	1.5
Middletown city *Butler Co.*	81.8	11.9	1.0	0.2	0.0	4.0	5.1
Newark city *Licking Co.*	92.8	2.9	0.6	0.1	0.0	3.2	1.0
Niles city *Trumbull Co.*	92.5	4.8	0.3	0.0	0.0	2.3	1.5
North Olmsted city *Cuyahoga Co.*	92.0	2.6	3.4	0.1	0.0	1.5	3.5
North Ridgeville city *Lorain Co.*	92.9	1.6	1.7	0.1	0.0	3.0	3.8
North Royalton city *Cuyahoga Co.*	93.4	1.5	3.5	0.1	0.0	1.4	2.0
Norwood city *Hamilton Co.*	87.8	9.3	0.4	0.0	0.0	1.5	4.1
Oregon city *Lucas Co.*	89.8	2.3	1.4	0.3	0.0	3.6	7.6
Oxford city *Butler Co.*	88.9	4.0	6.1	0.0	0.0	0.9	2.4
Painesville city *Lake Co.*	72.6	13.9	0.7	0.2	0.0	9.0	24.3
Parma city *Cuyahoga Co.*	91.6	3.1	2.0	0.2	0.0	2.0	5.6
Parma Heights city *Cuyahoga Co.*	86.7	7.3	2.8	0.2	0.0	2.6	4.7
Perrysburg city *Wood Co.*	91.3	1.9	3.7	0.2	0.0	2.4	3.2
Pickerington city *Fairfield Co.*	73.6	18.4	3.6	0.0	0.1	3.2	2.9
Piqua city *Miami Co.*	90.6	3.2	1.0	0.1	0.0	4.7	1.4
Portsmouth city *Scioto Co.*	90.0	5.7	1.2	0.4	0.0	2.0	1.1
Reynoldsburg city *Franklin Co.*	64.3	26.9	2.4	0.0	0.1	4.5	3.9
Riverside city *Montgomery Co.*	85.7	7.8	2.2	0.2	0.0	3.3	4.0
Rocky River city *Cuyahoga Co.*	96.1	1.8	0.7	0.0	0.0	1.2	2.8
Sandusky city *Erie Co.*	69.2	21.2	0.3	0.9	0.3	6.0	6.1
Shaker Heights city *Cuyahoga Co.*	54.7	34.3	5.9	0.2	0.0	4.3	2.4
Sidney city *Shelby Co.*	88.5	6.7	1.7	0.4	0.0	2.1	2.7
Solon city *Cuyahoga Co.*	72.6	11.4	12.5	0.2	0.1	3.1	1.3
South Euclid city *Cuyahoga Co.*	52.1	41.0	2.1	0.1	0.0	3.9	2.8
Springfield city *Clark Co.*	74.7	17.4	0.6	0.2	0.0	5.6	3.1
Stow city *Summit Co.*	92.7	3.1	2.0	0.2	0.0	1.7	1.7
Strongsville city *Cuyahoga Co.*	90.5	2.7	4.4	0.3	0.0	1.3	2.8
Sylvania city *Lucas Co.*	93.2	1.6	2.7	0.1	0.0	2.1	2.4
Toledo city *Lucas Co.*	63.5	27.2	1.4	0.3	0.0	4.9	8.2
Trotwood city *Montgomery Co.*	24.3	69.9	0.3	0.1	0.0	4.2	1.8
Troy city *Miami Co.*	89.6	4.2	2.7	0.3	0.0	3.2	1.7
Twinsburg city *Summit Co.*	75.5	13.9	6.3	0.2	0.1	2.9	2.8
Upper Arlington city *Franklin Co.*	91.9	1.3	4.3	0.2	0.0	2.1	2.5
Wadsworth city *Medina Co.*	95.7	1.4	0.7	0.3	0.0	1.7	1.3
Warren city *Trumbull Co.*	66.8	29.0	0.3	0.2	0.0	3.4	2.6
Westerville city *Franklin Co.*	86.3	7.8	2.0	0.0	0.1	3.2	2.4
Westlake city *Cuyahoga Co.*	89.9	2.1	5.1	0.0	0.1	2.2	3.2
White Oak CDP *Hamilton Co.*	83.8	8.7	5.4	0.0	0.0	1.9	0.9
Willoughby city *Lake Co.*	91.0	5.1	1.5	0.2	0.0	1.3	1.7
Wooster city *Wayne Co.*	90.3	3.2	3.1	0.5	0.0	2.5	2.2
Xenia city *Greene Co.*	81.9	14.5	0.3	0.0	0.0	3.2	1.6
Youngstown city *Mahoning Co.*	49.1	43.7	0.5	0.5	0.0	4.7	10.7
Zanesville city *Muskingum Co.*	85.0	8.0	0.5	0.3	0.0	6.0	1.3

NOTE: (1) Exclude multiple race combinations; (2) American Indian/Alaska Native; (3) Native Hawaiian/Other Pacific Islander; (4) May be of any race
SOURCE: U.S. Census Bureau, American Community Survey, 2012-2016 Five-Year Estimates

Average Household Size, Age, and Male/Female Ratio

Place	Average Household Size (persons)	Median Age (years)	Age Under 18 (%)	Age 65 and Over (%)	Males per 100 Females
Akron city *Summit Co.*	2.29	36.7	21.6	13.6	92.8
Alliance city *Stark Co.*	2.37	35.6	22.5	16.7	96.1
Ashland city *Ashland Co.*	2.25	37.6	20.0	18.3	92.5
Athens city *Athens Co.*	2.32	21.4	6.7	5.0	102.1
Austintown CDP *Mahoning Co.*	2.19	43.0	19.4	20.2	91.8
Avon city *Lorain Co.*	2.78	40.5	30.5	15.0	98.5
Avon Lake city *Lorain Co.*	2.55	43.4	26.0	17.2	92.7
Barberton city *Summit Co.*	2.44	39.8	22.7	18.2	85.5
Beavercreek city *Greene Co.*	2.45	41.1	20.4	16.4	104.4
Berea city *Cuyahoga Co.*	2.30	38.2	18.3	15.9	90.4
Boardman CDP *Mahoning Co.*	2.25	43.3	18.8	19.5	91.7
Bowling Green city *Wood Co.*	2.26	22.8	12.3	10.0	84.9
Broadview Heights city *Cuyahoga Co.*	2.52	41.7	23.2	14.8	90.6
Brook Park city *Cuyahoga Co.*	2.46	44.5	19.8	20.0	96.9
Brunswick city *Medina Co.*	2.55	39.6	22.4	14.8	94.6
Canton city *Stark Co.*	2.28	35.8	24.7	14.4	88.1
Centerville city *Montgomery Co.*	2.19	48.2	21.0	27.1	84.3
Chillicothe city *Ross Co.*	2.26	43.3	20.5	20.4	95.5
Cincinnati city *Hamilton Co.*	2.12	32.3	22.1	11.6	91.9
Cleveland city *Cuyahoga Co.*	2.25	35.8	23.0	13.0	92.6
Cleveland Heights city *Cuyahoga Co.*	2.32	36.1	21.9	15.0	89.1
Columbus city *Franklin Co.*	2.39	32.1	22.7	9.4	94.9
Cuyahoga Falls city *Summit Co.*	2.27	39.5	20.7	16.0	95.9
Dayton city *Montgomery Co.*	2.25	33.3	22.1	12.5	94.0
Delaware city *Delaware Co.*	2.52	34.0	25.5	11.2	92.9
Dublin city *Franklin Co.*	2.80	39.6	29.7	9.4	97.7
Elyria city *Lorain Co.*	2.35	37.8	23.1	14.4	92.6
Euclid city *Cuyahoga Co.*	2.12	40.6	22.2	15.2	83.9
Fairborn city *Greene Co.*	2.24	33.8	20.4	14.3	94.0
Fairfield city *Butler Co.*	2.50	38.1	20.9	14.5	101.1
Findlay city *Hancock Co.*	2.20	36.7	21.0	17.1	91.7
Forest Park city *Hamilton Co.*	2.61	37.1	24.9	13.0	96.5
Gahanna city *Franklin Co.*	2.59	39.0	24.2	13.5	93.1
Garfield Heights city *Cuyahoga Co.*	2.38	38.9	23.2	15.9	83.3
Green city *Summit Co.*	2.53	42.1	23.1	16.7	102.6
Grove City city *Franklin Co.*	2.57	39.0	25.4	13.6	93.7
Hamilton city *Butler Co.*	2.49	37.2	24.3	14.9	87.6
Hilliard city *Franklin Co.*	2.75	35.9	28.5	10.2	98.6
Huber Heights city *Montgomery Co.*	2.57	36.8	26.3	15.5	88.6
Hudson city *Summit Co.*	2.80	45.2	27.1	15.6	92.1
Kent city *Portage Co.*	2.43	23.5	15.4	8.1	93.7
Kettering city *Montgomery Co.*	2.20	40.7	21.2	18.2	88.6
Lakewood city *Cuyahoga Co.*	2.07	34.7	18.4	11.3	95.5
Lancaster city *Fairfield Co.*	2.40	38.8	22.5	16.7	93.2
Lebanon city *Warren Co.*	2.75	33.2	28.2	10.7	93.2
Lima city *Allen Co.*	2.48	33.2	25.7	11.2	111.0
Lorain city *Lorain Co.*	2.51	36.9	25.2	15.3	86.4
Mansfield city *Richland Co.*	2.28	37.7	20.9	16.3	117.7
Maple Heights city *Cuyahoga Co.*	2.41	37.6	22.8	13.5	76.2
Marion city *Marion Co.*	2.40	37.8	20.8	13.4	134.4

Place	Average Household Size (persons)	Median Age (years)	Age Under 18 (%)	Age 65 and Over (%)	Males per 100 Females
Marysville city *Union Co.*	2.59	34.8	24.7	9.8	78.3
Mason city *Warren Co.*	2.65	41.9	27.3	14.5	92.0
Massillon city *Stark Co.*	2.41	40.0	23.2	17.6	102.5
Mayfield Heights city *Cuyahoga Co.*	1.99	43.1	18.3	24.2	83.6
Medina city *Medina Co.*	2.56	37.9	26.6	13.1	91.3
Mentor city *Lake Co.*	2.38	46.7	19.2	19.1	93.7
Miamisburg city *Montgomery Co.*	2.43	41.1	23.3	17.4	95.1
Middletown city *Butler Co.*	2.45	37.8	24.0	15.0	92.5
Newark city *Licking Co.*	2.40	37.0	24.6	15.5	88.5
Niles city *Trumbull Co.*	2.24	42.4	21.5	18.4	84.5
North Olmsted city *Cuyahoga Co.*	2.42	45.2	18.9	19.9	95.9
North Ridgeville city *Lorain Co.*	2.58	41.7	22.9	19.5	102.0
North Royalton city *Cuyahoga Co.*	2.35	43.1	19.5	17.0	93.8
Norwood city *Hamilton Co.*	2.20	33.3	18.6	10.6	102.9
Oregon city *Lucas Co.*	2.44	42.8	22.1	17.4	94.3
Oxford city *Butler Co.*	2.42	21.2	5.7	6.9	95.5
Painesville city *Lake Co.*	2.54	32.5	25.7	10.4	101.4
Parma city *Cuyahoga Co.*	2.36	41.9	19.9	17.8	95.3
Parma Heights city *Cuyahoga Co.*	2.22	40.0	20.4	18.8	85.9
Perrysburg city *Wood Co.*	2.51	38.1	26.3	13.7	101.1
Pickerington city *Fairfield Co.*	2.91	35.5	30.5	9.3	96.2
Piqua city *Miami Co.*	2.45	37.9	24.4	17.0	93.3
Portsmouth city *Scioto Co.*	2.27	36.8	20.1	17.6	91.4
Reynoldsburg city *Franklin Co.*	2.55	35.9	24.4	11.2	96.0
Riverside city *Montgomery Co.*	2.43	35.7	23.7	14.3	102.6
Rocky River city *Cuyahoga Co.*	2.25	46.2	20.8	23.0	82.0
Sandusky city *Erie Co.*	2.20	39.4	22.3	17.0	91.3
Shaker Heights city *Cuyahoga Co.*	2.48	40.5	25.8	16.6	83.9
Sidney city *Shelby Co.*	2.47	38.8	24.4	14.5	94.7
Solon city *Cuyahoga Co.*	2.75	44.0	27.4	15.8	92.4
South Euclid city *Cuyahoga Co.*	2.41	38.0	20.4	14.0	85.3
Springfield city *Clark Co.*	2.32	36.7	23.9	16.2	89.9
Stow city *Summit Co.*	2.40	40.3	22.0	16.4	90.6
Strongsville city *Cuyahoga Co.*	2.52	45.9	21.2	19.1	93.5
Sylvania city *Lucas Co.*	2.43	42.8	22.8	19.6	91.5
Toledo city *Lucas Co.*	2.31	35.3	23.3	13.4	94.3
Trotwood city *Montgomery Co.*	2.30	41.8	21.4	19.4	81.2
Troy city *Miami Co.*	2.35	40.4	21.9	15.7	99.3
Twinsburg city *Summit Co.*	2.46	42.5	23.6	17.4	88.3
Upper Arlington city *Franklin Co.*	2.53	42.1	26.6	17.0	95.1
Wadsworth city *Medina Co.*	2.57	37.7	26.3	16.1	88.2
Warren city *Trumbull Co.*	2.17	38.8	23.5	17.5	93.2
Westerville city *Franklin Co.*	2.49	41.4	21.9	17.7	90.4
Westlake city *Cuyahoga Co.*	2.29	47.2	21.1	22.2	88.4
White Oak CDP *Hamilton Co.*	2.47	41.1	23.2	16.8	95.0
Willoughby city *Lake Co.*	2.06	44.0	18.3	20.4	88.0
Wooster city *Wayne Co.*	2.22	36.2	20.2	18.1	92.7
Xenia city *Greene Co.*	2.34	37.2	24.8	16.8	91.1
Youngstown city *Mahoning Co.*	2.23	39.0	22.3	16.4	95.3
Zanesville city *Muskingum Co.*	2.26	35.5	23.2	16.5	87.8

SOURCE: U.S. Census Bureau, American Community Survey, 2012-2016 Five-Year Estimates

Foreign Born, Language Spoken, Disabled Persons, and Veterans

Place	Foreign Born (%)	Speak English Only at Home (%)	With a Disability (%)	Veterans (%)
Akron city *Summit Co.*	5.50	93.3	15.1	8.4
Alliance city *Stark Co.*	2.00	97.1	18.8	8.2
Ashland city *Ashland Co.*	3.30	96.1	16.7	9.4
Athens city *Athens Co.*	10.20	88.5	7.3	2.8
Austintown CDP *Mahoning Co.*	2.70	96.1	14.6	11.4
Avon city *Lorain Co.*	3.30	92.9	8.2	7.0
Avon Lake city *Lorain Co.*	4.60	94.3	10.7	7.3
Barberton city *Summit Co.*	3.10	96.2	17.2	8.5
Beavercreek city *Greene Co.*	7.90	89.4	9.6	16.7
Berea city *Cuyahoga Co.*	2.90	94.1	13.3	6.3
Boardman CDP *Mahoning Co.*	3.50	94.1	13.1	8.8
Bowling Green city *Wood Co.*	5.00	92.6	8.6	4.3
Broadview Heights city *Cuyahoga Co.*	9.90	87.8	7.0	6.0
Brook Park city *Cuyahoga Co.*	4.80	92.4	17.7	10.8
Brunswick city *Medina Co.*	3.30	94.6	10.1	9.0
Canton city *Stark Co.*	2.40	96.1	16.4	8.5
Centerville city *Montgomery Co.*	5.80	92.7	14.5	12.0
Chillicothe city *Ross Co.*	1.10	97.9	23.1	11.9
Cincinnati city *Hamilton Co.*	5.10	92.4	14.1	5.9
Cleveland city *Cuyahoga Co.*	4.90	87.4	20.0	7.0
Cleveland Heights city *Cuyahoga Co.*	8.10	89.7	12.0	5.5
Columbus city *Franklin Co.*	11.60	85.3	11.9	6.4
Cuyahoga Falls city *Summit Co.*	4.20	95.2	12.3	8.8
Dayton city *Montgomery Co.*	4.50	93.3	18.5	8.6
Delaware city *Delaware Co.*	3.50	96.0	9.7	8.1
Dublin city *Franklin Co.*	16.50	81.8	5.7	6.8
Elyria city *Lorain Co.*	1.80	95.5	18.0	9.4
Euclid city *Cuyahoga Co.*	3.30	95.3	16.2	8.4
Fairborn city *Greene Co.*	6.00	92.5	15.7	14.3
Fairfield city *Butler Co.*	9.40	87.5	10.4	7.8
Findlay city *Hancock Co.*	4.90	92.7	13.0	8.9
Forest Park city *Hamilton Co.*	10.60	85.0	13.4	8.9
Gahanna city *Franklin Co.*	5.60	93.7	9.5	7.9
Garfield Heights city *Cuyahoga Co.*	2.90	93.9	14.4	8.8
Green city *Summit Co.*	3.70	94.1	10.9	7.8
Grove City city *Franklin Co.*	2.60	96.5	12.1	9.7
Hamilton city *Butler Co.*	3.40	94.4	16.4	8.3
Hilliard city *Franklin Co.*	6.20	89.8	7.7	7.3
Huber Heights city *Montgomery Co.*	4.00	93.5	14.1	14.1
Hudson city *Summit Co.*	6.60	93.1	6.7	5.4
Kent city *Portage Co.*	8.40	90.8	11.2	4.8
Kettering city *Montgomery Co.*	4.30	94.5	13.8	10.1
Lakewood city *Cuyahoga Co.*	7.30	89.9	11.8	6.2
Lancaster city *Fairfield Co.*	1.20	98.5	19.6	10.5
Lebanon city *Warren Co.*	4.30	95.3	10.6	7.0
Lima city *Allen Co.*	1.10	97.2	18.4	8.5
Lorain city *Lorain Co.*	3.00	81.6	20.1	9.0
Mansfield city *Richland Co.*	1.70	96.3	18.9	9.9
Maple Heights city *Cuyahoga Co.*	2.50	97.0	19.2	7.8
Marion city *Marion Co.*	1.60	95.0	23.2	10.0

Place	Foreign Born (%)	Speak English Only at Home (%)	With a Disability (%)	Veterans (%)
Marysville city *Union Co.*	3.60	96.6	12.2	8.3
Mason city *Warren Co.*	11.30	86.1	8.3	7.6
Massillon city *Stark Co.*	1.40	96.8	15.4	10.0
Mayfield Heights city *Cuyahoga Co.*	15.80	80.5	14.9	7.3
Medina city *Medina Co.*	2.30	96.3	10.7	8.6
Mentor city *Lake Co.*	4.10	95.1	11.8	8.7
Miamisburg city *Montgomery Co.*	2.30	97.3	13.8	9.0
Middletown city *Butler Co.*	3.10	94.6	19.6	7.8
Newark city *Licking Co.*	1.50	97.7	18.2	9.7
Niles city *Trumbull Co.*	0.70	96.9	17.8	10.0
North Olmsted city *Cuyahoga Co.*	9.10	87.1	12.7	8.0
North Ridgeville city *Lorain Co.*	4.70	93.5	10.7	9.8
North Royalton city *Cuyahoga Co.*	10.30	86.7	10.8	6.9
Norwood city *Hamilton Co.*	3.30	94.8	14.4	7.6
Oregon city *Lucas Co.*	2.60	95.4	12.7	8.8
Oxford city *Butler Co.*	7.80	91.4	5.8	2.4
Painesville city *Lake Co.*	12.30	79.7	14.2	8.1
Parma city *Cuyahoga Co.*	9.90	84.5	14.2	8.6
Parma Heights city *Cuyahoga Co.*	10.40	86.2	15.5	7.0
Perrysburg city *Wood Co.*	4.70	92.0	8.5	6.1
Pickerington city *Fairfield Co.*	5.20	93.3	8.0	10.3
Piqua city *Miami Co.*	1.10	97.5	17.3	8.4
Portsmouth city *Scioto Co.*	1.80	97.8	24.5	9.1
Reynoldsburg city *Franklin Co.*	6.00	93.0	10.5	10.0
Riverside city *Montgomery Co.*	4.50	94.4	15.6	14.0
Rocky River city *Cuyahoga Co.*	9.10	88.5	11.1	8.8
Sandusky city *Erie Co.*	2.40	96.3	17.0	10.4
Shaker Heights city *Cuyahoga Co.*	9.20	89.6	9.6	6.2
Sidney city *Shelby Co.*	3.20	94.6	15.9	9.4
Solon city *Cuyahoga Co.*	14.90	82.7	7.2	4.8
South Euclid city *Cuyahoga Co.*	6.70	92.5	9.0	6.4
Springfield city *Clark Co.*	1.70	95.7	18.5	10.0
Stow city *Summit Co.*	4.60	94.6	8.9	7.8
Strongsville city *Cuyahoga Co.*	8.60	88.2	9.8	8.5
Sylvania city *Lucas Co.*	4.20	95.0	10.8	7.5
Toledo city *Lucas Co.*	3.40	93.1	17.3	7.5
Trotwood city *Montgomery Co.*	1.50	96.9	19.2	12.0
Troy city *Miami Co.*	3.40	96.2	14.5	10.5
Twinsburg city *Summit Co.*	7.70	91.1	8.6	7.0
Upper Arlington city *Franklin Co.*	7.50	90.9	8.6	6.9
Wadsworth city *Medina Co.*	1.30	98.0	10.4	9.4
Warren city *Trumbull Co.*	1.40	96.5	17.9	10.9
Westerville city *Franklin Co.*	5.20	94.0	11.3	8.1
Westlake city *Cuyahoga Co.*	7.80	89.0	9.7	8.3
White Oak CDP *Hamilton Co.*	6.90	92.6	12.0	8.6
Willoughby city *Lake Co.*	5.00	93.6	13.0	8.9
Wooster city *Wayne Co.*	4.10	93.8	13.5	7.5
Xenia city *Greene Co.*	1.00	98.1	16.6	10.4
Youngstown city *Mahoning Co.*	3.10	90.1	20.6	8.8
Zanesville city *Muskingum Co.*	1.50	97.5	22.1	9.5

SOURCE: U.S. Census Bureau, American Community Survey, 2012-2016 Five-Year Estimates

Five Largest Ancestry Groups

Place	Group 1	Group 2	Group 3	Group 4	Group 5
Akron city *Summit Co.*	German (16.1%)	Irish (11.1%)	American (8.4%)	Italian (6.1%)	English (5.7%)
Alliance city *Stark Co.*	German (23.7%)	Irish (12.7%)	Italian (9.9%)	English (6.8%)	American (5.1%)
Ashland city *Ashland Co.*	German (30.5%)	Irish (11.7%)	English (9.6%)	American (7.6%)	Italian (5.1%)
Athens city *Athens Co.*	German (23.6%)	Irish (14.1%)	Italian (7.2%)	English (7.2%)	Polish (5.0%)
Austintown CDP *Mahoning Co.*	German (26.0%)	Irish (21.4%)	Italian (19.9%)	English (8.8%)	Slovak (6.8%)
Avon city *Lorain Co.*	German (26.7%)	Irish (21.3%)	Italian (13.9%)	English (12.1%)	Polish (8.9%)
Avon Lake city *Lorain Co.*	German (31.2%)	Irish (21.9%)	English (13.6%)	Italian (9.6%)	Polish (7.4%)
Barberton city *Summit Co.*	German (18.5%)	American (17.2%)	Irish (12.0%)	English (7.6%)	Italian (4.6%)
Beavercreek city *Greene Co.*	German (24.5%)	Irish (13.2%)	English (10.6%)	American (10.0%)	Italian (4.8%)
Berea city *Cuyahoga Co.*	German (28.0%)	Irish (20.9%)	English (11.4%)	Italian (10.3%)	Polish (9.7%)
Boardman CDP *Mahoning Co.*	Italian (25.7%)	German (20.7%)	Irish (18.0%)	Slovak (8.7%)	English (8.0%)
Bowling Green city *Wood Co.*	German (37.2%)	Irish (16.1%)	English (8.7%)	Polish (5.5%)	Italian (5.1%)
Broadview Heights city *Cuyahoga Co.*	German (23.5%)	Irish (16.6%)	Italian (16.0%)	Polish (15.8%)	Slovak (5.6%)
Brook Park city *Cuyahoga Co.*	German (25.8%)	Irish (19.3%)	Italian (12.8%)	Polish (10.7%)	English (8.2%)
Brunswick city *Medina Co.*	German (28.2%)	Irish (19.9%)	Polish (13.5%)	Italian (12.8%)	English (6.7%)
Canton city *Stark Co.*	German (22.0%)	Irish (12.6%)	Italian (8.8%)	English (5.4%)	American (4.3%)
Centerville city *Montgomery Co.*	German (32.5%)	Irish (18.1%)	English (11.1%)	Italian (7.1%)	American (6.2%)
Chillicothe city *Ross Co.*	German (24.3%)	Irish (14.6%)	American (11.7%)	English (9.5%)	Italian (2.5%)
Cincinnati city *Hamilton Co.*	German (19.5%)	Irish (10.4%)	English (5.0%)	Italian (3.7%)	American (3.7%)
Cleveland city *Cuyahoga Co.*	German (9.4%)	Irish (8.8%)	Italian (4.6%)	Polish (4.1%)	English (3.0%)
Cleveland Heights city *Cuyahoga Co.*	German (12.1%)	Irish (8.4%)	English (5.5%)	Italian (5.3%)	Polish (4.3%)
Columbus city *Franklin Co.*	German (19.3%)	Irish (11.2%)	English (6.5%)	Italian (5.1%)	American (4.3%)
Cuyahoga Falls city *Summit Co.*	German (24.6%)	Irish (15.4%)	American (12.7%)	Italian (11.1%)	English (10.2%)
Dayton city *Montgomery Co.*	German (15.4%)	Irish (9.5%)	English (4.6%)	American (4.4%)	Italian (3.1%)
Delaware city *Delaware Co.*	German (29.7%)	Irish (14.7%)	English (12.5%)	American (7.4%)	Italian (6.1%)
Dublin city *Franklin Co.*	German (27.3%)	Irish (14.1%)	English (10.7%)	Italian (7.2%)	American (6.3%)
Elyria city *Lorain Co.*	German (22.7%)	Irish (13.4%)	English (9.5%)	Polish (7.4%)	American (7.4%)
Euclid city *Cuyahoga Co.*	German (9.0%)	Irish (7.1%)	Italian (5.1%)	Slovene (4.1%)	English (3.5%)
Fairborn city *Greene Co.*	German (21.8%)	American (13.3%)	Irish (12.9%)	English (10.1%)	Italian (3.8%)
Fairfield city *Butler Co.*	German (26.8%)	Irish (11.1%)	American (8.0%)	English (7.1%)	Italian (5.6%)
Findlay city *Hancock Co.*	German (32.2%)	American (16.3%)	Irish (11.2%)	English (8.3%)	Italian (3.9%)
Forest Park city *Hamilton Co.*	German (8.9%)	Irish (3.8%)	English (2.6%)	American (2.5%)	(a) (1.8%)
Gahanna city *Franklin Co.*	German (27.6%)	Irish (16.3%)	English (11.0%)	Italian (7.5%)	American (5.6%)
Garfield Heights city *Cuyahoga Co.*	Polish (13.8%)	German (11.8%)	Irish (9.7%)	Italian (7.6%)	English (3.2%)
Green city *Summit Co.*	German (26.8%)	Irish (13.5%)	Italian (11.2%)	English (10.6%)	American (7.1%)
Grove City city *Franklin Co.*	German (32.3%)	Irish (17.5%)	English (8.7%)	American (8.6%)	Italian (5.4%)
Hamilton city *Butler Co.*	German (29.8%)	Irish (15.8%)	English (8.7%)	American (8.3%)	Italian (3.7%)
Hilliard city *Franklin Co.*	German (28.6%)	Irish (14.5%)	English (11.2%)	Italian (8.4%)	American (5.8%)
Huber Heights city *Montgomery Co.*	German (22.9%)	Irish (13.9%)	American (8.6%)	English (8.2%)	French (2.5%)
Hudson city *Summit Co.*	German (26.0%)	Irish (16.6%)	English (12.3%)	Italian (11.9%)	Polish (5.4%)
Kent city *Portage Co.*	German (28.2%)	Irish (17.9%)	Italian (11.6%)	English (7.4%)	Polish (6.4%)
Kettering city *Montgomery Co.*	German (30.4%)	Irish (14.7%)	English (11.7%)	American (7.5%)	Italian (4.7%)
Lakewood city *Cuyahoga Co.*	German (24.8%)	Irish (24.5%)	Italian (10.0%)	English (9.0%)	Polish (7.4%)
Lancaster city *Fairfield Co.*	German (29.5%)	Irish (16.7%)	American (10.3%)	English (9.4%)	Italian (3.9%)
Lebanon city *Warren Co.*	German (29.7%)	Irish (21.3%)	English (11.6%)	American (7.3%)	Italian (4.2%)
Lima city *Allen Co.*	German (24.9%)	Irish (10.9%)	English (5.8%)	American (4.8%)	Italian (3.7%)
Lorain city *Lorain Co.*	German (16.0%)	Irish (10.6%)	Italian (7.7%)	Polish (6.6%)	English (6.2%)
Mansfield city *Richland Co.*	German (27.3%)	Irish (12.1%)	English (9.5%)	American (6.0%)	Italian (5.2%)
Maple Heights city *Cuyahoga Co.*	Polish (5.1%)	German (5.0%)	Irish (3.6%)	Italian (3.3%)	Czech (1.9%)
Marion city *Marion Co.*	German (22.4%)	Irish (14.2%)	American (10.1%)	English (8.3%)	Italian (4.3%)

Place	Group 1	Group 2	Group 3	Group 4	Group 5
Marysville city *Union Co.*	German (29.8%)	Irish (16.4%)	American (10.8%)	English (9.0%)	Italian (4.5%)
Mason city *Warren Co.*	German (29.0%)	Irish (11.8%)	English (9.4%)	Italian (6.1%)	American (5.7%)
Massillon city *Stark Co.*	German (31.5%)	Irish (16.0%)	Italian (9.5%)	English (8.9%)	American (6.2%)
Mayfield Heights city *Cuyahoga Co.*	Italian (20.0%)	German (17.0%)	Irish (11.8%)	Polish (7.8%)	Russian (6.6%)
Medina city *Medina Co.*	German (31.0%)	Irish (19.6%)	Italian (11.5%)	English (10.0%)	Polish (8.9%)
Mentor city *Lake Co.*	German (27.9%)	Irish (19.9%)	Italian (15.9%)	English (10.8%)	Polish (8.0%)
Miamisburg city *Montgomery Co.*	German (31.3%)	Irish (16.8%)	English (12.3%)	American (8.6%)	Scottish (4.0%)
Middletown city *Butler Co.*	German (21.0%)	Irish (11.3%)	American (8.2%)	English (7.3%)	Italian (3.7%)
Newark city *Licking Co.*	German (25.5%)	Irish (14.8%)	American (10.0%)	English (9.1%)	Italian (6.2%)
Niles city *Trumbull Co.*	American (28.7%)	Italian (19.6%)	German (18.1%)	Irish (15.8%)	English (6.0%)
North Olmsted city *Cuyahoga Co.*	German (26.8%)	Irish (22.7%)	Italian (11.4%)	Polish (9.3%)	English (8.7%)
North Ridgeville city *Lorain Co.*	German (28.4%)	Irish (20.6%)	Italian (11.4%)	Polish (9.8%)	English (9.3%)
North Royalton city *Cuyahoga Co.*	German (24.4%)	Italian (17.2%)	Polish (16.6%)	Irish (14.7%)	English (8.3%)
Norwood city *Hamilton Co.*	German (26.8%)	Irish (16.5%)	English (7.9%)	American (7.4%)	Italian (5.1%)
Oregon city *Lucas Co.*	German (35.9%)	Irish (12.8%)	English (7.9%)	Polish (7.7%)	Hungarian (7.7%)
Oxford city *Butler Co.*	German (20.2%)	Irish (10.4%)	Italian (6.3%)	English (5.8%)	American (5.1%)
Painesville city *Lake Co.*	German (16.4%)	Irish (13.8%)	Italian (11.1%)	English (4.7%)	Hungarian (4.0%)
Parma city *Cuyahoga Co.*	German (24.1%)	Polish (15.9%)	Irish (15.2%)	Italian (13.1%)	Slovak (6.3%)
Parma Heights city *Cuyahoga Co.*	German (21.0%)	Irish (14.2%)	Polish (13.3%)	Italian (12.0%)	English (7.7%)
Perrysburg city *Wood Co.*	German (39.4%)	Irish (16.4%)	English (10.5%)	Polish (8.5%)	Italian (5.4%)
Pickerington city *Fairfield Co.*	German (24.0%)	Irish (14.3%)	English (11.6%)	Italian (5.5%)	American (4.5%)
Piqua city *Miami Co.*	German (27.3%)	Irish (16.1%)	American (8.6%)	English (7.9%)	Italian (4.2%)
Portsmouth city *Scioto Co.*	German (20.6%)	Irish (15.3%)	American (9.3%)	English (7.2%)	Italian (2.3%)
Reynoldsburg city *Franklin Co.*	German (20.2%)	Irish (13.5%)	English (7.3%)	American (5.1%)	Italian (5.0%)
Riverside city *Montgomery Co.*	German (22.6%)	Irish (14.8%)	American (7.8%)	English (5.6%)	Italian (3.6%)
Rocky River city *Cuyahoga Co.*	Irish (28.2%)	German (26.6%)	Italian (10.7%)	English (10.4%)	Polish (7.6%)
Sandusky city *Erie Co.*	German (30.2%)	Irish (14.3%)	Italian (7.9%)	English (5.9%)	American (4.3%)
Shaker Heights city *Cuyahoga Co.*	German (12.6%)	Irish (9.9%)	English (8.6%)	Italian (7.1%)	Polish (4.0%)
Sidney city *Shelby Co.*	German (27.3%)	American (10.0%)	Irish (8.1%)	English (7.9%)	French (3.5%)
Solon city *Cuyahoga Co.*	German (14.4%)	Italian (10.6%)	Irish (9.2%)	Polish (6.0%)	English (5.4%)
South Euclid city *Cuyahoga Co.*	German (11.3%)	Irish (10.0%)	Italian (9.6%)	Polish (4.8%)	American (3.5%)
Springfield city *Clark Co.*	German (19.9%)	Irish (13.4%)	English (7.1%)	American (6.8%)	Italian (3.1%)
Stow city *Summit Co.*	German (26.9%)	Irish (15.8%)	English (11.8%)	American (11.5%)	Italian (8.9%)
Strongsville city *Cuyahoga Co.*	German (24.5%)	Irish (16.6%)	Italian (13.2%)	Polish (12.1%)	English (9.3%)
Sylvania city *Lucas Co.*	German (34.9%)	Irish (15.7%)	Polish (13.4%)	English (12.4%)	French (6.1%)
Toledo city *Lucas Co.*	German (22.5%)	Irish (11.2%)	Polish (8.5%)	English (5.2%)	French (3.6%)
Trotwood city *Montgomery Co.*	German (6.2%)	Irish (3.8%)	American (3.4%)	African (2.1%)	English (2.0%)
Troy city *Miami Co.*	German (31.6%)	Irish (14.1%)	English (9.9%)	American (9.1%)	French (4.2%)
Twinsburg city *Summit Co.*	German (20.5%)	Italian (15.3%)	Irish (13.4%)	English (8.3%)	Polish (8.1%)
Upper Arlington city *Franklin Co.*	German (31.7%)	Irish (17.6%)	English (15.5%)	Italian (9.3%)	American (6.5%)
Wadsworth city *Medina Co.*	German (27.3%)	Irish (14.8%)	English (12.6%)	Italian (8.1%)	American (6.1%)
Warren city *Trumbull Co.*	American (21.6%)	German (11.5%)	Italian (8.1%)	Irish (8.0%)	English (5.1%)
Westerville city *Franklin Co.*	German (29.5%)	Irish (16.5%)	English (13.2%)	Italian (7.5%)	American (5.3%)
Westlake city *Cuyahoga Co.*	German (26.7%)	Irish (19.3%)	Italian (10.8%)	English (10.4%)	Polish (7.0%)
White Oak CDP *Hamilton Co.*	German (37.0%)	Irish (15.5%)	American (5.3%)	English (5.2%)	Italian (4.9%)
Willoughby city *Lake Co.*	German (23.0%)	Irish (20.8%)	Italian (19.4%)	English (9.9%)	Polish (7.1%)
Wooster city *Wayne Co.*	German (29.6%)	Irish (10.8%)	English (9.1%)	American (6.6%)	Italian (5.5%)
Xenia city *Greene Co.*	German (21.6%)	Irish (13.7%)	American (13.2%)	English (7.3%)	European (3.0%)
Youngstown city *Mahoning Co.*	German (10.6%)	Irish (10.4%)	Italian (10.2%)	American (8.2%)	African (5.2%)
Zanesville city *Muskingum Co.*	German (18.1%)	Irish (12.1%)	English (7.8%)	American (7.5%)	Italian (2.4%)

NOTE: "French" excludes Basque; (a) Other Subsaharan African; Please refer to the User Guide for more information.
SOURCE: U.S. Census Bureau, American Community Survey, 2012-2016 Five-Year Estimates

Marriage Status

Place	Never Married (%)	Now Married[1] (%)	Separated (%)	Widowed (%)	Divorced (%)
Akron city *Summit Co.*	42.8	36.6	2.4	6.3	14.3
Alliance city *Stark Co.*	36.3	38.5	2.6	8.9	16.2
Ashland city *Ashland Co.*	35.8	43.9	1.4	7.7	12.6
Athens city *Athens Co.*	80.1	14.7	0.3	1.6	3.6
Austintown CDP *Mahoning Co.*	30.5	48.7	0.9	8.1	12.8
Avon city *Lorain Co.*	26.1	59.0	1.1	6.7	8.2
Avon Lake city *Lorain Co.*	21.6	61.1	0.4	6.1	11.3
Barberton city *Summit Co.*	34.7	43.5	2.2	8.9	12.9
Beavercreek city *Greene Co.*	26.4	60.5	0.8	4.9	8.2
Berea city *Cuyahoga Co.*	40.5	40.2	0.9	5.4	13.9
Boardman CDP *Mahoning Co.*	29.6	49.3	1.3	7.9	13.1
Bowling Green city *Wood Co.*	61.7	28.5	1.1	3.8	6.0
Broadview Heights city *Cuyahoga Co.*	27.1	56.2	0.5	6.6	10.1
Brook Park city *Cuyahoga Co.*	30.0	47.6	1.1	8.7	13.7
Brunswick city *Medina Co.*	29.8	51.8	1.2	6.2	12.2
Canton city *Stark Co.*	40.7	35.2	2.3	7.5	16.6
Centerville city *Montgomery Co.*	24.3	56.1	1.2	8.7	10.9
Chillicothe city *Ross Co.*	29.0	42.6	2.7	9.2	19.2
Cincinnati city *Hamilton Co.*	51.6	30.5	2.7	5.5	12.5
Cleveland city *Cuyahoga Co.*	50.3	28.8	3.5	6.6	14.3
Cleveland Heights city *Cuyahoga Co.*	43.3	40.5	1.4	4.9	11.3
Columbus city *Franklin Co.*	44.3	38.8	2.3	4.4	12.5
Cuyahoga Falls city *Summit Co.*	30.1	49.8	1.1	6.8	13.3
Dayton city *Montgomery Co.*	47.7	31.1	3.0	6.3	15.0
Delaware city *Delaware Co.*	30.9	51.8	1.7	5.1	12.2
Dublin city *Franklin Co.*	21.6	68.2	0.4	3.0	7.2
Elyria city *Lorain Co.*	36.3	42.6	1.9	7.1	13.9
Euclid city *Cuyahoga Co.*	43.2	34.6	2.8	8.1	14.1
Fairborn city *Greene Co.*	36.4	43.8	1.9	6.1	13.7
Fairfield city *Butler Co.*	29.7	51.8	2.1	6.0	12.4
Findlay city *Hancock Co.*	31.9	47.4	2.0	7.9	12.8
Forest Park city *Hamilton Co.*	34.9	47.6	1.9	4.9	12.6
Gahanna city *Franklin Co.*	26.4	55.6	1.6	5.0	13.1
Garfield Heights city *Cuyahoga Co.*	41.8	37.0	2.0	7.3	13.9
Green city *Summit Co.*	26.0	58.6	1.0	6.5	8.9
Grove City city *Franklin Co.*	25.7	57.0	1.7	5.3	12.0
Hamilton city *Butler Co.*	33.4	42.7	3.0	7.3	16.6
Hilliard city *Franklin Co.*	26.7	60.4	1.3	5.0	8.0
Huber Heights city *Montgomery Co.*	27.0	54.1	2.1	6.5	12.3
Hudson city *Summit Co.*	20.3	69.7	0.5	4.2	5.8
Kent city *Portage Co.*	62.1	26.6	1.0	3.0	8.2
Kettering city *Montgomery Co.*	30.0	47.8	1.4	7.1	15.1
Lakewood city *Cuyahoga Co.*	43.8	38.6	1.5	4.9	12.7
Lancaster city *Fairfield Co.*	29.2	46.9	2.8	7.7	16.2
Lebanon city *Warren Co.*	29.9	51.6	1.0	5.9	12.6
Lima city *Allen Co.*	45.0	32.1	2.2	6.2	16.7
Lorain city *Lorain Co.*	36.7	42.3	3.2	7.3	13.7
Mansfield city *Richland Co.*	35.8	39.8	3.7	8.3	16.1
Maple Heights city *Cuyahoga Co.*	44.5	32.6	2.3	7.6	15.3
Marion city *Marion Co.*	34.4	41.7	3.0	7.2	16.7

Place	Never Married (%)	Now Married[1] (%)	Separated (%)	Widowed (%)	Divorced (%)
Marysville city *Union Co.*	31.5	48.7	2.1	5.5	14.2
Mason city *Warren Co.*	24.4	61.2	1.4	5.5	8.9
Massillon city *Stark Co.*	31.5	45.7	1.4	6.5	16.3
Mayfield Heights city *Cuyahoga Co.*	32.8	42.9	1.1	10.8	13.4
Medina city *Medina Co.*	29.6	52.1	1.5	6.5	11.9
Mentor city *Lake Co.*	24.5	57.5	0.6	7.3	10.7
Miamisburg city *Montgomery Co.*	23.0	53.8	1.4	9.0	14.2
Middletown city *Butler Co.*	31.3	45.1	3.3	7.2	16.4
Newark city *Licking Co.*	32.1	44.5	2.4	7.8	15.7
Niles city *Trumbull Co.*	32.6	42.5	2.7	8.0	17.0
North Olmsted city *Cuyahoga Co.*	29.6	54.2	1.2	6.5	9.6
North Ridgeville city *Lorain Co.*	21.7	61.9	1.3	6.7	9.6
North Royalton city *Cuyahoga Co.*	28.8	53.9	0.6	6.5	10.8
Norwood city *Hamilton Co.*	47.5	33.4	2.3	6.6	12.5
Oregon city *Lucas Co.*	30.2	49.4	1.4	6.9	13.6
Oxford city *Butler Co.*	78.9	16.2	0.8	1.6	3.4
Painesville city *Lake Co.*	40.3	42.4	2.4	4.8	12.5
Parma city *Cuyahoga Co.*	31.6	48.8	1.1	8.0	11.6
Parma Heights city *Cuyahoga Co.*	32.7	45.8	0.5	8.4	13.1
Perrysburg city *Wood Co.*	27.2	59.3	1.0	6.0	7.6
Pickerington city *Fairfield Co.*	26.1	59.8	1.2	4.4	9.7
Piqua city *Miami Co.*	31.4	42.3	1.3	9.3	17.0
Portsmouth city *Scioto Co.*	35.5	37.0	2.6	9.9	17.6
Reynoldsburg city *Franklin Co.*	33.6	47.2	1.8	4.5	14.6
Riverside city *Montgomery Co.*	30.6	47.1	1.8	7.7	14.6
Rocky River city *Cuyahoga Co.*	29.9	49.7	1.6	10.2	10.1
Sandusky city *Erie Co.*	37.7	38.2	2.9	8.6	15.5
Shaker Heights city *Cuyahoga Co.*	31.8	53.5	1.5	4.9	9.7
Sidney city *Shelby Co.*	28.4	49.5	1.8	8.4	13.8
Solon city *Cuyahoga Co.*	21.6	64.8	0.8	5.8	7.9
South Euclid city *Cuyahoga Co.*	40.8	43.7	1.4	5.2	10.3
Springfield city *Clark Co.*	36.4	38.6	3.1	8.8	16.1
Stow city *Summit Co.*	26.4	56.0	0.9	5.9	11.7
Strongsville city *Cuyahoga Co.*	22.6	60.6	0.6	7.0	9.8
Sylvania city *Lucas Co.*	26.3	55.6	0.9	8.0	10.1
Toledo city *Lucas Co.*	41.2	36.6	2.3	6.7	15.6
Trotwood city *Montgomery Co.*	40.2	36.0	2.8	8.4	15.4
Troy city *Miami Co.*	28.9	50.0	1.8	6.2	15.0
Twinsburg city *Summit Co.*	25.8	57.9	0.4	7.8	8.6
Upper Arlington city *Franklin Co.*	23.1	63.9	0.8	4.8	8.1
Wadsworth city *Medina Co.*	25.2	55.7	1.5	6.6	12.6
Warren city *Trumbull Co.*	41.0	34.5	2.3	8.7	15.8
Westerville city *Franklin Co.*	26.9	56.4	1.3	6.7	10.0
Westlake city *Cuyahoga Co.*	24.8	56.0	1.4	8.4	10.8
White Oak CDP *Hamilton Co.*	28.1	53.1	1.7	6.4	12.4
Willoughby city *Lake Co.*	30.7	47.0	1.2	8.8	13.5
Wooster city *Wayne Co.*	34.9	46.1	1.3	6.3	12.7
Xenia city *Greene Co.*	30.9	45.3	1.6	8.6	15.2
Youngstown city *Mahoning Co.*	44.9	30.8	2.9	8.8	15.6
Zanesville city *Muskingum Co.*	32.8	39.3	3.3	9.1	18.8

NOTE: (1) Includes separated.
SOURCE: U.S. Census Bureau, American Community Survey, 2012-2016 Five-Year Estimates

Employment by Occupation

Place	MBF[1] (%)	CES[2] (%)	ELCAM[3] (%)	HPT[4] (%)	S[5] (%)	SO[6] (%)	NRCM[7] (%)	PTMM[8] (%)
Akron city *Summit Co.*	10.2	3.6	9.8	5.1	21.7	26.8	6.2	16.6
Alliance city *Stark Co.*	7.3	3.3	6.6	3.6	22.1	23.8	6.7	26.6
Ashland city *Ashland Co.*	12.3	2.9	11.6	5.4	18.5	24.7	5.4	19.3
Athens city *Athens Co.*	7.5	5.7	25.6	3.0	28.4	21.8	2.5	5.4
Austintown CDP *Mahoning Co.*	11.1	2.4	9.6	7.3	21.2	23.2	8.3	16.8
Avon city *Lorain Co.*	23.4	6.5	11.2	8.4	12.7	27.5	4.7	5.7
Avon Lake city *Lorain Co.*	23.2	4.1	14.0	8.9	11.8	26.5	4.0	7.4
Barberton city *Summit Co.*	9.0	3.9	6.1	5.9	21.8	25.9	8.8	18.6
Beavercreek city *Greene Co.*	22.1	12.0	11.0	9.9	12.5	21.5	4.0	7.1
Berea city *Cuyahoga Co.*	14.6	6.8	12.7	4.5	15.9	27.2	6.7	11.6
Boardman CDP *Mahoning Co.*	13.7	3.3	10.9	8.8	16.2	27.6	7.7	11.8
Bowling Green city *Wood Co.*	8.8	3.0	17.6	2.6	27.1	25.0	5.1	10.8
Broadview Heights city *Cuyahoga Co.*	20.6	8.9	9.5	10.0	12.7	23.5	4.3	10.6
Brook Park city *Cuyahoga Co.*	8.8	2.6	6.7	5.7	17.6	29.8	9.2	19.7
Brunswick city *Medina Co.*	13.4	5.3	7.4	6.9	17.0	27.0	7.7	15.4
Canton city *Stark Co.*	8.1	2.9	8.0	5.4	26.6	22.6	8.0	18.4
Centerville city *Montgomery Co.*	20.0	7.7	13.3	9.6	13.6	25.1	2.9	7.6
Chillicothe city *Ross Co.*	7.7	2.9	8.2	8.0	23.9	24.8	8.4	16.0
Cincinnati city *Hamilton Co.*	14.3	6.5	12.5	6.4	21.4	22.2	4.7	12.0
Cleveland city *Cuyahoga Co.*	10.1	3.2	8.6	5.1	26.4	22.9	6.0	17.7
Cleveland Heights city *Cuyahoga Co.*	15.7	7.8	22.4	11.6	13.7	19.0	3.4	6.5
Columbus city *Franklin Co.*	15.5	6.9	11.1	5.9	18.2	25.4	5.0	12.1
Cuyahoga Falls city *Summit Co.*	13.5	6.8	10.9	6.7	15.5	27.5	7.7	11.4
Dayton city *Montgomery Co.*	9.2	4.8	9.9	4.8	24.9	23.3	6.8	16.4
Delaware city *Delaware Co.*	15.5	6.3	12.9	6.3	17.7	22.7	6.6	12.0
Dublin city *Franklin Co.*	30.1	15.6	10.8	9.2	7.9	21.1	1.5	3.8
Elyria city *Lorain Co.*	8.0	3.6	6.8	6.3	22.2	23.7	8.4	21.0
Euclid city *Cuyahoga Co.*	10.3	3.5	7.8	6.3	22.7	29.8	4.4	15.4
Fairborn city *Greene Co.*	11.0	7.6	8.8	5.7	17.3	29.4	6.6	13.6
Fairfield city *Butler Co.*	15.4	4.7	9.0	6.6	16.3	24.6	6.3	17.1
Findlay city *Hancock Co.*	15.4	5.8	8.1	4.2	19.1	19.1	6.8	21.4
Forest Park city *Hamilton Co.*	11.9	3.8	7.9	5.9	18.9	26.7	7.3	17.7
Gahanna city *Franklin Co.*	24.0	7.6	13.8	5.1	16.0	22.5	3.8	7.2
Garfield Heights city *Cuyahoga Co.*	10.0	3.5	8.1	5.6	19.6	29.9	7.1	16.2
Green city *Summit Co.*	15.8	5.7	12.2	7.2	15.1	25.9	6.4	11.8
Grove City city *Franklin Co.*	14.5	5.2	10.4	7.9	14.9	28.1	8.1	10.9
Hamilton city *Butler Co.*	8.9	3.0	6.7	6.5	21.8	25.9	8.7	18.6
Hilliard city *Franklin Co.*	22.8	10.3	12.4	8.4	12.4	24.4	2.4	6.8
Huber Heights city *Montgomery Co.*	12.9	6.9	7.7	7.6	18.0	24.0	5.9	17.0
Hudson city *Summit Co.*	30.3	7.1	16.4	6.5	10.0	23.0	2.1	4.5
Kent city *Portage Co.*	9.4	3.9	17.4	3.7	23.8	24.4	4.7	12.8
Kettering city *Montgomery Co.*	13.5	7.1	12.0	9.0	16.6	25.6	5.6	10.7
Lakewood city *Cuyahoga Co.*	18.0	5.6	15.9	7.9	15.1	23.2	5.5	8.8
Lancaster city *Fairfield Co.*	11.5	2.4	7.5	5.7	22.1	27.2	7.8	15.7
Lebanon city *Warren Co.*	12.7	5.8	9.3	6.1	16.7	27.3	8.6	13.4
Lima city *Allen Co.*	6.0	1.5	6.5	5.7	25.9	20.0	6.1	28.1
Lorain city *Lorain Co.*	8.7	2.6	7.3	4.9	21.3	23.4	9.3	22.5
Mansfield city *Richland Co.*	8.7	2.9	7.7	5.4	22.5	28.0	4.5	20.3
Maple Heights city *Cuyahoga Co.*	10.9	3.2	6.0	5.9	23.8	27.0	5.5	17.6
Marion city *Marion Co.*	6.8	2.2	6.4	5.0	20.9	21.0	7.3	30.3

Place	MBF[1] (%)	CES[2] (%)	ELCAM[3] (%)	HPT[4] (%)	S[5] (%)	SO[6] (%)	NRCM[7] (%)	PTMM[8] (%)
Marysville city *Union Co.*	15.8	9.5	7.6	4.9	17.5	21.2	7.4	16.0
Mason city *Warren Co.*	26.6	10.3	12.2	6.7	11.0	22.9	4.0	6.4
Massillon city *Stark Co.*	8.3	3.1	7.9	6.0	20.1	25.9	8.8	20.0
Mayfield Heights city *Cuyahoga Co.*	16.6	12.4	10.6	8.1	18.0	23.9	4.4	6.1
Medina city *Medina Co.*	15.7	5.0	10.0	6.1	14.3	29.7	8.0	11.3
Mentor city *Lake Co.*	17.8	7.2	9.1	6.7	14.3	26.9	6.2	11.7
Miamisburg city *Montgomery Co.*	16.2	7.4	8.6	6.3	17.4	23.2	5.9	15.0
Middletown city *Butler Co.*	9.9	3.4	7.7	5.0	20.1	25.1	8.1	20.8
Newark city *Licking Co.*	12.3	3.8	8.5	5.2	21.9	24.7	7.1	16.7
Niles city *Trumbull Co.*	7.3	1.7	8.4	6.8	23.6	24.7	9.5	18.1
North Olmsted city *Cuyahoga Co.*	14.6	6.9	9.6	6.1	16.7	26.8	7.2	12.1
North Ridgeville city *Lorain Co.*	16.3	5.8	10.6	8.8	14.1	26.3	6.5	11.5
North Royalton city *Cuyahoga Co.*	20.2	5.0	8.6	9.4	14.2	25.6	6.9	10.1
Norwood city *Hamilton Co.*	15.4	5.9	8.6	6.0	20.2	26.4	6.4	11.2
Oregon city *Lucas Co.*	9.1	3.9	7.2	9.2	17.2	23.3	10.9	19.4
Oxford city *Butler Co.*	10.3	4.0	22.6	2.8	32.2	18.0	3.1	6.9
Painesville city *Lake Co.*	8.7	3.5	8.4	3.0	24.0	20.5	8.6	23.3
Parma city *Cuyahoga Co.*	11.1	4.6	7.3	7.3	17.5	27.4	8.1	16.6
Parma Heights city *Cuyahoga Co.*	11.9	6.5	7.6	6.0	18.2	29.6	6.8	13.4
Perrysburg city *Wood Co.*	24.2	6.9	14.5	8.6	13.2	21.9	4.0	6.7
Pickerington city *Fairfield Co.*	19.4	5.4	10.4	8.2	16.9	25.9	5.6	8.2
Piqua city *Miami Co.*	6.3	4.6	7.3	3.9	19.6	23.8	8.0	26.6
Portsmouth city *Scioto Co.*	9.6	3.7	9.8	11.0	28.3	24.0	3.8	9.8
Reynoldsburg city *Franklin Co.*	14.9	6.8	10.3	4.3	16.6	30.2	7.2	9.7
Riverside city *Montgomery Co.*	12.5	7.3	5.7	6.5	19.6	23.3	8.8	16.3
Rocky River city *Cuyahoga Co.*	26.8	7.4	13.9	8.9	12.6	19.8	2.7	7.9
Sandusky city *Erie Co.*	8.6	1.1	7.3	4.7	29.5	22.4	5.2	21.3
Shaker Heights city *Cuyahoga Co.*	20.4	7.2	23.4	14.0	10.5	17.3	2.3	4.9
Sidney city *Shelby Co.*	10.8	4.6	6.8	3.9	18.5	20.5	5.6	29.4
Solon city *Cuyahoga Co.*	23.5	7.7	15.3	10.4	14.0	21.3	3.2	4.6
South Euclid city *Cuyahoga Co.*	15.0	5.5	11.5	8.3	19.5	25.1	4.7	10.2
Springfield city *Clark Co.*	9.2	2.1	8.9	4.5	23.4	23.8	5.7	22.3
Stow city *Summit Co.*	17.8	8.0	12.3	8.2	14.8	26.7	3.2	9.0
Strongsville city *Cuyahoga Co.*	21.8	7.8	10.6	7.5	12.8	26.8	4.2	8.5
Sylvania city *Lucas Co.*	20.2	7.2	13.9	10.1	14.1	22.5	3.9	8.1
Toledo city *Lucas Co.*	9.2	3.2	8.6	5.9	22.5	24.1	7.0	19.7
Trotwood city *Montgomery Co.*	9.7	2.6	7.3	5.3	26.4	23.7	4.5	20.6
Troy city *Miami Co.*	12.2	7.0	8.5	4.3	15.9	22.7	6.2	23.3
Twinsburg city *Summit Co.*	21.0	9.9	10.7	6.6	12.7	26.7	3.4	9.0
Upper Arlington city *Franklin Co.*	25.3	9.0	20.1	12.8	7.8	20.4	2.2	2.4
Wadsworth city *Medina Co.*	17.6	6.7	10.6	8.0	14.9	22.1	8.6	11.4
Warren city *Trumbull Co.*	9.5	2.6	7.9	6.5	23.6	24.9	5.7	19.3
Westerville city *Franklin Co.*	25.3	7.3	15.3	5.9	12.3	24.4	3.8	5.6
Westlake city *Cuyahoga Co.*	25.2	6.5	12.9	10.6	11.8	24.4	3.5	5.0
White Oak CDP *Hamilton Co.*	12.9	4.1	8.4	10.0	21.3	25.9	5.3	12.1
Willoughby city *Lake Co.*	14.8	6.2	10.3	7.8	16.4	24.7	6.5	13.2
Wooster city *Wayne Co.*	12.0	6.3	13.9	4.8	20.2	20.5	5.9	16.4
Xenia city *Greene Co.*	11.6	4.2	9.5	6.3	18.1	27.6	9.1	13.4
Youngstown city *Mahoning Co.*	6.6	1.8	8.0	5.4	27.3	24.4	6.9	19.5
Zanesville city *Muskingum Co.*	6.2	2.5	7.0	7.4	25.4	26.6	6.8	18.2

NOTES: (1) Management, business, and financial occupations; (2) Computer, engineering, and science occupations; (3) Education, legal, community service, arts, and media occupations; (4) Healthcare practitioners and technical occupations; (5) Service occupations; (6) Sales and office occupations; (7) Natural resources, construction, and maintenance occupations; (8) Production, transportation, and material moving occupations
SOURCE: U.S. Census Bureau, American Community Survey, 2012-2016 Five-Year Estimates

Educational Attainment

Place	Percent of Population 25 Years and Over with: High School Diploma or Higher[1]	Bachelor's Degree or Higher	Graduate/Professional Degree
Akron city *Summit Co.*	86.4	20.2	6.8
Alliance city *Stark Co.*	85.0	14.8	5.0
Ashland city *Ashland Co.*	87.0	26.8	10.1
Athens city *Athens Co.*	96.2	63.2	38.7
Austintown CDP *Mahoning Co.*	91.4	21.1	6.7
Avon city *Lorain Co.*	95.7	47.2	18.2
Avon Lake city *Lorain Co.*	96.3	51.5	20.0
Barberton city *Summit Co.*	84.2	12.7	3.1
Beavercreek city *Greene Co.*	97.3	50.0	25.0
Berea city *Cuyahoga Co.*	92.1	32.9	12.3
Boardman CDP *Mahoning Co.*	93.9	29.6	10.2
Bowling Green city *Wood Co.*	93.9	42.4	22.5
Broadview Heights city *Cuyahoga Co.*	96.2	45.7	19.9
Brook Park city *Cuyahoga Co.*	87.0	12.6	3.5
Brunswick city *Medina Co.*	91.7	23.5	6.7
Canton city *Stark Co.*	84.4	14.6	4.9
Centerville city *Montgomery Co.*	95.8	51.4	21.9
Chillicothe city *Ross Co.*	85.6	18.8	7.3
Cincinnati city *Hamilton Co.*	86.2	33.8	14.1
Cleveland city *Cuyahoga Co.*	78.4	16.1	5.9
Cleveland Heights city *Cuyahoga Co.*	93.7	51.0	26.8
Columbus city *Franklin Co.*	88.8	34.8	11.9
Cuyahoga Falls city *Summit Co.*	93.8	32.4	10.4
Dayton city *Montgomery Co.*	83.1	17.6	6.5
Delaware city *Delaware Co.*	93.6	34.3	13.3
Dublin city *Franklin Co.*	98.5	75.3	30.7
Elyria city *Lorain Co.*	86.7	15.4	5.2
Euclid city *Cuyahoga Co.*	89.3	20.6	6.6
Fairborn city *Greene Co.*	87.5	26.8	11.7
Fairfield city *Butler Co.*	91.3	28.2	10.1
Findlay city *Hancock Co.*	91.0	26.8	9.6
Forest Park city *Hamilton Co.*	89.1	27.2	8.1
Gahanna city *Franklin Co.*	95.2	46.1	17.1
Garfield Heights city *Cuyahoga Co.*	85.5	14.1	5.3
Green city *Summit Co.*	94.3	35.1	11.7
Grove City city *Franklin Co.*	94.5	29.9	8.4
Hamilton city *Butler Co.*	84.7	15.1	4.6
Hilliard city *Franklin Co.*	96.3	52.1	20.5
Huber Heights city *Montgomery Co.*	92.9	23.6	9.2
Hudson city *Summit Co.*	97.9	70.7	31.0
Kent city *Portage Co.*	94.1	42.1	19.9
Kettering city *Montgomery Co.*	94.1	33.6	14.0
Lakewood city *Cuyahoga Co.*	93.9	43.7	16.0
Lancaster city *Fairfield Co.*	87.6	16.5	5.3
Lebanon city *Warren Co.*	93.1	29.2	7.7
Lima city *Allen Co.*	83.7	11.5	4.1
Lorain city *Lorain Co.*	82.4	11.7	4.4
Mansfield city *Richland Co.*	83.5	13.8	4.2
Maple Heights city *Cuyahoga Co.*	89.0	15.4	4.6
Marion city *Marion Co.*	83.2	9.4	3.6

Place	Percent of Population 25 Years and Over with: High School Diploma or Higher[1]	Bachelor's Degree or Higher	Graduate/Professional Degree
Marysville city *Union Co.*	89.2	27.2	7.8
Mason city *Warren Co.*	97.5	59.3	26.0
Massillon city *Stark Co.*	89.3	16.3	6.1
Mayfield Heights city *Cuyahoga Co.*	93.5	37.2	15.3
Medina city *Medina Co.*	94.5	35.5	10.9
Mentor city *Lake Co.*	94.7	32.2	11.9
Miamisburg city *Montgomery Co.*	91.6	22.6	7.9
Middletown city *Butler Co.*	82.5	16.8	4.5
Newark city *Licking Co.*	87.1	18.1	6.0
Niles city *Trumbull Co.*	89.3	16.8	4.7
North Olmsted city *Cuyahoga Co.*	92.6	29.0	9.0
North Ridgeville city *Lorain Co.*	92.3	32.6	11.5
North Royalton city *Cuyahoga Co.*	93.1	36.0	13.7
Norwood city *Hamilton Co.*	84.0	28.3	8.2
Oregon city *Lucas Co.*	90.2	18.3	6.4
Oxford city *Butler Co.*	90.7	58.8	33.1
Painesville city *Lake Co.*	79.2	14.7	4.2
Parma city *Cuyahoga Co.*	90.1	20.0	6.4
Parma Heights city *Cuyahoga Co.*	90.9	22.6	6.5
Perrysburg city *Wood Co.*	97.1	51.0	20.9
Pickerington city *Fairfield Co.*	94.9	38.6	12.3
Piqua city *Miami Co.*	85.6	11.4	4.3
Portsmouth city *Scioto Co.*	80.7	16.7	5.9
Reynoldsburg city *Franklin Co.*	93.8	31.4	10.8
Riverside city *Montgomery Co.*	86.9	18.0	6.6
Rocky River city *Cuyahoga Co.*	95.7	55.2	25.7
Sandusky city *Erie Co.*	85.3	16.2	4.8
Shaker Heights city *Cuyahoga Co.*	96.2	64.9	39.9
Sidney city *Shelby Co.*	88.0	16.2	6.8
Solon city *Cuyahoga Co.*	96.9	62.0	31.6
South Euclid city *Cuyahoga Co.*	92.8	39.5	17.0
Springfield city *Clark Co.*	83.1	14.9	5.5
Stow city *Summit Co.*	94.9	42.9	16.1
Strongsville city *Cuyahoga Co.*	95.9	44.6	17.3
Sylvania city *Lucas Co.*	95.8	43.1	15.6
Toledo city *Lucas Co.*	85.7	18.0	6.4
Trotwood city *Montgomery Co.*	86.2	15.1	5.6
Troy city *Miami Co.*	88.5	23.3	6.9
Twinsburg city *Summit Co.*	95.1	45.8	16.8
Upper Arlington city *Franklin Co.*	98.7	74.0	35.4
Wadsworth city *Medina Co.*	94.6	35.4	12.1
Warren city *Trumbull Co.*	84.9	12.8	3.2
Westerville city *Franklin Co.*	96.7	52.5	19.5
Westlake city *Cuyahoga Co.*	96.4	52.5	21.1
White Oak CDP *Hamilton Co.*	88.6	25.4	9.0
Willoughby city *Lake Co.*	93.3	30.7	9.5
Wooster city *Wayne Co.*	90.1	28.7	12.8
Xenia city *Greene Co.*	87.9	19.5	7.6
Youngstown city *Mahoning Co.*	83.0	12.0	3.5
Zanesville city *Muskingum Co.*	80.8	12.1	4.3

NOTE: (1) Includes General Equivalency Diploma (GED)
SOURCE: U.S. Census Bureau, American Community Survey, 2012-2016 Five-Year Estimates

Health Insurance

Place	Percent of Total Population with: Any Insurance	Private Insurance	Public Insurance	No Insurance	Percent of Population[1] Under Age 18 without Health Insurance
Akron city *Summit Co.*	87.9	55.3	43.4	12.1	6.1
Alliance city *Stark Co.*	90.0	60.1	45.2	10.0	6.1
Ashland city *Ashland Co.*	92.4	72.0	35.4	7.6	3.0
Athens city *Athens Co.*	95.0	86.0	13.8	5.0	2.0
Austintown CDP *Mahoning Co.*	91.4	67.5	38.7	8.6	6.3
Avon city *Lorain Co.*	97.8	89.6	22.3	2.2	0.5
Avon Lake city *Lorain Co.*	97.3	87.7	23.0	2.7	0.7
Barberton city *Summit Co.*	87.4	57.7	41.9	12.6	10.5
Beavercreek city *Greene Co.*	96.6	88.0	23.4	3.4	3.2
Berea city *Cuyahoga Co.*	94.3	81.4	25.4	5.7	2.2
Boardman CDP *Mahoning Co.*	92.5	73.9	33.6	7.5	6.0
Bowling Green city *Wood Co.*	94.4	84.0	20.0	5.6	2.5
Broadview Heights city *Cuyahoga Co.*	93.9	83.1	22.2	6.1	3.7
Brook Park city *Cuyahoga Co.*	92.1	72.5	34.8	7.9	3.0
Brunswick city *Medina Co.*	94.3	80.5	26.4	5.7	0.9
Canton city *Stark Co.*	88.9	49.8	50.7	11.1	4.4
Centerville city *Montgomery Co.*	96.5	80.8	35.3	3.5	1.5
Chillicothe city *Ross Co.*	89.4	55.3	50.6	10.6	4.6
Cincinnati city *Hamilton Co.*	89.1	57.4	39.7	10.9	4.2
Cleveland city *Cuyahoga Co.*	87.8	43.1	53.9	12.2	3.7
Cleveland Heights city *Cuyahoga Co.*	93.2	69.3	35.9	6.8	4.7
Columbus city *Franklin Co.*	88.1	63.7	32.0	11.9	5.8
Cuyahoga Falls city *Summit Co.*	93.4	76.6	29.8	6.6	3.1
Dayton city *Montgomery Co.*	87.1	49.0	48.6	12.9	5.3
Delaware city *Delaware Co.*	92.9	77.5	25.4	7.1	3.0
Dublin city *Franklin Co.*	97.9	93.5	11.4	2.1	1.2
Elyria city *Lorain Co.*	90.4	62.5	41.8	9.6	2.4
Euclid city *Cuyahoga Co.*	89.8	61.3	40.8	10.2	5.3
Fairborn city *Greene Co.*	89.4	63.1	38.8	10.6	4.7
Fairfield city *Butler Co.*	88.7	73.4	25.7	11.3	3.8
Findlay city *Hancock Co.*	90.5	70.7	34.7	9.5	4.9
Forest Park city *Hamilton Co.*	89.7	65.8	34.1	10.3	0.9
Gahanna city *Franklin Co.*	94.7	81.6	23.4	5.3	3.3
Garfield Heights city *Cuyahoga Co.*	90.6	62.3	42.8	9.4	2.4
Green city *Summit Co.*	94.5	79.4	26.7	5.5	2.8
Grove City city *Franklin Co.*	93.6	80.7	23.7	6.4	3.3
Hamilton city *Butler Co.*	88.6	57.3	42.6	11.4	3.7
Hilliard city *Franklin Co.*	94.6	84.7	18.3	5.4	2.2
Huber Heights city *Montgomery Co.*	90.1	68.9	36.0	9.9	6.3
Hudson city *Summit Co.*	97.3	92.6	16.9	2.7	2.5
Kent city *Portage Co.*	89.5	70.8	25.9	10.5	6.4
Kettering city *Montgomery Co.*	92.2	73.0	33.1	7.8	4.2
Lakewood city *Cuyahoga Co.*	90.4	70.1	28.4	9.6	3.4
Lancaster city *Fairfield Co.*	91.4	59.5	45.1	8.6	1.1
Lebanon city *Warren Co.*	90.3	70.6	28.1	9.7	8.9
Lima city *Allen Co.*	86.4	53.0	46.2	13.6	4.4
Lorain city *Lorain Co.*	90.1	52.7	49.2	9.9	2.7
Mansfield city *Richland Co.*	88.9	54.4	49.9	11.1	3.9
Maple Heights city *Cuyahoga Co.*	92.1	57.9	47.1	7.9	0.9
Marion city *Marion Co.*	89.7	54.3	49.7	10.3	3.5

Place	Percent of Total Population with: Any Insurance	Private Insurance	Public Insurance	No Insurance	Percent of Population[1] Under Age 18 without Health Insurance
Marysville city *Union Co.*	94.2	79.8	24.8	5.8	2.1
Mason city *Warren Co.*	96.7	89.4	17.1	3.3	2.0
Massillon city *Stark Co.*	92.5	65.5	43.4	7.5	4.0
Mayfield Heights city *Cuyahoga Co.*	92.2	73.0	35.1	7.8	8.1
Medina city *Medina Co.*	92.9	78.3	24.6	7.1	4.5
Mentor city *Lake Co.*	95.8	84.1	27.3	4.2	2.2
Miamisburg city *Montgomery Co.*	93.8	71.1	37.0	6.2	1.2
Middletown city *Butler Co.*	88.5	51.7	48.9	11.5	4.2
Newark city *Licking Co.*	89.8	58.8	44.3	10.2	2.0
Niles city *Trumbull Co.*	87.0	59.8	41.8	13.0	11.3
North Olmsted city *Cuyahoga Co.*	92.9	77.1	31.5	7.1	4.3
North Ridgeville city *Lorain Co.*	95.5	83.1	27.6	4.5	1.6
North Royalton city *Cuyahoga Co.*	91.8	79.2	25.8	8.2	3.4
Norwood city *Hamilton Co.*	88.2	63.1	33.4	11.8	7.2
Oregon city *Lucas Co.*	93.6	75.1	34.3	6.4	3.2
Oxford city *Butler Co.*	95.6	89.2	11.6	4.4	1.7
Painesville city *Lake Co.*	87.3	56.9	38.2	12.7	6.7
Parma city *Cuyahoga Co.*	92.3	72.1	34.4	7.7	5.0
Parma Heights city *Cuyahoga Co.*	93.5	71.0	36.8	6.5	3.6
Perrysburg city *Wood Co.*	96.3	88.2	18.5	3.7	2.6
Pickerington city *Fairfield Co.*	96.9	86.0	19.8	3.1	1.2
Piqua city *Miami Co.*	90.0	62.9	44.2	10.0	2.7
Portsmouth city *Scioto Co.*	87.7	43.2	56.0	12.3	4.0
Reynoldsburg city *Franklin Co.*	92.3	76.2	27.1	7.7	4.2
Riverside city *Montgomery Co.*	88.8	63.3	38.4	11.2	5.6
Rocky River city *Cuyahoga Co.*	95.0	84.7	28.3	5.0	3.0
Sandusky city *Erie Co.*	89.4	54.5	50.0	10.6	4.5
Shaker Heights city *Cuyahoga Co.*	96.5	82.6	26.9	3.5	1.1
Sidney city *Shelby Co.*	92.9	70.7	37.3	7.1	2.7
Solon city *Cuyahoga Co.*	97.5	86.9	22.0	2.5	1.4
South Euclid city *Cuyahoga Co.*	92.1	75.9	26.5	7.9	3.8
Springfield city *Clark Co.*	90.5	53.1	51.3	9.5	1.6
Stow city *Summit Co.*	96.2	84.4	22.6	3.8	0.7
Strongsville city *Cuyahoga Co.*	96.3	84.5	25.7	3.7	1.0
Sylvania city *Lucas Co.*	96.2	83.4	27.3	3.8	1.7
Toledo city *Lucas Co.*	89.6	56.9	44.6	10.4	3.8
Trotwood city *Montgomery Co.*	90.0	53.4	51.9	10.0	4.3
Troy city *Miami Co.*	92.7	73.6	32.3	7.3	4.2
Twinsburg city *Summit Co.*	96.7	86.0	24.7	3.3	2.7
Upper Arlington city *Franklin Co.*	96.8	88.4	21.4	3.2	1.6
Wadsworth city *Medina Co.*	93.4	78.3	28.0	6.6	4.7
Warren city *Trumbull Co.*	90.1	45.9	56.6	9.9	1.9
Westerville city *Franklin Co.*	95.5	85.5	22.5	4.5	1.2
Westlake city *Cuyahoga Co.*	96.0	83.1	28.1	4.0	3.5
White Oak CDP *Hamilton Co.*	92.5	68.7	35.4	7.5	3.2
Willoughby city *Lake Co.*	93.2	78.4	28.9	6.8	3.0
Wooster city *Wayne Co.*	92.6	69.6	38.5	7.4	2.6
Xenia city *Greene Co.*	91.5	59.3	46.1	8.5	1.6
Youngstown city *Mahoning Co.*	89.1	40.0	60.7	10.9	3.0
Zanesville city *Muskingum Co.*	90.7	44.8	59.2	9.3	1.3

NOTE: (1) Civilian noninstitutionalized population.
SOURCE: U.S. Census Bureau, American Community Survey, 2012-2016 Five-Year Estimates

Income and Poverty

Place	Average Household Income ($)	Median Household Income ($)	Per Capita Income ($)	Households w/$100,000+ Income (%)	Poverty Rate (%)
Akron city *Summit Co.*	48,368	35,240	21,378	9.5	25.4
Alliance city *Stark Co.*	47,109	32,058	18,935	8.4	23.4
Ashland city *Ashland Co.*	52,911	39,417	21,897	12.0	16.4
Athens city *Athens Co.*	42,562	22,204	13,758	11.6	54.7
Austintown CDP *Mahoning Co.*	51,740	41,789	23,717	10.4	13.2
Avon city *Lorain Co.*	119,947	90,846	42,594	47.1	3.8
Avon Lake city *Lorain Co.*	106,163	80,884	41,668	40.2	3.8
Barberton city *Summit Co.*	50,545	39,456	21,163	8.7	18.0
Beavercreek city *Greene Co.*	99,010	82,956	40,639	39.7	4.8
Berea city *Cuyahoga Co.*	70,665	57,896	27,862	21.6	11.3
Boardman CDP *Mahoning Co.*	63,784	51,158	28,486	17.9	9.6
Bowling Green city *Wood Co.*	53,245	33,562	20,175	14.4	35.8
Broadview Heights city *Cuyahoga Co.*	105,617	77,480	42,092	38.0	4.1
Brook Park city *Cuyahoga Co.*	58,454	48,813	24,384	15.4	9.7
Brunswick city *Medina Co.*	75,976	64,706	30,391	24.8	8.0
Canton city *Stark Co.*	39,670	30,444	17,384	5.6	31.8
Centerville city *Montgomery Co.*	85,024	63,524	38,580	32.2	6.4
Chillicothe city *Ross Co.*	51,700	37,757	22,890	11.3	22.5
Cincinnati city *Hamilton Co.*	55,931	34,629	26,152	13.8	29.9
Cleveland city *Cuyahoga Co.*	40,057	26,583	18,003	7.0	36.0
Cleveland Heights city *Cuyahoga Co.*	73,782	53,901	31,887	22.9	20.2
Columbus city *Franklin Co.*	61,050	47,156	25,781	16.5	21.2
Cuyahoga Falls city *Summit Co.*	61,871	51,586	27,531	15.5	10.9
Dayton city *Montgomery Co.*	40,735	28,745	17,461	7.2	34.5
Delaware city *Delaware Co.*	73,259	58,472	28,129	23.5	9.8
Dublin city *Franklin Co.*	163,872	125,540	58,698	61.9	2.7
Elyria city *Lorain Co.*	50,422	40,967	21,727	10.7	22.2
Euclid city *Cuyahoga Co.*	46,671	35,949	22,471	9.3	21.5
Fairborn city *Greene Co.*	55,141	41,529	24,646	14.9	22.1
Fairfield city *Butler Co.*	70,398	60,336	28,653	20.9	7.6
Findlay city *Hancock Co.*	59,210	45,364	26,052	15.5	18.5
Forest Park city *Hamilton Co.*	59,749	52,750	23,286	14.1	16.4
Gahanna city *Franklin Co.*	96,031	73,535	37,283	35.0	6.3
Garfield Heights city *Cuyahoga Co.*	49,500	40,376	21,332	9.3	17.4
Green city *Summit Co.*	85,426	66,656	34,117	30.3	9.6
Grove City city *Franklin Co.*	77,947	65,277	30,632	27.2	7.8
Hamilton city *Butler Co.*	53,972	40,401	22,113	12.1	21.9
Hilliard city *Franklin Co.*	111,490	92,727	40,964	46.1	4.0
Huber Heights city *Montgomery Co.*	63,129	54,357	25,037	15.6	13.0
Hudson city *Summit Co.*	155,164	126,618	55,145	61.6	3.2
Kent city *Portage Co.*	53,253	36,539	19,872	13.8	34.4
Kettering city *Montgomery Co.*	67,143	51,441	30,579	17.7	12.6
Lakewood city *Cuyahoga Co.*	63,217	47,145	31,122	19.0	14.4
Lancaster city *Fairfield Co.*	51,321	38,625	21,740	12.5	20.5
Lebanon city *Warren Co.*	70,089	61,669	25,194	22.4	10.2
Lima city *Allen Co.*	42,178	30,953	16,705	6.2	28.5
Lorain city *Lorain Co.*	48,238	35,753	19,573	9.3	26.2
Mansfield city *Richland Co.*	46,386	33,257	18,476	8.0	25.6
Maple Heights city *Cuyahoga Co.*	46,843	37,911	19,983	7.9	21.1
Marion city *Marion Co.*	46,811	34,932	16,731	7.5	21.9

Place	Average Household Income ($)	Median Household Income ($)	Per Capita Income ($)	Households w/$100,000+ Income (%)	Poverty Rate (%)
Marysville city *Union Co.*	74,249	62,371	25,419	28.3	9.3
Mason city *Warren Co.*	121,969	92,819	46,005	46.5	2.6
Massillon city *Stark Co.*	54,490	42,808	22,548	12.5	18.3
Mayfield Heights city *Cuyahoga Co.*	58,682	45,875	29,955	14.2	9.3
Medina city *Medina Co.*	74,277	60,706	29,295	26.2	9.8
Mentor city *Lake Co.*	83,165	70,058	34,819	32.1	5.6
Miamisburg city *Montgomery Co.*	68,211	54,557	28,437	23.7	15.1
Middletown city *Butler Co.*	49,634	36,898	20,786	10.0	24.2
Newark city *Licking Co.*	53,000	38,913	22,226	12.6	21.8
Niles city *Trumbull Co.*	51,765	39,311	23,050	9.7	19.8
North Olmsted city *Cuyahoga Co.*	74,465	61,444	31,172	23.7	7.2
North Ridgeville city *Lorain Co.*	80,662	68,778	31,399	28.4	4.9
North Royalton city *Cuyahoga Co.*	85,697	66,189	36,649	30.6	5.3
Norwood city *Hamilton Co.*	54,207	40,306	25,030	13.5	22.0
Oregon city *Lucas Co.*	68,410	55,157	28,458	22.6	10.7
Oxford city *Butler Co.*	53,876	29,451	16,197	17.5	46.1
Painesville city *Lake Co.*	54,069	41,652	20,666	12.0	21.7
Parma city *Cuyahoga Co.*	59,920	51,383	25,715	15.1	10.2
Parma Heights city *Cuyahoga Co.*	53,903	44,564	24,654	11.2	11.2
Perrysburg city *Wood Co.*	104,476	84,508	41,668	40.1	5.0
Pickerington city *Fairfield Co.*	93,283	84,410	32,626	38.5	5.2
Piqua city *Miami Co.*	48,666	40,101	20,502	8.7	19.8
Portsmouth city *Scioto Co.*	43,185	27,769	18,701	7.8	34.2
Reynoldsburg city *Franklin Co.*	72,886	61,648	29,184	24.2	9.8
Riverside city *Montgomery Co.*	54,412	43,888	22,751	11.6	14.9
Rocky River city *Cuyahoga Co.*	108,531	65,226	48,301	34.3	4.7
Sandusky city *Erie Co.*	44,919	33,817	20,793	6.2	22.4
Shaker Heights city *Cuyahoga Co.*	130,025	79,519	52,441	39.7	8.1
Sidney city *Shelby Co.*	64,212	46,697	26,219	12.5	14.7
Solon city *Cuyahoga Co.*	134,570	96,976	49,223	48.7	4.8
South Euclid city *Cuyahoga Co.*	67,205	59,734	27,731	20.4	9.2
Springfield city *Clark Co.*	45,891	32,165	19,608	7.8	27.9
Stow city *Summit Co.*	79,639	66,079	33,475	27.9	5.5
Strongsville city *Cuyahoga Co.*	100,415	80,323	40,133	39.8	4.2
Sylvania city *Lucas Co.*	90,620	72,936	37,235	36.2	7.7
Toledo city *Lucas Co.*	46,477	34,548	20,317	9.2	27.5
Trotwood city *Montgomery Co.*	44,562	34,490	19,702	9.4	25.9
Troy city *Miami Co.*	62,328	47,743	27,279	17.2	12.2
Twinsburg city *Summit Co.*	87,382	73,314	35,955	35.3	5.9
Upper Arlington city *Franklin Co.*	144,048	102,094	57,331	50.9	5.1
Wadsworth city *Medina Co.*	74,086	62,607	29,035	24.9	6.8
Warren city *Trumbull Co.*	39,518	29,176	17,680	5.4	34.9
Westerville city *Franklin Co.*	99,308	85,230	38,779	42.0	6.5
Westlake city *Cuyahoga Co.*	118,080	80,989	51,230	39.4	4.9
White Oak CDP *Hamilton Co.*	74,749	60,264	30,620	23.3	12.6
Willoughby city *Lake Co.*	65,810	53,324	31,754	18.1	7.6
Wooster city *Wayne Co.*	57,804	41,703	24,311	12.5	19.3
Xenia city *Greene Co.*	51,563	38,426	21,867	9.6	24.6
Youngstown city *Mahoning Co.*	35,829	24,448	15,713	4.4	38.0
Zanesville city *Muskingum Co.*	37,551	26,039	16,858	4.9	30.8

SOURCE: U.S. Census Bureau, American Community Survey, 2012-2016 Five-Year Estimates

Housing

Place	Homeownership Rate (%)	Median Home Value ($)	Median Year Structure Built	Homeowner Vacancy Rate (%)	Median Gross Rent ($/month)	Rental Vacancy Rate (%)
Akron city *Summit Co.*	51.0	$80,000	1952	2.8	$693	7.8
Alliance city *Stark Co.*	52.1	$79,600	1952	1.9	$644	3.9
Ashland city *Ashland Co.*	60.0	$99,400	1961	2.8	$680	5.6
Athens city *Athens Co.*	29.4	$164,300	1970	1.8	$754	6.6
Austintown CDP *Mahoning Co.*	63.0	$93,800	1966	6.5	$614	13.7
Avon city *Lorain Co.*	80.9	$262,100	2000	0.6	$1,156	9.4
Avon Lake city *Lorain Co.*	79.7	$225,600	1988	2.0	$1,122	4.1
Barberton city *Summit Co.*	62.8	$85,800	1954	2.2	$676	7.9
Beavercreek city *Greene Co.*	71.2	$175,100	1980	1.2	$1,135	3.3
Berea city *Cuyahoga Co.*	67.7	$129,000	1960	0.5	$753	7.2
Boardman CDP *Mahoning Co.*	64.7	$112,100	1965	1.7	$630	4.9
Bowling Green city *Wood Co.*	39.3	$157,900	1978	1.5	$667	5.2
Broadview Heights city *Cuyahoga Co.*	81.0	$217,600	1981	2.4	$843	0.0
Brook Park city *Cuyahoga Co.*	76.7	$111,800	1961	1.2	$850	5.0
Brunswick city *Medina Co.*	77.2	$159,400	1977	1.4	$832	4.3
Canton city *Stark Co.*	49.2	$71,000	1948	2.2	$606	7.9
Centerville city *Montgomery Co.*	70.5	$179,600	1977	0.0	$853	7.9
Chillicothe city *Ross Co.*	58.4	$98,900	1954	4.4	$701	6.6
Cincinnati city *Hamilton Co.*	37.7	$120,300	1949	2.7	$662	7.5
Cleveland city *Cuyahoga Co.*	41.9	$67,500	Before 1940	3.0	$660	6.9
Cleveland Heights city *Cuyahoga Co.*	56.2	$127,700	Before 1940	3.3	$871	9.0
Columbus city *Franklin Co.*	45.0	$131,800	1976	1.8	$856	5.7
Cuyahoga Falls city *Summit Co.*	61.8	$120,000	1959	3.2	$798	7.3
Dayton city *Montgomery Co.*	48.4	$66,600	1948	4.5	$636	8.0
Delaware city *Delaware Co.*	62.5	$161,100	1988	1.2	$861	3.7
Dublin city *Franklin Co.*	75.7	$352,300	1993	0.7	$1,266	5.7
Elyria city *Lorain Co.*	58.3	$94,800	1965	2.6	$710	5.5
Euclid city *Cuyahoga Co.*	48.6	$80,700	1956	3.8	$734	13.1
Fairborn city *Greene Co.*	48.0	$109,700	1969	2.0	$762	5.3
Fairfield city *Butler Co.*	62.2	$146,800	1979	2.3	$844	6.8
Findlay city *Hancock Co.*	58.1	$123,800	1966	0.6	$715	4.9
Forest Park city *Hamilton Co.*	56.8	$111,300	1972	0.6	$881	9.0
Gahanna city *Franklin Co.*	71.5	$195,100	1984	0.6	$984	2.8
Garfield Heights city *Cuyahoga Co.*	67.0	$73,600	1954	1.1	$807	8.8
Green city *Summit Co.*	74.4	$173,600	1981	1.4	$772	4.5
Grove City city *Franklin Co.*	68.4	$162,400	1990	2.7	$912	3.0
Hamilton city *Butler Co.*	56.0	$99,900	1954	2.5	$749	6.9
Hilliard city *Franklin Co.*	77.3	$213,000	1993	0.8	$1,004	2.5
Huber Heights city *Montgomery Co.*	68.7	$102,500	1973	1.6	$887	4.0
Hudson city *Summit Co.*	86.1	$313,300	1981	1.1	$1,842	0.0
Kent city *Portage Co.*	39.6	$139,900	1971	0.9	$770	6.2
Kettering city *Montgomery Co.*	61.8	$125,700	1960	2.1	$758	3.0
Lakewood city *Cuyahoga Co.*	45.0	$134,000	Before 1940	2.1	$715	4.8
Lancaster city *Fairfield Co.*	52.3	$117,100	1963	1.8	$748	5.9
Lebanon city *Warren Co.*	60.4	$163,800	1990	0.0	$790	5.3
Lima city *Allen Co.*	45.2	$66,600	1952	3.3	$628	7.1
Lorain city *Lorain Co.*	57.9	$85,700	1960	1.7	$659	8.3
Mansfield city *Richland Co.*	52.7	$77,500	1958	2.1	$592	6.4
Maple Heights city *Cuyahoga Co.*	63.5	$71,800	1956	4.7	$841	7.3
Marion city *Marion Co.*	57.2	$73,200	1950	3.1	$681	6.4

Place	Homeownership Rate (%)	Median Home Value ($)	Median Year Structure Built	Homeowner Vacancy Rate (%)	Median Gross Rent ($/month)	Rental Vacancy Rate (%)
Marysville city *Union Co.*	63.0	$166,200	1992	0.7	$855	4.1
Mason city *Warren Co.*	81.4	$230,100	1994	0.0	$1,056	0.8
Massillon city *Stark Co.*	63.6	$98,700	1957	2.1	$670	3.8
Mayfield Heights city *Cuyahoga Co.*	50.7	$141,700	1962	3.1	$861	11.4
Medina city *Medina Co.*	65.2	$160,700	1979	3.3	$800	0.9
Mentor city *Lake Co.*	85.0	$167,100	1973	1.3	$925	8.4
Miamisburg city *Montgomery Co.*	70.5	$133,100	1970	2.3	$750	6.9
Middletown city *Butler Co.*	52.6	$91,300	1959	1.9	$745	7.5
Newark city *Licking Co.*	54.0	$114,500	1964	3.0	$702	5.4
Niles city *Trumbull Co.*	55.0	$78,700	1958	5.3	$649	4.4
North Olmsted city *Cuyahoga Co.*	74.0	$146,900	1966	1.5	$867	4.9
North Ridgeville city *Lorain Co.*	87.0	$160,300	1986	0.6	$1,071	5.1
North Royalton city *Cuyahoga Co.*	70.7	$193,100	1982	1.5	$820	0.8
Norwood city *Hamilton Co.*	47.8	$118,700	Before 1940	2.0	$706	4.8
Oregon city *Lucas Co.*	68.8	$130,200	1971	2.5	$620	3.2
Oxford city *Butler Co.*	32.3	$185,900	1978	4.1	$772	6.8
Painesville city *Lake Co.*	49.1	$100,300	1963	0.6	$734	5.9
Parma city *Cuyahoga Co.*	73.2	$107,500	1958	1.4	$778	5.6
Parma Heights city *Cuyahoga Co.*	55.2	$110,700	1960	1.4	$738	3.5
Perrysburg city *Wood Co.*	69.1	$194,200	1983	0.0	$888	2.5
Pickerington city *Fairfield Co.*	75.1	$184,500	2000	1.0	$1,033	0.0
Piqua city *Miami Co.*	60.4	$85,800	1956	1.3	$674	5.4
Portsmouth city *Scioto Co.*	49.9	$72,700	Before 1940	1.5	$562	8.2
Reynoldsburg city *Franklin Co.*	58.9	$142,600	1983	1.3	$948	5.2
Riverside city *Montgomery Co.*	54.7	$84,900	1962	3.4	$798	3.4
Rocky River city *Cuyahoga Co.*	72.7	$215,800	1958	1.7	$838	1.7
Sandusky city *Erie Co.*	52.0	$81,600	1952	4.8	$640	9.5
Shaker Heights city *Cuyahoga Co.*	63.1	$213,100	1941	3.7	$945	8.8
Sidney city *Shelby Co.*	56.6	$109,500	1971	2.4	$684	4.3
Solon city *Cuyahoga Co.*	83.7	$273,800	1981	1.8	$1,200	1.2
South Euclid city *Cuyahoga Co.*	73.9	$100,100	1954	2.8	$943	5.1
Springfield city *Clark Co.*	47.8	$77,000	1950	3.4	$675	4.8
Stow city *Summit Co.*	69.5	$166,200	1980	1.7	$920	6.2
Strongsville city *Cuyahoga Co.*	80.4	$194,000	1981	1.1	$908	2.3
Sylvania city *Lucas Co.*	72.1	$165,900	1975	0.0	$785	5.1
Toledo city *Lucas Co.*	52.3	$77,800	1953	2.4	$651	7.9
Trotwood city *Montgomery Co.*	50.2	$75,800	1966	2.5	$726	6.4
Troy city *Miami Co.*	57.8	$123,400	1968	1.4	$746	4.1
Twinsburg city *Summit Co.*	72.5	$210,100	1991	0.4	$1,027	1.1
Upper Arlington city *Franklin Co.*	80.4	$338,000	1958	0.9	$1,074	7.2
Wadsworth city *Medina Co.*	69.3	$162,300	1975	4.1	$814	9.6
Warren city *Trumbull Co.*	51.2	$61,200	1955	1.8	$594	7.6
Westerville city *Franklin Co.*	76.6	$207,900	1980	0.4	$927	4.1
Westlake city *Cuyahoga Co.*	75.2	$236,400	1982	1.1	$1,066	9.0
White Oak CDP *Hamilton Co.*	72.3	$136,300	1967	2.3	$709	12.5
Willoughby city *Lake Co.*	60.2	$144,300	1972	1.1	$864	6.1
Wooster city *Wayne Co.*	54.3	$126,300	1971	3.0	$684	4.9
Xenia city *Greene Co.*	61.6	$93,800	1969	2.4	$665	3.0
Youngstown city *Mahoning Co.*	56.5	$43,300	1948	9.0	$619	5.3
Zanesville city *Muskingum Co.*	43.3	$76,600	1946	3.8	$632	9.4

SOURCE: U.S. Census Bureau, American Community Survey, 2012-2016 Five-Year Estimates

Commute to Work

Place	Automobile (%)	Public Transportation (%)	Walk (%)	Work from Home (%)	Mean Travel Time to Work (minutes)
Akron city *Summit Co.*	90.8	4.2	2.4	2.0	21.4
Alliance city *Stark Co.*	91.1	0.8	4.9	2.2	19.6
Ashland city *Ashland Co.*	89.4	0.0	6.6	2.3	19.6
Athens city *Athens Co.*	51.6	1.4	35.9	6.7	13.9
Austintown CDP *Mahoning Co.*	96.5	0.4	0.5	2.2	21.7
Avon city *Lorain Co.*	88.1	0.3	0.4	8.9	25.1
Avon Lake city *Lorain Co.*	90.6	1.1	1.5	5.7	26.3
Barberton city *Summit Co.*	93.3	1.7	2.4	1.5	21.9
Beavercreek city *Greene Co.*	93.9	0.1	1.3	4.0	19.4
Berea city *Cuyahoga Co.*	86.5	0.7	6.1	4.6	22.0
Boardman CDP *Mahoning Co.*	94.8	0.6	0.8	3.1	20.2
Bowling Green city *Wood Co.*	79.7	0.7	14.6	2.5	15.5
Broadview Heights city *Cuyahoga Co.*	93.0	0.4	0.1	6.4	28.2
Brook Park city *Cuyahoga Co.*	94.9	1.1	1.6	1.8	21.8
Brunswick city *Medina Co.*	93.6	1.0	1.6	3.4	28.4
Canton city *Stark Co.*	89.4	4.3	2.9	2.4	20.3
Centerville city *Montgomery Co.*	91.9	0.9	0.7	6.3	20.5
Chillicothe city *Ross Co.*	92.7	0.8	2.9	2.3	20.3
Cincinnati city *Hamilton Co.*	80.3	7.9	5.7	4.4	22.6
Cleveland city *Cuyahoga Co.*	79.5	10.6	5.3	2.8	24.3
Cleveland Heights city *Cuyahoga Co.*	82.1	5.3	5.7	5.0	23.2
Columbus city *Franklin Co.*	88.6	3.2	3.0	3.5	21.5
Cuyahoga Falls city *Summit Co.*	95.0	0.6	1.5	2.6	22.3
Dayton city *Montgomery Co.*	82.7	6.1	7.0	2.5	20.8
Delaware city *Delaware Co.*	89.5	0.4	3.9	5.3	27.0
Dublin city *Franklin Co.*	90.3	0.4	0.5	7.2	24.4
Elyria city *Lorain Co.*	93.2	0.7	1.0	1.6	21.7
Euclid city *Cuyahoga Co.*	88.4	6.3	1.4	2.8	24.6
Fairborn city *Greene Co.*	93.6	0.3	3.0	2.3	19.8
Fairfield city *Butler Co.*	96.5	0.3	0.7	2.0	22.9
Findlay city *Hancock Co.*	92.2	0.4	3.2	3.3	15.5
Forest Park city *Hamilton Co.*	92.6	2.5	0.9	3.4	22.7
Gahanna city *Franklin Co.*	90.4	0.4	1.2	7.7	20.3
Garfield Heights city *Cuyahoga Co.*	91.6	4.0	1.6	2.2	23.7
Green city *Summit Co.*	95.3	0.4	0.2	3.7	21.4
Grove City city *Franklin Co.*	94.7	0.5	0.6	3.3	23.0
Hamilton city *Butler Co.*	94.2	0.4	2.4	1.7	25.3
Hilliard city *Franklin Co.*	92.5	0.4	1.0	5.2	22.1
Huber Heights city *Montgomery Co.*	93.7	1.5	1.5	1.6	22.2
Hudson city *Summit Co.*	87.7	0.5	1.9	9.0	27.6
Kent city *Portage Co.*	82.0	2.1	9.3	5.9	21.0
Kettering city *Montgomery Co.*	92.6	1.1	1.5	3.7	20.2
Lakewood city *Cuyahoga Co.*	86.2	5.2	2.8	3.8	23.4
Lancaster city *Fairfield Co.*	93.4	0.7	3.4	1.4	25.7
Lebanon city *Warren Co.*	94.3	0.3	1.8	3.6	23.1
Lima city *Allen Co.*	93.9	1.6	2.3	1.1	18.0
Lorain city *Lorain Co.*	92.5	0.7	1.6	1.7	22.4
Mansfield city *Richland Co.*	91.9	2.3	2.8	2.2	19.3
Maple Heights city *Cuyahoga Co.*	89.6	7.2	1.3	1.0	25.3
Marion city *Marion Co.*	94.0	1.2	1.7	1.4	19.4

Place	Automobile (%)	Public Transportation (%)	Walk (%)	Work from Home (%)	Mean Travel Time to Work (minutes)
Marysville city *Union Co.*	93.3	1.5	0.7	3.9	21.7
Mason city *Warren Co.*	92.2	0.6	0.7	6.2	24.5
Massillon city *Stark Co.*	93.7	1.8	1.3	2.6	20.1
Mayfield Heights city *Cuyahoga Co.*	93.5	1.5	1.1	3.6	20.9
Medina city *Medina Co.*	92.4	0.6	1.5	3.4	28.0
Mentor city *Lake Co.*	91.9	1.1	2.6	3.9	23.2
Miamisburg city *Montgomery Co.*	94.6	0.7	1.7	2.9	19.8
Middletown city *Butler Co.*	94.2	0.9	1.1	1.9	21.8
Newark city *Licking Co.*	92.8	0.5	2.4	2.7	21.1
Niles city *Trumbull Co.*	96.7	0.8	1.3	1.0	17.6
North Olmsted city *Cuyahoga Co.*	90.8	2.8	1.8	3.3	24.1
North Ridgeville city *Lorain Co.*	93.9	0.9	0.5	3.6	27.4
North Royalton city *Cuyahoga Co.*	93.8	0.6	0.5	4.6	27.3
Norwood city *Hamilton Co.*	91.9	2.3	2.1	1.5	19.6
Oregon city *Lucas Co.*	94.9	1.0	1.1	2.4	19.3
Oxford city *Butler Co.*	63.4	4.0	25.5	5.5	14.2
Painesville city *Lake Co.*	92.9	1.6	2.4	2.4	19.5
Parma city *Cuyahoga Co.*	93.5	1.7	1.4	2.4	24.8
Parma Heights city *Cuyahoga Co.*	94.2	1.1	2.0	2.2	26.4
Perrysburg city *Wood Co.*	94.0	0.2	1.3	4.1	19.8
Pickerington city *Fairfield Co.*	95.5	0.1	0.0	3.6	26.4
Piqua city *Miami Co.*	94.1	0.3	1.6	2.4	18.0
Portsmouth city *Scioto Co.*	87.5	0.4	7.0	3.3	16.0
Reynoldsburg city *Franklin Co.*	91.9	1.0	2.0	4.2	24.3
Riverside city *Montgomery Co.*	95.4	0.4	1.7	1.2	18.5
Rocky River city *Cuyahoga Co.*	88.0	4.1	1.1	5.8	24.3
Sandusky city *Erie Co.*	89.8	2.4	3.3	2.0	17.1
Shaker Heights city *Cuyahoga Co.*	83.7	5.0	1.4	7.9	22.8
Sidney city *Shelby Co.*	95.0	0.5	1.6	1.8	16.2
Solon city *Cuyahoga Co.*	92.9	0.4	0.4	5.9	25.3
South Euclid city *Cuyahoga Co.*	89.7	2.4	3.8	3.1	23.2
Springfield city *Clark Co.*	89.9	1.5	4.7	2.8	19.5
Stow city *Summit Co.*	95.8	0.6	0.6	2.9	23.9
Strongsville city *Cuyahoga Co.*	91.8	1.9	0.7	4.9	27.4
Sylvania city *Lucas Co.*	93.2	0.6	1.2	4.4	21.7
Toledo city *Lucas Co.*	91.4	2.4	2.6	2.1	19.6
Trotwood city *Montgomery Co.*	91.2	4.9	1.5	1.5	25.9
Troy city *Miami Co.*	93.5	0.9	2.6	2.5	19.2
Twinsburg city *Summit Co.*	92.2	0.1	0.6	6.0	25.5
Upper Arlington city *Franklin Co.*	90.1	0.8	1.5	5.9	19.7
Wadsworth city *Medina Co.*	95.5	0.3	1.2	1.9	23.7
Warren city *Trumbull Co.*	94.4	0.6	1.7	2.5	19.6
Westerville city *Franklin Co.*	90.1	0.6	2.1	6.1	21.1
Westlake city *Cuyahoga Co.*	90.0	1.5	0.9	7.1	25.3
White Oak CDP *Hamilton Co.*	93.9	0.6	1.1	3.2	23.3
Willoughby city *Lake Co.*	95.7	0.6	1.1	2.4	22.0
Wooster city *Wayne Co.*	84.1	0.0	9.5	3.5	18.1
Xenia city *Greene Co.*	93.3	1.3	2.6	1.9	22.2
Youngstown city *Mahoning Co.*	87.2	3.6	3.3	3.3	20.0
Zanesville city *Muskingum Co.*	93.8	0.6	1.1	2.6	20.3

SOURCE: U.S. Census Bureau, American Community Survey, 2012-2016 Five-Year Estimates

Crime

Place	Violent Crime Rate (crimes per 10,000 population)	Property Crime Rate (crimes per 10,000 population)
Akron city *Summit Co.*	61.6	438.3
Alliance city *Stark Co.*	45.0	349.8
Ashland city *Ashland Co.*	11.8	199.7
Athens city *Athens Co.*	10.7	183.3
Austintown CDP *Mahoning Co.*	14.6	229.3
Avon city *Lorain Co.*	n/a	n/a
Avon Lake city *Lorain Co.*	n/a	n/a
Barberton city *Summit Co.*	28.7	305.3
Beavercreek city *Greene Co.*	6.9	229.1
Berea city *Cuyahoga Co.*	5.9	96.3
Boardman CDP *Mahoning Co.*	n/a	n/a
Bowling Green city *Wood Co.*	13.4	178.3
Broadview Heights city *Cuyahoga Co.*	n/a	n/a
Brook Park city *Cuyahoga Co.*	n/a	n/a
Brunswick city *Medina Co.*	7.2	64.4
Canton city *Stark Co.*	94.5	511.4
Centerville city *Montgomery Co.*	5.5	147.6
Chillicothe city *Ross Co.*	43.3	805.4
Cincinnati city *Hamilton Co.*	91.0	514.7
Cleveland city *Cuyahoga Co.*	163.1	531.6
Cleveland Heights city *Cuyahoga Co.*	32.4	223.1
Columbus city *Franklin Co.*	52.2	407.0
Cuyahoga Falls city *Summit Co.*	13.7	233.0
Dayton city *Montgomery Co.*	100.0	515.8
Delaware city *Delaware Co.*	18.9	230.2
Dublin city *Franklin Co.*	4.8	112.7
Elyria city *Lorain Co.*	30.0	276.5
Euclid city *Cuyahoga Co.*	n/a	n/a
Fairborn city *Greene Co.*	25.0	270.3
Fairfield city *Butler Co.*	25.7	244.1
Findlay city *Hancock Co.*	n/a	n/a
Forest Park city *Hamilton Co.*	25.2	339.1
Gahanna city *Franklin Co.*	5.7	226.3
Garfield Heights city *Cuyahoga Co.*	n/a	n/a
Green city *Summit Co.*	n/a	n/a
Grove City city *Franklin Co.*	10.7	417.8
Hamilton city *Butler Co.*	51.3	531.2
Hilliard city *Franklin Co.*	9.5	98.8
Huber Heights city *Montgomery Co.*	22.0	332.6
Hudson city *Summit Co.*	1.8	40.9
Kent city *Portage Co.*	22.3	165.4
Kettering city *Montgomery Co.*	13.2	182.0
Lakewood city *Cuyahoga Co.*	12.5	174.0
Lancaster city *Fairfield Co.*	35.3	457.0
Lebanon city *Warren Co.*	10.6	174.2
Lima city *Allen Co.*	94.4	599.0
Lorain city *Lorain Co.*	n/a	n/a
Mansfield city *Richland Co.*	44.8	558.3
Maple Heights city *Cuyahoga Co.*	n/a	n/a
Marion city *Marion Co.*	29.5	363.9

Place	Violent Crime Rate (crimes per 10,000 population)	Property Crime Rate (crimes per 10,000 population)
Marysville city *Union Co.*	3.1	62.7
Mason city *Warren Co.*	1.8	99.9
Massillon city *Stark Co.*	n/a	n/a
Mayfield Heights city *Cuyahoga Co.*	n/a	n/a
Medina city *Medina Co.*	n/a	n/a
Mentor city *Lake Co.*	10.9	220.7
Miamisburg city *Montgomery Co.*	10.0	114.0
Middletown city *Butler Co.*	52.3	675.9
Newark city *Licking Co.*	n/a	n/a
Niles city *Trumbull Co.*	28.6	282.7
North Olmsted city *Cuyahoga Co.*	n/a	n/a
North Ridgeville city *Lorain Co.*	3.6	58.3
North Royalton city *Cuyahoga Co.*	n/a	n/a
Norwood city *Hamilton Co.*	25.9	504.9
Oregon city *Lucas Co.*	18.4	331.6
Oxford city *Butler Co.*	n/a	n/a
Painesville city *Lake Co.*	n/a	n/a
Parma city *Cuyahoga Co.*	13.6	138.5
Parma Heights city *Cuyahoga Co.*	n/a	n/a
Perrysburg city *Wood Co.*	3.7	113.2
Pickerington city *Fairfield Co.*	8.0	214.6
Piqua city *Miami Co.*	18.7	423.1
Portsmouth city *Scioto Co.*	n/a	n/a
Reynoldsburg city *Franklin Co.*	21.9	359.6
Riverside city *Montgomery Co.*	20.5	248.0
Rocky River city *Cuyahoga Co.*	3.4	39.7
Sandusky city *Erie Co.*	17.9	363.3
Shaker Heights city *Cuyahoga Co.*	n/a	n/a
Sidney city *Shelby Co.*	21.6	445.3
Solon city *Cuyahoga Co.*	4.8	76.2
South Euclid city *Cuyahoga Co.*	16.1	262.8
Springfield city *Clark Co.*	69.1	679.0
Stow city *Summit Co.*	8.6	184.5
Strongsville city *Cuyahoga Co.*	4.3	197.6
Sylvania city *Lucas Co.*	n/a	n/a
Toledo city *Lucas Co.*	119.2	402.0
Trotwood city *Montgomery Co.*	37.5	400.4
Troy city *Miami Co.*	8.5	281.2
Twinsburg city *Summit Co.*	10.6	69.4
Upper Arlington city *Franklin Co.*	4.6	152.2
Wadsworth city *Medina Co.*	11.0	218.6
Warren city *Trumbull Co.*	57.0	377.2
Westerville city *Franklin Co.*	5.4	240.9
Westlake city *Cuyahoga Co.*	4.3	142.5
White Oak CDP *Hamilton Co.*	n/a	n/a
Willoughby city *Lake Co.*	19.8	210.6
Wooster city *Wayne Co.*	27.2	288.7
Xenia city *Greene Co.*	20.4	315.3
Youngstown city *Mahoning Co.*	64.7	378.0
Zanesville city *Muskingum Co.*	36.5	505.2

NOTE: n/a not available.
SOURCE: Federal Bureau of Investigation, Uniform Crime Reports, 2016

Community Rankings

This section ranks incorporated places and CDPs (Census Designated Places) with populations of 2,500 or more. Unincorporated postal areas were not considered. For each topic below, you will find two tables, one in Descending Order—highest to lowest, and one in Ascending Order—lowest to highest. Seven topics are exceptions to this rule, and only include Descending Order—Water Area, Ancestry (five tables), American Indian/Alaska Native Population, Native Hawaiian/Other Pacific Islander, Homeowner Vacancy Rate, Rental Vacancy Rate, and Commute to Work: Public Transportation. This is because there are an extraordinarily large number of places that place at the bottom of these topics with zero numbers.

Land Area

Top 150 Places Ranked in *Descending* Order

State Rank	Sq. Miles	Place
1	217.169	**Columbus** (city) Franklin County
2	80.692	**Toledo** (city) Lucas County
3	77.942	**Cincinnati** (city) Hamilton County
4	77.697	**Cleveland** (city) Cuyahoga County
5	62.033	**Akron** (city) Summit County
6	55.652	**Dayton** (city) Montgomery County
7	33.955	**Youngstown** (city) Mahoning County
8	32.055	**Green** (city) Summit County
9	30.872	**Mansfield** (city) Richland County
10	30.494	**Trotwood** (city) Montgomery County
11	29.976	**Oregon** (city) Lucas County
12	28.617	**Pataskala** (city) Licking County
13	26.645	**Mentor** (city) Lake County
14	26.399	**Beavercreek** (city) Greene County
15	26.355	**Conneaut** (city) Ashtabula County
16	26.185	**Middletown** (city) Butler County
17	25.648	**Cuyahoga Falls** (city) Summit County
18	25.596	**Hudson** (city) Summit County
19	25.462	**Canton** (city) Stark County
20	25.294	**Springfield** (city) Clark County
21	25.036	**New Franklin** (city) Summit County
22	24.627	**Strongsville** (city) Cuyahoga County
23	24.437	**Dublin** (city) Franklin County
24	23.673	**Lorain** (city) Lorain County
25	23.459	**Streetsboro** (city) Portage County
26	23.438	**North Ridgeville** (city) Lorain County
27	23.137	**Lordstown** (village) Trumbull County
28	22.918	**Aurora** (city) Portage County
29	22.272	**Huber Heights** (city) Montgomery County
30	21.596	**Hamilton** (city) Butler County
31	21.310	**North Royalton** (city) Cuyahoga County
32	20.939	**Fairfield** (city) Butler County
33	20.884	**Newark** (city) Licking County
34	20.808	**Avon** (city) Lorain County
35	20.571	**Elyria** (city) Lorain County
36	20.361	**Solon** (city) Cuyahoga County
37	20.162	**Norton** (city) Summit County
38	20.024	**Parma** (city) Cuyahoga County
39	19.574	**Brecksville** (city) Cuyahoga County
40	19.134	**Findlay** (city) Hancock County
41	18.952	**Delaware** (city) Delaware County
42	18.841	**Lancaster** (city) Fairfield County
43	18.677	**Kettering** (city) Montgomery County
44	18.629	**Mason** (city) Warren County
45	18.578	**Massillon** (city) Stark County
46	18.554	**The Village of Indian Hill** (city) Hamilton County
47	18.506	**Clayton** (city) Montgomery County
48	17.088	**Stow** (city) Summit County
49	16.671	**Kirtland** (city) Lake County
50	16.310	**Wooster** (city) Wayne County
51	16.271	**Marysville** (city) Union County
52	16.196	**Grove City** (city) Franklin County
53	16.127	**Warren** (city) Trumbull County
54	15.926	**Westlake** (city) Cuyahoga County
55	15.873	**Monroe** (city) Butler County
56	15.121	**Boardman** (CDP) Mahoning County
57	13.996	**Tallmadge** (city) Summit County
58	13.769	**Twinsburg** (city) Summit County
59	13.565	**Lima** (city) Allen County
60	13.281	**Xenia** (city) Greene County
61	13.167	**Hilliard** (city) Franklin County
62	13.160	**Fairborn** (city) Greene County
63	13.048	**Broadview Heights** (city) Cuyahoga County
64	12.963	**Lebanon** (city) Warren County
65	12.916	**Brunswick** (city) Medina County
66	12.557	**Bowling Green** (city) Wood County
67	12.473	**Westerville** (city) Franklin County
68	12.427	**Gahanna** (city) Franklin County
69	12.344	**Vandalia** (city) Montgomery County
70	12.184	**Miamisburg** (city) Montgomery County
71	12.023	**Sidney** (city) Shelby County
72	11.865	**Calcutta** (CDP) Columbiana County
73	11.768	**Zanesville** (city) Muskingum County
74	11.736	**Marion** (city) Marion County
75	11.722	**Troy** (city) Miami County
76	11.674	**North Olmsted** (city) Cuyahoga County
77	11.630	**Austintown** (CDP) Mahoning County
78	11.620	**Piqua** (city) Miami County
79	11.617	**Defiance** (city) Defiance County
80	11.572	**Medina** (city) Medina County
81	11.557	**New Albany** (city) Franklin County
82	11.514	**Perrysburg** (city) Wood County
83	11.169	**Ashland** (city) Ashland County
84	11.157	**Reynoldsburg** (city) Franklin County
85	11.129	**Avon Lake** (city) Lorain County
86	11.084	**Ontario** (city) Richland County
87	10.922	**Heath** (city) Licking County
88	10.889	**Wilmington** (city) Clinton County
89	10.780	**Centerville** (city) Montgomery County
90	10.743	**Sheffield** (village) Lorain County
91	10.734	**Portsmouth** (city) Scioto County
92	10.729	**Willoughby Hills** (city) Lake County
93	10.655	**Vermilion** (city) Lorain County
94	10.630	**Euclid** (city) Cuyahoga County
95	10.621	**Wadsworth** (city) Medina County
96	10.545	**Steubenville** (city) Jefferson County
97	10.428	**Chillicothe** (city) Ross County
98	10.249	**Willoughby** (city) Lake County
99	10.036	**Bellefontaine** (city) Logan County
100	9.929	**Wright-Patterson AFB** (CDP) Greene County
101	9.886	**Maumee** (city) Lucas County
102	9.839	**Upper Arlington** (city) Franklin County
103	9.832	**Sharonville** (city) Hamilton County
104	9.827	**Athens** (city) Athens County
105	9.745	**Pickerington** (city) Fairfield County
106	9.726	**Sandusky** (city) Erie County
107	9.720	**Riverside** (city) Montgomery County
108	9.706	**Macedonia** (city) Summit County
109	9.540	**Independence** (city) Cuyahoga County
110	9.423	**Montrose-Ghent** (CDP) Summit County
111	9.408	**Mount Vernon** (city) Knox County
112	9.355	**Springboro** (city) Warren County
113	9.319	**Richfield** (village) Summit County
114	9.273	**Mack** (CDP) Hamilton County
115	9.251	**Moraine** (city) Montgomery County
116	9.174	**Kent** (city) Portage County
117	9.173	**Franklin** (city) Warren County
118	9.038	**Barberton** (city) Summit County
119	8.924	**Alliance** (city) Stark County
120	8.887	**Mount Orab** (village) Brown County
121	8.887	**North Kingsville** (village) Ashtabula County
122	8.870	**Norwalk** (city) Huron County
123	8.777	**Cadiz** (village) Harrison County
124	8.739	**Washington Court House** (city) Fayette County
125	8.611	**Niles** (city) Trumbull County
126	8.560	**Groveport** (city) Franklin County
127	8.523	**Northwood** (city) Wood County
128	8.448	**London** (city) Madison County
129	8.435	**Taylor Creek** (CDP) Hamilton County
130	8.433	**Marietta** (city) Washington County
131	8.367	**Champion Heights** (CDP) Trumbull County
132	8.346	**Fremont** (city) Sandusky County
133	8.232	**Jackson** (city) Jackson County
134	8.216	**New Philadelphia** (city) Tuscarawas County
135	8.107	**Cleveland Heights** (city) Cuyahoga County
136	8.084	**Coshocton** (city) Coshocton County
137	8.065	**Middleburg Heights** (city) Cuyahoga County
138	7.753	**Urbana** (city) Champaign County
139	7.735	**Ashtabula** (city) Ashtabula County
140	7.607	**Galion** (city) Crawford County
141	7.580	**Blue Ash** (city) Hamilton County
142	7.545	**Fostoria** (city) Seneca County
143	7.530	**Brook Park** (city) Cuyahoga County
144	7.529	**Tipp City** (city) Miami County
145	7.465	**Canal Winchester** (city) Franklin County
146	7.422	**Bucyrus** (city) Crawford County
147	7.325	**Van Wert** (city) Van Wert County
148	7.230	**Garfield Heights** (city) Cuyahoga County
149	7.208	**Fort Shawnee** (CDP) Allen County
150	7.149	**Moreland Hills** (village) Cuyahoga County

Note: *This section ranks incorporated places and CDPs (Census Designated Places) with populations of 2,500 or more. Unincorporated postal areas were not considered. Please refer to the User Guide for additional information.*

Land Area

Top 150 Places Ranked in *Ascending* Order

State Rank	Sq. Miles	Place
1	0.575	**Golf Manor** (village) Hamilton County
2	0.699	**Delshire** (CDP) Hamilton County
3	0.757	**Lincoln Heights** (village) Hamilton County
4	0.777	**Mount Healthy Heights** (CDP) Hamilton County
5	0.798	**Green Meadows** (CDP) Clark County
6	0.864	**Mariemont** (village) Hamilton County
7	0.874	**Deer Park** (city) Hamilton County
8	0.891	**Dillonvale** (CDP) Hamilton County
9	1.011	**Shadyside** (village) Belmont County
10	1.027	**Fairport Harbor** (village) Lake County
11	1.041	**Huber Ridge** (CDP) Franklin County
12	1.058	**Pleasant Run Farm** (CDP) Hamilton County
13	1.069	**Sherwood** (CDP) Hamilton County
14	1.083	**Northfield** (village) Summit County
15	1.112	**Silverton** (village) Hamilton County
16	1.116	**Sixteen Mile Stand** (CDP) Hamilton County
17	1.132	**Cherry Grove** (CDP) Hamilton County
18	1.168	**Cheviot** (city) Hamilton County
19	1.178	**Day Heights** (CDP) Clermont County
20	1.231	**Lockland** (village) Hamilton County
21	1.246	**Greenhills** (village) Hamilton County
22	1.275	**Fruit Hill** (CDP) Hamilton County
23	1.276	**Enon** (village) Clark County
24	1.282	**Cedarville** (village) Greene County
25	1.324	**Covington** (village) Miami County
26	1.332	**Grandview Heights** (city) Franklin County
27	1.349	**Dennison** (village) Tuscarawas County
28	1.388	**Strasburg** (village) Tuscarawas County
29	1.393	**Burlington** (CDP) Lawrence County
30	1.395	**Bethel** (village) Clermont County
31	1.406	**Mount Healthy** (city) Hamilton County
32	1.465	**Park Layne** (CDP) Clark County
33	1.476	**Lakemore** (village) Summit County
34	1.488	**Delhi Hills** (CDP) Hamilton County
35	1.546	**Saint Bernard** (city) Hamilton County
36	1.550	**Oak Harbor** (village) Ottawa County
37	1.583	**Cleves** (village) Hamilton County
38	1.590	**Mulberry** (CDP) Clermont County
39	1.604	**Saint Henry** (village) Mercer County
40	1.613	**Mentor-on-the-Lake** (city) Lake County
41	1.624	**Crooksville** (village) Perry County
42	1.626	**New Concord** (village) Muskingum County
43	1.634	**Poland** (village) Mahoning County
44	1.645	**Salem Heights** (CDP) Hamilton County
45	1.650	**Bellaire** (village) Belmont County
46	1.687	**Lisbon** (village) Columbiana County
47	1.688	**McDonald** (village) Trumbull County
48	1.791	**Amelia** (village) Clermont County
49	1.802	**Wellsville** (village) Columbiana County
50	1.820	**University Heights** (city) Cuyahoga County
51	1.826	**North College Hill** (city) Hamilton County
52	1.834	**Mount Carmel** (CDP) Clermont County
53	1.836	**Lincoln Village** (CDP) Franklin County
54	1.846	**Ottawa Hills** (village) Lucas County
55	1.858	**Toronto** (city) Jefferson County
56	1.867	**Versailles** (village) Darke County
57	1.875	**Doylestown** (village) Wayne County
58	1.891	**Blacklick Estates** (CDP) Franklin County
59	1.923	**Coldwater** (village) Mercer County
60	1.932	**Minster** (village) Auglaize County
61	1.943	**Barnesville** (village) Belmont County
62	1.947	**Williamsburg** (village) Clermont County
63	1.947	**New Lexington** (village) Perry County
64	1.949	**Northbrook** (CDP) Hamilton County
65	1.974	**Fredericktown** (village) Knox County
66	1.976	**Carey** (village) Wyandot County
67	2.000	**Buckeye Lake** (village) Licking County
68	2.016	**Yellow Springs** (village) Greene County
69	2.028	**Landen** (CDP) Warren County
70	2.033	**Mount Repose** (CDP) Clermont County
71	2.045	**New Lebanon** (village) Montgomery County
72	2.061	**Greenfield** (village) Highland County
73	2.069	**Pleasant Run** (CDP) Hamilton County
74	2.075	**Chagrin Falls** (village) Cuyahoga County
75	2.078	**Ada** (village) Hardin County
76	2.078	**Port Clinton** (city) Ottawa County
77	2.087	**Summerside** (CDP) Clermont County
78	2.090	**Baltimore** (village) Fairfield County
79	2.094	**Mogadore** (village) Summit County
80	2.145	**New Bremen** (village) Auglaize County
81	2.172	**Newtown** (village) Hamilton County
82	2.180	**Reminderville** (village) Summit County
83	2.186	**Walbridge** (village) Wood County
84	2.194	**Four Bridges** (CDP) Butler County
85	2.195	**Oakwood** (city) Montgomery County
86	2.205	**New London** (village) Huron County
87	2.217	**Millersburg** (village) Holmes County
88	2.230	**Minerva** (village) Stark County
89	2.246	**Lodi** (village) Medina County
90	2.277	**The Plains** (CDP) Athens County
91	2.304	**Kenwood** (CDP) Hamilton County
92	2.307	**Newton Falls** (village) Trumbull County
93	2.329	**Martins Ferry** (city) Belmont County
94	2.364	**Paulding** (village) Paulding County
95	2.377	**Waynesville** (village) Warren County
96	2.379	**Plain City** (village) Madison County
97	2.395	**Gibsonburg** (village) Sandusky County
98	2.418	**Saint Clairsville** (city) Belmont County
99	2.431	**Bexley** (city) Franklin County
100	2.447	**Carrollton** (village) Carroll County
101	2.471	**North Baltimore** (village) Wood County
102	2.477	**Sheffield Lake** (city) Lorain County
103	2.492	**Uniontown** (CDP) Stark County
104	2.496	**Sebring** (village) Mahoning County
105	2.507	**Ashville** (village) Pickaway County
106	2.513	**Garrettsville** (village) Portage County
107	2.519	**Jefferson** (village) Ashtabula County
108	2.530	**Northgate** (CDP) Hamilton County
109	2.536	**Willowick** (city) Lake County
110	2.570	**Woodlawn** (village) Hamilton County
111	2.576	**Hartville** (village) Stark County
112	2.599	**Loudonville** (village) Ashland County
113	2.603	**Seville** (village) Medina County
114	2.647	**South Lebanon** (village) Warren County
115	2.656	**Hicksville** (village) Defiance County
116	2.670	**Delta** (village) Fulton County
117	2.690	**Mingo Junction** (village) Jefferson County
118	2.703	**Ballville** (CDP) Sandusky County
119	2.718	**Munroe Falls** (city) Summit County
120	2.738	**New Carlisle** (city) Clark County
121	2.741	**Greentown** (CDP) Stark County
122	2.800	**Covedale** (CDP) Hamilton County
123	2.811	**Uhrichsville** (city) Tuscarawas County
124	2.831	**West Union** (village) Adams County
125	2.843	**Newcomerstown** (village) Tuscarawas County
126	2.860	**Lake Lakengren** (CDP) Preble County
127	2.863	**Perry Heights** (CDP) Stark County
128	2.868	**Wyoming** (city) Hamilton County
129	2.892	**Reading** (city) Hamilton County
130	2.904	**Johnstown** (village) Licking County
131	2.909	**Montpelier** (village) Williams County
132	2.939	**South Point** (village) Lawrence County
133	2.945	**Groesbeck** (CDP) Hamilton County
134	2.978	**Turpin Hills** (CDP) Hamilton County
135	3.021	**Middlefield** (village) Geauga County
136	3.051	**Northridge** (CDP) Clark County
137	3.068	**New Burlington** (CDP) Hamilton County
138	3.086	**East Cleveland** (city) Cuyahoga County
139	3.094	**Swanton** (village) Fulton County
140	3.117	**Withamsville** (CDP) Clermont County
141	3.117	**Ross** (CDP) Butler County
142	3.119	**Wintersville** (village) Jefferson County
143	3.125	**Bellbrook** (city) Greene County
144	3.128	**Richville** (CDP) Stark County
145	3.147	**Norwood** (city) Hamilton County
146	3.152	**East Palestine** (village) Columbiana County
147	3.166	**Crestline** (village) Crawford County
148	3.244	**West Milton** (village) Miami County
149	3.258	**Canal Fulton** (city) Stark County
150	3.263	**Mineral Ridge** (CDP) Trumbull County

***Note:** This section ranks incorporated places and CDPs (Census Designated Places) with populations of 2,500 or more. Unincorporated postal areas were not considered. Please refer to the User Guide for additional information.*

Water Area

Top 150 Places Ranked in *Descending* Order

State Rank	Sq. Miles	Place
1	12.175	**Sandusky** (city) Erie County
2	8.055	**Oregon** (city) Lucas County
3	5.936	**Columbus** (city) Franklin County
4	4.769	**Cleveland** (city) Cuyahoga County
5	3.432	**Toledo** (city) Lucas County
6	2.891	**Huron** (city) Erie County
7	2.488	**Bay Village** (city) Cuyahoga County
8	1.642	**New Franklin** (city) Summit County
9	1.604	**Cincinnati** (city) Hamilton County
10	1.479	**Green** (city) Summit County
11	1.353	**Mentor** (city) Lake County
12	1.159	**Lakewood** (city) Cuyahoga County
13	1.147	**Aurora** (city) Portage County
14	0.994	**Portage Lakes** (CDP) Summit County
15	0.902	**Streetsboro** (city) Portage County
16	0.873	**Rocky River** (city) Cuyahoga County
17	0.853	**Dayton** (city) Montgomery County
18	0.852	**Euclid** (city) Cuyahoga County
19	0.795	**Apple Valley** (CDP) Knox County
20	0.726	**Painesville** (city) Lake County
21	0.716	**Maumee** (city) Lucas County
22	0.635	**Youngstown** (city) Mahoning County
23	0.509	**Defiance** (city) Defiance County
24	0.486	**Newark** (city) Licking County
25	0.486	**Girard** (city) Trumbull County
26	0.479	**Hamilton** (city) Butler County
27	0.478	**Gibsonburg** (village) Sandusky County
28	0.474	**Lorain** (city) Lorain County
29	0.400	**Napoleon** (city) Henry County
30	0.373	**Zanesville** (city) Muskingum County
31	0.361	**Dublin** (city) Franklin County
32	0.340	**Akron** (city) Summit County
33	0.338	**Portsmouth** (city) Scioto County
34	0.331	**New London** (village) Huron County
35	0.327	**Norton** (city) Summit County
36	0.327	**Lake Lakengren** (CDP) Preble County
37	0.319	**Marietta** (city) Washington County
38	0.309	**New Richmond** (village) Clermont County
39	0.306	**Rossford** (city) Wood County
40	0.296	**Ironton** (city) Lawrence County
41	0.291	**Wellington** (village) Lorain County
42	0.291	**Marysville** (city) Union County
43	0.289	**South Point** (village) Lawrence County
44	0.289	**Celina** (city) Mercer County
45	0.282	**Norwalk** (city) Huron County
46	0.281	**Van Wert** (city) Van Wert County
47	0.276	**Toronto** (city) Jefferson County
48	0.274	**Elyria** (city) Lorain County
49	0.267	**Piqua** (city) Miami County
50	0.266	**Moraine** (city) Montgomery County
51	0.265	**Hudson** (city) Summit County
52	0.261	**Jackson** (city) Jackson County
53	0.235	**Middletown** (city) Butler County
54	0.233	**Stow** (city) Summit County
55	0.233	**Devola** (CDP) Washington County
56	0.229	**Lima** (city) Allen County
57	0.228	**Gallipolis** (village) Gallia County
58	0.227	**Groveport** (city) Franklin County
59	0.219	**Fremont** (city) Sandusky County
60	0.219	**Troy** (city) Miami County
61	0.219	**Athens** (city) Athens County
62	0.219	**Barberton** (city) Summit County
63	0.218	**West Carrollton** (city) Montgomery County
64	0.218	**Fostoria** (city) Seneca County
65	0.210	**Medina** (city) Medina County
66	0.205	**Springfield** (city) Clark County
67	0.205	**Ballville** (CDP) Sandusky County
68	0.201	**Port Clinton** (city) Ottawa County
69	0.199	**Newtown** (village) Hamilton County
70	0.198	**Carlisle** (village) Warren County
71	0.196	**East Liverpool** (city) Columbiana County
72	0.191	**Lakemore** (village) Summit County
73	0.188	**Waterville** (city) Lucas County
74	0.185	**Miamisburg** (city) Montgomery County
75	0.185	**Mount Vernon** (city) Knox County
76	0.183	**Upper Sandusky** (city) Wyandot County
77	0.181	**Massillon** (city) Stark County
78	0.172	**Boardman** (CDP) Mahoning County
79	0.171	**Ashtabula** (city) Ashtabula County
80	0.171	**Gahanna** (city) Franklin County
81	0.171	**Mingo Junction** (village) Jefferson County
82	0.170	**New Philadelphia** (city) Tuscarawas County
83	0.170	**Franklin** (city) Warren County
84	0.168	**Hilliard** (city) Franklin County
85	0.167	**Chillicothe** (city) Ross County
86	0.166	**Vermilion** (city) Lorain County
87	0.163	**Cadiz** (village) Harrison County
88	0.157	**Grove City** (city) Franklin County
89	0.153	**Oak Harbor** (village) Ottawa County
90	0.144	**New Albany** (city) Franklin County
91	0.144	**Obetz** (village) Franklin County
92	0.143	**Columbiana** (city) Columbiana County
93	0.142	**Shelby** (city) Richland County
94	0.140	**North Ridgeville** (city) Lorain County
95	0.139	**Archbold** (village) Fulton County
96	0.139	**Logan** (city) Hocking County
97	0.138	**Westerville** (city) Franklin County
98	0.136	**Canal Winchester** (city) Franklin County
99	0.136	**Tiffin** (city) Seneca County
100	0.132	**Sidney** (city) Shelby County
101	0.130	**Kirtland** (city) Lake County
102	0.130	**Eastlake** (city) Lake County
103	0.130	**Solon** (city) Cuyahoga County
104	0.124	**Coshocton** (city) Coshocton County
105	0.124	**Milford** (city) Clermont County
106	0.122	**Delaware** (city) Delaware County
107	0.121	**Circleville** (city) Pickaway County
108	0.121	**Fairfield** (city) Butler County
109	0.120	**Findlay** (city) Hancock County
110	0.118	**Bellevue** (city) Sandusky County
111	0.114	**Tipp City** (city) Miami County
112	0.113	**Brecksville** (city) Cuyahoga County
113	0.111	**Nelsonville** (city) Athens County
114	0.109	**Wellsville** (village) Columbiana County
115	0.109	**Kent** (city) Portage County
116	0.109	**Berea** (city) Cuyahoga County
117	0.103	**Dover** (city) Tuscarawas County
118	0.103	**Independence** (city) Cuyahoga County
119	0.102	**Fredericktown** (village) Knox County
120	0.099	**Cuyahoga Falls** (city) Summit County
121	0.098	**Paulding** (village) Paulding County
122	0.098	**Sheffield** (village) Lorain County
123	0.098	**West Milton** (village) Miami County
124	0.097	**Blanchester** (village) Clinton County
125	0.097	**Newcomerstown** (village) Tuscarawas County
126	0.096	**Pataskala** (city) Licking County
127	0.096	**Struthers** (city) Mahoning County
128	0.095	**The Village of Indian Hill** (city) Hamilton County
129	0.095	**Huber Heights** (city) Montgomery County
130	0.094	**Wheelersburg** (CDP) Scioto County
131	0.094	**Kenton** (city) Hardin County
132	0.092	**Munroe Falls** (city) Summit County
133	0.091	**Landen** (CDP) Warren County
134	0.091	**Montrose-Ghent** (CDP) Summit County
135	0.090	**Willoughby** (city) Lake County
136	0.089	**Clayton** (city) Montgomery County
137	0.085	**Willoughby Hills** (city) Lake County
138	0.084	**Wellston** (city) Jackson County
139	0.083	**Reynoldsburg** (city) Franklin County
140	0.083	**Belpre** (city) Washington County
141	0.082	**Steubenville** (city) Jefferson County
142	0.082	**Newton Falls** (village) Trumbull County
143	0.081	**Fairport Harbor** (village) Lake County
144	0.080	**Wright-Patterson AFB** (CDP) Greene County
145	0.079	**South Russell** (village) Geauga County
146	0.078	**Marion** (city) Marion County
147	0.078	**Moreland Hills** (village) Cuyahoga County
148	0.078	**Heath** (city) Licking County
149	0.076	**Worthington** (city) Franklin County
150	0.076	**Union** (city) Montgomery County

***Note:** This section ranks incorporated places and CDPs (Census Designated Places) with populations of 2,500 or more. Unincorporated postal areas were not considered. Please refer to the User Guide for additional information.*

Elevation

Top 150 Places Ranked in *Descending* Order

State Rank	Feet	Place
1	1,355	**Ontario** (city) Richland County
2	1,309	**Chardon** (city) Geauga County
3	1,273	**Barnesville** (village) Belmont County
4	1,266	**Cadiz** (village) Harrison County
4	1,266	**Saint Clairsville** (city) Belmont County
6	1,260	**Wintersville** (village) Jefferson County
7	1,247	**Doylestown** (village) Wayne County
8	1,243	**Bellefontaine** (city) Logan County
9	1,240	**Mansfield** (city) Richland County
10	1,227	**Salem** (city) Columbiana County
11	1,214	**Lexington** (village) Richland County
12	1,207	**Beechwood Trails** (CDP) Licking County
13	1,197	**Greentown** (CDP) Stark County
13	1,197	**North Royalton** (city) Cuyahoga County
15	1,191	**Broadview Heights** (city) Cuyahoga County
16	1,184	**Beachwood** (city) Cuyahoga County
17	1,171	**Wadsworth** (city) Medina County
18	1,168	**Bainbridge** (CDP) Geauga County
18	1,168	**Brunswick** (city) Medina County
18	1,168	**Galion** (city) Crawford County
18	1,168	**Hartville** (village) Stark County
22	1,158	**Alliance** (city) Stark County
22	1,158	**Johnstown** (village) Licking County
22	1,158	**North Canton** (city) Stark County
22	1,158	**Orange** (village) Cuyahoga County
26	1,152	**Richfield** (village) Summit County
27	1,148	**Canfield** (city) Mahoning County
27	1,148	**Columbiana** (city) Columbiana County
29	1,145	**Crestline** (village) Crawford County
29	1,145	**Mogadore** (village) Summit County
31	1,142	**Green** (city) Summit County
32	1,138	**Louisville** (city) Stark County
33	1,135	**Mount Gilead** (village) Morrow County
33	1,135	**Ravenna** (city) Portage County
35	1,132	**Hillsboro** (city) Highland County
36	1,129	**Aurora** (city) Portage County
36	1,129	**Austintown** (CDP) Mahoning County
36	1,129	**Streetsboro** (city) Portage County
39	1,125	**Apple Valley** (CDP) Knox County
39	1,125	**Middlefield** (village) Geauga County
41	1,122	**South Russell** (village) Geauga County
42	1,119	**Uniontown** (CDP) Stark County
43	1,112	**Boardman** (CDP) Mahoning County
43	1,112	**Calcutta** (CDP) Columbiana County
43	1,112	**Tallmadge** (city) Summit County
46	1,106	**Carrollton** (village) Carroll County
47	1,102	**Brimfield** (CDP) Portage County
47	1,102	**Sebring** (village) Mahoning County
49	1,099	**Perry Heights** (CDP) Stark County
49	1,099	**Shelby** (city) Richland County
51	1,096	**Fredericktown** (village) Knox County
52	1,089	**Lake Lakengren** (CDP) Preble County
52	1,089	**Medina** (city) Medina County
52	1,089	**New Franklin** (city) Summit County
52	1,089	**Stow** (city) Summit County
56	1,086	**Mayfield Heights** (city) Cuyahoga County
57	1,083	**Lakemore** (village) Summit County
58	1,079	**Northridge** (CDP) Clark County
59	1,066	**Ashland** (city) Ashland County
59	1,066	**Hudson** (city) Summit County
61	1,063	**Kent** (city) Portage County
62	1,060	**Norton** (city) Summit County
62	1,060	**Orrville** (city) Wayne County
62	1,060	**Richville** (CDP) Stark County
65	1,056	**Canton** (city) Stark County
65	1,056	**Minerva** (village) Stark County
65	1,056	**Pepper Pike** (city) Cuyahoga County
68	1,053	**London** (city) Madison County
68	1,053	**Portage Lakes** (CDP) Summit County
70	1,050	**Cedarville** (village) Greene County
70	1,050	**Northfield** (village) Summit County
70	1,050	**Shaker Heights** (city) Cuyahoga County
70	1,050	**Steubenville** (city) Jefferson County
70	1,050	**Urbana** (city) Champaign County
75	1,047	**Oakwood** (village) Cuyahoga County
76	1,043	**Greenville** (city) Darke County
76	1,043	**Poland** (village) Mahoning County
78	1,040	**Bedford Heights** (city) Cuyahoga County
78	1,040	**Eaton** (city) Preble County
78	1,040	**Moreland Hills** (village) Cuyahoga County
78	1,040	**Solon** (city) Cuyahoga County
82	1,037	**Warrensville Heights** (city) Cuyahoga County
83	1,033	**Campbell** (city) Mahoning County
83	1,033	**Lyndhurst** (city) Cuyahoga County
85	1,030	**Brookville** (city) Montgomery County
85	1,030	**Munroe Falls** (city) Summit County
87	1,027	**Cuyahoga Falls** (city) Summit County
87	1,027	**University Heights** (city) Cuyahoga County
89	1,024	**Cortland** (city) Trumbull County
89	1,024	**New Albany** (city) Franklin County
91	1,020	**Centerville** (city) Montgomery County
92	1,017	**Wilmington** (city) Clinton County
93	1,014	**Reminderville** (village) Summit County
94	1,007	**Fairlawn** (city) Summit County
94	1,007	**Struthers** (city) Mahoning County
96	1,004	**Kettering** (city) Montgomery County
96	1,004	**Mineral Ridge** (CDP) Trumbull County
96	1,004	**Mount Vernon** (city) Knox County
96	1,004	**Twinsburg** (city) Summit County
100	1,001	**Chagrin Falls** (village) Cuyahoga County
100	1,001	**Clayton** (city) Montgomery County
100	1,001	**Garrettsville** (village) Portage County
100	1,001	**Pataskala** (city) Licking County
104	997	**East Palestine** (village) Columbiana County
105	994	**Bucyrus** (city) Crawford County
105	994	**Marysville** (city) Union County
105	994	**Wooster** (city) Wayne County
108	991	**Kenton** (city) Hardin County
108	991	**Vandalia** (city) Montgomery County
110	988	**Macedonia** (city) Summit County
110	988	**Oakwood** (city) Montgomery County
110	988	**Seville** (village) Medina County
113	981	**Hubbard** (city) Trumbull County
113	981	**Marion** (city) Marion County
113	981	**New London** (village) Huron County
113	981	**Rittman** (city) Wayne County
113	981	**Versailles** (village) Darke County
118	978	**Washington Court House** (city) Fayette County
119	974	**Springfield** (city) Clark County
120	971	**Barberton** (city) Summit County
120	971	**Loudonville** (village) Ashland County
120	971	**Saint Henry** (village) Mercer County
123	968	**Blanchester** (village) Clinton County
123	968	**Sunbury** (village) Delaware County
125	965	**Lisbon** (village) Columbiana County
125	965	**Minster** (village) Auglaize County
127	961	**Ada** (village) Hardin County
127	961	**Akron** (city) Summit County
127	961	**Jefferson** (village) Ashtabula County
127	961	**McDonald** (village) Trumbull County
127	961	**Yellow Springs** (village) Greene County
132	958	**Granville** (village) Licking County
132	958	**New Lexington** (village) Perry County
132	958	**South Euclid** (city) Cuyahoga County
135	955	**Garfield Heights** (city) Cuyahoga County
135	955	**Lordstown** (village) Trumbull County
135	955	**Sidney** (city) Shelby County
138	951	**Canal Fulton** (city) Stark County
139	948	**Bedford** (city) Cuyahoga County
139	948	**Massillon** (city) Stark County
141	945	**New Bremen** (village) Auglaize County
141	945	**West Union** (village) Adams County
143	942	**Cleveland Heights** (city) Cuyahoga County
143	942	**Mount Orab** (village) Brown County
145	935	**Highland Heights** (city) Cuyahoga County
145	935	**Plain City** (village) Madison County
145	935	**Xenia** (city) Greene County
148	932	**Champion Heights** (CDP) Trumbull County
148	932	**Hilliard** (city) Franklin County
148	932	**Huber Heights** (city) Montgomery County

Note: *This section ranks incorporated places and CDPs (Census Designated Places) with populations of 2,500 or more. Unincorporated postal areas were not considered. Please refer to the User Guide for additional information.*

Elevation

Top 150 Places Ranked in *Ascending* Order

State Rank	Feet	Place
1	492	**New Richmond** (village) Clermont County
2	499	**Cleves** (village) Hamilton County
2	499	**Newtown** (village) Hamilton County
4	522	**Harrison** (city) Hamilton County
5	535	**Portsmouth** (city) Scioto County
6	551	**Ironton** (city) Lawrence County
6	551	**Milford** (city) Clermont County
8	554	**Ross** (CDP) Butler County
8	554	**Wheelersburg** (CDP) Scioto County
10	558	**Burlington** (CDP) Lawrence County
11	561	**Reading** (city) Hamilton County
11	561	**South Point** (village) Lawrence County
13	564	**The Village of Indian Hill** (city) Hamilton County
14	568	**Saint Bernard** (city) Hamilton County
15	571	**Gallipolis** (village) Gallia County
16	577	**Port Clinton** (city) Ottawa County
16	577	**Wyoming** (city) Hamilton County
18	581	**Lockland** (village) Hamilton County
19	584	**Mariemont** (village) Hamilton County
19	584	**Oak Harbor** (village) Ottawa County
21	587	**Huron** (city) Erie County
21	587	**Sharonville** (city) Hamilton County
21	587	**Woodlawn** (village) Hamilton County
24	594	**Evendale** (village) Hamilton County
24	594	**Fairfield** (city) Butler County
24	594	**Sandusky** (city) Erie County
27	597	**Hamilton** (city) Butler County
27	597	**Lincoln Heights** (village) Hamilton County
29	600	**Loveland** (city) Hamilton County
29	600	**Sheffield Lake** (city) Lorain County
31	604	**Oregon** (city) Lucas County
31	604	**Ottawa Hills** (village) Lucas County
33	610	**Avon Lake** (city) Lorain County
33	610	**Fairport Harbor** (village) Lake County
33	610	**Lorain** (city) Lorain County
33	610	**Northwood** (city) Wood County
33	610	**Toledo** (city) Lucas County
38	614	**Belpre** (city) Washington County
38	614	**Marietta** (city) Washington County
38	614	**Waterville** (city) Lucas County
41	617	**Eastlake** (city) Lake County
41	617	**Euclid** (city) Cuyahoga County
41	617	**Rossford** (city) Wood County
41	617	**Walbridge** (village) Wood County
41	617	**West Portsmouth** (CDP) Scioto County
46	623	**Ballville** (CDP) Sandusky County
46	623	**Willowick** (city) Lake County
48	627	**Cincinnati** (city) Hamilton County
48	627	**Fremont** (city) Sandusky County
48	627	**Mentor-on-the-Lake** (city) Lake County
51	630	**South Lebanon** (village) Warren County
52	633	**Bay Village** (city) Cuyahoga County
52	633	**Chillicothe** (city) Ross County
52	633	**Maumee** (city) Lucas County
52	633	**Perrysburg** (city) Wood County
56	650	**Conneaut** (city) Ashtabula County
56	650	**Trenton** (city) Butler County
56	650	**Turpin Hills** (CDP) Hamilton County
59	653	**Cleveland** (city) Cuyahoga County
59	653	**Norwood** (city) Hamilton County
59	653	**Whitehouse** (village) Lucas County
62	656	**Middletown** (city) Butler County
63	659	**Willoughby** (city) Lake County
64	663	**Golf Manor** (village) Hamilton County
65	666	**Bellaire** (village) Belmont County
65	666	**Kirtland** (city) Lake County
65	666	**Sylvania** (city) Lucas County
68	669	**Ashtabula** (city) Ashtabula County
68	669	**Avon** (city) Lorain County
68	669	**Sheffield** (village) Lorain County
71	673	**Geneva** (city) Ashtabula County
71	673	**North Madison** (CDP) Lake County
73	676	**Defiance** (city) Defiance County
73	676	**Painesville** (city) Lake County
73	676	**Zanesville** (city) Muskingum County
76	679	**Napoleon** (city) Henry County
76	679	**Nelsonville** (city) Athens County
78	682	**Edgewood** (CDP) Ashtabula County
78	682	**Franklin** (city) Warren County
78	682	**Gibsonburg** (village) Sandusky County
78	682	**Swanton** (village) Fulton County
82	686	**Devola** (CDP) Washington County
82	686	**East Cleveland** (city) Cuyahoga County
82	686	**Jackson** (city) Jackson County
85	689	**Amherst** (city) Lorain County
85	689	**Carlisle** (village) Warren County
85	689	**Shadyside** (village) Belmont County
88	692	**Bowling Green** (city) Wood County
88	692	**Mentor** (city) Lake County
88	692	**Rocky River** (city) Cuyahoga County
91	696	**Circleville** (city) Pickaway County
91	696	**Clyde** (city) Sandusky County
91	696	**Toronto** (city) Jefferson County
91	696	**Wellsville** (village) Columbiana County
95	702	**Lakewood** (city) Cuyahoga County
96	705	**Miamisburg** (city) Montgomery County
97	709	**Martins Ferry** (city) Belmont County
97	709	**North Kingsville** (village) Ashtabula County
97	709	**Westlake** (city) Cuyahoga County
100	712	**Ashville** (village) Pickaway County
101	715	**The Plains** (CDP) Athens County
101	715	**West Carrollton** (city) Montgomery County
103	718	**Athens** (city) Athens County
103	718	**Germantown** (city) Montgomery County
105	722	**Delta** (village) Fulton County
105	722	**Paulding** (village) Paulding County
107	725	**Ottawa** (village) Putnam County
107	725	**Sherwood** (CDP) Hamilton County
109	728	**Madison** (village) Lake County
109	728	**North Ridgeville** (city) Lorain County
109	728	**Norwalk** (city) Huron County
112	732	**Archbold** (village) Fulton County
112	732	**Fruit Hill** (CDP) Hamilton County
112	732	**North Baltimore** (village) Wood County
115	738	**Dayton** (city) Montgomery County
115	738	**Elyria** (city) Lorain County
115	738	**Moraine** (city) Montgomery County
115	738	**Springdale** (city) Hamilton County
115	738	**Wellston** (city) Jackson County
120	741	**Groveport** (city) Franklin County
120	741	**Logan** (city) Hocking County
122	745	**Fairview Park** (city) Cuyahoga County
122	745	**Salem Heights** (CDP) Hamilton County
122	745	**Tiffin** (city) Seneca County
125	748	**Obetz** (village) Franklin County
125	748	**Pleasant Run** (CDP) Hamilton County
127	751	**Bellevue** (city) Sandusky County
127	751	**Waynesville** (village) Warren County
129	755	**Berea** (city) Cuyahoga County
130	758	**Blacklick Estates** (CDP) Franklin County
131	761	**Canal Winchester** (city) Franklin County
131	761	**Hicksville** (village) Defiance County
131	761	**North Olmsted** (city) Cuyahoga County
134	764	**Brooklyn** (city) Cuyahoga County
134	764	**Madeira** (city) Hamilton County
134	764	**Pleasant Run Farm** (CDP) Hamilton County
134	764	**Wickliffe** (city) Lake County
138	768	**Bryan** (city) Williams County
138	768	**East Liverpool** (city) Columbiana County
138	768	**Wauseon** (city) Fulton County
141	771	**Grandview Heights** (city) Franklin County
141	771	**Lebanon** (city) Warren County
143	774	**Coshocton** (city) Coshocton County
143	774	**Delphos** (city) Allen County
143	774	**Findlay** (city) Hancock County
143	774	**Olmsted Falls** (city) Cuyahoga County
147	778	**Bellbrook** (city) Greene County
147	778	**Riverside** (city) Montgomery County
147	778	**Van Wert** (city) Van Wert County
150	781	**Columbus** (city) Franklin County

***Note:** This section ranks incorporated places and CDPs (Census Designated Places) with populations of 2,500 or more. Unincorporated postal areas were not considered. Please refer to the User Guide for additional information.*

Population

Top 150 Places Ranked in *Descending* Order

State Rank	Number	Place
1	837,038	**Columbus** (city) Franklin County
2	389,165	**Cleveland** (city) Cuyahoga County
3	298,011	**Cincinnati** (city) Hamilton County
4	280,854	**Toledo** (city) Lucas County
5	198,508	**Akron** (city) Summit County
6	141,143	**Dayton** (city) Montgomery County
7	80,088	**Parma** (city) Cuyahoga County
8	72,163	**Canton** (city) Stark County
9	65,161	**Youngstown** (city) Mahoning County
10	63,714	**Lorain** (city) Lorain County
11	62,259	**Hamilton** (city) Butler County
12	59,761	**Springfield** (city) Clark County
13	55,720	**Kettering** (city) Montgomery County
14	53,928	**Elyria** (city) Lorain County
15	50,866	**Lakewood** (city) Cuyahoga County
16	49,353	**Cuyahoga Falls** (city) Summit County
17	48,527	**Middletown** (city) Butler County
18	48,477	**Newark** (city) Licking County
19	47,863	**Euclid** (city) Cuyahoga County
20	46,902	**Mansfield** (city) Richland County
21	46,896	**Mentor** (city) Lake County
22	46,086	**Beavercreek** (city) Greene County
23	45,160	**Cleveland Heights** (city) Cuyahoga County
24	44,622	**Strongsville** (city) Cuyahoga County
25	43,874	**Dublin** (city) Franklin County
26	42,640	**Fairfield** (city) Butler County
27	41,412	**Findlay** (city) Hancock County
28	40,433	**Warren** (city) Trumbull County
29	39,483	**Lancaster** (city) Fairfield County
30	38,795	**Huber Heights** (city) Montgomery County
31	38,374	**Grove City** (city) Franklin County
32	38,089	**Westerville** (city) Franklin County
33	37,836	**Lima** (city) Allen County
34	37,554	**Delaware** (city) Delaware County
35	36,995	**Reynoldsburg** (city) Franklin County
36	36,568	**Marion** (city) Marion County
37	34,746	**Stow** (city) Summit County
38	34,717	**Boardman** (CDP) Mahoning County
39	34,675	**Upper Arlington** (city) Franklin County
40	34,578	**Brunswick** (city) Medina County
41	34,373	**Gahanna** (city) Franklin County
42	33,487	**Fairborn** (city) Greene County
43	33,108	**Hilliard** (city) Franklin County
44	32,408	**Westlake** (city) Cuyahoga County
45	32,268	**Massillon** (city) Stark County
46	32,108	**North Olmsted** (city) Cuyahoga County
47	32,025	**Mason** (city) Warren County
48	31,832	**North Ridgeville** (city) Lorain County
49	31,641	**Bowling Green** (city) Wood County
50	30,302	**North Royalton** (city) Cuyahoga County
51	29,761	**Kent** (city) Portage County
52	28,468	**Austintown** (CDP) Mahoning County
53	28,207	**Garfield Heights** (city) Cuyahoga County
54	27,773	**Shaker Heights** (city) Cuyahoga County
55	26,773	**Wooster** (city) Wayne County
56	26,445	**Medina** (city) Medina County
57	26,266	**Barberton** (city) Summit County
58	26,105	**Xenia** (city) Greene County
59	25,713	**Green** (city) Summit County
60	25,684	**Troy** (city) Miami County
61	25,467	**Zanesville** (city) Muskingum County
62	25,338	**Sandusky** (city) Erie County
63	25,036	**Riverside** (city) Montgomery County
64	24,372	**Trotwood** (city) Montgomery County
65	24,365	**Athens** (city) Athens County
66	23,899	**Centerville** (city) Montgomery County
67	23,221	**Avon Lake** (city) Lorain County
68	23,085	**Solon** (city) Cuyahoga County
69	22,860	**Marysville** (city) Union County
70	22,685	**Maple Heights** (city) Cuyahoga County
71	22,578	**Wadsworth** (city) Medina County
72	22,495	**Willoughby** (city) Lake County
73	22,289	**Avon** (city) Lorain County
74	22,282	**Hudson** (city) Summit County
75	22,121	**Alliance** (city) Stark County

State Rank	Number	Place
76	21,941	**Oxford** (city) Butler County
77	21,865	**South Euclid** (city) Cuyahoga County
78	21,748	**Chillicothe** (city) Ross County
79	21,367	**Perrysburg** (city) Wood County
80	20,761	**Sidney** (city) Shelby County
81	20,743	**Piqua** (city) Miami County
82	20,536	**Lebanon** (city) Warren County
83	20,419	**Ashland** (city) Ashland County
84	20,393	**Portsmouth** (city) Scioto County
85	20,311	**Parma Heights** (city) Cuyahoga County
86	20,211	**Rocky River** (city) Cuyahoga County
87	20,137	**Oregon** (city) Lucas County
88	20,069	**Miamisburg** (city) Montgomery County
89	19,735	**Painesville** (city) Lake County
90	19,462	**Norwood** (city) Hamilton County
91	19,379	**Pickerington** (city) Fairfield County
92	19,257	**Broadview Heights** (city) Cuyahoga County
93	19,068	**White Oak** (CDP) Hamilton County
94	18,949	**Berea** (city) Cuyahoga County
95	18,882	**Sylvania** (city) Lucas County
96	18,878	**Mayfield Heights** (city) Cuyahoga County
97	18,877	**Niles** (city) Trumbull County
98	18,875	**Brook Park** (city) Cuyahoga County
99	18,851	**Twinsburg** (city) Summit County
100	18,679	**Forest Park** (city) Hamilton County
101	18,596	**Whitehall** (city) Franklin County
102	18,540	**Ashtabula** (city) Ashtabula County
103	18,342	**Eastlake** (city) Lake County
104	18,305	**Steubenville** (city) Jefferson County
105	17,978	**Springboro** (city) Warren County
106	17,701	**Tiffin** (city) Seneca County
107	17,488	**Tallmadge** (city) Summit County
108	17,422	**North Canton** (city) Stark County
109	17,413	**East Cleveland** (city) Cuyahoga County
110	17,412	**New Philadelphia** (city) Tuscarawas County
111	16,862	**Norwalk** (city) Huron County
112	16,777	**Mount Vernon** (city) Knox County
113	16,725	**Defiance** (city) Defiance County
114	16,473	**Fairview Park** (city) Cuyahoga County
115	16,388	**Fremont** (city) Sandusky County
116	16,224	**Streetsboro** (city) Portage County
117	15,724	**Middleburg Heights** (city) Cuyahoga County
118	15,712	**Aurora** (city) Portage County
119	15,414	**Bay Village** (city) Cuyahoga County
120	15,225	**Pataskala** (city) Licking County
121	15,127	**Vandalia** (city) Montgomery County
122	14,195	**New Franklin** (city) Summit County
123	14,155	**Worthington** (city) Franklin County
124	14,150	**Bridgetown** (CDP) Hamilton County
125	14,131	**Willowick** (city) Lake County
126	14,115	**Washington Court House** (city) Fayette County
127	14,018	**Maumee** (city) Lucas County
128	13,912	**Marietta** (city) Washington County
129	13,782	**Sharonville** (city) Hamilton County
130	13,761	**Circleville** (city) Pickaway County
131	13,736	**Lyndhurst** (city) Cuyahoga County
132	13,552	**Monroe** (city) Butler County
133	13,534	**Bexley** (city) Franklin County
134	13,512	**Englewood** (city) Montgomery County
135	13,470	**Brecksville** (city) Cuyahoga County
136	13,397	**Fostoria** (city) Seneca County
137	13,293	**Warrensville Heights** (city) Cuyahoga County
138	13,273	**University Heights** (city) Cuyahoga County
139	13,211	**Bellefontaine** (city) Logan County
140	13,172	**Clayton** (city) Montgomery County
141	13,012	**West Carrollton** (city) Montgomery County
142	12,979	**Greenville** (city) Darke County
143	12,886	**Dover** (city) Tuscarawas County
144	12,850	**Monfort Heights** (CDP) Hamilton County
145	12,782	**Bedford** (city) Cuyahoga County
145	12,782	**Conneaut** (city) Ashtabula County
147	12,718	**Wickliffe** (city) Lake County
148	12,641	**Loveland** (city) Hamilton County
149	12,477	**Trenton** (city) Butler County
150	12,441	**Wilmington** (city) Clinton County

Note: *This section ranks incorporated places and CDPs (Census Designated Places) with populations of 2,500 or more. Unincorporated postal areas were not considered. Please refer to the User Guide for additional information.*

Population

Top 150 Places Ranked in *Ascending* Order

State Rank	Number	Place
1	2,505	**Seville** (village) Medina County
2	2,514	**Burlington** (CDP) Lawrence County
2	2,514	**Green Meadows** (CDP) Clark County
4	2,543	**Williamsburg** (village) Clermont County
5	2,546	**Crooksville** (village) Perry County
6	2,573	**Dry Ridge** (CDP) Hamilton County
7	2,590	**Devola** (CDP) Washington County
8	2,596	**Wright-Patterson AFB** (CDP) Greene County
9	2,599	**Day Heights** (CDP) Clermont County
10	2,604	**New Concord** (village) Muskingum County
11	2,607	**Covington** (village) Miami County
12	2,614	**New London** (village) Huron County
13	2,634	**Loudonville** (village) Ashland County
14	2,645	**New Richmond** (village) Clermont County
15	2,646	**Saint Henry** (village) Mercer County
16	2,648	**Enon** (village) Clark County
17	2,671	**Poland** (village) Mahoning County
18	2,683	**Newtown** (village) Hamilton County
19	2,687	**Dennison** (village) Tuscarawas County
20	2,690	**Versailles** (village) Darke County
21	2,709	**Middlefield** (village) Geauga County
22	2,717	**Gibsonburg** (village) Sandusky County
23	2,725	**Buckeye Lake** (village) Licking County
24	2,741	**Lisbon** (village) Columbiana County
24	2,741	**Oak Harbor** (village) Ottawa County
26	2,763	**Bethel** (village) Clermont County
27	2,769	**Evendale** (village) Hamilton County
28	2,784	**West Portsmouth** (CDP) Scioto County
29	2,789	**Lodi** (village) Medina County
30	2,846	**North Zanesville** (CDP) Muskingum County
31	2,859	**North Kingsville** (village) Ashtabula County
32	2,870	**Garrettsville** (village) Portage County
33	2,881	**Ballville** (CDP) Sandusky County
34	2,898	**Minster** (village) Auglaize County
35	2,918	**The Plains** (CDP) Athens County
36	2,952	**Carrollton** (village) Carroll County
37	2,963	**Baltimore** (village) Fairfield County
38	2,967	**Waynesville** (village) Warren County
39	2,994	**Beechwood Trails** (CDP) Licking County
40	2,998	**Hartville** (village) Stark County
41	3,007	**Strasburg** (village) Tuscarawas County
42	3,028	**West Union** (village) Adams County
43	3,064	**Lakemore** (village) Summit County
44	3,068	**Mount Healthy Heights** (CDP) Hamilton County
45	3,072	**Walbridge** (village) Wood County
46	3,081	**Fairport Harbor** (village) Lake County
47	3,084	**Fredericktown** (village) Knox County
48	3,089	**Doylestown** (village) Wayne County
49	3,092	**Delshire** (CDP) Hamilton County
50	3,096	**Bainbridge** (CDP) Geauga County
51	3,110	**Hicksville** (village) Defiance County
52	3,140	**Millersburg** (village) Holmes County
53	3,159	**New Bremen** (village) Auglaize County
54	3,166	**Madison** (village) Lake County
55	3,173	**McDonald** (village) Trumbull County
56	3,175	**Salem Heights** (CDP) Hamilton County
57	3,185	**Sixteen Mile Stand** (CDP) Hamilton County
58	3,229	**Taylor Creek** (CDP) Hamilton County
59	3,253	**Mingo Junction** (village) Jefferson County
60	3,268	**Cadiz** (village) Harrison County
61	3,271	**Delta** (village) Fulton County
62	3,279	**Woodlawn** (village) Hamilton County
63	3,288	**Orange** (village) Cuyahoga County
64	3,295	**Jefferson** (village) Ashtabula County
65	3,297	**Moreland Hills** (village) Cuyahoga County
66	3,304	**Richville** (CDP) Stark County
67	3,325	**Lordstown** (village) Trumbull County
68	3,341	**Brimfield** (CDP) Portage County
69	3,342	**Sherwood** (CDP) Hamilton County
70	3,359	**Four Bridges** (CDP) Butler County
71	3,360	**Lincoln Heights** (village) Hamilton County
72	3,371	**Cleves** (village) Hamilton County
73	3,400	**Mariemont** (village) Hamilton County
74	3,401	**Mayfield** (village) Cuyahoga County
75	3,407	**Mount Gilead** (village) Morrow County
76	3,414	**Dillonvale** (CDP) Hamilton County
77	3,435	**Lockland** (village) Hamilton County
78	3,436	**Wellsville** (village) Columbiana County
79	3,465	**Lake Lakengren** (CDP) Preble County
80	3,482	**Carey** (village) Wyandot County
81	3,514	**North Baltimore** (village) Wood County
82	3,543	**Calcutta** (CDP) Columbiana County
83	3,555	**Gallipolis** (village) Gallia County
84	3,588	**Golf Manor** (village) Hamilton County
85	3,591	**Greenhills** (village) Hamilton County
86	3,595	**Amberley** (village) Hamilton County
87	3,615	**Paulding** (village) Paulding County
88	3,624	**Uniontown** (CDP) Stark County
89	3,637	**Shadyside** (village) Belmont County
90	3,639	**South Point** (village) Lawrence County
91	3,651	**Richfield** (village) Summit County
92	3,662	**Mogadore** (village) Summit County
93	3,679	**Northfield** (village) Summit County
94	3,684	**Oakwood** (village) Cuyahoga County
95	3,693	**Ross** (CDP) Butler County
96	3,740	**Newcomerstown** (village) Tuscarawas County
97	3,743	**Fruit Hill** (CDP) Hamilton County
98	3,755	**Swanton** (village) Fulton County
99	3,784	**Yellow Springs** (village) Greene County
100	3,802	**Mulberry** (CDP) Clermont County
101	3,839	**South Russell** (village) Geauga County
102	3,860	**Mineral Ridge** (CDP) Trumbull County
103	3,862	**Reminderville** (village) Summit County
104	3,923	**Barnesville** (village) Belmont County
105	4,001	**Minerva** (village) Stark County
106	4,011	**Cedarville** (village) Greene County
107	4,024	**Montpelier** (village) Williams County
108	4,045	**Sheffield** (village) Lorain County
109	4,056	**Chagrin Falls** (village) Cuyahoga County
110	4,077	**Wintersville** (village) Jefferson County
111	4,088	**Greentown** (CDP) Stark County
112	4,130	**New Lebanon** (village) Montgomery County
113	4,142	**Ashville** (village) Pickaway County
114	4,159	**Mount Orab** (village) Brown County
115	4,163	**Blanchester** (village) Clinton County
116	4,189	**Bellaire** (village) Belmont County
117	4,285	**West Jefferson** (village) Madison County
118	4,294	**Sebring** (village) Mahoning County
119	4,349	**Coldwater** (village) Mercer County
120	4,352	**Saint Bernard** (city) Hamilton County
121	4,368	**Archbold** (village) Fulton County
122	4,374	**Waverly** (village) Pike County
123	4,376	**Bluffton** (village) Allen County
124	4,378	**Whitehouse** (village) Lucas County
125	4,389	**Edgewood** (CDP) Ashtabula County
126	4,392	**Lake Darby** (CDP) Franklin County
127	4,421	**Obetz** (village) Franklin County
128	4,430	**Ottawa** (village) Putnam County
129	4,444	**Plain City** (village) Madison County
130	4,463	**Crestline** (village) Crawford County
131	4,481	**Park Layne** (CDP) Clark County
132	4,497	**Ottawa Hills** (village) Lucas County
133	4,506	**New Burlington** (CDP) Hamilton County
134	4,539	**Cherry Grove** (CDP) Hamilton County
135	4,569	**Huber Ridge** (CDP) Franklin County
136	4,592	**Pleasant Run** (CDP) Hamilton County
137	4,598	**East Palestine** (village) Columbiana County
138	4,668	**Newton Falls** (village) Trumbull County
139	4,690	**West Milton** (village) Miami County
140	4,691	**Mount Repose** (CDP) Clermont County
141	4,740	**Miami Heights** (CDP) Hamilton County
142	4,746	**South Lebanon** (village) Warren County
143	4,766	**Silverton** (village) Hamilton County
144	4,776	**Montrose-Ghent** (CDP) Summit County
145	4,794	**Greenfield** (village) Highland County
146	4,810	**Georgetown** (village) Brown County
147	4,926	**Sunbury** (village) Delaware County
148	4,992	**New Lexington** (village) Perry County
149	4,999	**Johnstown** (village) Licking County
150	5,055	**Munroe Falls** (city) Summit County

Note: *This section ranks incorporated places and CDPs (Census Designated Places) with populations of 2,500 or more. Unincorporated postal areas were not considered. Please refer to the User Guide for additional information.*

Population Growth Since 2000

Top 150 Places Ranked in *Descending* Order

State Rank	Percent	Place
1	547.9	**New Franklin** (city) Summit County
2	163.9	**Grafton** (village) Lorain County
3	152.9	**New Albany** (city) Franklin County
4	125.3	**Withamsville** (CDP) Clermont County
5	99.1	**Powell** (city) Delaware County
6	97.9	**Pickerington** (city) Fairfield County
7	94.7	**Avon** (city) Lorain County
8	90.0	**Monroe** (city) Butler County
9	87.4	**Ross** (CDP) Butler County
10	87.3	**Sunbury** (village) Delaware County
11	87.0	**South Lebanon** (village) Warren County
12	86.5	**Amelia** (village) Clermont County
13	80.8	**Granville** (village) Licking County
14	80.3	**Mount Orab** (village) Brown County
15	73.6	**Canal Winchester** (city) Franklin County
16	64.6	**Reminderville** (village) Summit County
17	60.2	**Whitehouse** (village) Lucas County
18	57.2	**Fort Shawnee** (CDP) Allen County
19	56.9	**Plain City** (village) Madison County
20	48.8	**Delaware** (city) Delaware County
21	48.6	**Pataskala** (city) Licking County
22	45.5	**Mason** (city) Warren County
23	45.3	**Johnstown** (village) Licking County
24	45.2	**Springboro** (city) Warren County
25	44.0	**Dent** (CDP) Hamilton County
26	43.6	**White Oak** (CDP) Hamilton County
27	43.4	**Marysville** (city) Union County
28	42.7	**Trenton** (city) Butler County
29	42.5	**North Ridgeville** (city) Lorain County
30	42.3	**Groveport** (city) Franklin County
31	41.7	**Grove City** (city) Franklin County
32	40.5	**Harrison** (city) Hamilton County
33	39.8	**Dublin** (city) Franklin County
34	37.9	**Hartville** (village) Stark County
35	37.3	**Champion Heights** (CDP) Trumbull County
36	37.2	**Sheffield** (village) Lorain County
37	36.6	**Hilliard** (city) Franklin County
38	32.6	**Beechwood Trails** (CDP) Licking County
39	31.8	**Streetsboro** (city) Portage County
40	31.7	**Lexington** (village) Richland County
41	30.5	**Ashville** (village) Pickaway County
42	30.3	**Georgetown** (village) Brown County
43	30.2	**Strasburg** (village) Tuscarawas County
44	29.6	**Greentown** (CDP) Stark County
45	29.3	**Uniontown** (CDP) Stark County
46	28.0	**Avon Lake** (city) Lorain County
47	27.0	**Fredericktown** (village) Knox County
48	26.9	**Garrettsville** (village) Portage County
49	26.1	**Perrysburg** (city) Wood County
50	25.7	**Macedonia** (city) Summit County
51	22.8	**Heath** (city) Licking County
52	22.5	**Wadsworth** (city) Medina County
53	21.3	**Beavercreek** (city) Greene County
53	21.3	**Middlefield** (village) Geauga County
55	21.1	**Lebanon** (city) Warren County
55	21.1	**Mulberry** (CDP) Clermont County
57	20.8	**Cleves** (village) Hamilton County
58	20.7	**Walbridge** (village) Wood County
59	20.6	**Broadview Heights** (city) Cuyahoga County
60	19.6	**Lakemore** (village) Summit County
61	19.2	**New Richmond** (village) Clermont County
62	18.8	**Dry Run** (CDP) Hamilton County
63	17.9	**Union** (city) Montgomery County
64	17.8	**Lake Darby** (CDP) Franklin County
65	17.6	**Columbus** (city) Franklin County
66	17.5	**Mount Carmel** (CDP) Clermont County
67	16.8	**Troy** (city) Miami County
68	16.7	**Mount Vernon** (city) Knox County
69	16.5	**Saint Henry** (village) Mercer County
70	16.4	**Woodlawn** (village) Hamilton County
71	16.0	**Seville** (village) Medina County
71	16.0	**Waynesville** (village) Warren County
73	15.9	**Aurora** (city) Portage County
74	15.4	**Reynoldsburg** (city) Franklin County
75	15.3	**Ontario** (city) Richland County
76	14.7	**Columbiana** (city) Columbiana County
76	14.7	**London** (city) Madison County
78	14.4	**Mount Repose** (CDP) Clermont County
79	14.2	**Athens** (city) Athens County
80	13.8	**Waterville** (city) Lucas County
81	13.5	**Swanton** (village) Fulton County
82	13.3	**Brookville** (city) Montgomery County
83	12.8	**Painesville** (city) Lake County
84	12.7	**Germantown** (city) Montgomery County
84	12.7	**Green** (city) Summit County
86	12.3	**Bluffton** (village) Allen County
87	12.2	**Wellington** (village) Lorain County
88	11.7	**Lancaster** (city) Fairfield County
89	11.6	**Delta** (village) Fulton County
89	11.6	**Olmsted Falls** (city) Cuyahoga County
91	11.2	**Obetz** (village) Franklin County
92	11.1	**Richfield** (village) Summit County
93	10.9	**Newtown** (village) Hamilton County
94	10.8	**Twinsburg** (city) Summit County
95	10.5	**Willoughby Hills** (city) Lake County
96	10.4	**Doylestown** (village) Wayne County
96	10.4	**Englewood** (city) Montgomery County
98	8.7	**Milford** (city) Clermont County
99	8.6	**New Bremen** (village) Auglaize County
100	8.5	**Green Meadows** (CDP) Clark County
101	8.4	**Gibsonburg** (village) Sandusky County
101	8.4	**Madison** (village) Lake County
103	8.3	**Ada** (village) Hardin County
103	8.3	**Loveland** (city) Hamilton County
105	8.1	**Stow** (city) Summit County
106	8.0	**Canal Fulton** (city) Stark County
106	8.0	**Xenia** (city) Greene County
108	7.9	**Wooster** (city) Wayne County
109	7.8	**Westerville** (city) Franklin County
109	7.8	**Williamsburg** (village) Clermont County
111	7.6	**North Kingsville** (village) Ashtabula County
112	7.5	**Logan** (city) Hocking County
112	7.5	**Pleasant Run Farm** (CDP) Hamilton County
114	7.4	**Grandview Heights** (city) Franklin County
115	6.8	**Bowling Green** (city) Wood County
116	6.7	**Tallmadge** (city) Summit County
117	6.6	**Kent** (city) Portage County
117	6.6	**Tipp City** (city) Miami County
119	6.5	**New Lexington** (village) Perry County
120	6.4	**North Canton** (city) Stark County
121	6.3	**Findlay** (city) Hancock County
121	6.3	**Riverside** (city) Montgomery County
123	6.1	**Springdale** (city) Hamilton County
124	5.9	**Solon** (city) Cuyahoga County
124	5.9	**Upper Sandusky** (city) Wyandot County
126	5.8	**North Royalton** (city) Cuyahoga County
127	5.5	**Dover** (city) Tuscarawas County
128	5.3	**Gahanna** (city) Franklin County
129	5.2	**Medina** (city) Medina County
130	5.0	**Amberley** (village) Hamilton County
131	4.9	**Northridge** (CDP) Clark County
132	4.8	**Bethel** (village) Clermont County
132	4.8	**Cedarville** (village) Greene County
134	4.7	**Newark** (city) Licking County
135	4.6	**Louisville** (city) Stark County
135	4.6	**North Baltimore** (village) Wood County
137	4.5	**Fairborn** (city) Greene County
137	4.5	**Norton** (city) Summit County
139	4.4	**Turpin Hills** (CDP) Hamilton County
139	4.4	**Wilmington** (city) Clinton County
141	4.3	**West Union** (village) Adams County
142	4.2	**Lincoln Village** (CDP) Franklin County
143	4.0	**Oregon** (city) Lucas County
144	3.9	**Delphos** (city) Allen County
144	3.9	**Versailles** (village) Darke County
146	3.8	**Centerville** (city) Montgomery County
146	3.8	**Norwalk** (city) Huron County
148	3.7	**Minster** (village) Auglaize County
149	3.6	**Brunswick** (city) Medina County
149	3.6	**Clyde** (city) Sandusky County

Note: *This section ranks incorporated places and CDPs (Census Designated Places) with populations of 2,500 or more. Unincorporated postal areas were not considered. Please refer to the User Guide for additional information.*

Population Growth Since 2000

Top 150 Places Ranked in *Ascending* Order

State Rank	Percent	Place
1	-61.0	**Wright-Patterson AFB** (CDP) Greene County
2	-46.9	**Landen** (CDP) Warren County
3	-36.0	**East Cleveland** (city) Cuyahoga County
4	-31.3	**Portage Lakes** (CDP) Summit County
5	-20.6	**Youngstown** (city) Mahoning County
6	-19.5	**West Portsmouth** (CDP) Scioto County
7	-18.7	**Cleveland** (city) Cuyahoga County
8	-18.3	**Lincoln Heights** (village) Hamilton County
9	-16.9	**Wellsville** (village) Columbiana County
10	-16.6	**East Liverpool** (city) Columbiana County
11	-15.3	**Mount Healthy** (city) Hamilton County
12	-15.1	**Dayton** (city) Montgomery County
13	-15.0	**Campbell** (city) Mahoning County
13	-15.0	**Gallipolis** (village) Gallia County
15	-14.8	**Hicksville** (village) Defiance County
16	-14.4	**Bellaire** (village) Belmont County
17	-13.7	**Warren** (city) Trumbull County
18	-13.3	**Maple Heights** (city) Cuyahoga County
19	-12.8	**Pleasant Run** (CDP) Hamilton County
20	-12.6	**Sebring** (village) Mahoning County
21	-12.5	**Greenhills** (village) Hamilton County
22	-12.3	**Crestline** (village) Crawford County
23	-12.0	**Warrensville Heights** (city) Cuyahoga County
24	-11.8	**Girard** (city) Trumbull County
25	-11.6	**Ashtabula** (city) Ashtabula County
25	-11.6	**Huron** (city) Erie County
25	-11.6	**Saint Bernard** (city) Hamilton County
28	-11.5	**Ballville** (CDP) Sandusky County
29	-11.2	**Struthers** (city) Mahoning County
30	-11.1	**Mount Healthy Heights** (CDP) Hamilton County
30	-11.1	**Trotwood** (city) Montgomery County
32	-11.0	**Brook Park** (city) Cuyahoga County
33	-10.9	**Shelby** (city) Richland County
34	-10.7	**Canton** (city) Stark County
34	-10.7	**Carey** (village) Wyandot County
36	-10.6	**Buckeye Lake** (village) Licking County
37	-10.4	**Evendale** (village) Hamilton County
37	-10.4	**Mingo Junction** (village) Jefferson County
37	-10.4	**Toledo** (city) Lucas County
37	-10.4	**Toronto** (city) Jefferson County
41	-10.3	**Golf Manor** (village) Hamilton County
41	-10.3	**Willard** (city) Huron County
43	-10.2	**Dennison** (village) Tuscarawas County
43	-10.2	**Lakewood** (city) Cuyahoga County
43	-10.2	**Norwood** (city) Hamilton County
46	-10.1	**Bedford** (city) Cuyahoga County
46	-10.1	**Lyndhurst** (city) Cuyahoga County
48	-10.0	**Austintown** (CDP) Mahoning County
48	-10.0	**Burlington** (CDP) Lawrence County
48	-10.0	**Cincinnati** (city) Hamilton County
51	-9.8	**Niles** (city) Trumbull County
52	-9.7	**Galion** (city) Crawford County
53	-9.6	**Cleveland Heights** (city) Cuyahoga County
54	-9.4	**Bainbridge** (CDP) Geauga County
54	-9.4	**Eastlake** (city) Lake County
54	-9.4	**Loudonville** (village) Ashland County
57	-9.2	**Bucyrus** (city) Crawford County
57	-9.2	**Euclid** (city) Cuyahoga County
57	-9.2	**Montrose-Ghent** (CDP) Summit County
60	-9.0	**Finneytown** (CDP) Hamilton County
60	-9.0	**Sandusky** (city) Erie County
62	-8.9	**Cambridge** (city) Guernsey County
62	-8.9	**Lodi** (village) Medina County
62	-8.9	**Mentor-on-the-Lake** (city) Lake County
65	-8.8	**McDonald** (village) Trumbull County
66	-8.6	**Akron** (city) Summit County
66	-8.6	**Springfield** (city) Clark County
68	-8.5	**Lordstown** (village) Trumbull County
69	-8.4	**Reading** (city) Hamilton County
70	-8.3	**Wheelersburg** (CDP) Scioto County
71	-8.2	**Garfield Heights** (city) Cuyahoga County
72	-8.1	**Dillonvale** (CDP) Hamilton County
73	-8.0	**Maumee** (city) Lucas County
73	-8.0	**Moraine** (city) Montgomery County
73	-8.0	**Silverton** (village) Hamilton County
76	-7.9	**Day Heights** (CDP) Clermont County
76	-7.9	**Geneva** (city) Ashtabula County
76	-7.9	**Wellston** (city) Jackson County
79	-7.8	**Edgewood** (CDP) Ashtabula County
79	-7.8	**Jefferson** (village) Ashtabula County
81	-7.7	**Cheviot** (city) Hamilton County
82	-7.5	**Carrollton** (village) Carroll County
83	-7.4	**Kenton** (city) Hardin County
84	-7.3	**Lockland** (village) Hamilton County
84	-7.3	**North College Hill** (city) Hamilton County
86	-7.2	**Hubbard** (city) Trumbull County
86	-7.2	**Lorain** (city) Lorain County
88	-7.1	**Barnesville** (village) Belmont County
88	-7.1	**Napoleon** (city) Henry County
88	-7.1	**South Euclid** (city) Cuyahoga County
91	-7.0	**Northbrook** (CDP) Hamilton County
92	-6.9	**Montpelier** (village) Williams County
93	-6.8	**Poland** (village) Mahoning County
94	-6.7	**Boardman** (CDP) Mahoning County
94	-6.7	**Kenwood** (CDP) Hamilton County
94	-6.7	**Mentor** (city) Lake County
94	-6.7	**Newcomerstown** (village) Tuscarawas County
94	-6.7	**Newton Falls** (village) Trumbull County
99	-6.6	**Summerside** (CDP) Clermont County
100	-6.5	**Bedford Heights** (city) Cuyahoga County
100	-6.5	**Devola** (CDP) Washington County
100	-6.5	**East Palestine** (village) Columbiana County
100	-6.5	**Parma** (city) Cuyahoga County
104	-6.4	**Huber Ridge** (CDP) Franklin County
105	-6.3	**Fairview Park** (city) Cuyahoga County
106	-6.2	**Parma Heights** (city) Cuyahoga County
106	-6.2	**University Heights** (city) Cuyahoga County
108	-6.1	**Port Clinton** (city) Ottawa County
109	-6.0	**Middletown** (city) Butler County
110	-5.9	**Barberton** (city) Summit County
110	-5.9	**Mogadore** (village) Summit County
110	-5.9	**North Olmsted** (city) Cuyahoga County
113	-5.7	**Fremont** (city) Sandusky County
113	-5.7	**Martins Ferry** (city) Belmont County
113	-5.7	**Northgate** (CDP) Hamilton County
113	-5.7	**Wickliffe** (city) Lake County
117	-5.6	**Brooklyn** (city) Cuyahoga County
117	-5.6	**Lima** (city) Allen County
117	-5.6	**Millersburg** (village) Holmes County
117	-5.6	**Shaker Heights** (city) Cuyahoga County
121	-5.5	**North Zanesville** (CDP) Muskingum County
122	-5.2	**Blacklick Estates** (CDP) Franklin County
123	-5.1	**Fruit Hill** (CDP) Hamilton County
124	-5.0	**Mansfield** (city) Richland County
125	-4.9	**Alliance** (city) Stark County
125	-4.9	**Munroe Falls** (city) Summit County
127	-4.6	**Deer Park** (city) Hamilton County
127	-4.6	**Uhrichsville** (city) Tuscarawas County
129	-4.5	**South Russell** (village) Geauga County
130	-4.3	**Richmond Heights** (city) Cuyahoga County
131	-4.2	**Bay Village** (city) Cuyahoga County
131	-4.2	**Coshocton** (city) Coshocton County
131	-4.2	**Marietta** (city) Washington County
134	-4.0	**Forest Park** (city) Hamilton County
134	-4.0	**Vermilion** (city) Lorain County
136	-3.9	**Ashland** (city) Ashland County
136	-3.9	**Northfield** (village) Summit County
138	-3.8	**Fostoria** (city) Seneca County
139	-3.7	**Steubenville** (city) Jefferson County
140	-3.6	**Elyria** (city) Lorain County
141	-3.5	**Oak Harbor** (village) Ottawa County
142	-3.4	**Groesbeck** (CDP) Hamilton County
142	-3.4	**Sheffield Lake** (city) Lorain County
144	-3.3	**Beachwood** (city) Cuyahoga County
144	-3.3	**Forestville** (CDP) Hamilton County
146	-3.2	**Belpre** (city) Washington County
146	-3.2	**Seven Hills** (city) Cuyahoga County
146	-3.2	**Whitehall** (city) Franklin County
149	-3.1	**Fairport Harbor** (village) Lake County
149	-3.1	**Kettering** (city) Montgomery County

Note: *This section ranks incorporated places and CDPs (Census Designated Places) with populations of 2,500 or more. Unincorporated postal areas were not considered. Please refer to the User Guide for additional information.*

Population Density

Top 150 Places Ranked in *Descending* Order

State Rank	Pop./ Sq. Mi.	Place
1	9,190.8	**Lakewood** (city) Cuyahoga County
2	7,291.7	**University Heights** (city) Cuyahoga County
3	7,123.2	**Cheviot** (city) Hamilton County
4	6,531.0	**Deer Park** (city) Hamilton County
5	6,235.5	**Golf Manor** (village) Hamilton County
6	6,183.8	**Norwood** (city) Hamilton County
7	5,643.1	**East Cleveland** (city) Cuyahoga County
8	5,571.2	**Willowick** (city) Lake County
9	5,570.8	**Cleveland Heights** (city) Cuyahoga County
10	5,567.1	**Bexley** (city) Franklin County
11	5,400.0	**Grandview Heights** (city) Franklin County
12	5,382.8	**Lincoln Village** (CDP) Franklin County
13	5,284.1	**Northbrook** (CDP) Hamilton County
14	5,120.1	**North College Hill** (city) Hamilton County
15	5,008.8	**Cleveland** (city) Cuyahoga County
16	4,852.6	**Parma Heights** (city) Cuyahoga County
17	4,804.2	**Pleasant Run Farm** (CDP) Hamilton County
18	4,772.2	**Blacklick Estates** (CDP) Franklin County
19	4,701.5	**South Euclid** (city) Cuyahoga County
20	4,589.8	**Mentor-on-the-Lake** (city) Lake County
21	4,528.9	**Mayfield Heights** (city) Cuyahoga County
22	4,502.6	**Euclid** (city) Cuyahoga County
23	4,441.3	**Lincoln Heights** (village) Hamilton County
24	4,424.0	**Delshire** (CDP) Hamilton County
25	4,420.7	**Shaker Heights** (city) Cuyahoga County
26	4,387.8	**Huber Ridge** (CDP) Franklin County
27	4,386.0	**Maple Heights** (city) Cuyahoga County
28	4,305.2	**Mount Healthy** (city) Hamilton County
29	4,287.4	**Silverton** (village) Hamilton County
30	4,265.8	**Rocky River** (city) Cuyahoga County
31	4,135.4	**Oakwood** (city) Montgomery County
32	4,008.0	**Cherry Grove** (CDP) Hamilton County
33	3,999.5	**Parma** (city) Cuyahoga County
34	3,947.0	**Mount Healthy Heights** (CDP) Hamilton County
35	3,935.5	**Mariemont** (village) Hamilton County
36	3,901.5	**Garfield Heights** (city) Cuyahoga County
37	3,854.3	**Columbus** (city) Franklin County
38	3,833.2	**Dillonvale** (CDP) Hamilton County
39	3,823.5	**Cincinnati** (city) Hamilton County
40	3,656.2	**Sheffield Lake** (city) Lorain County
41	3,598.8	**Shadyside** (village) Belmont County
42	3,576.7	**Reading** (city) Hamilton County
43	3,556.1	**Delhi Hills** (CDP) Hamilton County
44	3,537.3	**Whitehall** (city) Franklin County
45	3,524.3	**Upper Arlington** (city) Franklin County
46	3,521.2	**Fairview Park** (city) Cuyahoga County
47	3,480.6	**Toledo** (city) Lucas County
48	3,398.3	**Northfield** (village) Summit County
49	3,376.0	**Bay Village** (city) Cuyahoga County
50	3,340.8	**Landen** (CDP) Warren County
51	3,315.8	**Reynoldsburg** (city) Franklin County
52	3,314.2	**Berea** (city) Cuyahoga County
53	3,286.3	**Oxford** (city) Butler County
54	3,273.6	**Bridgetown** (CDP) Hamilton County
55	3,243.9	**Kent** (city) Portage County
56	3,217.5	**Warrensville Heights** (city) Cuyahoga County
57	3,200.1	**Akron** (city) Summit County
58	3,149.8	**Green Meadows** (CDP) Clark County
59	3,140.1	**Painesville** (city) Lake County
60	3,128.6	**Cedarville** (village) Greene County
61	3,125.6	**Sherwood** (CDP) Hamilton County
62	3,115.9	**Marion** (city) Marion County
63	3,099.5	**Lyndhurst** (city) Cuyahoga County
64	3,092.1	**White Oak** (CDP) Hamilton County
65	3,059.6	**Park Layne** (CDP) Clark County
66	3,053.7	**Westerville** (city) Franklin County
67	3,050.4	**Perry Heights** (CDP) Stark County
68	3,026.3	**Finneytown** (CDP) Hamilton County
69	3,005.0	**Kenwood** (CDP) Hamilton County
70	2,999.8	**Fairport Harbor** (village) Lake County
71	2,989.3	**Northgate** (CDP) Hamilton County
72	2,983.3	**Kettering** (city) Montgomery County
73	2,958.3	**Wyoming** (city) Hamilton County
74	2,934.9	**Fruit Hill** (CDP) Hamilton County
75	2,925.7	**Martins Ferry** (city) Belmont County
76	2,915.0	**Sylvania** (city) Lucas County
77	2,909.3	**Ada** (village) Hardin County
78	2,906.1	**Barberton** (city) Summit County
79	2,888.9	**Port Clinton** (city) Ottawa County
80	2,882.9	**Hamilton** (city) Butler County
81	2,882.7	**Greenhills** (village) Hamilton County
82	2,882.6	**Forest Park** (city) Hamilton County
83	2,868.2	**Eastlake** (city) Lake County
84	2,867.8	**Struthers** (city) Mahoning County
85	2,865.4	**Amelia** (village) Clermont County
86	2,854.7	**Sixteen Mile Stand** (CDP) Hamilton County
87	2,850.7	**Forestville** (CDP) Hamilton County
88	2,834.1	**Canton** (city) Stark County
89	2,815.1	**Saint Bernard** (city) Hamilton County
90	2,790.1	**Lockland** (village) Hamilton County
91	2,789.3	**Lima** (city) Allen County
92	2,766.0	**Gahanna** (city) Franklin County
93	2,760.6	**Mount Carmel** (CDP) Clermont County
94	2,750.4	**North Olmsted** (city) Cuyahoga County
95	2,741.8	**Wickliffe** (city) Lake County
96	2,737.5	**Toronto** (city) Jefferson County
97	2,734.2	**Trenton** (city) Butler County
98	2,722.2	**North Canton** (city) Stark County
99	2,691.4	**Lorain** (city) Lorain County
100	2,677.2	**Brunswick** (city) Medina County
101	2,655.2	**Ironton** (city) Lawrence County
102	2,642.6	**Madeira** (city) Hamilton County
103	2,621.5	**Elyria** (city) Lorain County
104	2,617.1	**Tiffin** (city) Seneca County
105	2,605.3	**Sandusky** (city) Erie County
106	2,575.8	**Riverside** (city) Montgomery County
107	2,574.1	**Brooklyn** (city) Cuyahoga County
108	2,565.7	**Loveland** (city) Hamilton County
109	2,563.6	**New Lexington** (village) Perry County
110	2,552.8	**Worthington** (city) Franklin County
111	2,544.7	**Fairborn** (city) Greene County
112	2,538.6	**Bellaire** (village) Belmont County
113	2,536.2	**Dayton** (city) Montgomery County
114	2,521.7	**Powell** (city) Delaware County
115	2,519.7	**Bowling Green** (city) Wood County
116	2,514.5	**Hilliard** (city) Franklin County
117	2,507.1	**Warren** (city) Trumbull County
118	2,506.7	**Brook Park** (city) Cuyahoga County
119	2,479.4	**Athens** (city) Athens County
120	2,478.8	**Alliance** (city) Stark County
121	2,473.2	**Summerside** (CDP) Clermont County
122	2,447.9	**Austintown** (CDP) Mahoning County
123	2,435.5	**Ottawa Hills** (village) Lucas County
124	2,397.0	**Ashtabula** (city) Ashtabula County
125	2,393.2	**East Liverpool** (city) Columbiana County
126	2,391.0	**Mulberry** (CDP) Clermont County
127	2,388.7	**Bedford** (city) Cuyahoga County
128	2,383.5	**Seven Hills** (city) Cuyahoga County
129	2,369.3	**Grove City** (city) Franklin County
130	2,362.6	**Springfield** (city) Clark County
131	2,362.5	**Groesbeck** (CDP) Hamilton County
132	2,361.8	**Richmond Heights** (city) Cuyahoga County
133	2,356.0	**Northridge** (CDP) Clark County
134	2,346.4	**Bedford Heights** (city) Cuyahoga County
135	2,325.9	**Greenfield** (village) Highland County
136	2,321.3	**Newark** (city) Licking County
137	2,306.9	**Mount Repose** (CDP) Clermont County
138	2,295.9	**Boardman** (CDP) Mahoning County
139	2,285.3	**Medina** (city) Medina County
140	2,273.9	**Withamsville** (CDP) Clermont County
141	2,266.7	**Dover** (city) Tuscarawas County
142	2,265.9	**Bellbrook** (city) Greene County
143	2,261.1	**Coldwater** (village) Mercer County
144	2,257.8	**Springdale** (city) Hamilton County
145	2,219.3	**Pleasant Run** (CDP) Hamilton County
146	2,216.9	**Centerville** (city) Montgomery County
147	2,213.3	**Beachwood** (city) Cuyahoga County
148	2,212.4	**Covedale** (CDP) Hamilton County
149	2,206.0	**Day Heights** (CDP) Clermont County
150	2,194.8	**Willoughby** (city) Lake County

Note: *This section ranks incorporated places and CDPs (Census Designated Places) with populations of 2,500 or more. Unincorporated postal areas were not considered. Please refer to the User Guide for additional information.*

Population Density

Top 150 Places Ranked in *Ascending* Order

State Rank	Pop./ Sq. Mi.	Place
1	143.7	**Lordstown** (village) Trumbull County
2	261.5	**Wright-Patterson AFB** (CDP) Greene County
3	298.6	**Calcutta** (CDP) Columbiana County
4	312.8	**The Village of Indian Hill** (city) Hamilton County
5	321.7	**North Kingsville** (village) Ashtabula County
6	372.3	**Cadiz** (village) Harrison County
7	376.5	**Sheffield** (village) Lorain County
8	382.8	**Taylor Creek** (CDP) Hamilton County
9	391.8	**Richfield** (village) Summit County
10	408.0	**Kirtland** (city) Lake County
11	461.2	**Moreland Hills** (village) Cuyahoga County
12	468.0	**Mount Orab** (village) Brown County
13	485.0	**Conneaut** (city) Ashtabula County
14	504.4	**Devola** (CDP) Washington County
15	506.8	**Montrose-Ghent** (CDP) Summit County
16	532.0	**Pataskala** (city) Licking County
17	551.9	**Ontario** (city) Richland County
18	567.0	**New Franklin** (city) Summit County
19	583.9	**Evendale** (village) Hamilton County
20	591.7	**West Portsmouth** (CDP) Scioto County
21	597.4	**Norton** (city) Summit County
22	621.4	**Dry Ridge** (CDP) Hamilton County
23	622.4	**Madison** (village) Lake County
24	626.2	**Northwood** (city) Wood County
25	642.5	**Edgewood** (CDP) Ashtabula County
25	642.5	**Groveport** (city) Franklin County
27	671.8	**Oregon** (city) Lucas County
28	685.6	**Aurora** (city) Portage County
28	685.6	**Moraine** (city) Montgomery County
30	688.2	**Brecksville** (city) Cuyahoga County
31	691.6	**Streetsboro** (city) Portage County
32	711.8	**Clayton** (city) Montgomery County
33	745.8	**Independence** (city) Cuyahoga County
34	764.4	**Obetz** (village) Franklin County
35	765.7	**Beechwood Trails** (CDP) Licking County
36	770.9	**Jackson** (city) Jackson County
37	774.9	**New Richmond** (village) Clermont County
38	775.8	**Champion Heights** (CDP) Trumbull County
39	799.2	**Trotwood** (city) Montgomery County
40	801.2	**North Zanesville** (CDP) Muskingum County
41	802.2	**Green** (city) Summit County
42	802.7	**Wellston** (city) Jackson County
43	812.0	**New Albany** (city) Franklin County
44	840.7	**Fort Shawnee** (CDP) Allen County
45	841.5	**Brimfield** (CDP) Portage County
46	853.8	**Monroe** (city) Butler County
47	860.9	**Mayfield** (village) Cuyahoga County
48	864.6	**Orange** (village) Cuyahoga County
49	870.5	**Hudson** (city) Summit County
50	871.3	**Pepper Pike** (city) Cuyahoga County
51	883.5	**West Jefferson** (village) Madison County
52	885.2	**Willoughby Hills** (city) Lake County
53	885.7	**Archbold** (village) Fulton County
54	896.7	**Middlefield** (village) Geauga County
55	912.9	**Bainbridge** (CDP) Geauga County
56	925.4	**Apple Valley** (CDP) Knox County
57	931.8	**Union** (city) Montgomery County
58	943.4	**Ottawa** (village) Putnam County
59	958.7	**Heath** (city) Licking County
60	962.5	**Seville** (village) Medina County
61	984.6	**Vermilion** (city) Lorain County
62	986.6	**Upper Sandusky** (city) Wyandot County
63	988.2	**Gallipolis** (village) Gallia County
64	1,003.5	**Blanchester** (village) Clinton County
65	1,005.9	**Mount Gilead** (village) Morrow County
66	1,013.5	**Loudonville** (village) Ashland County
67	1,015.2	**Rittman** (city) Wayne County
68	1,020.0	**Whitehouse** (village) Lucas County
69	1,021.9	**Wheelersburg** (CDP) Scioto County
70	1,022.6	**South Russell** (village) Geauga County
71	1,027.5	**Amberley** (village) Hamilton County
72	1,041.3	**Canal Winchester** (city) Franklin County
73	1,056.1	**Richville** (CDP) Stark County
74	1,065.9	**Ballville** (CDP) Sandusky County
75	1,069.6	**West Union** (village) Adams County
76	1,071.2	**Avon** (city) Lorain County
77	1,072.0	**Oakwood** (village) Cuyahoga County
78	1,072.9	**Nelsonville** (city) Athens County
79	1,077.2	**Columbiana** (city) Columbiana County
80	1,133.8	**Solon** (city) Cuyahoga County
81	1,134.1	**Chardon** (city) Geauga County
82	1,134.3	**Gibsonburg** (village) Sandusky County
83	1,141.9	**Garrettsville** (village) Portage County
84	1,142.5	**Wilmington** (city) Clinton County
85	1,163.8	**Hartville** (village) Stark County
86	1,170.8	**Hicksville** (village) Defiance County
87	1,172.1	**Waterville** (city) Lucas County
88	1,183.1	**Mineral Ridge** (CDP) Trumbull County
89	1,184.9	**Ross** (CDP) Butler County
90	1,185.4	**New London** (village) Huron County
91	1,189.3	**Georgetown** (village) Brown County
92	1,190.6	**London** (city) Madison County
93	1,194.6	**Macedonia** (city) Summit County
94	1,206.5	**Carrollton** (village) Carroll County
95	1,209.5	**Mingo Junction** (village) Jefferson County
96	1,210.6	**Hillsboro** (city) Highland County
97	1,211.7	**Lake Lakengren** (CDP) Preble County
98	1,213.6	**Swanton** (village) Fulton County
99	1,224.6	**Granville** (village) Licking County
100	1,225.2	**Delta** (village) Fulton County
101	1,225.5	**Vandalia** (city) Montgomery County
102	1,233.8	**Bluffton** (village) Allen County
103	1,235.4	**Newtown** (village) Hamilton County
104	1,238.2	**South Point** (village) Lawrence County
105	1,239.7	**Mack** (CDP) Hamilton County
106	1,241.8	**Lodi** (village) Medina County
107	1,245.7	**Clyde** (city) Sandusky County
108	1,248.3	**Waynesville** (village) Warren County
109	1,249.5	**Tallmadge** (city) Summit County
110	1,268.2	**Lake Darby** (CDP) Franklin County
111	1,275.6	**Woodlawn** (village) Hamilton County
112	1,281.4	**The Plains** (CDP) Athens County
113	1,286.6	**Franklin** (city) Warren County
114	1,289.2	**Grafton** (village) Lorain County
115	1,291.1	**Germantown** (city) Montgomery County
116	1,298.0	**Rossford** (city) Wood County
117	1,306.1	**Tipp City** (city) Miami County
118	1,306.4	**Williamsburg** (village) Clermont County
119	1,307.0	**Wintersville** (village) Jefferson County
120	1,308.0	**Jefferson** (village) Ashtabula County
121	1,313.4	**Bellevue** (city) Sandusky County
122	1,315.7	**Newcomerstown** (village) Tuscarawas County
123	1,316.3	**Bellefontaine** (city) Logan County
124	1,335.7	**Eaton** (city) Preble County
125	1,346.8	**Galion** (city) Crawford County
126	1,349.5	**Miami Heights** (CDP) Hamilton County
127	1,358.1	**North Ridgeville** (city) Lorain County
128	1,362.6	**Buckeye Lake** (village) Licking County
129	1,365.8	**Wauseon** (city) Fulton County
130	1,369.0	**Twinsburg** (city) Summit County
131	1,378.6	**Shelby** (city) Richland County
132	1,383.2	**Montpelier** (village) Williams County
133	1,384.3	**Coshocton** (city) Coshocton County
134	1,399.8	**Napoleon** (city) Henry County
135	1,401.8	**Sharonville** (city) Hamilton County
136	1,404.9	**Marysville** (city) Union County
137	1,405.0	**Walbridge** (village) Wood County
138	1,408.2	**Wellington** (village) Lorain County
139	1,409.7	**Crestline** (village) Crawford County
140	1,416.3	**Millersburg** (village) Holmes County
141	1,417.7	**Baltimore** (village) Fairfield County
142	1,418.0	**Maumee** (city) Lucas County
143	1,422.0	**North Royalton** (city) Cuyahoga County
144	1,422.4	**North Baltimore** (village) Wood County
145	1,438.4	**Lexington** (village) Richland County
146	1,439.6	**Defiance** (city) Defiance County
147	1,441.0	**Versailles** (village) Darke County
148	1,445.7	**West Milton** (village) Miami County
149	1,450.0	**Carlisle** (village) Warren County
150	1,454.1	**Uniontown** (CDP) Stark County

Note: *This section ranks incorporated places and CDPs (Census Designated Places) with populations of 2,500 or more. Unincorporated postal areas were not considered. Please refer to the User Guide for additional information.*

White Population

Top 150 Places Ranked in *Descending* Order

State Rank	Percent	Place
1	100.0	**Strasburg** (village) Tuscarawas County
2	99.8	**Poland** (village) Mahoning County
3	99.6	**Sebring** (village) Mahoning County
4	99.5	**Day Heights** (CDP) Clermont County
5	99.4	**Mogadore** (village) Summit County
5	99.4	**Versailles** (village) Darke County
7	99.3	**Shadyside** (village) Belmont County
8	99.1	**Saint Henry** (village) Mercer County
9	99.0	**Columbiana** (city) Columbiana County
9	99.0	**South Russell** (village) Geauga County
11	98.9	**Kirtland** (city) Lake County
11	98.9	**Shelby** (city) Richland County
13	98.8	**Bellevue** (city) Sandusky County
13	98.8	**Fairport Harbor** (village) Lake County
13	98.8	**West Portsmouth** (CDP) Scioto County
16	98.7	**Ross** (CDP) Butler County
17	98.6	**Covington** (village) Miami County
17	98.6	**Greentown** (CDP) Stark County
17	98.6	**Harrison** (city) Hamilton County
17	98.6	**Johnstown** (village) Licking County
17	98.6	**McDonald** (village) Trumbull County
17	98.6	**Waynesville** (village) Warren County
17	98.6	**West Union** (village) Adams County
24	98.5	**Calcutta** (CDP) Columbiana County
25	98.4	**Champion Heights** (CDP) Trumbull County
26	98.3	**Beechwood Trails** (CDP) Licking County
26	98.3	**Brookville** (city) Montgomery County
26	98.3	**Mount Gilead** (village) Morrow County
26	98.3	**Salem Heights** (CDP) Hamilton County
26	98.3	**Union** (city) Montgomery County
31	98.2	**Baltimore** (village) Fairfield County
31	98.2	**Madison** (village) Lake County
31	98.2	**Vermilion** (city) Lorain County
34	98.1	**Carrollton** (village) Carroll County
34	98.1	**Uniontown** (CDP) Stark County
36	98.0	**Coldwater** (village) Mercer County
36	98.0	**Germantown** (city) Montgomery County
36	98.0	**Mount Carmel** (CDP) Clermont County
39	97.9	**Barnesville** (village) Belmont County
40	97.8	**Bellbrook** (city) Greene County
40	97.8	**Jackson** (city) Jackson County
40	97.8	**North Madison** (CDP) Lake County
40	97.8	**Richfield** (village) Summit County
40	97.8	**Walbridge** (village) Wood County
45	97.7	**Bainbridge** (CDP) Geauga County
45	97.7	**Bethel** (village) Clermont County
45	97.7	**Cortland** (city) Trumbull County
45	97.7	**Turpin Hills** (CDP) Hamilton County
49	97.6	**Fredericktown** (village) Knox County
49	97.6	**Loudonville** (village) Ashland County
51	97.5	**Carlisle** (village) Warren County
51	97.5	**Chagrin Falls** (village) Cuyahoga County
51	97.5	**Lisbon** (village) Columbiana County
51	97.5	**Mount Repose** (CDP) Clermont County
51	97.5	**Norton** (city) Summit County
56	97.4	**Cleves** (village) Hamilton County
56	97.4	**Crooksville** (village) Perry County
56	97.4	**Galion** (city) Crawford County
56	97.4	**Greenfield** (village) Highland County
56	97.4	**Independence** (city) Cuyahoga County
56	97.4	**New Lexington** (village) Perry County
56	97.4	**Olmsted Falls** (city) Cuyahoga County
56	97.4	**Summerside** (CDP) Clermont County
56	97.4	**Tipp City** (city) Miami County
65	97.3	**Whitehouse** (village) Lucas County
66	97.2	**Geneva** (city) Ashtabula County
66	97.2	**Kenton** (city) Hardin County
66	97.2	**Newcomerstown** (village) Tuscarawas County
66	97.2	**Wellston** (city) Jackson County
70	97.1	**Apple Valley** (CDP) Knox County
70	97.1	**Bryan** (city) Williams County
70	97.1	**Minster** (village) Auglaize County
70	97.1	**Struthers** (city) Mahoning County
70	97.1	**Uhrichsville** (city) Tuscarawas County
75	97.0	**Mariemont** (village) Hamilton County
75	97.0	**Newton Falls** (village) Trumbull County
75	97.0	**Swanton** (village) Fulton County
78	96.9	**Blanchester** (village) Clinton County
78	96.9	**Bridgetown** (CDP) Hamilton County
78	96.9	**Logan** (city) Hocking County
78	96.9	**Oakwood** (city) Montgomery County
82	96.8	**Millersburg** (village) Holmes County
83	96.7	**Bucyrus** (city) Crawford County
83	96.7	**Garrettsville** (village) Portage County
83	96.7	**Jefferson** (village) Ashtabula County
83	96.7	**Rittman** (city) Wayne County
87	96.6	**Enon** (village) Clark County
87	96.6	**Greenville** (city) Darke County
87	96.6	**Huron** (city) Erie County
87	96.6	**Mentor** (city) Lake County
87	96.6	**Mineral Ridge** (CDP) Trumbull County
87	96.6	**New Franklin** (city) Summit County
87	96.6	**Plain City** (village) Madison County
87	96.6	**Wapakoneta** (city) Auglaize County
95	96.5	**Delta** (village) Fulton County
95	96.5	**Dillonvale** (CDP) Hamilton County
95	96.5	**Louisville** (city) Stark County
95	96.5	**New Bremen** (village) Auglaize County
95	96.5	**Withamsville** (CDP) Clermont County
100	96.4	**Hubbard** (city) Trumbull County
100	96.4	**Miami Heights** (CDP) Hamilton County
100	96.4	**Northwood** (city) Wood County
100	96.4	**Oak Harbor** (village) Ottawa County
104	96.3	**Amherst** (city) Lorain County
104	96.3	**Lodi** (village) Medina County
104	96.3	**Mack** (CDP) Hamilton County
104	96.3	**Mount Orab** (village) Brown County
108	96.2	**Hartville** (village) Stark County
108	96.2	**Middlefield** (village) Geauga County
108	96.2	**North Canton** (city) Stark County
111	96.1	**Perry Heights** (CDP) Stark County
111	96.1	**Rocky River** (city) Cuyahoga County
111	96.1	**Upper Sandusky** (city) Wyandot County
114	96.0	**Eaton** (city) Preble County
114	96.0	**Northridge** (CDP) Clark County
114	96.0	**West Milton** (village) Miami County
117	95.9	**Bay Village** (city) Cuyahoga County
117	95.9	**Brunswick** (city) Medina County
119	95.8	**Amelia** (village) Clermont County
119	95.8	**Canal Fulton** (city) Stark County
119	95.8	**Clyde** (city) Sandusky County
119	95.8	**Loveland** (city) Hamilton County
119	95.8	**Mulberry** (CDP) Clermont County
119	95.8	**South Point** (village) Lawrence County
125	95.7	**Brecksville** (city) Cuyahoga County
125	95.7	**Carey** (village) Wyandot County
125	95.7	**Richville** (CDP) Stark County
125	95.7	**Wadsworth** (city) Medina County
129	95.6	**Lake Lakengren** (CDP) Preble County
129	95.6	**Portage Lakes** (CDP) Summit County
131	95.5	**Ballville** (CDP) Sandusky County
131	95.5	**Delhi Hills** (CDP) Hamilton County
131	95.5	**Mount Vernon** (city) Knox County
131	95.5	**New Richmond** (village) Clermont County
131	95.5	**Rossford** (city) Wood County
131	95.5	**Salem** (city) Columbiana County
131	95.5	**Seven Hills** (city) Cuyahoga County
138	95.4	**Bluffton** (village) Allen County
139	95.3	**Seville** (village) Medina County
139	95.3	**Williamsburg** (village) Clermont County
141	95.2	**New London** (village) Huron County
141	95.2	**Saint Marys** (city) Auglaize County
143	95.1	**Ashland** (city) Ashland County
143	95.1	**Coshocton** (city) Coshocton County
143	95.1	**Madeira** (city) Hamilton County
143	95.1	**Mentor-on-the-Lake** (city) Lake County
143	95.1	**New Carlisle** (city) Clark County
143	95.1	**Van Wert** (city) Van Wert County
149	95.0	**Franklin** (city) Warren County
149	95.0	**North Baltimore** (village) Wood County

Note: *This section ranks incorporated places and CDPs (Census Designated Places) with populations of 2,500 or more. Unincorporated postal areas were not considered. Please refer to the User Guide for additional information.*

White Population

Top 150 Places Ranked in *Ascending* Order

State Rank	Percent	Place
1	4.6	**Warrensville Heights** (city) Cuyahoga County
2	6.6	**East Cleveland** (city) Cuyahoga County
3	8.8	**Lincoln Heights** (village) Hamilton County
4	20.0	**Bedford Heights** (city) Cuyahoga County
5	23.9	**Maple Heights** (city) Cuyahoga County
6	24.3	**Trotwood** (city) Montgomery County
7	25.1	**Golf Manor** (village) Hamilton County
8	26.0	**Forest Park** (city) Hamilton County
9	27.6	**Woodlawn** (village) Hamilton County
10	36.1	**Oakwood** (village) Cuyahoga County
11	37.3	**Euclid** (city) Cuyahoga County
12	40.3	**Cleveland** (city) Cuyahoga County
13	41.1	**Bedford** (city) Cuyahoga County
14	43.3	**Silverton** (village) Hamilton County
15	45.7	**Richmond Heights** (city) Cuyahoga County
16	49.1	**Youngstown** (city) Mahoning County
17	49.3	**Cleveland Heights** (city) Cuyahoga County
18	50.4	**North College Hill** (city) Hamilton County
19	50.5	**Garfield Heights** (city) Cuyahoga County
20	50.7	**Cincinnati** (city) Hamilton County
20	50.7	**New Burlington** (CDP) Hamilton County
22	51.5	**Mount Healthy Heights** (CDP) Hamilton County
23	51.8	**Pleasant Run Farm** (CDP) Hamilton County
24	52.1	**South Euclid** (city) Cuyahoga County
25	52.2	**Whitehall** (city) Franklin County
26	53.3	**Lockland** (village) Hamilton County
27	53.4	**Mount Healthy** (city) Hamilton County
28	54.7	**Shaker Heights** (city) Cuyahoga County
29	54.8	**Springdale** (city) Hamilton County
30	54.9	**Dayton** (city) Montgomery County
31	57.1	**Finneytown** (CDP) Hamilton County
32	60.1	**Northbrook** (CDP) Hamilton County
33	61.1	**Akron** (city) Summit County
33	61.1	**Columbus** (city) Franklin County
35	63.5	**Toledo** (city) Lucas County
36	63.7	**Blacklick Estates** (CDP) Franklin County
37	64.2	**Grafton** (village) Lorain County
38	64.3	**Reynoldsburg** (city) Franklin County
39	66.8	**Warren** (city) Trumbull County
40	67.1	**Lima** (city) Allen County
41	68.1	**Canton** (city) Stark County
42	68.5	**Oberlin** (city) Lorain County
43	69.0	**Sixteen Mile Stand** (CDP) Hamilton County
44	69.2	**Sandusky** (city) Erie County
45	69.3	**Campbell** (city) Mahoning County
46	71.3	**Orange** (village) Cuyahoga County
47	72.6	**Painesville** (city) Lake County
47	72.6	**Solon** (city) Cuyahoga County
49	73.0	**Mansfield** (city) Richland County
50	73.4	**Lorain** (city) Lorain County
51	73.6	**Pickerington** (city) Fairfield County
52	73.8	**Groveport** (city) Franklin County
53	73.9	**University Heights** (city) Cuyahoga County
54	74.6	**Clayton** (city) Montgomery County
55	74.7	**Springfield** (city) Clark County
56	75.1	**Sharonville** (city) Hamilton County
57	75.2	**Groesbeck** (CDP) Hamilton County
58	75.5	**Twinsburg** (city) Summit County
59	76.0	**Northgate** (CDP) Hamilton County
60	76.4	**Dublin** (city) Franklin County
61	77.2	**Huber Heights** (city) Montgomery County
62	77.5	**Willoughby Hills** (city) Lake County
62	77.5	**Wyoming** (city) Hamilton County
64	77.8	**Beachwood** (city) Cuyahoga County
64	77.8	**Elyria** (city) Lorain County
66	78.3	**Blue Ash** (city) Hamilton County
66	78.3	**Pleasant Run** (CDP) Hamilton County
68	78.4	**Saint Bernard** (city) Hamilton County
69	78.5	**Reminderville** (village) Summit County
70	78.8	**Huber Ridge** (CDP) Franklin County
71	79.3	**Mayfield Heights** (city) Cuyahoga County
72	79.5	**Brooklyn** (city) Cuyahoga County
73	80.0	**Kent** (city) Portage County
74	80.1	**Fairfield** (city) Butler County
75	80.8	**Fremont** (city) Sandusky County
75	80.8	**Steubenville** (city) Jefferson County
77	80.9	**Northfield** (village) Summit County
78	81.4	**Gahanna** (city) Franklin County
79	81.8	**Middletown** (city) Butler County
80	81.9	**Xenia** (city) Greene County
81	82.0	**Fairborn** (city) Greene County
82	82.2	**Englewood** (city) Montgomery County
83	82.6	**Beckett Ridge** (CDP) Butler County
83	82.6	**West Carrollton** (city) Montgomery County
85	82.8	**Pepper Pike** (city) Cuyahoga County
86	83.0	**Greenhills** (village) Hamilton County
86	83.0	**Wright-Patterson AFB** (CDP) Greene County
88	83.2	**Cheviot** (city) Hamilton County
89	83.5	**Cedarville** (village) Greene County
90	83.6	**Macedonia** (city) Summit County
91	83.7	**Athens** (city) Athens County
91	83.7	**New Albany** (city) Franklin County
93	83.8	**Kenwood** (CDP) Hamilton County
93	83.8	**White Oak** (CDP) Hamilton County
95	84.0	**Yellow Springs** (village) Greene County
96	84.3	**Moraine** (city) Montgomery County
97	84.6	**Fairlawn** (city) Summit County
97	84.6	**Mason** (city) Warren County
99	84.7	**Hamilton** (city) Butler County
100	84.8	**Alliance** (city) Stark County
101	84.9	**Ontario** (city) Richland County
102	85.0	**Ashtabula** (city) Ashtabula County
102	85.0	**Zanesville** (city) Muskingum County
104	85.1	**Marion** (city) Marion County
105	85.3	**Mingo Junction** (village) Jefferson County
106	85.5	**Lincoln Village** (CDP) Franklin County
107	85.6	**Deer Park** (city) Hamilton County
107	85.6	**Wauseon** (city) Fulton County
109	85.7	**Middleburg Heights** (city) Cuyahoga County
109	85.7	**Obetz** (village) Franklin County
109	85.7	**Riverside** (city) Montgomery County
112	85.9	**Four Bridges** (CDP) Butler County
113	86.0	**Broadview Heights** (city) Cuyahoga County
113	86.0	**Powell** (city) Delaware County
115	86.3	**Westerville** (city) Franklin County
116	86.5	**Archbold** (village) Fulton County
117	86.6	**Streetsboro** (city) Portage County
118	86.7	**Parma Heights** (city) Cuyahoga County
118	86.7	**Paulding** (village) Paulding County
120	86.8	**Fostoria** (city) Seneca County
120	86.8	**Lakewood** (city) Cuyahoga County
122	87.0	**Defiance** (city) Defiance County
123	87.2	**Centerville** (city) Montgomery County
123	87.2	**Monfort Heights** (CDP) Hamilton County
125	87.3	**Dry Ridge** (CDP) Hamilton County
125	87.3	**Lyndhurst** (city) Cuyahoga County
127	87.4	**Beavercreek** (city) Greene County
128	87.5	**Austintown** (CDP) Mahoning County
128	87.5	**Evendale** (village) Hamilton County
130	87.6	**Wellsville** (village) Columbiana County
131	87.8	**Norwood** (city) Hamilton County
132	87.9	**Chillicothe** (city) Ross County
133	88.0	**Ottawa** (village) Putnam County
133	88.0	**The Village of Indian Hill** (city) Hamilton County
135	88.1	**Berea** (city) Cuyahoga County
135	88.1	**Granville** (village) Licking County
137	88.2	**Hilliard** (city) Franklin County
138	88.3	**Martins Ferry** (city) Belmont County
139	88.4	**Amberley** (village) Hamilton County
139	88.4	**Bowling Green** (city) Wood County
141	88.5	**Avon** (city) Lorain County
141	88.5	**Ottawa Hills** (village) Lucas County
141	88.5	**Sidney** (city) Shelby County
144	88.6	**Reading** (city) Hamilton County
145	88.7	**Gibsonburg** (village) Sandusky County
145	88.7	**Springboro** (city) Warren County
147	88.8	**Bexley** (city) Franklin County
147	88.8	**Montgomery** (city) Hamilton County
149	88.9	**Oxford** (city) Butler County
150	89.0	**Barberton** (city) Summit County

Note: *This section ranks incorporated places and CDPs (Census Designated Places) with populations of 2,500 or more. Unincorporated postal areas were not considered. Please refer to the User Guide for additional information.*

Black/African American Population

Top 150 Places Ranked in *Descending* Order

State Rank	Percent	Place
1	92.1	**Warrensville Heights** (city) Cuyahoga County
2	90.3	**East Cleveland** (city) Cuyahoga County
3	87.4	**Lincoln Heights** (village) Hamilton County
4	72.7	**Bedford Heights** (city) Cuyahoga County
5	72.1	**Maple Heights** (city) Cuyahoga County
6	69.9	**Trotwood** (city) Montgomery County
7	69.4	**Golf Manor** (village) Hamilton County
8	60.0	**Forest Park** (city) Hamilton County
9	59.5	**Euclid** (city) Cuyahoga County
10	59.2	**Oakwood** (village) Cuyahoga County
11	59.1	**Woodlawn** (village) Hamilton County
12	55.2	**Bedford** (city) Cuyahoga County
13	50.8	**Cleveland** (city) Cuyahoga County
14	50.4	**Silverton** (village) Hamilton County
15	46.2	**North College Hill** (city) Hamilton County
16	45.7	**Richmond Heights** (city) Cuyahoga County
17	45.3	**Garfield Heights** (city) Cuyahoga County
18	45.1	**New Burlington** (CDP) Hamilton County
19	44.6	**Mount Healthy Heights** (CDP) Hamilton County
19	44.6	**Pleasant Run Farm** (CDP) Hamilton County
21	43.7	**Youngstown** (city) Mahoning County
22	43.1	**Cincinnati** (city) Hamilton County
23	42.7	**Cleveland Heights** (city) Cuyahoga County
24	41.0	**South Euclid** (city) Cuyahoga County
25	39.8	**Dayton** (city) Montgomery County
26	39.7	**Mount Healthy** (city) Hamilton County
27	37.6	**Lockland** (village) Hamilton County
28	36.5	**Finneytown** (CDP) Hamilton County
29	34.3	**Shaker Heights** (city) Cuyahoga County
30	33.2	**Springdale** (city) Hamilton County
31	32.0	**Whitehall** (city) Franklin County
32	31.3	**Blacklick Estates** (CDP) Franklin County
32	31.3	**Northbrook** (CDP) Hamilton County
34	30.5	**Akron** (city) Summit County
35	30.4	**Grafton** (village) Lorain County
36	29.0	**Warren** (city) Trumbull County
37	28.0	**Columbus** (city) Franklin County
38	27.2	**Toledo** (city) Lucas County
39	26.9	**Reynoldsburg** (city) Franklin County
40	25.9	**Lima** (city) Allen County
41	24.3	**Canton** (city) Stark County
42	21.5	**Groveport** (city) Franklin County
43	21.4	**Campbell** (city) Mahoning County
44	21.2	**Sandusky** (city) Erie County
45	20.7	**Clayton** (city) Montgomery County
46	20.6	**University Heights** (city) Cuyahoga County
47	18.8	**Northgate** (CDP) Hamilton County
48	18.5	**Orange** (village) Cuyahoga County
49	18.4	**Pickerington** (city) Fairfield County
50	17.8	**Mansfield** (city) Richland County
51	17.6	**Saint Bernard** (city) Hamilton County
52	17.4	**Springfield** (city) Clark County
53	17.3	**Groesbeck** (CDP) Hamilton County
54	16.2	**Lorain** (city) Lorain County
55	15.7	**Pleasant Run** (CDP) Hamilton County
56	15.6	**Oberlin** (city) Lorain County
57	15.1	**Elyria** (city) Lorain County
58	15.0	**Willoughby Hills** (city) Lake County
59	14.8	**Wyoming** (city) Hamilton County
60	14.5	**Xenia** (city) Greene County
61	14.4	**Greenhills** (village) Hamilton County
62	13.9	**Mayfield Heights** (city) Cuyahoga County
62	13.9	**Painesville** (city) Lake County
62	13.9	**Steubenville** (city) Jefferson County
62	13.9	**Twinsburg** (city) Summit County
66	13.8	**Huber Heights** (city) Montgomery County
67	13.7	**Sharonville** (city) Hamilton County
68	13.6	**Cheviot** (city) Hamilton County
69	13.4	**Reminderville** (village) Summit County
70	13.1	**Fairfield** (city) Butler County
71	12.9	**Gahanna** (city) Franklin County
72	12.8	**Moraine** (city) Montgomery County
73	12.4	**West Carrollton** (city) Montgomery County
74	12.3	**Yellow Springs** (village) Greene County
75	11.9	**Middletown** (city) Butler County
76	11.8	**Huber Ridge** (CDP) Franklin County
76	11.8	**Wright-Patterson AFB** (CDP) Greene County
78	11.7	**Englewood** (city) Montgomery County
79	11.4	**Solon** (city) Cuyahoga County
80	10.7	**Cedarville** (village) Greene County
80	10.7	**Sixteen Mile Stand** (CDP) Hamilton County
82	10.4	**Monfort Heights** (CDP) Hamilton County
83	10.3	**Hamilton** (city) Butler County
84	10.2	**Beachwood** (city) Cuyahoga County
85	10.0	**Lyndhurst** (city) Cuyahoga County
86	9.9	**Alliance** (city) Stark County
86	9.9	**Kent** (city) Portage County
88	9.8	**Marion** (city) Marion County
89	9.5	**Amberley** (village) Hamilton County
89	9.5	**Austintown** (CDP) Mahoning County
91	9.3	**Kenwood** (CDP) Hamilton County
91	9.3	**Norwood** (city) Hamilton County
93	9.2	**Macedonia** (city) Summit County
93	9.2	**Reading** (city) Hamilton County
95	9.1	**Fremont** (city) Sandusky County
96	8.9	**Fairlawn** (city) Summit County
97	8.8	**Wintersville** (village) Jefferson County
98	8.7	**Avon** (city) Lorain County
98	8.7	**Lincoln Village** (CDP) Franklin County
98	8.7	**White Oak** (CDP) Hamilton County
101	8.6	**Ashtabula** (city) Ashtabula County
102	8.5	**Conneaut** (city) Ashtabula County
103	8.3	**Beckett Ridge** (CDP) Butler County
104	8.1	**Fairborn** (city) Greene County
105	8.0	**Cadiz** (village) Harrison County
105	8.0	**Zanesville** (city) Muskingum County
107	7.8	**Riverside** (city) Montgomery County
107	7.8	**Westerville** (city) Franklin County
109	7.7	**Obetz** (village) Franklin County
110	7.5	**Brooklyn** (city) Cuyahoga County
110	7.5	**Wilmington** (city) Clinton County
112	7.4	**Bellaire** (village) Belmont County
112	7.4	**Pataskala** (city) Licking County
112	7.4	**Streetsboro** (city) Portage County
115	7.3	**Parma Heights** (city) Cuyahoga County
116	7.2	**Lakemore** (village) Summit County
116	7.2	**Massillon** (city) Stark County
118	7.1	**Barberton** (city) Summit County
119	7.0	**Boardman** (CDP) Mahoning County
120	6.9	**Blue Ash** (city) Hamilton County
120	6.9	**Lakewood** (city) Cuyahoga County
122	6.7	**Sidney** (city) Shelby County
123	6.6	**Martins Ferry** (city) Belmont County
124	6.5	**Deer Park** (city) Hamilton County
125	6.4	**Berea** (city) Cuyahoga County
125	6.4	**Wellsville** (village) Columbiana County
127	6.3	**Montrose-Ghent** (CDP) Summit County
127	6.3	**Saint Clairsville** (city) Belmont County
129	6.2	**Ironton** (city) Lawrence County
129	6.2	**Vandalia** (city) Montgomery County
131	6.1	**Bowling Green** (city) Wood County
132	6.0	**Bexley** (city) Franklin County
132	6.0	**Centerville** (city) Montgomery County
132	6.0	**Sheffield** (village) Lorain County
135	5.9	**Canal Winchester** (city) Franklin County
136	5.8	**Fostoria** (city) Seneca County
136	5.8	**Pepper Pike** (city) Cuyahoga County
138	5.7	**Granville** (village) Licking County
138	5.7	**Portsmouth** (city) Scioto County
140	5.6	**East Liverpool** (city) Columbiana County
140	5.6	**Wickliffe** (city) Lake County
142	5.5	**Evendale** (village) Hamilton County
142	5.5	**New Albany** (city) Franklin County
144	5.3	**Four Bridges** (CDP) Butler County
145	5.2	**Lebanon** (city) Warren County
146	5.1	**Brook Park** (city) Cuyahoga County
146	5.1	**Burlington** (CDP) Lawrence County
146	5.1	**Mingo Junction** (village) Jefferson County
146	5.1	**Willoughby** (city) Lake County
150	5.0	**Chillicothe** (city) Ross County

Note: *This section ranks incorporated places and CDPs (Census Designated Places) with populations of 2,500 or more. Unincorporated postal areas were not considered. Please refer to the User Guide for additional information.*

Black/African American Population

Top 150 Places Ranked in *Ascending* Order

State Rank	Percent	Place
1	0.0	**Ashville** (village) Pickaway County
1	0.0	**Baltimore** (village) Fairfield County
1	0.0	**Buckeye Lake** (village) Licking County
1	0.0	**Canfield** (city) Mahoning County
1	0.0	**Clyde** (city) Sandusky County
1	0.0	**Covington** (village) Miami County
1	0.0	**Crooksville** (village) Perry County
1	0.0	**Day Heights** (CDP) Clermont County
1	0.0	**Delshire** (CDP) Hamilton County
1	0.0	**Dry Run** (CDP) Hamilton County
1	0.0	**Enon** (village) Clark County
1	0.0	**Germantown** (city) Montgomery County
1	0.0	**Hicksville** (village) Defiance County
1	0.0	**Johnstown** (village) Licking County
1	0.0	**Lake Lakengren** (CDP) Preble County
1	0.0	**Louisville** (city) Stark County
1	0.0	**Minster** (village) Auglaize County
1	0.0	**Mount Carmel** (CDP) Clermont County
1	0.0	**New Bremen** (village) Auglaize County
1	0.0	**New Carlisle** (city) Clark County
1	0.0	**Newton Falls** (village) Trumbull County
1	0.0	**North Baltimore** (village) Wood County
1	0.0	**Oak Harbor** (village) Ottawa County
1	0.0	**Oakwood** (city) Montgomery County
1	0.0	**Poland** (village) Mahoning County
1	0.0	**Ross** (CDP) Butler County
1	0.0	**South Russell** (village) Geauga County
1	0.0	**Strasburg** (village) Tuscarawas County
1	0.0	**Union** (city) Montgomery County
1	0.0	**Vermilion** (city) Lorain County
1	0.0	**Versailles** (village) Darke County
1	0.0	**Walbridge** (village) Wood County
1	0.0	**Wellston** (city) Jackson County
1	0.0	**West Milton** (village) Miami County
1	0.0	**West Portsmouth** (CDP) Scioto County
36	0.1	**Bethel** (village) Clermont County
36	0.1	**Bryan** (city) Williams County
36	0.1	**Galion** (city) Crawford County
36	0.1	**Harrison** (city) Hamilton County
36	0.1	**Mogadore** (village) Summit County
36	0.1	**Montpelier** (village) Williams County
36	0.1	**Shelby** (city) Richland County
36	0.1	**Wauseon** (city) Fulton County
44	0.2	**Bellbrook** (city) Greene County
44	0.2	**Bellevue** (city) Sandusky County
44	0.2	**Kirtland** (city) Lake County
44	0.2	**Miami Heights** (CDP) Hamilton County
44	0.2	**Northridge** (CDP) Clark County
44	0.2	**Plain City** (village) Madison County
44	0.2	**Shadyside** (village) Belmont County
44	0.2	**Upper Sandusky** (city) Wyandot County
44	0.2	**Wheelersburg** (CDP) Scioto County
53	0.3	**Amelia** (village) Clermont County
53	0.3	**Barnesville** (village) Belmont County
53	0.3	**Carlisle** (village) Warren County
53	0.3	**Carrollton** (village) Carroll County
53	0.3	**Chagrin Falls** (village) Cuyahoga County
53	0.3	**Cherry Grove** (CDP) Hamilton County
53	0.3	**Cleves** (village) Hamilton County
53	0.3	**Coldwater** (village) Mercer County
53	0.3	**Geneva** (city) Ashtabula County
53	0.3	**Independence** (city) Cuyahoga County
53	0.3	**Mack** (CDP) Hamilton County
53	0.3	**Mariemont** (village) Hamilton County
53	0.3	**Middlefield** (village) Geauga County
53	0.3	**New Lexington** (village) Perry County
53	0.3	**North Madison** (CDP) Lake County
68	0.4	**Brookville** (city) Montgomery County
68	0.4	**Devola** (CDP) Washington County
68	0.4	**Garrettsville** (village) Portage County
68	0.4	**Mount Gilead** (village) Morrow County
68	0.4	**Newcomerstown** (village) Tuscarawas County
68	0.4	**Northwood** (city) Wood County
68	0.4	**Saint Henry** (village) Mercer County
68	0.4	**Sebring** (village) Mahoning County
68	0.4	**Uniontown** (CDP) Stark County
77	0.5	**Amherst** (city) Lorain County
77	0.5	**Blanchester** (village) Clinton County
77	0.5	**Greentown** (CDP) Stark County
77	0.5	**Hubbard** (city) Trumbull County
77	0.5	**Mayfield** (village) Cuyahoga County
77	0.5	**McDonald** (village) Trumbull County
77	0.5	**Millersburg** (village) Holmes County
77	0.5	**New Franklin** (city) Summit County
77	0.5	**Seville** (village) Medina County
77	0.5	**Wapakoneta** (city) Auglaize County
77	0.5	**Waynesville** (village) Warren County
88	0.6	**Bay Village** (city) Cuyahoga County
88	0.6	**Calcutta** (CDP) Columbiana County
88	0.6	**Columbiana** (city) Columbiana County
88	0.6	**Cortland** (city) Trumbull County
88	0.6	**Fairport Harbor** (village) Lake County
88	0.6	**Kenton** (city) Hardin County
88	0.6	**Loudonville** (village) Ashland County
88	0.6	**Mentor** (city) Lake County
88	0.6	**Saint Marys** (city) Auglaize County
88	0.6	**Sheffield Lake** (city) Lorain County
98	0.7	**Canal Fulton** (city) Stark County
98	0.7	**Carey** (village) Wyandot County
98	0.7	**Mentor-on-the-Lake** (city) Lake County
98	0.7	**Mount Repose** (CDP) Clermont County
98	0.7	**Ottawa** (village) Putnam County
98	0.7	**Park Layne** (CDP) Clark County
98	0.7	**Salem Heights** (CDP) Hamilton County
98	0.7	**Tipp City** (city) Miami County
106	0.8	**Archbold** (village) Fulton County
106	0.8	**Delta** (village) Fulton County
106	0.8	**Fredericktown** (village) Knox County
106	0.8	**Gibsonburg** (village) Sandusky County
106	0.8	**Grandview Heights** (city) Franklin County
106	0.8	**Green Meadows** (CDP) Clark County
106	0.8	**Hartville** (village) Stark County
106	0.8	**Napoleon** (city) Henry County
106	0.8	**Olmsted Falls** (city) Cuyahoga County
106	0.8	**Richfield** (village) Summit County
106	0.8	**Rittman** (city) Wayne County
106	0.8	**Turpin Hills** (CDP) Hamilton County
106	0.8	**West Jefferson** (village) Madison County
119	0.9	**Brecksville** (city) Cuyahoga County
119	0.9	**Bucyrus** (city) Crawford County
119	0.9	**Huron** (city) Erie County
119	0.9	**Jefferson** (village) Ashtabula County
119	0.9	**Sherwood** (CDP) Hamilton County
119	0.9	**Uhrichsville** (city) Tuscarawas County
119	0.9	**Waverly** (village) Pike County
119	0.9	**Willard** (city) Huron County
127	1.0	**Apple Valley** (CDP) Knox County
127	1.0	**Eaton** (city) Preble County
127	1.0	**Madeira** (city) Hamilton County
127	1.0	**Madison** (village) Lake County
127	1.0	**Mount Orab** (village) Brown County
127	1.0	**Munroe Falls** (city) Summit County
127	1.0	**Wellington** (village) Lorain County
134	1.1	**Dillonvale** (CDP) Hamilton County
134	1.1	**Jackson** (city) Jackson County
134	1.1	**Lisbon** (village) Columbiana County
134	1.1	**Sunbury** (village) Delaware County
134	1.1	**West Union** (village) Adams County
139	1.2	**Brunswick** (city) Medina County
139	1.2	**Celina** (city) Mercer County
139	1.2	**Champion Heights** (CDP) Trumbull County
139	1.2	**East Palestine** (village) Columbiana County
139	1.2	**Logan** (city) Hocking County
139	1.2	**Richville** (CDP) Stark County
139	1.2	**Struthers** (city) Mahoning County
139	1.2	**Swanton** (village) Fulton County
139	1.2	**Waterville** (city) Lucas County
139	1.2	**Worthington** (city) Franklin County
149	1.3	**Delphos** (city) Allen County
149	1.3	**Franklin** (city) Warren County

Note: *This section ranks incorporated places and CDPs (Census Designated Places) with populations of 2,500 or more. Unincorporated postal areas were not considered. Please refer to the User Guide for additional information.*

Asian Population

Top 150 Places Ranked in *Descending* Order

State Rank	Percent	Place
1	16.9	**Dublin** (city) Franklin County
2	15.3	**Sixteen Mile Stand** (CDP) Hamilton County
3	12.5	**Solon** (city) Cuyahoga County
4	11.2	**Blue Ash** (city) Hamilton County
5	10.2	**The Village of Indian Hill** (city) Hamilton County
6	9.5	**Beachwood** (city) Cuyahoga County
7	9.2	**Powell** (city) Delaware County
8	9.0	**Pepper Pike** (city) Cuyahoga County
9	8.8	**Mason** (city) Warren County
10	8.5	**Middleburg Heights** (city) Cuyahoga County
11	8.2	**New Albany** (city) Franklin County
12	8.1	**Northfield** (village) Summit County
13	7.9	**Ontario** (city) Richland County
14	7.7	**Dry Ridge** (CDP) Hamilton County
14	7.7	**Mayfield** (village) Cuyahoga County
16	7.5	**Athens** (city) Athens County
17	7.2	**Orange** (village) Cuyahoga County
18	6.7	**Ottawa Hills** (village) Lucas County
19	6.5	**Hilliard** (city) Franklin County
20	6.4	**Montgomery** (city) Hamilton County
20	6.4	**Reminderville** (village) Summit County
20	6.4	**Sharonville** (city) Hamilton County
23	6.3	**Twinsburg** (city) Summit County
24	6.1	**Oxford** (city) Butler County
25	6.0	**Broadview Heights** (city) Cuyahoga County
26	5.9	**Shaker Heights** (city) Cuyahoga County
27	5.8	**Beckett Ridge** (CDP) Butler County
28	5.5	**Kent** (city) Portage County
29	5.4	**Brooklyn** (city) Cuyahoga County
29	5.4	**Forest Park** (city) Hamilton County
29	5.4	**Oberlin** (city) Lorain County
29	5.4	**Springdale** (city) Hamilton County
29	5.4	**White Oak** (CDP) Hamilton County
34	5.3	**Beavercreek** (city) Greene County
34	5.3	**North Kingsville** (village) Ashtabula County
36	5.2	**Willoughby Hills** (city) Lake County
37	5.1	**Highland Heights** (city) Cuyahoga County
37	5.1	**Springboro** (city) Warren County
37	5.1	**Westlake** (city) Cuyahoga County
40	5.0	**Dry Run** (CDP) Hamilton County
41	4.9	**Columbus** (city) Franklin County
41	4.9	**Woodlawn** (village) Hamilton County
43	4.5	**Mayfield Heights** (city) Cuyahoga County
44	4.4	**Evendale** (village) Hamilton County
44	4.4	**Strongsville** (city) Cuyahoga County
46	4.3	**Canfield** (city) Mahoning County
46	4.3	**Fairborn** (city) Greene County
46	4.3	**Munroe Falls** (city) Summit County
46	4.3	**Richmond Heights** (city) Cuyahoga County
46	4.3	**Upper Arlington** (city) Franklin County
51	4.2	**Ada** (village) Hardin County
51	4.2	**Cherry Grove** (CDP) Hamilton County
51	4.2	**Cleveland Heights** (city) Cuyahoga County
54	4.0	**Kenwood** (CDP) Hamilton County
55	3.7	**Four Bridges** (CDP) Butler County
55	3.7	**Perrysburg** (city) Wood County
57	3.6	**Akron** (city) Summit County
57	3.6	**Hudson** (city) Summit County
57	3.6	**Pickerington** (city) Fairfield County
60	3.5	**Aurora** (city) Portage County
60	3.5	**Centerville** (city) Montgomery County
60	3.5	**Granville** (village) Licking County
60	3.5	**Lake Darby** (CDP) Franklin County
60	3.5	**North Royalton** (city) Cuyahoga County
65	3.4	**North Olmsted** (city) Cuyahoga County
66	3.3	**New Concord** (village) Muskingum County
67	3.2	**Brecksville** (city) Cuyahoga County
67	3.2	**Groveport** (city) Franklin County
67	3.2	**Landen** (CDP) Warren County
67	3.2	**Moreland Hills** (village) Cuyahoga County
71	3.1	**Wooster** (city) Wayne County
71	3.1	**Wyoming** (city) Hamilton County
73	3.0	**The Plains** (CDP) Athens County
73	3.0	**Waterville** (city) Lucas County
75	2.9	**Devola** (CDP) Washington County
75	2.9	**Heath** (city) Licking County
75	2.9	**Macedonia** (city) Summit County
75	2.9	**Marysville** (city) Union County
75	2.9	**Montpelier** (village) Williams County
80	2.8	**Parma Heights** (city) Cuyahoga County
80	2.8	**South Lebanon** (village) Warren County
82	2.7	**Buckeye Lake** (village) Licking County
82	2.7	**Fruit Hill** (CDP) Hamilton County
82	2.7	**Mount Healthy** (city) Hamilton County
82	2.7	**Sylvania** (city) Lucas County
82	2.7	**Troy** (city) Miami County
87	2.6	**Canal Winchester** (city) Franklin County
87	2.6	**Findlay** (city) Hancock County
87	2.6	**Finneytown** (CDP) Hamilton County
87	2.6	**Gahanna** (city) Franklin County
87	2.6	**Grandview Heights** (city) Franklin County
92	2.5	**Berea** (city) Cuyahoga County
92	2.5	**Wright-Patterson AFB** (CDP) Greene County
94	2.4	**Reynoldsburg** (city) Franklin County
95	2.3	**Chardon** (city) Geauga County
95	2.3	**Englewood** (city) Montgomery County
95	2.3	**Fairfield** (city) Butler County
95	2.3	**Sheffield** (village) Lorain County
99	2.2	**Carey** (village) Wyandot County
99	2.2	**Forestville** (CDP) Hamilton County
99	2.2	**Kettering** (city) Montgomery County
99	2.2	**Portage Lakes** (CDP) Summit County
99	2.2	**Riverside** (city) Montgomery County
104	2.1	**Delta** (village) Fulton County
104	2.1	**Monroe** (city) Butler County
104	2.1	**South Euclid** (city) Cuyahoga County
104	2.1	**University Heights** (city) Cuyahoga County
108	2.0	**Cleveland** (city) Cuyahoga County
108	2.0	**Deer Park** (city) Hamilton County
108	2.0	**Green Meadows** (CDP) Clark County
108	2.0	**Parma** (city) Cuyahoga County
108	2.0	**Stow** (city) Summit County
108	2.0	**Westerville** (city) Franklin County
114	1.9	**Cedarville** (village) Greene County
114	1.9	**Cuyahoga Falls** (city) Summit County
114	1.9	**Fairlawn** (city) Summit County
114	1.9	**Green** (city) Summit County
114	1.9	**Huber Heights** (city) Montgomery County
114	1.9	**Lordstown** (village) Trumbull County
114	1.9	**Maumee** (city) Lucas County
114	1.9	**Seven Hills** (city) Cuyahoga County
122	1.8	**Cincinnati** (city) Hamilton County
122	1.8	**Dillonvale** (CDP) Hamilton County
122	1.8	**London** (city) Madison County
122	1.8	**Middlefield** (village) Geauga County
122	1.8	**Waverly** (village) Pike County
127	1.7	**North Ridgeville** (city) Lorain County
127	1.7	**Pleasant Run** (CDP) Hamilton County
127	1.7	**Sidney** (city) Shelby County
127	1.7	**Streetsboro** (city) Portage County
131	1.6	**Avon** (city) Lorain County
131	1.6	**Bowling Green** (city) Wood County
131	1.6	**Carrollton** (village) Carroll County
131	1.6	**Covedale** (CDP) Hamilton County
131	1.6	**Delaware** (city) Delaware County
131	1.6	**Lakewood** (city) Cuyahoga County
131	1.6	**Lebanon** (city) Warren County
131	1.6	**Madeira** (city) Hamilton County
131	1.6	**Mentor** (city) Lake County
131	1.6	**Monfort Heights** (CDP) Hamilton County
131	1.6	**New Bremen** (village) Auglaize County
131	1.6	**Plain City** (village) Madison County
143	1.5	**Bedford** (city) Cuyahoga County
143	1.5	**Howland Center** (CDP) Trumbull County
143	1.5	**Mingo Junction** (village) Jefferson County
143	1.5	**Northridge** (CDP) Clark County
143	1.5	**Willoughby** (city) Lake County
148	1.4	**Bedford Heights** (city) Cuyahoga County
148	1.4	**Fort Shawnee** (CDP) Allen County
148	1.4	**New Lebanon** (village) Montgomery County

Note: *This section ranks incorporated places and CDPs (Census Designated Places) with populations of 2,500 or more. Unincorporated postal areas were not considered. Please refer to the User Guide for additional information.*

Asian Population

Top 150 Places Ranked in *Ascending* Order

State Rank	Percent	Place
1	0.0	**Archbold** (village) Fulton County
1	0.0	**Ashville** (village) Pickaway County
1	0.0	**Bainbridge** (CDP) Geauga County
1	0.0	**Ballville** (CDP) Sandusky County
1	0.0	**Baltimore** (village) Fairfield County
1	0.0	**Bethel** (village) Clermont County
1	0.0	**Brimfield** (CDP) Portage County
1	0.0	**Burlington** (CDP) Lawrence County
1	0.0	**Cadiz** (village) Harrison County
1	0.0	**Calcutta** (CDP) Columbiana County
1	0.0	**Campbell** (city) Mahoning County
1	0.0	**Canal Fulton** (city) Stark County
1	0.0	**Cleves** (village) Hamilton County
1	0.0	**Coldwater** (village) Mercer County
1	0.0	**Cortland** (city) Trumbull County
1	0.0	**Crooksville** (village) Perry County
1	0.0	**Day Heights** (CDP) Clermont County
1	0.0	**Delshire** (CDP) Hamilton County
1	0.0	**East Liverpool** (city) Columbiana County
1	0.0	**Edgewood** (CDP) Ashtabula County
1	0.0	**Fairport Harbor** (village) Lake County
1	0.0	**Fredericktown** (village) Knox County
1	0.0	**Gallipolis** (village) Gallia County
1	0.0	**Geneva** (city) Ashtabula County
1	0.0	**Gibsonburg** (village) Sandusky County
1	0.0	**Greentown** (CDP) Stark County
1	0.0	**Harrison** (city) Hamilton County
1	0.0	**Hartville** (village) Stark County
1	0.0	**Hubbard** (city) Trumbull County
1	0.0	**Huron** (city) Erie County
1	0.0	**Johnstown** (village) Licking County
1	0.0	**Kenton** (city) Hardin County
1	0.0	**Lakemore** (village) Summit County
1	0.0	**Lincoln Heights** (village) Hamilton County
1	0.0	**Lisbon** (village) Columbiana County
1	0.0	**Lockland** (village) Hamilton County
1	0.0	**Lodi** (village) Medina County
1	0.0	**Louisville** (city) Stark County
1	0.0	**Martins Ferry** (city) Belmont County
1	0.0	**McDonald** (village) Trumbull County
1	0.0	**Millersburg** (village) Holmes County
1	0.0	**Mineral Ridge** (CDP) Trumbull County
1	0.0	**Minerva** (village) Stark County
1	0.0	**Mount Carmel** (CDP) Clermont County
1	0.0	**Mount Gilead** (village) Morrow County
1	0.0	**Mount Healthy Heights** (CDP) Hamilton County
1	0.0	**Mount Repose** (CDP) Clermont County
1	0.0	**New Burlington** (CDP) Hamilton County
1	0.0	**New Lexington** (village) Perry County
1	0.0	**North College Hill** (city) Hamilton County
1	0.0	**Poland** (village) Mahoning County
1	0.0	**Port Clinton** (city) Ottawa County
1	0.0	**Rittman** (city) Wayne County
1	0.0	**Ross** (CDP) Butler County
1	0.0	**Saint Bernard** (city) Hamilton County
1	0.0	**Salem Heights** (CDP) Hamilton County
1	0.0	**Sebring** (village) Mahoning County
1	0.0	**Sherwood** (CDP) Hamilton County
1	0.0	**Silverton** (village) Hamilton County
1	0.0	**South Russell** (village) Geauga County
1	0.0	**Strasburg** (village) Tuscarawas County
1	0.0	**Summerside** (CDP) Clermont County
1	0.0	**Swanton** (village) Fulton County
1	0.0	**Taylor Creek** (CDP) Hamilton County
1	0.0	**Trenton** (city) Butler County
1	0.0	**Versailles** (village) Darke County
1	0.0	**Walbridge** (village) Wood County
1	0.0	**Waynesville** (village) Warren County
1	0.0	**Wellston** (city) Jackson County
1	0.0	**Wellsville** (village) Columbiana County
1	0.0	**West Jefferson** (village) Madison County
1	0.0	**West Portsmouth** (CDP) Scioto County
1	0.0	**West Union** (village) Adams County
1	0.0	**Whitehouse** (village) Lucas County
1	0.0	**Williamsburg** (village) Clermont County

State Rank	Percent	Place
1	0.0	**Wintersville** (village) Jefferson County
77	0.1	**Bellevue** (city) Sandusky County
77	0.1	**Blacklick Estates** (CDP) Franklin County
77	0.1	**Circleville** (city) Pickaway County
77	0.1	**Conneaut** (city) Ashtabula County
77	0.1	**Fostoria** (city) Seneca County
77	0.1	**Greenfield** (village) Highland County
77	0.1	**Ironton** (city) Lawrence County
77	0.1	**Jackson** (city) Jackson County
77	0.1	**Mount Vernon** (city) Knox County
77	0.1	**New Carlisle** (city) Clark County
77	0.1	**New Richmond** (village) Clermont County
77	0.1	**North Baltimore** (village) Wood County
77	0.1	**Norwalk** (city) Huron County
77	0.1	**Olmsted Falls** (city) Cuyahoga County
77	0.1	**Rossford** (city) Wood County
77	0.1	**Salem** (city) Columbiana County
77	0.1	**Shelby** (city) Richland County
77	0.1	**Struthers** (city) Mahoning County
77	0.1	**Uhrichsville** (city) Tuscarawas County
96	0.2	**Amberley** (village) Hamilton County
96	0.2	**Ashtabula** (city) Ashtabula County
96	0.2	**Bridgetown** (CDP) Hamilton County
96	0.2	**Bryan** (city) Williams County
96	0.2	**Champion Heights** (CDP) Trumbull County
96	0.2	**Cheviot** (city) Hamilton County
96	0.2	**Covington** (village) Miami County
96	0.2	**Delphos** (city) Allen County
96	0.2	**East Cleveland** (city) Cuyahoga County
96	0.2	**Fremont** (city) Sandusky County
96	0.2	**Galion** (city) Crawford County
96	0.2	**Grafton** (village) Lorain County
96	0.2	**Groesbeck** (CDP) Hamilton County
96	0.2	**Lincoln Village** (CDP) Franklin County
96	0.2	**Mariemont** (village) Hamilton County
96	0.2	**Mogadore** (village) Summit County
96	0.2	**Oak Harbor** (village) Ottawa County
96	0.2	**Sheffield Lake** (city) Lorain County
96	0.2	**Toronto** (city) Jefferson County
96	0.2	**Willard** (city) Huron County
96	0.2	**Wilmington** (city) Clinton County
117	0.3	**Beechwood Trails** (CDP) Licking County
117	0.3	**Brookville** (city) Montgomery County
117	0.3	**Carlisle** (village) Warren County
117	0.3	**Columbiana** (city) Columbiana County
117	0.3	**Huber Ridge** (CDP) Franklin County
117	0.3	**Kirtland** (city) Lake County
117	0.3	**Lexington** (village) Richland County
117	0.3	**Loveland** (city) Hamilton County
117	0.3	**Marion** (city) Marion County
117	0.3	**Niles** (city) Trumbull County
117	0.3	**Park Layne** (CDP) Clark County
117	0.3	**Perry Heights** (CDP) Stark County
117	0.3	**Pleasant Run Farm** (CDP) Hamilton County
117	0.3	**Richfield** (village) Summit County
117	0.3	**Sandusky** (city) Erie County
117	0.3	**Trotwood** (city) Montgomery County
117	0.3	**Turpin Hills** (CDP) Hamilton County
117	0.3	**Uniontown** (CDP) Stark County
117	0.3	**Urbana** (city) Champaign County
117	0.3	**Vermilion** (city) Lorain County
117	0.3	**Warren** (city) Trumbull County
117	0.3	**Xenia** (city) Greene County
117	0.3	**Yellow Springs** (village) Greene County
140	0.4	**Alliance** (city) Stark County
140	0.4	**Amherst** (city) Lorain County
140	0.4	**Canton** (city) Stark County
140	0.4	**Clyde** (city) Sandusky County
140	0.4	**Defiance** (city) Defiance County
140	0.4	**Dennison** (village) Tuscarawas County
140	0.4	**Hicksville** (village) Defiance County
140	0.4	**Lake Lakengren** (CDP) Preble County
140	0.4	**New Franklin** (city) Summit County
140	0.4	**North Madison** (CDP) Lake County
140	0.4	**Norton** (city) Summit County

Note: *This section ranks incorporated places and CDPs (Census Designated Places) with populations of 2,500 or more. Unincorporated postal areas were not considered. Please refer to the User Guide for additional information.*

American Indian/Alaska Native Population

Top 150 Places Ranked in *Descending* Order

State Rank	Percent	Place
1	2.7	**The Plains** (CDP) Athens County
2	2.2	**Mingo Junction** (village) Jefferson County
2	2.2	**Park Layne** (CDP) Clark County
4	2.0	**Gallipolis** (village) Gallia County
5	1.6	**Buckeye Lake** (village) Licking County
6	1.4	**Marietta** (city) Washington County
7	1.2	**Golf Manor** (village) Hamilton County
7	1.2	**New Franklin** (city) Summit County
7	1.2	**Saint Marys** (city) Auglaize County
7	1.2	**West Portsmouth** (CDP) Scioto County
11	1.1	**Grafton** (village) Lorain County
11	1.1	**Hicksville** (village) Defiance County
11	1.1	**Huber Heights** (city) Montgomery County
11	1.1	**Sheffield** (village) Lorain County
15	1.0	**Campbell** (city) Mahoning County
15	1.0	**Lordstown** (village) Trumbull County
17	0.9	**Sandusky** (city) Erie County
18	0.8	**Amelia** (village) Clermont County
18	0.8	**Enon** (village) Clark County
18	0.8	**Walbridge** (village) Wood County
21	0.7	**Ashville** (village) Pickaway County
21	0.7	**Cleves** (village) Hamilton County
21	0.7	**Toronto** (city) Jefferson County
21	0.7	**Uhrichsville** (city) Tuscarawas County
25	0.6	**Louisville** (city) Stark County
25	0.6	**Middleburg Heights** (city) Cuyahoga County
25	0.6	**Richmond Heights** (city) Cuyahoga County
28	0.5	**Amherst** (city) Lorain County
28	0.5	**Brooklyn** (city) Cuyahoga County
28	0.5	**Canfield** (city) Mahoning County
28	0.5	**Cleveland** (city) Cuyahoga County
28	0.5	**Clyde** (city) Sandusky County
28	0.5	**Day Heights** (CDP) Clermont County
28	0.5	**Greenville** (city) Darke County
28	0.5	**Hamilton** (city) Butler County
28	0.5	**Lorain** (city) Lorain County
28	0.5	**Montpelier** (village) Williams County
28	0.5	**Mount Orab** (village) Brown County
28	0.5	**Mount Repose** (CDP) Clermont County
28	0.5	**New Philadelphia** (city) Tuscarawas County
28	0.5	**Orrville** (city) Wayne County
28	0.5	**Wooster** (city) Wayne County
28	0.5	**Youngstown** (city) Mahoning County
44	0.4	**Berea** (city) Cuyahoga County
44	0.4	**Broadview Heights** (city) Cuyahoga County
44	0.4	**Defiance** (city) Defiance County
44	0.4	**East Cleveland** (city) Cuyahoga County
44	0.4	**Eaton** (city) Preble County
44	0.4	**Green Meadows** (CDP) Clark County
44	0.4	**Kenwood** (CDP) Hamilton County
44	0.4	**Lima** (city) Allen County
44	0.4	**Medina** (city) Medina County
44	0.4	**Nelsonville** (city) Athens County
44	0.4	**New Albany** (city) Franklin County
44	0.4	**Northwood** (city) Wood County
44	0.4	**Oberlin** (city) Lorain County
44	0.4	**Port Clinton** (city) Ottawa County
44	0.4	**Portage Lakes** (CDP) Summit County
44	0.4	**Portsmouth** (city) Scioto County
44	0.4	**Sheffield Lake** (city) Lorain County
44	0.4	**Sidney** (city) Shelby County
62	0.3	**Apple Valley** (CDP) Knox County
62	0.3	**Ashtabula** (city) Ashtabula County
62	0.3	**Beckett Ridge** (CDP) Butler County
62	0.3	**Bellaire** (village) Belmont County
62	0.3	**Canton** (city) Stark County
62	0.3	**Carlisle** (village) Warren County
62	0.3	**Cedarville** (village) Greene County
62	0.3	**Coshocton** (city) Coshocton County
62	0.3	**Dayton** (city) Montgomery County
62	0.3	**Delshire** (CDP) Hamilton County
62	0.3	**Dublin** (city) Franklin County
62	0.3	**Franklin** (city) Warren County
62	0.3	**Garfield Heights** (city) Cuyahoga County
62	0.3	**Greenhills** (village) Hamilton County
62	0.3	**Hillsboro** (city) Highland County
62	0.3	**Lake Darby** (CDP) Franklin County
62	0.3	**Lodi** (village) Medina County
62	0.3	**Lyndhurst** (city) Cuyahoga County
62	0.3	**Mansfield** (city) Richland County
62	0.3	**North College Hill** (city) Hamilton County
62	0.3	**Northfield** (village) Summit County
62	0.3	**Oregon** (city) Lucas County
62	0.3	**Pataskala** (city) Licking County
62	0.3	**Paulding** (village) Paulding County
62	0.3	**Strongsville** (city) Cuyahoga County
62	0.3	**Sunbury** (village) Delaware County
62	0.3	**Toledo** (city) Lucas County
62	0.3	**Troy** (city) Miami County
62	0.3	**Wadsworth** (city) Medina County
62	0.3	**Wauseon** (city) Fulton County
62	0.3	**Zanesville** (city) Muskingum County
93	0.2	**Akron** (city) Summit County
93	0.2	**Austintown** (CDP) Mahoning County
93	0.2	**Ballville** (CDP) Sandusky County
93	0.2	**Baltimore** (village) Fairfield County
93	0.2	**Beavercreek** (city) Greene County
93	0.2	**Boardman** (CDP) Mahoning County
93	0.2	**Bryan** (city) Williams County
93	0.2	**Cambridge** (city) Guernsey County
93	0.2	**Cincinnati** (city) Hamilton County
93	0.2	**Circleville** (city) Pickaway County
93	0.2	**Cleveland Heights** (city) Cuyahoga County
93	0.2	**Columbus** (city) Franklin County
93	0.2	**Conneaut** (city) Ashtabula County
93	0.2	**Delta** (village) Fulton County
93	0.2	**Dent** (CDP) Hamilton County
93	0.2	**East Palestine** (village) Columbiana County
93	0.2	**Edgewood** (CDP) Ashtabula County
93	0.2	**Elyria** (city) Lorain County
93	0.2	**Fairborn** (city) Greene County
93	0.2	**Fairfield** (city) Butler County
93	0.2	**Fairview Park** (city) Cuyahoga County
93	0.2	**Girard** (city) Trumbull County
93	0.2	**Groveport** (city) Franklin County
93	0.2	**Heath** (city) Licking County
93	0.2	**Kettering** (city) Montgomery County
93	0.2	**Lancaster** (city) Fairfield County
93	0.2	**Lebanon** (city) Warren County
93	0.2	**Lexington** (village) Richland County
93	0.2	**London** (city) Madison County
93	0.2	**Maple Heights** (city) Cuyahoga County
93	0.2	**Marion** (city) Marion County
93	0.2	**Mayfield Heights** (city) Cuyahoga County
93	0.2	**Middletown** (city) Butler County
93	0.2	**North Baltimore** (village) Wood County
93	0.2	**Northridge** (CDP) Clark County
93	0.2	**Oakwood** (village) Cuyahoga County
93	0.2	**Ontario** (city) Richland County
93	0.2	**Painesville** (city) Lake County
93	0.2	**Parma** (city) Cuyahoga County
93	0.2	**Parma Heights** (city) Cuyahoga County
93	0.2	**Pepper Pike** (city) Cuyahoga County
93	0.2	**Perrysburg** (city) Wood County
93	0.2	**Plain City** (village) Madison County
93	0.2	**Rittman** (city) Wayne County
93	0.2	**Riverside** (city) Montgomery County
93	0.2	**Shaker Heights** (city) Cuyahoga County
93	0.2	**Solon** (city) Cuyahoga County
93	0.2	**Springfield** (city) Clark County
93	0.2	**Stow** (city) Summit County
93	0.2	**Swanton** (village) Fulton County
93	0.2	**Twinsburg** (city) Summit County
93	0.2	**Upper Arlington** (city) Franklin County
93	0.2	**Urbana** (city) Champaign County
93	0.2	**Van Wert** (city) Van Wert County
93	0.2	**Warren** (city) Trumbull County
93	0.2	**Waterville** (city) Lucas County
93	0.2	**Willoughby** (city) Lake County
93	0.2	**Willowick** (city) Lake County

Note: *This section ranks incorporated places and CDPs (Census Designated Places) with populations of 2,500 or more. Unincorporated postal areas were not considered. Please refer to the User Guide for additional information.*

Native Hawaiian/Other Pacific Islander Population

Top 150 Places Ranked in *Descending* Order

State Rank	Percent	Place
1	1.6	**Coldwater** (village) Mercer County
2	1.2	**New Lebanon** (village) Montgomery County
3	1.0	**Amelia** (village) Clermont County
4	0.8	**Gallipolis** (village) Gallia County
5	0.7	**Minerva** (village) Stark County
6	0.6	**Celina** (city) Mercer County
7	0.4	**Delhi Hills** (CDP) Hamilton County
7	0.4	**Fairlawn** (city) Summit County
7	0.4	**Groesbeck** (CDP) Hamilton County
10	0.3	**Hicksville** (village) Defiance County
10	0.3	**Sandusky** (city) Erie County
12	0.2	**Ashtabula** (city) Ashtabula County
12	0.2	**Austintown** (CDP) Mahoning County
12	0.2	**Beachwood** (city) Cuyahoga County
12	0.2	**Edgewood** (CDP) Ashtabula County
12	0.2	**Hamilton** (city) Butler County
12	0.2	**Urbana** (city) Champaign County
18	0.1	**Athens** (city) Athens County
18	0.1	**Bay Village** (city) Cuyahoga County
18	0.1	**Beckett Ridge** (CDP) Butler County
18	0.1	**Bexley** (city) Franklin County
18	0.1	**Blue Ash** (city) Hamilton County
18	0.1	**Bowling Green** (city) Wood County
18	0.1	**Brooklyn** (city) Cuyahoga County
18	0.1	**Bucyrus** (city) Crawford County
18	0.1	**Chillicothe** (city) Ross County
18	0.1	**Cuyahoga Falls** (city) Summit County
18	0.1	**Elyria** (city) Lorain County
18	0.1	**Fairborn** (city) Greene County
18	0.1	**Forest Park** (city) Hamilton County
18	0.1	**Green** (city) Summit County
18	0.1	**Hilliard** (city) Franklin County
18	0.1	**Lakewood** (city) Cuyahoga County
18	0.1	**Lebanon** (city) Warren County
18	0.1	**Marietta** (city) Washington County
18	0.1	**Maumee** (city) Lucas County
18	0.1	**Montpelier** (village) Williams County
18	0.1	**New London** (village) Huron County
18	0.1	**Pickerington** (city) Fairfield County
18	0.1	**Powell** (city) Delaware County
18	0.1	**Reynoldsburg** (city) Franklin County
18	0.1	**Solon** (city) Cuyahoga County
18	0.1	**Twinsburg** (city) Summit County
18	0.1	**West Carrollton** (city) Montgomery County
18	0.1	**Westerville** (city) Franklin County
18	0.1	**Westlake** (city) Cuyahoga County
18	0.1	**Willowick** (city) Lake County
18	0.1	**Wilmington** (city) Clinton County
49	0.0	**Ada** (village) Hardin County
49	0.0	**Akron** (city) Summit County
49	0.0	**Alliance** (city) Stark County
49	0.0	**Amberley** (village) Hamilton County
49	0.0	**Amherst** (city) Lorain County
49	0.0	**Apple Valley** (CDP) Knox County
49	0.0	**Archbold** (village) Fulton County
49	0.0	**Ashland** (city) Ashland County
49	0.0	**Ashville** (village) Pickaway County
49	0.0	**Aurora** (city) Portage County
49	0.0	**Avon** (city) Lorain County
49	0.0	**Avon Lake** (city) Lorain County
49	0.0	**Bainbridge** (CDP) Geauga County
49	0.0	**Ballville** (CDP) Sandusky County
49	0.0	**Baltimore** (village) Fairfield County
49	0.0	**Barberton** (city) Summit County
49	0.0	**Barnesville** (village) Belmont County
49	0.0	**Beavercreek** (city) Greene County
49	0.0	**Bedford** (city) Cuyahoga County
49	0.0	**Bedford Heights** (city) Cuyahoga County
49	0.0	**Beechwood Trails** (CDP) Licking County
49	0.0	**Bellaire** (village) Belmont County
49	0.0	**Bellbrook** (city) Greene County
49	0.0	**Bellefontaine** (city) Logan County
49	0.0	**Bellevue** (city) Sandusky County
49	0.0	**Belpre** (city) Washington County
49	0.0	**Berea** (city) Cuyahoga County
49	0.0	**Bethel** (village) Clermont County
49	0.0	**Blacklick Estates** (CDP) Franklin County
49	0.0	**Blanchester** (village) Clinton County
49	0.0	**Bluffton** (village) Allen County
49	0.0	**Boardman** (CDP) Mahoning County
49	0.0	**Brecksville** (city) Cuyahoga County
49	0.0	**Bridgetown** (CDP) Hamilton County
49	0.0	**Brimfield** (CDP) Portage County
49	0.0	**Broadview Heights** (city) Cuyahoga County
49	0.0	**Brook Park** (city) Cuyahoga County
49	0.0	**Brookville** (city) Montgomery County
49	0.0	**Brunswick** (city) Medina County
49	0.0	**Bryan** (city) Williams County
49	0.0	**Buckeye Lake** (village) Licking County
49	0.0	**Burlington** (CDP) Lawrence County
49	0.0	**Cadiz** (village) Harrison County
49	0.0	**Calcutta** (CDP) Columbiana County
49	0.0	**Cambridge** (city) Guernsey County
49	0.0	**Campbell** (city) Mahoning County
49	0.0	**Canal Fulton** (city) Stark County
49	0.0	**Canal Winchester** (city) Franklin County
49	0.0	**Canfield** (city) Mahoning County
49	0.0	**Canton** (city) Stark County
49	0.0	**Carey** (village) Wyandot County
49	0.0	**Carlisle** (village) Warren County
49	0.0	**Carrollton** (village) Carroll County
49	0.0	**Cedarville** (village) Greene County
49	0.0	**Centerville** (city) Montgomery County
49	0.0	**Chagrin Falls** (village) Cuyahoga County
49	0.0	**Champion Heights** (CDP) Trumbull County
49	0.0	**Chardon** (city) Geauga County
49	0.0	**Cherry Grove** (CDP) Hamilton County
49	0.0	**Cheviot** (city) Hamilton County
49	0.0	**Cincinnati** (city) Hamilton County
49	0.0	**Circleville** (city) Pickaway County
49	0.0	**Clayton** (city) Montgomery County
49	0.0	**Cleveland** (city) Cuyahoga County
49	0.0	**Cleveland Heights** (city) Cuyahoga County
49	0.0	**Cleves** (village) Hamilton County
49	0.0	**Clyde** (city) Sandusky County
49	0.0	**Columbiana** (city) Columbiana County
49	0.0	**Columbus** (city) Franklin County
49	0.0	**Conneaut** (city) Ashtabula County
49	0.0	**Cortland** (city) Trumbull County
49	0.0	**Coshocton** (city) Coshocton County
49	0.0	**Covedale** (CDP) Hamilton County
49	0.0	**Covington** (village) Miami County
49	0.0	**Crestline** (village) Crawford County
49	0.0	**Crooksville** (village) Perry County
49	0.0	**Day Heights** (CDP) Clermont County
49	0.0	**Dayton** (city) Montgomery County
49	0.0	**Deer Park** (city) Hamilton County
49	0.0	**Defiance** (city) Defiance County
49	0.0	**Delaware** (city) Delaware County
49	0.0	**Delphos** (city) Allen County
49	0.0	**Delshire** (CDP) Hamilton County
49	0.0	**Delta** (village) Fulton County
49	0.0	**Dennison** (village) Tuscarawas County
49	0.0	**Dent** (CDP) Hamilton County
49	0.0	**Devola** (CDP) Washington County
49	0.0	**Dillonvale** (CDP) Hamilton County
49	0.0	**Dover** (city) Tuscarawas County
49	0.0	**Doylestown** (village) Wayne County
49	0.0	**Dry Ridge** (CDP) Hamilton County
49	0.0	**Dry Run** (CDP) Hamilton County
49	0.0	**Dublin** (city) Franklin County
49	0.0	**East Cleveland** (city) Cuyahoga County
49	0.0	**East Liverpool** (city) Columbiana County
49	0.0	**East Palestine** (village) Columbiana County
49	0.0	**Eastlake** (city) Lake County
49	0.0	**Eaton** (city) Preble County
49	0.0	**Englewood** (city) Montgomery County
49	0.0	**Enon** (village) Clark County
49	0.0	**Euclid** (city) Cuyahoga County
49	0.0	**Evendale** (village) Hamilton County

Note: *This section ranks incorporated places and CDPs (Census Designated Places) with populations of 2,500 or more. Unincorporated postal areas were not considered. Please refer to the User Guide for additional information.*

Two or More Races

Top 150 Places Ranked in *Descending* Order

State Rank	Percent	Place
1	9.0	**Oberlin** (city) Lorain County
1	9.0	**Painesville** (city) Lake County
3	8.7	**Huber Ridge** (CDP) Franklin County
4	8.2	**Woodlawn** (village) Hamilton County
5	7.7	**Whitehall** (city) Franklin County
6	7.5	**Mansfield** (city) Richland County
7	7.1	**Northbrook** (CDP) Hamilton County
8	7.0	**Campbell** (city) Mahoning County
9	6.6	**Ravenna** (city) Portage County
9	6.6	**West Jefferson** (village) Madison County
11	6.4	**Ashville** (village) Pickaway County
12	6.2	**Groesbeck** (CDP) Hamilton County
12	6.2	**Silverton** (village) Hamilton County
14	6.1	**Canton** (city) Stark County
15	6.0	**North Zanesville** (CDP) Muskingum County
15	6.0	**Sandusky** (city) Erie County
15	6.0	**Wellsville** (village) Columbiana County
15	6.0	**Zanesville** (city) Muskingum County
19	5.9	**Mingo Junction** (village) Jefferson County
20	5.8	**Chillicothe** (city) Ross County
21	5.6	**Northfield** (village) Summit County
21	5.6	**Springfield** (city) Clark County
23	5.3	**Gibsonburg** (village) Sandusky County
23	5.3	**Wellington** (village) Lorain County
25	5.2	**Lorain** (city) Lorain County
26	5.1	**Elyria** (city) Lorain County
26	5.1	**Forest Park** (city) Hamilton County
26	5.1	**Lima** (city) Allen County
26	5.1	**Martins Ferry** (city) Belmont County
30	5.0	**Ashtabula** (city) Ashtabula County
30	5.0	**Huber Heights** (city) Montgomery County
32	4.9	**Fostoria** (city) Seneca County
32	4.9	**Lexington** (village) Richland County
32	4.9	**Toledo** (city) Lucas County
35	4.8	**Blacklick Estates** (CDP) Franklin County
36	4.7	**Bedford Heights** (city) Cuyahoga County
36	4.7	**Four Bridges** (CDP) Butler County
36	4.7	**Piqua** (city) Miami County
36	4.7	**Youngstown** (city) Mahoning County
40	4.6	**Fairborn** (city) Greene County
41	4.5	**Crestline** (village) Crawford County
41	4.5	**Reynoldsburg** (city) Franklin County
41	4.5	**Wheelersburg** (CDP) Scioto County
44	4.4	**Alliance** (city) Stark County
45	4.3	**Brimfield** (CDP) Portage County
45	4.3	**Heath** (city) Licking County
45	4.3	**Kent** (city) Portage County
45	4.3	**Macedonia** (city) Summit County
45	4.3	**Shaker Heights** (city) Cuyahoga County
50	4.2	**Moreland Hills** (village) Cuyahoga County
50	4.2	**New Burlington** (CDP) Hamilton County
50	4.2	**Steubenville** (city) Jefferson County
50	4.2	**Trotwood** (city) Montgomery County
50	4.2	**Wyoming** (city) Hamilton County
55	4.1	**Akron** (city) Summit County
55	4.1	**Columbus** (city) Franklin County
55	4.1	**Deer Park** (city) Hamilton County
55	4.1	**Lakewood** (city) Cuyahoga County
59	4.0	**Fairlawn** (city) Summit County
59	4.0	**Lake Darby** (CDP) Franklin County
59	4.0	**Lake Lakengren** (CDP) Preble County
59	4.0	**Middletown** (city) Butler County
59	4.0	**New Concord** (village) Muskingum County
59	4.0	**Sheffield Lake** (city) Lorain County
59	4.0	**Sixteen Mile Stand** (CDP) Hamilton County
66	3.9	**Bellefontaine** (city) Logan County
66	3.9	**Mount Healthy** (city) Hamilton County
66	3.9	**North Baltimore** (village) Wood County
66	3.9	**Sherwood** (CDP) Hamilton County
66	3.9	**South Euclid** (city) Cuyahoga County
71	3.8	**Athens** (city) Athens County
71	3.8	**Fort Shawnee** (CDP) Allen County
71	3.8	**Fremont** (city) Sandusky County
71	3.8	**Lincoln Heights** (village) Hamilton County
71	3.8	**Milford** (city) Clermont County
76	3.7	**Edgewood** (CDP) Ashtabula County
76	3.7	**Toronto** (city) Jefferson County
78	3.6	**Beavercreek** (city) Greene County
78	3.6	**Findlay** (city) Hancock County
78	3.6	**Golf Manor** (village) Hamilton County
78	3.6	**Oregon** (city) Lucas County
78	3.6	**Urbana** (city) Champaign County
78	3.6	**Wauseon** (city) Fulton County
84	3.5	**Cleveland** (city) Cuyahoga County
84	3.5	**Englewood** (city) Montgomery County
84	3.5	**Finneytown** (CDP) Hamilton County
84	3.5	**Saint Bernard** (city) Hamilton County
88	3.4	**Grafton** (village) Lorain County
88	3.4	**Marion** (city) Marion County
88	3.4	**Warren** (city) Trumbull County
88	3.4	**Yellow Springs** (village) Greene County
92	3.3	**Dayton** (city) Montgomery County
92	3.3	**Dublin** (city) Franklin County
92	3.3	**Minerva** (village) Stark County
92	3.3	**Orrville** (city) Wayne County
92	3.3	**Riverside** (city) Montgomery County
92	3.3	**Tallmadge** (city) Summit County
92	3.3	**Taylor Creek** (CDP) Hamilton County
92	3.3	**West Carrollton** (city) Montgomery County
100	3.2	**Defiance** (city) Defiance County
100	3.2	**East Liverpool** (city) Columbiana County
100	3.2	**Ironton** (city) Lawrence County
100	3.2	**Lordstown** (village) Trumbull County
100	3.2	**Newark** (city) Licking County
100	3.2	**Obetz** (village) Franklin County
100	3.2	**Pickerington** (city) Fairfield County
100	3.2	**Richmond Heights** (city) Cuyahoga County
100	3.2	**Troy** (city) Miami County
100	3.2	**Westerville** (city) Franklin County
100	3.2	**Xenia** (city) Greene County
111	3.1	**Barberton** (city) Summit County
111	3.1	**Cincinnati** (city) Hamilton County
111	3.1	**Dennison** (village) Tuscarawas County
111	3.1	**Marysville** (city) Union County
111	3.1	**Mount Healthy Heights** (CDP) Hamilton County
111	3.1	**Solon** (city) Cuyahoga County
111	3.1	**Vandalia** (city) Montgomery County
118	3.0	**Centerville** (city) Montgomery County
118	3.0	**London** (city) Madison County
118	3.0	**Nelsonville** (city) Athens County
118	3.0	**North College Hill** (city) Hamilton County
118	3.0	**North Ridgeville** (city) Lorain County
118	3.0	**Northgate** (CDP) Hamilton County
118	3.0	**The Plains** (CDP) Athens County
118	3.0	**Washington Court House** (city) Fayette County
126	2.9	**Canal Fulton** (city) Stark County
126	2.9	**Cleveland Heights** (city) Cuyahoga County
126	2.9	**Park Layne** (CDP) Clark County
126	2.9	**Sharonville** (city) Hamilton County
126	2.9	**Twinsburg** (city) Summit County
131	2.8	**Ada** (village) Hardin County
131	2.8	**Bexley** (city) Franklin County
131	2.8	**Bowling Green** (city) Wood County
131	2.8	**Brooklyn** (city) Cuyahoga County
131	2.8	**Clayton** (city) Montgomery County
131	2.8	**Girard** (city) Trumbull County
131	2.8	**Hamilton** (city) Butler County
131	2.8	**Hartville** (village) Stark County
131	2.8	**Hicksville** (village) Defiance County
131	2.8	**Lockland** (village) Hamilton County
131	2.8	**Massillon** (city) Stark County
131	2.8	**Oakwood** (village) Cuyahoga County
131	2.8	**Springboro** (city) Warren County
131	2.8	**Wellston** (city) Jackson County
131	2.8	**Wilmington** (city) Clinton County
146	2.7	**Mount Vernon** (city) Knox County
146	2.7	**New Richmond** (village) Clermont County
146	2.7	**Orange** (village) Cuyahoga County
146	2.7	**Ottawa Hills** (village) Lucas County
150	2.6	**Broadview Heights** (city) Cuyahoga County

Note: *This section ranks incorporated places and CDPs (Census Designated Places) with populations of 2,500 or more. Unincorporated postal areas were not considered. Please refer to the User Guide for additional information.*

Two or More Races

Top 150 Places Ranked in *Ascending* Order

State Rank	Percent	Place
1	0.0	**Ballville** (CDP) Sandusky County
1	0.0	**Beechwood Trails** (CDP) Licking County
1	0.0	**Carrollton** (village) Carroll County
1	0.0	**Champion Heights** (CDP) Trumbull County
1	0.0	**Coldwater** (village) Mercer County
1	0.0	**Columbiana** (city) Columbiana County
1	0.0	**Day Heights** (CDP) Clermont County
1	0.0	**Delta** (village) Fulton County
1	0.0	**Lakemore** (village) Summit County
1	0.0	**Minster** (village) Auglaize County
1	0.0	**Munroe Falls** (city) Summit County
1	0.0	**Portage Lakes** (CDP) Summit County
1	0.0	**Saint Henry** (village) Mercer County
1	0.0	**Sebring** (village) Mahoning County
1	0.0	**Seville** (village) Medina County
1	0.0	**Shadyside** (village) Belmont County
1	0.0	**Strasburg** (village) Tuscarawas County
1	0.0	**Summerside** (CDP) Clermont County
1	0.0	**Swanton** (village) Fulton County
1	0.0	**The Village of Indian Hill** (city) Hamilton County
1	0.0	**West Portsmouth** (CDP) Scioto County
22	0.2	**Brecksville** (city) Cuyahoga County
22	0.2	**Poland** (village) Mahoning County
22	0.2	**Union** (city) Montgomery County
22	0.2	**Waverly** (village) Pike County
26	0.3	**Madison** (village) Lake County
26	0.3	**Mogadore** (village) Summit County
26	0.3	**Mount Repose** (CDP) Clermont County
26	0.3	**Oak Harbor** (village) Ottawa County
26	0.3	**Sheffield** (village) Lorain County
26	0.3	**West Union** (village) Adams County
32	0.4	**Miami Heights** (CDP) Hamilton County
33	0.5	**Bellbrook** (city) Greene County
33	0.5	**Greenfield** (village) Highland County
33	0.5	**Jefferson** (village) Ashtabula County
33	0.5	**Newtown** (village) Hamilton County
33	0.5	**South Point** (village) Lawrence County
33	0.5	**Wintersville** (village) Jefferson County
39	0.6	**Chardon** (city) Geauga County
39	0.6	**Fairport Harbor** (village) Lake County
39	0.6	**Fruit Hill** (CDP) Hamilton County
39	0.6	**Kirtland** (city) Lake County
39	0.6	**Mineral Ridge** (CDP) Trumbull County
39	0.6	**New Lebanon** (village) Montgomery County
39	0.6	**New London** (village) Huron County
39	0.6	**Norton** (city) Summit County
39	0.6	**Versailles** (village) Darke County
48	0.7	**Bainbridge** (CDP) Geauga County
48	0.7	**Dillonvale** (CDP) Hamilton County
48	0.7	**Greenville** (city) Darke County
48	0.7	**Jackson** (city) Jackson County
48	0.7	**Lisbon** (village) Columbiana County
48	0.7	**Middleburg Heights** (city) Cuyahoga County
48	0.7	**Monfort Heights** (CDP) Hamilton County
48	0.7	**Shelby** (city) Richland County
56	0.8	**Avon** (city) Lorain County
56	0.8	**Bellevue** (city) Sandusky County
56	0.8	**Eastlake** (city) Lake County
56	0.8	**Germantown** (city) Montgomery County
56	0.8	**Harrison** (city) Hamilton County
56	0.8	**Lodi** (village) Medina County
56	0.8	**Mentor** (city) Lake County
56	0.8	**Reading** (city) Hamilton County
56	0.8	**Tipp City** (city) Miami County
56	0.8	**Wapakoneta** (city) Auglaize County
56	0.8	**Whitehouse** (village) Lucas County
56	0.8	**Withamsville** (CDP) Clermont County
68	0.9	**Amelia** (village) Clermont County
68	0.9	**Bellaire** (village) Belmont County
68	0.9	**Bluffton** (village) Allen County
68	0.9	**Delhi Hills** (CDP) Hamilton County
68	0.9	**Greentown** (CDP) Stark County
68	0.9	**Groveport** (city) Franklin County
68	0.9	**Loudonville** (village) Ashland County
68	0.9	**McDonald** (village) Trumbull County
68	0.9	**Oxford** (city) Butler County
68	0.9	**Waynesville** (village) Warren County
78	1.0	**Apple Valley** (CDP) Knox County
78	1.0	**Brookville** (city) Montgomery County
78	1.0	**Calcutta** (CDP) Columbiana County
78	1.0	**Chagrin Falls** (village) Cuyahoga County
78	1.0	**Fredericktown** (village) Knox County
78	1.0	**Georgetown** (village) Brown County
78	1.0	**Maumee** (city) Lucas County
78	1.0	**Mayfield** (village) Cuyahoga County
78	1.0	**Saint Clairsville** (city) Belmont County
78	1.0	**Salem** (city) Columbiana County
78	1.0	**Salem Heights** (CDP) Hamilton County
78	1.0	**South Russell** (village) Geauga County
90	1.1	**Barnesville** (village) Belmont County
90	1.1	**Covington** (village) Miami County
90	1.1	**Independence** (city) Cuyahoga County
90	1.1	**Logan** (city) Hocking County
90	1.1	**Northwood** (city) Wood County
90	1.1	**Perry Heights** (CDP) Stark County
90	1.1	**Port Clinton** (city) Ottawa County
90	1.1	**Seven Hills** (city) Cuyahoga County
90	1.1	**South Lebanon** (village) Warren County
90	1.1	**Springdale** (city) Hamilton County
90	1.1	**Walbridge** (village) Wood County
101	1.2	**Austintown** (CDP) Mahoning County
101	1.2	**Baltimore** (village) Fairfield County
101	1.2	**Carey** (village) Wyandot County
101	1.2	**Delphos** (city) Allen County
101	1.2	**Dent** (CDP) Hamilton County
101	1.2	**Galion** (city) Crawford County
101	1.2	**Mulberry** (CDP) Clermont County
101	1.2	**New Carlisle** (city) Clark County
101	1.2	**Ontario** (city) Richland County
101	1.2	**Richfield** (village) Summit County
101	1.2	**Rocky River** (city) Cuyahoga County
101	1.2	**Rossford** (city) Wood County
101	1.2	**Turpin Hills** (CDP) Hamilton County
101	1.2	**Uhrichsville** (city) Tuscarawas County
101	1.2	**Uniontown** (CDP) Stark County
101	1.2	**Van Wert** (city) Van Wert County
117	1.3	**Amberley** (village) Hamilton County
117	1.3	**Bedford** (city) Cuyahoga County
117	1.3	**Bridgetown** (CDP) Hamilton County
117	1.3	**Bucyrus** (city) Crawford County
117	1.3	**Cadiz** (village) Harrison County
117	1.3	**Landen** (CDP) Warren County
117	1.3	**Lyndhurst** (city) Cuyahoga County
117	1.3	**Montgomery** (city) Hamilton County
117	1.3	**Montpelier** (village) Williams County
117	1.3	**Mount Gilead** (village) Morrow County
117	1.3	**New Franklin** (city) Summit County
117	1.3	**North Madison** (CDP) Lake County
117	1.3	**Oakwood** (city) Montgomery County
117	1.3	**Powell** (city) Delaware County
117	1.3	**Ross** (CDP) Butler County
117	1.3	**Strongsville** (city) Cuyahoga County
117	1.3	**Upper Sandusky** (city) Wyandot County
117	1.3	**Willoughby** (city) Lake County
135	1.4	**Forestville** (CDP) Hamilton County
135	1.4	**Gallipolis** (village) Gallia County
135	1.4	**Hilliard** (city) Franklin County
135	1.4	**Johnstown** (village) Licking County
135	1.4	**Loveland** (city) Hamilton County
135	1.4	**New Albany** (city) Franklin County
135	1.4	**Newcomerstown** (village) Tuscarawas County
135	1.4	**North Royalton** (city) Cuyahoga County
135	1.4	**Plain City** (village) Madison County
135	1.4	**Struthers** (city) Mahoning County
135	1.4	**Williamsburg** (village) Clermont County
146	1.5	**Brunswick** (city) Medina County
146	1.5	**Cleves** (village) Hamilton County
146	1.5	**Doylestown** (village) Wayne County
146	1.5	**Mack** (CDP) Hamilton County
146	1.5	**Medina** (city) Medina County

Note: *This section ranks incorporated places and CDPs (Census Designated Places) with populations of 2,500 or more. Unincorporated postal areas were not considered. Please refer to the User Guide for additional information.*

Hispanic Population

Top 150 Places Ranked in *Descending* Order

State Rank	Percent	Place
1	28.3	**Lorain** (city) Lorain County
2	24.3	**Painesville** (city) Lake County
3	19.1	**New Carlisle** (city) Clark County
4	18.2	**Campbell** (city) Mahoning County
5	17.8	**Fremont** (city) Sandusky County
5	17.8	**Wauseon** (city) Fulton County
7	17.5	**Springdale** (city) Hamilton County
8	17.1	**Archbold** (village) Fulton County
9	15.0	**Willard** (city) Huron County
10	14.7	**Defiance** (city) Defiance County
11	14.0	**Whitehall** (city) Franklin County
12	13.7	**Lockland** (village) Hamilton County
13	12.9	**Ottawa** (village) Putnam County
14	12.7	**Gibsonburg** (village) Sandusky County
15	12.4	**Lincoln Village** (CDP) Franklin County
16	12.3	**Wright-Patterson AFB** (CDP) Greene County
17	11.8	**Brooklyn** (city) Cuyahoga County
18	11.6	**Hicksville** (village) Defiance County
19	10.8	**Cleveland** (city) Cuyahoga County
20	10.7	**Youngstown** (city) Mahoning County
21	9.9	**Fostoria** (city) Seneca County
21	9.9	**Sheffield Lake** (city) Lorain County
23	9.7	**Paulding** (village) Paulding County
24	9.6	**Port Clinton** (city) Ottawa County
25	9.1	**Norwalk** (city) Huron County
26	8.8	**Sheffield** (village) Lorain County
27	8.7	**Ashtabula** (city) Ashtabula County
28	8.3	**Delta** (village) Fulton County
29	8.2	**Geneva** (city) Ashtabula County
29	8.2	**Toledo** (city) Lucas County
31	7.8	**Fairfield** (city) Butler County
31	7.8	**Napoleon** (city) Henry County
31	7.8	**Northwood** (city) Wood County
31	7.8	**Swanton** (village) Fulton County
35	7.6	**Buckeye Lake** (village) Licking County
35	7.6	**Dover** (city) Tuscarawas County
35	7.6	**Oregon** (city) Lucas County
38	7.4	**Delshire** (CDP) Hamilton County
39	7.3	**Findlay** (city) Hancock County
39	7.3	**Newtown** (village) Hamilton County
41	6.6	**Johnstown** (village) Licking County
42	6.5	**Fairport Harbor** (village) Lake County
43	6.3	**Ballville** (CDP) Sandusky County
44	6.2	**Forest Park** (city) Hamilton County
45	6.1	**Sandusky** (city) Erie County
46	5.8	**Columbus** (city) Franklin County
46	5.8	**Middleburg Heights** (city) Cuyahoga County
48	5.7	**Bowling Green** (city) Wood County
48	5.7	**Groesbeck** (CDP) Hamilton County
48	5.7	**Turpin Hills** (CDP) Hamilton County
51	5.6	**Clyde** (city) Sandusky County
51	5.6	**Parma** (city) Cuyahoga County
53	5.5	**Dublin** (city) Franklin County
54	5.3	**Oak Harbor** (village) Ottawa County
54	5.3	**Van Wert** (city) Van Wert County
56	5.2	**Elyria** (city) Lorain County
57	5.1	**Amherst** (city) Lorain County
57	5.1	**Middletown** (city) Butler County
59	5.0	**Hamilton** (city) Butler County
60	4.9	**Lakewood** (city) Cuyahoga County
60	4.9	**North Baltimore** (village) Wood County
62	4.8	**Sebring** (village) Mahoning County
63	4.7	**Delphos** (city) Allen County
63	4.7	**Moreland Hills** (village) Cuyahoga County
63	4.7	**Orrville** (city) Wayne County
63	4.7	**Parma Heights** (city) Cuyahoga County
67	4.6	**Millersburg** (village) Holmes County
67	4.6	**North Kingsville** (village) Ashtabula County
67	4.6	**Pleasant Run** (CDP) Hamilton County
67	4.6	**Seville** (village) Medina County
71	4.5	**New Philadelphia** (city) Tuscarawas County
72	4.4	**Amberley** (village) Hamilton County
72	4.4	**Bryan** (city) Williams County
72	4.4	**Sharonville** (city) Hamilton County
75	4.3	**Beckett Ridge** (CDP) Butler County
75	4.3	**Greenhills** (village) Hamilton County
75	4.3	**Madeira** (city) Hamilton County
75	4.3	**Milford** (city) Clermont County
75	4.3	**Saint Henry** (village) Mercer County
75	4.3	**Walbridge** (village) Wood County
81	4.2	**Fairview Park** (city) Cuyahoga County
81	4.2	**Jackson** (city) Jackson County
83	4.1	**Boardman** (CDP) Mahoning County
83	4.1	**Northbrook** (CDP) Hamilton County
83	4.1	**Norwood** (city) Hamilton County
86	4.0	**Grafton** (village) Lorain County
86	4.0	**Oberlin** (city) Lorain County
86	4.0	**Riverside** (city) Montgomery County
89	3.9	**Dayton** (city) Montgomery County
89	3.9	**Fairborn** (city) Greene County
89	3.9	**Granville** (village) Licking County
89	3.9	**Huber Heights** (city) Montgomery County
89	3.9	**Reynoldsburg** (city) Franklin County
89	3.9	**Rossford** (city) Wood County
89	3.9	**Sherwood** (CDP) Hamilton County
89	3.9	**Tiffin** (city) Seneca County
89	3.9	**Waynesville** (village) Warren County
89	3.9	**Wellington** (village) Lorain County
99	3.8	**Edgewood** (CDP) Ashtabula County
99	3.8	**North Ridgeville** (city) Lorain County
99	3.8	**Obetz** (village) Franklin County
99	3.8	**Salem** (city) Columbiana County
99	3.8	**Wintersville** (village) Jefferson County
104	3.7	**Streetsboro** (city) Portage County
105	3.6	**Brook Park** (city) Cuyahoga County
105	3.6	**Devola** (CDP) Washington County
105	3.6	**Miami Heights** (CDP) Hamilton County
105	3.6	**Mingo Junction** (village) Jefferson County
109	3.5	**Blue Ash** (city) Hamilton County
109	3.5	**North Olmsted** (city) Cuyahoga County
111	3.4	**Athens** (city) Athens County
111	3.4	**Mason** (city) Warren County
111	3.4	**Monroe** (city) Butler County
111	3.4	**Montgomery** (city) Hamilton County
111	3.4	**Upper Sandusky** (city) Wyandot County
111	3.4	**Urbana** (city) Champaign County
117	3.3	**Bedford Heights** (city) Cuyahoga County
117	3.3	**Bellevue** (city) Sandusky County
117	3.3	**Berea** (city) Cuyahoga County
117	3.3	**Lima** (city) Allen County
117	3.3	**Marion** (city) Marion County
117	3.3	**Vermilion** (city) Lorain County
117	3.3	**Woodlawn** (village) Hamilton County
124	3.2	**Alliance** (city) Stark County
124	3.2	**Canton** (city) Stark County
124	3.2	**Cincinnati** (city) Hamilton County
124	3.2	**Highland Heights** (city) Cuyahoga County
124	3.2	**Perrysburg** (city) Wood County
124	3.2	**West Carrollton** (city) Montgomery County
124	3.2	**Westlake** (city) Cuyahoga County
131	3.1	**Avon** (city) Lorain County
131	3.1	**Deer Park** (city) Hamilton County
131	3.1	**Newcomerstown** (village) Tuscarawas County
131	3.1	**Springfield** (city) Clark County
135	3.0	**Conneaut** (city) Ashtabula County
135	3.0	**Gallipolis** (village) Gallia County
135	3.0	**Maumee** (city) Lucas County
135	3.0	**Middlefield** (village) Geauga County
139	2.9	**Dry Run** (CDP) Hamilton County
139	2.9	**Enon** (village) Clark County
139	2.9	**Girard** (city) Trumbull County
139	2.9	**Huber Ridge** (CDP) Franklin County
139	2.9	**London** (city) Madison County
139	2.9	**Park Layne** (CDP) Clark County
139	2.9	**Pickerington** (city) Fairfield County
139	2.9	**Struthers** (city) Mahoning County
139	2.9	**Wapakoneta** (city) Auglaize County
148	2.8	**Baltimore** (village) Fairfield County
148	2.8	**Beavercreek** (city) Greene County
148	2.8	**Lake Darby** (CDP) Franklin County

Note: *This section ranks incorporated places and CDPs (Census Designated Places) with populations of 2,500 or more. Unincorporated postal areas were not considered. Please refer to the User Guide for additional information.*

Hispanic Population

Top 150 Places Ranked in *Ascending* Order

State Rank	Percent	Place
1	0.0	**Amelia** (village) Clermont County
1	0.0	**Blanchester** (village) Clinton County
1	0.0	**Burlington** (CDP) Lawrence County
1	0.0	**Coldwater** (village) Mercer County
1	0.0	**Greenfield** (village) Highland County
1	0.0	**Lakemore** (village) Summit County
1	0.0	**Mount Carmel** (CDP) Clermont County
1	0.0	**Mount Gilead** (village) Morrow County
1	0.0	**Mount Healthy Heights** (CDP) Hamilton County
1	0.0	**North Zanesville** (CDP) Muskingum County
1	0.0	**Salem Heights** (CDP) Hamilton County
1	0.0	**Shadyside** (village) Belmont County
1	0.0	**Silverton** (village) Hamilton County
1	0.0	**Strasburg** (village) Tuscarawas County
1	0.0	**Taylor Creek** (CDP) Hamilton County
1	0.0	**Uniontown** (CDP) Stark County
1	0.0	**Versailles** (village) Darke County
1	0.0	**Wellston** (city) Jackson County
1	0.0	**West Portsmouth** (CDP) Scioto County
1	0.0	**West Union** (village) Adams County
21	0.1	**Barnesville** (village) Belmont County
21	0.1	**Rittman** (city) Wayne County
23	0.2	**Bridgetown** (CDP) Hamilton County
23	0.2	**Forestville** (CDP) Hamilton County
23	0.2	**Logan** (city) Hocking County
23	0.2	**Lordstown** (village) Trumbull County
23	0.2	**Monfort Heights** (CDP) Hamilton County
23	0.2	**Perry Heights** (CDP) Stark County
23	0.2	**Plain City** (village) Madison County
23	0.2	**Williamsburg** (village) Clermont County
31	0.3	**Delhi Hills** (CDP) Hamilton County
31	0.3	**Fort Shawnee** (CDP) Allen County
31	0.3	**Georgetown** (village) Brown County
31	0.3	**Hartville** (village) Stark County
31	0.3	**Lake Lakengren** (CDP) Preble County
31	0.3	**McDonald** (village) Trumbull County
31	0.3	**New Richmond** (village) Clermont County
31	0.3	**Northfield** (village) Summit County
31	0.3	**Richville** (CDP) Stark County
31	0.3	**Wheelersburg** (CDP) Scioto County
41	0.4	**Apple Valley** (CDP) Knox County
41	0.4	**Brecksville** (city) Cuyahoga County
41	0.4	**Cortland** (city) Trumbull County
41	0.4	**Englewood** (city) Montgomery County
41	0.4	**Evendale** (village) Hamilton County
41	0.4	**Landen** (CDP) Warren County
41	0.4	**Loudonville** (village) Ashland County
41	0.4	**Munroe Falls** (city) Summit County
41	0.4	**Northridge** (CDP) Clark County
41	0.4	**Saint Clairsville** (city) Belmont County
41	0.4	**Uhrichsville** (city) Tuscarawas County
52	0.5	**Cadiz** (village) Harrison County
52	0.5	**Day Heights** (CDP) Clermont County
52	0.5	**Howland Center** (CDP) Trumbull County
52	0.5	**Mineral Ridge** (CDP) Trumbull County
52	0.5	**New Franklin** (city) Summit County
52	0.5	**North Madison** (CDP) Lake County
52	0.5	**Reminderville** (village) Summit County
52	0.5	**West Jefferson** (village) Madison County
60	0.6	**Bellaire** (village) Belmont County
60	0.6	**Carlisle** (village) Warren County
60	0.6	**Crooksville** (village) Perry County
60	0.6	**Mount Healthy** (city) Hamilton County
60	0.6	**New Lexington** (village) Perry County
60	0.6	**Ottawa Hills** (village) Lucas County
60	0.6	**Powell** (city) Delaware County
60	0.6	**Ross** (CDP) Butler County
60	0.6	**Saint Bernard** (city) Hamilton County
60	0.6	**Saint Marys** (city) Auglaize County
60	0.6	**Tipp City** (city) Miami County
60	0.6	**Toronto** (city) Jefferson County
60	0.6	**Withamsville** (CDP) Clermont County
73	0.7	**Covedale** (CDP) Hamilton County
73	0.7	**Dillonvale** (CDP) Hamilton County
73	0.7	**Mogadore** (village) Summit County
73	0.7	**Mulberry** (CDP) Clermont County
73	0.7	**Summerside** (CDP) Clermont County
78	0.8	**Ashland** (city) Ashland County
78	0.8	**Eaton** (city) Preble County
78	0.8	**Fredericktown** (village) Knox County
78	0.8	**Golf Manor** (village) Hamilton County
78	0.8	**Mount Orab** (village) Brown County
78	0.8	**North College Hill** (city) Hamilton County
78	0.8	**Pleasant Run Farm** (CDP) Hamilton County
78	0.8	**Tallmadge** (city) Summit County
86	0.9	**Beechwood Trails** (CDP) Licking County
86	0.9	**Bellbrook** (city) Greene County
86	0.9	**Bethel** (village) Clermont County
86	0.9	**Canal Fulton** (city) Stark County
86	0.9	**Canfield** (city) Mahoning County
86	0.9	**Chagrin Falls** (village) Cuyahoga County
86	0.9	**Chillicothe** (city) Ross County
86	0.9	**Dennison** (village) Tuscarawas County
86	0.9	**East Cleveland** (city) Cuyahoga County
86	0.9	**Green** (city) Summit County
86	0.9	**Heath** (city) Licking County
86	0.9	**Mentor** (city) Lake County
86	0.9	**Warrensville Heights** (city) Cuyahoga County
86	0.9	**White Oak** (CDP) Hamilton County
100	1.0	**Brookville** (city) Montgomery County
100	1.0	**Bucyrus** (city) Crawford County
100	1.0	**Columbiana** (city) Columbiana County
100	1.0	**Greentown** (CDP) Stark County
100	1.0	**Hubbard** (city) Trumbull County
100	1.0	**Kirtland** (city) Lake County
100	1.0	**Mayfield** (village) Cuyahoga County
100	1.0	**New Lebanon** (village) Montgomery County
100	1.0	**Newark** (city) Licking County
100	1.0	**Portage Lakes** (CDP) Summit County
110	1.1	**Bainbridge** (CDP) Geauga County
110	1.1	**Champion Heights** (CDP) Trumbull County
110	1.1	**Finneytown** (CDP) Hamilton County
110	1.1	**Greenville** (city) Darke County
110	1.1	**Lyndhurst** (city) Cuyahoga County
110	1.1	**Madison** (village) Lake County
110	1.1	**Portsmouth** (city) Scioto County
117	1.2	**Martins Ferry** (city) Belmont County
117	1.2	**Nelsonville** (city) Athens County
117	1.2	**Pataskala** (city) Licking County
117	1.2	**Reading** (city) Hamilton County
117	1.2	**South Lebanon** (village) Warren County
122	1.3	**Ashville** (village) Pickaway County
122	1.3	**Belpre** (city) Washington County
122	1.3	**Bluffton** (village) Allen County
122	1.3	**Grove City** (city) Franklin County
122	1.3	**Groveport** (city) Franklin County
122	1.3	**Lexington** (village) Richland County
122	1.3	**Ravenna** (city) Portage County
122	1.3	**Solon** (city) Cuyahoga County
122	1.3	**South Russell** (village) Geauga County
122	1.3	**Wadsworth** (city) Medina County
122	1.3	**Zanesville** (city) Muskingum County
133	1.4	**Calcutta** (CDP) Columbiana County
133	1.4	**Carrollton** (village) Carroll County
133	1.4	**Crestline** (village) Crawford County
133	1.4	**Dry Ridge** (CDP) Hamilton County
133	1.4	**East Liverpool** (city) Columbiana County
133	1.4	**Euclid** (city) Cuyahoga County
133	1.4	**Fairlawn** (city) Summit County
133	1.4	**Germantown** (city) Montgomery County
133	1.4	**Huron** (city) Erie County
133	1.4	**Lodi** (village) Medina County
133	1.4	**Louisville** (city) Stark County
133	1.4	**Marietta** (city) Washington County
133	1.4	**Mayfield Heights** (city) Cuyahoga County
133	1.4	**Norton** (city) Summit County
133	1.4	**Oakwood** (city) Montgomery County
133	1.4	**Ontario** (city) Richland County
133	1.4	**Piqua** (city) Miami County
133	1.4	**Seven Hills** (city) Cuyahoga County

Note: *This section ranks incorporated places and CDPs (Census Designated Places) with populations of 2,500 or more. Unincorporated postal areas were not considered. Please refer to the User Guide for additional information.*

Average Household Size

Top 150 Places Ranked in *Descending* Order

State Rank	Persons	Place
1	3.20	**Dry Run** (CDP) Hamilton County
2	3.17	**New Albany** (city) Franklin County
3	3.12	**Wright-Patterson AFB** (CDP) Greene County
4	3.09	**Lake Darby** (CDP) Franklin County
5	3.01	**New London** (village) Huron County
5	3.01	**Powell** (city) Delaware County
7	2.98	**Cherry Grove** (CDP) Hamilton County
7	2.98	**Cleves** (village) Hamilton County
7	2.98	**Delshire** (CDP) Hamilton County
7	2.98	**Greentown** (CDP) Stark County
11	2.96	**Trenton** (city) Butler County
12	2.92	**Delhi Hills** (CDP) Hamilton County
12	2.92	**Park Layne** (CDP) Clark County
12	2.92	**Sunbury** (village) Delaware County
15	2.91	**Pickerington** (city) Fairfield County
16	2.89	**Amberley** (village) Hamilton County
16	2.89	**Ashville** (village) Pickaway County
16	2.89	**Day Heights** (CDP) Clermont County
16	2.89	**Pleasant Run Farm** (CDP) Hamilton County
20	2.88	**Huber Ridge** (CDP) Franklin County
20	2.88	**Mogadore** (village) Summit County
20	2.88	**Springboro** (city) Warren County
23	2.87	**Mack** (CDP) Hamilton County
24	2.86	**Mount Orab** (village) Brown County
25	2.85	**Saint Henry** (village) Mercer County
26	2.83	**Obetz** (village) Franklin County
26	2.83	**Ross** (CDP) Butler County
26	2.83	**Waterville** (city) Lucas County
29	2.81	**Amelia** (village) Clermont County
29	2.81	**Monroe** (city) Butler County
29	2.81	**Williamsburg** (village) Clermont County
32	2.80	**Dublin** (city) Franklin County
32	2.80	**Hudson** (city) Summit County
34	2.79	**Ottawa Hills** (village) Lucas County
35	2.78	**Avon** (city) Lorain County
35	2.78	**The Village of Indian Hill** (city) Hamilton County
37	2.77	**Garrettsville** (village) Portage County
38	2.76	**Wyoming** (city) Hamilton County
39	2.75	**Brimfield** (CDP) Portage County
39	2.75	**Gibsonburg** (village) Sandusky County
39	2.75	**Hilliard** (city) Franklin County
39	2.75	**Lebanon** (city) Warren County
39	2.75	**Pleasant Run** (CDP) Hamilton County
39	2.75	**Solon** (city) Cuyahoga County
45	2.74	**Blacklick Estates** (CDP) Franklin County
45	2.74	**Uniontown** (CDP) Stark County
47	2.73	**Turpin Hills** (CDP) Hamilton County
47	2.73	**Whitehouse** (village) Lucas County
49	2.72	**Fruit Hill** (CDP) Hamilton County
49	2.72	**South Lebanon** (village) Warren County
51	2.71	**Bexley** (city) Franklin County
51	2.71	**Mount Carmel** (CDP) Clermont County
51	2.71	**Pataskala** (city) Licking County
51	2.71	**Pepper Pike** (city) Cuyahoga County
55	2.70	**Carlisle** (village) Warren County
56	2.69	**Johnstown** (village) Licking County
56	2.69	**New Lexington** (village) Perry County
56	2.69	**Willard** (city) Huron County
59	2.68	**Lake Lakengren** (CDP) Preble County
59	2.68	**Mount Repose** (CDP) Clermont County
59	2.68	**New Carlisle** (city) Clark County
59	2.68	**North Baltimore** (village) Wood County
63	2.67	**Covington** (village) Miami County
63	2.67	**New Richmond** (village) Clermont County
65	2.66	**Baltimore** (village) Fairfield County
65	2.66	**Evendale** (village) Hamilton County
65	2.66	**Groesbeck** (CDP) Hamilton County
65	2.66	**Montgomery** (city) Hamilton County
65	2.66	**Northgate** (CDP) Hamilton County
70	2.65	**Mason** (city) Warren County
70	2.65	**North Madison** (CDP) Lake County
70	2.65	**South Russell** (village) Geauga County
70	2.65	**Waynesville** (village) Warren County
74	2.64	**Canal Winchester** (city) Franklin County
74	2.64	**Independence** (city) Cuyahoga County
74	2.64	**West Jefferson** (village) Madison County
77	2.63	**Clayton** (city) Montgomery County
77	2.63	**Highland Heights** (city) Cuyahoga County
77	2.63	**Monfort Heights** (CDP) Hamilton County
77	2.63	**Union** (city) Montgomery County
81	2.62	**Reminderville** (village) Summit County
82	2.61	**Forest Park** (city) Hamilton County
82	2.61	**Landen** (CDP) Warren County
82	2.61	**Lincoln Village** (CDP) Franklin County
82	2.61	**Madeira** (city) Hamilton County
82	2.61	**New Lebanon** (village) Montgomery County
82	2.61	**Summerside** (CDP) Clermont County
88	2.60	**Oakwood** (city) Montgomery County
89	2.59	**Gahanna** (city) Franklin County
89	2.59	**Germantown** (city) Montgomery County
89	2.59	**Marysville** (city) Union County
89	2.59	**Norton** (city) Summit County
89	2.59	**Richville** (CDP) Stark County
89	2.59	**Rittman** (city) Wayne County
89	2.59	**Swanton** (village) Fulton County
96	2.58	**Miami Heights** (CDP) Hamilton County
96	2.58	**Moraine** (city) Montgomery County
96	2.58	**Moreland Hills** (village) Cuyahoga County
96	2.58	**North Ridgeville** (city) Lorain County
96	2.58	**Sherwood** (CDP) Hamilton County
96	2.58	**Taylor Creek** (CDP) Hamilton County
102	2.57	**Grove City** (city) Franklin County
102	2.57	**Huber Heights** (city) Montgomery County
102	2.57	**Minster** (village) Auglaize County
102	2.57	**Newcomerstown** (village) Tuscarawas County
102	2.57	**Wadsworth** (city) Medina County
107	2.56	**Amherst** (city) Lorain County
107	2.56	**Bainbridge** (CDP) Geauga County
107	2.56	**Blanchester** (village) Clinton County
107	2.56	**Cadiz** (village) Harrison County
107	2.56	**Four Bridges** (CDP) Butler County
107	2.56	**Granville** (village) Licking County
107	2.56	**Harrison** (city) Hamilton County
107	2.56	**Loveland** (city) Hamilton County
107	2.56	**Macedonia** (city) Summit County
107	2.56	**Medina** (city) Medina County
107	2.56	**University Heights** (city) Cuyahoga County
118	2.55	**Avon Lake** (city) Lorain County
118	2.55	**Brunswick** (city) Medina County
118	2.55	**Clyde** (city) Sandusky County
118	2.55	**Covedale** (CDP) Hamilton County
118	2.55	**New Burlington** (CDP) Hamilton County
118	2.55	**New Franklin** (city) Summit County
118	2.55	**Reynoldsburg** (city) Franklin County
118	2.55	**Richfield** (village) Summit County
118	2.55	**Wellington** (village) Lorain County
127	2.54	**Archbold** (village) Fulton County
127	2.54	**Bellevue** (city) Sandusky County
127	2.54	**Finneytown** (CDP) Hamilton County
127	2.54	**New Concord** (village) Muskingum County
127	2.54	**Painesville** (city) Lake County
127	2.54	**Springdale** (city) Hamilton County
133	2.53	**Bay Village** (city) Cuyahoga County
133	2.53	**East Palestine** (village) Columbiana County
133	2.53	**Green** (city) Summit County
133	2.53	**Northbrook** (CDP) Hamilton County
133	2.53	**Orange** (village) Cuyahoga County
133	2.53	**Sheffield Lake** (city) Lorain County
133	2.53	**Sixteen Mile Stand** (CDP) Hamilton County
133	2.53	**Upper Arlington** (city) Franklin County
141	2.52	**Bellbrook** (city) Greene County
141	2.52	**Bethel** (village) Clermont County
141	2.52	**Broadview Heights** (city) Cuyahoga County
141	2.52	**Delaware** (city) Delaware County
141	2.52	**Jefferson** (village) Ashtabula County
141	2.52	**Strongsville** (city) Cuyahoga County
141	2.52	**Tallmadge** (city) Summit County
148	2.51	**Brecksville** (city) Cuyahoga County
148	2.51	**Lexington** (village) Richland County
148	2.51	**Lorain** (city) Lorain County

Note: *This section ranks incorporated places and CDPs (Census Designated Places) with populations of 2,500 or more. Unincorporated postal areas were not considered. Please refer to the User Guide for additional information.*

Average Household Size

Top 150 Places Ranked in *Ascending* Order

State Rank	Persons	Place
1	1.90	**Silverton** (village) Hamilton County
2	1.92	**Walbridge** (village) Wood County
3	1.99	**Mayfield Heights** (city) Cuyahoga County
4	2.00	**Newton Falls** (village) Trumbull County
5	2.02	**Mount Healthy** (city) Hamilton County
6	2.03	**Waverly** (village) Pike County
6	2.03	**Yellow Springs** (village) Greene County
8	2.05	**Bedford Heights** (city) Cuyahoga County
9	2.06	**West Union** (village) Adams County
9	2.06	**Willoughby** (city) Lake County
11	2.07	**East Cleveland** (city) Cuyahoga County
11	2.07	**Lakewood** (city) Cuyahoga County
13	2.09	**Brookville** (city) Montgomery County
13	2.09	**Columbiana** (city) Columbiana County
13	2.09	**Greenville** (city) Darke County
16	2.10	**Belpre** (city) Washington County
17	2.11	**Willoughby Hills** (city) Lake County
18	2.12	**Cincinnati** (city) Hamilton County
18	2.12	**Euclid** (city) Cuyahoga County
18	2.12	**Middlefield** (village) Geauga County
21	2.13	**Carrollton** (village) Carroll County
21	2.13	**Marietta** (city) Washington County
21	2.13	**Portage Lakes** (CDP) Summit County
24	2.14	**Fairlawn** (city) Summit County
24	2.14	**Hicksville** (village) Defiance County
24	2.14	**Richmond Heights** (city) Cuyahoga County
27	2.15	**Cheviot** (city) Hamilton County
27	2.15	**Deer Park** (city) Hamilton County
27	2.15	**Mulberry** (CDP) Clermont County
27	2.15	**Shadyside** (village) Belmont County
27	2.15	**West Carrollton** (city) Montgomery County
32	2.16	**Ada** (village) Hardin County
32	2.16	**Chagrin Falls** (village) Cuyahoga County
32	2.16	**Saint Clairsville** (city) Belmont County
32	2.16	**Warrensville Heights** (city) Cuyahoga County
36	2.17	**Jackson** (city) Jackson County
36	2.17	**Loudonville** (village) Ashland County
36	2.17	**Warren** (city) Trumbull County
39	2.18	**Bucyrus** (city) Crawford County
39	2.18	**Enon** (village) Clark County
39	2.18	**Milford** (city) Clermont County
42	2.19	**Austintown** (CDP) Mahoning County
42	2.19	**Centerville** (city) Montgomery County
42	2.19	**Wickliffe** (city) Lake County
45	2.20	**Brooklyn** (city) Cuyahoga County
45	2.20	**Fairport Harbor** (village) Lake County
45	2.20	**Findlay** (city) Hancock County
45	2.20	**Kettering** (city) Montgomery County
45	2.20	**Lyndhurst** (city) Cuyahoga County
45	2.20	**Norwood** (city) Hamilton County
45	2.20	**Port Clinton** (city) Ottawa County
45	2.20	**Sandusky** (city) Erie County
45	2.20	**Sebring** (village) Mahoning County
45	2.20	**Shelby** (city) Richland County
45	2.20	**Upper Sandusky** (city) Wyandot County
56	2.21	**Cedarville** (village) Greene County
56	2.21	**Hillsboro** (city) Highland County
56	2.21	**North College Hill** (city) Hamilton County
56	2.21	**Wilmington** (city) Clinton County
60	2.22	**Chardon** (city) Geauga County
60	2.22	**Millersburg** (village) Holmes County
60	2.22	**Mount Vernon** (city) Knox County
60	2.22	**North Canton** (city) Stark County
60	2.22	**Oberlin** (city) Lorain County
60	2.22	**Parma Heights** (city) Cuyahoga County
60	2.22	**Steubenville** (city) Jefferson County
60	2.22	**Wooster** (city) Wayne County
68	2.23	**Bedford** (city) Cuyahoga County
68	2.23	**Kenwood** (CDP) Hamilton County
68	2.23	**Logan** (city) Hocking County
68	2.23	**Youngstown** (city) Mahoning County
72	2.24	**Bryan** (city) Williams County
72	2.24	**Canal Fulton** (city) Stark County
72	2.24	**Fairborn** (city) Greene County
72	2.24	**Girard** (city) Trumbull County
72	2.24	**Middleburg Heights** (city) Cuyahoga County
72	2.24	**Niles** (city) Trumbull County
72	2.24	**Northridge** (CDP) Clark County
72	2.24	**Urbana** (city) Champaign County
72	2.24	**Woodlawn** (village) Hamilton County
81	2.25	**Ashland** (city) Ashland County
81	2.25	**Boardman** (CDP) Mahoning County
81	2.25	**Cleveland** (city) Cuyahoga County
81	2.25	**Dayton** (city) Montgomery County
81	2.25	**Fairview Park** (city) Cuyahoga County
81	2.25	**Ottawa** (village) Putnam County
81	2.25	**Rocky River** (city) Cuyahoga County
81	2.25	**Withamsville** (CDP) Clermont County
89	2.26	**Ballville** (CDP) Sandusky County
89	2.26	**Bowling Green** (city) Wood County
89	2.26	**Cambridge** (city) Guernsey County
89	2.26	**Chillicothe** (city) Ross County
89	2.26	**Cortland** (city) Trumbull County
89	2.26	**Dry Ridge** (CDP) Hamilton County
89	2.26	**Toronto** (city) Jefferson County
89	2.26	**Zanesville** (city) Muskingum County
97	2.27	**Cuyahoga Falls** (city) Summit County
97	2.27	**Devola** (CDP) Washington County
97	2.27	**Martins Ferry** (city) Belmont County
97	2.27	**Portsmouth** (city) Scioto County
97	2.27	**Ravenna** (city) Portage County
97	2.27	**The Plains** (CDP) Athens County
103	2.28	**Barnesville** (village) Belmont County
103	2.28	**Bellaire** (village) Belmont County
103	2.28	**Canton** (city) Stark County
103	2.28	**Conneaut** (city) Ashtabula County
103	2.28	**Mansfield** (city) Richland County
103	2.28	**Mayfield** (village) Cuyahoga County
103	2.28	**Wellsville** (village) Columbiana County
110	2.29	**Akron** (city) Summit County
110	2.29	**Coshocton** (city) Coshocton County
110	2.29	**Mineral Ridge** (CDP) Trumbull County
110	2.29	**Sharonville** (city) Hamilton County
110	2.29	**Vermilion** (city) Lorain County
110	2.29	**Westlake** (city) Cuyahoga County
116	2.30	**Berea** (city) Cuyahoga County
116	2.30	**Gallipolis** (village) Gallia County
116	2.30	**Mentor-on-the-Lake** (city) Lake County
116	2.30	**Mingo Junction** (village) Jefferson County
116	2.30	**Napoleon** (city) Henry County
116	2.30	**Trotwood** (city) Montgomery County
122	2.31	**Defiance** (city) Defiance County
122	2.31	**Englewood** (city) Montgomery County
122	2.31	**Hubbard** (city) Trumbull County
122	2.31	**Lordstown** (village) Trumbull County
122	2.31	**Toledo** (city) Lucas County
122	2.31	**Vandalia** (city) Montgomery County
128	2.32	**Athens** (city) Athens County
128	2.32	**Celina** (city) Mercer County
128	2.32	**Champion Heights** (CDP) Trumbull County
128	2.32	**Cleveland Heights** (city) Cuyahoga County
128	2.32	**Huron** (city) Erie County
128	2.32	**Springfield** (city) Clark County
128	2.32	**Washington Court House** (city) Fayette County
128	2.32	**Wheelersburg** (CDP) Scioto County
136	2.33	**Coldwater** (village) Mercer County
136	2.33	**Dillonvale** (CDP) Hamilton County
136	2.33	**Galion** (city) Crawford County
136	2.33	**Orrville** (city) Wayne County
136	2.33	**Strasburg** (village) Tuscarawas County
141	2.34	**Beachwood** (city) Cuyahoga County
141	2.34	**Blue Ash** (city) Hamilton County
141	2.34	**Eaton** (city) Preble County
141	2.34	**Edgewood** (CDP) Ashtabula County
141	2.34	**Lodi** (village) Medina County
141	2.34	**Mount Gilead** (village) Morrow County
141	2.34	**Reading** (city) Hamilton County
141	2.34	**Xenia** (city) Greene County
149	2.35	**Eastlake** (city) Lake County
149	2.35	**Elyria** (city) Lorain County

***Note:** This section ranks incorporated places and CDPs (Census Designated Places) with populations of 2,500 or more. Unincorporated postal areas were not considered. Please refer to the User Guide for additional information.*

Median Age

Top 150 Places Ranked in *Descending* Order

State Rank	Years	Place
1	53.9	**Columbiana** (city) Columbiana County
2	53.5	**Mulberry** (CDP) Clermont County
3	53.1	**Dry Ridge** (CDP) Hamilton County
4	52.6	**Walbridge** (village) Wood County
5	52.2	**Beechwood Trails** (CDP) Licking County
6	51.7	**Enon** (village) Clark County
7	51.5	**Ballville** (CDP) Sandusky County
8	51.3	**Mayfield** (village) Cuyahoga County
9	51.1	**The Village of Indian Hill** (city) Hamilton County
10	50.9	**Seven Hills** (city) Cuyahoga County
11	50.6	**Evendale** (village) Hamilton County
12	50.5	**Mingo Junction** (village) Jefferson County
13	50.3	**Beachwood** (city) Cuyahoga County
14	50.2	**Devola** (CDP) Washington County
15	49.8	**Montrose-Ghent** (CDP) Summit County
16	49.7	**Mount Gilead** (village) Morrow County
16	49.7	**Saint Clairsville** (city) Belmont County
16	49.7	**Strasburg** (village) Tuscarawas County
19	49.4	**Kirtland** (city) Lake County
20	49.3	**Canfield** (city) Mahoning County
20	49.3	**Loudonville** (village) Ashland County
22	49.2	**Pepper Pike** (city) Cuyahoga County
23	48.7	**Carrollton** (village) Carroll County
24	48.5	**Highland Heights** (city) Cuyahoga County
24	48.5	**Richmond Heights** (city) Cuyahoga County
26	48.4	**Yellow Springs** (village) Greene County
27	48.3	**Vermilion** (city) Lorain County
28	48.2	**Aurora** (city) Portage County
28	48.2	**Centerville** (city) Montgomery County
30	48.0	**Moreland Hills** (village) Cuyahoga County
30	48.0	**Sheffield** (village) Lorain County
32	47.9	**Brecksville** (city) Cuyahoga County
32	47.9	**Chagrin Falls** (village) Cuyahoga County
32	47.9	**New Franklin** (city) Summit County
35	47.7	**North Zanesville** (CDP) Muskingum County
35	47.7	**Richfield** (village) Summit County
37	47.3	**Calcutta** (CDP) Columbiana County
38	47.2	**Westlake** (city) Cuyahoga County
39	46.9	**Independence** (city) Cuyahoga County
40	46.8	**Lordstown** (village) Trumbull County
41	46.7	**Fairlawn** (city) Summit County
41	46.7	**Lyndhurst** (city) Cuyahoga County
41	46.7	**Mentor** (city) Lake County
41	46.7	**Northridge** (CDP) Clark County
45	46.5	**Montgomery** (city) Hamilton County
46	46.4	**Champion Heights** (CDP) Trumbull County
47	46.3	**Richville** (CDP) Stark County
47	46.3	**Sebring** (village) Mahoning County
49	46.2	**Middleburg Heights** (city) Cuyahoga County
49	46.2	**Rocky River** (city) Cuyahoga County
51	46.1	**Munroe Falls** (city) Summit County
51	46.1	**New Burlington** (CDP) Hamilton County
53	46.0	**Cortland** (city) Trumbull County
54	45.9	**Fort Shawnee** (CDP) Allen County
54	45.9	**Ontario** (city) Richland County
54	45.9	**Strongsville** (city) Cuyahoga County
54	45.9	**Waverly** (village) Pike County
58	45.7	**Orange** (village) Cuyahoga County
58	45.7	**Shadyside** (village) Belmont County
60	45.6	**Apple Valley** (CDP) Knox County
60	45.6	**Belpre** (city) Washington County
60	45.6	**South Russell** (village) Geauga County
63	45.5	**Bedford Heights** (city) Cuyahoga County
64	45.4	**Poland** (village) Mahoning County
65	45.3	**Tallmadge** (city) Summit County
66	45.2	**Hudson** (city) Summit County
66	45.2	**North Olmsted** (city) Cuyahoga County
68	45.1	**Barnesville** (village) Belmont County
68	45.1	**Englewood** (city) Montgomery County
68	45.1	**Huron** (city) Erie County
68	45.1	**Salem Heights** (CDP) Hamilton County
72	45.0	**Wintersville** (village) Jefferson County
73	44.9	**Macedonia** (city) Summit County
73	44.9	**Mack** (CDP) Hamilton County
75	44.8	**Fairport Harbor** (village) Lake County
75	44.8	**Lakemore** (village) Summit County
75	44.8	**Willoughby Hills** (city) Lake County
78	44.6	**Kenwood** (CDP) Hamilton County
79	44.5	**Amherst** (city) Lorain County
79	44.5	**Brook Park** (city) Cuyahoga County
79	44.5	**Miami Heights** (CDP) Hamilton County
82	44.4	**Canal Fulton** (city) Stark County
82	44.4	**Wickliffe** (city) Lake County
84	44.3	**Lodi** (village) Medina County
84	44.3	**North Kingsville** (village) Ashtabula County
86	44.2	**Seville** (village) Medina County
86	44.2	**Silverton** (village) Hamilton County
86	44.2	**Wyoming** (city) Hamilton County
89	44.1	**Burlington** (CDP) Lawrence County
89	44.1	**Martins Ferry** (city) Belmont County
91	44.0	**Bainbridge** (CDP) Geauga County
91	44.0	**North Canton** (city) Stark County
91	44.0	**Solon** (city) Cuyahoga County
91	44.0	**Willoughby** (city) Lake County
95	43.9	**Brookville** (city) Montgomery County
95	43.9	**East Cleveland** (city) Cuyahoga County
95	43.9	**Newton Falls** (village) Trumbull County
95	43.9	**Olmsted Falls** (city) Cuyahoga County
95	43.9	**Sherwood** (CDP) Hamilton County
100	43.8	**Bay Village** (city) Cuyahoga County
100	43.8	**Greenville** (city) Darke County
100	43.8	**Port Clinton** (city) Ottawa County
103	43.7	**Bucyrus** (city) Crawford County
104	43.5	**Amberley** (village) Hamilton County
104	43.5	**Brooklyn** (city) Cuyahoga County
104	43.5	**Perry Heights** (CDP) Stark County
107	43.4	**Avon Lake** (city) Lorain County
107	43.4	**Eastlake** (city) Lake County
109	43.3	**Boardman** (CDP) Mahoning County
109	43.3	**Chillicothe** (city) Ross County
109	43.3	**Jackson** (city) Jackson County
112	43.2	**Canal Winchester** (city) Franklin County
112	43.2	**Dover** (city) Tuscarawas County
112	43.2	**Forestville** (CDP) Hamilton County
112	43.2	**Norton** (city) Summit County
116	43.1	**Hubbard** (city) Trumbull County
116	43.1	**Mayfield Heights** (city) Cuyahoga County
116	43.1	**North Royalton** (city) Cuyahoga County
116	43.1	**Oakwood** (village) Cuyahoga County
116	43.1	**Worthington** (city) Franklin County
121	43.0	**Austintown** (CDP) Mahoning County
121	43.0	**Howland Center** (CDP) Trumbull County
121	43.0	**Millersburg** (village) Holmes County
121	43.0	**Vandalia** (city) Montgomery County
121	43.0	**Versailles** (village) Darke County
126	42.9	**Green Meadows** (CDP) Clark County
126	42.9	**Taylor Creek** (CDP) Hamilton County
128	42.8	**Groveport** (city) Franklin County
128	42.8	**Northgate** (CDP) Hamilton County
128	42.8	**Oregon** (city) Lucas County
128	42.8	**Sylvania** (city) Lucas County
132	42.7	**Blue Ash** (city) Hamilton County
132	42.7	**Withamsville** (CDP) Clermont County
134	42.6	**Oakwood** (city) Montgomery County
134	42.6	**Steubenville** (city) Jefferson County
134	42.6	**Turpin Hills** (CDP) Hamilton County
134	42.6	**West Union** (village) Adams County
138	42.5	**Coshocton** (city) Coshocton County
138	42.5	**Mineral Ridge** (CDP) Trumbull County
138	42.5	**Twinsburg** (city) Summit County
141	42.4	**Niles** (city) Trumbull County
142	42.3	**Clayton** (city) Montgomery County
142	42.3	**Monfort Heights** (CDP) Hamilton County
142	42.3	**Ottawa Hills** (village) Lucas County
145	42.2	**Bellbrook** (city) Greene County
145	42.2	**Doylestown** (village) Wayne County
145	42.2	**Milford** (city) Clermont County
148	42.1	**Covedale** (CDP) Hamilton County
148	42.1	**Green** (city) Summit County
148	42.1	**McDonald** (village) Trumbull County

Note: *This section ranks incorporated places and CDPs (Census Designated Places) with populations of 2,500 or more. Unincorporated postal areas were not considered. Please refer to the User Guide for additional information.*

Median Age

Top 150 Places Ranked in *Ascending* Order

State Rank	Years	Place
1	20.9	**Cedarville** (village) Greene County
2	21.2	**Oxford** (city) Butler County
3	21.4	**Athens** (city) Athens County
3	21.4	**New Concord** (village) Muskingum County
5	21.6	**Ada** (village) Hardin County
5	21.6	**Granville** (village) Licking County
7	22.8	**Bowling Green** (city) Wood County
7	22.8	**Wright-Patterson AFB** (CDP) Greene County
9	23.5	**Kent** (city) Portage County
10	24.5	**Oberlin** (city) Lorain County
11	28.2	**Nelsonville** (city) Athens County
12	29.9	**University Heights** (city) Cuyahoga County
13	30.1	**New London** (village) Huron County
14	30.9	**Trenton** (city) Butler County
15	31.6	**Gibsonburg** (village) Sandusky County
15	31.6	**Huber Ridge** (CDP) Franklin County
17	31.8	**Mount Carmel** (CDP) Clermont County
18	32.1	**Amelia** (village) Clermont County
18	32.1	**Columbus** (city) Franklin County
20	32.3	**Cincinnati** (city) Hamilton County
21	32.5	**Painesville** (city) Lake County
22	32.7	**Johnstown** (village) Licking County
23	32.9	**Dennison** (village) Tuscarawas County
23	32.9	**Golf Manor** (village) Hamilton County
25	33.0	**Whitehall** (city) Franklin County
26	33.2	**Lebanon** (city) Warren County
26	33.2	**Lima** (city) Allen County
26	33.2	**Summerside** (CDP) Clermont County
29	33.3	**Bellefontaine** (city) Logan County
29	33.3	**Dayton** (city) Montgomery County
29	33.3	**Norwood** (city) Hamilton County
32	33.5	**North Baltimore** (village) Wood County
33	33.8	**Fairborn** (city) Greene County
34	33.9	**Park Layne** (CDP) Clark County
35	34.0	**Cleves** (village) Hamilton County
35	34.0	**Delaware** (city) Delaware County
35	34.0	**Grandview Heights** (city) Franklin County
38	34.1	**Bexley** (city) Franklin County
38	34.1	**Mount Orab** (village) Brown County
40	34.2	**Northbrook** (CDP) Hamilton County
41	34.3	**Ashville** (village) Pickaway County
42	34.4	**Blacklick Estates** (CDP) Franklin County
42	34.4	**Willard** (city) Huron County
44	34.5	**Baltimore** (village) Fairfield County
44	34.5	**Wellsville** (village) Columbiana County
46	34.6	**Mount Healthy Heights** (CDP) Hamilton County
47	34.7	**Lakewood** (city) Cuyahoga County
47	34.7	**Monroe** (city) Butler County
47	34.7	**New Lexington** (village) Perry County
50	34.8	**Marysville** (city) Union County
50	34.8	**Saint Henry** (village) Mercer County
52	35.1	**Tiffin** (city) Seneca County
53	35.2	**Lake Darby** (CDP) Franklin County
54	35.3	**Toledo** (city) Lucas County
55	35.4	**Delshire** (CDP) Hamilton County
56	35.5	**Pickerington** (city) Fairfield County
56	35.5	**Zanesville** (city) Muskingum County
58	35.6	**Alliance** (city) Stark County
58	35.6	**Wilmington** (city) Clinton County
60	35.7	**Riverside** (city) Montgomery County
60	35.7	**Williamsburg** (village) Clermont County
62	35.8	**Canton** (city) Stark County
62	35.8	**Cleveland** (city) Cuyahoga County
62	35.8	**Mount Vernon** (city) Knox County
62	35.8	**Sunbury** (village) Delaware County
66	35.9	**Hilliard** (city) Franklin County
66	35.9	**Landen** (CDP) Warren County
66	35.9	**Moraine** (city) Montgomery County
66	35.9	**New Carlisle** (city) Clark County
66	35.9	**Obetz** (village) Franklin County
66	35.9	**Reynoldsburg** (city) Franklin County
72	36.0	**Cheviot** (city) Hamilton County
72	36.0	**Groesbeck** (CDP) Hamilton County
72	36.0	**Lockland** (village) Hamilton County
72	36.0	**New Lebanon** (village) Montgomery County
72	36.0	**Ross** (CDP) Butler County
72	36.0	**Swanton** (village) Fulton County
78	36.1	**Brimfield** (CDP) Portage County
78	36.1	**Cleveland Heights** (city) Cuyahoga County
78	36.1	**Fremont** (city) Sandusky County
81	36.2	**Georgetown** (village) Brown County
81	36.2	**Pleasant Run Farm** (CDP) Hamilton County
81	36.2	**Wapakoneta** (city) Auglaize County
81	36.2	**Wooster** (city) Wayne County
85	36.3	**Harrison** (city) Hamilton County
85	36.3	**Wauseon** (city) Fulton County
87	36.4	**Cherry Grove** (CDP) Hamilton County
87	36.4	**London** (city) Madison County
89	36.5	**Garrettsville** (village) Portage County
90	36.6	**West Carrollton** (city) Montgomery County
91	36.7	**Akron** (city) Summit County
91	36.7	**Crooksville** (village) Perry County
91	36.7	**Findlay** (city) Hancock County
91	36.7	**Springfield** (city) Clark County
95	36.8	**Fredericktown** (village) Knox County
95	36.8	**Huber Heights** (city) Montgomery County
95	36.8	**Portsmouth** (city) Scioto County
98	36.9	**Covington** (village) Miami County
98	36.9	**Jefferson** (village) Ashtabula County
98	36.9	**Lorain** (city) Lorain County
98	36.9	**Northfield** (village) Summit County
102	37.0	**Delhi Hills** (CDP) Hamilton County
102	37.0	**Newark** (city) Licking County
102	37.0	**Plain City** (village) Madison County
105	37.1	**Clyde** (city) Sandusky County
105	37.1	**Forest Park** (city) Hamilton County
107	37.2	**Fruit Hill** (CDP) Hamilton County
107	37.2	**Hamilton** (city) Butler County
107	37.2	**Uhrichsville** (city) Tuscarawas County
107	37.2	**Woodlawn** (village) Hamilton County
107	37.2	**Xenia** (city) Greene County
112	37.3	**Franklin** (city) Warren County
113	37.4	**Bellevue** (city) Sandusky County
113	37.4	**Pleasant Run** (CDP) Hamilton County
115	37.5	**Defiance** (city) Defiance County
115	37.5	**Marietta** (city) Washington County
115	37.5	**Minerva** (village) Stark County
115	37.5	**Pataskala** (city) Licking County
119	37.6	**Ashland** (city) Ashland County
119	37.6	**Maple Heights** (city) Cuyahoga County
119	37.6	**Sharonville** (city) Hamilton County
119	37.6	**Springboro** (city) Warren County
119	37.6	**Union** (city) Montgomery County
124	37.7	**Blanchester** (village) Clinton County
124	37.7	**Mansfield** (city) Richland County
124	37.7	**Salem** (city) Columbiana County
124	37.7	**Upper Sandusky** (city) Wyandot County
124	37.7	**Wadsworth** (city) Medina County
124	37.7	**Wellington** (village) Lorain County
130	37.8	**Elyria** (city) Lorain County
130	37.8	**Lexington** (village) Richland County
130	37.8	**Lincoln Village** (CDP) Franklin County
130	37.8	**Marion** (city) Marion County
130	37.8	**Middletown** (city) Butler County
130	37.8	**The Plains** (CDP) Athens County
136	37.9	**Greentown** (CDP) Stark County
136	37.9	**Medina** (city) Medina County
136	37.9	**New Philadelphia** (city) Tuscarawas County
136	37.9	**Paulding** (village) Paulding County
136	37.9	**Piqua** (city) Miami County
136	37.9	**Saint Bernard** (city) Hamilton County
142	38.0	**Archbold** (village) Fulton County
142	38.0	**Circleville** (city) Pickaway County
142	38.0	**Mariemont** (village) Hamilton County
142	38.0	**New Richmond** (village) Clermont County
142	38.0	**South Euclid** (city) Cuyahoga County
142	38.0	**Warrensville Heights** (city) Cuyahoga County
148	38.1	**Fairfield** (city) Butler County
148	38.1	**Greenfield** (village) Highland County
148	38.1	**Lake Lakengren** (CDP) Preble County

Note: *This section ranks incorporated places and CDPs (Census Designated Places) with populations of 2,500 or more. Unincorporated postal areas were not considered. Please refer to the User Guide for additional information.*

Population Under Age 18

Top 150 Places Ranked in *Descending* Order

State Rank	Percent	Place
1	36.3	**New Albany** (city) Franklin County
2	34.2	**Baltimore** (village) Fairfield County
3	33.7	**Powell** (city) Delaware County
4	32.9	**Dry Run** (CDP) Hamilton County
5	32.7	**Cleves** (village) Hamilton County
6	32.4	**Fruit Hill** (CDP) Hamilton County
7	31.8	**New London** (village) Huron County
8	31.2	**Mount Orab** (village) Brown County
9	31.1	**Trenton** (city) Butler County
10	30.6	**Springboro** (city) Warren County
10	30.6	**Sunbury** (village) Delaware County
12	30.5	**Avon** (city) Lorain County
12	30.5	**Pickerington** (city) Fairfield County
14	30.4	**Day Heights** (CDP) Clermont County
15	30.2	**Amelia** (village) Clermont County
15	30.2	**Garrettsville** (village) Portage County
15	30.2	**Landen** (CDP) Warren County
18	30.1	**Blacklick Estates** (CDP) Franklin County
18	30.1	**Gibsonburg** (village) Sandusky County
20	29.9	**Lake Darby** (CDP) Franklin County
21	29.7	**Dublin** (city) Franklin County
21	29.7	**Ross** (CDP) Butler County
23	29.6	**Amberley** (village) Hamilton County
24	29.4	**Park Layne** (CDP) Clark County
25	29.3	**New Carlisle** (city) Clark County
25	29.3	**Saint Henry** (village) Mercer County
27	29.2	**Oakwood** (city) Montgomery County
28	29.1	**North Madison** (CDP) Lake County
28	29.1	**Obetz** (village) Franklin County
30	29.0	**Four Bridges** (CDP) Butler County
30	29.0	**Pleasant Run Farm** (CDP) Hamilton County
32	28.9	**Springdale** (city) Hamilton County
32	28.9	**Uniontown** (CDP) Stark County
34	28.8	**Monroe** (city) Butler County
34	28.8	**Mount Repose** (CDP) Clermont County
34	28.8	**Wellsville** (village) Columbiana County
37	28.7	**Mount Healthy Heights** (CDP) Hamilton County
38	28.6	**Huber Ridge** (CDP) Franklin County
39	28.5	**Hilliard** (city) Franklin County
39	28.5	**Whitehall** (city) Franklin County
41	28.4	**Lexington** (village) Richland County
41	28.4	**Minster** (village) Auglaize County
41	28.4	**South Russell** (village) Geauga County
44	28.3	**Germantown** (city) Montgomery County
44	28.3	**North Baltimore** (village) Wood County
44	28.3	**Turpin Hills** (CDP) Hamilton County
47	28.2	**Lebanon** (city) Warren County
48	28.1	**Cherry Grove** (CDP) Hamilton County
49	28.0	**Summerside** (CDP) Clermont County
50	27.9	**Georgetown** (village) Brown County
50	27.9	**Golf Manor** (village) Hamilton County
50	27.9	**Ottawa Hills** (village) Lucas County
53	27.7	**Dennison** (village) Tuscarawas County
53	27.7	**Mariemont** (village) Hamilton County
53	27.7	**The Village of Indian Hill** (city) Hamilton County
53	27.7	**Waterville** (city) Lucas County
57	27.6	**Ashville** (village) Pickaway County
57	27.6	**Newcomerstown** (village) Tuscarawas County
59	27.5	**Willard** (city) Huron County
60	27.4	**Archbold** (village) Fulton County
60	27.4	**Solon** (city) Cuyahoga County
62	27.3	**Mason** (city) Warren County
62	27.3	**New Lexington** (village) Perry County
62	27.3	**Plain City** (village) Madison County
65	27.2	**Lake Lakengren** (CDP) Preble County
65	27.2	**Wyoming** (city) Hamilton County
67	27.1	**Harrison** (city) Hamilton County
67	27.1	**Hudson** (city) Summit County
67	27.1	**New Richmond** (village) Clermont County
70	27.0	**Carey** (village) Wyandot County
71	26.9	**New Lebanon** (village) Montgomery County
72	26.8	**Northbrook** (CDP) Hamilton County
72	26.8	**Whitehouse** (village) Lucas County
74	26.7	**Bainbridge** (CDP) Geauga County
75	26.6	**Buckeye Lake** (village) Licking County
75	26.6	**Medina** (city) Medina County
75	26.6	**Upper Arlington** (city) Franklin County
78	26.5	**Bellefontaine** (city) Logan County
78	26.5	**Delta** (village) Fulton County
78	26.5	**Fostoria** (city) Seneca County
81	26.4	**Clyde** (city) Sandusky County
81	26.4	**Delshire** (CDP) Hamilton County
81	26.4	**Fremont** (city) Sandusky County
81	26.4	**Groesbeck** (CDP) Hamilton County
85	26.3	**Huber Heights** (city) Montgomery County
85	26.3	**Madison** (village) Lake County
85	26.3	**Perrysburg** (city) Wood County
85	26.3	**Wadsworth** (city) Medina County
89	26.2	**Lincoln Village** (CDP) Franklin County
90	26.1	**Lincoln Heights** (village) Hamilton County
90	26.1	**Newtown** (village) Hamilton County
90	26.1	**Wapakoneta** (city) Auglaize County
93	26.0	**Avon Lake** (city) Lorain County
93	26.0	**Johnstown** (village) Licking County
93	26.0	**Madeira** (city) Hamilton County
96	25.9	**Bexley** (city) Franklin County
96	25.9	**East Liverpool** (city) Columbiana County
96	25.9	**Montgomery** (city) Hamilton County
96	25.9	**Moraine** (city) Montgomery County
96	25.9	**New Bremen** (village) Auglaize County
96	25.9	**Wauseon** (city) Fulton County
102	25.8	**Coldwater** (village) Mercer County
102	25.8	**Covington** (village) Miami County
102	25.8	**Fredericktown** (village) Knox County
102	25.8	**Shaker Heights** (city) Cuyahoga County
106	25.7	**Lima** (city) Allen County
106	25.7	**Painesville** (city) Lake County
108	25.6	**Pataskala** (city) Licking County
109	25.5	**Delaware** (city) Delaware County
109	25.5	**East Palestine** (village) Columbiana County
109	25.5	**Norwalk** (city) Huron County
109	25.5	**Williamsburg** (village) Clermont County
113	25.4	**Brimfield** (CDP) Portage County
113	25.4	**Grove City** (city) Franklin County
113	25.4	**McDonald** (village) Trumbull County
113	25.4	**Worthington** (city) Franklin County
117	25.3	**Blanchester** (village) Clinton County
117	25.3	**Pepper Pike** (city) Cuyahoga County
119	25.2	**Lorain** (city) Lorain County
119	25.2	**Mount Carmel** (CDP) Clermont County
119	25.2	**Reminderville** (village) Summit County
122	25.1	**Ashtabula** (city) Ashtabula County
122	25.1	**Union** (city) Montgomery County
124	25.0	**Canal Winchester** (city) Franklin County
124	25.0	**Greentown** (CDP) Stark County
124	25.0	**Ottawa** (village) Putnam County
124	25.0	**Paulding** (village) Paulding County
128	24.9	**Bay Village** (city) Cuyahoga County
128	24.9	**Forest Park** (city) Hamilton County
128	24.9	**Mogadore** (village) Summit County
128	24.9	**Versailles** (village) Darke County
132	24.8	**Doylestown** (village) Wayne County
132	24.8	**Rittman** (city) Wayne County
132	24.8	**Xenia** (city) Greene County
135	24.7	**Canton** (city) Stark County
135	24.7	**Forestville** (CDP) Hamilton County
135	24.7	**Geneva** (city) Ashtabula County
135	24.7	**Marysville** (city) Union County
135	24.7	**Miami Heights** (CDP) Hamilton County
140	24.6	**Bellevue** (city) Sandusky County
140	24.6	**Greenfield** (village) Highland County
140	24.6	**Newark** (city) Licking County
140	24.6	**West Portsmouth** (CDP) Scioto County
144	24.5	**Crestline** (village) Crawford County
144	24.5	**Franklin** (city) Warren County
144	24.5	**Jefferson** (village) Ashtabula County
144	24.5	**Logan** (city) Hocking County
144	24.5	**Pleasant Run** (CDP) Hamilton County
144	24.5	**Saint Marys** (city) Auglaize County
144	24.5	**Van Wert** (city) Van Wert County

Note: *This section ranks incorporated places and CDPs (Census Designated Places) with populations of 2,500 or more. Unincorporated postal areas were not considered. Please refer to the User Guide for additional information.*

Population Under Age 18

Top 150 Places Ranked in *Ascending* Order

State Rank	Percent	Place
1	5.7	**Oxford** (city) Butler County
2	6.4	**Cedarville** (village) Greene County
3	6.7	**Athens** (city) Athens County
4	7.6	**Grafton** (village) Lorain County
5	12.3	**Bowling Green** (city) Wood County
6	12.8	**Walbridge** (village) Wood County
7	13.9	**Portage Lakes** (CDP) Summit County
8	14.2	**Carrollton** (village) Carroll County
9	14.9	**New Concord** (village) Muskingum County
10	15.2	**Beechwood Trails** (CDP) Licking County
10	15.2	**Richmond Heights** (city) Cuyahoga County
10	15.2	**Withamsville** (CDP) Clermont County
13	15.4	**Enon** (village) Clark County
13	15.4	**Kent** (city) Portage County
13	15.4	**Oberlin** (city) Lorain County
16	15.5	**Willoughby Hills** (city) Lake County
17	15.6	**Mulberry** (CDP) Clermont County
18	15.7	**Mingo Junction** (village) Jefferson County
19	15.9	**Mayfield** (village) Cuyahoga County
20	16.0	**Ada** (village) Hardin County
20	16.0	**Seven Hills** (city) Cuyahoga County
22	16.1	**Belpre** (city) Washington County
22	16.1	**Brooklyn** (city) Cuyahoga County
22	16.1	**Shadyside** (village) Belmont County
25	16.2	**Loudonville** (village) Ashland County
26	16.7	**Granville** (village) Licking County
27	16.8	**Columbiana** (city) Columbiana County
28	17.1	**Dry Ridge** (CDP) Hamilton County
29	17.3	**Newton Falls** (village) Trumbull County
29	17.3	**Sebring** (village) Mahoning County
31	17.4	**North Canton** (city) Stark County
31	17.4	**Vermilion** (city) Lorain County
33	17.5	**Munroe Falls** (city) Summit County
33	17.5	**Ontario** (city) Richland County
35	17.6	**Saint Clairsville** (city) Belmont County
36	17.7	**Conneaut** (city) Ashtabula County
37	17.9	**Bedford Heights** (city) Cuyahoga County
37	17.9	**Lyndhurst** (city) Cuyahoga County
39	18.1	**Steubenville** (city) Jefferson County
40	18.2	**Devola** (CDP) Washington County
40	18.2	**Waverly** (village) Pike County
42	18.3	**Berea** (city) Cuyahoga County
42	18.3	**Lordstown** (village) Trumbull County
42	18.3	**Mayfield Heights** (city) Cuyahoga County
42	18.3	**Nelsonville** (city) Athens County
42	18.3	**Silverton** (village) Hamilton County
42	18.3	**Willoughby** (city) Lake County
48	18.4	**Lakewood** (city) Cuyahoga County
48	18.4	**Sheffield** (village) Lorain County
50	18.5	**Marietta** (city) Washington County
50	18.5	**Middleburg Heights** (city) Cuyahoga County
50	18.5	**New Franklin** (city) Summit County
50	18.5	**Northfield** (village) Summit County
54	18.6	**Fairlawn** (city) Summit County
54	18.6	**Norwood** (city) Hamilton County
56	18.7	**Cortland** (city) Trumbull County
56	18.7	**Strasburg** (village) Tuscarawas County
58	18.8	**Ballville** (CDP) Sandusky County
58	18.8	**Boardman** (CDP) Mahoning County
58	18.8	**Canfield** (city) Mahoning County
61	18.9	**North Olmsted** (city) Cuyahoga County
61	18.9	**Yellow Springs** (village) Greene County
63	19.0	**Kirtland** (city) Lake County
63	19.0	**Wickliffe** (city) Lake County
65	19.1	**Jackson** (city) Jackson County
65	19.1	**Mentor-on-the-Lake** (city) Lake County
67	19.2	**Lakemore** (village) Summit County
67	19.2	**Mentor** (city) Lake County
67	19.2	**Sixteen Mile Stand** (CDP) Hamilton County
70	19.3	**Oakwood** (village) Cuyahoga County
71	19.4	**Austintown** (CDP) Mahoning County
71	19.4	**Grandview Heights** (city) Franklin County
71	19.4	**Lodi** (village) Medina County
74	19.5	**North Royalton** (city) Cuyahoga County
75	19.6	**Deer Park** (city) Hamilton County
75	19.6	**West Union** (village) Adams County
77	19.7	**Richville** (CDP) Stark County
78	19.8	**Brook Park** (city) Cuyahoga County
78	19.8	**Evendale** (village) Hamilton County
78	19.8	**West Carrollton** (city) Montgomery County
78	19.8	**Wheelersburg** (CDP) Scioto County
82	19.9	**Parma** (city) Cuyahoga County
83	20.0	**Ashland** (city) Ashland County
83	20.0	**Coshocton** (city) Coshocton County
83	20.0	**Mineral Ridge** (CDP) Trumbull County
83	20.0	**South Lebanon** (village) Warren County
87	20.1	**Portsmouth** (city) Scioto County
87	20.1	**Wintersville** (village) Jefferson County
89	20.2	**Fairview Park** (city) Cuyahoga County
89	20.2	**Wooster** (city) Wayne County
91	20.3	**Blue Ash** (city) Hamilton County
91	20.3	**Eastlake** (city) Lake County
91	20.3	**Englewood** (city) Montgomery County
91	20.3	**Fort Shawnee** (CDP) Allen County
95	20.4	**Beachwood** (city) Cuyahoga County
95	20.4	**Beavercreek** (city) Greene County
95	20.4	**Bethel** (village) Clermont County
95	20.4	**Fairborn** (city) Greene County
95	20.4	**Parma Heights** (city) Cuyahoga County
95	20.4	**South Euclid** (city) Cuyahoga County
95	20.4	**Toronto** (city) Jefferson County
102	20.5	**Cadiz** (village) Harrison County
102	20.5	**Chillicothe** (city) Ross County
102	20.5	**Delhi Hills** (CDP) Hamilton County
102	20.5	**Girard** (city) Trumbull County
102	20.5	**Ravenna** (city) Portage County
107	20.6	**Martins Ferry** (city) Belmont County
107	20.6	**Millersburg** (village) Holmes County
107	20.6	**Tiffin** (city) Seneca County
110	20.7	**Cuyahoga Falls** (city) Summit County
110	20.7	**East Cleveland** (city) Cuyahoga County
110	20.7	**Northridge** (CDP) Clark County
113	20.8	**Canal Fulton** (city) Stark County
113	20.8	**Highland Heights** (city) Cuyahoga County
113	20.8	**Marion** (city) Marion County
113	20.8	**Rocky River** (city) Cuyahoga County
117	20.9	**Cheviot** (city) Hamilton County
117	20.9	**Fairfield** (city) Butler County
117	20.9	**Mansfield** (city) Richland County
117	20.9	**Salem Heights** (CDP) Hamilton County
117	20.9	**Streetsboro** (city) Portage County
122	21.0	**Centerville** (city) Montgomery County
122	21.0	**Circleville** (city) Pickaway County
122	21.0	**Findlay** (city) Hancock County
125	21.1	**Amherst** (city) Lorain County
125	21.1	**Brookville** (city) Montgomery County
125	21.1	**Howland Center** (CDP) Trumbull County
125	21.1	**Perry Heights** (CDP) Stark County
125	21.1	**Westlake** (city) Cuyahoga County
130	21.2	**Calcutta** (CDP) Columbiana County
130	21.2	**Green Meadows** (CDP) Clark County
130	21.2	**Kettering** (city) Montgomery County
130	21.2	**Mount Vernon** (city) Knox County
130	21.2	**Strongsville** (city) Cuyahoga County
135	21.3	**Apple Valley** (CDP) Knox County
135	21.3	**Champion Heights** (CDP) Trumbull County
135	21.3	**Edgewood** (CDP) Ashtabula County
135	21.3	**Greenville** (city) Darke County
139	21.4	**Trotwood** (city) Montgomery County
140	21.5	**Barnesville** (village) Belmont County
140	21.5	**Beckett Ridge** (CDP) Butler County
140	21.5	**Bellaire** (village) Belmont County
140	21.5	**Hicksville** (village) Defiance County
140	21.5	**Niles** (city) Trumbull County
140	21.5	**Saint Bernard** (city) Hamilton County
146	21.6	**Akron** (city) Summit County
146	21.6	**Bucyrus** (city) Crawford County
146	21.6	**Huron** (city) Erie County
146	21.6	**Lisbon** (village) Columbiana County
146	21.6	**Mount Gilead** (village) Morrow County

Note: *This section ranks incorporated places and CDPs (Census Designated Places) with populations of 2,500 or more. Unincorporated postal areas were not considered. Please refer to the User Guide for additional information.*

Population Age 65 and Over

Top 150 Places Ranked in *Descending* Order

State Rank	Percent	Place
1	33.0	**Mulberry** (CDP) Clermont County
2	30.9	**Columbiana** (city) Columbiana County
3	30.3	**Beachwood** (city) Cuyahoga County
4	29.9	**Walbridge** (village) Wood County
5	28.9	**Brookville** (city) Montgomery County
6	28.1	**Sebring** (village) Mahoning County
7	27.9	**Saint Clairsville** (city) Belmont County
8	27.1	**Centerville** (city) Montgomery County
9	27.0	**Mayfield** (village) Cuyahoga County
10	26.6	**Fairlawn** (city) Summit County
11	26.5	**Dry Ridge** (CDP) Hamilton County
12	26.2	**Waverly** (village) Pike County
13	26.0	**Carrollton** (village) Carroll County
14	25.9	**Ballville** (CDP) Sandusky County
15	25.8	**Burlington** (CDP) Lawrence County
16	25.5	**Calcutta** (CDP) Columbiana County
17	25.4	**Seven Hills** (city) Cuyahoga County
18	25.3	**Dover** (city) Tuscarawas County
18	25.3	**Enon** (village) Clark County
18	25.3	**Pepper Pike** (city) Cuyahoga County
21	25.2	**Strasburg** (village) Tuscarawas County
22	25.1	**Chagrin Falls** (village) Cuyahoga County
23	24.8	**Montrose-Ghent** (CDP) Summit County
24	24.7	**Apple Valley** (CDP) Knox County
25	24.3	**North Canton** (city) Stark County
26	24.2	**Devola** (CDP) Washington County
26	24.2	**Mayfield Heights** (city) Cuyahoga County
28	24.1	**Lyndhurst** (city) Cuyahoga County
28	24.1	**Mount Gilead** (village) Morrow County
30	23.9	**Lakemore** (village) Summit County
31	23.8	**Greenville** (city) Darke County
31	23.8	**Northridge** (CDP) Clark County
33	23.7	**Loudonville** (village) Ashland County
34	23.5	**Middleburg Heights** (city) Cuyahoga County
35	23.3	**North Zanesville** (CDP) Muskingum County
36	23.2	**Huron** (city) Erie County
36	23.2	**Vermilion** (city) Lorain County
36	23.2	**Versailles** (village) Darke County
39	23.1	**Belpre** (city) Washington County
39	23.1	**Kenwood** (CDP) Hamilton County
39	23.1	**Wintersville** (village) Jefferson County
42	23.0	**Rocky River** (city) Cuyahoga County
42	23.0	**Shadyside** (village) Belmont County
44	22.9	**Munroe Falls** (city) Summit County
45	22.8	**Champion Heights** (CDP) Trumbull County
45	22.8	**Howland Center** (CDP) Trumbull County
47	22.4	**Hubbard** (city) Trumbull County
48	22.2	**Cortland** (city) Trumbull County
48	22.2	**Westlake** (city) Cuyahoga County
50	22.1	**Richmond Heights** (city) Cuyahoga County
51	21.9	**Kirtland** (city) Lake County
51	21.9	**Lordstown** (village) Trumbull County
53	21.7	**Bucyrus** (city) Crawford County
54	21.6	**Hartville** (village) Stark County
55	21.5	**Montgomery** (city) Hamilton County
55	21.5	**West Union** (village) Adams County
55	21.5	**Yellow Springs** (village) Greene County
58	21.4	**Fort Shawnee** (CDP) Allen County
59	21.3	**Middlefield** (village) Geauga County
59	21.3	**Mingo Junction** (village) Jefferson County
61	21.2	**Day Heights** (CDP) Clermont County
61	21.2	**Moreland Hills** (village) Cuyahoga County
61	21.2	**Wickliffe** (city) Lake County
64	21.1	**Canal Fulton** (city) Stark County
64	21.1	**Newton Falls** (village) Trumbull County
66	21.0	**Aurora** (city) Portage County
66	21.0	**Canfield** (city) Mahoning County
66	21.0	**Englewood** (city) Montgomery County
69	20.9	**Evendale** (village) Hamilton County
69	20.9	**Steubenville** (city) Jefferson County
71	20.8	**Bridgetown** (CDP) Hamilton County
72	20.7	**Bluffton** (village) Allen County
72	20.7	**Milford** (city) Clermont County
74	20.6	**Bedford Heights** (city) Cuyahoga County
74	20.6	**Tallmadge** (city) Summit County
76	20.5	**Napoleon** (city) Henry County
76	20.5	**New Burlington** (CDP) Hamilton County
76	20.5	**Upper Sandusky** (city) Wyandot County
79	20.4	**Brooklyn** (city) Cuyahoga County
79	20.4	**Chillicothe** (city) Ross County
79	20.4	**Green Meadows** (CDP) Clark County
79	20.4	**Willoughby** (city) Lake County
83	20.3	**Coshocton** (city) Coshocton County
83	20.3	**The Village of Indian Hill** (city) Hamilton County
83	20.3	**Van Wert** (city) Van Wert County
86	20.2	**Austintown** (CDP) Mahoning County
86	20.2	**Heath** (city) Licking County
86	20.2	**New Franklin** (city) Summit County
86	20.2	**Ontario** (city) Richland County
90	20.1	**Barnesville** (village) Belmont County
91	20.0	**Brecksville** (city) Cuyahoga County
91	20.0	**Brook Park** (city) Cuyahoga County
91	20.0	**Cadiz** (village) Harrison County
91	20.0	**The Plains** (CDP) Athens County
91	20.0	**Worthington** (city) Franklin County
96	19.9	**Doylestown** (village) Wayne County
96	19.9	**North Olmsted** (city) Cuyahoga County
98	19.8	**Coldwater** (village) Mercer County
98	19.8	**Eaton** (city) Preble County
98	19.8	**Oakwood** (village) Cuyahoga County
98	19.8	**Springdale** (city) Hamilton County
102	19.7	**Highland Heights** (city) Cuyahoga County
102	19.7	**Hillsboro** (city) Highland County
102	19.7	**Orrville** (city) Wayne County
105	19.6	**Canal Winchester** (city) Franklin County
105	19.6	**Independence** (city) Cuyahoga County
105	19.6	**Sylvania** (city) Lucas County
108	19.5	**Boardman** (CDP) Mahoning County
108	19.5	**Circleville** (city) Pickaway County
108	19.5	**North Ridgeville** (city) Lorain County
108	19.5	**Richville** (CDP) Stark County
112	19.4	**Orange** (village) Cuyahoga County
112	19.4	**Trotwood** (city) Montgomery County
114	19.3	**Archbold** (village) Fulton County
114	19.3	**Galion** (city) Crawford County
116	19.2	**East Cleveland** (city) Cuyahoga County
116	19.2	**Minster** (village) Auglaize County
116	19.2	**Waynesville** (village) Warren County
119	19.1	**Martins Ferry** (city) Belmont County
119	19.1	**Mentor** (city) Lake County
119	19.1	**Mineral Ridge** (CDP) Trumbull County
119	19.1	**Salem Heights** (CDP) Hamilton County
119	19.1	**Shelby** (city) Richland County
119	19.1	**Strongsville** (city) Cuyahoga County
125	19.0	**Cambridge** (city) Guernsey County
125	19.0	**Minerva** (village) Stark County
125	19.0	**Toronto** (city) Jefferson County
125	19.0	**West Milton** (village) Miami County
129	18.9	**Amberley** (village) Hamilton County
129	18.9	**Ironton** (city) Lawrence County
131	18.8	**Forestville** (CDP) Hamilton County
131	18.8	**Parma Heights** (city) Cuyahoga County
131	18.8	**South Lebanon** (village) Warren County
131	18.8	**Willoughby Hills** (city) Lake County
135	18.7	**Geneva** (city) Ashtabula County
135	18.7	**Lodi** (village) Medina County
135	18.7	**Poland** (village) Mahoning County
138	18.6	**Four Bridges** (CDP) Butler County
138	18.6	**Marietta** (city) Washington County
138	18.6	**Warrensville Heights** (city) Cuyahoga County
138	18.6	**Wellington** (village) Lorain County
142	18.4	**Bryan** (city) Williams County
142	18.4	**Carlisle** (village) Warren County
142	18.4	**Mount Healthy** (city) Hamilton County
142	18.4	**Niles** (city) Trumbull County
142	18.4	**Swanton** (village) Fulton County
147	18.3	**Ashland** (city) Ashland County
147	18.3	**Conneaut** (city) Ashtabula County
147	18.3	**Dillonvale** (CDP) Hamilton County
147	18.3	**Norwalk** (city) Huron County

***Note:** This section ranks incorporated places and CDPs (Census Designated Places) with populations of 2,500 or more. Unincorporated postal areas were not considered. Please refer to the User Guide for additional information.*

Population Age 65 and Over

Top 150 Places Ranked in *Ascending* Order

State Rank	Percent	Place
1	3.9	**Wright-Patterson AFB** (CDP) Greene County
2	5.0	**Athens** (city) Athens County
3	5.9	**Lake Darby** (CDP) Franklin County
4	6.8	**Amelia** (village) Clermont County
5	6.9	**Oxford** (city) Butler County
6	7.6	**Sixteen Mile Stand** (CDP) Hamilton County
7	7.8	**Cedarville** (village) Greene County
8	8.1	**Cleves** (village) Hamilton County
8	8.1	**Kent** (city) Portage County
10	8.4	**Landen** (CDP) Warren County
11	8.5	**Ada** (village) Hardin County
11	8.5	**Nelsonville** (city) Athens County
13	8.6	**Grafton** (village) Lorain County
14	8.8	**Obetz** (village) Franklin County
15	9.0	**New Albany** (city) Franklin County
16	9.1	**Dry Run** (CDP) Hamilton County
17	9.2	**Ashville** (village) Pickaway County
18	9.3	**Pickerington** (city) Fairfield County
19	9.4	**Columbus** (city) Franklin County
19	9.4	**Dublin** (city) Franklin County
19	9.4	**Greentown** (CDP) Stark County
22	9.8	**Huber Ridge** (CDP) Franklin County
22	9.8	**Marysville** (city) Union County
24	10.0	**Bowling Green** (city) Wood County
24	10.0	**Grandview Heights** (city) Franklin County
24	10.0	**Trenton** (city) Butler County
27	10.2	**Hilliard** (city) Franklin County
28	10.3	**University Heights** (city) Cuyahoga County
29	10.4	**New London** (village) Huron County
29	10.4	**Painesville** (city) Lake County
29	10.4	**Powell** (city) Delaware County
32	10.6	**Blacklick Estates** (CDP) Franklin County
32	10.6	**Norwood** (city) Hamilton County
34	10.7	**Lebanon** (city) Warren County
35	10.8	**Park Layne** (CDP) Clark County
35	10.8	**Reminderville** (village) Summit County
37	10.9	**Lockland** (village) Hamilton County
38	11.0	**Bexley** (city) Franklin County
38	11.0	**Granville** (village) Licking County
38	11.0	**Whitehall** (city) Franklin County
41	11.1	**Saint Henry** (village) Mercer County
42	11.2	**Delaware** (city) Delaware County
42	11.2	**Delshire** (CDP) Hamilton County
42	11.2	**Lima** (city) Allen County
42	11.2	**Reynoldsburg** (city) Franklin County
46	11.3	**Lakewood** (city) Cuyahoga County
47	11.5	**Golf Manor** (village) Hamilton County
47	11.5	**Harrison** (city) Hamilton County
49	11.6	**Cincinnati** (city) Hamilton County
50	11.7	**Beckett Ridge** (CDP) Butler County
51	11.8	**Sunbury** (village) Delaware County
52	12.0	**Pleasant Run** (CDP) Hamilton County
52	12.0	**Williamsburg** (village) Clermont County
54	12.1	**Newtown** (village) Hamilton County
55	12.2	**Moraine** (city) Montgomery County
55	12.2	**Mount Healthy Heights** (CDP) Hamilton County
55	12.2	**New Concord** (village) Muskingum County
58	12.4	**Cherry Grove** (CDP) Hamilton County
58	12.4	**Saint Bernard** (city) Hamilton County
60	12.5	**Dayton** (city) Montgomery County
61	12.6	**Fruit Hill** (CDP) Hamilton County
61	12.6	**Gibsonburg** (village) Sandusky County
61	12.6	**Groesbeck** (CDP) Hamilton County
61	12.6	**Pataskala** (city) Licking County
65	12.7	**Springboro** (city) Warren County
65	12.7	**Union** (city) Montgomery County
67	12.8	**Delhi Hills** (CDP) Hamilton County
67	12.8	**Lincoln Village** (CDP) Franklin County
69	13.0	**Cleveland** (city) Cuyahoga County
69	13.0	**Forest Park** (city) Hamilton County
69	13.0	**Garrettsville** (village) Portage County
69	13.0	**North College Hill** (city) Hamilton County
69	13.0	**Ross** (CDP) Butler County
74	13.1	**Medina** (city) Medina County
74	13.1	**North Baltimore** (village) Wood County
74	13.1	**Rossford** (city) Wood County
77	13.2	**Mount Carmel** (CDP) Clermont County
77	13.2	**New Lexington** (village) Perry County
77	13.2	**Wellsville** (village) Columbiana County
80	13.3	**Cheviot** (city) Hamilton County
80	13.3	**Lincoln Heights** (village) Hamilton County
80	13.3	**Northbrook** (CDP) Hamilton County
83	13.4	**Bellefontaine** (city) Logan County
83	13.4	**Marion** (city) Marion County
83	13.4	**Northwood** (city) Wood County
83	13.4	**Toledo** (city) Lucas County
87	13.5	**Brimfield** (CDP) Portage County
87	13.5	**Gahanna** (city) Franklin County
87	13.5	**Loveland** (city) Hamilton County
87	13.5	**Maple Heights** (city) Cuyahoga County
91	13.6	**Akron** (city) Summit County
91	13.6	**Grove City** (city) Franklin County
91	13.6	**New Bremen** (village) Auglaize County
94	13.7	**Dennison** (village) Tuscarawas County
94	13.7	**Perrysburg** (city) Wood County
94	13.7	**Reading** (city) Hamilton County
97	13.8	**Crooksville** (village) Perry County
97	13.8	**Franklin** (city) Warren County
97	13.8	**Sheffield Lake** (city) Lorain County
100	13.9	**Pleasant Run Farm** (CDP) Hamilton County
101	14.0	**Lake Lakengren** (CDP) Preble County
101	14.0	**South Euclid** (city) Cuyahoga County
101	14.0	**Streetsboro** (city) Portage County
104	14.1	**Carey** (village) Wyandot County
104	14.1	**East Liverpool** (city) Columbiana County
104	14.1	**Summerside** (CDP) Clermont County
107	14.2	**Baltimore** (village) Fairfield County
107	14.2	**Montpelier** (village) Williams County
107	14.2	**Mount Orab** (village) Brown County
107	14.2	**Ottawa Hills** (village) Lucas County
107	14.2	**Turpin Hills** (CDP) Hamilton County
112	14.3	**Fairborn** (city) Greene County
112	14.3	**Riverside** (city) Montgomery County
114	14.4	**Canton** (city) Stark County
114	14.4	**Elyria** (city) Lorain County
114	14.4	**Madison** (village) Lake County
114	14.4	**Waterville** (city) Lucas County
114	14.4	**Woodlawn** (village) Hamilton County
119	14.5	**Fairfield** (city) Butler County
119	14.5	**Fairport Harbor** (village) Lake County
119	14.5	**Mack** (CDP) Hamilton County
119	14.5	**Mason** (city) Warren County
119	14.5	**Monroe** (city) Butler County
119	14.5	**Rittman** (city) Wayne County
119	14.5	**Sidney** (city) Shelby County
126	14.6	**Whitehouse** (village) Lucas County
127	14.7	**Bellevue** (city) Sandusky County
127	14.7	**Deer Park** (city) Hamilton County
127	14.7	**New Richmond** (village) Clermont County
127	14.7	**North Madison** (CDP) Lake County
127	14.7	**Sherwood** (CDP) Hamilton County
127	14.7	**South Russell** (village) Geauga County
133	14.8	**Broadview Heights** (city) Cuyahoga County
133	14.8	**Brunswick** (city) Medina County
133	14.8	**New Carlisle** (city) Clark County
136	14.9	**Fremont** (city) Sandusky County
136	14.9	**Hamilton** (city) Butler County
136	14.9	**Oakwood** (city) Montgomery County
139	15.0	**Avon** (city) Lorain County
139	15.0	**Cleveland Heights** (city) Cuyahoga County
139	15.0	**Middletown** (city) Butler County
139	15.0	**Mogadore** (village) Summit County
139	15.0	**North Kingsville** (village) Ashtabula County
139	15.0	**Willard** (city) Huron County
145	15.1	**Bainbridge** (CDP) Geauga County
145	15.1	**Johnstown** (village) Licking County
145	15.1	**Taylor Creek** (CDP) Hamilton County
148	15.2	**Bedford** (city) Cuyahoga County
148	15.2	**Euclid** (city) Cuyahoga County
148	15.2	**Georgetown** (village) Brown County

Note: *This section ranks incorporated places and CDPs (Census Designated Places) with populations of 2,500 or more. Unincorporated postal areas were not considered. Please refer to the User Guide for additional information.*

Males per 100 Females

Top 150 Places Ranked in *Descending* Order

State Rank	Ratio	Place
1	392.3	**Grafton** (village) Lorain County
2	128.2	**Wright-Patterson AFB** (CDP) Greene County
3	121.6	**Marion** (city) Marion County
4	121.2	**Nelsonville** (city) Athens County
5	119.5	**Conneaut** (city) Ashtabula County
6	112.6	**Mansfield** (city) Richland County
7	112.0	**Lima** (city) Allen County
8	105.5	**Lockland** (village) Hamilton County
9	103.4	**Ada** (village) Hardin County
10	102.3	**Day Heights** (CDP) Clermont County
10	102.3	**Sixteen Mile Stand** (CDP) Hamilton County
12	102.1	**Portage Lakes** (CDP) Summit County
13	101.5	**Richfield** (village) Summit County
14	101.4	**Apple Valley** (CDP) Knox County
15	101.2	**Cleves** (village) Hamilton County
15	101.2	**Painesville** (city) Lake County
17	100.8	**Lake Lakengren** (CDP) Preble County
17	100.8	**Richville** (CDP) Stark County
19	100.6	**Lake Darby** (CDP) Franklin County
20	100.5	**Fort Shawnee** (CDP) Allen County
20	100.5	**New Richmond** (village) Clermont County
22	100.1	**Mack** (CDP) Hamilton County
22	100.1	**Saint Henry** (village) Mercer County
24	100.0	**Athens** (city) Athens County
25	99.7	**Beavercreek** (city) Greene County
26	99.5	**Brecksville** (city) Cuyahoga County
26	99.5	**Dry Run** (CDP) Hamilton County
26	99.5	**Norwood** (city) Hamilton County
29	99.3	**New Bremen** (village) Auglaize County
30	99.1	**Ross** (CDP) Butler County
31	99.0	**South Russell** (village) Geauga County
32	98.7	**Greentown** (CDP) Stark County
32	98.7	**Minster** (village) Auglaize County
34	98.5	**Montrose-Ghent** (CDP) Summit County
35	98.4	**Taylor Creek** (CDP) Hamilton County
36	98.3	**Mayfield** (village) Cuyahoga County
36	98.3	**New Albany** (city) Franklin County
38	98.0	**New Franklin** (city) Summit County
39	97.9	**Sheffield Lake** (city) Lorain County
40	97.8	**Northfield** (village) Summit County
41	97.7	**Bellbrook** (city) Greene County
41	97.7	**Edgewood** (CDP) Ashtabula County
43	97.6	**Brimfield** (CDP) Portage County
43	97.6	**Delshire** (CDP) Hamilton County
43	97.6	**Dublin** (city) Franklin County
46	97.5	**Evendale** (village) Hamilton County
47	97.4	**Sheffield** (village) Lorain County
48	97.3	**Delhi Hills** (CDP) Hamilton County
49	97.2	**Eastlake** (city) Lake County
49	97.2	**Norton** (city) Summit County
49	97.2	**Rossford** (city) Wood County
52	97.1	**Carey** (village) Wyandot County
52	97.1	**Kirtland** (city) Lake County
52	97.1	**Moreland Hills** (village) Cuyahoga County
52	97.1	**North Madison** (CDP) Lake County
52	97.1	**Park Layne** (CDP) Clark County
57	97.0	**Highland Heights** (city) Cuyahoga County
57	97.0	**Powell** (city) Delaware County
59	96.9	**Saint Marys** (city) Auglaize County
59	96.9	**Youngstown** (city) Mahoning County
61	96.8	**Lincoln Village** (CDP) Franklin County
62	96.7	**Beckett Ridge** (CDP) Butler County
62	96.7	**Turpin Hills** (CDP) Hamilton County
64	96.6	**Brunswick** (city) Medina County
64	96.6	**Lakewood** (city) Cuyahoga County
66	96.5	**Pataskala** (city) Licking County
67	96.4	**Hudson** (city) Summit County
67	96.4	**Reading** (city) Hamilton County
67	96.4	**Sidney** (city) Shelby County
70	96.3	**North Ridgeville** (city) Lorain County
70	96.3	**Salem Heights** (CDP) Hamilton County
72	96.2	**East Palestine** (village) Columbiana County
72	96.2	**Green Meadows** (CDP) Clark County
72	96.2	**Lebanon** (city) Warren County
72	96.2	**Northwood** (city) Wood County
76	96.1	**Mount Repose** (CDP) Clermont County
77	96.0	**Blue Ash** (city) Hamilton County
77	96.0	**Groesbeck** (CDP) Hamilton County
77	96.0	**Mentor-on-the-Lake** (city) Lake County
77	96.0	**Obetz** (village) Franklin County
77	96.0	**Uniontown** (CDP) Stark County
82	95.9	**Clayton** (city) Montgomery County
82	95.9	**Maumee** (city) Lucas County
82	95.9	**Withamsville** (CDP) Clermont County
85	95.8	**Fairborn** (city) Greene County
85	95.8	**Tiffin** (city) Seneca County
87	95.7	**Moraine** (city) Montgomery County
87	95.7	**Rittman** (city) Wayne County
89	95.6	**Reminderville** (village) Summit County
89	95.6	**Springboro** (city) Warren County
89	95.6	**West Jefferson** (village) Madison County
92	95.5	**Ballville** (CDP) Sandusky County
92	95.5	**Geneva** (city) Ashtabula County
92	95.5	**Hilliard** (city) Franklin County
95	95.4	**Columbus** (city) Franklin County
95	95.4	**Hamilton** (city) Butler County
95	95.4	**Miami Heights** (CDP) Hamilton County
95	95.4	**Mineral Ridge** (CDP) Trumbull County
95	95.4	**Mount Carmel** (CDP) Clermont County
100	95.3	**North Kingsville** (village) Ashtabula County
100	95.3	**North Royalton** (city) Cuyahoga County
102	95.2	**Dennison** (village) Tuscarawas County
102	95.2	**North Baltimore** (village) Wood County
104	95.1	**Beechwood Trails** (CDP) Licking County
104	95.1	**Clyde** (city) Sandusky County
104	95.1	**Green** (city) Summit County
104	95.1	**Monroe** (city) Butler County
104	95.1	**Orrville** (city) Wayne County
104	95.1	**Solon** (city) Cuyahoga County
104	95.1	**Swanton** (village) Fulton County
104	95.1	**Waverly** (village) Pike County
112	95.0	**Blacklick Estates** (CDP) Franklin County
112	95.0	**Dayton** (city) Montgomery County
112	95.0	**Seven Hills** (city) Cuyahoga County
115	94.9	**Enon** (village) Clark County
115	94.9	**Fredericktown** (village) Knox County
115	94.9	**Harrison** (city) Hamilton County
115	94.9	**Munroe Falls** (city) Summit County
115	94.9	**Troy** (city) Miami County
120	94.8	**Strasburg** (village) Tuscarawas County
121	94.7	**Fairport Harbor** (village) Lake County
121	94.7	**Pickerington** (city) Fairfield County
121	94.7	**Strongsville** (city) Cuyahoga County
124	94.6	**Buckeye Lake** (village) Licking County
124	94.6	**Trenton** (city) Butler County
124	94.6	**Whitehall** (city) Franklin County
127	94.5	**Delphos** (city) Allen County
127	94.5	**Lordstown** (village) Trumbull County
127	94.5	**Vermilion** (city) Lorain County
127	94.5	**Whitehouse** (village) Lucas County
131	94.3	**Grandview Heights** (city) Franklin County
131	94.3	**Pleasant Run** (CDP) Hamilton County
133	94.2	**Carlisle** (village) Warren County
133	94.2	**Independence** (city) Cuyahoga County
133	94.2	**Mogadore** (village) Summit County
133	94.2	**Northgate** (CDP) Hamilton County
133	94.2	**Riverside** (city) Montgomery County
133	94.2	**Streetsboro** (city) Portage County
139	94.1	**Amelia** (village) Clermont County
139	94.1	**Ashville** (village) Pickaway County
139	94.1	**Macedonia** (city) Summit County
139	94.1	**Mason** (city) Warren County
139	94.1	**New Philadelphia** (city) Tuscarawas County
139	94.1	**Ottawa** (village) Putnam County
145	94.0	**Massillon** (city) Stark County
145	94.0	**Perrysburg** (city) Wood County
147	93.9	**Bellefontaine** (city) Logan County
147	93.9	**Delta** (village) Fulton County
147	93.9	**McDonald** (village) Trumbull County
147	93.9	**Sherwood** (CDP) Hamilton County

Note: *This section ranks incorporated places and CDPs (Census Designated Places) with populations of 2,500 or more. Unincorporated postal areas were not considered. Please refer to the User Guide for additional information.*

Males per 100 Females

Top 150 Places Ranked in *Ascending* Order

State Rank	Ratio	Place
1	74.4	**Warrensville Heights** (city) Cuyahoga County
2	74.9	**Marysville** (city) Union County
3	76.3	**Lincoln Heights** (village) Hamilton County
4	79.2	**Carrollton** (village) Carroll County
5	79.6	**Beachwood** (city) Cuyahoga County
6	79.9	**Trotwood** (city) Montgomery County
7	80.0	**The Plains** (CDP) Athens County
8	80.5	**Golf Manor** (village) Hamilton County
9	80.6	**Mulberry** (CDP) Clermont County
10	81.1	**Euclid** (city) Cuyahoga County
11	81.4	**Mount Healthy** (city) Hamilton County
12	81.5	**Richmond Heights** (city) Cuyahoga County
13	81.6	**Hillsboro** (city) Highland County
14	81.8	**Woodlawn** (village) Hamilton County
15	82.1	**East Cleveland** (city) Cuyahoga County
16	82.2	**Chardon** (city) Geauga County
17	82.4	**New Concord** (village) Muskingum County
18	82.5	**Mariemont** (village) Hamilton County
18	82.5	**Shaker Heights** (city) Cuyahoga County
20	82.6	**Milford** (city) Clermont County
21	82.7	**Mayfield Heights** (city) Cuyahoga County
22	82.9	**Middlefield** (village) Geauga County
23	83.2	**Mount Healthy Heights** (CDP) Hamilton County
24	83.4	**West Union** (village) Adams County
25	83.9	**Bluffton** (village) Allen County
25	83.9	**Jefferson** (village) Ashtabula County
25	83.9	**South Euclid** (city) Cuyahoga County
28	84.1	**Kenwood** (CDP) Hamilton County
29	84.2	**Sebring** (village) Mahoning County
30	84.4	**Bedford** (city) Cuyahoga County
31	84.7	**Shadyside** (village) Belmont County
32	84.9	**Bedford Heights** (city) Cuyahoga County
32	84.9	**Saint Clairsville** (city) Belmont County
34	85.1	**Oberlin** (city) Lorain County
34	85.1	**Yellow Springs** (village) Greene County
36	85.2	**Garfield Heights** (city) Cuyahoga County
37	85.3	**Lyndhurst** (city) Cuyahoga County
38	85.4	**Greenville** (city) Darke County
38	85.4	**Walbridge** (village) Wood County
40	85.5	**Rocky River** (city) Cuyahoga County
41	85.7	**Brookville** (city) Montgomery County
41	85.7	**Silverton** (village) Hamilton County
41	85.7	**Steubenville** (city) Jefferson County
44	85.8	**Burlington** (CDP) Lawrence County
45	85.9	**Barnesville** (village) Belmont County
45	85.9	**New Burlington** (CDP) Hamilton County
47	86.0	**Centerville** (city) Montgomery County
47	86.0	**Chagrin Falls** (village) Cuyahoga County
49	86.1	**Forestville** (CDP) Hamilton County
49	86.1	**Granville** (village) Licking County
49	86.1	**Maple Heights** (city) Cuyahoga County
49	86.1	**North Canton** (city) Stark County
53	86.2	**Doylestown** (village) Wayne County
53	86.2	**Kent** (city) Portage County
53	86.2	**Millersburg** (village) Holmes County
56	86.6	**Forest Park** (city) Hamilton County
56	86.6	**Portsmouth** (city) Scioto County
58	86.7	**Logan** (city) Hocking County
59	86.8	**Bethel** (village) Clermont County
59	86.8	**Louisville** (city) Stark County
59	86.8	**Oak Harbor** (village) Ottawa County
59	86.8	**Springdale** (city) Hamilton County
63	86.9	**Mount Vernon** (city) Knox County
64	87.0	**Cedarville** (village) Greene County
64	87.0	**Jackson** (city) Jackson County
64	87.0	**Parma Heights** (city) Cuyahoga County
64	87.0	**Pepper Pike** (city) Cuyahoga County
68	87.1	**Finneytown** (CDP) Hamilton County
69	87.2	**Cleveland Heights** (city) Cuyahoga County
69	87.2	**Englewood** (city) Montgomery County
69	87.2	**Paulding** (village) Paulding County
72	87.3	**Zanesville** (city) Muskingum County
73	87.4	**Cambridge** (city) Guernsey County
73	87.4	**Columbiana** (city) Columbiana County
73	87.4	**Summerside** (CDP) Clermont County

State Rank	Ratio	Place
76	87.5	**Belpre** (city) Washington County
77	87.6	**Loudonville** (village) Ashland County
77	87.6	**Olmsted Falls** (city) Cuyahoga County
79	87.7	**Girard** (city) Trumbull County
79	87.7	**Wilmington** (city) Clinton County
81	87.9	**Wintersville** (village) Jefferson County
82	88.0	**Coshocton** (city) Coshocton County
82	88.0	**Twinsburg** (city) Summit County
82	88.0	**Van Wert** (city) Van Wert County
82	88.0	**Wellston** (city) Jackson County
86	88.1	**Ashland** (city) Ashland County
86	88.1	**Martins Ferry** (city) Belmont County
86	88.1	**South Point** (village) Lawrence County
86	88.1	**Willoughby** (city) Lake County
90	88.2	**Toronto** (city) Jefferson County
90	88.2	**Upper Sandusky** (city) Wyandot County
90	88.2	**Wellsville** (village) Columbiana County
93	88.3	**London** (city) Madison County
94	88.4	**Bexley** (city) Franklin County
94	88.4	**Marietta** (city) Washington County
94	88.4	**Northbrook** (CDP) Hamilton County
94	88.4	**Waynesville** (village) Warren County
98	88.5	**Archbold** (village) Fulton County
98	88.5	**Westerville** (city) Franklin County
100	88.6	**Shelby** (city) Richland County
101	88.8	**Cortland** (city) Trumbull County
102	88.9	**Fairlawn** (city) Summit County
102	88.9	**Galion** (city) Crawford County
102	88.9	**Kenton** (city) Hardin County
102	88.9	**Ontario** (city) Richland County
102	88.9	**Plain City** (village) Madison County
107	89.0	**Blanchester** (village) Clinton County
107	89.0	**Covedale** (CDP) Hamilton County
109	89.1	**Ironton** (city) Lawrence County
109	89.1	**Urbana** (city) Champaign County
111	89.3	**Cadiz** (village) Harrison County
111	89.3	**Canal Winchester** (city) Franklin County
111	89.3	**Lakemore** (village) Summit County
111	89.3	**Worthington** (city) Franklin County
111	89.3	**Xenia** (city) Greene County
116	89.4	**Canal Fulton** (city) Stark County
116	89.4	**Greenhills** (village) Hamilton County
116	89.4	**Northridge** (CDP) Clark County
116	89.4	**Saint Bernard** (city) Hamilton County
116	89.4	**Wheelersburg** (CDP) Scioto County
121	89.5	**Eaton** (city) Preble County
122	89.6	**Hartville** (village) Stark County
122	89.6	**Howland Center** (CDP) Trumbull County
122	89.6	**Middleburg Heights** (city) Cuyahoga County
122	89.6	**New Lexington** (village) Perry County
126	89.7	**Cuyahoga Falls** (city) Summit County
126	89.7	**Devola** (CDP) Washington County
126	89.7	**Fostoria** (city) Seneca County
126	89.7	**Lisbon** (village) Columbiana County
126	89.7	**Sylvania** (city) Lucas County
131	89.8	**North College Hill** (city) Hamilton County
131	89.8	**Ottawa Hills** (village) Lucas County
131	89.8	**Uhrichsville** (city) Tuscarawas County
134	89.9	**Mount Gilead** (village) Morrow County
134	89.9	**Napoleon** (city) Henry County
136	90.0	**Bridgetown** (CDP) Hamilton County
136	90.0	**Campbell** (city) Mahoning County
136	90.0	**Canton** (city) Stark County
136	90.0	**Dry Ridge** (CDP) Hamilton County
136	90.0	**Reynoldsburg** (city) Franklin County
141	90.1	**Baltimore** (village) Fairfield County
141	90.1	**Deer Park** (city) Hamilton County
141	90.1	**Minerva** (village) Stark County
141	90.1	**Newcomerstown** (village) Tuscarawas County
141	90.1	**Sunbury** (village) Delaware County
146	90.2	**Oakwood** (city) Montgomery County
146	90.2	**Westlake** (city) Cuyahoga County
148	90.3	**Dover** (city) Tuscarawas County
148	90.3	**Johnstown** (village) Licking County
148	90.3	**Madison** (village) Lake County

Note: *This section ranks incorporated places and CDPs (Census Designated Places) with populations of 2,500 or more. Unincorporated postal areas were not considered. Please refer to the User Guide for additional information.*

Marriage Status: Never Married

Top 150 Places Ranked in *Descending* Order

State Rank	Percent	Place
1	80.1	**Athens** (city) Athens County
2	78.9	**Oxford** (city) Butler County
3	77.5	**Cedarville** (village) Greene County
4	62.7	**New Concord** (village) Muskingum County
5	62.1	**Kent** (city) Portage County
6	61.7	**Bowling Green** (city) Wood County
7	57.7	**Ada** (village) Hardin County
8	55.0	**Granville** (village) Licking County
8	55.0	**Nelsonville** (city) Athens County
10	54.2	**Oberlin** (city) Lorain County
11	51.6	**Cincinnati** (city) Hamilton County
12	51.3	**Wright-Patterson AFB** (CDP) Greene County
13	50.3	**Cleveland** (city) Cuyahoga County
14	49.3	**East Cleveland** (city) Cuyahoga County
15	47.7	**Dayton** (city) Montgomery County
16	47.5	**Norwood** (city) Hamilton County
17	46.8	**Grafton** (village) Lorain County
18	45.9	**Lincoln Heights** (village) Hamilton County
19	45.8	**Warrensville Heights** (city) Cuyahoga County
20	45.0	**Lima** (city) Allen County
21	44.9	**Youngstown** (city) Mahoning County
22	44.5	**Maple Heights** (city) Cuyahoga County
23	44.3	**Columbus** (city) Franklin County
24	43.8	**Lakewood** (city) Cuyahoga County
25	43.7	**Golf Manor** (village) Hamilton County
26	43.3	**Cleveland Heights** (city) Cuyahoga County
27	43.2	**Euclid** (city) Cuyahoga County
27	43.2	**University Heights** (city) Cuyahoga County
29	42.8	**Akron** (city) Summit County
29	42.8	**Lockland** (village) Hamilton County
31	41.8	**Garfield Heights** (city) Cuyahoga County
32	41.5	**Woodlawn** (village) Hamilton County
33	41.3	**North College Hill** (city) Hamilton County
34	41.2	**Toledo** (city) Lucas County
35	41.0	**Silverton** (village) Hamilton County
35	41.0	**Warren** (city) Trumbull County
37	40.8	**South Euclid** (city) Cuyahoga County
38	40.7	**Canton** (city) Stark County
39	40.5	**Berea** (city) Cuyahoga County
39	40.5	**Whitehall** (city) Franklin County
41	40.3	**Painesville** (city) Lake County
42	40.2	**Trotwood** (city) Montgomery County
43	39.3	**Cheviot** (city) Hamilton County
44	38.3	**Steubenville** (city) Jefferson County
45	37.9	**Fremont** (city) Sandusky County
45	37.9	**Richmond Heights** (city) Cuyahoga County
45	37.9	**Tiffin** (city) Seneca County
48	37.8	**Brimfield** (CDP) Portage County
48	37.8	**Marietta** (city) Washington County
50	37.7	**Sandusky** (city) Erie County
51	37.3	**Campbell** (city) Mahoning County
51	37.3	**Mount Carmel** (CDP) Clermont County
51	37.3	**Saint Bernard** (city) Hamilton County
54	37.2	**Bedford Heights** (city) Cuyahoga County
55	37.1	**Reading** (city) Hamilton County
56	36.9	**Mount Healthy** (city) Hamilton County
57	36.8	**Northfield** (village) Summit County
58	36.7	**Bexley** (city) Franklin County
58	36.7	**Lorain** (city) Lorain County
60	36.4	**Fairborn** (city) Greene County
60	36.4	**Springfield** (city) Clark County
62	36.3	**Alliance** (city) Stark County
62	36.3	**Elyria** (city) Lorain County
64	35.8	**Ashland** (city) Ashland County
64	35.8	**Mansfield** (city) Richland County
64	35.8	**Wellsville** (village) Columbiana County
67	35.7	**Brooklyn** (city) Cuyahoga County
68	35.5	**Portsmouth** (city) Scioto County
69	35.4	**Grandview Heights** (city) Franklin County
70	35.3	**Deer Park** (city) Hamilton County
71	35.1	**Blacklick Estates** (CDP) Franklin County
72	34.9	**Finneytown** (CDP) Hamilton County
72	34.9	**Forest Park** (city) Hamilton County
72	34.9	**London** (city) Madison County
72	34.9	**Wooster** (city) Wayne County
76	34.8	**Huber Ridge** (CDP) Franklin County
76	34.8	**Northbrook** (CDP) Hamilton County
78	34.7	**Barberton** (city) Summit County
78	34.7	**Oakwood** (village) Cuyahoga County
80	34.6	**Edgewood** (CDP) Ashtabula County
81	34.5	**Fairport Harbor** (village) Lake County
81	34.5	**Portage Lakes** (CDP) Summit County
81	34.5	**The Plains** (CDP) Athens County
84	34.4	**Marion** (city) Marion County
85	34.2	**Gibsonburg** (village) Sandusky County
86	34.1	**Bedford** (city) Cuyahoga County
87	34.0	**West Carrollton** (city) Montgomery County
88	33.8	**Ashtabula** (city) Ashtabula County
89	33.6	**Reynoldsburg** (city) Franklin County
90	33.4	**Hamilton** (city) Butler County
91	33.2	**Newton Falls** (village) Trumbull County
91	33.2	**Ravenna** (city) Portage County
93	33.0	**Mount Vernon** (city) Knox County
93	33.0	**Wilmington** (city) Clinton County
95	32.8	**Mayfield Heights** (city) Cuyahoga County
95	32.8	**Zanesville** (city) Muskingum County
97	32.7	**Mount Healthy Heights** (CDP) Hamilton County
97	32.7	**Parma Heights** (city) Cuyahoga County
99	32.6	**Lincoln Village** (CDP) Franklin County
99	32.6	**Niles** (city) Trumbull County
101	32.5	**Gallipolis** (village) Gallia County
102	32.4	**North Baltimore** (village) Wood County
103	32.3	**Bellaire** (village) Belmont County
103	32.3	**Mineral Ridge** (CDP) Trumbull County
103	32.3	**Pleasant Run** (CDP) Hamilton County
106	32.1	**New Lebanon** (village) Montgomery County
106	32.1	**Newark** (city) Licking County
106	32.1	**Struthers** (city) Mahoning County
106	32.1	**Willoughby Hills** (city) Lake County
110	31.9	**Findlay** (city) Hancock County
110	31.9	**Sheffield Lake** (city) Lorain County
112	31.8	**Bethel** (village) Clermont County
112	31.8	**Johnstown** (village) Licking County
112	31.8	**Shaker Heights** (city) Cuyahoga County
112	31.8	**Sharonville** (city) Hamilton County
116	31.6	**Circleville** (city) Pickaway County
116	31.6	**Lisbon** (village) Columbiana County
116	31.6	**Parma** (city) Cuyahoga County
119	31.5	**Defiance** (city) Defiance County
119	31.5	**Marysville** (city) Union County
119	31.5	**Massillon** (city) Stark County
119	31.5	**Williamsburg** (village) Clermont County
119	31.5	**Willowick** (city) Lake County
124	31.4	**Fairview Park** (city) Cuyahoga County
124	31.4	**Piqua** (city) Miami County
126	31.3	**Fostoria** (city) Seneca County
126	31.3	**Middletown** (city) Butler County
126	31.3	**New Lexington** (village) Perry County
129	31.2	**Mogadore** (village) Summit County
130	31.1	**New London** (village) Huron County
130	31.1	**Norwalk** (city) Huron County
132	31.0	**Northgate** (CDP) Hamilton County
132	31.0	**Urbana** (city) Champaign County
134	30.9	**Delaware** (city) Delaware County
134	30.9	**Delshire** (CDP) Hamilton County
134	30.9	**Willard** (city) Huron County
134	30.9	**Xenia** (city) Greene County
134	30.9	**Yellow Springs** (village) Greene County
139	30.7	**Eastlake** (city) Lake County
139	30.7	**Groesbeck** (CDP) Hamilton County
139	30.7	**Toronto** (city) Jefferson County
139	30.7	**Willoughby** (city) Lake County
143	30.6	**Bellefontaine** (city) Logan County
143	30.6	**Loveland** (city) Hamilton County
143	30.6	**Riverside** (city) Montgomery County
143	30.6	**Springdale** (city) Hamilton County
143	30.6	**Streetsboro** (city) Portage County
148	30.5	**Austintown** (CDP) Mahoning County
149	30.4	**Chardon** (city) Geauga County
149	30.4	**Conneaut** (city) Ashtabula County

Note: *This section ranks incorporated places and CDPs (Census Designated Places) with populations of 2,500 or more. Unincorporated postal areas were not considered. Please refer to the User Guide for additional information.*

Marriage Status: Never Married

Top 150 Places Ranked in *Ascending* Order

State Rank	Percent	Place
1	12.7	**The Village of Indian Hill** (city) Hamilton County
2	15.0	**South Russell** (village) Geauga County
3	15.4	**Montrose-Ghent** (CDP) Summit County
4	15.5	**Apple Valley** (CDP) Knox County
5	15.9	**Beechwood Trails** (CDP) Licking County
6	16.2	**North Zanesville** (CDP) Muskingum County
7	16.8	**Montgomery** (city) Hamilton County
8	17.1	**Barnesville** (village) Belmont County
9	17.7	**Powell** (city) Delaware County
9	17.7	**Uniontown** (CDP) Stark County
11	17.8	**Northwood** (city) Wood County
12	17.9	**Ballville** (CDP) Sandusky County
13	18.1	**Columbiana** (city) Columbiana County
13	18.1	**Moreland Hills** (village) Cuyahoga County
15	18.3	**Champion Heights** (CDP) Trumbull County
16	18.5	**Four Bridges** (CDP) Butler County
16	18.5	**Lake Lakengren** (CDP) Preble County
18	18.7	**Fort Shawnee** (CDP) Allen County
18	18.7	**Hicksville** (village) Defiance County
20	18.9	**Miami Heights** (CDP) Hamilton County
21	19.2	**Amberley** (village) Hamilton County
22	19.3	**New Albany** (city) Franklin County
22	19.3	**Orange** (village) Cuyahoga County
24	19.4	**Doylestown** (village) Wayne County
25	19.5	**Bellbrook** (city) Greene County
26	19.6	**Chagrin Falls** (village) Cuyahoga County
27	19.7	**Mulberry** (CDP) Clermont County
28	19.8	**Brookville** (city) Montgomery County
28	19.8	**Lake Darby** (CDP) Franklin County
28	19.8	**Ottawa Hills** (village) Lucas County
31	19.9	**Poland** (village) Mahoning County
32	20.0	**Sherwood** (CDP) Hamilton County
33	20.1	**West Portsmouth** (CDP) Scioto County
33	20.1	**Worthington** (city) Franklin County
35	20.2	**Beachwood** (city) Cuyahoga County
35	20.2	**Macedonia** (city) Summit County
37	20.3	**Hudson** (city) Summit County
38	20.5	**Newcomerstown** (village) Tuscarawas County
39	20.6	**Minster** (village) Auglaize County
39	20.6	**Springboro** (city) Warren County
41	20.7	**Enon** (village) Clark County
41	20.7	**Landen** (CDP) Warren County
43	20.9	**Union** (city) Montgomery County
43	20.9	**Versailles** (village) Darke County
45	21.1	**Saint Clairsville** (city) Belmont County
45	21.1	**Sheffield** (village) Lorain County
47	21.2	**Canfield** (city) Mahoning County
47	21.2	**Strasburg** (village) Tuscarawas County
49	21.3	**Day Heights** (CDP) Clermont County
50	21.5	**Evendale** (village) Hamilton County
51	21.6	**Avon Lake** (city) Lorain County
51	21.6	**Dublin** (city) Franklin County
51	21.6	**Solon** (city) Cuyahoga County
54	21.7	**Calcutta** (CDP) Columbiana County
54	21.7	**Cortland** (city) Trumbull County
54	21.7	**Devola** (CDP) Washington County
54	21.7	**Lordstown** (village) Trumbull County
54	21.7	**North Ridgeville** (city) Lorain County
54	21.7	**Northridge** (CDP) Clark County
54	21.7	**Waterville** (city) Lucas County
61	21.8	**Clyde** (city) Sandusky County
61	21.8	**Loudonville** (village) Ashland County
63	21.9	**Dry Ridge** (CDP) Hamilton County
63	21.9	**Harrison** (city) Hamilton County
65	22.0	**Aurora** (city) Portage County
65	22.0	**Bay Village** (city) Cuyahoga County
67	22.1	**Bainbridge** (CDP) Geauga County
67	22.1	**Greentown** (CDP) Stark County
67	22.1	**Wheelersburg** (CDP) Scioto County
70	22.3	**Dry Run** (CDP) Hamilton County
70	22.3	**Monroe** (city) Butler County
72	22.4	**Dover** (city) Tuscarawas County
72	22.4	**Pepper Pike** (city) Cuyahoga County
72	22.4	**Sunbury** (village) Delaware County
75	22.5	**Hubbard** (city) Trumbull County
75	22.5	**Oakwood** (city) Montgomery County
75	22.5	**Taylor Creek** (CDP) Hamilton County
78	22.6	**Ashville** (village) Pickaway County
78	22.6	**Fruit Hill** (CDP) Hamilton County
78	22.6	**Strongsville** (city) Cuyahoga County
81	22.8	**Van Wert** (city) Van Wert County
81	22.8	**Wellston** (city) Jackson County
83	22.9	**Burlington** (CDP) Lawrence County
83	22.9	**North Kingsville** (village) Ashtabula County
85	23.0	**Lyndhurst** (city) Cuyahoga County
85	23.0	**Miamisburg** (city) Montgomery County
85	23.0	**Vermilion** (city) Lorain County
88	23.1	**Salem Heights** (CDP) Hamilton County
88	23.1	**Upper Arlington** (city) Franklin County
90	23.2	**Lexington** (village) Richland County
90	23.2	**Trenton** (city) Butler County
92	23.3	**Carlisle** (village) Warren County
92	23.3	**Moraine** (city) Montgomery County
94	23.4	**Kirtland** (city) Lake County
94	23.4	**Ontario** (city) Richland County
96	23.5	**Minerva** (village) Stark County
96	23.5	**Norton** (city) Summit County
96	23.5	**Ross** (CDP) Butler County
96	23.5	**Turpin Hills** (CDP) Hamilton County
100	23.7	**Madeira** (city) Hamilton County
101	23.8	**Archbold** (village) Fulton County
101	23.8	**Kenton** (city) Hardin County
101	23.8	**Mount Gilead** (village) Morrow County
104	23.9	**Canal Winchester** (city) Franklin County
104	23.9	**Covedale** (CDP) Hamilton County
104	23.9	**New Franklin** (city) Summit County
107	24.0	**Forestville** (CDP) Hamilton County
107	24.0	**Mack** (CDP) Hamilton County
107	24.0	**Richville** (CDP) Stark County
107	24.0	**Wyoming** (city) Hamilton County
111	24.1	**Amherst** (city) Lorain County
111	24.1	**New Bremen** (village) Auglaize County
111	24.1	**Orrville** (city) Wayne County
111	24.1	**Plain City** (village) Madison County
115	24.2	**Richfield** (village) Summit County
115	24.2	**Shelby** (city) Richland County
117	24.3	**Blue Ash** (city) Hamilton County
117	24.3	**Centerville** (city) Montgomery County
117	24.3	**Georgetown** (village) Brown County
120	24.4	**Englewood** (city) Montgomery County
120	24.4	**Mason** (city) Warren County
122	24.5	**Franklin** (city) Warren County
122	24.5	**Mentor** (city) Lake County
124	24.6	**Coldwater** (village) Mercer County
124	24.6	**Dent** (CDP) Hamilton County
124	24.6	**Tipp City** (city) Miami County
127	24.7	**Belpre** (city) Washington County
127	24.7	**Olmsted Falls** (city) Cuyahoga County
129	24.8	**Swanton** (village) Fulton County
129	24.8	**Westlake** (city) Cuyahoga County
131	24.9	**Germantown** (city) Montgomery County
131	24.9	**Oak Harbor** (village) Ottawa County
133	25.0	**South Lebanon** (village) Warren County
133	25.0	**Walbridge** (village) Wood County
135	25.1	**Geneva** (city) Ashtabula County
135	25.1	**Upper Sandusky** (city) Wyandot County
137	25.2	**Coshocton** (city) Coshocton County
137	25.2	**Wadsworth** (city) Medina County
139	25.3	**South Point** (village) Lawrence County
140	25.5	**Cadiz** (village) Harrison County
140	25.5	**Carey** (village) Wyandot County
140	25.5	**Fredericktown** (village) Knox County
140	25.5	**Galion** (city) Crawford County
140	25.5	**Jackson** (city) Jackson County
140	25.5	**Washington Court House** (city) Fayette County
146	25.6	**Beckett Ridge** (CDP) Butler County
146	25.6	**Brecksville** (city) Cuyahoga County
146	25.6	**Seven Hills** (city) Cuyahoga County
149	25.7	**Grove City** (city) Franklin County
149	25.7	**Lakemore** (village) Summit County

Note: *This section ranks incorporated places and CDPs (Census Designated Places) with populations of 2,500 or more. Unincorporated postal areas were not considered. Please refer to the User Guide for additional information.*

Marriage Status: Now Married

Top 150 Places Ranked in *Descending* Order

State Rank	Percent	Place
1	80.7	**The Village of Indian Hill** (city) Hamilton County
2	73.5	**South Russell** (village) Geauga County
3	73.1	**Powell** (city) Delaware County
4	73.0	**Amberley** (village) Hamilton County
5	72.3	**Beechwood Trails** (CDP) Licking County
6	71.8	**Dry Run** (CDP) Hamilton County
7	70.6	**Montgomery** (city) Hamilton County
8	69.7	**Hudson** (city) Summit County
9	69.6	**New Albany** (city) Franklin County
10	69.5	**Greentown** (CDP) Stark County
11	69.1	**Moreland Hills** (village) Cuyahoga County
12	68.8	**Pepper Pike** (city) Cuyahoga County
13	68.5	**Day Heights** (CDP) Clermont County
13	68.5	**Evendale** (village) Hamilton County
15	68.2	**Apple Valley** (CDP) Knox County
15	68.2	**Dublin** (city) Franklin County
17	67.7	**Springboro** (city) Warren County
18	67.3	**Lake Lakengren** (CDP) Preble County
18	67.3	**Ottawa Hills** (village) Lucas County
20	67.2	**Ashville** (village) Pickaway County
20	67.2	**Lake Darby** (CDP) Franklin County
22	66.2	**Canfield** (city) Mahoning County
22	66.2	**Miami Heights** (CDP) Hamilton County
22	66.2	**Montrose-Ghent** (CDP) Summit County
25	66.0	**Ballville** (CDP) Sandusky County
26	65.9	**Sherwood** (CDP) Hamilton County
27	65.6	**Minster** (village) Auglaize County
28	65.3	**Saint Henry** (village) Mercer County
29	65.2	**Northwood** (city) Wood County
30	64.9	**Mack** (CDP) Hamilton County
31	64.8	**Solon** (city) Cuyahoga County
32	64.6	**Four Bridges** (CDP) Butler County
32	64.6	**Wyoming** (city) Hamilton County
34	64.5	**Turpin Hills** (CDP) Hamilton County
35	64.4	**Macedonia** (city) Summit County
36	64.3	**Cherry Grove** (CDP) Hamilton County
37	64.2	**Harrison** (city) Hamilton County
38	64.0	**Poland** (village) Mahoning County
39	63.9	**Upper Arlington** (city) Franklin County
40	63.5	**Bellbrook** (city) Greene County
41	63.3	**Bay Village** (city) Cuyahoga County
42	63.2	**Dry Ridge** (CDP) Hamilton County
43	63.0	**Bainbridge** (CDP) Geauga County
44	62.7	**Madeira** (city) Hamilton County
44	62.7	**New Bremen** (village) Auglaize County
44	62.7	**Sheffield** (village) Lorain County
47	62.6	**Cortland** (city) Trumbull County
47	62.6	**Kirtland** (city) Lake County
47	62.6	**Union** (city) Montgomery County
50	62.1	**Waterville** (city) Lucas County
51	62.0	**Highland Heights** (city) Cuyahoga County
52	61.9	**North Ridgeville** (city) Lorain County
53	61.8	**Doylestown** (village) Wayne County
53	61.8	**Strasburg** (village) Tuscarawas County
55	61.5	**Ross** (CDP) Butler County
56	61.4	**North Zanesville** (CDP) Muskingum County
56	61.4	**Oakwood** (city) Montgomery County
56	61.4	**Sunbury** (village) Delaware County
59	61.3	**Aurora** (city) Portage County
59	61.3	**Taylor Creek** (CDP) Hamilton County
61	61.2	**Devola** (CDP) Washington County
61	61.2	**Mason** (city) Warren County
61	61.2	**Worthington** (city) Franklin County
64	61.1	**Avon Lake** (city) Lorain County
64	61.1	**Delhi Hills** (CDP) Hamilton County
66	61.0	**Lordstown** (village) Trumbull County
66	61.0	**Orange** (village) Cuyahoga County
68	60.8	**Clyde** (city) Sandusky County
69	60.7	**Archbold** (village) Fulton County
70	60.6	**Strongsville** (city) Cuyahoga County
70	60.6	**Uniontown** (CDP) Stark County
72	60.5	**Beavercreek** (city) Greene County
72	60.5	**Carlisle** (village) Warren County
72	60.5	**Norton** (city) Summit County
75	60.4	**Hilliard** (city) Franklin County
76	60.3	**Beckett Ridge** (CDP) Butler County
76	60.3	**Richville** (CDP) Stark County
78	60.1	**Brecksville** (city) Cuyahoga County
78	60.1	**Dent** (CDP) Hamilton County
78	60.1	**Monroe** (city) Butler County
81	60.0	**Clayton** (city) Montgomery County
81	60.0	**Independence** (city) Cuyahoga County
81	60.0	**New Franklin** (city) Summit County
81	60.0	**South Lebanon** (village) Warren County
85	59.8	**Canal Winchester** (city) Franklin County
85	59.8	**Fort Shawnee** (CDP) Allen County
85	59.8	**Pickerington** (city) Fairfield County
88	59.6	**Blue Ash** (city) Hamilton County
88	59.6	**Columbiana** (city) Columbiana County
88	59.6	**Salem Heights** (CDP) Hamilton County
91	59.4	**Lexington** (village) Richland County
91	59.4	**Mariemont** (village) Hamilton County
91	59.4	**Richfield** (village) Summit County
94	59.3	**Perrysburg** (city) Wood County
95	59.2	**Champion Heights** (CDP) Trumbull County
95	59.2	**Monfort Heights** (CDP) Hamilton County
97	59.0	**Avon** (city) Lorain County
97	59.0	**North Kingsville** (village) Ashtabula County
97	59.0	**Trenton** (city) Butler County
100	58.8	**Covedale** (CDP) Hamilton County
100	58.8	**Fruit Hill** (CDP) Hamilton County
102	58.6	**Green** (city) Summit County
103	58.4	**Ontario** (city) Richland County
103	58.4	**Seven Hills** (city) Cuyahoga County
105	58.3	**Carey** (village) Wyandot County
105	58.3	**Munroe Falls** (city) Summit County
105	58.3	**Sixteen Mile Stand** (CDP) Hamilton County
108	58.2	**Landen** (CDP) Warren County
109	58.0	**Forestville** (CDP) Hamilton County
110	57.9	**Twinsburg** (city) Summit County
111	57.8	**Enon** (village) Clark County
112	57.7	**Wheelersburg** (CDP) Scioto County
113	57.6	**Versailles** (village) Darke County
114	57.5	**Mentor** (city) Lake County
115	57.4	**Northridge** (CDP) Clark County
116	57.2	**Lyndhurst** (city) Cuyahoga County
117	57.0	**Beachwood** (city) Cuyahoga County
117	57.0	**Grove City** (city) Franklin County
117	57.0	**Olmsted Falls** (city) Cuyahoga County
120	56.6	**Seville** (village) Medina County
121	56.4	**Mayfield** (village) Cuyahoga County
121	56.4	**Westerville** (city) Franklin County
123	56.2	**Broadview Heights** (city) Cuyahoga County
123	56.2	**Garrettsville** (village) Portage County
123	56.2	**Park Layne** (CDP) Clark County
126	56.1	**Centerville** (city) Montgomery County
127	56.0	**Chagrin Falls** (village) Cuyahoga County
127	56.0	**Hubbard** (city) Trumbull County
127	56.0	**North Madison** (CDP) Lake County
127	56.0	**Stow** (city) Summit County
127	56.0	**Westlake** (city) Cuyahoga County
132	55.9	**Fredericktown** (village) Knox County
133	55.8	**Cleves** (village) Hamilton County
134	55.7	**Amelia** (village) Clermont County
134	55.7	**Swanton** (village) Fulton County
134	55.7	**Tallmadge** (city) Summit County
134	55.7	**Wadsworth** (city) Medina County
138	55.6	**Bluffton** (village) Allen County
138	55.6	**Gahanna** (city) Franklin County
138	55.6	**Saint Clairsville** (city) Belmont County
138	55.6	**Sylvania** (city) Lucas County
142	55.4	**Amherst** (city) Lorain County
142	55.4	**Coldwater** (village) Mercer County
142	55.4	**Madison** (village) Lake County
145	55.3	**Calcutta** (CDP) Columbiana County
145	55.3	**Obetz** (village) Franklin County
147	55.2	**West Portsmouth** (CDP) Scioto County
148	55.0	**Moraine** (city) Montgomery County
148	55.0	**Orrville** (city) Wayne County
150	54.9	**Maumee** (city) Lucas County

Note: *This section ranks incorporated places and CDPs (Census Designated Places) with populations of 2,500 or more. Unincorporated postal areas were not considered. Please refer to the User Guide for additional information.*

Marriage Status: Now Married

Top 150 Places Ranked in *Ascending* Order

State Rank	Percent	Place
1	14.7	**Athens** (city) Athens County
2	16.2	**Oxford** (city) Butler County
3	16.5	**Cedarville** (village) Greene County
4	23.1	**Lincoln Heights** (village) Hamilton County
5	24.7	**New Concord** (village) Muskingum County
6	25.0	**Ada** (village) Hardin County
7	25.5	**East Cleveland** (city) Cuyahoga County
8	26.6	**Kent** (city) Portage County
9	27.8	**Lockland** (village) Hamilton County
9	27.8	**Nelsonville** (city) Athens County
11	28.5	**Bowling Green** (city) Wood County
12	28.8	**Cleveland** (city) Cuyahoga County
13	30.2	**Warrensville Heights** (city) Cuyahoga County
14	30.5	**Cincinnati** (city) Hamilton County
15	30.8	**Youngstown** (city) Mahoning County
16	31.1	**Dayton** (city) Montgomery County
17	31.4	**Grafton** (village) Lorain County
18	31.6	**Oberlin** (city) Lorain County
19	32.1	**Lima** (city) Allen County
20	32.5	**Silverton** (village) Hamilton County
21	32.6	**Maple Heights** (city) Cuyahoga County
22	33.3	**Mount Healthy** (city) Hamilton County
23	33.4	**Norwood** (city) Hamilton County
24	33.7	**Gallipolis** (village) Gallia County
25	34.0	**North College Hill** (city) Hamilton County
26	34.5	**Warren** (city) Trumbull County
27	34.6	**Euclid** (city) Cuyahoga County
28	35.2	**Canton** (city) Stark County
29	36.0	**Trotwood** (city) Montgomery County
30	36.4	**Golf Manor** (village) Hamilton County
31	36.6	**Akron** (city) Summit County
31	36.6	**Bedford Heights** (city) Cuyahoga County
31	36.6	**Toledo** (city) Lucas County
34	37.0	**Garfield Heights** (city) Cuyahoga County
34	37.0	**Portsmouth** (city) Scioto County
36	37.2	**Woodlawn** (village) Hamilton County
37	38.0	**West Union** (village) Adams County
38	38.2	**Sandusky** (city) Erie County
39	38.5	**Alliance** (city) Stark County
40	38.6	**Lakewood** (city) Cuyahoga County
40	38.6	**Springfield** (city) Clark County
40	38.6	**Steubenville** (city) Jefferson County
43	38.8	**Columbus** (city) Franklin County
44	39.1	**Ashtabula** (city) Ashtabula County
45	39.3	**Zanesville** (city) Muskingum County
46	39.5	**Fremont** (city) Sandusky County
46	39.5	**Granville** (village) Licking County
46	39.5	**Wellsville** (village) Columbiana County
49	39.6	**West Carrollton** (city) Montgomery County
50	39.8	**Mansfield** (city) Richland County
51	40.0	**Marietta** (city) Washington County
51	40.0	**Whitehall** (city) Franklin County
53	40.2	**Berea** (city) Cuyahoga County
53	40.2	**Burlington** (CDP) Lawrence County
55	40.3	**Campbell** (city) Mahoning County
55	40.3	**Newton Falls** (village) Trumbull County
57	40.5	**Cleveland Heights** (city) Cuyahoga County
57	40.5	**The Plains** (CDP) Athens County
57	40.5	**Waverly** (village) Pike County
60	40.8	**Fostoria** (city) Seneca County
61	41.1	**Fairport Harbor** (village) Lake County
61	41.1	**Greenfield** (village) Highland County
61	41.1	**New Lebanon** (village) Montgomery County
64	41.2	**Ravenna** (city) Portage County
65	41.6	**Millersburg** (village) Holmes County
66	41.7	**Marion** (city) Marion County
67	41.8	**Cheviot** (city) Hamilton County
67	41.8	**Deer Park** (city) Hamilton County
69	41.9	**Northfield** (village) Summit County
70	42.3	**Lorain** (city) Lorain County
70	42.3	**Piqua** (city) Miami County
72	42.4	**Painesville** (city) Lake County
73	42.5	**Bellaire** (village) Belmont County
73	42.5	**Niles** (city) Trumbull County
73	42.5	**Tiffin** (city) Seneca County
76	42.6	**Blacklick Estates** (CDP) Franklin County
76	42.6	**Chillicothe** (city) Ross County
76	42.6	**Elyria** (city) Lorain County
76	42.6	**Wright-Patterson AFB** (CDP) Greene County
80	42.7	**Hamilton** (city) Butler County
81	42.8	**London** (city) Madison County
82	42.9	**Greenville** (city) Darke County
82	42.9	**Mayfield Heights** (city) Cuyahoga County
84	43.1	**Bedford** (city) Cuyahoga County
84	43.1	**Urbana** (city) Champaign County
86	43.2	**Mount Carmel** (CDP) Clermont County
86	43.2	**Portage Lakes** (CDP) Summit County
88	43.3	**Brooklyn** (city) Cuyahoga County
89	43.4	**Jefferson** (village) Ashtabula County
90	43.5	**Barberton** (city) Summit County
90	43.5	**Reading** (city) Hamilton County
92	43.6	**Oakwood** (village) Cuyahoga County
93	43.7	**Mount Vernon** (city) Knox County
93	43.7	**South Euclid** (city) Cuyahoga County
95	43.8	**Fairborn** (city) Greene County
95	43.8	**Richmond Heights** (city) Cuyahoga County
97	43.9	**Ashland** (city) Ashland County
97	43.9	**Yellow Springs** (village) Greene County
99	44.2	**Bethel** (village) Clermont County
99	44.2	**Ironton** (city) Lawrence County
99	44.2	**Milford** (city) Clermont County
99	44.2	**Sebring** (village) Mahoning County
103	44.3	**New Carlisle** (city) Clark County
104	44.4	**Mineral Ridge** (CDP) Trumbull County
104	44.4	**Mount Gilead** (village) Morrow County
106	44.5	**Circleville** (city) Pickaway County
106	44.5	**Newark** (city) Licking County
108	44.8	**Uhrichsville** (city) Tuscarawas County
109	44.9	**Struthers** (city) Mahoning County
110	45.1	**Middletown** (city) Butler County
110	45.1	**Saint Bernard** (city) Hamilton County
112	45.2	**Wilmington** (city) Clinton County
113	45.3	**Xenia** (city) Greene County
114	45.6	**Cambridge** (city) Guernsey County
115	45.7	**Edgewood** (CDP) Ashtabula County
115	45.7	**Massillon** (city) Stark County
115	45.7	**Northbrook** (CDP) Hamilton County
115	45.7	**Port Clinton** (city) Ottawa County
119	45.8	**Hillsboro** (city) Highland County
119	45.8	**Parma Heights** (city) Cuyahoga County
121	45.9	**North Baltimore** (village) Wood County
122	46.0	**Norwalk** (city) Huron County
123	46.1	**Covington** (village) Miami County
123	46.1	**Lincoln Village** (CDP) Franklin County
123	46.1	**Wooster** (city) Wayne County
126	46.2	**Bucyrus** (city) Crawford County
126	46.2	**Middlefield** (village) Geauga County
126	46.2	**Mount Healthy Heights** (CDP) Hamilton County
129	46.3	**Eaton** (city) Preble County
130	46.4	**Green Meadows** (CDP) Clark County
130	46.4	**Mingo Junction** (village) Jefferson County
130	46.4	**University Heights** (city) Cuyahoga County
133	46.5	**Bryan** (city) Williams County
134	46.6	**Lodi** (village) Medina County
135	46.7	**Lisbon** (village) Columbiana County
135	46.7	**Waynesville** (village) Warren County
137	46.8	**Perry Heights** (CDP) Stark County
137	46.8	**Walbridge** (village) Wood County
139	46.9	**Lancaster** (city) Fairfield County
139	46.9	**Napoleon** (city) Henry County
141	47.0	**Bellefontaine** (city) Logan County
141	47.0	**Willoughby** (city) Lake County
143	47.1	**Riverside** (city) Montgomery County
144	47.2	**Reynoldsburg** (city) Franklin County
145	47.4	**Conneaut** (city) Ashtabula County
145	47.4	**Findlay** (city) Hancock County
147	47.5	**Shadyside** (village) Belmont County
148	47.6	**Brook Park** (city) Cuyahoga County
148	47.6	**Forest Park** (city) Hamilton County
148	47.6	**Toronto** (city) Jefferson County

Note: *This section ranks incorporated places and CDPs (Census Designated Places) with populations of 2,500 or more. Unincorporated postal areas were not considered. Please refer to the User Guide for additional information.*

Marriage Status: Separated

Top 150 Places Ranked in *Descending* Order

State Rank	Percent	Place
1	6.2	**Georgetown** (village) Brown County
1	6.2	**Lincoln Heights** (village) Hamilton County
3	5.7	**Mount Healthy Heights** (CDP) Hamilton County
4	5.4	**Bellaire** (village) Belmont County
5	5.2	**North College Hill** (city) Hamilton County
6	5.0	**Bellefontaine** (city) Logan County
6	5.0	**Cheviot** (city) Hamilton County
8	4.7	**Dennison** (village) Tuscarawas County
8	4.7	**Fruit Hill** (CDP) Hamilton County
10	4.6	**Carrollton** (village) Carroll County
11	4.5	**Bedford Heights** (city) Cuyahoga County
11	4.5	**Lexington** (village) Richland County
11	4.5	**Shelby** (city) Richland County
14	4.4	**Cambridge** (city) Guernsey County
15	4.3	**Greenfield** (village) Highland County
15	4.3	**Nelsonville** (city) Athens County
17	4.1	**Milford** (city) Clermont County
18	4.0	**East Cleveland** (city) Cuyahoga County
18	4.0	**Grafton** (village) Lorain County
20	3.9	**Lincoln Village** (CDP) Franklin County
21	3.8	**Ironton** (city) Lawrence County
21	3.8	**London** (city) Madison County
23	3.7	**Mansfield** (city) Richland County
23	3.7	**Martins Ferry** (city) Belmont County
23	3.7	**Park Layne** (CDP) Clark County
23	3.7	**Wellsville** (village) Columbiana County
27	3.6	**Bellevue** (city) Sandusky County
27	3.6	**Galion** (city) Crawford County
27	3.6	**Mount Carmel** (CDP) Clermont County
30	3.5	**Cleveland** (city) Cuyahoga County
30	3.5	**Washington Court House** (city) Fayette County
32	3.4	**East Palestine** (village) Columbiana County
32	3.4	**Walbridge** (village) Wood County
34	3.3	**Middletown** (city) Butler County
34	3.3	**Ravenna** (city) Portage County
34	3.3	**Wellston** (city) Jackson County
34	3.3	**Whitehall** (city) Franklin County
34	3.3	**Zanesville** (city) Muskingum County
39	3.2	**Blacklick Estates** (CDP) Franklin County
39	3.2	**Crestline** (village) Crawford County
39	3.2	**Lorain** (city) Lorain County
42	3.1	**Blanchester** (village) Clinton County
42	3.1	**Fort Shawnee** (CDP) Allen County
42	3.1	**Hicksville** (village) Defiance County
42	3.1	**Jackson** (city) Jackson County
42	3.1	**Northwood** (city) Wood County
42	3.1	**Springfield** (city) Clark County
48	3.0	**Baltimore** (village) Fairfield County
48	3.0	**Dayton** (city) Montgomery County
48	3.0	**Hamilton** (city) Butler County
48	3.0	**Hillsboro** (city) Highland County
48	3.0	**Marion** (city) Marion County
48	3.0	**Moraine** (city) Montgomery County
48	3.0	**Mount Vernon** (city) Knox County
48	3.0	**New Burlington** (CDP) Hamilton County
48	3.0	**Willard** (city) Huron County
57	2.9	**East Liverpool** (city) Columbiana County
57	2.9	**Fairport Harbor** (village) Lake County
57	2.9	**Sandusky** (city) Erie County
57	2.9	**Trenton** (city) Butler County
57	2.9	**Youngstown** (city) Mahoning County
62	2.8	**Carey** (village) Wyandot County
62	2.8	**Crooksville** (village) Perry County
62	2.8	**Euclid** (city) Cuyahoga County
62	2.8	**Groveport** (city) Franklin County
62	2.8	**Lancaster** (city) Fairfield County
62	2.8	**Northbrook** (CDP) Hamilton County
62	2.8	**Salem Heights** (CDP) Hamilton County
62	2.8	**Trotwood** (city) Montgomery County
62	2.8	**Wauseon** (city) Fulton County
62	2.8	**West Portsmouth** (CDP) Scioto County
62	2.8	**Williamsburg** (village) Clermont County
73	2.7	**Chillicothe** (city) Ross County
73	2.7	**Cincinnati** (city) Hamilton County
73	2.7	**Finneytown** (CDP) Hamilton County
73	2.7	**Niles** (city) Trumbull County
73	2.7	**Urbana** (city) Champaign County
78	2.6	**Alliance** (city) Stark County
78	2.6	**Lockland** (village) Hamilton County
78	2.6	**Portsmouth** (city) Scioto County
81	2.5	**Campbell** (city) Mahoning County
81	2.5	**Celina** (city) Mercer County
81	2.5	**Englewood** (city) Montgomery County
81	2.5	**Fremont** (city) Sandusky County
81	2.5	**Heath** (city) Licking County
81	2.5	**Minerva** (village) Stark County
81	2.5	**Obetz** (village) Franklin County
81	2.5	**Reading** (city) Hamilton County
81	2.5	**Shadyside** (village) Belmont County
81	2.5	**Upper Sandusky** (city) Wyandot County
81	2.5	**Wellington** (village) Lorain County
92	2.4	**Akron** (city) Summit County
92	2.4	**Circleville** (city) Pickaway County
92	2.4	**Franklin** (city) Warren County
92	2.4	**Groesbeck** (CDP) Hamilton County
92	2.4	**Newark** (city) Licking County
92	2.4	**Newcomerstown** (village) Tuscarawas County
92	2.4	**Painesville** (city) Lake County
92	2.4	**Struthers** (city) Mahoning County
92	2.4	**Willoughby Hills** (city) Lake County
92	2.4	**Withamsville** (CDP) Clermont County
92	2.4	**Woodlawn** (village) Hamilton County
103	2.3	**Bryan** (city) Williams County
103	2.3	**Canton** (city) Stark County
103	2.3	**Columbus** (city) Franklin County
103	2.3	**Kirtland** (city) Lake County
103	2.3	**Lisbon** (village) Columbiana County
103	2.3	**Loudonville** (village) Ashland County
103	2.3	**Maple Heights** (city) Cuyahoga County
103	2.3	**New Philadelphia** (city) Tuscarawas County
103	2.3	**Norwood** (city) Hamilton County
103	2.3	**Port Clinton** (city) Ottawa County
103	2.3	**Springdale** (city) Hamilton County
103	2.3	**Swanton** (village) Fulton County
103	2.3	**Toledo** (city) Lucas County
103	2.3	**Warren** (city) Trumbull County
103	2.3	**Warrensville Heights** (city) Cuyahoga County
103	2.3	**West Jefferson** (village) Madison County
103	2.3	**Wilmington** (city) Clinton County
120	2.2	**Barberton** (city) Summit County
120	2.2	**Germantown** (city) Montgomery County
120	2.2	**Girard** (city) Trumbull County
120	2.2	**Lima** (city) Allen County
120	2.2	**Mariemont** (village) Hamilton County
120	2.2	**Marietta** (city) Washington County
120	2.2	**New Lexington** (village) Perry County
120	2.2	**Northgate** (CDP) Hamilton County
120	2.2	**Ottawa** (village) Putnam County
120	2.2	**Pataskala** (city) Licking County
120	2.2	**Rittman** (city) Wayne County
120	2.2	**Streetsboro** (city) Portage County
120	2.2	**Van Wert** (city) Van Wert County
133	2.1	**Bedford** (city) Cuyahoga County
133	2.1	**Brookville** (city) Montgomery County
133	2.1	**Fairfield** (city) Butler County
133	2.1	**Forestville** (CDP) Hamilton County
133	2.1	**Fredericktown** (village) Knox County
133	2.1	**Huber Heights** (city) Montgomery County
133	2.1	**Logan** (city) Hocking County
133	2.1	**Marysville** (city) Union County
133	2.1	**Newton Falls** (village) Trumbull County
133	2.1	**Richmond Heights** (city) Cuyahoga County
133	2.1	**Silverton** (village) Hamilton County
144	2.0	**Cadiz** (village) Harrison County
144	2.0	**Conneaut** (city) Ashtabula County
144	2.0	**Eaton** (city) Preble County
144	2.0	**Findlay** (city) Hancock County
144	2.0	**Garfield Heights** (city) Cuyahoga County
144	2.0	**Geneva** (city) Ashtabula County
144	2.0	**Greenville** (city) Darke County

Note: *This section ranks incorporated places and CDPs (Census Designated Places) with populations of 2,500 or more. Unincorporated postal areas were not considered. Please refer to the User Guide for additional information.*

Marriage Status: Separated

Top 150 Places Ranked in *Ascending* Order

State Rank	Percent	Place
1	0.0	**Ada** (village) Hardin County
1	0.0	**Bainbridge** (CDP) Geauga County
1	0.0	**Ballville** (CDP) Sandusky County
1	0.0	**Cedarville** (village) Greene County
1	0.0	**Coldwater** (village) Mercer County
1	0.0	**Lakemore** (village) Summit County
1	0.0	**Madison** (village) Lake County
1	0.0	**Montrose-Ghent** (CDP) Summit County
1	0.0	**New Bremen** (village) Auglaize County
1	0.0	**Ontario** (city) Richland County
1	0.0	**Ross** (CDP) Butler County
1	0.0	**Saint Henry** (village) Mercer County
1	0.0	**Wright-Patterson AFB** (CDP) Greene County
14	0.1	**Apple Valley** (CDP) Knox County
15	0.2	**Granville** (village) Licking County
15	0.2	**Green Meadows** (CDP) Clark County
15	0.2	**Mack** (CDP) Hamilton County
15	0.2	**Ottawa Hills** (village) Lucas County
19	0.3	**Athens** (city) Athens County
19	0.3	**Edgewood** (CDP) Ashtabula County
19	0.3	**Greenhills** (village) Hamilton County
19	0.3	**Greentown** (CDP) Stark County
19	0.3	**Mineral Ridge** (CDP) Trumbull County
19	0.3	**Minster** (village) Auglaize County
19	0.3	**New Albany** (city) Franklin County
19	0.3	**Richville** (CDP) Stark County
19	0.3	**South Russell** (village) Geauga County
19	0.3	**Strasburg** (village) Tuscarawas County
19	0.3	**The Village of Indian Hill** (city) Hamilton County
19	0.3	**Turpin Hills** (CDP) Hamilton County
19	0.3	**Uniontown** (CDP) Stark County
32	0.4	**Amelia** (village) Clermont County
32	0.4	**Ashville** (village) Pickaway County
32	0.4	**Avon Lake** (city) Lorain County
32	0.4	**Barnesville** (village) Belmont County
32	0.4	**Canal Winchester** (city) Franklin County
32	0.4	**Dublin** (city) Franklin County
32	0.4	**Evendale** (village) Hamilton County
32	0.4	**Grandview Heights** (city) Franklin County
32	0.4	**Mogadore** (village) Summit County
32	0.4	**Montgomery** (city) Hamilton County
32	0.4	**Moreland Hills** (village) Cuyahoga County
32	0.4	**Rossford** (city) Wood County
32	0.4	**Seven Hills** (city) Cuyahoga County
32	0.4	**Springboro** (city) Warren County
32	0.4	**Twinsburg** (city) Summit County
32	0.4	**Wintersville** (village) Jefferson County
48	0.5	**Bay Village** (city) Cuyahoga County
48	0.5	**Blue Ash** (city) Hamilton County
48	0.5	**Broadview Heights** (city) Cuyahoga County
48	0.5	**Canfield** (city) Mahoning County
48	0.5	**Champion Heights** (CDP) Trumbull County
48	0.5	**Cortland** (city) Trumbull County
48	0.5	**Delta** (village) Fulton County
48	0.5	**Hudson** (city) Summit County
48	0.5	**Jefferson** (village) Ashtabula County
48	0.5	**Johnstown** (village) Licking County
48	0.5	**Kenwood** (CDP) Hamilton County
48	0.5	**New Concord** (village) Muskingum County
48	0.5	**Orrville** (city) Wayne County
48	0.5	**Parma Heights** (city) Cuyahoga County
48	0.5	**Plain City** (village) Madison County
48	0.5	**Richfield** (village) Summit County
48	0.5	**The Plains** (CDP) Athens County
48	0.5	**Waterville** (city) Lucas County
48	0.5	**West Milton** (village) Miami County
67	0.6	**Beachwood** (city) Cuyahoga County
67	0.6	**Beechwood Trails** (CDP) Licking County
67	0.6	**Bexley** (city) Franklin County
67	0.6	**Bluffton** (village) Allen County
67	0.6	**Brecksville** (city) Cuyahoga County
67	0.6	**Canal Fulton** (city) Stark County
67	0.6	**Covington** (village) Miami County
67	0.6	**Devola** (CDP) Washington County
67	0.6	**Dry Run** (CDP) Hamilton County
67	0.6	**Fairview Park** (city) Cuyahoga County
67	0.6	**Lake Darby** (CDP) Franklin County
67	0.6	**Mentor** (city) Lake County
67	0.6	**North Royalton** (city) Cuyahoga County
67	0.6	**South Point** (village) Lawrence County
67	0.6	**Strongsville** (city) Cuyahoga County
67	0.6	**University Heights** (city) Cuyahoga County
67	0.6	**Whitehouse** (village) Lucas County
84	0.7	**Columbiana** (city) Columbiana County
84	0.7	**Delhi Hills** (CDP) Hamilton County
84	0.7	**Dry Ridge** (CDP) Hamilton County
84	0.7	**Hartville** (village) Stark County
84	0.7	**Highland Heights** (city) Cuyahoga County
84	0.7	**Independence** (city) Cuyahoga County
84	0.7	**Lake Lakengren** (CDP) Preble County
84	0.7	**Lyndhurst** (city) Cuyahoga County
84	0.7	**Middlefield** (village) Geauga County
84	0.7	**Mount Healthy** (city) Hamilton County
84	0.7	**Mulberry** (CDP) Clermont County
84	0.7	**North Canton** (city) Stark County
84	0.7	**Oakwood** (city) Montgomery County
84	0.7	**Pleasant Run** (CDP) Hamilton County
84	0.7	**Poland** (village) Mahoning County
84	0.7	**Sharonville** (city) Hamilton County
84	0.7	**Vermilion** (city) Lorain County
84	0.7	**Wapakoneta** (city) Auglaize County
84	0.7	**Willowick** (city) Lake County
103	0.8	**Beavercreek** (city) Greene County
103	0.8	**Beckett Ridge** (CDP) Butler County
103	0.8	**Gibsonburg** (village) Sandusky County
103	0.8	**Madeira** (city) Hamilton County
103	0.8	**Munroe Falls** (city) Summit County
103	0.8	**Orange** (village) Cuyahoga County
103	0.8	**Oxford** (city) Butler County
103	0.8	**Solon** (city) Cuyahoga County
103	0.8	**Upper Arlington** (city) Franklin County
103	0.8	**Wheelersburg** (CDP) Scioto County
113	0.9	**Austintown** (CDP) Mahoning County
113	0.9	**Berea** (city) Cuyahoga County
113	0.9	**Brimfield** (CDP) Portage County
113	0.9	**Buckeye Lake** (village) Licking County
113	0.9	**Clayton** (city) Montgomery County
113	0.9	**Clyde** (city) Sandusky County
113	0.9	**Covedale** (CDP) Hamilton County
113	0.9	**Garrettsville** (village) Portage County
113	0.9	**Louisville** (city) Stark County
113	0.9	**Macedonia** (city) Summit County
113	0.9	**McDonald** (village) Trumbull County
113	0.9	**Monfort Heights** (CDP) Hamilton County
113	0.9	**Mount Orab** (village) Brown County
113	0.9	**Northfield** (village) Summit County
113	0.9	**Seville** (village) Medina County
113	0.9	**Stow** (city) Summit County
113	0.9	**Sylvania** (city) Lucas County
113	0.9	**Tallmadge** (city) Summit County
113	0.9	**Uhrichsville** (city) Tuscarawas County
113	0.9	**Worthington** (city) Franklin County
133	1.0	**Bridgetown** (CDP) Hamilton County
133	1.0	**Burlington** (CDP) Lawrence County
133	1.0	**Delshire** (CDP) Hamilton County
133	1.0	**Eastlake** (city) Lake County
133	1.0	**Green** (city) Summit County
133	1.0	**Hubbard** (city) Trumbull County
133	1.0	**Kent** (city) Portage County
133	1.0	**Landen** (CDP) Warren County
133	1.0	**Lebanon** (city) Warren County
133	1.0	**New Franklin** (city) Summit County
133	1.0	**North Kingsville** (village) Ashtabula County
133	1.0	**Perrysburg** (city) Wood County
133	1.0	**Powell** (city) Delaware County
133	1.0	**Summerside** (CDP) Clermont County
133	1.0	**Wickliffe** (city) Lake County
148	1.1	**Avon** (city) Lorain County
148	1.1	**Bellbrook** (city) Greene County
148	1.1	**Bowling Green** (city) Wood County

Note: *This section ranks incorporated places and CDPs (Census Designated Places) with populations of 2,500 or more. Unincorporated postal areas were not considered. Please refer to the User Guide for additional information.*

Marriage Status: Widowed

Top 150 Places Ranked in *Descending* Order

State Rank	Percent	Place
1	17.4	**Burlington** (CDP) Lawrence County
2	16.8	**Sebring** (village) Mahoning County
3	14.3	**Mount Gilead** (village) Morrow County
4	13.9	**Coldwater** (village) Mercer County
5	13.6	**Beachwood** (city) Cuyahoga County
6	13.4	**Greenville** (city) Darke County
7	13.2	**Brookville** (city) Montgomery County
8	13.1	**Calcutta** (CDP) Columbiana County
9	13.0	**West Union** (village) Adams County
10	12.7	**Waverly** (village) Pike County
11	12.6	**Mulberry** (CDP) Clermont County
12	12.4	**Mount Healthy** (city) Hamilton County
13	12.3	**Georgetown** (village) Brown County
14	12.0	**Walbridge** (village) Wood County
15	11.7	**Milford** (city) Clermont County
16	11.5	**Waynesville** (village) Warren County
17	11.4	**Barnesville** (village) Belmont County
17	11.4	**Greenfield** (village) Highland County
19	11.3	**Dover** (city) Tuscarawas County
19	11.3	**Ironton** (city) Lawrence County
19	11.3	**Middlefield** (village) Geauga County
22	11.2	**Jefferson** (village) Ashtabula County
22	11.2	**Shelby** (city) Richland County
24	11.1	**Bucyrus** (city) Crawford County
25	10.9	**Four Bridges** (CDP) Butler County
25	10.9	**Napoleon** (city) Henry County
25	10.9	**Upper Sandusky** (city) Wyandot County
28	10.8	**Mayfield Heights** (city) Cuyahoga County
29	10.7	**Bridgetown** (CDP) Hamilton County
29	10.7	**Columbiana** (city) Columbiana County
29	10.7	**Urbana** (city) Champaign County
32	10.5	**Kenwood** (CDP) Hamilton County
32	10.5	**Mayfield** (village) Cuyahoga County
32	10.5	**Uhrichsville** (city) Tuscarawas County
35	10.4	**Saint Clairsville** (city) Belmont County
36	10.3	**Eaton** (city) Preble County
36	10.3	**Loudonville** (village) Ashland County
36	10.3	**Springdale** (city) Hamilton County
39	10.2	**Minerva** (village) Stark County
39	10.2	**Rocky River** (city) Cuyahoga County
41	10.1	**Kenton** (city) Hardin County
41	10.1	**Wellston** (city) Jackson County
43	10.0	**Fostoria** (city) Seneca County
43	10.0	**Shadyside** (village) Belmont County
45	9.9	**Newton Falls** (village) Trumbull County
45	9.9	**Portsmouth** (city) Scioto County
45	9.9	**Saint Marys** (city) Auglaize County
48	9.8	**Coshocton** (city) Coshocton County
48	9.8	**Marietta** (city) Washington County
50	9.7	**Cambridge** (city) Guernsey County
50	9.7	**Chagrin Falls** (village) Cuyahoga County
50	9.7	**Hillsboro** (city) Highland County
50	9.7	**Paulding** (village) Paulding County
54	9.6	**Canal Fulton** (city) Stark County
54	9.6	**Crestline** (village) Crawford County
54	9.6	**North Canton** (city) Stark County
54	9.6	**Swanton** (village) Fulton County
54	9.6	**Versailles** (village) Darke County
59	9.4	**Fairlawn** (city) Summit County
59	9.4	**Struthers** (city) Mahoning County
61	9.3	**Bryan** (city) Williams County
61	9.3	**Piqua** (city) Miami County
63	9.2	**Chillicothe** (city) Ross County
63	9.2	**Devola** (CDP) Washington County
63	9.2	**Minster** (village) Auglaize County
63	9.2	**Oak Harbor** (village) Ottawa County
63	9.2	**Wapakoneta** (city) Auglaize County
63	9.2	**Wauseon** (city) Fulton County
69	9.1	**Apple Valley** (CDP) Knox County
69	9.1	**Bellaire** (village) Belmont County
69	9.1	**Deer Park** (city) Hamilton County
69	9.1	**Delphos** (city) Allen County
69	9.1	**Silverton** (village) Hamilton County
69	9.1	**Wickliffe** (city) Lake County
69	9.1	**Zanesville** (city) Muskingum County
76	9.0	**Geneva** (city) Ashtabula County
76	9.0	**Lisbon** (village) Columbiana County
76	9.0	**Miamisburg** (city) Montgomery County
76	9.0	**Ontario** (city) Richland County
76	9.0	**Vermilion** (city) Lorain County
81	8.9	**Alliance** (city) Stark County
81	8.9	**Barberton** (city) Summit County
81	8.9	**East Palestine** (village) Columbiana County
81	8.9	**Mingo Junction** (village) Jefferson County
81	8.9	**Perry Heights** (CDP) Stark County
81	8.9	**Ross** (CDP) Butler County
87	8.8	**Champion Heights** (CDP) Trumbull County
87	8.8	**Circleville** (city) Pickaway County
87	8.8	**Doylestown** (village) Wayne County
87	8.8	**Lincoln Heights** (village) Hamilton County
87	8.8	**Logan** (city) Hocking County
87	8.8	**Mount Vernon** (city) Knox County
87	8.8	**Springfield** (city) Clark County
87	8.8	**Willoughby** (city) Lake County
87	8.8	**Youngstown** (city) Mahoning County
96	8.7	**Brook Park** (city) Cuyahoga County
96	8.7	**Centerville** (city) Montgomery County
96	8.7	**Lyndhurst** (city) Cuyahoga County
96	8.7	**Mogadore** (village) Summit County
96	8.7	**Orrville** (city) Wayne County
96	8.7	**Steubenville** (city) Jefferson County
96	8.7	**Warren** (city) Trumbull County
103	8.6	**Englewood** (city) Montgomery County
103	8.6	**Franklin** (city) Warren County
103	8.6	**Galion** (city) Crawford County
103	8.6	**Martins Ferry** (city) Belmont County
103	8.6	**Monroe** (city) Butler County
103	8.6	**Salem** (city) Columbiana County
103	8.6	**Sandusky** (city) Erie County
103	8.6	**Seven Hills** (city) Cuyahoga County
103	8.6	**Xenia** (city) Greene County
112	8.5	**Bellevue** (city) Sandusky County
112	8.5	**Gallipolis** (village) Gallia County
112	8.5	**Hicksville** (village) Defiance County
112	8.5	**Middleburg Heights** (city) Cuyahoga County
112	8.5	**New Carlisle** (city) Clark County
117	8.4	**Hubbard** (city) Trumbull County
117	8.4	**Huron** (city) Erie County
117	8.4	**Mount Healthy Heights** (CDP) Hamilton County
117	8.4	**North College Hill** (city) Hamilton County
117	8.4	**Parma Heights** (city) Cuyahoga County
117	8.4	**Sidney** (city) Shelby County
117	8.4	**The Plains** (CDP) Athens County
117	8.4	**Trotwood** (city) Montgomery County
117	8.4	**West Milton** (village) Miami County
117	8.4	**Westlake** (city) Cuyahoga County
117	8.4	**Wilmington** (city) Clinton County
128	8.3	**Dennison** (village) Tuscarawas County
128	8.3	**Dry Ridge** (CDP) Hamilton County
128	8.3	**East Cleveland** (city) Cuyahoga County
128	8.3	**Enon** (village) Clark County
128	8.3	**Madison** (village) Lake County
128	8.3	**Mansfield** (city) Richland County
128	8.3	**Mineral Ridge** (CDP) Trumbull County
135	8.2	**Campbell** (city) Mahoning County
135	8.2	**Fort Shawnee** (CDP) Allen County
135	8.2	**Macedonia** (city) Summit County
135	8.2	**New Philadelphia** (city) Tuscarawas County
135	8.2	**Sheffield Lake** (city) Lorain County
135	8.2	**Willowick** (city) Lake County
141	8.1	**Ashtabula** (city) Ashtabula County
141	8.1	**Austintown** (CDP) Mahoning County
141	8.1	**Belpre** (city) Washington County
141	8.1	**Brooklyn** (city) Cuyahoga County
141	8.1	**Cortland** (city) Trumbull County
141	8.1	**Euclid** (city) Cuyahoga County
141	8.1	**Fairport Harbor** (village) Lake County
141	8.1	**Lakemore** (village) Summit County
141	8.1	**Louisville** (city) Stark County
150	8.0	**Defiance** (city) Defiance County

Note: *This section ranks incorporated places and CDPs (Census Designated Places) with populations of 2,500 or more. Unincorporated postal areas were not considered. Please refer to the User Guide for additional information.*

Marriage Status: Widowed

Top 150 Places Ranked in *Ascending* Order

State Rank	Percent	Place
1	1.2	**Granville** (village) Licking County
1	1.2	**Wright-Patterson AFB** (CDP) Greene County
3	1.6	**Athens** (city) Athens County
3	1.6	**Oxford** (city) Butler County
5	2.1	**Powell** (city) Delaware County
6	2.2	**Sherwood** (CDP) Hamilton County
6	2.2	**Sixteen Mile Stand** (CDP) Hamilton County
8	2.4	**Turpin Hills** (CDP) Hamilton County
9	2.5	**Lake Darby** (CDP) Franklin County
10	2.6	**The Village of Indian Hill** (city) Hamilton County
11	2.7	**Cedarville** (village) Greene County
12	2.8	**Grandview Heights** (city) Franklin County
13	2.9	**Ashville** (village) Pickaway County
14	3.0	**Bexley** (city) Franklin County
14	3.0	**Dry Run** (CDP) Hamilton County
14	3.0	**Dublin** (city) Franklin County
14	3.0	**Kent** (city) Portage County
18	3.1	**Greentown** (CDP) Stark County
19	3.2	**Springboro** (city) Warren County
20	3.3	**Cleves** (village) Hamilton County
20	3.3	**Reminderville** (village) Summit County
22	3.4	**Beechwood Trails** (CDP) Licking County
22	3.4	**New Albany** (city) Franklin County
24	3.5	**Obetz** (village) Franklin County
25	3.7	**Beckett Ridge** (CDP) Butler County
25	3.7	**Huber Ridge** (CDP) Franklin County
25	3.7	**Moreland Hills** (village) Cuyahoga County
25	3.7	**Taylor Creek** (CDP) Hamilton County
29	3.8	**Bowling Green** (city) Wood County
29	3.8	**Day Heights** (CDP) Clermont County
29	3.8	**New Bremen** (village) Auglaize County
32	3.9	**Evendale** (village) Hamilton County
32	3.9	**Garrettsville** (village) Portage County
32	3.9	**South Lebanon** (village) Warren County
32	3.9	**University Heights** (city) Cuyahoga County
36	4.0	**Fruit Hill** (CDP) Hamilton County
37	4.1	**Grafton** (village) Lorain County
37	4.1	**Wyoming** (city) Hamilton County
39	4.2	**Hudson** (city) Summit County
39	4.2	**Trenton** (city) Butler County
39	4.2	**Union** (city) Montgomery County
42	4.3	**Amberley** (village) Hamilton County
43	4.4	**Brimfield** (CDP) Portage County
43	4.4	**Columbus** (city) Franklin County
43	4.4	**New London** (village) Huron County
43	4.4	**Pickerington** (city) Fairfield County
47	4.5	**Mack** (CDP) Hamilton County
47	4.5	**North Madison** (CDP) Lake County
47	4.5	**Reynoldsburg** (city) Franklin County
50	4.6	**Brecksville** (city) Cuyahoga County
50	4.6	**Harrison** (city) Hamilton County
50	4.6	**Landen** (CDP) Warren County
50	4.6	**Saint Henry** (village) Mercer County
54	4.7	**Newtown** (village) Hamilton County
55	4.8	**Carey** (village) Wyandot County
55	4.8	**Chardon** (city) Geauga County
55	4.8	**Clyde** (city) Sandusky County
55	4.8	**Delhi Hills** (CDP) Hamilton County
55	4.8	**Painesville** (city) Lake County
55	4.8	**Rossford** (city) Wood County
55	4.8	**Upper Arlington** (city) Franklin County
55	4.8	**Whitehall** (city) Franklin County
63	4.9	**Beavercreek** (city) Greene County
63	4.9	**Cherry Grove** (CDP) Hamilton County
63	4.9	**Clayton** (city) Montgomery County
63	4.9	**Cleveland Heights** (city) Cuyahoga County
63	4.9	**Forest Park** (city) Hamilton County
63	4.9	**Lakewood** (city) Cuyahoga County
63	4.9	**Shaker Heights** (city) Cuyahoga County
63	4.9	**Willoughby Hills** (city) Lake County
71	5.0	**Amelia** (village) Clermont County
71	5.0	**Bay Village** (city) Cuyahoga County
71	5.0	**Gahanna** (city) Franklin County
71	5.0	**Hilliard** (city) Franklin County
71	5.0	**Ottawa Hills** (village) Lucas County
71	5.0	**Williamsburg** (village) Clermont County
77	5.1	**Ada** (village) Hardin County
77	5.1	**Delaware** (city) Delaware County
77	5.1	**Dent** (CDP) Hamilton County
77	5.1	**South Russell** (village) Geauga County
77	5.1	**Withamsville** (CDP) Clermont County
82	5.2	**Bainbridge** (CDP) Geauga County
82	5.2	**Delshire** (CDP) Hamilton County
82	5.2	**Highland Heights** (city) Cuyahoga County
82	5.2	**South Euclid** (city) Cuyahoga County
86	5.3	**Carrollton** (village) Carroll County
86	5.3	**Cheviot** (city) Hamilton County
86	5.3	**Grove City** (city) Franklin County
89	5.4	**Berea** (city) Cuyahoga County
89	5.4	**Lexington** (village) Richland County
89	5.4	**North Kingsville** (village) Ashtabula County
89	5.4	**Northbrook** (CDP) Hamilton County
89	5.4	**Pataskala** (city) Licking County
89	5.4	**Sunbury** (village) Delaware County
95	5.5	**Bellbrook** (city) Greene County
95	5.5	**Cincinnati** (city) Hamilton County
95	5.5	**Madeira** (city) Hamilton County
95	5.5	**Marysville** (city) Union County
95	5.5	**Mason** (city) Warren County
95	5.5	**Nelsonville** (city) Athens County
95	5.5	**Orange** (village) Cuyahoga County
95	5.5	**Pepper Pike** (city) Cuyahoga County
103	5.6	**Edgewood** (CDP) Ashtabula County
104	5.7	**Blue Ash** (city) Hamilton County
104	5.7	**Buckeye Lake** (village) Licking County
104	5.7	**Montpelier** (village) Williams County
104	5.7	**Oakwood** (city) Montgomery County
108	5.8	**Canfield** (city) Mahoning County
108	5.8	**Crooksville** (village) Perry County
108	5.8	**Golf Manor** (village) Hamilton County
108	5.8	**Maumee** (city) Lucas County
108	5.8	**Monfort Heights** (CDP) Hamilton County
108	5.8	**Northwood** (city) Wood County
108	5.8	**Solon** (city) Cuyahoga County
115	5.9	**Fairview Park** (city) Cuyahoga County
115	5.9	**Lebanon** (city) Warren County
115	5.9	**Portage Lakes** (CDP) Summit County
115	5.9	**Richville** (CDP) Stark County
115	5.9	**Stow** (city) Summit County
115	5.9	**Waterville** (city) Lucas County
121	6.0	**Fairfield** (city) Butler County
121	6.0	**Johnstown** (village) Licking County
121	6.0	**Newcomerstown** (village) Tuscarawas County
121	6.0	**Perrysburg** (city) Wood County
121	6.0	**Streetsboro** (city) Portage County
126	6.1	**Avon Lake** (city) Lorain County
126	6.1	**Fairborn** (city) Greene County
126	6.1	**Oberlin** (city) Lorain County
126	6.1	**Pleasant Run** (CDP) Hamilton County
126	6.1	**Strasburg** (village) Tuscarawas County
126	6.1	**Tiffin** (city) Seneca County
126	6.1	**West Portsmouth** (CDP) Scioto County
133	6.2	**Brunswick** (city) Medina County
133	6.2	**Hartville** (village) Stark County
133	6.2	**Lima** (city) Allen County
133	6.2	**Summerside** (CDP) Clermont County
133	6.2	**Troy** (city) Miami County
133	6.2	**Vandalia** (city) Montgomery County
139	6.3	**Akron** (city) Summit County
139	6.3	**Dayton** (city) Montgomery County
139	6.3	**Groesbeck** (CDP) Hamilton County
139	6.3	**Lake Lakengren** (CDP) Preble County
139	6.3	**Mentor-on-the-Lake** (city) Lake County
139	6.3	**Millersburg** (village) Holmes County
139	6.3	**New Burlington** (CDP) Hamilton County
139	6.3	**New Lexington** (village) Perry County
139	6.3	**Norton** (city) Summit County
139	6.3	**Wooster** (city) Wayne County
149	6.4	**Finneytown** (CDP) Hamilton County
149	6.4	**Gibsonburg** (village) Sandusky County

***Note:** This section ranks incorporated places and CDPs (Census Designated Places) with populations of 2,500 or more. Unincorporated postal areas were not considered. Please refer to the User Guide for additional information.*

Marriage Status: Divorced

Top 150 Places Ranked in *Descending* Order

State Rank	Percent	Place
1	25.3	**Gallipolis** (village) Gallia County
2	22.9	**Lockland** (village) Hamilton County
2	22.9	**Millersburg** (village) Holmes County
4	22.2	**Lincoln Heights** (village) Hamilton County
5	20.8	**New Carlisle** (city) Clark County
6	20.2	**Newcomerstown** (village) Tuscarawas County
7	20.1	**Barnesville** (village) Belmont County
8	19.6	**West Union** (village) Adams County
9	19.4	**Burlington** (CDP) Lawrence County
10	19.3	**Bedford Heights** (city) Cuyahoga County
11	19.2	**Chillicothe** (city) Ross County
12	19.0	**Ashtabula** (city) Ashtabula County
12	19.0	**Greenfield** (village) Highland County
14	18.9	**New Lebanon** (village) Montgomery County
14	18.9	**Washington Court House** (city) Fayette County
16	18.8	**Zanesville** (city) Muskingum County
17	18.6	**Cambridge** (city) Guernsey County
17	18.6	**West Portsmouth** (CDP) Scioto County
19	18.5	**West Carrollton** (city) Montgomery County
20	18.3	**Kenton** (city) Hardin County
20	18.3	**Yellow Springs** (village) Greene County
22	18.1	**Covington** (village) Miami County
22	18.1	**Van Wert** (city) Van Wert County
24	18.0	**Hicksville** (village) Defiance County
25	17.9	**Fostoria** (city) Seneca County
25	17.9	**Ravenna** (city) Portage County
27	17.8	**Grafton** (village) Lorain County
27	17.8	**Perry Heights** (CDP) Stark County
29	17.7	**Lodi** (village) Medina County
30	17.6	**Bryan** (city) Williams County
30	17.6	**Portsmouth** (city) Scioto County
32	17.5	**Mount Gilead** (village) Morrow County
33	17.4	**Port Clinton** (city) Ottawa County
33	17.4	**Silverton** (village) Hamilton County
35	17.3	**Green Meadows** (CDP) Clark County
35	17.3	**Mount Healthy** (city) Hamilton County
35	17.3	**Uhrichsville** (city) Tuscarawas County
38	17.2	**Wauseon** (city) Fulton County
38	17.2	**Waverly** (village) Pike County
40	17.0	**Hillsboro** (city) Highland County
40	17.0	**Niles** (city) Trumbull County
40	17.0	**Piqua** (city) Miami County
43	16.9	**East Cleveland** (city) Cuyahoga County
43	16.9	**Plain City** (village) Madison County
45	16.8	**Jackson** (city) Jackson County
45	16.8	**Wellsville** (village) Columbiana County
47	16.7	**Eaton** (city) Preble County
47	16.7	**Lima** (city) Allen County
47	16.7	**Marion** (city) Marion County
47	16.7	**Mingo Junction** (village) Jefferson County
51	16.6	**Bethel** (village) Clermont County
51	16.6	**Buckeye Lake** (village) Licking County
51	16.6	**Canton** (city) Stark County
51	16.6	**Hamilton** (city) Butler County
51	16.6	**Newton Falls** (village) Trumbull County
56	16.5	**Greenville** (city) Darke County
56	16.5	**Landen** (CDP) Warren County
56	16.5	**Logan** (city) Hocking County
56	16.5	**The Plains** (CDP) Athens County
56	16.5	**Warrensville Heights** (city) Cuyahoga County
61	16.4	**Fairport Harbor** (village) Lake County
61	16.4	**Franklin** (city) Warren County
61	16.4	**Middletown** (city) Butler County
64	16.3	**Massillon** (city) Stark County
64	16.3	**North College Hill** (city) Hamilton County
64	16.3	**Portage Lakes** (CDP) Summit County
64	16.3	**Walbridge** (village) Wood County
68	16.2	**Alliance** (city) Stark County
68	16.2	**Lancaster** (city) Fairfield County
70	16.1	**Baltimore** (village) Fairfield County
70	16.1	**Bellaire** (village) Belmont County
70	16.1	**Mansfield** (city) Richland County
70	16.1	**New Richmond** (village) Clermont County
70	16.1	**Norwalk** (city) Huron County
70	16.1	**Shelby** (city) Richland County
70	16.1	**Springfield** (city) Clark County
77	15.9	**Heath** (city) Licking County
78	15.8	**Blacklick Estates** (CDP) Franklin County
78	15.8	**London** (city) Madison County
78	15.8	**New London** (village) Huron County
78	15.8	**Warren** (city) Trumbull County
78	15.8	**Williamsburg** (village) Clermont County
83	15.7	**Newark** (city) Licking County
84	15.6	**Coshocton** (city) Coshocton County
84	15.6	**Toledo** (city) Lucas County
84	15.6	**Youngstown** (city) Mahoning County
87	15.5	**Hartville** (village) Stark County
87	15.5	**Jefferson** (village) Ashtabula County
87	15.5	**McDonald** (village) Trumbull County
87	15.5	**Sandusky** (city) Erie County
87	15.5	**Wellston** (city) Jackson County
92	15.4	**Bellefontaine** (city) Logan County
92	15.4	**Delta** (village) Fulton County
92	15.4	**Fremont** (city) Sandusky County
92	15.4	**Middlefield** (village) Geauga County
92	15.4	**Mulberry** (CDP) Clermont County
92	15.4	**North Zanesville** (CDP) Muskingum County
92	15.4	**Trotwood** (city) Montgomery County
99	15.3	**Bedford** (city) Cuyahoga County
99	15.3	**Maple Heights** (city) Cuyahoga County
99	15.3	**Urbana** (city) Champaign County
102	15.2	**Bucyrus** (city) Crawford County
102	15.2	**Crooksville** (village) Perry County
102	15.2	**Xenia** (city) Greene County
105	15.1	**Circleville** (city) Pickaway County
105	15.1	**Kettering** (city) Montgomery County
105	15.1	**Mentor-on-the-Lake** (city) Lake County
105	15.1	**Obetz** (village) Franklin County
105	15.1	**Reminderville** (village) Summit County
105	15.1	**West Jefferson** (village) Madison County
111	15.0	**Dayton** (city) Montgomery County
111	15.0	**Mineral Ridge** (CDP) Trumbull County
111	15.0	**Troy** (city) Miami County
114	14.9	**Georgetown** (village) Brown County
114	14.9	**Lincoln Village** (CDP) Franklin County
114	14.9	**Loudonville** (village) Ashland County
117	14.8	**Dover** (city) Tuscarawas County
117	14.8	**Wintersville** (village) Jefferson County
119	14.7	**Chagrin Falls** (village) Cuyahoga County
119	14.7	**Geneva** (city) Ashtabula County
119	14.7	**Germantown** (city) Montgomery County
119	14.7	**Minerva** (village) Stark County
119	14.7	**Summerside** (CDP) Clermont County
119	14.7	**Tipp City** (city) Miami County
119	14.7	**Whitehall** (city) Franklin County
126	14.6	**Fruit Hill** (CDP) Hamilton County
126	14.6	**North Baltimore** (village) Wood County
126	14.6	**Reynoldsburg** (city) Franklin County
126	14.6	**Riverside** (city) Montgomery County
126	14.6	**Uniontown** (CDP) Stark County
131	14.5	**Celina** (city) Mercer County
131	14.5	**Milford** (city) Clermont County
131	14.5	**Mount Vernon** (city) Knox County
131	14.5	**Oakwood** (village) Cuyahoga County
135	14.4	**Belpre** (city) Washington County
135	14.4	**Shadyside** (village) Belmont County
135	14.4	**Steubenville** (city) Jefferson County
138	14.3	**Akron** (city) Summit County
138	14.3	**Cleveland** (city) Cuyahoga County
138	14.3	**Conneaut** (city) Ashtabula County
138	14.3	**Englewood** (city) Montgomery County
138	14.3	**Ironton** (city) Lawrence County
143	14.2	**Campbell** (city) Mahoning County
143	14.2	**Edgewood** (CDP) Ashtabula County
143	14.2	**Marysville** (city) Union County
143	14.2	**Miamisburg** (city) Montgomery County
143	14.2	**Oak Harbor** (village) Ottawa County
143	14.2	**Orange** (village) Cuyahoga County
149	14.1	**Chardon** (city) Geauga County
149	14.1	**Euclid** (city) Cuyahoga County

Note: *This section ranks incorporated places and CDPs (Census Designated Places) with populations of 2,500 or more. Unincorporated postal areas were not considered. Please refer to the User Guide for additional information.*

Marriage Status: Divorced

Top 150 Places Ranked in *Ascending* Order

State Rank	Percent	Place
1	2.9	**Dry Run** (CDP) Hamilton County
2	3.2	**Pepper Pike** (city) Cuyahoga County
3	3.3	**Cedarville** (village) Greene County
4	3.4	**Oxford** (city) Butler County
4	3.4	**Saint Henry** (village) Mercer County
6	3.5	**Amberley** (village) Hamilton County
7	3.6	**Athens** (city) Athens County
8	3.8	**Cherry Grove** (CDP) Hamilton County
9	4.0	**The Village of Indian Hill** (city) Hamilton County
10	4.3	**Granville** (village) Licking County
11	4.6	**Minster** (village) Auglaize County
12	4.9	**Delhi Hills** (CDP) Hamilton County
12	4.9	**Wright-Patterson AFB** (CDP) Greene County
14	5.1	**New Concord** (village) Muskingum County
15	5.2	**Highland Heights** (city) Cuyahoga County
16	5.3	**Greentown** (CDP) Stark County
16	5.3	**Montgomery** (city) Hamilton County
18	5.7	**Mayfield** (village) Cuyahoga County
19	5.8	**Hudson** (city) Summit County
20	6.0	**Bowling Green** (city) Wood County
20	6.0	**Four Bridges** (CDP) Butler County
20	6.0	**Independence** (city) Cuyahoga County
23	6.1	**Coldwater** (village) Mercer County
23	6.1	**Evendale** (village) Hamilton County
23	6.1	**Ross** (CDP) Butler County
26	6.4	**Day Heights** (CDP) Clermont County
27	6.5	**South Russell** (village) Geauga County
27	6.5	**University Heights** (city) Cuyahoga County
29	6.6	**Dry Ridge** (CDP) Hamilton County
29	6.6	**Kirtland** (city) Lake County
31	6.7	**Mack** (CDP) Hamilton County
32	6.8	**Canfield** (city) Mahoning County
33	7.0	**Powell** (city) Delaware County
34	7.2	**Dublin** (city) Franklin County
34	7.2	**Macedonia** (city) Summit County
34	7.2	**Mariemont** (village) Hamilton County
37	7.3	**Apple Valley** (CDP) Knox County
38	7.4	**Ashville** (village) Pickaway County
38	7.4	**Seven Hills** (city) Cuyahoga County
38	7.4	**Wyoming** (city) Hamilton County
41	7.6	**Cortland** (city) Trumbull County
41	7.6	**Miami Heights** (CDP) Hamilton County
41	7.6	**Perrysburg** (city) Wood County
44	7.7	**New Albany** (city) Franklin County
45	7.8	**Ottawa Hills** (village) Lucas County
46	7.9	**Devola** (CDP) Washington County
46	7.9	**Lake Lakengren** (CDP) Preble County
46	7.9	**Madison** (village) Lake County
46	7.9	**Monfort Heights** (CDP) Hamilton County
46	7.9	**Solon** (city) Cuyahoga County
51	8.0	**Archbold** (village) Fulton County
51	8.0	**Hilliard** (city) Franklin County
51	8.0	**Oberlin** (city) Lorain County
54	8.1	**Madeira** (city) Hamilton County
54	8.1	**Upper Arlington** (city) Franklin County
56	8.2	**Avon** (city) Lorain County
56	8.2	**Beavercreek** (city) Greene County
56	8.2	**Bexley** (city) Franklin County
56	8.2	**Kent** (city) Portage County
60	8.4	**Beechwood Trails** (CDP) Licking County
61	8.5	**Springboro** (city) Warren County
62	8.6	**Carlisle** (village) Warren County
62	8.6	**Poland** (village) Mahoning County
62	8.6	**Twinsburg** (city) Summit County
65	8.7	**Munroe Falls** (city) Summit County
66	8.9	**Aurora** (city) Portage County
66	8.9	**Clayton** (city) Montgomery County
66	8.9	**Green** (city) Summit County
66	8.9	**Mason** (city) Warren County
66	8.9	**Monroe** (city) Butler County
71	9.0	**Moreland Hills** (village) Cuyahoga County
72	9.1	**Ontario** (city) Richland County
73	9.2	**Beachwood** (city) Cuyahoga County
73	9.2	**Harrison** (city) Hamilton County
73	9.2	**Mogadore** (village) Summit County
73	9.2	**Ottawa** (village) Putnam County
77	9.3	**Brimfield** (CDP) Portage County
77	9.3	**New Franklin** (city) Summit County
77	9.3	**Richfield** (village) Summit County
77	9.3	**Sheffield** (village) Lorain County
81	9.4	**Ballville** (CDP) Sandusky County
81	9.4	**Delshire** (CDP) Hamilton County
81	9.4	**Sixteen Mile Stand** (CDP) Hamilton County
81	9.4	**West Milton** (village) Miami County
85	9.5	**Grandview Heights** (city) Franklin County
85	9.5	**New Bremen** (village) Auglaize County
87	9.6	**Bay Village** (city) Cuyahoga County
87	9.6	**North Olmsted** (city) Cuyahoga County
87	9.6	**North Ridgeville** (city) Lorain County
87	9.6	**Tallmadge** (city) Summit County
87	9.6	**Turpin Hills** (CDP) Hamilton County
92	9.7	**Bainbridge** (CDP) Geauga County
92	9.7	**Bluffton** (village) Allen County
92	9.7	**Brecksville** (city) Cuyahoga County
92	9.7	**Norton** (city) Summit County
92	9.7	**Park Layne** (CDP) Clark County
92	9.7	**Pickerington** (city) Fairfield County
92	9.7	**Shaker Heights** (city) Cuyahoga County
99	9.8	**Canal Winchester** (city) Franklin County
99	9.8	**Strongsville** (city) Cuyahoga County
101	9.9	**Calcutta** (CDP) Columbiana County
101	9.9	**Richville** (CDP) Stark County
101	9.9	**Swanton** (village) Fulton County
104	10.0	**Doylestown** (village) Wayne County
104	10.0	**Finneytown** (CDP) Hamilton County
104	10.0	**Seville** (village) Medina County
104	10.0	**Springdale** (city) Hamilton County
104	10.0	**Westerville** (city) Franklin County
109	10.1	**Broadview Heights** (city) Cuyahoga County
109	10.1	**Rocky River** (city) Cuyahoga County
109	10.1	**Sylvania** (city) Lucas County
112	10.2	**Dent** (CDP) Hamilton County
112	10.2	**Waterville** (city) Lucas County
114	10.3	**Gibsonburg** (village) Sandusky County
114	10.3	**Greenhills** (village) Hamilton County
114	10.3	**Lordstown** (village) Trumbull County
114	10.3	**Loveland** (city) Hamilton County
114	10.3	**Mount Orab** (village) Brown County
114	10.3	**Saint Bernard** (city) Hamilton County
114	10.3	**Salem Heights** (CDP) Hamilton County
114	10.3	**South Euclid** (city) Cuyahoga County
122	10.4	**Beckett Ridge** (CDP) Butler County
122	10.4	**Blue Ash** (city) Hamilton County
122	10.4	**Covedale** (CDP) Hamilton County
122	10.4	**Fairlawn** (city) Summit County
122	10.4	**Oakwood** (city) Montgomery County
122	10.4	**Paulding** (village) Paulding County
128	10.5	**Lake Darby** (CDP) Franklin County
128	10.5	**Pleasant Run** (CDP) Hamilton County
128	10.5	**Richmond Heights** (city) Cuyahoga County
131	10.6	**Bridgetown** (CDP) Hamilton County
132	10.7	**Mentor** (city) Lake County
133	10.8	**Forestville** (CDP) Hamilton County
133	10.8	**Mount Repose** (CDP) Clermont County
133	10.8	**North Royalton** (city) Cuyahoga County
133	10.8	**Sunbury** (village) Delaware County
133	10.8	**Westlake** (city) Cuyahoga County
138	10.9	**Centerville** (city) Montgomery County
138	10.9	**Fredericktown** (village) Knox County
138	10.9	**Strasburg** (village) Tuscarawas County
141	11.0	**Dillonvale** (CDP) Hamilton County
141	11.0	**Johnstown** (village) Licking County
141	11.0	**South Lebanon** (village) Warren County
144	11.1	**Lyndhurst** (city) Cuyahoga County
145	11.2	**Defiance** (city) Defiance County
146	11.3	**Avon Lake** (city) Lorain County
146	11.3	**Carey** (village) Wyandot County
146	11.3	**Cleveland Heights** (city) Cuyahoga County
146	11.3	**Huber Ridge** (CDP) Franklin County
146	11.3	**Northwood** (city) Wood County

Note: *This section ranks incorporated places and CDPs (Census Designated Places) with populations of 2,500 or more. Unincorporated postal areas were not considered. Please refer to the User Guide for additional information.*

Foreign Born

Top 150 Places Ranked in *Descending* Order

State Rank	Percent	Place
1	18.2	**Mayfield** (village) Cuyahoga County
2	17.8	**Willoughby Hills** (city) Lake County
3	16.5	**Dublin** (city) Franklin County
3	16.5	**Sixteen Mile Stand** (CDP) Hamilton County
5	16.3	**Beachwood** (city) Cuyahoga County
6	15.8	**Mayfield Heights** (city) Cuyahoga County
7	15.7	**Springdale** (city) Hamilton County
8	14.9	**Solon** (city) Cuyahoga County
9	14.8	**Lockland** (village) Hamilton County
10	14.1	**Blue Ash** (city) Hamilton County
11	13.9	**Middleburg Heights** (city) Cuyahoga County
12	13.8	**Brooklyn** (city) Cuyahoga County
13	13.1	**Pepper Pike** (city) Cuyahoga County
14	12.9	**Orange** (village) Cuyahoga County
15	12.5	**Whitehall** (city) Franklin County
16	12.3	**Painesville** (city) Lake County
17	11.8	**Highland Heights** (city) Cuyahoga County
18	11.6	**Columbus** (city) Franklin County
19	11.3	**Mason** (city) Warren County
20	11.2	**Moreland Hills** (village) Cuyahoga County
21	11.0	**Sharonville** (city) Hamilton County
22	10.6	**Forest Park** (city) Hamilton County
23	10.4	**Parma Heights** (city) Cuyahoga County
23	10.4	**Richmond Heights** (city) Cuyahoga County
25	10.3	**North Royalton** (city) Cuyahoga County
26	10.2	**Athens** (city) Athens County
27	10.1	**Beckett Ridge** (CDP) Butler County
28	9.9	**Broadview Heights** (city) Cuyahoga County
28	9.9	**Parma** (city) Cuyahoga County
28	9.9	**The Village of Indian Hill** (city) Hamilton County
31	9.5	**Seven Hills** (city) Cuyahoga County
32	9.4	**Fairfield** (city) Butler County
32	9.4	**Montgomery** (city) Hamilton County
34	9.3	**New Carlisle** (city) Clark County
35	9.2	**Shaker Heights** (city) Cuyahoga County
36	9.1	**North Olmsted** (city) Cuyahoga County
36	9.1	**Rocky River** (city) Cuyahoga County
38	8.6	**Ottawa Hills** (village) Lucas County
38	8.6	**Powell** (city) Delaware County
38	8.6	**Strongsville** (city) Cuyahoga County
41	8.4	**Kent** (city) Portage County
41	8.4	**Wyoming** (city) Hamilton County
43	8.1	**Cleveland Heights** (city) Cuyahoga County
44	8.0	**University Heights** (city) Cuyahoga County
45	7.9	**Beavercreek** (city) Greene County
46	7.8	**Amberley** (village) Hamilton County
46	7.8	**Oberlin** (city) Lorain County
46	7.8	**Oxford** (city) Butler County
46	7.8	**Westlake** (city) Cuyahoga County
50	7.7	**Lyndhurst** (city) Cuyahoga County
50	7.7	**Montrose-Ghent** (CDP) Summit County
50	7.7	**Twinsburg** (city) Summit County
53	7.6	**Lincoln Village** (CDP) Franklin County
54	7.5	**Fairview Park** (city) Cuyahoga County
54	7.5	**Upper Arlington** (city) Franklin County
56	7.3	**Lakewood** (city) Cuyahoga County
57	7.1	**Four Bridges** (CDP) Butler County
58	6.9	**Northfield** (village) Summit County
58	6.9	**Ontario** (city) Richland County
58	6.9	**White Oak** (CDP) Hamilton County
61	6.8	**Brecksville** (city) Cuyahoga County
61	6.8	**New Albany** (city) Franklin County
63	6.7	**South Euclid** (city) Cuyahoga County
63	6.7	**Streetsboro** (city) Portage County
65	6.6	**Hudson** (city) Summit County
65	6.6	**Kenwood** (CDP) Hamilton County
67	6.5	**Woodlawn** (village) Hamilton County
68	6.3	**Aurora** (city) Portage County
68	6.3	**Reminderville** (village) Summit County
70	6.2	**Hilliard** (city) Franklin County
70	6.2	**West Carrollton** (city) Montgomery County
72	6.1	**Evendale** (village) Hamilton County
73	6.0	**Dry Run** (CDP) Hamilton County
73	6.0	**Fairborn** (city) Greene County
73	6.0	**Reynoldsburg** (city) Franklin County
76	5.9	**Bexley** (city) Franklin County
76	5.9	**Lake Darby** (CDP) Franklin County
78	5.8	**Centerville** (city) Montgomery County
78	5.8	**Munroe Falls** (city) Summit County
80	5.7	**Independence** (city) Cuyahoga County
80	5.7	**New Concord** (village) Muskingum County
82	5.6	**Cherry Grove** (CDP) Hamilton County
82	5.6	**Dry Ridge** (CDP) Hamilton County
82	5.6	**Gahanna** (city) Franklin County
85	5.5	**Akron** (city) Summit County
86	5.4	**Canfield** (city) Mahoning County
87	5.3	**Devola** (CDP) Washington County
87	5.3	**Forestville** (CDP) Hamilton County
87	5.3	**Huber Ridge** (CDP) Franklin County
87	5.3	**Willowick** (city) Lake County
91	5.2	**Clayton** (city) Montgomery County
91	5.2	**Madeira** (city) Hamilton County
91	5.2	**Pickerington** (city) Fairfield County
91	5.2	**Westerville** (city) Franklin County
95	5.1	**Cincinnati** (city) Hamilton County
95	5.1	**Sebring** (village) Mahoning County
97	5.0	**Bowling Green** (city) Wood County
97	5.0	**Willoughby** (city) Lake County
99	4.9	**Cleveland** (city) Cuyahoga County
99	4.9	**Findlay** (city) Hancock County
101	4.8	**Brook Park** (city) Cuyahoga County
101	4.8	**Finneytown** (CDP) Hamilton County
101	4.8	**Landen** (CDP) Warren County
101	4.8	**Sherwood** (CDP) Hamilton County
105	4.7	**Granville** (village) Licking County
105	4.7	**Kirtland** (city) Lake County
105	4.7	**North Ridgeville** (city) Lorain County
105	4.7	**Perrysburg** (city) Wood County
105	4.7	**Sheffield** (village) Lorain County
105	4.7	**South Lebanon** (village) Warren County
111	4.6	**Avon Lake** (city) Lorain County
111	4.6	**Bedford Heights** (city) Cuyahoga County
111	4.6	**Dover** (city) Tuscarawas County
111	4.6	**Northbrook** (CDP) Hamilton County
111	4.6	**Stow** (city) Summit County
111	4.6	**Wintersville** (village) Jefferson County
117	4.5	**Dayton** (city) Montgomery County
117	4.5	**Fairlawn** (city) Summit County
117	4.5	**Girard** (city) Trumbull County
117	4.5	**Oakwood** (village) Cuyahoga County
117	4.5	**Reading** (city) Hamilton County
117	4.5	**Riverside** (city) Montgomery County
117	4.5	**Springboro** (city) Warren County
117	4.5	**Wickliffe** (city) Lake County
125	4.4	**Campbell** (city) Mahoning County
125	4.4	**Wright-Patterson AFB** (CDP) Greene County
127	4.3	**Ada** (village) Hardin County
127	4.3	**Eastlake** (city) Lake County
127	4.3	**Hicksville** (village) Defiance County
127	4.3	**Kettering** (city) Montgomery County
127	4.3	**Lebanon** (city) Warren County
127	4.3	**Macedonia** (city) Summit County
127	4.3	**Norwalk** (city) Huron County
134	4.2	**Cuyahoga Falls** (city) Summit County
134	4.2	**Delshire** (CDP) Hamilton County
134	4.2	**Sylvania** (city) Lucas County
137	4.1	**Mentor** (city) Lake County
137	4.1	**Milford** (city) Clermont County
137	4.1	**Paulding** (village) Paulding County
137	4.1	**Wooster** (city) Wayne County
141	4.0	**Huber Heights** (city) Montgomery County
141	4.0	**Orrville** (city) Wayne County
141	4.0	**Warrensville Heights** (city) Cuyahoga County
144	3.9	**Mariemont** (village) Hamilton County
144	3.9	**Tallmadge** (city) Summit County
146	3.7	**Green** (city) Summit County
146	3.7	**Groveport** (city) Franklin County
148	3.6	**Apple Valley** (CDP) Knox County
148	3.6	**Deer Park** (city) Hamilton County
148	3.6	**Marysville** (city) Union County

Note: *This section ranks incorporated places and CDPs (Census Designated Places) with populations of 2,500 or more. Unincorporated postal areas were not considered. Please refer to the User Guide for additional information.*

Foreign Born

Top 150 Places Ranked in *Ascending* Order

State Rank	Percent	Place
1	0.0	**Barnesville** (village) Belmont County
1	0.0	**Fredericktown** (village) Knox County
1	0.0	**Mount Carmel** (CDP) Clermont County
1	0.0	**Mount Healthy Heights** (CDP) Hamilton County
1	0.0	**Ross** (CDP) Butler County
1	0.0	**Walbridge** (village) Wood County
1	0.0	**Wellsville** (village) Columbiana County
1	0.0	**West Portsmouth** (CDP) Scioto County
1	0.0	**Whitehouse** (village) Lucas County
10	0.1	**Greenfield** (village) Highland County
10	0.1	**New Richmond** (village) Clermont County
10	0.1	**Versailles** (village) Darke County
13	0.2	**Crooksville** (village) Perry County
13	0.2	**Gibsonburg** (village) Sandusky County
13	0.2	**Minerva** (village) Stark County
13	0.2	**Oak Harbor** (village) Ottawa County
13	0.2	**South Point** (village) Lawrence County
13	0.2	**Williamsburg** (village) Clermont County
19	0.3	**Baltimore** (village) Fairfield County
19	0.3	**Bethel** (village) Clermont County
19	0.3	**Harrison** (city) Hamilton County
19	0.3	**Shelby** (city) Richland County
19	0.3	**Wellston** (city) Jackson County
24	0.4	**Crestline** (village) Crawford County
24	0.4	**Loudonville** (village) Ashland County
24	0.4	**Uhrichsville** (city) Tuscarawas County
24	0.4	**West Jefferson** (village) Madison County
24	0.4	**West Union** (village) Adams County
29	0.5	**Bellaire** (village) Belmont County
29	0.5	**Cadiz** (village) Harrison County
29	0.5	**Circleville** (city) Pickaway County
29	0.5	**Columbiana** (city) Columbiana County
29	0.5	**Covington** (village) Miami County
29	0.5	**Ironton** (city) Lawrence County
29	0.5	**Kenton** (city) Hardin County
29	0.5	**North Baltimore** (village) Wood County
37	0.6	**Blanchester** (village) Clinton County
37	0.6	**Brookville** (city) Montgomery County
37	0.6	**Edgewood** (CDP) Ashtabula County
37	0.6	**Greenville** (city) Darke County
37	0.6	**Lisbon** (village) Columbiana County
37	0.6	**Newton Falls** (village) Trumbull County
37	0.6	**Perry Heights** (CDP) Stark County
37	0.6	**Taylor Creek** (CDP) Hamilton County
37	0.6	**Toronto** (city) Jefferson County
46	0.7	**Carlisle** (village) Warren County
46	0.7	**Clyde** (city) Sandusky County
46	0.7	**Fostoria** (city) Seneca County
46	0.7	**Geneva** (city) Ashtabula County
46	0.7	**Lexington** (village) Richland County
46	0.7	**Niles** (city) Trumbull County
46	0.7	**Northwood** (city) Wood County
46	0.7	**Strasburg** (village) Tuscarawas County
46	0.7	**Trenton** (city) Butler County
46	0.7	**Union** (city) Montgomery County
56	0.8	**Ballville** (CDP) Sandusky County
56	0.8	**Buckeye Lake** (village) Licking County
56	0.8	**Cleves** (village) Hamilton County
56	0.8	**Lincoln Heights** (village) Hamilton County
56	0.8	**Mount Orab** (village) Brown County
56	0.8	**New London** (village) Huron County
56	0.8	**Park Layne** (CDP) Clark County
56	0.8	**Port Clinton** (city) Ottawa County
56	0.8	**Saint Bernard** (city) Hamilton County
56	0.8	**South Russell** (village) Geauga County
66	0.9	**Mount Gilead** (village) Morrow County
66	0.9	**New Lexington** (village) Perry County
66	0.9	**Salem Heights** (CDP) Hamilton County
66	0.9	**Silverton** (village) Hamilton County
66	0.9	**West Milton** (village) Miami County
71	1.0	**Bridgetown** (CDP) Hamilton County
71	1.0	**Burlington** (CDP) Lawrence County
71	1.0	**Celina** (city) Mercer County
71	1.0	**Coshocton** (city) Coshocton County
71	1.0	**Day Heights** (CDP) Clermont County
71	1.0	**East Liverpool** (city) Columbiana County
71	1.0	**Gallipolis** (village) Gallia County
71	1.0	**Hubbard** (city) Trumbull County
71	1.0	**Lakemore** (village) Summit County
71	1.0	**Mineral Ridge** (CDP) Trumbull County
71	1.0	**Ravenna** (city) Portage County
71	1.0	**Rittman** (city) Wayne County
71	1.0	**Summerside** (CDP) Clermont County
71	1.0	**Swanton** (village) Fulton County
71	1.0	**Van Wert** (city) Van Wert County
71	1.0	**Xenia** (city) Greene County
87	1.1	**Champion Heights** (CDP) Trumbull County
87	1.1	**Chillicothe** (city) Ross County
87	1.1	**Conneaut** (city) Ashtabula County
87	1.1	**Delta** (village) Fulton County
87	1.1	**Georgetown** (village) Brown County
87	1.1	**Grafton** (village) Lorain County
87	1.1	**Lima** (city) Allen County
87	1.1	**Lodi** (village) Medina County
87	1.1	**Piqua** (city) Miami County
87	1.1	**Saint Marys** (city) Auglaize County
87	1.1	**Sheffield Lake** (city) Lorain County
98	1.2	**Bucyrus** (city) Crawford County
98	1.2	**Huron** (city) Erie County
98	1.2	**Lancaster** (city) Fairfield County
98	1.2	**Mount Vernon** (city) Knox County
98	1.2	**Turpin Hills** (CDP) Hamilton County
98	1.2	**Wapakoneta** (city) Auglaize County
104	1.3	**Belpre** (city) Washington County
104	1.3	**Coldwater** (village) Mercer County
104	1.3	**Dennison** (village) Tuscarawas County
104	1.3	**Nelsonville** (city) Athens County
104	1.3	**North Madison** (CDP) Lake County
104	1.3	**Ottawa** (village) Putnam County
104	1.3	**Pleasant Run Farm** (CDP) Hamilton County
104	1.3	**Poland** (village) Mahoning County
104	1.3	**Struthers** (city) Mahoning County
104	1.3	**Tipp City** (city) Miami County
104	1.3	**Urbana** (city) Champaign County
104	1.3	**Wadsworth** (city) Medina County
104	1.3	**Wellington** (village) Lorain County
117	1.4	**Ashville** (village) Pickaway County
117	1.4	**Cambridge** (city) Guernsey County
117	1.4	**Canal Fulton** (city) Stark County
117	1.4	**East Palestine** (village) Columbiana County
117	1.4	**Eaton** (city) Preble County
117	1.4	**Logan** (city) Hocking County
117	1.4	**Massillon** (city) Stark County
117	1.4	**Miami Heights** (CDP) Hamilton County
117	1.4	**Mogadore** (village) Summit County
117	1.4	**Napoleon** (city) Henry County
117	1.4	**Newcomerstown** (village) Tuscarawas County
117	1.4	**Saint Clairsville** (city) Belmont County
117	1.4	**Seville** (village) Medina County
117	1.4	**Shadyside** (village) Belmont County
117	1.4	**Warren** (city) Trumbull County
132	1.5	**Carey** (village) Wyandot County
132	1.5	**Germantown** (city) Montgomery County
132	1.5	**Greentown** (CDP) Stark County
132	1.5	**Hartville** (village) Stark County
132	1.5	**Hillsboro** (city) Highland County
132	1.5	**Johnstown** (village) Licking County
132	1.5	**McDonald** (village) Trumbull County
132	1.5	**Mingo Junction** (village) Jefferson County
132	1.5	**Minster** (village) Auglaize County
132	1.5	**Newark** (city) Licking County
132	1.5	**Trotwood** (city) Montgomery County
132	1.5	**Zanesville** (city) Muskingum County
144	1.6	**Bellevue** (city) Sandusky County
144	1.6	**Brimfield** (CDP) Portage County
144	1.6	**Fairport Harbor** (village) Lake County
144	1.6	**Fort Shawnee** (CDP) Allen County
144	1.6	**Franklin** (city) Warren County
144	1.6	**Garrettsville** (village) Portage County
144	1.6	**Jefferson** (village) Ashtabula County

Note: *This section ranks incorporated places and CDPs (Census Designated Places) with populations of 2,500 or more. Unincorporated postal areas were not considered. Please refer to the User Guide for additional information.*

Speak English Only at Home

Top 150 Places Ranked in *Descending* Order

State Rank	Percent	Place
1	100.0	**Barnesville** (village) Belmont County
1	100.0	**Mount Healthy Heights** (CDP) Hamilton County
1	100.0	**Ross** (CDP) Butler County
4	99.8	**Versailles** (village) Darke County
5	99.7	**West Portsmouth** (CDP) Scioto County
6	99.6	**Loudonville** (village) Ashland County
7	99.5	**Uhrichsville** (city) Tuscarawas County
7	99.5	**West Jefferson** (village) Madison County
9	99.4	**Cadiz** (village) Harrison County
9	99.4	**Champion Heights** (CDP) Trumbull County
9	99.4	**Lakemore** (village) Summit County
12	99.3	**Brookville** (city) Montgomery County
13	99.2	**Blanchester** (village) Clinton County
13	99.2	**Carlisle** (village) Warren County
13	99.2	**Crooksville** (village) Perry County
13	99.2	**Mogadore** (village) Summit County
13	99.2	**Mount Orab** (village) Brown County
13	99.2	**West Union** (village) Adams County
19	99.1	**East Palestine** (village) Columbiana County
19	99.1	**Garrettsville** (village) Portage County
21	99.0	**Crestline** (village) Crawford County
21	99.0	**Edgewood** (CDP) Ashtabula County
21	99.0	**Mount Gilead** (village) Morrow County
21	99.0	**North Baltimore** (village) Wood County
21	99.0	**Wellington** (village) Lorain County
21	99.0	**Wheelersburg** (CDP) Scioto County
27	98.9	**Burlington** (CDP) Lawrence County
27	98.9	**Covington** (village) Miami County
27	98.9	**Fredericktown** (village) Knox County
27	98.9	**Huron** (city) Erie County
27	98.9	**Trenton** (city) Butler County
32	98.8	**Cleves** (village) Hamilton County
32	98.8	**Greenfield** (village) Highland County
32	98.8	**Logan** (city) Hocking County
35	98.7	**Columbiana** (city) Columbiana County
35	98.7	**Silverton** (village) Hamilton County
35	98.7	**South Point** (village) Lawrence County
35	98.7	**South Russell** (village) Geauga County
39	98.6	**Bethel** (village) Clermont County
39	98.6	**Mount Carmel** (CDP) Clermont County
39	98.6	**Williamsburg** (village) Clermont County
42	98.5	**Coldwater** (village) Mercer County
42	98.5	**Lancaster** (city) Fairfield County
42	98.5	**Newton Falls** (village) Trumbull County
42	98.5	**Park Layne** (CDP) Clark County
46	98.4	**Apple Valley** (CDP) Knox County
46	98.4	**Bellevue** (city) Sandusky County
46	98.4	**Buckeye Lake** (village) Licking County
46	98.4	**Bucyrus** (city) Crawford County
46	98.4	**Clyde** (city) Sandusky County
46	98.4	**Germantown** (city) Montgomery County
46	98.4	**Kenton** (city) Hardin County
46	98.4	**New Richmond** (village) Clermont County
46	98.4	**Perry Heights** (CDP) Stark County
46	98.4	**Ravenna** (city) Portage County
46	98.4	**Toronto** (city) Jefferson County
46	98.4	**Vermilion** (city) Lorain County
58	98.3	**Day Heights** (CDP) Clermont County
58	98.3	**East Liverpool** (city) Columbiana County
58	98.3	**Galion** (city) Crawford County
58	98.3	**Gallipolis** (village) Gallia County
58	98.3	**Greentown** (CDP) Stark County
58	98.3	**Hartville** (village) Stark County
58	98.3	**Martins Ferry** (city) Belmont County
58	98.3	**Minerva** (village) Stark County
58	98.3	**North Madison** (CDP) Lake County
58	98.3	**Shelby** (city) Richland County
68	98.2	**Bluffton** (village) Allen County
68	98.2	**Greenville** (city) Darke County
68	98.2	**Mineral Ridge** (CDP) Trumbull County
68	98.2	**New London** (village) Huron County
68	98.2	**Pleasant Run Farm** (CDP) Hamilton County
73	98.1	**Coshocton** (city) Coshocton County
73	98.1	**Lake Lakengren** (CDP) Preble County
73	98.1	**Saint Henry** (village) Mercer County
73	98.1	**Union** (city) Montgomery County
73	98.1	**Van Wert** (city) Van Wert County
73	98.1	**Whitehouse** (village) Lucas County
73	98.1	**Withamsville** (CDP) Clermont County
73	98.1	**Xenia** (city) Greene County
81	98.0	**Circleville** (city) Pickaway County
81	98.0	**Lincoln Heights** (village) Hamilton County
81	98.0	**Lisbon** (village) Columbiana County
81	98.0	**New Franklin** (city) Summit County
81	98.0	**New Lebanon** (village) Montgomery County
81	98.0	**Tipp City** (city) Miami County
81	98.0	**Wadsworth** (city) Medina County
81	98.0	**Wellsville** (village) Columbiana County
89	97.9	**Bellaire** (village) Belmont County
89	97.9	**Canal Fulton** (city) Stark County
89	97.9	**Chillicothe** (city) Ross County
89	97.9	**Delhi Hills** (CDP) Hamilton County
89	97.9	**Dennison** (village) Tuscarawas County
89	97.9	**Georgetown** (village) Brown County
89	97.9	**Mount Vernon** (city) Knox County
89	97.9	**Mulberry** (CDP) Clermont County
89	97.9	**Nelsonville** (city) Athens County
89	97.9	**Saint Clairsville** (city) Belmont County
89	97.9	**Walbridge** (village) Wood County
100	97.8	**Bellbrook** (city) Greene County
100	97.8	**Conneaut** (city) Ashtabula County
100	97.8	**Fort Shawnee** (CDP) Allen County
100	97.8	**Golf Manor** (village) Hamilton County
100	97.8	**Harrison** (city) Hamilton County
100	97.8	**Portsmouth** (city) Scioto County
100	97.8	**Saint Marys** (city) Auglaize County
100	97.8	**Wellston** (city) Jackson County
108	97.7	**Cambridge** (city) Guernsey County
108	97.7	**Madison** (village) Lake County
108	97.7	**Newark** (city) Licking County
111	97.6	**Bridgetown** (CDP) Hamilton County
111	97.6	**Franklin** (city) Warren County
111	97.6	**McDonald** (village) Trumbull County
111	97.6	**Salem Heights** (CDP) Hamilton County
111	97.6	**Summerside** (CDP) Clermont County
111	97.6	**Uniontown** (CDP) Stark County
117	97.5	**Hubbard** (city) Trumbull County
117	97.5	**Lexington** (village) Richland County
117	97.5	**Minster** (village) Auglaize County
117	97.5	**Piqua** (city) Miami County
117	97.5	**Rittman** (city) Wayne County
117	97.5	**Zanesville** (city) Muskingum County
123	97.4	**Calcutta** (CDP) Columbiana County
123	97.4	**Enon** (village) Clark County
123	97.4	**Hillsboro** (city) Highland County
123	97.4	**New Burlington** (CDP) Hamilton County
123	97.4	**Newcomerstown** (village) Tuscarawas County
123	97.4	**Portage Lakes** (CDP) Summit County
129	97.3	**Baltimore** (village) Fairfield County
129	97.3	**Heath** (city) Licking County
129	97.3	**Miamisburg** (city) Montgomery County
129	97.3	**Turpin Hills** (CDP) Hamilton County
133	97.2	**Johnstown** (village) Licking County
133	97.2	**Lima** (city) Allen County
133	97.2	**Monfort Heights** (CDP) Hamilton County
133	97.2	**Northwood** (city) Wood County
133	97.2	**Seville** (village) Medina County
133	97.2	**Shadyside** (village) Belmont County
133	97.2	**Urbana** (city) Champaign County
133	97.2	**West Milton** (village) Miami County
141	97.1	**Alliance** (city) Stark County
141	97.1	**Eaton** (city) Preble County
141	97.1	**Oak Harbor** (village) Ottawa County
141	97.1	**Strasburg** (village) Tuscarawas County
141	97.1	**Taylor Creek** (CDP) Hamilton County
141	97.1	**Wapakoneta** (city) Auglaize County
141	97.1	**Wintersville** (village) Jefferson County
148	97.0	**Maple Heights** (city) Cuyahoga County
148	97.0	**New Bremen** (village) Auglaize County
148	97.0	**Waynesville** (village) Warren County

Note: *This section ranks incorporated places and CDPs (Census Designated Places) with populations of 2,500 or more. Unincorporated postal areas were not considered. Please refer to the User Guide for additional information.*

Speak English Only at Home

Top 150 Places Ranked in *Ascending* Order

State Rank	Percent	Place
1	75.2	**Lockland** (village) Hamilton County
2	77.2	**Springdale** (city) Hamilton County
3	77.5	**Brooklyn** (city) Cuyahoga County
4	78.0	**Sixteen Mile Stand** (CDP) Hamilton County
5	79.2	**Beachwood** (city) Cuyahoga County
6	79.7	**Painesville** (city) Lake County
7	80.0	**Mayfield** (village) Cuyahoga County
8	80.5	**Mayfield Heights** (city) Cuyahoga County
8	80.5	**Middleburg Heights** (city) Cuyahoga County
10	80.6	**Willoughby Hills** (city) Lake County
11	80.8	**Whitehall** (city) Franklin County
12	81.6	**Lorain** (city) Lorain County
13	81.7	**Campbell** (city) Mahoning County
13	81.7	**Orange** (village) Cuyahoga County
15	81.8	**Dublin** (city) Franklin County
16	82.7	**Solon** (city) Cuyahoga County
17	82.8	**New Carlisle** (city) Clark County
18	82.9	**Pepper Pike** (city) Cuyahoga County
19	83.1	**Highland Heights** (city) Cuyahoga County
20	84.5	**Parma** (city) Cuyahoga County
21	85.0	**Blue Ash** (city) Hamilton County
21	85.0	**Forest Park** (city) Hamilton County
23	85.1	**Sharonville** (city) Hamilton County
24	85.3	**Columbus** (city) Franklin County
25	86.1	**Mason** (city) Warren County
26	86.2	**Lincoln Village** (CDP) Franklin County
26	86.2	**Parma Heights** (city) Cuyahoga County
28	86.7	**North Royalton** (city) Cuyahoga County
29	87.1	**North Olmsted** (city) Cuyahoga County
30	87.2	**Seven Hills** (city) Cuyahoga County
31	87.4	**Cleveland** (city) Cuyahoga County
32	87.5	**Fairfield** (city) Butler County
33	87.7	**Richmond Heights** (city) Cuyahoga County
34	87.8	**Broadview Heights** (city) Cuyahoga County
35	88.1	**Wyoming** (city) Hamilton County
36	88.2	**Strongsville** (city) Cuyahoga County
37	88.5	**Athens** (city) Athens County
37	88.5	**Rocky River** (city) Cuyahoga County
39	88.7	**Granville** (village) Licking County
40	88.8	**Fairview Park** (city) Cuyahoga County
40	88.8	**Moreland Hills** (village) Cuyahoga County
42	89.0	**Westlake** (city) Cuyahoga County
42	89.0	**Willard** (city) Huron County
44	89.1	**Montgomery** (city) Hamilton County
44	89.1	**Wauseon** (city) Fulton County
46	89.4	**Beavercreek** (city) Greene County
47	89.6	**Ontario** (city) Richland County
47	89.6	**Shaker Heights** (city) Cuyahoga County
49	89.7	**Cleveland Heights** (city) Cuyahoga County
50	89.8	**Hilliard** (city) Franklin County
50	89.8	**Powell** (city) Delaware County
52	89.9	**Delshire** (CDP) Hamilton County
52	89.9	**Lakewood** (city) Cuyahoga County
52	89.9	**Lyndhurst** (city) Cuyahoga County
55	90.0	**University Heights** (city) Cuyahoga County
56	90.1	**Northfield** (village) Summit County
56	90.1	**The Village of Indian Hill** (city) Hamilton County
56	90.1	**Youngstown** (city) Mahoning County
59	90.4	**Dry Ridge** (CDP) Hamilton County
60	90.8	**Kent** (city) Portage County
60	90.8	**Lake Darby** (CDP) Franklin County
62	90.9	**Oberlin** (city) Lorain County
62	90.9	**Sherwood** (CDP) Hamilton County
62	90.9	**Upper Arlington** (city) Franklin County
65	91.0	**Amberley** (village) Hamilton County
65	91.0	**Fremont** (city) Sandusky County
67	91.1	**Twinsburg** (city) Summit County
68	91.4	**Brecksville** (city) Cuyahoga County
68	91.4	**Oxford** (city) Butler County
68	91.4	**Paulding** (village) Paulding County
71	91.5	**Fairport Harbor** (village) Lake County
71	91.5	**Huber Ridge** (CDP) Franklin County
71	91.5	**Independence** (city) Cuyahoga County
71	91.5	**Ottawa Hills** (village) Lucas County
75	91.6	**Beckett Ridge** (CDP) Butler County
76	91.7	**Sheffield** (village) Lorain County
77	91.8	**New Albany** (city) Franklin County
78	91.9	**Geneva** (city) Ashtabula County
79	92.0	**Perrysburg** (city) Wood County
80	92.1	**Madeira** (city) Hamilton County
80	92.1	**Millersburg** (village) Holmes County
82	92.2	**Landen** (CDP) Warren County
83	92.4	**Brook Park** (city) Cuyahoga County
83	92.4	**Cincinnati** (city) Hamilton County
83	92.4	**South Lebanon** (village) Warren County
86	92.5	**Fairborn** (city) Greene County
86	92.5	**Kenwood** (CDP) Hamilton County
86	92.5	**Norwalk** (city) Huron County
86	92.5	**Oakwood** (village) Cuyahoga County
86	92.5	**South Euclid** (city) Cuyahoga County
91	92.6	**Bowling Green** (city) Wood County
91	92.6	**West Carrollton** (city) Montgomery County
91	92.6	**White Oak** (CDP) Hamilton County
91	92.6	**Wright-Patterson AFB** (CDP) Greene County
95	92.7	**Bedford Heights** (city) Cuyahoga County
95	92.7	**Centerville** (city) Montgomery County
95	92.7	**Dover** (city) Tuscarawas County
95	92.7	**Fairlawn** (city) Summit County
95	92.7	**Findlay** (city) Hancock County
95	92.7	**Montrose-Ghent** (CDP) Summit County
101	92.8	**Archbold** (village) Fulton County
101	92.8	**Woodlawn** (village) Hamilton County
103	92.9	**Avon** (city) Lorain County
104	93.0	**New Concord** (village) Muskingum County
104	93.0	**Reynoldsburg** (city) Franklin County
104	93.0	**Richfield** (village) Summit County
107	93.1	**Aurora** (city) Portage County
107	93.1	**Canfield** (city) Mahoning County
107	93.1	**Chagrin Falls** (village) Cuyahoga County
107	93.1	**Forestville** (CDP) Hamilton County
107	93.1	**Hicksville** (village) Defiance County
107	93.1	**Hudson** (city) Summit County
107	93.1	**Toledo** (city) Lucas County
114	93.2	**Munroe Falls** (city) Summit County
115	93.3	**Akron** (city) Summit County
115	93.3	**Ashtabula** (city) Ashtabula County
115	93.3	**Dayton** (city) Montgomery County
115	93.3	**Pickerington** (city) Fairfield County
119	93.4	**Ada** (village) Hardin County
119	93.4	**Howland Center** (CDP) Trumbull County
121	93.5	**Evendale** (village) Hamilton County
121	93.5	**Girard** (city) Trumbull County
121	93.5	**Huber Heights** (city) Montgomery County
121	93.5	**North Ridgeville** (city) Lorain County
121	93.5	**Streetsboro** (city) Portage County
126	93.6	**Kirtland** (city) Lake County
126	93.6	**Willoughby** (city) Lake County
128	93.7	**Cheviot** (city) Hamilton County
128	93.7	**Gahanna** (city) Franklin County
130	93.8	**Dry Run** (CDP) Hamilton County
130	93.8	**Sebring** (village) Mahoning County
130	93.8	**Wickliffe** (city) Lake County
130	93.8	**Wooster** (city) Wayne County
134	93.9	**Garfield Heights** (city) Cuyahoga County
134	93.9	**Monroe** (city) Butler County
134	93.9	**Northbrook** (CDP) Hamilton County
137	94.0	**Eastlake** (city) Lake County
137	94.0	**Greenhills** (village) Hamilton County
137	94.0	**Newtown** (village) Hamilton County
137	94.0	**Reminderville** (village) Summit County
137	94.0	**Westerville** (city) Franklin County
142	94.1	**Berea** (city) Cuyahoga County
142	94.1	**Boardman** (CDP) Mahoning County
142	94.1	**Defiance** (city) Defiance County
142	94.1	**Green** (city) Summit County
142	94.1	**Willowick** (city) Lake County
147	94.2	**Grafton** (village) Lorain County
147	94.2	**Pleasant Run** (CDP) Hamilton County
149	94.3	**Avon Lake** (city) Lorain County
149	94.3	**Doylestown** (village) Wayne County

***Note:** This section ranks incorporated places and CDPs (Census Designated Places) with populations of 2,500 or more. Unincorporated postal areas were not considered. Please refer to the User Guide for additional information.*

Individuals with a Disability

Top 150 Places Ranked in *Descending* Order

State Rank	Percent	Place
1	27.1	**Gallipolis** (village) Gallia County
2	27.0	**The Plains** (CDP) Athens County
2	27.0	**West Union** (village) Adams County
4	25.9	**Belpre** (city) Washington County
5	24.5	**Portsmouth** (city) Scioto County
6	24.4	**Ironton** (city) Lawrence County
7	24.3	**Barnesville** (village) Belmont County
8	23.5	**West Portsmouth** (CDP) Scioto County
9	23.2	**Marion** (city) Marion County
9	23.2	**Waverly** (village) Pike County
11	23.1	**Chillicothe** (city) Ross County
12	23.0	**Greenfield** (village) Highland County
13	22.9	**Campbell** (city) Mahoning County
13	22.9	**Mount Gilead** (village) Morrow County
15	22.3	**Lodi** (village) Medina County
16	22.2	**Marietta** (city) Washington County
17	22.1	**Zanesville** (city) Muskingum County
18	22.0	**Sebring** (village) Mahoning County
19	21.8	**East Cleveland** (city) Cuyahoga County
19	21.8	**Jackson** (city) Jackson County
21	21.7	**Galion** (city) Crawford County
22	21.5	**Enon** (village) Clark County
22	21.5	**Logan** (city) Hocking County
22	21.5	**New Lebanon** (village) Montgomery County
25	21.4	**East Liverpool** (city) Columbiana County
26	21.2	**Greenville** (city) Darke County
26	21.2	**Hillsboro** (city) Highland County
28	21.1	**Crooksville** (village) Perry County
29	20.9	**Eaton** (city) Preble County
30	20.8	**Nelsonville** (city) Athens County
31	20.7	**Steubenville** (city) Jefferson County
32	20.6	**Youngstown** (city) Mahoning County
33	20.4	**Cheviot** (city) Hamilton County
33	20.4	**North Zanesville** (CDP) Muskingum County
35	20.3	**Wellston** (city) Jackson County
36	20.2	**Bellaire** (village) Belmont County
37	20.1	**Lorain** (city) Lorain County
37	20.1	**Mingo Junction** (village) Jefferson County
39	20.0	**Cleveland** (city) Cuyahoga County
39	20.0	**Toronto** (city) Jefferson County
41	19.8	**Bethel** (village) Clermont County
42	19.6	**Cambridge** (city) Guernsey County
42	19.6	**Lancaster** (city) Fairfield County
42	19.6	**Middletown** (city) Butler County
45	19.4	**London** (city) Madison County
46	19.3	**Lisbon** (village) Columbiana County
46	19.3	**Urbana** (city) Champaign County
48	19.2	**Maple Heights** (city) Cuyahoga County
48	19.2	**Trotwood** (city) Montgomery County
50	19.1	**Burlington** (CDP) Lawrence County
51	18.9	**Mansfield** (city) Richland County
51	18.9	**Mount Healthy** (city) Hamilton County
51	18.9	**Mount Vernon** (city) Knox County
51	18.9	**New Burlington** (CDP) Hamilton County
55	18.8	**Alliance** (city) Stark County
55	18.8	**Heath** (city) Licking County
55	18.8	**Millersburg** (village) Holmes County
58	18.5	**Dayton** (city) Montgomery County
58	18.5	**Springfield** (city) Clark County
58	18.5	**Van Wert** (city) Van Wert County
58	18.5	**Wilmington** (city) Clinton County
62	18.4	**Lima** (city) Allen County
62	18.4	**Withamsville** (CDP) Clermont County
64	18.3	**Brookville** (city) Montgomery County
64	18.3	**Lincoln Village** (CDP) Franklin County
64	18.3	**Northwood** (city) Wood County
64	18.3	**Uhrichsville** (city) Tuscarawas County
68	18.2	**Newark** (city) Licking County
69	18.1	**Ashtabula** (city) Ashtabula County
69	18.1	**Napoleon** (city) Henry County
69	18.1	**Obetz** (village) Franklin County
69	18.1	**Wellsville** (village) Columbiana County
73	18.0	**Buckeye Lake** (village) Licking County
73	18.0	**Elyria** (city) Lorain County
73	18.0	**Newcomerstown** (village) Tuscarawas County
73	18.0	**South Point** (village) Lawrence County
77	17.9	**Circleville** (city) Pickaway County
77	17.9	**Lakemore** (village) Summit County
77	17.9	**Milford** (city) Clermont County
77	17.9	**Warren** (city) Trumbull County
81	17.8	**Fostoria** (city) Seneca County
81	17.8	**Loudonville** (village) Ashland County
81	17.8	**Niles** (city) Trumbull County
84	17.7	**Brook Park** (city) Cuyahoga County
84	17.7	**Kenton** (city) Hardin County
84	17.7	**Paulding** (village) Paulding County
87	17.6	**Bryan** (city) Williams County
87	17.6	**Ravenna** (city) Portage County
87	17.6	**Washington Court House** (city) Fayette County
90	17.5	**East Palestine** (village) Columbiana County
90	17.5	**Green Meadows** (CDP) Clark County
92	17.4	**Brooklyn** (city) Cuyahoga County
93	17.3	**Geneva** (city) Ashtabula County
93	17.3	**Piqua** (city) Miami County
93	17.3	**Shadyside** (village) Belmont County
93	17.3	**Toledo** (city) Lucas County
97	17.2	**Barberton** (city) Summit County
97	17.2	**Bucyrus** (city) Crawford County
97	17.2	**Wauseon** (city) Fulton County
100	17.0	**Crestline** (village) Crawford County
100	17.0	**Sandusky** (city) Erie County
100	17.0	**Vermilion** (city) Lorain County
100	17.0	**Willard** (city) Huron County
104	16.9	**Dover** (city) Tuscarawas County
105	16.8	**Mentor-on-the-Lake** (city) Lake County
106	16.7	**Ashland** (city) Ashland County
107	16.6	**Georgetown** (village) Brown County
107	16.6	**Mineral Ridge** (CDP) Trumbull County
107	16.6	**Xenia** (city) Greene County
110	16.5	**Delphos** (city) Allen County
110	16.5	**Sheffield Lake** (city) Lorain County
112	16.4	**Canton** (city) Stark County
112	16.4	**Hamilton** (city) Butler County
112	16.4	**Strasburg** (village) Tuscarawas County
112	16.4	**Williamsburg** (village) Clermont County
116	16.3	**Bellefontaine** (city) Logan County
116	16.3	**Martins Ferry** (city) Belmont County
116	16.3	**New Richmond** (village) Clermont County
116	16.3	**Northridge** (CDP) Clark County
120	16.2	**Euclid** (city) Cuyahoga County
121	16.1	**Edgewood** (CDP) Ashtabula County
121	16.1	**Wellington** (village) Lorain County
123	16.0	**Columbiana** (city) Columbiana County
124	15.9	**Carlisle** (village) Warren County
124	15.9	**Sidney** (city) Shelby County
126	15.8	**Celina** (city) Mercer County
126	15.8	**Coshocton** (city) Coshocton County
126	15.8	**Oberlin** (city) Lorain County
126	15.8	**Richmond Heights** (city) Cuyahoga County
126	15.8	**Struthers** (city) Mahoning County
131	15.7	**Fairborn** (city) Greene County
131	15.7	**Franklin** (city) Warren County
131	15.7	**Moraine** (city) Montgomery County
131	15.7	**Walbridge** (village) Wood County
131	15.7	**Wheelersburg** (CDP) Scioto County
131	15.7	**Yellow Springs** (village) Greene County
137	15.6	**Chardon** (city) Geauga County
137	15.6	**Lincoln Heights** (village) Hamilton County
137	15.6	**Norwalk** (city) Huron County
137	15.6	**Oak Harbor** (village) Ottawa County
137	15.6	**Riverside** (city) Montgomery County
142	15.5	**Clyde** (city) Sandusky County
142	15.5	**Fremont** (city) Sandusky County
142	15.5	**Girard** (city) Trumbull County
142	15.5	**Parma Heights** (city) Cuyahoga County
146	15.4	**Massillon** (city) Stark County
147	15.3	**Conneaut** (city) Ashtabula County
147	15.3	**Dennison** (village) Tuscarawas County
147	15.3	**Port Clinton** (city) Ottawa County
150	15.2	**McDonald** (village) Trumbull County

Note: *This section ranks incorporated places and CDPs (Census Designated Places) with populations of 2,500 or more. Unincorporated postal areas were not considered. Please refer to the User Guide for additional information.*

Individuals with a Disability

Top 150 Places Ranked in *Ascending* Order

State Rank	Percent	Place
1	2.9	**Mariemont** (village) Hamilton County
2	3.9	**New Albany** (city) Franklin County
3	4.0	**Bainbridge** (CDP) Geauga County
4	4.5	**Greentown** (CDP) Stark County
5	4.7	**Granville** (village) Licking County
5	4.7	**Powell** (city) Delaware County
7	5.3	**Landen** (CDP) Warren County
8	5.6	**Saint Henry** (village) Mercer County
8	5.6	**South Russell** (village) Geauga County
10	5.7	**Dublin** (city) Franklin County
11	5.8	**Beckett Ridge** (CDP) Butler County
11	5.8	**Oxford** (city) Butler County
13	5.9	**Dry Run** (CDP) Hamilton County
14	6.0	**Grandview Heights** (city) Franklin County
15	6.4	**Bexley** (city) Franklin County
15	6.4	**Canfield** (city) Mahoning County
17	6.5	**Beechwood Trails** (CDP) Licking County
18	6.6	**Mogadore** (village) Summit County
18	6.6	**Springboro** (city) Warren County
20	6.7	**Brecksville** (city) Cuyahoga County
20	6.7	**Hudson** (city) Summit County
22	6.9	**Highland Heights** (city) Cuyahoga County
22	6.9	**Ottawa** (village) Putnam County
22	6.9	**Waterville** (city) Lucas County
25	7.0	**Broadview Heights** (city) Cuyahoga County
26	7.1	**Cedarville** (village) Greene County
26	7.1	**Madeira** (city) Hamilton County
26	7.1	**Oakwood** (city) Montgomery County
29	7.2	**Fruit Hill** (CDP) Hamilton County
29	7.2	**Solon** (city) Cuyahoga County
31	7.3	**Athens** (city) Athens County
31	7.3	**Worthington** (city) Franklin County
33	7.4	**Evendale** (village) Hamilton County
33	7.4	**Salem Heights** (CDP) Hamilton County
35	7.7	**Cleves** (village) Hamilton County
35	7.7	**Hilliard** (city) Franklin County
37	7.8	**Ottawa Hills** (village) Lucas County
37	7.8	**University Heights** (city) Cuyahoga County
39	7.9	**Miami Heights** (CDP) Hamilton County
40	8.0	**Pickerington** (city) Fairfield County
41	8.1	**Wyoming** (city) Hamilton County
42	8.2	**Avon** (city) Lorain County
42	8.2	**Bay Village** (city) Cuyahoga County
44	8.3	**Ada** (village) Hardin County
44	8.3	**Cherry Grove** (CDP) Hamilton County
44	8.3	**Mason** (city) Warren County
44	8.3	**Mount Repose** (CDP) Clermont County
44	8.3	**Rossford** (city) Wood County
49	8.4	**Bellbrook** (city) Greene County
49	8.4	**Poland** (village) Mahoning County
49	8.4	**Reminderville** (village) Summit County
49	8.4	**Richfield** (village) Summit County
53	8.5	**New Bremen** (village) Auglaize County
53	8.5	**Perrysburg** (city) Wood County
55	8.6	**Bowling Green** (city) Wood County
55	8.6	**Lake Darby** (CDP) Franklin County
55	8.6	**Twinsburg** (city) Summit County
55	8.6	**Upper Arlington** (city) Franklin County
59	8.8	**Mack** (CDP) Hamilton County
59	8.8	**Turpin Hills** (CDP) Hamilton County
61	8.9	**Howland Center** (CDP) Trumbull County
61	8.9	**Mayfield** (village) Cuyahoga County
61	8.9	**Stow** (city) Summit County
64	9.0	**Sixteen Mile Stand** (CDP) Hamilton County
64	9.0	**South Euclid** (city) Cuyahoga County
66	9.1	**Lake Lakengren** (CDP) Preble County
67	9.2	**Newtown** (village) Hamilton County
67	9.2	**Sherwood** (CDP) Hamilton County
69	9.4	**Loveland** (city) Hamilton County
69	9.4	**Orange** (village) Cuyahoga County
69	9.4	**The Village of Indian Hill** (city) Hamilton County
72	9.5	**Coldwater** (village) Mercer County
72	9.5	**Delhi Hills** (CDP) Hamilton County
72	9.5	**Gahanna** (city) Franklin County
75	9.6	**Beavercreek** (city) Greene County

State Rank	Percent	Place
75	9.6	**Shaker Heights** (city) Cuyahoga County
77	9.7	**Delaware** (city) Delaware County
77	9.7	**Dent** (CDP) Hamilton County
77	9.7	**Devola** (CDP) Washington County
77	9.7	**Dry Ridge** (CDP) Hamilton County
77	9.7	**Monroe** (city) Butler County
77	9.7	**Montgomery** (city) Hamilton County
77	9.7	**Seville** (village) Medina County
77	9.7	**Westlake** (city) Cuyahoga County
85	9.8	**Minster** (village) Auglaize County
85	9.8	**Strongsville** (city) Cuyahoga County
87	9.9	**Ashville** (village) Pickaway County
87	9.9	**Lexington** (village) Richland County
87	9.9	**Newton Falls** (village) Trumbull County
87	9.9	**Uniontown** (CDP) Stark County
87	9.9	**Whitehouse** (village) Lucas County
92	10.0	**Amberley** (village) Hamilton County
92	10.0	**Bluffton** (village) Allen County
92	10.0	**Fairlawn** (city) Summit County
95	10.1	**Brunswick** (city) Medina County
95	10.1	**Huber Ridge** (CDP) Franklin County
95	10.1	**Kirtland** (city) Lake County
95	10.1	**Olmsted Falls** (city) Cuyahoga County
99	10.2	**Covington** (village) Miami County
99	10.2	**Greenhills** (village) Hamilton County
99	10.2	**Montrose-Ghent** (CDP) Summit County
99	10.2	**Willoughby Hills** (city) Lake County
103	10.4	**Dillonvale** (CDP) Hamilton County
103	10.4	**Fairfield** (city) Butler County
103	10.4	**Macedonia** (city) Summit County
103	10.4	**Wadsworth** (city) Medina County
107	10.5	**Plain City** (village) Madison County
107	10.5	**Reynoldsburg** (city) Franklin County
109	10.6	**Blue Ash** (city) Hamilton County
109	10.6	**Four Bridges** (CDP) Butler County
109	10.6	**Hartville** (village) Stark County
109	10.6	**Lebanon** (city) Warren County
109	10.6	**Moreland Hills** (village) Cuyahoga County
109	10.6	**Pepper Pike** (city) Cuyahoga County
109	10.6	**Perry Heights** (CDP) Stark County
116	10.7	**Avon Lake** (city) Lorain County
116	10.7	**Independence** (city) Cuyahoga County
116	10.7	**Maumee** (city) Lucas County
116	10.7	**Medina** (city) Medina County
116	10.7	**North Ridgeville** (city) Lorain County
116	10.7	**South Lebanon** (village) Warren County
116	10.7	**Tipp City** (city) Miami County
123	10.8	**Munroe Falls** (city) Summit County
123	10.8	**North Royalton** (city) Cuyahoga County
123	10.8	**Sunbury** (village) Delaware County
123	10.8	**Sylvania** (city) Lucas County
127	10.9	**Aurora** (city) Portage County
127	10.9	**Garrettsville** (village) Portage County
127	10.9	**Green** (city) Summit County
127	10.9	**Pleasant Run** (CDP) Hamilton County
131	11.1	**North Kingsville** (village) Ashtabula County
131	11.1	**Rocky River** (city) Cuyahoga County
133	11.2	**Kent** (city) Portage County
134	11.3	**Clayton** (city) Montgomery County
134	11.3	**Pataskala** (city) Licking County
134	11.3	**Westerville** (city) Franklin County
137	11.4	**Woodlawn** (village) Hamilton County
138	11.6	**Canal Winchester** (city) Franklin County
138	11.6	**Richville** (CDP) Stark County
138	11.6	**Versailles** (village) Darke County
141	11.7	**Monfort Heights** (CDP) Hamilton County
142	11.8	**Doylestown** (village) Wayne County
142	11.8	**Fairview Park** (city) Cuyahoga County
142	11.8	**Lakewood** (city) Cuyahoga County
142	11.8	**Mentor** (city) Lake County
142	11.8	**Pleasant Run Farm** (CDP) Hamilton County
147	11.9	**Ballville** (CDP) Sandusky County
147	11.9	**Columbus** (city) Franklin County
147	11.9	**Sharonville** (city) Hamilton County
147	11.9	**Union** (city) Montgomery County

Note: *This section ranks incorporated places and CDPs (Census Designated Places) with populations of 2,500 or more. Unincorporated postal areas were not considered. Please refer to the User Guide for additional information.*

Veterans

Top 150 Places Ranked in *Descending* Order

State Rank	Percent	Place
1	32.5	**Wright-Patterson AFB** (CDP) Greene County
2	21.6	**Enon** (village) Clark County
3	17.7	**Northridge** (CDP) Clark County
4	17.1	**Green Meadows** (CDP) Clark County
5	16.7	**Beavercreek** (city) Greene County
6	15.3	**Mingo Junction** (village) Jefferson County
7	14.9	**Columbiana** (city) Columbiana County
8	14.4	**Mulberry** (CDP) Clermont County
8	14.4	**Saint Clairsville** (city) Belmont County
10	14.3	**Bellbrook** (city) Greene County
10	14.3	**Doylestown** (village) Wayne County
10	14.3	**Fairborn** (city) Greene County
13	14.1	**Chardon** (city) Geauga County
13	14.1	**Huber Heights** (city) Montgomery County
15	14.0	**Riverside** (city) Montgomery County
16	13.7	**Blanchester** (village) Clinton County
16	13.7	**Shadyside** (village) Belmont County
18	13.5	**Buckeye Lake** (village) Licking County
18	13.5	**Grafton** (village) Lorain County
20	13.4	**Mineral Ridge** (CDP) Trumbull County
21	13.2	**Loudonville** (village) Ashland County
22	13.1	**Canal Winchester** (city) Franklin County
23	13.0	**Canal Fulton** (city) Stark County
24	12.9	**Belpre** (city) Washington County
24	12.9	**Obetz** (village) Franklin County
26	12.7	**Mogadore** (village) Summit County
27	12.6	**Lodi** (village) Medina County
27	12.6	**Ross** (CDP) Butler County
29	12.5	**Union** (city) Montgomery County
30	12.4	**Apple Valley** (CDP) Knox County
30	12.4	**Champion Heights** (CDP) Trumbull County
30	12.4	**Dover** (city) Tuscarawas County
30	12.4	**North Kingsville** (village) Ashtabula County
34	12.2	**Crestline** (village) Crawford County
34	12.2	**West Portsmouth** (CDP) Scioto County
36	12.1	**Vermilion** (city) Lorain County
37	12.0	**Centerville** (city) Montgomery County
37	12.0	**Geneva** (city) Ashtabula County
37	12.0	**Trotwood** (city) Montgomery County
40	11.9	**Calcutta** (CDP) Columbiana County
40	11.9	**Chillicothe** (city) Ross County
40	11.9	**Garrettsville** (village) Portage County
40	11.9	**Pleasant Run Farm** (CDP) Hamilton County
44	11.8	**Versailles** (village) Darke County
45	11.7	**Logan** (city) Hocking County
46	11.6	**Brimfield** (CDP) Portage County
46	11.6	**Coshocton** (city) Coshocton County
48	11.5	**Lincoln Village** (CDP) Franklin County
48	11.5	**Perry Heights** (CDP) Stark County
48	11.5	**Van Wert** (city) Van Wert County
51	11.4	**Austintown** (CDP) Mahoning County
52	11.3	**Greentown** (CDP) Stark County
52	11.3	**Louisville** (city) Stark County
54	11.2	**Baltimore** (village) Fairfield County
54	11.2	**Huron** (city) Erie County
54	11.2	**Pataskala** (city) Licking County
54	11.2	**Upper Sandusky** (city) Wyandot County
54	11.2	**Waverly** (village) Pike County
59	11.1	**Clayton** (city) Montgomery County
59	11.1	**Hubbard** (city) Trumbull County
59	11.1	**Northwood** (city) Wood County
59	11.1	**Strasburg** (village) Tuscarawas County
59	11.1	**Taylor Creek** (CDP) Hamilton County
64	11.0	**Day Heights** (CDP) Clermont County
64	11.0	**Girard** (city) Trumbull County
64	11.0	**Greenfield** (village) Highland County
64	11.0	**Harrison** (city) Hamilton County
64	11.0	**Hicksville** (village) Defiance County
64	11.0	**Lordstown** (village) Trumbull County
64	11.0	**Uniontown** (CDP) Stark County
71	10.9	**Ashtabula** (city) Ashtabula County
71	10.9	**Cambridge** (city) Guernsey County
71	10.9	**Hillsboro** (city) Highland County
71	10.9	**Mentor-on-the-Lake** (city) Lake County
71	10.9	**New Burlington** (CDP) Hamilton County
71	10.9	**Park Layne** (CDP) Clark County
71	10.9	**Richville** (CDP) Stark County
71	10.9	**Warren** (city) Trumbull County
79	10.8	**Brook Park** (city) Cuyahoga County
79	10.8	**Clyde** (city) Sandusky County
79	10.8	**Fostoria** (city) Seneca County
79	10.8	**North Madison** (CDP) Lake County
79	10.8	**South Lebanon** (village) Warren County
84	10.7	**Campbell** (city) Mahoning County
84	10.7	**Germantown** (city) Montgomery County
84	10.7	**Mount Repose** (CDP) Clermont County
84	10.7	**Walbridge** (village) Wood County
84	10.7	**Wellsville** (village) Columbiana County
89	10.6	**Heath** (city) Licking County
89	10.6	**Milford** (city) Clermont County
89	10.6	**Ottawa** (village) Putnam County
89	10.6	**Reading** (city) Hamilton County
89	10.6	**Trenton** (city) Butler County
94	10.5	**Cadiz** (village) Harrison County
94	10.5	**Fort Shawnee** (CDP) Allen County
94	10.5	**Johnstown** (village) Licking County
94	10.5	**Lancaster** (city) Fairfield County
94	10.5	**Minerva** (village) Stark County
94	10.5	**New Franklin** (city) Summit County
94	10.5	**Rossford** (city) Wood County
94	10.5	**Sheffield Lake** (city) Lorain County
94	10.5	**Troy** (city) Miami County
103	10.4	**Bucyrus** (city) Crawford County
103	10.4	**Montpelier** (village) Williams County
103	10.4	**Salem** (city) Columbiana County
103	10.4	**Sandusky** (city) Erie County
103	10.4	**Whitehouse** (village) Lucas County
103	10.4	**Xenia** (city) Greene County
109	10.3	**Bedford Heights** (city) Cuyahoga County
109	10.3	**Conneaut** (city) Ashtabula County
109	10.3	**Galion** (city) Crawford County
109	10.3	**Howland Center** (CDP) Trumbull County
109	10.3	**New Richmond** (village) Clermont County
109	10.3	**Newcomerstown** (village) Tuscarawas County
109	10.3	**Pickerington** (city) Fairfield County
109	10.3	**Uhrichsville** (city) Tuscarawas County
109	10.3	**West Milton** (village) Miami County
118	10.2	**Amelia** (village) Clermont County
118	10.2	**Aurora** (city) Portage County
118	10.2	**Barnesville** (village) Belmont County
118	10.2	**East Liverpool** (city) Columbiana County
118	10.2	**Greenville** (city) Darke County
118	10.2	**Middleburg Heights** (city) Cuyahoga County
118	10.2	**Napoleon** (city) Henry County
118	10.2	**New Carlisle** (city) Clark County
126	10.1	**Kettering** (city) Montgomery County
126	10.1	**Lincoln Heights** (village) Hamilton County
126	10.1	**Norwalk** (city) Huron County
126	10.1	**Springdale** (city) Hamilton County
130	10.0	**Bridgetown** (CDP) Hamilton County
130	10.0	**Brookville** (city) Montgomery County
130	10.0	**Edgewood** (CDP) Ashtabula County
130	10.0	**Fredericktown** (village) Knox County
130	10.0	**Georgetown** (village) Brown County
130	10.0	**Marion** (city) Marion County
130	10.0	**Massillon** (city) Stark County
130	10.0	**Niles** (city) Trumbull County
130	10.0	**Northgate** (CDP) Hamilton County
130	10.0	**Reynoldsburg** (city) Franklin County
130	10.0	**Sheffield** (village) Lorain County
130	10.0	**Springfield** (city) Clark County
130	10.0	**Wickliffe** (city) Lake County
143	9.9	**Blacklick Estates** (CDP) Franklin County
143	9.9	**Delta** (village) Fulton County
143	9.9	**Mansfield** (city) Richland County
143	9.9	**Monroe** (city) Butler County
143	9.9	**Oak Harbor** (village) Ottawa County
143	9.9	**Portage Lakes** (CDP) Summit County
143	9.9	**Rittman** (city) Wayne County
143	9.9	**Tallmadge** (city) Summit County

Note: *This section ranks incorporated places and CDPs (Census Designated Places) with populations of 2,500 or more. Unincorporated postal areas were not considered. Please refer to the User Guide for additional information.*

Veterans

Top 150 Places Ranked in *Ascending* Order

State Rank	Percent	Place
1	2.4	**Oxford** (city) Butler County
2	2.6	**Cedarville** (village) Greene County
3	2.8	**Athens** (city) Athens County
4	3.1	**New Concord** (village) Muskingum County
5	3.2	**Silverton** (village) Hamilton County
6	3.7	**New Lexington** (village) Perry County
7	4.1	**Granville** (village) Licking County
7	4.1	**Pepper Pike** (city) Cuyahoga County
7	4.1	**Reminderville** (village) Summit County
7	4.1	**Waynesville** (village) Warren County
7	4.1	**Wyoming** (city) Hamilton County
12	4.2	**Ada** (village) Hardin County
12	4.2	**University Heights** (city) Cuyahoga County
14	4.3	**Bowling Green** (city) Wood County
15	4.6	**Cheviot** (city) Hamilton County
16	4.8	**Kent** (city) Portage County
16	4.8	**Solon** (city) Cuyahoga County
18	4.9	**Bexley** (city) Franklin County
19	5.1	**Dry Run** (CDP) Hamilton County
19	5.1	**Ottawa Hills** (village) Lucas County
21	5.2	**Woodlawn** (village) Hamilton County
22	5.3	**South Russell** (village) Geauga County
23	5.4	**Hudson** (city) Summit County
24	5.5	**Cleveland Heights** (city) Cuyahoga County
24	5.5	**North Zanesville** (CDP) Muskingum County
26	5.6	**Bainbridge** (CDP) Geauga County
26	5.6	**Sixteen Mile Stand** (CDP) Hamilton County
28	5.7	**New Albany** (city) Franklin County
29	5.8	**Grandview Heights** (city) Franklin County
29	5.8	**Mariemont** (village) Hamilton County
29	5.8	**Minster** (village) Auglaize County
29	5.8	**Sunbury** (village) Delaware County
33	5.9	**Cincinnati** (city) Hamilton County
33	5.9	**Kenwood** (CDP) Hamilton County
33	5.9	**Oberlin** (city) Lorain County
36	6.0	**Broadview Heights** (city) Cuyahoga County
36	6.0	**Moreland Hills** (village) Cuyahoga County
36	6.0	**Powell** (city) Delaware County
36	6.0	**Saint Henry** (village) Mercer County
40	6.1	**Bryan** (city) Williams County
40	6.1	**Perrysburg** (city) Wood County
40	6.1	**West Union** (village) Adams County
43	6.2	**Lakewood** (city) Cuyahoga County
43	6.2	**New Bremen** (village) Auglaize County
43	6.2	**Shaker Heights** (city) Cuyahoga County
43	6.2	**Wellington** (village) Lorain County
47	6.3	**Berea** (city) Cuyahoga County
47	6.3	**Golf Manor** (village) Hamilton County
47	6.3	**Greenhills** (village) Hamilton County
47	6.3	**The Village of Indian Hill** (city) Hamilton County
51	6.4	**Columbus** (city) Franklin County
51	6.4	**South Euclid** (city) Cuyahoga County
51	6.4	**Struthers** (city) Mahoning County
54	6.5	**Bluffton** (village) Allen County
54	6.5	**Gibsonburg** (village) Sandusky County
54	6.5	**Newton Falls** (village) Trumbull County
57	6.6	**Mount Healthy** (city) Hamilton County
57	6.6	**Sherwood** (CDP) Hamilton County
57	6.6	**Willard** (city) Huron County
60	6.7	**Beachwood** (city) Cuyahoga County
60	6.7	**Blue Ash** (city) Hamilton County
60	6.7	**Richfield** (village) Summit County
63	6.8	**Dublin** (city) Franklin County
63	6.8	**Lexington** (village) Richland County
65	6.9	**Madison** (village) Lake County
65	6.9	**Moraine** (city) Montgomery County
65	6.9	**North Royalton** (city) Cuyahoga County
65	6.9	**Salem Heights** (CDP) Hamilton County
65	6.9	**Upper Arlington** (city) Franklin County
70	7.0	**Avon** (city) Lorain County
70	7.0	**Cleveland** (city) Cuyahoga County
70	7.0	**Lebanon** (city) Warren County
70	7.0	**Parma Heights** (city) Cuyahoga County
70	7.0	**Ravenna** (city) Portage County
70	7.0	**Saint Bernard** (city) Hamilton County
70	7.0	**Twinsburg** (city) Summit County
77	7.1	**Beckett Ridge** (CDP) Butler County
77	7.1	**Carrollton** (village) Carroll County
77	7.1	**Martins Ferry** (city) Belmont County
77	7.1	**Northfield** (village) Summit County
77	7.1	**Urbana** (city) Champaign County
77	7.1	**Waterville** (city) Lucas County
83	7.2	**Bellevue** (city) Sandusky County
83	7.2	**Fruit Hill** (CDP) Hamilton County
83	7.2	**Mack** (CDP) Hamilton County
83	7.2	**Madeira** (city) Hamilton County
87	7.3	**Avon Lake** (city) Lorain County
87	7.3	**Crooksville** (village) Perry County
87	7.3	**Evendale** (village) Hamilton County
87	7.3	**Hilliard** (city) Franklin County
87	7.3	**Jackson** (city) Jackson County
87	7.3	**Mayfield Heights** (city) Cuyahoga County
93	7.4	**Archbold** (village) Fulton County
93	7.4	**Delhi Hills** (CDP) Hamilton County
93	7.4	**Lockland** (village) Hamilton County
93	7.4	**Munroe Falls** (city) Summit County
93	7.4	**Wheelersburg** (CDP) Scioto County
93	7.4	**Yellow Springs** (village) Greene County
99	7.5	**Highland Heights** (city) Cuyahoga County
99	7.5	**Sylvania** (city) Lucas County
99	7.5	**Toledo** (city) Lucas County
99	7.5	**Wooster** (city) Wayne County
103	7.6	**Bellefontaine** (city) Logan County
103	7.6	**Chagrin Falls** (village) Cuyahoga County
103	7.6	**Franklin** (city) Warren County
103	7.6	**Mason** (city) Warren County
103	7.6	**Millersburg** (village) Holmes County
103	7.6	**Montgomery** (city) Hamilton County
103	7.6	**Mount Carmel** (CDP) Clermont County
103	7.6	**Nelsonville** (city) Athens County
103	7.6	**Norwood** (city) Hamilton County
103	7.6	**Seven Hills** (city) Cuyahoga County
103	7.6	**Wapakoneta** (city) Auglaize County
114	7.7	**Bay Village** (city) Cuyahoga County
114	7.7	**Jefferson** (village) Ashtabula County
114	7.7	**Maumee** (city) Lucas County
114	7.7	**Worthington** (city) Franklin County
118	7.8	**Fairfield** (city) Butler County
118	7.8	**Fairview Park** (city) Cuyahoga County
118	7.8	**Green** (city) Summit County
118	7.8	**Lakemore** (village) Summit County
118	7.8	**Maple Heights** (city) Cuyahoga County
118	7.8	**Middletown** (city) Butler County
118	7.8	**Port Clinton** (city) Ottawa County
118	7.8	**Stow** (city) Summit County
126	7.9	**Bethel** (village) Clermont County
126	7.9	**Covedale** (CDP) Hamilton County
126	7.9	**Gahanna** (city) Franklin County
126	7.9	**Saint Marys** (city) Auglaize County
130	8.0	**Delshire** (CDP) Hamilton County
130	8.0	**Ironton** (city) Lawrence County
130	8.0	**North Olmsted** (city) Cuyahoga County
130	8.0	**Poland** (village) Mahoning County
130	8.0	**Wellston** (city) Jackson County
135	8.1	**Delaware** (city) Delaware County
135	8.1	**Loveland** (city) Hamilton County
135	8.1	**Middlefield** (village) Geauga County
135	8.1	**Mount Orab** (village) Brown County
135	8.1	**New London** (village) Huron County
135	8.1	**Newtown** (village) Hamilton County
135	8.1	**Painesville** (city) Lake County
135	8.1	**Richmond Heights** (city) Cuyahoga County
135	8.1	**Westerville** (city) Franklin County
135	8.1	**Willowick** (city) Lake County
145	8.2	**Alliance** (city) Stark County
145	8.2	**Mayfield** (village) Cuyahoga County
145	8.2	**The Plains** (CDP) Athens County
145	8.2	**Whitehall** (city) Franklin County
145	8.2	**Willoughby Hills** (city) Lake County
150	8.3	**Amberley** (village) Hamilton County

Note: *This section ranks incorporated places and CDPs (Census Designated Places) with populations of 2,500 or more. Unincorporated postal areas were not considered. Please refer to the User Guide for additional information.*

Ancestry: German

Top 150 Places Ranked in *Descending* Order

State Rank	Percent	Place
1	73.3	**Addison** (town) Washington County
2	71.0	**Jackson** (town) Washington County
3	70.1	**Dyersville** (city) Dubuque County
4	69.9	**Howards Grove** (village) Sheboygan County
5	69.4	**Chilton** (city) Calumet County
6	69.3	**Polk** (town) Washington County
7	69.1	**Kiel** (city) Manitowoc County
8	67.9	**Harrison** (town) Calumet County
8	67.9	**Saint Henry** (village) Mercer County
10	67.1	**Minster** (village) Auglaize County
11	66.8	**Trenton** (town) Washington County
12	66.1	**Wakefield** (township) Stearns County
13	65.8	**Empire** (town) Fond du Lac County
14	65.6	**Medford** (town) Taylor County
15	65.4	**Mayville** (city) Dodge County
15	65.4	**New Bremen** (village) Auglaize County
17	65.0	**Hartford** (town) Washington County
18	64.9	**Sheboygan** (town) Sheboygan County
19	64.6	**Coldwater** (village) Mercer County
20	64.3	**Springfield** (town) Dane County
21	64.2	**Barton** (town) Washington County
22	64.0	**Albany** (city) Stearns County
22	64.0	**Plymouth** (town) Sheboygan County
24	63.9	**Kewaskum** (village) Washington County
25	63.3	**Taycheedah** (town) Fond du Lac County
26	63.1	**Brillion** (city) Calumet County
27	63.0	**New Ulm** (city) Brown County
28	62.5	**Auburn** (town) Fond du Lac County
29	62.4	**Cold Spring** (city) Stearns County
30	62.3	**Plymouth** (city) Sheboygan County
31	61.9	**Mandan** (city) Morton County
32	61.8	**Center** (town) Outagamie County
33	61.5	**Miami Heights** (CDP) Hamilton County
34	61.4	**Breese** (city) Clinton County
34	61.4	**Hortonville** (village) Outagamie County
36	61.2	**Merrill** (town) Lincoln County
37	61.1	**Farmington** (town) Washington County
38	60.7	**Lodi** (town) Columbia County
39	59.6	**Fayette** (township) Juniata County
40	59.5	**Friendship** (town) Fond du Lac County
41	59.3	**Columbus** (city) Columbia County
41	59.3	**Sheboygan Falls** (city) Sheboygan County
43	59.2	**Carroll** (city) Carroll County
44	59.1	**Dale** (town) Outagamie County
44	59.1	**Saint Augusta** (city) Stearns County
46	58.9	**Caledonia** (city) Houston County
46	58.9	**Shelby** (town) La Crosse County
48	58.8	**Mukwa** (town) Waupaca County
49	58.7	**Merrill** (city) Lincoln County
50	58.6	**Germantown** (village) Washington County
51	58.5	**Lake Crystal** (city) Blue Earth County
51	58.5	**Oakland** (town) Jefferson County
53	58.4	**Clintonville** (city) Waupaca County
54	58.3	**Pelican** (town) Oneida County
54	58.3	**Saint Marys** (city) Elk County
56	58.1	**Horicon** (city) Dodge County
56	58.1	**Jackson** (village) Washington County
56	58.1	**Wausau** (town) Marathon County
59	58.0	**Beaver Dam** (town) Dodge County
60	57.9	**West Bend** (town) Washington County
61	57.7	**Richfield** (village) Washington County
61	57.7	**Saukville** (village) Ozaukee County
63	57.5	**Delhi Hills** (CDP) Hamilton County
64	57.4	**Grundy Center** (city) Grundy County
64	57.4	**Ripon** (city) Fond du Lac County
64	57.4	**West Bend** (city) Washington County
67	57.2	**Sherwood** (village) Calumet County
67	57.2	**Wescott** (town) Shawano County
69	57.0	**Merton** (village) Waukesha County
70	56.9	**Grafton** (town) Ozaukee County
70	56.9	**Lake Wisconsin** (CDP) Columbia County
72	56.8	**Ixonia** (town) Jefferson County
73	56.5	**Wales** (village) Waukesha County
74	56.4	**Ashippun** (town) Dodge County
74	56.4	**Sebewaing** (township) Huron County
76	56.3	**Delphos** (city) Allen County
76	56.3	**New Holstein** (city) Calumet County
78	56.2	**Alsace** (township) Berks County
78	56.2	**Mack** (CDP) Hamilton County
80	56.1	**Horace** (city) Cass County
80	56.1	**Monticello** (city) Jones County
80	56.1	**Sleepy Eye** (city) Brown County
83	56.0	**Milbank** (city) Grant County
83	56.0	**Sauk City** (village) Sauk County
83	56.0	**Washington** (township) Schuylkill County
86	55.9	**Jordan** (city) Scott County
86	55.9	**Oregon** (town) Dane County
86	55.9	**Sussex** (village) Waukesha County
89	55.8	**Centre** (township) Berks County
90	55.7	**Johnson Creek** (village) Jefferson County
90	55.7	**Sauk Centre** (city) Stearns County
92	55.4	**Belle Plaine** (city) Scott County
93	55.3	**Norwood Young America** (city) Carver County
94	55.2	**Lisbon** (town) Waukesha County
95	55.1	**Harrison** (city) Hamilton County
95	55.1	**Oak Harbor** (village) Ottawa County
97	55.0	**Hegins** (township) Schuylkill County
98	54.9	**Fond du Lac** (town) Fond du Lac County
98	54.9	**Stettin** (town) Marathon County
100	54.8	**Bismarck** (city) Burleigh County
100	54.8	**Brockway** (township) Stearns County
100	54.8	**Wayne** (city) Wayne County
103	54.7	**Beulah** (city) Mercer County
103	54.7	**Muskego** (city) Waukesha County
105	54.6	**Jamestown** (city) Stutsman County
106	54.3	**Lake Wazeecha** (CDP) Wood County
106	54.3	**Merton** (town) Waukesha County
108	54.1	**Cottage Grove** (town) Dane County
109	54.0	**Hays** (city) Ellis County
109	54.0	**Kronenwetter** (village) Marathon County
109	54.0	**Menasha** (town) Winnebago County
112	53.8	**De Witt** (city) Clinton County
113	53.7	**Denmark** (township) Tuscola County
113	53.7	**Millstadt** (village) Saint Clair County
113	53.7	**New Prague** (city) Scott County
116	53.6	**Marshfield** (city) Wood County
117	53.5	**Lincoln** (city) Burleigh County
117	53.5	**North Mankato** (city) Nicollet County
117	53.5	**Watertown** (city) Jefferson County
120	53.4	**Hallam** (borough) York County
120	53.4	**Spring Valley** (city) Fillmore County
122	53.3	**Glencoe** (city) McLeod County
122	53.3	**Oconomowoc** (town) Waukesha County
122	53.3	**Reedsburg** (city) Sauk County
125	53.2	**Poynette** (village) Columbia County
126	53.1	**Beaver Dam** (city) Dodge County
126	53.1	**Dent** (CDP) Hamilton County
126	53.1	**Winneconne** (village) Winnebago County
129	53.0	**Aberdeen** (city) Brown County
129	53.0	**Hartford** (city) Washington County
129	53.0	**Menasha** (city) Winnebago County
129	53.0	**Oshkosh** (city) Winnebago County
129	53.0	**Vernon** (town) Waukesha County
134	52.9	**Brookfield** (town) Waukesha County
134	52.9	**Frankenmuth** (city) Saginaw County
134	52.9	**Marysville** (city) Marshall County
134	52.9	**Pewaukee** (city) Waukesha County
134	52.9	**Rockland** (township) Berks County
139	52.8	**Algoma** (city) Kewaunee County
139	52.8	**West Union** (city) Fayette County
141	52.7	**Halifax** (township) Dauphin County
141	52.7	**Sparta** (town) Monroe County
143	52.6	**Cross Plains** (village) Dane County
144	52.5	**Alexandria** (township) Douglas County
144	52.5	**Rock Rapids** (city) Lyon County
144	52.5	**Wheatland** (town) Kenosha County
147	52.4	**North Fond du Lac** (village) Fond du Lac County
147	52.4	**Rothsville** (CDP) Lancaster County
149	52.3	**Reserve** (township) Allegheny County
150	52.2	**Covedale** (CDP) Hamilton County

Note: *This section ranks incorporated places and CDPs (Census Designated Places) with populations of 2,500 or more. Unincorporated postal areas were not considered. Please refer to the User Guide for additional information.*

Ancestry: English

Top 150 Places Ranked in *Descending* Order

State Rank	Percent	Place
1	77.3	**Hildale** (city) Washington County
2	66.0	**Colorado City** (town) Mohave County
3	47.8	**Monroe** (city) Sevier County
4	42.4	**McCall** (city) Valley County
5	42.3	**Manti** (city) Sanpete County
6	40.9	**Beaver** (city) Beaver County
6	40.9	**Highland** (city) Utah County
8	39.3	**Indian Springs** (CDP) Catoosa County
9	38.7	**Sheridan** (city) Grant County
10	38.0	**Alpine** (city) Utah County
11	37.9	**Hopkinton** (town) Merrimack County
12	37.7	**Mapleton** (city) Utah County
13	37.6	**Centerville** (city) Davis County
14	37.2	**Fruit Heights** (city) Davis County
15	36.4	**Cedar Hills** (city) Utah County
15	36.4	**Elk Ridge** (city) Utah County
17	36.3	**Hyde Park** (city) Cache County
18	36.1	**Boothbay** (town) Lincoln County
19	36.0	**Farr West** (city) Weber County
20	35.3	**Rockport** (town) Knox County
20	35.3	**Wellsville** (city) Cache County
22	34.5	**Mountain Green** (CDP) Morgan County
23	34.4	**Hooper** (city) Weber County
23	34.4	**South Beach** (CDP) Indian River County
25	34.2	**Tamworth** (town) Carroll County
26	34.1	**Providence** (city) Cache County
27	33.8	**Midway** (city) Wasatch County
28	33.6	**Bountiful** (city) Davis County
28	33.6	**Wolfeboro** (CDP) Carroll County
30	33.5	**Farmingdale** (town) Kennebec County
31	33.4	**Pleasant View** (city) Weber County
31	33.4	**Salem** (city) Utah County
33	33.2	**White Hall** (city) Jefferson County
34	33.1	**Poland** (town) Androscoggin County
35	33.0	**Freeport** (town) Cumberland County
35	33.0	**Hyrum** (city) Cache County
37	32.9	**Kaysville** (city) Davis County
37	32.9	**North Logan** (city) Cache County
39	32.4	**West Bountiful** (city) Davis County
40	32.3	**Morgan** (city) Morgan County
41	32.0	**Trent Woods** (town) Craven County
42	31.9	**Rexburg** (city) Madison County
43	31.8	**Bristol** (town) Lincoln County
44	31.6	**Yarmouth** (town) Cumberland County
45	31.5	**Harrison** (town) Cumberland County
46	31.4	**Holladay** (city) Salt Lake County
47	31.3	**Parowan** (city) Iron County
48	31.2	**Farmington** (city) Davis County
49	31.1	**Kennebunkport** (town) York County
50	30.6	**Oakland** (CDP) Kennebec County
51	30.5	**Herriman** (city) Salt Lake County
51	30.5	**Woolwich** (town) Sagadahoc County
51	30.5	**Yarmouth** (CDP) Cumberland County
54	30.4	**Charlestown** (town) Sullivan County
54	30.4	**South Jordan** (city) Salt Lake County
56	30.1	**American Fork** (city) Utah County
56	30.1	**Harpswell** (town) Cumberland County
56	30.1	**Oxford** (town) Oxford County
59	30.0	**Fryeburg** (town) Oxford County
59	30.0	**Saint George** (town) Knox County
61	29.9	**Chichester** (town) Merrimack County
62	29.8	**Santa Clara** (city) Washington County
62	29.8	**Woodstock** (town) Windsor County
64	29.7	**Monmouth** (town) Kennebec County
64	29.7	**Saint George** (city) Washington County
66	29.6	**Alamo** (town) Wheeler County
66	29.6	**Eagle Mountain** (city) Utah County
66	29.6	**Santaquin** (city) Utah County
69	29.5	**Bridgton** (town) Cumberland County
69	29.5	**Indian River Shores** (town) Indian River County
69	29.5	**Lehi** (city) Utah County
69	29.5	**Manchester** (town) Kennebec County
69	29.5	**Smithfield** (city) Cache County
74	29.4	**Wolfeboro** (town) Carroll County
75	29.3	**Kanab** (city) Kane County
76	29.2	**Camden** (town) Knox County
76	29.2	**Delta** (city) Millard County
76	29.2	**Spanish Fork** (city) Utah County
79	29.1	**Bluffdale** (city) Salt Lake County
79	29.1	**Richmond** (city) Cache County
81	29.0	**Lindon** (city) Utah County
81	29.0	**Preston** (city) Franklin County
81	29.0	**Waldoboro** (town) Lincoln County
84	28.8	**Grantsville** (city) Tooele County
84	28.8	**Madison** (town) Carroll County
84	28.8	**Oneida** (town) Scott County
87	28.7	**Springville** (city) Utah County
88	28.5	**Draper** (city) Salt Lake County
88	28.5	**Ivins** (city) Washington County
88	28.5	**Nephi** (city) Juab County
88	28.5	**North Ogden** (city) Weber County
92	28.4	**Riverton** (city) Salt Lake County
92	28.4	**White City** (CDP) Salt Lake County
94	28.2	**Lake San Marcos** (CDP) San Diego County
94	28.2	**Maeser** (CDP) Uintah County
96	28.1	**Hanover** (township) Jackson County
96	28.1	**Nibley** (city) Cache County
96	28.1	**Somerset** (township) Hillsdale County
99	28.0	**Saratoga Springs** (city) Utah County
99	28.0	**Snowflake** (town) Navajo County
99	28.0	**Thetford** (town) Orange County
99	28.0	**Woods Cross** (city) Davis County
103	27.9	**Cedar City** (city) Iron County
103	27.9	**Helena** (city) Telfair County
105	27.8	**Spring Arbor** (township) Jackson County
106	27.7	**East Bloomfield** (town) Ontario County
107	27.6	**Bethel** (town) Oxford County
107	27.6	**Nicholls** (city) Coffee County
107	27.6	**Syracuse** (city) Davis County
110	27.5	**Bradford** (town) Orange County
110	27.5	**Orem** (city) Utah County
110	27.5	**Sandy** (city) Salt Lake County
113	27.4	**Hillsborough** (town) Hillsborough County
113	27.4	**New Durham** (town) Strafford County
113	27.4	**Washington Terrace** (city) Weber County
116	27.3	**Bartlett** (town) Carroll County
116	27.3	**Pleasant Grove** (city) Utah County
118	27.2	**Hope** (township) Barry County
118	27.2	**North Yarmouth** (town) Cumberland County
118	27.2	**Plainfield** (town) Sullivan County
121	27.1	**Ammon** (city) Bonneville County
122	27.0	**Anson** (town) Somerset County
123	26.9	**Northfield** (town) Franklin County
124	26.8	**Harrisville** (city) Weber County
124	26.8	**South Eliot** (CDP) York County
124	26.8	**Walpole** (town) Cheshire County
127	26.7	**China** (town) Kennebec County
127	26.7	**Fillmore** (city) Millard County
127	26.7	**Jefferson** (town) Lincoln County
130	26.6	**Holden** (town) Penobscot County
131	26.5	**Lake Monticello** (CDP) Fluvanna County
132	26.4	**Strafford** (town) Strafford County
133	26.3	**Cottonwood Heights** (city) Salt Lake County
133	26.3	**Plain City** (city) Weber County
133	26.3	**Richmond** (town) Sagadahoc County
136	26.2	**Enoch** (city) Iron County
136	26.2	**Hartland** (town) Windsor County
136	26.2	**Horse Shoe** (CDP) Henderson County
136	26.2	**Pavilion** (town) Genesee County
140	26.1	**Arundel** (town) York County
140	26.1	**Bowdoin** (town) Sagadahoc County
140	26.1	**Fairfield** (town) Somerset County
140	26.1	**Little Compton** (town) Newport County
140	26.1	**Washington** (city) Washington County
145	26.0	**Cordova** (city) Valdez-Cordova Census Area
145	26.0	**Millcreek** (CDP) Salt Lake County
145	26.0	**West Haven** (city) Weber County
148	25.9	**Buxton** (town) York County
148	25.9	**McRae** (city) Telfair County
150	25.8	**Concord** (township) Jackson County

Note: *This section ranks incorporated places and CDPs (Census Designated Places) with populations of 2,500 or more. Unincorporated postal areas were not considered. Please refer to the User Guide for additional information.*

Ancestry: American

Top 150 Places Ranked in *Descending* Order

State Rank	Percent	Place
1	63.6	**La Follette** (city) Campbell County
2	61.6	**Gloverville** (CDP) Aiken County
3	58.6	**Healdton** (city) Carter County
4	57.7	**Caryville** (town) Campbell County
5	48.2	**Bonifay** (city) Holmes County
6	47.0	**Dresden** (town) Weakley County
6	47.0	**Summerville** (city) Chattooga County
8	46.2	**Clearwater** (CDP) Aiken County
9	45.9	**Pell City** (city) Saint Clair County
10	45.5	**New Tazewell** (town) Claiborne County
11	45.0	**Hartford** (city) Ohio County
12	44.7	**North Wilkesboro** (town) Wilkes County
13	44.5	**Treasure Lake** (CDP) Clearfield County
14	44.4	**Eaton** (town) Madison County
15	44.3	**Harrogate** (city) Claiborne County
16	43.8	**Rockwood** (city) Roane County
17	43.5	**Atkins** (city) Pope County
18	42.9	**Nassau Village-Ratliff** (CDP) Nassau County
19	42.7	**Wrightsville Beach** (town) New Hanover County
20	42.6	**Temple** (city) Carroll County
21	42.3	**Church Hill** (city) Hawkins County
21	42.3	**De Funiak Springs** (city) Walton County
23	41.5	**Morehead** (city) Rowan County
24	41.1	**Mascot** (CDP) Knox County
25	40.9	**Bremen** (city) Haralson County
26	40.8	**Junction City** (city) Boyle County
27	40.7	**Taylor** (town) Houston County
28	40.5	**Wilkesboro** (town) Wilkes County
29	40.1	**Margaret** (town) Saint Clair County
30	40.0	**Stanton** (city) Powell County
31	39.8	**Bean Station** (city) Grainger County
32	39.4	**Eagle Lake** (city) Polk County
33	39.3	**Weyers Cave** (CDP) Augusta County
34	39.1	**Bloomingdale** (CDP) Sullivan County
35	39.0	**Chincoteague** (town) Accomack County
36	38.7	**Jan Phyl Village** (CDP) Polk County
37	38.2	**Georgetown** (city) Vermilion County
38	38.1	**Oliver Springs** (town) Anderson County
39	38.0	**Algood** (city) Putnam County
40	37.8	**Hilliard** (town) Nassau County
41	37.4	**Mount Carmel** (CDP) Clermont County
41	37.4	**West Tisbury** (town) Dukes County
41	37.4	**Williamsburg** (village) Clermont County
44	37.3	**Somerset** (city) Pulaski County
45	37.2	**Bethel** (village) Clermont County
45	37.2	**Dawson Springs** (city) Hopkins County
45	37.2	**Harlem** (CDP) Hendry County
45	37.2	**Stanford** (city) Lincoln County
49	37.0	**Gray Summit** (CDP) Franklin County
50	36.7	**Hooks** (city) Bowie County
51	36.6	**Cullowhee** (CDP) Jackson County
52	36.3	**Lancaster** (city) Garrard County
53	36.2	**Brooks** (CDP) Bullitt County
53	36.2	**Livingston** (town) Overton County
55	35.8	**Blue Hill** (town) Hancock County
56	35.7	**Bayou Vista** (CDP) Saint Mary Parish
56	35.7	**Waynesville** (town) Haywood County
58	35.6	**Blennerhassett** (CDP) Wood County
59	35.4	**Beaver Dam** (city) Ohio County
59	35.4	**Colonial Heights** (CDP) Sullivan County
61	35.3	**Lake of the Woods** (CDP) Champaign County
62	35.0	**Mount Vernon** (city) Rockcastle County
63	34.7	**Broadway** (town) Rockingham County
63	34.7	**Middlesborough** (city) Bell County
65	34.6	**Cookeville** (city) Putnam County
66	34.5	**Madison** (town) Madison County
66	34.5	**Sylva** (town) Jackson County
68	34.4	**Inverness Highlands North** (CDP) Citrus County
68	34.4	**Pearisburg** (town) Giles County
70	34.3	**Shepherdsville** (city) Bullitt County
71	34.2	**Lone Grove** (city) Carter County
72	34.0	**Pike Road** (town) Montgomery County
73	33.9	**Withamsville** (CDP) Clermont County
74	33.8	**Grantville** (city) Coweta County
75	33.6	**Burnettown** (town) Aiken County
75	33.6	**Harriman** (city) Roane County
75	33.6	**Rogersville** (town) Hawkins County
78	33.5	**Canton** (town) Haywood County
78	33.5	**Galena** (city) Cherokee County
80	33.4	**LaFayette** (city) Walker County
81	33.3	**Ball** (town) Rapides Parish
82	33.2	**Amelia** (village) Clermont County
82	33.2	**Dundee** (town) Polk County
82	33.2	**Oak Grove** (CDP) Washington County
85	33.1	**Park City** (CDP) Lincoln County
86	33.0	**England** (city) Lonoke County
86	33.0	**Tallapoosa** (city) Haralson County
88	32.7	**Fairview** (CDP) Walker County
88	32.7	**Honea Path** (town) Anderson County
90	32.6	**Miramar Beach** (CDP) Walton County
91	32.5	**Crab Orchard** (CDP) Raleigh County
92	32.4	**Edgartown** (town) Dukes County
93	32.3	**Flemingsburg** (city) Fleming County
94	32.1	**Ward** (city) Lonoke County
94	32.1	**West Liberty** (city) Morgan County
96	32.0	**Mountain City** (town) Johnson County
96	32.0	**Pittsburg** (city) Crawford County
96	32.0	**Robertsdale** (city) Baldwin County
96	32.0	**Sandy** (township) Clearfield County
100	31.9	**Jena** (town) La Salle Parish
100	31.9	**Suncoast Estates** (CDP) Lee County
102	31.8	**Chelan** (city) Chelan County
102	31.8	**Mary Esther** (city) Okaloosa County
102	31.8	**Sullivan** (city) Franklin County
105	31.7	**North Terre Haute** (CDP) Vigo County
106	31.6	**Unicoi** (town) Unicoi County
107	31.5	**Mills** (town) Natrona County
108	31.4	**Haynesville** (town) Claiborne Parish
108	31.4	**Richlands** (town) Tazewell County
110	31.3	**Hamilton** (town) Madison County
111	31.2	**Mount Carmel** (town) Hawkins County
111	31.2	**Moyock** (CDP) Currituck County
113	31.1	**Cypress Gardens** (CDP) Polk County
113	31.1	**Pigeon Forge** (city) Sevier County
115	30.9	**Beacon Square** (CDP) Pasco County
116	30.8	**Bayshore** (CDP) New Hanover County
116	30.8	**Hannahs Mill** (CDP) Upson County
116	30.8	**Odenville** (town) Saint Clair County
119	30.7	**Crestview** (city) Okaloosa County
119	30.7	**Westville** (village) Vermilion County
121	30.6	**Chipley** (city) Washington County
121	30.6	**Greenville** (city) Muhlenberg County
123	30.4	**Wellsville** (village) Columbiana County
124	30.3	**Bradford** (township) Clearfield County
125	30.2	**Red Bay** (city) Franklin County
126	30.1	**Inwood** (CDP) Polk County
127	30.0	**Byron** (city) Peach County
127	30.0	**Destin** (city) Okaloosa County
129	29.9	**Central City** (city) Muhlenberg County
130	29.8	**Owensboro** (city) Daviess County
131	29.7	**Clinton** (city) Anderson County
131	29.7	**Hamilton** (city) Marion County
131	29.7	**Monterey** (town) Putnam County
131	29.7	**Timberville** (town) Rockingham County
131	29.7	**Yulee** (CDP) Nassau County
136	29.6	**Hillview** (city) Bullitt County
136	29.6	**Moody** (city) Saint Clair County
136	29.6	**Niceville** (city) Okaloosa County
136	29.6	**Peru** (city) Miami County
136	29.6	**Salem** (city) Washington County
141	29.5	**Bawcomville** (CDP) Ouachita Parish
141	29.5	**Bessemer City** (city) Gaston County
141	29.5	**Selmer** (town) McNairy County
144	29.4	**Fort Scott** (city) Bourbon County
144	29.4	**Lake Lorraine** (CDP) Okaloosa County
144	29.4	**Lynchburg-Moore County** (metropolitan government) Moore County
144	29.4	**Malabar** (town) Brevard County
144	29.4	**Mount Orab** (village) Brown County
149	29.3	**Winchester** (city) Clark County
150	29.2	**Fort Valley** (city) Peach County

Note: *This section ranks incorporated places and CDPs (Census Designated Places) with populations of 2,500 or more. Unincorporated postal areas were not considered. Please refer to the User Guide for additional information.*

Ancestry: Irish

Top 150 Places Ranked in *Descending* Order

State Rank	Percent	Place
1	49.2	**Pearl River** (CDP) Rockland County
2	48.5	**Walpole** (CDP) Norfolk County
3	47.9	**Spring Lake Heights** (borough) Monmouth County
4	47.4	**Ocean Bluff-Brant Rock** (CDP) Plymouth County
4	47.4	**Rockledge** (borough) Montgomery County
6	46.8	**Green Harbor-Cedar Crest** (CDP) Plymouth County
7	46.7	**Scituate** (town) Plymouth County
8	46.0	**Scituate** (CDP) Plymouth County
9	45.7	**Hanover** (town) Plymouth County
10	45.5	**North Scituate** (CDP) Plymouth County
11	45.1	**Marshfield** (town) Plymouth County
12	44.3	**Ridley Park** (borough) Delaware County
13	44.0	**North Wildwood** (city) Cape May County
13	44.0	**Norwell** (town) Plymouth County
15	43.6	**Glenside** (CDP) Montgomery County
16	43.1	**North Middletown** (CDP) Monmouth County
17	42.8	**Littleton Common** (CDP) Middlesex County
18	42.4	**Oak Valley** (CDP) Gloucester County
19	42.3	**Braintree Town** (city) Norfolk County
20	42.2	**Whitman** (town) Plymouth County
21	41.9	**East Sandwich** (CDP) Barnstable County
22	41.8	**Walpole** (town) Norfolk County
23	41.7	**Brielle** (borough) Monmouth County
23	41.7	**Manasquan** (borough) Monmouth County
25	41.6	**Churchville** (CDP) Bucks County
26	41.3	**Spring Lake** (borough) Monmouth County
27	41.2	**Marshfield** (CDP) Plymouth County
27	41.2	**Springfield** (township) Delaware County
29	41.1	**Glenolden** (borough) Delaware County
30	41.0	**Abington** (cdp/town) Plymouth County
31	40.9	**Eddystone** (borough) Delaware County
31	40.9	**National Park** (borough) Gloucester County
33	40.5	**Cohasset** (town) Norfolk County
34	40.4	**Norwood** (borough) Delaware County
35	40.3	**Hingham** (town) Plymouth County
36	40.2	**Weymouth Town** (city) Norfolk County
37	40.1	**Wynantskill** (CDP) Rensselaer County
38	39.9	**Sayville** (CDP) Suffolk County
39	39.8	**Fairview** (CDP) Monmouth County
40	39.7	**East Bridgewater** (town) Plymouth County
40	39.7	**Folsom** (CDP) Delaware County
40	39.7	**Nahant** (cdp/town) Essex County
43	39.6	**Foxborough** (town) Norfolk County
44	39.4	**Bridgewater** (CDP) Plymouth County
44	39.4	**Mystic Island** (CDP) Ocean County
44	39.4	**Tinicum** (township) Delaware County
47	39.0	**Notre Dame** (CDP) Saint Joseph County
48	38.6	**Barrington** (borough) Camden County
48	38.6	**Gloucester City** (city) Camden County
48	38.6	**Rockland** (town) Plymouth County
51	38.3	**East Douglas** (CDP) Worcester County
51	38.3	**Hull** (cdp/town) Plymouth County
53	38.2	**Haverford** (township) Delaware County
54	38.1	**North Reading** (town) Middlesex County
55	37.9	**Haddon Heights** (borough) Camden County
55	37.9	**Hanson** (town) Plymouth County
55	37.9	**Woodbury Heights** (borough) Gloucester County
58	37.8	**Milton** (cdp/town) Norfolk County
59	37.6	**Highlands** (borough) Monmouth County
60	37.5	**Hingham** (CDP) Plymouth County
61	37.3	**Buzzards Bay** (CDP) Barnstable County
62	37.2	**Ridley** (township) Delaware County
63	37.1	**Canton** (town) Norfolk County
64	37.0	**Holbrook** (cdp/town) Norfolk County
65	36.9	**Garden City** (village) Nassau County
66	36.8	**Foxborough** (CDP) Norfolk County
67	36.6	**Kingston** (town) Plymouth County
68	36.5	**Drexel Hill** (CDP) Delaware County
69	36.4	**Ramtown** (CDP) Monmouth County
70	36.2	**Bridgewater** (town) Plymouth County
70	36.2	**West Brandywine** (township) Chester County
72	36.1	**Atkinson** (town) Rockingham County
72	36.1	**Wanamassa** (CDP) Monmouth County
74	36.0	**Norwood** (cdp/town) Norfolk County
75	35.9	**Western Springs** (village) Cook County
76	35.8	**Upton** (CDP) Worcester County
76	35.8	**Westvale** (CDP) Onondaga County
78	35.7	**East Greenbush** (CDP) Rensselaer County
79	35.6	**Avon** (town) Norfolk County
79	35.6	**Chester** (city) Hancock County
79	35.6	**Medfield** (CDP) Norfolk County
79	35.6	**Wakefield** (cdp/town) Middlesex County
83	35.5	**Aston** (township) Delaware County
84	35.4	**Green Island** (town/village) Albany County
85	35.3	**Duxbury** (town) Plymouth County
85	35.3	**Fair Haven** (borough) Monmouth County
87	35.2	**Connerton** (CDP) Pasco County
87	35.2	**Hopedale** (CDP) Worcester County
87	35.2	**Mansfield Center** (CDP) Bristol County
90	35.1	**Shrewsbury** (borough) Monmouth County
90	35.1	**Wilmington** (cdp/town) Middlesex County
92	35.0	**North Hampton** (town) Rockingham County
92	35.0	**Turnersville** (CDP) Gloucester County
94	34.9	**Aldan** (borough) Delaware County
94	34.9	**Audubon** (borough) Camden County
94	34.9	**Blue Point** (CDP) Suffolk County
94	34.9	**North Cape May** (CDP) Cape May County
94	34.9	**North Plymouth** (CDP) Plymouth County
99	34.8	**Wrentham** (town) Norfolk County
100	34.7	**Skaneateles** (village) Onondaga County
100	34.7	**West Bridgewater** (town) Plymouth County
102	34.6	**Little Egg Harbor** (township) Ocean County
102	34.6	**Prospect Park** (borough) Delaware County
104	34.5	**East Islip** (CDP) Suffolk County
104	34.5	**Plainville** (town) Norfolk County
104	34.5	**Washington** (town) Dutchess County
107	34.4	**Glendora** (CDP) Camden County
107	34.4	**Newtown** (township) Delaware County
107	34.4	**Tyngsborough** (town) Middlesex County
107	34.4	**Wall** (township) Monmouth County
111	34.3	**Port Monmouth** (CDP) Monmouth County
111	34.3	**Tewksbury** (town) Middlesex County
113	34.2	**Mansfield** (town) Bristol County
114	34.1	**North Wales** (borough) Montgomery County
114	34.1	**Pembroke** (town) Plymouth County
114	34.1	**Rockville Centre** (village) Nassau County
114	34.1	**Seabrook** (town) Rockingham County
118	34.0	**Cape Neddick** (CDP) York County
118	34.0	**Village Green-Green Ridge** (CDP) Delaware County
118	34.0	**Wanakah** (CDP) Erie County
118	34.0	**West Sayville** (CDP) Suffolk County
122	33.9	**Bellingham** (town) Norfolk County
122	33.9	**Clinton** (town) Dutchess County
124	33.8	**Haddon** (township) Camden County
124	33.8	**Marcellus** (town) Onondaga County
126	33.7	**Roseland** (borough) Essex County
127	33.6	**Bellingham** (CDP) Norfolk County
127	33.6	**Plymouth** (town) Plymouth County
129	33.5	**Bethel** (township) Delaware County
129	33.5	**Centreville** (town) Queen Anne's County
129	33.5	**East Bradford** (township) Chester County
129	33.5	**Gilford** (town) Belknap County
129	33.5	**Haddonfield** (borough) Camden County
129	33.5	**Medford Lakes** (borough) Burlington County
129	33.5	**Norton** (town) Bristol County
136	33.4	**Williston Park** (village) Nassau County
137	33.3	**Atlantic Highlands** (borough) Monmouth County
137	33.3	**Clementon** (borough) Camden County
137	33.3	**Hopkinton** (CDP) Middlesex County
137	33.3	**Melrose** (city) Middlesex County
137	33.3	**Trevose** (CDP) Bucks County
142	33.2	**Brightwaters** (village) Suffolk County
142	33.2	**Clinton** (town) Worcester County
142	33.2	**Horsham** (CDP) Montgomery County
142	33.2	**Massapequa Park** (village) Nassau County
142	33.2	**Medfield** (town) Norfolk County
142	33.2	**Rumson** (borough) Monmouth County
148	33.1	**Blauvelt** (CDP) Rockland County
148	33.1	**Clinton** (CDP) Worcester County
148	33.1	**New Britain** (borough) Bucks County

Note: *This section ranks incorporated places and CDPs (Census Designated Places) with populations of 2,500 or more. Unincorporated postal areas were not considered. Please refer to the User Guide for additional information.*

Ancestry: Italian

Top 150 Places Ranked in *Descending* Order

State Rank	Percent	Place
1	50.3	**Fairfield** (township) Essex County
2	49.5	**Johnston** (town) Providence County
3	47.8	**North Massapequa** (CDP) Nassau County
4	46.9	**Thornwood** (CDP) Westchester County
5	46.7	**Halesite** (CDP) Suffolk County
6	46.3	**Beach Haven West** (CDP) Ocean County
7	45.8	**Eastchester** (CDP) Westchester County
8	45.6	**Massapequa** (CDP) Nassau County
9	44.4	**Massapequa Park** (village) Nassau County
10	43.9	**North Branford** (town) New Haven County
11	43.7	**Hawthorne** (CDP) Westchester County
12	43.6	**East Haven** (cdp/town) New Haven County
13	43.2	**Hammonton** (town) Atlantic County
14	43.1	**Watertown** (CDP) Litchfield County
15	43.0	**Turnersville** (CDP) Gloucester County
16	42.3	**West Islip** (CDP) Suffolk County
17	42.1	**Frankfort** (village) Herkimer County
18	41.3	**East Hanover** (township) Morris County
18	41.3	**East Norwich** (CDP) Nassau County
20	41.2	**Islip Terrace** (CDP) Suffolk County
20	41.2	**North Haven** (cdp/town) New Haven County
22	41.1	**Glendora** (CDP) Camden County
23	40.8	**Cedar Grove** (township) Essex County
23	40.8	**Jefferson Valley-Yorktown** (CDP) Westchester County
23	40.8	**Miller Place** (CDP) Suffolk County
26	40.7	**Marlboro** (CDP) Ulster County
27	40.6	**Wood-Ridge** (borough) Bergen County
28	40.4	**Franklin Square** (CDP) Nassau County
29	40.3	**Nesconset** (CDP) Suffolk County
30	40.1	**Gibbstown** (CDP) Gloucester County
31	40.0	**Bayville** (village) Nassau County
32	39.7	**Richwood** (CDP) Gloucester County
33	39.6	**Saint James** (CDP) Suffolk County
34	39.1	**Lake Grove** (village) Suffolk County
35	38.9	**Dunmore** (borough) Lackawanna County
35	38.9	**North Providence** (town) Providence County
37	38.5	**Saugus** (cdp/town) Essex County
38	38.4	**Blackwood** (CDP) Camden County
38	38.4	**Jenkins** (township) Luzerne County
40	38.3	**South Farmingdale** (CDP) Nassau County
41	38.0	**East Islip** (CDP) Suffolk County
41	38.0	**Seaford** (CDP) Nassau County
43	37.9	**West Pittston** (borough) Luzerne County
44	37.8	**Old Forge** (borough) Lackawanna County
44	37.8	**Smithtown** (CDP) Suffolk County
46	37.5	**Prospect** (town) New Haven County
47	37.4	**Plainedge** (CDP) Nassau County
48	37.3	**Greenwich** (township) Gloucester County
48	37.3	**Manorville** (CDP) Suffolk County
50	37.0	**Watertown** (town) Litchfield County
51	36.4	**Smithtown** (town) Suffolk County
52	36.3	**Nutley** (township) Essex County
52	36.3	**Pittston** (city) Luzerne County
54	36.1	**Hauppauge** (CDP) Suffolk County
54	36.1	**Ronkonkoma** (CDP) Suffolk County
56	36.0	**Jessup** (borough) Lackawanna County
56	36.0	**Lyncourt** (CDP) Onondaga County
56	36.0	**Washington** (township) Gloucester County
59	35.9	**Eastchester** (town) Westchester County
59	35.9	**Frankfort** (town) Herkimer County
59	35.9	**Verona** (township) Essex County
62	35.8	**Barnegat** (CDP) Ocean County
62	35.8	**Centerport** (CDP) Suffolk County
64	35.7	**North Great River** (CDP) Suffolk County
64	35.7	**Oakdale** (CDP) Suffolk County
66	35.4	**North Babylon** (CDP) Suffolk County
66	35.4	**Pelham Manor** (village) Westchester County
68	35.2	**Bohemia** (CDP) Suffolk County
68	35.2	**Union Vale** (town) Dutchess County
68	35.2	**Yorktown** (town) Westchester County
71	35.1	**Center Moriches** (CDP) Suffolk County
71	35.1	**Selden** (CDP) Suffolk County
73	35.0	**Caldwell** (borough) Essex County
74	34.8	**Holbrook** (CDP) Suffolk County
74	34.8	**Holtsville** (CDP) Suffolk County
74	34.8	**Port Jefferson Station** (CDP) Suffolk County
77	34.7	**Holiday City-Berkeley** (CDP) Ocean County
77	34.7	**Oyster Bay** (CDP) Nassau County
77	34.7	**Stoneham** (cdp/town) Middlesex County
80	34.6	**Malverne** (village) Nassau County
81	34.5	**Brightwaters** (village) Suffolk County
81	34.5	**Hasbrouck Heights** (borough) Bergen County
81	34.5	**Lynnfield** (cdp/town) Essex County
84	34.4	**Bethpage** (CDP) Nassau County
84	34.4	**East Fishkill** (town) Dutchess County
84	34.4	**East Freehold** (CDP) Monmouth County
84	34.4	**Hazlet** (township) Monmouth County
84	34.4	**Kenmore** (village) Erie County
89	34.2	**Farmingville** (CDP) Suffolk County
89	34.2	**Moonachie** (borough) Bergen County
89	34.2	**Oceanport** (borough) Monmouth County
92	34.1	**Glen Head** (CDP) Nassau County
92	34.1	**Lacey** (township) Ocean County
94	33.9	**Bayport** (CDP) Suffolk County
94	33.9	**Deer Park** (CDP) Suffolk County
94	33.9	**Garden City South** (CDP) Nassau County
94	33.9	**Ocean Acres** (CDP) Ocean County
94	33.9	**West Babylon** (CDP) Suffolk County
99	33.8	**Carmel** (town) Putnam County
99	33.8	**Commack** (CDP) Suffolk County
99	33.8	**Neshannock** (township) Lawrence County
99	33.8	**Old Brookville** (village) Nassau County
103	33.7	**Blue Point** (CDP) Suffolk County
103	33.7	**Centereach** (CDP) Suffolk County
103	33.7	**Fort Salonga** (CDP) Suffolk County
103	33.7	**Kings Park** (CDP) Suffolk County
103	33.7	**Oakland** (borough) Bergen County
103	33.7	**Putnam Lake** (CDP) Putnam County
109	33.6	**Kensington** (CDP) Hartford County
109	33.6	**Lindenhurst** (village) Suffolk County
109	33.6	**Mechanicville** (city) Saratoga County
109	33.6	**Shirley** (CDP) Suffolk County
109	33.6	**Woodland Park** (borough) Passaic County
114	33.5	**Netcong** (borough) Morris County
115	33.3	**Elwood** (CDP) Suffolk County
115	33.3	**Mount Arlington** (borough) Morris County
115	33.3	**Somers** (town) Westchester County
115	33.3	**South Hackensack** (township) Bergen County
119	33.2	**Marlborough** (town) Ulster County
120	33.1	**Babylon** (village) Suffolk County
120	33.1	**Pine Lake Park** (CDP) Ocean County
120	33.1	**West Caldwell** (township) Essex County
123	33.0	**Lake Ronkonkoma** (CDP) Suffolk County
123	33.0	**Rotterdam** (CDP) Schenectady County
123	33.0	**Toms River** (township) Ocean County
126	32.9	**East Massapequa** (CDP) Nassau County
127	32.8	**Branford** (town) New Haven County
127	32.8	**North Patchogue** (CDP) Suffolk County
127	32.8	**Oakville** (CDP) Litchfield County
130	32.7	**Berkeley** (township) Ocean County
130	32.7	**Toms River** (CDP) Ocean County
130	32.7	**Washington** (township) Bergen County
133	32.6	**Greece** (CDP) Monroe County
133	32.6	**Mount Sinai** (CDP) Suffolk County
133	32.6	**Terryville** (CDP) Suffolk County
133	32.6	**Yaphank** (CDP) Suffolk County
137	32.5	**Emerson** (borough) Bergen County
137	32.5	**Point Pleasant** (borough) Ocean County
137	32.5	**West Long Branch** (borough) Monmouth County
140	32.4	**Cranston** (city) Providence County
140	32.4	**Fairview** (CDP) Monmouth County
140	32.4	**Lincroft** (CDP) Monmouth County
140	32.4	**Stafford** (township) Ocean County
140	32.4	**Totowa** (borough) Passaic County
140	32.4	**Wolcott** (town) New Haven County
146	32.3	**Middletown** (township) Monmouth County
147	32.2	**Berlin** (town) Hartford County
147	32.2	**Branford Center** (CDP) New Haven County
147	32.2	**Garden City** (village) Nassau County
147	32.2	**Highland Lakes** (CDP) Sussex County

Note: *This section ranks incorporated places and CDPs (Census Designated Places) with populations of 2,500 or more. Unincorporated postal areas were not considered. Please refer to the User Guide for additional information.*

Employment: Management, Business, and Financial Occupations

Top 150 Places Ranked in *Descending* Order

State Rank	Percent	Place
1	36.3	**Moreland Hills** (village) Cuyahoga County
2	35.4	**The Village of Indian Hill** (city) Hamilton County
3	32.2	**New Albany** (city) Franklin County
4	31.3	**Dry Run** (CDP) Hamilton County
5	31.1	**Powell** (city) Delaware County
6	30.9	**Beachwood** (city) Cuyahoga County
7	30.8	**Chagrin Falls** (village) Cuyahoga County
8	30.3	**Hudson** (city) Summit County
9	30.1	**Dublin** (city) Franklin County
10	30.0	**South Russell** (village) Geauga County
11	29.2	**Turpin Hills** (CDP) Hamilton County
12	28.9	**Amberley** (village) Hamilton County
13	28.2	**Grandview Heights** (city) Franklin County
13	28.2	**Ottawa Hills** (village) Lucas County
15	28.1	**Montgomery** (city) Hamilton County
16	27.8	**Wyoming** (city) Hamilton County
17	27.0	**Dillonvale** (CDP) Hamilton County
17	27.0	**Sixteen Mile Stand** (CDP) Hamilton County
19	26.8	**Rocky River** (city) Cuyahoga County
20	26.7	**Evendale** (village) Hamilton County
21	26.6	**Bay Village** (city) Cuyahoga County
21	26.6	**Mason** (city) Warren County
23	26.5	**Four Bridges** (CDP) Butler County
24	26.1	**Bexley** (city) Franklin County
25	25.9	**Oakwood** (city) Montgomery County
26	25.8	**Independence** (city) Cuyahoga County
27	25.7	**Day Heights** (CDP) Clermont County
27	25.7	**Montrose-Ghent** (CDP) Summit County
29	25.3	**Brecksville** (city) Cuyahoga County
29	25.3	**Upper Arlington** (city) Franklin County
29	25.3	**Westerville** (city) Franklin County
32	25.2	**Westlake** (city) Cuyahoga County
33	25.1	**Aurora** (city) Portage County
34	25.0	**Madeira** (city) Hamilton County
35	24.7	**Orange** (village) Cuyahoga County
36	24.6	**Beckett Ridge** (CDP) Butler County
36	24.6	**Forestville** (CDP) Hamilton County
38	24.5	**Newtown** (village) Hamilton County
39	24.4	**Reminderville** (village) Summit County
39	24.4	**Richfield** (village) Summit County
41	24.3	**Canal Winchester** (city) Franklin County
41	24.3	**Plain City** (village) Madison County
41	24.3	**South Lebanon** (village) Warren County
44	24.2	**Perrysburg** (city) Wood County
45	24.0	**Gahanna** (city) Franklin County
46	23.6	**Worthington** (city) Franklin County
47	23.5	**Pepper Pike** (city) Cuyahoga County
47	23.5	**Solon** (city) Cuyahoga County
49	23.4	**Avon** (city) Lorain County
50	23.3	**Highland Heights** (city) Cuyahoga County
51	23.2	**Avon Lake** (city) Lorain County
52	23.1	**Dry Ridge** (CDP) Hamilton County
53	23.0	**Mariemont** (village) Hamilton County
53	23.0	**Springboro** (city) Warren County
55	22.8	**Fruit Hill** (CDP) Hamilton County
55	22.8	**Hilliard** (city) Franklin County
55	22.8	**Kenwood** (CDP) Hamilton County
58	22.3	**Sunbury** (village) Delaware County
59	22.1	**Beavercreek** (city) Greene County
60	21.8	**Strongsville** (city) Cuyahoga County
61	21.3	**Miami Heights** (CDP) Hamilton County
62	21.2	**Munroe Falls** (city) Summit County
63	21.0	**Macedonia** (city) Summit County
63	21.0	**Twinsburg** (city) Summit County
65	20.8	**Monroe** (city) Butler County
66	20.6	**Broadview Heights** (city) Cuyahoga County
67	20.5	**Mayfield** (village) Cuyahoga County
68	20.4	**Shaker Heights** (city) Cuyahoga County
69	20.3	**Landen** (CDP) Warren County
70	20.2	**North Royalton** (city) Cuyahoga County
70	20.2	**Sylvania** (city) Lucas County
72	20.0	**Canfield** (city) Mahoning County
72	20.0	**Centerville** (city) Montgomery County
72	20.0	**Loveland** (city) Hamilton County
72	20.0	**Mack** (CDP) Hamilton County
72	20.0	**University Heights** (city) Cuyahoga County
77	19.9	**Seven Hills** (city) Cuyahoga County
78	19.8	**Salem Heights** (CDP) Hamilton County
79	19.7	**Kirtland** (city) Lake County
79	19.7	**Monfort Heights** (CDP) Hamilton County
81	19.6	**Blue Ash** (city) Hamilton County
82	19.4	**Pickerington** (city) Fairfield County
83	19.1	**Uniontown** (CDP) Stark County
84	18.6	**Lyndhurst** (city) Cuyahoga County
84	18.6	**Sharonville** (city) Hamilton County
84	18.6	**Sherwood** (CDP) Hamilton County
87	18.4	**Fairlawn** (city) Summit County
87	18.4	**Huber Ridge** (CDP) Franklin County
89	18.2	**Covedale** (CDP) Hamilton County
89	18.2	**Deer Park** (city) Hamilton County
89	18.2	**Whitehouse** (village) Lucas County
92	18.0	**Lakewood** (city) Cuyahoga County
92	18.0	**Pataskala** (city) Licking County
94	17.9	**Sheffield** (village) Lorain County
95	17.8	**Mentor** (city) Lake County
95	17.8	**Middleburg Heights** (city) Cuyahoga County
95	17.8	**Stow** (city) Summit County
98	17.7	**Dent** (CDP) Hamilton County
98	17.7	**Huron** (city) Erie County
98	17.7	**New Bremen** (village) Auglaize County
98	17.7	**Taylor Creek** (CDP) Hamilton County
102	17.6	**Wadsworth** (city) Medina County
103	17.5	**Bainbridge** (CDP) Geauga County
104	17.4	**Granville** (village) Licking County
104	17.4	**Olmsted Falls** (city) Cuyahoga County
106	17.3	**Bluffton** (village) Allen County
106	17.3	**South Point** (village) Lawrence County
106	17.3	**Summerside** (CDP) Clermont County
109	17.2	**Greenhills** (village) Hamilton County
109	17.2	**Lake Darby** (CDP) Franklin County
111	17.1	**Apple Valley** (CDP) Knox County
111	17.1	**Withamsville** (CDP) Clermont County
113	17.0	**Waterville** (city) Lucas County
114	16.9	**Bellbrook** (city) Greene County
115	16.8	**Fairview Park** (city) Cuyahoga County
116	16.6	**Devola** (CDP) Washington County
116	16.6	**Doylestown** (village) Wayne County
116	16.6	**Mayfield Heights** (city) Cuyahoga County
119	16.3	**North Ridgeville** (city) Lorain County
120	16.2	**Beechwood Trails** (CDP) Licking County
120	16.2	**Miamisburg** (city) Montgomery County
122	15.8	**Ashville** (village) Pickaway County
122	15.8	**Chardon** (city) Geauga County
122	15.8	**Green** (city) Summit County
122	15.8	**Marysville** (city) Union County
122	15.8	**Portage Lakes** (CDP) Summit County
127	15.7	**Clayton** (city) Montgomery County
127	15.7	**Cleveland Heights** (city) Cuyahoga County
127	15.7	**Columbiana** (city) Columbiana County
127	15.7	**Cortland** (city) Trumbull County
127	15.7	**Medina** (city) Medina County
127	15.7	**North Kingsville** (village) Ashtabula County
127	15.7	**Oak Harbor** (village) Ottawa County
134	15.6	**Champion Heights** (CDP) Trumbull County
134	15.6	**Cleves** (village) Hamilton County
134	15.6	**Mount Repose** (CDP) Clermont County
134	15.6	**Versailles** (village) Darke County
138	15.5	**Columbus** (city) Franklin County
138	15.5	**Delaware** (city) Delaware County
140	15.4	**Fairfield** (city) Butler County
140	15.4	**Findlay** (city) Hancock County
140	15.4	**Norwood** (city) Hamilton County
143	15.1	**Mulberry** (CDP) Clermont County
144	15.0	**Greentown** (CDP) Stark County
144	15.0	**South Euclid** (city) Cuyahoga County
146	14.9	**Hartville** (village) Stark County
146	14.9	**Reynoldsburg** (city) Franklin County
148	14.8	**Willoughby** (city) Lake County
149	14.7	**Vandalia** (city) Montgomery County
150	14.6	**Berea** (city) Cuyahoga County

Note: *This section ranks incorporated places and CDPs (Census Designated Places) with populations of 2,500 or more. Unincorporated postal areas were not considered. Please refer to the User Guide for additional information.*

Employment: Management, Business, and Financial Occupations

Top 150 Places Ranked in *Ascending* Order

State Rank	Percent	Place
1	3.5	**Wellsville** (village) Columbiana County
2	3.6	**Sebring** (village) Mahoning County
3	3.9	**Bethel** (village) Clermont County
4	4.0	**Campbell** (city) Mahoning County
4	4.0	**Park Layne** (CDP) Clark County
6	4.1	**Mount Healthy Heights** (CDP) Hamilton County
7	4.3	**The Plains** (CDP) Athens County
8	4.4	**Uhrichsville** (city) Tuscarawas County
9	4.6	**Jefferson** (village) Ashtabula County
10	4.8	**Bellaire** (village) Belmont County
10	4.8	**Lodi** (village) Medina County
12	5.0	**Burlington** (CDP) Lawrence County
12	5.0	**Milford** (city) Clermont County
12	5.0	**New Lebanon** (village) Montgomery County
15	5.1	**Fostoria** (city) Seneca County
15	5.1	**Williamsburg** (village) Clermont County
17	5.2	**Blanchester** (village) Clinton County
17	5.2	**Jackson** (city) Jackson County
17	5.2	**Mount Orab** (village) Brown County
17	5.2	**Paulding** (village) Paulding County
21	5.4	**Lincoln Heights** (village) Hamilton County
22	5.5	**Covington** (village) Miami County
22	5.5	**Crooksville** (village) Perry County
22	5.5	**Logan** (city) Hocking County
25	5.7	**Mount Healthy** (city) Hamilton County
26	5.8	**Clyde** (city) Sandusky County
26	5.8	**Ironton** (city) Lawrence County
26	5.8	**New London** (village) Huron County
29	5.9	**Barnesville** (village) Belmont County
30	6.0	**Lima** (city) Allen County
30	6.0	**Van Wert** (city) Van Wert County
32	6.1	**Minerva** (village) Stark County
33	6.2	**Golf Manor** (village) Hamilton County
33	6.2	**Zanesville** (city) Muskingum County
35	6.3	**Fremont** (city) Sandusky County
35	6.3	**Piqua** (city) Miami County
37	6.4	**Carlisle** (village) Warren County
37	6.4	**Georgetown** (village) Brown County
37	6.4	**Urbana** (city) Champaign County
40	6.5	**East Cleveland** (city) Cuyahoga County
40	6.5	**Lockland** (village) Hamilton County
42	6.6	**Youngstown** (city) Mahoning County
43	6.7	**Eaton** (city) Preble County
43	6.7	**Greenfield** (village) Highland County
43	6.7	**London** (city) Madison County
43	6.7	**Mogadore** (village) Summit County
47	6.8	**Marion** (city) Marion County
47	6.8	**Newton Falls** (village) Trumbull County
49	6.9	**Northbrook** (CDP) Hamilton County
50	7.0	**Calcutta** (CDP) Columbiana County
50	7.0	**Cedarville** (village) Greene County
50	7.0	**Newcomerstown** (village) Tuscarawas County
50	7.0	**West Milton** (village) Miami County
50	7.0	**Willard** (city) Huron County
55	7.2	**Nelsonville** (city) Athens County
56	7.3	**Ada** (village) Hardin County
56	7.3	**Alliance** (city) Stark County
56	7.3	**Martins Ferry** (city) Belmont County
56	7.3	**New Carlisle** (city) Clark County
56	7.3	**Niles** (city) Trumbull County
61	7.4	**North Zanesville** (CDP) Muskingum County
61	7.4	**Walbridge** (village) Wood County
63	7.5	**Athens** (city) Athens County
63	7.5	**Wauseon** (city) Fulton County
65	7.6	**Conneaut** (city) Ashtabula County
65	7.6	**Mount Gilead** (village) Morrow County
65	7.6	**Silverton** (village) Hamilton County
68	7.7	**Cadiz** (village) Harrison County
68	7.7	**Chillicothe** (city) Ross County
68	7.7	**Coshocton** (city) Coshocton County
68	7.7	**Delphos** (city) Allen County
72	7.8	**Saint Bernard** (city) Hamilton County
73	7.9	**Bellevue** (city) Sandusky County
73	7.9	**Kenton** (city) Hardin County
75	8.0	**Bucyrus** (city) Crawford County
75	8.0	**Elyria** (city) Lorain County
77	8.1	**Belpre** (city) Washington County
77	8.1	**Canton** (city) Stark County
77	8.1	**Millersburg** (village) Holmes County
77	8.1	**New Lexington** (village) Perry County
77	8.1	**Northwood** (city) Wood County
82	8.2	**Crestline** (village) Crawford County
82	8.2	**Greenville** (city) Darke County
82	8.2	**Norwalk** (city) Huron County
82	8.2	**Struthers** (city) Mahoning County
86	8.3	**Dover** (city) Tuscarawas County
86	8.3	**East Palestine** (village) Columbiana County
86	8.3	**Massillon** (city) Stark County
89	8.4	**Whitehall** (city) Franklin County
90	8.5	**Amelia** (village) Clermont County
90	8.5	**Bedford** (city) Cuyahoga County
90	8.5	**Carey** (village) Wyandot County
90	8.5	**Lisbon** (village) Columbiana County
90	8.5	**Strasburg** (village) Tuscarawas County
95	8.6	**Cambridge** (city) Guernsey County
95	8.6	**Edgewood** (CDP) Ashtabula County
95	8.6	**Geneva** (city) Ashtabula County
95	8.6	**Loudonville** (village) Ashland County
95	8.6	**Mineral Ridge** (CDP) Trumbull County
95	8.6	**Sandusky** (city) Erie County
101	8.7	**Bryan** (city) Williams County
101	8.7	**Dennison** (village) Tuscarawas County
101	8.7	**Lorain** (city) Lorain County
101	8.7	**Mansfield** (city) Richland County
101	8.7	**Oberlin** (city) Lorain County
101	8.7	**Painesville** (city) Lake County
101	8.7	**Shelby** (city) Richland County
108	8.8	**Ashtabula** (city) Ashtabula County
108	8.8	**Bowling Green** (city) Wood County
108	8.8	**Brook Park** (city) Cuyahoga County
108	8.8	**East Liverpool** (city) Columbiana County
108	8.8	**Gibsonburg** (village) Sandusky County
113	8.9	**Hamilton** (city) Butler County
113	8.9	**Ross** (CDP) Butler County
115	9.0	**Barberton** (city) Summit County
115	9.0	**Ravenna** (city) Portage County
115	9.0	**Washington Court House** (city) Fayette County
118	9.1	**North College Hill** (city) Hamilton County
118	9.1	**Oregon** (city) Lucas County
118	9.1	**Tiffin** (city) Seneca County
121	9.2	**Dayton** (city) Montgomery County
121	9.2	**Lincoln Village** (CDP) Franklin County
121	9.2	**Northridge** (CDP) Clark County
121	9.2	**Orrville** (city) Wayne County
121	9.2	**Springfield** (city) Clark County
121	9.2	**Toledo** (city) Lucas County
127	9.3	**Saint Marys** (city) Auglaize County
127	9.3	**Springdale** (city) Hamilton County
127	9.3	**West Portsmouth** (CDP) Scioto County
130	9.4	**Bellefontaine** (city) Logan County
130	9.4	**Kent** (city) Portage County
132	9.5	**Baltimore** (village) Fairfield County
132	9.5	**Montpelier** (village) Williams County
132	9.5	**North Baltimore** (village) Wood County
132	9.5	**Salem** (city) Columbiana County
132	9.5	**Warren** (city) Trumbull County
132	9.5	**Wellston** (city) Jackson County
132	9.5	**West Carrollton** (city) Montgomery County
132	9.5	**Wilmington** (city) Clinton County
140	9.6	**Circleville** (city) Pickaway County
140	9.6	**New Philadelphia** (city) Tuscarawas County
140	9.6	**Portsmouth** (city) Scioto County
143	9.7	**Lake Lakengren** (CDP) Preble County
143	9.7	**Trotwood** (city) Montgomery County
145	9.8	**Shadyside** (village) Belmont County
146	9.9	**Defiance** (city) Defiance County
146	9.9	**Hillsboro** (city) Highland County
146	9.9	**Middletown** (city) Butler County
149	10.0	**Garfield Heights** (city) Cuyahoga County
149	10.0	**Hicksville** (village) Defiance County

Note: *This section ranks incorporated places and CDPs (Census Designated Places) with populations of 2,500 or more. Unincorporated postal areas were not considered. Please refer to the User Guide for additional information.*

Employment: Computer, Engineering, and Science Occupations

Top 150 Places Ranked in *Descending* Order

State Rank	Percent	Place
1	16.1	**Bellbrook** (city) Greene County
2	15.6	**Dublin** (city) Franklin County
3	15.1	**Woodlawn** (village) Hamilton County
4	12.9	**Beckett Ridge** (CDP) Butler County
5	12.4	**Mayfield Heights** (city) Cuyahoga County
6	12.3	**Greentown** (CDP) Stark County
7	12.0	**Beavercreek** (city) Greene County
8	11.9	**Yellow Springs** (village) Greene County
9	11.8	**Doylestown** (village) Wayne County
10	11.6	**Blue Ash** (city) Hamilton County
11	11.2	**Orange** (village) Cuyahoga County
11	11.2	**Wright-Patterson AFB** (CDP) Greene County
13	11.0	**Reminderville** (village) Summit County
14	10.7	**Willoughby Hills** (city) Lake County
15	10.5	**South Lebanon** (village) Warren County
16	10.4	**Sharonville** (city) Hamilton County
16	10.4	**Sixteen Mile Stand** (CDP) Hamilton County
18	10.3	**Hilliard** (city) Franklin County
18	10.3	**Mason** (city) Warren County
20	9.9	**Fairlawn** (city) Summit County
20	9.9	**Seven Hills** (city) Cuyahoga County
20	9.9	**Springboro** (city) Warren County
20	9.9	**Twinsburg** (city) Summit County
24	9.8	**Four Bridges** (CDP) Butler County
25	9.7	**Cherry Grove** (CDP) Hamilton County
26	9.6	**Powell** (city) Delaware County
27	9.5	**Marysville** (city) Union County
28	9.4	**Mack** (CDP) Hamilton County
28	9.4	**Pleasant Run Farm** (CDP) Hamilton County
30	9.3	**New Bremen** (village) Auglaize County
31	9.1	**Deer Park** (city) Hamilton County
31	9.1	**Oakwood** (city) Montgomery County
33	9.0	**Upper Arlington** (city) Franklin County
34	8.9	**Broadview Heights** (city) Cuyahoga County
34	8.9	**Kirtland** (city) Lake County
34	8.9	**Springdale** (city) Hamilton County
37	8.8	**Dry Ridge** (CDP) Hamilton County
37	8.8	**Middleburg Heights** (city) Cuyahoga County
39	8.7	**Beachwood** (city) Cuyahoga County
40	8.6	**Covedale** (CDP) Hamilton County
41	8.3	**Enon** (village) Clark County
41	8.3	**Madeira** (city) Hamilton County
41	8.3	**Sherwood** (CDP) Hamilton County
44	8.1	**Lyndhurst** (city) Cuyahoga County
45	8.0	**Grandview Heights** (city) Franklin County
45	8.0	**Monroe** (city) Butler County
45	8.0	**Montgomery** (city) Hamilton County
45	8.0	**Stow** (city) Summit County
45	8.0	**Summerside** (CDP) Clermont County
50	7.9	**Highland Heights** (city) Cuyahoga County
50	7.9	**Landen** (CDP) Warren County
50	7.9	**Worthington** (city) Franklin County
50	7.9	**Wyoming** (city) Hamilton County
54	7.8	**Cleveland Heights** (city) Cuyahoga County
54	7.8	**Forestville** (CDP) Hamilton County
54	7.8	**Strongsville** (city) Cuyahoga County
57	7.7	**Centerville** (city) Montgomery County
57	7.7	**Solon** (city) Cuyahoga County
59	7.6	**Fairborn** (city) Greene County
59	7.6	**Gahanna** (city) Franklin County
61	7.5	**Garrettsville** (village) Portage County
62	7.4	**Miami Heights** (CDP) Hamilton County
62	7.4	**Miamisburg** (city) Montgomery County
62	7.4	**Richmond Heights** (city) Cuyahoga County
62	7.4	**Rocky River** (city) Cuyahoga County
66	7.3	**Mount Healthy** (city) Hamilton County
66	7.3	**Riverside** (city) Montgomery County
66	7.3	**The Plains** (CDP) Athens County
66	7.3	**Turpin Hills** (CDP) Hamilton County
66	7.3	**Westerville** (city) Franklin County
71	7.2	**Dent** (CDP) Hamilton County
71	7.2	**Mayfield** (village) Cuyahoga County
71	7.2	**Mentor** (city) Lake County
71	7.2	**Minster** (village) Auglaize County
71	7.2	**New Richmond** (village) Clermont County
71	7.2	**Shaker Heights** (city) Cuyahoga County
71	7.2	**Sylvania** (city) Lucas County
71	7.2	**Tipp City** (city) Miami County
79	7.1	**Devola** (CDP) Washington County
79	7.1	**Green Meadows** (CDP) Clark County
79	7.1	**Hudson** (city) Summit County
79	7.1	**Kettering** (city) Montgomery County
83	7.0	**Bainbridge** (CDP) Geauga County
83	7.0	**Brecksville** (city) Cuyahoga County
83	7.0	**Mount Repose** (CDP) Clermont County
83	7.0	**Troy** (city) Miami County
87	6.9	**Amelia** (village) Clermont County
87	6.9	**Aurora** (city) Portage County
87	6.9	**Brookville** (city) Montgomery County
87	6.9	**Columbus** (city) Franklin County
87	6.9	**Fairview Park** (city) Cuyahoga County
87	6.9	**Huber Heights** (city) Montgomery County
87	6.9	**North Olmsted** (city) Cuyahoga County
87	6.9	**Perrysburg** (city) Wood County
95	6.8	**Berea** (city) Cuyahoga County
95	6.8	**Cuyahoga Falls** (city) Summit County
95	6.8	**Macedonia** (city) Summit County
95	6.8	**Milford** (city) Clermont County
95	6.8	**Reynoldsburg** (city) Franklin County
100	6.7	**Lake Darby** (CDP) Franklin County
100	6.7	**Reading** (city) Hamilton County
100	6.7	**Wadsworth** (city) Medina County
103	6.6	**Loveland** (city) Hamilton County
104	6.5	**Avon** (city) Lorain County
104	6.5	**Cincinnati** (city) Hamilton County
104	6.5	**Dillonvale** (CDP) Hamilton County
104	6.5	**Golf Manor** (village) Hamilton County
104	6.5	**Parma Heights** (city) Cuyahoga County
104	6.5	**Plain City** (village) Madison County
104	6.5	**Richfield** (village) Summit County
104	6.5	**Westlake** (city) Cuyahoga County
104	6.5	**Wickliffe** (city) Lake County
113	6.4	**Canal Winchester** (city) Franklin County
113	6.4	**Montrose-Ghent** (CDP) Summit County
113	6.4	**Mount Gilead** (village) Morrow County
116	6.3	**Cortland** (city) Trumbull County
116	6.3	**Day Heights** (CDP) Clermont County
116	6.3	**Delaware** (city) Delaware County
116	6.3	**Finneytown** (CDP) Hamilton County
116	6.3	**Moreland Hills** (village) Cuyahoga County
116	6.3	**Mulberry** (CDP) Clermont County
116	6.3	**University Heights** (city) Cuyahoga County
116	6.3	**Wooster** (city) Wayne County
124	6.2	**Munroe Falls** (city) Summit County
124	6.2	**Willoughby** (city) Lake County
126	6.1	**Burlington** (CDP) Lawrence County
126	6.1	**Olmsted Falls** (city) Cuyahoga County
126	6.1	**Poland** (village) Mahoning County
129	6.0	**Clayton** (city) Montgomery County
129	6.0	**Newtown** (village) Hamilton County
131	5.9	**Germantown** (city) Montgomery County
131	5.9	**Norwood** (city) Hamilton County
131	5.9	**The Village of Indian Hill** (city) Hamilton County
134	5.8	**Evendale** (village) Hamilton County
134	5.8	**Findlay** (city) Hancock County
134	5.8	**Lebanon** (city) Warren County
134	5.8	**North Canton** (city) Stark County
134	5.8	**North Ridgeville** (city) Lorain County
139	5.7	**Athens** (city) Athens County
139	5.7	**Carlisle** (village) Warren County
139	5.7	**Edgewood** (CDP) Ashtabula County
139	5.7	**Englewood** (city) Montgomery County
139	5.7	**Green** (city) Summit County
139	5.7	**Groesbeck** (CDP) Hamilton County
139	5.7	**Huber Ridge** (CDP) Franklin County
139	5.7	**Mariemont** (village) Hamilton County
139	5.7	**New Albany** (city) Franklin County
139	5.7	**Sunbury** (village) Delaware County
139	5.7	**Willowick** (city) Lake County
150	5.6	**Beechwood Trails** (CDP) Licking County

***Note:** This section ranks incorporated places and CDPs (Census Designated Places) with populations of 2,500 or more. Unincorporated postal areas were not considered. Please refer to the User Guide for additional information.*

Employment: Computer, Engineering, and Science Occupations

Top 150 Places Ranked in *Ascending* Order

State Rank	Percent	Place
1	0.0	**Lincoln Heights** (village) Hamilton County
1	0.0	**Wellsville** (village) Columbiana County
1	0.0	**West Union** (village) Adams County
4	0.3	**Bellaire** (village) Belmont County
4	0.3	**Lodi** (village) Medina County
6	0.4	**Willard** (city) Huron County
7	0.5	**Calcutta** (CDP) Columbiana County
7	0.5	**New Concord** (village) Muskingum County
9	0.6	**Campbell** (city) Mahoning County
10	0.7	**Geneva** (city) Ashtabula County
10	0.7	**Lordstown** (village) Trumbull County
10	0.7	**New London** (village) Huron County
13	0.8	**Sebring** (village) Mahoning County
14	0.9	**Hillsboro** (city) Highland County
15	1.0	**Kenton** (city) Hardin County
15	1.0	**New Lebanon** (village) Montgomery County
15	1.0	**Washington Court House** (city) Fayette County
18	1.1	**Crooksville** (village) Perry County
18	1.1	**Lexington** (village) Richland County
18	1.1	**Mount Orab** (village) Brown County
18	1.1	**Sandusky** (city) Erie County
18	1.1	**Toronto** (city) Jefferson County
23	1.2	**McDonald** (village) Trumbull County
23	1.2	**Upper Sandusky** (city) Wyandot County
23	1.2	**Warrensville Heights** (city) Cuyahoga County
26	1.3	**Barnesville** (village) Belmont County
26	1.3	**Cadiz** (village) Harrison County
26	1.3	**Huron** (city) Erie County
26	1.3	**New Lexington** (village) Perry County
30	1.4	**Buckeye Lake** (village) Licking County
30	1.4	**Circleville** (city) Pickaway County
30	1.4	**Nelsonville** (city) Athens County
30	1.4	**Newton Falls** (village) Trumbull County
34	1.5	**Blanchester** (village) Clinton County
34	1.5	**Lima** (city) Allen County
34	1.5	**Strasburg** (village) Tuscarawas County
34	1.5	**Uhrichsville** (city) Tuscarawas County
34	1.5	**Urbana** (city) Champaign County
39	1.6	**East Cleveland** (city) Cuyahoga County
39	1.6	**Montpelier** (village) Williams County
39	1.6	**Shadyside** (village) Belmont County
39	1.6	**Wauseon** (city) Fulton County
39	1.6	**West Milton** (village) Miami County
44	1.7	**Carrollton** (village) Carroll County
44	1.7	**Clyde** (city) Sandusky County
44	1.7	**Niles** (city) Trumbull County
44	1.7	**Shelby** (city) Richland County
44	1.7	**Wellston** (city) Jackson County
49	1.8	**South Point** (village) Lawrence County
49	1.8	**Union** (city) Montgomery County
49	1.8	**Youngstown** (city) Mahoning County
52	1.9	**Crestline** (village) Crawford County
52	1.9	**Fostoria** (city) Seneca County
52	1.9	**Ironton** (city) Lawrence County
52	1.9	**Minerva** (village) Stark County
52	1.9	**Napoleon** (city) Henry County
52	1.9	**Vermilion** (city) Lorain County
58	2.0	**Ashtabula** (city) Ashtabula County
58	2.0	**Gallipolis** (village) Gallia County
58	2.0	**Greenfield** (village) Highland County
58	2.0	**Mingo Junction** (village) Jefferson County
62	2.1	**Blacklick Estates** (CDP) Franklin County
62	2.1	**Cedarville** (village) Greene County
62	2.1	**Coshocton** (city) Coshocton County
62	2.1	**Jefferson** (village) Ashtabula County
62	2.1	**Northbrook** (CDP) Hamilton County
62	2.1	**Oak Harbor** (village) Ottawa County
62	2.1	**Salem** (city) Columbiana County
62	2.1	**Springfield** (city) Clark County
70	2.2	**Defiance** (city) Defiance County
70	2.2	**Eaton** (city) Preble County
70	2.2	**Greenville** (city) Darke County
70	2.2	**Lisbon** (village) Columbiana County
70	2.2	**Marion** (city) Marion County
75	2.3	**Archbold** (village) Fulton County
75	2.3	**Chardon** (city) Geauga County
75	2.3	**Middlefield** (village) Geauga County
78	2.4	**Austintown** (CDP) Mahoning County
78	2.4	**Lancaster** (city) Fairfield County
78	2.4	**Mount Carmel** (CDP) Clermont County
78	2.4	**Newcomerstown** (village) Tuscarawas County
78	2.4	**North Baltimore** (village) Wood County
78	2.4	**North College Hill** (city) Hamilton County
78	2.4	**Northwood** (city) Wood County
78	2.4	**Saint Marys** (city) Auglaize County
78	2.4	**Steubenville** (city) Jefferson County
78	2.4	**West Jefferson** (village) Madison County
88	2.5	**Lockland** (village) Hamilton County
88	2.5	**Logan** (city) Hocking County
88	2.5	**New Philadelphia** (city) Tuscarawas County
88	2.5	**Northgate** (CDP) Hamilton County
88	2.5	**Ravenna** (city) Portage County
88	2.5	**Waverly** (village) Pike County
88	2.5	**Zanesville** (city) Muskingum County
95	2.6	**Brook Park** (city) Cuyahoga County
95	2.6	**Lincoln Village** (CDP) Franklin County
95	2.6	**Lorain** (city) Lorain County
95	2.6	**Martins Ferry** (city) Belmont County
95	2.6	**New Burlington** (CDP) Hamilton County
95	2.6	**Tiffin** (city) Seneca County
95	2.6	**Trotwood** (city) Montgomery County
95	2.6	**Warren** (city) Trumbull County
103	2.7	**Conneaut** (city) Ashtabula County
103	2.7	**Delta** (village) Fulton County
103	2.7	**Girard** (city) Trumbull County
103	2.7	**Loudonville** (village) Ashland County
103	2.7	**Millersburg** (village) Holmes County
103	2.7	**Moraine** (city) Montgomery County
103	2.7	**Walbridge** (village) Wood County
110	2.8	**Bedford** (city) Cuyahoga County
110	2.8	**Brimfield** (CDP) Portage County
110	2.8	**Bucyrus** (city) Crawford County
110	2.8	**East Liverpool** (city) Columbiana County
110	2.8	**Hartville** (village) Stark County
110	2.8	**Mount Healthy Heights** (CDP) Hamilton County
116	2.9	**Ashland** (city) Ashland County
116	2.9	**Cambridge** (city) Guernsey County
116	2.9	**Canton** (city) Stark County
116	2.9	**Chillicothe** (city) Ross County
116	2.9	**Mansfield** (city) Richland County
116	2.9	**Struthers** (city) Mahoning County
122	3.0	**Bowling Green** (city) Wood County
122	3.0	**Dennison** (village) Tuscarawas County
122	3.0	**East Palestine** (village) Columbiana County
122	3.0	**Fremont** (city) Sandusky County
122	3.0	**Galion** (city) Crawford County
122	3.0	**Hamilton** (city) Butler County
122	3.0	**Van Wert** (city) Van Wert County
122	3.0	**Whitehall** (city) Franklin County
130	3.1	**Bellevue** (city) Sandusky County
130	3.1	**Celina** (city) Mercer County
130	3.1	**Coldwater** (village) Mercer County
130	3.1	**Jackson** (city) Jackson County
130	3.1	**Massillon** (city) Stark County
130	3.1	**North Kingsville** (village) Ashtabula County
130	3.1	**Seville** (village) Medina County
137	3.2	**Cleveland** (city) Cuyahoga County
137	3.2	**Maple Heights** (city) Cuyahoga County
137	3.2	**Mogadore** (village) Summit County
137	3.2	**Sheffield Lake** (city) Lorain County
137	3.2	**Toledo** (city) Lucas County
137	3.2	**Wheelersburg** (CDP) Scioto County
143	3.3	**Alliance** (city) Stark County
143	3.3	**Ballville** (CDP) Sandusky County
143	3.3	**Boardman** (CDP) Mahoning County
143	3.3	**Mentor-on-the-Lake** (city) Lake County
143	3.3	**Northfield** (village) Summit County
143	3.3	**Northridge** (CDP) Clark County
143	3.3	**Norwalk** (city) Huron County
143	3.3	**Vandalia** (city) Montgomery County

Note: *This section ranks incorporated places and CDPs (Census Designated Places) with populations of 2,500 or more. Unincorporated postal areas were not considered. Please refer to the User Guide for additional information.*

Employment: Education, Legal, Community Service, Arts, and Media Occupations

Top 150 Places Ranked in *Descending* Order

State Rank	Percent	Place
1	29.7	**Oberlin** (city) Lorain County
2	29.3	**Granville** (village) Licking County
3	27.2	**Yellow Springs** (village) Greene County
4	25.6	**Athens** (city) Athens County
5	23.4	**Shaker Heights** (city) Cuyahoga County
6	23.1	**Bexley** (city) Franklin County
7	22.6	**Oxford** (city) Butler County
8	22.4	**Cleveland Heights** (city) Cuyahoga County
9	22.3	**Worthington** (city) Franklin County
10	21.7	**Oakwood** (city) Montgomery County
11	21.0	**University Heights** (city) Cuyahoga County
12	20.7	**Fruit Hill** (CDP) Hamilton County
12	20.7	**The Plains** (CDP) Athens County
14	20.4	**Wyoming** (city) Hamilton County
15	20.2	**Mayfield** (village) Cuyahoga County
16	20.1	**Bluffton** (village) Allen County
16	20.1	**Upper Arlington** (city) Franklin County
18	19.9	**Cedarville** (village) Greene County
19	19.5	**Ottawa Hills** (village) Lucas County
20	19.4	**Bay Village** (city) Cuyahoga County
21	19.3	**Grandview Heights** (city) Franklin County
21	19.3	**North Zanesville** (CDP) Muskingum County
23	18.6	**Bainbridge** (CDP) Geauga County
24	18.1	**Amberley** (village) Hamilton County
25	17.9	**Pepper Pike** (city) Cuyahoga County
26	17.6	**Bowling Green** (city) Wood County
26	17.6	**The Village of Indian Hill** (city) Hamilton County
28	17.4	**Kent** (city) Portage County
29	17.2	**Salem Heights** (CDP) Hamilton County
30	17.1	**Turpin Hills** (CDP) Hamilton County
31	16.8	**Fairlawn** (city) Summit County
31	16.8	**South Russell** (village) Geauga County
33	16.7	**Madeira** (city) Hamilton County
34	16.4	**Hudson** (city) Summit County
35	16.2	**Beachwood** (city) Cuyahoga County
35	16.2	**Canfield** (city) Mahoning County
35	16.2	**Dry Run** (CDP) Hamilton County
35	16.2	**Montgomery** (city) Hamilton County
39	15.9	**Forestville** (CDP) Hamilton County
39	15.9	**Lakewood** (city) Cuyahoga County
39	15.9	**Newtown** (village) Hamilton County
42	15.8	**Landen** (CDP) Warren County
43	15.6	**Poland** (village) Mahoning County
44	15.4	**Jackson** (city) Jackson County
45	15.3	**Beechwood Trails** (CDP) Licking County
45	15.3	**Montrose-Ghent** (CDP) Summit County
45	15.3	**Solon** (city) Cuyahoga County
45	15.3	**South Lebanon** (village) Warren County
45	15.3	**Westerville** (city) Franklin County
50	15.1	**New Albany** (city) Franklin County
51	14.9	**North Canton** (city) Stark County
52	14.7	**Kenwood** (CDP) Hamilton County
52	14.7	**Whitehouse** (village) Lucas County
54	14.5	**Perrysburg** (city) Wood County
55	14.3	**Mineral Ridge** (CDP) Trumbull County
56	14.2	**Ada** (village) Hardin County
56	14.2	**Apple Valley** (CDP) Knox County
56	14.2	**Blue Ash** (city) Hamilton County
56	14.2	**Brecksville** (city) Cuyahoga County
56	14.2	**Cherry Grove** (CDP) Hamilton County
61	14.1	**Greenhills** (village) Hamilton County
62	14.0	**Avon Lake** (city) Lorain County
62	14.0	**Brookville** (city) Montgomery County
64	13.9	**Bellbrook** (city) Greene County
64	13.9	**Orange** (village) Cuyahoga County
64	13.9	**Orrville** (city) Wayne County
64	13.9	**Rocky River** (city) Cuyahoga County
64	13.9	**Springboro** (city) Warren County
64	13.9	**Sylvania** (city) Lucas County
64	13.9	**Wooster** (city) Wayne County
71	13.8	**Gahanna** (city) Franklin County
71	13.8	**Greentown** (CDP) Stark County
71	13.8	**Seville** (village) Medina County
74	13.6	**Oakwood** (village) Cuyahoga County
74	13.6	**Saint Clairsville** (city) Belmont County
74	13.6	**Sunbury** (village) Delaware County
77	13.5	**South Point** (village) Lawrence County
78	13.4	**Mulberry** (CDP) Clermont County
79	13.3	**Centerville** (city) Montgomery County
79	13.3	**Evendale** (village) Hamilton County
81	13.1	**Macedonia** (city) Summit County
81	13.1	**Sixteen Mile Stand** (CDP) Hamilton County
83	13.0	**New Lexington** (village) Perry County
84	12.9	**Delaware** (city) Delaware County
84	12.9	**Lake Lakengren** (CDP) Preble County
84	12.9	**Mount Gilead** (village) Morrow County
84	12.9	**Westlake** (city) Cuyahoga County
88	12.7	**Berea** (city) Cuyahoga County
89	12.5	**Cincinnati** (city) Hamilton County
89	12.5	**Lyndhurst** (city) Cuyahoga County
89	12.5	**Steubenville** (city) Jefferson County
92	12.4	**Archbold** (village) Fulton County
92	12.4	**Hilliard** (city) Franklin County
94	12.3	**Four Bridges** (CDP) Butler County
94	12.3	**Pleasant Run Farm** (CDP) Hamilton County
94	12.3	**Stow** (city) Summit County
97	12.2	**Cortland** (city) Trumbull County
97	12.2	**Fort Shawnee** (CDP) Allen County
97	12.2	**Green** (city) Summit County
97	12.2	**Logan** (city) Hocking County
97	12.2	**Mason** (city) Warren County
102	12.1	**Chagrin Falls** (village) Cuyahoga County
102	12.1	**Dent** (CDP) Hamilton County
102	12.1	**Minster** (village) Auglaize County
102	12.1	**New Concord** (village) Muskingum County
102	12.1	**Silverton** (village) Hamilton County
107	12.0	**Kettering** (city) Montgomery County
108	11.9	**Calcutta** (CDP) Columbiana County
108	11.9	**Garrettsville** (village) Portage County
108	11.9	**Madison** (village) Lake County
111	11.8	**Covedale** (CDP) Hamilton County
111	11.8	**Highland Heights** (city) Cuyahoga County
111	11.8	**Ironton** (city) Lawrence County
111	11.8	**Reminderville** (village) Summit County
115	11.7	**Seven Hills** (city) Cuyahoga County
116	11.6	**Ashland** (city) Ashland County
117	11.5	**Kenton** (city) Hardin County
117	11.5	**South Euclid** (city) Cuyahoga County
119	11.4	**Grafton** (village) Lorain County
119	11.4	**Richfield** (village) Summit County
119	11.4	**Waterville** (city) Lucas County
122	11.3	**Enon** (village) Clark County
122	11.3	**Fairview Park** (city) Cuyahoga County
122	11.3	**Munroe Falls** (city) Summit County
122	11.3	**Olmsted Falls** (city) Cuyahoga County
122	11.3	**Ontario** (city) Richland County
122	11.3	**Wickliffe** (city) Lake County
128	11.2	**Avon** (city) Lorain County
128	11.2	**Uniontown** (CDP) Stark County
128	11.2	**Wright-Patterson AFB** (CDP) Greene County
131	11.1	**Columbus** (city) Franklin County
131	11.1	**Sheffield** (village) Lorain County
133	11.0	**Aurora** (city) Portage County
133	11.0	**Beavercreek** (city) Greene County
133	11.0	**Lake Darby** (CDP) Franklin County
136	10.9	**Boardman** (CDP) Mahoning County
136	10.9	**Cuyahoga Falls** (city) Summit County
136	10.9	**Kirtland** (city) Lake County
136	10.9	**Mariemont** (village) Hamilton County
136	10.9	**Tipp City** (city) Miami County
141	10.8	**Dublin** (city) Franklin County
141	10.8	**Norton** (city) Summit County
141	10.8	**Shelby** (city) Richland County
144	10.7	**Howland Center** (CDP) Trumbull County
144	10.7	**Loveland** (city) Hamilton County
144	10.7	**Streetsboro** (city) Portage County
144	10.7	**Twinsburg** (city) Summit County
148	10.6	**Brooklyn** (city) Cuyahoga County
148	10.6	**Finneytown** (CDP) Hamilton County
148	10.6	**Mayfield Heights** (city) Cuyahoga County

Note: *This section ranks incorporated places and CDPs (Census Designated Places) with populations of 2,500 or more. Unincorporated postal areas were not considered. Please refer to the User Guide for additional information.*

Employment: Education, Legal, Community Service, Arts, and Media Occupations

Top 150 Places Ranked in *Ascending* Order

State Rank	Percent	Place
1	0.4	**Mount Healthy Heights** (CDP) Hamilton County
2	1.1	**Lockland** (village) Hamilton County
3	1.5	**Millersburg** (village) Holmes County
4	1.9	**Park Layne** (CDP) Clark County
5	2.0	**Moraine** (city) Montgomery County
6	2.2	**New Lebanon** (village) Montgomery County
7	2.4	**Newton Falls** (village) Trumbull County
8	2.8	**Wellsville** (village) Columbiana County
9	3.1	**Hicksville** (village) Defiance County
9	3.1	**Pleasant Run** (CDP) Hamilton County
9	3.1	**Richville** (CDP) Stark County
12	3.2	**Paulding** (village) Paulding County
13	3.4	**Lincoln Village** (CDP) Franklin County
13	3.4	**North Baltimore** (village) Wood County
13	3.4	**Sebring** (village) Mahoning County
16	3.6	**New Burlington** (CDP) Hamilton County
17	3.8	**Carey** (village) Wyandot County
18	3.9	**Northfield** (village) Summit County
18	3.9	**West Milton** (village) Miami County
20	4.0	**Crooksville** (village) Perry County
20	4.0	**Mingo Junction** (village) Jefferson County
20	4.0	**New Carlisle** (city) Clark County
23	4.1	**Ross** (CDP) Butler County
24	4.2	**Bellaire** (village) Belmont County
24	4.2	**Blacklick Estates** (CDP) Franklin County
24	4.2	**Day Heights** (CDP) Clermont County
24	4.2	**Wauseon** (city) Fulton County
24	4.2	**Wellington** (village) Lorain County
29	4.4	**Edgewood** (CDP) Ashtabula County
30	4.5	**Greenville** (city) Darke County
30	4.5	**North Madison** (CDP) Lake County
32	4.7	**Taylor Creek** (CDP) Hamilton County
33	4.8	**Delta** (village) Fulton County
33	4.8	**West Carrollton** (city) Montgomery County
35	5.1	**Plain City** (village) Madison County
36	5.2	**Blanchester** (village) Clinton County
36	5.2	**Burlington** (CDP) Lawrence County
36	5.2	**Dillonvale** (CDP) Hamilton County
36	5.2	**Lincoln Heights** (village) Hamilton County
36	5.2	**Perry Heights** (CDP) Stark County
41	5.3	**Dennison** (village) Tuscarawas County
41	5.3	**Newcomerstown** (village) Tuscarawas County
41	5.3	**Toronto** (city) Jefferson County
44	5.4	**Carlisle** (village) Warren County
45	5.5	**Coldwater** (village) Mercer County
46	5.6	**Ashtabula** (city) Ashtabula County
46	5.6	**Cadiz** (village) Harrison County
46	5.6	**Franklin** (city) Warren County
46	5.6	**Johnstown** (village) Licking County
46	5.6	**Northbrook** (CDP) Hamilton County
46	5.6	**West Union** (village) Adams County
52	5.7	**Brimfield** (CDP) Portage County
52	5.7	**Riverside** (city) Montgomery County
54	5.8	**Doylestown** (village) Wayne County
54	5.8	**Geneva** (city) Ashtabula County
56	5.9	**Campbell** (city) Mahoning County
56	5.9	**Montpelier** (village) Williams County
58	6.0	**Champion Heights** (CDP) Trumbull County
58	6.0	**Conneaut** (city) Ashtabula County
58	6.0	**Eastlake** (city) Lake County
58	6.0	**Harrison** (city) Hamilton County
58	6.0	**Maple Heights** (city) Cuyahoga County
63	6.1	**Barberton** (city) Summit County
63	6.1	**Cheviot** (city) Hamilton County
63	6.1	**Rittman** (city) Wayne County
63	6.1	**Whitehall** (city) Franklin County
67	6.2	**Lodi** (village) Medina County
67	6.2	**Nelsonville** (city) Athens County
67	6.2	**Norwalk** (city) Huron County
67	6.2	**Salem** (city) Columbiana County
71	6.3	**Canal Fulton** (city) Stark County
71	6.3	**East Palestine** (village) Columbiana County
71	6.3	**Portage Lakes** (CDP) Summit County
71	6.3	**Van Wert** (city) Van Wert County
75	6.4	**Clyde** (city) Sandusky County

State Rank	Percent	Place
75	6.4	**Marion** (city) Marion County
75	6.4	**Struthers** (city) Mahoning County
78	6.5	**Bridgetown** (CDP) Hamilton County
78	6.5	**Lima** (city) Allen County
78	6.5	**Northgate** (CDP) Hamilton County
78	6.5	**West Jefferson** (village) Madison County
82	6.6	**Alliance** (city) Stark County
82	6.6	**Fostoria** (city) Seneca County
84	6.7	**Brook Park** (city) Cuyahoga County
84	6.7	**Hamilton** (city) Butler County
84	6.7	**Martins Ferry** (city) Belmont County
84	6.7	**Mentor-on-the-Lake** (city) Lake County
84	6.7	**Minerva** (village) Stark County
84	6.7	**Port Clinton** (city) Ottawa County
84	6.7	**Summerside** (CDP) Clermont County
84	6.7	**Withamsville** (CDP) Clermont County
92	6.8	**Elyria** (city) Lorain County
92	6.8	**Monroe** (city) Butler County
92	6.8	**New London** (village) Huron County
92	6.8	**New Richmond** (village) Clermont County
92	6.8	**Sidney** (city) Shelby County
92	6.8	**Wapakoneta** (city) Auglaize County
98	6.9	**Eaton** (city) Preble County
98	6.9	**Lordstown** (village) Trumbull County
98	6.9	**Saint Marys** (city) Auglaize County
98	6.9	**Versailles** (village) Darke County
102	7.0	**Girard** (city) Trumbull County
102	7.0	**Woodlawn** (village) Hamilton County
102	7.0	**Zanesville** (city) Muskingum County
105	7.1	**Cambridge** (city) Guernsey County
105	7.1	**London** (city) Madison County
105	7.1	**Louisville** (city) Stark County
108	7.2	**Oregon** (city) Lucas County
108	7.2	**Wheelersburg** (CDP) Scioto County
110	7.3	**Belpre** (city) Washington County
110	7.3	**Hillsboro** (city) Highland County
110	7.3	**Lorain** (city) Lorain County
110	7.3	**North Kingsville** (village) Ashtabula County
110	7.3	**Parma** (city) Cuyahoga County
110	7.3	**Piqua** (city) Miami County
110	7.3	**Sandusky** (city) Erie County
110	7.3	**Trotwood** (city) Montgomery County
110	7.3	**Wintersville** (village) Jefferson County
119	7.4	**Brunswick** (city) Medina County
119	7.4	**Delhi Hills** (CDP) Hamilton County
119	7.4	**Groesbeck** (CDP) Hamilton County
119	7.4	**Oak Harbor** (village) Ottawa County
119	7.4	**Upper Sandusky** (city) Wyandot County
119	7.4	**Washington Court House** (city) Fayette County
125	7.5	**Lancaster** (city) Fairfield County
125	7.5	**New Philadelphia** (city) Tuscarawas County
125	7.5	**Northwood** (city) Wood County
128	7.6	**East Liverpool** (city) Columbiana County
128	7.6	**Fremont** (city) Sandusky County
128	7.6	**Marysville** (city) Union County
128	7.6	**Parma Heights** (city) Cuyahoga County
128	7.6	**Saint Bernard** (city) Hamilton County
128	7.6	**Saint Henry** (village) Mercer County
128	7.6	**Trenton** (city) Butler County
128	7.6	**Vermilion** (city) Lorain County
128	7.6	**Willard** (city) Huron County
137	7.7	**Bedford Heights** (city) Cuyahoga County
137	7.7	**Columbiana** (city) Columbiana County
137	7.7	**Delphos** (city) Allen County
137	7.7	**Huber Heights** (city) Montgomery County
137	7.7	**Mansfield** (city) Richland County
137	7.7	**Middletown** (city) Butler County
137	7.7	**Mount Orab** (village) Brown County
137	7.7	**Pataskala** (city) Licking County
137	7.7	**Uhrichsville** (city) Tuscarawas County
146	7.8	**Celina** (city) Mercer County
146	7.8	**Coshocton** (city) Coshocton County
146	7.8	**Euclid** (city) Cuyahoga County
146	7.8	**Greenfield** (village) Highland County
146	7.8	**Jefferson** (village) Ashtabula County

Note: *This section ranks incorporated places and CDPs (Census Designated Places) with populations of 2,500 or more. Unincorporated postal areas were not considered. Please refer to the User Guide for additional information.*

Employment: Healthcare Practitioners

Top 150 Places Ranked in *Descending* Order

State Rank	Percent	Place
1	21.0	**The Village of Indian Hill** (city) Hamilton County
2	18.2	**Montrose-Ghent** (CDP) Summit County
3	15.9	**Pepper Pike** (city) Cuyahoga County
4	15.3	**Highland Heights** (city) Cuyahoga County
5	14.9	**Amberley** (village) Hamilton County
6	14.0	**Shaker Heights** (city) Cuyahoga County
7	13.1	**Lexington** (village) Richland County
8	13.0	**Orange** (village) Cuyahoga County
8	13.0	**Ottawa Hills** (village) Lucas County
10	12.9	**Oakwood** (city) Montgomery County
10	12.9	**Pleasant Run Farm** (CDP) Hamilton County
12	12.8	**Upper Arlington** (city) Franklin County
13	12.6	**Cadiz** (village) Harrison County
13	12.6	**Saint Clairsville** (city) Belmont County
13	12.6	**Waterville** (city) Lucas County
13	12.6	**Wright-Patterson AFB** (CDP) Greene County
17	12.4	**Canal Fulton** (city) Stark County
18	12.3	**Barnesville** (village) Belmont County
19	12.2	**Willoughby Hills** (city) Lake County
20	12.0	**Mariemont** (village) Hamilton County
21	11.8	**Moreland Hills** (village) Cuyahoga County
21	11.8	**Whitehouse** (village) Lucas County
23	11.6	**Cleveland Heights** (city) Cuyahoga County
23	11.6	**Mount Gilead** (village) Morrow County
25	11.5	**Jackson** (city) Jackson County
26	11.4	**Burlington** (CDP) Lawrence County
27	11.3	**Kenwood** (CDP) Hamilton County
27	11.3	**Lyndhurst** (city) Cuyahoga County
29	11.2	**Wheelersburg** (CDP) Scioto County
29	11.2	**Yellow Springs** (village) Greene County
31	11.0	**Portsmouth** (city) Scioto County
31	11.0	**Powell** (city) Delaware County
33	10.9	**Fairlawn** (city) Summit County
34	10.8	**Cherry Grove** (CDP) Hamilton County
35	10.6	**Westlake** (city) Cuyahoga County
35	10.6	**Wintersville** (village) Jefferson County
37	10.5	**Doylestown** (village) Wayne County
37	10.5	**Dry Run** (CDP) Hamilton County
37	10.5	**Grandview Heights** (city) Franklin County
40	10.4	**Poland** (village) Mahoning County
40	10.4	**Solon** (city) Cuyahoga County
42	10.3	**Monfort Heights** (CDP) Hamilton County
43	10.1	**Munroe Falls** (city) Summit County
43	10.1	**Sylvania** (city) Lucas County
45	10.0	**Beachwood** (city) Cuyahoga County
45	10.0	**Broadview Heights** (city) Cuyahoga County
45	10.0	**Newcomerstown** (village) Tuscarawas County
45	10.0	**South Point** (village) Lawrence County
45	10.0	**White Oak** (CDP) Hamilton County
50	9.9	**Ballville** (CDP) Sandusky County
50	9.9	**Beavercreek** (city) Greene County
50	9.9	**Canfield** (city) Mahoning County
53	9.8	**Bellaire** (village) Belmont County
53	9.8	**Englewood** (city) Montgomery County
53	9.8	**Groesbeck** (CDP) Hamilton County
53	9.8	**Mayfield** (village) Cuyahoga County
53	9.8	**New Albany** (city) Franklin County
53	9.8	**University Heights** (city) Cuyahoga County
59	9.7	**Canal Winchester** (city) Franklin County
59	9.7	**Hillsboro** (city) Highland County
59	9.7	**Montgomery** (city) Hamilton County
62	9.6	**Centerville** (city) Montgomery County
62	9.6	**Covedale** (CDP) Hamilton County
64	9.5	**Fort Shawnee** (CDP) Allen County
64	9.5	**Landen** (CDP) Warren County
64	9.5	**Mack** (CDP) Hamilton County
64	9.5	**Springboro** (city) Warren County
68	9.4	**Blue Ash** (city) Hamilton County
68	9.4	**Mingo Junction** (village) Jefferson County
68	9.4	**North Royalton** (city) Cuyahoga County
71	9.3	**Brecksville** (city) Cuyahoga County
71	9.3	**Columbiana** (city) Columbiana County
71	9.3	**North Madison** (CDP) Lake County
71	9.3	**Pleasant Run** (CDP) Hamilton County
71	9.3	**Turpin Hills** (CDP) Hamilton County
76	9.2	**Cortland** (city) Trumbull County
76	9.2	**Dent** (CDP) Hamilton County
76	9.2	**Dublin** (city) Franklin County
76	9.2	**Oregon** (city) Lucas County
76	9.2	**South Russell** (village) Geauga County
81	9.1	**Beckett Ridge** (CDP) Butler County
81	9.1	**Germantown** (city) Montgomery County
81	9.1	**Monroe** (city) Butler County
81	9.1	**Wellston** (city) Jackson County
85	9.0	**Kettering** (city) Montgomery County
85	9.0	**Minster** (village) Auglaize County
85	9.0	**Northridge** (CDP) Clark County
85	9.0	**Shadyside** (village) Belmont County
85	9.0	**Waynesville** (village) Warren County
90	8.9	**Avon Lake** (city) Lorain County
90	8.9	**Bainbridge** (CDP) Geauga County
90	8.9	**Milford** (city) Clermont County
90	8.9	**Mineral Ridge** (CDP) Trumbull County
90	8.9	**Rocky River** (city) Cuyahoga County
90	8.9	**Wellsville** (village) Columbiana County
96	8.8	**Apple Valley** (CDP) Knox County
96	8.8	**Boardman** (CDP) Mahoning County
96	8.8	**North Ridgeville** (city) Lorain County
96	8.8	**Olmsted Falls** (city) Cuyahoga County
96	8.8	**Taylor Creek** (CDP) Hamilton County
101	8.7	**Edgewood** (CDP) Ashtabula County
101	8.7	**Georgetown** (village) Brown County
101	8.7	**Maumee** (city) Lucas County
101	8.7	**Miami Heights** (CDP) Hamilton County
101	8.7	**Sheffield Lake** (city) Lorain County
106	8.6	**Bridgetown** (CDP) Hamilton County
106	8.6	**Delhi Hills** (CDP) Hamilton County
106	8.6	**Geneva** (city) Ashtabula County
106	8.6	**Macedonia** (city) Summit County
106	8.6	**Oakwood** (village) Cuyahoga County
106	8.6	**Perrysburg** (city) Wood County
106	8.6	**Wyoming** (city) Hamilton County
113	8.5	**Worthington** (city) Franklin County
114	8.4	**Avon** (city) Lorain County
114	8.4	**Delta** (village) Fulton County
114	8.4	**Hilliard** (city) Franklin County
114	8.4	**Lake Lakengren** (CDP) Preble County
114	8.4	**North Canton** (city) Stark County
114	8.4	**Seven Hills** (city) Cuyahoga County
114	8.4	**Sixteen Mile Stand** (CDP) Hamilton County
121	8.3	**Bellbrook** (city) Greene County
121	8.3	**South Euclid** (city) Cuyahoga County
123	8.2	**Dover** (city) Tuscarawas County
123	8.2	**Moraine** (city) Montgomery County
123	8.2	**Pickerington** (city) Fairfield County
123	8.2	**Stow** (city) Summit County
123	8.2	**Sunbury** (village) Delaware County
123	8.2	**Waverly** (village) Pike County
129	8.1	**Forestville** (CDP) Hamilton County
129	8.1	**Gallipolis** (village) Gallia County
129	8.1	**Golf Manor** (village) Hamilton County
129	8.1	**Greentown** (CDP) Stark County
129	8.1	**Mayfield Heights** (city) Cuyahoga County
129	8.1	**Uniontown** (CDP) Stark County
135	8.0	**Chillicothe** (city) Ross County
135	8.0	**Four Bridges** (CDP) Butler County
135	8.0	**Independence** (city) Cuyahoga County
135	8.0	**Wadsworth** (city) Medina County
139	7.9	**Beechwood Trails** (CDP) Licking County
139	7.9	**Grove City** (city) Franklin County
139	7.9	**Lakewood** (city) Cuyahoga County
139	7.9	**Norton** (city) Summit County
139	7.9	**Reminderville** (village) Summit County
139	7.9	**Vermilion** (city) Lorain County
139	7.9	**West Union** (village) Adams County
146	7.8	**Dry Ridge** (CDP) Hamilton County
146	7.8	**Hubbard** (city) Trumbull County
146	7.8	**Kirtland** (city) Lake County
146	7.8	**Silverton** (village) Hamilton County
146	7.8	**Willoughby** (city) Lake County

Note: *This section ranks incorporated places and CDPs (Census Designated Places) with populations of 2,500 or more. Unincorporated postal areas were not considered. Please refer to the User Guide for additional information.*

Employment: Healthcare Practitioners

Top 150 Places Ranked in *Ascending* Order

State Rank	Percent	Place
1	0.7	**Green Meadows** (CDP) Clark County
2	1.0	**Summerside** (CDP) Clermont County
3	1.4	**Kenton** (city) Hardin County
4	1.6	**Brimfield** (CDP) Portage County
5	1.7	**Hicksville** (village) Defiance County
5	1.7	**West Jefferson** (village) Madison County
7	1.9	**Lincoln Heights** (village) Hamilton County
8	2.0	**Dillonvale** (CDP) Hamilton County
9	2.1	**Lodi** (village) Medina County
9	2.1	**Montpelier** (village) Williams County
11	2.2	**New Lebanon** (village) Montgomery County
12	2.3	**Fremont** (city) Sandusky County
13	2.4	**Lockland** (village) Hamilton County
13	2.4	**Oberlin** (city) Lorain County
15	2.5	**Millersburg** (village) Holmes County
16	2.6	**Bowling Green** (city) Wood County
16	2.6	**New Burlington** (CDP) Hamilton County
18	2.7	**Whitehall** (city) Franklin County
19	2.8	**Blanchester** (village) Clinton County
19	2.8	**Carrollton** (village) Carroll County
19	2.8	**Loudonville** (village) Ashland County
19	2.8	**Ottawa** (village) Putnam County
19	2.8	**Oxford** (city) Butler County
19	2.8	**Streetsboro** (city) Portage County
25	2.9	**Delphos** (city) Allen County
25	2.9	**Strasburg** (village) Tuscarawas County
27	3.0	**Athens** (city) Athens County
27	3.0	**Cleves** (village) Hamilton County
27	3.0	**Painesville** (city) Lake County
27	3.0	**Shelby** (city) Richland County
31	3.1	**Northfield** (village) Summit County
32	3.3	**Ashville** (village) Pickaway County
32	3.3	**Nelsonville** (city) Athens County
34	3.4	**Mogadore** (village) Summit County
35	3.5	**Celina** (city) Mercer County
35	3.5	**Coldwater** (village) Mercer County
35	3.5	**Delshire** (CDP) Hamilton County
38	3.6	**Alliance** (city) Stark County
38	3.6	**Greenfield** (village) Highland County
38	3.6	**Lincoln Village** (CDP) Franklin County
41	3.7	**Amelia** (village) Clermont County
41	3.7	**Fostoria** (city) Seneca County
41	3.7	**Girard** (city) Trumbull County
41	3.7	**Greenville** (city) Darke County
41	3.7	**Kent** (city) Portage County
41	3.7	**The Plains** (CDP) Athens County
47	3.8	**Ashtabula** (city) Ashtabula County
47	3.8	**Enon** (village) Clark County
47	3.8	**Fredericktown** (village) Knox County
47	3.8	**Hartville** (village) Stark County
47	3.8	**Heath** (city) Licking County
47	3.8	**Plain City** (village) Madison County
47	3.8	**Warrensville Heights** (city) Cuyahoga County
54	3.9	**Northgate** (CDP) Hamilton County
54	3.9	**Piqua** (city) Miami County
54	3.9	**Sidney** (city) Shelby County
57	4.0	**Calcutta** (CDP) Columbiana County
57	4.0	**Lisbon** (village) Columbiana County
57	4.0	**Minerva** (village) Stark County
60	4.1	**Brooklyn** (city) Cuyahoga County
60	4.1	**London** (city) Madison County
60	4.1	**Loveland** (city) Hamilton County
60	4.1	**Tiffin** (city) Seneca County
64	4.2	**Findlay** (city) Hancock County
64	4.2	**Mount Carmel** (CDP) Clermont County
64	4.2	**New Carlisle** (city) Clark County
64	4.2	**Seville** (village) Medina County
68	4.3	**Baltimore** (village) Fairfield County
68	4.3	**Bedford** (city) Cuyahoga County
68	4.3	**Blacklick Estates** (CDP) Franklin County
68	4.3	**Bryan** (city) Williams County
68	4.3	**Defiance** (city) Defiance County
68	4.3	**Reynoldsburg** (city) Franklin County
68	4.3	**Troy** (city) Miami County
75	4.4	**Cedarville** (village) Greene County
75	4.4	**Oak Harbor** (village) Ottawa County
75	4.4	**South Lebanon** (village) Warren County
78	4.5	**Berea** (city) Cuyahoga County
78	4.5	**Huber Ridge** (CDP) Franklin County
78	4.5	**Springfield** (city) Clark County
81	4.6	**Coshocton** (city) Coshocton County
82	4.7	**Clyde** (city) Sandusky County
82	4.7	**Devola** (CDP) Washington County
82	4.7	**Louisville** (city) Stark County
82	4.7	**New Lexington** (village) Perry County
82	4.7	**Park Layne** (CDP) Clark County
82	4.7	**Sandusky** (city) Erie County
82	4.7	**Urbana** (city) Champaign County
82	4.7	**Wapakoneta** (city) Auglaize County
90	4.8	**Dayton** (city) Montgomery County
90	4.8	**East Liverpool** (city) Columbiana County
90	4.8	**Mentor-on-the-Lake** (city) Lake County
90	4.8	**Ontario** (city) Richland County
90	4.8	**Wooster** (city) Wayne County
95	4.9	**Ada** (village) Hardin County
95	4.9	**Lorain** (city) Lorain County
95	4.9	**Marysville** (city) Union County
95	4.9	**North Zanesville** (CDP) Muskingum County
95	4.9	**Obetz** (village) Franklin County
95	4.9	**Port Clinton** (city) Ottawa County
95	4.9	**Wilmington** (city) Clinton County
102	5.0	**Bethel** (village) Clermont County
102	5.0	**Dennison** (village) Tuscarawas County
102	5.0	**Marion** (city) Marion County
102	5.0	**Middletown** (city) Butler County
102	5.0	**Willard** (city) Huron County
102	5.0	**Williamsburg** (village) Clermont County
108	5.1	**Akron** (city) Summit County
108	5.1	**Cleveland** (city) Cuyahoga County
108	5.1	**Gahanna** (city) Franklin County
108	5.1	**Granville** (village) Licking County
108	5.1	**Mount Repose** (CDP) Clermont County
108	5.1	**Uhrichsville** (city) Tuscarawas County
114	5.2	**Galion** (city) Crawford County
114	5.2	**Lake Darby** (CDP) Franklin County
114	5.2	**Newark** (city) Licking County
114	5.2	**North Baltimore** (village) Wood County
114	5.2	**Wauseon** (city) Fulton County
114	5.2	**West Milton** (village) Miami County
120	5.3	**Bellefontaine** (city) Logan County
120	5.3	**Middleburg Heights** (city) Cuyahoga County
120	5.3	**Mount Healthy** (city) Hamilton County
120	5.3	**Mount Vernon** (city) Knox County
120	5.3	**Norwalk** (city) Huron County
120	5.3	**Trotwood** (city) Montgomery County
126	5.4	**Ashland** (city) Ashland County
126	5.4	**Canton** (city) Stark County
126	5.4	**Mansfield** (city) Richland County
126	5.4	**Rittman** (city) Wayne County
126	5.4	**Tallmadge** (city) Summit County
126	5.4	**Youngstown** (city) Mahoning County
132	5.5	**Finneytown** (CDP) Hamilton County
132	5.5	**Johnstown** (village) Licking County
132	5.5	**Madison** (village) Lake County
132	5.5	**Orrville** (city) Wayne County
132	5.5	**Saint Marys** (city) Auglaize County
132	5.5	**Sebring** (village) Mahoning County
138	5.6	**Buckeye Lake** (village) Licking County
138	5.6	**Bucyrus** (city) Crawford County
138	5.6	**Garfield Heights** (city) Cuyahoga County
138	5.6	**Groveport** (city) Franklin County
138	5.6	**McDonald** (village) Trumbull County
138	5.6	**Swanton** (village) Fulton County
144	5.7	**Brook Park** (city) Cuyahoga County
144	5.7	**Fairborn** (city) Greene County
144	5.7	**Gibsonburg** (village) Sandusky County
144	5.7	**Lancaster** (city) Fairfield County
144	5.7	**Lima** (city) Allen County
144	5.7	**Logan** (city) Hocking County
144	5.7	**Salem Heights** (CDP) Hamilton County

Note: *This section ranks incorporated places and CDPs (Census Designated Places) with populations of 2,500 or more. Unincorporated postal areas were not considered. Please refer to the User Guide for additional information.*

Employment: Service Occupations

Top 150 Places Ranked in *Descending* Order

State Rank	Percent	Place
1	33.8	**New Concord** (village) Muskingum County
2	32.2	**Oxford** (city) Butler County
3	31.7	**Lincoln Heights** (village) Hamilton County
4	31.4	**Cedarville** (village) Greene County
5	30.7	**East Cleveland** (city) Cuyahoga County
6	30.2	**Lodi** (village) Medina County
7	29.7	**Nelsonville** (city) Athens County
8	29.5	**Dennison** (village) Tuscarawas County
8	29.5	**Sandusky** (city) Erie County
10	29.4	**Toronto** (city) Jefferson County
11	28.9	**Saint Bernard** (city) Hamilton County
12	28.7	**Ada** (village) Hardin County
13	28.4	**Athens** (city) Athens County
14	28.3	**Portsmouth** (city) Scioto County
15	28.2	**Bellaire** (village) Belmont County
16	27.9	**Georgetown** (village) Brown County
17	27.3	**Youngstown** (city) Mahoning County
18	27.2	**Ashtabula** (city) Ashtabula County
19	27.1	**Bowling Green** (city) Wood County
20	27.0	**East Liverpool** (city) Columbiana County
21	26.6	**Canton** (city) Stark County
22	26.4	**Cleveland** (city) Cuyahoga County
22	26.4	**Middlefield** (village) Geauga County
22	26.4	**Trotwood** (city) Montgomery County
25	26.3	**Jefferson** (village) Ashtabula County
26	26.2	**Baltimore** (village) Fairfield County
27	26.0	**Millersburg** (village) Holmes County
28	25.9	**Lima** (city) Allen County
28	25.9	**Martins Ferry** (city) Belmont County
30	25.5	**Mount Orab** (village) Brown County
31	25.4	**Ravenna** (city) Portage County
31	25.4	**Zanesville** (city) Muskingum County
33	25.2	**Delshire** (CDP) Hamilton County
34	25.0	**Warrensville Heights** (city) Cuyahoga County
35	24.9	**Dayton** (city) Montgomery County
35	24.9	**Waynesville** (village) Warren County
37	24.8	**Canal Fulton** (city) Stark County
38	24.6	**Mount Vernon** (city) Knox County
39	24.5	**Logan** (city) Hocking County
39	24.5	**New London** (village) Huron County
41	24.4	**Walbridge** (village) Wood County
42	24.3	**Silverton** (village) Hamilton County
43	24.2	**Ironton** (city) Lawrence County
44	24.0	**Lake Lakengren** (CDP) Preble County
44	24.0	**Ontario** (city) Richland County
44	24.0	**Painesville** (city) Lake County
44	24.0	**Park Layne** (CDP) Clark County
48	23.9	**Chillicothe** (city) Ross County
48	23.9	**Oberlin** (city) Lorain County
48	23.9	**Uhrichsville** (city) Tuscarawas County
51	23.8	**Golf Manor** (village) Hamilton County
51	23.8	**Kent** (city) Portage County
51	23.8	**Maple Heights** (city) Cuyahoga County
51	23.8	**Northfield** (village) Summit County
55	23.7	**Crestline** (village) Crawford County
55	23.7	**Lincoln Village** (CDP) Franklin County
55	23.7	**Marietta** (city) Washington County
58	23.6	**Cheviot** (city) Hamilton County
58	23.6	**Mingo Junction** (village) Jefferson County
58	23.6	**Niles** (city) Trumbull County
58	23.6	**Perry Heights** (CDP) Stark County
58	23.6	**Warren** (city) Trumbull County
58	23.6	**West Milton** (village) Miami County
64	23.4	**North College Hill** (city) Hamilton County
64	23.4	**Springfield** (city) Clark County
64	23.4	**Waverly** (village) Pike County
67	23.2	**Carlisle** (village) Warren County
68	23.0	**Tiffin** (city) Seneca County
69	22.8	**Hartville** (village) Stark County
70	22.7	**Bethel** (village) Clermont County
70	22.7	**Euclid** (city) Cuyahoga County
70	22.7	**Lisbon** (village) Columbiana County
70	22.7	**London** (city) Madison County
74	22.6	**Fredericktown** (village) Knox County
74	22.6	**New Burlington** (CDP) Hamilton County
76	22.5	**Campbell** (city) Mahoning County
76	22.5	**Coshocton** (city) Coshocton County
76	22.5	**Eaton** (city) Preble County
76	22.5	**Mansfield** (city) Richland County
76	22.5	**Toledo** (city) Lucas County
81	22.3	**Hillsboro** (city) Highland County
82	22.2	**Edgewood** (CDP) Ashtabula County
82	22.2	**Elyria** (city) Lorain County
82	22.2	**Milford** (city) Clermont County
82	22.2	**Pleasant Run** (CDP) Hamilton County
86	22.1	**Alliance** (city) Stark County
86	22.1	**Carrollton** (village) Carroll County
86	22.1	**Lancaster** (city) Fairfield County
86	22.1	**Steubenville** (city) Jefferson County
90	22.0	**Whitehall** (city) Franklin County
91	21.9	**Newark** (city) Licking County
91	21.9	**Wilmington** (city) Clinton County
93	21.8	**Barberton** (city) Summit County
93	21.8	**Hamilton** (city) Butler County
93	21.8	**Huron** (city) Erie County
93	21.8	**Mount Healthy** (city) Hamilton County
93	21.8	**Salem** (city) Columbiana County
98	21.7	**Akron** (city) Summit County
98	21.7	**Fostoria** (city) Seneca County
98	21.7	**Mount Healthy Heights** (CDP) Hamilton County
101	21.6	**Mount Carmel** (CDP) Clermont County
101	21.6	**Seville** (village) Medina County
101	21.6	**Streetsboro** (city) Portage County
101	21.6	**Struthers** (city) Mahoning County
105	21.5	**Heath** (city) Licking County
105	21.5	**Mentor-on-the-Lake** (city) Lake County
107	21.4	**Cambridge** (city) Guernsey County
107	21.4	**Cincinnati** (city) Hamilton County
107	21.4	**New Lexington** (village) Perry County
110	21.3	**Johnstown** (village) Licking County
110	21.3	**Lorain** (city) Lorain County
110	21.3	**Shadyside** (village) Belmont County
110	21.3	**Wellsville** (village) Columbiana County
110	21.3	**White Oak** (CDP) Hamilton County
115	21.2	**Austintown** (CDP) Mahoning County
115	21.2	**Northbrook** (CDP) Hamilton County
117	21.1	**Bucyrus** (city) Crawford County
117	21.1	**Burlington** (CDP) Lawrence County
119	21.0	**Lakemore** (village) Summit County
119	21.0	**McDonald** (village) Trumbull County
121	20.9	**Marion** (city) Marion County
121	20.9	**Richmond Heights** (city) Cuyahoga County
123	20.8	**South Point** (village) Lawrence County
124	20.6	**Fruit Hill** (CDP) Hamilton County
125	20.5	**Union** (city) Montgomery County
125	20.5	**West Portsmouth** (CDP) Scioto County
127	20.4	**Archbold** (village) Fulton County
127	20.4	**New Carlisle** (city) Clark County
129	20.3	**Doylestown** (village) Wayne County
130	20.2	**Delta** (village) Fulton County
130	20.2	**Galion** (city) Crawford County
130	20.2	**Moraine** (city) Montgomery County
130	20.2	**Norwood** (city) Hamilton County
130	20.2	**Port Clinton** (city) Ottawa County
130	20.2	**Springdale** (city) Hamilton County
130	20.2	**Wooster** (city) Wayne County
137	20.1	**Girard** (city) Trumbull County
137	20.1	**Massillon** (city) Stark County
137	20.1	**Middletown** (city) Butler County
140	20.0	**Geneva** (city) Ashtabula County
141	19.8	**New Philadelphia** (city) Tuscarawas County
142	19.6	**Garfield Heights** (city) Cuyahoga County
142	19.6	**Piqua** (city) Miami County
142	19.6	**Riverside** (city) Montgomery County
145	19.5	**Eastlake** (city) Lake County
145	19.5	**Lordstown** (village) Trumbull County
145	19.5	**Mount Repose** (CDP) Clermont County
145	19.5	**South Euclid** (city) Cuyahoga County
145	19.5	**Van Wert** (city) Van Wert County
150	19.4	**Munroe Falls** (city) Summit County

Note: *This section ranks incorporated places and CDPs (Census Designated Places) with populations of 2,500 or more. Unincorporated postal areas were not considered. Please refer to the User Guide for additional information.*

Employment: Service Occupations

Top 150 Places Ranked in *Ascending* Order

State Rank	Percent	Place
1	2.9	**The Village of Indian Hill** (city) Hamilton County
2	4.7	**Amberley** (village) Hamilton County
2	4.7	**Oakwood** (city) Montgomery County
4	4.8	**Orange** (village) Cuyahoga County
5	4.9	**Montrose-Ghent** (CDP) Summit County
5	4.9	**Powell** (city) Delaware County
7	6.0	**Four Bridges** (CDP) Butler County
8	7.0	**Pepper Pike** (city) Cuyahoga County
9	7.2	**Ottawa Hills** (village) Lucas County
10	7.4	**Mayfield** (village) Cuyahoga County
11	7.8	**Upper Arlington** (city) Franklin County
12	7.9	**Dublin** (city) Franklin County
13	8.3	**Bainbridge** (CDP) Geauga County
13	8.3	**Dry Run** (CDP) Hamilton County
15	8.6	**Worthington** (city) Franklin County
16	9.0	**Bay Village** (city) Cuyahoga County
16	9.0	**Bryan** (city) Williams County
16	9.0	**Mariemont** (village) Hamilton County
19	9.1	**Kenwood** (CDP) Hamilton County
19	9.1	**Montgomery** (city) Hamilton County
21	9.3	**Apple Valley** (CDP) Knox County
21	9.3	**Turpin Hills** (CDP) Hamilton County
23	9.4	**Bellbrook** (city) Greene County
23	9.4	**Grandview Heights** (city) Franklin County
25	9.6	**New Albany** (city) Franklin County
26	9.7	**Carey** (village) Wyandot County
26	9.7	**Delhi Hills** (CDP) Hamilton County
28	9.8	**Beachwood** (city) Cuyahoga County
28	9.8	**Dry Ridge** (CDP) Hamilton County
30	10.0	**Fort Shawnee** (CDP) Allen County
30	10.0	**Hudson** (city) Summit County
30	10.0	**Macedonia** (city) Summit County
30	10.0	**Moreland Hills** (village) Cuyahoga County
30	10.0	**Poland** (village) Mahoning County
30	10.0	**Wyoming** (city) Hamilton County
36	10.1	**Canfield** (city) Mahoning County
36	10.1	**Greentown** (CDP) Stark County
38	10.2	**Plain City** (village) Madison County
39	10.4	**Landen** (CDP) Warren County
40	10.5	**Forestville** (CDP) Hamilton County
40	10.5	**Madeira** (city) Hamilton County
40	10.5	**Shaker Heights** (city) Cuyahoga County
43	10.7	**Covedale** (CDP) Hamilton County
43	10.7	**Mack** (CDP) Hamilton County
43	10.7	**Wellston** (city) Jackson County
46	10.8	**Fairlawn** (city) Summit County
46	10.8	**Garrettsville** (village) Portage County
46	10.8	**Olmsted Falls** (city) Cuyahoga County
46	10.8	**Seven Hills** (city) Cuyahoga County
50	10.9	**South Russell** (village) Geauga County
51	11.0	**Mason** (city) Warren County
52	11.1	**Taylor Creek** (CDP) Hamilton County
53	11.4	**Highland Heights** (city) Cuyahoga County
54	11.5	**Newton Falls** (village) Trumbull County
54	11.5	**Springboro** (city) Warren County
56	11.6	**Chardon** (city) Geauga County
56	11.6	**Kirtland** (city) Lake County
58	11.7	**Cortland** (city) Trumbull County
59	11.8	**Avon Lake** (city) Lorain County
59	11.8	**Day Heights** (CDP) Clermont County
59	11.8	**Westlake** (city) Cuyahoga County
62	11.9	**Brecksville** (city) Cuyahoga County
63	12.0	**Richfield** (village) Summit County
63	12.0	**Uniontown** (CDP) Stark County
65	12.1	**Chagrin Falls** (village) Cuyahoga County
65	12.1	**New Bremen** (village) Auglaize County
67	12.2	**Beckett Ridge** (CDP) Butler County
67	12.2	**Bexley** (city) Franklin County
67	12.2	**Versailles** (village) Darke County
70	12.3	**Minster** (village) Auglaize County
70	12.3	**Westerville** (city) Franklin County
72	12.4	**Hilliard** (city) Franklin County
72	12.4	**Saint Henry** (village) Mercer County
74	12.5	**Beavercreek** (city) Greene County
75	12.6	**Rocky River** (city) Cuyahoga County
76	12.7	**Avon** (city) Lorain County
76	12.7	**Broadview Heights** (city) Cuyahoga County
76	12.7	**Fairport Harbor** (village) Lake County
76	12.7	**Twinsburg** (city) Summit County
80	12.8	**South Lebanon** (village) Warren County
80	12.8	**Strongsville** (city) Cuyahoga County
82	12.9	**North Madison** (CDP) Lake County
83	13.0	**Ballville** (CDP) Sandusky County
83	13.0	**Lyndhurst** (city) Cuyahoga County
85	13.1	**Dent** (CDP) Hamilton County
85	13.1	**Grafton** (village) Lorain County
85	13.1	**Salem Heights** (CDP) Hamilton County
88	13.2	**Belpre** (city) Washington County
88	13.2	**Cherry Grove** (CDP) Hamilton County
88	13.2	**Perrysburg** (city) Wood County
88	13.2	**Sharonville** (city) Hamilton County
88	13.2	**Sherwood** (CDP) Hamilton County
88	13.2	**Trenton** (city) Butler County
88	13.2	**West Union** (village) Adams County
95	13.3	**Franklin** (city) Warren County
96	13.4	**Brimfield** (CDP) Portage County
96	13.4	**Sixteen Mile Stand** (CDP) Hamilton County
98	13.5	**Blue Ash** (city) Hamilton County
98	13.5	**Groveport** (city) Franklin County
98	13.5	**The Plains** (CDP) Athens County
98	13.5	**Willoughby Hills** (city) Lake County
102	13.6	**Centerville** (city) Montgomery County
102	13.6	**Independence** (city) Cuyahoga County
102	13.6	**Strasburg** (village) Tuscarawas County
105	13.7	**Champion Heights** (CDP) Trumbull County
105	13.7	**Cleveland Heights** (city) Cuyahoga County
105	13.7	**Oakwood** (village) Cuyahoga County
108	13.8	**Newtown** (village) Hamilton County
108	13.8	**Obetz** (village) Franklin County
110	13.9	**Aurora** (city) Portage County
110	13.9	**Delphos** (city) Allen County
110	13.9	**Northridge** (CDP) Clark County
110	13.9	**Saint Clairsville** (city) Belmont County
114	14.0	**Solon** (city) Cuyahoga County
114	14.0	**University Heights** (city) Cuyahoga County
116	14.1	**Dillonvale** (CDP) Hamilton County
116	14.1	**Mount Gilead** (village) Morrow County
116	14.1	**North Ridgeville** (city) Lorain County
116	14.1	**Sylvania** (city) Lucas County
120	14.2	**Evendale** (village) Hamilton County
120	14.2	**North Royalton** (city) Cuyahoga County
120	14.2	**Pleasant Run Farm** (CDP) Hamilton County
123	14.3	**Barnesville** (village) Belmont County
123	14.3	**Devola** (CDP) Washington County
123	14.3	**Medina** (city) Medina County
123	14.3	**Mentor** (city) Lake County
127	14.4	**Brookville** (city) Montgomery County
127	14.4	**Reminderville** (village) Summit County
129	14.5	**Sunbury** (village) Delaware County
130	14.6	**Beechwood Trails** (CDP) Licking County
130	14.6	**Woodlawn** (village) Hamilton County
132	14.7	**Buckeye Lake** (village) Licking County
132	14.7	**Miami Heights** (CDP) Hamilton County
132	14.7	**Norton** (city) Summit County
135	14.8	**Fairview Park** (city) Cuyahoga County
135	14.8	**North Kingsville** (village) Ashtabula County
135	14.8	**Stow** (city) Summit County
135	14.8	**Willowick** (city) Lake County
139	14.9	**Grove City** (city) Franklin County
139	14.9	**Paulding** (village) Paulding County
139	14.9	**Wadsworth** (city) Medina County
142	15.0	**Jackson** (city) Jackson County
142	15.0	**Northwood** (city) Wood County
144	15.1	**Bellefontaine** (city) Logan County
144	15.1	**Green** (city) Summit County
144	15.1	**Lakewood** (city) Cuyahoga County
144	15.1	**Monfort Heights** (CDP) Hamilton County
148	15.2	**Maumee** (city) Lucas County
149	15.3	**North Zanesville** (CDP) Muskingum County
149	15.3	**Waterville** (city) Lucas County

Note: *This section ranks incorporated places and CDPs (Census Designated Places) with populations of 2,500 or more. Unincorporated postal areas were not considered. Please refer to the User Guide for additional information.*

Employment: Sales and Office Occupations

Top 150 Places Ranked in *Descending* Order

State Rank	Percent	Place
1	37.3	**Belpre** (city) Washington County
1	37.3	**Chardon** (city) Geauga County
3	35.9	**Delhi Hills** (CDP) Hamilton County
4	33.9	**North Zanesville** (CDP) Muskingum County
5	32.7	**Brimfield** (CDP) Portage County
6	32.2	**West Jefferson** (village) Madison County
7	31.6	**Northbrook** (CDP) Hamilton County
8	31.4	**Sherwood** (CDP) Hamilton County
9	31.3	**Nelsonville** (city) Athens County
10	31.2	**Dillonvale** (CDP) Hamilton County
10	31.2	**New Lebanon** (village) Montgomery County
12	30.9	**Dent** (CDP) Hamilton County
12	30.9	**Park Layne** (CDP) Clark County
14	30.8	**Mogadore** (village) Summit County
15	30.6	**Gallipolis** (village) Gallia County
16	30.4	**Ashville** (village) Pickaway County
16	30.4	**Burlington** (CDP) Lawrence County
16	30.4	**Mariemont** (village) Hamilton County
19	30.3	**Warrensville Heights** (city) Cuyahoga County
20	30.2	**Reynoldsburg** (city) Franklin County
21	30.0	**Bridgetown** (CDP) Hamilton County
21	30.0	**Day Heights** (CDP) Clermont County
21	30.0	**New Burlington** (CDP) Hamilton County
24	29.9	**Garfield Heights** (city) Cuyahoga County
25	29.8	**Brook Park** (city) Cuyahoga County
25	29.8	**Euclid** (city) Cuyahoga County
27	29.7	**Grafton** (village) Lorain County
27	29.7	**Medina** (city) Medina County
29	29.6	**Groveport** (city) Franklin County
29	29.6	**Parma Heights** (city) Cuyahoga County
31	29.4	**Fairborn** (city) Greene County
31	29.4	**Harrison** (city) Hamilton County
33	29.2	**Blacklick Estates** (CDP) Franklin County
33	29.2	**Milford** (city) Clermont County
33	29.2	**Minerva** (village) Stark County
36	29.1	**Canfield** (city) Mahoning County
37	28.9	**Germantown** (city) Montgomery County
38	28.8	**Carrollton** (village) Carroll County
39	28.7	**Bedford** (city) Cuyahoga County
39	28.7	**Girard** (city) Trumbull County
39	28.7	**Greentown** (CDP) Stark County
42	28.6	**Groesbeck** (CDP) Hamilton County
43	28.5	**Chagrin Falls** (village) Cuyahoga County
43	28.5	**Mount Healthy Heights** (CDP) Hamilton County
45	28.4	**Sheffield Lake** (city) Lorain County
46	28.3	**Delshire** (CDP) Hamilton County
46	28.3	**Northwood** (city) Wood County
46	28.3	**Pleasant Run** (CDP) Hamilton County
49	28.2	**Bainbridge** (CDP) Geauga County
50	28.1	**Grove City** (city) Franklin County
50	28.1	**Olmsted Falls** (city) Cuyahoga County
52	28.0	**Mansfield** (city) Richland County
53	27.8	**Pataskala** (city) Licking County
53	27.8	**Tallmadge** (city) Summit County
55	27.7	**Amelia** (village) Clermont County
55	27.7	**Covedale** (CDP) Hamilton County
55	27.7	**Devola** (CDP) Washington County
55	27.7	**Lincoln Village** (CDP) Franklin County
55	27.7	**Union** (city) Montgomery County
60	27.6	**Boardman** (CDP) Mahoning County
60	27.6	**Cherry Grove** (CDP) Hamilton County
60	27.6	**Struthers** (city) Mahoning County
60	27.6	**Xenia** (city) Greene County
64	27.5	**Avon** (city) Lorain County
64	27.5	**Cuyahoga Falls** (city) Summit County
64	27.5	**Rossford** (city) Wood County
67	27.4	**Aurora** (city) Portage County
67	27.4	**Cheviot** (city) Hamilton County
67	27.4	**Ironton** (city) Lawrence County
67	27.4	**Kenwood** (CDP) Hamilton County
67	27.4	**Parma** (city) Cuyahoga County
67	27.4	**Perry Heights** (CDP) Stark County
67	27.4	**Strasburg** (village) Tuscarawas County
74	27.3	**Dry Ridge** (CDP) Hamilton County
74	27.3	**Englewood** (city) Montgomery County
74	27.3	**Lebanon** (city) Warren County
74	27.3	**Portage Lakes** (CDP) Summit County
74	27.3	**Streetsboro** (city) Portage County
79	27.2	**Berea** (city) Cuyahoga County
79	27.2	**Greenfield** (village) Highland County
79	27.2	**Lancaster** (city) Fairfield County
79	27.2	**Ontario** (city) Richland County
83	27.1	**McDonald** (village) Trumbull County
83	27.1	**Vandalia** (city) Montgomery County
83	27.1	**Woodlawn** (village) Hamilton County
86	27.0	**Brunswick** (city) Medina County
86	27.0	**Calcutta** (CDP) Columbiana County
86	27.0	**Maple Heights** (city) Cuyahoga County
89	26.9	**Amherst** (city) Lorain County
89	26.9	**Mentor** (city) Lake County
89	26.9	**Mount Healthy** (city) Hamilton County
92	26.8	**Akron** (city) Summit County
92	26.8	**Carlisle** (village) Warren County
92	26.8	**North Olmsted** (city) Cuyahoga County
92	26.8	**Strongsville** (city) Cuyahoga County
96	26.7	**Forest Park** (city) Hamilton County
96	26.7	**Landen** (CDP) Warren County
96	26.7	**Stow** (city) Summit County
96	26.7	**Twinsburg** (city) Summit County
100	26.6	**Plain City** (village) Madison County
100	26.6	**The Plains** (CDP) Athens County
100	26.6	**Wilmington** (city) Clinton County
100	26.6	**Zanesville** (city) Muskingum County
104	26.5	**Avon Lake** (city) Lorain County
104	26.5	**Fairview Park** (city) Cuyahoga County
104	26.5	**Louisville** (city) Stark County
104	26.5	**Powell** (city) Delaware County
104	26.5	**Saint Bernard** (city) Hamilton County
104	26.5	**Sheffield** (village) Lorain County
104	26.5	**Washington Court House** (city) Fayette County
111	26.4	**Campbell** (city) Mahoning County
111	26.4	**Finneytown** (CDP) Hamilton County
111	26.4	**New Franklin** (city) Summit County
111	26.4	**Norwood** (city) Hamilton County
115	26.3	**Martins Ferry** (city) Belmont County
115	26.3	**North Ridgeville** (city) Lorain County
117	26.2	**Lodi** (village) Medina County
117	26.2	**Norton** (city) Summit County
119	26.1	**Ballville** (CDP) Sandusky County
119	26.1	**Bethel** (village) Clermont County
119	26.1	**Whitehall** (city) Franklin County
122	26.0	**Mack** (CDP) Hamilton County
122	26.0	**Trenton** (city) Butler County
124	25.9	**Barberton** (city) Summit County
124	25.9	**Delta** (village) Fulton County
124	25.9	**Green** (city) Summit County
124	25.9	**Greenville** (city) Darke County
124	25.9	**Hamilton** (city) Butler County
124	25.9	**Jackson** (city) Jackson County
124	25.9	**Massillon** (city) Stark County
124	25.9	**Maumee** (city) Lucas County
124	25.9	**Pickerington** (city) Fairfield County
124	25.9	**Summerside** (CDP) Clermont County
124	25.9	**White Oak** (CDP) Hamilton County
135	25.8	**Four Bridges** (CDP) Butler County
135	25.8	**Hillsboro** (city) Highland County
135	25.8	**Hubbard** (city) Trumbull County
135	25.8	**Jefferson** (village) Ashtabula County
135	25.8	**Logan** (city) Hocking County
135	25.8	**Mulberry** (CDP) Clermont County
141	25.7	**Hartville** (village) Stark County
141	25.7	**Silverton** (village) Hamilton County
143	25.6	**Brookville** (city) Montgomery County
143	25.6	**Kettering** (city) Montgomery County
143	25.6	**Miami Heights** (CDP) Hamilton County
143	25.6	**North Royalton** (city) Cuyahoga County
147	25.5	**Bedford Heights** (city) Cuyahoga County
147	25.5	**Dover** (city) Tuscarawas County
147	25.5	**Moraine** (city) Montgomery County
147	25.5	**Richmond Heights** (city) Cuyahoga County

Note: *This section ranks incorporated places and CDPs (Census Designated Places) with populations of 2,500 or more. Unincorporated postal areas were not considered. Please refer to the User Guide for additional information.*

Employment: Sales and Office Occupations

Top 150 Places Ranked in *Ascending* Order

State Rank	Percent	Place
1	11.5	**Yellow Springs** (village) Greene County
2	13.9	**Napoleon** (city) Henry County
3	14.6	**Doylestown** (village) Wayne County
4	14.9	**The Village of Indian Hill** (city) Hamilton County
5	15.2	**Willard** (city) Huron County
6	15.3	**Crestline** (village) Crawford County
7	15.5	**Carey** (village) Wyandot County
8	15.8	**Lincoln Heights** (village) Hamilton County
9	15.9	**South Lebanon** (village) Warren County
10	16.1	**Versailles** (village) Darke County
11	16.4	**Upper Sandusky** (city) Wyandot County
12	16.5	**Lake Lakengren** (CDP) Preble County
13	16.9	**Beechwood Trails** (CDP) Licking County
14	17.0	**North Baltimore** (village) Wood County
15	17.1	**Archbold** (village) Fulton County
15	17.1	**Grandview Heights** (city) Franklin County
17	17.3	**Loudonville** (village) Ashland County
17	17.3	**New London** (village) Huron County
17	17.3	**Shaker Heights** (city) Cuyahoga County
20	17.4	**Fostoria** (city) Seneca County
20	17.4	**Lordstown** (village) Trumbull County
22	17.5	**Montpelier** (village) Williams County
23	17.6	**Shadyside** (village) Belmont County
24	17.7	**Dennison** (village) Tuscarawas County
25	17.8	**Bluffton** (village) Allen County
25	17.8	**Eaton** (city) Preble County
25	17.8	**Wauseon** (city) Fulton County
28	17.9	**Celina** (city) Mercer County
28	17.9	**Tipp City** (city) Miami County
30	18.0	**Oxford** (city) Butler County
30	18.0	**West Union** (village) Adams County
32	18.1	**New Bremen** (village) Auglaize County
33	18.2	**Bellevue** (city) Sandusky County
33	18.2	**Fruit Hill** (CDP) Hamilton County
35	18.4	**Coldwater** (village) Mercer County
35	18.4	**Millersburg** (village) Holmes County
37	18.5	**Mount Vernon** (city) Knox County
38	18.8	**Clyde** (city) Sandusky County
38	18.8	**East Liverpool** (city) Columbiana County
38	18.8	**Fairlawn** (city) Summit County
38	18.8	**Green Meadows** (CDP) Clark County
38	18.8	**Madison** (village) Lake County
43	18.9	**Whitehouse** (village) Lucas County
44	19.0	**Bellefontaine** (city) Logan County
44	19.0	**Cleveland Heights** (city) Cuyahoga County
44	19.0	**Oakwood** (city) Montgomery County
47	19.1	**Findlay** (city) Hancock County
48	19.2	**Fremont** (city) Sandusky County
48	19.2	**Van Wert** (city) Van Wert County
50	19.4	**Newtown** (village) Hamilton County
51	19.5	**Saint Marys** (city) Auglaize County
52	19.7	**Reminderville** (village) Summit County
53	19.8	**Covington** (village) Miami County
53	19.8	**Rocky River** (city) Cuyahoga County
55	20.0	**Coshocton** (city) Coshocton County
55	20.0	**Lima** (city) Allen County
57	20.1	**Ada** (village) Hardin County
58	20.2	**Bellaire** (village) Belmont County
58	20.2	**Newton Falls** (village) Trumbull County
58	20.2	**Wellston** (city) Jackson County
61	20.3	**Blue Ash** (city) Hamilton County
61	20.3	**Galion** (city) Crawford County
61	20.3	**Hicksville** (village) Defiance County
61	20.3	**Tiffin** (city) Seneca County
61	20.3	**Williamsburg** (village) Clermont County
66	20.4	**Enon** (village) Clark County
66	20.4	**Lisbon** (village) Columbiana County
66	20.4	**North Kingsville** (village) Ashtabula County
66	20.4	**South Point** (village) Lawrence County
66	20.4	**Upper Arlington** (city) Franklin County
71	20.5	**Painesville** (city) Lake County
71	20.5	**Sidney** (city) Shelby County
71	20.5	**Wapakoneta** (city) Auglaize County
71	20.5	**Wooster** (city) Wayne County
75	20.6	**Canal Winchester** (city) Franklin County
75	20.6	**Sebring** (village) Mahoning County
77	20.7	**New Carlisle** (city) Clark County
77	20.7	**New Richmond** (village) Clermont County
79	20.8	**Beachwood** (city) Cuyahoga County
79	20.8	**Mineral Ridge** (CDP) Trumbull County
79	20.8	**Paulding** (village) Paulding County
82	20.9	**New Albany** (city) Franklin County
82	20.9	**Newcomerstown** (village) Tuscarawas County
84	21.0	**Marion** (city) Marion County
84	21.0	**Springboro** (city) Warren County
84	21.0	**Urbana** (city) Champaign County
87	21.1	**Dublin** (city) Franklin County
87	21.1	**Oberlin** (city) Lorain County
87	21.1	**Wyoming** (city) Hamilton County
90	21.2	**Marysville** (city) Union County
90	21.2	**Middlefield** (village) Geauga County
90	21.2	**Reading** (city) Hamilton County
93	21.3	**Oak Harbor** (village) Ottawa County
93	21.3	**Solon** (city) Cuyahoga County
93	21.3	**University Heights** (city) Cuyahoga County
96	21.4	**Granville** (village) Licking County
96	21.4	**Ottawa** (village) Putnam County
98	21.5	**Beavercreek** (city) Greene County
98	21.5	**Bexley** (city) Franklin County
98	21.5	**Champion Heights** (CDP) Trumbull County
101	21.6	**Cadiz** (village) Harrison County
101	21.6	**Huron** (city) Erie County
101	21.6	**Montgomery** (city) Hamilton County
101	21.6	**Rittman** (city) Wayne County
101	21.6	**Saint Henry** (village) Mercer County
106	21.8	**Athens** (city) Athens County
106	21.8	**Baltimore** (village) Fairfield County
106	21.8	**Canal Fulton** (city) Stark County
106	21.8	**Highland Heights** (city) Cuyahoga County
106	21.8	**Johnstown** (village) Licking County
106	21.8	**Montrose-Ghent** (CDP) Summit County
112	21.9	**Bellbrook** (city) Greene County
112	21.9	**Brecksville** (city) Cuyahoga County
112	21.9	**Oakwood** (village) Cuyahoga County
112	21.9	**Orrville** (city) Wayne County
112	21.9	**Perrysburg** (city) Wood County
112	21.9	**Uniontown** (CDP) Stark County
118	22.0	**Bucyrus** (city) Crawford County
118	22.0	**Kirtland** (city) Lake County
118	22.0	**Seville** (village) Medina County
118	22.0	**Swanton** (village) Fulton County
122	22.1	**Greenhills** (village) Hamilton County
122	22.1	**Ottawa Hills** (village) Lucas County
122	22.1	**Sunbury** (village) Delaware County
122	22.1	**Wadsworth** (city) Medina County
126	22.2	**Cincinnati** (city) Hamilton County
126	22.2	**Minster** (village) Auglaize County
126	22.2	**Sharonville** (city) Hamilton County
129	22.3	**Ashtabula** (city) Ashtabula County
129	22.3	**West Milton** (village) Miami County
131	22.4	**Dry Run** (CDP) Hamilton County
131	22.4	**Gibsonburg** (village) Sandusky County
131	22.4	**Lockland** (village) Hamilton County
131	22.4	**Mount Repose** (CDP) Clermont County
131	22.4	**Munroe Falls** (city) Summit County
131	22.4	**Sandusky** (city) Erie County
137	22.5	**Gahanna** (city) Franklin County
137	22.5	**Sylvania** (city) Lucas County
137	22.5	**Wheelersburg** (CDP) Scioto County
140	22.6	**Canton** (city) Stark County
140	22.6	**Garrettsville** (village) Portage County
140	22.6	**Independence** (city) Cuyahoga County
140	22.6	**Vermilion** (city) Lorain County
144	22.7	**Delaware** (city) Delaware County
144	22.7	**Troy** (city) Miami County
146	22.8	**Amberley** (village) Hamilton County
146	22.8	**Howland Center** (CDP) Trumbull County
146	22.8	**Norwalk** (city) Huron County
146	22.8	**Walbridge** (village) Wood County
146	22.8	**Wickliffe** (city) Lake County

Note: *This section ranks incorporated places and CDPs (Census Designated Places) with populations of 2,500 or more. Unincorporated postal areas were not considered. Please refer to the User Guide for additional information.*

Employment: Natural Resources, Construction, and Maintenance Occupations

Top 150 Places Ranked in *Descending* Order

State Rank	Percent	Place
1	21.5	**New Lebanon** (village) Montgomery County
2	19.6	**Cadiz** (village) Harrison County
3	18.6	**Sebring** (village) Mahoning County
4	17.6	**New Richmond** (village) Clermont County
5	17.1	**Green Meadows** (CDP) Clark County
6	16.4	**Ross** (CDP) Butler County
6	16.4	**West Union** (village) Adams County
8	15.5	**New Carlisle** (city) Clark County
9	15.3	**Barnesville** (village) Belmont County
10	15.2	**Amelia** (village) Clermont County
10	15.2	**Bellaire** (village) Belmont County
10	15.2	**Paulding** (village) Paulding County
13	15.1	**Wellsville** (village) Columbiana County
14	14.8	**Johnstown** (village) Licking County
14	14.8	**Shadyside** (village) Belmont County
16	14.6	**Williamsburg** (village) Clermont County
17	14.3	**Taylor Creek** (CDP) Hamilton County
18	14.2	**Obetz** (village) Franklin County
19	14.0	**Wellston** (city) Jackson County
20	13.2	**Mount Healthy Heights** (CDP) Hamilton County
21	12.8	**Beechwood Trails** (CDP) Licking County
21	12.8	**Cleves** (village) Hamilton County
21	12.8	**Upper Sandusky** (city) Wyandot County
24	12.7	**Northgate** (CDP) Hamilton County
25	12.6	**Blanchester** (village) Clinton County
25	12.6	**West Milton** (village) Miami County
25	12.6	**Wheelersburg** (CDP) Scioto County
28	12.5	**Coldwater** (village) Mercer County
28	12.5	**East Palestine** (village) Columbiana County
28	12.5	**West Jefferson** (village) Madison County
31	12.4	**Brimfield** (CDP) Portage County
31	12.4	**Norwalk** (city) Huron County
31	12.4	**Pleasant Run** (CDP) Hamilton County
34	12.3	**Loudonville** (village) Ashland County
34	12.3	**Vermilion** (city) Lorain County
36	12.1	**Buckeye Lake** (village) Licking County
36	12.1	**Lordstown** (village) Trumbull County
38	12.0	**Swanton** (village) Fulton County
39	11.8	**Champion Heights** (CDP) Trumbull County
39	11.8	**Mount Orab** (village) Brown County
41	11.7	**Moraine** (city) Montgomery County
42	11.5	**Franklin** (city) Warren County
43	11.3	**North Madison** (CDP) Lake County
43	11.3	**Wintersville** (village) Jefferson County
45	11.2	**Lisbon** (village) Columbiana County
46	11.1	**Gallipolis** (village) Gallia County
46	11.1	**Greenhills** (village) Hamilton County
46	11.1	**Hicksville** (village) Defiance County
46	11.1	**Norton** (city) Summit County
46	11.1	**The Plains** (CDP) Athens County
51	11.0	**New Franklin** (city) Summit County
52	10.9	**Oregon** (city) Lucas County
52	10.9	**Plain City** (village) Madison County
52	10.9	**Poland** (village) Mahoning County
52	10.9	**Saint Clairsville** (city) Belmont County
56	10.8	**Crooksville** (village) Perry County
56	10.8	**Newcomerstown** (village) Tuscarawas County
56	10.8	**Port Clinton** (city) Ottawa County
56	10.8	**Rossford** (city) Wood County
60	10.7	**Campbell** (city) Mahoning County
60	10.7	**Lincoln Village** (CDP) Franklin County
60	10.7	**West Carrollton** (city) Montgomery County
63	10.6	**Conneaut** (city) Ashtabula County
63	10.6	**Tipp City** (city) Miami County
65	10.5	**Delshire** (CDP) Hamilton County
65	10.5	**Martins Ferry** (city) Belmont County
67	10.4	**Amherst** (city) Lorain County
67	10.4	**Saint Henry** (village) Mercer County
69	10.3	**Clyde** (city) Sandusky County
69	10.3	**Greenville** (city) Darke County
69	10.3	**Lodi** (village) Medina County
69	10.3	**Ottawa** (village) Putnam County
73	10.2	**Bellevue** (city) Sandusky County
74	10.1	**Rittman** (city) Wayne County
75	10.0	**Portage Lakes** (CDP) Summit County
76	9.9	**Brooklyn** (city) Cuyahoga County
76	9.9	**Millersburg** (village) Holmes County
76	9.9	**Napoleon** (city) Henry County
79	9.7	**Bethel** (village) Clermont County
79	9.7	**Louisville** (city) Stark County
79	9.7	**Withamsville** (CDP) Clermont County
82	9.6	**Coshocton** (city) Coshocton County
82	9.6	**Mentor-on-the-Lake** (city) Lake County
84	9.5	**Niles** (city) Trumbull County
84	9.5	**Park Layne** (CDP) Clark County
84	9.5	**Strasburg** (village) Tuscarawas County
87	9.4	**Delhi Hills** (CDP) Hamilton County
87	9.4	**Eastlake** (city) Lake County
87	9.4	**Galion** (city) Crawford County
87	9.4	**London** (city) Madison County
87	9.4	**Oakwood** (village) Cuyahoga County
92	9.3	**Crestline** (village) Crawford County
92	9.3	**Grafton** (village) Lorain County
92	9.3	**Lorain** (city) Lorain County
92	9.3	**North Kingsville** (village) Ashtabula County
96	9.2	**Brook Park** (city) Cuyahoga County
96	9.2	**Oak Harbor** (village) Ottawa County
98	9.1	**Celina** (city) Mercer County
98	9.1	**Geneva** (city) Ashtabula County
98	9.1	**New London** (village) Huron County
98	9.1	**Xenia** (city) Greene County
102	9.0	**Harrison** (city) Hamilton County
102	9.0	**Tallmadge** (city) Summit County
102	9.0	**Trenton** (city) Butler County
105	8.9	**Garrettsville** (village) Portage County
105	8.9	**Toronto** (city) Jefferson County
105	8.9	**Versailles** (village) Darke County
108	8.8	**Barberton** (city) Summit County
108	8.8	**Covington** (village) Miami County
108	8.8	**Gibsonburg** (village) Sandusky County
108	8.8	**Madison** (village) Lake County
108	8.8	**Massillon** (city) Stark County
108	8.8	**Mingo Junction** (village) Jefferson County
108	8.8	**Riverside** (city) Montgomery County
108	8.8	**Washington Court House** (city) Fayette County
116	8.7	**Hamilton** (city) Butler County
116	8.7	**Pataskala** (city) Licking County
116	8.7	**Sheffield Lake** (city) Lorain County
116	8.7	**Willowick** (city) Lake County
120	8.6	**Baltimore** (village) Fairfield County
120	8.6	**Carlisle** (village) Warren County
120	8.6	**Howland Center** (CDP) Trumbull County
120	8.6	**Lebanon** (city) Warren County
120	8.6	**Logan** (city) Hocking County
120	8.6	**Mogadore** (village) Summit County
120	8.6	**Painesville** (city) Lake County
120	8.6	**Wadsworth** (city) Medina County
128	8.5	**Reading** (city) Hamilton County
128	8.5	**Silverton** (village) Hamilton County
130	8.4	**Chillicothe** (city) Ross County
130	8.4	**Elyria** (city) Lorain County
130	8.4	**Hartville** (village) Stark County
130	8.4	**New Lexington** (village) Perry County
134	8.3	**Austintown** (CDP) Mahoning County
134	8.3	**Bryan** (city) Williams County
134	8.3	**Cheviot** (city) Hamilton County
134	8.3	**Fremont** (city) Sandusky County
138	8.2	**Deer Park** (city) Hamilton County
138	8.2	**Richville** (CDP) Stark County
138	8.2	**Whitehall** (city) Franklin County
141	8.1	**Chardon** (city) Geauga County
141	8.1	**Grove City** (city) Franklin County
141	8.1	**Kenton** (city) Hardin County
141	8.1	**Middletown** (city) Butler County
141	8.1	**Parma** (city) Cuyahoga County
141	8.1	**Tiffin** (city) Seneca County
141	8.1	**Wapakoneta** (city) Auglaize County
148	8.0	**Canton** (city) Stark County
148	8.0	**Delta** (village) Fulton County
148	8.0	**Medina** (city) Medina County

Note: *This section ranks incorporated places and CDPs (Census Designated Places) with populations of 2,500 or more. Unincorporated postal areas were not considered. Please refer to the User Guide for additional information.*

Employment: Natural Resources, Construction, and Maintenance Occupations

Top 150 Places Ranked in *Ascending* Order

State Rank	Percent	Place
1	0.0	**Turpin Hills** (CDP) Hamilton County
2	0.6	**The Village of Indian Hill** (city) Hamilton County
3	1.0	**Evendale** (village) Hamilton County
4	1.1	**South Russell** (village) Geauga County
5	1.2	**Fruit Hill** (CDP) Hamilton County
6	1.3	**University Heights** (city) Cuyahoga County
7	1.4	**Sixteen Mile Stand** (CDP) Hamilton County
7	1.4	**Wright-Patterson AFB** (CDP) Greene County
7	1.4	**Wyoming** (city) Hamilton County
10	1.5	**Dublin** (city) Franklin County
10	1.5	**New Albany** (city) Franklin County
12	1.8	**Beachwood** (city) Cuyahoga County
12	1.8	**Bexley** (city) Franklin County
12	1.8	**Moreland Hills** (village) Cuyahoga County
12	1.8	**Ottawa Hills** (village) Lucas County
16	1.9	**Golf Manor** (village) Hamilton County
17	2.0	**Amberley** (village) Hamilton County
17	2.0	**Day Heights** (CDP) Clermont County
17	2.0	**Highland Heights** (city) Cuyahoga County
20	2.1	**Hudson** (city) Summit County
21	2.2	**Oakwood** (city) Montgomery County
21	2.2	**Upper Arlington** (city) Franklin County
23	2.3	**Granville** (village) Licking County
23	2.3	**Powell** (city) Delaware County
23	2.3	**Shaker Heights** (city) Cuyahoga County
26	2.4	**Dry Run** (CDP) Hamilton County
26	2.4	**Grandview Heights** (city) Franklin County
26	2.4	**Hilliard** (city) Franklin County
26	2.4	**Worthington** (city) Franklin County
30	2.5	**Athens** (city) Athens County
30	2.5	**Beckett Ridge** (CDP) Butler County
30	2.5	**Canal Winchester** (city) Franklin County
30	2.5	**Chagrin Falls** (village) Cuyahoga County
34	2.6	**Aurora** (city) Portage County
34	2.6	**Orange** (village) Cuyahoga County
36	2.7	**Pepper Pike** (city) Cuyahoga County
36	2.7	**Rocky River** (city) Cuyahoga County
38	2.9	**Centerville** (city) Montgomery County
39	3.0	**Canal Fulton** (city) Stark County
39	3.0	**Edgewood** (CDP) Ashtabula County
39	3.0	**Montgomery** (city) Hamilton County
42	3.1	**Blue Ash** (city) Hamilton County
42	3.1	**Forestville** (CDP) Hamilton County
42	3.1	**Madeira** (city) Hamilton County
42	3.1	**Mount Gilead** (village) Morrow County
42	3.1	**Oxford** (city) Butler County
42	3.1	**Sunbury** (village) Delaware County
48	3.2	**Canfield** (city) Mahoning County
48	3.2	**Munroe Falls** (city) Summit County
48	3.2	**Solon** (city) Cuyahoga County
48	3.2	**Stow** (city) Summit County
52	3.3	**Mariemont** (village) Hamilton County
52	3.3	**Springboro** (city) Warren County
54	3.4	**Cleveland Heights** (city) Cuyahoga County
54	3.4	**Twinsburg** (city) Summit County
56	3.5	**Dillonvale** (CDP) Hamilton County
56	3.5	**Montrose-Ghent** (CDP) Summit County
56	3.5	**Westlake** (city) Cuyahoga County
59	3.6	**Bucyrus** (city) Crawford County
59	3.6	**Dry Ridge** (CDP) Hamilton County
59	3.6	**Hubbard** (city) Trumbull County
59	3.6	**Pleasant Run Farm** (CDP) Hamilton County
59	3.6	**Richmond Heights** (city) Cuyahoga County
64	3.7	**Lexington** (village) Richland County
65	3.8	**Gahanna** (city) Franklin County
65	3.8	**Portsmouth** (city) Scioto County
65	3.8	**Westerville** (city) Franklin County
68	3.9	**Cortland** (city) Trumbull County
68	3.9	**Sylvania** (city) Lucas County
70	4.0	**Avon Lake** (city) Lorain County
70	4.0	**Beavercreek** (city) Greene County
70	4.0	**Fairlawn** (city) Summit County
70	4.0	**Mason** (city) Warren County
70	4.0	**Perrysburg** (city) Wood County
70	4.0	**Sharonville** (city) Hamilton County
70	4.0	**South Lebanon** (village) Warren County
77	4.1	**Bay Village** (city) Cuyahoga County
77	4.1	**Lakemore** (village) Summit County
77	4.1	**Landen** (CDP) Warren County
77	4.1	**Yellow Springs** (village) Greene County
81	4.2	**Ballville** (CDP) Sandusky County
81	4.2	**Bluffton** (village) Allen County
81	4.2	**Dent** (CDP) Hamilton County
81	4.2	**East Cleveland** (city) Cuyahoga County
81	4.2	**Finneytown** (CDP) Hamilton County
81	4.2	**Monroe** (city) Butler County
81	4.2	**New Concord** (village) Muskingum County
81	4.2	**Oberlin** (city) Lorain County
81	4.2	**Strongsville** (city) Cuyahoga County
81	4.2	**Walbridge** (village) Wood County
91	4.3	**Ada** (village) Hardin County
91	4.3	**Broadview Heights** (city) Cuyahoga County
91	4.3	**Calcutta** (CDP) Columbiana County
91	4.3	**Lyndhurst** (city) Cuyahoga County
91	4.3	**Waynesville** (village) Warren County
96	4.4	**Euclid** (city) Cuyahoga County
96	4.4	**Mayfield Heights** (city) Cuyahoga County
96	4.4	**Milford** (city) Clermont County
96	4.4	**Sheffield** (village) Lorain County
100	4.5	**Mansfield** (city) Richland County
100	4.5	**New Bremen** (village) Auglaize County
100	4.5	**Ontario** (city) Richland County
100	4.5	**Trotwood** (city) Montgomery County
104	4.6	**Germantown** (city) Montgomery County
104	4.6	**Kenwood** (CDP) Hamilton County
104	4.6	**Sherwood** (CDP) Hamilton County
104	4.6	**Streetsboro** (city) Portage County
104	4.6	**Willoughby Hills** (city) Lake County
109	4.7	**Avon** (city) Lorain County
109	4.7	**Cincinnati** (city) Hamilton County
109	4.7	**Hillsboro** (city) Highland County
109	4.7	**Kent** (city) Portage County
109	4.7	**Miami Heights** (CDP) Hamilton County
109	4.7	**South Euclid** (city) Cuyahoga County
115	4.8	**Fostoria** (city) Seneca County
116	4.9	**Brecksville** (city) Cuyahoga County
116	4.9	**Cedarville** (village) Greene County
116	4.9	**North Canton** (city) Stark County
116	4.9	**Reminderville** (village) Summit County
116	4.9	**Steubenville** (city) Jefferson County
116	4.9	**Vandalia** (city) Montgomery County
122	5.0	**Columbiana** (city) Columbiana County
122	5.0	**Columbus** (city) Franklin County
124	5.1	**Bowling Green** (city) Wood County
124	5.1	**Middleburg Heights** (city) Cuyahoga County
124	5.1	**Richfield** (village) Summit County
124	5.1	**Warrensville Heights** (city) Cuyahoga County
128	5.2	**Groesbeck** (CDP) Hamilton County
128	5.2	**Sandusky** (city) Erie County
130	5.3	**Archbold** (village) Fulton County
130	5.3	**Belpre** (city) Washington County
130	5.3	**Van Wert** (city) Van Wert County
130	5.3	**White Oak** (CDP) Hamilton County
130	5.3	**Woodlawn** (village) Hamilton County
135	5.4	**Ashland** (city) Ashland County
135	5.4	**Jefferson** (village) Ashtabula County
135	5.4	**North College Hill** (city) Hamilton County
138	5.5	**Bellbrook** (city) Greene County
138	5.5	**Blacklick Estates** (CDP) Franklin County
138	5.5	**Doylestown** (village) Wayne County
138	5.5	**Lakewood** (city) Cuyahoga County
138	5.5	**Maple Heights** (city) Cuyahoga County
143	5.6	**Fairport Harbor** (village) Lake County
143	5.6	**Kettering** (city) Montgomery County
143	5.6	**Orrville** (city) Wayne County
143	5.6	**Pickerington** (city) Fairfield County
143	5.6	**Sidney** (city) Shelby County
148	5.7	**Bedford Heights** (city) Cuyahoga County
148	5.7	**Fairview Park** (city) Cuyahoga County
148	5.7	**McDonald** (village) Trumbull County

Note: *This section ranks incorporated places and CDPs (Census Designated Places) with populations of 2,500 or more. Unincorporated postal areas were not considered. Please refer to the User Guide for additional information.*

Employment: Production, Transportation, and Material Moving Occupations

Top 150 Places Ranked in *Descending* Order

State Rank	Percent	Place
1	45.0	**Carey** (village) Wyandot County
2	44.5	**Newton Falls** (village) Trumbull County
3	40.4	**Montpelier** (village) Williams County
4	39.3	**North Baltimore** (village) Wood County
5	38.8	**Fostoria** (city) Seneca County
5	38.8	**Willard** (city) Huron County
7	38.7	**Lockland** (village) Hamilton County
8	37.1	**Wauseon** (city) Fulton County
9	36.5	**Fremont** (city) Sandusky County
10	35.0	**Van Wert** (city) Van Wert County
11	34.0	**Hicksville** (village) Defiance County
12	33.5	**Clyde** (city) Sandusky County
13	33.2	**Bryan** (city) Williams County
14	32.7	**Lincoln Heights** (village) Hamilton County
15	32.5	**Saint Marys** (city) Auglaize County
16	32.2	**Urbana** (city) Champaign County
17	31.7	**Blanchester** (village) Clinton County
18	31.6	**Delphos** (city) Allen County
19	31.3	**Bellefontaine** (city) Logan County
20	31.0	**Paulding** (village) Paulding County
21	30.9	**Versailles** (village) Darke County
22	30.8	**Millersburg** (village) Holmes County
22	30.8	**Minerva** (village) Stark County
24	30.7	**Napoleon** (city) Henry County
25	30.5	**Celina** (city) Mercer County
26	30.3	**Covington** (village) Miami County
26	30.3	**Marion** (city) Marion County
28	30.1	**Greenfield** (village) Highland County
29	30.0	**New London** (village) Huron County
30	29.4	**Sidney** (city) Shelby County
31	29.1	**Sebring** (village) Mahoning County
32	28.9	**Bucyrus** (city) Crawford County
33	28.8	**Eaton** (city) Preble County
33	28.8	**Loudonville** (village) Ashland County
33	28.8	**Shelby** (city) Richland County
33	28.8	**Wapakoneta** (city) Auglaize County
37	28.7	**Crooksville** (village) Perry County
38	28.1	**Lima** (city) Allen County
39	27.4	**Coldwater** (village) Mercer County
39	27.4	**Greenville** (city) Darke County
41	27.3	**Bellevue** (city) Sandusky County
41	27.3	**Newcomerstown** (village) Tuscarawas County
43	27.2	**Calcutta** (CDP) Columbiana County
43	27.2	**West Union** (village) Adams County
45	27.0	**Uhrichsville** (city) Tuscarawas County
46	26.9	**Strasburg** (village) Tuscarawas County
47	26.6	**Alliance** (city) Stark County
47	26.6	**Piqua** (city) Miami County
49	26.4	**Gibsonburg** (village) Sandusky County
49	26.4	**Kenton** (city) Hardin County
51	25.8	**Crestline** (village) Crawford County
51	25.8	**Richville** (CDP) Stark County
51	25.8	**Upper Sandusky** (city) Wyandot County
54	25.7	**Coshocton** (city) Coshocton County
54	25.7	**Saint Henry** (village) Mercer County
56	25.4	**Defiance** (city) Defiance County
57	25.3	**Wellington** (village) Lorain County
58	25.2	**Conneaut** (city) Ashtabula County
59	25.1	**Norwalk** (city) Huron County
60	25.0	**Archbold** (village) Fulton County
60	25.0	**Lordstown** (village) Trumbull County
62	24.7	**Blacklick Estates** (CDP) Franklin County
62	24.7	**Dennison** (village) Tuscarawas County
62	24.7	**New Philadelphia** (city) Tuscarawas County
65	24.5	**Ashtabula** (city) Ashtabula County
65	24.5	**Wellston** (city) Jackson County
67	24.4	**East Palestine** (village) Columbiana County
67	24.4	**Walbridge** (village) Wood County
69	24.3	**Franklin** (city) Warren County
69	24.3	**Ottawa** (village) Putnam County
71	23.9	**Geneva** (city) Ashtabula County
71	23.9	**New Carlisle** (city) Clark County
71	23.9	**Wellsville** (village) Columbiana County
74	23.8	**West Milton** (village) Miami County
75	23.6	**Campbell** (city) Mahoning County
75	23.6	**Whitehall** (city) Franklin County
77	23.5	**Fairport Harbor** (village) Lake County
77	23.5	**Northwood** (city) Wood County
79	23.4	**Buckeye Lake** (village) Licking County
80	23.3	**Painesville** (city) Lake County
80	23.3	**Troy** (city) Miami County
82	23.1	**Bedford Heights** (city) Cuyahoga County
82	23.1	**London** (city) Madison County
82	23.1	**North Madison** (CDP) Lake County
82	23.1	**Tiffin** (city) Seneca County
86	23.0	**Northfield** (village) Summit County
87	22.7	**Williamsburg** (village) Clermont County
88	22.6	**Edgewood** (CDP) Ashtabula County
88	22.6	**Orrville** (city) Wayne County
90	22.5	**East Liverpool** (city) Columbiana County
90	22.5	**Lorain** (city) Lorain County
90	22.5	**Mount Healthy Heights** (CDP) Hamilton County
90	22.5	**North Kingsville** (village) Ashtabula County
90	22.5	**Trenton** (city) Butler County
95	22.4	**Washington Court House** (city) Fayette County
96	22.3	**Galion** (city) Crawford County
96	22.3	**Springfield** (city) Clark County
98	22.1	**Cambridge** (city) Guernsey County
99	22.0	**Circleville** (city) Pickaway County
99	22.0	**New Bremen** (village) Auglaize County
101	21.9	**Ballville** (CDP) Sandusky County
101	21.9	**Lisbon** (village) Columbiana County
103	21.8	**Northridge** (CDP) Clark County
103	21.8	**Oak Harbor** (village) Ottawa County
105	21.6	**Fort Shawnee** (CDP) Allen County
105	21.6	**Salem** (city) Columbiana County
107	21.4	**Findlay** (city) Hancock County
108	21.3	**Sandusky** (city) Erie County
109	21.2	**Champion Heights** (CDP) Trumbull County
109	21.2	**Rittman** (city) Wayne County
111	21.1	**Garrettsville** (village) Portage County
111	21.1	**Jefferson** (village) Ashtabula County
113	21.0	**Elyria** (city) Lorain County
114	20.8	**Middletown** (city) Butler County
115	20.6	**Girard** (city) Trumbull County
115	20.6	**Obetz** (village) Franklin County
115	20.6	**Park Layne** (CDP) Clark County
115	20.6	**Trotwood** (city) Montgomery County
119	20.4	**Bedford** (city) Cuyahoga County
119	20.4	**Mineral Ridge** (CDP) Trumbull County
121	20.3	**Dover** (city) Tuscarawas County
121	20.3	**Mansfield** (city) Richland County
123	20.2	**New Lexington** (village) Perry County
124	20.0	**Enon** (village) Clark County
124	20.0	**Massillon** (city) Stark County
126	19.9	**Golf Manor** (village) Hamilton County
126	19.9	**Lodi** (village) Medina County
126	19.9	**Mogadore** (village) Summit County
126	19.9	**West Carrollton** (city) Montgomery County
130	19.7	**Brook Park** (city) Cuyahoga County
130	19.7	**Mount Vernon** (city) Knox County
130	19.7	**Struthers** (city) Mahoning County
130	19.7	**Toledo** (city) Lucas County
134	19.6	**Bethel** (village) Clermont County
134	19.6	**Port Clinton** (city) Ottawa County
136	19.5	**Mount Gilead** (village) Morrow County
136	19.5	**Youngstown** (city) Mahoning County
138	19.4	**Brimfield** (CDP) Portage County
138	19.4	**Hillsboro** (city) Highland County
138	19.4	**Oregon** (city) Lucas County
141	19.3	**Ashland** (city) Ashland County
141	19.3	**Carrollton** (village) Carroll County
141	19.3	**Heath** (city) Licking County
141	19.3	**Warren** (city) Trumbull County
145	19.1	**Northgate** (CDP) Hamilton County
146	19.0	**Lincoln Village** (CDP) Franklin County
146	19.0	**Mentor-on-the-Lake** (city) Lake County
148	18.9	**New Lebanon** (village) Montgomery County
148	18.9	**North College Hill** (city) Hamilton County
150	18.8	**Madison** (village) Lake County

Note: *This section ranks incorporated places and CDPs (Census Designated Places) with populations of 2,500 or more. Unincorporated postal areas were not considered. Please refer to the User Guide for additional information.*

Employment: Production, Transportation, and Material Moving Occupations

Top 150 Places Ranked in *Ascending* Order

State Rank	Percent	Place
1	1.7	**The Village of Indian Hill** (city) Hamilton County
2	1.9	**Beachwood** (city) Cuyahoga County
3	2.1	**Moreland Hills** (village) Cuyahoga County
4	2.4	**Upper Arlington** (city) Franklin County
5	2.5	**Turpin Hills** (CDP) Hamilton County
6	2.9	**Wyoming** (city) Hamilton County
7	3.2	**Bexley** (city) Franklin County
7	3.2	**Sixteen Mile Stand** (CDP) Hamilton County
7	3.2	**South Russell** (village) Geauga County
10	3.4	**Chagrin Falls** (village) Cuyahoga County
11	3.5	**Mayfield** (village) Cuyahoga County
11	3.5	**Worthington** (city) Franklin County
13	3.8	**Dublin** (city) Franklin County
13	3.8	**Granville** (village) Licking County
15	3.9	**Ottawa Hills** (village) Lucas County
16	4.1	**Fruit Hill** (CDP) Hamilton County
16	4.1	**Powell** (city) Delaware County
18	4.2	**Montrose-Ghent** (CDP) Summit County
19	4.3	**Greentown** (CDP) Stark County
19	4.3	**Montgomery** (city) Hamilton County
21	4.5	**Dry Run** (CDP) Hamilton County
21	4.5	**Hudson** (city) Summit County
21	4.5	**Oakwood** (city) Montgomery County
24	4.6	**Solon** (city) Cuyahoga County
25	4.7	**Pepper Pike** (city) Cuyahoga County
26	4.8	**Amberley** (village) Hamilton County
26	4.8	**Beckett Ridge** (CDP) Butler County
28	4.9	**Four Bridges** (CDP) Butler County
28	4.9	**Shaker Heights** (city) Cuyahoga County
30	5.0	**Bay Village** (city) Cuyahoga County
30	5.0	**Westlake** (city) Cuyahoga County
32	5.2	**Bainbridge** (CDP) Geauga County
32	5.2	**Grandview Heights** (city) Franklin County
32	5.2	**Landen** (CDP) Warren County
35	5.3	**New Albany** (city) Franklin County
36	5.4	**Athens** (city) Athens County
36	5.4	**Kenwood** (CDP) Hamilton County
38	5.5	**Brecksville** (city) Cuyahoga County
38	5.5	**Orange** (village) Cuyahoga County
40	5.6	**Dent** (CDP) Hamilton County
40	5.6	**Westerville** (city) Franklin County
42	5.7	**Avon** (city) Lorain County
42	5.7	**Cherry Grove** (CDP) Hamilton County
44	5.8	**Madeira** (city) Hamilton County
44	5.8	**Mariemont** (village) Hamilton County
44	5.8	**Reminderville** (village) Summit County
47	6.0	**Cedarville** (village) Greene County
48	6.1	**Mayfield Heights** (city) Cuyahoga County
48	6.1	**Sherwood** (CDP) Hamilton County
50	6.2	**Oberlin** (city) Lorain County
51	6.3	**Munroe Falls** (city) Summit County
51	6.3	**University Heights** (city) Cuyahoga County
53	6.4	**Mason** (city) Warren County
54	6.5	**Cleveland Heights** (city) Cuyahoga County
55	6.6	**Covedale** (CDP) Hamilton County
55	6.6	**Highland Heights** (city) Cuyahoga County
57	6.7	**Forestville** (CDP) Hamilton County
57	6.7	**Greenhills** (village) Hamilton County
57	6.7	**Perrysburg** (city) Wood County
60	6.8	**Aurora** (city) Portage County
60	6.8	**Hilliard** (city) Franklin County
62	6.9	**Oxford** (city) Butler County
62	6.9	**Yellow Springs** (village) Greene County
64	7.1	**Beavercreek** (city) Greene County
65	7.2	**Gahanna** (city) Franklin County
66	7.4	**Avon Lake** (city) Lorain County
66	7.4	**Evendale** (village) Hamilton County
68	7.6	**Centerville** (city) Montgomery County
69	7.7	**Canfield** (city) Mahoning County
70	7.8	**Delshire** (CDP) Hamilton County
70	7.8	**Lyndhurst** (city) Cuyahoga County
72	7.9	**Rocky River** (city) Cuyahoga County
73	8.0	**Bellbrook** (city) Greene County
73	8.0	**Springboro** (city) Warren County
75	8.1	**Sylvania** (city) Lucas County
76	8.2	**Blue Ash** (city) Hamilton County
76	8.2	**Newtown** (village) Hamilton County
76	8.2	**Pickerington** (city) Fairfield County
79	8.3	**Seven Hills** (city) Cuyahoga County
80	8.4	**Silverton** (village) Hamilton County
81	8.5	**Richfield** (village) Summit County
81	8.5	**Strongsville** (city) Cuyahoga County
83	8.7	**Chardon** (city) Geauga County
83	8.7	**North Canton** (city) Stark County
85	8.8	**Lakewood** (city) Cuyahoga County
86	8.9	**Mack** (CDP) Hamilton County
86	8.9	**Whitehouse** (village) Lucas County
88	9.0	**Independence** (city) Cuyahoga County
88	9.0	**Miami Heights** (CDP) Hamilton County
88	9.0	**Stow** (city) Summit County
88	9.0	**Twinsburg** (city) Summit County
92	9.1	**Dry Ridge** (CDP) Hamilton County
92	9.1	**New Concord** (village) Muskingum County
94	9.2	**North Zanesville** (CDP) Muskingum County
95	9.3	**Canal Winchester** (city) Franklin County
96	9.4	**Salem Heights** (CDP) Hamilton County
96	9.4	**Waterville** (city) Lucas County
98	9.5	**Deer Park** (city) Hamilton County
98	9.5	**Macedonia** (city) Summit County
100	9.6	**Pleasant Run** (CDP) Hamilton County
100	9.6	**South Point** (village) Lawrence County
102	9.7	**Reynoldsburg** (city) Franklin County
103	9.8	**Portsmouth** (city) Scioto County
103	9.8	**Wintersville** (village) Jefferson County
105	10.1	**North Royalton** (city) Cuyahoga County
105	10.1	**Pataskala** (city) Licking County
107	10.2	**Saint Clairsville** (city) Belmont County
107	10.2	**South Euclid** (city) Cuyahoga County
109	10.3	**Delhi Hills** (CDP) Hamilton County
110	10.4	**Fairlawn** (city) Summit County
111	10.5	**Dillonvale** (CDP) Hamilton County
111	10.5	**New Richmond** (village) Clermont County
111	10.5	**Olmsted Falls** (city) Cuyahoga County
114	10.6	**Broadview Heights** (city) Cuyahoga County
114	10.6	**Sunbury** (village) Delaware County
116	10.7	**Kettering** (city) Montgomery County
116	10.7	**Waynesville** (village) Warren County
116	10.7	**Wright-Patterson AFB** (CDP) Greene County
119	10.8	**Beechwood Trails** (CDP) Licking County
119	10.8	**Bowling Green** (city) Wood County
119	10.8	**Pleasant Run Farm** (CDP) Hamilton County
119	10.8	**Poland** (village) Mahoning County
123	10.9	**Groesbeck** (CDP) Hamilton County
123	10.9	**Grove City** (city) Franklin County
125	11.0	**Loveland** (city) Hamilton County
126	11.2	**Cleves** (village) Hamilton County
126	11.2	**Fairview Park** (city) Cuyahoga County
126	11.2	**Norwood** (city) Hamilton County
129	11.3	**Medina** (city) Medina County
130	11.4	**Cuyahoga Falls** (city) Summit County
130	11.4	**Wadsworth** (city) Medina County
130	11.4	**Woodlawn** (village) Hamilton County
133	11.5	**North Ridgeville** (city) Lorain County
134	11.6	**Berea** (city) Cuyahoga County
134	11.6	**Tallmadge** (city) Summit County
136	11.7	**Englewood** (city) Montgomery County
136	11.7	**Mentor** (city) Lake County
136	11.7	**Portage Lakes** (CDP) Summit County
139	11.8	**Boardman** (CDP) Mahoning County
139	11.8	**Green** (city) Summit County
139	11.8	**Mulberry** (CDP) Clermont County
142	11.9	**Amherst** (city) Lorain County
142	11.9	**Bridgetown** (CDP) Hamilton County
144	12.0	**Cincinnati** (city) Hamilton County
144	12.0	**Delaware** (city) Delaware County
144	12.0	**Kirtland** (city) Lake County
144	12.0	**Monroe** (city) Butler County
148	12.1	**Columbus** (city) Franklin County
148	12.1	**Georgetown** (village) Brown County
148	12.1	**North Olmsted** (city) Cuyahoga County

Note: *This section ranks incorporated places and CDPs (Census Designated Places) with populations of 2,500 or more. Unincorporated postal areas were not considered. Please refer to the User Guide for additional information.*

Per Capita Income

Top 150 Places Ranked in *Descending* Order

State Rank	Dollars	Place
1	112,391	**The Village of Indian Hill** (city) Hamilton County
2	86,786	**Pepper Pike** (city) Cuyahoga County
3	78,776	**Moreland Hills** (village) Cuyahoga County
4	73,900	**New Albany** (city) Franklin County
5	69,113	**Montrose-Ghent** (CDP) Summit County
6	69,103	**Ottawa Hills** (village) Lucas County
7	63,340	**Chagrin Falls** (village) Cuyahoga County
8	61,700	**South Russell** (village) Geauga County
9	58,698	**Dublin** (city) Franklin County
10	58,054	**Amberley** (village) Hamilton County
11	57,789	**Wyoming** (city) Hamilton County
12	57,619	**Orange** (village) Cuyahoga County
13	57,331	**Upper Arlington** (city) Franklin County
14	56,653	**Evendale** (village) Hamilton County
15	55,306	**Grandview Heights** (city) Franklin County
16	55,145	**Hudson** (city) Summit County
17	55,133	**Dry Run** (CDP) Hamilton County
18	55,024	**Sixteen Mile Stand** (CDP) Hamilton County
19	54,809	**Montgomery** (city) Hamilton County
20	54,162	**Mariemont** (village) Hamilton County
21	52,991	**Powell** (city) Delaware County
22	52,441	**Shaker Heights** (city) Cuyahoga County
23	51,230	**Westlake** (city) Cuyahoga County
24	50,988	**Brecksville** (city) Cuyahoga County
25	50,733	**Oakwood** (city) Montgomery County
26	50,525	**Beachwood** (city) Cuyahoga County
27	50,461	**Dry Ridge** (CDP) Hamilton County
28	50,415	**Turpin Hills** (CDP) Hamilton County
29	49,654	**Worthington** (city) Franklin County
30	49,223	**Solon** (city) Cuyahoga County
31	48,498	**Mayfield** (village) Cuyahoga County
32	48,301	**Rocky River** (city) Cuyahoga County
33	47,990	**Bay Village** (city) Cuyahoga County
34	47,960	**Four Bridges** (CDP) Butler County
35	47,706	**Beckett Ridge** (CDP) Butler County
36	46,864	**Highland Heights** (city) Cuyahoga County
37	46,821	**Bexley** (city) Franklin County
38	46,005	**Mason** (city) Warren County
39	45,454	**Kirtland** (city) Lake County
40	45,269	**Aurora** (city) Portage County
41	44,499	**Bainbridge** (CDP) Geauga County
42	44,374	**Blue Ash** (city) Hamilton County
43	44,056	**Sherwood** (CDP) Hamilton County
44	43,623	**Kenwood** (CDP) Hamilton County
45	43,468	**Macedonia** (city) Summit County
46	42,659	**Yellow Springs** (village) Greene County
47	42,594	**Avon** (city) Lorain County
48	42,097	**Richfield** (village) Summit County
49	42,092	**Broadview Heights** (city) Cuyahoga County
50	41,668	**Avon Lake** (city) Lorain County
50	41,668	**Perrysburg** (city) Wood County
52	41,507	**Madeira** (city) Hamilton County
53	41,425	**Independence** (city) Cuyahoga County
54	41,364	**Newtown** (village) Hamilton County
55	40,964	**Hilliard** (city) Franklin County
56	40,881	**Fairlawn** (city) Summit County
57	40,639	**Beavercreek** (city) Greene County
58	40,133	**Strongsville** (city) Cuyahoga County
59	39,906	**Canfield** (city) Mahoning County
60	39,714	**Salem Heights** (CDP) Hamilton County
61	38,779	**Westerville** (city) Franklin County
62	38,580	**Centerville** (city) Montgomery County
63	38,466	**Landen** (CDP) Warren County
64	38,270	**Poland** (village) Mahoning County
65	38,216	**Mack** (CDP) Hamilton County
66	38,049	**Lyndhurst** (city) Cuyahoga County
67	37,951	**Forestville** (CDP) Hamilton County
68	37,674	**Fruit Hill** (CDP) Hamilton County
69	37,657	**Dent** (CDP) Hamilton County
70	37,498	**Beechwood Trails** (CDP) Licking County
71	37,477	**Springboro** (city) Warren County
72	37,283	**Gahanna** (city) Franklin County
73	37,235	**Sylvania** (city) Lucas County
74	37,046	**Taylor Creek** (CDP) Hamilton County
75	36,838	**Loveland** (city) Hamilton County
76	36,659	**Whitehouse** (village) Lucas County
77	36,649	**North Royalton** (city) Cuyahoga County
78	36,614	**Howland Center** (CDP) Trumbull County
79	36,568	**Monfort Heights** (CDP) Hamilton County
80	36,283	**Seven Hills** (city) Cuyahoga County
81	36,228	**Mulberry** (CDP) Clermont County
82	35,998	**Bellbrook** (city) Greene County
83	35,955	**Twinsburg** (city) Summit County
84	35,911	**Willoughby Hills** (city) Lake County
85	35,808	**South Lebanon** (village) Warren County
86	35,564	**Devola** (CDP) Washington County
87	35,440	**Fort Shawnee** (CDP) Allen County
88	35,122	**Sheffield** (village) Lorain County
89	34,929	**Miami Heights** (CDP) Hamilton County
90	34,819	**Mentor** (city) Lake County
91	34,784	**Huron** (city) Erie County
92	34,635	**Saint Clairsville** (city) Belmont County
93	34,117	**Green** (city) Summit County
94	33,817	**Munroe Falls** (city) Summit County
95	33,612	**Maumee** (city) Lucas County
96	33,475	**Stow** (city) Summit County
97	33,402	**Reminderville** (village) Summit County
98	33,272	**Tipp City** (city) Miami County
99	33,144	**Delhi Hills** (CDP) Hamilton County
100	33,037	**Covedale** (CDP) Hamilton County
101	32,879	**New Bremen** (village) Auglaize County
102	32,842	**Olmsted Falls** (city) Cuyahoga County
103	32,834	**Green Meadows** (CDP) Clark County
104	32,832	**Granville** (village) Licking County
105	32,626	**Pickerington** (city) Fairfield County
106	32,602	**New Franklin** (city) Summit County
107	32,401	**Clayton** (city) Montgomery County
108	32,358	**Enon** (village) Clark County
109	32,171	**Fairview Park** (city) Cuyahoga County
110	32,165	**Canal Winchester** (city) Franklin County
111	32,118	**Chardon** (city) Geauga County
112	32,111	**Seville** (village) Medina County
113	31,887	**Cleveland Heights** (city) Cuyahoga County
114	31,754	**Willoughby** (city) Lake County
115	31,649	**Cherry Grove** (CDP) Hamilton County
116	31,498	**Sharonville** (city) Hamilton County
117	31,399	**North Ridgeville** (city) Lorain County
118	31,346	**Middleburg Heights** (city) Cuyahoga County
119	31,279	**Lake Darby** (CDP) Franklin County
120	31,182	**Day Heights** (CDP) Clermont County
121	31,177	**Cortland** (city) Trumbull County
122	31,172	**North Olmsted** (city) Cuyahoga County
123	31,155	**Plain City** (village) Madison County
124	31,148	**Greentown** (CDP) Stark County
125	31,122	**Lakewood** (city) Cuyahoga County
126	31,085	**North Zanesville** (CDP) Muskingum County
127	30,951	**Waterville** (city) Lucas County
128	30,835	**Saint Henry** (village) Mercer County
129	30,656	**Amherst** (city) Lorain County
130	30,632	**Grove City** (city) Franklin County
131	30,620	**White Oak** (CDP) Hamilton County
132	30,579	**Kettering** (city) Montgomery County
133	30,559	**Portage Lakes** (CDP) Summit County
134	30,493	**Columbiana** (city) Columbiana County
135	30,488	**Pataskala** (city) Licking County
136	30,399	**North Canton** (city) Stark County
137	30,391	**Brunswick** (city) Medina County
138	30,368	**Monroe** (city) Butler County
139	30,298	**University Heights** (city) Cuyahoga County
140	30,280	**Germantown** (city) Montgomery County
141	30,153	**Deer Park** (city) Hamilton County
142	30,144	**Tallmadge** (city) Summit County
143	29,987	**Rossford** (city) Wood County
144	29,955	**Mayfield Heights** (city) Cuyahoga County
145	29,852	**Vermilion** (city) Lorain County
146	29,729	**Bluffton** (village) Allen County
147	29,674	**Doylestown** (village) Wayne County
148	29,644	**Apple Valley** (CDP) Knox County
149	29,534	**Greenhills** (village) Hamilton County
150	29,341	**Uniontown** (CDP) Stark County

Note: *This section ranks incorporated places and CDPs (Census Designated Places) with populations of 2,500 or more. Unincorporated postal areas were not considered. Please refer to the User Guide for additional information.*

Per Capita Income

Top 150 Places Ranked in *Ascending* Order

State Rank	Dollars	Place
1	11,724	**Cedarville** (village) Greene County
2	12,019	**Lincoln Heights** (village) Hamilton County
3	13,218	**Nelsonville** (city) Athens County
4	13,758	**Athens** (city) Athens County
5	14,390	**Grafton** (village) Lorain County
6	15,002	**Greenfield** (village) Highland County
7	15,089	**East Cleveland** (city) Cuyahoga County
8	15,097	**New Concord** (village) Muskingum County
9	15,282	**Wellsville** (village) Columbiana County
10	15,485	**Ada** (village) Hardin County
11	15,713	**Youngstown** (city) Mahoning County
12	15,746	**New Lexington** (village) Perry County
13	16,106	**Crooksville** (village) Perry County
14	16,171	**Ashtabula** (city) Ashtabula County
15	16,191	**Dennison** (village) Tuscarawas County
16	16,197	**Oxford** (city) Butler County
17	16,360	**Campbell** (city) Mahoning County
18	16,556	**New Carlisle** (city) Clark County
19	16,670	**Lockland** (village) Hamilton County
20	16,673	**West Union** (village) Adams County
21	16,705	**Lima** (city) Allen County
22	16,731	**Marion** (city) Marion County
23	16,858	**Zanesville** (city) Muskingum County
24	17,302	**New London** (village) Huron County
25	17,324	**East Liverpool** (city) Columbiana County
26	17,333	**Newcomerstown** (village) Tuscarawas County
27	17,384	**Canton** (city) Stark County
28	17,412	**Uhrichsville** (city) Tuscarawas County
29	17,461	**Dayton** (city) Montgomery County
30	17,578	**Georgetown** (village) Brown County
31	17,680	**Warren** (city) Trumbull County
32	17,733	**The Plains** (CDP) Athens County
33	17,892	**Bellaire** (village) Belmont County
34	18,003	**Cleveland** (city) Cuyahoga County
35	18,132	**Park Layne** (CDP) Clark County
36	18,207	**Logan** (city) Hocking County
37	18,287	**Conneaut** (city) Ashtabula County
38	18,327	**West Portsmouth** (CDP) Scioto County
39	18,398	**Cambridge** (city) Guernsey County
40	18,476	**Mansfield** (city) Richland County
41	18,701	**Portsmouth** (city) Scioto County
42	18,756	**Obetz** (village) Franklin County
43	18,782	**Willard** (city) Huron County
44	18,935	**Alliance** (city) Stark County
45	19,042	**Lisbon** (village) Columbiana County
46	19,277	**Mount Orab** (village) Brown County
47	19,342	**Whitehall** (city) Franklin County
48	19,347	**Ironton** (city) Lawrence County
49	19,473	**New Lebanon** (village) Montgomery County
50	19,538	**Bethel** (village) Clermont County
51	19,561	**Hillsboro** (city) Highland County
52	19,573	**Lorain** (city) Lorain County
53	19,608	**Springfield** (city) Clark County
54	19,701	**Struthers** (city) Mahoning County
55	19,702	**Trotwood** (city) Montgomery County
56	19,728	**Mount Vernon** (city) Knox County
57	19,843	**Paulding** (village) Paulding County
58	19,872	**Kent** (city) Portage County
59	19,894	**Baltimore** (village) Fairfield County
60	19,916	**Hicksville** (village) Defiance County
61	19,962	**Crestline** (village) Crawford County
62	19,983	**Maple Heights** (city) Cuyahoga County
63	20,059	**Fremont** (city) Sandusky County
64	20,074	**Urbana** (city) Champaign County
65	20,175	**Bowling Green** (city) Wood County
65	20,175	**East Palestine** (village) Columbiana County
67	20,180	**Blacklick Estates** (CDP) Franklin County
68	20,185	**Mount Healthy Heights** (CDP) Hamilton County
69	20,200	**Fostoria** (city) Seneca County
70	20,225	**Millersburg** (village) Holmes County
71	20,291	**Galion** (city) Crawford County
72	20,317	**Toledo** (city) Lucas County
73	20,345	**Kenton** (city) Hardin County
74	20,379	**Covington** (village) Miami County
75	20,391	**Ravenna** (city) Portage County
76	20,393	**Gibsonburg** (village) Sandusky County
77	20,464	**Toronto** (city) Jefferson County
78	20,497	**Jefferson** (village) Ashtabula County
79	20,502	**Piqua** (city) Miami County
80	20,584	**Steubenville** (city) Jefferson County
81	20,648	**Tiffin** (city) Seneca County
82	20,650	**Williamsburg** (village) Clermont County
83	20,662	**Moraine** (city) Montgomery County
84	20,666	**Painesville** (city) Lake County
85	20,742	**Barnesville** (village) Belmont County
86	20,753	**Martins Ferry** (city) Belmont County
87	20,786	**Middletown** (city) Butler County
88	20,793	**Sandusky** (city) Erie County
89	20,830	**Warrensville Heights** (city) Cuyahoga County
90	20,866	**Sebring** (village) Mahoning County
91	20,877	**Van Wert** (city) Van Wert County
92	20,886	**Loudonville** (village) Ashland County
93	20,898	**Wilmington** (city) Clinton County
94	20,925	**Lodi** (village) Medina County
95	21,043	**Jackson** (city) Jackson County
96	21,057	**Mount Healthy** (city) Hamilton County
97	21,061	**Golf Manor** (village) Hamilton County
98	21,162	**Minerva** (village) Stark County
99	21,163	**Barberton** (city) Summit County
100	21,256	**Circleville** (city) Pickaway County
101	21,281	**Edgewood** (CDP) Ashtabula County
102	21,332	**Garfield Heights** (city) Cuyahoga County
103	21,370	**Blanchester** (village) Clinton County
104	21,378	**Akron** (city) Summit County
105	21,434	**Greenville** (city) Darke County
106	21,475	**Lincoln Village** (CDP) Franklin County
107	21,538	**Montpelier** (village) Williams County
108	21,550	**Bucyrus** (city) Crawford County
109	21,605	**Northbrook** (CDP) Hamilton County
110	21,658	**Amelia** (village) Clermont County
111	21,665	**West Carrollton** (city) Montgomery County
112	21,700	**North Baltimore** (village) Wood County
113	21,712	**Shelby** (city) Richland County
114	21,727	**Elyria** (city) Lorain County
115	21,740	**Lancaster** (city) Fairfield County
116	21,745	**Rittman** (city) Wayne County
117	21,773	**Washington Court House** (city) Fayette County
118	21,867	**Xenia** (city) Greene County
119	21,897	**Ashland** (city) Ashland County
120	21,939	**Bryan** (city) Williams County
121	21,978	**Upper Sandusky** (city) Wyandot County
122	22,093	**Mount Gilead** (village) Morrow County
123	22,113	**Hamilton** (city) Butler County
124	22,176	**Saint Marys** (city) Auglaize County
125	22,226	**Newark** (city) Licking County
126	22,250	**Coshocton** (city) Coshocton County
127	22,261	**Delphos** (city) Allen County
128	22,276	**Geneva** (city) Ashtabula County
129	22,298	**Oberlin** (city) Lorain County
130	22,401	**Norwalk** (city) Huron County
131	22,434	**Wauseon** (city) Fulton County
132	22,471	**Euclid** (city) Cuyahoga County
133	22,493	**North College Hill** (city) Hamilton County
134	22,508	**Wapakoneta** (city) Auglaize County
135	22,520	**North Madison** (CDP) Lake County
136	22,534	**Celina** (city) Mercer County
137	22,548	**Massillon** (city) Stark County
138	22,572	**Cheviot** (city) Hamilton County
139	22,614	**West Jefferson** (village) Madison County
140	22,673	**Eaton** (city) Preble County
141	22,691	**Delshire** (CDP) Hamilton County
142	22,751	**Riverside** (city) Montgomery County
143	22,890	**Chillicothe** (city) Ross County
144	23,002	**McDonald** (village) Trumbull County
145	23,050	**Niles** (city) Trumbull County
146	23,092	**West Milton** (village) Miami County
147	23,128	**Brimfield** (CDP) Portage County
148	23,150	**Wellington** (village) Lorain County
149	23,189	**Mogadore** (village) Summit County
150	23,217	**New Philadelphia** (city) Tuscarawas County

Note: *This section ranks incorporated places and CDPs (Census Designated Places) with populations of 2,500 or more. Unincorporated postal areas were not considered. Please refer to the User Guide for additional information.*

Median Household Income

Top 150 Places Ranked in *Descending* Order

State Rank	Dollars	Place
1	205,221	**The Village of Indian Hill** (city) Hamilton County
2	191,375	**New Albany** (city) Franklin County
3	164,471	**Pepper Pike** (city) Cuyahoga County
4	139,539	**Moreland Hills** (village) Cuyahoga County
5	137,543	**Dry Run** (CDP) Hamilton County
6	132,917	**Powell** (city) Delaware County
7	126,618	**Hudson** (city) Summit County
8	125,540	**Dublin** (city) Franklin County
9	120,676	**Wyoming** (city) Hamilton County
10	118,700	**Ottawa Hills** (village) Lucas County
11	115,703	**Amberley** (village) Hamilton County
12	114,973	**Turpin Hills** (CDP) Hamilton County
13	113,875	**Evendale** (village) Hamilton County
14	108,469	**Montgomery** (city) Hamilton County
15	107,250	**South Russell** (village) Geauga County
16	105,000	**Four Bridges** (CDP) Butler County
17	103,208	**Bainbridge** (CDP) Geauga County
18	102,109	**Orange** (village) Cuyahoga County
19	102,094	**Upper Arlington** (city) Franklin County
20	101,884	**Montrose-Ghent** (CDP) Summit County
21	101,875	**Highland Heights** (city) Cuyahoga County
22	101,736	**Bexley** (city) Franklin County
23	99,364	**Springboro** (city) Warren County
24	98,345	**Brecksville** (city) Cuyahoga County
25	96,976	**Solon** (city) Cuyahoga County
26	96,790	**Oakwood** (city) Montgomery County
27	95,938	**Grandview Heights** (city) Franklin County
28	93,220	**Bay Village** (city) Cuyahoga County
29	92,819	**Mason** (city) Warren County
30	92,727	**Hilliard** (city) Franklin County
31	92,216	**Mariemont** (village) Hamilton County
32	92,109	**Granville** (village) Licking County
33	91,810	**Madeira** (city) Hamilton County
34	91,075	**Worthington** (city) Franklin County
35	90,846	**Avon** (city) Lorain County
36	90,139	**Sherwood** (CDP) Hamilton County
37	89,632	**Delhi Hills** (CDP) Hamilton County
38	88,478	**Beechwood Trails** (CDP) Licking County
39	88,287	**Beachwood** (city) Cuyahoga County
40	87,152	**Lake Darby** (CDP) Franklin County
41	86,061	**Macedonia** (city) Summit County
42	85,994	**Mack** (CDP) Hamilton County
43	85,930	**Sixteen Mile Stand** (CDP) Hamilton County
44	85,230	**Westerville** (city) Franklin County
45	84,958	**Beckett Ridge** (CDP) Butler County
46	84,944	**Greentown** (CDP) Stark County
47	84,900	**Independence** (city) Cuyahoga County
48	84,508	**Perrysburg** (city) Wood County
49	84,410	**Pickerington** (city) Fairfield County
50	84,135	**Aurora** (city) Portage County
51	82,956	**Beavercreek** (city) Greene County
52	82,763	**Wright-Patterson AFB** (CDP) Greene County
53	81,204	**Miami Heights** (CDP) Hamilton County
54	80,989	**Westlake** (city) Cuyahoga County
55	80,884	**Avon Lake** (city) Lorain County
56	80,323	**Strongsville** (city) Cuyahoga County
57	80,203	**Salem Heights** (CDP) Hamilton County
58	79,600	**Landen** (CDP) Warren County
59	79,519	**Shaker Heights** (city) Cuyahoga County
60	79,293	**Waterville** (city) Lucas County
61	78,718	**Canal Winchester** (city) Franklin County
62	78,173	**Cherry Grove** (CDP) Hamilton County
63	77,480	**Broadview Heights** (city) Cuyahoga County
64	76,691	**Kirtland** (city) Lake County
65	76,576	**Bellbrook** (city) Greene County
66	76,133	**Whitehouse** (village) Lucas County
67	76,127	**Devola** (CDP) Washington County
68	75,461	**Sheffield** (village) Lorain County
69	75,313	**Saint Henry** (village) Mercer County
70	75,260	**Chagrin Falls** (village) Cuyahoga County
71	74,545	**Covedale** (CDP) Hamilton County
72	74,197	**Monfort Heights** (CDP) Hamilton County
73	73,948	**Seven Hills** (city) Cuyahoga County
74	73,618	**Fruit Hill** (CDP) Hamilton County
75	73,535	**Gahanna** (city) Franklin County
76	73,314	**Twinsburg** (city) Summit County
77	73,132	**Bluffton** (village) Allen County
78	72,982	**Monroe** (city) Butler County
79	72,946	**Taylor Creek** (CDP) Hamilton County
80	72,936	**Sylvania** (city) Lucas County
81	72,628	**Blue Ash** (city) Hamilton County
82	72,318	**Day Heights** (CDP) Clermont County
83	72,176	**Dent** (CDP) Hamilton County
84	72,156	**Mayfield** (village) Cuyahoga County
85	71,911	**Clayton** (city) Montgomery County
86	71,417	**Reminderville** (village) Summit County
87	71,321	**Poland** (village) Mahoning County
88	70,731	**Ross** (CDP) Butler County
89	70,478	**Minster** (village) Auglaize County
90	70,473	**Newtown** (village) Hamilton County
91	70,265	**Forestville** (CDP) Hamilton County
92	70,122	**New Bremen** (village) Auglaize County
93	70,058	**Mentor** (city) Lake County
94	69,671	**Sunbury** (village) Delaware County
95	69,574	**Pataskala** (city) Licking County
96	69,355	**Loveland** (city) Hamilton County
97	68,778	**North Ridgeville** (city) Lorain County
98	68,234	**Saint Clairsville** (city) Belmont County
99	68,161	**New Franklin** (city) Summit County
100	67,875	**Richfield** (village) Summit County
101	66,731	**Amherst** (city) Lorain County
102	66,716	**Canfield** (city) Mahoning County
103	66,656	**Green** (city) Summit County
104	66,419	**Dry Ridge** (CDP) Hamilton County
105	66,386	**Kenwood** (CDP) Hamilton County
106	66,189	**North Royalton** (city) Cuyahoga County
107	66,079	**Stow** (city) Summit County
108	65,921	**Lyndhurst** (city) Cuyahoga County
109	65,625	**Ashville** (village) Pickaway County
110	65,521	**Fairlawn** (city) Summit County
111	65,277	**Grove City** (city) Franklin County
112	65,226	**Rocky River** (city) Cuyahoga County
113	65,222	**Pleasant Run** (CDP) Hamilton County
114	65,143	**University Heights** (city) Cuyahoga County
115	65,060	**Pleasant Run Farm** (CDP) Hamilton County
116	64,897	**Lake Lakengren** (CDP) Preble County
117	64,848	**Cleves** (village) Hamilton County
118	64,706	**Brunswick** (city) Medina County
119	64,608	**Union** (city) Montgomery County
120	64,337	**Dillonvale** (CDP) Hamilton County
121	64,167	**Mulberry** (CDP) Clermont County
122	63,864	**Northgate** (CDP) Hamilton County
123	63,618	**Trenton** (city) Butler County
124	63,524	**Centerville** (city) Montgomery County
125	63,493	**Cortland** (city) Trumbull County
126	63,349	**Tipp City** (city) Miami County
127	63,043	**Maumee** (city) Lucas County
128	63,024	**Howland Center** (CDP) Trumbull County
129	62,855	**Munroe Falls** (city) Summit County
130	62,607	**Wadsworth** (city) Medina County
131	62,514	**Fort Shawnee** (CDP) Allen County
132	62,500	**Yellow Springs** (village) Greene County
133	62,477	**Mogadore** (village) Summit County
134	62,371	**Marysville** (city) Union County
135	62,355	**Norton** (city) Summit County
136	62,058	**Olmsted Falls** (city) Cuyahoga County
137	62,000	**Uniontown** (CDP) Stark County
138	61,958	**Plain City** (village) Madison County
139	61,957	**South Lebanon** (village) Warren County
140	61,669	**Lebanon** (city) Warren County
141	61,648	**Reynoldsburg** (city) Franklin County
142	61,555	**North Kingsville** (village) Ashtabula County
143	61,485	**Rossford** (city) Wood County
144	61,444	**North Olmsted** (city) Cuyahoga County
145	61,343	**Harrison** (city) Hamilton County
146	61,276	**Willoughby Hills** (city) Lake County
147	61,092	**Doylestown** (village) Wayne County
148	61,005	**Waynesville** (village) Warren County
149	60,845	**Chardon** (city) Geauga County
150	60,750	**North Zanesville** (CDP) Muskingum County

Note: *This section ranks incorporated places and CDPs (Census Designated Places) with populations of 2,500 or more. Unincorporated postal areas were not considered. Please refer to the User Guide for additional information.*

Median Household Income

Top 150 Places Ranked in *Ascending* Order

State Rank	Dollars	Place
1	19,953	**East Cleveland** (city) Cuyahoga County
2	20,479	**West Union** (village) Adams County
3	22,204	**Athens** (city) Athens County
4	23,494	**Lincoln Heights** (village) Hamilton County
5	24,448	**Youngstown** (city) Mahoning County
6	25,594	**Bellaire** (village) Belmont County
7	25,735	**Nelsonville** (city) Athens County
8	26,039	**Zanesville** (city) Muskingum County
9	26,361	**Greenfield** (village) Highland County
10	26,583	**Cleveland** (city) Cuyahoga County
11	27,769	**Portsmouth** (city) Scioto County
12	28,171	**Wellsville** (village) Columbiana County
13	28,745	**Dayton** (city) Montgomery County
14	28,865	**Ashtabula** (city) Ashtabula County
15	28,917	**Dennison** (village) Tuscarawas County
16	28,952	**Campbell** (city) Mahoning County
17	29,176	**Warren** (city) Trumbull County
18	29,451	**Oxford** (city) Butler County
19	30,291	**East Liverpool** (city) Columbiana County
20	30,444	**Canton** (city) Stark County
21	30,795	**Cambridge** (city) Guernsey County
22	30,953	**Lima** (city) Allen County
23	31,096	**Logan** (city) Hocking County
24	31,250	**Crooksville** (village) Perry County
25	31,742	**Lockland** (village) Hamilton County
26	32,058	**Alliance** (city) Stark County
27	32,165	**Springfield** (city) Clark County
28	32,266	**Newcomerstown** (village) Tuscarawas County
29	32,663	**Uhrichsville** (city) Tuscarawas County
30	32,721	**Galion** (city) Crawford County
31	33,051	**Hillsboro** (city) Highland County
32	33,207	**The Plains** (CDP) Athens County
33	33,257	**Mansfield** (city) Richland County
34	33,355	**Barnesville** (village) Belmont County
35	33,369	**Steubenville** (city) Jefferson County
36	33,379	**West Portsmouth** (CDP) Scioto County
37	33,456	**Martins Ferry** (city) Belmont County
38	33,562	**Bowling Green** (city) Wood County
39	33,563	**New Lexington** (village) Perry County
40	33,670	**Marietta** (city) Washington County
41	33,704	**Gallipolis** (village) Gallia County
42	33,817	**Sandusky** (city) Erie County
43	33,845	**Wilmington** (city) Clinton County
44	34,140	**Ironton** (city) Lawrence County
45	34,167	**Fremont** (city) Sandusky County
46	34,404	**Mount Healthy** (city) Hamilton County
47	34,490	**Bryan** (city) Williams County
47	34,490	**Trotwood** (city) Montgomery County
49	34,548	**Toledo** (city) Lucas County
50	34,566	**Sebring** (village) Mahoning County
51	34,569	**Georgetown** (village) Brown County
52	34,629	**Cincinnati** (city) Hamilton County
53	34,688	**Edgewood** (CDP) Ashtabula County
54	34,698	**Mount Vernon** (city) Knox County
55	34,750	**Silverton** (village) Hamilton County
56	34,856	**Conneaut** (city) Ashtabula County
57	34,932	**Marion** (city) Marion County
58	35,022	**Ada** (village) Hardin County
59	35,168	**Fostoria** (city) Seneca County
60	35,240	**Akron** (city) Summit County
61	35,471	**Greenville** (city) Darke County
62	35,733	**Warrensville Heights** (city) Cuyahoga County
63	35,753	**Lorain** (city) Lorain County
64	35,949	**Euclid** (city) Cuyahoga County
65	36,087	**Ravenna** (city) Portage County
66	36,207	**Lodi** (village) Medina County
67	36,230	**Bucyrus** (city) Crawford County
68	36,303	**Mount Gilead** (village) Morrow County
69	36,487	**Eaton** (city) Preble County
70	36,539	**Kent** (city) Portage County
71	36,581	**Lisbon** (village) Columbiana County
72	36,736	**Urbana** (city) Champaign County
73	36,829	**Millersburg** (village) Holmes County
74	36,898	**Middletown** (city) Butler County
75	37,118	**Belpre** (city) Washington County
76	37,143	**Crestline** (village) Crawford County
77	37,344	**Loudonville** (village) Ashland County
78	37,426	**Girard** (city) Trumbull County
79	37,431	**Struthers** (city) Mahoning County
80	37,476	**Jackson** (city) Jackson County
81	37,671	**Whitehall** (city) Franklin County
82	37,692	**Bedford Heights** (city) Cuyahoga County
83	37,757	**Chillicothe** (city) Ross County
84	37,798	**New Carlisle** (city) Clark County
85	37,814	**West Carrollton** (city) Montgomery County
86	37,905	**Washington Court House** (city) Fayette County
87	37,911	**Maple Heights** (city) Cuyahoga County
88	37,929	**New Lebanon** (village) Montgomery County
89	38,015	**Waverly** (village) Pike County
90	38,310	**Coshocton** (city) Coshocton County
91	38,359	**Buckeye Lake** (village) Licking County
92	38,418	**Milford** (city) Clermont County
93	38,426	**Xenia** (city) Greene County
94	38,438	**Toronto** (city) Jefferson County
95	38,624	**Salem** (city) Columbiana County
96	38,625	**Lancaster** (city) Fairfield County
97	38,913	**Newark** (city) Licking County
98	39,311	**Niles** (city) Trumbull County
99	39,398	**Wellston** (city) Jackson County
100	39,417	**Ashland** (city) Ashland County
101	39,456	**Barberton** (city) Summit County
102	39,826	**Walbridge** (village) Wood County
103	39,980	**Newton Falls** (village) Trumbull County
104	40,026	**Kenton** (city) Hardin County
105	40,101	**Piqua** (city) Miami County
106	40,276	**Circleville** (city) Pickaway County
107	40,306	**Norwood** (city) Hamilton County
108	40,361	**Golf Manor** (village) Hamilton County
109	40,376	**Garfield Heights** (city) Cuyahoga County
110	40,397	**Upper Sandusky** (city) Wyandot County
111	40,401	**Hamilton** (city) Butler County
112	40,673	**Fredericktown** (village) Knox County
113	40,677	**Bethel** (village) Clermont County
114	40,854	**East Palestine** (village) Columbiana County
115	40,864	**Willard** (city) Huron County
116	40,967	**Elyria** (city) Lorain County
117	41,037	**Tiffin** (city) Seneca County
118	41,077	**Shelby** (city) Richland County
119	41,080	**Blanchester** (village) Clinton County
120	41,101	**Montpelier** (village) Williams County
121	41,285	**Bedford** (city) Cuyahoga County
122	41,289	**Cheviot** (city) Hamilton County
123	41,316	**Norwalk** (city) Huron County
124	41,372	**Hicksville** (village) Defiance County
125	41,380	**Hubbard** (city) Trumbull County
126	41,529	**Fairborn** (city) Greene County
127	41,556	**Middlefield** (village) Geauga County
128	41,640	**Geneva** (city) Ashtabula County
129	41,652	**Painesville** (city) Lake County
130	41,683	**New London** (village) Huron County
131	41,703	**Wooster** (city) Wayne County
132	41,753	**New Philadelphia** (city) Tuscarawas County
133	41,789	**Austintown** (CDP) Mahoning County
134	41,841	**North College Hill** (city) Hamilton County
134	41,841	**Saint Marys** (city) Auglaize County
136	41,844	**Lakemore** (village) Summit County
137	41,900	**Van Wert** (city) Van Wert County
138	41,956	**Perry Heights** (CDP) Stark County
139	42,227	**Rittman** (city) Wayne County
140	42,263	**Celina** (city) Mercer County
141	42,394	**Oak Harbor** (village) Ottawa County
142	42,415	**Mount Orab** (village) Brown County
143	42,442	**Mount Healthy Heights** (CDP) Hamilton County
144	42,471	**Bellefontaine** (city) Logan County
145	42,609	**Cedarville** (village) Greene County
146	42,614	**Covington** (village) Miami County
147	42,808	**Massillon** (city) Stark County
148	43,208	**Baltimore** (village) Fairfield County
149	43,250	**New Concord** (village) Muskingum County
150	43,415	**Mount Carmel** (CDP) Clermont County

Note: *This section ranks incorporated places and CDPs (Census Designated Places) with populations of 2,500 or more. Unincorporated postal areas were not considered. Please refer to the User Guide for additional information.*

Average Household Income

Top 150 Places Ranked in *Descending* Order

State Rank	Dollars	Place
1	314,077	**The Village of Indian Hill** (city) Hamilton County
2	248,753	**Pepper Pike** (city) Cuyahoga County
3	232,615	**New Albany** (city) Franklin County
4	203,660	**Moreland Hills** (village) Cuyahoga County
5	192,525	**Ottawa Hills** (village) Lucas County
6	176,372	**Dry Run** (CDP) Hamilton County
7	166,166	**Amberley** (village) Hamilton County
8	165,574	**Montrose-Ghent** (CDP) Summit County
9	163,872	**Dublin** (city) Franklin County
10	161,216	**South Russell** (village) Geauga County
11	159,435	**Wyoming** (city) Hamilton County
12	159,361	**Powell** (city) Delaware County
13	155,164	**Hudson** (city) Summit County
14	148,986	**Evendale** (village) Hamilton County
15	148,522	**Montgomery** (city) Hamilton County
16	145,301	**Orange** (village) Cuyahoga County
17	144,048	**Upper Arlington** (city) Franklin County
18	138,885	**Chagrin Falls** (village) Cuyahoga County
19	138,147	**Sixteen Mile Stand** (CDP) Hamilton County
20	137,652	**Bexley** (city) Franklin County
21	136,838	**Turpin Hills** (CDP) Hamilton County
22	134,570	**Solon** (city) Cuyahoga County
23	130,304	**Oakwood** (city) Montgomery County
24	130,025	**Shaker Heights** (city) Cuyahoga County
25	129,583	**Mariemont** (village) Hamilton County
26	128,428	**Granville** (village) Licking County
27	127,450	**Four Bridges** (CDP) Butler County
28	126,923	**Brecksville** (city) Cuyahoga County
28	126,923	**Grandview Heights** (city) Franklin County
30	124,009	**Beachwood** (city) Cuyahoga County
31	122,786	**Highland Heights** (city) Cuyahoga County
32	121,969	**Mason** (city) Warren County
33	121,516	**Bay Village** (city) Cuyahoga County
34	120,388	**Worthington** (city) Franklin County
35	119,947	**Avon** (city) Lorain County
36	118,080	**Westlake** (city) Cuyahoga County
37	116,170	**Beckett Ridge** (CDP) Butler County
38	114,894	**Kirtland** (city) Lake County
39	114,249	**Bainbridge** (CDP) Geauga County
40	113,102	**Dry Ridge** (CDP) Hamilton County
41	111,898	**Sherwood** (CDP) Hamilton County
42	111,490	**Hilliard** (city) Franklin County
43	110,765	**Madeira** (city) Hamilton County
44	110,317	**Aurora** (city) Portage County
45	110,207	**Macedonia** (city) Summit County
46	108,723	**Mack** (CDP) Hamilton County
47	108,531	**Rocky River** (city) Cuyahoga County
48	108,456	**Springboro** (city) Warren County
49	108,395	**Richfield** (village) Summit County
50	108,189	**Mayfield** (village) Cuyahoga County
51	107,851	**Independence** (city) Cuyahoga County
52	106,163	**Avon Lake** (city) Lorain County
53	105,617	**Broadview Heights** (city) Cuyahoga County
54	104,476	**Perrysburg** (city) Wood County
55	103,655	**Blue Ash** (city) Hamilton County
56	102,624	**Newtown** (village) Hamilton County
57	100,803	**Fruit Hill** (CDP) Hamilton County
58	100,415	**Strongsville** (city) Cuyahoga County
59	99,959	**Whitehouse** (village) Lucas County
60	99,762	**Landen** (CDP) Warren County
61	99,308	**Westerville** (city) Franklin County
62	99,010	**Beavercreek** (city) Greene County
63	99,000	**Kenwood** (CDP) Hamilton County
64	96,327	**Lake Darby** (CDP) Franklin County
65	96,031	**Gahanna** (city) Franklin County
66	95,507	**South Lebanon** (village) Warren County
67	95,116	**Salem Heights** (CDP) Hamilton County
68	94,974	**Delhi Hills** (CDP) Hamilton County
69	94,959	**Taylor Creek** (CDP) Hamilton County
70	94,836	**Monfort Heights** (CDP) Hamilton County
71	94,183	**Canfield** (city) Mahoning County
72	93,425	**Loveland** (city) Hamilton County
73	93,283	**Pickerington** (city) Fairfield County
74	93,087	**Cherry Grove** (CDP) Hamilton County
75	92,029	**Wright-Patterson AFB** (CDP) Greene County
76	91,663	**Poland** (village) Mahoning County
77	91,652	**Greentown** (CDP) Stark County
78	91,566	**Dent** (CDP) Hamilton County
79	91,234	**Forestville** (CDP) Hamilton County
80	90,768	**Miami Heights** (CDP) Hamilton County
81	90,620	**Sylvania** (city) Lucas County
82	89,858	**Beechwood Trails** (CDP) Licking County
83	89,852	**Fairlawn** (city) Summit County
84	89,639	**Saint Henry** (village) Mercer County
85	89,457	**Bellbrook** (city) Greene County
86	88,626	**Day Heights** (CDP) Clermont County
87	88,188	**Howland Center** (CDP) Trumbull County
88	88,030	**Yellow Springs** (village) Greene County
89	87,382	**Twinsburg** (city) Summit County
90	87,295	**Waterville** (city) Lucas County
91	87,172	**University Heights** (city) Cuyahoga County
92	86,109	**Reminderville** (village) Summit County
93	85,697	**North Royalton** (city) Cuyahoga County
94	85,426	**Green** (city) Summit County
95	85,377	**Sheffield** (village) Lorain County
96	85,144	**Devola** (CDP) Washington County
97	85,048	**Seven Hills** (city) Cuyahoga County
98	85,024	**Centerville** (city) Montgomery County
99	84,925	**Clayton** (city) Montgomery County
100	84,731	**Fort Shawnee** (CDP) Allen County
101	84,423	**Monroe** (city) Butler County
102	84,383	**Canal Winchester** (city) Franklin County
103	83,165	**Mentor** (city) Lake County
104	82,979	**Covedale** (CDP) Hamilton County
105	82,891	**Lyndhurst** (city) Cuyahoga County
106	81,925	**Pataskala** (city) Licking County
107	81,082	**Mulberry** (CDP) Clermont County
108	80,798	**New Franklin** (city) Summit County
109	80,662	**North Ridgeville** (city) Lorain County
110	80,284	**Munroe Falls** (city) Summit County
111	80,134	**Huron** (city) Erie County
112	79,639	**Stow** (city) Summit County
113	79,603	**Uniontown** (CDP) Stark County
114	79,574	**Maumee** (city) Lucas County
115	79,519	**Seville** (village) Medina County
116	79,398	**Cleves** (village) Hamilton County
117	79,393	**New Bremen** (village) Auglaize County
118	78,315	**Tipp City** (city) Miami County
119	78,199	**Olmsted Falls** (city) Cuyahoga County
120	78,169	**Pleasant Run Farm** (CDP) Hamilton County
121	78,144	**Green Meadows** (CDP) Clark County
122	77,947	**Grove City** (city) Franklin County
123	77,712	**Amherst** (city) Lorain County
124	77,420	**Germantown** (city) Montgomery County
125	77,056	**Saint Clairsville** (city) Belmont County
126	76,710	**Plain City** (village) Madison County
127	76,338	**North Zanesville** (CDP) Muskingum County
128	76,276	**Willoughby Hills** (city) Lake County
129	75,976	**Brunswick** (city) Medina County
130	75,604	**Sunbury** (village) Delaware County
131	75,526	**Minster** (village) Auglaize County
132	75,209	**Tallmadge** (city) Summit County
133	74,749	**White Oak** (CDP) Hamilton County
134	74,744	**Ross** (CDP) Butler County
135	74,724	**Union** (city) Montgomery County
136	74,465	**North Olmsted** (city) Cuyahoga County
137	74,464	**Bluffton** (village) Allen County
138	74,277	**Medina** (city) Medina County
139	74,249	**Marysville** (city) Union County
140	74,086	**Wadsworth** (city) Medina County
141	73,782	**Cleveland Heights** (city) Cuyahoga County
142	73,577	**Apple Valley** (CDP) Knox County
143	73,259	**Delaware** (city) Delaware County
144	72,901	**Norton** (city) Summit County
145	72,886	**Reynoldsburg** (city) Franklin County
146	72,300	**Chardon** (city) Geauga County
147	72,109	**Doylestown** (village) Wayne County
148	72,005	**Mount Repose** (CDP) Clermont County
149	71,516	**Sharonville** (city) Hamilton County
150	71,460	**Pleasant Run** (CDP) Hamilton County

Note: *This section ranks incorporated places and CDPs (Census Designated Places) with populations of 2,500 or more. Unincorporated postal areas were not considered. Please refer to the User Guide for additional information.*

Average Household Income

Top 150 Places Ranked in *Ascending* Order

State Rank	Dollars	Place
1	28,357	**Lincoln Heights** (village) Hamilton County
2	30,188	**East Cleveland** (city) Cuyahoga County
3	34,119	**Nelsonville** (city) Athens County
4	34,582	**West Union** (village) Adams County
5	34,838	**Wellsville** (village) Columbiana County
6	34,930	**Greenfield** (village) Highland County
7	35,829	**Youngstown** (city) Mahoning County
8	37,516	**Ashtabula** (city) Ashtabula County
9	37,551	**Zanesville** (city) Muskingum County
10	37,580	**Lockland** (village) Hamilton County
11	37,762	**Dennison** (village) Tuscarawas County
12	38,544	**Campbell** (city) Mahoning County
13	38,996	**Crooksville** (village) Perry County
14	39,237	**Bellaire** (village) Belmont County
15	39,518	**Warren** (city) Trumbull County
16	39,670	**Canton** (city) Stark County
17	40,057	**Cleveland** (city) Cuyahoga County
18	40,735	**Dayton** (city) Montgomery County
19	40,827	**The Plains** (CDP) Athens County
20	41,077	**Logan** (city) Hocking County
21	41,292	**Cambridge** (city) Guernsey County
22	41,566	**Uhrichsville** (city) Tuscarawas County
23	41,646	**New Lexington** (village) Perry County
24	41,724	**Georgetown** (village) Brown County
25	42,178	**Lima** (city) Allen County
26	42,213	**East Liverpool** (city) Columbiana County
27	42,420	**Mount Healthy** (city) Hamilton County
28	42,562	**Athens** (city) Athens County
29	42,966	**Hicksville** (village) Defiance County
30	43,185	**Portsmouth** (city) Scioto County
31	43,331	**West Portsmouth** (CDP) Scioto County
32	43,469	**Warrensville Heights** (city) Cuyahoga County
33	43,475	**New Carlisle** (city) Clark County
34	43,614	**Newcomerstown** (village) Tuscarawas County
35	43,819	**Hillsboro** (city) Highland County
36	44,318	**Martins Ferry** (city) Belmont County
37	44,367	**Greenville** (city) Darke County
38	44,406	**Conneaut** (city) Ashtabula County
39	44,487	**Jackson** (city) Jackson County
40	44,562	**Trotwood** (city) Montgomery County
41	44,919	**Sandusky** (city) Erie County
42	45,046	**Ravenna** (city) Portage County
43	45,402	**Millersburg** (village) Holmes County
44	45,434	**Toronto** (city) Jefferson County
45	45,437	**Sebring** (village) Mahoning County
46	45,561	**Ironton** (city) Lawrence County
47	45,678	**Whitehall** (city) Franklin County
48	45,712	**Mount Vernon** (city) Knox County
49	45,891	**Springfield** (city) Clark County
50	45,897	**Loudonville** (village) Ashland County
51	45,998	**West Carrollton** (city) Montgomery County
52	46,386	**Mansfield** (city) Richland County
53	46,422	**Ada** (village) Hardin County
54	46,477	**Toledo** (city) Lucas County
55	46,498	**Crestline** (village) Crawford County
56	46,530	**Barnesville** (village) Belmont County
57	46,550	**Urbana** (city) Champaign County
58	46,671	**Euclid** (city) Cuyahoga County
59	46,811	**Marion** (city) Marion County
60	46,831	**Bethel** (village) Clermont County
61	46,843	**Maple Heights** (city) Cuyahoga County
62	46,901	**Fremont** (city) Sandusky County
63	47,109	**Alliance** (city) Stark County
64	47,125	**Paulding** (village) Paulding County
65	47,135	**Lisbon** (village) Columbiana County
66	47,361	**Shelby** (city) Richland County
67	47,512	**Bucyrus** (city) Crawford County
68	47,749	**Lodi** (village) Medina County
69	47,844	**Galion** (city) Crawford County
69	47,844	**Kenton** (city) Hardin County
71	47,899	**Cheviot** (city) Hamilton County
72	47,927	**Newton Falls** (village) Trumbull County
73	47,967	**Fostoria** (city) Seneca County
74	48,176	**Walbridge** (village) Wood County
75	48,238	**Lorain** (city) Lorain County
76	48,336	**Struthers** (city) Mahoning County
77	48,368	**Akron** (city) Summit County
78	48,410	**Bedford Heights** (city) Cuyahoga County
79	48,666	**Piqua** (city) Miami County
80	48,826	**Silverton** (village) Hamilton County
81	48,851	**North College Hill** (city) Hamilton County
82	48,861	**Steubenville** (city) Jefferson County
83	48,862	**Edgewood** (CDP) Ashtabula County
84	49,145	**Wilmington** (city) Clinton County
85	49,153	**Waverly** (village) Pike County
86	49,177	**Upper Sandusky** (city) Wyandot County
87	49,309	**Mount Healthy Heights** (CDP) Hamilton County
88	49,500	**Garfield Heights** (city) Cuyahoga County
89	49,634	**Bryan** (city) Williams County
89	49,634	**Middletown** (city) Butler County
91	49,653	**Golf Manor** (village) Hamilton County
92	49,750	**Van Wert** (city) Van Wert County
93	49,869	**Willard** (city) Huron County
94	50,188	**Cedarville** (village) Greene County
95	50,218	**New Lebanon** (village) Montgomery County
96	50,422	**Elyria** (city) Lorain County
97	50,545	**Barberton** (city) Summit County
98	50,630	**East Palestine** (village) Columbiana County
99	50,781	**Middlefield** (village) Geauga County
100	50,790	**Coshocton** (city) Coshocton County
101	51,317	**Minerva** (village) Stark County
102	51,321	**Lancaster** (city) Fairfield County
103	51,401	**Washington Court House** (city) Fayette County
104	51,563	**Xenia** (city) Greene County
105	51,627	**Brooklyn** (city) Cuyahoga County
106	51,686	**Obetz** (village) Franklin County
107	51,700	**Chillicothe** (city) Ross County
108	51,704	**Mount Gilead** (village) Morrow County
109	51,740	**Austintown** (CDP) Mahoning County
110	51,765	**Niles** (city) Trumbull County
111	51,774	**Baltimore** (village) Fairfield County
112	51,919	**Circleville** (city) Pickaway County
113	52,002	**New London** (village) Huron County
114	52,053	**Geneva** (city) Ashtabula County
115	52,157	**Marietta** (city) Washington County
116	52,199	**Montpelier** (village) Williams County
117	52,295	**Belpre** (city) Washington County
118	52,369	**Park Layne** (CDP) Clark County
119	52,563	**Jefferson** (village) Ashtabula County
120	52,641	**Gallipolis** (village) Gallia County
121	52,659	**Moraine** (city) Montgomery County
122	52,752	**Tiffin** (city) Seneca County
123	52,858	**Delphos** (city) Allen County
124	52,871	**Girard** (city) Trumbull County
125	52,911	**Ashland** (city) Ashland County
126	52,981	**Bedford** (city) Cuyahoga County
127	53,000	**Newark** (city) Licking County
128	53,031	**Celina** (city) Mercer County
129	53,088	**Covington** (village) Miami County
130	53,100	**Eaton** (city) Preble County
131	53,245	**Bowling Green** (city) Wood County
132	53,253	**Kent** (city) Portage County
133	53,610	**Northbrook** (CDP) Hamilton County
134	53,849	**Blacklick Estates** (CDP) Franklin County
135	53,876	**Oxford** (city) Butler County
136	53,903	**Parma Heights** (city) Cuyahoga County
137	53,972	**Hamilton** (city) Butler County
138	53,996	**Port Clinton** (city) Ottawa County
139	54,069	**Painesville** (city) Lake County
140	54,180	**Saint Marys** (city) Auglaize County
141	54,203	**Lincoln Village** (CDP) Franklin County
142	54,207	**Norwood** (city) Hamilton County
143	54,294	**Carrollton** (village) Carroll County
144	54,412	**Riverside** (city) Montgomery County
145	54,490	**Massillon** (city) Stark County
146	54,606	**Perry Heights** (CDP) Stark County
147	54,866	**McDonald** (village) Trumbull County
148	54,880	**West Milton** (village) Miami County
149	54,980	**Wapakoneta** (city) Auglaize County
150	54,991	**Blanchester** (village) Clinton County

***Note:** This section ranks incorporated places and CDPs (Census Designated Places) with populations of 2,500 or more. Unincorporated postal areas were not considered. Please refer to the User Guide for additional information.*

Households with Income of $100,000 or More

Top 150 Places Ranked in *Descending* Order

State Rank	Percent	Place
1	74.6	**The Village of Indian Hill** (city) Hamilton County
2	73.9	**New Albany** (city) Franklin County
3	70.2	**Pepper Pike** (city) Cuyahoga County
4	69.5	**Powell** (city) Delaware County
5	69.2	**Dry Run** (CDP) Hamilton County
6	61.9	**Dublin** (city) Franklin County
7	61.7	**Moreland Hills** (village) Cuyahoga County
8	61.6	**Hudson** (city) Summit County
9	59.6	**Amberley** (village) Hamilton County
10	59.2	**Wyoming** (city) Hamilton County
11	58.1	**Turpin Hills** (CDP) Hamilton County
12	57.1	**Ottawa Hills** (village) Lucas County
13	56.0	**Evendale** (village) Hamilton County
14	54.8	**Four Bridges** (CDP) Butler County
15	54.3	**Montgomery** (city) Hamilton County
16	52.9	**Bainbridge** (CDP) Geauga County
17	52.7	**South Russell** (village) Geauga County
18	52.6	**Montrose-Ghent** (CDP) Summit County
19	52.0	**Highland Heights** (city) Cuyahoga County
20	51.1	**Orange** (village) Cuyahoga County
21	50.9	**Upper Arlington** (city) Franklin County
22	50.8	**Bexley** (city) Franklin County
23	49.8	**Springboro** (city) Warren County
24	49.1	**Brecksville** (city) Cuyahoga County
25	48.8	**Oakwood** (city) Montgomery County
26	48.7	**Solon** (city) Cuyahoga County
27	48.4	**Grandview Heights** (city) Franklin County
28	47.1	**Avon** (city) Lorain County
28	47.1	**Worthington** (city) Franklin County
30	46.8	**Granville** (village) Licking County
31	46.6	**Greentown** (CDP) Stark County
32	46.5	**Mason** (city) Warren County
33	46.2	**Bay Village** (city) Cuyahoga County
34	46.1	**Hilliard** (city) Franklin County
35	45.9	**Mariemont** (village) Hamilton County
36	45.3	**Madeira** (city) Hamilton County
37	44.7	**Sixteen Mile Stand** (CDP) Hamilton County
38	44.1	**Beckett Ridge** (CDP) Butler County
39	43.2	**Macedonia** (city) Summit County
39	43.2	**Mack** (CDP) Hamilton County
41	43.0	**Beachwood** (city) Cuyahoga County
42	42.4	**Sherwood** (CDP) Hamilton County
43	42.0	**Independence** (city) Cuyahoga County
43	42.0	**Westerville** (city) Franklin County
45	41.6	**Richfield** (village) Summit County
46	41.5	**Kirtland** (city) Lake County
47	41.2	**Landen** (CDP) Warren County
48	40.4	**Aurora** (city) Portage County
49	40.3	**Delhi Hills** (CDP) Hamilton County
50	40.2	**Avon Lake** (city) Lorain County
51	40.1	**Perrysburg** (city) Wood County
52	39.8	**Strongsville** (city) Cuyahoga County
53	39.7	**Beavercreek** (city) Greene County
53	39.7	**Shaker Heights** (city) Cuyahoga County
55	39.4	**Westlake** (city) Cuyahoga County
56	39.3	**Chagrin Falls** (village) Cuyahoga County
57	39.2	**Cherry Grove** (CDP) Hamilton County
58	39.1	**Forestville** (CDP) Hamilton County
59	38.5	**Pickerington** (city) Fairfield County
60	38.3	**Dry Ridge** (CDP) Hamilton County
61	38.2	**Miami Heights** (CDP) Hamilton County
62	38.1	**Wright-Patterson AFB** (CDP) Greene County
63	38.0	**Broadview Heights** (city) Cuyahoga County
64	37.7	**Fruit Hill** (CDP) Hamilton County
65	37.3	**Sheffield** (village) Lorain County
66	37.1	**Beechwood Trails** (CDP) Licking County
67	36.8	**Waterville** (city) Lucas County
68	36.2	**Sylvania** (city) Lucas County
69	36.0	**Dent** (CDP) Hamilton County
69	36.0	**Taylor Creek** (CDP) Hamilton County
71	35.8	**Whitehouse** (village) Lucas County
72	35.6	**Covedale** (CDP) Hamilton County
73	35.4	**Blue Ash** (city) Hamilton County
74	35.3	**Twinsburg** (city) Summit County
75	35.0	**Gahanna** (city) Franklin County
75	35.0	**South Lebanon** (village) Warren County
77	34.9	**Bellbrook** (city) Greene County
78	34.3	**Rocky River** (city) Cuyahoga County
79	34.1	**Reminderville** (village) Summit County
80	34.0	**Day Heights** (CDP) Clermont County
80	34.0	**Seven Hills** (city) Cuyahoga County
82	33.7	**Loveland** (city) Hamilton County
83	33.6	**Lake Darby** (CDP) Franklin County
83	33.6	**Mayfield** (village) Cuyahoga County
83	33.6	**Poland** (village) Mahoning County
86	33.3	**Yellow Springs** (village) Greene County
87	32.9	**Canal Winchester** (city) Franklin County
88	32.7	**Kenwood** (CDP) Hamilton County
89	32.6	**Canfield** (city) Mahoning County
90	32.2	**Centerville** (city) Montgomery County
91	32.1	**Mentor** (city) Lake County
91	32.1	**Newtown** (village) Hamilton County
93	31.2	**Salem Heights** (CDP) Hamilton County
94	30.6	**North Royalton** (city) Cuyahoga County
95	30.5	**Monroe** (city) Butler County
96	30.4	**Fairlawn** (city) Summit County
96	30.4	**Sunbury** (village) Delaware County
98	30.3	**Green** (city) Summit County
98	30.3	**New Bremen** (village) Auglaize County
98	30.3	**Saint Henry** (village) Mercer County
101	30.0	**Amherst** (city) Lorain County
102	29.9	**Clayton** (city) Montgomery County
103	29.8	**University Heights** (city) Cuyahoga County
104	29.5	**Devola** (CDP) Washington County
105	28.6	**Cleves** (village) Hamilton County
106	28.4	**Monfort Heights** (CDP) Hamilton County
106	28.4	**North Ridgeville** (city) Lorain County
108	28.3	**Marysville** (city) Union County
108	28.3	**Mulberry** (CDP) Clermont County
108	28.3	**Olmsted Falls** (city) Cuyahoga County
111	28.1	**Lyndhurst** (city) Cuyahoga County
111	28.1	**Minster** (village) Auglaize County
113	28.0	**Saint Clairsville** (city) Belmont County
114	27.9	**Pataskala** (city) Licking County
114	27.9	**Stow** (city) Summit County
116	27.4	**New Franklin** (city) Summit County
117	27.2	**Grove City** (city) Franklin County
118	26.9	**Uniontown** (CDP) Stark County
119	26.7	**Ross** (CDP) Butler County
120	26.6	**Plain City** (village) Madison County
121	26.2	**Medina** (city) Medina County
122	25.8	**Enon** (village) Clark County
122	25.8	**Munroe Falls** (city) Summit County
122	25.8	**North Zanesville** (CDP) Muskingum County
125	25.5	**Willoughby Hills** (city) Lake County
126	25.3	**Germantown** (city) Montgomery County
126	25.3	**Rossford** (city) Wood County
128	25.0	**Groesbeck** (CDP) Hamilton County
128	25.0	**Pleasant Run Farm** (CDP) Hamilton County
128	25.0	**Tallmadge** (city) Summit County
131	24.9	**Wadsworth** (city) Medina County
132	24.8	**Brunswick** (city) Medina County
133	24.7	**Harrison** (city) Hamilton County
134	24.5	**Howland Center** (CDP) Trumbull County
135	24.4	**Maumee** (city) Lucas County
136	24.3	**Seville** (village) Medina County
137	24.2	**Reynoldsburg** (city) Franklin County
138	23.9	**Finneytown** (CDP) Hamilton County
139	23.7	**Miamisburg** (city) Montgomery County
139	23.7	**North Olmsted** (city) Cuyahoga County
139	23.7	**Tipp City** (city) Miami County
142	23.5	**Delaware** (city) Delaware County
143	23.4	**Garrettsville** (village) Portage County
144	23.3	**White Oak** (CDP) Hamilton County
145	23.2	**Lexington** (village) Richland County
145	23.2	**Middleburg Heights** (city) Cuyahoga County
147	22.9	**Cleveland Heights** (city) Cuyahoga County
148	22.7	**Norton** (city) Summit County
149	22.6	**Oregon** (city) Lucas County
150	22.5	**Mount Repose** (CDP) Clermont County

Note: *This section ranks incorporated places and CDPs (Census Designated Places) with populations of 2,500 or more. Unincorporated postal areas were not considered. Please refer to the User Guide for additional information.*

Households with Income of $100,000 or More

Top 150 Places Ranked in *Ascending* Order

State Rank	Percent	Place
1	2.3	**Lincoln Heights** (village) Hamilton County
2	2.5	**Hicksville** (village) Defiance County
3	2.9	**Wellsville** (village) Columbiana County
4	3.6	**East Cleveland** (city) Cuyahoga County
5	3.9	**Dennison** (village) Tuscarawas County
6	4.2	**Ashtabula** (city) Ashtabula County
7	4.3	**Campbell** (city) Mahoning County
7	4.3	**New Lexington** (village) Perry County
9	4.4	**Youngstown** (city) Mahoning County
10	4.6	**Nelsonville** (city) Athens County
11	4.7	**Crooksville** (village) Perry County
11	4.7	**Greenfield** (village) Highland County
11	4.7	**Warrensville Heights** (city) Cuyahoga County
14	4.8	**Paulding** (village) Paulding County
15	4.9	**Zanesville** (city) Muskingum County
16	5.3	**Newcomerstown** (village) Tuscarawas County
17	5.4	**Georgetown** (village) Brown County
17	5.4	**Uhrichsville** (city) Tuscarawas County
17	5.4	**Warren** (city) Trumbull County
20	5.6	**Canton** (city) Stark County
20	5.6	**West Union** (village) Adams County
22	5.8	**Newton Falls** (village) Trumbull County
23	6.2	**Lima** (city) Allen County
23	6.2	**Lockland** (village) Hamilton County
23	6.2	**Sandusky** (city) Erie County
26	6.4	**Millersburg** (village) Holmes County
27	6.5	**Lodi** (village) Medina County
28	6.7	**Ada** (village) Hardin County
28	6.7	**Hillsboro** (city) Highland County
30	6.9	**Greenville** (city) Darke County
31	7.0	**Cleveland** (city) Cuyahoga County
31	7.0	**Conneaut** (city) Ashtabula County
31	7.0	**Logan** (city) Hocking County
31	7.0	**Ravenna** (city) Portage County
31	7.0	**Whitehall** (city) Franklin County
36	7.1	**Fostoria** (city) Seneca County
36	7.1	**Galion** (city) Crawford County
36	7.1	**The Plains** (CDP) Athens County
39	7.2	**Bellaire** (village) Belmont County
39	7.2	**Dayton** (city) Montgomery County
39	7.2	**Jackson** (city) Jackson County
42	7.4	**Kenton** (city) Hardin County
42	7.4	**Mount Vernon** (city) Knox County
44	7.5	**Marion** (city) Marion County
44	7.5	**New Carlisle** (city) Clark County
46	7.6	**Bryan** (city) Williams County
46	7.6	**Fremont** (city) Sandusky County
48	7.8	**Portsmouth** (city) Scioto County
48	7.8	**Springfield** (city) Clark County
48	7.8	**Urbana** (city) Champaign County
51	7.9	**Bucyrus** (city) Crawford County
51	7.9	**Maple Heights** (city) Cuyahoga County
53	8.0	**Barnesville** (village) Belmont County
53	8.0	**Mansfield** (city) Richland County
55	8.1	**Blacklick Estates** (CDP) Franklin County
56	8.3	**Crestline** (village) Crawford County
56	8.3	**East Liverpool** (city) Columbiana County
56	8.3	**Mount Healthy** (city) Hamilton County
56	8.3	**Struthers** (city) Mahoning County
60	8.4	**Alliance** (city) Stark County
60	8.4	**West Carrollton** (city) Montgomery County
62	8.5	**Bethel** (village) Clermont County
62	8.5	**Cambridge** (city) Guernsey County
62	8.5	**Shelby** (city) Richland County
65	8.6	**North College Hill** (city) Hamilton County
65	8.6	**Sebring** (village) Mahoning County
67	8.7	**Barberton** (city) Summit County
67	8.7	**Martins Ferry** (city) Belmont County
67	8.7	**Piqua** (city) Miami County
70	8.8	**Van Wert** (city) Van Wert County
71	8.9	**Upper Sandusky** (city) Wyandot County
72	9.0	**Belpre** (city) Washington County
73	9.2	**Toledo** (city) Lucas County
74	9.3	**Celina** (city) Mercer County
74	9.3	**Delphos** (city) Allen County
74	9.3	**Euclid** (city) Cuyahoga County
74	9.3	**Garfield Heights** (city) Cuyahoga County
74	9.3	**Lorain** (city) Lorain County
74	9.3	**Loudonville** (village) Ashland County
80	9.4	**Trotwood** (city) Montgomery County
80	9.4	**Washington Court House** (city) Fayette County
82	9.5	**Akron** (city) Summit County
83	9.6	**Fredericktown** (village) Knox County
83	9.6	**Xenia** (city) Greene County
85	9.7	**Ironton** (city) Lawrence County
85	9.7	**Niles** (city) Trumbull County
87	9.8	**Northbrook** (CDP) Hamilton County
87	9.8	**Toronto** (city) Jefferson County
89	9.9	**Bedford Heights** (city) Cuyahoga County
89	9.9	**Girard** (city) Trumbull County
89	9.9	**Tiffin** (city) Seneca County
92	10.0	**Gallipolis** (village) Gallia County
92	10.0	**Middletown** (city) Butler County
94	10.1	**Wellston** (city) Jackson County
95	10.2	**Brooklyn** (city) Cuyahoga County
95	10.2	**East Palestine** (village) Columbiana County
95	10.2	**Lake Lakengren** (CDP) Preble County
98	10.3	**New London** (village) Huron County
99	10.4	**Austintown** (CDP) Mahoning County
100	10.5	**Gibsonburg** (village) Sandusky County
100	10.5	**Walbridge** (village) Wood County
100	10.5	**Willard** (city) Huron County
103	10.6	**Lincoln Village** (CDP) Franklin County
103	10.6	**Wapakoneta** (city) Auglaize County
103	10.6	**West Portsmouth** (CDP) Scioto County
106	10.7	**Eaton** (city) Preble County
106	10.7	**Elyria** (city) Lorain County
108	10.8	**McDonald** (village) Trumbull County
109	10.9	**Carrollton** (village) Carroll County
110	11.0	**Burlington** (CDP) Lawrence County
110	11.0	**Cedarville** (village) Greene County
112	11.1	**Covington** (village) Miami County
112	11.1	**Lisbon** (village) Columbiana County
114	11.2	**Heath** (city) Licking County
114	11.2	**Marietta** (city) Washington County
114	11.2	**Parma Heights** (city) Cuyahoga County
114	11.2	**Steubenville** (city) Jefferson County
114	11.2	**Waverly** (village) Pike County
119	11.3	**Cheviot** (city) Hamilton County
119	11.3	**Chillicothe** (city) Ross County
119	11.3	**Circleville** (city) Pickaway County
119	11.3	**Wilmington** (city) Clinton County
119	11.3	**Woodlawn** (village) Hamilton County
124	11.4	**Geneva** (city) Ashtabula County
125	11.5	**Golf Manor** (village) Hamilton County
125	11.5	**Rittman** (city) Wayne County
127	11.6	**Athens** (city) Athens County
127	11.6	**Jefferson** (village) Ashtabula County
127	11.6	**Riverside** (city) Montgomery County
127	11.6	**Salem** (city) Columbiana County
131	11.7	**Hubbard** (city) Trumbull County
131	11.7	**Montpelier** (village) Williams County
131	11.7	**Mount Healthy Heights** (CDP) Hamilton County
131	11.7	**Norwalk** (city) Huron County
135	11.8	**Middlefield** (village) Geauga County
135	11.8	**Minerva** (village) Stark County
137	11.9	**New Lebanon** (village) Montgomery County
138	12.0	**Ashland** (city) Ashland County
138	12.0	**Painesville** (city) Lake County
140	12.1	**Defiance** (city) Defiance County
140	12.1	**Hamilton** (city) Butler County
140	12.1	**Northfield** (village) Summit County
143	12.3	**Buckeye Lake** (village) Licking County
143	12.3	**Port Clinton** (city) Ottawa County
145	12.4	**Perry Heights** (CDP) Stark County
145	12.4	**Sheffield Lake** (city) Lorain County
147	12.5	**Lancaster** (city) Fairfield County
147	12.5	**Massillon** (city) Stark County
147	12.5	**Sidney** (city) Shelby County
147	12.5	**Wooster** (city) Wayne County

***Note:** This section ranks incorporated places and CDPs (Census Designated Places) with populations of 2,500 or more. Unincorporated postal areas were not considered. Please refer to the User Guide for additional information.*

Poverty Rate

Top 150 Places Ranked in *Descending* Order

State Rank	Percent	Place
1	54.7	**Athens** (city) Athens County
2	46.1	**Oxford** (city) Butler County
3	44.1	**West Union** (village) Adams County
4	41.8	**East Cleveland** (city) Cuyahoga County
4	41.8	**Lincoln Heights** (village) Hamilton County
6	40.0	**Nelsonville** (city) Athens County
7	38.0	**Youngstown** (city) Mahoning County
8	36.0	**Cleveland** (city) Cuyahoga County
9	35.8	**Bowling Green** (city) Wood County
10	35.6	**Lockland** (village) Hamilton County
11	34.9	**Warren** (city) Trumbull County
12	34.5	**Dayton** (city) Montgomery County
13	34.4	**Kent** (city) Portage County
14	34.3	**Ashtabula** (city) Ashtabula County
15	34.2	**Portsmouth** (city) Scioto County
16	33.8	**Bellaire** (village) Belmont County
17	33.7	**Greenfield** (village) Highland County
18	33.5	**Wellsville** (village) Columbiana County
19	32.6	**Gallipolis** (village) Gallia County
20	32.3	**Lisbon** (village) Columbiana County
21	31.8	**Canton** (city) Stark County
22	31.2	**Cambridge** (city) Guernsey County
23	30.8	**Zanesville** (city) Muskingum County
24	30.7	**Uhrichsville** (city) Tuscarawas County
25	30.6	**Fostoria** (city) Seneca County
25	30.6	**The Plains** (CDP) Athens County
27	30.0	**Dennison** (village) Tuscarawas County
28	29.9	**Cincinnati** (city) Hamilton County
29	29.2	**Campbell** (city) Mahoning County
30	29.0	**New Lexington** (village) Perry County
31	28.5	**Lima** (city) Allen County
32	27.9	**Springfield** (city) Clark County
33	27.5	**Toledo** (city) Lucas County
34	26.9	**Steubenville** (city) Jefferson County
35	26.3	**East Liverpool** (city) Columbiana County
35	26.3	**New Lebanon** (village) Montgomery County
37	26.2	**Lorain** (city) Lorain County
38	25.9	**Trotwood** (city) Montgomery County
39	25.8	**Crestline** (village) Crawford County
39	25.8	**Marietta** (city) Washington County
41	25.6	**Mansfield** (city) Richland County
42	25.5	**Hillsboro** (city) Highland County
43	25.4	**Akron** (city) Summit County
43	25.4	**Wellston** (city) Jackson County
45	25.2	**Georgetown** (village) Brown County
46	24.9	**Fruit Hill** (CDP) Hamilton County
47	24.6	**Xenia** (city) Greene County
48	24.5	**New Concord** (village) Muskingum County
49	24.2	**Middletown** (city) Butler County
50	24.1	**Lodi** (village) Medina County
51	23.8	**Fremont** (city) Sandusky County
52	23.7	**New Burlington** (CDP) Hamilton County
53	23.6	**Williamsburg** (village) Clermont County
54	23.5	**Mount Vernon** (city) Knox County
54	23.5	**New London** (village) Huron County
56	23.4	**Ada** (village) Hardin County
56	23.4	**Alliance** (city) Stark County
58	23.3	**Salem** (city) Columbiana County
59	23.2	**Edgewood** (CDP) Ashtabula County
59	23.2	**Willard** (city) Huron County
61	22.9	**Buckeye Lake** (village) Licking County
61	22.9	**Newcomerstown** (village) Tuscarawas County
61	22.9	**Whitehall** (city) Franklin County
64	22.8	**Eaton** (city) Preble County
64	22.8	**Martins Ferry** (city) Belmont County
66	22.6	**Logan** (city) Hocking County
67	22.5	**Chillicothe** (city) Ross County
68	22.4	**Crooksville** (village) Perry County
68	22.4	**Sandusky** (city) Erie County
68	22.4	**Washington Court House** (city) Fayette County
71	22.3	**Ravenna** (city) Portage County
72	22.2	**Elyria** (city) Lorain County
73	22.1	**Fairborn** (city) Greene County
74	22.0	**Norwood** (city) Hamilton County
75	21.9	**Hamilton** (city) Butler County
75	21.9	**Marion** (city) Marion County
77	21.8	**Newark** (city) Licking County
78	21.7	**Cedarville** (village) Greene County
78	21.7	**Painesville** (city) Lake County
80	21.5	**Euclid** (city) Cuyahoga County
81	21.4	**Wilmington** (city) Clinton County
82	21.2	**Columbus** (city) Franklin County
82	21.2	**Golf Manor** (village) Hamilton County
82	21.2	**Jefferson** (village) Ashtabula County
82	21.2	**Milford** (city) Clermont County
86	21.1	**Maple Heights** (city) Cuyahoga County
87	21.0	**Ironton** (city) Lawrence County
87	21.0	**Obetz** (village) Franklin County
89	20.9	**Bellefontaine** (city) Logan County
89	20.9	**Toronto** (city) Jefferson County
91	20.8	**Jackson** (city) Jackson County
91	20.8	**New Carlisle** (city) Clark County
93	20.7	**Cheviot** (city) Hamilton County
93	20.7	**Urbana** (city) Champaign County
95	20.6	**Oberlin** (city) Lorain County
96	20.5	**Lancaster** (city) Fairfield County
97	20.4	**Belpre** (city) Washington County
97	20.4	**Circleville** (city) Pickaway County
97	20.4	**Mount Healthy Heights** (CDP) Hamilton County
100	20.2	**Cleveland Heights** (city) Cuyahoga County
101	20.0	**Van Wert** (city) Van Wert County
102	19.9	**Warrensville Heights** (city) Cuyahoga County
102	19.9	**West Carrollton** (city) Montgomery County
102	19.9	**West Portsmouth** (CDP) Scioto County
105	19.8	**Niles** (city) Trumbull County
105	19.8	**Piqua** (city) Miami County
107	19.6	**Mount Carmel** (CDP) Clermont County
108	19.5	**Newton Falls** (village) Trumbull County
109	19.4	**Mount Healthy** (city) Hamilton County
110	19.3	**Wooster** (city) Wayne County
111	19.2	**Montpelier** (village) Williams County
111	19.2	**North College Hill** (city) Hamilton County
113	18.8	**Defiance** (city) Defiance County
113	18.8	**Springdale** (city) Hamilton County
115	18.6	**Gibsonburg** (village) Sandusky County
115	18.6	**Kenton** (city) Hardin County
115	18.6	**Moraine** (city) Montgomery County
118	18.5	**Findlay** (city) Hancock County
118	18.5	**Perry Heights** (CDP) Stark County
120	18.4	**Conneaut** (city) Ashtabula County
121	18.3	**Massillon** (city) Stark County
122	18.2	**Covington** (village) Miami County
123	18.0	**Barberton** (city) Summit County
124	17.8	**Bucyrus** (city) Crawford County
125	17.7	**Galion** (city) Crawford County
125	17.7	**Greenville** (city) Darke County
127	17.6	**East Palestine** (village) Columbiana County
128	17.4	**Garfield Heights** (city) Cuyahoga County
128	17.4	**Waverly** (village) Pike County
128	17.4	**Woodlawn** (village) Hamilton County
131	17.3	**Mount Orab** (village) Brown County
131	17.3	**Upper Sandusky** (city) Wyandot County
133	17.2	**Baltimore** (village) Fairfield County
133	17.2	**Fairport Harbor** (village) Lake County
133	17.2	**Norwalk** (city) Huron County
136	17.0	**Tiffin** (city) Seneca County
137	16.9	**Franklin** (city) Warren County
138	16.8	**Barnesville** (village) Belmont County
139	16.7	**Napoleon** (city) Henry County
140	16.6	**Park Layne** (CDP) Clark County
141	16.5	**Blanchester** (village) Clinton County
141	16.5	**Wauseon** (city) Fulton County
143	16.4	**Ashland** (city) Ashland County
143	16.4	**Bedford Heights** (city) Cuyahoga County
143	16.4	**Forest Park** (city) Hamilton County
143	16.4	**Loudonville** (village) Ashland County
143	16.4	**New Philadelphia** (city) Tuscarawas County
143	16.4	**Oakwood** (village) Cuyahoga County
149	16.3	**Cadiz** (village) Harrison County
149	16.3	**Millersburg** (village) Holmes County

Note: *This section ranks incorporated places and CDPs (Census Designated Places) with populations of 2,500 or more. Unincorporated postal areas were not considered. Please refer to the User Guide for additional information.*

Poverty Rate

Top 150 Places Ranked in *Ascending* Order

State Rank	Percent	Place
1	0.0	**Beechwood Trails** (CDP) Licking County
2	0.2	**Dry Run** (CDP) Hamilton County
3	0.3	**Powell** (city) Delaware County
4	0.7	**South Russell** (village) Geauga County
5	1.3	**Landen** (CDP) Warren County
6	1.9	**Evendale** (village) Hamilton County
6	1.9	**Macedonia** (city) Summit County
8	2.0	**Grandview Heights** (city) Franklin County
8	2.0	**Turpin Hills** (CDP) Hamilton County
8	2.0	**Wyoming** (city) Hamilton County
11	2.1	**Madeira** (city) Hamilton County
12	2.3	**Bainbridge** (CDP) Geauga County
12	2.3	**Mariemont** (village) Hamilton County
14	2.4	**Ottawa Hills** (village) Lucas County
15	2.5	**Independence** (city) Cuyahoga County
15	2.5	**Ross** (CDP) Butler County
17	2.6	**Mason** (city) Warren County
17	2.6	**Springboro** (city) Warren County
19	2.7	**Chagrin Falls** (village) Cuyahoga County
19	2.7	**Dublin** (city) Franklin County
19	2.7	**Four Bridges** (CDP) Butler County
19	2.7	**New Albany** (city) Franklin County
19	2.7	**Salem Heights** (CDP) Hamilton County
24	2.8	**Brecksville** (city) Cuyahoga County
24	2.8	**Canal Winchester** (city) Franklin County
24	2.8	**Kirtland** (city) Lake County
24	2.8	**Moreland Hills** (village) Cuyahoga County
24	2.8	**Orange** (village) Cuyahoga County
29	2.9	**Beachwood** (city) Cuyahoga County
29	2.9	**Mayfield** (village) Cuyahoga County
29	2.9	**Richfield** (village) Summit County
32	3.0	**Olmsted Falls** (city) Cuyahoga County
32	3.0	**Seville** (village) Medina County
34	3.1	**Devola** (CDP) Washington County
34	3.1	**The Village of Indian Hill** (city) Hamilton County
36	3.2	**Bellbrook** (city) Greene County
36	3.2	**Hudson** (city) Summit County
36	3.2	**Miami Heights** (CDP) Hamilton County
39	3.3	**Amberley** (village) Hamilton County
40	3.5	**Bay Village** (city) Cuyahoga County
40	3.5	**Beckett Ridge** (CDP) Butler County
42	3.6	**Highland Heights** (city) Cuyahoga County
43	3.7	**Green Meadows** (CDP) Clark County
43	3.7	**Saint Henry** (village) Mercer County
45	3.8	**Avon** (city) Lorain County
45	3.8	**Avon Lake** (city) Lorain County
45	3.8	**Worthington** (city) Franklin County
48	3.9	**Montgomery** (city) Hamilton County
49	4.0	**Hilliard** (city) Franklin County
49	4.0	**Poland** (village) Mahoning County
51	4.1	**Broadview Heights** (city) Cuyahoga County
51	4.1	**Middleburg Heights** (city) Cuyahoga County
51	4.1	**Pepper Pike** (city) Cuyahoga County
51	4.1	**Sixteen Mile Stand** (CDP) Hamilton County
55	4.2	**Delhi Hills** (CDP) Hamilton County
55	4.2	**Strongsville** (city) Cuyahoga County
57	4.3	**Waterville** (city) Lucas County
58	4.4	**Mulberry** (CDP) Clermont County
58	4.4	**Sherwood** (CDP) Hamilton County
60	4.5	**Seven Hills** (city) Cuyahoga County
61	4.6	**Greentown** (CDP) Stark County
62	4.7	**Cherry Grove** (CDP) Hamilton County
62	4.7	**Dry Ridge** (CDP) Hamilton County
62	4.7	**Lyndhurst** (city) Cuyahoga County
62	4.7	**New Franklin** (city) Summit County
62	4.7	**Pleasant Run** (CDP) Hamilton County
62	4.7	**Reminderville** (village) Summit County
62	4.7	**Rocky River** (city) Cuyahoga County
69	4.8	**Beavercreek** (city) Greene County
69	4.8	**Northridge** (CDP) Clark County
69	4.8	**Saint Clairsville** (city) Belmont County
69	4.8	**Solon** (city) Cuyahoga County
73	4.9	**North Ridgeville** (city) Lorain County
73	4.9	**Westlake** (city) Cuyahoga County
75	5.0	**Perrysburg** (city) Wood County
76	5.1	**Groveport** (city) Franklin County
76	5.1	**Sheffield** (village) Lorain County
76	5.1	**Upper Arlington** (city) Franklin County
79	5.2	**Aurora** (city) Portage County
79	5.2	**Pickerington** (city) Fairfield County
81	5.3	**North Royalton** (city) Cuyahoga County
82	5.4	**Louisville** (city) Stark County
83	5.5	**Stow** (city) Summit County
84	5.6	**Blue Ash** (city) Hamilton County
84	5.6	**Brookville** (city) Montgomery County
84	5.6	**Mentor** (city) Lake County
84	5.6	**Montrose-Ghent** (CDP) Summit County
84	5.6	**North Canton** (city) Stark County
89	5.7	**Canfield** (city) Mahoning County
90	5.8	**North Madison** (CDP) Lake County
91	5.9	**Dillonvale** (CDP) Hamilton County
91	5.9	**Monroe** (city) Butler County
91	5.9	**Twinsburg** (city) Summit County
94	6.0	**Bluffton** (village) Allen County
94	6.0	**Fairlawn** (city) Summit County
94	6.0	**Mack** (CDP) Hamilton County
97	6.1	**Ballville** (CDP) Sandusky County
97	6.1	**Coldwater** (village) Mercer County
97	6.1	**Minster** (village) Auglaize County
97	6.1	**New Bremen** (village) Auglaize County
97	6.1	**Uniontown** (CDP) Stark County
102	6.3	**Gahanna** (city) Franklin County
102	6.3	**Lake Darby** (CDP) Franklin County
102	6.3	**Norton** (city) Summit County
102	6.3	**Oakwood** (city) Montgomery County
102	6.3	**Taylor Creek** (CDP) Hamilton County
107	6.4	**Centerville** (city) Montgomery County
108	6.5	**Ashville** (village) Pickaway County
108	6.5	**Doylestown** (village) Wayne County
108	6.5	**Lake Lakengren** (CDP) Preble County
108	6.5	**Monfort Heights** (CDP) Hamilton County
108	6.5	**Rossford** (city) Wood County
108	6.5	**Westerville** (city) Franklin County
108	6.5	**Willowick** (city) Lake County
115	6.6	**Dent** (CDP) Hamilton County
115	6.6	**Harrison** (city) Hamilton County
117	6.8	**Covedale** (CDP) Hamilton County
117	6.8	**Wadsworth** (city) Medina County
117	6.8	**Wickliffe** (city) Lake County
117	6.8	**Wright-Patterson AFB** (CDP) Greene County
121	6.9	**Mount Repose** (CDP) Clermont County
121	6.9	**North Kingsville** (village) Ashtabula County
121	6.9	**Tipp City** (city) Miami County
124	7.1	**Munroe Falls** (city) Summit County
125	7.2	**North Olmsted** (city) Cuyahoga County
126	7.3	**Calcutta** (CDP) Columbiana County
127	7.4	**Ontario** (city) Richland County
128	7.5	**Clayton** (city) Montgomery County
128	7.5	**Northgate** (CDP) Hamilton County
130	7.6	**Fairfield** (city) Butler County
130	7.6	**Northwood** (city) Wood County
130	7.6	**Willoughby** (city) Lake County
133	7.7	**Apple Valley** (CDP) Knox County
133	7.7	**Kenwood** (CDP) Hamilton County
133	7.7	**Sylvania** (city) Lucas County
136	7.8	**Grove City** (city) Franklin County
136	7.8	**Versailles** (village) Darke County
136	7.8	**Whitehouse** (village) Lucas County
139	7.9	**Canal Fulton** (city) Stark County
139	7.9	**Maumee** (city) Lucas County
141	8.0	**Brunswick** (city) Medina County
141	8.0	**Howland Center** (CDP) Trumbull County
141	8.0	**West Milton** (village) Miami County
144	8.1	**Deer Park** (city) Hamilton County
144	8.1	**Middlefield** (village) Geauga County
144	8.1	**Shaker Heights** (city) Cuyahoga County
144	8.1	**Sunbury** (village) Delaware County
148	8.2	**Amherst** (city) Lorain County
148	8.2	**Richville** (CDP) Stark County
148	8.2	**Union** (city) Montgomery County

Note: *This section ranks incorporated places and CDPs (Census Designated Places) with populations of 2,500 or more. Unincorporated postal areas were not considered. Please refer to the User Guide for additional information.*

Educational Attainment: High School Diploma or Higher

Top 150 Places Ranked in *Descending* Order

State Rank	Percent	Place
1	99.8	**Powell** (city) Delaware County
2	99.6	**Mariemont** (village) Hamilton County
3	99.5	**Turpin Hills** (CDP) Hamilton County
4	99.3	**Grandview Heights** (city) Franklin County
4	99.3	**Moreland Hills** (village) Cuyahoga County
6	99.2	**Bainbridge** (CDP) Geauga County
6	99.2	**Sixteen Mile Stand** (CDP) Hamilton County
8	98.9	**Greentown** (CDP) Stark County
9	98.8	**Fruit Hill** (CDP) Hamilton County
9	98.8	**Granville** (village) Licking County
9	98.8	**South Russell** (village) Geauga County
12	98.7	**New Albany** (city) Franklin County
12	98.7	**The Village of Indian Hill** (city) Hamilton County
12	98.7	**Upper Arlington** (city) Franklin County
15	98.5	**Dublin** (city) Franklin County
16	98.4	**Amberley** (village) Hamilton County
16	98.4	**Worthington** (city) Franklin County
18	98.3	**Beckett Ridge** (CDP) Butler County
18	98.3	**Oakwood** (city) Montgomery County
20	98.1	**Landen** (CDP) Warren County
20	98.1	**Wyoming** (city) Hamilton County
22	97.9	**Hudson** (city) Summit County
23	97.8	**Bexley** (city) Franklin County
23	97.8	**Dry Run** (CDP) Hamilton County
23	97.8	**Montrose-Ghent** (CDP) Summit County
23	97.8	**Poland** (village) Mahoning County
27	97.7	**Cherry Grove** (CDP) Hamilton County
27	97.7	**Montgomery** (city) Hamilton County
29	97.6	**Canfield** (city) Mahoning County
29	97.6	**Orange** (village) Cuyahoga County
29	97.6	**Pepper Pike** (city) Cuyahoga County
32	97.5	**Bay Village** (city) Cuyahoga County
32	97.5	**Mason** (city) Warren County
34	97.4	**Brecksville** (city) Cuyahoga County
34	97.4	**Whitehouse** (village) Lucas County
36	97.3	**Beavercreek** (city) Greene County
36	97.3	**Chagrin Falls** (village) Cuyahoga County
38	97.1	**Fairlawn** (city) Summit County
38	97.1	**New Bremen** (village) Auglaize County
38	97.1	**Perrysburg** (city) Wood County
41	97.0	**Evendale** (village) Hamilton County
41	97.0	**Mack** (CDP) Hamilton County
41	97.0	**Reminderville** (village) Summit County
44	96.9	**Bellbrook** (city) Greene County
44	96.9	**Solon** (city) Cuyahoga County
46	96.7	**Westerville** (city) Franklin County
46	96.7	**Yellow Springs** (village) Greene County
48	96.6	**Beechwood Trails** (CDP) Licking County
49	96.5	**Garrettsville** (village) Portage County
49	96.5	**Lake Darby** (CDP) Franklin County
51	96.4	**Macedonia** (city) Summit County
51	96.4	**Springboro** (city) Warren County
51	96.4	**Westlake** (city) Cuyahoga County
54	96.3	**Avon Lake** (city) Lorain County
54	96.3	**Hilliard** (city) Franklin County
54	96.3	**Kenwood** (CDP) Hamilton County
54	96.3	**University Heights** (city) Cuyahoga County
58	96.2	**Athens** (city) Athens County
58	96.2	**Broadview Heights** (city) Cuyahoga County
58	96.2	**Ottawa Hills** (village) Lucas County
58	96.2	**Shaker Heights** (city) Cuyahoga County
62	96.1	**Salem Heights** (CDP) Hamilton County
63	96.0	**Cedarville** (village) Greene County
63	96.0	**Four Bridges** (CDP) Butler County
63	96.0	**Shadyside** (village) Belmont County
66	95.9	**Madeira** (city) Hamilton County
66	95.9	**Mingo Junction** (village) Jefferson County
66	95.9	**Strongsville** (city) Cuyahoga County
66	95.9	**Waterville** (city) Lucas County
70	95.8	**Bluffton** (village) Allen County
70	95.8	**Brimfield** (CDP) Portage County
70	95.8	**Centerville** (city) Montgomery County
70	95.8	**Devola** (CDP) Washington County
70	95.8	**Maumee** (city) Lucas County
70	95.8	**Sheffield** (village) Lorain County
70	95.8	**Sylvania** (city) Lucas County
77	95.7	**Avon** (city) Lorain County
77	95.7	**Blue Ash** (city) Hamilton County
77	95.7	**Rocky River** (city) Cuyahoga County
77	95.7	**Sherwood** (CDP) Hamilton County
77	95.7	**Sunbury** (village) Delaware County
82	95.6	**Beachwood** (city) Cuyahoga County
82	95.6	**New Concord** (village) Muskingum County
84	95.5	**Day Heights** (CDP) Clermont County
85	95.4	**Fairview Park** (city) Cuyahoga County
85	95.4	**Highland Heights** (city) Cuyahoga County
85	95.4	**Lyndhurst** (city) Cuyahoga County
88	95.3	**Union** (city) Montgomery County
89	95.2	**Gahanna** (city) Franklin County
90	95.1	**Lexington** (village) Richland County
90	95.1	**Saint Clairsville** (city) Belmont County
90	95.1	**Twinsburg** (city) Summit County
93	95.0	**Clayton** (city) Montgomery County
93	95.0	**Olmsted Falls** (city) Cuyahoga County
95	94.9	**Columbiana** (city) Columbiana County
95	94.9	**Mayfield** (village) Cuyahoga County
95	94.9	**Pickerington** (city) Fairfield County
95	94.9	**Stow** (city) Summit County
99	94.8	**Forestville** (CDP) Hamilton County
99	94.8	**Greenhills** (village) Hamilton County
99	94.8	**Rossford** (city) Wood County
102	94.7	**Aurora** (city) Portage County
102	94.7	**Dent** (CDP) Hamilton County
102	94.7	**Mentor** (city) Lake County
105	94.6	**Canal Winchester** (city) Franklin County
105	94.6	**Loveland** (city) Hamilton County
105	94.6	**Wadsworth** (city) Medina County
108	94.5	**Cortland** (city) Trumbull County
108	94.5	**Grove City** (city) Franklin County
108	94.5	**Independence** (city) Cuyahoga County
108	94.5	**Kirtland** (city) Lake County
108	94.5	**Medina** (city) Medina County
113	94.4	**Huron** (city) Erie County
113	94.4	**North Canton** (city) Stark County
115	94.3	**Dry Ridge** (CDP) Hamilton County
115	94.3	**Green** (city) Summit County
115	94.3	**Minster** (village) Auglaize County
115	94.3	**Northridge** (CDP) Clark County
115	94.3	**Richfield** (village) Summit County
120	94.2	**Monfort Heights** (CDP) Hamilton County
121	94.1	**Ballville** (CDP) Sandusky County
121	94.1	**Kent** (city) Portage County
121	94.1	**Kettering** (city) Montgomery County
124	94.0	**Delhi Hills** (CDP) Hamilton County
125	93.9	**Boardman** (CDP) Mahoning County
125	93.9	**Bowling Green** (city) Wood County
125	93.9	**Lakewood** (city) Cuyahoga County
128	93.8	**Cuyahoga Falls** (city) Summit County
128	93.8	**Groveport** (city) Franklin County
128	93.8	**Mount Repose** (CDP) Clermont County
128	93.8	**Reynoldsburg** (city) Franklin County
132	93.7	**Cleveland Heights** (city) Cuyahoga County
132	93.7	**Oak Harbor** (village) Ottawa County
134	93.6	**Delaware** (city) Delaware County
134	93.6	**Howland Center** (CDP) Trumbull County
134	93.6	**Mulberry** (CDP) Clermont County
134	93.6	**Wintersville** (village) Jefferson County
138	93.5	**Englewood** (city) Montgomery County
138	93.5	**Green Meadows** (CDP) Clark County
138	93.5	**Hubbard** (city) Trumbull County
138	93.5	**Mayfield Heights** (city) Cuyahoga County
138	93.5	**Mount Gilead** (village) Morrow County
138	93.5	**Oberlin** (city) Lorain County
144	93.4	**Fort Shawnee** (CDP) Allen County
144	93.4	**Harrison** (city) Hamilton County
144	93.4	**North Zanesville** (CDP) Muskingum County
144	93.4	**Pleasant Run** (CDP) Hamilton County
144	93.4	**Swanton** (village) Fulton County
144	93.4	**Tallmadge** (city) Summit County
150	93.3	**Chardon** (city) Geauga County

***Note:** This section ranks incorporated places and CDPs (Census Designated Places) with populations of 2,500 or more. Unincorporated postal areas were not considered. Please refer to the User Guide for additional information.*

Educational Attainment: High School Diploma or Higher

Top 150 Places Ranked in *Ascending* Order

State Rank	Percent	Place
1	75.6	**Lockland** (village) Hamilton County
2	78.4	**Cleveland** (city) Cuyahoga County
2	78.4	**West Union** (village) Adams County
4	79.2	**Painesville** (city) Lake County
5	79.6	**Bellaire** (village) Belmont County
6	79.8	**Grafton** (village) Lorain County
6	79.8	**Park Layne** (CDP) Clark County
6	79.8	**Uhrichsville** (city) Tuscarawas County
6	79.8	**Willard** (city) Huron County
10	80.0	**Ashtabula** (city) Ashtabula County
11	80.2	**Buckeye Lake** (village) Licking County
12	80.3	**Lincoln Village** (CDP) Franklin County
13	80.4	**Hicksville** (village) Defiance County
14	80.7	**Portsmouth** (city) Scioto County
14	80.7	**Whitehall** (city) Franklin County
16	80.8	**New Carlisle** (city) Clark County
16	80.8	**Zanesville** (city) Muskingum County
18	81.2	**Mount Orab** (village) Brown County
19	81.5	**Gallipolis** (village) Gallia County
19	81.5	**Montpelier** (village) Williams County
21	81.6	**New Lexington** (village) Perry County
21	81.6	**New Richmond** (village) Clermont County
23	81.8	**Wellston** (city) Jackson County
24	81.9	**Franklin** (city) Warren County
25	82.0	**East Liverpool** (city) Columbiana County
26	82.1	**East Cleveland** (city) Cuyahoga County
27	82.4	**Lorain** (city) Lorain County
28	82.5	**Middletown** (city) Butler County
29	82.7	**Hillsboro** (city) Highland County
29	82.7	**Williamsburg** (village) Clermont County
31	82.8	**Lincoln Heights** (village) Hamilton County
32	83.0	**Campbell** (city) Mahoning County
32	83.0	**Youngstown** (city) Mahoning County
34	83.1	**Dayton** (city) Montgomery County
34	83.1	**Springfield** (city) Clark County
34	83.1	**Waverly** (village) Pike County
37	83.2	**Marion** (city) Marion County
38	83.4	**Obetz** (village) Franklin County
39	83.5	**Greenfield** (village) Highland County
39	83.5	**Mansfield** (city) Richland County
41	83.7	**Lima** (city) Allen County
42	84.0	**Blanchester** (village) Clinton County
42	84.0	**Dennison** (village) Tuscarawas County
42	84.0	**Norwood** (city) Hamilton County
45	84.1	**Covington** (village) Miami County
46	84.2	**Barberton** (city) Summit County
46	84.2	**Sebring** (village) Mahoning County
48	84.3	**Lisbon** (village) Columbiana County
49	84.4	**Canton** (city) Stark County
49	84.4	**Circleville** (city) Pickaway County
51	84.5	**Paulding** (village) Paulding County
52	84.6	**Mount Carmel** (CDP) Clermont County
53	84.7	**Hamilton** (city) Butler County
53	84.7	**New London** (village) Huron County
55	84.8	**Oakwood** (village) Cuyahoga County
55	84.8	**West Portsmouth** (CDP) Scioto County
57	84.9	**Crestline** (village) Crawford County
57	84.9	**Newcomerstown** (village) Tuscarawas County
57	84.9	**Warren** (city) Trumbull County
60	85.0	**Alliance** (city) Stark County
60	85.0	**Mount Healthy Heights** (CDP) Hamilton County
62	85.1	**Urbana** (city) Champaign County
62	85.1	**Wellsville** (village) Columbiana County
64	85.2	**Mineral Ridge** (CDP) Trumbull County
64	85.2	**Wauseon** (city) Fulton County
66	85.3	**Bethel** (village) Clermont County
66	85.3	**Georgetown** (village) Brown County
66	85.3	**Sandusky** (city) Erie County
66	85.3	**The Plains** (CDP) Athens County
70	85.4	**Cambridge** (city) Guernsey County
71	85.5	**Crooksville** (village) Perry County
71	85.5	**Garfield Heights** (city) Cuyahoga County
71	85.5	**Nelsonville** (city) Athens County
74	85.6	**Chillicothe** (city) Ross County
74	85.6	**Piqua** (city) Miami County
74	85.6	**Wilmington** (city) Clinton County
77	85.7	**Fremont** (city) Sandusky County
77	85.7	**Moraine** (city) Montgomery County
77	85.7	**Toledo** (city) Lucas County
80	86.0	**Salem** (city) Columbiana County
81	86.1	**Brooklyn** (city) Cuyahoga County
81	86.1	**London** (city) Madison County
81	86.1	**Ravenna** (city) Portage County
84	86.2	**Cincinnati** (city) Hamilton County
84	86.2	**Millersburg** (village) Holmes County
84	86.2	**Trotwood** (city) Montgomery County
87	86.4	**Akron** (city) Summit County
87	86.4	**Gibsonburg** (village) Sandusky County
89	86.5	**Conneaut** (city) Ashtabula County
89	86.5	**Dover** (city) Tuscarawas County
91	86.6	**Groesbeck** (CDP) Hamilton County
91	86.6	**Ironton** (city) Lawrence County
91	86.6	**Springdale** (city) Hamilton County
91	86.6	**Washington Court House** (city) Fayette County
91	86.6	**West Jefferson** (village) Madison County
96	86.7	**Amelia** (village) Clermont County
96	86.7	**Elyria** (city) Lorain County
96	86.7	**Shelby** (city) Richland County
99	86.8	**Belpre** (city) Washington County
99	86.8	**Girard** (city) Trumbull County
99	86.8	**New Philadelphia** (city) Tuscarawas County
102	86.9	**Riverside** (city) Montgomery County
103	87.0	**Ashland** (city) Ashland County
103	87.0	**Brook Park** (city) Cuyahoga County
103	87.0	**Summerside** (CDP) Clermont County
106	87.1	**Fostoria** (city) Seneca County
106	87.1	**Newark** (city) Licking County
108	87.2	**Northbrook** (CDP) Hamilton County
108	87.2	**West Milton** (village) Miami County
110	87.3	**Newton Falls** (village) Trumbull County
111	87.4	**Rittman** (city) Wayne County
112	87.5	**Cheviot** (city) Hamilton County
112	87.5	**Fairborn** (city) Greene County
112	87.5	**Greenville** (city) Darke County
112	87.5	**Milford** (city) Clermont County
112	87.5	**Reading** (city) Hamilton County
117	87.6	**Lancaster** (city) Fairfield County
117	87.6	**Norwalk** (city) Huron County
117	87.6	**Steubenville** (city) Jefferson County
120	87.7	**Mount Vernon** (city) Knox County
121	87.8	**Bucyrus** (city) Crawford County
121	87.8	**Calcutta** (CDP) Columbiana County
123	87.9	**Logan** (city) Hocking County
123	87.9	**Xenia** (city) Greene County
125	88.0	**Sidney** (city) Shelby County
125	88.0	**Silverton** (village) Hamilton County
125	88.0	**Vermilion** (city) Lorain County
128	88.1	**Bellefontaine** (city) Logan County
128	88.1	**Eaton** (city) Preble County
130	88.2	**Coldwater** (village) Mercer County
131	88.3	**Ada** (village) Hardin County
131	88.3	**Kenton** (city) Hardin County
133	88.4	**Coshocton** (city) Coshocton County
133	88.4	**East Palestine** (village) Columbiana County
133	88.4	**Galion** (city) Crawford County
133	88.4	**Port Clinton** (city) Ottawa County
137	88.5	**Carlisle** (village) Warren County
137	88.5	**New Lebanon** (village) Montgomery County
137	88.5	**Troy** (city) Miami County
140	88.6	**White Oak** (CDP) Hamilton County
141	88.7	**Bedford Heights** (city) Cuyahoga County
142	88.8	**Cadiz** (village) Harrison County
142	88.8	**Columbus** (city) Franklin County
142	88.8	**Loudonville** (village) Ashland County
142	88.8	**Saint Marys** (city) Auglaize County
146	88.9	**Blacklick Estates** (CDP) Franklin County
146	88.9	**Martins Ferry** (city) Belmont County
148	89.0	**Maple Heights** (city) Cuyahoga County
148	89.0	**Ross** (CDP) Butler County
150	89.1	**Doylestown** (village) Wayne County

Note: *This section ranks incorporated places and CDPs (Census Designated Places) with populations of 2,500 or more. Unincorporated postal areas were not considered. Please refer to the User Guide for additional information.*

Educational Attainment: Bachelor's Degree or Higher

Top 150 Places Ranked in *Descending* Order

State Rank	Percent	Place
1	88.1	**The Village of Indian Hill** (city) Hamilton County
2	78.4	**South Russell** (village) Geauga County
3	77.4	**Ottawa Hills** (village) Lucas County
4	77.0	**New Albany** (city) Franklin County
5	76.7	**Mariemont** (village) Hamilton County
6	75.3	**Dublin** (city) Franklin County
6	75.3	**Pepper Pike** (city) Cuyahoga County
8	74.5	**Moreland Hills** (village) Cuyahoga County
9	74.1	**Bexley** (city) Franklin County
10	74.0	**Upper Arlington** (city) Franklin County
11	73.9	**Dry Run** (CDP) Hamilton County
12	73.4	**Powell** (city) Delaware County
13	71.0	**Grandview Heights** (city) Franklin County
14	70.7	**Hudson** (city) Summit County
15	70.6	**Oakwood** (city) Montgomery County
16	69.6	**Wyoming** (city) Hamilton County
17	69.3	**Orange** (village) Cuyahoga County
18	69.1	**Montgomery** (city) Hamilton County
19	68.5	**Amberley** (village) Hamilton County
20	68.4	**Worthington** (city) Franklin County
21	68.3	**Sixteen Mile Stand** (CDP) Hamilton County
22	68.0	**Turpin Hills** (CDP) Hamilton County
23	66.0	**Granville** (village) Licking County
24	65.4	**Chagrin Falls** (village) Cuyahoga County
25	64.9	**Shaker Heights** (city) Cuyahoga County
26	64.4	**Bainbridge** (CDP) Geauga County
27	64.0	**Bay Village** (city) Cuyahoga County
28	63.2	**Athens** (city) Athens County
29	62.6	**Montrose-Ghent** (CDP) Summit County
30	62.0	**Solon** (city) Cuyahoga County
31	61.2	**Yellow Springs** (village) Greene County
32	61.1	**Madeira** (city) Hamilton County
33	60.0	**Evendale** (village) Hamilton County
34	59.3	**Mason** (city) Warren County
35	58.8	**Oxford** (city) Butler County
36	58.1	**Kenwood** (CDP) Hamilton County
37	57.0	**University Heights** (city) Cuyahoga County
38	56.9	**Beachwood** (city) Cuyahoga County
39	56.5	**Four Bridges** (CDP) Butler County
40	56.3	**Beckett Ridge** (CDP) Butler County
41	55.4	**Blue Ash** (city) Hamilton County
42	55.2	**Rocky River** (city) Cuyahoga County
43	55.1	**Highland Heights** (city) Cuyahoga County
44	54.1	**Sherwood** (CDP) Hamilton County
45	53.8	**Brecksville** (city) Cuyahoga County
46	53.0	**Landen** (CDP) Warren County
47	52.5	**Westerville** (city) Franklin County
47	52.5	**Westlake** (city) Cuyahoga County
49	52.4	**Mayfield** (village) Cuyahoga County
50	52.1	**Hilliard** (city) Franklin County
51	51.8	**Forestville** (CDP) Hamilton County
52	51.5	**Avon Lake** (city) Lorain County
53	51.4	**Centerville** (city) Montgomery County
53	51.4	**Fairlawn** (city) Summit County
55	51.0	**Cleveland Heights** (city) Cuyahoga County
55	51.0	**Perrysburg** (city) Wood County
57	50.1	**Aurora** (city) Portage County
58	50.0	**Beavercreek** (city) Greene County
59	49.9	**South Lebanon** (village) Warren County
60	48.7	**Springboro** (city) Warren County
61	48.3	**Lyndhurst** (city) Cuyahoga County
62	47.3	**Fruit Hill** (CDP) Hamilton County
63	47.2	**Avon** (city) Lorain County
64	46.1	**Gahanna** (city) Franklin County
65	45.8	**Oberlin** (city) Lorain County
65	45.8	**Twinsburg** (city) Summit County
67	45.7	**Broadview Heights** (city) Cuyahoga County
68	45.1	**Wright-Patterson AFB** (CDP) Greene County
69	44.8	**Poland** (village) Mahoning County
70	44.6	**Strongsville** (city) Cuyahoga County
71	44.5	**Bellbrook** (city) Greene County
72	44.0	**Bluffton** (village) Allen County
72	44.0	**Macedonia** (city) Summit County
74	43.9	**Canfield** (city) Mahoning County
75	43.8	**Newtown** (village) Hamilton County
76	43.7	**Lakewood** (city) Cuyahoga County
77	43.1	**Cherry Grove** (CDP) Hamilton County
77	43.1	**Sylvania** (city) Lucas County
79	42.9	**Stow** (city) Summit County
80	42.4	**Bowling Green** (city) Wood County
81	42.3	**Cedarville** (village) Greene County
82	42.1	**Kent** (city) Portage County
83	42.0	**Reminderville** (village) Summit County
84	41.9	**Richfield** (village) Summit County
85	41.7	**Dry Ridge** (CDP) Hamilton County
86	41.6	**Loveland** (city) Hamilton County
87	41.0	**Kirtland** (city) Lake County
88	40.8	**Salem Heights** (CDP) Hamilton County
88	40.8	**Waterville** (city) Lucas County
90	40.5	**Greentown** (CDP) Stark County
90	40.5	**Mack** (CDP) Hamilton County
92	40.3	**Independence** (city) Cuyahoga County
93	39.6	**Covedale** (CDP) Hamilton County
94	39.5	**South Euclid** (city) Cuyahoga County
95	39.0	**Sharonville** (city) Hamilton County
96	38.6	**Pickerington** (city) Fairfield County
97	37.8	**Willoughby Hills** (city) Lake County
98	37.2	**Mayfield Heights** (city) Cuyahoga County
98	37.2	**Mulberry** (CDP) Clermont County
100	37.1	**Dent** (CDP) Hamilton County
100	37.1	**Maumee** (city) Lucas County
102	36.9	**Fairview Park** (city) Cuyahoga County
102	36.9	**Woodlawn** (village) Hamilton County
104	36.8	**Sunbury** (village) Delaware County
105	36.4	**Munroe Falls** (city) Summit County
106	36.1	**Whitehouse** (village) Lucas County
107	36.0	**North Royalton** (city) Cuyahoga County
108	35.8	**Canal Winchester** (city) Franklin County
109	35.7	**New Concord** (village) Muskingum County
110	35.5	**Medina** (city) Medina County
111	35.4	**Wadsworth** (city) Medina County
112	35.3	**Monfort Heights** (CDP) Hamilton County
112	35.3	**North Canton** (city) Stark County
114	35.2	**Beechwood Trails** (CDP) Licking County
115	35.1	**Green** (city) Summit County
116	34.9	**Devola** (CDP) Washington County
117	34.8	**Columbus** (city) Franklin County
117	34.8	**Lake Darby** (CDP) Franklin County
119	34.6	**Finneytown** (CDP) Hamilton County
119	34.6	**Miami Heights** (CDP) Hamilton County
119	34.6	**Middleburg Heights** (city) Cuyahoga County
119	34.6	**Richmond Heights** (city) Cuyahoga County
123	34.5	**Seven Hills** (city) Cuyahoga County
124	34.3	**Clayton** (city) Montgomery County
124	34.3	**Delaware** (city) Delaware County
126	34.0	**Olmsted Falls** (city) Cuyahoga County
127	33.8	**Cincinnati** (city) Hamilton County
127	33.8	**Huron** (city) Erie County
127	33.8	**North Zanesville** (CDP) Muskingum County
130	33.6	**Kettering** (city) Montgomery County
131	33.3	**Greenhills** (village) Hamilton County
132	32.9	**Berea** (city) Cuyahoga County
133	32.6	**North Ridgeville** (city) Lorain County
134	32.4	**Cuyahoga Falls** (city) Summit County
135	32.2	**Mentor** (city) Lake County
136	32.1	**Springdale** (city) Hamilton County
136	32.1	**Tipp City** (city) Miami County
138	31.5	**Cortland** (city) Trumbull County
139	31.4	**Dillonvale** (CDP) Hamilton County
139	31.4	**Reynoldsburg** (city) Franklin County
141	31.3	**Portage Lakes** (CDP) Summit County
142	30.8	**Monroe** (city) Butler County
143	30.7	**New Bremen** (village) Auglaize County
143	30.7	**Willoughby** (city) Lake County
145	30.4	**Milford** (city) Clermont County
145	30.4	**Plain City** (village) Madison County
145	30.4	**Pleasant Run Farm** (CDP) Hamilton County
148	30.2	**Mount Repose** (CDP) Clermont County
149	30.0	**Howland Center** (CDP) Trumbull County
150	29.9	**Grove City** (city) Franklin County

Note: *This section ranks incorporated places and CDPs (Census Designated Places) with populations of 2,500 or more. Unincorporated postal areas were not considered. Please refer to the User Guide for additional information.*

Educational Attainment: Bachelor's Degree or Higher

Top 150 Places Ranked in *Ascending* Order

State Rank	Percent	Place
1	5.4	**Lockland** (village) Hamilton County
1	5.4	**Uhrichsville** (city) Tuscarawas County
1	5.4	**Wellsville** (village) Columbiana County
4	5.5	**Blanchester** (village) Clinton County
5	6.4	**Newton Falls** (village) Trumbull County
6	6.5	**Grafton** (village) Lorain County
7	6.6	**New Lebanon** (village) Montgomery County
8	7.2	**Bellaire** (village) Belmont County
9	7.5	**Park Layne** (CDP) Clark County
10	7.7	**West Jefferson** (village) Madison County
11	7.9	**New Lexington** (village) Perry County
11	7.9	**West Portsmouth** (CDP) Scioto County
13	8.0	**Campbell** (city) Mahoning County
14	8.2	**Hicksville** (village) Defiance County
15	8.5	**Crooksville** (village) Perry County
16	8.7	**Dennison** (village) Tuscarawas County
16	8.7	**Kenton** (city) Hardin County
18	9.1	**Lakemore** (village) Summit County
19	9.3	**Fostoria** (city) Seneca County
19	9.3	**Lodi** (village) Medina County
19	9.3	**Mount Healthy Heights** (CDP) Hamilton County
19	9.3	**Newcomerstown** (village) Tuscarawas County
23	9.4	**Ashtabula** (city) Ashtabula County
23	9.4	**Burlington** (CDP) Lawrence County
23	9.4	**Marion** (city) Marion County
26	9.6	**Covington** (village) Miami County
26	9.6	**Lincoln Heights** (village) Hamilton County
26	9.6	**Toronto** (city) Jefferson County
29	9.9	**Galion** (city) Crawford County
29	9.9	**Greenfield** (village) Highland County
29	9.9	**Paulding** (village) Paulding County
32	10.0	**Millersburg** (village) Holmes County
33	10.1	**New London** (village) Huron County
34	10.2	**Conneaut** (city) Ashtabula County
35	10.5	**Crestline** (village) Crawford County
35	10.5	**Lincoln Village** (CDP) Franklin County
35	10.5	**North Baltimore** (village) Wood County
38	10.7	**East Liverpool** (city) Columbiana County
38	10.7	**Fremont** (city) Sandusky County
38	10.7	**Perry Heights** (CDP) Stark County
41	10.9	**Carey** (village) Wyandot County
41	10.9	**Nelsonville** (city) Athens County
43	11.0	**Montpelier** (village) Williams County
44	11.1	**Mount Orab** (village) Brown County
45	11.2	**Geneva** (city) Ashtabula County
46	11.4	**Blacklick Estates** (CDP) Franklin County
46	11.4	**Piqua** (city) Miami County
48	11.5	**Lima** (city) Allen County
49	11.6	**Baltimore** (village) Fairfield County
49	11.6	**Saint Marys** (city) Auglaize County
49	11.6	**West Union** (village) Adams County
52	11.7	**Greenville** (city) Darke County
52	11.7	**Lorain** (city) Lorain County
54	11.8	**Eaton** (city) Preble County
54	11.8	**Georgetown** (village) Brown County
54	11.8	**New Carlisle** (city) Clark County
54	11.8	**Willard** (city) Huron County
58	11.9	**Obetz** (village) Franklin County
58	11.9	**Richville** (CDP) Stark County
60	12.0	**Youngstown** (city) Mahoning County
61	12.1	**Zanesville** (city) Muskingum County
62	12.4	**East Cleveland** (city) Cuyahoga County
63	12.5	**Bucyrus** (city) Crawford County
64	12.6	**Brook Park** (city) Cuyahoga County
64	12.6	**Franklin** (city) Warren County
66	12.7	**Barberton** (city) Summit County
66	12.7	**East Palestine** (village) Columbiana County
66	12.7	**Jefferson** (village) Ashtabula County
66	12.7	**Whitehall** (city) Franklin County
70	12.8	**Bethel** (village) Clermont County
70	12.8	**Cambridge** (city) Guernsey County
70	12.8	**Loudonville** (village) Ashland County
70	12.8	**Warren** (city) Trumbull County
74	13.0	**Carlisle** (village) Warren County
75	13.1	**Gibsonburg** (village) Sandusky County
76	13.3	**Salem** (city) Columbiana County
77	13.4	**Bryan** (city) Williams County
77	13.4	**Clyde** (city) Sandusky County
79	13.5	**Walbridge** (village) Wood County
80	13.6	**Edgewood** (CDP) Ashtabula County
80	13.6	**Lisbon** (village) Columbiana County
80	13.6	**Moraine** (city) Montgomery County
83	13.7	**Wapakoneta** (city) Auglaize County
84	13.8	**Mansfield** (city) Richland County
84	13.8	**West Carrollton** (city) Montgomery County
86	13.9	**Bellevue** (city) Sandusky County
86	13.9	**Mingo Junction** (village) Jefferson County
88	14.0	**Cadiz** (village) Harrison County
88	14.0	**London** (city) Madison County
90	14.1	**Garfield Heights** (city) Cuyahoga County
91	14.4	**Minerva** (village) Stark County
92	14.6	**Canton** (city) Stark County
92	14.6	**Williamsburg** (village) Clermont County
94	14.7	**Logan** (city) Hocking County
94	14.7	**Painesville** (city) Lake County
94	14.7	**Struthers** (city) Mahoning County
97	14.8	**Alliance** (city) Stark County
97	14.8	**Northfield** (village) Summit County
97	14.8	**Trenton** (city) Butler County
100	14.9	**Springfield** (city) Clark County
101	15.0	**Amelia** (village) Clermont County
101	15.0	**Washington Court House** (city) Fayette County
103	15.1	**Hamilton** (city) Butler County
103	15.1	**Martins Ferry** (city) Belmont County
103	15.1	**Napoleon** (city) Henry County
103	15.1	**Trotwood** (city) Montgomery County
107	15.2	**Ironton** (city) Lawrence County
108	15.4	**Calcutta** (CDP) Columbiana County
108	15.4	**Elyria** (city) Lorain County
108	15.4	**Lordstown** (village) Trumbull County
108	15.4	**Maple Heights** (city) Cuyahoga County
108	15.4	**Urbana** (city) Champaign County
113	15.5	**Belpre** (city) Washington County
113	15.5	**Northwood** (city) Wood County
115	15.6	**Buckeye Lake** (village) Licking County
116	15.7	**Circleville** (city) Pickaway County
117	15.8	**Mentor-on-the-Lake** (city) Lake County
117	15.8	**Northbrook** (CDP) Hamilton County
117	15.8	**Norwalk** (city) Huron County
117	15.8	**Rittman** (city) Wayne County
121	16.0	**Celina** (city) Mercer County
121	16.0	**Coshocton** (city) Coshocton County
121	16.0	**Ravenna** (city) Portage County
124	16.1	**Cleveland** (city) Cuyahoga County
124	16.1	**Shelby** (city) Richland County
126	16.2	**Sandusky** (city) Erie County
126	16.2	**Sidney** (city) Shelby County
128	16.3	**Eastlake** (city) Lake County
128	16.3	**Massillon** (city) Stark County
128	16.3	**McDonald** (village) Trumbull County
128	16.3	**North Madison** (CDP) Lake County
128	16.3	**Strasburg** (village) Tuscarawas County
128	16.3	**Wellston** (city) Jackson County
134	16.4	**Delphos** (city) Allen County
134	16.4	**Tiffin** (city) Seneca County
136	16.5	**Bedford Heights** (city) Cuyahoga County
136	16.5	**Lancaster** (city) Fairfield County
136	16.5	**Van Wert** (city) Van Wert County
139	16.6	**Sebring** (village) Mahoning County
139	16.6	**Waverly** (village) Pike County
141	16.7	**Brooklyn** (city) Cuyahoga County
141	16.7	**Pleasant Run** (CDP) Hamilton County
141	16.7	**Portsmouth** (city) Scioto County
141	16.7	**Union** (city) Montgomery County
141	16.7	**Upper Sandusky** (city) Wyandot County
146	16.8	**Gallipolis** (village) Gallia County
146	16.8	**Middletown** (city) Butler County
146	16.8	**Niles** (city) Trumbull County
146	16.8	**Wellington** (village) Lorain County
150	16.9	**Hillsboro** (city) Highland County

Note: *This section ranks incorporated places and CDPs (Census Designated Places) with populations of 2,500 or more. Unincorporated postal areas were not considered. Please refer to the User Guide for additional information.*

Educational Attainment: Graduate/Professional Degree or Higher

Top 150 Places Ranked in *Descending* Order

State Rank	Percent	Place
1	45.0	**The Village of Indian Hill** (city) Hamilton County
2	43.3	**Pepper Pike** (city) Cuyahoga County
3	40.2	**Granville** (village) Licking County
4	39.9	**Shaker Heights** (city) Cuyahoga County
5	39.3	**Ottawa Hills** (village) Lucas County
6	38.7	**Athens** (city) Athens County
7	37.4	**Wyoming** (city) Hamilton County
8	37.3	**Oakwood** (city) Montgomery County
9	36.3	**Yellow Springs** (village) Greene County
10	36.2	**New Albany** (city) Franklin County
11	35.8	**Bexley** (city) Franklin County
12	35.4	**Upper Arlington** (city) Franklin County
13	34.6	**Moreland Hills** (village) Cuyahoga County
14	33.7	**Mariemont** (village) Hamilton County
15	33.2	**Amberley** (village) Hamilton County
15	33.2	**Orange** (village) Cuyahoga County
17	33.1	**Oxford** (city) Butler County
18	32.3	**Beachwood** (city) Cuyahoga County
19	32.1	**Powell** (city) Delaware County
20	31.6	**Solon** (city) Cuyahoga County
21	31.0	**Hudson** (city) Summit County
22	30.8	**Montgomery** (city) Hamilton County
22	30.8	**Oberlin** (city) Lorain County
24	30.7	**Dublin** (city) Franklin County
24	30.7	**Grandview Heights** (city) Franklin County
26	30.3	**University Heights** (city) Cuyahoga County
27	29.8	**Worthington** (city) Franklin County
28	29.1	**Sixteen Mile Stand** (CDP) Hamilton County
29	28.5	**Bainbridge** (CDP) Geauga County
29	28.5	**Dry Run** (CDP) Hamilton County
29	28.5	**Kenwood** (CDP) Hamilton County
32	27.8	**Highland Heights** (city) Cuyahoga County
33	27.7	**Montrose-Ghent** (CDP) Summit County
34	27.3	**Madeira** (city) Hamilton County
35	26.8	**Cleveland Heights** (city) Cuyahoga County
36	26.7	**Chagrin Falls** (village) Cuyahoga County
37	26.2	**Blue Ash** (city) Hamilton County
38	26.0	**Mason** (city) Warren County
39	25.9	**South Russell** (village) Geauga County
40	25.8	**Turpin Hills** (CDP) Hamilton County
41	25.7	**Rocky River** (city) Cuyahoga County
42	25.0	**Bay Village** (city) Cuyahoga County
42	25.0	**Beavercreek** (city) Greene County
44	24.9	**Evendale** (village) Hamilton County
45	24.6	**Wright-Patterson AFB** (CDP) Greene County
46	23.1	**Bluffton** (village) Allen County
46	23.1	**Mayfield** (village) Cuyahoga County
48	22.5	**Bowling Green** (city) Wood County
48	22.5	**Four Bridges** (CDP) Butler County
50	22.4	**Brecksville** (city) Cuyahoga County
51	22.1	**Poland** (village) Mahoning County
52	21.9	**Centerville** (city) Montgomery County
53	21.7	**Forestville** (CDP) Hamilton County
54	21.3	**Landen** (CDP) Warren County
55	21.1	**Westlake** (city) Cuyahoga County
56	20.9	**Perrysburg** (city) Wood County
57	20.5	**Hilliard** (city) Franklin County
58	20.3	**Reminderville** (village) Summit County
59	20.0	**Avon Lake** (city) Lorain County
60	19.9	**Broadview Heights** (city) Cuyahoga County
60	19.9	**Kent** (city) Portage County
60	19.9	**Lyndhurst** (city) Cuyahoga County
63	19.8	**Beckett Ridge** (CDP) Butler County
64	19.5	**Kirtland** (city) Lake County
64	19.5	**Westerville** (city) Franklin County
66	19.2	**Sherwood** (CDP) Hamilton County
67	19.0	**Aurora** (city) Portage County
68	18.7	**Bellbrook** (city) Greene County
69	18.3	**Macedonia** (city) Summit County
70	18.2	**Avon** (city) Lorain County
70	18.2	**Waterville** (city) Lucas County
72	18.1	**Fairlawn** (city) Summit County
73	18.0	**Canfield** (city) Mahoning County
74	17.9	**Springboro** (city) Warren County
75	17.7	**Canal Winchester** (city) Franklin County
76	17.6	**Mulberry** (CDP) Clermont County
77	17.4	**North Zanesville** (CDP) Muskingum County
78	17.3	**Strongsville** (city) Cuyahoga County
79	17.1	**Gahanna** (city) Franklin County
80	17.0	**South Euclid** (city) Cuyahoga County
81	16.8	**Twinsburg** (city) Summit County
82	16.6	**Cedarville** (village) Greene County
83	16.1	**Stow** (city) Summit County
84	16.0	**Lakewood** (city) Cuyahoga County
85	15.9	**Dry Ridge** (CDP) Hamilton County
86	15.7	**New Concord** (village) Muskingum County
87	15.6	**Sylvania** (city) Lucas County
88	15.5	**Loveland** (city) Hamilton County
88	15.5	**Sharonville** (city) Hamilton County
90	15.4	**Whitehouse** (village) Lucas County
91	15.3	**Mayfield Heights** (city) Cuyahoga County
92	15.2	**Fruit Hill** (CDP) Hamilton County
93	15.1	**Finneytown** (CDP) Hamilton County
93	15.1	**North Canton** (city) Stark County
95	15.0	**Richfield** (village) Summit County
96	14.7	**Willoughby Hills** (city) Lake County
97	14.4	**Ada** (village) Hardin County
97	14.4	**Independence** (city) Cuyahoga County
99	14.3	**Devola** (CDP) Washington County
100	14.2	**Clayton** (city) Montgomery County
100	14.2	**Maumee** (city) Lucas County
102	14.1	**Cincinnati** (city) Hamilton County
103	14.0	**Kettering** (city) Montgomery County
104	13.8	**Enon** (village) Clark County
105	13.7	**North Royalton** (city) Cuyahoga County
105	13.7	**Sheffield** (village) Lorain County
107	13.6	**Greentown** (CDP) Stark County
108	13.5	**Newtown** (village) Hamilton County
108	13.5	**Richmond Heights** (city) Cuyahoga County
110	13.3	**Delaware** (city) Delaware County
110	13.3	**Munroe Falls** (city) Summit County
112	13.0	**Covedale** (CDP) Hamilton County
112	13.0	**Middleburg Heights** (city) Cuyahoga County
112	13.0	**Monfort Heights** (CDP) Hamilton County
115	12.8	**Waynesville** (village) Warren County
115	12.8	**Wooster** (city) Wayne County
117	12.7	**Fairview Park** (city) Cuyahoga County
118	12.6	**Beechwood Trails** (CDP) Licking County
118	12.6	**Sunbury** (village) Delaware County
120	12.3	**Berea** (city) Cuyahoga County
120	12.3	**Huron** (city) Erie County
120	12.3	**Pickerington** (city) Fairfield County
123	12.1	**Howland Center** (CDP) Trumbull County
123	12.1	**Tipp City** (city) Miami County
123	12.1	**Wadsworth** (city) Medina County
126	12.0	**Mount Repose** (CDP) Clermont County
127	11.9	**Columbus** (city) Franklin County
127	11.9	**Mentor** (city) Lake County
129	11.8	**Mack** (CDP) Hamilton County
130	11.7	**Fairborn** (city) Greene County
130	11.7	**Green** (city) Summit County
130	11.7	**Uniontown** (CDP) Stark County
133	11.5	**Cherry Grove** (CDP) Hamilton County
133	11.5	**Miami Heights** (CDP) Hamilton County
133	11.5	**North Ridgeville** (city) Lorain County
133	11.5	**Seven Hills** (city) Cuyahoga County
137	11.4	**Greenhills** (village) Hamilton County
138	11.3	**Dent** (CDP) Hamilton County
138	11.3	**Milford** (city) Clermont County
138	11.3	**Olmsted Falls** (city) Cuyahoga County
141	11.2	**New Bremen** (village) Auglaize County
142	11.1	**The Plains** (CDP) Athens County
143	10.9	**Ballville** (CDP) Sandusky County
143	10.9	**Medina** (city) Medina County
145	10.8	**Reynoldsburg** (city) Franklin County
145	10.8	**Saint Clairsville** (city) Belmont County
147	10.6	**Minster** (village) Auglaize County
148	10.5	**Doylestown** (village) Wayne County
149	10.4	**Cuyahoga Falls** (city) Summit County
149	10.4	**Oakwood** (village) Cuyahoga County

Note: *This section ranks incorporated places and CDPs (Census Designated Places) with populations of 2,500 or more. Unincorporated postal areas were not considered. Please refer to the User Guide for additional information.*

Educational Attainment: Graduate/Professional Degree or Higher

Top 150 Places Ranked in *Ascending* Order

State Rank	Percent	Place
1	0.3	**Wellsville** (village) Columbiana County
2	0.6	**Park Layne** (CDP) Clark County
3	0.8	**New Lebanon** (village) Montgomery County
4	1.2	**Blacklick Estates** (CDP) Franklin County
4	1.2	**Hicksville** (village) Defiance County
4	1.2	**Mount Healthy Heights** (CDP) Hamilton County
7	1.3	**Lockland** (village) Hamilton County
8	1.4	**Dennison** (village) Tuscarawas County
9	1.6	**West Portsmouth** (CDP) Scioto County
10	1.7	**Uhrichsville** (city) Tuscarawas County
10	1.7	**West Jefferson** (village) Madison County
12	1.9	**Blanchester** (village) Clinton County
12	1.9	**New Carlisle** (city) Clark County
14	2.0	**Mount Orab** (village) Brown County
15	2.1	**Nelsonville** (city) Athens County
16	2.2	**Crooksville** (village) Perry County
16	2.2	**Grafton** (village) Lorain County
16	2.2	**Lincoln Village** (CDP) Franklin County
19	2.3	**Lincoln Heights** (village) Hamilton County
19	2.3	**Struthers** (city) Mahoning County
21	2.4	**Amelia** (village) Clermont County
21	2.4	**Obetz** (village) Franklin County
23	2.5	**Campbell** (city) Mahoning County
24	2.6	**Bellaire** (village) Belmont County
24	2.6	**Crestline** (village) Crawford County
24	2.6	**Kenton** (city) Hardin County
24	2.6	**New London** (village) Huron County
24	2.6	**Richville** (CDP) Stark County
29	2.8	**Covington** (village) Miami County
29	2.8	**Fostoria** (city) Seneca County
29	2.8	**North Baltimore** (village) Wood County
29	2.8	**Willard** (city) Huron County
33	2.9	**Burlington** (CDP) Lawrence County
33	2.9	**Lodi** (village) Medina County
33	2.9	**Saint Marys** (city) Auglaize County
33	2.9	**Toronto** (city) Jefferson County
33	2.9	**Washington Court House** (city) Fayette County
38	3.0	**Baltimore** (village) Fairfield County
38	3.0	**East Palestine** (village) Columbiana County
38	3.0	**Moraine** (city) Montgomery County
38	3.0	**Newcomerstown** (village) Tuscarawas County
42	3.1	**Barberton** (city) Summit County
42	3.1	**Bucyrus** (city) Crawford County
42	3.1	**Pleasant Run** (CDP) Hamilton County
45	3.2	**Warren** (city) Trumbull County
45	3.2	**West Carrollton** (city) Montgomery County
45	3.2	**Whitehall** (city) Franklin County
48	3.3	**Millersburg** (village) Holmes County
48	3.3	**Newton Falls** (village) Trumbull County
48	3.3	**Perry Heights** (CDP) Stark County
51	3.4	**Carey** (village) Wyandot County
51	3.4	**Conneaut** (city) Ashtabula County
51	3.4	**Franklin** (city) Warren County
54	3.5	**Bethel** (village) Clermont County
54	3.5	**Brook Park** (city) Cuyahoga County
54	3.5	**Fremont** (city) Sandusky County
54	3.5	**Greenfield** (village) Highland County
54	3.5	**Northfield** (village) Summit County
54	3.5	**Youngstown** (city) Mahoning County
60	3.6	**Edgewood** (CDP) Ashtabula County
60	3.6	**London** (city) Madison County
60	3.6	**Marion** (city) Marion County
60	3.6	**Montpelier** (village) Williams County
64	3.7	**Barnesville** (village) Belmont County
64	3.7	**Coldwater** (village) Mercer County
64	3.7	**East Liverpool** (city) Columbiana County
64	3.7	**Geneva** (city) Ashtabula County
64	3.7	**Mentor-on-the-Lake** (city) Lake County
69	3.8	**Greenville** (city) Darke County
70	3.9	**Eaton** (city) Preble County
70	3.9	**Loudonville** (village) Ashland County
70	3.9	**Trenton** (city) Butler County
73	4.0	**Rittman** (city) Wayne County
74	4.1	**Belpre** (city) Washington County
74	4.1	**Lima** (city) Allen County
74	4.1	**Withamsville** (CDP) Clermont County
77	4.2	**Ashtabula** (city) Ashtabula County
77	4.2	**Carlisle** (village) Warren County
77	4.2	**Galion** (city) Crawford County
77	4.2	**Gibsonburg** (village) Sandusky County
77	4.2	**Mansfield** (city) Richland County
77	4.2	**Middlefield** (village) Geauga County
77	4.2	**Mount Carmel** (CDP) Clermont County
77	4.2	**New Richmond** (village) Clermont County
77	4.2	**Painesville** (city) Lake County
77	4.2	**Paulding** (village) Paulding County
87	4.3	**Bryan** (city) Williams County
87	4.3	**Northwood** (city) Wood County
87	4.3	**Piqua** (city) Miami County
87	4.3	**Zanesville** (city) Muskingum County
91	4.4	**Clyde** (city) Sandusky County
91	4.4	**Lorain** (city) Lorain County
91	4.4	**Lordstown** (village) Trumbull County
91	4.4	**Northbrook** (CDP) Hamilton County
91	4.4	**Salem** (city) Columbiana County
96	4.5	**Georgetown** (village) Brown County
96	4.5	**Middletown** (city) Butler County
96	4.5	**Wauseon** (city) Fulton County
99	4.6	**East Cleveland** (city) Cuyahoga County
99	4.6	**Hamilton** (city) Butler County
99	4.6	**Maple Heights** (city) Cuyahoga County
102	4.7	**McDonald** (village) Trumbull County
102	4.7	**Niles** (city) Trumbull County
102	4.7	**Northgate** (CDP) Hamilton County
102	4.7	**Sebring** (village) Mahoning County
106	4.8	**Cambridge** (city) Guernsey County
106	4.8	**Coshocton** (city) Coshocton County
106	4.8	**Lakemore** (village) Summit County
106	4.8	**Sandusky** (city) Erie County
106	4.8	**Wapakoneta** (city) Auglaize County
111	4.9	**Canton** (city) Stark County
111	4.9	**Girard** (city) Trumbull County
113	5.0	**Alliance** (city) Stark County
113	5.0	**Bedford Heights** (city) Cuyahoga County
113	5.0	**Champion Heights** (CDP) Trumbull County
113	5.0	**Ironton** (city) Lawrence County
113	5.0	**Logan** (city) Hocking County
113	5.0	**North College Hill** (city) Hamilton County
113	5.0	**Sheffield Lake** (city) Lorain County
113	5.0	**Union** (city) Montgomery County
113	5.0	**Williamsburg** (village) Clermont County
122	5.1	**Heath** (city) Licking County
122	5.1	**Ross** (CDP) Butler County
124	5.2	**Elyria** (city) Lorain County
124	5.2	**Mount Gilead** (village) Morrow County
124	5.2	**New Lexington** (village) Perry County
127	5.3	**Circleville** (city) Pickaway County
127	5.3	**Garfield Heights** (city) Cuyahoga County
127	5.3	**Golf Manor** (village) Hamilton County
127	5.3	**Green Meadows** (CDP) Clark County
127	5.3	**Lancaster** (city) Fairfield County
127	5.3	**New Philadelphia** (city) Tuscarawas County
127	5.3	**Upper Sandusky** (city) Wyandot County
127	5.3	**Wellston** (city) Jackson County
135	5.4	**Bellevue** (city) Sandusky County
136	5.5	**Brooklyn** (city) Cuyahoga County
136	5.5	**Huber Ridge** (CDP) Franklin County
136	5.5	**Lisbon** (village) Columbiana County
136	5.5	**Martins Ferry** (city) Belmont County
136	5.5	**Springfield** (city) Clark County
136	5.5	**Urbana** (city) Champaign County
142	5.6	**Trotwood** (city) Montgomery County
142	5.6	**Walbridge** (village) Wood County
144	5.7	**Northridge** (CDP) Clark County
144	5.7	**Ravenna** (city) Portage County
146	5.8	**Eastlake** (city) Lake County
146	5.8	**Hubbard** (city) Trumbull County
146	5.8	**Mingo Junction** (village) Jefferson County
149	5.9	**Cadiz** (village) Harrison County
149	5.9	**Cleveland** (city) Cuyahoga County

Note: *This section ranks incorporated places and CDPs (Census Designated Places) with populations of 2,500 or more. Unincorporated postal areas were not considered. Please refer to the User Guide for additional information.*

Homeownership Rate

Top 150 Places Ranked in *Descending* Order

State Rank	Percent	Place
1	100.0	**Beechwood Trails** (CDP) Licking County
2	97.2	**Dry Run** (CDP) Hamilton County
3	96.7	**Dry Ridge** (CDP) Hamilton County
4	96.6	**The Village of Indian Hill** (city) Hamilton County
5	96.5	**Pepper Pike** (city) Cuyahoga County
6	95.8	**Powell** (city) Delaware County
7	95.4	**Seven Hills** (city) Cuyahoga County
8	95.2	**Mack** (CDP) Hamilton County
9	94.4	**Miami Heights** (CDP) Hamilton County
10	94.2	**Independence** (city) Cuyahoga County
11	93.6	**Amberley** (village) Hamilton County
12	93.4	**Lake Darby** (CDP) Franklin County
13	93.1	**Day Heights** (CDP) Clermont County
13	93.1	**Highland Heights** (city) Cuyahoga County
15	92.9	**Moreland Hills** (village) Cuyahoga County
16	92.7	**Delhi Hills** (CDP) Hamilton County
17	92.5	**Evendale** (village) Hamilton County
18	92.4	**Apple Valley** (CDP) Knox County
19	92.3	**Macedonia** (city) Summit County
20	92.0	**Cherry Grove** (CDP) Hamilton County
21	91.9	**Sherwood** (CDP) Hamilton County
22	91.8	**New Franklin** (city) Summit County
23	91.7	**Salem Heights** (CDP) Hamilton County
24	91.2	**South Russell** (village) Geauga County
25	91.1	**Bay Village** (city) Cuyahoga County
26	90.6	**Bainbridge** (CDP) Geauga County
27	88.8	**Pleasant Run** (CDP) Hamilton County
28	88.6	**Ballville** (CDP) Sandusky County
28	88.6	**Lake Lakengren** (CDP) Preble County
30	88.3	**Montgomery** (city) Hamilton County
30	88.3	**Orange** (village) Cuyahoga County
32	88.1	**New Albany** (city) Franklin County
33	87.9	**Poland** (village) Mahoning County
34	87.5	**Montrose-Ghent** (CDP) Summit County
34	87.5	**Ross** (CDP) Butler County
36	87.4	**Fort Shawnee** (CDP) Allen County
37	87.3	**Madeira** (city) Hamilton County
37	87.3	**Richfield** (village) Summit County
39	87.2	**Devola** (CDP) Washington County
40	87.0	**North Ridgeville** (city) Lorain County
41	86.4	**North Zanesville** (CDP) Muskingum County
42	86.2	**Wyoming** (city) Hamilton County
43	86.1	**Hudson** (city) Summit County
43	86.1	**North Kingsville** (village) Ashtabula County
45	86.0	**Bellbrook** (city) Greene County
45	86.0	**Covedale** (CDP) Hamilton County
47	85.6	**Greentown** (CDP) Stark County
48	85.5	**Taylor Creek** (CDP) Hamilton County
49	85.0	**Mentor** (city) Lake County
49	85.0	**Springboro** (city) Warren County
51	84.8	**Union** (city) Montgomery County
52	84.6	**Norton** (city) Summit County
53	84.5	**Brecksville** (city) Cuyahoga County
53	84.5	**Clayton** (city) Montgomery County
53	84.5	**Northwood** (city) Wood County
56	84.3	**Mount Repose** (CDP) Clermont County
57	83.8	**Reminderville** (village) Summit County
58	83.7	**Solon** (city) Cuyahoga County
59	83.3	**Fruit Hill** (CDP) Hamilton County
59	83.3	**Uniontown** (CDP) Stark County
61	83.1	**Dillonvale** (CDP) Hamilton County
62	83.0	**Ottawa Hills** (village) Lucas County
63	82.8	**Waterville** (city) Lucas County
64	82.3	**Pleasant Run Farm** (CDP) Hamilton County
65	82.2	**Canal Winchester** (city) Franklin County
66	82.0	**Green Meadows** (CDP) Clark County
67	81.7	**Kirtland** (city) Lake County
68	81.6	**Lyndhurst** (city) Cuyahoga County
69	81.4	**Mason** (city) Warren County
69	81.4	**Richville** (CDP) Stark County
71	81.2	**Amherst** (city) Lorain County
72	81.0	**Broadview Heights** (city) Cuyahoga County
72	81.0	**Wickliffe** (city) Lake County
74	80.9	**Avon** (city) Lorain County
75	80.8	**Lordstown** (village) Trumbull County
75	80.8	**Olmsted Falls** (city) Cuyahoga County
77	80.4	**Bridgetown** (CDP) Hamilton County
77	80.4	**Minster** (village) Auglaize County
77	80.4	**Strongsville** (city) Cuyahoga County
77	80.4	**Upper Arlington** (city) Franklin County
81	80.1	**Mingo Junction** (village) Jefferson County
81	80.1	**Northridge** (CDP) Clark County
83	80.0	**Aurora** (city) Portage County
84	79.9	**Canfield** (city) Mahoning County
84	79.9	**Lakemore** (village) Summit County
84	79.9	**New Bremen** (village) Auglaize County
87	79.7	**Avon Lake** (city) Lorain County
88	79.5	**Worthington** (city) Franklin County
89	79.4	**Calcutta** (CDP) Columbiana County
90	79.3	**Delta** (village) Fulton County
91	79.2	**Turpin Hills** (CDP) Hamilton County
92	79.1	**Oakwood** (city) Montgomery County
93	79.0	**Champion Heights** (CDP) Trumbull County
93	79.0	**Saint Henry** (village) Mercer County
95	78.6	**Seville** (village) Medina County
96	78.4	**Tallmadge** (city) Summit County
97	78.2	**Dent** (CDP) Hamilton County
97	78.2	**Whitehouse** (village) Lucas County
99	77.9	**McDonald** (village) Trumbull County
100	77.4	**Monfort Heights** (CDP) Hamilton County
101	77.3	**Hilliard** (city) Franklin County
102	77.2	**Beckett Ridge** (CDP) Butler County
102	77.2	**Brunswick** (city) Medina County
104	76.7	**Brimfield** (CDP) Portage County
104	76.7	**Brook Park** (city) Cuyahoga County
106	76.6	**Westerville** (city) Franklin County
107	76.5	**Willowick** (city) Lake County
108	76.2	**Groesbeck** (CDP) Hamilton County
109	76.0	**Bexley** (city) Franklin County
110	75.7	**Carlisle** (village) Warren County
110	75.7	**Dublin** (city) Franklin County
110	75.7	**West Portsmouth** (CDP) Scioto County
113	75.5	**Finneytown** (CDP) Hamilton County
113	75.5	**Versailles** (village) Darke County
115	75.3	**Monroe** (city) Butler County
116	75.2	**Westlake** (city) Cuyahoga County
117	75.1	**Howland Center** (CDP) Trumbull County
117	75.1	**Mineral Ridge** (CDP) Trumbull County
117	75.1	**Pickerington** (city) Fairfield County
120	75.0	**Harrison** (city) Hamilton County
121	74.8	**Vermilion** (city) Lorain County
122	74.5	**Enon** (village) Clark County
123	74.4	**Doylestown** (village) Wayne County
123	74.4	**Green** (city) Summit County
125	74.2	**Forestville** (CDP) Hamilton County
126	74.1	**North Madison** (CDP) Lake County
126	74.1	**Sunbury** (village) Delaware County
128	74.0	**Madison** (village) Lake County
128	74.0	**North Olmsted** (city) Cuyahoga County
130	73.9	**South Euclid** (city) Cuyahoga County
130	73.9	**Walbridge** (village) Wood County
132	73.7	**Shadyside** (village) Belmont County
133	73.5	**Granville** (village) Licking County
134	73.3	**Grafton** (village) Lorain County
134	73.3	**Munroe Falls** (city) Summit County
136	73.2	**Landen** (CDP) Warren County
136	73.2	**Parma** (city) Cuyahoga County
138	72.9	**Fairview Park** (city) Cuyahoga County
138	72.9	**Groveport** (city) Franklin County
138	72.9	**Hubbard** (city) Trumbull County
141	72.8	**Mogadore** (village) Summit County
142	72.7	**Loveland** (city) Hamilton County
142	72.7	**Rocky River** (city) Cuyahoga County
142	72.7	**Rossford** (city) Wood County
145	72.5	**Delshire** (CDP) Hamilton County
145	72.5	**Oakwood** (village) Cuyahoga County
145	72.5	**Plain City** (village) Madison County
145	72.5	**Struthers** (city) Mahoning County
145	72.5	**Twinsburg** (city) Summit County
150	72.3	**Maumee** (city) Lucas County

Note: *This section ranks incorporated places and CDPs (Census Designated Places) with populations of 2,500 or more. Unincorporated postal areas were not considered. Please refer to the User Guide for additional information.*

Homeownership Rate

Top 150 Places Ranked in *Ascending* Order

State Rank	Percent	Place
1	1.0	**Wright-Patterson AFB** (CDP) Greene County
2	29.4	**Athens** (city) Athens County
3	32.3	**Oxford** (city) Butler County
4	32.7	**East Cleveland** (city) Cuyahoga County
5	34.5	**Lincoln Heights** (village) Hamilton County
6	36.4	**Whitehall** (city) Franklin County
7	37.7	**Cincinnati** (city) Hamilton County
8	39.3	**Bowling Green** (city) Wood County
9	39.6	**Kent** (city) Portage County
10	39.8	**West Union** (village) Adams County
11	40.4	**Lockland** (village) Hamilton County
12	41.3	**Warrensville Heights** (city) Cuyahoga County
13	41.9	**Cleveland** (city) Cuyahoga County
14	42.3	**Nelsonville** (city) Athens County
15	42.5	**Wilmington** (city) Clinton County
16	43.3	**Zanesville** (city) Muskingum County
17	43.7	**Mount Healthy** (city) Hamilton County
18	43.9	**The Plains** (CDP) Athens County
19	44.6	**Milford** (city) Clermont County
20	45.0	**Columbus** (city) Franklin County
20	45.0	**Lakewood** (city) Cuyahoga County
20	45.0	**Waverly** (village) Pike County
23	45.2	**Lima** (city) Allen County
24	45.3	**Woodlawn** (village) Hamilton County
25	46.0	**Ada** (village) Hardin County
26	46.7	**Greenfield** (village) Highland County
27	47.4	**Ashtabula** (city) Ashtabula County
28	47.6	**Williamsburg** (village) Clermont County
29	47.7	**Gallipolis** (village) Gallia County
30	47.8	**Cheviot** (city) Hamilton County
30	47.8	**Norwood** (city) Hamilton County
30	47.8	**Springfield** (city) Clark County
33	48.0	**Fairborn** (city) Greene County
34	48.1	**Cedarville** (village) Greene County
35	48.2	**Bethel** (village) Clermont County
36	48.4	**Dayton** (city) Montgomery County
37	48.6	**Euclid** (city) Cuyahoga County
38	48.8	**Dennison** (village) Tuscarawas County
39	49.1	**Bedford Heights** (city) Cuyahoga County
39	49.1	**Painesville** (city) Lake County
41	49.2	**Canton** (city) Stark County
41	49.2	**Ravenna** (city) Portage County
43	49.3	**Golf Manor** (village) Hamilton County
44	49.4	**Willard** (city) Huron County
45	49.6	**Mount Carmel** (CDP) Clermont County
46	49.7	**Mount Vernon** (city) Knox County
47	49.8	**Georgetown** (village) Brown County
47	49.8	**Wellsville** (village) Columbiana County
49	49.9	**Portsmouth** (city) Scioto County
49	49.9	**Washington Court House** (city) Fayette County
51	50.0	**Millersburg** (village) Holmes County
52	50.1	**New Lebanon** (village) Montgomery County
52	50.1	**Sixteen Mile Stand** (CDP) Hamilton County
54	50.2	**Hillsboro** (city) Highland County
54	50.2	**Trotwood** (city) Montgomery County
54	50.2	**Willoughby Hills** (city) Lake County
57	50.3	**Springdale** (city) Hamilton County
58	50.7	**Mayfield Heights** (city) Cuyahoga County
59	50.8	**Bedford** (city) Cuyahoga County
60	50.9	**New Lexington** (village) Perry County
61	51.0	**Akron** (city) Summit County
62	51.2	**Warren** (city) Trumbull County
63	51.3	**London** (city) Madison County
64	52.0	**Sandusky** (city) Erie County
65	52.1	**Alliance** (city) Stark County
66	52.3	**Lancaster** (city) Fairfield County
66	52.3	**Toledo** (city) Lucas County
68	52.4	**Bellaire** (village) Belmont County
69	52.5	**Greenville** (city) Darke County
70	52.6	**Middletown** (city) Butler County
70	52.6	**North College Hill** (city) Hamilton County
72	52.7	**Crooksville** (village) Perry County
72	52.7	**Mansfield** (city) Richland County
74	53.1	**West Carrollton** (city) Montgomery County
75	53.4	**Urbana** (city) Champaign County
76	53.7	**Cambridge** (city) Guernsey County
76	53.7	**Logan** (city) Hocking County
78	53.8	**Middlefield** (village) Geauga County
79	54.0	**Newark** (city) Licking County
80	54.1	**Marietta** (city) Washington County
81	54.3	**Wooster** (city) Wayne County
82	54.4	**Circleville** (city) Pickaway County
82	54.4	**Sebring** (village) Mahoning County
82	54.4	**Wellington** (village) Lorain County
85	54.7	**Riverside** (city) Montgomery County
86	54.9	**East Liverpool** (city) Columbiana County
86	54.9	**Oberlin** (city) Lorain County
88	55.0	**Bellefontaine** (city) Logan County
88	55.0	**Niles** (city) Trumbull County
90	55.1	**Steubenville** (city) Jefferson County
90	55.1	**Withamsville** (CDP) Clermont County
92	55.2	**Parma Heights** (city) Cuyahoga County
93	55.5	**New Concord** (village) Muskingum County
93	55.5	**Newton Falls** (village) Trumbull County
95	55.7	**Lodi** (village) Medina County
96	55.9	**Uhrichsville** (city) Tuscarawas County
97	56.0	**Hamilton** (city) Butler County
98	56.2	**Cleveland Heights** (city) Cuyahoga County
98	56.2	**Silverton** (village) Hamilton County
100	56.3	**Jackson** (city) Jackson County
100	56.3	**Upper Sandusky** (city) Wyandot County
102	56.5	**Youngstown** (city) Mahoning County
103	56.6	**Sidney** (city) Shelby County
104	56.7	**Franklin** (city) Warren County
105	56.8	**Forest Park** (city) Hamilton County
106	56.9	**Fremont** (city) Sandusky County
107	57.2	**Baltimore** (village) Fairfield County
107	57.2	**Marion** (city) Marion County
109	57.5	**Brooklyn** (city) Cuyahoga County
110	57.6	**Ottawa** (village) Putnam County
111	57.8	**Troy** (city) Miami County
112	57.9	**Lorain** (city) Lorain County
113	58.1	**Findlay** (city) Hancock County
114	58.2	**Eaton** (city) Preble County
114	58.2	**Portage Lakes** (CDP) Summit County
116	58.3	**Elyria** (city) Lorain County
117	58.4	**Chillicothe** (city) Ross County
118	58.5	**Chardon** (city) Geauga County
118	58.5	**Wauseon** (city) Fulton County
120	58.6	**Moraine** (city) Montgomery County
120	58.6	**Salem** (city) Columbiana County
122	58.8	**Lisbon** (village) Columbiana County
122	58.8	**Mount Healthy Heights** (CDP) Hamilton County
124	58.9	**Reynoldsburg** (city) Franklin County
125	59.5	**Saint Bernard** (city) Hamilton County
126	59.7	**Amelia** (village) Clermont County
127	59.8	**Kenwood** (CDP) Hamilton County
128	59.9	**Blanchester** (village) Clinton County
129	60.0	**Ashland** (city) Ashland County
130	60.1	**New Philadelphia** (city) Tuscarawas County
131	60.2	**Willoughby** (city) Lake County
131	60.2	**Wintersville** (village) Jefferson County
133	60.4	**Lebanon** (city) Warren County
133	60.4	**Mount Gilead** (village) Morrow County
133	60.4	**Piqua** (city) Miami County
136	60.5	**New London** (village) Huron County
136	60.5	**Newcomerstown** (village) Tuscarawas County
136	60.5	**Sharonville** (city) Hamilton County
139	60.6	**Celina** (city) Mercer County
139	60.6	**Girard** (city) Trumbull County
139	60.6	**Tiffin** (city) Seneca County
142	60.7	**Bryan** (city) Williams County
143	60.9	**Norwalk** (city) Huron County
144	61.0	**Waynesville** (village) Warren County
145	61.1	**Galion** (city) Crawford County
145	61.1	**Johnstown** (village) Licking County
147	61.2	**Newtown** (village) Hamilton County
148	61.3	**Coshocton** (city) Coshocton County
148	61.3	**Vandalia** (city) Montgomery County
150	61.4	**Covington** (village) Miami County

***Note:** This section ranks incorporated places and CDPs (Census Designated Places) with populations of 2,500 or more. Unincorporated postal areas were not considered. Please refer to the User Guide for additional information.*

Median Home Value

Top 150 Places Ranked in *Descending* Order

State Rank	Dollars	Place
1	922,500	**The Village of Indian Hill** (city) Hamilton County
2	492,400	**New Albany** (city) Franklin County
3	421,500	**Pepper Pike** (city) Cuyahoga County
4	383,800	**Four Bridges** (CDP) Butler County
5	379,400	**Moreland Hills** (village) Cuyahoga County
6	364,900	**Mariemont** (village) Hamilton County
7	353,200	**Sixteen Mile Stand** (CDP) Hamilton County
8	352,300	**Dublin** (city) Franklin County
9	348,000	**Powell** (city) Delaware County
10	338,000	**Upper Arlington** (city) Franklin County
11	332,900	**Montgomery** (city) Hamilton County
12	328,100	**Chagrin Falls** (village) Cuyahoga County
13	323,400	**Granville** (village) Licking County
14	317,800	**South Russell** (village) Geauga County
15	313,300	**Hudson** (city) Summit County
16	311,300	**Dry Run** (CDP) Hamilton County
17	305,900	**Wyoming** (city) Hamilton County
18	305,500	**Amberley** (village) Hamilton County
19	301,000	**Montrose-Ghent** (CDP) Summit County
20	299,800	**Turpin Hills** (CDP) Hamilton County
21	295,400	**Grandview Heights** (city) Franklin County
22	291,900	**Bexley** (city) Franklin County
23	291,800	**Orange** (village) Cuyahoga County
24	274,400	**Beachwood** (city) Cuyahoga County
24	274,400	**Kenwood** (CDP) Hamilton County
26	273,800	**Solon** (city) Cuyahoga County
27	273,400	**Ottawa Hills** (village) Lucas County
28	271,400	**Kirtland** (city) Lake County
29	264,200	**Evendale** (village) Hamilton County
30	263,100	**Bainbridge** (CDP) Geauga County
31	262,100	**Avon** (city) Lorain County
32	256,000	**Brecksville** (city) Cuyahoga County
33	251,400	**Worthington** (city) Franklin County
34	249,700	**Madeira** (city) Hamilton County
35	246,700	**Highland Heights** (city) Cuyahoga County
36	244,100	**Willoughby Hills** (city) Lake County
37	241,800	**Aurora** (city) Portage County
38	236,400	**Westlake** (city) Cuyahoga County
39	234,200	**Mayfield** (village) Cuyahoga County
40	233,200	**Blue Ash** (city) Hamilton County
41	230,300	**South Lebanon** (village) Warren County
42	230,100	**Mason** (city) Warren County
43	228,700	**Oakwood** (city) Montgomery County
44	225,900	**Richfield** (village) Summit County
45	225,600	**Avon Lake** (city) Lorain County
46	222,600	**Independence** (city) Cuyahoga County
47	217,600	**Broadview Heights** (city) Cuyahoga County
48	215,800	**Rocky River** (city) Cuyahoga County
49	215,300	**Mack** (CDP) Hamilton County
50	215,100	**Bay Village** (city) Cuyahoga County
51	213,100	**Shaker Heights** (city) Cuyahoga County
52	213,000	**Hilliard** (city) Franklin County
53	210,900	**Yellow Springs** (village) Greene County
54	210,100	**Twinsburg** (city) Summit County
55	208,500	**Miami Heights** (CDP) Hamilton County
56	207,900	**Westerville** (city) Franklin County
57	207,500	**Springboro** (city) Warren County
58	204,200	**Beckett Ridge** (CDP) Butler County
59	204,000	**Forestville** (CDP) Hamilton County
60	201,100	**Taylor Creek** (CDP) Hamilton County
61	195,100	**Gahanna** (city) Franklin County
62	194,800	**Dry Ridge** (CDP) Hamilton County
63	194,200	**Perrysburg** (city) Wood County
64	194,000	**Strongsville** (city) Cuyahoga County
65	193,100	**North Royalton** (city) Cuyahoga County
66	192,900	**Plain City** (village) Madison County
67	189,700	**Macedonia** (city) Summit County
68	189,500	**Greentown** (CDP) Stark County
69	188,600	**Landen** (CDP) Warren County
70	187,100	**Beechwood Trails** (CDP) Licking County
71	186,400	**Sunbury** (village) Delaware County
72	185,900	**Oxford** (city) Butler County
73	184,900	**Whitehouse** (village) Lucas County
74	184,500	**Pickerington** (city) Fairfield County
75	184,400	**Sherwood** (CDP) Hamilton County
76	183,200	**Sheffield** (village) Lorain County
77	180,500	**Dent** (CDP) Hamilton County
78	179,600	**Centerville** (city) Montgomery County
79	176,000	**Devola** (CDP) Washington County
80	175,500	**Waterville** (city) Lucas County
81	175,100	**Beavercreek** (city) Greene County
82	174,700	**Fairlawn** (city) Summit County
83	173,900	**Canal Winchester** (city) Franklin County
84	173,600	**Green** (city) Summit County
85	172,900	**Loveland** (city) Hamilton County
86	172,700	**Reminderville** (village) Summit County
87	169,100	**Minster** (village) Auglaize County
88	168,700	**Cherry Grove** (CDP) Hamilton County
89	167,500	**Chardon** (city) Geauga County
90	167,100	**Mentor** (city) Lake County
91	166,900	**Saint Henry** (village) Mercer County
92	166,200	**Marysville** (city) Union County
92	166,200	**Stow** (city) Summit County
94	165,900	**Sylvania** (city) Lucas County
95	165,700	**Monfort Heights** (CDP) Hamilton County
96	164,800	**Fruit Hill** (CDP) Hamilton County
97	164,300	**Athens** (city) Athens County
98	164,100	**Seven Hills** (city) Cuyahoga County
99	163,800	**Lebanon** (city) Warren County
100	162,900	**Pataskala** (city) Licking County
101	162,800	**Monroe** (city) Butler County
102	162,400	**Grove City** (city) Franklin County
103	162,300	**Wadsworth** (city) Medina County
104	162,000	**New Bremen** (village) Auglaize County
105	161,600	**Canfield** (city) Mahoning County
106	161,100	**Delaware** (city) Delaware County
107	160,900	**Waynesville** (village) Warren County
108	160,700	**Medina** (city) Medina County
109	160,300	**North Ridgeville** (city) Lorain County
110	160,200	**Bellbrook** (city) Greene County
110	160,200	**Munroe Falls** (city) Summit County
112	159,400	**Brunswick** (city) Medina County
113	158,700	**Ross** (CDP) Butler County
114	158,100	**Tipp City** (city) Miami County
115	157,900	**Bowling Green** (city) Wood County
116	157,500	**Middleburg Heights** (city) Cuyahoga County
116	157,500	**Middlefield** (village) Geauga County
118	156,700	**North Zanesville** (CDP) Muskingum County
119	156,400	**Tallmadge** (city) Summit County
120	155,800	**Ottawa** (village) Putnam County
121	155,100	**Covedale** (CDP) Hamilton County
121	155,100	**Day Heights** (CDP) Clermont County
123	154,600	**University Heights** (city) Cuyahoga County
124	152,700	**Milford** (city) Clermont County
125	152,200	**Huron** (city) Erie County
126	152,000	**Wheelersburg** (CDP) Scioto County
127	151,600	**Garrettsville** (village) Portage County
128	150,600	**Johnstown** (village) Licking County
129	150,000	**Salem Heights** (CDP) Hamilton County
130	148,400	**Uniontown** (CDP) Stark County
131	148,300	**Ashville** (village) Pickaway County
132	148,200	**Mulberry** (CDP) Clermont County
133	147,100	**Ballville** (CDP) Sandusky County
134	146,900	**North Olmsted** (city) Cuyahoga County
135	146,800	**Fairfield** (city) Butler County
136	146,700	**New Richmond** (village) Clermont County
137	146,200	**Amherst** (city) Lorain County
138	145,900	**Newtown** (village) Hamilton County
139	145,700	**Olmsted Falls** (city) Cuyahoga County
140	145,500	**Fairview Park** (city) Cuyahoga County
141	145,100	**Withamsville** (CDP) Clermont County
142	145,000	**Oberlin** (city) Lorain County
143	144,800	**Apple Valley** (CDP) Knox County
144	144,300	**Groveport** (city) Franklin County
144	144,300	**Streetsboro** (city) Portage County
144	144,300	**Willoughby** (city) Lake County
147	143,900	**Saint Clairsville** (city) Belmont County
148	142,700	**Enon** (village) Clark County
149	142,600	**Reynoldsburg** (city) Franklin County
150	142,400	**Cleves** (village) Hamilton County

Note: *This section ranks incorporated places and CDPs (Census Designated Places) with populations of 2,500 or more. Unincorporated postal areas were not considered. Please refer to the User Guide for additional information.*

Median Home Value

Top 150 Places Ranked in *Ascending* Order

State Rank	Dollars	Place
1	43,300	**Youngstown** (city) Mahoning County
2	51,200	**Bellaire** (village) Belmont County
3	54,200	**Wellsville** (village) Columbiana County
4	55,300	**East Liverpool** (city) Columbiana County
5	58,500	**East Cleveland** (city) Cuyahoga County
6	59,600	**Crooksville** (village) Perry County
7	61,200	**Warren** (city) Trumbull County
8	61,600	**Campbell** (city) Mahoning County
9	62,900	**Fostoria** (city) Seneca County
10	66,600	**Dayton** (city) Montgomery County
10	66,600	**Lima** (city) Allen County
12	67,500	**Cleveland** (city) Cuyahoga County
13	68,600	**Galion** (city) Crawford County
14	68,800	**Crestline** (village) Crawford County
14	68,800	**Uhrichsville** (city) Tuscarawas County
16	70,600	**Ashtabula** (city) Ashtabula County
16	70,600	**Dennison** (village) Tuscarawas County
18	71,000	**Canton** (city) Stark County
19	71,800	**Maple Heights** (city) Cuyahoga County
19	71,800	**West Portsmouth** (CDP) Scioto County
21	71,900	**Struthers** (city) Mahoning County
22	72,700	**Portsmouth** (city) Scioto County
23	73,200	**Marion** (city) Marion County
24	73,600	**Garfield Heights** (city) Cuyahoga County
24	73,600	**Park Layne** (CDP) Clark County
26	74,300	**Kenton** (city) Hardin County
27	74,900	**Greenfield** (village) Highland County
28	75,000	**Montpelier** (village) Williams County
29	75,200	**West Union** (village) Adams County
30	75,400	**Lincoln Heights** (village) Hamilton County
31	75,800	**Trotwood** (city) Montgomery County
32	76,000	**Martins Ferry** (city) Belmont County
32	76,000	**New Lexington** (village) Perry County
34	76,400	**Newcomerstown** (village) Tuscarawas County
35	76,600	**Zanesville** (city) Muskingum County
36	77,000	**Springfield** (city) Clark County
37	77,500	**Mansfield** (city) Richland County
38	77,700	**Nelsonville** (city) Athens County
39	77,800	**Toledo** (city) Lucas County
40	78,100	**New Lebanon** (village) Montgomery County
41	78,600	**Lisbon** (village) Columbiana County
42	78,700	**Niles** (city) Trumbull County
42	78,700	**Northbrook** (CDP) Hamilton County
44	79,600	**Alliance** (city) Stark County
44	79,600	**Bucyrus** (city) Crawford County
44	79,600	**Paulding** (village) Paulding County
47	79,700	**Mingo Junction** (village) Jefferson County
48	79,900	**Sebring** (village) Mahoning County
49	80,000	**Akron** (city) Summit County
49	80,000	**North Baltimore** (village) Wood County
51	80,400	**Warrensville Heights** (city) Cuyahoga County
52	80,700	**Euclid** (city) Cuyahoga County
53	80,900	**Fremont** (city) Sandusky County
54	81,000	**Moraine** (city) Montgomery County
55	81,100	**East Palestine** (village) Columbiana County
55	81,100	**Lockland** (village) Hamilton County
55	81,100	**New London** (village) Huron County
58	81,200	**Girard** (city) Trumbull County
59	81,600	**Sandusky** (city) Erie County
60	81,700	**Edgewood** (CDP) Ashtabula County
61	82,200	**Toronto** (city) Jefferson County
62	82,400	**Van Wert** (city) Van Wert County
63	82,500	**Hicksville** (village) Defiance County
64	83,000	**Willard** (city) Huron County
65	83,200	**Barnesville** (village) Belmont County
65	83,200	**Whitehall** (city) Franklin County
67	83,400	**North College Hill** (city) Hamilton County
68	83,500	**Ada** (village) Hardin County
69	84,000	**Coshocton** (city) Coshocton County
70	84,600	**Mount Healthy** (city) Hamilton County
71	84,700	**Bethel** (village) Clermont County
71	84,700	**Minerva** (village) Stark County
73	84,900	**Riverside** (city) Montgomery County
74	85,000	**Cambridge** (city) Guernsey County
74	85,000	**Hillsboro** (city) Highland County
76	85,500	**Newton Falls** (village) Trumbull County
77	85,700	**Lorain** (city) Lorain County
77	85,700	**Wellston** (city) Jackson County
79	85,800	**Barberton** (city) Summit County
79	85,800	**Buckeye Lake** (village) Licking County
79	85,800	**Piqua** (city) Miami County
82	86,500	**Delphos** (city) Allen County
83	86,800	**Steubenville** (city) Jefferson County
84	87,600	**Greenville** (city) Darke County
85	87,900	**Conneaut** (city) Ashtabula County
86	88,200	**Blanchester** (village) Clinton County
87	88,300	**Lodi** (village) Medina County
88	88,500	**McDonald** (village) Trumbull County
89	88,900	**Loudonville** (village) Ashland County
90	89,000	**Walbridge** (village) Wood County
91	89,200	**Golf Manor** (village) Hamilton County
92	89,300	**Tiffin** (city) Seneca County
93	89,500	**Blacklick Estates** (CDP) Franklin County
94	90,100	**Cheviot** (city) Hamilton County
94	90,100	**Shelby** (city) Richland County
96	90,700	**Gibsonburg** (village) Sandusky County
96	90,700	**West Carrollton** (city) Montgomery County
98	90,800	**Lincoln Village** (CDP) Franklin County
98	90,800	**New Carlisle** (city) Clark County
100	91,300	**Middletown** (city) Butler County
101	91,400	**Covington** (village) Miami County
101	91,400	**Ironton** (city) Lawrence County
101	91,400	**Union** (city) Montgomery County
104	91,500	**Bedford** (city) Cuyahoga County
105	92,500	**Cadiz** (village) Harrison County
106	92,600	**Shadyside** (village) Belmont County
107	92,900	**Hubbard** (city) Trumbull County
108	93,100	**Mount Healthy Heights** (CDP) Hamilton County
109	93,500	**Salem** (city) Columbiana County
110	93,700	**Saint Bernard** (city) Hamilton County
111	93,800	**Austintown** (CDP) Mahoning County
111	93,800	**Carey** (village) Wyandot County
111	93,800	**Xenia** (city) Greene County
114	94,100	**Bryan** (city) Williams County
115	94,500	**Jackson** (city) Jackson County
116	94,800	**Elyria** (city) Lorain County
117	95,500	**Geneva** (city) Ashtabula County
118	95,600	**Washington Court House** (city) Fayette County
119	95,800	**Upper Sandusky** (city) Wyandot County
120	95,900	**Jefferson** (village) Ashtabula County
121	96,200	**Woodlawn** (village) Hamilton County
122	96,700	**Eaton** (city) Preble County
123	96,900	**Bellevue** (city) Sandusky County
124	97,800	**Bedford Heights** (city) Cuyahoga County
125	98,300	**Perry Heights** (CDP) Stark County
126	98,500	**Belpre** (city) Washington County
126	98,500	**Urbana** (city) Champaign County
128	98,600	**Logan** (city) Hocking County
129	98,700	**Marietta** (city) Washington County
129	98,700	**Massillon** (city) Stark County
131	98,800	**Wilmington** (city) Clinton County
132	98,900	**Chillicothe** (city) Ross County
132	98,900	**Defiance** (city) Defiance County
134	99,400	**Ashland** (city) Ashland County
135	99,600	**Ravenna** (city) Portage County
136	99,900	**Hamilton** (city) Butler County
137	100,000	**Clyde** (city) Sandusky County
138	100,100	**South Euclid** (city) Cuyahoga County
139	100,300	**Painesville** (city) Lake County
140	100,600	**Fredericktown** (village) Knox County
141	100,700	**Millersburg** (village) Holmes County
142	100,800	**Waverly** (village) Pike County
143	101,300	**Bellefontaine** (city) Logan County
143	101,300	**Georgetown** (village) Brown County
145	101,900	**Mount Vernon** (city) Knox County
146	102,500	**Burlington** (CDP) Lawrence County
146	102,500	**Franklin** (city) Warren County
146	102,500	**Huber Heights** (city) Montgomery County
149	103,100	**Napoleon** (city) Henry County
149	103,100	**Saint Marys** (city) Auglaize County

Note: *This section ranks incorporated places and CDPs (Census Designated Places) with populations of 2,500 or more. Unincorporated postal areas were not considered. Please refer to the User Guide for additional information.*

Median Year Structure Built

Top 150 Places Ranked in *Descending* Order

State Rank	Year	Place
1	2004	**Four Bridges** (CDP) Butler County
2	2003	**New Albany** (city) Franklin County
2	2003	**South Lebanon** (village) Warren County
4	2000	**Avon** (city) Lorain County
4	2000	**Pickerington** (city) Fairfield County
4	2000	**Powell** (city) Delaware County
7	1999	**Canal Winchester** (city) Franklin County
8	1997	**Amelia** (village) Clermont County
8	1997	**Miami Heights** (CDP) Hamilton County
8	1997	**Monroe** (city) Butler County
11	1995	**Apple Valley** (CDP) Knox County
12	1994	**Mason** (city) Warren County
12	1994	**Mount Orab** (village) Brown County
12	1994	**Sheffield** (village) Lorain County
15	1993	**Dublin** (city) Franklin County
15	1993	**Hilliard** (city) Franklin County
15	1993	**Lake Lakengren** (CDP) Preble County
15	1993	**Pataskala** (city) Licking County
15	1993	**Springboro** (city) Warren County
20	1992	**Ashville** (village) Pickaway County
20	1992	**Dent** (CDP) Hamilton County
20	1992	**Dry Ridge** (CDP) Hamilton County
20	1992	**Marysville** (city) Union County
24	1991	**Beckett Ridge** (CDP) Butler County
24	1991	**Sunbury** (village) Delaware County
24	1991	**Twinsburg** (city) Summit County
27	1990	**Greentown** (CDP) Stark County
27	1990	**Grove City** (city) Franklin County
27	1990	**Lake Darby** (CDP) Franklin County
27	1990	**Lebanon** (city) Warren County
27	1990	**Plain City** (village) Madison County
32	1989	**Macedonia** (city) Summit County
32	1989	**Mulberry** (CDP) Clermont County
34	1988	**Avon Lake** (city) Lorain County
34	1988	**Beechwood Trails** (CDP) Licking County
34	1988	**Delaware** (city) Delaware County
34	1988	**The Plains** (CDP) Athens County
34	1988	**Whitehouse** (village) Lucas County
39	1987	**Sixteen Mile Stand** (CDP) Hamilton County
39	1987	**Streetsboro** (city) Portage County
41	1986	**Aurora** (city) Portage County
41	1986	**North Ridgeville** (city) Lorain County
43	1985	**Dry Run** (CDP) Hamilton County
43	1985	**Trenton** (city) Butler County
45	1984	**Gahanna** (city) Franklin County
45	1984	**Ontario** (city) Richland County
45	1984	**Taylor Creek** (CDP) Hamilton County
45	1984	**Woodlawn** (village) Hamilton County
49	1983	**Landen** (CDP) Warren County
49	1983	**Perrysburg** (city) Wood County
49	1983	**Reynoldsburg** (city) Franklin County
52	1982	**Buckeye Lake** (village) Licking County
52	1982	**Harrison** (city) Hamilton County
52	1982	**North Royalton** (city) Cuyahoga County
52	1982	**Waynesville** (village) Warren County
52	1982	**Westlake** (city) Cuyahoga County
57	1981	**Broadview Heights** (city) Cuyahoga County
57	1981	**Forestville** (CDP) Hamilton County
57	1981	**Green** (city) Summit County
57	1981	**Hudson** (city) Summit County
57	1981	**Middlefield** (village) Geauga County
57	1981	**Solon** (city) Cuyahoga County
57	1981	**Strongsville** (city) Cuyahoga County
64	1980	**Beavercreek** (city) Greene County
64	1980	**Newtown** (village) Hamilton County
64	1980	**Obetz** (village) Franklin County
64	1980	**Reminderville** (village) Summit County
64	1980	**Saint Henry** (village) Mercer County
64	1980	**Seville** (village) Medina County
64	1980	**Sharonville** (city) Hamilton County
64	1980	**Stow** (city) Summit County
64	1980	**Westerville** (city) Franklin County
73	1979	**Blue Ash** (city) Hamilton County
73	1979	**Evendale** (village) Hamilton County
73	1979	**Fairfield** (city) Butler County
73	1979	**Heath** (city) Licking County
73	1979	**Medina** (city) Medina County
78	1978	**Bowling Green** (city) Wood County
78	1978	**Brecksville** (city) Cuyahoga County
78	1978	**Cortland** (city) Trumbull County
78	1978	**Olmsted Falls** (city) Cuyahoga County
78	1978	**Oxford** (city) Butler County
78	1978	**Ross** (CDP) Butler County
84	1977	**Brunswick** (city) Medina County
84	1977	**Burlington** (CDP) Lawrence County
84	1977	**Canal Fulton** (city) Stark County
84	1977	**Canfield** (city) Mahoning County
84	1977	**Centerville** (city) Montgomery County
84	1977	**Groveport** (city) Franklin County
84	1977	**Mount Repose** (CDP) Clermont County
84	1977	**Summerside** (CDP) Clermont County
84	1977	**Tipp City** (city) Miami County
84	1977	**Withamsville** (CDP) Clermont County
94	1976	**Carlisle** (village) Warren County
94	1976	**Columbus** (city) Franklin County
94	1976	**Lordstown** (village) Trumbull County
94	1976	**Loveland** (city) Hamilton County
94	1976	**Monfort Heights** (CDP) Hamilton County
94	1976	**South Point** (village) Lawrence County
94	1976	**Turpin Hills** (CDP) Hamilton County
94	1976	**West Union** (village) Adams County
102	1975	**Highland Heights** (city) Cuyahoga County
102	1975	**Mack** (CDP) Hamilton County
102	1975	**Montgomery** (city) Hamilton County
102	1975	**Moraine** (city) Montgomery County
102	1975	**Ottawa** (village) Putnam County
102	1975	**Pleasant Run Farm** (CDP) Hamilton County
102	1975	**South Russell** (village) Geauga County
102	1975	**Sylvania** (city) Lucas County
102	1975	**Wadsworth** (city) Medina County
111	1974	**Englewood** (city) Montgomery County
111	1974	**Johnstown** (village) Licking County
111	1974	**London** (city) Madison County
111	1974	**Munroe Falls** (city) Summit County
111	1974	**Strasburg** (village) Tuscarawas County
111	1974	**Union** (city) Montgomery County
111	1974	**Waterville** (city) Lucas County
118	1973	**Bainbridge** (CDP) Geauga County
118	1973	**Celina** (city) Mercer County
118	1973	**Devola** (CDP) Washington County
118	1973	**Georgetown** (village) Brown County
118	1973	**Grafton** (village) Lorain County
118	1973	**Hartville** (village) Stark County
118	1973	**Huber Heights** (city) Montgomery County
118	1973	**Louisville** (city) Stark County
118	1973	**Madison** (village) Lake County
118	1973	**Mentor** (city) Lake County
118	1973	**Milford** (city) Clermont County
118	1973	**Northridge** (CDP) Clark County
118	1973	**Orange** (village) Cuyahoga County
118	1973	**Pleasant Run** (CDP) Hamilton County
118	1973	**Wheelersburg** (CDP) Scioto County
118	1973	**Willoughby Hills** (city) Lake County
134	1972	**Cherry Grove** (CDP) Hamilton County
134	1972	**Coldwater** (village) Mercer County
134	1972	**Delhi Hills** (CDP) Hamilton County
134	1972	**Fairlawn** (city) Summit County
134	1972	**Forest Park** (city) Hamilton County
134	1972	**Jefferson** (village) Ashtabula County
134	1972	**Middleburg Heights** (city) Cuyahoga County
134	1972	**Mineral Ridge** (CDP) Trumbull County
134	1972	**New Burlington** (CDP) Hamilton County
134	1972	**Oakwood** (village) Cuyahoga County
134	1972	**Uniontown** (CDP) Stark County
134	1972	**West Carrollton** (city) Montgomery County
134	1972	**Willoughby** (city) Lake County
147	1971	**Blanchester** (village) Clinton County
147	1971	**Clayton** (city) Montgomery County
147	1971	**Enon** (village) Clark County
147	1971	**Howland Center** (CDP) Trumbull County

Note: *This section ranks incorporated places and CDPs (Census Designated Places) with populations of 2,500 or more. Unincorporated postal areas were not considered. Please refer to the User Guide for additional information.*

Median Year Structure Built

Top 150 Places Ranked in *Ascending* Order

State Rank	Year	Place
1	<1940	**Bellaire** (village) Belmont County
1	<1940	**Cleveland** (city) Cuyahoga County
1	<1940	**Cleveland Heights** (city) Cuyahoga County
1	<1940	**Dennison** (village) Tuscarawas County
1	<1940	**East Cleveland** (city) Cuyahoga County
1	<1940	**East Palestine** (village) Columbiana County
1	<1940	**Grandview Heights** (city) Franklin County
1	<1940	**Lakewood** (city) Cuyahoga County
1	<1940	**Lisbon** (village) Columbiana County
1	<1940	**Montpelier** (village) Williams County
1	<1940	**Norwood** (city) Hamilton County
1	<1940	**Oakwood** (city) Montgomery County
1	<1940	**Portsmouth** (city) Scioto County
1	<1940	**Saint Bernard** (city) Hamilton County
1	<1940	**Wellsville** (village) Columbiana County
16	1941	**Crooksville** (village) Perry County
16	1941	**East Liverpool** (city) Columbiana County
16	1941	**Shaker Heights** (city) Cuyahoga County
19	1942	**Cheviot** (city) Hamilton County
20	1943	**Bexley** (city) Franklin County
20	1943	**Fremont** (city) Sandusky County
20	1943	**Lockland** (village) Hamilton County
23	1944	**Coshocton** (city) Coshocton County
24	1945	**Mariemont** (village) Hamilton County
24	1945	**Martins Ferry** (city) Belmont County
26	1946	**Barnesville** (village) Belmont County
26	1946	**Gibsonburg** (village) Sandusky County
26	1946	**Zanesville** (city) Muskingum County
29	1947	**Deer Park** (city) Hamilton County
29	1947	**Marietta** (city) Washington County
31	1948	**Canton** (city) Stark County
31	1948	**Conneaut** (city) Ashtabula County
31	1948	**Dayton** (city) Montgomery County
31	1948	**Geneva** (city) Ashtabula County
31	1948	**Uhrichsville** (city) Tuscarawas County
31	1948	**Youngstown** (city) Mahoning County
37	1949	**Cincinnati** (city) Hamilton County
37	1949	**University Heights** (city) Cuyahoga County
39	1950	**Cambridge** (city) Guernsey County
39	1950	**Covington** (village) Miami County
39	1950	**Marion** (city) Marion County
39	1950	**Springfield** (city) Clark County
43	1951	**Ashtabula** (city) Ashtabula County
43	1951	**Fostoria** (city) Seneca County
43	1951	**Loudonville** (village) Ashland County
43	1951	**New Lexington** (village) Perry County
43	1951	**Oak Harbor** (village) Ottawa County
43	1951	**Shadyside** (village) Belmont County
43	1951	**Silverton** (village) Hamilton County
50	1952	**Akron** (city) Summit County
50	1952	**Alliance** (city) Stark County
50	1952	**Campbell** (city) Mahoning County
50	1952	**Greenfield** (village) Highland County
50	1952	**Ironton** (city) Lawrence County
50	1952	**Lima** (city) Allen County
50	1952	**North College Hill** (city) Hamilton County
50	1952	**Poland** (village) Mahoning County
50	1952	**Ravenna** (city) Portage County
50	1952	**Sandusky** (city) Erie County
50	1952	**Struthers** (city) Mahoning County
50	1952	**Tiffin** (city) Seneca County
50	1952	**Versailles** (village) Darke County
63	1953	**Gallipolis** (village) Gallia County
63	1953	**Toledo** (city) Lucas County
63	1953	**Wyoming** (city) Hamilton County
66	1954	**Barberton** (city) Summit County
66	1954	**Bellevue** (city) Sandusky County
66	1954	**Cadiz** (village) Harrison County
66	1954	**Chillicothe** (city) Ross County
66	1954	**Fairport Harbor** (village) Lake County
66	1954	**Galion** (city) Crawford County
66	1954	**Garfield Heights** (city) Cuyahoga County
66	1954	**Golf Manor** (village) Hamilton County
66	1954	**Greenhills** (village) Hamilton County
66	1954	**Hamilton** (city) Butler County

State Rank	Year	Place
66	1954	**Newcomerstown** (village) Tuscarawas County
66	1954	**North Baltimore** (village) Wood County
66	1954	**Ottawa Hills** (village) Lucas County
66	1954	**South Euclid** (city) Cuyahoga County
66	1954	**Steubenville** (city) Jefferson County
81	1955	**Dillonvale** (CDP) Hamilton County
81	1955	**Girard** (city) Trumbull County
81	1955	**Jackson** (city) Jackson County
81	1955	**Kenton** (city) Hardin County
81	1955	**Minerva** (village) Stark County
81	1955	**New London** (village) Huron County
81	1955	**Toronto** (city) Jefferson County
81	1955	**Van Wert** (city) Van Wert County
81	1955	**Warren** (city) Trumbull County
81	1955	**Williamsburg** (village) Clermont County
91	1956	**Euclid** (city) Cuyahoga County
91	1956	**Madeira** (city) Hamilton County
91	1956	**Maple Heights** (city) Cuyahoga County
91	1956	**Piqua** (city) Miami County
91	1956	**Port Clinton** (city) Ottawa County
91	1956	**Sebring** (village) Mahoning County
97	1957	**Bay Village** (city) Cuyahoga County
97	1957	**Cedarville** (village) Greene County
97	1957	**Edgewood** (CDP) Ashtabula County
97	1957	**Fairview Park** (city) Cuyahoga County
97	1957	**Lyndhurst** (city) Cuyahoga County
97	1957	**Massillon** (city) Stark County
97	1957	**Mount Healthy** (city) Hamilton County
97	1957	**Rossford** (city) Wood County
97	1957	**Urbana** (city) Champaign County
97	1957	**Wickliffe** (city) Lake County
97	1957	**Willowick** (city) Lake County
108	1958	**Bedford** (city) Cuyahoga County
108	1958	**Bethel** (village) Clermont County
108	1958	**Bucyrus** (city) Crawford County
108	1958	**Chagrin Falls** (village) Cuyahoga County
108	1958	**Covedale** (CDP) Hamilton County
108	1958	**Delphos** (city) Allen County
108	1958	**Greenville** (city) Darke County
108	1958	**Hicksville** (village) Defiance County
108	1958	**Mansfield** (city) Richland County
108	1958	**Mingo Junction** (village) Jefferson County
108	1958	**Niles** (city) Trumbull County
108	1958	**Parma** (city) Cuyahoga County
108	1958	**Rocky River** (city) Cuyahoga County
108	1958	**Saint Marys** (city) Auglaize County
108	1958	**Salem** (city) Columbiana County
108	1958	**Upper Arlington** (city) Franklin County
108	1958	**West Portsmouth** (CDP) Scioto County
125	1959	**Amberley** (village) Hamilton County
125	1959	**Brooklyn** (city) Cuyahoga County
125	1959	**Carey** (village) Wyandot County
125	1959	**Cuyahoga Falls** (city) Summit County
125	1959	**Delta** (village) Fulton County
125	1959	**Finneytown** (CDP) Hamilton County
125	1959	**Fredericktown** (village) Knox County
125	1959	**Hubbard** (city) Trumbull County
125	1959	**Lakemore** (village) Summit County
125	1959	**Logan** (city) Hocking County
125	1959	**McDonald** (village) Trumbull County
125	1959	**Middletown** (city) Butler County
125	1959	**Mogadore** (village) Summit County
125	1959	**New Philadelphia** (city) Tuscarawas County
125	1959	**Reading** (city) Hamilton County
125	1959	**Rittman** (city) Wayne County
125	1959	**Shelby** (city) Richland County
125	1959	**Upper Sandusky** (city) Wyandot County
125	1959	**Willard** (city) Huron County
144	1960	**Baltimore** (village) Fairfield County
144	1960	**Bellefontaine** (city) Logan County
144	1960	**Berea** (city) Cuyahoga County
144	1960	**Bluffton** (village) Allen County
144	1960	**Bridgetown** (CDP) Hamilton County
144	1960	**Carrollton** (village) Carroll County
144	1960	**Defiance** (city) Defiance County

Note: *This section ranks incorporated places and CDPs (Census Designated Places) with populations of 2,500 or more. Unincorporated postal areas were not considered. Please refer to the User Guide for additional information.*

Homeowner Vacancy Rate

Top 150 Places Ranked in *Descending* Order

State Rank	Percent	Place
1	9.6	**New Lebanon** (village) Montgomery County
2	9.0	**Youngstown** (city) Mahoning County
3	8.8	**Mineral Ridge** (CDP) Trumbull County
3	8.8	**Minerva** (village) Stark County
5	8.5	**New Burlington** (CDP) Hamilton County
6	8.0	**Wellston** (city) Jackson County
7	7.9	**Wilmington** (city) Clinton County
8	7.2	**Johnstown** (village) Licking County
9	7.1	**Lake Darby** (CDP) Franklin County
10	6.9	**Mount Healthy Heights** (CDP) Hamilton County
10	6.9	**Wellsville** (village) Columbiana County
12	6.8	**Oakwood** (village) Cuyahoga County
13	6.6	**Mingo Junction** (village) Jefferson County
14	6.5	**Austintown** (CDP) Mahoning County
15	6.4	**New Carlisle** (city) Clark County
16	6.2	**Jackson** (city) Jackson County
17	6.1	**Saint Bernard** (city) Hamilton County
18	5.9	**Clyde** (city) Sandusky County
19	5.3	**Huron** (city) Erie County
19	5.3	**Niles** (city) Trumbull County
19	5.3	**Urbana** (city) Champaign County
22	5.2	**East Cleveland** (city) Cuyahoga County
22	5.2	**Mount Repose** (CDP) Clermont County
24	5.1	**Canfield** (city) Mahoning County
24	5.1	**Mayfield** (village) Cuyahoga County
26	5.0	**Chardon** (city) Geauga County
27	4.9	**Bedford Heights** (city) Cuyahoga County
27	4.9	**New Concord** (village) Muskingum County
29	4.8	**Delshire** (CDP) Hamilton County
29	4.8	**Sandusky** (city) Erie County
31	4.7	**Granville** (village) Licking County
31	4.7	**Harrison** (city) Hamilton County
31	4.7	**Maple Heights** (city) Cuyahoga County
34	4.6	**Lockland** (village) Hamilton County
34	4.6	**Sebring** (village) Mahoning County
34	4.6	**Van Wert** (city) Van Wert County
37	4.5	**Dayton** (city) Montgomery County
37	4.5	**Delphos** (city) Allen County
37	4.5	**Dennison** (village) Tuscarawas County
40	4.4	**Chillicothe** (city) Ross County
40	4.4	**Kenton** (city) Hardin County
42	4.3	**Bedford** (city) Cuyahoga County
42	4.3	**Fostoria** (city) Seneca County
42	4.3	**Girard** (city) Trumbull County
42	4.3	**Howland Center** (CDP) Trumbull County
42	4.3	**London** (city) Madison County
42	4.3	**Saint Marys** (city) Auglaize County
48	4.2	**Ashtabula** (city) Ashtabula County
48	4.2	**Mulberry** (CDP) Clermont County
50	4.1	**Oxford** (city) Butler County
50	4.1	**Toronto** (city) Jefferson County
50	4.1	**Wadsworth** (city) Medina County
50	4.1	**Waynesville** (village) Warren County
54	4.0	**Pleasant Run** (CDP) Hamilton County
55	3.9	**Conneaut** (city) Ashtabula County
55	3.9	**Northbrook** (CDP) Hamilton County
55	3.9	**Sheffield Lake** (city) Lorain County
58	3.8	**Euclid** (city) Cuyahoga County
58	3.8	**Zanesville** (city) Muskingum County
60	3.7	**Mount Vernon** (city) Knox County
60	3.7	**Shaker Heights** (city) Cuyahoga County
62	3.6	**Louisville** (city) Stark County
63	3.5	**Covedale** (CDP) Hamilton County
63	3.5	**Sunbury** (village) Delaware County
63	3.5	**Vermilion** (city) Lorain County
66	3.4	**Riverside** (city) Montgomery County
66	3.4	**Springfield** (city) Clark County
68	3.3	**Cleveland Heights** (city) Cuyahoga County
68	3.3	**Galion** (city) Crawford County
68	3.3	**Lima** (city) Allen County
68	3.3	**Medina** (city) Medina County
68	3.3	**Mount Orab** (village) Brown County
73	3.2	**Cuyahoga Falls** (city) Summit County
73	3.2	**Struthers** (city) Mahoning County
75	3.1	**East Liverpool** (city) Columbiana County
75	3.1	**Marion** (city) Marion County
75	3.1	**Mayfield Heights** (city) Cuyahoga County
75	3.1	**Nelsonville** (city) Athens County
75	3.1	**Oakwood** (city) Montgomery County
80	3.0	**Cherry Grove** (CDP) Hamilton County
80	3.0	**Cleveland** (city) Cuyahoga County
80	3.0	**Crestline** (village) Crawford County
80	3.0	**Eastlake** (city) Lake County
80	3.0	**Logan** (city) Hocking County
80	3.0	**Newark** (city) Licking County
80	3.0	**Salem** (city) Columbiana County
80	3.0	**Warrensville Heights** (city) Cuyahoga County
80	3.0	**Wooster** (city) Wayne County
89	2.9	**Garrettsville** (village) Portage County
89	2.9	**North College Hill** (city) Hamilton County
89	2.9	**North Zanesville** (CDP) Muskingum County
92	2.8	**Akron** (city) Summit County
92	2.8	**Ashland** (city) Ashland County
92	2.8	**Clayton** (city) Montgomery County
92	2.8	**East Palestine** (village) Columbiana County
92	2.8	**Milford** (city) Clermont County
92	2.8	**Pleasant Run Farm** (CDP) Hamilton County
92	2.8	**Rossford** (city) Wood County
92	2.8	**South Euclid** (city) Cuyahoga County
92	2.8	**West Portsmouth** (CDP) Scioto County
101	2.7	**Chagrin Falls** (village) Cuyahoga County
101	2.7	**Cincinnati** (city) Hamilton County
101	2.7	**Fairlawn** (city) Summit County
101	2.7	**Grove City** (city) Franklin County
101	2.7	**Williamsburg** (village) Clermont County
106	2.6	**Elyria** (city) Lorain County
106	2.6	**Wheelersburg** (CDP) Scioto County
106	2.6	**Wyoming** (city) Hamilton County
109	2.5	**Blue Ash** (city) Hamilton County
109	2.5	**Celina** (city) Mercer County
109	2.5	**Defiance** (city) Defiance County
109	2.5	**Gallipolis** (village) Gallia County
109	2.5	**Greenville** (city) Darke County
109	2.5	**Hamilton** (city) Butler County
109	2.5	**Heath** (city) Licking County
109	2.5	**Ironton** (city) Lawrence County
109	2.5	**Oregon** (city) Lucas County
109	2.5	**Richmond Heights** (city) Cuyahoga County
109	2.5	**Springdale** (city) Hamilton County
109	2.5	**Strasburg** (village) Tuscarawas County
109	2.5	**Trotwood** (city) Montgomery County
109	2.5	**University Heights** (city) Cuyahoga County
109	2.5	**West Carrollton** (city) Montgomery County
109	2.5	**West Jefferson** (village) Madison County
125	2.4	**Amberley** (village) Hamilton County
125	2.4	**Broadview Heights** (city) Cuyahoga County
125	2.4	**Doylestown** (village) Wayne County
125	2.4	**Gibsonburg** (village) Sandusky County
125	2.4	**Landen** (CDP) Warren County
125	2.4	**Pataskala** (city) Licking County
125	2.4	**Reminderville** (village) Summit County
125	2.4	**Sidney** (city) Shelby County
125	2.4	**Silverton** (village) Hamilton County
125	2.4	**Toledo** (city) Lucas County
125	2.4	**Xenia** (city) Greene County
136	2.3	**Bellevue** (city) Sandusky County
136	2.3	**Bridgetown** (CDP) Hamilton County
136	2.3	**Fairfield** (city) Butler County
136	2.3	**Highland Heights** (city) Cuyahoga County
136	2.3	**Lordstown** (village) Trumbull County
136	2.3	**Miamisburg** (city) Montgomery County
136	2.3	**Napoleon** (city) Henry County
136	2.3	**Ottawa Hills** (village) Lucas County
136	2.3	**Pepper Pike** (city) Cuyahoga County
136	2.3	**Seville** (village) Medina County
136	2.3	**Versailles** (village) Darke County
136	2.3	**Waterville** (city) Lucas County
136	2.3	**White Oak** (CDP) Hamilton County
149	2.2	**Barberton** (city) Summit County
149	2.2	**Canton** (city) Stark County

Note: *This section ranks incorporated places and CDPs (Census Designated Places) with populations of 2,500 or more. Unincorporated postal areas were not considered. Please refer to the User Guide for additional information.*

Median Selected Monthly Owner Costs: With Mortgage

Top 150 Places Ranked in *Descending* Order

State Rank	Dollars	Place
1	4,000+	**The Village of Indian Hill** (city) Hamilton County
2	3,286	**Pepper Pike** (city) Cuyahoga County
3	3,220	**New Albany** (city) Franklin County
4	2,529	**Four Bridges** (CDP) Butler County
5	2,479	**Dry Run** (CDP) Hamilton County
6	2,460	**Dublin** (city) Franklin County
7	2,405	**Moreland Hills** (village) Cuyahoga County
8	2,344	**Mariemont** (village) Hamilton County
9	2,342	**Powell** (city) Delaware County
10	2,275	**Ottawa Hills** (village) Lucas County
11	2,231	**Sixteen Mile Stand** (CDP) Hamilton County
12	2,224	**Chagrin Falls** (village) Cuyahoga County
13	2,149	**Hudson** (city) Summit County
13	2,149	**Wyoming** (city) Hamilton County
15	2,146	**Montgomery** (city) Hamilton County
16	2,139	**Granville** (village) Licking County
17	2,127	**Upper Arlington** (city) Franklin County
18	2,100	**Bexley** (city) Franklin County
19	2,097	**Amberley** (village) Hamilton County
20	2,087	**Turpin Hills** (CDP) Hamilton County
21	2,048	**Montrose-Ghent** (CDP) Summit County
22	2,039	**Orange** (village) Cuyahoga County
23	2,033	**Shaker Heights** (city) Cuyahoga County
24	2,022	**Oakwood** (city) Montgomery County
25	2,010	**Beachwood** (city) Cuyahoga County
26	2,007	**South Lebanon** (village) Warren County
27	1,996	**Solon** (city) Cuyahoga County
28	1,995	**Kirtland** (city) Lake County
29	1,967	**South Russell** (village) Geauga County
30	1,953	**Mayfield** (village) Cuyahoga County
31	1,943	**Highland Heights** (city) Cuyahoga County
32	1,931	**Grandview Heights** (city) Franklin County
33	1,851	**Brecksville** (city) Cuyahoga County
34	1,831	**Avon** (city) Lorain County
35	1,829	**Worthington** (city) Franklin County
36	1,791	**Bainbridge** (CDP) Geauga County
37	1,789	**Westlake** (city) Cuyahoga County
38	1,787	**Evendale** (village) Hamilton County
39	1,771	**Hilliard** (city) Franklin County
40	1,768	**Independence** (city) Cuyahoga County
41	1,750	**Richfield** (village) Summit County
42	1,734	**Broadview Heights** (city) Cuyahoga County
43	1,722	**Willoughby Hills** (city) Lake County
44	1,709	**Madeira** (city) Hamilton County
44	1,709	**Mason** (city) Warren County
46	1,701	**Westerville** (city) Franklin County
47	1,694	**Aurora** (city) Portage County
48	1,686	**Pickerington** (city) Fairfield County
49	1,683	**Mack** (CDP) Hamilton County
50	1,681	**Sherwood** (CDP) Hamilton County
51	1,659	**Gahanna** (city) Franklin County
52	1,657	**Avon Lake** (city) Lorain County
53	1,651	**Strongsville** (city) Cuyahoga County
54	1,645	**Greentown** (CDP) Stark County
55	1,642	**Kenwood** (CDP) Hamilton County
56	1,641	**Bay Village** (city) Cuyahoga County
57	1,635	**Perrysburg** (city) Wood County
58	1,623	**Rocky River** (city) Cuyahoga County
59	1,613	**Canal Winchester** (city) Franklin County
59	1,613	**Forestville** (CDP) Hamilton County
61	1,608	**Springboro** (city) Warren County
62	1,604	**Beavercreek** (city) Greene County
63	1,593	**Plain City** (village) Madison County
64	1,591	**Twinsburg** (city) Summit County
65	1,587	**Richmond Heights** (city) Cuyahoga County
66	1,576	**Dry Ridge** (CDP) Hamilton County
67	1,574	**University Heights** (city) Cuyahoga County
68	1,573	**Fruit Hill** (CDP) Hamilton County
69	1,570	**Beechwood Trails** (CDP) Licking County
70	1,560	**Beckett Ridge** (CDP) Butler County
70	1,560	**Miami Heights** (CDP) Hamilton County
72	1,558	**Lake Darby** (CDP) Franklin County
73	1,554	**Whitehouse** (village) Lucas County
74	1,550	**North Royalton** (city) Cuyahoga County
75	1,542	**Blue Ash** (city) Hamilton County
76	1,523	**Macedonia** (city) Summit County
77	1,522	**Centerville** (city) Montgomery County
78	1,515	**Sheffield** (village) Lorain County
79	1,506	**Bellbrook** (city) Greene County
79	1,506	**Taylor Creek** (CDP) Hamilton County
81	1,504	**Grove City** (city) Franklin County
82	1,493	**Dent** (CDP) Hamilton County
82	1,493	**Loveland** (city) Hamilton County
84	1,491	**Milford** (city) Clermont County
85	1,490	**Waterville** (city) Lucas County
86	1,485	**Green** (city) Summit County
87	1,477	**Monfort Heights** (CDP) Hamilton County
88	1,472	**North Zanesville** (CDP) Muskingum County
88	1,472	**Reminderville** (village) Summit County
90	1,468	**Marysville** (city) Union County
91	1,466	**Cherry Grove** (CDP) Hamilton County
92	1,465	**Cleveland Heights** (city) Cuyahoga County
93	1,462	**Pataskala** (city) Licking County
94	1,456	**Yellow Springs** (village) Greene County
95	1,441	**Delaware** (city) Delaware County
96	1,435	**Seven Hills** (city) Cuyahoga County
97	1,428	**Sunbury** (village) Delaware County
98	1,421	**Salem Heights** (CDP) Hamilton County
99	1,416	**Reynoldsburg** (city) Franklin County
100	1,415	**Olmsted Falls** (city) Cuyahoga County
101	1,408	**Monroe** (city) Butler County
101	1,408	**Stow** (city) Summit County
103	1,407	**North Olmsted** (city) Cuyahoga County
104	1,406	**Landen** (CDP) Warren County
105	1,402	**North Ridgeville** (city) Lorain County
106	1,400	**Bowling Green** (city) Wood County
106	1,400	**Fairlawn** (city) Summit County
106	1,400	**Newtown** (village) Hamilton County
109	1,393	**Amherst** (city) Lorain County
109	1,393	**Lakewood** (city) Cuyahoga County
111	1,390	**Garrettsville** (village) Portage County
111	1,390	**Sylvania** (city) Lucas County
113	1,389	**Canfield** (city) Mahoning County
114	1,387	**Uniontown** (CDP) Stark County
115	1,386	**Oakwood** (village) Cuyahoga County
116	1,383	**Groveport** (city) Franklin County
117	1,380	**Clayton** (city) Montgomery County
118	1,373	**Lyndhurst** (city) Cuyahoga County
119	1,371	**Medina** (city) Medina County
120	1,359	**Covedale** (CDP) Hamilton County
121	1,355	**Cleves** (village) Hamilton County
121	1,355	**Lordstown** (village) Trumbull County
123	1,353	**Streetsboro** (city) Portage County
124	1,349	**Chardon** (city) Geauga County
125	1,345	**Tallmadge** (city) Summit County
126	1,341	**Mentor** (city) Lake County
126	1,341	**Munroe Falls** (city) Summit County
128	1,332	**Devola** (CDP) Washington County
129	1,331	**Fairport Harbor** (village) Lake County
130	1,329	**Oxford** (city) Butler County
131	1,326	**Fairview Park** (city) Cuyahoga County
131	1,326	**Tipp City** (city) Miami County
133	1,325	**Minster** (village) Auglaize County
134	1,323	**Mayfield Heights** (city) Cuyahoga County
134	1,323	**Willoughby** (city) Lake County
136	1,322	**White Oak** (CDP) Hamilton County
137	1,318	**Huber Ridge** (CDP) Franklin County
138	1,317	**Wadsworth** (city) Medina County
139	1,315	**Middleburg Heights** (city) Cuyahoga County
140	1,311	**Day Heights** (CDP) Clermont County
141	1,310	**Lebanon** (city) Warren County
142	1,304	**Rossford** (city) Wood County
143	1,299	**Germantown** (city) Montgomery County
144	1,296	**Berea** (city) Cuyahoga County
144	1,296	**Waynesville** (village) Warren County
146	1,291	**Kent** (city) Portage County
147	1,290	**Mount Repose** (CDP) Clermont County
148	1,288	**Madison** (village) Lake County
149	1,287	**Springdale** (city) Hamilton County
150	1,286	**Northfield** (village) Summit County

Note: *This section ranks incorporated places and CDPs (Census Designated Places) with populations of 2,500 or more. Unincorporated postal areas were not considered. Please refer to the User Guide for additional information.*

Median Selected Monthly Owner Costs: With Mortgage

Top 150 Places Ranked in *Ascending* Order

State Rank	Dollars	Place
1	742	**Crooksville** (village) Perry County
2	769	**Campbell** (city) Mahoning County
3	771	**Youngstown** (city) Mahoning County
4	773	**Wellsville** (village) Columbiana County
5	783	**Fostoria** (city) Seneca County
6	786	**Buckeye Lake** (village) Licking County
7	790	**East Liverpool** (city) Columbiana County
8	792	**Toronto** (city) Jefferson County
9	793	**Loudonville** (village) Ashland County
10	799	**Dennison** (village) Tuscarawas County
11	807	**Sebring** (village) Mahoning County
12	811	**Greenfield** (village) Highland County
13	813	**Kenton** (city) Hardin County
14	815	**Barnesville** (village) Belmont County
15	818	**Struthers** (city) Mahoning County
15	818	**Warren** (city) Trumbull County
17	819	**Montpelier** (village) Williams County
18	827	**Uhrichsville** (city) Tuscarawas County
18	827	**Zanesville** (city) Muskingum County
20	828	**Willard** (city) Huron County
21	840	**Portsmouth** (city) Scioto County
22	841	**Ashtabula** (city) Ashtabula County
23	848	**East Palestine** (village) Columbiana County
23	848	**Lima** (city) Allen County
25	853	**Galion** (city) Crawford County
26	857	**Bucyrus** (city) Crawford County
26	857	**Girard** (city) Trumbull County
26	857	**Van Wert** (city) Van Wert County
29	864	**Newton Falls** (village) Trumbull County
30	866	**Shadyside** (village) Belmont County
31	868	**Coshocton** (city) Coshocton County
31	868	**Mingo Junction** (village) Jefferson County
33	870	**Greenville** (city) Darke County
33	870	**Ironton** (city) Lawrence County
33	870	**Lisbon** (village) Columbiana County
36	871	**Niles** (city) Trumbull County
36	871	**Springfield** (city) Clark County
38	872	**New Lexington** (village) Perry County
39	878	**Mansfield** (city) Richland County
40	881	**Bellaire** (village) Belmont County
41	884	**Hillsboro** (city) Highland County
42	885	**Cambridge** (city) Guernsey County
42	885	**Park Layne** (CDP) Clark County
42	885	**Sandusky** (city) Erie County
45	887	**Canton** (city) Stark County
46	888	**Georgetown** (village) Brown County
47	889	**Paulding** (village) Paulding County
48	895	**Barberton** (city) Summit County
48	895	**New Carlisle** (city) Clark County
50	900	**Bethel** (village) Clermont County
50	900	**Newcomerstown** (village) Tuscarawas County
52	901	**Martins Ferry** (city) Belmont County
53	902	**Marietta** (city) Washington County
54	904	**Alliance** (city) Stark County
55	905	**Ravenna** (city) Portage County
56	913	**Marion** (city) Marion County
57	919	**Walbridge** (village) Wood County
58	921	**Covington** (village) Miami County
59	922	**Logan** (city) Hocking County
60	923	**Fremont** (city) Sandusky County
61	924	**Bryan** (city) Williams County
61	924	**Conneaut** (city) Ashtabula County
63	925	**West Union** (village) Adams County
64	929	**Carey** (village) Wyandot County
64	929	**Crestline** (village) Crawford County
66	931	**Salem** (city) Columbiana County
67	934	**Wilmington** (city) Clinton County
68	937	**New Lebanon** (village) Montgomery County
69	942	**Minerva** (village) Stark County
70	944	**Millersburg** (village) Holmes County
70	944	**Steubenville** (city) Jefferson County
72	945	**Shelby** (city) Richland County
73	948	**Jackson** (city) Jackson County
74	949	**Tiffin** (city) Seneca County
75	951	**Mount Gilead** (village) Morrow County
76	952	**Piqua** (city) Miami County
77	955	**Dayton** (city) Montgomery County
78	957	**Eaton** (city) Preble County
79	961	**Belpre** (city) Washington County
79	961	**Upper Sandusky** (city) Wyandot County
81	962	**Urbana** (city) Champaign County
82	963	**Carrollton** (village) Carroll County
82	963	**Perry Heights** (CDP) Stark County
84	965	**Bellefontaine** (city) Logan County
84	965	**Burlington** (CDP) Lawrence County
86	968	**New London** (village) Huron County
87	969	**Lockland** (village) Hamilton County
87	969	**Nelsonville** (city) Athens County
89	970	**Akron** (city) Summit County
90	973	**Geneva** (city) Ashtabula County
90	973	**Wapakoneta** (city) Auglaize County
92	976	**Napoleon** (city) Henry County
93	980	**Bellevue** (city) Sandusky County
94	982	**Orrville** (city) Wayne County
95	984	**Edgewood** (CDP) Ashtabula County
95	984	**Waverly** (village) Pike County
97	985	**Hubbard** (city) Trumbull County
98	986	**Wellston** (city) Jackson County
99	987	**McDonald** (village) Trumbull County
100	988	**Hicksville** (village) Defiance County
101	989	**Mount Vernon** (city) Knox County
101	989	**Sidney** (city) Shelby County
103	990	**Delphos** (city) Allen County
104	992	**Coldwater** (village) Mercer County
104	992	**Gibsonburg** (village) Sandusky County
106	994	**Massillon** (city) Stark County
107	996	**Xenia** (city) Greene County
108	997	**Cedarville** (village) Greene County
109	998	**Northbrook** (CDP) Hamilton County
110	999	**Ashland** (city) Ashland County
110	999	**Strasburg** (village) Tuscarawas County
112	1,000	**Cleveland** (city) Cuyahoga County
113	1,005	**Washington Court House** (city) Fayette County
114	1,006	**Austintown** (CDP) Mahoning County
115	1,007	**Rittman** (city) Wayne County
116	1,008	**Lodi** (village) Medina County
117	1,009	**Brimfield** (CDP) Portage County
118	1,011	**Wintersville** (village) Jefferson County
119	1,015	**Toledo** (city) Lucas County
120	1,016	**Jefferson** (village) Ashtabula County
121	1,020	**Ada** (village) Hardin County
122	1,022	**Brookville** (city) Montgomery County
123	1,025	**Clyde** (city) Sandusky County
123	1,025	**West Portsmouth** (CDP) Scioto County
125	1,027	**Dover** (city) Tuscarawas County
125	1,027	**Hamilton** (city) Butler County
125	1,027	**North College Hill** (city) Hamilton County
125	1,027	**Whitehall** (city) Franklin County
129	1,031	**Maple Heights** (city) Cuyahoga County
130	1,034	**Green Meadows** (CDP) Clark County
131	1,035	**Defiance** (city) Defiance County
132	1,036	**Norwalk** (city) Huron County
133	1,037	**Lorain** (city) Lorain County
133	1,037	**New Philadelphia** (city) Tuscarawas County
135	1,039	**Chillicothe** (city) Ross County
135	1,039	**North Madison** (CDP) Lake County
135	1,039	**Port Clinton** (city) Ottawa County
135	1,039	**Riverside** (city) Montgomery County
139	1,046	**Cadiz** (village) Harrison County
139	1,046	**Fredericktown** (village) Knox County
141	1,048	**Oak Harbor** (village) Ottawa County
142	1,049	**West Carrollton** (city) Montgomery County
143	1,051	**Newark** (city) Licking County
144	1,052	**Middletown** (city) Butler County
145	1,056	**Delta** (village) Fulton County
145	1,056	**Elyria** (city) Lorain County
147	1,060	**Saint Marys** (city) Auglaize County
148	1,062	**Northridge** (CDP) Clark County
149	1,063	**Warrensville Heights** (city) Cuyahoga County
150	1,064	**Mount Healthy Heights** (CDP) Hamilton County

***Note:** This section ranks incorporated places and CDPs (Census Designated Places) with populations of 2,500 or more. Unincorporated postal areas were not considered. Please refer to the User Guide for additional information.*

Median Selected Monthly Owner Costs: Without Mortgage

Top 150 Places Ranked in *Descending* Order

State Rank	Dollars	Place
1	1,366	**The Village of Indian Hill** (city) Hamilton County
2	1,354	**New Albany** (city) Franklin County
3	1,325	**Mariemont** (village) Hamilton County
4	1,160	**Moreland Hills** (village) Cuyahoga County
5	1,117	**Pepper Pike** (city) Cuyahoga County
6	1,058	**Four Bridges** (CDP) Butler County
7	1,043	**Ottawa Hills** (village) Lucas County
8	1,029	**Dublin** (city) Franklin County
9	1,021	**Shaker Heights** (city) Cuyahoga County
10	1,018	**Amberley** (village) Hamilton County
11	948	**Powell** (city) Delaware County
12	928	**Sixteen Mile Stand** (CDP) Hamilton County
13	915	**Orange** (village) Cuyahoga County
14	895	**Chagrin Falls** (village) Cuyahoga County
15	874	**Wyoming** (city) Hamilton County
16	873	**Upper Arlington** (city) Franklin County
17	868	**Bexley** (city) Franklin County
18	846	**Bainbridge** (CDP) Geauga County
19	841	**Highland Heights** (city) Cuyahoga County
20	824	**South Russell** (village) Geauga County
21	818	**Beachwood** (city) Cuyahoga County
21	818	**Grandview Heights** (city) Franklin County
23	810	**Hudson** (city) Summit County
24	782	**Granville** (village) Licking County
25	769	**Worthington** (city) Franklin County
26	762	**Oakwood** (city) Montgomery County
27	758	**Brecksville** (city) Cuyahoga County
28	756	**Turpin Hills** (CDP) Hamilton County
29	752	**Dry Run** (CDP) Hamilton County
30	751	**Montrose-Ghent** (CDP) Summit County
31	750	**Hilliard** (city) Franklin County
32	743	**Madeira** (city) Hamilton County
33	737	**Solon** (city) Cuyahoga County
34	730	**Bay Village** (city) Cuyahoga County
35	705	**Canal Winchester** (city) Franklin County
36	703	**Aurora** (city) Portage County
37	702	**Montgomery** (city) Hamilton County
38	701	**Fruit Hill** (CDP) Hamilton County
39	699	**University Heights** (city) Cuyahoga County
40	689	**Rocky River** (city) Cuyahoga County
41	682	**Willoughby Hills** (city) Lake County
42	679	**Beechwood Trails** (CDP) Licking County
43	677	**Westerville** (city) Franklin County
44	661	**Landen** (CDP) Warren County
45	657	**Westlake** (city) Cuyahoga County
46	656	**Mayfield** (village) Cuyahoga County
47	646	**Beckett Ridge** (CDP) Butler County
48	641	**Gahanna** (city) Franklin County
49	638	**Evendale** (village) Hamilton County
50	636	**Avon Lake** (city) Lorain County
51	635	**Cleveland Heights** (city) Cuyahoga County
52	634	**Mason** (city) Warren County
53	632	**Beavercreek** (city) Greene County
54	629	**Forestville** (CDP) Hamilton County
55	628	**Blue Ash** (city) Hamilton County
56	622	**Taylor Creek** (CDP) Hamilton County
57	620	**Kenwood** (CDP) Hamilton County
58	618	**North Royalton** (city) Cuyahoga County
59	617	**Strongsville** (city) Cuyahoga County
60	615	**Lyndhurst** (city) Cuyahoga County
61	613	**Centerville** (city) Montgomery County
62	609	**Broadview Heights** (city) Cuyahoga County
63	608	**Lake Darby** (CDP) Franklin County
64	606	**Salem Heights** (CDP) Hamilton County
65	600	**Pickerington** (city) Fairfield County
66	599	**Avon** (city) Lorain County
67	595	**Bellbrook** (city) Greene County
68	594	**Mack** (CDP) Hamilton County
69	593	**Miami Heights** (CDP) Hamilton County
69	593	**Sherwood** (CDP) Hamilton County
71	592	**Fairlawn** (city) Summit County
71	592	**Lakewood** (city) Cuyahoga County
73	590	**Seven Hills** (city) Cuyahoga County
74	589	**Dry Ridge** (CDP) Hamilton County
74	589	**Kirtland** (city) Lake County
76	581	**Newtown** (village) Hamilton County
76	581	**South Lebanon** (village) Warren County
78	579	**Sylvania** (city) Lucas County
79	578	**Olmsted Falls** (city) Cuyahoga County
80	576	**Springboro** (city) Warren County
81	574	**Grove City** (city) Franklin County
81	574	**Richmond Heights** (city) Cuyahoga County
83	572	**North Olmsted** (city) Cuyahoga County
84	571	**Finneytown** (CDP) Hamilton County
85	570	**Twinsburg** (city) Summit County
86	564	**Monfort Heights** (CDP) Hamilton County
87	562	**Independence** (city) Cuyahoga County
88	560	**Yellow Springs** (village) Greene County
89	558	**New Burlington** (CDP) Hamilton County
90	557	**Middleburg Heights** (city) Cuyahoga County
91	555	**Clayton** (city) Montgomery County
92	551	**Fairview Park** (city) Cuyahoga County
92	551	**Perrysburg** (city) Wood County
94	548	**Day Heights** (CDP) Clermont County
95	545	**Huber Ridge** (CDP) Franklin County
95	545	**Reynoldsburg** (city) Franklin County
97	543	**Pataskala** (city) Licking County
97	543	**Sheffield** (village) Lorain County
99	541	**Macedonia** (city) Summit County
100	540	**Reminderville** (village) Summit County
100	540	**Silverton** (village) Hamilton County
102	537	**Streetsboro** (city) Portage County
103	535	**Chardon** (city) Geauga County
104	531	**Mayfield Heights** (city) Cuyahoga County
105	530	**Mulberry** (CDP) Clermont County
106	529	**Loveland** (city) Hamilton County
106	529	**Pleasant Run Farm** (CDP) Hamilton County
108	527	**Mount Repose** (CDP) Clermont County
109	525	**Covedale** (CDP) Hamilton County
110	524	**Lake Lakengren** (CDP) Preble County
110	524	**Miamisburg** (city) Montgomery County
112	518	**Dent** (CDP) Hamilton County
112	518	**Union** (city) Montgomery County
114	517	**Greenhills** (village) Hamilton County
114	517	**Greentown** (CDP) Stark County
116	514	**Stow** (city) Summit County
117	513	**Delaware** (city) Delaware County
117	513	**Groveport** (city) Franklin County
117	513	**Medina** (city) Medina County
120	512	**Tallmadge** (city) Summit County
121	511	**Cincinnati** (city) Hamilton County
122	510	**Sharonville** (city) Hamilton County
123	507	**Waterville** (city) Lucas County
124	504	**Rossford** (city) Wood County
125	501	**Canfield** (city) Mahoning County
126	499	**Obetz** (village) Franklin County
126	499	**South Euclid** (city) Cuyahoga County
128	497	**Northgate** (CDP) Hamilton County
128	497	**Saint Bernard** (city) Hamilton County
130	496	**Northwood** (city) Wood County
131	495	**Green** (city) Summit County
131	495	**North Ridgeville** (city) Lorain County
133	494	**Golf Manor** (village) Hamilton County
134	492	**White Oak** (CDP) Hamilton County
135	491	**Huron** (city) Erie County
136	490	**Berea** (city) Cuyahoga County
137	488	**Cortland** (city) Trumbull County
137	488	**Dillonvale** (CDP) Hamilton County
139	487	**Portage Lakes** (CDP) Summit County
140	486	**Cherry Grove** (CDP) Hamilton County
140	486	**Lebanon** (city) Warren County
140	486	**Maumee** (city) Lucas County
140	486	**Mentor** (city) Lake County
144	485	**Columbus** (city) Franklin County
144	485	**Kettering** (city) Montgomery County
146	484	**Deer Park** (city) Hamilton County
146	484	**Monroe** (city) Butler County
146	484	**Whitehouse** (village) Lucas County
149	483	**Oakwood** (village) Cuyahoga County
150	482	**Tipp City** (city) Miami County

Note: *This section ranks incorporated places and CDPs (Census Designated Places) with populations of 2,500 or more. Unincorporated postal areas were not considered. Please refer to the User Guide for additional information.*

Median Selected Monthly Owner Costs: Without Mortgage

Top 150 Places Ranked in *Ascending* Order

State Rank	Dollars	Place
1	292	**The Plains** (CDP) Athens County
2	294	**Newcomerstown** (village) Tuscarawas County
3	295	**Youngstown** (city) Mahoning County
4	298	**Barnesville** (village) Belmont County
5	302	**Van Wert** (city) Van Wert County
6	305	**Struthers** (city) Mahoning County
7	306	**Bellaire** (village) Belmont County
8	311	**Shadyside** (village) Belmont County
9	315	**Alliance** (city) Stark County
10	317	**Montpelier** (village) Williams County
11	318	**Dennison** (village) Tuscarawas County
12	320	**Bryan** (city) Williams County
13	321	**Sebring** (village) Mahoning County
14	322	**Georgetown** (village) Brown County
14	322	**Warren** (city) Trumbull County
16	324	**Greenfield** (village) Highland County
17	326	**Canton** (city) Stark County
18	332	**East Liverpool** (city) Columbiana County
18	332	**Marion** (city) Marion County
18	332	**New Carlisle** (city) Clark County
21	333	**Campbell** (city) Mahoning County
21	333	**New Lebanon** (village) Montgomery County
23	334	**Fremont** (city) Sandusky County
23	334	**Park Layne** (CDP) Clark County
25	336	**Ashtabula** (city) Ashtabula County
25	336	**Lima** (city) Allen County
27	337	**Gallipolis** (village) Gallia County
28	338	**Conneaut** (city) Ashtabula County
28	338	**Martins Ferry** (city) Belmont County
28	338	**Springfield** (city) Clark County
28	338	**Toronto** (city) Jefferson County
32	339	**Bucyrus** (city) Crawford County
32	339	**Cambridge** (city) Guernsey County
34	340	**Zanesville** (city) Muskingum County
35	341	**Loudonville** (village) Ashland County
35	341	**Salem** (city) Columbiana County
37	342	**Ravenna** (city) Portage County
38	343	**Marietta** (city) Washington County
38	343	**Wellsville** (village) Columbiana County
40	344	**Cadiz** (village) Harrison County
41	345	**Brimfield** (CDP) Portage County
41	345	**Hillsboro** (city) Highland County
41	345	**Kenton** (city) Hardin County
44	346	**Mansfield** (city) Richland County
44	346	**West Union** (village) Adams County
46	347	**Carrollton** (village) Carroll County
46	347	**Galion** (city) Crawford County
46	347	**Shelby** (city) Richland County
49	348	**Belpre** (city) Washington County
49	348	**Painesville** (city) Lake County
49	348	**Sandusky** (city) Erie County
49	348	**Wilmington** (city) Clinton County
53	350	**Troy** (city) Miami County
54	351	**Saint Marys** (city) Auglaize County
54	351	**Waverly** (village) Pike County
54	351	**Wellington** (village) Lorain County
57	352	**Lisbon** (village) Columbiana County
58	353	**Delta** (village) Fulton County
58	353	**Portsmouth** (city) Scioto County
58	353	**Washington Court House** (city) Fayette County
58	353	**Wellston** (city) Jackson County
62	354	**Bethel** (village) Clermont County
63	355	**Lorain** (city) Lorain County
64	356	**Barberton** (city) Summit County
64	356	**Doylestown** (village) Wayne County
64	356	**Greenville** (city) Darke County
64	356	**Willard** (city) Huron County
68	357	**North Kingsville** (village) Ashtabula County
69	358	**Austintown** (CDP) Mahoning County
69	358	**Williamsburg** (village) Clermont County
71	360	**Coshocton** (city) Coshocton County
71	360	**McDonald** (village) Trumbull County
71	360	**New London** (village) Huron County
74	361	**Lincoln Heights** (village) Hamilton County
74	361	**Nelsonville** (city) Athens County
76	362	**Oak Harbor** (village) Ottawa County
77	363	**Niles** (city) Trumbull County
78	364	**Mingo Junction** (village) Jefferson County
78	364	**Paulding** (village) Paulding County
78	364	**Uhrichsville** (city) Tuscarawas County
81	365	**Chillicothe** (city) Ross County
81	365	**Logan** (city) Hocking County
83	366	**Fostoria** (city) Seneca County
83	366	**Minerva** (village) Stark County
85	368	**Franklin** (city) Warren County
85	368	**Ironton** (city) Lawrence County
85	368	**Newton Falls** (village) Trumbull County
85	368	**Tiffin** (city) Seneca County
89	369	**Carey** (village) Wyandot County
89	369	**Cleveland** (city) Cuyahoga County
89	369	**Jefferson** (village) Ashtabula County
92	370	**Mount Orab** (village) Brown County
92	370	**West Milton** (village) Miami County
94	371	**Hamilton** (city) Butler County
95	372	**Blanchester** (village) Clinton County
95	372	**Covington** (village) Miami County
95	372	**New Lexington** (village) Perry County
95	372	**Piqua** (city) Miami County
99	373	**Brookville** (city) Montgomery County
99	373	**Newark** (city) Licking County
101	376	**East Palestine** (village) Columbiana County
101	376	**Gibsonburg** (village) Sandusky County
101	376	**Girard** (city) Trumbull County
104	377	**East Cleveland** (city) Cuyahoga County
104	377	**New Philadelphia** (city) Tuscarawas County
104	377	**Xenia** (city) Greene County
107	379	**Dayton** (city) Montgomery County
107	379	**Minster** (village) Auglaize County
109	380	**Bellefontaine** (city) Logan County
109	380	**Geneva** (city) Ashtabula County
111	382	**Crestline** (village) Crawford County
111	382	**Crooksville** (village) Perry County
113	383	**Germantown** (city) Montgomery County
113	383	**Wauseon** (city) Fulton County
115	384	**Lockland** (village) Hamilton County
115	384	**New Bremen** (village) Auglaize County
115	384	**Northridge** (CDP) Clark County
115	384	**Perry Heights** (CDP) Stark County
115	384	**Versailles** (village) Darke County
120	386	**Whitehall** (city) Franklin County
121	387	**Maple Heights** (city) Cuyahoga County
121	387	**Richville** (CDP) Stark County
121	387	**Toledo** (city) Lucas County
124	389	**Defiance** (city) Defiance County
124	389	**Delphos** (city) Allen County
124	389	**Rittman** (city) Wayne County
124	389	**South Point** (village) Lawrence County
124	389	**Walbridge** (village) Wood County
129	390	**Middletown** (city) Butler County
129	390	**North College Hill** (city) Hamilton County
131	391	**Clyde** (city) Sandusky County
131	391	**Coldwater** (village) Mercer County
131	391	**West Portsmouth** (CDP) Scioto County
134	392	**Celina** (city) Mercer County
134	392	**Champion Heights** (CDP) Trumbull County
134	392	**Mogadore** (village) Summit County
134	392	**Riverside** (city) Montgomery County
134	392	**Wapakoneta** (city) Auglaize County
139	393	**Akron** (city) Summit County
139	393	**Edgewood** (CDP) Ashtabula County
141	394	**Bellevue** (city) Sandusky County
141	394	**Mineral Ridge** (CDP) Trumbull County
141	394	**Port Clinton** (city) Ottawa County
141	394	**Upper Sandusky** (city) Wyandot County
145	395	**Hubbard** (city) Trumbull County
145	395	**Lancaster** (city) Fairfield County
145	395	**Louisville** (city) Stark County
148	396	**Mount Healthy Heights** (CDP) Hamilton County
149	399	**Ross** (CDP) Butler County
150	400	**Moraine** (city) Montgomery County

Note: *This section ranks incorporated places and CDPs (Census Designated Places) with populations of 2,500 or more. Unincorporated postal areas were not considered. Please refer to the User Guide for additional information.*

Median Gross Rent

Top 150 Places Ranked in *Descending* Order

State Rank	Dollars	Place
1	1,842	**Hudson** (city) Summit County
2	1,750	**Cherry Grove** (CDP) Hamilton County
3	1,675	**Powell** (city) Delaware County
4	1,667	**New Albany** (city) Franklin County
5	1,625	**Orange** (village) Cuyahoga County
6	1,597	**Montrose-Ghent** (CDP) Summit County
7	1,546	**Beachwood** (city) Cuyahoga County
8	1,461	**Aurora** (city) Portage County
9	1,452	**Brecksville** (city) Cuyahoga County
10	1,442	**Salem Heights** (CDP) Hamilton County
11	1,385	**Lake Darby** (CDP) Franklin County
12	1,377	**Four Bridges** (CDP) Butler County
13	1,375	**Moreland Hills** (village) Cuyahoga County
14	1,324	**Bainbridge** (CDP) Geauga County
15	1,311	**Kenwood** (CDP) Hamilton County
16	1,309	**Chagrin Falls** (village) Cuyahoga County
17	1,266	**Dublin** (city) Franklin County
18	1,250	**Evendale** (village) Hamilton County
19	1,247	**Wright-Patterson AFB** (CDP) Greene County
20	1,241	**Pepper Pike** (city) Cuyahoga County
21	1,222	**Dry Ridge** (CDP) Hamilton County
22	1,202	**Macedonia** (city) Summit County
23	1,200	**Solon** (city) Cuyahoga County
24	1,196	**Beckett Ridge** (CDP) Butler County
25	1,192	**Ottawa Hills** (village) Lucas County
26	1,189	**Pleasant Run** (CDP) Hamilton County
27	1,188	**Apple Valley** (CDP) Knox County
28	1,185	**Delhi Hills** (CDP) Hamilton County
29	1,165	**Amberley** (village) Hamilton County
29	1,165	**Seven Hills** (city) Cuyahoga County
31	1,164	**Sheffield** (village) Lorain County
32	1,161	**Day Heights** (CDP) Clermont County
33	1,158	**Sixteen Mile Stand** (CDP) Hamilton County
34	1,156	**Avon** (city) Lorain County
35	1,143	**Fruit Hill** (CDP) Hamilton County
36	1,142	**Landen** (CDP) Warren County
36	1,142	**Reminderville** (village) Summit County
38	1,135	**Beavercreek** (city) Greene County
39	1,122	**Avon Lake** (city) Lorain County
40	1,119	**Huber Ridge** (CDP) Franklin County
41	1,116	**Montgomery** (city) Hamilton County
42	1,106	**Lyndhurst** (city) Cuyahoga County
43	1,103	**Wyoming** (city) Hamilton County
44	1,102	**Madeira** (city) Hamilton County
45	1,092	**Grandview Heights** (city) Franklin County
46	1,075	**Newtown** (village) Hamilton County
47	1,074	**Sherwood** (CDP) Hamilton County
47	1,074	**Upper Arlington** (city) Franklin County
49	1,071	**North Ridgeville** (city) Lorain County
50	1,066	**Westlake** (city) Cuyahoga County
51	1,061	**Devola** (CDP) Washington County
52	1,058	**Woodlawn** (village) Hamilton County
53	1,056	**Mason** (city) Warren County
54	1,054	**Blue Ash** (city) Hamilton County
55	1,053	**Fairlawn** (city) Summit County
56	1,041	**Waterville** (city) Lucas County
57	1,040	**Blacklick Estates** (CDP) Franklin County
57	1,040	**Oakwood** (city) Montgomery County
59	1,036	**Monfort Heights** (CDP) Hamilton County
60	1,033	**Pickerington** (city) Fairfield County
61	1,027	**Twinsburg** (city) Summit County
62	1,022	**Highland Heights** (city) Cuyahoga County
63	1,021	**Covedale** (CDP) Hamilton County
64	1,019	**Mariemont** (village) Hamilton County
65	1,009	**Pataskala** (city) Licking County
66	1,004	**Hilliard** (city) Franklin County
66	1,004	**Sunbury** (village) Delaware County
68	998	**Mayfield** (village) Cuyahoga County
69	991	**Poland** (village) Mahoning County
70	989	**Springboro** (city) Warren County
71	988	**Bellbrook** (city) Greene County
72	987	**University Heights** (city) Cuyahoga County
73	984	**Gahanna** (city) Franklin County
74	977	**Monroe** (city) Butler County
75	976	**Bay Village** (city) Cuyahoga County
76	971	**Mack** (CDP) Hamilton County
77	967	**Streetsboro** (city) Portage County
78	950	**Union** (city) Montgomery County
79	948	**Reynoldsburg** (city) Franklin County
80	947	**Forestville** (CDP) Hamilton County
81	945	**Shaker Heights** (city) Cuyahoga County
82	943	**South Euclid** (city) Cuyahoga County
83	939	**Northbrook** (CDP) Hamilton County
84	936	**Trenton** (city) Butler County
85	935	**Northgate** (CDP) Hamilton County
86	931	**Lake Lakengren** (CDP) Preble County
87	927	**Westerville** (city) Franklin County
88	925	**Mentor** (city) Lake County
89	923	**Norton** (city) Summit County
90	921	**Sheffield Lake** (city) Lorain County
91	920	**Stow** (city) Summit County
92	916	**North Madison** (CDP) Lake County
93	914	**Pleasant Run Farm** (CDP) Hamilton County
94	913	**Bexley** (city) Franklin County
95	912	**Grove City** (city) Franklin County
96	908	**Sharonville** (city) Hamilton County
96	908	**Strongsville** (city) Cuyahoga County
98	904	**Baltimore** (village) Fairfield County
99	900	**Granville** (village) Licking County
100	898	**South Russell** (village) Geauga County
101	896	**Mogadore** (village) Summit County
102	891	**Taylor Creek** (CDP) Hamilton County
103	888	**Perrysburg** (city) Wood County
104	887	**Huber Heights** (city) Montgomery County
104	887	**New Burlington** (CDP) Hamilton County
106	882	**Worthington** (city) Franklin County
107	881	**Forest Park** (city) Hamilton County
108	880	**Springdale** (city) Hamilton County
109	878	**Richfield** (village) Summit County
110	876	**Wickliffe** (city) Lake County
111	875	**Dent** (CDP) Hamilton County
111	875	**Miami Heights** (CDP) Hamilton County
113	873	**Howland Center** (CDP) Trumbull County
114	871	**Cleveland Heights** (city) Cuyahoga County
115	867	**North Olmsted** (city) Cuyahoga County
116	864	**Willoughby** (city) Lake County
117	861	**Delaware** (city) Delaware County
117	861	**Mayfield Heights** (city) Cuyahoga County
119	859	**Germantown** (city) Montgomery County
120	857	**Greenhills** (village) Hamilton County
121	856	**Columbus** (city) Franklin County
122	855	**Marysville** (city) Union County
123	854	**Turpin Hills** (CDP) Hamilton County
124	853	**Centerville** (city) Montgomery County
124	853	**Mentor-on-the-Lake** (city) Lake County
126	850	**Brook Park** (city) Cuyahoga County
127	846	**Lakemore** (village) Summit County
128	845	**Amherst** (city) Lorain County
129	844	**Fairfield** (city) Butler County
130	843	**Broadview Heights** (city) Cuyahoga County
130	843	**Mount Healthy Heights** (CDP) Hamilton County
132	842	**Greentown** (CDP) Stark County
133	841	**Maple Heights** (city) Cuyahoga County
134	838	**Rocky River** (city) Cuyahoga County
135	836	**Heath** (city) Licking County
136	835	**Mulberry** (CDP) Clermont County
137	834	**North Kingsville** (village) Ashtabula County
137	834	**South Lebanon** (village) Warren County
139	833	**Willoughby Hills** (city) Lake County
140	832	**Brunswick** (city) Medina County
141	829	**Obetz** (village) Franklin County
142	828	**West Milton** (village) Miami County
143	825	**New Franklin** (city) Summit County
144	824	**Middleburg Heights** (city) Cuyahoga County
144	824	**Ross** (CDP) Butler County
146	823	**North College Hill** (city) Hamilton County
146	823	**Sebring** (village) Mahoning County
148	822	**Amelia** (village) Clermont County
149	820	**Fort Shawnee** (CDP) Allen County
149	820	**North Royalton** (city) Cuyahoga County

Note: *This section ranks incorporated places and CDPs (Census Designated Places) with populations of 2,500 or more. Unincorporated postal areas were not considered. Please refer to the User Guide for additional information.*

Median Gross Rent

Top 150 Places Ranked in *Ascending* Order

State Rank	Dollars	Place
1	442	**Wellsville** (village) Columbiana County
2	456	**Martins Ferry** (city) Belmont County
3	483	**Carrollton** (village) Carroll County
4	496	**West Union** (village) Adams County
5	506	**Barnesville** (village) Belmont County
6	514	**North Zanesville** (CDP) Muskingum County
7	520	**Mount Gilead** (village) Morrow County
8	527	**Burlington** (CDP) Lawrence County
9	529	**Georgetown** (village) Brown County
10	535	**Wellston** (city) Jackson County
11	539	**Hicksville** (village) Defiance County
11	539	**Mineral Ridge** (CDP) Trumbull County
13	543	**Lordstown** (village) Trumbull County
14	545	**Millersburg** (village) Holmes County
15	550	**Coldwater** (village) Mercer County
16	556	**North Baltimore** (village) Wood County
17	557	**Crooksville** (village) Perry County
18	559	**East Liverpool** (city) Columbiana County
19	562	**Portsmouth** (city) Scioto County
20	563	**Bellaire** (village) Belmont County
21	564	**Jefferson** (village) Ashtabula County
22	566	**Logan** (city) Hocking County
23	567	**Mingo Junction** (village) Jefferson County
24	568	**Carey** (village) Wyandot County
25	571	**Versailles** (village) Darke County
26	573	**Bethel** (village) Clermont County
26	573	**Lodi** (village) Medina County
28	575	**East Cleveland** (city) Cuyahoga County
29	576	**Cambridge** (city) Guernsey County
30	577	**Willard** (city) Huron County
31	578	**Crestline** (village) Crawford County
32	579	**Ironton** (city) Lawrence County
33	580	**Loudonville** (village) Ashland County
34	585	**Coshocton** (city) Coshocton County
34	585	**Steubenville** (city) Jefferson County
36	587	**Cadiz** (village) Harrison County
37	588	**Fostoria** (city) Seneca County
38	589	**Toronto** (city) Jefferson County
38	589	**Wapakoneta** (city) Auglaize County
40	590	**West Portsmouth** (CDP) Scioto County
41	591	**Conneaut** (city) Ashtabula County
42	592	**Mansfield** (city) Richland County
43	593	**Geneva** (city) Ashtabula County
44	594	**Lisbon** (village) Columbiana County
44	594	**New Bremen** (village) Auglaize County
44	594	**Warren** (city) Trumbull County
47	595	**Kenton** (city) Hardin County
47	595	**New Lexington** (village) Perry County
49	597	**Walbridge** (village) Wood County
50	598	**Paulding** (village) Paulding County
51	601	**Newton Falls** (village) Trumbull County
52	602	**Norwalk** (city) Huron County
53	603	**New Concord** (village) Muskingum County
54	604	**Silverton** (village) Hamilton County
55	605	**Delta** (village) Fulton County
56	606	**Belpre** (city) Washington County
56	606	**Canton** (city) Stark County
58	607	**Archbold** (village) Fulton County
59	608	**Port Clinton** (city) Ottawa County
60	609	**Greenfield** (village) Highland County
60	609	**Greenville** (city) Darke County
60	609	**Upper Sandusky** (city) Wyandot County
60	609	**Wheelersburg** (CDP) Scioto County
64	612	**Eaton** (city) Preble County
64	612	**Shadyside** (village) Belmont County
66	613	**Ottawa** (village) Putnam County
67	614	**Austintown** (CDP) Mahoning County
67	614	**Galion** (city) Crawford County
69	616	**Lockland** (village) Hamilton County
69	616	**Struthers** (city) Mahoning County
71	617	**Bluffton** (village) Allen County
72	618	**Calcutta** (CDP) Columbiana County
73	619	**Youngstown** (city) Mahoning County
74	620	**Munroe Falls** (city) Summit County
74	620	**Oregon** (city) Lucas County
76	621	**Ashtabula** (city) Ashtabula County
76	621	**Girard** (city) Trumbull County
76	621	**Montpelier** (village) Williams County
79	624	**Edgewood** (CDP) Ashtabula County
80	625	**Uhrichsville** (city) Tuscarawas County
81	626	**Bellevue** (city) Sandusky County
81	626	**Columbiana** (city) Columbiana County
83	628	**Fremont** (city) Sandusky County
83	628	**Lima** (city) Allen County
83	628	**Oakwood** (village) Cuyahoga County
86	629	**Dennison** (village) Tuscarawas County
87	630	**Boardman** (CDP) Mahoning County
87	630	**Hubbard** (city) Trumbull County
89	631	**Bucyrus** (city) Crawford County
89	631	**Wauseon** (city) Fulton County
91	632	**Hillsboro** (city) Highland County
91	632	**Zanesville** (city) Muskingum County
93	633	**Campbell** (city) Mahoning County
93	633	**Cedarville** (village) Greene County
93	633	**Van Wert** (city) Van Wert County
96	636	**Dayton** (city) Montgomery County
97	638	**Lincoln Heights** (village) Hamilton County
97	638	**Shelby** (city) Richland County
99	640	**New Lebanon** (village) Montgomery County
99	640	**Sandusky** (city) Erie County
101	641	**Gallipolis** (village) Gallia County
102	644	**Alliance** (city) Stark County
103	645	**Urbana** (city) Champaign County
103	645	**Williamsburg** (village) Clermont County
105	646	**Salem** (city) Columbiana County
106	647	**New Richmond** (village) Clermont County
107	649	**Niles** (city) Trumbull County
108	650	**Enon** (village) Clark County
108	650	**Minster** (village) Auglaize County
110	651	**Toledo** (city) Lucas County
111	653	**Minerva** (village) Stark County
111	653	**Nelsonville** (city) Athens County
113	654	**Bryan** (city) Williams County
113	654	**Plain City** (village) Madison County
115	655	**Cheviot** (city) Hamilton County
115	655	**Milford** (city) Clermont County
117	657	**Ravenna** (city) Portage County
117	657	**Reading** (city) Hamilton County
119	658	**Celina** (city) Mercer County
119	658	**Gibsonburg** (village) Sandusky County
119	658	**Swanton** (village) Fulton County
122	659	**Blanchester** (village) Clinton County
122	659	**Lorain** (city) Lorain County
122	659	**Mount Healthy** (city) Hamilton County
122	659	**Oak Harbor** (village) Ottawa County
126	660	**Cleveland** (city) Cuyahoga County
127	662	**Cincinnati** (city) Hamilton County
128	663	**Marietta** (city) Washington County
128	663	**Saint Marys** (city) Auglaize County
130	665	**Xenia** (city) Greene County
131	667	**Bowling Green** (city) Wood County
131	667	**Tiffin** (city) Seneca County
133	670	**Massillon** (city) Stark County
133	670	**Rossford** (city) Wood County
135	671	**Napoleon** (city) Henry County
136	673	**Groveport** (city) Franklin County
136	673	**Wilmington** (city) Clinton County
138	674	**Northfield** (village) Summit County
138	674	**Piqua** (city) Miami County
140	675	**Springfield** (city) Clark County
141	676	**Barberton** (city) Summit County
141	676	**Mount Vernon** (city) Knox County
143	677	**Brooklyn** (city) Cuyahoga County
144	678	**Northridge** (CDP) Clark County
144	678	**Saint Henry** (village) Mercer County
146	679	**Covington** (village) Miami County
147	680	**Ashland** (city) Ashland County
148	681	**Marion** (city) Marion County
149	682	**Garrettsville** (village) Portage County
149	682	**Hartville** (village) Stark County

Note: *This section ranks incorporated places and CDPs (Census Designated Places) with populations of 2,500 or more. Unincorporated postal areas were not considered. Please refer to the User Guide for additional information.*

Rental Vacancy Rate

Top 150 Places Ranked in *Descending* Order

State Rank	Percent	Place
1	25.8	**Mulberry** (CDP) Clermont County
2	22.4	**Fort Shawnee** (CDP) Allen County
3	20.2	**New Albany** (city) Franklin County
4	19.5	**The Village of Indian Hill** (city) Hamilton County
5	19.4	**Jefferson** (village) Ashtabula County
5	19.4	**Summerside** (CDP) Clermont County
7	19.2	**Nelsonville** (city) Athens County
8	18.3	**Richmond Heights** (city) Cuyahoga County
9	17.1	**Lincoln Village** (CDP) Franklin County
10	16.4	**Wyoming** (city) Hamilton County
11	16.3	**Salem Heights** (CDP) Hamilton County
12	14.9	**East Cleveland** (city) Cuyahoga County
13	14.8	**Beachwood** (city) Cuyahoga County
14	14.6	**Bedford Heights** (city) Cuyahoga County
15	14.0	**Madison** (village) Lake County
16	13.7	**Austintown** (CDP) Mahoning County
16	13.7	**New Franklin** (city) Summit County
16	13.7	**Silverton** (village) Hamilton County
19	13.6	**Bedford** (city) Cuyahoga County
20	13.5	**Moraine** (city) Montgomery County
21	13.1	**Euclid** (city) Cuyahoga County
21	13.1	**Tiffin** (city) Seneca County
23	12.9	**West Milton** (village) Miami County
24	12.7	**Port Clinton** (city) Ottawa County
25	12.5	**White Oak** (CDP) Hamilton County
26	12.4	**Lincoln Heights** (village) Hamilton County
26	12.4	**Mingo Junction** (village) Jefferson County
26	12.4	**Willard** (city) Huron County
29	12.3	**Steubenville** (city) Jefferson County
30	12.2	**Belpre** (city) Washington County
30	12.2	**Ironton** (city) Lawrence County
32	11.8	**Johnstown** (village) Licking County
33	11.6	**Versailles** (village) Darke County
33	11.6	**Warrensville Heights** (city) Cuyahoga County
35	11.4	**Mayfield Heights** (city) Cuyahoga County
36	11.3	**Fremont** (city) Sandusky County
36	11.3	**Mariemont** (village) Hamilton County
36	11.3	**Powell** (city) Delaware County
39	11.2	**Harrison** (city) Hamilton County
40	11.1	**Jackson** (city) Jackson County
41	11.0	**Lakemore** (village) Summit County
41	11.0	**Mount Healthy Heights** (CDP) Hamilton County
41	11.0	**Sebring** (village) Mahoning County
44	10.9	**Wheelersburg** (CDP) Scioto County
45	10.8	**Kenton** (city) Hardin County
45	10.8	**Ottawa Hills** (village) Lucas County
47	10.7	**Bellevue** (city) Sandusky County
47	10.7	**Cambridge** (city) Guernsey County
47	10.7	**Paulding** (village) Paulding County
50	10.5	**Shadyside** (village) Belmont County
51	10.4	**Waterville** (city) Lucas County
52	10.3	**Circleville** (city) Pickaway County
53	10.0	**Norwalk** (city) Huron County
54	9.9	**Portage Lakes** (CDP) Summit County
55	9.8	**Uniontown** (CDP) Stark County
55	9.8	**University Heights** (city) Cuyahoga County
57	9.7	**Lisbon** (village) Columbiana County
57	9.7	**Newtown** (village) Hamilton County
59	9.6	**Englewood** (city) Montgomery County
59	9.6	**Wadsworth** (city) Medina County
61	9.5	**Sandusky** (city) Erie County
62	9.4	**Avon** (city) Lorain County
62	9.4	**Taylor Creek** (CDP) Hamilton County
62	9.4	**Zanesville** (city) Muskingum County
65	9.2	**Carlisle** (village) Warren County
65	9.2	**Grandview Heights** (city) Franklin County
65	9.2	**West Portsmouth** (CDP) Scioto County
68	9.1	**Burlington** (CDP) Lawrence County
69	9.0	**Cleveland Heights** (city) Cuyahoga County
69	9.0	**Forest Park** (city) Hamilton County
69	9.0	**Westlake** (city) Cuyahoga County
69	9.0	**Willoughby Hills** (city) Lake County
69	9.0	**Wintersville** (village) Jefferson County
74	8.9	**West Carrollton** (city) Montgomery County
75	8.8	**Garfield Heights** (city) Cuyahoga County
75	8.8	**Shaker Heights** (city) Cuyahoga County
77	8.7	**Cleves** (village) Hamilton County
77	8.7	**Green Meadows** (CDP) Clark County
77	8.7	**North Canton** (city) Stark County
80	8.6	**Amelia** (village) Clermont County
80	8.6	**Coshocton** (city) Coshocton County
80	8.6	**Lyndhurst** (city) Cuyahoga County
80	8.6	**Oak Harbor** (village) Ottawa County
84	8.4	**Mentor** (city) Lake County
85	8.3	**Clyde** (city) Sandusky County
85	8.3	**Lorain** (city) Lorain County
87	8.2	**Ada** (village) Hardin County
87	8.2	**Blanchester** (village) Clinton County
87	8.2	**Hillsboro** (city) Highland County
87	8.2	**Portsmouth** (city) Scioto County
91	8.1	**Golf Manor** (village) Hamilton County
91	8.1	**Saint Bernard** (city) Hamilton County
91	8.1	**Waverly** (village) Pike County
94	8.0	**Clayton** (city) Montgomery County
94	8.0	**Dayton** (city) Montgomery County
96	7.9	**Barberton** (city) Summit County
96	7.9	**Brookville** (city) Montgomery County
96	7.9	**Canton** (city) Stark County
96	7.9	**Carrollton** (village) Carroll County
96	7.9	**Centerville** (city) Montgomery County
96	7.9	**Cheviot** (city) Hamilton County
96	7.9	**Seville** (village) Medina County
96	7.9	**Toledo** (city) Lucas County
96	7.9	**Woodlawn** (village) Hamilton County
105	7.8	**Akron** (city) Summit County
105	7.8	**Ashtabula** (city) Ashtabula County
105	7.8	**Calcutta** (CDP) Columbiana County
105	7.8	**Celina** (city) Mercer County
109	7.7	**Delta** (village) Fulton County
109	7.7	**Girard** (city) Trumbull County
109	7.7	**Lexington** (village) Richland County
112	7.6	**Ashville** (village) Pickaway County
112	7.6	**Reading** (city) Hamilton County
112	7.6	**Saint Marys** (city) Auglaize County
112	7.6	**Warren** (city) Trumbull County
116	7.5	**Cincinnati** (city) Hamilton County
116	7.5	**Middletown** (city) Butler County
118	7.4	**Conneaut** (city) Ashtabula County
118	7.4	**New London** (village) Huron County
118	7.4	**Newcomerstown** (village) Tuscarawas County
121	7.3	**Cuyahoga Falls** (city) Summit County
121	7.3	**Maple Heights** (city) Cuyahoga County
121	7.3	**Whitehouse** (village) Lucas County
124	7.2	**Berea** (city) Cuyahoga County
124	7.2	**Bethel** (village) Clermont County
124	7.2	**Delphos** (city) Allen County
124	7.2	**Norton** (city) Summit County
124	7.2	**Upper Arlington** (city) Franklin County
129	7.1	**Columbiana** (city) Columbiana County
129	7.1	**Crestline** (village) Crawford County
129	7.1	**Lima** (city) Allen County
129	7.1	**Salem** (city) Columbiana County
133	7.0	**Barnesville** (village) Belmont County
133	7.0	**Lockland** (village) Hamilton County
133	7.0	**The Plains** (CDP) Athens County
136	6.9	**Cleveland** (city) Cuyahoga County
136	6.9	**Greenville** (city) Darke County
136	6.9	**Hamilton** (city) Butler County
136	6.9	**Miamisburg** (city) Montgomery County
140	6.8	**Buckeye Lake** (village) Licking County
140	6.8	**Cadiz** (village) Harrison County
140	6.8	**Dover** (city) Tuscarawas County
140	6.8	**Fairfield** (city) Butler County
140	6.8	**Oxford** (city) Butler County
145	6.7	**Streetsboro** (city) Portage County
145	6.7	**Van Wert** (city) Van Wert County
147	6.6	**Athens** (city) Athens County
147	6.6	**Chillicothe** (city) Ross County
147	6.6	**Minster** (village) Auglaize County
147	6.6	**New Lebanon** (village) Montgomery County

Note: *This section ranks incorporated places and CDPs (Census Designated Places) with populations of 2,500 or more. Unincorporated postal areas were not considered. Please refer to the User Guide for additional information.*

Population with Health Insurance

Top 150 Places Ranked in *Descending* Order

State Rank	Percent	Place
1	99.6	**Powell** (city) Delaware County
2	98.9	**Independence** (city) Cuyahoga County
2	98.9	**The Village of Indian Hill** (city) Hamilton County
4	98.8	**Beachwood** (city) Cuyahoga County
5	98.7	**Pepper Pike** (city) Cuyahoga County
6	98.6	**Turpin Hills** (CDP) Hamilton County
7	98.5	**Four Bridges** (CDP) Butler County
8	98.4	**Day Heights** (CDP) Clermont County
8	98.4	**Mariemont** (village) Hamilton County
8	98.4	**Minster** (village) Auglaize County
8	98.4	**Whitehouse** (village) Lucas County
12	98.3	**Evendale** (village) Hamilton County
12	98.3	**Kirtland** (city) Lake County
12	98.3	**Montgomery** (city) Hamilton County
12	98.3	**Mulberry** (CDP) Clermont County
16	98.2	**Delta** (village) Fulton County
16	98.2	**Dry Run** (CDP) Hamilton County
16	98.2	**Seven Hills** (city) Cuyahoga County
19	98.0	**New Albany** (city) Franklin County
19	98.0	**New Bremen** (village) Auglaize County
19	98.0	**Springboro** (city) Warren County
22	97.9	**Dublin** (city) Franklin County
22	97.9	**Miami Heights** (CDP) Hamilton County
22	97.9	**Orange** (village) Cuyahoga County
22	97.9	**Wyoming** (city) Hamilton County
26	97.8	**Avon** (city) Lorain County
26	97.8	**Chagrin Falls** (village) Cuyahoga County
28	97.7	**Dent** (CDP) Hamilton County
28	97.7	**Mayfield** (village) Cuyahoga County
30	97.6	**Greentown** (CDP) Stark County
31	97.5	**Bay Village** (city) Cuyahoga County
31	97.5	**Ottawa Hills** (village) Lucas County
31	97.5	**Poland** (village) Mahoning County
31	97.5	**Solon** (city) Cuyahoga County
35	97.4	**Brookville** (city) Montgomery County
35	97.4	**Devola** (CDP) Washington County
35	97.4	**Montrose-Ghent** (CDP) Summit County
35	97.4	**South Russell** (village) Geauga County
39	97.3	**Avon Lake** (city) Lorain County
39	97.3	**Brecksville** (city) Cuyahoga County
39	97.3	**Hudson** (city) Summit County
39	97.3	**Summerside** (CDP) Clermont County
43	97.2	**Beechwood Trails** (CDP) Licking County
43	97.2	**Bexley** (city) Franklin County
43	97.2	**Highland Heights** (city) Cuyahoga County
43	97.2	**Macedonia** (city) Summit County
47	97.1	**Worthington** (city) Franklin County
48	97.0	**Canal Winchester** (city) Franklin County
48	97.0	**Landen** (CDP) Warren County
48	97.0	**Madeira** (city) Hamilton County
48	97.0	**Seville** (village) Medina County
52	96.9	**Cherry Grove** (CDP) Hamilton County
52	96.9	**Pickerington** (city) Fairfield County
52	96.9	**Saint Henry** (village) Mercer County
52	96.9	**Sunbury** (village) Delaware County
56	96.8	**Oakwood** (city) Montgomery County
56	96.8	**Reminderville** (village) Summit County
56	96.8	**Upper Arlington** (city) Franklin County
59	96.7	**Apple Valley** (CDP) Knox County
59	96.7	**Chardon** (city) Geauga County
59	96.7	**Granville** (village) Licking County
59	96.7	**Mack** (CDP) Hamilton County
59	96.7	**Mason** (city) Warren County
59	96.7	**McDonald** (village) Trumbull County
59	96.7	**Twinsburg** (city) Summit County
66	96.6	**Beavercreek** (city) Greene County
66	96.6	**Columbiana** (city) Columbiana County
68	96.5	**Amberley** (village) Hamilton County
68	96.5	**Centerville** (city) Montgomery County
68	96.5	**Shaker Heights** (city) Cuyahoga County
71	96.4	**Moreland Hills** (village) Cuyahoga County
71	96.4	**Richfield** (village) Summit County
73	96.3	**Bellbrook** (city) Greene County
73	96.3	**Forestville** (CDP) Hamilton County
73	96.3	**Mogadore** (village) Summit County
73	96.3	**Perrysburg** (city) Wood County
73	96.3	**Strongsville** (city) Cuyahoga County
78	96.2	**Canfield** (city) Mahoning County
78	96.2	**Stow** (city) Summit County
78	96.2	**Sylvania** (city) Lucas County
81	96.1	**Bainbridge** (CDP) Geauga County
81	96.1	**Lyndhurst** (city) Cuyahoga County
83	96.0	**Aurora** (city) Portage County
83	96.0	**Doylestown** (village) Wayne County
83	96.0	**Garrettsville** (village) Portage County
83	96.0	**Grafton** (village) Lorain County
83	96.0	**Westlake** (city) Cuyahoga County
88	95.9	**Baltimore** (village) Fairfield County
88	95.9	**Beckett Ridge** (CDP) Butler County
88	95.9	**Blue Ash** (city) Hamilton County
88	95.9	**Covedale** (CDP) Hamilton County
88	95.9	**Mount Repose** (CDP) Clermont County
88	95.9	**University Heights** (city) Cuyahoga County
88	95.9	**Waterville** (city) Lucas County
95	95.8	**Clyde** (city) Sandusky County
95	95.8	**Mentor** (city) Lake County
95	95.8	**Middleburg Heights** (city) Cuyahoga County
98	95.7	**Lake Lakengren** (CDP) Preble County
98	95.7	**The Plains** (CDP) Athens County
100	95.6	**Champion Heights** (CDP) Trumbull County
100	95.6	**Harrison** (city) Hamilton County
100	95.6	**Oxford** (city) Butler County
100	95.6	**Rossford** (city) Wood County
100	95.6	**Versailles** (village) Darke County
105	95.5	**Monfort Heights** (CDP) Hamilton County
105	95.5	**North Kingsville** (village) Ashtabula County
105	95.5	**North Ridgeville** (city) Lorain County
105	95.5	**Tallmadge** (city) Summit County
105	95.5	**Union** (city) Montgomery County
105	95.5	**Westerville** (city) Franklin County
111	95.4	**Lakemore** (village) Summit County
111	95.4	**Pleasant Run Farm** (CDP) Hamilton County
111	95.4	**Sherwood** (CDP) Hamilton County
111	95.4	**Strasburg** (village) Tuscarawas County
115	95.3	**Fairlawn** (city) Summit County
115	95.3	**Maumee** (city) Lucas County
117	95.2	**New Franklin** (city) Summit County
117	95.2	**North Zanesville** (CDP) Muskingum County
119	95.1	**Grandview Heights** (city) Franklin County
119	95.1	**North Canton** (city) Stark County
119	95.1	**Northridge** (CDP) Clark County
122	95.0	**Athens** (city) Athens County
122	95.0	**Rocky River** (city) Cuyahoga County
124	94.9	**Archbold** (village) Fulton County
124	94.9	**Ross** (CDP) Butler County
124	94.9	**Wickliffe** (city) Lake County
127	94.8	**Bridgetown** (CDP) Hamilton County
127	94.8	**Clayton** (city) Montgomery County
127	94.8	**Crestline** (village) Crawford County
127	94.8	**Middlefield** (village) Geauga County
127	94.8	**Oberlin** (city) Lorain County
127	94.8	**Sixteen Mile Stand** (CDP) Hamilton County
133	94.7	**Gahanna** (city) Franklin County
133	94.7	**Monroe** (city) Butler County
133	94.7	**Swanton** (village) Fulton County
133	94.7	**Wintersville** (village) Jefferson County
137	94.6	**Ballville** (CDP) Sandusky County
137	94.6	**Enon** (village) Clark County
137	94.6	**Fruit Hill** (CDP) Hamilton County
137	94.6	**Hilliard** (city) Franklin County
141	94.5	**Green** (city) Summit County
141	94.5	**Huron** (city) Erie County
141	94.5	**Olmsted Falls** (city) Cuyahoga County
141	94.5	**Uniontown** (CDP) Stark County
145	94.4	**Bowling Green** (city) Wood County
145	94.4	**Coshocton** (city) Coshocton County
147	94.3	**Berea** (city) Cuyahoga County
147	94.3	**Brunswick** (city) Medina County
147	94.3	**Calcutta** (CDP) Columbiana County
150	94.2	**Amherst** (city) Lorain County

Note: *This section ranks incorporated places and CDPs (Census Designated Places) with populations of 2,500 or more. Unincorporated postal areas were not considered. Please refer to the User Guide for additional information.*

Population with Health Insurance

Top 150 Places Ranked in *Ascending* Order

State Rank	Percent	Place
1	80.9	**Mount Orab** (village) Brown County
2	81.3	**New Carlisle** (city) Clark County
3	83.4	**Blacklick Estates** (CDP) Franklin County
4	84.1	**Whitehall** (city) Franklin County
5	84.2	**Lockland** (village) Hamilton County
6	84.8	**Lincoln Village** (CDP) Franklin County
7	85.2	**Lincoln Heights** (village) Hamilton County
8	86.2	**Fredericktown** (village) Knox County
9	86.3	**New Lexington** (village) Perry County
10	86.4	**Lima** (city) Allen County
11	86.7	**Crooksville** (village) Perry County
12	86.8	**Millersburg** (village) Holmes County
13	87.0	**Niles** (city) Trumbull County
13	87.0	**North College Hill** (city) Hamilton County
15	87.1	**Dayton** (city) Montgomery County
16	87.3	**Painesville** (city) Lake County
16	87.3	**Salem** (city) Columbiana County
18	87.4	**Barberton** (city) Summit County
18	87.4	**Buckeye Lake** (village) Licking County
20	87.5	**Bellaire** (village) Belmont County
21	87.6	**Ironton** (city) Lawrence County
22	87.7	**Portsmouth** (city) Scioto County
23	87.8	**Cleveland** (city) Cuyahoga County
23	87.8	**Williamsburg** (village) Clermont County
25	87.9	**Akron** (city) Summit County
25	87.9	**Delshire** (CDP) Hamilton County
25	87.9	**Fairport Harbor** (village) Lake County
25	87.9	**Logan** (city) Hocking County
29	88.0	**Wellsville** (village) Columbiana County
30	88.1	**Columbus** (city) Franklin County
30	88.1	**Springdale** (city) Hamilton County
32	88.2	**Milford** (city) Clermont County
32	88.2	**Norwood** (city) Hamilton County
32	88.2	**Oak Harbor** (village) Ottawa County
35	88.3	**Lexington** (village) Richland County
35	88.3	**West Jefferson** (village) Madison County
37	88.4	**Blanchester** (village) Clinton County
37	88.4	**East Cleveland** (city) Cuyahoga County
37	88.4	**Sharonville** (city) Hamilton County
40	88.5	**Bethel** (village) Clermont County
40	88.5	**East Liverpool** (city) Columbiana County
40	88.5	**Middletown** (city) Butler County
43	88.6	**Hamilton** (city) Butler County
43	88.6	**Oakwood** (village) Cuyahoga County
45	88.7	**Fairfield** (city) Butler County
45	88.7	**Kenton** (city) Hardin County
45	88.7	**Shadyside** (village) Belmont County
48	88.8	**Lordstown** (village) Trumbull County
48	88.8	**Northgate** (CDP) Hamilton County
48	88.8	**Riverside** (city) Montgomery County
51	88.9	**Canton** (city) Stark County
51	88.9	**Dennison** (village) Tuscarawas County
51	88.9	**Hillsboro** (city) Highland County
51	88.9	**Mansfield** (city) Richland County
55	89.0	**Moraine** (city) Montgomery County
56	89.1	**Cincinnati** (city) Hamilton County
56	89.1	**Nelsonville** (city) Athens County
56	89.1	**New Richmond** (village) Clermont County
56	89.1	**Obetz** (village) Franklin County
56	89.1	**West Union** (village) Adams County
56	89.1	**Youngstown** (city) Mahoning County
62	89.2	**London** (city) Madison County
62	89.2	**Napoleon** (city) Henry County
62	89.2	**Newton Falls** (village) Trumbull County
62	89.2	**Perry Heights** (CDP) Stark County
66	89.3	**Hicksville** (village) Defiance County
67	89.4	**Chillicothe** (city) Ross County
67	89.4	**Delphos** (city) Allen County
67	89.4	**Fairborn** (city) Greene County
67	89.4	**New Philadelphia** (city) Tuscarawas County
67	89.4	**Sandusky** (city) Erie County
72	89.5	**Bedford Heights** (city) Cuyahoga County
72	89.5	**Greenfield** (village) Highland County
72	89.5	**Kent** (city) Portage County
72	89.5	**Washington Court House** (city) Fayette County
76	89.6	**Circleville** (city) Pickaway County
76	89.6	**Covington** (village) Miami County
76	89.6	**New London** (village) Huron County
76	89.6	**Toledo** (city) Lucas County
80	89.7	**Forest Park** (city) Hamilton County
80	89.7	**Marion** (city) Marion County
80	89.7	**Newcomerstown** (village) Tuscarawas County
80	89.7	**West Carrollton** (city) Montgomery County
84	89.8	**Ashtabula** (city) Ashtabula County
84	89.8	**Euclid** (city) Cuyahoga County
84	89.8	**Newark** (city) Licking County
84	89.8	**Struthers** (city) Mahoning County
88	89.9	**Carlisle** (village) Warren County
88	89.9	**Dover** (city) Tuscarawas County
88	89.9	**Minerva** (village) Stark County
88	89.9	**Paulding** (village) Paulding County
88	89.9	**Toronto** (city) Jefferson County
93	90.0	**Alliance** (city) Stark County
93	90.0	**Burlington** (CDP) Lawrence County
93	90.0	**Northbrook** (CDP) Hamilton County
93	90.0	**Piqua** (city) Miami County
93	90.0	**Trotwood** (city) Montgomery County
98	90.1	**Bucyrus** (city) Crawford County
98	90.1	**Galion** (city) Crawford County
98	90.1	**Huber Heights** (city) Montgomery County
98	90.1	**Lorain** (city) Lorain County
98	90.1	**Marietta** (city) Washington County
98	90.1	**Mentor-on-the-Lake** (city) Lake County
98	90.1	**Warren** (city) Trumbull County
105	90.2	**Green Meadows** (CDP) Clark County
105	90.2	**Greenhills** (village) Hamilton County
105	90.2	**Uhrichsville** (city) Tuscarawas County
108	90.3	**Barnesville** (village) Belmont County
108	90.3	**Bellefontaine** (city) Logan County
108	90.3	**Lebanon** (city) Warren County
108	90.3	**Lisbon** (village) Columbiana County
108	90.3	**Van Wert** (city) Van Wert County
113	90.4	**Elyria** (city) Lorain County
113	90.4	**Lakewood** (city) Cuyahoga County
113	90.4	**Lodi** (village) Medina County
113	90.4	**Loudonville** (village) Ashland County
113	90.4	**Northfield** (village) Summit County
113	90.4	**Park Layne** (CDP) Clark County
113	90.4	**Reading** (city) Hamilton County
120	90.5	**Findlay** (city) Hancock County
120	90.5	**Sebring** (village) Mahoning County
120	90.5	**Springfield** (city) Clark County
123	90.6	**Garfield Heights** (city) Cuyahoga County
123	90.6	**North Baltimore** (village) Wood County
125	90.7	**Edgewood** (CDP) Ashtabula County
125	90.7	**Fostoria** (city) Seneca County
125	90.7	**Georgetown** (village) Brown County
125	90.7	**Saint Bernard** (city) Hamilton County
125	90.7	**Saint Clairsville** (city) Belmont County
125	90.7	**West Portsmouth** (CDP) Scioto County
125	90.7	**Zanesville** (city) Muskingum County
132	90.8	**Jefferson** (village) Ashtabula County
132	90.8	**Lake Darby** (CDP) Franklin County
132	90.8	**Martins Ferry** (city) Belmont County
132	90.8	**Mingo Junction** (village) Jefferson County
136	90.9	**Belpre** (city) Washington County
136	90.9	**Cheviot** (city) Hamilton County
136	90.9	**Cleves** (village) Hamilton County
136	90.9	**Newtown** (village) Hamilton County
136	90.9	**Ottawa** (village) Putnam County
141	91.0	**Celina** (city) Mercer County
141	91.0	**Cortland** (city) Trumbull County
141	91.0	**Fremont** (city) Sandusky County
141	91.0	**New Concord** (village) Muskingum County
141	91.0	**Pataskala** (city) Licking County
141	91.0	**South Point** (village) Lawrence County
141	91.0	**Wellston** (city) Jackson County
148	91.1	**Girard** (city) Trumbull County
148	91.1	**Silverton** (village) Hamilton County
150	91.2	**Geneva** (city) Ashtabula County

Note: *This section ranks incorporated places and CDPs (Census Designated Places) with populations of 2,500 or more. Unincorporated postal areas were not considered. Please refer to the User Guide for additional information.*

Population with Private Health Insurance

Top 150 Places Ranked in *Descending* Order

State Rank	Percent	Place
1	95.9	**Powell** (city) Delaware County
2	93.8	**Dry Run** (CDP) Hamilton County
3	93.5	**Dublin** (city) Franklin County
4	93.3	**Greentown** (CDP) Stark County
5	92.8	**New Albany** (city) Franklin County
6	92.6	**Hudson** (city) Summit County
7	92.4	**South Russell** (village) Geauga County
8	92.1	**Four Bridges** (CDP) Butler County
9	91.8	**Pepper Pike** (city) Cuyahoga County
10	91.3	**Bainbridge** (CDP) Geauga County
11	91.1	**Ottawa Hills** (village) Lucas County
12	90.9	**Granville** (village) Licking County
12	90.9	**Saint Henry** (village) Mercer County
14	90.8	**Grandview Heights** (city) Franklin County
15	90.5	**The Village of Indian Hill** (city) Hamilton County
16	90.1	**Kirtland** (city) Lake County
17	90.0	**Montgomery** (city) Hamilton County
18	89.7	**Bexley** (city) Franklin County
19	89.6	**Avon** (city) Lorain County
20	89.5	**New Bremen** (village) Auglaize County
20	89.5	**Sixteen Mile Stand** (CDP) Hamilton County
22	89.4	**Mason** (city) Warren County
23	89.2	**Chagrin Falls** (village) Cuyahoga County
23	89.2	**Evendale** (village) Hamilton County
23	89.2	**Independence** (city) Cuyahoga County
23	89.2	**Oxford** (city) Butler County
27	89.0	**Turpin Hills** (CDP) Hamilton County
28	88.9	**Worthington** (city) Franklin County
29	88.8	**Springboro** (city) Warren County
29	88.8	**Wright-Patterson AFB** (CDP) Greene County
31	88.5	**Oakwood** (city) Montgomery County
32	88.4	**Bay Village** (city) Cuyahoga County
32	88.4	**Devola** (CDP) Washington County
32	88.4	**Upper Arlington** (city) Franklin County
35	88.2	**Perrysburg** (city) Wood County
36	88.1	**Madeira** (city) Hamilton County
36	88.1	**Moreland Hills** (village) Cuyahoga County
36	88.1	**Seville** (village) Medina County
39	88.0	**Beavercreek** (city) Greene County
40	87.9	**Brecksville** (city) Cuyahoga County
40	87.9	**Macedonia** (city) Summit County
42	87.8	**Beachwood** (city) Cuyahoga County
43	87.7	**Avon Lake** (city) Lorain County
43	87.7	**Mariemont** (village) Hamilton County
43	87.7	**Minster** (village) Auglaize County
46	87.4	**Richfield** (village) Summit County
46	87.4	**Waterville** (city) Lucas County
48	87.1	**Landen** (CDP) Warren County
49	87.0	**Highland Heights** (city) Cuyahoga County
50	86.9	**Seven Hills** (city) Cuyahoga County
50	86.9	**Solon** (city) Cuyahoga County
52	86.6	**Mack** (CDP) Hamilton County
53	86.5	**Beckett Ridge** (CDP) Butler County
54	86.4	**Day Heights** (CDP) Clermont County
55	86.2	**Canal Winchester** (city) Franklin County
56	86.1	**Miami Heights** (CDP) Hamilton County
56	86.1	**Mogadore** (village) Summit County
56	86.1	**Reminderville** (village) Summit County
59	86.0	**Athens** (city) Athens County
59	86.0	**Beechwood Trails** (CDP) Licking County
59	86.0	**Pickerington** (city) Fairfield County
59	86.0	**Twinsburg** (city) Summit County
63	85.7	**Cherry Grove** (CDP) Hamilton County
63	85.7	**Dent** (CDP) Hamilton County
63	85.7	**Ross** (CDP) Butler County
63	85.7	**Rossford** (city) Wood County
67	85.5	**Westerville** (city) Franklin County
67	85.5	**Wyoming** (city) Hamilton County
69	85.0	**Aurora** (city) Portage County
69	85.0	**Sherwood** (CDP) Hamilton County
71	84.8	**Canfield** (city) Mahoning County
71	84.8	**Poland** (village) Mahoning County
73	84.7	**Hilliard** (city) Franklin County
73	84.7	**Rocky River** (city) Cuyahoga County
75	84.5	**Bluffton** (village) Allen County
75	84.5	**Strongsville** (city) Cuyahoga County
77	84.4	**Bellbrook** (city) Greene County
77	84.4	**Blue Ash** (city) Hamilton County
77	84.4	**Stow** (city) Summit County
80	84.3	**Mayfield** (village) Cuyahoga County
81	84.2	**Harrison** (city) Hamilton County
81	84.2	**Sunbury** (village) Delaware County
83	84.1	**Mentor** (city) Lake County
83	84.1	**Orange** (village) Cuyahoga County
85	84.0	**Bowling Green** (city) Wood County
86	83.8	**Lake Lakengren** (CDP) Preble County
86	83.8	**Montrose-Ghent** (CDP) Summit County
88	83.4	**Sylvania** (city) Lucas County
89	83.3	**Amberley** (village) Hamilton County
89	83.3	**Cedarville** (village) Greene County
89	83.3	**New Franklin** (city) Summit County
89	83.3	**Swanton** (village) Fulton County
93	83.2	**Lyndhurst** (city) Cuyahoga County
93	83.2	**North Canton** (city) Stark County
95	83.1	**Broadview Heights** (city) Cuyahoga County
95	83.1	**Monroe** (city) Butler County
95	83.1	**North Ridgeville** (city) Lorain County
95	83.1	**Westlake** (city) Cuyahoga County
99	82.8	**Northridge** (CDP) Clark County
99	82.8	**Salem Heights** (CDP) Hamilton County
101	82.7	**Mount Repose** (CDP) Clermont County
102	82.6	**Maumee** (city) Lucas County
102	82.6	**Shaker Heights** (city) Cuyahoga County
102	82.6	**Willoughby Hills** (city) Lake County
105	82.5	**Forestville** (CDP) Hamilton County
105	82.5	**Uniontown** (CDP) Stark County
107	82.0	**Clyde** (city) Sandusky County
108	81.9	**North Zanesville** (CDP) Muskingum County
108	81.9	**Sheffield** (village) Lorain County
110	81.7	**Coldwater** (village) Mercer County
110	81.7	**Fairlawn** (city) Summit County
112	81.6	**Carey** (village) Wyandot County
112	81.6	**Gahanna** (city) Franklin County
112	81.6	**University Heights** (city) Cuyahoga County
115	81.5	**Ballville** (CDP) Sandusky County
116	81.4	**Berea** (city) Cuyahoga County
117	81.3	**Brookville** (city) Montgomery County
118	81.0	**Ashville** (village) Pickaway County
118	81.0	**Middleburg Heights** (city) Cuyahoga County
120	80.9	**Mulberry** (CDP) Clermont County
120	80.9	**Olmsted Falls** (city) Cuyahoga County
122	80.8	**Centerville** (city) Montgomery County
123	80.7	**Doylestown** (village) Wayne County
123	80.7	**Grove City** (city) Franklin County
123	80.7	**Kenwood** (CDP) Hamilton County
126	80.6	**Monfort Heights** (CDP) Hamilton County
127	80.5	**Brunswick** (city) Medina County
128	80.3	**Dry Ridge** (CDP) Hamilton County
129	80.2	**Delhi Hills** (CDP) Hamilton County
129	80.2	**Oberlin** (city) Lorain County
131	80.1	**Saint Clairsville** (city) Belmont County
132	80.0	**Amherst** (city) Lorain County
132	80.0	**Canal Fulton** (city) Stark County
132	80.0	**Clayton** (city) Montgomery County
132	80.0	**New Concord** (village) Muskingum County
136	79.9	**Versailles** (village) Darke County
137	79.8	**Marysville** (city) Union County
138	79.6	**North Kingsville** (village) Ashtabula County
138	79.6	**Ontario** (city) Richland County
140	79.5	**Tipp City** (city) Miami County
141	79.4	**Green** (city) Summit County
142	79.2	**North Royalton** (city) Cuyahoga County
143	79.1	**Chardon** (city) Geauga County
144	79.0	**Garrettsville** (village) Portage County
144	79.0	**Portage Lakes** (CDP) Summit County
146	78.9	**Pleasant Run** (CDP) Hamilton County
146	78.9	**Wickliffe** (city) Lake County
148	78.6	**Bridgetown** (CDP) Hamilton County
149	78.4	**Whitehouse** (village) Lucas County
149	78.4	**Willoughby** (city) Lake County

Note: *This section ranks incorporated places and CDPs (Census Designated Places) with populations of 2,500 or more. Unincorporated postal areas were not considered. Please refer to the User Guide for additional information.*

Population with Private Health Insurance

Top 150 Places Ranked in *Ascending* Order

State Rank	Percent	Place
1	34.8	**East Cleveland** (city) Cuyahoga County
2	34.9	**Lincoln Heights** (village) Hamilton County
3	40.0	**Youngstown** (city) Mahoning County
4	41.4	**Greenfield** (village) Highland County
5	41.8	**Lockland** (village) Hamilton County
6	43.1	**Cleveland** (city) Cuyahoga County
7	43.2	**Portsmouth** (city) Scioto County
8	44.7	**Campbell** (city) Mahoning County
9	44.8	**Zanesville** (city) Muskingum County
10	45.5	**Buckeye Lake** (village) Licking County
11	45.7	**Ashtabula** (city) Ashtabula County
12	45.9	**Warren** (city) Trumbull County
13	46.3	**Whitehall** (city) Franklin County
14	47.0	**Wellsville** (village) Columbiana County
14	47.0	**West Union** (village) Adams County
16	47.9	**The Plains** (CDP) Athens County
17	48.1	**Uhrichsville** (city) Tuscarawas County
18	48.3	**New Carlisle** (city) Clark County
19	49.0	**Dayton** (city) Montgomery County
20	49.6	**East Liverpool** (city) Columbiana County
21	49.8	**Canton** (city) Stark County
22	49.9	**Georgetown** (village) Brown County
23	51.3	**Nelsonville** (city) Athens County
24	51.7	**Middletown** (city) Butler County
25	51.8	**Bellaire** (village) Belmont County
26	51.9	**Cambridge** (city) Guernsey County
27	52.7	**Lorain** (city) Lorain County
28	53.0	**Lima** (city) Allen County
28	53.0	**Lisbon** (village) Columbiana County
30	53.1	**Springfield** (city) Clark County
31	53.2	**Hillsboro** (city) Highland County
32	53.4	**New Lexington** (village) Perry County
32	53.4	**Trotwood** (city) Montgomery County
34	53.6	**Dennison** (village) Tuscarawas County
35	54.2	**Ironton** (city) Lawrence County
36	54.3	**Marion** (city) Marion County
37	54.4	**Mansfield** (city) Richland County
37	54.4	**Washington Court House** (city) Fayette County
39	54.5	**Sandusky** (city) Erie County
40	55.0	**Mount Vernon** (city) Knox County
41	55.3	**Akron** (city) Summit County
41	55.3	**Blacklick Estates** (CDP) Franklin County
41	55.3	**Chillicothe** (city) Ross County
44	55.6	**Lodi** (village) Medina County
44	55.6	**West Portsmouth** (CDP) Scioto County
46	56.0	**Gallipolis** (village) Gallia County
46	56.0	**Moraine** (city) Montgomery County
48	56.1	**Logan** (city) Hocking County
48	56.1	**Williamsburg** (village) Clermont County
50	56.2	**Wellston** (city) Jackson County
51	56.7	**Northbrook** (CDP) Hamilton County
51	56.7	**Park Layne** (CDP) Clark County
51	56.7	**Warrensville Heights** (city) Cuyahoga County
54	56.8	**Bethel** (village) Clermont County
54	56.8	**Kenton** (city) Hardin County
56	56.9	**Painesville** (city) Lake County
56	56.9	**Toledo** (city) Lucas County
58	57.1	**Crooksville** (village) Perry County
58	57.1	**Newcomerstown** (village) Tuscarawas County
60	57.2	**North College Hill** (city) Hamilton County
61	57.3	**Hamilton** (city) Butler County
62	57.4	**Cincinnati** (city) Hamilton County
62	57.4	**New London** (village) Huron County
64	57.5	**Lincoln Village** (CDP) Franklin County
64	57.5	**Mount Orab** (village) Brown County
66	57.7	**Barberton** (city) Summit County
67	57.9	**Maple Heights** (city) Cuyahoga County
67	57.9	**Salem** (city) Columbiana County
69	58.2	**Martins Ferry** (city) Belmont County
69	58.2	**New Lebanon** (village) Montgomery County
71	58.3	**Struthers** (city) Mahoning County
72	58.6	**Golf Manor** (village) Hamilton County
73	58.7	**Fairport Harbor** (village) Lake County
74	58.8	**Newark** (city) Licking County
75	58.9	**Fostoria** (city) Seneca County
76	59.3	**Xenia** (city) Greene County
77	59.5	**Lancaster** (city) Fairfield County
77	59.5	**Obetz** (village) Franklin County
79	59.7	**Marietta** (city) Washington County
80	59.8	**Niles** (city) Trumbull County
81	59.9	**Blanchester** (village) Clinton County
81	59.9	**Jefferson** (village) Ashtabula County
83	60.0	**Ravenna** (city) Portage County
83	60.0	**Springdale** (city) Hamilton County
85	60.1	**Alliance** (city) Stark County
86	60.4	**Montpelier** (village) Williams County
87	60.7	**Steubenville** (city) Jefferson County
87	60.7	**Toronto** (city) Jefferson County
89	60.8	**Mount Healthy** (city) Hamilton County
89	60.8	**New Burlington** (CDP) Hamilton County
91	60.9	**Greenville** (city) Darke County
91	60.9	**Sebring** (village) Mahoning County
93	61.0	**Circleville** (city) Pickaway County
94	61.2	**Galion** (city) Crawford County
95	61.3	**Eaton** (city) Preble County
95	61.3	**Euclid** (city) Cuyahoga County
97	61.4	**Fredericktown** (village) Knox County
98	61.5	**Crestline** (village) Crawford County
99	61.9	**Fremont** (city) Sandusky County
100	62.1	**Willard** (city) Huron County
101	62.3	**East Palestine** (village) Columbiana County
101	62.3	**Garfield Heights** (city) Cuyahoga County
101	62.3	**New Philadelphia** (city) Tuscarawas County
101	62.3	**West Carrollton** (city) Montgomery County
105	62.4	**Mount Gilead** (village) Morrow County
106	62.5	**Elyria** (city) Lorain County
107	62.8	**Mount Healthy Heights** (CDP) Hamilton County
108	62.9	**Piqua** (city) Miami County
109	63.0	**Van Wert** (city) Van Wert County
110	63.1	**Fairborn** (city) Greene County
110	63.1	**Norwood** (city) Hamilton County
110	63.1	**Wilmington** (city) Clinton County
113	63.2	**Bedford Heights** (city) Cuyahoga County
113	63.2	**Paulding** (village) Paulding County
115	63.3	**Amelia** (village) Clermont County
115	63.3	**Girard** (city) Trumbull County
115	63.3	**New Richmond** (village) Clermont County
115	63.3	**Riverside** (city) Montgomery County
119	63.5	**Baltimore** (village) Fairfield County
119	63.5	**Mingo Junction** (village) Jefferson County
121	63.6	**Bellefontaine** (city) Logan County
121	63.6	**Cheviot** (city) Hamilton County
123	63.7	**Columbus** (city) Franklin County
123	63.7	**Norwalk** (city) Huron County
125	63.8	**Delshire** (CDP) Hamilton County
125	63.8	**London** (city) Madison County
127	63.9	**Burlington** (CDP) Lawrence County
127	63.9	**Conneaut** (city) Ashtabula County
129	64.0	**Milford** (city) Clermont County
130	64.1	**Belpre** (city) Washington County
130	64.1	**Mentor-on-the-Lake** (city) Lake County
130	64.1	**Perry Heights** (CDP) Stark County
133	64.2	**Rittman** (city) Wayne County
134	64.4	**Newton Falls** (village) Trumbull County
135	64.7	**Franklin** (city) Warren County
135	64.7	**Lakemore** (village) Summit County
137	64.8	**Barnesville** (village) Belmont County
138	64.9	**Waverly** (village) Pike County
139	65.0	**Millersburg** (village) Holmes County
139	65.0	**Urbana** (city) Champaign County
141	65.1	**Coshocton** (city) Coshocton County
141	65.1	**Minerva** (village) Stark County
141	65.1	**Shelby** (city) Richland County
144	65.3	**Reading** (city) Hamilton County
145	65.5	**Bucyrus** (city) Crawford County
145	65.5	**Massillon** (city) Stark County
147	65.6	**Loudonville** (village) Ashland County
148	65.8	**Forest Park** (city) Hamilton County
149	66.7	**Saint Bernard** (city) Hamilton County
150	67.1	**Oakwood** (village) Cuyahoga County

Note: *This section ranks incorporated places and CDPs (Census Designated Places) with populations of 2,500 or more. Unincorporated postal areas were not considered. Please refer to the User Guide for additional information.*

Population with Public Health Insurance

Top 150 Places Ranked in *Descending* Order

State Rank	Percent	Place
1	66.5	**East Cleveland** (city) Cuyahoga County
2	61.9	**Lincoln Heights** (village) Hamilton County
3	60.7	**Youngstown** (city) Mahoning County
4	59.7	**Campbell** (city) Mahoning County
4	59.7	**Greenfield** (village) Highland County
6	59.2	**Zanesville** (city) Muskingum County
7	58.7	**The Plains** (CDP) Athens County
8	58.5	**West Union** (village) Adams County
9	56.7	**Ashtabula** (city) Ashtabula County
10	56.6	**Warren** (city) Trumbull County
11	56.0	**Portsmouth** (city) Scioto County
12	55.4	**Waverly** (village) Pike County
13	55.3	**Cambridge** (city) Guernsey County
14	54.4	**Wellsville** (village) Columbiana County
15	53.9	**Cleveland** (city) Cuyahoga County
16	53.6	**Lockland** (village) Hamilton County
17	52.8	**Uhrichsville** (city) Tuscarawas County
18	52.7	**Buckeye Lake** (village) Licking County
19	52.1	**Sebring** (village) Mahoning County
20	51.9	**Trotwood** (city) Montgomery County
21	51.6	**East Liverpool** (city) Columbiana County
22	51.3	**Springfield** (city) Clark County
23	50.7	**Canton** (city) Stark County
23	50.7	**Newcomerstown** (village) Tuscarawas County
25	50.6	**Chillicothe** (city) Ross County
25	50.6	**Lakemore** (village) Summit County
25	50.6	**Warrensville Heights** (city) Cuyahoga County
28	50.2	**Bellaire** (village) Belmont County
29	50.0	**Fostoria** (city) Seneca County
29	50.0	**Sandusky** (city) Erie County
31	49.9	**Mansfield** (city) Richland County
32	49.8	**Greenville** (city) Darke County
32	49.8	**Mount Vernon** (city) Knox County
34	49.7	**Marion** (city) Marion County
35	49.6	**Georgetown** (village) Brown County
36	49.5	**Hillsboro** (city) Highland County
37	49.3	**Gallipolis** (village) Gallia County
38	49.2	**Lorain** (city) Lorain County
39	48.9	**Dennison** (village) Tuscarawas County
39	48.9	**Middletown** (city) Butler County
41	48.6	**Dayton** (city) Montgomery County
41	48.6	**Nelsonville** (city) Athens County
41	48.6	**Ravenna** (city) Portage County
44	48.5	**Lisbon** (village) Columbiana County
45	48.3	**Washington Court House** (city) Fayette County
46	48.1	**Martins Ferry** (city) Belmont County
47	48.0	**Belpre** (city) Washington County
48	47.8	**Crestline** (village) Crawford County
48	47.8	**Ironton** (city) Lawrence County
50	47.7	**Crooksville** (village) Perry County
51	47.6	**New Lebanon** (village) Montgomery County
52	47.3	**Mount Gilead** (village) Morrow County
53	47.1	**Maple Heights** (city) Cuyahoga County
53	47.1	**New Burlington** (CDP) Hamilton County
55	46.9	**Eaton** (city) Preble County
56	46.8	**Steubenville** (city) Jefferson County
56	46.8	**Whitehall** (city) Franklin County
58	46.7	**Van Wert** (city) Van Wert County
59	46.6	**New Lexington** (village) Perry County
60	46.5	**Logan** (city) Hocking County
60	46.5	**Loudonville** (village) Ashland County
60	46.5	**West Portsmouth** (CDP) Scioto County
63	46.4	**Coshocton** (city) Coshocton County
64	46.3	**Lodi** (village) Medina County
65	46.2	**Lima** (city) Allen County
66	46.1	**Xenia** (city) Greene County
67	46.0	**Bethel** (village) Clermont County
68	45.7	**Golf Manor** (village) Hamilton County
69	45.3	**Huron** (city) Erie County
70	45.2	**Alliance** (city) Stark County
71	45.1	**Lancaster** (city) Fairfield County
72	45.0	**Baltimore** (village) Fairfield County
72	45.0	**Jackson** (city) Jackson County
72	45.0	**Kenton** (city) Hardin County
72	45.0	**Mingo Junction** (village) Jefferson County
76	44.9	**New Carlisle** (city) Clark County
76	44.9	**Willard** (city) Huron County
78	44.8	**Walbridge** (village) Wood County
79	44.6	**Toledo** (city) Lucas County
79	44.6	**Wellston** (city) Jackson County
79	44.6	**Wilmington** (city) Clinton County
82	44.5	**Bucyrus** (city) Crawford County
83	44.3	**Newark** (city) Licking County
83	44.3	**Urbana** (city) Champaign County
85	44.2	**Piqua** (city) Miami County
86	44.1	**Columbiana** (city) Columbiana County
86	44.1	**East Palestine** (village) Columbiana County
86	44.1	**Mount Healthy** (city) Hamilton County
89	43.7	**Circleville** (city) Pickaway County
89	43.7	**Galion** (city) Crawford County
89	43.7	**Norwalk** (city) Huron County
92	43.6	**Springdale** (city) Hamilton County
93	43.5	**Marietta** (city) Washington County
94	43.4	**Akron** (city) Summit County
94	43.4	**Massillon** (city) Stark County
96	43.3	**Toronto** (city) Jefferson County
97	43.2	**Struthers** (city) Mahoning County
98	43.1	**Jefferson** (village) Ashtabula County
98	43.1	**Northbrook** (CDP) Hamilton County
100	42.9	**Conneaut** (city) Ashtabula County
101	42.8	**Fremont** (city) Sandusky County
101	42.8	**Garfield Heights** (city) Cuyahoga County
101	42.8	**Williamsburg** (village) Clermont County
104	42.7	**Montpelier** (village) Williams County
105	42.6	**Hamilton** (city) Butler County
106	42.5	**Shelby** (city) Richland County
107	42.4	**West Carrollton** (city) Montgomery County
108	42.3	**Bedford Heights** (city) Cuyahoga County
109	42.1	**Dover** (city) Tuscarawas County
109	42.1	**Edgewood** (CDP) Ashtabula County
111	42.0	**Burlington** (CDP) Lawrence County
112	41.9	**Barberton** (city) Summit County
112	41.9	**Hartville** (village) Stark County
112	41.9	**New London** (village) Huron County
115	41.8	**Elyria** (city) Lorain County
115	41.8	**Niles** (city) Trumbull County
117	41.6	**Blanchester** (village) Clinton County
117	41.6	**Girard** (city) Trumbull County
117	41.6	**Salem** (city) Columbiana County
120	41.5	**Mount Healthy Heights** (CDP) Hamilton County
121	41.3	**Park Layne** (CDP) Clark County
121	41.3	**Rittman** (city) Wayne County
123	41.0	**Enon** (village) Clark County
123	41.0	**Hubbard** (city) Trumbull County
123	41.0	**Paulding** (village) Paulding County
126	40.8	**Euclid** (city) Cuyahoga County
127	40.7	**Defiance** (city) Defiance County
127	40.7	**Perry Heights** (CDP) Stark County
129	40.6	**Bellefontaine** (city) Logan County
130	40.5	**Bryan** (city) Williams County
131	40.1	**Minerva** (village) Stark County
132	39.9	**Newton Falls** (village) Trumbull County
132	39.9	**North College Hill** (city) Hamilton County
134	39.7	**Cincinnati** (city) Hamilton County
134	39.7	**Delta** (village) Fulton County
134	39.7	**Napoleon** (city) Henry County
137	39.6	**New Philadelphia** (city) Tuscarawas County
138	39.3	**Moraine** (city) Montgomery County
139	39.1	**Brooklyn** (city) Cuyahoga County
140	39.0	**Brookville** (city) Montgomery County
141	38.9	**Fairport Harbor** (village) Lake County
142	38.8	**Fairborn** (city) Greene County
142	38.8	**Fredericktown** (village) Knox County
142	38.8	**Mentor-on-the-Lake** (city) Lake County
145	38.7	**Austintown** (CDP) Mahoning County
145	38.7	**Vermilion** (city) Lorain County
147	38.6	**Franklin** (city) Warren County
147	38.6	**Strasburg** (village) Tuscarawas County
149	38.5	**London** (city) Madison County
149	38.5	**Wintersville** (village) Jefferson County

Note: *This section ranks incorporated places and CDPs (Census Designated Places) with populations of 2,500 or more. Unincorporated postal areas were not considered. Please refer to the User Guide for additional information.*

Population with Public Health Insurance

Top 150 Places Ranked in *Ascending* Order

State Rank	Percent	Place
1	11.2	**Grandview Heights** (city) Franklin County
2	11.4	**Dublin** (city) Franklin County
3	11.6	**Oxford** (city) Butler County
4	12.1	**Powell** (city) Delaware County
5	12.7	**Dry Run** (CDP) Hamilton County
6	12.9	**Granville** (village) Licking County
7	13.2	**Greentown** (CDP) Stark County
8	13.6	**New Albany** (city) Franklin County
9	13.8	**Athens** (city) Athens County
10	14.2	**Sixteen Mile Stand** (CDP) Hamilton County
11	15.3	**South Russell** (village) Geauga County
12	15.4	**Ottawa Hills** (village) Lucas County
12	15.4	**Saint Henry** (village) Mercer County
14	15.5	**Bainbridge** (CDP) Geauga County
15	15.6	**Cedarville** (village) Greene County
16	15.7	**Bexley** (city) Franklin County
17	15.8	**Lake Darby** (CDP) Franklin County
17	15.8	**Wright-Patterson AFB** (CDP) Greene County
19	16.9	**Hudson** (city) Summit County
20	17.1	**Landen** (CDP) Warren County
20	17.1	**Mason** (city) Warren County
22	17.3	**Waterville** (city) Lucas County
23	18.3	**Hilliard** (city) Franklin County
24	18.5	**Perrysburg** (city) Wood County
25	18.6	**Four Bridges** (CDP) Butler County
26	18.9	**Madeira** (city) Hamilton County
27	19.2	**Beckett Ridge** (CDP) Butler County
28	19.3	**Delhi Hills** (CDP) Hamilton County
28	19.3	**Turpin Hills** (CDP) Hamilton County
30	19.8	**Pickerington** (city) Fairfield County
31	20.0	**Bowling Green** (city) Wood County
32	20.1	**New Bremen** (village) Auglaize County
33	20.3	**Oakwood** (city) Montgomery County
33	20.3	**Sherwood** (CDP) Hamilton County
35	20.5	**Reminderville** (village) Summit County
36	20.6	**Springboro** (city) Warren County
37	20.8	**Mariemont** (village) Hamilton County
38	21.1	**Ashville** (village) Pickaway County
39	21.2	**Mack** (CDP) Hamilton County
39	21.2	**Rossford** (city) Wood County
41	21.4	**Upper Arlington** (city) Franklin County
42	21.6	**Pleasant Run** (CDP) Hamilton County
43	21.9	**Brecksville** (city) Cuyahoga County
44	22.0	**Solon** (city) Cuyahoga County
45	22.2	**Bay Village** (city) Cuyahoga County
45	22.2	**Beechwood Trails** (CDP) Licking County
45	22.2	**Broadview Heights** (city) Cuyahoga County
45	22.2	**Macedonia** (city) Summit County
49	22.3	**Avon** (city) Lorain County
50	22.4	**New Concord** (village) Muskingum County
50	22.4	**Seville** (village) Medina County
52	22.5	**Westerville** (city) Franklin County
53	22.6	**Stow** (city) Summit County
54	22.7	**Canal Winchester** (city) Franklin County
54	22.7	**Richfield** (village) Summit County
56	22.8	**Bellbrook** (city) Greene County
56	22.8	**Independence** (city) Cuyahoga County
58	22.9	**Wyoming** (city) Hamilton County
59	23.0	**Avon Lake** (city) Lorain County
60	23.2	**Kirtland** (city) Lake County
60	23.2	**University Heights** (city) Cuyahoga County
62	23.3	**Harrison** (city) Hamilton County
62	23.3	**Ross** (CDP) Butler County
62	23.3	**Sunbury** (village) Delaware County
65	23.4	**Beavercreek** (city) Greene County
65	23.4	**Gahanna** (city) Franklin County
65	23.4	**Monroe** (city) Butler County
68	23.5	**Ada** (village) Hardin County
69	23.7	**Grove City** (city) Franklin County
70	23.8	**Salem Heights** (CDP) Hamilton County
71	24.0	**Lake Lakengren** (CDP) Preble County
72	24.1	**Minster** (village) Auglaize County
73	24.2	**Bluffton** (village) Allen County
74	24.3	**Blue Ash** (city) Hamilton County
75	24.4	**Worthington** (city) Franklin County
76	24.5	**Dent** (CDP) Hamilton County
77	24.6	**Carey** (village) Wyandot County
77	24.6	**Medina** (city) Medina County
77	24.6	**The Village of Indian Hill** (city) Hamilton County
77	24.6	**Tipp City** (city) Miami County
81	24.7	**Brimfield** (CDP) Portage County
81	24.7	**Day Heights** (CDP) Clermont County
81	24.7	**Twinsburg** (city) Summit County
84	24.8	**Evendale** (village) Hamilton County
84	24.8	**Marysville** (city) Union County
86	24.9	**Devola** (CDP) Washington County
87	25.0	**Montgomery** (city) Hamilton County
88	25.1	**Canfield** (city) Mahoning County
89	25.2	**Newtown** (village) Hamilton County
89	25.2	**Willoughby Hills** (city) Lake County
91	25.3	**Miami Heights** (CDP) Hamilton County
91	25.3	**Swanton** (village) Fulton County
93	25.4	**Berea** (city) Cuyahoga County
93	25.4	**Delaware** (city) Delaware County
93	25.4	**Greenhills** (village) Hamilton County
93	25.4	**Mount Repose** (CDP) Clermont County
97	25.7	**Fairfield** (city) Butler County
97	25.7	**Highland Heights** (city) Cuyahoga County
97	25.7	**Strongsville** (city) Cuyahoga County
100	25.8	**Loveland** (city) Hamilton County
100	25.8	**North Royalton** (city) Cuyahoga County
100	25.8	**Poland** (village) Mahoning County
103	25.9	**Kent** (city) Portage County
103	25.9	**Pepper Pike** (city) Cuyahoga County
105	26.2	**Garrettsville** (village) Portage County
106	26.3	**Trenton** (city) Butler County
107	26.4	**Aurora** (city) Portage County
107	26.4	**Brunswick** (city) Medina County
107	26.4	**Coldwater** (village) Mercer County
107	26.4	**Uniontown** (CDP) Stark County
111	26.5	**South Euclid** (city) Cuyahoga County
112	26.6	**Cherry Grove** (CDP) Hamilton County
113	26.7	**Green** (city) Summit County
113	26.7	**Mogadore** (village) Summit County
115	26.8	**Monfort Heights** (CDP) Hamilton County
116	26.9	**Chagrin Falls** (village) Cuyahoga County
116	26.9	**Shaker Heights** (city) Cuyahoga County
118	27.1	**Moreland Hills** (village) Cuyahoga County
118	27.1	**Olmsted Falls** (city) Cuyahoga County
118	27.1	**Pataskala** (city) Licking County
118	27.1	**Reynoldsburg** (city) Franklin County
122	27.3	**Deer Park** (city) Hamilton County
122	27.3	**Mentor** (city) Lake County
122	27.3	**Orange** (village) Cuyahoga County
122	27.3	**Portage Lakes** (CDP) Summit County
122	27.3	**Sylvania** (city) Lucas County
122	27.3	**Withamsville** (CDP) Clermont County
128	27.4	**Maumee** (city) Lucas County
129	27.5	**Forestville** (CDP) Hamilton County
130	27.6	**North Ridgeville** (city) Lorain County
131	27.8	**Streetsboro** (city) Portage County
132	27.9	**Madison** (village) Lake County
132	27.9	**North Kingsville** (village) Ashtabula County
134	28.0	**Wadsworth** (city) Medina County
135	28.1	**Lebanon** (city) Warren County
135	28.1	**Westlake** (city) Cuyahoga County
137	28.2	**New Franklin** (city) Summit County
138	28.3	**Rocky River** (city) Cuyahoga County
139	28.4	**Lakewood** (city) Cuyahoga County
140	28.5	**Taylor Creek** (CDP) Hamilton County
141	28.6	**Covedale** (CDP) Hamilton County
141	28.6	**Dillonvale** (CDP) Hamilton County
143	28.7	**South Lebanon** (village) Warren County
144	28.8	**Doylestown** (village) Wayne County
144	28.8	**Fairview Park** (city) Cuyahoga County
146	28.9	**Willoughby** (city) Lake County
147	29.0	**Oberlin** (city) Lorain County
147	29.0	**Woodlawn** (village) Hamilton County
149	29.1	**Beachwood** (city) Cuyahoga County
149	29.1	**Kenwood** (CDP) Hamilton County

Note: *This section ranks incorporated places and CDPs (Census Designated Places) with populations of 2,500 or more. Unincorporated postal areas were not considered. Please refer to the User Guide for additional information.*

Population with No Health Insurance

Top 150 Places Ranked in *Descending* Order

State Rank	Percent	Place
1	19.1	**Mount Orab** (village) Brown County
2	18.7	**New Carlisle** (city) Clark County
3	16.6	**Blacklick Estates** (CDP) Franklin County
4	15.9	**Whitehall** (city) Franklin County
5	15.8	**Lockland** (village) Hamilton County
6	15.2	**Lincoln Village** (CDP) Franklin County
7	14.8	**Lincoln Heights** (village) Hamilton County
8	13.8	**Fredericktown** (village) Knox County
9	13.7	**New Lexington** (village) Perry County
10	13.6	**Lima** (city) Allen County
11	13.3	**Crooksville** (village) Perry County
12	13.2	**Millersburg** (village) Holmes County
13	13.0	**Niles** (city) Trumbull County
13	13.0	**North College Hill** (city) Hamilton County
15	12.9	**Dayton** (city) Montgomery County
16	12.7	**Painesville** (city) Lake County
16	12.7	**Salem** (city) Columbiana County
18	12.6	**Barberton** (city) Summit County
18	12.6	**Buckeye Lake** (village) Licking County
20	12.5	**Bellaire** (village) Belmont County
21	12.4	**Ironton** (city) Lawrence County
22	12.3	**Portsmouth** (city) Scioto County
23	12.2	**Cleveland** (city) Cuyahoga County
23	12.2	**Williamsburg** (village) Clermont County
25	12.1	**Akron** (city) Summit County
25	12.1	**Delshire** (CDP) Hamilton County
25	12.1	**Fairport Harbor** (village) Lake County
25	12.1	**Logan** (city) Hocking County
29	12.0	**Wellsville** (village) Columbiana County
30	11.9	**Columbus** (city) Franklin County
30	11.9	**Springdale** (city) Hamilton County
32	11.8	**Milford** (city) Clermont County
32	11.8	**Norwood** (city) Hamilton County
32	11.8	**Oak Harbor** (village) Ottawa County
35	11.7	**Lexington** (village) Richland County
35	11.7	**West Jefferson** (village) Madison County
37	11.6	**Blanchester** (village) Clinton County
37	11.6	**East Cleveland** (city) Cuyahoga County
37	11.6	**Sharonville** (city) Hamilton County
40	11.5	**Bethel** (village) Clermont County
40	11.5	**East Liverpool** (city) Columbiana County
40	11.5	**Middletown** (city) Butler County
43	11.4	**Hamilton** (city) Butler County
43	11.4	**Oakwood** (village) Cuyahoga County
45	11.3	**Fairfield** (city) Butler County
45	11.3	**Kenton** (city) Hardin County
45	11.3	**Shadyside** (village) Belmont County
48	11.2	**Lordstown** (village) Trumbull County
48	11.2	**Northgate** (CDP) Hamilton County
48	11.2	**Riverside** (city) Montgomery County
51	11.1	**Canton** (city) Stark County
51	11.1	**Dennison** (village) Tuscarawas County
51	11.1	**Hillsboro** (city) Highland County
51	11.1	**Mansfield** (city) Richland County
55	11.0	**Moraine** (city) Montgomery County
56	10.9	**Cincinnati** (city) Hamilton County
56	10.9	**Nelsonville** (city) Athens County
56	10.9	**New Richmond** (village) Clermont County
56	10.9	**Obetz** (village) Franklin County
56	10.9	**West Union** (village) Adams County
56	10.9	**Youngstown** (city) Mahoning County
62	10.8	**London** (city) Madison County
62	10.8	**Napoleon** (city) Henry County
62	10.8	**Newton Falls** (village) Trumbull County
62	10.8	**Perry Heights** (CDP) Stark County
66	10.7	**Hicksville** (village) Defiance County
67	10.6	**Chillicothe** (city) Ross County
67	10.6	**Delphos** (city) Allen County
67	10.6	**Fairborn** (city) Greene County
67	10.6	**New Philadelphia** (city) Tuscarawas County
67	10.6	**Sandusky** (city) Erie County
72	10.5	**Bedford Heights** (city) Cuyahoga County
72	10.5	**Greenfield** (village) Highland County
72	10.5	**Kent** (city) Portage County
72	10.5	**Washington Court House** (city) Fayette County
76	10.4	**Circleville** (city) Pickaway County
76	10.4	**Covington** (village) Miami County
76	10.4	**New London** (village) Huron County
76	10.4	**Toledo** (city) Lucas County
80	10.3	**Forest Park** (city) Hamilton County
80	10.3	**Marion** (city) Marion County
80	10.3	**Newcomerstown** (village) Tuscarawas County
80	10.3	**West Carrollton** (city) Montgomery County
84	10.2	**Ashtabula** (city) Ashtabula County
84	10.2	**Euclid** (city) Cuyahoga County
84	10.2	**Newark** (city) Licking County
84	10.2	**Struthers** (city) Mahoning County
88	10.1	**Carlisle** (village) Warren County
88	10.1	**Dover** (city) Tuscarawas County
88	10.1	**Minerva** (village) Stark County
88	10.1	**Paulding** (village) Paulding County
88	10.1	**Toronto** (city) Jefferson County
93	10.0	**Alliance** (city) Stark County
93	10.0	**Burlington** (CDP) Lawrence County
93	10.0	**Northbrook** (CDP) Hamilton County
93	10.0	**Piqua** (city) Miami County
93	10.0	**Trotwood** (city) Montgomery County
98	9.9	**Bucyrus** (city) Crawford County
98	9.9	**Galion** (city) Crawford County
98	9.9	**Huber Heights** (city) Montgomery County
98	9.9	**Lorain** (city) Lorain County
98	9.9	**Marietta** (city) Washington County
98	9.9	**Mentor-on-the-Lake** (city) Lake County
98	9.9	**Warren** (city) Trumbull County
105	9.8	**Green Meadows** (CDP) Clark County
105	9.8	**Greenhills** (village) Hamilton County
105	9.8	**Uhrichsville** (city) Tuscarawas County
108	9.7	**Barnesville** (village) Belmont County
108	9.7	**Bellefontaine** (city) Logan County
108	9.7	**Lebanon** (city) Warren County
108	9.7	**Lisbon** (village) Columbiana County
108	9.7	**Van Wert** (city) Van Wert County
113	9.6	**Elyria** (city) Lorain County
113	9.6	**Lakewood** (city) Cuyahoga County
113	9.6	**Lodi** (village) Medina County
113	9.6	**Loudonville** (village) Ashland County
113	9.6	**Northfield** (village) Summit County
113	9.6	**Park Layne** (CDP) Clark County
113	9.6	**Reading** (city) Hamilton County
120	9.5	**Findlay** (city) Hancock County
120	9.5	**Sebring** (village) Mahoning County
120	9.5	**Springfield** (city) Clark County
123	9.4	**Garfield Heights** (city) Cuyahoga County
123	9.4	**North Baltimore** (village) Wood County
125	9.3	**Edgewood** (CDP) Ashtabula County
125	9.3	**Fostoria** (city) Seneca County
125	9.3	**Georgetown** (village) Brown County
125	9.3	**Saint Bernard** (city) Hamilton County
125	9.3	**Saint Clairsville** (city) Belmont County
125	9.3	**West Portsmouth** (CDP) Scioto County
125	9.3	**Zanesville** (city) Muskingum County
132	9.2	**Jefferson** (village) Ashtabula County
132	9.2	**Lake Darby** (CDP) Franklin County
132	9.2	**Martins Ferry** (city) Belmont County
132	9.2	**Mingo Junction** (village) Jefferson County
136	9.1	**Belpre** (city) Washington County
136	9.1	**Cheviot** (city) Hamilton County
136	9.1	**Cleves** (village) Hamilton County
136	9.1	**Newtown** (village) Hamilton County
136	9.1	**Ottawa** (village) Putnam County
141	9.0	**Celina** (city) Mercer County
141	9.0	**Cortland** (city) Trumbull County
141	9.0	**Fremont** (city) Sandusky County
141	9.0	**New Concord** (village) Muskingum County
141	9.0	**Pataskala** (city) Licking County
141	9.0	**South Point** (village) Lawrence County
141	9.0	**Wellston** (city) Jackson County
148	8.9	**Girard** (city) Trumbull County
148	8.9	**Silverton** (village) Hamilton County
150	8.8	**Geneva** (city) Ashtabula County

***Note:** This section ranks incorporated places and CDPs (Census Designated Places) with populations of 2,500 or more. Unincorporated postal areas were not considered. Please refer to the User Guide for additional information.*

Population with No Health Insurance

Top 150 Places Ranked in *Ascending* Order

State Rank	Percent	Place
1	0.4	**Powell** (city) Delaware County
2	1.1	**Independence** (city) Cuyahoga County
2	1.1	**The Village of Indian Hill** (city) Hamilton County
4	1.2	**Beachwood** (city) Cuyahoga County
5	1.3	**Pepper Pike** (city) Cuyahoga County
6	1.4	**Turpin Hills** (CDP) Hamilton County
7	1.5	**Four Bridges** (CDP) Butler County
8	1.6	**Day Heights** (CDP) Clermont County
8	1.6	**Mariemont** (village) Hamilton County
8	1.6	**Minster** (village) Auglaize County
8	1.6	**Whitehouse** (village) Lucas County
12	1.7	**Evendale** (village) Hamilton County
12	1.7	**Kirtland** (city) Lake County
12	1.7	**Montgomery** (city) Hamilton County
12	1.7	**Mulberry** (CDP) Clermont County
16	1.8	**Delta** (village) Fulton County
16	1.8	**Dry Run** (CDP) Hamilton County
16	1.8	**Seven Hills** (city) Cuyahoga County
19	2.0	**New Albany** (city) Franklin County
19	2.0	**New Bremen** (village) Auglaize County
19	2.0	**Springboro** (city) Warren County
22	2.1	**Dublin** (city) Franklin County
22	2.1	**Miami Heights** (CDP) Hamilton County
22	2.1	**Orange** (village) Cuyahoga County
22	2.1	**Wyoming** (city) Hamilton County
26	2.2	**Avon** (city) Lorain County
26	2.2	**Chagrin Falls** (village) Cuyahoga County
28	2.3	**Dent** (CDP) Hamilton County
28	2.3	**Mayfield** (village) Cuyahoga County
30	2.4	**Greentown** (CDP) Stark County
31	2.5	**Bay Village** (city) Cuyahoga County
31	2.5	**Ottawa Hills** (village) Lucas County
31	2.5	**Poland** (village) Mahoning County
31	2.5	**Solon** (city) Cuyahoga County
35	2.6	**Brookville** (city) Montgomery County
35	2.6	**Devola** (CDP) Washington County
35	2.6	**Montrose-Ghent** (CDP) Summit County
35	2.6	**South Russell** (village) Geauga County
39	2.7	**Avon Lake** (city) Lorain County
39	2.7	**Brecksville** (city) Cuyahoga County
39	2.7	**Hudson** (city) Summit County
39	2.7	**Summerside** (CDP) Clermont County
43	2.8	**Beechwood Trails** (CDP) Licking County
43	2.8	**Bexley** (city) Franklin County
43	2.8	**Highland Heights** (city) Cuyahoga County
43	2.8	**Macedonia** (city) Summit County
47	2.9	**Worthington** (city) Franklin County
48	3.0	**Canal Winchester** (city) Franklin County
48	3.0	**Landen** (CDP) Warren County
48	3.0	**Madeira** (city) Hamilton County
48	3.0	**Seville** (village) Medina County
52	3.1	**Cherry Grove** (CDP) Hamilton County
52	3.1	**Pickerington** (city) Fairfield County
52	3.1	**Saint Henry** (village) Mercer County
52	3.1	**Sunbury** (village) Delaware County
56	3.2	**Oakwood** (city) Montgomery County
56	3.2	**Reminderville** (village) Summit County
56	3.2	**Upper Arlington** (city) Franklin County
59	3.3	**Apple Valley** (CDP) Knox County
59	3.3	**Chardon** (city) Geauga County
59	3.3	**Granville** (village) Licking County
59	3.3	**Mack** (CDP) Hamilton County
59	3.3	**Mason** (city) Warren County
59	3.3	**McDonald** (village) Trumbull County
59	3.3	**Twinsburg** (city) Summit County
66	3.4	**Beavercreek** (city) Greene County
66	3.4	**Columbiana** (city) Columbiana County
68	3.5	**Amberley** (village) Hamilton County
68	3.5	**Centerville** (city) Montgomery County
68	3.5	**Shaker Heights** (city) Cuyahoga County
71	3.6	**Moreland Hills** (village) Cuyahoga County
71	3.6	**Richfield** (village) Summit County
73	3.7	**Bellbrook** (city) Greene County
73	3.7	**Forestville** (CDP) Hamilton County
73	3.7	**Mogadore** (village) Summit County
73	3.7	**Perrysburg** (city) Wood County
73	3.7	**Strongsville** (city) Cuyahoga County
78	3.8	**Canfield** (city) Mahoning County
78	3.8	**Stow** (city) Summit County
78	3.8	**Sylvania** (city) Lucas County
81	3.9	**Bainbridge** (CDP) Geauga County
81	3.9	**Lyndhurst** (city) Cuyahoga County
83	4.0	**Aurora** (city) Portage County
83	4.0	**Doylestown** (village) Wayne County
83	4.0	**Garrettsville** (village) Portage County
83	4.0	**Grafton** (village) Lorain County
83	4.0	**Westlake** (city) Cuyahoga County
88	4.1	**Baltimore** (village) Fairfield County
88	4.1	**Beckett Ridge** (CDP) Butler County
88	4.1	**Blue Ash** (city) Hamilton County
88	4.1	**Covedale** (CDP) Hamilton County
88	4.1	**Mount Repose** (CDP) Clermont County
88	4.1	**University Heights** (city) Cuyahoga County
88	4.1	**Waterville** (city) Lucas County
95	4.2	**Clyde** (city) Sandusky County
95	4.2	**Mentor** (city) Lake County
95	4.2	**Middleburg Heights** (city) Cuyahoga County
98	4.3	**Lake Lakengren** (CDP) Preble County
98	4.3	**The Plains** (CDP) Athens County
100	4.4	**Champion Heights** (CDP) Trumbull County
100	4.4	**Harrison** (city) Hamilton County
100	4.4	**Oxford** (city) Butler County
100	4.4	**Rossford** (city) Wood County
100	4.4	**Versailles** (village) Darke County
105	4.5	**Monfort Heights** (CDP) Hamilton County
105	4.5	**North Kingsville** (village) Ashtabula County
105	4.5	**North Ridgeville** (city) Lorain County
105	4.5	**Tallmadge** (city) Summit County
105	4.5	**Union** (city) Montgomery County
105	4.5	**Westerville** (city) Franklin County
111	4.6	**Lakemore** (village) Summit County
111	4.6	**Pleasant Run Farm** (CDP) Hamilton County
111	4.6	**Sherwood** (CDP) Hamilton County
111	4.6	**Strasburg** (village) Tuscarawas County
115	4.7	**Fairlawn** (city) Summit County
115	4.7	**Maumee** (city) Lucas County
117	4.8	**New Franklin** (city) Summit County
117	4.8	**North Zanesville** (CDP) Muskingum County
119	4.9	**Grandview Heights** (city) Franklin County
119	4.9	**North Canton** (city) Stark County
119	4.9	**Northridge** (CDP) Clark County
122	5.0	**Athens** (city) Athens County
122	5.0	**Rocky River** (city) Cuyahoga County
124	5.1	**Archbold** (village) Fulton County
124	5.1	**Ross** (CDP) Butler County
124	5.1	**Wickliffe** (city) Lake County
127	5.2	**Bridgetown** (CDP) Hamilton County
127	5.2	**Clayton** (city) Montgomery County
127	5.2	**Crestline** (village) Crawford County
127	5.2	**Middlefield** (village) Geauga County
127	5.2	**Oberlin** (city) Lorain County
127	5.2	**Sixteen Mile Stand** (CDP) Hamilton County
133	5.3	**Gahanna** (city) Franklin County
133	5.3	**Monroe** (city) Butler County
133	5.3	**Swanton** (village) Fulton County
133	5.3	**Wintersville** (village) Jefferson County
137	5.4	**Ballville** (CDP) Sandusky County
137	5.4	**Enon** (village) Clark County
137	5.4	**Fruit Hill** (CDP) Hamilton County
137	5.4	**Hilliard** (city) Franklin County
141	5.5	**Green** (city) Summit County
141	5.5	**Huron** (city) Erie County
141	5.5	**Olmsted Falls** (city) Cuyahoga County
141	5.5	**Uniontown** (CDP) Stark County
145	5.6	**Bowling Green** (city) Wood County
145	5.6	**Coshocton** (city) Coshocton County
147	5.7	**Berea** (city) Cuyahoga County
147	5.7	**Brunswick** (city) Medina County
147	5.7	**Calcutta** (CDP) Columbiana County
150	5.8	**Amherst** (city) Lorain County

Note: *This section ranks incorporated places and CDPs (Census Designated Places) with populations of 2,500 or more. Unincorporated postal areas were not considered. Please refer to the User Guide for additional information.*

Population Under 18 Years Old with No Health Insurance

Top 150 Places Ranked in *Descending* Order

State Rank	Percent	Place
1	20.0	**Dry Ridge** (CDP) Hamilton County
2	15.2	**Lordstown** (village) Trumbull County
2	15.2	**New Carlisle** (city) Clark County
4	14.5	**Saint Clairsville** (city) Belmont County
5	14.3	**Fredericktown** (village) Knox County
6	13.6	**New Concord** (village) Muskingum County
7	12.7	**Delshire** (CDP) Hamilton County
8	12.6	**New Lexington** (village) Perry County
9	12.5	**Blacklick Estates** (CDP) Franklin County
9	12.5	**Enon** (village) Clark County
11	12.3	**Cortland** (city) Trumbull County
12	12.2	**Wright-Patterson AFB** (CDP) Greene County
13	11.6	**Mingo Junction** (village) Jefferson County
14	11.3	**Niles** (city) Trumbull County
15	10.5	**Barberton** (city) Summit County
16	10.3	**Paulding** (village) Paulding County
17	10.0	**Lincoln Village** (CDP) Franklin County
18	9.9	**Bluffton** (village) Allen County
19	9.4	**Newtown** (village) Hamilton County
20	9.0	**Napoleon** (city) Henry County
20	9.0	**Pleasant Run** (CDP) Hamilton County
22	8.9	**Lebanon** (city) Warren County
23	8.7	**Moraine** (city) Montgomery County
24	8.6	**Cedarville** (village) Greene County
24	8.6	**Sharonville** (city) Hamilton County
26	8.3	**Logan** (city) Hocking County
26	8.3	**Oakwood** (village) Cuyahoga County
28	8.2	**Heath** (city) Licking County
29	8.1	**Mayfield Heights** (city) Cuyahoga County
30	7.7	**Fort Shawnee** (CDP) Allen County
30	7.7	**Madison** (village) Lake County
32	7.6	**Mineral Ridge** (CDP) Trumbull County
33	7.5	**Dillonvale** (CDP) Hamilton County
33	7.5	**Fairport Harbor** (village) Lake County
33	7.5	**Tipp City** (city) Miami County
36	7.4	**West Jefferson** (village) Madison County
37	7.2	**Lake Darby** (CDP) Franklin County
37	7.2	**Norwood** (city) Hamilton County
39	7.1	**Coldwater** (village) Mercer County
40	7.0	**Delhi Hills** (CDP) Hamilton County
41	6.9	**Nelsonville** (city) Athens County
41	6.9	**Ottawa** (village) Putnam County
41	6.9	**Richville** (CDP) Stark County
44	6.8	**Munroe Falls** (city) Summit County
44	6.8	**Newcomerstown** (village) Tuscarawas County
44	6.8	**West Milton** (village) Miami County
47	6.7	**Painesville** (city) Lake County
48	6.6	**Blanchester** (village) Clinton County
49	6.5	**Van Wert** (city) Van Wert County
50	6.4	**Kent** (city) Portage County
50	6.4	**Uhrichsville** (city) Tuscarawas County
52	6.3	**Austintown** (CDP) Mahoning County
52	6.3	**Circleville** (city) Pickaway County
52	6.3	**Huber Heights** (city) Montgomery County
52	6.3	**Mount Healthy Heights** (CDP) Hamilton County
52	6.3	**Saint Bernard** (city) Hamilton County
57	6.2	**Delphos** (city) Allen County
57	6.2	**East Cleveland** (city) Cuyahoga County
57	6.2	**Groveport** (city) Franklin County
60	6.1	**Akron** (city) Summit County
60	6.1	**Alliance** (city) Stark County
60	6.1	**East Liverpool** (city) Columbiana County
60	6.1	**London** (city) Madison County
64	6.0	**Boardman** (CDP) Mahoning County
64	6.0	**Minerva** (village) Stark County
64	6.0	**Pataskala** (city) Licking County
64	6.0	**Waynesville** (village) Warren County
64	6.0	**Whitehall** (city) Franklin County
69	5.9	**Mount Orab** (village) Brown County
69	5.9	**Struthers** (city) Mahoning County
71	5.8	**Buckeye Lake** (village) Licking County
71	5.8	**Columbus** (city) Franklin County
71	5.8	**Covington** (village) Miami County
71	5.8	**Eaton** (city) Preble County
71	5.8	**Washington Court House** (city) Fayette County
76	5.6	**Brookville** (city) Montgomery County
76	5.6	**Rittman** (city) Wayne County
76	5.6	**Riverside** (city) Montgomery County
79	5.5	**Amherst** (city) Lorain County
79	5.5	**North College Hill** (city) Hamilton County
79	5.5	**Northwood** (city) Wood County
82	5.4	**Bridgetown** (CDP) Hamilton County
82	5.4	**Geneva** (city) Ashtabula County
82	5.4	**Lexington** (village) Richland County
82	5.4	**Willowick** (city) Lake County
86	5.3	**Dayton** (city) Montgomery County
86	5.3	**Euclid** (city) Cuyahoga County
86	5.3	**New Philadelphia** (city) Tuscarawas County
86	5.3	**Ross** (CDP) Butler County
90	5.2	**Salem** (city) Columbiana County
91	5.1	**Gibsonburg** (village) Sandusky County
92	5.0	**Deer Park** (city) Hamilton County
92	5.0	**Mentor-on-the-Lake** (city) Lake County
92	5.0	**Parma** (city) Cuyahoga County
95	4.9	**Findlay** (city) Hancock County
96	4.8	**Bedford Heights** (city) Cuyahoga County
96	4.8	**Plain City** (village) Madison County
96	4.8	**Salem Heights** (CDP) Hamilton County
96	4.8	**Wheelersburg** (CDP) Scioto County
100	4.7	**Canal Fulton** (city) Stark County
100	4.7	**Cleveland Heights** (city) Cuyahoga County
100	4.7	**Dover** (city) Tuscarawas County
100	4.7	**Fairborn** (city) Greene County
100	4.7	**Forestville** (CDP) Hamilton County
100	4.7	**Galion** (city) Crawford County
100	4.7	**Kenton** (city) Hardin County
100	4.7	**Perry Heights** (CDP) Stark County
100	4.7	**Wadsworth** (city) Medina County
109	4.6	**Ballville** (CDP) Sandusky County
109	4.6	**Chillicothe** (city) Ross County
109	4.6	**Kenwood** (CDP) Hamilton County
112	4.5	**Marietta** (city) Washington County
112	4.5	**Medina** (city) Medina County
112	4.5	**Sandusky** (city) Erie County
112	4.5	**Swanton** (village) Fulton County
116	4.4	**Canton** (city) Stark County
116	4.4	**Chardon** (city) Geauga County
116	4.4	**Lima** (city) Allen County
116	4.4	**Sherwood** (CDP) Hamilton County
120	4.3	**Green Meadows** (CDP) Clark County
120	4.3	**Howland Center** (CDP) Trumbull County
120	4.3	**Ironton** (city) Lawrence County
120	4.3	**North Madison** (CDP) Lake County
120	4.3	**North Olmsted** (city) Cuyahoga County
120	4.3	**Trotwood** (city) Montgomery County
126	4.2	**Cincinnati** (city) Hamilton County
126	4.2	**Fremont** (city) Sandusky County
126	4.2	**Hillsboro** (city) Highland County
126	4.2	**Kettering** (city) Montgomery County
126	4.2	**Middletown** (city) Butler County
126	4.2	**Reynoldsburg** (city) Franklin County
126	4.2	**Streetsboro** (city) Portage County
126	4.2	**Troy** (city) Miami County
134	4.1	**Cheviot** (city) Hamilton County
135	4.0	**Lockland** (village) Hamilton County
135	4.0	**Massillon** (city) Stark County
135	4.0	**Portsmouth** (city) Scioto County
135	4.0	**Steubenville** (city) Jefferson County
139	3.9	**Brooklyn** (city) Cuyahoga County
139	3.9	**Carlisle** (village) Warren County
139	3.9	**Crooksville** (village) Perry County
139	3.9	**Edgewood** (CDP) Ashtabula County
139	3.9	**Hartville** (village) Stark County
139	3.9	**Loveland** (city) Hamilton County
139	3.9	**Mansfield** (city) Richland County
139	3.9	**Montrose-Ghent** (CDP) Summit County
139	3.9	**Wickliffe** (city) Lake County
148	3.8	**Archbold** (village) Fulton County
148	3.8	**Bedford** (city) Cuyahoga County
148	3.8	**Bellevue** (city) Sandusky County

Note: *This section ranks incorporated places and CDPs (Census Designated Places) with populations of 2,500 or more. Unincorporated postal areas were not considered. Please refer to the User Guide for additional information.*

Population Under 18 Years Old with No Health Insurance

Top 150 Places Ranked in *Ascending* Order

State Rank	Percent	Place
1	0.0	**Ashville** (village) Pickaway County
1	0.0	**Bainbridge** (CDP) Geauga County
1	0.0	**Baltimore** (village) Fairfield County
1	0.0	**Beechwood Trails** (CDP) Licking County
1	0.0	**Bellbrook** (city) Greene County
1	0.0	**Brecksville** (city) Cuyahoga County
1	0.0	**Burlington** (CDP) Lawrence County
1	0.0	**Cadiz** (village) Harrison County
1	0.0	**Carrollton** (village) Carroll County
1	0.0	**Chagrin Falls** (village) Cuyahoga County
1	0.0	**Cherry Grove** (CDP) Hamilton County
1	0.0	**Columbiana** (city) Columbiana County
1	0.0	**Coshocton** (city) Coshocton County
1	0.0	**Crestline** (village) Crawford County
1	0.0	**Day Heights** (CDP) Clermont County
1	0.0	**Delta** (village) Fulton County
1	0.0	**Dennison** (village) Tuscarawas County
1	0.0	**Devola** (CDP) Washington County
1	0.0	**Dry Run** (CDP) Hamilton County
1	0.0	**Fairlawn** (city) Summit County
1	0.0	**Greenfield** (village) Highland County
1	0.0	**Greentown** (CDP) Stark County
1	0.0	**Highland Heights** (city) Cuyahoga County
1	0.0	**Jefferson** (village) Ashtabula County
1	0.0	**Kirtland** (city) Lake County
1	0.0	**Lakemore** (village) Summit County
1	0.0	**Landen** (CDP) Warren County
1	0.0	**Lincoln Heights** (village) Hamilton County
1	0.0	**Lodi** (village) Medina County
1	0.0	**Mack** (CDP) Hamilton County
1	0.0	**Mariemont** (village) Hamilton County
1	0.0	**Mayfield** (village) Cuyahoga County
1	0.0	**McDonald** (village) Trumbull County
1	0.0	**Minster** (village) Auglaize County
1	0.0	**Mogadore** (village) Summit County
1	0.0	**Mount Gilead** (village) Morrow County
1	0.0	**Mulberry** (CDP) Clermont County
1	0.0	**New Bremen** (village) Auglaize County
1	0.0	**New Lebanon** (village) Montgomery County
1	0.0	**Newton Falls** (village) Trumbull County
1	0.0	**North Kingsville** (village) Ashtabula County
1	0.0	**North Zanesville** (CDP) Muskingum County
1	0.0	**Orange** (village) Cuyahoga County
1	0.0	**Ottawa Hills** (village) Lucas County
1	0.0	**Pleasant Run Farm** (CDP) Hamilton County
1	0.0	**Portage Lakes** (CDP) Summit County
1	0.0	**Seville** (village) Medina County
1	0.0	**Silverton** (village) Hamilton County
1	0.0	**South Lebanon** (village) Warren County
1	0.0	**South Russell** (village) Geauga County
1	0.0	**Springboro** (city) Warren County
1	0.0	**Strasburg** (village) Tuscarawas County
1	0.0	**The Plains** (CDP) Athens County
1	0.0	**The Village of Indian Hill** (city) Hamilton County
1	0.0	**Urbana** (city) Champaign County
1	0.0	**Versailles** (village) Darke County
1	0.0	**Walbridge** (village) Wood County
1	0.0	**Waverly** (village) Pike County
1	0.0	**Wellington** (village) Lorain County
1	0.0	**West Portsmouth** (CDP) Scioto County
1	0.0	**West Union** (village) Adams County
62	0.2	**Beachwood** (city) Cuyahoga County
63	0.3	**Oberlin** (city) Lorain County
63	0.3	**Powell** (city) Delaware County
65	0.4	**Canal Winchester** (city) Franklin County
65	0.4	**Groesbeck** (CDP) Hamilton County
65	0.4	**Wellston** (city) Jackson County
68	0.5	**Avon** (city) Lorain County
68	0.5	**Bucyrus** (city) Crawford County
68	0.5	**Cleves** (village) Hamilton County
68	0.5	**Reminderville** (village) Summit County
68	0.5	**Whitehouse** (village) Lucas County
68	0.5	**Willard** (city) Huron County
74	0.6	**Champion Heights** (CDP) Trumbull County
74	0.6	**East Palestine** (village) Columbiana County
74	0.6	**Greenville** (city) Darke County
74	0.6	**Lyndhurst** (city) Cuyahoga County
74	0.6	**Northfield** (village) Summit County
74	0.6	**Yellow Springs** (village) Greene County
80	0.7	**Avon Lake** (city) Lorain County
80	0.7	**Greenhills** (village) Hamilton County
80	0.7	**Huron** (city) Erie County
80	0.7	**Montpelier** (village) Williams County
80	0.7	**New Richmond** (village) Clermont County
80	0.7	**Pepper Pike** (city) Cuyahoga County
80	0.7	**Shelby** (city) Richland County
80	0.7	**Stow** (city) Summit County
80	0.7	**Tallmadge** (city) Summit County
80	0.7	**Uniontown** (CDP) Stark County
80	0.7	**Wyoming** (city) Hamilton County
91	0.8	**Northgate** (CDP) Hamilton County
91	0.8	**Wilmington** (city) Clinton County
93	0.9	**Blue Ash** (city) Hamilton County
93	0.9	**Brunswick** (city) Medina County
93	0.9	**Forest Park** (city) Hamilton County
93	0.9	**Four Bridges** (CDP) Butler County
93	0.9	**Grandview Heights** (city) Franklin County
93	0.9	**Maple Heights** (city) Cuyahoga County
93	0.9	**Miami Heights** (CDP) Hamilton County
93	0.9	**Port Clinton** (city) Ottawa County
101	1.0	**Garrettsville** (village) Portage County
101	1.0	**Golf Manor** (village) Hamilton County
101	1.0	**Hubbard** (city) Trumbull County
101	1.0	**Lisbon** (village) Columbiana County
101	1.0	**Strongsville** (city) Cuyahoga County
101	1.0	**Summerside** (CDP) Clermont County
101	1.0	**Taylor Creek** (CDP) Hamilton County
101	1.0	**Union** (city) Montgomery County
101	1.0	**Warrensville Heights** (city) Cuyahoga County
101	1.0	**Worthington** (city) Franklin County
111	1.1	**Belpre** (city) Washington County
111	1.1	**Independence** (city) Cuyahoga County
111	1.1	**Lancaster** (city) Fairfield County
111	1.1	**New Albany** (city) Franklin County
111	1.1	**Shaker Heights** (city) Cuyahoga County
111	1.1	**Sunbury** (village) Delaware County
117	1.2	**Bexley** (city) Franklin County
117	1.2	**Campbell** (city) Mahoning County
117	1.2	**Carey** (village) Wyandot County
117	1.2	**Dublin** (city) Franklin County
117	1.2	**Loudonville** (village) Ashland County
117	1.2	**Miamisburg** (city) Montgomery County
117	1.2	**New London** (village) Huron County
117	1.2	**Pickerington** (city) Fairfield County
117	1.2	**Poland** (village) Mahoning County
117	1.2	**Sheffield Lake** (city) Lorain County
117	1.2	**South Point** (village) Lawrence County
117	1.2	**Turpin Hills** (CDP) Hamilton County
117	1.2	**Westerville** (city) Franklin County
130	1.3	**Englewood** (city) Montgomery County
130	1.3	**Mount Healthy** (city) Hamilton County
130	1.3	**Seven Hills** (city) Cuyahoga County
130	1.3	**Toronto** (city) Jefferson County
130	1.3	**Zanesville** (city) Muskingum County
135	1.4	**Cambridge** (city) Guernsey County
135	1.4	**Celina** (city) Mercer County
135	1.4	**Clayton** (city) Montgomery County
135	1.4	**Solon** (city) Cuyahoga County
135	1.4	**Withamsville** (CDP) Clermont County
140	1.5	**Centerville** (city) Montgomery County
140	1.5	**Georgetown** (village) Brown County
140	1.5	**Hicksville** (village) Defiance County
140	1.5	**Madeira** (city) Hamilton County
140	1.5	**Montgomery** (city) Hamilton County
140	1.5	**New Burlington** (CDP) Hamilton County
140	1.5	**Wintersville** (village) Jefferson County
147	1.6	**Bryan** (city) Williams County
147	1.6	**Dent** (CDP) Hamilton County
147	1.6	**Maumee** (city) Lucas County
147	1.6	**Middleburg Heights** (city) Cuyahoga County

***Note:** This section ranks incorporated places and CDPs (Census Designated Places) with populations of 2,500 or more. Unincorporated postal areas were not considered. Please refer to the User Guide for additional information.*

Commute to Work: Car

Top 150 Places Ranked in *Descending* Order

State Rank	Percent	Place
1	99.1	**Greentown** (CDP) Stark County
2	98.9	**Swanton** (village) Fulton County
3	98.5	**Ross** (CDP) Butler County
4	98.4	**Waverly** (village) Pike County
5	98.3	**Newcomerstown** (village) Tuscarawas County
6	98.2	**Lincoln Heights** (village) Hamilton County
6	98.2	**Newton Falls** (village) Trumbull County
6	98.2	**Woodlawn** (village) Hamilton County
9	98.1	**McDonald** (village) Trumbull County
10	98.0	**Fort Shawnee** (CDP) Allen County
10	98.0	**Mogadore** (village) Summit County
10	98.0	**Northridge** (CDP) Clark County
10	98.0	**Richville** (CDP) Stark County
10	98.0	**Saint Henry** (village) Mercer County
15	97.9	**Franklin** (city) Warren County
15	97.9	**North Baltimore** (village) Wood County
17	97.8	**Mount Healthy Heights** (CDP) Hamilton County
18	97.7	**Lake Darby** (CDP) Franklin County
19	97.6	**Harrison** (city) Hamilton County
19	97.6	**New Burlington** (CDP) Hamilton County
21	97.5	**North Madison** (CDP) Lake County
21	97.5	**Ontario** (city) Richland County
21	97.5	**Wellston** (city) Jackson County
24	97.3	**Portage Lakes** (CDP) Summit County
25	97.2	**Cortland** (city) Trumbull County
26	97.0	**West Portsmouth** (CDP) Scioto County
27	96.9	**Brookville** (city) Montgomery County
28	96.8	**Howland Center** (CDP) Trumbull County
28	96.8	**Lakemore** (village) Summit County
30	96.7	**Niles** (city) Trumbull County
30	96.7	**Sheffield Lake** (city) Lorain County
32	96.6	**Lexington** (village) Richland County
32	96.6	**New Lebanon** (village) Montgomery County
32	96.6	**Springdale** (city) Hamilton County
35	96.5	**Austintown** (CDP) Mahoning County
35	96.5	**Carlisle** (village) Warren County
35	96.5	**Fairfield** (city) Butler County
35	96.5	**Tallmadge** (city) Summit County
39	96.4	**Georgetown** (village) Brown County
39	96.4	**Wright-Patterson AFB** (CDP) Greene County
41	96.3	**Mingo Junction** (village) Jefferson County
41	96.3	**Obetz** (village) Franklin County
43	96.2	**Garrettsville** (village) Portage County
43	96.2	**Greenhills** (village) Hamilton County
43	96.2	**Kenton** (city) Hardin County
43	96.2	**Streetsboro** (city) Portage County
47	96.1	**Dry Ridge** (CDP) Hamilton County
47	96.1	**Ottawa** (village) Putnam County
47	96.1	**Reading** (city) Hamilton County
50	96.0	**Germantown** (city) Montgomery County
50	96.0	**Seven Hills** (city) Cuyahoga County
50	96.0	**Wintersville** (village) Jefferson County
53	95.9	**Calcutta** (CDP) Columbiana County
53	95.9	**Hillsboro** (city) Highland County
53	95.9	**Millersburg** (village) Holmes County
53	95.9	**South Lebanon** (village) Warren County
53	95.9	**Tipp City** (city) Miami County
53	95.9	**West Union** (village) Adams County
59	95.8	**Amherst** (city) Lorain County
59	95.8	**Belpre** (city) Washington County
59	95.8	**Burlington** (CDP) Lawrence County
59	95.8	**Englewood** (city) Montgomery County
59	95.8	**South Point** (village) Lawrence County
59	95.8	**Stow** (city) Summit County
59	95.8	**Struthers** (city) Mahoning County
59	95.8	**Trenton** (city) Butler County
59	95.8	**Union** (city) Montgomery County
59	95.8	**West Carrollton** (city) Montgomery County
69	95.7	**Bellefontaine** (city) Logan County
69	95.7	**Eastlake** (city) Lake County
69	95.7	**Huber Ridge** (CDP) Franklin County
69	95.7	**Jackson** (city) Jackson County
69	95.7	**Seville** (village) Medina County
69	95.7	**Willoughby** (city) Lake County
75	95.6	**Independence** (city) Cuyahoga County
75	95.6	**North Kingsville** (village) Ashtabula County
77	95.5	**Mentor-on-the-Lake** (city) Lake County
77	95.5	**Montpelier** (village) Williams County
77	95.5	**Norton** (city) Summit County
77	95.5	**Pickerington** (city) Fairfield County
77	95.5	**Wadsworth** (city) Medina County
77	95.5	**Whitehouse** (village) Lucas County
77	95.5	**Willoughby Hills** (city) Lake County
84	95.4	**Napoleon** (city) Henry County
84	95.4	**Northbrook** (CDP) Hamilton County
84	95.4	**Riverside** (city) Montgomery County
87	95.3	**Cleves** (village) Hamilton County
87	95.3	**Green** (city) Summit County
87	95.3	**Rossford** (city) Wood County
90	95.2	**Bridgetown** (CDP) Hamilton County
90	95.2	**Coldwater** (village) Mercer County
90	95.2	**Delphos** (city) Allen County
90	95.2	**Edgewood** (CDP) Ashtabula County
90	95.2	**Loudonville** (village) Ashland County
90	95.2	**Sebring** (village) Mahoning County
90	95.2	**Washington Court House** (city) Fayette County
97	95.1	**Delhi Hills** (CDP) Hamilton County
97	95.1	**East Liverpool** (city) Columbiana County
97	95.1	**Girard** (city) Trumbull County
97	95.1	**Summerside** (CDP) Clermont County
97	95.1	**Wickliffe** (city) Lake County
102	95.0	**Cuyahoga Falls** (city) Summit County
102	95.0	**Hubbard** (city) Trumbull County
102	95.0	**Loveland** (city) Hamilton County
102	95.0	**New Franklin** (city) Summit County
102	95.0	**Oakwood** (city) Montgomery County
102	95.0	**Oakwood** (village) Cuyahoga County
102	95.0	**Sidney** (city) Shelby County
109	94.9	**Brook Park** (city) Cuyahoga County
109	94.9	**Canfield** (city) Mahoning County
109	94.9	**Carey** (village) Wyandot County
109	94.9	**Clayton** (city) Montgomery County
109	94.9	**Oregon** (city) Lucas County
109	94.9	**Springboro** (city) Warren County
109	94.9	**The Plains** (CDP) Athens County
109	94.9	**Uniontown** (CDP) Stark County
109	94.9	**Wheelersburg** (CDP) Scioto County
118	94.8	**Boardman** (CDP) Mahoning County
118	94.8	**Waynesville** (village) Warren County
120	94.7	**Canal Fulton** (city) Stark County
120	94.7	**Champion Heights** (CDP) Trumbull County
120	94.7	**Clyde** (city) Sandusky County
120	94.7	**Dennison** (village) Tuscarawas County
120	94.7	**Grove City** (city) Franklin County
120	94.7	**Pataskala** (city) Licking County
120	94.7	**Urbana** (city) Champaign County
127	94.6	**Celina** (city) Mercer County
127	94.6	**Miamisburg** (city) Montgomery County
127	94.6	**Paulding** (village) Paulding County
127	94.6	**Rittman** (city) Wayne County
131	94.5	**Fremont** (city) Sandusky County
131	94.5	**Huron** (city) Erie County
131	94.5	**Maumee** (city) Lucas County
131	94.5	**Mayfield** (village) Cuyahoga County
131	94.5	**Mulberry** (CDP) Clermont County
131	94.5	**Northgate** (CDP) Hamilton County
131	94.5	**Ravenna** (city) Portage County
138	94.4	**Columbiana** (city) Columbiana County
138	94.4	**Grafton** (village) Lorain County
138	94.4	**Louisville** (city) Stark County
138	94.4	**Montrose-Ghent** (CDP) Summit County
138	94.4	**Saint Clairsville** (city) Belmont County
138	94.4	**Vermilion** (city) Lorain County
138	94.4	**Warren** (city) Trumbull County
138	94.4	**Williamsburg** (village) Clermont County
138	94.4	**Withamsville** (CDP) Clermont County
147	94.3	**Eaton** (city) Preble County
147	94.3	**Highland Heights** (city) Cuyahoga County
147	94.3	**Lebanon** (city) Warren County
147	94.3	**Vandalia** (city) Montgomery County

***Note:** This section ranks incorporated places and CDPs (Census Designated Places) with populations of 2,500 or more. Unincorporated postal areas were not considered. Please refer to the User Guide for additional information.*

Commute to Work: Car

Top 150 Places Ranked in *Ascending* Order

State Rank	Percent	Place
1	50.7	**Oberlin** (city) Lorain County
2	50.8	**Cedarville** (village) Greene County
3	50.9	**Granville** (village) Licking County
4	51.6	**Athens** (city) Athens County
5	63.4	**Oxford** (city) Butler County
6	70.7	**New Concord** (village) Muskingum County
7	71.0	**East Cleveland** (city) Cuyahoga County
8	76.6	**Yellow Springs** (village) Greene County
9	77.4	**Ada** (village) Hardin County
10	78.8	**Moreland Hills** (village) Cuyahoga County
11	79.4	**The Village of Indian Hill** (city) Hamilton County
12	79.5	**Cleveland** (city) Cuyahoga County
13	79.7	**Bowling Green** (city) Wood County
14	80.3	**Cincinnati** (city) Hamilton County
15	82.0	**Kent** (city) Portage County
16	82.1	**Cleveland Heights** (city) Cuyahoga County
17	82.2	**University Heights** (city) Cuyahoga County
18	82.3	**Steubenville** (city) Jefferson County
19	82.7	**Dayton** (city) Montgomery County
20	83.0	**Bexley** (city) Franklin County
20	83.0	**Bluffton** (village) Allen County
22	83.3	**Warrensville Heights** (city) Cuyahoga County
23	83.5	**Kenwood** (CDP) Hamilton County
24	83.7	**Shaker Heights** (city) Cuyahoga County
25	83.9	**Greenfield** (village) Highland County
26	84.1	**Wooster** (city) Wayne County
27	84.4	**Milford** (city) Clermont County
28	84.5	**Mount Orab** (village) Brown County
29	84.6	**Montgomery** (city) Hamilton County
30	85.2	**Wellington** (village) Lorain County
31	85.6	**Golf Manor** (village) Hamilton County
32	85.8	**Marietta** (city) Washington County
33	86.2	**Devola** (CDP) Washington County
33	86.2	**Lakewood** (city) Cuyahoga County
35	86.5	**Bay Village** (city) Cuyahoga County
35	86.5	**Berea** (city) Cuyahoga County
37	86.6	**Mariemont** (village) Hamilton County
37	86.6	**South Russell** (village) Geauga County
39	86.7	**Forestville** (CDP) Hamilton County
39	86.7	**Salem Heights** (CDP) Hamilton County
41	86.8	**Lincoln Village** (CDP) Franklin County
42	86.9	**Lockland** (village) Hamilton County
43	87.1	**Bainbridge** (CDP) Geauga County
44	87.2	**Pleasant Run Farm** (CDP) Hamilton County
44	87.2	**Youngstown** (city) Mahoning County
46	87.3	**Madeira** (city) Hamilton County
46	87.3	**Mount Vernon** (city) Knox County
48	87.4	**Nelsonville** (city) Athens County
48	87.4	**Tiffin** (city) Seneca County
50	87.5	**Chagrin Falls** (village) Cuyahoga County
50	87.5	**Portsmouth** (city) Scioto County
50	87.5	**Powell** (city) Delaware County
53	87.6	**Chardon** (city) Geauga County
54	87.7	**Hudson** (city) Summit County
54	87.7	**Wyoming** (city) Hamilton County
56	88.0	**Pepper Pike** (city) Cuyahoga County
56	88.0	**Rocky River** (city) Cuyahoga County
56	88.0	**Sherwood** (CDP) Hamilton County
59	88.1	**Avon** (city) Lorain County
59	88.1	**Bellaire** (village) Belmont County
61	88.3	**Covedale** (CDP) Hamilton County
61	88.3	**Heath** (city) Licking County
63	88.4	**Euclid** (city) Cuyahoga County
64	88.5	**West Milton** (village) Miami County
65	88.6	**Columbus** (city) Franklin County
65	88.6	**Four Bridges** (CDP) Butler County
67	88.9	**Moraine** (city) Montgomery County
67	88.9	**Worthington** (city) Franklin County
69	89.0	**Fruit Hill** (CDP) Hamilton County
70	89.1	**Wilmington** (city) Clinton County
71	89.2	**Silverton** (village) Hamilton County
72	89.3	**North Canton** (city) Stark County
73	89.4	**Ashland** (city) Ashland County
73	89.4	**Canton** (city) Stark County
73	89.4	**Richmond Heights** (city) Cuyahoga County
76	89.5	**Beckett Ridge** (CDP) Butler County
76	89.5	**Delaware** (city) Delaware County
78	89.6	**Crooksville** (village) Perry County
78	89.6	**Maple Heights** (city) Cuyahoga County
80	89.7	**Mount Healthy** (city) Hamilton County
80	89.7	**South Euclid** (city) Cuyahoga County
82	89.8	**Martins Ferry** (city) Belmont County
82	89.8	**New London** (village) Huron County
82	89.8	**North College Hill** (city) Hamilton County
82	89.8	**Sandusky** (city) Erie County
86	89.9	**Springfield** (city) Clark County
87	90.0	**Turpin Hills** (CDP) Hamilton County
87	90.0	**Westlake** (city) Cuyahoga County
89	90.1	**Beachwood** (city) Cuyahoga County
89	90.1	**Lyndhurst** (city) Cuyahoga County
89	90.1	**Upper Arlington** (city) Franklin County
89	90.1	**Westerville** (city) Franklin County
89	90.1	**Whitehall** (city) Franklin County
94	90.2	**Grandview Heights** (city) Franklin County
95	90.3	**Blanchester** (village) Clinton County
95	90.3	**Dublin** (city) Franklin County
95	90.3	**Finneytown** (CDP) Hamilton County
95	90.3	**Plain City** (village) Madison County
99	90.4	**Gahanna** (city) Franklin County
99	90.4	**New Albany** (city) Franklin County
101	90.5	**Coshocton** (city) Coshocton County
101	90.5	**Galion** (city) Crawford County
101	90.5	**Shadyside** (village) Belmont County
101	90.5	**Sixteen Mile Stand** (CDP) Hamilton County
105	90.6	**Archbold** (village) Fulton County
105	90.6	**Avon Lake** (city) Lorain County
105	90.6	**Dry Run** (CDP) Hamilton County
105	90.6	**Greenville** (city) Darke County
109	90.7	**Ottawa Hills** (village) Lucas County
110	90.8	**Akron** (city) Summit County
110	90.8	**North Olmsted** (city) Cuyahoga County
112	90.9	**Brecksville** (city) Cuyahoga County
112	90.9	**Richfield** (village) Summit County
114	91.0	**New Bremen** (village) Auglaize County
115	91.1	**Alliance** (city) Stark County
115	91.1	**Cadiz** (village) Harrison County
115	91.1	**Orange** (village) Cuyahoga County
118	91.2	**Buckeye Lake** (village) Licking County
118	91.2	**Cherry Grove** (CDP) Hamilton County
118	91.2	**Fairview Park** (city) Cuyahoga County
118	91.2	**Hartville** (village) Stark County
118	91.2	**Minster** (village) Auglaize County
118	91.2	**Sheffield** (village) Lorain County
118	91.2	**Trotwood** (city) Montgomery County
125	91.3	**Aurora** (city) Portage County
125	91.3	**Beechwood Trails** (CDP) Licking County
125	91.3	**Newtown** (village) Hamilton County
128	91.4	**Enon** (village) Clark County
128	91.4	**Logan** (city) Hocking County
128	91.4	**Madison** (village) Lake County
128	91.4	**Mount Repose** (CDP) Clermont County
128	91.4	**Toledo** (city) Lucas County
133	91.5	**Bedford Heights** (city) Cuyahoga County
133	91.5	**Mount Gilead** (village) Morrow County
135	91.6	**Dillonvale** (CDP) Hamilton County
135	91.6	**Garfield Heights** (city) Cuyahoga County
135	91.6	**Salem** (city) Columbiana County
138	91.7	**London** (city) Madison County
138	91.7	**Monroe** (city) Butler County
138	91.7	**Uhrichsville** (city) Tuscarawas County
141	91.8	**Norwalk** (city) Huron County
141	91.8	**Strongsville** (city) Cuyahoga County
141	91.8	**Wellsville** (village) Columbiana County
141	91.8	**Willard** (city) Huron County
145	91.9	**Centerville** (city) Montgomery County
145	91.9	**Covington** (village) Miami County
145	91.9	**Fredericktown** (village) Knox County
145	91.9	**Lake Lakengren** (CDP) Preble County
145	91.9	**Mansfield** (city) Richland County
145	91.9	**Mentor** (city) Lake County

Note: *This section ranks incorporated places and CDPs (Census Designated Places) with populations of 2,500 or more. Unincorporated postal areas were not considered. Please refer to the User Guide for additional information.*

Commute to Work: Public Transportation

Top 150 Places Ranked in *Descending* Order

State Rank	Percent	Place
1	20.1	**East Cleveland** (city) Cuyahoga County
2	11.9	**Warrensville Heights** (city) Cuyahoga County
3	10.6	**Cleveland** (city) Cuyahoga County
4	7.9	**Cincinnati** (city) Hamilton County
5	7.2	**Maple Heights** (city) Cuyahoga County
6	6.3	**Euclid** (city) Cuyahoga County
6	6.3	**Golf Manor** (village) Hamilton County
8	6.1	**Dayton** (city) Montgomery County
9	6.0	**North College Hill** (city) Hamilton County
10	5.3	**Cleveland Heights** (city) Cuyahoga County
10	5.3	**Moraine** (city) Montgomery County
12	5.2	**Lakewood** (city) Cuyahoga County
13	5.0	**Bedford Heights** (city) Cuyahoga County
13	5.0	**Shaker Heights** (city) Cuyahoga County
15	4.9	**Trotwood** (city) Montgomery County
16	4.3	**Canton** (city) Stark County
16	4.3	**Mineral Ridge** (CDP) Trumbull County
16	4.3	**Richmond Heights** (city) Cuyahoga County
19	4.2	**Akron** (city) Summit County
20	4.1	**Rocky River** (city) Cuyahoga County
21	4.0	**Garfield Heights** (city) Cuyahoga County
21	4.0	**Oxford** (city) Butler County
23	3.9	**Lockland** (village) Hamilton County
23	3.9	**Whitehall** (city) Franklin County
25	3.8	**Moreland Hills** (village) Cuyahoga County
26	3.7	**Finneytown** (CDP) Hamilton County
27	3.6	**Beachwood** (city) Cuyahoga County
27	3.6	**Cheviot** (city) Hamilton County
27	3.6	**Mount Healthy** (city) Hamilton County
27	3.6	**Pleasant Run Farm** (CDP) Hamilton County
27	3.6	**Youngstown** (city) Mahoning County
32	3.2	**Columbus** (city) Franklin County
32	3.2	**Forestville** (CDP) Hamilton County
34	3.1	**West Union** (village) Adams County
35	3.0	**Bedford** (city) Cuyahoga County
36	2.9	**Deer Park** (city) Hamilton County
37	2.8	**North Olmsted** (city) Cuyahoga County
37	2.8	**University Heights** (city) Cuyahoga County
39	2.6	**Madison** (village) Lake County
40	2.5	**Forest Park** (city) Hamilton County
40	2.5	**Kenwood** (CDP) Hamilton County
40	2.5	**Lincoln Village** (CDP) Franklin County
43	2.4	**Brooklyn** (city) Cuyahoga County
43	2.4	**Sandusky** (city) Erie County
43	2.4	**South Euclid** (city) Cuyahoga County
43	2.4	**Toledo** (city) Lucas County
47	2.3	**Mansfield** (city) Richland County
47	2.3	**Norwood** (city) Hamilton County
49	2.2	**Bay Village** (city) Cuyahoga County
49	2.2	**Edgewood** (CDP) Ashtabula County
49	2.2	**Mount Gilead** (village) Morrow County
49	2.2	**North Canton** (city) Stark County
49	2.2	**Silverton** (village) Hamilton County
54	2.1	**Delshire** (CDP) Hamilton County
54	2.1	**Geneva** (city) Ashtabula County
54	2.1	**Kent** (city) Portage County
54	2.1	**Oakwood** (village) Cuyahoga County
58	2.0	**Blacklick Estates** (CDP) Franklin County
58	2.0	**Greenfield** (village) Highland County
60	1.9	**Brecksville** (city) Cuyahoga County
60	1.9	**Martins Ferry** (city) Belmont County
60	1.9	**Steubenville** (city) Jefferson County
60	1.9	**Strongsville** (city) Cuyahoga County
64	1.8	**Amelia** (village) Clermont County
64	1.8	**Greenville** (city) Darke County
64	1.8	**Lyndhurst** (city) Cuyahoga County
64	1.8	**Massillon** (city) Stark County
68	1.7	**Barberton** (city) Summit County
68	1.7	**Macedonia** (city) Summit County
68	1.7	**Parma** (city) Cuyahoga County
68	1.7	**Willowick** (city) Lake County
72	1.6	**Gallipolis** (village) Gallia County
72	1.6	**Lima** (city) Allen County
72	1.6	**Painesville** (city) Lake County
72	1.6	**Summerside** (CDP) Clermont County

State Rank	Percent	Place
76	1.5	**Chagrin Falls** (village) Cuyahoga County
76	1.5	**Crestline** (village) Crawford County
76	1.5	**Dry Run** (CDP) Hamilton County
76	1.5	**Fairview Park** (city) Cuyahoga County
76	1.5	**Hicksville** (village) Defiance County
76	1.5	**Huber Heights** (city) Montgomery County
76	1.5	**Marysville** (city) Union County
76	1.5	**Mayfield Heights** (city) Cuyahoga County
76	1.5	**Montgomery** (city) Hamilton County
76	1.5	**New Burlington** (CDP) Hamilton County
76	1.5	**Reminderville** (village) Summit County
76	1.5	**Springfield** (city) Clark County
76	1.5	**Westlake** (city) Cuyahoga County
89	1.4	**Athens** (city) Athens County
89	1.4	**Bexley** (city) Franklin County
89	1.4	**Campbell** (city) Mahoning County
89	1.4	**Clyde** (city) Sandusky County
89	1.4	**Dillonvale** (CDP) Hamilton County
89	1.4	**Minster** (village) Auglaize County
89	1.4	**Northgate** (CDP) Hamilton County
96	1.3	**Enon** (village) Clark County
96	1.3	**Grandview Heights** (city) Franklin County
96	1.3	**Madeira** (city) Hamilton County
96	1.3	**Olmsted Falls** (city) Cuyahoga County
96	1.3	**Ross** (CDP) Butler County
96	1.3	**Sixteen Mile Stand** (CDP) Hamilton County
96	1.3	**Xenia** (city) Greene County
103	1.2	**Evendale** (village) Hamilton County
103	1.2	**Fairlawn** (city) Summit County
103	1.2	**Marion** (city) Marion County
103	1.2	**Port Clinton** (city) Ottawa County
103	1.2	**Turpin Hills** (CDP) Hamilton County
108	1.1	**Avon Lake** (city) Lorain County
108	1.1	**Beechwood Trails** (CDP) Licking County
108	1.1	**Brook Park** (city) Cuyahoga County
108	1.1	**Cambridge** (city) Guernsey County
108	1.1	**Independence** (city) Cuyahoga County
108	1.1	**Kettering** (city) Montgomery County
108	1.1	**Logan** (city) Hocking County
108	1.1	**Mentor** (city) Lake County
108	1.1	**Milford** (city) Clermont County
108	1.1	**Munroe Falls** (city) Summit County
108	1.1	**Parma Heights** (city) Cuyahoga County
108	1.1	**Pepper Pike** (city) Cuyahoga County
108	1.1	**Ravenna** (city) Portage County
121	1.0	**Bellaire** (village) Belmont County
121	1.0	**Brimfield** (CDP) Portage County
121	1.0	**Brunswick** (city) Medina County
121	1.0	**Clayton** (city) Montgomery County
121	1.0	**Dent** (CDP) Hamilton County
121	1.0	**Mount Orab** (village) Brown County
121	1.0	**North Zanesville** (CDP) Muskingum County
121	1.0	**Oregon** (city) Lucas County
121	1.0	**Reynoldsburg** (city) Franklin County
130	0.9	**Amberley** (village) Hamilton County
130	0.9	**Canal Fulton** (city) Stark County
130	0.9	**Centerville** (city) Montgomery County
130	0.9	**Covedale** (CDP) Hamilton County
130	0.9	**Dover** (city) Tuscarawas County
130	0.9	**East Liverpool** (city) Columbiana County
130	0.9	**Eastlake** (city) Lake County
130	0.9	**Grafton** (village) Lorain County
130	0.9	**Mariemont** (village) Hamilton County
130	0.9	**McDonald** (village) Trumbull County
130	0.9	**Mentor-on-the-Lake** (city) Lake County
130	0.9	**Middletown** (city) Butler County
130	0.9	**North Ridgeville** (city) Lorain County
130	0.9	**Troy** (city) Miami County
130	0.9	**Vandalia** (city) Montgomery County
130	0.9	**West Carrollton** (city) Montgomery County
130	0.9	**Wickliffe** (city) Lake County
130	0.9	**Williamsburg** (village) Clermont County
130	0.9	**Withamsville** (CDP) Clermont County
149	0.8	**Alliance** (city) Stark County
149	0.8	**Chillicothe** (city) Ross County

Note: *This section ranks incorporated places and CDPs (Census Designated Places) with populations of 2,500 or more. Unincorporated postal areas were not considered. Please refer to the User Guide for additional information.*

Commute to Work: Walk

Top 150 Places Ranked in *Descending* Order

State Rank	Percent	Place
1	39.6	**Oberlin** (city) Lorain County
2	35.9	**Athens** (city) Athens County
3	31.8	**Granville** (village) Licking County
4	30.6	**Cedarville** (village) Greene County
5	25.5	**Oxford** (city) Butler County
6	25.4	**New Concord** (village) Muskingum County
7	14.6	**Bowling Green** (city) Wood County
8	10.5	**Steubenville** (city) Jefferson County
9	10.3	**Greenfield** (village) Highland County
10	9.7	**Bellaire** (village) Belmont County
11	9.5	**Marietta** (city) Washington County
11	9.5	**Wooster** (city) Wayne County
13	9.3	**Kent** (city) Portage County
13	9.3	**Tiffin** (city) Seneca County
15	9.0	**Nelsonville** (city) Athens County
16	8.7	**University Heights** (city) Cuyahoga County
17	8.4	**Wellington** (village) Lorain County
18	8.0	**Ada** (village) Hardin County
19	7.9	**Blanchester** (village) Clinton County
20	7.8	**Crooksville** (village) Perry County
21	7.2	**Mount Vernon** (city) Knox County
22	7.0	**Dayton** (city) Montgomery County
22	7.0	**Portsmouth** (city) Scioto County
24	6.9	**West Milton** (village) Miami County
24	6.9	**Yellow Springs** (village) Greene County
26	6.8	**Bluffton** (village) Allen County
27	6.6	**Ashland** (city) Ashland County
28	6.5	**New London** (village) Huron County
29	6.4	**Bexley** (city) Franklin County
30	6.3	**Mount Healthy** (city) Hamilton County
30	6.3	**New Lexington** (village) Perry County
32	6.2	**Barnesville** (village) Belmont County
33	6.1	**Berea** (city) Cuyahoga County
33	6.1	**Wilmington** (city) Clinton County
35	5.8	**Chardon** (city) Geauga County
36	5.7	**Cincinnati** (city) Hamilton County
36	5.7	**Cleveland Heights** (city) Cuyahoga County
36	5.7	**Lockland** (village) Hamilton County
39	5.4	**Galion** (city) Crawford County
39	5.4	**Silverton** (village) Hamilton County
41	5.3	**Cleveland** (city) Cuyahoga County
41	5.3	**Wellsville** (village) Columbiana County
43	5.2	**Cadiz** (village) Harrison County
44	5.1	**Fostoria** (city) Seneca County
45	5.0	**East Cleveland** (city) Cuyahoga County
45	5.0	**Johnstown** (village) Licking County
47	4.9	**Alliance** (city) Stark County
47	4.9	**Devola** (CDP) Washington County
47	4.9	**Jefferson** (village) Ashtabula County
50	4.8	**Minerva** (village) Stark County
51	4.7	**Covington** (village) Miami County
51	4.7	**Springfield** (city) Clark County
53	4.6	**Lisbon** (village) Columbiana County
53	4.6	**New Carlisle** (city) Clark County
53	4.6	**Shelby** (city) Richland County
56	4.5	**Carrollton** (village) Carroll County
56	4.5	**Lodi** (village) Medina County
56	4.5	**Martins Ferry** (city) Belmont County
59	4.4	**Ballville** (CDP) Sandusky County
59	4.4	**Shadyside** (village) Belmont County
61	4.2	**Uhrichsville** (city) Tuscarawas County
62	4.0	**Northfield** (village) Summit County
63	3.9	**Cambridge** (city) Guernsey County
63	3.9	**Delaware** (city) Delaware County
65	3.8	**Coshocton** (city) Coshocton County
65	3.8	**East Palestine** (village) Columbiana County
65	3.8	**Fredericktown** (village) Knox County
65	3.8	**Salem** (city) Columbiana County
65	3.8	**South Euclid** (city) Cuyahoga County
65	3.8	**The Plains** (CDP) Athens County
65	3.8	**Urbana** (city) Champaign County
72	3.7	**Bethel** (village) Clermont County
72	3.7	**Defiance** (city) Defiance County
72	3.7	**Hicksville** (village) Defiance County
72	3.7	**Milford** (city) Clermont County
76	3.6	**Park Layne** (CDP) Clark County
76	3.6	**Willard** (city) Huron County
78	3.5	**Conneaut** (city) Ashtabula County
78	3.5	**Georgetown** (village) Brown County
78	3.5	**Strasburg** (village) Tuscarawas County
81	3.4	**Coldwater** (village) Mercer County
81	3.4	**Lancaster** (city) Fairfield County
81	3.4	**Montpelier** (village) Williams County
81	3.4	**New Lebanon** (village) Montgomery County
81	3.4	**Whitehall** (city) Franklin County
81	3.4	**Wright-Patterson AFB** (CDP) Greene County
87	3.3	**Crestline** (village) Crawford County
87	3.3	**Madison** (village) Lake County
87	3.3	**Sandusky** (city) Erie County
87	3.3	**Vermilion** (city) Lorain County
87	3.3	**Walbridge** (village) Wood County
87	3.3	**Youngstown** (city) Mahoning County
93	3.2	**Findlay** (city) Hancock County
94	3.1	**Covedale** (CDP) Hamilton County
94	3.1	**Golf Manor** (village) Hamilton County
94	3.1	**Pleasant Run** (CDP) Hamilton County
94	3.1	**Sharonville** (city) Hamilton County
94	3.1	**Versailles** (village) Darke County
99	3.0	**Columbus** (city) Franklin County
99	3.0	**Fairborn** (city) Greene County
99	3.0	**Lake Lakengren** (CDP) Preble County
99	3.0	**Logan** (city) Hocking County
99	3.0	**New Bremen** (village) Auglaize County
99	3.0	**Upper Sandusky** (city) Wyandot County
105	2.9	**Bucyrus** (city) Crawford County
105	2.9	**Canton** (city) Stark County
105	2.9	**Chillicothe** (city) Ross County
105	2.9	**Delphos** (city) Allen County
105	2.9	**Gallipolis** (village) Gallia County
105	2.9	**London** (city) Madison County
105	2.9	**Munroe Falls** (city) Summit County
105	2.9	**Wauseon** (city) Fulton County
113	2.8	**Columbiana** (city) Columbiana County
113	2.8	**Lakewood** (city) Cuyahoga County
113	2.8	**Mansfield** (city) Richland County
113	2.8	**Minster** (village) Auglaize County
113	2.8	**Paulding** (village) Paulding County
118	2.7	**Clyde** (city) Sandusky County
118	2.7	**Mount Carmel** (CDP) Clermont County
118	2.7	**North Canton** (city) Stark County
118	2.7	**North College Hill** (city) Hamilton County
122	2.6	**Circleville** (city) Pickaway County
122	2.6	**Doylestown** (village) Wayne County
122	2.6	**East Liverpool** (city) Columbiana County
122	2.6	**Garrettsville** (village) Portage County
122	2.6	**Greenville** (city) Darke County
122	2.6	**Ironton** (city) Lawrence County
122	2.6	**Mentor** (city) Lake County
122	2.6	**Saint Bernard** (city) Hamilton County
122	2.6	**Toledo** (city) Lucas County
122	2.6	**Troy** (city) Miami County
122	2.6	**Xenia** (city) Greene County
133	2.5	**Archbold** (village) Fulton County
133	2.5	**Carey** (village) Wyandot County
133	2.5	**Loudonville** (village) Ashland County
133	2.5	**Madeira** (city) Hamilton County
133	2.5	**New Philadelphia** (city) Tuscarawas County
133	2.5	**North Zanesville** (CDP) Muskingum County
133	2.5	**Norwalk** (city) Huron County
133	2.5	**Perry Heights** (CDP) Stark County
133	2.5	**Wapakoneta** (city) Auglaize County
133	2.5	**Waynesville** (village) Warren County
143	2.4	**Akron** (city) Summit County
143	2.4	**Barberton** (city) Summit County
143	2.4	**Delshire** (CDP) Hamilton County
143	2.4	**Eaton** (city) Preble County
143	2.4	**Hamilton** (city) Butler County
143	2.4	**Kenton** (city) Hardin County
143	2.4	**Louisville** (city) Stark County
143	2.4	**Mariemont** (village) Hamilton County

Note: *This section ranks incorporated places and CDPs (Census Designated Places) with populations of 2,500 or more. Unincorporated postal areas were not considered. Please refer to the User Guide for additional information.*

Commute to Work: Walk

Top 150 Places Ranked in *Ascending* Order

State Rank	Percent	Place
1	0.0	**Apple Valley** (CDP) Knox County
1	0.0	**Beechwood Trails** (CDP) Licking County
1	0.0	**Brimfield** (CDP) Portage County
1	0.0	**Burlington** (CDP) Lawrence County
1	0.0	**Canfield** (city) Mahoning County
1	0.0	**Champion Heights** (CDP) Trumbull County
1	0.0	**Cortland** (city) Trumbull County
1	0.0	**Delhi Hills** (CDP) Hamilton County
1	0.0	**Dry Ridge** (CDP) Hamilton County
1	0.0	**Four Bridges** (CDP) Butler County
1	0.0	**Germantown** (city) Montgomery County
1	0.0	**Greentown** (CDP) Stark County
1	0.0	**Harrison** (city) Hamilton County
1	0.0	**Huber Ridge** (CDP) Franklin County
1	0.0	**Lakemore** (village) Summit County
1	0.0	**Lexington** (village) Richland County
1	0.0	**Lordstown** (village) Trumbull County
1	0.0	**Macedonia** (city) Summit County
1	0.0	**Mack** (CDP) Hamilton County
1	0.0	**Mayfield** (village) Cuyahoga County
1	0.0	**Mineral Ridge** (CDP) Trumbull County
1	0.0	**Montrose-Ghent** (CDP) Summit County
1	0.0	**Mount Healthy Heights** (CDP) Hamilton County
1	0.0	**Mount Orab** (village) Brown County
1	0.0	**New Burlington** (CDP) Hamilton County
1	0.0	**Newcomerstown** (village) Tuscarawas County
1	0.0	**Northridge** (CDP) Clark County
1	0.0	**Oakwood** (city) Montgomery County
1	0.0	**Oakwood** (village) Cuyahoga County
1	0.0	**Ontario** (city) Richland County
1	0.0	**Orange** (village) Cuyahoga County
1	0.0	**Pickerington** (city) Fairfield County
1	0.0	**Richville** (CDP) Stark County
1	0.0	**Ross** (CDP) Butler County
1	0.0	**Salem Heights** (CDP) Hamilton County
1	0.0	**Sebring** (village) Mahoning County
1	0.0	**South Point** (village) Lawrence County
1	0.0	**South Russell** (village) Geauga County
1	0.0	**Summerside** (CDP) Clermont County
1	0.0	**Sunbury** (village) Delaware County
1	0.0	**Swanton** (village) Fulton County
1	0.0	**Turpin Hills** (CDP) Hamilton County
1	0.0	**Union** (city) Montgomery County
1	0.0	**Waverly** (village) Pike County
1	0.0	**West Union** (village) Adams County
1	0.0	**Willoughby Hills** (city) Lake County
1	0.0	**Wintersville** (village) Jefferson County
1	0.0	**Woodlawn** (village) Hamilton County
49	0.1	**Broadview Heights** (city) Cuyahoga County
49	0.1	**Howland Center** (CDP) Trumbull County
49	0.1	**North Madison** (CDP) Lake County
49	0.1	**Sheffield** (village) Lorain County
49	0.1	**South Lebanon** (village) Warren County
54	0.2	**Amherst** (city) Lorain County
54	0.2	**Dent** (CDP) Hamilton County
54	0.2	**Green** (city) Summit County
54	0.2	**Landen** (CDP) Warren County
54	0.2	**New Richmond** (village) Clermont County
54	0.2	**Springboro** (city) Warren County
60	0.3	**Carlisle** (village) Warren County
60	0.3	**Dry Run** (CDP) Hamilton County
60	0.3	**Fort Shawnee** (CDP) Allen County
60	0.3	**New Franklin** (city) Summit County
60	0.3	**North Kingsville** (village) Ashtabula County
60	0.3	**Vandalia** (city) Montgomery County
66	0.4	**Avon** (city) Lorain County
66	0.4	**Brookville** (city) Montgomery County
66	0.4	**Clayton** (city) Montgomery County
66	0.4	**Geneva** (city) Ashtabula County
66	0.4	**Kenwood** (CDP) Hamilton County
66	0.4	**Lake Darby** (CDP) Franklin County
66	0.4	**North Baltimore** (village) Wood County
66	0.4	**Obetz** (village) Franklin County
66	0.4	**Powell** (city) Delaware County
66	0.4	**Seven Hills** (city) Cuyahoga County

State Rank	Percent	Place
66	0.4	**Solon** (city) Cuyahoga County
66	0.4	**Withamsville** (CDP) Clermont County
78	0.5	**Austintown** (CDP) Mahoning County
78	0.5	**Cherry Grove** (CDP) Hamilton County
78	0.5	**Dublin** (city) Franklin County
78	0.5	**Greenhills** (village) Hamilton County
78	0.5	**Mogadore** (village) Summit County
78	0.5	**North Ridgeville** (city) Lorain County
78	0.5	**North Royalton** (city) Cuyahoga County
78	0.5	**Richmond Heights** (city) Cuyahoga County
78	0.5	**Seville** (village) Medina County
87	0.6	**Franklin** (city) Warren County
87	0.6	**Grove City** (city) Franklin County
87	0.6	**Hubbard** (city) Trumbull County
87	0.6	**Independence** (city) Cuyahoga County
87	0.6	**Mulberry** (CDP) Clermont County
87	0.6	**Plain City** (village) Madison County
87	0.6	**Reminderville** (village) Summit County
87	0.6	**Stow** (city) Summit County
87	0.6	**Streetsboro** (city) Portage County
87	0.6	**Tallmadge** (city) Summit County
87	0.6	**Tipp City** (city) Miami County
87	0.6	**Twinsburg** (city) Summit County
87	0.6	**Wyoming** (city) Hamilton County
100	0.7	**Bay Village** (city) Cuyahoga County
100	0.7	**Beachwood** (city) Cuyahoga County
100	0.7	**Centerville** (city) Montgomery County
100	0.7	**Cleves** (village) Hamilton County
100	0.7	**Fairfield** (city) Butler County
100	0.7	**Groveport** (city) Franklin County
100	0.7	**Marysville** (city) Union County
100	0.7	**Mason** (city) Warren County
100	0.7	**McDonald** (village) Trumbull County
100	0.7	**Northgate** (CDP) Hamilton County
100	0.7	**Sherwood** (CDP) Hamilton County
100	0.7	**Strongsville** (city) Cuyahoga County
100	0.7	**Whitehouse** (village) Lucas County
113	0.8	**Ashville** (village) Pickaway County
113	0.8	**Boardman** (CDP) Mahoning County
113	0.8	**Brecksville** (city) Cuyahoga County
113	0.8	**Campbell** (city) Mahoning County
113	0.8	**Delta** (village) Fulton County
113	0.8	**Highland Heights** (city) Cuyahoga County
113	0.8	**Mingo Junction** (village) Jefferson County
113	0.8	**Moraine** (city) Montgomery County
113	0.8	**Springdale** (city) Hamilton County
113	0.8	**Worthington** (city) Franklin County
123	0.9	**Amberley** (village) Hamilton County
123	0.9	**Aurora** (city) Portage County
123	0.9	**Blue Ash** (city) Hamilton County
123	0.9	**Canal Winchester** (city) Franklin County
123	0.9	**Fairport Harbor** (village) Lake County
123	0.9	**Forest Park** (city) Hamilton County
123	0.9	**Hartville** (village) Stark County
123	0.9	**Maumee** (city) Lucas County
123	0.9	**Mentor-on-the-Lake** (city) Lake County
123	0.9	**Monroe** (city) Butler County
123	0.9	**New Albany** (city) Franklin County
123	0.9	**Newton Falls** (village) Trumbull County
123	0.9	**Pleasant Run Farm** (CDP) Hamilton County
123	0.9	**Portage Lakes** (CDP) Summit County
123	0.9	**Saint Henry** (village) Mercer County
123	0.9	**Westlake** (city) Cuyahoga County
139	1.0	**Bedford Heights** (city) Cuyahoga County
139	1.0	**Bridgetown** (CDP) Hamilton County
139	1.0	**Elyria** (city) Lorain County
139	1.0	**Englewood** (city) Montgomery County
139	1.0	**Hilliard** (city) Franklin County
139	1.0	**Kirtland** (city) Lake County
139	1.0	**Lincoln Heights** (village) Hamilton County
139	1.0	**Mount Repose** (CDP) Clermont County
139	1.0	**Struthers** (city) Mahoning County
139	1.0	**Wellston** (city) Jackson County
139	1.0	**Wickliffe** (city) Lake County
150	1.1	**Belpre** (city) Washington County

Note: *This section ranks incorporated places and CDPs (Census Designated Places) with populations of 2,500 or more. Unincorporated postal areas were not considered. Please refer to the User Guide for additional information.*

Commute to Work: Work from Home

Top 150 Places Ranked in *Descending* Order

State Rank	Percent	Place
1	18.2	**Cedarville** (village) Greene County
2	16.6	**Granville** (village) Licking County
3	16.0	**The Village of Indian Hill** (city) Hamilton County
4	14.5	**Mount Orab** (village) Brown County
5	14.3	**Moreland Hills** (village) Cuyahoga County
6	13.9	**Ada** (village) Hardin County
7	13.4	**South Russell** (village) Geauga County
8	12.1	**Yellow Springs** (village) Greene County
9	11.7	**Montgomery** (city) Hamilton County
10	11.1	**Salem Heights** (CDP) Hamilton County
11	10.9	**Wyoming** (city) Hamilton County
12	10.8	**Four Bridges** (CDP) Butler County
13	10.6	**Powell** (city) Delaware County
14	10.4	**Bainbridge** (CDP) Geauga County
15	9.9	**Sherwood** (CDP) Hamilton County
16	9.8	**Bay Village** (city) Cuyahoga County
16	9.8	**Kenwood** (CDP) Hamilton County
18	9.7	**Milford** (city) Clermont County
19	9.2	**Fruit Hill** (CDP) Hamilton County
20	9.0	**Hudson** (city) Summit County
21	8.9	**Avon** (city) Lorain County
22	8.8	**Turpin Hills** (CDP) Hamilton County
23	8.7	**Chagrin Falls** (village) Cuyahoga County
24	8.4	**Pepper Pike** (city) Cuyahoga County
25	8.3	**Devola** (CDP) Washington County
25	8.3	**Pleasant Run Farm** (CDP) Hamilton County
25	8.3	**Worthington** (city) Franklin County
28	8.2	**Beckett Ridge** (CDP) Butler County
28	8.2	**Madeira** (city) Hamilton County
28	8.2	**Mariemont** (village) Hamilton County
28	8.2	**Orange** (village) Cuyahoga County
32	7.9	**Shaker Heights** (city) Cuyahoga County
33	7.8	**Apple Valley** (CDP) Knox County
33	7.8	**Sheffield** (village) Lorain County
35	7.7	**Gahanna** (city) Franklin County
36	7.6	**Beechwood Trails** (CDP) Licking County
36	7.6	**Cherry Grove** (CDP) Hamilton County
36	7.6	**Forestville** (CDP) Hamilton County
39	7.5	**New Albany** (city) Franklin County
40	7.2	**Dublin** (city) Franklin County
40	7.2	**New Richmond** (village) Clermont County
42	7.1	**Westlake** (city) Cuyahoga County
43	7.0	**Bexley** (city) Franklin County
43	7.0	**Dry Run** (CDP) Hamilton County
43	7.0	**Monroe** (city) Butler County
46	6.9	**Plain City** (village) Madison County
47	6.7	**Athens** (city) Athens County
47	6.7	**Hartville** (village) Stark County
49	6.6	**Aurora** (city) Portage County
50	6.5	**Lincoln Village** (CDP) Franklin County
51	6.4	**Broadview Heights** (city) Cuyahoga County
51	6.4	**Mount Repose** (CDP) Clermont County
53	6.3	**Centerville** (city) Montgomery County
53	6.3	**Covedale** (CDP) Hamilton County
55	6.2	**Lyndhurst** (city) Cuyahoga County
55	6.2	**Mason** (city) Warren County
57	6.1	**Green Meadows** (CDP) Clark County
57	6.1	**Sunbury** (village) Delaware County
57	6.1	**Westerville** (city) Franklin County
60	6.0	**Brecksville** (city) Cuyahoga County
60	6.0	**Twinsburg** (city) Summit County
62	5.9	**Kent** (city) Portage County
62	5.9	**Solon** (city) Cuyahoga County
62	5.9	**Upper Arlington** (city) Franklin County
65	5.8	**Rocky River** (city) Cuyahoga County
65	5.8	**Sixteen Mile Stand** (CDP) Hamilton County
67	5.7	**Avon Lake** (city) Lorain County
67	5.7	**Bluffton** (village) Allen County
69	5.6	**Montrose-Ghent** (CDP) Summit County
70	5.5	**Amberley** (village) Hamilton County
70	5.5	**Ashville** (village) Pickaway County
70	5.5	**Canal Winchester** (city) Franklin County
70	5.5	**North Canton** (city) Stark County
70	5.5	**Oxford** (city) Butler County
75	5.4	**Mack** (CDP) Hamilton County
76	5.3	**Delaware** (city) Delaware County
76	5.3	**Lordstown** (village) Trumbull County
76	5.3	**Richfield** (village) Summit County
76	5.3	**Richmond Heights** (city) Cuyahoga County
76	5.3	**University Heights** (city) Cuyahoga County
81	5.2	**Beachwood** (city) Cuyahoga County
81	5.2	**Hilliard** (city) Franklin County
81	5.2	**Kirtland** (city) Lake County
81	5.2	**Oberlin** (city) Lorain County
85	5.1	**Champion Heights** (CDP) Trumbull County
86	5.0	**Cleveland Heights** (city) Cuyahoga County
86	5.0	**Dillonvale** (CDP) Hamilton County
86	5.0	**Enon** (village) Clark County
86	5.0	**Miami Heights** (CDP) Hamilton County
90	4.9	**Blue Ash** (city) Hamilton County
90	4.9	**Dent** (CDP) Hamilton County
90	4.9	**Groveport** (city) Franklin County
90	4.9	**Mulberry** (CDP) Clermont County
90	4.9	**Oakwood** (city) Montgomery County
90	4.9	**Strongsville** (city) Cuyahoga County
96	4.8	**Delta** (village) Fulton County
96	4.8	**Grandview Heights** (city) Franklin County
96	4.8	**Saint Bernard** (city) Hamilton County
99	4.7	**Fairlawn** (city) Summit County
99	4.7	**Landen** (CDP) Warren County
99	4.7	**Steubenville** (city) Jefferson County
102	4.6	**Berea** (city) Cuyahoga County
102	4.6	**Day Heights** (CDP) Clermont County
102	4.6	**Macedonia** (city) Summit County
102	4.6	**North Royalton** (city) Cuyahoga County
106	4.5	**Baltimore** (village) Fairfield County
106	4.5	**Ottawa Hills** (village) Lucas County
108	4.4	**Bellbrook** (city) Greene County
108	4.4	**Cincinnati** (city) Hamilton County
108	4.4	**Newtown** (village) Hamilton County
108	4.4	**Sebring** (village) Mahoning County
108	4.4	**Sylvania** (city) Lucas County
113	4.3	**Highland Heights** (city) Cuyahoga County
114	4.2	**Bethel** (village) Clermont County
114	4.2	**Burlington** (CDP) Lawrence County
114	4.2	**Fairport Harbor** (village) Lake County
114	4.2	**Reynoldsburg** (city) Franklin County
114	4.2	**Sharonville** (city) Hamilton County
114	4.2	**Waterville** (city) Lucas County
120	4.1	**Fairview Park** (city) Cuyahoga County
120	4.1	**Perrysburg** (city) Wood County
120	4.1	**Pleasant Run** (CDP) Hamilton County
120	4.1	**Reminderville** (village) Summit County
124	4.0	**Beavercreek** (city) Greene County
124	4.0	**Germantown** (city) Montgomery County
124	4.0	**Heath** (city) Licking County
124	4.0	**Monfort Heights** (CDP) Hamilton County
124	4.0	**New Concord** (village) Muskingum County
129	3.9	**Amelia** (village) Clermont County
129	3.9	**Canfield** (city) Mahoning County
129	3.9	**Delhi Hills** (CDP) Hamilton County
129	3.9	**Dry Ridge** (CDP) Hamilton County
129	3.9	**Loveland** (city) Hamilton County
129	3.9	**Marysville** (city) Union County
129	3.9	**Mentor** (city) Lake County
129	3.9	**Moraine** (city) Montgomery County
129	3.9	**North Zanesville** (CDP) Muskingum County
129	3.9	**Port Clinton** (city) Ottawa County
129	3.9	**Springboro** (city) Warren County
140	3.8	**Lakewood** (city) Cuyahoga County
140	3.8	**Poland** (village) Mahoning County
140	3.8	**Wintersville** (village) Jefferson County
143	3.7	**Conneaut** (city) Ashtabula County
143	3.7	**Green** (city) Summit County
143	3.7	**Greenfield** (village) Highland County
143	3.7	**Kettering** (city) Montgomery County
143	3.7	**Salem** (city) Columbiana County
143	3.7	**Seville** (village) Medina County
143	3.7	**West Jefferson** (village) Madison County
150	3.6	**Coshocton** (city) Coshocton County

Note: *This section ranks incorporated places and CDPs (Census Designated Places) with populations of 2,500 or more. Unincorporated postal areas were not considered. Please refer to the User Guide for additional information.*

Commute to Work: Work from Home

Top 150 Places Ranked in *Ascending* Order

State Rank	Percent	Place
1	0.0	**Barnesville** (village) Belmont County
1	0.0	**Georgetown** (village) Brown County
1	0.0	**New Lebanon** (village) Montgomery County
1	0.0	**New Lexington** (village) Perry County
1	0.0	**Newcomerstown** (village) Tuscarawas County
6	0.1	**Wright-Patterson AFB** (CDP) Greene County
7	0.2	**Ross** (CDP) Butler County
8	0.3	**McDonald** (village) Trumbull County
8	0.3	**Napoleon** (city) Henry County
8	0.3	**Sheffield Lake** (city) Lorain County
11	0.4	**Mount Healthy** (city) Hamilton County
11	0.4	**Newton Falls** (village) Trumbull County
11	0.4	**Struthers** (city) Mahoning County
14	0.5	**Covington** (village) Miami County
14	0.5	**East Palestine** (village) Columbiana County
14	0.5	**Waverly** (village) Pike County
17	0.6	**Brookville** (city) Montgomery County
17	0.6	**Cheviot** (city) Hamilton County
17	0.6	**Coldwater** (village) Mercer County
17	0.6	**Crestline** (village) Crawford County
17	0.6	**Edgewood** (CDP) Ashtabula County
17	0.6	**Richville** (CDP) Stark County
17	0.6	**Rossford** (city) Wood County
17	0.6	**Shelby** (city) Richland County
17	0.6	**Swanton** (village) Fulton County
17	0.6	**Wellsville** (village) Columbiana County
27	0.7	**Celina** (city) Mercer County
27	0.7	**Hicksville** (village) Defiance County
27	0.7	**Montpelier** (village) Williams County
27	0.7	**Park Layne** (CDP) Clark County
31	0.8	**Lincoln Heights** (village) Hamilton County
31	0.8	**Van Wert** (city) Van Wert County
31	0.8	**West Portsmouth** (CDP) Scioto County
34	0.9	**Garrettsville** (village) Portage County
34	0.9	**Greentown** (CDP) Stark County
34	0.9	**Minerva** (village) Stark County
34	0.9	**New Burlington** (CDP) Hamilton County
34	0.9	**Versailles** (village) Darke County
39	1.0	**Bellaire** (village) Belmont County
39	1.0	**Carey** (village) Wyandot County
39	1.0	**Delphos** (city) Allen County
39	1.0	**East Liverpool** (city) Columbiana County
39	1.0	**Maple Heights** (city) Cuyahoga County
39	1.0	**Niles** (city) Trumbull County
39	1.0	**North Madison** (CDP) Lake County
39	1.0	**Reading** (city) Hamilton County
39	1.0	**West Carrollton** (city) Montgomery County
39	1.0	**West Union** (village) Adams County
49	1.1	**Bedford Heights** (city) Cuyahoga County
49	1.1	**Belpre** (city) Washington County
49	1.1	**Franklin** (city) Warren County
49	1.1	**Kenton** (city) Hardin County
49	1.1	**Lima** (city) Allen County
49	1.1	**New Carlisle** (city) Clark County
49	1.1	**New Philadelphia** (city) Tuscarawas County
49	1.1	**North College Hill** (city) Hamilton County
49	1.1	**Saint Henry** (village) Mercer County
58	1.2	**Cambridge** (city) Guernsey County
58	1.2	**Clyde** (city) Sandusky County
58	1.2	**Crooksville** (village) Perry County
58	1.2	**Riverside** (city) Montgomery County
58	1.2	**Upper Sandusky** (city) Wyandot County
58	1.2	**Wauseon** (city) Fulton County
58	1.2	**Woodlawn** (village) Hamilton County
65	1.3	**Bryan** (city) Williams County
65	1.3	**Fort Shawnee** (CDP) Allen County
65	1.3	**Munroe Falls** (city) Summit County
65	1.3	**North Baltimore** (village) Wood County
65	1.3	**Ottawa** (village) Putnam County
65	1.3	**The Plains** (CDP) Athens County
65	1.3	**Tiffin** (city) Seneca County
72	1.4	**Ballville** (CDP) Sandusky County
72	1.4	**Blanchester** (village) Clinton County
72	1.4	**Calcutta** (CDP) Columbiana County
72	1.4	**Lancaster** (city) Fairfield County
72	1.4	**Marion** (city) Marion County
72	1.4	**Millersburg** (village) Holmes County
72	1.4	**Mineral Ridge** (CDP) Trumbull County
72	1.4	**Mogadore** (village) Summit County
72	1.4	**Saint Clairsville** (city) Belmont County
72	1.4	**Urbana** (city) Champaign County
72	1.4	**Williamsburg** (village) Clermont County
83	1.5	**Barberton** (city) Summit County
83	1.5	**Madison** (village) Lake County
83	1.5	**Norwood** (city) Hamilton County
83	1.5	**Trotwood** (city) Montgomery County
83	1.5	**Wellston** (city) Jackson County
83	1.5	**Willard** (city) Huron County
89	1.6	**Campbell** (city) Mahoning County
89	1.6	**Elyria** (city) Lorain County
89	1.6	**Huber Heights** (city) Montgomery County
89	1.6	**Springdale** (city) Hamilton County
89	1.6	**Vermilion** (city) Lorain County
89	1.6	**Whitehall** (city) Franklin County
95	1.7	**Delshire** (CDP) Hamilton County
95	1.7	**Hamilton** (city) Butler County
95	1.7	**Johnstown** (village) Licking County
95	1.7	**Lake Darby** (CDP) Franklin County
95	1.7	**Lorain** (city) Lorain County
95	1.7	**Northridge** (CDP) Clark County
95	1.7	**Oak Harbor** (village) Ottawa County
95	1.7	**Portage Lakes** (CDP) Summit County
103	1.8	**Brook Park** (city) Cuyahoga County
103	1.8	**Carlisle** (village) Warren County
103	1.8	**Eastlake** (city) Lake County
103	1.8	**Fostoria** (city) Seneca County
103	1.8	**Galion** (city) Crawford County
103	1.8	**Geneva** (city) Ashtabula County
103	1.8	**Lockland** (village) Hamilton County
103	1.8	**Loudonville** (village) Ashland County
103	1.8	**Sidney** (city) Shelby County
112	1.9	**Bedford** (city) Cuyahoga County
112	1.9	**Bellefontaine** (city) Logan County
112	1.9	**Bucyrus** (city) Crawford County
112	1.9	**Jefferson** (village) Ashtabula County
112	1.9	**Lake Lakengren** (CDP) Preble County
112	1.9	**Middletown** (city) Butler County
112	1.9	**Saint Marys** (city) Auglaize County
112	1.9	**Tallmadge** (city) Summit County
112	1.9	**Wadsworth** (city) Medina County
112	1.9	**Wapakoneta** (city) Auglaize County
112	1.9	**Xenia** (city) Greene County
123	2.0	**Akron** (city) Summit County
123	2.0	**Archbold** (village) Fulton County
123	2.0	**Brooklyn** (city) Cuyahoga County
123	2.0	**Fairfield** (city) Butler County
123	2.0	**Martins Ferry** (city) Belmont County
123	2.0	**Mentor-on-the-Lake** (city) Lake County
123	2.0	**Middleburg Heights** (city) Cuyahoga County
123	2.0	**Minster** (village) Auglaize County
123	2.0	**Oakwood** (village) Cuyahoga County
123	2.0	**Ontario** (city) Richland County
123	2.0	**Sandusky** (city) Erie County
134	2.1	**Chardon** (city) Geauga County
134	2.1	**Circleville** (city) Pickaway County
134	2.1	**Cleves** (village) Hamilton County
134	2.1	**Deer Park** (city) Hamilton County
134	2.1	**Defiance** (city) Defiance County
134	2.1	**Lodi** (village) Medina County
134	2.1	**Ravenna** (city) Portage County
134	2.1	**Toledo** (city) Lucas County
134	2.1	**Walbridge** (village) Wood County
143	2.2	**Alliance** (city) Stark County
143	2.2	**Austintown** (CDP) Mahoning County
143	2.2	**Bridgetown** (CDP) Hamilton County
143	2.2	**Eaton** (city) Preble County
143	2.2	**Englewood** (city) Montgomery County
143	2.2	**Fremont** (city) Sandusky County
143	2.2	**Garfield Heights** (city) Cuyahoga County
143	2.2	**Jackson** (city) Jackson County

Note: *This section ranks incorporated places and CDPs (Census Designated Places) with populations of 2,500 or more. Unincorporated postal areas were not considered. Please refer to the User Guide for additional information.*

Mean Travel Time to Work

Top 150 Places Ranked in *Descending* Order

State Rank	Minutes	Place
1	35.2	**Apple Valley** (CDP) Knox County
2	34.8	**Mount Orab** (village) Brown County
3	33.5	**Amelia** (village) Clermont County
4	33.2	**Georgetown** (village) Brown County
5	32.1	**Bethel** (village) Clermont County
6	32.0	**Williamsburg** (village) Clermont County
7	31.0	**Baltimore** (village) Fairfield County
8	30.8	**North Madison** (CDP) Lake County
9	30.6	**South Russell** (village) Geauga County
10	30.3	**Lake Lakengren** (CDP) Preble County
11	29.9	**West Portsmouth** (CDP) Scioto County
12	29.6	**Wintersville** (village) Jefferson County
13	29.4	**Wellington** (village) Lorain County
13	29.4	**West Union** (village) Adams County
15	29.3	**Sheffield Lake** (city) Lorain County
16	29.2	**Garrettsville** (village) Portage County
16	29.2	**Golf Manor** (village) Hamilton County
16	29.2	**Olmsted Falls** (city) Cuyahoga County
19	29.1	**Blanchester** (village) Clinton County
20	29.0	**Covedale** (CDP) Hamilton County
21	28.9	**Ashville** (village) Pickaway County
21	28.9	**Johnstown** (village) Licking County
23	28.7	**Crooksville** (village) Perry County
24	28.6	**Newton Falls** (village) Trumbull County
24	28.6	**Wellston** (city) Jackson County
26	28.5	**Trenton** (city) Butler County
27	28.4	**Beechwood Trails** (CDP) Licking County
27	28.4	**Brunswick** (city) Medina County
27	28.4	**North College Hill** (city) Hamilton County
30	28.3	**Withamsville** (CDP) Clermont County
31	28.2	**Broadview Heights** (city) Cuyahoga County
31	28.2	**Lake Darby** (CDP) Franklin County
31	28.2	**New Richmond** (village) Clermont County
34	28.1	**Turpin Hills** (CDP) Hamilton County
35	28.0	**Medina** (city) Medina County
35	28.0	**Minerva** (village) Stark County
37	27.6	**Aurora** (city) Portage County
37	27.6	**Hudson** (city) Summit County
37	27.6	**Miami Heights** (CDP) Hamilton County
37	27.6	**New Lebanon** (village) Montgomery County
37	27.6	**New London** (village) Huron County
42	27.5	**Mack** (CDP) Hamilton County
42	27.5	**Vermilion** (city) Lorain County
44	27.4	**Delhi Hills** (CDP) Hamilton County
44	27.4	**North Ridgeville** (city) Lorain County
44	27.4	**Strongsville** (city) Cuyahoga County
47	27.3	**Dry Run** (CDP) Hamilton County
47	27.3	**Newcomerstown** (village) Tuscarawas County
47	27.3	**North Royalton** (city) Cuyahoga County
50	27.2	**East Palestine** (village) Columbiana County
50	27.2	**Mingo Junction** (village) Jefferson County
50	27.2	**Reminderville** (village) Summit County
53	27.1	**Delshire** (CDP) Hamilton County
53	27.1	**Geneva** (city) Ashtabula County
55	27.0	**Delaware** (city) Delaware County
56	26.9	**Day Heights** (CDP) Clermont County
56	26.9	**Delta** (village) Fulton County
56	26.9	**Germantown** (city) Montgomery County
56	26.9	**Monroe** (city) Butler County
56	26.9	**New Lexington** (village) Perry County
61	26.8	**Canal Winchester** (city) Franklin County
61	26.8	**Lockland** (village) Hamilton County
63	26.7	**Cherry Grove** (CDP) Hamilton County
64	26.6	**Madison** (village) Lake County
64	26.6	**Uniontown** (CDP) Stark County
66	26.5	**Northgate** (CDP) Hamilton County
67	26.4	**Hartville** (village) Stark County
67	26.4	**Parma Heights** (city) Cuyahoga County
67	26.4	**Pickerington** (city) Fairfield County
67	26.4	**Seven Hills** (city) Cuyahoga County
71	26.3	**Avon Lake** (city) Lorain County
71	26.3	**Moreland Hills** (village) Cuyahoga County
71	26.3	**Newtown** (village) Hamilton County
74	26.2	**Grafton** (village) Lorain County
74	26.2	**Hillsboro** (city) Highland County
74	26.2	**Summerside** (CDP) Clermont County
77	26.1	**Macedonia** (city) Summit County
77	26.1	**Ross** (CDP) Butler County
79	26.0	**Cheviot** (city) Hamilton County
79	26.0	**Cleves** (village) Hamilton County
79	26.0	**Pataskala** (city) Licking County
79	26.0	**Seville** (village) Medina County
83	25.9	**Harrison** (city) Hamilton County
83	25.9	**Lincoln Heights** (village) Hamilton County
83	25.9	**Mount Repose** (CDP) Clermont County
83	25.9	**Poland** (village) Mahoning County
83	25.9	**Trotwood** (city) Montgomery County
83	25.9	**Warrensville Heights** (city) Cuyahoga County
89	25.8	**Greenfield** (village) Highland County
90	25.7	**Lancaster** (city) Fairfield County
90	25.7	**New Burlington** (CDP) Hamilton County
92	25.6	**East Cleveland** (city) Cuyahoga County
92	25.6	**Fredericktown** (village) Knox County
92	25.6	**Kirtland** (city) Lake County
92	25.6	**Mount Gilead** (village) Morrow County
96	25.5	**Mulberry** (CDP) Clermont County
96	25.5	**Rittman** (city) Wayne County
96	25.5	**Twinsburg** (city) Summit County
99	25.4	**Bainbridge** (CDP) Geauga County
99	25.4	**Barnesville** (village) Belmont County
99	25.4	**Chagrin Falls** (village) Cuyahoga County
99	25.4	**Sunbury** (village) Delaware County
103	25.3	**Cortland** (city) Trumbull County
103	25.3	**Hamilton** (city) Butler County
103	25.3	**Maple Heights** (city) Cuyahoga County
103	25.3	**Richfield** (village) Summit County
103	25.3	**Solon** (city) Cuyahoga County
103	25.3	**Westlake** (city) Cuyahoga County
109	25.2	**Green Meadows** (CDP) Clark County
109	25.2	**Jackson** (city) Jackson County
109	25.2	**South Lebanon** (village) Warren County
112	25.1	**Avon** (city) Lorain County
112	25.1	**Calcutta** (CDP) Columbiana County
112	25.1	**Wellsville** (village) Columbiana County
115	25.0	**Bay Village** (city) Cuyahoga County
115	25.0	**Greentown** (CDP) Stark County
115	25.0	**Louisville** (city) Stark County
115	25.0	**Mentor-on-the-Lake** (city) Lake County
115	25.0	**Streetsboro** (city) Portage County
120	24.9	**Fairview Park** (city) Cuyahoga County
120	24.9	**Lakemore** (village) Summit County
120	24.9	**Powell** (city) Delaware County
120	24.9	**Richmond Heights** (city) Cuyahoga County
124	24.8	**Circleville** (city) Pickaway County
124	24.8	**Fairlawn** (city) Summit County
124	24.8	**Parma** (city) Cuyahoga County
127	24.7	**Plain City** (village) Madison County
127	24.7	**Union** (city) Montgomery County
129	24.6	**Euclid** (city) Cuyahoga County
129	24.6	**Forestville** (CDP) Hamilton County
129	24.6	**Groesbeck** (CDP) Hamilton County
132	24.5	**Buckeye Lake** (village) Licking County
132	24.5	**Logan** (city) Hocking County
132	24.5	**Mariemont** (village) Hamilton County
132	24.5	**Mason** (city) Warren County
132	24.5	**Mineral Ridge** (CDP) Trumbull County
132	24.5	**Toronto** (city) Jefferson County
132	24.5	**Whitehouse** (village) Lucas County
139	24.4	**Chardon** (city) Geauga County
139	24.4	**Dublin** (city) Franklin County
139	24.4	**Mount Healthy Heights** (CDP) Hamilton County
139	24.4	**Pleasant Run Farm** (CDP) Hamilton County
139	24.4	**Swanton** (village) Fulton County
144	24.3	**Campbell** (city) Mahoning County
144	24.3	**Cleveland** (city) Cuyahoga County
144	24.3	**Northridge** (CDP) Clark County
144	24.3	**Reynoldsburg** (city) Franklin County
144	24.3	**Rocky River** (city) Cuyahoga County
144	24.3	**Sherwood** (CDP) Hamilton County
144	24.3	**Waterville** (city) Lucas County

Note: *This section ranks incorporated places and CDPs (Census Designated Places) with populations of 2,500 or more. Unincorporated postal areas were not considered. Please refer to the User Guide for additional information.*

Mean Travel Time to Work

Top 150 Places Ranked in *Ascending* Order

State Rank	Minutes	Place
1	12.6	**Wright-Patterson AFB** (CDP) Greene County
2	13.9	**Athens** (city) Athens County
3	14.1	**Marietta** (city) Washington County
4	14.2	**Oxford** (city) Butler County
5	14.9	**Oberlin** (city) Lorain County
6	15.0	**Ballville** (CDP) Sandusky County
6	15.0	**Cedarville** (village) Greene County
6	15.0	**Coldwater** (village) Mercer County
6	15.0	**The Plains** (CDP) Athens County
10	15.2	**Coshocton** (city) Coshocton County
11	15.4	**Walbridge** (village) Wood County
12	15.5	**Bowling Green** (city) Wood County
12	15.5	**Findlay** (city) Hancock County
14	15.6	**Cambridge** (city) Guernsey County
15	15.8	**Bryan** (city) Williams County
15	15.8	**Ironton** (city) Lawrence County
17	15.9	**Saint Henry** (village) Mercer County
18	16.0	**Portsmouth** (city) Scioto County
19	16.1	**Van Wert** (city) Van Wert County
20	16.2	**Celina** (city) Mercer County
20	16.2	**Saint Marys** (city) Auglaize County
20	16.2	**Sidney** (city) Shelby County
23	16.3	**Fremont** (city) Sandusky County
24	16.4	**Archbold** (village) Fulton County
25	16.5	**Minster** (village) Auglaize County
25	16.5	**Tiffin** (city) Seneca County
27	16.8	**Millersburg** (village) Holmes County
27	16.8	**North Zanesville** (CDP) Muskingum County
29	16.9	**Defiance** (city) Defiance County
30	17.0	**Edgewood** (CDP) Ashtabula County
31	17.1	**Devola** (CDP) Washington County
31	17.1	**Sandusky** (city) Erie County
33	17.3	**Ontario** (city) Richland County
34	17.4	**Grandview Heights** (city) Franklin County
35	17.6	**Mount Vernon** (city) Knox County
35	17.6	**Niles** (city) Trumbull County
37	17.8	**Clyde** (city) Sandusky County
38	17.9	**Bellaire** (village) Belmont County
38	17.9	**Steubenville** (city) Jefferson County
40	18.0	**Lima** (city) Allen County
40	18.0	**Montpelier** (village) Williams County
40	18.0	**Piqua** (city) Miami County
40	18.0	**Versailles** (village) Darke County
44	18.1	**Delphos** (city) Allen County
44	18.1	**Napoleon** (city) Henry County
44	18.1	**North Kingsville** (village) Ashtabula County
44	18.1	**Upper Sandusky** (city) Wyandot County
44	18.1	**Urbana** (city) Champaign County
44	18.1	**Wooster** (city) Wayne County
50	18.2	**Ada** (village) Hardin County
50	18.2	**Bexley** (city) Franklin County
50	18.2	**Heath** (city) Licking County
50	18.2	**New Bremen** (village) Auglaize County
50	18.2	**Orrville** (city) Wayne County
55	18.3	**Carrollton** (village) Carroll County
56	18.4	**Bucyrus** (city) Crawford County
57	18.5	**Riverside** (city) Montgomery County
58	18.6	**Saint Clairsville** (city) Belmont County
59	18.7	**London** (city) Madison County
59	18.7	**Ottawa** (village) Putnam County
61	18.8	**Greenville** (city) Darke County
61	18.8	**Ottawa Hills** (village) Lucas County
63	18.9	**Bellefontaine** (city) Logan County
63	18.9	**Lisbon** (village) Columbiana County
63	18.9	**Port Clinton** (city) Ottawa County
66	19.0	**Northwood** (city) Wood County
67	19.1	**Fort Shawnee** (CDP) Allen County
67	19.1	**Granville** (village) Licking County
67	19.1	**Maumee** (city) Lucas County
67	19.1	**New Concord** (village) Muskingum County
67	19.1	**Reading** (city) Hamilton County
67	19.1	**Woodlawn** (village) Hamilton County
73	19.2	**Bluffton** (village) Allen County
73	19.2	**Oakwood** (city) Montgomery County
73	19.2	**Obetz** (village) Franklin County
73	19.2	**Troy** (city) Miami County
77	19.3	**Bellevue** (city) Sandusky County
77	19.3	**Mansfield** (city) Richland County
77	19.3	**Oregon** (city) Lucas County
80	19.4	**Beavercreek** (city) Greene County
80	19.4	**Marion** (city) Marion County
82	19.5	**Evendale** (village) Hamilton County
82	19.5	**Martins Ferry** (city) Belmont County
82	19.5	**Norwalk** (city) Huron County
82	19.5	**Painesville** (city) Lake County
82	19.5	**Springdale** (city) Hamilton County
82	19.5	**Springfield** (city) Clark County
88	19.6	**Alliance** (city) Stark County
88	19.6	**Ashland** (city) Ashland County
88	19.6	**Ashtabula** (city) Ashtabula County
88	19.6	**Fostoria** (city) Seneca County
88	19.6	**North Canton** (city) Stark County
88	19.6	**Norwood** (city) Hamilton County
88	19.6	**Toledo** (city) Lucas County
88	19.6	**Warren** (city) Trumbull County
96	19.7	**Columbiana** (city) Columbiana County
96	19.7	**Upper Arlington** (city) Franklin County
98	19.8	**Crestline** (village) Crawford County
98	19.8	**Fairborn** (city) Greene County
98	19.8	**Miamisburg** (city) Montgomery County
98	19.8	**Mogadore** (village) Summit County
98	19.8	**Perrysburg** (city) Wood County
98	19.8	**Richville** (CDP) Stark County
104	19.9	**Deer Park** (city) Hamilton County
104	19.9	**Nelsonville** (city) Athens County
104	19.9	**Tipp City** (city) Miami County
104	19.9	**Wilmington** (city) Clinton County
108	20.0	**Burlington** (CDP) Lawrence County
108	20.0	**Madeira** (city) Hamilton County
108	20.0	**Sebring** (village) Mahoning County
108	20.0	**Vandalia** (city) Montgomery County
108	20.0	**Youngstown** (city) Mahoning County
113	20.1	**Dover** (city) Tuscarawas County
113	20.1	**Gallipolis** (village) Gallia County
113	20.1	**Massillon** (city) Stark County
113	20.1	**Paulding** (village) Paulding County
113	20.1	**Rossford** (city) Wood County
113	20.1	**Sharonville** (city) Hamilton County
119	20.2	**Boardman** (CDP) Mahoning County
119	20.2	**Kettering** (city) Montgomery County
119	20.2	**Wapakoneta** (city) Auglaize County
119	20.2	**Willard** (city) Huron County
123	20.3	**Canton** (city) Stark County
123	20.3	**Chillicothe** (city) Ross County
123	20.3	**Gahanna** (city) Franklin County
123	20.3	**Uhrichsville** (city) Tuscarawas County
123	20.3	**Zanesville** (city) Muskingum County
128	20.4	**Orange** (village) Cuyahoga County
129	20.5	**Bellbrook** (city) Greene County
129	20.5	**Centerville** (city) Montgomery County
129	20.5	**Fairport Harbor** (village) Lake County
129	20.5	**Perry Heights** (CDP) Stark County
129	20.5	**West Carrollton** (city) Montgomery County
134	20.6	**Groveport** (city) Franklin County
134	20.6	**Independence** (city) Cuyahoga County
134	20.6	**Mount Carmel** (CDP) Clermont County
134	20.6	**New Albany** (city) Franklin County
134	20.6	**New Philadelphia** (city) Tuscarawas County
134	20.6	**Saint Bernard** (city) Hamilton County
134	20.6	**Willowick** (city) Lake County
141	20.7	**Cadiz** (village) Harrison County
141	20.7	**Waverly** (village) Pike County
143	20.8	**Dayton** (city) Montgomery County
143	20.8	**McDonald** (village) Trumbull County
143	20.8	**Moraine** (city) Montgomery County
143	20.8	**Shelby** (city) Richland County
143	20.8	**South Point** (village) Lawrence County
143	20.8	**Whitehall** (city) Franklin County
149	20.9	**Kenton** (city) Hardin County
149	20.9	**Lordstown** (village) Trumbull County

Note: *This section ranks incorporated places and CDPs (Census Designated Places) with populations of 2,500 or more. Unincorporated postal areas were not considered. Please refer to the User Guide for additional information.*

Violent Crime Rate per 10,000 Population

Top 150 Places Ranked in *Descending* Order

State Rank	Rate	Place
1	163.1	**Cleveland** (city) Cuyahoga County
2	119.2	**Toledo** (city) Lucas County
3	100.0	**Dayton** (city) Montgomery County
4	94.5	**Canton** (city) Stark County
5	94.4	**Lima** (city) Allen County
6	91.0	**Cincinnati** (city) Hamilton County
7	81.4	**Whitehall** (city) Franklin County
8	69.1	**Springfield** (city) Clark County
9	64.7	**Youngstown** (city) Mahoning County
10	64.4	**East Cleveland** (city) Cuyahoga County
11	61.6	**Akron** (city) Summit County
12	58.4	**Lockland** (village) Hamilton County
13	57.0	**Warren** (city) Trumbull County
14	53.4	**Loudonville** (village) Ashland County
15	53.3	**Moraine** (city) Montgomery County
16	52.3	**Middletown** (city) Butler County
17	52.2	**Columbus** (city) Franklin County
18	51.4	**Mount Healthy** (city) Hamilton County
19	51.3	**Hamilton** (city) Butler County
20	45.6	**Oberlin** (city) Lorain County
21	45.5	**Mingo Junction** (village) Jefferson County
22	45.3	**New Richmond** (village) Clermont County
23	45.0	**Alliance** (city) Stark County
24	44.8	**Mansfield** (city) Richland County
25	43.3	**Chillicothe** (city) Ross County
26	37.5	**Trotwood** (city) Montgomery County
27	36.5	**Zanesville** (city) Muskingum County
28	36.2	**Cheviot** (city) Hamilton County
29	35.3	**Lancaster** (city) Fairfield County
30	35.2	**Montpelier** (village) Williams County
31	34.3	**University Heights** (city) Cuyahoga County
32	33.9	**Greenville** (city) Darke County
33	33.1	**Steubenville** (city) Jefferson County
34	33.0	**Wellston** (city) Jackson County
35	32.4	**Cleveland Heights** (city) Cuyahoga County
36	32.2	**North College Hill** (city) Hamilton County
37	30.0	**Elyria** (city) Lorain County
38	29.5	**Marion** (city) Marion County
39	29.1	**Gallipolis** (village) Gallia County
40	28.7	**Barberton** (city) Summit County
41	28.6	**Niles** (city) Trumbull County
42	27.2	**Wooster** (city) Wayne County
43	26.9	**Van Wert** (city) Van Wert County
44	26.8	**Brooklyn** (city) Cuyahoga County
45	26.6	**Circleville** (city) Pickaway County
46	26.5	**Washington Court House** (city) Fayette County
47	26.4	**Bedford Heights** (city) Cuyahoga County
48	26.2	**Struthers** (city) Mahoning County
49	25.9	**Norwood** (city) Hamilton County
49	25.9	**Richmond Heights** (city) Cuyahoga County
51	25.7	**Fairfield** (city) Butler County
52	25.4	**New Lexington** (village) Perry County
53	25.2	**Forest Park** (city) Hamilton County
53	25.2	**North Baltimore** (village) Wood County
55	25.0	**Fairborn** (city) Greene County
56	24.1	**Fredericktown** (village) Knox County
57	23.7	**Bedford** (city) Cuyahoga County
58	23.2	**Kenton** (city) Hardin County
59	22.5	**New Lebanon** (village) Montgomery County
60	22.3	**Kent** (city) Portage County
61	22.0	**Huber Heights** (city) Montgomery County
62	21.9	**Port Clinton** (city) Ottawa County
62	21.9	**Reynoldsburg** (city) Franklin County
64	21.8	**Heath** (city) Licking County
65	21.7	**Evendale** (village) Hamilton County
66	21.6	**Bellaire** (village) Belmont County
66	21.6	**Bethel** (village) Clermont County
66	21.6	**Sidney** (city) Shelby County
69	21.5	**Cadiz** (village) Harrison County
70	21.3	**Nelsonville** (city) Athens County
71	21.1	**Logan** (city) Hocking County
72	20.5	**Riverside** (city) Montgomery County
73	20.4	**Crestline** (village) Crawford County
73	20.4	**Xenia** (city) Greene County
75	20.3	**Bucyrus** (city) Crawford County
76	19.8	**Willoughby** (city) Lake County
77	19.7	**Fremont** (city) Sandusky County
78	19.6	**Fairview Park** (city) Cuyahoga County
79	19.5	**Franklin** (city) Warren County
80	19.4	**Newton Falls** (village) Trumbull County
81	19.3	**Ironton** (city) Lawrence County
82	18.9	**Bexley** (city) Franklin County
82	18.9	**Delaware** (city) Delaware County
82	18.9	**Shelby** (city) Richland County
85	18.8	**Orrville** (city) Wayne County
86	18.7	**Piqua** (city) Miami County
87	18.4	**Oregon** (city) Lucas County
87	18.4	**Upper Sandusky** (city) Wyandot County
89	18.2	**Woodlawn** (village) Hamilton County
90	17.9	**Sandusky** (city) Erie County
91	17.7	**Martins Ferry** (city) Belmont County
92	17.6	**Bellefontaine** (city) Logan County
93	17.0	**Belpre** (city) Washington County
93	17.0	**West Carrollton** (city) Montgomery County
95	16.9	**Galion** (city) Crawford County
96	16.2	**Fairport Harbor** (village) Lake County
97	16.1	**Jackson** (city) Jackson County
97	16.1	**South Euclid** (city) Cuyahoga County
99	15.9	**Deer Park** (city) Hamilton County
100	15.8	**West Union** (village) Adams County
101	15.4	**Independence** (city) Cuyahoga County
101	15.4	**Louisville** (city) Stark County
103	15.1	**Monroe** (city) Butler County
104	15.0	**Defiance** (city) Defiance County
105	14.6	**Austintown** (CDP) Mahoning County
106	14.5	**Wilmington** (city) Clinton County
107	14.1	**Blanchester** (village) Clinton County
108	13.7	**Cuyahoga Falls** (city) Summit County
108	13.7	**Mount Orab** (village) Brown County
110	13.6	**Chardon** (city) Geauga County
110	13.6	**Mentor-on-the-Lake** (city) Lake County
110	13.6	**Minerva** (village) Stark County
110	13.6	**Parma** (city) Cuyahoga County
110	13.6	**Wickliffe** (city) Lake County
115	13.5	**Cambridge** (city) Guernsey County
116	13.4	**Bowling Green** (city) Wood County
117	13.2	**East Palestine** (village) Columbiana County
117	13.2	**Greenfield** (village) Highland County
117	13.2	**Kettering** (city) Montgomery County
117	13.2	**Newcomerstown** (village) Tuscarawas County
121	13.1	**Hubbard** (city) Trumbull County
121	13.1	**Tallmadge** (city) Summit County
123	13.0	**Milford** (city) Clermont County
124	12.8	**Napoleon** (city) Henry County
125	12.5	**Lakewood** (city) Cuyahoga County
126	12.4	**Toronto** (city) Jefferson County
127	12.2	**Hillsboro** (city) Highland County
127	12.2	**Urbana** (city) Champaign County
129	12.1	**Johnstown** (village) Licking County
130	11.9	**Brookville** (city) Montgomery County
131	11.8	**Ashland** (city) Ashland County
132	11.7	**Williamsburg** (village) Clermont County
133	11.4	**Covington** (village) Miami County
134	11.3	**Georgetown** (village) Brown County
134	11.3	**Newtown** (village) Hamilton County
136	11.2	**Northwood** (city) Wood County
137	11.0	**Wadsworth** (city) Medina County
138	10.9	**Germantown** (city) Montgomery County
138	10.9	**Mentor** (city) Lake County
140	10.8	**Maumee** (city) Lucas County
141	10.7	**Athens** (city) Athens County
141	10.7	**Grove City** (city) Franklin County
143	10.6	**Lebanon** (city) Warren County
143	10.6	**Twinsburg** (city) Summit County
145	10.3	**Lyndhurst** (city) Cuyahoga County
146	10.2	**Mount Vernon** (city) Knox County
146	10.2	**Wapakoneta** (city) Auglaize County
148	10.0	**Chagrin Falls** (village) Cuyahoga County
148	10.0	**Miamisburg** (city) Montgomery County
150	9.7	**Englewood** (city) Montgomery County

Note: *This section ranks incorporated places and CDPs (Census Designated Places) with populations of 2,500 or more. Unincorporated postal areas were not considered. Please refer to the User Guide for additional information.*

Violent Crime Rate per 10,000 Population

Top 150 Places Ranked in *Ascending* Order

State Rank	Rate	Place
1	0.0	**Amelia** (village) Clermont County
1	0.0	**Carey** (village) Wyandot County
1	0.0	**Granville** (village) Licking County
1	0.0	**Harrison** (city) Hamilton County
1	0.0	**Lexington** (village) Richland County
1	0.0	**Lisbon** (village) Columbiana County
1	0.0	**Middlefield** (village) Geauga County
1	0.0	**New Concord** (village) Muskingum County
1	0.0	**Powell** (city) Delaware County
1	0.0	**Reminderville** (village) Summit County
1	0.0	**Shadyside** (village) Belmont County
1	0.0	**Strasburg** (village) Tuscarawas County
1	0.0	**Sunbury** (village) Delaware County
14	1.2	**Highland Heights** (city) Cuyahoga County
15	1.3	**Grandview Heights** (city) Franklin County
16	1.4	**Canfield** (city) Mahoning County
17	1.5	**Cortland** (city) Trumbull County
18	1.6	**Pepper Pike** (city) Cuyahoga County
19	1.7	**Ada** (village) Hardin County
19	1.7	**New Philadelphia** (city) Tuscarawas County
21	1.8	**Hudson** (city) Summit County
21	1.8	**Mason** (city) Warren County
23	2.2	**Whitehouse** (village) Lucas County
24	2.3	**Ottawa Hills** (village) Lucas County
25	2.4	**Ashville** (village) Pickaway County
25	2.4	**Barnesville** (village) Belmont County
25	2.4	**Bluffton** (village) Allen County
28	2.6	**Mogadore** (village) Summit County
29	2.7	**Wintersville** (village) Jefferson County
30	2.8	**Amberley** (village) Hamilton County
30	2.8	**Greenhills** (village) Hamilton County
32	2.9	**Delphos** (city) Allen County
32	2.9	**Mariemont** (village) Hamilton County
32	2.9	**Vermilion** (city) Lorain County
35	3.0	**Brecksville** (city) Cuyahoga County
35	3.0	**Moreland Hills** (village) Cuyahoga County
37	3.1	**Marysville** (city) Union County
38	3.4	**Baltimore** (village) Fairfield County
38	3.4	**Hartville** (village) Stark County
38	3.4	**Olmsted Falls** (city) Cuyahoga County
38	3.4	**Rocky River** (city) Cuyahoga County
38	3.4	**Seven Hills** (city) Cuyahoga County
38	3.4	**Worthington** (city) Franklin County
44	3.6	**Canal Fulton** (city) Stark County
44	3.6	**North Ridgeville** (city) Lorain County
44	3.6	**Waterville** (city) Lucas County
47	3.7	**Oak Harbor** (village) Ottawa County
47	3.7	**Perrysburg** (city) Wood County
47	3.7	**Streetsboro** (city) Portage County
50	3.8	**Montgomery** (city) Hamilton County
51	4.0	**Munroe Falls** (city) Summit County
51	4.0	**Poland** (village) Mahoning County
53	4.2	**Bellbrook** (city) Greene County
53	4.2	**Norton** (city) Summit County
55	4.3	**Strongsville** (city) Cuyahoga County
55	4.3	**Westlake** (city) Cuyahoga County
57	4.4	**Kirtland** (city) Lake County
58	4.6	**Clayton** (city) Montgomery County
58	4.6	**Upper Arlington** (city) Franklin County
60	4.7	**Loveland** (city) Hamilton County
61	4.8	**Clyde** (city) Sandusky County
61	4.8	**Columbiana** (city) Columbiana County
61	4.8	**Dublin** (city) Franklin County
61	4.8	**New Albany** (city) Franklin County
61	4.8	**Solon** (city) Cuyahoga County
66	5.0	**Campbell** (city) Mahoning County
67	5.2	**North Canton** (city) Stark County
67	5.2	**South Russell** (village) Geauga County
67	5.2	**Yellow Springs** (village) Greene County
70	5.4	**Westerville** (city) Franklin County
71	5.5	**Centerville** (city) Montgomery County
71	5.5	**Eastlake** (city) Lake County
71	5.5	**Northfield** (village) Summit County
74	5.6	**Uhrichsville** (city) Tuscarawas County
75	5.7	**Gahanna** (city) Franklin County
76	5.8	**Amherst** (city) Lorain County
77	5.9	**Berea** (city) Cuyahoga County
77	5.9	**Wyoming** (city) Hamilton County
79	6.0	**Norwalk** (city) Huron County
79	6.0	**Springboro** (city) Warren County
79	6.0	**Uniontown** (CDP) Stark County
82	6.1	**Rittman** (city) Wayne County
82	6.1	**Saint Marys** (city) Auglaize County
84	6.3	**New Franklin** (city) Summit County
85	6.6	**Grafton** (village) Lorain County
85	6.6	**Willard** (city) Huron County
87	6.8	**Macedonia** (city) Summit County
88	6.9	**Aurora** (city) Portage County
88	6.9	**Beavercreek** (city) Greene County
88	6.9	**London** (city) Madison County
91	7.0	**Tipp City** (city) Miami County
91	7.0	**West Jefferson** (village) Madison County
93	7.1	**Waverly** (village) Pike County
94	7.2	**Brunswick** (city) Medina County
95	7.4	**Tiffin** (city) Seneca County
96	7.5	**Carlisle** (village) Warren County
96	7.5	**Salem** (city) Columbiana County
98	7.6	**Dennison** (village) Tuscarawas County
99	7.7	**Swanton** (village) Fulton County
100	7.9	**Saint Clairsville** (city) Belmont County
101	8.0	**Pickerington** (city) Fairfield County
102	8.2	**Ontario** (city) Richland County
103	8.5	**Troy** (city) Miami County
104	8.6	**Groveport** (city) Franklin County
104	8.6	**Stow** (city) Summit County
106	9.0	**Blue Ash** (city) Hamilton County
107	9.2	**Archbold** (village) Fulton County
108	9.3	**Dover** (city) Tuscarawas County
108	9.3	**Vandalia** (city) Montgomery County
110	9.4	**Sebring** (village) Mahoning County
111	9.5	**Hilliard** (city) Franklin County
111	9.5	**Millersburg** (village) Holmes County
113	9.6	**Wauseon** (city) Fulton County
114	9.7	**Englewood** (city) Montgomery County
115	10.0	**Chagrin Falls** (village) Cuyahoga County
115	10.0	**Miamisburg** (city) Montgomery County
117	10.2	**Mount Vernon** (city) Knox County
117	10.2	**Wapakoneta** (city) Auglaize County
119	10.3	**Lyndhurst** (city) Cuyahoga County
120	10.6	**Lebanon** (city) Warren County
120	10.6	**Twinsburg** (city) Summit County
122	10.7	**Athens** (city) Athens County
122	10.7	**Grove City** (city) Franklin County
124	10.8	**Maumee** (city) Lucas County
125	10.9	**Germantown** (city) Montgomery County
125	10.9	**Mentor** (city) Lake County
127	11.0	**Wadsworth** (city) Medina County
128	11.2	**Northwood** (city) Wood County
129	11.3	**Georgetown** (village) Brown County
129	11.3	**Newtown** (village) Hamilton County
131	11.4	**Covington** (village) Miami County
132	11.7	**Williamsburg** (village) Clermont County
133	11.8	**Ashland** (city) Ashland County
134	11.9	**Brookville** (city) Montgomery County
135	12.1	**Johnstown** (village) Licking County
136	12.2	**Hillsboro** (city) Highland County
136	12.2	**Urbana** (city) Champaign County
138	12.4	**Toronto** (city) Jefferson County
139	12.5	**Lakewood** (city) Cuyahoga County
140	12.8	**Napoleon** (city) Henry County
141	13.0	**Milford** (city) Clermont County
142	13.1	**Hubbard** (city) Trumbull County
142	13.1	**Tallmadge** (city) Summit County
144	13.2	**East Palestine** (village) Columbiana County
144	13.2	**Greenfield** (village) Highland County
144	13.2	**Kettering** (city) Montgomery County
144	13.2	**Newcomerstown** (village) Tuscarawas County
148	13.4	**Bowling Green** (city) Wood County
149	13.5	**Cambridge** (city) Guernsey County
150	13.6	**Chardon** (city) Geauga County

Note: *This section ranks incorporated places and CDPs (Census Designated Places) with populations of 2,500 or more. Unincorporated postal areas were not considered. Please refer to the User Guide for additional information.*

Property Crime Rate per 10,000 Population

Top 150 Places Ranked in *Descending* Order

State Rank	Rate	Place
1	1,286.8	**Gallipolis** (village) Gallia County
2	1,071.3	**Moraine** (city) Montgomery County
3	860.4	**Evendale** (village) Hamilton County
4	805.4	**Chillicothe** (city) Ross County
5	679.0	**Springfield** (city) Clark County
6	675.9	**Middletown** (city) Butler County
7	630.7	**Heath** (city) Licking County
8	620.8	**Brooklyn** (city) Cuyahoga County
9	618.5	**Whitehall** (city) Franklin County
10	607.5	**Ontario** (city) Richland County
11	599.0	**Lima** (city) Allen County
12	598.2	**Steubenville** (city) Jefferson County
13	558.3	**Mansfield** (city) Richland County
14	531.6	**Cleveland** (city) Cuyahoga County
15	531.2	**Hamilton** (city) Butler County
16	519.3	**Fremont** (city) Sandusky County
17	515.8	**Dayton** (city) Montgomery County
18	514.7	**Cincinnati** (city) Hamilton County
19	511.4	**Canton** (city) Stark County
20	506.2	**Kenton** (city) Hardin County
21	505.2	**Zanesville** (city) Muskingum County
22	504.9	**Norwood** (city) Hamilton County
23	500.7	**Willard** (city) Huron County
24	483.8	**Circleville** (city) Pickaway County
25	468.0	**Cambridge** (city) Guernsey County
26	464.5	**Wilmington** (city) Clinton County
27	460.0	**Franklin** (city) Warren County
28	457.0	**Lancaster** (city) Fairfield County
29	445.3	**Sidney** (city) Shelby County
30	438.3	**Akron** (city) Summit County
31	437.6	**Washington Court House** (city) Fayette County
32	429.7	**Mount Healthy** (city) Hamilton County
33	423.1	**Piqua** (city) Miami County
34	417.8	**Grove City** (city) Franklin County
35	415.0	**Bucyrus** (city) Crawford County
36	407.6	**Mount Vernon** (city) Knox County
37	407.0	**Columbus** (city) Franklin County
38	402.0	**Toledo** (city) Lucas County
39	400.4	**Trotwood** (city) Montgomery County
40	398.2	**New Lexington** (village) Perry County
41	378.0	**Nelsonville** (city) Athens County
41	378.0	**Youngstown** (city) Mahoning County
43	377.2	**Warren** (city) Trumbull County
44	366.8	**Montpelier** (village) Williams County
45	365.8	**Urbana** (city) Champaign County
46	363.9	**Marion** (city) Marion County
47	363.3	**Sandusky** (city) Erie County
48	359.6	**Reynoldsburg** (city) Franklin County
49	353.6	**Lockland** (village) Hamilton County
50	351.4	**Sebring** (village) Mahoning County
51	349.8	**Alliance** (city) Stark County
52	349.3	**Woodlawn** (village) Hamilton County
53	342.0	**Logan** (city) Hocking County
54	341.5	**Bethel** (village) Clermont County
55	339.2	**Galion** (city) Crawford County
56	339.1	**Forest Park** (city) Hamilton County
57	334.3	**Milford** (city) Clermont County
58	333.7	**North College Hill** (city) Hamilton County
59	332.6	**Huber Heights** (city) Montgomery County
60	331.6	**Oregon** (city) Lucas County
61	329.8	**Fairport Harbor** (village) Lake County
62	327.0	**Van Wert** (city) Van Wert County
63	315.3	**Xenia** (city) Greene County
64	310.1	**Hillsboro** (city) Highland County
65	309.0	**Bellefontaine** (city) Logan County
66	306.7	**Cheviot** (city) Hamilton County
67	306.2	**Groveport** (city) Franklin County
68	305.3	**Barberton** (city) Summit County
69	304.0	**Englewood** (city) Montgomery County
70	294.9	**Wellston** (city) Jackson County
71	289.9	**New Lebanon** (village) Montgomery County
72	288.7	**Wooster** (city) Wayne County
73	286.7	**Millersburg** (village) Holmes County
74	286.3	**Shelby** (city) Richland County
75	286.2	**Port Clinton** (city) Ottawa County
76	282.8	**Harrison** (city) Hamilton County
77	282.7	**Niles** (city) Trumbull County
78	281.4	**London** (city) Madison County
79	281.2	**Troy** (city) Miami County
80	279.1	**New Richmond** (village) Clermont County
81	276.6	**West Carrollton** (city) Montgomery County
82	276.5	**Elyria** (city) Lorain County
83	273.9	**Maumee** (city) Lucas County
84	273.7	**Bedford Heights** (city) Cuyahoga County
85	273.6	**Monroe** (city) Butler County
86	270.3	**Fairborn** (city) Greene County
87	269.5	**Wauseon** (city) Fulton County
88	263.0	**Blue Ash** (city) Hamilton County
89	262.8	**South Euclid** (city) Cuyahoga County
90	262.0	**Norwalk** (city) Huron County
91	260.6	**Bexley** (city) Franklin County
92	259.6	**Salem** (city) Columbiana County
93	257.6	**Mount Orab** (village) Brown County
94	254.1	**Oberlin** (city) Lorain County
95	248.7	**Ironton** (city) Lawrence County
96	248.0	**Riverside** (city) Montgomery County
97	247.4	**Northwood** (city) Wood County
98	246.1	**Williamsburg** (village) Clermont County
99	244.1	**Fairfield** (city) Butler County
100	243.9	**Eastlake** (city) Lake County
101	243.2	**Uniontown** (CDP) Stark County
102	243.1	**Jackson** (city) Jackson County
103	243.0	**Greenville** (city) Darke County
104	240.9	**Westerville** (city) Franklin County
105	238.4	**Richmond Heights** (city) Cuyahoga County
106	237.4	**Clyde** (city) Sandusky County
107	237.0	**Tiffin** (city) Seneca County
108	236.6	**Struthers** (city) Mahoning County
109	235.4	**West Jefferson** (village) Madison County
110	234.8	**Upper Sandusky** (city) Wyandot County
111	233.0	**Cuyahoga Falls** (city) Summit County
112	232.3	**University Heights** (city) Cuyahoga County
113	230.3	**Tallmadge** (city) Summit County
114	230.2	**Delaware** (city) Delaware County
115	230.0	**Napoleon** (city) Henry County
116	229.9	**Georgetown** (village) Brown County
117	229.3	**Austintown** (CDP) Mahoning County
118	229.1	**Beavercreek** (city) Greene County
119	226.3	**Gahanna** (city) Franklin County
120	223.7	**Greenfield** (village) Highland County
121	223.1	**Cleveland Heights** (city) Cuyahoga County
122	222.6	**Crestline** (village) Crawford County
123	220.7	**Mentor** (city) Lake County
124	218.9	**Waverly** (village) Pike County
125	218.6	**Wadsworth** (city) Medina County
126	217.6	**Vandalia** (city) Montgomery County
127	216.4	**Newcomerstown** (village) Tuscarawas County
128	215.4	**Delphos** (city) Allen County
129	214.6	**Pickerington** (city) Fairfield County
130	210.6	**Willoughby** (city) Lake County
131	207.6	**Rittman** (city) Wayne County
132	204.8	**Yellow Springs** (village) Greene County
133	204.2	**Defiance** (city) Defiance County
134	201.1	**Bedford** (city) Cuyahoga County
135	199.7	**Ashland** (city) Ashland County
136	198.8	**Newton Falls** (village) Trumbull County
137	198.7	**Bluffton** (village) Allen County
138	198.4	**East Cleveland** (city) Cuyahoga County
139	197.6	**Strongsville** (city) Cuyahoga County
140	191.9	**Grandview Heights** (city) Franklin County
141	189.1	**Wyoming** (city) Hamilton County
142	187.8	**North Baltimore** (village) Wood County
143	186.3	**Wickliffe** (city) Lake County
144	184.5	**Stow** (city) Summit County
145	184.3	**Cadiz** (village) Harrison County
146	183.3	**Athens** (city) Athens County
147	182.1	**Tipp City** (city) Miami County
148	182.0	**Kettering** (city) Montgomery County
149	179.3	**Loudonville** (village) Ashland County
150	178.3	**Bowling Green** (city) Wood County

Note: *This section ranks incorporated places and CDPs (Census Designated Places) with populations of 2,500 or more. Unincorporated postal areas were not considered. Please refer to the User Guide for additional information.*

Property Crime Rate per 10,000 Population

Top 150 Places Ranked in *Ascending* Order

State Rank	Rate	Place
1	10.5	**South Russell** (village) Geauga County
2	10.6	**Lexington** (village) Richland County
3	14.0	**Carey** (village) Wyandot County
4	16.2	**Shadyside** (village) Belmont County
5	17.7	**Saint Clairsville** (city) Belmont County
6	30.3	**Moreland Hills** (village) Cuyahoga County
7	33.0	**Toronto** (city) Jefferson County
8	33.9	**Olmsted Falls** (city) Cuyahoga County
9	34.0	**Barnesville** (village) Belmont County
10	39.7	**Rocky River** (city) Cuyahoga County
11	39.8	**Kirtland** (city) Lake County
12	40.3	**Brecksville** (city) Cuyahoga County
13	40.9	**Hudson** (city) Summit County
14	44.5	**Poland** (village) Mahoning County
15	45.5	**Dennison** (village) Tuscarawas County
16	47.0	**Carlisle** (village) Warren County
17	50.4	**Amelia** (village) Clermont County
18	51.2	**Pepper Pike** (city) Cuyahoga County
19	51.7	**Campbell** (city) Mahoning County
20	52.6	**Waterville** (city) Lucas County
21	54.9	**Seven Hills** (city) Cuyahoga County
22	56.0	**Springboro** (city) Warren County
23	58.3	**North Ridgeville** (city) Lorain County
24	62.2	**Grafton** (village) Lorain County
25	62.7	**Marysville** (city) Union County
26	64.4	**Brunswick** (city) Medina County
27	64.7	**New Concord** (village) Muskingum County
28	65.7	**Ada** (village) Hardin County
29	66.3	**Whitehouse** (village) Lucas County
30	67.4	**Chagrin Falls** (village) Cuyahoga County
31	69.4	**Twinsburg** (city) Summit County
32	71.2	**Granville** (village) Licking County
33	72.0	**Swanton** (village) Fulton County
34	72.8	**Germantown** (city) Montgomery County
35	73.2	**Reminderville** (village) Summit County
36	74.4	**Dover** (city) Tuscarawas County
37	76.2	**Solon** (city) Cuyahoga County
38	77.0	**New Franklin** (city) Summit County
39	78.0	**Strasburg** (village) Tuscarawas County
40	79.8	**Munroe Falls** (city) Summit County
41	79.9	**Powell** (city) Delaware County
42	80.6	**Bellbrook** (city) Greene County
43	81.9	**Canfield** (city) Mahoning County
44	83.3	**Uhrichsville** (city) Tuscarawas County
45	83.5	**Ottawa Hills** (village) Lucas County
46	84.2	**Baltimore** (village) Fairfield County
47	96.3	**Berea** (city) Cuyahoga County
48	98.8	**Hilliard** (city) Franklin County
49	99.9	**Mason** (city) Warren County
50	100.0	**Brookville** (city) Montgomery County
51	100.3	**Greenhills** (village) Hamilton County
52	102.8	**Clayton** (city) Montgomery County
52	102.8	**Vermilion** (city) Lorain County
54	104.0	**Loveland** (city) Hamilton County
55	104.6	**Mogadore** (village) Summit County
56	105.7	**Aurora** (city) Portage County
57	106.8	**Sunbury** (village) Delaware County
58	107.3	**New Philadelphia** (city) Tuscarawas County
59	110.1	**Covington** (village) Miami County
60	110.3	**Bellaire** (village) Belmont County
61	111.7	**Cortland** (city) Trumbull County
62	112.3	**Norton** (city) Summit County
63	112.7	**Dublin** (city) Franklin County
64	113.2	**Perrysburg** (city) Wood County
65	114.0	**Miamisburg** (city) Montgomery County
66	116.4	**Newtown** (village) Hamilton County
67	117.8	**Highland Heights** (city) Cuyahoga County
68	119.7	**Amberley** (village) Hamilton County
69	123.4	**Mentor-on-the-Lake** (city) Lake County
70	125.1	**Louisville** (city) Stark County
71	125.3	**Minerva** (village) Stark County
72	126.7	**Northfield** (village) Summit County
73	127.9	**Chardon** (city) Geauga County
74	130.4	**Orrville** (city) Wayne County
75	130.5	**Deer Park** (city) Hamilton County
76	131.2	**Mariemont** (village) Hamilton County
77	133.0	**Canal Fulton** (city) Stark County
78	133.4	**Mingo Junction** (village) Jefferson County
79	133.6	**Archbold** (village) Fulton County
80	136.3	**East Palestine** (village) Columbiana County
81	138.5	**Parma** (city) Cuyahoga County
82	138.9	**West Union** (village) Adams County
83	139.1	**Fairview Park** (city) Cuyahoga County
84	140.2	**Montgomery** (city) Hamilton County
85	140.4	**Columbiana** (city) Columbiana County
86	142.4	**Lyndhurst** (city) Cuyahoga County
87	142.5	**Westlake** (city) Cuyahoga County
88	144.0	**Lisbon** (village) Columbiana County
89	146.7	**Wapakoneta** (city) Auglaize County
90	147.6	**Centerville** (city) Montgomery County
91	149.1	**Streetsboro** (city) Portage County
92	151.2	**Wintersville** (village) Jefferson County
93	152.2	**Upper Arlington** (city) Franklin County
94	154.7	**Amherst** (city) Lorain County
95	155.3	**Oak Harbor** (village) Ottawa County
96	155.4	**North Canton** (city) Stark County
97	157.5	**Saint Marys** (city) Auglaize County
98	158.6	**Worthington** (city) Franklin County
99	158.9	**Johnstown** (village) Licking County
100	159.3	**Ashville** (village) Pickaway County
101	162.7	**Martins Ferry** (city) Belmont County
102	163.3	**Middlefield** (village) Geauga County
103	164.4	**New Albany** (city) Franklin County
104	164.9	**Fredericktown** (village) Knox County
105	165.0	**Belpre** (city) Washington County
106	165.4	**Kent** (city) Portage County
107	167.0	**Macedonia** (city) Summit County
108	168.3	**Independence** (city) Cuyahoga County
109	174.0	**Lakewood** (city) Cuyahoga County
110	174.2	**Lebanon** (city) Warren County
111	174.8	**Hubbard** (city) Trumbull County
112	176.5	**Blanchester** (village) Clinton County
113	178.2	**Hartville** (village) Stark County
114	178.3	**Bowling Green** (city) Wood County
115	179.3	**Loudonville** (village) Ashland County
116	182.0	**Kettering** (city) Montgomery County
117	182.1	**Tipp City** (city) Miami County
118	183.3	**Athens** (city) Athens County
119	184.3	**Cadiz** (village) Harrison County
120	184.5	**Stow** (city) Summit County
121	186.3	**Wickliffe** (city) Lake County
122	187.8	**North Baltimore** (village) Wood County
123	189.1	**Wyoming** (city) Hamilton County
124	191.9	**Grandview Heights** (city) Franklin County
125	197.6	**Strongsville** (city) Cuyahoga County
126	198.4	**East Cleveland** (city) Cuyahoga County
127	198.7	**Bluffton** (village) Allen County
128	198.8	**Newton Falls** (village) Trumbull County
129	199.7	**Ashland** (city) Ashland County
130	201.1	**Bedford** (city) Cuyahoga County
131	204.2	**Defiance** (city) Defiance County
132	204.8	**Yellow Springs** (village) Greene County
133	207.6	**Rittman** (city) Wayne County
134	210.6	**Willoughby** (city) Lake County
135	214.6	**Pickerington** (city) Fairfield County
136	215.4	**Delphos** (city) Allen County
137	216.4	**Newcomerstown** (village) Tuscarawas County
138	217.6	**Vandalia** (city) Montgomery County
139	218.6	**Wadsworth** (city) Medina County
140	218.9	**Waverly** (village) Pike County
141	220.7	**Mentor** (city) Lake County
142	222.6	**Crestline** (village) Crawford County
143	223.1	**Cleveland Heights** (city) Cuyahoga County
144	223.7	**Greenfield** (village) Highland County
145	226.3	**Gahanna** (city) Franklin County
146	229.1	**Beavercreek** (city) Greene County
147	229.3	**Austintown** (CDP) Mahoning County
148	229.9	**Georgetown** (village) Brown County
149	230.0	**Napoleon** (city) Henry County
150	230.2	**Delaware** (city) Delaware County

Note: *This section ranks incorporated places and CDPs (Census Designated Places) with populations of 2,500 or more. Unincorporated postal areas were not considered. Please refer to the User Guide for additional information.*

Education

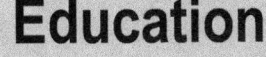

Ohio Public School Educational Profile

Category	Value
Schools *(2013-2014)*	3,675
Instructional Level	
Primary	1,916
Middle	719
High	861
Other/Not Reported	179
Curriculum	
Regular	3,552
Special Education	50
Vocational	69
Alternative	4
Type	
Magnet	0
Charter	408
Title I Eligible	2,899
School-wide Title I	2,242
Students *(2013-2014)*	1,723,619
Gender (%)	
Male	51.4
Female	48.6
Race/Ethnicity (%)	
White, Non-Hispanic	72.6
Black, Non-Hispanic	16.2
Asian, Non-Hispanic	1.9
American Indian/Alaska Native, Non-Hispanic	0.1
Hawaiian Native/Pacific Islander, Non-Hispanic	0.1
Two or More Races, Non-Hispanic	4.5
Hispanic of Any Race	4.5
Special Programs (%)	
Individual Education Program (IEP)	14.7
English Language Learner (ELL)	2.5
Eligible for Free Lunch Program	39.6
Eligible for Reduced-Price Lunch Program	5.0
Adjusted Cohort Graduation Rate (%) *(2013-2014)*	
All Students	82
White, Non-Hispanic	87
Black, Non-Hispanic	63
Asian/Pacific Islander, Non-Hispanic	88
American Indian/Alaska Native, Non-Hispanic	74
Hispanic of Any Race	n/a
Students with Disabilities	68
Limited English Proficient	66
Economically Disadvantaged	69

Category	Value
Averaged Freshman Graduation Rate (%) *(2011-2012)*	
All Students	84
Female	89
Male	84
Event Dropout Rate (%) *(2011-2012)*	
All Students	4.6
Staff *(2013-2014)*	
Teachers (FTE)	106,004.1
Salary[1] ($)	56,410
Librarians/Media Specialists (FTE)	920.0
Guidance Counselors (FTE)	3,734.5
Ratios *(2013-2014)*	
Number of Students per Teacher	16.3 to 1
Number of Students per Librarian	1,873.5 to 1
Number of Students per Guidance Counselor	461.5 to 1
Finances *(2012-2013)*	
Expenditures ($ per student)	
Total Expenditures	13,105
Current Expenditures	11,276
Instruction	6,438
Support Services	4,449
Non-Instruction	389
Net Current per Attendance for Title I	11,444
Revenue ($ per student)	
Total Revenue	13,070
From Federal Sources	1,124
From State Sources	5,683
From Local Sources	6,263
From Intermediate Sources	81
College Entrance Exam Scores	
SAT Reasoning Test™ *(2015)*	
Test Takers	17,253
Mean Combined Score	1,657
Mean Critical Reading Score	557
Mean Math Score	563
Mean Writing Score	537
ACT *(2015)*	
Participation Rate (%)	73
Mean Composite Score	22.0
Mean English Score	21.4
Mean Math Score	21.7
Mean Reading Score	22.5
Mean Science Score	22.1

Note: *For an explanation of data, please refer to the User Guide in the front of the book; (1) Average salary for classroom teachers in 2015-16*

Number of Schools

Rank	Number	District Name	City
1	115	Columbus City SD	Columbus
2	98	Cleveland Municipal	Cleveland
3	56	Cincinnati City	Cincinnati
4	52	Toledo City	Toledo
5	49	Akron City	Akron
6	33	South-Western City	Grove City
7	30	Dayton City	Dayton
8	24	Canton City	Canton
9	23	Hilliard City	Columbus
9	23	Olentangy Local	Lewis Center
11	22	Westerville City	Westerville
12	20	Lakota Local	Liberty Twp
13	19	Dublin City	Dublin
14	18	Worthington City	Worthington
15	16	Springfield City	Springfield
16	15	Lorain City	Lorain
16	15	Parma City	Parma
18	14	Pickerington Local	Pickerington
18	14	Reynoldsburg City	Reynoldsburg
20	13	Mentor Exempted Village	Mentor
20	13	Northwest Local	Cincinnati
22	12	Centerville City	Centerville
22	12	Elyria City Schools	Elyria
22	12	Findlay City	Findlay
22	12	Hamilton City	Hamilton
22	12	Kettering City	Kettering
22	12	Sylvania City	Sylvania
22	12	West Clermont Local	Cincinnati
22	12	Willoughby-Eastlake City	Willoughby
22	12	Youngstown City Schools	Youngstown
31	11	Brunswick City	Brunswick
31	11	Cleveland Heights-Univ Hgts City	University Hgts
31	11	Gahanna-Jefferson City	Gahanna
31	11	Lancaster City	Lancaster
31	11	Medina City SD	Medina
31	11	Newark City	Newark
31	11	Strongsville City	Strongsville
31	11	Washington Local	Toledo
39	10	Groveport Madison Local	Groveport
39	10	Lakewood City	Lakewood
39	10	Miamisburg City	Miamisburg
39	10	Middletown City	Middletown
39	10	Northmont City	Englewood
39	10	Princeton City	Cincinnati
39	10	Switzerland of Ohio Local	Woodsfield
46	9	Beavercreek City	Beavercreek
46	9	Cuyahoga Falls City	Cuyahoga Falls
46	9	East Holmes Local	Berlin
46	9	Fairfield City	Fairfield
46	9	Forest Hills Local	Cincinnati
46	9	Fremont City	Fremont
46	9	Lima City	Lima
46	9	Mansfield City	Mansfield
46	9	Milford Exempted Village	Milford
46	9	North Olmsted City	North Olmsted
46	9	Oak Hills Local	Cincinnati
46	9	Piqua City	Piqua
46	9	Plain Local	Canton
46	9	Stow-Munroe Falls City SD	Stow
46	9	Troy City	Troy
61	8	Ashtabula Area City	Ashtabula
61	8	Delaware City	Delaware
61	8	Euclid City	Euclid
61	8	Franklin City	Franklin
61	8	Gallia County Local	Gallipolis
61	8	Huber Heights City	Huber Heights
61	8	Mad River Local	Dayton
61	8	Marion City	Marion
61	8	Marysville Exempted Village	Marysville
61	8	Mount Vernon City	Mount Vernon
61	8	Perry Local	Massillon
61	8	Ravenna City	Ravenna
61	8	Riverside Local	Painesville
61	8	Shaker Heights City	Shaker Heights
61	8	Upper Arlington City	Upper Arlington
61	8	Wadsworth City	Wadsworth
61	8	Xenia Community City	Xenia
78	7	Adams County/Ohio Valley Local	West Union
78	7	Athens City	The Plains
78	7	Avon Lake City	Avon Lake
78	7	Berea City	Berea
78	7	Boardman Local	Youngstown
78	7	Celina City	Celina
78	7	Clark-Shawnee Local	Springfield
78	7	Claymont City	Dennison
78	7	East Cleveland City SD	East Cleveland
78	7	Kent City	Kent
78	7	Logan-Hocking Local	Logan
78	7	Mayfield City	Mayfield Hgts
78	7	New Philadel. City	New Philadel.
78	7	North Canton City	North Canton
78	7	N Ridgeville City	N Ridgeville
78	7	Northeastern Local	Springfield
78	7	Sandusky City	Sandusky
78	7	Solon City	Solon
78	7	Sycamore Community City	Blue Ash
78	7	Teays Valley Local	Ashville
78	7	West Carrollton City	West Carrollton
78	7	West Holmes Local	Millersburg
78	7	Westlake City	Westlake
78	7	Wooster City	Wooster
102	6	Alliance City	Alliance
102	6	Anthony Wayne Local	Whitehouse
102	6	Ashland City	Ashland
102	6	Avon Local	Avon
102	6	Bedford City	Bedford
102	6	Big Walnut Local	Sunbury
102	6	Bowling Green City SD	Bowling Green
102	6	Brecksville-Broadview Heights City	Brecksville
102	6	Chardon Local	Chardon
102	6	Chillicothe City	Chillicothe
102	6	East Muskingum Local	New Concord
102	6	Howland Local	Warren
102	6	Hudson City	Hudson
102	6	Jackson Local	Massillon
102	6	Kenton City	Kenton
102	6	Kings Local	Kings Mills
102	6	Lebanon City	Lebanon
102	6	Little Miami Local	Maineville
102	6	Logan Elm Local	Circleville
102	6	Loveland City	Loveland
102	6	Madison Local	Mansfield
102	6	Marietta City	Marietta
102	6	Massillon City	Massillon
102	6	Nordonia Hills City	Northfield
102	6	North Royalton City	North Royalton
102	6	Norwalk City	Norwalk
102	6	Norwood City	Norwood
102	6	Oregon City	Oregon
102	6	Painesville City Local	Painesville
102	6	Perrysburg Exempted Village	Perrysburg
102	6	Poland Local	Poland
102	6	River View Local	Warsaw
102	6	Sheffield-Sheffield Lake City	Sheffield Vllg
102	6	Sidney City	Sidney
102	6	South Euclid-Lyndhurst City	Lyndhurst
102	6	Southwest Local	Harrison
102	6	Springboro Community City	Springboro
102	6	Springfield Local	Holland
102	6	Tecumseh Local	New Carlisle
102	6	Tri-Valley Local	Dresden
102	6	Whitehall City	Whitehall
102	6	Winton Woods City	Cincinnati
102	6	Zanesville City	Zanesville
145	5	Amherst Exempted Village	Amherst
145	5	Beaver Local	Lisbon
145	5	Bellbrook-Sugarcreek Local SD	Bellbrook
145	5	Bexley City	Bexley
145	5	Bryan City	Bryan
145	5	Buckeye Local	Dillonvale
145	5	Cambridge City	Cambridge
145	5	Carrollton Exempted Village	Carrollton
145	5	Circleville City	Circleville
145	5	Copley-Fairlawn City	Copley
145	5	Crestwood Local	Mantua
145	5	Dover City	Dover
145	5	East Liverpool City	East Liverpool
145	5	Edgewood City	Trenton
145	5	Gallipolis City	Gallipolis
145	5	Garfield Hgts City Schools	Garfield Hgts
145	5	Geneva Area City	Geneva
145	5	Green Local	Uniontown
145	5	Greenfield Exempted Village	Greenfield
145	5	Greenville City	Greenville
145	5	Highland Local	Medina
145	5	Hillsboro City	Hillsboro
145	5	Indian Creek Local	Wintersville
145	5	Jackson City	Jackson
145	5	Jonathan Alder Local	Plain City
145	5	Lake Local	Uniontown
145	5	Lexington Local	Lexington
145	5	Licking Heights Local	Pataskala
145	5	Madison Local	Madison
145	5	Maple Heights City	Maple Heights
145	5	Marlington Local	Alliance
145	5	Mason City SD	Mason
145	5	Maumee City	Maumee
145	5	Midview Local	Grafton
145	5	Morgan Local	Mc Connelsville
145	5	Napoleon Area City	Napoleon
145	5	New Richmond Exempted Village	New Richmond
145	5	Northern Local	Thornville
145	5	Norton City	Norton
145	5	Oakwood City	Dayton
145	5	Olmsted Falls City	Olmsted Falls
145	5	Rolling Hills Local	Cambridge
145	5	Rossford Exempted Village	Rossford
145	5	Salem City	Salem
145	5	Southwest Licking Local	Pataskala
145	5	Steubenville City	Steubenville
145	5	Streetsboro City	Streetsboro
145	5	Talawanda City	Oxford
145	5	Tiffin City	Tiffin
145	5	Tipp City Exempted Village	Tipp City
145	5	Triway Local	Wooster
145	5	Trotwood-Madison City	Trotwood
145	5	Twinsburg City	Twinsburg
145	5	Upper Sandusky Exempted Village	Upper Sandusky
145	5	Urbana City	Urbana
145	5	Vandalia-Butler City	Vandalia
145	5	Vinton County Local	Mc Arthur
145	5	Wapakoneta City	Wapakoneta
145	5	Warren City	Warren
145	5	Wilmington City	Wilmington
145	5	Wyoming City	Wyoming
206	4	Amanda-Clearcreek Local	Amanda
206	4	Aurora City	Aurora
206	4	Austintown Local	Youngstown
206	4	Barberton City	Barberton
206	4	Bay Village City	Bay Village
206	4	Bellefontaine City	Bellefontaine
206	4	Bethel-Tate Local	Bethel
206	4	Blanchester Local	Blanchester
206	4	Bloom-Carroll Local	Carroll
206	4	Buckeye Local	Ashtabula
206	4	Buckeye Local	Medina
206	4	Buckeye Valley Local	Delaware
206	4	Canal Wnchstr Local	Canal Wnchstr
206	4	Canfield Local	Canfield
206	4	Carlisle Local	Carlisle
206	4	Chagrin Falls Exempted Village	Chagrin Falls
206	4	Clear Fork Valley Local	Bellville
206	4	Clyde-Green Springs Exempted Village	Clyde
206	4	Conneaut Area City	Conneaut
206	4	Coventry Local	Akron
206	4	Eaton Community City	Eaton
206	4	Edison Local	Hammondsville
206	4	Fairborn City	Fairborn
206	4	Fairfield Union Local	Lancaster
206	4	Fairland Local	Proctorville
206	4	Fairview Park City	Fairview Park
206	4	Field Local	Mogadore
206	4	Fostoria City	Fostoria
206	4	Franklin Local	Duncan Falls
206	4	Galion City	Galion
206	4	Girard City SD	Girard
206	4	Goshen Local	Goshen
206	4	Granville Exempted Village	Granville
206	4	Greenon Local	Enon
206	4	Hamilton Local	Columbus
206	4	Heath City	Heath
206	4	Indian Hill Exempted Village	Cincinnati
206	4	Indian Valley Local Schools	Gnadenhutten
206	4	Jefferson Area Local	Jefferson
206	4	Johnstown-Monroe Local	Johnstown
206	4	Kenston Local	Chagrin Falls
206	4	Lakewood Local	Hebron
206	4	Louisville City	Louisville
206	4	Mariemont City	Cincinnati

Note: This section only includes districts with 1,500 or more students; All categories are ranked from high to low

206	4	Meigs Local	Pomeroy
206	4	Mt Healthy City	Cincinnati
206	4	New Albany-Plain Local	New Albany
206	4	New Lexington City	New Lexington
206	4	Niles City	Niles
206	4	North Fork Local	Utica
206	4	Northridge Local	Dayton
206	4	Northwest Local	Canal Fulton
206	4	Orange City	Cleveland
206	4	Ottawa-Glandorf Local	Ottawa
206	4	Perkins Local	Sandusky
206	4	Port Clinton City	Port Clinton
206	4	Reading Community City	Reading
206	4	Revere Local	Bath
206	4	River Valley Local	Caledonia
206	4	Rocky River City	Rocky River
206	4	Ross Local	Hamilton
206	4	Shawnee Local	Lima
206	4	Shelby City	Shelby
206	4	South Point Local	South Point
206	4	Southeast Local	Ravenna
206	4	Springfield Local	Akron
206	4	Saint Marys City	Saint Marys
206	4	Struthers City	Struthers
206	4	Tallmadge City	Tallmadge
206	4	Valley View Local	Germantown
206	4	Van Wert City	Van Wert
206	4	Warren Local	Vincent
206	4	Washington CH City	Washington CH
206	4	Wauseon Exempted Village	Wauseon
206	4	Waverly City	Waverly
206	4	West Branch Local	Beloit
206	4	West Geauga Local	Chesterland
206	4	West Muskingum Local	Zanesville
206	4	Western Brown Local	Mount Orab
206	4	Willard City	Willard
206	4	Woodridge Local	Peninsula
287	3	Batavia Local	Batavia
287	3	Bath Local	Lima
287	3	Bellevue City	Bellevue
287	3	Benjamin Logan Local	Bellefontaine
287	3	Benton Carroll Salem Local	Oak Harbor
287	3	Canton Local	Canton
287	3	Clearview Local	Lorain
287	3	Clermont Northeastern Local	Batavia
287	3	Clinton-Massie Local	Clarksville
287	3	Cloverleaf Local	Lodi
287	3	Defiance City	Defiance
287	3	Edison Local (Formerly Berlin-Milan)	Milan
287	3	Elida Local	Elida
287	3	Fairless Local	Navarre
287	3	Firelands Local	South Amherst
287	3	Graham Local	Saint Paris
287	3	Harrison Hills City	Cadiz
287	3	Highland Local	Sparta
287	3	Hubbard Exempted Village	Hubbard
287	3	Indian Lake Local	Lewistown
287	3	Keystone Local	Lagrange
287	3	Lake Local	Millbury
287	3	Lakeview Local	Cortland
287	3	Licking Valley Local	Newark
287	3	London City	London
287	3	Madison Local	Middletown
287	3	Maysville Local	Zanesville
287	3	Miami Trace Local	Washington CH
287	3	Minerva Local	Minerva
287	3	Minford Local	Minford
287	3	Monroe Local SD	Monroe
287	3	North College Hill City	Cincinnati
287	3	Northwest Local	Mc Dermott
287	3	Ontario Local	Mansfield
287	3	Orrville City	Orrville
287	3	Perry Local	Perry
287	3	Portsmouth City	Portsmouth
287	3	Saint Clairsville-Richland City	Saint Clairsville
287	3	Union-Scioto Local	Chillicothe
287	3	Vermilion Local	Vermilion
287	3	Westfall Local	Williamsport
287	3	Wheelersburg Local	Wheelersburg
329	2	Alexander Local	Albany
329	2	Coshocton City	Coshocton
329	2	Northwestern Local	Springfield
329	2	Three Rivers Local	Cleves
333	1	Alternative Education Academy	Toledo
333	1	Electronic Classroom of Tomorrow	Columbus
333	1	Ohio Connections Academy, Inc	Cleveland
333	1	Ohio Virtual Academy	Maumee
333	1	Treca Digital Academy	Marion

Number of Teachers

Rank	Number	District Name	City
1	3,073.8	Columbus City SD	Columbus
2	2,469.5	Cleveland Municipal	Cleveland
3	1,947.1	Cincinnati City	Cincinnati
4	1,409.8	Toledo City	Toledo
5	1,379.5	Akron City	Akron
6	1,120.9	South-Western City	Grove City
7	944.1	Dayton City	Dayton
8	921.9	Olentangy Local	Lewis Center
9	842.5	Dublin City	Dublin
10	842.0	Hilliard City	Columbus
11	743.0	Westerville City	Westerville
12	724.3	Lakota Local	Liberty Twp
13	680.2	Parma City	Parma
14	626.6	Worthington City	Worthington
15	560.7	Canton City	Canton
16	519.7	Mason City SD	Mason
17	508.9	Cleveland Heights-Univ Hgts City	University Hgts
18	507.4	Hamilton City	Hamilton
19	504.6	Pickerington Local	Pickerington
20	498.8	Fairfield City	Fairfield
21	484.9	Centerville City	Centerville
22	465.9	Willoughby-Eastlake City	Willoughby
23	463.7	Springfield City	Springfield
24	450.3	Gahanna-Jefferson City	Gahanna
25	449.9	Mentor Exempted Village	Mentor
26	446.1	Northwest Local	Cincinnati
27	438.5	Sylvania City	Sylvania
28	432.1	Kettering City	Kettering
29	416.3	Oak Hills Local	Cincinnati
30	416.2	Washington Local	Toledo
31	398.7	West Clermont Local	Cincinnati
32	394.7	Forest Hills Local	Cincinnati
33	393.3	Berea City	Berea
34	389.9	Beavercreek City	Beavercreek
35	388.8	Brunswick City	Brunswick
36	380.6	Middletown City	Middletown
37	378.0	Lorain City	Lorain
38	377.5	Electronic Classroom of Tomorrow	Columbus
39	375.4	Elyria City Schools	Elyria
40	363.8	Strongsville City	Strongsville
41	357.4	Upper Arlington City	Upper Arlington
42	356.4	Youngstown City Schools	Youngstown
43	354.8	Euclid City	Euclid
44	353.7	Newark City	Newark
45	346.8	Lancaster City	Lancaster
46	345.3	Marion City	Marion
47	341.4	Lakewood City	Lakewood
48	341.3	Shaker Heights City	Shaker Heights
49	333.6	Findlay City	Findlay
50	332.4	Cuyahoga Falls City	Cuyahoga Falls
51	332.3	Milford Exempted Village	Milford
52	318.7	Medina City SD	Medina
53	317.4	Miamisburg City	Miamisburg
54	315.4	Princeton City	Cincinnati
55	313.8	Sycamore Community City	Blue Ash
56	313.3	Groveport Madison Local	Groveport
57	313.1	Delaware City	Delaware
58	311.8	Springboro Community City	Springboro
59	307.0	Ohio Virtual Academy	Maumee
60	305.6	Northmont City	Englewood
61	301.4	Huber Heights City	Huber Heights
62	294.7	Warren City	Warren
63	294.1	Stow-Munroe Falls City SD	Stow
64	285.5	New Albany-Plain Local	New Albany
65	281.9	Perry Local	Massillon
66	281.8	Reynoldsburg City	Reynoldsburg
67	281.0	Austintown Local	Youngstown
68	280.7	Mayfield City	Mayfield Hgts
69	277.9	North Canton City	North Canton
70	277.7	Plain Local	Canton
71	275.9	Marysville Exempted Village	Marysville
72	275.6	Hudson City	Hudson
73	273.3	Mansfield City	Mansfield
74	270.3	Solon City	Solon
75	267.0	Kent City	Kent
76	265.8	Jackson Local	Massillon
77	263.0	Lima City	Lima
78	254.6	Boardman Local	Youngstown
79	250.6	Lebanon City	Lebanon
80	245.9	Perrysburg Exempted Village	Perrysburg
81	245.7	Westlake City	Westlake
82	245.6	Fremont City	Fremont
83	243.7	Massillon City	Massillon
84	241.5	Mount Vernon City	Mount Vernon
85	240.4	North Royalton City	North Royalton
86	239.1	Fairborn City	Fairborn
87	236.9	Southwest Licking Local	Pataskala
88	234.2	Logan-Hocking Local	Logan
89	234.0	Troy City	Troy
90	231.2	Wooster City	Wooster
91	229.2	North Olmsted City	North Olmsted
92	228.4	South Euclid-Lyndhurst City	Lyndhurst
93	228.0	Kings Local	Kings Mills
94	227.5	Green Local	Uniontown
95	227.4	Wadsworth City	Wadsworth
96	225.8	Loveland City	Loveland
97	224.3	Xenia Community City	Xenia
98	223.3	Adams County/Ohio Valley Local	West Union
99	222.5	East Cleveland City SD	East Cleveland
100	222.1	Riverside Local	Painesville
101	219.8	Sandusky City	Sandusky
102	219.2	Bedford City	Bedford
103	218.0	Madison Local	Mansfield
104	216.0	Amherst Exempted Village	Amherst
105	215.8	N Ridgeville City	N Ridgeville
106	214.9	Garfield Hgts City Schools	Garfield Hgts
107	211.9	Oregon City	Oregon
108	210.0	Maple Heights City	Maple Heights
109	208.7	Avon Local	Avon
110	206.6	Mad River Local	Dayton
111	205.7	Greenville City	Greenville
112	205.0	Brecksville-Broadview Heights City	Brecksville
113	204.5	West Carrollton City	West Carrollton
114	203.5	Avon Lake City	Avon Lake
115	203.4	Nordonia Hills City	Northfield
116	202.0	Barberton City	Barberton
117	200.1	Winton Woods City	Cincinnati
118	199.4	Springfield Local	Holland
119	197.6	Anthony Wayne Local	Whitehouse
120	197.2	Licking Heights Local	Pataskala
121	195.8	Alliance City	Alliance
121	195.8	Athens City	The Plains
123	195.4	Kenston Local	Chagrin Falls
123	195.4	Twinsburg City	Twinsburg
125	195.0	New Philadel. City	New Philadel.
125	195.0	Olmsted Falls City	Olmsted Falls
127	193.9	Northeastern Local	Springfield
128	193.7	Lake Local	Uniontown
129	193.5	Little Miami Local	Maineville
130	191.7	Canal Wnchstr Local	Canal Wnchstr
131	191.3	Midview Local	Grafton
132	187.0	Ashland City	Ashland
133	186.6	Ashtabula Area City	Ashtabula
134	185.4	Celina City	Celina
135	184.4	Mt Healthy City	Cincinnati
136	182.8	Teays Valley Local	Ashville
137	181.6	Zanesville City	Zanesville
138	181.0	Franklin City	Franklin
139	179.0	Copley-Fairlawn City	Copley
140	178.8	Piqua City	Piqua
141	176.0	Edgewood City	Trenton
142	175.4	Talawanda City	Oxford
143	172.1	Howland Local	Warren
144	172.0	East Liverpool City	East Liverpool
145	170.5	Chardon Local	Chardon
146	169.0	Whitehall City	Whitehall
147	168.1	Chillicothe City	Chillicothe
148	167.6	Revere Local	Bath
149	167.3	Madison Local	Madison
150	163.7	Painesville City Local	Painesville
151	163.3	Sidney City	Sidney
152	162.9	Ravenna City	Ravenna
153	162.3	Vinton County Local	Mc Arthur
154	161.4	Steubenville City	Steubenville
155	161.2	Big Walnut Local	Sunbury
156	160.2	Marietta City	Marietta
157	160.0	Niles City	Niles
158	159.4	Orange City	Cleveland
159	159.3	Tecumseh Local	New Carlisle

Note: This section only includes districts with 1,500 or more students; All categories are ranked from high to low

160	158.2	Aurora City	Aurora
160	158.2	Jackson City	Jackson
162	157.2	Canfield Local	Canfield
163	156.9	Rocky River City	Rocky River
164	155.8	Vandalia-Butler City	Vandalia
165	155.6	Hamilton Local	Columbus
166	155.2	Trotwood-Madison City	Trotwood
167	154.4	Bowling Green City SD	Bowling Green
168	153.8	Highland Local	Medina
168	153.8	Southwest Local	Harrison
170	153.7	Bellefontaine City	Bellefontaine
171	152.9	Switzerland of Ohio Local	Woodsfield
172	152.0	Tri-Valley Local	Dresden
173	151.8	Bay Village City	Bay Village
174	151.2	Buckeye Local	Dillonvale
175	149.6	Tallmadge City	Tallmadge
176	149.1	Louisville City	Louisville
176	149.1	Norwalk City	Norwalk
178	148.6	Hillsboro City	Hillsboro
179	147.6	Lakewood Local	Hebron
180	146.9	West Branch Local	Beloit
181	146.4	Field Local	Mogadore
182	146.2	Buckeye Valley Local	Delaware
182	146.2	Maumee City	Maumee
184	145.6	Indian Hill Exempted Village	Cincinnati
185	144.7	Maysville Local	Zanesville
186	144.6	Wapakoneta City	Wapakoneta
187	144.3	Defiance City	Defiance
188	143.6	Dover City	Dover
189	143.5	Granville Exempted Village	Granville
190	143.4	Wilmington City	Wilmington
191	141.7	New Richmond Exempted Village	New Richmond
192	140.8	Batavia Local	Batavia
193	140.6	Tipp City Exempted Village	Tipp City
194	140.3	Miami Trace Local	Washington CH
194	140.3	Ross Local	Hamilton
196	140.2	Lexington Local	Lexington
197	139.8	Springfield Local	Akron
198	139.7	Shawnee Local	Lima
199	138.7	Norton City	Norton
200	138.6	Morgan Local	Mc Connelsville
201	138.5	Clyde-Green Springs Exempted Village	Clyde
202	138.3	Goshen Local	Goshen
203	138.2	Marlington Local	Alliance
204	137.3	Cambridge City	Cambridge
205	136.8	Franklin Local	Duncan Falls
206	136.6	Bexley City	Bexley
206	136.6	East Muskingum Local	New Concord
208	136.1	Chagrin Falls Exempted Village	Chagrin Falls
208	136.1	Warren Local	Vincent
210	135.0	Gallia County Local	Gallipolis
211	134.5	Norwood City	Norwood
212	133.5	Claymont City	Dennison
213	133.4	Cloverleaf Local	Lodi
214	132.9	Poland Local	Poland
215	132.4	Perkins Local	Sandusky
216	132.0	Western Brown Local	Mount Orab
217	131.8	Oakwood City	Dayton
218	131.0	Bellbrook-Sugarcreek Local SD	Bellbrook
219	130.4	Indian Creek Local	Wintersville
220	130.1	West Holmes Local	Millersburg
221	129.9	Tiffin City	Tiffin
222	129.6	Coventry Local	Akron
223	129.4	Washington CH City	Washington CH
224	128.0	River View Local	Warsaw
224	128.0	Wyoming City	Wyoming
226	127.4	Elida Local	Elida
227	126.9	Circleville City	Circleville
228	126.8	Logan Elm Local	Circleville
229	126.6	Union-Scioto Local	Chillicothe
230	125.6	Streetsboro City	Streetsboro
231	124.7	Triway Local	Wooster
232	124.4	Crestwood Local	Mantua
233	124.3	Woodridge Local	Peninsula
234	124.2	Geneva Area City	Geneva
234	124.2	London City	London
236	124.1	Canton Local	Canton
237	124.0	Van Wert City	Van Wert
238	123.8	Kenton City	Kenton
239	122.7	Gallipolis City	Gallipolis
240	122.0	Salem City	Salem
241	120.8	Licking Valley Local	Newark
242	120.2	Bryan City	Bryan
243	119.7	Northern Local	Thornville
244	118.9	Carrollton Exempted Village	Carrollton
245	118.4	Buckeye Local	Medina
246	117.6	Port Clinton City	Port Clinton
247	117.5	Urbana City	Urbana
248	115.7	New Lexington City	New Lexington
249	114.6	Bellevue City	Bellevue
250	114.0	Napoleon Area City	Napoleon
251	113.6	Monroe Local SD	Monroe
252	113.3	Fostoria City	Fostoria
253	113.0	Beaver Local	Lisbon
254	112.7	Portsmouth City	Portsmouth
255	112.5	Galion City	Galion
256	112.4	West Geauga Local	Chesterland
257	112.0	Meigs Local	Pomeroy
258	111.8	Saint Marys City	Saint Marys
259	111.7	Eaton Community City	Eaton
260	111.3	Struthers City	Struthers
261	111.2	Rossford Exempted Village	Rossford
262	110.0	Valley View Local	Germantown
263	109.4	Hubbard Exempted Village	Hubbard
264	108.5	Wauseon Exempted Village	Wauseon
265	108.4	Greenfield Exempted Village	Greenfield
266	108.2	East Holmes Local	Berlin
266	108.2	Perry Local	Perry
268	108.0	Clinton-Massie Local	Clarksville
269	107.8	Jonathan Alder Local	Plain City
269	107.8	Sheffield-Sheffield Lake City	Sheffield Vllg
271	107.5	Highland Local	Sparta
272	107.0	Rolling Hills Local	Cambridge
273	106.5	Southeast Local	Ravenna
274	105.5	Northridge Local	Dayton
275	105.2	Coshocton City	Coshocton
276	104.0	Northwest Local	Canal Fulton
277	103.6	Clark-Shawnee Local	Springfield
278	103.5	Graham Local	Saint Paris
279	103.4	Clear Fork Valley Local	Bellville
280	103.0	Indian Lake Local	Lewistown
281	102.1	Indian Valley Local Schools	Gnadenhutten
282	102.0	Vermilion Local	Vermilion
283	101.7	Shelby City	Shelby
284	101.2	Fairfield Union Local	Lancaster
285	101.0	Westfall Local	Williamsport
286	100.5	Benjamin Logan Local	Bellefontaine
287	99.7	Buckeye Local	Ashtabula
288	99.3	West Muskingum Local	Zanesville
289	99.0	Fairland Local	Proctorville
290	98.7	Girard City SD	Girard
291	98.5	Alexander Local	Albany
291	98.5	Northwest Local	Mc Dermott
293	98.4	Bath Local	Lima
293	98.4	Lake Local	Millbury
295	98.3	Conneaut Area City	Conneaut
296	97.7	Fairview Park City	Fairview Park
297	97.6	Three Rivers Local	Cleves
298	97.2	Carlisle Local	Carlisle
299	97.1	River Valley Local	Caledonia
300	96.2	Willard City	Willard
301	95.9	Bethel-Tate Local	Bethel
302	95.2	Firelands Local	South Amherst
303	94.7	Minerva Local	Minerva
303	94.7	North Fork Local	Utica
303	94.7	Orrville City	Orrville
303	94.7	Waverly City	Waverly
307	94.5	Amanda-Clearcreek Local	Amanda
308	94.3	South Point Local	South Point
309	94.0	Ohio Connections Academy, Inc	Cleveland
310	93.7	Johnstown-Monroe Local	Johnstown
310	93.7	Mariemont City	Cincinnati
310	93.7	Ontario Local	Mansfield
313	93.2	Saint Clairsville-Richland City	Saint Clairsville
314	92.8	Fairless Local	Navarre
314	92.8	Greenon Local	Enon
316	92.7	Edison Local (Formerly Berlin-Milan)	Milan
317	92.3	Blanchester Local	Blanchester
318	92.2	Upper Sandusky Exempted Village	Upper Sandusky
319	91.7	Reading Community City	Reading
320	91.0	Heath City	Heath
321	90.6	Keystone Local	Lagrange
322	89.5	Benton Carroll Salem Local	Oak Harbor
323	88.9	Northwestern Local	Springfield
324	87.9	Lakeview Local	Cortland
325	87.0	Bloom-Carroll Local	Carroll
326	86.9	Minford Local	Minford
327	85.7	Clearview Local	Lorain
327	85.7	Edison Local	Hammondsville
329	83.2	Ottawa-Glandorf Local	Ottawa
330	83.0	Harrison Hills City	Cadiz
331	82.7	Wheelersburg Local	Wheelersburg
332	79.5	North College Hill City	Cincinnati
333	79.2	Jefferson Area Local	Jefferson
334	78.4	Madison Local	Middletown
335	78.2	Clermont Northeastern Local	Batavia
336	56.0	Alternative Education Academy	Toledo
337	17.6	Treca Digital Academy	Marion

Number of Students

Rank	Number	District Name	City
1	50,478	Columbus City SD	Columbus
2	38,562	Cleveland Municipal	Cleveland
3	31,801	Cincinnati City	Cincinnati
4	21,708	Akron City	Akron
5	21,669	Toledo City	Toledo
6	21,107	South-Western City	Grove City
7	17,988	Olentangy Local	Lewis Center
8	16,223	Lakota Local	Liberty Twp
9	15,566	Hilliard City	Columbus
10	14,733	Dublin City	Dublin
11	14,595	Westerville City	Westerville
12	14,209	Dayton City	Dayton
13	12,974	Electronic Classroom of Tomorrow	Columbus
14	12,920	Ohio Virtual Academy	Maumee
15	11,164	Parma City	Parma
16	10,683	Mason City SD	Mason
17	10,076	Pickerington Local	Pickerington
18	10,033	Hamilton City	Hamilton
19	9,708	Fairfield City	Fairfield
20	9,529	Worthington City	Worthington
21	9,465	Canton City	Canton
22	9,176	Northwest Local	Cincinnati
23	8,362	Willoughby-Eastlake City	Willoughby
24	8,283	Centerville City	Centerville
25	8,200	West Clermont Local	Cincinnati
26	7,948	Oak Hills Local	Cincinnati
27	7,899	Mentor Exempted Village	Mentor
28	7,709	Kettering City	Kettering
29	7,498	Springfield City	Springfield
30	7,469	Forest Hills Local	Cincinnati
31	7,464	Sylvania City	Sylvania
32	7,454	Beavercreek City	Beavercreek
33	7,236	Brunswick City	Brunswick
34	7,135	Gahanna-Jefferson City	Gahanna
35	6,995	Medina City SD	Medina
36	6,880	Berea City	Berea
37	6,838	Washington Local	Toledo
38	6,572	Milford Exempted Village	Milford
39	6,550	Lorain City	Lorain
40	6,522	Reynoldsburg City	Reynoldsburg
41	6,418	Elyria City Schools	Elyria
42	6,307	Newark City	Newark
43	6,272	Middletown City	Middletown
44	6,194	Lancaster City	Lancaster
45	6,059	Plain Local	Canton
46	5,935	Jackson Local	Massillon
47	5,930	Huber Heights City	Huber Heights
48	5,888	Strongsville City	Strongsville
49	5,850	Springboro Community City	Springboro
50	5,802	Findlay City	Findlay
51	5,782	Cleveland Heights-Univ Hgts City	University Hgts
52	5,756	Upper Arlington City	Upper Arlington
53	5,602	Lakewood City	Lakewood
54	5,517	Euclid City	Euclid
55	5,484	Miamisburg City	Miamisburg
56	5,436	Groveport Madison Local	Groveport
57	5,430	Princeton City	Cincinnati
58	5,429	Lebanon City	Lebanon
59	5,408	Youngstown City Schools	Youngstown
60	5,401	Delaware City	Delaware
61	5,322	Shaker Heights City	Shaker Heights
62	5,299	Sycamore Community City	Blue Ash
63	5,252	Stow-Munroe Falls City SD	Stow
64	5,247	Austintown Local	Youngstown
65	5,153	Marysville Exempted Village	Marysville
66	5,119	Northmont City	Englewood
67	5,097	Warren City	Warren
68	4,951	Perry Local	Massillon
69	4,918	Cuyahoga Falls City	Cuyahoga Falls

Note: This section only includes districts with 1,500 or more students; All categories are ranked from high to low

70	4,872	Wadsworth City	Wadsworth
71	4,833	Solon City	Solon
72	4,702	New Albany-Plain Local	New Albany
73	4,697	Loveland City	Loveland
74	4,679	Perrysburg Exempted Village	Perrysburg
75	4,625	North Royalton City	North Royalton
76	4,602	North Canton City	North Canton
77	4,557	Hudson City	Hudson
78	4,496	Riverside Local	Painesville
79	4,462	Mayfield City	Mayfield Hgts
80	4,397	Boardman Local	Youngstown
81	4,332	Troy City	Troy
82	4,293	Anthony Wayne Local	Whitehouse
83	4,267	Xenia Community City	Xenia
84	4,223	Fairborn City	Fairborn
85	4,221	Twinsburg City	Twinsburg
86	4,197	Green Local	Uniontown
87	4,185	Marion City	Marion
88	4,155	Avon Local	Avon
89	4,117	Brecksville-Broadview Heights City	Brecksville
90	4,102	Fremont City	Fremont
91	4,092	N Ridgeville City	N Ridgeville
92	4,050	Kings Local	Kings Mills
93	4,036	North Olmsted City	North Olmsted
94	4,001	Little Miami Local	Maineville
95	3,980	Massillon City	Massillon
96	3,954	Logan-Hocking Local	Logan
97	3,939	Adams County/Ohio Valley Local	West Union
98	3,924	Barberton City	Barberton
99	3,910	Springfield Local	Holland
100	3,880	Amherst Exempted Village	Amherst
101	3,879	Westlake City	Westlake
102	3,876	Mad River Local	Dayton
103	3,865	Lima City	Lima
104	3,854	West Carrollton City	West Carrollton
105	3,838	South Euclid-Lyndhurst City	Lyndhurst
106	3,788	Mount Vernon City	Mount Vernon
107	3,786	Olmsted Falls City	Olmsted Falls
108	3,773	Southwest Licking Local	Pataskala
109	3,758	Garfield Hgts City Schools	Garfield Hgts
110	3,732	Nordonia Hills City	Northfield
111	3,730	Avon Lake City	Avon Lake
112	3,723	Ashtabula Area City	Ashtabula
113	3,721	Teays Valley Local	Ashville
114	3,710	Oregon City	Oregon
115	3,694	Maple Heights City	Maple Heights
116	3,671	Licking Heights Local	Pataskala
117	3,639	Mansfield City	Mansfield
118	3,627	Wooster City	Wooster
119	3,613	Canal Wnchstr Local	Canal Wnchstr
120	3,603	Edgewood City	Trenton
121	3,540	Kent City	Kent
122	3,517	Southwest Local	Harrison
123	3,506	Northeastern Local	Springfield
124	3,488	Lake Local	Uniontown
125	3,470	Bedford City	Bedford
126	3,442	Piqua City	Piqua
127	3,410	Zanesville City	Zanesville
128	3,378	Winton Woods City	Cincinnati
129	3,343	Ohio Connections Academy, Inc	Cleveland
130	3,318	Madison Local	Madison
131	3,300	Sidney City	Sidney
132	3,264	Sandusky City	Sandusky
133	3,245	Ashland City	Ashland
134	3,213	Mt Healthy City	Cincinnati
135	3,200	Whitehall City	Whitehall
136	3,197	Hamilton Local	Columbus
137	3,182	Highland Local	Medina
138	3,141	Copley-Fairlawn City	Copley
139	3,132	Western Brown Local	Mount Orab
140	3,124	Vandalia-Butler City	Vandalia
141	3,116	Madison Local	Mansfield
142	3,111	Big Walnut Local	Sunbury
143	3,099	Painesville City Local	Painesville
144	3,051	Wapakoneta City	Wapakoneta
145	3,028	Alliance City	Alliance
146	3,008	Tecumseh Local	New Carlisle
147	3,007	Wilmington City	Wilmington
148	2,995	Louisville City	Louisville
149	2,994	Tri-Valley Local	Dresden
150	2,985	Kenston Local	Chagrin Falls
151	2,982	Bowling Green City SD	Bowling Green
152	2,980	New Philadel. City	New Philadel.
153	2,970	Chardon Local	Chardon
154	2,968	Midview Local	Grafton
155	2,964	Talawanda City	Oxford
156	2,929	Chillicothe City	Chillicothe
157	2,928	Franklin City	Franklin
158	2,924	Aurora City	Aurora
159	2,877	Howland Local	Warren
160	2,838	Norwalk City	Norwalk
161	2,775	Dover City	Dover
162	2,756	Canfield Local	Canfield
163	2,753	Tiffin City	Tiffin
164	2,730	Ravenna City	Ravenna
165	2,726	Ross Local	Hamilton
166	2,721	Athens City	The Plains
167	2,720	Marietta City	Marietta
168	2,702	Celina City	Celina
169	2,679	Rocky River City	Rocky River
170	2,650	Goshen Local	Goshen
171	2,641	Greenville City	Greenville
172	2,613	Revere Local	Bath
173	2,570	Norton City	Norton
174	2,564	Hillsboro City	Hillsboro
175	2,535	Geneva Area City	Geneva
176	2,534	Bellbrook-Sugarcreek Local SD	Bellbrook
177	2,531	Bay Village City	Bay Village
178	2,526	Trotwood-Madison City	Trotwood
179	2,503	Miami Trace Local	Washington CH
179	2,503	Monroe Local SD	Monroe
181	2,501	Bellefontaine City	Bellefontaine
182	2,491	Shawnee Local	Lima
183	2,490	Defiance City	Defiance
184	2,484	East Cleveland City SD	East Cleveland
184	2,484	Tipp City Exempted Village	Tipp City
186	2,481	Cloverleaf Local	Lodi
187	2,471	Jackson City	Jackson
188	2,469	Granville Exempted Village	Granville
189	2,465	Elida Local	Elida
190	2,462	Maumee City	Maumee
191	2,445	Tallmadge City	Tallmadge
192	2,436	Steubenville City	Steubenville
193	2,429	Niles City	Niles
194	2,414	Springfield Local	Akron
195	2,405	Marlington Local	Alliance
196	2,398	New Richmond Exempted Village	New Richmond
197	2,382	West Holmes Local	Millersburg
198	2,378	Lexington Local	Lexington
199	2,359	Switzerland of Ohio Local	Woodsfield
200	2,300	Vinton County Local	Mc Arthur
201	2,284	Washington CH City	Washington CH
202	2,282	Perkins Local	Sandusky
203	2,275	Maysville Local	Zanesville
204	2,239	Buckeye Local	Medina
205	2,237	East Liverpool City	East Liverpool
206	2,220	Carrollton Exempted Village	Carrollton
206	2,220	Clyde-Green Springs Exempted Village	Clyde
208	2,217	Jonathan Alder Local	Plain City
209	2,202	Buckeye Valley Local	Delaware
209	2,202	Orange City	Cleveland
211	2,177	Batavia Local	Batavia
212	2,176	Streetsboro City	Streetsboro
213	2,168	Union-Scioto Local	Chillicothe
214	2,160	Bexley City	Bexley
215	2,156	West Geauga Local	Chesterland
216	2,154	Canton Local	Canton
217	2,152	Indian Creek Local	Wintersville
218	2,147	Gallipolis City	Gallipolis
219	2,146	Warren Local	Vincent
220	2,133	Coventry Local	Akron
220	2,133	East Muskingum Local	New Concord
222	2,131	Northern Local	Thornville
223	2,122	Eaton Community City	Eaton
224	2,110	Cambridge City	Cambridge
225	2,104	Saint Marys City	Saint Marys
226	2,093	Gallia County Local	Gallipolis
227	2,090	Clark-Shawnee Local	Springfield
228	2,089	Claymont City	Dennison
229	2,087	Oakwood City	Dayton
230	2,078	Poland Local	Poland
231	2,074	West Branch Local	Beloit
232	2,073	Salem City	Salem
233	2,052	Bellevue City	Bellevue
234	2,049	Woodridge Local	Peninsula
235	2,046	River View Local	Warsaw
236	2,042	Graham Local	Saint Paris
237	2,040	Circleville City	Circleville
238	2,039	Greenfield Exempted Village	Greenfield
239	2,031	Urbana City	Urbana
239	2,031	Van Wert City	Van Wert
241	2,017	Morgan Local	Mc Connelsville
242	2,015	Norwood City	Norwood
243	2,011	Chagrin Falls Exempted Village	Chagrin Falls
244	2,001	Licking Valley Local	Newark
245	2,000	Three Rivers Local	Cleves
246	1,980	Field Local	Mogadore
247	1,974	London City	London
248	1,970	Napoleon Area City	Napoleon
249	1,965	Franklin Local	Duncan Falls
250	1,964	Bryan City	Bryan
251	1,955	Logan Elm Local	Circleville
252	1,952	Fairfield Union Local	Lancaster
253	1,944	Kenton City	Kenton
254	1,934	River Valley Local	Caledonia
255	1,929	Crestwood Local	Mantua
256	1,919	Northwest Local	Canal Fulton
257	1,913	Wyoming City	Wyoming
258	1,907	Hubbard Exempted Village	Hubbard
259	1,906	Vermilion Local	Vermilion
260	1,902	Struthers City	Struthers
261	1,897	Buckeye Local	Dillonvale
262	1,890	Lakewood Local	Hebron
263	1,888	Ontario Local	Mansfield
264	1,883	Clinton-Massie Local	Clarksville
265	1,881	Indian Hill Exempted Village	Cincinnati
266	1,874	Beaver Local	Lisbon
267	1,872	Alternative Education Academy	Toledo
268	1,862	Waverly City	Waverly
269	1,856	Galion City	Galion
270	1,851	Valley View Local	Germantown
271	1,845	Portsmouth City	Portsmouth
272	1,842	Bloom-Carroll Local	Carroll
272	1,842	Shelby City	Shelby
272	1,842	Wauseon Exempted Village	Wauseon
275	1,840	Highland Local	Sparta
276	1,837	New Lexington City	New Lexington
277	1,817	Minerva Local	Minerva
278	1,811	Indian Valley Local Schools	Gnadenhutten
279	1,804	Fostoria City	Fostoria
280	1,800	Bath Local	Lima
281	1,792	Meigs Local	Pomeroy
282	1,783	Fairview Park City	Fairview Park
283	1,774	East Holmes Local	Berlin
284	1,765	Clear Fork Valley Local	Bellville
285	1,761	Perry Local	Perry
286	1,760	Buckeye Local	Ashtabula
287	1,758	Lakeview Local	Cortland
288	1,753	Sheffield-Sheffield Lake City	Sheffield Vllg
289	1,751	Northridge Local	Dayton
290	1,746	Benjamin Logan Local	Bellefontaine
291	1,742	Northwestern Local	Springfield
292	1,722	Port Clinton City	Port Clinton
293	1,711	Girard City SD	Girard
294	1,710	Greenon Local	Enon
295	1,705	Conneaut Area City	Conneaut
296	1,703	Blanchester Local	Blanchester
297	1,697	Clearview Local	Lorain
298	1,696	Triway Local	Wooster
299	1,685	Treca Digital Academy	Marion
300	1,684	Mariemont City	Cincinnati
301	1,682	Rossford Exempted Village	Rossford
302	1,679	Southeast Local	Ravenna
303	1,678	Jefferson Area Local	Jefferson
304	1,677	Firelands Local	South Amherst
305	1,676	Saint Clairsville-Richland City	Saint Clairsville
306	1,670	Indian Lake Local	Lewistown
307	1,656	Fairland Local	Proctorville
308	1,650	Heath City	Heath
309	1,639	South Point Local	South Point
310	1,637	Keystone Local	Lagrange
311	1,635	Willard City	Willard
312	1,626	Bethel-Tate Local	Bethel
312	1,626	Upper Sandusky Exempted Village	Upper Sandusky
314	1,623	Rolling Hills Local	Cambridge
315	1,606	Benton Carroll Salem Local	Oak Harbor
315	1,606	Reading Community City	Reading
317	1,601	North Fork Local	Utica
318	1,600	Amanda-Clearcreek Local	Amanda
319	1,592	Carlisle Local	Carlisle
320	1,583	North College Hill City	Cincinnati
321	1,578	Lake Local	Millbury

Note: This section only includes districts with 1,500 or more students; All categories are ranked from high to low

322	1,577	Coshocton City	Coshocton
323	1,569	Johnstown-Monroe Local	Johnstown
324	1,565	Harrison Hills City	Cadiz
325	1,563	Edison Local (Formerly Berlin-Milan)	Milan
326	1,562	Edison Local	Hammondsville
327	1,556	Northwest Local	Mc Dermott
328	1,536	Madison Local	Middletown
329	1,535	Alexander Local	Albany
330	1,534	Ottawa-Glandorf Local	Ottawa
331	1,532	Wheelersburg Local	Wheelersburg
332	1,530	Westfall Local	Williamsport
333	1,519	Clermont Northeastern Local	Batavia
334	1,513	Orrville City	Orrville
335	1,511	Minford Local	Minford
336	1,504	Fairless Local	Navarre
337	1,502	West Muskingum Local	Zanesville

Male Students

Rank	Percent	District Name	City
1	54.2	Coshocton City	Coshocton
2	54.1	Big Walnut Local	Sunbury
2	54.1	Saint Marys City	Saint Marys
4	54.0	Minford Local	Minford
5	53.8	Buckeye Valley Local	Delaware
6	53.4	Lake Local	Uniontown
6	53.4	Mansfield City	Mansfield
8	53.2	Morgan Local	Mc Connelsville
8	53.2	Wauseon Exempted Village	Wauseon
10	53.1	Amanda-Clearcreek Local	Amanda
10	53.1	Bellefontaine City	Bellefontaine
10	53.1	Claymont City	Dennison
10	53.1	Dover City	Dover
10	53.1	Groveport Madison Local	Groveport
10	53.1	Lakewood Local	Hebron
10	53.1	Monroe Local SD	Monroe
10	53.1	Napoleon Area City	Napoleon
10	53.1	North College Hill City	Cincinnati
10	53.1	Northmont City	Englewood
20	53.0	Fostoria City	Fostoria
20	53.0	Highland Local	Sparta
20	53.0	Marlington Local	Alliance
20	53.0	Massillon City	Massillon
20	53.0	Mt Healthy City	Cincinnati
20	53.0	N Ridgeville City	N Ridgeville
20	53.0	Norwood City	Norwood
20	53.0	Reynoldsburg City	Reynoldsburg
20	53.0	Sidney City	Sidney
20	53.0	Toledo City	Toledo
30	52.9	Fairfield Union Local	Lancaster
30	52.9	Marion City	Marion
30	52.9	Miami Trace Local	Washington CH
30	52.9	Painesville City Local	Painesville
34	52.8	Clinton-Massie Local	Clarksville
34	52.8	Fairborn City	Fairborn
34	52.8	Graham Local	Saint Paris
34	52.8	Huber Heights City	Huber Heights
34	52.8	Northern Local	Thornville
34	52.8	Sycamore Community City	Blue Ash
34	52.8	Willoughby-Eastlake City	Willoughby
41	52.7	Copley-Fairlawn City	Copley
41	52.7	London City	London
41	52.7	Lorain City	Lorain
41	52.7	Mayfield City	Mayfield Hgts
41	52.7	New Lexington City	New Lexington
41	52.7	Revere Local	Bath
47	52.6	Green Local	Uniontown
47	52.6	Wooster City	Wooster
49	52.5	Bexley City	Bexley
49	52.5	Gallipolis City	Gallipolis
49	52.5	Goshen Local	Goshen
49	52.5	Indian Valley Local Schools	Gnadenhutten
49	52.5	Licking Valley Local	Newark
49	52.5	Meigs Local	Pomeroy
49	52.5	Orrville City	Orrville
49	52.5	Perkins Local	Sandusky
57	52.4	Blanchester Local	Blanchester
57	52.4	Buckeye Local	Medina
57	52.4	Jackson City	Jackson
57	52.4	Kenton City	Kenton
57	52.4	Kettering City	Kettering
57	52.4	Marysville Exempted Village	Marysville
57	52.4	Milford Exempted Village	Milford
57	52.4	North Canton City	North Canton
57	52.4	Northeastern Local	Springfield
57	52.4	Southwest Licking Local	Pataskala
57	52.4	Struthers City	Struthers
68	52.3	Chillicothe City	Chillicothe
68	52.3	Clark-Shawnee Local	Springfield
68	52.3	Coventry Local	Akron
68	52.3	Dublin City	Dublin
68	52.3	Euclid City	Euclid
68	52.3	River Valley Local	Caledonia
68	52.3	Wadsworth City	Wadsworth
75	52.2	Bryan City	Bryan
75	52.2	Elyria City Schools	Elyria
75	52.2	Lancaster City	Lancaster
75	52.2	Lima City	Lima
75	52.2	Parma City	Parma
75	52.2	Westfall Local	Williamsport
81	52.1	Boardman Local	Youngstown
81	52.1	Canton Local	Canton
81	52.1	Cleveland Municipal	Cleveland
81	52.1	Findlay City	Findlay
81	52.1	Johnstown-Monroe Local	Johnstown
81	52.1	Maumee City	Maumee
81	52.1	Olmsted Falls City	Olmsted Falls
81	52.1	Ontario Local	Mansfield
81	52.1	Ottawa-Glandorf Local	Ottawa
81	52.1	Portsmouth City	Portsmouth
81	52.1	Salem City	Salem
81	52.1	Tipp City Exempted Village	Tipp City
81	52.1	Waverly City	Waverly
81	52.1	West Geauga Local	Chesterland
95	52.0	Beavercreek City	Beavercreek
95	52.0	Berea City	Berea
95	52.0	Eaton Community City	Eaton
95	52.0	Geneva Area City	Geneva
95	52.0	Lebanon City	Lebanon
95	52.0	Piqua City	Piqua
95	52.0	Rossford Exempted Village	Rossford
95	52.0	Sheffield-Sheffield Lake City	Sheffield Vllg
95	52.0	Springfield Local	Akron
95	52.0	Sylvania City	Sylvania
105	51.9	Centerville City	Centerville
105	51.9	Defiance City	Defiance
105	51.9	East Liverpool City	East Liverpool
105	51.9	Galion City	Galion
105	51.9	Hamilton Local	Columbus
105	51.9	Little Miami Local	Maineville
105	51.9	Madison Local	Mansfield
105	51.9	Mason City SD	Mason
105	51.9	Riverside Local	Painesville
105	51.9	Three Rivers Local	Cleves
105	51.9	Tiffin City	Tiffin
105	51.9	Vandalia-Butler City	Vandalia
105	51.9	Vermilion Local	Vermilion
105	51.9	West Carrollton City	West Carrollton
105	51.9	West Muskingum Local	Zanesville
105	51.9	Westerville City	Westerville
121	51.8	Aurora City	Aurora
121	51.8	Batavia Local	Batavia
121	51.8	Benjamin Logan Local	Bellefontaine
121	51.8	Cambridge City	Cambridge
121	51.8	Clyde-Green Springs Exempted Village	Clyde
121	51.8	Dayton City	Dayton
121	51.8	Firelands Local	South Amherst
121	51.8	Garfield Hgts City Schools	Garfield Hgts
121	51.8	Jefferson Area Local	Jefferson
121	51.8	Keystone Local	Lagrange
121	51.8	Lakeview Local	Cortland
121	51.8	Licking Heights Local	Pataskala
121	51.8	Logan-Hocking Local	Logan
121	51.8	Mad River Local	Dayton
121	51.8	North Royalton City	North Royalton
121	51.8	Ravenna City	Ravenna
121	51.8	Southeast Local	Ravenna
121	51.8	Van Wert City	Van Wert
139	51.7	Hamilton City	Hamilton
139	51.7	Logan Elm Local	Circleville
139	51.7	Loveland City	Loveland
139	51.7	Mentor Exempted Village	Mentor
139	51.7	Southwest Local	Harrison
139	51.7	Saint Clairsville-Richland City	Saint Clairsville
139	51.7	Streetsboro City	Streetsboro
139	51.7	Vinton County Local	Mc Arthur
139	51.7	Whitehall City	Whitehall
139	51.7	Winton Woods City	Cincinnati
149	51.6	Ashtabula Area City	Ashtabula
149	51.6	Barberton City	Barberton
149	51.6	Brecksville-Broadview Heights City	Brecksville
149	51.6	Cloverleaf Local	Lodi
149	51.6	Field Local	Mogadore
149	51.6	Hilliard City	Columbus
149	51.6	Indian Creek Local	Wintersville
149	51.6	Kings Local	Kings Mills
149	51.6	Mount Vernon City	Mount Vernon
149	51.6	New Richmond Exempted Village	New Richmond
149	51.6	North Fork Local	Utica
149	51.6	Orange City	Cleveland
149	51.6	Plain Local	Canton
149	51.6	West Clermont Local	Cincinnati
163	51.5	Alexander Local	Albany
163	51.5	Avon Lake City	Avon Lake
163	51.5	Franklin Local	Duncan Falls
163	51.5	Heath City	Heath
163	51.5	Mariemont City	Cincinnati
163	51.5	Northwest Local	Cincinnati
163	51.5	Shaker Heights City	Shaker Heights
163	51.5	South Point Local	South Point
163	51.5	South-Western City	Grove City
163	51.5	Trotwood-Madison City	Trotwood
163	51.5	Washington CH City	Washington CH
163	51.5	West Holmes Local	Millersburg
163	51.5	Youngstown City Schools	Youngstown
163	51.5	Zanesville City	Zanesville
177	51.4	Akron City	Akron
177	51.4	Amherst Exempted Village	Amherst
177	51.4	Buckeye Local	Dillonvale
177	51.4	Greenville City	Greenville
177	51.4	Harrison Hills City	Cadiz
177	51.4	Hubbard Exempted Village	Hubbard
177	51.4	Lexington Local	Lexington
177	51.4	Norton City	Norton
177	51.4	Perrysburg Exempted Village	Perrysburg
177	51.4	Pickerington Local	Pickerington
177	51.4	Poland Local	Poland
177	51.4	River View Local	Warsaw
177	51.4	Shelby City	Shelby
177	51.4	Washington Local	Toledo
191	51.3	Alliance City	Alliance
191	51.3	Athens City	The Plains
191	51.3	Carlisle Local	Carlisle
191	51.3	Cuyahoga Falls City	Cuyahoga Falls
191	51.3	Fairless Local	Navarre
191	51.3	Maple Heights City	Maple Heights
191	51.3	North Olmsted City	North Olmsted
191	51.3	Perry Local	Massillon
191	51.3	Springfield City	Springfield
191	51.3	Stow-Munroe Falls City SD	Stow
191	51.3	Strongsville City	Strongsville
202	51.2	Beaver Local	Lisbon
202	51.2	Canton City	Canton
202	51.2	Columbus City SD	Columbus
202	51.2	Kent City	Kent
202	51.2	Madison Local	Madison
202	51.2	Oregon City	Oregon
202	51.2	Reading Community City	Reading
202	51.2	Solon City	Solon
202	51.2	Teays Valley Local	Ashville
202	51.2	Upper Arlington City	Upper Arlington
212	51.1	Gahanna-Jefferson City	Gahanna
212	51.1	Highland Local	Medina
212	51.1	New Philadel. City	New Philadel.
212	51.1	Newark City	Newark
212	51.1	Norwalk City	Norwalk
212	51.1	Olentangy Local	Lewis Center
212	51.1	Ross Local	Hamilton
212	51.1	Steubenville City	Steubenville
212	51.1	Talawanda City	Oxford
212	51.1	Tecumseh Local	New Carlisle
212	51.1	Triway Local	Wooster
212	51.1	Twinsburg City	Twinsburg
212	51.1	Woodridge Local	Peninsula
225	51.0	Brunswick City	Brunswick
225	51.0	Canal Wnchstr Local	Canal Wnchstr
225	51.0	Cleveland Heights-Univ Hgts City	University Hgts
225	51.0	Forest Hills Local	Cincinnati
225	51.0	Fremont City	Fremont
225	51.0	Girard City SD	Girard
225	51.0	Granville Exempted Village	Granville

Note: This section only includes districts with 1,500 or more students; All categories are ranked from high to low

225	51.0	Medina City SD	Medina
225	51.0	Springfield Local	Holland
225	51.0	Switzerland of Ohio Local	Woodsfield
225	51.0	Tri-Valley Local	Dresden
225	51.0	Upper Sandusky Exempted Village	Upper Sandusky
225	51.0	Wheelersburg Local	Wheelersburg
225	51.0	Worthington City	Worthington
225	51.0	Xenia Community City	Xenia
240	50.9	Ashland City	Ashland
240	50.9	Delaware City	Delaware
240	50.9	Edgewood City	Trenton
240	50.9	Fairfield City	Fairfield
240	50.9	Greenfield Exempted Village	Greenfield
240	50.9	Howland Local	Warren
240	50.9	Hudson City	Hudson
240	50.9	Niles City	Niles
240	50.9	Northwestern Local	Springfield
240	50.9	Perry Local	Perry
240	50.9	Sandusky City	Sandusky
251	50.8	Bloom-Carroll Local	Carroll
251	50.8	Bowling Green City SD	Bowling Green
251	50.8	Carrollton Exempted Village	Carrollton
251	50.8	Chagrin Falls Exempted Village	Chagrin Falls
251	50.8	Kenston Local	Chagrin Falls
251	50.8	Middletown City	Middletown
251	50.8	Nordonia Hills City	Northfield
251	50.8	Oakwood City	Dayton
251	50.8	Urbana City	Urbana
251	50.8	Wapakoneta City	Wapakoneta
261	50.7	Avon Local	Avon
261	50.7	Conneaut Area City	Conneaut
261	50.7	Edison Local	Hammondsville
261	50.7	Lakewood City	Lakewood
261	50.7	Madison Local	Middletown
261	50.7	Midview Local	Grafton
261	50.7	Northridge Local	Dayton
261	50.7	Rolling Hills Local	Cambridge
261	50.7	South Euclid-Lyndhurst City	Lyndhurst
261	50.7	Wilmington City	Wilmington
271	50.6	Clermont Northeastern Local	Batavia
271	50.6	Lake Local	Millbury
271	50.6	Northwest Local	Mc Dermott
271	50.6	Princeton City	Cincinnati
271	50.6	Troy City	Troy
271	50.6	Western Brown Local	Mount Orab
277	50.5	Austintown Local	Youngstown
277	50.5	Bedford City	Bedford
277	50.5	Bellevue City	Bellevue
277	50.5	Benton Carroll Salem Local	Oak Harbor
277	50.5	Elida Local	Elida
277	50.5	Fairland Local	Proctorville
277	50.5	Franklin City	Franklin
277	50.5	Greenon Local	Enon
277	50.5	Hillsboro City	Hillsboro
277	50.5	Oak Hills Local	Cincinnati
277	50.5	Springboro Community City	Springboro
277	50.5	Westlake City	Westlake
289	50.4	Celina City	Celina
289	50.4	Clear Fork Valley Local	Bellville
289	50.4	Jackson Local	Massillon
289	50.4	Lakota Local	Liberty Twp
289	50.4	New Albany-Plain Local	New Albany
289	50.4	Valley View Local	Germantown
295	50.3	Adams County/Ohio Valley Local	West Union
295	50.3	Buckeye Local	Ashtabula
295	50.3	Fairview Park City	Fairview Park
295	50.3	Wyoming City	Wyoming
299	50.2	Canfield Local	Canfield
299	50.2	East Holmes Local	Berlin
299	50.2	Jonathan Alder Local	Plain City
299	50.2	Maysville Local	Zanesville
299	50.2	Warren City	Warren
299	50.2	Warren Local	Vincent
299	50.2	West Branch Local	Beloit
306	50.1	East Muskingum Local	New Concord
306	50.1	Indian Lake Local	Lewistown
306	50.1	Louisville City	Louisville
306	50.1	Marietta City	Marietta
310	50.0	Chardon Local	Chardon
310	50.0	Cincinnati City	Cincinnati
310	50.0	Rocky River City	Rocky River
313	49.9	Bethel-Tate Local	Bethel
313	49.9	Port Clinton City	Port Clinton
313	49.9	Union-Scioto Local	Chillicothe
313	49.9	Willard City	Willard
317	49.8	Northwest Local	Canal Fulton
318	49.7	Circleville City	Circleville
318	49.7	East Cleveland City SD	East Cleveland
318	49.7	Edison Local (Formerly Berlin-Milan)	Milan
318	49.7	Indian Hill Exempted Village	Cincinnati
322	49.6	Bath Local	Lima
323	49.5	Gallia County Local	Gallipolis
323	49.5	Shawnee Local	Lima
323	49.5	Tallmadge City	Tallmadge
326	49.4	Anthony Wayne Local	Whitehouse
326	49.4	Bellbrook-Sugarcreek Local SD	Bellbrook
326	49.4	Minerva Local	Minerva
329	49.2	Bay Village City	Bay Village
330	48.8	Miamisburg City	Miamisburg
331	48.7	Clearview Local	Lorain
331	48.7	Crestwood Local	Mantua
333	48.4	Ohio Virtual Academy	Maumee
334	47.2	Alternative Education Academy	Toledo
335	47.0	Ohio Connections Academy, Inc	Cleveland
336	46.0	Electronic Classroom of Tomorrow	Columbus
337	45.3	Treca Digital Academy	Marion

Female Students

Rank	Percent	District Name	City
1	54.7	Treca Digital Academy	Marion
2	54.0	Electronic Classroom of Tomorrow	Columbus
3	53.0	Ohio Connections Academy, Inc	Cleveland
4	52.8	Alternative Education Academy	Toledo
5	51.6	Ohio Virtual Academy	Maumee
6	51.3	Clearview Local	Lorain
6	51.3	Crestwood Local	Mantua
8	51.2	Miamisburg City	Miamisburg
9	50.8	Bay Village City	Bay Village
10	50.6	Anthony Wayne Local	Whitehouse
10	50.6	Bellbrook-Sugarcreek Local SD	Bellbrook
10	50.6	Minerva Local	Minerva
13	50.5	Gallia County Local	Gallipolis
13	50.5	Shawnee Local	Lima
13	50.5	Tallmadge City	Tallmadge
16	50.4	Bath Local	Lima
17	50.3	Circleville City	Circleville
17	50.3	East Cleveland City SD	East Cleveland
17	50.3	Edison Local (Formerly Berlin-Milan)	Milan
17	50.3	Indian Hill Exempted Village	Cincinnati
21	50.2	Northwest Local	Canal Fulton
22	50.1	Bethel-Tate Local	Bethel
22	50.1	Port Clinton City	Port Clinton
22	50.1	Union-Scioto Local	Chillicothe
22	50.1	Willard City	Willard
26	50.0	Chardon Local	Chardon
26	50.0	Cincinnati City	Cincinnati
26	50.0	Rocky River City	Rocky River
29	49.9	East Muskingum Local	New Concord
29	49.9	Indian Lake Local	Lewistown
29	49.9	Louisville City	Louisville
29	49.9	Marietta City	Marietta
33	49.8	Canfield Local	Canfield
33	49.8	East Holmes Local	Berlin
33	49.8	Jonathan Alder Local	Plain City
33	49.8	Maysville Local	Zanesville
33	49.8	Warren City	Warren
33	49.8	Warren Local	Vincent
33	49.8	West Branch Local	Beloit
40	49.7	Adams County/Ohio Valley Local	West Union
40	49.7	Buckeye Local	Ashtabula
40	49.7	Fairview Park City	Fairview Park
40	49.7	Wyoming City	Wyoming
44	49.6	Celina City	Celina
44	49.6	Clear Fork Valley Local	Bellville
44	49.6	Jackson Local	Massillon
44	49.6	Lakota Local	Liberty Twp
44	49.6	New Albany-Plain Local	New Albany
44	49.6	Valley View Local	Germantown
50	49.5	Austintown Local	Youngstown
50	49.5	Bedford City	Bedford
50	49.5	Bellevue City	Bellevue
50	49.5	Benton Carroll Salem Local	Oak Harbor
50	49.5	Elida Local	Elida
50	49.5	Fairland Local	Proctorville
50	49.5	Franklin City	Franklin
50	49.5	Greenon Local	Enon
50	49.5	Hillsboro City	Hillsboro
50	49.5	Oak Hills Local	Cincinnati
50	49.5	Springboro Community City	Springboro
50	49.5	Westlake City	Westlake
62	49.4	Clermont Northeastern Local	Batavia
62	49.4	Lake Local	Millbury
62	49.4	Northwest Local	Mc Dermott
62	49.4	Princeton City	Cincinnati
62	49.4	Troy City	Troy
62	49.4	Western Brown Local	Mount Orab
68	49.3	Avon Local	Avon
68	49.3	Conneaut Area City	Conneaut
68	49.3	Edison Local	Hammondsville
68	49.3	Lakewood City	Lakewood
68	49.3	Madison Local	Middletown
68	49.3	Midview Local	Grafton
68	49.3	Northridge Local	Dayton
68	49.3	Rolling Hills Local	Cambridge
68	49.3	South Euclid-Lyndhurst City	Lyndhurst
68	49.3	Wilmington City	Wilmington
78	49.2	Bloom-Carroll Local	Carroll
78	49.2	Bowling Green City SD	Bowling Green
78	49.2	Carrollton Exempted Village	Carrollton
78	49.2	Chagrin Falls Exempted Village	Chagrin Falls
78	49.2	Kenston Local	Chagrin Falls
78	49.2	Middletown City	Middletown
78	49.2	Nordonia Hills City	Northfield
78	49.2	Oakwood City	Dayton
78	49.2	Urbana City	Urbana
78	49.2	Wapakoneta City	Wapakoneta
88	49.1	Ashland City	Ashland
88	49.1	Delaware City	Delaware
88	49.1	Edgewood City	Trenton
88	49.1	Fairfield City	Fairfield
88	49.1	Greenfield Exempted Village	Greenfield
88	49.1	Howland Local	Warren
88	49.1	Hudson City	Hudson
88	49.1	Niles City	Niles
88	49.1	Northwestern Local	Springfield
88	49.1	Perry Local	Perry
88	49.1	Sandusky City	Sandusky
99	49.0	Brunswick City	Brunswick
99	49.0	Canal Wnchstr Local	Canal Wnchstr
99	49.0	Cleveland Heights-Univ Hgts City	University Hgts
99	49.0	Forest Hills Local	Cincinnati
99	49.0	Fremont City	Fremont
99	49.0	Girard City SD	Girard
99	49.0	Granville Exempted Village	Granville
99	49.0	Medina City SD	Medina
99	49.0	Springfield Local	Holland
99	49.0	Switzerland of Ohio Local	Woodsfield
99	49.0	Tri-Valley Local	Dresden
99	49.0	Upper Sandusky Exempted Village	Upper Sandusky
99	49.0	Wheelersburg Local	Wheelersburg
99	49.0	Worthington City	Worthington
99	49.0	Xenia Community City	Xenia
114	48.9	Gahanna-Jefferson City	Gahanna
114	48.9	Highland Local	Medina
114	48.9	New Philadel. City	New Philadel.
114	48.9	Newark City	Newark
114	48.9	Norwalk City	Norwalk
114	48.9	Olentangy Local	Lewis Center
114	48.9	Ross Local	Hamilton
114	48.9	Steubenville City	Steubenville
114	48.9	Talawanda City	Oxford
114	48.9	Tecumseh Local	New Carlisle
114	48.9	Triway Local	Wooster
114	48.9	Twinsburg City	Twinsburg
114	48.9	Woodridge Local	Peninsula
127	48.8	Beaver Local	Lisbon
127	48.8	Canton City	Canton
127	48.8	Columbus City SD	Columbus
127	48.8	Kent City	Kent
127	48.8	Madison Local	Madison
127	48.8	Oregon City	Oregon
127	48.8	Reading Community City	Reading
127	48.8	Solon City	Solon
127	48.8	Teays Valley Local	Ashville
127	48.8	Upper Arlington City	Upper Arlington
137	48.7	Alliance City	Alliance
137	48.7	Athens City	The Plains
137	48.7	Carlisle Local	Carlisle
137	48.7	Cuyahoga Falls City	Cuyahoga Falls
137	48.7	Fairless Local	Navarre

Note: This section only includes districts with 1,500 or more students; All categories are ranked from high to low

137	48.7	Maple Heights City	Maple Heights
137	48.7	North Olmsted City	North Olmsted
137	48.7	Perry Local	Massillon
137	48.7	Springfield City	Springfield
137	48.7	Stow-Munroe Falls City SD	Stow
137	48.7	Strongsville City	Strongsville
148	48.6	Akron City	Akron
148	48.6	Amherst Exempted Village	Amherst
148	48.6	Buckeye Local	Dillonvale
148	48.6	Greenville City	Greenville
148	48.6	Harrison Hills City	Cadiz
148	48.6	Hubbard Exempted Village	Hubbard
148	48.6	Lexington Local	Lexington
148	48.6	Norton City	Norton
148	48.6	Perrysburg Exempted Village	Perrysburg
148	48.6	Pickerington Local	Pickerington
148	48.6	Poland Local	Poland
148	48.6	River View Local	Warsaw
148	48.6	Shelby City	Shelby
148	48.6	Washington Local	Toledo
162	48.5	Alexander Local	Albany
162	48.5	Avon Lake City	Avon Lake
162	48.5	Franklin Local	Duncan Falls
162	48.5	Heath City	Heath
162	48.5	Mariemont City	Cincinnati
162	48.5	Northwest Local	Cincinnati
162	48.5	Shaker Heights City	Shaker Heights
162	48.5	South Point Local	South Point
162	48.5	South-Western City	Grove City
162	48.5	Trotwood-Madison City	Trotwood
162	48.5	Washington CH City	Washington CH
162	48.5	West Holmes Local	Millersburg
162	48.5	Youngstown City Schools	Youngstown
162	48.5	Zanesville City	Zanesville
176	48.4	Ashtabula Area City	Ashtabula
176	48.4	Barberton City	Barberton
176	48.4	Brecksville-Broadview Heights City	Brecksville
176	48.4	Cloverleaf Local	Lodi
176	48.4	Field Local	Mogadore
176	48.4	Hilliard City	Columbus
176	48.4	Indian Creek Local	Wintersville
176	48.4	Kings Local	Kings Mills
176	48.4	Mount Vernon City	Mount Vernon
176	48.4	New Richmond Exempted Village	New Richmond
176	48.4	North Fork Local	Utica
176	48.4	Orange City	Cleveland
176	48.4	Plain Local	Canton
176	48.4	West Clermont Local	Cincinnati
190	48.3	Hamilton City	Hamilton
190	48.3	Logan Elm Local	Circleville
190	48.3	Loveland City	Loveland
190	48.3	Mentor Exempted Village	Mentor
190	48.3	Southwest Local	Harrison
190	48.3	Saint Clairsville-Richland City	Saint Clairsville
190	48.3	Streetsboro City	Streetsboro
190	48.3	Vinton County Local	Mc Arthur
190	48.3	Whitehall City	Whitehall
190	48.3	Winton Woods City	Cincinnati
200	48.2	Aurora City	Aurora
200	48.2	Batavia Local	Batavia
200	48.2	Benjamin Logan Local	Bellefontaine
200	48.2	Cambridge City	Cambridge
200	48.2	Clyde-Green Springs Exempted Village	Clyde
200	48.2	Dayton City	Dayton
200	48.2	Firelands Local	South Amherst
200	48.2	Garfield Hgts City Schools	Garfield Hgts
200	48.2	Jefferson Area Local	Jefferson
200	48.2	Keystone Local	Lagrange
200	48.2	Lakeview Local	Cortland
200	48.2	Licking Heights Local	Pataskala
200	48.2	Logan-Hocking Local	Logan
200	48.2	Mad River Local	Dayton
200	48.2	North Royalton City	North Royalton
200	48.2	Ravenna City	Ravenna
200	48.2	Southeast Local	Ravenna
200	48.2	Van Wert City	Van Wert
218	48.1	Centerville City	Centerville
218	48.1	Defiance City	Defiance
218	48.1	East Liverpool City	East Liverpool
218	48.1	Galion City	Galion
218	48.1	Hamilton Local	Columbus
218	48.1	Little Miami Local	Maineville
218	48.1	Madison Local	Mansfield
218	48.1	Mason City SD	Mason
218	48.1	Riverside Local	Painesville
218	48.1	Three Rivers Local	Cleves
218	48.1	Tiffin City	Tiffin
218	48.1	Vandalia-Butler City	Vandalia
218	48.1	Vermilion Local	Vermilion
218	48.1	West Carrollton City	West Carrollton
218	48.1	West Muskingum Local	Zanesville
218	48.1	Westerville City	Westerville
234	48.0	Beavercreek City	Beavercreek
234	48.0	Berea City	Berea
234	48.0	Eaton Community City	Eaton
234	48.0	Geneva Area City	Geneva
234	48.0	Lebanon City	Lebanon
234	48.0	Piqua City	Piqua
234	48.0	Rossford Exempted Village	Rossford
234	48.0	Sheffield-Sheffield Lake City	Sheffield Vllg
234	48.0	Springfield Local	Akron
234	48.0	Sylvania City	Sylvania
244	47.9	Boardman Local	Youngstown
244	47.9	Canton Local	Canton
244	47.9	Cleveland Municipal	Cleveland
244	47.9	Findlay City	Findlay
244	47.9	Johnstown-Monroe Local	Johnstown
244	47.9	Maumee City	Maumee
244	47.9	Olmsted Falls City	Olmsted Falls
244	47.9	Ontario Local	Mansfield
244	47.9	Ottawa-Glandorf Local	Ottawa
244	47.9	Portsmouth City	Portsmouth
244	47.9	Salem City	Salem
244	47.9	Tipp City Exempted Village	Tipp City
244	47.9	Waverly City	Waverly
244	47.9	West Geauga Local	Chesterland
258	47.8	Bryan City	Bryan
258	47.8	Elyria City Schools	Elyria
258	47.8	Lancaster City	Lancaster
258	47.8	Lima City	Lima
258	47.8	Parma City	Parma
258	47.8	Westfall Local	Williamsport
264	47.7	Chillicothe City	Chillicothe
264	47.7	Clark-Shawnee Local	Springfield
264	47.7	Coventry Local	Akron
264	47.7	Dublin City	Dublin
264	47.7	Euclid City	Euclid
264	47.7	River Valley Local	Caledonia
264	47.7	Wadsworth City	Wadsworth
271	47.6	Blanchester Local	Blanchester
271	47.6	Buckeye Local	Medina
271	47.6	Jackson City	Jackson
271	47.6	Kenton City	Kenton
271	47.6	Kettering City	Kettering
271	47.6	Marysville Exempted Village	Marysville
271	47.6	Milford Exempted Village	Milford
271	47.6	North Canton City	North Canton
271	47.6	Northeastern Local	Springfield
271	47.6	Southwest Licking Local	Pataskala
271	47.6	Struthers City	Struthers
282	47.5	Bexley City	Bexley
282	47.5	Gallipolis City	Gallipolis
282	47.5	Goshen Local	Goshen
282	47.5	Indian Valley Local Schools	Gnadenhutten
282	47.5	Licking Valley Local	Newark
282	47.5	Meigs Local	Pomeroy
282	47.5	Orrville City	Orrville
282	47.5	Perkins Local	Sandusky
290	47.4	Green Local	Uniontown
290	47.4	Wooster City	Wooster
292	47.3	Copley-Fairlawn City	Copley
292	47.3	London City	London
292	47.3	Lorain City	Lorain
292	47.3	Mayfield City	Mayfield Hgts
292	47.3	New Lexington City	New Lexington
292	47.3	Revere Local	Bath
298	47.2	Clinton-Massie Local	Clarksville
298	47.2	Fairborn City	Fairborn
298	47.2	Graham Local	Saint Paris
298	47.2	Huber Heights City	Huber Heights
298	47.2	Northern Local	Thornville
298	47.2	Sycamore Community City	Blue Ash
298	47.2	Willoughby-Eastlake City	Willoughby
305	47.1	Fairfield Union Local	Lancaster
305	47.1	Marion City	Marion
305	47.1	Miami Trace Local	Washington CH
305	47.1	Painesville City Local	Painesville
309	47.0	Fostoria City	Fostoria
309	47.0	Highland Local	Sparta
309	47.0	Marlington Local	Alliance
309	47.0	Massillon City	Massillon
309	47.0	Mt Healthy City	Cincinnati
309	47.0	N Ridgeville City	N Ridgeville
309	47.0	Norwood City	Norwood
309	47.0	Reynoldsburg City	Reynoldsburg
309	47.0	Sidney City	Sidney
309	47.0	Toledo City	Toledo
319	46.9	Amanda-Clearcreek Local	Amanda
319	46.9	Bellefontaine City	Bellefontaine
319	46.9	Claymont City	Dennison
319	46.9	Dover City	Dover
319	46.9	Groveport Madison Local	Groveport
319	46.9	Lakewood Local	Hebron
319	46.9	Monroe Local SD	Monroe
319	46.9	Napoleon Area City	Napoleon
319	46.9	North College Hill City	Cincinnati
319	46.9	Northmont City	Englewood
329	46.8	Morgan Local	Mc Connelsville
329	46.8	Wauseon Exempted Village	Wauseon
331	46.6	Lake Local	Uniontown
331	46.6	Mansfield City	Mansfield
333	46.2	Buckeye Valley Local	Delaware
334	46.0	Minford Local	Minford
335	45.9	Big Walnut Local	Sunbury
335	45.9	Saint Marys City	Saint Marys
337	45.8	Coshocton City	Coshocton

White Students

Rank	Percent	District Name	City
1	98.3	Switzerland of Ohio Local	Woodsfield
1	98.3	Western Brown Local	Mount Orab
3	98.2	Southeast Local	Ravenna
3	98.2	Vinton County Local	Mc Arthur
5	98.1	Adams County/Ohio Valley Local	West Union
5	98.1	Northern Local	Thornville
7	97.8	West Holmes Local	Millersburg
8	97.7	Edison Local	Hammondsville
9	97.6	East Holmes Local	Berlin
10	97.5	Alexander Local	Albany
10	97.5	Carrollton Exempted Village	Carrollton
12	97.4	Indian Valley Local Schools	Gnadenhutten
12	97.4	Logan Elm Local	Circleville
12	97.4	Northwest Local	Mc Dermott
15	97.3	Amanda-Clearcreek Local	Amanda
16	97.2	Fairfield Union Local	Lancaster
16	97.2	Ross Local	Hamilton
18	97.1	Bethel-Tate Local	Bethel
18	97.1	Louisville City	Louisville
18	97.1	West Branch Local	Beloit
18	97.1	Westfall Local	Williamsport
22	97.0	Minford Local	Minford
22	97.0	New Lexington City	New Lexington
24	96.9	Beaver Local	Lisbon
24	96.9	Blanchester Local	Blanchester
26	96.8	Fairless Local	Navarre
26	96.8	Licking Valley Local	Newark
26	96.8	North Fork Local	Utica
29	96.7	Buckeye Local	Dillonvale
29	96.7	Franklin Local	Duncan Falls
31	96.5	Bloom-Carroll Local	Carroll
31	96.5	Meigs Local	Pomeroy
33	96.4	Clinton-Massie Local	Clarksville
33	96.4	Jackson City	Jackson
35	96.3	Crestwood Local	Mantua
35	96.3	Gallia County Local	Gallipolis
35	96.3	Madison Local	Middletown
38	96.2	Logan-Hocking Local	Logan
39	96.1	Clermont Northeastern Local	Batavia
39	96.1	Northwest Local	Canal Fulton
39	96.1	Wapakoneta City	Wapakoneta
42	96.0	Warren Local	Vincent
43	95.9	Highland Local	Sparta
44	95.8	Clear Fork Valley Local	Bellville
44	95.8	Minerva Local	Minerva
44	95.8	Triway Local	Wooster
47	95.7	Fairland Local	Proctorville
48	95.6	East Muskingum Local	New Concord
49	95.5	Cloverleaf Local	Lodi
49	95.5	Graham Local	Saint Paris
49	95.5	Highland Local	Medina

Note: This section only includes districts with 1,500 or more students; All categories are ranked from high to low

52	95.4	Lake Local	Uniontown
52	95.4	River View Local	Warsaw
52	95.4	Shelby City	Shelby
55	95.3	Greenfield Exempted Village	Greenfield
56	95.2	Tri-Valley Local	Dresden
56	95.2	Valley View Local	Germantown
58	95.1	Jefferson Area Local	Jefferson
59	95.0	Galion City	Galion
60	94.8	Franklin City	Franklin
60	94.8	Teays Valley Local	Ashville
62	94.6	Buckeye Local	Medina
62	94.6	Johnstown-Monroe Local	Johnstown
62	94.6	Keystone Local	Lagrange
62	94.6	Wheelersburg Local	Wheelersburg
66	94.5	Salem City	Salem
66	94.5	Southwest Local	Harrison
68	94.4	Carlisle Local	Carlisle
68	94.4	Harrison Hills City	Cadiz
68	94.4	Poland Local	Poland
71	94.3	Edgewood City	Trenton
71	94.3	Lakewood Local	Hebron
71	94.3	Rolling Hills Local	Cambridge
71	94.3	Saint Marys City	Saint Marys
75	94.2	Claymont City	Dennison
75	94.2	Granville Exempted Village	Granville
75	94.2	New Richmond Exempted Village	New Richmond
75	94.2	Three Rivers Local	Cleves
79	94.0	Chagrin Falls Exempted Village	Chagrin Falls
79	94.0	Jonathan Alder Local	Plain City
79	94.0	Marietta City	Marietta
82	93.9	Chardon Local	Chardon
82	93.9	Lakeview Local	Cortland
82	93.9	Lancaster City	Lancaster
82	93.9	Tipp City Exempted Village	Tipp City
82	93.9	Wadsworth City	Wadsworth
87	93.7	Greenville City	Greenville
87	93.7	Maysville Local	Zanesville
87	93.7	Waverly City	Waverly
90	93.5	Eaton Community City	Eaton
90	93.5	Indian Lake Local	Lewistown
90	93.5	Kenton City	Kenton
93	93.3	Bay Village City	Bay Village
93	93.3	West Geauga Local	Chesterland
95	93.2	Goshen Local	Goshen
96	93.0	Buckeye Valley Local	Delaware
96	93.0	North Canton City	North Canton
96	93.0	Northwestern Local	Springfield
96	93.0	Vermilion Local	Vermilion
100	92.9	Avon Lake City	Avon Lake
100	92.9	Canfield Local	Canfield
100	92.9	West Muskingum Local	Zanesville
103	92.8	Marysville Exempted Village	Marysville
104	92.7	Firelands Local	South Amherst
105	92.6	Benjamin Logan Local	Bellefontaine
105	92.6	Hubbard Exempted Village	Hubbard
105	92.6	Norton City	Norton
108	92.5	Green Local	Uniontown
109	92.3	Greenon Local	Enon
110	92.2	Big Walnut Local	Sunbury
110	92.2	Indian Creek Local	Wintersville
110	92.2	Little Miami Local	Maineville
110	92.2	Olmsted Falls City	Olmsted Falls
110	92.2	Springfield Local	Akron
115	92.1	Field Local	Mogadore
115	92.1	West Clermont Local	Cincinnati
117	92.0	Ashland City	Ashland
117	92.0	Edison Local (Formerly Berlin-Milan)	Milan
119	91.9	Celina City	Celina
119	91.9	Oak Hills Local	Cincinnati
119	91.9	Saint Clairsville-Richland City	Saint Clairsville
122	91.8	Bellevue City	Bellevue
123	91.7	Conneaut Area City	Conneaut
124	91.6	Benton Carroll Salem Local	Oak Harbor
124	91.6	Brunswick City	Brunswick
124	91.6	Loveland City	Loveland
127	91.5	Cambridge City	Cambridge
127	91.5	Mariemont City	Cincinnati
127	91.5	Marlington Local	Alliance
130	91.3	Upper Sandusky Exempted Village	Upper Sandusky
131	91.2	Coshocton City	Coshocton
131	91.2	Mentor Exempted Village	Mentor
131	91.2	Milford Exempted Village	Milford
131	91.2	Van Wert City	Van Wert
135	91.1	Miami Trace Local	Washington CH
135	91.1	River Valley Local	Caledonia
135	91.1	Springboro Community City	Springboro
138	91.0	Medina City SD	Medina
139	90.9	Northeastern Local	Springfield
140	90.7	Dover City	Dover
141	90.6	Anthony Wayne Local	Whitehouse
141	90.6	Buckeye Local	Ashtabula
141	90.6	Coventry Local	Akron
141	90.6	Gallipolis City	Gallipolis
145	90.5	Bryan City	Bryan
145	90.5	Forest Hills Local	Cincinnati
147	90.4	Circleville City	Circleville
147	90.4	Rocky River City	Rocky River
149	90.3	Madison Local	Madison
149	90.3	Mount Vernon City	Mount Vernon
151	90.2	Hillsboro City	Hillsboro
151	90.2	Midview Local	Grafton
153	90.1	N Ridgeville City	N Ridgeville
153	90.1	Talawanda City	Oxford
155	89.9	Kenston Local	Chagrin Falls
155	89.9	Lexington Local	Lexington
155	89.9	Morgan Local	Mc Connelsville
158	89.8	Jackson Local	Massillon
159	89.7	Hudson City	Hudson
159	89.7	Oakwood City	Dayton
161	89.6	Tiffin City	Tiffin
162	89.4	Stow-Munroe Falls City SD	Stow
163	89.3	Southwest Licking Local	Pataskala
164	89.1	Perry Local	Massillon
164	89.1	Revere Local	Bath
166	89.0	Geneva Area City	Geneva
167	88.9	Aurora City	Aurora
168	88.7	Clark-Shawnee Local	Springfield
168	88.7	Madison Local	Mansfield
168	88.7	New Philadel. City	New Philadel.
171	88.4	Avon Local	Avon
171	88.4	Union-Scioto Local	Chillicothe
173	88.3	North Royalton City	North Royalton
174	88.2	Niles City	Niles
174	88.2	Perry Local	Perry
176	88.1	Bath Local	Lima
177	88.0	Lebanon City	Lebanon
178	87.9	Upper Arlington City	Upper Arlington
179	87.7	Riverside Local	Painesville
180	87.6	Batavia Local	Batavia
181	87.5	London City	London
181	87.5	Washington CH City	Washington CH
183	87.4	Cuyahoga Falls City	Cuyahoga Falls
183	87.4	East Liverpool City	East Liverpool
185	87.3	Bellbrook-Sugarcreek Local SD	Bellbrook
186	87.0	Howland Local	Warren
186	87.0	Tallmadge City	Tallmadge
188	86.8	Brecksville-Broadview Heights City	Brecksville
189	86.7	Heath City	Heath
189	86.7	Kettering City	Kettering
189	86.7	Kings Local	Kings Mills
192	86.6	South Point Local	South Point
193	86.5	Canton Local	Canton
194	86.4	Fairview Park City	Fairview Park
195	86.0	Clyde-Green Springs Exempted Village	Clyde
196	85.9	Reading Community City	Reading
196	85.9	Willoughby-Eastlake City	Willoughby
196	85.9	Wooster City	Wooster
199	85.8	Napoleon Area City	Napoleon
199	85.8	Piqua City	Piqua
201	85.6	Ontario Local	Mansfield
201	85.6	Strongsville City	Strongsville
203	85.4	Girard City SD	Girard
203	85.4	Newark City	Newark
203	85.4	Ottawa-Glandorf Local	Ottawa
206	85.3	Athens City	The Plains
207	85.2	Perrysburg Exempted Village	Perrysburg
208	85.0	Sylvania City	Sylvania
209	84.9	Monroe Local SD	Monroe
209	84.9	North Olmsted City	North Olmsted
211	84.6	Urbana City	Urbana
211	84.6	Westlake City	Westlake
213	84.2	Beavercreek City	Beavercreek
213	84.2	Sheffield-Sheffield Lake City	Sheffield Vllg
215	84.1	Rossford Exempted Village	Rossford
216	84.0	Delaware City	Delaware
217	83.6	Troy City	Troy
218	83.5	Oregon City	Oregon
218	83.5	Parma City	Parma
220	83.4	Ohio Virtual Academy	Maumee
220	83.4	Struthers City	Struthers
220	83.4	Wilmington City	Wilmington
223	83.2	Bexley City	Bexley
223	83.2	Tecumseh Local	New Carlisle
225	83.1	Indian Hill Exempted Village	Cincinnati
225	83.1	Perkins Local	Sandusky
225	83.1	Shawnee Local	Lima
225	83.1	Treca Digital Academy	Marion
229	83.0	Lake Local	Millbury
229	83.0	Miamisburg City	Miamisburg
231	82.9	Sidney City	Sidney
232	82.8	Norwalk City	Norwalk
232	82.8	Vandalia-Butler City	Vandalia
234	82.4	Bellefontaine City	Bellefontaine
235	81.9	Port Clinton City	Port Clinton
236	81.8	Findlay City	Findlay
237	81.1	Austintown Local	Youngstown
238	81.0	Olentangy Local	Lewis Center
239	80.9	Barberton City	Barberton
240	80.7	Maumee City	Maumee
241	80.4	Marion City	Marion
242	80.0	Amherst Exempted Village	Amherst
243	79.4	Portsmouth City	Portsmouth
244	79.3	Bowling Green City SD	Bowling Green
244	79.3	Streetsboro City	Streetsboro
246	79.2	Ravenna City	Ravenna
247	79.0	Centerville City	Centerville
248	78.7	Nordonia Hills City	Northfield
248	78.7	Ohio Connections Academy, Inc	Cleveland
248	78.7	Orrville City	Orrville
251	78.6	Fairborn City	Fairborn
252	78.4	Berea City	Berea
253	78.3	Wauseon Exempted Village	Wauseon
254	78.1	Hamilton Local	Columbus
255	77.8	Mad River Local	Dayton
256	77.5	Chillicothe City	Chillicothe
257	76.9	Wyoming City	Wyoming
258	76.5	Boardman Local	Youngstown
259	76.4	Hilliard City	Columbus
260	75.7	Massillon City	Massillon
261	75.0	Elida Local	Elida
262	74.8	Plain Local	Canton
263	74.1	Alternative Education Academy	Toledo
263	74.1	Electronic Classroom of Tomorrow	Columbus
265	73.9	New Albany-Plain Local	New Albany
265	73.9	Xenia Community City	Xenia
267	73.8	Copley-Fairlawn City	Copley
267	73.8	Washington Local	Toledo
269	73.6	Lakewood City	Lakewood
270	73.4	Norwood City	Norwood
271	73.3	Lakota Local	Liberty Twp
272	72.8	Kent City	Kent
273	72.2	Hamilton City	Hamilton
274	71.4	Alliance City	Alliance
275	70.5	Worthington City	Worthington
276	70.4	Mason City SD	Mason
276	70.4	Willard City	Willard
278	70.3	Mayfield City	Mayfield Hgts
279	70.1	Northmont City	Englewood
280	69.8	Canal Wnchstr Local	Canal Wnchstr
281	69.6	West Carrollton City	West Carrollton
282	68.7	Zanesville City	Zanesville
283	68.5	Fairfield City	Fairfield
284	68.2	Defiance City	Defiance
285	68.1	Northridge Local	Dayton
286	68.0	Sycamore Community City	Blue Ash
287	67.5	South-Western City	Grove City
288	66.7	Ashtabula Area City	Ashtabula
289	66.6	Dublin City	Dublin
290	66.1	Woodridge Local	Peninsula
291	65.1	Orange City	Cleveland
292	64.8	Springfield Local	Holland
293	64.6	Gahanna-Jefferson City	Gahanna
293	64.6	Middletown City	Middletown
293	64.6	Pickerington Local	Pickerington
296	63.8	Huber Heights City	Huber Heights
297	63.6	Solon City	Solon
298	62.1	Westerville City	Westerville
299	61.9	Twinsburg City	Twinsburg
300	60.6	Licking Heights Local	Pataskala
301	60.0	Fremont City	Fremont
301	60.0	Springfield City	Springfield
303	59.8	Northwest Local	Cincinnati

Note: This section only includes districts with 1,500 or more students; All categories are ranked from high to low

304	59.7	Steubenville City	Steubenville
305	59.3	Fostoria City	Fostoria
306	55.5	Elyria City Schools	Elyria
307	53.9	Mansfield City	Mansfield
308	50.0	Groveport Madison Local	Groveport
309	46.8	Canton City	Canton
310	46.4	Reynoldsburg City	Reynoldsburg
311	46.0	Clearview Local	Lorain
312	45.6	Warren City	Warren
313	41.7	Sandusky City	Sandusky
314	39.1	Toledo City	Toledo
315	39.0	Lima City	Lima
316	38.7	Whitehall City	Whitehall
317	38.6	Shaker Heights City	Shaker Heights
318	38.3	Akron City	Akron
319	30.2	Princeton City	Cincinnati
320	28.3	Garfield Hgts City Schools	Garfield Hgts
321	28.0	South Euclid-Lyndhurst City	Lyndhurst
322	27.5	Painesville City Local	Painesville
323	26.5	Dayton City	Dayton
323	26.5	Lorain City	Lorain
325	26.2	Columbus City SD	Columbus
326	25.6	Cincinnati City	Cincinnati
327	18.2	Mt Healthy City	Cincinnati
328	17.4	Cleveland Heights-Univ Hgts City	University Hgts
329	14.9	Cleveland Municipal	Cleveland
329	14.9	Youngstown City Schools	Youngstown
331	13.4	Winton Woods City	Cincinnati
332	13.3	North College Hill City	Cincinnati
333	12.5	Euclid City	Euclid
334	10.8	Bedford City	Bedford
335	6.5	Trotwood-Madison City	Trotwood
336	2.4	Maple Heights City	Maple Heights
337	0.3	East Cleveland City SD	East Cleveland

Black Students

Rank	Percent	District Name	City
1	98.6	East Cleveland City SD	East Cleveland
2	92.4	Maple Heights City	Maple Heights
3	89.4	Trotwood-Madison City	Trotwood
4	82.0	Euclid City	Euclid
5	80.5	Bedford City	Bedford
6	76.8	North College Hill City	Cincinnati
7	73.1	Cleveland Heights-Univ Hgts City	University Hgts
8	70.3	Mt Healthy City	Cincinnati
9	66.4	Cleveland Municipal	Cleveland
10	65.2	Youngstown City Schools	Youngstown
11	64.3	Dayton City	Dayton
12	63.7	Winton Woods City	Cincinnati
13	63.4	Cincinnati City	Cincinnati
14	62.4	Garfield Hgts City Schools	Garfield Hgts
15	61.3	South Euclid-Lyndhurst City	Lyndhurst
16	56.4	Columbus City SD	Columbus
17	48.2	Shaker Heights City	Shaker Heights
18	45.4	Akron City	Akron
19	41.5	Princeton City	Cincinnati
20	40.9	Toledo City	Toledo
21	40.4	Lima City	Lima
22	39.3	Groveport Madison Local	Groveport
23	38.5	Warren City	Warren
24	37.5	Sandusky City	Sandusky
25	36.7	Reynoldsburg City	Reynoldsburg
26	35.0	Whitehall City	Whitehall
27	34.7	Canton City	Canton
28	30.2	Mansfield City	Mansfield
29	27.8	Licking Heights Local	Pataskala
30	27.5	Lorain City	Lorain
31	26.2	Northwest Local	Cincinnati
32	26.1	Steubenville City	Steubenville
33	23.8	Springfield City	Springfield
34	23.7	Northridge Local	Dayton
35	23.2	Twinsburg City	Twinsburg
36	22.8	Westerville City	Westerville
37	21.8	Orange City	Cleveland
38	21.0	Elyria City Schools	Elyria
39	20.5	Pickerington Local	Pickerington
40	20.4	Woodridge Local	Peninsula
41	19.8	Gahanna-Jefferson City	Gahanna
42	19.3	Northmont City	Englewood
43	19.0	Huber Heights City	Huber Heights
44	17.7	Canal Wnchstr Local	Canal Wnchstr
45	17.5	Springfield Local	Holland
46	16.9	Mayfield City	Mayfield Hgts
47	16.8	Middletown City	Middletown
48	16.7	West Carrollton City	West Carrollton
49	15.8	Fairfield City	Fairfield
50	15.6	Painesville City Local	Painesville
51	14.6	Copley-Fairlawn City	Copley
52	14.4	Solon City	Solon
53	14.1	Electronic Classroom of Tomorrow	Columbus
54	13.4	Streetsboro City	Streetsboro
55	13.3	Plain Local	Canton
56	13.2	Xenia Community City	Xenia
57	13.1	Alternative Education Academy	Toledo
58	12.4	Alliance City	Alliance
59	12.2	Norwood City	Norwood
60	12.1	Kent City	Kent
60	12.1	Ohio Virtual Academy	Maumee
62	12.0	Clearview Local	Lorain
63	11.9	Massillon City	Massillon
63	11.9	Wyoming City	Wyoming
65	11.7	Hamilton City	Hamilton
65	11.7	South-Western City	Grove City
67	11.6	Nordonia Hills City	Northfield
68	11.2	Barberton City	Barberton
68	11.2	Zanesville City	Zanesville
70	11.1	Austintown Local	Youngstown
70	11.1	Elida Local	Elida
72	10.6	Hamilton Local	Columbus
73	10.2	Lakota Local	Liberty Twp
74	9.8	Ohio Connections Academy, Inc	Cleveland
75	9.1	Boardman Local	Youngstown
76	9.0	Fairborn City	Fairborn
77	8.8	Washington Local	Toledo
78	8.7	Reading Community City	Reading
79	8.5	Lakewood City	Lakewood
79	8.5	Ravenna City	Ravenna
81	8.2	Worthington City	Worthington
82	8.1	Mad River Local	Dayton
83	8.0	Maumee City	Maumee
84	7.9	Willoughby-Eastlake City	Willoughby
85	7.8	Ashtabula Area City	Ashtabula
85	7.8	Fremont City	Fremont
85	7.8	Sycamore Community City	Blue Ash
88	7.7	Miamisburg City	Miamisburg
89	7.4	Bexley City	Bexley
90	7.2	Chillicothe City	Chillicothe
91	6.7	New Albany-Plain Local	New Albany
91	6.7	Portsmouth City	Portsmouth
93	6.6	Marion City	Marion
94	6.4	Girard City SD	Girard
94	6.4	Treca Digital Academy	Marion
96	6.3	Centerville City	Centerville
96	6.3	Defiance City	Defiance
98	6.2	Canton Local	Canton
98	6.2	South Point Local	South Point
100	6.1	Vandalia-Butler City	Vandalia
101	6.0	Hilliard City	Columbus
102	5.9	Shawnee Local	Lima
103	5.8	Perkins Local	Sandusky
104	5.7	Berea City	Berea
105	5.2	Sylvania City	Sylvania
106	5.0	Howland Local	Warren
107	4.9	East Liverpool City	East Liverpool
108	4.8	Bath Local	Lima
108	4.8	Delaware City	Delaware
108	4.8	Kettering City	Kettering
111	4.7	Fostoria City	Fostoria
111	4.7	Struthers City	Struthers
113	4.6	Gallipolis City	Gallipolis
114	4.4	Dublin City	Dublin
114	4.4	Kenston Local	Chagrin Falls
116	4.3	Orrville City	Orrville
117	4.2	London City	London
117	4.2	Sidney City	Sidney
119	4.1	Niles City	Niles
119	4.1	Ontario Local	Mansfield
119	4.1	Troy City	Troy
119	4.1	Urbana City	Urbana
123	4.0	Madison Local	Mansfield
123	4.0	Parma City	Parma
125	3.9	Wilmington City	Wilmington
126	3.8	Bellefontaine City	Bellefontaine
126	3.8	Coventry Local	Akron
126	3.8	Mason City SD	Mason
126	3.8	Newark City	Newark
126	3.8	Olentangy Local	Lewis Center
131	3.7	Cuyahoga Falls City	Cuyahoga Falls
131	3.7	Hubbard Exempted Village	Hubbard
131	3.7	Tallmadge City	Tallmadge
131	3.7	West Muskingum Local	Zanesville
135	3.6	Aurora City	Aurora
136	3.5	Indian Hill Exempted Village	Cincinnati
136	3.5	Stow-Munroe Falls City SD	Stow
138	3.4	Beavercreek City	Beavercreek
138	3.4	Bellbrook-Sugarcreek Local SD	Bellbrook
138	3.4	Clark-Shawnee Local	Springfield
138	3.4	Morgan Local	Mc Connelsville
138	3.4	North Olmsted City	North Olmsted
143	3.3	Cambridge City	Cambridge
143	3.3	Perry Local	Massillon
143	3.3	Wooster City	Wooster
146	3.2	Fairview Park City	Fairview Park
146	3.2	Monroe Local SD	Monroe
148	3.1	Heath City	Heath
148	3.1	Piqua City	Piqua
150	3.0	Bowling Green City SD	Bowling Green
150	3.0	Washington CH City	Washington CH
152	2.9	Avon Local	Avon
153	2.8	Medina City SD	Medina
153	2.8	Southwest Licking Local	Pataskala
153	2.8	Springfield Local	Akron
156	2.6	Field Local	Mogadore
156	2.6	Hillsboro City	Hillsboro
156	2.6	Riverside Local	Painesville
159	2.5	Findlay City	Findlay
159	2.5	Indian Creek Local	Wintersville
161	2.4	Norton City	Norton
162	2.3	Batavia Local	Batavia
162	2.3	Mentor Exempted Village	Mentor
162	2.3	Union-Scioto Local	Chillicothe
162	2.3	West Geauga Local	Chesterland
166	2.2	Amherst Exempted Village	Amherst
166	2.2	Athens City	The Plains
166	2.2	Midview Local	Grafton
166	2.2	Sheffield-Sheffield Lake City	Sheffield Vllg
170	2.1	Brecksville-Broadview Heights City	Brecksville
170	2.1	Port Clinton City	Port Clinton
172	2.0	Kings Local	Kings Mills
172	2.0	Marlington Local	Alliance
172	2.0	Milford Exempted Village	Milford
172	2.0	Oregon City	Oregon
172	2.0	Strongsville City	Strongsville
177	1.9	Loveland City	Loveland
177	1.9	Oak Hills Local	Cincinnati
177	1.9	Waverly City	Waverly
180	1.8	Coshocton City	Coshocton
180	1.8	Jackson Local	Massillon
180	1.8	N Ridgeville City	N Ridgeville
180	1.8	North Royalton City	North Royalton
180	1.8	Rossford Exempted Village	Rossford
180	1.8	Westlake City	Westlake
186	1.7	Buckeye Local	Ashtabula
186	1.7	Green Local	Uniontown
186	1.7	Lancaster City	Lancaster
186	1.7	Lebanon City	Lebanon
186	1.7	Mariemont City	Cincinnati
186	1.7	Northeastern Local	Springfield
186	1.7	Perrysburg Exempted Village	Perrysburg
186	1.7	Talawanda City	Oxford
186	1.7	Tiffin City	Tiffin
195	1.6	Gallia County Local	Gallipolis
195	1.6	Little Miami Local	Maineville
195	1.6	Maysville Local	Zanesville
195	1.6	Olmsted Falls City	Olmsted Falls
195	1.6	Revere Local	Bath
195	1.6	Springboro Community City	Springboro
201	1.5	Brunswick City	Brunswick
201	1.5	North Canton City	North Canton
203	1.4	Claymont City	Dennison
203	1.4	Dover City	Dover
203	1.4	Forest Hills Local	Cincinnati
203	1.4	Jackson City	Jackson
203	1.4	Lake Local	Millbury
203	1.4	Norwalk City	Norwalk
203	1.4	River Valley Local	Caledonia
210	1.3	Anthony Wayne Local	Whitehouse
210	1.3	Big Walnut Local	Sunbury
210	1.3	Chagrin Falls Exempted Village	Chagrin Falls
210	1.3	Conneaut Area City	Conneaut

Note: This section only includes districts with 1,500 or more students; All categories are ranked from high to low

210	1.3	Marysville Exempted Village	Marysville
210	1.3	Northwest Local	Canal Fulton
210	1.3	River View Local	Warsaw
210	1.3	Saint Clairsville-Richland City	Saint Clairsville
218	1.2	Buckeye Local	Medina
218	1.2	Harrison Hills City	Cadiz
218	1.2	Miami Trace Local	Washington CH
218	1.2	Rocky River City	Rocky River
218	1.2	Warren Local	Vincent
223	1.1	Circleville City	Circleville
223	1.1	Edgewood City	Trenton
223	1.1	Geneva Area City	Geneva
223	1.1	Hudson City	Hudson
223	1.1	Logan Elm Local	Circleville
223	1.1	Mount Vernon City	Mount Vernon
223	1.1	Perry Local	Perry
223	1.1	Wauseon Exempted Village	Wauseon
223	1.1	West Clermont Local	Cincinnati
232	1.0	Ashland City	Ashland
232	1.0	Celina City	Celina
232	1.0	Lexington Local	Lexington
232	1.0	Licking Valley Local	Newark
232	1.0	Meigs Local	Pomeroy
232	1.0	Napoleon Area City	Napoleon
232	1.0	North Fork Local	Utica
232	1.0	Northwestern Local	Springfield
232	1.0	Oakwood City	Dayton
232	1.0	Tri-Valley Local	Dresden
232	1.0	Westfall Local	Williamsport
243	0.9	Galion City	Galion
243	0.9	Goshen Local	Goshen
243	0.9	Greenfield Exempted Village	Greenfield
243	0.9	New Richmond Exempted Village	New Richmond
243	0.9	Tecumseh Local	New Carlisle
243	0.9	Upper Arlington City	Upper Arlington
249	0.8	Avon Lake City	Avon Lake
249	0.8	Bay Village City	Bay Village
249	0.8	Canfield Local	Canfield
249	0.8	Carlisle Local	Carlisle
249	0.8	Clyde-Green Springs Exempted Village	Clyde
249	0.8	East Muskingum Local	New Concord
249	0.8	Franklin City	Franklin
249	0.8	Greenon Local	Enon
249	0.8	Marietta City	Marietta
249	0.8	Minerva Local	Minerva
249	0.8	New Philadel. City	New Philadel.
249	0.8	Teays Valley Local	Ashville
249	0.8	Tipp City Exempted Village	Tipp City
249	0.8	Wadsworth City	Wadsworth
249	0.8	Wheelersburg Local	Wheelersburg
264	0.7	Buckeye Local	Dillonvale
264	0.7	Chardon Local	Chardon
264	0.7	Eaton Community City	Eaton
264	0.7	Edison Local (Formerly Berlin-Milan)	Milan
264	0.7	Fairless Local	Navarre
264	0.7	Franklin Local	Duncan Falls
264	0.7	Jonathan Alder Local	Plain City
264	0.7	Kenton City	Kenton
264	0.7	Lakeview Local	Cortland
264	0.7	Van Wert City	Van Wert
274	0.6	Amanda-Clearcreek Local	Amanda
274	0.6	Beaver Local	Lisbon
274	0.6	Clear Fork Valley Local	Bellville
274	0.6	Cloverleaf Local	Lodi
274	0.6	Graham Local	Saint Paris
274	0.6	Granville Exempted Village	Granville
274	0.6	Greenville City	Greenville
274	0.6	Lakewood Local	Hebron
274	0.6	Logan-Hocking Local	Logan
274	0.6	Madison Local	Madison
274	0.6	Rolling Hills Local	Cambridge
274	0.6	Southeast Local	Ravenna
274	0.6	Three Rivers Local	Cleves
274	0.6	Willard City	Willard
288	0.5	Bloom-Carroll Local	Carroll
288	0.5	Bryan City	Bryan
288	0.5	Buckeye Valley Local	Delaware
288	0.5	Crestwood Local	Mantua
288	0.5	Fairland Local	Proctorville
288	0.5	Highland Local	Sparta
288	0.5	Jefferson Area Local	Jefferson
288	0.5	Madison Local	Middletown
288	0.5	Upper Sandusky Exempted Village	Upper Sandusky
288	0.5	Valley View Local	Germantown
298	0.4	Alexander Local	Albany
298	0.4	Benton Carroll Salem Local	Oak Harbor
298	0.4	Blanchester Local	Blanchester
298	0.4	Highland Local	Medina
298	0.4	Minford Local	Minford
298	0.4	Northwest Local	Mc Dermott
298	0.4	Poland Local	Poland
298	0.4	Vermilion Local	Vermilion
306	0.3	Adams County/Ohio Valley Local	West Union
306	0.3	East Holmes Local	Berlin
306	0.3	Edison Local	Hammondsville
306	0.3	Firelands Local	South Amherst
306	0.3	Indian Lake Local	Lewistown
306	0.3	Indian Valley Local Schools	Gnadenhutten
306	0.3	Johnstown-Monroe Local	Johnstown
306	0.3	Northern Local	Thornville
306	0.3	Ottawa-Glandorf Local	Ottawa
306	0.3	Salem City	Salem
306	0.3	Southwest Local	Harrison
306	0.3	Switzerland of Ohio Local	Woodsfield
306	0.3	Vinton County Local	Mc Arthur
306	0.3	West Branch Local	Beloit
320	0.2	Bellevue City	Bellevue
320	0.2	Carrollton Exempted Village	Carrollton
320	0.2	Clinton-Massie Local	Clarksville
320	0.2	Keystone Local	Lagrange
320	0.2	Lake Local	Uniontown
320	0.2	Louisville City	Louisville
320	0.2	New Lexington City	New Lexington
320	0.2	Ross Local	Hamilton
320	0.2	Saint Marys City	Saint Marys
320	0.2	Triway Local	Wooster
320	0.2	Wapakoneta City	Wapakoneta
320	0.2	Western Brown Local	Mount Orab
332	0.1	Benjamin Logan Local	Bellefontaine
332	0.1	Clermont Northeastern Local	Batavia
332	0.1	Shelby City	Shelby
332	0.1	West Holmes Local	Millersburg
336	0.0	Bethel-Tate Local	Bethel
336	0.0	Fairfield Union Local	Lancaster

Asian Students

Rank	Percent	District Name	City
1	18.0	Dublin City	Dublin
2	17.4	Mason City SD	Mason
3	15.8	Solon City	Solon
4	13.6	Sycamore Community City	Blue Ash
5	11.7	New Albany-Plain Local	New Albany
6	8.8	Olentangy Local	Lewis Center
7	8.5	Centerville City	Centerville
8	7.5	Twinsburg City	Twinsburg
9	7.3	Indian Hill Exempted Village	Cincinnati
10	6.8	Hilliard City	Columbus
11	6.4	Beavercreek City	Beavercreek
12	6.2	Upper Arlington City	Upper Arlington
13	6.1	Lakota Local	Liberty Twp
14	6.0	Mayfield City	Mayfield Hgts
14	6.0	Worthington City	Worthington
16	5.9	Brecksville-Broadview Heights City	Brecksville
17	5.6	Copley-Fairlawn City	Copley
17	5.6	Westlake City	Westlake
19	5.4	Orange City	Cleveland
20	5.3	Akron City	Akron
20	5.3	Strongsville City	Strongsville
22	5.2	Revere Local	Bath
23	4.9	Hudson City	Hudson
23	4.9	Lakewood City	Lakewood
25	4.8	Athens City	The Plains
26	4.3	North Royalton City	North Royalton
27	4.1	Shaker Heights City	Shaker Heights
27	4.1	Sylvania City	Sylvania
29	3.9	Nordonia Hills City	Northfield
30	3.7	Jackson Local	Massillon
30	3.7	Perrysburg Exempted Village	Perrysburg
32	3.6	Oakwood City	Dayton
33	3.5	Berea City	Berea
34	3.4	Woodridge Local	Peninsula
35	3.3	Gahanna-Jefferson City	Gahanna
36	3.2	Boardman Local	Youngstown
36	3.2	Pickerington Local	Pickerington
36	3.2	Springboro Community City	Springboro
39	3.1	Aurora City	Aurora
39	3.1	Avon Local	Avon
39	3.1	Princeton City	Cincinnati
39	3.1	Wyoming City	Wyoming
43	2.9	Columbus City SD	Columbus
44	2.8	Troy City	Troy
45	2.7	Miamisburg City	Miamisburg
45	2.7	Talawanda City	Oxford
47	2.6	Canfield Local	Canfield
47	2.6	Findlay City	Findlay
47	2.6	Westerville City	Westerville
50	2.5	Cuyahoga Falls City	Cuyahoga Falls
50	2.5	Forest Hills Local	Cincinnati
50	2.5	Kings Local	Kings Mills
50	2.5	Ontario Local	Mansfield
54	2.4	South-Western City	Grove City
55	2.3	Fairfield City	Fairfield
55	2.3	Fairview Park City	Fairview Park
55	2.3	Marysville Exempted Village	Marysville
55	2.3	Northmont City	Englewood
55	2.3	Parma City	Parma
60	2.2	North Olmsted City	North Olmsted
60	2.2	Springfield Local	Holland
60	2.2	Stow-Munroe Falls City SD	Stow
63	2.1	Bellbrook-Sugarcreek Local SD	Bellbrook
63	2.1	Green Local	Uniontown
63	2.1	Groveport Madison Local	Groveport
63	2.1	Kent City	Kent
63	2.1	Orrville City	Orrville
68	2.0	Highland Local	Medina
68	2.0	Huber Heights City	Huber Heights
68	2.0	Maumee City	Maumee
68	2.0	Rocky River City	Rocky River
68	2.0	Shawnee Local	Lima
68	2.0	South Euclid-Lyndhurst City	Lyndhurst
74	1.9	Celina City	Celina
74	1.9	Loveland City	Loveland
74	1.9	Mad River Local	Dayton
74	1.9	Monroe Local SD	Monroe
74	1.9	Northwest Local	Cincinnati
74	1.9	Vandalia-Butler City	Vandalia
74	1.9	Willoughby-Eastlake City	Willoughby
81	1.8	Bexley City	Bexley
81	1.8	Bowling Green City SD	Bowling Green
81	1.8	Lexington Local	Lexington
81	1.8	Mentor Exempted Village	Mentor
81	1.8	Olmsted Falls City	Olmsted Falls
81	1.8	Perkins Local	Sandusky
87	1.7	Anthony Wayne Local	Whitehouse
87	1.7	Bath Local	Lima
87	1.7	Cleveland Heights-Univ Hgts City	University Hgts
87	1.7	Milford Exempted Village	Milford
87	1.7	North Canton City	North Canton
87	1.7	Sidney City	Sidney
87	1.7	Winton Woods City	Cincinnati
87	1.7	Wooster City	Wooster
95	1.6	Field Local	Mogadore
95	1.6	Granville Exempted Village	Granville
97	1.5	Canal Wnchstr Local	Canal Wnchstr
97	1.5	Coventry Local	Akron
97	1.5	Garfield Hgts City Schools	Garfield Hgts
97	1.5	Reynoldsburg City	Reynoldsburg
97	1.5	West Clermont Local	Cincinnati
102	1.4	Buckeye Valley Local	Delaware
102	1.4	Hamilton Local	Columbus
102	1.4	Kettering City	Kettering
102	1.4	Lakeview Local	Cortland
102	1.4	Mariemont City	Cincinnati
102	1.4	N Ridgeville City	N Ridgeville
102	1.4	Ohio Virtual Academy	Maumee
102	1.4	River Valley Local	Caledonia
102	1.4	Sheffield-Sheffield Lake City	Sheffield Vllg
111	1.3	Brunswick City	Brunswick
111	1.3	Fairborn City	Fairborn
111	1.3	Norton City	Norton
111	1.3	Poland Local	Poland
111	1.3	Springfield Local	Akron
111	1.3	Streetsboro City	Streetsboro
111	1.3	Washington CH City	Washington CH
111	1.3	West Carrollton City	West Carrollton
119	1.2	Alternative Education Academy	Toledo
119	1.2	Avon Lake City	Avon Lake
119	1.2	Chagrin Falls Exempted Village	Chagrin Falls
119	1.2	Cincinnati City	Cincinnati
119	1.2	Eaton Community City	Eaton

Note: This section only includes districts with 1,500 or more students; All categories are ranked from high to low

119	1.2	Oak Hills Local	Cincinnati
119	1.2	West Geauga Local	Chesterland
126	1.1	Bay Village City	Bay Village
126	1.1	Big Walnut Local	Sunbury
126	1.1	Bryan City	Bryan
126	1.1	Greenon Local	Enon
126	1.1	Greenville City	Greenville
126	1.1	Kenston Local	Chagrin Falls
126	1.1	Little Miami Local	Maineville
126	1.1	Medina City SD	Medina
126	1.1	Rossford Exempted Village	Rossford
126	1.1	West Muskingum Local	Zanesville
126	1.1	Whitehall City	Whitehall
137	1.0	Amherst Exempted Village	Amherst
137	1.0	Batavia Local	Batavia
137	1.0	Bellefontaine City	Bellefontaine
137	1.0	Cleveland Municipal	Cleveland
137	1.0	Gallipolis City	Gallipolis
137	1.0	Heath City	Heath
137	1.0	Howland Local	Warren
137	1.0	Lebanon City	Lebanon
137	1.0	London City	London
137	1.0	Ohio Connections Academy, Inc	Cleveland
137	1.0	Oregon City	Oregon
137	1.0	Tipp City Exempted Village	Tipp City
149	0.9	Ashland City	Ashland
149	0.9	Chardon Local	Chardon
149	0.9	Delaware City	Delaware
149	0.9	East Muskingum Local	New Concord
149	0.9	Fairland Local	Proctorville
149	0.9	Riverside Local	Painesville
149	0.9	Tallmadge City	Tallmadge
149	0.9	Upper Sandusky Exempted Village	Upper Sandusky
157	0.8	Carlisle Local	Carlisle
157	0.8	Circleville City	Circleville
157	0.8	Elida Local	Elida
157	0.8	Licking Heights Local	Pataskala
157	0.8	Northeastern Local	Springfield
157	0.8	Northwest Local	Canal Fulton
157	0.8	Piqua City	Piqua
157	0.8	South Point Local	South Point
157	0.8	Van Wert City	Van Wert
157	0.8	Wadsworth City	Wadsworth
157	0.8	Waverly City	Waverly
168	0.7	Austintown Local	Youngstown
168	0.7	Bloom-Carroll Local	Carroll
168	0.7	Buckeye Local	Ashtabula
168	0.7	Clark-Shawnee Local	Springfield
168	0.7	Marietta City	Marietta
168	0.7	Midview Local	Grafton
168	0.7	Mount Vernon City	Mount Vernon
168	0.7	Mt Healthy City	Cincinnati
168	0.7	Napoleon Area City	Napoleon
168	0.7	Plain Local	Canton
168	0.7	Southwest Licking Local	Pataskala
168	0.7	Three Rivers Local	Cleves
168	0.7	Valley View Local	Germantown
168	0.7	Washington Local	Toledo
168	0.7	Wauseon Exempted Village	Wauseon
168	0.7	Wilmington City	Wilmington
184	0.6	Alliance City	Alliance
184	0.6	Coshocton City	Coshocton
184	0.6	Defiance City	Defiance
184	0.6	Fostoria City	Fostoria
184	0.6	Franklin City	Franklin
184	0.6	Johnstown-Monroe Local	Johnstown
184	0.6	Lake Local	Millbury
184	0.6	New Philadel. City	New Philadel.
184	0.6	Perry Local	Perry
184	0.6	Perry Local	Massillon
184	0.6	Springfield City	Springfield
184	0.6	Teays Valley Local	Ashville
184	0.6	Union-Scioto Local	Chillicothe
197	0.5	Barberton City	Barberton
197	0.5	Benjamin Logan Local	Bellefontaine
197	0.5	Buckeye Local	Medina
197	0.5	Chillicothe City	Chillicothe
197	0.5	Cloverleaf Local	Lodi
197	0.5	Conneaut Area City	Conneaut
197	0.5	Elyria City Schools	Elyria
197	0.5	Fremont City	Fremont
197	0.5	Kenton City	Kenton
197	0.5	Lancaster City	Lancaster
197	0.5	Newark City	Newark
197	0.5	Niles City	Niles
197	0.5	Northwestern Local	Springfield
197	0.5	Ottawa-Glandorf Local	Ottawa
197	0.5	Saint Clairsville-Richland City	Saint Clairsville
197	0.5	Tecumseh Local	New Carlisle
197	0.5	Tiffin City	Tiffin
197	0.5	Toledo City	Toledo
197	0.5	Triway Local	Wooster
197	0.5	Vermilion Local	Vermilion
197	0.5	Wheelersburg Local	Wheelersburg
197	0.5	Xenia Community City	Xenia
219	0.4	Bedford City	Bedford
219	0.4	Clinton-Massie Local	Clarksville
219	0.4	Dover City	Dover
219	0.4	East Holmes Local	Berlin
219	0.4	Electronic Classroom of Tomorrow	Columbus
219	0.4	Geneva Area City	Geneva
219	0.4	Hamilton City	Hamilton
219	0.4	Jonathan Alder Local	Plain City
219	0.4	Keystone Local	Lagrange
219	0.4	Lake Local	Uniontown
219	0.4	Lakewood Local	Hebron
219	0.4	Lima City	Lima
219	0.4	Louisville City	Louisville
219	0.4	Madison Local	Madison
219	0.4	Mansfield City	Mansfield
219	0.4	Maple Heights City	Maple Heights
219	0.4	Middletown City	Middletown
219	0.4	New Richmond Exempted Village	New Richmond
219	0.4	North College Hill City	Cincinnati
219	0.4	Struthers City	Struthers
219	0.4	Tri-Valley Local	Dresden
219	0.4	Wapakoneta City	Wapakoneta
219	0.4	Zanesville City	Zanesville
242	0.3	Ashtabula Area City	Ashtabula
242	0.3	Beaver Local	Lisbon
242	0.3	Buckeye Local	Dillonvale
242	0.3	Canton Local	Canton
242	0.3	Clyde-Green Springs Exempted Village	Clyde
242	0.3	Dayton City	Dayton
242	0.3	Edgewood City	Trenton
242	0.3	Edison Local (Formerly Berlin-Milan)	Milan
242	0.3	Fairless Local	Navarre
242	0.3	Firelands Local	South Amherst
242	0.3	Franklin Local	Duncan Falls
242	0.3	Graham Local	Saint Paris
242	0.3	Harrison Hills City	Cadiz
242	0.3	Highland Local	Sparta
242	0.3	Hillsboro City	Hillsboro
242	0.3	Indian Creek Local	Wintersville
242	0.3	Indian Lake Local	Lewistown
242	0.3	Jackson City	Jackson
242	0.3	Logan-Hocking Local	Logan
242	0.3	Lorain City	Lorain
242	0.3	Madison Local	Mansfield
242	0.3	Madison Local	Middletown
242	0.3	New Lexington City	New Lexington
242	0.3	Norwalk City	Norwalk
242	0.3	Painesville City Local	Painesville
242	0.3	Portsmouth City	Portsmouth
242	0.3	Ross Local	Hamilton
242	0.3	Salem City	Salem
242	0.3	Sandusky City	Sandusky
242	0.3	Shelby City	Shelby
242	0.3	Southwest Local	Harrison
242	0.3	Saint Marys City	Saint Marys
242	0.3	Urbana City	Urbana
242	0.3	Warren Local	Vincent
242	0.3	Willard City	Willard
277	0.2	Adams County/Ohio Valley Local	West Union
277	0.2	Blanchester Local	Blanchester
277	0.2	Cambridge City	Cambridge
277	0.2	Canton City	Canton
277	0.2	Carrollton Exempted Village	Carrollton
277	0.2	Claymont City	Dennison
277	0.2	Clear Fork Valley Local	Bellville
277	0.2	Clearview Local	Lorain
277	0.2	Crestwood Local	Mantua
277	0.2	Edison Local	Hammondsville
277	0.2	Euclid City	Euclid
277	0.2	Galion City	Galion
277	0.2	Hubbard Exempted Village	Hubbard
277	0.2	Logan Elm Local	Circleville
277	0.2	Marlington Local	Alliance
277	0.2	Massillon City	Massillon
277	0.2	Miami Trace Local	Washington CH
277	0.2	Minerva Local	Minerva
277	0.2	Northridge Local	Dayton
277	0.2	Port Clinton City	Port Clinton
277	0.2	Ravenna City	Ravenna
277	0.2	Reading Community City	Reading
277	0.2	River View Local	Warsaw
277	0.2	Steubenville City	Steubenville
277	0.2	Vinton County Local	Mc Arthur
277	0.2	West Holmes Local	Millersburg
277	0.2	Western Brown Local	Mount Orab
304	0.1	Amanda-Clearcreek Local	Amanda
304	0.1	Benton Carroll Salem Local	Oak Harbor
304	0.1	Bethel-Tate Local	Bethel
304	0.1	Clermont Northeastern Local	Batavia
304	0.1	East Liverpool City	East Liverpool
304	0.1	Fairfield Union Local	Lancaster
304	0.1	Girard City SD	Girard
304	0.1	Goshen Local	Goshen
304	0.1	Greenfield Exempted Village	Greenfield
304	0.1	Jefferson Area Local	Jefferson
304	0.1	Licking Valley Local	Newark
304	0.1	Marion City	Marion
304	0.1	Maysville Local	Zanesville
304	0.1	Minford Local	Minford
304	0.1	North Fork Local	Utica
304	0.1	Northern Local	Thornville
304	0.1	Northwest Local	Mc Dermott
304	0.1	Norwood City	Norwood
304	0.1	Treca Digital Academy	Marion
304	0.1	Trotwood-Madison City	Trotwood
304	0.1	Warren City	Warren
304	0.1	West Branch Local	Beloit
304	0.1	Westfall Local	Williamsport
304	0.1	Youngstown City Schools	Youngstown
328	0.0	Alexander Local	Albany
328	0.0	Bellevue City	Bellevue
328	0.0	East Cleveland City SD	East Cleveland
328	0.0	Gallia County Local	Gallipolis
328	0.0	Indian Valley Local Schools	Gnadenhutten
328	0.0	Meigs Local	Pomeroy
328	0.0	Morgan Local	Mc Connelsville
328	0.0	Rolling Hills Local	Cambridge
328	0.0	Southeast Local	Ravenna
328	0.0	Switzerland of Ohio Local	Woodsfield

American Indian/Alaska Native Students

Rank	Percent	District Name	City
1	0.7	Sheffield-Sheffield Lake City	Sheffield Vlg
2	0.5	Ohio Virtual Academy	Maumee
3	0.4	Big Walnut Local	Sunbury
3	0.4	Carrollton Exempted Village	Carrollton
3	0.4	Edison Local (Formerly Berlin-Milan)	Milan
3	0.4	Elida Local	Elida
3	0.4	Hillsboro City	Hillsboro
3	0.4	Indian Lake Local	Lewistown
3	0.4	Keystone Local	Lagrange
3	0.4	Meigs Local	Pomeroy
3	0.4	Midview Local	Grafton
3	0.4	Minford Local	Minford
3	0.4	Ohio Connections Academy, Inc	Cleveland
3	0.4	Struthers City	Struthers
15	0.3	Alternative Education Academy	Toledo
15	0.3	Barberton City	Barberton
15	0.3	Beaver Local	Lisbon
15	0.3	Circleville City	Circleville
15	0.3	Electronic Classroom of Tomorrow	Columbus
15	0.3	Johnstown-Monroe Local	Johnstown
15	0.3	Licking Valley Local	Newark
15	0.3	Mount Vernon City	Mount Vernon
15	0.3	New Lexington City	New Lexington
15	0.3	Northridge Local	Dayton
15	0.3	Ontario Local	Mansfield
15	0.3	Oregon City	Oregon
15	0.3	Perkins Local	Sandusky
15	0.3	Piqua City	Piqua
15	0.3	Southwest Licking Local	Pataskala
15	0.3	Vermilion Local	Vermilion
15	0.3	Washington Local	Toledo
15	0.3	Wauseon Exempted Village	Wauseon
15	0.3	Waverly City	Waverly

Note: This section only includes districts with 1,500 or more students; All categories are ranked from high to low

15	0.3	West Carrollton City	West Carrollton
35	0.2	Amanda-Clearcreek Local	Amanda
35	0.2	Amherst Exempted Village	Amherst
35	0.2	Austintown Local	Youngstown
35	0.2	Beavercreek City	Beavercreek
35	0.2	Bellbrook-Sugarcreek Local SD	Bellbrook
35	0.2	Bellefontaine City	Bellefontaine
35	0.2	Benjamin Logan Local	Bellefontaine
35	0.2	Benton Carroll Salem Local	Oak Harbor
35	0.2	Buckeye Valley Local	Delaware
35	0.2	Canal Wnchstr Local	Canal Wnchstr
35	0.2	Canfield Local	Canfield
35	0.2	Canton City	Canton
35	0.2	Canton Local	Canton
35	0.2	Centerville City	Centerville
35	0.2	Chardon Local	Chardon
35	0.2	Claymont City	Dennison
35	0.2	Clearview Local	Lorain
35	0.2	Clermont Northeastern Local	Batavia
35	0.2	Cleveland Municipal	Cleveland
35	0.2	Cloverleaf Local	Lodi
35	0.2	Columbus City SD	Columbus
35	0.2	Copley-Fairlawn City	Copley
35	0.2	Coventry Local	Akron
35	0.2	East Liverpool City	East Liverpool
35	0.2	Elyria City Schools	Elyria
35	0.2	Fairfield Union Local	Lancaster
35	0.2	Field Local	Mogadore
35	0.2	Gahanna-Jefferson City	Gahanna
35	0.2	Heath City	Heath
35	0.2	Highland Local	Sparta
35	0.2	Hilliard City	Columbus
35	0.2	Howland Local	Warren
35	0.2	Indian Valley Local Schools	Gnadenhutten
35	0.2	Jonathan Alder Local	Plain City
35	0.2	Kent City	Kent
35	0.2	Kettering City	Kettering
35	0.2	Lake Local	Uniontown
35	0.2	Lakeview Local	Cortland
35	0.2	Lakewood Local	Hebron
35	0.2	Lancaster City	Lancaster
35	0.2	Lexington Local	Lexington
35	0.2	Lorain City	Lorain
35	0.2	Mad River Local	Dayton
35	0.2	Marietta City	Marietta
35	0.2	Mason City SD	Mason
35	0.2	Morgan Local	Mc Connelsville
35	0.2	Newark City	Newark
35	0.2	Niles City	Niles
35	0.2	Nordonia Hills City	Northfield
35	0.2	North College Hill City	Cincinnati
35	0.2	North Fork Local	Utica
35	0.2	Northwestern Local	Springfield
35	0.2	Norton City	Norton
35	0.2	Oak Hills Local	Cincinnati
35	0.2	Olmsted Falls City	Olmsted Falls
35	0.2	Orange City	Cleveland
35	0.2	Painesville City Local	Painesville
35	0.2	Pickerington Local	Pickerington
35	0.2	Plain Local	Canton
35	0.2	Poland Local	Poland
35	0.2	Portsmouth City	Portsmouth
35	0.2	Princeton City	Cincinnati
35	0.2	Ravenna City	Ravenna
35	0.2	River Valley Local	Caledonia
35	0.2	Rocky River City	Rocky River
35	0.2	Sandusky City	Sandusky
35	0.2	Shelby City	Shelby
35	0.2	Southwest Local	Harrison
35	0.2	Tallmadge City	Tallmadge
35	0.2	Tecumseh Local	New Carlisle
35	0.2	Triway Local	Wooster
35	0.2	Twinsburg City	Twinsburg
35	0.2	Union-Scioto Local	Chillicothe
35	0.2	Upper Sandusky Exempted Village	Upper Sandusky
35	0.2	Valley View Local	Germantown
35	0.2	Vandalia-Butler City	Vandalia
35	0.2	Westerville City	Westerville
35	0.2	Whitehall City	Whitehall
35	0.2	Willoughby-Eastlake City	Willoughby
35	0.2	Zanesville City	Zanesville
115	0.1	Adams County/Ohio Valley Local	West Union
115	0.1	Akron City	Akron
115	0.1	Alliance City	Alliance
115	0.1	Anthony Wayne Local	Whitehouse
115	0.1	Ashtabula Area City	Ashtabula
115	0.1	Athens City	The Plains
115	0.1	Avon Lake City	Avon Lake
115	0.1	Batavia Local	Batavia
115	0.1	Bath Local	Lima
115	0.1	Bay Village City	Bay Village
115	0.1	Bedford City	Bedford
115	0.1	Berea City	Berea
115	0.1	Boardman Local	Youngstown
115	0.1	Bowling Green City SD	Bowling Green
115	0.1	Brecksville-Broadview Heights City	Brecksville
115	0.1	Brunswick City	Brunswick
115	0.1	Bryan City	Bryan
115	0.1	Buckeye Local	Ashtabula
115	0.1	Cambridge City	Cambridge
115	0.1	Celina City	Celina
115	0.1	Chagrin Falls Exempted Village	Chagrin Falls
115	0.1	Chillicothe City	Chillicothe
115	0.1	Cincinnati City	Cincinnati
115	0.1	Clark-Shawnee Local	Springfield
115	0.1	Clinton-Massie Local	Clarksville
115	0.1	Conneaut Area City	Conneaut
115	0.1	Dayton City	Dayton
115	0.1	Delaware City	Delaware
115	0.1	Dublin City	Dublin
115	0.1	East Holmes Local	Berlin
115	0.1	East Muskingum Local	New Concord
115	0.1	Euclid City	Euclid
115	0.1	Fairborn City	Fairborn
115	0.1	Fairfield City	Fairfield
115	0.1	Fairless Local	Navarre
115	0.1	Fairview Park City	Fairview Park
115	0.1	Findlay City	Findlay
115	0.1	Firelands Local	South Amherst
115	0.1	Fostoria City	Fostoria
115	0.1	Franklin City	Franklin
115	0.1	Franklin Local	Duncan Falls
115	0.1	Fremont City	Fremont
115	0.1	Gallia County Local	Gallipolis
115	0.1	Garfield Hgts City Schools	Garfield Hgts
115	0.1	Geneva Area City	Geneva
115	0.1	Goshen Local	Goshen
115	0.1	Graham Local	Saint Paris
115	0.1	Green Local	Uniontown
115	0.1	Greenfield Exempted Village	Greenfield
115	0.1	Greenon Local	Enon
115	0.1	Greenville City	Greenville
115	0.1	Groveport Madison Local	Groveport
115	0.1	Hamilton City	Hamilton
115	0.1	Harrison Hills City	Cadiz
115	0.1	Hubbard Exempted Village	Hubbard
115	0.1	Huber Heights City	Huber Heights
115	0.1	Hudson City	Hudson
115	0.1	Indian Creek Local	Wintersville
115	0.1	Jackson Local	Massillon
115	0.1	Kings Local	Kings Mills
115	0.1	Lakewood City	Lakewood
115	0.1	Lakota Local	Liberty Twp
115	0.1	Lebanon City	Lebanon
115	0.1	Lima City	Lima
115	0.1	Little Miami Local	Maineville
115	0.1	Logan-Hocking Local	Logan
115	0.1	London City	London
115	0.1	Madison Local	Mansfield
115	0.1	Madison Local	Middletown
115	0.1	Madison Local	Madison
115	0.1	Maple Heights City	Maple Heights
115	0.1	Mariemont City	Cincinnati
115	0.1	Marysville Exempted Village	Marysville
115	0.1	Massillon City	Massillon
115	0.1	Medina City SD	Medina
115	0.1	Mentor Exempted Village	Mentor
115	0.1	Miamisburg City	Miamisburg
115	0.1	Middletown City	Middletown
115	0.1	Minerva Local	Minerva
115	0.1	Mt Healthy City	Cincinnati
115	0.1	Napoleon Area City	Napoleon
115	0.1	New Albany-Plain Local	New Albany
115	0.1	New Richmond Exempted Village	New Richmond
115	0.1	North Olmsted City	North Olmsted
115	0.1	N Ridgeville City	N Ridgeville
115	0.1	Northmont City	Englewood
115	0.1	Northwest Local	Cincinnati
115	0.1	Northwest Local	Mc Dermott
115	0.1	Norwalk City	Norwalk
115	0.1	Olentangy Local	Lewis Center
115	0.1	Orrville City	Orrville
115	0.1	Parma City	Parma
115	0.1	Perry Local	Perry
115	0.1	Perry Local	Massillon
115	0.1	Perrysburg Exempted Village	Perrysburg
115	0.1	Port Clinton City	Port Clinton
115	0.1	Reading Community City	Reading
115	0.1	River View Local	Warsaw
115	0.1	Rolling Hills Local	Cambridge
115	0.1	Ross Local	Hamilton
115	0.1	Rossford Exempted Village	Rossford
115	0.1	Shawnee Local	Lima
115	0.1	Sidney City	Sidney
115	0.1	South Point Local	South Point
115	0.1	South-Western City	Grove City
115	0.1	Southeast Local	Ravenna
115	0.1	Springfield City	Springfield
115	0.1	Springfield Local	Holland
115	0.1	Saint Clairsville-Richland City	Saint Clairsville
115	0.1	Saint Marys City	Saint Marys
115	0.1	Steubenville City	Steubenville
115	0.1	Stow-Munroe Falls City SD	Stow
115	0.1	Strongsville City	Strongsville
115	0.1	Sylvania City	Sylvania
115	0.1	Talawanda City	Oxford
115	0.1	Teays Valley Local	Ashville
115	0.1	Three Rivers Local	Cleves
115	0.1	Tipp City Exempted Village	Tipp City
115	0.1	Toledo City	Toledo
115	0.1	Treca Digital Academy	Marion
115	0.1	Tri-Valley Local	Dresden
115	0.1	Troy City	Troy
115	0.1	Upper Arlington City	Upper Arlington
115	0.1	Van Wert City	Van Wert
115	0.1	Wadsworth City	Wadsworth
115	0.1	Wapakoneta City	Wapakoneta
115	0.1	Washington CH City	Washington CH
115	0.1	West Branch Local	Beloit
115	0.1	West Geauga Local	Chesterland
115	0.1	West Muskingum Local	Zanesville
115	0.1	Westlake City	Westlake
115	0.1	Willard City	Willard
115	0.1	Wilmington City	Wilmington
115	0.1	Winton Woods City	Cincinnati
115	0.1	Woodridge Local	Peninsula
115	0.1	Wooster City	Wooster
115	0.1	Worthington City	Worthington
115	0.1	Xenia Community City	Xenia
115	0.1	Youngstown City Schools	Youngstown
254	0.0	Alexander Local	Albany
254	0.0	Ashland City	Ashland
254	0.0	Aurora City	Aurora
254	0.0	Avon Local	Avon
254	0.0	Bellevue City	Bellevue
254	0.0	Bethel-Tate Local	Bethel
254	0.0	Bexley City	Bexley
254	0.0	Blanchester Local	Blanchester
254	0.0	Bloom-Carroll Local	Carroll
254	0.0	Buckeye Local	Medina
254	0.0	Buckeye Local	Dillonvale
254	0.0	Carlisle Local	Carlisle
254	0.0	Clear Fork Valley Local	Bellville
254	0.0	Cleveland Heights-Univ Hgts City	University Hgts
254	0.0	Clyde-Green Springs Exempted Village	Clyde
254	0.0	Coshocton City	Coshocton
254	0.0	Crestwood Local	Mantua
254	0.0	Cuyahoga Falls City	Cuyahoga Falls
254	0.0	Defiance City	Defiance
254	0.0	Dover City	Dover
254	0.0	East Cleveland City SD	East Cleveland
254	0.0	Eaton Community City	Eaton
254	0.0	Edgewood City	Trenton
254	0.0	Edison Local	Hammondsville
254	0.0	Fairland Local	Proctorville
254	0.0	Forest Hills Local	Cincinnati
254	0.0	Galion City	Galion
254	0.0	Gallipolis City	Gallipolis
254	0.0	Girard City SD	Girard
254	0.0	Granville Exempted Village	Granville
254	0.0	Hamilton Local	Columbus
254	0.0	Highland Local	Medina

Note: This section only includes districts with 1,500 or more students; All categories are ranked from high to low

254	0.0	Indian Hill Exempted Village	Cincinnati
254	0.0	Jackson City	Jackson
254	0.0	Jefferson Area Local	Jefferson
254	0.0	Kenston Local	Chagrin Falls
254	0.0	Kenton City	Kenton
254	0.0	Lake Local	Millbury
254	0.0	Licking Heights Local	Pataskala
254	0.0	Logan Elm Local	Circleville
254	0.0	Louisville City	Louisville
254	0.0	Loveland City	Loveland
254	0.0	Mansfield City	Mansfield
254	0.0	Marion City	Marion
254	0.0	Marlington Local	Alliance
254	0.0	Maumee City	Maumee
254	0.0	Mayfield City	Mayfield Hgts
254	0.0	Maysville Local	Zanesville
254	0.0	Miami Trace Local	Washington CH
254	0.0	Milford Exempted Village	Milford
254	0.0	Monroe Local SD	Monroe
254	0.0	New Philadel. City	New Philadel.
254	0.0	North Canton City	North Canton
254	0.0	North Royalton City	North Royalton
254	0.0	Northeastern Local	Springfield
254	0.0	Northern Local	Thornville
254	0.0	Northwest Local	Canal Fulton
254	0.0	Norwood City	Norwood
254	0.0	Oakwood City	Dayton
254	0.0	Ottawa-Glandorf Local	Ottawa
254	0.0	Revere Local	Bath
254	0.0	Reynoldsburg City	Reynoldsburg
254	0.0	Riverside Local	Painesville
254	0.0	Salem City	Salem
254	0.0	Shaker Heights City	Shaker Heights
254	0.0	Solon City	Solon
254	0.0	South Euclid-Lyndhurst City	Lyndhurst
254	0.0	Springboro Community City	Springboro
254	0.0	Springfield Local	Akron
254	0.0	Streetsboro City	Streetsboro
254	0.0	Switzerland of Ohio Local	Woodsfield
254	0.0	Sycamore Community City	Blue Ash
254	0.0	Tiffin City	Tiffin
254	0.0	Trotwood-Madison City	Trotwood
254	0.0	Urbana City	Urbana
254	0.0	Vinton County Local	Mc Arthur
254	0.0	Warren City	Warren
254	0.0	Warren Local	Vincent
254	0.0	West Clermont Local	Cincinnati
254	0.0	West Holmes Local	Millersburg
254	0.0	Western Brown Local	Mount Orab
254	0.0	Westfall Local	Williamsport
254	0.0	Wheelersburg Local	Wheelersburg
254	0.0	Wyoming City	Wyoming

Native Hawaiian/Pacific Islander Students

Rank	Percent	District Name	City
1	0.8	Princeton City	Cincinnati
2	0.6	Hamilton City	Hamilton
2	0.6	Winton Woods City	Cincinnati
4	0.5	Celina City	Celina
4	0.5	Orange City	Cleveland
6	0.4	Field Local	Mogadore
6	0.4	Westlake City	Westlake
8	0.3	West Muskingum Local	Zanesville
9	0.2	Ashland City	Ashland
9	0.2	Aurora City	Aurora
9	0.2	Bath Local	Lima
9	0.2	Berea City	Berea
9	0.2	Circleville City	Circleville
9	0.2	Edison Local (Formerly Berlin-Milan)	Milan
9	0.2	Groveport Madison Local	Groveport
9	0.2	Huber Heights City	Huber Heights
9	0.2	Kings Local	Kings Mills
9	0.2	Mad River Local	Dayton
9	0.2	Madison Local	Middletown
9	0.2	Miami Trace Local	Washington CH
9	0.2	Northridge Local	Dayton
9	0.2	Northwestern Local	Springfield
9	0.2	Olmsted Falls City	Olmsted Falls
9	0.2	Ontario Local	Mansfield
9	0.2	Sidney City	Sidney
9	0.2	Streetsboro City	Streetsboro
9	0.2	Talawanda City	Oxford
9	0.2	Tallmadge City	Tallmadge
29	0.1	Adams County/Ohio Valley Local	West Union
29	0.1	Akron City	Akron
29	0.1	Alternative Education Academy	Toledo
29	0.1	Amanda-Clearcreek Local	Amanda
29	0.1	Austintown Local	Youngstown
29	0.1	Batavia Local	Batavia
29	0.1	Bay Village City	Bay Village
29	0.1	Beaver Local	Lisbon
29	0.1	Beavercreek City	Beavercreek
29	0.1	Bellefontaine City	Bellefontaine
29	0.1	Bellevue City	Bellevue
29	0.1	Benjamin Logan Local	Bellefontaine
29	0.1	Blanchester Local	Blanchester
29	0.1	Boardman Local	Youngstown
29	0.1	Brunswick City	Brunswick
29	0.1	Buckeye Local	Ashtabula
29	0.1	Canal Wnchstr Local	Canal Wnchstr
29	0.1	Canton City	Canton
29	0.1	Cincinnati City	Cincinnati
29	0.1	Clark-Shawnee Local	Springfield
29	0.1	Clear Fork Valley Local	Bellville
29	0.1	Cleveland Municipal	Cleveland
29	0.1	Clyde-Green Springs Exempted Village	Clyde
29	0.1	Conneaut Area City	Conneaut
29	0.1	Coventry Local	Akron
29	0.1	Dover City	Dover
29	0.1	Dublin City	Dublin
29	0.1	Electronic Classroom of Tomorrow	Columbus
29	0.1	Fairborn City	Fairborn
29	0.1	Fairfield Union Local	Lancaster
29	0.1	Findlay City	Findlay
29	0.1	Franklin City	Franklin
29	0.1	Galion City	Galion
29	0.1	Garfield Hgts City Schools	Garfield Hgts
29	0.1	Geneva Area City	Geneva
29	0.1	Graham Local	Saint Paris
29	0.1	Highland Local	Medina
29	0.1	Hilliard City	Columbus
29	0.1	Hubbard Exempted Village	Hubbard
29	0.1	Indian Hill Exempted Village	Cincinnati
29	0.1	Indian Valley Local Schools	Gnadenhutten
29	0.1	Kettering City	Kettering
29	0.1	Lake Local	Uniontown
29	0.1	Lake Local	Millbury
29	0.1	Lakeview Local	Cortland
29	0.1	Lakewood City	Lakewood
29	0.1	Lakota Local	Liberty Twp
29	0.1	Lancaster City	Lancaster
29	0.1	Lexington Local	Lexington
29	0.1	London City	London
29	0.1	Madison Local	Madison
29	0.1	Mansfield City	Mansfield
29	0.1	Mariemont City	Cincinnati
29	0.1	Mason City SD	Mason
29	0.1	Miamisburg City	Miamisburg
29	0.1	Middletown City	Middletown
29	0.1	Minerva Local	Minerva
29	0.1	Morgan Local	Mc Connelsville
29	0.1	Mount Vernon City	Mount Vernon
29	0.1	Mt Healthy City	Cincinnati
29	0.1	New Albany-Plain Local	New Albany
29	0.1	New Lexington City	New Lexington
29	0.1	New Richmond Exempted Village	New Richmond
29	0.1	Newark City	Newark
29	0.1	N Ridgeville City	N Ridgeville
29	0.1	Northeastern Local	Springfield
29	0.1	Northmont City	Englewood
29	0.1	Northwest Local	Cincinnati
29	0.1	Northwest Local	Canal Fulton
29	0.1	Ohio Connections Academy, Inc	Cleveland
29	0.1	Ohio Virtual Academy	Maumee
29	0.1	Oregon City	Oregon
29	0.1	Perkins Local	Sandusky
29	0.1	Piqua City	Piqua
29	0.1	Plain Local	Canton
29	0.1	Port Clinton City	Port Clinton
29	0.1	Portsmouth City	Portsmouth
29	0.1	Reading Community City	Reading
29	0.1	River Valley Local	Caledonia
29	0.1	Riverside Local	Painesville
29	0.1	Rolling Hills Local	Cambridge
29	0.1	Sheffield-Sheffield Lake City	Sheffield Vllg
29	0.1	Solon City	Solon
29	0.1	South Point Local	South Point
29	0.1	Southwest Licking Local	Pataskala
29	0.1	Springfield City	Springfield
29	0.1	Springfield Local	Holland
29	0.1	Springfield Local	Akron
29	0.1	Strongsville City	Strongsville
29	0.1	Sylvania City	Sylvania
29	0.1	Tecumseh Local	New Carlisle
29	0.1	Treca Digital Academy	Marion
29	0.1	Troy City	Troy
29	0.1	Twinsburg City	Twinsburg
29	0.1	Valley View Local	Germantown
29	0.1	Vandalia-Butler City	Vandalia
29	0.1	Vermilion Local	Vermilion
29	0.1	Wapakoneta City	Wapakoneta
29	0.1	Waverly City	Waverly
29	0.1	West Carrollton City	West Carrollton
29	0.1	Westerville City	Westerville
29	0.1	Willoughby-Eastlake City	Willoughby
29	0.1	Wilmington City	Wilmington
29	0.1	Wooster City	Wooster
29	0.1	Worthington City	Worthington
29	0.1	Wyoming City	Wyoming
135	0.0	Alexander Local	Albany
135	0.0	Alliance City	Alliance
135	0.0	Amherst Exempted Village	Amherst
135	0.0	Anthony Wayne Local	Whitehouse
135	0.0	Ashtabula Area City	Ashtabula
135	0.0	Athens City	The Plains
135	0.0	Avon Lake City	Avon Lake
135	0.0	Avon Local	Avon
135	0.0	Barberton City	Barberton
135	0.0	Bedford City	Bedford
135	0.0	Bellbrook-Sugarcreek Local SD	Bellbrook
135	0.0	Benton Carroll Salem Local	Oak Harbor
135	0.0	Bethel-Tate Local	Bethel
135	0.0	Bexley City	Bexley
135	0.0	Big Walnut Local	Sunbury
135	0.0	Bloom-Carroll Local	Carroll
135	0.0	Bowling Green City SD	Bowling Green
135	0.0	Brecksville-Broadview Heights City	Brecksville
135	0.0	Bryan City	Bryan
135	0.0	Buckeye Local	Medina
135	0.0	Buckeye Local	Dillonvale
135	0.0	Buckeye Valley Local	Delaware
135	0.0	Cambridge City	Cambridge
135	0.0	Canfield Local	Canfield
135	0.0	Canton Local	Canton
135	0.0	Carlisle Local	Carlisle
135	0.0	Carrollton Exempted Village	Carrollton
135	0.0	Centerville City	Centerville
135	0.0	Chagrin Falls Exempted Village	Chagrin Falls
135	0.0	Chardon Local	Chardon
135	0.0	Chillicothe City	Chillicothe
135	0.0	Claymont City	Dennison
135	0.0	Clearview Local	Lorain
135	0.0	Clermont Northeastern Local	Batavia
135	0.0	Cleveland Heights-Univ Hgts City	University Hgts
135	0.0	Clinton-Massie Local	Clarksville
135	0.0	Cloverleaf Local	Lodi
135	0.0	Columbus City SD	Columbus
135	0.0	Copley-Fairlawn City	Copley
135	0.0	Coshocton City	Coshocton
135	0.0	Crestwood Local	Mantua
135	0.0	Cuyahoga Falls City	Cuyahoga Falls
135	0.0	Dayton City	Dayton
135	0.0	Defiance City	Defiance
135	0.0	Delaware City	Delaware
135	0.0	East Cleveland City SD	East Cleveland
135	0.0	East Holmes Local	Berlin
135	0.0	East Liverpool City	East Liverpool
135	0.0	East Muskingum Local	New Concord
135	0.0	Eaton Community City	Eaton
135	0.0	Edgewood City	Trenton
135	0.0	Edison Local	Hammondsville
135	0.0	Elida Local	Elida
135	0.0	Elyria City Schools	Elyria
135	0.0	Euclid City	Euclid
135	0.0	Fairfield City	Fairfield
135	0.0	Fairland Local	Proctorville
135	0.0	Fairless Local	Navarre
135	0.0	Fairview Park City	Fairview Park
135	0.0	Firelands Local	South Amherst

Note: This section only includes districts with 1,500 or more students; All categories are ranked from high to low

135	0.0	Forest Hills Local	Cincinnati
135	0.0	Fostoria City	Fostoria
135	0.0	Franklin Local	Duncan Falls
135	0.0	Fremont City	Fremont
135	0.0	Gahanna-Jefferson City	Gahanna
135	0.0	Gallia County Local	Gallipolis
135	0.0	Gallipolis City	Gallipolis
135	0.0	Girard City SD	Girard
135	0.0	Goshen Local	Goshen
135	0.0	Granville Exempted Village	Granville
135	0.0	Green Local	Uniontown
135	0.0	Greenfield Exempted Village	Greenfield
135	0.0	Greenon Local	Enon
135	0.0	Greenville City	Greenville
135	0.0	Hamilton Local	Columbus
135	0.0	Harrison Hills City	Cadiz
135	0.0	Heath City	Heath
135	0.0	Highland Local	Sparta
135	0.0	Hillsboro City	Hillsboro
135	0.0	Howland Local	Warren
135	0.0	Hudson City	Hudson
135	0.0	Indian Creek Local	Wintersville
135	0.0	Indian Lake Local	Lewistown
135	0.0	Jackson City	Jackson
135	0.0	Jackson Local	Massillon
135	0.0	Jefferson Area Local	Jefferson
135	0.0	Johnstown-Monroe Local	Johnstown
135	0.0	Jonathan Alder Local	Plain City
135	0.0	Kenston Local	Chagrin Falls
135	0.0	Kent City	Kent
135	0.0	Kenton City	Kenton
135	0.0	Keystone Local	Lagrange
135	0.0	Lakewood Local	Hebron
135	0.0	Lebanon City	Lebanon
135	0.0	Licking Heights Local	Pataskala
135	0.0	Licking Valley Local	Newark
135	0.0	Lima City	Lima
135	0.0	Little Miami Local	Maineville
135	0.0	Logan Elm Local	Circleville
135	0.0	Logan-Hocking Local	Logan
135	0.0	Lorain City	Lorain
135	0.0	Louisville City	Louisville
135	0.0	Loveland City	Loveland
135	0.0	Madison Local	Mansfield
135	0.0	Maple Heights City	Maple Heights
135	0.0	Marietta City	Marietta
135	0.0	Marion City	Marion
135	0.0	Marlington Local	Alliance
135	0.0	Marysville Exempted Village	Marysville
135	0.0	Massillon City	Massillon
135	0.0	Maumee City	Maumee
135	0.0	Mayfield City	Mayfield Hgts
135	0.0	Maysville Local	Zanesville
135	0.0	Medina City SD	Medina
135	0.0	Meigs Local	Pomeroy
135	0.0	Mentor Exempted Village	Mentor
135	0.0	Midview Local	Grafton
135	0.0	Milford Exempted Village	Milford
135	0.0	Minford Local	Minford
135	0.0	Monroe Local SD	Monroe
135	0.0	Napoleon Area City	Napoleon
135	0.0	New Philadel. City	New Philadel.
135	0.0	Niles City	Niles
135	0.0	Nordonia Hills City	Northfield
135	0.0	North Canton City	North Canton
135	0.0	North College Hill City	Cincinnati
135	0.0	North Fork Local	Utica
135	0.0	North Olmsted City	North Olmsted
135	0.0	North Royalton City	North Royalton
135	0.0	Northern Local	Thornville
135	0.0	Northwest Local	Mc Dermott
135	0.0	Norton City	Norton
135	0.0	Norwalk City	Norwalk
135	0.0	Norwood City	Norwood
135	0.0	Oak Hills Local	Cincinnati
135	0.0	Oakwood City	Dayton
135	0.0	Olentangy Local	Lewis Center
135	0.0	Orrville City	Orrville
135	0.0	Ottawa-Glandorf Local	Ottawa
135	0.0	Painesville City Local	Painesville
135	0.0	Parma City	Parma
135	0.0	Perry Local	Perry
135	0.0	Perry Local	Massillon
135	0.0	Perrysburg Exempted Village	Perrysburg
135	0.0	Pickerington Local	Pickerington
135	0.0	Poland Local	Poland
135	0.0	Ravenna City	Ravenna
135	0.0	Revere Local	Bath
135	0.0	Reynoldsburg City	Reynoldsburg
135	0.0	River View Local	Warsaw
135	0.0	Rocky River City	Rocky River
135	0.0	Ross Local	Hamilton
135	0.0	Rossford Exempted Village	Rossford
135	0.0	Salem City	Salem
135	0.0	Sandusky City	Sandusky
135	0.0	Shaker Heights City	Shaker Heights
135	0.0	Shawnee Local	Lima
135	0.0	Shelby City	Shelby
135	0.0	South Euclid-Lyndhurst City	Lyndhurst
135	0.0	South-Western City	Grove City
135	0.0	Southeast Local	Ravenna
135	0.0	Southwest Local	Harrison
135	0.0	Springboro Community City	Springboro
135	0.0	Saint Clairsville-Richland City	Saint Clairsville
135	0.0	Saint Marys City	Saint Marys
135	0.0	Steubenville City	Steubenville
135	0.0	Stow-Munroe Falls City SD	Stow
135	0.0	Struthers City	Struthers
135	0.0	Switzerland of Ohio Local	Woodsfield
135	0.0	Sycamore Community City	Blue Ash
135	0.0	Teays Valley Local	Ashville
135	0.0	Three Rivers Local	Cleves
135	0.0	Tiffin City	Tiffin
135	0.0	Tipp City Exempted Village	Tipp City
135	0.0	Toledo City	Toledo
135	0.0	Tri-Valley Local	Dresden
135	0.0	Triway Local	Wooster
135	0.0	Trotwood-Madison City	Trotwood
135	0.0	Union-Scioto Local	Chillicothe
135	0.0	Upper Arlington City	Upper Arlington
135	0.0	Upper Sandusky Exempted Village	Upper Sandusky
135	0.0	Urbana City	Urbana
135	0.0	Van Wert City	Van Wert
135	0.0	Vinton County Local	Mc Arthur
135	0.0	Wadsworth City	Wadsworth
135	0.0	Warren City	Warren
135	0.0	Warren Local	Vincent
135	0.0	Washington CH City	Washington CH
135	0.0	Washington Local	Toledo
135	0.0	Wauseon Exempted Village	Wauseon
135	0.0	West Branch Local	Beloit
135	0.0	West Clermont Local	Cincinnati
135	0.0	West Geauga Local	Chesterland
135	0.0	West Holmes Local	Millersburg
135	0.0	Western Brown Local	Mount Orab
135	0.0	Westfall Local	Williamsport
135	0.0	Wheelersburg Local	Wheelersburg
135	0.0	Whitehall City	Whitehall
135	0.0	Willard City	Willard
135	0.0	Woodridge Local	Peninsula
135	0.0	Xenia Community City	Xenia
135	0.0	Youngstown City Schools	Youngstown
135	0.0	Zanesville City	Zanesville

Students who are Two or More Races

Rank	Percent	District Name	City
1	17.9	Zanesville City	Zanesville
2	17.7	Sandusky City	Sandusky
3	17.6	Fostoria City	Fostoria
4	15.9	Lima City	Lima
5	14.2	Canton City	Canton
6	13.4	Elyria City Schools	Elyria
7	13.2	Alliance City	Alliance
8	12.9	Warren City	Warren
9	12.6	Mansfield City	Mansfield
9	12.6	Steubenville City	Steubenville
11	12.0	Clearview Local	Lorain
12	11.8	Chillicothe City	Chillicothe
13	11.5	Ashtabula Area City	Ashtabula
14	11.0	Bellefontaine City	Bellefontaine
15	10.5	Springfield City	Springfield
16	10.3	Fremont City	Fremont
17	10.1	Painesville City Local	Painesville
18	9.8	Kent City	Kent
18	9.8	Middletown City	Middletown
18	9.8	Reynoldsburg City	Reynoldsburg
18	9.8	Xenia Community City	Xenia
22	9.5	Portsmouth City	Portsmouth
23	9.4	Huber Heights City	Huber Heights
23	9.4	Massillon City	Massillon
23	9.4	Springfield Local	Holland
26	9.1	Lorain City	Lorain
27	9.0	Northwest Local	Cincinnati
28	8.9	Ravenna City	Ravenna
29	8.8	Sidney City	Sidney
30	8.6	Urbana City	Urbana
30	8.6	Winton Woods City	Cincinnati
32	8.4	Elida Local	Elida
32	8.4	Newark City	Newark
34	8.3	North College Hill City	Cincinnati
35	8.2	Toledo City	Toledo
36	7.9	Orrville City	Orrville
36	7.9	Piqua City	Piqua
38	7.7	Mt Healthy City	Cincinnati
38	7.7	Washington Local	Toledo
40	7.5	Canal Wnchstr Local	Canal Wnchstr
40	7.5	Plain Local	Canton
40	7.5	Whitehall City	Whitehall
43	7.4	Akron City	Akron
44	7.2	Marion City	Marion
44	7.2	Worthington City	Worthington
46	7.1	Fairborn City	Fairborn
46	7.1	Gahanna-Jefferson City	Gahanna
46	7.1	Licking Heights Local	Pataskala
46	7.1	Pickerington Local	Pickerington
46	7.1	Wilmington City	Wilmington
51	6.9	Heath City	Heath
51	6.9	Woodridge Local	Peninsula
53	6.8	Troy City	Troy
54	6.7	Mad River Local	Dayton
54	6.7	South Euclid-Lyndhurst City	Lyndhurst
54	6.7	Westerville City	Westerville
57	6.6	Lakewood City	Lakewood
57	6.6	Perkins Local	Sandusky
57	6.6	Port Clinton City	Port Clinton
57	6.6	Shaker Heights City	Shaker Heights
61	6.5	Batavia Local	Batavia
62	6.4	Vandalia-Butler City	Vandalia
62	6.4	West Carrollton City	West Carrollton
64	6.3	Bowling Green City SD	Bowling Green
64	6.3	Delaware City	Delaware
64	6.3	Northmont City	Englewood
67	6.2	Alternative Education Academy	Toledo
67	6.2	Princeton City	Cincinnati
67	6.2	Union-Scioto Local	Chillicothe
70	6.1	Morgan Local	Mc Connelsville
70	6.1	Shawnee Local	Lima
70	6.1	Wooster City	Wooster
73	6.0	Wyoming City	Wyoming
74	5.9	Cincinnati City	Cincinnati
74	5.9	Electronic Classroom of Tomorrow	Columbus
74	5.9	Hamilton Local	Columbus
77	5.8	East Liverpool City	East Liverpool
77	5.8	Findlay City	Findlay
77	5.8	Ohio Connections Academy, Inc	Cleveland
77	5.8	Sycamore Community City	Blue Ash
77	5.8	Youngstown City Schools	Youngstown
82	5.7	Berea City	Berea
82	5.7	Bexley City	Bexley
82	5.7	Canton Local	Canton
82	5.7	Ontario Local	Mansfield
86	5.6	Niles City	Niles
86	5.6	Struthers City	Struthers
88	5.5	Barberton City	Barberton
88	5.5	Dublin City	Dublin
88	5.5	South Point Local	South Point
88	5.5	Treca Digital Academy	Marion
92	5.4	Columbus City SD	Columbus
92	5.4	Fairfield City	Fairfield
92	5.4	Girard City SD	Girard
92	5.4	Howland Local	Warren
96	5.3	Boardman Local	Youngstown
96	5.3	Circleville City	Circleville
96	5.3	London City	London
96	5.3	Orange City	Cleveland
100	5.2	Bedford City	Bedford
100	5.2	Clark-Shawnee Local	Springfield
100	5.2	Maumee City	Maumee
100	5.2	Washington CH City	Washington CH
104	5.1	Benjamin Logan Local	Bellefontaine

Note: This section only includes districts with 1,500 or more students; All categories are ranked from high to low

104	5.1	Cleveland Heights-Univ Hgts City	University Hgts
106	5.0	Coshocton City	Coshocton
106	5.0	Saint Clairsville-Richland City	Saint Clairsville
108	4.9	Dayton City	Dayton
108	4.9	Garfield Hgts City Schools	Garfield Hgts
108	4.9	Hillsboro City	Hillsboro
108	4.9	Tallmadge City	Tallmadge
112	4.8	Cuyahoga Falls City	Cuyahoga Falls
112	4.8	Madison Local	Mansfield
112	4.8	Norwood City	Norwood
112	4.8	Southwest Licking Local	Pataskala
116	4.7	Euclid City	Euclid
116	4.7	Lexington Local	Lexington
116	4.7	Mayfield City	Mayfield Hgts
119	4.6	Athens City	The Plains
119	4.6	Kettering City	Kettering
119	4.6	Miami Trace Local	Washington CH
119	4.6	North Olmsted City	North Olmsted
119	4.6	Perry Local	Massillon
119	4.6	Twinsburg City	Twinsburg
125	4.5	Lakota Local	Liberty Twp
125	4.5	Northridge Local	Dayton
125	4.5	South-Western City	Grove City
128	4.4	New Albany-Plain Local	New Albany
129	4.3	Buckeye Local	Ashtabula
129	4.3	Hilliard City	Columbus
129	4.3	Indian Creek Local	Wintersville
129	4.3	Mason City SD	Mason
129	4.3	Mount Vernon City	Mount Vernon
134	4.2	Northeastern Local	Springfield
134	4.2	Solon City	Solon
136	4.1	Ashland City	Ashland
136	4.1	Tiffin City	Tiffin
138	4.0	Amherst Exempted Village	Amherst
138	4.0	Centerville City	Centerville
138	4.0	Madison Local	Madison
138	4.0	Rossford Exempted Village	Rossford
142	3.9	Conneaut Area City	Conneaut
142	3.9	Copley-Fairlawn City	Copley
142	3.9	Hamilton City	Hamilton
142	3.9	Indian Hill Exempted Village	Cincinnati
142	3.9	Lake Local	Millbury
142	3.9	Maysville Local	Zanesville
142	3.9	Nordonia Hills City	Northfield
142	3.9	Norwalk City	Norwalk
142	3.9	Riverside Local	Painesville
151	3.8	Fairview Park City	Fairview Park
151	3.8	Lebanon City	Lebanon
151	3.8	River Valley Local	Caledonia
154	3.7	Miamisburg City	Miamisburg
154	3.7	Olentangy Local	Lewis Center
154	3.7	Strongsville City	Strongsville
157	3.6	Bellevue City	Bellevue
157	3.6	Greenon Local	Enon
157	3.6	Upper Arlington City	Upper Arlington
160	3.5	Groveport Madison Local	Groveport
160	3.5	Harrison Hills City	Cadiz
160	3.5	Kings Local	Kings Mills
160	3.5	Rolling Hills Local	Cambridge
164	3.4	Beavercreek City	Beavercreek
164	3.4	Cambridge City	Cambridge
164	3.4	Clyde-Green Springs Exempted Village	Clyde
164	3.4	Streetsboro City	Streetsboro
164	3.4	Willoughby-Eastlake City	Willoughby
169	3.3	Forest Hills Local	Cincinnati
169	3.3	Indian Lake Local	Lewistown
169	3.3	Midview Local	Grafton
169	3.3	Monroe Local SD	Monroe
169	3.3	Oak Hills Local	Cincinnati
169	3.3	Saint Marys City	Saint Marys
169	3.3	Van Wert City	Van Wert
169	3.3	Wauseon Exempted Village	Wauseon
177	3.2	Bellbrook-Sugarcreek Local SD	Bellbrook
177	3.2	Benton Carroll Salem Local	Oak Harbor
177	3.2	Firelands Local	South Amherst
177	3.2	Mariemont City	Cincinnati
177	3.2	Reading Community City	Reading
177	3.2	Stow-Munroe Falls City SD	Stow
177	3.2	Westlake City	Westlake
184	3.1	Goshen Local	Goshen
184	3.1	Jackson Local	Massillon
184	3.1	Maple Heights City	Maple Heights
184	3.1	Medina City SD	Medina
184	3.1	Rocky River City	Rocky River
184	3.1	Sylvania City	Sylvania
184	3.1	Talawanda City	Oxford
191	3.0	Gallipolis City	Gallipolis
191	3.0	Greenville City	Greenville
191	3.0	Kenston Local	Chagrin Falls
191	3.0	Marietta City	Marietta
191	3.0	Parma City	Parma
191	3.0	Sheffield-Sheffield Lake City	Sheffield Vllg
191	3.0	West Clermont Local	Cincinnati
198	2.9	Austintown Local	Youngstown
198	2.9	Big Walnut Local	Sunbury
198	2.9	Brunswick City	Brunswick
198	2.9	Claymont City	Dennison
198	2.9	Defiance City	Defiance
198	2.9	Eaton Community City	Eaton
198	2.9	Geneva Area City	Geneva
198	2.9	New Philadel. City	New Philadel.
198	2.9	New Richmond Exempted Village	New Richmond
198	2.9	Willard City	Willard
208	2.8	Cleveland Municipal	Cleveland
208	2.8	Edgewood City	Trenton
208	2.8	Kenton City	Kenton
208	2.8	Mentor Exempted Village	Mentor
208	2.8	N Ridgeville City	N Ridgeville
208	2.8	Northwestern Local	Springfield
208	2.8	Oakwood City	Dayton
208	2.8	Perrysburg Exempted Village	Perrysburg
208	2.8	Revere Local	Bath
208	2.8	Tecumseh Local	New Carlisle
208	2.8	Three Rivers Local	Cleves
219	2.7	Brecksville-Broadview Heights City	Brecksville
219	2.7	Clermont Northeastern Local	Batavia
219	2.7	Keystone Local	Lagrange
219	2.7	Milford Exempted Village	Milford
219	2.7	North Royalton City	North Royalton
219	2.7	Tri-Valley Local	Dresden
219	2.7	Trotwood-Madison City	Trotwood
219	2.7	Wheelersburg Local	Wheelersburg
227	2.6	Lakeview Local	Cortland
227	2.6	Springboro Community City	Springboro
229	2.5	Avon Lake City	Avon Lake
229	2.5	Greenfield Exempted Village	Greenfield
229	2.5	Hudson City	Hudson
229	2.5	Lakewood Local	Hebron
229	2.5	Lancaster City	Lancaster
229	2.5	Perry Local	Perry
229	2.5	Springfield Local	Akron
229	2.5	Wadsworth City	Wadsworth
237	2.4	Edison Local (Formerly Berlin-Milan)	Milan
237	2.4	Field Local	Mogadore
237	2.4	Franklin City	Franklin
237	2.4	Galion City	Galion
237	2.4	Jefferson Area Local	Jefferson
237	2.4	Marysville Exempted Village	Marysville
237	2.4	Napoleon Area City	Napoleon
237	2.4	Oregon City	Oregon
245	2.3	Anthony Wayne Local	Whitehouse
245	2.3	Bay Village City	Bay Village
245	2.3	Buckeye Valley Local	Delaware
245	2.3	Coventry Local	Akron
245	2.3	Crestwood Local	Mantua
245	2.3	Norton City	Norton
245	2.3	Teays Valley Local	Ashville
252	2.2	Green Local	Uniontown
252	2.2	Little Miami Local	Maineville
252	2.2	Marlington Local	Alliance
255	2.1	Aurora City	Aurora
255	2.1	Avon Local	Avon
255	2.1	Buckeye Local	Medina
255	2.1	Fairland Local	Proctorville
255	2.1	Granville Exempted Village	Granville
255	2.1	Lake Local	Uniontown
255	2.1	Logan-Hocking Local	Logan
255	2.1	North Canton City	North Canton
255	2.1	Salem City	Salem
255	2.1	Tipp City Exempted Village	Tipp City
255	2.1	Valley View Local	Germantown
255	2.1	Waverly City	Waverly
267	2.0	Bryan City	Bryan
267	2.0	Cloverleaf Local	Lodi
267	2.0	Franklin Local	Duncan Falls
267	2.0	Hubbard Exempted Village	Hubbard
267	2.0	Loveland City	Loveland
267	2.0	Southwest Local	Harrison
273	1.9	Buckeye Local	Dillonvale
273	1.9	Carlisle Local	Carlisle
273	1.9	Celina City	Celina
273	1.9	Chagrin Falls Exempted Village	Chagrin Falls
273	1.9	Vermilion Local	Vermilion
273	1.9	West Branch Local	Beloit
279	1.8	Alexander Local	Albany
279	1.8	Madison Local	Middletown
279	1.8	Meigs Local	Pomeroy
279	1.8	Minerva Local	Minerva
279	1.8	Olmsted Falls City	Olmsted Falls
279	1.8	Poland Local	Poland
279	1.8	Shelby City	Shelby
279	1.8	Upper Sandusky Exempted Village	Upper Sandusky
287	1.7	Bath Local	Lima
287	1.7	Bloom-Carroll Local	Carroll
287	1.7	Canfield Local	Canfield
287	1.7	Chardon Local	Chardon
287	1.7	Johnstown-Monroe Local	Johnstown
287	1.7	Jonathan Alder Local	Plain City
287	1.7	Louisville City	Louisville
287	1.7	Ottawa-Glandorf Local	Ottawa
287	1.7	Triway Local	Wooster
296	1.6	Clear Fork Valley Local	Bellville
296	1.6	East Muskingum Local	New Concord
296	1.6	Graham Local	Saint Paris
296	1.6	Licking Valley Local	Newark
296	1.6	River View Local	Warsaw
296	1.6	Warren Local	Vincent
302	1.5	Bethel-Tate Local	Bethel
302	1.5	Blanchester Local	Blanchester
302	1.5	Dover City	Dover
302	1.5	Fairfield Union Local	Lancaster
302	1.5	Fairless Local	Navarre
302	1.5	Jackson City	Jackson
302	1.5	Minford Local	Minford
302	1.5	New Lexington City	New Lexington
310	1.3	Beaver Local	Lisbon
310	1.3	Gallia County Local	Gallipolis
310	1.3	Indian Valley Local Schools	Gnadenhutten
310	1.3	Northern Local	Thornville
310	1.3	Wapakoneta City	Wapakoneta
315	1.2	Highland Local	Medina
315	1.2	Ross Local	Hamilton
317	1.1	Carrollton Exempted Village	Carrollton
317	1.1	Clinton-Massie Local	Clarksville
317	1.1	Highland Local	Sparta
317	1.1	West Muskingum Local	Zanesville
321	1.0	Switzerland of Ohio Local	Woodsfield
321	1.0	Vinton County Local	Mc Arthur
321	1.0	West Geauga Local	Chesterland
324	0.9	Amanda-Clearcreek Local	Amanda
324	0.9	Edison Local	Hammondsville
324	0.9	North Fork Local	Utica
324	0.9	Northwest Local	Canal Fulton
324	0.9	Ohio Virtual Academy	Maumee
324	0.9	West Holmes Local	Millersburg
324	0.9	Western Brown Local	Mount Orab
324	0.9	Westfall Local	Williamsport
332	0.8	East Holmes Local	Berlin
332	0.8	Logan Elm Local	Circleville
332	0.8	Northwest Local	Mc Dermott
335	0.6	Adams County/Ohio Valley Local	West Union
335	0.6	East Cleveland City SD	East Cleveland
337	0.3	Southeast Local	Ravenna

Hispanic Students

Rank	Percent	District Name	City
1	46.4	Painesville City Local	Painesville
2	36.4	Lorain City	Lorain
3	29.7	Clearview Local	Lorain
4	25.8	Willard City	Willard
5	22.0	Defiance City	Defiance
6	21.2	Fremont City	Fremont
7	18.0	Princeton City	Cincinnati
8	17.7	Fostoria City	Fostoria
9	17.6	Whitehall City	Whitehall
10	16.2	Wauseon Exempted Village	Wauseon
11	14.7	Cleveland Municipal	Cleveland
12	13.9	Youngstown City Schools	Youngstown
13	13.8	South-Western City	Grove City
14	13.6	Ashtabula Area City	Ashtabula

Note: This section only includes districts with 1,500 or more students; All categories are ranked from high to low

15	12.6	Amherst Exempted Village	Amherst
16	12.3	Tecumseh Local	New Carlisle
17	12.1	Ottawa-Glandorf Local	Ottawa
18	11.9	Winton Woods City	Cincinnati
19	11.5	Norwalk City	Norwalk
20	11.2	Toledo City	Toledo
21	11.0	Hamilton City	Hamilton
21	11.0	Lake Local	Millbury
23	10.8	Oregon City	Oregon
24	9.9	Napoleon Area City	Napoleon
25	9.5	Norwood City	Norwood
26	9.4	Bowling Green City SD	Bowling Green
26	9.4	Clyde-Green Springs Exempted Village	Clyde
28	9.3	Elyria City Schools	Elyria
29	9.1	Port Clinton City	Port Clinton
30	9.0	Rossford Exempted Village	Rossford
31	8.8	Columbus City SD	Columbus
32	8.7	Washington Local	Toledo
33	8.4	Sheffield-Sheffield Lake City	Sheffield Vllg
34	8.2	Middletown City	Middletown
35	7.9	Worthington City	Worthington
36	7.8	Fairfield City	Fairfield
37	7.5	Perry Local	Perry
38	7.2	Findlay City	Findlay
39	7.0	New Philadel. City	New Philadel.
39	7.0	Orrville City	Orrville
39	7.0	Parma City	Parma
42	6.6	Monroe Local SD	Monroe
42	6.6	Perrysburg Exempted Village	Perrysburg
44	6.5	Geneva Area City	Geneva
45	6.3	Berea City	Berea
46	6.2	Hilliard City	Columbus
46	6.2	Lakewood City	Lakewood
48	5.9	Springfield Local	Holland
49	5.8	Bryan City	Bryan
49	5.8	Dover City	Dover
51	5.7	Marion City	Marion
52	5.6	Boardman Local	Youngstown
52	5.6	Lakota Local	Liberty Twp
52	5.6	West Carrollton City	West Carrollton
55	5.5	Huber Heights City	Huber Heights
55	5.5	Reynoldsburg City	Reynoldsburg
55	5.5	Struthers City	Struthers
58	5.4	Dublin City	Dublin
58	5.4	Lebanon City	Lebanon
58	5.4	Westerville City	Westerville
61	5.3	Electronic Classroom of Tomorrow	Columbus
61	5.3	Upper Sandusky Exempted Village	Upper Sandusky
63	5.0	Alternative Education Academy	Toledo
63	5.0	Gahanna-Jefferson City	Gahanna
63	5.0	Kings Local	Kings Mills
63	5.0	Mad River Local	Dayton
63	5.0	Springfield City	Springfield
68	4.8	Groveport Madison Local	Groveport
68	4.8	Riverside Local	Painesville
68	4.8	Treca Digital Academy	Marion
71	4.7	North Olmsted City	North Olmsted
71	4.7	Sycamore Community City	Blue Ash
71	4.7	Wilmington City	Wilmington
74	4.5	Benton Carroll Salem Local	Oak Harbor
74	4.5	Madison Local	Madison
76	4.4	Pickerington Local	Pickerington
77	4.3	Bellevue City	Bellevue
77	4.3	Ohio Connections Academy, Inc	Cleveland
77	4.3	Westlake City	Westlake
80	4.2	Fairview Park City	Fairview Park
80	4.2	Lima City	Lima
82	4.1	Anthony Wayne Local	Whitehouse
82	4.1	Elida Local	Elida
82	4.1	Marlington Local	Alliance
82	4.1	Maumee City	Maumee
86	4.0	Austintown Local	Youngstown
86	4.0	Delaware City	Delaware
86	4.0	Edison Local (Formerly Berlin-Milan)	Milan
86	4.0	Tiffin City	Tiffin
90	3.9	Bellbrook-Sugarcreek Local SD	Bellbrook
90	3.9	Hamilton Local	Columbus
90	3.9	Portsmouth City	Portsmouth
90	3.9	Vermilion Local	Vermilion
94	3.8	Canton City	Canton
94	3.8	Dayton City	Dayton
94	3.8	Fairborn City	Fairborn
94	3.8	Mason City SD	Mason
94	3.8	Van Wert City	Van Wert
99	3.7	Cincinnati City	Cincinnati
99	3.7	Licking Heights Local	Pataskala
101	3.6	N Ridgeville City	N Ridgeville
102	3.5	Bath Local	Lima
103	3.4	Akron City	Akron
103	3.4	Avon Local	Avon
103	3.4	Firelands Local	South Amherst
106	3.3	Canal Wnchstr Local	Canal Wnchstr
106	3.3	Midview Local	Grafton
106	3.3	Mount Vernon City	Mount Vernon
106	3.3	Plain Local	Canton
110	3.2	Strongsville City	Strongsville
111	3.1	Athens City	The Plains
111	3.1	Kent City	Kent
111	3.1	Ravenna City	Ravenna
111	3.1	Rocky River City	Rocky River
115	3.0	Bedford City	Bedford
115	3.0	Jonathan Alder Local	Plain City
115	3.0	Mt Healthy City	Cincinnati
115	3.0	New Albany-Plain Local	New Albany
115	3.0	Northridge Local	Dayton
115	3.0	Oakwood City	Dayton
115	3.0	Tallmadge City	Tallmadge
115	3.0	Woodridge Local	Peninsula
123	2.9	North Royalton City	North Royalton
123	2.9	Northwest Local	Cincinnati
125	2.8	Chillicothe City	Chillicothe
125	2.8	Mansfield City	Mansfield
125	2.8	Miamisburg City	Miamisburg
125	2.8	Salem City	Salem
125	2.8	Shawnee Local	Lima
125	2.8	Warren City	Warren
125	2.8	Washington CH City	Washington CH
125	2.8	Wooster City	Wooster
133	2.7	Celina City	Celina
133	2.7	Garfield Hgts City Schools	Garfield Hgts
133	2.7	Girard City SD	Girard
133	2.7	Little Miami Local	Maineville
133	2.7	Southwest Local	Harrison
138	2.6	Buckeye Valley Local	Delaware
138	2.6	Chardon Local	Chardon
138	2.6	Cleveland Heights-Univ Hgts City	University Hgts
138	2.6	Goshen Local	Goshen
138	2.6	Massillon City	Massillon
138	2.6	Miami Trace Local	Washington CH
138	2.6	Olentangy Local	Lewis Center
138	2.6	Sandusky City	Sandusky
146	2.5	Avon Lake City	Avon Lake
146	2.5	Brunswick City	Brunswick
146	2.5	Buckeye Local	Ashtabula
146	2.5	Conneaut Area City	Conneaut
146	2.5	Johnstown-Monroe Local	Johnstown
146	2.5	Kenton City	Kenton
146	2.5	Loveland City	Loveland
146	2.5	Streetsboro City	Streetsboro
146	2.5	Sylvania City	Sylvania
146	2.5	Twinsburg City	Twinsburg
146	2.5	Vandalia-Butler City	Vandalia
146	2.5	Xenia Community City	Xenia
158	2.4	Batavia Local	Batavia
158	2.4	Beavercreek City	Beavercreek
158	2.4	Brecksville-Broadview Heights City	Brecksville
158	2.4	Lexington Local	Lexington
158	2.4	Milford Exempted Village	Milford
158	2.4	Northwestern Local	Springfield
158	2.4	Perry Local	Massillon
158	2.4	Shaker Heights City	Shaker Heights
158	2.4	Troy City	Troy
167	2.3	Alliance City	Alliance
167	2.3	Bay Village City	Bay Village
167	2.3	Forest Hills Local	Cincinnati
167	2.3	Indian Lake Local	Lewistown
167	2.3	Northeastern Local	Springfield
172	2.2	Big Walnut Local	Sunbury
172	2.2	Indian Hill Exempted Village	Cincinnati
172	2.2	Kettering City	Kettering
172	2.2	Mayfield City	Mayfield Hgts
172	2.2	Olmsted Falls City	Olmsted Falls
172	2.2	Perkins Local	Sandusky
172	2.2	Sidney City	Sidney
172	2.2	Union-Scioto Local	Chillicothe
172	2.2	Urbana City	Urbana
181	2.1	Aurora City	Aurora
181	2.1	Carlisle Local	Carlisle
181	2.1	Greenon Local	Enon
181	2.1	Heath City	Heath
181	2.1	Madison Local	Mansfield
181	2.1	River Valley Local	Caledonia
181	2.1	Shelby City	Shelby
181	2.1	Tipp City Exempted Village	Tipp City
181	2.1	West Clermont Local	Cincinnati
181	2.1	West Geauga Local	Chesterland
191	2.0	Centerville City	Centerville
191	2.0	Highland Local	Sparta
191	2.0	Jefferson Area Local	Jefferson
191	2.0	Lakewood Local	Hebron
191	2.0	Piqua City	Piqua
191	2.0	South Euclid-Lyndhurst City	Lyndhurst
191	2.0	Talawanda City	Oxford
191	2.0	Wyoming City	Wyoming
199	1.9	Ashland City	Ashland
199	1.9	Bexley City	Bexley
199	1.9	Circleville City	Circleville
199	1.9	Clinton-Massie Local	Clarksville
199	1.9	Mariemont City	Cincinnati
199	1.9	Medina City SD	Medina
199	1.9	Poland Local	Poland
199	1.9	Solon City	Solon
199	1.9	Southwest Licking Local	Pataskala
208	1.8	Canfield Local	Canfield
208	1.8	Clark-Shawnee Local	Springfield
208	1.8	Clear Fork Valley Local	Bellville
208	1.8	Copley-Fairlawn City	Copley
208	1.8	London City	London
208	1.8	Mentor Exempted Village	Mentor
208	1.8	Northmont City	Englewood
208	1.8	Reading Community City	Reading
208	1.8	Saint Marys City	Saint Marys
208	1.8	Wadsworth City	Wadsworth
218	1.7	Graham Local	Saint Paris
218	1.7	Hudson City	Hudson
218	1.7	Keystone Local	Lagrange
218	1.7	Newark City	Newark
218	1.7	Nordonia Hills City	Northfield
218	1.7	North Canton City	North Canton
218	1.7	Orange City	Cleveland
218	1.7	Three Rivers Local	Cleves
218	1.7	Wapakoneta City	Wapakoneta
227	1.6	Barberton City	Barberton
227	1.6	Bellefontaine City	Bellefontaine
227	1.6	Buckeye Local	Medina
227	1.6	Cuyahoga Falls City	Cuyahoga Falls
227	1.6	East Liverpool City	East Liverpool
227	1.6	Eaton Community City	Eaton
227	1.6	Hillsboro City	Hillsboro
227	1.6	Kenston Local	Chagrin Falls
227	1.6	Lake Local	Uniontown
227	1.6	Maple Heights City	Maple Heights
227	1.6	Ohio Virtual Academy	Maumee
227	1.6	Ontario Local	Mansfield
227	1.6	Stow-Munroe Falls City SD	Stow
227	1.6	Triway Local	Wooster
227	1.6	Zanesville City	Zanesville
242	1.5	Benjamin Logan Local	Bellefontaine
242	1.5	Cambridge City	Cambridge
242	1.5	Chagrin Falls Exempted Village	Chagrin Falls
242	1.5	Coventry Local	Akron
242	1.5	Galion City	Galion
242	1.5	Granville Exempted Village	Granville
242	1.5	Greenville City	Greenville
242	1.5	Hubbard Exempted Village	Hubbard
242	1.5	Oak Hills Local	Cincinnati
251	1.4	Coshocton City	Coshocton
251	1.4	Edgewood City	Trenton
251	1.4	Howland Local	Warren
251	1.4	Jackson Local	Massillon
251	1.4	New Richmond Exempted Village	New Richmond
251	1.4	River View Local	Warsaw
251	1.4	Rolling Hills Local	Cambridge
251	1.4	Springboro Community City	Springboro
251	1.4	Steubenville City	Steubenville
251	1.4	Teays Valley Local	Ashville
251	1.4	Upper Arlington City	Upper Arlington
262	1.3	Bethel-Tate Local	Bethel
262	1.3	Lancaster City	Lancaster
262	1.3	Marietta City	Marietta
262	1.3	Minerva Local	Minerva
262	1.3	Niles City	Niles

Note: This section only includes districts with 1,500 or more students; All categories are ranked from high to low

262	1.3	Northwest Local	Mc Dermott
262	1.3	Revere Local	Bath
262	1.3	Saint Clairsville-Richland City	Saint Clairsville
270	1.2	Green Local	Uniontown
270	1.2	Lakeview Local	Cortland
270	1.2	Springfield Local	Akron
270	1.2	Trotwood-Madison City	Trotwood
270	1.2	Valley View Local	Germantown
270	1.2	Wheelersburg Local	Wheelersburg
276	1.1	Canton Local	Canton
276	1.1	Claymont City	Dennison
276	1.1	Cloverleaf Local	Lodi
276	1.1	Franklin City	Franklin
276	1.1	North College Hill City	Cincinnati
276	1.1	Norton City	Norton
276	1.1	Waverly City	Waverly
283	1.0	East Muskingum Local	New Concord
283	1.0	Edison Local	Hammondsville
283	1.0	Fairfield Union Local	Lancaster
283	1.0	Greenfield Exempted Village	Greenfield
283	1.0	Marysville Exempted Village	Marysville
283	1.0	Ross Local	Hamilton
283	1.0	West Holmes Local	Millersburg
290	0.9	Amanda-Clearcreek Local	Amanda
290	0.9	Blanchester Local	Blanchester
290	0.9	North Fork Local	Utica
293	0.8	Clermont Northeastern Local	Batavia
293	0.8	East Holmes Local	Berlin
293	0.8	Field Local	Mogadore
293	0.8	Highland Local	Medina
293	0.8	Indian Valley Local Schools	Gnadenhutten
293	0.8	Madison Local	Middletown
293	0.8	Northwest Local	Canal Fulton
293	0.8	Southeast Local	Ravenna
293	0.8	Warren Local	Vincent
293	0.8	Westfall Local	Williamsport
303	0.7	Adams County/Ohio Valley Local	West Union
303	0.7	Bloom-Carroll Local	Carroll
303	0.7	Crestwood Local	Mantua
303	0.7	Fairland Local	Proctorville
303	0.7	Fairless Local	Navarre
303	0.7	Gallipolis City	Gallipolis
303	0.7	Logan-Hocking Local	Logan
303	0.7	New Lexington City	New Lexington
303	0.7	South Point Local	South Point
303	0.7	West Muskingum Local	Zanesville
313	0.6	Beaver Local	Lisbon
313	0.6	Carrollton Exempted Village	Carrollton
313	0.6	Gallia County Local	Gallipolis
313	0.6	Harrison Hills City	Cadiz
313	0.6	Logan Elm Local	Circleville
313	0.6	Louisville City	Louisville
313	0.6	Maysville Local	Zanesville
313	0.6	Minford Local	Minford
313	0.6	Willoughby-Eastlake City	Willoughby
322	0.5	East Cleveland City SD	East Cleveland
322	0.5	Euclid City	Euclid
322	0.5	Indian Creek Local	Wintersville
322	0.5	Jackson City	Jackson
322	0.5	Switzerland of Ohio Local	Woodsfield
322	0.5	Tri-Valley Local	Dresden
322	0.5	Western Brown Local	Mount Orab
329	0.4	Buckeye Local	Dillonvale
329	0.4	West Branch Local	Beloit
331	0.3	Alexander Local	Albany
331	0.3	Meigs Local	Pomeroy
331	0.3	Vinton County Local	Mc Arthur
334	0.2	Franklin Local	Duncan Falls
334	0.2	Licking Valley Local	Newark
334	0.2	Morgan Local	Mc Connelsville
334	0.2	Northern Local	Thornville

Individual Education Program Students

Rank	Percent	District Name	City
1	26.8	Mansfield City	Mansfield
1	26.8	Portsmouth City	Portsmouth
3	24.6	Zanesville City	Zanesville
4	24.1	Youngstown City Schools	Youngstown
5	23.8	Ashtabula Area City	Ashtabula
6	23.6	Sidney City	Sidney
7	23.3	Coshocton City	Coshocton
8	23.2	Lima City	Lima
9	23.0	Cambridge City	Cambridge
10	22.9	Lorain City	Lorain
11	22.2	Harrison Hills City	Cadiz
12	22.1	Port Clinton City	Port Clinton
13	22.0	Gallipolis City	Gallipolis
14	21.8	Mt Healthy City	Cincinnati
15	21.6	Urbana City	Urbana
16	21.3	Electronic Classroom of Tomorrow	Columbus
17	21.1	Marion City	Marion
17	21.1	Treca Digital Academy	Marion
19	21.0	Cleveland Municipal	Cleveland
20	20.6	Galion City	Galion
21	20.5	East Liverpool City	East Liverpool
22	20.4	Claymont City	Dennison
22	20.4	Rolling Hills Local	Cambridge
24	20.3	Alexander Local	Albany
25	19.8	Orrville City	Orrville
25	19.8	Ravenna City	Ravenna
25	19.8	West Holmes Local	Millersburg
28	19.7	Dayton City	Dayton
28	19.7	Washington CH City	Washington CH
30	19.6	Middletown City	Middletown
31	19.4	Switzerland of Ohio Local	Woodsfield
32	19.3	Mount Vernon City	Mount Vernon
32	19.3	Toledo City	Toledo
34	19.2	Newark City	Newark
35	19.1	Akron City	Akron
35	19.1	Fairless Local	Navarre
37	19.0	Massillon City	Massillon
38	18.9	Reading Community City	Reading
39	18.8	Celina City	Celina
40	18.6	Tiffin City	Tiffin
40	18.6	Van Wert City	Van Wert
42	18.5	Alliance City	Alliance
42	18.5	Cincinnati City	Cincinnati
44	18.4	Napoleon Area City	Napoleon
44	18.4	River View Local	Warsaw
44	18.4	Springfield City	Springfield
47	18.3	Marysville Exempted Village	Marysville
48	18.2	Edison Local	Hammondsville
48	18.2	Southeast Local	Ravenna
48	18.2	Three Rivers Local	Cleves
51	18.0	Barberton City	Barberton
51	18.0	Clermont Northeastern Local	Batavia
51	18.0	East Cleveland City SD	East Cleveland
51	18.0	Warren City	Warren
55	17.9	Euclid City	Euclid
55	17.9	Vermilion Local	Vermilion
57	17.8	Fostoria City	Fostoria
58	17.7	Piqua City	Piqua
59	17.6	Cleveland Heights-Univ Hgts City	University Hgts
59	17.6	Saint Marys City	Saint Marys
61	17.5	Adams County/Ohio Valley Local	West Union
61	17.5	Carrollton Exempted Village	Carrollton
61	17.5	Fremont City	Fremont
61	17.5	Goshen Local	Goshen
65	17.4	Defiance City	Defiance
65	17.4	Parma City	Parma
65	17.4	South Euclid-Lyndhurst City	Lyndhurst
68	17.2	Franklin City	Franklin
68	17.2	Northwest Local	Canal Fulton
68	17.2	Springfield Local	Akron
71	17.1	Beaver Local	Lisbon
71	17.1	Logan Elm Local	Circleville
71	17.1	Northwest Local	Mc Dermott
71	17.1	Winton Woods City	Cincinnati
71	17.1	Wooster City	Wooster
76	17.0	Bellefontaine City	Bellefontaine
76	17.0	Columbus City SD	Columbus
76	17.0	Logan-Hocking Local	Logan
79	16.9	Elyria City Schools	Elyria
79	16.9	Gallia County Local	Gallipolis
79	16.9	Hamilton City	Hamilton
82	16.8	Canton City	Canton
82	16.8	Conneaut Area City	Conneaut
82	16.8	Greenville City	Greenville
85	16.7	Bedford City	Bedford
85	16.7	Findlay City	Findlay
87	16.6	Xenia Community City	Xenia
88	16.5	Indian Creek Local	Wintersville
88	16.5	London City	London
88	16.5	Salem City	Salem
88	16.5	Sandusky City	Sandusky
88	16.5	Vandalia-Butler City	Vandalia
93	16.4	Circleville City	Circleville
93	16.4	New Philadel. City	New Philadel.
93	16.4	Northwest Local	Cincinnati
93	16.4	Southwest Local	Harrison
97	16.3	Bryan City	Bryan
97	16.3	Fairland Local	Proctorville
97	16.3	Gahanna-Jefferson City	Gahanna
97	16.3	Maumee City	Maumee
101	16.1	Clyde-Green Springs Exempted Village	Clyde
101	16.1	Marietta City	Marietta
101	16.1	North Fork Local	Utica
101	16.1	Upper Sandusky Exempted Village	Upper Sandusky
105	16.0	Buckeye Local	Dillonvale
105	16.0	Shelby City	Shelby
105	16.0	South Point Local	South Point
108	15.9	Amherst Exempted Village	Amherst
108	15.9	Garfield Hgts City Schools	Garfield Hgts
110	15.8	Oak Hills Local	Cincinnati
111	15.7	Groveport Madison Local	Groveport
111	15.7	Huber Heights City	Huber Heights
111	15.7	Kenton City	Kenton
111	15.7	Vinton County Local	Mc Arthur
115	15.6	Girard City SD	Girard
115	15.6	Lancaster City	Lancaster
115	15.6	Miamisburg City	Miamisburg
115	15.6	North College Hill City	Cincinnati
115	15.6	Tri-Valley Local	Dresden
120	15.5	Fairborn City	Fairborn
120	15.5	Willoughby-Eastlake City	Willoughby
122	15.4	Hudson City	Hudson
122	15.4	New Richmond Exempted Village	New Richmond
122	15.4	Painesville City Local	Painesville
122	15.4	Trotwood-Madison City	Trotwood
126	15.3	Lakewood Local	Hebron
126	15.3	Norwood City	Norwood
126	15.3	Springfield Local	Holland
129	15.2	Beavercreek City	Beavercreek
129	15.2	Dover City	Dover
129	15.2	Graham Local	Saint Paris
129	15.2	Madison Local	Mansfield
129	15.2	Plain Local	Canton
129	15.2	Waverly City	Waverly
129	15.2	West Carrollton City	West Carrollton
136	15.1	Jefferson Area Local	Jefferson
136	15.1	New Lexington City	New Lexington
136	15.1	Wapakoneta City	Wapakoneta
136	15.1	Westlake City	Westlake
140	15.0	Benton Carroll Salem Local	Oak Harbor
140	15.0	Minerva Local	Minerva
140	15.0	West Muskingum Local	Zanesville
143	14.9	Batavia Local	Batavia
143	14.9	Boardman Local	Youngstown
143	14.9	Niles City	Niles
143	14.9	Princeton City	Cincinnati
143	14.9	Willard City	Willard
148	14.8	Berea City	Berea
148	14.8	Delaware City	Delaware
150	14.7	Athens City	The Plains
150	14.7	Bowling Green City SD	Bowling Green
150	14.7	Maysville Local	Zanesville
150	14.7	Meigs Local	Pomeroy
150	14.7	Steubenville City	Steubenville
150	14.7	West Clermont Local	Cincinnati
156	14.6	Edgewood City	Trenton
156	14.6	Shaker Heights City	Shaker Heights
156	14.6	Struthers City	Struthers
159	14.5	Cuyahoga Falls City	Cuyahoga Falls
159	14.5	Southwest Licking Local	Pataskala
161	14.3	Bellevue City	Bellevue
161	14.3	Kettering City	Kettering
161	14.3	Lexington Local	Lexington
164	14.2	Clear Fork Valley Local	Bellville
164	14.2	Indian Valley Local Schools	Gnadenhutten
164	14.2	Northmont City	Englewood
164	14.2	Westerville City	Westerville
168	14.1	Bay Village City	Bay Village
168	14.1	Kings Local	Kings Mills
168	14.1	Louisville City	Louisville
168	14.1	Pickerington Local	Pickerington
168	14.1	South-Western City	Grove City
168	14.1	Tecumseh Local	New Carlisle
174	14.0	Field Local	Mogadore
174	14.0	Jackson City	Jackson
174	14.0	N Ridgeville City	N Ridgeville

Note: This section only includes districts with 1,500 or more students; All categories are ranked from high to low

174	14.0	Western Brown Local	Mount Orab
178	13.9	Buckeye Local	Ashtabula
178	13.9	Morgan Local	Mc Connelsville
178	13.9	Whitehall City	Whitehall
181	13.8	Hillsboro City	Hillsboro
181	13.8	Miami Trace Local	Washington CH
183	13.7	Bethel-Tate Local	Bethel
183	13.7	Geneva Area City	Geneva
183	13.7	Maple Heights City	Maple Heights
183	13.7	Streetsboro City	Streetsboro
183	13.7	West Geauga Local	Chesterland
188	13.6	Marlington Local	Alliance
189	13.5	Centerville City	Centerville
189	13.5	Coventry Local	Akron
189	13.5	Kent City	Kent
189	13.5	Norwalk City	Norwalk
193	13.4	Austintown Local	Youngstown
193	13.4	Mayfield City	Mayfield Hgts
193	13.4	Minford Local	Minford
193	13.4	Tipp City Exempted Village	Tipp City
193	13.4	Valley View Local	Germantown
198	13.3	Chardon Local	Chardon
198	13.3	Sylvania City	Sylvania
200	13.2	Milford Exempted Village	Milford
200	13.2	North Olmsted City	North Olmsted
200	13.2	Worthington City	Worthington
203	13.1	Chillicothe City	Chillicothe
203	13.1	Edison Local (Formerly Berlin-Milan)	Milan
205	13.0	Benjamin Logan Local	Bellefontaine
205	13.0	Green Local	Uniontown
207	12.9	Canton Local	Canton
207	12.9	Franklin Local	Duncan Falls
207	12.9	Little Miami Local	Maineville
210	12.8	East Muskingum Local	New Concord
210	12.8	Northridge Local	Dayton
212	12.7	Cloverleaf Local	Lodi
212	12.7	Lakewood City	Lakewood
212	12.7	Orange City	Cleveland
215	12.6	Indian Lake Local	Lewistown
215	12.6	Medina City SD	Medina
217	12.5	Fairview Park City	Fairview Park
217	12.5	Ottawa-Glandorf Local	Ottawa
219	12.4	Blanchester Local	Blanchester
219	12.4	Upper Arlington City	Upper Arlington
221	12.3	Crestwood Local	Mantua
221	12.3	Fairfield City	Fairfield
221	12.3	Hilliard City	Columbus
221	12.3	Loveland City	Loveland
221	12.3	Ohio Virtual Academy	Maumee
221	12.3	Troy City	Troy
227	12.2	Ashland City	Ashland
227	12.2	Lake Local	Millbury
227	12.2	Mentor Exempted Village	Mentor
227	12.2	Northwestern Local	Springfield
227	12.2	Tallmadge City	Tallmadge
227	12.2	West Branch Local	Beloit
233	12.1	Greenon Local	Enon
233	12.1	Lake Local	Uniontown
233	12.1	Rossford Exempted Village	Rossford
236	12.0	Highland Local	Medina
236	12.0	Olmsted Falls City	Olmsted Falls
236	12.0	Washington Local	Toledo
239	11.9	Granville Exempted Village	Granville
240	11.8	Greenfield Exempted Village	Greenfield
240	11.8	Hubbard Exempted Village	Hubbard
240	11.8	Lebanon City	Lebanon
240	11.8	Warren Local	Vincent
244	11.7	Avon Local	Avon
244	11.7	Canal Wnchstr Local	Canal Wnchstr
244	11.7	Teays Valley Local	Ashville
247	11.6	Buckeye Local	Medina
247	11.6	Keystone Local	Lagrange
247	11.6	Midview Local	Grafton
247	11.6	Oakwood City	Dayton
247	11.6	Reynoldsburg City	Reynoldsburg
252	11.5	Canfield Local	Canfield
252	11.5	Eaton Community City	Eaton
252	11.5	Sycamore Community City	Blue Ash
255	11.4	Clinton-Massie Local	Clarksville
255	11.4	Mad River Local	Dayton
255	11.4	Woodridge Local	Peninsula
258	11.3	Big Walnut Local	Sunbury
258	11.3	East Holmes Local	Berlin
258	11.3	Lakeview Local	Cortland
258	11.3	Mariemont City	Cincinnati
258	11.3	Riverside Local	Painesville
258	11.3	Rocky River City	Rocky River
258	11.3	Triway Local	Wooster
258	11.3	Union-Scioto Local	Chillicothe
258	11.3	Wilmington City	Wilmington
267	11.2	Brunswick City	Brunswick
267	11.2	Lakota Local	Liberty Twp
267	11.2	Northern Local	Thornville
267	11.2	Oregon City	Oregon
267	11.2	Stow-Munroe Falls City SD	Stow
272	11.1	Brecksville-Broadview Heights City	Brecksville
272	11.1	Howland Local	Warren
272	11.1	Monroe Local SD	Monroe
272	11.1	Norton City	Norton
272	11.1	Perrysburg Exempted Village	Perrysburg
272	11.1	Ross Local	Hamilton
272	11.1	Wheelersburg Local	Wheelersburg
279	11.0	Clark-Shawnee Local	Springfield
279	11.0	Licking Heights Local	Pataskala
279	11.0	North Canton City	North Canton
279	11.0	Olentangy Local	Lewis Center
279	11.0	Springboro Community City	Springboro
284	10.9	River Valley Local	Caledonia
285	10.8	Copley-Fairlawn City	Copley
285	10.8	Johnstown-Monroe Local	Johnstown
285	10.8	Perry Local	Perry
288	10.7	Bath Local	Lima
288	10.7	Indian Hill Exempted Village	Cincinnati
288	10.7	New Albany-Plain Local	New Albany
288	10.7	Wadsworth City	Wadsworth
292	10.6	Chagrin Falls Exempted Village	Chagrin Falls
292	10.6	Elida Local	Elida
294	10.5	Alternative Education Academy	Toledo
294	10.5	Highland Local	Sparta
294	10.5	Jonathan Alder Local	Plain City
294	10.5	Perkins Local	Sandusky
298	10.4	Avon Lake City	Avon Lake
298	10.4	Kenston Local	Chagrin Falls
298	10.4	Perry Local	Massillon
301	10.3	Amanda-Clearcreek Local	Amanda
302	10.2	Buckeye Valley Local	Delaware
302	10.2	Madison Local	Middletown
302	10.2	North Royalton City	North Royalton
302	10.2	Ontario Local	Mansfield
302	10.2	Strongsville City	Strongsville
307	10.1	Carlisle Local	Carlisle
307	10.1	Dublin City	Dublin
307	10.1	Hamilton Local	Columbus
307	10.1	Nordonia Hills City	Northfield
311	10.0	Ohio Connections Academy, Inc	Cleveland
311	10.0	Solon City	Solon
313	9.9	Fairfield Union Local	Lancaster
313	9.9	Saint Clairsville-Richland City	Saint Clairsville
315	9.8	Firelands Local	South Amherst
316	9.7	Forest Hills Local	Cincinnati
316	9.7	Heath City	Heath
316	9.7	Westfall Local	Williamsport
319	9.6	Anthony Wayne Local	Whitehouse
319	9.6	Bloom-Carroll Local	Carroll
321	9.5	Madison Local	Madison
321	9.5	Talawanda City	Oxford
323	9.4	Twinsburg City	Twinsburg
324	9.3	Jackson Local	Massillon
325	9.2	Wauseon Exempted Village	Wauseon
326	9.1	Bellbrook-Sugarcreek Local SD	Bellbrook
326	9.1	Bexley City	Bexley
326	9.1	Shawnee Local	Lima
329	8.9	Mason City SD	Mason
329	8.9	Poland Local	Poland
331	8.8	Northeastern Local	Springfield
332	8.6	Aurora City	Aurora
333	8.2	Clearview Local	Lorain
334	8.0	Licking Valley Local	Newark
335	7.9	Sheffield-Sheffield Lake City	Sheffield Vllg
336	7.8	Wyoming City	Wyoming
337	7.7	Revere Local	Bath

English Language Learner Students

Rank	Percent	District Name	City
1	34.2	East Holmes Local	Berlin
2	28.8	Painesville City Local	Painesville
3	16.1	Princeton City	Cincinnati
4	13.5	Whitehall City	Whitehall
5	12.7	Columbus City SD	Columbus
6	12.2	South-Western City	Grove City
7	11.1	Winton Woods City	Cincinnati
8	8.5	Lakewood City	Lakewood
9	8.4	Dublin City	Dublin
10	8.3	Westerville City	Westerville
11	8.2	Tecumseh Local	New Carlisle
12	7.6	Licking Heights Local	Pataskala
13	7.2	Cleveland Municipal	Cleveland
14	6.9	Hilliard City	Columbus
15	6.2	Lorain City	Lorain
16	5.9	Ashtabula Area City	Ashtabula
17	5.8	Westlake City	Westlake
18	5.7	Reynoldsburg City	Reynoldsburg
19	5.4	Akron City	Akron
19	5.4	Hamilton City	Hamilton
19	5.4	North Olmsted City	North Olmsted
22	5.3	Fairfield City	Fairfield
22	5.3	Lakota Local	Liberty Twp
24	5.2	Sycamore Community City	Blue Ash
24	5.2	Worthington City	Worthington
26	4.7	Cincinnati City	Cincinnati
26	4.7	Norwood City	Norwood
28	4.5	Dayton City	Dayton
29	4.4	Norwalk City	Norwalk
30	4.2	Monroe Local SD	Monroe
31	4.1	Dover City	Dover
31	4.1	Mason City SD	Mason
31	4.1	New Philadel. City	New Philadel.
34	4.0	Fremont City	Fremont
34	4.0	Orrville City	Orrville
34	4.0	Youngstown City Schools	Youngstown
37	3.8	Middletown City	Middletown
38	3.7	Perry Local	Perry
38	3.7	West Carrollton City	West Carrollton
40	3.6	Copley-Fairlawn City	Copley
40	3.6	Groveport Madison Local	Groveport
42	3.5	Marlington Local	Alliance
42	3.5	Solon City	Solon
44	3.4	Mayfield City	Mayfield Hgts
44	3.4	Pickerington Local	Pickerington
44	3.4	Woodridge Local	Peninsula
47	3.3	Gahanna-Jefferson City	Gahanna
48	3.0	Strongsville City	Strongsville
49	2.9	Beavercreek City	Beavercreek
49	2.9	North Royalton City	North Royalton
49	2.9	Springfield City	Springfield
52	2.8	Fairview Park City	Fairview Park
52	2.8	Rocky River City	Rocky River
54	2.7	Field Local	Mogadore
54	2.7	Northwest Local	Cincinnati
54	2.7	Riverside Local	Painesville
54	2.7	Twinsburg City	Twinsburg
58	2.6	Athens City	The Plains
58	2.6	New Albany-Plain Local	New Albany
58	2.6	Shaker Heights City	Shaker Heights
61	2.4	Kings Local	Kings Mills
61	2.4	Talawanda City	Oxford
63	2.3	Cuyahoga Falls City	Cuyahoga Falls
63	2.3	Geneva Area City	Geneva
65	2.2	Boardman Local	Youngstown
65	2.2	Canal Wnchstr Local	Canal Wnchstr
65	2.2	Huber Heights City	Huber Heights
65	2.2	Salem City	Salem
65	2.2	Wauseon Exempted Village	Wauseon
70	2.1	Lebanon City	Lebanon
70	2.1	Mad River Local	Dayton
70	2.1	Northmont City	Englewood
70	2.1	Sidney City	Sidney
74	2.0	Cleveland Heights-Univ Hgts City	University Hgts
74	2.0	Fairborn City	Fairborn
76	1.9	Centerville City	Centerville
77	1.8	Avon Local	Avon
77	1.8	Bedford City	Bedford
77	1.8	Berea City	Berea
77	1.8	Brecksville-Broadview Heights City	Brecksville
77	1.8	Nordonia Hills City	Northfield
77	1.8	Parma City	Parma
77	1.8	Troy City	Troy
84	1.7	Jonathan Alder Local	Plain City
84	1.7	Mentor Exempted Village	Mentor
84	1.7	Miamisburg City	Miamisburg

Note: This section only includes districts with 1,500 or more students; All categories are ranked from high to low

84	1.7	Mt Healthy City	Cincinnati
84	1.7	Olentangy Local	Lewis Center
89	1.6	Clearview Local	Lorain
89	1.6	Elyria City Schools	Elyria
89	1.6	Findlay City	Findlay
89	1.6	Kent City	Kent
89	1.6	Orange City	Cleveland
89	1.6	South Euclid-Lyndhurst City	Lyndhurst
89	1.6	Sylvania City	Sylvania
96	1.5	Bowling Green City SD	Bowling Green
96	1.5	Kettering City	Kettering
96	1.5	Ontario Local	Mansfield
96	1.5	Tipp City Exempted Village	Tipp City
96	1.5	Toledo City	Toledo
96	1.5	Willoughby-Eastlake City	Willoughby
102	1.4	Bellbrook-Sugarcreek Local SD	Bellbrook
102	1.4	London City	London
102	1.4	Olmsted Falls City	Olmsted Falls
102	1.4	Upper Sandusky Exempted Village	Upper Sandusky
102	1.4	West Clermont Local	Cincinnati
107	1.3	Celina City	Celina
107	1.3	Streetsboro City	Streetsboro
109	1.2	Aurora City	Aurora
109	1.2	Fostoria City	Fostoria
109	1.2	Granville Exempted Village	Granville
109	1.2	Maumee City	Maumee
109	1.2	Milford Exempted Village	Milford
109	1.2	N Ridgeville City	N Ridgeville
109	1.2	Stow-Munroe Falls City SD	Stow
109	1.2	Tallmadge City	Tallmadge
109	1.2	Triway Local	Wooster
109	1.2	Upper Arlington City	Upper Arlington
109	1.2	Washington Local	Toledo
120	1.1	Canton City	Canton
120	1.1	Delaware City	Delaware
120	1.1	Forest Hills Local	Cincinnati
120	1.1	Marion City	Marion
120	1.1	North College Hill City	Cincinnati
120	1.1	Wilmington City	Wilmington
126	1.0	Amherst Exempted Village	Amherst
126	1.0	Bexley City	Bexley
126	1.0	Chagrin Falls Exempted Village	Chagrin Falls
126	1.0	Coventry Local	Akron
126	1.0	Loveland City	Loveland
126	1.0	Madison Local	Madison
126	1.0	Miami Trace Local	Washington CH
126	1.0	Napoleon Area City	Napoleon
126	1.0	North Canton City	North Canton
126	1.0	Revere Local	Bath
126	1.0	Springfield Local	Holland
137	0.9	Chardon Local	Chardon
137	0.9	Jackson Local	Massillon
137	0.9	Johnstown-Monroe Local	Johnstown
137	0.9	Lake Local	Uniontown
137	0.9	Lexington Local	Lexington
137	0.9	Little Miami Local	Maineville
137	0.9	Sandusky City	Sandusky
144	0.8	Barberton City	Barberton
144	0.8	Bath Local	Lima
144	0.8	Heath City	Heath
144	0.8	Howland Local	Warren
144	0.8	Hudson City	Hudson
144	0.8	Massillon City	Massillon
144	0.8	Mount Vernon City	Mount Vernon
144	0.8	Ottawa-Glandorf Local	Ottawa
144	0.8	Plain Local	Canton
144	0.8	Valley View Local	Germantown
144	0.8	Washington CH City	Washington CH
155	0.7	Brunswick City	Brunswick
155	0.7	Eaton Community City	Eaton
155	0.7	Garfield Hgts City Schools	Garfield Hgts
155	0.7	Green Local	Uniontown
155	0.7	Greenville City	Greenville
155	0.7	Highland Local	Medina
155	0.7	Indian Hill Exempted Village	Cincinnati
155	0.7	Lake Local	Millbury
155	0.7	Marysville Exempted Village	Marysville
155	0.7	Oak Hills Local	Cincinnati
155	0.7	Perrysburg Exempted Village	Perrysburg
155	0.7	Reading Community City	Reading
155	0.7	Vandalia-Butler City	Vandalia
168	0.6	Anthony Wayne Local	Whitehouse
168	0.6	Ashland City	Ashland
168	0.6	Austintown Local	Youngstown
168	0.6	Batavia Local	Batavia
168	0.6	Edison Local (Formerly Berlin-Milan)	Milan
168	0.6	Goshen Local	Goshen
168	0.6	Hamilton Local	Columbus
168	0.6	Mariemont City	Cincinnati
168	0.6	Medina City SD	Medina
168	0.6	Northridge Local	Dayton
168	0.6	Norton City	Norton
168	0.6	Perkins Local	Sandusky
168	0.6	Perry Local	Massillon
168	0.6	Poland Local	Poland
168	0.6	West Geauga Local	Chesterland
168	0.6	Wooster City	Wooster
184	0.5	Avon Lake City	Avon Lake
184	0.5	Bellefontaine City	Bellefontaine
184	0.5	Big Walnut Local	Sunbury
184	0.5	Buckeye Valley Local	Delaware
184	0.5	Euclid City	Euclid
184	0.5	Kenston Local	Chagrin Falls
184	0.5	Newark City	Newark
184	0.5	Northwest Local	Canal Fulton
184	0.5	Oregon City	Oregon
184	0.5	Ravenna City	Ravenna
184	0.5	Springboro Community City	Springboro
184	0.5	Springfield Local	Akron
184	0.5	West Holmes Local	Millersburg
184	0.5	West Muskingum Local	Zanesville
184	0.5	Xenia Community City	Xenia
199	0.4	Alliance City	Alliance
199	0.4	Bay Village City	Bay Village
199	0.4	Bryan City	Bryan
199	0.4	Conneaut Area City	Conneaut
199	0.4	Coshocton City	Coshocton
199	0.4	Elida Local	Elida
199	0.4	Franklin City	Franklin
199	0.4	Jefferson Area Local	Jefferson
199	0.4	Lima City	Lima
199	0.4	Ohio Virtual Academy	Maumee
199	0.4	Southwest Licking Local	Pataskala
199	0.4	Treca Digital Academy	Marion
199	0.4	West Branch Local	Beloit
199	0.4	Westfall Local	Williamsport
213	0.3	Bloom-Carroll Local	Carroll
213	0.3	Cambridge City	Cambridge
213	0.3	Canfield Local	Canfield
213	0.3	Clark-Shawnee Local	Springfield
213	0.3	Defiance City	Defiance
213	0.3	Electronic Classroom of Tomorrow	Columbus
213	0.3	Galion City	Galion
213	0.3	Lakeview Local	Cortland
213	0.3	Louisville City	Louisville
213	0.3	Mansfield City	Mansfield
213	0.3	Niles City	Niles
213	0.3	River Valley Local	Caledonia
213	0.3	Shawnee Local	Lima
213	0.3	Wapakoneta City	Wapakoneta
213	0.3	Warren City	Warren
213	0.3	Wyoming City	Wyoming
229	0.2	Amanda-Clearcreek Local	Amanda
229	0.2	Benton Carroll Salem Local	Oak Harbor
229	0.2	Buckeye Local	Ashtabula
229	0.2	Clear Fork Valley Local	Bellville
229	0.2	Clyde-Green Springs Exempted Village	Clyde
229	0.2	Crestwood Local	Mantua
229	0.2	Edgewood City	Trenton
229	0.2	Greenon Local	Enon
229	0.2	Lancaster City	Lancaster
229	0.2	Maple Heights City	Maple Heights
229	0.2	Midview Local	Grafton
229	0.2	Minerva Local	Minerva
229	0.2	Ohio Connections Academy, Inc	Cleveland
229	0.2	Piqua City	Piqua
229	0.2	Ross Local	Hamilton
229	0.2	South Point Local	South Point
229	0.2	Southwest Local	Harrison
229	0.2	Saint Marys City	Saint Marys
229	0.2	Struthers City	Struthers
229	0.2	Three Rivers Local	Cleves
229	0.2	Tiffin City	Tiffin
229	0.2	Trotwood-Madison City	Trotwood
229	0.2	Union-Scioto Local	Chillicothe
229	0.2	Van Wert City	Van Wert
229	0.2	Vermilion Local	Vermilion
229	0.2	Wadsworth City	Wadsworth
255	0.1	Benjamin Logan Local	Bellefontaine
255	0.1	Bethel-Tate Local	Bethel
255	0.1	Blanchester Local	Blanchester
255	0.1	Claymont City	Dennison
255	0.1	Cloverleaf Local	Lodi
255	0.1	East Cleveland City SD	East Cleveland
255	0.1	East Muskingum Local	New Concord
255	0.1	Highland Local	Sparta
255	0.1	Hillsboro City	Hillsboro
255	0.1	Hubbard Exempted Village	Hubbard
255	0.1	Indian Creek Local	Wintersville
255	0.1	Keystone Local	Lagrange
255	0.1	Lakewood Local	Hebron
255	0.1	Marietta City	Marietta
255	0.1	New Lexington City	New Lexington
255	0.1	Northeastern Local	Springfield
255	0.1	Northwestern Local	Springfield
255	0.1	Port Clinton City	Port Clinton
255	0.1	Portsmouth City	Portsmouth
255	0.1	Rossford Exempted Village	Rossford
255	0.1	Shelby City	Shelby
255	0.1	Saint Clairsville-Richland City	Saint Clairsville
255	0.1	Switzerland of Ohio Local	Woodsfield
255	0.1	Teays Valley Local	Ashville
255	0.1	Zanesville City	Zanesville
280	0.0	Adams County/Ohio Valley Local	West Union
280	0.0	Alexander Local	Albany
280	0.0	Alternative Education Academy	Toledo
280	0.0	Beaver Local	Lisbon
280	0.0	Bellevue City	Bellevue
280	0.0	Buckeye Local	Medina
280	0.0	Buckeye Local	Dillonvale
280	0.0	Canton Local	Canton
280	0.0	Carlisle Local	Carlisle
280	0.0	Carrollton Exempted Village	Carrollton
280	0.0	Chillicothe City	Chillicothe
280	0.0	Circleville City	Circleville
280	0.0	Clermont Northeastern Local	Batavia
280	0.0	Clinton-Massie Local	Clarksville
280	0.0	East Liverpool City	East Liverpool
280	0.0	Edison Local	Hammondsville
280	0.0	Fairfield Union Local	Lancaster
280	0.0	Fairland Local	Proctorville
280	0.0	Fairless Local	Navarre
280	0.0	Firelands Local	South Amherst
280	0.0	Franklin Local	Duncan Falls
280	0.0	Gallia County Local	Gallipolis
280	0.0	Gallipolis City	Gallipolis
280	0.0	Girard City SD	Girard
280	0.0	Graham Local	Saint Paris
280	0.0	Greenfield Exempted Village	Greenfield
280	0.0	Harrison Hills City	Cadiz
280	0.0	Indian Lake Local	Lewistown
280	0.0	Indian Valley Local Schools	Gnadenhutten
280	0.0	Jackson City	Jackson
280	0.0	Kenton City	Kenton
280	0.0	Licking Valley Local	Newark
280	0.0	Logan Elm Local	Circleville
280	0.0	Logan-Hocking Local	Logan
280	0.0	Madison Local	Mansfield
280	0.0	Madison Local	Middletown
280	0.0	Maysville Local	Zanesville
280	0.0	Meigs Local	Pomeroy
280	0.0	Minford Local	Minford
280	0.0	Morgan Local	Mc Connelsville
280	0.0	New Richmond Exempted Village	New Richmond
280	0.0	North Fork Local	Utica
280	0.0	Northern Local	Thornville
280	0.0	Northwest Local	Mc Dermott
280	0.0	Oakwood City	Dayton
280	0.0	River View Local	Warsaw
280	0.0	Rolling Hills Local	Cambridge
280	0.0	Sheffield-Sheffield Lake City	Sheffield Vllg
280	0.0	Southeast Local	Ravenna
280	0.0	Steubenville City	Steubenville
280	0.0	Tri-Valley Local	Dresden
280	0.0	Urbana City	Urbana
280	0.0	Vinton County Local	Mc Arthur
280	0.0	Warren Local	Vincent
280	0.0	Waverly City	Waverly
280	0.0	Western Brown Local	Mount Orab
280	0.0	Wheelersburg Local	Wheelersburg
n/a	n/a	Willard City	Willard

Note: This section only includes districts with 1,500 or more students; All categories are ranked from high to low

Students Eligible for Free Lunch

Rank	Percent	District Name	City
1	99.2	East Cleveland City SD	East Cleveland
2	97.4	Warren City	Warren
3	95.9	Portsmouth City	Portsmouth
4	91.5	Lima City	Lima
5	91.2	Dayton City	Dayton
6	89.7	Middletown City	Middletown
7	87.7	Cleveland Municipal	Cleveland
8	86.8	Maple Heights City	Maple Heights
9	84.7	Springfield City	Springfield
10	83.1	Lorain City	Lorain
11	81.3	Youngstown City Schools	Youngstown
12	80.7	Marion City	Marion
13	79.8	Steubenville City	Steubenville
14	79.4	Northridge Local	Dayton
15	78.9	Painesville City Local	Painesville
16	78.2	Mansfield City	Mansfield
17	77.6	Akron City	Akron
18	77.0	Mt Healthy City	Cincinnati
19	74.9	Vinton County Local	Mc Arthur
20	73.3	Canton City	Canton
21	70.6	Circleville City	Circleville
22	70.0	Zanesville City	Zanesville
23	69.5	Fostoria City	Fostoria
24	67.9	Northwest Local	Mc Dermott
25	66.8	Columbus City SD	Columbus
25	66.8	Euclid City	Euclid
27	66.7	Ashtabula Area City	Ashtabula
28	65.7	Toledo City	Toledo
29	65.2	Alliance City	Alliance
30	64.6	Clearview Local	Lorain
31	64.2	Whitehall City	Whitehall
32	63.9	Groveport Madison Local	Groveport
33	63.4	Coshocton City	Coshocton
34	63.3	Chillicothe City	Chillicothe
35	63.1	East Liverpool City	East Liverpool
36	63.0	Garfield Hgts City Schools	Garfield Hgts
36	63.0	Hamilton City	Hamilton
38	62.5	New Lexington City	New Lexington
39	62.2	Meigs Local	Pomeroy
40	62.0	Winton Woods City	Cincinnati
41	61.9	Cincinnati City	Cincinnati
42	61.2	Sandusky City	Sandusky
43	59.6	Elyria City Schools	Elyria
44	59.1	Norwood City	Norwood
45	59.0	Switzerland of Ohio Local	Woodsfield
46	58.5	West Carrollton City	West Carrollton
47	58.4	Princeton City	Cincinnati
48	58.2	Niles City	Niles
49	57.2	Logan-Hocking Local	Logan
50	57.0	Waverly City	Waverly
51	56.9	Struthers City	Struthers
52	56.7	South Point Local	South Point
53	56.5	Cleveland Heights-Univ Hgts City	University Hgts
54	56.1	Fremont City	Fremont
55	56.0	Cambridge City	Cambridge
56	55.8	Gallia County Local	Gallipolis
57	55.6	Mount Vernon City	Mount Vernon
58	55.4	Bedford City	Bedford
59	55.3	Newark City	Newark
60	54.9	West Muskingum Local	Zanesville
61	54.5	Conneaut Area City	Conneaut
62	54.0	Western Brown Local	Mount Orab
63	53.5	Maysville Local	Zanesville
64	53.4	Hamilton Local	Columbus
65	53.2	Washington CH City	Washington CH
66	53.1	Willard City	Willard
67	52.8	Tecumseh Local	New Carlisle
68	52.6	North College Hill City	Cincinnati
69	52.5	Buckeye Local	Dillonvale
70	52.4	Ravenna City	Ravenna
71	52.2	Massillon City	Massillon
72	51.8	Rolling Hills Local	Cambridge
73	51.5	Fairborn City	Fairborn
73	51.5	Goshen Local	Goshen
73	51.5	Kenton City	Kenton
76	51.2	Mad River Local	Dayton
76	51.2	Madison Local	Mansfield
78	50.9	Harrison Hills City	Cadiz
78	50.9	Sidney City	Sidney
80	50.6	Defiance City	Defiance
81	50.2	Galion City	Galion
82	50.0	Lancaster City	Lancaster
83	49.8	Washington Local	Toledo
84	49.5	Jackson City	Jackson
85	49.4	Piqua City	Piqua
85	49.4	Wilmington City	Wilmington
87	49.2	Gallipolis City	Gallipolis
87	49.2	Morgan Local	Mc Connelsville
89	49.0	Fairland Local	Proctorville
90	48.8	Girard City SD	Girard
91	48.5	Reading Community City	Reading
92	48.3	Claymont City	Dennison
93	48.2	South-Western City	Grove City
94	48.0	Indian Creek Local	Wintersville
95	47.7	Austintown Local	Youngstown
96	47.6	Minerva Local	Minerva
97	47.4	Urbana City	Urbana
98	47.0	Barberton City	Barberton
99	46.7	Canton Local	Canton
99	46.7	Salem City	Salem
101	46.2	Xenia Community City	Xenia
102	46.1	Adams County/Ohio Valley Local	West Union
103	46.0	Lakewood Local	Hebron
104	45.9	River View Local	Warsaw
105	45.8	Batavia Local	Batavia
105	45.8	Bellefontaine City	Bellefontaine
105	45.8	Edison Local	Hammondsville
108	45.6	Miami Trace Local	Washington CH
108	45.6	Union-Scioto Local	Chillicothe
110	45.5	Trotwood-Madison City	Trotwood
111	45.3	Lakewood City	Lakewood
112	44.7	Norwalk City	Norwalk
113	44.6	Reynoldsburg City	Reynoldsburg
114	44.4	Van Wert City	Van Wert
115	44.2	Minford Local	Minford
115	44.2	Northwest Local	Cincinnati
117	44.0	Marietta City	Marietta
118	43.8	Springfield Local	Akron
119	43.7	Buckeye Local	Ashtabula
120	43.6	Orrville City	Orrville
121	42.7	Clark-Shawnee Local	Springfield
122	42.6	Westfall Local	Williamsport
123	42.5	Springfield Local	Holland
124	42.1	Kent City	Kent
125	42.0	Alexander Local	Albany
125	42.0	Port Clinton City	Port Clinton
127	41.8	Franklin City	Franklin
128	41.4	Sheffield-Sheffield Lake City	Sheffield Vllg
129	41.3	Hillsboro City	Hillsboro
129	41.3	Tri-Valley Local	Dresden
131	41.2	Elida Local	Elida
131	41.2	Fairless Local	Navarre
133	40.8	Huber Heights City	Huber Heights
133	40.8	Indian Lake Local	Lewistown
135	40.6	Tiffin City	Tiffin
135	40.6	Wapakoneta City	Wapakoneta
137	40.4	Jefferson Area Local	Jefferson
138	40.3	Parma City	Parma
139	40.1	Beaver Local	Lisbon
140	39.8	London City	London
141	39.7	Bath Local	Lima
141	39.7	Geneva Area City	Geneva
143	39.5	Franklin Local	Duncan Falls
144	39.2	Blanchester Local	Blanchester
145	39.0	Shelby City	Shelby
146	38.7	South Euclid-Lyndhurst City	Lyndhurst
147	38.6	Bryan City	Bryan
148	38.5	Southwest Local	Harrison
149	38.4	Ashland City	Ashland
150	38.3	New Richmond Exempted Village	New Richmond
150	38.3	Three Rivers Local	Cleves
152	38.2	Greenon Local	Enon
153	38.0	Greenfield Exempted Village	Greenfield
153	38.0	Rossford Exempted Village	Rossford
153	38.0	Wooster City	Wooster
156	37.9	Southeast Local	Ravenna
157	37.8	Clermont Northeastern Local	Batavia
157	37.8	Northern Local	Thornville
159	37.4	Clyde-Green Springs Exempted Village	Clyde
159	37.4	Vermilion Local	Vermilion
161	37.2	Plain Local	Canton
162	36.8	Carrollton Exempted Village	Carrollton
163	36.2	Bethel-Tate Local	Bethel
164	36.1	Indian Valley Local Schools	Gnadenhutten
165	36.0	Logan Elm Local	Circleville
166	35.9	Hubbard Exempted Village	Hubbard
167	35.8	Woodridge Local	Peninsula
168	35.5	Athens City	The Plains
168	35.5	Findlay City	Findlay
170	35.4	Greenville City	Greenville
171	35.2	Fairfield Union Local	Lancaster
172	35.1	Edison Local (Formerly Berlin-Milan)	Milan
173	35.0	Edgewood City	Trenton
174	34.9	West Holmes Local	Millersburg
175	34.8	Marlington Local	Alliance
176	34.7	Cloverleaf Local	Lodi
176	34.7	Eaton Community City	Eaton
178	34.5	Lake Local	Millbury
178	34.5	North Fork Local	Utica
180	34.3	Napoleon Area City	Napoleon
181	34.2	Wheelersburg Local	Wheelersburg
182	34.1	Bellevue City	Bellevue
183	33.9	Wauseon Exempted Village	Wauseon
184	33.4	West Branch Local	Beloit
185	33.3	New Philadel. City	New Philadel.
186	33.2	Oregon City	Oregon
186	33.2	Saint Marys City	Saint Marys
188	33.1	Amanda-Clearcreek Local	Amanda
188	33.1	Madison Local	Middletown
188	33.1	Miamisburg City	Miamisburg
191	33.0	Cuyahoga Falls City	Cuyahoga Falls
191	33.0	Highland Local	Sparta
191	33.0	Northwestern Local	Springfield
191	33.0	Shaker Heights City	Shaker Heights
195	32.7	Boardman Local	Youngstown
196	32.6	Celina City	Celina
196	32.6	Graham Local	Saint Paris
198	32.5	North Olmsted City	North Olmsted
198	32.5	West Clermont Local	Cincinnati
200	32.4	Kettering City	Kettering
201	32.2	Bowling Green City SD	Bowling Green
202	32.1	Warren Local	Vincent
203	32.0	Troy City	Troy
204	31.7	Licking Valley Local	Newark
204	31.7	Madison Local	Madison
206	31.3	Licking Heights Local	Pataskala
207	31.0	Heath City	Heath
208	30.8	Fairfield City	Fairfield
209	30.5	Maumee City	Maumee
210	30.4	Upper Sandusky Exempted Village	Upper Sandusky
211	30.1	Clear Fork Valley Local	Bellville
212	30.0	East Muskingum Local	New Concord
213	29.9	Louisville City	Louisville
214	29.8	Triway Local	Wooster
215	29.6	Canal Wnchstr Local	Canal Wnchstr
216	29.4	Coventry Local	Akron
216	29.4	Perry Local	Massillon
218	29.3	Delaware City	Delaware
219	29.2	Midview Local	Grafton
220	29.1	Buckeye Local	Medina
221	28.8	Benton Carroll Salem Local	Oak Harbor
222	28.7	River Valley Local	Caledonia
223	28.5	Talawanda City	Oxford
224	27.7	Willoughby-Eastlake City	Willoughby
225	27.3	Saint Clairsville-Richland City	Saint Clairsville
226	27.2	Dover City	Dover
227	26.9	Westerville City	Westerville
228	26.8	Norton City	Norton
228	26.8	Perkins Local	Sandusky
230	26.6	Monroe Local SD	Monroe
231	26.5	Firelands Local	South Amherst
232	26.3	Teays Valley Local	Ashville
233	26.1	Tallmadge City	Tallmadge
234	26.0	Northmont City	Englewood
235	25.9	Carlisle Local	Carlisle
236	25.7	Clinton-Massie Local	Clarksville
237	25.4	Howland Local	Warren
238	25.1	Field Local	Mogadore
239	24.7	Streetsboro City	Streetsboro
240	24.3	Lebanon City	Lebanon
241	24.1	Southwest Licking Local	Pataskala
242	23.8	Jonathan Alder Local	Plain City
243	23.7	Northeastern Local	Springfield
244	23.6	Crestwood Local	Mantua
245	23.2	Shawnee Local	Lima
246	23.1	Milford Exempted Village	Milford
247	22.8	Johnstown-Monroe Local	Johnstown
248	22.7	Keystone Local	Lagrange
248	22.7	Northwest Local	Canal Fulton

Note: This section only includes districts with 1,500 or more students; All categories are ranked from high to low

248	22.7	Perry Local	Perry
251	22.4	Marysville Exempted Village	Marysville
252	22.1	Lakeview Local	Cortland
253	21.7	Valley View Local	Germantown
254	21.6	Gahanna-Jefferson City	Gahanna
255	21.3	Sylvania City	Sylvania
256	21.2	Vandalia-Butler City	Vandalia
257	20.7	Berea City	Berea
258	20.5	Ottawa-Glandorf Local	Ottawa
259	20.2	Hilliard City	Columbus
260	20.1	Lexington Local	Lexington
260	20.1	Worthington City	Worthington
262	20.0	Pickerington Local	Pickerington
263	19.5	Buckeye Valley Local	Delaware
264	19.4	Benjamin Logan Local	Bellefontaine
264	19.4	Mentor Exempted Village	Mentor
266	19.3	Green Local	Uniontown
267	18.8	Lakota Local	Liberty Twp
267	18.8	Ross Local	Hamilton
269	18.2	East Holmes Local	Berlin
270	17.6	Wadsworth City	Wadsworth
271	17.5	N Ridgeville City	N Ridgeville
272	17.2	Mayfield City	Mayfield Hgts
273	17.1	Little Miami Local	Maineville
274	16.7	Amherst Exempted Village	Amherst
274	16.7	Chardon Local	Chardon
276	16.6	Riverside Local	Painesville
277	16.5	Nordonia Hills City	Northfield
278	16.4	Kings Local	Kings Mills
279	15.9	Fairview Park City	Fairview Park
280	15.8	Twinsburg City	Twinsburg
281	15.7	Brunswick City	Brunswick
282	15.6	Bloom-Carroll Local	Carroll
283	15.5	Medina City SD	Medina
284	15.4	Westlake City	Westlake
285	15.3	Olmsted Falls City	Olmsted Falls
286	15.0	Tipp City Exempted Village	Tipp City
287	14.9	Big Walnut Local	Sunbury
287	14.9	Stow-Munroe Falls City SD	Stow
289	14.8	Sycamore Community City	Blue Ash
290	14.6	Strongsville City	Strongsville
291	14.5	Copley-Fairlawn City	Copley
292	14.2	Lake Local	Uniontown
292	14.2	North Canton City	North Canton
294	14.0	Bellbrook-Sugarcreek Local SD	Bellbrook
295	13.6	North Royalton City	North Royalton
296	13.5	Ontario Local	Mansfield
297	12.8	Centerville City	Centerville
298	12.3	Dublin City	Dublin
298	12.3	Jackson Local	Massillon
298	12.3	Loveland City	Loveland
301	12.0	Oak Hills Local	Cincinnati
301	12.0	Poland Local	Poland
303	11.9	Canfield Local	Canfield
304	11.3	Bexley City	Bexley
305	11.1	Beavercreek City	Beavercreek
305	11.1	Orange City	Cleveland
307	10.7	Solon City	Solon
308	10.5	West Geauga Local	Chesterland
309	10.3	Brecksville-Broadview Heights City	Brecksville
310	10.0	Anthony Wayne Local	Whitehouse
311	9.6	Avon Local	Avon
312	9.1	Forest Hills Local	Cincinnati
312	9.1	Perrysburg Exempted Village	Perrysburg
314	9.0	Avon Lake City	Avon Lake
315	8.2	Kenston Local	Chagrin Falls
316	7.5	Highland Local	Medina
317	7.4	Mariemont City	Cincinnati
318	7.2	Rocky River City	Rocky River
319	7.1	Aurora City	Aurora
320	6.7	New Albany-Plain Local	New Albany
321	6.5	Wyoming City	Wyoming
322	6.4	Bay Village City	Bay Village
323	5.7	Mason City SD	Mason
324	5.4	Granville Exempted Village	Granville
324	5.4	Olentangy Local	Lewis Center
326	5.0	Revere Local	Bath
327	4.2	Hudson City	Hudson
328	4.0	Indian Hill Exempted Village	Cincinnati
329	3.2	Chagrin Falls Exempted Village	Chagrin Falls
330	2.8	Springboro Community City	Springboro
331	2.5	Oakwood City	Dayton
332	1.5	Upper Arlington City	Upper Arlington
333	0.0	Alternative Education Academy	Toledo
333	0.0	Electronic Classroom of Tomorrow	Columbus
333	0.0	Ohio Connections Academy, Inc	Cleveland
333	0.0	Ohio Virtual Academy	Maumee
333	0.0	Treca Digital Academy	Marion

Students Eligible for Reduced-Price Lunch

Rank	Percent	District Name	City
1	15.8	Fairless Local	Navarre
2	14.1	East Holmes Local	Berlin
3	13.0	Galion City	Galion
4	12.2	Sidney City	Sidney
5	12.1	Minerva Local	Minerva
5	12.1	West Holmes Local	Millersburg
7	11.8	Elida Local	Elida
7	11.8	Hamilton Local	Columbus
9	11.4	Defiance City	Defiance
10	11.1	Bedford City	Bedford
11	11.0	Fairland Local	Proctorville
11	11.0	Upper Sandusky Exempted Village	Upper Sandusky
11	11.0	Van Wert City	Van Wert
14	10.9	Mad River Local	Dayton
14	10.9	Sheffield-Sheffield Lake City	Sheffield Vllg
16	10.7	Carrollton Exempted Village	Carrollton
16	10.7	Clear Fork Valley Local	Bellville
18	10.5	Clearview Local	Lorain
18	10.5	Northwest Local	Mc Dermott
20	10.4	Ashland City	Ashland
21	10.3	Celina City	Celina
21	10.3	Orrville City	Orrville
21	10.3	Piqua City	Piqua
24	10.2	Clyde-Green Springs Exempted Village	Clyde
25	10.1	Edison Local	Hammondsville
25	10.1	Fremont City	Fremont
25	10.1	Marlington Local	Alliance
28	10.0	Blanchester Local	Blanchester
28	10.0	Niles City	Niles
30	9.9	Rossford Exempted Village	Rossford
31	9.8	Huber Heights City	Huber Heights
32	9.7	Buckeye Local	Ashtabula
32	9.7	Kenton City	Kenton
32	9.7	Saint Marys City	Saint Marys
32	9.7	West Carrollton City	West Carrollton
36	9.6	Parma City	Parma
36	9.6	Rolling Hills Local	Cambridge
38	9.5	Wapakoneta City	Wapakoneta
39	9.4	Shelby City	Shelby
39	9.4	Wheelersburg Local	Wheelersburg
41	9.3	Alliance City	Alliance
41	9.3	Madison Local	Mansfield
43	9.2	Bryan City	Bryan
43	9.2	Indian Valley Local Schools	Gnadenhutten
43	9.2	Logan-Hocking Local	Logan
43	9.2	Morgan Local	Mc Connelsville
47	9.1	Cloverleaf Local	Lodi
48	9.0	Carlisle Local	Carlisle
48	9.0	Cuyahoga Falls City	Cuyahoga Falls
48	9.0	Fostoria City	Fostoria
51	8.9	Austintown Local	Youngstown
51	8.9	Bellefontaine City	Bellefontaine
51	8.9	Norwalk City	Norwalk
51	8.9	River View Local	Warsaw
55	8.8	Harrison Hills City	Cadiz
55	8.8	Midview Local	Grafton
55	8.8	Perry Local	Massillon
58	8.7	Conneaut Area City	Conneaut
58	8.7	Edgewood City	Trenton
58	8.7	Lake Local	Millbury
58	8.7	North Fork Local	Utica
62	8.6	Gallia County Local	Gallipolis
62	8.6	Geneva Area City	Geneva
62	8.6	Hubbard Exempted Village	Hubbard
62	8.6	Northwest Local	Cincinnati
62	8.6	Triway Local	Wooster
67	8.5	Bath Local	Lima
67	8.5	Elyria City Schools	Elyria
69	8.4	Claymont City	Dennison
69	8.4	Tecumseh Local	New Carlisle
69	8.4	Wauseon Exempted Village	Wauseon
72	8.3	Louisville City	Louisville
72	8.3	Northmont City	Englewood
72	8.3	Shawnee Local	Lima
72	8.3	West Branch Local	Beloit
76	8.2	Cambridge City	Cambridge
76	8.2	Greenville City	Greenville
76	8.2	Warren Local	Vincent
79	8.1	East Liverpool City	East Liverpool
79	8.1	Edison Local (Formerly Berlin-Milan)	Milan
79	8.1	Licking Valley Local	Newark
79	8.1	Sandusky City	Sandusky
79	8.1	Streetsboro City	Streetsboro
79	8.1	Struthers City	Struthers
85	8.0	Clermont Northeastern Local	Batavia
85	8.0	Northwest Local	Canal Fulton
87	7.9	Hamilton City	Hamilton
87	7.9	Western Brown Local	Mount Orab
89	7.8	Adams County/Ohio Valley Local	West Union
89	7.8	Bethel-Tate Local	Bethel
89	7.8	Canton Local	Canton
89	7.8	East Muskingum Local	New Concord
89	7.8	Kettering City	Kettering
89	7.8	Maumee City	Maumee
89	7.8	Ravenna City	Ravenna
89	7.8	South Point Local	South Point
89	7.8	Springfield Local	Akron
89	7.8	Tiffin City	Tiffin
99	7.7	Canfield Local	Canfield
99	7.7	Delaware City	Delaware
99	7.7	Highland Local	Sparta
99	7.7	Indian Creek Local	Wintersville
99	7.7	Jackson City	Jackson
99	7.7	Southeast Local	Ravenna
99	7.7	Xenia Community City	Xenia
106	7.6	Wooster City	Wooster
107	7.5	Maysville Local	Zanesville
108	7.4	Lexington Local	Lexington
108	7.4	Miami Trace Local	Washington CH
108	7.4	Tri-Valley Local	Dresden
111	7.3	Barberton City	Barberton
111	7.3	Bellevue City	Bellevue
111	7.3	Euclid City	Euclid
111	7.3	Garfield Hgts City Schools	Garfield Hgts
111	7.3	Northern Local	Thornville
111	7.3	Washington Local	Toledo
117	7.2	Fairborn City	Fairborn
117	7.2	Franklin Local	Duncan Falls
117	7.2	Madison Local	Madison
117	7.2	Tallmadge City	Tallmadge
121	7.1	Buckeye Local	Dillonvale
121	7.1	Graham Local	Saint Paris
121	7.1	Keystone Local	Lagrange
121	7.1	Perkins Local	Sandusky
121	7.1	Whitehall City	Whitehall
126	7.0	Benjamin Logan Local	Bellefontaine
126	7.0	Benton Carroll Salem Local	Oak Harbor
126	7.0	Poland Local	Poland
126	7.0	River Valley Local	Caledonia
130	6.9	Franklin City	Franklin
130	6.9	Winton Woods City	Cincinnati
132	6.8	Howland Local	Warren
132	6.8	Monroe Local SD	Monroe
132	6.8	Mt Healthy City	Cincinnati
132	6.8	Saint Clairsville-Richland City	Saint Clairsville
132	6.8	Willard City	Willard
132	6.8	Wilmington City	Wilmington
138	6.7	Clark-Shawnee Local	Springfield
138	6.7	Eaton Community City	Eaton
138	6.7	Mount Vernon City	Mount Vernon
138	6.7	Willoughby-Eastlake City	Willoughby
142	6.6	Dover City	Dover
142	6.6	Northridge Local	Dayton
142	6.6	Port Clinton City	Port Clinton
145	6.5	Coshocton City	Coshocton
145	6.5	Field Local	Mogadore
145	6.5	Princeton City	Cincinnati
145	6.5	Urbana City	Urbana
149	6.4	Beaver Local	Lisbon
149	6.4	Groveport Madison Local	Groveport
149	6.4	Lancaster City	Lancaster
149	6.4	Mansfield City	Mansfield
149	6.4	Marietta City	Marietta
149	6.4	Union-Scioto Local	Chillicothe
155	6.3	Indian Lake Local	Lewistown
155	6.3	Loveland City	Loveland
155	6.3	Massillon City	Massillon
155	6.3	North Olmsted City	North Olmsted

Note: This section only includes districts with 1,500 or more students; All categories are ranked from high to low

155	6.3	Northwestern Local	Springfield
155	6.3	Vermilion Local	Vermilion
161	6.2	Fairfield Union Local	Lancaster
161	6.2	Heath City	Heath
161	6.2	Norton City	Norton
161	6.2	Teays Valley Local	Ashville
161	6.2	West Clermont Local	Cincinnati
166	6.1	Amanda-Clearcreek Local	Amanda
166	6.1	Jefferson Area Local	Jefferson
166	6.1	Mayfield City	Mayfield Hgts
166	6.1	Oregon City	Oregon
166	6.1	South Euclid-Lyndhurst City	Lyndhurst
171	6.0	Batavia Local	Batavia
171	6.0	Licking Heights Local	Pataskala
171	6.0	New Philadel. City	New Philadel.
171	6.0	Newark City	Newark
171	6.0	Troy City	Troy
171	6.0	Westfall Local	Williamsport
177	5.9	Canton City	Canton
178	5.8	Firelands Local	South Amherst
178	5.8	Logan Elm Local	Circleville
178	5.8	Nordonia Hills City	Northfield
178	5.8	South-Western City	Grove City
178	5.8	Washington CH City	Washington CH
183	5.7	Buckeye Valley Local	Delaware
183	5.7	Fairfield City	Fairfield
183	5.7	Findlay City	Findlay
183	5.7	Lakewood Local	Hebron
183	5.7	Plain Local	Canton
183	5.7	Valley View Local	Germantown
189	5.6	Salem City	Salem
189	5.6	Southwest Licking Local	Pataskala
191	5.5	Gahanna-Jefferson City	Gahanna
191	5.5	Kent City	Kent
191	5.5	Reading Community City	Reading
191	5.5	Southwest Local	Harrison
191	5.5	Vandalia-Butler City	Vandalia
191	5.5	West Muskingum Local	Zanesville
197	5.4	Goshen Local	Goshen
197	5.4	Greenon Local	Enon
197	5.4	Mentor Exempted Village	Mentor
197	5.4	Ross Local	Hamilton
201	5.3	Boardman Local	Youngstown
201	5.3	Jonathan Alder Local	Plain City
201	5.3	North Canton City	North Canton
204	5.2	Madison Local	Middletown
204	5.2	Woodridge Local	Peninsula
206	5.1	Ottawa-Glandorf Local	Ottawa
206	5.1	Perry Local	Perry
206	5.1	Wadsworth City	Wadsworth
206	5.1	West Geauga Local	Chesterland
210	5.0	Bowling Green City SD	Bowling Green
210	5.0	Coventry Local	Akron
210	5.0	Lakeview Local	Cortland
210	5.0	Reynoldsburg City	Reynoldsburg
210	5.0	Stow-Munroe Falls City SD	Stow
210	5.0	Talawanda City	Oxford
210	5.0	Zanesville City	Zanesville
217	4.8	Clinton-Massie Local	Clarksville
217	4.8	Northeastern Local	Springfield
217	4.8	Norwood City	Norwood
217	4.8	Worthington City	Worthington
221	4.7	Amherst Exempted Village	Amherst
221	4.7	Lebanon City	Lebanon
221	4.7	Pickerington Local	Pickerington
224	4.6	Chardon Local	Chardon
224	4.6	Cleveland Heights-Univ Hgts City	University Hgts
224	4.6	London City	London
224	4.6	Miamisburg City	Miamisburg
224	4.6	Springfield Local	Holland
229	4.5	Crestwood Local	Mantua
229	4.5	Kings Local	Kings Mills
229	4.5	Lakewood City	Lakewood
229	4.5	Sycamore Community City	Blue Ash
233	4.4	Fairview Park City	Fairview Park
233	4.4	New Richmond Exempted Village	New Richmond
233	4.4	Ontario Local	Mansfield
236	4.3	Ashtabula Area City	Ashtabula
236	4.3	Lake Local	Uniontown
236	4.3	Riverside Local	Painesville
236	4.3	Sylvania City	Sylvania
240	4.2	Berea City	Berea
240	4.2	Milford Exempted Village	Milford
240	4.2	N Ridgeville City	N Ridgeville
243	4.1	Johnstown-Monroe Local	Johnstown
244	4.0	Brunswick City	Brunswick
244	4.0	Little Miami Local	Maineville
244	4.0	Olmsted Falls City	Olmsted Falls
247	3.9	Bloom-Carroll Local	Carroll
247	3.9	Gallipolis City	Gallipolis
247	3.9	Girard City SD	Girard
247	3.9	Marysville Exempted Village	Marysville
247	3.9	Napoleon Area City	Napoleon
252	3.8	Shaker Heights City	Shaker Heights
252	3.8	Toledo City	Toledo
254	3.7	Three Rivers Local	Cleves
255	3.6	Athens City	The Plains
255	3.6	Hilliard City	Columbus
255	3.6	New Lexington City	New Lexington
255	3.6	Perrysburg Exempted Village	Perrysburg
255	3.6	Westerville City	Westerville
260	3.5	Beavercreek City	Beavercreek
260	3.5	Twinsburg City	Twinsburg
262	3.4	Brecksville-Broadview Heights City	Brecksville
262	3.4	Canal Wnchstr Local	Canal Wnchstr
262	3.4	Hillsboro City	Hillsboro
262	3.4	Tipp City Exempted Village	Tipp City
266	3.3	Bellbrook-Sugarcreek Local SD	Bellbrook
266	3.3	Jackson Local	Massillon
266	3.3	Strongsville City	Strongsville
269	3.2	Copley-Fairlawn City	Copley
270	3.1	Kenston Local	Chagrin Falls
271	3.0	Big Walnut Local	Sunbury
271	3.0	Vinton County Local	Mc Arthur
273	2.9	Columbus City SD	Columbus
273	2.9	Medina City SD	Medina
275	2.8	Centerville City	Centerville
275	2.8	North College Hill City	Cincinnati
275	2.8	Solon City	Solon
278	2.7	Chillicothe City	Chillicothe
278	2.7	Westlake City	Westlake
280	2.6	Cincinnati City	Cincinnati
280	2.6	Circleville City	Circleville
280	2.6	North Royalton City	North Royalton
283	2.5	Avon Lake City	Avon Lake
283	2.5	Lakota Local	Liberty Twp
283	2.5	Orange City	Cleveland
286	2.3	Highland Local	Medina
286	2.3	Revere Local	Bath
288	2.2	Forest Hills Local	Cincinnati
289	2.1	Avon Local	Avon
289	2.1	Dublin City	Dublin
289	2.1	Green Local	Uniontown
292	2.0	Buckeye Local	Medina
292	2.0	Minford Local	Minford
294	1.9	Bay Village City	Bay Village
294	1.9	Oak Hills Local	Cincinnati
296	1.7	Anthony Wayne Local	Whitehouse
296	1.7	Bexley City	Bexley
296	1.7	Mariemont City	Cincinnati
296	1.7	New Albany-Plain Local	New Albany
300	1.6	Greenfield Exempted Village	Greenfield
300	1.6	Lorain City	Lorain
302	1.5	Mason City SD	Mason
303	1.4	Alexander Local	Albany
303	1.4	Olentangy Local	Lewis Center
305	1.2	Aurora City	Aurora
305	1.2	Chagrin Falls Exempted Village	Chagrin Falls
305	1.2	Rocky River City	Rocky River
305	1.2	Waverly City	Waverly
305	1.2	Wyoming City	Wyoming
310	1.0	Hudson City	Hudson
311	0.9	Granville Exempted Village	Granville
312	0.7	Springboro Community City	Springboro
313	0.6	Indian Hill Exempted Village	Cincinnati
314	0.2	Oakwood City	Dayton
314	0.2	Upper Arlington City	Upper Arlington
316	0.0	Akron City	Akron
316	0.0	Alternative Education Academy	Toledo
316	0.0	Cleveland Municipal	Cleveland
316	0.0	Dayton City	Dayton
316	0.0	East Cleveland City SD	East Cleveland
316	0.0	Electronic Classroom of Tomorrow	Columbus
316	0.0	Lima City	Lima
316	0.0	Maple Heights City	Maple Heights
316	0.0	Marion City	Marion
316	0.0	Meigs Local	Pomeroy
316	0.0	Middletown City	Middletown
316	0.0	Ohio Connections Academy, Inc	Cleveland
316	0.0	Ohio Virtual Academy	Maumee
316	0.0	Painesville City Local	Painesville
316	0.0	Portsmouth City	Portsmouth
316	0.0	Springfield City	Springfield
316	0.0	Steubenville City	Steubenville
316	0.0	Switzerland of Ohio Local	Woodsfield
316	0.0	Treca Digital Academy	Marion
316	0.0	Trotwood-Madison City	Trotwood
316	0.0	Warren City	Warren
316	0.0	Youngstown City Schools	Youngstown

Student/Teacher Ratio

(number of students per teacher)

Rank	Number	District Name	City
1	11.2	East Cleveland City SD	East Cleveland
2	11.4	Cleveland Heights-Univ Hgts City	University Hgts
3	12.1	Marion City	Marion
4	12.5	Buckeye Local	Dillonvale
5	12.8	Greenville City	Greenville
5	12.8	Lakewood Local	Hebron
7	12.9	Indian Hill Exempted Village	Cincinnati
8	13.0	East Liverpool City	East Liverpool
9	13.3	Kent City	Kent
9	13.3	Mansfield City	Mansfield
11	13.5	Field Local	Mogadore
12	13.6	Triway Local	Wooster
13	13.8	Orange City	Cleveland
14	13.9	Athens City	The Plains
15	14.1	West Branch Local	Beloit
16	14.2	Vinton County Local	Mc Arthur
17	14.3	Madison Local	Mansfield
18	14.4	Franklin Local	Duncan Falls
19	14.5	Morgan Local	Mc Connelsville
20	14.6	Celina City	Celina
20	14.6	Port Clinton City	Port Clinton
22	14.7	Lima City	Lima
23	14.8	Chagrin Falls Exempted Village	Chagrin Falls
23	14.8	Cuyahoga Falls City	Cuyahoga Falls
23	14.8	Sandusky City	Sandusky
26	14.9	Wyoming City	Wyoming
27	15.0	Coshocton City	Coshocton
27	15.0	Norwood City	Norwood
29	15.1	Buckeye Valley Local	Delaware
29	15.1	Dayton City	Dayton
29	15.1	Rossford Exempted Village	Rossford
29	15.1	Steubenville City	Steubenville
29	15.1	West Muskingum Local	Zanesville
29	15.1	Westfall Local	Williamsport
35	15.2	Niles City	Niles
35	15.2	Rolling Hills Local	Cambridge
35	15.2	Worthington City	Worthington
35	15.2	Youngstown City Schools	Youngstown
39	15.3	Kenston Local	Chagrin Falls
39	15.3	New Philadel. City	New Philadel.
41	15.4	Cambridge City	Cambridge
41	15.4	Logan Elm Local	Circleville
41	15.4	Switzerland of Ohio Local	Woodsfield
41	15.4	Toledo City	Toledo
45	15.5	Alliance City	Alliance
45	15.5	Batavia Local	Batavia
45	15.5	Crestwood Local	Mantua
45	15.5	Euclid City	Euclid
45	15.5	Gallia County Local	Gallipolis
45	15.5	Midview Local	Grafton
51	15.6	Alexander Local	Albany
51	15.6	Claymont City	Dennison
51	15.6	Cleveland Municipal	Cleveland
51	15.6	East Muskingum Local	New Concord
51	15.6	Jackson City	Jackson
51	15.6	Poland Local	Poland
51	15.6	Revere Local	Bath
51	15.6	Shaker Heights City	Shaker Heights
59	15.7	Akron City	Akron
59	15.7	Kenton City	Kenton
59	15.7	Maysville Local	Zanesville
59	15.7	Mount Vernon City	Mount Vernon
59	15.7	Wooster City	Wooster
64	15.8	Bedford City	Bedford
64	15.8	Bexley City	Bexley
64	15.8	Gahanna-Jefferson City	Gahanna
64	15.8	Northwest Local	Mc Dermott

Note: This section only includes districts with 1,500 or more students; All categories are ranked from high to low

64	15.8	Oakwood City	Dayton
64	15.8	Southeast Local	Ravenna
64	15.8	Warren Local	Vincent
64	15.8	Westlake City	Westlake
72	15.9	Fostoria City	Fostoria
72	15.9	London City	London
72	15.9	Mayfield City	Mayfield Hgts
72	15.9	New Lexington City	New Lexington
72	15.9	Southwest Licking Local	Pataskala
77	16.0	Clyde-Green Springs Exempted Village	Clyde
77	16.0	Lake Local	Millbury
77	16.0	Meigs Local	Pomeroy
77	16.0	Orrville City	Orrville
77	16.0	River View Local	Warsaw
82	16.1	Circleville City	Circleville
82	16.1	Upper Arlington City	Upper Arlington
84	16.2	Fairless Local	Navarre
84	16.2	Franklin City	Franklin
84	16.2	Indian Lake Local	Lewistown
84	16.2	Springfield City	Springfield
84	16.2	Strongsville City	Strongsville
89	16.3	Bellefontaine City	Bellefontaine
89	16.3	Bryan City	Bryan
89	16.3	Cincinnati City	Cincinnati
89	16.3	Massillon City	Massillon
89	16.3	Perry Local	Perry
89	16.3	Sheffield-Sheffield Lake City	Sheffield Vllg
89	16.3	Tallmadge City	Tallmadge
89	16.3	Trotwood-Madison City	Trotwood
97	16.4	Carlisle Local	Carlisle
97	16.4	Columbus City SD	Columbus
97	16.4	East Holmes Local	Berlin
97	16.4	Lakewood City	Lakewood
97	16.4	Parma City	Parma
97	16.4	Portsmouth City	Portsmouth
97	16.4	Van Wert City	Van Wert
97	16.4	Washington Local	Toledo
105	16.5	Coventry Local	Akron
105	16.5	Galion City	Galion
105	16.5	Hudson City	Hudson
105	16.5	Indian Creek Local	Wintersville
105	16.5	Middletown City	Middletown
105	16.5	New Albany-Plain Local	New Albany
105	16.5	Woodridge Local	Peninsula
112	16.6	Beaver Local	Lisbon
112	16.6	Licking Valley Local	Newark
112	16.6	North Canton City	North Canton
112	16.6	Northridge Local	Dayton
116	16.7	Bay Village City	Bay Village
116	16.7	Fairland Local	Proctorville
116	16.7	Fremont City	Fremont
116	16.7	Howland Local	Warren
120	16.8	Johnstown-Monroe Local	Johnstown
120	16.8	Maumee City	Maumee
120	16.8	Northmont City	Englewood
120	16.8	Ravenna City	Ravenna
120	16.8	South Euclid-Lyndhurst City	Lyndhurst
120	16.8	Valley View Local	Germantown
126	16.9	Amanda-Clearcreek Local	Amanda
126	16.9	Canton City	Canton
126	16.9	Edison Local (Formerly Berlin-Milan)	Milan
126	16.9	Logan-Hocking Local	Logan
126	16.9	New Richmond Exempted Village	New Richmond
126	16.9	North Fork Local	Utica
126	16.9	Sycamore Community City	Blue Ash
126	16.9	Talawanda City	Oxford
126	16.9	Winton Woods City	Cincinnati
135	17.0	Bethel-Tate Local	Bethel
135	17.0	Lexington Local	Lexington
135	17.0	Marietta City	Marietta
135	17.0	Salem City	Salem
135	17.0	Sylvania City	Sylvania
135	17.0	Wauseon Exempted Village	Wauseon
135	17.0	Willard City	Willard
142	17.1	Centerville City	Centerville
142	17.1	Clear Fork Valley Local	Bellville
142	17.1	Elyria City Schools	Elyria
142	17.1	Highland Local	Sparta
142	17.1	Rocky River City	Rocky River
142	17.1	Struthers City	Struthers
142	17.1	Union-Scioto Local	Chillicothe
149	17.2	Granville Exempted Village	Granville
149	17.2	Perkins Local	Sandusky
149	17.2	Princeton City	Cincinnati
152	17.3	Boardman Local	Youngstown
152	17.3	Conneaut Area City	Conneaut
152	17.3	Defiance City	Defiance
152	17.3	Delaware City	Delaware
152	17.3	Girard City SD	Girard
152	17.3	Hillsboro City	Hillsboro
152	17.3	Lorain City	Lorain
152	17.3	Miamisburg City	Miamisburg
152	17.3	Napoleon Area City	Napoleon
152	17.3	Springfield Local	Akron
152	17.3	Streetsboro City	Streetsboro
152	17.3	Urbana City	Urbana
152	17.3	Warren City	Warren
165	17.4	Ashland City	Ashland
165	17.4	Benjamin Logan Local	Bellefontaine
165	17.4	Canton Local	Canton
165	17.4	Chardon Local	Chardon
165	17.4	Chillicothe City	Chillicothe
165	17.4	Clinton-Massie Local	Clarksville
165	17.4	Findlay City	Findlay
165	17.4	Groveport Madison Local	Groveport
165	17.4	Hubbard Exempted Village	Hubbard
165	17.4	Marlington Local	Alliance
165	17.4	Minford Local	Minford
165	17.4	Mt Healthy City	Cincinnati
165	17.4	South Point Local	South Point
178	17.5	Berea City	Berea
178	17.5	Canfield Local	Canfield
178	17.5	Dublin City	Dublin
178	17.5	Gallipolis City	Gallipolis
178	17.5	Garfield Hgts City Schools	Garfield Hgts
178	17.5	Oregon City	Oregon
178	17.5	Reading Community City	Reading
185	17.6	Adams County/Ohio Valley Local	West Union
185	17.6	Copley-Fairlawn City	Copley
185	17.6	Firelands Local	South Amherst
185	17.6	Maple Heights City	Maple Heights
185	17.6	Mentor Exempted Village	Mentor
185	17.6	North Olmsted City	North Olmsted
185	17.6	Perry Local	Massillon
185	17.6	Upper Sandusky Exempted Village	Upper Sandusky
185	17.6	Washington CH City	Washington CH
194	17.7	Buckeye Local	Ashtabula
194	17.7	Fairborn City	Fairborn
194	17.7	Indian Valley Local Schools	Gnadenhutten
194	17.7	Tipp City Exempted Village	Tipp City
198	17.8	Kettering City	Kettering
198	17.8	Kings Local	Kings Mills
198	17.8	Miami Trace Local	Washington CH
198	17.8	Newark City	Newark
198	17.8	Northern Local	Thornville
198	17.8	Shawnee Local	Lima
204	17.9	Bellevue City	Bellevue
204	17.9	Benton Carroll Salem Local	Oak Harbor
204	17.9	Lancaster City	Lancaster
204	17.9	Solon City	Solon
204	17.9	Stow-Munroe Falls City SD	Stow
204	17.9	Willoughby-Eastlake City	Willoughby
210	18.0	Amherst Exempted Village	Amherst
210	18.0	Lake Local	Uniontown
210	18.0	Mariemont City	Cincinnati
210	18.0	Saint Clairsville-Richland City	Saint Clairsville
214	18.1	Heath City	Heath
214	18.1	Keystone Local	Lagrange
214	18.1	Northeastern Local	Springfield
214	18.1	Shelby City	Shelby
218	18.2	Edison Local	Hammondsville
218	18.2	Fairview Park City	Fairview Park
220	18.3	Avon Lake City	Avon Lake
220	18.3	Bath Local	Lima
220	18.3	Nordonia Hills City	Northfield
220	18.3	West Holmes Local	Millersburg
224	18.4	Blanchester Local	Blanchester
224	18.4	Green Local	Uniontown
224	18.4	Greenon Local	Enon
224	18.4	Ottawa-Glandorf Local	Ottawa
228	18.5	Aurora City	Aurora
228	18.5	Hilliard City	Columbus
228	18.5	Northwest Local	Canal Fulton
228	18.5	Norton City	Norton
228	18.5	Troy City	Troy
228	18.5	Wheelersburg Local	Wheelersburg
234	18.6	Brunswick City	Brunswick
234	18.6	Cloverleaf Local	Lodi
234	18.6	Licking Heights Local	Pataskala
237	18.7	Austintown Local	Youngstown
237	18.7	Carrollton Exempted Village	Carrollton
237	18.7	Marysville Exempted Village	Marysville
237	18.7	Vermilion Local	Vermilion
241	18.8	Canal Wnchstr Local	Canal Wnchstr
241	18.8	Greenfield Exempted Village	Greenfield
241	18.8	Mad River Local	Dayton
241	18.8	South-Western City	Grove City
241	18.8	Springboro Community City	Springboro
241	18.8	Saint Marys City	Saint Marys
241	18.8	West Carrollton City	West Carrollton
241	18.8	Zanesville City	Zanesville
249	18.9	Buckeye Local	Medina
249	18.9	Forest Hills Local	Cincinnati
249	18.9	Harrison Hills City	Cadiz
249	18.9	Painesville City Local	Painesville
249	18.9	Tecumseh Local	New Carlisle
249	18.9	Whitehall City	Whitehall
255	19.0	Eaton Community City	Eaton
255	19.0	N Ridgeville City	N Ridgeville
255	19.0	Norwalk City	Norwalk
255	19.0	Perrysburg Exempted Village	Perrysburg
255	19.0	Xenia Community City	Xenia
260	19.1	Beavercreek City	Beavercreek
260	19.1	Oak Hills Local	Cincinnati
262	19.2	Goshen Local	Goshen
262	19.2	Minerva Local	Minerva
262	19.2	North Royalton City	North Royalton
262	19.2	West Geauga Local	Chesterland
266	19.3	Bellbrook-Sugarcreek Local SD	Bellbrook
266	19.3	Big Walnut Local	Sunbury
266	19.3	Bowling Green City SD	Bowling Green
266	19.3	Dover City	Dover
266	19.3	Elida Local	Elida
266	19.3	Fairfield Union Local	Lancaster
266	19.3	Piqua City	Piqua
273	19.4	Barberton City	Barberton
273	19.4	Clermont Northeastern Local	Batavia
273	19.4	Olmsted Falls City	Olmsted Falls
273	19.4	Ross Local	Hamilton
277	19.5	Fairfield City	Fairfield
277	19.5	Olentangy Local	Lewis Center
279	19.6	Madison Local	Middletown
279	19.6	Northwestern Local	Springfield
279	19.6	Springfield Local	Holland
279	19.6	Westerville City	Westerville
283	19.7	Graham Local	Saint Paris
283	19.7	Huber Heights City	Huber Heights
283	19.7	Tri-Valley Local	Dresden
283	19.7	Waverly City	Waverly
287	19.8	Clearview Local	Lorain
287	19.8	Hamilton City	Hamilton
287	19.8	Madison Local	Madison
287	19.8	Milford Exempted Village	Milford
291	19.9	Avon Local	Avon
291	19.9	North College Hill City	Cincinnati
291	19.9	River Valley Local	Caledonia
294	20.0	Ashtabula Area City	Ashtabula
294	20.0	Lakeview Local	Cortland
294	20.0	Pickerington Local	Pickerington
297	20.1	Brecksville-Broadview Heights City	Brecksville
297	20.1	Louisville City	Louisville
297	20.1	Ontario Local	Mansfield
297	20.1	Vandalia-Butler City	Vandalia
301	20.2	Clark-Shawnee Local	Springfield
301	20.2	Riverside Local	Painesville
301	20.2	Sidney City	Sidney
304	20.4	Geneva Area City	Geneva
304	20.4	Teays Valley Local	Ashville
306	20.5	Edgewood City	Trenton
306	20.5	Hamilton Local	Columbus
306	20.5	Three Rivers Local	Cleves
309	20.6	Jonathan Alder Local	Plain City
309	20.6	Mason City SD	Mason
309	20.6	Northwest Local	Cincinnati
309	20.6	West Clermont Local	Cincinnati
313	20.7	Highland Local	Medina
313	20.7	Little Miami Local	Maineville
315	20.8	Loveland City	Loveland
316	21.0	Wilmington City	Wilmington
317	21.1	Wapakoneta City	Wapakoneta
318	21.2	Bloom-Carroll Local	Carroll
318	21.2	Jefferson Area Local	Jefferson

Note: This section only includes districts with 1,500 or more students; All categories are ranked from high to low

318	21.2	Tiffin City	Tiffin
321	21.4	Wadsworth City	Wadsworth
322	21.6	Twinsburg City	Twinsburg
323	21.7	Anthony Wayne Local	Whitehouse
323	21.7	Lebanon City	Lebanon
325	21.8	Plain Local	Canton
326	22.0	Medina City SD	Medina
326	22.0	Monroe Local SD	Monroe
328	22.3	Jackson Local	Massillon
329	22.4	Lakota Local	Liberty Twp
330	22.9	Southwest Local	Harrison
331	23.1	Reynoldsburg City	Reynoldsburg
332	23.7	Western Brown Local	Mount Orab
333	33.4	Alternative Education Academy	Toledo
334	34.4	Electronic Classroom of Tomorrow	Columbus
335	35.6	Ohio Connections Academy, Inc	Cleveland
336	42.1	Ohio Virtual Academy	Maumee
337	95.8	Treca Digital Academy	Marion

Student/Librarian Ratio

(number of students per librarian)

Rank	Number	District Name	City
1	440.4	Orange City	Cleveland
2	456.9	Chardon Local	Chardon
3	459.3	New Lexington City	New Lexington
4	470.3	Indian Hill Exempted Village	Cincinnati
5	493.8	Granville Exempted Village	Granville
6	519.5	Poland Local	Poland
7	540.0	Bexley City	Bexley
8	591.3	Shaker Heights City	Shaker Heights
9	597.3	Meigs Local	Pomeroy
10	638.0	Westlake City	Westlake
11	640.6	Dublin City	Dublin
12	671.7	New Albany-Plain Local	New Albany
13	680.6	Worthington City	Worthington
14	708.0	Kent City	Kent
15	719.5	Olentangy Local	Lewis Center
15	719.5	Upper Arlington City	Upper Arlington
17	722.7	Union-Scioto Local	Chillicothe
18	755.5	Minford Local	Minford
19	766.0	Wheelersburg Local	Wheelersburg
20	768.0	Madison Local	Middletown
21	790.8	Logan-Hocking Local	Logan
22	815.2	Sycamore Community City	Blue Ash
23	823.7	Jackson City	Jackson
24	826.0	Cleveland Heights-Univ Hgts City	University Hgts
25	828.0	East Cleveland City SD	East Cleveland
25	828.0	Fairland Local	Proctorville
27	829.9	Forest Hills Local	Cincinnati
28	839.4	Gahanna-Jefferson City	Gahanna
29	841.0	Rossford Exempted Village	Rossford
30	862.4	West Geauga Local	Chesterland
31	879.0	Lakeview Local	Cortland
32	889.5	Hilliard City	Columbus
33	906.0	Groveport Madison Local	Groveport
34	910.0	Ravenna City	Ravenna
35	911.4	Hudson City	Hudson
36	918.7	Canfield Local	Canfield
37	922.5	Portsmouth City	Portsmouth
38	944.0	Ontario Local	Mansfield
39	953.5	Hubbard Exempted Village	Hubbard
40	956.5	Wyoming City	Wyoming
41	976.1	Licking Valley Local	Newark
42	985.0	Napoleon Area City	Napoleon
43	994.0	Bowling Green City SD	Bowling Green
44	1,005.5	Chagrin Falls Exempted Village	Chagrin Falls
45	1,019.4	Warren City	Warren
46	1,020.0	Circleville City	Circleville
47	1,046.5	Gallia County Local	Gallipolis
48	1,065.5	Northern Local	Thornville
49	1,066.5	East Muskingum Local	New Concord
50	1,066.7	Whitehall City	Whitehall
51	1,076.0	Indian Creek Local	Wintersville
52	1,081.6	Youngstown City Schools	Youngstown
53	1,085.4	Akron City	Akron
54	1,101.8	Cleveland Municipal	Cleveland
55	1,118.5	East Liverpool City	East Liverpool
56	1,135.2	Norwalk City	Norwalk
57	1,137.5	Maysville Local	Zanesville
58	1,162.7	Lake Local	Uniontown
59	1,168.7	Northeastern Local	Springfield
60	1,177.6	Strongsville City	Strongsville
61	1,204.3	Canal Wnchstr Local	Canal Wnchstr
62	1,229.5	Cuyahoga Falls City	Cuyahoga Falls
63	1,242.0	Tipp City Exempted Village	Tipp City
64	1,251.7	Westerville City	Westerville
65	1,306.5	Revere Local	Bath
66	1,320.0	Field Local	Mogadore
67	1,323.1	Berea City	Berea
68	1,357.3	Lebanon City	Lebanon
69	1,464.0	Franklin City	Franklin
70	1,478.0	Solon City	Solon
71	1,484.0	Midview Local	Grafton
72	1,504.0	Fairless Local	Navarre
72	1,504.0	Tecumseh Local	New Carlisle
74	1,514.0	Alliance City	Alliance
75	1,530.0	Westfall Local	Williamsport
76	1,556.0	Northwest Local	Mc Dermott
77	1,558.0	Madison Local	Mansfield
78	1,562.0	Edison Local	Hammondsville
79	1,569.0	Johnstown-Monroe Local	Johnstown
80	1,570.5	Copley-Fairlawn City	Copley
81	1,577.0	Coshocton City	Coshocton
82	1,583.0	North College Hill City	Cincinnati
83	1,592.0	Carlisle Local	Carlisle
84	1,600.6	Lakewood City	Lakewood
85	1,616.2	Clearview Local	Lorain
86	1,626.0	Upper Sandusky Exempted Village	Upper Sandusky
87	1,637.0	Keystone Local	Lagrange
88	1,639.0	South Point Local	South Point
89	1,650.0	Heath City	Heath
90	1,666.8	Toledo City	Toledo
91	1,668.7	Miami Trace Local	Washington CH
92	1,672.4	Willoughby-Eastlake City	Willoughby
93	1,677.0	Firelands Local	South Amherst
94	1,678.0	Jefferson Area Local	Jefferson
95	1,679.0	Southeast Local	Ravenna
96	1,684.0	Mariemont City	Cincinnati
97	1,696.0	Triway Local	Wooster
98	1,703.0	Blanchester Local	Blanchester
99	1,719.3	Orrville City	Orrville
100	1,726.1	West Holmes Local	Millersburg
101	1,742.0	Northwestern Local	Springfield
102	1,746.0	Benjamin Logan Local	Bellefontaine
103	1,750.7	Stow-Munroe Falls City SD	Stow
104	1,753.0	Sheffield-Sheffield Lake City	Sheffield Vllg
105	1,760.0	Buckeye Local	Ashtabula
106	1,761.0	Perry Local	Perry
107	1,765.0	Clear Fork Valley Local	Bellville
108	1,777.4	Columbus City SD	Columbus
109	1,783.0	Fairview Park City	Fairview Park
110	1,800.0	Bath Local	Lima
111	1,800.3	Delaware City	Delaware
112	1,804.0	Fostoria City	Fostoria
113	1,809.0	Brunswick City	Brunswick
114	1,810.0	Princeton City	Cincinnati
115	1,813.3	Marietta City	Marietta
116	1,819.5	Mansfield City	Mansfield
117	1,840.0	Highland Local	Sparta
118	1,842.0	Bloom-Carroll Local	Carroll
119	1,851.0	Valley View Local	Germantown
120	1,856.0	Galion City	Galion
121	1,862.0	Waverly City	Waverly
122	1,866.0	Sylvania City	Sylvania
123	1,874.5	Springfield City	Springfield
124	1,890.0	Lakewood Local	Hebron
125	1,894.0	Mount Vernon City	Mount Vernon
126	1,902.0	Struthers City	Struthers
127	1,906.0	Vermilion Local	Vermilion
128	1,919.0	South Euclid-Lyndhurst City	Lyndhurst
129	1,952.0	Fairfield Union Local	Lancaster
130	1,955.0	Logan Elm Local	Circleville
131	1,969.5	Adams County/Ohio Valley Local	West Union
132	1,974.0	London City	London
133	1,978.3	Jackson Local	Massillon
134	1,990.0	Massillon City	Massillon
135	2,000.0	Three Rivers Local	Cleves
136	2,000.5	Little Miami Local	Maineville
137	2,011.4	Teays Valley Local	Ashville
138	2,017.0	Morgan Local	Mc Connelsville
139	2,025.0	Kings Local	Kings Mills
140	2,029.9	Dayton City	Dayton
141	2,031.0	Van Wert City	Van Wert
142	2,039.0	Greenfield Exempted Village	Greenfield
143	2,042.0	Graham Local	Saint Paris
144	2,049.0	Woodridge Local	Peninsula
145	2,051.0	Fremont City	Fremont
146	2,051.7	Cincinnati City	Cincinnati
147	2,058.5	Brecksville-Broadview Heights City	Brecksville
148	2,064.7	Lancaster City	Lancaster
149	2,066.7	River View Local	Warsaw
150	2,073.0	Salem City	Salem
151	2,074.0	West Branch Local	Beloit
152	2,087.0	Oakwood City	Dayton
153	2,089.0	Claymont City	Dennison
154	2,092.5	Marion City	Marion
155	2,104.0	Saint Marys City	Saint Marys
156	2,146.0	Warren Local	Vincent
157	2,146.5	Anthony Wayne Local	Whitehouse
158	2,175.2	Washington CH City	Washington CH
159	2,176.0	Streetsboro City	Streetsboro
160	2,184.8	Northwest Local	Cincinnati
161	2,202.0	Buckeye Valley Local	Delaware
162	2,205.7	Northwest Local	Canal Fulton
163	2,217.0	Jonathan Alder Local	Plain City
164	2,220.0	Clyde-Green Springs Exempted Village	Clyde
165	2,231.0	Mayfield City	Mayfield Hgts
166	2,300.0	Vinton County Local	Mc Arthur
167	2,312.5	North Royalton City	North Royalton
168	2,405.0	Marlington Local	Alliance
169	2,410.5	Bay Village City	Bay Village
170	2,414.0	Springfield Local	Akron
171	2,429.0	Niles City	Niles
172	2,445.0	Tallmadge City	Tallmadge
173	2,462.0	Maumee City	Maumee
174	2,467.8	Gallipolis City	Gallipolis
175	2,481.0	Cloverleaf Local	Lodi
176	2,490.0	Defiance City	Defiance
177	2,503.0	Monroe Local SD	Monroe
178	2,508.3	Hamilton City	Hamilton
179	2,519.0	Pickerington Local	Pickerington
180	2,526.0	Trotwood-Madison City	Trotwood
181	2,564.0	Hillsboro City	Hillsboro
182	2,621.9	Tiffin City	Tiffin
183	2,679.0	Rocky River City	Rocky River
184	2,702.0	Celina City	Celina
185	2,721.0	Athens City	The Plains
186	2,726.0	Ross Local	Hamilton
187	2,729.2	East Holmes Local	Berlin
188	2,775.0	Dover City	Dover
189	2,798.8	Buckeye Local	Medina
190	2,877.0	Howland Local	Warren
191	2,924.0	Aurora City	Aurora
192	2,925.0	Springboro Community City	Springboro
193	2,964.0	Talawanda City	Oxford
194	2,980.0	New Philadel. City	New Philadel.
195	2,985.0	Kenston Local	Chagrin Falls
196	2,995.0	Louisville City	Louisville
197	3,006.1	Elida Local	Elida
198	3,038.0	Clermont Northeastern Local	Batavia
199	3,051.0	Wapakoneta City	Wapakoneta
200	3,099.0	Painesville City Local	Painesville
201	3,111.0	Big Walnut Local	Sunbury
202	3,122.8	Medina City SD	Medina
203	3,132.0	Western Brown Local	Mount Orab
204	3,153.5	Newark City	Newark
205	3,213.0	Mt Healthy City	Cincinnati
206	3,245.0	Ashland City	Ashland
207	3,261.0	Reynoldsburg City	Reynoldsburg
208	3,264.0	Sandusky City	Sandusky
209	3,286.0	Milford Exempted Village	Milford
210	3,300.0	Sidney City	Sidney
211	3,378.0	Winton Woods City	Cincinnati
212	3,387.5	Bethel-Tate Local	Bethel
213	3,419.0	Washington Local	Toledo
214	3,470.0	Bedford City	Bedford
215	3,496.5	Wilmington City	Wilmington
216	3,603.0	Edgewood City	Trenton
217	3,613.0	Avon Local	Avon
218	3,627.0	Wooster City	Wooster
219	3,671.0	Licking Heights Local	Pataskala
220	3,680.6	Goshen Local	Goshen
221	3,694.0	Maple Heights City	Maple Heights
222	3,710.0	Oregon City	Oregon
223	3,721.3	Parma City	Parma
224	3,730.0	Avon Lake City	Avon Lake
225	3,732.0	Nordonia Hills City	Northfield
226	3,758.0	Garfield Hgts City Schools	Garfield Hgts
227	3,773.0	Southwest Licking Local	Pataskala
228	3,786.0	Olmsted Falls City	Olmsted Falls

Note: This section only includes districts with 1,500 or more students; All categories are ranked from high to low

229	3,854.0	West Carrollton City	West Carrollton
230	3,876.0	Mad River Local	Dayton
231	3,910.0	Springfield Local	Holland
232	3,924.0	Barberton City	Barberton
233	4,036.0	North Olmsted City	North Olmsted
234	4,100.0	West Clermont Local	Cincinnati
235	4,141.5	Centerville City	Centerville
236	4,197.0	Green Local	Uniontown
237	4,223.0	Fairborn City	Fairborn
238	4,267.0	Xenia Community City	Xenia
239	4,332.0	Troy City	Troy
240	4,397.0	Boardman Local	Youngstown
241	4,494.2	Lima City	Lima
242	4,496.0	Riverside Local	Painesville
243	4,602.0	North Canton City	North Canton
244	4,679.0	Perrysburg Exempted Village	Perrysburg
245	4,697.0	Loveland City	Loveland
246	4,732.5	Canton City	Canton
247	4,951.0	Perry Local	Massillon
248	5,119.0	Northmont City	Englewood
249	5,153.0	Marysville Exempted Village	Marysville
250	5,276.8	South-Western City	Grove City
251	5,341.5	Mason City SD	Mason
252	5,484.0	Miamisburg City	Miamisburg
253	5,517.0	Euclid City	Euclid
254	5,802.0	Findlay City	Findlay
255	5,930.0	Huber Heights City	Huber Heights
256	6,272.0	Middletown City	Middletown
257	6,550.0	Lorain City	Lorain
258	7,454.0	Beavercreek City	Beavercreek
259	7,709.0	Kettering City	Kettering
260	7,899.0	Mentor Exempted Village	Mentor
261	7,948.0	Oak Hills Local	Cincinnati
262	8,111.5	Lakota Local	Liberty Twp
263	8,184.0	N Ridgeville City	N Ridgeville
264	9,700.0	Amherst Exempted Village	Amherst
265	12,974.0	Electronic Classroom of Tomorrow	Columbus
n/a	n/a	Alexander Local	Albany
n/a	n/a	Alternative Education Academy	Toledo
n/a	n/a	Amanda-Clearcreek Local	Amanda
n/a	n/a	Ashtabula Area City	Ashtabula
n/a	n/a	Austintown Local	Youngstown
n/a	n/a	Batavia Local	Batavia
n/a	n/a	Beaver Local	Lisbon
n/a	n/a	Bellbrook-Sugarcreek Local SD	Bellbrook
n/a	n/a	Bellefontaine City	Bellefontaine
n/a	n/a	Bellevue City	Bellevue
n/a	n/a	Benton Carroll Salem Local	Oak Harbor
n/a	n/a	Bryan City	Bryan
n/a	n/a	Buckeye Local	Dillonvale
n/a	n/a	Cambridge City	Cambridge
n/a	n/a	Canton Local	Canton
n/a	n/a	Carrollton Exempted Village	Carrollton
n/a	n/a	Chillicothe City	Chillicothe
n/a	n/a	Clark-Shawnee Local	Springfield
n/a	n/a	Clinton-Massie Local	Clarksville
n/a	n/a	Conneaut Area City	Conneaut
n/a	n/a	Coventry Local	Akron
n/a	n/a	Crestwood Local	Mantua
n/a	n/a	Eaton Community City	Eaton
n/a	n/a	Edison Local (Formerly Berlin-Milan)	Milan
n/a	n/a	Elyria City Schools	Elyria
n/a	n/a	Fairfield City	Fairfield
n/a	n/a	Franklin Local	Duncan Falls
n/a	n/a	Geneva Area City	Geneva
n/a	n/a	Girard City SD	Girard
n/a	n/a	Greenon Local	Enon
n/a	n/a	Greenville City	Greenville
n/a	n/a	Hamilton Local	Columbus
n/a	n/a	Harrison Hills City	Cadiz
n/a	n/a	Highland Local	Medina
n/a	n/a	Indian Lake Local	Lewistown
n/a	n/a	Indian Valley Local Schools	Gnadenhutten
n/a	n/a	Kenton City	Kenton
n/a	n/a	Lake Local	Millbury
n/a	n/a	Lexington Local	Lexington
n/a	n/a	Madison Local	Madison
n/a	n/a	Minerva Local	Minerva
n/a	n/a	New Richmond Exempted Village	New Richmond
n/a	n/a	North Fork Local	Utica
n/a	n/a	Northridge Local	Dayton
n/a	n/a	Norton City	Norton
n/a	n/a	Norwood City	Norwood
n/a	n/a	Ohio Connections Academy, Inc	Cleveland
n/a	n/a	Ohio Virtual Academy	Maumee
n/a	n/a	Ottawa-Glandorf Local	Ottawa
n/a	n/a	Perkins Local	Sandusky
n/a	n/a	Piqua City	Piqua
n/a	n/a	Plain Local	Canton
n/a	n/a	Port Clinton City	Port Clinton
n/a	n/a	Reading Community City	Reading
n/a	n/a	River Valley Local	Caledonia
n/a	n/a	Rolling Hills Local	Cambridge
n/a	n/a	Shawnee Local	Lima
n/a	n/a	Shelby City	Shelby
n/a	n/a	Southwest Local	Harrison
n/a	n/a	Saint Clairsville-Richland City	Saint Clairsville
n/a	n/a	Steubenville City	Steubenville
n/a	n/a	Switzerland of Ohio Local	Woodsfield
n/a	n/a	Treca Digital Academy	Marion
n/a	n/a	Tri-Valley Local	Dresden
n/a	n/a	Twinsburg City	Twinsburg
n/a	n/a	Urbana City	Urbana
n/a	n/a	Vandalia-Butler City	Vandalia
n/a	n/a	Wadsworth City	Wadsworth
n/a	n/a	Wauseon Exempted Village	Wauseon
n/a	n/a	West Muskingum Local	Zanesville
n/a	n/a	Willard City	Willard
n/a	n/a	Zanesville City	Zanesville

Student/Counselor Ratio

(number of students per counselor)

Rank	Number	District Name	City
1	180.7	Union-Scioto Local	Chillicothe
2	200.4	Tallmadge City	Tallmadge
3	216.0	Kenton City	Kenton
4	217.0	Kings Local	Kings Mills
5	221.3	Indian Hill Exempted Village	Cincinnati
6	228.0	Bellevue City	Bellevue
7	229.4	Shawnee Local	Lima
8	237.8	Struthers City	Struthers
9	246.2	Whitehall City	Whitehall
10	246.3	Napoleon Area City	Napoleon
11	248.2	Cleveland Heights-Univ Hgts City	University Hgts
12	248.6	East Liverpool City	East Liverpool
13	251.4	Chagrin Falls Exempted Village	Chagrin Falls
14	259.8	Poland Local	Poland
15	264.1	Greenville City	Greenville
16	270.6	Barberton City	Barberton
17	275.3	Alliance City	Alliance
18	280.6	Bryan City	Bryan
19	285.5	Copley-Fairlawn City	Copley
20	297.9	Bexley City	Bexley
21	300.7	Fostoria City	Fostoria
22	301.0	Cambridge City	Cambridge
23	302.2	Minford Local	Minford
24	307.8	Maumee City	Maumee
25	312.1	Cloverleaf Local	Lodi
26	314.2	Groveport Madison Local	Groveport
27	314.6	Orange City	Cleveland
28	315.5	Canton City	Canton
29	319.6	North Canton City	North Canton
30	319.8	Revere Local	Bath
30	319.8	South Euclid-Lyndhurst City	Lyndhurst
32	321.2	Reading Community City	Reading
33	322.7	Kenston Local	Chagrin Falls
34	327.4	Keystone Local	Lagrange
35	335.8	Norwood City	Norwood
36	336.4	Rossford Exempted Village	Rossford
37	337.8	Elyria City Schools	Elyria
38	338.0	Youngstown City Schools	Youngstown
39	338.5	Urbana City	Urbana
40	341.5	Woodridge Local	Peninsula
41	341.8	Fremont City	Fremont
42	342.2	Girard City SD	Girard
43	342.4	Westlake City	Westlake
44	344.2	Western Brown Local	Mount Orab
45	345.7	Upper Arlington City	Upper Arlington
46	347.0	Bedford City	Bedford
47	348.4	Oakwood City	Dayton
48	350.8	Dublin City	Dublin
49	351.6	Lakeview Local	Cortland
50	353.3	Sycamore Community City	Blue Ash
51	353.6	Perry Local	Massillon
52	354.0	Kent City	Kent
53	355.8	North Royalton City	North Royalton
54	356.8	Mariemont City	Cincinnati
55	358.4	Meigs Local	Pomeroy
56	359.3	West Geauga Local	Chesterland
57	360.2	Fairview Park City	Fairview Park
58	360.9	Trotwood-Madison City	Trotwood
59	361.7	Hudson City	Hudson
60	362.0	Bellbrook-Sugarcreek Local SD	Bellbrook
61	366.7	Sidney City	Sidney
62	366.9	North Olmsted City	North Olmsted
62	366.9	Perry Local	Perry
64	368.0	Strongsville City	Strongsville
65	369.0	Portsmouth City	Portsmouth
66	370.5	Talawanda City	Oxford
67	370.8	Cleveland Municipal	Cleveland
68	372.2	Bay Village City	Bay Village
69	373.2	Nordonia Hills City	Northfield
70	373.3	Kettering City	Kettering
71	375.1	Wyoming City	Wyoming
72	377.3	Southwest Licking Local	Pataskala
73	377.7	Brecksville-Broadview Heights City	Brecksville
74	379.9	Washington Local	Toledo
75	381.5	Green Local	Uniontown
76	382.5	Westfall Local	Williamsport
77	383.5	Ottawa-Glandorf Local	Ottawa
78	383.8	Alexander Local	Albany
79	384.0	Madison Local	Middletown
80	386.0	Celina City	Celina
81	389.0	Northwest Local	Mc Dermott
82	389.4	Tiffin City	Tiffin
83	389.8	Columbus City SD	Columbus
84	392.3	Beavercreek City	Beavercreek
85	393.9	Northeastern Local	Springfield
86	394.5	Lake Local	Millbury
87	400.0	Amanda-Clearcreek Local	Amanda
88	400.6	Avon Lake City	Avon Lake
89	402.8	Solon City	Solon
90	403.0	Wooster City	Wooster
91	403.9	Plain Local	Canton
92	404.8	Niles City	Niles
93	406.0	Mayfield City	Mayfield Hgts
94	407.9	Washington CH City	Washington CH
95	408.0	Sandusky City	Sandusky
96	411.5	Granville Exempted Village	Granville
97	414.0	Fairland Local	Proctorville
97	414.0	Tipp City Exempted Village	Tipp City
99	414.8	West Branch Local	Beloit
100	414.9	Saint Clairsville-Richland City	Saint Clairsville
101	417.5	Indian Lake Local	Lewistown
102	417.7	Aurora City	Aurora
103	418.3	Franklin City	Franklin
104	419.8	Southeast Local	Ravenna
105	420.8	Saint Marys City	Saint Marys
106	421.3	Treca Digital Academy	Marion
107	424.4	Eaton Community City	Eaton
108	424.8	Warren City	Warren
109	425.4	Perrysburg Exempted Village	Perrysburg
110	426.0	Bowling Green City SD	Bowling Green
111	426.5	Sylvania City	Sylvania
112	427.9	Louisville City	Louisville
113	428.9	Oregon City	Oregon
114	429.3	Anthony Wayne Local	Whitehouse
115	430.5	Port Clinton City	Port Clinton
116	430.8	Canton Local	Canton
117	433.2	Troy City	Troy
118	435.6	Firelands Local	South Amherst
119	435.9	Centerville City	Centerville
119	435.9	Wapakoneta City	Wapakoneta
121	436.5	Benjamin Logan Local	Bellefontaine
122	437.0	Westerville City	Westerville
123	437.3	Austintown Local	Youngstown
124	438.3	Sheffield-Sheffield Lake City	Sheffield Vllg
125	438.6	Wauseon Exempted Village	Wauseon
126	439.7	Boardman Local	Youngstown
127	442.2	Toledo City	Toledo
128	443.5	Shaker Heights City	Shaker Heights
129	444.0	Clyde-Green Springs Exempted Village	Clyde
130	445.1	Madison Local	Mansfield
131	446.5	Rocky River City	Rocky River
132	447.1	Cuyahoga Falls City	Cuyahoga Falls
133	449.0	Northmont City	Englewood
134	450.0	Bath Local	Lima
135	450.1	Delaware City	Delaware
136	452.3	Akron City	Akron
137	454.3	Ross Local	Hamilton

Note: This section only includes districts with 1,500 or more students; All categories are ranked from high to low

138	455.3	Clark-Shawnee Local	Springfield
139	456.4	Perkins Local	Sandusky
140	456.5	Jackson Local	Massillon
141	456.6	Midview Local	Grafton
142	458.0	Pickerington Local	Pickerington
143	458.7	Berea City	Berea
144	458.9	Licking Heights Local	Pataskala
145	459.0	Mt Healthy City	Cincinnati
146	459.3	New Lexington City	New Lexington
147	460.5	Shelby City	Shelby
148	461.2	Olentangy Local	Lewis Center
149	463.6	Ashland City	Ashland
150	465.1	Lake Local	Uniontown
151	466.6	Massillon City	Massillon
152	468.5	Marysville Exempted Village	Marysville
153	470.2	New Albany-Plain Local	New Albany
154	470.6	Forest Hills Local	Cincinnati
155	470.8	Clinton-Massie Local	Clarksville
155	470.8	Licking Valley Local	Newark
157	471.3	Hillsboro City	Hillsboro
158	472.0	Ontario Local	Mansfield
159	474.3	Buckeye Local	Dillonvale
160	476.8	Hubbard Exempted Village	Hubbard
161	477.7	Vermilion Local	Vermilion
162	478.2	Gahanna-Jefferson City	Gahanna
163	478.5	Highland Local	Medina
164	478.8	Worthington City	Worthington
165	479.5	Howland Local	Warren
166	479.8	Northwest Local	Canal Fulton
167	482.3	Crestwood Local	Mantua
168	482.7	Marion City	Marion
169	487.2	Steubenville City	Steubenville
170	488.8	Springfield Local	Holland
171	493.7	Mentor Exempted Village	Mentor
172	493.8	Findlay City	Findlay
173	496.8	East Cleveland City SD	East Cleveland
174	498.0	Defiance City	Defiance
175	499.9	Springfield City	Springfield
176	500.2	Bellefontaine City	Bellefontaine
177	500.6	Miami Trace Local	Washington CH
178	504.5	Miamisburg City	Miamisburg
179	504.6	Lakota Local	Liberty Twp
180	507.8	Van Wert City	Van Wert
181	510.0	Circleville City	Circleville
182	510.7	Wheelersburg Local	Wheelersburg
183	511.6	Olmsted Falls City	Olmsted Falls
184	515.0	Lakewood Local	Hebron
185	516.5	Painesville City Local	Painesville
186	517.2	Vandalia-Butler City	Vandalia
187	522.3	Claymont City	Dennison
188	525.3	Orrville City	Orrville
189	525.7	Coshocton City	Coshocton
190	527.6	Twinsburg City	Twinsburg
191	527.7	Maple Heights City	Maple Heights
192	530.0	Goshen Local	Goshen
193	530.7	Carlisle Local	Carlisle
194	533.7	North Fork Local	Utica
195	534.2	Mason City SD	Mason
196	535.3	Benton Carroll Salem Local	Oak Harbor
197	536.9	Garfield Hgts City Schools	Garfield Hgts
198	538.0	Indian Creek Local	Wintersville
199	539.1	Huber Heights City	Huber Heights
200	541.0	Rolling Hills Local	Cambridge
201	541.1	Mount Vernon City	Mount Vernon
202	542.0	Upper Sandusky Exempted Village	Upper Sandusky
203	542.9	Lebanon City	Lebanon
204	544.0	Marietta City	Marietta
205	544.2	Athens City	The Plains
206	544.3	Hilliard City	Columbus
207	545.0	Willard City	Willard
208	546.0	Ravenna City	Ravenna
209	546.1	Buckeye Local	Medina
210	550.5	Buckeye Valley Local	Delaware
211	551.7	Euclid City	Euclid
212	552.1	Lima City	Lima
213	556.4	Clearview Local	Lorain
214	557.7	Fairfield Union Local	Lancaster
215	562.6	Wadsworth City	Wadsworth
216	564.0	London City	London
217	565.3	Triway Local	Wooster
218	568.8	Maysville Local	Zanesville
219	569.5	Valley View Local	Germantown
220	570.0	Greenon Local	Enon
221	572.8	Loveland City	Loveland
222	574.9	Parma City	Parma
223	575.0	Vinton County Local	Mc Arthur
224	578.3	Wilmington City	Wilmington
225	582.6	Northwestern Local	Springfield
226	583.6	Stow-Munroe Falls City SD	Stow
227	585.0	Springboro Community City	Springboro
228	586.2	Southwest Local	Harrison
229	586.7	Buckeye Local	Ashtabula
230	589.8	Switzerland of Ohio Local	Woodsfield
231	594.0	Chardon Local	Chardon
232	599.5	New Richmond Exempted Village	New Richmond
232	599.5	Riverside Local	Painesville
234	600.5	Edgewood City	Trenton
235	602.2	Canal Wnchstr Local	Canal Wnchstr
236	602.8	Marlington Local	Alliance
237	603.3	Princeton City	Cincinnati
238	603.5	Springfield Local	Akron
239	603.9	Bloom-Carroll Local	Carroll
240	604.8	Middletown City	Middletown
241	605.7	Minerva Local	Minerva
242	606.5	Mansfield City	Mansfield
243	609.6	Xenia Community City	Xenia
244	613.3	Highland Local	Sparta
245	620.2	Teays Valley Local	Ashville
246	622.2	Big Walnut Local	Sunbury
247	629.2	Brunswick City	Brunswick
248	632.9	Electronic Classroom of Tomorrow	Columbus
249	633.4	Jonathan Alder Local	Plain City
250	642.3	West Carrollton City	West Carrollton
251	642.5	Norton City	Norton
252	644.7	River Valley Local	Caledonia
253	646.7	Amherst Exempted Village	Amherst
254	651.7	Logan Elm Local	Circleville
255	655.0	Franklin Local	Duncan Falls
256	655.4	Northwest Local	Cincinnati
257	659.0	Logan-Hocking Local	Logan
258	663.6	Madison Local	Madison
259	666.7	Three Rivers Local	Cleves
260	666.8	Little Miami Local	Maineville
261	668.6	Ohio Connections Academy, Inc	Cleveland
262	675.6	Winton Woods City	Cincinnati
263	679.7	Greenfield Exempted Village	Greenfield
264	680.7	Graham Local	Saint Paris
265	682.0	N Ridgeville City	N Ridgeville
266	688.4	Piqua City	Piqua
267	691.0	Salem City	Salem
268	693.8	Dover City	Dover
269	697.7	Gallia County Local	Gallipolis
270	698.0	Fairborn City	Fairborn
271	707.3	Mad River Local	Dayton
272	709.5	Norwalk City	Norwalk
273	710.3	Northern Local	Thornville
274	711.0	Coventry Local	Akron
275	715.3	Warren Local	Vincent
276	715.7	Gallipolis City	Gallipolis
277	716.6	Hamilton City	Hamilton
278	725.3	Streetsboro City	Streetsboro
279	730.5	East Muskingum Local	New Concord
280	732.3	Chillicothe City	Chillicothe
281	735.9	Oak Hills Local	Cincinnati
282	740.0	Carrollton Exempted Village	Carrollton
283	742.4	Galion City	Galion
284	745.0	New Philadel. City	New Philadel.
285	746.8	Fairfield City	Fairfield
286	748.5	Tri-Valley Local	Dresden
287	751.0	West Muskingum Local	Zanesville
288	752.0	Fairless Local	Navarre
288	752.0	Tecumseh Local	New Carlisle
290	757.8	Zanesville City	Zanesville
291	759.5	Clermont Northeastern Local	Batavia
292	760.2	Willoughby-Eastlake City	Willoughby
293	770.4	Hamilton Local	Columbus
294	774.3	Lancaster City	Lancaster
295	776.8	South Point Local	South Point
296	781.0	Edison Local	Hammondsville
297	781.5	Edison Local (Formerly Berlin-Milan)	Milan
298	784.5	Johnstown-Monroe Local	Johnstown
299	792.7	Lexington Local	Lexington
300	794.0	West Holmes Local	Millersburg
301	807.5	Ohio Virtual Academy	Maumee
302	813.0	Bethel-Tate Local	Bethel
303	818.8	Lorain City	Lorain
304	823.7	Jackson City	Jackson
305	831.0	Avon Local	Avon
306	844.3	South-Western City	Grove City
307	845.0	Geneva Area City	Geneva
308	851.5	Blanchester Local	Blanchester
309	852.5	Conneaut Area City	Conneaut
310	861.8	Lakewood City	Lakewood
311	887.0	East Holmes Local	Berlin
312	905.5	Indian Valley Local Schools	Gnadenhutten
313	918.7	Canfield Local	Canfield
314	930.8	Ashtabula Area City	Ashtabula
315	936.0	Alternative Education Academy	Toledo
316	937.0	Beaver Local	Lisbon
317	938.9	Milford Exempted Village	Milford
318	984.8	Adams County/Ohio Valley Local	West Union
319	990.0	Field Local	Mogadore
320	1,008.5	Morgan Local	Mc Connelsville
321	1,023.0	River View Local	Warsaw
322	1,025.0	West Clermont Local	Cincinnati
323	1,035.2	Reynoldsburg City	Reynoldsburg
324	1,055.3	North College Hill City	Cincinnati
325	1,088.5	Batavia Local	Batavia
326	1,093.0	Dayton City	Dayton
327	1,103.1	Clear Fork Valley Local	Bellville
328	1,167.3	Northridge Local	Dayton
329	1,216.5	Medina City SD	Medina
330	1,232.5	Elida Local	Elida
331	1,251.5	Monroe Local SD	Monroe
332	1,392.3	Newark City	Newark
333	1,486.5	Heath City	Heath
334	1,565.0	Harrison Hills City	Cadiz
335	1,656.3	Cincinnati City	Cincinnati
336	1,678.0	Jefferson Area Local	Jefferson
337	1,862.0	Waverly City	Waverly

Current Expenditures per Student

Rank	Dollars	District Name	City
1	20,387	Orange City	Cleveland
2	18,334	East Cleveland City SD	East Cleveland
3	17,620	Cleveland Heights-Univ Hgts City	University Hgts
4	16,030	Shaker Heights City	Shaker Heights
5	15,609	Youngstown City Schools	Youngstown
6	15,488	Indian Hill Exempted Village	Cincinnati
7	14,562	Upper Arlington City	Upper Arlington
8	14,446	Bexley City	Bexley
9	14,078	Mansfield City	Mansfield
10	13,994	Rossford Exempted Village	Rossford
11	13,980	Cleveland Municipal	Cleveland
12	13,832	Sycamore Community City	Blue Ash
13	13,794	Columbus City SD	Columbus
14	13,556	Perry Local	Perry
15	13,500	South Euclid-Lyndhurst City	Lyndhurst
16	13,434	Dayton City	Dayton
17	13,200	Westlake City	Westlake
18	13,107	Hudson City	Hudson
19	13,013	Princeton City	Cincinnati
20	12,984	Akron City	Akron
21	12,838	Mayfield City	Mayfield Hgts
22	12,710	Kent City	Kent
23	12,683	Euclid City	Euclid
24	12,638	Solon City	Solon
25	12,593	Revere Local	Bath
26	12,514	North Olmsted City	North Olmsted
27	12,479	Worthington City	Worthington
28	12,389	Chagrin Falls Exempted Village	Chagrin Falls
29	12,361	Cincinnati City	Cincinnati
30	12,356	Rocky River City	Rocky River
31	12,221	Berea City	Berea
32	12,213	Warren City	Warren
33	12,199	Bedford City	Bedford
34	12,190	Sandusky City	Sandusky
35	12,182	Mariemont City	Cincinnati
36	12,179	Portsmouth City	Portsmouth
37	12,085	Dublin City	Dublin
38	11,973	Mentor Exempted Village	Mentor
39	11,964	Toledo City	Toledo
40	11,856	Trotwood-Madison City	Trotwood
41	11,848	Athens City	The Plains
42	11,831	Wyoming City	Wyoming
43	11,798	New Albany-Plain Local	New Albany
44	11,751	Parma City	Parma
45	11,581	Oakwood City	Dayton
46	11,565	Kenston Local	Chagrin Falls
47	11,534	Maumee City	Maumee

Note: This section only includes districts with 1,500 or more students; All categories are ranked from high to low

48	11,485	Winton Woods City	Cincinnati
49	11,472	Brecksville-Broadview Heights City	Brecksville
50	11,432	Norwood City	Norwood
51	11,427	Lakewood City	Lakewood
52	11,270	Sheffield-Sheffield Lake City	Sheffield Vllg
53	11,235	Port Clinton City	Port Clinton
54	11,200	Bay Village City	Bay Village
55	11,186	Springfield City	Springfield
56	11,175	Fostoria City	Fostoria
57	11,131	Celina City	Celina
58	11,120	Benton Carroll Salem Local	Oak Harbor
59	11,073	Meigs Local	Pomeroy
60	11,062	Canton City	Canton
61	11,048	Gahanna-Jefferson City	Gahanna
62	11,003	Strongsville City	Strongsville
63	10,981	Hilliard City	Columbus
64	10,967	East Liverpool City	East Liverpool
65	10,953	Lorain City	Lorain
66	10,932	Talawanda City	Oxford
67	10,929	Northridge Local	Dayton
68	10,886	Lima City	Lima
69	10,879	Centerville City	Centerville
70	10,834	Avon Lake City	Avon Lake
71	10,824	West Geauga Local	Chesterland
72	10,818	Woodridge Local	Peninsula
73	10,792	Wooster City	Wooster
74	10,790	Kettering City	Kettering
75	10,727	Marion City	Marion
76	10,725	Willoughby-Eastlake City	Willoughby
77	10,708	Vermilion Local	Vermilion
78	10,695	Canton Local	Canton
79	10,656	Switzerland of Ohio Local	Woodsfield
80	10,630	Circleville City	Circleville
81	10,602	Sylvania City	Sylvania
82	10,580	Washington Local	Toledo
83	10,574	Vinton County Local	Mc Arthur
84	10,571	Elyria City Schools	Elyria
85	10,527	New Lexington City	New Lexington
86	10,506	Middletown City	Middletown
87	10,437	Oregon City	Oregon
88	10,422	New Richmond Exempted Village	New Richmond
89	10,412	Aurora City	Aurora
90	10,408	Bryan City	Bryan
91	10,406	Shelby City	Shelby
92	10,402	Northmont City	Englewood
93	10,396	Gallia County Local	Gallipolis
94	10,344	Buckeye Local	Dillonvale
95	10,304	Fairview Park City	Fairview Park
96	10,293	Nordonia Hills City	Northfield
97	10,279	Franklin Local	Duncan Falls
98	10,273	North Royalton City	North Royalton
99	10,256	Urbana City	Urbana
100	10,231	Springfield Local	Akron
101	10,207	Rolling Hills Local	Cambridge
102	10,199	Northern Local	Thornville
103	10,149	Bowling Green City SD	Bowling Green
104	10,148	Copley-Fairlawn City	Copley
105	10,119	Mt Healthy City	Cincinnati
105	10,119	Three Rivers Local	Cleves
107	10,104	Whitehall City	Whitehall
108	10,089	Olmsted Falls City	Olmsted Falls
109	10,086	Groveport Madison Local	Groveport
110	10,071	Northwest Local	Mc Dermott
111	10,067	Morgan Local	Mc Connelsville
112	10,050	Coshocton City	Coshocton
113	10,033	Mason City SD	Mason
114	10,030	Vandalia-Butler City	Vandalia
115	10,026	Crestwood Local	Mantua
116	9,999	Lakewood Local	Hebron
117	9,989	Conneaut Area City	Conneaut
118	9,985	River View Local	Warsaw
119	9,960	Kings Local	Kings Mills
120	9,954	Massillon City	Massillon
121	9,950	Westerville City	Westerville
122	9,931	Napoleon Area City	Napoleon
123	9,928	Cambridge City	Cambridge
124	9,917	Madison Local	Mansfield
125	9,910	Tallmadge City	Tallmadge
126	9,903	Garfield Hgts City Schools	Garfield Hgts
127	9,886	Zanesville City	Zanesville
128	9,877	West Carrollton City	West Carrollton
129	9,842	Perkins Local	Sandusky
130	9,836	Fairless Local	Navarre
131	9,829	Harrison Hills City	Cadiz
132	9,828	Benjamin Logan Local	Bellefontaine
133	9,826	Van Wert City	Van Wert
134	9,810	Alliance City	Alliance
135	9,798	South-Western City	Grove City
136	9,788	West Holmes Local	Millersburg
137	9,785	Buckeye Valley Local	Delaware
138	9,773	Goshen Local	Goshen
139	9,771	Ravenna City	Ravenna
140	9,759	Willard City	Willard
141	9,755	North Fork Local	Utica
142	9,753	Logan-Hocking Local	Logan
143	9,749	Streetsboro City	Streetsboro
144	9,701	Huber Heights City	Huber Heights
145	9,689	Orrville City	Orrville
146	9,687	Buckeye Local	Ashtabula
147	9,664	Franklin City	Franklin
148	9,663	Xenia Community City	Xenia
149	9,646	Troy City	Troy
150	9,638	Gallipolis City	Gallipolis
151	9,635	Indian Lake Local	Lewistown
152	9,622	Triway Local	Wooster
153	9,613	Bellbrook-Sugarcreek Local SD	Bellbrook
154	9,607	Forest Hills Local	Cincinnati
155	9,572	Newark City	Newark
156	9,564	Granville Exempted Village	Granville
157	9,544	Olentangy Local	Lewis Center
158	9,541	Big Walnut Local	Sunbury
159	9,532	Southeast Local	Ravenna
160	9,527	Painesville City Local	Painesville
161	9,522	Bellefontaine City	Bellefontaine
162	9,520	Fairborn City	Fairborn
163	9,491	Chardon Local	Chardon
164	9,485	Ashland City	Ashland
165	9,482	Logan Elm Local	Circleville
166	9,474	East Holmes Local	Berlin
167	9,463	Miami Trace Local	Washington CH
168	9,451	Maple Heights City	Maple Heights
169	9,430	Westfall Local	Williamsport
170	9,418	Upper Sandusky Exempted Village	Upper Sandusky
171	9,398	Firelands Local	South Amherst
172	9,393	Reynoldsburg City	Reynoldsburg
173	9,385	Beavercreek City	Beavercreek
174	9,354	Twinsburg City	Twinsburg
175	9,350	Loveland City	Loveland
176	9,329	Pickerington Local	Pickerington
177	9,326	Cloverleaf Local	Lodi
178	9,321	Alexander Local	Albany
179	9,319	Mad River Local	Dayton
180	9,315	Stow-Munroe Falls City SD	Stow
181	9,310	Lancaster City	Lancaster
182	9,303	Medina City SD	Medina
183	9,300	Canal Wnchstr Local	Canal Wnchstr
184	9,292	Marysville Exempted Village	Marysville
185	9,280	Hubbard Exempted Village	Hubbard
186	9,269	Perrysburg Exempted Village	Perrysburg
187	9,266	Girard City SD	Girard
188	9,258	Findlay City	Findlay
189	9,257	Greenville City	Greenville
190	9,251	Clermont Northeastern Local	Batavia
191	9,233	Fairland Local	Proctorville
192	9,224	North Canton City	North Canton
193	9,212	Brunswick City	Brunswick
194	9,195	West Branch Local	Beloit
195	9,188	Valley View Local	Germantown
196	9,186	Carlisle Local	Carlisle
197	9,181	Fairfield Union Local	Lancaster
198	9,165	Fremont City	Fremont
199	9,153	Keystone Local	Lagrange
200	9,151	Salem City	Salem
201	9,147	Reading Community City	Reading
202	9,146	Kenton City	Kenton
203	9,134	Barberton City	Barberton
204	9,119	Edison Local (Formerly Berlin-Milan)	Milan
205	9,107	Shawnee Local	Lima
206	9,101	Poland Local	Poland
207	9,092	Heath City	Heath
208	9,089	Licking Valley Local	Newark
209	9,075	Tecumseh Local	New Carlisle
210	9,049	West Muskingum Local	Zanesville
211	9,038	Marietta City	Marietta
212	9,030	Ashtabula Area City	Ashtabula
213	9,021	Howland Local	Warren
214	9,020	Bellevue City	Bellevue
215	9,014	Springfield Local	Holland
216	9,012	Delaware City	Delaware
217	8,988	Miamisburg City	Miamisburg
218	8,975	Piqua City	Piqua
219	8,974	Saint Marys City	Saint Marys
220	8,972	Greenfield Exempted Village	Greenfield
221	8,971	New Philadel. City	New Philadel.
222	8,960	Wauseon Exempted Village	Wauseon
223	8,955	Amherst Exempted Village	Amherst
224	8,944	Marlington Local	Alliance
225	8,939	Northwest Local	Cincinnati
226	8,921	Steubenville City	Steubenville
227	8,918	Bath Local	Lima
228	8,915	Cuyahoga Falls City	Cuyahoga Falls
229	8,909	East Muskingum Local	New Concord
230	8,899	Maysville Local	Zanesville
231	8,886	Teays Valley Local	Ashville
232	8,878	Beaver Local	Lisbon
233	8,842	Highland Local	Sparta
234	8,839	Greenon Local	Enon
235	8,835	Clearview Local	Lorain
236	8,832	Galion City	Galion
237	8,820	Green Local	Uniontown
237	8,820	Jackson City	Jackson
239	8,818	Claymont City	Dennison
240	8,816	Lakeview Local	Cortland
240	8,816	Lakota Local	Liberty Twp
242	8,815	Coventry Local	Akron
243	8,811	Lexington Local	Lexington
244	8,806	Boardman Local	Youngstown
245	8,805	Milford Exempted Village	Milford
246	8,787	Northwest Local	Canal Fulton
247	8,771	Perry Local	Massillon
248	8,751	Midview Local	Grafton
249	8,745	Oak Hills Local	Cincinnati
250	8,732	Eaton Community City	Eaton
251	8,715	Southwest Local	Harrison
252	8,714	Hamilton City	Hamilton
253	8,696	Adams County/Ohio Valley Local	West Union
254	8,690	Mount Vernon City	Mount Vernon
255	8,689	Southwest Licking Local	Pataskala
256	8,681	Ontario Local	Mansfield
257	8,679	Niles City	Niles
258	8,649	London City	London
259	8,643	Chillicothe City	Chillicothe
260	8,638	Madison Local	Middletown
261	8,635	Northwestern Local	Springfield
262	8,632	Clyde-Green Springs Exempted Village	Clyde
263	8,629	Tipp City Exempted Village	Tipp City
264	8,625	South Point Local	South Point
265	8,623	Edison Local	Hammondsville
266	8,619	Bloom-Carroll Local	Carroll
267	8,609	Indian Valley Local Schools	Gnadenhutten
268	8,598	Hillsboro City	Hillsboro
269	8,564	Canfield Local	Canfield
270	8,552	Tri-Valley Local	Dresden
271	8,534	Clark-Shawnee Local	Springfield
272	8,531	Minford Local	Minford
273	8,519	Carrollton Exempted Village	Carrollton
274	8,515	Struthers City	Struthers
275	8,508	Minerva Local	Minerva
276	8,479	Edgewood City	Trenton
277	8,474	Anthony Wayne Local	Whitehouse
278	8,450	Louisville City	Louisville
279	8,431	Highland Local	Medina
280	8,427	Amanda-Clearcreek Local	Amanda
280	8,427	Jefferson Area Local	Jefferson
282	8,414	Jonathan Alder Local	Plain City
283	8,380	Indian Creek Local	Wintersville
284	8,372	Northeastern Local	Springfield
285	8,366	Norwalk City	Norwalk
286	8,359	Ross Local	Hamilton
287	8,355	Dover City	Dover
288	8,352	Defiance City	Defiance
289	8,325	North College Hill City	Cincinnati
290	8,309	Waverly City	Waverly
291	8,299	Little Miami Local	Maineville
292	8,288	Hamilton Local	Columbus
293	8,229	Clear Fork Valley Local	Bellville
294	8,220	Norton City	Norton
295	8,218	Washington CH City	Washington CH
296	8,193	Warren Local	Vincent
297	8,178	Electronic Classroom of Tomorrow	Columbus
297	8,178	Sidney City	Sidney
299	8,162	Madison Local	Madison

Note: This section only includes districts with 1,500 or more students; All categories are ranked from high to low

300	8,146	Geneva Area City	Geneva
301	8,132	Lake Local	Millbury
302	8,126	Clinton-Massie Local	Clarksville
303	8,123	Elida Local	Elida
304	8,112	Johnstown-Monroe Local	Johnstown
305	8,106	Lake Local	Uniontown
306	8,084	Ottawa-Glandorf Local	Ottawa
307	8,082	Batavia Local	Batavia
308	8,062	Jackson Local	Massillon
309	8,040	Field Local	Mogadore
310	8,035	Blanchester Local	Blanchester
311	8,015	Bethel-Tate Local	Bethel
312	8,005	Buckeye Local	Medina
313	7,997	Plain Local	Canton
314	7,993	West Clermont Local	Cincinnati
315	7,982	Western Brown Local	Mount Orab
316	7,956	Wapakoneta City	Wapakoneta
317	7,928	Wadsworth City	Wadsworth
318	7,921	Wheelersburg Local	Wheelersburg
319	7,861	Saint Clairsville-Richland City	Saint Clairsville
319	7,861	Union-Scioto Local	Chillicothe
321	7,845	Austintown Local	Youngstown
322	7,813	Springboro Community City	Springboro
323	7,808	Ohio Connections Academy, Inc	Cleveland
324	7,806	Licking Heights Local	Pataskala
325	7,733	River Valley Local	Caledonia
326	7,691	Riverside Local	Painesville
327	7,656	Wilmington City	Wilmington
328	7,580	Avon Local	Avon
329	7,531	Lebanon City	Lebanon
330	7,487	Fairfield City	Fairfield
331	7,449	Monroe Local SD	Monroe
332	7,417	N Ridgeville City	N Ridgeville
333	7,366	Graham Local	Saint Paris
334	7,337	Alternative Education Academy	Toledo
335	7,221	Tiffin City	Tiffin
336	6,836	Ohio Virtual Academy	Maumee
337	6,699	Treca Digital Academy	Marion

Total General Revenue per Student

Rank	Dollars	District Name	City
1	25,472	Orange City	Cleveland
2	25,207	Chagrin Falls Exempted Village	Chagrin Falls
3	21,793	Youngstown City Schools	Youngstown
4	20,412	Indian Hill Exempted Village	Cincinnati
5	20,325	Cleveland Municipal	Cleveland
6	19,873	Cleveland Heights-Univ Hgts City	University Hgts
7	18,976	Circleville City	Circleville
8	18,364	Dayton City	Dayton
9	18,323	Cincinnati City	Cincinnati
10	18,182	Bexley City	Bexley
11	18,122	Eaton Community City	Eaton
12	18,103	East Cleveland City SD	East Cleveland
13	18,100	Shaker Heights City	Shaker Heights
14	17,016	Willard City	Willard
15	16,985	Columbus City SD	Columbus
16	16,882	South Euclid-Lyndhurst City	Lyndhurst
17	16,863	Orrville City	Orrville
18	16,343	Princeton City	Cincinnati
19	16,234	Toledo City	Toledo
20	16,177	Mayfield City	Mayfield Hgts
21	15,912	Rocky River City	Rocky River
22	15,795	Solon City	Solon
23	15,781	Hudson City	Hudson
24	15,698	Mansfield City	Mansfield
25	15,676	Akron City	Akron
26	15,653	Westlake City	Westlake
27	15,635	Upper Arlington City	Upper Arlington
28	15,605	Sycamore Community City	Blue Ash
29	15,317	Perry Local	Perry
30	15,143	Portsmouth City	Portsmouth
31	14,983	Revere Local	Bath
32	14,943	Wyoming City	Wyoming
33	14,857	Northwestern Local	Springfield
34	14,791	Mariemont City	Cincinnati
35	14,748	Lorain City	Lorain
36	14,738	Worthington City	Worthington
37	14,611	Sandusky City	Sandusky
38	14,468	Lakewood City	Lakewood
39	14,400	Keystone Local	Lagrange
40	14,388	Trotwood-Madison City	Trotwood
41	14,383	Euclid City	Euclid
42	14,147	Port Clinton City	Port Clinton
43	14,028	North Olmsted City	North Olmsted
44	14,018	New Albany-Plain Local	New Albany
45	14,004	Norwood City	Norwood
46	13,928	Bay Village City	Bay Village
47	13,915	Switzerland of Ohio Local	Woodsfield
48	13,901	Parma City	Parma
49	13,814	Maumee City	Maumee
50	13,803	Coshocton City	Coshocton
51	13,733	Winton Woods City	Cincinnati
52	13,692	Dublin City	Dublin
53	13,687	Wooster City	Wooster
54	13,650	Kent City	Kent
55	13,631	Bedford City	Bedford
56	13,595	West Geauga Local	Chesterland
57	13,575	Napoleon Area City	Napoleon
58	13,573	Rossford Exempted Village	Rossford
59	13,571	Lima City	Lima
60	13,569	Gallia County Local	Gallipolis
61	13,528	Warren City	Warren
62	13,493	Kenston Local	Chagrin Falls
63	13,487	Fairview Park City	Fairview Park
64	13,376	Jefferson Area Local	Jefferson
65	13,310	Talawanda City	Oxford
66	13,079	Springfield City	Springfield
67	13,060	Little Miami Local	Maineville
68	12,999	Kenton City	Kenton
69	12,979	Northmont City	Englewood
70	12,945	Nordonia Hills City	Northfield
71	12,883	Strongsville City	Strongsville
72	12,843	Elyria City Schools	Elyria
73	12,839	Franklin Local	Duncan Falls
74	12,834	Northridge Local	Dayton
75	12,802	Mt Healthy City	Cincinnati
76	12,780	Mentor Exempted Village	Mentor
77	12,774	Brecksville-Broadview Heights City	Brecksville
78	12,764	Springfield Local	Akron
79	12,752	Athens City	The Plains
79	12,752	Canton City	Canton
81	12,747	South-Western City	Grove City
82	12,738	Van Wert City	Van Wert
83	12,615	Hilliard City	Columbus
84	12,614	Kettering City	Kettering
85	12,606	Gahanna-Jefferson City	Gahanna
86	12,599	Piqua City	Piqua
87	12,557	Vermilion Local	Vermilion
88	12,545	Berea City	Berea
89	12,526	Reynoldsburg City	Reynoldsburg
90	12,513	Xenia Community City	Xenia
91	12,510	Oakwood City	Dayton
92	12,482	Three Rivers Local	Cleves
93	12,479	Lancaster City	Lancaster
94	12,462	Miami Trace Local	Washington CH
95	12,452	Marion City	Marion
96	12,433	New Richmond Exempted Village	New Richmond
97	12,430	Groveport Madison Local	Groveport
98	12,428	Fostoria City	Fostoria
99	12,403	West Muskingum Local	Zanesville
100	12,399	Olentangy Local	Lewis Center
101	12,395	Middletown City	Middletown
102	12,382	Niles City	Niles
103	12,375	Harrison Hills City	Cadiz
104	12,345	Indian Lake Local	Lewistown
105	12,330	Benton Carroll Salem Local	Oak Harbor
106	12,325	Sylvania City	Sylvania
107	12,312	Fairfield Union Local	Lancaster
108	12,306	Waverly City	Waverly
109	12,277	Northwest Local	Canal Fulton
110	12,275	Maple Heights City	Maple Heights
111	12,267	Beaver Local	Lisbon
112	12,261	Meigs Local	Pomeroy
113	12,254	Woodridge Local	Peninsula
114	12,240	Celina City	Celina
115	12,195	Zanesville City	Zanesville
116	12,150	Southeast Local	Ravenna
117	12,143	Westerville City	Westerville
118	12,102	Garfield Hgts City Schools	Garfield Hgts
119	12,101	Pickerington Local	Pickerington
120	12,063	Sheffield-Sheffield Lake City	Sheffield Vllg
121	12,047	Copley-Fairlawn City	Copley
122	12,045	Aurora City	Aurora
123	11,965	London City	London
124	11,954	Canal Wnchstr Local	Canal Wnchstr
125	11,942	Newark City	Newark
125	11,942	Tallmadge City	Tallmadge
127	11,892	Lake Local	Millbury
128	11,844	Oregon City	Oregon
129	11,833	Madison Local	Mansfield
130	11,828	Whitehall City	Whitehall
131	11,761	Lakewood Local	Hebron
132	11,757	Westfall Local	Williamsport
133	11,718	Washington Local	Toledo
134	11,713	Cloverleaf Local	Lodi
135	11,709	Findlay City	Findlay
136	11,703	Marysville Exempted Village	Marysville
136	11,703	Northern Local	Thornville
138	11,676	Buckeye Valley Local	Delaware
139	11,675	Morgan Local	Mc Connelsville
140	11,666	Streetsboro City	Streetsboro
141	11,661	North Royalton City	North Royalton
142	11,638	Olmsted Falls City	Olmsted Falls
143	11,635	East Liverpool City	East Liverpool
144	11,615	Medina City SD	Medina
145	11,589	Canton Local	Canton
146	11,575	Massillon City	Massillon
147	11,561	Barberton City	Barberton
148	11,542	Centerville City	Centerville
149	11,532	Bellbrook-Sugarcreek Local SD	Bellbrook
150	11,521	Huber Heights City	Huber Heights
151	11,516	Kings Local	Kings Mills
152	11,489	Shelby City	Shelby
153	11,484	Painesville City Local	Painesville
154	11,483	Troy City	Troy
155	11,476	Ashtabula Area City	Ashtabula
156	11,467	Bellevue City	Bellevue
157	11,462	North Fork Local	Utica
158	11,459	Urbana City	Urbana
159	11,454	Rolling Hills Local	Cambridge
160	11,436	Big Walnut Local	Sunbury
161	11,406	Clermont Northeastern Local	Batavia
162	11,382	Firelands Local	South Amherst
163	11,358	Avon Lake City	Avon Lake
164	11,268	Beavercreek City	Beavercreek
165	11,267	Granville Exempted Village	Granville
166	11,238	Alexander Local	Albany
167	11,235	Stow-Munroe Falls City SD	Stow
168	11,213	Bryan City	Bryan
169	11,210	New Lexington City	New Lexington
169	11,210	Willoughby-Eastlake City	Willoughby
171	11,202	Crestwood Local	Mantua
172	11,192	Bellefontaine City	Bellefontaine
173	11,164	Chillicothe City	Chillicothe
174	11,109	Gallipolis City	Gallipolis
175	11,098	Bowling Green City SD	Bowling Green
176	11,081	Vinton County Local	Mc Arthur
177	11,069	Miamisburg City	Miamisburg
178	11,067	Delaware City	Delaware
179	11,057	Fairless Local	Navarre
180	11,053	River View Local	Warsaw
181	11,051	Bloom-Carroll Local	Carroll
182	11,046	Sidney City	Sidney
183	11,035	Highland Local	Medina
184	11,011	Edgewood City	Trenton
185	10,999	Mad River Local	Dayton
186	10,940	Alliance City	Alliance
186	10,940	Perrysburg Exempted Village	Perrysburg
188	10,934	Northwest Local	Mc Dermott
189	10,926	Perkins Local	Sandusky
190	10,918	Mason City SD	Mason
190	10,918	Ravenna City	Ravenna
192	10,913	Chardon Local	Chardon
193	10,887	Benjamin Logan Local	Bellefontaine
194	10,861	Fairborn City	Fairborn
195	10,858	Twinsburg City	Twinsburg
196	10,857	Buckeye Local	Dillonvale
197	10,845	Jackson City	Jackson
197	10,845	Union-Scioto Local	Chillicothe
199	10,824	Field Local	Mogadore
200	10,794	Geneva Area City	Geneva
201	10,783	Wadsworth City	Wadsworth
202	10,776	Springfield Local	Holland
203	10,767	Cambridge City	Cambridge
204	10,741	Edison Local	Hammondsville
205	10,719	Adams County/Ohio Valley Local	West Union
206	10,718	Greenville City	Greenville
207	10,687	Vandalia-Butler City	Vandalia
208	10,684	Conneaut Area City	Conneaut
209	10,679	Cuyahoga Falls City	Cuyahoga Falls

Note: This section only includes districts with 1,500 or more students; All categories are ranked from high to low

210	10,671	Buckeye Local	Medina
211	10,614	Goshen Local	Goshen
212	10,609	Reading Community City	Reading
213	10,580	South Point Local	South Point
214	10,568	Franklin City	Franklin
215	10,562	Loveland City	Loveland
216	10,539	Jackson Local	Massillon
217	10,537	Ashland City	Ashland
218	10,525	Ross Local	Hamilton
219	10,515	Minerva Local	Minerva
220	10,495	Green Local	Uniontown
221	10,487	Amherst Exempted Village	Amherst
222	10,480	West Carrollton City	West Carrollton
223	10,473	Galion City	Galion
224	10,454	Saint Marys City	Saint Marys
225	10,450	Southwest Licking Local	Pataskala
226	10,442	Elida Local	Elida
227	10,436	Hubbard Exempted Village	Hubbard
228	10,410	Logan-Hocking Local	Logan
229	10,398	Salem City	Salem
230	10,394	Wauseon Exempted Village	Wauseon
231	10,392	Indian Creek Local	Wintersville
232	10,382	Clyde-Green Springs Exempted Village	Clyde
233	10,361	Amanda-Clearcreek Local	Amanda
234	10,339	Northwest Local	Cincinnati
235	10,337	Wheelersburg Local	Wheelersburg
236	10,331	Johnstown-Monroe Local	Johnstown
237	10,324	Monroe Local SD	Monroe
238	10,268	Triway Local	Wooster
239	10,264	Fremont City	Fremont
240	10,252	Austintown Local	Youngstown
241	10,249	West Holmes Local	Millersburg
242	10,229	Logan Elm Local	Circleville
243	10,206	Milford Exempted Village	Milford
244	10,185	Struthers City	Struthers
245	10,184	Greenfield Exempted Village	Greenfield
246	10,180	Poland Local	Poland
247	10,177	Defiance City	Defiance
247	10,177	Lexington Local	Lexington
249	10,166	Southwest Local	Harrison
250	10,158	Indian Valley Local Schools	Gnadenhutten
251	10,148	Boardman Local	Youngstown
252	10,140	Midview Local	Grafton
253	10,136	Howland Local	Warren
254	10,127	Madison Local	Middletown
255	10,117	Licking Valley Local	Newark
256	10,092	Ontario Local	Mansfield
256	10,092	Washington CH City	Washington CH
258	10,059	Tecumseh Local	New Carlisle
259	10,051	Teays Valley Local	Ashville
260	10,036	Lakeview Local	Cortland
261	10,025	Marlington Local	Alliance
262	10,019	Tipp City Exempted Village	Tipp City
263	10,001	Marietta City	Marietta
264	9,993	Madison Local	Madison
265	9,973	Upper Sandusky Exempted Village	Upper Sandusky
266	9,936	Bath Local	Lima
267	9,918	Steubenville City	Steubenville
268	9,916	Girard City SD	Girard
269	9,905	Buckeye Local	Ashtabula
270	9,900	Edison Local (Formerly Berlin-Milan)	Milan
271	9,898	Carlisle Local	Carlisle
272	9,885	Hillsboro City	Hillsboro
273	9,878	Minford Local	Minford
274	9,873	North Canton City	North Canton
275	9,856	Batavia Local	Batavia
276	9,843	Plain Local	Canton
277	9,839	Brunswick City	Brunswick
278	9,790	East Muskingum Local	New Concord
279	9,789	West Branch Local	Beloit
280	9,788	Avon Local	Avon
281	9,773	Coventry Local	Akron
282	9,757	Shawnee Local	Lima
283	9,742	Ottawa-Glandorf Local	Ottawa
284	9,736	Lakota Local	Liberty Twp
285	9,721	Hamilton City	Hamilton
286	9,719	Heath City	Heath
287	9,711	Jonathan Alder Local	Plain City
287	9,711	Lebanon City	Lebanon
289	9,701	West Clermont Local	Cincinnati
290	9,683	Greenon Local	Enon
291	9,653	Claymont City	Dennison
292	9,651	Forest Hills Local	Cincinnati
293	9,647	Warren Local	Vincent
294	9,646	Western Brown Local	Mount Orab
295	9,641	Valley View Local	Germantown
296	9,628	Riverside Local	Painesville
297	9,592	Graham Local	Saint Paris
298	9,569	Licking Heights Local	Pataskala
299	9,559	Springboro Community City	Springboro
300	9,557	Wapakoneta City	Wapakoneta
301	9,552	Hamilton Local	Columbus
302	9,544	Blanchester Local	Blanchester
303	9,543	Fairfield City	Fairfield
304	9,501	Lake Local	Uniontown
305	9,498	Tiffin City	Tiffin
306	9,470	North College Hill City	Cincinnati
307	9,469	Canfield Local	Canfield
308	9,454	Bethel-Tate Local	Bethel
309	9,450	Highland Local	Sparta
310	9,388	East Holmes Local	Berlin
311	9,350	Louisville City	Louisville
312	9,332	Perry Local	Massillon
313	9,327	River Valley Local	Caledonia
314	9,324	Tri-Valley Local	Dresden
315	9,323	Clinton-Massie Local	Clarksville
316	9,300	Clark-Shawnee Local	Springfield
317	9,279	Clearview Local	Lorain
318	9,272	Saint Clairsville-Richland City	Saint Clairsville
319	9,231	N Ridgeville City	N Ridgeville
320	9,206	Anthony Wayne Local	Whitehouse
321	9,173	Maysville Local	Zanesville
322	9,168	Norwalk City	Norwalk
323	9,149	Mount Vernon City	Mount Vernon
324	9,146	Carrollton Exempted Village	Carrollton
325	9,102	Fairland Local	Proctorville
326	9,070	Clear Fork Valley Local	Bellville
327	8,932	Wilmington City	Wilmington
328	8,816	Norton City	Norton
329	8,790	Dover City	Dover
330	8,738	Northeastern Local	Springfield
331	8,584	New Philadel. City	New Philadel.
332	8,544	Oak Hills Local	Cincinnati
333	7,701	Electronic Classroom of Tomorrow	Columbus
334	7,286	Treca Digital Academy	Marion
335	6,969	Ohio Connections Academy, Inc	Cleveland
336	6,899	Alternative Education Academy	Toledo
337	6,840	Ohio Virtual Academy	Maumee

Long-Term Debt per Student (end of FY)

Rank	Dollars	District Name	City
1	0	Adams County/Ohio Valley Local	West Union
1	0	Akron City	Akron
1	0	Alexander Local	Albany
1	0	Alliance City	Alliance
1	0	Alternative Education Academy	Toledo
1	0	Amanda-Clearcreek Local	Amanda
1	0	Amherst Exempted Village	Amherst
1	0	Anthony Wayne Local	Whitehouse
1	0	Ashland City	Ashland
1	0	Ashtabula Area City	Ashtabula
1	0	Athens City	The Plains
1	0	Aurora City	Aurora
1	0	Austintown Local	Youngstown
1	0	Avon Lake City	Avon Lake
1	0	Avon Local	Avon
1	0	Barberton City	Barberton
1	0	Batavia Local	Batavia
1	0	Bath Local	Lima
1	0	Bay Village City	Bay Village
1	0	Beaver Local	Lisbon
1	0	Beavercreek City	Beavercreek
1	0	Bedford City	Bedford
1	0	Bellbrook-Sugarcreek Local SD	Bellbrook
1	0	Bellefontaine City	Bellefontaine
1	0	Bellevue City	Bellevue
1	0	Benjamin Logan Local	Bellefontaine
1	0	Benton Carroll Salem Local	Oak Harbor
1	0	Berea City	Berea
1	0	Bethel-Tate Local	Bethel
1	0	Bexley City	Bexley
1	0	Big Walnut Local	Sunbury
1	0	Blanchester Local	Blanchester
1	0	Bloom-Carroll Local	Carroll
1	0	Boardman Local	Youngstown
1	0	Bowling Green City SD	Bowling Green
1	0	Brecksville-Broadview Heights City	Brecksville
1	0	Brunswick City	Brunswick
1	0	Bryan City	Bryan
1	0	Buckeye Local	Ashtabula
1	0	Buckeye Local	Medina
1	0	Buckeye Local	Dillonvale
1	0	Buckeye Valley Local	Delaware
1	0	Cambridge City	Cambridge
1	0	Canal Wnchstr Local	Canal Wnchstr
1	0	Canfield Local	Canfield
1	0	Canton City	Canton
1	0	Canton Local	Canton
1	0	Carlisle Local	Carlisle
1	0	Carrollton Exempted Village	Carrollton
1	0	Celina City	Celina
1	0	Centerville City	Centerville
1	0	Chagrin Falls Exempted Village	Chagrin Falls
1	0	Chardon Local	Chardon
1	0	Chillicothe City	Chillicothe
1	0	Cincinnati City	Cincinnati
1	0	Circleville City	Circleville
1	0	Clark-Shawnee Local	Springfield
1	0	Claymont City	Dennison
1	0	Clear Fork Valley Local	Bellville
1	0	Clearview Local	Lorain
1	0	Clermont Northeastern Local	Batavia
1	0	Cleveland Heights-Univ Hgts City	University Hgts
1	0	Cleveland Municipal	Cleveland
1	0	Clinton-Massie Local	Clarksville
1	0	Cloverleaf Local	Lodi
1	0	Clyde-Green Springs Exempted Village	Clyde
1	0	Columbus City SD	Columbus
1	0	Conneaut Area City	Conneaut
1	0	Copley-Fairlawn City	Copley
1	0	Coshocton City	Coshocton
1	0	Coventry Local	Akron
1	0	Crestwood Local	Mantua
1	0	Cuyahoga Falls City	Cuyahoga Falls
1	0	Dayton City	Dayton
1	0	Defiance City	Defiance
1	0	Delaware City	Delaware
1	0	Dover City	Dover
1	0	Dublin City	Dublin
1	0	East Cleveland City SD	East Cleveland
1	0	East Holmes Local	Berlin
1	0	East Liverpool City	East Liverpool
1	0	East Muskingum Local	New Concord
1	0	Eaton Community City	Eaton
1	0	Edgewood City	Trenton
1	0	Edison Local	Hammondsville
1	0	Edison Local (Formerly Berlin-Milan)	Milan
1	0	Electronic Classroom of Tomorrow	Columbus
1	0	Elida Local	Elida
1	0	Elyria City Schools	Elyria
1	0	Euclid City	Euclid
1	0	Fairborn City	Fairborn
1	0	Fairfield City	Fairfield
1	0	Fairfield Union Local	Lancaster
1	0	Fairland Local	Proctorville
1	0	Fairless Local	Navarre
1	0	Fairview Park City	Fairview Park
1	0	Field Local	Mogadore
1	0	Findlay City	Findlay
1	0	Firelands Local	South Amherst
1	0	Forest Hills Local	Cincinnati
1	0	Fostoria City	Fostoria
1	0	Franklin City	Franklin
1	0	Franklin Local	Duncan Falls
1	0	Fremont City	Fremont
1	0	Gahanna-Jefferson City	Gahanna
1	0	Galion City	Galion
1	0	Gallia County Local	Gallipolis
1	0	Gallipolis City	Gallipolis
1	0	Garfield Hgts City Schools	Garfield Hgts
1	0	Geneva Area City	Geneva
1	0	Girard City SD	Girard
1	0	Goshen Local	Goshen
1	0	Graham Local	Saint Paris
1	0	Granville Exempted Village	Granville
1	0	Green Local	Uniontown
1	0	Greenfield Exempted Village	Greenfield
1	0	Greenon Local	Enon
1	0	Greenville City	Greenville
1	0	Groveport Madison Local	Groveport

Note: This section only includes districts with 1,500 or more students; All categories are ranked from high to low

1	0	Hamilton City	Hamilton
1	0	Hamilton Local	Columbus
1	0	Harrison Hills City	Cadiz
1	0	Heath City	Heath
1	0	Highland Local	Sparta
1	0	Highland Local	Medina
1	0	Hilliard City	Columbus
1	0	Hillsboro City	Hillsboro
1	0	Howland Local	Warren
1	0	Hubbard Exempted Village	Hubbard
1	0	Huber Heights City	Huber Heights
1	0	Hudson City	Hudson
1	0	Indian Creek Local	Wintersville
1	0	Indian Hill Exempted Village	Cincinnati
1	0	Indian Lake Local	Lewistown
1	0	Indian Valley Local Schools	Gnadenhutten
1	0	Jackson City	Jackson
1	0	Jackson Local	Massillon
1	0	Jefferson Area Local	Jefferson
1	0	Johnstown-Monroe Local	Johnstown
1	0	Jonathan Alder Local	Plain City
1	0	Kenston Local	Chagrin Falls
1	0	Kent City	Kent
1	0	Kenton City	Kenton
1	0	Kettering City	Kettering
1	0	Keystone Local	Lagrange
1	0	Kings Local	Kings Mills
1	0	Lake Local	Uniontown
1	0	Lake Local	Millbury
1	0	Lakeview Local	Cortland
1	0	Lakewood City	Lakewood
1	0	Lakewood Local	Hebron
1	0	Lakota Local	Liberty Twp
1	0	Lancaster City	Lancaster
1	0	Lebanon City	Lebanon
1	0	Lexington Local	Lexington
1	0	Licking Heights Local	Pataskala
1	0	Licking Valley Local	Newark
1	0	Lima City	Lima
1	0	Little Miami Local	Maineville
1	0	Logan Elm Local	Circleville
1	0	Logan-Hocking Local	Logan
1	0	London City	London
1	0	Lorain City	Lorain
1	0	Louisville City	Louisville
1	0	Loveland City	Loveland
1	0	Mad River Local	Dayton
1	0	Madison Local	Mansfield
1	0	Madison Local	Middletown
1	0	Madison Local	Madison
1	0	Mansfield City	Mansfield
1	0	Maple Heights City	Maple Heights
1	0	Mariemont City	Cincinnati
1	0	Marietta City	Marietta
1	0	Marion City	Marion
1	0	Marlington Local	Alliance
1	0	Marysville Exempted Village	Marysville
1	0	Mason City SD	Mason
1	0	Massillon City	Massillon
1	0	Maumee City	Maumee
1	0	Mayfield City	Mayfield Hgts
1	0	Maysville Local	Zanesville
1	0	Medina City SD	Medina
1	0	Meigs Local	Pomeroy
1	0	Mentor Exempted Village	Mentor
1	0	Miami Trace Local	Washington CH
1	0	Miamisburg City	Miamisburg
1	0	Middletown City	Middletown
1	0	Midview Local	Grafton
1	0	Milford Exempted Village	Milford
1	0	Minerva Local	Minerva
1	0	Minford Local	Minford
1	0	Monroe Local SD	Monroe
1	0	Morgan Local	Mc Connelsville
1	0	Mount Vernon City	Mount Vernon
1	0	Mt Healthy City	Cincinnati
1	0	Napoleon Area City	Napoleon
1	0	New Albany-Plain Local	New Albany
1	0	New Lexington City	New Lexington
1	0	New Philadel. City	New Philadel.
1	0	New Richmond Exempted Village	New Richmond
1	0	Newark City	Newark
1	0	Niles City	Niles
1	0	Nordonia Hills City	Northfield
1	0	North Canton City	North Canton
1	0	North College Hill City	Cincinnati
1	0	North Fork Local	Utica
1	0	North Olmsted City	North Olmsted
1	0	N Ridgeville City	N Ridgeville
1	0	North Royalton City	North Royalton
1	0	Northeastern Local	Springfield
1	0	Northern Local	Thornville
1	0	Northmont City	Englewood
1	0	Northridge Local	Dayton
1	0	Northwest Local	Cincinnati
1	0	Northwest Local	Canal Fulton
1	0	Northwest Local	Mc Dermott
1	0	Northwestern Local	Springfield
1	0	Norton City	Norton
1	0	Norwalk City	Norwalk
1	0	Norwood City	Norwood
1	0	Oak Hills Local	Cincinnati
1	0	Oakwood City	Dayton
1	0	Ohio Connections Academy, Inc	Cleveland
1	0	Ohio Virtual Academy	Maumee
1	0	Olentangy Local	Lewis Center
1	0	Olmsted Falls City	Olmsted Falls
1	0	Ontario Local	Mansfield
1	0	Orange City	Cleveland
1	0	Oregon City	Oregon
1	0	Orrville City	Orrville
1	0	Ottawa-Glandorf Local	Ottawa
1	0	Painesville City Local	Painesville
1	0	Parma City	Parma
1	0	Perkins Local	Sandusky
1	0	Perry Local	Perry
1	0	Perry Local	Massillon
1	0	Perrysburg Exempted Village	Perrysburg
1	0	Pickerington Local	Pickerington
1	0	Piqua City	Piqua
1	0	Plain Local	Canton
1	0	Poland Local	Poland
1	0	Port Clinton City	Port Clinton
1	0	Portsmouth City	Portsmouth
1	0	Princeton City	Cincinnati
1	0	Ravenna City	Ravenna
1	0	Reading Community City	Reading
1	0	Revere Local	Bath
1	0	Reynoldsburg City	Reynoldsburg
1	0	River Valley Local	Caledonia
1	0	River View Local	Warsaw
1	0	Riverside Local	Painesville
1	0	Rocky River City	Rocky River
1	0	Rolling Hills Local	Cambridge
1	0	Ross Local	Hamilton
1	0	Rossford Exempted Village	Rossford
1	0	Salem City	Salem
1	0	Sandusky City	Sandusky
1	0	Shaker Heights City	Shaker Heights
1	0	Shawnee Local	Lima
1	0	Sheffield-Sheffield Lake City	Sheffield Vllg
1	0	Shelby City	Shelby
1	0	Sidney City	Sidney
1	0	Solon City	Solon
1	0	South Euclid-Lyndhurst City	Lyndhurst
1	0	South Point Local	South Point
1	0	South-Western City	Grove City
1	0	Southeast Local	Ravenna
1	0	Southwest Licking Local	Pataskala
1	0	Southwest Local	Harrison
1	0	Springboro Community City	Springboro
1	0	Springfield City	Springfield
1	0	Springfield Local	Holland
1	0	Springfield Local	Akron
1	0	Saint Clairsville-Richland City	Saint Clairsville
1	0	Saint Marys City	Saint Marys
1	0	Steubenville City	Steubenville
1	0	Stow-Munroe Falls City SD	Stow
1	0	Streetsboro City	Streetsboro
1	0	Strongsville City	Strongsville
1	0	Struthers City	Struthers
1	0	Switzerland of Ohio Local	Woodsfield
1	0	Sycamore Community City	Blue Ash
1	0	Sylvania City	Sylvania
1	0	Talawanda City	Oxford
1	0	Tallmadge City	Tallmadge
1	0	Teays Valley Local	Ashville
1	0	Tecumseh Local	New Carlisle
1	0	Three Rivers Local	Cleves
1	0	Tiffin City	Tiffin
1	0	Tipp City Exempted Village	Tipp City
1	0	Toledo City	Toledo
1	0	Treca Digital Academy	Marion
1	0	Tri-Valley Local	Dresden
1	0	Triway Local	Wooster
1	0	Trotwood-Madison City	Trotwood
1	0	Troy City	Troy
1	0	Twinsburg City	Twinsburg
1	0	Union-Scioto Local	Chillicothe
1	0	Upper Arlington City	Upper Arlington
1	0	Upper Sandusky Exempted Village	Upper Sandusky
1	0	Urbana City	Urbana
1	0	Valley View Local	Germantown
1	0	Van Wert City	Van Wert
1	0	Vandalia-Butler City	Vandalia
1	0	Vermilion Local	Vermilion
1	0	Vinton County Local	Mc Arthur
1	0	Wadsworth City	Wadsworth
1	0	Wapakoneta City	Wapakoneta
1	0	Warren City	Warren
1	0	Warren Local	Vincent
1	0	Washington CH City	Washington CH
1	0	Washington Local	Toledo
1	0	Wauseon Exempted Village	Wauseon
1	0	Waverly City	Waverly
1	0	West Branch Local	Beloit
1	0	West Carrollton City	West Carrollton
1	0	West Clermont Local	Cincinnati
1	0	West Geauga Local	Chesterland
1	0	West Holmes Local	Millersburg
1	0	West Muskingum Local	Zanesville
1	0	Western Brown Local	Mount Orab
1	0	Westerville City	Westerville
1	0	Westfall Local	Williamsport
1	0	Westlake City	Westlake
1	0	Wheelersburg Local	Wheelersburg
1	0	Whitehall City	Whitehall
1	0	Willard City	Willard
1	0	Willoughby-Eastlake City	Willoughby
1	0	Wilmington City	Wilmington
1	0	Winton Woods City	Cincinnati
1	0	Woodridge Local	Peninsula
1	0	Wooster City	Wooster
1	0	Worthington City	Worthington
1	0	Wyoming City	Wyoming
1	0	Xenia Community City	Xenia
1	0	Youngstown City Schools	Youngstown
1	0	Zanesville City	Zanesville

Note: This section only includes districts with 1,500 or more students; All categories are ranked from high to low

The Nation's Report Card

2017 Mathematics State Snapshot Report
Ohio • Grade 4 • Public Schools

Overall Results

- In 2017, the average score of fourth-grade students in Ohio was 241. This was not significantly different from the average score of 239 for public school students in the nation.
- The average score for students in Ohio in 2017 (241) was not significantly different from their average score in 2015 (244) and was higher than their average score in 2000 (230).
- The percentage of students in Ohio who performed at or above the NAEP *Proficient* level was 41 percent in 2017. This percentage was not significantly different from that in 2015 (45 percent) and was greater than that in 2000 (25 percent).
- The percentage of students in Ohio who performed at or above the NAEP *Basic* level was 81 percent in 2017. This percentage was smaller than that in 2015 (85 percent) and was greater than that in 2000 (73 percent).

Achievement-Level Percentages and Average Score Results

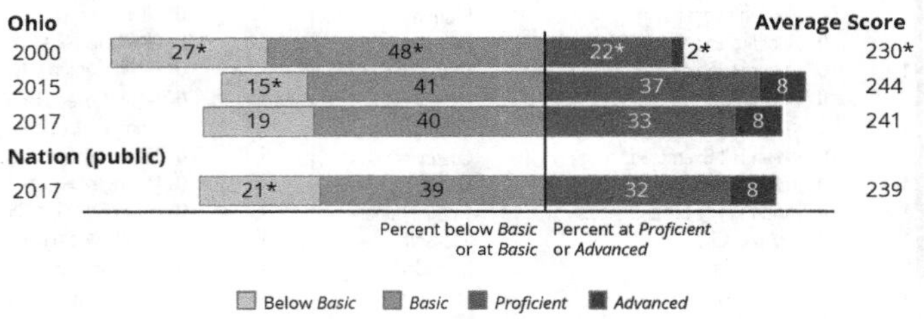

* Significantly different ($p < .05$) from state's results in 2017. Significance tests were performed using unrounded numbers.
NOTE: Detail may not sum to totals because of rounding.

Compare the Average Score in 2017 to Other States/Jurisdictions

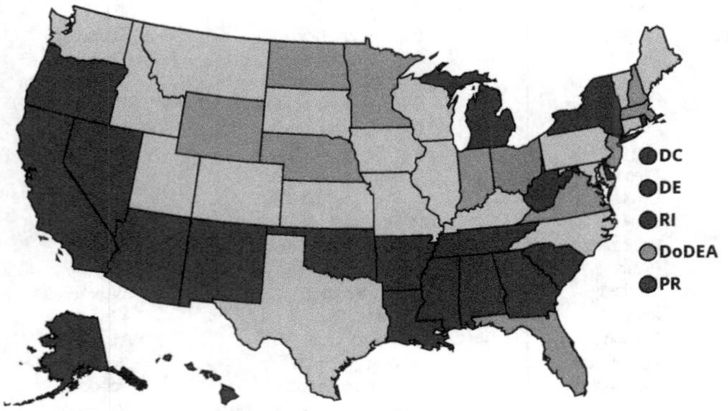

In 2017, the average score in Ohio (241) was
- lower than those in 11 states/jurisdictions
- higher than those in 22 states/jurisdictions
- not significantly different from those in 19 states/jurisdictions

DoDEA = Department of Defense Education Activity (overseas and domestic schools)

Average Scores for State/Jurisdiction and Nation (public)

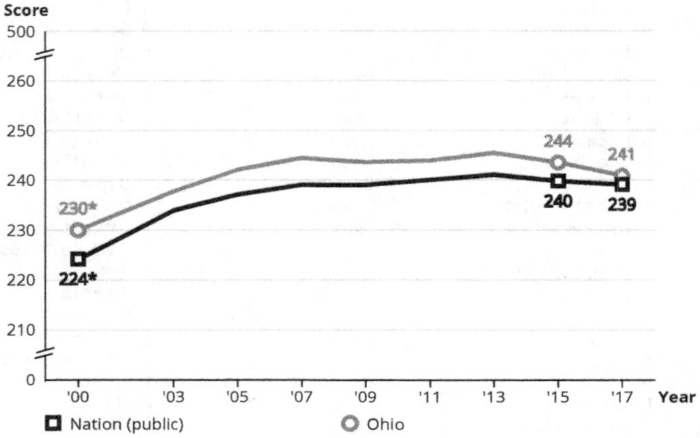

* Significantly different ($p < .05$) from 2017. Significance tests were performed using unrounded numbers.

Results for Student Groups in 2017

Reporting Groups	Percentage of students	Avg. score	Percentage at or above *Basic*	Percentage at or above *Proficient*	Percentage at *Advanced*
Race/Ethnicity					
White	70	246	87	48	10
Black	18	220	59	15	1
Hispanic	5	229	71	24	3
Asian	3	264	91	70	36
American Indian/Alaska Native	#	‡	‡	‡	‡
Native Hawaiian/Pacific Islander	#	‡	‡	‡	‡
Two or more races	5	237	80	36	4
Gender					
Male	51	241	81	41	9
Female	49	240	81	41	7
National School Lunch Program					
Eligible	51	228	70	24	2
Not eligible	49	254	93	60	14

\# Rounds to zero.
‡ Reporting standards not met.
NOTE: Detail may not sum to totals because of rounding, and because the "Information not available" category for the National School Lunch Program, which provides free/reduced-price lunches, is not displayed. Black includes African American and Hispanic includes Latino. Race categories exclude Hispanic origin.

Score Gaps for Student Groups

- In 2017, Black students had an average score that was 26 points lower than that for White students. This performance gap was not significantly different from that in 2000 (29 points).
- In 2017, Hispanic students had an average score that was 17 points lower than that for White students. Data are not reported for Hispanic students in 2000, because reporting standards were not met.
- In 2017, male students in Ohio had an average score that was not significantly different from that for female students.
- In 2017, students who were eligible for free/reduced-price school lunch, an indicator of low family income, had an average score that was 26 points lower than that for students who were not eligible. This performance gap was not significantly different from that in 2000 (22 points).

ies NATIONAL CENTER FOR EDUCATION STATISTICS
Institute of Education Sciences

NOTE: The NAEP mathematics scale ranges from 0 to 500. Statistical comparisons are calculated on the basis of unrounded scale scores or percentages. Read more about how to interpret NAEP results from the mathematics assessment at https://nces.ed.gov/nationsreportcard/mathematics/interpret_results.aspx.
SOURCE: U.S. Department of Education, Institute of Education Sciences, National Center for Education Statistics, National Assessment of Educational Progress (NAEP), various years, 2000-2017 Mathematics Assessments.

The Nation's Report Card

2017 Mathematics State Snapshot Report
Ohio • Grade 8 • Public Schools

Overall Results

- In 2017, the average score of eighth-grade students in Ohio was 288. This was higher than the average score of 282 for public school students in the nation.
- The average score for students in Ohio in 2017 (288) was not significantly different from their average score in 2015 (285) and was higher than their average score in 2000 (281).
- The percentage of students in Ohio who performed at or above the NAEP *Proficient* level was 40 percent in 2017. This percentage was not significantly different from that in 2015 (35 percent) and was greater than that in 2000 (30 percent).
- The percentage of students in Ohio who performed at or above the NAEP *Basic* level was 74 percent in 2017. This percentage was not significantly different from that in 2015 (75 percent) and in 2000 (73 percent).

Compare the Average Score in 2017 to Other States/Jurisdictions

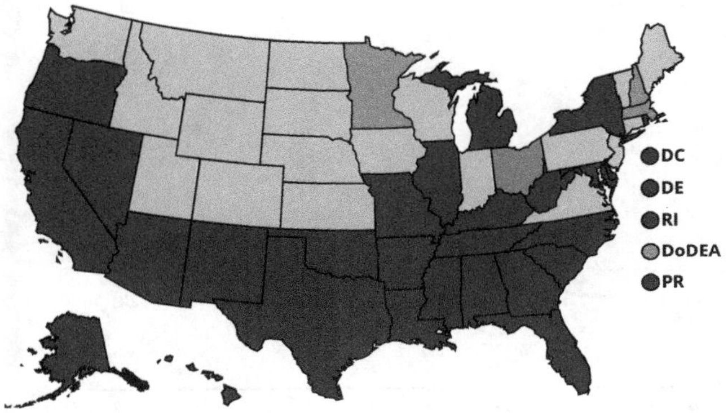

In 2017, the average score in Ohio (288) was
- lower than those in 4 states/jurisdictions
- higher than those in 29 states/jurisdictions
- not significantly different from those in 19 states/jurisdictions

DoDEA = Department of Defense Education Activity (overseas and domestic schools)

Results for Student Groups in 2017

Reporting Groups	Percentage of students	Avg. score	Percentage at or above *Basic*	Percentage at or above *Proficient*	Percentage at *Advanced*
Race/Ethnicity					
White	72	295	82	47	15
Black	16	254	41	12	1
Hispanic	4	279	68	28	5
Asian	2	‡	‡	‡	‡
American Indian/Alaska Native	#	‡	‡	‡	‡
Native Hawaiian/Pacific Islander	#	‡	‡	‡	‡
Two or more races	5	274	61	25	8
Gender					
Male	51	288	74	40	13
Female	49	288	74	41	12
National School Lunch Program					
Eligible	44	267	54	21	4
Not eligible	54	303	89	55	19

Rounds to zero.
‡ Reporting standards not met.
NOTE: Detail may not sum to totals because of rounding, and because the "Information not available" category for the National School Lunch Program, which provides free/reduced-price lunches, is not displayed. Black includes African American and Hispanic includes Latino. Race categories exclude Hispanic origin.

Achievement-Level Percentages and Average Score Results

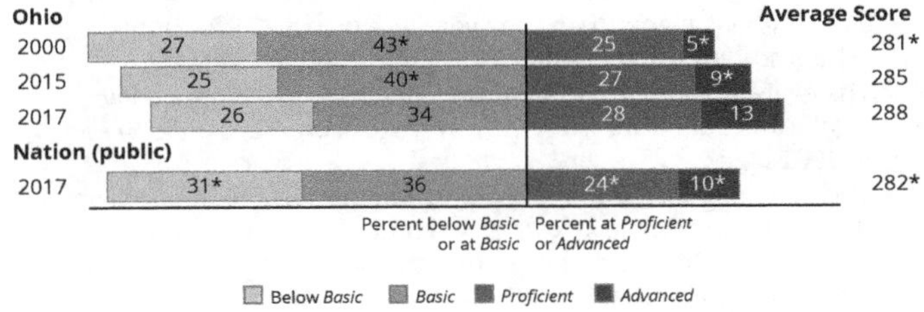

* Significantly different ($p < .05$) from state's results in 2017. Significance tests were performed using unrounded numbers.
NOTE: Detail may not sum to totals because of rounding.

Average Scores for State/Jurisdiction and Nation (public)

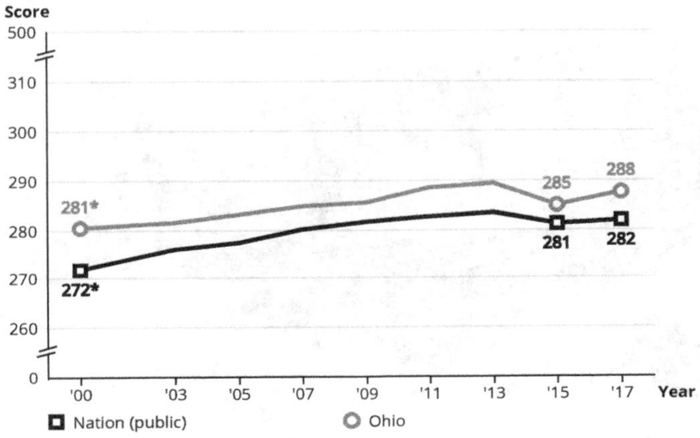

* Significantly different ($p < .05$) from 2017. Significance tests were performed using unrounded numbers.

Score Gaps for Student Groups

- In 2017, Black students had an average score that was 41 points lower than that for White students. This performance gap was not significantly different from that in 2000 (34 points).
- In 2017, Hispanic students had an average score that was 17 points lower than that for White students. Data are not reported for Hispanic students in 2000, because reporting standards were not met.
- In 2017, male students in Ohio had an average score that was not significantly different from that for female students.
- In 2017, students who were eligible for free/reduced-price school lunch, an indicator of low family income, had an average score that was 36 points lower than that for students who were not eligible. This performance gap was not significantly different from that in 2000 (30 points).

ies NATIONAL CENTER FOR EDUCATION STATISTICS
Institute of Education Sciences

NOTE: The NAEP mathematics scale ranges from 0 to 500. Statistical comparisons are calculated on the basis of unrounded scale scores or percentages. Read more about how to interpret NAEP results from the mathematics assessment at https://nces.ed.gov/nationsreportcard/mathematics/interpret_results.aspx.
SOURCE: U.S. Department of Education, Institute of Education Sciences, National Center for Education Statistics, National Assessment of Educational Progress (NAEP), various years, 2000-2017 Mathematics Assessments.

The Nation's Report Card

2017 Reading State Snapshot Report
Ohio • Grade 4 • Public Schools

Overall Results

- In 2017, the average score of fourth-grade students in Ohio was 225. This was higher than the average score of 221 for public school students in the nation.
- The average score for students in Ohio in 2017 (225) was not significantly different from their average score in 2015 (225) and in 2002 (222).
- The percentage of students in Ohio who performed at or above the NAEP *Proficient* level was 39 percent in 2017. This percentage was not significantly different from that in 2015 (38 percent) and was greater than that in 2002 (34 percent).
- The percentage of students in Ohio who performed at or above the NAEP *Basic* level was 71 percent in 2017. This percentage was not significantly different from that in 2015 (72 percent) and in 2002 (68 percent).

Achievement-Level Percentages and Average Score Results

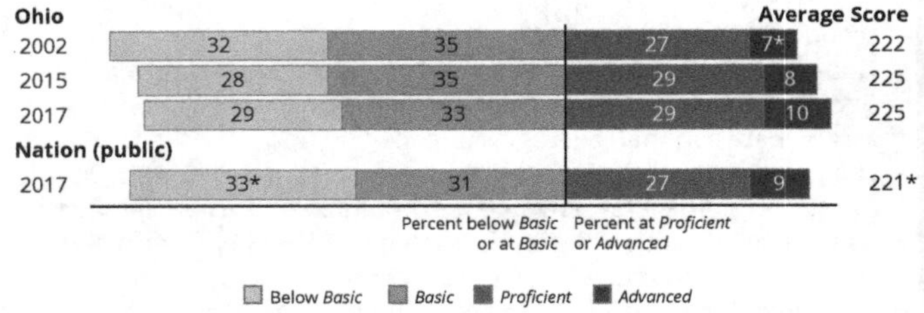

* Significantly different ($p < .05$) from state's results in 2017. Significance tests were performed using unrounded numbers.
NOTE: Detail may not sum to totals because of rounding.

Compare the Average Score in 2017 to Other States/Jurisdictions

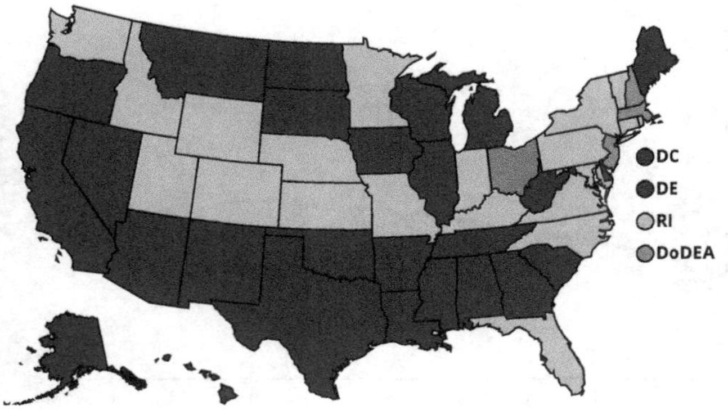

In 2017, the average score in Ohio (225) was
- lower than those in 4 states/jurisdictions
- higher than those in 27 states/jurisdictions
- not significantly different from those in 20 states/jurisdictions

DoDEA = Department of Defense Education Activity (overseas and domestic schools)

Average Scores for State/Jurisdiction and Nation (public)

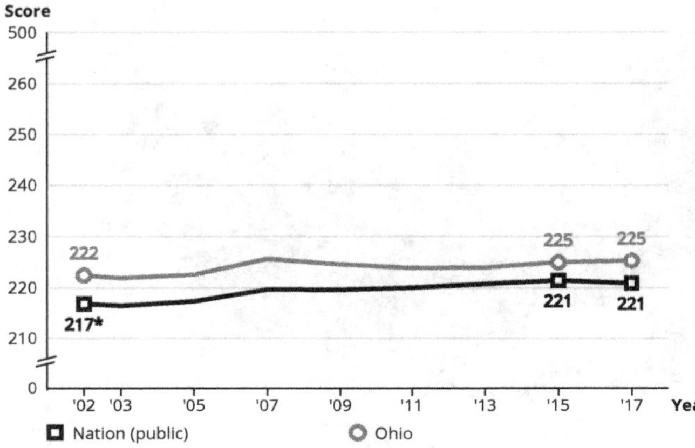

* Significantly different ($p < .05$) from 2017. Significance tests were performed using unrounded numbers.

Results for Student Groups in 2017

Reporting Groups	Percentage of students	Avg. score	Percentage at or above *Basic*	Percentage at or above *Proficient*	Percentage at *Advanced*
Race/Ethnicity					
White	70	231	78	44	11
Black	17	203	47	15	2
Hispanic	5	216	61	26	5
Asian	3	243	87	60	20
American Indian/Alaska Native	#	‡	‡	‡	‡
Native Hawaiian/Pacific Islander	#	‡	‡	‡	‡
Two or more races	5	224	70	38	9
Gender					
Male	51	223	69	38	10
Female	49	227	74	39	10
National School Lunch Program					
Eligible	53	213	59	24	4
Not eligible	47	239	85	55	16

Rounds to zero.
‡ Reporting standards not met.
NOTE: Detail may not sum to totals because of rounding, and because the "Information not available" category for the National School Lunch Program, which provides free/reduced-price lunches, is not displayed. Black includes African American and Hispanic includes Latino. Race categories exclude Hispanic origin.

Score Gaps for Student Groups

- In 2017, Black students had an average score that was 28 points lower than that for White students. This performance gap was not significantly different from that in 2002 (27 points).
- In 2017, Hispanic students had an average score that was 15 points lower than that for White students. Data are not reported for Hispanic students in 2002, because reporting standards were not met.
- In 2017, female students in Ohio had an average score that was higher than that for male students by 4 points.
- In 2017, students who were eligible for free/reduced-price school lunch, an indicator of low family income, had an average score that was 27 points lower than that for students who were not eligible. This performance gap was not significantly different from that in 2002 (24 points).

ies NATIONAL CENTER FOR EDUCATION STATISTICS
Institute of Education Sciences

NOTE: The NAEP reading scale ranges from 0 to 500. Statistical comparisons are calculated on the basis of unrounded scale scores or percentages. Read more about how to interpret NAEP results from the reading assessment at https://nces.ed.gov/nationsreportcard/reading/interpret_results.aspx.
SOURCE: U.S. Department of Education, Institute of Education Sciences, National Center for Education Statistics, National Assessment of Educational Progress (NAEP), various years, 2002-2017 Reading Assessments.

The Nation's Report Card

2017 Reading State Snapshot Report
Ohio • Grade 8 • Public Schools

Overall Results

- In 2017, the average score of eighth-grade students in Ohio was 268. This was not significantly different from the average score of 265 for public school students in the nation.
- The average score for students in Ohio in 2017 (268) was not significantly different from their average score in 2015 (266) and in 2002 (268).
- The percentage of students in Ohio who performed at or above the NAEP *Proficient* level was 39 percent in 2017. This percentage was not significantly different from that in 2015 (36 percent) and in 2002 (35 percent).
- The percentage of students in Ohio who performed at or above the NAEP *Basic* level was 77 percent in 2017. This percentage was not significantly different from that in 2015 (76 percent) and in 2002 (82 percent).

Compare the Average Score in 2017 to Other States/Jurisdictions

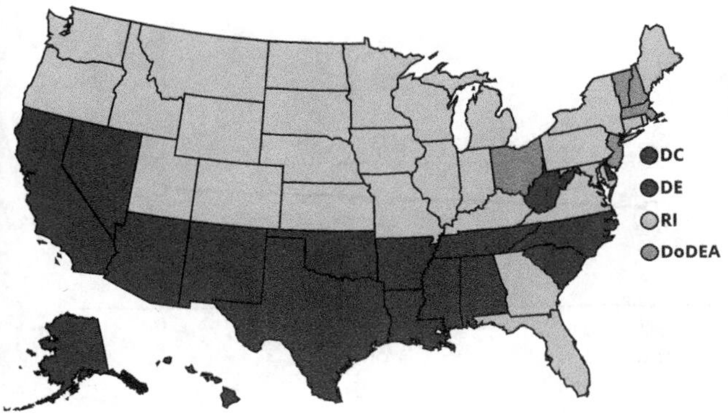

In 2017, the average score in Ohio (268) was
- lower than those in 5 states/jurisdictions
- higher than those in 18 states/jurisdictions
- not significantly different from those in 28 states/jurisdictions

DoDEA = Department of Defense Education Activity (overseas and domestic schools)

Results for Student Groups in 2017

Reporting Groups	Percentage of students	Avg. score	Percentage at or above *Basic*	Percentage at or above *Proficient*	Percentage at *Advanced*
Race/Ethnicity					
White	72	274	83	45	6
Black	16	244	51	15	1
Hispanic	4	260	71	26	2
Asian	2	281	80	56	16
American Indian/Alaska Native	#	‡	‡	‡	‡
Native Hawaiian/Pacific Islander	#	‡	‡	‡	‡
Two or more races	5	264	72	34	4
Gender					
Male	51	263	72	34	3
Female	49	274	81	45	7
National School Lunch Program					
Eligible	44	251	61	20	1
Not eligible	54	282	89	54	8

Rounds to zero.
‡ Reporting standards not met.
NOTE: Detail may not sum to totals because of rounding, and because the "Information not available" category for the National School Lunch Program, which provides free/reduced-price lunches, is not displayed. Black includes African American and Hispanic includes Latino. Race categories exclude Hispanic origin.

Achievement-Level Percentages and Average Score Results

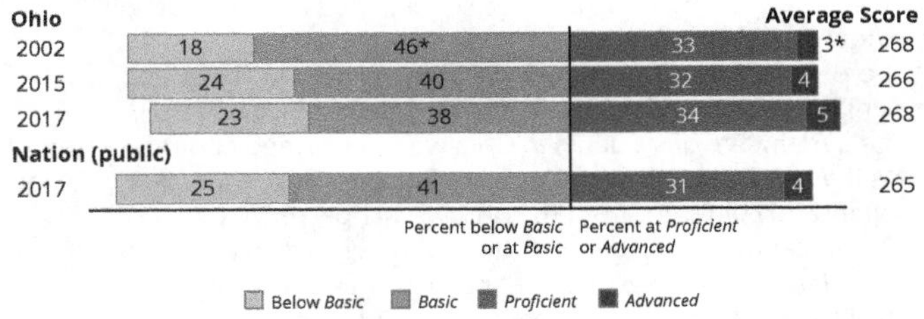

* Significantly different ($p < .05$) from state's results in 2017. Significance tests were performed using unrounded numbers.
NOTE: Detail may not sum to totals because of rounding.

Average Scores for State/Jurisdiction and Nation (public)

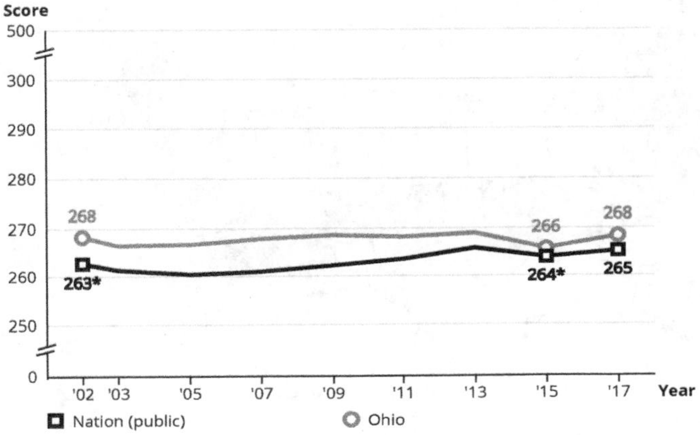

* Significantly different ($p < .05$) from 2017. Significance tests were performed using unrounded numbers.

Score Gaps for Student Groups

- In 2017, Black students had an average score that was 30 points lower than that for White students. This performance gap was not significantly different from that in 2002 (27 points).
- In 2017, Hispanic students had an average score that was 15 points lower than that for White students. Data are not reported for Hispanic students in 2002, because reporting standards were not met.
- In 2017, female students in Ohio had an average score that was higher than that for male students by 10 points.
- In 2017, students who were eligible for free/reduced-price school lunch, an indicator of low family income, had an average score that was 31 points lower than that for students who were not eligible. This performance gap was wider than that in 2002 (16 points).

ies NATIONAL CENTER FOR EDUCATION STATISTICS
Institute of Education Sciences

NOTE: The NAEP reading scale ranges from 0 to 500. Statistical comparisons are calculated on the basis of unrounded scale scores or percentages. Read more about how to interpret NAEP results from the reading assessment at https://nces.ed.gov/nationsreportcard/reading/interpret_results.aspx.
SOURCE: U.S. Department of Education, Institute of Education Sciences, National Center for Education Statistics, National Assessment of Educational Progress (NAEP), various years, 2002-2017 Reading Assessments.

The Nation's Report Card

2015 Science State Snapshot Report
Ohio • Grade 4 • Public Schools

Overall Results

- In 2015, the average score of fourth-grade students in Ohio was 157. This was higher than the average score of 153 for public school students in the nation.
- The average score for students in Ohio in 2015 (157) was not significantly different from their average score in 2009 (157).
- The percentage of students in Ohio who performed at or above the NAEP *Proficient* level was 41 percent in 2015. This percentage was not significantly different from that in 2009 (41 percent).
- The percentage of students in Ohio who performed at or above the NAEP *Basic* level was 81 percent in 2015. This percentage was not significantly different from that in 2009 (79 percent).

Achievement-Level Percentages and Average Score Results

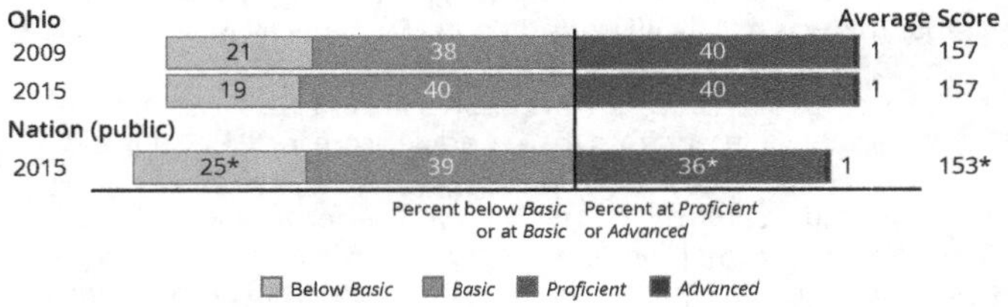

* Significantly different ($p < .05$) from state's results in 2015. Significance tests were performed using unrounded numbers.
NOTE: Detail may not sum to totals because of rounding.

Compare the Average Score in 2015 to Other States/Jurisdictions

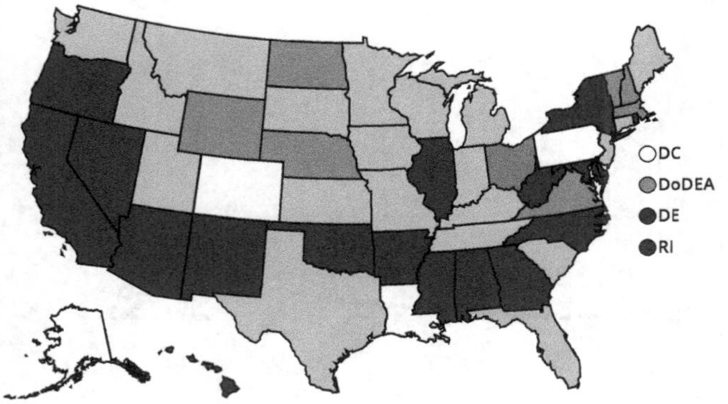

In 2015, the average score in Ohio (157) was
- lower than those in 8 states/jurisdictions
- higher than those in 18 states/jurisdictions
- not significantly different from those in 20 states/jurisdictions

- 5 states/jurisdictions did not participate in 2015

DoDEA = Department of Defense Education Activity (overseas and domestic schools)

Average Scores for State/Jurisdiction and Nation (public)

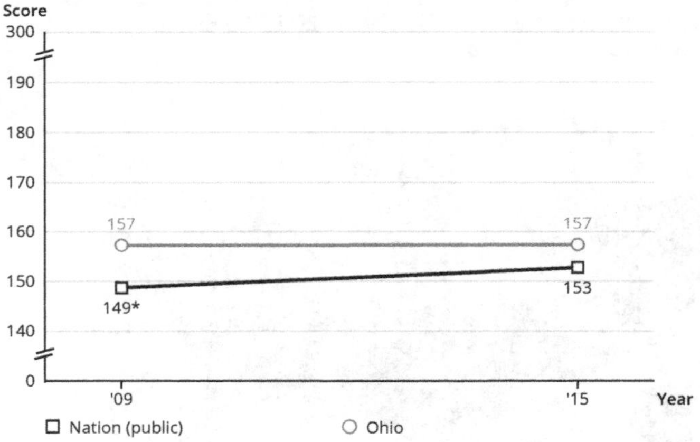

* Significantly different ($p < .05$) from 2015. Significance tests were performed using unrounded numbers.

Results for Student Groups in 2015

Reporting Groups	Percentage of students	Avg. score	Percentage at or above *Basic*	Percentage at or above *Proficient*	Percentage at *Advanced*
Race/Ethnicity					
White	72	164	89	48	1
Black	16	127	46	9	#
Hispanic	5	144	65	28	#
Asian	2	‡	‡	‡	‡
American Indian/Alaska Native	#	‡	‡	‡	‡
Native Hawaiian/Pacific Islander	#	‡	‡	‡	‡
Two or more races	5	159	80	40	2
Gender					
Male	51	159	81	43	1
Female	49	156	80	39	#
National School Lunch Program					
Eligible	47	143	67	23	#
Not eligible	51	170	93	57	1

\# Rounds to zero.
‡ Reporting standards not met.
NOTE: Detail may not sum to totals because of rounding, and because the "Information not available" category for the National School Lunch Program, which provides free/reduced-price lunches, is not displayed. Black includes African American and Hispanic includes Latino. Race categories exclude Hispanic origin.

Score Gaps for Student Groups

- In 2015, Black students had an average score that was 37 points lower than that for White students. This performance gap was not significantly different from that in 2009 (37 points).
- In 2015, Hispanic students had an average score that was 20 points lower than that for White students. This performance gap was not significantly different from that in 2009 (25 points).
- In 2015, male students in Ohio had an average score that was not significantly different from that for female students.
- In 2015, students who were eligible for free/reduced-price school lunch, an indicator of low family income, had an average score that was 27 points lower than that for students who were not eligible. This performance gap was not significantly different from that in 2009 (30 points).

ies NATIONAL CENTER FOR EDUCATION STATISTICS
Institute of Education Sciences

NOTE: The NAEP science scale ranges from 0 to 300. Statistical comparisons are calculated on the basis of unrounded scale scores or percentages.
SOURCE: U.S. Department of Education, Institute of Education Sciences, National Center for Education Statistics, National Assessment of Educational Progress (NAEP), 2009 and 2015 Science Assessments.

The Nation's Report Card

2015 Science State Snapshot Report

Ohio • Grade 8 • Public Schools

Overall Results

- In 2015, the average score of eighth-grade students in Ohio was 157. This was higher than the average score of 153 for public school students in the nation.
- The average score for students in Ohio in 2015 (157) was not significantly different from their average score in 2011 (158) and in 2009 (158).
- The percentage of students in Ohio who performed at or above the NAEP *Proficient* level was 38 percent in 2015. This percentage was not significantly different from that in 2011 (38 percent) and in 2009 (37 percent).
- The percentage of students in Ohio who performed at or above the NAEP *Basic* level was 72 percent in 2015. This percentage was not significantly different from that in 2011 (73 percent) and in 2009 (73 percent).

Achievement-Level Percentages and Average Score Results

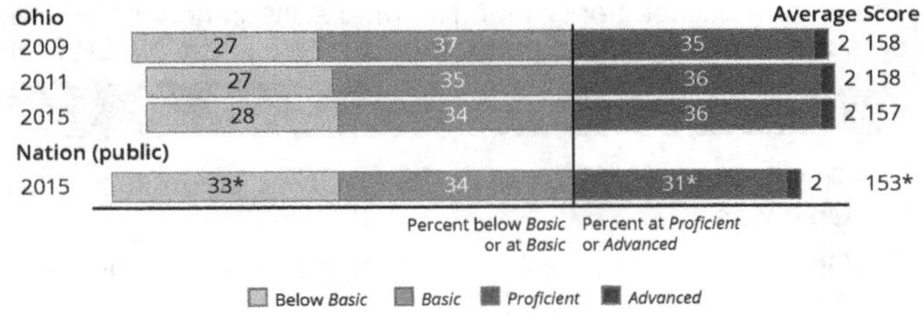

* Significantly different ($p < .05$) from state's results in 2015. Significance tests were performed using unrounded numbers.
NOTE: Detail may not sum to totals because of rounding.

Compare the Average Score in 2015 to Other States/Jurisdictions

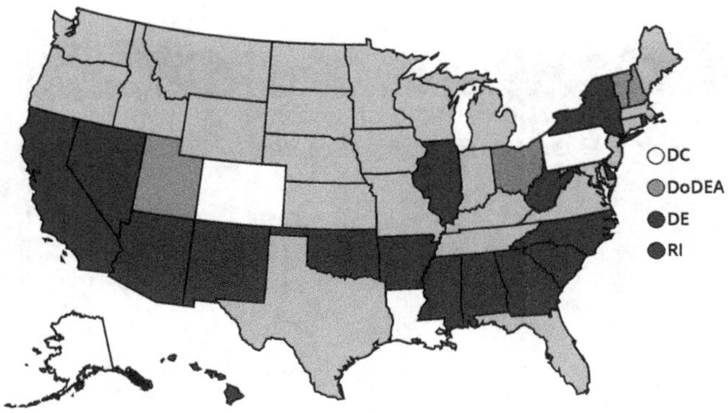

In 2015, the average score in Ohio (157) was
- lower than those in 4 states/jurisdictions
- higher than those in 17 states/jurisdictions
- not significantly different from those in 25 states/jurisdictions

- 5 states/jurisdictions did not participate in 2015

DoDEA = Department of Defense Education Activity (overseas and domestic schools)

Average Scores for State/Jurisdiction and Nation (public)

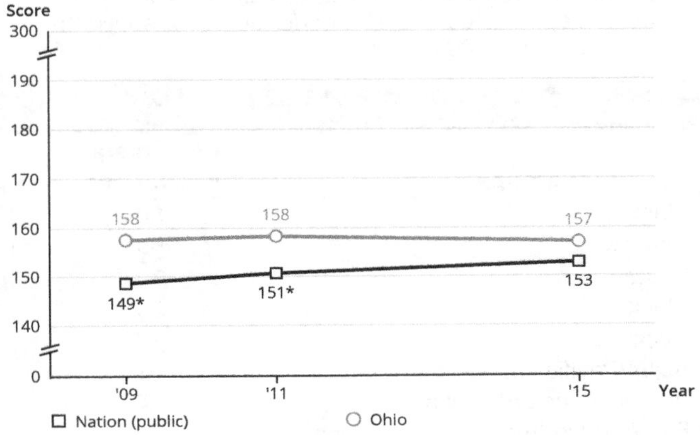

* Significantly different ($p < .05$) from 2015. Significance tests were performed using unrounded numbers.

Results for Student Groups in 2015

Reporting Groups	Percentage of students	Avg. score	Percentage at or above *Basic*	Percentage at or above *Proficient*	Percentage at *Advanced*
Race/Ethnicity					
White	74	165	81	45	3
Black	16	127	37	10	#
Hispanic	3	142	60	27	1
Asian	2	‡	‡	‡	‡
American Indian/Alaska Native	#	‡	‡	‡	‡
Native Hawaiian/Pacific Islander	#	‡	‡	‡	‡
Two or more races	4	155	70	34	1
Gender					
Male	52	159	73	41	3
Female	48	155	71	35	1
National School Lunch Program					
Eligible	48	143	56	22	1
Not eligible	52	170	87	53	3

Rounds to zero.
‡ Reporting standards not met.
NOTE: Detail may not sum to totals because of rounding, and because the "Information not available" category for the National School Lunch Program, which provides free/reduced-price lunches, is not displayed. Black includes African American and Hispanic includes Latino. Race categories exclude Hispanic origin.

Score Gaps for Student Groups

- In 2015, Black students had an average score that was 37 points lower than that for White students. This performance gap was not significantly different from that in 2009 (38 points).
- In 2015, Hispanic students had an average score that was 22 points not significantly different from that for White students. This performance gap was not significantly different from that in 2009 (24 points).
- In 2015, male students in Ohio had an average score that was not significantly different from that for female students.
- In 2015, students who were eligible for free/reduced-price school lunch, an indicator of low family income, had an average score that was 27 points lower than that for students who were not eligible. This performance gap was not significantly different from that in 2009 (24 points).

ies NATIONAL CENTER FOR EDUCATION STATISTICS Institute of Education Sciences

NOTE: The NAEP science scale ranges from 0 to 300. Statistical comparisons are calculated on the basis of unrounded scale scores or percentages.
SOURCE: U.S. Department of Education, Institute of Education Sciences, National Center for Education Statistics, National Assessment of Educational Progress (NAEP), various years, 2009-2015 Science Assessments.

NCES National Center for Education Statistics — The Nation's Report Card NAEP

The Nation's Report Card
State **Writing 2002**

Ohio
Grade 4
Public School

Snapshot Report

NCES 2003-532OH4

The writing assessment of the National Assessment of Educational Progress (NAEP) measures narrative, informative, and persuasive writing–three purposes identified in the NAEP framework. The NAEP writing scale ranges from 0 to 300.

Overall Writing Results for Ohio

- The average scale score for fourth-grade students in Ohio was 157.
- Ohio's average score (157) was higher[1] than that of the nation's public schools (153).
- Students' average scale scores in Ohio were higher than those in 26 jurisdictions[2], not significantly different from those in 17 jurisdictions, and lower than those in 4 jurisdictions.
- The percentage of students who performed at or above the NAEP *Proficient* level was 28 percent. The percentage of students who performed at or above the *Basic* level was 90 percent.

Student Percentage at Each Achievement Level

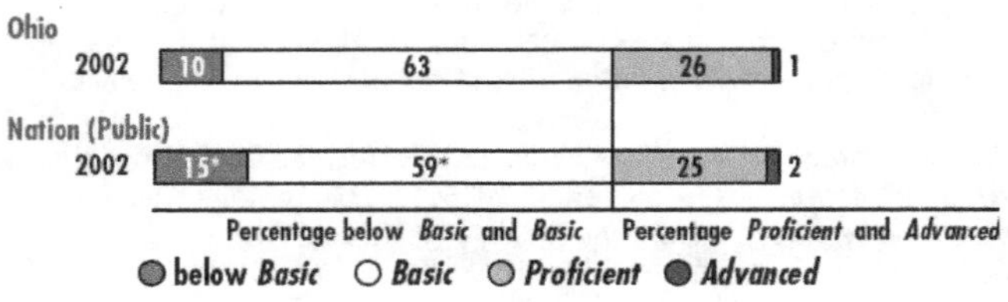

Performance of NAEP Reporting Groups in Ohio

Reporting groups	Percentage of students	Average Score	Below *Basic*	*Basic*	*Proficient*	Advanced
Male	50	150 ↑	13 ↓	67 ↑	19	1
Female	50	164	6 ↓	59	33	2
White	76	162	7 ↓	61 ↑	31	2
Black	20	140	20	68	11	#
Hispanic	2	---	---	---	---	---
Asian/Pacific Islander	1	---	---	---	---	---
American Indian/Alaska Native	#	---	---	---	---	---
Free/reduced-priced school lunch						
Eligible	32	143	18 ↓	69 ↑	14	#
Not eligible	61	164	5 ↓	60	33	2
Information not available	7	158	8	64	26	2

(Columns Below *Basic* through Advanced: Percentage of students at)

Average Score Gaps Between Selected Groups

- Female students in Ohio had an average score that was higher than that of male students (14 points). This performance gap was not significantly different from that of the Nation (18 points).
- White students had an average score that was higher than that of Black students (22 points). This performance gap was not significantly different from that of the Nation (20 points).
- The sample size was not sufficient to permit a reliable estimate for Hispanic students in Ohio.
- Students who were not eligible for free/reduced-price school lunch had an average score that was higher than that of students who were eligible (21 points). This performance gap was not significantly different from that of the Nation (22 points).

Writing Scale Scores at Selected Percentiles

Scale Score Distribution

	25th Percentile	50th Percentile	75th Percentile
Ohio	*135* ↑	*157* ↑	*179*
Nation (Public)	*128*	*153*	*178*

An examination of scores at different percentiles on the 0-300 NAEP writing scale at each grade indicates how well students at lower, middle, and higher levels of the distribution performed. For example, the data above shows that 75 percent of students in public schools nationally scored below *178,* while 75 percent of students in Ohio scored below *179*.

Percentage rounds to zero.
--- Reporting standards not met; sample size insufficient to permit a reliable estimate.
* Significantly different from Ohio.
↑ Significantly higher than, ↓ lower than appropriate subgroup in the nation (public).
[1] Comparisons (higher/lower/not different) are based on statistical tests. The .05 level was used for testing statistical significance.
[2] "Jurisdictions" includes participating states and other jurisdictions (such as Guam or the District of Columbia).
NOTE: Detail may not sum to totals because of rounding. Score gaps are calculated based on differences between unrounded average scale scores.
Visit http://nces.ed.gov/nationsreportcard/states/ for additional results and detailed information.
SOURCE: U.S. Department of Education, Institute of Education Sciences, National Center for Education Statistics, National Assessment of Educational Progress (NAEP), 2002 Writing Assessment.

ies NATIONAL CENTER FOR EDUCATION STATISTICS Institute of Education Sciences

NCES 2008-470OH8

The Nation's Report Card Writing 2007 State Snapshot Report

Ohio
Grade 8
Public Schools

The National Assessment of Educational Progress (NAEP) assesses writing for three purposes identified in the NAEP framework: narrative, informative, and persuasive. The NAEP writing scale ranges from 0 to 300.

Overall Writing Results for Ohio

- In 2007, the average scale score for eighth-grade students in Ohio was 156. This was not significantly different from their average score in 2002 (160).[1]
- Ohio's average score (156) in 2007 was not significantly different from that of the nation's public schools (154).
- Of the 45 states and one other jurisdiction that participated in the 2007 eighth-grade assessment, students' average scale score in Ohio was higher than those in 15 jurisdictions, not significantly different from those in 22 jurisdictions, and lower than those in 8 jurisdictions.[2]
- The percentage of students in Ohio who performed at or above the NAEP *Proficient* level was 32 percent in 2007. This percentage was smaller than that in 2002 (38 percent).
- The percentage of students in Ohio who performed at or above the NAEP *Basic* level was 90 percent in 2007. This percentage was not significantly different from that in 2002 (89 percent).

Percentages at NAEP Achievement Levels and Average Score

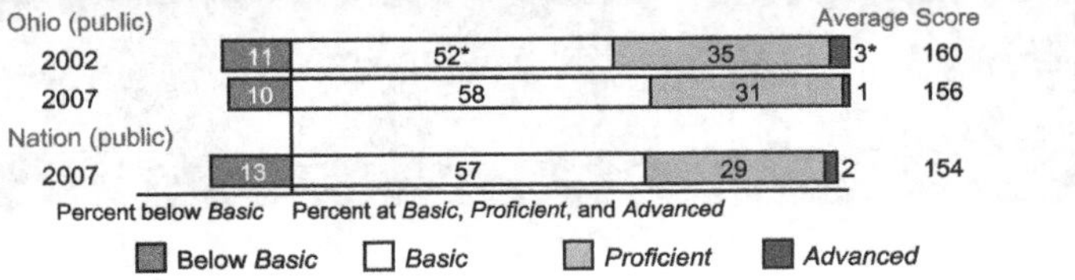

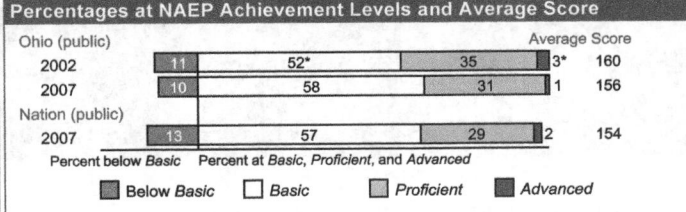

NOTE: The NAEP grade 8 writing achievement levels correspond to the following scale points: Below *Basic*, 113 or lower; *Basic*, 114–172; *Proficient*, 173–223; *Advanced*, 224 or above.

Performance of NAEP Reporting Groups in Ohio: 2007

Reporting groups	Percent of students	Average score	Percent below *Basic*	Percent of students at or above *Basic*	Percent of students at or above *Proficient*	Percent *Advanced*
Male	52	147	15	85	21	#
Female	48	166	5	95	43	2↓
White	76	160	8	92	36	1↓
Black	19	138	20	80	13	#
Hispanic	2	141	26	74	22	#
Asian/Pacific Islander	1	‡	‡	‡	‡	‡
American Indian/Alaska Native	#	‡	‡	‡	‡	‡
Eligible for National School Lunch Program	32	140	19	81	15	#
Not eligible for National School Lunch Program	66	163	6	94	39	1↓

Average Score Gaps Between Selected Groups

- In 2007, male students in Ohio had an average score that was lower than that of female students by 19 points. This performance gap was not significantly different from that of 2002 (20 points).
- In 2007, Black students had an average score that was lower than that of White students by 22 points. This performance gap was not significantly different from that of 2002 (33 points).
- In 2007, Hispanic students had an average score that was lower than that of White students by 20 points. Data are not reported for Hispanic students in 2002, because reporting standards were not met. Therefore, the performance gap results are not reported.
- In 2007, students who were eligible for free/reduced-price school lunch, an indicator of poverty, had an average score that was lower than that of students who were not eligible for free/reduced-price school lunch by 23 points. This performance gap was the same as that of 2002 (23 points).
- In 2007, the score gap between students at the 75th percentile and students at the 25th percentile was 44 points. This performance gap was not significantly different from that of 2002 (47 points).

Writing Scores at Selected Percentiles in Ohio

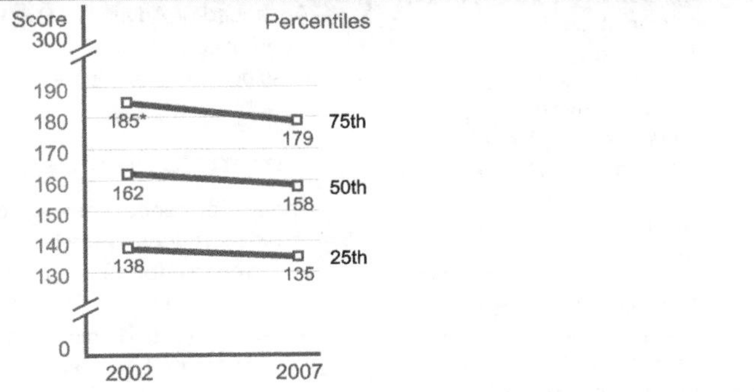

NOTE: Scores at selected percentiles on the NAEP writing scale indicate how well students at lower, middle, and higher levels performed.

Rounds to zero.
‡ Reporting standards not met.
* Significantly different from 2007.
↑ Significantly higher than 2002. ↓ Significantly lower than 2002.

[1] Comparisons (higher/lower/narrower/wider/not different) are based on statistical tests. The .05 level with appropriate adjustments for multiple comparisons was used for testing statistical significance. Statistical comparisons are calculated on the basis of unrounded scale scores or percentages. Comparisons across jurisdictions and comparisons with the nation or within a jurisdiction across years may be affected by differences in exclusion rates for students with disabilities (SD) and English language learners (ELL). The exclusion rates for SD and ELL in Ohio were 4 percent and "percentage rounds to zero" in 2007, respectively. For more information on NAEP significance testing, see http://nces.ed.gov/nationsreportcard/writing/interpret-results.asp#statistical.

[2] "Jurisdiction" refers to states, the District of Columbia, and the Department of Defense Education Activity schools.

NOTE: Detail may not sum to totals because of rounding and because the "Information not available" category for the National School Lunch Program, which provides free and reduced-price lunches, and the "Unclassified" category for race/ethnicity are not displayed. Visit http://nces.ed.gov/nationsreportcard/states/ for additional results and detailed information.

SOURCE: U.S. Department of Education, Institute of Education Sciences, National Center for Education Statistics, National Assessment of Educational Progress (NAEP), 2002 and 2007 Writing Assessments.

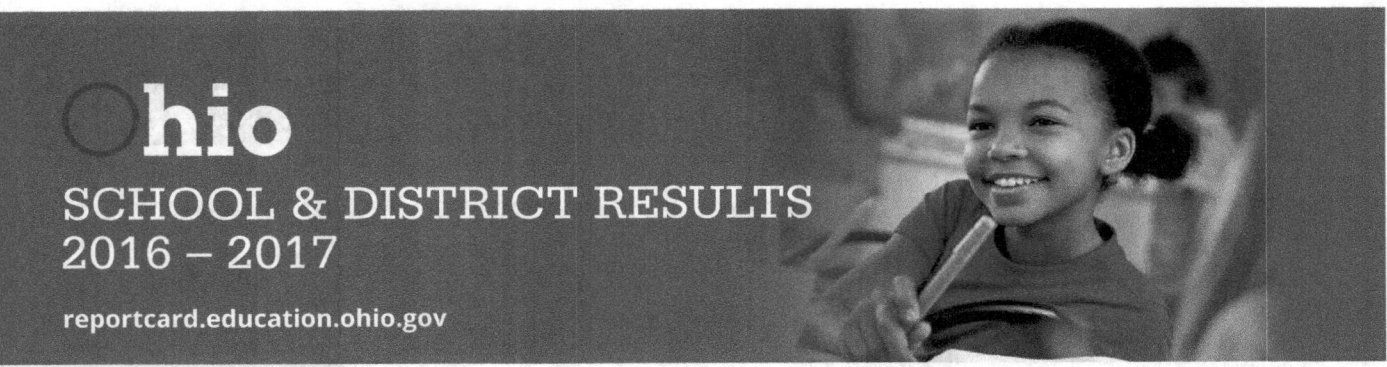

Ohio
SCHOOL & DISTRICT RESULTS 2016 – 2017

reportcard.education.ohio.gov

SUPERINTENDENT'S MESSAGE

Paolo DeMaria
Superintendent of Public Instruction

Colleges and employers are demanding greater knowledge and skills from our graduates than ever before. As Ohio continues to help students in meeting higher expectations for what they should know and be able to do, student achievement is higher statewide. Here is a snapshot of the state results on the 2016-2017 report card.

Schools and districts will use these report cards to have discussions about performance and make decisions about instruction and improvement. Remember, however, that report cards are just one element of what is happening in a district or school. To get a fuller picture, we encourage people to visit schools and talk to teachers, administrators, parents and students. A lot of great things are happening every day.

Achievement is increasing across the state, in all subjects and with all subgroups

Ohio's education system is helping more and more students meet the bar even when we set high expectations. From 2016 to 2017, **every subject area had an increase in first-time test takers scoring proficient and higher.** All high school subject areas, except one, saw an increase in the percent of students scoring proficient or better in their first attempts. Similarly, for elementary and middle school, in every grade and subject except fifth grade math, higher rates of students scored proficient or better.

Additionally, when looking at students scoring at higher levels (Accelerated, Advanced or Advanced Plus), another trend becomes clear: more students are passing at *higher levels* of proficiency.

Performance Index

The Performance Index is a composite measure reflecting the level of achievement for each student on each state test. There are six levels of achievement, and points are awarded for each student at each achievement level.

Over time, the Performance Index has steadily increased since it was first calculated in 2001. Recently, Ohio implemented higher expectations for students, including new assessments. Not surprisingly, during this transition period, the Performance Index saw a sharp decrease, as new assessments based on higher standards were introduced. The 2015-2016 Performance Index forms a new baseline at 81.6.

State Level Proficiency 2016-2017

GRADE	SUBJECT	2016	2017	
3	English Language Arts	54.9%	63.7%	↑
	Mathematics	65.8%	70.7%	↑
4	English Language Arts	57.5%	62.8%	↑
	Mathematics	69.2%	72.4%	↑
	Social Studies	75.8%	77.5%	↑
5	English Language Arts	60.2%	67.7%	↑
	Mathematics	62.4%	61.6%	↓
	Science	67.5%	68.3%	↑
6	English Language Arts	54.0%	60.2%	↑
	Mathematics	56.7%	60.2%	↑
	Social Studies	61.2%	64.0%	↑
7	English Language Arts	53.6%	59.2%	↑
	Mathematics	55.3%	56.1%	↑
8	English Language Arts	47.5%	50.3%	↑
	Mathematics	52.7%	54.9%	↑
	Science	64.9%	65.8%	↑
High School	Government	68.0%	73.1%	↑
	History	76.3%	74.5%	↓
	English I	60.0%	69.2%	↑
	English II	53.4%	63.3%	↑
	Algebra I	53.0%	56.2%	↑
	Geometry	49.4%	49.7%	↑
	Math I	46.9%	47.6%	↑
	Math II	36.0%	37.4%	↑
	Biology	65.4%	65.7%	↑

Note: retakes excluded from analysis

Year	Performance Index
2015-2016	81.6
2016-2017	84.1 ↑

As students and teachers adjust to the more rigorous standards and with the new assessments in place for a second consecutive year, the **Performance Index increased 2.46 points, which is the third largest increase since it was first calculated.**

To find a school or district report card, go to reportcard.education.ohio.gov.

Ohio | Department of Education

All subgroups improved in English language arts and math

Ohio wants to ensure that all students are making gains, regardless of income, race, ethnicity or disability. **In 2016-2017, all subgroups improved their proficiency rates in English language arts and math compared to last year.** There is still much work to do to close achievement gaps.

Graduation Rate continues its upward trajectory

The Graduation Rate measures how many students are successfully finishing high school with a diploma in four or five years. Since 2010, the four- and five-year graduation rates have trended upward. The four-year rate reached a high of 83.4 percent for the 2016 graduating class and the five-year 85.6 percent for the 2015 graduating class. **The graduation rate has demonstrated consistent growth since the state began reporting four-year and five-year cohort graduation rates.**

More students are prepared for success, future results should continue to improve

Whether training in a technical field or preparing for work or college, the Prepared for Success component looks at how well prepared Ohio's students are for all future opportunities. Students can meet the college and career readiness mark by scoring remediation free on the ACT or SAT, earning an honors diploma or earning an industry-recognized credential or group of credentials in one of 13 high-demand career fields. Bonus points also can be earned for those college and career ready students who do well on Advanced Placement or International Baccalaureate tests or earn college credit through the growing College Credit Plus program.

Ohio has made gains in this area from 2016 to 2017, as more than 3,000 Ohio students met the Prepared for Success criteria, and nearly 6,000 more earned a "bonus point" compared to last year.

Additionally, almost every element of Prepared for Success had increases over last year. For example, nearly 4 percent more students earned three or more college credits.

Outcomes are improving as expectations have significantly increased

Ohio School Report Cards are still in transition. Measures continue to evolve as the new system replaces the old and as schools and districts adjust. Generally, achievement and student outcomes increased. This played out with improved grades in several measures (Performance Index, K-3 Literacy, Gap Closing). So, even though outcomes improved, some grades, such as Prepared for Success, reflected the raised expectations.

English Language Arts and Math Proficiency Rates by Demographic Group

	ENGLISH LANGUAGE ARTS		MATH	
DEMOGRAPHIC GROUP	15-16	16-17	15-16	16-17
All Students	54.3%	60.9% ↑	58.9%	60.8% ↑
American Indian or Alaskan Native	49.1%	56.6% ↑	49.8%	54.2% ↑
Asian or Pacific Islander	70.1%	73.7% ↑	77.9%	78.4% ↑
Black	28.3%	34.2% ↑	29.6%	31.5% ↑
Students w/Disabilities	20.8%	25.2% ↑	25.6%	27.3% ↑
Economically Disadvantaged	38.7%	45.7% ↑	43.6%	45.8% ↑
Hispanic	40.5%	47.3% ↑	45.4%	48.0% ↑
English Learner	33.1%	37.8% ↑	42.9%	44.1% ↑
Multiracial	49.0%	56.2% ↑	51.9%	54.3% ↑
White	60.9%	68.0% ↑	66.3%	68.4% ↑

Third Grade Reading Promotion Percent

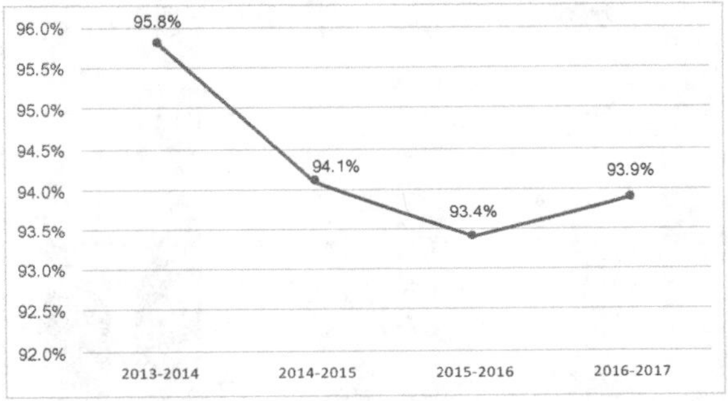

Graduation Rate Trend for Ohio Schools

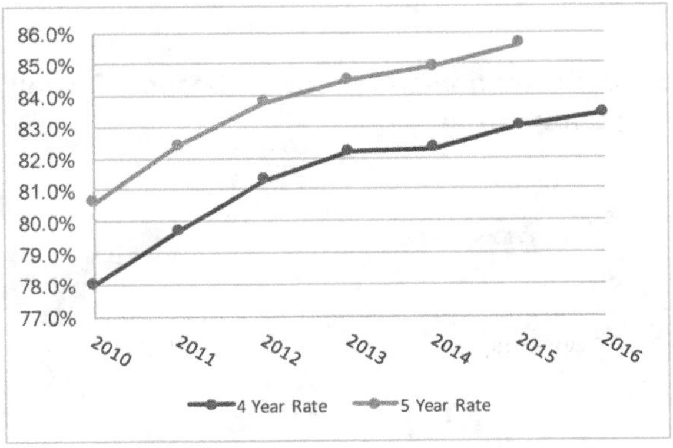

Year	Students meeting Prepared for Success expectation
2015-2016	34.2%
2016-2017	36.1% ↑

Chronic absenteeism is an issue the state is addressing

It is important for every student in Ohio to attend school every day. Missing too much school has long-term, negative effects on students, such as lower achievement and graduation rates. Students are chronically absent if they miss 10 percent or more of a school year.

Recent state legislation requires schools to take more proactive approaches and work with community partners to address chronic absenteeism.

Students can be absent for many reasons, including health concerns, dental/vision needs, bullying, school safety and more. The data reveal important trends.

16.4% of Ohio students are chronically absent.

2.5x Economically disadvantaged students are 2.5 times more likely to be chronically absent than non-disadvantaged students.

27% of African-American students were chronically absent last year.

30% of seniors were chronically absent last year.

District Report Card Grade Component Comparison 2016 and 2017

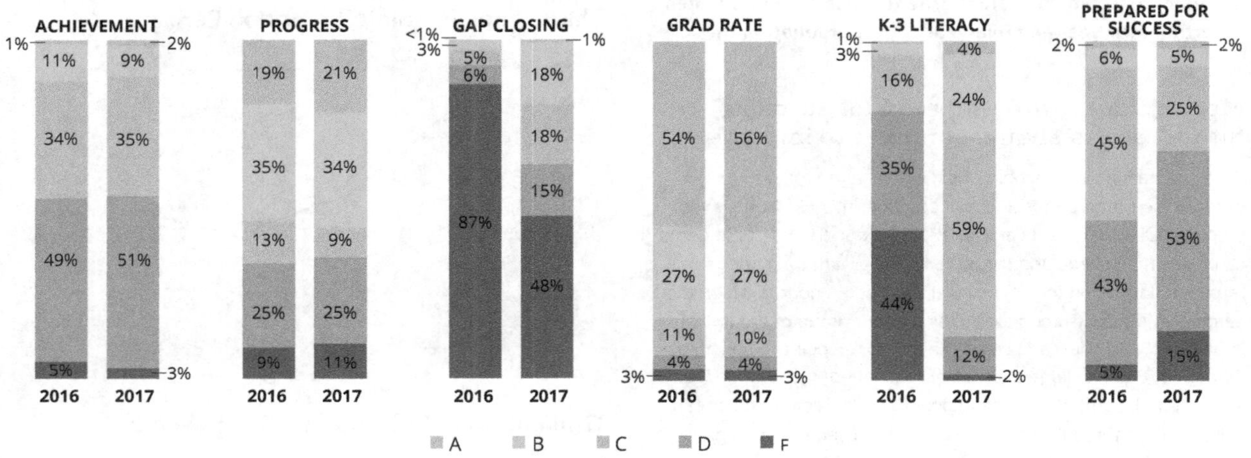

Dropout Prevention and Recovery Schools Overall Rating Comparison

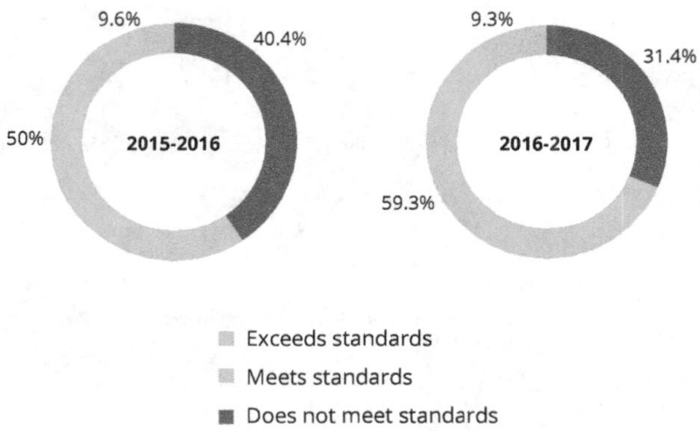

Report Card Component Grade for Career Technical Planning District Schools for 2016 and 2017

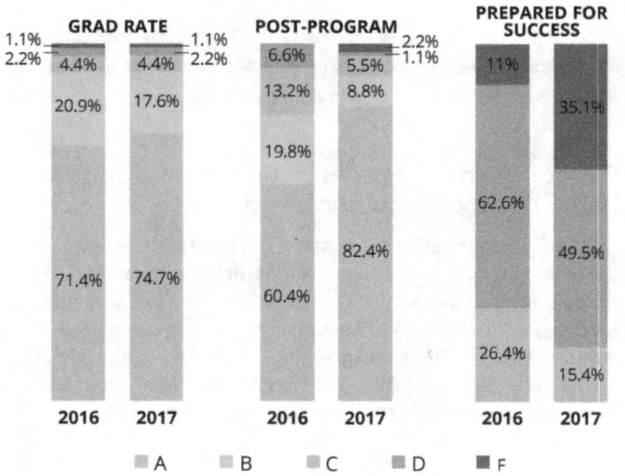

Ancestry and Ethnicity

Ohio State Profile

Population: 11,536,504

Ancestry	Population	%
Afghan (334)	403	<0.01
African, Sub-Saharan (86,101)	98,709	0.86
African (56,965)	66,657	0.58
Cape Verdean (145)	396	<0.01
Ethiopian (4,654)	5,039	0.04
Ghanaian (2,800)	2,919	0.03
Kenyan (805)	948	0.01
Liberian (846)	939	0.01
Nigerian (4,600)	5,051	0.04
Senegalese (438)	537	<0.01
Sierra Leonean (530)	558	<0.01
Somalian (9,821)	10,078	0.09
South African (814)	1,304	0.01
Sudanese (348)	385	<0.01
Ugandan (139)	139	<0.01
Zimbabwean (381)	381	<0.01
Other Sub-Saharan African (2,815)	3,378	0.03
Albanian (3,200)	4,061	0.04
Alsatian (213)	705	0.01
American (911,201)	911,201	7.91
Arab (41,613)	65,834	0.57
Arab (7,980)	10,035	0.09
Egyptian (3,921)	4,801	0.04
Iraqi (1,205)	1,346	0.01
Jordanian (2,350)	2,833	0.02
Lebanese (14,495)	30,056	0.26
Moroccan (1,055)	1,497	0.01
Palestinian (4,116)	4,705	0.04
Syrian (2,939)	6,042	0.05
Other Arab (3,552)	4,519	0.04
Armenian (1,768)	4,333	0.04
Assyrian/Chaldean/Syriac (288)	389	<0.01
Australian (662)	2,134	0.02
Austrian (6,767)	28,071	0.24
Basque (8)	63	<0.01
Belgian (2,787)	10,037	0.09
Brazilian (1,749)	2,500	0.02
British (19,024)	42,018	0.36
Bulgarian (1,401)	2,864	0.02
Cajun (205)	558	<0.01
Canadian (6,805)	15,625	0.14
Carpatho Rusyn (539)	959	0.01
Celtic (1,001)	1,824	0.02
Croatian (15,181)	41,430	0.36
Cypriot (116)	141	<0.01
Czech (19,585)	73,775	0.64
Czechoslovakian (8,047)	18,742	0.16
Danish (4,624)	18,632	0.16
Dutch (34,625)	207,492	1.80
Eastern European (9,338)	10,672	0.09
English (362,859)	1,112,280	9.66
Estonian (461)	663	0.01
European (87,969)	98,058	0.85
Finnish (5,944)	19,872	0.17
French, ex. Basque (46,200)	284,589	2.47
French Canadian (11,090)	32,522	0.28
German (1,247,503)	3,220,180	27.97
German Russian (164)	481	<0.01
Greek (27,899)	58,649	0.51
Guyanese (907)	1,203	0.01
Hungarian (69,178)	210,625	1.83
Icelander (252)	808	0.01
Iranian (3,084)	4,038	0.04
Irish (413,997)	1,666,746	14.48
Israeli (907)	1,650	0.01
Italian (282,256)	748,397	6.50
Latvian (1,324)	2,580	0.02
Lithuanian (8,194)	24,321	0.21
Luxemburger (165)	665	0.01
Macedonian (2,762)	4,613	0.04
Maltese (204)	516	<0.01
New Zealander (154)	387	<0.01
Northern European (3,525)	3,939	0.03
Norwegian (12,651)	42,773	0.37
Pennsylvania German (24,371)	32,246	0.28
Polish (156,163)	462,815	4.02
Portuguese (3,847)	9,658	0.08
Romanian (13,078)	29,751	0.26
Russian (29,493)	80,848	0.70
Scandinavian (3,490)	8,810	0.08
Scotch-Irish (70,567)	190,369	1.65
Scottish (65,322)	229,371	1.99
Serbian (8,080)	17,530	0.15
Slavic (2,824)	8,235	0.07
Slovak (51,528)	144,300	1.25
Slovene (19,901)	55,482	0.48
Soviet Union (23)	36	<0.01
Swedish (17,992)	78,498	0.68
Swiss (19,738)	78,114	0.68
Turkish (2,941)	4,399	0.04
Ukrainian (22,564)	46,993	0.41
Welsh (28,763)	135,998	1.18
West Indian, ex. Hispanic (11,019)	17,473	0.15
Bahamian (276)	396	<0.01
Barbadian (223)	480	<0.01
Belizean (133)	214	<0.01
Bermudan (59)	128	<0.01
British West Indian (323)	457	<0.01
Dutch West Indian (156)	676	0.01
Haitian (2,297)	2,912	0.03
Jamaican (5,799)	8,744	0.08
Trinidadian/Tobagonian (541)	938	0.01
U.S. Virgin Islander (35)	56	<0.01
West Indian (1,168)	2,428	0.02
Other West Indian (9)	44	<0.01
Yugoslavian (6,948)	12,485	0.11

Hispanic Origin	Population	%
Hispanic or Latino (of any race)	354,674	3.07
Central American, ex. Mexican	22,756	0.20
Costa Rican	1,093	0.01
Guatemalan	8,680	0.08
Honduran	3,699	0.03
Nicaraguan	1,383	0.01
Panamanian	2,055	0.02
Salvadoran	5,627	0.05
Other Central American	219	<0.01
Cuban	7,523	0.07
Dominican Republic	6,453	0.06
Mexican	172,029	1.49
Puerto Rican	94,965	0.82
South American	17,571	0.15
Argentinean	1,921	0.02
Bolivian	649	0.01
Chilean	1,065	0.01
Colombian	5,247	0.05
Ecuadorian	2,090	0.02
Paraguayan	205	<0.01
Peruvian	3,741	0.03
Uruguayan	291	<0.01
Venezuelan	2,190	0.02
Other South American	172	<0.01
Other Hispanic or Latino	33,377	0.29

Race*	Population	%
African-American/Black (1,407,681)	1,541,771	13.36
Not Hispanic (1,389,115)	1,511,035	13.10
Hispanic (18,566)	30,736	0.27
American Indian/Alaska Native (25,292)	90,124	0.78
Not Hispanic (20,906)	79,872	0.69
Hispanic (4,386)	10,252	0.09
Alaska Athabascan *(Ala. Nat.)* (47)	100	<0.01
Aleut *(Alaska Native)* (43)	88	<0.01
Apache (362)	1,325	0.01
Arapaho (21)	95	<0.01
Blackfeet (642)	4,916	0.04
Canadian/French Am. Ind. (143)	338	<0.01
Central American Ind. (372)	458	<0.01
Cherokee (5,386)	26,584	0.23
Cheyenne (57)	236	<0.01
Chickasaw (111)	289	<0.01
Chippewa (807)	1,599	0.01
Choctaw (339)	1,194	0.01
Colville (5)	11	<0.01
Comanche (84)	237	<0.01
Cree (64)	194	<0.01
Creek (169)	579	0.01
Crow (38)	204	<0.01
Delaware (252)	608	0.01
Hopi (35)	105	<0.01
Houma (9)	22	<0.01
Inupiat *(Alaska Native)* (56)	115	<0.01
Iroquois (570)	1,807	0.02
Kiowa (33)	70	<0.01
Lumbee (235)	406	<0.01
Menominee (48)	66	<0.01
Mexican American Ind. (862)	1,472	0.01
Navajo (310)	809	0.01
Osage (47)	125	<0.01
Ottawa (91)	229	<0.01
Paiute (21)	39	<0.01
Pima (15)	27	<0.01
Potawatomi (125)	276	<0.01
Pueblo (75)	163	<0.01
Puget Sound Salish (24)	32	<0.01
Seminole (87)	460	<0.01
Shoshone (28)	99	<0.01
Sioux (613)	2,069	0.02
South American Ind. (287)	650	0.01
Spanish American Ind. (81)	124	<0.01
Tlingit-Haida *(Alaska Native)* (48)	77	<0.01
Tohono O'Odham (22)	41	<0.01
Tsimshian *(Alaska Native)* (12)	28	<0.01
Ute (5)	32	<0.01
Yakama (9)	19	<0.01
Yaqui (29)	73	<0.01
Yuman (13)	31	<0.01
Yup'ik *(Alaska Native)* (27)	47	<0.01
Asian (192,233)	238,292	2.07
Not Hispanic (190,765)	234,053	2.03
Hispanic (1,468)	4,239	0.04
Bangladeshi (928)	1,052	0.01
Bhutanese (703)	865	0.01
Burmese (1,258)	1,356	0.01
Cambodian (3,744)	4,570	0.04
Chinese, ex. Taiwanese (41,006)	47,861	0.41
Filipino (16,899)	27,661	0.24
Hmong (539)	589	0.01
Indian (64,187)	71,211	0.62
Indonesian (862)	1,354	0.01
Japanese (10,162)	16,995	0.15
Korean (15,281)	21,207	0.18
Laotian (3,355)	4,183	0.04
Malaysian (335)	528	<0.01
Nepalese (819)	992	0.01
Pakistani (4,644)	5,330	0.05
Sri Lankan (882)	1,029	0.01
Taiwanese (2,672)	3,172	0.03
Thai (2,535)	4,024	0.03
Vietnamese (13,121)	15,639	0.14
Hawaii Native/Pacific Islander (4,066)	10,525	0.09
Not Hispanic (3,400)	8,702	0.08
Hispanic (666)	1,823	0.02
Fijian (46)	90	<0.01
Guamanian/Chamorro (1,145)	1,977	0.02
Marshallese (99)	124	<0.01
Native Hawaiian (928)	3,037	0.03
Samoan (702)	1,278	0.01
Tongan (30)	81	<0.01
White (9,539,437)	9,751,547	84.53
Not Hispanic (9,359,263)	9,543,218	82.72
Hispanic (180,174)	208,329	1.81

*Notes: † The Census 2010 population figure is used to calculate the percentages in the Hispanic Origin and Race categories. Ancestry percentages are based on the 2006-2010 American Community Survey population (not shown); ‡ Numbers in parentheses indicate the number of people reporting a single ancestry; * Numbers in parentheses indicate the number of persons reporting this race alone, not in combination with any other race; Please refer to the User Guide for more information.*

County Profiles

Allen County

Population: 106,331

Ancestry	Population	%
Afghan (0)	0	<0.01
African, Sub-Saharan (1,284)	1,341	1.26
African (1,030)	1,087	1.02
Cape Verdean (0)	0	<0.01
Ethiopian (0)	0	<0.01
Ghanaian (193)	193	0.18
Kenyan (0)	0	<0.01
Liberian (0)	0	<0.01
Nigerian (17)	17	0.02
Senegalese (0)	0	<0.01
Sierra Leonean (0)	0	<0.01
Somalian (34)	34	0.03
South African (0)	0	<0.01
Sudanese (10)	10	0.01
Ugandan (0)	0	<0.01
Zimbabwean (0)	0	<0.01
Other Sub-Saharan African (0)	0	<0.01
Albanian (0)	0	<0.01
Alsatian (15)	15	0.01
American (10,384)	10,384	9.74
Arab (187)	315	0.30
Arab (38)	93	0.09
Egyptian (9)	9	0.01
Iraqi (11)	11	0.01
Jordanian (0)	0	<0.01
Lebanese (102)	158	0.15
Moroccan (0)	0	<0.01
Palestinian (14)	14	0.01
Syrian (13)	30	0.03
Other Arab (0)	0	<0.01
Armenian (0)	0	<0.01
Assyrian/Chaldean/Syriac (0)	0	<0.01
Australian (0)	24	0.02
Austrian (46)	167	0.16
Basque (0)	0	<0.01
Belgian (39)	71	0.07
Brazilian (0)	0	<0.01
British (68)	320	0.30
Bulgarian (7)	7	0.01
Cajun (0)	0	<0.01
Canadian (60)	105	0.10
Carpatho Rusyn (0)	0	<0.01
Celtic (8)	8	0.01
Croatian (8)	28	0.03
Cypriot (0)	0	<0.01
Czech (133)	337	0.32
Czechoslovakian (68)	111	0.10
Danish (10)	39	0.04
Dutch (381)	2,356	2.21
Eastern European (8)	8	0.01
English (2,554)	7,586	7.12
Estonian (0)	0	<0.01
European (738)	750	0.70
Finnish (44)	119	0.11
French, ex. Basque (423)	2,710	2.54
French Canadian (61)	231	0.22
German (17,813)	37,029	34.74
German Russian (0)	0	<0.01
Greek (169)	297	0.28
Guyanese (0)	0	<0.01
Hungarian (188)	436	0.41
Icelander (0)	10	0.01
Iranian (0)	0	<0.01
Irish (3,143)	13,434	12.60
Israeli (0)	0	<0.01
Italian (1,426)	4,111	3.86
Latvian (0)	0	<0.01
Lithuanian (47)	110	0.10
Luxemburger (0)	13	0.01
Macedonian (4)	4	<0.01
Maltese (0)	0	<0.01
New Zealander (0)	0	<0.01
Northern European (69)	69	0.06
Norwegian (21)	207	0.19
Pennsylvania German (56)	77	0.07
Polish (464)	1,589	1.49
Portuguese (10)	47	0.04
Romanian (0)	14	0.01
Russian (82)	343	0.32
Scandinavian (13)	121	0.11
Scotch-Irish (572)	1,491	1.40
Scottish (443)	1,650	1.55
Serbian (0)	34	0.03
Slavic (15)	45	0.04
Slovak (31)	187	0.18
Slovene (10)	10	0.01
Soviet Union (0)	0	<0.01
Swedish (128)	534	0.50
Swiss (570)	1,717	1.61
Turkish (0)	0	<0.01
Ukrainian (54)	70	0.07
Welsh (617)	1,982	1.86
West Indian, ex. Hispanic (130)	240	0.23
Bahamian (14)	14	0.01
Barbadian (0)	0	<0.01
Belizean (0)	0	<0.01
Bermudan (0)	0	<0.01
British West Indian (0)	0	<0.01
Dutch West Indian (0)	0	<0.01
Haitian (14)	56	0.05
Jamaican (91)	159	0.15
Trinidadian/Tobagonian (11)	11	0.01
U.S. Virgin Islander (0)	0	<0.01
West Indian (0)	0	<0.01
Other West Indian (0)	0	<0.01
Yugoslavian (0)	24	0.02

Hispanic Origin	Population	%
Hispanic or Latino (of any race)	2,513	2.36
Central American, ex. Mexican	74	0.07
Costa Rican	17	0.02
Guatemalan	13	0.01
Honduran	7	0.01
Nicaraguan	7	0.01
Panamanian	8	0.01
Salvadoran	22	0.02
Other Central American	0	<0.01
Cuban	54	0.05
Dominican Republic	4	<0.01
Mexican	1,614	1.52
Puerto Rican	202	0.19
South American	55	0.05
Argentinean	3	<0.01
Bolivian	9	0.01
Chilean	9	0.01
Colombian	14	0.01
Ecuadorian	9	0.01
Paraguayan	0	<0.01
Peruvian	5	<0.01
Uruguayan	0	<0.01
Venezuelan	6	0.01
Other South American	0	<0.01
Other Hispanic or Latino	510	0.48

Race*	Population	%
African-American/Black (12,639)	14,616	13.75
Not Hispanic (12,508)	14,331	13.48
Hispanic (131)	285	0.27
American Indian/Alaska Native (207)	790	0.74
Not Hispanic (162)	672	0.63
Hispanic (45)	118	0.11
Alaska Athabascan (*Ala. Nat.*) (0)	0	<0.01
Aleut (*Alaska Native*) (0)	0	<0.01
Apache (6)	15	0.01
Arapaho (0)	0	<0.01
Blackfeet (1)	31	0.03
Canadian/French Am. Ind. (1)	8	0.01
Central American Ind. (0)	0	<0.01
Cherokee (32)	227	0.21
Cheyenne (1)	3	<0.01
Chickasaw (1)	2	<0.01
Chippewa (9)	28	0.03
Choctaw (2)	7	0.01
Colville (0)	0	<0.01
Comanche (0)	0	<0.01
Cree (0)	0	<0.01
Creek (0)	6	0.01
Crow (0)	0	<0.01
Delaware (3)	4	<0.01
Hopi (0)	0	<0.01
Houma (0)	0	<0.01
Inupiat (*Alaska Native*) (0)	1	<0.01
Iroquois (5)	13	0.01
Kiowa (0)	0	<0.01
Lumbee (0)	0	<0.01
Menominee (4)	5	<0.01
Mexican American Ind. (6)	16	0.02
Navajo (0)	3	<0.01
Osage (2)	4	<0.01
Ottawa (0)	0	<0.01
Paiute (0)	0	<0.01
Pima (0)	0	<0.01
Potawatomi (0)	1	<0.01
Pueblo (0)	0	<0.01
Puget Sound Salish (0)	0	<0.01
Seminole (0)	3	<0.01
Shoshone (0)	0	<0.01
Sioux (4)	19	0.02
South American Ind. (5)	5	<0.01
Spanish American Ind. (0)	0	<0.01
Tlingit-Haida (*Alaska Native*) (0)	0	<0.01
Tohono O'Odham (0)	0	<0.01
Tsimshian (*Alaska Native*) (0)	0	<0.01
Ute (0)	0	<0.01
Yakama (0)	0	<0.01
Yaqui (0)	0	<0.01
Yuman (0)	0	<0.01
Yup'ik (*Alaska Native*) (0)	0	<0.01
Asian (740)	1,043	0.98
Not Hispanic (725)	1,004	0.94
Hispanic (15)	39	0.04
Bangladeshi (1)	1	<0.01
Bhutanese (0)	0	<0.01
Burmese (0)	0	<0.01
Cambodian (5)	5	<0.01
Chinese, ex. Taiwanese (83)	134	0.13
Filipino (124)	187	0.18
Hmong (3)	4	<0.01
Indian (224)	258	0.24
Indonesian (1)	2	<0.01
Japanese (37)	69	0.06
Korean (74)	124	0.12
Laotian (37)	50	0.05
Malaysian (0)	0	<0.01
Nepalese (4)	4	<0.01
Pakistani (9)	12	0.01
Sri Lankan (0)	0	<0.01
Taiwanese (11)	16	0.02
Thai (8)	22	0.02
Vietnamese (61)	87	0.08
Hawaii Native/Pacific Islander (15)	71	0.07
Not Hispanic (13)	64	0.06
Hispanic (2)	7	0.01
Fijian (0)	0	<0.01
Guamanian/Chamorro (4)	12	0.01
Marshallese (0)	0	<0.01
Native Hawaiian (5)	22	0.02
Samoan (5)	7	0.01
Tongan (0)	0	<0.01
White (89,089)	91,659	86.20
Not Hispanic (87,708)	89,974	84.62
Hispanic (1,381)	1,685	1.58

*Notes: † The Census 2010 population figure is used to calculate the percentages in the Hispanic Origin and Race categories. Ancestry percentages are based on the 2006-2010 American Community Survey population (not shown); ‡ Numbers in parentheses indicate the number of people reporting a single ancestry; * Numbers in parentheses indicate the number of persons reporting this race alone, not in combination with any other race; Please refer to the User Guide for more information.*

Ashtabula County

Population: 101,497

Ancestry	Population	%
Afghan (0)	0	<0.01
African, Sub-Saharan (119)	195	0.19
African (119)	186	0.18
Cape Verdean (0)	0	<0.01
Ethiopian (0)	9	0.01
Ghanaian (0)	0	<0.01
Kenyan (0)	0	<0.01
Liberian (0)	0	<0.01
Nigerian (0)	0	<0.01
Senegalese (0)	0	<0.01
Sierra Leonean (0)	0	<0.01
Somalian (0)	0	<0.01
South African (0)	0	<0.01
Sudanese (0)	0	<0.01
Ugandan (0)	0	<0.01
Zimbabwean (0)	0	<0.01
Other Sub-Saharan African (0)	0	<0.01
Albanian (0)	11	0.01
Alsatian (0)	0	<0.01
American (10,204)	10,204	10.02
Arab (150)	268	0.26
Arab (0)	0	<0.01
Egyptian (0)	0	<0.01
Iraqi (0)	0	<0.01
Jordanian (0)	0	<0.01
Lebanese (126)	221	0.22
Moroccan (0)	0	<0.01
Palestinian (0)	0	<0.01
Syrian (24)	47	0.05
Other Arab (0)	0	<0.01
Armenian (0)	0	<0.01
Assyrian/Chaldean/Syriac (0)	0	<0.01
Australian (4)	10	0.01
Austrian (145)	359	0.35
Basque (0)	0	<0.01
Belgian (48)	100	0.10
Brazilian (0)	21	0.02
British (98)	163	0.16
Bulgarian (0)	0	<0.01
Cajun (0)	0	<0.01
Canadian (6)	36	0.04
Carpatho Rusyn (0)	0	<0.01
Celtic (0)	14	0.01
Croatian (142)	409	0.40
Cypriot (0)	0	<0.01
Czech (171)	765	0.75
Czechoslovakian (155)	297	0.29
Danish (36)	186	0.18
Dutch (135)	1,900	1.87
Eastern European (0)	10	0.01
English (3,641)	12,816	12.58
Estonian (0)	0	<0.01
European (936)	1,037	1.02
Finnish (995)	3,193	3.13
French, ex. Basque (366)	2,039	2.00
French Canadian (76)	350	0.34
German (7,153)	25,350	24.89
German Russian (0)	0	<0.01
Greek (103)	320	0.31
Guyanese (0)	0	<0.01
Hungarian (1,198)	4,254	4.18
Icelander (0)	0	<0.01
Iranian (21)	21	0.02
Irish (3,195)	16,053	15.76
Israeli (0)	9	0.01
Italian (5,075)	11,334	11.13
Latvian (11)	46	0.05
Lithuanian (88)	270	0.27
Luxemburger (0)	0	<0.01
Macedonian (0)	8	0.01
Maltese (0)	0	<0.01
New Zealander (0)	0	<0.01
Northern European (0)	0	<0.01
Norwegian (101)	425	0.42
Pennsylvania German (701)	836	0.82
Polish (2,107)	5,897	5.79
Portuguese (154)	348	0.34
Romanian (51)	339	0.33
Russian (231)	832	0.82
Scandinavian (91)	91	0.09
Scotch-Irish (476)	2,033	2.00
Scottish (301)	2,062	2.02
Serbian (27)	109	0.11
Slavic (51)	164	0.16
Slovak (612)	1,747	1.71
Slovene (678)	1,392	1.37
Soviet Union (0)	0	<0.01
Swedish (530)	2,018	1.98
Swiss (201)	487	0.48
Turkish (0)	0	<0.01
Ukrainian (55)	145	0.14
Welsh (200)	1,102	1.08
West Indian, ex. Hispanic (40)	40	0.04
Bahamian (0)	0	<0.01
Barbadian (0)	0	<0.01
Belizean (0)	0	<0.01
Bermudan (0)	0	<0.01
British West Indian (0)	0	<0.01
Dutch West Indian (0)	0	<0.01
Haitian (0)	0	<0.01
Jamaican (40)	40	0.04
Trinidadian/Tobagonian (0)	0	<0.01
U.S. Virgin Islander (0)	0	<0.01
West Indian (0)	0	<0.01
Other West Indian (0)	0	<0.01
Yugoslavian (32)	106	0.10

Hispanic Origin	Population	%
Hispanic or Latino (of any race)	3,441	3.39
Central American, ex. Mexican	132	0.13
Costa Rican	1	<0.01
Guatemalan	16	0.02
Honduran	96	0.09
Nicaraguan	1	<0.01
Panamanian	10	0.01
Salvadoran	7	0.01
Other Central American	1	<0.01
Cuban	31	0.03
Dominican Republic	11	0.01
Mexican	948	0.93
Puerto Rican	2,065	2.03
South American	46	0.05
Argentinean	1	<0.01
Bolivian	3	<0.01
Chilean	1	<0.01
Colombian	22	0.02
Ecuadorian	3	<0.01
Paraguayan	1	<0.01
Peruvian	9	0.01
Uruguayan	0	<0.01
Venezuelan	1	<0.01
Other South American	5	<0.01
Other Hispanic or Latino	208	0.20

Race*	Population	%
African-American/Black (3,586)	4,820	4.75
Not Hispanic (3,467)	4,620	4.55
Hispanic (119)	200	0.20
American Indian/Alaska Native (241)	870	0.86
Not Hispanic (208)	779	0.77
Hispanic (33)	91	0.09
Alaska Athabascan *(Ala. Nat.)* (0)	0	<0.01
Aleut *(Alaska Native)* (0)	0	<0.01
Apache (1)	12	0.01
Arapaho (0)	0	<0.01
Blackfeet (4)	50	0.05
Canadian/French Am. Ind. (2)	7	0.01
Central American Ind. (0)	0	<0.01
Cherokee (67)	274	0.27
Cheyenne (1)	2	<0.01
Chickasaw (0)	6	0.01
Chippewa (14)	28	0.03
Choctaw (6)	9	0.01
Colville (0)	0	<0.01
Comanche (0)	1	<0.01
Cree (1)	1	<0.01
Creek (0)	4	<0.01
Crow (0)	5	<0.01
Delaware (4)	15	0.01
Hopi (1)	2	<0.01
Houma (0)	0	<0.01
Inupiat *(Alaska Native)* (1)	1	<0.01
Iroquois (9)	14	0.01
Kiowa (0)	0	<0.01
Lumbee (0)	0	<0.01
Menominee (0)	0	<0.01
Mexican American Ind. (6)	7	0.01
Navajo (2)	7	0.01
Osage (1)	1	<0.01
Ottawa (0)	0	<0.01
Paiute (0)	2	<0.01
Pima (0)	0	<0.01
Potawatomi (0)	1	<0.01
Pueblo (0)	0	<0.01
Puget Sound Salish (0)	0	<0.01
Seminole (1)	3	<0.01
Shoshone (0)	0	<0.01
Sioux (3)	12	0.01
South American Ind. (1)	1	<0.01
Spanish American Ind. (1)	1	<0.01
Tlingit-Haida *(Alaska Native)* (0)	0	<0.01
Tohono O'Odham (0)	3	<0.01
Tsimshian *(Alaska Native)* (0)	0	<0.01
Ute (0)	1	<0.01
Yakama (0)	0	<0.01
Yaqui (0)	1	<0.01
Yuman (0)	0	<0.01
Yup'ik *(Alaska Native)* (0)	0	<0.01
Asian (375)	588	0.58
Not Hispanic (372)	572	0.56
Hispanic (3)	16	0.02
Bangladeshi (3)	3	<0.01
Bhutanese (0)	0	<0.01
Burmese (0)	0	<0.01
Cambodian (1)	3	<0.01
Chinese, ex. Taiwanese (59)	90	0.09
Filipino (62)	127	0.13
Hmong (0)	0	<0.01
Indian (69)	97	0.10
Indonesian (0)	2	<0.01
Japanese (33)	68	0.07
Korean (61)	95	0.09
Laotian (2)	3	<0.01
Malaysian (0)	0	<0.01
Nepalese (0)	0	<0.01
Pakistani (2)	2	<0.01
Sri Lankan (9)	9	0.01
Taiwanese (3)	4	<0.01
Thai (9)	11	0.01
Vietnamese (37)	48	0.05
Hawaii Native/Pacific Islander (22)	76	0.07
Not Hispanic (17)	61	0.06
Hispanic (5)	15	0.01
Fijian (0)	0	<0.01
Guamanian/Chamorro (8)	19	0.02
Marshallese (0)	0	<0.01
Native Hawaiian (10)	29	0.03
Samoan (1)	4	<0.01
Tongan (0)	0	<0.01
White (94,041)	96,058	94.64
Not Hispanic (92,126)	93,866	92.48
Hispanic (1,915)	2,192	2.16

*Notes: † The Census 2010 population figure is used to calculate the percentages in the Hispanic Origin and Race categories. Ancestry percentages are based on the 2006-2010 American Community Survey population (not shown); ‡ Numbers in parentheses indicate the number of people reporting a single ancestry; * Numbers in parentheses indicate the number of persons reporting this race alone, not in combination with any other race; Please refer to the User Guide for more information.*

Butler County

Population: 368,130

Ancestry	Population	%
Afghan (0)	0	<0.01
African, Sub-Saharan (2,444)	2,728	0.75
African (1,625)	1,909	0.53
Cape Verdean (0)	0	<0.01
Ethiopian (47)	47	0.01
Ghanaian (376)	376	0.10
Kenyan (0)	0	<0.01
Liberian (0)	0	<0.01
Nigerian (250)	250	0.07
Senegalese (0)	0	<0.01
Sierra Leonean (0)	0	<0.01
Somalian (0)	0	<0.01
South African (0)	0	<0.01
Sudanese (0)	0	<0.01
Ugandan (8)	8	<0.01
Zimbabwean (19)	19	0.01
Other Sub-Saharan African (119)	119	0.03
Albanian (0)	12	<0.01
Alsatian (0)	0	<0.01
American (53,925)	53,925	14.84
Arab (1,006)	1,229	0.34
Arab (248)	260	0.07
Egyptian (75)	75	0.02
Iraqi (8)	8	<0.01
Jordanian (80)	97	0.03
Lebanese (295)	396	0.11
Moroccan (165)	235	0.06
Palestinian (17)	17	<0.01
Syrian (76)	76	0.02
Other Arab (42)	65	0.02
Armenian (43)	52	0.01
Assyrian/Chaldean/Syriac (0)	0	<0.01
Australian (0)	27	0.01
Austrian (191)	767	0.21
Basque (0)	0	<0.01
Belgian (32)	252	0.07
Brazilian (82)	146	0.04
British (731)	1,647	0.45
Bulgarian (32)	68	0.02
Cajun (12)	12	<0.01
Canadian (110)	295	0.08
Carpatho Rusyn (17)	17	<0.01
Celtic (13)	40	0.01
Croatian (40)	164	0.05
Cypriot (0)	0	<0.01
Czech (352)	1,431	0.39
Czechoslovakian (143)	319	0.09
Danish (309)	603	0.17
Dutch (959)	5,753	1.58
Eastern European (74)	115	0.03
English (12,989)	35,175	9.68
Estonian (79)	79	0.02
European (3,647)	4,103	1.13
Finnish (171)	582	0.16
French, ex. Basque (1,876)	8,367	2.30
French Canadian (320)	628	0.17
German (43,445)	98,300	27.05
German Russian (0)	0	<0.01
Greek (498)	1,102	0.30
Guyanese (0)	0	<0.01
Hungarian (616)	1,949	0.54
Icelander (14)	24	0.01
Iranian (14)	63	0.02
Irish (11,925)	49,474	13.61
Israeli (13)	24	0.01
Italian (6,157)	16,823	4.63
Latvian (35)	46	0.01
Lithuanian (213)	383	0.11
Luxemburger (0)	0	<0.01
Macedonian (16)	16	<0.01
Maltese (0)	0	<0.01
New Zealander (0)	8	<0.01
Northern European (102)	102	0.03
Norwegian (604)	1,864	0.51
Pennsylvania German (55)	69	0.02
Polish (1,561)	6,159	1.69
Portuguese (47)	214	0.06
Romanian (48)	269	0.07
Russian (718)	2,015	0.55
Scandinavian (152)	360	0.10
Scotch-Irish (2,105)	5,738	1.58
Scottish (2,061)	6,619	1.82
Serbian (22)	89	0.02
Slavic (25)	79	0.02
Slovak (280)	834	0.23
Slovene (48)	141	0.04
Soviet Union (0)	0	<0.01
Swedish (576)	2,229	0.61
Swiss (340)	1,054	0.29
Turkish (77)	155	0.04
Ukrainian (204)	577	0.16
Welsh (786)	2,921	0.80
West Indian, ex. Hispanic (165)	255	0.07
Bahamian (0)	0	<0.01
Barbadian (0)	0	<0.01
Belizean (0)	0	<0.01
Bermudan (0)	0	<0.01
British West Indian (0)	0	<0.01
Dutch West Indian (43)	70	0.02
Haitian (0)	0	<0.01
Jamaican (43)	76	0.02
Trinidadian/Tobagonian (59)	89	0.02
U.S. Virgin Islander (0)	0	<0.01
West Indian (20)	20	0.01
Other West Indian (0)	0	<0.01
Yugoslavian (117)	244	0.07

Hispanic Origin	Population	%
Hispanic or Latino (of any race)	14,670	3.99
Central American, ex. Mexican	1,493	0.41
Costa Rican	43	0.01
Guatemalan	824	0.22
Honduran	251	0.07
Nicaraguan	61	0.02
Panamanian	103	0.03
Salvadoran	206	0.06
Other Central American	5	<0.01
Cuban	382	0.10
Dominican Republic	880	0.24
Mexican	8,246	2.24
Puerto Rican	1,366	0.37
South American	990	0.27
Argentinean	63	0.02
Bolivian	17	<0.01
Chilean	38	0.01
Colombian	260	0.07
Ecuadorian	112	0.03
Paraguayan	13	<0.01
Peruvian	355	0.10
Uruguayan	16	<0.01
Venezuelan	105	0.03
Other South American	11	<0.01
Other Hispanic or Latino	1,313	0.36

Race*	Population	%
African-American/Black (26,972)	31,121	8.45
Not Hispanic (26,463)	30,315	8.23
Hispanic (509)	806	0.22
American Indian/Alaska Native (770)	2,496	0.68
Not Hispanic (606)	2,203	0.60
Hispanic (164)	293	0.08
Alaska Athabascan *(Ala. Nat.)* (1)	1	<0.01
Aleut *(Alaska Native)* (1)	4	<0.01
Apache (9)	20	0.01
Arapaho (0)	1	<0.01
Blackfeet (9)	86	0.02
Canadian/French Am. Ind. (16)	17	<0.01
Central American Ind. (12)	12	<0.01
Cherokee (185)	805	0.22
Cheyenne (2)	4	<0.01
Chickasaw (0)	1	<0.01
Chippewa (22)	39	0.01
Choctaw (13)	36	0.01
Colville (0)	0	<0.01
Comanche (6)	9	<0.01
Cree (3)	5	<0.01
Creek (4)	17	<0.01
Crow (1)	4	<0.01
Delaware (4)	6	<0.01
Hopi (0)	0	<0.01
Houma (0)	1	<0.01
Inupiat *(Alaska Native)* (2)	2	<0.01
Iroquois (19)	49	0.01
Kiowa (0)	3	<0.01
Lumbee (6)	6	<0.01
Menominee (0)	0	<0.01
Mexican American Ind. (54)	69	0.02
Navajo (12)	29	0.01
Osage (2)	4	<0.01
Ottawa (0)	0	<0.01
Paiute (0)	0	<0.01
Pima (0)	0	<0.01
Potawatomi (1)	4	<0.01
Pueblo (2)	3	<0.01
Puget Sound Salish (1)	1	<0.01
Seminole (6)	15	<0.01
Shoshone (0)	3	<0.01
Sioux (23)	65	0.02
South American Ind. (10)	18	<0.01
Spanish American Ind. (5)	13	<0.01
Tlingit-Haida *(Alaska Native)* (3)	3	<0.01
Tohono O'Odham (0)	0	<0.01
Tsimshian *(Alaska Native)* (0)	0	<0.01
Ute (0)	0	<0.01
Yakama (0)	5	<0.01
Yaqui (2)	3	<0.01
Yuman (0)	0	<0.01
Yup'ik *(Alaska Native)* (0)	0	<0.01
Asian (8,811)	10,555	2.87
Not Hispanic (8,759)	10,414	2.83
Hispanic (52)	141	0.04
Bangladeshi (28)	34	0.01
Bhutanese (0)	0	<0.01
Burmese (8)	12	<0.01
Cambodian (249)	289	0.08
Chinese, ex. Taiwanese (1,781)	2,042	0.55
Filipino (715)	1,137	0.31
Hmong (5)	5	<0.01
Indian (2,966)	3,272	0.89
Indonesian (23)	42	0.01
Japanese (272)	533	0.14
Korean (520)	740	0.20
Laotian (39)	44	0.01
Malaysian (13)	21	0.01
Nepalese (31)	34	0.01
Pakistani (228)	270	0.07
Sri Lankan (64)	73	0.02
Taiwanese (86)	128	0.03
Thai (113)	169	0.05
Vietnamese (1,351)	1,469	0.40
Hawaii Native/Pacific Islander (288)	503	0.14
Not Hispanic (239)	426	0.12
Hispanic (49)	77	0.02
Fijian (2)	4	<0.01
Guamanian/Chamorro (79)	113	0.03
Marshallese (7)	15	<0.01
Native Hawaiian (46)	101	0.03
Samoan (10)	33	0.01
Tongan (6)	7	<0.01
White (316,667)	323,820	87.96
Not Hispanic (310,183)	316,333	85.93
Hispanic (6,484)	7,487	2.03

*Notes: † The Census 2010 population figure is used to calculate the percentages in the Hispanic Origin and Race categories. Ancestry percentages are based on the 2006-2010 American Community Survey population (not shown); ‡ Numbers in parentheses indicate the number of people reporting a single ancestry; * Numbers in parentheses indicate the number of persons reporting this race alone, not in combination with any other race; Please refer to the User Guide for more information.*

Clark County

Population: 138,333

Ancestry	Population	%
Afghan (0)	0	<0.01
African, Sub-Saharan (670)	776	0.56
African (639)	738	0.53
Cape Verdean (6)	13	0.01
Ethiopian (0)	0	<0.01
Ghanaian (0)	0	<0.01
Kenyan (0)	0	<0.01
Liberian (0)	0	<0.01
Nigerian (25)	25	0.02
Senegalese (0)	0	<0.01
Sierra Leonean (0)	0	<0.01
Somalian (0)	0	<0.01
South African (0)	0	<0.01
Sudanese (0)	0	<0.01
Ugandan (0)	0	<0.01
Zimbabwean (0)	0	<0.01
Other Sub-Saharan African (0)	0	<0.01
Albanian (0)	0	<0.01
Alsatian (5)	5	<0.01
American (19,231)	19,231	13.80
Arab (62)	112	0.08
Arab (0)	0	<0.01
Egyptian (0)	0	<0.01
Iraqi (0)	0	<0.01
Jordanian (27)	35	0.03
Lebanese (0)	29	0.02
Moroccan (0)	0	<0.01
Palestinian (0)	0	<0.01
Syrian (0)	5	<0.01
Other Arab (35)	43	0.03
Armenian (6)	18	0.01
Assyrian/Chaldean/Syriac (0)	0	<0.01
Australian (9)	40	0.03
Austrian (3)	81	0.06
Basque (0)	0	<0.01
Belgian (26)	144	0.10
Brazilian (8)	8	0.01
British (227)	436	0.31
Bulgarian (9)	39	0.03
Cajun (0)	0	<0.01
Canadian (104)	194	0.14
Carpatho Rusyn (0)	0	<0.01
Celtic (12)	12	0.01
Croatian (24)	77	0.06
Cypriot (0)	0	<0.01
Czech (22)	246	0.18
Czechoslovakian (59)	106	0.08
Danish (20)	139	0.10
Dutch (622)	3,291	2.36
Eastern European (0)	0	<0.01
English (5,879)	14,578	10.46
Estonian (0)	0	<0.01
European (1,180)	1,255	0.90
Finnish (126)	163	0.12
French, ex. Basque (678)	2,901	2.08
French Canadian (75)	353	0.25
German (14,560)	35,228	25.28
German Russian (0)	0	<0.01
Greek (199)	537	0.39
Guyanese (0)	0	<0.01
Hungarian (228)	701	0.50
Icelander (8)	8	0.01
Iranian (28)	57	0.04
Irish (6,572)	20,947	15.03
Israeli (0)	0	<0.01
Italian (1,835)	4,266	3.06
Latvian (8)	8	0.01
Lithuanian (64)	150	0.11
Luxemburger (0)	0	<0.01
Macedonian (111)	266	0.19
Maltese (0)	0	<0.01
New Zealander (0)	0	<0.01
Northern European (38)	38	0.03
Norwegian (170)	572	0.41
Pennsylvania German (175)	175	0.13
Polish (638)	1,899	1.36
Portuguese (113)	155	0.11
Romanian (85)	179	0.13
Russian (107)	312	0.22
Scandinavian (76)	94	0.07
Scotch-Irish (1,119)	2,810	2.02
Scottish (1,099)	3,182	2.28
Serbian (0)	0	<0.01
Slavic (0)	53	0.04
Slovak (57)	393	0.28
Slovene (18)	54	0.04
Soviet Union (0)	0	<0.01
Swedish (335)	1,275	0.91
Swiss (110)	354	0.25
Turkish (0)	0	<0.01
Ukrainian (22)	119	0.09
Welsh (426)	1,414	1.01
West Indian, ex. Hispanic (49)	112	0.08
Bahamian (0)	0	<0.01
Barbadian (0)	0	<0.01
Belizean (0)	0	<0.01
Bermudan (0)	0	<0.01
British West Indian (0)	0	<0.01
Dutch West Indian (9)	44	0.03
Haitian (6)	6	<0.01
Jamaican (34)	62	0.04
Trinidadian/Tobagonian (0)	0	<0.01
U.S. Virgin Islander (0)	0	<0.01
West Indian (0)	0	<0.01
Other West Indian (0)	0	<0.01
Yugoslavian (24)	35	0.03

Hispanic Origin	Population	%
Hispanic or Latino (of any race)	3,805	2.75
Central American, ex. Mexican	142	0.10
Costa Rican	3	<0.01
Guatemalan	39	0.03
Honduran	30	0.02
Nicaraguan	19	0.01
Panamanian	23	0.02
Salvadoran	28	0.02
Other Central American	0	<0.01
Cuban	51	0.04
Dominican Republic	22	0.02
Mexican	2,961	2.14
Puerto Rican	204	0.15
South American	31	0.02
Argentinean	0	<0.01
Bolivian	1	<0.01
Chilean	3	<0.01
Colombian	14	0.01
Ecuadorian	3	<0.01
Paraguayan	2	<0.01
Peruvian	4	<0.01
Uruguayan	0	<0.01
Venezuelan	4	<0.01
Other South American	0	<0.01
Other Hispanic or Latino	394	0.28

Race*	Population	%
African-American/Black (12,128)	14,415	10.42
Not Hispanic (11,999)	14,145	10.23
Hispanic (129)	270	0.20
American Indian/Alaska Native (351)	1,287	0.93
Not Hispanic (302)	1,159	0.84
Hispanic (49)	128	0.09
Alaska Athabascan *(Ala. Nat.)* (0)	3	<0.01
Aleut *(Alaska Native)* (1)	1	<0.01
Apache (6)	16	0.01
Arapaho (0)	0	<0.01
Blackfeet (12)	62	0.04
Canadian/French Am. Ind. (0)	4	<0.01
Central American Ind. (0)	1	<0.01
Cherokee (70)	401	0.29
Cheyenne (3)	7	0.01
Chickasaw (1)	2	<0.01
Chippewa (8)	11	0.01
Choctaw (11)	17	0.01
Colville (0)	0	<0.01
Comanche (5)	7	0.01
Cree (1)	2	<0.01
Creek (4)	10	0.01
Crow (1)	2	<0.01
Delaware (2)	12	0.01
Hopi (0)	5	<0.01
Houma (0)	0	<0.01
Inupiat *(Alaska Native)* (1)	4	<0.01
Iroquois (7)	24	0.02
Kiowa (0)	0	<0.01
Lumbee (2)	2	<0.01
Menominee (0)	0	<0.01
Mexican American Ind. (7)	17	0.01
Navajo (0)	3	<0.01
Osage (0)	6	<0.01
Ottawa (1)	1	<0.01
Paiute (0)	0	<0.01
Pima (0)	0	<0.01
Potawatomi (1)	4	<0.01
Pueblo (0)	0	<0.01
Puget Sound Salish (0)	0	<0.01
Seminole (0)	7	0.01
Shoshone (0)	0	<0.01
Sioux (9)	28	0.02
South American Ind. (0)	0	<0.01
Spanish American Ind. (2)	2	<0.01
Tlingit-Haida *(Alaska Native)* (0)	0	<0.01
Tohono O'Odham (3)	3	<0.01
Tsimshian *(Alaska Native)* (0)	0	<0.01
Ute (0)	0	<0.01
Yakama (0)	0	<0.01
Yaqui (1)	1	<0.01
Yuman (0)	0	<0.01
Yup'ik *(Alaska Native)* (0)	0	<0.01
Asian (858)	1,294	0.94
Not Hispanic (849)	1,243	0.90
Hispanic (9)	51	0.04
Bangladeshi (0)	0	<0.01
Bhutanese (0)	0	<0.01
Burmese (0)	0	<0.01
Cambodian (3)	6	<0.01
Chinese, ex. Taiwanese (154)	207	0.15
Filipino (131)	220	0.16
Hmong (0)	0	<0.01
Indian (244)	293	0.21
Indonesian (3)	8	0.01
Japanese (67)	137	0.10
Korean (87)	156	0.11
Laotian (19)	26	0.02
Malaysian (1)	1	<0.01
Nepalese (0)	0	<0.01
Pakistani (46)	51	0.04
Sri Lankan (3)	4	<0.01
Taiwanese (2)	11	0.01
Thai (28)	60	0.04
Vietnamese (33)	63	0.05
Hawaii Native/Pacific Islander (51)	152	0.11
Not Hispanic (47)	123	0.09
Hispanic (4)	29	0.02
Fijian (19)	24	0.02
Guamanian/Chamorro (4)	12	0.01
Marshallese (2)	2	<0.01
Native Hawaiian (6)	29	0.02
Samoan (8)	16	0.01
Tongan (0)	2	<0.01
White (119,440)	122,670	88.68
Not Hispanic (117,976)	120,876	87.38
Hispanic (1,464)	1,794	1.30

*Notes: † The Census 2010 population figure is used to calculate the percentages in the Hispanic Origin and Race categories. Ancestry percentages are based on the 2006-2010 American Community Survey population (not shown); ‡ Numbers in parentheses indicate the number of people reporting a single ancestry; * Numbers in parentheses indicate the number of persons reporting this race alone, not in combination with any other race; Please refer to the User Guide for more information.*

Clermont County

Population: 197,363

Ancestry	Population	%
Afghan (0)	0	<0.01
African, Sub-Saharan (206)	244	0.12
African (192)	230	0.12
Cape Verdean (0)	0	<0.01
Ethiopian (0)	0	<0.01
Ghanaian (14)	14	0.01
Kenyan (0)	0	<0.01
Liberian (0)	0	<0.01
Nigerian (0)	0	<0.01
Senegalese (0)	0	<0.01
Sierra Leonean (0)	0	<0.01
Somalian (0)	0	<0.01
South African (0)	0	<0.01
Sudanese (0)	0	<0.01
Ugandan (0)	0	<0.01
Zimbabwean (0)	0	<0.01
Other Sub-Saharan African (0)	0	<0.01
Albanian (0)	0	<0.01
Alsatian (0)	4	<0.01
American (23,411)	23,411	11.99
Arab (277)	623	0.32
Arab (44)	54	0.03
Egyptian (7)	14	0.01
Iraqi (0)	0	<0.01
Jordanian (14)	14	0.01
Lebanese (113)	423	0.22
Moroccan (0)	0	<0.01
Palestinian (0)	19	0.01
Syrian (0)	0	<0.01
Other Arab (99)	99	0.05
Armenian (0)	16	0.01
Assyrian/Chaldean/Syriac (0)	0	<0.01
Australian (54)	54	0.03
Austrian (101)	505	0.26
Basque (0)	0	<0.01
Belgian (20)	149	0.08
Brazilian (26)	26	0.01
British (548)	971	0.50
Bulgarian (42)	42	0.02
Cajun (0)	0	<0.01
Canadian (107)	327	0.17
Carpatho Rusyn (0)	0	<0.01
Celtic (28)	75	0.04
Croatian (77)	174	0.09
Cypriot (0)	0	<0.01
Czech (68)	427	0.22
Czechoslovakian (22)	134	0.07
Danish (119)	421	0.22
Dutch (589)	3,615	1.85
Eastern European (57)	69	0.04
English (7,598)	21,648	11.08
Estonian (0)	0	<0.01
European (1,949)	2,158	1.10
Finnish (23)	215	0.11
French, ex. Basque (871)	5,377	2.75
French Canadian (230)	522	0.27
German (26,679)	66,435	34.01
German Russian (0)	0	<0.01
Greek (306)	772	0.40
Guyanese (0)	0	<0.01
Hungarian (314)	1,216	0.62
Icelander (0)	31	0.02
Iranian (31)	31	0.02
Irish (7,947)	35,329	18.09
Israeli (11)	11	0.01
Italian (2,963)	8,369	4.28
Latvian (0)	0	<0.01
Lithuanian (84)	287	0.15
Luxemburger (0)	0	<0.01
Macedonian (0)	15	0.01
Maltese (0)	0	<0.01
New Zealander (0)	0	<0.01
Northern European (67)	67	0.03
Norwegian (468)	1,002	0.51
Pennsylvania German (73)	106	0.05
Polish (1,205)	3,481	1.78
Portuguese (15)	137	0.07
Romanian (231)	301	0.15
Russian (325)	710	0.36
Scandinavian (64)	226	0.12
Scotch-Irish (1,192)	3,090	1.58
Scottish (1,598)	4,770	2.44
Serbian (62)	112	0.06
Slavic (0)	188	0.10
Slovak (74)	262	0.13
Slovene (12)	52	0.03
Soviet Union (0)	0	<0.01
Swedish (214)	1,409	0.72
Swiss (118)	560	0.29
Turkish (33)	39	0.02
Ukrainian (300)	500	0.26
Welsh (299)	1,461	0.75
West Indian, ex. Hispanic (50)	194	0.10
Bahamian (0)	0	<0.01
Barbadian (0)	0	<0.01
Belizean (0)	0	<0.01
Bermudan (0)	0	<0.01
British West Indian (0)	23	0.01
Dutch West Indian (0)	0	<0.01
Haitian (38)	79	0.04
Jamaican (0)	23	0.01
Trinidadian/Tobagonian (0)	0	<0.01
U.S. Virgin Islander (0)	0	<0.01
West Indian (12)	69	0.04
Other West Indian (0)	0	<0.01
Yugoslavian (59)	74	0.04

Hispanic Origin	Population	%
Hispanic or Latino (of any race)	2,896	1.47
Central American, ex. Mexican	260	0.13
Costa Rican	45	0.02
Guatemalan	69	0.03
Honduran	41	0.02
Nicaraguan	9	<0.01
Panamanian	40	0.02
Salvadoran	52	0.03
Other Central American	4	<0.01
Cuban	109	0.06
Dominican Republic	36	0.02
Mexican	1,504	0.76
Puerto Rican	407	0.21
South American	244	0.12
Argentinean	17	0.01
Bolivian	13	0.01
Chilean	16	0.01
Colombian	71	0.04
Ecuadorian	24	0.01
Paraguayan	4	<0.01
Peruvian	52	0.03
Uruguayan	3	<0.01
Venezuelan	41	0.02
Other South American	3	<0.01
Other Hispanic or Latino	336	0.17

Race*	Population	%
African-American/Black (2,284)	3,297	1.67
Not Hispanic (2,234)	3,202	1.62
Hispanic (50)	95	0.05
American Indian/Alaska Native (403)	1,343	0.68
Not Hispanic (349)	1,236	0.63
Hispanic (54)	107	0.05
Alaska Athabascan *(Ala. Nat.)* (0)	0	<0.01
Aleut *(Alaska Native)* (0)	3	<0.01
Apache (6)	26	0.01
Arapaho (0)	1	<0.01
Blackfeet (10)	78	0.04
Canadian/French Am. Ind. (0)	2	<0.01
Central American Ind. (2)	2	<0.01
Cherokee (127)	519	0.26
Cheyenne (0)	1	<0.01
Chickasaw (0)	0	<0.01
Chippewa (11)	21	0.01
Choctaw (4)	12	0.01
Colville (0)	0	<0.01
Comanche (0)	2	<0.01
Cree (0)	1	<0.01
Creek (5)	8	<0.01
Crow (5)	8	<0.01
Delaware (1)	4	<0.01
Hopi (1)	1	<0.01
Houma (0)	0	<0.01
Inupiat *(Alaska Native)* (0)	0	<0.01
Iroquois (2)	9	<0.01
Kiowa (0)	0	<0.01
Lumbee (2)	2	<0.01
Menominee (2)	2	<0.01
Mexican American Ind. (11)	15	0.01
Navajo (1)	2	<0.01
Osage (8)	8	<0.01
Ottawa (3)	5	<0.01
Paiute (0)	0	<0.01
Pima (0)	1	<0.01
Potawatomi (7)	7	<0.01
Pueblo (0)	0	<0.01
Puget Sound Salish (0)	1	<0.01
Seminole (1)	8	<0.01
Shoshone (0)	0	<0.01
Sioux (8)	26	0.01
South American Ind. (4)	5	<0.01
Spanish American Ind. (0)	0	<0.01
Tlingit-Haida *(Alaska Native)* (1)	1	<0.01
Tohono O'Odham (0)	0	<0.01
Tsimshian *(Alaska Native)* (0)	3	<0.01
Ute (0)	0	<0.01
Yakama (0)	0	<0.01
Yaqui (0)	0	<0.01
Yuman (0)	0	<0.01
Yup'ik *(Alaska Native)* (0)	0	<0.01
Asian (1,920)	2,544	1.29
Not Hispanic (1,900)	2,509	1.27
Hispanic (20)	35	0.02
Bangladeshi (12)	13	0.01
Bhutanese (0)	0	<0.01
Burmese (0)	0	<0.01
Cambodian (23)	39	0.02
Chinese, ex. Taiwanese (369)	441	0.22
Filipino (205)	388	0.20
Hmong (0)	0	<0.01
Indian (692)	797	0.40
Indonesian (14)	20	0.01
Japanese (84)	176	0.09
Korean (107)	178	0.09
Laotian (1)	3	<0.01
Malaysian (1)	1	<0.01
Nepalese (0)	0	<0.01
Pakistani (25)	31	0.02
Sri Lankan (11)	12	0.01
Taiwanese (17)	20	0.01
Thai (57)	70	0.04
Vietnamese (226)	263	0.13
Hawaii Native/Pacific Islander (61)	138	0.07
Not Hispanic (58)	123	0.06
Hispanic (3)	15	0.01
Fijian (0)	1	<0.01
Guamanian/Chamorro (3)	8	<0.01
Marshallese (2)	2	<0.01
Native Hawaiian (22)	45	0.02
Samoan (14)	32	0.02
Tongan (1)	1	<0.01
White (189,250)	191,819	97.19
Not Hispanic (187,331)	189,662	96.10
Hispanic (1,919)	2,157	1.09

*Notes: † The Census 2010 population figure is used to calculate the percentages in the Hispanic Origin and Race categories. Ancestry percentages are based on the 2006-2010 American Community Survey population (not shown); ‡ Numbers in parentheses indicate the number of people reporting a single ancestry; * Numbers in parentheses indicate the number of persons reporting this race alone, not in combination with any other race; Please refer to the User Guide for more information.*

Columbiana County

Population: 107,841

Ancestry	Population	%
Afghan (0)	0	<0.01
African, Sub-Saharan (120)	134	0.12
African (103)	117	0.11
Cape Verdean (8)	8	0.01
Ethiopian (0)	0	<0.01
Ghanaian (0)	0	<0.01
Kenyan (0)	0	<0.01
Liberian (0)	0	<0.01
Nigerian (9)	9	0.01
Senegalese (0)	0	<0.01
Sierra Leonean (0)	0	<0.01
Somalian (0)	0	<0.01
South African (0)	0	<0.01
Sudanese (0)	0	<0.01
Ugandan (0)	0	<0.01
Zimbabwean (0)	0	<0.01
Other Sub-Saharan African (0)	0	<0.01
Albanian (13)	13	0.01
Alsatian (0)	0	<0.01
American (8,280)	8,280	7.62
Arab (31)	166	0.15
Arab (8)	8	0.01
Egyptian (0)	0	<0.01
Iraqi (0)	0	<0.01
Jordanian (0)	0	<0.01
Lebanese (5)	127	0.12
Moroccan (18)	18	0.02
Palestinian (0)	0	<0.01
Syrian (0)	13	0.01
Other Arab (0)	0	<0.01
Armenian (0)	0	<0.01
Assyrian/Chaldean/Syriac (0)	0	<0.01
Australian (0)	0	<0.01
Austrian (83)	245	0.23
Basque (0)	0	<0.01
Belgian (80)	150	0.14
Brazilian (21)	57	0.05
British (171)	308	0.28
Bulgarian (0)	0	<0.01
Cajun (0)	0	<0.01
Canadian (76)	136	0.13
Carpatho Rusyn (0)	12	0.01
Celtic (57)	79	0.07
Croatian (116)	357	0.33
Cypriot (0)	0	<0.01
Czech (120)	464	0.43
Czechoslovakian (107)	216	0.20
Danish (42)	121	0.11
Dutch (320)	2,422	2.23
Eastern European (9)	9	0.01
English (5,017)	15,893	14.63
Estonian (0)	0	<0.01
European (529)	541	0.50
Finnish (19)	19	0.02
French, ex. Basque (366)	2,166	1.99
French Canadian (80)	340	0.31
German (10,044)	31,734	29.22
German Russian (0)	0	<0.01
Greek (106)	222	0.20
Guyanese (10)	10	0.01
Hungarian (374)	1,020	0.94
Icelander (0)	0	<0.01
Iranian (0)	0	<0.01
Irish (4,371)	19,269	17.74
Israeli (0)	0	<0.01
Italian (4,242)	9,830	9.05
Latvian (11)	11	0.01
Lithuanian (87)	147	0.14
Luxemburger (0)	0	<0.01
Macedonian (0)	0	<0.01
Maltese (0)	0	<0.01
New Zealander (0)	0	<0.01
Northern European (0)	0	<0.01
Norwegian (118)	490	0.45
Pennsylvania German (226)	481	0.44
Polish (846)	3,535	3.25
Portuguese (14)	20	0.02
Romanian (103)	434	0.40
Russian (91)	418	0.38
Scandinavian (0)	18	0.02
Scotch-Irish (1,485)	3,602	3.32
Scottish (816)	3,106	2.86
Serbian (111)	329	0.30
Slavic (52)	162	0.15
Slovak (572)	1,437	1.32
Slovene (65)	92	0.08
Soviet Union (0)	0	<0.01
Swedish (180)	783	0.72
Swiss (505)	1,442	1.33
Turkish (0)	0	<0.01
Ukrainian (144)	429	0.39
Welsh (485)	1,979	1.82
West Indian, ex. Hispanic (30)	65	0.06
Bahamian (14)	14	0.01
Barbadian (0)	0	<0.01
Belizean (0)	0	<0.01
Bermudan (0)	0	<0.01
British West Indian (0)	0	<0.01
Dutch West Indian (0)	0	<0.01
Haitian (0)	0	<0.01
Jamaican (16)	33	0.03
Trinidadian/Tobagonian (0)	18	0.02
U.S. Virgin Islander (0)	0	<0.01
West Indian (0)	0	<0.01
Other West Indian (0)	0	<0.01
Yugoslavian (95)	226	0.21

Hispanic Origin	Population	%
Hispanic or Latino (of any race)	1,348	1.25
Central American, ex. Mexican	189	0.18
Costa Rican	1	<0.01
Guatemalan	155	0.14
Honduran	6	0.01
Nicaraguan	1	<0.01
Panamanian	15	0.01
Salvadoran	9	0.01
Other Central American	2	<0.01
Cuban	30	0.03
Dominican Republic	40	0.04
Mexican	616	0.57
Puerto Rican	269	0.25
South American	54	0.05
Argentinean	2	<0.01
Bolivian	2	<0.01
Chilean	4	<0.01
Colombian	26	0.02
Ecuadorian	6	0.01
Paraguayan	0	<0.01
Peruvian	12	0.01
Uruguayan	0	<0.01
Venezuelan	2	<0.01
Other South American	0	<0.01
Other Hispanic or Latino	150	0.14

Race*	Population	%
African-American/Black (2,405)	3,123	2.90
Not Hispanic (2,323)	3,014	2.79
Hispanic (82)	109	0.10
American Indian/Alaska Native (202)	710	0.66
Not Hispanic (164)	644	0.60
Hispanic (38)	66	0.06
Alaska Athabascan *(Ala. Nat.)* (1)	1	<0.01
Aleut *(Alaska Native)* (0)	1	<0.01
Apache (5)	14	0.01
Arapaho (0)	0	<0.01
Blackfeet (7)	47	0.04
Canadian/French Am. Ind. (6)	6	0.01
Central American Ind. (0)	1	<0.01
Cherokee (34)	227	0.21
Cheyenne (1)	2	<0.01
Chickasaw (1)	5	<0.01
Chippewa (10)	18	0.02
Choctaw (4)	10	0.01
Colville (0)	0	<0.01
Comanche (2)	2	<0.01
Cree (2)	8	0.01
Creek (0)	1	<0.01
Crow (0)	3	<0.01
Delaware (10)	16	0.01
Hopi (0)	0	<0.01
Houma (0)	0	<0.01
Inupiat *(Alaska Native)* (1)	1	<0.01
Iroquois (4)	10	0.01
Kiowa (0)	0	<0.01
Lumbee (4)	6	0.01
Menominee (0)	0	<0.01
Mexican American Ind. (7)	14	0.01
Navajo (0)	4	<0.01
Osage (0)	0	<0.01
Ottawa (2)	5	<0.01
Paiute (0)	1	<0.01
Pima (0)	0	<0.01
Potawatomi (0)	0	<0.01
Pueblo (0)	0	<0.01
Puget Sound Salish (0)	0	<0.01
Seminole (0)	4	<0.01
Shoshone (0)	0	<0.01
Sioux (9)	21	0.02
South American Ind. (6)	12	0.01
Spanish American Ind. (0)	0	<0.01
Tlingit-Haida *(Alaska Native)* (0)	0	<0.01
Tohono O'Odham (0)	0	<0.01
Tsimshian *(Alaska Native)* (0)	0	<0.01
Ute (0)	0	<0.01
Yakama (0)	1	<0.01
Yaqui (3)	3	<0.01
Yuman (0)	0	<0.01
Yup'ik *(Alaska Native)* (0)	0	<0.01
Asian (322)	500	0.46
Not Hispanic (319)	489	0.45
Hispanic (3)	11	0.01
Bangladeshi (0)	0	<0.01
Bhutanese (0)	0	<0.01
Burmese (0)	0	<0.01
Cambodian (0)	1	<0.01
Chinese, ex. Taiwanese (85)	102	0.09
Filipino (80)	139	0.13
Hmong (3)	3	<0.01
Indian (50)	66	0.06
Indonesian (0)	1	<0.01
Japanese (15)	44	0.04
Korean (21)	52	0.05
Laotian (3)	3	<0.01
Malaysian (0)	0	<0.01
Nepalese (0)	0	<0.01
Pakistani (22)	25	0.02
Sri Lankan (0)	0	<0.01
Taiwanese (0)	1	<0.01
Thai (3)	5	<0.01
Vietnamese (20)	27	0.03
Hawaii Native/Pacific Islander (27)	65	0.06
Not Hispanic (20)	57	0.05
Hispanic (7)	8	0.01
Fijian (0)	0	<0.01
Guamanian/Chamorro (11)	18	0.02
Marshallese (0)	0	<0.01
Native Hawaiian (15)	31	0.03
Samoan (0)	3	<0.01
Tongan (0)	0	<0.01
White (102,959)	104,291	96.71
Not Hispanic (102,326)	103,554	96.02
Hispanic (633)	737	0.68

*Notes: † The Census 2010 population figure is used to calculate the percentages in the Hispanic Origin and Race categories. Ancestry percentages are based on the 2006-2010 American Community Survey population (not shown); ‡ Numbers in parentheses indicate the number of people reporting a single ancestry; * Numbers in parentheses indicate the number of persons reporting this race alone, not in combination with any other race; Please refer to the User Guide for more information.*

Cuyahoga County

Population: 1,280,122

Ancestry	Population	%
Afghan (0)	0	<0.01
African, Sub-Saharan (9,385)	11,464	0.89
African (6,600)	8,154	0.63
Cape Verdean (19)	58	<0.01
Ethiopian (21)	31	<0.01
Ghanaian (229)	244	0.02
Kenyan (89)	120	0.01
Liberian (248)	253	0.02
Nigerian (1,014)	1,093	0.08
Senegalese (17)	39	<0.01
Sierra Leonean (36)	36	<0.01
Somalian (212)	246	0.02
South African (179)	326	0.03
Sudanese (117)	117	0.01
Ugandan (29)	29	<0.01
Zimbabwean (0)	0	<0.01
Other Sub-Saharan African (575)	718	0.06
Albanian (1,946)	2,139	0.17
Alsatian (0)	15	<0.01
American (35,629)	35,629	2.75
Arab (12,072)	17,189	1.33
Arab (2,129)	2,644	0.20
Egyptian (1,223)	1,360	0.11
Iraqi (238)	238	0.02
Jordanian (433)	495	0.04
Lebanese (4,616)	8,193	0.63
Moroccan (202)	260	0.02
Palestinian (1,654)	1,741	0.13
Syrian (965)	1,513	0.12
Other Arab (612)	745	0.06
Armenian (458)	958	0.07
Assyrian/Chaldean/Syriac (15)	20	<0.01
Australian (70)	199	0.02
Austrian (942)	5,359	0.41
Basque (0)	12	<0.01
Belgian (149)	762	0.06
Brazilian (178)	240	0.02
British (1,174)	3,030	0.23
Bulgarian (373)	640	0.05
Cajun (37)	46	<0.01
Canadian (458)	1,902	0.15
Carpatho Rusyn (214)	256	0.02
Celtic (79)	125	0.01
Croatian (3,695)	9,707	0.75
Cypriot (12)	12	<0.01
Czech (6,762)	22,584	1.75
Czechoslovakian (1,730)	3,395	0.26
Danish (563)	2,158	0.17
Dutch (1,191)	10,463	0.81
Eastern European (3,823)	4,024	0.31
English (18,135)	80,962	6.26
Estonian (97)	150	0.01
European (6,840)	7,776	0.60
Finnish (491)	2,144	0.17
French, ex. Basque (1,631)	18,173	1.40
French Canadian (892)	2,785	0.22
German (54,613)	225,136	17.40
German Russian (72)	125	0.01
Greek (4,765)	9,414	0.73
Guyanese (337)	403	0.03
Hungarian (14,725)	44,605	3.45
Icelander (51)	95	0.01
Iranian (554)	816	0.06
Irish (42,280)	168,679	13.04
Israeli (331)	648	0.05
Italian (47,317)	118,489	9.16
Latvian (486)	897	0.07
Lithuanian (2,405)	6,678	0.52
Luxemburger (6)	18	<0.01
Macedonian (155)	304	0.02
Maltese (30)	30	<0.01
New Zealander (41)	87	0.01
Northern European (304)	341	0.03
Norwegian (823)	3,363	0.26
Pennsylvania German (189)	547	0.04
Polish (41,516)	111,245	8.60
Portuguese (369)	1,075	0.08
Romanian (4,309)	7,213	0.56
Russian (9,338)	21,861	1.69
Scandinavian (294)	776	0.06
Scotch-Irish (4,893)	15,009	1.16
Scottish (3,655)	16,982	1.31
Serbian (3,085)	5,164	0.40
Slavic (426)	1,177	0.09
Slovak (15,574)	43,131	3.33
Slovene (6,974)	19,262	1.49
Soviet Union (0)	0	<0.01
Swedish (1,524)	7,938	0.61
Swiss (453)	3,615	0.28
Turkish (707)	942	0.07
Ukrainian (10,616)	17,407	1.35
Welsh (1,137)	8,613	0.67
West Indian, ex. Hispanic (3,010)	4,624	0.36
Bahamian (11)	26	<0.01
Barbadian (44)	128	0.01
Belizean (30)	46	<0.01
Bermudan (32)	90	0.01
British West Indian (55)	65	0.01
Dutch West Indian (0)	0	<0.01
Haitian (103)	195	0.02
Jamaican (2,303)	3,087	0.24
Trinidadian/Tobagonian (78)	185	0.01
U.S. Virgin Islander (12)	12	<0.01
West Indian (342)	790	0.06
Other West Indian (0)	0	<0.01
Yugoslavian (978)	1,617	0.12

Hispanic Origin	Population	%
Hispanic or Latino (of any race)	61,270	4.79
Central American, ex. Mexican	3,371	0.26
Costa Rican	108	0.01
Guatemalan	1,187	0.09
Honduran	455	0.04
Nicaraguan	195	0.02
Panamanian	278	0.02
Salvadoran	1,119	0.09
Other Central American	29	<0.01
Cuban	1,153	0.09
Dominican Republic	1,643	0.13
Mexican	8,797	0.69
Puerto Rican	39,068	3.05
South American	3,175	0.25
Argentinean	380	0.03
Bolivian	28	<0.01
Chilean	196	0.02
Colombian	920	0.07
Ecuadorian	280	0.02
Paraguayan	49	<0.01
Peruvian	872	0.07
Uruguayan	105	0.01
Venezuelan	302	0.02
Other South American	43	<0.01
Other Hispanic or Latino	4,063	0.32

Race*	Population	%
African-American/Black (380,198)	396,157	30.95
Not Hispanic (374,968)	388,386	30.34
Hispanic (5,230)	7,771	0.61
American Indian/Alaska Native (2,578)	8,991	0.70
Not Hispanic (2,018)	7,571	0.59
Hispanic (560)	1,420	0.11
Alaska Athabascan *(Ala. Nat.)* (5)	11	<0.01
Aleut *(Alaska Native)* (1)	1	<0.01
Apache (30)	106	0.01
Arapaho (1)	9	<0.01
Blackfeet (75)	560	0.04
Canadian/French Am. Ind. (12)	27	<0.01
Central American Ind. (35)	46	<0.01
Cherokee (297)	2,013	0.16
Cheyenne (12)	23	<0.01
Chickasaw (21)	53	<0.01
Chippewa (87)	146	0.01
Choctaw (49)	178	0.01
Colville (1)	3	<0.01
Comanche (2)	12	<0.01
Cree (2)	8	<0.01
Creek (12)	65	0.01
Crow (4)	14	<0.01
Delaware (8)	28	<0.01
Hopi (0)	5	<0.01
Houma (0)	0	<0.01
Inupiat *(Alaska Native)* (10)	15	<0.01
Iroquois (62)	195	0.02
Kiowa (8)	14	<0.01
Lumbee (18)	38	<0.01
Menominee (2)	4	<0.01
Mexican American Ind. (84)	126	0.01
Navajo (44)	100	0.01
Osage (2)	5	<0.01
Ottawa (8)	17	<0.01
Paiute (0)	0	<0.01
Pima (0)	1	<0.01
Potawatomi (6)	16	<0.01
Pueblo (21)	32	<0.01
Puget Sound Salish (1)	1	<0.01
Seminole (20)	87	0.01
Shoshone (5)	10	<0.01
Sioux (66)	223	0.02
South American Ind. (66)	167	0.01
Spanish American Ind. (11)	13	<0.01
Tlingit-Haida *(Alaska Native)* (13)	21	<0.01
Tohono O'Odham (7)	7	<0.01
Tsimshian *(Alaska Native)* (1)	4	<0.01
Ute (0)	0	<0.01
Yakama (0)	0	<0.01
Yaqui (0)	5	<0.01
Yuman (1)	2	<0.01
Yup'ik *(Alaska Native)* (1)	4	<0.01
Asian (32,883)	39,136	3.06
Not Hispanic (32,615)	38,506	3.01
Hispanic (268)	630	0.05
Bangladeshi (99)	127	0.01
Bhutanese (175)	246	0.02
Burmese (241)	257	0.02
Cambodian (560)	652	0.05
Chinese, ex. Taiwanese (8,541)	9,633	0.75
Filipino (3,308)	4,758	0.37
Hmong (3)	8	<0.01
Indian (11,778)	12,960	1.01
Indonesian (85)	136	0.01
Japanese (947)	1,671	0.13
Korean (2,181)	2,765	0.22
Laotian (169)	221	0.02
Malaysian (27)	47	<0.01
Nepalese (171)	226	0.02
Pakistani (659)	743	0.06
Sri Lankan (92)	127	0.01
Taiwanese (432)	494	0.04
Thai (343)	457	0.04
Vietnamese (2,023)	2,355	0.18
Hawaii Native/Pacific Islander (285)	1,203	0.09
Not Hispanic (217)	896	0.07
Hispanic (68)	307	0.02
Fijian (2)	3	<0.01
Guamanian/Chamorro (87)	155	0.01
Marshallese (2)	2	<0.01
Native Hawaiian (80)	306	0.02
Samoan (14)	58	<0.01
Tongan (10)	19	<0.01
White (814,103)	835,527	65.27
Not Hispanic (785,977)	803,437	62.76
Hispanic (28,126)	32,090	2.51

*Notes: † The Census 2010 population figure is used to calculate the percentages in the Hispanic Origin and Race categories. Ancestry percentages are based on the 2006-2010 American Community Survey population (not shown); ‡ Numbers in parentheses indicate the number of people reporting a single ancestry; * Numbers in parentheses indicate the number of persons reporting this race alone, not in combination with any other race; Please refer to the User Guide for more information.*

Delaware County

Population: 174,214

Ancestry	Population	%
Afghan (9)	44	0.03
African, Sub-Saharan (838)	934	0.56
African (369)	414	0.25
Cape Verdean (0)	0	<0.01
Ethiopian (145)	145	0.09
Ghanaian (18)	31	0.02
Kenyan (0)	0	<0.01
Liberian (0)	0	<0.01
Nigerian (293)	293	0.18
Senegalese (0)	0	<0.01
Sierra Leonean (0)	0	<0.01
Somalian (13)	51	0.03
South African (0)	0	<0.01
Sudanese (0)	0	<0.01
Ugandan (0)	0	<0.01
Zimbabwean (0)	0	<0.01
Other Sub-Saharan African (0)	0	<0.01
Albanian (6)	6	<0.01
Alsatian (0)	9	0.01
American (9,422)	9,422	5.67
Arab (490)	905	0.54
Arab (72)	121	0.07
Egyptian (0)	0	<0.01
Iraqi (39)	58	0.03
Jordanian (24)	82	0.05
Lebanese (260)	465	0.28
Moroccan (0)	0	<0.01
Palestinian (7)	11	0.01
Syrian (15)	71	0.04
Other Arab (73)	97	0.06
Armenian (87)	144	0.09
Assyrian/Chaldean/Syriac (50)	50	0.03
Australian (0)	43	0.03
Austrian (75)	349	0.21
Basque (0)	0	<0.01
Belgian (58)	205	0.12
Brazilian (77)	116	0.07
British (469)	1,224	0.74
Bulgarian (0)	47	0.03
Cajun (0)	0	<0.01
Canadian (269)	461	0.28
Carpatho Rusyn (28)	28	0.02
Celtic (0)	39	0.02
Croatian (145)	514	0.31
Cypriot (37)	37	0.02
Czech (282)	978	0.59
Czechoslovakian (72)	205	0.12
Danish (59)	314	0.19
Dutch (573)	3,085	1.86
Eastern European (154)	197	0.12
English (7,225)	23,193	13.96
Estonian (9)	35	0.02
European (2,102)	2,445	1.47
Finnish (146)	292	0.18
French, ex. Basque (815)	4,571	2.75
French Canadian (292)	547	0.33
German (20,334)	56,848	34.22
German Russian (0)	0	<0.01
Greek (432)	1,038	0.62
Guyanese (0)	0	<0.01
Hungarian (755)	2,137	1.29
Icelander (0)	24	0.01
Iranian (185)	234	0.14
Irish (5,844)	27,048	16.28
Israeli (0)	0	<0.01
Italian (4,570)	13,511	8.13
Latvian (0)	63	0.04
Lithuanian (46)	353	0.21
Luxemburger (6)	6	<0.01
Macedonian (105)	150	0.09
Maltese (0)	0	<0.01
New Zealander (29)	29	0.02
Northern European (66)	66	0.04
Norwegian (341)	1,188	0.72
Pennsylvania German (33)	113	0.07
Polish (1,920)	6,886	4.15
Portuguese (28)	131	0.08
Romanian (121)	451	0.27
Russian (413)	1,131	0.68
Scandinavian (198)	282	0.17
Scotch-Irish (1,350)	3,495	2.10
Scottish (1,605)	5,292	3.19
Serbian (51)	178	0.11
Slavic (60)	158	0.10
Slovak (359)	1,042	0.63
Slovene (104)	335	0.20
Soviet Union (0)	0	<0.01
Swedish (415)	1,715	1.03
Swiss (126)	722	0.43
Turkish (25)	98	0.06
Ukrainian (125)	375	0.23
Welsh (892)	3,864	2.33
West Indian, ex. Hispanic (149)	192	0.12
Bahamian (0)	0	<0.01
Barbadian (0)	0	<0.01
Belizean (0)	0	<0.01
Bermudan (0)	0	<0.01
British West Indian (9)	9	0.01
Dutch West Indian (0)	12	0.01
Haitian (54)	75	0.05
Jamaican (70)	75	0.05
Trinidadian/Tobagonian (16)	21	0.01
U.S. Virgin Islander (0)	0	<0.01
West Indian (0)	0	<0.01
Other West Indian (0)	0	<0.01
Yugoslavian (83)	185	0.11

Hispanic Origin	Population	%
Hispanic or Latino (of any race)	3,669	2.11
Central American, ex. Mexican	326	0.19
Costa Rican	24	0.01
Guatemalan	100	0.06
Honduran	37	0.02
Nicaraguan	36	0.02
Panamanian	36	0.02
Salvadoran	92	0.05
Other Central American	1	<0.01
Cuban	128	0.07
Dominican Republic	61	0.04
Mexican	1,800	1.03
Puerto Rican	481	0.28
South American	489	0.28
Argentinean	28	0.02
Bolivian	20	0.01
Chilean	16	0.01
Colombian	195	0.11
Ecuadorian	49	0.03
Paraguayan	7	<0.01
Peruvian	72	0.04
Uruguayan	4	<0.01
Venezuelan	95	0.05
Other South American	3	<0.01
Other Hispanic or Latino	384	0.22

Race*	Population	%
African-American/Black (5,837)	7,133	4.09
Not Hispanic (5,756)	6,974	4.00
Hispanic (81)	159	0.09
American Indian/Alaska Native (252)	1,001	0.57
Not Hispanic (216)	890	0.51
Hispanic (36)	111	0.06
Alaska Athabascan *(Ala. Nat.)* (2)	2	<0.01
Aleut *(Alaska Native)* (0)	0	<0.01
Apache (5)	17	0.01
Arapaho (0)	0	<0.01
Blackfeet (4)	34	0.02
Canadian/French Am. Ind. (1)	5	<0.01
Central American Ind. (6)	6	<0.01
Cherokee (56)	292	0.17
Cheyenne (0)	1	<0.01
Chickasaw (2)	2	<0.01
Chippewa (8)	16	0.01
Choctaw (1)	5	<0.01
Colville (0)	0	<0.01
Comanche (0)	0	<0.01
Cree (0)	2	<0.01
Creek (1)	10	0.01
Crow (0)	0	<0.01
Delaware (1)	6	<0.01
Hopi (0)	0	<0.01
Houma (0)	0	<0.01
Inupiat *(Alaska Native)* (1)	1	<0.01
Iroquois (1)	31	0.02
Kiowa (1)	1	<0.01
Lumbee (5)	20	0.01
Menominee (0)	0	<0.01
Mexican American Ind. (12)	19	0.01
Navajo (8)	15	0.01
Osage (0)	0	<0.01
Ottawa (0)	2	<0.01
Paiute (0)	1	<0.01
Pima (0)	0	<0.01
Potawatomi (2)	2	<0.01
Pueblo (0)	1	<0.01
Puget Sound Salish (0)	0	<0.01
Seminole (0)	4	<0.01
Shoshone (0)	0	<0.01
Sioux (6)	29	0.02
South American Ind. (1)	6	<0.01
Spanish American Ind. (3)	4	<0.01
Tlingit-Haida *(Alaska Native)* (0)	0	<0.01
Tohono O'Odham (0)	0	<0.01
Tsimshian *(Alaska Native)* (0)	0	<0.01
Ute (0)	0	<0.01
Yakama (0)	0	<0.01
Yaqui (0)	3	<0.01
Yuman (1)	1	<0.01
Yup'ik *(Alaska Native)* (0)	0	<0.01
Asian (7,436)	8,690	4.99
Not Hispanic (7,393)	8,599	4.94
Hispanic (43)	91	0.05
Bangladeshi (50)	51	0.03
Bhutanese (0)	0	<0.01
Burmese (3)	11	0.01
Cambodian (67)	88	0.05
Chinese, ex. Taiwanese (1,548)	1,818	1.04
Filipino (357)	544	0.31
Hmong (0)	1	<0.01
Indian (3,401)	3,648	2.09
Indonesian (43)	62	0.04
Japanese (272)	455	0.26
Korean (605)	779	0.45
Laotian (59)	83	0.05
Malaysian (10)	27	0.02
Nepalese (7)	7	<0.01
Pakistani (137)	149	0.09
Sri Lankan (30)	39	0.02
Taiwanese (74)	105	0.06
Thai (45)	83	0.05
Vietnamese (514)	620	0.36
Hawaii Native/Pacific Islander (51)	152	0.09
Not Hispanic (47)	126	0.07
Hispanic (4)	26	0.01
Fijian (0)	0	<0.01
Guamanian/Chamorro (12)	33	0.02
Marshallese (0)	1	<0.01
Native Hawaiian (21)	59	0.03
Samoan (3)	9	0.01
Tongan (0)	1	<0.01
White (156,328)	159,242	91.41
Not Hispanic (153,969)	156,608	89.89
Hispanic (2,359)	2,634	1.51

*Notes: † The Census 2010 population figure is used to calculate the percentages in the Hispanic Origin and Race categories. Ancestry percentages are based on the 2006-2010 American Community Survey population (not shown); ‡ Numbers in parentheses indicate the number of people reporting a single ancestry; * Numbers in parentheses indicate the number of persons reporting this race alone, not in combination with any other race; Please refer to the User Guide for more information.*

Fairfield County

Population: 146,156

Ancestry	Population	%
Afghan (0)	0	<0.01
African, Sub-Saharan (537)	666	0.46
African (332)	435	0.30
Cape Verdean (0)	0	<0.01
Ethiopian (63)	63	0.04
Ghanaian (0)	8	0.01
Kenyan (0)	0	<0.01
Liberian (7)	15	0.01
Nigerian (0)	0	<0.01
Senegalese (0)	0	<0.01
Sierra Leonean (0)	0	<0.01
Somalian (9)	9	0.01
South African (0)	10	0.01
Sudanese (0)	0	<0.01
Ugandan (0)	0	<0.01
Zimbabwean (0)	0	<0.01
Other Sub-Saharan African (126)	126	0.09
Albanian (16)	35	0.02
Alsatian (0)	0	<0.01
American (12,393)	12,393	8.61
Arab (424)	749	0.52
Arab (50)	79	0.05
Egyptian (82)	82	0.06
Iraqi (0)	0	<0.01
Jordanian (167)	167	0.12
Lebanese (31)	243	0.17
Moroccan (5)	67	0.05
Palestinian (0)	0	<0.01
Syrian (89)	111	0.08
Other Arab (0)	0	<0.01
Armenian (0)	0	<0.01
Assyrian/Chaldean/Syriac (0)	12	0.01
Australian (0)	0	<0.01
Austrian (98)	250	0.17
Basque (0)	0	<0.01
Belgian (66)	147	0.10
Brazilian (52)	118	0.08
British (338)	706	0.49
Bulgarian (0)	0	<0.01
Cajun (14)	36	0.03
Canadian (96)	160	0.11
Carpatho Rusyn (0)	0	<0.01
Celtic (0)	0	<0.01
Croatian (79)	308	0.21
Cypriot (0)	0	<0.01
Czech (125)	459	0.32
Czechoslovakian (46)	153	0.11
Danish (51)	186	0.13
Dutch (641)	3,641	2.53
Eastern European (44)	49	0.03
English (5,465)	16,787	11.66
Estonian (0)	0	<0.01
European (1,394)	1,427	0.99
Finnish (9)	50	0.03
French, ex. Basque (687)	3,594	2.50
French Canadian (133)	328	0.23
German (17,469)	44,962	31.23
German Russian (0)	0	<0.01
Greek (221)	468	0.33
Guyanese (0)	36	0.03
Hungarian (761)	1,436	1.00
Icelander (0)	0	<0.01
Iranian (12)	24	0.02
Irish (6,142)	23,293	16.18
Israeli (0)	0	<0.01
Italian (2,857)	7,503	5.21
Latvian (0)	0	<0.01
Lithuanian (42)	118	0.08
Luxemburger (0)	4	<0.01
Macedonian (169)	262	0.18
Maltese (0)	0	<0.01
New Zealander (14)	14	0.01
Northern European (119)	135	0.09
Norwegian (253)	683	0.47
Pennsylvania German (62)	102	0.07
Polish (672)	2,996	2.08
Portuguese (0)	43	0.03
Romanian (27)	308	0.21
Russian (276)	655	0.46
Scandinavian (58)	105	0.07
Scotch-Irish (1,296)	2,544	1.77
Scottish (927)	3,376	2.35
Serbian (4)	55	0.04
Slavic (11)	69	0.05
Slovak (128)	432	0.30
Slovene (0)	58	0.04
Soviet Union (0)	0	<0.01
Swedish (412)	1,055	0.73
Swiss (157)	675	0.47
Turkish (0)	0	<0.01
Ukrainian (76)	255	0.18
Welsh (414)	2,475	1.72
West Indian, ex. Hispanic (363)	393	0.27
Bahamian (100)	100	0.07
Barbadian (0)	0	<0.01
Belizean (0)	0	<0.01
Bermudan (0)	0	<0.01
British West Indian (0)	0	<0.01
Dutch West Indian (0)	6	<0.01
Haitian (238)	238	0.17
Jamaican (25)	25	0.02
Trinidadian/Tobagonian (0)	0	<0.01
U.S. Virgin Islander (0)	0	<0.01
West Indian (0)	24	0.02
Other West Indian (0)	0	<0.01
Yugoslavian (44)	176	0.12

Hispanic Origin	Population	%
Hispanic or Latino (of any race)	2,510	1.72
Central American, ex. Mexican	208	0.14
Costa Rican	21	0.01
Guatemalan	63	0.04
Honduran	40	0.03
Nicaraguan	4	<0.01
Panamanian	45	0.03
Salvadoran	29	0.02
Other Central American	6	<0.01
Cuban	97	0.07
Dominican Republic	101	0.07
Mexican	1,184	0.81
Puerto Rican	411	0.28
South American	167	0.11
Argentinean	14	0.01
Bolivian	6	<0.01
Chilean	7	<0.01
Colombian	54	0.04
Ecuadorian	20	0.01
Paraguayan	0	<0.01
Peruvian	34	0.02
Uruguayan	6	<0.01
Venezuelan	20	0.01
Other South American	6	<0.01
Other Hispanic or Latino	342	0.23

Race*	Population	%
African-American/Black (8,702)	10,097	6.91
Not Hispanic (8,609)	9,927	6.79
Hispanic (93)	170	0.12
American Indian/Alaska Native (309)	1,253	0.86
Not Hispanic (278)	1,153	0.79
Hispanic (31)	100	0.07
Alaska Athabascan *(Ala. Nat.)* (4)	8	0.01
Aleut *(Alaska Native)* (1)	3	<0.01
Apache (9)	35	0.02
Arapaho (0)	0	<0.01
Blackfeet (6)	63	0.04
Canadian/French Am. Ind. (0)	6	<0.01
Central American Ind. (4)	4	<0.01
Cherokee (55)	361	0.25
Cheyenne (0)	3	<0.01
Chickasaw (0)	0	<0.01
Chippewa (10)	18	0.01
Choctaw (3)	10	0.01
Colville (0)	0	<0.01
Comanche (0)	3	<0.01
Cree (1)	1	<0.01
Creek (2)	19	0.01
Crow (0)	2	<0.01
Delaware (0)	6	<0.01
Hopi (0)	1	<0.01
Houma (0)	0	<0.01
Inupiat *(Alaska Native)* (0)	0	<0.01
Iroquois (7)	28	0.02
Kiowa (0)	0	<0.01
Lumbee (2)	6	<0.01
Menominee (0)	0	<0.01
Mexican American Ind. (9)	16	0.01
Navajo (1)	12	0.01
Osage (0)	0	<0.01
Ottawa (0)	0	<0.01
Paiute (1)	4	<0.01
Pima (0)	0	<0.01
Potawatomi (4)	9	0.01
Pueblo (0)	0	<0.01
Puget Sound Salish (0)	0	<0.01
Seminole (1)	6	<0.01
Shoshone (0)	0	<0.01
Sioux (8)	35	0.02
South American Ind. (1)	1	<0.01
Spanish American Ind. (0)	0	<0.01
Tlingit-Haida *(Alaska Native)* (0)	0	<0.01
Tohono O'Odham (0)	0	<0.01
Tsimshian *(Alaska Native)* (0)	0	<0.01
Ute (0)	0	<0.01
Yakama (0)	0	<0.01
Yaqui (0)	0	<0.01
Yuman (0)	0	<0.01
Yup'ik *(Alaska Native)* (3)	3	<0.01
Asian (1,645)	2,311	1.58
Not Hispanic (1,626)	2,260	1.55
Hispanic (19)	51	0.03
Bangladeshi (2)	4	<0.01
Bhutanese (0)	0	<0.01
Burmese (8)	8	0.01
Cambodian (34)	42	0.03
Chinese, ex. Taiwanese (318)	414	0.28
Filipino (165)	323	0.22
Hmong (4)	6	<0.01
Indian (391)	473	0.32
Indonesian (11)	19	0.01
Japanese (96)	197	0.13
Korean (87)	185	0.13
Laotian (87)	107	0.07
Malaysian (5)	9	0.01
Nepalese (1)	4	<0.01
Pakistani (153)	167	0.11
Sri Lankan (12)	18	0.01
Taiwanese (7)	11	0.01
Thai (28)	71	0.05
Vietnamese (141)	172	0.12
Hawaii Native/Pacific Islander (45)	137	0.09
Not Hispanic (39)	123	0.08
Hispanic (6)	14	0.01
Fijian (1)	2	<0.01
Guamanian/Chamorro (4)	20	0.01
Marshallese (0)	0	<0.01
Native Hawaiian (20)	67	0.05
Samoan (6)	8	0.01
Tongan (0)	0	<0.01
White (131,830)	134,451	91.99
Not Hispanic (130,377)	132,756	90.83
Hispanic (1,453)	1,695	1.16

*Notes: † The Census 2010 population figure is used to calculate the percentages in the Hispanic Origin and Race categories. Ancestry percentages are based on the 2006-2010 American Community Survey population (not shown); ‡ Numbers in parentheses indicate the number of people reporting a single ancestry; * Numbers in parentheses indicate the number of persons reporting this race alone, not in combination with any other race; Please refer to the User Guide for more information.*

Franklin County

Population: 1,163,414

Ancestry	Population	%
Afghan (87)	109	0.01
African, Sub-Saharan (28,783)	30,900	2.71
African (11,345)	12,661	1.11
Cape Verdean (28)	28	<0.01
Ethiopian (2,910)	3,037	0.27
Ghanaian (1,550)	1,575	0.14
Kenyan (490)	574	0.05
Liberian (379)	446	0.04
Nigerian (930)	1,120	0.10
Senegalese (104)	104	0.01
Sierra Leonean (471)	499	0.04
Somalian (9,515)	9,670	0.85
South African (124)	142	0.01
Sudanese (103)	140	0.01
Ugandan (88)	88	0.01
Zimbabwean (125)	125	0.01
Other Sub-Saharan African (621)	691	0.06
Albanian (425)	479	0.04
Alsatian (0)	67	0.01
American (57,318)	57,318	5.02
Arab (5,994)	8,707	0.76
Arab (1,280)	1,476	0.13
Egyptian (1,197)	1,478	0.13
Iraqi (279)	334	0.03
Jordanian (492)	507	0.04
Lebanese (807)	2,288	0.20
Moroccan (396)	513	0.04
Palestinian (785)	914	0.08
Syrian (238)	565	0.05
Other Arab (520)	632	0.06
Armenian (183)	328	0.03
Assyrian/Chaldean/Syriac (148)	148	0.01
Australian (60)	357	0.03
Austrian (645)	2,554	0.22
Basque (0)	0	<0.01
Belgian (447)	1,043	0.09
Brazilian (469)	601	0.05
British (2,691)	6,035	0.53
Bulgarian (110)	261	0.02
Cajun (0)	56	<0.01
Canadian (839)	2,087	0.18
Carpatho Rusyn (12)	45	<0.01
Celtic (97)	178	0.02
Croatian (521)	1,761	0.15
Cypriot (0)	14	<0.01
Czech (1,425)	5,115	0.45
Czechoslovakian (459)	1,339	0.12
Danish (479)	1,925	0.17
Dutch (3,171)	17,752	1.56
Eastern European (1,201)	1,436	0.13
English (32,516)	104,384	9.15
Estonian (39)	53	<0.01
European (11,463)	12,844	1.13
Finnish (495)	1,723	0.15
French, ex. Basque (4,674)	23,955	2.10
French Canadian (1,234)	3,189	0.28
German (99,605)	276,500	24.23
German Russian (33)	62	0.01
Greek (2,545)	6,069	0.53
Guyanese (101)	135	0.01
Hungarian (2,928)	10,887	0.95
Icelander (15)	51	<0.01
Iranian (769)	911	0.08
Irish (47,953)	164,857	14.45
Israeli (125)	220	0.02
Italian (23,468)	63,246	5.54
Latvian (206)	359	0.03
Lithuanian (466)	1,729	0.15
Luxemburger (28)	49	<0.01
Macedonian (568)	702	0.06
Maltese (0)	29	<0.01
New Zealander (62)	62	0.01
Northern European (504)	549	0.05
Norwegian (1,682)	5,861	0.51
Pennsylvania German (370)	716	0.06
Polish (8,491)	29,037	2.54
Portuguese (960)	1,993	0.17
Romanian (759)	1,923	0.17
Russian (4,085)	9,141	0.80
Scandinavian (703)	1,618	0.14
Scotch-Irish (7,654)	20,404	1.79
Scottish (7,727)	24,642	2.16
Serbian (228)	741	0.06
Slavic (275)	783	0.07
Slovak (1,643)	5,279	0.46
Slovene (771)	2,005	0.18
Soviet Union (0)	0	<0.01
Swedish (1,856)	8,493	0.74
Swiss (903)	5,061	0.44
Turkish (685)	881	0.08
Ukrainian (1,565)	3,428	0.30
Welsh (4,053)	18,461	1.62
West Indian, ex. Hispanic (3,018)	4,506	0.39
Bahamian (82)	156	0.01
Barbadian (106)	179	0.02
Belizean (28)	42	<0.01
Bermudan (0)	11	<0.01
British West Indian (157)	173	0.02
Dutch West Indian (0)	84	0.01
Haitian (1,306)	1,547	0.14
Jamaican (833)	1,602	0.14
Trinidadian/Tobagonian (213)	292	0.03
U.S. Virgin Islander (15)	27	<0.01
West Indian (278)	393	0.03
Other West Indian (0)	0	<0.01
Yugoslavian (779)	1,106	0.10

Hispanic Origin	Population	%
Hispanic or Latino (of any race)	55,718	4.79
Central American, ex. Mexican	5,203	0.45
Costa Rican	204	0.02
Guatemalan	845	0.07
Honduran	993	0.09
Nicaraguan	227	0.02
Panamanian	372	0.03
Salvadoran	2,503	0.22
Other Central American	59	0.01
Cuban	1,285	0.11
Dominican Republic	1,879	0.16
Mexican	31,905	2.74
Puerto Rican	6,443	0.55
South American	3,830	0.33
Argentinean	498	0.04
Bolivian	159	0.01
Chilean	183	0.02
Colombian	1,073	0.09
Ecuadorian	597	0.05
Paraguayan	19	<0.01
Peruvian	736	0.06
Uruguayan	56	<0.01
Venezuelan	483	0.04
Other South American	26	<0.01
Other Hispanic or Latino	5,173	0.44

Race*	Population	%
African-American/Black (247,225)	268,432	23.07
Not Hispanic (244,200)	263,683	22.66
Hispanic (3,025)	4,749	0.41
American Indian/Alaska Native (2,852)	11,292	0.97
Not Hispanic (2,280)	9,913	0.85
Hispanic (572)	1,379	0.12
Alaska Athabascan *(Ala. Nat.)* (10)	15	<0.01
Aleut *(Alaska Native)* (6)	15	<0.01
Apache (32)	137	0.01
Arapaho (3)	11	<0.01
Blackfeet (57)	670	0.06
Canadian/French Am. Ind. (4)	27	<0.01
Central American Ind. (11)	19	<0.01
Cherokee (471)	2,950	0.25
Cheyenne (6)	22	<0.01
Chickasaw (11)	29	<0.01
Chippewa (60)	158	0.01
Choctaw (36)	129	0.01
Colville (0)	1	<0.01
Comanche (5)	31	<0.01
Cree (9)	26	<0.01
Creek (14)	70	0.01
Crow (2)	15	<0.01
Delaware (19)	76	0.01
Hopi (3)	11	<0.01
Houma (4)	7	<0.01
Inupiat *(Alaska Native)* (3)	5	<0.01
Iroquois (74)	193	0.02
Kiowa (0)	1	<0.01
Lumbee (58)	90	0.01
Menominee (3)	3	<0.01
Mexican American Ind. (145)	263	0.02
Navajo (37)	89	0.01
Osage (6)	14	<0.01
Ottawa (9)	19	<0.01
Paiute (4)	4	<0.01
Pima (0)	4	<0.01
Potawatomi (10)	31	<0.01
Pueblo (12)	22	<0.01
Puget Sound Salish (0)	1	<0.01
Seminole (4)	60	0.01
Shoshone (3)	10	<0.01
Sioux (56)	235	0.02
South American Ind. (27)	68	0.01
Spanish American Ind. (16)	20	<0.01
Tlingit-Haida *(Alaska Native)* (11)	14	<0.01
Tohono O'Odham (2)	5	<0.01
Tsimshian *(Alaska Native)* (3)	5	<0.01
Ute (2)	6	<0.01
Yakama (0)	0	<0.01
Yaqui (1)	3	<0.01
Yuman (0)	3	<0.01
Yup'ik *(Alaska Native)* (3)	5	<0.01
Asian (44,996)	53,189	4.57
Not Hispanic (44,723)	52,482	4.51
Hispanic (273)	707	0.06
Bangladeshi (436)	476	0.04
Bhutanese (71)	97	0.01
Burmese (219)	233	0.02
Cambodian (1,814)	2,153	0.19
Chinese, ex. Taiwanese (8,824)	10,162	0.87
Filipino (2,353)	3,974	0.34
Hmong (46)	52	<0.01
Indian (14,789)	16,029	1.38
Indonesian (329)	441	0.04
Japanese (2,870)	4,124	0.35
Korean (3,763)	4,788	0.41
Laotian (1,454)	1,771	0.15
Malaysian (101)	140	0.01
Nepalese (202)	230	0.02
Pakistani (1,140)	1,332	0.11
Sri Lankan (248)	273	0.02
Taiwanese (805)	928	0.08
Thai (546)	830	0.07
Vietnamese (2,383)	2,914	0.25
Hawaii Native/Pacific Islander (746)	1,756	0.15
Not Hispanic (676)	1,535	0.13
Hispanic (70)	221	0.02
Fijian (5)	10	<0.01
Guamanian/Chamorro (105)	215	0.02
Marshallese (2)	3	<0.01
Native Hawaiian (113)	419	0.04
Samoan (424)	550	0.05
Tongan (0)	2	<0.01
White (805,617)	835,249	71.79
Not Hispanic (783,048)	809,006	69.54
Hispanic (22,569)	26,243	2.26

*Notes: † The Census 2010 population figure is used to calculate the percentages in the Hispanic Origin and Race categories. Ancestry percentages are based on the 2006-2010 American Community Survey population (not shown); ‡ Numbers in parentheses indicate the number of people reporting a single ancestry; * Numbers in parentheses indicate the number of persons reporting this race alone, not in combination with any other race; Please refer to the User Guide for more information.*

Greene County

Population: 161,573

Ancestry	Population	%
Afghan (0)	0	<0.01
African, Sub-Saharan (487)	550	0.34
African (325)	372	0.23
Cape Verdean (12)	28	0.02
Ethiopian (0)	0	<0.01
Ghanaian (0)	0	<0.01
Kenyan (12)	12	0.01
Liberian (0)	0	<0.01
Nigerian (111)	111	0.07
Senegalese (0)	0	<0.01
Sierra Leonean (0)	0	<0.01
Somalian (0)	0	<0.01
South African (13)	13	0.01
Sudanese (0)	0	<0.01
Ugandan (0)	0	<0.01
Zimbabwean (0)	0	<0.01
Other Sub-Saharan African (14)	14	0.01
Albanian (0)	0	<0.01
Alsatian (0)	0	<0.01
American (25,183)	25,183	15.75
Arab (342)	613	0.38
Arab (17)	79	0.05
Egyptian (24)	34	0.02
Iraqi (0)	0	<0.01
Jordanian (0)	0	<0.01
Lebanese (127)	207	0.13
Moroccan (0)	0	<0.01
Palestinian (9)	9	0.01
Syrian (0)	32	0.02
Other Arab (165)	252	0.16
Armenian (11)	45	0.03
Assyrian/Chaldean/Syriac (0)	0	<0.01
Australian (39)	57	0.04
Austrian (28)	285	0.18
Basque (0)	0	<0.01
Belgian (13)	84	0.05
Brazilian (19)	19	0.01
British (597)	1,427	0.89
Bulgarian (0)	0	<0.01
Cajun (15)	32	0.02
Canadian (117)	251	0.16
Carpatho Rusyn (0)	0	<0.01
Celtic (16)	25	0.02
Croatian (72)	112	0.07
Cypriot (0)	0	<0.01
Czech (161)	742	0.46
Czechoslovakian (45)	185	0.12
Danish (107)	333	0.21
Dutch (646)	3,086	1.93
Eastern European (128)	142	0.09
English (6,488)	17,505	10.94
Estonian (0)	12	0.01
European (1,652)	1,853	1.16
Finnish (46)	101	0.06
French, ex. Basque (844)	4,562	2.85
French Canadian (192)	494	0.31
German (16,801)	42,247	26.41
German Russian (0)	0	<0.01
Greek (269)	492	0.31
Guyanese (0)	0	<0.01
Hungarian (558)	1,680	1.05
Icelander (0)	0	<0.01
Iranian (7)	37	0.02
Irish (5,856)	20,815	13.01
Israeli (10)	50	0.03
Italian (1,941)	5,598	3.50
Latvian (15)	52	0.03
Lithuanian (59)	257	0.16
Luxemburger (0)	0	<0.01
Macedonian (0)	20	0.01
Maltese (11)	11	0.01
New Zealander (0)	0	<0.01
Northern European (119)	133	0.08
Norwegian (312)	1,046	0.65
Pennsylvania German (95)	107	0.07
Polish (1,075)	3,427	2.14
Portuguese (160)	287	0.18
Romanian (132)	260	0.16
Russian (120)	597	0.37
Scandinavian (83)	352	0.22
Scotch-Irish (1,205)	3,287	2.06
Scottish (1,592)	4,603	2.88
Serbian (0)	0	<0.01
Slavic (0)	68	0.04
Slovak (177)	465	0.29
Slovene (9)	119	0.07
Soviet Union (0)	0	<0.01
Swedish (398)	1,438	0.90
Swiss (141)	594	0.37
Turkish (43)	43	0.03
Ukrainian (73)	327	0.20
Welsh (422)	1,975	1.23
West Indian, ex. Hispanic (0)	7	<0.01
Bahamian (0)	0	<0.01
Barbadian (0)	0	<0.01
Belizean (0)	0	<0.01
Bermudan (0)	0	<0.01
British West Indian (0)	0	<0.01
Dutch West Indian (0)	0	<0.01
Haitian (0)	0	<0.01
Jamaican (0)	7	<0.01
Trinidadian/Tobagonian (0)	0	<0.01
U.S. Virgin Islander (0)	0	<0.01
West Indian (0)	0	<0.01
Other West Indian (0)	0	<0.01
Yugoslavian (76)	148	0.09

Hispanic Origin	Population	%
Hispanic or Latino (of any race)	3,439	2.13
Central American, ex. Mexican	254	0.16
Costa Rican	21	0.01
Guatemalan	86	0.05
Honduran	35	0.02
Nicaraguan	26	0.02
Panamanian	60	0.04
Salvadoran	16	0.01
Other Central American	10	0.01
Cuban	137	0.08
Dominican Republic	41	0.03
Mexican	1,577	0.98
Puerto Rican	660	0.41
South American	304	0.19
Argentinean	40	0.02
Bolivian	24	0.01
Chilean	20	0.01
Colombian	115	0.07
Ecuadorian	27	0.02
Paraguayan	2	<0.01
Peruvian	50	0.03
Uruguayan	2	<0.01
Venezuelan	19	0.01
Other South American	5	<0.01
Other Hispanic or Latino	466	0.29

Race*	Population	%
African-American/Black (11,681)	13,716	8.49
Not Hispanic (11,506)	13,419	8.31
Hispanic (175)	297	0.18
American Indian/Alaska Native (428)	1,567	0.97
Not Hispanic (367)	1,416	0.88
Hispanic (61)	151	0.09
Alaska Athabascan *(Ala. Nat.)* (0)	0	<0.01
Aleut *(Alaska Native)* (1)	1	<0.01
Apache (9)	15	0.01
Arapaho (0)	4	<0.01
Blackfeet (9)	49	0.03
Canadian/French Am. Ind. (3)	9	0.01
Central American Ind. (3)	3	<0.01
Cherokee (89)	463	0.29
Cheyenne (0)	0	<0.01
Chickasaw (5)	6	<0.01
Chippewa (24)	47	0.03
Choctaw (9)	33	0.02
Colville (0)	0	<0.01
Comanche (0)	4	<0.01
Cree (0)	2	<0.01
Creek (5)	19	0.01
Crow (1)	2	<0.01
Delaware (1)	6	<0.01
Hopi (1)	3	<0.01
Houma (0)	0	<0.01
Inupiat *(Alaska Native)* (0)	0	<0.01
Iroquois (4)	29	0.02
Kiowa (5)	7	<0.01
Lumbee (0)	1	<0.01
Menominee (0)	0	<0.01
Mexican American Ind. (25)	29	0.02
Navajo (4)	5	<0.01
Osage (2)	5	<0.01
Ottawa (0)	0	<0.01
Paiute (1)	4	<0.01
Pima (0)	0	<0.01
Potawatomi (3)	6	<0.01
Pueblo (1)	6	<0.01
Puget Sound Salish (0)	0	<0.01
Seminole (3)	21	0.01
Shoshone (1)	3	<0.01
Sioux (12)	35	0.02
South American Ind. (2)	4	<0.01
Spanish American Ind. (0)	0	<0.01
Tlingit-Haida *(Alaska Native)* (1)	1	<0.01
Tohono O'Odham (0)	0	<0.01
Tsimshian *(Alaska Native)* (1)	1	<0.01
Ute (0)	1	<0.01
Yakama (1)	1	<0.01
Yaqui (1)	1	<0.01
Yuman (0)	0	<0.01
Yup'ik *(Alaska Native)* (1)	1	<0.01
Asian (4,703)	5,967	3.69
Not Hispanic (4,663)	5,876	3.64
Hispanic (40)	91	0.06
Bangladeshi (15)	15	0.01
Bhutanese (0)	0	<0.01
Burmese (5)	5	<0.01
Cambodian (37)	54	0.03
Chinese, ex. Taiwanese (829)	970	0.60
Filipino (476)	788	0.49
Hmong (1)	1	<0.01
Indian (1,646)	1,807	1.12
Indonesian (8)	13	0.01
Japanese (243)	494	0.31
Korean (603)	798	0.49
Laotian (13)	15	0.01
Malaysian (6)	11	0.01
Nepalese (7)	14	0.01
Pakistani (152)	160	0.10
Sri Lankan (28)	35	0.02
Taiwanese (65)	72	0.04
Thai (72)	130	0.08
Vietnamese (328)	394	0.24
Hawaii Native/Pacific Islander (89)	245	0.15
Not Hispanic (81)	221	0.14
Hispanic (8)	24	0.01
Fijian (2)	6	<0.01
Guamanian/Chamorro (25)	52	0.03
Marshallese (0)	0	<0.01
Native Hawaiian (36)	95	0.06
Samoan (9)	21	0.01
Tongan (0)	0	<0.01
White (139,670)	143,414	88.76
Not Hispanic (137,440)	140,906	87.21
Hispanic (2,230)	2,508	1.55

*Notes: † The Census 2010 population figure is used to calculate the percentages in the Hispanic Origin and Race categories. Ancestry percentages are based on the 2006-2010 American Community Survey population (not shown); ‡ Numbers in parentheses indicate the number of people reporting a single ancestry; * Numbers in parentheses indicate the number of persons reporting this race alone, not in combination with any other race; Please refer to the User Guide for more information.*

Hamilton County

Population: 802,374

Ancestry	Population	%
Afghan (0)	0	<0.01
African, Sub-Saharan (20,067)	21,746	2.71
African (16,797)	18,085	2.25
Cape Verdean (0)	0	<0.01
Ethiopian (774)	902	0.11
Ghanaian (150)	150	0.02
Kenyan (50)	50	0.01
Liberian (73)	73	0.01
Nigerian (786)	786	0.10
Senegalese (289)	358	0.04
Sierra Leonean (0)	0	<0.01
Somalian (0)	0	<0.01
South African (56)	92	0.01
Sudanese (63)	63	0.01
Ugandan (0)	0	<0.01
Zimbabwean (225)	225	0.03
Other Sub-Saharan African (804)	962	0.12
Albanian (0)	0	<0.01
Alsatian (83)	209	0.03
American (52,671)	52,671	6.57
Arab (2,021)	3,515	0.44
Arab (483)	613	0.08
Egyptian (123)	149	0.02
Iraqi (29)	29	<0.01
Jordanian (225)	240	0.03
Lebanese (799)	1,736	0.22
Moroccan (65)	65	0.01
Palestinian (204)	219	0.03
Syrian (11)	292	0.04
Other Arab (82)	172	0.02
Armenian (107)	320	0.04
Assyrian/Chaldean/Syriac (0)	9	<0.01
Australian (154)	193	0.02
Austrian (355)	1,909	0.24
Basque (0)	17	<0.01
Belgian (115)	482	0.06
Brazilian (203)	253	0.03
British (1,795)	3,407	0.42
Bulgarian (81)	81	0.01
Cajun (0)	41	0.01
Canadian (581)	1,055	0.13
Carpatho Rusyn (0)	0	<0.01
Celtic (14)	77	0.01
Croatian (118)	416	0.05
Cypriot (0)	0	<0.01
Czech (591)	2,237	0.28
Czechoslovakian (154)	538	0.07
Danish (259)	1,281	0.16
Dutch (1,696)	10,817	1.35
Eastern European (584)	711	0.09
English (19,015)	61,903	7.72
Estonian (77)	104	0.01
European (7,230)	7,844	0.98
Finnish (123)	491	0.06
French, ex. Basque (2,367)	18,863	2.35
French Canadian (473)	1,508	0.19
German (110,301)	248,340	30.96
German Russian (10)	87	0.01
Greek (2,072)	3,954	0.49
Guyanese (107)	128	0.02
Hungarian (1,340)	4,734	0.59
Icelander (0)	35	<0.01
Iranian (202)	254	0.03
Irish (25,494)	117,831	14.69
Israeli (226)	320	0.04
Italian (12,262)	36,726	4.58
Latvian (80)	151	0.02
Lithuanian (355)	927	0.12
Luxemburger (26)	159	0.02
Macedonian (217)	304	0.04
Maltese (0)	38	<0.01
New Zealander (0)	0	<0.01
Northern European (265)	315	0.04
Norwegian (833)	2,814	0.35
Pennsylvania German (111)	202	0.03
Polish (3,259)	11,895	1.48
Portuguese (156)	451	0.06
Romanian (324)	1,259	0.16
Russian (2,457)	6,004	0.75
Scandinavian (321)	647	0.08
Scotch-Irish (3,677)	10,796	1.35
Scottish (3,616)	13,159	1.64
Serbian (112)	270	0.03
Slavic (136)	329	0.04
Slovak (453)	1,659	0.21
Slovene (139)	513	0.06
Soviet Union (15)	15	<0.01
Swedish (924)	3,936	0.49
Swiss (602)	2,633	0.33
Turkish (130)	155	0.02
Ukrainian (475)	1,053	0.13
Welsh (1,148)	5,952	0.74
West Indian, ex. Hispanic (701)	1,149	0.14
Bahamian (33)	40	<0.01
Barbadian (11)	41	0.01
Belizean (0)	0	<0.01
Bermudan (0)	0	<0.01
British West Indian (16)	36	<0.01
Dutch West Indian (0)	0	<0.01
Haitian (57)	61	0.01
Jamaican (477)	657	0.08
Trinidadian/Tobagonian (29)	127	0.02
U.S. Virgin Islander (0)	0	<0.01
West Indian (69)	168	0.02
Other West Indian (9)	19	<0.01
Yugoslavian (378)	598	0.07

Hispanic Origin	Population	%
Hispanic or Latino (of any race)	20,607	2.57
Central American, ex. Mexican	3,802	0.47
Costa Rican	99	0.01
Guatemalan	2,381	0.30
Honduran	509	0.06
Nicaraguan	178	0.02
Panamanian	198	0.02
Salvadoran	392	0.05
Other Central American	45	0.01
Cuban	682	0.08
Dominican Republic	324	0.04
Mexican	9,583	1.19
Puerto Rican	2,111	0.26
South American	1,785	0.22
Argentinean	206	0.03
Bolivian	48	0.01
Chilean	103	0.01
Colombian	505	0.06
Ecuadorian	142	0.02
Paraguayan	12	<0.01
Peruvian	454	0.06
Uruguayan	12	<0.01
Venezuelan	285	0.04
Other South American	18	<0.01
Other Hispanic or Latino	2,320	0.29

Race*	Population	%
African-American/Black (205,952)	216,782	27.02
Not Hispanic (204,748)	214,889	26.78
Hispanic (1,204)	1,893	0.24
American Indian/Alaska Native (1,617)	5,806	0.72
Not Hispanic (1,219)	5,029	0.63
Hispanic (398)	777	0.10
Alaska Athabascan *(Ala. Nat.)* (1)	11	<0.01
Aleut *(Alaska Native)* (7)	13	<0.01
Apache (27)	88	0.01
Arapaho (1)	8	<0.01
Blackfeet (28)	294	0.04
Canadian/French Am. Ind. (10)	18	<0.01
Central American Ind. (121)	142	0.02
Cherokee (253)	1,605	0.20
Cheyenne (0)	12	<0.01
Chickasaw (8)	18	<0.01
Chippewa (32)	72	0.01
Choctaw (21)	71	0.01
Colville (0)	3	<0.01
Comanche (8)	18	<0.01
Cree (1)	15	<0.01
Creek (19)	40	<0.01
Crow (0)	6	<0.01
Delaware (6)	11	<0.01
Hopi (2)	2	<0.01
Houma (0)	0	<0.01
Inupiat *(Alaska Native)* (1)	3	<0.01
Iroquois (16)	48	0.01
Kiowa (1)	2	<0.01
Lumbee (9)	10	<0.01
Menominee (2)	2	<0.01
Mexican American Ind. (90)	142	0.02
Navajo (32)	81	0.01
Osage (9)	15	<0.01
Ottawa (3)	10	<0.01
Paiute (1)	1	<0.01
Pima (2)	2	<0.01
Potawatomi (13)	26	<0.01
Pueblo (3)	5	<0.01
Puget Sound Salish (0)	0	<0.01
Seminole (4)	34	<0.01
Shoshone (0)	2	<0.01
Sioux (33)	125	0.02
South American Ind. (10)	39	<0.01
Spanish American Ind. (9)	10	<0.01
Tlingit-Haida *(Alaska Native)* (3)	6	<0.01
Tohono O'Odham (1)	7	<0.01
Tsimshian *(Alaska Native)* (0)	1	<0.01
Ute (0)	2	<0.01
Yakama (0)	1	<0.01
Yaqui (1)	4	<0.01
Yuman (2)	2	<0.01
Yup'ik *(Alaska Native)* (0)	0	<0.01
Asian (16,182)	20,016	2.49
Not Hispanic (16,080)	19,665	2.45
Hispanic (102)	351	0.04
Bangladeshi (43)	53	0.01
Bhutanese (120)	133	0.02
Burmese (87)	89	0.01
Cambodian (525)	644	0.08
Chinese, ex. Taiwanese (3,277)	3,987	0.50
Filipino (1,385)	2,314	0.29
Hmong (0)	3	<0.01
Indian (5,612)	6,253	0.78
Indonesian (33)	83	0.01
Japanese (841)	1,353	0.17
Korean (1,344)	1,745	0.22
Laotian (48)	67	0.01
Malaysian (13)	20	<0.01
Nepalese (118)	137	0.02
Pakistani (319)	372	0.05
Sri Lankan (127)	142	0.02
Taiwanese (322)	368	0.05
Thai (214)	305	0.04
Vietnamese (1,142)	1,323	0.16
Hawaii Native/Pacific Islander (603)	1,075	0.13
Not Hispanic (474)	868	0.11
Hispanic (129)	207	0.03
Fijian (3)	6	<0.01
Guamanian/Chamorro (231)	292	0.04
Marshallese (9)	10	<0.01
Native Hawaiian (87)	234	0.03
Samoan (35)	83	0.01
Tongan (2)	3	<0.01
White (552,330)	567,032	70.67
Not Hispanic (542,273)	555,532	69.24
Hispanic (10,057)	11,500	1.43

*Notes: † The Census 2010 population figure is used to calculate the percentages in the Hispanic Origin and Race categories. Ancestry percentages are based on the 2006-2010 American Community Survey population (not shown); ‡ Numbers in parentheses indicate the number of people reporting a single ancestry; * Numbers in parentheses indicate the number of persons reporting this race alone, not in combination with any other race; Please refer to the User Guide for more information.*

Lake County

Population: 230,041

Ancestry	Population	%
Afghan (8)	8	<0.01
African, Sub-Saharan (56)	118	0.05
African (24)	74	0.03
Cape Verdean (0)	0	<0.01
Ethiopian (0)	0	<0.01
Ghanaian (0)	0	<0.01
Kenyan (0)	12	0.01
Liberian (0)	0	<0.01
Nigerian (0)	0	<0.01
Senegalese (0)	0	<0.01
Sierra Leonean (0)	0	<0.01
Somalian (15)	15	0.01
South African (17)	17	0.01
Sudanese (0)	0	<0.01
Ugandan (0)	0	<0.01
Zimbabwean (0)	0	<0.01
Other Sub-Saharan African (0)	0	<0.01
Albanian (141)	215	0.09
Alsatian (9)	53	0.02
American (9,031)	9,031	3.94
Arab (313)	711	0.31
Arab (24)	47	0.02
Egyptian (0)	0	<0.01
Iraqi (0)	0	<0.01
Jordanian (10)	10	<0.01
Lebanese (232)	593	0.26
Moroccan (0)	0	<0.01
Palestinian (0)	0	<0.01
Syrian (22)	36	0.02
Other Arab (25)	25	0.01
Armenian (51)	76	0.03
Assyrian/Chaldean/Syriac (0)	0	<0.01
Australian (0)	35	0.02
Austrian (228)	903	0.39
Basque (0)	0	<0.01
Belgian (21)	87	0.04
Brazilian (0)	24	0.01
British (344)	659	0.29
Bulgarian (25)	25	0.01
Cajun (0)	0	<0.01
Canadian (158)	394	0.17
Carpatho Rusyn (11)	11	<0.01
Celtic (15)	15	0.01
Croatian (3,374)	6,869	2.99
Cypriot (0)	0	<0.01
Czech (686)	2,952	1.29
Czechoslovakian (309)	648	0.28
Danish (115)	547	0.24
Dutch (376)	3,156	1.38
Eastern European (245)	270	0.12
English (6,191)	26,409	11.51
Estonian (17)	17	0.01
European (1,444)	1,645	0.72
Finnish (920)	2,815	1.23
French, ex. Basque (560)	5,340	2.33
French Canadian (368)	1,386	0.60
German (15,119)	60,669	26.44
German Russian (0)	0	<0.01
Greek (541)	1,103	0.48
Guyanese (0)	9	<0.01
Hungarian (4,431)	12,343	5.38
Icelander (4)	4	<0.01
Iranian (28)	28	0.01
Irish (9,514)	43,284	18.87
Israeli (0)	0	<0.01
Italian (13,636)	37,567	16.37
Latvian (29)	46	0.02
Lithuanian (970)	2,468	1.08
Luxemburger (22)	44	0.02
Macedonian (6)	10	<0.01
Maltese (0)	0	<0.01
New Zealander (8)	8	<0.01
Northern European (42)	51	0.02
Norwegian (293)	1,050	0.46
Pennsylvania German (138)	288	0.13
Polish (5,388)	17,548	7.65
Portuguese (53)	257	0.11
Romanian (295)	805	0.35
Russian (830)	2,724	1.19
Scandinavian (85)	139	0.06
Scotch-Irish (1,694)	4,962	2.16
Scottish (1,215)	5,929	2.58
Serbian (173)	491	0.21
Slavic (256)	636	0.28
Slovak (2,193)	6,095	2.66
Slovene (5,406)	14,255	6.21
Soviet Union (0)	0	<0.01
Swedish (461)	2,475	1.08
Swiss (71)	534	0.23
Turkish (15)	53	0.02
Ukrainian (505)	1,413	0.62
Welsh (435)	2,661	1.16
West Indian, ex. Hispanic (0)	7	<0.01
Bahamian (0)	0	<0.01
Barbadian (0)	0	<0.01
Belizean (0)	7	<0.01
Bermudan (0)	0	<0.01
British West Indian (0)	0	<0.01
Dutch West Indian (0)	0	<0.01
Haitian (0)	0	<0.01
Jamaican (0)	0	<0.01
Trinidadian/Tobagonian (0)	0	<0.01
U.S. Virgin Islander (0)	0	<0.01
West Indian (0)	0	<0.01
Other West Indian (0)	0	<0.01
Yugoslavian (756)	893	0.39

Hispanic Origin	Population	%
Hispanic or Latino (of any race)	7,825	3.40
Central American, ex. Mexican	186	0.08
Costa Rican	17	0.01
Guatemalan	55	0.02
Honduran	38	0.02
Nicaraguan	10	<0.01
Panamanian	19	0.01
Salvadoran	47	0.02
Other Central American	0	<0.01
Cuban	115	0.05
Dominican Republic	31	0.01
Mexican	5,378	2.34
Puerto Rican	1,289	0.56
South American	309	0.13
Argentinean	51	0.02
Bolivian	2	<0.01
Chilean	39	0.02
Colombian	86	0.04
Ecuadorian	9	<0.01
Paraguayan	4	<0.01
Peruvian	66	0.03
Uruguayan	7	<0.01
Venezuelan	41	0.02
Other South American	4	<0.01
Other Hispanic or Latino	517	0.22

Race*	Population	%
African-American/Black (7,306)	9,106	3.96
Not Hispanic (7,156)	8,813	3.83
Hispanic (150)	293	0.13
American Indian/Alaska Native (273)	1,141	0.50
Not Hispanic (234)	1,032	0.45
Hispanic (39)	109	0.05
Alaska Athabascan *(Ala. Nat.)* (0)	0	<0.01
Aleut *(Alaska Native)* (1)	1	<0.01
Apache (4)	27	0.01
Arapaho (0)	0	<0.01
Blackfeet (7)	65	0.03
Canadian/French Am. Ind. (3)	5	<0.01
Central American Ind. (2)	3	<0.01
Cherokee (56)	329	0.14
Cheyenne (0)	1	<0.01
Chickasaw (2)	7	<0.01
Chippewa (5)	23	0.01
Choctaw (3)	13	0.01
Colville (0)	0	<0.01
Comanche (0)	1	<0.01
Cree (1)	1	<0.01
Creek (3)	9	<0.01
Crow (0)	3	<0.01
Delaware (2)	5	<0.01
Hopi (0)	1	<0.01
Houma (0)	0	<0.01
Inupiat *(Alaska Native)* (5)	10	<0.01
Iroquois (10)	35	0.02
Kiowa (0)	1	<0.01
Lumbee (3)	3	<0.01
Menominee (0)	0	<0.01
Mexican American Ind. (8)	26	0.01
Navajo (8)	22	0.01
Osage (2)	4	<0.01
Ottawa (5)	5	<0.01
Paiute (0)	0	<0.01
Pima (0)	0	<0.01
Potawatomi (2)	5	<0.01
Pueblo (3)	6	<0.01
Puget Sound Salish (0)	1	<0.01
Seminole (1)	5	<0.01
Shoshone (0)	3	<0.01
Sioux (4)	15	0.01
South American Ind. (5)	6	<0.01
Spanish American Ind. (0)	0	<0.01
Tlingit-Haida *(Alaska Native)* (0)	0	<0.01
Tohono O'Odham (6)	7	<0.01
Tsimshian *(Alaska Native)* (0)	0	<0.01
Ute (0)	0	<0.01
Yakama (0)	0	<0.01
Yaqui (0)	0	<0.01
Yuman (0)	0	<0.01
Yup'ik *(Alaska Native)* (0)	0	<0.01
Asian (2,611)	3,388	1.47
Not Hispanic (2,586)	3,317	1.44
Hispanic (25)	71	0.03
Bangladeshi (2)	2	<0.01
Bhutanese (0)	0	<0.01
Burmese (8)	13	0.01
Cambodian (5)	11	<0.01
Chinese, ex. Taiwanese (503)	620	0.27
Filipino (289)	478	0.21
Hmong (5)	5	<0.01
Indian (998)	1,124	0.49
Indonesian (6)	8	<0.01
Japanese (157)	299	0.13
Korean (245)	344	0.15
Laotian (54)	61	0.03
Malaysian (4)	7	<0.01
Nepalese (7)	9	<0.01
Pakistani (41)	42	0.02
Sri Lankan (3)	3	<0.01
Taiwanese (10)	13	0.01
Thai (28)	49	0.02
Vietnamese (156)	187	0.08
Hawaii Native/Pacific Islander (35)	156	0.07
Not Hispanic (31)	128	0.06
Hispanic (4)	28	0.01
Fijian (2)	3	<0.01
Guamanian/Chamorro (9)	26	0.01
Marshallese (1)	1	<0.01
Native Hawaiian (5)	55	0.02
Samoan (3)	17	0.01
Tongan (0)	1	<0.01
White (212,713)	215,963	93.88
Not Hispanic (208,994)	211,827	92.08
Hispanic (3,719)	4,136	1.80

*Notes: † The Census 2010 population figure is used to calculate the percentages in the Hispanic Origin and Race categories. Ancestry percentages are based on the 2006-2010 American Community Survey population (not shown); ‡ Numbers in parentheses indicate the number of people reporting a single ancestry; * Numbers in parentheses indicate the number of persons reporting this race alone, not in combination with any other race; Please refer to the User Guide for more information.*

Licking County

Population: 166,492

Ancestry	Population	%
Afghan (0)	0	<0.01
African, Sub-Saharan (317)	356	0.22
African (220)	256	0.16
Cape Verdean (0)	0	<0.01
Ethiopian (39)	42	0.03
Ghanaian (0)	0	<0.01
Kenyan (0)	0	<0.01
Liberian (58)	58	0.04
Nigerian (0)	0	<0.01
Senegalese (0)	0	<0.01
Sierra Leonean (0)	0	<0.01
Somalian (0)	0	<0.01
South African (0)	0	<0.01
Sudanese (0)	0	<0.01
Ugandan (0)	0	<0.01
Zimbabwean (0)	0	<0.01
Other Sub-Saharan African (0)	0	<0.01
Albanian (0)	0	<0.01
Alsatian (0)	0	<0.01
American (17,654)	17,654	10.78
Arab (170)	239	0.15
Arab (70)	70	0.04
Egyptian (20)	20	0.01
Iraqi (0)	0	<0.01
Jordanian (0)	0	<0.01
Lebanese (15)	49	0.03
Moroccan (0)	0	<0.01
Palestinian (0)	0	<0.01
Syrian (0)	35	0.02
Other Arab (65)	65	0.04
Armenian (24)	66	0.04
Assyrian/Chaldean/Syriac (0)	0	<0.01
Australian (8)	101	0.06
Austrian (92)	296	0.18
Basque (0)	0	<0.01
Belgian (32)	165	0.10
Brazilian (0)	0	<0.01
British (287)	711	0.43
Bulgarian (0)	21	0.01
Cajun (0)	0	<0.01
Canadian (95)	198	0.12
Carpatho Rusyn (9)	9	0.01
Celtic (19)	19	0.01
Croatian (8)	81	0.05
Cypriot (0)	0	<0.01
Czech (98)	485	0.30
Czechoslovakian (36)	153	0.09
Danish (31)	187	0.11
Dutch (616)	3,931	2.40
Eastern European (78)	78	0.05
English (9,053)	21,334	13.03
Estonian (0)	0	<0.01
European (2,067)	2,271	1.39
Finnish (0)	125	0.08
French, ex. Basque (747)	3,832	2.34
French Canadian (180)	376	0.23
German (17,842)	48,283	29.49
German Russian (0)	0	<0.01
Greek (185)	440	0.27
Guyanese (0)	0	<0.01
Hungarian (548)	1,246	0.76
Icelander (13)	26	0.02
Iranian (41)	57	0.03
Irish (7,125)	26,219	16.02
Israeli (10)	23	0.01
Italian (3,245)	8,958	5.47
Latvian (0)	0	<0.01
Lithuanian (23)	96	0.06
Luxemburger (12)	12	0.01
Macedonian (135)	214	0.13
Maltese (0)	0	<0.01
New Zealander (0)	15	0.01
Northern European (51)	51	0.03
Norwegian (144)	696	0.43
Pennsylvania German (221)	315	0.19
Polish (1,157)	3,439	2.10
Portuguese (139)	219	0.13
Romanian (52)	155	0.09
Russian (265)	886	0.54
Scandinavian (70)	145	0.09
Scotch-Irish (1,300)	3,286	2.01
Scottish (1,441)	4,018	2.45
Serbian (54)	144	0.09
Slavic (24)	151	0.09
Slovak (71)	502	0.31
Slovene (37)	265	0.16
Soviet Union (8)	8	<0.01
Swedish (232)	1,373	0.84
Swiss (83)	700	0.43
Turkish (17)	32	0.02
Ukrainian (156)	334	0.20
Welsh (794)	3,351	2.05
West Indian, ex. Hispanic (157)	279	0.17
Bahamian (0)	0	<0.01
Barbadian (0)	0	<0.01
Belizean (0)	0	<0.01
Bermudan (0)	0	<0.01
British West Indian (0)	31	0.02
Dutch West Indian (0)	40	0.02
Haitian (110)	123	0.08
Jamaican (47)	77	0.05
Trinidadian/Tobagonian (0)	0	<0.01
U.S. Virgin Islander (0)	0	<0.01
West Indian (0)	0	<0.01
Other West Indian (0)	8	<0.01
Yugoslavian (12)	60	0.04

Hispanic Origin	Population	%
Hispanic or Latino (of any race)	2,312	1.39
Central American, ex. Mexican	144	0.09
Costa Rican	12	0.01
Guatemalan	32	0.02
Honduran	18	0.01
Nicaraguan	7	<0.01
Panamanian	19	0.01
Salvadoran	56	0.03
Other Central American	0	<0.01
Cuban	72	0.04
Dominican Republic	43	0.03
Mexican	1,197	0.72
Puerto Rican	400	0.24
South American	174	0.10
Argentinean	14	0.01
Bolivian	7	<0.01
Chilean	18	0.01
Colombian	71	0.04
Ecuadorian	11	0.01
Paraguayan	4	<0.01
Peruvian	26	0.02
Uruguayan	0	<0.01
Venezuelan	23	0.01
Other South American	0	<0.01
Other Hispanic or Latino	282	0.17

Race*	Population	%
African-American/Black (5,701)	7,309	4.39
Not Hispanic (5,643)	7,167	4.30
Hispanic (58)	142	0.09
American Indian/Alaska Native (462)	1,454	0.87
Not Hispanic (436)	1,380	0.83
Hispanic (26)	74	0.04
Alaska Athabascan *(Ala. Nat.)* (0)	0	<0.01
Aleut *(Alaska Native)* (0)	0	<0.01
Apache (11)	21	0.01
Arapaho (0)	0	<0.01
Blackfeet (9)	94	0.06
Canadian/French Am. Ind. (6)	12	0.01
Central American Ind. (0)	0	<0.01
Cherokee (114)	462	0.28
Cheyenne (1)	2	<0.01
Chickasaw (2)	3	<0.01
Chippewa (19)	33	0.02
Choctaw (8)	18	0.01
Colville (0)	0	<0.01
Comanche (4)	5	<0.01
Cree (1)	8	<0.01
Creek (5)	10	0.01
Crow (0)	2	<0.01
Delaware (10)	18	0.01
Hopi (0)	0	<0.01
Houma (0)	0	<0.01
Inupiat *(Alaska Native)* (0)	3	<0.01
Iroquois (12)	22	0.01
Kiowa (0)	1	<0.01
Lumbee (6)	10	0.01
Menominee (0)	0	<0.01
Mexican American Ind. (3)	7	<0.01
Navajo (6)	9	0.01
Osage (0)	1	<0.01
Ottawa (3)	3	<0.01
Paiute (0)	0	<0.01
Pima (0)	0	<0.01
Potawatomi (2)	2	<0.01
Pueblo (1)	1	<0.01
Puget Sound Salish (0)	0	<0.01
Seminole (1)	9	0.01
Shoshone (0)	4	<0.01
Sioux (21)	49	0.03
South American Ind. (0)	2	<0.01
Spanish American Ind. (0)	0	<0.01
Tlingit-Haida *(Alaska Native)* (0)	0	<0.01
Tohono O'Odham (0)	0	<0.01
Tsimshian *(Alaska Native)* (0)	0	<0.01
Ute (0)	1	<0.01
Yakama (0)	0	<0.01
Yaqui (0)	0	<0.01
Yuman (0)	0	<0.01
Yup'ik *(Alaska Native)* (0)	1	<0.01
Asian (1,237)	1,787	1.07
Not Hispanic (1,224)	1,741	1.05
Hispanic (13)	46	0.03
Bangladeshi (2)	2	<0.01
Bhutanese (0)	0	<0.01
Burmese (0)	0	<0.01
Cambodian (26)	46	0.03
Chinese, ex. Taiwanese (291)	378	0.23
Filipino (159)	284	0.17
Hmong (0)	0	<0.01
Indian (219)	305	0.18
Indonesian (7)	17	0.01
Japanese (76)	166	0.10
Korean (148)	219	0.13
Laotian (66)	85	0.05
Malaysian (2)	4	<0.01
Nepalese (3)	5	<0.01
Pakistani (21)	26	0.02
Sri Lankan (5)	6	<0.01
Taiwanese (18)	23	0.01
Thai (36)	81	0.05
Vietnamese (80)	123	0.07
Hawaii Native/Pacific Islander (36)	124	0.07
Not Hispanic (33)	105	0.06
Hispanic (3)	19	0.01
Fijian (0)	0	<0.01
Guamanian/Chamorro (11)	24	0.01
Marshallese (0)	0	<0.01
Native Hawaiian (10)	38	0.02
Samoan (1)	4	<0.01
Tongan (4)	8	<0.01
White (155,190)	158,164	95.00
Not Hispanic (153,811)	156,500	94.00
Hispanic (1,379)	1,664	1.00

*Notes: † The Census 2010 population figure is used to calculate the percentages in the Hispanic Origin and Race categories. Ancestry percentages are based on the 2006-2010 American Community Survey population (not shown); ‡ Numbers in parentheses indicate the number of people reporting a single ancestry; * Numbers in parentheses indicate the number of persons reporting this race alone, not in combination with any other race; Please refer to the User Guide for more information.*

Lorain County

Population: 301,356

Ancestry	Population	%
Afghan (0)	0	<0.01
African, Sub-Saharan (518)	843	0.28
African (418)	705	0.24
Cape Verdean (0)	0	<0.01
Ethiopian (10)	14	<0.01
Ghanaian (0)	11	<0.01
Kenyan (35)	35	0.01
Liberian (0)	0	<0.01
Nigerian (0)	11	<0.01
Senegalese (0)	0	<0.01
Sierra Leonean (0)	0	<0.01
Somalian (0)	0	<0.01
South African (0)	12	<0.01
Sudanese (55)	55	0.02
Ugandan (0)	0	<0.01
Zimbabwean (0)	0	<0.01
Other Sub-Saharan African (0)	0	<0.01
Albanian (3)	12	<0.01
Alsatian (0)	13	<0.01
American (18,528)	18,528	6.18
Arab (683)	1,464	0.49
Arab (309)	322	0.11
Egyptian (23)	23	0.01
Iraqi (0)	0	<0.01
Jordanian (30)	30	0.01
Lebanese (161)	762	0.25
Moroccan (41)	46	0.02
Palestinian (59)	82	0.03
Syrian (60)	185	0.06
Other Arab (0)	14	<0.01
Armenian (37)	103	0.03
Assyrian/Chaldean/Syriac (0)	0	<0.01
Australian (12)	26	0.01
Austrian (240)	1,125	0.38
Basque (0)	0	<0.01
Belgian (0)	76	0.03
Brazilian (0)	28	0.01
British (626)	1,177	0.39
Bulgarian (80)	145	0.05
Cajun (20)	32	0.01
Canadian (195)	487	0.16
Carpatho Rusyn (36)	50	0.02
Celtic (20)	60	0.02
Croatian (637)	1,774	0.59
Cypriot (0)	0	<0.01
Czech (522)	2,564	0.86
Czechoslovakian (321)	1,118	0.37
Danish (206)	734	0.24
Dutch (707)	4,971	1.66
Eastern European (300)	342	0.11
English (7,830)	32,511	10.85
Estonian (5)	17	0.01
European (1,534)	1,671	0.56
Finnish (159)	486	0.16
French, ex. Basque (748)	5,830	1.95
French Canadian (377)	1,229	0.41
German (22,162)	79,530	26.54
German Russian (18)	21	0.01
Greek (966)	2,176	0.73
Guyanese (0)	0	<0.01
Hungarian (5,551)	15,474	5.16
Icelander (0)	0	<0.01
Iranian (57)	57	0.02
Irish (12,155)	50,160	16.74
Israeli (16)	37	0.01
Italian (7,768)	24,705	8.25
Latvian (9)	96	0.03
Lithuanian (191)	836	0.28
Luxemburger (0)	0	<0.01
Macedonian (174)	280	0.09
Maltese (0)	0	<0.01
New Zealander (0)	0	<0.01
Northern European (61)	89	0.03
Norwegian (327)	1,503	0.50
Pennsylvania German (194)	386	0.13
Polish (8,652)	25,192	8.41
Portuguese (25)	247	0.08
Romanian (497)	1,042	0.35
Russian (717)	2,669	0.89
Scandinavian (53)	107	0.04
Scotch-Irish (1,508)	5,015	1.67
Scottish (1,629)	6,620	2.21
Serbian (373)	881	0.29
Slavic (71)	240	0.08
Slovak (3,466)	10,981	3.67
Slovene (614)	2,540	0.85
Soviet Union (0)	0	<0.01
Swedish (460)	2,004	0.67
Swiss (123)	1,198	0.40
Turkish (40)	62	0.02
Ukrainian (885)	2,512	0.84
Welsh (462)	3,341	1.12
West Indian, ex. Hispanic (118)	218	0.07
Bahamian (0)	0	<0.01
Barbadian (0)	0	<0.01
Belizean (0)	0	<0.01
Bermudan (0)	0	<0.01
British West Indian (9)	9	<0.01
Dutch West Indian (0)	0	<0.01
Haitian (43)	43	0.01
Jamaican (53)	116	0.04
Trinidadian/Tobagonian (0)	0	<0.01
U.S. Virgin Islander (0)	0	<0.01
West Indian (13)	50	0.02
Other West Indian (0)	0	<0.01
Yugoslavian (91)	259	0.09

Hispanic Origin	Population	%
Hispanic or Latino (of any race)	25,290	8.39
Central American, ex. Mexican	343	0.11
Costa Rican	27	0.01
Guatemalan	100	0.03
Honduran	53	0.02
Nicaraguan	43	0.01
Panamanian	62	0.02
Salvadoran	57	0.02
Other Central American	1	<0.01
Cuban	236	0.08
Dominican Republic	169	0.06
Mexican	5,490	1.82
Puerto Rican	17,580	5.83
South American	399	0.13
Argentinean	46	0.02
Bolivian	11	<0.01
Chilean	57	0.02
Colombian	111	0.04
Ecuadorian	41	0.01
Paraguayan	5	<0.01
Peruvian	74	0.02
Uruguayan	4	<0.01
Venezuelan	43	0.01
Other South American	7	<0.01
Other Hispanic or Latino	1,073	0.36

Race*	Population	%
African-American/Black (25,799)	30,995	10.29
Not Hispanic (24,289)	28,443	9.44
Hispanic (1,510)	2,552	0.85
American Indian/Alaska Native (883)	3,062	1.02
Not Hispanic (635)	2,468	0.82
Hispanic (248)	594	0.20
Alaska Athabascan *(Ala. Nat.)* (0)	0	<0.01
Aleut *(Alaska Native)* (2)	2	<0.01
Apache (9)	34	0.01
Arapaho (3)	3	<0.01
Blackfeet (21)	183	0.06
Canadian/French Am. Ind. (6)	12	<0.01
Central American Ind. (7)	12	<0.01
Cherokee (159)	861	0.29
Cheyenne (0)	6	<0.01
Chickasaw (8)	19	0.01
Chippewa (26)	48	0.02
Choctaw (16)	47	0.02
Colville (0)	0	<0.01
Comanche (0)	1	<0.01
Cree (2)	3	<0.01
Creek (1)	15	<0.01
Crow (2)	10	<0.01
Delaware (5)	10	<0.01
Hopi (6)	9	<0.01
Houma (0)	1	<0.01
Inupiat *(Alaska Native)* (0)	2	<0.01
Iroquois (24)	90	0.03
Kiowa (1)	3	<0.01
Lumbee (11)	22	0.01
Menominee (0)	0	<0.01
Mexican American Ind. (25)	41	0.01
Navajo (9)	41	0.01
Osage (0)	5	<0.01
Ottawa (3)	4	<0.01
Paiute (3)	4	<0.01
Pima (0)	0	<0.01
Potawatomi (6)	8	<0.01
Pueblo (11)	22	0.01
Puget Sound Salish (0)	1	<0.01
Seminole (7)	13	<0.01
Shoshone (3)	3	<0.01
Sioux (23)	79	0.03
South American Ind. (37)	96	0.03
Spanish American Ind. (1)	1	<0.01
Tlingit-Haida *(Alaska Native)* (4)	6	<0.01
Tohono O'Odham (0)	1	<0.01
Tsimshian *(Alaska Native)* (0)	0	<0.01
Ute (0)	0	<0.01
Yakama (0)	0	<0.01
Yaqui (0)	1	<0.01
Yuman (0)	0	<0.01
Yup'ik *(Alaska Native)* (0)	1	<0.01
Asian (2,811)	3,976	1.32
Not Hispanic (2,758)	3,782	1.25
Hispanic (53)	194	0.06
Bangladeshi (5)	5	<0.01
Bhutanese (0)	0	<0.01
Burmese (1)	8	<0.01
Cambodian (35)	42	0.01
Chinese, ex. Taiwanese (532)	722	0.24
Filipino (540)	878	0.29
Hmong (6)	6	<0.01
Indian (751)	893	0.30
Indonesian (18)	30	0.01
Japanese (154)	337	0.11
Korean (305)	482	0.16
Laotian (0)	5	<0.01
Malaysian (4)	4	<0.01
Nepalese (3)	3	<0.01
Pakistani (72)	78	0.03
Sri Lankan (9)	15	<0.01
Taiwanese (29)	41	0.01
Thai (32)	56	0.02
Vietnamese (217)	267	0.09
Hawaii Native/Pacific Islander (49)	267	0.09
Not Hispanic (35)	148	0.05
Hispanic (14)	119	0.04
Fijian (0)	0	<0.01
Guamanian/Chamorro (12)	31	0.01
Marshallese (1)	1	<0.01
Native Hawaiian (9)	64	0.02
Samoan (11)	23	0.01
Tongan (0)	3	<0.01
White (255,410)	263,438	87.42
Not Hispanic (241,543)	247,632	82.17
Hispanic (13,867)	15,806	5.24

*Notes: † The Census 2010 population figure is used to calculate the percentages in the Hispanic Origin and Race categories. Ancestry percentages are based on the 2006-2010 American Community Survey population (not shown); ‡ Numbers in parentheses indicate the number of people reporting a single ancestry; * Numbers in parentheses indicate the number of persons reporting this race alone, not in combination with any other race; Please refer to the User Guide for more information.*

Lucas County

Population: 441,815

Ancestry	Population	%
Afghan (187)	187	0.04
African, Sub-Saharan (3,067)	3,959	0.89
African (2,136)	2,868	0.65
Cape Verdean (0)	46	0.01
Ethiopian (229)	229	0.05
Ghanaian (69)	69	0.02
Kenyan (19)	19	<0.01
Liberian (0)	0	<0.01
Nigerian (536)	650	0.15
Senegalese (15)	15	<0.01
Sierra Leonean (0)	0	<0.01
Somalian (0)	0	<0.01
South African (27)	27	0.01
Sudanese (0)	0	<0.01
Ugandan (0)	0	<0.01
Zimbabwean (0)	0	<0.01
Other Sub-Saharan African (36)	36	0.01
Albanian (0)	28	0.01
Alsatian (0)	6	<0.01
American (17,015)	17,015	3.83
Arab (4,410)	5,952	1.34
Arab (930)	990	0.22
Egyptian (180)	210	0.05
Iraqi (15)	28	0.01
Jordanian (249)	293	0.07
Lebanese (2,016)	3,005	0.68
Moroccan (0)	0	<0.01
Palestinian (254)	310	0.07
Syrian (342)	648	0.15
Other Arab (424)	468	0.11
Armenian (86)	357	0.08
Assyrian/Chaldean/Syriac (27)	27	0.01
Australian (9)	9	<0.01
Austrian (229)	1,015	0.23
Basque (0)	0	<0.01
Belgian (184)	746	0.17
Brazilian (7)	7	<0.01
British (521)	1,427	0.32
Bulgarian (140)	372	0.08
Cajun (0)	0	<0.01
Canadian (424)	1,003	0.23
Carpatho Rusyn (6)	15	<0.01
Celtic (57)	73	0.02
Croatian (29)	310	0.07
Cypriot (0)	11	<0.01
Czech (341)	1,689	0.38
Czechoslovakian (229)	697	0.16
Danish (151)	893	0.20
Dutch (910)	6,731	1.52
Eastern European (142)	192	0.04
English (8,967)	35,376	7.97
Estonian (30)	30	0.01
European (2,910)	3,204	0.72
Finnish (175)	566	0.13
French, ex. Basque (2,735)	23,487	5.29
French Canadian (1,034)	3,609	0.81
German (48,514)	132,503	29.84
German Russian (0)	0	<0.01
Greek (862)	1,898	0.43
Guyanese (60)	60	0.01
Hungarian (3,663)	11,178	2.52
Icelander (13)	44	0.01
Iranian (123)	160	0.04
Irish (12,847)	58,662	13.21
Israeli (28)	35	0.01
Italian (5,132)	17,011	3.83
Latvian (80)	118	0.03
Lithuanian (158)	603	0.14
Luxemburger (12)	58	0.01
Macedonian (20)	30	0.01
Maltese (23)	49	0.01
New Zealander (0)	0	<0.01
Northern European (120)	120	0.03
Norwegian (360)	1,759	0.40
Pennsylvania German (179)	372	0.08
Polish (18,012)	42,924	9.67
Portuguese (58)	182	0.04
Romanian (166)	752	0.17
Russian (673)	2,219	0.50
Scandinavian (12)	113	0.03
Scotch-Irish (1,494)	4,371	0.98
Scottish (1,722)	7,222	1.63
Serbian (151)	238	0.05
Slavic (27)	110	0.02
Slovak (494)	1,650	0.37
Slovene (109)	322	0.07
Soviet Union (0)	0	<0.01
Swedish (496)	2,805	0.63
Swiss (321)	2,347	0.53
Turkish (193)	373	0.08
Ukrainian (328)	990	0.22
Welsh (531)	2,337	0.53
West Indian, ex. Hispanic (868)	1,151	0.26
Bahamian (0)	0	<0.01
Barbadian (0)	0	<0.01
Belizean (19)	19	<0.01
Bermudan (0)	0	<0.01
British West Indian (22)	22	<0.01
Dutch West Indian (9)	18	<0.01
Haitian (64)	97	0.02
Jamaican (714)	926	0.21
Trinidadian/Tobagonian (11)	11	<0.01
U.S. Virgin Islander (0)	9	<0.01
West Indian (29)	49	0.01
Other West Indian (0)	0	<0.01
Yugoslavian (99)	183	0.04

Hispanic Origin	Population	%
Hispanic or Latino (of any race)	26,974	6.11
Central American, ex. Mexican	396	0.09
Costa Rican	20	<0.01
Guatemalan	114	0.03
Honduran	36	0.01
Nicaraguan	113	0.03
Panamanian	70	0.02
Salvadoran	38	0.01
Other Central American	5	<0.01
Cuban	388	0.09
Dominican Republic	90	0.02
Mexican	22,028	4.99
Puerto Rican	1,482	0.34
South American	460	0.10
Argentinean	55	0.01
Bolivian	11	<0.01
Chilean	40	0.01
Colombian	90	0.02
Ecuadorian	38	0.01
Paraguayan	24	0.01
Peruvian	89	0.02
Uruguayan	5	<0.01
Venezuelan	95	0.02
Other South American	13	<0.01
Other Hispanic or Latino	2,130	0.48

Race*	Population	%
African-American/Black (83,926)	92,260	20.88
Not Hispanic (82,541)	89,631	20.29
Hispanic (1,385)	2,629	0.60
American Indian/Alaska Native (1,349)	4,246	0.96
Not Hispanic (955)	3,390	0.77
Hispanic (394)	856	0.19
Alaska Athabascan *(Ala. Nat.)* (1)	2	<0.01
Aleut *(Alaska Native)* (1)	3	<0.01
Apache (23)	80	0.02
Arapaho (0)	7	<0.01
Blackfeet (38)	187	0.04
Canadian/French Am. Ind. (8)	30	0.01
Central American Ind. (0)	0	<0.01
Cherokee (201)	968	0.22
Cheyenne (1)	8	<0.01
Chickasaw (5)	9	<0.01
Chippewa (104)	200	0.05
Choctaw (19)	69	0.02
Colville (0)	0	<0.01
Comanche (1)	3	<0.01
Cree (5)	15	<0.01
Creek (2)	26	0.01
Crow (1)	10	<0.01
Delaware (9)	11	<0.01
Hopi (4)	5	<0.01
Houma (0)	0	<0.01
Inupiat *(Alaska Native)* (2)	7	<0.01
Iroquois (20)	55	0.01
Kiowa (0)	1	<0.01
Lumbee (6)	16	<0.01
Menominee (9)	11	<0.01
Mexican American Ind. (49)	133	0.03
Navajo (15)	36	0.01
Osage (0)	3	<0.01
Ottawa (11)	54	0.01
Paiute (0)	0	<0.01
Pima (0)	0	<0.01
Potawatomi (15)	36	0.01
Pueblo (7)	16	<0.01
Puget Sound Salish (0)	0	<0.01
Seminole (5)	20	<0.01
Shoshone (1)	7	<0.01
Sioux (23)	57	0.01
South American Ind. (20)	33	0.01
Spanish American Ind. (4)	8	<0.01
Tlingit-Haida *(Alaska Native)* (1)	2	<0.01
Tohono O'Odham (0)	0	<0.01
Tsimshian *(Alaska Native)* (0)	0	<0.01
Ute (0)	1	<0.01
Yakama (0)	0	<0.01
Yaqui (5)	6	<0.01
Yuman (0)	0	<0.01
Yup'ik *(Alaska Native)* (0)	0	<0.01
Asian (6,764)	8,801	1.99
Not Hispanic (6,676)	8,493	1.92
Hispanic (88)	308	0.07
Bangladeshi (23)	26	0.01
Bhutanese (0)	0	<0.01
Burmese (14)	20	<0.01
Cambodian (14)	25	0.01
Chinese, ex. Taiwanese (1,883)	2,174	0.49
Filipino (613)	999	0.23
Hmong (5)	7	<0.01
Indian (2,028)	2,289	0.52
Indonesian (19)	40	0.01
Japanese (194)	464	0.11
Korean (534)	803	0.18
Laotian (110)	162	0.04
Malaysian (23)	42	0.01
Nepalese (37)	45	0.01
Pakistani (306)	354	0.08
Sri Lankan (23)	27	0.01
Taiwanese (62)	84	0.02
Thai (121)	197	0.04
Vietnamese (428)	533	0.12
Hawaii Native/Pacific Islander (113)	382	0.09
Not Hispanic (91)	308	0.07
Hispanic (22)	74	0.02
Fijian (2)	2	<0.01
Guamanian/Chamorro (26)	48	0.01
Marshallese (0)	0	<0.01
Native Hawaiian (29)	119	0.03
Samoan (23)	54	0.01
Tongan (1)	2	<0.01
White (326,868)	339,206	76.78
Not Hispanic (313,596)	322,945	73.10
Hispanic (13,272)	16,261	3.68

*Notes: † The Census 2010 population figure is used to calculate the percentages in the Hispanic Origin and Race categories. Ancestry percentages are based on the 2006-2010 American Community Survey population (not shown); ‡ Numbers in parentheses indicate the number of people reporting a single ancestry; * Numbers in parentheses indicate the number of persons reporting this race alone, not in combination with any other race; Please refer to the User Guide for more information.*

Mahoning County

Population: 238,823

Ancestry	Population	%
Afghan (0)	0	<0.01
African, Sub-Saharan (3,001)	3,338	1.38
African (2,932)	3,188	1.32
Cape Verdean (0)	0	<0.01
Ethiopian (14)	65	0.03
Ghanaian (0)	0	<0.01
Kenyan (0)	0	<0.01
Liberian (0)	0	<0.01
Nigerian (0)	0	<0.01
Senegalese (0)	0	<0.01
Sierra Leonean (0)	0	<0.01
Somalian (0)	0	<0.01
South African (0)	30	0.01
Sudanese (0)	0	<0.01
Ugandan (0)	0	<0.01
Zimbabwean (0)	0	<0.01
Other Sub-Saharan African (55)	55	0.02
Albanian (23)	73	0.03
Alsatian (0)	0	<0.01
American (10,247)	10,247	4.24
Arab (1,473)	2,445	1.01
Arab (556)	696	0.29
Egyptian (146)	196	0.08
Iraqi (0)	0	<0.01
Jordanian (135)	135	0.06
Lebanese (464)	1,098	0.45
Moroccan (0)	0	<0.01
Palestinian (80)	97	0.04
Syrian (14)	141	0.06
Other Arab (78)	82	0.03
Armenian (8)	78	0.03
Assyrian/Chaldean/Syriac (0)	0	<0.01
Australian (0)	79	0.03
Austrian (63)	359	0.15
Basque (0)	0	<0.01
Belgian (0)	122	0.05
Brazilian (0)	0	<0.01
British (317)	544	0.22
Bulgarian (59)	119	0.05
Cajun (0)	0	<0.01
Canadian (45)	145	0.06
Carpatho Rusyn (78)	118	0.05
Celtic (52)	65	0.03
Croatian (1,430)	4,200	1.74
Cypriot (21)	21	0.01
Czech (225)	1,304	0.54
Czechoslovakian (229)	378	0.16
Danish (0)	267	0.11
Dutch (536)	3,379	1.40
Eastern European (71)	96	0.04
English (4,980)	21,540	8.90
Estonian (16)	16	0.01
European (1,104)	1,190	0.49
Finnish (70)	389	0.16
French, ex. Basque (450)	3,826	1.58
French Canadian (186)	570	0.24
German (13,004)	51,681	21.36
German Russian (0)	1	<0.01
Greek (2,071)	4,074	1.68
Guyanese (0)	0	<0.01
Hungarian (2,227)	7,298	3.02
Icelander (0)	0	<0.01
Iranian (10)	29	0.01
Irish (7,655)	40,063	16.56
Israeli (0)	0	<0.01
Italian (19,058)	44,626	18.45
Latvian (0)	0	<0.01
Lithuanian (109)	462	0.19
Luxemburger (0)	7	<0.01
Macedonian (39)	80	0.03
Maltese (0)	152	0.06
New Zealander (0)	0	<0.01
Northern European (121)	143	0.06
Norwegian (126)	475	0.20
Pennsylvania German (382)	859	0.36
Polish (3,620)	11,693	4.83
Portuguese (10)	100	0.04
Romanian (815)	1,741	0.72
Russian (524)	1,838	0.76
Scandinavian (24)	90	0.04
Scotch-Irish (1,401)	3,735	1.54
Scottish (640)	3,641	1.51
Serbian (259)	702	0.29
Slavic (108)	274	0.11
Slovak (6,975)	17,550	7.26
Slovene (150)	418	0.17
Soviet Union (0)	0	<0.01
Swedish (769)	2,630	1.09
Swiss (273)	1,061	0.44
Turkish (12)	12	<0.01
Ukrainian (1,439)	3,465	1.43
Welsh (578)	5,295	2.19
West Indian, ex. Hispanic (115)	238	0.10
Bahamian (0)	0	<0.01
Barbadian (0)	8	<0.01
Belizean (0)	0	<0.01
Bermudan (0)	0	<0.01
British West Indian (0)	0	<0.01
Dutch West Indian (0)	0	<0.01
Haitian (9)	43	0.02
Jamaican (106)	154	0.06
Trinidadian/Tobagonian (0)	0	<0.01
U.S. Virgin Islander (0)	0	<0.01
West Indian (0)	33	0.01
Other West Indian (0)	0	<0.01
Yugoslavian (103)	197	0.08

Hispanic Origin	Population	%
Hispanic or Latino (of any race)	11,136	4.66
Central American, ex. Mexican	265	0.11
Costa Rican	11	<0.01
Guatemalan	72	0.03
Honduran	78	0.03
Nicaraguan	9	<0.01
Panamanian	29	0.01
Salvadoran	65	0.03
Other Central American	1	<0.01
Cuban	172	0.07
Dominican Republic	321	0.13
Mexican	2,326	0.97
Puerto Rican	6,904	2.89
South American	294	0.12
Argentinean	24	0.01
Bolivian	4	<0.01
Chilean	16	0.01
Colombian	130	0.05
Ecuadorian	24	0.01
Paraguayan	5	<0.01
Peruvian	59	0.02
Uruguayan	6	<0.01
Venezuelan	23	0.01
Other South American	3	<0.01
Other Hispanic or Latino	854	0.36

Race*	Population	%
African-American/Black (37,433)	40,500	16.96
Not Hispanic (36,400)	38,901	16.29
Hispanic (1,033)	1,599	0.67
American Indian/Alaska Native (491)	1,808	0.76
Not Hispanic (392)	1,498	0.63
Hispanic (99)	310	0.13
Alaska Athabascan *(Ala. Nat.)* (1)	5	<0.01
Aleut *(Alaska Native)* (2)	2	<0.01
Apache (2)	29	0.01
Arapaho (0)	4	<0.01
Blackfeet (12)	116	0.05
Canadian/French Am. Ind. (1)	1	<0.01
Central American Ind. (1)	2	<0.01
Cherokee (110)	502	0.21
Cheyenne (0)	1	<0.01
Chickasaw (1)	1	<0.01
Chippewa (8)	20	0.01
Choctaw (3)	19	0.01
Colville (0)	0	<0.01
Comanche (3)	7	<0.01
Cree (0)	1	<0.01
Creek (1)	4	<0.01
Crow (0)	3	<0.01
Delaware (6)	9	<0.01
Hopi (3)	3	<0.01
Houma (0)	0	<0.01
Inupiat *(Alaska Native)* (1)	2	<0.01
Iroquois (11)	45	0.02
Kiowa (0)	0	<0.01
Lumbee (2)	2	<0.01
Menominee (0)	1	<0.01
Mexican American Ind. (16)	38	0.02
Navajo (3)	12	0.01
Osage (0)	0	<0.01
Ottawa (0)	0	<0.01
Paiute (0)	0	<0.01
Pima (0)	1	<0.01
Potawatomi (2)	4	<0.01
Pueblo (0)	0	<0.01
Puget Sound Salish (0)	0	<0.01
Seminole (2)	10	<0.01
Shoshone (1)	1	<0.01
Sioux (9)	35	0.01
South American Ind. (15)	32	0.01
Spanish American Ind. (3)	3	<0.01
Tlingit-Haida *(Alaska Native)* (1)	5	<0.01
Tohono O'Odham (0)	2	<0.01
Tsimshian *(Alaska Native)* (0)	0	<0.01
Ute (1)	1	<0.01
Yakama (0)	0	<0.01
Yaqui (2)	2	<0.01
Yuman (0)	0	<0.01
Yup'ik *(Alaska Native)* (0)	0	<0.01
Asian (1,682)	2,364	0.99
Not Hispanic (1,647)	2,264	0.95
Hispanic (35)	100	0.04
Bangladeshi (11)	14	0.01
Bhutanese (0)	0	<0.01
Burmese (0)	0	<0.01
Cambodian (11)	16	0.01
Chinese, ex. Taiwanese (278)	367	0.15
Filipino (172)	311	0.13
Hmong (5)	11	<0.01
Indian (564)	653	0.27
Indonesian (6)	8	<0.01
Japanese (69)	152	0.06
Korean (153)	255	0.11
Laotian (7)	12	0.01
Malaysian (5)	5	<0.01
Nepalese (14)	15	0.01
Pakistani (98)	113	0.05
Sri Lankan (3)	4	<0.01
Taiwanese (6)	7	<0.01
Thai (34)	59	0.02
Vietnamese (154)	197	0.08
Hawaii Native/Pacific Islander (51)	180	0.08
Not Hispanic (36)	128	0.05
Hispanic (15)	52	0.02
Fijian (0)	0	<0.01
Guamanian/Chamorro (13)	24	0.01
Marshallese (0)	0	<0.01
Native Hawaiian (14)	50	0.02
Samoan (7)	15	0.01
Tongan (0)	1	<0.01
White (190,848)	195,006	81.65
Not Hispanic (185,230)	188,538	78.94
Hispanic (5,618)	6,468	2.71

*Notes: † The Census 2010 population figure is used to calculate the percentages in the Hispanic Origin and Race categories. Ancestry percentages are based on the 2006-2010 American Community Survey population (not shown); ‡ Numbers in parentheses indicate the number of people reporting a single ancestry; * Numbers in parentheses indicate the number of persons reporting this race alone, not in combination with any other race; Please refer to the User Guide for more information.*

Medina County

Population: 172,332

Ancestry	Population	%
Afghan (0)	0	<0.01
African, Sub-Saharan (151)	198	0.12
African (130)	155	0.09
Cape Verdean (8)	16	0.01
Ethiopian (0)	0	<0.01
Ghanaian (0)	0	<0.01
Kenyan (0)	0	<0.01
Liberian (0)	0	<0.01
Nigerian (0)	0	<0.01
Senegalese (13)	13	0.01
Sierra Leonean (0)	0	<0.01
Somalian (0)	14	0.01
South African (0)	0	<0.01
Sudanese (0)	0	<0.01
Ugandan (0)	0	<0.01
Zimbabwean (0)	0	<0.01
Other Sub-Saharan African (0)	0	<0.01
Albanian (0)	14	0.01
Alsatian (0)	0	<0.01
American (12,543)	12,543	7.37
Arab (504)	1,097	0.64
Arab (29)	62	0.04
Egyptian (10)	31	0.02
Iraqi (0)	0	<0.01
Jordanian (82)	82	0.05
Lebanese (208)	647	0.38
Moroccan (0)	0	<0.01
Palestinian (152)	188	0.11
Syrian (23)	87	0.05
Other Arab (0)	0	<0.01
Armenian (61)	213	0.13
Assyrian/Chaldean/Syriac (0)	0	<0.01
Australian (0)	0	<0.01
Austrian (164)	647	0.38
Basque (0)	0	<0.01
Belgian (0)	90	0.05
Brazilian (0)	0	<0.01
British (277)	537	0.32
Bulgarian (36)	72	0.04
Cajun (0)	0	<0.01
Canadian (176)	221	0.13
Carpatho Rusyn (0)	38	0.02
Celtic (19)	28	0.02
Croatian (306)	1,083	0.64
Cypriot (0)	0	<0.01
Czech (645)	3,358	1.97
Czechoslovakian (156)	576	0.34
Danish (106)	599	0.35
Dutch (500)	2,909	1.71
Eastern European (34)	71	0.04
English (5,191)	19,753	11.61
Estonian (11)	11	0.01
European (1,146)	1,250	0.73
Finnish (74)	373	0.22
French, ex. Basque (832)	5,622	3.30
French Canadian (131)	702	0.41
German (16,103)	55,560	32.66
German Russian (0)	15	0.01
Greek (484)	1,330	0.78
Guyanese (10)	25	0.01
Hungarian (2,690)	7,887	4.64
Icelander (0)	0	<0.01
Iranian (94)	144	0.08
Irish (6,101)	31,210	18.34
Israeli (11)	11	0.01
Italian (5,370)	18,275	10.74
Latvian (64)	78	0.05
Lithuanian (135)	438	0.26
Luxemburger (0)	0	<0.01
Macedonian (296)	328	0.19
Maltese (9)	37	0.02
New Zealander (0)	0	<0.01
Northern European (47)	65	0.04
Norwegian (161)	886	0.52
Pennsylvania German (301)	465	0.27
Polish (5,177)	17,719	10.41
Portuguese (405)	609	0.36
Romanian (513)	870	0.51
Russian (391)	2,091	1.23
Scandinavian (78)	171	0.10
Scotch-Irish (1,017)	2,972	1.75
Scottish (1,122)	4,219	2.48
Serbian (369)	915	0.54
Slavic (125)	304	0.18
Slovak (2,484)	7,074	4.16
Slovene (321)	1,377	0.81
Soviet Union (0)	0	<0.01
Swedish (322)	1,366	0.80
Swiss (331)	1,698	1.00
Turkish (63)	238	0.14
Ukrainian (837)	2,197	1.29
Welsh (392)	1,943	1.14
West Indian, ex. Hispanic (0)	43	0.03
Bahamian (0)	0	<0.01
Barbadian (0)	0	<0.01
Belizean (0)	0	<0.01
Bermudan (0)	0	<0.01
British West Indian (0)	0	<0.01
Dutch West Indian (0)	10	0.01
Haitian (0)	0	<0.01
Jamaican (0)	33	0.02
Trinidadian/Tobagonian (0)	0	<0.01
U.S. Virgin Islander (0)	0	<0.01
West Indian (0)	0	<0.01
Other West Indian (0)	0	<0.01
Yugoslavian (141)	418	0.25

Hispanic Origin	Population	%
Hispanic or Latino (of any race)	2,747	1.59
Central American, ex. Mexican	193	0.11
Costa Rican	10	0.01
Guatemalan	86	0.05
Honduran	19	0.01
Nicaraguan	15	0.01
Panamanian	28	0.02
Salvadoran	34	0.02
Other Central American	1	<0.01
Cuban	67	0.04
Dominican Republic	25	0.01
Mexican	950	0.55
Puerto Rican	1,016	0.59
South American	193	0.11
Argentinean	37	0.02
Bolivian	1	<0.01
Chilean	13	0.01
Colombian	57	0.03
Ecuadorian	17	0.01
Paraguayan	3	<0.01
Peruvian	39	0.02
Uruguayan	1	<0.01
Venezuelan	25	0.01
Other South American	0	<0.01
Other Hispanic or Latino	303	0.18

Race*	Population	%
African-American/Black (2,027)	2,834	1.64
Not Hispanic (1,982)	2,714	1.57
Hispanic (45)	120	0.07
American Indian/Alaska Native (247)	944	0.55
Not Hispanic (216)	865	0.50
Hispanic (31)	79	0.05
Alaska Athabascan *(Ala. Nat.)* (0)	1	<0.01
Aleut *(Alaska Native)* (0)	0	<0.01
Apache (10)	18	0.01
Arapaho (0)	1	<0.01
Blackfeet (9)	86	0.05
Canadian/French Am. Ind. (2)	5	<0.01
Central American Ind. (1)	4	<0.01
Cherokee (64)	334	0.19
Cheyenne (0)	3	<0.01
Chickasaw (0)	5	<0.01
Chippewa (13)	23	0.01
Choctaw (1)	12	0.01
Colville (0)	0	<0.01
Comanche (4)	8	<0.01
Cree (0)	1	<0.01
Creek (0)	4	<0.01
Crow (0)	4	<0.01
Delaware (0)	4	<0.01
Hopi (0)	1	<0.01
Houma (0)	0	<0.01
Inupiat *(Alaska Native)* (0)	3	<0.01
Iroquois (2)	19	0.01
Kiowa (0)	0	<0.01
Lumbee (8)	13	0.01
Menominee (0)	0	<0.01
Mexican American Ind. (5)	8	<0.01
Navajo (2)	6	<0.01
Osage (0)	0	<0.01
Ottawa (1)	1	<0.01
Paiute (0)	0	<0.01
Pima (0)	0	<0.01
Potawatomi (1)	6	<0.01
Pueblo (0)	2	<0.01
Puget Sound Salish (0)	0	<0.01
Seminole (0)	1	<0.01
Shoshone (0)	0	<0.01
Sioux (11)	30	0.02
South American Ind. (2)	4	<0.01
Spanish American Ind. (0)	0	<0.01
Tlingit-Haida *(Alaska Native)* (0)	0	<0.01
Tohono O'Odham (0)	0	<0.01
Tsimshian *(Alaska Native)* (0)	0	<0.01
Ute (0)	1	<0.01
Yakama (0)	0	<0.01
Yaqui (0)	0	<0.01
Yuman (2)	4	<0.01
Yup'ik *(Alaska Native)* (0)	0	<0.01
Asian (1,660)	2,154	1.25
Not Hispanic (1,638)	2,108	1.22
Hispanic (22)	46	0.03
Bangladeshi (0)	0	<0.01
Bhutanese (0)	0	<0.01
Burmese (0)	0	<0.01
Cambodian (8)	13	0.01
Chinese, ex. Taiwanese (269)	311	0.18
Filipino (233)	373	0.22
Hmong (12)	12	0.01
Indian (532)	629	0.36
Indonesian (12)	14	0.01
Japanese (74)	163	0.09
Korean (193)	265	0.15
Laotian (38)	44	0.03
Malaysian (1)	1	<0.01
Nepalese (0)	0	<0.01
Pakistani (18)	27	0.02
Sri Lankan (0)	1	<0.01
Taiwanese (23)	26	0.02
Thai (10)	15	0.01
Vietnamese (149)	167	0.10
Hawaii Native/Pacific Islander (18)	60	0.03
Not Hispanic (17)	52	0.03
Hispanic (1)	8	<0.01
Fijian (0)	0	<0.01
Guamanian/Chamorro (2)	5	<0.01
Marshallese (1)	1	<0.01
Native Hawaiian (4)	21	0.01
Samoan (3)	4	<0.01
Tongan (0)	0	<0.01
White (165,642)	167,628	97.27
Not Hispanic (163,794)	165,548	96.06
Hispanic (1,848)	2,080	1.21

*Notes: † The Census 2010 population figure is used to calculate the percentages in the Hispanic Origin and Race categories. Ancestry percentages are based on the 2006-2010 American Community Survey population (not shown); ‡ Numbers in parentheses indicate the number of people reporting a single ancestry; * Numbers in parentheses indicate the number of persons reporting this race alone, not in combination with any other race; Please refer to the User Guide for more information.*

Miami County

Population: 102,506

Ancestry	Population	%
Afghan (0)	0	<0.01
African, Sub-Saharan (113)	145	0.14
African (113)	145	0.14
Cape Verdean (0)	0	<0.01
Ethiopian (0)	0	<0.01
Ghanaian (0)	0	<0.01
Kenyan (0)	0	<0.01
Liberian (0)	0	<0.01
Nigerian (0)	0	<0.01
Senegalese (0)	0	<0.01
Sierra Leonean (0)	0	<0.01
Somalian (0)	0	<0.01
South African (0)	0	<0.01
Sudanese (0)	0	<0.01
Ugandan (0)	0	<0.01
Zimbabwean (0)	0	<0.01
Other Sub-Saharan African (0)	0	<0.01
Albanian (24)	30	0.03
Alsatian (0)	7	0.01
American (9,988)	9,988	9.76
Arab (42)	137	0.13
Arab (19)	19	0.02
Egyptian (0)	0	<0.01
Iraqi (0)	0	<0.01
Jordanian (0)	0	<0.01
Lebanese (9)	104	0.10
Moroccan (0)	0	<0.01
Palestinian (0)	0	<0.01
Syrian (14)	14	0.01
Other Arab (0)	0	<0.01
Armenian (0)	0	<0.01
Assyrian/Chaldean/Syriac (0)	0	<0.01
Australian (11)	25	0.02
Austrian (73)	160	0.16
Basque (0)	0	<0.01
Belgian (0)	44	0.04
Brazilian (0)	0	<0.01
British (195)	443	0.43
Bulgarian (0)	0	<0.01
Cajun (0)	0	<0.01
Canadian (95)	137	0.13
Carpatho Rusyn (0)	0	<0.01
Celtic (0)	7	0.01
Croatian (26)	78	0.08
Cypriot (0)	0	<0.01
Czech (90)	274	0.27
Czechoslovakian (98)	151	0.15
Danish (51)	155	0.15
Dutch (445)	2,246	2.20
Eastern European (65)	65	0.06
English (4,240)	10,409	10.17
Estonian (0)	0	<0.01
European (1,110)	1,207	1.18
Finnish (23)	31	0.03
French, ex. Basque (823)	3,488	3.41
French Canadian (97)	209	0.20
German (17,407)	35,267	34.47
German Russian (0)	0	<0.01
Greek (89)	198	0.19
Guyanese (0)	0	<0.01
Hungarian (187)	603	0.59
Icelander (0)	9	0.01
Iranian (0)	0	<0.01
Irish (4,138)	13,801	13.49
Israeli (0)	0	<0.01
Italian (910)	2,915	2.85
Latvian (13)	13	0.01
Lithuanian (0)	83	0.08
Luxemburger (0)	12	0.01
Macedonian (0)	8	0.01
Maltese (10)	10	0.01
New Zealander (0)	0	<0.01
Northern European (49)	80	0.08
Norwegian (83)	348	0.34
Pennsylvania German (134)	189	0.18
Polish (671)	1,928	1.88
Portuguese (34)	86	0.08
Romanian (66)	98	0.10
Russian (72)	169	0.17
Scandinavian (31)	31	0.03
Scotch-Irish (646)	1,966	1.92
Scottish (1,088)	2,588	2.53
Serbian (0)	0	<0.01
Slavic (18)	54	0.05
Slovak (31)	115	0.11
Slovene (0)	47	0.05
Soviet Union (0)	0	<0.01
Swedish (37)	601	0.59
Swiss (62)	510	0.50
Turkish (0)	0	<0.01
Ukrainian (64)	96	0.09
Welsh (300)	1,252	1.22
West Indian, ex. Hispanic (0)	10	0.01
Bahamian (0)	10	0.01
Barbadian (0)	0	<0.01
Belizean (0)	0	<0.01
Bermudan (0)	0	<0.01
British West Indian (0)	0	<0.01
Dutch West Indian (0)	0	<0.01
Haitian (0)	0	<0.01
Jamaican (0)	0	<0.01
Trinidadian/Tobagonian (0)	0	<0.01
U.S. Virgin Islander (0)	0	<0.01
West Indian (0)	0	<0.01
Other West Indian (0)	0	<0.01
Yugoslavian (32)	104	0.10

Hispanic Origin	Population	%
Hispanic or Latino (of any race)	1,341	1.31
Central American, ex. Mexican	57	0.06
Costa Rican	1	<0.01
Guatemalan	42	0.04
Honduran	8	0.01
Nicaraguan	2	<0.01
Panamanian	3	<0.01
Salvadoran	1	<0.01
Other Central American	0	<0.01
Cuban	33	0.03
Dominican Republic	9	0.01
Mexican	855	0.83
Puerto Rican	130	0.13
South American	56	0.05
Argentinean	1	<0.01
Bolivian	2	<0.01
Chilean	5	<0.01
Colombian	23	0.02
Ecuadorian	7	0.01
Paraguayan	0	<0.01
Peruvian	10	0.01
Uruguayan	0	<0.01
Venezuelan	7	0.01
Other South American	1	<0.01
Other Hispanic or Latino	201	0.20

Race*	Population	%
African-American/Black (2,084)	3,137	3.06
Not Hispanic (2,063)	3,087	3.01
Hispanic (21)	50	0.05
American Indian/Alaska Native (189)	665	0.65
Not Hispanic (173)	635	0.62
Hispanic (16)	30	0.03
Alaska Athabascan *(Ala. Nat.)* (0)	1	<0.01
Aleut *(Alaska Native)* (0)	0	<0.01
Apache (0)	2	<0.01
Arapaho (1)	1	<0.01
Blackfeet (7)	36	0.04
Canadian/French Am. Ind. (1)	7	0.01
Central American Ind. (3)	3	<0.01
Cherokee (58)	227	0.22
Cheyenne (0)	2	<0.01
Chickasaw (0)	0	<0.01
Chippewa (4)	7	0.01
Choctaw (4)	6	0.01
Colville (0)	0	<0.01
Comanche (0)	0	<0.01
Cree (0)	0	<0.01
Creek (1)	2	<0.01
Crow (0)	0	<0.01
Delaware (2)	5	<0.01
Hopi (1)	1	<0.01
Houma (0)	0	<0.01
Inupiat *(Alaska Native)* (0)	0	<0.01
Iroquois (7)	14	0.01
Kiowa (0)	0	<0.01
Lumbee (0)	5	<0.01
Menominee (0)	1	<0.01
Mexican American Ind. (3)	5	<0.01
Navajo (0)	2	<0.01
Osage (0)	0	<0.01
Ottawa (0)	0	<0.01
Paiute (0)	0	<0.01
Pima (0)	0	<0.01
Potawatomi (0)	1	<0.01
Pueblo (0)	1	<0.01
Puget Sound Salish (0)	0	<0.01
Seminole (1)	2	<0.01
Shoshone (0)	0	<0.01
Sioux (5)	16	0.02
South American Ind. (0)	0	<0.01
Spanish American Ind. (1)	1	<0.01
Tlingit-Haida *(Alaska Native)* (0)	0	<0.01
Tohono O'Odham (0)	0	<0.01
Tsimshian *(Alaska Native)* (0)	0	<0.01
Ute (0)	0	<0.01
Yakama (0)	0	<0.01
Yaqui (0)	1	<0.01
Yuman (0)	0	<0.01
Yup'ik *(Alaska Native)* (0)	0	<0.01
Asian (1,218)	1,494	1.46
Not Hispanic (1,213)	1,479	1.44
Hispanic (5)	15	0.01
Bangladeshi (7)	7	0.01
Bhutanese (0)	0	<0.01
Burmese (0)	0	<0.01
Cambodian (3)	3	<0.01
Chinese, ex. Taiwanese (167)	186	0.18
Filipino (147)	237	0.23
Hmong (0)	0	<0.01
Indian (334)	355	0.35
Indonesian (7)	13	0.01
Japanese (324)	390	0.38
Korean (74)	108	0.11
Laotian (3)	3	<0.01
Malaysian (1)	3	<0.01
Nepalese (3)	3	<0.01
Pakistani (3)	5	<0.01
Sri Lankan (7)	8	0.01
Taiwanese (13)	13	0.01
Thai (16)	26	0.03
Vietnamese (64)	80	0.08
Hawaii Native/Pacific Islander (15)	42	0.04
Not Hispanic (13)	34	0.03
Hispanic (2)	8	0.01
Fijian (0)	0	<0.01
Guamanian/Chamorro (3)	6	0.01
Marshallese (0)	0	<0.01
Native Hawaiian (5)	18	0.02
Samoan (1)	3	<0.01
Tongan (0)	0	<0.01
White (96,722)	98,447	96.04
Not Hispanic (95,908)	97,527	95.14
Hispanic (814)	920	0.90

*Notes: † The Census 2010 population figure is used to calculate the percentages in the Hispanic Origin and Race categories. Ancestry percentages are based on the 2006-2010 American Community Survey population (not shown); ‡ Numbers in parentheses indicate the number of people reporting a single ancestry; * Numbers in parentheses indicate the number of persons reporting this race alone, not in combination with any other race; Please refer to the User Guide for more information.*

Montgomery County

Population: 535,153

Ancestry	Population	%
Afghan (12)	12	<0.01
African, Sub-Saharan (3,349)	4,246	0.79
African (2,457)	3,166	0.59
Cape Verdean (18)	94	0.02
Ethiopian (87)	103	0.02
Ghanaian (59)	70	0.01
Kenyan (10)	10	<0.01
Liberian (0)	0	<0.01
Nigerian (420)	465	0.09
Senegalese (0)	0	<0.01
Sierra Leonean (0)	0	<0.01
Somalian (0)	0	<0.01
South African (45)	76	0.01
Sudanese (0)	0	<0.01
Ugandan (0)	0	<0.01
Zimbabwean (0)	0	<0.01
Other Sub-Saharan African (253)	262	0.05
Albanian (144)	144	0.03
Alsatian (13)	26	<0.01
American (52,457)	52,457	9.74
Arab (1,900)	2,858	0.53
Arab (387)	398	0.07
Egyptian (165)	251	0.05
Iraqi (401)	401	0.07
Jordanian (150)	279	0.05
Lebanese (342)	922	0.17
Moroccan (66)	94	0.02
Palestinian (219)	239	0.04
Syrian (72)	135	0.03
Other Arab (98)	139	0.03
Armenian (51)	65	0.01
Assyrian/Chaldean/Syriac (25)	44	0.01
Australian (9)	120	0.02
Austrian (231)	853	0.16
Basque (0)	0	<0.01
Belgian (54)	385	0.07
Brazilian (82)	93	0.02
British (1,012)	2,510	0.47
Bulgarian (86)	216	0.04
Cajun (31)	76	0.01
Canadian (207)	547	0.10
Carpatho Rusyn (0)	0	<0.01
Celtic (6)	16	<0.01
Croatian (253)	497	0.09
Cypriot (0)	0	<0.01
Czech (309)	1,310	0.24
Czechoslovakian (231)	625	0.12
Danish (166)	910	0.17
Dutch (1,834)	9,203	1.71
Eastern European (361)	471	0.09
English (17,233)	47,269	8.78
Estonian (0)	39	0.01
European (5,187)	5,893	1.09
Finnish (167)	456	0.08
French, ex. Basque (2,036)	12,340	2.29
French Canadian (620)	1,589	0.30
German (55,815)	134,170	24.92
German Russian (0)	0	<0.01
Greek (1,061)	2,164	0.40
Guyanese (123)	157	0.03
Hungarian (1,753)	4,146	0.77
Icelander (9)	61	0.01
Iranian (121)	166	0.03
Irish (17,193)	68,965	12.81
Israeli (45)	45	0.01
Italian (6,606)	18,464	3.43
Latvian (29)	142	0.03
Lithuanian (278)	1,098	0.20
Luxemburger (0)	13	<0.01
Macedonian (9)	218	0.04
Maltese (0)	0	<0.01
New Zealander (0)	11	<0.01
Northern European (140)	152	0.03
Norwegian (790)	2,193	0.41
Pennsylvania German (269)	486	0.09
Polish (3,463)	10,812	2.01
Portuguese (37)	299	0.06
Romanian (275)	683	0.13
Russian (980)	2,173	0.40
Scandinavian (223)	647	0.12
Scotch-Irish (3,718)	8,851	1.64
Scottish (3,709)	10,342	1.92
Serbian (20)	175	0.03
Slavic (43)	125	0.02
Slovak (432)	1,181	0.22
Slovene (81)	308	0.06
Soviet Union (0)	0	<0.01
Swedish (1,036)	3,796	0.70
Swiss (437)	1,953	0.36
Turkish (208)	276	0.05
Ukrainian (263)	585	0.11
Welsh (1,083)	4,789	0.89
West Indian, ex. Hispanic (517)	977	0.18
Bahamian (0)	0	<0.01
Barbadian (23)	23	<0.01
Belizean (27)	27	0.01
Bermudan (18)	18	<0.01
British West Indian (16)	16	<0.01
Dutch West Indian (37)	107	0.02
Haitian (81)	105	0.02
Jamaican (173)	310	0.06
Trinidadian/Tobagonian (62)	62	0.01
U.S. Virgin Islander (0)	0	<0.01
West Indian (80)	309	0.06
Other West Indian (0)	0	<0.01
Yugoslavian (201)	340	0.06

Hispanic Origin	Population	%
Hispanic or Latino (of any race)	12,177	2.28
Central American, ex. Mexican	839	0.16
Costa Rican	164	0.03
Guatemalan	188	0.04
Honduran	142	0.03
Nicaraguan	39	0.01
Panamanian	159	0.03
Salvadoran	140	0.03
Other Central American	7	<0.01
Cuban	447	0.08
Dominican Republic	183	0.03
Mexican	6,544	1.22
Puerto Rican	1,854	0.35
South American	931	0.17
Argentinean	59	0.01
Bolivian	61	0.01
Chilean	49	0.01
Colombian	215	0.04
Ecuadorian	342	0.06
Paraguayan	7	<0.01
Peruvian	133	0.02
Uruguayan	11	<0.01
Venezuelan	50	0.01
Other South American	4	<0.01
Other Hispanic or Latino	1,379	0.26

Race*	Population	%
African-American/Black (111,870)	119,559	22.34
Not Hispanic (111,105)	118,252	22.10
Hispanic (765)	1,307	0.24
American Indian/Alaska Native (1,242)	4,628	0.86
Not Hispanic (1,096)	4,245	0.79
Hispanic (146)	383	0.07
Alaska Athabascan *(Ala. Nat.)* (1)	2	<0.01
Aleut *(Alaska Native)* (5)	9	<0.01
Apache (21)	52	0.01
Arapaho (3)	11	<0.01
Blackfeet (43)	242	0.05
Canadian/French Am. Ind. (5)	12	<0.01
Central American Ind. (2)	7	<0.01
Cherokee (288)	1,458	0.27
Cheyenne (0)	9	<0.01
Chickasaw (6)	9	<0.01
Chippewa (28)	79	0.01
Choctaw (20)	47	0.01
Colville (0)	0	<0.01
Comanche (7)	10	<0.01
Cree (2)	5	<0.01
Creek (15)	43	0.01
Crow (1)	13	<0.01
Delaware (2)	5	<0.01
Hopi (2)	3	<0.01
Houma (0)	0	<0.01
Inupiat *(Alaska Native)* (3)	5	<0.01
Iroquois (19)	61	0.01
Kiowa (0)	0	<0.01
Lumbee (6)	8	<0.01
Menominee (1)	7	<0.01
Mexican American Ind. (22)	45	0.01
Navajo (20)	45	0.01
Osage (1)	2	<0.01
Ottawa (9)	16	<0.01
Paiute (0)	0	<0.01
Pima (5)	6	<0.01
Potawatomi (6)	7	<0.01
Pueblo (1)	9	<0.01
Puget Sound Salish (2)	4	<0.01
Seminole (5)	28	0.01
Shoshone (3)	6	<0.01
Sioux (35)	114	0.02
South American Ind. (12)	30	0.01
Spanish American Ind. (3)	6	<0.01
Tlingit-Haida *(Alaska Native)* (1)	2	<0.01
Tohono O'Odham (0)	0	<0.01
Tsimshian *(Alaska Native)* (3)	3	<0.01
Ute (1)	5	<0.01
Yakama (0)	0	<0.01
Yaqui (0)	0	<0.01
Yuman (1)	1	<0.01
Yup'ik *(Alaska Native)* (5)	5	<0.01
Asian (9,273)	12,254	2.29
Not Hispanic (9,195)	11,992	2.24
Hispanic (78)	262	0.05
Bangladeshi (30)	38	0.01
Bhutanese (0)	0	<0.01
Burmese (17)	21	<0.01
Cambodian (88)	114	0.02
Chinese, ex. Taiwanese (1,404)	1,716	0.32
Filipino (1,187)	1,996	0.37
Hmong (2)	2	<0.01
Indian (3,182)	3,507	0.66
Indonesian (40)	89	0.02
Japanese (487)	972	0.18
Korean (699)	1,152	0.22
Laotian (45)	69	0.01
Malaysian (21)	23	<0.01
Nepalese (15)	16	<0.01
Pakistani (241)	278	0.05
Sri Lankan (36)	41	0.01
Taiwanese (126)	152	0.03
Thai (148)	247	0.05
Vietnamese (1,178)	1,330	0.25
Hawaii Native/Pacific Islander (177)	548	0.10
Not Hispanic (163)	496	0.09
Hispanic (14)	52	0.01
Fijian (0)	5	<0.01
Guamanian/Chamorro (62)	133	0.02
Marshallese (1)	5	<0.01
Native Hawaiian (64)	195	0.04
Samoan (23)	58	0.01
Tongan (0)	3	<0.01
White (395,272)	406,488	75.96
Not Hispanic (388,917)	399,143	74.58
Hispanic (6,355)	7,345	1.37

*Notes: † The Census 2010 population figure is used to calculate the percentages in the Hispanic Origin and Race categories. Ancestry percentages are based on the 2006-2010 American Community Survey population (not shown); ‡ Numbers in parentheses indicate the number of people reporting a single ancestry; * Numbers in parentheses indicate the number of persons reporting this race alone, not in combination with any other race; Please refer to the User Guide for more information.*

Portage County

Population: 161,419

Ancestry	Population	%
Afghan (0)	0	<0.01
African, Sub-Saharan (177)	363	0.23
African (8)	61	0.04
Cape Verdean (0)	0	<0.01
Ethiopian (0)	0	<0.01
Ghanaian (57)	93	0.06
Kenyan (0)	0	<0.01
Liberian (0)	0	<0.01
Nigerian (76)	76	0.05
Senegalese (0)	0	<0.01
Sierra Leonean (23)	23	0.01
Somalian (0)	0	<0.01
South African (13)	19	0.01
Sudanese (0)	0	<0.01
Ugandan (0)	0	<0.01
Zimbabwean (0)	0	<0.01
Other Sub-Saharan African (0)	91	0.06
Albanian (1)	1	<0.01
Alsatian (0)	0	<0.01
American (9,158)	9,158	5.73
Arab (511)	1,086	0.68
Arab (37)	174	0.11
Egyptian (59)	85	0.05
Iraqi (0)	0	<0.01
Jordanian (94)	94	0.06
Lebanese (147)	251	0.16
Moroccan (0)	63	0.04
Palestinian (18)	146	0.09
Syrian (63)	111	0.07
Other Arab (93)	162	0.10
Armenian (17)	27	0.02
Assyrian/Chaldean/Syriac (0)	0	<0.01
Australian (0)	6	<0.01
Austrian (123)	514	0.32
Basque (0)	0	<0.01
Belgian (59)	262	0.16
Brazilian (29)	29	0.02
British (300)	806	0.50
Bulgarian (0)	14	0.01
Cajun (0)	11	0.01
Canadian (36)	236	0.15
Carpatho Rusyn (16)	65	0.04
Celtic (12)	26	0.02
Croatian (196)	744	0.47
Cypriot (0)	0	<0.01
Czech (555)	2,099	1.31
Czechoslovakian (203)	502	0.31
Danish (121)	387	0.24
Dutch (569)	3,617	2.26
Eastern European (96)	128	0.08
English (4,544)	18,433	11.52
Estonian (0)	0	<0.01
European (1,073)	1,227	0.77
Finnish (66)	258	0.16
French, ex. Basque (584)	4,050	2.53
French Canadian (147)	485	0.30
German (14,445)	49,152	30.73
German Russian (0)	0	<0.01
Greek (317)	830	0.52
Guyanese (16)	16	0.01
Hungarian (1,620)	6,159	3.85
Icelander (0)	10	0.01
Iranian (10)	55	0.03
Irish (6,142)	27,355	17.10
Israeli (0)	0	<0.01
Italian (6,334)	17,622	11.02
Latvian (30)	52	0.03
Lithuanian (134)	512	0.32
Luxemburger (0)	13	0.01
Macedonian (0)	15	0.01
Maltese (0)	0	<0.01
New Zealander (0)	0	<0.01
Northern European (18)	18	0.01
Norwegian (148)	723	0.45
Pennsylvania German (352)	485	0.30
Polish (3,519)	10,497	6.56
Portuguese (15)	46	0.03
Romanian (267)	645	0.40
Russian (406)	1,485	0.93
Scandinavian (23)	90	0.06
Scotch-Irish (1,176)	3,355	2.10
Scottish (919)	4,128	2.58
Serbian (18)	222	0.14
Slavic (133)	224	0.14
Slovak (1,063)	3,826	2.39
Slovene (523)	1,139	0.71
Soviet Union (0)	0	<0.01
Swedish (572)	1,768	1.11
Swiss (164)	1,081	0.68
Turkish (33)	65	0.04
Ukrainian (319)	813	0.51
Welsh (652)	3,117	1.95
West Indian, ex. Hispanic (91)	120	0.08
Bahamian (0)	0	<0.01
Barbadian (0)	0	<0.01
Belizean (0)	0	<0.01
Bermudan (0)	0	<0.01
British West Indian (0)	0	<0.01
Dutch West Indian (0)	0	<0.01
Haitian (0)	0	<0.01
Jamaican (91)	120	0.08
Trinidadian/Tobagonian (0)	0	<0.01
U.S. Virgin Islander (0)	0	<0.01
West Indian (0)	0	<0.01
Other West Indian (0)	0	<0.01
Yugoslavian (90)	326	0.20

Hispanic Origin	Population	%
Hispanic or Latino (of any race)	2,073	1.28
Central American, ex. Mexican	152	0.09
Costa Rican	20	0.01
Guatemalan	40	0.02
Honduran	32	0.02
Nicaraguan	11	0.01
Panamanian	17	0.01
Salvadoran	31	0.02
Other Central American	1	<0.01
Cuban	96	0.06
Dominican Republic	16	0.01
Mexican	875	0.54
Puerto Rican	496	0.31
South American	144	0.09
Argentinean	19	0.01
Bolivian	3	<0.01
Chilean	12	0.01
Colombian	59	0.04
Ecuadorian	11	0.01
Paraguayan	0	<0.01
Peruvian	22	0.01
Uruguayan	3	<0.01
Venezuelan	15	0.01
Other South American	0	<0.01
Other Hispanic or Latino	294	0.18

Race*	Population	%
African-American/Black (6,687)	8,080	5.01
Not Hispanic (6,611)	7,910	4.90
Hispanic (76)	170	0.11
American Indian/Alaska Native (296)	1,136	0.70
Not Hispanic (274)	1,063	0.66
Hispanic (22)	73	0.05
Alaska Athabascan *(Ala. Nat.)* (4)	4	<0.01
Aleut *(Alaska Native)* (0)	0	<0.01
Apache (4)	14	0.01
Arapaho (0)	2	<0.01
Blackfeet (17)	70	0.04
Canadian/French Am. Ind. (2)	2	<0.01
Central American Ind. (0)	0	<0.01
Cherokee (73)	352	0.22
Cheyenne (0)	7	<0.01
Chickasaw (0)	2	<0.01
Chippewa (21)	38	0.02
Choctaw (4)	17	0.01
Colville (0)	0	<0.01
Comanche (0)	2	<0.01
Cree (2)	6	<0.01
Creek (0)	7	<0.01
Crow (0)	3	<0.01
Delaware (0)	5	<0.01
Hopi (0)	0	<0.01
Houma (0)	1	<0.01
Inupiat *(Alaska Native)* (2)	2	<0.01
Iroquois (6)	30	0.02
Kiowa (0)	0	<0.01
Lumbee (4)	6	<0.01
Menominee (1)	1	<0.01
Mexican American Ind. (3)	6	<0.01
Navajo (3)	11	0.01
Osage (0)	2	<0.01
Ottawa (0)	0	<0.01
Paiute (0)	0	<0.01
Pima (1)	1	<0.01
Potawatomi (1)	4	<0.01
Pueblo (0)	0	<0.01
Puget Sound Salish (0)	0	<0.01
Seminole (2)	5	<0.01
Shoshone (0)	2	<0.01
Sioux (15)	32	0.02
South American Ind. (3)	5	<0.01
Spanish American Ind. (0)	0	<0.01
Tlingit-Haida *(Alaska Native)* (0)	0	<0.01
Tohono O'Odham (0)	0	<0.01
Tsimshian *(Alaska Native)* (0)	0	<0.01
Ute (0)	0	<0.01
Yakama (0)	0	<0.01
Yaqui (1)	1	<0.01
Yuman (3)	3	<0.01
Yup'ik *(Alaska Native)* (1)	1	<0.01
Asian (2,305)	2,884	1.79
Not Hispanic (2,283)	2,844	1.76
Hispanic (22)	40	0.02
Bangladeshi (6)	7	<0.01
Bhutanese (16)	16	0.01
Burmese (5)	6	<0.01
Cambodian (4)	8	<0.01
Chinese, ex. Taiwanese (746)	816	0.51
Filipino (180)	307	0.19
Hmong (8)	8	<0.01
Indian (676)	765	0.47
Indonesian (11)	13	0.01
Japanese (84)	182	0.11
Korean (174)	236	0.15
Laotian (11)	21	0.01
Malaysian (14)	16	0.01
Nepalese (55)	55	0.03
Pakistani (37)	41	0.03
Sri Lankan (21)	24	0.01
Taiwanese (51)	59	0.04
Thai (24)	32	0.02
Vietnamese (109)	135	0.08
Hawaii Native/Pacific Islander (40)	136	0.08
Not Hispanic (33)	121	0.07
Hispanic (7)	15	0.01
Fijian (1)	3	<0.01
Guamanian/Chamorro (12)	38	0.02
Marshallese (0)	0	<0.01
Native Hawaiian (5)	36	0.02
Samoan (5)	11	0.01
Tongan (0)	0	<0.01
White (148,936)	151,473	93.84
Not Hispanic (147,527)	149,826	92.82
Hispanic (1,409)	1,647	1.02

*Notes: † The Census 2010 population figure is used to calculate the percentages in the Hispanic Origin and Race categories. Ancestry percentages are based on the 2006-2010 American Community Survey population (not shown); ‡ Numbers in parentheses indicate the number of people reporting a single ancestry; * Numbers in parentheses indicate the number of persons reporting this race alone, not in combination with any other race; Please refer to the User Guide for more information.*

Richland County

Population: 124,475

Ancestry	Population	%
Afghan (0)	0	<0.01
African, Sub-Saharan (751)	950	0.75
African (732)	914	0.73
Cape Verdean (0)	0	<0.01
Ethiopian (0)	0	<0.01
Ghanaian (19)	19	0.02
Kenyan (0)	0	<0.01
Liberian (0)	0	<0.01
Nigerian (0)	0	<0.01
Senegalese (0)	8	0.01
Sierra Leonean (0)	0	<0.01
Somalian (0)	0	<0.01
South African (0)	0	<0.01
Sudanese (0)	0	<0.01
Ugandan (0)	0	<0.01
Zimbabwean (0)	0	<0.01
Other Sub-Saharan African (0)	9	0.01
Albanian (29)	29	0.02
Alsatian (0)	0	<0.01
American (10,022)	10,022	7.96
Arab (212)	217	0.17
Arab (177)	177	0.14
Egyptian (0)	0	<0.01
Iraqi (4)	4	<0.01
Jordanian (18)	18	0.01
Lebanese (0)	0	<0.01
Moroccan (0)	0	<0.01
Palestinian (13)	18	0.01
Syrian (0)	0	<0.01
Other Arab (0)	0	<0.01
Armenian (11)	43	0.03
Assyrian/Chaldean/Syriac (0)	0	<0.01
Australian (20)	80	0.06
Austrian (121)	597	0.47
Basque (0)	0	<0.01
Belgian (12)	80	0.06
Brazilian (23)	64	0.05
British (154)	416	0.33
Bulgarian (6)	15	0.01
Cajun (0)	0	<0.01
Canadian (51)	79	0.06
Carpatho Rusyn (0)	43	0.03
Celtic (13)	13	0.01
Croatian (51)	169	0.13
Cypriot (3)	3	<0.01
Czech (171)	348	0.28
Czechoslovakian (106)	410	0.33
Danish (62)	224	0.18
Dutch (402)	2,808	2.23
Eastern European (18)	18	0.01
English (7,367)	15,829	12.56
Estonian (0)	0	<0.01
European (614)	634	0.50
Finnish (42)	97	0.08
French, ex. Basque (601)	2,831	2.25
French Canadian (157)	274	0.22
German (17,415)	38,612	30.65
German Russian (0)	0	<0.01
Greek (215)	419	0.33
Guyanese (0)	0	<0.01
Hungarian (415)	1,475	1.17
Icelander (0)	0	<0.01
Iranian (0)	0	<0.01
Irish (4,037)	16,794	13.33
Israeli (0)	0	<0.01
Italian (1,609)	4,341	3.45
Latvian (8)	30	0.02
Lithuanian (96)	235	0.19
Luxemburger (0)	4	<0.01
Macedonian (71)	103	0.08
Maltese (26)	26	0.02
New Zealander (0)	0	<0.01
Northern European (0)	0	<0.01
Norwegian (241)	521	0.41
Pennsylvania German (470)	794	0.63
Polish (1,004)	2,803	2.22
Portuguese (12)	12	0.01
Romanian (53)	175	0.14
Russian (55)	215	0.17
Scandinavian (0)	69	0.05
Scotch-Irish (756)	2,632	2.09
Scottish (668)	2,475	1.96
Serbian (32)	140	0.11
Slavic (22)	51	0.04
Slovak (82)	235	0.19
Slovene (12)	29	0.02
Soviet Union (0)	0	<0.01
Swedish (171)	698	0.55
Swiss (606)	1,639	1.30
Turkish (0)	9	0.01
Ukrainian (15)	110	0.09
Welsh (218)	1,327	1.05
West Indian, ex. Hispanic (146)	226	0.18
Bahamian (0)	0	<0.01
Barbadian (0)	40	0.03
Belizean (0)	0	<0.01
Bermudan (0)	0	<0.01
British West Indian (0)	0	<0.01
Dutch West Indian (0)	0	<0.01
Haitian (9)	9	0.01
Jamaican (129)	169	0.13
Trinidadian/Tobagonian (0)	0	<0.01
U.S. Virgin Islander (0)	0	<0.01
West Indian (8)	8	0.01
Other West Indian (0)	0	<0.01
Yugoslavian (319)	777	0.62

Hispanic Origin	Population	%
Hispanic or Latino (of any race)	1,732	1.39
Central American, ex. Mexican	67	0.05
Costa Rican	2	<0.01
Guatemalan	21	0.02
Honduran	4	<0.01
Nicaraguan	8	0.01
Panamanian	20	0.02
Salvadoran	7	0.01
Other Central American	5	<0.01
Cuban	46	0.04
Dominican Republic	18	0.01
Mexican	978	0.79
Puerto Rican	282	0.23
South American	93	0.07
Argentinean	21	0.02
Bolivian	0	<0.01
Chilean	2	<0.01
Colombian	35	0.03
Ecuadorian	7	0.01
Paraguayan	0	<0.01
Peruvian	22	0.02
Uruguayan	0	<0.01
Venezuelan	6	<0.01
Other South American	0	<0.01
Other Hispanic or Latino	248	0.20

Race*	Population	%
African-American/Black (11,709)	13,120	10.54
Not Hispanic (11,612)	12,948	10.40
Hispanic (97)	172	0.14
American Indian/Alaska Native (240)	956	0.77
Not Hispanic (218)	899	0.72
Hispanic (22)	57	0.05
Alaska Athabascan *(Ala. Nat.)* (0)	0	<0.01
Aleut *(Alaska Native)* (0)	1	<0.01
Apache (1)	19	0.02
Arapaho (0)	2	<0.01
Blackfeet (12)	42	0.03
Canadian/French Am. Ind. (1)	6	<0.01
Central American Ind. (0)	0	<0.01
Cherokee (53)	321	0.26
Cheyenne (0)	6	<0.01
Chickasaw (0)	2	<0.01
Chippewa (8)	11	0.01
Choctaw (1)	21	0.02
Colville (0)	0	<0.01
Comanche (0)	2	<0.01
Cree (0)	0	<0.01
Creek (0)	12	0.01
Crow (0)	2	<0.01
Delaware (0)	1	<0.01
Hopi (2)	4	<0.01
Houma (0)	0	<0.01
Inupiat *(Alaska Native)* (0)	0	<0.01
Iroquois (11)	24	0.02
Kiowa (0)	0	<0.01
Lumbee (1)	1	<0.01
Menominee (5)	5	<0.01
Mexican American Ind. (8)	8	0.01
Navajo (2)	4	<0.01
Osage (0)	0	<0.01
Ottawa (0)	2	<0.01
Paiute (0)	0	<0.01
Pima (0)	0	<0.01
Potawatomi (0)	0	<0.01
Pueblo (1)	1	<0.01
Puget Sound Salish (1)	1	<0.01
Seminole (0)	1	<0.01
Shoshone (0)	1	<0.01
Sioux (4)	22	0.02
South American Ind. (0)	0	<0.01
Spanish American Ind. (0)	0	<0.01
Tlingit-Haida *(Alaska Native)* (0)	0	<0.01
Tohono O'Odham (1)	1	<0.01
Tsimshian *(Alaska Native)* (0)	0	<0.01
Ute (0)	0	<0.01
Yakama (2)	4	<0.01
Yaqui (0)	0	<0.01
Yuman (0)	0	<0.01
Yup'ik *(Alaska Native)* (1)	1	<0.01
Asian (808)	1,097	0.88
Not Hispanic (800)	1,078	0.87
Hispanic (8)	19	0.02
Bangladeshi (0)	0	<0.01
Bhutanese (0)	0	<0.01
Burmese (3)	3	<0.01
Cambodian (2)	3	<0.01
Chinese, ex. Taiwanese (106)	141	0.11
Filipino (102)	171	0.14
Hmong (0)	0	<0.01
Indian (264)	300	0.24
Indonesian (2)	2	<0.01
Japanese (63)	109	0.09
Korean (103)	166	0.13
Laotian (5)	5	<0.01
Malaysian (0)	0	<0.01
Nepalese (2)	2	<0.01
Pakistani (13)	17	0.01
Sri Lankan (2)	3	<0.01
Taiwanese (15)	23	0.02
Thai (7)	13	0.01
Vietnamese (75)	85	0.07
Hawaii Native/Pacific Islander (37)	112	0.09
Not Hispanic (32)	101	0.08
Hispanic (5)	11	0.01
Fijian (0)	0	<0.01
Guamanian/Chamorro (15)	35	0.03
Marshallese (0)	0	<0.01
Native Hawaiian (9)	26	0.02
Samoan (6)	22	0.02
Tongan (0)	0	<0.01
White (108,870)	111,108	89.26
Not Hispanic (107,726)	109,824	88.23
Hispanic (1,144)	1,284	1.03

*Notes: † The Census 2010 population figure is used to calculate the percentages in the Hispanic Origin and Race categories. Ancestry percentages are based on the 2006-2010 American Community Survey population (not shown); ‡ Numbers in parentheses indicate the number of people reporting a single ancestry; * Numbers in parentheses indicate the number of persons reporting this race alone, not in combination with any other race; Please refer to the User Guide for more information.*

Stark County

Population: 375,586

Ancestry	Population	%
Afghan (0)	0	<0.01
African, Sub-Saharan (3,722)	4,085	1.09
African (3,501)	3,854	1.02
Cape Verdean (46)	56	0.01
Ethiopian (57)	57	0.02
Ghanaian (0)	0	<0.01
Kenyan (0)	0	<0.01
Liberian (38)	38	0.01
Nigerian (0)	0	<0.01
Senegalese (0)	0	<0.01
Sierra Leonean (0)	0	<0.01
Somalian (0)	0	<0.01
South African (61)	61	0.02
Sudanese (0)	0	<0.01
Ugandan (0)	0	<0.01
Zimbabwean (0)	0	<0.01
Other Sub-Saharan African (19)	19	0.01
Albanian (102)	247	0.07
Alsatian (0)	8	<0.01
American (28,916)	28,916	7.68
Arab (1,165)	2,453	0.65
Arab (280)	408	0.11
Egyptian (9)	50	0.01
Iraqi (15)	15	<0.01
Jordanian (0)	70	0.02
Lebanese (552)	1,314	0.35
Moroccan (0)	0	<0.01
Palestinian (0)	0	<0.01
Syrian (300)	530	0.14
Other Arab (9)	66	0.02
Armenian (9)	127	0.03
Assyrian/Chaldean/Syriac (0)	0	<0.01
Australian (30)	53	0.01
Austrian (417)	1,239	0.33
Basque (0)	0	<0.01
Belgian (16)	379	0.10
Brazilian (154)	154	0.04
British (597)	1,141	0.30
Bulgarian (11)	66	0.02
Cajun (15)	15	<0.01
Canadian (342)	558	0.15
Carpatho Rusyn (0)	13	<0.01
Celtic (32)	83	0.02
Croatian (371)	1,701	0.45
Cypriot (43)	43	0.01
Czech (452)	1,822	0.48
Czechoslovakian (254)	504	0.13
Danish (124)	784	0.21
Dutch (1,226)	9,341	2.48
Eastern European (192)	237	0.06
English (10,395)	38,102	10.12
Estonian (0)	0	<0.01
European (2,258)	2,452	0.65
Finnish (124)	349	0.09
French, ex. Basque (2,120)	14,425	3.83
French Canadian (295)	904	0.24
German (42,182)	126,329	33.57
German Russian (0)	0	<0.01
Greek (2,068)	3,895	1.03
Guyanese (0)	0	<0.01
Hungarian (2,389)	7,189	1.91
Icelander (0)	0	<0.01
Iranian (85)	85	0.02
Irish (13,451)	58,384	15.51
Israeli (0)	0	<0.01
Italian (15,557)	37,971	10.09
Latvian (14)	28	0.01
Lithuanian (201)	695	0.18
Luxemburger (13)	23	0.01
Macedonian (276)	401	0.11
Maltese (0)	0	<0.01
New Zealander (0)	0	<0.01
Northern European (80)	102	0.03
Norwegian (258)	1,065	0.28
Pennsylvania German (779)	1,397	0.37
Polish (3,271)	11,279	3.00
Portuguese (262)	573	0.15
Romanian (1,292)	3,717	0.99
Russian (599)	2,217	0.59
Scandinavian (39)	139	0.04
Scotch-Irish (2,713)	7,885	2.10
Scottish (1,947)	7,932	2.11
Serbian (420)	849	0.23
Slavic (75)	267	0.07
Slovak (1,626)	4,539	1.21
Slovene (229)	585	0.16
Soviet Union (0)	13	<0.01
Swedish (587)	3,093	0.82
Swiss (1,532)	6,978	1.85
Turkish (25)	45	0.01
Ukrainian (687)	1,515	0.40
Welsh (1,219)	6,556	1.74
West Indian, ex. Hispanic (35)	139	0.04
Bahamian (16)	16	<0.01
Barbadian (0)	0	<0.01
Belizean (0)	0	<0.01
Bermudan (0)	0	<0.01
British West Indian (0)	10	<0.01
Dutch West Indian (0)	0	<0.01
Haitian (0)	16	<0.01
Jamaican (19)	67	0.02
Trinidadian/Tobagonian (0)	0	<0.01
U.S. Virgin Islander (0)	0	<0.01
West Indian (0)	30	0.01
Other West Indian (0)	0	<0.01
Yugoslavian (229)	460	0.12

Hispanic Origin	Population	%
Hispanic or Latino (of any race)	5,965	1.59
Central American, ex. Mexican	730	0.19
Costa Rican	18	<0.01
Guatemalan	306	0.08
Honduran	212	0.06
Nicaraguan	40	0.01
Panamanian	57	0.02
Salvadoran	83	0.02
Other Central American	14	<0.01
Cuban	165	0.04
Dominican Republic	64	0.02
Mexican	2,413	0.64
Puerto Rican	924	0.25
South American	279	0.07
Argentinean	56	0.01
Bolivian	14	<0.01
Chilean	11	<0.01
Colombian	99	0.03
Ecuadorian	26	0.01
Paraguayan	4	<0.01
Peruvian	42	0.01
Uruguayan	3	<0.01
Venezuelan	24	0.01
Other South American	0	<0.01
Other Hispanic or Latino	1,390	0.37

Race*	Population	%
African-American/Black (28,537)	34,010	9.06
Not Hispanic (28,272)	33,503	8.92
Hispanic (265)	507	0.13
American Indian/Alaska Native (961)	3,253	0.87
Not Hispanic (808)	2,950	0.79
Hispanic (153)	303	0.08
Alaska Athabascan *(Ala. Nat.)* (0)	1	<0.01
Aleut *(Alaska Native)* (0)	0	<0.01
Apache (9)	44	0.01
Arapaho (0)	0	<0.01
Blackfeet (17)	208	0.06
Canadian/French Am. Ind. (2)	9	<0.01
Central American Ind. (73)	73	0.02
Cherokee (218)	934	0.25
Cheyenne (2)	14	<0.01
Chickasaw (7)	16	<0.01
Chippewa (13)	39	0.01
Choctaw (7)	43	0.01
Colville (0)	0	<0.01
Comanche (1)	13	<0.01
Cree (1)	6	<0.01
Creek (11)	18	<0.01
Crow (1)	13	<0.01
Delaware (84)	147	0.04
Hopi (1)	5	<0.01
Houma (2)	2	<0.01
Inupiat *(Alaska Native)* (6)	8	<0.01
Iroquois (30)	104	0.03
Kiowa (2)	8	<0.01
Lumbee (19)	23	0.01
Menominee (3)	4	<0.01
Mexican American Ind. (33)	43	0.01
Navajo (8)	31	0.01
Osage (0)	4	<0.01
Ottawa (4)	15	<0.01
Paiute (0)	0	<0.01
Pima (1)	2	<0.01
Potawatomi (6)	17	<0.01
Pueblo (2)	4	<0.01
Puget Sound Salish (0)	0	<0.01
Seminole (2)	20	0.01
Shoshone (0)	0	<0.01
Sioux (15)	62	0.02
South American Ind. (4)	11	<0.01
Spanish American Ind. (2)	4	<0.01
Tlingit-Haida *(Alaska Native)* (1)	1	<0.01
Tohono O'Odham (0)	0	<0.01
Tsimshian *(Alaska Native)* (0)	0	<0.01
Ute (0)	0	<0.01
Yakama (0)	0	<0.01
Yaqui (1)	1	<0.01
Yuman (1)	9	<0.01
Yup'ik *(Alaska Native)* (0)	0	<0.01
Asian (2,764)	3,754	1.00
Not Hispanic (2,736)	3,683	0.98
Hispanic (28)	71	0.02
Bangladeshi (8)	8	<0.01
Bhutanese (0)	0	<0.01
Burmese (2)	3	<0.01
Cambodian (1)	5	<0.01
Chinese, ex. Taiwanese (617)	727	0.19
Filipino (364)	671	0.18
Hmong (10)	10	<0.01
Indian (855)	969	0.26
Indonesian (5)	7	<0.01
Japanese (139)	294	0.08
Korean (272)	412	0.11
Laotian (28)	35	0.01
Malaysian (5)	11	<0.01
Nepalese (2)	2	<0.01
Pakistani (96)	106	0.03
Sri Lankan (13)	13	<0.01
Taiwanese (17)	22	0.01
Thai (37)	83	0.02
Vietnamese (194)	245	0.07
Hawaii Native/Pacific Islander (85)	244	0.06
Not Hispanic (63)	197	0.05
Hispanic (22)	47	0.01
Fijian (0)	1	<0.01
Guamanian/Chamorro (32)	58	0.02
Marshallese (0)	0	<0.01
Native Hawaiian (21)	86	0.02
Samoan (3)	14	<0.01
Tongan (0)	2	<0.01
White (333,191)	340,942	90.78
Not Hispanic (329,497)	336,694	89.64
Hispanic (3,694)	4,248	1.13

*Notes: † The Census 2010 population figure is used to calculate the percentages in the Hispanic Origin and Race categories. Ancestry percentages are based on the 2006-2010 American Community Survey population (not shown); ‡ Numbers in parentheses indicate the number of people reporting a single ancestry; * Numbers in parentheses indicate the number of persons reporting this race alone, not in combination with any other race; Please refer to the User Guide for more information.*

Summit County

Population: 541,781

Ancestry	Population	%
Afghan (13)	13	<0.01
African, Sub-Saharan (2,025)	2,791	0.51
African (1,804)	2,372	0.44
Cape Verdean (0)	33	0.01
Ethiopian (14)	42	0.01
Ghanaian (0)	0	<0.01
Kenyan (30)	46	0.01
Liberian (29)	29	0.01
Nigerian (12)	24	<0.01
Senegalese (0)	0	<0.01
Sierra Leonean (0)	0	<0.01
Somalian (23)	23	<0.01
South African (58)	103	0.02
Sudanese (0)	0	<0.01
Ugandan (0)	0	<0.01
Zimbabwean (12)	12	<0.01
Other Sub-Saharan African (43)	107	0.02
Albanian (272)	390	0.07
Alsatian (17)	74	0.01
American (24,520)	24,520	4.51
Arab (2,893)	4,596	0.85
Arab (318)	447	0.08
Egyptian (199)	244	0.04
Iraqi (58)	65	0.01
Jordanian (11)	57	0.01
Lebanese (1,229)	2,545	0.47
Moroccan (0)	13	<0.01
Palestinian (447)	447	0.08
Syrian (147)	285	0.05
Other Arab (484)	493	0.09
Armenian (181)	517	0.10
Assyrian/Chaldean/Syriac (0)	0	<0.01
Australian (0)	103	0.02
Austrian (349)	1,705	0.31
Basque (0)	0	<0.01
Belgian (173)	320	0.06
Brazilian (16)	68	0.01
British (838)	1,803	0.33
Bulgarian (54)	107	0.02
Cajun (9)	61	0.01
Canadian (509)	987	0.18
Carpatho Rusyn (56)	111	0.02
Celtic (6)	24	<0.01
Croatian (1,360)	3,314	0.61
Cypriot (0)	0	<0.01
Czech (1,502)	5,935	1.09
Czechoslovakian (809)	1,368	0.25
Danish (212)	1,047	0.19
Dutch (1,318)	9,167	1.69
Eastern European (564)	677	0.12
English (15,823)	57,459	10.58
Estonian (22)	29	0.01
European (4,981)	5,585	1.03
Finnish (318)	956	0.18
French, ex. Basque (1,649)	12,241	2.25
French Canadian (524)	1,401	0.26
German (38,453)	135,453	24.94
German Russian (0)	78	0.01
Greek (1,777)	3,595	0.66
Guyanese (0)	0	<0.01
Hungarian (5,700)	19,645	3.62
Icelander (29)	51	0.01
Iranian (176)	201	0.04
Irish (19,719)	83,267	15.33
Israeli (19)	50	0.01
Italian (21,644)	55,039	10.13
Latvian (68)	115	0.02
Lithuanian (626)	1,553	0.29
Luxemburger (21)	31	0.01
Macedonian (90)	288	0.05
Maltese (0)	0	<0.01
New Zealander (0)	32	0.01
Northern European (413)	500	0.09
Norwegian (606)	1,840	0.34
Pennsylvania German (661)	1,257	0.23
Polish (8,553)	27,447	5.05
Portuguese (295)	546	0.10
Romanian (1,106)	2,246	0.41
Russian (1,746)	4,648	0.86
Scandinavian (93)	310	0.06
Scotch-Irish (3,976)	10,172	1.87
Scottish (2,691)	11,673	2.15
Serbian (1,641)	3,098	0.57
Slavic (260)	653	0.12
Slovak (3,751)	10,163	1.87
Slovene (1,358)	3,802	0.70
Soviet Union (0)	0	<0.01
Swedish (916)	4,472	0.82
Swiss (682)	3,119	0.57
Turkish (205)	314	0.06
Ukrainian (920)	2,431	0.45
Welsh (1,358)	7,018	1.29
West Indian, ex. Hispanic (267)	469	0.09
Bahamian (0)	0	<0.01
Barbadian (5)	5	<0.01
Belizean (0)	0	<0.01
Bermudan (9)	9	<0.01
British West Indian (39)	39	0.01
Dutch West Indian (0)	0	<0.01
Haitian (9)	36	0.01
Jamaican (133)	287	0.05
Trinidadian/Tobagonian (0)	9	<0.01
U.S. Virgin Islander (0)	0	<0.01
West Indian (72)	84	0.02
Other West Indian (0)	0	<0.01
Yugoslavian (1,235)	1,878	0.35

Hispanic Origin	Population	%
Hispanic or Latino (of any race)	8,660	1.60
Central American, ex. Mexican	658	0.12
Costa Rican	42	0.01
Guatemalan	205	0.04
Honduran	141	0.03
Nicaraguan	59	0.01
Panamanian	76	0.01
Salvadoran	130	0.02
Other Central American	5	<0.01
Cuban	306	0.06
Dominican Republic	87	0.02
Mexican	3,704	0.68
Puerto Rican	2,006	0.37
South American	755	0.14
Argentinean	88	0.02
Bolivian	27	<0.01
Chilean	69	0.01
Colombian	259	0.05
Ecuadorian	75	0.01
Paraguayan	10	<0.01
Peruvian	125	0.02
Uruguayan	14	<0.01
Venezuelan	82	0.02
Other South American	6	<0.01
Other Hispanic or Latino	1,144	0.21

Race*	Population	%
African-American/Black (78,120)	85,046	15.70
Not Hispanic (77,373)	83,851	15.48
Hispanic (747)	1,195	0.22
American Indian/Alaska Native (1,015)	4,185	0.77
Not Hispanic (901)	3,836	0.71
Hispanic (114)	349	0.06
Alaska Athabascan *(Ala. Nat.)* (5)	8	<0.01
Aleut *(Alaska Native)* (1)	1	<0.01
Apache (8)	46	0.01
Arapaho (0)	4	<0.01
Blackfeet (27)	228	0.04
Canadian/French Am. Ind. (18)	27	<0.01
Central American Ind. (3)	3	<0.01
Cherokee (216)	1,218	0.22
Cheyenne (5)	17	<0.01
Chickasaw (5)	19	<0.01
Chippewa (36)	59	0.01
Choctaw (20)	89	0.02
Colville (3)	3	<0.01
Comanche (2)	7	<0.01
Cree (6)	13	<0.01
Creek (6)	24	<0.01
Crow (1)	13	<0.01
Delaware (11)	26	<0.01
Hopi (0)	0	<0.01
Houma (0)	0	<0.01
Inupiat *(Alaska Native)* (2)	6	<0.01
Iroquois (28)	121	0.02
Kiowa (0)	1	<0.01
Lumbee (8)	11	<0.01
Menominee (0)	0	<0.01
Mexican American Ind. (22)	43	0.01
Navajo (11)	38	0.01
Osage (1)	4	<0.01
Ottawa (5)	9	<0.01
Paiute (1)	1	<0.01
Pima (4)	5	<0.01
Potawatomi (4)	5	<0.01
Pueblo (2)	3	<0.01
Puget Sound Salish (0)	0	<0.01
Seminole (4)	29	0.01
Shoshone (4)	14	<0.01
Sioux (33)	112	0.02
South American Ind. (5)	13	<0.01
Spanish American Ind. (2)	6	<0.01
Tlingit-Haida *(Alaska Native)* (0)	2	<0.01
Tohono O'Odham (0)	0	<0.01
Tsimshian *(Alaska Native)* (1)	2	<0.01
Ute (0)	1	<0.01
Yakama (0)	0	<0.01
Yaqui (2)	13	<0.01
Yuman (0)	0	<0.01
Yup'ik *(Alaska Native)* (3)	3	<0.01
Asian (11,885)	14,311	2.64
Not Hispanic (11,841)	14,170	2.62
Hispanic (44)	141	0.03
Bangladeshi (70)	82	0.02
Bhutanese (320)	372	0.07
Burmese (597)	615	0.11
Cambodian (77)	107	0.02
Chinese, ex. Taiwanese (2,126)	2,473	0.46
Filipino (797)	1,316	0.24
Hmong (410)	426	0.08
Indian (3,727)	4,154	0.77
Indonesian (47)	79	0.01
Japanese (416)	728	0.13
Korean (874)	1,154	0.21
Laotian (413)	481	0.09
Malaysian (16)	27	<0.01
Nepalese (72)	106	0.02
Pakistani (161)	175	0.03
Sri Lankan (48)	49	0.01
Taiwanese (171)	195	0.04
Thai (161)	249	0.05
Vietnamese (828)	936	0.17
Hawaii Native/Pacific Islander (133)	373	0.07
Not Hispanic (118)	328	0.06
Hispanic (15)	45	0.01
Fijian (0)	0	<0.01
Guamanian/Chamorro (23)	58	0.01
Marshallese (2)	2	<0.01
Native Hawaiian (59)	150	0.03
Samoan (9)	28	0.01
Tongan (1)	1	<0.01
White (436,487)	446,769	82.46
Not Hispanic (431,624)	441,092	81.42
Hispanic (4,863)	5,677	1.05

*Notes: † The Census 2010 population figure is used to calculate the percentages in the Hispanic Origin and Race categories. Ancestry percentages are based on the 2006-2010 American Community Survey population (not shown); ‡ Numbers in parentheses indicate the number of people reporting a single ancestry; * Numbers in parentheses indicate the number of persons reporting this race alone, not in combination with any other race; Please refer to the User Guide for more information.*

Trumbull County

Population: 210,312

Ancestry	Population	%
Afghan (0)	0	<0.01
African, Sub-Saharan (327)	475	0.22
African (205)	353	0.17
Cape Verdean (0)	0	<0.01
Ethiopian (122)	122	0.06
Ghanaian (0)	0	<0.01
Kenyan (0)	0	<0.01
Liberian (0)	0	<0.01
Nigerian (0)	0	<0.01
Senegalese (0)	0	<0.01
Sierra Leonean (0)	0	<0.01
Somalian (0)	0	<0.01
South African (0)	0	<0.01
Sudanese (0)	0	<0.01
Ugandan (0)	0	<0.01
Zimbabwean (0)	0	<0.01
Other Sub-Saharan African (0)	0	<0.01
Albanian (14)	39	0.02
Alsatian (0)	0	<0.01
American (35,115)	35,115	16.50
Arab (538)	1,014	0.48
Arab (57)	143	0.07
Egyptian (49)	49	0.02
Iraqi (0)	0	<0.01
Jordanian (11)	11	0.01
Lebanese (265)	618	0.29
Moroccan (17)	17	0.01
Palestinian (118)	118	0.06
Syrian (21)	58	0.03
Other Arab (0)	0	<0.01
Armenian (0)	8	<0.01
Assyrian/Chaldean/Syriac (0)	0	<0.01
Australian (12)	12	0.01
Austrian (104)	295	0.14
Basque (0)	0	<0.01
Belgian (38)	189	0.09
Brazilian (72)	72	0.03
British (89)	400	0.19
Bulgarian (0)	10	<0.01
Cajun (13)	13	0.01
Canadian (113)	229	0.11
Carpatho Rusyn (54)	69	0.03
Celtic (39)	88	0.04
Croatian (890)	2,594	1.22
Cypriot (0)	0	<0.01
Czech (210)	1,093	0.51
Czechoslovakian (154)	429	0.20
Danish (23)	181	0.09
Dutch (518)	4,149	1.95
Eastern European (80)	89	0.04
English (6,026)	22,460	10.56
Estonian (0)	0	<0.01
European (643)	728	0.34
Finnish (337)	1,139	0.54
French, ex. Basque (441)	3,486	1.64
French Canadian (94)	494	0.23
German (11,879)	46,006	21.62
German Russian (0)	0	<0.01
Greek (1,318)	2,767	1.30
Guyanese (0)	0	<0.01
Hungarian (2,269)	6,552	3.08
Icelander (0)	0	<0.01
Iranian (74)	74	0.03
Irish (6,169)	30,396	14.29
Israeli (0)	0	<0.01
Italian (13,208)	29,089	13.67
Latvian (12)	12	0.01
Lithuanian (237)	586	0.28
Luxemburger (0)	17	0.01
Macedonian (11)	121	0.06
Maltese (0)	0	<0.01
New Zealander (0)	0	<0.01
Northern European (37)	37	0.02
Norwegian (7)	178	0.08
Pennsylvania German (1,510)	2,069	0.97
Polish (2,756)	9,735	4.58
Portuguese (0)	46	0.02
Romanian (670)	1,351	0.63
Russian (481)	1,626	0.76
Scandinavian (27)	132	0.06
Scotch-Irish (1,006)	3,638	1.71
Scottish (951)	4,070	1.91
Serbian (259)	689	0.32
Slavic (65)	145	0.07
Slovak (2,964)	8,417	3.96
Slovene (339)	883	0.41
Soviet Union (0)	0	<0.01
Swedish (410)	1,475	0.69
Swiss (219)	907	0.43
Turkish (0)	0	<0.01
Ukrainian (765)	1,747	0.82
Welsh (838)	5,069	2.38
West Indian, ex. Hispanic (106)	166	0.08
Bahamian (0)	0	<0.01
Barbadian (0)	8	<0.01
Belizean (0)	0	<0.01
Bermudan (0)	0	<0.01
British West Indian (0)	0	<0.01
Dutch West Indian (0)	0	<0.01
Haitian (12)	12	0.01
Jamaican (37)	75	0.04
Trinidadian/Tobagonian (0)	6	<0.01
U.S. Virgin Islander (0)	0	<0.01
West Indian (57)	65	0.03
Other West Indian (0)	0	<0.01
Yugoslavian (101)	207	0.10

Hispanic Origin	Population	%
Hispanic or Latino (of any race)	2,801	1.33
Central American, ex. Mexican	98	0.05
Costa Rican	0	<0.01
Guatemalan	43	0.02
Honduran	13	0.01
Nicaraguan	8	<0.01
Panamanian	15	0.01
Salvadoran	19	0.01
Other Central American	0	<0.01
Cuban	89	0.04
Dominican Republic	40	0.02
Mexican	1,027	0.49
Puerto Rican	1,023	0.49
South American	112	0.05
Argentinean	10	<0.01
Bolivian	0	<0.01
Chilean	12	0.01
Colombian	40	0.02
Ecuadorian	9	<0.01
Paraguayan	0	<0.01
Peruvian	28	0.01
Uruguayan	0	<0.01
Venezuelan	13	0.01
Other South American	0	<0.01
Other Hispanic or Latino	412	0.20

Race*	Population	%
African-American/Black (17,417)	19,704	9.37
Not Hispanic (17,200)	19,327	9.19
Hispanic (217)	377	0.18
American Indian/Alaska Native (360)	1,456	0.69
Not Hispanic (326)	1,348	0.64
Hispanic (34)	108	0.05
Alaska Athabascan *(Ala. Nat.)* (2)	4	<0.01
Aleut *(Alaska Native)* (0)	0	<0.01
Apache (5)	22	0.01
Arapaho (0)	2	<0.01
Blackfeet (14)	88	0.04
Canadian/French Am. Ind. (0)	1	<0.01
Central American Ind. (1)	2	<0.01
Cherokee (90)	493	0.23
Cheyenne (1)	7	<0.01
Chickasaw (1)	2	<0.01
Chippewa (3)	15	0.01
Choctaw (2)	21	0.01
Colville (0)	0	<0.01
Comanche (1)	9	<0.01
Cree (6)	10	<0.01
Creek (4)	10	<0.01
Crow (2)	2	<0.01
Delaware (3)	5	<0.01
Hopi (4)	8	<0.01
Houma (0)	0	<0.01
Inupiat *(Alaska Native)* (0)	2	<0.01
Iroquois (7)	55	0.03
Kiowa (0)	0	<0.01
Lumbee (1)	1	<0.01
Menominee (0)	0	<0.01
Mexican American Ind. (5)	9	<0.01
Navajo (5)	18	0.01
Osage (1)	1	<0.01
Ottawa (2)	2	<0.01
Paiute (0)	5	<0.01
Pima (0)	0	<0.01
Potawatomi (1)	2	<0.01
Pueblo (0)	0	<0.01
Puget Sound Salish (0)	0	<0.01
Seminole (1)	2	<0.01
Shoshone (1)	1	<0.01
Sioux (10)	36	0.02
South American Ind. (0)	1	<0.01
Spanish American Ind. (0)	0	<0.01
Tlingit-Haida *(Alaska Native)* (0)	2	<0.01
Tohono O'Odham (0)	0	<0.01
Tsimshian *(Alaska Native)* (0)	0	<0.01
Ute (0)	0	<0.01
Yakama (0)	0	<0.01
Yaqui (0)	0	<0.01
Yuman (0)	0	<0.01
Yup'ik *(Alaska Native)* (0)	0	<0.01
Asian (984)	1,469	0.70
Not Hispanic (979)	1,424	0.68
Hispanic (5)	45	0.02
Bangladeshi (3)	3	<0.01
Bhutanese (1)	1	<0.01
Burmese (1)	1	<0.01
Cambodian (3)	3	<0.01
Chinese, ex. Taiwanese (196)	255	0.12
Filipino (130)	236	0.11
Hmong (0)	0	<0.01
Indian (311)	379	0.18
Indonesian (8)	10	<0.01
Japanese (51)	145	0.07
Korean (103)	178	0.08
Laotian (1)	7	<0.01
Malaysian (7)	8	<0.01
Nepalese (3)	5	<0.01
Pakistani (8)	20	0.01
Sri Lankan (5)	5	<0.01
Taiwanese (4)	7	<0.01
Thai (24)	47	0.02
Vietnamese (64)	86	0.04
Hawaii Native/Pacific Islander (41)	118	0.06
Not Hispanic (36)	93	0.04
Hispanic (5)	25	0.01
Fijian (0)	0	<0.01
Guamanian/Chamorro (15)	18	0.01
Marshallese (0)	1	<0.01
Native Hawaiian (9)	39	0.02
Samoan (8)	18	0.01
Tongan (0)	3	<0.01
White (187,113)	190,582	90.62
Not Hispanic (185,388)	188,576	89.66
Hispanic (1,725)	2,006	0.95

*Notes: † The Census 2010 population figure is used to calculate the percentages in the Hispanic Origin and Race categories. Ancestry percentages are based on the 2006-2010 American Community Survey population (not shown); ‡ Numbers in parentheses indicate the number of people reporting a single ancestry; * Numbers in parentheses indicate the number of persons reporting this race alone, not in combination with any other race; Please refer to the User Guide for more information.*

Warren County

Population: 212,693

Ancestry	Population	%
Afghan (0)	12	0.01
African, Sub-Saharan (366)	610	0.29
African (209)	453	0.22
Cape Verdean (0)	0	<0.01
Ethiopian (91)	91	0.04
Ghanaian (0)	0	<0.01
Kenyan (0)	0	<0.01
Liberian (6)	6	<0.01
Nigerian (30)	30	0.01
Senegalese (0)	0	<0.01
Sierra Leonean (0)	0	<0.01
Somalian (0)	0	<0.01
South African (0)	0	<0.01
Sudanese (0)	0	<0.01
Ugandan (0)	0	<0.01
Zimbabwean (0)	0	<0.01
Other Sub-Saharan African (30)	30	0.01
Albanian (10)	20	0.01
Alsatian (0)	8	<0.01
American (24,038)	24,038	11.57
Arab (350)	826	0.40
Arab (57)	118	0.06
Egyptian (105)	113	0.05
Iraqi (0)	0	<0.01
Jordanian (18)	26	0.01
Lebanese (80)	335	0.16
Moroccan (11)	20	0.01
Palestinian (15)	15	0.01
Syrian (24)	64	0.03
Other Arab (40)	135	0.06
Armenian (0)	79	0.04
Assyrian/Chaldean/Syriac (0)	21	0.01
Australian (19)	19	0.01
Austrian (149)	413	0.20
Basque (0)	0	<0.01
Belgian (52)	203	0.10
Brazilian (49)	94	0.05
British (621)	1,206	0.58
Bulgarian (0)	25	0.01
Cajun (0)	0	<0.01
Canadian (150)	331	0.16
Carpatho Rusyn (0)	0	<0.01
Celtic (42)	42	0.02
Croatian (51)	184	0.09
Cypriot (0)	0	<0.01
Czech (100)	673	0.32
Czechoslovakian (16)	138	0.07
Danish (81)	461	0.22
Dutch (739)	3,919	1.89
Eastern European (205)	218	0.10
English (10,025)	24,983	12.02
Estonian (9)	9	<0.01
European (2,731)	3,094	1.49
Finnish (138)	417	0.20
French, ex. Basque (730)	4,785	2.30
French Canadian (102)	422	0.20
German (22,765)	59,637	28.70
German Russian (0)	0	<0.01
Greek (437)	1,118	0.54
Guyanese (0)	0	<0.01
Hungarian (370)	1,377	0.66
Icelander (11)	33	0.02
Iranian (119)	119	0.06
Irish (7,210)	29,249	14.08
Israeli (31)	62	0.03
Italian (3,105)	10,403	5.01
Latvian (12)	31	0.01
Lithuanian (147)	307	0.15
Luxemburger (6)	6	<0.01
Macedonian (14)	14	0.01
Maltese (31)	31	0.01
New Zealander (0)	0	<0.01
Northern European (32)	49	0.02
Norwegian (275)	1,113	0.54
Pennsylvania German (74)	100	0.05
Polish (1,497)	5,547	2.67
Portuguese (12)	125	0.06
Romanian (78)	155	0.07
Russian (891)	1,525	0.73
Scandinavian (92)	198	0.10
Scotch-Irish (1,554)	3,368	1.62
Scottish (1,351)	5,065	2.44
Serbian (25)	165	0.08
Slavic (15)	80	0.04
Slovak (139)	468	0.23
Slovene (29)	198	0.10
Soviet Union (0)	0	<0.01
Swedish (351)	1,671	0.80
Swiss (47)	666	0.32
Turkish (74)	112	0.05
Ukrainian (190)	582	0.28
Welsh (401)	1,691	0.81
West Indian, ex. Hispanic (162)	193	0.09
Bahamian (0)	0	<0.01
Barbadian (22)	36	0.02
Belizean (0)	0	<0.01
Bermudan (0)	0	<0.01
British West Indian (0)	0	<0.01
Dutch West Indian (0)	0	<0.01
Haitian (0)	17	0.01
Jamaican (11)	11	0.01
Trinidadian/Tobagonian (0)	0	<0.01
U.S. Virgin Islander (0)	0	<0.01
West Indian (129)	129	0.06
Other West Indian (0)	0	<0.01
Yugoslavian (154)	220	0.11

Hispanic Origin	Population	%
Hispanic or Latino (of any race)	4,784	2.25
Central American, ex. Mexican	387	0.18
Costa Rican	42	0.02
Guatemalan	152	0.07
Honduran	50	0.02
Nicaraguan	42	0.02
Panamanian	33	0.02
Salvadoran	67	0.03
Other Central American	1	<0.01
Cuban	210	0.10
Dominican Republic	50	0.02
Mexican	2,449	1.15
Puerto Rican	651	0.31
South American	663	0.31
Argentinean	35	0.02
Bolivian	27	0.01
Chilean	21	0.01
Colombian	207	0.10
Ecuadorian	59	0.03
Paraguayan	0	<0.01
Peruvian	95	0.04
Uruguayan	10	<0.01
Venezuelan	206	0.10
Other South American	3	<0.01
Other Hispanic or Latino	374	0.18

Race*	Population	%
African-American/Black (6,940)	8,004	3.76
Not Hispanic (6,838)	7,827	3.68
Hispanic (102)	177	0.08
American Indian/Alaska Native (341)	1,151	0.54
Not Hispanic (289)	1,026	0.48
Hispanic (52)	125	0.06
Alaska Athabascan *(Ala. Nat.)* (0)	1	<0.01
Aleut *(Alaska Native)* (1)	3	<0.01
Apache (6)	22	0.01
Arapaho (0)	0	<0.01
Blackfeet (3)	48	0.02
Canadian/French Am. Ind. (4)	4	<0.01
Central American Ind. (1)	3	<0.01
Cherokee (78)	386	0.18
Cheyenne (0)	9	<0.01
Chickasaw (3)	3	<0.01
Chippewa (22)	25	0.01
Choctaw (8)	25	0.01
Colville (0)	0	<0.01
Comanche (3)	4	<0.01
Cree (0)	0	<0.01
Creek (5)	13	0.01
Crow (0)	4	<0.01
Delaware (0)	0	<0.01
Hopi (0)	2	<0.01
Houma (0)	0	<0.01
Inupiat *(Alaska Native)* (0)	1	<0.01
Iroquois (21)	32	0.02
Kiowa (0)	0	<0.01
Lumbee (0)	2	<0.01
Menominee (0)	0	<0.01
Mexican American Ind. (19)	21	0.01
Navajo (10)	27	0.01
Osage (1)	1	<0.01
Ottawa (0)	0	<0.01
Paiute (0)	0	<0.01
Pima (1)	1	<0.01
Potawatomi (0)	3	<0.01
Pueblo (1)	2	<0.01
Puget Sound Salish (0)	0	<0.01
Seminole (0)	5	<0.01
Shoshone (0)	2	<0.01
Sioux (5)	13	0.01
South American Ind. (2)	7	<0.01
Spanish American Ind. (5)	8	<0.01
Tlingit-Haida *(Alaska Native)* (3)	3	<0.01
Tohono O'Odham (0)	0	<0.01
Tsimshian *(Alaska Native)* (1)	6	<0.01
Ute (1)	4	<0.01
Yakama (0)	0	<0.01
Yaqui (0)	0	<0.01
Yuman (0)	0	<0.01
Yup'ik *(Alaska Native)* (0)	0	<0.01
Asian (8,284)	9,550	4.49
Not Hispanic (8,261)	9,483	4.46
Hispanic (23)	67	0.03
Bangladeshi (22)	22	0.01
Bhutanese (0)	0	<0.01
Burmese (8)	18	0.01
Cambodian (31)	42	0.02
Chinese, ex. Taiwanese (1,734)	1,964	0.92
Filipino (375)	642	0.30
Hmong (0)	0	<0.01
Indian (4,142)	4,373	2.06
Indonesian (8)	23	0.01
Japanese (405)	578	0.27
Korean (445)	632	0.30
Laotian (19)	36	0.02
Malaysian (6)	28	0.01
Nepalese (9)	12	0.01
Pakistani (333)	359	0.17
Sri Lankan (29)	35	0.02
Taiwanese (103)	125	0.06
Thai (42)	71	0.03
Vietnamese (357)	406	0.19
Hawaii Native/Pacific Islander (99)	220	0.10
Not Hispanic (93)	206	0.10
Hispanic (6)	14	0.01
Fijian (0)	0	<0.01
Guamanian/Chamorro (17)	38	0.02
Marshallese (5)	5	<0.01
Native Hawaiian (23)	64	0.03
Samoan (1)	4	<0.01
Tongan (0)	0	<0.01
White (192,431)	195,373	91.86
Not Hispanic (189,305)	191,943	90.24
Hispanic (3,126)	3,430	1.61

*Notes: † The Census 2010 population figure is used to calculate the percentages in the Hispanic Origin and Race categories. Ancestry percentages are based on the 2006-2010 American Community Survey population (not shown); ‡ Numbers in parentheses indicate the number of people reporting a single ancestry; * Numbers in parentheses indicate the number of persons reporting this race alone, not in combination with any other race; Please refer to the User Guide for more information.*

Wayne County

Population: 114,520

Ancestry	Population	%
Afghan (0)	0	<0.01
African, Sub-Saharan (140)	242	0.21
African (124)	208	0.18
Cape Verdean (0)	0	<0.01
Ethiopian (0)	0	<0.01
Ghanaian (16)	16	0.01
Kenyan (0)	0	<0.01
Liberian (0)	0	<0.01
Nigerian (0)	0	<0.01
Senegalese (0)	0	<0.01
Sierra Leonean (0)	0	<0.01
Somalian (0)	0	<0.01
South African (0)	18	0.02
Sudanese (0)	0	<0.01
Ugandan (0)	0	<0.01
Zimbabwean (0)	0	<0.01
Other Sub-Saharan African (0)	0	<0.01
Albanian (0)	0	<0.01
Alsatian (0)	0	<0.01
American (15,164)	15,164	13.25
Arab (100)	177	0.15
Arab (0)	0	<0.01
Egyptian (10)	10	0.01
Iraqi (0)	0	<0.01
Jordanian (0)	0	<0.01
Lebanese (58)	135	0.12
Moroccan (11)	11	0.01
Palestinian (0)	0	<0.01
Syrian (0)	0	<0.01
Other Arab (21)	21	0.02
Armenian (0)	69	0.06
Assyrian/Chaldean/Syriac (0)	0	<0.01
Australian (0)	0	<0.01
Austrian (128)	458	0.40
Basque (0)	0	<0.01
Belgian (0)	37	0.03
Brazilian (0)	8	0.01
British (57)	170	0.15
Bulgarian (25)	66	0.06
Cajun (7)	7	0.01
Canadian (48)	138	0.12
Carpatho Rusyn (0)	0	<0.01
Celtic (9)	19	0.02
Croatian (115)	223	0.19
Cypriot (0)	0	<0.01
Czech (62)	539	0.47
Czechoslovakian (109)	190	0.17
Danish (3)	58	0.05
Dutch (484)	2,735	2.39
Eastern European (18)	18	0.02
English (3,643)	10,250	8.96
Estonian (0)	0	<0.01
European (1,342)	1,471	1.29
Finnish (53)	196	0.17
French, ex. Basque (567)	3,668	3.21
French Canadian (165)	260	0.23
German (15,883)	39,012	34.09
German Russian (0)	0	<0.01
Greek (181)	373	0.33
Guyanese (0)	0	<0.01
Hungarian (591)	1,848	1.61
Icelander (0)	0	<0.01
Iranian (0)	19	0.02
Irish (3,476)	14,717	12.86
Israeli (0)	0	<0.01
Italian (2,066)	5,444	4.76
Latvian (0)	0	<0.01
Lithuanian (9)	146	0.13
Luxemburger (0)	0	<0.01
Macedonian (0)	2	<0.01
Maltese (0)	9	0.01
New Zealander (0)	0	<0.01
Northern European (30)	30	0.03
Norwegian (29)	267	0.23
Pennsylvania German (3,063)	3,330	2.91
Polish (802)	2,823	2.47
Portuguese (0)	104	0.09
Romanian (54)	124	0.11
Russian (126)	572	0.50
Scandinavian (9)	30	0.03
Scotch-Irish (664)	2,007	1.75
Scottish (730)	2,498	2.18
Serbian (0)	42	0.04
Slavic (0)	47	0.04
Slovak (258)	822	0.72
Slovene (60)	161	0.14
Soviet Union (0)	0	<0.01
Swedish (329)	1,134	0.99
Swiss (2,904)	7,223	6.31
Turkish (15)	23	0.02
Ukrainian (83)	181	0.16
Welsh (325)	1,043	0.91
West Indian, ex. Hispanic (83)	97	0.08
Bahamian (0)	0	<0.01
Barbadian (0)	0	<0.01
Belizean (0)	0	<0.01
Bermudan (0)	0	<0.01
British West Indian (0)	0	<0.01
Dutch West Indian (0)	10	0.01
Haitian (45)	45	0.04
Jamaican (38)	42	0.04
Trinidadian/Tobagonian (0)	0	<0.01
U.S. Virgin Islander (0)	0	<0.01
West Indian (0)	0	<0.01
Other West Indian (0)	0	<0.01
Yugoslavian (97)	163	0.14

Hispanic Origin	Population	%
Hispanic or Latino (of any race)	1,800	1.57
Central American, ex. Mexican	174	0.15
Costa Rican	16	0.01
Guatemalan	52	0.05
Honduran	40	0.03
Nicaraguan	4	<0.01
Panamanian	5	<0.01
Salvadoran	53	0.05
Other Central American	4	<0.01
Cuban	71	0.06
Dominican Republic	20	0.02
Mexican	927	0.81
Puerto Rican	235	0.21
South American	125	0.11
Argentinean	9	0.01
Bolivian	13	0.01
Chilean	13	0.01
Colombian	37	0.03
Ecuadorian	24	0.02
Paraguayan	2	<0.01
Peruvian	15	0.01
Uruguayan	3	<0.01
Venezuelan	9	0.01
Other South American	0	<0.01
Other Hispanic or Latino	248	0.22

Race*	Population	%
African-American/Black (1,712)	2,490	2.17
Not Hispanic (1,689)	2,429	2.12
Hispanic (23)	61	0.05
American Indian/Alaska Native (183)	693	0.61
Not Hispanic (152)	629	0.55
Hispanic (31)	64	0.06
Alaska Athabascan *(Ala. Nat.)* (1)	1	<0.01
Aleut *(Alaska Native)* (0)	0	<0.01
Apache (2)	9	0.01
Arapaho (0)	0	<0.01
Blackfeet (2)	38	0.03
Canadian/French Am. Ind. (1)	2	<0.01
Central American Ind. (2)	5	<0.01
Cherokee (58)	248	0.22
Cheyenne (0)	1	<0.01
Chickasaw (0)	0	<0.01
Chippewa (6)	18	0.02
Choctaw (4)	17	0.01
Colville (0)	0	<0.01
Comanche (1)	1	<0.01
Cree (2)	3	<0.01
Creek (5)	5	<0.01
Crow (1)	1	<0.01
Delaware (0)	8	0.01
Hopi (0)	4	<0.01
Houma (1)	3	<0.01
Inupiat *(Alaska Native)* (1)	2	<0.01
Iroquois (4)	18	0.02
Kiowa (0)	0	<0.01
Lumbee (0)	0	<0.01
Menominee (4)	4	<0.01
Mexican American Ind. (4)	10	0.01
Navajo (1)	7	0.01
Osage (1)	1	<0.01
Ottawa (0)	0	<0.01
Paiute (0)	0	<0.01
Pima (0)	0	<0.01
Potawatomi (2)	2	<0.01
Pueblo (0)	0	<0.01
Puget Sound Salish (0)	0	<0.01
Seminole (0)	0	<0.01
Shoshone (0)	0	<0.01
Sioux (10)	19	0.02
South American Ind. (2)	2	<0.01
Spanish American Ind. (1)	3	<0.01
Tlingit-Haida *(Alaska Native)* (2)	4	<0.01
Tohono O'Odham (0)	0	<0.01
Tsimshian *(Alaska Native)* (0)	0	<0.01
Ute (0)	0	<0.01
Yakama (0)	0	<0.01
Yaqui (0)	0	<0.01
Yuman (0)	0	<0.01
Yup'ik *(Alaska Native)* (0)	0	<0.01
Asian (874)	1,148	1.00
Not Hispanic (864)	1,122	0.98
Hispanic (10)	26	0.02
Bangladeshi (0)	1	<0.01
Bhutanese (0)	0	<0.01
Burmese (0)	0	<0.01
Cambodian (2)	2	<0.01
Chinese, ex. Taiwanese (184)	220	0.19
Filipino (84)	161	0.14
Hmong (0)	0	<0.01
Indian (226)	264	0.23
Indonesian (5)	7	0.01
Japanese (28)	74	0.06
Korean (103)	125	0.11
Laotian (128)	155	0.14
Malaysian (0)	1	<0.01
Nepalese (5)	5	<0.01
Pakistani (14)	15	0.01
Sri Lankan (0)	1	<0.01
Taiwanese (2)	3	<0.01
Thai (17)	22	0.02
Vietnamese (50)	70	0.06
Hawaii Native/Pacific Islander (26)	80	0.07
Not Hispanic (22)	73	0.06
Hispanic (4)	7	0.01
Fijian (0)	0	<0.01
Guamanian/Chamorro (10)	25	0.02
Marshallese (0)	0	<0.01
Native Hawaiian (4)	28	0.02
Samoan (4)	8	0.01
Tongan (0)	0	<0.01
White (109,543)	111,077	96.99
Not Hispanic (108,450)	109,832	95.91
Hispanic (1,093)	1,245	1.09

*Notes: † The Census 2010 population figure is used to calculate the percentages in the Hispanic Origin and Race categories. Ancestry percentages are based on the 2006-2010 American Community Survey population (not shown); ‡ Numbers in parentheses indicate the number of people reporting a single ancestry; * Numbers in parentheses indicate the number of persons reporting this race alone, not in combination with any other race; Please refer to the User Guide for more information.*

Wood County

Population: 125,488

Ancestry	Population	%
Afghan (0)	0	<0.01
African, Sub-Saharan (212)	317	0.25
African (154)	227	0.18
Cape Verdean (0)	16	0.01
Ethiopian (0)	0	<0.01
Ghanaian (21)	21	0.02
Kenyan (0)	0	<0.01
Liberian (0)	0	<0.01
Nigerian (20)	20	0.02
Senegalese (0)	0	<0.01
Sierra Leonean (0)	0	<0.01
Somalian (0)	0	<0.01
South African (17)	17	0.01
Sudanese (0)	0	<0.01
Ugandan (0)	0	<0.01
Zimbabwean (0)	0	<0.01
Other Sub-Saharan African (0)	16	0.01
Albanian (0)	0	<0.01
Alsatian (0)	0	<0.01
American (6,552)	6,552	5.23
Arab (370)	602	0.48
Arab (26)	48	0.04
Egyptian (12)	12	0.01
Iraqi (0)	0	<0.01
Jordanian (0)	0	<0.01
Lebanese (159)	327	0.26
Moroccan (24)	24	0.02
Palestinian (0)	0	<0.01
Syrian (75)	114	0.09
Other Arab (74)	77	0.06
Armenian (51)	70	0.06
Assyrian/Chaldean/Syriac (0)	0	<0.01
Australian (14)	32	0.03
Austrian (102)	305	0.24
Basque (0)	18	0.01
Belgian (101)	261	0.21
Brazilian (0)	0	<0.01
British (147)	469	0.37
Bulgarian (45)	65	0.05
Cajun (0)	0	<0.01
Canadian (35)	183	0.15
Carpatho Rusyn (0)	0	<0.01
Celtic (3)	3	<0.01
Croatian (36)	277	0.22
Cypriot (0)	0	<0.01
Czech (262)	1,037	0.83
Czechoslovakian (76)	347	0.28
Danish (92)	379	0.30
Dutch (487)	2,672	2.13
Eastern European (51)	85	0.07
English (3,102)	13,032	10.40
Estonian (0)	0	<0.01
European (1,039)	1,086	0.87
Finnish (91)	181	0.14
French, ex. Basque (744)	4,979	3.97
French Canadian (140)	863	0.69
German (22,082)	51,154	40.83
German Russian (0)	0	<0.01
Greek (178)	554	0.44
Guyanese (0)	0	<0.01
Hungarian (1,147)	3,343	2.67
Icelander (31)	70	0.06
Iranian (68)	68	0.05
Irish (3,606)	17,993	14.36
Israeli (14)	14	0.01
Italian (1,865)	5,664	4.52
Latvian (0)	0	<0.01
Lithuanian (70)	248	0.20
Luxemburger (0)	0	<0.01
Macedonian (17)	38	0.03
Maltese (12)	39	0.03
New Zealander (0)	0	<0.01
Northern European (2)	5	<0.01
Norwegian (266)	710	0.57
Pennsylvania German (105)	208	0.17
Polish (3,125)	8,421	6.72
Portuguese (0)	14	0.01
Romanian (30)	240	0.19
Russian (130)	511	0.41
Scandinavian (35)	93	0.07
Scotch-Irish (523)	1,850	1.48
Scottish (846)	3,070	2.45
Serbian (15)	53	0.04
Slavic (12)	62	0.05
Slovak (537)	1,052	0.84
Slovene (2)	105	0.08
Soviet Union (0)	0	<0.01
Swedish (178)	824	0.66
Swiss (220)	976	0.78
Turkish (207)	207	0.17
Ukrainian (94)	277	0.22
Welsh (180)	1,348	1.08
West Indian, ex. Hispanic (11)	37	0.03
Bahamian (0)	14	0.01
Barbadian (0)	0	<0.01
Belizean (0)	0	<0.01
Bermudan (0)	0	<0.01
British West Indian (0)	0	<0.01
Dutch West Indian (0)	12	0.01
Haitian (0)	0	<0.01
Jamaican (0)	0	<0.01
Trinidadian/Tobagonian (0)	0	<0.01
U.S. Virgin Islander (0)	0	<0.01
West Indian (11)	11	0.01
Other West Indian (0)	0	<0.01
Yugoslavian (0)	29	0.02

Hispanic Origin	Population	%
Hispanic or Latino (of any race)	5,663	4.51
Central American, ex. Mexican	91	0.07
Costa Rican	5	<0.01
Guatemalan	43	0.03
Honduran	8	0.01
Nicaraguan	9	0.01
Panamanian	13	0.01
Salvadoran	13	0.01
Other Central American	0	<0.01
Cuban	74	0.06
Dominican Republic	14	0.01
Mexican	4,502	3.59
Puerto Rican	291	0.23
South American	172	0.14
Argentinean	28	0.02
Bolivian	16	0.01
Chilean	5	<0.01
Colombian	53	0.04
Ecuadorian	11	0.01
Paraguayan	9	0.01
Peruvian	23	0.02
Uruguayan	1	<0.01
Venezuelan	26	0.02
Other South American	0	<0.01
Other Hispanic or Latino	519	0.41

Race*	Population	%
African-American/Black (3,022)	3,799	3.03
Not Hispanic (2,906)	3,582	2.85
Hispanic (116)	217	0.17
American Indian/Alaska Native (286)	919	0.73
Not Hispanic (232)	766	0.61
Hispanic (54)	153	0.12
Alaska Athabascan *(Ala. Nat.)* (0)	0	<0.01
Aleut *(Alaska Native)* (2)	2	<0.01
Apache (9)	21	0.02
Arapaho (1)	2	<0.01
Blackfeet (6)	44	0.04
Canadian/French Am. Ind. (0)	1	<0.01
Central American Ind. (0)	0	<0.01
Cherokee (81)	283	0.23
Cheyenne (1)	2	<0.01
Chickasaw (0)	1	<0.01
Chippewa (12)	28	0.02
Choctaw (1)	7	0.01
Colville (0)	0	<0.01
Comanche (2)	5	<0.01
Cree (0)	2	<0.01
Creek (0)	2	<0.01
Crow (0)	4	<0.01
Delaware (3)	4	<0.01
Hopi (0)	1	<0.01
Houma (1)	3	<0.01
Inupiat *(Alaska Native)* (3)	3	<0.01
Iroquois (12)	28	0.02
Kiowa (0)	0	<0.01
Lumbee (2)	2	<0.01
Menominee (1)	1	<0.01
Mexican American Ind. (11)	20	0.02
Navajo (6)	8	0.01
Osage (1)	1	<0.01
Ottawa (2)	2	<0.01
Paiute (0)	0	<0.01
Pima (0)	0	<0.01
Potawatomi (3)	6	<0.01
Pueblo (0)	0	<0.01
Puget Sound Salish (0)	0	<0.01
Seminole (0)	1	<0.01
Shoshone (1)	3	<0.01
Sioux (11)	27	0.02
South American Ind. (1)	2	<0.01
Spanish American Ind. (0)	0	<0.01
Tlingit-Haida *(Alaska Native)* (0)	0	<0.01
Tohono O'Odham (0)	0	<0.01
Tsimshian *(Alaska Native)* (0)	0	<0.01
Ute (0)	0	<0.01
Yakama (0)	0	<0.01
Yaqui (1)	1	<0.01
Yuman (0)	0	<0.01
Yup'ik *(Alaska Native)* (0)	0	<0.01
Asian (1,943)	2,472	1.97
Not Hispanic (1,924)	2,418	1.93
Hispanic (19)	54	0.04
Bangladeshi (14)	19	0.02
Bhutanese (0)	0	<0.01
Burmese (0)	1	<0.01
Cambodian (6)	9	0.01
Chinese, ex. Taiwanese (546)	619	0.49
Filipino (181)	293	0.23
Hmong (0)	1	<0.01
Indian (503)	581	0.46
Indonesian (12)	17	0.01
Japanese (88)	136	0.11
Korean (201)	276	0.22
Laotian (41)	62	0.05
Malaysian (5)	5	<0.01
Nepalese (10)	10	0.01
Pakistani (91)	110	0.09
Sri Lankan (13)	15	0.01
Taiwanese (12)	16	0.01
Thai (51)	80	0.06
Vietnamese (69)	86	0.07
Hawaii Native/Pacific Islander (37)	82	0.07
Not Hispanic (30)	66	0.05
Hispanic (7)	16	0.01
Fijian (0)	1	<0.01
Guamanian/Chamorro (6)	10	0.01
Marshallese (0)	1	<0.01
Native Hawaiian (12)	23	0.02
Samoan (4)	10	0.01
Tongan (0)	0	<0.01
White (116,422)	118,442	94.39
Not Hispanic (113,021)	114,519	91.26
Hispanic (3,401)	3,923	3.13

*Notes: † The Census 2010 population figure is used to calculate the percentages in the Hispanic Origin and Race categories. Ancestry percentages are based on the 2006-2010 American Community Survey population (not shown); ‡ Numbers in parentheses indicate the number of people reporting a single ancestry; * Numbers in parentheses indicate the number of persons reporting this race alone, not in combination with any other race; Please refer to the User Guide for more information.*

Place Profiles

Akron

Place Type: City
County: Summit
Population: 199,110

Ancestry	Population	%
Afghan (0)	0	<0.01
African, Sub-Saharan (1,717)	2,290	1.13
African (1,579)	2,027	1.00
Cape Verdean (0)	33	0.02
Ethiopian (14)	42	0.02
Ghanaian (0)	0	<0.01
Kenyan (0)	0	<0.01
Liberian (29)	29	0.01
Nigerian (0)	0	<0.01
Senegalese (0)	0	<0.01
Sierra Leonean (0)	0	<0.01
Somalian (23)	23	0.01
South African (17)	17	0.01
Sudanese (0)	0	<0.01
Ugandan (0)	0	<0.01
Zimbabwean (12)	12	0.01
Other Sub-Saharan African (43)	107	0.05
Albanian (214)	304	0.15
Alsatian (0)	26	0.01
American (8,242)	8,242	4.06
Arab (714)	1,396	0.69
Arab (30)	159	0.08
Egyptian (124)	137	0.07
Iraqi (0)	7	<0.01
Jordanian (0)	0	<0.01
Lebanese (407)	914	0.45
Moroccan (0)	0	<0.01
Palestinian (10)	10	<0.01
Syrian (0)	26	0.01
Other Arab (143)	143	0.07
Armenian (26)	82	0.04
Assyrian/Chaldean/Syriac (0)	0	<0.01
Australian (0)	21	0.01
Austrian (108)	450	0.22
Basque (0)	0	<0.01
Belgian (58)	109	0.05
Brazilian (0)	27	0.01
British (201)	508	0.25
Bulgarian (11)	32	0.02
Cajun (0)	27	0.01
Canadian (102)	196	0.10
Carpatho Rusyn (7)	25	0.01
Celtic (0)	0	<0.01
Croatian (225)	584	0.29
Cypriot (0)	0	<0.01
Czech (236)	919	0.45
Czechoslovakian (176)	233	0.11
Danish (76)	260	0.13
Dutch (352)	2,805	1.38
Eastern European (115)	138	0.07
English (4,635)	15,829	7.80
Estonian (0)	0	<0.01
European (1,068)	1,390	0.69
Finnish (12)	84	0.04
French, ex. Basque (524)	3,698	1.82
French Canadian (143)	320	0.16
German (11,486)	39,722	19.59
German Russian (0)	78	0.04
Greek (609)	1,127	0.56
Guyanese (0)	0	<0.01
Hungarian (1,222)	4,508	2.22
Icelander (19)	19	0.01
Iranian (36)	36	0.02
Irish (6,958)	26,458	13.05
Israeli (11)	11	0.01
Italian (5,897)	15,000	7.40
Latvian (27)	27	0.01
Lithuanian (87)	239	0.12
Luxemburger (0)	0	<0.01
Macedonian (43)	56	0.03
Maltese (0)	0	<0.01
New Zealander (0)	0	<0.01
Northern European (103)	103	0.05
Norwegian (220)	541	0.27
Pennsylvania German (177)	444	0.22
Polish (1,639)	4,998	2.46
Portuguese (210)	293	0.14
Romanian (344)	564	0.28
Russian (294)	893	0.44
Scandinavian (49)	130	0.06
Scotch-Irish (1,292)	3,342	1.65
Scottish (734)	2,974	1.47
Serbian (522)	945	0.47
Slavic (25)	106	0.05
Slovak (960)	2,164	1.07
Slovene (180)	588	0.29
Soviet Union (0)	0	<0.01
Swedish (292)	1,161	0.57
Swiss (161)	690	0.34
Turkish (27)	61	0.03
Ukrainian (304)	693	0.34
Welsh (376)	2,022	1.00
West Indian, ex. Hispanic (142)	240	0.12
Bahamian (0)	0	<0.01
Barbadian (5)	5	<0.01
Belizean (0)	0	<0.01
Bermudan (0)	0	<0.01
British West Indian (39)	39	0.02
Dutch West Indian (0)	0	<0.01
Haitian (9)	36	0.02
Jamaican (30)	89	0.04
Trinidadian/Tobagonian (0)	0	<0.01
U.S. Virgin Islander (0)	0	<0.01
West Indian (59)	71	0.04
Other West Indian (0)	0	<0.01
Yugoslavian (858)	1,145	0.56

Hispanic Origin	Population	%
Hispanic or Latino (of any race)	4,255	2.14
Central American, ex. Mexican	341	0.17
Costa Rican	10	0.01
Guatemalan	80	0.04
Honduran	93	0.05
Nicaraguan	38	0.02
Panamanian	47	0.02
Salvadoran	69	0.03
Other Central American	4	<0.01
Cuban	148	0.07
Dominican Republic	50	0.03
Mexican	1,784	0.90
Puerto Rican	1,091	0.55
South American	251	0.13
Argentinean	23	0.01
Bolivian	6	<0.01
Chilean	18	0.01
Colombian	101	0.05
Ecuadorian	39	0.02
Paraguayan	0	<0.01
Peruvian	24	0.01
Uruguayan	6	<0.01
Venezuelan	31	0.02
Other South American	3	<0.01
Other Hispanic or Latino	590	0.30

Race*	Population	%
African-American/Black (62,648)	67,240	33.77
Not Hispanic (62,095)	66,385	33.34
Hispanic (553)	855	0.43
American Indian/Alaska Native (486)	2,083	1.05
Not Hispanic (425)	1,899	0.95
Hispanic (61)	184	0.09
Alaska Athabascan *(Ala. Nat.)* (0)	0	<0.01
Aleut *(Alaska Native)* (1)	1	<0.01
Apache (3)	16	0.01
Arapaho (0)	3	<0.01
Blackfeet (11)	115	0.06
Canadian/French Am. Ind. (12)	18	0.01
Central American Ind. (0)	0	<0.01
Cherokee (91)	534	0.27
Cheyenne (4)	14	0.01
Chickasaw (3)	9	<0.01
Chippewa (13)	20	0.01
Choctaw (10)	42	0.02
Colville (0)	0	<0.01
Comanche (2)	5	<0.01
Cree (4)	8	<0.01
Creek (5)	16	0.01
Crow (0)	6	<0.01
Delaware (5)	17	0.01
Hopi (0)	0	<0.01
Houma (0)	0	<0.01
Inupiat *(Alaska Native)* (2)	4	<0.01
Iroquois (6)	41	0.02
Kiowa (0)	0	<0.01
Lumbee (2)	5	<0.01
Menominee (0)	0	<0.01
Mexican American Ind. (1)	14	0.01
Navajo (3)	15	0.01
Osage (0)	3	<0.01
Ottawa (3)	4	<0.01
Paiute (0)	0	<0.01
Pima (4)	5	<0.01
Potawatomi (2)	2	<0.01
Pueblo (0)	1	<0.01
Puget Sound Salish (0)	0	<0.01
Seminole (1)	17	0.01
Shoshone (4)	10	0.01
Sioux (14)	55	0.03
South American Ind. (4)	7	<0.01
Spanish American Ind. (2)	4	<0.01
Tlingit-Haida *(Alaska Native)* (0)	1	<0.01
Tohono O'Odham (0)	0	<0.01
Tsimshian *(Alaska Native)* (0)	0	<0.01
Ute (0)	1	<0.01
Yakama (0)	0	<0.01
Yaqui (1)	9	<0.01
Yuman (0)	0	<0.01
Yup'ik *(Alaska Native)* (0)	0	<0.01
Asian (4,218)	5,081	2.55
Not Hispanic (4,201)	5,008	2.52
Hispanic (17)	73	0.04
Bangladeshi (15)	15	0.01
Bhutanese (267)	318	0.16
Burmese (585)	603	0.30
Cambodian (55)	69	0.03
Chinese, ex. Taiwanese (486)	607	0.30
Filipino (174)	317	0.16
Hmong (351)	362	0.18
Indian (713)	874	0.44
Indonesian (12)	20	0.01
Japanese (68)	207	0.10
Korean (174)	252	0.13
Laotian (346)	388	0.19
Malaysian (6)	9	<0.01
Nepalese (54)	85	0.04
Pakistani (19)	22	0.01
Sri Lankan (17)	18	0.01
Taiwanese (50)	54	0.03
Thai (77)	116	0.06
Vietnamese (427)	474	0.24
Hawaii Native/Pacific Islander (52)	189	0.09
Not Hispanic (49)	164	0.08
Hispanic (3)	25	0.01
Fijian (0)	0	<0.01
Guamanian/Chamorro (12)	27	0.01
Marshallese (0)	0	<0.01
Native Hawaiian (20)	84	0.04
Samoan (5)	14	0.01
Tongan (1)	1	<0.01
White (123,879)	129,298	64.94
Not Hispanic (121,946)	126,928	63.75
Hispanic (1,933)	2,370	1.19

*Notes: † The Census 2010 population figure is used to calculate the percentages in the Hispanic Origin and Race categories. Ancestry percentages are based on the 2006-2010 American Community Survey population (not shown); ‡ Numbers in parentheses indicate the number of people reporting a single ancestry; * Numbers in parentheses indicate the number of persons reporting this race alone, not in combination with any other race; Please refer to the User Guide for more information.*

Canton

Place Type: City
County: Stark
Population: 73,007

Ancestry	Population	%
Afghan (0)	0	<0.01
African, Sub-Saharan (2,636)	2,852	3.83
African (2,507)	2,713	3.64
Cape Verdean (46)	56	0.08
Ethiopian (0)	0	<0.01
Ghanaian (0)	0	<0.01
Kenyan (0)	0	<0.01
Liberian (38)	38	0.05
Nigerian (0)	0	<0.01
Senegalese (0)	0	<0.01
Sierra Leonean (0)	0	<0.01
Somalian (0)	0	<0.01
South African (45)	45	0.06
Sudanese (0)	0	<0.01
Ugandan (0)	0	<0.01
Zimbabwean (0)	0	<0.01
Other Sub-Saharan African (0)	0	<0.01
Albanian (14)	30	0.04
Alsatian (0)	0	<0.01
American (5,025)	5,025	6.75
Arab (443)	577	0.78
Arab (13)	23	0.03
Egyptian (0)	5	0.01
Iraqi (15)	15	0.02
Jordanian (0)	0	<0.01
Lebanese (278)	358	0.48
Moroccan (0)	0	<0.01
Palestinian (0)	0	<0.01
Syrian (137)	164	0.22
Other Arab (0)	12	0.02
Armenian (9)	35	0.05
Assyrian/Chaldean/Syriac (0)	0	<0.01
Australian (0)	0	<0.01
Austrian (99)	143	0.19
Basque (0)	0	<0.01
Belgian (6)	152	0.20
Brazilian (0)	0	<0.01
British (75)	146	0.20
Bulgarian (11)	11	0.01
Cajun (0)	0	<0.01
Canadian (17)	41	0.06
Carpatho Rusyn (0)	13	0.02
Celtic (0)	39	0.05
Croatian (66)	279	0.37
Cypriot (0)	0	<0.01
Czech (192)	342	0.46
Czechoslovakian (30)	51	0.07
Danish (25)	176	0.24
Dutch (88)	1,441	1.94
Eastern European (0)	0	<0.01
English (1,447)	5,256	7.06
Estonian (0)	0	<0.01
European (341)	358	0.48
Finnish (0)	27	0.04
French, ex. Basque (135)	1,697	2.28
French Canadian (37)	122	0.16
German (5,392)	18,990	25.51
German Russian (0)	0	<0.01
Greek (747)	1,154	1.55
Guyanese (0)	0	<0.01
Hungarian (330)	917	1.23
Icelander (0)	0	<0.01
Iranian (0)	0	<0.01
Irish (2,411)	9,815	13.18
Israeli (0)	0	<0.01
Italian (2,380)	5,958	8.00
Latvian (0)	0	<0.01
Lithuanian (29)	99	0.13
Luxemburger (0)	0	<0.01
Macedonian (0)	0	<0.01
Maltese (0)	0	<0.01
New Zealander (0)	0	<0.01
Northern European (80)	80	0.11
Norwegian (51)	143	0.19
Pennsylvania German (125)	212	0.28
Polish (447)	1,434	1.93
Portuguese (253)	367	0.49
Romanian (171)	682	0.92
Russian (185)	603	0.81
Scandinavian (0)	0	<0.01
Scotch-Irish (392)	1,161	1.56
Scottish (250)	1,294	1.74
Serbian (10)	67	0.09
Slavic (25)	87	0.12
Slovak (197)	577	0.78
Slovene (5)	28	0.04
Soviet Union (0)	0	<0.01
Swedish (57)	420	0.56
Swiss (41)	577	0.78
Turkish (0)	9	0.01
Ukrainian (128)	214	0.29
Welsh (91)	631	0.85
West Indian, ex. Hispanic (22)	32	0.04
Bahamian (16)	16	0.02
Barbadian (0)	0	<0.01
Belizean (0)	0	<0.01
Bermudan (0)	0	<0.01
British West Indian (0)	10	0.01
Dutch West Indian (0)	0	<0.01
Haitian (0)	0	<0.01
Jamaican (6)	6	0.01
Trinidadian/Tobagonian (0)	0	<0.01
U.S. Virgin Islander (0)	0	<0.01
West Indian (0)	0	<0.01
Other West Indian (0)	0	<0.01
Yugoslavian (36)	48	0.06

Hispanic Origin	Population	%
Hispanic or Latino (of any race)	1,899	2.60
Central American, ex. Mexican	348	0.48
Costa Rican	2	<0.01
Guatemalan	138	0.19
Honduran	139	0.19
Nicaraguan	5	0.01
Panamanian	8	0.01
Salvadoran	42	0.06
Other Central American	14	0.02
Cuban	49	0.07
Dominican Republic	27	0.04
Mexican	666	0.91
Puerto Rican	356	0.49
South American	66	0.09
Argentinean	14	0.02
Bolivian	3	<0.01
Chilean	0	<0.01
Colombian	25	0.03
Ecuadorian	6	0.01
Paraguayan	0	<0.01
Peruvian	13	0.02
Uruguayan	1	<0.01
Venezuelan	4	0.01
Other South American	0	<0.01
Other Hispanic or Latino	387	0.53

Race*	Population	%
African-American/Black (17,666)	20,377	27.91
Not Hispanic (17,501)	20,069	27.49
Hispanic (165)	308	0.42
American Indian/Alaska Native (349)	1,243	1.70
Not Hispanic (274)	1,102	1.51
Hispanic (75)	141	0.19
Alaska Athabascan *(Ala. Nat.)* (0)	0	<0.01
Aleut *(Alaska Native)* (0)	0	<0.01
Apache (3)	20	0.03
Arapaho (0)	0	<0.01
Blackfeet (4)	100	0.14
Canadian/French Am. Ind. (2)	5	0.01
Central American Ind. (45)	45	0.06
Cherokee (64)	327	0.45
Cheyenne (2)	5	0.01
Chickasaw (0)	2	<0.01
Chippewa (5)	5	0.01
Choctaw (1)	6	0.01
Colville (0)	0	<0.01
Comanche (1)	5	0.01
Cree (0)	0	<0.01
Creek (4)	5	0.01
Crow (0)	3	<0.01
Delaware (30)	57	0.08
Hopi (1)	4	0.01
Houma (1)	1	<0.01
Inupiat *(Alaska Native)* (1)	2	<0.01
Iroquois (4)	31	0.04
Kiowa (0)	0	<0.01
Lumbee (4)	5	0.01
Menominee (0)	0	<0.01
Mexican American Ind. (19)	24	0.03
Navajo (3)	16	0.02
Osage (0)	0	<0.01
Ottawa (0)	1	<0.01
Paiute (0)	0	<0.01
Pima (0)	0	<0.01
Potawatomi (3)	3	<0.01
Pueblo (1)	1	<0.01
Puget Sound Salish (0)	0	<0.01
Seminole (2)	13	0.02
Shoshone (0)	0	<0.01
Sioux (0)	8	0.01
South American Ind. (0)	4	0.01
Spanish American Ind. (1)	1	<0.01
Tlingit-Haida *(Alaska Native)* (0)	0	<0.01
Tohono O'Odham (0)	0	<0.01
Tsimshian *(Alaska Native)* (0)	0	<0.01
Ute (0)	0	<0.01
Yakama (0)	0	<0.01
Yaqui (0)	0	<0.01
Yuman (1)	5	0.01
Yup'ik *(Alaska Native)* (0)	0	<0.01
Asian (253)	461	0.63
Not Hispanic (243)	442	0.61
Hispanic (10)	19	0.03
Bangladeshi (1)	1	<0.01
Bhutanese (0)	0	<0.01
Burmese (0)	1	<0.01
Cambodian (0)	0	<0.01
Chinese, ex. Taiwanese (55)	78	0.11
Filipino (53)	112	0.15
Hmong (1)	1	<0.01
Indian (43)	58	0.08
Indonesian (0)	0	<0.01
Japanese (22)	60	0.08
Korean (38)	80	0.11
Laotian (2)	2	<0.01
Malaysian (0)	0	<0.01
Nepalese (0)	0	<0.01
Pakistani (1)	1	<0.01
Sri Lankan (1)	1	<0.01
Taiwanese (0)	0	<0.01
Thai (5)	17	0.02
Vietnamese (22)	28	0.04
Hawaii Native/Pacific Islander (35)	93	0.13
Not Hispanic (21)	65	0.09
Hispanic (14)	28	0.04
Fijian (0)	0	<0.01
Guamanian/Chamorro (17)	28	0.04
Marshallese (0)	0	<0.01
Native Hawaiian (8)	32	0.04
Samoan (2)	9	0.01
Tongan (0)	0	<0.01
White (50,458)	53,661	73.50
Not Hispanic (49,591)	52,555	71.99
Hispanic (867)	1,106	1.51

*Notes: † The Census 2010 population figure is used to calculate the percentages in the Hispanic Origin and Race categories. Ancestry percentages are based on the 2006-2010 American Community Survey population (not shown); ‡ Numbers in parentheses indicate the number of people reporting a single ancestry; * Numbers in parentheses indicate the number of persons reporting this race alone, not in combination with any other race; Please refer to the User Guide for more information.*

Cincinnati

Place Type: City
County: Hamilton
Population: 296,943

Ancestry	Population	%
Afghan (0)	0	<0.01
African, Sub-Saharan (16,040)	17,006	5.67
African (14,780)	15,631	5.21
Cape Verdean (0)	0	<0.01
Ethiopian (432)	458	0.15
Ghanaian (23)	23	0.01
Kenyan (12)	12	<0.01
Liberian (26)	26	0.01
Nigerian (158)	158	0.05
Senegalese (144)	195	0.06
Sierra Leonean (0)	0	<0.01
Somalian (0)	0	<0.01
South African (13)	13	<0.01
Sudanese (63)	63	0.02
Ugandan (0)	0	<0.01
Zimbabwean (53)	53	0.02
Other Sub-Saharan African (336)	374	0.12
Albanian (0)	0	<0.01
Alsatian (9)	67	0.02
American (18,156)	18,156	6.05
Arab (941)	1,405	0.47
Arab (142)	199	0.07
Egyptian (107)	133	0.04
Iraqi (14)	14	<0.01
Jordanian (112)	127	0.04
Lebanese (408)	704	0.23
Moroccan (65)	65	0.02
Palestinian (40)	55	0.02
Syrian (0)	38	0.01
Other Arab (53)	70	0.02
Armenian (30)	82	0.03
Assyrian/Chaldean/Syriac (0)	9	<0.01
Australian (45)	50	0.02
Austrian (82)	502	0.17
Basque (0)	0	<0.01
Belgian (48)	185	0.06
Brazilian (16)	23	0.01
British (770)	1,314	0.44
Bulgarian (13)	13	<0.01
Cajun (0)	41	0.01
Canadian (144)	275	0.09
Carpatho Rusyn (0)	0	<0.01
Celtic (0)	29	0.01
Croatian (60)	146	0.05
Cypriot (0)	0	<0.01
Czech (240)	704	0.23
Czechoslovakian (64)	180	0.06
Danish (99)	439	0.15
Dutch (627)	2,867	0.96
Eastern European (147)	172	0.06
English (4,893)	16,011	5.33
Estonian (69)	86	0.03
European (2,291)	2,521	0.84
Finnish (7)	175	0.06
French, ex. Basque (685)	5,247	1.75
French Canadian (127)	503	0.17
German (23,192)	59,441	19.80
German Russian (0)	34	0.01
Greek (499)	840	0.28
Guyanese (77)	77	0.03
Hungarian (350)	1,319	0.44
Icelander (0)	0	<0.01
Iranian (47)	69	0.02
Irish (8,007)	32,799	10.93
Israeli (75)	118	0.04
Italian (3,201)	9,502	3.17
Latvian (36)	67	0.02
Lithuanian (86)	212	0.07
Luxemburger (0)	0	<0.01
Macedonian (13)	46	0.02
Maltese (0)	18	0.01
New Zealander (0)	0	<0.01
Northern European (69)	69	0.02
Norwegian (302)	1,024	0.34
Pennsylvania German (46)	63	0.02
Polish (972)	3,782	1.26
Portuguese (10)	142	0.05
Romanian (46)	356	0.12
Russian (598)	1,528	0.51
Scandinavian (168)	293	0.10
Scotch-Irish (988)	3,249	1.08
Scottish (987)	3,828	1.28
Serbian (10)	10	<0.01
Slavic (9)	63	0.02
Slovak (229)	659	0.22
Slovene (19)	90	0.03
Soviet Union (15)	15	<0.01
Swedish (193)	1,245	0.41
Swiss (128)	796	0.27
Turkish (75)	75	0.02
Ukrainian (128)	313	0.10
Welsh (405)	2,038	0.68
West Indian, ex. Hispanic (270)	478	0.16
Bahamian (33)	33	0.01
Barbadian (0)	0	<0.01
Belizean (0)	0	<0.01
Bermudan (0)	0	<0.01
British West Indian (0)	20	0.01
Dutch West Indian (0)	0	<0.01
Haitian (41)	41	0.01
Jamaican (153)	292	0.10
Trinidadian/Tobagonian (29)	29	0.01
U.S. Virgin Islander (0)	0	<0.01
West Indian (14)	53	0.02
Other West Indian (0)	10	<0.01
Yugoslavian (128)	158	0.05

Hispanic Origin	Population	%
Hispanic or Latino (of any race)	8,308	2.80
Central American, ex. Mexican	1,860	0.63
Costa Rican	39	0.01
Guatemalan	1,257	0.42
Honduran	230	0.08
Nicaraguan	90	0.03
Panamanian	78	0.03
Salvadoran	132	0.04
Other Central American	34	0.01
Cuban	320	0.11
Dominican Republic	119	0.04
Mexican	3,244	1.09
Puerto Rican	973	0.33
South American	668	0.22
Argentinean	83	0.03
Bolivian	14	<0.01
Chilean	50	0.02
Colombian	215	0.07
Ecuadorian	45	0.02
Paraguayan	6	<0.01
Peruvian	138	0.05
Uruguayan	1	<0.01
Venezuelan	107	0.04
Other South American	9	<0.01
Other Hispanic or Latino	1,124	0.38

Race*	Population	%
African-American/Black (133,039)	138,296	46.57
Not Hispanic (132,307)	137,223	46.21
Hispanic (732)	1,073	0.36
American Indian/Alaska Native (759)	2,658	0.90
Not Hispanic (549)	2,276	0.77
Hispanic (210)	382	0.13
Alaska Athabascan *(Ala. Nat.)* (1)	3	<0.01
Aleut *(Alaska Native)* (4)	8	<0.01
Apache (10)	44	0.01
Arapaho (0)	4	<0.01
Blackfeet (16)	160	0.05
Canadian/French Am. Ind. (3)	6	<0.01
Central American Ind. (95)	98	0.03
Cherokee (85)	652	0.22
Cheyenne (0)	0	<0.01
Chickasaw (5)	11	<0.01
Chippewa (13)	29	0.01
Choctaw (6)	26	0.01
Colville (0)	0	<0.01
Comanche (5)	7	<0.01
Cree (0)	6	<0.01
Creek (6)	23	0.01
Crow (0)	5	<0.01
Delaware (2)	5	<0.01
Hopi (0)	0	<0.01
Houma (0)	0	<0.01
Inupiat *(Alaska Native)* (1)	1	<0.01
Iroquois (6)	18	0.01
Kiowa (0)	0	<0.01
Lumbee (4)	4	<0.01
Menominee (1)	1	<0.01
Mexican American Ind. (25)	38	0.01
Navajo (11)	31	0.01
Osage (2)	3	<0.01
Ottawa (0)	1	<0.01
Paiute (0)	0	<0.01
Pima (0)	0	<0.01
Potawatomi (1)	10	<0.01
Pueblo (3)	4	<0.01
Puget Sound Salish (0)	0	<0.01
Seminole (3)	20	0.01
Shoshone (0)	2	<0.01
Sioux (12)	56	0.02
South American Ind. (2)	18	0.01
Spanish American Ind. (6)	6	<0.01
Tlingit-Haida *(Alaska Native)* (0)	0	<0.01
Tohono O'Odham (1)	7	<0.01
Tsimshian *(Alaska Native)* (0)	1	<0.01
Ute (0)	0	<0.01
Yakama (0)	1	<0.01
Yaqui (0)	2	<0.01
Yuman (2)	2	<0.01
Yup'ik *(Alaska Native)* (0)	0	<0.01
Asian (5,481)	6,875	2.32
Not Hispanic (5,434)	6,728	2.27
Hispanic (47)	147	0.05
Bangladeshi (25)	25	0.01
Bhutanese (74)	74	0.02
Burmese (12)	13	<0.01
Cambodian (169)	212	0.07
Chinese, ex. Taiwanese (1,267)	1,558	0.52
Filipino (411)	718	0.24
Hmong (0)	3	<0.01
Indian (1,805)	2,036	0.69
Indonesian (10)	31	0.01
Japanese (222)	399	0.13
Korean (514)	674	0.23
Laotian (9)	14	<0.01
Malaysian (4)	5	<0.01
Nepalese (59)	77	0.03
Pakistani (98)	125	0.04
Sri Lankan (75)	82	0.03
Taiwanese (112)	122	0.04
Thai (108)	143	0.05
Vietnamese (303)	359	0.12
Hawaii Native/Pacific Islander (251)	465	0.16
Not Hispanic (168)	344	0.12
Hispanic (83)	121	0.04
Fijian (1)	1	<0.01
Guamanian/Chamorro (171)	202	0.07
Marshallese (1)	2	<0.01
Native Hawaiian (15)	70	0.02
Samoan (21)	51	0.02
Tongan (0)	0	<0.01
White (146,435)	152,515	51.36
Not Hispanic (142,831)	148,354	49.96
Hispanic (3,604)	4,161	1.40

*Notes: † The Census 2010 population figure is used to calculate the percentages in the Hispanic Origin and Race categories. Ancestry percentages are based on the 2006-2010 American Community Survey population (not shown); ‡ Numbers in parentheses indicate the number of people reporting a single ancestry; * Numbers in parentheses indicate the number of persons reporting this race alone, not in combination with any other race; Please refer to the User Guide for more information.*

Cleveland

Place Type: City
County: Cuyahoga
Population: 396,815

Ancestry	Population	%
Afghan (0)	0	<0.01
African, Sub-Saharan (4,355)	5,454	1.33
African (3,344)	4,279	1.05
Cape Verdean (19)	58	0.01
Ethiopian (21)	21	0.01
Ghanaian (79)	79	0.02
Kenyan (0)	10	<0.01
Liberian (128)	128	0.03
Nigerian (352)	352	0.09
Senegalese (17)	17	<0.01
Sierra Leonean (0)	0	<0.01
Somalian (41)	41	0.01
South African (19)	68	0.02
Sudanese (86)	86	0.02
Ugandan (0)	0	<0.01
Zimbabwean (0)	0	<0.01
Other Sub-Saharan African (249)	315	0.08
Albanian (130)	139	0.03
Alsatian (0)	0	<0.01
American (9,836)	9,836	2.40
Arab (2,382)	3,346	0.82
Arab (466)	663	0.16
Egyptian (318)	326	0.08
Iraqi (85)	85	0.02
Jordanian (115)	115	0.03
Lebanese (551)	1,147	0.28
Moroccan (37)	75	0.02
Palestinian (553)	553	0.14
Syrian (77)	155	0.04
Other Arab (180)	227	0.06
Armenian (61)	91	0.02
Assyrian/Chaldean/Syriac (5)	5	<0.01
Australian (24)	39	0.01
Austrian (85)	589	0.14
Basque (0)	0	<0.01
Belgian (0)	96	0.02
Brazilian (80)	80	0.02
British (102)	474	0.12
Bulgarian (29)	54	0.01
Cajun (29)	29	0.01
Canadian (124)	343	0.08
Carpatho Rusyn (0)	0	<0.01
Celtic (8)	18	<0.01
Croatian (509)	1,547	0.38
Cypriot (0)	0	<0.01
Czech (881)	2,835	0.69
Czechoslovakian (319)	553	0.14
Danish (54)	230	0.06
Dutch (180)	2,881	0.70
Eastern European (140)	140	0.03
English (4,019)	13,765	3.36
Estonian (0)	0	<0.01
European (887)	1,116	0.27
Finnish (79)	376	0.09
French, ex. Basque (428)	4,063	0.99
French Canadian (146)	425	0.10
German (9,110)	40,200	9.82
German Russian (18)	18	<0.01
Greek (536)	1,435	0.35
Guyanese (304)	370	0.09
Hungarian (2,360)	6,822	1.67
Icelander (11)	25	0.01
Iranian (26)	26	0.01
Irish (9,753)	37,296	9.11
Israeli (10)	10	<0.01
Italian (7,160)	19,033	4.65
Latvian (62)	99	0.02
Lithuanian (435)	1,180	0.29
Luxemburger (0)	0	<0.01
Macedonian (0)	10	<0.01
Maltese (0)	0	<0.01
New Zealander (0)	0	<0.01
Northern European (48)	48	0.01
Norwegian (77)	435	0.11
Pennsylvania German (89)	157	0.04
Polish (6,968)	18,227	4.45
Portuguese (73)	277	0.07
Romanian (904)	1,296	0.32
Russian (692)	2,395	0.59
Scandinavian (29)	127	0.03
Scotch-Irish (927)	2,928	0.72
Scottish (682)	3,093	0.76
Serbian (241)	529	0.13
Slavic (72)	232	0.06
Slovak (2,328)	7,074	1.73
Slovene (1,381)	3,214	0.79
Soviet Union (0)	0	<0.01
Swedish (186)	1,163	0.28
Swiss (55)	405	0.10
Turkish (45)	53	0.01
Ukrainian (858)	2,072	0.51
Welsh (131)	1,575	0.38
West Indian, ex. Hispanic (1,118)	1,835	0.45
Bahamian (0)	0	<0.01
Barbadian (0)	0	<0.01
Belizean (0)	16	<0.01
Bermudan (11)	11	<0.01
British West Indian (21)	31	0.01
Dutch West Indian (0)	0	<0.01
Haitian (22)	31	0.01
Jamaican (904)	1,281	0.31
Trinidadian/Tobagonian (45)	94	0.02
U.S. Virgin Islander (7)	7	<0.01
West Indian (108)	364	0.09
Other West Indian (0)	0	<0.01
Yugoslavian (168)	287	0.07

Hispanic Origin	Population	%
Hispanic or Latino (of any race)	39,534	9.96
Central American, ex. Mexican	2,085	0.53
Costa Rican	45	0.01
Guatemalan	786	0.20
Honduran	324	0.08
Nicaraguan	82	0.02
Panamanian	89	0.02
Salvadoran	738	0.19
Other Central American	21	0.01
Cuban	463	0.12
Dominican Republic	1,140	0.29
Mexican	3,593	0.91
Puerto Rican	29,286	7.38
South American	959	0.24
Argentinean	70	0.02
Bolivian	3	<0.01
Chilean	62	0.02
Colombian	320	0.08
Ecuadorian	113	0.03
Paraguayan	8	<0.01
Peruvian	276	0.07
Uruguayan	28	0.01
Venezuelan	54	0.01
Other South American	25	0.01
Other Hispanic or Latino	2,008	0.51

Race*	Population	%
African-American/Black (211,672)	219,027	55.20
Not Hispanic (208,208)	213,920	53.91
Hispanic (3,464)	5,107	1.29
American Indian/Alaska Native (1,340)	4,008	1.01
Not Hispanic (997)	3,202	0.81
Hispanic (343)	806	0.20
Alaska Athabascan *(Ala. Nat.)* (0)	2	<0.01
Aleut *(Alaska Native)* (0)	0	<0.01
Apache (10)	43	0.01
Arapaho (0)	7	<0.01
Blackfeet (39)	240	0.06
Canadian/French Am. Ind. (2)	7	<0.01
Central American Ind. (24)	32	0.01
Cherokee (140)	865	0.22
Cheyenne (5)	7	<0.01
Chickasaw (14)	34	0.01
Chippewa (38)	54	0.01
Choctaw (29)	83	0.02
Colville (1)	3	<0.01
Comanche (1)	3	<0.01
Cree (1)	3	<0.01
Creek (7)	23	0.01
Crow (3)	10	<0.01
Delaware (3)	10	<0.01
Hopi (0)	4	<0.01
Houma (0)	0	<0.01
Inupiat *(Alaska Native)* (3)	6	<0.01
Iroquois (27)	62	0.02
Kiowa (6)	11	<0.01
Lumbee (6)	9	<0.01
Menominee (0)	0	<0.01
Mexican American Ind. (44)	60	0.02
Navajo (16)	31	0.01
Osage (0)	0	<0.01
Ottawa (6)	7	<0.01
Paiute (0)	0	<0.01
Pima (0)	1	<0.01
Potawatomi (1)	4	<0.01
Pueblo (13)	13	<0.01
Puget Sound Salish (0)	0	<0.01
Seminole (9)	30	0.01
Shoshone (3)	4	<0.01
Sioux (34)	91	0.02
South American Ind. (39)	105	0.03
Spanish American Ind. (2)	3	<0.01
Tlingit-Haida *(Alaska Native)* (2)	2	<0.01
Tohono O'Odham (7)	7	<0.01
Tsimshian *(Alaska Native)* (0)	0	<0.01
Ute (0)	0	<0.01
Yakama (0)	0	<0.01
Yaqui (0)	0	<0.01
Yuman (0)	0	<0.01
Yup'ik *(Alaska Native)* (1)	3	<0.01
Asian (7,327)	8,705	2.19
Not Hispanic (7,213)	8,422	2.12
Hispanic (114)	283	0.07
Bangladeshi (8)	11	<0.01
Bhutanese (70)	94	0.02
Burmese (63)	69	0.02
Cambodian (275)	328	0.08
Chinese, ex. Taiwanese (2,620)	2,916	0.73
Filipino (643)	937	0.24
Hmong (2)	7	<0.01
Indian (1,412)	1,649	0.42
Indonesian (18)	25	0.01
Japanese (158)	349	0.09
Korean (418)	533	0.13
Laotian (87)	108	0.03
Malaysian (6)	12	<0.01
Nepalese (79)	108	0.03
Pakistani (55)	61	0.02
Sri Lankan (14)	18	<0.01
Taiwanese (94)	102	0.03
Thai (89)	121	0.03
Vietnamese (882)	990	0.25
Hawaii Native/Pacific Islander (120)	582	0.15
Not Hispanic (70)	347	0.09
Hispanic (50)	235	0.06
Fijian (0)	0	<0.01
Guamanian/Chamorro (47)	73	0.02
Marshallese (0)	0	<0.01
Native Hawaiian (25)	127	0.03
Samoan (7)	24	0.01
Tongan (4)	6	<0.01
White (147,929)	156,136	39.35
Not Hispanic (132,710)	138,590	34.93
Hispanic (15,219)	17,546	4.42

*Notes: † The Census 2010 population figure is used to calculate the percentages in the Hispanic Origin and Race categories. Ancestry percentages are based on the 2006-2010 American Community Survey population (not shown); ‡ Numbers in parentheses indicate the number of people reporting a single ancestry; * Numbers in parentheses indicate the number of persons reporting this race alone, not in combination with any other race; Please refer to the User Guide for more information.*

Columbus

Place Type: City
County: Franklin
Population: 787,033

Ancestry	Population	%
Afghan (67)	89	0.01
African, Sub-Saharan (25,127)	26,987	3.50
African (9,844)	10,986	1.43
Cape Verdean (28)	28	<0.01
Ethiopian (2,080)	2,207	0.29
Ghanaian (1,270)	1,303	0.17
Kenyan (433)	517	0.07
Liberian (376)	384	0.05
Nigerian (703)	861	0.11
Senegalese (104)	104	0.01
Sierra Leonean (433)	461	0.06
Somalian (8,938)	9,093	1.18
South African (97)	115	0.01
Sudanese (53)	90	0.01
Ugandan (0)	0	<0.01
Zimbabwean (125)	125	0.02
Other Sub-Saharan African (643)	713	0.09
Albanian (261)	292	0.04
Alsatian (0)	29	<0.01
American (31,925)	31,925	4.14
Arab (4,438)	6,451	0.84
Arab (974)	1,109	0.14
Egyptian (669)	911	0.12
Iraqi (279)	334	0.04
Jordanian (602)	617	0.08
Lebanese (518)	1,656	0.21
Moroccan (222)	308	0.04
Palestinian (576)	604	0.08
Syrian (163)	415	0.05
Other Arab (435)	497	0.06
Armenian (111)	163	0.02
Assyrian/Chaldean/Syriac (97)	97	0.01
Australian (43)	154	0.02
Austrian (325)	1,440	0.19
Basque (0)	0	<0.01
Belgian (320)	699	0.09
Brazilian (263)	284	0.04
British (1,471)	3,242	0.42
Bulgarian (55)	130	0.02
Cajun (0)	56	0.01
Canadian (509)	1,023	0.13
Carpatho Rusyn (12)	35	<0.01
Celtic (17)	95	0.01
Croatian (428)	1,158	0.15
Cypriot (0)	14	<0.01
Czech (836)	2,996	0.39
Czechoslovakian (251)	819	0.11
Danish (332)	1,200	0.16
Dutch (1,747)	10,822	1.40
Eastern European (701)	867	0.11
English (18,279)	58,155	7.55
Estonian (20)	20	<0.01
European (6,242)	7,099	0.92
Finnish (224)	858	0.11
French, ex. Basque (3,125)	14,605	1.90
French Canadian (763)	1,886	0.24
German (59,347)	163,383	21.21
German Russian (33)	33	<0.01
Greek (1,110)	2,987	0.39
Guyanese (101)	135	0.02
Hungarian (1,716)	6,569	0.85
Icelander (15)	51	0.01
Iranian (408)	466	0.06
Irish (30,407)	99,000	12.85
Israeli (63)	138	0.02
Italian (14,391)	38,883	5.05
Latvian (150)	214	0.03
Lithuanian (193)	1,022	0.13
Luxemburger (14)	23	<0.01
Macedonian (235)	307	0.04
Maltese (0)	29	<0.01
New Zealander (48)	48	0.01
Northern European (188)	220	0.03
Norwegian (1,070)	3,594	0.47
Pennsylvania German (141)	359	0.05
Polish (5,407)	17,936	2.33
Portuguese (819)	1,667	0.22
Romanian (458)	1,256	0.16
Russian (2,348)	5,392	0.70
Scandinavian (453)	1,042	0.14
Scotch-Irish (4,412)	12,017	1.56
Scottish (4,099)	13,797	1.79
Serbian (189)	511	0.07
Slavic (192)	458	0.06
Slovak (1,091)	3,380	0.44
Slovene (592)	1,380	0.18
Soviet Union (0)	0	<0.01
Swedish (985)	4,492	0.58
Swiss (563)	2,745	0.36
Turkish (530)	601	0.08
Ukrainian (989)	1,935	0.25
Welsh (2,202)	10,220	1.33
West Indian, ex. Hispanic (2,879)	3,944	0.51
Bahamian (82)	93	0.01
Barbadian (88)	132	0.02
Belizean (28)	42	0.01
Bermudan (0)	11	<0.01
British West Indian (149)	165	0.02
Dutch West Indian (0)	54	0.01
Haitian (1,450)	1,655	0.21
Jamaican (757)	1,305	0.17
Trinidadian/Tobagonian (68)	103	0.01
U.S. Virgin Islander (15)	27	<0.01
West Indian (242)	357	0.05
Other West Indian (0)	0	<0.01
Yugoslavian (660)	883	0.11

Hispanic Origin	Population	%
Hispanic or Latino (of any race)	44,359	5.64
Central American, ex. Mexican	4,017	0.51
Costa Rican	129	0.02
Guatemalan	645	0.08
Honduran	784	0.10
Nicaraguan	157	0.02
Panamanian	294	0.04
Salvadoran	1,954	0.25
Other Central American	54	0.01
Cuban	922	0.12
Dominican Republic	1,553	0.20
Mexican	25,973	3.30
Puerto Rican	5,034	0.64
South American	2,730	0.35
Argentinean	273	0.03
Bolivian	81	0.01
Chilean	112	0.01
Colombian	797	0.10
Ecuadorian	491	0.06
Paraguayan	9	<0.01
Peruvian	543	0.07
Uruguayan	47	0.01
Venezuelan	355	0.05
Other South American	22	<0.01
Other Hispanic or Latino	4,130	0.52

Race*	Population	%
African-American/Black (220,241)	237,077	30.12
Not Hispanic (217,694)	233,108	29.62
Hispanic (2,547)	3,969	0.50
American Indian/Alaska Native (2,105)	8,353	1.06
Not Hispanic (1,643)	7,286	0.93
Hispanic (462)	1,067	0.14
Alaska Athabascan *(Ala. Nat.)* (8)	11	<0.01
Aleut *(Alaska Native)* (4)	9	<0.01
Apache (21)	109	0.01
Arapaho (0)	3	<0.01
Blackfeet (49)	539	0.07
Canadian/French Am. Ind. (3)	21	<0.01
Central American Ind. (11)	18	<0.01
Cherokee (333)	2,100	0.27
Cheyenne (3)	15	<0.01
Chickasaw (11)	23	<0.01
Chippewa (44)	112	0.01
Choctaw (17)	72	0.01
Colville (0)	1	<0.01
Comanche (3)	17	<0.01
Cree (6)	17	<0.01
Creek (8)	47	0.01
Crow (0)	12	<0.01
Delaware (5)	40	0.01
Hopi (3)	9	<0.01
Houma (0)	0	<0.01
Inupiat *(Alaska Native)* (2)	3	<0.01
Iroquois (50)	126	0.02
Kiowa (0)	1	<0.01
Lumbee (37)	56	0.01
Menominee (3)	3	<0.01
Mexican American Ind. (114)	203	0.03
Navajo (24)	68	0.01
Osage (5)	7	<0.01
Ottawa (6)	13	<0.01
Paiute (1)	1	<0.01
Pima (0)	3	<0.01
Potawatomi (5)	13	<0.01
Pueblo (9)	16	<0.01
Puget Sound Salish (0)	1	<0.01
Seminole (3)	42	0.01
Shoshone (3)	5	<0.01
Sioux (41)	182	0.02
South American Ind. (24)	51	0.01
Spanish American Ind. (14)	18	<0.01
Tlingit-Haida *(Alaska Native)* (9)	10	<0.01
Tohono O'Odham (2)	5	<0.01
Tsimshian *(Alaska Native)* (1)	1	<0.01
Ute (1)	4	<0.01
Yakama (0)	0	<0.01
Yaqui (0)	1	<0.01
Yuman (0)	2	<0.01
Yup'ik *(Alaska Native)* (0)	2	<0.01
Asian (31,965)	37,743	4.80
Not Hispanic (31,734)	37,170	4.72
Hispanic (231)	573	0.07
Bangladeshi (334)	366	0.05
Bhutanese (71)	96	0.01
Burmese (198)	204	0.03
Cambodian (1,521)	1,794	0.23
Chinese, ex. Taiwanese (5,887)	6,780	0.86
Filipino (1,713)	2,827	0.36
Hmong (45)	51	0.01
Indian (10,495)	11,364	1.44
Indonesian (245)	326	0.04
Japanese (1,474)	2,331	0.30
Korean (2,612)	3,330	0.42
Laotian (1,161)	1,412	0.18
Malaysian (92)	121	0.02
Nepalese (163)	190	0.02
Pakistani (787)	927	0.12
Sri Lankan (188)	202	0.03
Taiwanese (535)	626	0.08
Thai (375)	594	0.08
Vietnamese (1,922)	2,319	0.29
Hawaii Native/Pacific Islander (512)	1,346	0.17
Not Hispanic (462)	1,149	0.15
Hispanic (50)	197	0.03
Fijian (4)	7	<0.01
Guamanian/Chamorro (77)	181	0.02
Marshallese (0)	0	<0.01
Native Hawaiian (78)	336	0.04
Samoan (298)	399	0.05
Tongan (0)	2	<0.01
White (483,677)	505,454	64.22
Not Hispanic (466,615)	485,567	61.70
Hispanic (17,062)	19,887	2.53

*Notes: † The Census 2010 population figure is used to calculate the percentages in the Hispanic Origin and Race categories. Ancestry percentages are based on the 2006-2010 American Community Survey population (not shown); ‡ Numbers in parentheses indicate the number of people reporting a single ancestry; * Numbers in parentheses indicate the number of persons reporting this race alone, not in combination with any other race; Please refer to the User Guide for more information.*

Dayton

Place Type: City
County: Montgomery
Population: 141,527

Ancestry	Population	%
Afghan (0)	0	<0.01
African, Sub-Saharan (2,085)	2,395	1.64
African (1,718)	1,956	1.34
Cape Verdean (0)	0	<0.01
Ethiopian (78)	94	0.06
Ghanaian (0)	0	<0.01
Kenyan (10)	10	0.01
Liberian (0)	0	<0.01
Nigerian (104)	138	0.09
Senegalese (0)	0	<0.01
Sierra Leonean (0)	0	<0.01
Somalian (0)	0	<0.01
South African (9)	22	0.02
Sudanese (0)	0	<0.01
Ugandan (0)	0	<0.01
Zimbabwean (0)	0	<0.01
Other Sub-Saharan African (166)	175	0.12
Albanian (0)	0	<0.01
Alsatian (13)	13	0.01
American (16,035)	16,035	11.01
Arab (256)	474	0.33
Arab (39)	39	0.03
Egyptian (28)	46	0.03
Iraqi (123)	123	0.08
Jordanian (0)	39	0.03
Lebanese (51)	184	0.13
Moroccan (0)	28	0.02
Palestinian (15)	15	0.01
Syrian (0)	0	<0.01
Other Arab (0)	0	<0.01
Armenian (0)	0	<0.01
Assyrian/Chaldean/Syriac (0)	0	<0.01
Australian (9)	22	0.02
Austrian (11)	93	0.06
Basque (0)	0	<0.01
Belgian (35)	105	0.07
Brazilian (0)	0	<0.01
British (397)	727	0.50
Bulgarian (62)	125	0.09
Cajun (0)	0	<0.01
Canadian (19)	116	0.08
Carpatho Rusyn (0)	0	<0.01
Celtic (0)	0	<0.01
Croatian (37)	81	0.06
Cypriot (0)	0	<0.01
Czech (69)	231	0.16
Czechoslovakian (27)	179	0.12
Danish (13)	94	0.06
Dutch (260)	1,660	1.14
Eastern European (0)	54	0.04
English (2,681)	7,108	4.88
Estonian (0)	0	<0.01
European (968)	1,113	0.76
Finnish (53)	144	0.10
French, ex. Basque (165)	2,130	1.46
French Canadian (137)	280	0.19
German (8,595)	23,171	15.91
German Russian (0)	0	<0.01
Greek (227)	451	0.31
Guyanese (0)	0	<0.01
Hungarian (312)	792	0.54
Icelander (0)	0	<0.01
Iranian (0)	0	<0.01
Irish (3,119)	14,086	9.67
Israeli (29)	29	0.02
Italian (1,474)	4,059	2.79
Latvian (9)	9	0.01
Lithuanian (47)	244	0.17
Luxemburger (0)	0	<0.01
Macedonian (0)	14	0.01
Maltese (0)	0	<0.01
New Zealander (0)	0	<0.01
Northern European (0)	0	<0.01
Norwegian (78)	346	0.24
Pennsylvania German (21)	80	0.05
Polish (614)	2,017	1.39
Portuguese (0)	45	0.03
Romanian (11)	177	0.12
Russian (121)	358	0.25
Scandinavian (42)	93	0.06
Scotch-Irish (817)	1,768	1.21
Scottish (514)	1,758	1.21
Serbian (7)	30	0.02
Slavic (10)	31	0.02
Slovak (16)	154	0.11
Slovene (14)	132	0.09
Soviet Union (0)	0	<0.01
Swedish (371)	927	0.64
Swiss (84)	346	0.24
Turkish (158)	203	0.14
Ukrainian (79)	150	0.10
Welsh (162)	856	0.59
West Indian, ex. Hispanic (175)	267	0.18
Bahamian (0)	0	<0.01
Barbadian (0)	0	<0.01
Belizean (0)	0	<0.01
Bermudan (0)	0	<0.01
British West Indian (0)	0	<0.01
Dutch West Indian (0)	0	<0.01
Haitian (32)	32	0.02
Jamaican (81)	173	0.12
Trinidadian/Tobagonian (62)	62	0.04
U.S. Virgin Islander (0)	0	<0.01
West Indian (0)	0	<0.01
Other West Indian (0)	0	<0.01
Yugoslavian (28)	28	0.02

Hispanic Origin	Population	%
Hispanic or Latino (of any race)	4,180	2.95
Central American, ex. Mexican	269	0.19
Costa Rican	87	0.06
Guatemalan	51	0.04
Honduran	59	0.04
Nicaraguan	14	0.01
Panamanian	37	0.03
Salvadoran	20	0.01
Other Central American	1	<0.01
Cuban	147	0.10
Dominican Republic	58	0.04
Mexican	2,541	1.80
Puerto Rican	515	0.36
South American	217	0.15
Argentinean	11	0.01
Bolivian	11	0.01
Chilean	8	0.01
Colombian	34	0.02
Ecuadorian	115	0.08
Paraguayan	1	<0.01
Peruvian	25	0.02
Uruguayan	7	<0.01
Venezuelan	5	<0.01
Other South American	0	<0.01
Other Hispanic or Latino	433	0.31

Race*	Population	%
African-American/Black (60,705)	63,535	44.89
Not Hispanic (60,342)	62,972	44.49
Hispanic (363)	563	0.40
American Indian/Alaska Native (417)	1,579	1.12
Not Hispanic (373)	1,460	1.03
Hispanic (44)	119	0.08
Alaska Athabascan *(Ala. Nat.)* (0)	0	<0.01
Aleut *(Alaska Native)* (4)	4	<0.01
Apache (5)	18	0.01
Arapaho (3)	10	0.01
Blackfeet (19)	100	0.07
Canadian/French Am. Ind. (0)	1	<0.01
Central American Ind. (1)	1	<0.01
Cherokee (90)	435	0.31
Cheyenne (0)	4	<0.01
Chickasaw (0)	1	<0.01
Chippewa (9)	23	0.02
Choctaw (1)	9	0.01
Colville (0)	0	<0.01
Comanche (1)	2	<0.01
Cree (0)	0	<0.01
Creek (6)	17	0.01
Crow (0)	0	<0.01
Delaware (0)	1	<0.01
Hopi (0)	1	<0.01
Houma (0)	0	<0.01
Inupiat *(Alaska Native)* (0)	0	<0.01
Iroquois (4)	19	0.01
Kiowa (0)	0	<0.01
Lumbee (1)	2	<0.01
Menominee (1)	6	<0.01
Mexican American Ind. (7)	12	0.01
Navajo (3)	13	0.01
Osage (0)	1	<0.01
Ottawa (2)	6	<0.01
Paiute (0)	0	<0.01
Pima (1)	2	<0.01
Potawatomi (2)	3	<0.01
Pueblo (0)	5	<0.01
Puget Sound Salish (0)	2	<0.01
Seminole (2)	10	0.01
Shoshone (1)	1	<0.01
Sioux (10)	31	0.02
South American Ind. (1)	5	<0.01
Spanish American Ind. (2)	2	<0.01
Tlingit-Haida *(Alaska Native)* (0)	0	<0.01
Tohono O'Odham (0)	0	<0.01
Tsimshian *(Alaska Native)* (0)	0	<0.01
Ute (0)	4	<0.01
Yakama (0)	0	<0.01
Yaqui (0)	0	<0.01
Yuman (0)	0	<0.01
Yup'ik *(Alaska Native)* (0)	0	<0.01
Asian (1,206)	1,864	1.32
Not Hispanic (1,195)	1,813	1.28
Hispanic (11)	51	0.04
Bangladeshi (3)	8	0.01
Bhutanese (0)	0	<0.01
Burmese (2)	2	<0.01
Cambodian (43)	59	0.04
Chinese, ex. Taiwanese (252)	324	0.23
Filipino (196)	334	0.24
Hmong (0)	0	<0.01
Indian (220)	281	0.20
Indonesian (5)	16	0.01
Japanese (51)	147	0.10
Korean (96)	184	0.13
Laotian (0)	1	<0.01
Malaysian (9)	9	0.01
Nepalese (4)	4	<0.01
Pakistani (24)	30	0.02
Sri Lankan (8)	9	0.01
Taiwanese (10)	12	0.01
Thai (30)	54	0.04
Vietnamese (188)	220	0.16
Hawaii Native/Pacific Islander (52)	166	0.12
Not Hispanic (47)	148	0.10
Hispanic (5)	18	0.01
Fijian (0)	0	<0.01
Guamanian/Chamorro (7)	31	0.02
Marshallese (0)	4	<0.01
Native Hawaiian (17)	57	0.04
Samoan (15)	34	0.02
Tongan (0)	2	<0.01
White (73,193)	76,680	54.18
Not Hispanic (71,458)	74,600	52.71
Hispanic (1,735)	2,080	1.47

*Notes: † The Census 2010 population figure is used to calculate the percentages in the Hispanic Origin and Race categories. Ancestry percentages are based on the 2006-2010 American Community Survey population (not shown); ‡ Numbers in parentheses indicate the number of people reporting a single ancestry; * Numbers in parentheses indicate the number of persons reporting this race alone, not in combination with any other race; Please refer to the User Guide for more information.*

Elyria

Place Type: City
County: Lorain
Population: 54,533

Ancestry	Population	%
Afghan (0)	0	<0.01
African, Sub-Saharan (102)	138	0.25
African (29)	65	0.12
Cape Verdean (0)	0	<0.01
Ethiopian (0)	0	<0.01
Ghanaian (0)	0	<0.01
Kenyan (18)	18	0.03
Liberian (0)	0	<0.01
Nigerian (0)	0	<0.01
Senegalese (0)	0	<0.01
Sierra Leonean (0)	0	<0.01
Somalian (0)	0	<0.01
South African (0)	0	<0.01
Sudanese (55)	55	0.10
Ugandan (0)	0	<0.01
Zimbabwean (0)	0	<0.01
Other Sub-Saharan African (0)	0	<0.01
Albanian (0)	0	<0.01
Alsatian (0)	0	<0.01
American (5,042)	5,042	9.17
Arab (31)	112	0.20
Arab (1)	1	<0.01
Egyptian (0)	0	<0.01
Iraqi (0)	0	<0.01
Jordanian (30)	30	0.05
Lebanese (0)	72	0.13
Moroccan (0)	0	<0.01
Palestinian (0)	0	<0.01
Syrian (0)	9	0.02
Other Arab (0)	0	<0.01
Armenian (0)	10	0.02
Assyrian/Chaldean/Syriac (0)	0	<0.01
Australian (0)	0	<0.01
Austrian (30)	154	0.28
Basque (0)	0	<0.01
Belgian (0)	21	0.04
Brazilian (0)	0	<0.01
British (72)	137	0.25
Bulgarian (0)	0	<0.01
Cajun (0)	0	<0.01
Canadian (11)	100	0.18
Carpatho Rusyn (0)	0	<0.01
Celtic (0)	0	<0.01
Croatian (33)	123	0.22
Cypriot (0)	0	<0.01
Czech (85)	556	1.01
Czechoslovakian (26)	312	0.57
Danish (39)	183	0.33
Dutch (123)	1,082	1.97
Eastern European (31)	31	0.06
English (1,799)	6,659	12.11
Estonian (0)	0	<0.01
European (78)	88	0.16
Finnish (6)	36	0.07
French, ex. Basque (74)	896	1.63
French Canadian (78)	376	0.68
German (3,671)	13,579	24.69
German Russian (0)	0	<0.01
Greek (203)	317	0.58
Guyanese (0)	0	<0.01
Hungarian (968)	2,358	4.29
Icelander (0)	0	<0.01
Iranian (0)	0	<0.01
Irish (1,823)	8,207	14.92
Israeli (0)	0	<0.01
Italian (1,155)	3,507	6.38
Latvian (0)	0	<0.01
Lithuanian (64)	132	0.24
Luxemburger (0)	0	<0.01
Macedonian (74)	95	0.17
Maltese (0)	0	<0.01
New Zealander (0)	0	<0.01
Northern European (0)	28	0.05
Norwegian (52)	234	0.43
Pennsylvania German (68)	68	0.12
Polish (1,483)	4,359	7.93
Portuguese (8)	58	0.11
Romanian (89)	165	0.30
Russian (131)	599	1.09
Scandinavian (20)	20	0.04
Scotch-Irish (311)	730	1.33
Scottish (316)	1,571	2.86
Serbian (8)	57	0.10
Slavic (0)	43	0.08
Slovak (531)	1,549	2.82
Slovene (57)	165	0.30
Soviet Union (0)	0	<0.01
Swedish (196)	509	0.93
Swiss (32)	318	0.58
Turkish (0)	0	<0.01
Ukrainian (6)	229	0.42
Welsh (149)	612	1.11
West Indian, ex. Hispanic (10)	22	0.04
Bahamian (0)	0	<0.01
Barbadian (0)	0	<0.01
Belizean (0)	0	<0.01
Bermudan (0)	0	<0.01
British West Indian (0)	0	<0.01
Dutch West Indian (0)	0	<0.01
Haitian (0)	0	<0.01
Jamaican (10)	22	0.04
Trinidadian/Tobagonian (0)	0	<0.01
U.S. Virgin Islander (0)	0	<0.01
West Indian (0)	0	<0.01
Other West Indian (0)	0	<0.01
Yugoslavian (11)	41	0.07

Hispanic Origin	Population	%
Hispanic or Latino (of any race)	2,649	4.86
Central American, ex. Mexican	34	0.06
Costa Rican	3	0.01
Guatemalan	16	0.03
Honduran	3	0.01
Nicaraguan	1	<0.01
Panamanian	3	0.01
Salvadoran	7	0.01
Other Central American	1	<0.01
Cuban	28	0.05
Dominican Republic	18	0.03
Mexican	578	1.06
Puerto Rican	1,719	3.15
South American	50	0.09
Argentinean	2	<0.01
Bolivian	1	<0.01
Chilean	3	0.01
Colombian	16	0.03
Ecuadorian	8	0.01
Paraguayan	0	<0.01
Peruvian	13	0.02
Uruguayan	0	<0.01
Venezuelan	5	0.01
Other South American	2	<0.01
Other Hispanic or Latino	222	0.41

Race*	Population	%
African-American/Black (8,441)	10,098	18.52
Not Hispanic (8,161)	9,622	17.64
Hispanic (280)	476	0.87
American Indian/Alaska Native (162)	631	1.16
Not Hispanic (131)	531	0.97
Hispanic (31)	100	0.18
Alaska Athabascan (*Ala. Nat.*) (0)	0	<0.01
Aleut (*Alaska Native*) (1)	1	<0.01
Apache (0)	6	0.01
Arapaho (1)	1	<0.01
Blackfeet (7)	44	0.08
Canadian/French Am. Ind. (0)	0	<0.01
Central American Ind. (0)	0	<0.01
Cherokee (32)	197	0.36
Cheyenne (0)	4	0.01
Chickasaw (0)	3	0.01
Chippewa (7)	11	0.02
Choctaw (0)	3	0.01
Colville (0)	0	<0.01
Comanche (0)	0	<0.01
Cree (0)	0	<0.01
Creek (0)	0	<0.01
Crow (0)	0	<0.01
Delaware (0)	1	<0.01
Hopi (0)	0	<0.01
Houma (0)	0	<0.01
Inupiat (*Alaska Native*) (0)	1	<0.01
Iroquois (7)	17	0.03
Kiowa (0)	0	<0.01
Lumbee (5)	8	0.01
Menominee (0)	0	<0.01
Mexican American Ind. (3)	4	0.01
Navajo (0)	6	0.01
Osage (0)	1	<0.01
Ottawa (0)	0	<0.01
Paiute (0)	1	<0.01
Pima (0)	0	<0.01
Potawatomi (1)	2	<0.01
Pueblo (1)	1	<0.01
Puget Sound Salish (0)	1	<0.01
Seminole (3)	4	0.01
Shoshone (0)	0	<0.01
Sioux (4)	11	0.02
South American Ind. (3)	3	0.01
Spanish American Ind. (0)	0	<0.01
Tlingit-Haida (*Alaska Native*) (0)	0	<0.01
Tohono O'Odham (0)	0	<0.01
Tsimshian (*Alaska Native*) (0)	0	<0.01
Ute (0)	0	<0.01
Yakama (0)	0	<0.01
Yaqui (0)	0	<0.01
Yuman (0)	0	<0.01
Yup'ik (*Alaska Native*) (0)	0	<0.01
Asian (435)	628	1.15
Not Hispanic (421)	590	1.08
Hispanic (14)	38	0.07
Bangladeshi (0)	0	<0.01
Bhutanese (0)	0	<0.01
Burmese (0)	0	<0.01
Cambodian (0)	1	<0.01
Chinese, ex. Taiwanese (60)	78	0.14
Filipino (185)	273	0.50
Hmong (0)	0	<0.01
Indian (70)	88	0.16
Indonesian (1)	2	<0.01
Japanese (16)	33	0.06
Korean (39)	76	0.14
Laotian (0)	0	<0.01
Malaysian (2)	2	<0.01
Nepalese (0)	0	<0.01
Pakistani (6)	7	0.01
Sri Lankan (2)	8	0.01
Taiwanese (3)	3	0.01
Thai (6)	13	0.02
Vietnamese (25)	31	0.06
Hawaii Native/Pacific Islander (4)	65	0.12
Not Hispanic (3)	45	0.08
Hispanic (1)	20	0.04
Fijian (0)	0	<0.01
Guamanian/Chamorro (2)	13	0.02
Marshallese (0)	0	<0.01
Native Hawaiian (1)	16	0.03
Samoan (1)	5	0.01
Tongan (0)	0	<0.01
White (42,601)	44,643	81.86
Not Hispanic (41,226)	42,979	78.81
Hispanic (1,375)	1,664	3.05

*Notes: † The Census 2010 population figure is used to calculate the percentages in the Hispanic Origin and Race categories. Ancestry percentages are based on the 2006-2010 American Community Survey population (not shown); ‡ Numbers in parentheses indicate the number of people reporting a single ancestry; * Numbers in parentheses indicate the number of persons reporting this race alone, not in combination with any other race; Please refer to the User Guide for more information.*

Hamilton

Place Type: City
County: Butler
Population: 62,477

Ancestry	Population	%
Afghan (0)	0	<0.01
African, Sub-Saharan (289)	348	0.56
African (289)	348	0.56
Cape Verdean (0)	0	<0.01
Ethiopian (0)	0	<0.01
Ghanaian (0)	0	<0.01
Kenyan (0)	0	<0.01
Liberian (0)	0	<0.01
Nigerian (0)	0	<0.01
Senegalese (0)	0	<0.01
Sierra Leonean (0)	0	<0.01
Somalian (0)	0	<0.01
South African (0)	0	<0.01
Sudanese (0)	0	<0.01
Ugandan (0)	0	<0.01
Zimbabwean (0)	0	<0.01
Other Sub-Saharan African (0)	0	<0.01
Albanian (0)	0	<0.01
Alsatian (0)	0	<0.01
American (15,067)	15,067	24.12
Arab (81)	81	0.13
Arab (0)	0	<0.01
Egyptian (0)	0	<0.01
Iraqi (8)	8	0.01
Jordanian (58)	58	0.09
Lebanese (0)	0	<0.01
Moroccan (0)	0	<0.01
Palestinian (0)	0	<0.01
Syrian (0)	0	<0.01
Other Arab (15)	15	0.02
Armenian (0)	0	<0.01
Assyrian/Chaldean/Syriac (0)	0	<0.01
Australian (0)	10	0.02
Austrian (49)	93	0.15
Basque (0)	0	<0.01
Belgian (0)	16	0.03
Brazilian (0)	0	<0.01
British (139)	270	0.43
Bulgarian (0)	0	<0.01
Cajun (0)	0	<0.01
Canadian (0)	0	<0.01
Carpatho Rusyn (0)	0	<0.01
Celtic (0)	0	<0.01
Croatian (0)	0	<0.01
Cypriot (0)	0	<0.01
Czech (10)	114	0.18
Czechoslovakian (0)	36	0.06
Danish (48)	48	0.08
Dutch (179)	873	1.40
Eastern European (24)	24	0.04
English (1,890)	4,631	7.41
Estonian (0)	0	<0.01
European (327)	357	0.57
Finnish (0)	49	0.08
French, ex. Basque (188)	844	1.35
French Canadian (9)	19	0.03
German (6,035)	13,275	21.25
German Russian (0)	0	<0.01
Greek (26)	71	0.11
Guyanese (0)	0	<0.01
Hungarian (64)	193	0.31
Icelander (0)	0	<0.01
Iranian (0)	0	<0.01
Irish (1,930)	6,846	10.96
Israeli (0)	0	<0.01
Italian (1,003)	2,251	3.60
Latvian (0)	0	<0.01
Lithuanian (16)	16	0.03
Luxemburger (0)	0	<0.01
Macedonian (0)	0	<0.01
Maltese (0)	0	<0.01
New Zealander (0)	8	0.01
Northern European (28)	28	0.04
Norwegian (139)	199	0.32
Pennsylvania German (24)	24	0.04
Polish (70)	477	0.76
Portuguese (0)	18	0.03
Romanian (0)	34	0.05
Russian (45)	206	0.33
Scandinavian (0)	0	<0.01
Scotch-Irish (276)	655	1.05
Scottish (239)	801	1.28
Serbian (0)	0	<0.01
Slavic (8)	8	0.01
Slovak (33)	59	0.09
Slovene (0)	0	<0.01
Soviet Union (0)	0	<0.01
Swedish (28)	142	0.23
Swiss (160)	202	0.32
Turkish (0)	0	<0.01
Ukrainian (47)	47	0.08
Welsh (52)	242	0.39
West Indian, ex. Hispanic (29)	29	0.05
Bahamian (0)	0	<0.01
Barbadian (0)	0	<0.01
Belizean (0)	0	<0.01
Bermudan (0)	0	<0.01
British West Indian (0)	0	<0.01
Dutch West Indian (0)	0	<0.01
Haitian (0)	0	<0.01
Jamaican (17)	17	0.03
Trinidadian/Tobagonian (12)	12	0.02
U.S. Virgin Islander (0)	0	<0.01
West Indian (0)	0	<0.01
Other West Indian (0)	0	<0.01
Yugoslavian (0)	15	0.02

Hispanic Origin	Population	%
Hispanic or Latino (of any race)	3,981	6.37
Central American, ex. Mexican	166	0.27
Costa Rican	3	<0.01
Guatemalan	41	0.07
Honduran	64	0.10
Nicaraguan	2	<0.01
Panamanian	3	<0.01
Salvadoran	50	0.08
Other Central American	3	<0.01
Cuban	48	0.08
Dominican Republic	300	0.48
Mexican	2,897	4.64
Puerto Rican	209	0.33
South American	60	0.10
Argentinean	4	0.01
Bolivian	2	<0.01
Chilean	3	<0.01
Colombian	18	0.03
Ecuadorian	5	0.01
Paraguayan	4	0.01
Peruvian	20	0.03
Uruguayan	0	<0.01
Venezuelan	3	<0.01
Other South American	1	<0.01
Other Hispanic or Latino	301	0.48

Race*	Population	%
African-American/Black (5,336)	6,394	10.23
Not Hispanic (5,232)	6,226	9.97
Hispanic (104)	168	0.27
American Indian/Alaska Native (150)	518	0.83
Not Hispanic (113)	451	0.72
Hispanic (37)	67	0.11
Alaska Athabascan *(Ala. Nat.)* (0)	0	<0.01
Aleut *(Alaska Native)* (1)	4	0.01
Apache (1)	6	0.01
Arapaho (0)	1	<0.01
Blackfeet (1)	16	0.03
Canadian/French Am. Ind. (0)	0	<0.01
Central American Ind. (1)	1	<0.01
Cherokee (33)	172	0.28
Cheyenne (1)	2	<0.01
Chickasaw (0)	1	<0.01
Chippewa (0)	4	0.01
Choctaw (6)	6	0.01
Colville (0)	0	<0.01
Comanche (1)	2	<0.01
Cree (2)	2	<0.01
Creek (0)	6	0.01
Crow (0)	0	<0.01
Delaware (0)	0	<0.01
Hopi (0)	0	<0.01
Houma (0)	0	<0.01
Inupiat *(Alaska Native)* (0)	0	<0.01
Iroquois (2)	11	0.02
Kiowa (0)	2	<0.01
Lumbee (0)	0	<0.01
Menominee (0)	0	<0.01
Mexican American Ind. (10)	11	0.02
Navajo (2)	4	0.01
Osage (0)	0	<0.01
Ottawa (0)	0	<0.01
Paiute (0)	0	<0.01
Pima (0)	0	<0.01
Potawatomi (0)	0	<0.01
Pueblo (0)	0	<0.01
Puget Sound Salish (0)	0	<0.01
Seminole (2)	3	<0.01
Shoshone (0)	0	<0.01
Sioux (3)	14	0.02
South American Ind. (1)	5	0.01
Spanish American Ind. (3)	3	<0.01
Tlingit-Haida *(Alaska Native)* (0)	0	<0.01
Tohono O'Odham (0)	0	<0.01
Tsimshian *(Alaska Native)* (0)	0	<0.01
Ute (0)	0	<0.01
Yakama (0)	5	0.01
Yaqui (0)	1	<0.01
Yuman (0)	0	<0.01
Yup'ik *(Alaska Native)* (0)	0	<0.01
Asian (384)	576	0.92
Not Hispanic (379)	552	0.88
Hispanic (5)	24	0.04
Bangladeshi (0)	0	<0.01
Bhutanese (0)	0	<0.01
Burmese (0)	0	<0.01
Cambodian (9)	12	0.02
Chinese, ex. Taiwanese (48)	65	0.10
Filipino (118)	164	0.26
Hmong (0)	0	<0.01
Indian (50)	73	0.12
Indonesian (7)	11	0.02
Japanese (23)	52	0.08
Korean (20)	56	0.09
Laotian (0)	0	<0.01
Malaysian (0)	0	<0.01
Nepalese (3)	3	<0.01
Pakistani (2)	9	0.01
Sri Lankan (0)	1	<0.01
Taiwanese (1)	1	<0.01
Thai (5)	19	0.03
Vietnamese (83)	98	0.16
Hawaii Native/Pacific Islander (46)	104	0.17
Not Hispanic (40)	82	0.13
Hispanic (6)	22	0.04
Fijian (0)	0	<0.01
Guamanian/Chamorro (18)	30	0.05
Marshallese (0)	5	0.01
Native Hawaiian (8)	22	0.04
Samoan (2)	9	0.01
Tongan (6)	7	0.01
White (52,487)	54,183	86.72
Not Hispanic (51,198)	52,579	84.16
Hispanic (1,289)	1,604	2.57

*Notes: † The Census 2010 population figure is used to calculate the percentages in the Hispanic Origin and Race categories. Ancestry percentages are based on the 2006-2010 American Community Survey population (not shown); ‡ Numbers in parentheses indicate the number of people reporting a single ancestry; * Numbers in parentheses indicate the number of persons reporting this race alone, not in combination with any other race; Please refer to the User Guide for more information.*

Kettering

Place Type: City
County: Montgomery
Population: 56,163

Ancestry	Population	%
Afghan (0)	0	<0.01
African, Sub-Saharan (11)	42	0.07
African (0)	31	0.06
Cape Verdean (0)	0	<0.01
Ethiopian (0)	0	<0.01
Ghanaian (0)	0	<0.01
Kenyan (0)	0	<0.01
Liberian (0)	0	<0.01
Nigerian (0)	0	<0.01
Senegalese (0)	0	<0.01
Sierra Leonean (0)	0	<0.01
Somalian (0)	0	<0.01
South African (0)	0	<0.01
Sudanese (0)	0	<0.01
Ugandan (0)	0	<0.01
Zimbabwean (0)	0	<0.01
Other Sub-Saharan African (11)	11	0.02
Albanian (15)	15	0.03
Alsatian (0)	13	0.02
American (4,961)	4,961	8.83
Arab (345)	458	0.82
Arab (0)	11	0.02
Egyptian (10)	10	0.02
Iraqi (0)	0	<0.01
Jordanian (78)	78	0.14
Lebanese (184)	251	0.45
Moroccan (0)	0	<0.01
Palestinian (0)	0	<0.01
Syrian (56)	81	0.14
Other Arab (17)	27	0.05
Armenian (0)	0	<0.01
Assyrian/Chaldean/Syriac (0)	0	<0.01
Australian (0)	4	0.01
Austrian (36)	160	0.28
Basque (0)	0	<0.01
Belgian (19)	63	0.11
Brazilian (59)	59	0.11
British (119)	352	0.63
Bulgarian (0)	0	<0.01
Cajun (31)	66	0.12
Canadian (28)	58	0.10
Carpatho Rusyn (0)	0	<0.01
Celtic (0)	0	<0.01
Croatian (13)	58	0.10
Cypriot (0)	0	<0.01
Czech (53)	220	0.39
Czechoslovakian (36)	136	0.24
Danish (20)	174	0.31
Dutch (254)	1,420	2.53
Eastern European (95)	104	0.19
English (2,059)	6,441	11.46
Estonian (0)	39	0.07
European (633)	692	1.23
Finnish (23)	84	0.15
French, ex. Basque (480)	2,149	3.83
French Canadian (69)	237	0.42
German (8,550)	20,845	37.10
German Russian (0)	0	<0.01
Greek (100)	224	0.40
Guyanese (0)	0	<0.01
Hungarian (298)	714	1.27
Icelander (0)	0	<0.01
Iranian (9)	9	0.02
Irish (2,170)	9,275	16.51
Israeli (0)	0	<0.01
Italian (1,188)	2,845	5.06
Latvian (0)	0	<0.01
Lithuanian (46)	202	0.36
Luxemburger (0)	0	<0.01
Macedonian (0)	0	<0.01
Maltese (0)	0	<0.01
New Zealander (0)	0	<0.01
Northern European (18)	18	0.03
Norwegian (112)	264	0.47
Pennsylvania German (81)	118	0.21
Polish (395)	1,457	2.59
Portuguese (8)	22	0.04
Romanian (55)	70	0.12
Russian (91)	238	0.42
Scandinavian (42)	120	0.21
Scotch-Irish (467)	1,103	1.96
Scottish (452)	1,568	2.79
Serbian (0)	12	0.02
Slavic (0)	15	0.03
Slovak (51)	208	0.37
Slovene (11)	41	0.07
Soviet Union (0)	0	<0.01
Swedish (77)	648	1.15
Swiss (63)	263	0.47
Turkish (0)	0	<0.01
Ukrainian (55)	157	0.28
Welsh (170)	757	1.35
West Indian, ex. Hispanic (8)	74	0.13
Bahamian (0)	0	<0.01
Barbadian (0)	0	<0.01
Belizean (0)	0	<0.01
Bermudan (0)	0	<0.01
British West Indian (0)	0	<0.01
Dutch West Indian (0)	0	<0.01
Haitian (0)	9	0.02
Jamaican (8)	8	0.01
Trinidadian/Tobagonian (0)	0	<0.01
U.S. Virgin Islander (0)	0	<0.01
West Indian (0)	57	0.10
Other West Indian (0)	0	<0.01
Yugoslavian (60)	81	0.14

Hispanic Origin	Population	%
Hispanic or Latino (of any race)	1,178	2.10
Central American, ex. Mexican	116	0.21
Costa Rican	29	0.05
Guatemalan	28	0.05
Honduran	11	0.02
Nicaraguan	5	0.01
Panamanian	28	0.05
Salvadoran	15	0.03
Other Central American	0	<0.01
Cuban	84	0.15
Dominican Republic	7	0.01
Mexican	542	0.97
Puerto Rican	151	0.27
South American	125	0.22
Argentinean	7	0.01
Bolivian	13	0.02
Chilean	5	0.01
Colombian	44	0.08
Ecuadorian	18	0.03
Paraguayan	3	0.01
Peruvian	15	0.03
Uruguayan	3	0.01
Venezuelan	15	0.03
Other South American	2	<0.01
Other Hispanic or Latino	153	0.27

Race*	Population	%
African-American/Black (1,840)	2,386	4.25
Not Hispanic (1,806)	2,323	4.14
Hispanic (34)	63	0.11
American Indian/Alaska Native (106)	414	0.74
Not Hispanic (98)	382	0.68
Hispanic (8)	32	0.06
Alaska Athabascan *(Ala. Nat.)* (0)	0	<0.01
Aleut *(Alaska Native)* (0)	1	<0.01
Apache (1)	5	0.01
Arapaho (0)	0	<0.01
Blackfeet (4)	15	0.03
Canadian/French Am. Ind. (2)	2	<0.01
Central American Ind. (0)	0	<0.01
Cherokee (18)	134	0.24
Cheyenne (0)	0	<0.01
Chickasaw (0)	0	<0.01
Chippewa (4)	8	0.01
Choctaw (3)	5	0.01
Colville (0)	0	<0.01
Comanche (1)	1	<0.01
Cree (0)	0	<0.01
Creek (4)	8	0.01
Crow (0)	1	<0.01
Delaware (0)	0	<0.01
Hopi (0)	0	<0.01
Houma (0)	0	<0.01
Inupiat *(Alaska Native)* (1)	1	<0.01
Iroquois (1)	2	<0.01
Kiowa (0)	0	<0.01
Lumbee (1)	1	<0.01
Menominee (0)	0	<0.01
Mexican American Ind. (0)	1	<0.01
Navajo (3)	6	0.01
Osage (0)	0	<0.01
Ottawa (1)	1	<0.01
Paiute (0)	0	<0.01
Pima (0)	0	<0.01
Potawatomi (0)	0	<0.01
Pueblo (0)	0	<0.01
Puget Sound Salish (0)	0	<0.01
Seminole (0)	1	<0.01
Shoshone (0)	0	<0.01
Sioux (4)	14	0.02
South American Ind. (0)	6	0.01
Spanish American Ind. (0)	3	0.01
Tlingit-Haida *(Alaska Native)* (0)	0	<0.01
Tohono O'Odham (0)	0	<0.01
Tsimshian *(Alaska Native)* (0)	0	<0.01
Ute (1)	1	<0.01
Yakama (0)	0	<0.01
Yaqui (0)	0	<0.01
Yuman (1)	1	<0.01
Yup'ik *(Alaska Native)* (0)	0	<0.01
Asian (752)	1,101	1.96
Not Hispanic (745)	1,080	1.92
Hispanic (7)	21	0.04
Bangladeshi (1)	3	0.01
Bhutanese (0)	0	<0.01
Burmese (7)	7	0.01
Cambodian (20)	23	0.04
Chinese, ex. Taiwanese (161)	197	0.35
Filipino (120)	213	0.38
Hmong (0)	0	<0.01
Indian (148)	182	0.32
Indonesian (2)	13	0.02
Japanese (55)	119	0.21
Korean (58)	124	0.22
Laotian (7)	7	0.01
Malaysian (3)	3	0.01
Nepalese (0)	0	<0.01
Pakistani (14)	21	0.04
Sri Lankan (2)	2	<0.01
Taiwanese (13)	15	0.03
Thai (13)	26	0.05
Vietnamese (96)	116	0.21
Hawaii Native/Pacific Islander (12)	46	0.08
Not Hispanic (12)	45	0.08
Hispanic (0)	1	<0.01
Fijian (0)	0	<0.01
Guamanian/Chamorro (2)	6	0.01
Marshallese (0)	0	<0.01
Native Hawaiian (5)	15	0.03
Samoan (2)	4	0.01
Tongan (0)	0	<0.01
White (51,982)	53,090	94.53
Not Hispanic (51,191)	52,203	92.95
Hispanic (791)	887	1.58

*Notes: † The Census 2010 population figure is used to calculate the percentages in the Hispanic Origin and Race categories. Ancestry percentages are based on the 2006-2010 American Community Survey population (not shown); ‡ Numbers in parentheses indicate the number of people reporting a single ancestry; * Numbers in parentheses indicate the number of persons reporting this race alone, not in combination with any other race; Please refer to the User Guide for more information.*

Lakewood

Place Type: City
County: Cuyahoga
Population: 52,131

Ancestry	Population	%
Afghan (0)	0	<0.01
African, Sub-Saharan (363)	406	0.77
African (159)	169	0.32
Cape Verdean (0)	0	<0.01
Ethiopian (0)	0	<0.01
Ghanaian (67)	67	0.13
Kenyan (13)	13	0.02
Liberian (0)	0	<0.01
Nigerian (19)	52	0.10
Senegalese (0)	0	<0.01
Sierra Leonean (0)	0	<0.01
Somalian (0)	0	<0.01
South African (0)	0	<0.01
Sudanese (23)	23	0.04
Ugandan (9)	9	0.02
Zimbabwean (0)	0	<0.01
Other Sub-Saharan African (73)	73	0.14
Albanian (741)	766	1.45
Alsatian (0)	0	<0.01
American (1,234)	1,234	2.34
Arab (997)	1,450	2.75
Arab (151)	218	0.41
Egyptian (172)	172	0.33
Iraqi (0)	0	<0.01
Jordanian (0)	0	<0.01
Lebanese (360)	706	1.34
Moroccan (0)	0	<0.01
Palestinian (105)	116	0.22
Syrian (207)	213	0.40
Other Arab (2)	25	0.05
Armenian (13)	29	0.06
Assyrian/Chaldean/Syriac (0)	0	<0.01
Australian (0)	10	0.02
Austrian (22)	233	0.44
Basque (0)	0	<0.01
Belgian (24)	53	0.10
Brazilian (0)	21	0.04
British (64)	313	0.59
Bulgarian (23)	23	0.04
Cajun (0)	0	<0.01
Canadian (0)	16	0.03
Carpatho Rusyn (12)	25	0.05
Celtic (0)	0	<0.01
Croatian (108)	563	1.07
Cypriot (12)	12	0.02
Czech (240)	758	1.44
Czechoslovakian (38)	126	0.24
Danish (61)	219	0.42
Dutch (59)	553	1.05
Eastern European (107)	129	0.24
English (1,284)	5,509	10.46
Estonian (9)	9	0.02
European (373)	385	0.73
Finnish (77)	386	0.73
French, ex. Basque (16)	1,255	2.38
French Canadian (55)	227	0.43
German (2,948)	14,246	27.05
German Russian (0)	0	<0.01
Greek (343)	607	1.15
Guyanese (0)	0	<0.01
Hungarian (632)	2,499	4.74
Icelander (0)	0	<0.01
Iranian (0)	118	0.22
Irish (3,451)	12,740	24.19
Israeli (14)	14	0.03
Italian (2,167)	6,124	11.63
Latvian (44)	60	0.11
Lithuanian (140)	291	0.55
Luxemburger (0)	0	<0.01
Macedonian (11)	11	0.02
Maltese (30)	30	0.06
New Zealander (0)	0	<0.01
Northern European (9)	9	0.02
Norwegian (64)	366	0.69
Pennsylvania German (12)	12	0.02
Polish (907)	4,284	8.13
Portuguese (8)	31	0.06
Romanian (147)	293	0.56
Russian (209)	673	1.28
Scandinavian (11)	66	0.13
Scotch-Irish (447)	1,371	2.60
Scottish (236)	1,113	2.11
Serbian (85)	183	0.35
Slavic (27)	47	0.09
Slovak (795)	2,432	4.62
Slovene (199)	761	1.44
Soviet Union (0)	0	<0.01
Swedish (94)	528	1.00
Swiss (29)	154	0.29
Turkish (222)	222	0.42
Ukrainian (235)	528	1.00
Welsh (121)	657	1.25
West Indian, ex. Hispanic (90)	193	0.37
Bahamian (0)	0	<0.01
Barbadian (0)	0	<0.01
Belizean (0)	0	<0.01
Bermudan (0)	0	<0.01
British West Indian (0)	0	<0.01
Dutch West Indian (0)	0	<0.01
Haitian (13)	27	0.05
Jamaican (69)	158	0.30
Trinidadian/Tobagonian (0)	0	<0.01
U.S. Virgin Islander (0)	0	<0.01
West Indian (8)	8	0.02
Other West Indian (0)	0	<0.01
Yugoslavian (87)	109	0.21

Hispanic Origin	Population	%
Hispanic or Latino (of any race)	2,147	4.12
Central American, ex. Mexican	98	0.19
Costa Rican	5	0.01
Guatemalan	21	0.04
Honduran	16	0.03
Nicaraguan	17	0.03
Panamanian	13	0.02
Salvadoran	26	0.05
Other Central American	0	<0.01
Cuban	80	0.15
Dominican Republic	82	0.16
Mexican	442	0.85
Puerto Rican	1,077	2.07
South American	179	0.34
Argentinean	32	0.06
Bolivian	1	<0.01
Chilean	11	0.02
Colombian	37	0.07
Ecuadorian	5	0.01
Paraguayan	1	<0.01
Peruvian	31	0.06
Uruguayan	7	0.01
Venezuelan	52	0.10
Other South American	2	<0.01
Other Hispanic or Latino	189	0.36

Race*	Population	%
African-American/Black (3,340)	4,052	7.77
Not Hispanic (3,238)	3,858	7.40
Hispanic (102)	194	0.37
American Indian/Alaska Native (149)	503	0.96
Not Hispanic (127)	428	0.82
Hispanic (22)	75	0.14
Alaska Athabascan *(Ala. Nat.)* (2)	2	<0.01
Aleut *(Alaska Native)* (1)	1	<0.01
Apache (1)	4	0.01
Arapaho (0)	0	<0.01
Blackfeet (7)	27	0.05
Canadian/French Am. Ind. (0)	1	<0.01
Central American Ind. (3)	3	0.01
Cherokee (26)	132	0.25
Cheyenne (0)	2	<0.01
Chickasaw (2)	6	0.01
Chippewa (9)	11	0.02
Choctaw (1)	9	0.02
Colville (0)	0	<0.01
Comanche (1)	1	<0.01
Cree (1)	1	<0.01
Creek (0)	7	0.01
Crow (0)	0	<0.01
Delaware (2)	4	0.01
Hopi (0)	0	<0.01
Houma (0)	0	<0.01
Inupiat *(Alaska Native)* (0)	0	<0.01
Iroquois (1)	10	0.02
Kiowa (0)	0	<0.01
Lumbee (0)	0	<0.01
Menominee (0)	0	<0.01
Mexican American Ind. (4)	9	0.02
Navajo (5)	13	0.02
Osage (0)	0	<0.01
Ottawa (0)	0	<0.01
Paiute (0)	0	<0.01
Pima (0)	0	<0.01
Potawatomi (1)	1	<0.01
Pueblo (1)	1	<0.01
Puget Sound Salish (0)	0	<0.01
Seminole (1)	7	0.01
Shoshone (0)	0	<0.01
Sioux (15)	35	0.07
South American Ind. (0)	2	<0.01
Spanish American Ind. (5)	5	0.01
Tlingit-Haida *(Alaska Native)* (1)	2	<0.01
Tohono O'Odham (0)	0	<0.01
Tsimshian *(Alaska Native)* (1)	2	<0.01
Ute (0)	0	<0.01
Yakama (0)	0	<0.01
Yaqui (0)	0	<0.01
Yuman (0)	1	<0.01
Yup'ik *(Alaska Native)* (0)	0	<0.01
Asian (988)	1,344	2.58
Not Hispanic (977)	1,323	2.54
Hispanic (11)	21	0.04
Bangladeshi (5)	8	0.02
Bhutanese (29)	49	0.09
Burmese (146)	146	0.28
Cambodian (6)	7	0.01
Chinese, ex. Taiwanese (150)	189	0.36
Filipino (73)	137	0.26
Hmong (0)	0	<0.01
Indian (217)	277	0.53
Indonesian (13)	21	0.04
Japanese (49)	95	0.18
Korean (68)	96	0.18
Laotian (3)	6	0.01
Malaysian (0)	0	<0.01
Nepalese (16)	29	0.06
Pakistani (68)	75	0.14
Sri Lankan (1)	1	<0.01
Taiwanese (8)	8	0.02
Thai (34)	47	0.09
Vietnamese (49)	62	0.12
Hawaii Native/Pacific Islander (9)	41	0.08
Not Hispanic (9)	37	0.07
Hispanic (0)	4	0.01
Fijian (0)	0	<0.01
Guamanian/Chamorro (3)	5	0.01
Marshallese (0)	0	<0.01
Native Hawaiian (4)	8	0.02
Samoan (0)	0	<0.01
Tongan (0)	0	<0.01
White (45,598)	46,836	89.84
Not Hispanic (44,341)	45,393	87.07
Hispanic (1,257)	1,443	2.77

*Notes: † The Census 2010 population figure is used to calculate the percentages in the Hispanic Origin and Race categories. Ancestry percentages are based on the 2006-2010 American Community Survey population (not shown); ‡ Numbers in parentheses indicate the number of people reporting a single ancestry; * Numbers in parentheses indicate the number of persons reporting this race alone, not in combination with any other race; Please refer to the User Guide for more information.*

Lorain

Place Type: City
County: Lorain
Population: 64,097

Ancestry	Population	%
Afghan (0)	0	<0.01
African, Sub-Saharan (258)	473	0.73
African (258)	451	0.69
Cape Verdean (0)	0	<0.01
Ethiopian (0)	0	<0.01
Ghanaian (0)	11	0.02
Kenyan (0)	0	<0.01
Liberian (0)	0	<0.01
Nigerian (0)	11	0.02
Senegalese (0)	0	<0.01
Sierra Leonean (0)	0	<0.01
Somalian (0)	0	<0.01
South African (0)	0	<0.01
Sudanese (0)	0	<0.01
Ugandan (0)	0	<0.01
Zimbabwean (0)	0	<0.01
Other Sub-Saharan African (0)	0	<0.01
Albanian (0)	0	<0.01
Alsatian (0)	0	<0.01
American (2,165)	2,165	3.32
Arab (222)	383	0.59
Arab (211)	211	0.32
Egyptian (0)	0	<0.01
Iraqi (0)	0	<0.01
Jordanian (0)	0	<0.01
Lebanese (0)	153	0.23
Moroccan (0)	0	<0.01
Palestinian (0)	0	<0.01
Syrian (11)	19	0.03
Other Arab (0)	0	<0.01
Armenian (0)	0	<0.01
Assyrian/Chaldean/Syriac (0)	0	<0.01
Australian (0)	0	<0.01
Austrian (24)	110	0.17
Basque (0)	0	<0.01
Belgian (0)	31	0.05
Brazilian (0)	0	<0.01
British (85)	93	0.14
Bulgarian (15)	15	0.02
Cajun (0)	0	<0.01
Canadian (8)	26	0.04
Carpatho Rusyn (26)	26	0.04
Celtic (0)	0	<0.01
Croatian (319)	569	0.87
Cypriot (0)	0	<0.01
Czech (32)	104	0.16
Czechoslovakian (64)	186	0.29
Danish (18)	53	0.08
Dutch (46)	824	1.26
Eastern European (156)	156	0.24
English (581)	3,807	5.84
Estonian (0)	0	<0.01
European (77)	87	0.13
Finnish (11)	23	0.04
French, ex. Basque (190)	1,057	1.62
French Canadian (4)	42	0.06
German (2,443)	9,408	14.42
German Russian (18)	18	0.03
Greek (160)	365	0.56
Guyanese (0)	0	<0.01
Hungarian (1,136)	3,113	4.77
Icelander (0)	0	<0.01
Iranian (0)	0	<0.01
Irish (1,573)	7,298	11.19
Israeli (0)	0	<0.01
Italian (1,682)	4,912	7.53
Latvian (0)	23	0.04
Lithuanian (25)	66	0.10
Luxemburger (0)	0	<0.01
Macedonian (62)	97	0.15
Maltese (0)	0	<0.01
New Zealander (0)	0	<0.01
Northern European (0)	0	<0.01
Norwegian (25)	71	0.11
Pennsylvania German (25)	25	0.04
Polish (1,803)	4,052	6.21
Portuguese (0)	0	<0.01
Romanian (44)	135	0.21
Russian (81)	399	0.61
Scandinavian (0)	33	0.05
Scotch-Irish (232)	1,107	1.70
Scottish (77)	613	0.94
Serbian (95)	206	0.32
Slavic (7)	15	0.02
Slovak (769)	1,882	2.89
Slovene (175)	546	0.84
Soviet Union (0)	0	<0.01
Swedish (27)	125	0.19
Swiss (11)	115	0.18
Turkish (0)	0	<0.01
Ukrainian (284)	521	0.80
Welsh (50)	314	0.48
West Indian, ex. Hispanic (78)	122	0.19
Bahamian (0)	0	<0.01
Barbadian (0)	0	<0.01
Belizean (0)	0	<0.01
Bermudan (0)	0	<0.01
British West Indian (0)	0	<0.01
Dutch West Indian (0)	0	<0.01
Haitian (43)	43	0.07
Jamaican (22)	29	0.04
Trinidadian/Tobagonian (0)	0	<0.01
U.S. Virgin Islander (0)	0	<0.01
West Indian (13)	50	0.08
Other West Indian (0)	0	<0.01
Yugoslavian (0)	23	0.04

Hispanic Origin	Population	%
Hispanic or Latino (of any race)	16,177	25.24
Central American, ex. Mexican	118	0.18
Costa Rican	4	0.01
Guatemalan	32	0.05
Honduran	17	0.03
Nicaraguan	8	0.01
Panamanian	28	0.04
Salvadoran	29	0.05
Other Central American	0	<0.01
Cuban	79	0.12
Dominican Republic	115	0.18
Mexican	2,934	4.58
Puerto Rican	12,413	19.37
South American	60	0.09
Argentinean	9	0.01
Bolivian	4	0.01
Chilean	3	<0.01
Colombian	12	0.02
Ecuadorian	12	0.02
Paraguayan	0	<0.01
Peruvian	10	0.02
Uruguayan	0	<0.01
Venezuelan	10	0.02
Other South American	0	<0.01
Other Hispanic or Latino	458	0.71

Race*	Population	%
African-American/Black (11,262)	13,512	21.08
Not Hispanic (10,245)	11,803	18.41
Hispanic (1,017)	1,709	2.67
American Indian/Alaska Native (324)	966	1.51
Not Hispanic (177)	651	1.02
Hispanic (147)	315	0.49
Alaska Athabascan *(Ala. Nat.)* (0)	0	<0.01
Aleut *(Alaska Native)* (0)	0	<0.01
Apache (2)	13	0.02
Arapaho (2)	2	<0.01
Blackfeet (8)	54	0.08
Canadian/French Am. Ind. (1)	1	<0.01
Central American Ind. (6)	9	0.01
Cherokee (41)	227	0.35
Cheyenne (0)	1	<0.01
Chickasaw (4)	5	0.01
Chippewa (6)	11	0.02
Choctaw (1)	6	0.01
Colville (0)	0	<0.01
Comanche (0)	1	<0.01
Cree (1)	1	<0.01
Creek (0)	4	0.01
Crow (0)	0	<0.01
Delaware (0)	2	<0.01
Hopi (0)	1	<0.01
Houma (0)	0	<0.01
Inupiat *(Alaska Native)* (0)	0	<0.01
Iroquois (3)	14	0.02
Kiowa (1)	2	<0.01
Lumbee (0)	2	<0.01
Menominee (0)	0	<0.01
Mexican American Ind. (10)	16	0.02
Navajo (2)	7	0.01
Osage (0)	0	<0.01
Ottawa (2)	2	<0.01
Paiute (0)	0	<0.01
Pima (0)	0	<0.01
Potawatomi (3)	3	<0.01
Pueblo (7)	14	0.02
Puget Sound Salish (0)	0	<0.01
Seminole (0)	1	<0.01
Shoshone (0)	0	<0.01
Sioux (8)	26	0.04
South American Ind. (31)	79	0.12
Spanish American Ind. (1)	1	<0.01
Tlingit-Haida *(Alaska Native)* (0)	0	<0.01
Tohono O'Odham (0)	0	<0.01
Tsimshian *(Alaska Native)* (0)	0	<0.01
Ute (0)	0	<0.01
Yakama (0)	0	<0.01
Yaqui (0)	1	<0.01
Yuman (0)	0	<0.01
Yup'ik *(Alaska Native)* (0)	0	<0.01
Asian (228)	428	0.67
Not Hispanic (206)	342	0.53
Hispanic (22)	86	0.13
Bangladeshi (0)	0	<0.01
Bhutanese (0)	0	<0.01
Burmese (0)	0	<0.01
Cambodian (0)	3	<0.01
Chinese, ex. Taiwanese (36)	70	0.11
Filipino (70)	131	0.20
Hmong (6)	6	0.01
Indian (38)	59	0.09
Indonesian (4)	5	0.01
Japanese (11)	29	0.05
Korean (25)	53	0.08
Laotian (0)	0	<0.01
Malaysian (0)	0	<0.01
Nepalese (1)	1	<0.01
Pakistani (5)	7	0.01
Sri Lankan (0)	0	<0.01
Taiwanese (0)	0	<0.01
Thai (11)	13	0.02
Vietnamese (13)	22	0.03
Hawaii Native/Pacific Islander (9)	88	0.14
Not Hispanic (4)	27	0.04
Hispanic (5)	61	0.10
Fijian (0)	0	<0.01
Guamanian/Chamorro (4)	6	0.01
Marshallese (0)	0	<0.01
Native Hawaiian (1)	15	0.02
Samoan (1)	4	0.01
Tongan (0)	0	<0.01
White (43,505)	46,446	72.46
Not Hispanic (35,269)	37,080	57.85
Hispanic (8,236)	9,366	14.61

*Notes: † The Census 2010 population figure is used to calculate the percentages in the Hispanic Origin and Race categories. Ancestry percentages are based on the 2006-2010 American Community Survey population (not shown); ‡ Numbers in parentheses indicate the number of people reporting a single ancestry; * Numbers in parentheses indicate the number of persons reporting this race alone, not in combination with any other race; Please refer to the User Guide for more information.*

Parma

Place Type: City
County: Cuyahoga
Population: 81,601

Ancestry	Population	%
Afghan (0)	0	<0.01
African, Sub-Saharan (341)	341	0.42
African (122)	122	0.15
Cape Verdean (0)	0	<0.01
Ethiopian (0)	0	<0.01
Ghanaian (0)	0	<0.01
Kenyan (31)	31	0.04
Liberian (0)	0	<0.01
Nigerian (180)	180	0.22
Senegalese (0)	0	<0.01
Sierra Leonean (0)	0	<0.01
Somalian (0)	0	<0.01
South African (0)	0	<0.01
Sudanese (0)	0	<0.01
Ugandan (8)	8	0.01
Zimbabwean (0)	0	<0.01
Other Sub-Saharan African (0)	0	<0.01
Albanian (26)	41	0.05
Alsatian (0)	0	<0.01
American (3,084)	3,084	3.77
Arab (743)	1,340	1.64
Arab (55)	184	0.22
Egyptian (0)	0	<0.01
Iraqi (153)	153	0.19
Jordanian (0)	0	<0.01
Lebanese (356)	813	0.99
Moroccan (83)	83	0.10
Palestinian (34)	34	0.04
Syrian (62)	62	0.08
Other Arab (0)	11	0.01
Armenian (35)	80	0.10
Assyrian/Chaldean/Syriac (0)	0	<0.01
Australian (0)	44	0.05
Austrian (64)	283	0.35
Basque (0)	0	<0.01
Belgian (0)	163	0.20
Brazilian (0)	0	<0.01
British (66)	189	0.23
Bulgarian (52)	73	0.09
Cajun (0)	0	<0.01
Canadian (43)	85	0.10
Carpatho Rusyn (95)	116	0.14
Celtic (0)	0	<0.01
Croatian (256)	1,112	1.36
Cypriot (0)	0	<0.01
Czech (648)	2,231	2.72
Czechoslovakian (215)	299	0.37
Danish (0)	32	0.04
Dutch (49)	589	0.72
Eastern European (91)	102	0.12
English (959)	5,050	6.17
Estonian (0)	0	<0.01
European (367)	420	0.51
Finnish (20)	42	0.05
French, ex. Basque (83)	1,339	1.64
French Canadian (46)	178	0.22
German (5,153)	21,335	26.05
German Russian (0)	0	<0.01
Greek (712)	1,087	1.33
Guyanese (0)	0	<0.01
Hungarian (1,279)	4,239	5.18
Icelander (0)	0	<0.01
Iranian (24)	24	0.03
Irish (2,406)	11,502	14.04
Israeli (0)	0	<0.01
Italian (3,782)	11,434	13.96
Latvian (24)	24	0.03
Lithuanian (183)	613	0.75
Luxemburger (0)	0	<0.01
Macedonian (10)	10	0.01
Maltese (0)	0	<0.01
New Zealander (0)	0	<0.01
Northern European (0)	0	<0.01
Norwegian (43)	152	0.19
Pennsylvania German (12)	25	0.03
Polish (5,990)	14,703	17.95
Portuguese (50)	97	0.12
Romanian (460)	761	0.93
Russian (437)	1,152	1.41
Scandinavian (0)	0	<0.01
Scotch-Irish (230)	831	1.01
Scottish (146)	883	1.08
Serbian (1,540)	1,778	2.17
Slavic (56)	145	0.18
Slovak (2,503)	6,760	8.25
Slovene (501)	1,677	2.05
Soviet Union (0)	0	<0.01
Swedish (58)	382	0.47
Swiss (36)	206	0.25
Turkish (0)	0	<0.01
Ukrainian (3,660)	4,857	5.93
Welsh (76)	411	0.50
West Indian, ex. Hispanic (139)	160	0.20
Bahamian (0)	0	<0.01
Barbadian (44)	44	0.05
Belizean (0)	0	<0.01
Bermudan (0)	0	<0.01
British West Indian (0)	0	<0.01
Dutch West Indian (0)	0	<0.01
Haitian (0)	21	0.03
Jamaican (0)	0	<0.01
Trinidadian/Tobagonian (0)	0	<0.01
U.S. Virgin Islander (5)	5	0.01
West Indian (90)	90	0.11
Other West Indian (0)	0	<0.01
Yugoslavian (264)	332	0.41

Hispanic Origin	Population	%
Hispanic or Latino (of any race)	2,915	3.57
Central American, ex. Mexican	117	0.14
Costa Rican	6	0.01
Guatemalan	34	0.04
Honduran	19	0.02
Nicaraguan	13	0.02
Panamanian	8	0.01
Salvadoran	37	0.05
Other Central American	0	<0.01
Cuban	58	0.07
Dominican Republic	64	0.08
Mexican	566	0.69
Puerto Rican	1,665	2.04
South American	252	0.31
Argentinean	19	0.02
Bolivian	0	<0.01
Chilean	4	<0.01
Colombian	45	0.06
Ecuadorian	44	0.05
Paraguayan	1	<0.01
Peruvian	129	0.16
Uruguayan	0	<0.01
Venezuelan	7	0.01
Other South American	3	<0.01
Other Hispanic or Latino	193	0.24

Race*	Population	%
African-American/Black (1,887)	2,340	2.87
Not Hispanic (1,797)	2,211	2.71
Hispanic (90)	129	0.16
American Indian/Alaska Native (151)	435	0.53
Not Hispanic (121)	368	0.45
Hispanic (30)	67	0.08
Alaska Athabascan *(Ala. Nat.)* (1)	3	<0.01
Aleut *(Alaska Native)* (0)	0	<0.01
Apache (6)	13	0.02
Arapaho (0)	0	<0.01
Blackfeet (5)	27	0.03
Canadian/French Am. Ind. (0)	0	<0.01
Central American Ind. (3)	3	<0.01
Cherokee (18)	115	0.14
Cheyenne (2)	5	0.01
Chickasaw (0)	1	<0.01
Chippewa (1)	6	0.01
Choctaw (8)	15	0.02
Colville (0)	0	<0.01
Comanche (0)	3	<0.01
Cree (0)	0	<0.01
Creek (0)	0	<0.01
Crow (0)	1	<0.01
Delaware (0)	0	<0.01
Hopi (0)	0	<0.01
Houma (0)	0	<0.01
Inupiat *(Alaska Native)* (1)	2	<0.01
Iroquois (3)	13	0.02
Kiowa (0)	0	<0.01
Lumbee (1)	3	<0.01
Menominee (0)	0	<0.01
Mexican American Ind. (3)	5	0.01
Navajo (7)	13	0.02
Osage (0)	1	<0.01
Ottawa (0)	0	<0.01
Paiute (0)	0	<0.01
Pima (0)	0	<0.01
Potawatomi (0)	3	<0.01
Pueblo (1)	2	<0.01
Puget Sound Salish (0)	0	<0.01
Seminole (0)	0	<0.01
Shoshone (0)	0	<0.01
Sioux (0)	9	0.01
South American Ind. (8)	10	0.01
Spanish American Ind. (1)	1	<0.01
Tlingit-Haida *(Alaska Native)* (5)	6	0.01
Tohono O'Odham (0)	0	<0.01
Tsimshian *(Alaska Native)* (0)	2	<0.01
Ute (0)	0	<0.01
Yakama (0)	0	<0.01
Yaqui (0)	0	<0.01
Yuman (0)	0	<0.01
Yup'ik *(Alaska Native)* (0)	0	<0.01
Asian (1,511)	1,920	2.35
Not Hispanic (1,497)	1,891	2.32
Hispanic (14)	29	0.04
Bangladeshi (0)	1	<0.01
Bhutanese (0)	0	<0.01
Burmese (0)	0	<0.01
Cambodian (52)	54	0.07
Chinese, ex. Taiwanese (174)	218	0.27
Filipino (392)	515	0.63
Hmong (0)	0	<0.01
Indian (543)	630	0.77
Indonesian (1)	4	<0.01
Japanese (48)	86	0.11
Korean (60)	86	0.11
Laotian (16)	18	0.02
Malaysian (0)	0	<0.01
Nepalese (5)	5	0.01
Pakistani (20)	21	0.03
Sri Lankan (5)	8	0.01
Taiwanese (2)	4	<0.01
Thai (12)	16	0.02
Vietnamese (149)	176	0.22
Hawaii Native/Pacific Islander (13)	79	0.10
Not Hispanic (11)	71	0.09
Hispanic (2)	8	0.01
Fijian (0)	0	<0.01
Guamanian/Chamorro (4)	8	0.01
Marshallese (0)	0	<0.01
Native Hawaiian (6)	16	0.02
Samoan (1)	9	0.01
Tongan (0)	0	<0.01
White (75,921)	77,034	94.40
Not Hispanic (74,186)	75,053	91.98
Hispanic (1,735)	1,981	2.43

*Notes: † The Census 2010 population figure is used to calculate the percentages in the Hispanic Origin and Race categories. Ancestry percentages are based on the 2006-2010 American Community Survey population (not shown); ‡ Numbers in parentheses indicate the number of people reporting a single ancestry; * Numbers in parentheses indicate the number of persons reporting this race alone, not in combination with any other race; Please refer to the User Guide for more information.*

Springfield

Place Type: City
County: Clark
Population: 60,608

Ancestry	Population	%
Afghan (0)	0	<0.01
African, Sub-Saharan (658)	729	1.19
African (627)	691	1.12
Cape Verdean (6)	13	0.02
Ethiopian (0)	0	<0.01
Ghanaian (0)	0	<0.01
Kenyan (0)	0	<0.01
Liberian (0)	0	<0.01
Nigerian (25)	25	0.04
Senegalese (0)	0	<0.01
Sierra Leonean (0)	0	<0.01
Somalian (0)	0	<0.01
South African (0)	0	<0.01
Sudanese (0)	0	<0.01
Ugandan (0)	0	<0.01
Zimbabwean (0)	0	<0.01
Other Sub-Saharan African (0)	0	<0.01
Albanian (0)	0	<0.01
Alsatian (0)	0	<0.01
American (8,078)	8,078	13.14
Arab (35)	35	0.06
Arab (0)	0	<0.01
Egyptian (0)	0	<0.01
Iraqi (0)	0	<0.01
Jordanian (0)	0	<0.01
Lebanese (0)	0	<0.01
Moroccan (0)	0	<0.01
Palestinian (0)	0	<0.01
Syrian (0)	0	<0.01
Other Arab (35)	35	0.06
Armenian (0)	12	0.02
Assyrian/Chaldean/Syriac (0)	0	<0.01
Australian (0)	0	<0.01
Austrian (0)	11	0.02
Basque (0)	0	<0.01
Belgian (12)	12	0.02
Brazilian (0)	0	<0.01
British (25)	83	0.13
Bulgarian (0)	22	0.04
Cajun (0)	0	<0.01
Canadian (22)	61	0.10
Carpatho Rusyn (0)	0	<0.01
Celtic (12)	12	0.02
Croatian (0)	0	<0.01
Cypriot (0)	0	<0.01
Czech (16)	153	0.25
Czechoslovakian (15)	15	0.02
Danish (0)	35	0.06
Dutch (186)	1,199	1.95
Eastern European (0)	0	<0.01
English (1,994)	4,701	7.64
Estonian (0)	0	<0.01
European (473)	473	0.77
Finnish (78)	106	0.17
French, ex. Basque (201)	1,220	1.98
French Canadian (19)	177	0.29
German (5,064)	13,145	21.37
German Russian (0)	0	<0.01
Greek (123)	244	0.40
Guyanese (0)	0	<0.01
Hungarian (85)	267	0.43
Icelander (0)	0	<0.01
Iranian (28)	28	0.05
Irish (2,254)	7,564	12.30
Israeli (0)	0	<0.01
Italian (754)	1,570	2.55
Latvian (8)	8	0.01
Lithuanian (26)	84	0.14
Luxemburger (0)	0	<0.01
Macedonian (55)	145	0.24
Maltese (0)	0	<0.01
New Zealander (0)	0	<0.01
Northern European (11)	11	0.02
Norwegian (25)	151	0.25
Pennsylvania German (9)	9	0.01
Polish (134)	661	1.07
Portuguese (87)	116	0.19
Romanian (38)	60	0.10
Russian (81)	192	0.31
Scandinavian (59)	67	0.11
Scotch-Irish (557)	1,143	1.86
Scottish (545)	1,400	2.28
Serbian (0)	0	<0.01
Slavic (0)	14	0.02
Slovak (20)	139	0.23
Slovene (0)	0	<0.01
Soviet Union (0)	0	<0.01
Swedish (212)	498	0.81
Swiss (12)	63	0.10
Turkish (0)	0	<0.01
Ukrainian (0)	41	0.07
Welsh (182)	505	0.82
West Indian, ex. Hispanic (40)	103	0.17
Bahamian (0)	0	<0.01
Barbadian (0)	0	<0.01
Belizean (0)	0	<0.01
Bermudan (0)	0	<0.01
British West Indian (0)	0	<0.01
Dutch West Indian (0)	35	0.06
Haitian (6)	6	0.01
Jamaican (34)	62	0.10
Trinidadian/Tobagonian (0)	0	<0.01
U.S. Virgin Islander (0)	0	<0.01
West Indian (0)	0	<0.01
Other West Indian (0)	0	<0.01
Yugoslavian (0)	11	0.02

Hispanic Origin	Population	%
Hispanic or Latino (of any race)	1,824	3.01
Central American, ex. Mexican	77	0.13
Costa Rican	3	<0.01
Guatemalan	26	0.04
Honduran	10	0.02
Nicaraguan	13	0.02
Panamanian	11	0.02
Salvadoran	14	0.02
Other Central American	0	<0.01
Cuban	40	0.07
Dominican Republic	13	0.02
Mexican	1,342	2.21
Puerto Rican	115	0.19
South American	19	0.03
Argentinean	0	<0.01
Bolivian	0	<0.01
Chilean	0	<0.01
Colombian	12	0.02
Ecuadorian	2	<0.01
Paraguayan	1	<0.01
Peruvian	2	<0.01
Uruguayan	0	<0.01
Venezuelan	2	<0.01
Other South American	0	<0.01
Other Hispanic or Latino	218	0.36

Race*	Population	%
African-American/Black (10,981)	12,807	21.13
Not Hispanic (10,876)	12,597	20.78
Hispanic (105)	210	0.35
American Indian/Alaska Native (201)	748	1.23
Not Hispanic (167)	660	1.09
Hispanic (34)	88	0.15
Alaska Athabascan (*Ala. Nat.*) (0)	0	<0.01
Aleut (*Alaska Native*) (0)	0	<0.01
Apache (4)	9	0.01
Arapaho (0)	0	<0.01
Blackfeet (5)	47	0.08
Canadian/French Am. Ind. (0)	3	<0.01
Central American Ind. (0)	1	<0.01
Cherokee (46)	230	0.38
Cheyenne (2)	4	0.01
Chickasaw (0)	0	<0.01
Chippewa (1)	2	<0.01
Choctaw (7)	9	0.01
Colville (0)	0	<0.01
Comanche (4)	6	0.01
Cree (1)	2	<0.01
Creek (4)	7	0.01
Crow (1)	2	<0.01
Delaware (0)	6	0.01
Hopi (0)	5	0.01
Houma (0)	0	<0.01
Inupiat (*Alaska Native*) (0)	0	<0.01
Iroquois (2)	6	0.01
Kiowa (0)	0	<0.01
Lumbee (1)	1	<0.01
Menominee (0)	0	<0.01
Mexican American Ind. (1)	8	0.01
Navajo (0)	2	<0.01
Osage (0)	6	0.01
Ottawa (1)	1	<0.01
Paiute (0)	0	<0.01
Pima (0)	0	<0.01
Potawatomi (1)	4	0.01
Pueblo (0)	0	<0.01
Puget Sound Salish (0)	0	<0.01
Seminole (0)	7	0.01
Shoshone (0)	0	<0.01
Sioux (3)	12	0.02
South American Ind. (0)	0	<0.01
Spanish American Ind. (2)	2	<0.01
Tlingit-Haida (*Alaska Native*) (0)	0	<0.01
Tohono O'Odham (3)	3	<0.01
Tsimshian (*Alaska Native*) (0)	0	<0.01
Ute (0)	0	<0.01
Yakama (0)	0	<0.01
Yaqui (1)	1	<0.01
Yuman (0)	0	<0.01
Yup'ik (*Alaska Native*) (0)	0	<0.01
Asian (455)	667	1.10
Not Hispanic (446)	634	1.05
Hispanic (9)	33	0.05
Bangladeshi (0)	0	<0.01
Bhutanese (0)	0	<0.01
Burmese (0)	0	<0.01
Cambodian (3)	6	0.01
Chinese, ex. Taiwanese (76)	97	0.16
Filipino (64)	102	0.17
Hmong (0)	0	<0.01
Indian (163)	196	0.32
Indonesian (1)	6	0.01
Japanese (36)	68	0.11
Korean (18)	48	0.08
Laotian (16)	22	0.04
Malaysian (0)	0	<0.01
Nepalese (0)	0	<0.01
Pakistani (35)	38	0.06
Sri Lankan (2)	2	<0.01
Taiwanese (1)	2	<0.01
Thai (5)	16	0.03
Vietnamese (17)	38	0.06
Hawaii Native/Pacific Islander (25)	96	0.16
Not Hispanic (21)	73	0.12
Hispanic (4)	23	0.04
Fijian (7)	11	0.02
Guamanian/Chamorro (4)	12	0.02
Marshallese (1)	1	<0.01
Native Hawaiian (4)	16	0.03
Samoan (6)	10	0.02
Tongan (0)	2	<0.01
White (45,607)	47,786	78.84
Not Hispanic (44,946)	46,921	77.42
Hispanic (661)	865	1.43

*Notes: † The Census 2010 population figure is used to calculate the percentages in the Hispanic Origin and Race categories. Ancestry percentages are based on the 2006-2010 American Community Survey population (not shown); ‡ Numbers in parentheses indicate the number of people reporting a single ancestry; * Numbers in parentheses indicate the number of persons reporting this race alone, not in combination with any other race; Please refer to the User Guide for more information.*

Toledo

Place Type: City
County: Lucas
Population: 287,208

Ancestry	Population	%
Afghan (0)	0	<0.01
African, Sub-Saharan (2,462)	3,260	1.12
African (1,781)	2,419	0.83
Cape Verdean (0)	46	0.02
Ethiopian (0)	0	<0.01
Ghanaian (69)	69	0.02
Kenyan (19)	19	0.01
Liberian (0)	0	<0.01
Nigerian (528)	642	0.22
Senegalese (15)	15	0.01
Sierra Leonean (0)	0	<0.01
Somalian (0)	0	<0.01
South African (27)	27	0.01
Sudanese (0)	0	<0.01
Ugandan (0)	0	<0.01
Zimbabwean (0)	0	<0.01
Other Sub-Saharan African (23)	23	0.01
Albanian (0)	0	<0.01
Alsatian (0)	6	<0.01
American (10,051)	10,051	3.44
Arab (2,777)	3,428	1.17
Arab (592)	614	0.21
Egyptian (9)	28	0.01
Iraqi (15)	28	0.01
Jordanian (201)	201	0.07
Lebanese (1,284)	1,656	0.57
Moroccan (0)	0	<0.01
Palestinian (183)	216	0.07
Syrian (209)	381	0.13
Other Arab (284)	304	0.10
Armenian (48)	234	0.08
Assyrian/Chaldean/Syriac (27)	27	0.01
Australian (9)	9	<0.01
Austrian (103)	628	0.22
Basque (0)	0	<0.01
Belgian (34)	215	0.07
Brazilian (0)	0	<0.01
British (325)	785	0.27
Bulgarian (66)	217	0.07
Cajun (0)	0	<0.01
Canadian (235)	521	0.18
Carpatho Rusyn (6)	15	0.01
Celtic (57)	73	0.03
Croatian (0)	125	0.04
Cypriot (0)	11	<0.01
Czech (143)	833	0.29
Czechoslovakian (116)	304	0.10
Danish (101)	499	0.17
Dutch (454)	3,569	1.22
Eastern European (63)	63	0.02
English (5,068)	18,826	6.45
Estonian (19)	19	0.01
European (1,540)	1,626	0.56
Finnish (95)	295	0.10
French, ex. Basque (1,553)	13,787	4.72
French Canadian (664)	2,025	0.69
German (27,798)	76,635	26.26
German Russian (0)	0	<0.01
Greek (510)	910	0.31
Guyanese (60)	60	0.02
Hungarian (2,245)	6,352	2.18
Icelander (13)	44	0.02
Iranian (73)	73	0.03
Irish (8,029)	34,827	11.93
Israeli (28)	35	0.01
Italian (3,020)	9,356	3.21
Latvian (21)	21	0.01
Lithuanian (38)	264	0.09
Luxemburger (0)	0	<0.01
Macedonian (8)	18	0.01
Maltese (9)	17	0.01
New Zealander (0)	0	<0.01
Northern European (13)	13	<0.01
Norwegian (197)	1,161	0.40
Pennsylvania German (65)	245	0.08
Polish (10,864)	25,480	8.73
Portuguese (48)	154	0.05
Romanian (114)	436	0.15
Russian (227)	959	0.33
Scandinavian (12)	101	0.03
Scotch-Irish (695)	2,388	0.82
Scottish (805)	3,645	1.25
Serbian (35)	69	0.02
Slavic (0)	58	0.02
Slovak (237)	945	0.32
Slovene (70)	149	0.05
Soviet Union (0)	0	<0.01
Swedish (278)	1,344	0.46
Swiss (165)	1,134	0.39
Turkish (120)	120	0.04
Ukrainian (159)	499	0.17
Welsh (246)	1,296	0.44
West Indian, ex. Hispanic (812)	1,077	0.37
Bahamian (0)	0	<0.01
Barbadian (0)	0	<0.01
Belizean (19)	19	0.01
Bermudan (0)	0	<0.01
British West Indian (22)	22	0.01
Dutch West Indian (0)	0	<0.01
Haitian (64)	97	0.03
Jamaican (667)	879	0.30
Trinidadian/Tobagonian (11)	11	<0.01
U.S. Virgin Islander (0)	0	<0.01
West Indian (29)	49	0.02
Other West Indian (0)	0	<0.01
Yugoslavian (75)	115	0.04

Hispanic Origin	Population	%
Hispanic or Latino (of any race)	21,231	7.39
Central American, ex. Mexican	240	0.08
Costa Rican	15	0.01
Guatemalan	61	0.02
Honduran	26	0.01
Nicaraguan	72	0.03
Panamanian	33	0.01
Salvadoran	33	0.01
Other Central American	0	<0.01
Cuban	299	0.10
Dominican Republic	69	0.02
Mexican	17,576	6.12
Puerto Rican	1,143	0.40
South American	219	0.08
Argentinean	24	0.01
Bolivian	4	<0.01
Chilean	18	0.01
Colombian	49	0.02
Ecuadorian	27	0.01
Paraguayan	6	<0.01
Peruvian	51	0.02
Uruguayan	0	<0.01
Venezuelan	32	0.01
Other South American	8	<0.01
Other Hispanic or Latino	1,685	0.59

Race*	Population	%
African-American/Black (78,073)	85,254	29.68
Not Hispanic (76,820)	82,886	28.86
Hispanic (1,253)	2,368	0.82
American Indian/Alaska Native (1,065)	3,359	1.17
Not Hispanic (755)	2,675	0.93
Hispanic (310)	684	0.24
Alaska Athabascan *(Ala. Nat.)* (1)	2	<0.01
Aleut *(Alaska Native)* (1)	2	<0.01
Apache (21)	66	0.02
Arapaho (0)	6	<0.01
Blackfeet (25)	158	0.06
Canadian/French Am. Ind. (7)	23	0.01
Central American Ind. (0)	0	<0.01
Cherokee (163)	784	0.27
Cheyenne (0)	6	<0.01
Chickasaw (3)	7	<0.01
Chippewa (77)	139	0.05
Choctaw (13)	59	0.02
Colville (0)	0	<0.01
Comanche (1)	3	<0.01
Cree (1)	6	<0.01
Creek (2)	23	0.01
Crow (0)	5	<0.01
Delaware (9)	11	<0.01
Hopi (3)	4	<0.01
Houma (0)	0	<0.01
Inupiat *(Alaska Native)* (2)	3	<0.01
Iroquois (15)	39	0.01
Kiowa (0)	1	<0.01
Lumbee (5)	14	<0.01
Menominee (9)	11	<0.01
Mexican American Ind. (38)	96	0.03
Navajo (13)	30	0.01
Osage (0)	3	<0.01
Ottawa (10)	41	0.01
Paiute (0)	0	<0.01
Pima (0)	0	<0.01
Potawatomi (13)	33	0.01
Pueblo (6)	15	0.01
Puget Sound Salish (0)	0	<0.01
Seminole (1)	9	<0.01
Shoshone (0)	3	<0.01
Sioux (14)	39	0.01
South American Ind. (14)	17	0.01
Spanish American Ind. (2)	6	<0.01
Tlingit-Haida *(Alaska Native)* (1)	2	<0.01
Tohono O'Odham (0)	0	<0.01
Tsimshian *(Alaska Native)* (0)	0	<0.01
Ute (0)	0	<0.01
Yakama (0)	0	<0.01
Yaqui (3)	4	<0.01
Yuman (0)	0	<0.01
Yup'ik *(Alaska Native)* (0)	0	<0.01
Asian (3,264)	4,559	1.59
Not Hispanic (3,204)	4,312	1.50
Hispanic (60)	247	0.09
Bangladeshi (2)	5	<0.01
Bhutanese (0)	0	<0.01
Burmese (5)	5	<0.01
Cambodian (2)	7	<0.01
Chinese, ex. Taiwanese (1,015)	1,177	0.41
Filipino (355)	610	0.21
Hmong (4)	4	<0.01
Indian (836)	995	0.35
Indonesian (14)	28	0.01
Japanese (84)	272	0.09
Korean (216)	382	0.13
Laotian (91)	129	0.04
Malaysian (11)	22	0.01
Nepalese (32)	36	0.01
Pakistani (81)	97	0.03
Sri Lankan (16)	18	0.01
Taiwanese (26)	30	0.01
Thai (72)	116	0.04
Vietnamese (236)	286	0.10
Hawaii Native/Pacific Islander (77)	275	0.10
Not Hispanic (64)	220	0.08
Hispanic (13)	55	0.02
Fijian (2)	2	<0.01
Guamanian/Chamorro (13)	28	0.01
Marshallese (0)	0	<0.01
Native Hawaiian (23)	86	0.03
Samoan (17)	34	0.01
Tongan (1)	2	<0.01
White (186,188)	195,953	68.23
Not Hispanic (176,468)	183,797	63.99
Hispanic (9,720)	12,156	4.23

*Notes: † The Census 2010 population figure is used to calculate the percentages in the Hispanic Origin and Race categories. Ancestry percentages are based on the 2006-2010 American Community Survey population (not shown); ‡ Numbers in parentheses indicate the number of people reporting a single ancestry; * Numbers in parentheses indicate the number of persons reporting this race alone, not in combination with any other race; Please refer to the User Guide for more information.*

Youngstown

Place Type: City
County: Mahoning
Population: 66,982

Ancestry	Population	%
Afghan (0)	0	<0.01
African, Sub-Saharan (2,618)	2,765	3.97
African (2,559)	2,655	3.82
Cape Verdean (0)	0	<0.01
Ethiopian (14)	65	0.09
Ghanaian (0)	0	<0.01
Kenyan (0)	0	<0.01
Liberian (0)	0	<0.01
Nigerian (0)	0	<0.01
Senegalese (0)	0	<0.01
Sierra Leonean (0)	0	<0.01
Somalian (0)	0	<0.01
South African (0)	0	<0.01
Sudanese (0)	0	<0.01
Ugandan (0)	0	<0.01
Zimbabwean (0)	0	<0.01
Other Sub-Saharan African (45)	45	0.06
Albanian (10)	22	0.03
Alsatian (0)	0	<0.01
American (2,278)	2,278	3.27
Arab (104)	274	0.39
Arab (84)	110	0.16
Egyptian (0)	0	<0.01
Iraqi (0)	0	<0.01
Jordanian (0)	0	<0.01
Lebanese (20)	139	0.20
Moroccan (0)	0	<0.01
Palestinian (0)	0	<0.01
Syrian (0)	25	0.04
Other Arab (0)	0	<0.01
Armenian (0)	11	0.02
Assyrian/Chaldean/Syriac (0)	0	<0.01
Australian (0)	18	0.03
Austrian (0)	0	<0.01
Basque (0)	0	<0.01
Belgian (0)	0	<0.01
Brazilian (0)	0	<0.01
British (82)	115	0.17
Bulgarian (10)	33	0.05
Cajun (0)	0	<0.01
Canadian (11)	46	0.07
Carpatho Rusyn (0)	20	0.03
Celtic (0)	0	<0.01
Croatian (314)	688	0.99
Cypriot (0)	0	<0.01
Czech (28)	160	0.23
Czechoslovakian (24)	32	0.05
Danish (0)	141	0.20
Dutch (72)	662	0.95
Eastern European (11)	11	0.02
English (656)	3,017	4.34
Estonian (0)	0	<0.01
European (103)	119	0.17
Finnish (0)	29	0.04
French, ex. Basque (130)	542	0.78
French Canadian (58)	106	0.15
German (1,840)	7,654	11.00
German Russian (0)	1	<0.01
Greek (110)	312	0.45
Guyanese (0)	0	<0.01
Hungarian (389)	1,409	2.02
Icelander (0)	0	<0.01
Iranian (0)	0	<0.01
Irish (1,479)	6,661	9.57
Israeli (0)	0	<0.01
Italian (3,495)	7,337	10.54
Latvian (0)	0	<0.01
Lithuanian (33)	79	0.11
Luxemburger (0)	0	<0.01
Macedonian (0)	0	<0.01
Maltese (0)	0	<0.01
New Zealander (0)	0	<0.01
Northern European (7)	7	0.01
Norwegian (7)	22	0.03
Pennsylvania German (19)	113	0.16
Polish (807)	2,036	2.93
Portuguese (10)	25	0.04
Romanian (146)	267	0.38
Russian (152)	351	0.50
Scandinavian (0)	0	<0.01
Scotch-Irish (218)	730	1.05
Scottish (79)	466	0.67
Serbian (16)	43	0.06
Slavic (9)	16	0.02
Slovak (1,477)	3,113	4.47
Slovene (20)	44	0.06
Soviet Union (0)	0	<0.01
Swedish (128)	228	0.33
Swiss (12)	96	0.14
Turkish (12)	12	0.02
Ukrainian (218)	533	0.77
Welsh (70)	877	1.26
West Indian, ex. Hispanic (86)	152	0.22
Bahamian (0)	0	<0.01
Barbadian (0)	8	0.01
Belizean (0)	0	<0.01
Bermudan (0)	0	<0.01
British West Indian (0)	0	<0.01
Dutch West Indian (0)	0	<0.01
Haitian (9)	19	0.03
Jamaican (77)	125	0.18
Trinidadian/Tobagonian (0)	0	<0.01
U.S. Virgin Islander (0)	0	<0.01
West Indian (0)	0	<0.01
Other West Indian (0)	0	<0.01
Yugoslavian (7)	34	0.05

Hispanic Origin	Population	%
Hispanic or Latino (of any race)	6,207	9.27
Central American, ex. Mexican	152	0.23
Costa Rican	5	0.01
Guatemalan	26	0.04
Honduran	46	0.07
Nicaraguan	7	0.01
Panamanian	19	0.03
Salvadoran	49	0.07
Other Central American	0	<0.01
Cuban	98	0.15
Dominican Republic	239	0.36
Mexican	1,270	1.90
Puerto Rican	3,836	5.73
South American	155	0.23
Argentinean	9	0.01
Bolivian	2	<0.01
Chilean	3	<0.01
Colombian	104	0.16
Ecuadorian	7	0.01
Paraguayan	0	<0.01
Peruvian	18	0.03
Uruguayan	1	<0.01
Venezuelan	9	0.01
Other South American	2	<0.01
Other Hispanic or Latino	457	0.68

Race*	Population	%
African-American/Black (30,257)	32,093	47.91
Not Hispanic (29,448)	30,939	46.19
Hispanic (809)	1,154	1.72
American Indian/Alaska Native (237)	870	1.30
Not Hispanic (183)	715	1.07
Hispanic (54)	155	0.23
Alaska Athabascan (*Ala. Nat.*) (0)	3	<0.01
Aleut (*Alaska Native*) (0)	0	<0.01
Apache (1)	19	0.03
Arapaho (0)	4	0.01
Blackfeet (9)	60	0.09
Canadian/French Am. Ind. (0)	0	<0.01
Central American Ind. (0)	0	<0.01
Cherokee (55)	234	0.35
Cheyenne (0)	0	<0.01
Chickasaw (1)	1	<0.01
Chippewa (0)	7	0.01
Choctaw (3)	14	0.02
Colville (0)	0	<0.01
Comanche (2)	6	0.01
Cree (0)	0	<0.01
Creek (0)	1	<0.01
Crow (0)	2	<0.01
Delaware (0)	1	<0.01
Hopi (2)	2	<0.01
Houma (0)	0	<0.01
Inupiat (*Alaska Native*) (1)	2	<0.01
Iroquois (6)	11	0.02
Kiowa (0)	0	<0.01
Lumbee (2)	2	<0.01
Menominee (0)	1	<0.01
Mexican American Ind. (8)	19	0.03
Navajo (2)	3	<0.01
Osage (0)	0	<0.01
Ottawa (0)	0	<0.01
Paiute (0)	0	<0.01
Pima (0)	0	<0.01
Potawatomi (0)	0	<0.01
Pueblo (0)	0	<0.01
Puget Sound Salish (0)	0	<0.01
Seminole (2)	6	0.01
Shoshone (1)	1	<0.01
Sioux (2)	11	0.02
South American Ind. (8)	15	0.02
Spanish American Ind. (3)	3	<0.01
Tlingit-Haida (*Alaska Native*) (0)	1	<0.01
Tohono O'Odham (0)	0	<0.01
Tsimshian (*Alaska Native*) (0)	0	<0.01
Ute (1)	1	<0.01
Yakama (0)	0	<0.01
Yaqui (2)	2	<0.01
Yuman (0)	0	<0.01
Yup'ik (*Alaska Native*) (0)	0	<0.01
Asian (297)	499	0.74
Not Hispanic (283)	449	0.67
Hispanic (14)	50	0.07
Bangladeshi (0)	1	<0.01
Bhutanese (0)	0	<0.01
Burmese (0)	0	<0.01
Cambodian (7)	9	0.01
Chinese, ex. Taiwanese (31)	43	0.06
Filipino (34)	74	0.11
Hmong (3)	3	<0.01
Indian (100)	128	0.19
Indonesian (1)	1	<0.01
Japanese (8)	27	0.04
Korean (19)	59	0.09
Laotian (7)	10	0.01
Malaysian (0)	0	<0.01
Nepalese (6)	7	0.01
Pakistani (11)	12	0.02
Sri Lankan (0)	1	<0.01
Taiwanese (3)	3	<0.01
Thai (1)	3	<0.01
Vietnamese (50)	67	0.10
Hawaii Native/Pacific Islander (17)	87	0.13
Not Hispanic (7)	54	0.08
Hispanic (10)	33	0.05
Fijian (0)	0	<0.01
Guamanian/Chamorro (3)	10	0.01
Marshallese (0)	0	<0.01
Native Hawaiian (5)	25	0.04
Samoan (2)	6	0.01
Tongan (0)	0	<0.01
White (31,508)	33,448	49.94
Not Hispanic (28,918)	30,411	45.40
Hispanic (2,590)	3,037	4.53

*Notes: † The Census 2010 population figure is used to calculate the percentages in the Hispanic Origin and Race categories. Ancestry percentages are based on the 2006-2010 American Community Survey population (not shown); ‡ Numbers in parentheses indicate the number of people reporting a single ancestry; * Numbers in parentheses indicate the number of persons reporting this race alone, not in combination with any other race; Please refer to the User Guide for more information.*

Ancestry Group Rankings

Afghan

Top 10 Places Sorted by Population
Based on all places, regardless of total population

Place	Population	%
Columbus (city) Franklin County	89	0.01
Dublin (city) Franklin County	38	0.10
Tallmadge (city) Summit County	13	0.07
Lebanon (city) Warren County	12	0.06
Wickliffe (city) Lake County	8	0.06
Aberdeen (village) Brown County	0	0.00
Ada (village) Hardin County	0	0.00
Adamsville (village) Muskingum County	0	0.00
Addyston (village) Hamilton County	0	0.00
Adelphi (village) Ross County	0	0.00

Top 10 Places Sorted by Percent of Total Population
Based on all places, regardless of total population

Place	Population	%
Dublin (city) Franklin County	38	0.10
Tallmadge (city) Summit County	13	0.07
Lebanon (city) Warren County	12	0.06
Wickliffe (city) Lake County	8	0.06
Columbus (city) Franklin County	89	0.01
Aberdeen (village) Brown County	0	0.00
Ada (village) Hardin County	0	0.00
Adamsville (village) Muskingum County	0	0.00
Addyston (village) Hamilton County	0	0.00
Adelphi (village) Ross County	0	0.00

Top 10 Places Sorted by Percent of Total Population
Based on places with total population of 50,000 or more

Place	Population	%
Columbus (city) Franklin County	89	0.01
Akron (city) Summit County	0	0.00
Canton (city) Stark County	0	0.00
Cincinnati (city) Hamilton County	0	0.00
Cleveland (city) Cuyahoga County	0	0.00
Dayton (city) Montgomery County	0	0.00
Elyria (city) Lorain County	0	0.00
Hamilton (city) Butler County	0	0.00
Kettering (city) Montgomery County	0	0.00
Lakewood (city) Cuyahoga County	0	0.00

African, Sub-Saharan

Top 10 Places Sorted by Population
Based on all places, regardless of total population

Place	Population	%
Columbus (city) Franklin County	26,987	3.50
Cincinnati (city) Hamilton County	17,006	5.67
Cleveland (city) Cuyahoga County	5,454	1.33
Toledo (city) Lucas County	3,260	1.12
Canton (city) Stark County	2,852	3.83
Youngstown (city) Mahoning County	2,765	3.97
Dayton (city) Montgomery County	2,395	1.64
Akron (city) Summit County	2,290	1.13
Fairfield (city) Butler County	1,080	2.53
Lima (city) Allen County	1,042	2.68

Top 10 Places Sorted by Percent of Total Population
Based on all places, regardless of total population

Place	Population	%
Urbancrest (village) Franklin County	284	27.76
Lockland (village) Hamilton County	451	13.02
Skyline Acres (cdp) Hamilton County	152	7.81
Chesterhill (village) Morgan County	16	6.40
Cincinnati (city) Hamilton County	17,006	5.67
Whitehall (city) Franklin County	932	5.13
Mount Healthy (city) Hamilton County	276	4.53
Kenwood (cdp) Hamilton County	326	4.51
Huber Ridge (cdp) Franklin County	196	4.39
Youngstown (city) Mahoning County	2,765	3.97

Top 10 Places Sorted by Percent of Total Population
Based on places with total population of 50,000 or more

Place	Population	%
Cincinnati (city) Hamilton County	17,006	5.67
Youngstown (city) Mahoning County	2,765	3.97
Canton (city) Stark County	2,852	3.83
Columbus (city) Franklin County	26,987	3.50
Dayton (city) Montgomery County	2,395	1.64
Cleveland (city) Cuyahoga County	5,454	1.33
Springfield (city) Clark County	729	1.19
Akron (city) Summit County	2,290	1.13
Toledo (city) Lucas County	3,260	1.12
Lakewood (city) Cuyahoga County	406	0.77

African, Sub-Saharan: African

Top 10 Places Sorted by Population
Based on all places, regardless of total population

Place	Population	%
Cincinnati (city) Hamilton County	15,631	5.21
Columbus (city) Franklin County	10,986	1.43
Cleveland (city) Cuyahoga County	4,279	1.05
Canton (city) Stark County	2,713	3.64
Youngstown (city) Mahoning County	2,655	3.82
Toledo (city) Lucas County	2,419	0.83
Akron (city) Summit County	2,027	1.00
Dayton (city) Montgomery County	1,956	1.34
Lima (city) Allen County	995	2.56
Mansfield (city) Richland County	827	1.69

Top 10 Places Sorted by Percent of Total Population
Based on all places, regardless of total population

Place	Population	%
Skyline Acres (cdp) Hamilton County	152	7.81
Chesterhill (village) Morgan County	16	6.40
Cincinnati (city) Hamilton County	15,631	5.21
Urbancrest (village) Franklin County	45	4.40
Youngstown (city) Mahoning County	2,655	3.82
Canton (city) Stark County	2,713	3.64
Maplewood Park (cdp) Trumbull County	10	3.44
Addyston (village) Hamilton County	24	3.38
New Weston (village) Darke County	6	3.28
Mount Healthy (city) Hamilton County	193	3.17

Top 10 Places Sorted by Percent of Total Population
Based on places with total population of 50,000 or more

Place	Population	%
Cincinnati (city) Hamilton County	15,631	5.21
Youngstown (city) Mahoning County	2,655	3.82
Canton (city) Stark County	2,713	3.64
Columbus (city) Franklin County	10,986	1.43
Dayton (city) Montgomery County	1,956	1.34
Springfield (city) Clark County	691	1.12
Cleveland (city) Cuyahoga County	4,279	1.05
Akron (city) Summit County	2,027	1.00
Toledo (city) Lucas County	2,419	0.83
Lorain (city) Lorain County	451	0.69

African, Sub-Saharan: Cape Verdean

Top 10 Places Sorted by Population
Based on all places, regardless of total population

Place	Population	%
Englewood (city) Montgomery County	94	0.71
Cleveland (city) Cuyahoga County	58	0.01
Canton (city) Stark County	56	0.08
Toledo (city) Lucas County	46	0.02
Akron (city) Summit County	33	0.02
Fairborn (city) Greene County	28	0.09
Columbus (city) Franklin County	28	<0.01
Springfield (city) Clark County	13	0.02
Aberdeen (village) Brown County	0	0.00
Ada (village) Hardin County	0	0.00

Top 10 Places Sorted by Percent of Total Population
Based on all places, regardless of total population

Place	Population	%
Englewood (city) Montgomery County	94	0.71
Fairborn (city) Greene County	28	0.09
Canton (city) Stark County	56	0.08
Toledo (city) Lucas County	46	0.02
Akron (city) Summit County	33	0.02
Springfield (city) Clark County	13	0.02
Cleveland (city) Cuyahoga County	58	0.01
Columbus (city) Franklin County	28	<0.01
Aberdeen (village) Brown County	0	0.00
Ada (village) Hardin County	0	0.00

Top 10 Places Sorted by Percent of Total Population
Based on places with total population of 50,000 or more

Place	Population	%
Canton (city) Stark County	56	0.08
Toledo (city) Lucas County	46	0.02
Akron (city) Summit County	33	0.02
Springfield (city) Clark County	13	0.02
Cleveland (city) Cuyahoga County	58	0.01
Columbus (city) Franklin County	28	<0.01
Cincinnati (city) Hamilton County	0	0.00
Dayton (city) Montgomery County	0	0.00
Elyria (city) Lorain County	0	0.00
Hamilton (city) Butler County	0	0.00

African, Sub-Saharan: Ethiopian

Top 10 Places Sorted by Population
Based on all places, regardless of total population

Place	Population	%
Columbus (city) Franklin County	2,207	0.29
Whitehall (city) Franklin County	565	3.11
Cincinnati (city) Hamilton County	458	0.15
Reynoldsburg (city) Franklin County	297	0.85
Pleasant Run Farm (cdp) Hamilton County	141	3.19
Forestville (cdp) Hamilton County	96	0.88
Forest Park (city) Hamilton County	96	0.51
Dayton (city) Montgomery County	94	0.06
Kenwood (cdp) Hamilton County	87	1.20
Westerville (city) Franklin County	68	0.19

Top 10 Places Sorted by Percent of Total Population
Based on all places, regardless of total population

Place	Population	%
Pleasant Run Farm (cdp) Hamilton County	141	3.19
Whitehall (city) Franklin County	565	3.11
Urbancrest (village) Franklin County	16	1.56
Kenwood (cdp) Hamilton County	87	1.20
Forestville (cdp) Hamilton County	96	0.88
Reynoldsburg (city) Franklin County	297	0.85
Forest Park (city) Hamilton County	96	0.51
Hartford (village) Licking County	3	0.51
Columbus (city) Franklin County	2,207	0.29
Westerville (city) Franklin County	68	0.19

Top 10 Places Sorted by Percent of Total Population
Based on places with total population of 50,000 or more

Place	Population	%
Columbus (city) Franklin County	2,207	0.29
Cincinnati (city) Hamilton County	458	0.15
Youngstown (city) Mahoning County	65	0.09
Dayton (city) Montgomery County	94	0.06
Akron (city) Summit County	42	0.02
Cleveland (city) Cuyahoga County	21	0.01
Canton (city) Stark County	0	0.00
Elyria (city) Lorain County	0	0.00
Hamilton (city) Butler County	0	0.00
Kettering (city) Montgomery County	0	0.00

African, Sub-Saharan: Ghanaian

Top 10 Places Sorted by Population
Based on all places, regardless of total population

Place	Population	%
Columbus (city) Franklin County	1,303	0.17
Fairfield (city) Butler County	368	0.86
Westerville (city) Franklin County	262	0.73
Cleveland (city) Cuyahoga County	79	0.02
Toledo (city) Lucas County	69	0.02
Lakewood (city) Cuyahoga County	67	0.13
Mount Healthy (city) Hamilton County	42	0.69
Forest Park (city) Hamilton County	39	0.21
South Euclid (city) Cuyahoga County	39	0.17
Solon (city) Cuyahoga County	34	0.15

Top 10 Places Sorted by Percent of Total Population
Based on all places, regardless of total population

Place	Population	%
Fairfield (city) Butler County	368	0.86
Westerville (city) Franklin County	262	0.73
Mount Healthy (city) Hamilton County	42	0.69
Mulberry (cdp) Clermont County	14	0.43
North College Hill (city) Hamilton County	33	0.35
Oakwood (village) Cuyahoga County	10	0.27
Forest Park (city) Hamilton County	39	0.21
Northgate (cdp) Hamilton County	13	0.20
Ada (village) Hardin County	12	0.20
Columbus (city) Franklin County	1,303	0.17

Top 10 Places Sorted by Percent of Total Population
Based on places with total population of 50,000 or more

Place	Population	%
Columbus (city) Franklin County	1,303	0.17
Lakewood (city) Cuyahoga County	67	0.13
Cleveland (city) Cuyahoga County	79	0.02
Toledo (city) Lucas County	69	0.02
Lorain (city) Lorain County	11	0.02
Cincinnati (city) Hamilton County	23	0.01
Akron (city) Summit County	0	0.00
Canton (city) Stark County	0	0.00
Dayton (city) Montgomery County	0	0.00
Elyria (city) Lorain County	0	0.00

African, Sub-Saharan: Kenyan

Top 10 Places Sorted by Population
Based on all places, regardless of total population

Place	Population	%
Columbus (city) Franklin County	517	0.07
Reynoldsburg (city) Franklin County	57	0.16
Garfield Heights (city) Cuyahoga County	51	0.18
Green (city) Summit County	46	0.18
Pleasant Run (cdp) Hamilton County	38	0.80
Parma (city) Cuyahoga County	31	0.04
Toledo (city) Lucas County	19	0.01
Elyria (city) Lorain County	18	0.03
Oberlin (city) Lorain County	17	0.20
Lakewood (city) Cuyahoga County	13	0.02

Top 10 Places Sorted by Percent of Total Population
Based on all places, regardless of total population

Place	Population	%
Pleasant Run (cdp) Hamilton County	38	0.80
North Randall (village) Cuyahoga County	3	0.35
Oberlin (city) Lorain County	17	0.20
Garfield Heights (city) Cuyahoga County	51	0.18
Green (city) Summit County	46	0.18
Reynoldsburg (city) Franklin County	57	0.16
Beachwood (city) Cuyahoga County	12	0.10
Columbus (city) Franklin County	517	0.07
Wilmington (city) Clinton County	9	0.07
Painesville (city) Lake County	12	0.06

Top 10 Places Sorted by Percent of Total Population
Based on places with total population of 50,000 or more

Place	Population	%
Columbus (city) Franklin County	517	0.07
Parma (city) Cuyahoga County	31	0.04
Elyria (city) Lorain County	18	0.03
Lakewood (city) Cuyahoga County	13	0.02
Toledo (city) Lucas County	19	0.01
Dayton (city) Montgomery County	10	0.01
Cincinnati (city) Hamilton County	12	<0.01
Cleveland (city) Cuyahoga County	10	<0.01
Akron (city) Summit County	0	0.00
Canton (city) Stark County	0	0.00

African, Sub-Saharan: Liberian

Top 10 Places Sorted by Population
Based on all places, regardless of total population

Place	Population	%
Columbus (city) Franklin County	384	0.05
Cleveland (city) Cuyahoga County	128	0.03
Richmond Heights (city) Cuyahoga County	65	0.61
Pataskala (city) Licking County	58	0.41
Huber Ridge (cdp) Franklin County	56	1.25
Lockland (village) Hamilton County	47	1.36
Canton (city) Stark County	38	0.05
Akron (city) Summit County	29	0.01
Cleveland Heights (city) Cuyahoga County	28	0.06
Cincinnati (city) Hamilton County	26	0.01

Top 10 Places Sorted by Percent of Total Population
Based on all places, regardless of total population

Place	Population	%
Lockland (village) Hamilton County	47	1.36
Huber Ridge (cdp) Franklin County	56	1.25
Richmond Heights (city) Cuyahoga County	65	0.61
Pataskala (city) Licking County	58	0.41
University Heights (city) Cuyahoga County	25	0.18
Landen (cdp) Warren County	6	0.09
Cleveland Heights (city) Cuyahoga County	28	0.06
Columbus (city) Franklin County	384	0.05
Canton (city) Stark County	38	0.05
Zanesville (city) Muskingum County	13	0.05

Top 10 Places Sorted by Percent of Total Population
Based on places with total population of 50,000 or more

Place	Population	%
Columbus (city) Franklin County	384	0.05
Canton (city) Stark County	38	0.05
Cleveland (city) Cuyahoga County	128	0.03
Akron (city) Summit County	29	0.01
Cincinnati (city) Hamilton County	26	0.01
Dayton (city) Montgomery County	0	0.00
Elyria (city) Lorain County	0	0.00
Hamilton (city) Butler County	0	0.00
Kettering (city) Montgomery County	0	0.00
Lakewood (city) Cuyahoga County	0	0.00

African, Sub-Saharan: Nigerian

Top 10 Places Sorted by Population
Based on all places, regardless of total population

Place	Population	%
Columbus (city) Franklin County	861	0.11
Toledo (city) Lucas County	642	0.22
Cleveland (city) Cuyahoga County	352	0.09
Kenwood (cdp) Hamilton County	239	3.31
Lockland (village) Hamilton County	204	5.89
Parma (city) Cuyahoga County	180	0.22
Solon (city) Cuyahoga County	168	0.73
Cincinnati (city) Hamilton County	158	0.05
Trotwood (city) Montgomery County	153	0.61
Dayton (city) Montgomery County	138	0.09

Top 10 Places Sorted by Percent of Total Population
Based on all places, regardless of total population

Place	Population	%
Lockland (village) Hamilton County	204	5.89
Kenwood (cdp) Hamilton County	239	3.31
Canal Winchester (village) Franklin County	77	1.14
Twinsburg Heights (cdp) Summit County	12	1.07
North Randall (village) Cuyahoga County	9	1.04
Newtown (village) Hamilton County	24	0.92
Solon (city) Cuyahoga County	168	0.73
Trotwood (city) Montgomery County	153	0.61
Bergholz (village) Jefferson County	4	0.60
Blacklick Estates (cdp) Franklin County	44	0.51

Top 10 Places Sorted by Percent of Total Population
Based on places with total population of 50,000 or more

Place	Population	%
Toledo (city) Lucas County	642	0.22
Parma (city) Cuyahoga County	180	0.22
Columbus (city) Franklin County	861	0.11
Lakewood (city) Cuyahoga County	52	0.10
Cleveland (city) Cuyahoga County	352	0.09
Dayton (city) Montgomery County	138	0.09
Cincinnati (city) Hamilton County	158	0.05
Springfield (city) Clark County	25	0.04
Lorain (city) Lorain County	11	0.02
Akron (city) Summit County	0	0.00

African, Sub-Saharan: Senegalese

Top 10 Places Sorted by Population
Based on all places, regardless of total population

Place	Population	%
Cincinnati (city) Hamilton County	195	0.06
Finneytown (cdp) Hamilton County	131	1.01
Columbus (city) Franklin County	104	0.01
Bedford Heights (city) Cuyahoga County	22	0.20
Cleveland (city) Cuyahoga County	17	<0.01
Toledo (city) Lucas County	15	0.01
Northbrook (cdp) Hamilton County	14	0.14
Medina (city) Medina County	13	0.05
Mansfield (city) Richland County	8	0.02
Aberdeen (village) Brown County	0	0.00

Top 10 Places Sorted by Percent of Total Population
Based on all places, regardless of total population

Place	Population	%
Finneytown (cdp) Hamilton County	131	1.01
Bedford Heights (city) Cuyahoga County	22	0.20
Northbrook (cdp) Hamilton County	14	0.14
Cincinnati (city) Hamilton County	195	0.06
Medina (city) Medina County	13	0.05
Mansfield (city) Richland County	8	0.02
Columbus (city) Franklin County	104	0.01
Toledo (city) Lucas County	15	0.01
Cleveland (city) Cuyahoga County	17	<0.01
Aberdeen (village) Brown County	0	0.00

Top 10 Places Sorted by Percent of Total Population
Based on places with total population of 50,000 or more

Place	Population	%
Cincinnati (city) Hamilton County	195	0.06
Columbus (city) Franklin County	104	0.01
Toledo (city) Lucas County	15	0.01
Cleveland (city) Cuyahoga County	17	<0.01
Akron (city) Summit County	0	0.00
Canton (city) Stark County	0	0.00
Dayton (city) Montgomery County	0	0.00
Elyria (city) Lorain County	0	0.00
Hamilton (city) Butler County	0	0.00
Kettering (city) Montgomery County	0	0.00

African, Sub-Saharan: Sierra Leonean

Top 10 Places Sorted by Population
Based on all places, regardless of total population

Place	Population	%
Columbus (city) Franklin County	461	0.06
Lake Darby (cdp) Franklin County	38	0.82
Olmsted Falls (city) Cuyahoga County	36	0.41
Streetsboro (city) Portage County	23	0.15
Aberdeen (village) Brown County	0	0.00
Ada (village) Hardin County	0	0.00
Adamsville (village) Muskingum County	0	0.00
Addyston (village) Hamilton County	0	0.00
Adelphi (village) Ross County	0	0.00
Adena (village) Jefferson County	0	0.00

Top 10 Places Sorted by Percent of Total Population
Based on all places, regardless of total population

Place	Population	%
Lake Darby (cdp) Franklin County	38	0.82
Olmsted Falls (city) Cuyahoga County	36	0.41
Streetsboro (city) Portage County	23	0.15

Columbus (city) Franklin County	461	0.06
Aberdeen (village) Brown County	0	0.00
Ada (village) Hardin County	0	0.00
Adamsville (village) Muskingum County	0	0.00
Addyston (village) Hamilton County	0	0.00
Adelphi (village) Ross County	0	0.00
Adena (village) Jefferson County	0	0.00

Top 10 Places Sorted by Percent of Total Population
Based on places with total population of 50,000 or more

Place	Population	%
Columbus (city) Franklin County	461	0.06
Akron (city) Summit County	0	0.00
Canton (city) Stark County	0	0.00
Cincinnati (city) Hamilton County	0	0.00
Cleveland (city) Cuyahoga County	0	0.00
Dayton (city) Montgomery County	0	0.00
Elyria (city) Lorain County	0	0.00
Hamilton (city) Butler County	0	0.00
Kettering (city) Montgomery County	0	0.00
Lakewood (city) Cuyahoga County	0	0.00

African, Sub-Saharan: Somalian

Top 10 Places Sorted by Population
Based on all places, regardless of total population

Place	Population	%
Columbus (city) Franklin County	9,093	1.18
Urbancrest (village) Franklin County	223	21.80
Hilliard (city) Franklin County	130	0.47
Warrensville Heights (city) Cuyahoga County	119	0.87
Dublin (city) Franklin County	77	0.20
Westlake (city) Cuyahoga County	76	0.23
Huber Ridge (cdp) Franklin County	57	1.28
Cleveland (city) Cuyahoga County	41	0.01
Whitehall (city) Franklin County	37	0.20
Lima (city) Allen County	34	0.09

Top 10 Places Sorted by Percent of Total Population
Based on all places, regardless of total population

Place	Population	%
Urbancrest (village) Franklin County	223	21.80
Huber Ridge (cdp) Franklin County	57	1.28
Columbus (city) Franklin County	9,093	1.18
Warrensville Heights (city) Cuyahoga County	119	0.87
Hilliard (city) Franklin County	130	0.47
Westlake (city) Cuyahoga County	76	0.23
Dublin (city) Franklin County	77	0.20
Whitehall (city) Franklin County	37	0.20
Lima (city) Allen County	34	0.09
Grove City (city) Franklin County	28	0.08

Top 10 Places Sorted by Percent of Total Population
Based on places with total population of 50,000 or more

Place	Population	%
Columbus (city) Franklin County	9,093	1.18
Cleveland (city) Cuyahoga County	41	0.01
Akron (city) Summit County	23	0.01
Canton (city) Stark County	0	0.00
Cincinnati (city) Hamilton County	0	0.00
Dayton (city) Montgomery County	0	0.00
Elyria (city) Lorain County	0	0.00
Hamilton (city) Butler County	0	0.00
Kettering (city) Montgomery County	0	0.00
Lakewood (city) Cuyahoga County	0	0.00

African, Sub-Saharan: South African

Top 10 Places Sorted by Population
Based on all places, regardless of total population

Place	Population	%
Columbus (city) Franklin County	115	0.01
Beachwood (city) Cuyahoga County	79	0.66
Greenville (city) Darke County	75	0.57
Cleveland (city) Cuyahoga County	68	0.02
Findlay (city) Hancock County	51	0.12
Montrose-Ghent (cdp) Summit County	46	0.90
Canton (city) Stark County	45	0.06
Monfort Heights (cdp) Hamilton County	36	0.31
Shaker Heights (city) Cuyahoga County	35	0.12
Cleveland Heights (city) Cuyahoga County	35	0.07

Top 10 Places Sorted by Percent of Total Population
Based on all places, regardless of total population

Place	Population	%
Montrose-Ghent (cdp) Summit County	46	0.90
Orange (village) Cuyahoga County	28	0.85
Lockland (village) Hamilton County	25	0.72
Northfield (village) Summit County	26	0.70
Beachwood (city) Cuyahoga County	79	0.66
Greenville (city) Darke County	75	0.57
Brimfield (cdp) Portage County	13	0.39
Monfort Heights (cdp) Hamilton County	36	0.31
New Concord (village) Muskingum County	4	0.16
West Carrollton (city) Montgomery County	18	0.14

Top 10 Places Sorted by Percent of Total Population
Based on places with total population of 50,000 or more

Place	Population	%
Canton (city) Stark County	45	0.06
Cleveland (city) Cuyahoga County	68	0.02
Dayton (city) Montgomery County	22	0.02
Columbus (city) Franklin County	115	0.01
Toledo (city) Lucas County	27	0.01
Akron (city) Summit County	17	0.01
Cincinnati (city) Hamilton County	13	<0.01
Elyria (city) Lorain County	0	0.00
Hamilton (city) Butler County	0	0.00
Kettering (city) Montgomery County	0	0.00

African, Sub-Saharan: Sudanese

Top 10 Places Sorted by Population
Based on all places, regardless of total population

Place	Population	%
Columbus (city) Franklin County	90	0.01
Cleveland (city) Cuyahoga County	86	0.02
Cincinnati (city) Hamilton County	63	0.02
Elyria (city) Lorain County	55	0.10
Whitehall (city) Franklin County	50	0.28
Lakewood (city) Cuyahoga County	23	0.04
Bluffton (village) Allen County	10	0.24
Mayfield Heights (city) Cuyahoga County	8	0.04
Aberdeen (village) Brown County	0	0.00
Ada (village) Hardin County	0	0.00

Top 10 Places Sorted by Percent of Total Population
Based on all places, regardless of total population

Place	Population	%
Whitehall (city) Franklin County	50	0.28
Bluffton (village) Allen County	10	0.24
Elyria (city) Lorain County	55	0.10
Lakewood (city) Cuyahoga County	23	0.04
Mayfield Heights (city) Cuyahoga County	8	0.04
Cleveland (city) Cuyahoga County	86	0.02
Cincinnati (city) Hamilton County	63	0.02
Columbus (city) Franklin County	90	0.01
Aberdeen (village) Brown County	0	0.00
Ada (village) Hardin County	0	0.00

Top 10 Places Sorted by Percent of Total Population
Based on places with total population of 50,000 or more

Place	Population	%
Elyria (city) Lorain County	55	0.10
Lakewood (city) Cuyahoga County	23	0.04
Cleveland (city) Cuyahoga County	86	0.02
Cincinnati (city) Hamilton County	63	0.02
Columbus (city) Franklin County	90	0.01
Akron (city) Summit County	0	0.00
Canton (city) Stark County	0	0.00
Dayton (city) Montgomery County	0	0.00
Hamilton (city) Butler County	0	0.00
Kettering (city) Montgomery County	0	0.00

African, Sub-Saharan: Ugandan

Top 10 Places Sorted by Population
Based on all places, regardless of total population

Place	Population	%
Cleveland Heights (city) Cuyahoga County	12	0.03
Lakewood (city) Cuyahoga County	9	0.02
Oxford (city) Butler County	8	0.04
Parma (city) Cuyahoga County	8	0.01
Athens (city) Athens County	6	0.03
Aberdeen (village) Brown County	0	0.00
Ada (village) Hardin County	0	0.00
Adamsville (village) Muskingum County	0	0.00
Addyston (village) Hamilton County	0	0.00
Adelphi (village) Ross County	0	0.00

Top 10 Places Sorted by Percent of Total Population
Based on all places, regardless of total population

Place	Population	%
Oxford (city) Butler County	8	0.04
Cleveland Heights (city) Cuyahoga County	12	0.03
Athens (city) Athens County	6	0.03
Lakewood (city) Cuyahoga County	9	0.02
Parma (city) Cuyahoga County	8	0.01
Aberdeen (village) Brown County	0	0.00
Ada (village) Hardin County	0	0.00
Adamsville (village) Muskingum County	0	0.00
Addyston (village) Hamilton County	0	0.00
Adelphi (village) Ross County	0	0.00

Top 10 Places Sorted by Percent of Total Population
Based on places with total population of 50,000 or more

Place	Population	%
Lakewood (city) Cuyahoga County	9	0.02
Parma (city) Cuyahoga County	8	0.01
Akron (city) Summit County	0	0.00
Canton (city) Stark County	0	0.00
Cincinnati (city) Hamilton County	0	0.00
Cleveland (city) Cuyahoga County	0	0.00
Columbus (city) Franklin County	0	0.00
Dayton (city) Montgomery County	0	0.00
Elyria (city) Lorain County	0	0.00
Hamilton (city) Butler County	0	0.00

African, Sub-Saharan: Zimbabwean

Top 10 Places Sorted by Population
Based on all places, regardless of total population

Place	Population	%
Blue Ash (city) Hamilton County	172	1.43
Columbus (city) Franklin County	125	0.02
Cincinnati (city) Hamilton County	53	0.02
Akron (city) Summit County	12	0.01
Aberdeen (village) Brown County	0	0.00
Ada (village) Hardin County	0	0.00
Adamsville (village) Muskingum County	0	0.00
Addyston (village) Hamilton County	0	0.00
Adelphi (village) Ross County	0	0.00
Adena (village) Jefferson County	0	0.00

Top 10 Places Sorted by Percent of Total Population
Based on all places, regardless of total population

Place	Population	%
Blue Ash (city) Hamilton County	172	1.43
Columbus (city) Franklin County	125	0.02
Cincinnati (city) Hamilton County	53	0.02
Akron (city) Summit County	12	0.01
Aberdeen (village) Brown County	0	0.00
Ada (village) Hardin County	0	0.00
Adamsville (village) Muskingum County	0	0.00
Addyston (village) Hamilton County	0	0.00
Adelphi (village) Ross County	0	0.00
Adena (village) Jefferson County	0	0.00

Top 10 Places Sorted by Percent of Total Population
Based on places with total population of 50,000 or more

Place	Population	%
Columbus (city) Franklin County	125	0.02
Cincinnati (city) Hamilton County	53	0.02
Akron (city) Summit County	12	0.01
Canton (city) Stark County	0	0.00
Cleveland (city) Cuyahoga County	0	0.00
Dayton (city) Montgomery County	0	0.00
Elyria (city) Lorain County	0	0.00
Hamilton (city) Butler County	0	0.00
Kettering (city) Montgomery County	0	0.00
Lakewood (city) Cuyahoga County	0	0.00

African, Sub-Saharan: Other

Top 10 Places Sorted by Population
Based on all places, regardless of total population

Place	Population	%
Columbus (city) Franklin County	713	0.09
Cincinnati (city) Hamilton County	374	0.12
Forest Park (city) Hamilton County	366	1.96
Cleveland (city) Cuyahoga County	315	0.08
Dayton (city) Montgomery County	175	0.12
Akron (city) Summit County	107	0.05
Euclid (city) Cuyahoga County	105	0.21
Lockland (village) Hamilton County	93	2.69
Parma Heights (city) Cuyahoga County	91	0.44
Streetsboro (city) Portage County	82	0.53

Top 10 Places Sorted by Percent of Total Population
Based on all places, regardless of total population

Place	Population	%
Lockland (village) Hamilton County	93	2.69
Forest Park (city) Hamilton County	366	1.96
Turpin Hills (cdp) Hamilton County	45	0.91
North Randall (village) Cuyahoga County	7	0.81
Hiram (village) Portage County	9	0.73
Baltic (village) Tuscarawas County	3	0.58
Streetsboro (city) Portage County	82	0.53
Parma Heights (city) Cuyahoga County	91	0.44
Beach City (village) Stark County	4	0.36
Sidney (city) Shelby County	64	0.30

Top 10 Places Sorted by Percent of Total Population
Based on places with total population of 50,000 or more

Place	Population	%
Lakewood (city) Cuyahoga County	73	0.14
Cincinnati (city) Hamilton County	374	0.12
Dayton (city) Montgomery County	175	0.12
Columbus (city) Franklin County	713	0.09
Cleveland (city) Cuyahoga County	315	0.08
Youngstown (city) Mahoning County	45	0.06
Akron (city) Summit County	107	0.05
Kettering (city) Montgomery County	11	0.02
Toledo (city) Lucas County	23	0.01
Canton (city) Stark County	0	0.00

Albanian

Top 10 Places Sorted by Population
Based on all places, regardless of total population

Place	Population	%
Lakewood (city) Cuyahoga County	766	1.45
Rocky River (city) Cuyahoga County	328	1.62
Akron (city) Summit County	304	0.15
Columbus (city) Franklin County	292	0.04
Fairview Park (city) Cuyahoga County	223	1.32
North Olmsted (city) Cuyahoga County	176	0.54
Parma Heights (city) Cuyahoga County	164	0.79
Cleveland (city) Cuyahoga County	139	0.03
Willowick (city) Lake County	132	0.93
West Carrollton (city) Montgomery County	129	0.97

Top 10 Places Sorted by Percent of Total Population
Based on all places, regardless of total population

Place	Population	%
Peninsula (village) Summit County	16	2.79
Lake Mohawk (cdp) Carroll County	48	2.76
McKinley Heights (cdp) Trumbull County	25	2.29
Rocky River (city) Cuyahoga County	328	1.62
Lakewood (city) Cuyahoga County	766	1.45
Fairview Park (city) Cuyahoga County	223	1.32
West Carrollton (city) Montgomery County	129	0.97
Willowick (city) Lake County	132	0.93
Montrose-Ghent (cdp) Summit County	42	0.82
Parma Heights (city) Cuyahoga County	164	0.79

Top 10 Places Sorted by Percent of Total Population
Based on places with total population of 50,000 or more

Place	Population	%
Lakewood (city) Cuyahoga County	766	1.45
Akron (city) Summit County	304	0.15
Parma (city) Cuyahoga County	41	0.05
Columbus (city) Franklin County	292	0.04
Canton (city) Stark County	30	0.04
Cleveland (city) Cuyahoga County	139	0.03
Youngstown (city) Mahoning County	22	0.03
Kettering (city) Montgomery County	15	0.03
Cincinnati (city) Hamilton County	0	0.00
Dayton (city) Montgomery County	0	0.00

Alsatian

Top 10 Places Sorted by Population
Based on all places, regardless of total population

Place	Population	%
Ashland (city) Ashland County	69	0.33
Cincinnati (city) Hamilton County	67	0.02
Dent (cdp) Hamilton County	30	0.31
Grove City (city) Franklin County	30	0.09
Columbus (city) Franklin County	29	<0.01
Akron (city) Summit County	26	0.01
Salem Heights (cdp) Hamilton County	25	0.63
Archbold (village) Fulton County	24	0.57
Athens (city) Athens County	21	0.09
White Oak (cdp) Hamilton County	20	0.11

Top 10 Places Sorted by Percent of Total Population
Based on all places, regardless of total population

Place	Population	%
Lake Waynoka (cdp) Brown County	11	1.21
Silver Lake (village) Summit County	17	0.66
Salem Heights (cdp) Hamilton County	25	0.63
Archbold (village) Fulton County	24	0.57
Moreland Hills (village) Cuyahoga County	15	0.45
Sherwood (cdp) Hamilton County	14	0.40
Fredericktown (village) Knox County	10	0.40
Ashland (city) Ashland County	69	0.33
Dent (cdp) Hamilton County	30	0.31
Gibsonburg (village) Sandusky County	6	0.23

Top 10 Places Sorted by Percent of Total Population
Based on places with total population of 50,000 or more

Place	Population	%
Cincinnati (city) Hamilton County	67	0.02
Kettering (city) Montgomery County	13	0.02
Akron (city) Summit County	26	0.01
Dayton (city) Montgomery County	13	0.01
Columbus (city) Franklin County	29	<0.01
Toledo (city) Lucas County	6	<0.01
Canton (city) Stark County	0	0.00
Cleveland (city) Cuyahoga County	0	0.00
Elyria (city) Lorain County	0	0.00
Hamilton (city) Butler County	0	0.00

American

Top 10 Places Sorted by Population
Based on all places, regardless of total population

Place	Population	%
Columbus (city) Franklin County	31,925	4.14
Cincinnati (city) Hamilton County	18,156	6.05
Dayton (city) Montgomery County	16,035	11.01
Hamilton (city) Butler County	15,067	24.12
Toledo (city) Lucas County	10,051	3.44
Cleveland (city) Cuyahoga County	9,836	2.40
Akron (city) Summit County	8,242	4.06
Springfield (city) Clark County	8,078	13.14
Warren (city) Trumbull County	7,537	17.66
Fairborn (city) Greene County	6,052	18.82

Top 10 Places Sorted by Percent of Total Population
Based on all places, regardless of total population

Place	Population	%
Flat Rock (cdp) Seneca County	86	61.87
Kanauga (cdp) Gallia County	75	59.52
Octa (village) Fayette County	28	58.33
Kansas (cdp) Seneca County	166	56.27
Somerville (village) Butler County	147	55.89
Olde West Chester (cdp) Butler County	95	46.57
Cynthiana (cdp) Pike County	26	46.43
Congress (village) Wayne County	78	45.61
Hanging Rock (village) Lawrence County	74	42.77
Darbyville (village) Pickaway County	89	42.38

Top 10 Places Sorted by Percent of Total Population
Based on places with total population of 50,000 or more

Place	Population	%
Hamilton (city) Butler County	15,067	24.12
Springfield (city) Clark County	8,078	13.14
Dayton (city) Montgomery County	16,035	11.01
Elyria (city) Lorain County	5,042	9.17
Kettering (city) Montgomery County	4,961	8.83
Canton (city) Stark County	5,025	6.75
Cincinnati (city) Hamilton County	18,156	6.05
Columbus (city) Franklin County	31,925	4.14
Akron (city) Summit County	8,242	4.06
Parma (city) Cuyahoga County	3,084	3.77

Arab: Total

Top 10 Places Sorted by Population
Based on all places, regardless of total population

Place	Population	%
Columbus (city) Franklin County	6,451	0.84
Toledo (city) Lucas County	3,428	1.17
Cleveland (city) Cuyahoga County	3,346	0.82
Lakewood (city) Cuyahoga County	1,450	2.75
Cincinnati (city) Hamilton County	1,405	0.47
Akron (city) Summit County	1,396	0.69
Parma (city) Cuyahoga County	1,340	1.64
North Olmsted (city) Cuyahoga County	1,223	3.73
Westlake (city) Cuyahoga County	1,183	3.66
Strongsville (city) Cuyahoga County	988	2.23

Top 10 Places Sorted by Percent of Total Population
Based on all places, regardless of total population

Place	Population	%
Damascus (cdp) Mahoning County	23	9.27
Port William (village) Clinton County	17	6.67
Lake Tomahawk (cdp) Columbiana County	21	4.59
Bloomingburg (village) Fayette County	44	4.51
Rosemount (cdp) Scioto County	90	4.09
Olmsted Falls (city) Cuyahoga County	343	3.92
Middleburg Heights (city) Cuyahoga County	596	3.77
North Olmsted (city) Cuyahoga County	1,223	3.73
Linndale (village) Cuyahoga County	5	3.68
Westlake (city) Cuyahoga County	1,183	3.66

Top 10 Places Sorted by Percent of Total Population
Based on places with total population of 50,000 or more

Place	Population	%
Lakewood (city) Cuyahoga County	1,450	2.75
Parma (city) Cuyahoga County	1,340	1.64
Toledo (city) Lucas County	3,428	1.17
Columbus (city) Franklin County	6,451	0.84
Cleveland (city) Cuyahoga County	3,346	0.82
Kettering (city) Montgomery County	458	0.82
Canton (city) Stark County	577	0.78
Akron (city) Summit County	1,396	0.69
Lorain (city) Lorain County	383	0.59
Cincinnati (city) Hamilton County	1,405	0.47

Arab: Arab

Top 10 Places Sorted by Population
Based on all places, regardless of total population

Place	Population	%
Columbus (city) Franklin County	1,109	0.14
Cleveland (city) Cuyahoga County	663	0.16
Toledo (city) Lucas County	614	0.21
North Olmsted (city) Cuyahoga County	447	1.36
Westlake (city) Cuyahoga County	344	1.06
Lakewood (city) Cuyahoga County	218	0.41
Lorain (city) Lorain County	211	0.32
Cincinnati (city) Hamilton County	199	0.07
Boardman (cdp) Mahoning County	198	0.56
Parma (city) Cuyahoga County	184	0.22

Top 10 Places Sorted by Percent of Total Population
Based on all places, regardless of total population

Place	Population	%
Lexington (village) Richland County	168	3.25
Moreland Hills (village) Cuyahoga County	52	1.57
Linndale (village) Cuyahoga County	2	1.47

Lincoln Heights (village) Hamilton County	49	1.44
North Olmsted (city) Cuyahoga County	447	1.36
Craig Beach (village) Mahoning County	12	1.07
Westlake (city) Cuyahoga County	344	1.06
Mogadore (village) Summit County	43	1.06
Williamsburg (village) Clermont County	25	1.04
Gates Mills (village) Cuyahoga County	18	0.83

Top 10 Places Sorted by Percent of Total Population
Based on places with total population of 50,000 or more

Place	Population	%
Lakewood (city) Cuyahoga County	218	0.41
Lorain (city) Lorain County	211	0.32
Parma (city) Cuyahoga County	184	0.22
Toledo (city) Lucas County	614	0.21
Cleveland (city) Cuyahoga County	663	0.16
Youngstown (city) Mahoning County	110	0.16
Columbus (city) Franklin County	1,109	0.14
Akron (city) Summit County	159	0.08
Cincinnati (city) Hamilton County	199	0.07
Dayton (city) Montgomery County	39	0.03

Arab: Egyptian

Top 10 Places Sorted by Population
Based on all places, regardless of total population

Place	Population	%
Columbus (city) Franklin County	911	0.12
Cleveland (city) Cuyahoga County	326	0.08
Strongsville (city) Cuyahoga County	179	0.40
Lakewood (city) Cuyahoga County	172	0.33
Dublin (city) Franklin County	164	0.42
Akron (city) Summit County	137	0.07
Cincinnati (city) Hamilton County	133	0.04
Sylvania (city) Lucas County	114	0.60
Westlake (city) Cuyahoga County	111	0.34
Parma Heights (city) Cuyahoga County	110	0.53

Top 10 Places Sorted by Percent of Total Population
Based on all places, regardless of total population

Place	Population	%
Orange (village) Cuyahoga County	56	1.70
Maineville (village) Warren County	8	0.97
New Albany (village) Franklin County	62	0.87
Sylvania (city) Lucas County	114	0.60
Parma Heights (city) Cuyahoga County	110	0.53
Independence (city) Cuyahoga County	36	0.51
Delta (village) Fulton County	15	0.50
Dublin (city) Franklin County	164	0.42
Elida (village) Allen County	9	0.42
Strongsville (city) Cuyahoga County	179	0.40

Top 10 Places Sorted by Percent of Total Population
Based on places with total population of 50,000 or more

Place	Population	%
Lakewood (city) Cuyahoga County	172	0.33
Columbus (city) Franklin County	911	0.12
Cleveland (city) Cuyahoga County	326	0.08
Akron (city) Summit County	137	0.07
Cincinnati (city) Hamilton County	133	0.04
Dayton (city) Montgomery County	46	0.03
Kettering (city) Montgomery County	10	0.02
Toledo (city) Lucas County	28	0.01
Canton (city) Stark County	5	0.01
Elyria (city) Lorain County	0	0.00

Arab: Iraqi

Top 10 Places Sorted by Population
Based on all places, regardless of total population

Place	Population	%
Columbus (city) Franklin County	334	0.04
Centerville (city) Montgomery County	264	1.11
Parma (city) Cuyahoga County	153	0.19
Dayton (city) Montgomery County	123	0.08
Cleveland (city) Cuyahoga County	85	0.02
Delaware (city) Delaware County	58	0.17
Stow (city) Summit County	44	0.13
Toledo (city) Lucas County	28	0.01
Canton (city) Stark County	15	0.02
Miamisburg (city) Montgomery County	14	0.07

Top 10 Places Sorted by Percent of Total Population
Based on all places, regardless of total population

Place	Population	%
Centerville (city) Montgomery County	264	1.11
Bluffton (village) Allen County	11	0.27
Parma (city) Cuyahoga County	153	0.19
Delaware (city) Delaware County	58	0.17
Stow (city) Summit County	44	0.13
Dayton (city) Montgomery County	123	0.08
Miamisburg (city) Montgomery County	14	0.07
Barberton (city) Summit County	14	0.05
Columbus (city) Franklin County	334	0.04
Cleveland (city) Cuyahoga County	85	0.02

Top 10 Places Sorted by Percent of Total Population
Based on places with total population of 50,000 or more

Place	Population	%
Parma (city) Cuyahoga County	153	0.19
Dayton (city) Montgomery County	123	0.08
Columbus (city) Franklin County	334	0.04
Cleveland (city) Cuyahoga County	85	0.02
Canton (city) Stark County	15	0.02
Toledo (city) Lucas County	28	0.01
Hamilton (city) Butler County	8	0.01
Cincinnati (city) Hamilton County	14	<0.01
Akron (city) Summit County	7	<0.01
Elyria (city) Lorain County	0	0.00

Arab: Jordanian

Top 10 Places Sorted by Population
Based on all places, regardless of total population

Place	Population	%
Columbus (city) Franklin County	617	0.08
Toledo (city) Lucas County	201	0.07
Cincinnati (city) Hamilton County	127	0.04
Cleveland (city) Cuyahoga County	115	0.03
Fairview Park (city) Cuyahoga County	107	0.63
Miamisburg (city) Montgomery County	105	0.53
New Burlington (cdp) Hamilton County	99	1.87
Ravenna (city) Portage County	94	0.80
Bellefontaine (city) Logan County	83	0.63
Kettering (city) Montgomery County	78	0.14

Top 10 Places Sorted by Percent of Total Population
Based on all places, regardless of total population

Place	Population	%
New Burlington (cdp) Hamilton County	99	1.87
Ravenna (city) Portage County	94	0.80
Park Layne (cdp) Clark County	35	0.78
Fairview Park (city) Cuyahoga County	107	0.63
Bellefontaine (city) Logan County	83	0.63
Olmsted Falls (city) Cuyahoga County	48	0.55
Miamisburg (city) Montgomery County	105	0.53
Shawnee Hills (village) Delaware County	4	0.51
Rocky River (city) Cuyahoga County	62	0.31
Glendale (village) Hamilton County	7	0.30

Top 10 Places Sorted by Percent of Total Population
Based on places with total population of 50,000 or more

Place	Population	%
Kettering (city) Montgomery County	78	0.14
Hamilton (city) Butler County	58	0.09
Columbus (city) Franklin County	617	0.08
Toledo (city) Lucas County	201	0.07
Elyria (city) Lorain County	30	0.05
Cincinnati (city) Hamilton County	127	0.04
Cleveland (city) Cuyahoga County	115	0.03
Dayton (city) Montgomery County	39	0.03
Akron (city) Summit County	0	0.00
Canton (city) Stark County	0	0.00

Arab: Lebanese

Top 10 Places Sorted by Population
Based on all places, regardless of total population

Place	Population	%
Toledo (city) Lucas County	1,656	0.57
Columbus (city) Franklin County	1,656	0.21
Cleveland (city) Cuyahoga County	1,147	0.28
Akron (city) Summit County	914	0.45
Parma (city) Cuyahoga County	813	0.99
Lakewood (city) Cuyahoga County	706	1.34
Cincinnati (city) Hamilton County	704	0.23
Middleburg Heights (city) Cuyahoga County	479	3.03
Westlake (city) Cuyahoga County	431	1.33
Strongsville (city) Cuyahoga County	410	0.92

Top 10 Places Sorted by Percent of Total Population
Based on all places, regardless of total population

Place	Population	%
Damascus (cdp) Mahoning County	23	9.27
Port William (village) Clinton County	17	6.67
Lake Tomahawk (cdp) Columbiana County	21	4.59
Bloomingburg (village) Fayette County	44	4.51
Five Points (cdp) Warren County	65	3.37
Mulberry (cdp) Clermont County	109	3.35
Middleburg Heights (city) Cuyahoga County	479	3.03
Marble Cliff (village) Franklin County	17	2.91
Savannah (village) Ashland County	7	2.29
Mount Repose (cdp) Clermont County	94	2.21

Top 10 Places Sorted by Percent of Total Population
Based on places with total population of 50,000 or more

Place	Population	%
Lakewood (city) Cuyahoga County	706	1.34
Parma (city) Cuyahoga County	813	0.99
Toledo (city) Lucas County	1,656	0.57
Canton (city) Stark County	358	0.48
Akron (city) Summit County	914	0.45
Kettering (city) Montgomery County	251	0.45
Cleveland (city) Cuyahoga County	1,147	0.28
Cincinnati (city) Hamilton County	704	0.23
Lorain (city) Lorain County	153	0.23
Columbus (city) Franklin County	1,656	0.21

Arab: Moroccan

Top 10 Places Sorted by Population
Based on all places, regardless of total population

Place	Population	%
Columbus (city) Franklin County	308	0.04
Parma (city) Cuyahoga County	83	0.10
Cleveland Heights (city) Cuyahoga County	82	0.18
Cleveland (city) Cuyahoga County	75	0.02
Cincinnati (city) Hamilton County	65	0.02
Aurora (city) Portage County	63	0.41
Englewood (city) Montgomery County	39	0.30
Dublin (city) Franklin County	39	0.10
Bexley (city) Franklin County	38	0.29
Dayton (city) Montgomery County	28	0.02

Top 10 Places Sorted by Percent of Total Population
Based on all places, regardless of total population

Place	Population	%
South Amherst (village) Lorain County	10	0.54
New Holland (village) Pickaway County	3	0.44
Aurora (city) Portage County	63	0.41
Englewood (city) Montgomery County	39	0.30
Bexley (city) Franklin County	38	0.29
South Lebanon (village) Warren County	11	0.29
Amherst (city) Lorain County	27	0.22
Cleveland Heights (city) Cuyahoga County	82	0.18
Grafton (village) Lorain County	9	0.14
Orrville (city) Wayne County	11	0.13

Top 10 Places Sorted by Percent of Total Population
Based on places with total population of 50,000 or more

Place	Population	%
Parma (city) Cuyahoga County	83	0.10
Columbus (city) Franklin County	308	0.04
Cleveland (city) Cuyahoga County	75	0.02
Cincinnati (city) Hamilton County	65	0.02
Dayton (city) Montgomery County	28	0.02
Akron (city) Summit County	0	0.00
Canton (city) Stark County	0	0.00
Elyria (city) Lorain County	0	0.00
Hamilton (city) Butler County	0	0.00
Kettering (city) Montgomery County	0	0.00

Arab: Palestinian

Top 10 Places Sorted by Population
Based on all places, regardless of total population

Place	Population	%
Columbus (city) Franklin County	604	0.08
Cleveland (city) Cuyahoga County	553	0.14
North Olmsted (city) Cuyahoga County	331	1.01
Toledo (city) Lucas County	216	0.07
Macedonia (city) Summit County	213	1.96
Strongsville (city) Cuyahoga County	211	0.48
Tallmadge (city) Summit County	199	1.15
Westlake (city) Cuyahoga County	145	0.45
Lakewood (city) Cuyahoga County	116	0.22
Miamisburg (city) Montgomery County	104	0.52

Top 10 Places Sorted by Percent of Total Population
Based on all places, regardless of total population

Place	Population	%
Lowellville (village) Mahoning County	33	2.86
Salem Heights (cdp) Hamilton County	90	2.26
Macedonia (city) Summit County	213	1.96
Huber Ridge (cdp) Franklin County	83	1.86
Tallmadge (city) Summit County	199	1.15
North Olmsted (city) Cuyahoga County	331	1.01
New Albany (village) Franklin County	59	0.83
Fairview Park (city) Cuyahoga County	94	0.56
Miamisburg (city) Montgomery County	104	0.52
Pepper Pike (city) Cuyahoga County	31	0.52

Top 10 Places Sorted by Percent of Total Population
Based on places with total population of 50,000 or more

Place	Population	%
Lakewood (city) Cuyahoga County	116	0.22
Cleveland (city) Cuyahoga County	553	0.14
Columbus (city) Franklin County	604	0.08
Toledo (city) Lucas County	216	0.07
Parma (city) Cuyahoga County	34	0.04
Cincinnati (city) Hamilton County	55	0.02
Dayton (city) Montgomery County	15	0.01
Akron (city) Summit County	10	<0.01
Canton (city) Stark County	0	0.00
Elyria (city) Lorain County	0	0.00

Arab: Syrian

Top 10 Places Sorted by Population
Based on all places, regardless of total population

Place	Population	%
Columbus (city) Franklin County	415	0.05
Toledo (city) Lucas County	381	0.13
Lakewood (city) Cuyahoga County	213	0.40
Olmsted Falls (city) Cuyahoga County	210	2.40
Canton (city) Stark County	164	0.22
Cleveland (city) Cuyahoga County	155	0.04
Westlake (city) Cuyahoga County	126	0.39
Fairview Park (city) Cuyahoga County	123	0.73
Parma Heights (city) Cuyahoga County	93	0.45
Rocky River (city) Cuyahoga County	89	0.44

Top 10 Places Sorted by Percent of Total Population
Based on all places, regardless of total population

Place	Population	%
Rosemount (cdp) Scioto County	77	3.50
Olmsted Falls (city) Cuyahoga County	210	2.40
Walbridge (village) Wood County	71	2.30
Waterville (village) Lucas County	64	1.18
Clay Center (village) Ottawa County	3	1.06
Waite Hill (village) Lake County	5	1.03
Middlefield (village) Geauga County	26	0.99
Chagrin Falls (village) Cuyahoga County	37	0.91
Caldwell (village) Noble County	12	0.86
Dent (cdp) Hamilton County	82	0.84

Top 10 Places Sorted by Percent of Total Population
Based on places with total population of 50,000 or more

Place	Population	%
Lakewood (city) Cuyahoga County	213	0.40
Canton (city) Stark County	164	0.22
Kettering (city) Montgomery County	81	0.14
Toledo (city) Lucas County	381	0.13
Parma (city) Cuyahoga County	62	0.08
Columbus (city) Franklin County	415	0.05
Cleveland (city) Cuyahoga County	155	0.04
Youngstown (city) Mahoning County	25	0.04
Lorain (city) Lorain County	19	0.03
Elyria (city) Lorain County	9	0.02

Arab: Other

Top 10 Places Sorted by Population
Based on all places, regardless of total population

Place	Population	%
Columbus (city) Franklin County	497	0.06
Toledo (city) Lucas County	304	0.10
Cleveland (city) Cuyahoga County	227	0.06
Cleveland Heights (city) Cuyahoga County	200	0.43
Cuyahoga Falls (city) Summit County	149	0.30
Athens (city) Athens County	148	0.63
Akron (city) Summit County	143	0.07
Findlay (city) Hancock County	137	0.33
Bellbrook (city) Greene County	131	1.87
Beavercreek (city) Greene County	121	0.27

Top 10 Places Sorted by Percent of Total Population
Based on all places, regardless of total population

Place	Population	%
Haskins (village) Wood County	29	2.53
Bellbrook (city) Greene County	131	1.87
Greentown (cdp) Stark County	45	1.40
Frankfort (village) Ross County	12	1.09
Waynesville (village) Warren County	29	1.01
Cherry Grove (cdp) Hamilton County	38	0.84
Higginsport (village) Brown County	2	0.80
Athens (city) Athens County	148	0.63
Mariemont (village) Hamilton County	21	0.62
Streetsboro (city) Portage County	93	0.60

Top 10 Places Sorted by Percent of Total Population
Based on places with total population of 50,000 or more

Place	Population	%
Toledo (city) Lucas County	304	0.10
Akron (city) Summit County	143	0.07
Columbus (city) Franklin County	497	0.06
Cleveland (city) Cuyahoga County	227	0.06
Springfield (city) Clark County	35	0.06
Kettering (city) Montgomery County	27	0.05
Lakewood (city) Cuyahoga County	25	0.05
Cincinnati (city) Hamilton County	70	0.02
Hamilton (city) Butler County	15	0.02
Canton (city) Stark County	12	0.02

Armenian

Top 10 Places Sorted by Population
Based on all places, regardless of total population

Place	Population	%
Toledo (city) Lucas County	234	0.08
Columbus (city) Franklin County	163	0.02
Portsmouth (city) Scioto County	126	0.62
Pepper Pike (city) Cuyahoga County	112	1.88
Cleveland (city) Cuyahoga County	91	0.02
Golf Manor (village) Hamilton County	86	2.36
Akron (city) Summit County	82	0.04
Cincinnati (city) Hamilton County	82	0.03
Parma (city) Cuyahoga County	80	0.10
Northfield (village) Summit County	73	1.97

Top 10 Places Sorted by Percent of Total Population
Based on all places, regardless of total population

Place	Population	%
Malinta (village) Henry County	10	3.36
Bradner (village) Wood County	33	2.67
Golf Manor (village) Hamilton County	86	2.36
Northfield (village) Summit County	73	1.97
Pepper Pike (city) Cuyahoga County	112	1.88
Sebring (village) Mahoning County	59	1.31
Hunting Valley (village) Cuyahoga County	7	1.09
Frankfort (village) Ross County	11	1.00
Chagrin Falls (village) Cuyahoga County	37	0.91
Granville (village) Licking County	42	0.75

Top 10 Places Sorted by Percent of Total Population
Based on places with total population of 50,000 or more

Place	Population	%
Parma (city) Cuyahoga County	80	0.10
Toledo (city) Lucas County	234	0.08
Lakewood (city) Cuyahoga County	29	0.06
Canton (city) Stark County	35	0.05
Akron (city) Summit County	82	0.04
Cincinnati (city) Hamilton County	82	0.03
Columbus (city) Franklin County	163	0.02
Cleveland (city) Cuyahoga County	91	0.02
Springfield (city) Clark County	12	0.02
Youngstown (city) Mahoning County	11	0.02

Assyrian/Chaldean/Syriac

Top 10 Places Sorted by Population
Based on all places, regardless of total population

Place	Population	%
Columbus (city) Franklin County	97	0.01
Upper Arlington (city) Franklin County	51	0.15
Toledo (city) Lucas County	27	0.01
Circleville (city) Pickaway County	13	0.10
Pickerington (city) Fairfield County	12	0.07
Highland Heights (city) Cuyahoga County	10	0.12
Englewood (city) Montgomery County	10	0.08
Defiance (city) Defiance County	10	0.06
Dublin (city) Franklin County	10	0.03
Cincinnati (city) Hamilton County	9	<0.01

Top 10 Places Sorted by Percent of Total Population
Based on all places, regardless of total population

Place	Population	%
Upper Arlington (city) Franklin County	51	0.15
Highland Heights (city) Cuyahoga County	10	0.12
Circleville (city) Pickaway County	13	0.10
Englewood (city) Montgomery County	10	0.08
Pickerington (city) Fairfield County	12	0.07
Defiance (city) Defiance County	10	0.06
Dublin (city) Franklin County	10	0.03
Columbus (city) Franklin County	97	0.01
Toledo (city) Lucas County	27	0.01
Euclid (city) Cuyahoga County	5	0.01

Top 10 Places Sorted by Percent of Total Population
Based on places with total population of 50,000 or more

Place	Population	%
Columbus (city) Franklin County	97	0.01
Toledo (city) Lucas County	27	0.01
Cincinnati (city) Hamilton County	9	<0.01
Cleveland (city) Cuyahoga County	5	<0.01
Akron (city) Summit County	0	0.00
Canton (city) Stark County	0	0.00
Dayton (city) Montgomery County	0	0.00
Elyria (city) Lorain County	0	0.00
Hamilton (city) Butler County	0	0.00
Kettering (city) Montgomery County	0	0.00

Australian

Top 10 Places Sorted by Population
Based on all places, regardless of total population

Place	Population	%
Whitehall (city) Franklin County	156	0.86
Columbus (city) Franklin County	154	0.02
Marion (city) Marion County	59	0.16
Cincinnati (city) Hamilton County	50	0.02
Parma (city) Cuyahoga County	44	0.05
Struthers (city) Mahoning County	42	0.39
Lexington (village) Richland County	41	0.79
Kenwood (cdp) Hamilton County	40	0.55
Mansfield (city) Richland County	39	0.08
Cleveland (city) Cuyahoga County	39	0.01

Top 10 Places Sorted by Percent of Total Population
Based on all places, regardless of total population

Place	Population	%
Lafayette (village) Allen County	13	4.55
Brice (village) Franklin County	3	2.70
Dellroy (village) Carroll County	3	1.01

Whitehall (city) Franklin County	156	0.86
Lexington (village) Richland County	41	0.79
Four Bridges (cdp) Butler County	17	0.73
Orwell (village) Ashtabula County	10	0.68
Fayetteville (village) Brown County	2	0.68
Sherwood (cdp) Hamilton County	23	0.66
Newtown (village) Hamilton County	16	0.61

Top 10 Places Sorted by Percent of Total Population

Based on places with total population of 50,000 or more

Place	Population	%
Parma (city) Cuyahoga County	44	0.05
Youngstown (city) Mahoning County	18	0.03
Columbus (city) Franklin County	154	0.02
Cincinnati (city) Hamilton County	50	0.02
Dayton (city) Montgomery County	22	0.02
Hamilton (city) Butler County	10	0.02
Lakewood (city) Cuyahoga County	10	0.02
Cleveland (city) Cuyahoga County	39	0.01
Akron (city) Summit County	21	0.01
Kettering (city) Montgomery County	4	0.01

Austrian

Top 10 Places Sorted by Population

Based on all places, regardless of total population

Place	Population	%
Columbus (city) Franklin County	1,440	0.19
Toledo (city) Lucas County	628	0.22
Cleveland (city) Cuyahoga County	589	0.14
Cincinnati (city) Hamilton County	502	0.17
Akron (city) Summit County	450	0.22
Solon (city) Cuyahoga County	300	1.31
Parma (city) Cuyahoga County	283	0.35
Hilliard (city) Franklin County	255	0.93
Cleveland Heights (city) Cuyahoga County	255	0.54
Mansfield (city) Richland County	253	0.52

Top 10 Places Sorted by Percent of Total Population

Based on all places, regardless of total population

Place	Population	%
Lafferty (cdp) Belmont County	33	15.07
Port Washington (village) Tuscarawas County	33	6.21
Belle Valley (village) Noble County	19	5.31
Gilboa (village) Putnam County	7	5.00
Rock Creek (village) Ashtabula County	31	4.34
Wetherington (cdp) Butler County	60	4.18
Stone Creek (village) Tuscarawas County	7	3.78
Lake Tomahawk (cdp) Columbiana County	16	3.49
Waite Hill (village) Lake County	15	3.10
Malinta (village) Henry County	9	3.02

Top 10 Places Sorted by Percent of Total Population

Based on places with total population of 50,000 or more

Place	Population	%
Lakewood (city) Cuyahoga County	233	0.44
Parma (city) Cuyahoga County	283	0.35
Kettering (city) Montgomery County	160	0.28
Elyria (city) Lorain County	154	0.28
Toledo (city) Lucas County	628	0.22
Akron (city) Summit County	450	0.22
Columbus (city) Franklin County	1,440	0.19
Canton (city) Stark County	143	0.19
Cincinnati (city) Hamilton County	502	0.17
Lorain (city) Lorain County	110	0.17

Basque

Top 10 Places Sorted by Population

Based on all places, regardless of total population

Place	Population	%
Bowling Green (city) Wood County	18	0.06
Dent (cdp) Hamilton County	17	0.17
Chagrin Falls (village) Cuyahoga County	12	0.29
Aberdeen (village) Brown County	0	0.00
Ada (village) Hardin County	0	0.00
Adamsville (village) Muskingum County	0	0.00
Addyston (village) Hamilton County	0	0.00
Adelphi (village) Ross County	0	0.00
Adena (village) Jefferson County	0	0.00
Akron (city) Summit County	0	0.00

Top 10 Places Sorted by Percent of Total Population

Based on all places, regardless of total population

Place	Population	%
Chagrin Falls (village) Cuyahoga County	12	0.29
Dent (cdp) Hamilton County	17	0.17
Bowling Green (city) Wood County	18	0.06
Aberdeen (village) Brown County	0	0.00
Ada (village) Hardin County	0	0.00
Adamsville (village) Muskingum County	0	0.00
Addyston (village) Hamilton County	0	0.00
Adelphi (village) Ross County	0	0.00
Adena (village) Jefferson County	0	0.00
Akron (city) Summit County	0	0.00

Top 10 Places Sorted by Percent of Total Population

Based on places with total population of 50,000 or more

Place	Population	%
Akron (city) Summit County	0	0.00
Canton (city) Stark County	0	0.00
Cincinnati (city) Hamilton County	0	0.00
Cleveland (city) Cuyahoga County	0	0.00
Columbus (city) Franklin County	0	0.00
Dayton (city) Montgomery County	0	0.00
Elyria (city) Lorain County	0	0.00
Hamilton (city) Butler County	0	0.00
Kettering (city) Montgomery County	0	0.00
Lakewood (city) Cuyahoga County	0	0.00

Belgian

Top 10 Places Sorted by Population

Based on all places, regardless of total population

Place	Population	%
Columbus (city) Franklin County	699	0.09
Toledo (city) Lucas County	215	0.07
Cincinnati (city) Hamilton County	185	0.06
Parma (city) Cuyahoga County	163	0.20
Canton (city) Stark County	152	0.20
Plain City (village) Madison County	145	3.81
Findlay (city) Hancock County	116	0.28
Akron (city) Summit County	109	0.05
Bowling Green (city) Wood County	107	0.35
Dayton (city) Montgomery County	105	0.07

Top 10 Places Sorted by Percent of Total Population

Based on all places, regardless of total population

Place	Population	%
Plumwood (cdp) Madison County	43	24.02
Martinsburg (village) Knox County	10	5.43
Plain City (village) Madison County	145	3.81
Berkey (village) Lucas County	8	3.03
Highland Holiday (cdp) Highland County	11	2.78
Kings Mills (cdp) Warren County	32	2.56
Helena (village) Sandusky County	6	2.39
Bethel (village) Clermont County	58	2.13
Mount Gilead (village) Morrow County	80	2.11
Mutual (village) Champaign County	3	2.07

Top 10 Places Sorted by Percent of Total Population

Based on places with total population of 50,000 or more

Place	Population	%
Parma (city) Cuyahoga County	163	0.20
Canton (city) Stark County	152	0.20
Kettering (city) Montgomery County	63	0.11
Lakewood (city) Cuyahoga County	53	0.10
Columbus (city) Franklin County	699	0.09
Toledo (city) Lucas County	215	0.07
Dayton (city) Montgomery County	105	0.07
Cincinnati (city) Hamilton County	185	0.06
Akron (city) Summit County	109	0.05
Lorain (city) Lorain County	31	0.05

Brazilian

Top 10 Places Sorted by Population

Based on all places, regardless of total population

Place	Population	%
Columbus (city) Franklin County	284	0.04
Dublin (city) Franklin County	155	0.39
Forest Park (city) Hamilton County	135	0.72
Fairfield (city) Butler County	131	0.31
Pickerington (city) Fairfield County	118	0.69
Cleveland (city) Cuyahoga County	80	0.02
Upper Arlington (city) Franklin County	72	0.21
Athens (city) Athens County	68	0.29
Kettering (city) Montgomery County	59	0.11
Arcanum (village) Darke County	53	2.21

Top 10 Places Sorted by Percent of Total Population

Based on all places, regardless of total population

Place	Population	%
Fairview (village) Guernsey County	4	6.56
Arcanum (village) Darke County	53	2.21
West Mansfield (village) Logan County	13	1.88
East Palestine (city) Columbiana County	53	1.11
Fayetteville (village) Brown County	3	1.03
Hanoverton (village) Columbiana County	4	0.97
Forest Park (city) Hamilton County	135	0.72
Pickerington (city) Fairfield County	118	0.69
Canal Fulton (city) Stark County	28	0.52
Fairlawn (city) Summit County	32	0.43

Top 10 Places Sorted by Percent of Total Population

Based on places with total population of 50,000 or more

Place	Population	%
Kettering (city) Montgomery County	59	0.11
Columbus (city) Franklin County	284	0.04
Lakewood (city) Cuyahoga County	21	0.04
Cleveland (city) Cuyahoga County	80	0.02
Akron (city) Summit County	27	0.01
Cincinnati (city) Hamilton County	23	0.01
Canton (city) Stark County	0	0.00
Dayton (city) Montgomery County	0	0.00
Elyria (city) Lorain County	0	0.00
Hamilton (city) Butler County	0	0.00

British

Top 10 Places Sorted by Population

Based on all places, regardless of total population

Place	Population	%
Columbus (city) Franklin County	3,242	0.42
Cincinnati (city) Hamilton County	1,314	0.44
Toledo (city) Lucas County	785	0.27
Dayton (city) Montgomery County	727	0.50
Westerville (city) Franklin County	538	1.50
Akron (city) Summit County	508	0.25
Cleveland (city) Cuyahoga County	474	0.12
Upper Arlington (city) Franklin County	394	1.17
Kettering (city) Montgomery County	352	0.63
Grove City (city) Franklin County	324	0.95

Top 10 Places Sorted by Percent of Total Population

Based on all places, regardless of total population

Place	Population	%
Oceola (cdp) Crawford County	100	45.66
Canal Lewisville (cdp) Coshocton County	23	6.65
Pleasant Plain (village) Warren County	9	6.16
Sherwood (village) Defiance County	31	5.61
Concorde Hills (cdp) Hamilton County	26	5.30
Lafayette (village) Allen County	13	4.55
Old Washington (village) Guernsey County	12	3.99
North Perry (village) Lake County	37	3.85
Bellbrook (city) Greene County	254	3.63
New Straitsville (village) Perry County	17	3.47

Top 10 Places Sorted by Percent of Total Population

Based on places with total population of 50,000 or more

Place	Population	%
Kettering (city) Montgomery County	352	0.63
Lakewood (city) Cuyahoga County	313	0.59
Dayton (city) Montgomery County	727	0.50
Cincinnati (city) Hamilton County	1,314	0.44
Hamilton (city) Butler County	270	0.43
Columbus (city) Franklin County	3,242	0.42
Toledo (city) Lucas County	785	0.27
Akron (city) Summit County	508	0.25
Elyria (city) Lorain County	137	0.25
Parma (city) Cuyahoga County	189	0.23

Bulgarian

Top 10 Places Sorted by Population
Based on all places, regardless of total population

Place	Population	%
Toledo (city) Lucas County	217	0.07
Columbus (city) Franklin County	130	0.02
Dayton (city) Montgomery County	125	0.09
Parma Heights (city) Cuyahoga County	112	0.54
Fairview Park (city) Cuyahoga County	107	0.63
Avon (city) Lorain County	84	0.43
Oregon (city) Lucas County	77	0.38
Parma (city) Cuyahoga County	73	0.09
Upper Arlington (city) Franklin County	67	0.20
Cleveland (city) Cuyahoga County	54	0.01

Top 10 Places Sorted by Percent of Total Population
Based on all places, regardless of total population

Place	Population	%
Woodmere (village) Cuyahoga County	36	3.91
Monroeville (village) Huron County	27	2.02
Gambier (village) Knox County	33	1.50
Belle Valley (village) Noble County	5	1.40
Lyons (village) Fulton County	4	0.78
Northwood (city) Wood County	35	0.66
Oak Harbor (village) Ottawa County	18	0.65
Newtown (village) Hamilton County	17	0.65
Fairview Park (city) Cuyahoga County	107	0.63
Windham (village) Portage County	14	0.61

Top 10 Places Sorted by Percent of Total Population
Based on places with total population of 50,000 or more

Place	Population	%
Dayton (city) Montgomery County	125	0.09
Parma (city) Cuyahoga County	73	0.09
Toledo (city) Lucas County	217	0.07
Youngstown (city) Mahoning County	33	0.05
Lakewood (city) Cuyahoga County	23	0.04
Springfield (city) Clark County	22	0.04
Columbus (city) Franklin County	130	0.02
Akron (city) Summit County	32	0.02
Lorain (city) Lorain County	15	0.02
Cleveland (city) Cuyahoga County	54	0.01

Cajun

Top 10 Places Sorted by Population
Based on all places, regardless of total population

Place	Population	%
Kettering (city) Montgomery County	66	0.12
Columbus (city) Franklin County	56	0.01
Cincinnati (city) Hamilton County	41	0.01
Beavercreek (city) Greene County	29	0.07
Cleveland (city) Cuyahoga County	29	0.01
Akron (city) Summit County	27	0.01
Montrose-Ghent (cdp) Summit County	19	0.37
Green (city) Summit County	15	0.06
Lithopolis (village) Fairfield County	14	2.22
North Ridgeville (city) Lorain County	13	0.05

Top 10 Places Sorted by Percent of Total Population
Based on all places, regardless of total population

Place	Population	%
Lithopolis (village) Fairfield County	14	2.22
Smithville (village) Wayne County	7	0.55
Montrose-Ghent (cdp) Summit County	19	0.37
Kettering (city) Montgomery County	66	0.12
Highland Heights (city) Cuyahoga County	8	0.10
Beavercreek (city) Greene County	29	0.07
Cedarville (village) Greene County	3	0.07
Green (city) Summit County	15	0.06
North Ridgeville (city) Lorain County	13	0.05
Kent (city) Portage County	11	0.04

Top 10 Places Sorted by Percent of Total Population
Based on places with total population of 50,000 or more

Place	Population	%
Kettering (city) Montgomery County	66	0.12
Columbus (city) Franklin County	56	0.01
Cincinnati (city) Hamilton County	41	0.01
Cleveland (city) Cuyahoga County	29	0.01
Akron (city) Summit County	27	0.01
Canton (city) Stark County	0	0.00
Dayton (city) Montgomery County	0	0.00
Elyria (city) Lorain County	0	0.00
Hamilton (city) Butler County	0	0.00
Lakewood (city) Cuyahoga County	0	0.00

Canadian

Top 10 Places Sorted by Population
Based on all places, regardless of total population

Place	Population	%
Columbus (city) Franklin County	1,023	0.13
Toledo (city) Lucas County	521	0.18
Cleveland (city) Cuyahoga County	343	0.08
Cincinnati (city) Hamilton County	275	0.09
Cleveland Heights (city) Cuyahoga County	210	0.45
Hudson (city) Summit County	201	0.90
Akron (city) Summit County	196	0.10
Westerville (city) Franklin County	187	0.52
Hilliard (city) Franklin County	170	0.62
Gahanna (city) Franklin County	157	0.48

Top 10 Places Sorted by Percent of Total Population
Based on all places, regardless of total population

Place	Population	%
Negley (cdp) Columbiana County	40	16.74
Huntsville (village) Logan County	44	11.08
Yankee Lake (village) Trumbull County	4	5.80
Clarksville (village) Clinton County	26	4.26
Kings Mills (cdp) Warren County	48	3.84
Day Heights (cdp) Clermont County	73	2.69
Amberley (village) Hamilton County	95	2.68
Shawnee (cdp) Hamilton County	18	2.49
Green Meadows (cdp) Clark County	58	2.45
St. Paris (village) Champaign County	48	2.42

Top 10 Places Sorted by Percent of Total Population
Based on places with total population of 50,000 or more

Place	Population	%
Toledo (city) Lucas County	521	0.18
Elyria (city) Lorain County	100	0.18
Columbus (city) Franklin County	1,023	0.13
Akron (city) Summit County	196	0.10
Parma (city) Cuyahoga County	85	0.10
Springfield (city) Clark County	61	0.10
Kettering (city) Montgomery County	58	0.10
Cincinnati (city) Hamilton County	275	0.09
Cleveland (city) Cuyahoga County	343	0.08
Dayton (city) Montgomery County	116	0.08

Carpatho Rusyn

Top 10 Places Sorted by Population
Based on all places, regardless of total population

Place	Population	%
Parma (city) Cuyahoga County	116	0.14
Aurora (city) Portage County	65	0.43
Tallmadge (city) Summit County	51	0.29
Mansfield (city) Richland County	43	0.09
Canfield (city) Mahoning County	41	0.55
Columbus (city) Franklin County	35	<0.01
Fairview Park (city) Cuyahoga County	30	0.18
Westerville (city) Franklin County	28	0.08
Lorain (city) Lorain County	26	0.04
Lakewood (city) Cuyahoga County	25	0.05

Top 10 Places Sorted by Percent of Total Population
Based on all places, regardless of total population

Place	Population	%
Canfield (city) Mahoning County	41	0.55
Aurora (city) Portage County	65	0.43
Pleasant City (village) Guernsey County	2	0.43
Tallmadge (city) Summit County	51	0.29
Campbell (city) Mahoning County	17	0.20
Wellington (village) Lorain County	10	0.20
Brooklyn Heights (village) Cuyahoga County	3	0.20
Fairview Park (city) Cuyahoga County	30	0.18
Shadyside (village) Belmont County	7	0.18
Oberlin (city) Lorain County	14	0.17

Top 10 Places Sorted by Percent of Total Population
Based on places with total population of 50,000 or more

Place	Population	%
Parma (city) Cuyahoga County	116	0.14
Lakewood (city) Cuyahoga County	25	0.05
Lorain (city) Lorain County	26	0.04
Youngstown (city) Mahoning County	20	0.03
Canton (city) Stark County	13	0.02
Akron (city) Summit County	25	0.01
Toledo (city) Lucas County	15	0.01
Columbus (city) Franklin County	35	<0.01
Cincinnati (city) Hamilton County	0	0.00
Cleveland (city) Cuyahoga County	0	0.00

Celtic

Top 10 Places Sorted by Population
Based on all places, regardless of total population

Place	Population	%
Columbus (city) Franklin County	95	0.01
Toledo (city) Lucas County	73	0.03
Toronto (city) Jefferson County	70	1.40
Niles (city) Trumbull County	64	0.33
Mount Repose (cdp) Clermont County	60	1.41
Struthers (city) Mahoning County	51	0.47
Gahanna (city) Franklin County	51	0.16
Rocky River (city) Cuyahoga County	42	0.21
Canton (city) Stark County	39	0.05
North Ridgeville (city) Lorain County	31	0.11

Top 10 Places Sorted by Percent of Total Population
Based on all places, regardless of total population

Place	Population	%
Mount Repose (cdp) Clermont County	60	1.41
Toronto (city) Jefferson County	70	1.40
Sugar Bush Knolls (village) Portage County	2	1.32
Laura (village) Miami County	7	1.20
Granville South (cdp) Licking County	19	1.19
Beloit (village) Mahoning County	14	1.13
Riverlea (village) Franklin County	5	1.04
Walton Hills (village) Cuyahoga County	22	0.97
Richfield (village) Summit County	18	0.50
Milford Center (village) Union County	3	0.50

Top 10 Places Sorted by Percent of Total Population
Based on places with total population of 50,000 or more

Place	Population	%
Canton (city) Stark County	39	0.05
Toledo (city) Lucas County	73	0.03
Springfield (city) Clark County	12	0.02
Columbus (city) Franklin County	95	0.01
Cincinnati (city) Hamilton County	29	0.01
Cleveland (city) Cuyahoga County	18	<0.01
Akron (city) Summit County	0	0.00
Dayton (city) Montgomery County	0	0.00
Elyria (city) Lorain County	0	0.00
Hamilton (city) Butler County	0	0.00

Croatian

Top 10 Places Sorted by Population
Based on all places, regardless of total population

Place	Population	%
Mentor (city) Lake County	1,797	3.77
Cleveland (city) Cuyahoga County	1,547	0.38
Columbus (city) Franklin County	1,158	0.15
Parma (city) Cuyahoga County	1,112	1.36
Euclid (city) Cuyahoga County	1,084	2.20
Willoughby (city) Lake County	769	3.46
Boardman (cdp) Mahoning County	733	2.07
Willowick (city) Lake County	705	4.96
Eastlake (city) Lake County	689	3.65
Youngstown (city) Mahoning County	688	0.99

Top 10 Places Sorted by Percent of Total Population
Based on all places, regardless of total population

Place	Population	%
Yankee Lake (village) Trumbull County	10	14.49
Radnor (cdp) Delaware County	16	11.35
McKinley Heights (cdp) Trumbull County	75	6.88

Willoughby Hills (city) Lake County	505	5.38
Lakeline (village) Lake County	8	5.30
Waite Hill (village) Lake County	25	5.17
Willowick (city) Lake County	705	4.96
Austinburg (cdp) Ashtabula County	40	4.96
Wickliffe (city) Lake County	580	4.51
Newburgh Heights (village) Cuyahoga County	91	4.32

Top 10 Places Sorted by Percent of Total Population
Based on places with total population of 50,000 or more

Place	Population	%
Parma (city) Cuyahoga County	1,112	1.36
Lakewood (city) Cuyahoga County	563	1.07
Youngstown (city) Mahoning County	688	0.99
Lorain (city) Lorain County	569	0.87
Cleveland (city) Cuyahoga County	1,547	0.38
Canton (city) Stark County	279	0.37
Akron (city) Summit County	584	0.29
Elyria (city) Lorain County	123	0.22
Columbus (city) Franklin County	1,158	0.15
Kettering (city) Montgomery County	58	0.10

Cypriot

Top 10 Places Sorted by Population
Based on all places, regardless of total population

Place	Population	%
North Canton (city) Stark County	15	0.09
Columbus (city) Franklin County	14	<0.01
Lakewood (city) Cuyahoga County	12	0.02
Boardman (cdp) Mahoning County	11	0.03
Toledo (city) Lucas County	11	<0.01
Plymouth (village) Richland County	3	0.15
Aberdeen (village) Brown County	0	0.00
Ada (village) Hardin County	0	0.00
Adamsville (village) Muskingum County	0	0.00
Addyston (village) Hamilton County	0	0.00

Top 10 Places Sorted by Percent of Total Population
Based on all places, regardless of total population

Place	Population	%
Plymouth (village) Richland County	3	0.15
North Canton (city) Stark County	15	0.09
Boardman (cdp) Mahoning County	11	0.03
Lakewood (city) Cuyahoga County	12	0.02
Columbus (city) Franklin County	14	<0.01
Toledo (city) Lucas County	11	<0.01
Aberdeen (village) Brown County	0	0.00
Ada (village) Hardin County	0	0.00
Adamsville (village) Muskingum County	0	0.00
Addyston (village) Hamilton County	0	0.00

Top 10 Places Sorted by Percent of Total Population
Based on places with total population of 50,000 or more

Place	Population	%
Lakewood (city) Cuyahoga County	12	0.02
Columbus (city) Franklin County	14	<0.01
Toledo (city) Lucas County	11	<0.01
Akron (city) Summit County	0	0.00
Canton (city) Stark County	0	0.00
Cincinnati (city) Hamilton County	0	0.00
Cleveland (city) Cuyahoga County	0	0.00
Dayton (city) Montgomery County	0	0.00
Elyria (city) Lorain County	0	0.00
Hamilton (city) Butler County	0	0.00

Czech

Top 10 Places Sorted by Population
Based on all places, regardless of total population

Place	Population	%
Columbus (city) Franklin County	2,996	0.39
Cleveland (city) Cuyahoga County	2,835	0.69
Parma (city) Cuyahoga County	2,231	2.72
North Royalton (city) Cuyahoga County	1,263	4.21
Strongsville (city) Cuyahoga County	1,236	2.79
North Olmsted (city) Cuyahoga County	982	2.99
Garfield Heights (city) Cuyahoga County	945	3.25
Akron (city) Summit County	919	0.45
Toledo (city) Lucas County	833	0.29
Brunswick (city) Medina County	824	2.39

Top 10 Places Sorted by Percent of Total Population
Based on all places, regardless of total population

Place	Population	%
Tippecanoe (cdp) Harrison County	47	60.26
Blakeslee (village) Williams County	7	10.61
Put-in-Bay (village) Ottawa County	13	9.35
Independence (city) Cuyahoga County	531	7.50
Lansing (cdp) Belmont County	27	7.32
Neffs (cdp) Belmont County	72	7.29
Brooklyn Heights (village) Cuyahoga County	98	6.56
West Rushville (village) Fairfield County	7	6.48
Bourneville (cdp) Ross County	11	6.47
Seven Hills (city) Cuyahoga County	756	6.41

Top 10 Places Sorted by Percent of Total Population
Based on places with total population of 50,000 or more

Place	Population	%
Parma (city) Cuyahoga County	2,231	2.72
Lakewood (city) Cuyahoga County	758	1.44
Elyria (city) Lorain County	556	1.01
Cleveland (city) Cuyahoga County	2,835	0.69
Canton (city) Stark County	342	0.46
Akron (city) Summit County	919	0.45
Columbus (city) Franklin County	2,996	0.39
Kettering (city) Montgomery County	220	0.39
Toledo (city) Lucas County	833	0.29
Springfield (city) Clark County	153	0.25

Czechoslovakian

Top 10 Places Sorted by Population
Based on all places, regardless of total population

Place	Population	%
Columbus (city) Franklin County	819	0.11
Cleveland (city) Cuyahoga County	553	0.14
Elyria (city) Lorain County	312	0.57
Toledo (city) Lucas County	304	0.10
Parma (city) Cuyahoga County	299	0.37
Mansfield (city) Richland County	260	0.53
Akron (city) Summit County	233	0.11
Cuyahoga Falls (city) Summit County	222	0.45
Strongsville (city) Cuyahoga County	217	0.49
Westlake (city) Cuyahoga County	204	0.63

Top 10 Places Sorted by Percent of Total Population
Based on all places, regardless of total population

Place	Population	%
Buffalo (cdp) Guernsey County	18	4.68
Kidron (cdp) Wayne County	33	3.17
Leavittsburg (cdp) Trumbull County	50	2.57
Bloomingburg (village) Fayette County	24	2.46
Hannibal (cdp) Monroe County	12	2.45
Jefferson (village) Ashtabula County	73	2.26
Burgoon (village) Sandusky County	4	2.13
Whites Landing (cdp) Erie County	7	1.84
Montpelier (village) Williams County	71	1.71
Adena (village) Jefferson County	14	1.66

Top 10 Places Sorted by Percent of Total Population
Based on places with total population of 50,000 or more

Place	Population	%
Elyria (city) Lorain County	312	0.57
Parma (city) Cuyahoga County	299	0.37
Lorain (city) Lorain County	186	0.29
Kettering (city) Montgomery County	136	0.24
Lakewood (city) Cuyahoga County	126	0.24
Cleveland (city) Cuyahoga County	553	0.14
Dayton (city) Montgomery County	179	0.12
Columbus (city) Franklin County	819	0.11
Akron (city) Summit County	233	0.11
Toledo (city) Lucas County	304	0.10

Danish

Top 10 Places Sorted by Population
Based on all places, regardless of total population

Place	Population	%
Columbus (city) Franklin County	1,200	0.16
Toledo (city) Lucas County	499	0.17
Cincinnati (city) Hamilton County	439	0.15
Cleveland Heights (city) Cuyahoga County	271	0.58
Akron (city) Summit County	260	0.13
Cleveland (city) Cuyahoga County	230	0.06
Lakewood (city) Cuyahoga County	219	0.42
Elyria (city) Lorain County	183	0.33
Canton (city) Stark County	176	0.24
Kettering (city) Montgomery County	174	0.31

Top 10 Places Sorted by Percent of Total Population
Based on all places, regardless of total population

Place	Population	%
Tarlton (village) Pickaway County	20	6.21
Reno (cdp) Washington County	41	4.47
Lewistown (cdp) Logan County	14	3.89
Swanton (village) Fulton County	133	3.49
Sardis (cdp) Monroe County	10	3.02
Concorde Hills (cdp) Hamilton County	12	2.44
Butler (village) Richland County	25	2.43
Caledonia (village) Marion County	12	1.87
Chesterland (cdp) Geauga County	44	1.82
Gratis (village) Preble County	18	1.80

Top 10 Places Sorted by Percent of Total Population
Based on places with total population of 50,000 or more

Place	Population	%
Lakewood (city) Cuyahoga County	219	0.42
Elyria (city) Lorain County	183	0.33
Kettering (city) Montgomery County	174	0.31
Canton (city) Stark County	176	0.24
Youngstown (city) Mahoning County	141	0.20
Toledo (city) Lucas County	499	0.17
Columbus (city) Franklin County	1,200	0.16
Cincinnati (city) Hamilton County	439	0.15
Akron (city) Summit County	260	0.13
Lorain (city) Lorain County	53	0.08

Dutch

Top 10 Places Sorted by Population
Based on all places, regardless of total population

Place	Population	%
Columbus (city) Franklin County	10,822	1.40
Toledo (city) Lucas County	3,569	1.22
Cleveland (city) Cuyahoga County	2,881	0.70
Cincinnati (city) Hamilton County	2,867	0.96
Akron (city) Summit County	2,805	1.38
Dayton (city) Montgomery County	1,660	1.14
Canton (city) Stark County	1,441	1.94
Kettering (city) Montgomery County	1,420	2.53
Lancaster (city) Fairfield County	1,384	3.58
Springfield (city) Clark County	1,199	1.95

Top 10 Places Sorted by Percent of Total Population
Based on all places, regardless of total population

Place	Population	%
Celeryville (cdp) Huron County	59	44.36
Pulaski (cdp) Williams County	26	39.39
Fairview (village) Guernsey County	16	26.23
Elgin (village) Van Wert County	6	26.09
Beulah Beach (cdp) Erie County	9	25.71
East Liberty (cdp) Logan County	81	25.23
Otway (village) Scioto County	26	21.49
Crystal Lakes (cdp) Clark County	229	18.79
Neville (village) Clermont County	20	18.69
Derby (cdp) Pickaway County	76	17.92

Top 10 Places Sorted by Percent of Total Population
Based on places with total population of 50,000 or more

Place	Population	%
Kettering (city) Montgomery County	1,420	2.53
Elyria (city) Lorain County	1,082	1.97
Springfield (city) Clark County	1,199	1.95
Canton (city) Stark County	1,441	1.94
Columbus (city) Franklin County	10,822	1.40
Hamilton (city) Butler County	873	1.40
Akron (city) Summit County	2,805	1.38
Lorain (city) Lorain County	824	1.26
Toledo (city) Lucas County	3,569	1.22
Dayton (city) Montgomery County	1,660	1.14

Eastern European

Top 10 Places Sorted by Population
Based on all places, regardless of total population

Place	Population	%
Columbus (city) Franklin County	867	0.11
Beachwood (city) Cuyahoga County	546	4.58
Shaker Heights (city) Cuyahoga County	545	1.92
Cleveland Heights (city) Cuyahoga County	475	1.02
University Heights (city) Cuyahoga County	457	3.37
Solon (city) Cuyahoga County	420	1.83
Pepper Pike (city) Cuyahoga County	227	3.81
Cincinnati (city) Hamilton County	172	0.06
Lorain (city) Lorain County	156	0.24
Bexley (city) Franklin County	151	1.16

Top 10 Places Sorted by Percent of Total Population
Based on all places, regardless of total population

Place	Population	%
Beachwood (city) Cuyahoga County	546	4.58
Aquilla (village) Geauga County	14	3.83
Pepper Pike (city) Cuyahoga County	227	3.81
University Heights (city) Cuyahoga County	457	3.37
Orange (village) Cuyahoga County	105	3.20
Bentleyville (village) Cuyahoga County	31	2.93
Nellie (village) Coshocton County	3	2.59
Moreland Hills (village) Cuyahoga County	75	2.27
Shaker Heights (city) Cuyahoga County	545	1.92
Hunting Valley (village) Cuyahoga County	12	1.87

Top 10 Places Sorted by Percent of Total Population
Based on places with total population of 50,000 or more

Place	Population	%
Lorain (city) Lorain County	156	0.24
Lakewood (city) Cuyahoga County	129	0.24
Kettering (city) Montgomery County	104	0.19
Parma (city) Cuyahoga County	102	0.12
Columbus (city) Franklin County	867	0.11
Akron (city) Summit County	138	0.07
Cincinnati (city) Hamilton County	172	0.06
Elyria (city) Lorain County	31	0.06
Dayton (city) Montgomery County	54	0.04
Hamilton (city) Butler County	24	0.04

English

Top 10 Places Sorted by Population
Based on all places, regardless of total population

Place	Population	%
Columbus (city) Franklin County	58,155	7.55
Toledo (city) Lucas County	18,826	6.45
Cincinnati (city) Hamilton County	16,011	5.33
Akron (city) Summit County	15,829	7.80
Cleveland (city) Cuyahoga County	13,765	3.36
Dayton (city) Montgomery County	7,108	4.88
Elyria (city) Lorain County	6,659	12.11
Cuyahoga Falls (city) Summit County	6,483	13.04
Kettering (city) Montgomery County	6,441	11.46
Mentor (city) Lake County	6,049	12.70

Top 10 Places Sorted by Percent of Total Population
Based on all places, regardless of total population

Place	Population	%
Cynthiana (cdp) Pike County	30	53.57
Dundee (cdp) Tuscarawas County	174	43.28
Rocky Fork Point (cdp) Highland County	237	43.25
Tuppers Plains (cdp) Meigs County	112	42.42
Brice (village) Franklin County	47	42.34
East Fultonham (cdp) Muskingum County	63	40.13
Howard (cdp) Knox County	136	38.53
Gann (village) Knox County	42	37.84
Old Fort (cdp) Seneca County	39	35.45
Lakeside (cdp) Ottawa County	224	34.09

Top 10 Places Sorted by Percent of Total Population
Based on places with total population of 50,000 or more

Place	Population	%
Elyria (city) Lorain County	6,659	12.11
Kettering (city) Montgomery County	6,441	11.46
Lakewood (city) Cuyahoga County	5,509	10.46
Akron (city) Summit County	15,829	7.80
Springfield (city) Clark County	4,701	7.64
Columbus (city) Franklin County	58,155	7.55
Hamilton (city) Butler County	4,631	7.41
Canton (city) Stark County	5,256	7.06
Toledo (city) Lucas County	18,826	6.45
Parma (city) Cuyahoga County	5,050	6.17

Estonian

Top 10 Places Sorted by Population
Based on all places, regardless of total population

Place	Population	%
Cincinnati (city) Hamilton County	86	0.03
Kettering (city) Montgomery County	39	0.07
North Royalton (city) Cuyahoga County	35	0.12
University Heights (city) Cuyahoga County	30	0.22
Broadview Heights (city) Cuyahoga County	27	0.14
Oxford (city) Butler County	27	0.13
Columbus (city) Franklin County	20	<0.01
Toledo (city) Lucas County	19	0.01
Norwalk (city) Huron County	17	0.10
Mentor (city) Lake County	17	0.04

Top 10 Places Sorted by Percent of Total Population
Based on all places, regardless of total population

Place	Population	%
Marble Cliff (village) Franklin County	3	0.51
Ballville (cdp) Sandusky County	11	0.35
University Heights (city) Cuyahoga County	30	0.22
Richfield (village) Summit County	7	0.19
Archbold (village) Fulton County	7	0.17
Broadview Heights (city) Cuyahoga County	27	0.14
Oxford (city) Butler County	27	0.13
North Royalton (city) Cuyahoga County	35	0.12
Norwalk (city) Huron County	17	0.10
Mount Vernon (city) Knox County	15	0.09

Top 10 Places Sorted by Percent of Total Population
Based on places with total population of 50,000 or more

Place	Population	%
Kettering (city) Montgomery County	39	0.07
Cincinnati (city) Hamilton County	86	0.03
Lakewood (city) Cuyahoga County	9	0.02
Toledo (city) Lucas County	19	0.01
Columbus (city) Franklin County	20	<0.01
Akron (city) Summit County	0	0.00
Canton (city) Stark County	0	0.00
Cleveland (city) Cuyahoga County	0	0.00
Dayton (city) Montgomery County	0	0.00
Elyria (city) Lorain County	0	0.00

European

Top 10 Places Sorted by Population
Based on all places, regardless of total population

Place	Population	%
Columbus (city) Franklin County	7,099	0.92
Cincinnati (city) Hamilton County	2,521	0.84
Toledo (city) Lucas County	1,626	0.56
Akron (city) Summit County	1,390	0.69
Cleveland (city) Cuyahoga County	1,116	0.27
Dayton (city) Montgomery County	1,113	0.76
Newark (city) Licking County	901	1.89
Findlay (city) Hancock County	845	2.05
Dublin (city) Franklin County	836	2.13
Westerville (city) Franklin County	733	2.04

Top 10 Places Sorted by Percent of Total Population
Based on all places, regardless of total population

Place	Population	%
Homeworth (cdp) Columbiana County	163	17.70
Camp Dennison (cdp) Hamilton County	61	13.01
Ithaca (village) Darke County	10	12.82
Richmond Dale (cdp) Ross County	26	12.62
Rawson (village) Hancock County	46	9.64
Fort Seneca (cdp) Seneca County	40	9.55
Wilson (village) Monroe County	10	8.70
Granville South (cdp) Licking County	132	8.26
Pancoastburg (cdp) Fayette County	8	8.08
Plainville (cdp) Hamilton County	15	6.73

Top 10 Places Sorted by Percent of Total Population
Based on places with total population of 50,000 or more

Place	Population	%
Kettering (city) Montgomery County	692	1.23
Columbus (city) Franklin County	7,099	0.92
Cincinnati (city) Hamilton County	2,521	0.84
Springfield (city) Clark County	473	0.77
Dayton (city) Montgomery County	1,113	0.76
Lakewood (city) Cuyahoga County	385	0.73
Akron (city) Summit County	1,390	0.69
Hamilton (city) Butler County	357	0.57
Toledo (city) Lucas County	1,626	0.56
Parma (city) Cuyahoga County	420	0.51

Finnish

Top 10 Places Sorted by Population
Based on all places, regardless of total population

Place	Population	%
Ashtabula (city) Ashtabula County	914	4.69
Columbus (city) Franklin County	858	0.11
Conneaut (city) Ashtabula County	688	5.38
Lakewood (city) Cuyahoga County	386	0.73
Cleveland (city) Cuyahoga County	376	0.09
Fairport Harbor (village) Lake County	356	11.40
Toledo (city) Lucas County	295	0.10
Painesville (city) Lake County	290	1.51
Mentor (city) Lake County	280	0.59
North Madison (cdp) Lake County	226	2.51

Top 10 Places Sorted by Percent of Total Population
Based on all places, regardless of total population

Place	Population	%
Austinburg (cdp) Ashtabula County	97	12.02
Fairport Harbor (village) Lake County	356	11.40
North Kingsville (village) Ashtabula County	179	6.22
Conneaut (city) Ashtabula County	688	5.38
Ashtabula (city) Ashtabula County	914	4.69
Madison (village) Lake County	137	4.37
Jefferson (village) Ashtabula County	133	4.11
Peninsula (village) Summit County	21	3.66
Put-in-Bay (village) Ottawa County	5	3.60
North Madison (cdp) Lake County	226	2.51

Top 10 Places Sorted by Percent of Total Population
Based on places with total population of 50,000 or more

Place	Population	%
Lakewood (city) Cuyahoga County	386	0.73
Springfield (city) Clark County	106	0.17
Kettering (city) Montgomery County	84	0.15
Columbus (city) Franklin County	858	0.11
Toledo (city) Lucas County	295	0.10
Dayton (city) Montgomery County	144	0.10
Cleveland (city) Cuyahoga County	376	0.09
Hamilton (city) Butler County	49	0.08
Elyria (city) Lorain County	36	0.07
Cincinnati (city) Hamilton County	175	0.06

French, except Basque

Top 10 Places Sorted by Population
Based on all places, regardless of total population

Place	Population	%
Columbus (city) Franklin County	14,605	1.90
Toledo (city) Lucas County	13,787	4.72
Cincinnati (city) Hamilton County	5,247	1.75
Cleveland (city) Cuyahoga County	4,063	0.99
Akron (city) Summit County	3,698	1.82
Kettering (city) Montgomery County	2,149	3.83
Dayton (city) Montgomery County	2,130	1.46
Beavercreek (city) Greene County	1,789	4.06
Canton (city) Stark County	1,697	2.28
Oregon (city) Lucas County	1,492	7.42

Top 10 Places Sorted by Percent of Total Population
Based on all places, regardless of total population

Place	Population	%
Maplewood Park (cdp) Trumbull County	112	38.49
Russia (village) Shelby County	243	38.15
Versailles (village) Darke County	895	33.76

North Star (village) Darke County	71	33.02
Remington (cdp) Hamilton County	71	29.71
Mifflin (village) Ashland County	28	23.93
Haviland (village) Paulding County	23	18.70
New Hampshire (cdp) Auglaize County	21	15.56
Osgood (village) Darke County	42	15.50
Stony Ridge (cdp) Wood County	55	14.86

Top 10 Places Sorted by Percent of Total Population
Based on places with total population of 50,000 or more

Place	Population	%
Toledo (city) Lucas County	13,787	4.72
Kettering (city) Montgomery County	2,149	3.83
Lakewood (city) Cuyahoga County	1,255	2.38
Canton (city) Stark County	1,697	2.28
Springfield (city) Clark County	1,220	1.98
Columbus (city) Franklin County	14,605	1.90
Akron (city) Summit County	3,698	1.82
Cincinnati (city) Hamilton County	5,247	1.75
Parma (city) Cuyahoga County	1,339	1.64
Elyria (city) Lorain County	896	1.63

French Canadian

Top 10 Places Sorted by Population
Based on all places, regardless of total population

Place	Population	%
Toledo (city) Lucas County	2,025	0.69
Columbus (city) Franklin County	1,886	0.24
Cincinnati (city) Hamilton County	503	0.17
Cleveland (city) Cuyahoga County	425	0.10
Oregon (city) Lucas County	417	2.07
Elyria (city) Lorain County	376	0.68
Mentor (city) Lake County	326	0.68
Akron (city) Summit County	320	0.16
Dayton (city) Montgomery County	280	0.19
Sylvania (city) Lucas County	266	1.40

Top 10 Places Sorted by Percent of Total Population
Based on all places, regardless of total population

Place	Population	%
East Fultonham (cdp) Muskingum County	25	15.92
Trinway (cdp) Muskingum County	40	9.39
Montezuma (village) Mercer County	13	8.39
Caledonia (village) Marion County	37	5.76
Millbury (village) Wood County	77	5.64
Alger (village) Hardin County	45	5.55
Berkey (village) Lucas County	13	4.92
Jerusalem (village) Monroe County	6	4.80
Burgoon (village) Sandusky County	9	4.79
Buckland (village) Auglaize County	9	3.85

Top 10 Places Sorted by Percent of Total Population
Based on places with total population of 50,000 or more

Place	Population	%
Toledo (city) Lucas County	2,025	0.69
Elyria (city) Lorain County	376	0.68
Lakewood (city) Cuyahoga County	227	0.43
Kettering (city) Montgomery County	237	0.42
Springfield (city) Clark County	177	0.29
Columbus (city) Franklin County	1,886	0.24
Parma (city) Cuyahoga County	178	0.22
Dayton (city) Montgomery County	280	0.19
Cincinnati (city) Hamilton County	503	0.17
Akron (city) Summit County	320	0.16

German

Top 10 Places Sorted by Population
Based on all places, regardless of total population

Place	Population	%
Columbus (city) Franklin County	163,383	21.21
Toledo (city) Lucas County	76,635	26.26
Cincinnati (city) Hamilton County	59,441	19.80
Cleveland (city) Cuyahoga County	40,200	9.82
Akron (city) Summit County	39,722	19.59
Dayton (city) Montgomery County	23,171	15.91
Parma (city) Cuyahoga County	21,335	26.05
Kettering (city) Montgomery County	20,845	37.10
Canton (city) Stark County	18,990	25.51
Findlay (city) Hancock County	16,605	40.31

Top 10 Places Sorted by Percent of Total Population
Based on all places, regardless of total population

Place	Population	%
Miamiville (cdp) Clermont County	226	100.00
Miltonsburg (village) Monroe County	7	100.00
Walnut Creek (cdp) Holmes County	373	96.38
Holiday City (village) Williams County	45	91.84
Glandorf (village) Putnam County	869	86.99
Miller City (village) Putnam County	87	84.47
Fort Jennings (village) Putnam County	440	83.81
St Johns (cdp) Auglaize County	60	83.33
Newport (cdp) Shelby County	238	82.64
Kalida (village) Putnam County	836	82.20

Top 10 Places Sorted by Percent of Total Population
Based on places with total population of 50,000 or more

Place	Population	%
Kettering (city) Montgomery County	20,845	37.10
Lakewood (city) Cuyahoga County	14,246	27.05
Toledo (city) Lucas County	76,635	26.26
Parma (city) Cuyahoga County	21,335	26.05
Canton (city) Stark County	18,990	25.51
Elyria (city) Lorain County	13,579	24.69
Springfield (city) Clark County	13,145	21.37
Hamilton (city) Butler County	13,275	21.25
Columbus (city) Franklin County	163,383	21.21
Cincinnati (city) Hamilton County	59,441	19.80

German Russian

Top 10 Places Sorted by Population
Based on all places, regardless of total population

Place	Population	%
Akron (city) Summit County	78	0.04
Maple Heights (city) Cuyahoga County	68	0.29
Cincinnati (city) Hamilton County	34	0.01
Columbus (city) Franklin County	33	<0.01
Grove City (city) Franklin County	29	0.09
Garfield Heights (city) Cuyahoga County	28	0.10
Washington Court House (city) Fayette County	23	0.16
Ashland (city) Ashland County	22	0.11
Lorain (city) Lorain County	18	0.03
Cleveland (city) Cuyahoga County	18	<0.01

Top 10 Places Sorted by Percent of Total Population
Based on all places, regardless of total population

Place	Population	%
North Randall (village) Cuyahoga County	11	1.27
Ridgeway (village) Hardin County	4	0.85
Valley Hi (village) Logan County	2	0.81
West Liberty (village) Logan County	7	0.38
Maple Heights (city) Cuyahoga County	68	0.29
Silverton (city) Hamilton County	14	0.29
Washington Court House (city) Fayette County	23	0.16
South Amherst (village) Lorain County	3	0.16
Ashland (city) Ashland County	22	0.11
Garfield Heights (city) Cuyahoga County	28	0.10

Top 10 Places Sorted by Percent of Total Population
Based on places with total population of 50,000 or more

Place	Population	%
Akron (city) Summit County	78	0.04
Lorain (city) Lorain County	18	0.03
Cincinnati (city) Hamilton County	34	0.01
Columbus (city) Franklin County	33	<0.01
Cleveland (city) Cuyahoga County	18	<0.01
Youngstown (city) Mahoning County	1	<0.01
Canton (city) Stark County	0	0.00
Dayton (city) Montgomery County	0	0.00
Elyria (city) Lorain County	0	0.00
Hamilton (city) Butler County	0	0.00

Greek

Top 10 Places Sorted by Population
Based on all places, regardless of total population

Place	Population	%
Columbus (city) Franklin County	2,987	0.39
Cleveland (city) Cuyahoga County	1,435	0.35
Campbell (city) Mahoning County	1,393	16.50
Canton (city) Stark County	1,154	1.55
Akron (city) Summit County	1,127	0.56
Parma (city) Cuyahoga County	1,087	1.33
Toledo (city) Lucas County	910	0.31
Warren (city) Trumbull County	876	2.05
Cincinnati (city) Hamilton County	840	0.28
Boardman (cdp) Mahoning County	783	2.21

Top 10 Places Sorted by Percent of Total Population
Based on all places, regardless of total population

Place	Population	%
Campbell (city) Mahoning County	1,393	16.50
Lake Mohawk (cdp) Carroll County	187	10.77
Lake Buckhorn (cdp) Holmes County	32	9.30
Mount Orab (village) Brown County	334	8.47
Yorkville (village) Jefferson County	86	6.71
Miami Heights (cdp) Hamilton County	241	5.27
Rayland (village) Jefferson County	18	4.64
Arcadia (village) Hancock County	26	4.46
Linndale (village) Cuyahoga County	6	4.41
Aquilla (village) Geauga County	16	4.37

Top 10 Places Sorted by Percent of Total Population
Based on places with total population of 50,000 or more

Place	Population	%
Canton (city) Stark County	1,154	1.55
Parma (city) Cuyahoga County	1,087	1.33
Lakewood (city) Cuyahoga County	607	1.15
Elyria (city) Lorain County	317	0.58
Akron (city) Summit County	1,127	0.56
Lorain (city) Lorain County	365	0.56
Youngstown (city) Mahoning County	312	0.45
Springfield (city) Clark County	244	0.40
Kettering (city) Montgomery County	224	0.40
Columbus (city) Franklin County	2,987	0.39

Guyanese

Top 10 Places Sorted by Population
Based on all places, regardless of total population

Place	Population	%
Cleveland (city) Cuyahoga County	370	0.09
Columbus (city) Franklin County	135	0.02
Centerville (city) Montgomery County	123	0.52
Mount Vernon (city) Knox County	120	0.71
Ballville (cdp) Sandusky County	88	2.77
Cincinnati (city) Hamilton County	77	0.03
Toledo (city) Lucas County	60	0.02
Middleburg Heights (city) Cuyahoga County	33	0.21
White Oak (cdp) Hamilton County	22	0.12
Springdale (city) Hamilton County	21	0.19

Top 10 Places Sorted by Percent of Total Population
Based on all places, regardless of total population

Place	Population	%
Ballville (cdp) Sandusky County	88	2.77
Mount Vernon (city) Knox County	120	0.71
Centerville (city) Montgomery County	123	0.52
Sixteen Mile Stand (cdp) Hamilton County	8	0.27
Middleburg Heights (city) Cuyahoga County	33	0.21
Springdale (city) Hamilton County	21	0.19
White Oak (cdp) Hamilton County	22	0.12
Cleveland (city) Cuyahoga County	370	0.09
Kent (city) Portage County	16	0.06
Eastlake (city) Lake County	9	0.05

Top 10 Places Sorted by Percent of Total Population
Based on places with total population of 50,000 or more

Place	Population	%
Cleveland (city) Cuyahoga County	370	0.09
Cincinnati (city) Hamilton County	77	0.03
Columbus (city) Franklin County	135	0.02
Toledo (city) Lucas County	60	0.02
Akron (city) Summit County	0	0.00
Canton (city) Stark County	0	0.00
Dayton (city) Montgomery County	0	0.00
Elyria (city) Lorain County	0	0.00
Hamilton (city) Butler County	0	0.00
Kettering (city) Montgomery County	0	0.00

Hungarian

Top 10 Places Sorted by Population
Based on all places, regardless of total population

Place	Population	%
Cleveland (city) Cuyahoga County	6,822	1.67
Columbus (city) Franklin County	6,569	0.85
Toledo (city) Lucas County	6,352	2.18
Akron (city) Summit County	4,508	2.22
Parma (city) Cuyahoga County	4,239	5.18
Lorain (city) Lorain County	3,113	4.77
Mentor (city) Lake County	2,998	6.29
Lakewood (city) Cuyahoga County	2,499	4.74
Elyria (city) Lorain County	2,358	4.29
Brunswick (city) Medina County	1,802	5.24

Top 10 Places Sorted by Percent of Total Population
Based on all places, regardless of total population

Place	Population	%
East Fultonham (cdp) Muskingum County	47	29.94
Williston (cdp) Ottawa County	75	20.27
Crystal Rock (cdp) Erie County	14	19.72
Pigeon Creek (cdp) Summit County	135	18.96
Fairport Harbor (village) Lake County	487	15.59
Bolivar (village) Tuscarawas County	144	11.94
Clifton (village) Greene County	27	11.64
Yankee Lake (village) Trumbull County	8	11.59
Moreland Hills (village) Cuyahoga County	373	11.27
Rayland (village) Jefferson County	42	10.82

Top 10 Places Sorted by Percent of Total Population
Based on places with total population of 50,000 or more

Place	Population	%
Parma (city) Cuyahoga County	4,239	5.18
Lorain (city) Lorain County	3,113	4.77
Lakewood (city) Cuyahoga County	2,499	4.74
Elyria (city) Lorain County	2,358	4.29
Akron (city) Summit County	4,508	2.22
Toledo (city) Lucas County	6,352	2.18
Youngstown (city) Mahoning County	1,409	2.02
Cleveland (city) Cuyahoga County	6,822	1.67
Kettering (city) Montgomery County	714	1.27
Canton (city) Stark County	917	1.23

Icelander

Top 10 Places Sorted by Population
Based on all places, regardless of total population

Place	Population	%
Gambier (village) Knox County	75	3.41
Columbus (city) Franklin County	51	0.01
Toledo (city) Lucas County	44	0.02
Miamisburg (city) Montgomery County	43	0.22
Northwood (city) Wood County	37	0.69
Monfort Heights (cdp) Hamilton County	35	0.30
Westlake (city) Cuyahoga County	33	0.10
Stow (city) Summit County	32	0.09
Strongsville (city) Cuyahoga County	29	0.07
Cleveland (city) Cuyahoga County	25	0.01

Top 10 Places Sorted by Percent of Total Population
Based on all places, regardless of total population

Place	Population	%
Gambier (village) Knox County	75	3.41
Waite Hill (village) Lake County	4	0.83
Northwood (city) Wood County	37	0.69
Beechwood Trails (cdp) Licking County	13	0.40
Monfort Heights (cdp) Hamilton County	35	0.30
Granville (village) Licking County	13	0.23
Miamisburg (city) Montgomery County	43	0.22
Fostoria (city) Seneca County	24	0.18
West Carrollton (city) Montgomery County	18	0.14
Delphos (city) Allen County	10	0.14

Top 10 Places Sorted by Percent of Total Population
Based on places with total population of 50,000 or more

Place	Population	%
Toledo (city) Lucas County	44	0.02
Columbus (city) Franklin County	51	0.01
Cleveland (city) Cuyahoga County	25	0.01
Akron (city) Summit County	19	0.01
Canton (city) Stark County	0	0.00
Cincinnati (city) Hamilton County	0	0.00
Dayton (city) Montgomery County	0	0.00
Elyria (city) Lorain County	0	0.00
Hamilton (city) Butler County	0	0.00
Kettering (city) Montgomery County	0	0.00

Iranian

Top 10 Places Sorted by Population
Based on all places, regardless of total population

Place	Population	%
Columbus (city) Franklin County	466	0.06
Upper Arlington (city) Franklin County	161	0.48
Lakewood (city) Cuyahoga County	118	0.22
Dublin (city) Franklin County	98	0.25
Shaker Heights (city) Cuyahoga County	96	0.34
Springboro (city) Warren County	86	0.50
Strongsville (city) Cuyahoga County	85	0.19
Oakwood (city) Montgomery County	77	0.84
Toledo (city) Lucas County	73	0.03
Cincinnati (city) Hamilton County	69	0.02

Top 10 Places Sorted by Percent of Total Population
Based on all places, regardless of total population

Place	Population	%
Remington (cdp) Hamilton County	8	3.35
Moreland Hills (village) Cuyahoga County	43	1.30
Mayfield (village) Cuyahoga County	42	1.23
Montrose-Ghent (cdp) Summit County	52	1.01
Hunting Valley (village) Cuyahoga County	6	0.93
Oakwood (city) Montgomery County	77	0.84
Brooklyn Heights (village) Cuyahoga County	12	0.80
Ottawa Hills (village) Lucas County	33	0.73
Mariemont (village) Hamilton County	24	0.71
New Albany (village) Franklin County	46	0.65

Top 10 Places Sorted by Percent of Total Population
Based on places with total population of 50,000 or more

Place	Population	%
Lakewood (city) Cuyahoga County	118	0.22
Columbus (city) Franklin County	466	0.06
Springfield (city) Clark County	28	0.05
Toledo (city) Lucas County	73	0.03
Parma (city) Cuyahoga County	24	0.03
Cincinnati (city) Hamilton County	69	0.02
Akron (city) Summit County	36	0.02
Kettering (city) Montgomery County	9	0.02
Cleveland (city) Cuyahoga County	26	0.01
Canton (city) Stark County	0	0.00

Irish

Top 10 Places Sorted by Population
Based on all places, regardless of total population

Place	Population	%
Columbus (city) Franklin County	99,000	12.85
Cleveland (city) Cuyahoga County	37,296	9.11
Toledo (city) Lucas County	34,827	11.93
Cincinnati (city) Hamilton County	32,799	10.93
Akron (city) Summit County	26,458	13.05
Dayton (city) Montgomery County	14,086	9.67
Lakewood (city) Cuyahoga County	12,740	24.19
Parma (city) Cuyahoga County	11,502	14.04
Canton (city) Stark County	9,815	13.18
Cuyahoga Falls (city) Summit County	9,658	19.43

Top 10 Places Sorted by Percent of Total Population
Based on all places, regardless of total population

Place	Population	%
Miltonsburg (village) Monroe County	7	100.00
Kilbourne (cdp) Delaware County	136	74.73
Miamiville (cdp) Clermont County	166	73.45
Pulaski (cdp) Williams County	44	66.67
Wightmans Grove (cdp) Sandusky County	20	60.61
Vaughnsville (cdp) Putnam County	82	59.85
Stockdale (cdp) Pike County	91	52.60
Buford (cdp) Highland County	146	52.33
Glencoe (cdp) Belmont County	45	52.33
East Fultonham (cdp) Muskingum County	80	50.96

Top 10 Places Sorted by Percent of Total Population
Based on places with total population of 50,000 or more

Place	Population	%
Lakewood (city) Cuyahoga County	12,740	24.19
Kettering (city) Montgomery County	9,275	16.51
Elyria (city) Lorain County	8,207	14.92
Parma (city) Cuyahoga County	11,502	14.04
Canton (city) Stark County	9,815	13.18
Akron (city) Summit County	26,458	13.05
Columbus (city) Franklin County	99,000	12.85
Springfield (city) Clark County	7,564	12.30
Toledo (city) Lucas County	34,827	11.93
Lorain (city) Lorain County	7,298	11.19

Israeli

Top 10 Places Sorted by Population
Based on all places, regardless of total population

Place	Population	%
Columbus (city) Franklin County	138	0.02
Lyndhurst (city) Cuyahoga County	136	0.96
Solon (city) Cuyahoga County	124	0.54
Cincinnati (city) Hamilton County	118	0.04
North Olmsted (city) Cuyahoga County	80	0.24
South Euclid (city) Cuyahoga County	69	0.31
Blue Ash (city) Hamilton County	50	0.41
Beavercreek (city) Greene County	50	0.11
Cleveland Heights (city) Cuyahoga County	49	0.10
Kenwood (cdp) Hamilton County	47	0.65

Top 10 Places Sorted by Percent of Total Population
Based on all places, regardless of total population

Place	Population	%
Lyndhurst (city) Cuyahoga County	136	0.96
Kenwood (cdp) Hamilton County	47	0.65
Solon (city) Cuyahoga County	124	0.54
Oberlin (city) Lorain County	37	0.45
Reminderville (village) Summit County	14	0.43
Blue Ash (city) Hamilton County	50	0.41
South Euclid (city) Cuyahoga County	69	0.31
Silver Lake (village) Summit County	8	0.31
University Heights (city) Cuyahoga County	38	0.28
Westfield Center (village) Medina County	3	0.28

Top 10 Places Sorted by Percent of Total Population
Based on places with total population of 50,000 or more

Place	Population	%
Cincinnati (city) Hamilton County	118	0.04
Lakewood (city) Cuyahoga County	14	0.03
Columbus (city) Franklin County	138	0.02
Dayton (city) Montgomery County	29	0.02
Toledo (city) Lucas County	35	0.01
Akron (city) Summit County	11	0.01
Cleveland (city) Cuyahoga County	10	<0.01
Canton (city) Stark County	0	0.00
Elyria (city) Lorain County	0	0.00
Hamilton (city) Butler County	0	0.00

Italian

Top 10 Places Sorted by Population
Based on all places, regardless of total population

Place	Population	%
Columbus (city) Franklin County	38,883	5.05
Cleveland (city) Cuyahoga County	19,033	4.65
Akron (city) Summit County	15,000	7.40
Parma (city) Cuyahoga County	11,434	13.96
Cincinnati (city) Hamilton County	9,502	3.17
Toledo (city) Lucas County	9,356	3.21
Boardman (cdp) Mahoning County	8,683	24.53
Mentor (city) Lake County	8,526	17.90
Youngstown (city) Mahoning County	7,337	10.54
Cuyahoga Falls (city) Summit County	6,168	12.41

Top 10 Places Sorted by Percent of Total Population
Based on all places, regardless of total population

Place	Population	%
Kilbourne (cdp) Delaware County	123	67.58
Wightmans Grove (cdp) Sandusky County	20	60.61
Lafferty (cdp) Belmont County	102	46.58

Lowellville (village) Mahoning County	506	43.81
McKinley Heights (cdp) Trumbull County	410	37.61
Poland (village) Mahoning County	825	31.72
New Middletown (village) Mahoning County	565	30.59
Summitville (village) Columbiana County	49	30.43
Brookfield Center (cdp) Trumbull County	427	29.01
Lockbourne (village) Franklin County	112	28.72

Top 10 Places Sorted by Percent of Total Population
Based on places with total population of 50,000 or more

Place	Population	%
Parma (city) Cuyahoga County	11,434	13.96
Lakewood (city) Cuyahoga County	6,124	11.63
Youngstown (city) Mahoning County	7,337	10.54
Canton (city) Stark County	5,958	8.00
Lorain (city) Lorain County	4,912	7.53
Akron (city) Summit County	15,000	7.40
Elyria (city) Lorain County	3,507	6.38
Kettering (city) Montgomery County	2,845	5.06
Columbus (city) Franklin County	38,883	5.05
Cleveland (city) Cuyahoga County	19,033	4.65

Latvian

Top 10 Places Sorted by Population
Based on all places, regardless of total population

Place	Population	%
Columbus (city) Franklin County	214	0.03
Cleveland (city) Cuyahoga County	99	0.02
Middleburg Heights (city) Cuyahoga County	94	0.60
Cincinnati (city) Hamilton County	67	0.02
Shaker Heights (city) Cuyahoga County	63	0.22
Lakewood (city) Cuyahoga County	60	0.11
Waterville (village) Lucas County	59	1.09
Brook Park (city) Cuyahoga County	55	0.28
Hilliard (city) Franklin County	51	0.19
Gahanna (city) Franklin County	48	0.15

Top 10 Places Sorted by Percent of Total Population
Based on all places, regardless of total population

Place	Population	%
Waterville (village) Lucas County	59	1.09
Bentleyville (village) Cuyahoga County	10	0.95
Jamestown (village) Greene County	15	0.80
Moreland Hills (village) Cuyahoga County	22	0.66
Gambier (village) Knox County	14	0.64
Middleburg Heights (city) Cuyahoga County	94	0.60
Ney (village) Defiance County	2	0.60
Bailey Lakes (village) Ashland County	2	0.53
Pepper Pike (city) Cuyahoga County	29	0.49
Hunting Valley (village) Cuyahoga County	3	0.47

Top 10 Places Sorted by Percent of Total Population
Based on places with total population of 50,000 or more

Place	Population	%
Lakewood (city) Cuyahoga County	60	0.11
Lorain (city) Lorain County	23	0.04
Columbus (city) Franklin County	214	0.03
Parma (city) Cuyahoga County	24	0.03
Cleveland (city) Cuyahoga County	99	0.02
Cincinnati (city) Hamilton County	67	0.02
Akron (city) Summit County	27	0.01
Toledo (city) Lucas County	21	0.01
Dayton (city) Montgomery County	9	0.01
Springfield (city) Clark County	8	0.01

Lithuanian

Top 10 Places Sorted by Population
Based on all places, regardless of total population

Place	Population	%
Cleveland (city) Cuyahoga County	1,180	0.29
Columbus (city) Franklin County	1,022	0.13
Parma (city) Cuyahoga County	613	0.75
Euclid (city) Cuyahoga County	568	1.15
Mentor (city) Lake County	497	1.04
Willoughby (city) Lake County	338	1.52
Willowick (city) Lake County	316	2.22
Beachwood (city) Cuyahoga County	299	2.51
Lakewood (city) Cuyahoga County	291	0.55
Eastlake (city) Lake County	286	1.51

Top 10 Places Sorted by Percent of Total Population
Based on all places, regardless of total population

Place	Population	%
Deersville (village) Harrison County	6	5.26
Kettlersville (village) Shelby County	9	4.39
Mount Eaton (village) Wayne County	10	4.15
Timberlake (village) Lake County	22	3.49
Kirtland Hills (village) Lake County	25	3.27
Lockington (village) Shelby County	5	2.98
Cortland (city) Trumbull County	191	2.72
Beachwood (city) Cuyahoga County	299	2.51
South Russell (village) Geauga County	96	2.48
Orange (village) Cuyahoga County	80	2.43

Top 10 Places Sorted by Percent of Total Population
Based on places with total population of 50,000 or more

Place	Population	%
Parma (city) Cuyahoga County	613	0.75
Lakewood (city) Cuyahoga County	291	0.55
Kettering (city) Montgomery County	202	0.36
Cleveland (city) Cuyahoga County	1,180	0.29
Elyria (city) Lorain County	132	0.24
Dayton (city) Montgomery County	244	0.17
Springfield (city) Clark County	84	0.14
Columbus (city) Franklin County	1,022	0.13
Canton (city) Stark County	99	0.13
Akron (city) Summit County	239	0.12

Luxemburger

Top 10 Places Sorted by Population
Based on all places, regardless of total population

Place	Population	%
Tiffin (city) Seneca County	56	0.31
Steubenville (city) Jefferson County	54	0.29
Mentor (city) Lake County	44	0.09
Dry Run (cdp) Hamilton County	29	0.44
Columbus (city) Franklin County	23	<0.01
Greenhills (village) Hamilton County	19	0.52
McKinley Heights (cdp) Trumbull County	17	1.56
Taylor Creek (cdp) Hamilton County	17	0.48
Green (city) Summit County	14	0.06
Aurora (city) Portage County	13	0.09

Top 10 Places Sorted by Percent of Total Population
Based on all places, regardless of total population

Place	Population	%
McKinley Heights (cdp) Trumbull County	17	1.56
Sugar Grove (village) Fairfield County	4	0.82
Greenhills (village) Hamilton County	19	0.52
Taylor Creek (cdp) Hamilton County	17	0.48
Dry Run (cdp) Hamilton County	29	0.44
Terrace Park (village) Hamilton County	9	0.40
Butler (village) Richland County	4	0.39
Tiffin (city) Seneca County	56	0.31
Carey (village) Wyandot County	12	0.31
Steubenville (city) Jefferson County	54	0.29

Top 10 Places Sorted by Percent of Total Population
Based on places with total population of 50,000 or more

Place	Population	%
Columbus (city) Franklin County	23	<0.01
Akron (city) Summit County	0	0.00
Canton (city) Stark County	0	0.00
Cincinnati (city) Hamilton County	0	0.00
Cleveland (city) Cuyahoga County	0	0.00
Dayton (city) Montgomery County	0	0.00
Elyria (city) Lorain County	0	0.00
Hamilton (city) Butler County	0	0.00
Kettering (city) Montgomery County	0	0.00
Lakewood (city) Cuyahoga County	0	0.00

Macedonian

Top 10 Places Sorted by Population
Based on all places, regardless of total population

Place	Population	%
Columbus (city) Franklin County	307	0.04
Brunswick (city) Medina County	222	0.65
Springfield (city) Clark County	145	0.24
White Oak (cdp) Hamilton County	123	0.65
Johnstown (village) Licking County	122	2.47
Pickerington (city) Fairfield County	116	0.68
Gahanna (city) Franklin County	103	0.32
Lorain (city) Lorain County	97	0.15
Elyria (city) Lorain County	95	0.17
Norwalk (city) Huron County	76	0.45

Top 10 Places Sorted by Percent of Total Population
Based on all places, regardless of total population

Place	Population	%
West Manchester (village) Preble County	17	3.82
Johnstown (village) Licking County	122	2.47
Lake Mohawk (cdp) Carroll County	24	1.38
Churchill (cdp) Trumbull County	22	0.83
Pickerington (city) Fairfield County	116	0.68
Brunswick (city) Medina County	222	0.65
White Oak (cdp) Hamilton County	123	0.65
Mack (cdp) Hamilton County	72	0.63
New Albany (village) Franklin County	44	0.62
Poland (village) Mahoning County	16	0.62

Top 10 Places Sorted by Percent of Total Population
Based on places with total population of 50,000 or more

Place	Population	%
Springfield (city) Clark County	145	0.24
Elyria (city) Lorain County	95	0.17
Lorain (city) Lorain County	97	0.15
Columbus (city) Franklin County	307	0.04
Akron (city) Summit County	56	0.03
Cincinnati (city) Hamilton County	46	0.02
Lakewood (city) Cuyahoga County	11	0.02
Toledo (city) Lucas County	18	0.01
Dayton (city) Montgomery County	14	0.01
Parma (city) Cuyahoga County	10	0.01

Maltese

Top 10 Places Sorted by Population
Based on all places, regardless of total population

Place	Population	%
Boardman (cdp) Mahoning County	152	0.43
Perrysburg (city) Wood County	39	0.19
Lakewood (city) Cuyahoga County	30	0.06
Columbus (city) Franklin County	29	<0.01
Mansfield (city) Richland County	26	0.05
Evendale (village) Hamilton County	20	0.71
Ballville (cdp) Sandusky County	19	0.60
Cincinnati (city) Hamilton County	18	0.01
Toledo (city) Lucas County	17	0.01
Norwalk (city) Huron County	11	0.06

Top 10 Places Sorted by Percent of Total Population
Based on all places, regardless of total population

Place	Population	%
Evendale (village) Hamilton County	20	0.71
Ballville (cdp) Sandusky County	19	0.60
Boardman (cdp) Mahoning County	152	0.43
Doylestown (village) Wayne County	9	0.30
Perrysburg (city) Wood County	39	0.19
Union City (village) Darke County	3	0.18
Lakewood (city) Cuyahoga County	30	0.06
Norwalk (city) Huron County	11	0.06
Mansfield (city) Richland County	26	0.05
Sylvania (city) Lucas County	7	0.04

Top 10 Places Sorted by Percent of Total Population
Based on places with total population of 50,000 or more

Place	Population	%
Lakewood (city) Cuyahoga County	30	0.06
Cincinnati (city) Hamilton County	18	0.01
Toledo (city) Lucas County	17	0.01
Columbus (city) Franklin County	29	<0.01
Akron (city) Summit County	0	0.00
Canton (city) Stark County	0	0.00
Cleveland (city) Cuyahoga County	0	0.00
Dayton (city) Montgomery County	0	0.00
Elyria (city) Lorain County	0	0.00
Hamilton (city) Butler County	0	0.00

New Zealander

Top 10 Places Sorted by Population
Based on all places, regardless of total population

Place	Population	%
Ballville (cdp) Sandusky County	62	1.95
Chagrin Falls (village) Cuyahoga County	55	1.35
Columbus (city) Franklin County	48	0.01
Cuyahoga Falls (city) Summit County	32	0.06
Delaware (city) Delaware County	29	0.09
University Heights (city) Cuyahoga County	22	0.16
Granville (village) Licking County	15	0.27
Gahanna (city) Franklin County	14	0.04
Oakwood (city) Montgomery County	11	0.12
Cleveland Heights (city) Cuyahoga County	10	0.02

Top 10 Places Sorted by Percent of Total Population
Based on all places, regardless of total population

Place	Population	%
Ballville (cdp) Sandusky County	62	1.95
Chagrin Falls (village) Cuyahoga County	55	1.35
Granville (village) Licking County	15	0.27
University Heights (city) Cuyahoga County	22	0.16
Oakwood (city) Montgomery County	11	0.12
Delaware (city) Delaware County	29	0.09
Willoughby Hills (city) Lake County	8	0.09
Cuyahoga Falls (city) Summit County	32	0.06
Gahanna (city) Franklin County	14	0.04
Cleveland Heights (city) Cuyahoga County	10	0.02

Top 10 Places Sorted by Percent of Total Population
Based on places with total population of 50,000 or more

Place	Population	%
Columbus (city) Franklin County	48	0.01
Hamilton (city) Butler County	8	0.01
Akron (city) Summit County	0	0.00
Canton (city) Stark County	0	0.00
Cincinnati (city) Hamilton County	0	0.00
Cleveland (city) Cuyahoga County	0	0.00
Dayton (city) Montgomery County	0	0.00
Elyria (city) Lorain County	0	0.00
Kettering (city) Montgomery County	0	0.00
Lakewood (city) Cuyahoga County	0	0.00

Northern European

Top 10 Places Sorted by Population
Based on all places, regardless of total population

Place	Population	%
Columbus (city) Franklin County	220	0.03
Boardman (cdp) Mahoning County	109	0.31
Akron (city) Summit County	103	0.05
Grove City (city) Franklin County	80	0.24
Canton (city) Stark County	80	0.11
Beavercreek (city) Greene County	79	0.18
Dublin (city) Franklin County	77	0.20
Cuyahoga Falls (city) Summit County	73	0.15
Cincinnati (city) Hamilton County	69	0.02
Shaker Heights (city) Cuyahoga County	55	0.19

Top 10 Places Sorted by Percent of Total Population
Based on all places, regardless of total population

Place	Population	%
Duncan Falls (cdp) Muskingum County	22	2.57
Silver Lake (village) Summit County	39	1.52
Sixteen Mile Stand (cdp) Hamilton County	35	1.19
Glendale (village) Hamilton County	24	1.04
Chagrin Falls (village) Cuyahoga County	36	0.88
Newcomerstown (village) Tuscarawas County	34	0.88
Richfield (village) Summit County	30	0.83
Kenwood (cdp) Hamilton County	50	0.69
Millersport (village) Fairfield County	6	0.63
Cherry Grove (cdp) Hamilton County	26	0.57

Top 10 Places Sorted by Percent of Total Population
Based on places with total population of 50,000 or more

Place	Population	%
Canton (city) Stark County	80	0.11
Akron (city) Summit County	103	0.05
Elyria (city) Lorain County	28	0.05
Hamilton (city) Butler County	28	0.04
Columbus (city) Franklin County	220	0.03
Kettering (city) Montgomery County	18	0.03
Cincinnati (city) Hamilton County	69	0.02
Springfield (city) Clark County	11	0.02
Lakewood (city) Cuyahoga County	9	0.02
Cleveland (city) Cuyahoga County	48	0.01

Norwegian

Top 10 Places Sorted by Population
Based on all places, regardless of total population

Place	Population	%
Columbus (city) Franklin County	3,594	0.47
Toledo (city) Lucas County	1,161	0.40
Cincinnati (city) Hamilton County	1,024	0.34
Akron (city) Summit County	541	0.27
Cleveland (city) Cuyahoga County	435	0.11
Upper Arlington (city) Franklin County	392	1.17
Lakewood (city) Cuyahoga County	366	0.69
Beavercreek (city) Greene County	349	0.79
Dayton (city) Montgomery County	346	0.24
Mason (city) Warren County	338	1.13

Top 10 Places Sorted by Percent of Total Population
Based on all places, regardless of total population

Place	Population	%
Mount Blanchard (village) Hancock County	34	6.18
Wright-Patterson AFB (cdp) Greene County	180	5.71
Tuppers Plains (cdp) Meigs County	13	4.92
Casstown (village) Miami County	12	4.40
New Straitsville (village) Perry County	20	4.08
Lewistown (cdp) Logan County	14	3.89
Luckey (village) Wood County	39	3.87
Mount Gilead (village) Morrow County	139	3.67
Johnstown (village) Licking County	170	3.45
Clifton (village) Greene County	7	3.02

Top 10 Places Sorted by Percent of Total Population
Based on places with total population of 50,000 or more

Place	Population	%
Lakewood (city) Cuyahoga County	366	0.69
Columbus (city) Franklin County	3,594	0.47
Kettering (city) Montgomery County	264	0.47
Elyria (city) Lorain County	234	0.43
Toledo (city) Lucas County	1,161	0.40
Cincinnati (city) Hamilton County	1,024	0.34
Hamilton (city) Butler County	199	0.32
Akron (city) Summit County	541	0.27
Springfield (city) Clark County	151	0.25
Dayton (city) Montgomery County	346	0.24

Pennsylvania German

Top 10 Places Sorted by Population
Based on all places, regardless of total population

Place	Population	%
Akron (city) Summit County	444	0.22
Columbus (city) Franklin County	359	0.05
Ashland (city) Ashland County	283	1.37
Boardman (cdp) Mahoning County	275	0.78
Toledo (city) Lucas County	245	0.08
Canton (city) Stark County	212	0.28
Newark (city) Licking County	202	0.42
Cleveland (city) Cuyahoga County	157	0.04
Kent (city) Portage County	156	0.54
Ontario (city) Richland County	153	2.51

Top 10 Places Sorted by Percent of Total Population
Based on all places, regardless of total population

Place	Population	%
Whites Landing (cdp) Erie County	136	35.70
Jacksonburg (village) Butler County	4	6.25
West Millgrove (village) Wood County	8	5.71
North Robinson (village) Crawford County	10	5.21
Hartville (village) Stark County	138	4.82
Holmesville (village) Holmes County	19	4.68
Green Camp (village) Marion County	13	4.42
New Haven (cdp) Huron County	11	4.12
Walnut Creek (cdp) Holmes County	14	3.62
Shiloh (village) Richland County	17	3.49

Top 10 Places Sorted by Percent of Total Population
Based on places with total population of 50,000 or more

Place	Population	%
Canton (city) Stark County	212	0.28
Akron (city) Summit County	444	0.22
Kettering (city) Montgomery County	118	0.21
Youngstown (city) Mahoning County	113	0.16
Elyria (city) Lorain County	68	0.12
Toledo (city) Lucas County	245	0.08
Columbus (city) Franklin County	359	0.05
Dayton (city) Montgomery County	80	0.05
Cleveland (city) Cuyahoga County	157	0.04
Lorain (city) Lorain County	25	0.04

Polish

Top 10 Places Sorted by Population
Based on all places, regardless of total population

Place	Population	%
Toledo (city) Lucas County	25,480	8.73
Cleveland (city) Cuyahoga County	18,227	4.45
Columbus (city) Franklin County	17,936	2.33
Parma (city) Cuyahoga County	14,703	17.95
Garfield Heights (city) Cuyahoga County	6,009	20.68
Strongsville (city) Cuyahoga County	5,938	13.39
North Royalton (city) Cuyahoga County	5,749	19.19
Brunswick (city) Medina County	5,132	14.92
Akron (city) Summit County	4,998	2.46
Elyria (city) Lorain County	4,359	7.93

Top 10 Places Sorted by Percent of Total Population
Based on all places, regardless of total population

Place	Population	%
Plumwood (cdp) Madison County	73	40.78
Cuyahoga Heights (village) Cuyahoga County	216	39.49
Independence (city) Cuyahoga County	2,591	36.60
Newburgh Heights (village) Cuyahoga County	706	33.49
Hockingport (cdp) Athens County	26	31.33
Valley View (village) Cuyahoga County	531	27.29
Brooklyn Heights (village) Cuyahoga County	357	23.90
Neapolis (cdp) Lucas County	112	23.88
Lansing (cdp) Belmont County	88	23.85
Rocky Ridge (village) Ottawa County	96	22.97

Top 10 Places Sorted by Percent of Total Population
Based on places with total population of 50,000 or more

Place	Population	%
Parma (city) Cuyahoga County	14,703	17.95
Toledo (city) Lucas County	25,480	8.73
Lakewood (city) Cuyahoga County	4,284	8.13
Elyria (city) Lorain County	4,359	7.93
Lorain (city) Lorain County	4,052	6.21
Cleveland (city) Cuyahoga County	18,227	4.45
Youngstown (city) Mahoning County	2,036	2.93
Kettering (city) Montgomery County	1,457	2.59
Akron (city) Summit County	4,998	2.46
Columbus (city) Franklin County	17,936	2.33

Portuguese

Top 10 Places Sorted by Population
Based on all places, regardless of total population

Place	Population	%
Columbus (city) Franklin County	1,667	0.22
Canton (city) Stark County	367	0.49
Akron (city) Summit County	293	0.14
Cleveland (city) Cuyahoga County	277	0.07
Medina (city) Medina County	214	0.80
Newark (city) Licking County	186	0.39
Mentor (city) Lake County	184	0.39
Wadsworth (city) Medina County	170	0.80
Toledo (city) Lucas County	154	0.05
Cincinnati (city) Hamilton County	142	0.05

Top 10 Places Sorted by Percent of Total Population
Based on all places, regardless of total population

Place	Population	%
Bolivar (village) Tuscarawas County	85	7.05
Wilson (village) Monroe County	4	3.48
St. Paris (village) Champaign County	60	3.02

Summerfield (village) Noble County	7	2.33
Union City (village) Darke County	37	2.22
Fort Recovery (village) Mercer County	24	2.13
Kipton (village) Lorain County	6	1.90
Leesburg (village) Highland County	28	1.87
East Liberty (cdp) Logan County	6	1.87
Mendon (village) Mercer County	10	1.78

Top 10 Places Sorted by Percent of Total Population
Based on places with total population of 50,000 or more

Place	Population	%
Canton (city) Stark County	367	0.49
Columbus (city) Franklin County	1,667	0.22
Springfield (city) Clark County	116	0.19
Akron (city) Summit County	293	0.14
Parma (city) Cuyahoga County	97	0.12
Elyria (city) Lorain County	58	0.11
Cleveland (city) Cuyahoga County	277	0.07
Lakewood (city) Cuyahoga County	31	0.06
Toledo (city) Lucas County	154	0.05
Cincinnati (city) Hamilton County	142	0.05

Romanian

Top 10 Places Sorted by Population
Based on all places, regardless of total population

Place	Population	%
Cleveland (city) Cuyahoga County	1,296	0.32
Columbus (city) Franklin County	1,256	0.16
Parma (city) Cuyahoga County	761	0.93
Canton (city) Stark County	682	0.92
Akron (city) Summit County	564	0.28
Parma Heights (city) Cuyahoga County	549	2.64
Strongsville (city) Cuyahoga County	468	1.06
Toledo (city) Lucas County	436	0.15
North Olmsted (city) Cuyahoga County	398	1.21
Warren (city) Trumbull County	372	0.87

Top 10 Places Sorted by Percent of Total Population
Based on all places, regardless of total population

Place	Population	%
Remington (cdp) Hamilton County	16	6.69
Vienna Center (cdp) Trumbull County	44	6.14
Celeryville (cdp) Huron County	7	5.26
North Robinson (village) Crawford County	8	4.17
Pepper Pike (city) Cuyahoga County	243	4.08
Fairlawn (city) Summit County	254	3.40
Newburgh Heights (village) Cuyahoga County	66	3.13
Parma Heights (city) Cuyahoga County	549	2.64
Brimfield (cdp) Portage County	85	2.56
Sixteen Mile Stand (cdp) Hamilton County	70	2.39

Top 10 Places Sorted by Percent of Total Population
Based on places with total population of 50,000 or more

Place	Population	%
Parma (city) Cuyahoga County	761	0.93
Canton (city) Stark County	682	0.92
Lakewood (city) Cuyahoga County	293	0.56
Youngstown (city) Mahoning County	267	0.38
Cleveland (city) Cuyahoga County	1,296	0.32
Elyria (city) Lorain County	165	0.30
Akron (city) Summit County	564	0.28
Lorain (city) Lorain County	135	0.21
Columbus (city) Franklin County	1,256	0.16
Toledo (city) Lucas County	436	0.15

Russian

Top 10 Places Sorted by Population
Based on all places, regardless of total population

Place	Population	%
Columbus (city) Franklin County	5,392	0.70
Cleveland (city) Cuyahoga County	2,395	0.59
Beachwood (city) Cuyahoga County	1,926	16.14
Cincinnati (city) Hamilton County	1,528	0.51
Solon (city) Cuyahoga County	1,498	6.52
Cleveland Heights (city) Cuyahoga County	1,231	2.63
Bexley (city) Franklin County	1,210	9.29
Mayfield Heights (city) Cuyahoga County	1,185	6.20
Parma (city) Cuyahoga County	1,152	1.41
Shaker Heights (city) Cuyahoga County	1,019	3.58

Top 10 Places Sorted by Percent of Total Population
Based on all places, regardless of total population

Place	Population	%
East Liberty (cdp) Logan County	81	25.23
Beachwood (city) Cuyahoga County	1,926	16.14
Loveland Park (cdp) Warren County	146	12.09
Pepper Pike (city) Cuyahoga County	675	11.34
New Pittsburg (cdp) Wayne County	28	10.53
Amberley (village) Hamilton County	367	10.36
Bexley (city) Franklin County	1,210	9.29
Sixteen Mile Stand (cdp) Hamilton County	265	9.04
Moreland Hills (village) Cuyahoga County	275	8.31
Woodmere (village) Cuyahoga County	74	8.03

Top 10 Places Sorted by Percent of Total Population
Based on places with total population of 50,000 or more

Place	Population	%
Parma (city) Cuyahoga County	1,152	1.41
Lakewood (city) Cuyahoga County	673	1.28
Elyria (city) Lorain County	599	1.09
Canton (city) Stark County	603	0.81
Columbus (city) Franklin County	5,392	0.70
Lorain (city) Lorain County	399	0.61
Cleveland (city) Cuyahoga County	2,395	0.59
Cincinnati (city) Hamilton County	1,528	0.51
Youngstown (city) Mahoning County	351	0.50
Akron (city) Summit County	893	0.44

Scandinavian

Top 10 Places Sorted by Population
Based on all places, regardless of total population

Place	Population	%
Columbus (city) Franklin County	1,042	0.14
Cincinnati (city) Hamilton County	293	0.10
Beavercreek (city) Greene County	156	0.35
Akron (city) Summit County	130	0.06
Huber Heights (city) Montgomery County	128	0.34
Cleveland (city) Cuyahoga County	127	0.03
Wright-Patterson AFB (cdp) Greene County	121	3.84
Dublin (city) Franklin County	121	0.31
Kettering (city) Montgomery County	120	0.21
Newark (city) Licking County	102	0.21

Top 10 Places Sorted by Percent of Total Population
Based on all places, regardless of total population

Place	Population	%
Wilkesville (village) Vinton County	4	3.92
Wright-Patterson AFB (cdp) Greene County	121	3.84
Shiloh (village) Richland County	13	2.67
Warsaw (village) Coshocton County	22	2.43
Venedocia (village) Van Wert County	2	1.77
Caledonia (village) Marion County	11	1.71
Williamsburg (village) Clermont County	40	1.66
Geneva-on-the-Lake (village) Ashtabula County	22	1.58
Tuscarawas (village) Tuscarawas County	14	1.40
Fairfax (village) Hamilton County	22	1.25

Top 10 Places Sorted by Percent of Total Population
Based on places with total population of 50,000 or more

Place	Population	%
Kettering (city) Montgomery County	120	0.21
Columbus (city) Franklin County	1,042	0.14
Lakewood (city) Cuyahoga County	66	0.13
Springfield (city) Clark County	67	0.11
Cincinnati (city) Hamilton County	293	0.10
Akron (city) Summit County	130	0.06
Dayton (city) Montgomery County	93	0.06
Lorain (city) Lorain County	33	0.05
Elyria (city) Lorain County	20	0.04
Cleveland (city) Cuyahoga County	127	0.03

Scotch-Irish

Top 10 Places Sorted by Population
Based on all places, regardless of total population

Place	Population	%
Columbus (city) Franklin County	12,017	1.56
Akron (city) Summit County	3,342	1.65
Cincinnati (city) Hamilton County	3,249	1.08
Cleveland (city) Cuyahoga County	2,928	0.72
Toledo (city) Lucas County	2,388	0.82
Dayton (city) Montgomery County	1,768	1.21
Lakewood (city) Cuyahoga County	1,371	2.60
Cuyahoga Falls (city) Summit County	1,222	2.46
Newark (city) Licking County	1,163	2.44
Canton (city) Stark County	1,161	1.56

Top 10 Places Sorted by Percent of Total Population
Based on all places, regardless of total population

Place	Population	%
Hessville (cdp) Sandusky County	17	21.52
Kunkle (cdp) Williams County	29	20.42
Newport (cdp) Shelby County	53	18.40
Stewart (cdp) Athens County	12	17.65
Elgin (village) Van Wert County	4	17.39
Tuppers Plains (cdp) Meigs County	41	15.53
Lansing (cdp) Belmont County	57	15.45
Pottery Addition (cdp) Jefferson County	25	13.02
Salesville (village) Guernsey County	24	12.90
Sulphur Springs (cdp) Crawford County	32	11.43

Top 10 Places Sorted by Percent of Total Population
Based on places with total population of 50,000 or more

Place	Population	%
Lakewood (city) Cuyahoga County	1,371	2.60
Kettering (city) Montgomery County	1,103	1.96
Springfield (city) Clark County	1,143	1.86
Lorain (city) Lorain County	1,107	1.70
Akron (city) Summit County	3,342	1.65
Columbus (city) Franklin County	12,017	1.56
Canton (city) Stark County	1,161	1.56
Elyria (city) Lorain County	730	1.33
Dayton (city) Montgomery County	1,768	1.21
Cincinnati (city) Hamilton County	3,249	1.08

Scottish

Top 10 Places Sorted by Population
Based on all places, regardless of total population

Place	Population	%
Columbus (city) Franklin County	13,797	1.79
Cincinnati (city) Hamilton County	3,828	1.28
Toledo (city) Lucas County	3,645	1.25
Cleveland (city) Cuyahoga County	3,093	0.76
Akron (city) Summit County	2,974	1.47
Dayton (city) Montgomery County	1,758	1.21
Elyria (city) Lorain County	1,571	2.86
Kettering (city) Montgomery County	1,568	2.79
Mentor (city) Lake County	1,464	3.07
Westerville (city) Franklin County	1,430	3.98

Top 10 Places Sorted by Percent of Total Population
Based on all places, regardless of total population

Place	Population	%
Vickery (cdp) Sandusky County	43	47.25
Gann (village) Knox County	31	27.93
Plainville (cdp) Hamilton County	54	24.22
Raymond (cdp) Union County	52	19.77
Howard (cdp) Knox County	68	19.26
Minford (cdp) Scioto County	96	18.60
Sandyville (cdp) Tuscarawas County	48	15.43
Rosewood (cdp) Champaign County	39	14.66
Glenford (village) Perry County	33	12.99
Polk (village) Ashland County	38	12.71

Top 10 Places Sorted by Percent of Total Population
Based on places with total population of 50,000 or more

Place	Population	%
Elyria (city) Lorain County	1,571	2.86
Kettering (city) Montgomery County	1,568	2.79
Springfield (city) Clark County	1,400	2.28
Lakewood (city) Cuyahoga County	1,113	2.11
Columbus (city) Franklin County	13,797	1.79
Canton (city) Stark County	1,294	1.74
Akron (city) Summit County	2,974	1.47
Cincinnati (city) Hamilton County	3,828	1.28
Hamilton (city) Butler County	801	1.28
Toledo (city) Lucas County	3,645	1.25

Serbian

Top 10 Places Sorted by Population

Based on all places, regardless of total population

Place	Population	%
Parma (city) Cuyahoga County	1,778	2.17
Akron (city) Summit County	945	0.47
Cleveland (city) Cuyahoga County	529	0.13
Columbus (city) Franklin County	511	0.07
North Royalton (city) Cuyahoga County	433	1.45
Brunswick (city) Medina County	399	1.16
Barberton (city) Summit County	358	1.33
Cuyahoga Falls (city) Summit County	264	0.53
Parma Heights (city) Cuyahoga County	234	1.13
Broadview Heights (city) Cuyahoga County	230	1.23

Top 10 Places Sorted by Percent of Total Population

Based on all places, regardless of total population

Place	Population	%
Plainville (cdp) Hamilton County	18	8.07
Silver Lake (village) Summit County	70	2.73
Franklin Furnace (cdp) Scioto County	37	2.21
Parma (city) Cuyahoga County	1,778	2.17
Mingo Junction (village) Jefferson County	74	2.14
Orange (village) Cuyahoga County	67	2.04
Orangeville (village) Trumbull County	3	1.96
Lindsey (village) Sandusky County	9	1.91
Kipton (village) Lorain County	6	1.90
Antwerp (village) Paulding County	31	1.84

Top 10 Places Sorted by Percent of Total Population

Based on places with total population of 50,000 or more

Place	Population	%
Parma (city) Cuyahoga County	1,778	2.17
Akron (city) Summit County	945	0.47
Lakewood (city) Cuyahoga County	183	0.35
Lorain (city) Lorain County	206	0.32
Cleveland (city) Cuyahoga County	529	0.13
Elyria (city) Lorain County	57	0.10
Canton (city) Stark County	67	0.09
Columbus (city) Franklin County	511	0.07
Youngstown (city) Mahoning County	43	0.06
Toledo (city) Lucas County	69	0.02

Slavic

Top 10 Places Sorted by Population

Based on all places, regardless of total population

Place	Population	%
Columbus (city) Franklin County	458	0.06
Cleveland (city) Cuyahoga County	232	0.06
Parma (city) Cuyahoga County	145	0.18
Cuyahoga Falls (city) Summit County	132	0.27
Brunswick (city) Medina County	117	0.34
Mentor (city) Lake County	112	0.24
Zanesville (city) Muskingum County	108	0.42
Akron (city) Summit County	106	0.05
Willoughby (city) Lake County	94	0.42
Eastlake (city) Lake County	91	0.48

Top 10 Places Sorted by Percent of Total Population

Based on all places, regardless of total population

Place	Population	%
Lafferty (cdp) Belmont County	35	15.98
Cinnamon Lake (cdp) Ashland County	74	8.15
Washingtonville (village) Columbiana County	62	6.87
Marshallville (village) Wayne County	21	2.62
Alexandria (village) Licking County	4	1.67
Mingo Junction (village) Jefferson County	50	1.44
Oak Harbor (village) Ottawa County	35	1.26
Richfield (village) Summit County	44	1.22
Peninsula (village) Summit County	7	1.22
Blue Jay (cdp) Hamilton County	14	1.17

Top 10 Places Sorted by Percent of Total Population

Based on places with total population of 50,000 or more

Place	Population	%
Parma (city) Cuyahoga County	145	0.18
Canton (city) Stark County	87	0.12
Lakewood (city) Cuyahoga County	47	0.09
Elyria (city) Lorain County	43	0.08
Columbus (city) Franklin County	458	0.06
Cleveland (city) Cuyahoga County	232	0.06
Akron (city) Summit County	106	0.05
Kettering (city) Montgomery County	15	0.03
Cincinnati (city) Hamilton County	63	0.02
Toledo (city) Lucas County	58	0.02

Slovak

Top 10 Places Sorted by Population

Based on all places, regardless of total population

Place	Population	%
Cleveland (city) Cuyahoga County	7,074	1.73
Parma (city) Cuyahoga County	6,760	8.25
Columbus (city) Franklin County	3,380	0.44
Youngstown (city) Mahoning County	3,113	4.47
Strongsville (city) Cuyahoga County	2,962	6.68
Boardman (cdp) Mahoning County	2,764	7.81
Lakewood (city) Cuyahoga County	2,432	4.62
Austintown (cdp) Mahoning County	2,267	7.50
Akron (city) Summit County	2,164	1.07
North Olmsted (city) Cuyahoga County	2,024	6.17

Top 10 Places Sorted by Percent of Total Population

Based on all places, regardless of total population

Place	Population	%
Yankee Lake (village) Trumbull County	18	26.09
Brookfield Center (cdp) Trumbull County	244	16.58
New Middletown (village) Mahoning County	293	15.86
Put-in-Bay (village) Ottawa County	20	14.39
Struthers (city) Mahoning County	1,441	13.23
Lowellville (village) Mahoning County	148	12.81
Stratton (village) Jefferson County	35	12.59
Mingo Junction (village) Jefferson County	385	11.12
Marblehead (village) Ottawa County	86	10.71
Campbell (city) Mahoning County	892	10.56

Top 10 Places Sorted by Percent of Total Population

Based on places with total population of 50,000 or more

Place	Population	%
Parma (city) Cuyahoga County	6,760	8.25
Lakewood (city) Cuyahoga County	2,432	4.62
Youngstown (city) Mahoning County	3,113	4.47
Lorain (city) Lorain County	1,882	2.89
Elyria (city) Lorain County	1,549	2.82
Cleveland (city) Cuyahoga County	7,074	1.73
Akron (city) Summit County	2,164	1.07
Canton (city) Stark County	577	0.78
Columbus (city) Franklin County	3,380	0.44
Kettering (city) Montgomery County	208	0.37

Slovene

Top 10 Places Sorted by Population

Based on all places, regardless of total population

Place	Population	%
Cleveland (city) Cuyahoga County	3,214	0.79
Mentor (city) Lake County	3,037	6.38
Euclid (city) Cuyahoga County	2,895	5.87
Willoughby (city) Lake County	1,861	8.37
Parma (city) Cuyahoga County	1,677	2.05
Eastlake (city) Lake County	1,595	8.45
Columbus (city) Franklin County	1,380	0.18
Willowick (city) Lake County	1,273	8.96
Wickliffe (city) Lake County	1,137	8.85
Lakewood (city) Cuyahoga County	761	1.44

Top 10 Places Sorted by Percent of Total Population

Based on all places, regardless of total population

Place	Population	%
Lakeline (village) Lake County	22	14.57
Grand River (village) Lake County	48	13.68
Kirtland Hills (village) Lake County	94	12.30
Willowick (city) Lake County	1,273	8.96
Mayfield (village) Cuyahoga County	305	8.90
Wickliffe (city) Lake County	1,137	8.85
Kirtland (city) Lake County	581	8.50
Eastlake (city) Lake County	1,595	8.45
Willoughby (city) Lake County	1,861	8.37
Mentor-on-the-Lake (city) Lake County	601	7.92

Top 10 Places Sorted by Percent of Total Population

Based on places with total population of 50,000 or more

Place	Population	%
Parma (city) Cuyahoga County	1,677	2.05
Lakewood (city) Cuyahoga County	761	1.44
Lorain (city) Lorain County	546	0.84
Cleveland (city) Cuyahoga County	3,214	0.79
Elyria (city) Lorain County	165	0.30
Akron (city) Summit County	588	0.29
Columbus (city) Franklin County	1,380	0.18
Dayton (city) Montgomery County	132	0.09
Kettering (city) Montgomery County	41	0.07
Youngstown (city) Mahoning County	44	0.06

Soviet Union

Top 10 Places Sorted by Population

Based on all places, regardless of total population

Place	Population	%
Cincinnati (city) Hamilton County	15	<0.01
Perry Heights (cdp) Stark County	13	0.15
Aberdeen (village) Brown County	0	0.00
Ada (village) Hardin County	0	0.00
Adamsville (village) Muskingum County	0	0.00
Addyston (village) Hamilton County	0	0.00
Adelphi (village) Ross County	0	0.00
Adena (village) Jefferson County	0	0.00
Akron (city) Summit County	0	0.00
Albany (village) Athens County	0	0.00

Top 10 Places Sorted by Percent of Total Population

Based on all places, regardless of total population

Place	Population	%
Perry Heights (cdp) Stark County	13	0.15
Cincinnati (city) Hamilton County	15	<0.01
Aberdeen (village) Brown County	0	0.00
Ada (village) Hardin County	0	0.00
Adamsville (village) Muskingum County	0	0.00
Addyston (village) Hamilton County	0	0.00
Adelphi (village) Ross County	0	0.00
Adena (village) Jefferson County	0	0.00
Akron (city) Summit County	0	0.00
Albany (village) Athens County	0	0.00

Top 10 Places Sorted by Percent of Total Population

Based on places with total population of 50,000 or more

Place	Population	%
Cincinnati (city) Hamilton County	15	<0.01
Akron (city) Summit County	0	0.00
Canton (city) Stark County	0	0.00
Cleveland (city) Cuyahoga County	0	0.00
Columbus (city) Franklin County	0	0.00
Dayton (city) Montgomery County	0	0.00
Elyria (city) Lorain County	0	0.00
Hamilton (city) Butler County	0	0.00
Kettering (city) Montgomery County	0	0.00
Lakewood (city) Cuyahoga County	0	0.00

Swedish

Top 10 Places Sorted by Population

Based on all places, regardless of total population

Place	Population	%
Columbus (city) Franklin County	4,492	0.58
Toledo (city) Lucas County	1,344	0.46
Cincinnati (city) Hamilton County	1,245	0.41
Cleveland (city) Cuyahoga County	1,163	0.28
Akron (city) Summit County	1,161	0.57
Dublin (city) Franklin County	978	2.49
Dayton (city) Montgomery County	927	0.64
Kettering (city) Montgomery County	648	1.15
Cuyahoga Falls (city) Summit County	642	1.29
Austintown (cdp) Mahoning County	579	1.91

Top 10 Places Sorted by Percent of Total Population

Based on all places, regardless of total population

Place	Population	%
Pleasant Grove (cdp) Muskingum County	271	14.23
Congress (village) Wayne County	21	12.28
Darbydale (cdp) Franklin County	57	9.98

New Bavaria (village) Henry County	5	7.25
Ridgeville Corners (cdp) Henry County	21	6.75
Plainville (cdp) Hamilton County	14	6.28
Hartford (village) Licking County	36	6.09
Brimfield (cdp) Portage County	175	5.27
Gratiot (village) Licking County	15	5.23
La Croft (cdp) Columbiana County	60	5.17

Top 10 Places Sorted by Percent of Total Population
Based on places with total population of 50,000 or more

Place	Population	%
Kettering (city) Montgomery County	648	1.15
Lakewood (city) Cuyahoga County	528	1.00
Elyria (city) Lorain County	509	0.93
Springfield (city) Clark County	498	0.81
Dayton (city) Montgomery County	927	0.64
Columbus (city) Franklin County	4,492	0.58
Akron (city) Summit County	1,161	0.57
Canton (city) Stark County	420	0.56
Parma (city) Cuyahoga County	382	0.47
Toledo (city) Lucas County	1,344	0.46

Swiss

Top 10 Places Sorted by Population
Based on all places, regardless of total population

Place	Population	%
Columbus (city) Franklin County	2,745	0.36
Toledo (city) Lucas County	1,134	0.39
Cincinnati (city) Hamilton County	796	0.27
Wooster (city) Wayne County	722	2.77
Akron (city) Summit County	690	0.34
Orrville (city) Wayne County	622	7.37
New Philadelphia (city) Tuscarawas County	620	3.59
Canton (city) Stark County	577	0.78
Dover (city) Tuscarawas County	541	4.23
Alliance (city) Stark County	540	2.40

Top 10 Places Sorted by Percent of Total Population
Based on all places, regardless of total population

Place	Population	%
Berlin (cdp) Holmes County	390	41.40
Mount Eaton (village) Wayne County	70	29.05
Sterling (cdp) Wayne County	96	28.24
Kidron (cdp) Wayne County	253	24.33
Antioch (village) Monroe County	50	23.04
Wilmot (village) Stark County	51	21.98
Walnut Creek (cdp) Holmes County	82	21.19
Sugarcreek (village) Tuscarawas County	448	20.06
Pandora (village) Putnam County	205	17.95
Gilboa (village) Putnam County	24	17.14

Top 10 Places Sorted by Percent of Total Population
Based on places with total population of 50,000 or more

Place	Population	%
Canton (city) Stark County	577	0.78
Elyria (city) Lorain County	318	0.58
Kettering (city) Montgomery County	263	0.47
Toledo (city) Lucas County	1,134	0.39
Columbus (city) Franklin County	2,745	0.36
Akron (city) Summit County	690	0.34
Hamilton (city) Butler County	202	0.32
Lakewood (city) Cuyahoga County	154	0.29
Cincinnati (city) Hamilton County	796	0.27
Parma (city) Cuyahoga County	206	0.25

Turkish

Top 10 Places Sorted by Population
Based on all places, regardless of total population

Place	Population	%
Columbus (city) Franklin County	601	0.08
Lakewood (city) Cuyahoga County	222	0.42
Dayton (city) Montgomery County	203	0.14
Medina (city) Medina County	199	0.75
Perrysburg (city) Wood County	176	0.87
Stow (city) Summit County	152	0.44
Toledo (city) Lucas County	120	0.04
Solon (city) Cuyahoga County	112	0.49
Westlake (city) Cuyahoga County	83	0.26
Richmond Heights (city) Cuyahoga County	75	0.71

Top 10 Places Sorted by Percent of Total Population
Based on all places, regardless of total population

Place	Population	%
Van Buren (village) Hancock County	7	2.12
Newtonsville (village) Clermont County	6	1.99
West Union (village) Adams County	28	1.00
Perrysburg (city) Wood County	176	0.87
Medina (city) Medina County	199	0.75
Richmond Heights (city) Cuyahoga County	75	0.71
Bailey Lakes (village) Ashland County	2	0.53
Beachwood (city) Cuyahoga County	60	0.50
Solon (city) Cuyahoga County	112	0.49
Stow (city) Summit County	152	0.44

Top 10 Places Sorted by Percent of Total Population
Based on places with total population of 50,000 or more

Place	Population	%
Lakewood (city) Cuyahoga County	222	0.42
Dayton (city) Montgomery County	203	0.14
Columbus (city) Franklin County	601	0.08
Toledo (city) Lucas County	120	0.04
Akron (city) Summit County	61	0.03
Cincinnati (city) Hamilton County	75	0.02
Youngstown (city) Mahoning County	12	0.02
Cleveland (city) Cuyahoga County	53	0.01
Canton (city) Stark County	9	0.01
Elyria (city) Lorain County	0	0.00

Ukrainian

Top 10 Places Sorted by Population
Based on all places, regardless of total population

Place	Population	%
Parma (city) Cuyahoga County	4,857	5.93
Cleveland (city) Cuyahoga County	2,072	0.51
Columbus (city) Franklin County	1,935	0.25
North Royalton (city) Cuyahoga County	1,113	3.71
Parma Heights (city) Cuyahoga County	883	4.25
Strongsville (city) Cuyahoga County	741	1.67
Akron (city) Summit County	693	0.34
Austintown (cdp) Mahoning County	666	2.20
Boardman (cdp) Mahoning County	653	1.84
Mayfield Heights (city) Cuyahoga County	649	3.40

Top 10 Places Sorted by Percent of Total Population
Based on all places, regardless of total population

Place	Population	%
Negley (cdp) Columbiana County	48	20.08
Collins (cdp) Huron County	41	7.84
Parma (city) Cuyahoga County	4,857	5.93
Independence (city) Cuyahoga County	390	5.51
Kipton (village) Lorain County	17	5.38
Parma Heights (city) Cuyahoga County	883	4.25
Marne (cdp) Licking County	23	3.99
North Royalton (city) Cuyahoga County	1,113	3.71
Highland Hills (village) Cuyahoga County	56	3.67
Loveland Park (cdp) Warren County	44	3.64

Top 10 Places Sorted by Percent of Total Population
Based on places with total population of 50,000 or more

Place	Population	%
Parma (city) Cuyahoga County	4,857	5.93
Lakewood (city) Cuyahoga County	528	1.00
Lorain (city) Lorain County	521	0.80
Youngstown (city) Mahoning County	533	0.77
Cleveland (city) Cuyahoga County	2,072	0.51
Elyria (city) Lorain County	229	0.42
Akron (city) Summit County	693	0.34
Canton (city) Stark County	214	0.29
Kettering (city) Montgomery County	157	0.28
Columbus (city) Franklin County	1,935	0.25

Welsh

Top 10 Places Sorted by Population
Based on all places, regardless of total population

Place	Population	%
Columbus (city) Franklin County	10,220	1.33
Cincinnati (city) Hamilton County	2,038	0.68
Akron (city) Summit County	2,022	1.00
Cleveland (city) Cuyahoga County	1,575	0.38
Toledo (city) Lucas County	1,296	0.44
Boardman (cdp) Mahoning County	1,078	3.04
Delaware (city) Delaware County	998	2.96
Upper Arlington (city) Franklin County	983	2.92
Gahanna (city) Franklin County	927	2.84
Niles (city) Trumbull County	898	4.61

Top 10 Places Sorted by Percent of Total Population
Based on all places, regardless of total population

Place	Population	%
Glencoe (cdp) Belmont County	37	43.02
Vaughnsville (cdp) Putnam County	32	23.36
Venedocia (village) Van Wert County	16	14.16
Sandyville (cdp) Tuscarawas County	38	12.22
Bannock (cdp) Belmont County	25	12.02
Radnor (cdp) Delaware County	15	10.64
Oak Hill (village) Jackson County	182	10.30
Cardington (village) Morrow County	221	10.18
Yankee Lake (village) Trumbull County	7	10.14
Senecaville (village) Guernsey County	32	9.82

Top 10 Places Sorted by Percent of Total Population
Based on places with total population of 50,000 or more

Place	Population	%
Kettering (city) Montgomery County	757	1.35
Columbus (city) Franklin County	10,220	1.33
Youngstown (city) Mahoning County	877	1.26
Lakewood (city) Cuyahoga County	657	1.25
Elyria (city) Lorain County	612	1.11
Akron (city) Summit County	2,022	1.00
Canton (city) Stark County	631	0.85
Springfield (city) Clark County	505	0.82
Cincinnati (city) Hamilton County	2,038	0.68
Dayton (city) Montgomery County	856	0.59

West Indian, excluding Hispanic

Top 10 Places Sorted by Population
Based on all places, regardless of total population

Place	Population	%
Columbus (city) Franklin County	3,944	0.51
Cleveland (city) Cuyahoga County	1,835	0.45
Toledo (city) Lucas County	1,077	0.37
Cincinnati (city) Hamilton County	478	0.16
Cleveland Heights (city) Cuyahoga County	351	0.75
Reynoldsburg (city) Franklin County	270	0.77
Dayton (city) Montgomery County	267	0.18
Strongsville (city) Cuyahoga County	250	0.56
Bedford Heights (city) Cuyahoga County	249	2.31
Akron (city) Summit County	240	0.12

Top 10 Places Sorted by Percent of Total Population
Based on all places, regardless of total population

Place	Population	%
Oceola (cdp) Crawford County	22	10.05
Mount Healthy Heights (cdp) Hamilton County	214	6.15
Woodmere (village) Cuyahoga County	50	5.43
Moreland Hills (village) Cuyahoga County	94	2.84
Sciotodale (cdp) Scioto County	19	2.55
North Randall (village) Cuyahoga County	21	2.42
Bedford Heights (city) Cuyahoga County	249	2.31
Holland (village) Lucas County	39	2.01
Nelsonville (city) Athens County	79	1.51
Aquilla (village) Geauga County	5	1.37

Top 10 Places Sorted by Percent of Total Population
Based on places with total population of 50,000 or more

Place	Population	%
Columbus (city) Franklin County	3,944	0.51
Cleveland (city) Cuyahoga County	1,835	0.45
Toledo (city) Lucas County	1,077	0.37
Lakewood (city) Cuyahoga County	193	0.37
Youngstown (city) Mahoning County	152	0.22
Parma (city) Cuyahoga County	160	0.20
Lorain (city) Lorain County	122	0.19
Dayton (city) Montgomery County	267	0.18
Springfield (city) Clark County	103	0.17
Cincinnati (city) Hamilton County	478	0.16

West Indian: Bahamian, excluding Hispanic

Top 10 Places Sorted by Population
Based on all places, regardless of total population

Place	Population	%
Pickerington (city) Fairfield County	100	0.59
Columbus (city) Franklin County	93	0.01
Worthington (city) Franklin County	63	0.46
Cincinnati (city) Hamilton County	33	0.01
Canton (city) Stark County	16	0.02
Euclid (city) Cuyahoga County	15	0.03
Fort Shawnee (village) Allen County	14	0.37
Bowling Green (city) Wood County	14	0.05
Warrensville Heights (city) Cuyahoga County	11	0.08
Troy (city) Miami County	10	0.04

Top 10 Places Sorted by Percent of Total Population
Based on all places, regardless of total population

Place	Population	%
Pickerington (city) Fairfield County	100	0.59
Worthington (city) Franklin County	63	0.46
Fort Shawnee (village) Allen County	14	0.37
Warrensville Heights (city) Cuyahoga County	11	0.08
Bowling Green (city) Wood County	14	0.05
Troy (city) Miami County	10	0.04
Euclid (city) Cuyahoga County	15	0.03
Tiffin (city) Seneca County	6	0.03
Canton (city) Stark County	16	0.02
Columbus (city) Franklin County	93	0.01

Top 10 Places Sorted by Percent of Total Population
Based on places with total population of 50,000 or more

Place	Population	%
Canton (city) Stark County	16	0.02
Columbus (city) Franklin County	93	0.01
Cincinnati (city) Hamilton County	33	0.01
Akron (city) Summit County	0	0.00
Cleveland (city) Cuyahoga County	0	0.00
Dayton (city) Montgomery County	0	0.00
Elyria (city) Lorain County	0	0.00
Hamilton (city) Butler County	0	0.00
Kettering (city) Montgomery County	0	0.00
Lakewood (city) Cuyahoga County	0	0.00

West Indian: Barbadian, excluding Hispanic

Top 10 Places Sorted by Population
Based on all places, regardless of total population

Place	Population	%
Columbus (city) Franklin County	132	0.02
North Olmsted (city) Cuyahoga County	74	0.23
Reynoldsburg (city) Franklin County	47	0.13
Parma (city) Cuyahoga County	44	0.05
Wyoming (city) Hamilton County	41	0.49
Mansfield (city) Richland County	40	0.08
Middletown (city) Butler County	36	0.07
West Carrollton (city) Montgomery County	10	0.08
Euclid (city) Cuyahoga County	10	0.02
Defiance (city) Defiance County	8	0.05

Top 10 Places Sorted by Percent of Total Population
Based on all places, regardless of total population

Place	Population	%
Wyoming (city) Hamilton County	41	0.49
North Olmsted (city) Cuyahoga County	74	0.23
Reynoldsburg (city) Franklin County	47	0.13
Mansfield (city) Richland County	40	0.08
West Carrollton (city) Montgomery County	10	0.08
Middletown (city) Butler County	36	0.07
Parma (city) Cuyahoga County	44	0.05
Defiance (city) Defiance County	8	0.05
Columbus (city) Franklin County	132	0.02
Euclid (city) Cuyahoga County	10	0.02

Top 10 Places Sorted by Percent of Total Population
Based on places with total population of 50,000 or more

Place	Population	%
Parma (city) Cuyahoga County	44	0.05
Columbus (city) Franklin County	132	0.02
Youngstown (city) Mahoning County	8	0.01
Akron (city) Summit County	5	<0.01
Canton (city) Stark County	0	0.00
Cincinnati (city) Hamilton County	0	0.00
Cleveland (city) Cuyahoga County	0	0.00
Dayton (city) Montgomery County	0	0.00
Elyria (city) Lorain County	0	0.00
Hamilton (city) Butler County	0	0.00

West Indian: Belizean, excluding Hispanic

Top 10 Places Sorted by Population
Based on all places, regardless of total population

Place	Population	%
Columbus (city) Franklin County	42	0.01
Marysville (city) Union County	20	0.09
Toledo (city) Lucas County	19	0.01
Cleveland (city) Cuyahoga County	16	<0.01
Bay Village (city) Cuyahoga County	12	0.08
Euclid (city) Cuyahoga County	10	0.02
Bedford Heights (city) Cuyahoga County	8	0.07
North Madison (cdp) Lake County	7	0.08
Aberdeen (village) Brown County	0	0.00
Ada (village) Hardin County	0	0.00

Top 10 Places Sorted by Percent of Total Population
Based on all places, regardless of total population

Place	Population	%
Marysville (city) Union County	20	0.09
Bay Village (city) Cuyahoga County	12	0.08
North Madison (cdp) Lake County	7	0.08
Bedford Heights (city) Cuyahoga County	8	0.07
Euclid (city) Cuyahoga County	10	0.02
Columbus (city) Franklin County	42	0.01
Toledo (city) Lucas County	19	0.01
Cleveland (city) Cuyahoga County	16	<0.01
Aberdeen (village) Brown County	0	0.00
Ada (village) Hardin County	0	0.00

Top 10 Places Sorted by Percent of Total Population
Based on places with total population of 50,000 or more

Place	Population	%
Columbus (city) Franklin County	42	0.01
Toledo (city) Lucas County	19	0.01
Cleveland (city) Cuyahoga County	16	<0.01
Akron (city) Summit County	0	0.00
Canton (city) Stark County	0	0.00
Cincinnati (city) Hamilton County	0	0.00
Dayton (city) Montgomery County	0	0.00
Elyria (city) Lorain County	0	0.00
Hamilton (city) Butler County	0	0.00
Kettering (city) Montgomery County	0	0.00

West Indian: Bermudan, excluding Hispanic

Top 10 Places Sorted by Population
Based on all places, regardless of total population

Place	Population	%
North Royalton (city) Cuyahoga County	45	0.15
Clayton (city) Montgomery County	18	0.14
Berea (city) Cuyahoga County	13	0.07
Cleveland Heights (city) Cuyahoga County	11	0.02
Cleveland (city) Cuyahoga County	11	<0.01
Columbus (city) Franklin County	11	<0.01
Shaker Heights (city) Cuyahoga County	10	0.04
Macedonia (city) Summit County	9	0.08
Aberdeen (village) Brown County	0	0.00
Ada (village) Hardin County	0	0.00

Top 10 Places Sorted by Percent of Total Population
Based on all places, regardless of total population

Place	Population	%
North Royalton (city) Cuyahoga County	45	0.15
Clayton (city) Montgomery County	18	0.14
Macedonia (city) Summit County	9	0.08
Berea (city) Cuyahoga County	13	0.07
Shaker Heights (city) Cuyahoga County	10	0.04
Cleveland Heights (city) Cuyahoga County	11	0.02
Cleveland (city) Cuyahoga County	11	<0.01
Columbus (city) Franklin County	11	<0.01
Aberdeen (village) Brown County	0	0.00
Ada (village) Hardin County	0	0.00

Top 10 Places Sorted by Percent of Total Population
Based on places with total population of 50,000 or more

Place	Population	%
Cleveland (city) Cuyahoga County	11	<0.01
Columbus (city) Franklin County	11	<0.01
Akron (city) Summit County	0	0.00
Canton (city) Stark County	0	0.00
Cincinnati (city) Hamilton County	0	0.00
Dayton (city) Montgomery County	0	0.00
Elyria (city) Lorain County	0	0.00
Hamilton (city) Butler County	0	0.00
Kettering (city) Montgomery County	0	0.00
Lakewood (city) Cuyahoga County	0	0.00

West Indian: British West Indian, excluding Hispanic

Top 10 Places Sorted by Population
Based on all places, regardless of total population

Place	Population	%
Columbus (city) Franklin County	165	0.02
Akron (city) Summit County	39	0.02
Bedford Heights (city) Cuyahoga County	34	0.31
Heath (city) Licking County	31	0.31
Cleveland (city) Cuyahoga County	31	0.01
Toledo (city) Lucas County	22	0.01
Cincinnati (city) Hamilton County	20	0.01
Dent (cdp) Hamilton County	16	0.16
Rosemount (cdp) Scioto County	15	0.68
Canton (city) Stark County	10	0.01

Top 10 Places Sorted by Percent of Total Population
Based on all places, regardless of total population

Place	Population	%
Rosemount (cdp) Scioto County	15	0.68
Bedford Heights (city) Cuyahoga County	34	0.31
Heath (city) Licking County	31	0.31
Dent (cdp) Hamilton County	16	0.16
Grafton (village) Lorain County	9	0.14
Delaware (city) Delaware County	9	0.03
Hilliard (city) Franklin County	8	0.03
Columbus (city) Franklin County	165	0.02
Akron (city) Summit County	39	0.02
Cleveland (city) Cuyahoga County	31	0.01

Top 10 Places Sorted by Percent of Total Population
Based on places with total population of 50,000 or more

Place	Population	%
Columbus (city) Franklin County	165	0.02
Akron (city) Summit County	39	0.02
Cleveland (city) Cuyahoga County	31	0.01
Toledo (city) Lucas County	22	0.01
Cincinnati (city) Hamilton County	20	0.01
Canton (city) Stark County	10	0.01
Dayton (city) Montgomery County	0	0.00
Elyria (city) Lorain County	0	0.00
Hamilton (city) Butler County	0	0.00
Kettering (city) Montgomery County	0	0.00

West Indian: Dutch West Indian, excluding Hispanic

Top 10 Places Sorted by Population
Based on all places, regardless of total population

Place	Population	%
Columbus (city) Franklin County	54	0.01
Huber Heights (city) Montgomery County	43	0.11
Springfield (city) Clark County	35	0.06
Nelsonville (city) Athens County	26	0.50
Riverside (city) Montgomery County	26	0.10
Hilliard (city) Franklin County	21	0.08
Maumee (city) Lucas County	18	0.12
Choctaw Lake (cdp) Madison County	17	1.09
Upper Sandusky (city) Wyandot County	13	0.20
Washington Court House (city) Fayette County	13	0.09

Top 10 Places Sorted by Percent of Total Population

Based on all places, regardless of total population

Place	Population	%
Choctaw Lake (cdp) Madison County	17	1.09
Bainbridge (village) Ross County	7	0.82
Nelsonville (city) Athens County	26	0.50
Buchtel (village) Athens County	3	0.50
Mount Sterling (village) Madison County	8	0.44
Bremen (village) Fairfield County	6	0.42
Cadiz (village) Harrison County	9	0.27
Northwood (city) Wood County	12	0.23
Upper Sandusky (city) Wyandot County	13	0.20
St. Paris (village) Champaign County	3	0.15

Top 10 Places Sorted by Percent of Total Population

Based on places with total population of 50,000 or more

Place	Population	%
Springfield (city) Clark County	35	0.06
Columbus (city) Franklin County	54	0.01
Akron (city) Summit County	0	0.00
Canton (city) Stark County	0	0.00
Cincinnati (city) Hamilton County	0	0.00
Cleveland (city) Cuyahoga County	0	0.00
Dayton (city) Montgomery County	0	0.00
Elyria (city) Lorain County	0	0.00
Hamilton (city) Butler County	0	0.00
Kettering (city) Montgomery County	0	0.00

West Indian: Haitian, excluding Hispanic

Top 10 Places Sorted by Population

Based on all places, regardless of total population

Place	Population	%
Columbus (city) Franklin County	1,655	0.21
Reynoldsburg (city) Franklin County	145	0.41
Toledo (city) Lucas County	97	0.03
Lima (city) Allen County	52	0.13
Euclid (city) Cuyahoga County	49	0.10
Lorain (city) Lorain County	43	0.07
Cincinnati (city) Hamilton County	41	0.01
Akron (city) Summit County	36	0.02
Dayton (city) Montgomery County	32	0.02
Chillicothe (city) Ross County	31	0.14

Top 10 Places Sorted by Percent of Total Population

Based on all places, regardless of total population

Place	Population	%
Dunkirk (village) Hardin County	11	1.20
Richville (cdp) Stark County	16	0.47
Reynoldsburg (city) Franklin County	145	0.41
McDonald (village) Trumbull County	12	0.36
North Randall (village) Cuyahoga County	3	0.35
Granville (village) Licking County	13	0.23
Dillonvale (cdp) Hamilton County	8	0.23
Castalia (village) Erie County	2	0.23
Columbus (city) Franklin County	1,655	0.21
Fruit Hill (cdp) Hamilton County	8	0.20

Top 10 Places Sorted by Percent of Total Population

Based on places with total population of 50,000 or more

Place	Population	%
Columbus (city) Franklin County	1,655	0.21
Lorain (city) Lorain County	43	0.07
Lakewood (city) Cuyahoga County	27	0.05
Toledo (city) Lucas County	97	0.03
Parma (city) Cuyahoga County	21	0.03
Youngstown (city) Mahoning County	19	0.03
Akron (city) Summit County	36	0.02
Dayton (city) Montgomery County	32	0.02
Kettering (city) Montgomery County	9	0.02
Cincinnati (city) Hamilton County	41	0.01

West Indian: Jamaican, excluding Hispanic

Top 10 Places Sorted by Population

Based on all places, regardless of total population

Place	Population	%
Columbus (city) Franklin County	1,305	0.17
Cleveland (city) Cuyahoga County	1,281	0.31
Toledo (city) Lucas County	879	0.30
Cleveland Heights (city) Cuyahoga County	315	0.67
Cincinnati (city) Hamilton County	292	0.10
Strongsville (city) Cuyahoga County	236	0.53
Mount Healthy Heights (cdp) Hamilton County	214	6.15
Maple Heights (city) Cuyahoga County	182	0.77
Dayton (city) Montgomery County	173	0.12
Mansfield (city) Richland County	169	0.35

Top 10 Places Sorted by Percent of Total Population

Based on all places, regardless of total population

Place	Population	%
Mount Healthy Heights (cdp) Hamilton County	214	6.15
Woodmere (village) Cuyahoga County	40	4.34
Moreland Hills (village) Cuyahoga County	94	2.84
Sciotodale (cdp) Scioto County	19	2.55
Holland (village) Lucas County	39	2.01
North Randall (village) Cuyahoga County	15	1.73
Bedford Heights (city) Cuyahoga County	155	1.44
Aquilla (village) Geauga County	5	1.37
Midvale (village) Tuscarawas County	6	1.14
Nelsonville (city) Athens County	53	1.01

Top 10 Places Sorted by Percent of Total Population

Based on places with total population of 50,000 or more

Place	Population	%
Cleveland (city) Cuyahoga County	1,281	0.31
Toledo (city) Lucas County	879	0.30
Lakewood (city) Cuyahoga County	158	0.30
Youngstown (city) Mahoning County	125	0.18
Columbus (city) Franklin County	1,305	0.17
Dayton (city) Montgomery County	173	0.12
Cincinnati (city) Hamilton County	292	0.10
Springfield (city) Clark County	62	0.10
Akron (city) Summit County	89	0.04
Lorain (city) Lorain County	29	0.04

West Indian: Trinidadian and Tobagonian, excluding Hispanic

Top 10 Places Sorted by Population

Based on all places, regardless of total population

Place	Population	%
Columbus (city) Franklin County	103	0.01
Springdale (city) Hamilton County	98	0.89
Cleveland (city) Cuyahoga County	94	0.02
Dayton (city) Montgomery County	62	0.04
Warrensville Heights (city) Cuyahoga County	33	0.24
Ballville (cdp) Sandusky County	31	0.98
Reynoldsburg (city) Franklin County	29	0.08
Cincinnati (city) Hamilton County	29	0.01
Blacklick Estates (cdp) Franklin County	25	0.29
Chillicothe (city) Ross County	23	0.10

Top 10 Places Sorted by Percent of Total Population

Based on all places, regardless of total population

Place	Population	%
Oceola (cdp) Crawford County	22	10.05
Ballville (cdp) Sandusky County	31	0.98
Springdale (city) Hamilton County	98	0.89
Highland Hills (village) Cuyahoga County	7	0.46
Blacklick Estates (cdp) Franklin County	25	0.29
Warrensville Heights (city) Cuyahoga County	33	0.24
Chillicothe (city) Ross County	23	0.10
Reynoldsburg (city) Franklin County	29	0.08
Berea (city) Cuyahoga County	16	0.08
Shaker Heights (city) Cuyahoga County	21	0.07

Top 10 Places Sorted by Percent of Total Population

Based on places with total population of 50,000 or more

Place	Population	%
Dayton (city) Montgomery County	62	0.04
Cleveland (city) Cuyahoga County	94	0.02
Hamilton (city) Butler County	12	0.02
Columbus (city) Franklin County	103	0.01
Cincinnati (city) Hamilton County	29	0.01
Toledo (city) Lucas County	11	<0.01
Akron (city) Summit County	0	0.00
Canton (city) Stark County	0	0.00
Elyria (city) Lorain County	0	0.00
Kettering (city) Montgomery County	0	0.00

West Indian: U.S. Virgin Islander, excluding Hispanic

Top 10 Places Sorted by Population

Based on all places, regardless of total population

Place	Population	%
Columbus (city) Franklin County	27	<0.01
Findlay (city) Hancock County	8	0.02
Cleveland (city) Cuyahoga County	7	<0.01
Parma (city) Cuyahoga County	5	0.01
Aberdeen (village) Brown County	0	0.00
Ada (village) Hardin County	0	0.00
Adamsville (village) Muskingum County	0	0.00
Addyston (village) Hamilton County	0	0.00
Adelphi (village) Ross County	0	0.00
Adena (village) Jefferson County	0	0.00

Top 10 Places Sorted by Percent of Total Population

Based on all places, regardless of total population

Place	Population	%
Findlay (city) Hancock County	8	0.02
Parma (city) Cuyahoga County	5	0.01
Columbus (city) Franklin County	27	<0.01
Cleveland (city) Cuyahoga County	7	<0.01
Aberdeen (village) Brown County	0	0.00
Ada (village) Hardin County	0	0.00
Adamsville (village) Muskingum County	0	0.00
Addyston (village) Hamilton County	0	0.00
Adelphi (village) Ross County	0	0.00
Adena (village) Jefferson County	0	0.00

Top 10 Places Sorted by Percent of Total Population

Based on places with total population of 50,000 or more

Place	Population	%
Parma (city) Cuyahoga County	5	0.01
Columbus (city) Franklin County	27	<0.01
Cleveland (city) Cuyahoga County	7	<0.01
Akron (city) Summit County	0	0.00
Canton (city) Stark County	0	0.00
Cincinnati (city) Hamilton County	0	0.00
Dayton (city) Montgomery County	0	0.00
Elyria (city) Lorain County	0	0.00
Hamilton (city) Butler County	0	0.00
Kettering (city) Montgomery County	0	0.00

West Indian: West Indian, excluding Hispanic

Top 10 Places Sorted by Population

Based on all places, regardless of total population

Place	Population	%
Cleveland (city) Cuyahoga County	364	0.09
Columbus (city) Franklin County	357	0.05
Franklin (city) Warren County	129	1.08
Trotwood (city) Montgomery County	121	0.49
Euclid (city) Cuyahoga County	108	0.22
Parma (city) Cuyahoga County	90	0.11
Sandusky (city) Erie County	72	0.28
Akron (city) Summit County	71	0.04
Warren (city) Trumbull County	65	0.15
Kettering (city) Montgomery County	57	0.10

Top 10 Places Sorted by Percent of Total Population

Based on all places, regardless of total population

Place	Population	%
Woodmere (village) Cuyahoga County	10	1.09
Franklin (city) Warren County	129	1.08
Richwood (village) Union County	16	0.72
Columbiana (city) Columbiana County	33	0.52
Trotwood (city) Montgomery County	121	0.49
Bedford Heights (city) Cuyahoga County	52	0.48
Milford (city) Clermont County	28	0.42
North Randall (village) Cuyahoga County	3	0.35
Vandalia (city) Montgomery County	51	0.34
Greenwich (village) Huron County	4	0.30

Top 10 Places Sorted by Percent of Total Population

Based on places with total population of 50,000 or more

Place	Population	%
Parma (city) Cuyahoga County	90	0.11

Kettering (city) Montgomery County	57	0.10
Cleveland (city) Cuyahoga County	364	0.09
Lorain (city) Lorain County	50	0.08
Columbus (city) Franklin County	357	0.05
Akron (city) Summit County	71	0.04
Cincinnati (city) Hamilton County	53	0.02
Toledo (city) Lucas County	49	0.02
Lakewood (city) Cuyahoga County	8	0.02
Canton (city) Stark County	0	0.00

West Indian: Other, excluding Hispanic

Top 10 Places Sorted by Population

Based on all places, regardless of total population

Place	Population	%
Ashland (city) Ashland County	17	0.08
Cincinnati (city) Hamilton County	10	<0.01
Montgomery (city) Hamilton County	9	0.09
Newark (city) Licking County	8	0.02
Aberdeen (village) Brown County	0	0.00
Ada (village) Hardin County	0	0.00
Adamsville (village) Muskingum County	0	0.00
Addyston (village) Hamilton County	0	0.00
Adelphi (village) Ross County	0	0.00
Adena (village) Jefferson County	0	0.00

Top 10 Places Sorted by Percent of Total Population

Based on all places, regardless of total population

Place	Population	%
Montgomery (city) Hamilton County	9	0.09
Ashland (city) Ashland County	17	0.08
Newark (city) Licking County	8	0.02
Cincinnati (city) Hamilton County	10	<0.01
Aberdeen (village) Brown County	0	0.00
Ada (village) Hardin County	0	0.00
Adamsville (village) Muskingum County	0	0.00
Addyston (village) Hamilton County	0	0.00
Adelphi (village) Ross County	0	0.00
Adena (village) Jefferson County	0	0.00

Top 10 Places Sorted by Percent of Total Population

Based on places with total population of 50,000 or more

Place	Population	%
Cincinnati (city) Hamilton County	10	<0.01
Akron (city) Summit County	0	0.00
Canton (city) Stark County	0	0.00
Cleveland (city) Cuyahoga County	0	0.00
Columbus (city) Franklin County	0	0.00
Dayton (city) Montgomery County	0	0.00
Elyria (city) Lorain County	0	0.00
Hamilton (city) Butler County	0	0.00
Kettering (city) Montgomery County	0	0.00
Lakewood (city) Cuyahoga County	0	0.00

Yugoslavian

Top 10 Places Sorted by Population

Based on all places, regardless of total population

Place	Population	%
Akron (city) Summit County	1,145	0.56
Columbus (city) Franklin County	883	0.11
Parma (city) Cuyahoga County	332	0.41
Mansfield (city) Richland County	307	0.63
Cleveland (city) Cuyahoga County	287	0.07
Medina (city) Medina County	278	1.04
Eastlake (city) Lake County	265	1.40
Mentor (city) Lake County	241	0.51
Barberton (city) Summit County	178	0.66
Cincinnati (city) Hamilton County	158	0.05

Top 10 Places Sorted by Percent of Total Population

Based on all places, regardless of total population

Place	Population	%
Frankfort (village) Ross County	53	4.83
North Lawrence (cdp) Stark County	8	4.47
Hayesville (village) Ashland County	8	2.27
Four Bridges (cdp) Butler County	43	1.84
Mount Pleasant (village) Jefferson County	8	1.66
North Randall (village) Cuyahoga County	14	1.61
Thurston (village) Fairfield County	9	1.57
Mount Sterling (village) Madison County	26	1.43
Eastlake (city) Lake County	265	1.40
Dalton (village) Wayne County	27	1.40

Top 10 Places Sorted by Percent of Total Population

Based on places with total population of 50,000 or more

Place	Population	%
Akron (city) Summit County	1,145	0.56
Parma (city) Cuyahoga County	332	0.41
Lakewood (city) Cuyahoga County	109	0.21
Kettering (city) Montgomery County	81	0.14
Columbus (city) Franklin County	883	0.11
Cleveland (city) Cuyahoga County	287	0.07
Elyria (city) Lorain County	41	0.07
Canton (city) Stark County	48	0.06
Cincinnati (city) Hamilton County	158	0.05
Youngstown (city) Mahoning County	34	0.05

Hispanic Origin Rankings

Hispanic or Latino (of any race)

Top 10 Places Sorted by Population
Based on all places, regardless of total population

Place	Population	%
Columbus (city) Franklin County	44,359	5.64
Cleveland (city) Cuyahoga County	39,534	9.96
Toledo (city) Lucas County	21,231	7.39
Lorain (city) Lorain County	16,177	25.24
Cincinnati (city) Hamilton County	8,308	2.80
Youngstown (city) Mahoning County	6,207	9.27
Painesville (city) Lake County	4,298	21.97
Akron (city) Summit County	4,255	2.14
Dayton (city) Montgomery County	4,180	2.95
Hamilton (city) Butler County	3,981	6.37

Top 10 Places Sorted by Percent of Total Population
Based on all places, regardless of total population

Place	Population	%
Leipsic (village) Putnam County	656	31.34
Tedrow (cdp) Fulton County	53	30.64
West Leipsic (village) Putnam County	61	29.61
Belmore (village) Putnam County	42	29.37
Brecon (cdp) Hamilton County	69	28.28
Hessville (cdp) Sandusky County	55	25.70
Lorain (city) Lorain County	16,177	25.24
Milton Center (village) Wood County	33	22.92
Painesville (city) Lake County	4,298	21.97
Hamler (village) Henry County	124	21.53

Top 10 Places Sorted by Percent of Total Population
Based on places with total population of 50,000 or more

Place	Population	%
Lorain (city) Lorain County	16,177	25.24
Cleveland (city) Cuyahoga County	39,534	9.96
Youngstown (city) Mahoning County	6,207	9.27
Toledo (city) Lucas County	21,231	7.39
Hamilton (city) Butler County	3,981	6.37
Columbus (city) Franklin County	44,359	5.64
Elyria (city) Lorain County	2,649	4.86
Lakewood (city) Cuyahoga County	2,147	4.12
Parma (city) Cuyahoga County	2,915	3.57
Springfield (city) Clark County	1,824	3.01

Central American, excluding Mexican

Top 10 Places Sorted by Population
Based on all places, regardless of total population

Place	Population	%
Columbus (city) Franklin County	4,017	0.51
Cleveland (city) Cuyahoga County	2,085	0.53
Cincinnati (city) Hamilton County	1,860	0.63
Springdale (city) Hamilton County	613	5.46
New Philadelphia (city) Tuscarawas County	365	2.11
Canton (city) Stark County	348	0.48
Akron (city) Summit County	341	0.17
Whitehall (city) Franklin County	338	1.87
Fairfield (city) Butler County	299	0.70
Dover (city) Tuscarawas County	280	2.18

Top 10 Places Sorted by Percent of Total Population
Based on all places, regardless of total population

Place	Population	%
Springdale (city) Hamilton County	613	5.46
Parral (village) Tuscarawas County	5	2.29
Dover (city) Tuscarawas County	280	2.18
New Philadelphia (city) Tuscarawas County	365	2.11
North Robinson (village) Crawford County	4	1.95
Whitehall (city) Franklin County	338	1.87
Sugar Bush Knolls (village) Portage County	3	1.69
Brecon (cdp) Hamilton County	4	1.64
Sandyville (cdp) Tuscarawas County	6	1.63
Wilson (village) Monroe County	2	1.60

Top 10 Places Sorted by Percent of Total Population
Based on places with total population of 50,000 or more

Place	Population	%
Cincinnati (city) Hamilton County	1,860	0.63
Cleveland (city) Cuyahoga County	2,085	0.53
Columbus (city) Franklin County	4,017	0.51
Canton (city) Stark County	348	0.48
Hamilton (city) Butler County	166	0.27
Youngstown (city) Mahoning County	152	0.23
Kettering (city) Montgomery County	116	0.21
Dayton (city) Montgomery County	269	0.19
Lakewood (city) Cuyahoga County	98	0.19
Lorain (city) Lorain County	118	0.18

Central American: Costa Rican

Top 10 Places Sorted by Population
Based on all places, regardless of total population

Place	Population	%
Columbus (city) Franklin County	129	0.02
Dayton (city) Montgomery County	87	0.06
Cleveland (city) Cuyahoga County	45	0.01
Cincinnati (city) Hamilton County	39	0.01
Kettering (city) Montgomery County	29	0.05
Toledo (city) Lucas County	15	0.01
Hudson (city) Summit County	14	0.06
Whitehall (city) Franklin County	13	0.07
North Ridgeville (city) Lorain County	11	0.04
Fairborn (city) Greene County	11	0.03

Top 10 Places Sorted by Percent of Total Population
Based on all places, regardless of total population

Place	Population	%
Waldo (village) Marion County	2	0.59
Coldstream (cdp) Hamilton County	3	0.26
Fredericksburg (village) Wayne County	1	0.24
Loveland Park (cdp) Warren County	3	0.20
Pettisville (cdp) Fulton County	1	0.20
Marble Cliff (village) Franklin County	1	0.17
Kidron (cdp) Wayne County	1	0.11
Canal Winchester (village) Franklin County	7	0.10
Apple Valley (cdp) Knox County	5	0.10
Turpin Hills (cdp) Hamilton County	5	0.10

Top 10 Places Sorted by Percent of Total Population
Based on places with total population of 50,000 or more

Place	Population	%
Dayton (city) Montgomery County	87	0.06
Kettering (city) Montgomery County	29	0.05
Columbus (city) Franklin County	129	0.02
Cleveland (city) Cuyahoga County	45	0.01
Cincinnati (city) Hamilton County	39	0.01
Toledo (city) Lucas County	15	0.01
Akron (city) Summit County	10	0.01
Parma (city) Cuyahoga County	6	0.01
Lakewood (city) Cuyahoga County	5	0.01
Youngstown (city) Mahoning County	5	0.01

Central American: Guatemalan

Top 10 Places Sorted by Population
Based on all places, regardless of total population

Place	Population	%
Cincinnati (city) Hamilton County	1,257	0.42
Cleveland (city) Cuyahoga County	786	0.20
Columbus (city) Franklin County	645	0.08
Springdale (city) Hamilton County	562	5.01
New Philadelphia (city) Tuscarawas County	353	2.04
Dover (city) Tuscarawas County	273	2.13
Forest Park (city) Hamilton County	148	0.79
Canton (city) Stark County	138	0.19
Salem (city) Columbiana County	133	1.08
Fairfield (city) Butler County	133	0.31

Top 10 Places Sorted by Percent of Total Population
Based on all places, regardless of total population

Place	Population	%
Springdale (city) Hamilton County	562	5.01
Parral (village) Tuscarawas County	5	2.29
Dover (city) Tuscarawas County	273	2.13
New Philadelphia (city) Tuscarawas County	353	2.04
Brecon (cdp) Hamilton County	4	1.64
Sandyville (cdp) Tuscarawas County	6	1.63
Plumwood (cdp) Madison County	4	1.25
Leipsic (village) Putnam County	25	1.19
Salem (city) Columbiana County	133	1.08
South Vienna (village) Clark County	4	1.04

Top 10 Places Sorted by Percent of Total Population
Based on places with total population of 50,000 or more

Place	Population	%
Cincinnati (city) Hamilton County	1,257	0.42
Cleveland (city) Cuyahoga County	786	0.20
Canton (city) Stark County	138	0.19
Columbus (city) Franklin County	645	0.08
Hamilton (city) Butler County	41	0.07
Lorain (city) Lorain County	32	0.05
Kettering (city) Montgomery County	28	0.05
Akron (city) Summit County	80	0.04
Dayton (city) Montgomery County	51	0.04
Parma (city) Cuyahoga County	34	0.04

Central American: Honduran

Top 10 Places Sorted by Population
Based on all places, regardless of total population

Place	Population	%
Columbus (city) Franklin County	784	0.10
Cleveland (city) Cuyahoga County	324	0.08
Cincinnati (city) Hamilton County	230	0.08
Canton (city) Stark County	139	0.19
Akron (city) Summit County	93	0.05
Norwood (city) Hamilton County	81	0.42
Fairfield (city) Butler County	79	0.19
Hamilton (city) Butler County	64	0.10
Dayton (city) Montgomery County	59	0.04
Youngstown (city) Mahoning County	46	0.07

Top 10 Places Sorted by Percent of Total Population
Based on all places, regardless of total population

Place	Population	%
Midway (village) Madison County	5	1.55
Valleyview (village) Franklin County	9	1.45
Hooven (cdp) Hamilton County	3	0.56
Fredericksburg (village) Wayne County	2	0.47
Norwood (city) Hamilton County	81	0.42
Riverlea (village) Franklin County	2	0.37
Lincoln Village (cdp) Franklin County	32	0.35
Geneva-on-the-Lake (village) Ashtabula County	4	0.31
Robertsville (cdp) Stark County	1	0.30
Crystal Lakes (cdp) Clark County	4	0.27

Top 10 Places Sorted by Percent of Total Population
Based on places with total population of 50,000 or more

Place	Population	%
Canton (city) Stark County	139	0.19
Columbus (city) Franklin County	784	0.10
Hamilton (city) Butler County	64	0.10
Cleveland (city) Cuyahoga County	324	0.08
Cincinnati (city) Hamilton County	230	0.08
Youngstown (city) Mahoning County	46	0.07
Akron (city) Summit County	93	0.05
Dayton (city) Montgomery County	59	0.04
Lorain (city) Lorain County	17	0.03
Lakewood (city) Cuyahoga County	16	0.03

Central American: Nicaraguan

Top 10 Places Sorted by Population
Based on all places, regardless of total population

Place	Population	%
Columbus (city) Franklin County	157	0.02
Cincinnati (city) Hamilton County	90	0.03
Cleveland (city) Cuyahoga County	82	0.02
Toledo (city) Lucas County	72	0.03
Akron (city) Summit County	38	0.02
Norwood (city) Hamilton County	25	0.13
Reynoldsburg (city) Franklin County	22	0.06
North Ridgeville (city) Lorain County	18	0.06
Middletown (city) Butler County	18	0.04
Beavercreek (city) Greene County	17	0.04

Top 10 Places Sorted by Percent of Total Population
Based on all places, regardless of total population

Place	Population	%
Kipton (village) Lorain County	1	0.41
Flushing (village) Belmont County	3	0.34
New Marshfield (cdp) Athens County	1	0.31
Spring Valley (village) Greene County	1	0.21
Willard (city) Huron County	11	0.18
Rossmoyne (cdp) Hamilton County	4	0.18
Napoleon (city) Henry County	14	0.16
Greentown (cdp) Stark County	6	0.16
Etna (cdp) Licking County	2	0.16
Ostrander (village) Delaware County	1	0.16

Top 10 Places Sorted by Percent of Total Population
Based on places with total population of 50,000 or more

Place	Population	%
Cincinnati (city) Hamilton County	90	0.03
Toledo (city) Lucas County	72	0.03
Lakewood (city) Cuyahoga County	17	0.03
Columbus (city) Franklin County	157	0.02
Cleveland (city) Cuyahoga County	82	0.02
Akron (city) Summit County	38	0.02
Parma (city) Cuyahoga County	13	0.02
Springfield (city) Clark County	13	0.02
Dayton (city) Montgomery County	14	0.01
Lorain (city) Lorain County	8	0.01

Central American: Panamanian

Top 10 Places Sorted by Population
Based on all places, regardless of total population

Place	Population	%
Columbus (city) Franklin County	294	0.04
Cleveland (city) Cuyahoga County	89	0.02
Cincinnati (city) Hamilton County	78	0.03
Middletown (city) Butler County	47	0.10
Akron (city) Summit County	47	0.02
Dayton (city) Montgomery County	37	0.03
Toledo (city) Lucas County	33	0.01
Beavercreek (city) Greene County	30	0.07
Kettering (city) Montgomery County	28	0.05
Lorain (city) Lorain County	28	0.04

Top 10 Places Sorted by Percent of Total Population
Based on all places, regardless of total population

Place	Population	%
North Robinson (village) Crawford County	4	1.95
Wilson (village) Monroe County	2	1.60
Hanging Rock (village) Lawrence County	3	1.36
Barnhill (village) Tuscarawas County	5	1.26
Hills and Dales (village) Stark County	1	0.45
Mount Blanchard (village) Hancock County	2	0.41
Atwater (cdp) Portage County	3	0.40
Jeromesville (village) Ashland County	2	0.36
Woodmere (village) Cuyahoga County	3	0.34
Seaman (village) Adams County	3	0.32

Top 10 Places Sorted by Percent of Total Population
Based on places with total population of 50,000 or more

Place	Population	%
Kettering (city) Montgomery County	28	0.05
Columbus (city) Franklin County	294	0.04
Lorain (city) Lorain County	28	0.04
Cincinnati (city) Hamilton County	78	0.03
Dayton (city) Montgomery County	37	0.03
Youngstown (city) Mahoning County	19	0.03
Cleveland (city) Cuyahoga County	89	0.02
Akron (city) Summit County	47	0.02
Lakewood (city) Cuyahoga County	13	0.02
Springfield (city) Clark County	11	0.02

Central American: Salvadoran

Top 10 Places Sorted by Population
Based on all places, regardless of total population

Place	Population	%
Columbus (city) Franklin County	1,954	0.25
Cleveland (city) Cuyahoga County	738	0.19
Whitehall (city) Franklin County	236	1.31
Cincinnati (city) Hamilton County	132	0.04
Forest Park (city) Hamilton County	93	0.50
Grove City (city) Franklin County	77	0.22
Akron (city) Summit County	69	0.03
Fairfield (city) Butler County	62	0.15
Cleveland Heights (city) Cuyahoga County	61	0.13
Lincoln Village (cdp) Franklin County	54	0.60

Top 10 Places Sorted by Percent of Total Population
Based on all places, regardless of total population

Place	Population	%
Sugar Bush Knolls (village) Portage County	3	1.69
Chatfield (village) Crawford County	3	1.59
Whitehall (city) Franklin County	236	1.31
Hooven (cdp) Hamilton County	5	0.94
Willard (city) Huron County	50	0.80
New Haven (cdp) Huron County	3	0.75
Minerva Park (village) Franklin County	8	0.63
Lincoln Village (cdp) Franklin County	54	0.60
Linndale (village) Cuyahoga County	1	0.56
Forest Park (city) Hamilton County	93	0.50

Top 10 Places Sorted by Percent of Total Population
Based on places with total population of 50,000 or more

Place	Population	%
Columbus (city) Franklin County	1,954	0.25
Cleveland (city) Cuyahoga County	738	0.19
Hamilton (city) Butler County	50	0.08
Youngstown (city) Mahoning County	49	0.07
Canton (city) Stark County	42	0.06
Parma (city) Cuyahoga County	37	0.05
Lorain (city) Lorain County	29	0.05
Lakewood (city) Cuyahoga County	26	0.05
Cincinnati (city) Hamilton County	132	0.04
Akron (city) Summit County	69	0.03

Central American: Other Central American

Top 10 Places Sorted by Population
Based on all places, regardless of total population

Place	Population	%
Columbus (city) Franklin County	54	0.01
Cincinnati (city) Hamilton County	34	0.01
Cleveland (city) Cuyahoga County	21	0.01
Canton (city) Stark County	14	0.02
Beavercreek (city) Greene County	6	0.01
Cheviot (city) Hamilton County	5	0.06
Dublin (city) Franklin County	5	0.01
Mansfield (city) Richland County	5	0.01
Bellefontaine (city) Logan County	4	0.03
Middleburg Heights (city) Cuyahoga County	4	0.03

Top 10 Places Sorted by Percent of Total Population
Based on all places, regardless of total population

Place	Population	%
Cheviot (city) Hamilton County	5	0.06
Oakwood (village) Cuyahoga County	2	0.05
Ottawa Hills (village) Lucas County	2	0.04
Bellefontaine (city) Logan County	4	0.03
Middleburg Heights (city) Cuyahoga County	4	0.03
North Kingsville (village) Ashtabula County	1	0.03
Canton (city) Stark County	14	0.02
Forest Park (city) Hamilton County	4	0.02
Wooster (city) Wayne County	4	0.02
Springdale (city) Hamilton County	2	0.02

Top 10 Places Sorted by Percent of Total Population
Based on places with total population of 50,000 or more

Place	Population	%
Canton (city) Stark County	14	0.02
Columbus (city) Franklin County	54	0.01
Cincinnati (city) Hamilton County	34	0.01
Cleveland (city) Cuyahoga County	21	0.01
Akron (city) Summit County	4	<0.01
Hamilton (city) Butler County	3	<0.01
Dayton (city) Montgomery County	1	<0.01
Elyria (city) Lorain County	1	<0.01
Kettering (city) Montgomery County	0	0.00
Lakewood (city) Cuyahoga County	0	0.00

Cuban

Top 10 Places Sorted by Population
Based on all places, regardless of total population

Place	Population	%
Columbus (city) Franklin County	922	0.12
Cleveland (city) Cuyahoga County	463	0.12
Cincinnati (city) Hamilton County	320	0.11
Toledo (city) Lucas County	299	0.10
Akron (city) Summit County	148	0.07
Dayton (city) Montgomery County	147	0.10
Youngstown (city) Mahoning County	98	0.15
Kettering (city) Montgomery County	84	0.15
Lakewood (city) Cuyahoga County	80	0.15
Lorain (city) Lorain County	79	0.12

Top 10 Places Sorted by Percent of Total Population
Based on all places, regardless of total population

Place	Population	%
Amesville (village) Athens County	4	2.60
Olde West Chester (cdp) Butler County	4	1.67
Millfield (cdp) Athens County	5	1.47
Orangeville (village) Trumbull County	2	1.02
Vanlue (village) Hancock County	3	0.84
Clay Center (village) Ottawa County	2	0.72
Woodmere (village) Cuyahoga County	6	0.68
Amsterdam (village) Jefferson County	3	0.59
Sixteen Mile Stand (cdp) Hamilton County	15	0.51
Marne (cdp) Licking County	4	0.51

Top 10 Places Sorted by Percent of Total Population
Based on places with total population of 50,000 or more

Place	Population	%
Youngstown (city) Mahoning County	98	0.15
Kettering (city) Montgomery County	84	0.15
Lakewood (city) Cuyahoga County	80	0.15
Columbus (city) Franklin County	922	0.12
Cleveland (city) Cuyahoga County	463	0.12
Lorain (city) Lorain County	79	0.12
Cincinnati (city) Hamilton County	320	0.11
Toledo (city) Lucas County	299	0.10
Dayton (city) Montgomery County	147	0.10
Hamilton (city) Butler County	48	0.08

Dominican Republic

Top 10 Places Sorted by Population
Based on all places, regardless of total population

Place	Population	%
Columbus (city) Franklin County	1,553	0.20
Cleveland (city) Cuyahoga County	1,140	0.29
Hamilton (city) Butler County	300	0.48
Youngstown (city) Mahoning County	239	0.36
Fairfield (city) Butler County	233	0.55
Middletown (city) Butler County	182	0.37
Cincinnati (city) Hamilton County	119	0.04
Lorain (city) Lorain County	115	0.18
Reynoldsburg (city) Franklin County	109	0.30
Lakewood (city) Cuyahoga County	82	0.16

Top 10 Places Sorted by Percent of Total Population
Based on all places, regardless of total population

Place	Population	%
Fairfield (city) Butler County	233	0.55
Hamilton (city) Butler County	300	0.48
Lincoln Village (cdp) Franklin County	38	0.42

Middletown (city) Butler County	182	0.37
Youngstown (city) Mahoning County	239	0.36
New Burlington (cdp) Hamilton County	18	0.36
Phillipsburg (village) Montgomery County	2	0.36
Willard (city) Huron County	22	0.35
Meyers Lake (village) Stark County	2	0.35
Lake Lorelei (cdp) Brown County	4	0.34

Top 10 Places Sorted by Percent of Total Population

Based on places with total population of 50,000 or more

Place	Population	%
Hamilton (city) Butler County	300	0.48
Youngstown (city) Mahoning County	239	0.36
Cleveland (city) Cuyahoga County	1,140	0.29
Columbus (city) Franklin County	1,553	0.20
Lorain (city) Lorain County	115	0.18
Lakewood (city) Cuyahoga County	82	0.16
Parma (city) Cuyahoga County	64	0.08
Cincinnati (city) Hamilton County	119	0.04
Dayton (city) Montgomery County	58	0.04
Canton (city) Stark County	27	0.04

Mexican

Top 10 Places Sorted by Population

Based on all places, regardless of total population

Place	Population	%
Columbus (city) Franklin County	25,973	3.30
Toledo (city) Lucas County	17,576	6.12
Painesville (city) Lake County	3,614	18.47
Cleveland (city) Cuyahoga County	3,593	0.91
Cincinnati (city) Hamilton County	3,244	1.09
Lorain (city) Lorain County	2,934	4.58
Hamilton (city) Butler County	2,897	4.64
Dayton (city) Montgomery County	2,541	1.80
Fremont (city) Sandusky County	2,331	13.93
Findlay (city) Hancock County	1,926	4.67

Top 10 Places Sorted by Percent of Total Population

Based on all places, regardless of total population

Place	Population	%
Tedrow (cdp) Fulton County	53	30.64
West Leipsic (village) Putnam County	61	29.61
Belmore (village) Putnam County	42	29.37
Leipsic (village) Putnam County	547	26.13
Brecon (cdp) Hamilton County	63	25.82
Hessville (cdp) Sandusky County	54	25.23
Milton Center (village) Wood County	32	22.22
Hamler (village) Henry County	118	20.49
Painesville (city) Lake County	3,614	18.47
Holgate (village) Henry County	179	16.14

Top 10 Places Sorted by Percent of Total Population

Based on places with total population of 50,000 or more

Place	Population	%
Toledo (city) Lucas County	17,576	6.12
Hamilton (city) Butler County	2,897	4.64
Lorain (city) Lorain County	2,934	4.58
Columbus (city) Franklin County	25,973	3.30
Springfield (city) Clark County	1,342	2.21
Youngstown (city) Mahoning County	1,270	1.90
Dayton (city) Montgomery County	2,541	1.80
Cincinnati (city) Hamilton County	3,244	1.09
Elyria (city) Lorain County	578	1.06
Kettering (city) Montgomery County	542	0.97

Puerto Rican

Top 10 Places Sorted by Population

Based on all places, regardless of total population

Place	Population	%
Cleveland (city) Cuyahoga County	29,286	7.38
Lorain (city) Lorain County	12,413	19.37
Columbus (city) Franklin County	5,034	0.64
Youngstown (city) Mahoning County	3,836	5.73
Elyria (city) Lorain County	1,719	3.15
Parma (city) Cuyahoga County	1,665	2.04
Ashtabula (city) Ashtabula County	1,156	6.04
Toledo (city) Lucas County	1,143	0.40
Akron (city) Summit County	1,091	0.55
Campbell (city) Mahoning County	1,090	13.24

Top 10 Places Sorted by Percent of Total Population

Based on all places, regardless of total population

Place	Population	%
Lorain (city) Lorain County	12,413	19.37
Linndale (village) Cuyahoga County	29	16.20
Campbell (city) Mahoning County	1,090	13.24
Brooklyn (city) Cuyahoga County	896	8.02
Cleveland (city) Cuyahoga County	29,286	7.38
Ashtabula (city) Ashtabula County	1,156	6.04
Youngstown (city) Mahoning County	3,836	5.73
Summitville (village) Columbiana County	6	4.44
Geneva (city) Ashtabula County	246	3.96
Beulah Beach (cdp) Erie County	2	3.77

Top 10 Places Sorted by Percent of Total Population

Based on places with total population of 50,000 or more

Place	Population	%
Lorain (city) Lorain County	12,413	19.37
Cleveland (city) Cuyahoga County	29,286	7.38
Youngstown (city) Mahoning County	3,836	5.73
Elyria (city) Lorain County	1,719	3.15
Lakewood (city) Cuyahoga County	1,077	2.07
Parma (city) Cuyahoga County	1,665	2.04
Columbus (city) Franklin County	5,034	0.64
Akron (city) Summit County	1,091	0.55
Canton (city) Stark County	356	0.49
Toledo (city) Lucas County	1,143	0.40

South American

Top 10 Places Sorted by Population

Based on all places, regardless of total population

Place	Population	%
Columbus (city) Franklin County	2,730	0.35
Cleveland (city) Cuyahoga County	959	0.24
Cincinnati (city) Hamilton County	668	0.22
Parma (city) Cuyahoga County	252	0.31
Akron (city) Summit County	251	0.13
Fairfield (city) Butler County	250	0.59
Toledo (city) Lucas County	219	0.08
Dayton (city) Montgomery County	217	0.15
Lakewood (city) Cuyahoga County	179	0.34
Mason (city) Warren County	172	0.56

Top 10 Places Sorted by Percent of Total Population

Based on all places, regardless of total population

Place	Population	%
Cloverdale (village) Putnam County	4	2.38
Concorde Hills (cdp) Hamilton County	14	2.11
Pettisville (cdp) Fulton County	10	2.01
Hills and Dales (village) Stark County	3	1.36
Sixteen Mile Stand (cdp) Hamilton County	28	0.96
Moraine (city) Montgomery County	52	0.82
Kenwood (cdp) Hamilton County	53	0.76
Gambier (village) Knox County	18	0.75
West Rushville (village) Fairfield County	1	0.75
Proctorville (village) Lawrence County	4	0.70

Top 10 Places Sorted by Percent of Total Population

Based on places with total population of 50,000 or more

Place	Population	%
Columbus (city) Franklin County	2,730	0.35
Lakewood (city) Cuyahoga County	179	0.34
Parma (city) Cuyahoga County	252	0.31
Cleveland (city) Cuyahoga County	959	0.24
Youngstown (city) Mahoning County	155	0.23
Cincinnati (city) Hamilton County	668	0.22
Kettering (city) Montgomery County	125	0.22
Dayton (city) Montgomery County	217	0.15
Akron (city) Summit County	251	0.13
Hamilton (city) Butler County	60	0.10

South American: Argentinean

Top 10 Places Sorted by Population

Based on all places, regardless of total population

Place	Population	%
Columbus (city) Franklin County	273	0.03
Whitehall (city) Franklin County	100	0.55
Cincinnati (city) Hamilton County	83	0.03
Cleveland (city) Cuyahoga County	70	0.02
Upper Arlington (city) Franklin County	35	0.10
Shaker Heights (city) Cuyahoga County	32	0.11
Lakewood (city) Cuyahoga County	32	0.06
Beavercreek (city) Greene County	24	0.05
Toledo (city) Lucas County	24	0.01
Akron (city) Summit County	23	0.01

Top 10 Places Sorted by Percent of Total Population

Based on all places, regardless of total population

Place	Population	%
Whitehall (city) Franklin County	100	0.55
Spencer (village) Medina County	4	0.53
Port William (village) Clinton County	1	0.39
Gambier (village) Knox County	6	0.25
Stony Ridge (cdp) Wood County	1	0.24
Dry Ridge (cdp) Hamilton County	5	0.18
Rossmoyne (cdp) Hamilton County	4	0.18
Amberley (village) Hamilton County	6	0.17
Morrow (village) Warren County	2	0.17
Fairport Harbor (village) Lake County	5	0.16

Top 10 Places Sorted by Percent of Total Population

Based on places with total population of 50,000 or more

Place	Population	%
Lakewood (city) Cuyahoga County	32	0.06
Columbus (city) Franklin County	273	0.03
Cincinnati (city) Hamilton County	83	0.03
Cleveland (city) Cuyahoga County	70	0.02
Parma (city) Cuyahoga County	19	0.02
Canton (city) Stark County	14	0.02
Toledo (city) Lucas County	24	0.01
Akron (city) Summit County	23	0.01
Dayton (city) Montgomery County	11	0.01
Lorain (city) Lorain County	9	0.01

South American: Bolivian

Top 10 Places Sorted by Population

Based on all places, regardless of total population

Place	Population	%
Columbus (city) Franklin County	81	0.01
Wauseon (city) Fulton County	36	0.49
Dublin (city) Franklin County	14	0.03
Cincinnati (city) Hamilton County	14	<0.01
Beavercreek (city) Greene County	13	0.03
Kettering (city) Montgomery County	13	0.02
Burlington (cdp) Lawrence County	11	0.41
Upper Arlington (city) Franklin County	11	0.03
Dayton (city) Montgomery County	11	0.01
Westerville (city) Franklin County	10	0.03

Top 10 Places Sorted by Percent of Total Population

Based on all places, regardless of total population

Place	Population	%
Pettisville (cdp) Fulton County	9	1.81
Wauseon (city) Fulton County	36	0.49
Burlington (cdp) Lawrence County	11	0.41
Fletcher (village) Miami County	1	0.21
Smithville (village) Wayne County	2	0.16
Elmwood Place (village) Hamilton County	3	0.14
Napoleon (city) Henry County	7	0.08
Grandview Heights (city) Franklin County	5	0.08
Amberley (village) Hamilton County	3	0.08
West Carrollton (city) Montgomery County	9	0.07

Top 10 Places Sorted by Percent of Total Population

Based on places with total population of 50,000 or more

Place	Population	%
Kettering (city) Montgomery County	13	0.02
Columbus (city) Franklin County	81	0.01
Dayton (city) Montgomery County	11	0.01
Lorain (city) Lorain County	4	0.01
Cincinnati (city) Hamilton County	14	<0.01
Akron (city) Summit County	6	<0.01
Toledo (city) Lucas County	4	<0.01
Canton (city) Stark County	3	<0.01
Cleveland (city) Cuyahoga County	3	<0.01
Hamilton (city) Butler County	2	<0.01

South American: Chilean

Top 10 Places Sorted by Population

Based on all places, regardless of total population

Place	Population	%
Columbus (city) Franklin County	112	0.01
Cleveland (city) Cuyahoga County	62	0.02
Cincinnati (city) Hamilton County	50	0.02
North Ridgeville (city) Lorain County	24	0.08
Huber Heights (city) Montgomery County	22	0.06
Akron (city) Summit County	18	0.01
Toledo (city) Lucas County	18	0.01
Athens (city) Athens County	16	0.07
Hudson (city) Summit County	16	0.07
Cleveland Heights (city) Cuyahoga County	16	0.03

Top 10 Places Sorted by Percent of Total Population

Based on all places, regardless of total population

Place	Population	%
Cloverdale (village) Putnam County	4	2.38
Hunting Valley (village) Cuyahoga County	2	0.28
Sixteen Mile Stand (cdp) Hamilton County	8	0.27
Ottawa Hills (village) Lucas County	8	0.18
Timberlake (village) Lake County	1	0.15
Wellston (city) Jackson County	7	0.12
Covedale (cdp) Hamilton County	6	0.09
Green Meadows (cdp) Clark County	2	0.09
West Hill (cdp) Trumbull County	2	0.09
North Ridgeville (city) Lorain County	24	0.08

Top 10 Places Sorted by Percent of Total Population

Based on places with total population of 50,000 or more

Place	Population	%
Cleveland (city) Cuyahoga County	62	0.02
Cincinnati (city) Hamilton County	50	0.02
Lakewood (city) Cuyahoga County	11	0.02
Columbus (city) Franklin County	112	0.01
Akron (city) Summit County	18	0.01
Toledo (city) Lucas County	18	0.01
Dayton (city) Montgomery County	8	0.01
Kettering (city) Montgomery County	5	0.01
Elyria (city) Lorain County	3	0.01
Parma (city) Cuyahoga County	4	<0.01

South American: Colombian

Top 10 Places Sorted by Population

Based on all places, regardless of total population

Place	Population	%
Columbus (city) Franklin County	797	0.10
Cleveland (city) Cuyahoga County	320	0.08
Cincinnati (city) Hamilton County	215	0.07
Youngstown (city) Mahoning County	104	0.16
Akron (city) Summit County	101	0.05
Beavercreek (city) Greene County	53	0.12
Westlake (city) Cuyahoga County	51	0.16
Toledo (city) Lucas County	49	0.02
Dublin (city) Franklin County	47	0.11
Fairfield (city) Butler County	47	0.11

Top 10 Places Sorted by Percent of Total Population

Based on all places, regardless of total population

Place	Population	%
Hills and Dales (village) Stark County	3	1.36
Zoar (village) Tuscarawas County	1	0.59
Celeryville (cdp) Huron County	1	0.48
Milan (village) Erie County	5	0.37
Marble Cliff (village) Franklin County	2	0.35
Thurston (village) Fairfield County	2	0.33
Sixteen Mile Stand (cdp) Hamilton County	9	0.31
Wetherington (cdp) Butler County	4	0.31
Kenwood (cdp) Hamilton County	20	0.29
Beckett Ridge (cdp) Butler County	26	0.28

Top 10 Places Sorted by Percent of Total Population

Based on places with total population of 50,000 or more

Place	Population	%
Youngstown (city) Mahoning County	104	0.16
Columbus (city) Franklin County	797	0.10
Cleveland (city) Cuyahoga County	320	0.08
Kettering (city) Montgomery County	44	0.08
Cincinnati (city) Hamilton County	215	0.07
Lakewood (city) Cuyahoga County	37	0.07
Parma (city) Cuyahoga County	45	0.06
Akron (city) Summit County	101	0.05
Canton (city) Stark County	25	0.03
Hamilton (city) Butler County	18	0.03

South American: Ecuadorian

Top 10 Places Sorted by Population

Based on all places, regardless of total population

Place	Population	%
Columbus (city) Franklin County	491	0.06
Dayton (city) Montgomery County	115	0.08
Cleveland (city) Cuyahoga County	113	0.03
Moraine (city) Montgomery County	48	0.76
Cincinnati (city) Hamilton County	45	0.02
Parma (city) Cuyahoga County	44	0.05
Akron (city) Summit County	39	0.02
Huber Heights (city) Montgomery County	27	0.07
Toledo (city) Lucas County	27	0.01
Fairfield (city) Butler County	25	0.06

Top 10 Places Sorted by Percent of Total Population

Based on all places, regardless of total population

Place	Population	%
Moraine (city) Montgomery County	48	0.76
West Rushville (village) Fairfield County	1	0.75
Killbuck (village) Holmes County	4	0.49
Newtown (village) Hamilton County	7	0.26
South Amherst (village) Lorain County	4	0.24
New Concord (village) Muskingum County	5	0.20
Canal Winchester (village) Franklin County	13	0.18
Craig Beach (village) Mahoning County	2	0.17
Marble Cliff (village) Franklin County	1	0.17
Orange (village) Cuyahoga County	5	0.15

Top 10 Places Sorted by Percent of Total Population

Based on places with total population of 50,000 or more

Place	Population	%
Dayton (city) Montgomery County	115	0.08
Columbus (city) Franklin County	491	0.06
Parma (city) Cuyahoga County	44	0.05
Cleveland (city) Cuyahoga County	113	0.03
Kettering (city) Montgomery County	18	0.03
Cincinnati (city) Hamilton County	45	0.02
Akron (city) Summit County	39	0.02
Lorain (city) Lorain County	12	0.02
Toledo (city) Lucas County	27	0.01
Elyria (city) Lorain County	8	0.01

South American: Paraguayan

Top 10 Places Sorted by Population

Based on all places, regardless of total population

Place	Population	%
Columbus (city) Franklin County	9	<0.01
Fairview Park (city) Cuyahoga County	8	0.05
Cleveland (city) Cuyahoga County	8	<0.01
Strongsville (city) Cuyahoga County	7	0.02
Perrysburg (city) Wood County	6	0.03
Sylvania (city) Lucas County	6	0.03
Cincinnati (city) Hamilton County	6	<0.01
Toledo (city) Lucas County	6	<0.01
Athens (city) Athens County	5	0.02
North Royalton (city) Cuyahoga County	5	0.02

Top 10 Places Sorted by Percent of Total Population

Based on all places, regardless of total population

Place	Population	%
Phillipsburg (village) Montgomery County	1	0.18
Malta (village) Morgan County	1	0.15
Coldstream (cdp) Hamilton County	1	0.09
Fairview Park (city) Cuyahoga County	8	0.05
Edgerton (village) Williams County	1	0.05
Glendale (village) Hamilton County	1	0.05
Fairlawn (city) Summit County	3	0.04
Highland Heights (city) Cuyahoga County	3	0.04
Kirtland (city) Lake County	3	0.04
Oberlin (city) Lorain County	3	0.04

Top 10 Places Sorted by Percent of Total Population

Based on places with total population of 50,000 or more

Place	Population	%
Hamilton (city) Butler County	4	0.01
Kettering (city) Montgomery County	3	0.01
Columbus (city) Franklin County	9	<0.01
Cleveland (city) Cuyahoga County	8	<0.01
Cincinnati (city) Hamilton County	6	<0.01
Toledo (city) Lucas County	6	<0.01
Dayton (city) Montgomery County	1	<0.01
Lakewood (city) Cuyahoga County	1	<0.01
Parma (city) Cuyahoga County	1	<0.01
Springfield (city) Clark County	1	<0.01

South American: Peruvian

Top 10 Places Sorted by Population

Based on all places, regardless of total population

Place	Population	%
Columbus (city) Franklin County	543	0.07
Cleveland (city) Cuyahoga County	276	0.07
Fairfield (city) Butler County	145	0.34
Cincinnati (city) Hamilton County	138	0.05
Parma (city) Cuyahoga County	129	0.16
Toledo (city) Lucas County	51	0.02
Mentor (city) Lake County	33	0.07
Shaker Heights (city) Cuyahoga County	31	0.11
Lakewood (city) Cuyahoga County	31	0.06
Strongsville (city) Cuyahoga County	30	0.07

Top 10 Places Sorted by Percent of Total Population

Based on all places, regardless of total population

Place	Population	%
Proctorville (village) Lawrence County	4	0.70
Austinburg (cdp) Ashtabula County	3	0.58
Fairfield (city) Butler County	145	0.34
Hebron (village) Licking County	7	0.30
Pleasant Run (cdp) Hamilton County	14	0.28
Pleasant Run Farm (cdp) Hamilton County	12	0.26
Campbell (city) Mahoning County	20	0.24
Landen (cdp) Warren County	16	0.24
Bedford Heights (city) Cuyahoga County	25	0.23
Salem Heights (cdp) Hamilton County	9	0.23

Top 10 Places Sorted by Percent of Total Population

Based on places with total population of 50,000 or more

Place	Population	%
Parma (city) Cuyahoga County	129	0.16
Columbus (city) Franklin County	543	0.07
Cleveland (city) Cuyahoga County	276	0.07
Lakewood (city) Cuyahoga County	31	0.06
Cincinnati (city) Hamilton County	138	0.05
Hamilton (city) Butler County	20	0.03
Youngstown (city) Mahoning County	18	0.03
Kettering (city) Montgomery County	15	0.03
Toledo (city) Lucas County	51	0.02
Dayton (city) Montgomery County	25	0.02

South American: Uruguayan

Top 10 Places Sorted by Population

Based on all places, regardless of total population

Place	Population	%
Columbus (city) Franklin County	47	0.01
Cleveland (city) Cuyahoga County	28	0.01
Mayfield Heights (city) Cuyahoga County	15	0.08
Shaker Heights (city) Cuyahoga County	12	0.04
Richmond Heights (city) Cuyahoga County	10	0.09
Lakewood (city) Cuyahoga County	7	0.01
Dayton (city) Montgomery County	7	<0.01
Oxford (city) Butler County	6	0.03
Euclid (city) Cuyahoga County	6	0.01
Akron (city) Summit County	6	<0.01

Top 10 Places Sorted by Percent of Total Population

Based on all places, regardless of total population

Place	Population	%
Terrace Park (village) Hamilton County	3	0.13
Richmond Heights (city) Cuyahoga County	10	0.09
Mayfield Heights (city) Cuyahoga County	15	0.08

Highland Heights (city) Cuyahoga County	4	0.05
Windham (village) Portage County	1	0.05
Shaker Heights (city) Cuyahoga County	12	0.04
Gambier (village) Knox County	1	0.04
Oxford (city) Butler County	6	0.03
Groesbeck (cdp) Hamilton County	2	0.03
New Albany (village) Franklin County	2	0.03

Top 10 Places Sorted by Percent of Total Population
Based on places with total population of 50,000 or more

Place	Population	%
Columbus (city) Franklin County	47	0.01
Cleveland (city) Cuyahoga County	28	0.01
Lakewood (city) Cuyahoga County	7	0.01
Kettering (city) Montgomery County	3	0.01
Dayton (city) Montgomery County	7	<0.01
Akron (city) Summit County	6	<0.01
Canton (city) Stark County	1	<0.01
Cincinnati (city) Hamilton County	1	<0.01
Youngstown (city) Mahoning County	1	<0.01
Elyria (city) Lorain County	0	0.00

South American: Venezuelan

Top 10 Places Sorted by Population
Based on all places, regardless of total population

Place	Population	%
Columbus (city) Franklin County	355	0.05
Cincinnati (city) Hamilton County	107	0.04
Mason (city) Warren County	78	0.25
Cleveland (city) Cuyahoga County	54	0.01
Lakewood (city) Cuyahoga County	52	0.10
Dublin (city) Franklin County	37	0.09
Toledo (city) Lucas County	32	0.01
Akron (city) Summit County	31	0.02
Beachwood (city) Cuyahoga County	22	0.18
Upper Arlington (city) Franklin County	21	0.06

Top 10 Places Sorted by Percent of Total Population
Based on all places, regardless of total population

Place	Population	%
Concorde Hills (cdp) Hamilton County	13	1.96
Miamiville (cdp) Clermont County	1	0.41
The Village of Indian Hill (city) Hamilton County	20	0.35
East Liberty (cdp) Logan County	1	0.27
Mason (city) Warren County	78	0.25
Kenwood (cdp) Hamilton County	16	0.23
Sixteen Mile Stand (cdp) Hamilton County	6	0.20
Pettisville (cdp) Fulton County	1	0.20
Beachwood (city) Cuyahoga County	22	0.18
Nelsonville (city) Athens County	9	0.17

Top 10 Places Sorted by Percent of Total Population
Based on places with total population of 50,000 or more

Place	Population	%
Lakewood (city) Cuyahoga County	52	0.10
Columbus (city) Franklin County	355	0.05
Cincinnati (city) Hamilton County	107	0.04
Kettering (city) Montgomery County	15	0.03
Akron (city) Summit County	31	0.02
Lorain (city) Lorain County	10	0.02
Cleveland (city) Cuyahoga County	54	0.01
Toledo (city) Lucas County	32	0.01
Youngstown (city) Mahoning County	9	0.01
Parma (city) Cuyahoga County	7	0.01

South American: Other South American

Top 10 Places Sorted by Population
Based on all places, regardless of total population

Place	Population	%
Cleveland (city) Cuyahoga County	25	0.01
Columbus (city) Franklin County	22	<0.01
Cincinnati (city) Hamilton County	9	<0.01
Toledo (city) Lucas County	8	<0.01
Ashtabula (city) Ashtabula County	4	0.02
Mentor-on-the-Lake (city) Lake County	3	0.04
Cambridge (city) Guernsey County	3	0.03
Sheffield Lake (city) Lorain County	3	0.03
Lyndhurst (city) Cuyahoga County	3	0.02
Pickerington (city) Fairfield County	3	0.02

Top 10 Places Sorted by Percent of Total Population
Based on all places, regardless of total population

Place	Population	%
East Liberty (cdp) Logan County	1	0.27
Jamestown (village) Greene County	2	0.10
Lincoln Heights (village) Hamilton County	2	0.06
Mentor-on-the-Lake (city) Lake County	3	0.04
Wilberforce (cdp) Greene County	1	0.04
Cambridge (city) Guernsey County	3	0.03
Sheffield Lake (city) Lorain County	3	0.03
Deer Park (city) Hamilton County	2	0.03
Ashtabula (city) Ashtabula County	4	0.02
Lyndhurst (city) Cuyahoga County	3	0.02

Top 10 Places Sorted by Percent of Total Population
Based on places with total population of 50,000 or more

Place	Population	%
Cleveland (city) Cuyahoga County	25	0.01
Columbus (city) Franklin County	22	<0.01
Cincinnati (city) Hamilton County	9	<0.01
Toledo (city) Lucas County	8	<0.01
Akron (city) Summit County	3	<0.01
Parma (city) Cuyahoga County	3	<0.01
Elyria (city) Lorain County	2	<0.01
Kettering (city) Montgomery County	2	<0.01
Lakewood (city) Cuyahoga County	2	<0.01
Youngstown (city) Mahoning County	2	<0.01

Other Hispanic or Latino

Top 10 Places Sorted by Population
Based on all places, regardless of total population

Place	Population	%
Columbus (city) Franklin County	4,130	0.52
Cleveland (city) Cuyahoga County	2,008	0.51
Toledo (city) Lucas County	1,685	0.59
Cincinnati (city) Hamilton County	1,124	0.38
Akron (city) Summit County	590	0.30
Lorain (city) Lorain County	458	0.71
Youngstown (city) Mahoning County	457	0.68
Dayton (city) Montgomery County	433	0.31
Canton (city) Stark County	387	0.53
Lima (city) Allen County	380	0.98

Top 10 Places Sorted by Percent of Total Population
Based on all places, regardless of total population

Place	Population	%
Portage (village) Wood County	17	3.88
Leipsic (village) Putnam County	81	3.87
Ithaca (village) Darke County	5	3.68
Tontogany (village) Wood County	12	3.27
South Vienna (village) Clark County	11	2.86
Gilboa (village) Putnam County	5	2.72
St Johns (cdp) Auglaize County	5	2.70
Holgate (village) Henry County	26	2.34
Buckland (village) Auglaize County	5	2.15
Old Fort (cdp) Seneca County	4	2.15

Top 10 Places Sorted by Percent of Total Population
Based on places with total population of 50,000 or more

Place	Population	%
Lorain (city) Lorain County	458	0.71
Youngstown (city) Mahoning County	457	0.68
Toledo (city) Lucas County	1,685	0.59
Canton (city) Stark County	387	0.53
Columbus (city) Franklin County	4,130	0.52
Cleveland (city) Cuyahoga County	2,008	0.51
Hamilton (city) Butler County	301	0.48
Elyria (city) Lorain County	222	0.41
Cincinnati (city) Hamilton County	1,124	0.38
Springfield (city) Clark County	218	0.36

Racial Group Rankings

African-American/Black

Top 10 Places Sorted by Population
Based on all places, regardless of total population

Place	Population	%
Columbus (city) Franklin County	237,077	30.12
Cleveland (city) Cuyahoga County	219,027	55.20
Cincinnati (city) Hamilton County	138,296	46.57
Toledo (city) Lucas County	85,254	29.68
Akron (city) Summit County	67,240	33.77
Dayton (city) Montgomery County	63,535	44.89
Youngstown (city) Mahoning County	32,093	47.91
Euclid (city) Cuyahoga County	26,672	54.52
Cleveland Heights (city) Cuyahoga County	20,487	44.42
Canton (city) Stark County	20,377	27.91

Top 10 Places Sorted by Percent of Total Population
Based on all places, regardless of total population

Place	Population	%
Lincoln Heights (village) Hamilton County	3,203	97.47
Warrensville Heights (city) Cuyahoga County	12,909	95.33
East Cleveland (city) Cuyahoga County	16,901	94.72
Twinsburg Heights (cdp) Summit County	810	87.57
North Randall (village) Cuyahoga County	898	87.44
Wilberforce (cdp) Greene County	1,950	85.87
Skyline Acres (cdp) Hamilton County	1,435	83.58
Bedford Heights (city) Cuyahoga County	8,458	78.67
Highland Hills (village) Cuyahoga County	858	75.93
Golf Manor (village) Hamilton County	2,698	74.72

Top 10 Places Sorted by Percent of Total Population
Based on places with total population of 50,000 or more

Place	Population	%
Cleveland (city) Cuyahoga County	219,027	55.20
Youngstown (city) Mahoning County	32,093	47.91
Cincinnati (city) Hamilton County	138,296	46.57
Dayton (city) Montgomery County	63,535	44.89
Akron (city) Summit County	67,240	33.77
Columbus (city) Franklin County	237,077	30.12
Toledo (city) Lucas County	85,254	29.68
Canton (city) Stark County	20,377	27.91
Springfield (city) Clark County	12,807	21.13
Lorain (city) Lorain County	13,512	21.08

African-American/Black: Not Hispanic

Top 10 Places Sorted by Population
Based on all places, regardless of total population

Place	Population	%
Columbus (city) Franklin County	233,108	29.62
Cleveland (city) Cuyahoga County	213,920	53.91
Cincinnati (city) Hamilton County	137,223	46.21
Toledo (city) Lucas County	82,886	28.86
Akron (city) Summit County	66,385	33.34
Dayton (city) Montgomery County	62,972	44.49
Youngstown (city) Mahoning County	30,939	46.19
Euclid (city) Cuyahoga County	26,370	53.90
Cleveland Heights (city) Cuyahoga County	20,266	43.94
Canton (city) Stark County	20,069	27.49

Top 10 Places Sorted by Percent of Total Population
Based on all places, regardless of total population

Place	Population	%
Lincoln Heights (village) Hamilton County	3,193	97.17
Warrensville Heights (city) Cuyahoga County	12,764	94.25
East Cleveland (city) Cuyahoga County	16,770	93.99
North Randall (village) Cuyahoga County	897	87.34
Twinsburg Heights (cdp) Summit County	800	86.49
Wilberforce (cdp) Greene County	1,917	84.41
Skyline Acres (cdp) Hamilton County	1,433	83.46
Bedford Heights (city) Cuyahoga County	8,383	77.97
Highland Hills (village) Cuyahoga County	851	75.31
Golf Manor (village) Hamilton County	2,677	74.13

Top 10 Places Sorted by Percent of Total Population
Based on places with total population of 50,000 or more

Place	Population	%
Cleveland (city) Cuyahoga County	213,920	53.91
Cincinnati (city) Hamilton County	137,223	46.21
Youngstown (city) Mahoning County	30,939	46.19
Dayton (city) Montgomery County	62,972	44.49
Akron (city) Summit County	66,385	33.34
Columbus (city) Franklin County	233,108	29.62
Toledo (city) Lucas County	82,886	28.86
Canton (city) Stark County	20,069	27.49
Springfield (city) Clark County	12,597	20.78
Lorain (city) Lorain County	11,803	18.41

African-American/Black: Hispanic

Top 10 Places Sorted by Population
Based on all places, regardless of total population

Place	Population	%
Cleveland (city) Cuyahoga County	5,107	1.29
Columbus (city) Franklin County	3,969	0.50
Toledo (city) Lucas County	2,368	0.82
Lorain (city) Lorain County	1,709	2.67
Youngstown (city) Mahoning County	1,154	1.72
Cincinnati (city) Hamilton County	1,073	0.36
Akron (city) Summit County	855	0.43
Dayton (city) Montgomery County	563	0.40
Elyria (city) Lorain County	476	0.87
Canton (city) Stark County	308	0.42

Top 10 Places Sorted by Percent of Total Population
Based on all places, regardless of total population

Place	Population	%
Lorain (city) Lorain County	1,709	2.67
Campbell (city) Mahoning County	154	1.87
Youngstown (city) Mahoning County	1,154	1.72
Summitville (village) Columbiana County	2	1.48
Wilberforce (cdp) Greene County	33	1.45
Woodmere (village) Cuyahoga County	12	1.36
Oakwood (village) Paulding County	8	1.32
Drexel (cdp) Montgomery County	27	1.30
Cleveland (city) Cuyahoga County	5,107	1.29
Fairview (village) Guernsey County	1	1.20

Top 10 Places Sorted by Percent of Total Population
Based on places with total population of 50,000 or more

Place	Population	%
Lorain (city) Lorain County	1,709	2.67
Youngstown (city) Mahoning County	1,154	1.72
Cleveland (city) Cuyahoga County	5,107	1.29
Elyria (city) Lorain County	476	0.87
Toledo (city) Lucas County	2,368	0.82
Columbus (city) Franklin County	3,969	0.50
Akron (city) Summit County	855	0.43
Canton (city) Stark County	308	0.42
Dayton (city) Montgomery County	563	0.40
Lakewood (city) Cuyahoga County	194	0.37

American Indian/Alaska Native

Top 10 Places Sorted by Population
Based on all places, regardless of total population

Place	Population	%
Columbus (city) Franklin County	8,353	1.06
Cleveland (city) Cuyahoga County	4,008	1.01
Toledo (city) Lucas County	3,359	1.17
Cincinnati (city) Hamilton County	2,658	0.90
Akron (city) Summit County	2,083	1.05
Dayton (city) Montgomery County	1,579	1.12
Canton (city) Stark County	1,243	1.70
Lorain (city) Lorain County	966	1.51
Youngstown (city) Mahoning County	870	1.30
Springfield (city) Clark County	748	1.23

Top 10 Places Sorted by Percent of Total Population
Based on all places, regardless of total population

Place	Population	%
Rendville (village) Perry County	4	11.11
Graysville (village) Monroe County	8	10.53
Chesterhill (village) Morgan County	21	7.27
Otway (village) Scioto County	5	5.75
Latty (village) Paulding County	10	5.18
Jacksonburg (village) Butler County	3	4.76
Rome (village) Adams County	4	4.26
Yorkshire (village) Darke County	4	4.17
Whites Landing (cdp) Erie County	15	4.00
Clifton (village) Greene County	6	3.95

Top 10 Places Sorted by Percent of Total Population
Based on places with total population of 50,000 or more

Place	Population	%
Canton (city) Stark County	1,243	1.70
Lorain (city) Lorain County	966	1.51
Youngstown (city) Mahoning County	870	1.30
Springfield (city) Clark County	748	1.23
Toledo (city) Lucas County	3,359	1.17
Elyria (city) Lorain County	631	1.16
Dayton (city) Montgomery County	1,579	1.12
Columbus (city) Franklin County	8,353	1.06
Akron (city) Summit County	2,083	1.05
Cleveland (city) Cuyahoga County	4,008	1.01

American Indian/Alaska Native: Not Hispanic

Top 10 Places Sorted by Population
Based on all places, regardless of total population

Place	Population	%
Columbus (city) Franklin County	7,286	0.93
Cleveland (city) Cuyahoga County	3,202	0.81
Toledo (city) Lucas County	2,675	0.93
Cincinnati (city) Hamilton County	2,276	0.77
Akron (city) Summit County	1,899	0.95
Dayton (city) Montgomery County	1,460	1.03
Canton (city) Stark County	1,102	1.51
Youngstown (city) Mahoning County	715	1.07
Springfield (city) Clark County	660	1.09
Lorain (city) Lorain County	651	1.02

Top 10 Places Sorted by Percent of Total Population
Based on all places, regardless of total population

Place	Population	%
Rendville (village) Perry County	4	11.11
Graysville (village) Monroe County	8	10.53
Chesterhill (village) Morgan County	21	7.27
Otway (village) Scioto County	5	5.75
Jacksonburg (village) Butler County	3	4.76
Rome (village) Adams County	4	4.26
Yorkshire (village) Darke County	4	4.17
Whites Landing (cdp) Erie County	15	4.00
Clifton (village) Greene County	6	3.95
Potsdam (village) Miami County	11	3.82

Top 10 Places Sorted by Percent of Total Population
Based on places with total population of 50,000 or more

Place	Population	%
Canton (city) Stark County	1,102	1.51
Springfield (city) Clark County	660	1.09
Youngstown (city) Mahoning County	715	1.07
Dayton (city) Montgomery County	1,460	1.03
Lorain (city) Lorain County	651	1.02
Elyria (city) Lorain County	531	0.97
Akron (city) Summit County	1,899	0.95
Columbus (city) Franklin County	7,286	0.93
Toledo (city) Lucas County	2,675	0.93
Lakewood (city) Cuyahoga County	428	0.82

American Indian/Alaska Native: Hispanic

Top 10 Places Sorted by Population

Based on all places, regardless of total population

Place	Population	%
Columbus (city) Franklin County	1,067	0.14
Cleveland (city) Cuyahoga County	806	0.20
Toledo (city) Lucas County	684	0.24
Cincinnati (city) Hamilton County	382	0.13
Lorain (city) Lorain County	315	0.49
Akron (city) Summit County	184	0.09
Youngstown (city) Mahoning County	155	0.23
Canton (city) Stark County	141	0.19
Dayton (city) Montgomery County	119	0.08
Elyria (city) Lorain County	100	0.18

Top 10 Places Sorted by Percent of Total Population

Based on all places, regardless of total population

Place	Population	%
Latty (village) Paulding County	6	3.11
New Bloomington (village) Marion County	11	2.14
Hooven (cdp) Hamilton County	9	1.69
Valley Hi (village) Logan County	3	1.42
Milton Center (village) Wood County	2	1.39
Highland (village) Highland County	3	1.18
Oakwood (village) Paulding County	6	0.99
Wayne (village) Wood County	8	0.90
Jeromesville (village) Ashland County	5	0.89
Rudolph (cdp) Wood County	4	0.87

Top 10 Places Sorted by Percent of Total Population

Based on places with total population of 50,000 or more

Place	Population	%
Lorain (city) Lorain County	315	0.49
Toledo (city) Lucas County	684	0.24
Youngstown (city) Mahoning County	155	0.23
Cleveland (city) Cuyahoga County	806	0.20
Canton (city) Stark County	141	0.19
Elyria (city) Lorain County	100	0.18
Springfield (city) Clark County	88	0.15
Columbus (city) Franklin County	1,067	0.14
Lakewood (city) Cuyahoga County	75	0.14
Cincinnati (city) Hamilton County	382	0.13

Alaska Native: Alaska Athabascan

Top 10 Places Sorted by Population

Based on all places, regardless of total population

Place	Population	%
Columbus (city) Franklin County	11	<0.01
Pleasant Run Farm (cdp) Hamilton County	5	0.11
Hudson (city) Summit County	4	0.02
Minerva (village) Stark County	3	0.08
Jackson (city) Jackson County	3	0.05
Groesbeck (cdp) Hamilton County	3	0.04
Northridge (cdp) Clark County	3	0.04
Circleville (city) Pickaway County	3	0.02
Tallmadge (city) Summit County	3	0.02
Shaker Heights (city) Cuyahoga County	3	0.01

Top 10 Places Sorted by Percent of Total Population

Based on all places, regardless of total population

Place	Population	%
Pleasant Run Farm (cdp) Hamilton County	5	0.11
Minerva (village) Stark County	3	0.08
North Lewisburg (village) Champaign County	1	0.07
Jackson (city) Jackson County	3	0.05
Leipsic (village) Putnam County	1	0.05
Groesbeck (cdp) Hamilton County	3	0.04
Northridge (cdp) Clark County	3	0.04
Richfield (village) Summit County	1	0.03
Hudson (city) Summit County	4	0.02
Circleville (city) Pickaway County	3	0.02

Top 10 Places Sorted by Percent of Total Population

Based on places with total population of 50,000 or more

Place	Population	%
Columbus (city) Franklin County	11	<0.01
Cincinnati (city) Hamilton County	3	<0.01
Parma (city) Cuyahoga County	3	<0.01
Youngstown (city) Mahoning County	3	<0.01
Cleveland (city) Cuyahoga County	2	<0.01
Lakewood (city) Cuyahoga County	2	<0.01
Toledo (city) Lucas County	2	<0.01
Akron (city) Summit County	0	0.00
Canton (city) Stark County	0	0.00
Dayton (city) Montgomery County	0	0.00

Alaska Native: Aleut

Top 10 Places Sorted by Population

Based on all places, regardless of total population

Place	Population	%
Columbus (city) Franklin County	9	<0.01
Cincinnati (city) Hamilton County	8	<0.01
Milford Center (village) Union County	4	0.51
Hamilton (city) Butler County	4	0.01
Dayton (city) Montgomery County	4	<0.01
Minerva (village) Stark County	3	0.08
Wilmington (city) Clinton County	3	0.02
Lockland (village) Hamilton County	2	0.06
Milford (city) Clermont County	2	0.03
Boardman (cdp) Mahoning County	2	0.01

Top 10 Places Sorted by Percent of Total Population

Based on all places, regardless of total population

Place	Population	%
Milford Center (village) Union County	4	0.51
West Manchester (village) Preble County	1	0.21
Minerva (village) Stark County	3	0.08
Fayette (village) Fulton County	1	0.08
Grandview (cdp) Hamilton County	1	0.07
Lockland (village) Hamilton County	2	0.06
Franklin Furnace (cdp) Scioto County	1	0.06
South Bloomfield (village) Pickaway County	1	0.06
Milford (city) Clermont County	2	0.03
Wellsville (village) Columbiana County	1	0.03

Top 10 Places Sorted by Percent of Total Population

Based on places with total population of 50,000 or more

Place	Population	%
Hamilton (city) Butler County	4	0.01
Columbus (city) Franklin County	9	<0.01
Cincinnati (city) Hamilton County	8	<0.01
Dayton (city) Montgomery County	4	<0.01
Toledo (city) Lucas County	2	<0.01
Akron (city) Summit County	1	<0.01
Elyria (city) Lorain County	1	<0.01
Kettering (city) Montgomery County	1	<0.01
Lakewood (city) Cuyahoga County	1	<0.01
Canton (city) Stark County	0	0.00

American Indian: Apache

Top 10 Places Sorted by Population

Based on all places, regardless of total population

Place	Population	%
Columbus (city) Franklin County	109	0.01
Toledo (city) Lucas County	66	0.02
Cincinnati (city) Hamilton County	44	0.01
Cleveland (city) Cuyahoga County	43	0.01
Canton (city) Stark County	20	0.03
Sandusky (city) Erie County	19	0.07
Lancaster (city) Fairfield County	19	0.05
Youngstown (city) Mahoning County	19	0.03
Dayton (city) Montgomery County	18	0.01
Akron (city) Summit County	16	0.01

Top 10 Places Sorted by Percent of Total Population

Based on all places, regardless of total population

Place	Population	%
Whites Landing (cdp) Erie County	5	1.33
Dunkirk (village) Hardin County	8	0.91
College Corner (village) Preble County	3	0.74
Milton Center (village) Wood County	1	0.69
Gilboa (village) Putnam County	1	0.54
Camp Dennison (cdp) Hamilton County	2	0.53
Wren (village) Van Wert County	1	0.52
La Rue (village) Marion County	3	0.40
Glenmont (village) Holmes County	1	0.37
Russells Point (village) Logan County	5	0.36

Top 10 Places Sorted by Percent of Total Population

Based on places with total population of 50,000 or more

Place	Population	%
Canton (city) Stark County	20	0.03
Youngstown (city) Mahoning County	19	0.03
Toledo (city) Lucas County	66	0.02
Lorain (city) Lorain County	13	0.02
Parma (city) Cuyahoga County	13	0.02
Columbus (city) Franklin County	109	0.01
Cincinnati (city) Hamilton County	44	0.01
Cleveland (city) Cuyahoga County	43	0.01
Dayton (city) Montgomery County	18	0.01
Akron (city) Summit County	16	0.01

American Indian: Arapaho

Top 10 Places Sorted by Population

Based on all places, regardless of total population

Place	Population	%
Dayton (city) Montgomery County	10	0.01
Cleveland (city) Cuyahoga County	7	<0.01
Toledo (city) Lucas County	6	<0.01
Youngstown (city) Mahoning County	4	0.01
Cincinnati (city) Hamilton County	4	<0.01
Uhrichsville (city) Tuscarawas County	3	0.06
Montgomery (city) Hamilton County	3	0.03
Upper Arlington (city) Franklin County	3	0.01
Zanesville (city) Muskingum County	3	0.01
Akron (city) Summit County	3	<0.01

Top 10 Places Sorted by Percent of Total Population

Based on all places, regardless of total population

Place	Population	%
Otway (village) Scioto County	1	1.15
Uhrichsville (city) Tuscarawas County	3	0.06
Manchester (village) Adams County	1	0.05
Montgomery (city) Hamilton County	3	0.03
Mulberry (cdp) Clermont County	1	0.03
North Baltimore (village) Wood County	1	0.03
Reminderville (village) Summit County	1	0.03
London (city) Madison County	2	0.02
Dayton (city) Montgomery County	10	0.01
Youngstown (city) Mahoning County	4	0.01

Top 10 Places Sorted by Percent of Total Population

Based on places with total population of 50,000 or more

Place	Population	%
Dayton (city) Montgomery County	10	0.01
Youngstown (city) Mahoning County	4	0.01
Cleveland (city) Cuyahoga County	7	<0.01
Toledo (city) Lucas County	6	<0.01
Cincinnati (city) Hamilton County	4	<0.01
Akron (city) Summit County	3	<0.01
Columbus (city) Franklin County	3	<0.01
Lorain (city) Lorain County	2	<0.01
Elyria (city) Lorain County	1	<0.01
Hamilton (city) Butler County	1	<0.01

American Indian: Blackfeet

Top 10 Places Sorted by Population

Based on all places, regardless of total population

Place	Population	%
Columbus (city) Franklin County	539	0.07
Cleveland (city) Cuyahoga County	240	0.06
Cincinnati (city) Hamilton County	160	0.05
Toledo (city) Lucas County	158	0.06
Akron (city) Summit County	115	0.06
Canton (city) Stark County	100	0.14
Dayton (city) Montgomery County	100	0.07
Youngstown (city) Mahoning County	60	0.09
Lorain (city) Lorain County	54	0.08
Springfield (city) Clark County	47	0.08

Top 10 Places Sorted by Percent of Total Population

Based on all places, regardless of total population

Place	Population	%
Hollansburg (village) Darke County	3	1.32
Millfield (cdp) Athens County	4	1.17
Harveysburg (village) Warren County	6	1.10

Camp Dennison (cdp) Hamilton County	4	1.07
Trinway (cdp) Muskingum County	3	0.82
Stewart (cdp) Athens County	2	0.81
Magnetic Springs (village) Union County	2	0.75
Pleasant City (village) Guernsey County	3	0.67
Cloverdale (village) Putnam County	1	0.60
Maple Ridge (cdp) Mahoning County	4	0.53

Top 10 Places Sorted by Percent of Total Population
Based on places with total population of 50,000 or more

Place	Population	%
Canton (city) Stark County	100	0.14
Youngstown (city) Mahoning County	60	0.09
Lorain (city) Lorain County	54	0.08
Springfield (city) Clark County	47	0.08
Elyria (city) Lorain County	44	0.08
Columbus (city) Franklin County	539	0.07
Dayton (city) Montgomery County	100	0.07
Cleveland (city) Cuyahoga County	240	0.06
Toledo (city) Lucas County	158	0.06
Akron (city) Summit County	115	0.06

American Indian: Canadian/French American Indian

Top 10 Places Sorted by Population
Based on all places, regardless of total population

Place	Population	%
Toledo (city) Lucas County	23	0.01
Columbus (city) Franklin County	21	<0.01
Akron (city) Summit County	18	0.01
Cleveland (city) Cuyahoga County	7	<0.01
Salem (city) Columbiana County	6	0.05
Cincinnati (city) Hamilton County	6	<0.01
Amherst (city) Lorain County	5	0.04
Canton (city) Stark County	5	0.01
Euclid (city) Cuyahoga County	5	0.01
Findlay (city) Hancock County	5	0.01

Top 10 Places Sorted by Percent of Total Population
Based on all places, regardless of total population

Place	Population	%
Rushville (village) Fairfield County	4	1.32
McGuffey (village) Hardin County	2	0.40
Sherwood (cdp) Hamilton County	4	0.11
Shawnee Hills (cdp) Greene County	2	0.09
Fairport Harbor (village) Lake County	2	0.06
Salem (city) Columbiana County	6	0.05
Northfield (village) Summit County	2	0.05
LaGrange (village) Lorain County	1	0.05
Leipsic (village) Putnam County	1	0.05
Amherst (city) Lorain County	5	0.04

Top 10 Places Sorted by Percent of Total Population
Based on places with total population of 50,000 or more

Place	Population	%
Toledo (city) Lucas County	23	0.01
Akron (city) Summit County	18	0.01
Canton (city) Stark County	5	0.01
Columbus (city) Franklin County	21	<0.01
Cleveland (city) Cuyahoga County	7	<0.01
Cincinnati (city) Hamilton County	6	<0.01
Springfield (city) Clark County	3	<0.01
Kettering (city) Montgomery County	2	<0.01
Dayton (city) Montgomery County	1	<0.01
Lakewood (city) Cuyahoga County	1	<0.01

American Indian: Central American Indian

Top 10 Places Sorted by Population
Based on all places, regardless of total population

Place	Population	%
Cincinnati (city) Hamilton County	98	0.03
Canton (city) Stark County	45	0.06
New Philadelphia (city) Tuscarawas County	35	0.20
Dover (city) Tuscarawas County	33	0.26
Cleveland (city) Cuyahoga County	32	0.01
Massillon (city) Stark County	27	0.08
Columbus (city) Franklin County	18	<0.01
Springdale (city) Hamilton County	14	0.12
Northbrook (cdp) Hamilton County	10	0.09
Lorain (city) Lorain County	9	0.01

Top 10 Places Sorted by Percent of Total Population
Based on all places, regardless of total population

Place	Population	%
Dover (city) Tuscarawas County	33	0.26
New Philadelphia (city) Tuscarawas County	35	0.20
Cleves (village) Hamilton County	5	0.15
Crestline (city) Crawford County	6	0.13
Springdale (city) Hamilton County	14	0.12
Northbrook (cdp) Hamilton County	10	0.09
Massillon (city) Stark County	27	0.08
Canton (city) Stark County	45	0.06
Norwood (city) Hamilton County	8	0.04
Sharonville (city) Hamilton County	6	0.04

Top 10 Places Sorted by Percent of Total Population
Based on places with total population of 50,000 or more

Place	Population	%
Canton (city) Stark County	45	0.06
Cincinnati (city) Hamilton County	98	0.03
Cleveland (city) Cuyahoga County	32	0.01
Lorain (city) Lorain County	9	0.01
Lakewood (city) Cuyahoga County	3	0.01
Columbus (city) Franklin County	18	<0.01
Parma (city) Cuyahoga County	3	<0.01
Dayton (city) Montgomery County	1	<0.01
Hamilton (city) Butler County	1	<0.01
Springfield (city) Clark County	1	<0.01

American Indian: Cherokee

Top 10 Places Sorted by Population
Based on all places, regardless of total population

Place	Population	%
Columbus (city) Franklin County	2,100	0.27
Cleveland (city) Cuyahoga County	865	0.22
Toledo (city) Lucas County	784	0.27
Cincinnati (city) Hamilton County	652	0.22
Akron (city) Summit County	534	0.27
Dayton (city) Montgomery County	435	0.31
Canton (city) Stark County	327	0.45
Youngstown (city) Mahoning County	234	0.35
Springfield (city) Clark County	230	0.38
Lorain (city) Lorain County	227	0.35

Top 10 Places Sorted by Percent of Total Population
Based on all places, regardless of total population

Place	Population	%
Jacksonburg (village) Butler County	3	4.76
Rendville (village) Perry County	1	2.78
Graysville (village) Monroe County	2	2.63
West Millgrove (village) Wood County	4	2.30
Summitville (village) Columbiana County	3	2.22
Rome (village) Adams County	2	2.13
Richmond Dale (cdp) Ross County	8	2.12
Beaver (village) Pike County	9	2.00
North Robinson (village) Crawford County	4	1.95
Malinta (village) Henry County	5	1.89

Top 10 Places Sorted by Percent of Total Population
Based on places with total population of 50,000 or more

Place	Population	%
Canton (city) Stark County	327	0.45
Springfield (city) Clark County	230	0.38
Elyria (city) Lorain County	197	0.36
Youngstown (city) Mahoning County	234	0.35
Lorain (city) Lorain County	227	0.35
Dayton (city) Montgomery County	435	0.31
Hamilton (city) Butler County	172	0.28
Columbus (city) Franklin County	2,100	0.27
Toledo (city) Lucas County	784	0.27
Akron (city) Summit County	534	0.27

American Indian: Cheyenne

Top 10 Places Sorted by Population
Based on all places, regardless of total population

Place	Population	%
Columbus (city) Franklin County	15	<0.01
Akron (city) Summit County	14	0.01
Franklin (city) Warren County	7	0.06
Cleveland (city) Cuyahoga County	7	<0.01
Zanesville (city) Muskingum County	6	0.02
Warren (city) Trumbull County	6	0.01
Toledo (city) Lucas County	6	<0.01
Tuppers Plains (cdp) Meigs County	5	1.08
Canton (city) Stark County	5	0.01
Parma (city) Cuyahoga County	5	0.01

Top 10 Places Sorted by Percent of Total Population
Based on all places, regardless of total population

Place	Population	%
Tuppers Plains (cdp) Meigs County	5	1.08
South Vienna (village) Clark County	2	0.52
Rocky Ridge (village) Ottawa County	1	0.24
Coolville (village) Athens County	1	0.20
Brookside (village) Belmont County	1	0.16
Smithfield (village) Jefferson County	1	0.12
Franklin (city) Warren County	7	0.06
Logan (city) Hocking County	4	0.06
Holland (village) Lucas County	1	0.06
Pleasant Grove (cdp) Muskingum County	1	0.06

Top 10 Places Sorted by Percent of Total Population
Based on places with total population of 50,000 or more

Place	Population	%
Akron (city) Summit County	14	0.01
Canton (city) Stark County	5	0.01
Parma (city) Cuyahoga County	5	0.01
Elyria (city) Lorain County	4	0.01
Springfield (city) Clark County	4	0.01
Columbus (city) Franklin County	15	<0.01
Cleveland (city) Cuyahoga County	7	<0.01
Toledo (city) Lucas County	6	<0.01
Dayton (city) Montgomery County	4	<0.01
Hamilton (city) Butler County	2	<0.01

American Indian: Chickasaw

Top 10 Places Sorted by Population
Based on all places, regardless of total population

Place	Population	%
Cleveland (city) Cuyahoga County	34	0.01
Columbus (city) Franklin County	23	<0.01
Cincinnati (city) Hamilton County	11	<0.01
Akron (city) Summit County	9	<0.01
Napoleon (city) Henry County	8	0.09
Toledo (city) Lucas County	7	<0.01
Lakewood (city) Cuyahoga County	6	0.01
Nevada (village) Wyandot County	5	0.66
Fairborn (city) Greene County	5	0.02
Lorain (city) Lorain County	5	0.01

Top 10 Places Sorted by Percent of Total Population
Based on all places, regardless of total population

Place	Population	%
Nevada (village) Wyandot County	5	0.66
Latty (village) Paulding County	1	0.52
Holiday Lakes (cdp) Huron County	1	0.13
Napoleon (city) Henry County	8	0.09
Crestline (city) Crawford County	4	0.09
Tuscarawas (village) Tuscarawas County	1	0.09
Crystal Lakes (cdp) Clark County	1	0.07
McArthur (village) Vinton County	1	0.06
Elmwood Place (village) Hamilton County	1	0.05
Oberlin (city) Lorain County	3	0.04

Top 10 Places Sorted by Percent of Total Population
Based on places with total population of 50,000 or more

Place	Population	%
Cleveland (city) Cuyahoga County	34	0.01
Lakewood (city) Cuyahoga County	6	0.01
Lorain (city) Lorain County	5	0.01
Elyria (city) Lorain County	3	0.01
Columbus (city) Franklin County	23	<0.01
Cincinnati (city) Hamilton County	11	<0.01
Akron (city) Summit County	9	<0.01
Toledo (city) Lucas County	7	<0.01
Canton (city) Stark County	2	<0.01
Dayton (city) Montgomery County	1	<0.01

American Indian: Chippewa

Top 10 Places Sorted by Population
Based on all places, regardless of total population

Place	Population	%
Toledo (city) Lucas County	139	0.05
Columbus (city) Franklin County	112	0.01
Cleveland (city) Cuyahoga County	54	0.01
Cincinnati (city) Hamilton County	29	0.01
Dayton (city) Montgomery County	23	0.02
Akron (city) Summit County	20	0.01
Lima (city) Allen County	12	0.03
Cuyahoga Falls (city) Summit County	12	0.02
Oregon (city) Lucas County	11	0.05
Elyria (city) Lorain County	11	0.02

Top 10 Places Sorted by Percent of Total Population
Based on all places, regardless of total population

Place	Population	%
Port William (village) Clinton County	3	1.18
Castine (village) Darke County	1	0.77
Cherry Fork (village) Adams County	1	0.65
Plumwood (cdp) Madison County	2	0.63
Lake Tomahawk (cdp) Columbiana County	2	0.41
Orwell (village) Ashtabula County	4	0.24
Skyline Acres (cdp) Hamilton County	4	0.23
Portage (village) Wood County	1	0.23
Mount Pleasant (village) Jefferson County	1	0.21
Spring Valley (village) Greene County	1	0.21

Top 10 Places Sorted by Percent of Total Population
Based on places with total population of 50,000 or more

Place	Population	%
Toledo (city) Lucas County	139	0.05
Dayton (city) Montgomery County	23	0.02
Elyria (city) Lorain County	11	0.02
Lakewood (city) Cuyahoga County	11	0.02
Lorain (city) Lorain County	11	0.02
Columbus (city) Franklin County	112	0.01
Cleveland (city) Cuyahoga County	54	0.01
Cincinnati (city) Hamilton County	29	0.01
Akron (city) Summit County	20	0.01
Kettering (city) Montgomery County	8	0.01

American Indian: Choctaw

Top 10 Places Sorted by Population
Based on all places, regardless of total population

Place	Population	%
Cleveland (city) Cuyahoga County	83	0.02
Columbus (city) Franklin County	72	0.01
Toledo (city) Lucas County	59	0.02
Akron (city) Summit County	42	0.02
Cincinnati (city) Hamilton County	26	0.01
Parma (city) Cuyahoga County	15	0.02
Youngstown (city) Mahoning County	14	0.02
Gahanna (city) Franklin County	13	0.04
Warren (city) Trumbull County	13	0.03
Shaker Heights (city) Cuyahoga County	11	0.04

Top 10 Places Sorted by Percent of Total Population
Based on all places, regardless of total population

Place	Population	%
South Amherst (village) Lorain County	9	0.53
Brady Lake (village) Portage County	2	0.43
Christiansburg (village) Champaign County	2	0.38
Commercial Point (village) Pickaway County	5	0.32
Gibsonburg (village) Sandusky County	7	0.27
Bloomville (village) Seneca County	2	0.21
North Randall (village) Cuyahoga County	2	0.19
Cairo (village) Allen County	1	0.19
Dry Ridge (cdp) Hamilton County	5	0.18
Harveysburg (village) Warren County	1	0.18

Top 10 Places Sorted by Percent of Total Population
Based on places with total population of 50,000 or more

Place	Population	%
Cleveland (city) Cuyahoga County	83	0.02
Toledo (city) Lucas County	59	0.02
Akron (city) Summit County	42	0.02
Parma (city) Cuyahoga County	15	0.02
Youngstown (city) Mahoning County	14	0.02
Lakewood (city) Cuyahoga County	9	0.02
Columbus (city) Franklin County	72	0.01
Cincinnati (city) Hamilton County	26	0.01
Dayton (city) Montgomery County	9	0.01
Springfield (city) Clark County	9	0.01

American Indian: Colville

Top 10 Places Sorted by Population
Based on all places, regardless of total population

Place	Population	%
Dent (cdp) Hamilton County	3	0.03
Cleveland (city) Cuyahoga County	3	<0.01
Hudson (city) Summit County	2	0.01
Silver Lake (village) Summit County	1	0.04
Jackson (city) Jackson County	1	0.02
Columbus (city) Franklin County	1	<0.01
Aberdeen (village) Brown County	0	0.00
Ada (village) Hardin County	0	0.00
Adamsville (village) Muskingum County	0	0.00
Addyston (village) Hamilton County	0	0.00

Top 10 Places Sorted by Percent of Total Population
Based on all places, regardless of total population

Place	Population	%
Silver Lake (village) Summit County	1	0.04
Dent (cdp) Hamilton County	3	0.03
Jackson (city) Jackson County	1	0.02
Hudson (city) Summit County	2	0.01
Cleveland (city) Cuyahoga County	3	<0.01
Columbus (city) Franklin County	1	<0.01
Aberdeen (village) Brown County	0	0.00
Ada (village) Hardin County	0	0.00
Adamsville (village) Muskingum County	0	0.00
Addyston (village) Hamilton County	0	0.00

Top 10 Places Sorted by Percent of Total Population
Based on places with total population of 50,000 or more

Place	Population	%
Cleveland (city) Cuyahoga County	3	<0.01
Columbus (city) Franklin County	1	<0.01
Akron (city) Summit County	0	0.00
Canton (city) Stark County	0	0.00
Cincinnati (city) Hamilton County	0	0.00
Dayton (city) Montgomery County	0	0.00
Elyria (city) Lorain County	0	0.00
Hamilton (city) Butler County	0	0.00
Kettering (city) Montgomery County	0	0.00
Lakewood (city) Cuyahoga County	0	0.00

American Indian: Comanche

Top 10 Places Sorted by Population
Based on all places, regardless of total population

Place	Population	%
Columbus (city) Franklin County	17	<0.01
Wadsworth (city) Medina County	8	0.04
Grove City (city) Franklin County	8	0.02
Cincinnati (city) Hamilton County	7	<0.01
Steubenville (city) Jefferson County	6	0.03
Springfield (city) Clark County	6	0.01
Warren (city) Trumbull County	6	0.01
Youngstown (city) Mahoning County	6	0.01
Canton (city) Stark County	5	0.01
Akron (city) Summit County	5	<0.01

Top 10 Places Sorted by Percent of Total Population
Based on all places, regardless of total population

Place	Population	%
Seaman (village) Adams County	1	0.11
Bethesda (village) Belmont County	1	0.08
Mariemont (village) Hamilton County	2	0.06
Lewisburg (village) Preble County	1	0.05
Newburgh Heights (village) Cuyahoga County	1	0.05
Wadsworth (city) Medina County	8	0.04
Celina (city) Mercer County	4	0.04
Heath (city) Licking County	4	0.04
Wellston (city) Jackson County	2	0.04
Gambier (village) Knox County	1	0.04

Top 10 Places Sorted by Percent of Total Population
Based on places with total population of 50,000 or more

Place	Population	%
Springfield (city) Clark County	6	0.01
Youngstown (city) Mahoning County	6	0.01
Canton (city) Stark County	5	0.01
Columbus (city) Franklin County	17	<0.01
Cincinnati (city) Hamilton County	7	<0.01
Akron (city) Summit County	5	<0.01
Cleveland (city) Cuyahoga County	3	<0.01
Parma (city) Cuyahoga County	3	<0.01
Toledo (city) Lucas County	3	<0.01
Dayton (city) Montgomery County	2	<0.01

American Indian: Cree

Top 10 Places Sorted by Population
Based on all places, regardless of total population

Place	Population	%
Columbus (city) Franklin County	17	<0.01
Akron (city) Summit County	8	<0.01
Zanesville (city) Muskingum County	6	0.02
Cincinnati (city) Hamilton County	6	<0.01
Toledo (city) Lucas County	6	<0.01
Newtown (village) Hamilton County	5	0.19
Warren (city) Trumbull County	5	0.01
McDermott (cdp) Scioto County	4	0.92
Bainbridge (cdp) Geauga County	3	0.09
Greenhills (village) Hamilton County	3	0.08

Top 10 Places Sorted by Percent of Total Population
Based on all places, regardless of total population

Place	Population	%
McDermott (cdp) Scioto County	4	0.92
Newtown (village) Hamilton County	5	0.19
Clarksville (village) Clinton County	1	0.18
Bainbridge (cdp) Geauga County	3	0.09
Greenhills (village) Hamilton County	3	0.08
Smithville (village) Wayne County	1	0.08
Hiram (village) Portage County	1	0.07
Peebles (village) Adams County	1	0.06
Union City (village) Darke County	1	0.06
Glenmoor (cdp) Columbiana County	1	0.05

Top 10 Places Sorted by Percent of Total Population
Based on places with total population of 50,000 or more

Place	Population	%
Columbus (city) Franklin County	17	<0.01
Akron (city) Summit County	8	<0.01
Cincinnati (city) Hamilton County	6	<0.01
Toledo (city) Lucas County	6	<0.01
Cleveland (city) Cuyahoga County	3	<0.01
Hamilton (city) Butler County	2	<0.01
Springfield (city) Clark County	2	<0.01
Lakewood (city) Cuyahoga County	1	<0.01
Lorain (city) Lorain County	1	<0.01
Canton (city) Stark County	0	0.00

American Indian: Creek

Top 10 Places Sorted by Population
Based on all places, regardless of total population

Place	Population	%
Columbus (city) Franklin County	47	0.01
Cincinnati (city) Hamilton County	23	0.01
Cleveland (city) Cuyahoga County	23	0.01
Toledo (city) Lucas County	23	0.01
Dayton (city) Montgomery County	17	0.01
Akron (city) Summit County	16	0.01
Lancaster (city) Fairfield County	12	0.03
Kettering (city) Montgomery County	8	0.01
Dennison (village) Tuscarawas County	7	0.26
Sheffield Lake (city) Lorain County	7	0.08

Top 10 Places Sorted by Percent of Total Population
Based on all places, regardless of total population

Place	Population	%
Lake Lorelei (cdp) Brown County	4	0.34
Thurston (village) Fairfield County	2	0.33
Pomeroy (village) Meigs County	5	0.27

Whites Landing (cdp) Erie County	1	0.27
Dennison (village) Tuscarawas County	7	0.26
Rocky Ridge (village) Ottawa County	1	0.24
Lake Waynoka (cdp) Brown County	2	0.17
Fredericktown (village) Knox County	4	0.16
Kinsman Center (cdp) Trumbull County	1	0.16
Buckeye Lake (village) Licking County	3	0.11

Top 10 Places Sorted by Percent of Total Population

Based on places with total population of 50,000 or more

Place	Population	%
Columbus (city) Franklin County	47	0.01
Cincinnati (city) Hamilton County	23	0.01
Cleveland (city) Cuyahoga County	23	0.01
Toledo (city) Lucas County	23	0.01
Dayton (city) Montgomery County	17	0.01
Akron (city) Summit County	16	0.01
Kettering (city) Montgomery County	8	0.01
Lakewood (city) Cuyahoga County	7	0.01
Springfield (city) Clark County	7	0.01
Hamilton (city) Butler County	6	0.01

American Indian: Crow

Top 10 Places Sorted by Population

Based on all places, regardless of total population

Place	Population	%
Columbus (city) Franklin County	12	<0.01
Cleveland (city) Cuyahoga County	10	<0.01
Alliance (city) Stark County	7	0.03
Akron (city) Summit County	6	<0.01
Centerville (city) Montgomery County	5	0.02
Cincinnati (city) Hamilton County	5	<0.01
Toledo (city) Lucas County	5	<0.01
Loveland (city) Hamilton County	4	0.03
Latty (village) Paulding County	3	1.55
Oakwood (city) Montgomery County	3	0.03

Top 10 Places Sorted by Percent of Total Population

Based on all places, regardless of total population

Place	Population	%
Latty (village) Paulding County	3	1.55
Collins (cdp) Huron County	1	0.16
Shawnee (village) Perry County	1	0.15
Woodsfield (village) Monroe County	2	0.08
Jackson Center (village) Shelby County	1	0.07
Gallipolis (village) Gallia County	2	0.05
Glenmoor (cdp) Columbiana County	1	0.05
Lucasville (cdp) Scioto County	1	0.04
Alliance (city) Stark County	7	0.03
Loveland (city) Hamilton County	4	0.03

Top 10 Places Sorted by Percent of Total Population

Based on places with total population of 50,000 or more

Place	Population	%
Columbus (city) Franklin County	12	<0.01
Cleveland (city) Cuyahoga County	10	<0.01
Akron (city) Summit County	6	<0.01
Cincinnati (city) Hamilton County	5	<0.01
Toledo (city) Lucas County	5	<0.01
Canton (city) Stark County	3	<0.01
Springfield (city) Clark County	2	<0.01
Youngstown (city) Mahoning County	2	<0.01
Kettering (city) Montgomery County	1	<0.01
Parma (city) Cuyahoga County	1	<0.01

American Indian: Delaware

Top 10 Places Sorted by Population

Based on all places, regardless of total population

Place	Population	%
Canton (city) Stark County	57	0.08
Columbus (city) Franklin County	40	0.01
Akron (city) Summit County	17	0.01
Zanesville (city) Muskingum County	12	0.05
Toledo (city) Lucas County	11	<0.01
Cleveland (city) Cuyahoga County	10	<0.01
New Philadelphia (city) Tuscarawas County	8	0.05
Massillon (city) Stark County	7	0.02
Newark (city) Licking County	7	0.01
Ashtabula (city) Ashtabula County	6	0.03

Top 10 Places Sorted by Percent of Total Population

Based on all places, regardless of total population

Place	Population	%
Bailey Lakes (village) Ashland County	4	1.08
Robertsville (cdp) Stark County	3	0.91
Dexter City (village) Noble County	1	0.78
Kimbolton (cdp) Guernsey County	1	0.69
Sherrodsville (village) Carroll County	2	0.66
Belle Valley (village) Noble County	1	0.45
Eaton Estates (cdp) Lorain County	5	0.41
Urbancrest (village) Franklin County	3	0.31
New Concord (village) Muskingum County	4	0.16
Rocky Fork Point (cdp) Highland County	1	0.16

Top 10 Places Sorted by Percent of Total Population

Based on places with total population of 50,000 or more

Place	Population	%
Canton (city) Stark County	57	0.08
Columbus (city) Franklin County	40	0.01
Akron (city) Summit County	17	0.01
Springfield (city) Clark County	6	0.01
Lakewood (city) Cuyahoga County	4	0.01
Toledo (city) Lucas County	11	<0.01
Cleveland (city) Cuyahoga County	10	<0.01
Cincinnati (city) Hamilton County	5	<0.01
Lorain (city) Lorain County	2	<0.01
Dayton (city) Montgomery County	1	<0.01

American Indian: Hopi

Top 10 Places Sorted by Population

Based on all places, regardless of total population

Place	Population	%
Columbus (city) Franklin County	9	<0.01
LaGrange (village) Lorain County	6	0.29
Latty (village) Paulding County	5	2.59
Jackson (city) Jackson County	5	0.08
Springfield (city) Clark County	5	0.01
Canton (city) Stark County	4	0.01
Cleveland (city) Cuyahoga County	4	<0.01
Toledo (city) Lucas County	4	<0.01
Columbus Grove (village) Putnam County	3	0.14
McDonald (village) Trumbull County	3	0.09

Top 10 Places Sorted by Percent of Total Population

Based on all places, regardless of total population

Place	Population	%
Latty (village) Paulding County	5	2.59
LaGrange (village) Lorain County	6	0.29
Columbus Grove (village) Putnam County	3	0.14
West Salem (village) Wayne County	2	0.14
McDonald (village) Trumbull County	3	0.09
Jackson (city) Jackson County	5	0.08
Eaton Estates (cdp) Lorain County	1	0.08
Yellow Springs (village) Greene County	2	0.06
Leavittsburg (cdp) Trumbull County	1	0.05
Leipsic (village) Putnam County	1	0.05

Top 10 Places Sorted by Percent of Total Population

Based on places with total population of 50,000 or more

Place	Population	%
Springfield (city) Clark County	5	0.01
Canton (city) Stark County	4	0.01
Columbus (city) Franklin County	9	<0.01
Cleveland (city) Cuyahoga County	4	<0.01
Toledo (city) Lucas County	4	<0.01
Youngstown (city) Mahoning County	2	<0.01
Dayton (city) Montgomery County	1	<0.01
Lorain (city) Lorain County	1	<0.01
Akron (city) Summit County	0	0.00
Cincinnati (city) Hamilton County	0	0.00

American Indian: Houma

Top 10 Places Sorted by Population

Based on all places, regardless of total population

Place	Population	%
Groveport (village) Franklin County	4	0.07
Vermilion (city) Lorain County	3	0.03
Reynoldsburg (city) Franklin County	3	0.01
Wooster (city) Wayne County	3	0.01
Bowling Green (city) Wood County	2	0.01
Risingsun (village) Wood County	1	0.17
Oberlin (city) Lorain County	1	0.01
Canton (city) Stark County	1	<0.01
Middletown (city) Butler County	1	<0.01
Aberdeen (village) Brown County	0	0.00

Top 10 Places Sorted by Percent of Total Population

Based on all places, regardless of total population

Place	Population	%
Risingsun (village) Wood County	1	0.17
Groveport (village) Franklin County	4	0.07
Vermilion (city) Lorain County	3	0.03
Reynoldsburg (city) Franklin County	3	0.01
Wooster (city) Wayne County	3	0.01
Bowling Green (city) Wood County	2	0.01
Oberlin (city) Lorain County	1	0.01
Canton (city) Stark County	1	<0.01
Middletown (city) Butler County	1	<0.01
Aberdeen (village) Brown County	0	0.00

Top 10 Places Sorted by Percent of Total Population

Based on places with total population of 50,000 or more

Place	Population	%
Canton (city) Stark County	1	<0.01
Akron (city) Summit County	0	0.00
Cincinnati (city) Hamilton County	0	0.00
Cleveland (city) Cuyahoga County	0	0.00
Columbus (city) Franklin County	0	0.00
Dayton (city) Montgomery County	0	0.00
Elyria (city) Lorain County	0	0.00
Hamilton (city) Butler County	0	0.00
Kettering (city) Montgomery County	0	0.00
Lakewood (city) Cuyahoga County	0	0.00

Alaska Native: Inupiat (Eskimo)

Top 10 Places Sorted by Population

Based on all places, regardless of total population

Place	Population	%
Willowick (city) Lake County	7	0.05
Fremont (city) Sandusky County	6	0.04
Cleveland (city) Cuyahoga County	6	<0.01
New Carlisle (city) Clark County	4	0.07
Sylvania (city) Lucas County	4	0.02
Akron (city) Summit County	4	<0.01
North Canton (city) Stark County	3	0.02
Perrysburg (city) Wood County	3	0.01
Columbus (city) Franklin County	3	<0.01
Toledo (city) Lucas County	3	<0.01

Top 10 Places Sorted by Percent of Total Population

Based on all places, regardless of total population

Place	Population	%
East Fultonham (cdp) Muskingum County	1	0.30
Williamsdale (cdp) Butler County	1	0.17
Monroeville (village) Huron County	2	0.14
New Carlisle (city) Clark County	4	0.07
Lodi (village) Medina County	2	0.07
Willowick (city) Lake County	7	0.05
Brewster (village) Stark County	1	0.05
Fremont (city) Sandusky County	6	0.04
Beechwood Trails (cdp) Licking County	1	0.03
Sylvania (city) Lucas County	4	0.02

Top 10 Places Sorted by Percent of Total Population

Based on places with total population of 50,000 or more

Place	Population	%
Cleveland (city) Cuyahoga County	6	<0.01
Akron (city) Summit County	4	<0.01
Columbus (city) Franklin County	3	<0.01
Toledo (city) Lucas County	3	<0.01
Canton (city) Stark County	2	<0.01
Parma (city) Cuyahoga County	2	<0.01
Youngstown (city) Mahoning County	2	<0.01
Cincinnati (city) Hamilton County	1	<0.01
Elyria (city) Lorain County	1	<0.01
Kettering (city) Montgomery County	1	<0.01

American Indian: Iroquois

Top 10 Places Sorted by Population
Based on all places, regardless of total population

Place	Population	%
Columbus (city) Franklin County	126	0.02
Cleveland (city) Cuyahoga County	62	0.02
Akron (city) Summit County	41	0.02
Toledo (city) Lucas County	39	0.01
Canton (city) Stark County	31	0.04
Dayton (city) Montgomery County	19	0.01
Cincinnati (city) Hamilton County	18	0.01
Elyria (city) Lorain County	17	0.03
Cleveland Heights (city) Cuyahoga County	15	0.03
Lorain (city) Lorain County	14	0.02

Top 10 Places Sorted by Percent of Total Population
Based on all places, regardless of total population

Place	Population	%
Stafford (village) Monroe County	1	1.23
Cygnet (village) Wood County	4	0.67
Matamoras (village) Washington County	4	0.45
Flat Rock (cdp) Seneca County	1	0.43
Miamiville (cdp) Clermont County	1	0.41
Marshallville (village) Wayne County	3	0.40
Maple Ridge (cdp) Mahoning County	3	0.39
Beverly (village) Washington County	5	0.38
Hamler (village) Henry County	2	0.35
Potsdam (village) Miami County	1	0.35

Top 10 Places Sorted by Percent of Total Population
Based on places with total population of 50,000 or more

Place	Population	%
Canton (city) Stark County	31	0.04
Elyria (city) Lorain County	17	0.03
Columbus (city) Franklin County	126	0.02
Cleveland (city) Cuyahoga County	62	0.02
Akron (city) Summit County	41	0.02
Lorain (city) Lorain County	14	0.02
Parma (city) Cuyahoga County	13	0.02
Hamilton (city) Butler County	11	0.02
Youngstown (city) Mahoning County	11	0.02
Lakewood (city) Cuyahoga County	10	0.02

American Indian: Kiowa

Top 10 Places Sorted by Population
Based on all places, regardless of total population

Place	Population	%
Cleveland (city) Cuyahoga County	11	<0.01
Yellow Springs (village) Greene County	5	0.14
Jackson (city) Jackson County	4	0.06
St. Marys (city) Auglaize County	4	0.05
Minerva (village) Stark County	3	0.08
Ironton (city) Lawrence County	3	0.03
Marysville (city) Union County	2	0.01
Xenia (city) Greene County	2	0.01
Hamilton (city) Butler County	2	<0.01
Lorain (city) Lorain County	2	<0.01

Top 10 Places Sorted by Percent of Total Population
Based on all places, regardless of total population

Place	Population	%
Yellow Springs (village) Greene County	5	0.14
Minerva (village) Stark County	3	0.08
Jackson (city) Jackson County	4	0.06
Anna (village) Shelby County	1	0.06
St. Marys (city) Auglaize County	4	0.05
Rossmoyne (cdp) Hamilton County	1	0.04
Ironton (city) Lawrence County	3	0.03
Sixteen Mile Stand (cdp) Hamilton County	1	0.03
Marysville (city) Union County	2	0.01
Xenia (city) Greene County	2	0.01

Top 10 Places Sorted by Percent of Total Population
Based on places with total population of 50,000 or more

Place	Population	%
Cleveland (city) Cuyahoga County	11	<0.01
Hamilton (city) Butler County	2	<0.01
Lorain (city) Lorain County	2	<0.01
Columbus (city) Franklin County	1	<0.01
Toledo (city) Lucas County	1	<0.01
Akron (city) Summit County	0	0.00
Canton (city) Stark County	0	0.00
Cincinnati (city) Hamilton County	0	0.00
Dayton (city) Montgomery County	0	0.00
Elyria (city) Lorain County	0	0.00

American Indian: Lumbee

Top 10 Places Sorted by Population
Based on all places, regardless of total population

Place	Population	%
Columbus (city) Franklin County	56	0.01
Toledo (city) Lucas County	14	<0.01
Strongsville (city) Cuyahoga County	12	0.03
Cleveland (city) Cuyahoga County	9	<0.01
Delaware (city) Delaware County	8	0.02
Elyria (city) Lorain County	8	0.01
London (city) Madison County	6	0.06
Middleport (village) Meigs County	5	0.20
Blanchester (village) Clinton County	5	0.12
Alliance (city) Stark County	5	0.02

Top 10 Places Sorted by Percent of Total Population
Based on all places, regardless of total population

Place	Population	%
Marseilles (village) Wyandot County	1	0.89
Gratis (village) Preble County	3	0.34
Middleport (village) Meigs County	5	0.20
Hamersville (village) Brown County	1	0.18
Jeffersonville (village) Fayette County	2	0.17
Proctorville (village) Lawrence County	1	0.17
Piketon (village) Pike County	3	0.14
Blanchester (village) Clinton County	5	0.12
Rio Grande (village) Gallia County	1	0.12
Greentown (cdp) Stark County	3	0.08

Top 10 Places Sorted by Percent of Total Population
Based on places with total population of 50,000 or more

Place	Population	%
Columbus (city) Franklin County	56	0.01
Elyria (city) Lorain County	8	0.01
Canton (city) Stark County	5	0.01
Toledo (city) Lucas County	14	<0.01
Cleveland (city) Cuyahoga County	9	<0.01
Akron (city) Summit County	5	<0.01
Cincinnati (city) Hamilton County	4	<0.01
Parma (city) Cuyahoga County	3	<0.01
Dayton (city) Montgomery County	2	<0.01
Lorain (city) Lorain County	2	<0.01

American Indian: Menominee

Top 10 Places Sorted by Population
Based on all places, regardless of total population

Place	Population	%
Toledo (city) Lucas County	11	<0.01
Dayton (city) Montgomery County	6	<0.01
Lima (city) Allen County	4	0.01
New Knoxville (village) Auglaize County	3	0.34
Columbus (city) Franklin County	3	<0.01
Martins Ferry (city) Belmont County	2	0.03
Euclid (city) Cuyahoga County	2	<0.01
Franklin Furnace (cdp) Scioto County	1	0.06
Northwood (city) Wood County	1	0.02
Bedford Heights (city) Cuyahoga County	1	0.01

Top 10 Places Sorted by Percent of Total Population
Based on all places, regardless of total population

Place	Population	%
New Knoxville (village) Auglaize County	3	0.34
Franklin Furnace (cdp) Scioto County	1	0.06
Martins Ferry (city) Belmont County	2	0.03
Northwood (city) Wood County	1	0.02
Lima (city) Allen County	4	0.01
Bedford Heights (city) Cuyahoga County	1	0.01
Greenville (city) Darke County	1	0.01
Marietta (city) Washington County	1	0.01
Monfort Heights (cdp) Hamilton County	1	0.01
Ravenna (city) Portage County	1	0.01

Top 10 Places Sorted by Percent of Total Population
Based on places with total population of 50,000 or more

Place	Population	%
Toledo (city) Lucas County	11	<0.01
Dayton (city) Montgomery County	6	<0.01
Columbus (city) Franklin County	3	<0.01
Cincinnati (city) Hamilton County	1	<0.01
Youngstown (city) Mahoning County	1	<0.01
Akron (city) Summit County	0	0.00
Canton (city) Stark County	0	0.00
Cleveland (city) Cuyahoga County	0	0.00
Elyria (city) Lorain County	0	0.00
Hamilton (city) Butler County	0	0.00

American Indian: Mexican American Indian

Top 10 Places Sorted by Population
Based on all places, regardless of total population

Place	Population	%
Columbus (city) Franklin County	203	0.03
Toledo (city) Lucas County	96	0.03
Cleveland (city) Cuyahoga County	60	0.02
Cincinnati (city) Hamilton County	38	0.01
Northbrook (cdp) Hamilton County	30	0.28
Canton (city) Stark County	24	0.03
New Philadelphia (city) Tuscarawas County	21	0.12
Youngstown (city) Mahoning County	19	0.03
Lorain (city) Lorain County	16	0.02
Akron (city) Summit County	14	0.01

Top 10 Places Sorted by Percent of Total Population
Based on all places, regardless of total population

Place	Population	%
Highland (village) Highland County	3	1.18
Beaverdam (village) Allen County	3	0.79
Hooven (cdp) Hamilton County	4	0.75
Castalia (village) Erie County	5	0.59
Hessville (cdp) Sandusky County	1	0.47
Alvordton (cdp) Williams County	1	0.46
Addyston (village) Hamilton County	4	0.43
Malinta (village) Henry County	1	0.38
Berlin (cdp) Holmes County	3	0.33
New Marshfield (cdp) Athens County	1	0.31

Top 10 Places Sorted by Percent of Total Population
Based on places with total population of 50,000 or more

Place	Population	%
Columbus (city) Franklin County	203	0.03
Toledo (city) Lucas County	96	0.03
Canton (city) Stark County	24	0.03
Youngstown (city) Mahoning County	19	0.03
Cleveland (city) Cuyahoga County	60	0.02
Lorain (city) Lorain County	16	0.02
Hamilton (city) Butler County	11	0.02
Lakewood (city) Cuyahoga County	9	0.02
Cincinnati (city) Hamilton County	38	0.01
Akron (city) Summit County	14	0.01

American Indian: Navajo

Top 10 Places Sorted by Population
Based on all places, regardless of total population

Place	Population	%
Columbus (city) Franklin County	68	0.01
Cincinnati (city) Hamilton County	31	0.01
Cleveland (city) Cuyahoga County	31	0.01
Toledo (city) Lucas County	30	0.01
Canton (city) Stark County	16	0.02
Akron (city) Summit County	15	0.01
Lakewood (city) Cuyahoga County	13	0.02
Parma (city) Cuyahoga County	13	0.02
Dayton (city) Montgomery County	13	0.01
Miamisburg (city) Montgomery County	11	0.05

Top 10 Places Sorted by Percent of Total Population
Based on all places, regardless of total population

Place	Population	%
Higginsport (village) Brown County	2	0.80
Quincy (village) Logan County	2	0.28

Place	Population	%
South Solon (village) Madison County	1	0.28
Weston (village) Wood County	4	0.25
Buffalo (cdp) Guernsey County	1	0.25
South Amherst (village) Lorain County	3	0.18
Highland Holiday (cdp) Highland County	1	0.18
The Plains (cdp) Athens County	5	0.16
Waynesville (village) Warren County	4	0.14
New Straitsville (village) Perry County	1	0.14

Top 10 Places Sorted by Percent of Total Population
Based on places with total population of 50,000 or more

Place	Population	%
Canton (city) Stark County	16	0.02
Lakewood (city) Cuyahoga County	13	0.02
Parma (city) Cuyahoga County	13	0.02
Columbus (city) Franklin County	68	0.01
Cincinnati (city) Hamilton County	31	0.01
Cleveland (city) Cuyahoga County	31	0.01
Toledo (city) Lucas County	30	0.01
Akron (city) Summit County	15	0.01
Dayton (city) Montgomery County	13	0.01
Lorain (city) Lorain County	7	0.01

American Indian: Osage

Top 10 Places Sorted by Population
Based on all places, regardless of total population

Place	Population	%
Columbus (city) Franklin County	7	<0.01
Springfield (city) Clark County	6	0.01
Zanesville (city) Muskingum County	5	0.02
Coldstream (cdp) Hamilton County	3	0.26
Minerva Park (village) Franklin County	3	0.24
Byesville (village) Guernsey County	3	0.12
Cleves (village) Hamilton County	3	0.09
Avon Lake (city) Lorain County	3	0.01
Beavercreek (city) Greene County	3	0.01
Lima (city) Allen County	3	0.01

Top 10 Places Sorted by Percent of Total Population
Based on all places, regardless of total population

Place	Population	%
New Haven (cdp) Hamilton County	2	0.34
Coldstream (cdp) Hamilton County	3	0.26
Minerva Park (village) Franklin County	3	0.24
Pioneer (village) Williams County	2	0.14
Byesville (village) Guernsey County	3	0.12
Cleves (village) Hamilton County	3	0.09
Williamsburg (village) Clermont County	1	0.04
Withamsville (cdp) Clermont County	2	0.03
Fort Shawnee (village) Allen County	1	0.03
Mount Healthy Heights (cdp) Hamilton County	1	0.03

Top 10 Places Sorted by Percent of Total Population
Based on places with total population of 50,000 or more

Place	Population	%
Springfield (city) Clark County	6	0.01
Columbus (city) Franklin County	7	<0.01
Akron (city) Summit County	3	<0.01
Cincinnati (city) Hamilton County	3	<0.01
Toledo (city) Lucas County	3	<0.01
Dayton (city) Montgomery County	1	<0.01
Elyria (city) Lorain County	1	<0.01
Parma (city) Cuyahoga County	1	<0.01
Canton (city) Stark County	0	0.00
Cleveland (city) Cuyahoga County	0	0.00

American Indian: Ottawa

Top 10 Places Sorted by Population
Based on all places, regardless of total population

Place	Population	%
Toledo (city) Lucas County	41	0.01
Columbus (city) Franklin County	13	<0.01
Sandusky (city) Erie County	9	0.03
Cleveland (city) Cuyahoga County	7	<0.01
Dayton (city) Montgomery County	6	<0.01
Germantown (village) Montgomery County	5	0.09
Pomeroy (village) Meigs County	4	0.22
Bedford Heights (city) Cuyahoga County	4	0.04
Cuyahoga Falls (city) Summit County	4	0.01
Akron (city) Summit County	4	<0.01

Top 10 Places Sorted by Percent of Total Population
Based on all places, regardless of total population

Place	Population	%
Crystal Rock (cdp) Erie County	1	0.57
Hooven (cdp) Hamilton County	3	0.56
Athalia (village) Lawrence County	1	0.27
Pomeroy (village) Meigs County	4	0.22
Bay View (village) Erie County	1	0.16
Ashley (village) Delaware County	2	0.15
Genoa (village) Ottawa County	3	0.13
Germantown (village) Montgomery County	5	0.09
Caldwell (village) Noble County	1	0.06
Plain City (village) Madison County	2	0.05

Top 10 Places Sorted by Percent of Total Population
Based on places with total population of 50,000 or more

Place	Population	%
Toledo (city) Lucas County	41	0.01
Columbus (city) Franklin County	13	<0.01
Cleveland (city) Cuyahoga County	7	<0.01
Dayton (city) Montgomery County	6	<0.01
Akron (city) Summit County	4	<0.01
Lorain (city) Lorain County	2	<0.01
Canton (city) Stark County	1	<0.01
Cincinnati (city) Hamilton County	1	<0.01
Kettering (city) Montgomery County	1	<0.01
Springfield (city) Clark County	1	<0.01

American Indian: Paiute

Top 10 Places Sorted by Population
Based on all places, regardless of total population

Place	Population	%
Warren (city) Trumbull County	5	0.01
Pickerington (city) Fairfield County	3	0.02
Beavercreek (city) Greene County	3	0.01
Wheelersburg (cdp) Scioto County	2	0.03
Amherst (city) Lorain County	2	0.02
Reynoldsburg (city) Franklin County	2	0.01
Roseville (village) Perry County	1	0.05
Munroe Falls (city) Summit County	1	0.02
Pleasant Run (cdp) Hamilton County	1	0.02
East Liverpool (city) Columbiana County	1	0.01

Top 10 Places Sorted by Percent of Total Population
Based on all places, regardless of total population

Place	Population	%
Roseville (village) Perry County	1	0.05
Wheelersburg (cdp) Scioto County	2	0.03
Pickerington (city) Fairfield County	3	0.02
Amherst (city) Lorain County	2	0.02
Munroe Falls (city) Summit County	1	0.02
Pleasant Run (cdp) Hamilton County	1	0.02
Warren (city) Trumbull County	5	0.01
Beavercreek (city) Greene County	3	0.01
Reynoldsburg (city) Franklin County	2	0.01
East Liverpool (city) Columbiana County	1	0.01

Top 10 Places Sorted by Percent of Total Population
Based on places with total population of 50,000 or more

Place	Population	%
Columbus (city) Franklin County	1	<0.01
Elyria (city) Lorain County	1	<0.01
Akron (city) Summit County	0	0.00
Canton (city) Stark County	0	0.00
Cincinnati (city) Hamilton County	0	0.00
Cleveland (city) Cuyahoga County	0	0.00
Dayton (city) Montgomery County	0	0.00
Hamilton (city) Butler County	0	0.00
Kettering (city) Montgomery County	0	0.00
Lakewood (city) Cuyahoga County	0	0.00

American Indian: Pima

Top 10 Places Sorted by Population
Based on all places, regardless of total population

Place	Population	%
Akron (city) Summit County	5	<0.01
Columbus (city) Franklin County	3	<0.01
Dayton (city) Montgomery County	2	<0.01
Lockland (village) Hamilton County	1	0.03
Aurora (city) Portage County	1	0.01
North Canton (city) Stark County	1	0.01
Sharonville (city) Hamilton County	1	0.01
Wilmington (city) Clinton County	1	0.01
Alliance (city) Stark County	1	<0.01
Boardman (cdp) Mahoning County	1	<0.01

Top 10 Places Sorted by Percent of Total Population
Based on all places, regardless of total population

Place	Population	%
Lockland (village) Hamilton County	1	0.03
Aurora (city) Portage County	1	0.01
North Canton (city) Stark County	1	0.01
Sharonville (city) Hamilton County	1	0.01
Wilmington (city) Clinton County	1	0.01
Akron (city) Summit County	5	<0.01
Columbus (city) Franklin County	3	<0.01
Dayton (city) Montgomery County	2	<0.01
Alliance (city) Stark County	1	<0.01
Boardman (cdp) Mahoning County	1	<0.01

Top 10 Places Sorted by Percent of Total Population
Based on places with total population of 50,000 or more

Place	Population	%
Akron (city) Summit County	5	<0.01
Columbus (city) Franklin County	3	<0.01
Dayton (city) Montgomery County	2	<0.01
Cleveland (city) Cuyahoga County	1	<0.01
Canton (city) Stark County	0	0.00
Cincinnati (city) Hamilton County	0	0.00
Elyria (city) Lorain County	0	0.00
Hamilton (city) Butler County	0	0.00
Kettering (city) Montgomery County	0	0.00
Lakewood (city) Cuyahoga County	0	0.00

American Indian: Potawatomi

Top 10 Places Sorted by Population
Based on all places, regardless of total population

Place	Population	%
Toledo (city) Lucas County	33	0.01
Columbus (city) Franklin County	13	<0.01
Cincinnati (city) Hamilton County	10	<0.01
Sandusky (city) Erie County	6	0.02
Hilliard (city) Franklin County	5	0.02
Xenia (city) Greene County	5	0.02
Upper Arlington (city) Franklin County	5	0.01
Amesville (village) Athens County	4	2.60
Brunswick (city) Medina County	4	0.01
Springfield (city) Clark County	4	0.01

Top 10 Places Sorted by Percent of Total Population
Based on all places, regardless of total population

Place	Population	%
Amesville (village) Athens County	4	2.60
Bremen (village) Fairfield County	3	0.21
Williston (cdp) Ottawa County	1	0.21
Reminderville (village) Summit County	3	0.09
Chesterland (cdp) Geauga County	2	0.08
Obetz (village) Franklin County	3	0.07
Lodi (village) Medina County	2	0.07
Wellston (city) Jackson County	3	0.05
Miami Heights (cdp) Hamilton County	2	0.04
Van Wert (city) Van Wert County	3	0.03

Top 10 Places Sorted by Percent of Total Population
Based on places with total population of 50,000 or more

Place	Population	%
Toledo (city) Lucas County	33	0.01
Springfield (city) Clark County	4	0.01
Columbus (city) Franklin County	13	<0.01
Cincinnati (city) Hamilton County	10	<0.01
Cleveland (city) Cuyahoga County	4	<0.01
Canton (city) Stark County	3	<0.01
Dayton (city) Montgomery County	3	<0.01
Lorain (city) Lorain County	3	<0.01
Parma (city) Cuyahoga County	3	<0.01
Akron (city) Summit County	2	<0.01

American Indian: Pueblo

Top 10 Places Sorted by Population
Based on all places, regardless of total population

Place	Population	%
Columbus (city) Franklin County	16	<0.01
Toledo (city) Lucas County	15	0.01
Lorain (city) Lorain County	14	0.02
Cleveland (city) Cuyahoga County	13	<0.01
North Madison (cdp) Lake County	5	0.06
Fairborn (city) Greene County	5	0.02
Rocky River (city) Cuyahoga County	5	0.02
Dayton (city) Montgomery County	5	<0.01
Middlefield (village) Geauga County	4	0.15
Cincinnati (city) Hamilton County	4	<0.01

Top 10 Places Sorted by Percent of Total Population
Based on all places, regardless of total population

Place	Population	%
Middlefield (village) Geauga County	4	0.15
Russells Point (village) Logan County	2	0.14
La Rue (village) Marion County	1	0.13
North Madison (cdp) Lake County	5	0.06
Sugarcreek (village) Tuscarawas County	1	0.05
New Lexington (village) Perry County	2	0.04
Gambier (village) Knox County	1	0.04
Grandview Heights (city) Franklin County	2	0.03
Ballville (cdp) Sandusky County	1	0.03
Yellow Springs (village) Greene County	1	0.03

Top 10 Places Sorted by Percent of Total Population
Based on places with total population of 50,000 or more

Place	Population	%
Lorain (city) Lorain County	14	0.02
Toledo (city) Lucas County	15	0.01
Columbus (city) Franklin County	16	<0.01
Cleveland (city) Cuyahoga County	13	<0.01
Dayton (city) Montgomery County	5	<0.01
Cincinnati (city) Hamilton County	4	<0.01
Parma (city) Cuyahoga County	2	<0.01
Akron (city) Summit County	1	<0.01
Canton (city) Stark County	1	<0.01
Elyria (city) Lorain County	1	<0.01

American Indian: Puget Sound Salish

Top 10 Places Sorted by Population
Based on all places, regardless of total population

Place	Population	%
Belmont (village) Belmont County	6	1.32
Findlay (city) Hancock County	4	0.01
Dayton (city) Montgomery County	2	<0.01
Batavia (village) Clermont County	1	0.07
Minster (village) Auglaize County	1	0.04
Napoleon (city) Henry County	1	0.01
Willoughby Hills (city) Lake County	1	0.01
Centerville (city) Montgomery County	1	<0.01
Cleveland Heights (city) Cuyahoga County	1	<0.01
Columbus (city) Franklin County	1	<0.01

Top 10 Places Sorted by Percent of Total Population
Based on all places, regardless of total population

Place	Population	%
Belmont (village) Belmont County	6	1.32
Batavia (village) Clermont County	1	0.07
Minster (village) Auglaize County	1	0.04
Findlay (city) Hancock County	4	0.01
Napoleon (city) Henry County	1	0.01
Willoughby Hills (city) Lake County	1	0.01
Dayton (city) Montgomery County	2	<0.01
Centerville (city) Montgomery County	1	<0.01
Cleveland Heights (city) Cuyahoga County	1	<0.01
Columbus (city) Franklin County	1	<0.01

Top 10 Places Sorted by Percent of Total Population
Based on places with total population of 50,000 or more

Place	Population	%
Dayton (city) Montgomery County	2	<0.01
Columbus (city) Franklin County	1	<0.01
Elyria (city) Lorain County	1	<0.01
Akron (city) Summit County	0	0.00
Canton (city) Stark County	0	0.00
Cincinnati (city) Hamilton County	0	0.00
Cleveland (city) Cuyahoga County	0	0.00
Hamilton (city) Butler County	0	0.00
Kettering (city) Montgomery County	0	0.00
Lakewood (city) Cuyahoga County	0	0.00

American Indian: Seminole

Top 10 Places Sorted by Population
Based on all places, regardless of total population

Place	Population	%
Columbus (city) Franklin County	42	0.01
Cleveland (city) Cuyahoga County	30	0.01
Cincinnati (city) Hamilton County	20	0.01
Akron (city) Summit County	17	0.01
Euclid (city) Cuyahoga County	13	0.03
Canton (city) Stark County	13	0.02
Cleveland Heights (city) Cuyahoga County	10	0.02
Dayton (city) Montgomery County	10	0.01
Toledo (city) Lucas County	9	<0.01
Wilberforce (cdp) Greene County	7	0.31

Top 10 Places Sorted by Percent of Total Population
Based on all places, regardless of total population

Place	Population	%
Antioch (village) Monroe County	1	1.16
Twinsburg Heights (cdp) Summit County	3	0.32
Wilberforce (cdp) Greene County	7	0.31
Athalia (village) Lawrence County	1	0.27
Pleasant Hills (cdp) Hamilton County	1	0.17
Smithfield (village) Jefferson County	1	0.12
Bridgeport (village) Belmont County	2	0.11
Sheffield Lake (city) Lorain County	7	0.08
Moraine (city) Montgomery County	5	0.08
New Vienna (village) Clinton County	1	0.08

Top 10 Places Sorted by Percent of Total Population
Based on places with total population of 50,000 or more

Place	Population	%
Canton (city) Stark County	13	0.02
Columbus (city) Franklin County	42	0.01
Cleveland (city) Cuyahoga County	30	0.01
Cincinnati (city) Hamilton County	20	0.01
Akron (city) Summit County	17	0.01
Dayton (city) Montgomery County	10	0.01
Lakewood (city) Cuyahoga County	7	0.01
Springfield (city) Clark County	7	0.01
Youngstown (city) Mahoning County	6	0.01
Elyria (city) Lorain County	4	0.01

American Indian: Shoshone

Top 10 Places Sorted by Population
Based on all places, regardless of total population

Place	Population	%
Akron (city) Summit County	10	0.01
Columbus (city) Franklin County	5	<0.01
Castalia (village) Erie County	4	0.47
Pataskala (city) Licking County	4	0.03
Garfield Heights (city) Cuyahoga County	4	0.01
Westerville (city) Franklin County	4	0.01
Cleveland (city) Cuyahoga County	4	<0.01
Avon (city) Lorain County	3	0.01
Toledo (city) Lucas County	3	<0.01
Reminderville (village) Summit County	2	0.06

Top 10 Places Sorted by Percent of Total Population
Based on all places, regardless of total population

Place	Population	%
Castalia (village) Erie County	4	0.47
Seaman (village) Adams County	1	0.11
Reminderville (village) Summit County	2	0.06
Yellow Springs (village) Greene County	2	0.06
Bolindale (cdp) Trumbull County	1	0.05
Pataskala (city) Licking County	4	0.03
Bellaire (village) Belmont County	1	0.02
Jackson (city) Jackson County	1	0.02
Nelsonville (city) Athens County	1	0.02
Upper Sandusky (city) Wyandot County	1	0.02

Top 10 Places Sorted by Percent of Total Population
Based on places with total population of 50,000 or more

Place	Population	%
Akron (city) Summit County	10	0.01
Columbus (city) Franklin County	5	<0.01
Cleveland (city) Cuyahoga County	4	<0.01
Toledo (city) Lucas County	3	<0.01
Cincinnati (city) Hamilton County	2	<0.01
Dayton (city) Montgomery County	1	<0.01
Youngstown (city) Mahoning County	1	<0.01
Canton (city) Stark County	0	0.00
Elyria (city) Lorain County	0	0.00
Hamilton (city) Butler County	0	0.00

American Indian: Sioux

Top 10 Places Sorted by Population
Based on all places, regardless of total population

Place	Population	%
Columbus (city) Franklin County	182	0.02
Cleveland (city) Cuyahoga County	91	0.02
Cincinnati (city) Hamilton County	56	0.02
Akron (city) Summit County	55	0.03
Toledo (city) Lucas County	39	0.01
Lakewood (city) Cuyahoga County	35	0.07
Dayton (city) Montgomery County	31	0.02
Lorain (city) Lorain County	26	0.04
Reynoldsburg (city) Franklin County	21	0.06
Beavercreek (city) Greene County	14	0.03

Top 10 Places Sorted by Percent of Total Population
Based on all places, regardless of total population

Place	Population	%
Clifton (village) Greene County	4	2.63
Potsdam (village) Miami County	4	1.39
Otway (village) Scioto County	1	1.15
Orient (village) Pickaway County	3	1.11
College Corner (village) Preble County	2	0.49
Jewett (village) Harrison County	3	0.43
Carbon Hill (cdp) Hocking County	1	0.43
Florida (village) Henry County	1	0.43
Christiansburg (village) Champaign County	2	0.38
Dundee (cdp) Tuscarawas County	1	0.34

Top 10 Places Sorted by Percent of Total Population
Based on places with total population of 50,000 or more

Place	Population	%
Lakewood (city) Cuyahoga County	35	0.07
Lorain (city) Lorain County	26	0.04
Akron (city) Summit County	55	0.03
Columbus (city) Franklin County	182	0.02
Cleveland (city) Cuyahoga County	91	0.02
Cincinnati (city) Hamilton County	56	0.02
Dayton (city) Montgomery County	31	0.02
Hamilton (city) Butler County	14	0.02
Kettering (city) Montgomery County	14	0.02
Springfield (city) Clark County	12	0.02

American Indian: South American Indian

Top 10 Places Sorted by Population
Based on all places, regardless of total population

Place	Population	%
Cleveland (city) Cuyahoga County	105	0.03
Lorain (city) Lorain County	79	0.12
Columbus (city) Franklin County	51	0.01
Cincinnati (city) Hamilton County	18	0.01
Toledo (city) Lucas County	17	0.01
Youngstown (city) Mahoning County	15	0.02
Parma (city) Cuyahoga County	10	0.01
Boardman (cdp) Mahoning County	9	0.03
Strongsville (city) Cuyahoga County	7	0.02
Upper Arlington (city) Franklin County	7	0.02

Top 10 Places Sorted by Percent of Total Population
Based on all places, regardless of total population

Place	Population	%
Jeromesville (village) Ashland County	5	0.89
Brooklyn Heights (village) Cuyahoga County	5	0.32
Rayland (village) Jefferson County	1	0.24

Pettisville (cdp) Fulton County	1	0.20
Malta (village) Morgan County	1	0.15
Lorain (city) Lorain County	79	0.12
Salem Heights (cdp) Hamilton County	4	0.10
The Village of Indian Hill (city) Hamilton County	5	0.09
Rockford (village) Mercer County	1	0.09
Devola (cdp) Washington County	2	0.08

Top 10 Places Sorted by Percent of Total Population
Based on places with total population of 50,000 or more

Place	Population	%
Lorain (city) Lorain County	79	0.12
Cleveland (city) Cuyahoga County	105	0.03
Youngstown (city) Mahoning County	15	0.02
Columbus (city) Franklin County	51	0.01
Cincinnati (city) Hamilton County	18	0.01
Toledo (city) Lucas County	17	0.01
Parma (city) Cuyahoga County	10	0.01
Kettering (city) Montgomery County	6	0.01
Hamilton (city) Butler County	5	0.01
Canton (city) Stark County	4	0.01

American Indian: Spanish American Indian

Top 10 Places Sorted by Population
Based on all places, regardless of total population

Place	Population	%
Columbus (city) Franklin County	18	<0.01
Cincinnati (city) Hamilton County	6	<0.01
Toledo (city) Lucas County	6	<0.01
Ottawa (village) Putnam County	5	0.11
Lakewood (city) Cuyahoga County	5	0.01
Bryan (city) Williams County	4	0.05
Defiance (city) Defiance County	4	0.02
Akron (city) Summit County	4	<0.01
Fairfield (city) Butler County	3	0.01
Kettering (city) Montgomery County	3	0.01

Top 10 Places Sorted by Percent of Total Population
Based on all places, regardless of total population

Place	Population	%
Port William (village) Clinton County	1	0.39
Wayne Lakes (village) Darke County	1	0.14
Ottawa (village) Putnam County	5	0.11
Hartville (village) Stark County	2	0.07
Bryan (city) Williams County	4	0.05
Defiance (city) Defiance County	4	0.02
Jackson (city) Jackson County	1	0.02
Pleasant Run (cdp) Hamilton County	1	0.02
Lakewood (city) Cuyahoga County	5	0.01
Fairfield (city) Butler County	3	0.01

Top 10 Places Sorted by Percent of Total Population
Based on places with total population of 50,000 or more

Place	Population	%
Lakewood (city) Cuyahoga County	5	0.01
Kettering (city) Montgomery County	3	0.01
Columbus (city) Franklin County	18	<0.01
Cincinnati (city) Hamilton County	6	<0.01
Toledo (city) Lucas County	6	<0.01
Akron (city) Summit County	4	<0.01
Cleveland (city) Cuyahoga County	3	<0.01
Hamilton (city) Butler County	3	<0.01
Youngstown (city) Mahoning County	3	<0.01
Dayton (city) Montgomery County	2	<0.01

Alaska Native: Tlingit-Haida

Top 10 Places Sorted by Population
Based on all places, regardless of total population

Place	Population	%
Columbus (city) Franklin County	10	<0.01
North Olmsted (city) Cuyahoga County	6	0.02
Parma (city) Cuyahoga County	6	0.01
LaGrange (village) Lorain County	3	0.14
Rittman (city) Wayne County	3	0.05
Berea (city) Cuyahoga County	3	0.02
Gahanna (city) Franklin County	2	0.01
Niles (city) Trumbull County	2	0.01
Cleveland (city) Cuyahoga County	2	<0.01
Lakewood (city) Cuyahoga County	2	<0.01

Top 10 Places Sorted by Percent of Total Population
Based on all places, regardless of total population

Place	Population	%
LaGrange (village) Lorain County	3	0.14
Rittman (city) Wayne County	3	0.05
North Olmsted (city) Cuyahoga County	6	0.02
Berea (city) Cuyahoga County	3	0.02
Ada (village) Hardin County	1	0.02
Nelsonville (city) Athens County	1	0.02
Parma (city) Cuyahoga County	6	0.01
Gahanna (city) Franklin County	2	0.01
Niles (city) Trumbull County	2	0.01
Blue Ash (city) Hamilton County	1	0.01

Top 10 Places Sorted by Percent of Total Population
Based on places with total population of 50,000 or more

Place	Population	%
Parma (city) Cuyahoga County	6	0.01
Columbus (city) Franklin County	10	<0.01
Cleveland (city) Cuyahoga County	2	<0.01
Lakewood (city) Cuyahoga County	2	<0.01
Toledo (city) Lucas County	2	<0.01
Akron (city) Summit County	1	<0.01
Youngstown (city) Mahoning County	1	<0.01
Canton (city) Stark County	0	0.00
Cincinnati (city) Hamilton County	0	0.00
Dayton (city) Montgomery County	0	0.00

American Indian: Tohono O'Odham

Top 10 Places Sorted by Population
Based on all places, regardless of total population

Place	Population	%
Cincinnati (city) Hamilton County	7	<0.01
Cleveland (city) Cuyahoga County	7	<0.01
Columbus (city) Franklin County	5	<0.01
Mentor-on-the-Lake (city) Lake County	3	0.04
Conneaut (city) Ashtabula County	3	0.02
Eastlake (city) Lake County	3	0.02
Springfield (city) Clark County	3	<0.01
Campbell (city) Mahoning County	2	0.02
Ashville (village) Pickaway County	1	0.02
Oberlin (city) Lorain County	1	0.01

Top 10 Places Sorted by Percent of Total Population
Based on all places, regardless of total population

Place	Population	%
Mentor-on-the-Lake (city) Lake County	3	0.04
Conneaut (city) Ashtabula County	3	0.02
Eastlake (city) Lake County	3	0.02
Campbell (city) Mahoning County	2	0.02
Ashville (village) Pickaway County	1	0.02
Oberlin (city) Lorain County	1	0.01
Tiffin (city) Seneca County	1	0.01
Wilmington (city) Clinton County	1	0.01
Cincinnati (city) Hamilton County	7	<0.01
Cleveland (city) Cuyahoga County	7	<0.01

Top 10 Places Sorted by Percent of Total Population
Based on places with total population of 50,000 or more

Place	Population	%
Cincinnati (city) Hamilton County	7	<0.01
Cleveland (city) Cuyahoga County	7	<0.01
Columbus (city) Franklin County	5	<0.01
Springfield (city) Clark County	3	<0.01
Akron (city) Summit County	0	0.00
Canton (city) Stark County	0	0.00
Dayton (city) Montgomery County	0	0.00
Elyria (city) Lorain County	0	0.00
Hamilton (city) Butler County	0	0.00
Kettering (city) Montgomery County	0	0.00

Alaska Native: Tsimshian

Top 10 Places Sorted by Population
Based on all places, regardless of total population

Place	Population	%
Brookville (city) Montgomery County	2	0.03
Gahanna (city) Franklin County	2	0.01
Green (city) Summit County	2	0.01
Lakewood (city) Cuyahoga County	2	<0.01
Parma (city) Cuyahoga County	2	<0.01
West Manchester (village) Preble County	1	0.21
Moraine (city) Montgomery County	1	0.02
Bellbrook (city) Greene County	1	0.01
Cincinnati (city) Hamilton County	1	<0.01
Columbus (city) Franklin County	1	<0.01

Top 10 Places Sorted by Percent of Total Population
Based on all places, regardless of total population

Place	Population	%
West Manchester (village) Preble County	1	0.21
Brookville (city) Montgomery County	2	0.03
Moraine (city) Montgomery County	1	0.02
Gahanna (city) Franklin County	2	0.01
Green (city) Summit County	2	0.01
Bellbrook (city) Greene County	1	0.01
Lakewood (city) Cuyahoga County	2	<0.01
Parma (city) Cuyahoga County	2	<0.01
Cincinnati (city) Hamilton County	1	<0.01
Columbus (city) Franklin County	1	<0.01

Top 10 Places Sorted by Percent of Total Population
Based on places with total population of 50,000 or more

Place	Population	%
Lakewood (city) Cuyahoga County	2	<0.01
Parma (city) Cuyahoga County	2	<0.01
Cincinnati (city) Hamilton County	1	<0.01
Columbus (city) Franklin County	1	<0.01
Akron (city) Summit County	0	0.00
Canton (city) Stark County	0	0.00
Cleveland (city) Cuyahoga County	0	0.00
Dayton (city) Montgomery County	0	0.00
Elyria (city) Lorain County	0	0.00
Hamilton (city) Butler County	0	0.00

American Indian: Ute

Top 10 Places Sorted by Population
Based on all places, regardless of total population

Place	Population	%
Franklin (city) Warren County	4	0.03
Columbus (city) Franklin County	4	<0.01
Dayton (city) Montgomery County	4	<0.01
St. Marys (city) Auglaize County	2	0.02
White Oak (cdp) Hamilton County	2	0.01
Edgewood (cdp) Ashtabula County	1	0.02
Delphos (city) Allen County	1	0.01
Akron (city) Summit County	1	<0.01
Brunswick (city) Medina County	1	<0.01
Kettering (city) Montgomery County	1	<0.01

Top 10 Places Sorted by Percent of Total Population
Based on all places, regardless of total population

Place	Population	%
Franklin (city) Warren County	4	0.03
St. Marys (city) Auglaize County	2	0.02
Edgewood (cdp) Ashtabula County	1	0.02
White Oak (cdp) Hamilton County	2	0.01
Delphos (city) Allen County	1	0.01
Columbus (city) Franklin County	4	<0.01
Dayton (city) Montgomery County	4	<0.01
Akron (city) Summit County	1	<0.01
Brunswick (city) Medina County	1	<0.01
Kettering (city) Montgomery County	1	<0.01

Top 10 Places Sorted by Percent of Total Population
Based on places with total population of 50,000 or more

Place	Population	%
Columbus (city) Franklin County	4	<0.01
Dayton (city) Montgomery County	4	<0.01
Akron (city) Summit County	1	<0.01
Kettering (city) Montgomery County	1	<0.01
Youngstown (city) Mahoning County	1	<0.01
Canton (city) Stark County	0	0.00
Cincinnati (city) Hamilton County	0	0.00
Cleveland (city) Cuyahoga County	0	0.00
Elyria (city) Lorain County	0	0.00
Hamilton (city) Butler County	0	0.00

American Indian: Yakama

Top 10 Places Sorted by Population
Based on all places, regardless of total population

Place	Population	%
Hamilton (city) Butler County	5	0.01
Mansfield (city) Richland County	4	0.01
Fremont (city) Sandusky County	2	0.01
Port Clinton (city) Ottawa County	1	0.02
Wheelersburg (cdp) Scioto County	1	0.02
Cincinnati (city) Hamilton County	1	<0.01
Aberdeen (village) Brown County	0	0.00
Ada (village) Hardin County	0	0.00
Adamsville (village) Muskingum County	0	0.00
Addyston (village) Hamilton County	0	0.00

Top 10 Places Sorted by Percent of Total Population
Based on all places, regardless of total population

Place	Population	%
Port Clinton (city) Ottawa County	1	0.02
Wheelersburg (cdp) Scioto County	1	0.02
Hamilton (city) Butler County	5	0.01
Mansfield (city) Richland County	4	0.01
Fremont (city) Sandusky County	2	0.01
Cincinnati (city) Hamilton County	1	<0.01
Aberdeen (village) Brown County	0	0.00
Ada (village) Hardin County	0	0.00
Adamsville (village) Muskingum County	0	0.00
Addyston (village) Hamilton County	0	0.00

Top 10 Places Sorted by Percent of Total Population
Based on places with total population of 50,000 or more

Place	Population	%
Hamilton (city) Butler County	5	0.01
Cincinnati (city) Hamilton County	1	<0.01
Akron (city) Summit County	0	0.00
Canton (city) Stark County	0	0.00
Cleveland (city) Cuyahoga County	0	0.00
Columbus (city) Franklin County	0	0.00
Dayton (city) Montgomery County	0	0.00
Elyria (city) Lorain County	0	0.00
Kettering (city) Montgomery County	0	0.00
Lakewood (city) Cuyahoga County	0	0.00

American Indian: Yaqui

Top 10 Places Sorted by Population
Based on all places, regardless of total population

Place	Population	%
Akron (city) Summit County	9	<0.01
Marietta (city) Washington County	4	0.03
Toledo (city) Lucas County	4	<0.01
Glenmoor (cdp) Columbiana County	3	0.15
Archbold (village) Fulton County	3	0.07
Barberton (city) Summit County	3	0.01
Strongsville (city) Cuyahoga County	3	0.01
Steubenville (city) Jefferson County	2	0.01
Cincinnati (city) Hamilton County	2	<0.01
Youngstown (city) Mahoning County	2	<0.01

Top 10 Places Sorted by Percent of Total Population
Based on all places, regardless of total population

Place	Population	%
Glenmoor (cdp) Columbiana County	3	0.15
Bloomville (village) Seneca County	1	0.10
Archbold (village) Fulton County	3	0.07
Orwell (village) Ashtabula County	1	0.06
Marietta (city) Washington County	4	0.03
Groveport (village) Franklin County	1	0.02
Miami Heights (cdp) Hamilton County	1	0.02
Port Clinton (city) Ottawa County	1	0.02
Barberton (city) Summit County	3	0.01
Strongsville (city) Cuyahoga County	3	0.01

Top 10 Places Sorted by Percent of Total Population
Based on places with total population of 50,000 or more

Place	Population	%
Akron (city) Summit County	9	<0.01
Toledo (city) Lucas County	4	<0.01
Cincinnati (city) Hamilton County	2	<0.01
Youngstown (city) Mahoning County	2	<0.01
Columbus (city) Franklin County	1	<0.01
Hamilton (city) Butler County	1	<0.01
Lorain (city) Lorain County	1	<0.01
Springfield (city) Clark County	1	<0.01
Canton (city) Stark County	0	0.00
Cleveland (city) Cuyahoga County	0	0.00

American Indian: Yuman

Top 10 Places Sorted by Population
Based on all places, regardless of total population

Place	Population	%
Canton (city) Stark County	5	0.01
Wadsworth (city) Medina County	4	0.02
Mogadore (village) Summit County	3	0.08
Cincinnati (city) Hamilton County	2	<0.01
Columbus (city) Franklin County	2	<0.01
McArthur (village) Vinton County	1	0.06
Bedford Heights (city) Cuyahoga County	1	0.01
Bexley (city) Franklin County	1	0.01
Kettering (city) Montgomery County	1	<0.01
Lakewood (city) Cuyahoga County	1	<0.01

Top 10 Places Sorted by Percent of Total Population
Based on all places, regardless of total population

Place	Population	%
Mogadore (village) Summit County	3	0.08
McArthur (village) Vinton County	1	0.06
Wadsworth (city) Medina County	4	0.02
Canton (city) Stark County	5	0.01
Bedford Heights (city) Cuyahoga County	1	0.01
Bexley (city) Franklin County	1	0.01
Cincinnati (city) Hamilton County	2	<0.01
Columbus (city) Franklin County	2	<0.01
Kettering (city) Montgomery County	1	<0.01
Lakewood (city) Cuyahoga County	1	<0.01

Top 10 Places Sorted by Percent of Total Population
Based on places with total population of 50,000 or more

Place	Population	%
Canton (city) Stark County	5	0.01
Cincinnati (city) Hamilton County	2	<0.01
Columbus (city) Franklin County	2	<0.01
Kettering (city) Montgomery County	1	<0.01
Lakewood (city) Cuyahoga County	1	<0.01
Akron (city) Summit County	0	0.00
Cleveland (city) Cuyahoga County	0	0.00
Dayton (city) Montgomery County	0	0.00
Elyria (city) Lorain County	0	0.00
Hamilton (city) Butler County	0	0.00

Alaska Native: Yup'ik

Top 10 Places Sorted by Population
Based on all places, regardless of total population

Place	Population	%
Huber Heights (city) Montgomery County	5	0.01
Green (city) Summit County	3	0.01
Sandusky (city) Erie County	3	0.01
Cleveland (city) Cuyahoga County	3	<0.01
Columbus (city) Franklin County	2	<0.01
Hebron (village) Licking County	1	0.04
Amherst (city) Lorain County	1	0.01
Berea (city) Cuyahoga County	1	0.01
Defiance (city) Defiance County	1	0.01
Marietta (city) Washington County	1	0.01

Top 10 Places Sorted by Percent of Total Population
Based on all places, regardless of total population

Place	Population	%
Hebron (village) Licking County	1	0.04
Huber Heights (city) Montgomery County	5	0.01
Green (city) Summit County	3	0.01
Sandusky (city) Erie County	3	0.01
Amherst (city) Lorain County	1	0.01
Berea (city) Cuyahoga County	1	0.01
Defiance (city) Defiance County	1	0.01
Marietta (city) Washington County	1	0.01
Cleveland (city) Cuyahoga County	3	<0.01
Columbus (city) Franklin County	2	<0.01

Top 10 Places Sorted by Percent of Total Population
Based on places with total population of 50,000 or more

Place	Population	%
Cleveland (city) Cuyahoga County	3	<0.01
Columbus (city) Franklin County	2	<0.01
Akron (city) Summit County	0	0.00
Canton (city) Stark County	0	0.00
Cincinnati (city) Hamilton County	0	0.00
Dayton (city) Montgomery County	0	0.00
Elyria (city) Lorain County	0	0.00
Hamilton (city) Butler County	0	0.00
Kettering (city) Montgomery County	0	0.00
Lakewood (city) Cuyahoga County	0	0.00

Asian

Top 10 Places Sorted by Population
Based on all places, regardless of total population

Place	Population	%
Columbus (city) Franklin County	37,743	4.80
Cleveland (city) Cuyahoga County	8,705	2.19
Dublin (city) Franklin County	6,891	16.50
Cincinnati (city) Hamilton County	6,875	2.32
Akron (city) Summit County	5,081	2.55
Toledo (city) Lucas County	4,559	1.59
Beavercreek (city) Greene County	3,170	7.01
Mason (city) Warren County	3,049	9.93
Solon (city) Cuyahoga County	2,491	10.67
Cleveland Heights (city) Cuyahoga County	2,267	4.92

Top 10 Places Sorted by Percent of Total Population
Based on all places, regardless of total population

Place	Population	%
Dublin (city) Franklin County	6,891	16.50
Sixteen Mile Stand (cdp) Hamilton County	435	14.86
Remington (cdp) Hamilton County	41	12.50
Blue Ash (city) Hamilton County	1,406	11.61
Glenwillow (village) Cuyahoga County	102	11.05
Solon (city) Cuyahoga County	2,491	10.67
Mason (city) Warren County	3,049	9.93
Powell (city) Delaware County	955	8.30
Beachwood (city) Cuyahoga County	939	7.86
New Albany (village) Franklin County	601	7.78

Top 10 Places Sorted by Percent of Total Population
Based on places with total population of 50,000 or more

Place	Population	%
Columbus (city) Franklin County	37,743	4.80
Lakewood (city) Cuyahoga County	1,344	2.58
Akron (city) Summit County	5,081	2.55
Parma (city) Cuyahoga County	1,920	2.35
Cincinnati (city) Hamilton County	6,875	2.32
Cleveland (city) Cuyahoga County	8,705	2.19
Kettering (city) Montgomery County	1,101	1.96
Toledo (city) Lucas County	4,559	1.59
Dayton (city) Montgomery County	1,864	1.32
Elyria (city) Lorain County	628	1.15

Asian: Not Hispanic

Top 10 Places Sorted by Population
Based on all places, regardless of total population

Place	Population	%
Columbus (city) Franklin County	37,170	4.72
Cleveland (city) Cuyahoga County	8,422	2.12
Dublin (city) Franklin County	6,866	16.45
Cincinnati (city) Hamilton County	6,728	2.27
Akron (city) Summit County	5,008	2.52
Toledo (city) Lucas County	4,312	1.50
Beavercreek (city) Greene County	3,130	6.93
Mason (city) Warren County	3,035	9.88
Solon (city) Cuyahoga County	2,482	10.63
Cleveland Heights (city) Cuyahoga County	2,236	4.85

Top 10 Places Sorted by Percent of Total Population
Based on all places, regardless of total population

Place	Population	%
Dublin (city) Franklin County	6,866	16.45
Sixteen Mile Stand (cdp) Hamilton County	433	14.79
Remington (cdp) Hamilton County	41	12.50

Blue Ash (city) Hamilton County	1,393	11.50
Glenwillow (village) Cuyahoga County	102	11.05
Solon (city) Cuyahoga County	2,482	10.63
Mason (city) Warren County	3,035	9.88
Powell (city) Delaware County	951	8.27
Beachwood (city) Cuyahoga County	937	7.84
New Albany (village) Franklin County	595	7.70

Top 10 Places Sorted by Percent of Total Population
Based on places with total population of 50,000 or more

Place	Population	%
Columbus (city) Franklin County	37,170	4.72
Lakewood (city) Cuyahoga County	1,323	2.54
Akron (city) Summit County	5,008	2.52
Parma (city) Cuyahoga County	1,891	2.32
Cincinnati (city) Hamilton County	6,728	2.27
Cleveland (city) Cuyahoga County	8,422	2.12
Kettering (city) Montgomery County	1,080	1.92
Toledo (city) Lucas County	4,312	1.50
Dayton (city) Montgomery County	1,813	1.28
Elyria (city) Lorain County	590	1.08

Asian: Hispanic

Top 10 Places Sorted by Population
Based on all places, regardless of total population

Place	Population	%
Columbus (city) Franklin County	573	0.07
Cleveland (city) Cuyahoga County	283	0.07
Toledo (city) Lucas County	247	0.09
Cincinnati (city) Hamilton County	147	0.05
Lorain (city) Lorain County	86	0.13
Akron (city) Summit County	73	0.04
Dayton (city) Montgomery County	51	0.04
Youngstown (city) Mahoning County	50	0.07
Beavercreek (city) Greene County	40	0.09
Elyria (city) Lorain County	38	0.07

Top 10 Places Sorted by Percent of Total Population
Based on all places, regardless of total population

Place	Population	%
Burgoon (village) Sandusky County	1	0.58
Congress (village) Wayne County	1	0.54
Woodmere (village) Cuyahoga County	4	0.45
Spencer (village) Medina County	3	0.40
Pettisville (cdp) Fulton County	2	0.40
North Fairfield (village) Huron County	2	0.36
Collins (cdp) Huron County	2	0.32
Rockford (village) Mercer County	3	0.27
Cumberland (village) Guernsey County	1	0.27
Whites Landing (cdp) Erie County	1	0.27

Top 10 Places Sorted by Percent of Total Population
Based on places with total population of 50,000 or more

Place	Population	%
Lorain (city) Lorain County	86	0.13
Toledo (city) Lucas County	247	0.09
Columbus (city) Franklin County	573	0.07
Cleveland (city) Cuyahoga County	283	0.07
Youngstown (city) Mahoning County	50	0.07
Elyria (city) Lorain County	38	0.07
Cincinnati (city) Hamilton County	147	0.05
Springfield (city) Clark County	33	0.05
Akron (city) Summit County	73	0.04
Dayton (city) Montgomery County	51	0.04

Asian: Bangladeshi

Top 10 Places Sorted by Population
Based on all places, regardless of total population

Place	Population	%
Columbus (city) Franklin County	366	0.05
Dublin (city) Franklin County	53	0.13
Hilliard (city) Franklin County	28	0.10
Cincinnati (city) Hamilton County	25	0.01
Akron (city) Summit County	15	0.01
Kenwood (cdp) Hamilton County	12	0.17
Twinsburg (city) Summit County	12	0.06
Fairborn (city) Greene County	12	0.04
Strongsville (city) Cuyahoga County	12	0.03
Parma Heights (city) Cuyahoga County	11	0.05

Top 10 Places Sorted by Percent of Total Population
Based on all places, regardless of total population

Place	Population	%
Peninsula (village) Summit County	3	0.53
Concorde Hills (cdp) Hamilton County	3	0.45
Pigeon Creek (cdp) Summit County	3	0.34
Woodmere (village) Cuyahoga County	2	0.23
Northfield (village) Summit County	8	0.22
Obetz (village) Franklin County	9	0.20
Kenwood (cdp) Hamilton County	12	0.17
Dublin (city) Franklin County	53	0.13
Hilliard (city) Franklin County	28	0.10
Lake Darby (cdp) Franklin County	4	0.09

Top 10 Places Sorted by Percent of Total Population
Based on places with total population of 50,000 or more

Place	Population	%
Columbus (city) Franklin County	366	0.05
Lakewood (city) Cuyahoga County	8	0.02
Cincinnati (city) Hamilton County	25	0.01
Akron (city) Summit County	15	0.01
Dayton (city) Montgomery County	8	0.01
Kettering (city) Montgomery County	3	0.01
Cleveland (city) Cuyahoga County	11	<0.01
Toledo (city) Lucas County	5	<0.01
Canton (city) Stark County	1	<0.01
Parma (city) Cuyahoga County	1	<0.01

Asian: Bhutanese

Top 10 Places Sorted by Population
Based on all places, regardless of total population

Place	Population	%
Akron (city) Summit County	318	0.16
Columbus (city) Franklin County	96	0.01
Cleveland (city) Cuyahoga County	94	0.02
Cincinnati (city) Hamilton County	74	0.02
South Euclid (city) Cuyahoga County	55	0.25
Cuyahoga Falls (city) Summit County	54	0.11
Lakewood (city) Cuyahoga County	49	0.09
Cleveland Heights (city) Cuyahoga County	48	0.10
Finneytown (cdp) Hamilton County	25	0.20
White Oak (cdp) Hamilton County	16	0.08

Top 10 Places Sorted by Percent of Total Population
Based on all places, regardless of total population

Place	Population	%
South Euclid (city) Cuyahoga County	55	0.25
Finneytown (cdp) Hamilton County	25	0.20
Akron (city) Summit County	318	0.16
Cuyahoga Falls (city) Summit County	54	0.11
Cleveland Heights (city) Cuyahoga County	48	0.10
Lakewood (city) Cuyahoga County	49	0.09
White Oak (cdp) Hamilton County	16	0.08
Hiram (village) Portage County	1	0.07
Kent (city) Portage County	15	0.05
Monfort Heights (cdp) Hamilton County	6	0.05

Top 10 Places Sorted by Percent of Total Population
Based on places with total population of 50,000 or more

Place	Population	%
Akron (city) Summit County	318	0.16
Lakewood (city) Cuyahoga County	49	0.09
Cleveland (city) Cuyahoga County	94	0.02
Cincinnati (city) Hamilton County	74	0.02
Columbus (city) Franklin County	96	0.01
Canton (city) Stark County	0	0.00
Dayton (city) Montgomery County	0	0.00
Elyria (city) Lorain County	0	0.00
Hamilton (city) Butler County	0	0.00
Kettering (city) Montgomery County	0	0.00

Asian: Burmese

Top 10 Places Sorted by Population
Based on all places, regardless of total population

Place	Population	%
Akron (city) Summit County	603	0.30
Columbus (city) Franklin County	204	0.03
Lakewood (city) Cuyahoga County	146	0.28
Cleveland (city) Cuyahoga County	69	0.02
Blue Ash (city) Hamilton County	26	0.21
Montgomery (city) Hamilton County	17	0.17
Cincinnati (city) Hamilton County	13	<0.01
Strongsville (city) Cuyahoga County	12	0.03
Dover (city) Tuscarawas County	10	0.08
Madeira (city) Hamilton County	9	0.10

Top 10 Places Sorted by Percent of Total Population
Based on all places, regardless of total population

Place	Population	%
Akron (city) Summit County	603	0.30
Lakewood (city) Cuyahoga County	146	0.28
Blue Ash (city) Hamilton County	26	0.21
Montgomery (city) Hamilton County	17	0.17
Hiram (village) Portage County	2	0.14
Madeira (city) Hamilton County	9	0.10
Deer Park (city) Hamilton County	5	0.09
Dover (city) Tuscarawas County	10	0.08
Lincoln Village (cdp) Franklin County	7	0.08
Pleasant Run (cdp) Hamilton County	4	0.08

Top 10 Places Sorted by Percent of Total Population
Based on places with total population of 50,000 or more

Place	Population	%
Akron (city) Summit County	603	0.30
Lakewood (city) Cuyahoga County	146	0.28
Columbus (city) Franklin County	204	0.03
Cleveland (city) Cuyahoga County	69	0.02
Kettering (city) Montgomery County	7	0.01
Cincinnati (city) Hamilton County	13	<0.01
Toledo (city) Lucas County	5	<0.01
Dayton (city) Montgomery County	2	<0.01
Canton (city) Stark County	1	<0.01
Elyria (city) Lorain County	0	0.00

Asian: Cambodian

Top 10 Places Sorted by Population
Based on all places, regardless of total population

Place	Population	%
Columbus (city) Franklin County	1,794	0.23
Cleveland (city) Cuyahoga County	328	0.08
Cincinnati (city) Hamilton County	212	0.07
Fairfield (city) Butler County	133	0.31
Grove City (city) Franklin County	87	0.24
Akron (city) Summit County	69	0.03
Dayton (city) Montgomery County	59	0.04
Strongsville (city) Cuyahoga County	56	0.13
Pleasant Run (cdp) Hamilton County	54	1.09
Parma (city) Cuyahoga County	54	0.07

Top 10 Places Sorted by Percent of Total Population
Based on all places, regardless of total population

Place	Population	%
Urbancrest (village) Franklin County	23	2.40
Pleasant Run (cdp) Hamilton County	54	1.09
West Elkton (village) Preble County	2	1.02
Rossmoyne (cdp) Hamilton County	17	0.76
Obetz (village) Franklin County	27	0.60
Pleasant Hills (cdp) Hamilton County	3	0.50
Mount Victory (village) Hardin County	3	0.48
Madeira (city) Hamilton County	40	0.46
Kenwood (cdp) Hamilton County	32	0.46
Northgate (cdp) Hamilton County	33	0.45

Top 10 Places Sorted by Percent of Total Population
Based on places with total population of 50,000 or more

Place	Population	%
Columbus (city) Franklin County	1,794	0.23
Cleveland (city) Cuyahoga County	328	0.08
Cincinnati (city) Hamilton County	212	0.07
Parma (city) Cuyahoga County	54	0.07
Dayton (city) Montgomery County	59	0.04
Kettering (city) Montgomery County	23	0.04
Akron (city) Summit County	69	0.03
Hamilton (city) Butler County	12	0.02
Youngstown (city) Mahoning County	9	0.01
Lakewood (city) Cuyahoga County	7	0.01

Asian: Chinese, except Taiwanese

Top 10 Places Sorted by Population
Based on all places, regardless of total population

Place	Population	%
Columbus (city) Franklin County	6,780	0.86
Cleveland (city) Cuyahoga County	2,916	0.73
Cincinnati (city) Hamilton County	1,558	0.52
Dublin (city) Franklin County	1,343	3.22
Toledo (city) Lucas County	1,177	0.41
Solon (city) Cuyahoga County	965	4.13
Athens (city) Athens County	900	3.78
Upper Arlington (city) Franklin County	758	2.24
Oxford (city) Butler County	716	3.35
Mason (city) Warren County	667	2.17

Top 10 Places Sorted by Percent of Total Population
Based on all places, regardless of total population

Place	Population	%
Glenwillow (village) Cuyahoga County	49	5.31
Remington (cdp) Hamilton County	15	4.57
Solon (city) Cuyahoga County	965	4.13
Athens (city) Athens County	900	3.78
Oxford (city) Butler County	716	3.35
Harbor View (village) Lucas County	4	3.25
Dublin (city) Franklin County	1,343	3.22
Beachwood (city) Cuyahoga County	303	2.53
Bairdstown (village) Wood County	3	2.31
Upper Arlington (city) Franklin County	758	2.24

Top 10 Places Sorted by Percent of Total Population
Based on places with total population of 50,000 or more

Place	Population	%
Columbus (city) Franklin County	6,780	0.86
Cleveland (city) Cuyahoga County	2,916	0.73
Cincinnati (city) Hamilton County	1,558	0.52
Toledo (city) Lucas County	1,177	0.41
Lakewood (city) Cuyahoga County	189	0.36
Kettering (city) Montgomery County	197	0.35
Akron (city) Summit County	607	0.30
Parma (city) Cuyahoga County	218	0.27
Dayton (city) Montgomery County	324	0.23
Springfield (city) Clark County	97	0.16

Asian: Filipino

Top 10 Places Sorted by Population
Based on all places, regardless of total population

Place	Population	%
Columbus (city) Franklin County	2,827	0.36
Cleveland (city) Cuyahoga County	937	0.24
Cincinnati (city) Hamilton County	718	0.24
Toledo (city) Lucas County	610	0.21
Parma (city) Cuyahoga County	515	0.63
Huber Heights (city) Montgomery County	382	1.00
Beavercreek (city) Greene County	347	0.77
Dayton (city) Montgomery County	334	0.24
Akron (city) Summit County	317	0.16
Elyria (city) Lorain County	273	0.50

Top 10 Places Sorted by Percent of Total Population
Based on all places, regardless of total population

Place	Population	%
Bairdstown (village) Wood County	5	3.85
Melmore (cdp) Seneca County	4	2.61
Wright-Patterson AFB (cdp) Greene County	43	2.36
Hills and Dales (village) Stark County	5	2.26
Beulah Beach (cdp) Erie County	1	1.89
Milledgeville (village) Fayette County	2	1.79
Vaughnsville (cdp) Putnam County	4	1.53
Lockington (village) Shelby County	2	1.42
Deersville (village) Harrison County	1	1.27
Pleasantville (village) Fairfield County	11	1.15

Top 10 Places Sorted by Percent of Total Population
Based on places with total population of 50,000 or more

Place	Population	%
Parma (city) Cuyahoga County	515	0.63
Elyria (city) Lorain County	273	0.50
Kettering (city) Montgomery County	213	0.38
Columbus (city) Franklin County	2,827	0.36
Hamilton (city) Butler County	164	0.26
Lakewood (city) Cuyahoga County	137	0.26
Cleveland (city) Cuyahoga County	937	0.24
Cincinnati (city) Hamilton County	718	0.24
Dayton (city) Montgomery County	334	0.24
Toledo (city) Lucas County	610	0.21

Asian: Hmong

Top 10 Places Sorted by Population
Based on all places, regardless of total population

Place	Population	%
Akron (city) Summit County	362	0.18
Columbus (city) Franklin County	51	0.01
Green (city) Summit County	31	0.12
New Franklin (city) Summit County	12	0.08
Medina (city) Medina County	7	0.03
Cleveland (city) Cuyahoga County	7	<0.01
Lorain (city) Lorain County	6	0.01
Tallmadge (city) Summit County	5	0.03
Athens (city) Athens County	5	0.02
Upper Arlington (city) Franklin County	4	0.01

Top 10 Places Sorted by Percent of Total Population
Based on all places, regardless of total population

Place	Population	%
Holloway (village) Belmont County	1	0.30
Akron (city) Summit County	362	0.18
Green (city) Summit County	31	0.12
New Franklin (city) Summit County	12	0.08
Silver Lake (village) Summit County	2	0.08
Hiram (village) Portage County	1	0.07
Fairport Harbor (village) Lake County	2	0.06
West Union (village) Adams County	2	0.06
Weston (village) Wood County	1	0.06
Medina (city) Medina County	7	0.03

Top 10 Places Sorted by Percent of Total Population
Based on places with total population of 50,000 or more

Place	Population	%
Akron (city) Summit County	362	0.18
Columbus (city) Franklin County	51	0.01
Lorain (city) Lorain County	6	0.01
Cleveland (city) Cuyahoga County	7	<0.01
Toledo (city) Lucas County	4	<0.01
Cincinnati (city) Hamilton County	3	<0.01
Youngstown (city) Mahoning County	3	<0.01
Canton (city) Stark County	1	<0.01
Dayton (city) Montgomery County	0	0.00
Elyria (city) Lorain County	0	0.00

Asian: Indian

Top 10 Places Sorted by Population
Based on all places, regardless of total population

Place	Population	%
Columbus (city) Franklin County	11,364	1.44
Dublin (city) Franklin County	2,986	7.15
Cincinnati (city) Hamilton County	2,036	0.69
Cleveland (city) Cuyahoga County	1,649	0.42
Mason (city) Warren County	1,384	4.51
Beavercreek (city) Greene County	1,127	2.49
Solon (city) Cuyahoga County	1,107	4.74
Toledo (city) Lucas County	995	0.35
Strongsville (city) Cuyahoga County	971	2.17
Akron (city) Summit County	874	0.44

Top 10 Places Sorted by Percent of Total Population
Based on all places, regardless of total population

Place	Population	%
Dublin (city) Franklin County	2,986	7.15
Blue Ash (city) Hamilton County	807	6.66
Sixteen Mile Stand (cdp) Hamilton County	185	6.32
Glenwillow (village) Cuyahoga County	50	5.42
Northfield (village) Summit County	179	4.87
Solon (city) Cuyahoga County	1,107	4.74
Powell (city) Delaware County	530	4.61
Mason (city) Warren County	1,384	4.51
Wetherington (cdp) Butler County	58	4.45
Mayfield Heights (city) Cuyahoga County	836	4.36

Top 10 Places Sorted by Percent of Total Population
Based on places with total population of 50,000 or more

Place	Population	%
Columbus (city) Franklin County	11,364	1.44
Parma (city) Cuyahoga County	630	0.77
Cincinnati (city) Hamilton County	2,036	0.69
Lakewood (city) Cuyahoga County	277	0.53
Akron (city) Summit County	874	0.44
Cleveland (city) Cuyahoga County	1,649	0.42
Toledo (city) Lucas County	995	0.35
Springfield (city) Clark County	196	0.32
Kettering (city) Montgomery County	182	0.32
Dayton (city) Montgomery County	281	0.20

Asian: Indonesian

Top 10 Places Sorted by Population
Based on all places, regardless of total population

Place	Population	%
Columbus (city) Franklin County	326	0.04
Athens (city) Athens County	41	0.17
Hilliard (city) Franklin County	38	0.13
Cincinnati (city) Hamilton County	31	0.01
Dublin (city) Franklin County	30	0.07
Toledo (city) Lucas County	28	0.01
Cleveland (city) Cuyahoga County	25	0.01
Upper Arlington (city) Franklin County	23	0.07
Lakewood (city) Cuyahoga County	21	0.04
Akron (city) Summit County	20	0.01

Top 10 Places Sorted by Percent of Total Population
Based on all places, regardless of total population

Place	Population	%
Amesville (village) Athens County	7	4.55
Glenwillow (village) Cuyahoga County	3	0.33
Lake Lorelei (cdp) Brown County	3	0.26
Clarktown (cdp) Scioto County	2	0.21
Highpoint (cdp) Hamilton County	3	0.20
Rushsylvania (village) Logan County	1	0.19
Athens (city) Athens County	41	0.17
McConnelsville (village) Morgan County	3	0.17
Hilliard (city) Franklin County	38	0.13
Atwater (cdp) Portage County	1	0.13

Top 10 Places Sorted by Percent of Total Population
Based on places with total population of 50,000 or more

Place	Population	%
Columbus (city) Franklin County	326	0.04
Lakewood (city) Cuyahoga County	21	0.04
Kettering (city) Montgomery County	13	0.02
Hamilton (city) Butler County	11	0.02
Cincinnati (city) Hamilton County	31	0.01
Toledo (city) Lucas County	28	0.01
Cleveland (city) Cuyahoga County	25	0.01
Akron (city) Summit County	20	0.01
Dayton (city) Montgomery County	16	0.01
Springfield (city) Clark County	6	0.01

Asian: Japanese

Top 10 Places Sorted by Population
Based on all places, regardless of total population

Place	Population	%
Columbus (city) Franklin County	2,331	0.30
Dublin (city) Franklin County	1,154	2.76
Cincinnati (city) Hamilton County	399	0.13
Cleveland (city) Cuyahoga County	349	0.09
Findlay (city) Hancock County	274	0.67
Toledo (city) Lucas County	272	0.09
Troy (city) Miami County	251	1.00
Beavercreek (city) Greene County	214	0.47
Akron (city) Summit County	207	0.10
Sidney (city) Shelby County	178	0.84

Top 10 Places Sorted by Percent of Total Population
Based on all places, regardless of total population

Place	Population	%
Batesville (village) Noble County	2	2.82
Dublin (city) Franklin County	1,154	2.76
Deersville (village) Harrison County	2	2.53

Sugar Bush Knolls (village) Portage County	4	2.26
Sixteen Mile Stand (cdp) Hamilton County	65	2.22
Hollansburg (village) Darke County	3	1.32
Melmore (cdp) Seneca County	2	1.31
Buckland (village) Auglaize County	3	1.29
Carbon Hill (cdp) Hocking County	3	1.29
Woodmere (village) Cuyahoga County	11	1.24

Top 10 Places Sorted by Percent of Total Population
Based on places with total population of 50,000 or more

Place	Population	%
Columbus (city) Franklin County	2,331	0.30
Kettering (city) Montgomery County	119	0.21
Lakewood (city) Cuyahoga County	95	0.18
Cincinnati (city) Hamilton County	399	0.13
Parma (city) Cuyahoga County	86	0.11
Springfield (city) Clark County	68	0.11
Akron (city) Summit County	207	0.10
Dayton (city) Montgomery County	147	0.10
Cleveland (city) Cuyahoga County	349	0.09
Toledo (city) Lucas County	272	0.09

Asian: Korean

Top 10 Places Sorted by Population
Based on all places, regardless of total population

Place	Population	%
Columbus (city) Franklin County	3,330	0.42
Cincinnati (city) Hamilton County	674	0.23
Dublin (city) Franklin County	611	1.46
Cleveland (city) Cuyahoga County	533	0.13
Beavercreek (city) Greene County	410	0.91
Toledo (city) Lucas County	382	0.13
Akron (city) Summit County	252	0.13
Upper Arlington (city) Franklin County	214	0.63
Mason (city) Warren County	192	0.63
Cleveland Heights (city) Cuyahoga County	186	0.40

Top 10 Places Sorted by Percent of Total Population
Based on all places, regardless of total population

Place	Population	%
Remington (cdp) Hamilton County	7	2.13
Sixteen Mile Stand (cdp) Hamilton County	53	1.81
Brice (village) Franklin County	2	1.75
Dublin (city) Franklin County	611	1.46
Lafayette (village) Allen County	6	1.35
Plumwood (cdp) Madison County	4	1.25
Sugar Bush Knolls (village) Portage County	2	1.13
Oberlin (city) Lorain County	85	1.03
West Elkton (village) Preble County	2	1.02
Beachwood (city) Cuyahoga County	110	0.92

Top 10 Places Sorted by Percent of Total Population
Based on places with total population of 50,000 or more

Place	Population	%
Columbus (city) Franklin County	3,330	0.42
Cincinnati (city) Hamilton County	674	0.23
Kettering (city) Montgomery County	124	0.22
Lakewood (city) Cuyahoga County	96	0.18
Elyria (city) Lorain County	76	0.14
Cleveland (city) Cuyahoga County	533	0.13
Toledo (city) Lucas County	382	0.13
Akron (city) Summit County	252	0.13
Dayton (city) Montgomery County	184	0.13
Parma (city) Cuyahoga County	86	0.11

Asian: Laotian

Top 10 Places Sorted by Population
Based on all places, regardless of total population

Place	Population	%
Columbus (city) Franklin County	1,412	0.18
Akron (city) Summit County	388	0.19
Findlay (city) Hancock County	133	0.32
Toledo (city) Lucas County	129	0.04
Cleveland (city) Cuyahoga County	108	0.03
Orrville (city) Wayne County	76	0.91
Reynoldsburg (city) Franklin County	70	0.20
Whitehall (city) Franklin County	56	0.31
Groveport (village) Franklin County	49	0.91
Blacklick Estates (cdp) Franklin County	47	0.54

Top 10 Places Sorted by Percent of Total Population
Based on all places, regardless of total population

Place	Population	%
Unionville Center (village) Union County	6	2.58
Maplewood Park (cdp) Trumbull County	3	1.07
Carey (village) Wyandot County	35	0.95
Orrville (city) Wayne County	76	0.91
Groveport (village) Franklin County	49	0.91
Montpelier (village) Williams County	37	0.91
Pettisville (cdp) Fulton County	4	0.80
Luckey (village) Wood County	8	0.79
New Haven (cdp) Huron County	3	0.75
Etna (cdp) Licking County	9	0.74

Top 10 Places Sorted by Percent of Total Population
Based on places with total population of 50,000 or more

Place	Population	%
Akron (city) Summit County	388	0.19
Columbus (city) Franklin County	1,412	0.18
Toledo (city) Lucas County	129	0.04
Springfield (city) Clark County	22	0.04
Cleveland (city) Cuyahoga County	108	0.03
Parma (city) Cuyahoga County	18	0.02
Youngstown (city) Mahoning County	10	0.01
Kettering (city) Montgomery County	7	0.01
Lakewood (city) Cuyahoga County	6	0.01
Cincinnati (city) Hamilton County	14	<0.01

Asian: Malaysian

Top 10 Places Sorted by Population
Based on all places, regardless of total population

Place	Population	%
Columbus (city) Franklin County	121	0.02
Toledo (city) Lucas County	22	0.01
Mason (city) Warren County	17	0.06
Athens (city) Athens County	12	0.05
Cleveland (city) Cuyahoga County	12	<0.01
Kent (city) Portage County	10	0.03
Dayton (city) Montgomery County	9	0.01
Akron (city) Summit County	9	<0.01
Beavercreek (city) Greene County	8	0.02
Oxford (city) Butler County	7	0.03

Top 10 Places Sorted by Percent of Total Population
Based on all places, regardless of total population

Place	Population	%
Northfield (village) Summit County	6	0.16
Bremen (village) Fairfield County	2	0.14
Chauncey (village) Athens County	1	0.10
Sunbury (village) Delaware County	4	0.09
Ada (village) Hardin County	4	0.07
Mason (city) Warren County	17	0.06
Athens (city) Athens County	12	0.05
Worthington (city) Franklin County	6	0.04
Montgomery (city) Hamilton County	4	0.04
Fairlawn (city) Summit County	3	0.04

Top 10 Places Sorted by Percent of Total Population
Based on places with total population of 50,000 or more

Place	Population	%
Columbus (city) Franklin County	121	0.02
Toledo (city) Lucas County	22	0.01
Dayton (city) Montgomery County	9	0.01
Kettering (city) Montgomery County	3	0.01
Cleveland (city) Cuyahoga County	12	<0.01
Akron (city) Summit County	9	<0.01
Cincinnati (city) Hamilton County	5	<0.01
Elyria (city) Lorain County	2	<0.01
Canton (city) Stark County	0	0.00
Hamilton (city) Butler County	0	0.00

Asian: Nepalese

Top 10 Places Sorted by Population
Based on all places, regardless of total population

Place	Population	%
Columbus (city) Franklin County	190	0.02
Cleveland (city) Cuyahoga County	108	0.03
Akron (city) Summit County	85	0.04
Cincinnati (city) Hamilton County	77	0.03
Kent (city) Portage County	39	0.13
Toledo (city) Lucas County	36	0.01
Cleveland Heights (city) Cuyahoga County	34	0.07
Lakewood (city) Cuyahoga County	29	0.06
Upper Arlington (city) Franklin County	23	0.07
South Euclid (city) Cuyahoga County	22	0.10

Top 10 Places Sorted by Percent of Total Population
Based on all places, regardless of total population

Place	Population	%
Derby (cdp) Pickaway County	4	0.98
Hiram (village) Portage County	13	0.92
Harrisburg (village) Franklin County	1	0.31
Kent (city) Portage County	39	0.13
South Euclid (city) Cuyahoga County	22	0.10
Oxford (city) Butler County	21	0.10
Sixteen Mile Stand (cdp) Hamilton County	3	0.10
Ottawa Hills (village) Lucas County	4	0.09
Montgomery (city) Hamilton County	8	0.08
Cleveland Heights (city) Cuyahoga County	34	0.07

Top 10 Places Sorted by Percent of Total Population
Based on places with total population of 50,000 or more

Place	Population	%
Lakewood (city) Cuyahoga County	29	0.06
Akron (city) Summit County	85	0.04
Cleveland (city) Cuyahoga County	108	0.03
Cincinnati (city) Hamilton County	77	0.03
Columbus (city) Franklin County	190	0.02
Toledo (city) Lucas County	36	0.01
Youngstown (city) Mahoning County	7	0.01
Parma (city) Cuyahoga County	5	0.01
Dayton (city) Montgomery County	4	<0.01
Hamilton (city) Butler County	3	<0.01

Asian: Pakistani

Top 10 Places Sorted by Population
Based on all places, regardless of total population

Place	Population	%
Columbus (city) Franklin County	927	0.12
Mason (city) Warren County	190	0.62
Hilliard (city) Franklin County	177	0.62
Cincinnati (city) Hamilton County	125	0.04
Beavercreek (city) Greene County	113	0.25
Dublin (city) Franklin County	105	0.25
Westlake (city) Cuyahoga County	98	0.30
Toledo (city) Lucas County	97	0.03
Pickerington (city) Fairfield County	89	0.49
Lakewood (city) Cuyahoga County	75	0.14

Top 10 Places Sorted by Percent of Total Population
Based on all places, regardless of total population

Place	Population	%
Mineral City (village) Tuscarawas County	7	0.96
Brady Lake (village) Portage County	4	0.86
Orange (village) Cuyahoga County	25	0.75
Mason (city) Warren County	190	0.62
Hilliard (city) Franklin County	177	0.62
Sixteen Mile Stand (cdp) Hamilton County	17	0.58
Etna (cdp) Licking County	7	0.58
Millbury (village) Wood County	6	0.50
Pickerington (city) Fairfield County	89	0.49
Bentleyville (village) Cuyahoga County	4	0.46

Top 10 Places Sorted by Percent of Total Population
Based on places with total population of 50,000 or more

Place	Population	%
Lakewood (city) Cuyahoga County	75	0.14
Columbus (city) Franklin County	927	0.12
Springfield (city) Clark County	38	0.06
Cincinnati (city) Hamilton County	125	0.04
Kettering (city) Montgomery County	21	0.04
Toledo (city) Lucas County	97	0.03
Parma (city) Cuyahoga County	21	0.03
Cleveland (city) Cuyahoga County	61	0.02
Dayton (city) Montgomery County	30	0.02
Youngstown (city) Mahoning County	12	0.02

Asian: Sri Lankan

Top 10 Places Sorted by Population

Based on all places, regardless of total population

Place	Population	%
Columbus (city) Franklin County	202	0.03
Cincinnati (city) Hamilton County	82	0.03
Dublin (city) Franklin County	35	0.08
Hilliard (city) Franklin County	21	0.07
Akron (city) Summit County	18	0.01
Toledo (city) Lucas County	18	0.01
Cleveland (city) Cuyahoga County	18	<0.01
Cleveland Heights (city) Cuyahoga County	17	0.04
Beavercreek (city) Greene County	16	0.04
Mason (city) Warren County	15	0.05

Top 10 Places Sorted by Percent of Total Population

Based on all places, regardless of total population

Place	Population	%
Fairfax (village) Hamilton County	9	0.53
Four Bridges (cdp) Butler County	11	0.38
Gates Mills (village) Cuyahoga County	4	0.18
Union City (village) Darke County	3	0.18
Kenwood (cdp) Hamilton County	9	0.13
Fairlawn (city) Summit County	9	0.12
Greentown (cdp) Stark County	4	0.11
Sixteen Mile Stand (cdp) Hamilton County	3	0.10
Dublin (city) Franklin County	35	0.08
Dry Run (cdp) Hamilton County	6	0.08

Top 10 Places Sorted by Percent of Total Population

Based on places with total population of 50,000 or more

Place	Population	%
Columbus (city) Franklin County	202	0.03
Cincinnati (city) Hamilton County	82	0.03
Akron (city) Summit County	18	0.01
Toledo (city) Lucas County	18	0.01
Dayton (city) Montgomery County	9	0.01
Elyria (city) Lorain County	8	0.01
Parma (city) Cuyahoga County	8	0.01
Cleveland (city) Cuyahoga County	18	<0.01
Kettering (city) Montgomery County	2	<0.01
Springfield (city) Clark County	2	<0.01

Asian: Taiwanese

Top 10 Places Sorted by Population

Based on all places, regardless of total population

Place	Population	%
Columbus (city) Franklin County	626	0.08
Cincinnati (city) Hamilton County	122	0.04
Dublin (city) Franklin County	121	0.29
Upper Arlington (city) Franklin County	109	0.32
Cleveland (city) Cuyahoga County	102	0.03
Cleveland Heights (city) Cuyahoga County	83	0.18
Mason (city) Warren County	56	0.18
Akron (city) Summit County	54	0.03
Solon (city) Cuyahoga County	52	0.22
Beavercreek (city) Greene County	52	0.12

Top 10 Places Sorted by Percent of Total Population

Based on all places, regardless of total population

Place	Population	%
Evendale (village) Hamilton County	18	0.65
Sixteen Mile Stand (cdp) Hamilton County	17	0.58
Pigeon Creek (cdp) Summit County	3	0.34
Upper Arlington (city) Franklin County	109	0.32
The Village of Indian Hill (city) Hamilton County	18	0.31
Dublin (city) Franklin County	121	0.29
Blue Ash (city) Hamilton County	31	0.26
Oberlin (city) Lorain County	21	0.25
Solon (city) Cuyahoga County	52	0.22
Wyoming (city) Hamilton County	18	0.21

Top 10 Places Sorted by Percent of Total Population

Based on places with total population of 50,000 or more

Place	Population	%
Columbus (city) Franklin County	626	0.08
Cincinnati (city) Hamilton County	122	0.04
Cleveland (city) Cuyahoga County	102	0.03
Akron (city) Summit County	54	0.03
Kettering (city) Montgomery County	15	0.03
Lakewood (city) Cuyahoga County	8	0.02
Toledo (city) Lucas County	30	0.01
Dayton (city) Montgomery County	12	0.01
Elyria (city) Lorain County	3	0.01
Parma (city) Cuyahoga County	4	<0.01

Asian: Thai

Top 10 Places Sorted by Population

Based on all places, regardless of total population

Place	Population	%
Columbus (city) Franklin County	594	0.08
Cincinnati (city) Hamilton County	143	0.05
Cleveland (city) Cuyahoga County	121	0.03
Akron (city) Summit County	116	0.06
Toledo (city) Lucas County	116	0.04
Cleveland Heights (city) Cuyahoga County	68	0.15
Fairborn (city) Greene County	63	0.19
Dayton (city) Montgomery County	54	0.04
Huber Heights (city) Montgomery County	49	0.13
Lakewood (city) Cuyahoga County	47	0.09

Top 10 Places Sorted by Percent of Total Population

Based on all places, regardless of total population

Place	Population	%
Kimbolton (cdp) Guernsey County	2	1.39
Etna (cdp) Licking County	6	0.49
Crown City (village) Gallia County	2	0.48
Hebron (village) Licking County	11	0.47
Albany (village) Athens County	3	0.36
Green Meadows (cdp) Clark County	8	0.34
New Vienna (village) Clinton County	4	0.33
Donnelsville (village) Clark County	1	0.33
Minerva Park (village) Franklin County	4	0.31
Urbancrest (village) Franklin County	3	0.31

Top 10 Places Sorted by Percent of Total Population

Based on places with total population of 50,000 or more

Place	Population	%
Lakewood (city) Cuyahoga County	47	0.09
Columbus (city) Franklin County	594	0.08
Akron (city) Summit County	116	0.06
Cincinnati (city) Hamilton County	143	0.05
Kettering (city) Montgomery County	26	0.05
Toledo (city) Lucas County	116	0.04
Dayton (city) Montgomery County	54	0.04
Cleveland (city) Cuyahoga County	121	0.03
Hamilton (city) Butler County	19	0.03
Springfield (city) Clark County	16	0.03

Asian: Vietnamese

Top 10 Places Sorted by Population

Based on all places, regardless of total population

Place	Population	%
Columbus (city) Franklin County	2,319	0.29
Cleveland (city) Cuyahoga County	990	0.25
Akron (city) Summit County	474	0.24
Cincinnati (city) Hamilton County	359	0.12
Huber Heights (city) Montgomery County	294	0.77
Toledo (city) Lucas County	286	0.10
Fairfield (city) Butler County	224	0.53
Dayton (city) Montgomery County	220	0.16
Brooklyn (city) Cuyahoga County	193	1.73
Beavercreek (city) Greene County	188	0.42

Top 10 Places Sorted by Percent of Total Population

Based on all places, regardless of total population

Place	Population	%
Brooklyn (city) Cuyahoga County	193	1.73
West Leipsic (village) Putnam County	3	1.46
Sheffield (village) Lorain County	50	1.26
Galena (village) Delaware County	7	1.07
Beckett Ridge (cdp) Butler County	92	1.00
Waldo (village) Marion County	3	0.89
Springdale (city) Hamilton County	92	0.82
Four Bridges (cdp) Butler County	23	0.79
Huber Heights (city) Montgomery County	294	0.77
Bettsville (village) Seneca County	5	0.76

Top 10 Places Sorted by Percent of Total Population

Based on places with total population of 50,000 or more

Place	Population	%
Columbus (city) Franklin County	2,319	0.29
Cleveland (city) Cuyahoga County	990	0.25
Akron (city) Summit County	474	0.24
Parma (city) Cuyahoga County	176	0.22
Kettering (city) Montgomery County	116	0.21
Dayton (city) Montgomery County	220	0.16
Hamilton (city) Butler County	98	0.16
Cincinnati (city) Hamilton County	359	0.12
Lakewood (city) Cuyahoga County	62	0.12
Toledo (city) Lucas County	286	0.10

Hawaii Native/Pacific Islander

Top 10 Places Sorted by Population

Based on all places, regardless of total population

Place	Population	%
Columbus (city) Franklin County	1,346	0.17
Cleveland (city) Cuyahoga County	582	0.15
Cincinnati (city) Hamilton County	465	0.16
Toledo (city) Lucas County	275	0.10
Akron (city) Summit County	189	0.09
Dayton (city) Montgomery County	166	0.12
Hamilton (city) Butler County	104	0.17
Dover (city) Tuscarawas County	100	0.78
Urbancrest (village) Franklin County	97	10.10
Springfield (city) Clark County	96	0.16

Top 10 Places Sorted by Percent of Total Population

Based on all places, regardless of total population

Place	Population	%
Urbancrest (village) Franklin County	97	10.10
Brecon (cdp) Hamilton County	5	2.05
Linndale (village) Cuyahoga County	3	1.68
Haydenville (cdp) Hocking County	6	1.57
Highpoint (cdp) Hamilton County	18	1.20
Kettlersville (village) Shelby County	2	1.12
Zanesfield (village) Logan County	2	1.02
Valleyview (village) Franklin County	6	0.97
Elmwood Place (village) Hamilton County	21	0.96
Plumwood (cdp) Madison County	3	0.94

Top 10 Places Sorted by Percent of Total Population

Based on places with total population of 50,000 or more

Place	Population	%
Columbus (city) Franklin County	1,346	0.17
Hamilton (city) Butler County	104	0.17
Cincinnati (city) Hamilton County	465	0.16
Springfield (city) Clark County	96	0.16
Cleveland (city) Cuyahoga County	582	0.15
Lorain (city) Lorain County	88	0.14
Canton (city) Stark County	93	0.13
Youngstown (city) Mahoning County	87	0.13
Dayton (city) Montgomery County	166	0.12
Elyria (city) Lorain County	65	0.12

Hawaii Native/Pacific Islander: Not Hispanic

Top 10 Places Sorted by Population

Based on all places, regardless of total population

Place	Population	%
Columbus (city) Franklin County	1,149	0.15
Cleveland (city) Cuyahoga County	347	0.09
Cincinnati (city) Hamilton County	344	0.12
Toledo (city) Lucas County	220	0.08
Akron (city) Summit County	164	0.08
Dayton (city) Montgomery County	148	0.10
Urbancrest (village) Franklin County	97	10.10
Hamilton (city) Butler County	82	0.13
Huber Heights (city) Montgomery County	74	0.19
Springfield (city) Clark County	73	0.12

Top 10 Places Sorted by Percent of Total Population

Based on all places, regardless of total population

Place	Population	%
Urbancrest (village) Franklin County	97	10.10
Brecon (cdp) Hamilton County	5	2.05

Linndale (village) Cuyahoga County	3	1.68
Highpoint (cdp) Hamilton County	18	1.20
Kettlersville (village) Shelby County	2	1.12
Zanesfield (village) Logan County	2	1.02
Valleyview (village) Franklin County	6	0.97
Elmwood Place (village) Hamilton County	21	0.96
Plumwood (cdp) Madison County	3	0.94
Polk (village) Ashland County	3	0.89

Top 10 Places Sorted by Percent of Total Population

Based on places with total population of 50,000 or more

Place	Population	%
Columbus (city) Franklin County	1,149	0.15
Hamilton (city) Butler County	82	0.13
Cincinnati (city) Hamilton County	344	0.12
Springfield (city) Clark County	73	0.12
Dayton (city) Montgomery County	148	0.10
Cleveland (city) Cuyahoga County	347	0.09
Parma (city) Cuyahoga County	71	0.09
Canton (city) Stark County	65	0.09
Toledo (city) Lucas County	220	0.08
Akron (city) Summit County	164	0.08

Hawaii Native/Pacific Islander: Hispanic

Top 10 Places Sorted by Population

Based on all places, regardless of total population

Place	Population	%
Cleveland (city) Cuyahoga County	235	0.06
Columbus (city) Franklin County	197	0.03
Cincinnati (city) Hamilton County	121	0.04
Lorain (city) Lorain County	61	0.10
Dover (city) Tuscarawas County	59	0.46
Toledo (city) Lucas County	55	0.02
New Philadelphia (city) Tuscarawas County	50	0.29
Youngstown (city) Mahoning County	33	0.05
Canton (city) Stark County	28	0.04
Akron (city) Summit County	25	0.01

Top 10 Places Sorted by Percent of Total Population

Based on all places, regardless of total population

Place	Population	%
Haydenville (cdp) Hocking County	6	1.57
Celeryville (cdp) Huron County	1	0.48
Dover (city) Tuscarawas County	59	0.46
New Philadelphia (city) Tuscarawas County	50	0.29
Spencer (village) Medina County	2	0.27
Strasburg (village) Tuscarawas County	6	0.23
Lake Tomahawk (cdp) Columbiana County	1	0.21
Hebron (village) Licking County	4	0.17
Calcutta (cdp) Columbiana County	6	0.16
Valley View (village) Cuyahoga County	3	0.15

Top 10 Places Sorted by Percent of Total Population

Based on places with total population of 50,000 or more

Place	Population	%
Lorain (city) Lorain County	61	0.10
Cleveland (city) Cuyahoga County	235	0.06
Youngstown (city) Mahoning County	33	0.05
Cincinnati (city) Hamilton County	121	0.04
Canton (city) Stark County	28	0.04
Springfield (city) Clark County	23	0.04
Hamilton (city) Butler County	22	0.04
Elyria (city) Lorain County	20	0.04
Columbus (city) Franklin County	197	0.03
Toledo (city) Lucas County	55	0.02

Hawaii Native/Pacific Islander: Fijian

Top 10 Places Sorted by Population

Based on all places, regardless of total population

Place	Population	%
Springfield (city) Clark County	11	0.02
Columbus (city) Franklin County	7	<0.01
Fremont (city) Sandusky County	6	0.04
Huber Heights (city) Montgomery County	5	0.01
Elmwood Place (village) Hamilton County	3	0.14
Middletown (city) Butler County	3	0.01
Chillicothe (city) Ross County	2	0.01
Gahanna (city) Franklin County	2	0.01
Painesville (city) Lake County	2	0.01
Toledo (city) Lucas County	2	<0.01

Top 10 Places Sorted by Percent of Total Population

Based on all places, regardless of total population

Place	Population	%
Elmwood Place (village) Hamilton County	3	0.14
Adena (village) Jefferson County	1	0.13
Bethesda (village) Belmont County	1	0.08
Fremont (city) Sandusky County	6	0.04
Fruit Hill (cdp) Hamilton County	1	0.03
Springfield (city) Clark County	11	0.02
St. Bernard (city) Hamilton County	1	0.02
Huber Heights (city) Montgomery County	5	0.01
Middletown (city) Butler County	3	0.01
Chillicothe (city) Ross County	2	0.01

Top 10 Places Sorted by Percent of Total Population

Based on places with total population of 50,000 or more

Place	Population	%
Springfield (city) Clark County	11	0.02
Columbus (city) Franklin County	7	<0.01
Toledo (city) Lucas County	2	<0.01
Cincinnati (city) Hamilton County	1	<0.01
Akron (city) Summit County	0	0.00
Canton (city) Stark County	0	0.00
Cleveland (city) Cuyahoga County	0	0.00
Dayton (city) Montgomery County	0	0.00
Elyria (city) Lorain County	0	0.00
Hamilton (city) Butler County	0	0.00

Hawaii Native/Pacific Islander: Guamanian or Chamorro

Top 10 Places Sorted by Population

Based on all places, regardless of total population

Place	Population	%
Cincinnati (city) Hamilton County	202	0.07
Columbus (city) Franklin County	181	0.02
Dover (city) Tuscarawas County	89	0.69
Cleveland (city) Cuyahoga County	73	0.02
New Philadelphia (city) Tuscarawas County	65	0.38
Huber Heights (city) Montgomery County	33	0.09
Dayton (city) Montgomery County	31	0.02
Hamilton (city) Butler County	30	0.05
Sidney (city) Shelby County	29	0.14
Canton (city) Stark County	28	0.04

Top 10 Places Sorted by Percent of Total Population

Based on all places, regardless of total population

Place	Population	%
Brice (village) Franklin County	1	0.88
Dover (city) Tuscarawas County	89	0.69
Strasburg (village) Tuscarawas County	15	0.58
Sulphur Springs (cdp) Crawford County	1	0.52
Bourneville (cdp) Ross County	1	0.50
New Philadelphia (city) Tuscarawas County	65	0.38
Grand Rapids (village) Wood County	3	0.31
Elmwood Place (village) Hamilton County	6	0.27
Whites Landing (cdp) Erie County	1	0.27
Willshire (village) Van Wert County	1	0.25

Top 10 Places Sorted by Percent of Total Population

Based on places with total population of 50,000 or more

Place	Population	%
Cincinnati (city) Hamilton County	202	0.07
Hamilton (city) Butler County	30	0.05
Canton (city) Stark County	28	0.04
Columbus (city) Franklin County	181	0.02
Cleveland (city) Cuyahoga County	73	0.02
Dayton (city) Montgomery County	31	0.02
Elyria (city) Lorain County	13	0.02
Springfield (city) Clark County	12	0.02
Toledo (city) Lucas County	28	0.01
Akron (city) Summit County	27	0.01

Hawaii Native/Pacific Islander: Marshallese

Top 10 Places Sorted by Population

Based on all places, regardless of total population

Place	Population	%
Celina (city) Mercer County	24	0.23
Coldwater (village) Mercer County	9	0.20
St. Marys (city) Auglaize County	6	0.07
Mount Healthy (city) Hamilton County	5	0.08
Hamilton (city) Butler County	5	0.01
Dayton (city) Montgomery County	4	<0.01
Zanesfield (village) Logan County	2	1.02
De Graff (village) Logan County	2	0.16
Wyoming (city) Hamilton County	2	0.02
Athens (city) Athens County	2	0.01

Top 10 Places Sorted by Percent of Total Population

Based on all places, regardless of total population

Place	Population	%
Zanesfield (village) Logan County	2	1.02
Celina (city) Mercer County	24	0.23
Coldwater (village) Mercer County	9	0.20
De Graff (village) Logan County	2	0.16
Mount Healthy (city) Hamilton County	5	0.08
St. Marys (city) Auglaize County	6	0.07
West Liberty (village) Logan County	1	0.06
Waynesville (village) Warren County	1	0.04
Greenhills (village) Hamilton County	1	0.03
Wyoming (city) Hamilton County	2	0.02

Top 10 Places Sorted by Percent of Total Population

Based on places with total population of 50,000 or more

Place	Population	%
Hamilton (city) Butler County	5	0.01
Dayton (city) Montgomery County	4	<0.01
Cincinnati (city) Hamilton County	2	<0.01
Springfield (city) Clark County	1	<0.01
Akron (city) Summit County	0	0.00
Canton (city) Stark County	0	0.00
Cleveland (city) Cuyahoga County	0	0.00
Columbus (city) Franklin County	0	0.00
Elyria (city) Lorain County	0	0.00
Kettering (city) Montgomery County	0	0.00

Hawaii Native/Pacific Islander: Native Hawaiian

Top 10 Places Sorted by Population

Based on all places, regardless of total population

Place	Population	%
Columbus (city) Franklin County	336	0.04
Cleveland (city) Cuyahoga County	127	0.03
Toledo (city) Lucas County	86	0.03
Akron (city) Summit County	84	0.04
Cincinnati (city) Hamilton County	70	0.02
Dayton (city) Montgomery County	57	0.04
Canton (city) Stark County	32	0.04
Fairborn (city) Greene County	30	0.09
Beavercreek (city) Greene County	29	0.06
Strongsville (city) Cuyahoga County	26	0.06

Top 10 Places Sorted by Percent of Total Population

Based on all places, regardless of total population

Place	Population	%
Linndale (village) Cuyahoga County	3	1.68
Plumwood (cdp) Madison County	3	0.94
Clarington (village) Monroe County	3	0.78
Cairo (village) Allen County	4	0.76
Elmwood Place (village) Hamilton County	12	0.55
Haviland (village) Paulding County	1	0.47
Portage (village) Wood County	2	0.46
Hollansburg (village) Darke County	1	0.44
Amanda (village) Fairfield County	3	0.41
Alexandria (village) Licking County	2	0.39

Top 10 Places Sorted by Percent of Total Population

Based on places with total population of 50,000 or more

Place	Population	%
Columbus (city) Franklin County	336	0.04

Akron (city) Summit County	84	0.04
Dayton (city) Montgomery County	57	0.04
Canton (city) Stark County	32	0.04
Youngstown (city) Mahoning County	25	0.04
Hamilton (city) Butler County	22	0.04
Cleveland (city) Cuyahoga County	127	0.03
Toledo (city) Lucas County	86	0.03
Elyria (city) Lorain County	16	0.03
Springfield (city) Clark County	16	0.03

Hawaii Native/Pacific Islander: Samoan

Top 10 Places Sorted by Population

Based on all places, regardless of total population

Place	Population	%
Columbus (city) Franklin County	399	0.05
Urbancrest (village) Franklin County	93	9.69
Cincinnati (city) Hamilton County	51	0.02
Dayton (city) Montgomery County	34	0.02
Toledo (city) Lucas County	34	0.01
Cleveland (city) Cuyahoga County	24	0.01
Mansfield (city) Richland County	14	0.03
Akron (city) Summit County	14	0.01
Springfield (city) Clark County	10	0.02
Blacklick Estates (cdp) Franklin County	9	0.10

Top 10 Places Sorted by Percent of Total Population

Based on all places, regardless of total population

Place	Population	%
Urbancrest (village) Franklin County	93	9.69
Valleyview (village) Franklin County	6	0.97
Hilltop (cdp) Trumbull County	3	0.56
New Riegel (village) Seneca County	1	0.40
Rosewood (cdp) Champaign County	1	0.39
Bethel (village) Clermont County	8	0.30
Mendon (village) Mercer County	2	0.30
Blacklick Estates (cdp) Franklin County	9	0.10
New Albany (village) Franklin County	8	0.10
Spencerville (village) Allen County	2	0.09

Top 10 Places Sorted by Percent of Total Population

Based on places with total population of 50,000 or more

Place	Population	%
Columbus (city) Franklin County	399	0.05
Cincinnati (city) Hamilton County	51	0.02
Dayton (city) Montgomery County	34	0.02
Springfield (city) Clark County	10	0.02
Toledo (city) Lucas County	34	0.01
Cleveland (city) Cuyahoga County	24	0.01
Akron (city) Summit County	14	0.01
Canton (city) Stark County	9	0.01
Hamilton (city) Butler County	9	0.01
Parma (city) Cuyahoga County	9	0.01

Hawaii Native/Pacific Islander: Tongan

Top 10 Places Sorted by Population

Based on all places, regardless of total population

Place	Population	%
Newark (city) Licking County	8	0.02
Hamilton (city) Butler County	7	0.01
Fremont (city) Sandusky County	6	0.04
Cleveland (city) Cuyahoga County	6	<0.01
Brook Park (city) Cuyahoga County	4	0.02
Middleburg Heights (city) Cuyahoga County	3	0.02
Avon (city) Lorain County	3	0.01
Cleveland Heights (city) Cuyahoga County	3	0.01
St. Bernard (city) Hamilton County	2	0.05
Wilmington (city) Clinton County	2	0.02

Top 10 Places Sorted by Percent of Total Population

Based on all places, regardless of total population

Place	Population	%
St. Bernard (city) Hamilton County	2	0.05
Fremont (city) Sandusky County	6	0.04
New Richmond (village) Clermont County	1	0.04
Fairport Harbor (village) Lake County	1	0.03
Newark (city) Licking County	8	0.02
Brook Park (city) Cuyahoga County	4	0.02
Middleburg Heights (city) Cuyahoga County	3	0.02
Wilmington (city) Clinton County	2	0.02
Chagrin Falls (village) Cuyahoga County	1	0.02
Hamilton (city) Butler County	7	0.01

Top 10 Places Sorted by Percent of Total Population

Based on places with total population of 50,000 or more

Place	Population	%
Hamilton (city) Butler County	7	0.01
Cleveland (city) Cuyahoga County	6	<0.01
Columbus (city) Franklin County	2	<0.01
Dayton (city) Montgomery County	2	<0.01
Springfield (city) Clark County	2	<0.01
Toledo (city) Lucas County	2	<0.01
Akron (city) Summit County	1	<0.01
Canton (city) Stark County	0	0.00
Cincinnati (city) Hamilton County	0	0.00
Elyria (city) Lorain County	0	0.00

White

Top 10 Places Sorted by Population

Based on all places, regardless of total population

Place	Population	%
Columbus (city) Franklin County	505,454	64.22
Toledo (city) Lucas County	195,953	68.23
Cleveland (city) Cuyahoga County	156,136	39.35
Cincinnati (city) Hamilton County	152,515	51.36
Akron (city) Summit County	129,298	64.94
Parma (city) Cuyahoga County	77,034	94.40
Dayton (city) Montgomery County	76,680	54.18
Hamilton (city) Butler County	54,183	86.72
Canton (city) Stark County	53,661	73.50
Kettering (city) Montgomery County	53,090	94.53

Top 10 Places Sorted by Percent of Total Population

Based on all places, regardless of total population

Place	Population	%
Scio (village) Harrison County	763	100.00
Russia (village) Shelby County	640	100.00
Stoutsville (village) Fairfield County	560	100.00
Verona (village) Preble County	494	100.00
McDermott (cdp) Scioto County	434	100.00
Harrod (village) Allen County	417	100.00
Beallsville (village) Monroe County	409	100.00
Hanoverton (village) Columbiana County	408	100.00
Bascom (cdp) Seneca County	390	100.00
Green Camp (village) Marion County	374	100.00

Top 10 Places Sorted by Percent of Total Population

Based on places with total population of 50,000 or more

Place	Population	%
Kettering (city) Montgomery County	53,090	94.53
Parma (city) Cuyahoga County	77,034	94.40
Lakewood (city) Cuyahoga County	46,836	89.84
Hamilton (city) Butler County	54,183	86.72
Elyria (city) Lorain County	44,643	81.86
Springfield (city) Clark County	47,786	78.84
Canton (city) Stark County	53,661	73.50
Lorain (city) Lorain County	46,446	72.46
Toledo (city) Lucas County	195,953	68.23
Akron (city) Summit County	129,298	64.94

White: Not Hispanic

Top 10 Places Sorted by Population

Based on all places, regardless of total population

Place	Population	%
Columbus (city) Franklin County	485,567	61.70
Toledo (city) Lucas County	183,797	63.99
Cincinnati (city) Hamilton County	148,354	49.96
Cleveland (city) Cuyahoga County	138,590	34.93
Akron (city) Summit County	126,928	63.75
Parma (city) Cuyahoga County	75,053	91.98
Dayton (city) Montgomery County	74,600	52.71
Hamilton (city) Butler County	52,579	84.16
Canton (city) Stark County	52,555	71.99
Kettering (city) Montgomery County	52,203	92.95

Top 10 Places Sorted by Percent of Total Population

Based on all places, regardless of total population

Place	Population	%
Verona (village) Preble County	494	100.00
Beallsville (village) Monroe County	409	100.00
Hanoverton (village) Columbiana County	408	100.00
Port Jefferson (village) Shelby County	371	100.00
Freeport (village) Harrison County	369	100.00
Winesburg (cdp) Holmes County	352	100.00
Conesville (village) Coshocton County	347	100.00
Somerville (village) Butler County	281	100.00
Casstown (village) Miami County	267	100.00
North Star (village) Darke County	236	100.00

Top 10 Places Sorted by Percent of Total Population

Based on places with total population of 50,000 or more

Place	Population	%
Kettering (city) Montgomery County	52,203	92.95
Parma (city) Cuyahoga County	75,053	91.98
Lakewood (city) Cuyahoga County	45,393	87.07
Hamilton (city) Butler County	52,579	84.16
Elyria (city) Lorain County	42,979	78.81
Springfield (city) Clark County	46,921	77.42
Canton (city) Stark County	52,555	71.99
Toledo (city) Lucas County	183,797	63.99
Akron (city) Summit County	126,928	63.75
Columbus (city) Franklin County	485,567	61.70

White: Hispanic

Top 10 Places Sorted by Population

Based on all places, regardless of total population

Place	Population	%
Columbus (city) Franklin County	19,887	2.53
Cleveland (city) Cuyahoga County	17,546	4.42
Toledo (city) Lucas County	12,156	4.23
Lorain (city) Lorain County	9,366	14.61
Cincinnati (city) Hamilton County	4,161	1.40
Youngstown (city) Mahoning County	3,037	4.53
Akron (city) Summit County	2,370	1.19
Dayton (city) Montgomery County	2,080	1.47
Parma (city) Cuyahoga County	1,981	2.43
Fremont (city) Sandusky County	1,724	10.30

Top 10 Places Sorted by Percent of Total Population

Based on all places, regardless of total population

Place	Population	%
Tedrow (cdp) Fulton County	41	23.70
Brecon (cdp) Hamilton County	50	20.49
Hessville (cdp) Sandusky County	41	19.16
Milton Center (village) Wood County	24	16.67
West Leipsic (village) Putnam County	33	16.02
Hamler (village) Henry County	87	15.10
Lorain (city) Lorain County	9,366	14.61
Leipsic (village) Putnam County	270	12.90
Willard (city) Huron County	803	12.88
Linndale (village) Cuyahoga County	22	12.29

Top 10 Places Sorted by Percent of Total Population

Based on places with total population of 50,000 or more

Place	Population	%
Lorain (city) Lorain County	9,366	14.61
Youngstown (city) Mahoning County	3,037	4.53
Cleveland (city) Cuyahoga County	17,546	4.42
Toledo (city) Lucas County	12,156	4.23
Elyria (city) Lorain County	1,664	3.05
Lakewood (city) Cuyahoga County	1,443	2.77
Hamilton (city) Butler County	1,604	2.57
Columbus (city) Franklin County	19,887	2.53
Parma (city) Cuyahoga County	1,981	2.43
Kettering (city) Montgomery County	887	1.58

Climate

Ohio Physical Features and Climate Narrative

PHYSICAL FEATURES AND GENERAL CLIMATE. The climate of Ohio is remarkably varied. Less than one-half of its area is occupied by typical plains, while most of eastern and much of southern Ohio is hilly. Topography ranges in elevation from 430 feet above sea level at the junction of the Great Miami and Ohio Rivers up to 1,550 feet on a summit near Bellefontaine. In addition to this high point there are innumerable other hills which rise above 1,400 feet (mean sea level). These are located mainly along the dividing line between the Ohio River and Lake Erie drainage basins. Large areas in the State have elevations above 1,000 feet. An extensive area in northwestern Ohio is occupied by a flat lake plain — once the bottom of glacial Lake Maumee which was much larger than the present Lake Erie. The greater part of eastern Ohio is within the Allegheny Plateau, an unglaciated area consisting of picturesque hills, many of which rise above 1,300 feet and comprise many winding rivers and streams.

The Ohio River, which forms the southern and southeastern boundaries of Ohio, and its tributaries drain the greater portion of the State. A number of streams drain northward into Lake Erie. Although this area comprises nearly a third of the State, the divide between the two drainages is only 20 to 40 miles from the lake shore for a distance of more than 100 miles until it dips south of the arrowhead-shaped Maumee Basin. The largest streams in this region are the Maumee, Sandusky, and Cuyahoga Rivers. Principal tributaries flowing southward into the Ohio River include the Muskingum in the east, the Scioto in the central section, and the Great Miami in the west. A small portion in the west-central region drains westward into the Wabash River basin of Indiana.

Located west of the Appalachian Mountains, Ohio has a climate essentially continental in nature, characterized by moderate extremes of heat and cold, and wetness and dryness. Summers are moderately warm and humid, with occasional days when temperatures exceed 100°F.; winters are reasonably cold, with an average of about two days of subzero weather; and autumns are predominately cool, dry, and invigorating. Spring is the wettest season and vegetation is lush and profuse.

PRECIPITATION. Annual precipitation is slightly in excess of the national average and is well distributed, though with peaks in early spring and summer. In spite of the relatively small range in latitude and the compact shape of Ohio, rainfall varies considerably in amount and seasonal distribution. This is accounted for not only by the presence of Lake Erie on the north, but also by its topography and proximity to rain producing storm paths. Annual precipitation averages about 38 inches, being most generous in spring (about four inches in April) and least in the fall (about 2.5 inches in October). Greatest amounts are measured in the southwest where Wilmington has an average of 44.36 inches; the lake shore is driest, with Gilbralter Island having a normal of only 29.06 inches.

The southern half of the State is visited more frequently by productive rainstorms which, together with the general roughness of terrain, accounts for the larger total precipitation. The lifting of moist air masses over the hills tends to increase the yield of rainfall, especially in winter and spring. There is a marked tendency during the cold season for northeastern counties to receive snowfall amounts substantially in excess of those measured elsewhere. Northerly winds have a long fetch across Lake Huron and the widest part of Lake Erie, thus picking up moisture and heat from the lakes. This moisture is then forced to condense as the air is lifted abruptly over the divide a short distance from the lake. Average snowfall ranges from 60 inches in parts of Lake and adjoining counties down to 16 inches or less along the Ohio River.

TEMPERATURE. The normal annual temperature for the State ranges from 49.6°F. at Hiram in Portage County up to 56.9°F. at Portsmouth on the Ohio River. Variations over the State are due mainly to differences in latitude and topography, but the immediate lake shore area experiences a moderating effect due to its proximity to a large body of water. Widest temperature ranges are found generally among the eastern hills. In an average year, 90°F. heat may be expected about 20 times in summer with 100°F. or more once or twice. Readings of zero or lower are generally to be expected on two to four days each winter, and these are just as likely to occur in the south as the north. However, one winter out of six or eight will pass without experiencing zero readings anywhere in the State.

OTHER CLIMATIC ELEMENTS. The growing season, as defined by the period 32°F. or higher, ranges widely because of latitude and proximity to Lake Erie. The longest is about 200 days on the lake shore and the shortest is in the northeastern valleys within the Ohio River drainage. Dates of the average last freezing temperature in spring range from April 15 to May 18 and the mean first freeze date in fall varies from September 30 to November 6, the latter being on the western lake shore.

Damaging windstorms are mostly associated with heavy thunderstorms or line squalls. Three or four tornadoes may be expected to strike in Ohio each year. Most tornadoes, however, are of limited effect having paths that are short and narrow.

Most floods in Ohio are caused by unusual precipitation. The storms causing floods may bring rainfall of unusual intensity or of unusual duration and extent. Some floods may be caused by a series of ordinary storms which follow one another in rapid succession. Others may result from rain falling at relatively high temperatures on snow-covered areas. At times, though infrequent, flood conditions are caused or aggravated by ice gorges, especially in the tributary streams. Severe thunderstorms frequently cause local flash flooding. General flooding occurs most frequently during January to March and rarely occurs during August to October.

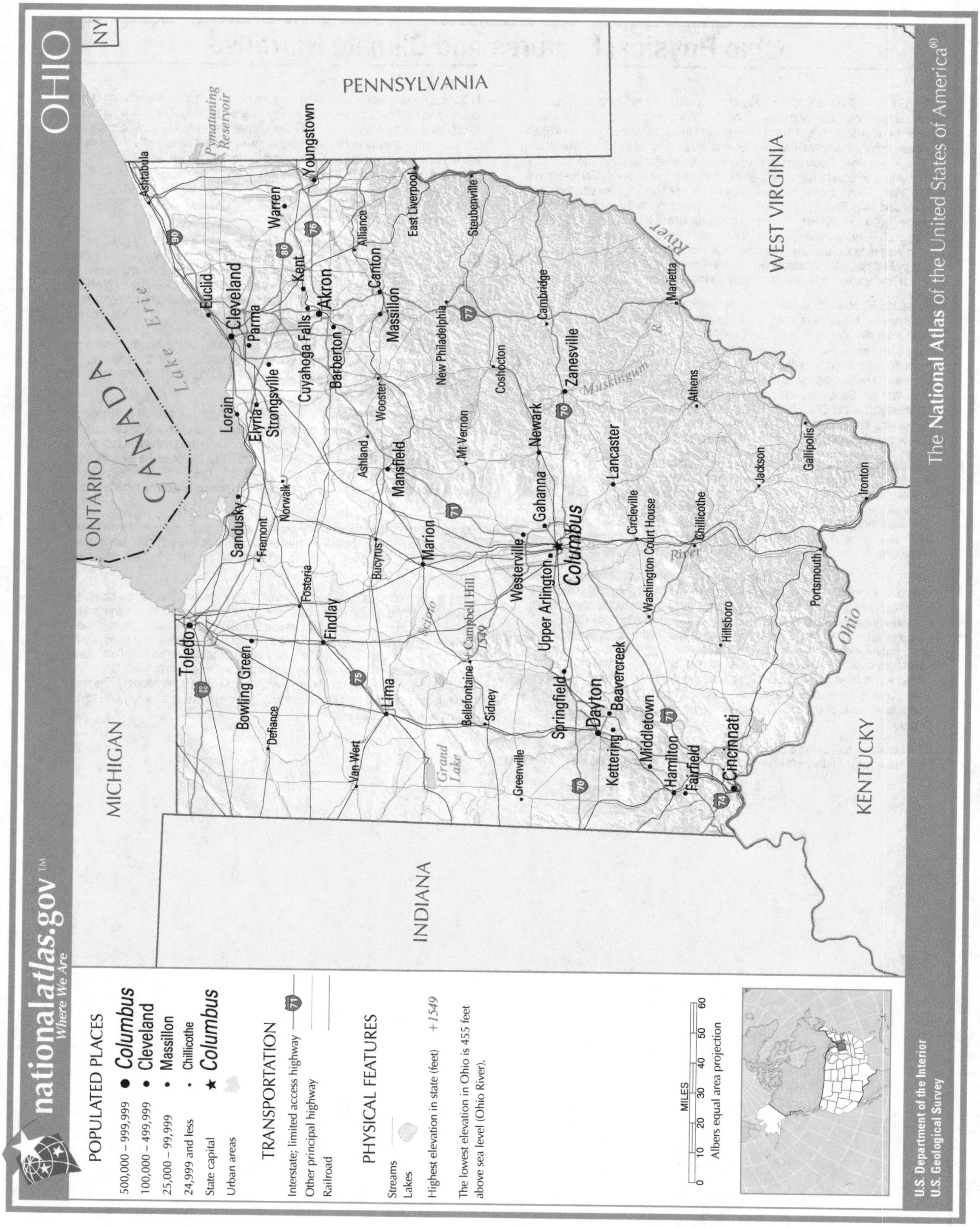
OHIO
nationalatlas.gov™
Where We Are
POPULATED PLACES
500,000 – 999,999 Columbus
100,000 – 499,999 Cleveland
25,000 – 99,999 Massillon
24,999 and less Chillicothe
State capital Columbus
Urban areas
TRANSPORTATION
Interstate; limited access highway 71
Other principal highway
Railroad
PHYSICAL FEATURES
Streams
Lakes
Highest elevation in state (feet) +1549
The lowest elevation in Ohio is 455 feet above sea level (Ohio River).
MILES
0 10 20 30 40 50 60
Albers equal area projection
U.S. Department of the Interior
U.S. Geological Survey
The National Atlas of the United States of America®
MICHIGAN
ONTARIO
CANADA
Lake Erie
NY
PENNSYLVANIA
WEST VIRGINIA
KENTUCKY
INDIANA
Pymatuning Reservoir
Ashtabula
Youngstown
Warren
Euclid
Cleveland
Parma
Kent
Akron
Alliance
Cuyahoga Falls
Barberton
Canton
Massillon
East Liverpool
Steubenville
Strongsville
Lorain
Elyria
Wooster
New Philadelphia
Cambridge
Marietta
Coshocton
Zanesville
Muskingum R.
Ohio River
Athens
Ashland
Mansfield
Mt Vernon
Newark
Lancaster
Gallipolis
Norwalk
Sandusky
Fremont
Jackson
Ironton
Gahanna
Columbus
Circleville
Chillicothe
Washington Court House
Bucyrus
Marion
Westerville
Upper Arlington
Portsmouth
Toledo
Fostoria
Findlay
Bowling Green
Scioto
Campbell Hill 1549
Hillsboro
Ohio
Bellefontaine
Sidney
Springfield
Dayton
Beavercreek
Kettering
Middletown
Hamilton
Fairfield
Cincinnati
Defiance
Lima
Van Wert
Grand Lake
Greenville
90
80
76
77
70
71
75
74

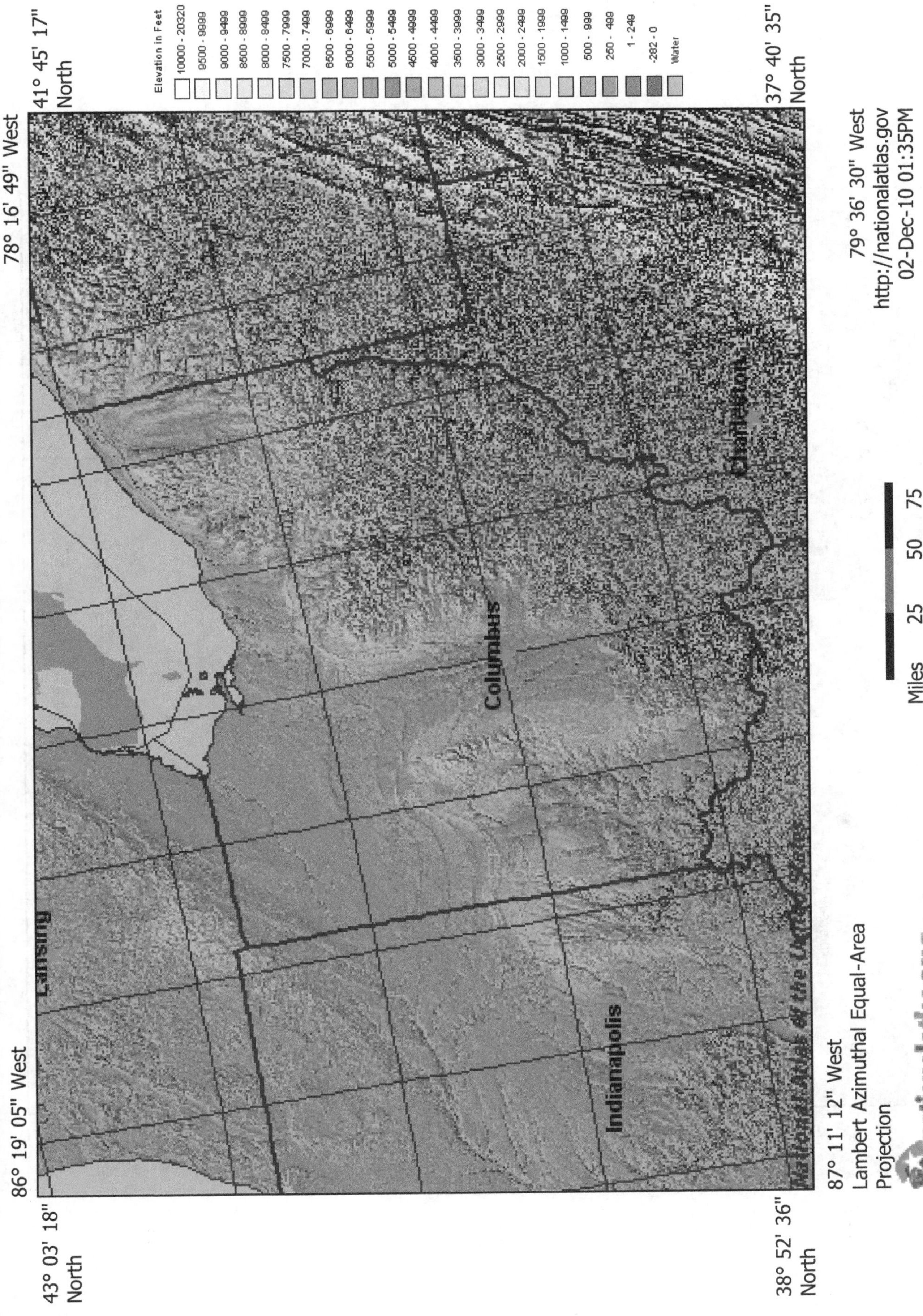
41° 45' 17" North
78° 16' 49" West
Elevation in Feet
10000 - 20320
9500 - 9999
9000 - 9499
8500 - 8999
8000 - 8499
7500 - 7999
7000 - 7499
6500 - 6999
6000 - 6499
5500 - 5999
5000 - 5499
4500 - 4999
4000 - 4499
3500 - 3999
3000 - 3499
2500 - 2999
2000 - 2499
1500 - 1999
1000 - 1499
500 - 999
250 - 499
1 - 249
-282 - 0
Water
37° 40' 35" North
79° 36' 30" West
http://nationalatlas.gov
02-Dec-10 01:35PM
Charleston
Columbus
Lansing
Indianapolis
Miles 25 50 75
43° 03' 18" North
86° 19' 05" West
38° 52' 36" North
87° 11' 12" West
Lambert Azimuthal Equal-Area Projection
nationalatlas.gov

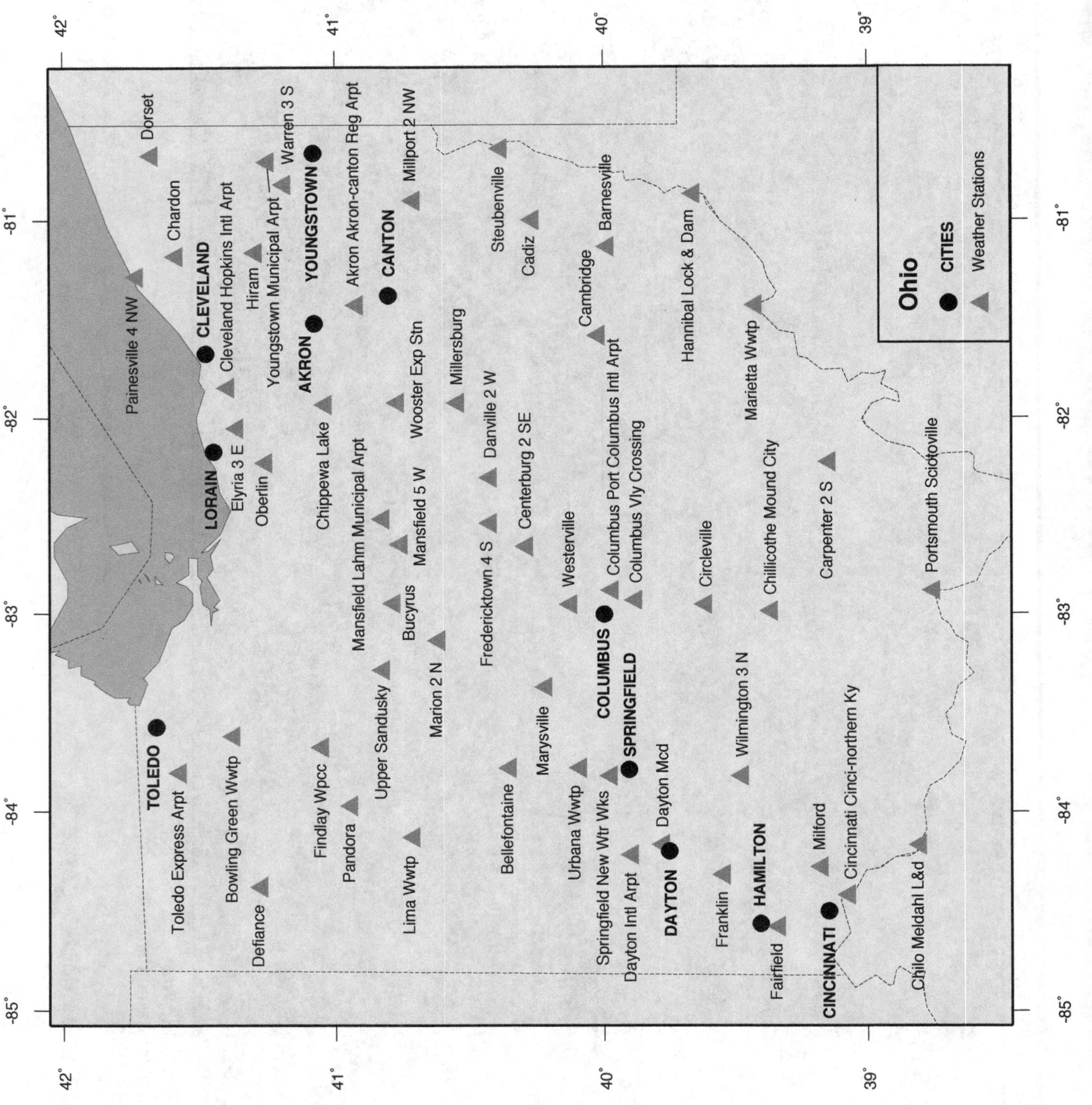
Ohio
CITIES
Weather Stations
42°
41°
40°
39°
-81°
-82°
-83°
-84°
-85°
TOLEDO
CLEVELAND
LORAIN
AKRON
YOUNGSTOWN
CANTON
COLUMBUS
SPRINGFIELD
DAYTON
HAMILTON
CINCINNATI
Dorset
Chardon
Painesville 4 NW
Cleveland Hopkins Intl Arpt
Hiram
Youngstown Municipal Arpt
Warren 3 S
Akron Akron-canton Reg Arpt
Millport 2 NW
Elyria 3 E
Oberlin
Chippewa Lake
Wooster Exp Stn
Millersburg
Steubenville
Cadiz
Barnesville
Cambridge
Hannibal Lock & Dam
Marietta Wwtp
Mansfield Lahm Municipal Arpt
Mansfield 5 W
Danville 2 W
Centerburg 2 SE
Fredericktown 4 S
Bucyrus
Marion 2 N
Westerville
Columbus Port Columbus Intl Arpt
Columbus Vly Crossing
Circleville
Chillicothe Mound City
Carpenter 2 S
Portsmouth Sciotoville
Toledo Express Arpt
Bowling Green Wwtp
Defiance
Findlay Wpcc
Pandora
Upper Sandusky
Lima Wwtp
Bellefontaine
Marysville
Urbana Wwtp
Springfield New Wtr Wks
Dayton Intl Arpt
Dayton Mcd
Wilmington 3 N
Franklin
Fairfield
Milford
Cincinnati Cinci-northern Ky
Chilo Meldahl L&d

Ohio Weather Stations by County

County	Station Name
Allen	Lima WWTP
Ashtabula	Dorset
Belmont	Barnesville
Boone	Cincinnati-Northern Kentucky
Butler	Fairfield
Champaign	Urbana WWTP
Clark	Springfield New Water Works
Clermont	Chilo Meldahl L&D Milford
Clinton	Wilmington 3 N
Columbiana	Millport 2 NW
Crawford	Bucyrus
Cuyahoga	Cleveland Hopkins Intl Arpt
Defiance	Defiance
Franklin	Columbus Valley Crossing Columbus-Port Columbus Intl Westerville
Geauga	Chardon
Guernsey	Cambridge
Hancock	Findlay Wpcc
Harrison	Cadiz
Holmes	Millersburg
Jefferson	Steubenville
Knox	Centerburg 2 SE Danville 2 W Fredericktown 4 S
Lake	Painesville 4 NW
Logan	Bellefontaine
Lorain	Elyria 3 E Oberlin
Lucas	Toledo Express Arpt
Marion	Marion 2 N
Medina	Chippewa Lake
Meigs	Carpenter 2 S
Monroe	Hannibal Lock & Dam

County	Station Name
Montgomery	Dayton Intl Arpt Dayton Mcd
Pickaway	Circleville
Portage	Hiram
Putnam	Pandora
Richland	Mansfield 5 W Mansfield Lahm Municipal Arpt
Ross	Chillicothe Mound City
Scioto	Portsmouth Sciotoville
Summit	Akron Akron-Canton Reg Arpt
Trumbull	Warren 3 S Youngstown Municipal Arpt
Union	Marysville
Warren	Franklin
Washington	Marietta Wwtp
Wayne	Wooster Exp Stn
Wood	Bowling Green WWTP
Wyandot	Upper Sandusky

See User Guide for station inclusion criteria.

Ohio Weather Stations by City

City	Station Name	Miles
Akron	Akron Akron-Canton Reg Arpt	11.9
	Chippewa Lake	21.7
	Hiram	24.6
Beavercreek	Dayton Mcd	6.9
	Dayton Intl Arpt	14.4
	Franklin	18.2
	Springfield New Water Works	21.1
	Wilmington 3 N	21.4
Boardman	Warren 3 S	13.9
	Youngstown Municipal Arpt	14.9
Brunswick	Chippewa Lake	14.8
	Cleveland Hopkins Intl Arpt	10.6
	Elyria 3 E	15.0
	Oberlin	20.5
Canton	Akron Akron-Canton Reg Arpt	7.9
Cincinnati	Cincinnati-Northern Kentucky	10.6
	Fairfield	14.8
	Milford	12.5
Cleveland	Cleveland Hopkins Intl Arpt	11.1
	Elyria 3 E	21.0
Cleveland Heights	Chardon	20.2
	Cleveland Hopkins Intl Arpt	16.8
	Painesville 4 NW	21.3
Columbus	Columbus Valley Crossing	7.6
	Columbus-Port Columbus Intl	6.0
	Westerville	9.5
Cuyahoga Falls	Akron Akron-Canton Reg Arpt	16.0
	Chippewa Lake	24.0
	Hiram	20.7
Dayton	Dayton Mcd	0.6
	Dayton Intl Arpt	9.6
	Franklin	16.1
	Springfield New Water Works	24.5
Delaware	Centerburg 2 SE	22.6
	Columbus-Port Columbus Intl	24.2
	Marion 2 N	22.1
	Marysville	15.9
	Westerville	13.3
Dublin	Columbus Valley Crossing	18.6
	Columbus-Port Columbus Intl	16.4
	Marysville	14.4
	Westerville	10.1
Elyria	Chippewa Lake	23.9
	Cleveland Hopkins Intl Arpt	13.1
	Elyria 3 E	2.7
	Oberlin	9.5
Euclid	Chardon	17.4
	Cleveland Hopkins Intl Arpt	21.8
	Painesville 4 NW	15.6

City	Station Name	Miles
Fairborn	Dayton Mcd	8.9
	Dayton Intl Arpt	12.3
	Franklin	23.5
	Springfield New Water Works	15.7
	Urbana WWTP	24.1
	Wilmington 3 N	24.6
Fairfield	Cincinnati-Northern Kentucky	20.2
	Fairfield	2.7
	Franklin	19.6
	Milford	17.1
Findlay	Bowling Green WWTP	23.4
	Findlay Wpcc	1.4
	Pandora	18.2
	Upper Sandusky	23.7
Gahanna	Centerburg 2 SE	22.1
	Columbus Valley Crossing	9.5
	Columbus-Port Columbus Intl	3.2
	Westerville	8.3
Grove City	Circleville	19.1
	Columbus Valley Crossing	7.8
	Columbus-Port Columbus Intl	12.6
	Westerville	19.0
Hamilton	Brookville, IN	24.0
	Cincinnati-Northern Kentucky	24.6
	Fairfield	3.4
	Franklin	17.0
	Milford	21.2
Huber Heights	Dayton Mcd	6.8
	Dayton Intl Arpt	5.7
	Franklin	23.4
	Springfield New Water Works	18.1
	Urbana WWTP	24.8
Kettering	Dayton Mcd	5.3
	Dayton Intl Arpt	14.7
	Franklin	13.5
	Wilmington 3 N	22.9
Lakewood	Cleveland Hopkins Intl Arpt	6.4
	Elyria 3 E	14.8
Lancaster	Circleville	19.9
	Columbus Valley Crossing	21.5
	Columbus-Port Columbus Intl	23.5
Lima	Lima WWTP	2.1
	Pandora	16.2
Lorain	Cleveland Hopkins Intl Arpt	16.9
	Elyria 3 E	7.6
	Oberlin	12.7
Mansfield	Bucyrus	23.5
	Danville 2 W	25.0
	Fredericktown 4 S	23.1
	Mansfield Lahm Municipal Arpt	4.5
	Mansfield 5 W	4.9

See User Guide for station inclusion criteria.

City	Station Name	Miles
Marion	Bucyrus	17.8
	Marion 2 N	2.0
	Upper Sandusky	18.8
Mason	Fairfield	14.4
	Franklin	13.5
	Milford	12.0
Massillon	Akron Akron-Canton Reg Arpt	9.5
	Wooster Exp Stn	20.6
Mentor	Chardon	10.9
	Painesville 4 NW	4.8
Middletown	Dayton Mcd	20.5
	Fairfield	15.6
	Franklin	4.2
	Milford	22.9
Newark	Centerburg 2 SE	20.3
North Olmsted	Cleveland Hopkins Intl Arpt	3.6
	Elyria 3 E	7.5
	Oberlin	18.9
Parma	Cleveland Hopkins Intl Arpt	6.5
	Elyria 3 E	16.8
Reynoldsburg	Centerburg 2 SE	24.9
	Circleville	24.9
	Columbus Valley Crossing	8.1
	Columbus-Port Columbus Intl	4.6
	Westerville	14.3
Springfield	Dayton Mcd	23.2
	Dayton Intl Arpt	22.2
	Springfield New Water Works	2.8
	Urbana WWTP	11.9
Stow	Akron Akron-Canton Reg Arpt	17.9
	Hiram	16.8
Strongsville	Chippewa Lake	18.9
	Cleveland Hopkins Intl Arpt	6.2
	Elyria 3 E	12.5
	Oberlin	20.3
Toledo	Bowling Green WWTP	19.5
	Toledo Express Arpt	12.5
Upper Arlington	Columbus Valley Crossing	11.1
	Columbus-Port Columbus Intl	10.2
	Marysville	21.4
	Westerville	9.9
Warren	Hiram	17.8
	Warren 3 S	2.7
	Youngstown Municipal Arpt	7.8
Westerville	Centerburg 2 SE	18.8
	Columbus Valley Crossing	15.3
	Columbus-Port Columbus Intl	9.7
	Marysville	25.0
	Westerville	1.9

City	Station Name	Miles
Westlake	Cleveland Hopkins Intl Arpt	5.3
	Elyria 3 E	8.0
	Oberlin	19.8
Youngstown	Warren 3 S	11.3
	Youngstown Municipal Arpt	11.0
	Mercer, PA	23.6

Note: Miles is the distance between the geographic center of the city and the weather station.

See User Guide for station inclusion criteria.

Ohio Weather Stations by Elevation

Feet	Station Name
1,350	Mansfield 5 W
1,294	Mansfield Lahm Municipal Arpt
1,259	Cadiz
1,240	Barnesville
1,229	Hiram
1,208	Akron Akron-Canton Reg Arpt
1,205	Centerburg 2 SE
1,185	Bellefontaine
1,180	Chippewa Lake
1,180	Youngstown Municipal Arpt
1,149	Millport 2 NW
1,129	Chardon
1,049	Fredericktown 4 S
1,029	Wilmington 3 N
1,020	Wooster Exp Stn
1,000	Dayton Intl Arpt
1,000	Marysville
1,000	Urbana WWTP
992	Steubenville
979	Dorset
970	Danville 2 W
964	Marion 2 N
955	Bucyrus
930	Springfield New Water Works
899	Warren 3 S
869	Cincinnati-Northern Kentucky
854	Upper Sandusky
850	Lima WWTP
821	Carpenter 2 S
818	Millersburg
815	Oberlin
810	Columbus-Port Columbus Intl
810	Westerville
799	Cambridge
770	Cleveland Hopkins Intl Arpt
770	Pandora
768	Findlay Wpcc
745	Dayton Mcd
734	Columbus Valley Crossing
729	Elyria 3 E
700	Defiance
674	Bowling Green WWTP
672	Circleville
669	Franklin
668	Toledo Express Arpt
649	Chillicothe Mound City
620	Hannibal Lock & Dam
600	Painesville 4 NW
580	Marietta Wwtp
575	Fairfield
540	Portsmouth Sciotoville
520	Milford
500	Chilo Meldahl L&D

See User Guide for station inclusion criteria.

Akron-Canton Regional Airport

The station at the Akron-Canton Airport is located about midway between Akron and Canton, a few miles south of the crest separating the Lake Erie and Muskingum River drainage areas. Precipitation at the station and southward drains through the Muskingum River into the Ohio, while northward of the crest the Cuyahoga and other streams flow into Lake Erie. The terrain is rolling with highest elevations near 1,300 feet above sea level and many small lakes provide water for local industry as well as recreational facilities for the densely populated region. The area is mainly industrial, agricultural operations having diminished rapidly in recent years.

Lake Erie has considerable influence on the area weather, tempering cold air masses during the late fall and winter, as well as contributing to the formation of brief, but heavy snow squalls until the lake freezes over.

The arrival of spring is late in this area, allowing growing of normally frost-susceptible fruits. Summers are moderately warm, but quite humid, while the months of September, October, and sometimes November are usually pleasant although with considerable morning fog. The average last occurrence of freezing temperatures in spring is the end of April, and the first occurrence in fall is late October. In past years, growing seasons for most vegetation has varied from 120 to 211 days. Temperatures and occurences of frost vary widely over the area because of the hilly terrain. Due to the influence of Lake Erie, snowfall is usually much heavier north of the station.

Akron-Canton Regional Airport *Summit County* Elevation: 1,208 ft. Latitude: 40° 55' N Longitude: 81° 26' W

	JAN	FEB	MAR	APR	MAY	JUN	JUL	AUG	SEP	OCT	NOV	DEC	YEAR
Mean Maximum Temp. (°F)	33.7	37.1	46.9	59.8	69.8	78.3	82.4	80.7	73.4	61.3	49.5	37.7	59.2
Mean Temp. (°F)	26.5	29.2	37.7	49.3	59.2	68.0	72.2	70.8	63.5	51.9	41.8	30.9	50.1
Mean Minimum Temp. (°F)	19.3	21.3	28.4	38.7	48.6	57.6	61.9	60.8	53.4	42.4	34.0	24.1	40.9
Extreme Maximum Temp. (°F)	68	72	81	88	93	100	101	97	93	86	76	76	101
Extreme Minimum Temp. (°F)	-25	-8	-3	15	27	33	43	41	33	22	8	-16	-25
Days Maximum Temp. ≥ 90°F	0	0	0	0	0	2	3	2	0	0	0	0	7
Days Maximum Temp. ≤ 32°F	14	10	4	0	0	0	0	0	0	0	1	10	39
Days Minimum Temp. ≤ 32°F	27	24	21	8	0	0	0	0	0	4	14	25	123
Days Minimum Temp. ≤ 0°F	2	1	0	0	0	0	0	0	0	0	0	1	4
Heating Degree Days (base 65°F)	1,186	1,005	841	472	214	47	5	12	110	407	690	1,050	6,039
Cooling Degree Days (base 65°F)	0	0	1	7	41	142	234	199	70	7	0	0	701
Mean Precipitation (in.)	2.60	2.26	3.03	3.58	4.32	3.76	4.12	3.67	3.38	2.83	3.19	2.84	39.58
Maximum Precipitation (in.)*	8.7	5.2	8.8	6.5	9.6	8.4	11.4	8.2	9.0	8.4	9.4	6.7	65.7
Minimum Precipitation (in.)*	0.7	0.3	1.0	0.9	1.0	0.4	0.7	0.5	0.2	0.4	0.6	0.3	23.8
Extreme Maximum Daily Precip. (in.)	2.04	1.66	1.48	1.99	2.29	2.31	3.98	3.67	3.70	2.07	2.31	1.71	3.98
Days With ≥ 0.1" Precipitation	7	6	8	8	9	8	7	6	6	6	8	8	87
Days With ≥ 0.5" Precipitation	1	1	2	2	3	3	3	2	2	2	2	1	24
Days With ≥ 1.0" Precipitation	0	0	0	1	1	1	1	1	1	0	0	0	6
Mean Snowfall (in.)	12.2	9.6	8.4	2.8	0.1	trace	0.0	trace	trace	0.5	2.9	9.9	46.4
Maximum Snowfall (in.)*	38	20	21	21	3	0	0	0	0	7	22	29	72
Maximum 24-hr. Snowfall (in.)*	9	10	8	20	3	0	0	0	0	4	7	16	20
Maximum Snow Depth (in.)	14	17	17	13	trace	trace	0	trace	trace	2	4	11	17
Days With ≥ 1.0" Snow Depth	15	12	6	1	0	0	0	0	0	0	1	10	45
Thunderstorm Days*	< 1	< 1	2	4	6	7	8	6	3	1	1	< 1	38
Foggy Days*	13	12	13	13	14	15	17	19	17	15	13	14	175
Predominant Sky Cover*	OVR	OVR	OVR	OVR	OVR	OVR	OVR	OVR	OVR	OVR	OVR	OVR	OVR
Mean Relative Humidity 7am (%)*	80	80	79	77	77	80	84	87	88	84	80	81	82
Mean Relative Humidity 4pm (%)*	69	65	59	53	52	54	54	55	56	56	64	70	59
Mean Dewpoint (°F)*	19	20	27	36	47	56	61	60	53	42	32	24	40
Prevailing Wind Direction*	SW	WSW	W	SW	SW	SW	SW	SW	S	S	S	WSW	SW
Prevailing Wind Speed (mph)*	13	12	13	12	10	9	8	8	8	9	12	13	10
Maximum Wind Gust (mph)*	76	58	64	60	56	63	68	62	52	51	58	61	76

Note: (*) Period of record is 1948-1995

Cincinnati Covington Airport

Greater Cincinnati Airport is located on a gently rolling plateau about 12 miles southwest of downtown Cincinnati and two miles south of the Ohio River at its nearest point. The river valley is rather narrow and steep-sided varying from one to three miles in width and the river bed is 500 feet below the level of the airport.

The climate is continental with a rather wide range of temperatures from winter to summer. A precipitation maximum occurs during winter and spring with a late summer and fall minimum. On the average, the maximum snowfall occurs during January, although the heaviest 24-hour amounts have been recorded during late November and February.

The heaviest precipitation, as well as the precipitation of the longest duration, is normally associated with low pressure disturbances moving in a general southwest to northeast direction through the Ohio valley and south of the Cincinnati area.

Summers are warm and rather humid. The temperature will reach 100 degrees or more in one year out of three. However, the temperature will reach 90 degrees or higher on about 19 days each year. Winters are moderately cold with frequent periods of extensive cloudiness.

The freeze free period lasts on the average 187 days from mid-April to the latter part of October.

Cincinnati Covington Airport *Boone County* Elevation: 869 ft. Latitude: 39° 03' N Longitude: 84° 40' W

	JAN	FEB	MAR	APR	MAY	JUN	JUL	AUG	SEP	OCT	NOV	DEC	YEAR
Mean Maximum Temp. (°F)	38.9	42.9	52.9	64.4	73.7	82.0	85.6	84.8	78.0	65.9	53.8	41.9	63.7
Mean Temp. (°F)	30.8	34.2	43.1	53.7	63.2	71.7	75.6	74.6	67.3	55.4	44.8	34.1	54.0
Mean Minimum Temp. (°F)	22.6	25.4	33.2	42.9	52.6	61.4	65.5	64.3	56.6	44.9	35.7	26.3	44.3
Extreme Maximum Temp. (°F)	70	75	84	87	91	102	103	101	97	91	81	75	103
Extreme Minimum Temp. (°F)	-24	-11	-11	15	30	41	47	43	31	20	10	-20	-24
Days Maximum Temp. ≥ 90°F	0	0	0	0	0	4	7	7	2	0	0	0	20
Days Maximum Temp. ≤ 32°F	9	6	1	0	0	0	0	0	0	0	0	7	23
Days Minimum Temp. ≤ 32°F	25	21	16	4	0	0	0	0	0	3	12	22	103
Days Minimum Temp. ≤ 0°F	2	1	0	0	0	0	0	0	0	0	0	1	4
Heating Degree Days (base 65°F)	1,055	866	674	350	125	15	0	2	60	312	602	951	5,012
Cooling Degree Days (base 65°F)	0	0	3	17	75	223	336	306	136	22	1	0	1,119
Mean Precipitation (in.)	3.01	2.77	3.99	3.89	4.90	3.94	3.86	3.51	2.67	3.36	3.28	3.35	42.53
Maximum Precipitation (in.)*	9.4	6.7	12.2	7.2	9.5	7.4	8.4	7.7	8.6	8.6	7.5	7.9	57.6
Minimum Precipitation (in.)*	0.6	0.3	1.1	1.0	1.1	0.9	1.2	0.3	0.2	0.3	0.4	0.5	28.0
Extreme Maximum Daily Precip. (in.)	3.23	2.84	3.25	2.41	2.96	3.04	3.11	3.52	2.55	4.30	1.87	2.47	4.30
Days With ≥ 0.1" Precipitation	6	6	8	8	9	7	7	6	5	6	7	7	82
Days With ≥ 0.5" Precipitation	2	1	2	3	3	3	3	2	2	2	2	2	27
Days With ≥ 1.0" Precipitation	1	1	1	1	1	1	1	1	1	1	1	1	12
Mean Snowfall (in.)	6.6	6.1	3.3	0.5	trace	trace	trace	trace	0.0	0.4	0.4	4.3	21.6
Maximum Snowfall (in.)*	32	20	13	4	trace	0	0	0	0	6	12	13	54
Maximum 24-hr. Snowfall (in.)*	8	9	10	3	trace	0	0	0	0	6	9	8	10
Maximum Snow Depth (in.)	14	14	11	5	trace	trace	trace	trace	0	4	1	9	14
Days With ≥ 1.0" Snow Depth	8	6	2	0	0	0	0	0	0	0	0	4	20
Thunderstorm Days*	1	1	3	4	6	7	8	6	3	1	1	< 1	41
Foggy Days*	13	12	12	9	12	13	16	19	16	14	12	14	162
Predominant Sky Cover*	OVR	OVR	OVR	OVR	OVR	OVR	OVR	OVR	OVR	OVR	OVR	OVR	OVR
Mean Relative Humidity 7am (%)*	80	79	77	76	80	82	85	88	87	83	79	80	81
Mean Relative Humidity 4pm (%)*	65	60	55	50	52	53	54	53	52	51	59	65	56
Mean Dewpoint (°F)*	22	24	31	40	51	60	64	63	56	44	34	26	43
Prevailing Wind Direction*	SSW	SSW	SSW	SSW	SSW	SSW	SW	SSW	SSW	SSW	SSW	SSW	SSW
Prevailing Wind Speed (mph)*	12	12	13	12	9	9	8	7	8	9	12	12	10
Maximum Wind Gust (mph)*	71	55	64	71	59	67	83	62	54	59	56	61	83

Note: (*) Period of record is 1948-1995

Cleveland Hopkins Int'l Airport

Cleveland is on the south shore of Lake Erie in northeast Ohio. The metropolitan area has a lake frontage of 3l miles. The surrounding terrain is generally level except for an abrupt ridge on the eastern edge of the city which rises some 500 feet above the shore terrain. The Cuyahoga River, which flows through a rather deep but narrow north-south valley, bisects the city.

Local climate is continental in character but with strong modifying influences by Lake Erie. West to northerly winds blowing off Lake Erie tend to lower daily high temperatures in summer and raise temperatures in winter. Temperatures at Hopkins Airport which is 5 miles south of the lakeshore average from two to four degrees higher than the lakeshore in summer, while overnight low temperatures average from two to four degrees lower than the lakefront during all seasons.

In this area, summers are moderately warm and humid with occasional days when temperatures exceed 90 degrees. Winters are relatively cold and cloudy with an average of five days with sub-zero temperatures. Weather changes occur every few days from the passing of cold fronts.

The daily range in temperature is usually greatest in late summer and least in winter. Annual extremes in temperature normally occur soon after late June and December. Maximum temperatures below freezing occur most often in December, January, and February. Temperatures of 100 degrees or higher are rare. On the average, freezing temperatures in fall are first recorded in October while the last freezing temperature in spring normally occurs in April.

As is characteristic of continental climates, precipitation varies widely from year to year. However, it is normally abundant and well distributed throughout the year with spring being the wettest season. Showers and thunderstorms account for most of the rainfall during the growing season. Thunderstorms are most frequent from April through August. Snowfall may fluctuate widely. Mean annual snowfall increases from west to east in Cuyahoga County ranging from about 45 inches in the west to more than 90 inches in the extreme east.

Damaging winds of 50 mph or greater are usually associated with thunderstorms. Tornadoes, one of the most destructive of all atmospheric storms, occasionally occur in Cuyahoga County.

Cleveland Hopkins Int'l Airport *Cuyahoga County* Elevation: 770 ft. Latitude: 41° 24' N Longitude: 81° 51' W

	JAN	FEB	MAR	APR	MAY	JUN	JUL	AUG	SEP	OCT	NOV	DEC	YEAR
Mean Maximum Temp. (°F)	34.2	37.1	46.0	58.5	69.1	78.2	82.3	80.5	73.7	61.9	50.4	38.2	59.2
Mean Temp. (°F)	27.3	29.6	37.4	48.8	59.0	68.3	72.7	71.3	64.3	53.0	43.1	31.8	50.5
Mean Minimum Temp. (°F)	20.3	22.1	28.7	39.0	48.8	58.4	63.1	62.0	54.8	44.0	35.7	25.3	41.9
Extreme Maximum Temp. (°F)	68	74	82	88	91	104	100	99	93	88	79	77	104
Extreme Minimum Temp. (°F)	-20	-10	-5	11	27	37	45	38	34	19	13	-15	-20
Days Maximum Temp. ≥ 90°F	0	0	0	0	0	2	4	3	0	0	0	0	9
Days Maximum Temp. ≤ 32°F	14	11	4	0	0	0	0	0	0	0	1	9	39
Days Minimum Temp. ≤ 32°F	27	24	21	7	0	0	0	0	0	2	12	24	117
Days Minimum Temp. ≤ 0°F	2	1	0	0	0	0	0	0	0	0	0	1	4
Heating Degree Days (base 65°F)	1,161	994	850	489	223	47	5	10	97	377	652	1,023	5,928
Cooling Degree Days (base 65°F)	0	0	2	9	43	153	250	211	82	11	1	0	762
Mean Precipitation (in.)	2.70	2.28	2.99	3.51	3.62	3.37	3.49	3.53	3.81	3.07	3.51	3.12	39.00
Maximum Precipitation (in.)*	7.0	4.7	6.1	6.6	9.1	9.1	9.1	9.0	7.3	9.5	8.8	8.6	53.8
Minimum Precipitation (in.)*	0.4	0.5	0.8	1.2	1.0	0.6	1.2	0.5	0.7	0.6	0.8	0.7	18.8
Extreme Maximum Daily Precip. (in.)	2.53	1.73	1.87	2.10	2.02	2.57	2.11	3.55	4.59	2.26	2.33	2.39	4.59
Days With ≥ 0.1" Precipitation	7	6	8	8	8	7	7	6	7	7	8	8	87
Days With ≥ 0.5" Precipitation	1	1	2	2	2	2	2	2	3	2	2	2	23
Days With ≥ 1.0" Precipitation	0	0	0	1	1	1	1	1	1	0	1	0	7
Mean Snowfall (in.)	18.4	14.5	12.6	3.3	trace	trace	trace	trace	trace	0.2	4.5	14.1	67.6
Maximum Snowfall (in.)*	43	39	26	13	2	0	0	0	0	8	22	30	97
Maximum 24-hr. Snowfall (in.)*	10	14	11	9	2	0	0	0	0	7	13	12	14
Maximum Snow Depth (in.)	17	22	15	14	trace	trace	trace	trace	trace	trace	9	14	22
Days With ≥ 1.0" Snow Depth	17	13	7	1	0	0	0	0	0	0	2	11	51
Thunderstorm Days*	< 1	< 1	2	3	5	6	6	5	3	2	1	< 1	33
Foggy Days*	13	12	13	12	13	11	12	14	12	11	12	13	148
Predominant Sky Cover*	OVR	OVR	OVR	OVR	OVR	OVR	OVR	OVR	OVR	OVR	OVR	OVR	OVR
Mean Relative Humidity 7am (%)*	79	79	79	76	77	79	81	85	84	81	78	78	80
Mean Relative Humidity 4pm (%)*	70	67	62	56	54	55	55	58	58	58	65	70	61
Mean Dewpoint (°F)*	19	21	27	37	47	57	61	61	54	43	33	24	40
Prevailing Wind Direction*	SW	SW	SW	S	N	SSW	SW	SW	S	SSW	SW	SW	SW
Prevailing Wind Speed (mph)*	13	13	14	13	9	10	9	8	9	10	13	13	12
Maximum Wind Gust (mph)*	82	64	63	78	55	77	67	51	58	54	59	71	82

Note: (*) Period of record is 1948-1995

Columbus-Port Columbus Int'l

Columbus is located in the center of the state and in the drainage area of the Ohio River. The airport is located at the eastern boundary of the city approximately seven miles from the center of the business district.

Four nearly parallel streams run through or adjacent to the city. The Scioto River is the principal stream and flows from the northwest into the center of the city and then flows straight south toward the Ohio River. The Olentangy River runs almost due south and empties into the Scioto just west of the business district. Alum Creek empties into the Big Walnut southeast of the city and the Big Walnut Creek empties into the Scioto a few miles downstream.

The narrow valleys associated with the streams flowing through the city supply the only variation in the micro-climate of the area. The city proper shows the typical metropolitan effect with shrubs and flowers blossoming earlier than in the immediate surroundings and in retarding light frost on clear quiet nights. Many small areas to the southeast and to the north and northeast show marked effects of air drainage as evidenced by the frequent formation of shallow ground fog at daybreak during the summer and fall months and the higher frequency of frost in the spring and fall.

The average occurrence of the last freezing temperature in the spring within the city proper is mid-April, and the first freeze in the fall is very late October, but in the immediate surroundings there is much variation. For example, at Valley Crossing located at the southeastern outskirts of the city, the average occurrence of the last 32 degree temperature in the spring is very early May, while the first 32 degree temperature in the fall is mid-October.

The records show a high frequency of calm or very low wind speeds during the late evening and early morning hours, from June through September. The rolling landscape is conducive to calm winds from the Weather Service location at the airport these are toward the northwest with the wind direction indicated as southeast, at speeds generally 4 mph or less.

Columbus is located in the area of changeable weather. Air masses from central and northwest Canada frequently invade this region. Air from the Gulf of Mexico often reaches central Ohio during the summer and to a much lesser extent in the fall and winter. There are also occasional weather changes brought about by cool outbreaks from the Hudson Bay region of Canada, especially during the spring months. At infrequent intervals the general circulation will bring showers or snow to Columbus from the Atlantic.

Columbus-Port Columbus Int'l *Franklin County* Elevation: 810 ft. Latitude: 39° 59' N Longitude: 82° 53' W

	JAN	FEB	MAR	APR	MAY	JUN	JUL	AUG	SEP	OCT	NOV	DEC	YEAR
Mean Maximum Temp. (°F)	36.7	40.6	50.9	63.2	72.9	81.4	84.8	83.7	77.0	64.9	52.4	40.4	62.4
Mean Temp. (°F)	29.3	32.4	41.3	52.4	62.1	71.0	74.9	73.6	66.5	54.5	43.9	33.3	52.9
Mean Minimum Temp. (°F)	21.9	24.2	31.7	41.6	51.3	60.5	64.8	63.5	55.9	44.1	35.4	26.2	43.4
Extreme Maximum Temp. (°F)	70	75	83	88	93	101	100	101	97	91	80	76	101
Extreme Minimum Temp. (°F)	-22	-10	-6	14	30	39	44	40	33	21	12	-17	-22
Days Maximum Temp. ≥ 90°F	0	0	0	0	0	4	6	5	1	0	0	0	16
Days Maximum Temp. ≤ 32°F	11	8	2	0	0	0	0	0	0	0	1	8	30
Days Minimum Temp. ≤ 32°F	26	22	18	5	0	0	0	0	0	3	12	22	108
Days Minimum Temp. ≤ 0°F	2	1	0	0	0	0	0	0	0	0	0	1	4
Heating Degree Days (base 65°F)	1,100	915	730	383	149	21	1	4	68	334	626	976	5,307
Cooling Degree Days (base 65°F)	0	0	2	12	66	207	313	278	118	16	1	0	1,013
Mean Precipitation (in.)	2.70	2.21	3.05	3.37	4.19	4.00	4.74	3.46	2.85	2.64	3.12	2.99	39.32
Maximum Precipitation (in.)*	8.3	5.1	9.6	6.4	9.1	9.8	12.4	8.6	6.8	5.2	10.7	7.0	53.2
Minimum Precipitation (in.)*	0.6	0.3	1.0	0.7	0.9	0.7	1.0	0.6	0.5	0.1	0.6	0.5	24.5
Extreme Maximum Daily Precip. (in.)	2.41	1.72	1.95	2.23	2.67	2.89	5.13	3.17	2.36	2.31	2.38	2.56	5.13
Days With ≥ 0.1" Precipitation	6	6	7	7	9	7	7	6	5	5	7	7	79
Days With ≥ 0.5" Precipitation	1	1	2	2	3	3	3	2	2	2	2	2	25
Days With ≥ 1.0" Precipitation	0	0	0	0	1	1	1	1	1	1	1	0	7
Mean Snowfall (in.)	9.3	6.3	4.4	1.1	trace	trace	trace	trace	trace	0.2	1.2	5.4	27.9
Maximum Snowfall (in.)*	34	16	14	13	1	0	0	0	trace	5	15	17	48
Maximum 24-hr. Snowfall (in.)*	7	9	9	12	1	0	0	0	trace	4	8	8	12
Maximum Snow Depth (in.)	13	13	18	10	trace	trace	trace	trace	trace	trace	5	7	18
Days With ≥ 1.0" Snow Depth	11	7	3	0	0	0	0	0	0	0	0	5	26
Thunderstorm Days*	< 1	1	2	4	6	8	8	6	3	1	1	< 1	40
Foggy Days*	13	11	12	10	13	14	16	19	15	14	12	14	163
Predominant Sky Cover*	OVR	OVR	OVR	OVR	OVR	OVR	OVR	SCT	OVR	OVR	OVR	OVR	OVR
Mean Relative Humidity 7am (%)*	78	78	76	76	79	81	84	87	87	83	80	80	81
Mean Relative Humidity 4pm (%)*	67	62	55	51	52	53	54	53	53	52	61	67	57
Mean Dewpoint (°F)*	20	22	29	38	49	59	63	62	55	43	34	25	42
Prevailing Wind Direction*	S	S	WNW	S	S	S	S	S	S	S	S	S	S
Prevailing Wind Speed (mph)*	9	9	12	9	8	8	7	7	8	8	9	9	9
Maximum Wind Gust (mph)*	69	58	62	78	76	68	67	66	62	53	53	61	78

Note: (*) Period of record is 1948-1995

Dayton Int'l Airport

Dayton is located near the center of the Miami River Valley, which is a nearly flat plain, 50 to 200 feet below the general elevation of the adjacent rolling country. Three Miami River tributaries, the Mad River, the Stillwater River, and Wolf Creek converge, fanwise, from the north to join the master stream within the city limits of Dayton. Heavy rains in March 1913 caused the worst flood disaster in the history of the Miami Valley. During the flood more than 400 people lost their lives and property damage amounted to $100 million. After the 1913 flood, dams were built on the streams north of Dayton, forming retarding basins. No floods have occurred at Dayton since the construction of these dams.

The elevation of the city of Dayton is about 750 feet. Terrain north of the city slopes gradually upward to about 1,100 feet at Indian Lake. Ten miles southeast of Indian Lake, near Bellefontaine, is the highest point in the state, with an elevation of about 1,550 feet. South of the city, the terrain slopes gradually downward to about 450 feet where the Miami River empties into the Ohio River.

Precipitation, which is rather evenly distributed throughout the year, and moderate temperatures help to make the Miami Valley a rich agricultural region. High relative humidities during much of the year cause some discomfort to people with allergies. Temperatures of zero or below will be experienced in about four years out of five, while 100 degrees or higher will be recorded in about one year out of five. Extreme temperatures are usually of short duration. The downward slope of about 700 feet in the 163 miles of the Miami River may have some moderating influence on the winter temperatures in the Miami Valley.

Based on the 1951-1980 period, the average last occurrence in the spring of freezing temperatures is mid-April, and the average first occurrence in the autumn is late October.

Cold, polar air, flowing across the Great Lakes, causes much cloudiness during the winter, and is accompanied by frequent snow flurries. These add little to the total snowfall.

Dayton Int'l Airport *Montgomery County* Elevation: 1,000 ft. Latitude: 39° 54' N Longitude: 84° 13' W

	JAN	FEB	MAR	APR	MAY	JUN	JUL	AUG	SEP	OCT	NOV	DEC	YEAR
Mean Maximum Temp. (°F)	35.3	39.4	49.8	62.1	71.9	80.7	84.4	83.1	76.4	64.0	51.4	38.9	61.4
Mean Temp. (°F)	27.8	31.2	40.4	51.6	61.6	70.7	74.4	73.0	65.6	53.9	43.0	31.7	52.1
Mean Minimum Temp. (°F)	20.3	23.0	31.0	41.1	51.2	60.6	64.4	62.8	54.9	43.8	34.6	24.5	42.7
Extreme Maximum Temp. (°F)	66	73	82	88	92	102	102	102	95	89	77	72	102
Extreme Minimum Temp. (°F)	-25	-12	-7	17	31	40	46	41	33	23	11	-20	-25
Days Maximum Temp. ≥ 90°F	0	0	0	0	0	3	6	5	1	0	0	0	15
Days Maximum Temp. ≤ 32°F	13	9	3	0	0	0	0	0	0	0	1	9	35
Days Minimum Temp. ≤ 32°F	27	23	18	6	0	0	0	0	0	3	14	24	115
Days Minimum Temp. ≤ 0°F	2	1	0	0	0	0	0	0	0	0	0	1	4
Heating Degree Days (base 65°F)	1,146	950	758	407	162	21	2	5	80	352	654	1,026	5,563
Cooling Degree Days (base 65°F)	0	0	2	12	62	197	300	259	106	14	0	0	952
Mean Precipitation (in.)	2.76	2.28	3.41	4.12	4.64	4.28	4.06	3.08	3.11	2.98	3.29	3.12	41.13
Maximum Precipitation (in.)*	9.9	5.8	7.6	6.8	9.0	10.9	8.5	8.0	5.7	6.3	8.1	10.0	59.8
Minimum Precipitation (in.)*	0.3	0.2	1.1	0.6	1.5	0.3	0.5	0.3	0.3	0.2	0.5	0.4	24.2
Extreme Maximum Daily Precip. (in.)	2.58	1.68	1.86	2.53	3.17	3.76	2.82	3.38	3.81	3.54	2.05	2.85	3.81
Days With ≥ 0.1" Precipitation	6	5	8	9	9	7	7	5	5	5	7	7	80
Days With ≥ 0.5" Precipitation	1	1	2	3	3	3	3	2	2	2	2	2	26
Days With ≥ 1.0" Precipitation	0	0	1	1	1	1	1	1	1	1	1	1	10
Mean Snowfall (in.)	8.0	6.3	4.1	0.6	trace	0.0	trace	trace	trace	0.4	0.8	5.1	25.3
Maximum Snowfall (in.)*	40	18	14	5	trace	0	0	0	0	6	13	16	53
Maximum 24-hr. Snowfall (in.)*	12	7	11	5	trace	0	0	0	0	5	8	6	12
Maximum Snow Depth (in.)	16	10	13	6	trace	0	trace	trace	trace	4	5	16	16
Days With ≥ 1.0" Snow Depth	10	8	3	0	0	0	0	0	0	0	0	6	27
Thunderstorm Days*	< 1	1	2	4	6	7	8	6	3	2	1	< 1	40
Foggy Days*	15	12	14	12	13	13	15	18	15	14	14	15	170
Predominant Sky Cover*	OVR	OVR	OVR	OVR	OVR	OVR	OVR	OVR	OVR	OVR	OVR	OVR	OVR
Mean Relative Humidity 7am (%)*	80	79	79	77	78	80	83	86	87	83	81	81	81
Mean Relative Humidity 4pm (%)*	68	64	59	53	52	52	53	53	52	52	63	69	57
Mean Dewpoint (°F)*	20	22	30	39	49	58	63	62	54	43	33	25	42
Prevailing Wind Direction*	W	WNW	WNW	SSW	SSW	SSW	SW	SW	SSW	SSW	SSW	SSW	SSW
Prevailing Wind Speed (mph)*	13	13	13	13	12	10	9	9	9	10	13	13	12
Maximum Wind Gust (mph)*	69	52	67	63	60	60	71	61	48	46	54	62	71

Note: (*) Period of record is 1948-1995

Mansfield Lahm Municipal Airport

Mansfield is in the north central highlands at the geographical and climatological junction of central Ohio, northwest Ohio, and northeast Ohio. The station is on a plateau 3 miles north of the city of Mansfield and surrounded by rolling open farmland. The general elevation ranges from around 1,300 to 1,400 feet above sea level with the 1,000-foot contour east to west some 15 miles to the north. The climate is continental, with the modifying effects of Lake Erie most pronounced in winter. Lake Erie is just 38 miles due north.

The lake influence, plus the elevation, produce cloudy skies and considerable snow shower activity from late November into April with any wind flow from northwest through northeast. Because of this, any windshift with a cold frontal passage in winter does not bring the clearing skies, indeed, more snow is often measured from the flurry activity behind the front than from the pre-frontal conditions. A frozen Lake Erie will allow clearing skies, but an open lake dictates overcast and snow flurries. Usually the lake is open enough to set off the flurries and cloudy conditions. The major snow producer will be an intense storm moving out of the southwest with the Gulf of Mexico moisture available. Snow cover is almost constant from December through March due to almost daily snow flurries, but the depth of cover is rarely more than 8 inches. Daytime winter temperatures are not above the freezing mark too often.

Spring is a short period of rapid transition from hard winter to summer conditions. April usually brings abundant shower activity and the crops and vegetation get a quick start.

Summer is a pleasant season with low humidities and no extremely high temperatures. Rarely does the temperature climb above the 90 degree point. Thunderstorms average about once every three days during the season from June through September. Highest winds are associated with the heavier thunderstorms, and while hail does not occur often, it is of major concern to the applegrowers in the area. Flooding problems are confined to the flash-flood type on the small streams in the area.

The growing season is normally about 153 days. Autumn usually produces many clear warm days and cool invigorating nights. Ground fog is at a maximum incidence during the autumn. Little rainfall occurs to interfere with harvest time and county fair time.

Mansfield Lahm Municipal Airport *Richland County* Elevation: 1,294 ft. Latitude: 40° 49' N Longitude: 82° 31' W

	JAN	FEB	MAR	APR	MAY	JUN	JUL	AUG	SEP	OCT	NOV	DEC	YEAR
Mean Maximum Temp. (°F)	33.2	36.3	46.2	59.2	69.4	78.0	81.7	80.0	73.4	61.5	49.3	37.0	58.8
Mean Temp. (°F)	26.1	28.6	37.3	48.9	58.9	67.8	71.8	70.3	63.3	52.0	41.6	30.3	49.7
Mean Minimum Temp. (°F)	18.9	20.9	28.3	38.6	48.4	57.6	61.8	60.6	53.2	42.4	33.8	23.5	40.7
Extreme Maximum Temp. (°F)	65	71	82	86	90	101	100	97	92	87	76	73	101
Extreme Minimum Temp. (°F)	-22	-11	-6	8	27	37	43	42	33	20	10	-17	-22
Days Maximum Temp. ≥ 90°F	0	0	0	0	0	1	2	2	0	0	0	0	5
Days Maximum Temp. ≤ 32°F	15	11	5	0	0	0	0	0	0	0	2	11	44
Days Minimum Temp. ≤ 32°F	28	24	21	9	0	0	0	0	0	4	15	25	126
Days Minimum Temp. ≤ 0°F	3	1	0	0	0	0	0	0	0	0	0	1	5
Heating Degree Days (base 65°F)	1,200	1,022	854	485	223	51	7	15	114	405	696	1,069	6,141
Cooling Degree Days (base 65°F)	0	0	1	8	42	142	224	187	70	9	0	0	683
Mean Precipitation (in.)	2.85	2.31	3.48	4.19	4.54	4.66	4.46	4.43	3.33	2.94	3.72	3.33	44.24
Maximum Precipitation (in.)*	11.5	5.4	7.0	7.0	8.8	10.0	13.2	8.6	7.8	6.4	12.8	11.2	67.2
Minimum Precipitation (in.)*	0.4	0.3	1.2	0.8	1.1	0.6	0.9	0.6	0.7	0.4	0.7	0.7	21.8
Extreme Maximum Daily Precip. (in.)	1.97	1.63	2.04	2.66	2.62	2.93	3.39	4.34	2.22	3.33	3.11	2.62	4.34
Days With ≥ 0.1" Precipitation	7	6	8	9	10	8	7	7	6	6	7	8	89
Days With ≥ 0.5" Precipitation	2	1	2	3	3	4	3	3	2	2	2	2	29
Days With ≥ 1.0" Precipitation	1	0	1	1	1	1	1	1	1	1	1	1	11
Mean Snowfall (in.)	13.1	10.3	8.0	2.7	trace	trace	0.0	0.0	0.0	0.6	2.5	10.5	47.7
Maximum Snowfall (in.)*	42	18	17	13	1	0	0	0	0	10	12	23	59
Maximum 24-hr. Snowfall (in.)*	10	9	8	12	1	0	0	0	0	8	5	12	12
Maximum Snow Depth (in.)	20	13	15	10	0	trace	0	0	0	2	4	15	20
Days With ≥ 1.0" Snow Depth	15	14	6	1	0	0	0	0	0	0	2	11	49
Thunderstorm Days*	< 1	< 1	2	3	5	6	7	6	3	1	1	< 1	34
Foggy Days*	13	12	14	13	14	13	14	17	15	13	13	15	166
Predominant Sky Cover*	OVR	OVR	OVR	OVR	OVR	OVR	SCT	SCT	OVR	OVR	OVR	OVR	OVR
Mean Relative Humidity 7am (%)*	82	81	81	78	78	81	83	87	87	83	82	83	82
Mean Relative Humidity 4pm (%)*	72	69	64	56	55	56	56	57	58	56	67	74	62
Mean Dewpoint (°F)*	20	21	28	37	47	58	62	61	54	42	33	24	40
Prevailing Wind Direction*	WSW	WSW	WSW	WSW	SSW	SSW	SW	SSW	S	S	SW	WSW	WSW
Prevailing Wind Speed (mph)*	15	14	15	14	13	12	10	10	9	10	14	14	13
Maximum Wind Gust (mph)*	62	59	62	68	60	68	81	69	61	53	69	69	81

Note: (*) Period of record is 1948-1995

Toledo Express Airport

Toledo is located on the western end of Lake Erie at the mouth of the Maumee River. Except for a bank up from the river about 30 feet, the terrain is generally level with only a slight slope toward the river and Lake Erie. The city has quite a diversified industrial section and excellent harbor facilities, making it a large transportation center for rail, water, and motor freight. Generally rich agricultural land is found in the surrounding area, especially up the Maumee Valley toward the Indiana state line.

Rainfall is usually sufficient for general agriculture. The terrain is level and drainage rather poor, therefore, a little less than the normal precipitation during the growing season is better than excessive amounts. Snowfall is generally light in this area, distributed throughout the winter from November to March with frequent thaws.

The nearness of Lake Erie and the other Great Lakes has a moderating effect on the temperature, and extremes are seldom recorded. On average, only fifteen days a year experience temperatures of 90 degrees or higher, and only eight days when it drops to zero or lower. The growing season averages 160 days, but has ranged from over 220 to less than 125 days.

Humidity is rather high throughout the year in this area, and there is an excessive amount of cloudiness. In the winter months the sun shines during only about 30 percent of the daylight hours. December and January, the cloudiest months, sometimes have as little as 16 percent of the possible hours of sunshine.

Severe windstorms, causing more than minor damage, occur infrequently. There are on the average twenty-three days per year having a sustained wind velocity of 32 mph or more.

Flooding in the Toledo area is produced by several factors. Heavy rains of one inch or more will cause a sudden rise in creeks and drainage ditches to the point of overflow. The western shores of Lake Erie are subject to flooding when the lake level is high and prolonged periods of east to northeast winds prevail.

Toledo Express Airport *Lucas County* Elevation: 668 ft. Latitude: 41° 35' N Longitude: 83° 48' W

	JAN	FEB	MAR	APR	MAY	JUN	JUL	AUG	SEP	OCT	NOV	DEC	YEAR
Mean Maximum Temp. (°F)	32.5	35.7	46.3	59.6	70.8	80.4	84.3	82.0	75.2	62.4	49.3	36.4	59.6
Mean Temp. (°F)	25.2	27.9	37.1	49.0	59.5	69.1	73.2	71.3	63.9	51.9	41.1	29.6	49.9
Mean Minimum Temp. (°F)	18.0	20.1	27.8	38.3	48.1	57.7	62.1	60.6	52.5	41.3	32.9	22.8	40.2
Extreme Maximum Temp. (°F)	66	71	81	88	94	104	104	99	96	89	80	70	104
Extreme Minimum Temp. (°F)	-20	-14	-6	8	25	37	40	34	30	16	9	-19	-20
Days Maximum Temp. ≥ 90°F	0	0	0	0	1	4	6	4	1	0	0	0	16
Days Maximum Temp. ≤ 32°F	16	11	4	0	0	0	0	0	0	0	1	11	43
Days Minimum Temp. ≤ 32°F	28	25	22	8	1	0	0	0	0	5	15	26	130
Days Minimum Temp. ≤ 0°F	3	2	0	0	0	0	0	0	0	0	0	1	6
Heating Degree Days (base 65°F)	1,226	1,041	859	482	209	37	3	12	108	409	710	1,090	6,186
Cooling Degree Days (base 65°F)	0	0	1	9	45	166	264	215	80	9	0	0	789
Mean Precipitation (in.)	2.05	2.03	2.52	3.13	3.48	3.54	3.21	3.26	2.78	2.62	2.78	2.71	34.11
Maximum Precipitation (in.)*	4.6	5.4	5.7	6.1	5.1	8.5	6.8	8.5	8.1	5.5	6.9	6.8	40.8
Minimum Precipitation (in.)*	0.3	0.3	0.6	0.9	1.0	0.3	0.3	0.4	0.6	0.3	0.5	0.5	22.0
Extreme Maximum Daily Precip. (in.)	1.30	2.59	2.60	2.81	1.85	3.12	3.15	2.21	2.70	2.88	2.71	2.51	3.15
Days With ≥ 0.1" Precipitation	5	5	7	7	7	6	6	6	5	5	6	7	72
Days With ≥ 0.5" Precipitation	1	1	1	2	2	2	2	2	2	2	2	2	21
Days With ≥ 1.0" Precipitation	0	0	0	0	1	1	1	1	1	1	1	0	7
Mean Snowfall (in.)	***11.3***	***8.6***	***5.9***	***1.4***	na	na	na	na	na	na	***1.9***	***7.4***	na
Maximum Snowfall (in.)*	31	17	18	12	1	0	0	0	trace	2	18	24	72
Maximum 24-hr. Snowfall (in.)*	10	8	9	7	1	0	0	0	trace	2	7	14	14
Maximum Snow Depth (in.)	***12***	***16***	***8***	***7***	***1***	na	na	na	na	na	***3***	***7***	na
Days With ≥ 1.0" Snow Depth	***15***	***13***	***6***	***1***	***0***	na	na	***0***	na	na	***1***	***10***	na
Thunderstorm Days*	< 1	1	2	4	5	7	7	6	4	1	1	< 1	38
Foggy Days*	13	11	14	12	12	11	14	18	15	13	14	15	162
Predominant Sky Cover*	OVR	OVR	OVR	OVR	OVR	OVR	SCT	SCT	OVR	OVR	OVR	OVR	OVR
Mean Relative Humidity 7am (%)*	80	80	81	80	80	82	86	91	91	86	83	83	84
Mean Relative Humidity 4pm (%)*	68	65	59	53	51	52	53	56	54	55	65	72	58
Mean Dewpoint (°F)*	17	19	27	36	47	57	62	61	54	42	32	23	40
Prevailing Wind Direction*	WSW	WSW	ENE	WSW	WSW	SW	SW	SW	SW	SW	WSW	WSW	WSW
Prevailing Wind Speed (mph)*	13	13	12	13	12	9	8	8	9	10	13	13	12
Maximum Wind Gust (mph)*	62	52	64	63	58	59	66	75	54	49	55	56	75

Note: (*) Period of record is 1955-1995

Youngstown Municipal Airport

The Youngstown Municipal Airport is located in northeastern Ohio approximately eight miles north of the city of Youngstown in Trumbull County. Airport elevation is 1,178 feet, about 200 feet higher than most communities in the Mahoning and Shenango River Valleys. There are numerous natural and man-made lakes in the region, including Lake Erie, 45 miles to the north. Drainage from the area flows southward through the Mahoning and Shenango Rivers which join to form the Beaver River at New Castle, Pennsylvania. The Beaver empties into the Ohio River at Rochester, Pennsylvania.

This entire area experiences frequent outbreaks of cold Canadian air masses which may be modified by passage over Lake Erie. This effect produces widespread cloudiness especially during the cool months of the year. The winter months are characterized by persistent cloudiness and intermittent snow flurries. The daily temperature range during most winter days is quite small. During most winters, the bulk of the snow falls as flurries of 2 inches or less per occurrence, although several snowstorms per year will produce amounts in the four to 10 inch range.

Destructive storms seldom occur, and tornadoes are not common. During recent years flood control projects have all but eliminated the threat of serious river flooding. Flash flooding of small streams and creeks rarely affects residential areas. Certain communities have well known areas of urban flooding during periods of prolonged heavy thunderstorms.

The climate of the Youngstown district has had an important role in the growth and development of this industrial area. Temperatures seldom reach extreme values especially during the summer months. However, high humidity during most days of the year tends to accentuate the temperature. Rainfall, reasonably well distributed throughout the year, provides a more than adequate supply of water for agriculture, industrial, and residential use.

Based on the 1951-1980 period, the average first occurrence of 32 degrees Fahrenheit in the fall is October 14 and the average last occurrence in the spring is May 6.

Youngstown Municipal Airport *Trumbull County* Elevation: 1,180 ft. Latitude: 41° 15' N Longitude: 80° 40' W

	JAN	FEB	MAR	APR	MAY	JUN	JUL	AUG	SEP	OCT	NOV	DEC	YEAR
Mean Maximum Temp. (°F)	33.2	36.6	46.1	59.3	69.5	77.9	81.9	80.5	73.0	61.0	49.3	37.3	58.8
Mean Temp. (°F)	26.1	28.6	36.7	48.6	58.0	66.6	70.8	69.4	62.2	51.2	41.6	30.6	49.2
Mean Minimum Temp. (°F)	19.0	20.5	27.4	37.7	46.5	55.1	59.6	58.3	51.4	41.3	33.9	23.9	39.6
Extreme Maximum Temp. (°F)	68	73	82	88	90	99	100	97	92	87	78	76	100
Extreme Minimum Temp. (°F)	-22	-8	-10	14	25	34	40	32	29	20	12	-12	-22
Days Maximum Temp. ≥ 90°F	0	0	0	0	0	1	3	2	0	0	0	0	6
Days Maximum Temp. ≤ 32°F	15	11	5	0	0	0	0	0	0	0	2	11	44
Days Minimum Temp. ≤ 32°F	27	24	22	10	1	0	0	0	0	4	15	26	129
Days Minimum Temp. ≤ 0°F	2	1	0	0	0	0	0	0	0	0	0	1	4
Heating Degree Days (base 65°F)	1,199	1,023	871	495	243	65	11	22	133	427	696	1,058	6,243
Cooling Degree Days (base 65°F)	0	0	1	8	34	118	197	166	57	7	0	0	588
Mean Precipitation (in.)	2.51	2.09	3.02	3.36	3.70	3.86	4.41	3.41	3.82	2.74	3.09	2.91	38.92
Maximum Precipitation (in.)*	7.6	5.3	6.2	6.4	6.2	10.7	9.7	7.9	6.1	8.6	9.1	6.5	48.6
Minimum Precipitation (in.)*	0.7	0.5	1.1	1.0	0.8	0.7	1.6	0.5	0.3	0.4	0.9	0.9	23.8
Extreme Maximum Daily Precip. (in.)	1.34	1.63	1.41	1.53	1.95	3.57	4.65	3.47	4.09	2.05	2.73	1.55	4.65
Days With ≥ 0.1" Precipitation	7	6	8	8	9	8	7	6	7	6	7	8	87
Days With ≥ 0.5" Precipitation	1	1	2	2	2	2	3	2	3	2	2	1	23
Days With ≥ 1.0" Precipitation	0	0	0	1	1	1	1	1	1	0	0	0	6
Mean Snowfall (in.)	15.9	11.9	10.8	3.0	trace	trace	trace	trace	trace	0.8	4.0	13.3	59.7
Maximum Snowfall (in.)*	36	23	31	12	5	0	0	0	trace	8	31	30	91
Maximum 24-hr. Snowfall (in.)*	17	9	15	12	5	0	0	0	trace	5	17	12	17
Maximum Snow Depth (in.)	18	14	11	10	trace	trace	trace	trace	trace	1	6	13	18
Days With ≥ 1.0" Snow Depth	17	14	7	1	0	0	0	0	0	0	2	13	54
Thunderstorm Days*	< 1	< 1	2	3	4	7	7	5	3	1	1	< 1	33
Foggy Days*	13	12	14	13	15	16	17	20	17	15	13	14	179
Predominant Sky Cover*	OVR	OVR	OVR	OVR	OVR	OVR	OVR	OVR	OVR	OVR	OVR	OVR	OVR
Mean Relative Humidity 7am (%)*	81	80	80	77	79	82	85	88	89	85	81	82	82
Mean Relative Humidity 4pm (%)*	70	66	60	54	52	54	55	55	57	57	66	72	60
Mean Dewpoint (°F)*	18	19	26	36	46	56	60	60	53	42	32	23	39
Prevailing Wind Direction*	WSW	WSW	W	SW	SW	SW	SW	SW	SW	SW	SW	WSW	SW
Prevailing Wind Speed (mph)*	14	13	13	13	12	9	9	8	9	10	12	14	12
Maximum Wind Gust (mph)*	67	54	78	75	70	58	66	58	62	51	53	62	78

Note: (*) Period of record is 1948-1995

Barnesville *Belmont County* Elevation: 1,240 ft. Latitude: 39° 59' N Longitude: 81° 09' W

	JAN	FEB	MAR	APR	MAY	JUN	JUL	AUG	SEP	OCT	NOV	DEC	YEAR
Mean Maximum Temp. (°F)	35.5	38.8	48.6	61.1	70.2	78.7	82.5	81.3	74.3	62.8	50.9	39.4	60.4
Mean Temp. (°F)	27.6	30.1	38.5	49.8	59.4	68.1	72.3	70.6	63.4	52.2	42.0	31.9	50.5
Mean Minimum Temp. (°F)	19.7	21.2	28.4	38.5	48.4	57.4	62.1	59.9	52.4	41.4	33.1	24.3	40.6
Extreme Maximum Temp. (°F)	71	76	82	87	90	96	100	97	93	85	76	75	100
Extreme Minimum Temp. (°F)	-23	-10	-5	15	26	33	45	38	30	18	na	-17	na
Days Maximum Temp. ≥ 90°F	0	0	0	0	0	1	2	3	1	0	0	0	7
Days Maximum Temp. ≤ 32°F	13	9	3	0	0	0	0	0	0	0	2	8	35
Days Minimum Temp. ≤ 32°F	27	24	21	9	1	0	0	0	0	5	15	24	126
Days Minimum Temp. ≤ 0°F	2	1	0	0	0	0	0	0	0	0	0	1	4
Heating Degree Days (base 65°F)	1,151	980	815	458	207	44	6	14	115	399	684	1,019	5,892
Cooling Degree Days (base 65°F)	0	0	2	9	40	144	239	196	72	8	0	0	710
Mean Precipitation (in.)	2.97	2.62	3.54	3.91	4.50	4.63	4.39	3.74	3.23	3.09	4.01	2.97	43.60
Extreme Maximum Daily Precip. (in.)	2.03	2.17	1.69	1.74	2.32	2.28	3.67	5.12	2.42	1.56	2.91	1.56	5.12
Days With ≥ 0.1" Precipitation	7	6	8	9	9	8	7	6	6	6	8	7	87
Days With ≥ 0.5" Precipitation	2	2	2	3	3	3	3	2	2	2	3	2	29
Days With ≥ 1.0" Precipitation	0	0	1	1	1	1	1	1	1	1	1	0	9
Mean Snowfall (in.)	10.1	7.7	4.9	1.2	trace	0.0	0.0	trace	0.0	0.1	1.8	5.8	31.6
Maximum Snow Depth (in.)	16	20	17	12	trace	0	0	trace	0	2	4	8	20
Days With ≥ 1.0" Snow Depth	12	9	4	0	0	0	0	0	0	0	2	7	34

Bellefontaine *Logan County* Elevation: 1,185 ft. Latitude: 40° 21' N Longitude: 83° 46' W

	JAN	FEB	MAR	APR	MAY	JUN	JUL	AUG	SEP	OCT	NOV	DEC	YEAR
Mean Maximum Temp. (°F)	33.4	37.5	47.6	60.6	71.1	79.5	82.9	81.8	75.9	63.4	50.4	37.6	60.2
Mean Temp. (°F)	25.7	28.9	38.1	49.8	60.4	69.3	72.8	71.6	64.8	52.8	41.8	30.1	50.5
Mean Minimum Temp. (°F)	17.9	20.2	28.5	38.9	49.6	59.0	62.6	61.4	53.8	42.2	33.0	22.6	40.8
Extreme Maximum Temp. (°F)	66	72	82	87	90	101	99	101	95	89	77	71	101
Extreme Minimum Temp. (°F)	-27	-13	-12	9	28	37	45	39	30	17	8	-22	-27
Days Maximum Temp. ≥ 90°F	0	0	0	0	0	2	4	3	1	0	0	0	10
Days Maximum Temp. ≤ 32°F	14	10	4	0	0	0	0	0	0	0	2	10	40
Days Minimum Temp. ≤ 32°F	28	24	21	8	1	0	0	0	0	5	16	26	129
Days Minimum Temp. ≤ 0°F	3	2	0	0	0	0	0	0	0	0	0	2	7
Heating Degree Days (base 65°F)	1,212	1,014	828	457	188	34	4	10	92	384	691	1,074	5,988
Cooling Degree Days (base 65°F)	0	0	1	8	50	169	253	222	94	13	0	0	810
Mean Precipitation (in.)	2.64	2.13	2.93	3.58	4.13	4.44	4.19	3.57	2.81	2.62	3.17	3.03	39.24
Extreme Maximum Daily Precip. (in.)	3.29	2.30	1.85	2.37	2.47	3.30	4.45	3.02	2.40	2.47	1.78	2.96	4.45
Days With ≥ 0.1" Precipitation	6	5	7	8	9	8	7	6	5	6	7	7	81
Days With ≥ 0.5" Precipitation	1	1	2	3	3	3	3	2	2	1	2	2	25
Days With ≥ 1.0" Precipitation	0	0	0	1	1	1	1	1	1	1	1	1	9
Mean Snowfall (in.)	na	3.2	1.2	0.2	0.0	0.0	0.0	0.0	0.0	0.2	0.4	2.5	na
Maximum Snow Depth (in.)	19	14	10	1	0	0	0	0	0	1	4	11	19
Days With ≥ 1.0" Snow Depth	7	4	1	0	0	0	0	0	0	0	0	3	15

Bowling Green WWTP *Wood County* Elevation: 674 ft. Latitude: 41° 23' N Longitude: 83° 37' W

	JAN	FEB	MAR	APR	MAY	JUN	JUL	AUG	SEP	OCT	NOV	DEC	YEAR
Mean Maximum Temp. (°F)	32.2	35.7	46.0	59.4	70.7	80.7	84.1	82.1	75.9	63.0	49.6	36.5	59.7
Mean Temp. (°F)	24.9	27.9	36.6	48.5	59.4	69.7	73.1	71.0	64.1	52.2	41.1	29.6	49.8
Mean Minimum Temp. (°F)	17.6	20.0	27.2	37.5	48.1	58.6	62.0	59.9	52.2	41.4	32.6	22.6	40.0
Extreme Maximum Temp. (°F)	66	72	80	88	92	104	101	98	95	90	78	70	104
Extreme Minimum Temp. (°F)	-20	-13	-5	8	28	39	45	38	30	21	11	-19	-20
Days Maximum Temp. ≥ 90°F	0	0	0	0	1	4	6	4	1	0	0	0	16
Days Maximum Temp. ≤ 32°F	16	11	4	0	0	0	0	0	0	0	1	11	43
Days Minimum Temp. ≤ 32°F	28	25	22	9	0	0	0	0	0	4	16	26	130
Days Minimum Temp. ≤ 0°F	4	2	0	0	0	0	0	0	0	0	0	1	7
Heating Degree Days (base 65°F)	1,238	1,044	873	496	211	32	3	13	103	402	710	1,090	6,215
Cooling Degree Days (base 65°F)	0	0	1	8	46	180	261	206	83	11	0	0	796
Mean Precipitation (in.)	1.91	1.84	2.17	3.14	3.76	3.37	3.66	3.64	2.61	2.82	2.57	2.43	33.92
Extreme Maximum Daily Precip. (in.)	1.47	2.00	1.68	1.90	2.66	4.25	4.08	3.31	2.49	3.37	2.12	2.11	4.25
Days With ≥ 0.1" Precipitation	5	4	6	7	8	7	7	6	5	6	6	6	73
Days With ≥ 0.5" Precipitation	1	1	1	2	2	2	3	2	2	2	2	1	21
Days With ≥ 1.0" Precipitation	0	0	0	1	1	1	1	1	1	1	0	0	7
Mean Snowfall (in.)	7.1	5.4	3.2	0.6	trace	0.0	0.0	0.0	0.0	0.0	0.6	4.7	21.6
Maximum Snow Depth (in.)	14	18	10	7	1	0	0	0	0	0	3	11	18
Days With ≥ 1.0" Snow Depth	14	11	5	0	0	0	0	0	0	0	1	7	38

Bucyrus *Crawford County* Elevation: 955 ft. Latitude: 40° 49' N Longitude: 82° 58' W

	JAN	FEB	MAR	APR	MAY	JUN	JUL	AUG	SEP	OCT	NOV	DEC	YEAR
Mean Maximum Temp. (°F)	32.6	35.7	45.6	59.6	70.2	79.5	83.1	81.4	74.8	61.9	49.2	36.6	59.2
Mean Temp. (°F)	25.2	27.6	36.3	48.5	58.8	68.4	72.3	70.5	63.4	51.4	40.8	29.7	49.4
Mean Minimum Temp. (°F)	17.8	19.5	26.9	37.4	47.4	57.3	61.4	59.6	52.0	40.8	32.4	22.7	39.6
Extreme Maximum Temp. (°F)	64	71	81	88	91	102	100	99	95	87	77	72	102
Extreme Minimum Temp. (°F)	-26	-18	-11	10	27	37	43	39	30	20	12	-18	-26
Days Maximum Temp. ≥ 90°F	0	0	0	0	0	3	4	3	1	0	0	0	11
Days Maximum Temp. ≤ 32°F	16	11	5	0	0	0	0	0	0	0	2	11	45
Days Minimum Temp. ≤ 32°F	27	25	23	10	0	0	0	0	0	5	16	26	132
Days Minimum Temp. ≤ 0°F	3	2	0	0	0	0	0	0	0	0	0	1	6
Heating Degree Days (base 65°F)	1,227	1,052	884	495	225	45	7	16	114	423	721	1,088	6,297
Cooling Degree Days (base 65°F)	0	0	1	7	40	154	240	195	74	9	0	0	720
Mean Precipitation (in.)	2.48	2.02	2.66	3.42	4.26	4.21	4.44	3.84	3.19	2.62	3.07	2.86	39.07
Extreme Maximum Daily Precip. (in.)	2.20	1.45	1.50	1.80	2.18	3.27	3.42	8.68	3.58	2.51	1.57	1.95	8.68
Days With ≥ 0.1" Precipitation	6	5	7	8	9	8	8	6	6	6	7	7	83
Days With ≥ 0.5" Precipitation	1	1	2	2	3	3	3	3	2	1	2	2	25
Days With ≥ 1.0" Precipitation	1	0	0	0	1	1	1	1	1	0	1	0	7
Mean Snowfall (in.)	7.4	4.6	3.4	0.9	0.1	0.0	0.0	0.0	0.0	0.1	0.9	5.1	22.5
Maximum Snow Depth (in.)	14	13	10	8	2	0	0	0	0	1	3	17	17
Days With ≥ 1.0" Snow Depth	12	7	3	0	0	0	0	0	0	0	1	6	29

The period of record for all cooperative weather station data is 1980 – 2009. See User Guide for detailed explanation of data.

Cadiz *Harrison County* Elevation: 1,259 ft. Latitude: 40° 16' N Longitude: 81° 00' W

	JAN	FEB	MAR	APR	MAY	JUN	JUL	AUG	SEP	OCT	NOV	DEC	YEAR
Mean Maximum Temp. (°F)	35.2	38.9	48.5	61.1	70.3	78.5	82.2	81.3	74.7	63.1	50.6	39.0	60.3
Mean Temp. (°F)	27.2	30.3	38.9	50.3	60.0	68.5	72.6	71.1	64.3	52.8	42.0	31.6	50.8
Mean Minimum Temp. (°F)	19.5	21.5	29.1	39.6	49.5	58.3	62.8	61.1	53.9	42.5	33.5	24.1	41.3
Extreme Maximum Temp. (°F)	69	76	81	89	89	95	101	97	94	87	79	75	101
Extreme Minimum Temp. (°F)	-24	-10	-6	14	26	35	47	40	35	22	10	-17	-24
Days Maximum Temp. ≥ 90°F	0	0	0	0	0	1	3	3	1	0	0	0	8
Days Maximum Temp. ≤ 32°F	14	9	4	0	0	0	0	0	0	0	1	9	37
Days Minimum Temp. ≤ 32°F	26	22	18	7	1	0	0	0	0	4	14	24	116
Days Minimum Temp. ≤ 0°F	2	1	0	0	0	0	0	0	0	0	0	1	4
Heating Degree Days (base 65°F)	1,168	978	805	446	196	38	4	11	99	381	683	1,031	5,840
Cooling Degree Days (base 65°F)	0	0	1	12	46	148	246	208	85	11	1	0	758
Mean Precipitation (in.)	3.02	2.37	3.17	3.48	4.39	4.27	4.31	3.80	3.43	2.75	3.37	2.90	41.26
Extreme Maximum Daily Precip. (in.)	2.07	1.75	1.64	2.00	2.32	5.00	3.28	2.70	5.09	1.93	2.90	2.05	5.09
Days With ≥ 0.1" Precipitation	7	6	8	9	9	8	8	6	6	6	7	7	87
Days With ≥ 0.5" Precipitation	2	1	2	2	3	3	3	3	2	2	2	2	27
Days With ≥ 1.0" Precipitation	0	0	0	1	1	1	1	1	1	1	0	0	7
Mean Snowfall (in.)	8.8	6.1	4.9	1.2	0.0	0.0	0.0	0.0	0.0	0.1	1.5	5.6	28.2
Maximum Snow Depth (in.)	***10***	***15***	***12***	2	0	0	0	0	0	***trace***	***3***	na	na
Days With ≥ 1.0" Snow Depth	***9***	6	3	0	0	0	0	0	0	0	1	***6***	***25***

Cambridge *Guernsey County* Elevation: 799 ft. Latitude: 40° 01' N Longitude: 81° 35' W

	JAN	FEB	MAR	APR	MAY	JUN	JUL	AUG	SEP	OCT	NOV	DEC	YEAR
Mean Maximum Temp. (°F)	38.0	42.6	52.9	65.7	74.2	82.0	85.2	84.2	77.6	66.0	53.8	41.6	63.6
Mean Temp. (°F)	30.0	33.3	42.0	53.3	62.0	70.2	74.1	73.0	66.0	54.4	44.1	33.7	53.0
Mean Minimum Temp. (°F)	21.8	23.9	31.0	40.8	49.7	58.4	63.0	61.7	54.4	42.7	34.5	25.7	42.3
Extreme Maximum Temp. (°F)	72	76	83	90	92	98	102	99	96	90	80	77	102
Extreme Minimum Temp. (°F)	-32	-12	-3	17	29	38	42	37	32	19	9	-17	-32
Days Maximum Temp. ≥ 90°F	0	0	0	0	0	3	6	5	1	0	0	0	15
Days Maximum Temp. ≤ 32°F	9	6	1	0	0	0	0	0	0	0	1	6	23
Days Minimum Temp. ≤ 32°F	25	22	18	6	1	0	0	0	0	5	13	23	113
Days Minimum Temp. ≤ 0°F	2	1	0	0	0	0	0	0	0	0	0	1	4
Heating Degree Days (base 65°F)	1,080	891	709	359	144	21	2	5	71	335	619	964	5,200
Cooling Degree Days (base 65°F)	0	0	2	14	57	185	292	259	107	13	0	0	929
Mean Precipitation (in.)	2.95	2.19	3.09	3.52	4.18	3.92	4.25	3.62	3.32	2.78	3.26	2.79	39.87
Extreme Maximum Daily Precip. (in.)	2.17	1.83	2.08	2.29	2.01	4.97	2.74	5.45	5.33	2.37	2.32	1.65	5.45
Days With ≥ 0.1" Precipitation	6	6	8	7	9	8	8	6	5	6	7	7	83
Days With ≥ 0.5" Precipitation	2	1	2	2	3	3	3	2	2	2	2	2	26
Days With ≥ 1.0" Precipitation	1	0	0	1	1	1	1	1	1	1	1	0	9
Mean Snowfall (in.)	6.3	4.5	2.8	0.7	trace	0.0	0.0	0.0	0.0	trace	0.7	3.2	18.2
Maximum Snow Depth (in.)	9	19	9	10	trace	0	0	0	0	trace	5	6	19
Days With ≥ 1.0" Snow Depth	11	7	2	0	0	0	0	0	0	0	0	5	25

Carpenter 2 S *Meigs County* Elevation: 821 ft. Latitude: 39° 09' N Longitude: 82° 13' W

	JAN	FEB	MAR	APR	MAY	JUN	JUL	AUG	SEP	OCT	NOV	DEC	YEAR
Mean Maximum Temp. (°F)	***39.0***	42.8	53.2	64.9	73.3	***81.2***	***84.7***	***84.0***	77.2	66.3	***54.6***	***42.9***	***63.7***
Mean Temp. (°F)	***30.2***	33.0	41.9	52.6	61.2	***69.5***	***73.3***	***72.1***	64.7	53.4	***43.9***	***33.9***	***52.5***
Mean Minimum Temp. (°F)	***21.3***	23.1	30.5	40.2	49.1	***57.7***	***61.9***	***60.2***	52.1	40.6	***33.2***	***24.9***	***41.2***
Extreme Maximum Temp. (°F)	***75***	***77***	***83***	***89***	***90***	***99***	***101***	***101***	***97***	***87***	***80***	***78***	***101***
Extreme Minimum Temp. (°F)	***-25***	***-11***	***-5***	***15***	***27***	***37***	***44***	***35***	***29***	***17***	***8***	***-4***	***-25***
Days Maximum Temp. ≥ 90°F	***0***	0	0	0	0	2	5	5	1	0	***0***	***0***	***13***
Days Maximum Temp. ≤ 32°F	***9***	6	1	0	0	0	0	0	0	0	***0***	***7***	***23***
Days Minimum Temp. ≤ 32°F	***26***	23	18	7	1	0	0	0	0	7	***15***	***23***	***120***
Days Minimum Temp. ≤ 0°F	***2***	1	0	0	0	0	0	0	0	0	***0***	***1***	***4***
Heating Degree Days (base 65°F)	***1,073***	899	714	381	163	***25***	***3***	***7***	93	364	***627***	***958***	***5,307***
Cooling Degree Days (base 65°F)	***0***	0	3	15	53	***167***	***267***	***234***	90	12	***2***	***0***	***843***
Mean Precipitation (in.)	***2.90***	***2.82***	3.67	3.55	4.39	3.76	4.47	3.32	3.22	2.90	***3.22***	***2.82***	***41.04***
Extreme Maximum Daily Precip. (in.)	***1.81***	***3.60***	***4.87***	***1.80***	***2.96***	***2.23***	***2.76***	***3.22***	***4.34***	***2.20***	***2.00***	na	na
Days With ≥ 0.1" Precipitation	***7***	***6***	7	8	8	***7***	8	6	6	6	***7***	***6***	***82***
Days With ≥ 0.5" Precipitation	***2***	***2***	3	2	3	***3***	3	2	2	2	***2***	***2***	***28***
Days With ≥ 1.0" Precipitation	***0***	***1***	1	1	1	1	1	1	1	1	***1***	***0***	***10***
Mean Snowfall (in.)	***6.9***	***4.4***	***2.7***	0.9	trace	0.0	0.0	0.0	0.0	trace	***0.6***	***3.1***	***18.6***
Maximum Snow Depth (in.)	na	na	na	na	na	na	na	na	na	na	na	na	na
Days With ≥ 1.0" Snow Depth	na	na	***1***	0	0	0	0	0	0	***0***	***0***	na	na

Centerburg 2 SE *Knox County* Elevation: 1,205 ft. Latitude: 40° 18' N Longitude: 82° 39' W

	JAN	FEB	MAR	APR	MAY	JUN	JUL	AUG	SEP	OCT	NOV	DEC	YEAR
Mean Maximum Temp. (°F)	33.7	37.3	47.6	60.9	70.6	79.2	82.6	81.4	74.7	62.6	50.3	37.3	59.8
Mean Temp. (°F)	25.8	28.4	37.8	49.9	59.6	68.6	72.2	70.8	63.5	51.6	41.3	29.7	49.9
Mean Minimum Temp. (°F)	17.4	19.6	28.0	38.6	48.6	57.9	61.6	60.0	52.2	40.6	32.3	22.3	39.9
Extreme Maximum Temp. (°F)	67	73	82	87	89	99	99	97	94	88	78	70	99
Extreme Minimum Temp. (°F)	-29	-16	-6	11	27	37	44	38	32	21	7	-23	-29
Days Maximum Temp. ≥ 90°F	0	0	0	0	0	2	3	3	1	0	0	0	9
Days Maximum Temp. ≤ 32°F	14	10	4	0	0	0	0	0	0	0	2	10	40
Days Minimum Temp. ≤ 32°F	28	25	21	8	1	0	0	0	0	6	16	26	131
Days Minimum Temp. ≤ 0°F	4	2	0	0	0	0	0	0	0	0	0	1	7
Heating Degree Days (base 65°F)	1,210	1,027	836	456	203	39	5	13	108	417	704	1,088	6,106
Cooling Degree Days (base 65°F)	0	0	1	9	42	152	234	201	70	8	0	0	717
Mean Precipitation (in.)	2.85	2.40	3.05	3.76	4.51	4.56	4.43	3.74	3.15	2.90	3.45	3.14	41.94
Extreme Maximum Daily Precip. (in.)	2.82	2.75	2.25	2.11	2.75	3.46	2.95	3.34	2.76	2.81	1.70	2.31	3.46
Days With ≥ 0.1" Precipitation	6	6	7	8	8	8	7	6	5	6	7	7	81
Days With ≥ 0.5" Precipitation	2	2	2	2	3	3	3	3	2	2	3	2	29
Days With ≥ 1.0" Precipitation	0	0	0	1	1	1	1	1	1	1	1	1	9
Mean Snowfall (in.)	4.6	2.1	2.1	0.2	trace	0.0	0.0	0.0	0.0	0.1	0.8	2.5	12.4
Maximum Snow Depth (in.)	23	9	10	7	1	0	0	0	0	1	4	10	23
Days With ≥ 1.0" Snow Depth	9	7	3	1	0	0	0	0	0	0	1	5	26

The period of record for all cooperative weather station data is 1980 – 2009. See User Guide for detailed explanation of data.

Chardon *Geauga County* Elevation: 1,129 ft. Latitude: 41° 35' N Longitude: 81° 11' W

	JAN	FEB	MAR	APR	MAY	JUN	JUL	AUG	SEP	OCT	NOV	DEC	YEAR
Mean Maximum Temp. (°F)	32.3	35.1	43.7	57.1	67.7	76.7	80.4	79.0	72.1	60.2	48.5	36.6	57.5
Mean Temp. (°F)	24.4	25.9	33.9	46.1	56.2	65.3	69.4	68.0	61.0	50.0	40.5	29.5	47.5
Mean Minimum Temp. (°F)	16.3	16.7	24.2	35.0	44.6	53.9	58.3	56.9	49.8	39.7	32.4	22.4	37.5
Extreme Maximum Temp. (°F)	67	73	82	88	90	100	98	96	92	85	79	73	100
Extreme Minimum Temp. (°F)	-23	-17	-17	5	23	33	40	33	29	17	4	-21	-23
Days Maximum Temp. ≥ 90°F	0	0	0	0	0	1	2	2	0	0	0	0	5
Days Maximum Temp. ≤ 32°F	16	13	7	0	0	0	0	0	0	0	2	11	49
Days Minimum Temp. ≤ 32°F	28	26	25	13	2	0	0	0	0	6	16	26	142
Days Minimum Temp. ≤ 0°F	4	3	1	0	0	0	0	0	0	0	0	1	9
Heating Degree Days (base 65°F)	1,253	1,099	956	565	290	86	24	36	160	463	729	1,093	6,754
Cooling Degree Days (base 65°F)	0	0	1	4	23	102	166	136	46	4	0	0	482
Mean Precipitation (in.)	3.59	2.79	3.27	4.03	4.42	4.46	4.38	4.24	4.30	4.06	4.30	4.40	48.24
Extreme Maximum Daily Precip. (in.)	1.78	2.33	2.25	2.30	3.13	3.66	5.50	3.75	2.65	2.00	2.89	2.14	5.50
Days With ≥ 0.1" Precipitation	10	8	9	10	9	8	8	7	8	9	10	12	108
Days With ≥ 0.5" Precipitation	2	1	2	3	3	3	3	3	3	3	3	3	32
Days With ≥ 1.0" Precipitation	0	0	0	1	1	1	1	1	1	1	1	1	9
Mean Snowfall (in.)	28.6	19.2	14.4	4.5	trace	0.0	0.0	0.0	0.0	0.9	9.5	25.7	102.8
Maximum Snow Depth (in.)	23	22	20	14	trace	0	0	0	0	7	47	23	47
Days With ≥ 1.0" Snow Depth	23	20	12	2	0	0	0	0	0	1	5	17	80

Chillicothe Mound City *Ross County* Elevation: 649 ft. Latitude: 39° 22' N Longitude: 83° 00' W

	JAN	FEB	MAR	APR	MAY	JUN	JUL	AUG	SEP	OCT	NOV	DEC	YEAR
Mean Maximum Temp. (°F)	***38.0***	***43.0***	***52.3***	***64.6***	***73.5***	82.5	***85.7***	***85.0***	***78.4***	***67.0***	***54.3***	***42.4***	***63.9***
Mean Temp. (°F)	***29.1***	***33.3***	***41.3***	***52.4***	***61.7***	***70.9***	***74.6***	***73.2***	***65.8***	***54.2***	***44.0***	***33.8***	***52.8***
Mean Minimum Temp. (°F)	***20.1***	***23.4***	***30.2***	***40.1***	***49.8***	***59.2***	***63.4***	***61.4***	***53.0***	***41.4***	***33.6***	***25.0***	***41.7***
Extreme Maximum Temp. (°F)	73	77	88	90	93	103	103	105	100	92	82	80	105
Extreme Minimum Temp. (°F)	-29	-14	-10	16	29	36	41	39	32	17	11	-21	-29
Days Maximum Temp. ≥ 90°F	0	0	0	0	0	4	7	6	2	0	0	0	19
Days Maximum Temp. ≤ 32°F	9	5	1	0	0	0	0	0	0	0	0	6	21
Days Minimum Temp. ≤ 32°F	25	22	18	6	0	0	0	0	0	5	14	22	112
Days Minimum Temp. ≤ 0°F	2	1	0	0	0	0	0	0	0	0	0	1	4
Heating Degree Days (base 65°F)	***1,107***	***891***	***729***	***387***	***157***	***21***	***1***	***6***	***83***	***341***	***625***	***960***	***5,308***
Cooling Degree Days (base 65°F)	***0***	***0***	***3***	***14***	***61***	***205***	***306***	***268***	***112***	***15***	***1***	***0***	***985***
Mean Precipitation (in.)	2.62	2.46	3.49	3.55	4.64	3.26	4.04	3.05	2.67	2.58	2.93	2.82	38.11
Extreme Maximum Daily Precip. (in.)	***1.95***	***2.21***	***1.96***	***3.05***	3.01	4.10	***2.45***	***3.98***	3.06	2.88	***2.04***	***1.72***	***4.10***
Days With ≥ 0.1" Precipitation	5	5	7	7	8	6	7	5	4	5	6	5	70
Days With ≥ 0.5" Precipitation	2	2	2	2	3	2	3	2	2	2	2	2	26
Days With ≥ 1.0" Precipitation	0	1	1	1	1	1	1	1	1	1	0	0	9
Mean Snowfall (in.)	5.2	4.0	2.4	0.4	trace	0.0	0.0	0.0	0.0	0.1	0.4	2.3	14.8
Maximum Snow Depth (in.)	11	10	9	11	trace	0	0	0	0	1	4	8	11
Days With ≥ 1.0" Snow Depth	8	5	2	0	0	0	0	0	0	0	0	3	18

Chilo Meldahl L&D *Clermont County* Elevation: 500 ft. Latitude: 38° 48' N Longitude: 84° 10' W

	JAN	FEB	MAR	APR	MAY	JUN	JUL	AUG	SEP	OCT	NOV	DEC	YEAR
Mean Maximum Temp. (°F)	39.9	43.8	53.8	65.5	73.7	82.3	86.0	85.6	79.5	67.9	55.6	43.7	64.8
Mean Temp. (°F)	31.2	34.2	42.8	53.5	62.4	71.2	75.4	74.8	68.0	56.4	45.6	35.2	54.2
Mean Minimum Temp. (°F)	22.6	24.4	31.7	41.5	51.0	60.1	64.8	63.9	56.3	44.8	35.7	26.6	43.6
Extreme Maximum Temp. (°F)	71	73	83	89	91	98	101	107	98	92	82	73	107
Extreme Minimum Temp. (°F)	-22	-6	-4	22	29	42	48	44	35	23	13	-15	-22
Days Maximum Temp. ≥ 90°F	0	0	0	0	0	3	8	7	2	0	0	0	20
Days Maximum Temp. ≤ 32°F	8	5	1	0	0	0	0	0	0	0	0	5	19
Days Minimum Temp. ≤ 32°F	26	22	18	4	0	0	0	0	0	2	12	23	107
Days Minimum Temp. ≤ 0°F	1	1	0	0	0	0	0	0	0	0	0	1	3
Heating Degree Days (base 65°F)	1,039	865	683	349	134	17	0	2	47	281	575	917	4,909
Cooling Degree Days (base 65°F)	0	0	1	12	59	209	332	313	143	21	0	0	1,090
Mean Precipitation (in.)	2.88	2.82	4.30	3.42	4.64	3.61	3.92	3.21	2.82	3.08	2.90	2.98	40.58
Extreme Maximum Daily Precip. (in.)	2.88	2.00	7.20	2.08	3.80	2.80	3.82	4.45	4.11	5.00	2.46	2.85	7.20
Days With ≥ 0.1" Precipitation	6	6	7	7	8	6	6	5	4	5	6	6	72
Days With ≥ 0.5" Precipitation	2	2	3	2	3	2	3	2	2	2	2	2	27
Days With ≥ 1.0" Precipitation	1	1	1	1	1	1	1	1	1	1	1	1	12
Mean Snowfall (in.)	***0.6***	na	***0.7***	0.0	0.0	0.0	0.0	0.0	0.0	0.0	trace	***1.3***	na
Maximum Snow Depth (in.)	***16***	***5***	***11***	0	0	0	0	***0***	0	***0***	***trace***	***3***	***16***
Days With ≥ 1.0" Snow Depth	***2***	***2***	***0***	0	0	0	0	0	0	0	0	***0***	***4***

Chippewa Lake *Medina County* Elevation: 1,180 ft. Latitude: 41° 03' N Longitude: 81° 56' W

	JAN	FEB	MAR	APR	MAY	JUN	JUL	AUG	SEP	OCT	NOV	DEC	YEAR
Mean Maximum Temp. (°F)	33.3	36.7	46.1	59.4	69.6	78.8	82.5	81.1	74.2	62.2	49.7	37.2	59.2
Mean Temp. (°F)	25.7	28.0	36.4	48.3	58.2	67.6	71.5	70.2	63.1	51.7	41.2	29.9	49.3
Mean Minimum Temp. (°F)	18.0	19.2	26.7	37.2	46.7	56.4	60.4	59.2	52.0	41.1	32.6	22.6	39.3
Extreme Maximum Temp. (°F)	68	74	83	88	90	102	102	99	92	88	78	75	102
Extreme Minimum Temp. (°F)	-26	-17	-14	8	25	34	39	34	31	16	8	-18	-26
Days Maximum Temp. ≥ 90°F	0	0	0	0	0	2	4	2	0	0	0	0	8
Days Maximum Temp. ≤ 32°F	15	11	5	0	0	0	0	0	0	0	2	11	44
Days Minimum Temp. ≤ 32°F	28	25	22	10	1	0	0	0	0	5	16	26	133
Days Minimum Temp. ≤ 0°F	3	2	0	0	0	0	0	0	0	0	0	1	6
Heating Degree Days (base 65°F)	1,213	1,039	880	500	236	51	8	16	118	413	708	1,081	6,263
Cooling Degree Days (base 65°F)	0	0	1	6	33	138	216	185	68	7	0	0	654
Mean Precipitation (in.)	2.54	2.12	2.94	3.46	3.98	3.89	4.21	3.66	3.44	2.79	3.29	3.00	39.32
Extreme Maximum Daily Precip. (in.)	1.93	1.83	1.44	1.63	2.72	2.25	3.91	4.30	3.40	2.29	2.16	2.45	4.30
Days With ≥ 0.1" Precipitation	7	6	8	9	9	7	7	6	6	7	8	7	87
Days With ≥ 0.5" Precipitation	1	1	2	2	2	3	3	3	2	2	2	2	25
Days With ≥ 1.0" Precipitation	0	0	0	1	1	1	1	1	1	0	0	0	6
Mean Snowfall (in.)	9.4	7.1	6.7	1.9	trace	0.0	0.0	0.0	0.0	0.1	2.6	8.1	35.9
Maximum Snow Depth (in.)	16	15	15	6	trace	0	0	0	0	1	7	24	24
Days With ≥ 1.0" Snow Depth	14	12	6	1	0	0	0	0	0	0	2	10	45

The period of record for all cooperative weather station data is 1980 – 2009. See User Guide for detailed explanation of data.

Circleville *Pickaway County* Elevation: 672 ft. Latitude: 39° 37' N Longitude: 82° 57' W

	JAN	FEB	MAR	APR	MAY	JUN	JUL	AUG	SEP	OCT	NOV	DEC	YEAR
Mean Maximum Temp. (°F)	37.6	40.9	51.3	63.9	73.2	81.8	85.0	84.1	78.0	66.2	53.6	41.1	63.1
Mean Temp. (°F)	29.8	32.2	41.0	52.2	61.9	70.8	74.2	72.9	66.1	54.6	44.0	33.4	52.8
Mean Minimum Temp. (°F)	21.9	23.5	30.6	40.5	50.5	59.9	63.5	61.7	54.2	42.9	34.4	25.6	42.4
Extreme Maximum Temp. (°F)	70	76	83	90	92	100	100	101	97	91	81	79	101
Extreme Minimum Temp. (°F)	-22	-14	-4	17	31	42	42	40	33	21	12	-19	-22
Days Maximum Temp. ≥ 90°F	0	0	0	0	0	4	7	6	1	0	0	0	18
Days Maximum Temp. ≤ 32°F	10	7	2	0	0	0	0	0	0	0	1	7	27
Days Minimum Temp. ≤ 32°F	25	22	19	6	0	0	0	0	0	4	14	23	113
Days Minimum Temp. ≤ 0°F	2	1	0	0	0	0	0	0	0	0	0	1	4
Heating Degree Days (base 65°F)	1,085	920	739	388	152	20	1	5	70	333	623	974	5,310
Cooling Degree Days (base 65°F)	0	0	2	13	61	201	295	259	112	18	1	0	962
Mean Precipitation (in.)	2.60	2.16	2.97	3.52	4.80	3.65	3.96	3.41	2.92	2.96	3.02	2.83	38.80
Extreme Maximum Daily Precip. (in.)	2.43	1.77	2.07	2.00	3.35	4.12	2.75	2.58	2.70	2.62	1.70	2.73	4.12
Days With ≥ 0.1" Precipitation	6	5	7	8	9	7	7	6	5	6	6	6	78
Days With ≥ 0.5" Precipitation	2	1	2	2	4	2	3	3	2	2	2	2	27
Days With ≥ 1.0" Precipitation	0	0	1	1	1	1	1	1	1	1	1	0	9
Mean Snowfall (in.)	5.5	3.9	1.7	0.4	0.0	0.0	0.0	0.0	0.0	0.0	0.3	2.1	13.9
Maximum Snow Depth (in.)	15	9	7	10	0	0	0	0	0	0	3	*7*	*15*
Days With ≥ 1.0" Snow Depth	7	6	2	0	0	0	0	0	0	0	0	4	19

Columbus Valley Crossing *Franklin County* Elevation: 734 ft. Latitude: 39° 54' N Longitude: 82° 56' W

	JAN	FEB	MAR	APR	MAY	JUN	JUL	AUG	SEP	OCT	NOV	DEC	YEAR
Mean Maximum Temp. (°F)	37.1	41.1	51.5	64.2	73.5	81.9	84.9	83.6	77.8	66.1	53.6	40.6	63.0
Mean Temp. (°F)	29.2	32.3	41.3	52.5	62.1	70.8	74.4	72.8	66.0	54.4	43.9	32.9	52.7
Mean Minimum Temp. (°F)	21.3	23.5	31.0	40.7	50.6	59.8	63.8	61.9	54.1	42.6	34.2	25.2	42.4
Extreme Maximum Temp. (°F)	70	75	83	90	92	100	100	100	96	91	79	76	100
Extreme Minimum Temp. (°F)	-28	-13	-2	17	29	39	45	38	28	20	10	-21	-28
Days Maximum Temp. ≥ 90°F	0	0	0	0	0	3	6	4	1	0	0	0	14
Days Maximum Temp. ≤ 32°F	10	6	2	0	0	0	0	0	0	0	1	7	26
Days Minimum Temp. ≤ 32°F	26	22	18	6	0	0	0	0	0	4	14	24	114
Days Minimum Temp. ≤ 0°F	2	1	0	0	0	0	0	0	0	0	0	1	4
Heating Degree Days (base 65°F)	1,103	917	728	379	144	19	1	4	72	337	627	987	5,318
Cooling Degree Days (base 65°F)	0	0	1	10	61	200	297	251	108	14	1	0	943
Mean Precipitation (in.)	2.93	2.13	3.30	3.74	4.46	4.00	4.45	3.30	3.00	2.85	3.22	3.01	40.39
Extreme Maximum Daily Precip. (in.)	2.34	1.43	2.07	2.76	2.16	3.46	3.77	3.72	2.76	2.36	1.74	2.16	3.77
Days With ≥ 0.1" Precipitation	6	5	7	7	8	6	7	5	5	5	7	6	74
Days With ≥ 0.5" Precipitation	2	1	2	3	3	3	3	2	2	2	2	2	27
Days With ≥ 1.0" Precipitation	1	0	0	1	1	1	1	1	1	1	1	0	9
Mean Snowfall (in.)	5.7	4.0	1.6	0.5	trace	0.0	0.0	0.0	0.0	trace	0.4	2.7	14.9
Maximum Snow Depth (in.)	13	*10*	10	5	trace	0	0	0	0	trace	trace	*6*	*13*
Days With ≥ 1.0" Snow Depth	6	3	1	0	0	0	0	0	0	0	0	3	13

Danville 2 W *Knox County* Elevation: 970 ft. Latitude: 40° 26' N Longitude: 82° 18' W

	JAN	FEB	MAR	APR	MAY	JUN	JUL	AUG	SEP	OCT	NOV	DEC	YEAR
Mean Maximum Temp. (°F)	34.8	38.7	48.9	61.4	71.0	79.8	83.4	82.5	75.7	63.8	51.4	39.0	60.9
Mean Temp. (°F)	25.9	28.7	37.5	48.3	58.0	67.2	71.0	69.7	62.3	50.5	40.8	30.3	49.2
Mean Minimum Temp. (°F)	16.9	18.5	26.2	35.2	44.9	54.6	58.6	56.9	48.9	37.2	30.1	21.5	37.5
Extreme Maximum Temp. (°F)	69	74	83	89	94	102	102	98	96	88	78	74	102
Extreme Minimum Temp. (°F)	-35	-22	-18	9	23	35	35	32	27	15	7	-22	-35
Days Maximum Temp. ≥ 90°F	0	0	0	0	0	2	4	3	1	0	0	0	10
Days Maximum Temp. ≤ 32°F	13	9	3	0	0	0	0	0	0	0	1	9	35
Days Minimum Temp. ≤ 32°F	28	25	23	13	3	0	0	0	1	12	19	26	150
Days Minimum Temp. ≤ 0°F	4	2	0	0	0	0	0	0	0	0	0	2	8
Heating Degree Days (base 65°F)	1,207	1,021	845	496	239	52	10	19	131	448	720	1,070	6,258
Cooling Degree Days (base 65°F)	0	0	0	3	30	125	204	171	58	6	0	0	597
Mean Precipitation (in.)	2.83	2.39	3.20	3.55	4.72	4.58	4.57	3.67	3.14	2.79	3.21	3.22	41.87
Extreme Maximum Daily Precip. (in.)	2.65	2.30	1.45	2.72	2.31	3.20	3.96	5.12	2.30	2.87	2.07	2.30	5.12
Days With ≥ 0.1" Precipitation	6	6	8	8	9	8	8	6	6	6	7	7	85
Days With ≥ 0.5" Precipitation	2	1	2	2	3	3	3	3	2	2	2	2	27
Days With ≥ 1.0" Precipitation	0	0	1	1	1	1	1	1	1	0	1	1	9
Mean Snowfall (in.)	12.2	8.5	6.2	1.8	trace	0.0	0.0	0.0	0.0	trace	2.2	8.2	39.1
Maximum Snow Depth (in.)	22	15	15	5	1	0	0	0	0	1	4	9	22
Days With ≥ 1.0" Snow Depth	15	11	5	1	0	0	0	0	0	0	2	9	43

Dayton Mcd *Montgomery County* Elevation: 745 ft. Latitude: 39° 46' N Longitude: 84° 11' W

	JAN	FEB	MAR	APR	MAY	JUN	JUL	AUG	SEP	OCT	NOV	DEC	YEAR
Mean Maximum Temp. (°F)	36.4	40.9	50.6	63.7	74.3	83.5	87.5	86.2	79.1	66.1	53.0	40.5	63.5
Mean Temp. (°F)	29.3	32.8	41.2	53.3	63.8	73.3	77.3	75.8	68.1	55.7	44.6	33.5	54.0
Mean Minimum Temp. (°F)	22.2	24.6	31.8	42.8	53.3	62.9	67.0	65.2	57.1	45.2	36.1	26.5	44.5
Extreme Maximum Temp. (°F)	69	77	84	90	95	103	104	103	99	92	81	75	104
Extreme Minimum Temp. (°F)	-21	-8	2	19	33	42	51	45	35	26	13	-16	-21
Days Maximum Temp. ≥ 90°F	0	0	0	0	2	8	12	10	3	0	0	0	35
Days Maximum Temp. ≤ 32°F	12	7	2	0	0	0	0	0	0	0	1	8	30
Days Minimum Temp. ≤ 32°F	25	22	17	3	0	0	0	0	0	2	12	22	103
Days Minimum Temp. ≤ 0°F	1	1	0	0	0	0	0	0	0	0	0	1	3
Heating Degree Days (base 65°F)	1,101	906	733	365	122	15	0	2	54	308	606	970	5,182
Cooling Degree Days (base 65°F)	0	0	3	20	92	269	387	342	154	26	1	0	1,294
Mean Precipitation (in.)	2.86	2.31	3.28	4.01	4.94	4.07	4.39	3.01	2.65	2.92	3.21	3.01	40.66
Extreme Maximum Daily Precip. (in.)	2.50	2.28	2.41	2.85	3.90	4.10	2.77	3.15	4.36	2.98	2.20	2.06	4.36
Days With ≥ 0.1" Precipitation	6	5	7	8	9	7	7	5	4	5	6	7	76
Days With ≥ 0.5" Precipitation	2	1	2	3	3	3	3	2	2	2	2	2	27
Days With ≥ 1.0" Precipitation	1	0	0	1	1	1	1	1	1	1	1	1	10
Mean Snowfall (in.)	4.8	2.7	1.6	0.1	0.0	0.0	0.0	0.0	0.0	trace	0.3	2.9	12.4
Maximum Snow Depth (in.)	12	10	7	2	0	0	0	0	0	1	6	7	12
Days With ≥ 1.0" Snow Depth	8	5	2	0	0	0	0	0	0	0	0	4	19

The period of record for all cooperative weather station data is 1980 – 2009. See User Guide for detailed explanation of data.

Defiance *Defiance County* Elevation: 700 ft. Latitude: 41° 17' N Longitude: 84° 23' W

	JAN	FEB	MAR	APR	MAY	JUN	JUL	AUG	SEP	OCT	NOV	DEC	YEAR
Mean Maximum Temp. (°F)	32.3	35.5	46.0	59.7	70.9	80.7	84.4	82.5	75.9	62.7	49.3	36.3	59.7
Mean Temp. (°F)	24.7	27.3	36.5	48.7	59.5	69.5	73.4	71.7	64.4	52.2	40.9	29.3	49.8
Mean Minimum Temp. (°F)	17.0	19.0	27.0	37.6	48.1	58.4	62.3	60.8	52.9	41.5	32.4	22.3	40.0
Extreme Maximum Temp. (°F)	65	73	80	89	93	104	101	99	95	90	78	70	104
Extreme Minimum Temp. (°F)	-22	-19	-5	4	28	39	46	43	32	18	11	-19	-22
Days Maximum Temp. ≥ 90°F	0	0	0	0	1	4	7	4	1	0	0	0	17
Days Maximum Temp. ≤ 32°F	15	12	4	0	0	0	0	0	0	0	1	11	43
Days Minimum Temp. ≤ 32°F	28	25	23	8	0	0	0	0	0	4	16	26	130
Days Minimum Temp. ≤ 0°F	4	3	0	0	0	0	0	0	0	0	0	2	9
Heating Degree Days (base 65°F)	1,243	1,060	877	491	208	35	3	10	99	402	716	1,100	6,244
Cooling Degree Days (base 65°F)	0	0	1	9	46	178	269	223	88	11	0	0	825
Mean Precipitation (in.)	2.01	2.09	2.47	3.36	3.87	3.59	4.10	3.17	3.30	2.98	2.97	2.73	36.64
Extreme Maximum Daily Precip. (in.)	1.93	2.19	1.90	1.87	1.95	2.65	3.37	3.02	2.58	3.89	3.13	2.14	3.89
Days With ≥ 0.1" Precipitation	5	5	6	7	8	7	7	6	6	6	7	7	77
Days With ≥ 0.5" Precipitation	1	1	2	2	3	2	3	2	2	2	2	2	24
Days With ≥ 1.0" Precipitation	0	0	0	1	1	1	1	1	1	1	1	0	8
Mean Snowfall (in.)	6.7	5.6	2.4	0.5	trace	0.0	0.0	0.0	0.0	0.1	0.9	4.5	20.7
Maximum Snow Depth (in.)	12	17	8	4	trace	0	0	0	0	trace	4	10	17
Days With ≥ 1.0" Snow Depth	14	11	4	0	0	0	0	0	0	0	1	8	38

Dorset *Ashtabula County* Elevation: 979 ft. Latitude: 41° 41' N Longitude: 80° 40' W

	JAN	FEB	MAR	APR	MAY	JUN	JUL	AUG	SEP	OCT	NOV	DEC	YEAR
Mean Maximum Temp. (°F)	32.6	35.5	44.6	57.9	68.5	77.3	81.3	79.9	73.5	61.4	49.2	37.0	58.2
Mean Temp. (°F)	24.5	26.2	34.7	46.5	56.5	65.5	69.5	68.2	61.7	50.6	40.9	29.7	47.9
Mean Minimum Temp. (°F)	16.2	16.9	24.7	35.1	44.4	53.6	57.7	56.6	49.9	39.8	32.5	22.3	37.5
Extreme Maximum Temp. (°F)	68	74	83	88	90	99	100	98	95	86	83	74	100
Extreme Minimum Temp. (°F)	-28	-21	-20	-4	22	30	39	30	26	17	4	-22	-28
Days Maximum Temp. ≥ 90°F	0	0	0	0	0	1	3	2	1	0	0	0	7
Days Maximum Temp. ≤ 32°F	16	12	6	0	0	0	0	0	0	0	1	10	45
Days Minimum Temp. ≤ 32°F	28	26	24	13	3	0	0	0	1	6	16	26	143
Days Minimum Temp. ≤ 0°F	4	3	1	0	0	0	0	0	0	0	0	1	9
Heating Degree Days (base 65°F)	1,250	1,091	933	552	284	83	25	34	149	443	716	1,088	6,648
Cooling Degree Days (base 65°F)	0	0	0	5	26	104	172	141	57	5	0	0	510
Mean Precipitation (in.)	2.63	2.15	2.88	3.59	3.94	4.51	4.80	3.82	4.40	3.96	3.72	3.18	43.58
Extreme Maximum Daily Precip. (in.)	1.65	1.85	2.04	1.63	2.50	3.22	3.60	2.80	2.98	2.23	4.29	2.00	4.29
Days With ≥ 0.1" Precipitation	7	6	7	9	8	8	8	7	8	9	9	8	94
Days With ≥ 0.5" Precipitation	1	1	2	2	3	4	3	3	3	3	2	2	29
Days With ≥ 1.0" Precipitation	0	0	0	1	1	1	1	1	1	1	0	0	7
Mean Snowfall (in.)	21.2	13.5	11.6	3.5	trace	0.0	0.0	0.0	0.0	0.5	8.3	20.4	79.0
Maximum Snow Depth (in.)	20	18	20	16	trace	0	0	0	0	4	15	18	20
Days With ≥ 1.0" Snow Depth	21	17	10	2	0	0	0	0	0	0	4	15	69

Elyria 3 E *Lorain County* Elevation: 729 ft. Latitude: 41° 23' N Longitude: 82° 03' W

	JAN	FEB	MAR	APR	MAY	JUN	JUL	AUG	SEP	OCT	NOV	DEC	YEAR
Mean Maximum Temp. (°F)	35.4	38.9	48.3	61.5	71.9	80.9	84.6	82.7	76.1	64.3	52.0	39.3	61.3
Mean Temp. (°F)	28.1	30.6	38.7	50.3	60.5	69.7	73.9	72.3	65.5	54.3	43.8	32.4	51.7
Mean Minimum Temp. (°F)	20.7	22.2	29.1	39.2	49.0	58.6	63.1	61.9	54.9	44.3	35.6	25.5	42.0
Extreme Maximum Temp. (°F)	68	76	84	89	93	104	102	100	94	90	80	76	104
Extreme Minimum Temp. (°F)	-22	-14	-10	11	28	38	44	40	32	18	14	-14	-22
Days Maximum Temp. ≥ 90°F	0	0	0	0	1	4	7	5	1	0	0	0	18
Days Maximum Temp. ≤ 32°F	12	8	3	0	0	0	0	0	0	0	0	8	31
Days Minimum Temp. ≤ 32°F	26	24	21	8	1	0	0	0	0	2	12	24	118
Days Minimum Temp. ≤ 0°F	2	1	0	0	0	0	0	0	0	0	0	1	4
Heating Degree Days (base 65°F)	1,137	967	809	445	186	31	2	7	77	338	629	1,003	5,631
Cooling Degree Days (base 65°F)	0	0	2	12	53	180	284	240	100	14	0	0	885
Mean Precipitation (in.)	2.56	2.25	2.82	3.40	3.72	3.75	3.79	3.82	3.69	3.10	3.27	3.20	39.37
Extreme Maximum Daily Precip. (in.)	1.66	1.92	1.79	2.06	2.45	3.28	2.80	3.25	5.75	3.10	1.80	2.30	5.75
Days With ≥ 0.1" Precipitation	7	7	7	8	9	7	7	7	7	7	8	8	89
Days With ≥ 0.5" Precipitation	1	1	2	2	2	2	3	3	3	2	2	2	25
Days With ≥ 1.0" Precipitation	0	0	0	0	1	1	1	1	1	1	1	0	7
Mean Snowfall (in.)	11.6	9.0	7.2	2.2	trace	trace	0.0	0.0	0.0	trace	2.4	8.6	41.0
Maximum Snow Depth (in.)	13	15	14	6	trace	trace	0	0	0	trace	3	13	15
Days With ≥ 1.0" Snow Depth	15	12	5	1	0	0	0	0	0	0	1	9	43

Fairfield *Butler County* Elevation: 575 ft. Latitude: 39° 21' N Longitude: 84° 35' W

	JAN	FEB	MAR	APR	MAY	JUN	JUL	AUG	SEP	OCT	NOV	DEC	YEAR
Mean Maximum Temp. (°F)	39.7	43.3	53.6	65.8	75.4	84.2	87.8	87.3	80.4	67.7	54.6	42.4	65.2
Mean Temp. (°F)	31.1	33.8	42.5	53.4	63.4	72.6	76.4	75.3	67.8	55.2	44.3	34.0	54.1
Mean Minimum Temp. (°F)	22.4	24.2	31.4	40.9	51.4	60.9	65.0	63.3	55.2	42.7	34.0	25.5	43.1
Extreme Maximum Temp. (°F)	69	76	85	90	93	103	103	104	101	93	82	74	104
Extreme Minimum Temp. (°F)	-23	-10	4	19	30	40	48	41	33	22	11	-19	-23
Days Maximum Temp. ≥ 90°F	0	0	0	0	1	8	12	11	3	0	0	0	35
Days Maximum Temp. ≤ 32°F	8	5	1	0	0	0	0	0	0	0	0	6	20
Days Minimum Temp. ≤ 32°F	25	22	18	5	0	0	0	0	0	4	14	23	111
Days Minimum Temp. ≤ 0°F	1	1	0	0	0	0	0	0	0	0	0	1	3
Heating Degree Days (base 65°F)	1,045	875	693	356	123	14	0	2	51	317	615	955	5,046
Cooling Degree Days (base 65°F)	0	0	3	15	81	248	360	329	142	20	1	0	1,199
Mean Precipitation (in.)	3.24	2.85	3.84	4.49	5.02	4.06	4.19	3.18	3.09	3.22	2.96	3.66	43.80
Extreme Maximum Daily Precip. (in.)	2.55	2.36	3.82	3.66	4.67	2.60	4.15	3.55	3.98	3.55	2.30	2.73	4.67
Days With ≥ 0.1" Precipitation	6	6	7	9	9	7	7	5	5	5	6	7	79
Days With ≥ 0.5" Precipitation	2	2	3	3	3	3	3	2	2	2	2	3	30
Days With ≥ 1.0" Precipitation	1	0	1	1	1	1	1	1	1	1	1	1	11
Mean Snowfall (in.)	3.1	2.1	0.8	0.0	0.0	0.0	0.0	0.0	0.0	0.2	0.1	1.5	7.8
Maximum Snow Depth (in.)	na	na	na	na	na	na	na	na	na	na	na	na	na
Days With ≥ 1.0" Snow Depth	na	na	0	0	0	0	0	0	0	0	0	na	na

The period of record for all cooperative weather station data is 1980 – 2009. See User Guide for detailed explanation of data.

Findlay Wpcc *Hancock County* Elevation: 768 ft. Latitude: 41° 03' N Longitude: 83° 40' W

	JAN	FEB	MAR	APR	MAY	JUN	JUL	AUG	SEP	OCT	NOV	DEC	YEAR
Mean Maximum Temp. (°F)	33.1	36.5	47.2	60.3	71.3	80.3	83.8	81.9	75.6	62.9	49.7	36.9	60.0
Mean Temp. (°F)	26.3	29.2	38.3	50.1	60.9	70.3	74.0	72.3	65.2	53.2	41.9	30.4	51.0
Mean Minimum Temp. (°F)	19.4	21.7	29.3	39.8	50.4	60.2	64.2	62.7	54.9	43.5	34.1	24.0	42.0
Extreme Maximum Temp. (°F)	66	73	81	86	93	104	101	99	95	90	78	70	104
Extreme Minimum Temp. (°F)	-20	-11	-11	8	29	40	47	42	33	21	9	-18	-20
Days Maximum Temp. ≥ 90°F	0	0	0	0	1	4	5	3	1	0	0	0	14
Days Maximum Temp. ≤ 32°F	15	11	4	0	0	0	0	0	0	0	1	11	42
Days Minimum Temp. ≤ 32°F	27	24	20	6	0	0	0	0	0	3	14	25	119
Days Minimum Temp. ≤ 0°F	2	1	0	0	0	0	0	0	0	0	0	1	4
Heating Degree Days (base 65°F)	1,193	1,007	823	451	178	28	2	7	86	371	685	1,064	5,895
Cooling Degree Days (base 65°F)	0	0	1	10	57	192	288	241	100	13	0	0	902
Mean Precipitation (in.)	2.32	2.08	2.63	3.43	4.06	4.17	3.99	3.77	2.72	2.65	2.85	2.77	37.44
Extreme Maximum Daily Precip. (in.)	2.30	2.04	2.70	1.94	3.80	4.47	2.76	5.62	2.95	2.40	1.54	1.33	5.62
Days With ≥ 0.1" Precipitation	6	5	7	8	8	8	7	6	5	6	6	7	79
Days With ≥ 0.5" Precipitation	1	1	2	2	2	3	3	2	2	2	2	2	24
Days With ≥ 1.0" Precipitation	0	0	0	1	1	1	1	1	1	0	1	0	7
Mean Snowfall (in.)	8.4	5.5	4.4	1.1	0.1	0.0	0.0	0.0	0.0	0.2	1.3	5.9	26.9
Maximum Snow Depth (in.)	14	14	12	4	trace	0	0	0	0	trace	7	12	14
Days With ≥ 1.0" Snow Depth	14	10	3	0	0	0	0	0	0	0	1	8	36

Franklin *Warren County* Elevation: 669 ft. Latitude: 39° 33' N Longitude: 84° 19' W

	JAN	FEB	MAR	APR	MAY	JUN	JUL	AUG	SEP	OCT	NOV	DEC	YEAR
Mean Maximum Temp. (°F)	37.4	41.4	51.5	63.4	73.3	81.8	85.4	84.7	78.1	65.6	53.3	41.0	63.1
Mean Temp. (°F)	28.8	31.9	40.8	51.5	61.5	70.4	74.1	72.9	65.4	53.0	43.3	32.6	52.2
Mean Minimum Temp. (°F)	20.2	22.4	30.0	39.5	49.7	58.9	62.8	61.1	52.6	40.4	33.1	24.2	41.2
Extreme Maximum Temp. (°F)	68	75	86	88	96	100	104	100	96	87	79	74	104
Extreme Minimum Temp. (°F)	-24	-12	-7	18	30	38	42	39	32	19	10	-21	-24
Days Maximum Temp. ≥ 90°F	0	0	0	0	0	4	7	6	2	0	0	0	19
Days Maximum Temp. ≤ 32°F	10	7	2	0	0	0	0	0	0	0	1	7	27
Days Minimum Temp. ≤ 32°F	26	23	19	7	0	0	0	0	0	6	15	24	120
Days Minimum Temp. ≤ 0°F	2	1	0	0	0	0	0	0	0	0	0	1	4
Heating Degree Days (base 65°F)	1,114	927	744	408	158	25	2	6	83	375	646	996	5,484
Cooling Degree Days (base 65°F)	0	0	2	9	57	193	291	258	101	10	0	0	921
Mean Precipitation (in.)	2.49	2.37	3.25	3.70	4.74	3.77	4.06	2.89	2.51	3.05	3.21	3.07	39.11
Extreme Maximum Daily Precip. (in.)	2.49	2.27	3.00	2.79	3.61	2.89	3.66	3.10	3.76	2.83	2.08	2.68	3.76
Days With ≥ 0.1" Precipitation	5	5	7	8	9	7	7	4	4	5	6	6	73
Days With ≥ 0.5" Precipitation	1	1	2	2	3	2	3	2	2	2	2	2	24
Days With ≥ 1.0" Precipitation	0	0	1	1	1	1	1	1	1	1	1	1	10
Mean Snowfall (in.)	***0.9***	***1.4***	***0.4***	trace	0.0	0.0	0.0	0.0	0.0	0.0	0.2	na	na
Maximum Snow Depth (in.)	***4***	na	***6***	3	0	0	0	***0***	0	***0***	***5***	na	na
Days With ≥ 1.0" Snow Depth	***3***	***3***	1	0	0	0	0	0	0	0	0	***1***	***8***

Fredericktown 4 S *Knox County* Elevation: 1,049 ft. Latitude: 40° 25' N Longitude: 82° 32' W

	JAN	FEB	MAR	APR	MAY	JUN	JUL	AUG	SEP	OCT	NOV	DEC	YEAR
Mean Maximum Temp. (°F)	33.2	37.2	46.9	60.1	70.0	78.9	82.3	80.9	74.8	62.7	50.5	38.5	59.7
Mean Temp. (°F)	24.2	27.6	36.3	47.9	57.9	67.0	70.6	68.6	61.7	50.1	40.4	30.3	48.5
Mean Minimum Temp. (°F)	15.2	18.0	25.7	35.7	45.7	55.2	58.8	56.2	48.7	37.4	30.2	22.0	37.4
Extreme Maximum Temp. (°F)	67	72	82	88	91	100	98	98	94	***86***	78	75	***100***
Extreme Minimum Temp. (°F)	-30	-26	-21	12	24	36	38	32	29	***17***	***4***	-20	***-30***
Days Maximum Temp. ≥ 90°F	0	0	0	0	0	2	3	2	1	0	0	0	8
Days Maximum Temp. ≤ 32°F	15	10	4	0	0	0	0	0	0	0	1	9	39
Days Minimum Temp. ≤ 32°F	28	26	24	12	2	0	0	0	1	10	19	25	147
Days Minimum Temp. ≤ 0°F	5	2	1	0	0	0	0	0	0	0	0	1	9
Heating Degree Days (base 65°F)	1,259	1,051	884	511	244	55	13	28	142	460	732	1,070	6,449
Cooling Degree Days (base 65°F)	0	0	0	5	30	122	192	145	50	4	0	0	548
Mean Precipitation (in.)	2.43	1.87	3.00	3.43	4.32	4.12	4.33	3.35	3.12	2.65	3.02	2.68	38.32
Extreme Maximum Daily Precip. (in.)	2.40	2.10	2.01	3.00	2.70	2.43	2.48	2.30	2.71	2.25	***1.60***	***1.80***	***3.00***
Days With ≥ 0.1" Precipitation	4	4	6	7	8	7	7	5	5	6	6	5	70
Days With ≥ 0.5" Precipitation	1	1	2	3	3	2	3	2	2	2	2	2	25
Days With ≥ 1.0" Precipitation	1	0	0	1	1	1	1	1	1	1	1	1	10
Mean Snowfall (in.)	8.7	5.5	3.5	0.6	trace	0.0	0.0	0.0	0.0	0.0	1.1	5.4	24.8
Maximum Snow Depth (in.)	na	na	na	***trace***	***0***	na	na	***0***	na	na	na	na	na
Days With ≥ 1.0" Snow Depth	na	na	0	0	0	0	0	0	0	0	0	***0***	na

Hannibal Lock & Dam *Monroe County* Elevation: 620 ft. Latitude: 39° 40' N Longitude: 80° 52' W

	JAN	FEB	MAR	APR	MAY	JUN	JUL	AUG	SEP	OCT	NOV	DEC	YEAR
Mean Maximum Temp. (°F)	38.5	42.0	51.1	63.6	72.3	80.5	83.7	83.1	76.6	65.3	53.9	42.1	62.7
Mean Temp. (°F)	29.9	32.5	40.1	51.0	60.2	68.8	73.1	72.6	65.6	54.0	43.8	33.8	52.1
Mean Minimum Temp. (°F)	21.2	22.9	29.0	38.5	48.0	57.0	62.3	61.9	54.6	42.7	33.6	25.6	41.4
Extreme Maximum Temp. (°F)	72	75	83	89	91	96	99	100	95	90	80	74	100
Extreme Minimum Temp. (°F)	-24	-10	-8	18	30	38	44	42	34	22	13	-14	-24
Days Maximum Temp. ≥ 90°F	0	0	0	0	0	2	4	4	1	0	0	0	11
Days Maximum Temp. ≤ 32°F	9	6	2	0	0	0	0	0	0	0	0	6	23
Days Minimum Temp. ≤ 32°F	26	23	21	8	1	0	0	0	0	3	15	23	120
Days Minimum Temp. ≤ 0°F	2	1	0	0	0	0	0	0	0	0	0	0	3
Heating Degree Days (base 65°F)	1,082	914	765	418	178	28	2	5	69	344	631	959	5,395
Cooling Degree Days (base 65°F)	0	0	0	6	37	149	258	246	94	10	0	0	800
Mean Precipitation (in.)	3.06	2.81	3.66	3.41	4.34	3.99	4.41	3.47	3.16	2.57	3.36	3.10	41.34
Extreme Maximum Daily Precip. (in.)	2.84	2.45	3.45	2.43	1.92	2.98	2.49	3.23	4.28	1.93	3.47	3.40	4.28
Days With ≥ 0.1" Precipitation	7	7	7	8	9	7	8	6	5	6	7	7	84
Days With ≥ 0.5" Precipitation	2	2	3	2	3	3	3	2	2	2	2	2	28
Days With ≥ 1.0" Precipitation	1	0	1	0	1	1	1	1	1	0	1	0	8
Mean Snowfall (in.)	na	na	1.9	trace	0.0	0.0	0.0	0.0	0.0	0.0	trace	0.5	na
Maximum Snow Depth (in.)	***15***	***23***	***4***	0	0	0	0	0	0	0	1	6	***23***
Days With ≥ 1.0" Snow Depth	***5***	2	0	0	0	0	0	0	0	0	0	3	***10***

The period of record for all cooperative weather station data is 1980 – 2009. See User Guide for detailed explanation of data.

Hiram *Portage County* Elevation: 1,229 ft. Latitude: 41° 18' N Longitude: 81° 09' W

	JAN	FEB	MAR	APR	MAY	JUN	JUL	AUG	SEP	OCT	NOV	DEC	YEAR
Mean Maximum Temp. (°F)	32.1	35.7	45.0	58.2	68.3	76.9	81.0	79.7	72.5	60.4	48.9	36.3	57.9
Mean Temp. (°F)	24.7	27.3	35.7	47.8	57.8	66.6	70.8	69.6	62.4	51.0	40.8	29.3	48.6
Mean Minimum Temp. (°F)	17.2	18.8	26.3	37.4	47.1	56.2	60.6	59.6	52.3	41.4	32.6	22.2	39.3
Extreme Maximum Temp. (°F)	69	72	81	87	90	100	99	95	91	85	77	73	100
Extreme Minimum Temp. (°F)	-25	-14	-6	12	27	37	41	38	32	22	4	-15	-25
Days Maximum Temp. ≥ 90°F	0	0	0	0	0	1	2	2	0	0	0	0	5
Days Maximum Temp. ≤ 32°F	16	12	5	0	0	0	0	0	0	0	1	12	46
Days Minimum Temp. ≤ 32°F	28	25	23	9	1	0	0	0	0	4	17	27	134
Days Minimum Temp. ≤ 0°F	3	2	0	0	0	0	0	0	0	0	0	1	6
Heating Degree Days (base 65°F)	1,243	1,060	902	515	248	63	11	19	127	434	720	1,100	6,442
Cooling Degree Days (base 65°F)	0	0	1	7	30	116	199	169	55	5	0	0	582
Mean Precipitation (in.)	3.03	2.42	3.32	3.77	4.06	4.00	4.05	3.72	3.82	3.44	3.59	3.45	42.67
Extreme Maximum Daily Precip. (in.)	1.71	1.64	2.93	1.76	2.19	3.22	4.05	3.42	3.30	2.13	2.41	1.98	4.05
Days With ≥ 0.1" Precipitation	8	7	8	9	9	9	7	6	7	8	8	9	95
Days With ≥ 0.5" Precipitation	2	1	2	2	3	2	3	2	3	2	2	2	26
Days With ≥ 1.0" Precipitation	0	0	0	1	1	1	1	1	1	1	0	0	7
Mean Snowfall (in.)	18.2	12.7	10.4	1.9	trace	0.0	0.0	0.0	0.0	0.4	5.3	14.3	63.2
Maximum Snow Depth (in.)	22	15	18	9	trace	0	0	0	0	2	16	16	22
Days With ≥ 1.0" Snow Depth	20	17	9	1	0	0	0	0	0	0	3	14	64

Lima WWTP *Allen County* Elevation: 850 ft. Latitude: 40° 43' N Longitude: 84° 08' W

	JAN	FEB	MAR	APR	MAY	JUN	JUL	AUG	SEP	OCT	NOV	DEC	YEAR
Mean Maximum Temp. (°F)	34.1	37.7	48.0	61.1	71.7	80.5	84.0	82.4	76.5	64.1	50.8	37.8	60.7
Mean Temp. (°F)	26.9	29.7	38.9	50.6	61.1	70.4	74.0	72.6	65.9	54.0	42.8	31.0	51.5
Mean Minimum Temp. (°F)	19.7	21.7	29.7	40.1	50.5	60.3	64.0	62.7	55.3	43.9	34.7	24.1	42.2
Extreme Maximum Temp. (°F)	66	72	81	89	93	97	100	99	95	90	77	70	100
Extreme Minimum Temp. (°F)	-21	-12	-3	8	30	39	46	42	31	19	9	-17	-21
Days Maximum Temp. ≥ 90°F	0	0	0	0	1	3	5	4	1	0	0	0	14
Days Maximum Temp. ≤ 32°F	14	10	3	0	0	0	0	0	0	0	1	10	38
Days Minimum Temp. ≤ 32°F	27	23	20	7	0	0	0	0	0	3	14	25	119
Days Minimum Temp. ≤ 0°F	3	1	0	0	0	0	0	0	0	0	0	1	5
Heating Degree Days (base 65°F)	1,174	989	804	437	174	26	2	7	75	349	657	1,047	5,741
Cooling Degree Days (base 65°F)	0	0	1	12	61	195	289	250	109	16	0	0	933
Mean Precipitation (in.)	2.44	2.18	2.71	3.44	4.16	3.87	4.34	3.50	3.15	2.72	3.26	2.78	38.55
Extreme Maximum Daily Precip. (in.)	2.08	1.98	1.95	2.15	2.50	4.38	2.97	5.08	2.78	3.03	2.10	2.96	5.08
Days With ≥ 0.1" Precipitation	6	5	6	8	9	7	8	6	6	6	7	6	80
Days With ≥ 0.5" Precipitation	1	2	1	2	3	3	3	2	2	2	2	2	25
Days With ≥ 1.0" Precipitation	0	0	0	1	1	1	1	1	1	0	0	0	6
Mean Snowfall (in.)	na	na	na	trace	0.0	0.0	0.0	0.0	0.0	0.0	***0.1***	na	na
Maximum Snow Depth (in.)	na	na	na	***1***	***0***	***0***	***0***	***0***	***0***	na	na	na	na
Days With ≥ 1.0" Snow Depth	na	na	na	0	0	0	0	0	0	0	***0***	na	na

Mansfield 5 W *Richland County* Elevation: 1,350 ft. Latitude: 40° 46' N Longitude: 82° 37' W

	JAN	FEB	MAR	APR	MAY	JUN	JUL	AUG	SEP	OCT	NOV	DEC	YEAR
Mean Maximum Temp. (°F)	32.5	36.2	46.1	59.3	69.7	78.3	81.6	80.2	73.6	61.0	48.8	36.6	58.7
Mean Temp. (°F)	24.5	27.7	36.4	48.4	58.5	67.2	70.9	69.5	62.7	50.8	40.4	29.2	48.8
Mean Minimum Temp. (°F)	16.5	19.2	26.6	37.3	47.2	56.0	60.1	58.8	51.8	40.5	32.0	21.7	39.0
Extreme Maximum Temp. (°F)	66	72	81	87	91	100	99	97	94	84	76	69	100
Extreme Minimum Temp. (°F)	-25	-15	-8	5	24	33	40	37	28	18	9	-19	-25
Days Maximum Temp. ≥ 90°F	0	0	0	0	0	2	2	2	0	0	0	0	6
Days Maximum Temp. ≤ 32°F	16	12	5	0	0	0	0	0	0	0	2	12	47
Days Minimum Temp. ≤ 32°F	28	25	22	11	1	0	0	0	0	7	16	26	136
Days Minimum Temp. ≤ 0°F	4	2	0	0	0	0	0	0	0	0	0	1	7
Heating Degree Days (base 65°F)	1,249	1,047	882	500	231	57	11	20	127	442	731	1,104	6,401
Cooling Degree Days (base 65°F)	0	0	1	8	36	128	200	169	66	7	0	0	615
Mean Precipitation (in.)	2.23	1.81	2.77	3.64	4.55	4.40	4.02	3.80	3.23	2.83	3.08	2.88	39.24
Extreme Maximum Daily Precip. (in.)	2.47	1.87	***2.04***	***1.80***	2.13	4.08	2.55	5.19	2.22	2.02	1.91	2.00	***5.19***
Days With ≥ 0.1" Precipitation	5	5	6	8	10	7	7	7	6	6	7	6	80
Days With ≥ 0.5" Precipitation	1	1	2	2	3	3	3	2	2	2	2	2	25
Days With ≥ 1.0" Precipitation	0	0	0	1	1	1	1	1	1	1	1	0	8
Mean Snowfall (in.)	na	na	na	0.4	0.0	0.0	0.0	0.0	0.0	trace	***0.4***	na	na
Maximum Snow Depth (in.)	na	na	na	***4***	***0***	***0***	***0***	***0***	***0***	na	na	na	na
Days With ≥ 1.0" Snow Depth	na	na	***1***	0	0	0	0	0	0	0	***0***	na	na

Marietta Wwtp *Washington County* Elevation: 580 ft. Latitude: 39° 25' N Longitude: 81° 26' W

	JAN	FEB	MAR	APR	MAY	JUN	JUL	AUG	SEP	OCT	NOV	DEC	YEAR
Mean Maximum Temp. (°F)	39.9	43.7	53.3	65.5	74.0	82.0	85.4	84.7	78.1	66.5	54.9	43.4	64.3
Mean Temp. (°F)	31.4	34.1	42.4	53.3	62.2	70.8	74.7	73.7	66.6	54.8	44.7	35.0	53.6
Mean Minimum Temp. (°F)	22.8	24.6	31.3	41.0	50.3	59.6	64.0	62.6	55.0	43.1	34.4	26.5	42.9
Extreme Maximum Temp. (°F)	74	77	85	91	93	99	102	100	97	91	81	78	102
Extreme Minimum Temp. (°F)	-23	-7	0	19	31	40	44	38	33	23	12	-11	-23
Days Maximum Temp. ≥ 90°F	0	0	0	0	1	4	7	6	1	0	0	0	19
Days Maximum Temp. ≤ 32°F	8	5	1	0	0	0	0	0	0	0	0	6	20
Days Minimum Temp. ≤ 32°F	25	22	18	5	0	0	0	0	0	4	14	22	110
Days Minimum Temp. ≤ 0°F	1	1	0	0	0	0	0	0	0	0	0	0	2
Heating Degree Days (base 65°F)	1,036	866	697	357	141	17	1	3	61	322	603	924	5,028
Cooling Degree Days (base 65°F)	0	0	1	12	59	199	309	278	114	14	1	0	987
Mean Precipitation (in.)	3.12	2.76	3.83	3.41	4.26	4.57	4.54	3.70	3.24	2.91	3.21	3.26	42.81
Extreme Maximum Daily Precip. (in.)	1.60	2.83	3.15	2.12	2.60	4.00	2.70	4.78	4.27	1.93	2.01	2.25	4.78
Days With ≥ 0.1" Precipitation	7	6	8	8	9	8	8	7	6	6	7	7	87
Days With ≥ 0.5" Precipitation	2	2	3	2	3	3	3	3	2	2	2	2	29
Days With ≥ 1.0" Precipitation	0	0	1	1	1	1	1	1	1	1	0	0	8
Mean Snowfall (in.)	7.0	4.6	3.0	0.6	0.0	0.0	0.0	0.0	0.0	trace	0.6	3.0	18.8
Maximum Snow Depth (in.)	19	16	20	10	0	0	0	0	0	trace	2	5	20
Days With ≥ 1.0" Snow Depth	7	4	1	0	0	0	0	0	0	0	0	3	15

The period of record for all cooperative weather station data is 1980 – 2009. See User Guide for detailed explanation of data.

Marion 2 N *Marion County* Elevation: 964 ft. Latitude: 40° 37' N Longitude: 83° 08' W

	JAN	FEB	MAR	APR	MAY	JUN	JUL	AUG	SEP	OCT	NOV	DEC	YEAR
Mean Maximum Temp. (°F)	33.2	37.0	46.9	60.4	70.5	80.0	83.4	82.0	75.6	63.3	50.4	37.5	60.0
Mean Temp. (°F)	25.5	28.5	37.3	49.2	59.6	69.3	72.9	71.1	64.0	52.2	41.5	30.1	50.1
Mean Minimum Temp. (°F)	17.7	20.0	27.6	38.0	48.6	58.6	62.3	60.2	52.3	41.1	32.6	22.7	40.1
Extreme Maximum Temp. (°F)	67	73	81	87	91	103	100	99	97	89	79	73	103
Extreme Minimum Temp. (°F)	-23	-20	-5	8	29	39	43	35	24	17	11	-19	-23
Days Maximum Temp. ≥ 90°F	0	0	0	0	0	3	5	4	1	0	0	0	13
Days Maximum Temp. ≤ 32°F	15	10	4	0	0	0	0	0	0	0	1	10	40
Days Minimum Temp. ≤ 32°F	28	25	22	9	0	0	0	0	0	5	16	25	130
Days Minimum Temp. ≤ 0°F	3	2	0	0	0	0	0	0	0	0	0	1	6
Heating Degree Days (base 65°F)	1,219	1,024	853	475	211	37	5	15	106	402	698	1,075	6,120
Cooling Degree Days (base 65°F)	0	0	2	8	49	174	256	212	82	12	0	0	795
Mean Precipitation (in.)	2.45	1.85	2.32	3.56	4.45	4.35	4.31	3.78	3.21	2.90	3.01	2.84	39.03
Extreme Maximum Daily Precip. (in.)	2.00	1.35	1.37	1.80	2.68	3.82	5.33	3.11	2.91	2.25	1.57	1.84	5.33
Days With ≥ 0.1" Precipitation	5	5	6	9	9	7	7	6	6	6	7	6	79
Days With ≥ 0.5" Precipitation	1	1	1	2	3	3	3	3	2	2	2	2	25
Days With ≥ 1.0" Precipitation	1	0	0	1	1	1	1	1	1	1	1	0	9
Mean Snowfall (in.)	7.6	5.2	3.5	0.6	0.0	0.0	0.0	0.0	0.0	trace	0.8	5.3	23.0
Maximum Snow Depth (in.)	15	15	13	2	0	0	0	0	0	trace	3	15	15
Days With ≥ 1.0" Snow Depth	11	9	2	0	0	0	0	0	0	0	0	5	27

Marysville *Union County* Elevation: 1,000 ft. Latitude: 40° 14' N Longitude: 83° 22' W

	JAN	FEB	MAR	APR	MAY	JUN	JUL	AUG	SEP	OCT	NOV	DEC	YEAR
Mean Maximum Temp. (°F)	34.5	38.6	49.2	62.0	72.3	80.8	84.3	82.9	76.3	63.9	50.8	38.3	61.2
Mean Temp. (°F)	27.2	30.4	39.5	51.2	61.4	70.2	74.0	72.4	65.2	53.4	42.4	31.2	51.5
Mean Minimum Temp. (°F)	19.8	22.3	29.8	40.2	50.4	59.5	63.6	61.9	54.0	42.8	34.0	24.1	41.9
Extreme Maximum Temp. (°F)	66	73	82	88	92	101	100	99	96	91	79	74	101
Extreme Minimum Temp. (°F)	-23	-18	-11	12	29	38	44	41	32	18	12	-20	-23
Days Maximum Temp. ≥ 90°F	0	0	0	0	0	3	6	4	1	0	0	0	14
Days Maximum Temp. ≤ 32°F	13	9	3	0	0	0	0	0	0	0	1	9	35
Days Minimum Temp. ≤ 32°F	26	24	20	6	0	0	0	0	0	3	14	24	117
Days Minimum Temp. ≤ 0°F	2	1	0	0	0	0	0	0	0	0	0	1	4
Heating Degree Days (base 65°F)	1,165	971	785	419	165	25	2	7	85	364	671	1,040	5,699
Cooling Degree Days (base 65°F)	0	0	1	11	59	187	287	244	97	11	0	0	897
Mean Precipitation (in.)	2.35	2.00	2.73	3.30	4.43	4.28	4.26	3.25	2.91	2.61	2.99	2.77	37.88
Extreme Maximum Daily Precip. (in.)	2.60	1.18	1.50	2.75	2.37	4.82	3.50	3.28	2.56	2.48	1.66	1.88	4.82
Days With ≥ 0.1" Precipitation	6	5	6	8	9	7	7	6	5	6	6	6	77
Days With ≥ 0.5" Precipitation	1	1	2	2	3	3	3	2	2	2	2	2	25
Days With ≥ 1.0" Precipitation	0	0	0	0	1	1	1	1	1	1	1	0	7
Mean Snowfall (in.)	6.2	4.6	3.8	0.4	0.0	0.0	0.0	0.0	0.0	0.1	0.9	4.5	20.5
Maximum Snow Depth (in.)	16	12	15	4	0	0	0	0	0	3	5	17	17
Days With ≥ 1.0" Snow Depth	12	8	4	0	0	0	0	0	0	0	1	6	31

Milford *Clermont County* Elevation: 520 ft. Latitude: 39° 11' N Longitude: 84° 17' W

	JAN	FEB	MAR	APR	MAY	JUN	JUL	AUG	SEP	OCT	NOV	DEC	YEAR
Mean Maximum Temp. (°F)	38.4	43.1	52.9	64.8	75.1	82.8	87.2	85.9	78.9	67.7	54.8	42.5	64.5
Mean Temp. (°F)	29.3	33.1	41.5	52.2	62.7	71.0	75.4	73.9	66.1	54.5	43.9	33.6	53.1
Mean Minimum Temp. (°F)	20.1	23.1	30.0	39.7	50.1	59.1	63.5	61.9	53.2	41.1	32.7	24.7	41.6
Extreme Maximum Temp. (°F)	72	76	84	89	93	96	104	101	98	87	81	75	104
Extreme Minimum Temp. (°F)	-23	-13	-10	19	31	36	45	41	26	20	12	-22	-23
Days Maximum Temp. ≥ 90°F	0	0	0	0	1	5	11	9	2	0	0	0	28
Days Maximum Temp. ≤ 32°F	9	6	1	0	0	0	0	0	0	0	0	6	22
Days Minimum Temp. ≤ 32°F	26	23	19	7	0	0	0	0	0	5	16	23	119
Days Minimum Temp. ≤ 0°F	2	1	0	0	0	0	0	0	0	0	0	1	4
Heating Degree Days (base 65°F)	1,101	896	724	390	136	19	1	3	75	334	626	966	5,271
Cooling Degree Days (base 65°F)	0	0	2	12	70	206	329	286	115	14	0	0	1,034
Mean Precipitation (in.)	3.06	2.62	3.73	4.14	5.55	4.35	4.27	4.10	3.01	2.96	3.60	3.33	44.72
Extreme Maximum Daily Precip. (in.)	3.10	2.38	2.03	2.50	3.55	2.86	4.45	4.63	3.34	2.53	2.45	2.41	4.63
Days With ≥ 0.1" Precipitation	6	6	7	9	9	8	7	6	5	6	7	6	82
Days With ≥ 0.5" Precipitation	2	2	3	3	4	3	3	3	2	2	3	2	32
Days With ≥ 1.0" Precipitation	1	0	1	1	1	1	1	1	1	1	1	1	11
Mean Snowfall (in.)	na	4.5	1.3	0.3	trace	0.0	0.0	trace	0.0	0.2	0.1	2.6	na
Maximum Snow Depth (in.)	na	na	na	trace	trace	na	0	na	na	na	na	na	na
Days With ≥ 1.0" Snow Depth	na	5	1	0	0	0	0	0	0	0	0	3	na

Millersburg *Holmes County* Elevation: 818 ft. Latitude: 40° 33' N Longitude: 81° 55' W

	JAN	FEB	MAR	APR	MAY	JUN	JUL	AUG	SEP	OCT	NOV	DEC	YEAR
Mean Maximum Temp. (°F)	36.2	38.9	49.1	61.7	71.1	80.4	83.8	82.6	75.9	63.9	51.6	39.3	61.2
Mean Temp. (°F)	27.3	29.1	37.9	48.9	58.3	68.1	71.8	70.4	63.0	51.0	41.2	30.8	49.8
Mean Minimum Temp. (°F)	18.4	19.3	26.7	36.1	45.5	55.7	59.7	58.2	50.1	38.1	30.8	22.2	38.4
Extreme Maximum Temp. (°F)	70	75	82	87	90	95	97	98	95	88	80	76	98
Extreme Minimum Temp. (°F)	-35	-13	-7	14	20	36	43	35	29	19	10	-24	-35
Days Maximum Temp. ≥ 90°F	0	0	0	0	0	3	5	4	1	0	0	0	13
Days Maximum Temp. ≤ 32°F	12	9	3	0	0	0	0	0	0	0	1	8	33
Days Minimum Temp. ≤ 32°F	27	25	23	12	2	0	0	0	0	9	18	26	142
Days Minimum Temp. ≤ 0°F	3	2	0	0	0	0	0	0	0	0	0	1	6
Heating Degree Days (base 65°F)	1,162	1,007	833	480	229	43	6	14	116	434	707	1,055	6,086
Cooling Degree Days (base 65°F)	0	0	0	5	29	142	223	188	61	6	0	0	654
Mean Precipitation (in.)	2.85	1.83	2.89	3.48	4.57	4.81	4.33	3.52	3.14	2.87	2.83	2.67	39.79
Extreme Maximum Daily Precip. (in.)	2.95	1.58	1.63	1.83	1.78	3.42	3.28	3.85	2.86	2.54	1.87	2.38	3.85
Days With ≥ 0.1" Precipitation	6	5	6	7	9	8	8	6	6	6	6	6	79
Days With ≥ 0.5" Precipitation	2	1	2	2	3	3	3	2	2	2	2	2	26
Days With ≥ 1.0" Precipitation	0	0	0	1	1	1	1	1	1	1	0	0	7
Mean Snowfall (in.)	6.3	3.8	2.5	0.3	trace	0.0	0.0	0.0	0.0	trace	0.7	3.9	17.5
Maximum Snow Depth (in.)	11	10	13	6	trace	0	0	0	0	1	4	7	13
Days With ≥ 1.0" Snow Depth	10	8	2	0	0	0	0	0	0	0	1	5	26

The period of record for all cooperative weather station data is 1980 – 2009. See User Guide for detailed explanation of data.

Millport 2 NW *Columbiana County* Elevation: 1,149 ft. Latitude: 40° 43' N Longitude: 80° 54' W

	JAN	FEB	MAR	APR	MAY	JUN	JUL	AUG	SEP	OCT	NOV	DEC	YEAR
Mean Maximum Temp. (°F)	35.7	39.9	49.6	62.1	71.5	79.9	83.6	82.4	75.6	63.9	51.2	39.1	61.2
Mean Temp. (°F)	26.9	29.9	38.2	49.4	58.6	67.3	71.2	69.8	62.8	51.5	41.3	30.7	49.8
Mean Minimum Temp. (°F)	18.1	19.9	26.7	36.7	45.7	54.7	58.9	57.0	49.9	39.1	31.3	22.2	38.4
Extreme Maximum Temp. (°F)	69	77	82	90	91	98	103	99	94	87	79	74	103
Extreme Minimum Temp. (°F)	-34	-19	-17	10	20	33	38	27	26	14	3	-20	-34
Days Maximum Temp. ≥ 90°F	0	0	0	0	0	2	5	4	1	0	0	0	12
Days Maximum Temp. ≤ 32°F	12	8	3	0	0	0	0	0	0	0	1	9	33
Days Minimum Temp. ≤ 32°F	27	25	22	11	3	0	0	0	1	9	17	26	141
Days Minimum Temp. ≤ 0°F	3	2	1	0	0	0	0	0	0	0	0	1	7
Heating Degree Days (base 65°F)	1,175	985	825	467	221	49	8	19	122	419	704	1,057	6,051
Cooling Degree Days (base 65°F)	0	0	0	6	30	125	209	174	61	7	0	0	612
Mean Precipitation (in.)	2.53	2.15	2.83	3.25	3.97	3.78	4.01	3.29	3.28	2.60	3.13	2.81	37.63
Extreme Maximum Daily Precip. (in.)	1.93	1.70	1.61	1.85	3.71	3.70	2.74	3.20	4.80	3.30	2.86	1.93	4.80
Days With ≥ 0.1" Precipitation	7	6	7	8	8	7	7	6	6	6	8	8	84
Days With ≥ 0.5" Precipitation	1	1	2	2	3	3	3	2	2	1	2	2	24
Days With ≥ 1.0" Precipitation	0	0	0	1	1	1	1	1	1	0	0	0	6
Mean Snowfall (in.)	8.0	6.6	5.1	1.5	trace	0.0	0.0	0.0	0.0	trace	1.6	5.9	28.7
Maximum Snow Depth (in.)	***12***	***15***	***6***	10	trace	0	0	0	0	***1***	***5***	***7***	***15***
Days With ≥ 1.0" Snow Depth	***4***	***6***	***1***	0	0	0	0	0	0	0	***1***	***3***	***15***

Oberlin *Lorain County* Elevation: 815 ft. Latitude: 41° 16' N Longitude: 82° 13' W

	JAN	FEB	MAR	APR	MAY	JUN	JUL	AUG	SEP	OCT	NOV	DEC	YEAR
Mean Maximum Temp. (°F)	33.6	36.8	45.9	59.3	70.0	79.2	83.2	81.4	75.0	62.7	50.0	37.6	59.6
Mean Temp. (°F)	25.7	28.2	36.6	48.4	58.8	68.2	72.3	70.4	63.4	51.9	41.6	30.2	49.6
Mean Minimum Temp. (°F)	17.8	19.5	27.3	37.5	47.5	57.1	61.5	59.4	51.7	41.0	33.2	22.8	39.7
Extreme Maximum Temp. (°F)	67	76	82	87	91	104	100	100	94	89	77	75	104
Extreme Minimum Temp. (°F)	-23	-18	-15	11	27	35	41	32	25	16	7	-18	-23
Days Maximum Temp. ≥ 90°F	0	0	0	0	0	3	5	3	1	0	0	0	12
Days Maximum Temp. ≤ 32°F	15	11	5	0	0	0	0	0	0	0	1	10	42
Days Minimum Temp. ≤ 32°F	28	25	22	10	1	0	0	0	0	5	15	25	131
Days Minimum Temp. ≤ 0°F	3	2	0	0	0	0	0	0	0	0	0	1	6
Heating Degree Days (base 65°F)	1,210	1,034	874	500	228	52	8	16	116	408	695	1,071	6,212
Cooling Degree Days (base 65°F)	0	0	1	8	42	153	241	192	74	9	0	0	720
Mean Precipitation (in.)	2.54	2.14	2.74	3.38	3.89	3.69	3.86	3.36	3.31	2.87	3.13	2.84	37.75
Extreme Maximum Daily Precip. (in.)	2.35	2.35	2.06	1.75	2.35	2.72	2.83	2.92	2.64	2.88	1.80	2.00	2.92
Days With ≥ 0.1" Precipitation	6	6	7	8	9	8	7	6	6	7	7	7	84
Days With ≥ 0.5" Precipitation	1	1	2	2	2	2	3	2	2	2	2	2	23
Days With ≥ 1.0" Precipitation	0	0	0	0	1	1	1	1	1	0	1	0	6
Mean Snowfall (in.)	13.3	10.0	8.6	2.2	trace	0.0	0.0	0.0	0.0	trace	2.1	9.6	45.8
Maximum Snow Depth (in.)	17	17	16	7	trace	0	0	0	0	trace	5	15	17
Days With ≥ 1.0" Snow Depth	18	14	7	1	0	0	0	0	0	0	2	11	53

Painesville 4 NW *Lake County* Elevation: 600 ft. Latitude: 41° 45' N Longitude: 81° 18' W

	JAN	FEB	MAR	APR	MAY	JUN	JUL	AUG	SEP	OCT	NOV	DEC	YEAR
Mean Maximum Temp. (°F)	35.2	37.2	45.3	56.8	67.3	76.6	80.9	79.8	74.2	63.0	51.5	39.7	58.9
Mean Temp. (°F)	28.7	30.0	37.2	48.2	58.5	68.1	72.9	71.9	65.8	55.0	44.7	33.6	51.2
Mean Minimum Temp. (°F)	22.2	22.8	29.0	39.5	49.8	59.6	64.8	64.0	57.3	47.0	37.9	27.5	43.4
Extreme Maximum Temp. (°F)	70	76	82	91	92	98	96	93	94	88	77	75	98
Extreme Minimum Temp. (°F)	-19	-4	0	17	30	40	47	39	33	24	16	-11	-19
Days Maximum Temp. ≥ 90°F	0	0	0	0	0	1	2	1	0	0	0	0	4
Days Maximum Temp. ≤ 32°F	13	10	4	0	0	0	0	0	0	0	0	7	34
Days Minimum Temp. ≤ 32°F	26	24	20	6	0	0	0	0	0	1	8	21	106
Days Minimum Temp. ≤ 0°F	1	0	0	0	0	0	0	0	0	0	0	0	1
Heating Degree Days (base 65°F)	1,119	983	857	505	229	42	2	4	67	317	604	966	5,695
Cooling Degree Days (base 65°F)	0	0	1	7	36	143	253	226	97	14	0	0	777
Mean Precipitation (in.)	2.40	1.98	2.80	3.31	3.31	3.66	3.80	3.39	4.03	3.47	3.50	2.98	38.63
Extreme Maximum Daily Precip. (in.)	2.25	2.10	1.97	3.64	2.02	3.10	4.57	2.41	2.51	2.97	2.37	2.70	4.57
Days With ≥ 0.1" Precipitation	7	5	7	8	7	7	7	6	7	8	8	8	85
Days With ≥ 0.5" Precipitation	1	1	2	2	2	2	3	2	3	2	2	1	23
Days With ≥ 1.0" Precipitation	0	0	0	0	1	1	1	1	1	0	1	0	6
Mean Snowfall (in.)	11.5	8.1	6.5	1.2	trace	0.0	0.0	0.0	0.0	trace	2.2	9.7	39.2
Maximum Snow Depth (in.)	24	25	25	7	trace	0	0	0	0	trace	16	15	25
Days With ≥ 1.0" Snow Depth	17	11	5	0	0	0	0	0	0	0	1	9	43

Pandora *Putnam County* Elevation: 770 ft. Latitude: 40° 57' N Longitude: 83° 58' W

	JAN	FEB	MAR	APR	MAY	JUN	JUL	AUG	SEP	OCT	NOV	DEC	YEAR
Mean Maximum Temp. (°F)	32.9	36.6	47.5	60.5	71.5	80.4	83.9	82.0	75.7	62.7	49.7	36.7	60.0
Mean Temp. (°F)	25.7	28.8	38.0	49.7	60.5	69.7	73.2	71.3	64.2	52.5	41.6	29.9	50.4
Mean Minimum Temp. (°F)	18.4	20.9	28.5	38.7	49.5	59.0	62.5	60.5	52.8	42.2	33.4	23.1	40.8
Extreme Maximum Temp. (°F)	67	73	82	89	94	103	101	100	96	90	78	71	103
Extreme Minimum Temp. (°F)	-21	-13	-13	6	26	38	44	40	29	19	8	-19	-21
Days Maximum Temp. ≥ 90°F	0	0	0	0	1	4	6	3	1	0	0	0	15
Days Maximum Temp. ≤ 32°F	15	11	4	0	0	0	0	0	0	0	1	11	42
Days Minimum Temp. ≤ 32°F	28	24	21	8	0	0	0	0	0	4	15	26	126
Days Minimum Temp. ≤ 0°F	4	2	0	0	0	0	0	0	0	0	0	1	7
Heating Degree Days (base 65°F)	1,212	1,018	831	464	189	31	3	12	100	393	696	1,080	6,029
Cooling Degree Days (base 65°F)	0	0	1	10	56	180	265	212	85	12	0	0	821
Mean Precipitation (in.)	2.26	2.01	2.65	3.47	3.94	4.10	3.95	3.43	2.98	2.67	3.07	2.66	37.19
Extreme Maximum Daily Precip. (in.)	1.83	1.76	3.01	1.73	3.41	3.69	2.58	6.19	2.54	2.80	1.91	1.31	6.19
Days With ≥ 0.1" Precipitation	6	5	7	8	8	7	7	6	6	6	7	6	79
Days With ≥ 0.5" Precipitation	1	1	1	2	3	3	3	3	2	2	2	2	25
Days With ≥ 1.0" Precipitation	0	0	0	0	1	1	1	1	1	0	1	0	6
Mean Snowfall (in.)	9.4	6.9	4.4	1.2	trace	0.0	0.0	0.0	trace	0.1	1.9	6.6	30.5
Maximum Snow Depth (in.)	13	16	10	7	trace	0	0	0	trace	trace	5	11	16
Days With ≥ 1.0" Snow Depth	14	11	4	0	0	0	0	0	0	0	1	9	39

The period of record for all cooperative weather station data is 1980 – 2009. See User Guide for detailed explanation of data.

Portsmouth Sciotoville *Scioto County* Elevation: 540 ft. Latitude: 38° 45' N Longitude: 82° 53' W

	JAN	FEB	MAR	APR	MAY	JUN	JUL	AUG	SEP	OCT	NOV	DEC	YEAR
Mean Maximum Temp. (°F)	40.6	44.9	54.9	66.5	75.3	83.2	86.6	86.0	79.8	68.4	56.3	44.4	65.6
Mean Temp. (°F)	31.7	35.0	43.8	54.2	63.4	71.7	75.3	73.9	67.0	55.4	45.3	35.4	54.3
Mean Minimum Temp. (°F)	22.7	25.0	32.7	42.1	51.5	60.1	63.9	61.9	54.0	42.5	34.2	26.3	43.1
Extreme Maximum Temp. (°F)	74	76	84	99	93	101	104	104	100	92	82	75	104
Extreme Minimum Temp. (°F)	-29	-8	0	12	28	38	40	35	31	22	10	-18	-29
Days Maximum Temp. ≥ 90°F	0	0	0	0	1	5	10	8	3	0	0	0	27
Days Maximum Temp. ≤ 32°F	7	4	1	0	0	0	0	0	0	0	0	4	16
Days Minimum Temp. ≤ 32°F	25	22	16	5	0	0	0	0	0	4	14	22	108
Days Minimum Temp. ≤ 0°F	1	1	0	0	0	0	0	0	0	0	0	1	3
Heating Degree Days (base 65°F)	1,025	842	652	333	119	14	1	5	61	306	585	912	4,855
Cooling Degree Days (base 65°F)	0	0	2	16	77	221	328	288	126	17	1	0	1,076
Mean Precipitation (in.)	3.06	2.77	3.76	3.61	4.71	3.42	4.39	3.78	2.57	2.62	3.05	3.19	40.93
Extreme Maximum Daily Precip. (in.)	2.52	2.42	3.74	3.95	2.18	2.50	3.69	5.20	2.82	2.17	1.86	2.50	5.20
Days With ≥ 0.1" Precipitation	7	6	8	8	9	7	8	6	5	5	6	7	82
Days With ≥ 0.5" Precipitation	2	2	3	2	3	2	3	2	2	2	2	2	27
Days With ≥ 1.0" Precipitation	1	1	1	1	1	1	1	1	1	0	1	0	10
Mean Snowfall (in.)	3.4	2.1	1.2	0.2	trace	0.0	0.0	0.0	0.0	0.0	0.1	1.0	8.0
Maximum Snow Depth (in.)	21	7	8	5	trace	0	0	0	0	0	1	5	21
Days With ≥ 1.0" Snow Depth	4	2	1	0	0	0	0	0	0	0	0	1	8

Springfield New Water Works *Clark County* Elevation: 930 ft. Latitude: 39° 58' N Longitude: 83° 49' W

	JAN	FEB	MAR	APR	MAY	JUN	JUL	AUG	SEP	OCT	NOV	DEC	YEAR
Mean Maximum Temp. (°F)	35.3	38.9	48.8	61.4	71.6	80.4	83.5	82.8	76.6	64.2	51.5	39.2	61.2
Mean Temp. (°F)	27.0	29.8	38.7	49.9	60.2	69.5	72.8	71.4	64.3	52.5	42.0	31.3	50.8
Mean Minimum Temp. (°F)	18.6	20.5	28.5	38.4	48.7	58.6	62.0	59.9	51.9	40.7	32.4	23.2	40.3
Extreme Maximum Temp. (°F)	68	74	81	87	91	98	98	100	95	89	79	72	100
Extreme Minimum Temp. (°F)	-26	-18	-13	14	29	37	46	39	29	16	10	-26	-26
Days Maximum Temp. ≥ 90°F	0	0	0	0	0	3	4	4	1	0	0	0	12
Days Maximum Temp. ≤ 32°F	12	9	3	0	0	0	0	0	0	0	1	9	34
Days Minimum Temp. ≤ 32°F	27	24	21	8	1	0	0	0	0	6	16	25	128
Days Minimum Temp. ≤ 0°F	3	2	0	0	0	0	0	0	0	0	0	1	6
Heating Degree Days (base 65°F)	1,172	991	810	453	191	33	4	10	100	393	683	1,040	5,880
Cooling Degree Days (base 65°F)	0	0	1	8	49	175	253	215	86	11	0	0	798
Mean Precipitation (in.)	2.40	1.79	2.43	3.41	4.68	4.38	4.60	3.34	3.08	2.82	2.94	2.70	38.57
Extreme Maximum Daily Precip. (in.)	2.51	2.26	1.73	2.80	3.09	3.60	3.78	3.60	3.14	2.65	2.55	2.68	3.78
Days With ≥ 0.1" Precipitation	5	5	6	7	9	8	7	5	5	5	6	6	74
Days With ≥ 0.5" Precipitation	1	1	2	2	4	3	3	2	2	2	2	2	26
Days With ≥ 1.0" Precipitation	0	0	0	1	1	1	1	1	1	1	1	1	9
Mean Snowfall (in.)	na	***2.7***	na	trace	0.0	0.0	0.0	0.0	0.0	trace	trace	***1.4***	na
Maximum Snow Depth (in.)	na	na	na	***trace***	***0***	***0***	***0***	***0***	***0***	***trace***	***trace***	na	na
Days With ≥ 1.0" Snow Depth	na	na	***0***	0	0	0	0	0	0	0	0	na	na

Steubenville *Jefferson County* Elevation: 992 ft. Latitude: 40° 23' N Longitude: 80° 38' W

	JAN	FEB	MAR	APR	MAY	JUN	JUL	AUG	SEP	OCT	NOV	DEC	YEAR
Mean Maximum Temp. (°F)	37.5	41.1	50.3	62.9	71.8	79.9	83.0	82.3	75.6	63.6	52.4	40.7	61.8
Mean Temp. (°F)	29.7	32.3	40.2	51.6	60.7	69.4	73.3	72.4	65.5	53.5	43.7	33.1	52.1
Mean Minimum Temp. (°F)	21.8	23.5	30.2	40.2	49.7	58.9	63.5	62.5	55.4	43.3	34.9	25.4	42.4
Extreme Maximum Temp. (°F)	72	77	83	89	91	97	102	96	93	85	80	77	102
Extreme Minimum Temp. (°F)	-22	-8	-1	16	29	39	46	42	34	22	12	-14	-22
Days Maximum Temp. ≥ 90°F	0	0	0	0	0	2	4	3	1	0	0	0	10
Days Maximum Temp. ≤ 32°F	11	7	2	0	0	0	0	0	0	0	1	8	29
Days Minimum Temp. ≤ 32°F	25	22	19	6	1	0	0	0	0	2	13	24	112
Days Minimum Temp. ≤ 0°F	1	1	0	0	0	0	0	0	0	0	0	0	2
Heating Degree Days (base 65°F)	1,088	917	763	406	174	29	2	6	75	360	634	984	5,438
Cooling Degree Days (base 65°F)	0	0	2	11	49	167	267	244	97	9	1	0	847
Mean Precipitation (in.)	3.00	2.31	3.27	3.41	4.35	4.21	4.38	3.96	3.37	2.81	3.47	2.98	41.52
Extreme Maximum Daily Precip. (in.)	1.75	1.32	1.48	1.56	2.25	3.14	3.42	2.72	5.36	2.37	2.90	1.80	5.36
Days With ≥ 0.1" Precipitation	7	6	8	8	9	8	8	7	6	6	8	7	88
Days With ≥ 0.5" Precipitation	2	1	2	2	3	3	3	3	2	2	2	2	27
Days With ≥ 1.0" Precipitation	1	0	0	0	1	1	1	1	1	0	1	0	7
Mean Snowfall (in.)	na	na	***0.4***	trace	0.0	0.0	0.0	0.0	0.0	0.2	0.2	na	na
Maximum Snow Depth (in.)	na	na	na	na	na	na	na	na	na	na	na	na	na
Days With ≥ 1.0" Snow Depth	na	na	***0***	0	0	0	0	0	0	0	0	na	na

Upper Sandusky *Wyandot County* Elevation: 854 ft. Latitude: 40° 50' N Longitude: 83° 17' W

	JAN	FEB	MAR	APR	MAY	JUN	JUL	AUG	SEP	OCT	NOV	DEC	YEAR
Mean Maximum Temp. (°F)	33.0	37.0	47.1	60.6	70.8	80.2	84.0	82.6	76.6	63.7	50.4	37.1	60.3
Mean Temp. (°F)	25.5	28.7	37.6	49.4	59.6	69.4	73.2	71.6	64.8	52.6	41.6	30.0	50.3
Mean Minimum Temp. (°F)	18.0	20.4	28.0	38.1	48.4	58.6	62.4	60.5	52.8	41.4	32.7	22.8	40.4
Extreme Maximum Temp. (°F)	67	73	82	87	91	104	102	99	97	89	79	72	104
Extreme Minimum Temp. (°F)	-23	-16	-8	9	27	38	43	40	29	18	9	-20	-23
Days Maximum Temp. ≥ 90°F	0	0	0	0	0	4	5	4	1	0	0	0	14
Days Maximum Temp. ≤ 32°F	14	10	4	0	0	0	0	0	0	0	1	10	39
Days Minimum Temp. ≤ 32°F	26	25	21	9	1	0	0	0	0	5	16	25	128
Days Minimum Temp. ≤ 0°F	3	1	0	0	0	0	0	0	0	0	0	1	5
Heating Degree Days (base 65°F)	1,217	1,022	844	472	208	36	4	11	94	393	696	1,078	6,075
Cooling Degree Days (base 65°F)	0	0	1	9	47	176	266	224	94	13	0	0	830
Mean Precipitation (in.)	1.98	1.89	2.50	3.51	4.52	3.92	4.46	3.49	3.13	2.36	3.20	2.56	37.52
Extreme Maximum Daily Precip. (in.)	1.78	1.60	2.05	1.74	2.27	3.21	2.50	9.35	3.74	2.46	2.00	2.05	9.35
Days With ≥ 0.1" Precipitation	5	5	6	8	9	7	7	6	5	6	7	6	77
Days With ≥ 0.5" Precipitation	1	1	1	2	3	3	3	2	2	1	2	1	22
Days With ≥ 1.0" Precipitation	0	0	0	1	1	1	2	1	1	0	1	0	8
Mean Snowfall (in.)	6.4	3.8	2.2	1.1	trace	0.0	0.0	0.0	0.0	trace	0.8	5.1	19.4
Maximum Snow Depth (in.)	12	11	13	9	0	0	0	0	0	trace	4	***19***	***19***
Days With ≥ 1.0" Snow Depth	9	6	2	0	0	0	0	0	0	0	1	4	22

The period of record for all cooperative weather station data is 1980 – 2009. See User Guide for detailed explanation of data.

Urbana WWTP *Champaign County* Elevation: 1,000 ft. Latitude: 40° 06' N Longitude: 83° 47' W

	JAN	FEB	MAR	APR	MAY	JUN	JUL	AUG	SEP	OCT	NOV	DEC	YEAR
Mean Maximum Temp. (°F)	34.5	38.6	47.9	60.8	71.0	80.4	84.1	82.9	76.2	63.5	50.9	38.2	60.7
Mean Temp. (°F)	26.7	30.1	38.3	50.0	60.2	69.5	73.1	71.5	64.3	52.4	42.0	30.8	50.7
Mean Minimum Temp. (°F)	19.0	21.6	28.7	39.1	49.3	58.6	62.0	60.0	52.4	41.2	33.1	23.3	40.7
Extreme Maximum Temp. (°F)	66	71	80	86	91	99	100	101	96	87	76	72	101
Extreme Minimum Temp. (°F)	-26	-18	-6	14	29	36	42	39	28	18	11	-22	-26
Days Maximum Temp. ≥ 90°F	0	0	0	0	0	3	6	4	1	0	0	0	14
Days Maximum Temp. ≤ 32°F	13	9	3	0	0	0	0	0	0	0	1	9	35
Days Minimum Temp. ≤ 32°F	27	24	20	7	0	0	0	0	0	6	15	25	124
Days Minimum Temp. ≤ 0°F	3	1	0	0	0	0	0	0	0	0	0	1	5
Heating Degree Days (base 65°F)	1,179	980	820	452	190	34	4	10	98	394	682	1,054	5,897
Cooling Degree Days (base 65°F)	0	0	0	7	47	175	261	218	84	9	0	0	801
Mean Precipitation (in.)	2.64	2.06	2.81	3.76	4.78	4.50	5.49	3.42	3.08	2.94	3.19	3.04	41.71
Extreme Maximum Daily Precip. (in.)	2.61	1.60	1.82	2.70	2.47	3.50	3.97	3.72	3.60	3.05	1.80	2.30	3.97
Days With ≥ 0.1" Precipitation	6	6	7	8	9	8	7	6	5	6	7	6	81
Days With ≥ 0.5" Precipitation	1	1	2	3	3	3	4	2	2	2	2	2	27
Days With ≥ 1.0" Precipitation	1	0	0	1	1	1	2	1	1	1	1	1	11
Mean Snowfall (in.)	na	na	na	0.1	0.0	0.0	0.0	0.0	0.0	0.0	trace	na	na
Maximum Snow Depth (in.)	na	na	na	*trace*	*0*	*0*	*0*	na	*0*	na	na	na	na
Days With ≥ 1.0" Snow Depth	na	na	na	0	0	0	0	0	0	0	0	na	na

Warren 3 S *Trumbull County* Elevation: 899 ft. Latitude: 41° 12' N Longitude: 80° 49' W

	JAN	FEB	MAR	APR	MAY	JUN	JUL	AUG	SEP	OCT	NOV	DEC	YEAR
Mean Maximum Temp. (°F)	34.7	37.9	47.4	60.6	70.7	79.3	83.1	81.7	74.5	62.6	50.7	38.7	60.2
Mean Temp. (°F)	26.1	28.1	36.4	48.0	57.6	66.6	70.7	69.4	62.1	50.8	41.1	30.5	48.9
Mean Minimum Temp. (°F)	17.3	18.3	25.3	35.3	44.4	53.9	58.2	57.0	49.7	38.9	31.4	22.3	37.7
Extreme Maximum Temp. (°F)	69	75	82	90	91	99	101	99	93	87	79	76	101
Extreme Minimum Temp. (°F)	-26	-13	-11	10	23	32	40	30	28	16	7	-17	-26
Days Maximum Temp. ≥ 90°F	0	0	0	0	0	2	4	3	0	0	0	0	9
Days Maximum Temp. ≤ 32°F	13	10	4	0	0	0	0	0	0	0	1	9	37
Days Minimum Temp. ≤ 32°F	28	25	24	13	3	0	0	0	1	8	18	26	146
Days Minimum Temp. ≤ 0°F	4	2	0	0	0	0	0	0	0	0	0	1	7
Heating Degree Days (base 65°F)	1,200	1,037	881	509	250	61	12	22	136	438	711	1,062	6,319
Cooling Degree Days (base 65°F)	0	0	0	5	28	116	195	164	55	4	0	0	567
Mean Precipitation (in.)	2.60	1.82	3.06	3.51	3.97	3.96	4.80	3.46	3.79	2.92	3.10	2.79	39.78
Extreme Maximum Daily Precip. (in.)	1.81	1.40	1.84	1.80	1.80	2.26	4.41	2.96	3.87	1.74	2.60	1.56	4.41
Days With ≥ 0.1" Precipitation	7	6	8	9	9	8	7	7	7	7	7	7	89
Days With ≥ 0.5" Precipitation	1	1	2	2	3	3	3	2	2	2	2	1	24
Days With ≥ 1.0" Precipitation	0	0	0	1	1	1	1	1	1	0	0	0	6
Mean Snowfall (in.)	11.5	6.9	5.2	0.4	0.0	0.0	0.0	0.0	0.0	trace	0.8	7.0	31.8
Maximum Snow Depth (in.)	16	14	15	6	0	0	0	0	0	trace	3	13	16
Days With ≥ 1.0" Snow Depth	13	9	4	0	0	0	0	0	0	0	1	8	35

Westerville *Franklin County* Elevation: 810 ft. Latitude: 40° 08' N Longitude: 82° 57' W

	JAN	FEB	MAR	APR	MAY	JUN	JUL	AUG	SEP	OCT	NOV	DEC	YEAR
Mean Maximum Temp. (°F)	36.9	41.5	52.1	65.0	74.2	82.4	85.4	84.4	78.2	66.4	53.4	40.7	63.4
Mean Temp. (°F)	28.9	32.3	41.4	52.8	62.2	70.8	74.3	73.2	66.3	54.7	44.2	33.1	52.9
Mean Minimum Temp. (°F)	20.9	23.1	30.7	40.5	50.2	59.2	63.2	61.9	54.3	43.0	34.9	25.5	42.3
Extreme Maximum Temp. (°F)	68	74	82	88	92	100	101	101	97	89	79	76	101
Extreme Minimum Temp. (°F)	-27	-20	-5	14	28	36	41	36	31	18	12	-25	-27
Days Maximum Temp. ≥ 90°F	0	0	0	0	0	4	7	6	2	0	0	0	19
Days Maximum Temp. ≤ 32°F	11	7	2	0	0	0	0	0	0	0	1	7	28
Days Minimum Temp. ≤ 32°F	25	23	18	7	1	0	0	0	0	4	13	23	114
Days Minimum Temp. ≤ 0°F	2	1	0	0	0	0	0	0	0	0	0	1	4
Heating Degree Days (base 65°F)	1,114	918	726	371	146	21	1	5	70	327	619	982	5,300
Cooling Degree Days (base 65°F)	0	0	2	13	67	202	298	265	115	16	0	0	978
Mean Precipitation (in.)	2.66	2.22	2.94	3.49	4.35	4.46	4.27	3.21	2.81	2.78	3.13	2.94	39.26
Extreme Maximum Daily Precip. (in.)	1.95	1.96	1.55	3.84	1.78	3.32	3.19	2.79	2.17	3.06	1.64	1.77	3.84
Days With ≥ 0.1" Precipitation	6	6	7	8	9	8	7	6	5	6	7	7	82
Days With ≥ 0.5" Precipitation	2	1	2	2	3	3	3	2	2	2	2	2	26
Days With ≥ 1.0" Precipitation	1	0	0	0	1	1	1	1	1	0	1	1	8
Mean Snowfall (in.)	6.9	4.6	2.5	0.5	trace	0.0	0.0	0.0	0.0	trace	0.3	3.7	18.5
Maximum Snow Depth (in.)	12	13	11	3	trace	0	0	0	0	trace	1	7	13
Days With ≥ 1.0" Snow Depth	10	6	2	0	0	0	0	0	0	0	0	5	23

Wilmington 3 N *Clinton County* Elevation: 1,029 ft. Latitude: 39° 29' N Longitude: 83° 49' W

	JAN	FEB	MAR	APR	MAY	JUN	JUL	AUG	SEP	OCT	NOV	DEC	YEAR
Mean Maximum Temp. (°F)	35.8	39.5	49.5	61.9	71.6	80.2	83.7	82.8	76.9	65.0	52.3	39.4	61.6
Mean Temp. (°F)	27.9	30.8	39.6	50.8	60.8	69.7	73.1	71.5	64.7	53.4	43.0	31.8	51.4
Mean Minimum Temp. (°F)	19.9	22.1	29.5	39.7	50.0	59.2	62.5	60.1	52.5	41.8	33.5	24.1	41.2
Extreme Maximum Temp. (°F)	69	73	81	87	90	99	99	99	95	91	78	73	99
Extreme Minimum Temp. (°F)	-25	-20	-10	17	29	39	40	37	32	17	11	-24	-25
Days Maximum Temp. ≥ 90°F	0	0	0	0	0	2	4	4	1	0	0	0	11
Days Maximum Temp. ≤ 32°F	12	9	3	0	0	0	0	0	0	0	1	9	34
Days Minimum Temp. ≤ 32°F	27	23	20	6	0	0	0	0	0	5	15	24	120
Days Minimum Temp. ≤ 0°F	3	2	0	0	0	0	0	0	0	0	0	1	6
Heating Degree Days (base 65°F)	1,144	960	783	429	173	29	3	10	90	366	655	1,022	5,664
Cooling Degree Days (base 65°F)	0	0	1	10	50	177	261	218	90	14	1	0	822
Mean Precipitation (in.)	2.81	2.35	3.50	3.92	5.22	3.79	4.19	3.02	2.82	3.10	3.13	2.95	40.80
Extreme Maximum Daily Precip. (in.)	3.42	2.23	1.67	2.85	2.14	2.53	3.03	3.39	2.43	2.83	1.70	2.40	3.42
Days With ≥ 0.1" Precipitation	6	5	7	9	9	8	8	5	5	6	7	7	82
Days With ≥ 0.5" Precipitation	2	1	2	3	4	2	3	2	2	2	2	2	27
Days With ≥ 1.0" Precipitation	1	0	1	1	1	1	1	1	1	1	1	0	10
Mean Snowfall (in.)	6.9	5.8	3.3	0.4	trace	0.0	0.0	0.0	0.0	0.2	0.9	3.5	21.0
Maximum Snow Depth (in.)	16	14	18	5	trace	0	0	0	0	2	5	7	18
Days With ≥ 1.0" Snow Depth	10	8	3	0	0	0	0	0	0	0	0	5	26

The period of record for all cooperative weather station data is 1980 – 2009. See User Guide for detailed explanation of data.

Wooster Exp Stn *Wayne County* Elevation: 1,020 ft. Latitude: 40° 47' N Longitude: 81° 55' W

	JAN	FEB	MAR	APR	MAY	JUN	JUL	AUG	SEP	OCT	NOV	DEC	YEAR
Mean Maximum Temp. (°F)	33.4	36.8	46.7	59.6	69.5	78.2	81.8	80.3	73.3	61.3	49.5	37.4	59.0
Mean Temp. (°F)	26.2	28.8	37.5	49.0	58.7	67.5	71.3	69.8	62.4	51.0	41.2	30.5	49.5
Mean Minimum Temp. (°F)	19.0	20.7	28.2	38.3	47.8	56.8	60.8	59.2	51.6	40.7	32.8	23.5	39.9
Extreme Maximum Temp. (°F)	69	71	80	86	90	100	101	96	94	88	76	74	101
Extreme Minimum Temp. (°F)	-24	-13	-6	14	26	37	41	36	30	17	9	-17	-24
Days Maximum Temp. ≥ 90°F	0	0	0	0	0	1	2	2	0	0	0	0	5
Days Maximum Temp. ≤ 32°F	15	11	4	0	0	0	0	0	0	0	1	11	42
Days Minimum Temp. ≤ 32°F	27	24	21	9	1	0	0	0	0	6	16	26	130
Days Minimum Temp. ≤ 0°F	3	1	0	0	0	0	0	0	0	0	0	1	5
Heating Degree Days (base 65°F)	1,195	1,019	847	480	223	51	8	18	128	432	707	1,064	6,172
Cooling Degree Days (base 65°F)	0	0	1	6	34	133	210	172	57	6	0	0	619
Mean Precipitation (in.)	2.29	1.95	2.83	3.66	4.43	4.34	4.24	4.10	3.36	3.03	3.06	2.70	39.99
Extreme Maximum Daily Precip. (in.)	2.59	1.39	1.63	1.96	2.37	2.47	2.95	3.60	3.25	2.37	2.09	2.08	3.60
Days With ≥ 0.1" Precipitation	6	5	7	8	9	8	7	6	6	6	7	6	81
Days With ≥ 0.5" Precipitation	1	1	2	3	3	3	3	3	2	2	2	2	27
Days With ≥ 1.0" Precipitation	0	0	0	1	1	1	1	1	1	1	0	0	7
Mean Snowfall (in.)	8.4	6.4	5.6	1.1	trace	0.0	0.0	trace	0.0	0.1	1.5	6.2	29.3
Maximum Snow Depth (in.)	13	17	13	8	0	0	0	trace	0	2	4	8	17
Days With ≥ 1.0" Snow Depth	15	12	6	1	0	0	0	0	0	0	1	10	45

The period of record for all cooperative weather station data is 1980 – 2009. See User Guide for detailed explanation of data.

Ohio Weather Station Rankings

Annual Extreme Maximum Temperature

Highest

Rank	Station Name	°F
1	Chilo Meldahl L&D	107
2	Chillicothe Mound City	105
3	Bowling Green WWTP	104
3	Cleveland Hopkins Intl Arpt	104
3	Dayton Mcd	104
3	Defiance	104
3	Elyria 3 E	104
3	Fairfield	***104***
3	Findlay Wpcc	104
3	Franklin	104
3	Milford	***104***
3	Oberlin	104
3	Portsmouth Sciotoville	104
3	Toledo Express Arpt	104
3	Upper Sandusky	104
16	Cincinnati-Northern Kentucky	103
16	Marion 2 N	103
16	Millport 2 NW	103
16	Pandora	103
20	Bucyrus	102
20	Cambridge	102
20	Chippewa Lake	102
20	Danville 2 W	102
20	Dayton Intl Arpt	102
20	Marietta Wwtp	102

Lowest

Rank	Station Name	°F
1	Millersburg	***98***
1	Painesville 4 NW	98
3	Centerburg 2 SE	99
3	Wilmington 3 N	99
5	Barnesville	***100***
5	Chardon	100
5	Columbus Valley Crossing	100
5	Dorset	100
5	Fredericktown 4 S	***100***
5	Hannibal Lock & Dam	100
5	Hiram	100
5	Lima WWTP	100
5	Mansfield 5 W	100
5	Springfield New Water Works	100
5	Youngstown Municipal Arpt	100
16	Akron Akron-Canton Reg Arpt	101
16	Bellefontaine	101
16	Cadiz	101
16	Carpenter 2 S	***101***
16	Circleville	101
16	Columbus-Port Columbus Intl	101
16	Mansfield Lahm Municipal Arpt	101
16	Marysville	101
16	Urbana WWTP	101
16	Warren 3 S	101

Annual Mean Maximum Temperature

Highest

Rank	Station Name	°F
1	Portsmouth Sciotoville	65.6
2	Fairfield	***65.2***
3	Chilo Meldahl L&D	64.8
4	Milford	***64.5***
5	Marietta Wwtp	64.3
6	Chillicothe Mound City	***63.9***
7	Carpenter 2 S	***63.7***
7	Cincinnati-Northern Kentucky	63.7
9	Cambridge	63.6
10	Dayton Mcd	63.5
11	Westerville	63.4
12	Circleville	63.1
12	Franklin	63.1
14	Columbus Valley Crossing	63.0
15	Hannibal Lock & Dam	62.7
16	Columbus-Port Columbus Intl	62.4
17	Steubenville	61.8
18	Wilmington 3 N	61.6
19	Dayton Intl Arpt	61.4
20	Elyria 3 E	61.3
21	Marysville	61.2
21	Millersburg	***61.2***
21	Millport 2 NW	61.2
21	Springfield New Water Works	61.2
25	Danville 2 W	60.9

Lowest

Rank	Station Name	°F
1	Chardon	57.5
2	Hiram	57.9
3	Dorset	58.2
4	Mansfield 5 W	58.7
5	Mansfield Lahm Municipal Arpt	58.8
5	Youngstown Municipal Arpt	58.8
7	Painesville 4 NW	59.0
7	Wooster Exp Stn	59.0
9	Akron Akron-Canton Reg Arpt	59.2
9	Bucyrus	59.2
9	Chippewa Lake	59.2
9	Cleveland Hopkins Intl Arpt	59.2
13	Oberlin	59.6
13	Toledo Express Arpt	59.6
15	Bowling Green WWTP	59.7
15	Defiance	59.7
15	Fredericktown 4 S	59.7
18	Centerburg 2 SE	59.8
19	Findlay Wpcc	60.0
19	Marion 2 N	60.0
19	Pandora	60.0
22	Bellefontaine	60.2
22	Warren 3 S	60.2
24	Cadiz	60.3
24	Upper Sandusky	60.3

Rankings include 25 highest/lowest stations. If state has less than 25 stations, all stations are included. The period of record is 1980–2009. See User Guide for detailed explanation of data.

Annual Mean Temperature

Highest

Rank	Station Name	°F
1	Portsmouth Sciotoville	54.4
2	Chilo Meldahl L&D	54.2
2	Fairfield	***54.2***
4	Cincinnati-Northern Kentucky	54.0
4	Dayton Mcd	54.0
6	Marietta Wwtp	53.6
7	Milford	***53.1***
8	Cambridge	53.0
9	Columbus-Port Columbus Intl	52.9
9	Westerville	52.9
11	Chillicothe Mound City	***52.8***
11	Circleville	52.8
13	Columbus Valley Crossing	52.7
14	Carpenter 2 S	***52.5***
15	Franklin	52.2
16	Dayton Intl Arpt	52.1
16	Hannibal Lock & Dam	52.1
16	Steubenville	52.1
19	Elyria 3 E	51.7
20	Lima WWTP	51.5
20	Marysville	51.5
22	Wilmington 3 N	51.4
23	Painesville 4 NW	51.2
24	Findlay Wpcc	51.0
25	Cadiz	50.8

Lowest

Rank	Station Name	°F
1	Chardon	47.5
2	Dorset	47.9
3	Fredericktown 4 S	48.5
4	Hiram	48.6
5	Mansfield 5 W	48.8
6	Warren 3 S	48.9
7	Danville 2 W	49.2
7	Youngstown Municipal Arpt	49.2
9	Chippewa Lake	49.3
10	Bucyrus	49.4
11	Wooster Exp Stn	49.5
12	Oberlin	49.6
13	Mansfield Lahm Municipal Arpt	49.7
14	Bowling Green WWTP	49.8
14	Defiance	49.8
14	Millersburg	***49.8***
14	Millport 2 NW	49.8
18	Centerburg 2 SE	49.9
18	Toledo Express Arpt	49.9
20	Akron Akron-Canton Reg Arpt	50.1
20	Marion 2 N	50.1
22	Upper Sandusky	50.3
23	Pandora	50.4
24	Barnesville	***50.5***
24	Bellefontaine	50.5

Annual Mean Minimum Temperature

Highest

Rank	Station Name	°F
1	Dayton Mcd	44.6
2	Cincinnati-Northern Kentucky	44.3
3	Chilo Meldahl L&D	43.6
4	Columbus-Port Columbus Intl	43.4
4	Painesville 4 NW	43.4
6	Fairfield	***43.1***
6	Portsmouth Sciotoville	43.1
8	Marietta Wwtp	42.9
9	Dayton Intl Arpt	42.7
10	Circleville	42.4
10	Columbus Valley Crossing	42.4
10	Steubenville	42.4
13	Cambridge	42.3
13	Westerville	42.3
15	Lima WWTP	42.2
16	Elyria 3 E	42.0
16	Findlay Wpcc	42.0
18	Cleveland Hopkins Intl Arpt	41.9
18	Marysville	41.9
20	Chillicothe Mound City	***41.7***
21	Milford	***41.6***
22	Hannibal Lock & Dam	41.4
23	Cadiz	41.3
23	Franklin	41.3
23	Wilmington 3 N	41.3

Lowest

Rank	Station Name	°F
1	Fredericktown 4 S	37.4
2	Chardon	37.5
2	Danville 2 W	37.5
2	Dorset	37.5
5	Warren 3 S	37.7
6	Millersburg	***38.4***
6	Millport 2 NW	38.4
8	Mansfield 5 W	39.0
9	Chippewa Lake	39.3
9	Hiram	39.3
11	Bucyrus	39.6
11	Youngstown Municipal Arpt	39.6
13	Oberlin	39.7
14	Centerburg 2 SE	39.9
15	Bowling Green WWTP	40.0
15	Defiance	40.0
15	Wooster Exp Stn	40.0
18	Marion 2 N	40.1
19	Toledo Express Arpt	40.2
20	Springfield New Water Works	40.3
21	Upper Sandusky	40.4
22	Barnesville	***40.6***
23	Mansfield Lahm Municipal Arpt	40.7
23	Urbana WWTP	40.7
25	Bellefontaine	40.8

Rankings include 25 highest/lowest stations. If state has less than 25 stations, all stations are included. The period of record is 1980–2009. See User Guide for detailed explanation of data.

Annual Extreme Minimum Temperature

Highest

Rank	Station Name	°F
1	Painesville 4 NW	-19
2	Bowling Green WWTP	-20
2	Cleveland Hopkins Intl Arpt	-20
2	Findlay Wpcc	-20
2	Toledo Express Arpt	-20
6	Dayton Mcd	-21
6	Lima WWTP	-21
6	Pandora	-21
9	Chilo Meldahl L&D	-22
9	Circleville	-22
9	Columbus-Port Columbus Intl	-22
9	Defiance	-22
9	Elyria 3 E	-22
9	Mansfield Lahm Municipal Arpt	-22
9	Steubenville	-22
9	Youngstown Municipal Arpt	-22
17	Chardon	-23
17	Fairfield	***-23***
17	Marietta Wwtp	-23
17	Marion 2 N	-23
17	Marysville	-23
17	Milford	***-23***
17	Oberlin	-23
17	Upper Sandusky	-23
25	Cadiz	-24

Lowest

Rank	Station Name	°F
1	Danville 2 W	-35
1	Millersburg	***-35***
3	Millport 2 NW	-34
4	Cambridge	-32
5	Fredericktown 4 S	***-30***
6	Centerburg 2 SE	-29
6	Chillicothe Mound City	-29
6	Portsmouth Sciotoville	-29
9	Columbus Valley Crossing	-28
9	Dorset	-28
11	Bellefontaine	-27
11	Westerville	-27
13	Bucyrus	-26
13	Chippewa Lake	-26
13	Springfield New Water Works	-26
13	Urbana WWTP	-26
13	Warren 3 S	-26
18	Akron Akron-Canton Reg Arpt	-25
18	Carpenter 2 S	***-25***
18	Dayton Intl Arpt	-25
18	Hiram	-25
18	Mansfield 5 W	-25
18	Wilmington 3 N	-25
24	Cadiz	-24
24	Cincinnati-Northern Kentucky	-24

July Mean Maximum Temperature

Highest

Rank	Station Name	°F
1	Fairfield	***87.8***
2	Dayton Mcd	87.5
3	Milford	***87.2***
4	Portsmouth Sciotoville	86.6
5	Chilo Meldahl L&D	86.0
6	Chillicothe Mound City	***85.7***
7	Cincinnati-Northern Kentucky	85.6
8	Franklin	85.4
8	Marietta Wwtp	85.4
8	Westerville	85.4
11	Cambridge	85.2
12	Circleville	85.0
13	Columbus Valley Crossing	84.9
14	Columbus-Port Columbus Intl	84.8
15	Carpenter 2 S	***84.7***
16	Elyria 3 E	84.6
17	Dayton Intl Arpt	84.4
17	Defiance	84.4
19	Marysville	84.3
19	Toledo Express Arpt	84.3
21	Bowling Green WWTP	84.1
21	Urbana WWTP	84.1
23	Lima WWTP	84.0
23	Upper Sandusky	84.0
25	Pandora	83.9

Lowest

Rank	Station Name	°F
1	Chardon	80.4
2	Painesville 4 NW	80.9
3	Hiram	81.0
4	Dorset	81.3
5	Mansfield 5 W	81.6
6	Mansfield Lahm Municipal Arpt	81.7
7	Wooster Exp Stn	81.8
8	Youngstown Municipal Arpt	81.9
9	Cadiz	82.2
10	Cleveland Hopkins Intl Arpt	82.3
10	Fredericktown 4 S	82.3
12	Akron Akron-Canton Reg Arpt	82.4
13	Barnesville	***82.5***
13	Chippewa Lake	82.5
15	Centerburg 2 SE	82.6
16	Bellefontaine	82.9
17	Steubenville	83.0
18	Bucyrus	83.1
18	Warren 3 S	83.1
20	Oberlin	83.2
21	Danville 2 W	83.4
21	Marion 2 N	83.4
23	Springfield New Water Works	83.5
24	Millport 2 NW	83.6
25	Hannibal Lock & Dam	83.7

Rankings include 25 highest/lowest stations. If state has less than 25 stations, all stations are included. The period of record is 1980–2009. See User Guide for detailed explanation of data.

January Mean Minimum Temperature

Highest

Rank	Station Name	°F
1	Marietta Wwtp	22.8
2	Portsmouth Sciotoville	22.7
3	Chilo Meldahl L&D	22.6
3	Cincinnati-Northern Kentucky	22.6
5	Fairfield	*22.4*
6	Dayton Mcd	22.2
6	Painesville 4 NW	22.2
8	Circleville	21.9
8	Columbus-Port Columbus Intl	21.9
10	Cambridge	21.8
10	Steubenville	21.8
12	Carpenter 2 S	*21.3*
12	Columbus Valley Crossing	21.3
14	Hannibal Lock & Dam	21.2
15	Westerville	20.9
16	Elyria 3 E	20.7
17	Cleveland Hopkins Intl Arpt	20.3
17	Dayton Intl Arpt	20.3
19	Franklin	20.2
20	Chillicothe Mound City	*20.1*
20	Milford	*20.1*
22	Wilmington 3 N	19.9
23	Lima WWTP	19.8
23	Marysville	19.8
25	Barnesville	*19.7*

Lowest

Rank	Station Name	°F
1	Fredericktown 4 S	15.2
2	Dorset	16.2
3	Chardon	16.3
4	Mansfield 5 W	16.5
5	Danville 2 W	16.9
6	Defiance	17.0
7	Hiram	17.2
8	Warren 3 S	17.3
9	Centerburg 2 SE	17.4
10	Bowling Green WWTP	17.6
11	Marion 2 N	17.7
12	Bucyrus	17.8
12	Oberlin	17.8
14	Bellefontaine	17.9
15	Chippewa Lake	18.0
15	Toledo Express Arpt	18.0
15	Upper Sandusky	18.0
18	Millport 2 NW	18.1
19	Millersburg	*18.4*
19	Pandora	18.4
21	Springfield New Water Works	18.6
22	Mansfield Lahm Municipal Arpt	18.9
23	Urbana WWTP	19.0
23	Wooster Exp Stn	19.0
23	Youngstown Municipal Arpt	19.0

Number of Days Annually Maximum Temperature ≥ 90°F

Highest

Rank	Station Name	Days
1	Dayton Mcd	35
1	Fairfield	*35*
3	Milford	*28*
4	Portsmouth Sciotoville	27
5	Chilo Meldahl L&D	20
5	Cincinnati-Northern Kentucky	20
7	Chillicothe Mound City	19
7	Franklin	19
7	Marietta Wwtp	19
7	Westerville	19
11	Circleville	18
11	Elyria 3 E	18
13	Defiance	17
14	Bowling Green WWTP	16
14	Columbus-Port Columbus Intl	16
14	Toledo Express Arpt	16
17	Cambridge	15
17	Dayton Intl Arpt	15
17	Pandora	15
20	Columbus Valley Crossing	14
20	Findlay Wpcc	14
20	Lima WWTP	14
20	Marysville	14
20	Upper Sandusky	14
20	Urbana WWTP	14

Lowest

Rank	Station Name	Days
1	Painesville 4 NW	4
2	Chardon	5
2	Hiram	5
2	Mansfield Lahm Municipal Arpt	5
2	Wooster Exp Stn	5
6	Mansfield 5 W	6
6	Youngstown Municipal Arpt	6
8	Akron Akron-Canton Reg Arpt	7
8	Barnesville	*7*
8	Dorset	7
11	Cadiz	8
11	Chippewa Lake	8
11	Fredericktown 4 S	8
14	Centerburg 2 SE	9
14	Cleveland Hopkins Intl Arpt	9
14	Warren 3 S	9
17	Bellefontaine	10
17	Danville 2 W	10
17	Steubenville	10
20	Bucyrus	11
20	Hannibal Lock & Dam	11
20	Wilmington 3 N	11
23	Millport 2 NW	12
23	Oberlin	12
23	Springfield New Water Works	12

Rankings include 25 highest/lowest stations. If state has less than 25 stations, all stations are included. The period of record is 1980–2009. See User Guide for detailed explanation of data.

Number of Days Annually Maximum Temperature ≤ 32°F

Highest			Lowest		
Rank	**Station Name**	**Days**	**Rank**	**Station Name**	**Days**
1	Chardon	49	1	Portsmouth Sciotoville	16
2	Mansfield 5 W	47	2	Chilo Meldahl L&D	19
3	Hiram	46	3	Fairfield	***20***
4	Bucyrus	45	3	Marietta Wwtp	20
4	Dorset	45	5	Chillicothe Mound City	21
6	Chippewa Lake	44	6	Milford	***22***
6	Mansfield Lahm Municipal Arpt	44	7	Cambridge	23
6	Youngstown Municipal Arpt	44	7	Carpenter 2 S	***23***
9	Bowling Green WWTP	43	7	Cincinnati-Northern Kentucky	23
9	Defiance	43	7	Hannibal Lock & Dam	23
9	Toledo Express Arpt	43	11	Columbus Valley Crossing	26
12	Findlay Wpcc	42	12	Circleville	27
12	Oberlin	42	12	Franklin	27
12	Pandora	42	14	Westerville	28
12	Wooster Exp Stn	42	15	Steubenville	29
16	Bellefontaine	40	16	Columbus-Port Columbus Intl	30
16	Centerburg 2 SE	40	16	Dayton Mcd	30
16	Marion 2 N	40	18	Elyria 3 E	31
19	Akron Akron-Canton Reg Arpt	39	19	Millersburg	***33***
19	Cleveland Hopkins Intl Arpt	39	19	Millport 2 NW	33
19	Fredericktown 4 S	39	21	Painesville 4 NW	34
19	Upper Sandusky	39	21	Springfield New Water Works	34
23	Lima WWTP	38	21	Wilmington 3 N	34
24	Cadiz	37	24	Barnesville	***35***
24	Warren 3 S	37	24	Danville 2 W	35

Number of Days Annually Minimum Temperature ≤ 32°F

Highest			Lowest		
Rank	**Station Name**	**Days**	**Rank**	**Station Name**	**Days**
1	Danville 2 W	150	1	Cincinnati-Northern Kentucky	103
2	Fredericktown 4 S	147	1	Dayton Mcd	103
3	Warren 3 S	146	3	Painesville 4 NW	106
4	Dorset	143	4	Chilo Meldahl L&D	107
5	Chardon	142	5	Columbus-Port Columbus Intl	108
5	Millersburg	***142***	5	Portsmouth Sciotoville	108
7	Millport 2 NW	141	7	Marietta Wwtp	110
8	Mansfield 5 W	136	8	Fairfield	***111***
9	Hiram	134	9	Chillicothe Mound City	112
10	Chippewa Lake	133	9	Steubenville	112
11	Bucyrus	132	11	Cambridge	113
12	Centerburg 2 SE	131	11	Circleville	113
12	Oberlin	131	13	Columbus Valley Crossing	114
14	Bowling Green WWTP	130	13	Westerville	114
14	Defiance	130	15	Dayton Intl Arpt	115
14	Marion 2 N	130	16	Cadiz	116
14	Toledo Express Arpt	130	17	Cleveland Hopkins Intl Arpt	117
14	Wooster Exp Stn	130	17	Marysville	117
19	Bellefontaine	129	19	Elyria 3 E	118
19	Youngstown Municipal Arpt	129	20	Findlay Wpcc	119
21	Springfield New Water Works	128	20	Lima WWTP	119
21	Upper Sandusky	128	20	Milford	***119***
23	Barnesville	***126***	23	Carpenter 2 S	***120***
23	Mansfield Lahm Municipal Arpt	126	23	Franklin	120
23	Pandora	126	23	Hannibal Lock & Dam	120

Rankings include 25 highest/lowest stations. If state has less than 25 stations, all stations are included. The period of record is 1980–2009. See User Guide for detailed explanation of data.

Number of Days Annually Minimum Temperature ≤ 0°F

Highest			Lowest		
Rank	Station Name	Days	Rank	Station Name	Days
1	Chardon	9	1	Painesville 4 NW	1
1	Defiance	9	2	Marietta Wwtp	2
1	Dorset	9	2	Steubenville	2
1	Fredericktown 4 S	9	4	Chilo Meldahl L&D	3
5	Danville 2 W	8	4	Dayton Mcd	3
6	Bellefontaine	7	4	Fairfield	*3*
6	Bowling Green WWTP	7	4	Hannibal Lock & Dam	3
6	Centerburg 2 SE	7	4	Portsmouth Sciotoville	3
6	Mansfield 5 W	7	9	Akron Akron-Canton Reg Arpt	4
6	Millport 2 NW	7	9	Barnesville	*4*
6	Pandora	7	9	Cadiz	4
6	Warren 3 S	7	9	Cambridge	4
13	Bucyrus	6	9	Carpenter 2 S	*4*
13	Chippewa Lake	6	9	Chillicothe Mound City	4
13	Hiram	6	9	Cincinnati-Northern Kentucky	4
13	Marion 2 N	6	9	Circleville	4
13	Millersburg	*6*	9	Cleveland Hopkins Intl Arpt	4
13	Oberlin	6	9	Columbus-Port Columbus Intl	4
13	Springfield New Water Works	6	9	Columbus Valley Crossing	4
13	Toledo Express Arpt	6	9	Dayton Intl Arpt	4
13	Wilmington 3 N	6	9	Elyria 3 E	4
22	Lima WWTP	5	9	Findlay Wpcc	4
22	Mansfield Lahm Municipal Arpt	5	9	Franklin	4
22	Upper Sandusky	5	9	Marysville	4
22	Urbana WWTP	5	9	Milford	*4*

Number of Annual Heating Degree Days

Highest			Lowest		
Rank	Station Name	Num.	Rank	Station Name	Num.
1	Chardon	6,754	1	Portsmouth Sciotoville	4,855
2	Dorset	6,648	2	Chilo Meldahl L&D	4,909
3	Fredericktown 4 S	6,449	3	Cincinnati-Northern Kentucky	5,012
4	Hiram	6,442	4	Marietta Wwtp	5,028
5	Mansfield 5 W	6,401	5	Fairfield	*5,046*
6	Warren 3 S	6,319	6	Dayton Mcd	5,182
7	Bucyrus	6,297	7	Cambridge	5,200
8	Chippewa Lake	6,263	8	Milford	*5,271*
9	Danville 2 W	6,258	9	Westerville	5,300
10	Defiance	6,244	10	Carpenter 2 S	*5,307*
11	Youngstown Municipal Arpt	6,243	10	Columbus-Port Columbus Intl	5,307
12	Bowling Green WWTP	6,215	12	Chillicothe Mound City	*5,308*
13	Oberlin	6,212	13	Circleville	5,310
14	Toledo Express Arpt	6,186	14	Columbus Valley Crossing	5,318
15	Wooster Exp Stn	6,172	15	Hannibal Lock & Dam	5,395
16	Mansfield Lahm Municipal Arpt	6,141	16	Steubenville	5,438
17	Marion 2 N	6,120	17	Franklin	5,484
18	Centerburg 2 SE	6,106	18	Dayton Intl Arpt	5,563
19	Millersburg	*6,086*	19	Elyria 3 E	5,631
20	Upper Sandusky	6,075	20	Wilmington 3 N	5,664
21	Millport 2 NW	6,051	21	Painesville 4 NW	5,695
22	Akron Akron-Canton Reg Arpt	6,039	22	Marysville	5,699
23	Pandora	6,029	23	Lima WWTP	5,741
24	Bellefontaine	5,988	24	Cadiz	5,840
25	Cleveland Hopkins Intl Arpt	5,928	25	Springfield New Water Works	5,880

Rankings include 25 highest/lowest stations. If state has less than 25 stations, all stations are included. The period of record is 1980–2009. See User Guide for detailed explanation of data.

Number of Annual Cooling Degree Days

Highest

Rank	Station Name	Num.
1	Dayton Mcd	1,294
2	Fairfield	***1,199***
3	Cincinnati-Northern Kentucky	1,119
4	Chilo Meldahl L&D	1,090
5	Portsmouth Sciotoville	1,076
6	Milford	***1,034***
7	Columbus-Port Columbus Intl	1,013
8	Marietta Wwtp	987
9	Chillicothe Mound City	***985***
10	Westerville	978
11	Circleville	962
12	Dayton Intl Arpt	952
13	Columbus Valley Crossing	943
14	Lima WWTP	933
15	Cambridge	929
16	Franklin	921
17	Findlay Wpcc	902
18	Marysville	897
19	Elyria 3 E	885
20	Steubenville	847
21	Carpenter 2 S	***843***
22	Upper Sandusky	830
23	Defiance	825
24	Wilmington 3 N	822
25	Pandora	821

Lowest

Rank	Station Name	Num.
1	Chardon	482
2	Dorset	510
3	Fredericktown 4 S	548
4	Warren 3 S	567
5	Hiram	582
6	Youngstown Municipal Arpt	588
7	Danville 2 W	597
8	Millport 2 NW	612
9	Mansfield 5 W	615
10	Wooster Exp Stn	619
11	Chippewa Lake	654
11	Millersburg	***654***
13	Mansfield Lahm Municipal Arpt	683
14	Akron Akron-Canton Reg Arpt	701
15	Barnesville	***710***
16	Centerburg 2 SE	717
17	Bucyrus	720
17	Oberlin	720
19	Cadiz	758
20	Cleveland Hopkins Intl Arpt	762
21	Painesville 4 NW	777
22	Toledo Express Arpt	789
23	Marion 2 N	795
24	Bowling Green WWTP	796
25	Springfield New Water Works	798

Annual Precipitation

Highest

Rank	Station Name	Inches
1	Chardon	48.24
2	Milford	***44.72***
3	Mansfield Lahm Municipal Arpt	44.24
4	Fairfield	***43.80***
5	Barnesville	***43.60***
6	Dorset	43.58
7	Marietta Wwtp	42.81
8	Hiram	42.67
9	Cincinnati-Northern Kentucky	42.53
10	Centerburg 2 SE	41.94
11	Danville 2 W	41.87
12	Urbana WWTP	41.71
13	Steubenville	41.52
14	Hannibal Lock & Dam	41.34
15	Cadiz	41.26
16	Dayton Intl Arpt	41.13
17	Carpenter 2 S	***41.04***
18	Portsmouth Sciotoville	40.93
19	Wilmington 3 N	40.80
20	Dayton Mcd	40.66
21	Chilo Meldahl L&D	40.58
22	Columbus Valley Crossing	40.39
23	Wooster Exp Stn	39.99
24	Cambridge	39.87
25	Millersburg	***39.79***

Lowest

Rank	Station Name	Inches
1	Bowling Green WWTP	33.92
2	Toledo Express Arpt	34.11
3	Defiance	36.64
4	Pandora	37.19
5	Findlay Wpcc	37.44
6	Upper Sandusky	37.52
7	Millport 2 NW	37.63
8	Oberlin	37.75
9	Marysville	37.88
10	Chillicothe Mound City	38.11
11	Fredericktown 4 S	38.32
12	Lima WWTP	38.55
13	Springfield New Water Works	38.57
14	Painesville 4 NW	38.63
15	Circleville	38.80
16	Youngstown Municipal Arpt	38.92
17	Cleveland Hopkins Intl Arpt	39.00
18	Marion 2 N	39.03
19	Bucyrus	39.07
20	Franklin	39.11
21	Bellefontaine	39.24
21	Mansfield 5 W	39.24
23	Westerville	39.26
24	Chippewa Lake	39.32
24	Columbus-Port Columbus Intl	39.32

Rankings include 25 highest/lowest stations. If state has less than 25 stations, all stations are included. The period of record is 1980–2009. See User Guide for detailed explanation of data.

Annual Extreme Maximum Daily Precipitation

Highest			Lowest		
Rank	Station Name	Inches	Rank	Station Name	Inches
1	Upper Sandusky	9.35	1	Oberlin	2.92
2	Bucyrus	8.68	2	Fredericktown 4 S	***3.00***
3	Chilo Meldahl L&D	7.20	3	Toledo Express Arpt	3.15
4	Pandora	6.19	4	Wilmington 3 N	3.42
5	Elyria 3 E	5.75	5	Centerburg 2 SE	3.46
6	Findlay Wpcc	5.62	6	Wooster Exp Stn	3.60
7	Chardon	5.50	7	Franklin	3.76
8	Cambridge	5.45	8	Columbus Valley Crossing	3.77
9	Steubenville	5.36	9	Springfield New Water Works	3.78
10	Marion 2 N	5.33	10	Dayton Intl Arpt	3.81
11	Portsmouth Sciotoville	5.20	11	Westerville	3.84
12	Mansfield 5 W	***5.19***	12	Millersburg	***3.85***
13	Columbus-Port Columbus Intl	5.13	13	Defiance	3.89
14	Barnesville	***5.12***	14	Urbana WWTP	3.97
14	Danville 2 W	5.12	15	Akron Akron-Canton Reg Arpt	3.98
16	Cadiz	5.09	16	Hiram	4.05
17	Lima WWTP	5.08	17	Chillicothe Mound City	***4.10***
18	Marysville	4.82	18	Circleville	4.12
19	Millport 2 NW	4.80	19	Bowling Green WWTP	4.25
20	Marietta Wwtp	4.78	20	Hannibal Lock & Dam	4.28
21	Fairfield	***4.67***	21	Dorset	4.29
22	Youngstown Municipal Arpt	4.65	22	Chippewa Lake	4.30
23	Milford	***4.63***	22	Cincinnati-Northern Kentucky	4.30
24	Cleveland Hopkins Intl Arpt	4.59	24	Mansfield Lahm Municipal Arpt	4.34
25	Painesville 4 NW	4.57	25	Dayton Mcd	4.36

Number of Days Annually With ≥ 0.1 Inches of Precipitation

Highest			Lowest		
Rank	Station Name	Days	Rank	Station Name	Days
1	Chardon	108	1	Chillicothe Mound City	70
2	Hiram	95	1	Fredericktown 4 S	70
3	Dorset	94	3	Chilo Meldahl L&D	72
4	Elyria 3 E	89	3	Toledo Express Arpt	72
4	Mansfield Lahm Municipal Arpt	89	5	Bowling Green WWTP	73
4	Warren 3 S	89	5	Franklin	73
7	Steubenville	88	7	Columbus Valley Crossing	74
8	Akron Akron-Canton Reg Arpt	87	7	Springfield New Water Works	74
8	Barnesville	***87***	9	Dayton Mcd	76
8	Cadiz	87	10	Defiance	77
8	Chippewa Lake	87	10	Marysville	77
8	Cleveland Hopkins Intl Arpt	87	10	Upper Sandusky	77
8	Marietta Wwtp	87	13	Circleville	78
8	Youngstown Municipal Arpt	87	14	Columbus-Port Columbus Intl	79
15	Danville 2 W	85	14	Fairfield	***79***
15	Painesville 4 NW	85	14	Findlay Wpcc	79
17	Hannibal Lock & Dam	84	14	Marion 2 N	79
17	Millport 2 NW	84	14	Millersburg	***79***
17	Oberlin	84	14	Pandora	79
20	Bucyrus	83	20	Dayton Intl Arpt	80
20	Cambridge	83	20	Lima WWTP	80
22	Carpenter 2 S	***82***	20	Mansfield 5 W	80
22	Cincinnati-Northern Kentucky	82	23	Bellefontaine	81
22	Milford	***82***	23	Centerburg 2 SE	81
22	Portsmouth Sciotoville	82	23	Urbana WWTP	81

Rankings include 25 highest/lowest stations. If state has less than 25 stations, all stations are included. The period of record is 1980–2009. See User Guide for detailed explanation of data.

Number of Days Annually With ≥ 0.5 Inches of Precipitation

Highest Rank	Station Name	Days	Lowest Rank	Station Name	Days
1	Chardon	32	1	Bowling Green WWTP	21
1	Milford	***32***	1	Toledo Express Arpt	21
3	Fairfield	***30***	3	Upper Sandusky	22
4	Barnesville	***29***	4	Cleveland Hopkins Intl Arpt	23
4	Centerburg 2 SE	29	4	Oberlin	23
4	Dorset	29	4	Painesville 4 NW	23
4	Mansfield Lahm Municipal Arpt	29	4	Youngstown Municipal Arpt	23
4	Marietta Wwtp	29	8	Akron Akron-Canton Reg Arpt	24
9	Carpenter 2 S	***28***	8	Defiance	24
9	Hannibal Lock & Dam	28	8	Findlay Wpcc	24
11	Cadiz	27	8	Franklin	24
11	Chilo Meldahl L&D	27	8	Millport 2 NW	24
11	Cincinnati-Northern Kentucky	27	8	Warren 3 S	24
11	Circleville	27	14	Bellefontaine	25
11	Columbus Valley Crossing	27	14	Bucyrus	25
11	Danville 2 W	27	14	Chippewa Lake	25
11	Dayton Mcd	27	14	Columbus-Port Columbus Intl	25
11	Portsmouth Sciotoville	27	14	Elyria 3 E	25
11	Steubenville	27	14	Fredericktown 4 S	25
11	Urbana WWTP	27	14	Lima WWTP	25
11	Wilmington 3 N	27	14	Mansfield 5 W	25
11	Wooster Exp Stn	27	14	Marion 2 N	25
23	Cambridge	26	14	Marysville	25
23	Chillicothe Mound City	26	14	Pandora	25
23	Dayton Intl Arpt	26	25	Cambridge	26

Number of Days Annually With ≥ 1.0 Inches of Precipitation

Highest Rank	Station Name	Days	Lowest Rank	Station Name	Days
1	Chilo Meldahl L&D	12	1	Akron Akron-Canton Reg Arpt	6
1	Cincinnati-Northern Kentucky	12	1	Chippewa Lake	6
3	Fairfield	***11***	1	Lima WWTP	6
3	Mansfield Lahm Municipal Arpt	11	1	Millport 2 NW	6
3	Milford	***11***	1	Oberlin	6
3	Urbana WWTP	11	1	Painesville 4 NW	6
7	Carpenter 2 S	***10***	1	Pandora	6
7	Dayton Intl Arpt	10	1	Warren 3 S	6
7	Dayton Mcd	10	1	Youngstown Municipal Arpt	6
7	Franklin	10	10	Bowling Green WWTP	7
7	Fredericktown 4 S	10	10	Bucyrus	7
7	Portsmouth Sciotoville	10	10	Cadiz	7
7	Wilmington 3 N	10	10	Cleveland Hopkins Intl Arpt	7
14	Barnesville	***9***	10	Columbus-Port Columbus Intl	7
14	Bellefontaine	9	10	Dorset	7
14	Cambridge	9	10	Elyria 3 E	7
14	Centerburg 2 SE	9	10	Findlay Wpcc	7
14	Chardon	9	10	Hiram	7
14	Chillicothe Mound City	9	10	Marysville	7
14	Circleville	9	10	Millersburg	***7***
14	Columbus Valley Crossing	9	10	Steubenville	7
14	Danville 2 W	9	10	Toledo Express Arpt	7
14	Marion 2 N	9	10	Wooster Exp Stn	7
14	Springfield New Water Works	9	24	Defiance	8
25	Defiance	8	24	Hannibal Lock & Dam	8

Rankings include 25 highest/lowest stations. If state has less than 25 stations, all stations are included. The period of record is 1980–2009. See User Guide for detailed explanation of data.

Annual Snowfall

Highest Rank	Station Name	Inches	Lowest Rank	Station Name	Inches
1	Chardon	102.8	1	Fairfield	***7.8***
2	Dorset	79.0	2	Portsmouth Sciotoville	8.0
3	Cleveland Hopkins Intl Arpt	67.6	3	Centerburg 2 SE	12.4
4	Hiram	63.2	3	Dayton Mcd	12.4
5	Youngstown Municipal Arpt	59.7	5	Circleville	13.9
6	Mansfield Lahm Municipal Arpt	47.7	6	Chillicothe Mound City	14.8
7	Akron Akron-Canton Reg Arpt	46.4	7	Columbus Valley Crossing	14.9
8	Oberlin	45.8	8	Millersburg	***17.5***
9	Elyria 3 E	41.0	9	Cambridge	18.2
10	Painesville 4 NW	39.2	10	Westerville	18.5
11	Danville 2 W	39.1	11	Carpenter 2 S	***18.6***
12	Chippewa Lake	35.9	12	Marietta Wwtp	18.8
13	Warren 3 S	31.8	13	Upper Sandusky	19.4
14	Barnesville	***31.6***	14	Marysville	20.5
15	Pandora	30.5	15	Defiance	20.7
16	Wooster Exp Stn	29.3	16	Wilmington 3 N	21.0
17	Millport 2 NW	28.7	17	Bowling Green WWTP	21.6
18	Cadiz	28.2	17	Cincinnati-Northern Kentucky	21.6
19	Columbus-Port Columbus Intl	27.9	19	Bucyrus	22.5
20	Findlay Wpcc	26.9	20	Marion 2 N	23.0
21	Dayton Intl Arpt	25.3	21	Fredericktown 4 S	24.8
22	Fredericktown 4 S	24.8	22	Dayton Intl Arpt	25.3
23	Marion 2 N	23.0	23	Findlay Wpcc	26.9
24	Bucyrus	22.5	24	Columbus-Port Columbus Intl	27.9
25	Bowling Green WWTP	21.6	25	Cadiz	28.2

Annual Maximum Snow Depth

Highest Rank	Station Name	Inches	Lowest Rank	Station Name	Inches
1	Chardon	47	1	Chillicothe Mound City	11
2	Painesville 4 NW	25	2	Dayton Mcd	12
3	Chippewa Lake	24	3	Columbus Valley Crossing	***13***
4	Centerburg 2 SE	23	3	Millersburg	***13***
4	Hannibal Lock & Dam	***23***	3	Westerville	13
6	Cleveland Hopkins Intl Arpt	22	6	Cincinnati-Northern Kentucky	14
6	Danville 2 W	22	6	Findlay Wpcc	14
6	Hiram	22	8	Circleville	***15***
9	Portsmouth Sciotoville	21	8	Elyria 3 E	15
10	Barnesville	***20***	8	Marion 2 N	***15***
10	Dorset	20	8	Millport 2 NW	***15***
10	Mansfield Lahm Municipal Arpt	20	12	Chilo Meldahl L&D	***16***
10	Marietta Wwtp	20	12	Dayton Intl Arpt	16
14	Bellefontaine	***19***	12	Pandora	16
14	Cambridge	19	12	Warren 3 S	16
14	Upper Sandusky	***19***	16	Akron Akron-Canton Reg Arpt	17
17	Bowling Green WWTP	18	16	Bucyrus	17
17	Columbus-Port Columbus Intl	18	16	Defiance	17
17	Wilmington 3 N	18	16	Marysville	17
17	Youngstown Municipal Arpt	18	16	Oberlin	17
21	Akron Akron-Canton Reg Arpt	17	16	Wooster Exp Stn	17
21	Bucyrus	17	22	Bowling Green WWTP	18
21	Defiance	17	22	Columbus-Port Columbus Intl	18
21	Marysville	17	22	Wilmington 3 N	18
21	Oberlin	17	22	Youngstown Municipal Arpt	18

Rankings include 25 highest/lowest stations. If state has less than 25 stations, all stations are included. The period of record is 1980–2009. See User Guide for detailed explanation of data.

Number of Days Annually With ≥ 1.0 Inch Snow Depth

Highest

Rank	Station Name	Days
1	Chardon	80
2	Dorset	69
3	Hiram	64
4	Youngstown Municipal Arpt	54
5	Oberlin	53
6	Cleveland Hopkins Intl Arpt	51
7	Mansfield Lahm Municipal Arpt	49
8	Akron Akron-Canton Reg Arpt	45
8	Chippewa Lake	45
8	Wooster Exp Stn	45
11	Danville 2 W	43
11	Elyria 3 E	43
11	Painesville 4 NW	43
14	Pandora	39
15	Bowling Green WWTP	38
15	Defiance	38
17	Findlay Wpcc	36
18	Warren 3 S	35
19	Barnesville	***34***
20	Marysville	31
21	Bucyrus	29
22	Dayton Intl Arpt	27
22	Marion 2 N	***27***
24	Centerburg 2 SE	26
24	Columbus-Port Columbus Intl	26

Lowest

Rank	Station Name	Days
1	Chilo Meldahl L&D	***4***
2	Franklin	***8***
2	Portsmouth Sciotoville	8
4	Hannibal Lock & Dam	***10***
5	Columbus Valley Crossing	13
6	Bellefontaine	***15***
6	Marietta Wwtp	15
6	Millport 2 NW	***15***
9	Chillicothe Mound City	18
10	Circleville	19
10	Dayton Mcd	19
12	Cincinnati-Northern Kentucky	20
13	Upper Sandusky	22
14	Westerville	23
15	Cadiz	***25***
15	Cambridge	25
17	Centerburg 2 SE	26
17	Columbus-Port Columbus Intl	26
17	Millersburg	***26***
17	Wilmington 3 N	26
21	Dayton Intl Arpt	27
21	Marion 2 N	***27***
23	Bucyrus	29
24	Marysville	31
25	Barnesville	***34***

Rankings include 25 highest/lowest stations. If state has less than 25 stations, all stations are included. The period of record is 1980–2009. See User Guide for detailed explanation of data.

Significant Storm Events in Ohio: 2000 – 2009

Location or County	Date	Type	Mag.	Deaths	Injuries	Property Damage ($mil.)	Crop Damage ($mil.)
Preble County	02/07/00	Fog	na	1	14	0.2	0.0
Greene	09/20/00	Tornado	F4	1	100	15.0	0.0
Montgomery	04/09/01	Hail	1.75 in.	0	0	70.0	0.0
Western and Southern Ohio	03/09/02	High Wind	84 mph	1	12	0.9	0.0
Stark	04/28/02	Tornado	F2	0	2	45.5	0.0
Van Wert	11/10/02	Tornado	F4	2	17	30.0	0.0
Franklin	04/20/03	Hail	1.75 in.	0	0	80.0	0.0
Delaware	04/20/03	Hail	1.50 in.	0	0	65.0	0.0
Summit	07/21/03	Flash Flood	na	3	0	100.0	0.0
Stark	07/27/03	Flash Flood	na	0	0	52.0	0.0
Northern Ohio	12/22/04	Winter Storm	na	0	0	54.9	0.0
Northern Ohio	01/05/05	Ice Storm	na	0	0	124.9	0.0
Lake	07/28/06	Flash Flood	na	1	0	320.0	0.0
Licking	10/04/06	Hail	1.75 in.	0	1	100.0	0.0
Franklin	10/04/06	Hail	2.00 in.	0	0	100.0	0.0
Franklin	10/11/06	Tornado	F2	0	0	50.0	0.0
Summit	06/08/07	Hail	4.25 in.	0	0	105.0	0.0
Hancock	08/21/07	Flash Flood	na	0	0	100.0	5.0
Richland	08/21/07	Flash Flood	na	0	0	70.0	5.0
Crawford	08/21/07	Flash Flood	na	0	0	62.0	3.0
Knox, Stark, and Trumbull Counties	03/07/08	Winter Storm	na	0	0	750.0	0.0
Franklin and Logan Counties	09/14/08	High Wind	75 mph	0	0	128.7	0.0
Hamilton County	09/14/08	High Wind	61 mph	1	0	96.6	0.0
Montgomery County	09/14/08	High Wind	69 mph	0	0	63.7	0.0

Note: Deaths, injuries, and damages are date and location specific.

Grey House Publishing

2018 Title List

Visit www.GreyHouse.com for Product Information, Table of Contents, and Sample Pages

General Reference

America's College Museums
American Environmental Leaders: From Colonial Times to the Present
Encyclopedia of African-American Writing
Encyclopedia of Constitutional Amendments
Encyclopedia of Human Rights and the United States
Encyclopedia of Invasions & Conquests
Encyclopedia of Prisoners of War & Internment
Encyclopedia of Religion & Law in America
Encyclopedia of Rural America
Encyclopedia of the Continental Congress
Encyclopedia of the United States Cabinet, 1789-2010
Encyclopedia of War Journalism
Encyclopedia of Warrior Peoples & Fighting Groups
The Environmental Debate: A Documentary History
The Evolution Wars: A Guide to the Debates
From Suffrage to the Senate: America's Political Women
Gun Debate: An Encyclopedia of Gun Rights & Gun Control in the U.S.
Opinions throughout History: National Security vs. Civil and Privacy Rights
Opinions throughout History: Immigration
Opinions throughout History: Drug Abuse & Drug Epidemics
Political Corruption in America
Privacy Rights in the Digital Era
The Religious Right: A Reference Handbook
Speakers of the House of Representatives, 1789-2009
This is Who We Were: 1880-1900
This is Who We Were: A Companion to the 1940 Census
This is Who We Were: In the 1900s
This is Who We Were: In the 1910s
This is Who We Were: In the 1920s
This is Who We Were: In the 1940s
This is Who We Were: In the 1950s
This is Who We Were: In the 1960s
This is Who We Were: In the 1970s
This is Who We Were: In the 1980s
This is Who We Were: In the 1990s
This is Who We Were: In the 2000s
U.S. Land & Natural Resource Policy
The Value of a Dollar 1600-1865: Colonial Era to the Civil War
The Value of a Dollar: 1860-2014
Working Americans 1770-1869 Vol. IX: Revolutionary War to the Civil War
Working Americans 1880-1999 Vol. I: The Working Class
Working Americans 1880-1999 Vol. II: The Middle Class
Working Americans 1880-1999 Vol. III: The Upper Class
Working Americans 1880-1999 Vol. IV: Their Children
Working Americans 1880-2015 Vol. V: Americans At War
Working Americans 1880-2005 Vol. VI: Women at Work
Working Americans 1880-2006 Vol. VII: Social Movements
Working Americans 1880-2007 Vol. VIII: Immigrants
Working Americans 1880-2009 Vol. X: Sports & Recreation
Working Americans 1880-2010 Vol. XI: Inventors & Entrepreneurs
Working Americans 1880-2011 Vol. XII: Our History through Music
Working Americans 1880-2012 Vol. XIII: Education & Educators
Working Americans 1880-2016 Vol. XIV: Industry Through the Ages
Working Americans 1880-2017 Vol. XV: Politics & Politicians
World Cultural Leaders of the 20th & 21st Centuries

Education Information

Charter School Movement
Comparative Guide to American Elementary & Secondary Schools
Complete Learning Disabilities Directory
Educators Resource Handbook
Special Education: Policy and Curriculum Development

Health Information

Comparative Guide to American Hospitals
Complete Directory for Pediatric Disorders
Complete Directory for People with Chronic Illness
Complete Directory for People with Disabilities
Complete Mental Health Directory
Diabetes in America: Analysis of an Epidemic
Guide to Health Care Group Purchasing Organizations
Guide to U.S. HMO's & PPO's
Medical Device Market Place
Older Americans Information Directory

Business Information

Complete Television, Radio & Cable Industry Directory
Directory of Business Information Resources
Directory of Mail Order Catalogs
Directory of Venture Capital & Private Equity Firms
Environmental Resource Handbook
Financial Literacy Starter Kit
Food & Beverage Market Place
Grey House Homeland Security Directory
Grey House Performing Arts Directory
Grey House Safety & Security Directory
Hudson's Washington News Media Contacts Directory
New York State Directory
Sports Market Place Directory

Statistics & Demographics

American Tally
America's Top-Rated Cities
America's Top-Rated Smaller Cities
Ancestry & Ethnicity in America
The Asian Databook
Comparative Guide to American Suburbs
The Hispanic Databook
Profiles of America
"Profiles of" Series - State Handbooks
Weather America

Financial Ratings Series

Financial Literacy Basics
TheStreet Ratings' Guide to Bond & Money Market Mutual Funds
TheStreet Ratings' Guide to Common Stocks
TheStreet Ratings' Guide to Exchange-Traded Funds
TheStreet Ratings' Guide to Stock Mutual Funds
TheStreet Ratings' Ultimate Guided Tour of Stock Investing
Weiss Ratings' Consumer Guides
Weiss Ratings' Financial Literary Basic Guides
Weiss Ratings' Guide to Banks
Weiss Ratings' Guide to Credit Unions
Weiss Ratings' Guide to Health Insurers
Weiss Ratings' Guide to Life & Annuity Insurers
Weiss Ratings' Guide to Property & Casualty Insurers

Bowker's Books In Print® Titles

American Book Publishing Record® Annual
American Book Publishing Record® Monthly
Books In Print®
Books In Print® Supplement
Books Out Loud™
Bowker's Complete Video Directory™
Children's Books In Print®
El-Hi Textbooks & Serials In Print®
Forthcoming Books®
Law Books & Serials In Print™
Medical & Health Care Books In Print™
Publishers, Distributors & Wholesalers of the US™
Subject Guide to Books In Print®
Subject Guide to Children's Books In Print®

Canadian General Reference

Associations Canada
Canadian Almanac & Directory
Canadian Environmental Resource Guide
Canadian Parliamentary Guide
Canadian Venture Capital & Private Equity Firms
Canadian Who's Who
Financial Post Directory of Directors
Financial Services Canada
Governments Canada
Health Guide Canada
The History of Canada
Libraries Canada
Major Canadian Cities

SALEM PRESS

SALEM PRESS

2018 Title List

Visit **www.SalemPress.com** for Product Information, Table of Contents, and Sample Pages

Science, Careers & Mathematics

Ancient Creatures
Applied Science
Applied Science: Engineering & Mathematics
Applied Science: Science & Medicine
Applied Science: Technology
Biomes and Ecosystems
Careers in the Arts: Fine, Performing & Visual
Careers in Building Construction
Careers in Business
Careers in Chemistry
Careers in Communications & Media
Careers in Environment & Conservation
Careers in Financial Services
Careers in Green Energy
Careers in Healthcare
Careers in Hospitality & Tourism
Careers in Human Services
Careers in Law, Criminal Justice & Emergency Services
Careers in Manufacturing
Careers in Outdoor Jobs
Careers in Overseas Jobs
Careers in Physics
Careers in Sales, Insurance & Real Estate
Careers in Science & Engineering
Careers in Sports & Fitness
Careers in Social Media
Careers in Sports Medicine & Training
Careers in Technology Services & Repair
Computer Technology Innovators
Contemporary Biographies in Business
Contemporary Biographies in Chemistry
Contemporary Biographies in Communications & Media
Contemporary Biographies in Environment & Conservation
Contemporary Biographies in Healthcare
Contemporary Biographies in Hospitality & Tourism
Contemporary Biographies in Law & Criminal Justice
Contemporary Biographies in Physics
Earth Science
Earth Science: Earth Materials & Resources
Earth Science: Earth's Surface and History
Earth Science: Physics & Chemistry of the Earth
Earth Science: Weather, Water & Atmosphere
Encyclopedia of Energy
Encyclopedia of Environmental Issues
Encyclopedia of Environmental Issues: Atmosphere and Air Pollution
Encyclopedia of Environmental Issues: Ecology and Ecosystems
Encyclopedia of Environmental Issues: Energy and Energy Use
Encyclopedia of Environmental Issues: Policy and Activism
Encyclopedia of Environmental Issues: Preservation/Wilderness Issues
Encyclopedia of Environmental Issues: Water and Water Pollution
Encyclopedia of Global Resources
Encyclopedia of Global Warming
Encyclopedia of Mathematics & Society
Encyclopedia of Mathematics & Society: Engineering, Tech, Medicine
Encyclopedia of Mathematics & Society: Great Mathematicians
Encyclopedia of Mathematics & Society: Math & Social Sciences
Encyclopedia of Mathematics & Society: Math Development/Concepts
Encyclopedia of Mathematics & Society: Math in Culture & Society
Encyclopedia of Mathematics & Society: Space, Science, Environment
Encyclopedia of the Ancient World
Forensic Science
Geography Basics
Internet Innovators
Inventions and Inventors
Magill's Encyclopedia of Science: Animal Life
Magill's Encyclopedia of Science: Plant life
Notable Natural Disasters
Principles of Artificial Intelligence & Robotics
Principles of Astronomy
Principles of Biology
Principles of Biotechnology
Principles of Chemistry
Principles of Climatology
Principles of Physical Science
Principles of Physics
Principles of Programming & Coding
Principles of Research Methods
Principles of Sustainability
Science and Scientists
Solar System
Solar System: Great Astronomers
Solar System: Study of the Universe
Solar System: The Inner Planets
Solar System: The Moon and Other Small Bodies
Solar System: The Outer Planets
Solar System: The Sun and Other Stars
World Geography

Literature

American Ethnic Writers
Classics of Science Fiction & Fantasy Literature
Critical Approaches: Feminist
Critical Approaches: Multicultural
Critical Approaches: Moral
Critical Approaches: Psychological
Critical Insights: Authors
Critical Insights: Film
Critical Insights: Literary Collection Bundles
Critical Insights: Themes
Critical Insights: Works
Critical Survey of American Literature
Critical Survey of Drama
Critical Survey of Graphic Novels: Heroes & Super Heroes
Critical Survey of Graphic Novels: History, Theme & Technique
Critical Survey of Graphic Novels: Independents/Underground Classics
Critical Survey of Graphic Novels: Manga
Critical Survey of Long Fiction
Critical Survey of Mystery & Detective Fiction
Critical Survey of Mythology and Folklore: Heroes and Heroines
Critical Survey of Mythology and Folklore: Love, Sexuality & Desire
Critical Survey of Mythology and Folklore: World Mythology
Critical Survey of Novels into Film
Critical Survey of Poetry
Critical Survey of Poetry: American Poets
Critical Survey of Poetry: British, Irish & Commonwealth Poets
Critical Survey of Poetry: Cumulative Index
Critical Survey of Poetry: European Poets
Critical Survey of Poetry: Topical Essays
Critical Survey of Poetry: World Poets
Critical Survey of Science Fiction & Fantasy
Critical Survey of Shakespeare's Plays
Critical Survey of Shakespeare's Sonnets
Critical Survey of Short Fiction
Critical Survey of Short Fiction: American Writers
Critical Survey of Short Fiction: British, Irish, Commonwealth Writers
Critical Survey of Short Fiction: Cumulative Index
Critical Survey of Short Fiction: European Writers
Critical Survey of Short Fiction: Topical Essays
Critical Survey of Short Fiction: World Writers
Critical Survey of World Literature
Critical Survey of Young Adult Literature
Cyclopedia of Literary Characters
Cyclopedia of Literary Places
Holocaust Literature
Introduction to Literary Context: American Poetry of the 20th Century
Introduction to Literary Context: American Post-Modernist Novels
Introduction to Literary Context: American Short Fiction
Introduction to Literary Context: English Literature
Introduction to Literary Context: Plays
Introduction to Literary Context: World Literature
Magill's Literary Annual 2018
Masterplots
Masterplots II: African American Literature
Masterplots II: American Fiction Series
Masterplots II: British & Commonwealth Fiction Series
Masterplots II: Christian Literature
Masterplots II: Drama Series
Masterplots II: Juvenile & Young Adult Literature, Supplement
Masterplots II: Nonfiction Series
Masterplots II: Poetry Series
Masterplots II: Short Story Series
Masterplots II: Women's Literature Series
Notable African American Writers
Notable American Novelists
Notable Playwrights
Notable Poets
Recommended Reading: 600 Classics Reviewed
Short Story Writers

 SALEM PRESS

2018 Title List

Visit www.SalemPress.com for Product Information, Table of Contents, and Sample Pages

History and Social Science

The 2000s in America
50 States
African American History
Agriculture in History
American First Ladies
American Heroes
American Indian Culture
American Indian History
American Indian Tribes
American Presidents
American Villains
America's Historic Sites
Ancient Greece
The Bill of Rights
The Civil Rights Movement
The Cold War
Countries, Peoples & Cultures
Countries, Peoples & Cultures: Central & South America
Countries, Peoples & Cultures: Central, South & Southeast Asia
Countries, Peoples & Cultures: East & South Africa
Countries, Peoples & Cultures: East Asia & the Pacific
Countries, Peoples & Cultures: Eastern Europe
Countries, Peoples & Cultures: Middle East & North Africa
Countries, Peoples & Cultures: North America & the Caribbean
Countries, Peoples & Cultures: West & Central Africa
Countries, Peoples & Cultures: Western Europe
Defining Documents: American Revolution
Defining Documents: American West
Defining Documents: Ancient World
Defining Documents: Asia
Defining Documents: Civil Rights
Defining Documents: Civil War
Defining Documents: Court Cases
Defining Documents: Dissent & Protest
Defining Documents: Emergence of Modern America
Defining Documents: Exploration & Colonial America
Defining Documents: Immigration & Immigrant Communities
Defining Documents: LGBTQ
Defining Documents: Manifest Destiny
Defining Documents: Middle Ages
Defining Documents: Middle East
Defining Documents: Nationalism & Populism
Defining Documents: Native Americans
Defining Documents: Political Campaigns, Candidates & Discourse
Defining Documents: Postwar 1940s
Defining Documents: Reconstruction
Defining Documents: Renaissance & Early Modern Era
Defining Documents: Secrets, Leaks & Scandals
Defining Documents: 1920s
Defining Documents: 1930s
Defining Documents: 1950s
Defining Documents: 1960s
Defining Documents: 1970s
Defining Documents: The 17th Century
Defining Documents: The 18th Century
Defining Documents: The 19th Century
Defining Documents: The 20th Century: 1900-1950
Defining Documents: Vietnam War
Defining Documents: Women
Defining Documents: World War I
Defining Documents: World War II
Education Today
The Eighties in America
Encyclopedia of American Immigration
Encyclopedia of Flight
Encyclopedia of the Ancient World
Fashion Innovators
The Fifties in America
The Forties in America
Great Athletes
Great Athletes: Baseball
Great Athletes: Basketball
Great Athletes: Boxing & Soccer
Great Athletes: Cumulative Index
Great Athletes: Football
Great Athletes: Golf & Tennis
Great Athletes: Olympics
Great Athletes: Racing & Individual Sports
Great Contemporary Athletes
Great Events from History: 17th Century
Great Events from History: 18th Century
Great Events from History: 19th Century
Great Events from History: 20th Century (1901-1940)
Great Events from History: 20th Century (1941-1970)
Great Events from History: 20th Century (1971-2000)
Great Events from History: 21st Century (2000-2016)
Great Events from History: African American History
Great Events from History: Cumulative Indexes
Great Events from History: LGBTG
Great Events from History: Middle Ages
Great Events from History: Secrets, Leaks & Scandals
Great Events from History: Renaissance & Early Modern Era
Great Lives from History: 17th Century
Great Lives from History: 18th Century
Great Lives from History: 19th Century
Great Lives from History: 20th Century
Great Lives from History: 21st Century (2000-2017)
Great Lives from History: American Women
Great Lives from History: Ancient World
Great Lives from History: Asian & Pacific Islander Americans
Great Lives from History: Cumulative Indexes
Great Lives from History: Incredibly Wealthy
Great Lives from History: Inventors & Inventions
Great Lives from History: Jewish Americans
Great Lives from History: Latinos
Great Lives from History: Notorious Lives
Great Lives from History: Renaissance & Early Modern Era
Great Lives from History: Scientists & Science
Historical Encyclopedia of American Business
Issues in U.S. Immigration
Magill's Guide to Military History
Milestone Documents in African American History
Milestone Documents in American History
Milestone Documents in World History
Milestone Documents of American Leaders
Milestone Documents of World Religions
Music Innovators
Musicians & Composers 20th Century
The Nineties in America
The Seventies in America
The Sixties in America
Sociology Today
Survey of American Industry and Careers
The Thirties in America
The Twenties in America
United States at War
U.S. Court Cases
U.S. Government Leaders
U.S. Laws, Acts, and Treaties
U.S. Legal System
U.S. Supreme Court
Weapons and Warfare
World Conflicts: Asia and the Middle East

Health

Addictions & Substance Abuse
Adolescent Health & Wellness
Cancer
Complementary & Alternative Medicine
Community & Family Health
Genetics & Inherited Conditions
Health Issues
Infectious Diseases & Conditions
Magill's Medical Guide
Nutrition
Nursing
Psychology & Behavioral Health
Psychology Basics

HW WILSON

HW WILSON

2018 Title List

Visit **www.HWWilsonInPrint.com** for Product Information, Table of Contents and Sample Pages

Current Biography
Current Biography Cumulative Index 1946-2013
Current Biography Monthly Magazine
Current Biography Yearbook: 2003
Current Biography Yearbook: 2004
Current Biography Yearbook: 2005
Current Biography Yearbook: 2006
Current Biography Yearbook: 2007
Current Biography Yearbook: 2008
Current Biography Yearbook: 2009
Current Biography Yearbook: 2010
Current Biography Yearbook: 2011
Current Biography Yearbook: 2012
Current Biography Yearbook: 2013
Current Biography Yearbook: 2014
Current Biography Yearbook: 2015
Current Biography Yearbook: 2016
Current Biography Yearbook: 2017

Core Collections
Children's Core Collection
Fiction Core Collection
Graphic Novels Core Collection
Middle & Junior High School Core
Public Library Core Collection: Nonfiction
Senior High Core Collection
Young Adult Fiction Core Collection

The Reference Shelf
Aging in America
Alternative Facts: Post Truth & the Information War
The American Dream
American Military Presence Overseas
The Arab Spring
Artificial Intelligence
The Brain
The Business of Food
Campaign Trends & Election Law
Conspiracy Theories
The Digital Age
Dinosaurs
Embracing New Paradigms in Education
Faith & Science
Families: Traditional and New Structures
The Future of U.S. Economic Relations: Mexico, Cuba, and Venezuela
Global Climate Change
Graphic Novels and Comic Books
Guns in America
Immigration
Immigration in the U.S.
Internet Abuses & Privacy Rights
Internet Safety
LGBTQ in the 21st Century
Marijuana Reform
The News and its Future
The Paranormal
Politics of the Ocean
Prescription Drug Abuse
Racial Tension in a "Postracial" Age
Reality Television
Representative American Speeches: 2008-2009
Representative American Speeches: 2009-2010
Representative American Speeches: 2010-2011
Representative American Speeches: 2011-2012
Representative American Speeches: 2012-2013
Representative American Speeches: 2013-2014
Representative American Speeches: 2014-2015
Representative American Speeches: 2015-2016
Representative American Speeches: 2016-2017
Representative American Speeches: 2017-2018
Rethinking Work
Revisiting Gender
Robotics
Russia
Social Networking
Social Services for the Poor
South China Seas Conflict
Space Exploration & Development
Sports in America
The Supreme Court
The Transformation of American Cities
U.S. Infrastructure
U.S. National Debate Topic: Educational Reform
U.S. National Debate Topic: Surveillance
U.S. National Debate Topic: The Ocean
U.S. National Debate Topic: Transportation Infrastructure
Whistleblowers

Readers' Guide
Abridged Readers' Guide to Periodical Literature
Readers' Guide to Periodical Literature

Indexes
Index to Legal Periodicals & Books
Short Story Index
Book Review Digest

Sears List
Sears List of Subject Headings
Sears: Lista de Encabezamientos de Materia

Facts About Series
Facts About American Immigration
Facts About China
Facts About the 20th Century
Facts About the Presidents
Facts About the World's Languages

Nobel Prize Winners
Nobel Prize Winners: 1901-1986
Nobel Prize Winners: 1987-1991
Nobel Prize Winners: 1992-1996
Nobel Prize Winners: 1997-2001

World Authors
World Authors: 1995-2000
World Authors: 2000-2005

Famous First Facts
Famous First Facts
Famous First Facts About American Politics
Famous First Facts About Sports
Famous First Facts About the Environment
Famous First Facts: International Edition

American Book of Days
The American Book of Days
The International Book of Days

Monographs
American Reformers
The Barnhart Dictionary of Etymology
Celebrate the World
Guide to the Ancient World
Indexing from A to Z
Nobel Prize Winners
The Poetry Break
Radical Change: Books for Youth in a Digital Age
Speeches of American Presidents

Wilson Chronology
Wilson Chronology of Asia and the Pacific
Wilson Chronology of Human Rights
Wilson Chronology of Ideas
Wilson Chronology of the Arts
Wilson Chronology of the World's Religions
Wilson Chronology of Women's Achievements